海上絲綢之路文獻集成

總主編　陳支平　陳春聲

科技與文化編

58

主編　王揚宗　葉　農

國家出版基金項目
NATIONAL PUBLICATION FOUNDATION

海峽出版發行集團
THE STRAITS PUBLISHING & DISTRIBUTING GROUP
福建人民出版社

本册目次

論語 大學 中庸

（*Confucian Analects, the Great Learning and the Doctrine of the Mean*）

〔英〕理雅各（James Legge）編譯

《論語　大學　中庸》，英國理雅各編譯。理雅各（James Legge，一八一五—一八九七），英國倫敦會傳教士，法國漢學儒蓮獎首位得主。生於蘇格蘭亞伯丁郡，一八四三年來華，任香港英華書院首任校長。一八七六至一八九七年任牛津大學首任漢學教授，逝於任上。於一八六一至一八七二年相繼出版《中國經典》（*The Chinese Classics*）五卷，含《論語》、《大學》、《中庸》、《孟子》、《書經》、《詩經》及《春秋左傳》；於一八七九至一八九一年相繼出版《中國聖書》（*The Sacred Books of China*）六卷，含《書經》、《詩經》、《孝經》、《易經》、《禮記》、《道德經》、《莊子》及《太上感應篇》。諸種中國經典譯作，被後世奉爲標準譯本。「四書」爲理雅各首先翻譯者。理雅各所譯各書，皆附以原文、注釋及長篇緒論。其中《論語》譯本於前人注疏多所參考，尤多取朱熹之説，亦採諸朱注以外各家注解，評價辨析，略陳己見。《大學》、《中庸》譯本善於運用複雜句式結構及豐富詞藻，沉穩厚重。據一八六一年香港版影印。

論語 大學 中庸

THE CHINESE CLASSICS.

VOL. I.

CONFUCIAN ANALECTS, THE GREAT LEARNING, AND THE DOCTRINE OF THE MEAN.

不以文害辭，不以辭害志，以意逆志，是爲得之。

MENCIUS, V. Pt. II. iv. 2.

論語 大學 中庸

THE

CHINESE CLASSICS:

WITH

A TRANSLATION, CRITICAL AND EXEGETICAL NOTES, PROLEGOMENA, AND COPIOUS INDEXES.

BY

JAMES LEGGE, D.D.,

OF THE LONDON MISSIONARY SOCIETY.

IN SEVEN VOLUMES.

VOL. I.,

CONTAINING

CONFUCIAN ANALECTS, THE GREAT LEARNING, AND THE DOCTRINE OF THE MEAN.

HONGKONG: AT THE AUTHOR'S.

LONDON: TRÜBNER & CO., 60, PATERNOSTER ROW.

1861.

HONGKONG:

PRINTED AT THE LONDON MISSIONARY SOCIETY'S

PRINTING OFFICE.

TO THE MEMORY

OF

THE HON. JOSEPH JARDINE, ESQ.,

BY WHOSE MUNIFICENT ASSISTANCE IT IS NOW PUBLISHED,

AND BUT FOR WHICH IT MIGHT NEVER HAVE BEEN PUBLISHED,

This Work is inscribed.

PREFACE.

THE author arrived in the East as a Missionary towards the end of 1839, and was stationed at Malacca for between three and four years. Before leaving England, he had enjoyed the benefit of a few months' instruction in Chinese from the late Professor Kidd at the University of London, and was able in the beginning of 1840 to commence the study of the first of the Works in the present publication. It seemed to him then—and the experience of one and twenty years gives its sanction to the correctness of the judgment—that he should not be able to consider himself qualified for the duties of his position, until he had thoroughly mastered the Classical Books of the Chinese, and had investigated for himself the whole field of thought through which the sages of China had ranged, and in which were to be found the foundations of the moral, social, and political life of the people. Under this conviction he addressed himself eagerly to the reading of the Confucian Analects, and proceeded from them to the other Works. Circumstances occurred in the Mission at Malacca to throw various engagements upon him, which left him little time to spend at his books, and he consequently sought about for all the assistance which he could find from the labours of men who had gone before.

In this respect he was favourably situated, the charge of the Anglo-Chinese College having devolved upon him, so that he had free access to all the treasures in its Library. He had translations and dictionaries in abundance, and they facilitated his progress. Yet he desiderated some Work upon the Classics, more critical, more full and exact, than any which he had the opportunity of consulting, and he sketched to himself the plan of its execution. This was distinctly before him in 1841, and for several years he hoped to hear that some experienced Chinese scholar was preparing to give to the public something of the kind. As time went on, and he began to feel assured as to his own progress in the language, it occurred to him that he might venture on such an undertaking himself. He studied, wrote out translations, and made notes, with the project in his mind. He hopes he can say that it did not divert him from the usual active labours of a Missionary in preaching and teaching, but it did not allow him to rest satisfied in any operations of the time then being.

In 1856, he first talked with some of his friends about his purpose, and among them was the Rev. Josiah Cox, of the Wesleyan Missionary Society. The question of the expense of publication came up. The author's idea was that by-and-by he would be able to digest his materials in readiness for the press, and that then he would be likely, on application, to meet with such encouragement from the British and other foreign merchants in China, as would enable him to go forward with his plan. Mr. Cox, soon after, without the slightest intimation of his intention, mentioned the whole matter to his friend, Mr. Joseph Jardine. In consequence of what he reported of Mr. Jardine's sentiments, the author had an interview with that gentleman, when he very generously undertook to bear the expense of carrying the Work through the press. His lamented death leaves the author at liberty to speak more freely on this point than he would otherwise have done. Mr. Jardine expressed himself favourably of the plan, and said, "I know the liberality of the merchants in China, and that many of them would readily give their help to such an undertaking, but you need not have the trouble of canvassing the community. If you are prepared for the toil of the publication, I will bear the expense of it. We make our money in China, and we should be glad to assist in whatever promises to be of benefit to it."

The author could not but be grateful to Mr. Jardine for his proffer, nor did he hesitate to accept it. The interruption of missionary labours, consequent on the breaking out of hostilities in the end of 1856, was favourable to retired and literary work, and he immediately set about preparing some of his materials for the press. A necessary visit to England in 1857, which kept him absent from the Colony for eighteen months, proved a serious interruption, but the first-fruits of his labours are now in a state to be presented to the public.

The first conception of the present work and the circumstances under which it is published have thus been detailed. Of the style and manner of its execution it is for others to judge. It originated in the author's feeling of his own wants. He has translated, annotated, and reasoned, always in the first place to satisfy himself. He hopes that the volumes will be of real service to Missionaries and other students of the Chinese language and literature. They have been foremost in his mind as those whom he wished to benefit. But he has thought also of the general reader. The Chinese is the largest family of mankind. Thoughtful minds in other parts of the world cannot but be anxious to know what the minds of this many-millioned people have had to live upon for thousands of years. The Work will enable them to draw their own conclusions on the subject. The author will give his views on the scope and value of their contents in his prolegomena to the several volumes. Some will agree with his opinions, and others will probably differ from them. He only hopes that he will be found to advance no judgment for which he does not render a reason. To think freely and for himself is a source to him of much happiness; his object is to supply to others the means of realizing the same for themselves, so far as the subjects here investigated are concerned. He hopes also that the time is not very remote, when among the Chinese themselves there will be found many men of intelligence, able and willing to read without prejudice what he may say about the teachings of their sages.

The title-page says that the Work will be in seven volumes,—two, that is, for the Four Books, and one for each of the Five King. It will be necessary, however, from their size, to publish more than one of the latter in two or more parts, so that to the eye the Work will present the appearance perhaps of ten volumes. Should life and health be spared, the author would like to give a supplementary volume or two, so as to embrace all the Books in "The Thirteen King." The second volume is two-thirds printed, and will appear, God willing, before the end of the present year He must then be permitted to rest for a time, before proceeding with the Shoo-king or The Book of History. His directly missionary labours are the chief business of his life, and require of course his chief attention. The fact that the Work is inscribed to the memory of Mr. Jardine impresses him deeply with the frailty of life and the uncertainty of all human plans. While he has been putting the finishing hand to this first volume, the same solemn truth has been still more realizingly forced upon him by the news of the death of his own eldest brother, the thought of giving pleasure to whom by the publication was one of the greatest stimuli under the toil of its preparation. Whether he shall be permitted to accomplish what he contemplates, the future alone can determine.

It would have been an easy matter to swell the volume now presented to double the size. In the Chinese Commentators he had abundant materials to do so; but the author's object has been to condense rather than expand. He has not sought to follow Choo He or any other authority. The text, and not the commentary, has been his study. He has read the varying views of scholars extensively, but only that he might the better understand what was written in the Book. He has also consulted the renderings of other translators, but never till he had made his own. He may have sometimes altered his own to adopt a happier expression from them, but the translation is independent. He has not made frequent mention in his notes of the labours of other scholars,—not because he undervalues them, but because there was no necessity to call attention to the circumstance, where he agreed with them, and where he differed, he thought it more seemly to avoid "doubtful disputations."

In expressing the sounds of proper names, the author has followed the orthography of Morrison and Medhurst; and in the index of Chinese characters he has given, in addition, that of Mr. Wade, taken from his "Peking Syllabary." Yet he is afraid that Mr. Wade may find some characters incorrectly represented, as the author could only fix their pronunciation by the analogy of others. It may seem strange also to some scholars, that where he has spoken in the notes of the tones of characters, he has assumed that in the Court dialect there are eight tones in the same way as in the dialect of Canton Province. The author has not paid sufficient attention to the Court dialect to justify his speaking on this point with positiveness. If K'ang-he's dictionary were to determine the question, it could be shown that a distinction of "upper" and "lower" is made in all the tones, and not in the first or "even" one only. The author, moreover, has fancied that he could detect that distinction in the pronunciation of teachers of the Court dialect. On this subject, however, he speaks with submission.

There are many deficiencies in the present volume in point of typographical execution, for which the author ventures to ask the indulgence of the reader. The only workmen employed upon it have been Chinese. He is under great obligation to his excellent friend, Mr. Hwang Shing, the superintendent of the Mission Printing Office; but well-skilled as he is in the English language, he could not perform the duties of proof-reader. The work of correction has mainly devolved on the author himself or members of his family, and has been done when the mind was otherwise occupied, or amid constant interruptions. The errors would have been much more numerous than they are but for the great kindness of Mr. Jeffrey, formerly of the "China Mail" Office, who has read nearly all the sheets before their finally going to press. To Mr. Low, of the same Office, and latterly to Mr. Dixson, the proprietor of the "China Mail," the author is glad to take this opportunity of expressing his thanks for their advice and help in many typographical matters. The more serious mistakes will be found corrected, it is hoped, in the subjoined lists. For others of smaller importance the circumstances just mentioned may form some apology; and where the sound of a Chinese character may in a few instances have been represented somewhat incorrectly, the character itself in a foot-note, or its sound in the 7th Index, will supply the necessary correction. The author has likewise to thank his friend, and former colleague in the Mission at Hongkong, the Rev. Mr. Chalmers, for the compilation of the indexes of Subjects and Proper Names.

HONGKONG, 26*th March* 1861.

CONTENTS.

I. THE PROLEGOMENA.

CHAPTER I.

OF THE CHINESE CLASSICS GENERALLY.

CHAPTER II.

OF THE CONFUCIAN ANALECTS.

CHAPTER III.

OF THE GREAT LEARNING.

CHAPTER IV.

THE DOCTRINE OF THE MEAN.

CHAPTER V.

CONFUCIUS AND HIS IMMEDIATE DISCIPLES.

目録

CHAPTER VI.

LIST OF THE PRINCIPAL WORKS WHICH HAVE BEEN CONSULTED IN THE PREPARATION OF THIS VOLUME.

II. THE BODY OF THE VOLUME.

III. INDEXES.

ERRATA.

I. IN THE CHINESE TEXT.

Page.	*Column.*		*Page.*	*Column.*	
3,	2,	for 人 read 仁.	185,	9,	for 湼 read 涅.
21,	1,	日 is inverted.	199,	5,	秐 " 芸.
70,	9,	for 祗 read 祇.	228,	8,	之 " 知
92,	4,	transpose 右 左.	230,	4,	裹 " 裏.
101,	2,	for 體 read 禮.	237,	9,	毋 " 毌.
114,	5,	仁 " 人.	256,	1,	致 " 至.
116,	2,	巳 " 矣.	273,	6,	事 " 士.
"	6,	爲 " 謂.	283,	2,	transpose 內 外.
130,	10,	日 is inverted.	285,	2,	for 洩 read 泄.
142,	10,	for 蔬 read 疏.	290,	4,	after 質 insert 諸.
143,	3,	舞 " 無.	295,	4,	for 曰 read 日.
181,	7,	典 " 與,			

PAGE 11, between the 6th and 7th Columns, for 篇 read 節.
" 25,..................... " " ,,..............., " *dele* 二節.
" 26,.....................1st and 2d..........., " 二節.
" " ....4th and 5th..........,for 三 read 二.
" 75,.....................3d and 4th............,by 成 insert 三節.
" 116,.....................6th and 7th........., after 乎 " 三節.
" 258,.....................3d and 4th. ....,for 二 read 三.
" 293,..................... " " " ...., " 五 " 四

II. CHINESE CHARACTERS IN THE NOTES.

Page.	Line.	Column.		
3,	29,	II.,	for 安	read 晏.
7,	10,	„	„ 約	„ 信.
49,	1,	„	„ 再	„ 冉.
52,	3,	I.,	„ 再	„ 冉.
88,	6,	II.,	„ 未	„ 末.
102,	9,	„	„ 溝	„ 講.
117,	6,	„	„ 讃	„ 譖.
138,	2,	„	„ 犀	„ 遲.
141,	3,	„	„ 堯	„ 澆.
152,	5,	„	„ 恩	„ 怨.
160,	2,	I.,	„ 狛	„ 狄.
173,	16,	II.,	„ 蕭	„ 肅.
182,	22,	I.,	for 明	read 日 月.
193,	2,	„	„ 以	„ 矣.
197,	4,	„	„ 澄	„ 證.
207,	1,	II.,	„ 酒	„ 洒.
227,	10,	„	„ 獻	„ 獻.
250,	12,	„ *et al.*,	„ 尼	„ 尼.
257,	3,	„	„ 照	„ 昭.
264,	12,	I.,	„ 栽	„ 栽.
269,	18,	„	„ 廬	„ 盧.
293,	15,	„	„ 貉	„ 貊.
294,	5,	„	„ 旦	„ 但.
—,	4,	II.,	„ 廬	„ 慮.

III. IN THE PROLEGOMENA.

Page.	Line.	
2,	24,	for Kuh Leang-ch'ih read Kuh-leang Ch'ih.
4,	6,	for 4... ... „ ... ... 6.
10,	24,	„ Lëang „ ... ... Lew.
15,	15,	„ 490 ... „ ... ... 430.
20,	11,	for P'ing read ... ... Ping.
40,	34,	„ transpose „ K'ung and Sung.
67,	14,	„ who „ ... ... which.
85,	15,	„ ages „ ... ... sages.

IV. IN THE TRANSLATION AND NOTES..

1,	3,	for pleasant read ... delightful.
130,	5,	„ government „ governments.
155,	6,	refer to char. 厲, Index vii.
183,	1,	for hing read ... ...shing.
201,	9,	„ no body „ ... ... nobody.
26,	17, col. II.,	for 540 read ... 642.
„	18, „ „	„ *p'a.* „ ... *pa.*
166,	26, „ I.,	„ BEAD „ ... HAND.
269,	6, „ I.,	„ ships „... ... slips.
271,	23, „ II.,	„ *Not, Lin, Sin,* read *Not. Lin. Sin.*

緒論

PROLEGOMENA.

CHAPTER I.

OF THE CHINESE CLASSICS GENERALLY.

SECTION I.

BOOKS INCLUDED UNDER THE NAME OF THE CHINESE CLASSICS.

1. The Books now recognized as of highest authority in China are comprehended under the denominations of "The five *King*,"[1] and "The four *Shoo*."[2] The term *King* is of textile origin, and signifies the warp threads of a web, and their adjustment. An easy application of it is to denote what is regular and insures regularity. As used with reference to books, it indicates their authority on the subjects of which they treat. "The five *King*" are the five *canonical* Works, containing the truth upon the highest subjects from the sages of China, and which should be received as law by all generations. The term *Shoo* simply means *Writings* or *Books*.

2. The five King are:—the *Yih*,[3] or, as it has been styled, "The Book of Changes;" the *Shoo*,[4] or "The Book of History;" the *She*,[5] or "The Book of Poetry;" the Le Ke,[6] or "Record of Rites;" and the Ch'un Ts'ew,[7] or "Spring and Autumn," a chronicle of events, extending from 721 to 480, B.C. The authorship, or compilation rather, of all these works is loosely attributed to Confucius. But much of the Le Ke is from later hands. Of the Yih, the Shoo, and the She, it is only in the first that we find additions from the philosopher himself, in the shape of appendixes. The Ch'un Ts'ew is the only one of the five King which can rightly be described as of his own "making."

[1] 五經. [2] 四書. [3] 易經. [4] 書經. [5] 詩經. [6] 禮記. [7] 春秋.

"The four Books" is an abbreviation for "The Books of the four Philosophers." [8] The first is the Lun Yu,[9] or "Digested Conversations," being occupied chiefly with the sayings of Confucius. He is the philosopher to whom it belongs. It appears in this Work under the title of "Confucian Analects." The second is the Ta Hëŏ,[10] or "Great Learning," now commonly attributed to Tsăng Sin,[11] a disciple of the sage. He is the philosopher of it. The third is the Chung Yung,[12] or "Doctrine of the Mean," ascribed to K'ung Keih,[13] the grandson of Confucius. He is the philosopher of it. The fourth contains the works of Mencius.

3. This arrangement of the Classical Books, which is commonly supposed to have originated with the scholars of the Sung dynasty, is defective. The *Great Learning* and the *Doctrine of the Mean* are both found in the Record of Rites, being the forty-second and thirty-first Books respectively of that compilation, according to the usual arrangement of it.

4. The oldest enumerations of the Classical Books specify only *the five King*. The Yŏ Ke, or "Record of Music,"[14] the remains of which now form one of the Books in the Le Ke, was sometimes added to those, making with them the *six King*. A division was also made into *nine King*, consisting of the Yih, the She, the Shoo, the Chow Le,[15] or "Ritual of Chow," the E Le,[16] or "Ceremonial Usages," the Le Ke, and the three annotated editions of the Ch'un Ts'ew,[17] by Tso-k'ew Ming,[18] Kung-yang Kaou,[19] and Kuh Lëang-ch'ih.[20] In the famous compilation of the classical Books, undertaken by order of T'ae-tsung, the second emperor of the T'ang dynasty (B.C. 627–649), and which appeared in the reign of his successor, there are *thirteen King*; viz., the Yih, the She, the Shoo, the three editions of the Ch'un Ts'ew, the Le Ke, the Chow Le, the E Le, the Confucian Analects, the Urh Ya,[21] a sort of ancient dictionary, the Heaou King,[22] or "Classic of Filial Piety," and the works of Mencius.

5. A distinction, however, was made among the Works thus comprehended under the same common name, and Mencius, the Lun Yu, the Ta Hëŏ, the Chung Yung, and the Heaou King were spoken of as the seaou King, or "smaller Classics." It thus appears,

[8] 四子之書. [9] 論語. [10] 大學. [11] 曾參. [12] 中庸. [13] 孔伋. [14] 樂記. [15] 周禮. [16] 儀禮. [17] 春秋三傳. [18] 左丘明. [19] 公羊高. [20] 穀梁赤. [21] 爾雅. [22] 孝經.

contrary to the ordinary opinion on the subject, that the Ta Hëŏ and Chung Yung had been published as separate treatises before the Sung dynasty, and that the Four Books, as distinguished from the greater King, had also previously found a place in the literature of China.[23]

SECTION II.

THE AUTHORITY OF THE CHINESE CLASSICS.

1. This subject will be discussed in connection with each separate Work, and it is only designed here to exhibit generally the evidence on which the Chinese Classics claim to be received as genuine productions of the time to which they are referred.

2. In the memoirs of the Former Han dynasty (B.C. 201—A.D. 24), we have one chapter which we may call the History of Literature.[1] It commences thus:—"After the death of Confucius,[2] there was an end of his exquisite words; and when his seventy disciples had passed away, violence began to be done to their meaning. It came about that there were five different editions of the Ch'un Ts'ew, four of the She, and several of the Yih. Amid the disorder and collision of the warring States (B.C. 480–221), truth and falsehood were still more in a state of warfare, and a sad confusion marked the words of the various scholars. Then came the calamity inflicted under the Ts'in dynasty (B.C. 220–200), when the literary monuments were destroyed by fire, in order to keep the people in ignorance. But, by-and-by, there arose the Han dynasty, which set itself to remedy the evil wrought by the Ts'in. Great efforts were made to collect slips and tablets,[3] and the way was thrown wide open for the bringing in of Books. In the time of the emperor Heaou-woo[4] (B.C. 139–86), portions of Books being wanting and tablets lost, so that ceremonies and music were suffering great

23 For the statements in the two last paragraphs, see 西河合集,大學證文,卷一.

1 前漢書,本志,第十卷,藝文志. 2 仲尼. 3 篇籍,—slips and tablets on bamboo, which supplied in those days the place of paper. 4 世宗孝武皇帝.

3]

damage, he was moved to sorrow, and said, 'I am very sad for this.' He therefore formed the plan of Repositories, in which the Books might be stored, and appointed officers to transcribe Books on an extensive scale, embracing the works of the various scholars, that they might all be placed in the Repositories. The emperor Shing[5] (B.C. 31–4), finding that a portion of the Books still continued dispersed or missing, commissioned Ch'in Nung, the superintendent of guests,[6] to search for undiscovered Books throughout the empire, and by special edict ordered the chief of the Banqueting House, Lew Heang,[7] to examine the classical Works, along with the commentaries on them, the writings of the scholars, and all poetical productions; the master-controller of infantry, Jin Hwang,[8] to examine the Books on the art of war; the grand historiographer, Yin Hëen,[9] to examine the Books treating of the art of numbers (*i.e.*, divination); and the imperial physician, Le Ch'oo-kŏ,[10] to examine the books on medicine. Whenever any Book was done with, Heang forthwith arranged it, indexed it, and made a digest of it, which was presented to the emperor. While the undertaking was in progress, Heang died, and the emperor Gae (B.C. 5—A.D.) appointed his son, Hin,[11] a master of the imperial carriages, to complete his father's work. On this, Hin collected all the books, and presented a report of them, under seven divisions."

The first of these divisions seems to have been a general catalogue,[12] containing perhaps only the titles of the works included in the other six. The second embraced the classical Works.[13] From the abstract of it, which is preserved in the chapter referred to, we find that there were 294 collections of the Yih-king, from 13 different individuals or editors;[14] 412 collections of the Shoo-king, from 9 different individuals; 416 volumes of the She-king, from 6 different individuals;[15] of the Books of Rites, 555 collections, from 13

5 孝成皇帝. 6 謁者陳農. 7 光祿大夫劉向. 8 步兵校尉任宏. 9 太史令尹咸. 10 侍醫李柱國. 11 侍中奉車都尉歆. 12 輯略. 13 六藝略. 14 凡易,十三家,二百九十四篇. How much of the whole Work was contained in each 篇, it is impossible for us to ascertain. P. Regis says:—"*Pien, quemadmodum Gallice dicimus 'des pieces d'eloquence, de poesie.'*" 15 詩,六家,四百一十六卷. The collections of the She-king are mentioned under the name of *Keuen*, 'sections,' 'portions.' Had *p'ëen* been used, it might have been understood of individual odes. This change of terms shows that by *p'ëen* in the other summaries, we are not to understand single blocks or chapters.

緒論

different individuals; of the Books on Music, 165 collections, from 6 different editors; 948 collections of History, under the heading of the Ch'un Ts'ew, from 23 different individuals; 229 collections of the Lun Yu, including the Analects and kindred fragments, from 12 different individuals; of the Heaou-king, embracing also the Urh Ya, and some other portions of the ancient literature, 59 collections, from 11 different individuals; and finally of the Lesser Learning, being works on the form of the characters, 45 collections, from 11 different individuals. The Works of Mencius were included in the second division,[16] among the Writings of what were deemed orthodox scholars,[17] of which there were 836 collections, from 53 different individuals.

3. The above important document is sufficient to show how the emperors of the Han dynasty, as soon as they had made good their possession of the empire, turned their attention to recover the ancient literature of the nation, the Classical Books engaging their first care, and how earnestly and effectively the scholars of the time responded to the wishes of their rulers. In addition to the facts specified in the preface to it, I may relate that the ordinance of the Ts'in dynasty against possessing the Classical Books (with the exception, as will appear in its proper place, of the Yih-king) was repealed by the second sovereign of the Han, the emperor Heaou Hwuy,[18] in the 4th year of his reign, B.C. 190, and that a large portion of the Shoo-king was recovered in the time of the third emperor, B.C. 178–156, while in the year B.C. 135, a special Board was constituted, consisting of literati who were put in charge of the five *King*.[19]

4. The collections reported on by Lew Hin suffered damage in the troubles which began A.D. 8, and continued till the rise of the second or eastern Han dynasty in the year 25. The founder of it (A.D. 25–57) zealously promoted the undertaking of his predecessors, and additional repositories were required for the books which were collected. His successors, the emperors, Heaou-ming[20] (58–75), Heaou-chang[21] (76–88), and Heaou-hwo[22] (89–105), took a part themselves in the studies and discussions of the literary tribunal,

16 諸子略. 17 儒家者流. 18 孝惠皇帝. 19 武帝建元五年, 初置五經博士. 20 顯宗孝明皇帝. 21 肅宗孝章皇帝. 22 孝和皇帝.

5]

and the emperor Heaou-ling,[23] between the years 172–178, had the text of the five *King*, as it had been fixed, cut in slabs of stone, in characters of three different forms.

5. Since the Han, the successive dynasties have considered the literary monuments of the country to be an object of their special care. Many of them have issued editions of the classics, embodying the commentaries of preceding generations. No dynasty has distinguished itself more in this line than the present Manchew possessors of the Empire. In fine, the evidence is complete that the Classical Books of China have come down from at least a century before our Christian era, substantially the same as we have them at present.

6. But it still remains to inquire in what condition we may suppose the Books were, when the scholars of the Han dynasty commenced their labours upon them. They acknowledge that the tablets—we cannot here speak of *manuscripts*—were mutilated and in disorder. Was the injury which they had received of such an extent that all the care and study put forth on the small remains would be of little use? This question can be answered satisfactorily, only by an examination of the evidence which is adduced for the text of each particular Classic; but it can be made apparent that there is nothing, in the nature of the case, to interfere with our believing that the materials were sufficient to enable the scholars to execute the work intrusted to them.

7. The burning of the ancient Books by order of the founder of the Ts'in dynasty is always referred to as the greatest disaster which they sustained, and with this is coupled the slaughter of many of the Literati by the same monarch.

The account which we have of these transactions in the Historical Records is the following:—[24]

"In his 34th year," (the 34th year, that is, after he had ascended the throne of Ts'in. It was only the 8th after he had been acknowledged Sovereign of the empire, coinciding with B.C. 212), the emperor, returning from a visit to the south, which had extended as far as Yuĕ, gave a feast in the palace of Heen-yang, when the Great

23 孝靈皇帝. 24 I have thought it well to endeavour to translate the whole of the passages. Father de Mailla merely constructs from them a narrative of his own; see *L'Histoire Generale de La Chine*, tome II., pp. 399-402. The 通鑑綱目 avoids the difficulties of the original by giving an abridgment of it.

緒論

Scholars, amounting to seventy men, appeared and wished him long life.[25] One of the principal ministers, Chow Ts'ing-shin,[26] came forward and said, 'Formerly, the State of Ts'in was only 1,000 le in extent, but Your Majesty, by your spirit-like efficacy and intelligent wisdom, has tranquillized and settled the whole empire, and driven away all barbarous tribes, so that, wherever the sun and moon shine, all appear before you as guests acknowledging subjection. You have formed the States of the various princes into provinces and districts, where the people enjoy a happy tranquillity, suffering no more from the calamities of war and contention. This condition of things will be transmitted for 10,000 generations. From the highest antiquity there has been no one in awful virtue like Your Majesty.'

"The Emperor was pleased with this flattery, when Shun Yuĕ,[27] one of the great scholars, a native of Ts'e, advanced and said, 'The sovereigns of Yin and Chow, for more than a thousand years, invested their sons and younger brothers, and meritorious ministers, with domains and rule, and could thus depend upon them for support and aid;—that I have heard. But now Your Majesty is in possession of all within the seas, and your sons and younger brothers are nothing but private individuals. The issue will be that some one will arise to play the part of T'een Chang,[28] or of the six nobles *of Tsin.* Without the support *of your own family*, where will you find the aid which you may require? That a state of things not modelled from the lessons of antiquity can long continue;—that is what I have not heard. Ts'ing is now showing himself to be a flatterer, who increases the errors of Your Majesty, and not a loyal minister.'

"The Emperor requested the opinions of others on this representation, when the premier, Le Sze,[29] said, 'The five emperors were not one the double of the other, nor did the three dynasties accept one another's ways. Each had a peculiar system of government, not for the sake of the contrariety, but as being required by the changed times. Now, Your Majesty has laid the foundations of imperial sway, so that it will last for 10,000 generations. This is

25 博士七十人前爲壽. The 博士 were not only 'great scholars,' but had an official rank. There was what we may call a college of them, consisting of seventy members. 26 僕射,周靑臣. 27 淳于越. 28 田常,—常 should probably be 恆, as it is given in the T'ung Këën. 29 丞相李斯.

7]

indeed beyond what a stupid scholar can understand. And, moreover, Yuĕ only talks of things belonging to the Three Dynasties, which are not fit to be models to you. At other times, when the princes were all striving together, they endeavoured to gather the wandering scholars about them; but now, the empire is in a stable condition, and laws and ordinances issue from one *supreme authority*. Let those of the people who abide in their homes give their strength to the toils of husbandry, and those who become scholars should study the various laws and prohibitions. Instead of doing this, however, the scholars do not learn what belongs to the present day, but study antiquity. They go on to condemn the present time, leading the masses of the people astray, and to disorder.

"At the risk of my life, I, the prime minister, say,—Formerly, when the empire was disunited and disturbed, there was no one who could give unity to it. The princes therefore stood up together; constant references were made to antiquity to the injury of the present state; baseless statements were dressed up to confound what was real, and men made a boast of their own peculiar learning to condemn what their rulers appointed. And now, when Your Majesty has consolidated the empire, and, distinguishing black from white, has constituted it a stable unity, they still honour their peculiar learning, and combine together; they teach men what is contrary to your laws. When they hear that an ordinance has been issued, every one sets to discussing it with his learning. In the court, they are dissatisfied in heart; out of it, they keep talking in the streets. While they make a pretence of vaunting their Master, they consider it fine to have extraordinary views of their own. And so they lead on the people to be guilty of murmuring and evil speaking. If these things are not prohibited, Your Majesty's authority will decline, and parties will be formed. The best way is to prohibit them. I pray that all the Records in charge of the Historiographers be burned, excepting those of Ts'in; that, with the exception of those officers belonging to the Board of Great Scholars, all throughout the empire who presume to keep copies of the She-king, or of the Shoo-king, or of the books of the Hundred Schools, be required to go with them to the officers in charge of the several districts, and burn them;[30] that all who may dare to speak together

30 悉詣守尉雜燒之

緒論

about the She and the Shoo be put to death, and their bodies exposed in the market place; that those who make mention of the past, so as to blame the present, be put to death along with their relatives; that officers who shall know of the violation of those rules and not inform against the offenders, be held equally guilty with them; and that whoever shall not have burned their Books within thirty days after the issuing of the ordinance, be branded and sent to labour on the wall for four years. The only Books which should be spared are those on medicine, divination, and husbandry. Whoever wants to learn the laws may go to the magistrates and learn of them.'

"The imperial decision was—'Approved.'"

The destruction of the scholars is related more briefly. In the year after the burning of the Books, the resentment of the emperor was excited by the remarks and flight of two scholars who had been favourites with him, and he determined to institute a strict inquiry about all of their class in Hëen-yang, to find out whether they had been making ominous speeches about him, and disturbing the minds of the people. The investigation was committed to the Censors,[31] and it being discovered that upwards of 460 scholars had violated the prohibitions, they were all buried alive in pits,[32] for a warning to the empire, while degradation and banishment were employed more strictly than before against all who fell under suspicion. The emperor's eldest son, Foo-soo, remonstrated with him, saying that such measures against those who repeated the words of Confucius and sought to imitate him, would alienate all the people from their infant dynasty, but his interference offended his father so much that he was sent off from court, to be with the general who was superintending the building of the great wall.

8. No attempts have been made by Chinese critics and historians to discredit the record of these events, though some have questioned the extent of the injury inflicted by them on the monuments of their ancient literature.[33] It is important to observe that the edict against the Books did not extend to the Yih-king, which was

31 御史悉案問諸生，諸生傳相告引. 32 自除犯禁者，四百六十餘人，皆阬之咸陽. The meaning of this passage as a whole is sufficiently plain, but I am unable to make out the force of the phrase 自除. 33 See the remarks of Ch'ing Këä-tse (夾際鄭氏), of the Sung dynasty, on the subject, in the 文獻通考, Bk. clxxiv. p. 5.

exempted as being a work on divination, nor did it extend to the other classics which were in charge of the Board of Great Scholars. It is still more important to note that the burning took place only three years before the death of the tyrant who commanded it. He died B.C. 209, and the feeble reign of his second son, who succeeded him, lasted only three years. A brief season of disorder and struggling between different chiefs for the supreme authority ensued, but the reign of the founder of the Han dynasty dates from B.C. 201. Thus, eleven years were all which intervened between the order for the burning of the Books and the rise of that family, which signalized itself by the care which it bestowed for their recovery; and from the edict of the tyrant of Ts'in against private individuals having copies in their keeping, to its express abrogation by the emperor Heaou Hwuy, there were only 22 years. We may believe, indeed, that vigorous efforts to carry the edict into effect would not be continued longer than the life of its author,—that is, not for more than about three years. The calamity inflicted on the ancient Books of China by the House of Ts'in could not have approached to anything like a complete destruction of them. There would be no occasion for the scholars of the Han dynasty, in regard to the bulk of their ancient literature, to undertake more than the work of recension and editing.

9. The idea of forgery by them on a large scale is out of the question. The catalogues of Leang Hin enumerated more than 13,000 volumes of a larger or smaller size, the productions of nearly 600 different writers, and arranged in 38 subdivisions of subjects.[34] In the third catalogue, the first subdivision contained the orthodox writers,[35] to the number of 53, with 836 Works or portions of their Works. Between Mencius and K'ung Keih, the grandson of Confucius, eight different authors have place. The second subdivision contained the Works of the Taouist school,[36] amounting to 993 collections, from 37 different authors. The sixth subdivision contained the Mihist writers,[37] to the number of 6, with their productions in 86 collections. I specify these two subdivisions, because they embraced the Works of schools or sects antagonist to that of Confucius, and some of them still hold a place in Chinese literature,

[34] 凡書六略，三十八種，五百九十六家，萬三千二百六十九卷. [35] 儒家者流. [36] 道家者流. [37] 墨家者流.

緒論

and contain many references to the five Classics, and to Confucius and his disciples.

10. The inquiry pursued in the above paragraphs conducts us to the conclusion that the materials from which the Classics, as they have come down to us, were compiled and edited in the two centuries preceding our Christian era, were genuine remains, going back to a still more remote period. The injury which they sustained from the dynasty of Ts'in was, I believe, the same in character as that to which they were exposed, during all the time of "the Warring States." It may have been more intense in degree, but the constant warfare which prevailed for some centuries among the different States which composed the empire was eminently unfavourable to the cultivation of literature. Mencius tells us how the princes had made away with many of the records of antiquity, from which their own usurpations and innovations might have been condemned.[38] Still the times were not unfruitful, either in scholars or statesmen, to whom the ways and monuments of antiquity were dear, and the space from the rise of the Ts'in dynasty to Confucius was not very great. It only amounted to 258 years. Between these two periods Mencius stands as a connecting link. Born probably in the year B.C. 371, he reached, by the intervention of K'ung Keih, back to the sage himself, and as his death happened B.C. 288, we are brought down to within nearly half a century of the Ts'in dynasty. From all these considerations we may proceed with confidence to consider each separate Work, believing that we have in these Classics and Books what the great sage of China and his disciples gave to their country more than 2,000 years ago.

38. See Mencius, V. Pt. II. ii. 2.

11]

CHAPTER II.

OF THE CONFUCIAN ANALECTS.

SECTION I.

FORMATION OF THE TEXT OF THE ANALECTS BY THE SCHOLARS OF THE HAN DYNASTY.

1. When the work of collecting and editing the remains of the Classical Books was undertaken by the scholars of Han, there appeared two different copies of the Analects, one from Loo, the native State of Confucius, and the other from Ts'e, the State adjoining. Between these there were considerable differences. The former consisted of twenty Books or Chapters, the same as those into which the Classic is now divided. The latter contained two Books in addition, and in the twenty Books, which they had in common, the chapters and sentences were somewhat more numerous than in the Loo exemplar.

2. The names of several individuals are given, who devoted themselves to the study of those two copies of the Classic. Among the patrons of the Loo copy are mentioned the names of Shing, the prince of Hea, grand-tutor of the heir-apparent, who died at the age of 90, and in the reign of the emperor Seuen (B.C. 72—48);[1] Seaou Wang-che,[2] a general officer, who died in the reign of the emperor Yuen, (B.C. 47–32); Wei Heen, who was premier of the empire from B.C. 70–66; and his son Heuen-shing.[3] As patrons of the Ts'e, copy, we have Wang K'ing, who was a censor in the year B.C. 99;[4] Yung Shang,[5] and Wang Keih,[6] a statesman who died in the beginning of the reign of the emperor Yuen.

3. But a third copy of the Analects was discovered about B.C. 150. One of the sons of the emperor King was appointed king of Loo,[7] in the year B.C. 153, and some time after, wishing to enlarge his palace, he proceeded to pull down the house of the K'ung family, known as that where Confucius himself had lived. While doing so,

[1] 太子大傅夏侯勝. [2] 前將軍,蕭望之. [3] 丞相,韋賢,及子,玄成. [4] 王卿. [5] 庸生. [6] 中尉王吉. [7] 魯王共(or 恭).

there were found in the wall copies of the Shoo-king, the Ch'un Ts'ew, the Heaou-king, and the Lun Yu or Analects, which had been deposited there, when the edict for the burning of the Books was issued. They were all written, however, in the most ancient form of the Chinese character,[8] which had fallen into disuse, and the king returned them to the K'ung family, the head of which, K'ung Gan-kwŏ,[9] gave himself to the study of them, and finally, in obedience to an imperial order, published a Work called "The Lun Yu, with Explanations of the Characters, and Exhibition of the Meaning."[10]

4. The recovery of this copy will be seen to be a most important circumstance in the history of the text of the Analects. It is referred to by Chinese writers, as "The old Lun Yu." In the historical narrative which we have of the affair, a circumstance is added which may appear to some minds to throw suspicion on the whole account. The king was finally arrested, we are told, in his purpose to destroy the house, by hearing the sounds of bells, musical stones, lutes, and harpsichords, as he was ascending the steps that led to the ancestral hall or temple. This incident was contrived, we may suppose, by the K'ung family, to preserve the house, or it may have been devised by the historian to glorify the sage, but we may not, on account of it, discredit the finding of the ancient copies of the Books. We have K'ung Gan-kwŏ's own account of their being committed to him, and of the ways which he took to decipher them. The work upon the Analects, mentioned above, has not indeed come down to us, but his labours on the Shoo-king still remain.

5. It has been already stated, that the Lun Yu of Ts'e contained two Books more than that of Loo. In this respect, the old Lun Yu agreed with the Loo exemplar. Those two books were wanting it in as well. The last book of the Loo Lun was divided in it, however, into two, the chapter beginning, "Yaou said," forming a whole Book by itself, and the remaining two chapters formed another Book beginning "Tsze-chang." With this trifling difference, the old and the Loo copies appear to have agreed together.

8 科斗文子,—lit., 'tadpole characters.' They were, it is said, the original forms devised by Ts'ang-Këĕ, with large heads and fine tails, like the creature from which they were named. See the notes to the preface to the Shoo-king in 'The thirteen Classics.' 9 孔安國. 10 論語訓解. See the Preface to the Lun Yu in 'The thirteen King.' It has been my principal authority in this Section.

6. Chang Yu, prince of Gan-ch'ang, who died B.C. 4, after having sustained several of the highest offices of the empire, instituted a comparison between the exemplars of Loo and Ts'e, with a view to determine the true text. The result of his labours appeared in twenty-one Books, which are mentioned in Lew Hin's catalogue. They were known as the Lun of the prince Chang,[12] and commanded general approbation. To Chang Yu is commonly ascribed the ejecting from the Classic the two additional books which the Ts'e exemplar contained, but Ma Twan-lin prefers to rest that circumstance on the authority of the old Lun, which we have seen was without them.[13] If we had the two Books, we might find sufficient reason from their contents to discredit them. That may have been sufficient for Chang Yu to condemn them as he did, but we can hardly suppose that he did not have before him the old Lun, which had come to light about a century before he published his Work.

7. In the course of the second century, a new edition of the Analects, with a commentary, was published by one of the greatest scholars which China has ever produced, Ch'ing Heuen, known also as Ch'ing K'ang-shing.[14] He died in the reign of the emperor Heen (A.D. 190–220) at the age of 74, and the amount of his labours on the ancient classical literature is almost incredible. While he adopted the Loo Lun as the received text of his time, he compared it minutely with those of Ts'e and the old exemplar. In the last section of this chapter will be found a list of the readings in his commentary different from those which are now acknowledged, in deference to the authority of Choo He, of the Sung dynasty. They are not many, and their importance is but trifling.

8. On the whole, the above statements will satisfy the reader of the care with which the text of the Lun Yu was fixed during the dynasty of Han.

SECTION II.

AT WHAT TIME, AND BY WHOM, THE ANALECTS WERE WRITTEN; THEIR PLAN; AND AUTHENTICITY.

1 At the commencement of the notes upon the first Book, under the heading—"The Title of the Work," I have given the received

11 安昌侯,張禹. 12 張侯論. 13 文獻通考, Bk. clxxxiv. p. 3.
14 鄭玄,字康成. 15 孝獻皇帝.

緒論

account of its authorship, taken from the "History of Literature" of the western Han dynasty. According to that, the Analects were compiled by the disciples of Confucius, coming together after his death, and digesting the memorials of his discourses and conversations which they had severally preserved. But this cannot be true. We may believe, indeed, that many of the disciples put on record conversations which they had had with their master, and notes about his manners and incidents of his life, and that these have been incorporated with the Work which we have, but that Work must have taken its present form at a period somewhat later.

In Book VIII., chapters iii. and iv., we have some notices of the last days of Tsăng Sin, and are told that he was visited on his death-bed by the officer Măng King. Now *King* was the posthumous title of Chung-sun Tsëĕ,[1] and we find him alive, (Le Ke, II. Pt. II. ii. 2) after the death of duke To of Loo,[2] which took place B.C. 490, about fifty years after the death of Confucius.

Again, Book XIX. is all occupied with the sayings of the disciples. Confucius personally does not appear in it. Parts of it, as chapters iii., xii., and xviii., carry us down to a time when the disciples had schools and followers of their own, and were accustomed to sustain their teachings by referring to the lessons which they had heard from the sage.

Thirdly, there is the second chapter of Book XI., the second paragraph of which is evidently a note by the compilers of the Work, enumerating ten of the principal disciples, and classifying them according to their distinguishing characteristics. We can hardly suppose it to have been written while any of the ten were alive. But there is among them the name of Tsze-hea, who lived to the age of about a hundred. We find him, B.C. 406, three quarters of a century after the death of Confucius, at the court of Wei, to the prince of which he is reported to have presented some of the Classical Books.[3]

2. We cannot therefore accept the above account of the origin of the Analects,—that they were compiled by the disciples of Confucius. Much more likely is the view that we owe the work to their disciples. In the note on I. ii. 1, a peculiarity is pointed out in the

1 See Choo He's commentary, *in loc.*—孟敬子，魯大夫，仲孫氏，名捷. 2 悼公. 3 晋魏斯受經於卜子夏; see the 歷代統紀表, Bk. i. p. 77.

use of the surnames of Yew Jŏ and Tsăng Sin, which has made some Chinese critics attribute the compilation to their followers. But this conclusion does not stand investigation. Others have assigned different portions to different schools. Thus, Book V. is given to the disciples of Tsze-kung; Book XI, to those of Min Tsze-k'een; Book XIV, to Yuen Heen; and Book XVI has been supposed to be interpolated from the Analects of Ts'e. Even if we were to acquiesce in these decisions, we should have accounted only for a small part of the Work. It is better to rest in the general conclusion, that it was compiled by the disciples of the disciples of the sage, making free use of the written memorials concerning him which they had received, and the oral statements which they had heard, from their several masters. And we shall not be far wrong, if we determine its date as about the end of the fourth, or the beginning of the fifth century before Christ.

3. In the critical work on the Four Books, called "Record of Remarks in the village of Yung,"[4] it is observed, "The Analects, in my opinion, were made by the disciples, just like this record of remarks. There they were recorded, and afterwards came a first-rate hand, who gave them the beautiful literary finish which we now witness, so that there is not a character which does not have its own indispensable place."[5] We have seen that the first of these statements contains only a small amount of truth with regard to the materials of the Analects, nor can we receive the second. If one hand or one mind had digested the materials provided by many, the arrangement and style of the work would have been different. We should not have had the same remark appearing in several Books, with little variation, and sometimes with none at all. Nor can we account on this supposition for such fragments as the last chapters of the 9th, 10th, and 16th Books, and many others. No definite plan has been kept in view throughout. A degree of unity appears to belong to some Books more than others, and in general to the first ten more than to those which follow, but there is no progress of thought or illustration of subject from Book to Book. And even in those where

4 榕村語錄,—榕村, 'the village of Yung,' is, I conceive, the writer's *nom de plume*.

5 論語想是門弟子,如語錄一般,記在那裏,後來有一高手,鍊成文理,這樣少,下字無一不渾.

緒論

the chapters have a common subject, they are thrown together at random more than on any plan.

4. When the Work was first called the Lun Yu, we cannot tell.[6] The evidence in the preceding section is sufficient to prove that when the Han scholars were engaged in collecting the ancient Books, it came before them, not in broken tablets, but complete, and arranged in Books or Sections, as we now have it. The old Lun was found deposited in the wall of the house which Confucius had occupied, and must have been placed there not later than B.C. 211, distant from the date which I have assigned to the compilation, not much more than a century and a half. That copy, written in the most ancient characters, was, possibly, the autograph of the compilers.

We have the Writings, or portions of the Writings, of several authors of the third and fourth centuries before Christ. Of these, in addition to "The Great Learning," "The Doctrine of the Mean," and "The Works of Mencius," I have looked over the Works of Seun K'ing[7] of the orthodox school, of the philosophers Chwang and Lëĕ of the Taouist school,[8] and of the heresiarch Mih.[9]

In The Great Learning, Commentary, chapter iv., we have the words of Ana. XII. xiii. In The Doctrine of the Mean, ch. iii., we have Ana. VI. xxvii.; and in ch. xxviii. 5, we have Ana. III. xxiv. In Mencius, II. Pt. I. ii. 19, we have Ana. VII. xxxiii., and in vii. 2, Ana. IV. i.; in III. Pt. I. iv. 11, Ana. VIII. xviii., xix.; in IV. Pt. I. xiv. 1, Ana. XI. xvi. 2; V. Pt. II. vii. 9, Ana. X. xiii. 4.; and in VII. Pt. II. xxxvii. 1, 2, 8, Ana. V. xxi., XIII. xxi., and XVII. xiii. These quotations, however, are introduced by "The Master said," or "Confucius said," no mention being made of any book called "The Lun Yu," or Analects. In The Great Learning, Commentary, x. 15, we have the words of Ana. IV. iii., and in Mencius, III. Pt. II. vii. 3, those of Ana. XVII. i, but without any notice of quotation.

6 In the continuation of the "General Examination of Records and Scholars. (續文獻通考), Bk. cxcviii. p. 17, it is said, indeed, on the authority of Wang Ch'ung (王充), a scholar of the 1st century, that when the Work came out of the wall it was named a Chuen or Record (傳), and that it was when K'ung Gan-kwŏ instructed a native of Tsin, named Foo-k'ing, in it, that it first got the name of Lun Yu:—武帝得論語于孔壁中, 皆名曰傳, 孔安國以古論教晉人扶卿, 始曰論語. If it were so, it is strange the circumstance is not mentioned in Ho An's preface. 7 荀卿. 8 莊子, 列子. 9 墨子.

In the Writings of Seun K'ing, Book I. page 2, we find the words of Ana. XV. xxx; p. 6, those of XIV. xxv. In Book VIII. p. 13. we have the words of Ana. II. xvii. But in these three instances there is no mark of quotation.

In the Writings of Chwang, I have noted only one passage where the words of the Analects are reproduced. Ana. XVIII. v. is found, but with large additions, and no reference of quotation, in his treatise on "The state of Men in the world, Intermediate,"[10] placed, that is, between Heaven and Earth. In all those Works, as well as in those of Lëĕ and Mih, the references to Confucius and his disciples, and to many circumstances of his life, are numerous.[11] The quotations of sayings of his not found in the Analects are likewise many, especially in the Doctrine of the Mean, in Mencius, and in the works of Chwang. Those in the latter are mostly burlesques, but those by the orthodox writers have more or less of classical authority. Some of them may be found in the Kea Yu,[12] or "Family Sayings," and in parts of the Le Ke, while others are only known to us by their occurrence in these Writings. Altogether, they do not supply the evidence, for which I am in quest, of the existence of the Analects as a distinct Work, bearing the name of the Lun Yu, prior to the Ts'in dynasty. They leave the presumption, however, in favour of those conclusions, which arises from the facts stated in the first section, undisturbed. They confirm it rather. They show that there was abundance of materials at hand to the scholars of Han, to compile a much larger Work with the same title, if they had felt it their duty to do the business of compilation, and not that of editing.

SECTION III.

OF COMMENTARIES UPON THE ANALECTS.

1. It would be a vast and unprofitable labour to attempt to give a list of the Commentaries which have been published on this Work. My object is merely to point out how zealously the business of interpretation was undertaken, as soon as the text had been recovered by the scholars of the Han dynasty, and with what industry it has been persevered in down to the present time.

10 人間世. 11 In Mih's chapter against the Literati, he mentions some of the characteristics of Confucius, in the very words of the 10th Book of the Analects. 12 家語.

緒論

2. Mention has been made, in Section I. 6, of the Lun of prince Chang, published in the half century before our era. Paou Heen,[1] a distinguished scholar and officer, of the reign of Kwang-woo,[2] the first emperor of the Eastern Han dynasty, A.D. 25–57, and another scholar of the surname Chow,[3] less known but of the same time, published Works, containing arrangements of this into chapters and sentences, with explanatory notes. The critical work of K'ung Gan-kwŏ on the old Lun Yu has been referred to. That was lost in consequence of suspicions under which Gan-kwŏ fell towards the close of the reign of the emperor Woo, but in the time of the emperor Shun, A.D. 126–144, another scholar, Ma Yung,[4] undertook the exposition of the characters in the old Lun, giving at the same time his views of the general meaning. The labours of Ch'ing Heuen in the second century have been mentioned. Not long after his death, there ensued a period of anarchy, when the empire was divided into three governments, well known from the celebrated historical romance, called "The Three States." The strongest of them, the House of Wei, patronized literature, and three of its high officers and scholars, Ch'in K'eun, Wang Suh, and Chow Shang-lëĕ,[5] in the first half, and probably the second quarter, of the third century, all gave to the world their notes on the Analects.

Very shortly after, five of the chief ministers of the Government of Wei, Sun Yung, Ch'ing Ch'ung, Tsaou He, Seun K'ae, and Ho An,[6] united in the production of one great Work, entitled, "A Collection of Explanations of the Lun Yu."[7] It embodied the labours of all the writers which have been mentioned, and having been frequently reprinted by succeeding dynasties, it still remains. The preface of the five compilers, in the form of a memorial to the emperor, so called, of the House of Wei, is published with it, and has been of much assistance to me in writing these sections. Ho An was the leader among them, and the work is commonly quoted as if it were the production of him alone.

1 包咸. 2 光武. 3 周氏. 4 至順帝時, 南郡太守, 馬融, 亦爲之訓說. 5 司農, 陳羣; 太常, 王肅; 博士, 周生列. 6 光祿大夫, 關內侯, 孫邕; 光祿大夫, 鄭沖; 散騎常侍, 中領軍, 安鄉亭侯, 曹羲; 侍中, 荀顗; 尙書, 駙馬都尉, 關內侯, 何晏. 7 論語集解.

3. From Ho An downwards, there has hardly been a dynasty which has not contributed its labourers to the illustration of the Analects. In the Leang, which occupied the throne a good part of the sixth century, there appeared the "Comments of Wang K'an,"[8] who to the seven authorities cited by Ho An added other thirteen, being scholars who had deserved well of the Classic during the intermediate time. Passing over other dynasties, we come to the Sung, A.D. 960–1279. An edition of the Classics was published by imperial authority, about the beginning of the 11th century, with the title of "The correct Meaning." The principal scholar engaged in the undertaking was Hing P'ing.[9] The portion of it on the Analects[10] is commonly reprinted in "The Thirteen Classics," after Ho An's explanations. But the names of the Sung dynasty are all thrown into the shade by that of Choo He, than whom China has not produced a greater scholar. He composed, in the 12th century, three Works on the Analects:—the first called "Collected Meanings,"[11] the second, "Collected Comments;"[12] and the third, "Queries."[13] Nothing could exceed the grace and clearness of his style, and the influence which he has exerted on the literature of China has been almost despotic.

The scholars of the present dynasty, however, seem inclined to question the correctness of his views and interpretations of the Classics, and the chief place among them is due to Maou K'e-ling,[14] known by the *nom de plume* of Se-ho.[15] His writings, under the name of "The collected Works of Se-ho,"[16] have been published in 80 volumes, containing between three and four hundred books or sections. He has nine treatises on The Four Books, or parts of them, and deserves to take rank with Ch'ing Heuen and Choo He at the head of Chinese scholars, though he is a vehement opponent of the latter. Most of his writings are to be found also in the great Work called "A collection of Works on the Classics, under the Imperial dynasty of Ts'ing,"[17] which contains 1,400 sections, and is a noble contribution by the present rulers of China to the illustration of its ancient literature.

8 皇侃論語疏. 9 邢昺. 10 論語正義. 11 論語集義. 12 論語集註. 13 論語或問. 14 毛奇齡 15 西河. 16 西河全集. 17 皇清經解.

20]

緒論

SECTION IV.

OF VARIOUS READINGS.

In "The Collection of Supplementary Observations on The Four Books,"[1] the second chapter contains a general view of commentaries on the Analects, and from it I extract the following list of various readings of the text found in the comments of Ch'ing Heuen, and referred to in the first section of this chapter.

Book II. i., 拱 for 共; viii., 餕 for 饌; xix., 措 for 錯; xxiii. 1, 十世可知, without 也, for 十世可知也. Book III. vii., in the clause 必也射乎, he makes a full stop at 也; xxi. 1, 主 for 社. Book IV. x., 敵 for 適, and 慕 for 莫. Book V. xxi., he puts a full stop at 子. Book VI. vii., he has not the characters 則 吾. Book VII. iv., 晏 for 燕; xxxiv., 子疾 simply, for 子疾病. Book IX. ix., 弁 for 冕. Book XI. xxv. 7, 僎 for 撰, and 饋 for 歸. Book XIII. iii. 3, 于往 for 迂; xviii. 1, 弓 for 躬. Book XIV. xxxi., 謗 for 方; xxxiv. 1, 何是栖栖者與 for 何爲是栖栖者與. Book XV. i. 2, 粻 for 糧. Book XVI. i. 13, 封 for 邦. Book XVII. i., 饋 for 歸; xxiv. 2, 絞 for 徼. Book XVIII. iv., 饋 for 歸; viii. 1, 侏 for 朱.

These various readings are exceedingly few, and in themselves insignificant. The student who wishes to pursue this subject at length, is provided with the means in the Work of Teih (? Chih) Keaou-show,[1] expressly devoted to it. It forms sections 449–473 of the Works on the Classics, mentioned at the close of the last section.

[1] 四書摭餘說. [2] 翟教授四書考異.

CHAPTER III.

OF THE GREAT LEARNING.

SECTION I.

HISTORY OF THE TEXT, AND THE DIFFERENT ARRANGEMENTS OF IT WHICH HAVE BEEN PROPOSED.

1. It has already been mentioned that "The Great Learning" forms one of the Chapters of the Le Ke, or "Record of Rites," the formation of the text of which will be treated of in its proper place. I will only say here, that the Book, or Books, of Rites had suffered much more, after the death of Confucius, than the other ancient Classics which had been collected and digested by him. They were in a more dilapidated condition at the time of the revival of the ancient literature under the Han dynasty, and were then published in three collections, only one of which—the Record of Rites—retains its place among the *King*.

The Record of Rites consists, according to the current arrangement, of 49 Chapters or Books. Lew Heang (see ch. I. sect. II. 2.) took the lead in its formation, and was followed by the two famous scholars, Tae Tih,[1] and his relative, Tae Shing.[2] The first of these reduced upwards of 200 chapters, collected by Heang, to 89, and Shing reduced these again to 46. The three other Books were added in the second century of our era, The Great Learning being one of them, by Ma Yung, mentioned in the last chapter, section III. 2. Since his time, the Work has not received any further additions.

2. In his note appended to what he calls the chapter of "Classical Text," Choo He says that the tablets of the "old copies" of the rest of The Great Learning were considerably out of order. By those old copies, he intends the Work of Ch'ing Heuen, who published his commentary on the Classic, soon after it was completed by the additions of Ma Yung; and it is possible that the tablets were in confusion, and had not been arranged with sufficient care; but such a thing

1 戴德. 2 戴聖. Shing was the son of a cousin of Tih's.

緒論

does not appear to have been suspected until the 12th century, nor can any authority from ancient monuments be adduced in its support.

I have related how the ancient Classics were cut on slabs of stone by imperial order, A.D. 175, the text being that which the various literati had determined, and which had been adopted by Ch'ing Heuen. The same work was performed about seventy years later, under the so-called dynasty of Wei, between the years 240 and 248, and the two sets of slabs were set up together. The only difference between them was, that whereas the Classics had been cut in the first instance in three different forms, called, the Seal character, the Pattern style, and the Imperfect form, there was substituted for the latter in the slabs of Wei the oldest form of the characters, similar to that which has been described in connection with the discovery of the old Lun Yu in the wall of Confucius' house. Amid the changes of dynasties, the slabs both of Han and Wei had perished, before the rise of the T'ang dynasty, A.D. 624; but under one of its emperors, in the year 836, a copy of the Classics was again cut on stone, though only in one form of the character. These slabs we can trace down through the Sung dynasty, when they were known as the tablets of Shen.[3] They were in exact conformity with the text of the Classics adopted by Ch'ing Heuen in his commentaries.

The Sung dynasty did not accomplish a similar work itself, nor has any one of the three which have followed it thought it necessary to engrave in stone in this way the ancient Classics. About the middle of the 16th century, however, the literary world in China was startled by a report that the slabs of Wei which contained The Great Learning had been discovered. But this was nothing more than the result of an impudent attempt at an imposition, for which it is difficult to a foreigner to assign any adequate cause. The treatise, as printed from these slabs, has some trifling additions, and many alterations in the order of the text, but differing from the arrangements proposed by Choo He, and by other scholars. There seems to be now no difference of opinion among Chinese critics that the whole affair was a forgery. The text of The Great Learning, as it appears in the Book of Rites with the commentary of Ch'ing

3 陝碑

Heuen, and was thrice engraved on stone, in three different dynasties, is, no doubt, that which was edited in the Han dynasty by Ma Yung.

3. I have said, that it is possible that the tablets containing the text were not arranged with sufficient care by him, and indeed, any one who studies the treatise attentively, will probably come to the conclusion that the part of it forming the first six chapters of commentary in the present Work is but a fragment. It would not be a difficult task to propose an arrangement of the text different from any which I have yet seen; but such an undertaking would not be interesting out of China. My object here is simply to mention the Chinese scholars who have rendered themselves famous or notorious in their own country, by what they have done in this way. The first was Ch'ing Haou, a native of Loh-yang in Ho-nan province, in the 11th century.[4] His designation was Pih-shun, but since his death he has been known chiefly by the style of Ming.taou,[5] which we may render the Wise-in-doctrine. The eulogies heaped on him by Choo He and others are extravagant, and he is placed immediately after Mencius in the list of great scholars. Doubtless he was a man of vast literary acquirements. The greatest change which he introduced into The Great Learning, was to read *sin*[6] for *ts'in*,[7] at the commencement, making the second object proposed in the treatise to be the *renovation* of the people, instead of *loving* them. This alteration and his various transpositions of the text are found in Maou Se-ho's treatise on "The attested text of The Great Learning."[8]

Hardly less illustrious than Ch'ing Haou was his younger brother Ch'ing E, known by the style of Ching-shuh,[9] and since his death by that of E-ch'uen.[10] He followed Haou in the adoption of the reading "*to renovate*," instead of "*to love*." But he transposed the text differently, more akin to the arrangement afterwards made by Choo He, suggesting also that there were some superfluous sentences in the old text which might conveniently be erased. The Work, as proposed to be read by him, will be found in the volume of Maou just referred to.

We come to the name of Choo He who entered into the labours of the brothers Ch'ing, the younger of whom he styles his Master, in his introductory note to The Great Learning. His arrangement of

4 程子顥,字伯淳,河南,洛陽人. 5 明道. 6 新. 7 親. 8 大學證文. 9 程子頤,字正叔,明道之弟. 10 伊川.

緒論

the text is that now current in all the editions of the Four Books, and it had nearly displaced the ancient text altogether. The sanction of Imperial approval was given to it during the Yuen and Ming dynasties. In the editions of the five *king* published by them, only the names of The Doctrine of the Mean and The Great Learning were preserved. No text of these Books was given, and Se-ho tells us that in the reign of Kea-tsing,[11] the most flourishing period of the Ming dynasty (A.D. 1522–1566), when Wang Wăn-shing,[12] published a copy of The Great Learning, taken from the T'ang edition of the Thirteen *King*, all the officers and scholars looked at one another in astonishment, and were inclined to suppose that the Work was a forgery. Besides adopting the reading of *sin* for *ts'in* from the Ch'ing, and modifying their arrangements of the text, Choo He made other innovations. He first divided the whole into one chapter of Classical text, which he assigned to Confucius, and ten chapters of Commentary, which he assigned to the disciple Tsăng. Previous to him, the whole had been published, indeed, without any specification of chapters and paragraphs. He undertook, moreover, to supply one whole chapter, which he supposed, after his master Ch'ing, to be missing.

Since the time of Choo He, many scholars have exercised their wit on The Great Learning. The Work of Maou Se-ho contains four arrangements of the text, proposed respectively by the scholars Wang Loo-chae,[13] Ke P'ang-san,[14] Kaou King-yih,[15] and Kŏ Hoo-chen.[16] The curious student may examine them there.

Under the present dynasty, the tendency has been to depreciate the labours of Choo He. The integrity of the text of Ch'ing Heuen is zealously maintained, and the simpler method of interpretation employed by him is advocated in preference to the more refined and ingenious schemes of the Sung scholars. I have referred several times in the notes to a Work published a few years ago, under the title of "The Old Text of the sacred *King*, with Commentary and Discussions, by Lo Chung-fan of Nan-hae."[17] I knew the man seventeen years ago. He was a fine scholar, and had taken the second degree, or that of *Keu-jin*. He applied to me in 1843 for Christian baptism, and offended by my hesitancy went and enrolled himself

11 嘉靖. 12 王文成. 13 王魯齋. 14 季彭山. 15 高景逸. 16 葛屺瞻. 17 聖經古本,南海羅仲藩註辨.

among the disciples of another Missionary. He soon, however, withdrew into seclusion, and spent the last years of his life in literary studies. His family have published the work on The Great Learning, and one or two others. He most vehemently impugns nearly every judgment of Choo He, but in his own exhibitions of the meaning he blends many ideas of the Supreme Being and of the condition of human nature, which he had learned from the Christian Scriptures.

SECTION II.

OF THE AUTHORSHIP, AND DISTINCTION OF THE TEXT INTO CLASSICAL TEXT AND COMMENTARY.

1. The authorship of The Great Learning is a very doubtful point, and one on which it does not appear possible to come to a decided conclusion. Choo He, as I have stated in the last section, determined that so much of it was *king*, or Classic, being the very words of Confucius, and that all the rest was *chuen*, or Commentary, being the views of Tsăng Sin upon the sage's words, recorded by *his* disciples. Thus, he does not expressly attribute the composition of the Treatise to Tsăng, as he is generally supposed to do. What he says, however, as it is destitute of external support, is contrary also to the internal evidence. The 4th chapter of commentary commences with "The Master said." Surely, if there were anything more, directly from Confucius, there would be an intimation of it in the same way. Or, if we may allow that short sayings of Confucius might be interwoven with the Work, as in the 15th paragraph of the 10th chapter, without referring them expressly to him, it is too much to ask us to receive the long chapter at the beginning as being from him. With regard to the Work having come from the disciples of Tsăng Sin, recording their master's views, the paragraph in chapter 6th, commencing with "The disciple Tsăng said," seems to be conclusive against that hypothesis. So much we may be sure is Tsăng's, and no more. Both of Choo He's judgments must be set aside. We cannot admit either the distinction of the contents into Classical text and Commentary, or that the Work was the production of Tsăng's disciples.

緒論

2. Who then was the author? An ancient tradition attributes it to K'ung Keih, the grandson of Confucius. In a notice published, at the time of their preparation, about the stone slabs of Wei, the following statement by Kea Kwei, a noted scholar of the 1st century is found:—"When K'ung Keih was living, and in straits, in Sung, being afraid lest the lessons of the former sages should become obscure, and the principles of the ancient emperors and kings fall to the ground, he therefore made The Great Learning as the warp of them, and The Doctrine of the Mean, as the woof."[1] This would seem, therefore, to have been the opinion of that early time, and I may say the only difficulty in admitting it is that no mention is made of it by Ch'ing Heuen. There certainly is that agreement between the two treatises, which makes their common authorship not at all unlikely.

3. Though we cannot positively assign the authorship of The Great Learning, there can be no hesitation in receiving it as a genuine monument of the Confucian school. There are not many words in it from the sage himself, but it is a faithful reflection of his teachings, written by some of his followers, not far removed from him by lapse of time. It must synchronize pretty nearly with the Analects, and may be safely referred to the fifth century before our era.

SECTION III.

ITS SCOPE AND VALUE.

1. The worth of The Great Learning has been celebrated in most extravagant terms by many Chinese writers, and there have been foreigners who have not yielded to them in their estimation of it. Pauthier, in the "Argument Philosophique," prefixed to his translation of the Work, says:—"It is evident that the aim of the Chinese philosopher is to exhibit the duties of political government as those of the perfecting of self, and of the practice of virtue by all men. He felt that he had a higher mission than that with which the greater part of ancient and modern philosophers have contented

[1] 唐氏奏疏有日,虞松校刻石經于魏表,引漢賈逵之言,曰,孔伋窮居于宋,懼先聖之學不明,而帝王之道墜,故作大學以經之,中庸以緯之; see the 大學證文,一, p. 5.

27]

themselves; and his immense love for the happiness of humanity, which dominated over all his other sentiments, has made of his philosophy a system of social perfectionating, which, we venture to say, has never been equalled."

Very different is the judgment passed upon the treatise by a writer in the Chinese Repository:—"The *Ta Hëö* is a short politico-moral discourse. *Ta Hëö*, or 'Superior Learning,' is at the same time both the name and the subject of the discourse; it is the *summum bonum* of the Chinese. In opening this Book, compiled by a disciple of Confucius, and containing his doctrines, we might expect to find a Work like Cicero's *De Officiis;* but we find a very different production, consisting of a few commonplace rules for the maintenance of a good government."[1]

My readers will perhaps think, after reading the present section, that the truth lies between these two representations.

2. I believe that the Book should be styled *T'ae Hëö*, and not *Ta Hëö*, and that it was so named as setting forth the higher and more extensive principles of moral science, which come into use and manifestation in the conduct of government. When Choo He endeavours to make the title mean—"The principles of Learning, which were taught in the higher schools of antiquity," and tells us how at the age of 15, all the sons of the emperor, with the legitimate sons of the nobles, and high officers, down to the more promising scions of the common people, all entered these seminaries, and were taught the difficult lessons here inculcated, we pity the ancient youth of China. Such "strong meat" is not adapted for the nourishment of youthful minds. But the evidence adduced for the existence of such educational institutions in ancient times is unsatisfactory, and from the older interpretation of the title we advance more easily to contemplate the object and method of the Work.

3. The *object* is stated definitely enough in the opening paragraph: —"What The Great Learning teaches, is—to illustrate illustrious virtue; to love the people; and to rest in the highest excellence." The political aim of the writer is here at once evident. He has before him on one side, *the people*, the masses of the empire, and over against them are those whose work and duty, delegated by Heaven,

1 Chinese Repository, vol. iii. p. 98. 2 太學, not 大學. See the note on the title of the Work, p. 219.

緒論

is to govern them, culminating, as a class, in "the son of Heaven,"[3] "the one man,"[4] the emperor. From the 4th and 5th paragraphs, we see that if the lessons of the treatise be learned and carried into practice, the result will be that "illustrious virtue will be illustrated throughout the empire," which will be brough t, through all its length and breadth, to a condition of happy tranquillity. This object is certainly both grand and good; and if a reasonable and likely method to secure it were proposed in the Work, language would hardly supply terms adequate to express its value.

4. But the above account of the object of The Great Learning leads us to the conclusion that the student of it should be an emperor. What interest can an ordinary man have in it? It is high up in the clouds, far beyond his reach. This is a serious objection to it, and quite unfits it for a place in schools, such as Choo He contends it once had. Intelligent Chinese, whose minds were somewhat quickened by Christianity, have spoken to me of this defect, and complained of the difficulty they felt in making the book a practical directory for their conduct. "It is so vague and vast," was the observation of one man. The writer, however, has made some provision for the general application of his instructions. He tells us that, from the emperor down to the mass of the people, all must consider the cultivation of the person to be the root, that is, the first thing to be attended to.[5] As in his method, moreover, he reaches from the cultivation of the person to the tranquillization of the Empire, through the intermediate steps of the regulation of the family, and the government of the State,[6] there is room for setting forth principles that parents and rulers generally may find adapted for their guidance.

5. The method which is laid down for the attainment of the great object proposed, consists of seven steps:—the investigation of things; the completion of knowledge; the sincerity of the thoughts; the rectifying of the heart; the cultivation of the person; the regulation of the family; and the government of the State. These form the steps of a climax, the end of which is the empire tranquillized. Pauthier calls the paragraphs where they occur instances of the sorites, or abridged syllogism. But they belong to *rhetoric*, and not to *logic*.

3 天子, Cl. Text, par. 6, 2. 4 一人, Comm. ix. 3. 5 Cl. Text, par. 6. 6 Cl. Text, parr. 4, 5.

6. In offering some observations on these steps, and the writer's treatment of them, it will be well to separate them into those preceding the cultivation of the person, and those following it; and to deal with the latter first.—Let us suppose that the cultivation of the person is all attained, every discordant mental element having been subdued and removed. It is assumed that the regulation of the family will necessarily flow from this. Two short paragraphs are all that are given to the illustration of the point, and they are vague generalities on the subject of men's being led astray by their feelings and affections.

The family being regulated, there will result from it the government of the State. First, the virtues taught in the family have their correspondencies in the wider sphere. Filial piety will appear as loyalty. Fraternal submission will be seen in respect and obedience to elders and superiors. Kindness is capable of universal application. Second, "From the loving example of one family, a whole State becomes loving, and from its courtesies the whole State becomes courteous."[7] Seven paragraphs suffice to illustrate these statements, and short as they are, the writer goes back to the topic of self-cultivation, returning from the family to the individual.

The State being governed, the whole empire will become peaceful and happy. There is even less of connection, however, in the treatment of this theme, between the premiss and the conclusion, than in the two previous chapters. Nothing is said about the relation between the whole empire, and its component States, or any one of them. It is said at once, "What is meant by 'The making the whole empire peaceful and happy depends on the government of the State,' is this.—When the sovereign behaves to his aged, as the aged should be behaved to, the people become filial; when the sovereign behaves to his elders, as elders should be behaved to, the people learn brotherly submission; when the sovereign treats compassionately the young and helpless, the people do the same."[8] This is nothing but a repetition of the preceding chapter, instead of that chapter's being made a step from which to go on to the splendid consummation of the good government of the whole empire.

The words which I have quoted are followed by a very striking enunciation of the golden rule in its negative form, and under the

7 See Comm. ix. 3. 8 See Comm. x. 1.

緒論

name of *the measuring square*, and all the lessons of the chapter are connected more or less closely with that. The application of this principle by a ruler, whose heart is in the first place in loving sympathy with the people, will guide him in all the exactions which he lays upon them, and in the selection of ministers, in such a way that he will secure the affections of his subjects, and his throne will be established, for "by gaining the people, the kingdom is gained, and, by losing the people, the kingdom is lost."[9] There are in this part of the treatise many valuable sentiments, and counsels for all in authority over others. The objection to it is, that, as the last step of the climax, it does not rise upon all the others with the accumulated force of their conclusions, but introduces us to new principles of action, and a new line of argument. Cut off the commencement of the first paragraph which connects it with the preceding chapters, and it would form a brief but admirable treatise by itself on the art of government.

This brief review of the writer's treatment of the concluding steps of his method will satisfy the reader that the execution is not equal to the design; and, moreover, underneath all the reasoning, and more especially apparent in the 8th and 9th chapters of commentary (according to the ordinary arrangement of the work), there lies the assumption that example is all but omnipotent. We find this principle pervading all the Confucian philosophy. And doubtless it is a truth, most important in education and government, that the influence of example is very great. I believe, and will insist upon it hereafter in these prolegomena, that we have come to overlook this element in our conduct of administration. It will be well if the study of the Chinese Classics should call attention to it. Yet in them the subject is pushed to an extreme, and represented in an extravagant manner. Proceeding from the view of human nature that it is entirely good, and led astray only by influences from without, the sage of China and his followers attribute to personal example and to instruction a power which we do not find that they actually possess.

7. The steps which precede the cultivation of the person are more briefly dealt with than those which we have just considered. "The cultivation of the person results from the rectifying the heart

9 Comm. x. 5.

or mind."[10] True, but in The Great Learning very inadequately set forth.

"The rectifying of the mind is realized when the thoughts are made sincere."[11] And the thoughts are sincere, when no self-deception is allowed, and we move without effort to what is right and wrong, "as we love what is beautiful, and as we hate a bad smell."[12] How are we to attain to this state? Here the Chinese moralist fails us. According to Choo He's arrangement of the Treatise, there is only one sentence from which we can frame a reply to the above question. "Therefore," it is said, "the superior man must be watchful over himself when he is alone."[13] Following Choo's 6th chapter of commentary, and forming, we may say, part of it, we have in the old arrangement of The Great Learning all the passages which he has distributed so as to form the previous five chapters. But even from the examination of them, we do not obtain the information which we desire on this momentous inquiry.

8. Indeed, the more I study the Work, the more satisfied I become, that from the conclusion of what is now called the chapter of Classical text to the sixth chapter of Commentary, we have only a few fragments, which it is of no use trying to arrange, so as fairly to exhibit the plan of the author. According to his method, the chapter on the connection between making the thoughts sincere and so rectifying the mental nature, should be preceded by one on the completion of knowledge as the means of making the thoughts sincere, and that again by one on the completion of knowledge by the investigation of things, or whatever else the phrase *kih wuh* may mean. I am less concerned for the loss and injury which this part of the Work has suffered, because the subject of the connection between intelligence and virtue is very fully exhibited in The Doctrine of the Mean, and will come under my notice in the review of that Treatise. The manner in which Choo He has endeavoured to supply the blank about the perfecting of knowledge by the investigation of things is too extravagant. "The Learning for Adults," he says, "at the outset of its lessons, instructs the learner, in regard to all things in the world, to proceed from what knowledge he has of their principles, and pursue his investigation of them, till he reaches the extreme point. After exerting himself for a long time, he will

10 Comm. vii. 1. 11 Comm. Ch. vi. 12 Comm. vi. 1. 13 Comm, vi. 2.

緒論

suddenly find himself possessed of a wide and far-reaching penetration. Then, the qualities of all things, whether external or internal, the subtle or the coarse, will be apprehended, and the mind, in its entire substance and its relations to things, will be perfectly intelligent. This is called the investigation of things. This is called the perfection of knowledge."[14] And knowledge must be thus perfected before we can achieve the sincerity of our thoughts, and the rectifying of our hearts! Verily this would be learning not for adults only, but even Methuselahs would not be able to compass it. Yet for centuries this has been accepted as the orthodox exposition of the Classic. Lo Chung-fan does not express himself too strongly when he says that such language is altogether incoherent. The author would only be "imposing on himself and others."

9. The orthodox doctrine of China concerning the connection between intelligence and virtue is most seriously erroneous, but I will not lay to the charge of the author of The Great Learning the wild representations of the commentator of the twelfth century, nor need I make here any remarks on what the doctrine really is. After the exhibition which I have given, my readers will probably conclude that the Work before us is far from developing, as Pauthier asserts, "a system of social perfectionating which has never been equalled."

10. The Treatise has undoubtedly great merits, but they are not to be sought in the severity of its logical processes, or the large-minded prosecution of any course of thought. We shall find them in the announcement of certain seminal principles, which, if recognized in government and the regulation of conduct, would conduce greatly to the happiness and virtue of mankind. I will conclude these observations by specifying four such principles.

First, The writer conceives nobly of the object of government, that it is to make its subjects happy and good. This may not be a sufficient account of that object, but it is much to have it so clearly laid down to "all kings and governors," that they are to love the people, ruling not for their own gratification, but for the good of those over whom they are exalted by Heaven. Very important also is the statement that rulers have no divine right but what springs from the discharge of their duty. "The decree does not always rest

14 Suppl. to Comm. Ch. v.

on them. Goodness obtains it, and the want of goodness loses it."[15]

Second, The insisting on personal excellence in all who have authority in the family, the State, and the empire, is a great moral and social principle. The influence of such personal excellence may be overstated, but by the requirement of its cultivation the writer deserved well of his country.

Third, Still more important than the requirement of such excellence, is the principle that it must be rooted in the state of the heart, and be the natural outgrowth of internal sincerity. "As a man thinketh in his heart, so is he." This is the teaching alike of Solomon and the author of The Great Learning.

Fourth, I mention last the striking exhibition which we have of the golden rule, though only in its negative form. "What a man dislikes in his superiors, let him not display in the treatment of his inferiors; what he dislikes in inferiors, let him not display in his service of his superiors; what he dislikes in those who are before him, let him not therewith precede those who are behind him; what he dislikes in those who are behind him, let him not therewith follow those who are before him; what he dislikes to receive on the right, let him not bestow on the left; what he dislikes to receive on the left, let him not bestow on the right:—this is what is called the principle with which, as with a measuring square, to regulate one's conduct."[16]

The Work which contains those principles cannot be thought meanly of. They are "commonplace," as the writer in the Chinese Repository calls them, but they are at the same time eternal verities.

15 Comm. x. 11. 16 Comm. x. 2.

緒論

CHAPTER IV.

THE DOCTRINE OF THE MEAN.

SECTION I.

ITS PLACE IN THE LE KE, AND ITS PUBLICATION SEPARATELY.

1. The Doctrine of the Mean was one of the treatises which came to light in connection with the labours of Lew Heang, and its place as the 31st Book in the Le Ke was finally determined by Ma Yung and Ch'ing Heuen.

2. But while it was thus made to form a part of the great collection of Works on Ceremonies, it maintained a separate footing of its own. In Lew Hin's catalogue of the Classical Works, we find "Two *p'ëen* of Observations on the Chung Yung."[1] In the Records of the dynasty of Suy (A.D. 589–617), in the chapter on the History of Literature,[2] there are mentioned three Works on the Chung Yung; —the first called "The Record of the Chung Yung," in two *keuen*, attributed to Tae Yung, a scholar who flourished about the middle of the 5th century; the second, "A Paraphrase and Commentary on the Chung Yung," attributed to the emperor 'Woo (A.D. 502–549) of the Leang dynasty, in one *keuen*, and the third, "A Private Record, Determining the Meaning of the Chung Yung," in five *keuen*, the author, or supposed author, of which is not mentioned.[3]

It thus appears, that the Chung Yung had been published and commented on separately, long before the time of the Sung dynasty. The scholars of that, however, devoted special attention to it, the way being led by the famous Chow Lëen-k'e.[4] He was followed by the two brothers Ch'ing, but neither of them published upon it. At last came Choo He, who produced his Work called "The Chung

[1] 中庸說二篇. [2] 隋書, 卷三十二, 志第二十七, 經籍, 一, p. 12. [3] 禮記中庸傳, 二卷, 宋散騎常侍戴顒撰; 中庸講疏, 一卷, 梁武帝撰; 私記制旨中庸義, 五卷. [4] 周濂溪.

35]

Yung, in Chapters and Sentences,"[5] which was made the text book of the Classic at the literary examinations, by the fourth Emperor of the Yuen dynasty (A.D. 1312–1320), and from that time the name merely of the Treatise was retained in editions of the Le Ke. Neither text nor ancient commentary was given.

Under the present dynasty it is not so. In the superb edition of "The Five *King*" edited by a numerous committee of scholars towards the end of K'ang He's reign, the Chung Yung is published in two parts, the ancient commentaries from "The Thirteen *King*" being given side by side with those of Choo He.

SECTION II.

ITS AUTHOR; AND SOME ACCOUNT OF HIM.

1. The composition of the Chung Yung is attributed to K'ung Keih, the grandson of Confucius. Chinese inquirers and critics are agreed on this point, and apparently on sufficient grounds. There is indeed no internal evidence in the Work to lead us to such a conclusion. Among the many quotations of Confucius' words and references to him, we might have expected to find some indication that the sage was the grandfather of the author, but nothing of the kind is given. The external evidence, however, or that from the testimony of authorities, is very strong. In Sze-ma Ts'een's Historical Records, published B.C. 103, it is expressly said that "Tsze-sze made the Chung Yung."[1] And we have a still stronger proof, a century earlier, from Tsze-sze's own descendant, K'ung Foo, whose words are, "Tsze-sze compiled the Chung Yung in 49 *p'ëen*."[2] We may, therefore, accept the received account without hesitation.

2. As Keih, spoken of chiefly by his designation of Tsze-sze, thus occupies a distinguished place in the classical literature of China, it

5 中庸章句

1 子思作中庸; see the 史記, 四十七, 孔子世家. 2 This K'ung Foo (孔鮒) was that descendant of Confucius, who hid several books in the wall of his house, on the issuing of the imperial edict for their burning. He was a writer himself, and his Works are referred to under the title of 孔叢子. I have not seen them, but the statement given above is found in the 四書摭餘說, art. 中庸.—孔叢子云, 子思撰中庸之書四十九篇.

36]

緒論

may not be out of place to bring together here a few notices of him gathered from reliable sources.

He was the son of Le, whose death took place B.C. 482, four years before that of the sage, his father. I have not found it recorded in what year he was born. Sze-ma Ts'een says he died at the age of 62. But this is evidently wrong, for we learn from Mencius that he was high in favour with the duke Muh of Loo,[3] whose accession to that principality dates in B.C. 408, seventy years after the death of Confucius. In the "Plates and Notices of the Worthies, sacrificed to in the Sage's Temples,"[4] it is supposed that the 62 in the Historical Records should be 82.[5] It is maintained by others that Tsze-sze's life was protracted beyond 100 years.[6] This variety of opinions simply shows that the point cannot be positively determined. To me it seems that the conjecture in the Sacrificial Canon must be pretty near the truth.[7]

During the years of his boyhood, then, Tsze-sze must have been with his grandfather, and received his instructions. It is related, that one day, when he was alone with the sage, and heard him sighing, he went up to him, and, bowing twice, inquired the reason of his grief. "Is it," said he, "because you think that your descendants, through not cultivating themselves, will be unworthy of you? Or is it that, in your admiration of the ways of Yaou and Shun, you are vexed that you fall short of them?" "Child," replied Confucius, "how is it that you know my thoughts?" "I have often," said Tsze-sze, "heard from you the lesson, that when the father has gathered and prepared the firewood, if the son cannot carry the bundle, he is to be pronounced degenerate and unworthy. The remark comes frequently into my thoughts, and fills me with great apprehensions." The sage was delighted. He smiled and said, "Now, indeed, shall

3 魯穆公. 4 聖廟祀典圖考. 5 或以六十二似八十二之誤. 82 and 62 may more easily be confounded, as written in Chinese than with the Roman figures. 6 See the 四書集證, on the preface to the Chung Yung,—年百餘歲卒. 7 Le himself was born in Confucius' 21st year, and if Tsze-sze had been born in Le's 21st year, he must have been 103 at the time of duke Muh's accession. But the tradition is, that Tsze-sze was a pupil of Tsang Sin who was born B.C. 504. We must place his birth therefore considerably later, and suppose him to have been quite young when his father died. I was talking once about the question with a Chinese friend, who observed:—"Le was 50 when he died, and his wife married again into a family of Wei. We can hardly think, therefore, that she was any thing like that age. Le could not have married so soon as his father did. Perhaps he was about 40 when Keih was born."

I be without anxiety! My undertakings will not come to nought. They will be carried on and flourish."[8]

After the death of Confucius, Keih became a pupil, it is said, of the philosopher Tsăng. But he received his instructions with discrimination, and in one instance which is recorded in the Le Ke, the pupil suddenly took the place of the master. We there read:—"Tsăng said to Tsze-sze, 'Keih, when I was engaged in mourning for my parents, neither congee nor water entered my mouth for seven days.' Tsze-sze answered, 'In ordering their rules of propriety, it was the design of the ancient kings that those who would go beyond them should stoop and keep by them, and that those who could hardly reach them should stand on tiptoe to do so. Thus it is that the superior man, in mourning for his parents, when he has been three days without water or congee, takes a staff to enable himself to rise."[9]

While he thus condemned the severe discipline of Tsăng, Tsze-sze appears in various incidents which are related of him, to have been himself more than sufficiently ascetic. As he was living in great poverty, a friend supplied him with grain, which he readily received. Another friend was emboldened by this to send him a bottle of wine, but he declined to receive it. "You receive your corn from other people," urged the donor, "and why should you decline my gift, which is of less value? You can assign no ground in reason for it, and if you wish to show your independence, you should do so completely." "I am so poor," was the reply, "as to be in want, and being afraid lest I should die and the sacrifices not be offered to my ancestors, I accept the grain as an alms. But the wine and the dried flesh which you offer to me are the appliances of a feast. For a poor man to be feasting is certainly unreasonable. This is the ground of my refusing your gift. I have no thought of asserting my independence."[10]

To the same effect is the account of Tsze-sze, which we have from Lew Heang. That scholar relates:—"When Keih was living in Wei, he wore a tattered coat, without any lining, and in 30 days had only 9 meals. T'ëen Tsze-fang having heard of his distress, sent a messenger to him with a coat of fox-fur, and being afraid that he might

8 See the 四書集證, in the place just quoted from. For the incident we are indebted to K'ung Foo; see note 2, 9. Le Ke, II. Pt. I. ii. 7. 10, 11 See the 四書集證, as above.

緒論

not receive it, he added the message,—'When I borrow from a man, I forget it; when I give a thing, I part with it freely as if I threw it away.' Tsze-sze declined the gift thus offered, and when Tsze-fang said, 'I have, and you have not; why will you not take it?' he replied, 'You give away so rashly, as if you were casting your things into a ditch. Poor as I am, I cannot think of my body as a ditch, and do not presume to accept your gift."[11]

Tsze-sze's mother married again, after Le's death, into a family of Wei. But this circumstance, which is not at all creditable in Chinese estimation, did not alienate his affections from her. He was in Loo when he heard of her death, and proceeded to weep in the temple of his family. A disciple came to him and said, "Your mother married again into the family of the Shoo, and do you weep for her in the temple of the K'ung?" "I am wrong," said Tsze-sze, "I am wrong;" and with these words he went to weep elsewhere.[12]

In his own married relation he does not seem to have been happy, and for some cause, which has not been transmitted to us, he divorced his wife, following in this, it would appear, the example of Confucius. On her death, her son, Tsze-shang,[13] did not undertake any mourning for her. Tsze-sze's disciples were surprised and questioned him. "Did not your father," they asked, "mourn for his mother who had been divorced?" "Yes," was the reply. "Then why do you not cause Pih[14] to mourn for his mother?" Tsze-sze answered, "My father failed in nothing to pursue the proper path. His observances increased or decreased as the case required. But I cannot attain to this. While she was my wife, she was Pih's mother; when she ceased to be my wife, she ceased to be Pih's mother." The custom of the K'ung family not to mourn for a mother who had left it herself, or been divorced, took its rise from Tsze-sze.[15]

These few notices of K'ung Keih in his more private relations bring him before us as a man of strong feeling and strong will, independent, and with a tendency to asceticism in his habits.

As a public character, we find him at the ducal courts of Wei, Sung, Loo, and Pe, and at each of them held in high esteem by the

12 See the Le Ke, II. Pt. II. iii. 15. 庶氏之母死 must be understood as I have done above, and not with Ch'ing Heuen,—"Your mother was born a Miss Shoo." 13 子上,—this was the designation of Tsze-sze's son. 14 白,—this was Tsze-shang's name. 15 See the Le Ke, II. Pt. I. i. 4.

rulers. To Wei he was carried probably by the fact of his mother having married into that State. We are told that the prince of Wei received him with great distinction and lodged him honourably. On one occasion he said to him, "An officer of the State of Loo, you have not despised this small and narrow Wei, but have bent your steps hither to comfort and preserve it;—vouchsafe to confer your benefits upon me." Tsze-sze replied, "If I should wish to requite your princely favour with money and silks, your treasuries are already full of them, and I am poor. If I should wish to requite it with good words, I am afraid that what I should say would not suit your ideas, so that I should speak in vain, and not be listened to. The only way in which I can requite it, is by recommending to your notice men of worth." The duke said, "Men of worth is exactly what I desire." "Nay," said Keih, "you are not able to appreciate them." "Nevertheless," was the reply, "I should like to hear whom you consider deserving that name." Tsze-sze replied, "Do you wish to select your officers for the name they may have, or for their reality?" "For their reality, certainly," said the duke. His guest then said, "In the eastern borders of your State, there is one Le Yin, who is a man of real worth." "What were his grandfather and father?" asked the duke. "They were husbandmen," was the reply, on which the duke broke into a loud laugh, saying, "I do not like husbandry. The son of a husbandman cannot be fit for me to employ. I do not put into office all the cadets of those families even in which office is hereditary." Tsze-sze observed, "I mention Le Yin because of his abilities; what has the fact of his forefathers being husbandmen to do with the case? And moreover, the duke of Chow was a great sage, and K'ang-shuh was a great worthy. Yet if you examine their beginnings, you will find that from the business of husbandry they came forth to found their States. I did certainly have my doubts that in the selection of your officers you did not have regard to their real character and capacity." With this the conversation ended. The duke was silent.[16]

Tsze-sze was naturally led to K'ung, as the Sung family originally sprang from that principality. One account, quoted in "The Four

[16] See the 氏姓譜, 卷一百二, 孔氏, 孔伋.

40]

緒論

Books, Text and Commentary, with Proofs and Illustrations,"[17] says that he went thither in his 16th year, and having foiled an officer of the State, named Yŏ Sŏ, in a conversation on the Shoo-king, his opponent was so irritated at the disgrace put on him by a youth, that he listened to the advice of evil counsellors, and made an attack on him to put him to death. The duke of Sung, hearing the tumult, hurried to the rescue, and when Keih found himself in safety, he said, "When king Wăn was imprisoned in Yew-le, he made the Yih of Chow. My grandfather made the Ch'un Ts'ew after he had been in danger in Ch'in and Ts'ae. Shall I not make something when rescued from such a risk in Sung?" Upon this he made the Chung Yung in 49 *p'ëen*.

According to this account, the Chung Yung was the work of Tsze-sze's early manhood, and the tradition has obtained a wonderful prevalence. The notice in "The Sacrificial Canon" says, on the contrary, that it was the work of his old age, when he had finally settled in Loo, which is much more likely.[18]

Of Tsze-sze in Pe, which could hardly be said to be out of Loo, we have only one short notice,—in Mencius, V. Pt. II. iii. 3, where the duke Hwuy of Pe is introduced as saying, "I treat Tsze-sze as my master."

We have fuller accounts of him in Loo where he spent all the latter years of his life, instructing his disciples to the number of several hundred,[19] and held in great reverence by the duke Muh. The duke indeed wanted to raise him to the highest office, but he declined this, and would only occupy the position of a "guide, philosopher, and friend." Of the attention which he demanded, however, instances will be found in Mencius, II. Pt. II. xi. 3; V. Pt. II. vi. 5, and vii. 3. In his intercourse with the duke he spoke the truth to him fearlessly. In the "Cyclopædia of Surnames,"[20] I find the following conversations, but I cannot tell from what source they are extracted into that Work.—"One day, the duke said to Tsze-sze, 'The officer

17 This is the Work so often referred to as the 四書集證, the full title being 四書經註集證. The passage here translated from it will be found in the place several times referred to in this section. 18 The author of the 四書摭餘說 adopts the view that the Work was composed in Sung. Some have advocated this from ch. xxviii. 5. compared with Ana. III. ix., "it being proper," they say, "that Tsze-sze, writing in Sung, should not depreciate it as Confucius had done, out of it!" 19 See in the 'Sacrificial Canon,' on Tsze-sze. 20 This is the Work referred to in note 14.

Heen told me that you do good without wishing for any praise from men;—is it so?' Tsze-sze replied, 'No, that is not my feeling. When I cultivate what is good, I wish men to know it, for when they know it and praise me, I feel encouraged to be more zealous in the cultivation. This is what I desire, and am not able to obtain. If I cultivate what is good, and men do not know it, it is likely that in their ignorance they will speak evil of me. So by my good-doing I only come to be evil spoken of. This is what I do not desire, but am not able to avoid. In the case of a man, who gets up at cock-crowing to practise what is good, and continues sedulous in the endeavour till midnight, and says at the same time that he does not wish men to know it, lest they should praise him, I must say of such a man, that if he be not deceitful he is stupid.'"

Another day, the duke asked Tsze-sze saying, "Can my State be made to flourish." "It may," was the reply. "And how?" Tsze-sze said, "O prince, if you and your ministers will only strive to realize the government of the duke of Chow and of Pih-k'in; practising their transforming principles, sending forth wide the favours of your ducal house, and not letting advantages flow in private channels;—if you will thus conciliate the affections of the people, and at the same time cultivate friendly relations with neighbouring States, your kingdom will soon begin to flourish."

On one occasion, the duke asked whether it had been the custom of old for ministers to go into mourning for a prince whose service and State they had left. Tsze-sze replied to him, "Of old, princes advanced their ministers to office according to propriety, and dismissed them in the same way, and hence there was that rule. But now-a-days, princes bring their ministers forward as if they were going to take them on their knees, and send them away as if they would cast them into an abyss. If they do not treat them as their greatest enemies, it is well.—How can you expect the ancient practice to be observed in such circumstances?"[21]

These instances may suffice to illustrate the character of Tsze-sze, as it was displayed in his intercourse with the princes of his time. We see the same independence which he affected in private life, and a dignity not unbecoming the grandson of Confucius. But we miss the reach of thought and capacity for administration which belonged

21 This conversation is given in the Le Ke, II. Pt. II. ii. 1.

緒
論

to the Sage. It is with him, however, as a thinker and writer that we have to do, and his rank in that capacity will appear from the examination of the Chung Yung in the section that follows. His place in the temples of the Sage has been that of one of his four assessors, since the year 1267. He ranks with Yen Hwuy, Tsăng Sin, and Mencius, and bears the title of "The Philosopher Tsze-sze, Transmitter of the Sage."[22]

22 述聖子思子.

SECTION III.

ITS INTEGRITY.

1. In the testimony of K'ung Foo, which has been adduced to prove the authorship of the Chung Yung, it is said that the Work consisted originally of 49 *p'ëen*. From this statement it is argued by some, that the arrangement of it in 33 chapters, which originated with Choo He, is wrong;[1] but this does not affect the question of integrity, and the character *p'ëen* is so vague and indefinite, that we cannot affirm that K'ung Foo meant to tell us by it that Tsze-sze himself divided his Treatise into so many paragraphs or chapters.

It is on the entry in Lew Hin's catalogue, quoted Section 1,—"Two *p'ëen* of observations on the Chung Yung," that the integrity of the present Work is called in question. Yen Sze-koo, of the T'ang dynasty, has a note on that entry to the effect:—"There is now the Chung Yung in the Le Ke in one *p'ëen*. But that is not the original Treatise here mentioned, but only a branch from it."[2] Wang Wei, a writer of the Ming dynasty, says:—"Anciently, the Chung Yung consisted of two *p'ëen*, as appears from the History of Literature of the Han dynasty, but in the Le Ke we have only one *p'ëen*, which Choo He, when he made his 'Chapters and Sentences,' divided into 33 chapters. The old Work in two *p'ëen* is not to be met with now."[3]

1 See the 四書摭餘說, art. 中庸. 2 顏師古曰, 今禮記有中庸一篇, 亦非本禮經, 蓋此之流. 3 王氏緯曰, 中庸古有二篇, 見漢藝文志, 而在禮記中者, 一篇而已, 朱子爲章句, 因其一篇者, 分爲三十三章, 而古所謂二篇者不可見矣.

43]

These views are based on a misinterpretation of the entry in the Catalogue. It does not speak of two *p'ëen* of the Chung Yung, but of *two p'ëen of Observations* thereon. The Great Learning carries on its front the evidence of being incomplete, but the student will not easily believe that the Doctrine of the Mean is so. I see no reason for calling its integrity in question, and no necessity therefore to recur to the ingenious device employed in the edition of the five *king* published by the imperial authority of K'ang He, to get over the difficulty which Wang Wei supposes. It there appears in two *p'ëen*, of which we have the following account from the author of "Supplemental Remarks upon the Four Books:"—"The proper course now is to consider the first 20 chapters in Choo He's arrangement as making up the first *p'ëen*, and the remaining 13 as forming the second. In this way we retain the old form of the Treatise, and do not come into collision with the views of Choo. For this suggestion we are indebted to Loo Wang-chae" (an author of the Sung dynasty).[4]

4 See the 四書摭餘說, art. 中庸.

SECTION IV.

ITS SCOPE AND VALUE.

1. The Doctrine of the Mean is a work not easy to understand. "It first," says the philosopher Ch'ing, "speaks of one principle; it next spreads this out and embraces all things; finally, it returns and gathers them up under the one principle. Unroll it, and it fills the universe; roll it up, and it retires and lies hid in secrecy."[1] There is this advantage, however, to the student of it, that, more than most other Chinese Treatises, it has a beginning, a middle, and an end. The first chapter stands to all that follows in the character of a text, containing several propositions of which we have the expansion or development. If that development were satisfactory, we should be able to bring our own minds *en rapport* with that of the author. Unfortunately it is not so. As a writer he belongs to the intuitional school more than to the logical. This is well put in the "Continuation of the General Examination of Literary Monuments and Learned Men,"—"The philosopher Tsăng reached his conclusions by following in the train of things, watching and examining;

1 See the Introductory note. pp. 246, 247.

緒論

whereas Tsze-sze proceeds directly and reaches to Heavenly virtue. His was a mysterious power of discernment, approaching to that of Yen Hwuy."[2] We must take the Book and the author, however, as we have them, and get to their meaning, if we can, by assiduous examination and reflection.

2. "Man has received his *nature* from *Heaven*. Conduct in accordance with that nature constitutes what is right and true,—is a pursuing of the proper *path*. The cultivation or regulation of that path is what is called *instruction*." It is with these axioms that the Treatise commences, and from such an introduction we might expect that the writer would go on to unfold the various principles of duty, derived from an analysis of man's moral constitution.

Confining himself, however, to the second axiom, he proceeds to say that "the path may not for an instant be left, and that the superior man is cautious and careful in reference to what he does not see, and fearful and apprehensive in reference to what he does not hear. There is nothing more visible than what is secret, and nothing more manifest than what is minute, and therefore the superior man is watchful over his *aloneness*." This is not all very plain. Comparing it with the 6th chapter of Commentary in the Great Learning, it seems to inculcate what is there called "making the thoughts sincere." The passage contains an admonition about equivalent to that of Solomon,—"Keep thy heart with all diligence, for out of it are the issues of life."

The next paragraph seems to speak of *the nature* and *the path* under other names. "While there are no movements of pleasure, anger, sorrow, or joy, we have what may be called the state of *equilibrium*. When those feelings have been moved, and they all act in the due degree, we have what may be called the state of *harmony*. This equilibrium is the great root of the world and this harmony is its universal path." What is here called "the state of equilibrium," is the same as the nature given by Heaven, considered absolutely in itself, without deflection or inclination. This nature acted on from without, and responding with the various emotions, so as always "to hit"[3] the mark with entire correctness, produces the state of harmony,

2 See the 續文獻通考, Bk. cxcix., art. 子思,—曾子得之于隨事省察,而子思之學,則直達天德:庶幾顏氏之妙悟.

3 中節.

and such harmonious response is the path along which all human activities should proceed.

Finally, "Let the states of equilibrium and harmony exist in perfection, and a happy order will prevail throughout heaven and earth, and all things will be nourished and flourish." Here we pass into the sphere of mystery and mysticism. The language, according to Choo He, "describes the meritorious achievements and transforming influence of sage and spiritual men in their highest extent." From the path of duty, where we tread on solid ground, the writer suddenly raises us aloft on wings of air, and will carry us we know not where, and to we know not what.

3. The paragraphs thus presented, and which constitute Choo He's first chapter, contain the sum of the whole Work. This is acknowledged by all;—by the critics who disown Choo He's interpretations of it, as freely as by him.[4] Revolving them in my own mind often and long, I collect from them the following as the ideas of the author:—1st, Man has received from Heaven a moral nature by which he is constituted a law to himself; 2d, Over this nature man requires to exercise a jealous watchfulness; and 3d, As he possesses it, absolutely and relatively, in perfection, or attains to such possession of it, he becomes invested with the highest dignity and power, and may say to himself—"I am a god; yea, I sit in the seat of God." I will not say here that there is blasphemy in the last of these ideas; but do we not have in them the same combination which we found in The Great Learning,—a combination of the ordinary and the extraordinary, the plain and the vague, which is very perplexing to the mind, and renders the Book unfit for the purposes of mental and moral discipline?

And here I may inquire whether we do right in calling the Treatise by any of the names which foreigners have hitherto used for it? In the note on the title, pp. 246, 247, I have entered a little into this question. The Work is not at all what a reader must expect to find in what he supposes to be a treatise on "The Golden Medium," "The Invariable Mean," or "The Doctrine of the Mean." Those names are descriptive only of a portion of it. Where the phrase *Chung Yung*

4 Compare Choo He's language in his concluding note to the 1st chapter:—楊氏所謂一篇之體要, and Maou Se-ho's, in his 中庸說卷一, p. 11:—此中庸一書之領要也.

緒論

occurs in the quotations from Confucius, in nearly every chapter from the 2d to the 11th, we do well to translate it by "the course of the Mean," or some similar terms; but the conception of it in Tsze-sze's mind was of a different kind, as the preceding analysis of the first chapter sufficiently shows.

4. I may return to this point of the proper title for the Work again, but in the mean time we must proceed with the analysis of it. —The ten chapters from the 2d to the 11th constitute the second part, and in them Tsze-sze quotes the words of Confucius, "for the purpose," according to Choo He, "of illustrating the meaning of the first chapter." Yet, as I have just intimated, they do not to my mind do this. Confucius bewails the rarity of the practice of the Mean, and graphically sets forth the difficulty of it. "The empire, with its component States and families, may be ruled; dignities and emoluments may be declined; naked weapons may be trampled under foot; but the course of the Mean can not be attained to."[5] "The knowing go beyond it, and the stupid do not come up to it."[6] Yet some have attained to it. Shun did so, humble and ever learning from people far inferior to himself;[7] and Yen Hwuy did so, holding fast whatever good he got hold of, and never letting it go?[8] Tsze-loo thought the Mean could be taken by storm, but Confucius taught him better.[9] And in fine, it is only the sage who can fully exemplify the Mean.[10]

All these citations do not throw any light on the ideas presented in the first chapter. On the contrary they interrupt the train of thought. Instead of showing us how virtue, or the path of duty is in accordance with our Heaven-given nature, they lead us to think of it as a mean between two extremes. Each extreme may be a violation of the law of our nature, but that is not made to appear. Confucius' sayings would be in place in illustrating the doctrine of the Peripatetics, "which placed all virtue in a medium between opposite vices."[11] Here in the Chung Yung of Tsze-sze I have always felt them to be out of place.

5. In the 12th chapter Tsze-sze speaks again himself, and we seem at once to know the voice. He begins by saying that "the way of the superior man reaches far and wide, and yet is secret,"

5 Ch. ix. 6 Ch. iv. 7 Ch. iv. 8 Ch. viii. 9 Ch. x. 10 Ch. xi. 11 Encyclopædia Britannica, Preliminary Dissertations, p. 318, latest edition

by which he means to tell us that the path of duty is to be pursued everywhere and at all times, while yet the secret spring and rule of it is near at hand, in the Heaven-conferred nature, the individual consciousness, with which no stranger can intermeddle. Choo He, as will be seen in the notes, gives a different interpretation of the utterance. But the view which I have adopted is maintained convincingly by Maou Se-ho in the second part of his "Observations on the Chung Yung." With this chapter commences the third part of the Work, which embraces also the eight chapters which follow. "It is designed," says Choo He, "to illustrate what is said in the first chapter that "the path may not be left." But more than that one sentence finds its illustration here. Tsze-sze had reference in it also to what he had said—"The superior man does not wait till he sees things to be cautious, nor till he hears things to be apprehensive. There is nothing more visible than what is secret, and nothing more manifest than what is minute. Therefore, the superior man is watchful over himself when he is alone."

It is in this portion of the Chung Yung that we find a good deal of moral instruction which is really valuable. Most of it consists of sayings of Confucius, but the sentiments of Tsze-sze himself in his own language are interspersed with them. The sage of China has no higher utterances than those which are given in the 13th chapter. —"The path is not far from man. When men try to pursue a course which is far from the common indications of consciousness, this course cannot be considered *the path*. In the Book of Poetry it is said—

> 'In hewing an axe-handle, in hewing an axe-handle,
> The pattern is not far off.'

We grasp one axe-handle to hew the other, and yet if we look askance from the one to the other, we may consider them as apart. Therefore, the superior man governs men according to their nature, with what is proper to them; and as soon as they change what is wrong, he stops. When one cultivates to the utmost the moral principles of his nature, and exercises them on the principle of reciprocity, he is not far from the path. What you do not like when done to yourself, do not do to others.

"In the way of the superior man there are four things, to none of which have I as yet attained.—To serve my father as I would

緒論

require my son to serve me: to this I have not attained; to serve my elder brother as I would require my younger brother to serve me: to this I have not attained; to serve my prince as I would require my minister to serve me: to this I have not attained; to set the example in behaving to a friend as I would require him to behave to me: to this I have not attained. Earnest in practising the ordinary virtues, and careful in speaking about them; if in his practice he has anything defective, the superior man dares not but exert himself, and if in his words he has any excess, he dares not allow himself such license. Thus his words have respect to his actions, and his actions have respect to his words;—is it not just an entire sincerity which marks the superior man?"

We have here the golden rule in its negative form expressly propounded:—"What you do not like when done to yourself, do not do to others." But in the paragraph which follows we have the rule virtually in its positive form. Confucius recognizes the duty of taking the initiative,—of behaving himself to others in the first instance as he would that they should behave to him. There is a certain narrowness, indeed, in that the sphere of its operations seems to be confined to the relations of society, which are spoken of more at large in the 20th chapter, but let us not grudge the tribute of our warm approbation to the sentiments.

This chapter is followed by two from Tsze-sze, to the effect that the superior man does what is proper in every change of his situation, always finding his rule in himself; and that in his practice there is an orderly advance from step to step,—from what is near to what is remote. Then follow five chapters from Confucius:—the first, on the operation and influence of spiritual beings, to show "the manifestness of what is minute, and the irrepressibleness of sincerity;" the second, on the filial piety of Shun, and how it was rewarded by Heaven with the empire, with enduring fame, and with long life; the third and fourth, on the kings Wăn and Woo, and the duke of Chow, celebrating them for their filial piety and other associate virtues; and the fifth, on the subject of government. These chapters are interesting enough in themselves, but when I go back from them, and examine whether I have from them any better understanding of the paragraphs in the first chapter which they are said to illustrate, I do not find that I have. Three of them, the 17th, 18th, and 19th, would be more in place in the Classic of Filial Piety than here in the Chung Yung. The meaning of the 16th is shadowy and undefined. After all the study which I have directed to it, there are some points in reference to which I have still doubts and difficulties.

The 20th chapter which concludes the third portion of the Work contains a full exposition of Confucius' views on government, though professedly descriptive only of that of the kings Wăn and Woo. Along with lessons proper for a ruler there are many also of universal application, but the mingling of them perplexes the mind. It tells us of "the five duties of universal application,"—those between sovereign and minister, husband and wife, father and son, elder and younger brother, and friends; of "the three virtues by which those duties are carried into effect," namely, knowledge, benevolence, and energy; and of "the one thing, by which those virtues are practised," which is singleness or sincerity.[10] It sets forth in detail the "nine standard rules for the administration of government," which are "the cultivation by the ruler of his own character; the honouring men of virtue and talents; affection to his relatives; respect towards the great ministers; kind and considerate treatment of the whole body of officers; cherishing the mass of the people as children; encouraging all classes of artizans; indulgent treatment of men from a distance; and the kindly cherishing of the princes of the States."[11] There are these and other equally interesting topics in this chapter; but, as they are in the Work, they distract the mind, instead of making the author's great object more clear to it, and I will not say more upon them here.

6. Doubtless it was the mention of "singleness," or "sincerity," in the 20th chapter, which made Tsze-sze introduce it into this Treatise, for from those terms he is able to go on to develope what he intended in saying that "if the states of Equilibrium and Harmony exist in perfection, a happy order will prevail throughout heaven and earth, and all things will be nourished and flourish." It is here, that now we are astonished at the audacity of the writer's assertions, and now lost in vain endeavours to ascertain his meaning I have quoted the words of Confucius that it is "singleness," by which the three virtues of knowledge, benevolence, and energy are able to carry into practice the duties of universal obligation. He

10 Par. 8. 11 Par. 12.

緒論

says also that it is this same "singleness" by which "the nine standard rules of government" can be effectively carried out.[12] This "singleness" is just a name for "the states of Equilibrium and Harmony existing in perfection." It denotes a character absolutely and relatively good, wanting nothing in itself, and correct in all its outgoings. "Sincerity" is another term for the same thing, and in speaking about it, Confucius makes a distinction between sincerity absolute and sincerity acquired. The former is born with some, and practised by them without any effort; the latter is attained by study and practised by strong endeavour.[13] The former is "the way of Heaven;" the latter is "the way of men."[14] "He who possesses sincerity,"—absolutely, that is,—"is he who without effort hits what is right, and apprehends without the exercise of thought;—he is the sage who naturally and easily embodies the right way. He who attains to sincerity, is he who chooses what is good and firmly holds it fast. And to this attainment there are requisite the extensive study of what is good, accurate inquiry about it, careful reflection on it, the clear discrimination of it, and the earnest practice of it."[15] In these passages Confucius unhesitatingly enunciates his belief that there are some men who are absolutely perfect, who come into the world as we may conceive the first man was, when he was created by God "in His own image," full of knowledge and righteousness, and who grow up as we know that Christ did, "increasing in wisdom and in stature." He disclaimed being considered to be such an one himself,[16] but the sages of China were such. And moreover, others who are not so naturally may make themselves to become so. Some will have to put forth more effort and to contend with greater struggles, but the end will be the possession of the knowledge and the achievement of the practice.

I need not say that these sentiments are contrary to the views of human nature which are presented in the Bible. The testimony of Revelation is that "there is not a just man upon earth that doeth good and sinneth not." "If we say that we have no sin," and in writing this term, I am thinking here not of sin against God, but, if we can conceive of it apart from that, of failures in regard to what ought to be in our regulation of ourselves, and in our behaviour to others;—"if we say that we have no sin, we deceive ourselves, and

12 Par. 15. 13 Par. 9. 14 Par. 18. 15 Parr. 18, 19. 16 Ana. VII. xix.

the truth is not in us." This language is appropriate in the lips of the learned as well as in those of the ignorant, to the highest sage as to the lowest child of the soil. Neither the scriptures of God nor the experience of man know of individuals absolutely perfect. The other sentiment that men can make themselves perfect is equally wide of the truth. Intelligence and goodness by no means stand to each other in the relation of cause and effect. The sayings of Ovid, "*Video meliora proboque, deteriora sequor,*" "*Nitimur in vetitum semper, cupimusque negata,*" are a more correct expression of the facts of human consciousness and conduct than the high-flown phrases of Confucius.

7. But Tsze-sze adopts the dicta of his grandfather without questioning them, and gives them forth in his own style at the commencement of the fourth part of his Treatise. "When we have intelligence resulting from sincerity, this condition is to be ascribed to nature; when we have sincerity resulting from intelligence, this condition is to be ascribed to instruction. But given the sincerity, and there shall be the intelligence; given the intelligence, and there shall be the sincerity."

Tsze-sze does more than adopt the dicta of Confucius. He applies them in a way which the sage never did, and which he would probably have shrunk from doing. The sincere, or perfect man of Confucius is he who satisfies completely all the requirements of duty in the various relations of Society, and in the exercise of government; but the sincere man of Tsze-sze is a potency in the universe. "Able to give its full development to his own nature, he can do the same to the nature of other men. Able to give its full development to the nature of other men, he can give their full development to the natures of animals and things. Able to give their full development to the natures of creatures and things, he can assist the transforming and nourishing powers of Heaven and Earth. Able to assist the transforming and nourishing powers of Heaven and Earth, he may with Heaven and Earth form a ternion."[18] Such are the results of sincerity natural. The case below this—of sincerity acquired, is as follows,—"The individual cultivates its shoots. From these he can attain to the possession of sincerity. This sincerity becomes apparent. From being apparent, it becomes manifest.

17 Ch. xxi. 18 Ch. xxii.

緒論

From being manifest, it becomes brilliant. Brilliant, it affects others. Affecting others, they are changed by it. Changed by it, they are transformed. It is only he who is possessed of the most complete sincerity that can exist under heaven, who can transform."[19] It may safely be affirmed, that when he thus expressed himself, Tsze-sze understood neither what he said nor whereof he affirmed. Maou Se-ho and some other modern writers explain away many of his predicates of sincerity, so that in their hands they become nothing but extravagant hyperboles, but the author himself would, I believe, have protested against such a mode of dealing with his words. True, his structures are castles in the air, but he had no idea himself that they were so.

In the 24th chapter there is a ridiculous descent from the sublimity of the two preceding. We are told that the possessor of entire sincerity is like a spirit and can foreknow, but the foreknowledge is only a judging by the milfoil and tortoise and other auguries! But the author recovers himself, and resumes his theme about sincerity as conducting to self-completion, and the completion of other men and things, describing it also as possessing all the qualities which can be predicated of Heaven and earth. Gradually the subject is made to converge to the person of Confucius, who is the ideal of the sage, as the sage is the ideal of humanity at large. An old account of the object of Tsze-sze in the Chung Yung is that he wrote it to celebrate the virtue of his grandfather."[20] He certainly contrives to do this in the course of it. The 30th, 31st, and 32d chapters contain his eulogium, and never has any other mortal been exalted in such terms. "He may be compared to heaven and earth in their supporting and containing, their overshadowing and curtaining all things; he may be compared to the four seasons in their alternating progress, and to the sun and moon in their successive shining." "Quick in apprehension, clear in discernment, of far-reaching intelligence, and all-embracing knowledge, he was fitted to exercise rule; magnanimous, generous, benign, and mild, he was fitted to exercise forbearance; impulsive, energetic, firm, and enduring, he was fitted to maintain a firm hold; self-adjusted, grave, never swerving from

19 Ch. xxiii. 20 唐陸德明釋文,謂孔子之孫,子思,作此以昭明祖德; see the 中庸唐說,一, p 1.

the Mean, and correct, he was fitted to command reverence; accomplished, distinctive, concentrative, and searching, he was fitted to exercise discrimination." "All-embracing and vast, he was like heaven; deep and active as a fountain, he was like the abyss." "Therefore his fame overspreads the Middle kingdom, and extends to all barbarous tribes. Wherever ships and carriages reach; wherever the strength of man penetrates; wherever the heavens overshadow and the earth sustains; wherever the sun and moon shine; wherever frosts and dews fall;—all who have blood and breath unfeignedly honour and love him. Hence it is said,—He is the equal of Heaven!" "Who can know him but he who is indeed quick in apprehension, clear in discernment, of far-reaching intelligence, and all-embracing knowledge, possessing all heavenly virtue?"

8. We have arrived at the concluding chapter of the Work, in which the author, according to Choo He, "having carried his descriptions to the highest point in the preceding chapters, turns back and examines the source of his subject; and then again from the work of the learner, free from all selfishness and watchful over himself when he is alone, he carries out his description, till by easy steps he brings it to the consummation of the whole empire tranquillized by simple and sincere reverentialness. He moreover eulogizes its mysteriousness, till he speaks of it at last as without sound or smell."[21] Between the first and last chapters there is a correspondency, and each of them may be considered as a summary of the whole treatise. The difference between them is, that in the first a commencement is made with the mention of Heaven as the conferrer of man's nature, while in this the progress of man in virtue is traced, step by step, till at last it is equal to that of High Heaven.

9. I have thus in the preceding paragraphs given a general and somewhat copious review of this Work. My object has been to seize, if I could, the train of thought, and to hold it up to the reader. Minor objections to it, arising from the confused use of terms and singular applications of passages from the older Classics, are noticed in the notes subjoined to the translation. I wished here that its scope should be seen, and the means be afforded of judging how far it is worthy of the high character attributed to it. "The relish of it," says the younger Ch'ing, "is inexhaustible. The whole of it is solid

21 See the concluding note by Choo He.

緒論

learning. When the skilful reader has explored it with delight till he has apprehended it, he may carry it into practice all his life, and will find that it cannot be exhausted."[22]

My own opinion of it is much less favourable. The names by which it has been called in translations of it have led to misconceptions of its character. Were it styled "The states of Equilibrium and Harmony," we should be prepared to expect something strange and probably extravagant. Assuredly we should expect nothing more strange or extravagant than what we have. It begins sufficiently well, but the author has hardly enunciated his preliminary apothegms, when he conducts into an obscurity where we can hardly grope our way, and when we emerge from that, it is to be bewildered by his gorgeous but unsubstantial pictures of sagely perfection. He has eminently contributed to nourish the pride of his countrymen. He has exalted their sages above all that is called God or is worshipped, and taught the masses of the people that with them they have need of nothing from without. In the mean time it is antagonistic to Christianity. By-and-by, when Christianity has prevailed in China, men will refer to it as a striking proof how their fathers by their wisdom knew neither God nor themselves

22 The Introductory note, p. 247.

CHAPTER V.

CONFUCIUS AND HIS IMMEDIATE DISCIPLES.

SECTION I.

LIFE OF CONFUCIUS.

His ancestry.

1. "And have you foreigners surnames as well?" This question has often been put to me by Chinese. It marks the ignorance which belongs to the people of all that is external to themselves, and the pride of antiquity which enters largely as an element into their character. If such a pride could in any case be justified, we might allow it to the family of the K'ung, the descendants of Confucius. In the reign of K'ang-he, twenty-one centuries and a half after the death of the sage, they amounted to eleven thousand males. But their ancestry is carried back through a period of equal extent, and genealogical tables are common, in which the descent of Confucius is traced down from Hwang-te, the inventor of the cycle, B.C. 2637.[1]

The more moderate writers, however, content themselves with exhibiting his ancestry back to the commencement of the Chow dynasty, B.C. 1121. Among the relatives of the tyrant Chow, the last emperor of the Yin dynasty, was an elder brother, by a concubine, named K'e,[2] who is celebrated by Confucius, Ana. XVIII. i., under the title of the viscount of Wei. Foreseeing the impending ruin of their family, K'e withdrew from the court; and subsequently, he was invested by the emperor Shing, the second of the house of Chow, with the principality of Sung, which embraced the eastern portion of the present province of Ho-nan, that he might there continue the sacrifices to the emperors of Yin. K'e was followed as duke of Sung by a younger brother, in whose line the succession

1 See Memoires concernant les Chinois, Tome XII, p. 447, *et seq.* Father Amiot states, p. 501, that he had seen the representative of the family, who succeeded to the dignity of 衍聖公 in the 9th year of K'ëen-lung, A.D. 1744. It is hardly necessary that I should say here, that the name Confucius is merely the Chinese characters 孔夫子 (K'ung Foo-tsze, 'The master, K'ung') latinized. 2 啟.

continued. His great-grandson, the duke Min,[3] was followed, B.C. 908, by a younger brother, leaving, however, two sons Fuh-foo Ho,[4] and Fang-sze.[5] Fuh Ho[6] resigned his right to the dukedom in favour of Fang-sze, who put his uncle to death in B.C. 893, and became master of the State. He is known as the duke Le,[7] and to his elder brother belongs the honour of having the sage among his descendants.

Three descents from Fuh Ho, we find Ching K'au-foo,[8] who was a distinguished officer under the dukes Tae, Woo, and Seuen[9] (B.C. 799—728). He is still celebrated for his humility, and for his literary tastes. We have accounts of him as being in communication with the Grand-historiographer of the empire, and engaged in researches about its ancient poetry, thus setting an example of one of the works to which Confucius gave himself.[10] K'aou gave birth to K'ung-foo Kea,[11] from whom the surname of K'ung took its rise. Five generations had now elapsed since the dukedom was held in the direct line of his ancestry, and it was according to the rule in such cases that the branch should cease its connection with the ducal stem, and merge among the people under a new surname. K'ung Kea was Master of the Horse in Sung, and an officer of well known loyalty and probity. Unfortunately for himself, he had a wife of surpassing beauty, of whom the chief minister of the State, by name Hwa Tuh,[12] happened on one occasion to get a glimpse. Determined to possess her, he commenced a series of intrigues, which, ended, B.C. 709, in the murder of Kea and the reigning duke Shang.[13] At the same time, Tuh secured the person of the lady, and hastened to his palace with the prize, but on the way she had strangled herself with her girdle.

An enmity was thus commenced between the two families of K'ung and Hwa which the lapse of time did not obliterate, and the latter being the more powerful of the two, Kea's great-grandson withdrew into the State of Loo to avoid their persecution. There he was appointed commandant of the city of Fang,[14] and is known in history

3 愍公. 4 弗父何. 5 魴 (al. 方) 祀. 6 I drop here the 父 (up. 2d tone), which seems to have been used in those times in a manner equivalent to our Mr. 7 厲公. 8 正考甫; 甫 is used in the same way as 父; see note 6. 9 戴, 武, 宣, 三公. 10. See the 魯語, and 商頌詩序; quoted in Keang Yung's (江永) Life of Confucius, which forms a part of the 鄉黨圖考. 11 孔父嘉. 12 華督. 13 殤公. 14 防.

by the name of Fang-shuh.[15] Fang-shuh gave birth to Pih-hea,[16] and from him came Shuh-leang Heih,[17] the father of Confucius. Heih appears in the history of the times as a soldier of great prowess and daring bravery. In the year B.C. 562, when serving at the siege of a place called Peih-yang,[18] a party of the assailants made their way in at a gate which had purposely been left open, and no sooner were they inside than the portcullis was dropped. Heih was just entering, and catching the massive structure with both his hands, he gradually by dint of main strength raised it and held it up, till his friends had made their escape.

Thus much on the ancestry of the sage. Doubtless he could trace his descent in the way which has been indicated up to the imperial house of Yin, nor was there one among his ancestors during the rule of Chow to whom he could not refer with satisfaction. They had been ministers and soldiers of Sung and Loo, all men of worth, and in Ching K'aou, both for his humility and literary researches, Confucius might have special complacency.

From his birth to his first public employments. B.C. 551—531.

2. Confucius was the child of Shuh-leang Heih's old age. The soldier had married in early life, but his wife brought him only daughters,—to the number of nine, and no son. By a concubine he had a son, named Măng-p'e and also Pih-ne,[1] who proved a cripple, so that, when he was over seventy years, Heih sought a second wife in the Yen family,[2] from which came subsequently Yen Hwuy, the favourite disciple of his son. There were three daughters in the family, the youngest being named Ching-tsae.[3] Their father said to them, "Here is the commandant of Tsow. His father and grandfather were only scholars, but his ancestors before them were descendants of the sage emperors. He is a man ten feet high,[4] and of extraordinary prowess, and I am very desirous of his alliance. Though he is old and austere, you need have no misgivings about him. Which of you three will be his wife?" The two elder daughters were silent, but Ching-tsae said, "Why do you ask us, father? It is for you to determine." "Very well," said her father in reply, "you will do."

15 防叔. 16 伯夏. 17 叔梁紇. 18 偪陽.

1 孟皮,一字伯尼. 2 顔氏. 3 徵在. 4 其人,身長十尺. See, on the length of the ancient foot, Ana. VIII. vi., but the point needs a more sifting investigation than it has yet received.

Ching-tsae, accordingly, became Heih's wife, and in due time gave birth to Confucius, who received the name of K'ew, and was subsequently styled Chung-ne.[5] The event happened on the 21st day of the 10th month of the 21st year of the duke Seang, of Loo, being the 20th year of the emperor Ling, B.C. 551. The birth-place was in the district of Tsow, of which Heih was the governor. It was somewhere within the limits of the present department of Yen-chow in Shan-tung, but the honour of being the exact spot is claimed for two places in two different districts of the department.

The notices which we have of Confucius' early years are very scanty. When he was in his third year his father died. It is related of

5 名邱字仲尼. The legends say that Ching-tsae, fearing lest she should not have a son, in consequence of her husband's age, privately ascended the Ne-k'ew hill to pray for the boon, and that when she had obtained it, she commemorated the fact in the names—K'ew and Chung-ne. But the cripple, Mang-p'e, had previously been styled Pih-ne. There was some reason, previous to Confucius' birth, for using the term *ne* in the family. As might be expected, the birth of the sage is surrounded with many prodigious occurrences. One account is, that the husband and wife prayed together for a son in a dell of mount Ne. As Ching-tsae went up the hill, the leaves of the trees and plants all erected themselves, and bent downwards on her return. That night she dreamt the Black *Te* appeared, and said to her, 'You shall have a son, a sage, and you must bring him forth in a hollow mulberry tree.' One day during her pregnancy, she fell into a dreamy state, and saw five old men in the hall, who called themselves the essences of the five planets, and led an animal which looked like a small cow with one horn, and was covered with scales like a dragon. This creature knelt before Ching-tsae, and cast forth from its mouth a slip of gem, on which was the inscription,—'The son of the essence of water shall succeed to the withering Chow, and be a throneless king.' Ching-tsae tied a piece of embroidered ribbon about its horn, and the vision disappeared. When Heih was told of it, he said, 'The creature must be the K'e-lin.' As her time drew near, Ching-tsae asked her husband if there was any place in the neighbourhood called 'The hollow mulberry tree.' He told her there was a dry cave in the south hill, which went by that name. Then she said, 'I will go and be confined there.' Her husband was surprised, but when made acquainted with her former dream, he made the necessary arrangements. On the night when the child was born, two dragons came and kept watch on the left and right of the hill, and two spirit-ladies appeared in the air, pouring out fragrant odours, as if to bathe Ching-tsae; and as soon as the birth took place, a spring of clear warm water bubbled up from the floor of the cave, which dried up again when the child had been washed in it. The child was of an extraordinary appearance; with a mouth like the sea, ox lips, a dragon's back, &c., &c. On the top of his head was a remarkable formation, in consequence of which he was named K'ew, &c. See the 列國志, Bk. lxxviii.—Sze-ma Ts'een seems to make Confucius to have been illegitimate, saying that Heih and Miss Yen cohabited in the wilderness (野合). Keang Yung says that the phrase has reference simply to the disparity of their ages.

6 Sze-ma Ts'een says that Confucius was born in the 22d year of duke Seang, B.C. 550. He is followed by Choo He in the short sketch of Confucius' life prefixed to the Lun Yu, and by 'The Annals of the Empire' (歷代統紀表), published with imperial sanction in the reign of Kea-k'ing. (To this latter work I have generally referred for my dates.) The year assigned in the text above rests on the authority of Kuh-lëang and Kung-yang, the two commentators on the Ts'un Ts'ew. With regard to the month, however, the 10th is that assigned by Kuh-lëang, while Kung-yang names the 11th. 7 Tsow is written 郰, 鄹, 陬, and 鄒

him, that as a boy he used to play at the arrangement of sacrificial vessels, and at postures of ceremony. Of his schooling we have no reliable account. There is a legend, indeed, that at seven he went to school to Gan P'ing-chung,[8] but it must be rejected as P'ing-chung belonged to the State of Ts'e. He tells us himself that at fifteen he bent his mind to learning;[9] but the condition of the family was one of poverty. At a subsequent period, when people were astonished at the variety of his knowledge, he explained it by saying "When I was young, my condition was low, and therefore I acquired my ability in many things; but they were mean matters."[10]

When he was nineteen, he married a lady from the State of Sung, of the Këen-kwan family,[11] and in the following year his son Le was born. On the occasion of this event, the duke Ch'aou sent him a present of a couple of carp. It was to signify his sense of his prince's favour, that he called his son Le (*The Carp*), and afterwards gave him the designation of Pih-yu[12] (*Fish Primus*). No mention is made of the birth of any other children, though we know, from Ana. V. i., that he had at least one daughter. The fact of the duke of Loo's sending him a gift on the occasion of Le's birth, shows that he was not unknown, but was already commanding public attention and the respect of the great.

It was about this time, probably in the year after his marriage, that Confucius took his first public employment, as keeper of the stores of grain,[13] and in the following year he was put in charge of the public fields and lands.[14] Mencius adduces these employments in illustration of his doctrine that the superior man may at times take office on account of his poverty, but must confine himself in such a case to places of small emolument, and aim at nothing but the discharge of their humble duties. According to him, Confucius as keeper of stores, said, "My calculations must all be right:—that is all I have to care about;" and when in charge of the public fields, he said, "The oxen and sheep must be fat and strong and superior:—that is all I have to care about."[15] It does not appear whether

[illegible]平仲. 9 Ana. II. iv. 10 Ana. IX. vi. 11 娶宋之幵官氏. [illegible]曰鯉, 而字伯魚. 13 爲委吏. This is Mencius' account. Sze-ma [illegible] says [illegible]爲季氏吏, but his subsequent words 料量平 show that the office [illegible] 14 Mencius calls this office 乘田, while Sze-ma Ts'een says 爲司職吏. [illegible] V. Pt. II. v. 4.

緒論

these offices were held by Confucius in the direct employment of the State, or as a dependent of the Ke family in whose jurisdiction he lived. The present of the carp from the duke may incline us to suppose the former.

3. In his twenty-second year, Confucius commenced his labours as a public teacher, and his house became a resort for young and enquiring spirits, who wished to learn the doctrines of antiquity.

Commencement of his labours as a teacher. The death of his mother. B.C. 530—526.

However small the fee his pupils were able to afford, he never refused his instructions.[1] All that he required, was an ardent desire for improvement, and some degree of capacity. "I do not open up the truth," he said, "to one who is not eager to get knowledge, nor help out any one who is not anxious to explain himself. When I have presented one corner of a subject to any one, and he cannot from it learn the other three, I do not repeat my lesson."[2]

His mother died in the year B.C. 528, and he resolved that her body should lie in the same grave with that of his father, and that their common resting place should be in Fang, the first home of the K'ung in Loo. But here a difficulty presented itself. His father's coffin had been for twenty years, where it had first been deposited, off the road of *The Five Fathers*, in the vicinity of Tsow:—would it be right in him to move it? He was relieved from this perplexity by an old woman of the neighbourhood, who told him that the coffin had only just been put into the ground, as a temporary arrangement, and not regularly buried. On learning this, he carried his purpose into execution. Both coffins were conveyed to Fang, and put in the ground together, with no intervening space between them, as was the custom in some States. And now came a new perplexity. He said to himself, "In old times, they had graves, but raised no tumulus over them. But I am a man, who belongs equally to the north and the south, the east and the west. I must have something by which I can remember the place." Accordingly he raised a mound, four feet high, over the grave, and returned home, leaving a party of his disciples to see everything properly completed. In the mean time there came on a heavy storm of rain, and it was a considerable time before the disciples joined him.

1 Ana. VII. vii. 2 Ana. VII. viii.

"What makes you so late?" he asked. "The grave in Fang fell down," they said. He made no reply, and they repeated their answer three times, when he burst into tears, and said, "Ah! they did not make their graves so in antiquity."[3]

Confucius mourned for his mother the regular period of three years,—three years nominally, but in fact only twenty-seven months. Five days after the mourning was expired, he played on his lute but could not sing. It required other five days before he could accompany an instrument with his voice.[4]

Some writers have represented Confucius as teaching his disciples important lessons from the manner in which he buried his mother, and having a design to correct irregularities in the ordinary funeral ceremonies of the time. These things are altogether "without book." We simply have a dutiful son paying the last tribute of affection to a good parent. In one point he departs from the ancient practice, raising a mound over the grave, and when the fresh earth gives way from a sudden rain, he is moved to tears, and seems to regret his innovation. This sets Confucius vividly before us,—a man of the past as much as of the present, whose own natural feelings were liable to be hampered in their development by the traditions of antiquity which he considered sacred. It is important, however, to observe the reason which he gave for rearing the mound. He had in it a presentiment of much of his future course. He was "a man of the north, the south, the east, and the west." He might not confine himself to any one State. He would travel, and his way might be directed to some "wise ruler," whom his counsels would conduct to a benevolent sway that would break forth on every side till it transformed the empire.

He learns music; visits the court of Chow; and returns to Loo. B.C. 526—517.

4. When the mourning for his mother was over, Confucius remained in Loo, but in what special capacity we do not know. Probably he continued to encourage the resort of inquirers to whom he communicated instruction, and pursued his own researches into the history, literature, and institutions of the empire. In the year B.C. 524, the chief of the small State of T'an,[1]

3 Le Ke, II. Pt. I. i. 10; Pt. II. iii. 30; Pt. I. i. 6. See also the discussion of those passages in Keang Yung's 'Life of Confucius.' 4 Le Ke, II. Pt. I. i. 22.

1 See the Ts'un Ts'ew, under the 7th year of duke Ch'aou.—秋,郯子來朝.

緒論

made his appearance at the court of Loo, and discoursed in a wonderful manner, at a feast given to him by the duke, about the names which the most ancient sovereigns, from Hwang-te downwards, gave to their ministers. The sacrifices to the emperor Shaou-haou, the next in descent from Hwang-te, were maintained in T'an, so that the chief fancied that he knew all about the abstruse subject on which he discoursed. Confucius, hearing about the matter, waited on the visitor, and learned from him all that he had to communicate.[2]

To the year B.C. 523, when Confucius was twenty-nine years old, is referred his studying music under a famous master of the name of Sëang.[3] He was approaching his 30th year when, as he tells us, "he stood"[4] firm, that is, in his convictions on the subjects of learning to which he had bent his mind fifteen years before. Five years more, however, were still to pass by, before the anticipation mentioned in the conclusion of the last paragraph began to receive its fulfilment,[5] though we may conclude from the way in which it was brought about that he was growing all the time in the estimation of the thinking minds in his native State.

In the 24th year of duke Ch'aou, B.C. 517, one of the principal ministers of Loo, known by the name of Măng He, died. Seventeen years before, he had painfully felt his ignorance of ceremonial observances, and had made it his subsequent business to make himself acquainted with them. On his deathbed, he addressed his chief officer, saying, "A knowledge of propriety is the stem of a man. Without it he has no means of standing firm. I have heard that there is one K'ung Kew, who is thoroughly versed in it. He is a descendant of Sages, and though the line of his family was extinguished in Sung, among his ancestors there were Fuh-foo Ho, who resigned the dukedom to his brother, and Ching K'aou-foo, who was

2 This rests on the respectable authority of Tso-k'ew Ming's annotations on the Ts'un Ts'ew, but I must consider it apocryphal. The legend-writers have fashioned a journey to T'an. The slightest historical intimation becomes a text with them, on which they enlarge to the glory of the sage. Amiot has reproduced and expanded their romancings, and others, such as Pauthier (Chine, pp. 121–183) and Thornton (History of China, vol. I. pp. 151–215) have followed in his wake. 3 師襄 See the 'Family Sayings,' 卷三, art. 辯樂解; but the account there given is not more credible than the chief of T'an's expositions. 4 Ana. II. iv.

5 The journey to Chow is placed by Sze-ma Ts'een before Confucius' holding of his first official employments, and Choo He and most other writers follow him. It is a great error, and arisen from a misunderstanding of the passage from the 左氏傳 upon the subject.

distinguished for his humility. Tsang Heih has observed that if sage men of intelligent virtue do not attain to eminence, distinguished men are sure to appear among their posterity. His words are now to be verified, I think, in K'ung K'ew. After my death, you must tell Ho-ke to go and study proprieties under him."[6] In consequence of this charge, Ho-ke,[7] Mang He's son, who appears in the Analects under the name of Mang E,[8] and a brother, or perhaps only a near relative, named Nan-kung King-shuh,[9] became disciples of Confucius. Their wealth and standing in the State gave him a position which he had not had before, and he told King-shuh of a wish which he had to visit the court of Chow, and especially to confer on the subject of ceremonies and music with Laou Tan. King-shuh represented the matter to the duke Ch'aou, who put a carriage and a pair of horses at Confucius' disposal for the expedition.[10]

At this time the court of Chow was in the city of Lŏ,[11] in the present department of Ho-nan of the province of the same name. The reigning emperor is known by the title of King,[12] but the sovereignty was little more than nominal. The state of China was then analogons to that of one of the European kingdoms during the prevalence of the feudal system. At the commencement of the dynasty, the various States of the empire had been assigned to the relatives and adherents of the reigning family. There were thirteen principalities of greater note, and a large number of smaller dependencies. During the vigorous youth of the dynasty, the emperor or lord paramount exercised an effective control over the various chiefs, but with the lapse of time there came weakness and decay. The chiefs—corresponding somewhat to the European dukes, earls, marquises, barons, &c.,—quarreled and warred among themselves, and the stronger among them barely acknowledged their subjection to the emperor. A similar condition of things prevailed in each particular State. There there were hereditary ministerial families, who were continually encroaching on the authority of their rulers, and the heads of those families again were frequently hard pressed by their inferior officers. Such was the state of China in Confucius' time. The

6 See 左氏傳, 昭公七年. 7 何忌. 8 孟懿子. 9 南宮敬叔. 10 The 家語 makes King-shuh accompany Confucius to Chow. It is difficult to understand this, if King-shuh were really a son of Mang He who had died that year. 11 洛. 12 敬王 (B.C. 518–475).

緒論

reader must have it clearly before him, if he would understand the position of the sage, and the reforms which, we shall find, it was subsequently his object to introduce.

Arrived at Chow, he had no intercourse with the court or any of the principal ministers. He was there not as a politician, but an inquirer about the ceremonies and maxims of the founders of the dynasty. Laou Tan,[13] whom he had wished to see, the acknowledged founder of the Taouists, or Rationalistic sect which has maintained its ground in opposition to the followers of Confucius, was then a treasury-keeper. They met and freely interchanged their views, but no reliable account of their conversations has been preserved. In the 5th Book of the Le Ke, which is headed, "The philosopher Tsăng asked," Confucius refers four times to the views of Laou-tsze on certain points of funeral ceremonies, and in the "Family Sayings," Book XXIV., he tells Ke K'ang what he had heard from him about "The Five Tes," but we may hope their conversation turned also on more important subjects. Sze-ma Ts'een, favourable to Laou-tsze, makes him lecture his visitor in the following style:—"Those whom you talk about are dead, and their bones are mouldered to dust; only their words remain. When the superior man gets his time, he mounts aloft; but when the time is against him, he moves as if his feet were entangled. I have heard that a good merchant, though he has rich treasures deeply stored, appears as if he were poor, and that the superior man whose virtue is complete, is yet to outward seeming stupid. Put away your proud air and many desires, your insinuating habit and wild will.[14] These are of no advantage to you. This is all which I have to tell you." On the other hand, Confucius is made to say to his disciples, "I know how birds can fly, how fishes can swim, and how animals can run. But the runner may be snared, the swimmer may be hooked, and the flyer may be shot by the arrow. But there is the dragon. I cannot tell how he mounts on the wind through the clouds, and rises to heaven. To-day I have seen Laou-tsze, and can only compare him to the dragon."[15]

13 According to Sze-ma Ts'een, Tan was the posthumous epithet of this individual, whose surname was Le (李), name Urh (耳), and designation Pih-yang (伯陽). 14 逸態與淫志. 15 See the 史記列傳第三, and compare the remarks attributed to Laou-tsze in the account of the K'ung family near the beginning.

While at Lŏ, Confucius walked over the grounds set apart for the great sacrifices to Heaven and Earth; inspected the pattern of the Hall of Light, built to give audience in to the princes of the empire; and examined all the arrangements of the ancestral temple and the court. From the whole he received a profound impression. "Now," said he with a sigh, "I know the sage wisdom of the duke of Chow, and how the house of Chow attained to the imperial sway."[16] On the walls of the Hall of Light were paintings of the ancient sovereigns from Yaou and Shun downwards, their characters appearing in the representations of them, and words of praise or warning being appended. There was also a picture of the duke of Chow sitting with his infant nephew, the king Shing, upon his knees, to give audience to all the princes. Confucius surveyed the scene with silent delight, and then said to his followers, "Here you see how Chow became so great. As we use a glass to examine the forms of things, so must we study antiquity in order to understand the present."[17] In the hall of the ancestral temple, there was a metal statue of a man with three clasps upon his mouth, and his back covered over with an enjoyable homily on the duty of keeping a watch upon the lips. Confucius turned to his disciples and said, "Observe it, my children. These words are true, and commend themselves to our feelings."[18]

About music he made inquiries at Ch'ang Hwang, to whom the following remarks are attributed:—"I have observed about Chung-ne many marks of a sage. His has river eyes and a dragon forehead,—the very characteristics of Hwang-te. His arms are long, his back is like a tortoise, and he is nine feet six inches in height,—the very semblance of T'ang the Completer. When he speaks, he praises the ancient kings. He moves along the path of humility and courtesy. He has heard of every subject, and retains with a strong memory. His knowledge of things seems inexhaustible.—Have we not in him the rising of a sage?"[19]

I have given these notices of Confucius at the court of Chow, more as being the only ones I could find, than because I put much faith in them. He did not remain there long, but returned the same year to Loo, and continued his work of teaching. His fame

16, 17, 18 See the 家語, 卷二, art. 觀周. 19 Quoted by Keang Yung from 'The Family Sayings.'

緒論

was greatly increased; disciples came to him from different parts, till their number amounted to three thousand. Several of those who have come down to us as the most distinguished among his followers, however, were yet unborn, and the statement just given may be considered as an exaggeration. We are not to conceive of the disciples as forming a community, and living together. Parties of them may have done so. We shall find Confucius hereafter always moving amid a company of admiring pupils; but the greater number must have had their proper avocations and ways of living, and would only resort to the master, when they wished specially to ask his counsel or to learn of him.

He withdraws to Ts'e, and returns to Loo the following year. B.C. 516, 515.

5. In the year succeeding the return to Loo, that State fell into great confusion. There were three Families in it, all connected irregularly with the ducal house, who had long kept the rulers in a condition of dependency. They appear frequently in the Analects as the Ke clan, the Shuh, and the Măng; and while Confucius freely spoke of their usurpations,[1] he was a sort of dependent of the Ke family, and appears in frequent communication with members of all the three. In the year B.C. 516, the duke Ch'aou came to open hostilities with them, and being worsted, fled into Ts'e, the State adjoining Loo on the north. Thither Confucius also repaired, that he might avoid the prevailing disorder of his native State. Ts'e was then under the government of a duke, afterwards styled King,[2] who "had a thousand teams, each of four horses, but on the day of his death the people did not praise him for a single virtue."[3] His chief minister, however, was Gan Ying,[4] a man of considerable ability and worth. At his court the music of the ancient sage-emperor, Shun, originally brought to T'se from the State of Ts'in,[5] was still preserved.

According to the "Family Sayings," an incident occurred on the way to Ts'e, which I may transfer to these pages as a good specimen of the way in which Confucius turned occurring matters to account, in his intercourse with his disciples. As he was passing by the side of the T'ae mountain, there was a woman weeping and wailing by a grave. Confucius bent forward in his carriage, and

1 See Analects, III. i., ii., *et al.* 2. 景公. 3 Ana. XVI. xii. 4 晏嬰. This is the same who was afterwards styled 晏平仲. 5 陳.

after listening to her for some time, sent Tsze-loo to ask the cause of her grief. "You weep, as if you had experienced sorrow upon sorrow," said Tsze-loo. The woman replied, "It is so. My husband's father was killed here by a tiger, and my husband also; and now my son has met the same fate." Confucius asked her why she did not remove from the place, and on her answering, "There is here no oppressive government," he turned to his disciples, and said, "My children, remember this. Oppressive government is fiercer than a tiger."[6]

As soon as he crossed the border from Loo, we are told he discovered from the gait and manners of a boy, whom he saw carrying a pitcher, the influence of the sage's music, and told the driver of his carriage to hurry on to the capital.[7] Arrived there, he heard the strain, and was so ravished with it, that for three months he did not know the taste of flesh. "I did not think," he said, "that music could have been made so excellent as this."[8] The duke King was pleased with the conferences which he had with him,[9] and proposed to assign to him the town of Lin-k'ew, from the revenues of which he might derive a sufficient support; but Confucius refused the gift, and said to his disciples, "A superior man will only receive reward for services which he has done. I have given advice to the duke King, but he has not yet obeyed it, and now he would endow me with this place! Very far is he from understanding me."[10]

On one occasion the duke asked about government, and received the characteristic reply, "There is government when the prince is prince, and the minister is minister; when the father is father, and the son is son."[11] I say that the reply is characteristic. Once, when Tsz-loo asked him what he would consider the first thing to be done if entrusted with the government of a State, Confucius answered, "What is necessary is to rectify names."[12] The disciple thought the

6 See the 家語, 卷四, art. 正論解. I have translated, however, from the Le Ke, II. Pt II. iii. 10, where the same incident is given, with some variations, and without saying when or where it occurred. 7 See the 說苑, 卷十九, p. 13. 8 Ana. VII. xiii.

9 Some of these are related in the Family Sayings;—about the burning of the ancestral shrine of the emperor 釐, and a one-footed bird which appeared hopping and flapping its wings in Ts'e. They are plainly fabulous, though quoted in proof of Confucius' sage wisdom. This reference to them is more than enough. 10 家語, 卷二, 六本. 11. Ana. XII. xi. 12 Ana. XIII. iii.

緒論

reply wide of the mark, but it was substantially the same with what he said to the duke King. There is a sufficient foundation in nature for government in the several relations of society, and if those be maintained and developed according to their relative significancy, it is sure to obtain. This was a first principle in the political ethics of Confucius.

Another day the duke got to a similar inquiry the reply that the art of government lay in an economical use of the revenues; and being pleased, he resumed his purpose of retaining the philosopher in his State, and proposed to assign to him the fields of Ne-k'e. His chief minister Gan Ying dissuaded him from the purpose, saying, "Those scholars are impracticable, and cannot be imitated. They are haughty and conceited of their own views, so that they will not be content in inferior positions. They set a high value on all funeral ceremonies, give way to their grief, and will waste their property on great burials, so that they would only be injurious to the common manners. This Mr K'ung has a thousand peculiarities. It would take generations to exhaust all that he knows about the ceremonies of going up and going down. This is not the time to examine into his rules of propriety. If you, prince, wish to employ him to change the customs of Ts'e, you will not be making the people your primary consideration."[13]

I had rather believe that these were not the words of Gan Ying, but they must represent pretty correctly the sentiments of many of the statesmen of the time about Confucius. The duke of Ts'e got tired ere long of having such a monitor about him, and observed, "I cannot treat him as I would the chief of the Ke family. I will treat him in a way between that accorded to the chief of the Ke, and that given to the chief of the Măng family." Finally he said, "I am old; I cannot use his doctrines."[14] These observations were made directly to Confucius, or came to his hearing.[15] It was not consistent with his self-respect to remain longer in Ts'e, and he returned to Loo.[16]

6. Returned to Loo, he remained for the long period of about

13 See the 史記, 孔子世家, p. 2. 14 Ana. XVIII. iii. 15 Sze-ma Ts'een makes the first observation to have been addressed directly to Confucius. 16 According to the above account Confucius was only once, and for a portion of two years, in Ts'e. For the refutation of contrary accounts, see Keang Yung's Life of the sage.

He remains without office in Loo, B.C. 515–501.

fifteen years without being engaged in any official employment. It was a time, indeed, of great disorder. The duke Ch'aou continued a refugee in Ts'e, the government being in the hands of the great Families, up to his death in B.C. 509, on which event the rightful heir was set aside, and another member of the ducal house, known to us by the title of Ting,[1] substituted in his place. The ruling authority of the principality became thus still more enfeebled than it had been before, and, on the other hand, the chiefs of the Ke, the Shuh, and the Măng, could hardly keep their ground against their own officers. Of those latter the two most conspicuous were Yang Hoo,[2] called also Yang Ho,[3] and Kung-shan Fuh-jaou.[4] At one time Ke Hwan, the most powerful of the chiefs, was kept a prisoner by Yang Hoo, and was obliged to make terms with him in order to secure his liberation. Confucius would give his countenance to none, as he disapproved of all, and he studiously kept aloof from them. Of how he comported himself among them we have a specimen in the incident related in the Analects, XVII. i.–" Yang Ho wished to see Confucius, but Confucius would not go to see him. On this, he sent a present of a pig to Confucius, who, having chosen a time when Ho was not at home, went to pay his respects for the gift. He met him, however, on the way. 'Come, let me speak with you,' said the officer. 'Can he be called benevolent, who keeps his jewel in his bosom, and leaves his country to confusion?' Confucius replied, 'No.' 'Can he be called wise, who is anxious to be engaged in public employment, and yet is constantly losing the opportunity of being so?' Confucius again said, 'No.' The other added, 'The days and months are passing away; the years do not wait for us.' Confucius said, 'Right; I will go into office.'" Chinese writers are eloquent in their praises of the sage for the combination of propriety, complaisance, and firmness, which they see in his behaviour in this matter. To myself there seems nothing remarkable in it but a somewhat questionable dexterity. But it was well for the fame of Confucius that his time was not occupied during those years with official services. He turned them to better account, prosecuting his researches into the poetry, history, ceremonies, and music of the empire. Many disciples continued to resort to him, and the legendary

1 定公. 2 陽虎. 3 陽貨. 4 公山弗擾(史記,狃).

緒論

writers tell us how he employed their services in digesting the results of his studies. I must repeat, however, that several of them, whose names are most famous, such as Tsăng Sin, were as yet children, and Min Sun[5] was not born till B.C. 500.

To this period we must refer the almost single instance which we have of the manner of Confucius' intercourse with his son Le. "Have you heard any lessons from your father different from what we have all heard?" asked one of the disciples once of Le. "No," said Le. "He was standing alone once, when I was passing through the court below with hasty steps, and said to me, 'Have you read the Odes?' On my replying, 'Not yet,' he added, 'If you do not learn the Odes, you will not be fit to converse with.' Another day, in the same place and the same way, he said to me, 'Have you read the rules of Propriety?' On my replying, 'Not yet,' he added, 'If you do not learn the rules of Propriety, your character cannot be established.' I have heard only these two things from him." The disciple was delighted and observed, "I asked one thing, and I have got three things. I have heard about the Odes. I have heard about the rules of Propriety. I have also heard that the superior man maintains a distant reserve towards his son"[6]

I can easily believe that this distant reserve was the rule which Confucius followed generally in his treatment of his son. A stern dignity is the quality which a father has to maintain upon his system, It is not to be without the element of kindness, but that must never go beyond the line of propriety. There is too little room left for the play and development of natural affection.

The divorce of his wife must also have taken place during these years, if it ever took place at all, which is a disputed point. The curious reader will find the question discussed in the notes on the second Book of the Le Ke. The evidence inclines, I think, against the supposition that Confucius did put his wife away. When she died, at a period subsequent to the present, Le kept on weeping aloud for her after the period for such a demonstration of grief had expired, when Confucius sent a message to him that his sorrow must be subdued, and the obedient son dried his tears.[7] We are glad to know that on one occasion—the death of his favourite disciple, Yen

5 閔損. 6. Ana XVI. xiii. 7 See the Le Ke II. Pt I. i. 27.

Hwuy—the tears of Confucius himself would flow over and above the measure of propriety.[8]

He holds office. B.C. 500–496.

7 We come to the short period of Confucius' official life. In the year B.C. 501, things had come to a head between the chiefs of the three Families and their ministers, and had resulted in the defeat of the latter. In B.C. 500, the resources of Yang Hoo were exhausted, and he fled into Ts'e, so that the State was delivered from its greatest troubler, and the way was made more clear for Confucius to go into office, should an opportunity occur. It soon presented itself. Towards the end of that year he was made chief magistrate of the town of Chung-too.[1]

Just before he received this appointment, a circumstance occured of which we do not well know what to make. When Yang-hoo fled into Ts'e, Kung-shan Fuh-jaou, who had been confederate with him, continued to maintain an attitude of rebellion, and held the city of Pe against the Ke family. Thence he sent a message to Confucius inviting him to join him, and the sage seemed so inclined to go that his disciple Tsze-loo remonstrated with him, saying, "Indeed you cannot go! why must you think of going to see Kung-shan?" Confucius replied, "Can it be without some reason that he has invited me? If any one employ me, may I not make an eastern Chow?"[2] The upshot, however, was that he did not go, and I cannot suppose that he had ever any serious intention of doing so. Amid the general gravity of his intercourse with his followers, there gleam out a few instances of quiet pleasantry, when he amused himself by playing with their notions about him. This was probably one of them.

As magistrate of Chung-too he produced a marvellous reformation of the manners of the people in a short time. According to the "Family Sayings," he enacted rules for the nourishing of the living and all observances to the dead. Different food was assigned to the old and the young, and different burdens to the strong and the weak. Males and females kept apart from each other in the streets. A

8 Ana. XI. ix.

1 中都宰. Amiot says this was 'la ville meme ou le Souverain tenoit sa Cour' (Vie de Confucius, p. 147). He is followed of course by Thornton and Pauthier. My reading has not shown me that such was the case. In the notes to K'ang-he's edition of the 'Five King,' Le Ke, II. Pt. I. iii. 4, it is simply said—'Chung-too,—the name of a town of Loo. It afterwards belonged to Ts'e when it was called P'ing-luh (平陸).' 2 Ana. XVII. v.

緒論

thing dropt on the road was not picked up. There was no fraudulent carving of vessels. Inner coffins were made four inches thick, and the outer ones five. Graves were made on the high grounds, no mounds being raised over them, and no trees planted about them. Within twelve months, the princes of the States all about wished to imitate his style of administration.[3]

The duke Ting, surprised at what he saw, asked whether his rules could be employed to govern a whole State, and Confucius told him that they might be applied to the whole empire. On this the duke appointed him assistant-superintendent of Works,[4] in which capacity he surveyed the lands of the State, and made many improvements in agriculture. From this he was quickly made minister of Crime,[5] and the appointment was enough to put an end to crime. There was no necessity to put the penal laws in execution. No offenders showed themselves.[6]

These indiscriminating eulogies are of little value. One incident, related in the annotations of Tso-k'ew on the Ts'un Ts'ew,[7] commends itself at once to our belief, as in harmony with Confucius' character. The chief of the Ke, pursuing with his enmity the duke Ch'aou, even after his death, had placed his grave apart from the graves of his predecessors; and Confucius surrounded the ducal cemetery with a ditch so as to include the solitary resting-place, boldly telling the chief that he did it to hide his disloyalty.[8] But he signalized himself most of all, in B.C. 499, by his behaviour at an interview between the dukes of Loo and Ts'e, at a place called Shih-k'e,[9] and Këă-kuh,[10] in the present district of Lae-woo, in the department of T'ae-gan.[11] Confucius was present as master of ceremonies on the part of Loo, and the meeting was professedly pacific. The two princes were to form a covenant of alliance. The principal officer on the part of Ts'e, however, despising Confucius as "a man of ceremonies, without courage," had advised his sovereign to make the duke of Loo a prisoner, and for this purpose a band of the half-savage original inhabitants of the place advanced with weapons to the stage where the two dukes were met. Confucius understood

3 家語, Bk I. 4 司空. This office, however, was held by the chief of the Măng family. We must understand that Confucius was only an assistant to him, or perhaps acted for him. 5 大司寇. 6 家語, Bk I. 7 左傳.定公元年. 8 家語, Bk I 9 實其. 10 夾谷 11 泰安府,萊蕪縣.

the scheme, and said to the opposite party, "Our two princes are met for a pacific object. For you to bring a band of savage vassals to disturb the meeting with their weapons, is not the way in which Ts'e can expect to give law to the princes of the empire. These barbarians have nothing to do with our Great Flowery land. Such vassals may not interfere with our covenant. Weapons are out of place at such a meeting. As before the spirits, such conduct is unpropitious. In point of virtue, it is contrary to right. As between man and man, it is not polite." The duke of Ts'e ordered the disturbers off, but Confucius withdrew, carrying the duke of Loo with him. The business proceeded, notwithstanding, and when the words of the alliance were being read on the part of Ts'e,—"So be it to Loo, if it contribute not 300 chariots of war to the help of Ts'e, when its army goes across its borders," a messenger from Confucius added,—"And so be it to us, if we obey your orders, unless you return to us the fields on the south of the Wăn." At the conclusion of the ceremonies, the prince of Ts'e wanted to give a grand entertainment, but Confucius demonstrated that such a thing would be contrary to the established rules of propriety, his real object being to keep his sovereign out of danger. In this way the two parties separated, they of Ts'e filled with shame at being foiled and disgraced by "the man of ceremonies," and the result was that the lands of Loo which had been appropriated by Ts'e were restored.[12]

For two years more Confucius held the office of minister of Crime. Some have supposed that he was further raised to the dignity of chief minister of the State,[13] but that was not the case. One instance of the manner in which he executed his functions is worth recording. When any matter came before him, he took the opinion of different individuals upon it, and in giving judgment would say, "I decide according to the view of so and so." There was an approach to our jury system in the plan, Confucius' object being to enlist general sympathy, and carry the public judgment with him in his administration of justice. A father having brought some charge against his son, Confucius kept them both in prison for three months, without

12 This meeting at Këă-kuh is related in Sze-ma Ts'een, the Family Sayings, and Kuh-leang, with many exaggerations. I have followed 左氏傳,定公十年. 13 The 家語 says, Bk II., 孔子爲魯司寇·攝相事. But he was a 相 only in the sense of an assistant of ceremonies, as at the meeting in Këă-kuh, described above.

making any difference in favour of the father, and then wished to dismiss them both. The head of the Ke was dissatisfied, and said, "You are playing with me, Sir minister of Crime. Formerly you told me that in a State or a family filial duty was the first thing to be insisted on. What hinders you now from putting to death this unfilial son as an example to all the people?" Confucius with a sigh replied, "When superiors fail in their duty, and yet go to put their inferiors to death, it is not right. This father has not taught his son to be filial;—to listen to his charge would be to slay the guiltless. The manners of the age have been long in a sad condition; we cannot expect the people not to be transgressing the laws."[14]

At this time two of his disciples, Tsze-loo and Tsze-yew, entered the employment of the Ke family, and lent their influence, the former especially, to forward the plans of their master. One great cause of disorder in the State was the fortified cities held by the three chiefs, in which they could defy the supreme authority, and were in turn defied themselves by their officers. Those cities were like the castles of the barons of England in the time of the Norman kings. Confucius had their destruction very much at heart, and partly by the influence of persuasion, and partly by the assisting counsels of Tsze-loo, he accomplished his object in regard to Pe,[15] the chief city of the Ke, and How,[16] the chief city of the Shuh.

It does not appear that he succeeded in the same way in dismantling Shing,[17] the chief city of the Mang;[18] but his authority in the State greatly increased. "He strengthened the ducal House and weakened the private Families. He exalted the sovereign, and depressed the ministers. A transforming government went abroad. Dishonesty and dissoluteness were ashamed and hid their heads. Loyalty and good faith became the characteristics of the men, and chastity and docility those of the women. Strangers came in crowds from other States."[19] Confucius became the idol of the people, and flew in songs through their mouths.[20]

14 See the 家語, Bk II. 15 費. 16 郈. 17 成. 18 In connection with these events, the Family Sayings and Sze-ma Ts'een mention the summary punishment inflicted by Confucius on an able but unscrupulous and insidious officer, the Shaou-ching, Maou (少正卯). His judgment and death occupy a conspicuous place in the legendary accounts. But the Analects, Tsze-sze, Mencius, and Tso-k'ew Ming are all silent about it, and Keang Yung rightly rejects it, as one of the many narratives invented to exalt the sage. 19 See the 家語, Bk II. 20 See 孔叢子, quoted by Keang Yung.

But this sky of bright promise was soon overcast. As the fame of the reformations in Loo went abroad, the neighbouring princes began to be afraid. The duke of Ts'e said, "With Confucius at the head of its government, Loo will become supreme among the States, and Ts'e which is nearest to it will be the first swallowed up. Let us propitiate it by a surrender of territory." One of his ministers proposed they should first try to separate between the sage and his sovereign, and to effect this, they hit upon the following scheme. Eighty beautiful girls, with musical and dancing accomplishments, were selected, and a hundred and twenty of the finest horses that could be found, and sent as a present to duke Ting. They were put up at first outside the city, and Ke Hwan having gone in disguise to see them, forgot the lessons of Confucius, and took the duke to look at the bait. They were both captivated. The women were received, and the sage was neglected. For three days the duke gave no audience to his ministers. "Master," said Tsze-loo to Confucius, "it is time for you to be going." But Confucius was very unwilling to leave. The spring was coming on, when the great sacrifice to Heaven would be offered, and he determined to wait and see whether the solemnity of that would bring the duke back to his right mind. No such result followed. The ceremony was hurried through, and portions of the offerings were not sent round to the various ministers, according to the established custom. Confucius regretfully took his departure, going away slowly and by easy stages.[21] He would have welcomed a messenger of recall. The duke continued in his abandonment, and the sage went forth to thirteen weary years of homeless wandering.

He wanders from State to State. B.C. 496—483.

8. On leaving Loo, Confucius first bent his steps westward to the State of Wei, situate about where the present provinces of Chih-le and Ho-nan adjoin. He was now in his 56th year, and felt depressed and melancholy. As he went along, he gave expression to his feelings in verse:—

"Fain would I still look towards Loo,
But this Kwei hill cuts off my view.
With an axe, I'd hew the thickets through.:—
Vain thought! 'gainst the hill I nought can do;"

21 史記,孔子世家, p. 5. See also Mencius, V. Pt. II. i. 4; *et al.*

緒論

and again,—

"Through the valley howls the blast,
Drizzling rain falls thick and fast.
Homeward goes the youthful bride,
O'er the wild, crowds by her side.
How is it, O azure Heaven,
From my home I thus am driven,
Through the land my way to trace,
With no certain dwelling-place?
Dark, dark, the minds of men!
Worth in vain comes to their ken.
Hastens on my term of years;
Old age, desolate, appears."[1]

A number of his disciples accompanied him, and his sadness infected them. When they arrived at the borders of Wei, at a place called E, the warden sought an interview, and on coming out from the sage, he tried to comfort the disciples, saying, "My friends, why are you distressed at your Master's loss of office? The empire has been long without the principles of truth and right; Heaven is going to use your master as a bell with its wooden tongue."[2] Such was the thought of this friendly stranger. The bell did indeed sound, but few had ears to hear.

Confucius' fame, however, had gone before him, and he was in little danger of having to suffer from want. On arriving at the capital of Wei, he lodged at first with a worthy officer, named Yen Ch'ow-yew.[3] The reigning duke, known to us by the epithet of Ling,[4] was a worthless, dissipated man, but he could not neglect a visitor of such eminence, and soon assigned to Confucius a revenue of 60,000 measures of grain.[5] Here he remained for ten months, and then for some reason left it to go to Ch'in.[6] On the way he had to pass by K'wang,[7] a place probably in the present department of K'ae-fung in Ho-nan, which had formerly suffered from Yang-hoo. It so happened that Confucius resembled Hoo, and the attention of the people being called to him by the movements of his carriage-driver, they thought it was their old enemy, and made an attack upon him. His

1 See Keang Yung's Life of Confucius, 去魯周遊考. 2 Ana. III. xxiv. 3 顏讐由. See Mencius, V. Pt. I. viii. 2. 4 靈公. 5 See the 史記, 孔子世家, p 5. 6 陳國. 7 匡.

followers were alarmed, but he was calm, and tried to assure them by declaring his belief that he had a divine mission. He said to them, "After the death of king Wăn, was not the cause of truth lodged here in me? If Heaven had wished to let this cause of truth perish, then I, a future mortal, should not have got such a relation to that cause. While Heaven does not let the cause of truth perish, what can the people of K'wang do to me?"[8] Having escaped from the hands of his assailants, he does not seem to have carried out his purpose of going to Ch'in, but returned to Wei.

On the way, he passed a house where he had formerly been lodged, and finding that the master was dead, and the funeral ceremonies going on, he went in to condole and weep. When he came out, he told Tsze-kung to take one of the horses from his carriage, and give it as a contribution to the expenses of the occasion. "You never did such a thing," Tsze-kung remonstrated, "at the funeral of any of your disciples; is it not too great a gift on this occasion of the death of an old host?" "When I went in," replied Confucius, "my presence brought a burst of grief from the chief mourner, and I joined him with my tears. I dislike the thought of my tears not being followed by any thing. Do it, my child."[9]

On reaching Wei, he lodged with Keu Pih-yuh, an officer of whom honourable mention is made in the Analects.[10] But this time he did not remain long in the State. The duke was married

B.C. 495.

to a lady of the house of Sung, known by the name of Nan-tsze, notorious for her intrigues and wickedness. She sought an interview with the sage, which he was obliged unwillingly to accord.[11] No doubt he was innocent of thought or act of evil, but it gave great dissatisfaction to Tsze-loo that his master should have been in company with such a woman, and Confucius, to assure him, swore an oath, saying, "Wherein I have done improperly, may Heaven reject me! May Heaven reject me!"[12] He could not well abide, however, about such a court. One day the duke rode out through the streets of his capital in the same carriage with Nan-tsze, and made Confucius follow them in another. Perhaps

8 Ana. IX. v. In Ana. XI. xxii., there is another reference to this time, in which Yen Hwuy is made to appear. 9 See the Le Ke, II. Pt. I. ii. 16. 10 Ana. XIV. xxvi.; XV. vi. 11 See the account in the 史記, 孔子世家 p. 6. 12 Ana. VI. xxvi.

緒論

he intended to honour the philosopher, but the people saw the incongruity, and cried out, "Lust in the front; virtue behind!" Confucius was ashamed, and made the observation, "I have not seen one who loves virtue as he loves beauty."[13] Wei was no place for him. He left it, and took his way towards Ch'in.

Ch'in which formed part of the present province of Ho-nan, lay south from Wei. After passing the small State of Ts'aou,[14] he approached the borders of Sung, occupying the present prefecture of Kwei-tih, and had some intentions of entering it, when an incident occurred, which it is not easy to understand from the meagre style in which it is related, but which gave occasion to a remarkable saying. Confucius was practising ceremonies with his disciples, we are told, under the shade of a large tree. Hwan T'uy, an ill-minded officer of Sung, heard of it, and sent a band of men to pull down the tree, and kill the philosopher, if they could get hold of him. The disciples were much alarmed, but Confucius observed, "Heaven has produced the virtue that is in me;—what can Hwan T'uy do to me?"[15] They all made their escape, but seem to have been driven westwards to the State of Ch'ing,[16] on arriving at the gate conducting into which from the east, Confucius found himself separated from his followers. Tsze-kung had arrived before him, and was told by a native of Ch'ing that there was a man standing by the east gate, with a forehead like Yaou, a neck like Kaou-yaou, his shoulders on a level with those of Tsze-ch'an, but wanting, below the waist, three inches of the height of Yu, and altogether having the disconsolate appearance of a stray dog." Tsze-kung knew it was the master, hastened to him, and repeated to his great amusement the description which the man had given. "The bodily appearance," said Confucius, "is but a small matter, but to say I was like a stray dog—capital! capital!"[17] The stay they made at Ch'ing was short, and by the end of B.C. 495, Confucius was in Ch'in.

All the next year he remained there lodging with the warder of the city wall, an officer of worth, of the name of Ching,[18] and we have no accounts of him which deserve to be related here.[19]

13 Ana. IX. xvii. 14 曹. 15 Ana. IX. xxii 16 鄭. 17 See the 史記, 孔家世字, p 6. 18 司城貞子. See Mencius, V. Pt I. viii. 3. 19 Keang Yung digests in this place two foolish stories,—about a large bone found in the State of Yuĕ, and a bird which appeared in Ch'in and died, shot through with a remarkable arrow. Confucius knew all about them.

In B.C. 493, Ch'in was much disturbed by attacks from Woo,[20] a large State, the capital of which was in the present department of Soo-chow, and Confucius determined to retrace his steps to Wei. On the way he was laid hold of at a place called P'oo,[21] which was held by a rebellious officer against Wei, and before he could get away, he was obliged to engage that he would not proceed thither. Thither, notwithstanding, he continued his route, and when Tsze-kung asked him whether it was right to violate the oath he had taken, he replied, "It was a forced oath. The spirits do not hear such."[22] The duke Ling received him with distinction, but paid no more attention to his lessons than before, and Confucius is said then to have uttered his complaint, "If there were any of the princes who would employ me, in the course of twelve months I should have done something considerable. In three years the government would be perfected."[23]

A circumstance occurred to direct his attention to the State of Tsin,[24] which occupied the southern part of the present Shan-se, and extended over the Yellow river into Ho-nan. An invitation came to Confucius, like that which he had formerly received from Kung-shan Fuh-jaou. Peih Heih, an officer of Tsin, who was holding the town of Chung-mow against his chief, invited him to visit him, and Confucius was inclined to go. Tsze-loo was always the mentor on such occasions. He said to him, "Master, I have heard you say, that when a man in his own person is guilty of doing evil, a superior man will not associate with him. Peih Heih is in rebellion; if you go to him, what shall be said?" Confucius replied, "Yes, I did use those words. But is it not said that if a thing be really hard, it may be ground without being made thin; and if it be really white, it may be steeped in a dark fluid without being made black? Am I a bitter gourd? Am I to be hung up out of the way of being eaten?"[25]

These sentiments sound strangely from his lips. After all, he did not go to Peih Heih; and having travelled as far as the Yellow river that he might see one of the principal ministers of Tsin, he heard of the violent death of two men of worth, and returned to

20 吳. 21 蒲. 22. This is related by Sze-ma Ts'een, 孔子世家, p. 7, and also in the Family Sayings. I would fain believe it is not true. The wonder is, that no Chinese critic should have set about disproving it. 23. Ana. XII. x. 24 晉. 25 Ana. XVII. vii.

海上絲綢之路文獻集成 科技與文化編

緒論

Wei, lamenting the fate which prevented him from crossing the stream, and trying to solace himself with poetry as he had done on leaving Loo. Again did he communicate with the duke, but as ineffectually, and disgusted at being questioned by him about military tactics, he left and went back to Ch'in.

He resided in Ch'in all the next year, B.C. 491, without anything occurring there which is worthy of note.[26] Events had transpired in Loo, however, which were to issue in his return to his native State. The duke Ting had deceased B.C. 494, and Ke Hwan, the chief of the Ke family, died in this year. On his deathbed, he felt remorse for his conduct to Confucius, and charged his successor, known to us in the Analects as Ke K'ang, to recall the sage; but the charge was not immediately fulfilled. Ke K'ang, by the advice of one of his officers, sent to Ch'in for the disciple Yen K'ew instead. Confucius willingly sent him off, and would gladly have accompanied him. "Let me return!" he said, "Let me return!"[27] But that was not to be for several years yet.

In B.C. 490, accompanied, as usual, by several of his disciples, he went from Ch'in to Ts'ae, a small dependency of the great fief of Ts'oo, which occupied a large part of the present provinces of Hoonan and Hoo-pih. On the way, between Ch'in and Ts'ae, their provisions became exhausted, and they were cut off somehow from obtaining a fresh supply. The disciples were quite overcome with want, and Tsze-loo said to the master, "Has the superior man indeed to endure in this way?" Confucius answered him, "The superior man may indeed have to endure want; but the mean man, when he is in want, gives way to unbridled license."[28] According to the "Family Sayings," the distress continued seven days, during which time Confucius retained his equanimity, and was even cheerful, playing on his lute and singing.[29] He retained, however, a strong impression of the perils of the season, and we find him afterwards recurring to it, and lamenting that of the friends that were with him in Ch'in and Ts'ae, there were none remaining to enter his door.[30]

Escaped from this strait, he remained in Ts'ae over B.C. 489, and in the following year we find him in Shĕ, another district of

26 Tso-k'ew Ming, indeed, relates a story of Confucius, on the report of a fire in Loo, telling whose ancestral temple had been destroyed by it. 27 Ana. V. xxi. 28 Ana. XV. i. 2, 3. 29 家語,卷二,在危二十篇. 30 Ana. XI. ii.

Ts'oo, the chief of which had usurped the title of duke. Puzzled about his visitor, he asked Tsze-loo what he should think of him, but the disciple did not venture a reply. When Confucius heard of it, he said to Tsze-loo, "Why did you not say to him,—He is simply a man who in his eager pursuit of knowledge forgets his food, who in the joy of its attainment forgets his sorrows, and who does not perceive that old age is coming on?"[31] Subsequently, the duke, in conversation with Confucius, asked him about government, and got the reply, dictated by some circumstances of which we are ignorant, "Good government obtains, when those who are near are made happy, and those who are far off are attracted."[32]

After a short stay in Shĕ, according to Sze-ma Ts'een, he returned to Ts'ae, and having to cross a river, he sent Tsze-loo to inquire for the ford of two men who were at work in a neighbouring field. They were recluses,—men who had withdrawn from public life in disgust at the waywardness of the times. One of them was called Ch'ang-tseu, and instead of giving Tsze-loo the information he wanted, he asked him, "Who is it that holds the reins in the carriage there?" "It is K'ung Kew." "K'ung Kew of Loo?" "Yes," was the reply, and then the man rejoined, "*He* knows the ford."

Tsze-loo applied to the other, who was called Këĕ-neih, but got for answer the question, "Who are you, Sir?" He replied, "I am Chung Yew." "Chung Yew, who is the disciple of K'ung Kew of Loo?" "Yes," again replied Tsze-loo, and Këĕ-neih addressed him, "Disorder, like a swelling flood, spreads over the whole empire, and who is he that will change it for you? Than follow one who merely withdraws from this one and that one, had you not better follow those who withdraw from the world altogether?" With this he fell to covering up the seed, and gave no more heed to the stranger. Tsze-loo went back and reported what they had said, when Confucius vindicated his own course, saying, "It is impossible to associate with birds and beasts as if they were the same with us. If I associate not with these people,—with mankind,—with whom shall I associate? If right principles prevailed through the empire, there would be no use for me to change its state."[33]

About the same time he had an encounter with another recluse, who was known as "The madman of Ts'oo." He passed by the

31 Ana. VII. xviii. 32 Ana. XIII. xvi. 33 Ana. XVIII. vi.

carriage of Confucius, singing out "O FUNG, O FUNG, how is your virtue degenerated! As to the past, reproof is useless, but the future may be provided against. Give up, give up your vain pursuit." Confucius alighted and wished to enter into conversation with him, but the man hastened away.[34]

But now the attention of the ruler of Ts'oo—king, as he styled himself—was directed to the illustrious stranger who was in his dominions, and he met Confucius and conducted him to his capital, which was in the present district of E-shing, in the department of Sëang-yang,[35] in Hoo-pih. After a time, he proposed endowing the philosopher with a considerable territory, but was dissuaded by his prime minister, who said to him, "Has your majesty any officer who could discharge the duties of an ambassador like Tsze-kung? or any one so qualified for a premier as Yen Hwuy? or any one to compare as a general with Tsze-loo? The kings Wăn and Woo, from their hereditary dominions of a hundred *le*, rose to the sovereignty of the empire. If K'ung K'ew, with such disciples to be his ministers, get the possession of any territory, it will not be to the prosperity of Ts'oo?[36] On this remonstrance the king gave up his purpose, and when he died in the same year, Confucius left the State, and went back again to Wei.

The duke Ling had died four years before, soon after Confucius

B.C 489. had last parted from him, and the reigning duke, known to us by the title of Ch'uh,[37] was his grandson, and was holding the principality against his own father. The relations between them were rather complicated. The father had been driven out in consequence of an attempt which he had instigated on the life of his mother, the notorious Nan-tsze, and the succession was given to his son. Subsequently, the father wanted to reclaim what he deemed his right, and an unseemly struggle ensued. The duke Ch'uh was conscious how much his cause would be strengthened by the support of Confucius, and hence when he got to Wei, Tsze-loo could say to him, "The prince of Wei has been waiting for you, in order with you to administer the government;—what will you consider the first thing to be done?"[38] The opinion of the philosopher, however,

34 Ana. XVII. v. 35 襄陽府宜城縣. 36 See the 史記, 孔子世家, p. 10. 37 出公. 38 Ana. XIII. iii. In the notes on this passage, I have given Choo He's opinion as to the time when Tsze-loo made this remark. It seems more correct, however, to refer it to Confucius' return to Wei from Ts'oo, as is done by Keang Yung.

was against the propriety of the duke's course,[39] and he declined taking office with him, though he remained in Wei for between five and six years. During all that time there is a blank in his history. In the very year of his return, according to the "Annals of the Empire," his most beloved disciple, Yen Hwuy died, on which occasion he exclaimed, "Alas! Heaven is destroying me! Heaven is destroying me!"[40] The death of his wife is assigned to B.C. 484, but nothing else is related which we can connect with this long period.

From his return to Loo to his death. B.C. 483—478.

9. His return to Loo was brought about by the disciple Yen Yew, who, we have seen, went into the service of Ke K'ang, in B.C. 491. In the year B.C. 483, Yew had the conduct of some military operations against Ts'e, and being successful, Ke K'ang asked him how he had obtained his military skill;—was it from nature, or by learning? He replied that he had learned it from Confucius, and entered into a glowing eulogy of the philosopher. The chief declared that he would bring Confucius home again to Loo. "If you do so," said the disciple, "see that you do not let mean men come between you and him." On this K'ang sent three officers with appropriate presents to Wei, to invite the wanderer home, and he returned with them accordingly.[1]

This event took place in the 11th year of the duke Gae,[2] who succeeded to Ting, and according to K'ung Foo, Confucius' descendant, the invitation proceeded from him.[3] We may suppose that while Ke K'ang was the mover and director of the proceeding, it was with the authority and approval of the duke. It is represented in the chronicle of Tso-k'ew Ming as having occurred at a very opportune time. The philosopher had been consulted a little before by K'ung Wăn,[4] an officer of Wei, about how he should conduct a feud with another officer, and disgusted at being referred to on such a subject, had ordered his carriage and prepared to leave the State, exclaiming, "The bird chooses its tree. The tree does not chase the bird." K'ung Wăn endeavoured to excuse himself, and to prevail on Confucius

39 Ana. VII. xiv. 40 Ana. XI. viii. In the notes on Ana. XI. vii. I have adverted to the chronological difficulty connected with the dates assigned respectively to the deaths of Yen Hwuy and Confucius' own son, Le. Keang Yung assigns Hwuy's death to B.C. 481.

1 See the 史記，孔子世家. 2 哀公. 3 See Keang Yung's memoir, *in loc.* 4 孔文子, the same who is mentioned in the Analects, V. xiv.

to remain in Wei, and just at this juncture the messengers from Loo arrived.[5]

Confucius was now in his 69th year. The world had not dealt kindly with him. In every State which he had visited he had met with disappointment and sorrow. Only five more years remained to him, nor were they of a brighter character than the past. He had, indeed, attained to that state, he tells us, in which "he could follow what his heart desired without transgressing what was right,"[6] but other people were not more inclined than they had been to abide by his counsels. The duke Gae and Ke K'ang often conversed with him, but he no longer had weight in the guidance of State affairs, and wisely addressed himself to the completion of his literary labours. He wrote a preface to the Shoo-king; carefully digested the rites and ceremonies determined by the wisdom of the more ancient ages and kings; collected and arranged the ancient poetry; and undertook the reform of music.[7] He has told us himself, "I returned from Wei to Loo, and then the music was reformed, and the pieces in the Imperial Songs and Praise Songs found all their proper place."[8] To the Yih-king he devoted much study, and Sze-ma Ts'een says that the leather thongs by which the tablets of his copy were bound together were thrice worn out. "If some years were added to my life," he said, "I would give fifty to the study of the Yih, and then I might come to be without great faults."[9] During this time also, we may suppose that he supplied Tsăng Sin with the materials of the classic of Filial Piety. The same year that he returned, Ke K'ang sent Yen Yew to ask his opinion about an additional impost which he wished to lay upon the people, but Confucius refused to give any reply, telling the disciple privately his disapproval of the proposed measure. It was carried out, however, in the following year, by the agency of Yen, on which occasion, I suppose, it was that Confucius said to the other disciples, "He is no disciple of mine; my little children, beat the drum and assail him."[10] The year B.C. 482 was marked by the death of his son Le, which he seems to have borne with more equanimity than he did that of his disciple Yen Hwuy, which some writers assign to the following year, though I have already mentioned it under the year B.C. 488.

5 See the 左傳, 哀公十一年. 6 Ana. II. iv. 6. 7 See the 史記, 孔子世家, p. 12. 8 Ana. IX. xiv. 9 Ana. VII. xvi. 10 Ana. XI. xvi.

海上絲綢之路文獻集成 科技與文化編

In the spring of B.C. 480, a servant of Ke K'ang caught a k'e-lin on a hunting excursion of the duke in the present district of Këa-ts'eang.[11] No person could tell what strange animal it was, and Confucius was called to look at it. He at once knew it to be a *lin*, and the legend-writers say that it bore on one of its horns the piece of ribbon, which his mother had attached to the one that appeared to her before his birth. According to the chronicle of Kung-yang, he was profoundly affected. He cried out, "For whom have you come? For whom have you come?" His tears flowed freely, and he added, "The course of my doctrines is run."[12]

Notwithstanding the appearance of the lin, the life of Confucius was still protracted for two years longer, though he took occasion to terminate with that event his history of the Ts'un Ts'ew. This Work according to Sze-ma Ts'een was altogether the production of this year, but we need not suppose that it was so. In it, from the standpoint of Loo, he briefly indicates the principal events occurring throughout the empire, every term being expressive, it is said, of the true character of the actors and events described. Confucius said himself, "It is the Spring and Autumn which will make men know me, and it is the Spring and Autumn which will make men condemn me."[13] Mencius makes the composition of it to have been an achievement as great as Yu's regulation of the waters of the deluge.—"Confucius completed the Spring and Autumn, and rebellious ministers and villainous sons were struck with terror."[14]

Towards the end of this year, word came to Loo that the duke of Ts'e had been murdered by one of his officers. Confucius was moved with indignation. Such an outrage, he felt, called for his solemn interference. He bathed, went to court, and represented the matter to the duke, saying, "Ch'in Hăng has slain his sovereign, I beg that you will undertake to punish him." The duke pleaded his incapacity, urging that Loo was weak compared with Ts'e, but Confucius replied, "One half the people of Ts'e are not consenting to the deed. If you add to the people of Loo one half the people of Ts'e, you are sure to overcome." But he could not infuse his spirit into the duke, who told him to go and lay the matter before the chiefs of the three Families. Sorely against his sense of propriety,

11 兗州府嘉祥縣. 12 公羊傳, 哀公十四年. According to Kung-yang, however, the lin was found by some wood-gatherers. 3 Mencius III. Pt. II. ix. 8. 14 Men., III. Pt. II. ix. 11.

86]

緒論

he did so, but they would not act, and he withdrew with the remark, "Following in the rear of the great officers, I did not dare not to represent such a matter."[15]

In the year B.C. 479, Confucius had to mourn the death of another of his disciples, one of those who had been longest with him,—the well-known Tsze-loo. He stands out a sort of Peter in the Confucian school, a man of impulse, prompt to speak and prompt to act. He gets many a check from the master, but there is evidently a strong sympathy between them. Tsze-loo uses a freedom with him on which none of the other disciples dares to venture, and there is not one among them all, for whom, if I may speak from my own feeling, the foreign student comes to form such a liking. A pleasant picture is presented to us in one passage of the Analects. It is said, "The disciple Min was standing by his side, looking bland and precise; Tsze-loo (named Yew), looking bold and soldierly; Yen Yew and Tsze-kung, with a free and straightforward manner. The master was pleased, but he observed, 'Yew there!—he will not die a natural death.'"[16]

This prediction was verified. When Confucius returned to Loo from Wei, he left Tsze-loo and Tsze-kaou[17] engaged there in official service. Troubles arose. News came to Loo, B.C. 479, that a revolution was in progress in Wei, and when Confucius heard it, he said, "Ch'ae will come here, but Yew will die."[18] So it turned out. When Tsze-kaou saw that matters were desperate he made his escape, but Tsze-loo would not forsake the chief who had treated him well. He threw himself into the melee, and was slain. Confucius wept sore for him, but his own death was not far off. It took place on the 11th day of the 4th month in the following year, B.C. 478.[19]

Early one morning, we are told, he got up, and with his hands behind his back, dragging his staff, he moved about by his door, crooning over,—

"The great mountain must crumble;
The strong beam must break;
And the wise man wither away like a plant."

15 See the 左傳, 哀公十四年, and Analects, XIV. xxii. 16 Ana. XI. xii. 17 子羔, by surname Kaou (高), and name Ch'ae (柴). 18 See the 左傳, 哀公十五年. 19 See the 左傳, 哀公十六年, and Keang Yung's Life of Confucius, *in loc.*

After a little, he entered the house and sat down opposite the door. Tsze-kung had heard his words, and said to himself, "If the great mountain crumble, to what shall I look up? If the strong beam break, and the wise man wither away, on whom shall I lean? The master, I fear, is going to be ill." With this he hastened into the house. Confucius said to him, "Ts'ze, what makes you so late? According to the statutes of Hea, the corpse was dressed and coffined at the top of the eastern steps, treating the dead as if he were still the host. Under the Yin, the ceremony was performed between the two pillars, as if the dead were both host and guest. The rule of Chow is to perform it at the top of the western steps, treating the dead as if he were a guest. I am a man of Yin, and last night I dreamt that I was sitting with offerings before me between the two pillars. No intelligent monarch arises; there is not one in the empire that will make me his master. My time has come to die." So it was. He went to his couch, and after seven days expired.[20]

Such is the account which we have of the last hours of the great philosopher of China. His end was not unimpressive, but it was melancholy. He sank behind a cloud. Disappointed hopes made his soul bitter. The great ones of the empire had not received his teachings. No wife nor child was by to do the kindly offices of affection for him. Nor were the expectations of another life present with him as he passed through the dark valley. He uttered no prayer, and he betrayed no apprehensions. Deep-treasured in his own heart may have been the thought that he had endeavoured to serve his generation by the will of God, but he gave no sign. "The mountain falling came to nought, and the rock was removed out of his place. So death prevailed against him and he passed; his countenance was changed, and he was sent away."

10. I flatter myself that the preceding paragraphs contain a more correct narrative of the principal incidents in the life of Confucius than has yet been given in any European language. They might easily have been expanded into a volume, but I did not wish to exhaust the subject, but only to furnish a sketch, which, while it might satisfy the general reader, would be of special assistance to the careful student of the classical Books. I had taken many notes of the manifest errors in regard to chronology and other matters in the

20 See the Le Ke, II. Pt. I. ii. 20.

緒論

"Family Sayings," and the chapter of Sze-ma Ts'een on the K'ung family, when the digest of Keang Yung, to which I have made frequent reference, attracted my attention. Conclusions to which I had come were confirmed, and a clue was furnished to difficulties which I was seeking to disentangle. I take the opportunity to acknowledge here my obligations to it. With a few notices of Confucius' habits and manners, I shall conclude this section.

Very little can be gathered from reliable sources on the personal appearance of the sage. The height of his father is stated, as I have noted, to have been ten feet, and though Confucius came short of this by four inches, he was often called "the tall man." It is allowed that the ancient foot or cubit was shorter than the modern, but it must be reduced more than any scholar I have consulted has yet done, to bring this statement within the range of credibility. The legends assign to his figure "nine-and-forty remarkable peculiarities,"[1] a tenth part of which would have made him more a monster than a man. Dr Morrison says that the images of him, which he had seen in the northern parts of China, represent him as of a dark swarthy colour.[2] It is not so with those common in the south. He was, no doubt, in size and complexion much the same as many of his descendants in the present day.

But if his disciples had nothing to chronicle of his personal appearance, they have gone very minutely into an account of many of his habits. The tenth book of the Analects is all occupied with his deportment, his eating, and his dress. In public, whether in the village, the temple, or the court, he was the man of rule and ceremony, but "at home he was not formal." Yet if not formal, he was particular. In bed even he did not forget himself;—"he did not lie like a corpse," and "he did not speak." "He required his sleeping dress to be half as long again as his body." "If he happened to be sick, and the prince came to visit him, he had his face to the east, made his court robes be put over him, and drew his girdle across them."

He was nice in his diet,—"not disliking to have his rice dressed fine, nor to have his minced meat cut small." "Anything at all

1 四十九表. 2 Chinese and English Dictionary, char. 孔. Sir John Davis also mentions seeing a figure of Confucius, in a temple near the Po-yang lake, of which the complexion was 'quite black.' (The Chinese, vol II. p. 66).

gone he would not touch." "He must have his meat cut properly, and to every kind its proper sauce; but he was not a great eater." "It was only in wine that he laid down no limit to himself, but he did not allow himself to be confused by it." "When the villagers were drinking together, on those who carried staves going out, he went out immediately after." There must always be ginger at the table, and "when eating, he did not converse." "Although his food might be coarse rice and poor soup, he would offer a little of it in sacrifice, with a grave respectful air."

"On occasion of a sudden clap of thunder, or a violent wind, he would change countenance. He would do the same, and rise up moreover, when he found himself a guest at a loaded board." "At the sight of a person in mourning, he would also change countenance, and if he happened to be in his carriage, he would bend forward with a respectful salutation." "His general way in his carriage was not to turn his head round, nor talk hastily, nor point with his hands." He was charitable. "When any of his friends died, if there were no relations who could be depended on for the necessary offices, he would say, 'I will bury him.'"

The disciples were so careful to record these and other characteristics of their master, it is said, because every act, of movement or of rest, was closely associated with the great principles which it was his object to inculcate. The detail of so many small matters, however, does not impress a foreigner so favourably. There is a want of freedom about the philosopher. Somehow he is less a sage to me, after I have seen him at his table, in his undress, in his bed, and in his carriage.

SECTION II.

HIS INFLUENCE AND OPINIONS.

Homage rendered to Confucius by the emperors of China.

1. Confucius died, we have seen, complaining that of all the princes of the empire there was not one who would adopt his principles and obey his lessons. He had hardly passed from the stage of life, when his merit began to be acknowledged. When the duke Gae heard of his death, he pronounced his eulogy in the words, "Heaven has not left to me the aged man. There is none now to

緒論

assist me on the throne. Woe is me! Alas! O venerable Ne!"[1] Tsze-kung complained of the inconsistency of this lamentation from one who could not use the master when he was alive, but the duke was probably sincere in his grief. He caused a temple to be erected, and ordered that sacrifice should be offered to the sage, at the four seasons of the year.[2]

The emperors of the tottering dynasty of Chow had not the intelligence, nor were they in a position, to do honour to the departed philosopher, but the facts detailed in the first chapter of these prolegomena, in connection with the attempt of the founder of the Ts'in dynasty to destroy the monuments of antiquity, show how the authority of Confucius had come by that time to prevail through the empire. The founder of the Han dynasty, in passing through Loo, B.C. 194, visited his tomb and offered an ox in sacrifice to him. Other emperors since then have often made pilgrimages to the spot. The most famous temple in the empire now rises over the place of the grave. K'ang-he, the second and greatest of the rulers of the present dynasty, in the 23d year of his reign, there set the example of kneeling thrice, and each time laying his forehead thrice in the dust, before the image of the sage.

In the year of our Lord 1, began the practice of conferring honorary designations on Confucius by imperial authority. The emperor P'ing[3] then styled him—"The duke Ne, all-complete and illustrious."[4] This was changed, in A.D. 492, to—"The venerable Ne, the accomplished Sage."[5] Other titles have supplanted this. Shun-che,[6] the first of the Man-chow dynasty, adopted, in his second year, A.D. 645, the style,—"K'ung, the ancient Teacher, accomplished and illustrious, all-complete, the perfect Sage;"[7] but twelve years later, a shorter title was introduced,—"K'ung, the ancient Teacher, the perfect Sage."[8] Since that year no further alteration has been made.

At first, the worship of Confucius was confined to the country of Loo, but in A.D. 57 it was enacted that sacrifices should be offered to him in the imperial college, and in all the colleges of the principal

1 Le Ke, II. Pt. I. iii. 43. This eulogy is found at greater length in the 左傳, immediately after the notice of the sage's death. 2 See the 聖廟祀典圖考, 卷一, art. on Confucius. I am indebted to this for most of the notices in this paragraph. 3 平帝. 4 成宣尼公. 5 文聖尼父. 6 順治. 7 大成至聖, 文宣先師, 孔子. 8 至聖先師孔子.

territorial divisions throughout the empire. In those sacrifices he was for some centuries associated with the duke of Chow, the legislator to whom Confucius made frequent reference, but in A.D. 609 separate temples were assigned to them, and in 628 our sage displaced the older worthy altogether. About the same time began the custom, which continues to the present day, of erecting temples to him,—separate structures, in connection with all the colleges, or examination-halls, of the country.

The sage is not alone in those temples. In a hall behind the principal one occupied by himself are the tablets—in some cases, the images—of several of his ancestors, and other worthies; while associated with himself are his principal disciples, and many who in subsequent times have signalized themselves as expounders and exemplifiers of his doctrines. On the first day of every month, offerings of fruits and vegetables are set forth, and on the fifteenth there is a solemn burning of incense. But twice a year, in the middle months of spring and autumn, when the first *ting* day[9] of the month comes round, the worship of Confucius is performed with peculiar solemnity. At the imperial college the emperor himself is required to attend in state, and is in fact the principal performer. After all the preliminary arrangements have been made, and the emperor has twice knelt and six times bowed his head to the earth, the presence of Confucius' spirit is invoked in the words, "Great art thou, O perfect sage! Thy virtue is full; thy doctrine is complete. Among mortal men there has not been thine equal. All kings honour thee. Thy statutes and laws have come gloriously down. Thou art the pattern in this imperial school. Reverently have the sacrificial vessels been set out. Full of awe, we sound our drums and bells."[10]

The spirit is supposed now to be present, and the service proceeds through various offerings, when the first of which has been set forth, an officer reads the following,[11] which is the prayer on the occasion:—"On this....month of this....year, I, *A.B.*, the emperor, offer a sacrifice to the philosopher K'ung, the ancient Teacher, the perfect Sage, and say,—O Teacher, in virtue equal to Heaven and Earth, whose doctrines embrace the past time and the present, thou didst digest and transmit the six classics, and didst hand down lessons for all generations!

9 上丁日. 10, 11 See the 大清通禮.卷十二.

92]

緒論

Now in this second month of spring (or autumn), in reverent observance of the old statutes, with victims, silks, spirits, and fruits, I carefully offer sacrifice to thee. With thee are associated the philosopher Yen, continuator of thee; the philosopher Tsăng, exhibiter of thy fundamental principles; the philosopher Tsze-sze, transmitter of thee; and the philosopher Măng, second to thee. May'st thou enjoy the offerings."

I need not go on to enlarge on the homage which the emperors of China render to Confucius. It could not be more complete. It is worship and not mere homage. He was unreasonably neglected when alive. He is now unreasonably venerated when dead. The estimation with which the rulers of China regard their sage, leads them to sin against God, and is a misfortune to the empire.

General appreciation of Confucius.

2. The rulers of China are not singular in this matter, but in entire sympathy with the mass of their people. It is the distinction of this empire that education has been highly prized in it from the earliest times. It was so before the era of Confucius, and we may be sure that the system met with his approbation. One of his remarkable sayings was,—"To lead an uninstructed people to war is to throw them away."[1] When he pronounced this judgment, he was not thinking of military training, but of education in the duties of life and citizenship. A people so taught, he thought, would be morally fitted to fight for their government. Mencius, when lecturing to the duke of T'ăng on the proper way of governing a kingdom, told him that he must provide the means of education for all, the poor as well as the rich. "Establish," said he, "*ts'eang*, *seu*, *heŏ*, and *heaou*,—all those educational institutions,—for the instruction of the people."[2]

At the present day, education is widely diffused throughout China. In no other country is the schoolmaster more abroad, and in all schools it is Confucius who is taught. The plan of competitive examinations, and the selection for civil offices only from those who have been successful candidates,—good so far as the competition is concerned, but injurious from the restricted range of subjects with which an acquaintance is required,—have obtained for more than twelve centuries. The classical works are the text books. It is from them almost exclusively that the themes proposed to determine

1 Ana. XIII. 30. 2 Mencius, III. Pt. I. iii 10.

the knowledge and ability of the students are chosen. The whole of the magistracy of China is thus versed in all that is recorded of the sage, and in the ancient literature which he preserved. His thoughts are familiar to every man in authority, and his character is more or less reproduced in him.

The official civilians of China, numerous as they are, are but a fraction of its students, and the students, or those who make literature a profession, are again but a fraction of those who attend school for a shorter or longer period. Yet so far as the studies have gone, they have been occupied with the Confucian writings. In many schoolrooms there is a tablet or inscription on the wall, sacred to the sage, and every pupil is required, on coming to school on the morning of the 1st and 15th of every month, to bow before it, the first thing, as an act of worship.[3] Thus all in China who receive the slightest tincture of learning do so at the fountain of Confucius. They learn of him and do homage to him at once. I have repeatedly quoted the statement that during his life-time he had three thousand disciples. Hundreds of millions are his disciples now. It is hardly necessary to make any allowance in this statement for the followers of Taouism and Buddhism, for, as Sir John Davis has observed, "whatever the other opinions or faith of a Chinese may be, he takes good care to treat Confucius with respect."[4] For two thousand years he has reigned supreme, the undisputed teacher of this most populous land.

The causes of his influence.

3. This position and influence of Confucius are to be ascribed, I conceive, chiefly to two causes:—his being the preserver, namely of the monuments of antiquity, and the exemplifier and expounder of the maxims of the golden age of China; and the devotion to him of his immediate disciples and their early followers. The national and the personal are thus blended in him, each in its highest degree of excellence. He was a Chinese of the Chinese; he is also represented, and all now believe him to have been, the *beau ideal* of humanity in its best and noblest estate.

4. It may be well to bring forward here Confucius' own estimate of himself, and of his doctrines. It will serve to illustrate the

3 During the present dynasty, the tablet of 文昌帝君, the god of literature, has to a considerable extent displaced that of Confucius in schools. Yet the worship of him does not clash with that of the other. He is 'the father' of composition only. 4 The Chinese, vol. II. p. 45.

緒論

His own estimate of himself and of his doctrines.

statements just made. The following are some of his sayings.—"The sage and the man of perfect virtue;—how dare I rank myself with them? It may simply be said of me, that I strive to become such without satiety, and teach others without weariness." "In letters I am perhaps equal to other men; but the character of the superior man, carrying out in his conduct what he professes, is what I have not yet attained to." "The leaving virtue without proper cultivation; the not thoroughly discussing what is learned; not being able to move towards righteousness of which a knowledge is gained; and not being able to change what is not good;—these are the things which occasion me solicitude." "I am not one who was born in the possession of knowledge; I am one who is fond of antiquity and earnest in seeking it there." "A transmitter and not a maker, believing in and loving the ancients, I venture to compare myself with our old P'ang."[1]

Confucius cannot be thought to speak of himself in these declarations more highly than he ought to do. Rather we may recognize in them the expressions of a genuine humility. He was conscious that personally he came short in many things, but he toiled after the character, which he saw, or fancied that he saw, in the ancient sages whom he acknowledged; and the lessons of government and morals which he laboured to diffuse were those which had already been inculcated and exhibited by them. Emphatically he was "a transmitter and not a maker." It is not to be understood that he was not fully satisfied of the truth of the principles which he had learned. He held them with the full approval and consent of his own understanding. He believed that if they were acted on, they would remedy the evils of his time. There was nothing to prevent rulers like Yaou and Shun and the great Yu from again arising, and a condition of happy tranquillity being realized throughout the empire under their sway.

If in any thing he thought himself "superior and alone," having attributes which others could not claim, it was in his possessing a divine commission as the conservator of ancient truth and rules. He does not speak very definitely on this point. It is noted that

1 All these passages are taken from the VIIth Book of the Analects. See chh. xxxiii; xxxii.; iii.; xix.; and i.

"the appointments of Heaven was one of the subjects on which he rarely touched."[2] His most remarkable utterance was that which I have already given in the sketch of his Life:—"When he was put in fear in K'wang, he said, 'After the death of king Wăn, was not the cause of truth lodged here in me? If Heaven had wished to let this cause of truth perish, then I, a future mortal, should not have got such a relation to that cause. While Heaven does not let the cause of truth perish, what can the people of Kwang do to me?'"[3] Confucius, then, did feel that he was in the world for a special purpose. But it was not to announce any new truths, or to initiate any new economy. It was to prevent what had previously been known from being lost. He followed in the wake of Yaou and Shun, of T'ang, and king Wăn. Distant from the last by a long interval of time, he would have said that he was distant from him also by a great inferiority of character, but still he had learned the principles on which they all happily governed the empire, and in their name he would lift up a standard against the prevailing lawlessness of his age.

Estimate of him by his disciples and their early followers.

5. The language employed with reference to Confucius by his disciples and their early followers presents a striking contrast with his own. I have already, in writing of the scope and value of "The Doctrine of the Mean," called attention to the extravagant eulogies of his grandson Tsze-sze. He only followed the example which had been set by those among whom the philosopher went in and out. We have the language of Yen Yuen, his favourite, which is comparatively moderate, and simply expresses the genuine admiration of a devoted pupil.[1] Tsze-kung on several occasions spoke in a different style. Having heard that one of the chiefs of Loo had said that he himself—Tsze-kung—was superior to Confucius, he observed, "Let me use the comparison of a house and its encompassing wall. My wall only reaches to the shoulders. One may peep over it, and see whatever is valuable in the apartments. The wall of my master is several fathoms high. If one do not find the door and enter by it, he cannot see the rich ancestral temple with its beauties, nor all the officers in their rich array. But I may assume

2 Ana. IX. i. 3 Ana. IX. iii.
1 Ana. IX. x.

緒論

that they are few who find the door. The remark of the chief was only what might have been expected."[2]

Another time, the same individual having spoken revilingly of Confucius, Tsze-kung said, "It is of no use doing so. Chung-ne cannot be reviled. The talents and virtue of other men are hillocks and mounds which may be stept over. Chung-ne is the sun or moon, which it is not possible to step over. Although a man may wish to cut himself off from the sage, what harm can he do to the sun and moon? He only shows that he does not know his own capacity."[3]

In conversation with a fellow-disciple, Tsze-kung took a still higher flight. Being charged by Tsze-k'in with being too modest, for that Confucius was not really superior to him, he replied, "For one word a man is often deemed to be wise, and for one word he is often deemed to be foolish. We ought to be careful indeed in what we say. Our master cannot be attained to, just in the same way as the heavens cannot be gone up to by the steps of a stair. Were our master in the position of the prince of a State, or the chief of a Family, we should find verified the description which has been given of a sage's rule:—He would plant the people, and forthwith they would be established; he would lead them on, and forthwith they would follow him; he would make them happy, and forthwith multitudes would resort to his dominions; he would stimulate them, and forthwith they would be harmonious. While he lived, he would be glorious. When he died, he would be bitterly lamented. How is it possible for him to be attained to?"[4]

From these representations of Tsze-kung, it was not a difficult step for Tsze-sze to make in exalting Confucius not only to the level of the ancient sages, but as "the equal of Heaven." And Mencius took up the theme. Being questioned by Kung-sun Ch'ow, one of his disciples, about two acknowledged sages, Pih-e and E Yin, whether they were to be placed in the same rank with Confucius, he replied, "No. Since there were living men until now, there never was another Confucius;" and then he proceeded to fortify his opinion by the concurring testimony of Tsae Go, Tsze-kung and Yew Jŏ, who all had wisdom, he thought, sufficient to know their master. Tsae Go's opinion was, "According to my view of our master, he is

2 Ana. XIX. xxiii. 3 Ana. XIX. xxiv. 4 Ana. XIX. xxv.

far superior to Yaou and Shun." Tsze-kung said, "By viewing the ceremonial ordinances of a prince, we know the character of his government. By hearing his music, we know the character of his virtue. From the distance of a hundred ages after, I can arrange, according to their merits, the kings of a hundred ages;—not one of them can escape me. From the birth of mankind till now, there has never been another like our master." Yew Jŏ said, "Is it only among men that it is so? There is the k'e-lin among quadrupeds; the fung-hwang among birds; the T'ae mountain among mounds and ant-hills; and rivers and seas among rain-pools. Though different in degree, they are the same in kind. So the sages among mankind are also the same in kind. But they stand out from their fellows, and rise above the level; and from the birth of mankind till now, there never has been one so complete as Confucius."[5] I will not indulge in farther illustration. The judgment of the sage's disciples, of Tsze-sze, and of Mencius, has been unchallenged by the mass of the scholars of China. Doubtless it pleases them to bow down at the shrine of the sage, for their profession of literature is thereby glorified. A reflection of the honour done to him falls upon themselves. And the powers that be, and the multitudes of the people, fall in with the judgment. Confucius is thus, in the empire of China, the one man by whom all possible personal excellence was exemplified, and by whom all possible lessons of social virtue and political wisdom are taught.

Subjects on which Confucius did not treat.—That he was unreligious, unspiritual, and open to the charge of insincerity.

6. The reader will be prepared by the preceding account not to expect to find any light thrown by Confucius on the great problems of the human condition and destiny. He did not speculate on the creation of things or the end of them. He was not troubled to account for the origin of man, nor did he seek to know about his hereafter. He meddled neither with physics nor metaphysics.[1] The testimony of the Analects about the subjects of his

5 Mencius, II. Pt. I. ii. 23—28.

1 The contents of the Yih-king, and Confucius' labours upon it, may be objected in opposition to this statement, and I must be understood to make it with some reservation. Six years ago, I spent all my leisure time for twelve months in the study of that Work, and wrote out a translation of it, but at the close I was only groping my way in darkness to lay hold of its scope and meaning, and up to this time I have not been able to master it so as to speak positively about it. It will come in due time, in its place, in the present Publication, and I do not think that what I here say of Confucius will require much, if any, modification.

緒論

teaching is the following:—"His frequent themes of discourse were the Book of Poetry, the Book of History, and the maintenance of the rules of Propriety." "He taught letters, ethics, devotion of soul, and truthfulness." "Extraordinary things; feats of strength; states of disorder; and spiritual beings; he did not like to talk about."[2]

Confucius is not to be blamed for his silence on the subjects here indicated. His ignorance of them was to a great extent his misfortune. He had not learned them. No report of them had come to him by the ear; no vision of them by the eye. And to his practical mind the toiling of thought amid uncertainties seemed worse than useless.

The question has, indeed, been raised, whether he did not make changes in the ancient creed of China,[3] but I cannot believe that he did so consciously and designedly. Had his idiosyncrasy been different, we might have had expositions of the ancient views on some points, the effect of which would have been more beneficial than the indefiniteness in which they are now left, and it may be doubted so far, whether Confucius was not unfaithful to his guides. But that he suppressed or added, in order to bring in articles of belief originating with himself, is a thing not to be charged against him.

I will mention two important subjects in regard to which there is a growing conviction in my mind that he came short of the faith of the older sages. The first is the doctrine of God. This name is common in the She-king, and Shoo-king. *Te* or *Shang Te* appears there as a personal being, ruling in heaven and on earth, the author of man's moral nature, the governor among the nations, by whom kings reign and princes decree justice, the rewarder of the good, and the punisher of the bad. Confucius preferred to speak of Heaven. Instances have already been given of this. Two others may be cited: —"He who offends against Heaven has none to whom he can pray?"[4] "Alas!" said he, "there is no one that knows me." Tsze-kung said, "What do you mean by thus saying that no one knows you?" He replied, "I do not murmur against Heaven. I do not grumble against men. My studies lie low, and my penetration rises high. But there is Heaven;—that knows me!"[5] Not once throughout the

2. Ana. VII. xvii; xxiv.; xx. 3 See Hardwick's 'Christ and other Masters,' Part III. pp. 18, 19, with his reference in a note to a passage from Meadows' 'The Chinese and their Rebellions.' 4 Ana. III. xiii. 5 Ana. XIV. xxxvii.

Analects does he use the personal name. I would say that he was unreligious rather than irreligious; yet by the coldness of his temperament and intellect in this matter, his influence is unfavourable to the development of true religious feeling among the Chinese people generally, and he prepared the way for the speculations of the literati of mediæval and modern times, which have exposed them to the charge of atheism.

Secondly, Along with the worship of God there existed in China, from the earliest historical times, the worship of other spiritual beings,—especially, and to every individual, the worship of departed ancestors. Confucius recognized this as an institution to be devoutly observed. "He sacrificed to the dead as if they were present; he sacrificed to the spirits as if the spirits were present. He said, 'I consider my not being present at the sacrifice as if I did not sacrifice.'"[6] The custom must have originated from a belief of the continued existence of the dead. We cannot suppose that they who instituted it thought that with the cessation of this life on earth there was a cessation also of all conscious being. But Confucius never spoke explicitly on this subject. He tried to evade it. "Ke Loo asked about serving the spirits of the dead, and the master said, 'While you are not able to serve men, how can you serve their spirits?' The disciple added, 'I venture to ask about death,' and he was answered, 'While you do not know life, how can you know about death.'"[7] Still more striking is a conversation with another disciple, recorded in the "Family Sayings." Tsze-kung asked him, saying, "Do the dead have knowledge (of our services, that is), or are they without knowledge?" The master replied, "If I were to say that the dead have such knowledge, I am afraid that filial sons and dutiful grandsons would injure their substance in paying the last offices to the departed; and if I were to say that the dead have not such knowledge, I am afraid lest unfilial sons should leave their parents unburied. You need not wish, Ts'ze, to know whether the dead have knowledge or not. There is no present urgency about the point. Hereafter you will know it for yourself."[8] Surely this was not the teaching proper to a sage. He said on one occasion that he had

6 Ana. III. xii. 7 Ana. XI. xi. 8 家語, 卷二, art. 致思, towards the end.

緒論

no concealments from his disciples.[9] Why did he not candidly tell his real thoughts on so interesting a subject? I incline to think that he doubted more than he believed. If the case were not so, it would be difficult to account for the answer which he returned to a question as to what constituted wisdom. "To give one's-self earnestly," said he, "to the duties due to men, and, while respecting spiritual beings, to keep aloof from them, may be called wisdom."[10] At any rate, as by his frequent references to Heaven, instead of following the phraseology of the older sages, he gave occasion to many of his professed followers to identify God with a principle of reason and the course of nature; so, in the point now in hand, he has led them to deny, like the Sadducees of old, the existence of any spirit at all, and to tell us that their sacrifices to the dead are but an outward form, the mode of expression which the principle of filial piety requires them to adopt, when its objects have departed this life.

It will not be supposed that I wish to advocate or to defend the practice of sacrificing to the dead. My object has been to point out how Confucius recognized it, without acknowledging the faith from which it must have originated, and how he enforced it as a matter of form or ceremony. It thus connects itself with the most serious charge that can be brought against him,—the charge of insincerity. Among the four things which it is said he taught, "truthfulness" is specified,[11] and many sayings might be quoted from him, in which "sincerity" is celebrated as highly and demanded as stringently as ever it has been by any Christian moralist; yet he was not altogether the truthful and true man to whom we accord our highest approbation. There was the case of Măng Che-fan, who boldly brought up the rear of the defeated troops of Loo, and attributed his occupying the place of honour to the backwardness of his horse. The action was gallant, but the apology for it was weak and wrong. And yet Confucius saw nothing in the whole but matter for praise.[12] He could excuse himself from seeing an unwelcome visitor on the ground that he was sick, when there was nothing the matter with him.[13] These perhaps were small matters, but what shall we say to the incident which I have given in the sketch of his Life, p. 80,—his deliberately breaking the oath which

9 Ana. VII. xxiii. 10 Ana. VI. xx. 11 See above, near the beginning of this paragraph. 12 Ana. VI. xiii. 13 Ana. XVII. xx.

he had sworn, simply on the ground that it had been forced from him? I should be glad if I could find evidence on which to deny the truth of that occurrence. But it rests on the same authority as most other statements about him, and it is accepted as a fact by the people and scholars of China. It must have had, and it must still have, a very injurious influence upon them. Foreigners charge, and with reason, a habit of deceitfulness upon the nation and its government. For every word of falsehood and every act of insincerity, the guilty party must bear his own burden, but we cannot but regret the example of Confucius in this particular. It is with the Chinese and their sage, as it was with the Jews of old and their teachers. He that leads them has caused them to err, and destroyed the way of their paths.[14]

But was not insincerity a natural result of the un-religion of Confucius? There are certain virtues which demand a true piety in order to their flourishing in the corrupt heart of man. Natural affection, the feeling of loyalty, and enlightened policy, may do much to build up and preserve a family and a State, but it requires more to maintain the love of truth, and make a lie, spoken or acted, to be shrunk from with shame. It requires in fact the living recognition of a God of truth, and all the sanctions of revealed religion. Unfortunately the Chinese have not had these, and the example of him to whom they bow down as the best and wisest of men, encourages them to act, to dissemble, to sin.

His views on government.

7. I go on to a brief discussion of Confucius' views on government, or what we may call his principles of political science. It could not be in his long intercourse with his disciples but that he should enunciate many maxims bearing on character and morals generally, but he never rested in the improvement of the individual. "The empire brought to a state of happy tranquillity"[1] was the grand object which he delighted to think of; that it might be brought about as easily as "one can look upon the palm of his hand," was the dream which it pleased him to indulge in.[2] He held that there was in men an adaptation and readiness to be governed, which only needed to be taken advantage of in the proper way. There must be the right administrators, but given those, and "the

14 Isaiah, iii. 12.

1 天下平. See the 大學, 經, parr. 4, 5; &c. 2 Ana. III. xi.; *et al.*

緒論

growth of government would be rapid, just as vegetation is rapid in the earth; yea, their government would display itself like an easily-growing rush."[3] The same sentiment was common from the lips of Mencius. Enforcing it one day, when conversing with one of the petty princes of his time, he said in his peculiar style, "Does your Majesty understand the way of the growing grain? During the seventh and eighth months, when drought prevails, the plants become dry. Then the clouds collect densely in the heavens, they send down torrents of rain, and the grain erects itself as if by a shoot. When it does so, who can keep it back?"[4] Such, he contended, would be the response of the mass of the people to any true "shepherd of men." It may be deemed unnecessary that I should specify this point, for it is a truth applicable to the people of all nations. Speaking generally, government is by no device or cunning craftiness; human nature demands it. But in no other family of mankind is the characteristic so largely developed as in the Chinese. The love of order and quiet, and a willingness to submit to "the powers that be", eminently distinguish them. Foreign writers have often taken notice of this, and have attributed it to the influence of Confucius' doctrines as inculcating subordination; but it existed previous to his time. The character of the people moulded his system, more than it was moulded by it.

This readiness to be governed arose, according to Confucius, from "the duties of universal obligation, or those between sovereign and minister, between father and son, between husband and wife, between elder brother and younger, and those belonging to the intercourse of friends."[5] Men as they are born into the world, and grow up in it, find themselves existing in those relations. They are the appointment of Heaven. And each relation has its reciprocal obligations, the recognition of which is proper to the Heaven-conferred nature. It only needs that the sacredness of the relations be maintained, and the duties belonging to them faithfully discharged, and the "happy tranquillity" will prevail all under heaven. As to the institutions of government, the laws and arrangements by which, as through a thousand channels, it should go forth to carry plenty and prosperity through the length and breadth of the country, it did not belong to Confucius, "the throneless king," to set them forth minutely. And

3 中庸, xx 3. 4 Mencius, I. Pt. I. vi. 6. 5 中庸, xx. 8

indeed they were existing in the records of "the ancient sovereigns." Nothing new was needed. It was only requisite to pursue the old paths, and raise up the old standards. "The government of Wăn and Woo," he said, "is displayed in the records,—the tablets of wood and bamboo. Let there be the men, and the government will flourish, but without the men, the government decays and ceases."[6] To the same effect was the reply which he gave to Yen Hwuy when asked by him how the government of a State should be administered. It seems very wide of the mark, until we read it in the light of the sage's veneration for ancient ordinances, and his opinion of their sufficiency. "Follow," he said, "the seasons of Hea. Ride in the state-carriages of Yin. Wear the ceremonial cap of Chow. Let the music be the Shaou with its pantomimes. Banish the songs of Ch'ing, and keep far from specious talkers."[7]

Confucius' idea then of a happy, well-governed State did not go beyond the flourishing of the five relations of society which have been mentioned; and we have not any condensed exhibition from him of their nature, or of the duties belonging to the several parties in them. Of the two first he spoke frequently, but all that he has said on the others would go into small compass. Mencius has said that "between father and son there should be affection; between sovereign and minister righteousness; between husband and wife attention to their separate functions; between old and young, a proper order; and between friends, fidelity."[8] Confucius, I apprehend, would hardly have accepted this account. It does not bring out sufficiently the authority which he claimed for the father and the sovereign, and the obedience which he exacted from the child and the minister. With regard to the relation of husband and wife, he was in no respect superior to the preceding sages who had enunciated their views of "propriety" on the subject. We have a somewhat detailed exposition of his opinions in the "Family Sayings.—"Man," said he, "is the representative of Heaven, and is supreme over all things. Woman yields obedience to the instructions of man, and helps to carry out his principles.[9] On this account she can determine nothing of herself, and is subject to the rule of the three

6 中庸, xx. 2. 7 Ana. XV. x. 8 Mencius, III. Pt. I. iv. 8. 9 男子者,任天道而長萬物者也;女子者,順男子之道,而長其理者也.

緒論

obediences. When young, she must obey her father and elder brother; when married, she must obey her husband; when her husband is dead, she must obey her son. She may not think of marrying a second time. No instructions or orders must issue from the harem. Woman's business is simply the preparation and supplying of wine and food. Beyond the threshold of her apartments she should not be known for evil or for good. She may not cross the boundaries of the State to accompany a funeral. She may take no step on her own motion, and may come to no conclusion on her own deliberation. There are five women who are not to be taken in marriage:—the daughter of a rebellious house; the daughter of a disorderly house; the daughter of a house which has produced criminals for more than one generation; the daughter of a leprous house; and the daughter who has lost her father and elder brother. A wife may be divorced for seven reasons, which may be overruled by three considerations. The grounds for divorce are disobedience to her husband's parents; not giving birth to a son; dissolute conduct; jealousy (of her husband's attentions, that is, to the other inmates of his harem); talkativeness; and thieving. The three considerations which may overrule these grounds are—first, if, while she was taken from a home, she has now no home to return to; second, if she have passed with her husband through the three years' mourning for his parents; third, if the husband have become rich from being poor. All these regulations were adopted by the sages in harmony with the natures of man and woman, and to give importance to the ordinance of marriage."[10]

With these ideas—not very enlarged—of the relations of society, Confucius dwelt much on the necessity of personal correctness of character on the part of those in authority, in order to secure the right fulfilment of the duties implied in them. This is one grand peculiarity of his teaching. I have adverted to it in the review of "The Great Learning," but it deserves some further exhibition, and there are three conversations with the chief Ke K'ang, in which it is very expressly set forth. "Ke K'ang asked about government, and Confucius replied, 'To govern means to rectify. If you lead on the people with correctness, who will dare not to be correct?'" "Ke K'ang, distressed about the number of thieves in the State, inquired

10 家語卷三,本命解.

of Confucius about how to do away with them. Confucius said, 'If you, sir, were not covetous, though you should reward them to do it, they would not steal.'" "Ke K'ang asked about government, saying, 'What do You say to killing the unprincipled for the good of the principled?' Confucius replied, 'Sir, in carrying on your government, why should you use killing at all? Let your evinced desires be for what is good, and the people will be good. The relation between superiors and inferiors is like that between the wind and the grass. The grass must bend, when the wind blows across it.'"[11]

Example is not so powerful as Confucius in these and many other passages represented it, but its influence is very great. Its virtue is recognized in the family, and it is demanded in the church of Christ. "A bishop"—and I quote the term with the simple meaning of overseer—"must be blameless." It seems to me, however, that in the progress of society in the West we have come to think less of the power of example in many departments of State than we ought to do. It is thought of too little in the army and the navy. We laugh at the "self-denying ordinance," and the "new model" of 1644, but there lay beneath them the principle which Confucius so broadly propounded,—the importance of personal virtue in all who are in authority. Now that Great Britain is the governing power over the masses of India, and that we are coming more and more into contact with tens of thousands of the Chinese, this maxim of our sage is deserving of serious consideration from all who bear rule, and especially from those on whom devolves the conduct of affairs. His words on the susceptibility of the people to be acted on by those above them ought not to prove as water spilt on the ground.

But to return to Confucius.—As he thus lays it down that the mainspring of the well-being of society is the personal character of the ruler, we look anxiously for what directions he has given for the cultivation of that. But here he is very defective. "Self-adjustment and purification," he said, "with careful regulation of his dress, and the not making a movement contrary to the rules of propriety;—this is the way for the ruler to cultivate his person."[12] This is laying too much stress on what is external; but even to attain to this

11 Analects, XII. xvii.; xviii.; xix. 12 中庸, xx. 14.

緒論

is beyond unassisted human strength. Confucius, however, never recognized a disturbance of the moral elements in the constitution of man. The people would move, according to him, to the virtue of their ruler as the grass bends to the wind, and that virtue would come to the ruler at his call. Many were the lamentations which he uttered over the degeneracy of his times; frequent were the confessions which he made of his own shortcomings. It seems strange that it never came distinctly before him, that there is a power of evil in the prince and the peasant, which no efforts of their own and no instructions of sages are effectual to subdue.

The government which Confucius taught was a despotism, but of a modified character. He allowed no "*jus divinum*," independent of personal virtue and a benevolent rule. He has not explicitly stated, indeed, wherein lies the ground of the great relation of the governor and the governed, but his views on the subject were, we may assume, in accordance with the language of the Shoo-king:—"Heaven and Earth are the parents of all things, and of all things men are the most intelligent. The man among them most distinguished for intelligence becomes chief ruler, and ought to prove himself the parent of the people."[13] And again, "Heaven, protecting the inferior people, has constituted for them rulers and teachers, who should be able to be assisting to God, extending favour and producing tranquillity throughout all parts of the empire."[14] The moment the ruler ceases to be a minister of God for good, and does not administer a government that is beneficial to the people, he forfeits the title by which he holds the throne, and perseverance in oppression will surely lead to his overthrow. Mencius inculcated this principle with a frequency and boldness which are remarkable. It was one of the things about which Confucius did not like to talk. Still he held it. It is conspicuous in the last chapter of "The Great Learning." Its tendency has been to check the violence of oppression, and maintain the self-respect of the people, all along the course of Chinese history.

I must bring these observations on Confucius' views of government to a close, and I do so with two remarks. First, they are adapted to a primitive, unsophisticated state of society. He is a good counsellor for the father of a family, the chief of a clan, and even the head of a small principality. But his views want the comprehen-

13, 14 See the Shoo-king, V. i. Sect. I. 2, 7.

sion which would make them of much service in a great empire. Within three centuries after his death, the government of China passed into a new phase. The founder of the Ts'in dynasty conceived the grand idea of abolishing all its feudal Kingdoms, and centralizing their administration in himself. He effected the revolution, and succeeding dynasties adopted his system, and gradually moulded it into the forms and proportions which are now existing. There has been a tendency to advance, and Confucius has all along been trying to carry the nation back. Principles have been needed, and not "proprieties." The consequence is that China has increased beyond its ancient dimensions, while there has been no corresponding development of thought. Its body politic has the size of giant, while it still retains the mind of a child. Its hoary age is but senility.

Second, Confucius makes no provision for the intercourse of his country with other and independent nations. He knew indeed of none such. China was to him "The middle Kingdom,"[15] "The multitude of Great States,"[16] "All under heaven."[17] Beyond it were only rude and barbarous tribes. He does not speak of them bitterly, as many Chinese have done since his time. In one place he contrasts them favourably with the prevailing anarchy of the empire, saying, "The rude tribes of the east and north have their princes, and are not like the States of our great land which are without them."[18] Another time, disgusted with the want of appreciation which he experienced, he was expressing his intention to go and live among the nine wild tribes of the east. Some one said, "They are rude. How can you do such a thing?" His reply was, "If a superior man dwelt among them, what rudeness would there be?"[19] But had he been an emperor-sage, he would not only have influenced them by his instructions, but brought them to acknowledge and submit to his sway, as the great Yu did.[20] The only passage of Confucius' teachings from which any rule can be gathered for dealing with foreigners, is that in the "Doctrine of the Mean," where "indulgent treatment of men from a distance" is laid down as one of the nine standard rules for the government of the empire.[21] But "the men from a distance" are understood to be *pin* and *leu*[22] simply,—"guests," that is, or officers of one State seeking employment in

15 中國. 16 諸夏; Ana. III. v. 17 天下; *passim*. 18 Ana. III. v. 19 Ana. IX. xiii. 20 書經, III. ii. 10; *et al.* 21 柔遠人. 22 賓旅.

緒論

another, or at the imperial court; and "visitors," or travelling merchants. Of independent nations the ancient classics have not any knowledge, nor has Confucius. So long as merchants from Europe and other parts of the world could have been content to appear in China as suppliants, seeking the privilege of trade, so long the government would have ranked them with the barbarous hordes of antiquity, and given them the benefit of the maxim about "indulgent treatment," according to its own understanding of it. But when their governments interfered, and claimed to treat with that of China on terms of equality, and that their subjects should be spoken to and of as being of the same clay with the Chinese themselves, an outrage was committed on tradition and prejudice, which it was necessary to resent with vehemence.

I do not charge the contemptuous arrogance of the Chinese government and people upon Confucius; what I deplore, is that he left no principles on record to check the development of such a spirit. His simple views of society and government were in a measure sufficient for the people while they dwelt apart from the rest of mankind. His practical lessons were better than if they had been left, which but for him they probably would have been, to fall a prey to the influences of Taouism and Buddhism, but they could only subsist while they were left alone. Of the earth earthy, China was sure to go to pieces when it came into collision with a Christianly-civilized power. Its sage had left it no preservative or restorative elements against such a case.

It is a rude awakening from its complacency of centuries which China has now received. Its ancient landmarks are swept away. Opinions will differ as to the justice or injustice of the grounds on which it has been assailed, and I do not feel called to judge or to pronounce here concerning them. In the progress of events, it could not be but that the collision should come; and when it did come, it could not be but that China should be broken and scattered. Disorganization will go on to destroy it more and more, and yet there is hope for the people, with their veneration of the relations of society, with their devotion to learning, and with their habits of industry and sobriety;—there is hope for them, if they will look away from all their ancient sages, and turn to Him, who sends them, along with the dissolution of their ancient state, the knowledge of Himself, the only living and true God, and of Jesus Christ whom He hath sent.

8. I have little more to add on the opinions of Confucius. Many of his sayings are pithy, and display much knowledge of character; but as they are contained in the body of the Work, I will not occupy the space here with a selection of those which have struck myself as most worthy of notice. The fourth Book of the Analects, which is on the subject of *jin*, or perfect virtue, has several utterances which are remarkable.

Thornton observes:—"It may excite surprise, and probably incredulity, to state that the golden rule of our Saviour, 'Do unto others as you would that they should do unto you,' which Mr. Locke designates as 'the most unshaken rule of morality, and foundation of all social virtue,' had been inculcated by Confucius, almost in the same words, four centuries before."[1] I have taken notice of this fact in reviewing both "The Great Learning," and "The Doctrine of the Mean." I would be far from grudging a tribute of admiration to Confucius for it. The maxim occurs also twice in the Analects. In Book XV. xxiii., Tsze-kung asks if there be one word which may serve as a rule of practice for all one's life, and is answered, "Is not reciprocity such a word? What you do not want done to yourself do not do to others." The same disciple appears in Book V. xi., telling Confucius that he was practising the lesson. He says, "What I do not wish men to do to me, I also wish not to do to men;" but the master tells him, "Ts'ze, you have not attained to that." It would appear from this reply, that he was aware of the difficulty of obeying the precept; and it is not found, in its condensed expression at least, in the older classics. The merit of it is Confucius' own.

When a comparison, however, is drawn between it and the rule laid down by Christ, it is proper to call attention to the positive form of the latter,—"All things whatsoever ye would that men should do unto you, do ye even so to them." The lesson of the gospel commands men to do what they feel to be right and good. It requires them to commence a course of such conduct, without regard to the conduct of others to themselves. The lesson of Confucius only forbids men to do what they feel to be wrong and hurtful. So far as the point of priority is concerned, moreover, Christ adds, "This is the law and the prophets." The maxim was to be found substantially in the earlier revelations of God.

1 History of China, vol. I. p. 209.

緒論

But the worth of the two maxims depends on the intention of the enunciators in regard to their application. Confucius, it seems to me, did not think of the reciprocity coming into action beyond the circle of his five relations of society. Possibly, he might have required its observance in dealings even with the rude tribes, which were the only specimens of mankind besides his own comtrymen of which he knew anything, for on one occasion, when asked about perfect virtue, he replied, "It is, in retirement, to be sedately grave; in the management of business, to be reverently attentive; in intercourse with others, to be strictly sincere. Though a man go among the rude uncultivated tribes, these qualities may not be neglected."[2] Still, Confucius delivered his rule to his countrymen only, and only for their guidance in their relations of which I have had so much occasion to speak. The rule of Christ is for man as man, having to do with other men, all with himself on the same platform, as the children and subjects of the one God and Father in heaven.

How far short Confucius came of the standard of Christian benevolence, may be seen from his remarks when asked what was to be thought of the principle that injury should be recompensed with kindness. He replied, "With what then will you recompense kindness? Recompense injury with justice, and recompense kindness with kindness."[3] The same deliverance is given in one of the Books of the Le Ke, where he adds that "he who recompenses injury with kindness is a man who is careful of his person."[4] Ch'ing Heuen, the commentator of the second century, says that such a course would be "incorrect in point of propriety."[5] This "propriety" was a great stumbling-block in the way of Confucius. His morality was the result of the balancings of his intellect, fettered by the decisions of men of old, and not the gushings of a loving heart, responsive to the promptings of Heaven, and in sympathy with erring and feeble humanity.

This subject leads me on to the last of the opinions of Confucius which I shall make the subject of remark in this place. A commentator observes, with reference to the inquiry about recompensing injury with kindness, that the questioner was asking only about trivial matters, which might be dealt with in the way he mentioned,

2 Analects, XIII. xix. 3 Ana. XXV. xxxvi. 4 禮記, 表記. par. 12. 5 非禮之正.

while great offences such as those against a sovereign or a father, could not be dealt with by such an inversion of the principles of justice.[6] In the second Book of the Le Ke there is the following passage:—"With the slayer of his father, a man may not live under the same heaven; against the slayer of his brother, a man must never have to go home to fetch a weapon; with the slayer of his friend, a man may not live in the same State."[7] The *lex talionis* is here laid down in its fullest extent. The Chow Le tells us of a provision made against the evil consequences of the principle, by the appointment of a minister called "The Reconciler."[8] The provision is very inferior to the cities of refuge which were set apart by Moses for the manslayer to flee to from the fury of the avenger. Such as it was, however, it existed, and it is remarkable that Confucius, when consulted on the subject, took no notice of it, but affirmed the duty of blood-revenge in the strongest and most unrestricted terms. His disciple Tsze-hea asked him, "What course is to be pursued in the case of the murder of a father or mother?" He replied, "The son must sleep upon a matting of grass, with his shield for his pillow; he must decline to take office; he must not live under the same heaven with the slayer. When he meets him in the market-place or the court, he must have his weapon ready to strike him." "And what is the course on the murder of a brother?" "The surviving brother must not take office in the same State with the slayer; yet if he go on his prince's service to the State where the slayer is, though he meet him, he must not fight with him." "And what is the course on the murder of an uncle or a cousin?" "In this case the nephew or cousin is not the principal. If the principal on whom the revenge devolves can take it, he has only to stand behind with his weapon in his hand, and support him."[9]

Sir John Davis has rightly called attention to this as one of the objectionable principles of Confucius.[10] The bad effects of it are evident even in the present day. Revenge is sweet to the Chinese. I have spoken of their readiness to submit to government, and wish to live in peace, yet they do not like to resign even to government the "inquisition for blood." Where the ruling authority is feeble,

6 See notes *in loc.*, p. 152. 7 禮記, I. Pt. I. v. 10. 8 周禮, 卷之十四, pp. 14—18. 9 禮記, II. Pt. I. ii. 24. See also the 家語, 卷四, 子貢問. 10 The Chinese, vol. II. p. 41.

緒論

as it is at present, individuals and clans take the law into their own hands, and whole districts are kept in a state of constant feud and warfare.

But I must now leave the sage. I hope I have not done him injustice; but after long study of his character and opinions, I am unable to regard him as a great man. He was not before his age, though he was above the mass of the officers and scholars of his time. He threw no new light on any of the questions which have a world-wide interest. He gave no impulse to religion. He had no sympathy with progress. His influence has been wonderful, but it will henceforth wane. My opinion is, that the faith of the nation in him will speedily and extensively pass away.

SECTION III.

HIS IMMEDIATE DISCIPLES.

Sze-ma Ts'een makes Confucius say:—"The disciples who received my instructions, and could comprehend them, were seventy-seven individuals. They were all scholars of extraordinary ability."[1] The common saying is, that the disciples of the sage were three thousand, while among them there were seventy-two worthies. I propose to give here a list of all those whose names have come down to us, as being his followers. Of the greater number it will be seen that we know nothing more than their names and surnames. My principal authorities will be the "Historical Records," the "Family Sayings," "The Sacrificial Canon for the Sage's Temple, with Plates," and the chapter on "The Disciples of Confucius" prefixed to the "Four Books, Text and Commentary, with Proofs and Illustrations." In giving a few notices of the better-known individuals, I will endeavour to avoid what may be gathered from the Analects.

1. Yen Hwuy, by designation Tsze-yuen (顏回，字子淵). He was a native of Loo, the favourite of his master, whose junior he was by 30 years, and whose disciple he became when he was quite a youth. "After I got Hwuy," Confucius remarked, "the disciples came closer to me." We are told that once, when he found himself on the Nung hill with Hwuy, Tsze-loo, and Tsze-kung, Confucius

[1] 孔子曰，受業身通者，七十有七人，皆異能之士也。

113]

asked them to tell him their different aims, and he would choose between them. Tsze-loo began, and when he had done, the master said, "It marks your bravery." Tsze-kung followed, on whose words the judgment was, "They show your discriminating eloquence." At last came Yen Yuen, who said, "I should like to find an intelligent king and sage ruler whom I might assist. I would diffuse among the people instructions on the five great points, and lead them on by the rules of propriety and music, so that they should not care to fortify their cities by walls and moats, but would fuse their swords and spears into implements of agriculture. They should send forth their flocks without fear into the plains and forests. There should be no sunderings of families, no widows or widowers. For a thousand years there would be no calamity of war. Yew would have no opportunity to display his bravery, or Ts'ze to display his oratory." The master pronounced, "How admirable is this virtue!"

When Hwuy was 29, his hair was all white, and in three years more he died. He was sacrificed to, along with Confucius, by the first emperor of the Han dynasty. The title which he now has in the sacrificial Canon,—"Continuator of the Sage," was conferred in the 9th year of the emperor, or, to speak more correctly, of the period, Kea-tsing, A.D. 1530. Almost all the present sacrificial titles of the worthies in the temple were fixed at that time. Hwuy's place is the first of the four Assessors, on the east of the sage.[2]

2. Min Sun, styled Tsze-k'een, (閔損,字子騫). He was a native of Loo, 15 years younger than Confucius, according to Sze-ma

2 I have referred briefly, at p. 92, to the temples of Confucius. The principal hall, called 大成殿, or 'Hall of the Great and Complete One,' is that in which is his own statue or the tablet of his spirit, having on each side of it, within a screen, the statues, or tablets, of his 'four Assessors.' On the east and west, along the walls of the same apartment are the two 序, the places of the 十二哲, or 'twelve Wise Ones,' those of his disciples, who, next to the 'Assessors,' are counted worthy of honour. Outside this apartment, and running in a line with the two 序, but along the external wall of the sacred inclosure, are the two 廡, or side-galleries, which I have sometimes called the ranges of the outer court. In each there are 64 tablets of the disciples and other worthies, having the same title, as the Wise Ones, that of 先賢, or 'Ancient Worthy,' or the inferior title of 先儒, 'Ancient Scholar.' Behind the principal hall is the 崇聖祠殿, sacred to Confucius' ancestors, whose tablets are in the centre, fronting the south, like that of Confucius. On each side are likewise the tablets of certain 'ancient Worthies,' and 'ancient Scholars.'

緒論

Ts'een, but 50 years younger, according to the "Family Sayings," which latter authority is followed in "The Annals of the Empire." When he first came to Confucius, we are told, he had a starved look,[1] which was by-and-by exchanged for one of fulness and satisfaction.[2] Tsze-kung asked him how the change had come about. He replied, "I came from the midst of my reeds and sedges into the school of the master. He trained my mind to filial piety, and set before me the examples of the ancient kings. I felt a pleasure in his instructions, but when I went abroad, and saw the people in authority, with their umbrellas and banners, and all the pomp and circumstance of their trains, I also felt pleasure in that show. These two things assaulted each other in my breast. I could not determine which to prefer, and so I wore that look of distress. But now the lessons of our master have penetrated deeply into my mind. My progress also has been helped by the example of you my fellow-disciples. I now know what I should follow and what I should avoid, and all the pomp of power is no more to me than the dust of the ground. It is on this account that I have that look of fulness and satisfaction." Tsze-k'een was high in Confucius' esteem. He was distinguished for his purity and filial affection. His place in the temple is the first, east, among "The Wise Ones," immediately after the four assessors. He was first sacrificed to along with Confucius, as is to be understood of the other "Wise Ones," excepting in the case of Yew Jŏ, in the 8th year of the style K'ae-yuen of the sixth emperor of the T'ang dynasty, A.D. 720. His title, the same as that of all but the Assessors is—"The ancient Worthy, the philosopher Min."

3. Yen Kăng, styled Pih-new (冉耕字白[*al.*, 百]牛). He was a native of Loo, and Confucius' junior only by seven years. When Confucius became Minister of Crime, he appointed Pih-new to the office, which he had himself formerly held, of commandant of Chung-too. His tablet is now fourth among "The Wise Ones," on the west.

4. Yen Yung, styled Chung-kung (冉雍字仲弓). He was of the same clan as Yen Kăng, and 29 years younger than Confucius. He had a bad father, but the master declared that was not to be counted to him, to detract from his admitted excellence. His place is among "The Wise Ones," the second, east.

[1] 菜色. [2] 芻豢之色.

5. Yen K'ew, styled Tsze-yew (冉求，字子有). He was related to the two former, and of the same age as Chung-kung. He was noted among the disciples for his versatile ability and many acquirements. Tsze-kung said of him, "Respectful to the old, and kind to the young; attentive to guests and visitors; fond of learning and skilled in many arts; diligent in his examination of things:—these are what belong to Yen K'ew." It has been noted in the life of Confucius that it was by the influence of Tsze-yew that he was finally restored to Loo. He occupies the third place, west, among "The Wise ones."

6. Chung Yew, styled Tsze-loo and Ke-loo (仲由，字子路，又字季路). He was a native of P'ëen (卞) in Loo, and only 9 years younger than Confucius. At their first interview, the master asked him what he was fond of, and he replied, "My long sword." Confucius said, "If to your present ability there were added the results of learning, you would be a very superior man." "Of what advantage would learning be to me?" asked Tsze-loo. "There is a bamboo on the southern hill, which is straight itself without being bent. If you cut it down and use it, you can send it though a rhinoceros' hide;—what is the use of learning?" "Yes," said the master; "but if you feather it and point it with steel, will it not penetrate more deeply?" Tsze-loo bowed twice, and said, "I will reverently receive your instructions." Confucius was wont to say, "From the time that I got Yew, bad words no more came to my ears." For some time Tsze-loo was chief magistrate of the district of P'oo (蒲), where his administration commanded the warm commendations of the master. He died finally in Wei, as has been related above, p. 87. His tablet is now the fourth, east, from those of the Assessors.

7. Tsae Yu, styled Tsze-go (宰予，字子我). He was a native of Loo, but nothing is mentioned of his age. He had "a sharp mouth," according to Sze-ma Ts'een. Once, when he was at the court of Ts'oo on some commission, the king Ch'aou offered him an easy carriage adorned with ivory for his master. Yu replied, "My master is a man who would rejoice in a government where right principles were carried out, and can find his joy in himself when that is not the case. Now right principles and virtue are as it were in a state of slumber. His wish is to rouse and put them in motion. Could he find a prince really anxious to rule according to them, he would walk on foot to his court, and be glad to do so. Why need

緒論

he receive such a valuable gift as this from so great a distance?" Confucius commended this reply; but where he is mentioned in the Analects, Tsze-go does not appear to great advantage. He took service in the State of Ts'e, and was chief magistrate of Lin-tsze, where he joined with T'een Chang in some disorderly movement,[1] which led to the destruction of his kindred, and made Confucius ashamed of him. His tablet is now the second, west, among "The Wise Ones."

8. Twan-muk Ts'ze, styled Tsze-kung (端木賜, 字子貢, [*al.*, 子贛]), whose place is now third, east, from the Assessors. He was a native of Wei (衞), and 31 years younger than Confucius. He had great quickness of natural ability, and appears in the Analects as one of the most forward talkers among the disciples. Confucius used to say, "From the time that I got Ts'ze, scholars from a distance came daily resorting to me." Several instances of the language which he used to express his admiration of the master have been given in the last section. Here is another:—The duke King of Ts'e asked Tsze-kung how Chung-ne was to be ranked as a sage. "I do not know," was the reply. "I have all my life had the heaven over my head, but I do not know its height, and the earth under my feet, but I do not know its thickness. In my serving of Confucius, I am like a thirsty man who goes with his pitcher to the river, and there he drinks his fill, without knowing the river's depth." He took leave of Confucius to become commandant of Sin-yang (信陽宰), when the master said to him, "In dealing with your subordinates, there is nothing like impartiality; and when wealth comes in your way, there is nothing like moderation. Hold fast these two things, and do not swerve from them. To conceal men's excellence is to obscure the worthy; and to proclaim people's wickedness is the part of a mean man. To speak evil of those whom you have not sought the opportunity to instruct, is not the way of friendship and harmony." Subsequently Tsze-kung was high in office both in Loo and Wei, and finally died in Ts'e. We saw how he was in attendance on Confucius at the time of the sage's death. Many of the disciples built huts near the master's grave, and mourned for him three years, but Tsze-kung remained sorrowing alone for three years more.

9. Yen Yen, styled Tsze-yew (言偃, 字子游), now the 4th in the western range of "The Wise Ones." He was a native of Woo

1 與田常作亂. See above, p. 7.

(吳), 45 years younger than Confucius, and distinguished for his literary acquirements. Being made commandant of Woo-shing, he transformed the character of the people by "proprieties" and music, and was praised by the master. After the death of Confucius, Ke K'ang asked Yen how that event had made no sensation in Loo like that which was made by the death of Tsze-ch'an, when the men laid aside their bowstring rings and girdle ornaments, and the women laid aside their pearls and ear-rings, and the voice of weeping was heard in the lanes for three months. Yen replied, "The influences of Tsze-ch'an and my master might be compared to those of overflowing water and the fattening rain. Wherever the water in its overflow reaches, men take knowledge of it, while the fattening rain falls unobserved."

10. Puh Shang, styled Tsze-hea (卜商, 字子夏). It is not certain to what State he belonged, his birth being assigned to Wei (衛), to Wei (魏), and to Wăn (溫). He was 45 years younger than Confucius, and lived to a great age, for we find him, B.C. 406, at the court of the prince Wăn of Wei (魏), to whom he gave copies of some of the classical Books. He is represented as a scholar extensively read and exact, but without great comprehension of mind. What is called Maou's She-king (毛詩) is said to contain the views of Tsze-hea. Kung-yang Kaou and Kuh-lëang Ch'ih are also said to have studied the Ch'un Ts'ew with him. On the occasion of the death of his son he wept himself blind. His place is the 5th, east, among "The Wise Ones."

11. Twan-sun Sze, styled Tsze-chang (端孫師, 字子張), has his tablet, corresponding to that of the preceding, on the west. He was a native of Ch'in (陳), and 48 years younger than Confucius. Tsze-kung said, "Not to boast of his admirable merit; not to signify joy on account of noble station; neither insolent nor indolent; showing no pride to the dependent:—these are the characteristics of Twan-sun Sze." When he was sick, he called Shin Ts'eang to him, and said, "We speak of his *end* in the case of a superior man, and of his *death* in the case of a mean man. May I think that it is going to be the former with me to-day?"

12. Tsăng Sin [or Ts'an], styled Tsze-yu (曾參, 字子輿, [*al.*, 子與]). He was a native of south Woo-shing, and 46 years younger than Confucius. In his 16th year he was sent by his father into

118]

緒論

Ts'oo, where Confucius then was, to learn under the sage. Excepting perhaps Yen Hwuy, there is not a name of greater note in the Confucian school. Tsze-kung said of him, "There is no subject which he has not studied. His appearance is respectful. His virtue is solid. His words command credence. Before great men he draws himself up in the pride of self-respect. His eyebrows are those of longevity." He was noted for his filial piety, and after the death of his parents, he could not read the rites of mourning without being led to think of them, and moved to tears. He was a voluminous writer. Ten Books of his composition are said to be contained in the "Rites of the elder Tae" (大戴禮). The classic of Filial Piety he is said to have made under the eye of Confucius. On his connection with "The Great Learning," see above, Ch. III. Sect. II. He was first associated with the sacrifices to Confucius in A.D. 668, but in 1267 he was advanced to be one of the sage's four Assessors. His title—"Exhibiter of the Fundamental Principles of the Sage," dates from the period of Kea-tsing, as mentioned in speaking of Yen Hwuy.

13. Tan-t'ae Mëĕ-ming, styled Tsze-yu (澹臺滅明,字子羽). He was a native of Woo-shing, 39 years younger than Confucius, according to the "Historical Records," but 49, according to the "Family Sayings." He was excessively ugly, and Confucius thought meanly of his talents in consequence, on his first application to him. After completing his studies, he travelled to the south as far as the Yang-tsze. Traces of his presence in that part of the country are still pointed out in the department of Soo-chow. He was followed by about three hundred disciples, to whom he laid down rules for their guidance in their intercourse with the princes. When Confucius heard of his success, he confessed how he had been led by his bad looks to misjudge him. He, with nearly all the disciples whose names follow, first had a place assigned to him in the sacrifices to Confucius in A.D. 739. The place of his tablet is the second, east, in the outer court, beyond that of the "Assessors" and "Wise Ones."

14. Corresponding to the preceding, on the west, is the tablet of Fuk Puh-ts'e, styled Tsze-tseen (宓 [*al.*, 密 and 虙, all=伏] 不齊, 字子賤). He was a native of Loo, and, according to different accounts, 30, 40, and 49 years younger than Confucius. He was commandant of Tan-foo (單父宰), and hardly needed to put forth any personal effort. Wo-ma K'e had been in the same office, and

had succeeded by dint of the greatest industry and toil. He asked Puh-ts'e how he managed so easily for himself, and was answered, "I employ men; you employ men's strength." People pronounced Fuh to be a superior man. He was also a writer, and his works are mentioned in Lew Hin's catalogue.

15. Next to that of Mëë-ming is the tablet of Yuen Hëen, styled Tsze-sze (原憲, 字子思) a native of Sung, or, according to Ch'ing Heuen, of Loo, and younger than Confucius by 36 years. He was noted for his purity and modesty, and for his happiness in the principles of the master amid deep poverty. After the death of Confucius, he lived in obscurity in Wei. In the notes to Ana. VI. iii., I have referred to an interview which he had with Tsze-kung.

16. Kung-yay Chang [*al.*, Che], styled Tsze-Ch'ang [*al.*, Tsze-che], (公冶長 [*al.*, 芝], 字子長, [*al.*, 子之]), has his tablet next to that of Pih-ts'e. He was son-in-law to Confucius. His nativity is assigned both to Loo and to Ts'e.

17. Nan-kung Kwŏ, styled Tsze-yung (南宮括 [*al.*, 适, and, in the "Family Sayings," 縚 (T'aou)], 字子容), has the place at the east next to Yuen Hëen. It is a question much debated whether he was the same with Nan-kung King-shuh, who accompanied Confucius to the court of Chow, or not. On occasion of a fire breaking out in the palace of duke Gae, while others were intent on securing the contents of the Treasury, Nan-kung directed his efforts to save the Library, and to him was owing the preservation of the copy of the Chow Le which was in Loo, and other ancient monuments.

18. Kung-seih Gae, styled Ke-ts'ze [*al.*, Ke-ch'in] (公晳哀, 字季次 [*al.*, 季沉]). His tablet follows that of Kung-yay. He was a native of Loo, or of Ts'e. Confucius commended him for refusing to take office with any of the Families which were encroaching on the authority of the princes of the States, and for choosing to endure the severest poverty rather than sacrifice a tittle of his principles.

19. Tsăng Tëen, styled Seih (曾蒧 [*al.*, 點], 字晳). He was the father of Tsăng Ts'an. His place in the temples is the hall to Confucius' ancestors, where his tablet is the first, west.

20. Yen Woo-yaou, styled Loo (顏無繇, 字路). He was the father of Yen Hwuy, younger than Confucius by six years. His sacrificial place is the first, east, in the same hall as the last.

21. Following the tablet of Nan-kung Kwŏ is that of Shang Keu,

緒論

styled Tsze-muh (商瞿，字子木). To him, it is said, we are indebted for the preservation of the Yih-king, which he received from Confucius. Its transmission step by step, from Keu down to the Han dynasty, is minutely set forth.

22. Next to Kung-seih Gae is the place of Kaou Ch'ae, styled Tsze-kaou and Ke-kaou (高柴，字子羔，[*al.*, 季羔; for 羔 moreover, we find 皐, and 睾]), a native of Ts'e, according to the "Family Sayings," but of Wei, according to Sze-ma Ts'een and Ch'ing Heuen. He was 30 (some say 40) years younger than Confucius, dwarfish and ugly, but of great worth and ability. At one time he was criminal judge of Wei, and in the execution of his office condemned a prisoner to lose his feet. Afterwards that same man saved his life, when he was flying from the State. Confucius praised Ch'ae for being able to administer stern justice with such a spirit of benevolence as to disarm resentment.

23. Shang Keu is followed by Tseih-teaou K'ae [prop. K'e], styled Tsze-k'ae, Tsze-jŏ, and Tsze-sew (漆雕開 [pr. 啟]，字子開，子若，and 子脩), a native of Ts'ae (蔡), or, acc. to Heuen, of Loo. We only know him as a reader of the Shoo-king, and refusing to go into office.

24. Kung-pih Leaou, styled Tsze-chow (公伯僚，字子周). He appears in the Analects XIV. xxxiii., slandering Tsze-loo. It is doubtful whether he should have a place among the disciples.

25. Sze-ma Kăng, styled Tsze-new (司馬耕，字子牛), follows Tseih-teaou K'ae. He was a great talker, a native of Sung, and a brother of Hwan T'uy, to escape from whom seems to have been the labour of his life.

26. The place next Kaou Ch'ae is occupied by Fan Seu, styled Tsze-ch'e (樊須，字子遲), a native of Ts'e, or, acc. to others, of Loo, and whose age is given as 36 or 46 years younger than Confucius. When young, he distinguished himself in a military command under the Ke family.

27. Yew Jŏ, styled Tsze-jŏ (有若，字子若). He was a native of Loo, and his age is stated very variously. He was noted among the disciples for his great memory and fondness for antiquity. After the death of Confucius, the rest of the disciples, because of the likeness of Jŏ's voice to the Master's, wished to render the same observances to him which they had done to Confucius, but on

T'ăng Sin's demurring to the thing, they abandoned the purpose. The tablet of Tsze-jŏ is now the 6th, east, among "The Wise Ones," to which place it was promoted in the 3d year of K'ëen-lung of the present dynasty. This was done in compliance with a memorial from the president of one of the Boards, who said he was moved by a dream to make the request. We may suppose that his real motives were—a wish to do justice to the merits of Tsze-jŏ, and to restore the symmetry of the tablets in the "Hall of the Great and Complete One," which had been disturbed by the introduction of the tablet of Choo He in the preceding reign.

28. Kung-se Ch'ih, styled Tsze-hwa (公西赤，字子華), a native of Loo, younger than Confucius by 42 years, whose place is the 4th, west, in the outer court. He was noted for his knowledge of ceremonies, and the other disciples devolved on him all the arrangements about the funeral of the Master.

29. Woo-ma She [or K'e], styled Tsze-K'e (巫馬施[*al.*, 期],字子期[*al.*, 子旗]), a native of Ch'in, or, acc. to Ch'ing Heuen, of Loo, 30 years younger than Confucius. His tablet is on the east, next to that of Sze-ma Kăng. It is related that on one occasion, when Confucius was about to set out with a company of the disciples on a walk or journey, he told them to take umbrellas. They met with a heavy shower, and Woo-ma asked him, saying, "There were no clouds in the morning, but after the sun had risen, you told us to take umbrellas. How did you know that it would rain?" Confucius said, "The moon last evening was in the constellation Peih, and is it not said in the She-king, 'When the moon is in Peih, there will be heavy rain?' It was thus I knew it."

30. Lëang Chen [*al.*, Le], styled Shuh-yu (梁鱣[*al.* 鯉] 字 叔魚), occupies the eighth place, west, among the tablets of the outer court. He was a man of Ts'e, and his age is stated as 29 and 39 years younger than Confucius. The following story is told in connection with him.—When he was thirty, being disappointed that he had no son, he was minded to put away his wife. "Do not do so," said Shang Keu to him. "I was 38 before I had a son, and my mother was then about to take another wife for me, when the Master proposed sending me to Ts'e. My mother was unwilling that I should go, but Confucius said, 'Don't be anxious. Keu will have five sons

緒論

after he is forty.' It has turned out so, and I apprehend it is your fault, and not your wife's, that you have no son yet." Chen took this advice, and in the second year after, he had a son.

31. Yen Hing [*al.*, Sin, Lew, and Wei], styled Tsze-lew (顏幸 [*al.* 辛, 柳, and 韋], 字子柳), occupies the place, east, after Woo-ma She. He was a native of Loo, and 46 years younger than Confucius.

32. Leang Chen is followed on the west by Yen Joo, styled Tsze-Loo [*al.*, Tsze-tsăng and Tsze-yu] (冉孺 [*al.*, 儒] 字子魯 [*al.*, 子曾 and 子魚]), a native of Loo, and 50 years younger than Confucius.

33. Yen Hing is followed on the east by Ts'aou Seuh, styled Tsze-seun (曹卹, 字子循), a native of Ts'ae, 50 years younger than Confucius.

34. Next on the west is Pih K'ëen, styled Tsze-seih, or, in the current copies of the "Family Sayings," Tsze-k'ëae (伯虔, 字子晳 [*al.*, 子析] or 子楷), a native of Loo, 50 years younger than Confucius.

35. Following Tsze-seun is Kung-sun Lung [*al.*, Ch'ung], styled Tsze-shih (公孫龍 [*al.* 寵], 字子石) whose birth is assigned by different writers to Wei, Ts'oo, and Chaou (趙). He was 53 years younger than Confucius. We have the following account:—"Tsze-kung asked Tsze-shih, saying, 'Have you not studied the Book of Poetry?' Tsze-shih replied, 'What leisure have I to do so? My parents require me to be filial; my brothers require me to be submissive; and my friends require me to be sincere. What leisure have I for anything else?' 'Come to my Master,' said Tsze-kung, 'and learn of him.'"

Sze-ma Ts'een here observes:—"Of the thirty-five disciples which precede, we have some details. Their age and other particulars are found in the Books and Records. It is not so, however, in regard to the fifty-two which follow."

36. Yen Ke, styled Tsze-ch'an [*al.* Ke-ch'an and Tsze-tă], (冉季, 字子產 [*al.* 季產 and 子達]), a native of Loo whose place is the eleventh, west, next to Pih K'ëen.

37. Kung-tsoo Kow-tsze or simply Tsze, styled Tsze-che (公祖勾茲 [or simply 茲], 字子之), a native of Loo. His tablet is the 23d, east, in the outer court.

38. Ts'in Tsoo, styled Tsze-nan (秦祖, 字子南), a native of Ts'in. His tablet precedes that of the last, two places.

123]

39. Tseih-teaou Ch'e, styled Tsze-lëen (漆雕哆 [*al.*, 侈], 字子歛), a native of Loo. His tablet is the 13th, west.

40. Yen Kaou, styled Tsze-Keaou (顏高字子驕). According to the "Family Sayings," he was the same as Yen K'ih (刻, or 尅) who drove the carriage, when Confucius rode in Wei after the duke and Nan-tsze. But this seems doubtful. Other authorities make his name Ch'an (產), and style him Tsze-tsing (子精). His tablet is the 13th, east.

41. Tseih-teaou T'oo-foo [*al*,. Ts'ung], styled Tsze-yew, Tsze-k'e and Tsze-wăn], 漆雕徒父 [*al.* 從], 字子有 or 子友 [*al.*, 子期 and 子文]) a native of Loo, whose tablet precedes that of Tseih-teaou Ch'e.

42. Jang Sze-ch'ih, styled Tsze-t'oo, or Tsze-ts'ung (壤 [*al.* 穰] 駟赤, 字子徒 [*al.* 子從]), a native of Ts'in. Some consider Jang-sze (壤駟) to be a double surname. His tablet comes after that of No. 40.

43. Shang Tsih, styled Tsze-ke and Tsze-sew (商澤, 字子季 [*al.*, 子秀]), a native of Loo. His tablet is immediately after that of Fan Seu, No. 26.

44. Shih Tsŏ [*al.*, Che and Tsze]-shuh, styled Tsze-ming (石作 [*al.*, 之 and 子]-蜀, 字子明). Some take Shih-tsŏ (石作) as a double surname. His tablet follows that of No. 42.

45. Jin Puh-ts'e, styled Seuen (任不齊, 字選), a native of Ts'oo, whose tablet is next to that of No. 28.

46. Kung Leang Joo, styled Tsze-ching (公良孺 [*al.*, 儒], 字子正), a native of Ch'in, follows the preceding in the temples. The "Sacrificial Canon" says:—"Tsze-ching was a man of worth and bravery. When Confucius was surrounded and stopt in P'oo, Tsze-ching fought so desperately, that the people of P'oo were afraid, and let the Master go, on his swearing that he would not proceed to Wei."

47. How [*al.*, Shih] Ch'oo [*al.*, K'ëen], styled Tsze-le [*al.*, Le-che], (后 [*al.*, 石] 處 [*al.*, 虔], 字子里 [*al.*, 里之]), a native of Ts'e, having his tablet the 17th, east.

48. Ts'in Yen, styled K'ae (秦冉, 字開), a native of Ts'ae. He is not given in the list of the "Family Sayings," and on this account his tablet was put out of the temples in the 9th year of Kea-tsing. It was restored, however, in the second year of Yung-ching, A.D. 1724, and is the thirty-third, east, in the outer court.

緒論

49. Kung-hea Show, styled Shing [and Tsze-shing], (公夏首 [*al.*, 守], 字乘 [and 子乘]), a native of Loo, whose tablet is next that of No. 44.

50. He Yung-tëen [or simply Tëen,] styled Tsze-seih [*al.*, Tsze-keae, and Tsze-k'eae], (系容蒧 [or 點], 字子皙 [*al.*, 子偕 and 子楷]), a native of Wei, having his tablet the 18th, east.

51. Kung Këen-ting [*al.*, Kung Yew], styled Tsze-chung (公肩 [*al.*, 堅] 定 [*al.*, 公有], 字子仲, [*al.*, 中, and 忠]). His nativity is assigned to Loo, to Wei, and to Tsin (晉). He follows No. 46.

52. Yen Tsoo [*al.*, Seang], styled Sëang, and Tsze-seang (顏祖 [*al.*, 相], 字襄, and 子襄), a native of Loo, with his tablet following that of No. 50.

53. Heaou Tan [*al.*, Woo], styled Tsze-këa (鄡單 [*al.*, 鄔], 字子家), a native of Loo. His place is next to that of No. 51.

54. Keu [*al.*, Kow] Tsing-keang [and simply Tsing] styled Tsze-keang [*al.*, Tsze-keae and Tsze-măng], (句 [*al.*, 勾 and 鉤] 井疆 [and simply 井], 字子疆 [*al.*, 子界, and 子孟]), a native of Wei, following No. 52.

55. Han [*al.*, Tsae]-foo Hih, styled Tsze-hih [*al.*, Tsze-sŏ and Tsze-soo], (罕 [*al.*, 宰] 父黑, 字子黑 [*al.*, 子索, and 子素]), a native of Loo, whose tablet is next to that of No. 53.

56. Ts'in Shang, styled Tsze-p'ei [*al.*, P'ei-tsze, and Puh-tsze], (秦商, 字子丕 [*al.*, 丕茲, and 不茲]), a native of Loo, or, according to Ch'ing Heuen, of Ts'oo. He was 40 years younger than Confucius. One authority, however, says he was only 4 years younger, and that his father and Confucius' father were both celebrated for their strength. His tablet is the 12th, east.

57. Shin Tang, styled Chow (申黨字周). In the "Family Sayings" there is a Shin Tseih, styled Tsze-chow (申績, 字子周). The name is given by others as T'ang (堂 and 儻), and Tsuh (續), with the designation Tsze-tsuh (子續). These are probably the same person mentioned in the Analects as Shin Ch'ang (申棖). Prior to the Ming dynasty they were sacrificed to as two, but in A.D. 1530, the name of Tang was expunged from the sacrificial list, and only that of Ch'ang left. His tablet is the 31st, east.

58. Yen Che-puh, styled Tsze-shuh [or simply Shuh], (顏之僕, 字子叔 [or simply 叔]), a native of Loo, who occupies the 29th place, east.

59. Yung K'e, styled Tsze-k'e [*al.*, Tsze-yen], (榮旂 [or 祈], 字子旗 or 子祺, [*al.*, 子顏]), a native of Loo, whose tablet is the 20th, west.

60. Hëen Shing, styled Tsze-k'e [*al.*, Tsze-hwang], (縣成, 字子祺 [*al.*, 子横]), a native of Loo. His place is the 22d, east.

61. Tso Jin-ying, [or simply Ying], styled Hing and Tsze-hing (左人郢 [or simply 郢], 字行 and 子行), a native of Loo. His tablet follows that of No. 59.

62. Yen Keih, styled Yin [*al.*, Tsze-sze], (燕伋 [or 級], 字思 [*al.*, 子思], a native of Ts'in. His tablet is the 24th, east.

63. Ch'ing Kwŏ, styled Tsze-t'oo (鄭國, 字子徒), a native of Loo. This is understood to be the same with the Sëĕ Pang, styled Tsze-ts'ung (薛邦字子從), of the "Family Sayings." His tablet follows No. 61.

64. Ts'in Fei, styled Tsze-che (秦非, 字子之), a native of Loo, having his tablet the 31st, west.

65. She Che-chang, styled Tsze-hăng [*al.*, chang], 施之常, 字子恆 [*al.*, 常]), a native of Loo. His tablet is the 30th, east.

66. Yen K'wae, styled Tsze-shing, (顔噲, 字子聲), a native of Loo. His tablet is the next to that of No. 64.

67. Poo Shuh-shing, styled Tsze-keu (步叔乘 [in the "Family Sayings" we have 椉, an old form of 乘], 字子車), a native of Ts'e. Sometimes for Poo (步) we find Shaou (少). His tablet is the 30th, west.

68. Yuen K'ang, styled Tsze-tseih (原亢, 字子籍), a native of Loo. Sze-ma Ts'een calls him Yuen K'ang-tseih, not mentioning any designation. The "Family Sayings" makes him Yuen K'ang (抗), styled Tseih. His tablet is the 23d, west.

69. Yŏ Kae [*al.*, Hin], styled Tsze-shing, (樂欬 [*al.*, 欣], 字子聲), a native of Loo. His tablet is the 25th, east.

70. Lëen Këĕ, styled Yung and Tsze-yung [*al.*, Tsze-ts'aou], (廉潔, 字庸 and 子庸 [*al.*, 子曹]), a native of Wei, or of Ts'e. His tablet is next to that of No. 68.

71. Shuh-chung Hwuy [*al.*, K'wae], styled Tsze-k'e (叔仲會 [*al.*, 噲], 字子期), a native of Loo, or, according to Ch'ing Heuen, of Tsin. He was younger than Confucius by 54 years. It is said that he and another youth, called K'ung Seuen (孔琁), attended by turns with their pencils, and acted as amanuenses to the sage, and

126]

緒論

when Măng Woo-pih expressed a doubt of their competency, Confucius declared his satisfaction with them. He follows Lëen Këĕ in the temples.

72. Yen Ho, styled Yen (顏何, 字冉), a native of Loo. The present copies of the "Family Sayings" do not contain this name, and in A.D. 1588 Yen was displaced from his place in the temples. His tablet, however, has been restored during the present dynasty. It is the 33d, west.

73. Teih Hih, styled Chĕ [*al.*, Tsze-chĕ and Chĕ-che] (狄黑, 字晳 [*al.*, 子晳 and 晳之]), a native of Wei, or of Loo. His tablet is the 26th, east.

74. Kwei [*al.*, Pang] Sun, styled Tsze-lëen [*al.*, Tsze-yin] (邽 [*al.*, 邦] 巽, 字子歛 [*al.*, 子飲]), a native of Loo. His tablet is the 27th, west.

75. K'ung Chung, styled Tsze-mëĕ (孔忠, 字子蔑). This was the son, it is said, of Confucius' elder brother, the cripple Măng-p'e. His tablet is next to that of No. 73. His sacrificial title is "The ancient Worthy, the philosopher Mëĕ."

76. Kung-se Yu-joo [*al.*, Yu], styled Tsze-shang (公西輿如 [*al.*, 輿], 字子上), a native of Loo. His place is the 26th, west.

77. Kung-se Tëen, styled Tsze-shang (公西蒧 [or 點], 字子上 [*al.*, 子尙]), a native of Loo. His tablet is the 28th, east.

78. Kin Chang [*al.*, Laou], styled Tsze-k'ae (琴張 [*al.*, 牢], 字子開), a native of Wei. His tablet is the 29th, west.

79. Ch'in K'ang, styled Tsze-k'ang [*al.*, Tsze-k'in] (陳亢, 字子亢 [*al.*, 子禽]), a native of Ch'in. See notes on Ana. I. x.

80. Hëen T'an [*al.*, T'an-foo, and Fung], styled Tsze-seang (縣亶 [*al.*, 亶父, and 豐], 字子象]), a native of Loo. Some suppose that this is the same as No. 53. The advisers of the present dynasty in such matters, however, have considered them to be different, and in 1724, a tablet was assigned to Heen Tan, the 34th, west.

The three preceding names are given in the "Family Sayings."

The research of scholars has added about twenty others.

81. Lin Fang, styled Tsze-k'ew (林放, 字子邱), a native of Loo. The only thing known of him is from the Ana. III. iv. His tablet was displaced under the Ming, but has been restored by the present dynasty. It is the first, west.

82. Keu Yuen, styled Pih-yuh (蘧瑗, 字伯玉), an officer of

Wei, and, as appears from the Analects and Mencius, an intimate friend of Confucius. Still his tablet has shared the same changes as that of Lin Fang. It is now the first, east.

83. and 84. Shin Ch'ang (申棖), and Shin T'ang (申堂). See No. 57.

85. Muh Pei (牧皮), mentioned by Mencius, VII. Pt. II. xxxvii. 4. His entrance into the temple has been under the present dynasty. His tablet is the 34th, east.

86. Tso-k'ew Ming or Tso K'ew-ming (左丘明) has the 32d place, east. His title was fixed in A.D. 1530 to be—"The Ancient Scholar," but in 1642 it was raised to that of "Ancient Worthy." To him we owe the most distinguished of the annotated editions of the Ch'un Ts'ew. But whether he really was a disciple of Confucius, and in presonal communication with him, is much debated.

The above are the only names and surnames of those of the disciples who now share in the sacrifices to the sage. Those who wish to exhaust the subject, mention in addition, on the authority of Tso-k'ew Ming, Chung-sun Ho-ke (仲孫何忌), a son of Măng He (see p. 63), and Chung-sun Shwŏ (仲孫說), also a son of Măng He, supposed by many to be the same with No. 17; Joo Pei, (孺悲), mentioned in the Analects XVII. xx., and in the Le Ke, XVIII. Pt. II. ii. 21; Kung-wang Che-k'ew (公罔之裘) and Tseu Tëen (序點), mentioned in the Le Ke, XLI. 7; Pin-mow Këa (賓牟賈), mentioned in the Le Ke, XVII. iii. 16; K'ung Seuen (孔璇) and Hwuy Shuh-lan (惠叔蘭), on the authority of the Family Sayings; Chang Ke (常季), mentioned by Chwang-tsze; Keŭh Yu (鞠語), mentioned by Gan-tsze (晏子); Leen-yu (廉瑀), and Loo Tseun (魯峻), on the authority of 文翁石室; and finally Tsze-fuk Ho (子服何), the Tsze-fuk King-pih (子服景伯) of the Analects, XIV. xxxviii.

緒論

CHAPTER VI.

LIST OF THE PRINCIPAL WORKS WHICH HAVE BEEN CONSULTED IN THE PREPARATION OF THIS VOLUME.

SECTION I.

CHINESE WORKS, WITH BRIEF NOTICES.

十三經註疏, "The Thirteen King, with Commentary and Explanations." This is the great repertory of ancient lore upon the Classics. On the Analects, it contains the "Collection of Explanations of the Lun Yu," by Ho An and others (see p. 19), and "The Correct Meaning," or Paraphrase of Hing Ping (see p. 20). On the Great Learning and the Doctrine of the Mean, it contains the comments and glosses of Ch'ing Heuen, and K'ung Ying-tă (孔穎達) of the T'ang dynasty.

新刻批點四書讀本, "A new edition of the Four Books,. Punctuated and Annotated, for Reading." This work was published in the 7th year of T'aou-kwang (1827) by a Kaou Lin (高琳). It is the finest edition of the Four Books which I have seen, in point of typographical execution. It is indeed a volume for reading. It contains the ordinary "Collected Comments" of Choo He on the Analects, and his "Chapters and Sentences" of the Great Learning and Doctrine of the Mean. The editor's own notes are at the top and bottom of the page, in rubric.

四書朱子本義匯參, "The Proper Meaning of the Four Books as determined by Choo He, Compared with, and Illustrated from, other Commentators." This is a most voluminous work, published in the tenth year of K'ëen-lung, A.D. 1745, by Wang Poots'ing (王步靑), a member of the Han-lin College. On the Great Learning and the Doctrine of the Mean, the "Queries" (或問) of Choo He are given in the same text as the standard commentary.

四書經註集證, "The Four Books, Text and Commentary, with Proofs and Illustrations." The copy of this Work which I have was edited by a Wang T'ing-ke (汪廷機), in the 3d year of

Këa-k'ing, A.D. 1798. It may be called a commentary on the commentary. The research in all matters of Geography, History, Biography, Natural History, &c., is immense.

四書諸儒輯要, "A Collection of the most important Comments of Scholars on the Four Books." By Le P'ei-lin (李沛霖); published in the 57th year of K'ang-he, A.D. 1718. This Work is about as voluminous as the 滙參, but on a different plan. Every chapter is preceded by a critical discussion of its general meaning, and the logical connection of its several paragraphs. This is followed by the text, and Choo He's standard commentary. We have then a paraphrase, full and generally perspicuous. Next, there is a selection of approved comments, from a great variety of authors; and finally, the reader finds a number of critical remarks and ingenious views, differing often from the common interpretation, which are submitted for his examination.

四書翼註論文, "A Supplemental Commentary, and Literary Discussions, on the Four Books." By Chang K'ëen-t'aou [*al.*, T'eih-gan] (張甄陶 [*al.*, 惕菴]), a member of the Han-lin college, in the early part, apparently, of the reign of K'ëen-lung. The work is on a peculiar plan. The reader is supposed to be acquainted with Choo He's commentary, which is not given; but the author generally supports his views, and defends them against the criticisms of some of the early scholars of this dynasty. His own exercitations are of the nature of essays more than of commentary. It is a book for the student who is somewhat advanced, rather than for the learner. I have often perused it with interest and advantage.

四書遵註合講, "The Four Books, according to the Commentary, with Paraphrase." Published in the 8th year of Yung Ching, A.D. 1730, by Ung Fuh [*al.*, K'ih-foo] (翁復 [*al.*, 克夫]). Every page is divided into two parts. Below, we have the text and Choo He's commentary. Above, we have an analysis of every chapter, followed by a paraphrase of the several paragraphs. To the paraphrase of each paragraph are subjoined critical notes, digested from a great variety of scholars, but without the mention of their names. A list of 116 is given who are thus laid under contribution. In addition, there are maps and illustrative figures at the commencement; and to each Book there are prefixed biographical notices, explanations of peculiar allusions, &c.

新增四書補註附考備旨, "The Four Books, with a complete Digest of Supplements to the Commentary, and additional Suggestions. A new edition, with Additions." By Too Ting-ke (杜定基). Published A.D. 1779. The original of this Work was by T'ăng Lin (鄧林), a scholar of the Ming dynasty. It is perhaps the best of all editions of the Four Books for a learner. Each page is divided into three parts. Below, is the text divided into sentences and members of sentences, which are followed by short glosses. The text is followed by the usual commentary, and that by a paraphrase, to which are subjoined the Supplements and Suggestions. The middle division contains a critical analysis of the chapters and paragraphs; and above, there are the necessary biographical and other notes.

四書味根錄, "The Four Books, with the Relish of the Radical Meaning." This is a new Work, published in 1852. It is the production of Kin Ch'ing, styled Ts'ew-t'an (金澂,字秋潭), an officer and scholar, who, returning, apparently to Canton province, from the North in 1836, occupied his retirement with reviewing his literary studies of former years, and employed his sons to transcribe his notes. The writer is fully up in all the commentaries on the classics, and pays particular attention to the labours of the scholars of the present dynasty. To the Analects, for instance, there is prefixed Keang Yung's History of Confucius, with criticisms on it by the author himself. Each chapter is preceded by a critical analysis. Then follows the text with the standard commentary, carefully divided into sentences, often with glosses, original and selected, between them. To the commentary there succeeds a paraphrase, which is not copied by the author from those of his predecessors. After the paraphrase we have Explanations (解). The Book is beautifully printed, and in small type, so that it is really a *multum in parvo*, with considerable freshness.

日講書四義解, "A Paraphrase for Daily Lessons, Explaining the Meaning of the Four Books." This work was produced in 1677, by a multitude of the members of the Han-lin college, in obedience to an Imperial rescript. The paraphrase is full, perspicuous, and elegant.

御製周易折中;書經傳說彙纂;詩經傳說彙纂;禮記義疏;春秋傳說彙纂. These works form together a superb edition of the Five King, published by imperial authority in the reigns of K'ang-he and his successor, Yung-ching. They contain the standard views (傳); various opinions (說); critical decisions of the editors (案); prolegomena; plates or cuts; and other apparatus for the student.

毛西河先生全集. "The Collected Writings of Maou Se-ho." See prolegomena, p. 20. The voluminousness of his Writings is understated there. Of 經集, or Writings on the Classics, there are 236 sections, while his 文集, or other literary compositions, amount to 257 sections. His treatises on the Great Learning and the Doctrine of the Mean have been especially helpful to me. He is a great opponent of Choo He, and would be a much more effective one, if he possessed the same graces of style as that "prince of literature."

四書摭餘說, "A collection of Supplemental Observations on the Four Books." The preface of the author, Ts'aou Che-shing (曹之升), is dated in 1795, the last year of the reign of K'ëen-lung. The work contains what we may call prolegomena on each of the Four Books, and then excursus on the most difficult and disputed passages. The tone is moderate, and the learning displayed ? extensive and solid. The views of Choo He are frequently well defended from the assaults of Maou Se-ho. I have found the Work very instructive.

鄉黨圖考, "On the Tenth Book of the Analects, with Plates." This Work was published by the author, Keang Yung (江永), in the 21st year of K'ëen-lung, A.D. 1761, when he was 76 years old. It is devoted to the illustration of the above portion of the Analects, and is divided into ten Sections, the first of which consists of woodcuts and tables. The second contains the Life of Confucius, of which I have largely availed myself in the last Chapter. The whole is a remarkable specimen of the minute care with which Chinese scholars have illustrated the Classical Books.

四書釋地;四書釋地續;四書釋地又續;四書釋地三續. We may call these volumes—"The Topography of the Four Books; with three Supplements." The Author's name is Yen Jŏ-keu (閻若璩). The first volume was published in 1698, and the second in 1700. I have not been able to find the dates of publication of the other two, in which there is more biographical and general matter than topographical. The author apologizes for the inappropriateness of their titles by saying that he could not help calling them Supplements to the Topography, which was his "first love."

皇淸經解, "Explanations of the Classics, under the Imperial dynasty of Ts'ing." See above, p. 20. The Work, however, was not published, as I have there supposed, by Imperial authority, but under the superintendence, and at the expense (aided by other officers), of Yuen Yuen (阮 元), Governor-general of K'wang-tung and K'wang-se, in the 9th year of the last reign, 1829. The publication of so extensive a Work shows a public spirit and zeal for literature among the high officers of China, which should keep foreigners from thinking meanly of them.

孔子家語, "Family Sayings of Confucius." Family is to be taken in the sense of Sect or School. In Lew Hin's Catalogue, in the subdivision devoted to the Lun Yu, we find the entry:—"Family Sayings of Confucius, 27 Books," with a note by Yen Sze-koo of the T'ang dynasty,—"Not the existing Work called the Family Sayings." The original Work was among the treasures found in the wall of Confucius' old house, and was deciphered and edited by K'ung Gan-kwŏ. The present Work is by Wang-suh of the Wei (魏) dynasty, grounded professedly on the older one, the blocks of which had suffered great dilapidation during the intervening centuries. It is allowed also, that, since Suh's time, the Work has suffered more than any of the acknowledged Classics. Yet it is a very valuable fragment of antiquity, and it would be worth while to incorporate it with the Analects. My copy is the edition of Le Yung (李容), published in 1780.

聖廟祀典圖考, "Sacrificial Canon of the Sage's Temples, with Plates." This Work, published in 1826, by Koo Yuen, styled Seang-chow (顧沅, 字湘舟), is a very pains-taking account of all the Names sacrificed to in the temples of Confucius, the dates of their attaining to that honour, &c. There are appended to it Memoirs of Confucius and Mencius, which are not of so much value.

十子全書, "The complete Works of the Ten *Tsze*." See Morrison's Dictionary, under the character 子. I have only had occasion, in connection with this Work, to refer to the writings of Chwang-tsze (莊子) and Lëĕ-tsze (列子). My copy is an edition of 1804.

歷代名賢列女氏姓譜, "A Cyclopædia of Surnames, or Biographical Dictionary, of the Famous Men and Virtuous Women of the successive Dynasties." This is a very notable work of its class; published in 1793, by 蕭智漢, and extending through 157 chapters or Books.

文獻通考, "General Examination of Records and Scholars." This astonishing Work, which cost its author, Ma Twan-lin (馬端臨), twenty years' labour, was first published in 1321. Remusat says—"This excellent Work is a library in itself, and if Chinese literature possessed no other, the language would be worth learning for the sake of reading this alone." It does indeed display all but incredible research into every subject connected with the Government, History, Literature, Religion, &c., of the empire of China. The author's researches are digested in 348 Books. I have had occasion to consult principally those on the Literary Monuments, embraced in 76 Books, from the 174th to the 249th.

續文獻通考, "A Continuation of the General Examination of Records and Scholars." This Work, which is in 254 Books, and nearly as extensive as the former, was the production of Wang K'e (王圻), who dates his preface in 1586, the 14th year of Wan-leih, the style of the reign of the 14th emperor of the Ming dynasty. Wang K'e brings down the Work of his predecessor to his own times. He also frequently goes over the same ground, and puts things in a clearer light. I have found this to be the case in the chapters on the classical and other Books.

二十三史, "The twenty-three Histories." These are the imperially-authorized records of the empire, commencing with the "Historical Records," the work of Sze-ma Ts'een, and ending with the History of the Ming dynasty, which appeared in 1742, the result of the joint labours of 145 officers and scholars of the present dynasty. The extent of the collection may be understood from this, that my copy, bound in English fashion, makes fifty-five volumes, each one larger than this. No nation has a history so thoroughly digested; and on the whole it is trustworthy. In preparing this volume, my necessities have been confined mostly to the Works of Sze-ma Ts'een, and his successor, Pan Koo (班固), the Historian of the first Han dynasty.

歷代統記表, "The Annals of the Empire." Published by imperial authority in 1803, the 8th year of Kea-k'ing. This Work is invaluable to a student, being, indeed, a collection of chronological tables, where every year from the rise of the Chow dynasty, B.C. 1121, has a distinct column to itself, in which, in different compartments, the most important events are noted. Beyond that date,

緒論

it ascends to the commencement of the cycles in the 61st year of Hwang-te, giving not every year, but the years of which any thing has been mentioned in history. From Hwang-te also, it ascends through the dateless ages up to P'wan-koo, the first of mortals.

歷代疆域表, "The Boundaries of the Empire in the successive Dynasties." This Work by the same author, and published in 1817, does for the boundaries of the empire the same service which the preceding renders to its chronology.

SECTION II.

TRANSLATIONS AND OTHER WORKS.

CONFUCIUS SINARUM PHILOSOPHUS; sive Scientia Sinensis Latine Exposita. Studio et opera Prosperi Intorcetta, Christiani Herdritch, Francisci Rougemont, Philippi Couplet, Patrum Societatis JESU. Jussu Ludovici Magni. Parisiis: MDCLXXXVII.

THE WORKS OF CONFUCIUS; containing the Original Text, with a Translation. Vol. I. By J. Marshman. Serampore: 1809.

THE FOUR BOOKS, Translated into English, by Rev. David Collie, of the London Missionary Society. Malacca: 1828.

L'INVARIABLE MILIEU, Ouvrage Moral de Tseu-sse, en Chinois et en Mandchou, avec une Version litterale Latine, une Traduction Françoise, &c., &c. Par M. Abel-Rémusat. A Paris: 1817.

LE TA HIO, OU LA GRANDE ETUDE: Traduit en François, avec une Version Latine, &c. Par G. Pauthier. Paris: 1837.

Y-KING, Antiquissimus Sinarum Liber, quem ex Latina Interpretatione P. Regis, aliorumque ex Soc. JESU PP. edidit Julius Mohl. 1839: Stuttgartiæ et Tubingæ.

MEMOIRES concernant L'Histoire, Les Sciences, Les Arts, Les Mœurs, Les Usages, &c., des Chinois. Par les Missionnaires de Pekin. A Paris: 1776—1814.

HISTOIRE GENERALE DE LA CHINE; ou Annales de cet Empire, Traduites du Tong-Kien-Kang-Mou. Par le feu Pere Joseph-Annie-Marie de Moyriac de Mailla, Jesuite François, Missionnaire a Pekin. A Paris: 1776—1785.

NOTITIA LINGUÆ SINICÆ. Auctore P. Premare. Malaccæ: cura Academiæ Anglo-Sinensis. MDCCCXXXI.

THE CHINESE REPOSITORY. Canton, China. 20 vols. 1832—1851.

DICTIONNAIRE DES NOMS, Anciens et Modernes, des Villes et Arrondissements de Premier, Deuxieme, et Troisieme ordre, compris dans L'Empire Chinois, &c. Par Edouard Biot, Membre du Conseil de la Societé Asiatique. Paris: 1842.

THE CHINESE. By John Francis Davis, Esq., F.R.S., &c. In two volumes. London: 1836.

CHINA: its State and Prospeets. By W. H. Medhurst, D.D., of the London Missionary Society. London: 1838.

L'UNIVERS: Histoire et Description des tous les Peuples. Chine. Par M. G. Pauthier. Paris: 1838.

HISTORY OF CHINA, from the earliest Records to the Treaty with Great Britain in 1842. By Thomas Thornton, Esq., Member of the Royal Asiatic Society. In two volumes. London: 1844.

THE MIDDLE KINGDOM: A Survey of the Geography, Government, Education, Social Life, Arts, Religion, &c., of the Chinese Empire. By S. Wells Williams, LL.D. In two volumes. New York and London: 1848.

THE RELIGIOUS CONDITION OF THE CHINESE. By Rev. Joseph Edkins, B. A., of the London Missionary Society. London: 1859.

CHRIST AND OTHER MASTERS. By Charles Hardwick, M.A., Christian Advocate in the University of Cambridge. Part III. Religions of China, America, and Oceanica. Cambridge: 1858.

CONFUCIAN ANALECTS.

BOOK I. HEŎ URH.

論語

學而第一

第一章 子曰、一節 學而時習之、不亦說乎。二節 有朋自遠方來、不亦樂乎。三節 人不知而不慍、不亦君子乎。

CHAPTER I. 1. The Master said, "Is it not pleasant to learn with a constant perseverance and application?

2. "Is it not pleasant to have friends coming from distant quarters?

3. "Is he not a man of complete virtue, who feels no discomposure though men may take no note of him?"

TITLE OF THE WORK.—論語, 'Discourses and Dialogues;' that is, the discourses or discussions of Confucius with his disciples and others on various topics, and his replies to their inquiries. Many chapters, however, and one whole book, are the sayings, not of the sage himself, but of some of his disciples. The characters may also be rendered 'Digested Conversations,' and this appears to be the more ancient signification attached to them, the account being, that, after the death of Confucius, his disciples collected together and compared the memoranda of his conversations which they had severally preserved, digesting them into the twenty books which compose the work. Hence the title—論語, 'Discussed Sayings,' or 'Digested Conversations.' See 論語註疏解經序. I have styled the work 'Confucian Analects,' as being more descriptive of its character than any other name I could think of.

HEADING OF THIS BOOK.—學而第一. The two first characters in the book, after the introductory—'The Master said,' are adopted as its heading. This is similar to the custom of the Jews, who name many books in the Bible from the first word in them. 第一, 'The first;' that is, of the twenty books composing the whole work. In some of the books we find a unity or analogy of subjects, which evidently guided the compilers in grouping the chapters together. Others seem devoid of any such principle of combination. The sixteen chapters of this book are occupied, it is said, with the fundamental subjects which ought to engage the attention of the learner, and the great matters of human practice. The word 學, '*learn*,' rightly occupies the forefront in the studies of a nation, of which its educational system has so long been the distinction and glory.

1. THE WHOLE WORK AND ACHIEVEMENT OF THE LEARNER, FIRST PERFECTING HIS KNOWLEDGE, THEN ATTRACTING BY HIS FAME LIKE-MINDED INDIVIDUALS, AND FINALLY COMPLETE IN HIMSELF. 1. 子, at the commencement, indicates Confucius. 子, 'a son,' is also the common designation of males,—especially of virtuous men. We find it, in conversations, used in the same way as our 'Sir.' When it *follows* the surname, it is equivalent to our 'Mr.,' or may be rendered 'the philosopher,' 'the scholar,' 'the officer,' &c. Often, however, it is better to leave it untranslated. When it *precedes* the surname, it indicates that the person spoken of was the master of the writer, as 子沈子, 'my master, the philosopher 沈.' Standing single and alone, as in the text, it denotes Confucius, *the philosopher*, or, rather, *the master*. If we render the term by Confucius, as all preceding translators have done, we miss the indication which it gives of the handiwork of his disciples, and the reverence

第二章 一節 有子曰、其爲人也孝弟、而好犯上者鮮矣、不好犯上、而好作亂者、未之有也。二節 君子務本、本立、而道生、孝

CHAPTER II. 1. The philosopher Yew said, "They are few who, being filial and fraternal, are fond of offending against their superiors. There have been none, who, not liking to offend against their superiors, have been fond of stirring up confusion.

2. "The superior man bends his attention to what is radical. That being established, all practical courses naturally grow up.

which it bespeaks for him. 學, in the old commentators, is explained by 誦, 'to read chantingly,' 'to discuss.' Choo He interprets it by 效, 'to imitate,' and makes its results to be 明善而復初, 'the understanding of all excellence, and the bringing back original goodness.' Subsequent scholars profess, for the most part, great admiration of this explanation. It is an illustration, to my mind, of the way in which Choo He and his followers are continually being wise above what is written in the classical books. 習 is the rapid and frequent motion of the wings of a bird in flying, used for 'to repeat,' 'to practise.' 之 is the obj. of the third pers. pronoun, and its antecedent is to be found in the pregnant meaning of 學. 不亦 is explained by 豈不, 'is it not?' See 四書補註備旨. To bring out the force of 'also' in 亦, some say thus:—"The occasions for pleasure are many, *is this not also one?*" 說, read *yuĕ*, as always when it has the 4th tone marked, stands for 悅. What is learned becomes by practice and application one's own, and hence arises complacent pleasure in the mastering mind. 悅 as distinguished from 樂, *lŏh*, in the next par., is the internal, individual, feeling of pleasure, and the other, its external manifestation, implying also companionship. 2. 朋, properly, 'fellow-students;' but, generally, individuals of the same class and character, like-minded. 3. 君子 I translate here—'a man of complete virtue.' Literally, it is—'a princely man.' See on 子, above. It is a technical term in Chin. moral writers, for which there is no exact correspondency in English, and which cannot be rendered always in the same way. See Morrison's Dictionary, char. 子. Its opposite is 小人, 'a small, mean, man.' 人不知, 'Men do not know him,' but anciently some explained—'men do not know,' that is, are stupid under his teaching. The interpretation in the text is doubtless the correct one.

2. FILIAL PIETY AND FRATERNAL SUBMISSION ARE THE FOUNDATION OF ALL VIRTUOUS PRACTICE. 1. Yew, named 若, and styled 子有, and 子若, a native of 魯, was famed among the other disciples of Confucius for his strong memory, and love for the doctrines of antiquity. In personal appearance he resembled the sage. See Mencius, III. Pt. II. iv. 13. 有子 is 'Yew, the philosopher,' and he and Tsăng Ts'an (or Sin) are the only two of Confucius' disciples who are mentioned in this style in the *Lun Yu*. This has led to an opinion on the part of some, that the work was compiled by their disciples. This may not be sufficiently supported, but I have not found the peculiarity pointed out satisfactorily explained. The tablet of Yew's spirit is now in the same apartment of the sage's temples as that of the sage himself, occupying the 6th place in the eastern range of 'the wise ones.' To this position it was promoted in the 3d year of K'een-lung of the present dynasty. A degree of activity enters into the meaning of 爲 in 爲人,='playing the man,' 'as men, showing themselves filial,' &c. 弟, here=悌, 'to be submissive as a younger brother,' is in the low. 3d tone. With its proper signification, it was anciently in the 2d tone. 而='and yet,' different from its simple conjunctive use='and,' in the prec. ch. 好, a verb, 'to love,' in the up. 3d tone, diff. from the same char. in the 2d tone, an adj.,='good.' 鮮, up. 2d tone,='few.' On the idiom—未之有, see Premare's gram. p. 156. 2.

弟也者、其爲人之本與。

第三章 子曰、巧言令色、鮮矣仁。

第四章 曾子曰、吾日三省吾身、爲人謀而不忠乎、與朋友交而不信乎、傳不習乎。

Filial piety and fraternal submission!—are they not the root of all benevolent actions?"

CHAPTER III. The Master said, "Fine words and an insinuating appearance are seldom associated with true virtue."

CHAPTER IV. The philosopher Tsăng said, "I daily examine myself on three points:—whether, in transacting business for others, I may have been not faithful;—whether, in intercourse with friends, I may have been not sincere;—whether I may have not mastered and practised the instructions of my teacher."

君子 has a less intense singnification here than in the last chap. I translate—'The superior man,' for want of a better term. 本, 'the root,' 'what is radical,' is here said of filial and fraternal duties, and 道, 'ways' or 'courses,' of all that is intended by 爲(=行) 仁, below. The particles 也者 resume the discourse about 孝弟, and introduce some further description of them. See Prem., p. 158. 與, in the lower 1st tone, is half interrogative, an answer in the affirmative being implied. 仁 is explained here as 'the principle of love,' 'the virtue of the heart.' Mencius says—仁也者人也, '仁 is man,' in accordance with which, Julien translates it by *humanitas*. *Benevolence* often comes near it, but, as has been said before of 君子, we cannot give a uniform rendering of this term.

3. FAIR APPEARANCES ARE SUSPICIOUS. 巧言令色,—see Shoo-king, II. iii. 2. 巧, 'skill in workmanship;' then, 'skill,' 'cleverness,' generally, and sometimes with a bad meaning, as here,='artful,' 'hypocritical.' 令 'a law,' 'an order,' also 'good,' and here like 巧, with a bad meaning,='pretending to be good.' 色, 'the manifestation of the feelings in the colour of the countenance,' is here used for the appearance generally.

4. HOW THE PHILOSOPHER TSANG DAILY EXAMINED HIMSELF, TO GUARD AGAINST HIS BEING GUILTY OF ANY IMPOSITION. *Tsăng*, whose name was 參, (*Ts'an*, now commonly read *Sin*,) and his designation 子輿, was one of the principal disciples of Confucius. A follower of the sage from his 16th year, though inferior in natural ability to some others, by his filial piety and other moral qualities, he entirely won the Master's esteem, and by persevering attention mastered his doctrines. Confucius employed him in the composition of the 孝經, or 'Classic of Filial Piety.' The authorship of the 大學, 'The Great Learning,' is also ascribed to him, though incorrectly, as we shall see. Ten books, moreover, of his composition are preserved in the Le-ke. His spirit tablet among the sage's four assessors, occupying the first place on the west, has precedence of that of Mencius. 省, read *sing*, 'to examine.' 三省 is naturally understood of 'three times,' but the context and consent of commentators make us assent to the interpretation—'on three points.' 身, 'the body,' 'one's personality;' 吾身=*myself*. 爲 is in low. 3d tone,='for. So, frequently, below. 忠 from 中, 'middle,' 'the centre,' and 心, 'the heart,'=loyalty, faithfulness, action with and from the heart. 朋, see ch. 1. 友, 'two hands joined,' denoting union. 朋友, 'friends.' 傳不習 is very enigmatical. The translation follows Choo He. 何安 explained quite differently:—'whether I have given instruction in what I had not studied and practised?' It does seem more correct to take

第五章 子曰、道千乘之國、敬事而信、節用而愛人、使民以時。

第六章 子曰、弟子、入則孝、出則弟、謹而信、汎愛衆、而親仁、行有餘力、則以學文。

第七章 子夏曰、賢賢易色、事父母、能竭其力、事君、能致其身、

CHAPTER V. The Master said, "To rule a country of a thousand chariots, there must be reverent attention to business, and sincerity; economy in expenditure, and love for men; and the employment of the people at the proper seasons."

CHAPTER VI. The Master said, "A youth, when at home, should be filial, and, abroad, respectful to his elders. He should be earnest and truthful. He should overflow in love to all, and cultivate the friendship of the good. When he has time and opportunity, after the performance of these things, he should employ them in polite studies."

CHAPTER VII. Tsze-hea said, "If a man withdraws his mind from the love of beauty, and applies it as sincerely to the love of the virtuous; if, in serving his parents, he can exert his utmost

傳 actively, 'to give instruction,' rather than passively, 'to receive instruction.' See 四書改錯, XV. 17.

5. FUNDAMENTAL PRINCIPLES FOR THE GOVERNMENT OF A LARGE STATE. 道 is used for 導, 'to rule,' 'to lead,' and is marked in the 3d tone, to distinguish it from 道, the noun, which was anciently read with the 2d tone. It is diff. from 治, which refers to the actual business of government, while 導 is the duty and purpose thereof, apprehended by the prince. The standpoint of the principles is the prince's mind. 乘, in low. 3d tone, 'a chariot,' diff. from its meaning in the 1st tone, 'to ride.' A country of 1000 chariots is one of the largest fiefs of the empire, which could bring such an armament into the field. The last principle,—使民以時, means that the people should not be called from their husbandry at improper seasons, to do service on military expeditions and public works.

6. RULES FOR THE TRAINING OF THE YOUNG:—DUTY FIRST AND THEN ACCOMPLISHMENTS. 弟子, 'younger brothers and sons,' taken together, =*youths, a youth*. The 2d 弟 is for 悌, as in ch. 2. 入出, 'coming in, going out,'=at home, abroad. 汎 is explained by Choo He by 廣, 'wide,' 'widely;' its proper meaning is 'the rush or overflow of water.' 力, 'strength,' here embracing the idea of *leisure*. 學文, not *literary studies* merely, but all the accomplishments of a gentleman also:—ceremonies, music, archery, horsemanship, writing, and numbers.

7. TSZE-HEA'S VIEWS OF THE SUBSTANCE OF LEARNING. Tsze-hea was the designation of 卜商, another of the sage's distinguished disciples, and now placed 5th in the eastern range of 'the wise ones.' He was greatly famed for his learning, and his views on the *She-king* and the *Ch'un Ts'ew* are said to be preserved in the comm. of 毛, and of 公羊高 and 穀梁赤. He wept himself blind on the death of his son, but lived to a great age, and was much esteemed by the people and princes of the time. With regard to the scope of this chapter, there

論語

與朋友交、言而有信、雖曰未學、吾必謂之學矣。

第八章 子曰、一節 君子不重、則不威、學則不固。二節 主忠信。三節 無友不如己者。四節 過則勿憚改。

第九章 曾子曰、慎終追遠、民德歸厚矣。

strength, if, in serving his prince, he can devote his life; if, in his intercourse with his friends, his words are sincere:—although men say that he has not learned, I will certainly say that he has."

CHAPTER VIII. 1. The Master said, "If the scholar be not grave, he will not call forth any veneration, and his learning will not be solid.

2. "Hold faithfulness and sincerity as first principles.

3. "Have no friends not equal to yourself.

4. "When you have faults, do not fear to abandon them."

CHAPTER IX. The philosopher Tsăng said, "Let there be a careful attention *to perform the funeral rites* to parents, and let them be followed when long gone *with the ceremonies of sacrifice*;—then the virtue of the people will resume its proper excellence."

is some truth in what the comm. Woo, 吳, says,—that Tsze-hea's words may be wrested to depreciate learning, while those of the Master in the prec. ch. hit exactly the due medium. The 2d 賢 is a concrete noun. Written in full, 賢, it is composed of the characters for a *minister*, *loyal*, and *a precious shell*. It conveys the ideas of *talents* and *worth* in the concrete, but it is not easy to render it uniformly by any one term of another language. The 1st 賢 is a verb, =' to treat as a *hëen*.' 色 has a diff. meaning from that in the 3d ch. Here it means 'sensual pleasure.' Literally rendered, the first sentence would be, 'esteeming properly the virtuous, and changing the love of woman,' and great fault is found by some, as in 四書改錯, XIII. 1, with Choo He's interpretation which I have followed; but there is force in what his adherents say, that the passage is not to be understood as if the individual spoken of had ever been given to pleasure, but simply signifies the sincerity of his love for the virtuous. 致 here =委, 'to give to,' 'to devote.'

8. PRINCIPLES OF SELF-CULTIVATION. 1. 君子 has here its lightest meaning,=*a student*, one who wishes to be a *keun-tsze*. 孔安國, of the Han dynasty, in the 1st half of the 2d century, took 固, in the sense of 'obscured,' 'dulled,' and interprets—'Let him learn, and he will not fall into error.' The received interpretation, as in the transl., is better. 2. 主, as a verb, 'to hold to be chief.' It is often used thus. 3. The object of friendship, with Chinese moralists, is to improve one's knowledge and virtue;—hence, this seemingly selfish maxim.

9. THE GOOD EFFECT OF ATTENTION ON THE PART OF PRINCES TO THE OFFICES TO THE DEAD:—AN ADMONITION OF TSANG SIN. 終, 'the end,' =death, and 遠, 'distant,' have both the force of adjectives,=' the dead,' and 'the departed,' or 'the long gone.' 慎 and 追 mean, 'to be careful of,' 'to follow,' but their application is as in the translation. 厚, 'thick,' in opposition to 薄, 'thin;' metaphorically,=*good*, *excellent*. The force of 歸, 'to return,' is to shew that this virtue is naturally proper to the people.

第十章 一節 子禽問於子貢曰、夫子至於是邦也、必聞其政、求之與、抑與之與。二節 子貢曰、夫子溫、良、恭、儉、讓、以得之、夫子之求之也、其諸異乎人之求之與。

第十一章 子曰、父在、觀其志、父沒、觀其行、三年無改於父之道、可謂孝矣。

CHAPTER X. 1. Tsze-k'in asked Tsze-kung, saying, "When our master comes to any country, he does not fail to learn all about its government. Does he ask his information? or is it given to him?"

2. Tsze-kung said, "Our master is benign, upright, courteous, temperate, and complaisant, and thus he gets his information. The Master's mode of asking information!—is it not different from that of other men?"

CHAPTER XI. The Master said, "While a man's father is alive, look at the bent of his will; when his father is dead, look at his conduct. If for three years he does not alter from the way of his father, he may be called filial."

10. CHARACTERISTICS OF CONFUCIUS, AND THEIR INFLUENCE ON THE PRINCES OF THE TIME. 1. Tsze-k'in, and Tsze-k'ang (亢), are designations of 陳亢, one of the minor disciples of Confucius. His tablet occupies the 28th place, on the west, in the outer hall of the temples. A good story is related of him. On the death of his brother, his wife and major-domo wished to bury some living persons with him, to serve him in the regions below. The thing being referred to Tsze-k'in, he proposed that the wife and steward should themselves submit to the immolation, which made them stop the matter. Tsze-kung, with the double surname 端木, and named 賜, occupies a higher place in the Confucian ranks, and is now the third on the east, among 'the wise ones.' He is conspicuous in this work for his readiness and smartness in reply, and displayed on several occasions practical and political ability. 夫, 'a general design ation for males,'=a man. 夫子,—a common designation for a teacher or master. 是邦, 'this country'=*any* country. 必, 'must,' =*does not fail to.* The antecedent to both the 之 is the whole clause 聞其政. Obs. the diff. in 與, up. 2d tone,='to give,' and often a preposition, 'with,' 'to,' and 與, low. 1st tone, as in ch. 2. 2. The force of 其諸 is well enough expressed by the dash in English, the previous 也 indicating a pause in the discourse, which the 其, 'it,' resumes.

11. ON FILIAL DUTY. 行 is in the low. 3d tone, explained by 行迹, 'traces of walking,' =*conduct.* It is to be understood that the way of the father had not been very bad. An old interpretation, that the three years are to be understood of the three years of mourning for the father, is now rightly rejected.

〔十二章〕一節 有子曰、禮之用、和爲貴、先王之道、斯爲美、小大由之。〇二節 有所不行、知和而和、不以禮節之、亦不可行也。

〔十三章〕有子曰、信近於義、言可復也、恭近於禮、遠恥辱也、因不失其親、亦可宗也。

〔十四章〕子曰、君子食無求

CHAPTER XII. 1. The philosopher Yew said, "In practising the rules of propriety, a natural ease is to be prized. In the ways prescribed by the ancient kings, this is the excellent quality, and in things small and great we follow them.

2. "Yet it is not to be observed in all cases. If one, knowing *how* such ease *should be prized*, manifests it, without regulating it by the rules of propriety, this likewise is not to be done."

CHAPTER XIII. The philosopher Yew said, "When agreements are made according to what is right, what is spoken can be made good. When respect is shown according to what is proper, one keeps far from shame and disgrace. When the parties upon whom a man leans are proper persons to be intimate with, he can make them his guides and masters."

CHAPTER XIV. The Master said, "He who aims to be a man of complete virtue, in his food does not seek to gratify his appetite,

12. IN CEREMONIES A NATURAL EASE IS TO BE PRIZED, AND YET TO BE SUBORDINATE TO THE END OF CEREMONIES,—THE REVERENTIAL OBSERVANCE OF PROPRIETY. 1. 禮 is not easily rendered in another language. There underlies it the idea of *what is proper*. It is 事之宜, 'the fitness of things,' what reason calls for in the performance of duties towards superior beings, and between man and man. Our term 'ceremonies' comes near its meaning here. 道 is here a name for 禮, as indicating the *courses* or *ways* to be pursued by men. In 小大由之, the antecedent to 之 is not 和, but 禮 or 道. 2. Obs. the force of the 亦, 'also,' in the last clause, and how it affirms the general principle enunciated in the first paragraph.

13. TO SAVE FROM FUTURE REPENTANCE, WE MUST BE CAREFUL IN OUR FIRST STEPS. A diff. view of the scope of this ch. is taken by Ho An. It illustrates, according to him, the difference between being sincere and righteousness, between being respectful and propriety, and how a man's conduct may be venerated. The later view commends itself, the only difficulty being with 近於, 'near to,' which we must accept as a *meiosis* for 合乎, 'agreeing with.' 約=信約, 'a covenant,' 'agreement.' 遠, up. 3d tone, 'to keep away from.' The force of the 亦='he can *go on* to make them his masters,' 宗 being taken as an active verb.

14. WITH WHAT MIND ONE AIMING TO BE A KEUN-TSZE PURSUES HIS LEARNING. He may be well, even luxuriously, fed and lodged, but,

飽、居無求安、敏於事、而愼於言、就有道、而正焉、可謂好學也已。

〔十五〕子一節貢曰、貧而無諂、富而無驕、何如。子曰、可也、未若貧而樂、富而好禮者也。子二節貢曰、詩云、如切如磋、如琢如磨、其斯之謂與。子三節曰、賜也、始可與言詩

nor in his dwelling-place does he seek the appliances of ease; he is earnest in what he is doing, and careful in his speech; he frequents the company of men of principle that he may be rectified:—such a person may be said indeed to love to learn."

CHAPTER XV. 1. Tsze-kung said, "What do you pronounce concerning the poor man who yet does not flatter, and the rich man who is not proud?" The Master replied, "They will do; but they are not equal to him, who, though poor, is yet cheerful, and to him, who, though rich, loves the rules of propriety."

2. Tsze-kung replied, "It is said in the Book of Poetry, 'As you cut and then file, as you carve and then polish.'—The meaning is the same, I apprehend, as that which you have just expressed."

3. The Master said, "With one like Tsze, I can begin to talk about the Odes. I told him one point, and he knew its proper sequence."

with his higher aim, these things are not his seeking,—無求. A nominative to 可謂 must be supposed,—*all this*, or *such a person*. The closing particles, 也已, give emphasis to the preceding sentence,=*yes indeed*.

15. AN ILLUSTRATION OF THE SUCCESSIVE STEPS IN SELF-CULTIVATION. 1. Tsze-kung had been poor, and then did not cringe. He became rich, and was not proud. He asked Confucius about the style of char. to which he had attained. Conf. allowed its worth, but sent him to higher attainments. 而, here,='and yet.' 何如, 'what as?'='what do you say— what is to be thought,—of this?' Obs. the force of the 未, 'not yet. 2. The ode quoted is the first of the songs of Wei (衛), praising the prince Woo, who had dealt with himself as an ivory-worker who first cuts the bone, and then files it smooth, or a lapidary whose hammer and chisel are followed by all the appliances for smoothing and polishing. See the She-king, I. v. Ode I. st. 2. In 其斯之謂, the antecedent to 其 is the passage of the ode, and that to 斯 is the reply of Confucius. 之謂, see Premare, p. 156. 3. Intorcetta and his co-adjutors translate this par. as if 賜 were in the 2d person. But the Chin. comm. put it in the 3d, and correctly. Premare, on the char. 也, says, '*Fere semper adjungitur nominibus propriis. Sic in libro Lun Yu, Confucius loquens de suis discipulis, Yeou, Keou, Hoei, vel ipsos alloquens, dicit* 由也, 求也, 回也.' With the example in III. 17, before us, it is not to be denied that the name before 也 is sometimes in the 2d person, but generally it is in the 3d, and the force of the

已矣、告諸往而知來者。

〔十六章〕子曰、不患人之不己知、患不知人也。

CHAPTER XVI. The Master said, "I will not be afflicted at men's not knowing me; I will be afflicted that I do not know men."

也=*quoad*. 賜也, *quoad Tsze*. 已矣, nearly=也已, in ch. 14. 已, the final part. (see Prem. p. 185), is thus marked with a tone, to distinguish it from 己, 'self,' as in next ch. The last clause may be given—'Tell him the past, and he knows the future,' but the connection determines the meaning as in the transltion. 諸, as in ch. 10, is a particle, a mere 語助, as it is called, 'a helping' or supporting sound.

16. PERSONAL ATTAINMENT SHOULD BE OUR CHIEF AIM. Comp. ch. 1. p. 3. Obs. the transposition in 己知, which is more elegant than 知己 would be. 己, 'self,' the person depending on the context. We cannot translate 'do not be afflicted,' because 不 is not used imperatively, like 勿. A nominative to 患 has to be assumed,-我, 'I,' or 君子, 'the superior man.'

BOOK II. WEI CHING.

為政第二

〔第一章〕子曰、為政以德、譬如北辰、居其所、而衆星共之。

CHAPTER I. The Master said, "He who exercises government by means of his virtue, may be compared to the north polar star, which keeps its place and all the stars turn towards it."

HEADING OF THIS BOOK.—為政第二. This second book contains twenty four chapters, and is named 為政, 'The practice of government.' That is ihe object to which learning, treated of in the last book, should lead, and here we have the qualities which constitute, and the character of the men who administer, good government.

1. THE INFLUENCE OF VIRTUE IN A RULER. 德 is explained by 得, but the old comm. say 物得以生謂之德, 'what creatures get in order to their birth is called their virtue,' while Choo He makes it=行道而有得於心, 'the practice of truth and acquisition thereof in the heart.' Choo's view of the comparison is that it sets forth the illimitable influence which virtue in a ruler exercises without his using any effort. This is extravagant. His opponents say that virtue is the polar star, and the various departments of government the other stars. This is far-fetched. We must be content to accept the vague utterance without minutely determining its meaning. 北辰 is, no doubt, 'the north polar star,' anciently believed to coincide exactly with the place of the real pole. 共 is up. 2d tone, used for 拱, 'to fold the hands in saluting,' here='to turn respectfully towards.'

第二章 子曰、詩三百、一言以蔽之、曰、思無邪。

第三章 子一節曰、道之以政、齊之以刑、民免而無恥。二節道之以德、齊之以禮、有恥且格。

第四章 子一節曰、吾十有五、而志于學。二節三十而立。三節四十而不惑。四節五

CHAPTER II. The Master said, "In the Book of Poetry are three hundred pieces, but the design of them all may be embraced in one sentence—'Have no depraved thoughts.'"

CHAPTER III. 1. The Master said, "If the people be led by laws, and uniformity sought to be given them by punishments, they will try to avoid *the punishment*, but have no sense of shame.

2. "If they be led by virtue, and uniformity sought to be given them by the rules of propriety, they will have the sense of shame, and moreover will become good."

CHAPTER IV. 1. The Master said, "At fifteen, I had my mind bent on learning.

2. "At thirty, I stood firm.

3. "At forty, I had no doubts.

2. THE PURE DESIGN OF THE BOOK OF POETRY. The number of compositions in the She-king is rather more than the round number here given. 一言=一句, 'one sentence.' 蔽=蓋, 'to cover,' 'to embrace.' 思無邪, see She-king, IV. ii. 1. st. 4. The sentence there is indicative, and in praise of the duke He, who had no depraved thoughts. The sage would seem to have been intending his own design in compiling the *She*. Individual pieces are calculated to have a diff. effect.

3. HOW RULERS SHOULD PREFER MORAL APPLIANCES. 1. 道, as in I. 5. 之, 'them,' ref. to 民, below. 政, as oppos. to 德,=laws and prohibitions. 齊, 'corn earing evenly;' hence, what is level, equal, adjusted, and here with the corresponding verbal force. 民免, 'The people will avoid,' that is, avoid breaking the laws thro. fear of the punishment. 2. 格 has the signif. of 'to come to,' and 'to correct,' from either of which the text may be explained, —'will come to good,' or 'will correct themselves.' Obs. the diff. of 且 and 而 in p. 1. 而='but;' 且='moreover.'

4. CONFUCIUS' OWN ACCOUNT OF HIS GRADUAL PROGRESS AND ATTAINMENTS. Chin. comm. are perplexed with this ch. Holding of Confucius that 生而知之, 安而行之, 'he was born with knowledge, and did what was right with entire ease,' they say that he here conceals his sagehood, and puts himself on the level of common men, to set before them a stimulating example. We may believe that the compilers of the Analects, the sage's immediate disciples, did not think of him so extravagantly as later men have done. It is to be wished, however, that he had been more definite and diffuse in his account of himself. 1. 有, in low. 3d tone,='and.' The 'learning,' to which, at 15, Conf. gave himself, is to be understood of the subjects of the 'Superior Learning.' See Choo He's preliminary essay to the Ta Hëŏ. 2. The 'standing firm' probably indicates that he no more needed to bend his will. 3. The 'no doubts' may have been concerning what was proper in all circumstances and

論語

十而知天命。五節六十而耳順。六節七十而從心所欲、不踰矩。

第五章 一節 孟懿子問孝、子曰、無違。二節 樊遲御、子告之曰、孟孫問孝於我、我對曰、無違。三節 樊遲曰、何謂也、子曰、生事之以禮、死葬之以禮、祭之以禮。

4. "At fifty, I knew the decrees of heaven.

5. "At sixty, my ear was an obedient organ *for the reception of truth.*

6. "At seventy, I could follow what my heart desired, without transgressing what was right".

CHAPTER V. Măng E asked what filial piety was. The Master said, "It is not being disobedient."

2. *Soon after*, as Fan Ch'e was driving him, the Master told him, saying, 'Măng-sun asked me what filial piety was, and I answered him,—'not being disobedient."

3. Fan Ch'e said, "What did you mean?" The Master replied, "That parents, when alive, should be served according to propriety; that, when dead, they should be buried according to propriety; and that they should be sacrificed to according to propriety."

events. 4. 'The decrees of Heaven,'=the things decreed by Heaven, the constitution of things making what was proper to be so. 5. 'The ear obedient' is the mind receiving as by intuition the truth from the ear. 6. 矩, 'an instrument for determining the square.' 不踰矩, 'without transgressing the square.'

5. FILIAL PIETY MUST BE SHOWN ACCORDING TO THE RULES OF PROPRIETY. 1. Mang E was a great officer of the state of Loo, by name Ho-ke (何忌), and the chief of one of the three great families by which in the time of Conf. the authority of that state was grasped. Those families were descended from three brothers, the sons by a concubine of the duke Hwan (B. C. 710-693), who were distinguished at first by the prenomens of 仲, 叔, and 季. To these was subsequently added the character 孫, 'grandson,' to indicate their princely descent, and 仲孫, 叔孫, and 季孫, became the respective surnames of the families. 仲孫 was changed into 孟孫, by the father of Mang E, on a principle of humility, as he thereby only claimed to be the eldest of the inferior sons or their representatives, and avoided the presumption of seeming to be a younger full brother of the reigning duke. 懿, 'mild and virtuous,' was the posthumous honorary title given to Ho-ke. On 子, see I. 1.1. Fan, by name 須, and designated 子遲, was a minor disciple of the sage. Conf. repeated his remark to Fan, that he might report the explanation of it to his friend Mang E, or Mang-sun, and thus prevent him from supposing that all the sage intended was disobedience to parents.

第六章 孟武伯問孝、子曰、父母唯其疾之憂。

第七章 子游問孝、子曰、今之孝者、是謂能養、至於犬馬、皆能有養、不敬、何以別乎。

第八章 子夏問孝、子曰、色難、有事、弟子服其勞、有酒食、先生饌、曾是以爲孝乎。

CHAPTER VI. Măng Woo asked what filial piety was. The Master said, "Parents are anxious lest their children should be sick."

CHAPTER VII. Tsze-yew asked what filial piety was. The Master said, "The filial piety of now-a-days means the support of one's parents. But dogs and horses likewise are able to do something in the way of support;-without reverence, what is there to distinguish the one support given from the other?"

CHAPTER VIII. Tsze-hea asked what filial piety was. The Master said, "The difficulty is with the countenance. If, when *their elders* have any *troublesome* affairs, the young take the toil of them, and if, when *the young* have wine and food, they set them before their elders, is THIS to be consdered filial piety?"

6. THE ANXIETY OF PARENTS ABOUT THEIR CHILDREN AN ARGUMENT FOR FILIAL PIETY. This engmatical sentence has been interpreted in two ways. Choo He takes 唯 (=惟) not in the sense of 'only,' but of 'thinking anxiously.'-'Parents have the sorrow of thinking anxiously about their-*i. e* their children's-being unwell. Therefore children should take care of their persons.' The old comm. again take 唯 in the sense of 'only.'-'Let parents have only the sorrow of their children's illness. Let them have no other occasion for sorrow. This will be filial piety.' Mang Woo (the hon. epithet,='Bold and of straightforward principle,') was the son of Mang E, and by name 彘. 伯 merely indicates that he was the eldest son.

HOW THERE MUST BE REVERENCE IN FILIAL DUTY. Tsze-yew was the designaiion of 言偃, a native of 吳, and distinguished among the disciples of Conf. for his knowl. of the rules of propriety, and for his learning. He is now 4th on the west among 'the wise ones.' 養 is in low. 3d tone,='to minister support to,' the act of an inferior to a superior. In low. 2d tone, it='to nourish,' 'bring up.' Choo He gives a different turn to the sentiment.-'But dogs and horses likewise manage to get their support.' The other and older interpr. is better. 至於, 'Coming to,'=as to, *quoad*. 別, up. 4th tone, 'to discriminate,' 'distinguish.' In low. tone, 別='to leave,' 'separate from.'

8. THE DUTIES OF FILIAL PIETY MUST BE PERFORMED WITH A CHEERFUL COUNTENANCE. 色, here, nearly analogous to I. 3. 事 followed by 勞, =the '*troublesome* affairs' in the transl. 弟子, as in I. 6. The use of the phrase here extends filial duty to elders generally,—to the 父兄 as well as to the 父母. We have in transl. to supply their respective nom. to the two 有. 食, read *tsze*, 'rice,' and then, food generally. 先生饌,=與先生 (earlier born=elders)饌之. 曾, low. 1st tone,=則,

論語

第九章 子曰、吾與回言終日、不違、如愚、退而省其私、亦足以發、回也不愚。

第十章 一節 子曰、視其所以。○二節 觀其所由。○三節 察其所安。○四節 人焉廋哉、人焉廋哉。

第十一章 子曰、溫故而知新、可以爲師矣。

CHAPTER IX. The Master said, "I have talked with Hwuy for a whole day, and he has not made any objection *to any thing I said*;—as if he were stupid. He has retired, and I have examined his conduct when away from me, and found him able to illustrate *my teachings*. Hwuy!—He is not stupid."

CHAPTER X. 1. The Master said, "See what a man does.

2. "Mark his motives.

3. "Examine in what things he rests.

4. "How can a man conceal his character!

5. "How can a man conceal his character!"

CHAPTER XI. The Master said, "If a man keeps cherishing his old knowledge, so as continually to be acquiring new, he may be a teacher of others."

'then,' a transition particle. To these diff. interrogatories about filial duty, the sage, we are told, made answer according to the character of the questioner, as each one needed instruction.

9. THE QUIET RECEPTIVITY OF THE DISCIPLE HWUY. Yen Hwuy (顔回), styled 子淵, was Confucius' favourite disciple, and is now honoured with the first place east among his four assessors in his temples, and with the title of 復聖顔子, 'The second sage, the philosopher Yen.' At 29 his hair was entirely white, and at 33 he died to the excessive grief of the sage. The subject of 退 is 回, and that of 省 (as in I. 4.) is 吾. 其私, 'his privacy,' not meaning his conduct in secret, but only his way when not with the master. 亦 'also,' takes up 如愚,—He was so, and also so. 回也, see I, 15.

10. HOW TO DETERMINE THE CHARACTERS OF MEN. 1. 以 is explained as=行, or 行用, 'does.' The same, tho' not its comm. meaning, is the first given to it in the Dict. For the noun to which the three 其 refer, we must go down to 人 in the 4th par. There is a climax in 所以, 所由 ('what from'), and 所安, and a corresponding one in the verbs 視, 觀, and 察. 4, 焉, gen. a final particle, in low. 1st tone, is here in up. 1st., an interrogative,=how? Its interrog. force blends with the exclamatory of 哉 at the end.

11. TO BE ABLE TO TEACH OTHERS ONE MUST FROM HIS OLD STORES BE CONTINUALLY DEVELOPING THINGS NEW. 溫 is exp. in the Dict. by 燖, and, with ref. to this very pass. it is said, 'one's old learning being thorough, again constantly to practise it, is called 溫.' Mod. comm. say that the 'new learning is in the old.' The idea probably is that of assimilating old acquisitions and new, the mind's harmonizing them. Comp. 中庸, XXVII. 1.

十二 子曰、君子不器。

十三 子貢問君子、子曰、先行其言、而後從之。

十四 子曰、君子周而不比、小人比而不周。

十五 子曰、學而不思則罔、思而不學則殆。

十六 子曰、攻乎異端、斯害也已。

CHAPTER XII. The Master said, "The accomplished scholar is not an utensil."

CHAPTER XIII. Tsze-kung asked what constituted the superior man. The Master said, "He acts before he speaks, and afterwards speaks according to his actions."

CHAPTER XIV. The Master said, "The superior man is catholic and no partizan. The mean man is a partizan and not catholic."

CHAPTER XV. The Master said, "Learning without thought is labour lost; thought without learning is perilous."

CHAPTER XVI. The Master said, "The study of strange doctrines is injurious indeed!"

12. THE GENERAL APTITUDE OF THE KEUN-TSZE. This is not like our Eng. saying, that 'such a man is a machine,'—a blind instrument. A utensil has its particular use. It answers for that and no other. Not so with the superior man, who is *ad omnia paratus*.

13. HOW WITH THE SUPERIOR MAN WORDS FOLLOW ACTIONS. The reply is literally;—'He first acts his words and afterwards follows them.' A translator's diffic. is with the latter clause. What is the antecedent to 之? It would seem to be 其言, but in that case there is no room for words at all. Nor is there according to the old comm. In the interpretation I have given, Choo He follows the famous Chow Leen-k'e, (周濂溪).

14. THE DIFFERENCE BETWEEN THE KEUN-TSZE AND THE SMALL MAN. 比, here low. 3d tone, 'partial,' 'partizanly.' The sent. is this—'With the Keun-tsze, it is principles not men; with the small man, the reverse.'

15. IN LEARNING, READING AND THOUGHT MUST BE COMBINED. 罔, 'a net,' used also in the sense of 'not,' as an adverb, and here as an adj. The old comm. makes 殆, 'perilous,' simply='wearisome to the body.'

16. STRANGE DOCTRINES ARE NOT TO BE STUDIED. 攻, often 'to attack,' as an enemy, here='to apply one's-self to,' 'to study.' 端, 'correct;' then, 'beginnings,' 'first principles;' here='doctrines.' 也已, as in I. 14. In Conf. time Buddhism was not in China, and we can hardly suppose him to intend Taouism. Indeed, we are ignorant to what doctrines he referred, but his maxim is of gen. application.

論語

十七章 子曰、由、誨女知之乎、知之爲知之、不知爲不知、是知也。

十八章 一節 子張學干祿。二節 子曰、多聞闕疑、愼言其餘、則寡尤、多見闕殆、愼行其餘、則寡悔、言寡尤、行寡悔、祿在其中矣。

CHAPTER XVII. The Master said, "Yew, shall I teach you what knowledge is? When you know a thing, to hold that you know it; and when you do not know a thing, to allow that you do not know it;—this is knowledge."

CHAPTER XVIII. 1. Tsze-chang was learning with a view to official emolument.

2. "The Master said, "Hear much and put aside the points of which you stand in doubt, while you speak cautiously at the same time of the others:—then you will afford few occasions for blame. See much and put aside the things which seem perilous, while you are cautious at the same time in carrying the others into practice:—then you will have few occasions for repentance. When one gives few occasions for blame in his words, and few occasions for repentance in his conduct, he is in the way to get emolument."

17. THERE SHOULD BE NO PRETENCE IN THE PROFESSION OF KNOWLEDGE, OR THE DENIAL OF IGNORANCE. 由, by surname 仲, and generally known by his designation of *Tsze-loo* (子路), was one of the most famous disciples of Confucius, and now occupies in the temples the 4th place east in the sage's own hall. He was noted for his courage and forwardness, a man of impulse rather than reflection. Conf. had foretold that he would come to an untimely end, and so it happened. He was killed through his own rashness in a revolution in the state of Wei. The tassel of his cap being cut off when he received his death-wound, he quoted a saying—'The superior man must not die without his cap,' tied on the tassel, adjusted the cap, and expired. This action—結纓禮全, is much lauded. Of the six 知, the 1st and 6th are knowledge subjective, the other four are knowledge objective. The first 知之= 知之之道. In the other two cases, 之= 'any one thing.' 爲=以爲, 'to take to be,' 'to consider,' 'to allow.' 女, thus marked with a tone, is used for 汝, 'you.'

18. THE END IN LEARNING SHOULD BE ONE'S OWN IMPROVEMENT, AND NOT EMOLUMENT. 1. Tsze-chang, named 師, with the double surname 顓孫, a native of Ch'in (陳), was not undistinguished in the Confucian school. Tsze-kung praised him as a man of merit without boasting, humble in a high position, and not arrogant to the helpless. From this ch., however, it would appear that inferior mot. did sometimes rule him. 學='was learning,' *i. e.*, at some particular time. 干=求, 'to seek for.' 2. 闕 is explained in the comm. as in transl.,—姑舍置, but this mean. of it is not found in the Dict. 祿在其中, 'Emolument is herein,' *i. e.*, it will come without

【十九章】哀公問曰、何爲則民服。孔子對曰、舉直錯諸枉、則民服、舉枉錯諸直、則民不服。

【二十章】季康子問使民敬忠以勸、如之何。子曰、臨之以莊、則敬、孝慈、則忠、舉善而教不能、則勸。

【廿一章】一節 或謂孔子曰、子奚

CHAPTER XIX. The duke Gae asked, saying, "What should be done in order to secure the submission of the people?" Confucius replied, "Advance the upright and set aside the crooked, then the people will submit. Advance the crooked and set aside the upright, then the people will not submit."

CHAPTER XX. Ke K'ang asked how to cause the people to reverence *their ruler*, to be faithful to him, and to urge themselves to virtue. The Master said, "Let him preside over them with gravity;—then they will reverence him. Let him be filial and kind to all;—then they will be faithful to him. Let him advance the good and teach the incompetent;—then they will eagerly seek to be virtuous."

CHAPTER XXI. 1. Some one addressed Confucius, saying, "Sir, why are you not engaged in the government?"

seeking; the individual is on the way to it. The lesson is that we are to do what is right, and not be anxious about temporal concerns.

19. HOW A PRINCE BY THE RIGHT EMPLOYMENT OF HIS OFFICERS MAY SECURE THE REAL SUBMISSION OF HIS SUBJECTS. Gae was the honorary epithet of 蔣, duke of Loo (B. C. 494-367). Conf. died in his 16th year. Accord. to the laws for posthumous titles, 哀 denotes 'the respectful and benevolent, early cut off.' 哀公='The to-be-lamented duke.' 錯, up. 3d tone,=置, 'to set aside.' 諸 is partly euphonious, but also indicates the plural. 孔子對曰, 'The philosopher K'ung replied.' Here, for the first time, the sage is called by his surname, and, 對 is used, as indicating the reply of an inferior to a superior.

20. EXAMPLE IN SUPERIORS IS MORE POWERFUL THAN FORCE. K'ang, 'easy and pleasant, people-soother,' was the honorary epithet of Ke-sun Fei (肥), the head of one of the three great families of Loo; see ch. 5. His idea is seen in 使, 'to cause,' the power of force; that of Conf. appears in 則, 'then,' the power of influence. In 以勸, 以 is said to=與, 'together with,' 'mutually.' 勸, 'to advise,' 'to teach,' has also in the Dict. the meaning-'to rejoice to follow,' which is its force here, 爲善, 'the practice of goodness,' being understood.

21. CONFUCIUS' EXPLANATION OF HIS NOT BEING IN ANY OFFICE. 1. 或謂孔子,—The surname indic. that the questioner was not a disciple. Conf. had his reason for not being in office at the time, but it was not expedient to tell. He replied therefore, as in par. 2. 2. See Shoo-king xxii. 1. But the text is neither correctly applied nor exactly quoted. The old

不爲政。二節子曰、書云孝乎、惟孝友于兄弟、施於有政、是亦爲政、奚其爲爲政。

二十二子曰、人而無信、不知其可也、大車無輗、小車無軏、其何以行之哉。

二十三子張問十世、可知也。二節子曰、殷因於夏禮、

2. The Master said, "What does the Shoo-king say of filial piety?—'You are filial, you discharge your brotherly duties. These qualities are displayed in government.' This then also constitutes the exercise of government. Why must there be THAT to make one be in the government."

CHAPTER XXII. The Master said, "I do not know how a man without truthfulness is to get on. How can a large carriage be made to go without the cross bar for yoking the oxen to, or a small carriage without the arrangement for yoking the horses?"

CHAPTER XXIII. 1. Tsze-chang asked whether *the affairs of* ten ages *after* could be known.

2. Confucius said, "The Yin dynasty followed the regulations of the Hea: wherein it took from or added to them may be known. The Chow dynasty has followed the regulations of the Yin: wherein it took from or added to them may be known. Some other may follow the Chow, but though it be should be at the distance of a hundred ages, its affairs may be known."

inter. read in one sentence 孝乎惟孝, 'O filial piety! nothing but filial piety!' Choo He, however, pauses at 乎, and commences rightly the quotation with 惟孝. A western may think that the philosopher might have made a happier evasion. 奚其爲爲政, the 1st 爲=以爲, and 其 referring to the thought in the man's question, that *office* was necessary to one's being in government.

22. THE NECESSITY TO A MAN OF BEING TRUTHFUL AND SINCERE. 輗 and 軏 are explained in the Dict. in the same way—'the cross bar at the end of the carriage pole.' But there was a difference. Choo He says, 'In the light carriage the end of the pole curved upwards, and the cross bar was suspended from a hook.' This would give it more elasticity.

23. THE GREAT PRINCIPLES GOVERNING SOCIETY ARE UNCHANGEABLE. 1. 世 may be taken as an age='a century,' or as a generation=30 years, which is its radical meaning, being formed from *three tens* and *one* (卅 and 一). Both meanings are in the Dict. Conf. made no pretension to supernatural powers, and all comm. are agreed that the things here asked about were not what we would call contingent or indifferent events. He merely says that the great principles of morality and relations of society had continued the same and would ever do so. 也=乎. 2. The Hea, Yin, and Chow are now spoken of as the 三代, 'The three

所損益、可知也、周因於殷禮、所損益、可知也、其或繼周者、雖百世、可知也。

廿四章 子曰、非其鬼而祭之、諂也。二節 見義不爲、無勇也。

CHAPTER XXIV. 1. The Master said, "For a man to sacrifice to a spirit which does not belong to him is flattery."

2. To see what is right and not to do it is want of courage."

changes,' *i. e.*, the three great dynasties. The first Emperor of the Hea was 'The great Yu,' B. C. 2204, of the Yin, T'ang, B. C. 1765, and of Chow, Woo, B. C. 1121.

24. NEITHER IN SACRIFICE NOR IN OTHER PRACTICE MAY A MAN DO ANYTHING BUT WHAT IS RIGHT. 1. 人神曰鬼, 'The human spirit (*i. e.*, of the dead) is called 鬼.' The 鬼 of which a man may say that they are his, are those only of his ancestors, and to them only he may sacrifice. The ritual of China provides for sacrifices to three classes of objects—天神, 地示, 人鬼, 'spirits of heaven, of the earth, of men.' This ch. is not to be extended to all the three. It has reference only to the manes of departed men.

BOOK III. PĂ YIH.

八佾第三

第一章 孔子謂季氏、八佾舞於庭、是可忍也、孰不可忍也。

CHAPTER I. Confucius said of the head of the Ke family, who had eight rows of pantomimes in his area, "If he can bear to do this, what may he not bear to do?"

HEADING OF THIS BOOK.—八佾第三. The last book treated of the practice of government, and therein no things, according to Chinese ideas, are more important than ceremonial rites and music. With those topics therefore, the twenty six chapters of this book are occupied, and 'eight rows,' the principal words in the first chapter, are adopted as its heading.

1. CONFUCIUS' INDIGNATION AT THE USURPATION OF IMPERIAL RITES. 季氏, by contraction for 季孫氏; see II. 5. 氏 and 姓 are now used without distinction, meaning 'surname,' only that the 氏 of a woman is always spoken of, and not her 姓. Originally the 氏 appears to have been used to denote the branch families of one surname. 季氏, 'The Ke family,' with special reference to its head, '*The* Ke,' as we should say. 佾, 'a row of dancers,' or pantomimes rather, who kept time in the temple services, in the 庭, the front space before the raised portion in the principal hall, moving or brandishing feathers, flags, or other articles. In his ancestral temple, the Emperor had 8 rows, each row consisting of eight men, a duke or prince had 6, and a great officer only 4. For the Ke, therefore, to use 8 rows was a

第二章 三家者、以雍徹。子曰、相維辟公、天子穆穆、奚取於三家之堂。

第三章 子曰、人而不仁、如禮何、人而不仁、如樂何。

第四章 一節 林放問禮之本。二節 子曰、大哉問。三節 禮與其奢也、寧

CHAPTER II. The three families used the YUNG ode, while the vessels were being removed, *at the conclusion of the sacrifice.* The Master said, "'Assisting are the princes;—the emperor looks profound and grave:'—what application can these words have in the hall of the three families?"

CHAPTER III. The Master said, "If a man be without the virtues proper to humanity, what has he to do with the rites of propriety? If a man be without the virtues proper to humanity, what has he to do with music?"

CHAPTER IV. Lin Fang asked what was the first thing to be attended to in ceremonies.

2. The Master said, "A great question indeed!"

usurpation, for tho' it may be argued, that to the ducal family of Loo imperial rites were conceded, and that the offshoots of it (II. 5) might use the same, still great officers were confined to the ordinances proper to their rank. 謂 is used here, as frequently, in the sense—'to speak of.' Conf. remark may also be translated, 'If this be endured, what may not be endured?' And this is probably the correct interpretation, for there is force in the observations of the author of the 四書翼註, that this remark and the following must be assigned to the sage during the short time that he held high office in Loo.

2. AGAIN AGAINST USURPED RITES. 三家者. '*Those* belonging to the three families.' They assembled together, as being the descendants of duke Hwan (II. 5), in one temple. To this temple belonged the 庭 in the last ch., which is called 季氏庭, because circumstances had concurred to make the Ke the chief of the three families; see 四書改錯, viii. 7. For the Yung ode, see She-king, II. ii. Ode. II. st. 7. It was, properly, sung in the imperial temples of the Chow dynasty, at the 徹, 'the clearing away,' of the sacrificial apparatus, and contains the lines quoted by Confucius, which of course were quite inappropriate to the circumstances of the three families. 辟,—up. 4th tone, without an aspirate. 相, up. 3d tone, 'assistant,' 'assisting.'

3. CEREMONIES AND MUSIC VAIN WITHOUT VIRTUE. 仁, see I. 2. I don't know how to render it here, otherwise than in the transla. Comm. define it—心之全德, 'the entire virtue of the heart.' As referred to 禮, it indicates the feeling of reverence; as referred to 樂 (*yŏ*), it indicates harmoniousness.

4. THE OBJECT OF CEREMONIES SHOULD REGULATE THEM:—AGAINST FORMALISM. 1. Lin Fang, styled 子邱, was a man of Loo, supposed to have been a disciple of Conf., and whose tablet is now placed first, on the west, in the outer court of the temples. He is known only by the question in this ch. Acc. to Choo He, 本 here is not 根本, 'the radical idea,' 'the essence;' but as 初, 'the beginning,' opposed to 末,='the first thing to be attended to.' 3. 禮 has not the gen. meaning of the char. in the 1st par. As opposed to 喪 (up. 1st tone), it must indicate the festive or fortunate (吉) ceremonies,—capping, marriage, and sacrifices.

儉、喪、與其易也、寧戚。

第五章 子曰、夷狄之有君、不如諸夏之亡也。

第六章 季氏旅於泰山。子謂冉有曰、女弗能救與。對曰、不能。子曰、嗚呼、曾謂泰山、不如林放乎。

3. In *festive* ceremonies, it is better to be sparing than extravagant. In the ceremonies of mourning, it is better that there be deep sorrow than a minute attention to observances."

CHAPTER V. The Master said, "The rude tribes of the east and north have their princes, and are not like the States of our great land which are without them."

CHAPTER VI. The chief of the Ke family was about to sacrifice to the T'ae mountain. The Master said to Yen-yew, "Can you not save him from this?" He answered, "I cannot." Confucius said, "Alas! will you say that the T'ae mountain is not so discerning as Lin Fang?"

易, read *e*, low 3d tone. Choo He explains it by 治, as in Mencius—易其田疇, 'to cleanse and dress the fields,' and interprets as in the transl. The old comm. take the meaning—和易, 'harmony and ease,' *i. e.*, not being overmuch troubled.

5. THE ANARCHY OF CONFUCIUS' TIME. The 夷 were the barbarians on the east of China, and 狄, those on the north. See 禮記, 王制, iii. 14. The two are here used for the barbarous tribes about China generally. 諸夏 is a name for China because of the *multitude* of its people (諸), and its *greatness* (夏). 華夏, 'The flowery and great,' is still a common designation of it. Choo He takes 如 as simply=似, and hence the sentiment in the transl. Ho An's comm. is to this effect:—'The rude tribes with their princes are still not equal to China with its anarchy.' 亡, read *woo*, and=無.

6. ON THE FOLLY OF USURPED SACRIFICES. 旅 is said to be the name appropriate to sacrifices to mountains, but we find it applied also to sacrifices to God. The T'ae mountain is the first of the 'five mountains' (五嶽), which are celebrated in Chinese literature, and have always received religious honours. It was in Loo, or rather on the borders between Loo and Ts'e, about 2 miles north of the present district city of T'ae-gan (泰安), in the department of Tse-nan (濟南), in Shan-tung. According to the ritual of China, sacrifice could only be offered to these mountains by the emperor, and princes in whose States any of them happened to be. For the chief of the Ke family, therefore, to sacrifice to the T'ae mountain, was a great usurpation. 女 as in II. 7,=汝, and 曾 as in II. 8,=則, or we may take it as=經, 'Have you said,' &c. 泰山=泰山之神, 'The spirit of the T'ae mountain.' Lin Fang,—see ch. 4, from which the reason of this reference to him may be understood. Yen Yew, named (求), and by designation 子有, was one of the disciples of Conf., and is now third, in the hall, on the west. He entered the service of the Ke family, and was a man of ability and resources.

第七章 子曰、君子無所爭、必也射乎、揖讓而升、下而飲、其爭也君子。

第八章 一節 子夏問曰、巧笑倩兮、美目盼兮、素以爲絢兮、何謂也。二節 子曰、繪事後素。三節 曰、禮後乎。子曰、起予者商也、始可與言詩已矣。

CHAPTER VII. The Master said, "The student of virtue has no contentions. If it be said he cannot avoid them, shall this be in archery? *But* he bows complaisantly *to his competitors;* thus he ascends *the hall*, descends, and exacts the forfeit of drinking. In his contention, he is still the Keun-tsze."

CHAPTER VIII. 1. Tsze-hea asked, saying, "What is the meaning of the passage—'The pretty dimples of her artful smile! The well defined black and white of her eye! The plain ground for the colours'?"

2. The Master said, "The business of laying on the colours follows the preparation of the plain ground."

3. "Ceremonies then are a subsequent thing." The Master said, "It is Shang who can bring out my meaning! Now I can begin to talk about the odes with him"

7. THE SUPERIOR MAN AVOIDS ALL CONTENTIOUS STRIVING. Here 君子=尙德之人, 'the man who prefers virtue.' 必也射乎 lit., 'if he must, shall it be archery?' 揖讓, according to Choo He, extend over all the verbs, 升, 下, 飲. 下 is marked in the 3d tone, anciently appropriate to it as a verb. 飲, up. 3d tone, 'to give to drink,' here=to exact from the vanquished the forfeit cup. In Conf. time there were three principal exercises of archery:—the great archery, under the eye of the Emperor, the guests' archery, which might be at the imperial court or at the visits of the princes among themselves, and the festive archery, for amusement. The regulations for the archers were substantially the same in them all, and served to prove their virtue, instead of giving occasion to quarreling. There is no end to the controversies among comm. on minor points.

8. CEREMONIES ARE SECONDARY AND ORNAMENTAL. 1. The sentences quoted by Tsze-hea are from a 逸詩, one of the poems which Conf. did not admit into the She-king. The two first lines, however, are found in it, I. v. 3. The disciple's inquiry turns on the meaning of 以爲 in the last line, which he took to mean—'The plain ground is to be regarded as the colouring.' 2. Conf., in his reply, makes 後 a verb, governing 素,='comes after the plain ground.' 3. 禮後乎, Tsze-hea's remark is an exclamation rather than a question. 起予者, 'He who stirs me up,'='He who brings out my meaning.' On the last sentence, see I. 15.—The above interpretation, especially as to the meaning of 繪事後素, after Choo He, is quite the opposite of that of the old interpreters. Their view is of course strongly supported by the author of 四書改錯, VIII. 3.

第九章 子曰、夏禮吾能言之、杞不足徵也、殷禮吾能言之、宋不足徵也、文獻不足故也、足則吾能徵之矣。

第十章 子曰、禘自既灌而往者、吾不欲觀之矣。

第十一章 或問禘之說。子曰、不知也、知其說者之於天下也、其如示諸

CHAPTER IX. The Master said, "I am able to describe the ceremonies of the Hea dynasty, but Ke cannot sufficiently attest my words. I am able to describe the ceremonies of the Yin dynasty, but Sung cannot sufficiently attest my words. They cannot do so because of the insufficiency of their records and wise men. If those were sufficient, I could adduce them in support of my words."

CHAPTER X. The Master said, "At the great sacrifice, after the pouring out of the libation, I have no wish to look on."

CHAPTER XI. Some one asked the meaning of the great sacrifice. The Master said, "I do not know. He who knew its meaning would

9. THE DECAY OF THE MONUMENTS OF ANTIQUITY. Of Hea and Yin, see II. 23. In the small state of Ke (originally what is now the district of the same name in K'ae-fung dep. in Ho-nan, but in Conf. time a part of Shan-tung), the sacrifices to the emperors of the Hea dynasty were maintained by their descendants. So with the Yin dynasty and Sung, a part of the present Ho-nan. But the 文, 'literary monuments' of those countries, and their 獻 (=賢, so in the Shoo-king, v. vii. 5, *et al.*) 'wise men' had become few. Had Conf. therefore delivered all his knowledge about the two dynasties, he would have exposed his truthfulness to suspicion, 徵, in the sense of 證, 'to witness,' and, at the end, 'to appeal to for evidence.' The old comm., however take 徵 in the sense of 成, 'to complete,' and interpret the whole differently.—We see from the chapter how in the time of Confucius many of the records of antiquity had perished.

10. THE SAGE'S DISSATISFACTION AT THE WANT OF PROPRIETY OF AND IN CEREMONIES. 禘 is the name belonging to different sacrifices, but here indicating the 大祭, 'great sacrifice,' which could properly be celebrated only by the Emperor. The individual sacrificed to in it was the remotest ancestor from whom the founder of the reigning dynasty traced his descent. As to who were his assessors in the sacrifice and how often it was offered;—these are disputed points. See K'ang-he's dict. char. 禘. Comp. also 四書改錯, VII. 8, and 四書摭餘說, I. 18. An imperial rite, its use in Loo was wrong (see next ch.), but there was something in the service after the early act of libation inviting the descent of the spirits, which more particularly moved the anger of Conf. 而往=以後, diff. from 往 in I. 15.

11. THE PROFOUND MEANING OF THE GREAT SACRIFICE. This ch. is akin to II. 21. Conf. evades replying to his questioner, it being contrary to Chinese propriety to speak in a country of the faults of its government or rulers. If he had entered into an account of the 禘 sacrifice, he must have condemned the use of an imperial rite in Loo. 說 'explanation,'=*meaning*. The antecedent to the second 其 is the whole of the preceding clause:—'The relation to the empire of him who knew its meaning;—

斯乎。指其掌。〔十二〕一節祭如在、祭神如神在。二節子曰、吾不與祭、如不祭。〔十三〕一節王孫賈問曰、與其媚於奧、寧媚於竈、何謂也。二節子曰、不然、獲罪於天、無所禱也。

find it as easy to govern the empire as to look on this;"—pointing to his palm.

CHAPTER XII. 1. He sacrificed *to the dead*, as if they were present. He sacrificed to the spirits, as if the spirits were present.

2. The Master said, "I consider my not being present at the sacrifice, as if I did not sacrifice."

CHAPTER XIII. 1. Wang-sun Kea asked, saying, "What is the meaning of the saying, 'It is better to pay court to the furnace than to the south-west corner'?"

2 The Master said, "Not so. He who offends against Heaven has none to whom he can pray."

that would be as to look on this.' 乎, interjective, more than interrogative. 示=視, 'to see.' 天下, 'under heaven,' an ambitious designation for the Chinese empire, as ἡ οἰκουμένη and *orbis* were used by the Greeks and Romans.

12. CONFUCIUS' OWN SINCERITY IN SACRIFICING. 1. 祭 here is historical and not to be translated in the imperative. We have to supply an object. to the first 祭, viz. 先祖, *the dead*, his forefathers, as contrasted with 神 in the next clause,=all the 'spirits' to which in his official capacity he would have to sacrifice. 2. Obs. 與 in low 3d tone, 'to be present at,' 'to take part in.'

13. THAT THERE IS NO RESOURCE AGAINST THE CONSEQUENCES OF VIOLATING THE RIGHT. 1. Kea was a great officer of Wei (衛), and having the power of the state in his hands insinuated to Confucius that it would be for his advantage to pay court to him. The 奧, or south west corner, was from the structure of ancient houses the cosiest nook, and the place of honour. Choo He explains the proverb by reference to the customs of sacrifice. The furnace was comparatively a mean place, but when the spirit of the furnace was sacrificed to, then the rank of the two places was changed for the time, and the proverb quoted was in vogue. But there does not seem much force in this explanation. The *door*, or *well*, or any other of the five things in the regular sacrifices, might take the place of the *furnace*. The old explanation which makes no reference to sacrifice is simpler. 奧 might be the more retired and honourable place, but the 竈 was the more important for the support and comfort of the household. The prince and his immediate attendants might be more honourable than such a minister as Kea, but more benefit might be got from him. 媚, from *woman* and *eyebrows*,='to ogle,' 'to flatter.' 2. Confucius' reply was in a high tone. Choo He says, 天卽理也, 'Heaven means principle.' But why should Heaven mean principle, if there were not in such a use of the term an instinctive recognition of a supreme government of intelligence and righteousness? We find 天 explained in the 撫餘說 by 高高在上者, 'The lofty one who is on high.'

〔十四章〕子曰、周監於二代、郁郁乎文哉、吾從周。

〔十五章〕子入大廟、每事問。或曰、孰謂鄹人之子知禮乎、入大廟、每事問。子聞之曰、是禮也。

〔十六章〕子曰、射不主皮、爲力不同科、古之道也。

CHAPTER XIV. The Master said, "Chow had the advantage of viewing the two past dynasties. How complete and elegant are its regulations! I follow Chow."

CHAPTER XV. The Master, when he entered the grand temple, asked about every thing. Some one said, "Who will say that the son of the man of Tsow knows the rules of propriety. He has entered the grand temple and asks about every thing." The Master heard the remark, and said, "This is a rule of propriety."

CHAPTER XVI. The Master said, "In archery it is not *going through* the leather which is the principal thing;—because people's strength is not equal. This was the old way."

14. THE COMPLETENESS AND ELEGANCE OF THE INSTITUTIONS OF THE CHOW DYNASTY. By the 周 we are specially to undersand the founders of the power and polity of the dynasty—the kings Wan and Woo, and the duke of Chow. The two past dynasties are of course the Hea and the Shang or Yin. 文 is an adj.

15. CONFUCIUS IN THE GRAND TEMPLE. 大(=太)廟 was the temple dedicated to the duke of Chow (周公), and where he was worshipped with imperial rites. The thing is supposed to have taken place, at the begin. of Conf. official service in Loo, when he went into the temple with other officers to assist at the sacrifice. He had studied all about ceremonies, and was famed for his knowledge of them, but he thought it a mark of sincerity and earnestness to make minute inquiries about them on the occasion spoken of. 鄹 was the name of the town in Loo of which Conf. father had been governor, who was known therefore as 'the man of Tsow.' We may suppose that Conf. would be styled as in the text, only in his early life, or by very ordinary people.

16. HOW THE ANCIENTS MADE ARCHERY A DISCIPLINE OF VIRTUE. We are not to understand 射不主皮 of all archery among the ancients. The char. are found in the 儀禮, 鄉射, par. 315, preceded by the char. 禮. There were trials of archery where the strength was tested. Probably Conf. was speaking of the 禮射 of his times, when the strength which could go through the 皮, 'skin,' or leather, in the middle of the target, was esteemed more than the skill which could hit it.

論語

〔十七章〕一節 子貢欲去告朔之餼羊。二節 子曰、賜也、爾愛其羊、我愛其禮。

〔十八章〕子曰、事君盡禮、人以爲諂也。

〔十九章〕一節 定公問君使臣、臣事君、如之何。二節 孔子對曰、君使臣以禮、臣事君以忠。

〔二十章〕子曰、關雎樂而不淫、哀而不傷。

CHAPTER XVII. 1. Tsze-kung wished to do away with the offering of a sheep connected with the inauguration of the first day of each month.

2. The Master said, "Tsze, you love the sheep; I love the ceremony."

CHAPTER XVIII. The Master said, "The full observance of the rules of propriety in serving one's prince is accounted by people to be flattery."

CHAPTER XIX. The duke Ting asked how a prince should employ his ministers, and how ministers should serve their prince. Confucius replied, "A prince should employ his ministers according to the rules of propriety; ministers should serve their prince with faithfulness."

CHAPTER XX. The Master said, "The Kwan Ts'eu is expressive of enjoyment without being licentious, and of grief without being hurtfully excessive."

17. HOW CONFUCIUS CLEAVED TO ANCIENT RITES. 1. The emperor in the last month of the year gave out to the princes a calendar for the 1st days of the 12 months of the year ensuing. This was kept in their ancestral temples, and on the 1st of every month, they offered a sheep and announced the day, requesting sanction for the duties of the month. This idea of requesting sanction is indicated by 告, read *kuh*, up. 4th tone. The dukes of Loo neglected now their part of this ceremony, but the sheep was still offered:—a meaningless formality, it seemed to Tsze-kung. Conf., however, thought that while any part of the cer. was retained, there was a better chance of restor. the whole. 去, up. 3d tone, an act. verb, 'to put away.' It is disputed whether 餼, in the text, mean a *living* sheep, or a sheep killed but not roasted. 2. 愛, in the sense of 愛惜, 'to grudge,' it is said. But this is hardly necessary.

18. HOW PRINCES SHOULD BE SERVED:—AGAINST THE SPIRIT OF THE TIMES.

19. THE GUIDING PRINCIPLES IN THE RELATION OF PRINCE AND MINISTER. 定, 'Greatly anxious, tranquillizer of the people,' was the posthumous epithet of 宋, prince of Loo, B.C. 508–494. 如之何, 'As it what,' 之 referring to the two points inquired about.

20. THE PRAISE OF THE FIRST OF THE ODES. 關雎 is the name of the first ode in the She-king, and may be translated.—'The murmuring of the *ts'eu*.' See She-king, I. i. 1.

【二十一章】一節 哀公問社於宰我。二節 宰我對曰、夏后氏以松、殷人以栢、周人以栗、曰、使民戰栗。三節 子聞之曰、成事不說、遂事不諫、既往不咎。

【二十二章】一節 子曰、管仲之器小哉。二節 或曰、管仲儉乎。三節 曰、管氏有三歸、

CHAPTER XXI. The duke Gae asked Tsae Go about the altars of the spirits of the land. Tsae Go replied, "The Hea sovereign used the pine tree; the man of the Yin used the cypress; and the man of the Chow used the chestnut tree, meaning thereby to cause the people to be in awe."

2. When the Master heard it, he said, "Things that are done, it is needless to speak about; things that have had their course, it is needless to remonstrate about; things that are past, it is needless to blame."

CHAPTER XXII. The Master said, "Small indeed was the capacity of Kwan Chung!"

2. Some one said, "Was Kwan Chung parsimonious?" "Kwan," was the reply, "had the *San Kwei*, and his officers performed no double duties; how can he be considered parsimonious?"

21. A RASH REPLY OF TSAE GO ABOUT THE ALTARS TO THE SPIRITS OF THE LAND, AND LAMENT OF CONFUCIUS THEREON. 哀公, see II. 19. Tsae Go, by name 予, and styled 子我, was an eloquent disciple of the sage, a native of Loo. His place is the second west among 'the wise ones.' 社, from 示, K'e, 'spirit or spirits of the earth,' and 土, 'the soil,' means 土地神主, 'the resting place or altars of the spirits of the land or ground.' Go simply tells the duke that the founders of the several dynasties planted such and such trees about those altars. The reason was that the soil suited such trees, but as 栗, 'the chestnut tree,' the tree of the existing dynasty, is used in the sense of 慄, 'to be afraid,' he suggested a reason for its planting which might lead the duke to severe measures against his people to be carried into effect at the altars. Comp. Shoo-king, IV. ii. 5, 'I will put you to death before the 社.' 夏后氏 is the Great Yu, called 后, to distinguish him from his predecessors, the 帝, and 夏氏, to distinguish him from 舜, who was 虞氏, while they were descended from the same ancestor. See ch. 1, on 氏. 殷人 and 周人, in parallelism with 夏后氏, must mean the founders of those dynasties; why they are simply styled 人, 'man,' or 'men,' I have not found clearly explained, though comm. feel it necess. to say something on the point. 2. This is all directed against Go's reply. He had spoken, and his words could not be recalled.

22. CONFUCIUS' OPINION OF KWAN-CHUNG;—AGAINST HIM. 1. Kwan-chung, by name 夷吾, is one of the most famous names in Chin. history. He was chief minister to the duke 桓 of 齊 (B. C. 683-540), the first and greatest of the five *p'a* (伯 or 霸), leaders of the princes of the empire under the Chow dynasty. In the times of Conf. and Men., people thought

官事不攝、焉得儉。○四節然則管仲知禮乎。○五節曰、邦君樹塞門、管氏亦樹塞門、邦君爲兩君之好、有反坫、管氏亦有反坫、管氏而知禮、孰不知禮。

〔二十三〕子語魯大師樂曰、樂其可知也、始作、翕如也、從之、純如也、皦如也、繹如也、以成。

3. "Then, did Kwan Chung know the rules of propriety?" The Master said, "The princes of states have a screen intercepting the view at their gates. Kwan had likewise a screen at his gate. The princes of states on any friendly meeting between two of them, had a stand on which to place their inverted cups. Kwan had also such a stand. If Kwan knew the rules of propriety, who does not know them?"

CHAPTER XXIII. The Master instructing the Grand music-master of Loo said, "How to play music may be known. At the commencement of the piece, all the parts should sound together. As it proceeds, they should be in harmony, severally distinct and flowing without break, and thus on to the conclusion."

more of Kwan, than those sages, no hero-worshippers, would allow. 器 see II. 12, but its signif. here is different, and=our *measure* or *capacity*. 2. 三歸, in the Dict., and the approved comm. of Choo He, was the name of an extravagant tower built by Kwan. There are other views of the phrase, the oldest, and the best supported appar., being that it means 'three wives.' (A woman's marriage is called 歸.) The *San Kwei* and having no pluralists among his officers proved suff. that he could not be parsimonious. 焉, up. 1st tone, 'how.' 3. 樹 'a tree,' here in the sense of 屏, 'a screen,' the screen of a prince, usurped by Kwan, who was only entitled to the 簾 of a great officer. 好 up. 3d tone,=好會, 'a friendly meeting.' The 坫, from 土 and 占, was a stand, made originally of earth and turf. Kwan usurped the use of it, as he did of the screen. This showed him to be as regardless of prescribed forms, as in par.2 he appears of expense, and he came far short therefore of the Confucian idea of the *Keun-tsze*.

23. ON THE PLAYING OF MUSIC. 語, low. 3d tone,=告, 'to tell,' 'to instruct.' 大 (=太) 師樂, was the title of the grand music-master. 樂其可知也, 'music, it may be known,' but the subject is not of the principles, but the performance of music. Observe the 如. Premare says, '*adjectivis addita sensum auget et exprimit modum.*' It is our *ly* or *like*, —翕如, 'blended-like.' 從, up. 3d tone, the same as 縱=放, 'let go,' *i. e.*, proceeding, swelling on.

二十四 儀封人請見、曰、君子之至於斯也、吾未嘗不得見也。從者見之、出曰、二三子、何患於喪乎、天下之無道也久矣、天將以夫子爲木鐸。

二十五 子謂韶、盡美矣、又盡善也、謂武、盡美矣、未盡善也。

二十六 子曰、居上不寬、爲禮

CHAPTER XXIV. The border-warden at E requested to be introduced to the Master, saying, "When men of superior virtue have come to this, I have never been denied the privilege of seeing them." The followers *of the sage* introduced him, and when he came out from the interview, he said, "My friends, why are you distressed by your master's loss of office? The empire has long been without the principles *of truth and right;* Heaven is going to use your master as a bell with its wooden tongue."

CHAPTER XXV. The Master said of the Shaou that it was perfectly beautiful and also perfectly good. He said of the Woo that it was perfectly beautiful but not perfectly good.

CHAPTER XXVI. The Master said, "High station filled without indulgent generosity; ceremonies performed without reverence; mourning conducted without sorrow;—wherewith should I contemplate such ways?"

24. A STRANGER'S VIEW OF THE VOCATION OF CONFUCIUS. E was a small town on the borders of Wei, referred to a place in the present dis. of 蘭陽, dep. 開封, Honan prov. Conf. was retiring from Wei, the prince of which could not employ him. This was the 喪 (up. 3d tone),=失位. The 1st and 3d 見 are read *heen*, low. 3d tone,=通使得見, 'to introduce,' or 'to be introduced.' 之 in 君子之至於斯也, has its prop. poss. power,—'In the case of a Keun-tsze's coming to this.' 從, low. 3d tone, 'to attend upon.' 二三子, 'Two or three sons,' or 'gentlemen,'=' my friends.' The same idiom occurs elsewhere. The 木鐸 was a metal bell with a wooden tongue, shaken to call attention to announcements, or along the ways to call people together. Heaven would employ Conf. to proclaim and call men's attention to the truth and right (道).

25. THE COMPARATIVE MERITS OF THE MUSIC OF SHUN AND WOO. 韶 was the name of the music made by Shun, perfect in melody and sentiment. 武 was the music of king Woo, also perfect in melody, but breathing the martial air, indicative of its author.

26. THE DISREGARD OF WHAT IS ESSENTIAL VITIATES ALL SERVICES. The meaning of the ch. turns upon 何以=何有, or 以何者, 'wherewith.' 寬 is ess. to rulers, 敬 to ceremonies, and 哀 to mourning. If they be wanting, one has no standpoint to view what are only shams or semblances.

論語

BOOK IV. LE JIN.

不敬、臨喪不哀、吾何以觀之哉。

里仁第四

第一章 子曰、里仁爲美、擇不處仁、焉得知。

第二章 子曰、不仁者、不可以久處約、不可以長處樂、仁者安仁、知者利仁。

CHAPTER I. The Master said, "It is virtuous manners which constitute the excellence of a neighbourhood. If a man in selecting a residence, do not fix on one where such prevail, how can he be wise?"

CHAPTER II. The Master said, "Those who are without virtue, cannot abide long either in a condition of poverty and hardship, or in a condition of enjoyment. The virtuous rest in virtue; the wise desire virtue."

HEADING OF THIS BOOK.—里仁第四. 'Virtue in a neighbourhood—No. IV.'—Such is the title of this fourth Book, which is mostly occupied with the subject of 仁. To render that term invariably by *benevolence*, would by no means suit many of the chapters. See II. 1, 2. *Virtue*, as a general term, would answer better. The embodiment of virtue demands an acquaintance with ceremonies and music, treated of in the last book; and this, it is said, is the reason why the one subject immediately follows the other.

1. RULE FOR THE SELECTION OF A RESIDENCE. According to the 周禮, 5 families made a 鄰, and 5 鄰 a 里, which we might style, therefore, *a hamlet* or *village*. There are other estimates of the number of its component households. 處, up. 2d tone, a verb, 'to dwell in.' 知, up, 3d tone, is the same as 智, 'wise,' 'wisdom.' So, not unfrequently, below. Friendship, we have seen, is for the aid of virtue (I. 8, 3), and the same should be the object desired in selecting a residence.

2. ONLY TRUE VIRTUE ADAPTS A MAN FOR THE VARIED CONDITIONS OF LIFE. 約, 'to bind,' is used for what binds, as an oath, a covenant; and here, the metaphor being otherwise directed, it denotes a condition of poverty and distress. 利, 'gain,' 'profit,' used as a verb,=貪, 'to desire,' 'to covet.' 安仁, 'to rest in virtue,' being virtuous without effort. 利仁, 'to desire virtue,' being virtuous because it is the best policy. Obs. how 者 following 仁 and 知 makes those terms adjectives. 不可, 'may not,'=不能, 'cannot.' The inability is moral.

〔第三章〕子曰、惟仁者、能好人、能惡人。

〔第四章〕子曰、苟志於仁矣、無惡也。

〔第五章〕子曰、富與貴、是人之所欲也、不以其道得之、不處也。貧與賤、是人之所惡也、不以其道得之、不去也。○二節 君子去仁、惡乎成名。○三節 君子無終食之閒

CHAPTER III. The Master said, "It is only the truly virtuous man, who can love, or who can hate, others."

CHAPTER IV. The Master said, "If the will be set on virtue, there will be no practice of wickedness."

CHAPTER V. 1. The Master said, "Riches and honours are what men desire. If it cannot be obtained in the proper way, they should not be held. Poverty and meanness are what men dislike. If it cannot be obtained in the proper way, they should not be avoided.

2. "If a superior man abandon virtue, how can he fulfil the requirements of that name?

3. "The superior man does not, even for the space of a single meal, act contrary to virtue. In moments of haste, he cleaves to it. In seasons of danger, he cleaves to it."

3. ONLY IN THE GOOD MAN ARE EMOTIONS OF LOVE AND HATRED RIGHT. This ch. containing an important truth, is incorporated with the 大學傳, x. 15. 好 and 惡 (read *woo*) are both verbs, up. 3d tone.

4. THE VIRTUOUS WILL PRESERVES FROM ALL WICKEDNESS. 苟=誠, not merely—'if,' but 'if really.' Comp. the apostle's sentiment, 1. John, iii. 9, 'Whosoever is born of God doth not commit sin.'

5. THE DEVOTION OF THE KEUN-TSZE TO VIRTUE. 1. For the antecedent to 之 in the recurring 得之, we are to look to the foll. verbs, 處 (up. 2d tone) and 去. We might translate the first 不以道得之, 'if *they* cannot be obtained, &c.,' but this would not suit the second case. 其道, '*the* way,' *i. e.*, the proper way. If we supply a nom. to 處 and 去, it must be 君子.—He will not 'abide in,' nor 'go away from,' riches and honours. 2. 惡, read *woo*, up. 1st tone, 'how.' 名, 'name,' not reputation, but the name of a *keun-tsze*, which he bears. 3. 終食之閒, 'The space in which a meal can be *finished*;' 造次 (interch. with 草次) and 顛沛 are well-known expressions, the former for haste and confusion, the latter for change and danger, but it is not easy to trace the attaching of those meanings to the characters. 顛, 'to fall down,' and 沛, the same, but the for. with the face up, the other with the face down. 必於是, Comp. Horace's '*Omnis in hoc sum.*'

違仁、造次必於是、顛沛必於是。

第六章 子曰、一節 我未見好仁者、惡不仁者、好仁者、無以尙之、惡不仁者、其爲仁矣、不使不仁者、加乎其身、二節 有能一日用其力於仁矣乎、我未見力不足者。三節 蓋有之矣、我未之見也。

第七章 子曰、人之過也、各於其黨、觀過、斯知仁矣。

CHAPTER VI. 1. The Master said, "I have not seen a person who loved virtue, or one who hated what was not virtuous. He who loved virtue, would esteem nothing above it. He who hated what is not virtuous, would practise virtue in such a way that he would not allow any thing that is not virtuous to approach his person.

2. "Is any one able for one day to apply his strength to virtue? I have not seen the case in which his strength would be insufficient.

3. "Should there possibly be any such case, I have not seen it."

CHAPTER VII. The Master said, "The faults of men are characteristic of the class to which they belong. By observing a man's faults, it may be known that he is virtuous."

6. A LAMENT BECAUSE OF THE RARITY OF THE LOVE OF VIRTUE; AND ENCOURAGEMENT TO PRACTISE VIRTUE. 1. The first four 者 belong to the verbs 好 and 惡, and give them the force of participles. In 使不仁者, 者 belongs to 不仁, and 不仁者=不仁之事. Commonly, 者='he or these who,' but sometimes also='that or those things which.' 尙=加, 'to add to.' Morr., char. 尙, translates the sentence wrongly—'He who loves virtue and benevolence can have nothing more said in his praise.' 3. 蓋 here is 疑辭 'a particle of doubt.' 未之有, a transpos., as in I. 26.

7. A MAN IS NOT TO BE UTTERLY CONDEMNED BECAUSE HE HAS FAULTS. Such is the sentiment found in this ch., in which we may say, however, that Conf. is liable to the charge brought against Taze-hea, I. 7. 人之過也 stands absolutely,—'As to the faults of men.' 各=各人, and 於=從,—'Each man follows his class.' Obs. the force of 過, 'what goes beyond.' The faults are the excesses of the general tendencies. Comp. Goldsmith's line, 'And even his failings leant to virtue's side.'

第八章 子曰、朝聞道、夕死、可矣。

第九章 子曰、士志於道、而恥惡衣惡食者、未足與議也。

第十章 子曰、君子之於天下也、無適也、無莫也、義之與比。

第十一章 子曰、君子懷德、小人懷土、君子懷刑、小

CHAPTER VIII. The Master said, "If a man in the morning hear the right way, he may die in the evening without regret."

CHAPTER IX. The Master said, "A scholar, whose mind is set on truth, and who is ashamed of bad clothes and bad food, is not fit to be discoursed with."

CHAPTER X. The Master said, "The superior man, in the world, does not set his mind either for any thing, or against any thing; what is right he will follow."

CHAPTER XI. The Master said, "The superior man thinks of virtue; the small man thinks of comfort. The superior man thinks of the sanctions of law; the small man thinks of favours *which he may receive.*"

8. THE IMPORTANCE OF KNOWING THE RIGHT WAY. One is perplexed to translate 道 here. Choo defines it—事物當然之理 'the principles of what is right in events and things.' Better is the expl. in 四書翼註,—道即率性之道, '道 is the path'—*i. e., of action*—'which is in accordance with our nature.' Man is formed for this, and if he die without coming to the knowledge of it, his death is no better than that of a beast. One would fain recognize, in such sentences as this, a vague apprehension of some higher truth or 道, than Chi. sages have been able to propound. —Ho An takes a diff. view of the whole ch., and makes it a lament of Confucius that he was likely to die without hearing of right principles prevailing in the world.—'Could I once hear of the prevalence of right principles, I could die the same evening.'

9. THE PURSUIT OF TRUTH SHOULD RAISE A MAN ABOVE BEING ASHAMED OF POVERTY. 與議,—'to be discoursed with,' *i. e.*, about 道, or 'truth,' which perhaps is the best translation of the term in places like this.

10. RIGHTEOUSNESS IS THE RULE OF THE KEUN-TSZE'S PRACTICE. 君子之云云, 'The relation of the *keun-tsze* to the world,' *i. e.*, to all things presenting themselves to him. 適, read *teih*, is explained by 專主, 'to set the mind exclusively on.' We may take the last clause thus:—'his is the according with, and keeping near to (比, low. 3d tone,=從 or 親) righteousness.' This gives each char. its signification.

11. THE DIFFERENT MINDINGS OF THE SUPERIOR AND THE SMALL MAN. 懷 is here emphatic, ='*cherishes* and plans about.' 土, 'earth,' 'the ground,' is here defined—所處之安, 'the rest or comforts one dwells amidst.' May it not be used somewhat in our sense of earthly?—'thinks of what is earthly.'

論語

人懷惠。

【十二章】子曰、放於利而行、多怨。

【十三章】子曰、能以禮讓為國乎、何有、不能以禮讓為國、如禮何。

【十四章】子曰、不患無位、患所以立、不患莫己知、求為可知也。

【十五章】子曰、參乎、吾道一以貫之。曾子曰、唯。一節 子出、門人問 二節

CHAPTER XII. The Master said, "He who acts with a constant view to his own advantage will be much murmured against."

CHAPTER XIII. The Master said, "Is *a prince* able to govern his kingdom with the complaisance proper to the rules of propriety, what difficulty will he have? If he cannot govern it with that complaisance, what has he to do with the rules of propriety?"

CHAPTER XIV. The Master said, "*A man should say*, I am not concerned that I have no place, I am concerned how I may fit myself for one. I am not concerned that I am not known, I seek to be worthy to be known."

CHAPTER XV. 1. The Master said, "Sin, my doctrine is that of an all-pervading unity." The disciple Tsăng replied, "Yes."

2. The Master went out, and the *other* disciples asked, saying,

12. THE CONSEQUENCE OF SELFISH CONDUCT. 放, up. 2d tone,=依, 'to accord with,' 'to lie alongside.'—'He who acts along the line of gain.'

13. THE INFLUENCE IN GOVERNMENT OF CEREMONIES OBSERVED IN THEIR PROPER SPIRIT. 禮讓字是二是一, *i. e.*, they are a hendiadys. 讓=禮之實, 'the sincer. and subs. of cer.,' the *spirit* of it, as we should say. Comp. 和 in I. 12. 爲=治, 'to govern.' This mean. is found in the Dict. 如禮何, see III. 3.

14. ADVISING TO SELF-CUTIVATION. Comp. I. 16. Here, as there, 不 not being imper. we must supply a nominative. 位, 'a place,' *i. e.* an official situation. 所以立 is to be completed 所以立乎其位.

15. CONFUCIUS' DOCTRINE THAT OF A PERVADING UNITY. This chap. is said to be the most profound in the *Lun Yu*. 1. 吾道一以貫之;—To myself it occurs to translate, 'my doctrines have one thing which goes thro. them,' but such an expos. has not been approved by any Chin. comm. 一以貫之 are made to contain the copula and predicate of 吾道, and 之, it is said, 指萬事萬物, 'refers to all affairs and all things.' The 2d par. shows us clearly enough what the one thing or unity intended by Conf. was. It was the heart, man's nature, of which all the relations and duties of life are only the development and outgo-

曰、何謂也。曾子曰、夫子之道、忠恕而已矣。

十六 子曰、君子喻於義、小人喻於利。

十七 子曰、見賢思齊焉、見不賢而內自省也。

十八 子曰、事父母幾諫、見志不從、又敬

,'What do his words mean?" Tsăng said, "The doctrine of our master is to be true to the principles of our nature and the benevolent exercise of them to others,—this and nothing more."

CHAPTER XVI. The Master said, "The mind of the superior man is conversant with righteousness; the mind of the mean man is conversant with gain."

CHAPTER XVII. The Master said, "When we see men of worth, we should think of equalling them; when we see men of a contrary character, we should turn inwards and examine ourselves."

CHAPTER XVIII. The Master said, "In serving his parents, *a son* may remonstrate with them, but gently; when he sees that they do not incline to follow *his advice*, he shows an increased degree of reverence, but does not abandon *his purpose;* and should they punish him, he does not allow himself to murmur."

ings. 忠 and 恕, which seem to be two things, are both formed from 心, 'the heart,' 忠 being compounded of 中, 'middle,' 'centre,' and 心, and 恕 of 如 'as,' and 心. The 'centre heart'=I, the *ego*, and the 'as heart'=the I in sympathy' with others. 忠 is duty-doing, on a consideration, or from the impulse, of one's own self; 恕 is duty doing, on the principle of reciprocity. The ch. is important, showing that Conf. only claimed to unfold and enforce duties indicated by man's mental constitution. He was simply a moral philosopher. Obs. 唯, up. 2d tone,='yes.' Some say that 門人 must mean Tsang's own disciples, and that had they been those of Conf., we should have read 弟子. The criticism can't be depended on. 而已矣 is a very emphatic—'and nothing more.'

16. HOW RIGHTEOUSNESS AND SELFISHNESS DISTINGUISH THE SUPERIOR MAN AND THE SMALL MAN. 喻=曉, 'to understand.' 於 is here to be dwelt on and may be compared with the Hebrew *eth*.

17. THE LESSONS TO BE LEARNED FROM OBSERVING MEN OF DIFFERENT CHARACTERS. Of the final particles 焉 and 也, it is said, 二字頗有抑揚警醒意, 'they have something of a repressive, expansive, warning force.'

18. HOW A SON MAY REMONSTRATE WITH HIS PARENTS ON THEIR FAULTS. See the 禮記, XII. i. 15. 幾, up. 1st tone, 'mildly,'=the 下氣, 怡色, 柔聲 of the 內則. 志 is the will of the parents. 又敬=更加孝敬, 'again increasing his filial reverence,' the 起敬起孝 of the 內則. 不違 is not abandoning his purpose of remonstrance, and not as 包咸 says in the

不違、勞而不怨。

十九章 子曰、父母在、不遠遊、遊必有方。

二十章 子曰、三年無改於父之道、可謂孝矣。

廿一章 子曰、父母之年、不可不知也、一則以喜、一則以懼。

廿二章 子曰、古者言之不出、恥躬之不逮也。

廿三章 子曰、以約、失之者鮮矣。

CHAPTER XIX. The Master said, "While his parents are alive, *the son* may not go abroad to a distance. If he does go abroad, he must have a fixed place to which he goes."

CHAPTER XX. The Master said, "If the son for three years does not alter from the way of his father, he may be called filial."

CHAPTER XXI. The Master said, "The years of parents may by no means not be kept in the memory, as an occasion at once for joy and for fear."

CHAPTER XXII. The Master said, "The reason why the ancients did not readily give utterance to their words, was that they feared lest their actions should not come up to them."

CHAPTER XXIII. The Master said, "The cautious seldom err."

comment given by Ho An, 不敢違父母意, 'not daring to go against the mind of his parents.' 勞='toiled and pained,' what the 內則 says, 撻之流血, 'should they beat him till the blood flows.'

19. A SON OUGHT NOT TO GO TO A DISTANCE WHERE HE WILL NOT BE ABLE TO PAY THE DUE SERVICES TO HIS PARENTS. 方=一定向, 'a fixed direction or quarter,' whence he may be recalled, if necessary.

20. A REPETITION OF PART OF I. 11.

21. WHAT EFFECT THE AGE OF PARENTS SHOULD HAVE ON THEIR CHILDREN. 知, it is said, conveys here 念念不忘意, 'the meaning of unforgetting thoughtfulness.'

22. THE VIRTUE OF THE ANCIENTS SEEN IN THEIR SLOWNESS TO SPEAK. Obs. the force of the two 之.—'The not coming forth of the words of the ancients was shame about the not coming up to them of their actions.'

23. ADVANTAGE OF CAUTION. Collie's version, which I have adopt., is here happy. 約, see ch. 2. The 'binding' here is of one's-self, self-restraint,='caution.' 失之, 'loses *it*,' 之 referring to whatev. bus. the cautious may be engaged in. 之, foll. an act. verb, often makes it neuter; at least, a neuter verb renders the expression best in English.

〔二十四章〕子曰、君子欲訥於言、而敏於行。

〔二十五章〕子曰、德不孤、必有鄰。

〔二十六章〕子游曰、事君數、斯辱矣、朋友數、斯疏矣。

CHAPTER XXIV. The Master said, "The superior man wishes to be slow in his words and earnest in his conduct."

CHAPTER XXV. The Master said, "Virtue is not left to stand alone. *He who practises it* will have neighbours."

CHAPTER XXVI. Tsze-yew said, "In serving a prince, frequent remonstrances lead to disgrace. Between friends, frequent reproofs make the friendship distant."

24. RULE OF THE KEUN-TSZE ABOUT HIS WORDS AND ACTIONS.

25. THE VIRTUOUS ARE NOT LEFT ALONE;—AN ENCOURAGEMENT TO VIRTUE. 孤, 'fatherless;' here=solitary, friendless. 德不孤=德無孤立之理, 'it is not the nature of virtue to be left to stand alone.' 鄰, see ch. I; here, generally, for friends, associates of like mind.

26. A LESSON TO COUNSELLORS AND FRIENDS. 數, up. 4th tone, read *shŏ*, 'frequently,' understood here in ref. to remonstrating or reproving.

BOOK V. KUNG-YAY CH'ANG.

公冶長第五

〔第一章〕子〔一節〕謂公冶長、可妻也、雖在縲紲之中、非其罪也。以其子妻之。〔二節〕子謂南容、

CHAPTER I. 1. The Master said of Kung-yay Ch'ang that he might be wived; although he was put in bonds, he had not been guilty of any crime. *Accordingly*, he gave him his own daughter to wife.

2. Of Nan Yung he said that if the country were well governed, he

HEADING OF THIS BOOK.—公冶長第五. Kung-yay Ch'ang, the surname and name of the first individual spoken of in it, heads this book, which is chiefly occupied with the judgment of the sage on the character of several of his disciples and others. As the decision frequently turns on their being possessed of that *jin*, or perfect virtue, which is so conspicuous in the last book, this is the reason, it is said, why the one immediately follows the other. As Tsze-kung appears in the book several times, some have fancied that it was compiled by his disciples.

邦有道不廢、邦無道免於刑戮。以其兄之子妻之。

第二章 子謂子賤、君子哉若人、魯無君子者、斯焉取斯。

第三章 子貢問曰、賜也何如。子曰、女器也。曰、何器也。曰、瑚璉也。

would not be out of office, and if it were ill governed, he would escape punishment and disgrace. He gave him the daughter of his own elder brother to wife.

CHAPTER II. The Master said, of Tsze-tseen, "Of superior virtue indeed is such a man! If there were not virtuous men in Loo, how could this man have acquired this character?"

CHAPTER III. Tsze-kung asked, "What do you say of me, Tsze? The Master said, "You are an utensil." "What utensil?" "A gemmed sacrificial utensil."

1. CONFUCIUS IN MARRIAGE-MAKING WAS GUIDED BY CHARACTER, AND NOT BY FORTUNE. 1. Of Kung-yay Ch'ang, tho' the son-in-law of Conf., nothing certain is known, and his tablet is only 3d on the west, among the οἱ πολλοί. Silly legends are told of his being put in prison from his bringing suspicion on himself by his knowl. of the language of birds. Choo He approves the interpr. of 縲 as mean. 'a black rope,' with which criminals were anciently bound (絏) in prison. 妻, and in par. 2, up. 3d tone, 'to wive,' 'to give to to wife.' 子, in both par.,='a daughter.' 2. Nan Yung, another of the disciples, is now 4th, east, in the outer hall. The discussions about who he was, and whether he is to be identified with 南宮适, and several other *aliases*, are very perplexing. See 四書改錯, I. 10, 11, and 摭餘說, I. 24. 廢, 'to lay, or be laid aside,' here, *i. e.*, *from office*. 戮, 'to put to death,' has also the lighter meaning of 'disgrace.' We cannot tell whether Conf. is giving his impress. of Yung's char., or referring to events that had taken place.

2. THE KEUN-TSZE FORMED BY INTERCOURSE WITH OTHER KEUN-TSZE. Tsze-tseen, by surname 宓 (=虙, and said to be *i. q.* 伏), and named 不齊, appears to have been of some note among the disci. of Conf., both as an administrator and writer, tho' his tablet is now only 2d west, in the outer hall. What chiefly disting. him, as appears here, was his cultivation of the friendship of men of ability and virtue, 若人 is more than '*this* man.' It is 若此人, 'a man such as this.' See the 註疏 *in loc.* The first 斯 is 'this *man*;' the second, 'this *virtue*.' The paraphrasts complete the last clause thus:—斯將何所取以成斯德乎, 'what friends could this man have chosen to complete this virtue?'

3. WHERETO TSZE-KUNG HAD ATTAINED. See I. 10, II. 12. The 瑚璉 were vessels richly adorned, used to contain grain-offerings in the Imper. ancestral temples. Under the Hea dyn., they were called 瑚, and 璉, under the Yin. See the Le Ke, XIV. 27. While the sage did not grant to Tsze that he was a *Keun-tsze* (II. 12), he made him 'a vessel of honour,' valuable and fit for use on high occasions.

第四章 一節 或曰、雍也仁、而不佞。二節 子曰、焉用佞、禦人以口給、屢憎於人、不知其仁、焉用佞。

第五章 子使漆雕開仕。對曰、吾斯之未能信。子說。

第六章 子曰、道不行、乘桴浮于海、從我者、

CHAPTER IV. 1. Some one said, "Yung is truly virtuous, but he is not ready with his tongue."

2. The Master said, "What is the good of being ready with the tongue? They who meet men with smartnesses of speech, for the most part procure themselves hatred. I know not whether he be truly virtuous, but why should he show readiness of the tongue?"

CHAPTER V. The Master was wishing Tseih-teaou K'ae to enter on official employment. He replied, "I am not yet able to rest in the assurance of THIS." The Master was pleased.

CHAPTER VI. The Master said, "My doctrines make no way. I will get upon a raft, and float about on the sea. He that will accompany me will be Yew, I dare to say." Tsze-loo hearing this was

4. OF YEN YUNG. READINESS WITH THE TONGUE NO PART OF VIRTUE. 1. 冉雍, styled 仲弓, has his tablet the second, on the east of Conf. own tablet, among 'the wise ones.' His father was a worthless character (see VI. 4), but he himself was the opposite. 佞 means 'ability,' generally, then 'ability of speech,' often, though not here, with the bad sense of artfulness and flattery. 2. Conf. would not grant that Yung was 仁, but his not being 佞 was in his favour rather than otherwise. 口給 (read *keĕ*. See Dict.), 'smartnesses of speech.' 焉 is here 'why,' rather than 'how.' The first 焉用仁 is a gen. statement, not having, like the sec., special reference to Yen Yung. In the 註疏, 不知其仁焉用佞, is read as one sentence;—'I do not know how the virtuous should also use readiness of speech.' This is not so good as the received interpretation.

5. TSEIH-TEAOU K'AE'S OPINION OF THE QUALIFICATIONS NECESSARY TO TAKING OFFICE. Tseih-teaou, now 6th, on the east, in the out. hall, was styled 子若. His name originally was 啟, changed into 開, on the accession of the Emperor 孝景, A. D. 155, whose name was also 啟. The diff. in the ch. is with 斯—what does it refer to? and with 信—what is its force? In the ch. about the disciples in the 家語, it is said that K'ae was reading in the Shoo-king, when Conf. spoke to him about taking office, and he pointed to the book, or some particular passage in it, saying, 'I am not yet able to rest in the assurance of (信=眞知確見) *this*.' It may have been so. Obs. the force of the 之;—'There is as yet my want of faith of this.'

6. CONFUCIUS PROPOSING TO WITHDRAW FROM THE WORLD:—A LESSON TO TSZE-LOO. Tsze-loo supposed his master really meant to leave the world, and the idea of floating along the coasts, pleased his ardent temper, while he was delighted with the compliment paid to himself. But Conf. only expressed in this way his regret at the backwardness of men to receive his doctrines. 無所取材 is diff. of interpretation. Choo He takes 材 as being for 裁, 'to cut out clothes,' 'to estimate, discrimi-

論語

其由與。子路聞之喜。子曰、由也、好勇過我、無所取材。

第七章 一節 孟武伯問子路仁乎。子曰、不知也。二節 又問。子曰、由也、千乘之國、可使治其賦也、不知其仁也。三節 求也何如。子曰、求也、千室之邑、百乘之家、可使爲之宰也、不知其仁也。四節 赤也何如。子曰、赤也、束帶立於朝、可使與賓客言也、不知其仁也。

glad, upon which the Master said, "Yew is fonder of daring than I am. He does not exercise his judgment upon matters."

CHAPTER VII. 1. Măng Woo asked about Tsze-loo, whether he was perfectly virtuous. The Master said, "I do not know."

2. He asked again, when the Master replied, "In a kingdom of a thousand chariots, Yew might be employed to manage the military levies, but I do not know whether he be perfectly virtuous."

3. "And what do you say of K'ew?" The Master replied, "In a city of a thousand families, or a house of a hundred chariots, K'ew might be employed as governor, but I do not know whether he is perfectly virtuous."

4. "What do you say of Ch'ih?" The Master replied, "With his sash girt and standing in a court, Ch'ih might be employed to converse with the visitors and guests, but I do not know whether he is perfectly virtuous."

nate,' and hence the mean. in the transl. An old comm., 鄭玄, keeping the mean. of 材, explains— 無所取於桴材, ='my meaning is not to be found in the raft.' Another old writer makes 材=哉, and putting a stop at 勇 expl.—'Yew is fond of daring; He cannot go beyond himself to find my meaning.' 與, here='I dare to say.'

7. OF TSZE-LOO, TSZE-YEW, AND TSZE-HWA. 1. 孟武伯, See II. 6. 2. 千乘之國, see I. 5. 賦, properly, 'revenues,' 'taxes,' but the quota of soldiers contributed being regul. by the amt. of the rev., the term is used here for the forces, or *military levies*. 3. 求 see III. 6. 百乘之家, in opp. to 千乘之國, was the secondary fief, the territory appropriated to the highest nobles or officers in a 國 or state, suppos. also to comprehend 1000 fami-

第八章 一節 子謂子貢曰、女與回也、孰愈。二節 對曰、賜也、何敢望回、回也、聞一以知十、賜也、聞一以知二。三節 子曰、弗如也、吾與女、弗如也。

第九章 一節 宰予晝寢。子曰、朽木不可雕也、糞土之牆、不可杇也、於予與何誅。二節 子曰、始吾於人也、聽其言而信其行、今吾於人也、

CHAPTER VIII. 1. The Master said to Tsze-kung, "Which do you consider superior, yourself or Hwuy?"

2. Tsze-kung replied, "How dare I compare myself with Hwuy? Hwuy hears one point and knows all about a subject; I hear one point and know a second."

3. The Master said, "You are not equal to him. I grant you, you are not equal to him."

CHAPTER IX. 1. Tsae Yu being asleep during the day time, the Master said, "Rotten wood cannot be carved; a wall of dirty earth will not receive the trowel. This Yu!—what is the use of my reproving him?"

2. The Master said, "At first, my way with men was to hear their words, and give them credit for their conduct. Now my way is to hear their words, and look at their conduct. It is from Yu that I have learned to make this change."

lies. 爲之宰, 'To be its governor.' This is a pec. idiom. 4. Ch'ih, surnamed 公西, and styled 子華, having now the 14th place, west, in the out. hall, was famous among the disciples for his knowl. of rules of cer., and those especially relating to dress and intercourse. 朝, low. 1st tone. 賓 and 客 may be distinguished, the former indicating neighbouring princes visiting the court, the lat. ministers and officers of the state present as guests.

8. SUPERIORITY OF YEN HWUY TO TSZE-KUNG. 2. 望, 'to look to,' 'to look up to,' here =比, 'to compare with.' 'One' is the begin. of numbers, and 'ten' the completion; hence the mean. of 聞一以知十, as in the transl. 3. 與=許, 'to allow,' 'to grant to.' Ho An gives here the comm. of 包咸, (about A. D. 50), who interprets strangely,—'I and you are both not equal to him,' saying that Conf. thus comforted Tsze-kung.

9. THE IDLENESS OF TSAE YU AND ITS REPROOF. 1. 於予與, 'In the case of Yu!' 與 has here the force of an exclam.; so, below. 誅, a strong term, to mark the severity of the reproof. 2. 子曰 is superfluous. The char. were probably added by a transcriber. If not, they should head another chapter.

聽其言而觀其行、於予與改是。

第十章 子曰、吾未見剛者。或對曰、申棖。子曰、棖也慾、焉得剛。

十一章 子貢曰、我不欲人之加諸我也、吾亦欲無加諸人。子曰、賜也、非爾所及也。

十二章 子貢曰、夫子之文章、

CHAPTER X. The Master said, "I have not seen a firm and unbending man." Some one replied, "There is Shin Ch'ang." "Ch'ang," said the Master, "is under the influence of his passions; how can he be pronounced firm and unbending?"

CHAPTER XI. Tsze-kung said, "What I do not wish men to do to me, I also wish not to do to men." The Master said, "Tsze, you have not attained to that."

CHAPTER XII. Tsze-kung said, "The Master's *personal* displays *of his principles*, and *ordinary* descriptions of them may be heard. His discourses about *man's* nature, and the way of Heaven, cannot be heard."

10. UNBENDING VIRTUE CANNOT COEXIST WITH INDULGENCE OF THE PASSIONS. Shin Ch'ang (there are several *aliases*, but they are disputed,) was one of the minor disciples, of whom little or nothing is known. He was styled 子周, and his place is 31st, east, in the out. ranges. 剛 is to be understood with reference to virtue. 慾 is 情所好, 'what the passions love,' 'lusts.' 焉得 are said to=不是, and not 不能. I have transl. accordingly.

11. THE DIFFICULTY OF ATTAINING TO THE NOT WISHING TO DO TO OTHERS AS WE WISH THEM NOT TO DO TO US. It is said—此章見無我之不易及, 'this ch. shows that the *no I* (freed. from selfishness) is not easily reached.' In the 中庸, XIII. 3, it is said—施諸己而不願亦勿施諸人, 'what you do not like when done to yourself, do not do to others.' The diff. between it and the sent. here is said to be that of 恕, 'reciprocity,' and 仁, 'benevolence,' or the highest virtue, appar. in the adv. 勿 and 無, the one prohibitive, and the other a simple, unconstrained, negation. The golden rule of the Gospel is higher than both,—'Do ye unto others as ye would that others should do unto you.' 諸=於; 加諸, or 加於, 'to add upon,' 'to do to.'

12. THE GRADUAL WAY IN WHICH CONFUCIUS COMMUNICATED HIS DOCTRINES. So the lesson of this ch. is summed up, but there is hardly another more perplexing to a transl. 文章 is the comm. name for essays, elegant literary compositions. Of course that mean. is out of the question. Whatever is *figured* and *brilliant* is 文, whatever is *orderly* and *defined* is 章. The comm., accordingly, make 文 to be the deportment and manners of the sage, and 章 his ordin. discourses, but 聞 is an inapprop. term

可得而聞也、夫子之言性與天道、不可得而聞也。

十三章 子路有聞、未之能行、唯恐有聞。

十四章 子貢問曰、孔文子、何以謂之文也。子曰、敏而好學、不恥下問、是以謂之文也。

十五章 子謂子產、有君子之道四焉、其行己也恭、其事上也敬、其養民也惠、其使民

CHAPTER XIII. When Tsze-loo heard anything, if he had not yet carried it into practice, he was only afraid lest he should hear *something else.*

CHAPTER XIV. Tsze-kung asked saying, "On what ground did Kung-wăn get that title of WAN?" The Master said, "He was of an active nature and yet fond of learning, and he was not ashamed to ask *and learn of* his inferiors!—On these grounds he has been styled WAN."

CHAPTER XV. The Master said of Tsze-ch'an that he had four of the characteristics of a superior man:—in his conduct of himself, he was humble; in serving his superiors, he was respectful; in nourishing the people, he was kind; in ordering the people, he was just."

with reference to the former. These things, however, were level to the cap. of the disci. generally, and they had the benefit of them. As to his views about man's nature, the gift of Heaven, and the way of Heaven generally;—these he only commun. to those who were prepared to receive them, and Tsze-kung is supposed to have expressed himself thus, after being on some occasion so privileged.

13. THE ARDOUR OF TSZE-LOO IN PRACTISING THE MASTER'S INSTRUCTIONS. The concl. 唯恐有聞 is to be completed 唯恐復有所聞, as in the translation.

14. AN EXAMPLE OF THE PRINCIPLE ON WHICH HONORARY POSTHUMOUS TITLES WERE CONFERRED. 文, corresponding nearly to our 'accomplished,' was the posthum. title given to 子圉, an officer of the state of Wei, and a contempor. of Conf. Many of his actions had been of a doubtful char., which made Tsze-kung stumble at the applica. to him of so hon. an epithet. But Conf. shows that, whatever he might otherwise be, he *had* those qualities, which justified his being so denominated. The rule for posth. titles in China has been, and is, very much—'*De mortuis nil nisi bonum.*'

15. THE EXCELLENT QUALITIES OF TSZE-CH'AN. Tsze-ch'an, named 公孫僑, was the chief min. of the state of Ching (鄭), the ablest perhaps, and most upright, of all the statesmen among Conf. contemporaries. The sage wept when he heard of his death. The old interpret. take 使 in the sense of 'employing,' but it seems to express more, and = 'ordering,' 'regulating.'

論語

也義。

十六 子曰、晏平仲、善與人交、久而敬之。

十七 子曰、臧文仲、居蔡、山節藻梲、何如其知也。

十八 子張問曰、令尹子文、三仕爲令尹、無喜色、三已之、無慍色、舊令尹之政、必以告新令尹、何如。子曰、忠矣。曰、仁矣乎。曰、

CHAPTER XVI. The Master said, "Gan P'ing knew well how to maintain friendly intercourse. The acquaintance might be long, but he showed the *same* respect *as at first*."

CHAPTER XVII. The Master said, "Tsang Wăn kept a large tortoise in a house, on the capitals of the pillars of which he had hills made, with representations of duckweed on the small pillars *above the beams supporting the rafters*.—Of what sort was his wisdom?"

CHAPTER XVIII. 1. Tsze-chang asked, saying, "The minister Tsze-wăn, thrice took office, and manifested no joy in his countenance. Thrice he retired from office, and manifested no displeasure. He made it a point to inform the new minister of the way in which he had conducted the government;—what do you say of him?" "The Master replied, "He was loyal." "Was he perfectly virtuous?" "I do not know. How can he be pronounced perfectly virtuous?"

16. HOW TO MAINTAIN FRIENDSHIP. 'Familiarity breeds contempt,' and with contempt friendship ends. It was not so with Gan P'ing, another of the worthies of Confucius' times. He was a prin. minister of Ts'e (齊), by name 嬰. P'ing (=' Ruling and averting calamity') was his posth. title. If we were to render 仲, the name would be 'Gan P'ing, *secundus*.' Obs. the anteced. to 之 is 人.

17. THE SUPERSTITION OF TSANG WAN. Tsang Wăn (wăn is the hon. epithet, and 仲, see last ch.) had been a great off. in Loo, and left a reputation for wisdom, which Conf. did not think was deserved. His full name was 臧孫辰. He was descended from the duke 孝 (B. C. 794-767), whose son was styled 子臧. This Tsang was taken by his descendants as their surname. This is mentioned to shew one of the ways in which surnames were formed among the Chinese. 蔡 'a large tortoise,' so called, because the state of that name was famous for its tortoises. 居 is used as an act. verb, =藏. The 節=柱頭斗栱, 'the capitals of the pillars.' The 梲 may be seen in any Ch. house. There being no ceilings, the whole structure of the roof is displayed, and these small pillars are very conspicuous. The old interpr. make the keep. such a tortoise an act of usurpa. on the part of Tsang Wăn. Choo He finds the point of Conf. words in the keeping it in such a style.

18. THE PRAISE OF PERFECT VIRTUE IS NOT TO BE LIGHTLY ACCORDED. 1. Ling yin, lit.. 'good corrector,' was the name given to the chief min. of Tsoo (楚). 尹 is still applied to officers;

未知、焉得仁。二節 崔子弑齊君、陳文子有馬十乘、棄而違之、至於他邦、則曰、猶吾大夫崔子也、違之、之一邦、則又曰、猶吾大夫崔子也、違之、何如。子曰、清矣。曰、仁矣乎。曰、未知、焉得仁。

十九章 季文子三思而後行。子聞之曰、再、斯可矣。

二十章 子曰、甯武子、邦有道、則

2. *Tsze-chang* proceeded, "When the officer Ts'uy killed the prince of Ts'e, Ch'in Wăn, though he was the owner of forty horses, abandoned them and left the country. Coming to another state, he said, 'They are here like our great officer, Ts'uy,' and left it. He came to a second state, and with the same observation left it also;—what do you say of him?" The Master replied, "He was pure." "Was he perfectly virtuous?" "I do not know. How can he be pronounced perfectly virtuous?"

CHAPTER XIX. Ke Wăn thought thrice, and then acted. When the Master was informed of it, he said, "Twice may do."

CHAPTER XX. The Master said, "When good order prevailed in his country, Ning Woo acted the part of a wise man. When his country was in disorder, he acted the part of a stupid man. Others may equal his wisdom, but they cannot equal his stupidity."

e. *g.*, the prefect of a department is called 府尹. Tsze-wăn, surnamed 鬬, and named 穀於菟 ('suckled by a tiger'), had been noted for the things mentioned by Tsze-chang, but the sage would not concede that he was therefore 仁. 2. 崔 was a great officer of Ts'e. Gan P'ing (ch. 16), distinguished himself on the occasion of the murder (B. C. 547) here referred to. Chin Wăn was likewise an officer of Ts'e. 之一邦, 之 is a verb, =往. 乘, low. 3d tone, as in I. 5, but with a diff. meaning, 'a team of four horses.'

19. PROMPT DECISION GOOD. Wăn was the posth. title of 季行父, a faithful and disinterested officer of Loo. 三, up. 3d tone, 'three times,' but some say it=二 三, 'again and again.' Comp. Robert Hall's remark,—'In matters of conscience first thoughts are best.'

20. THE UNCOMMON BUT ADMIRABLE STUPIDITY OF NING WOO. Ning Woo (武, hon. ep. See II. 6). was an officer of Wei in the times of Wăn, (B. C. 635-627), the second of the five *pa*. (III. 22). In the first part of his official life, the state was quiet and prosperous, and he 'wisely' acquitted himself of his duties. Afterwards came confusion. The prince was driven from the throne, and Ning Yu (俞 was his name) might, like other wise men, have retired from the danger. But he 'foolishly,' as it seem-

知、邦無道、則愚、其知可及也、其愚不可及也。

二十一 子在陳曰、歸與歸與、吾黨之小子、狂簡、斐然成章、不知所以裁之。

二十二 子曰、伯夷叔齊、不念舊惡、怨是用希。

二十三 子曰、孰謂微生高

CHAPTER XXI. When the Master was in Ch'in, he said, "Let me return! Let me return! The little children of my school are ambitious and too hasty. They are accomplished and complete so far, but they do not know how to restrict and shape themselves."

CHAPTER XXII. The Master said, "Pih-e and Shuh-ts'e did not keep the former wickednesses of men in mind, and hence the resentments directed towards them were few."

CHAPTER XXIII. The Master said, "Who says of Wei-shang Kaou that he is upright? One begged some vinegar of him, and he begged it of a neighbour and gave it him."

ed, chose to follow the fortunes of his prince, and yet adroitly brought it about in the end, that the prince was reinstated and order restored.

21. THE ANXIETY OF CONFUCIUS ABOUT THE TRAINING OF HIS DISCIPLES. Confucius was thrice in Ch'in. It must have been the 3d time, when he thus expressed himself. He was then over 60 years, and being convinced that he was not to see for himself the triumph of his principles, he became the more anxious about their transmission, and the train. of the disci. in order to that. Such is the com. view of the ch. Some say, however, that it is not to be understood of all the disciples. Comp. Mencius, VII. ii. 37. 吾黨之小子, an affectionate way of speaking of the disciples. 狂, 'mad,' also, 'extravagant,' 'highminded.' The 狂 are naturally 簡, hasty and careless of minutiæ. 斐然, 'accomplished-like.' 章, see ch. 12. 成章, 'something complete.' 裁, see ch. 6, but its applica. here is somewhat diff. The anteced. to 之 is all the preced. description.

22. THE GENEROSITY OF PIH-E AND SHUH-TS'E, AND ITS EFFECTS. These were ancient worthies of the closing period of the Shang dynasty. Comp. Mencius, II.i.2, 9, *et al.* They were brothers, sons of the king of Koo-chuh (孤竹), named respectively 允 and 致. E and Ts'e are their hon. epithets, and 伯 and 叔 only indicate their relation to each other as elder and younger. Pih-e and Shuh-ts'e, however, are in effect their names in the mouths and writings of the Chinese. Koo-chuh was a small state, included in the pres. depart. of 永平, in Pih-chih-le. Their father left his kingdom to Shuh-ts'e, who refused to take the place of his elder brother. Pih-e in turn declined the throne, so they both abandoned it, and retired into obscurity. When king Woo was taking his measures against the tyrant Chow, they made their appearance, and remonstrated against his course. Finally, they died of hunger, rather than live under the new dynasty. They were celebrated for their purity, and aversion to men whom they considered bad, but Conf. here brings out their generosity. 怨是用希=怨是以希, 'Resentments thereby were few.'

23. SMALL MEANNESSES INCONSISTENT WITH UPRIGHTNESS. It is implied that Kaou gave the vinegar as from himself.

直、或乞醯焉、乞諸其鄰而與之。

二十四章 子曰、巧言令色、足恭、左丘明恥之、丘亦恥之、匿怨而友其人、左丘明恥之、丘亦恥之。

二十五章 顏淵季路侍。子曰、盍各言爾志。一節 子路曰、願車馬、衣輕裘、與朋友共、敝之而無憾。二節 顏淵曰、願無

CHAPTER XXIV. The Master said, "Fine words, an insinuating appearance, and excessive respect;—Tso-k'ew Ming was ashamed of them. I also am ashamed of them. To conceal resentment against a person, and appear friendly with him;— Tso-k'ew Ming was ashamed of such conduct. I also am ashamed of it."

CHAPTER XXV. 1. Yen Yuen and Ke Loo being by his side, the Master said to them, "Come, let each of you tell his wishes."

2. Tsze-loo said, "I should like, having chariots and horses, and light fur dresses, to share them with my friends, and though they should spoil them, I would not be displeased."

3. Yen Yuen said, "I should like not to boast of my excellence, nor to make a display of my meritorious deeds."

4. Tsze-loo then said, "I should like, sir, to hear your wishes." The Master said, "*They are*, in regard to the aged, to give them rest; in regard to friends, to show them sincerity; in regard to the young, to treat them tenderly."

24. PRAISE OF SINCERITY, AND OF TSO-K'EW MING. 巧言令色, see I. 3. 足恭, 'excessive respect,' 足 being in 3d tone, read *tseu*. Some of the old comm., keeping the usual tone and meaning of 足, interpret the phrase of movements of the 'feet' to indicate respect. The discussions about Tso-k'ew Ming are endless. See 撫餘說, I. 30. It is sufficient for us to rest in the judgment of the comm. 程, that he was an ancient of reputation.' It is not to be received that he was a disciple of Conf. 丘 was the name of Conf. The Chinese decline pronouncing it, always substituting *mow* (某), 'such an one,' for it.

25. THE DIFFERENT WISHES OF YEN YUEN, TSZE-LOO, AND CONFUCIUS. 1. 盍各言爾志, 'why not each tell your will?' 2. A student is apt to translate—'I should like to have chariots and horses, &c,' but 共 is the import. word in the par., and under the regimen of 願. 衣, up. 3d tone, 'to wear.' Several writers carry the reg. of 願 on to 之, and removing the comma at 共, read 共敝 together, but this constr. is not so good. 3. In Ho An's compilation 施勞 is interpr.—'not to impose troublesome affairs on others.' Choo He's view is better. Comp. the Yih-king, 繫

伐善、無施勞。四節子路曰、願聞子之志。子曰、老者安之、朋友信之、少者懷之。

廿六章子曰、已矣乎、吾未見能見其過、而內自訟者也。

廿七章子曰、十室之邑、必有忠信、如丘者焉、不如丘之好學也。

CHAPTER XXVI. The Master said, "It is all over! I have not yet seen one who could perceive his faults, and inwardly accuse himself."

CHAPTER XXVII. The Master said, "In a hamlet of ten families, there may be found one honourable and sincere as I am, but not so fond of learning."

辭, I. ii. 10. 4. 信之=與之以信, 'To be with them with sincerity.'—The Master and the disci., it is said, agreed in being devoid of selfishness. Hwuy's, however, was seen in a higher style of mind and object than Yew's. In the sage, there was an unconsciousness of self, and without any effort, he propos. acting in regard to his classification of men just as they ought severally to be acted to.

26. A LAMENT OVER MEN'S PERSISTENCE IN ERROR. The 乎 has an exclamat. force. 訟, 'to litigate.' 內自訟者, 'one who brings himself before the bar of his conscience.' The remark affirms a fact, inexplicable on Conf. view of the nature of man. But perhaps such an exclamation should not be pressed too closely.

27. THE HUMBLE CLAIM OF CONFUCIUS FOR HIMSELF. 邑 (人聚會之稱也) is 'the designation of the place where men are collected together,' and may be applied from a hamlet upwards to a city. 忠=忠厚, 'honourable,' 'substantial.' Confucius thus did not claim higher natural and moral qualities than others, but sought to perfect himself by learning.

BOOK VI. YUNG YAY.

雍也第六

第一章 子(一節)曰、雍也、可使南面。(二節)仲弓問子桑伯子。子曰、可也、簡。(三節)仲弓曰、居敬而行簡、以臨其民、不亦可乎、居簡而行簡、無乃大簡乎。(四節)子曰、雍之言然。

CHAPTER I. 1. The Master said, "There is Yung!—He might occupy the place of a prince."

2. Chung-kung asked about Tsze-sang Pih-tsze. The Master said, "He may pass. He does not mind small matters."

3. Chung-kung said, "If a man cherish in himself a reverential feeling *of the necessity of attention to business*, though he may be easy in small matters, in his government of the people, that may be allowed. But if he cherish in himself that easy feeling, and also carry it out in his practice, is not such an easy mode of procedure excessive?"

4. The Master said, "Yung's words are right."

HEADING OF THIS BOOK.—雍也第六. 'There is Yung!' commences the first ch., and stands as the title of the book. Its subjects are much akin to those of the preceding book, and therefore, it is said, they are in juxtaposition.

1. THE CHARACTERS OF YEN YUNG AND TSZE-SANG PIH-TSZE, AS REGARDS THEIR ADAPTATION FOR GOVERNMENT. 1. 可使南面, 'might be employed with his face to the south.' In China, the emperor sits facing the south. So did the princes of the states in their several courts in Conf. time. An explan. of the practice is attempted in the Yih-King, 說卦 ch. 9, 離也者明也, 萬物皆相見, 南方之卦也, 聖人南面而聽天下, 向明而治, 蓋取此也, 'The diagram Le conveys the idea of brightness, when all things are exhibited to one another. It is the diagram of the south. The custom of the sages (*i. e.*, monarchs) to sit with their faces to the south, *and listen to the representations* of the empire, governing towards the bright region, was taken from this.' 2. Obs. Chung-kung was the designation of Yen Yung, see V. 4. 簡 has here substantially the same meaning as in V. 21,=不煩 'not troubling,' *i. e.*, one's self about small matters. With ref. to that place, however, the Dict., after the old comm., explains it by 大, 'great.' 3. Of Tsze-sang Pih-tsze, we know nothing certain but what is here stated. Choo He seems to be wrong in approving the identifica. of him with a Tsze-sang Hoo. 居敬, 'to dwell in respect,' to have the mind imbued with it. 敬=敬事 in I. 5.

論語

第二章 一節 哀公問弟子孰爲好學。二節 孔子對曰、有顏回者好學、不遷怒、不貳過、不幸短命死矣、今也則亡、未聞好學者也。

第三章 一節 子華使於齊、冉子爲其母請粟。子曰、與之釜。請益。曰、與之庾。冉子與之粟五秉。二節 子曰、赤之適齊也、乘肥馬、衣輕裘、吾

CHAPTER II. The duke Gae asked which of the disciples loved to learn. Confucius replied to him, "There was Yen Hwuy; HE loved to learn. He did not transfer his anger; he did not repeat a fault. Unfortunately, his appointed time was short and he died; and now there is not *such another*. I have not yet heard of any one who loves to learn *as he did*."

CHAPTER III. 1. Tsze hwa being employed on a mission to Ts'e, the disciple Yen requested grain for his mother. The Master said, "Give her a *foo*." *Yen* requested more. "Give her an *yu*," said the Master, Yen gave her five *ping*.

2. The Master said, "When Ch'ih was proceeding to Ts'e, he had fat horses to his carriage, and wore light furs. I have heard

2. THE RARITY OF A TRUE LOVE TO LEARN. HWUY'S SUPERIORITY TO THE OTHER DISCIPLES. In 有顏回者, 者='that.'—'There was that Yen Hwuy.' 'He did not transfer his anger,' *i. e.*, his anger was no tumultuary passion in the mind, but was excited by some specific cause, to which alone it was directed. 短命死矣,='He died an early death,' but 命 conveys also the idea in the transl. The two last clauses are completed thus:—今也,則亡 (read as, and=無) 是人,未聞如是之好學者也.

3. DISCRIMINATION OF CONFUCIUS IN REWARDING OR SALARYING OFFICERS. 1. 使, up. 3d tone, 'to commission,' or 'to be commissioned.' Choo He says the commission was a private one from Confucius, but this is not likely. The old interpretation makes it a public one from the court of Loo; see 四書改錯, III. 9. 冉子, 'The disciple Yen'; see III. 6. Yen is here styled 子, like 有子, in I. 2, but only in narrative, not as introducing any wise utterance. A *foo* contained 6 *tow* (斗), and 4 *shing* (升), or 64 *shing*. The *Yu* contained 160 *shing*, and the *ping* 16 *hŏ* (斛), or 1600 *shing*. A *shing* of the present day is about ¼th less than an English pint. 2. The 之 in 吾聞之, refers to what follows. 3. In He An's edition, another chapter commences here. Yuen Sze, named 憲, is now the third, east, in the outer hall of the temples. He was noted for his pursuit of truth, and carelessness of worldly advantages. After the death of Conf., he withdrew into retirement in Wei. It is related that Tsze-kung, high in official station, came one day in great style to visit him. Sze received him in a tattered coat, and Tsze-kung asking

聞之也、君子周急、不繼富。〇三節原思爲之宰、與之粟九百、辭。〇四節子曰、毋、以與爾鄰里鄉黨乎。

第四章 子謂仲弓曰、犂牛之子、騂且角、雖欲勿用、山川其舍諸。

第五章 子曰、回也、其心三月不違仁、其餘、則日月至焉而已矣。

that a superior man helps the distressed, but does not add to the wealth of the rich."

3. Yuen Sze being made governor *of his town by the Master*, he gave him nine hundred measures of grain, but Sze declined them.

4. The Master said, "Do not decline them. May you not give them away in the neighbourhoods, hamlets, towns, and villages?"

CHAPTER IV. The Master, speaking of Chung-kung, said, "If the calf of a brindled cow be red and horned, although man may not wish to use it, would *the spirits of* the mountains and rivers put it aside?"

CHAPTER V. The Master said, "Such was Hwuy that for three months there would be nothing in his mind contrary to perfect virtue. The others may attain to this on some days or in some months, but nothing more."

him if he were ill, he replied, 'I have heard that to have no money is to be poor, and that to study truth and not be able to find it is to be ill.' This answer sent Tsze-kung away in confusion. The 900 measures (whatever they were) was the proper allowance for an officer of Sze's station. 爲之宰, See V. 7, though it is not easy to give the 之 the same reference here as in that passage. 4. According to ancient statutes, a *lin*, a *le*, a *heang*, and a *tang*, have each their specific number of component families, but the meaning is no more than—'the poor about you.' 乎 makes the remark='may you not, &c.'

4. THE VICES OF A FATHER SHOULD NOT DISCREDIT A VIRTUOUS SON. The father of Chung-kung (see V. 2) was a man of bad character,' and some would have visited this upon his son, which drew forth Conf. remark. The rules of the Chow dyn. required that sacrific. victims should be red, and have good horns. An animal with those qual., tho' it might spring from one not possessing them, would certainly not be unacceptable on that account to the spirits sacrificed to. I translate 子 by 'calf,' but it is not implied that the victim was young. 舍, up. 2d tone,=捨, 'to lay aside,' 'to put away.' 其舍諸=其舍之乎.

5. THE SUPERIORITY OF HWUY TO THE OTHER DISCIPLES. It is impossible to say whether we should translate here about Hwuy in the past or present tense. 違 here is not 違背, 'to oppose,' but 違去, 'to depart from.' 日月至, 'come to it,' *i. e.*, the line of perfect virtue, 'in the course of a day, or a month.' 日月 may also be, 'for a day or a month.' So in the 註疏.

論語

第六章 季康子問仲由、可使從政也與。子曰、由也果、於從政乎何有。曰、賜也、可使從政也與。曰、賜也達、於從政乎何有。曰、求也、可使從政也與。曰、求也藝、於從政乎何有。

第七章 季氏使閔子騫爲費宰、閔子騫曰、善爲我辭焉、如有復我者、則吾必在汶上矣。

CHAPTER VI. Ke K'ang asked, "Is Chung-yew fit to be employed as an officer of government?" The Master said, "Yew is a man of decision; what difficulty would he find in being an officer of government?" *K'ang* asked, "Is Tsze fit to be employed as an officer of government?" and was answered, "Tsze is a man of intelligence; what difficulty would he find in being an officer of government?" And to the same question about K'ew the Master gave the same reply, saying, "K'ew is a man of various ability."

CHAPTER VII. The chief of the Ke family sent to ask Min Tsze-k'een to be governor of Pe. Min Tsze-k'een said, "Decline the offer for me politely. If any one come again to me with a second invitation, I shall be *obliged to go and live* on the banks of the Wăn."

6. THE QUALITIES OF TSZE-LOO, TSZE-KUNG, AND TSZE-YEW, AND THEIR COMPETENCY TO ASSIST IN GOVERNMENT. The prince is called 爲政者, 'the *doer* of government;' his ministers and officers are styled 從政者, 'the *followers* of government.' 也與 and 何有 are set, the one expression against the other, the former indicating a doubt of the competency of the disciples, the latter affirming their more than competency.

7. MIN TSZE-K'EEN REFUSES TO SERVE THE KE FAMILY. The tablet of Tsze-k'een (his name was 損) is now the first on the east among 'the wise ones' of the temple. He was among the foremost of the disciples. Conf. praises his filial piety, and we see here, how he could stand firm in his virtue, and refuse the proffers of powerful but unprincipled families of his time. 使=使人來召, in the transl., and in 復 (*fow*, low. 3d tone) 我者, we must similarly understand, 復來召我者. 費, read *Pe*, was a place belonging to the Ke family. Its name is still preserved in 費縣 in the depart. of 沂州, in Shan-tung. The Wăn stream divided Ts'e and Loo. Tsze-k'een threatens, if he should be troubled again to retreat to Ts'e, where the Ke family could not reach him.

第八章 伯牛有疾、子問之、自牖執其手、曰、亡之、命矣夫、斯人也、而有斯疾也、斯人也、而有斯疾也。

第九章 子曰、賢哉回也、一簞食、一瓢飲、在陋巷、人不堪其憂、回也不改其樂、賢哉回也。

第十章 冉求曰、非不說子之道、力不足也。子曰、力不

CHAPTER VIII. Pih-new being sick, the Master went to ask for him. He took hold of his hand through the window, and said, "It is killing him. It is the appointment *of Heaven*, alas! That such a man should have such a sickness! That such a man should have such a sickness!"

CHAPTER IX. The Master said, "Admirable indeed was the virtue of Hwuy! With a single bamboo dish of rice, a single gourd dish of drink, and living in his mean narrow lane, while others could not have endured the distress, he did not allow his joy to be affected by it. Admirable indeed was the virtue of Hwuy!"

CHAPTER X. Yen K'ew said, "It is not that I do not delight in your doctrines, but my strength is insufficient." The Master said, "Those whose strength is insufficient give over in the middle of the way, but now you limit yourself."

8. LAMENT OF CONFUCIUS OVER THE MORTAL SICKNESS OF PIH-NEW. Pih-new, 'elder or uncle New,' was the denomination of 冉耕 who had an honourable place among the disciples of the sage. In the old interpr., his sickness is said to have been 惡疾, 'an evil disease,' by which name leprosy, called 癩, is intended, though that char. is now employed for 'itch.' Suffering from such a disease, Pih-new would not see people, and Confucius took his hand through the window. A differ. explanation of that circumstance is given by Choo He. He says that sick persons were usually placed on the north side of the apartment, but when the prince visited them, in order that he might appear to them with his face to the south (see ch. 1), they were moved to the south. On this occasion, Pih-new's friends wanted to receive Conf. after this royal fashion, which he avoided by not entering the house. 亡 appears as an act. verb 亡之, 'It is killing him,' 夫, low. 1st tone, generally an initial particle='now.' It is here final, and='alas!'

9. THE HAPPINESS OF HWUY INDEPENDENT OF POVERTY. The 簞 was simply a piece of the stem of a bamboo, and the 瓢 half of a gourd cut into two. 食, See II. 8. The eulogy turns much on 其 in 其樂, as opposed to 其憂, '*his* joy,' the delight which he had in the doctrines of his master, contrasted with the grief others would have felt under such poverty.

10. A HIGH AIM AND PERSEVERANCE PROPER TO A STUDENT. Conf. would not admit K'ew's apology for not attempting more than he did. 'Give over in the middle of the way,' *i. e.*, they go as long and as far as they can, they are pursuing when they stop.

足者、中道而廢、今女畫。

十一 子謂子夏曰、女爲君子儒、無爲小人儒。

十二 子游爲武城宰、子曰、女得人焉耳乎。曰、有澹臺滅明者、行不由徑、非公事、未嘗至於偃之室也。

十三 子曰、孟之反不伐、奔而殿、將入門、策其馬、曰、非敢後也、馬不進也。

CHAPTER XI. The Master said to Tsze-hea, "Do you be a scholar after the style of the superior man, and not after that of the mean man."

CHAPTER XII. Tsze-yew being governor of Woo-shing, the Master said to him, "Have you got *good* men *there*?" He answered, "There is Tan-t'ae Mëë-ming, who never in walking takes a short cut, and never comes to my office, excepting on public business."

CHAPTER XIII. The Master said, "Măng Che-fan does not boast of his merit. Being in the rear on an occasion of flight, when they were about to enter the gate, he whipt up his horse saying, 'It is not that I dare to be last. My horse would not advance.'"

11. HOW LEARNING SHOULD BE PURSUED. 君子 and 小人 here=adjectives, qualifying 儒. The 君子, it is said, learns 爲己, for his own real improvement and from duty; the 小人 learning 爲人, 'for men,' with a view to their opinion, and for his own material benefit.

12. THE CHARACTER OF TAN-T'AE MEE-MING. The ch. shows, according to Chinese comm., the advantage to people in authority of their having good men about them. In this way after their usual fashion, they seek for a profound meaning in the remark of Conf. Tan-t'ae Mëë-ming, who was styled 子羽, has his tablet the 2d east outside the hall. The accounts of him are very conflicting. Acc. to one, he was very good-looking, while another says he was so bad-looking that Conf. at first formed an unfavourable opinion of him, an error which he afterwards confessed on Mëë-ming's becoming eminent. He travelled southwards with not a few followers, and places near Soo-chow and elsewhere retain names indicative of his presence. 焉爾乎, three particles coming together are said to indicate the slow and deliberate manner in which the sage spoke. 滅明者, Comp. 顏回者 in ch. 2. 室 is said to=公堂.

13. THE VIRTUE OF MANG CHE-FAN IN CONCEALING HIS MERIT. But where was his virtue in deviating from the truth? And how could Conf. commend him for doing so? These questions have never troubled the commentators. Mang Che-fan, named 側, was an officer of Loo. The defeat, after which he thus distinguished himself was in the 11th year of duke Gae, B. C. 483. To lead the van of an army is called 啟, to bring up the rear is 殿. In retreat, the rear is of course the place of honour. 伐, see V. 25, 4.

【十四章】子曰、不有祝鮀之佞、而有宋朝之美、難乎免於今之世矣。

【十五章】子曰、誰能出不由戶、何莫由斯道也。

【十六章】子曰、質勝文則野、文勝質則史、文質彬彬、然後君子。

【十七章】子曰、人之生也直、罔之生也、幸而免。

CHAPTER XIV. The Master said, "Without the specious speech of the litanist T'o, and the beauty of *the prince* Chaou of Sung, it is difficult to escape in the present age."

CHAPTER XV. The Master said, "Who can go out but by the door? How is it that men will not walk according to these ways?"

CHAPTER XVI. The Master said, "Where the solid qualities are in excess of accomplishments, we have rusticity; where the accomplishments are in excess of the solid qualities, we have the manners of a clerk. When the accomplishments and solid qualities are equally blended, we then have the man of complete virtue."

CHAPTER XVII. The Master said, "Man is born for uprightness. If a man lose his uprightness, and yet live, his escape *from death* is the effect of mere good fortune."

14. THE DEGENERACY OF THE AGE ESTEEMING GLIBNESS OF TONGUE AND BEAUTY OF PERSON. 祝, 'to pray,' 'prayers;' here, in the concrete, the officer charged with the prayers in the ancestral temple. I have coined the word *litanist* to come as near to the meaning as possible. This T'o was an officer of the state of Wei, styled 子魚. Prince Chaou had been guilty of incest with his sister Nan-tsze (see ch. 26), and afterwards, when she was married to the duke Ling of Wei, he served as an officer there, carrying on his wickedness. He was celebrated for his beauty of person. 而 is a simple connective, =與, and the 不 is made to belong to both clauses. This seems the correct construction, tho' unusual. The old comm. construe differently:—'If a man have not the speech of T'o, though he may have the beauty of Chaou, &c.,' making the degeneracy of the age all turn on its fondness for specious talk. This can't be right.

15. A LAMENT OVER THE WAYWARDNESS OF MEN'S CONDUCT. 斯道, 'These ways,' in a moral sense;—not deep doctrines, but rules of life.

16. THE EQUAL BLENDING OF SOLID EXCELLENCE AND ORNAMENTAL ACCOMPLISHMENTS IN A COMPLETE CHARACTER. 史, 'an historian,' an officer of importance in China. The term, however, is to be understood here of 'a clerk,' 'a scrivener in a public office,' one that is of a class sharp and well informed, but insincere.

17. LIFE WITHOUT UPRIGHTNESS IS NOT TRUE LIFE, AND CANNOT BE CALCULATED ON. 'No more serious warning than this,' says one comm., 'was ever addressed to men by Confucius.' A distinction is made by Choo He and others between the two 生, that the 1st is 始生, 'birth,' or 'the beginning of life,' and the 2d is 生存, 'preservation in life.' 人之生也直, 'The being born of man is upright,' which may mean either that man at his birth is upright, or that he is born for uprightness. I prefer the latter view. 罔之生也, 'The living without it,' if we take 罔=無, or 'to

十八章 子曰、知之者、不如好之者、好之者、不如樂之者。

十九章 子曰、中人以上、可以語上也、中人以下、不可以語上也。

二十章 樊遲問知。子曰、務民之義、敬鬼神而遠之、可謂知矣。問仁。曰、仁者先難而後獲、可

CHAPTER XVIII. The Master said, "They who know *the truth* are not equal to those who love it, and they who love it are not equal to those who find pleasure in it."

CHAPTER XIX. The Master said, "To those whose talents are above mediocrity, the highest subjects may be announced. To those who are below mediocrity, the highest subjects may not be announced."

CHAPTER XX. Fan Ch'e asked what constituted wisdom. The Master said, "To give one's-self earnestly to the duties due to men, and, while respecting spiritual beings, to keep aloof from them, may be called wisdom." He asked about perfect virtue. The Master said, "The man of virtue makes the difficulty *to be overcome* his first business, and success only a subsequent consideration;—this may be called perfect virtue."

defame it,' if 罔=誣. We long here as elsewhere for more perspicuity and fuller development of view. An important truth struggles here for expression, but only finds it imperfectly. Without uprightness the end of man's existence is not fulfilled, but his preservation in such case is not merely a fortunate accident.

18. DIFFERENT STAGES OF ATTAINMENT. The four 之 have all one reference, which must be 道 or 理, the subject spoken of.

19. TEACHERS MUST BE GUIDED IN COMMUNICATING KNOWLEDGE BY THE SUSCEPTIVITY OF THE LEARNERS. In 以上, 上 is read up. 2d tone, a verbal word, and not the prep. 'upon,' so the 下 in 以下 is also verbal as in III. 7. The 中人, 'or mediocre people,' may have all classes of subjects announced to them, I suppose.

20. CHIEF ELEMENTS IN WISDOM AND VIRTUE. The modern comm. take 民 here as=人, and 民之義 as=人道之宜, 'what is right according to the principles of humanity.' With some hesitation, I have assented to this view, though 民 properly means 'the multitude,' 'the people,' and the old interpr. explain—'Strive to perfect the righteousness of the people.' We may suppose from the second clause that Fan Ch'e was striving after what was uncommon and superhuman. For a full exhibition of the phrase 鬼神, see 中庸, XVI. Here it='spiritual beings,' *manes* and others. 遠, up. 3d tone. 遠之, 'Keep at a distance from them,' not 'keep them at a distance.' The sage's advice therefore is—'attend to what are plainly human duties, and do not be superstitious.' 先, and 後 are, as frequently elsewhere, verbs, 'put first,' 'put last.' The old interpreters take them differently, but not so well.

謂仁矣。
〔二十一〕子曰、知者樂水、仁者樂山、知者動、仁者靜、知者樂、仁者壽。
〔二十二〕子曰、齊一變、至於魯、魯一變、至於道。
〔二十三〕子曰、觚不觚、觚哉觚哉。
〔二十四〕宰我問曰、仁者雖告之曰、井有仁焉、其從之

CHAPTER XXI. The Master said, "The wise find pleasure in water; the virtuous find pleasure in hills. The wise are active; the virtuous are tranquil. The wise are joyful, the virtuous are long-lived."

CHAPTER XXII. The Master said, "Ts'e, by one change, would come to the state of Loo. Loo, by one change, would come to a state where true principles predominated."

CHAPTER XXIII. The Master said, "A cornered vessel without corners.—A strange cornered vessel! A strange cornered vessel!"

CHAPTER XXIV. Tsae Go asked, saying, "A benevolent man, though it be told him,—'There is a man in the well,' will go in after him, I suppose." Confucius said, "Why should he do so? A supe-

21. CONTRASTS OF THE WISE AND THE VIRTUOUS. The two first 樂 are read *ngaou*, low. 3d tone,=喜好, 'to find pleasure in.' The wise or knowing are active and restless, like the waters of a stream, ceaselessly flowing and advancing. The virtuous are tranquil and firm, like the stable mountains. The pursuit of knowledge brings joy. The life of the virtuous may be expected to glide calmly on and long. After all, the saying is not very comprehensible.

22. THE CONDITION OF THE STATES TS'E AND LOO. Ts'e and Loo were both within the present Shan-tung. Ts'e lay along the coast on the north, embracing the present dep. of 青州 and other territory. Loo was on the south, the larger portion of it being formed by the present dep. of 兗州. At the rise of the Chow dynasty, king Woo invested 太公望, 'the great duke Wang,' with the principality of Ts'e, while his successor, king Shing, constituted the son of his uncle, the famous duke of Chow, prince of Loo. In Conf. time, Ts'e had degenerated more than Loo. 道 is 先王盡善盡美之道, 'the entirely good and admirable ways of the former kings.'

23. THE NAME WITHOUT THE REALITY IS FOLLY. This was spoken (see the 註疏) with ref. to the governments of the time, retaining ancient names without ancient principles. The 觚 was a drinking vessel; others say a wooden tablet. The latter was a later use of the term. It was made with corners as appears from the composition of the character, which is formed from 角, 'a horn,' 'a sharp corner.' In Conf. time, the form was changed, while the name was kept.

24. THE BENEVOLENT EXERCISE THEIR BENEVOLENCE WITH PRUDENCE. Tsae Go could see no limitation to acting on the impulses of benevolence. We are not to suppose with modern

也。子曰、何爲其然也、君子可逝也、不可陷也、可欺也、不可罔也。

【二十五章】子曰、君子博學於文、約之以禮、亦可以弗畔矣夫。

【二十六章】子見南子、子路不說、夫子矢之曰、予所否者、天厭之、天厭之。

【二十七章】子曰、中庸之爲德也、其至矣乎、民鮮久矣。

rior man may be made to go *to the well*, but he cannot be made to go down into it. He may be imposed upon, but he cannot be befooled."

CHAPTER XXV. The Master said, "The superior man, extensively studying all learning, and keeping himself under the restraint of the rules of propriety, may thus likewise not overstep what is right."

CHAPTER XXVI. The Master having visited Nan-tsze, Tsze-loo was displeased, on which the Master swore, saying, "Wherein I have done improperly, may Heaven reject me! may Heaven reject me!"

CHAPTER XXVII. The Master said, "Perfect is the virtue which is according to the Constant Mean! Rare for a long time has been its practice among the people."

comm. that he wished to show that benevolence was impracticable. 雖 belongs to the whole following clause, especially to the mention of a well. The second 仁 is for 人. 其—也 indicate some doubt in Go's mind. Obs. the *hophal* force of 逝 and 陷.

25. THE HAPPY EFFECT OF LEARNING AND PROPRIETY COMBINED. 君子 has here its lighter meaning,—'the student of what is right and true.' The 之 in 約之 we naturally refer to 文, but comparing IX. 10, 2—約我以禮,—we may assent to the observa. that 我指已身, '*I* refers to the learner's own person.' See note on IV. 23. 畔, 'the boundary of a field;' then, 'to overstep that boundary.' 矣夫, as in V. 26, but the force here is more 'ah!' than 'alas!'

26. CONFUCIUS VINDICATES HIMSELF FOR VISITING THE UNWORTHY NAN-TSZE. Nan-tsze was the wife of the duke of Wei, and sister of prince Chaou, mentioned ch. 14. Her lewd character was well known, and hence Tsze-loo was displeased, thinking an interview with her was disgraceful to the Master. Great pains are taken to explain the incident. 'Nan-tsze,' says one, 'sought the interview from the stirrings of her natural conscience.' 'It was a rule,' says another, 'that officers in a state should visit the prince's wife.' 'Nan-tsze,' argues a third, 'had all influence with her husband, and Confucius wished to get currency by her means for his doctrine.' Whether 矢 is to be understood in the sense of 'to swear,'=誓, or 'to make a declaration'=陳, is much debated. Evidently, the thing is an oath, or solemn protestation against the suspicions of Tsze-loo.

27. THE DEFECTIVE PRACTICE OF THE PEOPLE IN CONFUCIUS' TIMES. See 中庸, III.

廿八 子一節貢曰、如有博施於民、而能濟衆、何如、可謂仁乎。子曰、何事於仁、必也聖乎、堯舜其猶病諸。○二節夫仁者、己欲立而立人、己欲達而達人。○三節能近取譬、可謂仁之方也已。

CHAPTER XXVIII. 1. Tsze-kung said, "Suppose the case of a man extensively conferring benefits on the people, and able to assist all, what would you say of him? Might he be called perfectly virtuous?" The Master said, "Why speak only of virtue in connection with him? Must he not have the qualities of a sage? Even Yaou and Shun were still solicitous about this.

2. "Now the man of perfect virtue, wishing to be established himself, seeks also to establish others; wishing to be enlarged himself, he seeks also to enlarge others.

3. "To be able to judge *of others* by what is nigh *in ourselves*;—this may be called the art of virtue."

28. THE TRUE NATURE AND ART OF VIRTUE. There are no higher sayings in the Analects than we have here. 1. 施, up 3d tone, 'to confer benefits.' 聖乎,—乎 is said to be 'a particle of doubt and uncertainty,' but it is rather the interrogative affirmation of opinion. Tsze-kung appears to have thought that great doings were necessary to virtue, and propounds a case which would transcend the achievements of Yaou and Shun. From such extravagant views the Master recalls him. 2. This is the description of 仁者之心體, 'the mind of the perfectly virtuous man' as void of all selfishness. 3. It is to be wished that the idea intended by 能近取譬 had been more clearly expressed. Still we seem to have here a near approach to a positive enunciation of 'the golden rule.'

論語

BOOK VII. SHUH URH.

述而第七

第一章 子曰、述而不作、信而好古、竊比於我老彭。

第二章 子曰、默而識之、學而不厭、誨人不倦、何有於我哉。

第三章 子曰、德之不脩、學之不講、聞義不能徙、不善不能改、

CHAPTER I. The Master said, "A transmitter and not a maker, believing in and loving the ancients, I venture to compare myself with our old P'ang."

CHAPTER II. The Master said, "The silent treasuring up of knowledge; learning without satiety; and instructing others without being wearied:—what one of these things belongs to me?"

CHAPTER III. The Master said, "The leaving virtue without proper cultivation; the not thoroughly discussing what is learned; not being able to move towards righteousness of which a knowledge is gained; and not being able to change what is not good:—these are the things which occasion me solicitude."

HEADING OF THIS BOOK.—述而第七. 'A transmitter, and ——Book VII.' We have in this book much information of a personal character about Confucius, both from his own lips, and from the descriptions of his disciples. The two preceding books treat of the disciples and other worthies, and here, in contrast with them, we have the sage himself exhibited.

1. CONFUCIUS DISCLAIMS BEING AN ORIGINATOR OR MAKER. 述=傳舊而已, 'simply to hand down the old.' Comm. say the master's language here is from his extreme humility. But we must hold that it expresses his true sense of his position and work. Who the individual called endearingly 'our old P'ang' was, can hardly be ascertained. Choo He adopts the view that he was a worthy officer of the Shang dynasty. But that individual's history is a mass of fables. Others make 老彭 to be Laou-tsze, the founder of the Taou sect, and others again make two individuals, one this Laou-tsze, and the other that 彭祖.

2. CONFUCIUS' HUMBLE ESTIMATE OF HIMSELF. 識, here by most scholars read *che*, up. 3d tone, 'to remember.' 之 refers, it is said, to 理, 'principles,' the subjects of the silent observation and reflection. 何有於我哉, cannot be—'what difficulty do these occasion me?' but=何者能有於我, as in the transl. 'The language,' says Choo He, 'is that of humility upon humility.' Some insert, in their expl., 此外 before 何—'Besides these, what is there in me?' But this is quite arbitrary. The profession may be inconsistent with what we find in other passages, but the inconsistency must stand rather than violence be done to the language. Ho An gives the singular exposition of 鄭康成 (about A. D. 150—200)—'Other men have not these things, I only have them.'

3. CONFUCIUS' ANXIETY ABOUT HIS SELF-CULTIVATION:—ANOTHER HUMBLE ESTIMATE OF HIMSELF. Here again, comm. find only the expressions of humility, but there can be no reason why we should not admit that Confucius was anxious lest these things, which are only put forth as possibilities, should become in his case actual

是吾憂也。

第四章 子之燕居、申申如也、夭夭如也。

第五章 子曰、甚矣吾衰也、久矣、吾不復夢見周公。

第六章 一節 子曰、志於道。二節 據於德。三節 依於仁。四節 游於藝。

CHAPTER IV. When the Master was unoccupied with business, his manner was easy, and he looked pleased.

CHAPTER V. The Master said, "Extreme is my decay. For a long time, I have not dreamed, as I was wont to do, that I saw the duke of Chow."

CHAPTER VI. 1. The Master said, "Let the will be set on the path of duty.

2. "Let every attainment in what is good be firmly grasped.

3. "Let perfect virtue be accorded with.

4. "Let relaxation and enjoyment be found in the polite arts."

facts. 講 is in the sense explained in the Dict. by the terms 習 and 究, 'practising,' 'examining.'

4. THE MANNER OF CONFUCIUS WHEN UNOCCUPIED. The first clause, which is the subject of the other two, is literally—'The master's dwelling at ease.' Obs. 燕, up. 3d tone; 夭, up. 1st tone; 如, as in III, 23.

5. HOW THE DISAPPOINTMENT OF CONFUCIUS' HOPES AFFECTED EVEN HIS DREAMS. 周公 (Chow-kung) is now to all intents a proper name, but the characters mean 'the duke of Chow.' Chow was the name of the seat of the family from which the dynasty so called sprang, and on the enlargement of this territory, king Wăn divided the original seat between his sons 旦 (Tan) and 奭 (Shih). Tan was *Chow kung*, in wisdom and politics, what his elder brother, the first emperor, Woo, was in arms. Confucius had longed to bring the principles and institutions of Chow-kung into practice, and in his earlier years, while hope animated him, had often dreamt of the former sage. The orig. territory of Chow was what is now the dis. of K'e-shan (岐山), dep. of Fung-tseang (鳳翔), in Shen-se.

6. RULES FOR THE FULL MATURING OF CHARACTER. 2. 德 might be translated virtue, but 仁='perfect virtue' following, we require another term. 4. 游, 'to ramble for amusement,' here='to seek recreation.' 藝, see note on 文, in I. 6. A full enumeration makes 'six arts,' viz., ceremonies, music, archery, charioteering, the study of characters or language, and figures or arithmetic. The ceremonies were ranged in five classes: lucky or sacrifices, unlucky or the mourning cer., military, those of host and guest, and festive. Music required the study of the music of Hwang-te, of Yaou, of Shun, of Yu, of T'ang, and of Woo. Archery had a five-fold classification. Charioteering had the same. The study of the characters required the examination of them, to determine whether there predominated in their formation resemblance to the object, combination of ideas, indication of properties, a phonetic principle, a principle of contrariety, or metaphorical accommodation. Figures were managed according to nine rules, as the object was the measurement of land, capacity, &c. These six subjects were the business of the highest and most liberal education, but we need not suppose that Conf. had them all in view here.

第七章 子曰、自行束脩以上、吾未嘗無誨焉。

第八章 子曰、不憤不啟、不悱不發、舉一隅、不以三隅反、則不復也。

第九章 一節 子食於有喪者之側、未嘗飽也。二節 子於是日哭、則不歌。

第十章 一節 子謂顏淵曰、用之則行、舍之則藏、惟我

CHAPTER VII. The Master said, "From the man bringing his bundle of dried flesh *for my teaching* upwards, I have never refused instruction to any one."

CHAPTER VIII. The Master said, "I do not open up the truth to one who is not eager *to get knowledge*, nor help out any one who is not anxious to explain himself. When I have presented one corner of a subject to any one, and he cannot from it learn the other three, I do not repeat my lesson."

CHAPTER IX. 1. When the Master was eating by the side of a mourner, he never ate to the full.

2. He did not sing on the same day in which he had been weeping.

CHAPTER X. 1. The Master said to Yen Yuen, "When called to office to undertake its duties; when not so called, to lie retired;—it is only I and you who have attained to this."

7. THE READINESS OF CONFUCIUS TO IMPART INSTRUCTION. It was the rule anciently that when one party waited on another, he should carry some present or offering with him. Pupils did so when they first waited on their teacher. Of such offerings, one of the lowest was a bundle of 脩, 'dried flesh.' The wages of a teacher are now called 脩金, 'the money of the dried flesh.' However small the offering brought to the sage, let him only see the indication of a wish to learn, and he imparted his instructions. 以上, may be translated 'upwards,' *i. e.*, 'to such a man and others with larger gifts,' 上 being up. 2d tone, or the char. may be understood in the sense of 'attending my instructions,' with its usual tone. I prefer the former interpretation.

8. CONFUCIUS REQUIRED A REAL DESIRE AND ABILITY IN HIS DISCIPLES. The last ch. tells of the sage's readiness to teach, this shows that he did not teach where his teaching was likely to prove of no avail. 悱, in the comm. and dict., is explained 口欲言而未能之貌, 'the appearance of one with mouth wishing to speak and yet not able to do so.' This being the meaning, we might have expected the character to be 啡. 反, 'to turn,' is explained 還以相證之義, 'going round for mutual testimony.' 不復=不復有所告, 'I tell him nothing more.'

9. CONFUCIUS' SYMPATHY WITH MOURNERS. The weeping is understood to be on occasion of offering his condolences to a mourner, which was 'a rule of propriety.'

10. THE ATTAINMENTS OF HWUY LIKE THOSE OF CONFUCIUS. THE EXCESSIVE BOLDNESS OF TSZE-LOO. 1. In 用之, 舍之, 之 is ex-

與爾有是夫。〔二〕子路曰、子行三軍則誰與。〔三〕子曰、暴虎馮河、死而無悔者、吾不與也。必也臨事而懼、好謀而成者也。

〔十一章〕子曰、富而可求也、雖執鞭之士、吾亦爲之。如不可求、從吾所好。

〔十二章〕子之所愼、齊、戰、疾。

2. Tsze-loo said, "If you had the conduct of the armies of a great state, whom would you have to act with you?"

3. The Master said, "I would not have him to act with me, who will unarmed attack a tiger, or cross a river without a boat, dying without any regret. My associate must be the man who proceeds to action full of solicitude, who is fond of adjusting his plans, and then carries them into execution."

CHAPTER XI. The Master said, "If the search for riches is sure to be successful, though I should become a groom with whip in hand to get them, I will do so. As the search may not be successful, I will follow after that which I love."

CHAPTER XII. The things in reference to which the Master exercised the greatest caution were—fasting, war, and sickness.

plained by 我, but we have seen that 之 foll. active verbs imparts to them a sort of neuter signification. 用之='used.' 舍之='neglected.' 2. A *Keun*, acc. to the 周禮, consisted of 12,500 men. The imperial forces consisted of six such bodies, and those of a great state of three. 3. 暴虎馮河, see She-king, II. ii. 1, st. 5. 懼 does not indicate *timidity*, but *solicitude*.—Tsze-loo, it would appear, was jealous of the praise conferred on Hwuy, and pluming himself on his bravery, put in for a share of the Master's approbation. But he only brought on himself this rebuke.

11. THE UNCERTAINTY AND FOLLY OF THE PURSUIT OF RICHES. It occurs to a student to understand the first clause—'If it be *proper* to search for riches,' and the third—'I will do it.' But the transl. is acc. to the modern comm., and the conclusion agrees better with it. In expl. 執鞭之士, some refer us to the attendants who cleared the street with their whips when the prince went abroad, but we need not seek any particular allusion of the kind. Obs. 而=若, 'if,' and then, 如='since.'—An objection to the pursuit of wealth may be made on the ground of righteousness, or on that of its uncertainty. It is the latter on which Confucius here rests.

12. WHAT THINGS CONFUCIUS WAS PARTICULARLY CAREFUL ABOUT. 齊, read *Chae*, and=齋, 'to fast,' or, rather, denoting the whole religious adjustment, enjoined before the offering of sacrifice, and extending over the ten days previous to the great sacrificial seasons. 齊 means 'to equalize' (see II. 3), and the effect of those previous exercises was 齊不齊以

〔十三章〕子在齊聞韶、三月不知肉味、曰、不圖爲樂之至於斯也。

〔十四章〕一節 冉有曰、夫子爲衛君乎。子貢曰、諾、吾將問之。二節 入曰、伯夷叔齊、何人也。曰、古之賢人也。曰、怨乎。曰、求仁而得仁、又何怨。出曰、夫子不爲也。

CHAPTER XIII. When the Master was in Ts‘e, he heard the Shaou, and for three months did not know the taste of flesh. "I did not think," he said, "that music could have been made so excellent as this."

CHAPTER XIV. 1. Yen Yew said, "Is our Master for the prince of Wei?" Tsze-kung said, "Oh! I will ask him."

2. He went in *accordingly*, and said, "What sort of men were Pih-e and Shuh-ts‘e?" "They were ancient worthies," said the Master. "Did they have any repinings *because of their course*?" The Master again replied, "They sought to act virtuously, and they did so; what was there for them to repine about?" On this, *Tsze-kung* went out and said, "Our Master is not for him."

致齊, 'to adjust what was not adjusted, to produce a perfect adjustment.' Sacrifices presented in such a state of mind were sure to be acceptable. Other people, it is said, might be heedless in refer. to sacrifices, to war, and to sickness, but not so the sage.

13. THE EFFECT OF MUSIC ON CONFUCIUS. The *shaou*, see II. 25. This incident must have happened in the 36th year of Conf., when he followed the duke Ch‘aou in his flight from Loo to Ts‘e. As related in the 史記, 'Historical Records,' before the characters 三月, we have 學之, 'he learned it three months,' which may relieve us from the necessity of extending the three months over all the time in which he did not know the taste of his food. In Ho An's compilation, the 不知 is expl. by 忽忘, 'he was careless about and forgot.' The last clause is also explained there—'I did not think that this music had reached this country of Ts‘e.'

14. CONFUCIUS DID NOT APPROVE OF A SON OPPOSING HIS FATHER. 1. The eldest son of duke Ling of Wei had planned to kill his mother (? stepmother), the notorious Nan-tsze (VI. 26). For this he had to flee the country, and his son, on the death of Ling, became duke (出公), and subsequently opposed his father's attempts to wrest the sovereignty from him. This was the matter argued among the disciples,—Was Confucius for (爲 low. 3d tone), the son, the reigning duke? 2. In Wei it would not have been acc. to *propriety* to speak by name of its ruler, and therefore Tsze-kung put the case of Pih-e and Shuh-ts‘e, see V. 22. They having given up a throne, and finally their lives, rather than do what they thought wrong, and Confucius fully approving of their conduct, it was plain he could not approve of a son's holding by force what was the rightful inheritance of the father. 求仁而得仁, 'They sought for virtue, and they got virtue;' *i.e.*, such was the character of their conduct.

（十五）子曰、飯疏食飲水、曲肱而枕之、樂亦在其中矣、不義而富且貴、於我如浮雲。

（十六）子曰、加我數年、五十以學易、可以無大過矣。

（十七）子所雅言、詩、書、執禮、皆雅言也。

CHAPTER XV. The Master said, "With coarse rice to eat, with water to drink, and my bended arm for a pillow;—I have still joy in the midst of these things. Riches and honours acquired by unrighteousness are to me as a floating cloud."

CHAPTER XVI. The Master said, "If some years were added to my life, I would give fifty to the study of the YIH, and then I might come to be without great faults."

CHAPTER XVII. The Master's frequent themes of discourse were —the Odes, the History, and the maintenance of the Rules of propriety. On all these he frequently discoursed.

15. THE JOY OF CONFUCIUS INDEPENDENT OF OUTWARD CIRCUMSTANCES. 飯, low. 2d tone, 'a meal,' also, as here, a verb, 'to eat.' 枕, up. 3d tone, 'to pillow,' 'to use as a pillow.' Critics call attention to 亦, making the sentiment='My joy is everywhere. It is amid other circumstances. It is *also* here.' 不義云云,='By unrighteousness I might get riches and honours, but such riches and honours are to me as a floating cloud. It is vain to grasp at them, so uncertain and unsubstantial.'

16. THE VALUE WHICH CONFUCIUS SET UPON THE STUDY OF THE YIH. Choo He supposes that this was spoken when Conf. was about seventy, as he was in his 68th year when he ceased his wanderings, and settled in Loo to the adjustment and compilation of the Yih and other *king*. If the remark be referred to that time, an error may well be found in 五十, for he would hardly be speaking at 70 of having 50 years added to his life. Choo also mentions the report of a certain individual that he had seen a copy of the Lun Yu, which read 假 for 加, and 卒 for 五十. Amended thus, the meaning would be—'If I had some *more* years to finish the study of the Yih, &c.' Ho An interprets the chapter quite differently. Referring to the saying, II. 4, 4, 'At fifty, I knew the decrees of heaven,' he supposes this to have been spoken when Conf. was 47, and explains—'In a few years more I will be fifty, and have finished the Yih, when I may be without great faults.' —One thing remains upon both views:—Confucius never claimed, what his followers do for him, to be a perfect man.

17. CONFUCIUS' MOST COMMON TOPICS. 書, 'The History,' *i. e.*, the historical documents which he compiled into the Shoo-king that has come down to us in a mutilated condition. 詩 also, and much less 禮, must not be understood of the now existing She-king and Le-ke. Choo He explains 雅 (low. 2d tone) by 常, 'constantly.' The old interpr. Ch'ing, explains it by 正 'correctly,'—'Conf. would speak of the Odes, &c., with attention, to the correct enunciation of the characters.' This does not seem so good.

十八章 葉公問孔子於子路、子路不對。子曰、女奚不曰、其爲人也、發憤忘食、樂以忘憂、不知老之將至云爾。

十九章 子曰、我非生而知之者、好古、敏以求之者也。

二十章 子不語、怪、力、亂、神。

CHAPTER XVIII. 1. The duke of Shě asked Tsze-loo about Confucius, and Tsze-loo did not answer him.

2. The Master said, "Why did you not say to him,—He is simply a man, who in his eager pursuit of knowledge forgets his food, who in the joy *of its attainment* forgets his sorrows, and who does not perceive that old age is coming on?"

CHAPTER XIX. The Master said, "I am not one who was born in the possession of knowledge; I am one who is fond of antiquity, and earnest in seeking it *there*."

CHAPTER XX. The subjects on which the Master did not talk, were—extraordinary things, feats of strength, disorder, and spiritual beings.

18. CONFUCIUS' DESCRIPTION OF HIS CHARACTER, AS BEING SIMPLY A MOST EARNEST LEARNER. 1. 葉 (read *shě*) was a district of Tsoo (楚), the governor or prefect of which had usurped the title of *kung*. Its name is still preserved in a district of the dep. of 南陽, in the south of Ho-nan. 2. 云 sometimes finishes a sentence (Premare, '*claudit orationem*'), as here. The 爾 after it=耳, imparting to all the preceding description a meaning indicated by our *simply* or *only*.

19. CONFUCIUS' KNOWLEDGE NOT CONNATE, BUT THE RESULT OF HIS STUDY OF ANTIQUITY. Here again, acc. to comm., is a wonderful instance of the sage's humility disclaiming what he really had. The comment of 尹和靖, subjoined to Choo He's own, is to the effect that the knowledge born with a man is only 義 and 理, while ceremonies, music, names of things, history, &c., must be learned. This would make what we may call connate or innate knowledge the moral sense, and those intuitive principles of reason, on and by which all knowledge is built up. But Confucius could not mean to deny his being possessed of these. 'I love antiquity;' *i. e.*, the ancients and all their works.

20. SUBJECTS AVOIDED BY CONFUCIUS IN CONVERSATION. 亂, 'confusion,' meaning rebellious disorder, parricide, regicide, and such crimes. Choo He makes 神 here=鬼神造化之迹, 'the mysterious, or spiritual operations apparent in the course of nature.' 王肅 (died A. D. 266), as given by Ho An, simply says—鬼神之事, 'the affairs of spiritual beings.' For an instance of Conf. avoiding such a subject, see XI. 11.

〔二十一〕子曰、三人行、必有我師焉、擇其善者而從之、其不善者而改之。

〔二十二〕子曰、天生德於予、桓魋其如予何。

〔二十三〕子曰、二三子、以我爲隱乎、吾無隱乎爾、吾無行而不與二三子者、是丘也、

〔二十四〕子以四教、文、行、忠、信。

CHAPTER XXI. The Master said, "When I walk along with two others, they may serve me as my teachers. I will select their good qualities and follow them, their bad qualities and avoid them."

CHAPTER XXII. The Master said, "Heaven produced the virtue that is in me. Hwan T'uy—what can he do to me?"

CHAPTER XXIII. The Master said, "Do you think, my disciples, that I have any concealments? I conceal nothing from you. There is nothing which I do that is not shown to you, my disciples;—that is my way."

CHAPTER XXIV. There were four things which the Master taught,—letters, ethics, devotion of soul, and truthfulness.

21. HOW A MAN MAY FIND INSTRUCTORS FOR HIMSELF. 三人行, 'Three men walking;' but it is implied that the speaker is himself one of them. The comm. all take 擇 in the sense of 'to distinguish,' 'to determine.'—'I will determine the one who is good, and follow him, &c.' I prefer to understand as in the translation. 改之, 'change them,' *i. e.*, correct them in myself, avoid them.

22. CONFUCIUS CALM IN DANGER, THROUGH THE ASSURANCE OF HAVING A DIVINE MISSION. Acc. to the historical accounts. Conf. was passing through Sung in his way from Wei to Ch'in, and was practising ceremonies with his disciples under a large tree, when they were set upon by emissaries of Hwan T'uy, a high officer of Sung. These pulled down the tree, and wanted to kill the sage. His disciples urged him to make haste and escape, when he calmed their fears by these words. At the same time, he disguised himself till he had got past Sung. This story may be apocryphal, but the saying remains,—a remarkable one.

23. CONFUCIUS PRACTISED NO CONCEALMENT WITH HIS DISCIPLES. 二三子, see III. 24. 與 is explained by Choo He by 示, 'to show,' as if the meaning were, 'There is not one of my doings in which I am not showing my doctrines to you.' But the common signif. of 與 may be retained, as in Ho An,—'which is not given to, shared with, you.' To what the concealment has reference we cannot tell. Observe the force of 者 foll. by 也 at the end;—'To have none of my actions not shared with you,—*that* is I, Hew.'

24. THE SUBJECTS OF CONFUCIUS TEACHING. 以四教, 'took four things and taught.' There were four things which—not four ways in which—Confucius taught. 文 here=our use of *letters*. 行=人倫日用, 'what is daily used in the relations of life.' 忠=無一念之不盡, 'not a single thought not ex-

〔廿五章〕子曰、聖人吾不得而見之矣、得見君子者、斯可矣。二節子曰、善人吾不得而見之矣、得見有恆者、斯可矣。三節亡而爲有、虛而爲盈、約而爲泰、難乎有恆矣。

〔廿六章〕子釣而不綱、弋不射宿。

〔廿七章〕子曰、蓋有不知而作

CHAPTER XXV. 1. The Master said, "A sage it is not mine to see; could I see a man of real talent and virtue, that would satisfy me."

2. The Master said, "A good man it is not mine to see; could I see a man possessed of constancy, that would satisfy me.

3. "Having not and yet affecting to have, empty and yet affecting to be full, straitened and yet affecting to be at ease:—it is difficult with such characteristics to have constancy."

CHAPTER XXVI. The Master angled,—but did not use a net. He shot,—but not at birds perching.

CHAPTER XXVII. The Master said, "There may be those who act without knowing why. I do not do so. Hearing much and selecting what is good and following it, seeing much and keeping it in memory:—this is the second style of knowledge."

hausted.' 信=無一事之不實, 'not a single thing without its reality.' These are the explanations in the 四書備旨. I confess to apprehend but vaguely the two latter subjects as distinguished from the second.

25. THE PAUCITY OF TRUE MEN IN, AND THE PRETENTIOUSNESS OF, CONFUCIUS' TIME. 子曰, par. 2, is supposed by some to be an addition to the text. That being so, we have in the ch. a climax of character:—the man of constancy, or the single-hearted, stedfast man; the good man, who on his single-heartedness has built up his virtue; the *Keun-tsze*, the man of virtue in large proportions, and intellectually able besides; and the sage, or highest style of man. 聖, from 耳, 口, and 壬, 'ear, mouth, and good,'= intuitively apprehensive of truth, and correct in utterance and action. Comp. Mencius, VII. ii. 24.

26. THE HUMANITY OF CONFUCIUS. 綱 is properly the large rope attached to a net, by means of which it may be drawn so as to sweep a stream. 弋, 'to shoot with a string tied to the arrow, by which it may be drawn back again.' 射, applied to such shooting, lower 4th tone, read *shih*. Confucius would only destroy what life was necessary for his use, and in taking that he would not take advantage of the inferior creatures. This ch. is said to be descriptive of him in his early life.

27. AGAINST ACTING HEEDLESSLY. Paou Heen, in Ho An, says that this was spoken with ref. to heedless compilers of records. Choo He makes 作之 simply=作事, 'to do things,' 'to act.' The paraphrasts make the latter part descriptive of Confucius—'I hear much, &c.' This is not necessary, and the transl. had better be as indefinite as the original.

之者、我無是也。多聞、擇其善者而從之、多見而識之、知之次也。

廿八章 一節 互鄉難與言、童子見、門人惑。二節 子曰、與其進也、不與其退也、唯何甚、人潔己以進、與其潔也、不保其往也、

廿九章 子曰、仁遠乎哉、我欲仁、斯仁至矣。

三十章 一節 陳司敗問昭公知禮乎。孔子曰、知禮。二節 孔子退、揖巫馬期而進

CHAPTER XXVIII. 1. It was difficult to talk with the people of Hoo-heang, and a lad of that place having had an interview with the Master, the disciples doubted.

2. The Master said, "I admit people's approach to me without committing myself *as to what they may do* when they have retired. Why must one be so severe? If a man purify himself to wait upon me, I receive him so purified, without guaranteeing his past conduct."

CHAPTER XXIX. The Master said, "Is virtue a thing remote? I wish to be virtuous, and lo! virtue is at hand."

CHAPTER XXX. 1. The minister of crime of Ch'in asked whether the duke Ch'aou knew propriety, and Confucius said, "He knew propriety."

28. THE READINESS OF CONFUCIUS TO MEET APPROACHES TO HIM THOUGH MADE BY THE UNLIKELY. 1. In 互鄉, the 鄉 appears to be like our local termination *ham*.—'The people of Hoo-ham.' Its site is now sought in three different places. 2. Choo He would here transpose the order of the text, and read 人潔已云云 immediately after 子曰. He also supposes some characters lost in the sentence 唯何甚. This is hardly necessary. 與, as in V. 8, 3, =許, 'to allow,' 'to concede to.'

29. VIRTUE IS NOT FAR TO SEEK. 哉, after 乎, implies the negative answer to be given.

30. HOW CONFUCIUS ACKNOWLEDGED HIS ERROR. 1. Ch'in, one of the states of China in Conf. time, is to be referred probably to the present department of Ch'in-chow in Ho-nan province. 司敗 was the name given in Ch'in and Tsoo to the minister elsewhere called 司寇, which terms Morrison and Medhurst translate—'criminal judge.' But *judge* does not come up to his functions, which were legislative as well as executive. He was the adviser of his sovereign on all matters relating to

論語

之、曰、吾聞君子不黨、君子亦黨乎、君取於吳爲同姓、謂之吳孟子、君而知禮、孰不知禮。○三節巫馬期以告。子曰、丘也幸、苟有過、人必知之。

卅一章 子與人歌而善、必使反之、而後和之。

卅二章 子曰、文、莫吾猶人

2. Confucius having retired, the minister bowed to Woo-ma K'e to come forward, and said, "I have heard that the superior man is not a partizan. May the superior man be a partizan also? The prince married a daughter of *the house of* Woo, of the same surname with himself, and called her,—'The elder *lady* Tsze of Woo'. If the prince knew propriety, who does not know it?"

3. Woo-ma K'e reported these remarks, and the Master said, "I am fortunate! If I have any errors, people are sure to know them."

CHAPTER XXXI. When the Master was in company with a person who was singing, if he sang well, he would make him repeat the song, while he accompanied it with his own voice.

CHAPTER XXXII. The Master said, "In letters I am perhaps equal to other men, but *the character of* the superior man, carrying out in his conduct what he professes, is what I have not yet attained to."

crime. See the 周禮 秋官司寇. Ch'aou was the hon. ep. of Chow (裯), duke of Loo, B. C. 541-509. He had a reputation for the knowledge and observance of ceremonies, and Conf. answered the minister's question accordingly, the more readily that he was speaking to the officer of another state, and was bound, therefore, to hide any failings that his own sovereign might have had. 2. With all his knowledge of proprieties, the duke Ch'aou had violated an import. rule,—that which forbids the intermarriage of parties of the same surname. The ruling houses of Loo and Woo were branches of the imperial house of Chow, and consequently had the same surname—*Ke* (姬). To conceal his violation of the rule, Ch'aou called his wife by the surname *Tsze* (子), as if she had belonged to the ducal house of Sung. 取, up. 3d tone=娶. 3. Conf. takes the criticism of his questioner very lightly.

31. THE GOOD FELLOWSHIP OF CONFUCIUS. On this chapter, see the 四書合講, which states very distinctly the interpretation which I have followed, making only two singings and not three. 和, lower 3d tone, here='to sing in unison with.'

32. ACKNOWLEDGMENT OF CONFUCIUS IN ESTIMATING HIMSELF. 莫 here occasions some difficulty. Ho An takes it, as it often is,=無, and explains, 'I am not better than others in letters.' In the dict., with ref. to this pass., it is explained by 强, so that the meaning would be—'By effort, I can equal other men in letters.' Choo He makes it 疑辭 a 'particle of doubt,' ='perhaps.' But this is formed for the occasion. 躬行君子, 'an-in-person-acting *keun-tsze*.'

也、躬行君子、則吾未之有得。

三十三 子曰、若聖與仁、則吾豈敢、抑爲之不厭、誨人不倦、則可謂云爾已矣。公西華曰、正唯弟子不能學也。

三十四 子疾病。子路請禱。子曰、有諸。子路對曰、有之、誄曰、禱爾于上下神祇。子曰、丘之禱久矣。

CHAPTER XXXIII. The Master said, "The sage and the man of perfect virtue;—how dare I *rank myself with them?* It may simply be said of me, that I strive to become such without satiety, and teach others without weariness." Kung-se Hwa said, "This is just what we, the disciples, cannot imitate you in."

CHAPTER XXXIV. The Master being very sick, Tsze-loo asked leave to pray for him. He said, "May such a thing be done?" Tsze-loo replied, "It may. In the Prayers it is said, 'Prayer has been made to the spirits of the upper and lower worlds.'" The Master said, "My praying has been for a long time."

33. WHAT CONFUCIUS DECLINED TO BE CONSIDERED, AND WHAT HE CLAIMED. 若 and 抑 are said to be correlatives, in which case they= our 'although' and 'yet.' More naturally, we may join 若 directly with 聖與人, and take 抑 as=our 'but.' 云爾, see ch. 18, 2. 已矣, added to 云爾, increases its emphasis,='just this and nothing more.'

34. CONFUCIUS DECLINES TO BE PRAYED FOR. 疾,病 together mean 'very sick.' 有諸, 諸 is interrogative, as we find it frequently in Mencius. 誄, 'To write a eulogy, and confer the posthumous honorary title;' also, 'to eulogize in prayer,' *i. e.*, to recite one's excellencies as the ground of supplication. Tsze-loo must have been referring to some well known collection of such prayers. In 禱爾, 爾 seems rather to be an expletive than the pronoun. 上下=heaven and earth, 神 being the approp. desig. of the spirits of the former, and 祇 of the latter.—Choo He says, 'Prayer is the expression of repentance and promise of amendment, to supplicate the help of the spirits. If there may not be those things, then there is no need for praying. In the case of the sage, he had committed no errors, and admitted of no amendment. In all his conduct he had been in harmony with the spiritual intelligences, and therefore he said,—*my praying has been for a long time.*' We may demur to some of these expressions, but the declining to be prayed for, and concluding remark, do indicate the satisfaction of Confucius with himself. Here, as in other places, we wish that our information about him were not so stinted and fragmentary.

〔卅五章〕子曰、奢則不孫、儉則固、與其不孫也、寧固。

〔卅六章〕子曰、君子坦蕩蕩、小人長戚戚。

〔卅七章〕子溫而厲、威而不猛、恭而安。

CHAPTER XXXV. The Master said, "Extravagance leads to insubordination, and parsimony to meanness. It is better to be mean than to be insubordinate."

CHAPTER XXXVI. The Master said, "The superior man is satisfied and composed; the mean man is always full of distress."

CHAPTER XXXVII. The Master was mild, and yet dignified; majestic, and yet not fierce; respectful, and yet easy.

35. MEANNESS NOT SO BAD AS INSUBORDINATION. 孫, read *shun*, like 遜, and with the same meaning.

36. CONTRAST IN THEIR FEELINGS BETWEEN THE KEUN-TSZE AND THE MEAN MAN. 坦, 'a level plain' used adverbially with 然,='lightsomely.' This is its force here. 長=常時, 'constantly.'

37. HOW VARIOUS ELEMENTS MODIFIED ONE ANOTHER IN THE CHARACTER OF CONFUCIUS.

BOOK VIII. T'AE-PIH.

泰伯第八

〔第一章〕子曰、泰伯其可謂至德也已矣、三以天下讓、民無得而稱焉。

CHAPTER I. The Master said, "T'ae-pih may be said to have reached the highest point of virtuous action. Thrice he declined the empire, and the people *in ignorance of his motives* could not express their approbation of his conduct."

THE HEADING OF THIS BOOK.—泰伯第八, 'T'ae-pih, Book eighth.' As in other cases, the first words of the book give name to it. The subjects of the chapter are miscellaneous, but it begins and ends with the character and deeds of ancient sages and worthies, and on this account it follows the seventh chapter, where we have Confucius himself described.

1. THE EXCEEDING VIRTUE OF T'AE-PIH. T'ae-pih was the eldest son of king T'ae (大), the grandfather of Wăn, the founder of the Chow dynasty. T'ae had formed the intention of upsetting the Yin dyn., of which T'ae-pih disapproved. T'ae moreover, because of the sage virtues of his grandson Ch'ang (昌), who afterwards became king Wăn, wished to hand

第二章 子曰、恭而無禮則勞、愼而無禮則葸、勇而無禮則亂、直而無禮則絞。○二節 君子篤於親、則民興於仁、故舊不遺、則民不偷。

第三章 曾子有疾、召門弟子曰、啟予

CHAPTER II. 1. The Master said, "Respectfulness, without the rules of propriety, becomes laborious bustle; carefulness, without the rules of propriety, becomes timidity; boldness, without the rules of propriety, becomes insubordination; straightforwardness, without the rules of propriety, becomes rudeness.

2. "When those who are in high stations perform well all their duties to their relations, the people are aroused to virtue. When old friends are not neglected by them, the people are preserved from meanness."

CHAPTER III. The philosopher Tsăng being sick, he called to him the disciples of his school, and said, "Uncover my feet, uncover my hands. It is said in the Book of Poetry, 'We should be apprehensive and cautious, as if on the brink of a deep gulf, as if treading on thin ice,' *and so have I been.* Now and hereafter, I know my escape *from all injury to my person,* O ye, my little children."

down his principality to his 3d son, Ch'ang's father. T'ae-pih observing this, and to escape opposing his father's purpose, retired with his second brother among the barbarous tribes of the south, and left their youngest brother in possession of the state. The motives of his conduct T'ae-pih kept to himself, so that the people 不得而稱之, 'could not find how to praise him.' There is a difficulty in making out the refusal of the empire *three* times, there being different accounts of the times and ways in which he did so. Choo He cuts the knot, by making 'thrice'='firmly,' in which solution we may acquiesce. There is as great difficulty to find out a declining of the *empire* in T'ae-pih's withdrawing from the petty state of Chow. It may be added that king Woo, the first emperor of the Chow dyn., subsequently conferred on T'ae-pih the posthumous title of Chief of Woo (吳), the country to which he had withdrawn, and whose rude inhabitants gathered round him. His second brother succeeded him in the government of them, and hence the ruling house of Woo had the same surname as the imperial house of Chow, that namely of Tsze (子). See VII. 30. 也已矣 give emphasis to the preceding declaration. Comp. I. 14.

2. THE VALUE OF THE RULES OF PROPRIETY; AND OF EXAMPLE IN THOSE IN HIGH STATIONS. 1. We must bear in mind that the ceremonies, or rules of propriety, spoken of in these books, are not mere conventionalities, but the ordinations of man's moral and intelligent nature in the line of what is *proper.* 絞, 'to strangle,' is here explained by Chow He by 急切. Ho An, after Ma Yung (early part of 2d century), makes it =絞刺, 'sarcasm.' 2. There does not seem any connection between the for. paragraph and this, and hence this is by many considered to be a new chap., and assigned to the philosopher Tsăng. 君子, diff. here from its previous usage, having reference more to the 位 or station of the individuals indicated, than to their 德 or virtue. 故舊=舊臣舊交, 'old ministers and old intimacies' 偷, often a verb, 'to steal;' here an adj., 'mean.'

3. THE PHILOSOPHER TSANG'S FILIAL PIETY SEEN IN HIS CARE OF HIS PERSON. We get our bodies perfect from our parents, and should so preserve them to the last. This is a great branch of filial piety with the Ch., and this ch. is said to illustrate how Tsăng-tsze had made

論語

足、啟予手、詩云、戰戰兢兢、如臨深淵、如履薄冰、而今而後、吾知免夫、小子。

第四章 一節 曾子有疾、孟敬子問之。二節 曾子言曰、鳥之將死、其鳴也哀、人之將死、其言也善。三節 君子所貴乎道者三、動容貌、斯遠暴慢矣、正顏色、斯近信矣、出辭氣、斯遠鄙倍矣、籩豆之事、則有司存。

CHAPTER IV. 1. The philosopher Tsăng being sick, Mang King went to ask how he was.

2. Tsăng said to him, "When a bird is about to die, its notes are mournful; when a man is about to die, his words are good.

3. "There are three principles of conduct which the man of high rank should consider specially important:—that in his deportment and manner he keep from violence and heedlessness; that in regulating his countenance he keep near to sincerity; and that in his words and tones he keep far from lowness and impropriety. As to such matters as attending to the sacrificial vessels, there are the proper officers for them."

this his life-long study. He made the disci. uncover his hands and feet to show them in what preservation those members were. 詩云,—see the She-king, II. v.i.st. 6. In 而今, we must take 而=自. The whole clause indicates, comm. say, not so much Tsăng's satisfaction in the preservation of his person, as the anxiety which he had had, and would continue to have, if life were prolonged, in preserving it.

4. THE PHILOSOPHER TSANG'S DYING COUNSELS TO A MAN OF HIGH RANK. 1. 敬 was the hon. epi. of 仲孫捷, a great officer of Loo, and son of Mang-woo, II. 6. From the conclusion of this chapter, we may suppose that he descended to small matters below his rank. 之 refers to 疾. 2. 言, in 曾子言曰, intimates that Tsăng commenced the conversation. 3. 動, 正, and 出 are all verbs governing the nouns following. 倍 is read like 背, and with the same meaning, 'to rebel against,' 'to be contrary to,' that here opposed being 道, 'the truth and right.' 籩 was a bamboo dish with a stand, made to hold fruits and seeds at sacrifice; 豆 was like it, and of the same size, only made of wood, and used to contain pickled vegetables and sauces. 君子 is used as in ch. 2.—In Ho An's compilation, the three clauses, begin. 斯遠, are taken differently, and='thus he will not suffer from men's being violent and insulting, &c., &c.' I prefer the modern view.

第五章 曾子曰、以能問於不能、以多問於寡、有若無、實若虛、犯而不校、昔者吾友、嘗從事於斯矣。

第六章 曾子曰、可以託六尺之孤、可以寄百里之命、臨大節、而不可奪也、君子人與、君子人也。

第七章 一節 曾子曰、士、不可以不弘毅、任重而道遠。二節 仁以爲己

CHAPTER V. The philosopher Tsăng said, "Gifted with ability, and yet putting questions to those who were not so; possessed of much, and yet putting questions to those possessed of little; having, as though he had not; full, and yet counting himself as empty; offended against, and yet entering into no altercation:—formerly I had a friend who pursued this style of conduct."

CHAPTER VI. The philosopher Tsăng said, "Suppose that there is an individual who can be entrusted with the charge of a young orphan *prince*, and can be commissioned with authority over *a state of* a hundred *le*, and whom no emergency however great can drive from his principles:—is such a man a superior man? He is a superior man indeed."

CHAPTER VII. 1. The philsopher Tsăng said, "The scholar may not be without breadth of mind and vigorous endurance. His burden is heavy and his course is long.

5. THE ADMIRABLE SIMPLICITY AND FREEDOM FROM EGOTISM OF A FRIEND OF THE PHILOSOPHER TSANG. This friend is supposed to have been Yen Yuen. 校, 'imprisonment by means of wood,' 'stocks.' The Dict., after the old interpr., explains it with reference to this passage, by 角也, 報也 'altercation,' 'recompensing.' 從事於斯, lit., 'followed things in this way.'

6. A COMBINATION OF TALENTS AND VIRTUE CONSTITUTING A KEUN TSZE. 六尺之孤, 'an orphan of six cubits.' By a comparison of a passage in the Chow Le and other references to the subject, it seems to be established that 'of six cubits' is here equivalent to 'of 15 years,' and that for every cubit more or less we should add or deduct five years. See the 經註集證, where it is also said that the ancient cubit was shorter than the modern, and only=7.4 in., so that 6 cubits=4.44 cubits of the present day. But this estimate of the ancient cubit is probably still too high. King Wăn, it is said, was 10 cubits high, '*i. e.*, 7.4 modern cubits or more than 8½ English feet. 百里之命, see Men. V. ii. 2. 與 amounts nearly to a question, and is answered by 也,—'Yes, indeed.'

7. THE NECESSITY TO THE SCHOLAR OF COMPASS AND VIGOUR OF MIND. 士, 'a learned

論語

任、不亦重乎、死而後已、不亦遠乎。

第八章 子曰、一節 興於詩。二節 立於禮。成於樂。

第九章 子曰、民可使由之、不可使知之。

第十章 子曰、好勇疾貧、亂也、人而不仁、疾之已甚、亂也。

2. "Perfect virtue is the burden which he considers it is his to sustain;—is it not heavy? Only with death does his course stop;—is it not long?"

CHAPTER VIII. 1. The Master said, "It is by the Odes that the mind is aroused.

2. "It is by the Rules of propriety that the character is established.

3. "It is from Music that the finish is received."

CHAPTER IX. The Master said, "The people may be made to follow a path of action, but they may not be made to understand it."

CHAPTER X. The Master said, "The man who is fond of daring and is dissatisfied with poverty, will proceed to insubordination. So will the man who is not virtuous, when you carry your dislike of him to an extreme."

man,' 'a scholar,' but in all ages learning has been the qualification for, and passport to, official employment in China, hence it is also a general designation for 'an officer.' 任, low. 3d tone, a noun,='an office,' 'a burden borne;' with the 1st tone, it is the verb 'to bear.'

8. THE EFFECTS OF POETRY, PROPRIETIES, AND MUSIC. These three short sentences are in form like the four, 志於道, &c., in VII. 6, but must be interpreted differently. There the first term in each sentence is a verb in the imperative mood; here it is in the indicative. There the 於 is to be joined closely to the 1st character and here to the 3d. There it=our prepos. *to*; here it=*by*. The terms 詩, 禮, 樂, have all specific reference.

9. WHAT MAY, AND WHAT MAY NOT BE ATTAINED TO WITH THE PEOPLE. According to Choo He, the first 之 is 理之所當然,—*duty*, what principles require, and the second is 理之所以然, 'the *principle* of duty.' He also takes 可 and 不可 as=能 and 不能. If the meaning were so, then the sentiment would be much too broadly expressed. See 四書改錯, XVI. 15. As often in other places, the 翼註 gives the meaning here happily; viz., that a knowledge of the reasons and principles of what they are called to do need not be required from the people,—不可責之民.

10. DIFFERENT CAUSES OF INSUBORDINATION —A LESSON TO RULERS.

十一章 子曰、如有周公之才之美、使驕且吝、其餘不足觀也已。

十二章 子曰、三年學、不至於穀、不易得也。

十三章 一節 子曰、篤信好學、守死善道。二節 危邦不入、亂邦不居、天下有道則見、無道則隱。三節 邦有道、貧且賤焉、恥也、邦無道、富且貴焉、恥也。

CHAPTER XI. The Master said, "Though a man have abilities as admirable as those of the duke of Chow, yet if he be proud and niggardly, those other things are really not worth being looked at."

CHAPTER XII. The Master said, "It is not easy to find a man who has learned for three years without coming to be good."

CHAPTER XIII. 1. The Master said, "With sincere faith he unites the love of learning; holding firm to death, he is perfecting the excellence of his course.

2. "*Such an one* will not enter a tottering state, nor dwell in a disorganized one. When right principles of government prevail in the empire, he will show himself; when they are prostrated, he will keep concealed.

3. "When a country is well governed, poverty and a mean condition are things to be ashamed of. When a country is ill governed, riches and honour are things to be ashamed of."

11. THE WORTHLESSNESS OF TALENT WITHOUT VIRTUE. 'The duke of Chow;'—see VII. 5. 其餘, 'the overplus,' 'the superfluity,' referring to the 'talents,' and indicating that ability is not the 本, or root of character, not what is essential. 也已, as in ch. 1.

12. HOW QUICKLY LEARNING LEADS TO GOOD. This is the interpretation of K'ung Gan-kwŏ, who takes 穀 in the sense of 善. Choo He takes the term in the sense of 祿, 'emolument,' and would change 至 into 志, making the whole a lamentation over the rarity of the disinterested pursuit of learning. But we are not at liberty to admit alterations of the text, unless, as received, it be absolutely unintelligible.

13. THE QUALIFICATIONS OF AN OFFICER, WHO WILL ALWAYS ACT RIGHT IN ACCEPTING AND DECLINING OFFICE. 1. This par. is to be taken as descriptive of character, the effects of whose presence we have in the next, and of its absence in the last. 2. 見 in oppos. to 隱, read *heen*, low. 3d tone. The whole ch. seems to want the warmth of generous principle and feeling. In fact, I doubt whether its parts bear the relation and connection which they are supposed to have.

十四章 子曰、不在其位、不謀其政。

十五章 子曰、師摯之始、關雎之亂、洋洋乎、盈耳哉。

十六章 子曰、狂而不直、侗而不愿、悾悾而不信、吾不知之矣。

十七章 子曰、學如不及、猶恐失之。

十八章 子曰、巍巍乎、舜禹之

CHAPTER XIV. The Master said, "He who is not in any particular office, has nothing to do with plans for the administration of its duties."

CHAPTER XV. The Master said, "When the music-master, Che, first entered on his office, the finish with the Kwan Ts'eu was magnificent;—how it filled the ears!"

CHAPTER XVI. The Master said, "Ardent and yet not upright; stupid and yet not attentive; simple and yet not sincere:—such persons I do not understand."

CHAPTER XVII. The Master said, "Learn as if you could not reach your object, and were *always* fearing also lest you should lose it."

CHAPTER XVIII. The Master said, "How majestic was the manner in which Shun and Yu held possession of the empire, as if it were nothing to them!"

14. EVERY MAN SHOULD MIND HIS OWN BUSINESS. So the sentiment of this ch. is generalized by the paraphrasts, and perhaps correctly. Its letter, however, has doubtless operated to prevent the spread of right notions about political liberty in China.

15. THE PRAISE OF THE MUSIC-MASTER CHE. Neither Morrison nor Medhurst gives what appears to be the meaning of 亂 in this ch. K'ang-he's dict. has it—樂之卒章曰亂. 'The last part in the musical services is called *lwan*.' The programme on those occasions consisted of four parts, in the last of which a number of pieces from the *fung* or national songs was sung, commencing with the *Kwan-ts'eu*. The name *lwan* was also given to a sort of refrain, at the end of each song.—The old interpreters explain differently. —'when the music-master Che first corrected the confusion of the Kwan-ts'eu,' &c.

16. A LAMENTATION OVER MORAL ERROR ADDED TO NATURAL DEFECT. 吾不知之, 'I do not know them,' that is, say comm., natural defects of endowment are generally associated with certain redeeming qualities, as hastiness with straightforwardness, &c. In the parties Conf. had in view, those redeeming qualities were absent. He did not understand them, and could do nothing for them.

17. WITH WHAT EARNESTNESS AND CONTINUOUSNESS LEARNING SHOULD BE PURSUED.

18. THE LOFTY CHARACTER OF SHUN AND YU. Shun received the empire from Yaou, B. C. 2254, and Yu received it from Shun, B. C. 2204. The throne came to them not by inheritance. They were called to it by their talents and virtue. And yet the possession of empire did not affect them at all. 不與,—'It did not concern them,' was as if nothing to them. He

有天下也、而不與焉。

十九章 一節 子曰、大哉、堯之爲君也、巍巍乎、唯天爲大、唯堯則之、蕩蕩乎、民無能名焉、二節 巍巍乎、其有成功也、煥乎、其有文章。

二十章 一節 舜有臣五人、而天下治、二節 武王曰、予有亂臣十人、三節 孔子曰、才難、不其然乎、唐虞之際、於斯爲盛、

CHAPTER XIX. 1. The Master said, "Great indeed was Yaou as a sovereign! How majestic was he! It is only Heaven that is grand, and only Yaou corresponded to it. How vast *was his virtue!* The people could find no name for it.

2. "How majestic was he in the works which he accomplished! How glorious in the elegant regulations which he instituted!"

CHAPTER XX. 1. Shun had five ministers, and the empire was well governed.

2. King Woo said, "I have ten able ministers."

3. Confucius said, "Is not *the saying* that talents are difficult to find, true? *Only* when the dynasties of T'ang and Yu met, were they more abundant than in this *of Chow, yet* there was a woman among them. *The able ministers* were no more than nine men."

An takes 與=求—'They had the empire without seeking for it.' This is not according to usage.

19. THE PRAISE OF YAOU. 1. No doubt, Yaou, as he appears in Chinese annals, is a fit object of admiration, but if Confucius had had a right knowledge of, and reverence for, Heaven, he could not have spoken as he does here. Grant that it is only the visible heaven overspreading all, to which he compares Yaou, even that is sufficiently absurd. 則之, not simply=法之, 'imitated it,' but 能與之準, 'could equalize with it.' 2. 其有成功=其所有之成功, the great achievements of his goverment. 文章 (see V. 12)=the music, ceremonies, &c., of which he was the author.

20. THE SCARCITY OF MEN OF TALENT, AND PRAISE OF THE HOUSE OF CHOW. 1. Shun's five ministers were 禹, superintendent of works, 稷, superintendent of agriculture, 契 (sëë), minister of instruction, 皐陶, minister of justice, and 伯益, warden of woods and marshes. Those five, as being eminent above all their compeers, are mentioned. 2. See the Shoo-king, V. i. sect. ii. 6. 亂臣, 'governing, *i. e.,* able ministers.' In the dict., the first meaning given of 亂 is 'to regulate,' and the second is just the opposite,—'to confound,' 'confusion.' Of the ten ministers, the most distinguished of course was the duke of Chow. One of them, it is said next par., was a woman, but whether she was the mother of king Wăn, or his wife, is much disputed. 3. Instead of the usual 'the master said,' we have here 孔子曰, 'The philosopher K'ung said.' This

有婦人焉、九人而已。四節三分天下有其二、以服事殷、周之德、其可謂至德也已矣。

二十一章子曰、禹吾無間然矣、菲飲食、而致孝乎鬼神、惡衣服、而致美乎黻冕、卑宮室、而盡力乎溝洫、禹吾無間然矣。

4. "*King Wăn* possessed two of the three parts of the empire, and with those he served the dynasty of Yin. The virtue of the house of Chow may be said to have reached the highest point indeed."

CHAPTER XXI. The Master said, "I can find no flaw in the character of Yu. He used himself coarse food and drink, but displayed the utmost filial piety towards the spirits. His ordinary garments were poor, but he displayed the utmost elegance in his sacrificial cap and apron. He lived in a low mean house, but expended all his strength on the ditches and water-channels. I can find nothing like a flaw in Yu."

is accounted for on the ground that the words of *king* Woo having been quoted immediately before, it would not have done to crown the sage with his usual title of 'the *Master*.' The style of the whole chapter, however, is different from that of any previous one, and we may suspect that it is corrupted. 才難 is a sort of proverb, or common saying, which Conf. quotes and illustrates. 唐虞之際, (Yaou is called T'ang, having ascended the throne from the marquisate of that name, and Yu became the accepted surname or style of Shun.) 於斯爲盛 is understood by Choo He as in the transl., while the old comm. take exactly the opposite view. The whole is obscure. 4. This par. must be spoken of King Wăn.

21. THE PRAISE OF YU. 閒, read *Këen*, up. 3d tone, 'a crevice,' 'a crack,' 禹吾無閒然矣, '*In* Yu, *I find* no crevice so,' *i. e.*, I find nothing in him to which I can point as a flaw. 鬼神 is interpreted of the spirits of heaven and earth, as well as those sacrificed to in the ancestral temple, but the saying that the rich offerings were filial (孝) would seem to restrict the phrase to the latter. The 黻 was an apron made of leather, and coming down over the knees, and the 冕 was a sort of cap or crown, flat on the top, and projecting before and behind, with a long fringe on which gems and pearls were strung. They were both used in sacrificing. 溝洫, generally the water-channels by which the boundaries of the fields were determined, and provision made for their irrigation, and to carry off the water of floods. The 溝 were 4 cubits wide and deep, and arranged so as to flow into the 洫, which were double the size.

BOOK IX. TSZE HAN.

子罕第九

第一章 子罕言、利、與命、與仁。

第二章 一節 達巷黨人曰、大哉孔子、博學而無所成名。二節 子聞之、謂門弟子曰、吾何執、執御乎、執射乎、吾執御矣。

CHAPTER I. The subjects of which the Master seldom spoke were—profitableness, and also the appointments *of Heaven*, and perfect virtue.

CHAPTER II. 1. A man of the village of Tă-heang said, "Great indeed is the philosopher K'ung! His learning is extensive, and yet he does not render his name famous by any *particular* thing."

2. The Master heard the observation, and said to his disciples, "What shall I practise? Shall I practise charioteering, or shall I practise archery? I will practise charioteering."

HEADING OF THIS BOOK.—子罕第九. 'The Master seldom, No. 9.' The thirty chapters of this Book are much akin to those of the seventh. They are mostly occupied with the doctrine, character, and ways of Confucius himself.

1. SUBJECTS SELDOM SPOKEN OF BY CONFUCIUS. 利 is mostly taken here in a good sense, not as selfish gain, but as it is defined under the first of the diagrams in the Yih-king,—義之和, 'the harmoniousness of all that is righteous;' that is, how what is right is really what is truly profitable. Comp. Mencius, I. i. 1. Yet even in this sense Conf. seldom spoke of it, as he would not have the consideration of the profitable introduced into conduct at all. With his not speaking of 仁 there is a difficulty which I know not how to solve. The IVth book is nearly all occupied with it, and no doubt it was a prominent topic in Conf. teachings. 命 is not=our *fate*, unless in the primary meaning of that term,—'*Fatum est quod dii fantur*.' Nor is it *decree*, or antecedent purpose and determination, but the decree embodied and realized in its object.

2. AMUSEMENT OF CONFUCIUS AT THE REMARK OF AN IGNORANT MAN ABOUT HIM. Comm., old and new, say that the ch. shows the exceeding humility of the sage, educed by his being praised, but his observation on the man's remark was evidently ironical. 1. For want of another word, I render 黨 'by village.' According to the statutes of Chow, 'five families made a 比, four *pe* a 閭, and five *leu* or 500 families a *tang*.' Who the villager was is not recorded, though some would have him to be the same with 項橐, the boy of whom it is said in the 三字經, 昔仲尼師項橐, 'of old Confucius was a scholar to Heang T'ŏ.' The man was able to see that Confucius was very extensively learned, but his idea of fame, common to the age, was that it must be acquired by excellence in some one particular art. In his lips, 孔子 was not more than our 'Mr. K'ung.'

第三章 一節 子曰、麻冕、禮也、今也純、儉、吾從衆。二節 拜下、禮也、今拜乎上、泰也、雖違衆、吾從下。

第四章 子絕四、毋意、毋必、毋固、毋我。

第五章 一節 子畏於匡。二節 曰、文王既沒、文不在茲乎。三節 天之將喪斯文也、後死者、不得與於斯文也、

CHAPTER III. 1. The Master said, "The linen cap is that prescribed by the rules of ceremony, but now a silk one is worn. It is economical, and I follow the common practice.

2. "The rules of ceremony prescribe the bowing below *the hall*, but now the practice is to bow *only* after ascending it. That is arrogant. I *continue to* bow below the hall, though I oppose the common practice."

CHAPTER IV. There were four things from which the Master was entirely free. He had no foregone conclusions, no arbitrary predeterminations, no obstinacy, and no egoism.

CHAPTER V. 1. The Master was put in fear in K'wang.

2. He said, "After the death of king Wăn, was not the cause of truth lodged here *in me*?

3. SOME COMMON PRACTICES INDIFFERENT AND OTHERS NOT. 1. The cap here spoken of was that prescribed to be worn in the ancestral temple, and made of very fine linen dyed of a deep dark colour. There are long discussions about the number of threads that went into its warp. It had fallen into disuse, and was superseded by a simpler one of silk. Rather than be singular, Confucius gave in to a practice, which involved no principle of right, and was economical. 2. Choo He explains the 拜下, 拜乎上, thus: 'In the ceremonial intercourse between ministers and their prince, it was proper for them to bow below the raised hall. This the prince declined, on which they ascended and completed the homage.' See this illustrated in the 經註集證, *in loc.* The prevailing disregard of the first part of the cer. Conf. considered inconsistent with the proper distance to be observed between prince and minister, and therefore he would be singular in adhering to the rule.

4. FRAILTIES FROM WHICH CONFUCIUS WAS FREE. 毋, it is said, is not prohibitive here, but simply negative, = 無. This criticism is made to make it appear that it was not by any effort, as 絕 and 毋 more naturally suggest, that Confucius attained to these things.

5. CONFUCIUS ASSURED IN A TIME OF DANGER BY HIS CONVICTION OF A DIVINE MISSION. Comp. VII. 22, but the adventure to which this ch. refers is placed in the sage's history before the other, and seems to have occurred in his 57th year, not long after he had resigned office, and left Loo. 1. There are different opinions as to what state K'wang belonged to. The most likely is that it was a border town of Ch'ing, and its site is now to be found in the dep. of K'ae-fung in Ho-nan. The account is that K'wang had suffered from 陽虎, an officer of Loo, to whom Conf. bore a resemblance. As he passed by the place moreover, a disciple, 顏刻, who had been associated with Yang Foo in his operations against K'wang, was driving him. These circum. made the people think that Conf. was their old enemy, so they attacked him, and kept him prisoner for five days. The accounts of his escape vary, some of them being evidently

天之未喪斯文也、匡人其如予何。

第六章 一節 大宰問於子貢、曰、夫子聖者與、何其多能也。二節 子貢曰、固天縱之將聖、又多能也。三節 子聞之曰、大宰知我乎、吾少也賤、故多能、鄙事、君子多乎哉、不多也。四節 牢曰、子云、吾不試、故藝。

3. "If Heaven had wished to let this cause of truth perish, then I, a future mortal, should not have got such a relation to that cause. While Heaven does not let the cause of truth perish, what can the people of K'wang do to me?"

CHAPTER VI. 1. A high officer asked Tsze-kung saying, "May we not say that your Master is a sage? How various is his ability!"

2. Tsze Kung said, "Certainly Heaven has endowed him unlimitedly. He is about a sage. And, moreover, his ability is various."

3. The Master heard of the conversation and said, "Does the high officer know me? When I was young, my condition was low, and therefore I acquired my ability in many things, but they were mean matters. Must the superior man have such variety of ability? He does not need variety of ability."

4. Laou said, "The Master said, 'Having no official employment, I acquired many arts.'"

fabulous. The disciples were in fear. 畏 would indicate that Confucius himself was so, but this is denied. 2. 文,—I render by 'the cause of truth.' More exactly, it is the truth embodied in literature, ceremonies, &c., and its use instead of 道, 'truth in its principles,' is attributed to Conf. modesty. 在茲, 'in this,' ref. to himself. 3. There may be modesty in his use of 文, but he here identifies himself with the line of the great sages, to whom Heaven has intrusted the instruction of men. In all the six centuries between himself and king Wăn, he does not admit of such another. 後死者, 'he who dies afterwards,'=a future mortal.

6. ON THE VARIOUS ABILITY OF CONFUCIUS:—HIS SAGEHOOD NOT THEREIN. 1. According to the 周禮, the 大宰 was the chief of the six great officers of state, but the use of the designation in Conf. times was confined to the states of Woo and Sung, and hence the officer in the text must have belonged to one of them. See the 註疏, *in loc.* The force of 與 is as appears in the transl. 2. 與 is responded to by Tsze-kung with 固, 'certainly,' while yet by the use of 將 he gives his answer an air of hesitancy. 縱之, 'lets him go,' *i. e.*, does not restrict him at all. The officer had found the sagehood of Conf. in his various ability;—by

論語

第七章 子曰、吾有知乎哉、無知也、有鄙夫問於我、空空如也、我叩其兩端而竭焉。

第八章 子曰、鳳鳥不至、河不出圖、吾已矣夫。

第九章 子見齊衰者、冕衣裳者、與瞽者、見之、雖少必作、過之必趨。

CHAPTER VII. The Master said, "Am I indeed possessed of knowledge? I am not knowing. But if a mean person, who appears quite empty-like, ask anything of me, I set it forth from one end to the other, and exhaust it."

CHAPTER VIII. The Master said, "The FUNG bird does not come; the river sends forth no map:—it is all over with me."

CHAPTER IX. When the Master saw a person in a mourning dress, or any one with the cap and upper and lower garments of full dress, or a blind person, on observing them *approaching*, though they were younger than himself, he would rise up, and if he had to pass by them, he would do so hastily.

the 又, 'moreover,' Tsze-kung makes that ability only an addit. circum. 3. Conf. explains his possess. of various ability, and repudiates its being essen. to the sage, or even to the *Keun-tsze*. 4. Laou was a disciple, by surname K'in (琴), and styled Tsze-k'ae (子開), or Tsze-chang (子張). It is supposed that when these conversations were being digested into their present form, some one remembered that Laou had been in the habit of mentioning the remark given, and accordingly it was appended to the chapter. 子云 indicates that it was a frequent saying of Confucius.

7. CONFUCIUS DISCLAIMS THE KNOWLEDGE ATTRIBUTED TO HIM, AND DECLARES HIS EARNESTNESS IN TEACHING. The first sentence here was probably an exclamation with reference to some remark upon himself as having extraordinary knowledge. 叩其兩端, 'exhibit (叩=發動, 'to agitate,') its two ends,' *i. e.*, discuss it from beginning to end.

8. FOR WANT OF AUSPICIOUS OMENS, CONFUCIUS GIVES UP THE HOPE OF THE TRIUMPH OF HIS DOCTRINES. The *fung* is the male of a fabulous bird, which has been called the Chinese phœnix, said to appear when a sage ascends the throne or when right principles are going to triumph thro' the empire. The female is called 凰. In the days of Shun, they gambolled in his hall, and were heard singing on mount K'e, in the time of king Wǎn. The river and the map carry us farther back still,—to the time of Fuh-he, to whom a monster with the head of a dragon, and the body of a horse, rose from the water, being marked on the back so as to give that first of the sages the idea of his diagrams. Conf. indorses these fables. 吾已矣夫,—see V. 26, and obs. how 乎 and 夫 are interchanged.

9. CONFUCIUS' SYMPATHY WITH SORROW, RESPECT FOR RANK, AND PITY FOR MISFORTUNE. 齊, read *tsze*, is 'the lower edge of a garment' and joined with 衰, read *ts'uy*, 'mourning garments,' the two char. indicate the mourning of the second degree of intensity, where the edge is unhemmed, but cut *even*, instead of being ragged, the terms for which are 斬衰. The phrase, however, seems to be for 'in mourning' generally. 少, up. 3d tone, 'young.'

第十章 一節 顏淵喟然歎曰、仰之彌高、鑽之彌堅、瞻之在前、忽焉在後。二節 夫子循循然善誘人、博我以文、約我以禮。三節 欲罷不能、既竭吾才、如有所立卓爾、雖欲從之、末由也已。

第十一章 一節 子疾病、子路使門人爲臣。二節 病間曰、久矣哉、由之行詐也、無臣而爲有

CHAPTER X. 1. Yen Yuen, *in admiration of the Master's doctrines,* sighed and said, "I looked up to them, and they *seemed to become* more high; I tried to penetrate them, and they *seemed to become* more firm; I looked at them before me, and suddenly they *seemed to be* behind.

2. "The Master, by orderly method, skilfully leads men on. He enlarged my mind with learning, and taught me the restraints of propriety.

3. "When I wish to give over *the study of his doctrines,* I cannot do so, and having exerted all my ability, there seems something to stand right up before me; but though I wish to follow *and lay hold of it,* I really find no way to do so."

CHAPTER XI. 1. The Master being very ill, Tsze-loo wished the disciples to act as ministers to him.

2. During a remission of his illness, he said, "Long has the con- luct of Yew been deceitful! By pretending to have ministers when have them not, whom should I impose upon? Should I impose ›on Heaven?

'. YEN YUEN'S ADMIRATION OF HIS MASTER'S 'RINES, AND HIS OWN PROGRESS IN THEM. 然歎, 'sighingly sighed.' 仰 and ıer verbs here are to be translated in the ıse, as the ch. seems to give an account rogress of Hwuy's mind. 忽焉=忽 ldenly.' 2. 誘=引進, 'to lead for- 我云云,—comp. VI. 25. 3. 卓然, an adv., 'uprightly,' 'loftily.' o follow it,' *i. e.,* to advance there- 末, in the sense of 無. 末由=無所由以用其力, 'I have not the means whereby to use my strength.' 也已, 'yea, indeed.'—It was this which made him sigh.

11. CONFUCIUS' DISLIKE OF PRETENSION, AND CONTENTMENT WITH HIS CONDITION. 1. 使, 'was causing,' or wanted to cause. Conf. had been a great officer, and enjoyed the services of ministers, as in a petty court. Tsze-loo would have surrounded him in his great sickness (疾病), with the illusions of his former state, and

論語

臣、吾誰欺、欺天乎。(三節) 且予與其死於臣之手也、無寧死於二三子之手乎、且予縱不得大葬、予死於道路乎。

(十二章) 子貢曰、有美玉於斯、韞匵而藏諸、求善賈而沽諸。子曰、沽之哉、沽之哉、我待賈者也。

(十三章) (一節) 子欲居九夷。(二節) 或曰、陋、如之何。子曰、君子居之、何陋之有。

(十四章) 子曰、吾自衞反魯、然後樂

3. "Moreover, than that I should die in the hands of ministers, is it not better that I should die in the hands of you, my disciples? And though I may not get a great burial, shall I die upon the road?"

CHAPTER XII. Tsze-kung said, "There is a beautiful gem here. Should I lay it up in a case and keep it? or should I seek for a good price and sell it?" The Master said, "Sell it! Sell it! But I would wait till the price was offered."

CHAPTER XIII. 1. The Master was wishing to go and live among the nine wild tribes of the east.

2. Some one said, "They are rude. How can you do such a thing?" The Master said, "If a superior man dwelt among them, what rudeness would there be?"

CHAPTER XIV. The Master said, "I returned from Wei to Loo, and then the music was reformed, and the pieces in the Imperial songs and Praise songs found all their proper place."

brought on himself this rebuke. 3. 縱=縱然, a conjunction, 'letting it be that,'=although.

12. HOW THE DESIRE FOR OFFICE SHOULD BE QUALIFIED BY SELF-RESPECT. 諸 is interrog. here, as in VII. 25. There being no nominative to 韞, like the 'I' in the transl., we might render, 'should it be put, &c.' 賈, read *kea*, up. 3d tone,=價, 'price,' 'value.' The disciple wanted to elicit from Conf. why he declined office so much, and insinuated the subject in this way.

13. HOW BARBARIANS CAN BE CIVILIZED. This ch. is to be understood, it is said like V. 6, not as if Conf. really wished to go among the E, but that he thus expressed his regret that his doctr. did not find accept. in China. 1. 夷, see III. 5. There were nine tribes or varieties (種) of them, the yellow, white, red, &c. 2. 如之何,—the 之 refers to his purpose to go among the E.

14. CONFUCIUS' SERVICES IN CORRECTING THE MUSIC OF HIS NATIVE STATE AND ADJUSTING THE

正雅頌各得其所。

十五 子曰、出則事公卿、入則事父兄、喪事不敢不勉、不爲酒困、何有於我哉。

十六 子在川上曰、逝者如斯夫、不舍晝夜。

十七 子曰、吾未見好德如好色者也。

十八 子曰、譬如爲山、未成一簣、止、吾止也、譬如平地、雖

CHAPTER XV. The Master said, "Abroad, to serve the high ministers and officers; at home, to serve one's father and elder brother; in all duties to the dead, not to dare not to exert one's-self; and not to be overcome of wine:—what one of these things do I attain to?"

CHAPTER XVI. The Master standing by a stream, said, "It passes on just like this, not ceasing day or night!"

CHAPTER XVII. The Master said, "I have not seen one who loves virtue as he loves beauty."

CHAPTER XVIII. The Master said, "*The prosecution of learning* may be compared to what may happen in raising a mound. If there want but one basket *of earth* to complete the work, and I stop,

BOOK OF POETRY. Conf. returned from Wei to Loo in his 69th year, and died 5 years after. The 雅, (read *nga*, low. 2d tone), and the 頌, are the names of two, or rather three, of the divisions of the She-king, the former being the 'elegant' or 'correct' odes, to be used with music at imperial festivals, and the praise-songs, celebrating principally the virtues of the founders of different dynasties, to be used in the services of the ancestral temple.

15. CONFUCIUS' VERY HUMBLE ESTIMATE OF HIMSELF. Comp. VII. 2, but the things which Confucius here disclaims are of a still lower char. than those there mentioned. Very remarkable is the last, as from the sage. The old interpr. treat 何有於我哉, as they do in VII. 12. 公卿 stand together, indicat. men of superior rank. If we disting. between them, the 公 may express the princes, high officers in the imperial court, and the 卿, the high officers in the princes' courts.

16. HOW CONFUCIUS WAS AFFECTED BY A RUNNING STREAM. What does the *it* in the transl. refer to? 者 and 如 indicate something in the sage's mind, suggested by the ceaseless move. of the water. Choo He makes it 天地之化,=our 'course of nature.' In the 註疏 we find for it 時事, 'events,' 'the things of time.' Probably Choo He is correct. Comp. Mencius, IV. ii. 18.

17. THE RARITY OF A SINCERE LOVE OF VIRTUE. 色, as in I. 7.

18. THAT LEARNERS SHOULD NOT CEASE NOR INTERMIT THEIR LABOURS. This is a fragment, like many other chapters, of some conversation, and the subject thus illustrated must be supplied, after the mod. comm., as in the translation, or, after the old, by 'the following of virtue.' See the Shoo-king, V. v. 9, where the subject is virtuous consistency. We might expect 平 in 平地, to be a verb, like 爲

論語

覆一簣、進、吾往也。

十九章 子曰、語之而不惰者、其回也與。

二十章 子謂顏淵曰、惜乎、吾見其進也、未見其止也。

廿一章 子曰、苗而不秀者、有矣夫、秀而不實者、有矣夫。

廿二章 子曰、後生可畏、焉知來者之不如今也、四十五十而無聞焉、斯亦不足畏也已。

the stopping is my own work. It may be compared to *throwing down the earth* on the level ground. Though *but* one basketful is thrown *at a time*, the advancing with it is my own going forward."

CHAPTER XIX. The Master said, "Never flagging when I set forth anything to him;—ah! that is Hwuy."

CHAPTER XX. The Master said of Yen Yuen, "Alas! I saw his constant advance. I never saw him stop in his progress."

CHAPTER XXI. The Master said, "There are cases in which the blade springs, but the plant does not go on to flower! There are cases where it flowers, but no fruit is subsequently produced!"

CHAPTER XXII. The Master said, "A youth is to be regarded with respect. How do we know that his future will not be equal to our present? If he reach the age of forty or fifty, and has not made himself heard of, then indeed he will not be worth being regarded with respect."

in 爲山, but a good sense cannot be made out by taking it so. 雖,='tho' *only*,' as many take it in VI. 24. The lesson of the ch. is—that repeated acquisitions individually small will ultimately amount to much, and that the learner is never to give over.

19. HWUY THE EARNEST STUDENT.

20. CONFUCIUS' FOND RECOLLECTION OF HWUY AS A MODEL STUDENT. This is said to have been spoken after Hwuy's death. 惜乎 looks as if it were so. The 未, 'not yet,' would rather make us think differently.

21. IT IS THE END WHICH CROWNS THE WORK.

22. HOW AND WHY A YOUTH SHOULD BE REGARDED WITH RESPECT. The same person is spoken of throughout the ch., as is shown by the 亦 in the last sentence. This is not very conclusive, but it brings out a good enough meaning. With Conf. remark compare that of John Trebonius, Luther's schoolmaster at Eisenach, who used to raise his cap to his pupils on entering the schoolroom, and gave as the reason—

〔二十三〕子曰、法語之言、能無從乎、改之爲貴、巽與之言、能無說乎、繹之爲貴、說而不繹、從而不改、吾末如之何也已矣。

〔二十四〕子曰、主忠信、毋友不如己者、過則勿憚改。

〔二十五〕子曰、三軍可奪帥也、匹夫不可奪志也。

CHAPTER XXIII. The Master said, "Can men refuse to assent to the words of strict admonition? But it is reforming the conduct because of them which is valuable. Can men refuse to be pleased with words of gentle advice? But it is unfolding their aim which is valuable. If a man be pleased with these words, but does not unfold their aim, and assents to those, but does not reform his conduct, I can really do nothing with him."

CHAPTER XXIV. The Master said, "Hold faithfulness and sincerity as first principles. Have no friends not equal to yourself. When you have faults, do not fear to abandon them."

CHAPTER XXV. The Master said, "The commander of the forces of a large state may be carried off, but the will of even a common man cannot be taken from him."

'There are among these boys men of whom God will one day make burgomasters, chancellors, doctors, and magistrates. Although you do not yet see them with the badges of their dignity, it is right that you should treat them with respect.' 後生, 'after born,' a youth. See 先生, II. 8.

23. THE HOPELESSNESS OF THE CASE OF THOSE WHO ASSENT AND APPROVE WITHOUT REFORMATION OR SERIOUS THOUGHT. 法語之言, 'words of law-like admonition.' 巽, is the name of the diagram, to which the element of 'wind' is attached. Wind enters everywhere, hence the char. is interpreted by 'entering,' and also by 'mildness,' 'yielding.' 巽與之言, 'words of gentle insinuation.' In 繹之爲貴, an anteced. to 之 is readily found in the prec. 言, but in 改之爲貴, such an anteced. can only be found in a roundabout way. This is one of the cases which shows the inapplicability to Chinese composition of our strict syntactical apparatus. 末 as in ch. 10.

24. This is a repetition of part of I. 8.

25. THE WILL UNSUBDUABLE. 三軍, see VII. 10. 帥, read *shwae*, lower 3d tone,=將帥, 'a general.' 匹, 'mate.' We find in the dict.—'Husband and wife of the common people are a pair (相匹),' and the applica. of the term being thus fixed, an individual man is called 匹夫, an individual woman 匹婦.

[二十六章]子曰、[一節]衣敝縕袍、與衣狐貉者立、而不恥者、其由也與。[二節]不忮不求、何用不臧。[三節]子路終身誦之、子曰、是道也、何足以臧。

[二十七章]子曰、歲寒、然後知松柏之後彫也。

[二十八章]子曰、知者不惑、仁者不憂、勇者不懼。

[二十九章]子曰、可與共學、未可與

CHAPTER XXVI. 1. The Master said, "Dressed himself in a tattered robe quilted with hemp, yet standing by the side of men dressed in furs, and not ashamed;—ah! it is Yew who is equal to this.

2. "'He dislikes none, he courts nothing;—what can he do but what is good?'"

3. Tsze-loo kept continually repeating these *words of the ode*, when the Master said, "Those things are by no means sufficient to constitute perfect excellence."

CHAPTER XXVII. The Master said, "When the year becomes cold, then we know how the pine and the cypress are the last to lose their leaves."

CHAPTER XXVIII. The Master said, "The wise are free from perplexities; the virtuous from anxiety; and the bold from fear."

CHAPTER XXIX. The Master said, "There are some with whom we may study in common, but we shall find them unable to go along with us to principles. *Perhaps* we may go on with them to prin-

26. TSZE-LOO'S BRAVE CONTENTMENT IN POVERTY, BUT FAILURE TO SEEK THE HIGHEST AIMS. 1. On the constr. of this par., comp. ch. 19. The 狐 is the fox. The 貉, read *hŏ*, is probably the badger. It is described as nocturnal in its habits, yielding a soft, warm, fur. It sleeps much, and is carnivorous. This last characteristic is not altogether inapplicable to the badger. See the 本草, 獸部. 2 See the She-king, I. iii. 8. st. 4. 3. 終身, not 'all his life,' as frequently, but 'continually.' Tsze-loo was a man of impulse, with many fine points, but not sufficiently reflective.

27. MEN ARE KNOWN IN TIMES OF ADVERSITY. 後彫, 'the after-withering,' a meiosis for their being evergreens.

28. SEQUENCES OF WISDOM, VIRTUE, AND BRAVERY. 仁者不憂,—this is one of the sayings about virtue, which is only true of pious trust in God.

29. HOW DIFFERENT INDIVIDUALS STOP AT DIFFERENT STAGES OF PROGRESS. More literally rendered, this ch. would be—'It may be possible with *some parties* together to study, *but* it may not yet be possible with them to go on to principles, &c.' 權, the weight of a steel-yard,

適道、可與適道、未可與立、可與立、未可與權。

三十 一節 唐棣之華、偏其反而、豈不爾思、室是遠而。二節 子曰、未之思也、夫何遠之有。

ciples, but we shall find them unable to get established in those along with us. Or if we may get so established along with them, we shall find them unable to weigh *occurring events* along with us."

CHAPTER XXX. 1. How the flowers of the aspen-plum flutter and turn! Do I not think of you? But your house is distant.

2. The Master said, "It is the want of thought about it. How is it distant?"

then 'to weigh.' It is used here with ref. to occurring events,—to weigh them and determine the application of principles to them. In the old comm., 權 is used here in opposition to 經, the latter being that which is always, and everywhere right, the former a deviation from that in particular circumstances, to bring things right. This meaning of the term here is denied. The ancients adopted it probably from their interpretation of the second clause in the next ch., which they made one with this.

30. THE NECESSITY OF REFLECTION. 1. This is from one of the pieces of poetry, which Conf. did not admit into his collection, and no more of it being preserved than what we have here, it is not altogether intelligible. There are long disputes about the 唐棣. Choo He makes it a kind of small plum or cherry tree, whose leaves are constantly quivering, even when there is no wind, and adopting a reading, in a book of the Tsin (晉) dyn., of 翩 for 偏, and changing 反 into 翻, he makes out the meaning in the transl. The old comm. keep the text, and interpret,—'How perversely contrary are the flowers of the T'ang-tae!' saying that those flowers are first open and then shut. This view made them take 權 in the last ch., as we have noticed. Who or what is meant by 爾 in 爾思, we cannot tell. The two 而 are mere expletives, completing the rhythm. 2. With this par. Choo He compares VII. 30.—The whole ch. is like the 20th of the last book, and suggests the thought of its being an addition by another hand to the original compilation.

論語

BOOK X. HEANG TANG.

鄉黨第十

第一章 一節 孔子於鄉黨、恂恂如也、似不能言者。二節 其在宗廟朝廷、便便言、唯謹爾。

第二章 一節 朝與下大夫言、侃侃如也、與上大夫言、誾誾如也。二節 君在、踧踖如也、與與如也。

CHAPTER I. 1. Confucius, in his village, looked simple and sincere, and as if he were not able to speak.

2. When he was in the *prince's* ancestorial temple, or in the court, he spoke minutely on every point, but cautiously.

CHAPTER II. 1. When he was waiting at court, in speaking with the officers of the lower grade, he spake freely, but in a straightforward manner; in speaking with the officers of the higher grade, he did so blandly, but precisely.

2. When the prince was present, his manner displayed respectful uneasiness; it was grave, but self-possessed.

HEADING OF THIS BOOK.—鄉黨第十. 'The village, No 10.' This book is different in its character from all the others in the work. It contains hardly any sayings of Confucius, but is descriptive of his ways and demeanour in a variety of places and circumstances. It is not uninteresting, but, as a whole, it does not heighten our veneration for the sage. We seem to know him better from it, and to Western minds, after being viewed in his bedchamber, his undress, and at his meals, he becomes divested of a good deal of his dignity and reputation. There is something remarkable about the style. Only in one passage is he styled 子, '*The Master*.' He appears either as 孔子, 'The philosopher, K'ung,' or as 君子, 'The superior man.' A suspicion is thus raised that the chronicler had not the same relation to him as the compilers of the other books. Anciently, the book formed only one chapter, but it is now arranged under seventeen divisions. Those divisions, for convenience in the translation, I continue to denominate chapters, which is done also in some native editions.

1. DEMEANOUR OF CONFUCIUS IN HIS VILLAGE, IN THE ANCESTRAL TEMPLE, AND IN THE COURT. 1. In the dict., quoting from a record of 'the former Han dyn., the 鄉 contained 2,500 families, and the 黨 only 500, but the two terms are to be taken here together, indicating the residence of the Sage's relatives. His native place in Loo is doubtless intended, and perhaps the original seat of his family in Sung. 恂恂如 is expl. by Wang Suh 'mild-like,' and by Choo He, as in the transl., thinking probably that, with that meaning, it suited the next clause better. 2. 便, read *p'een*, lower 1st tone =辯, 'to debate,' 'to discriminate accurately.' 爾=耳. In those two places of high ceremony and of government, it became the sage, it is said, to be precise and particular. Comp. III. 15.

2. DEMEANOUR OF CONFUCIUS AT COURT WITH OTHER OFFICERS, AND BEFORE THE PRINCE. 1. 朝 may be taken here as a verb, lit.='courting.' It was the custom for all the officers to repair at daybreak to the court, and wait for the prince to give them audience. 大夫, 'great officer,' was a general name, applicable

三章 一節 君召使擯、色勃如也、足躩如也。二節 揖所與立、右左手、衣前後、襜如也。三節 趨進、翼如也。四節 賓退、必復命曰、賓不顧矣。

四章 一節 入公門、鞠

CHAPTER III. 1. When the prince called him to employ him in the reception of a visitor, his countenance appeared to change, and his legs to bend beneath him.

2. He inclined himself to the *other officers* among whom he stood, moving his left or right arm, *as their position required*, but keeping the skirts of his robe before and behind evenly adjusted.

3. He hastened forward, *with his arms* like the wings of a bird.

4. When the guest had retired, he would report to the prince, "The visitor is not turning round any more."

CHAPTER IV. 1. When he entered the palace gate, he seemed to bend his body, as if it were not sufficient to admit him.

to all the higher ministers in a court. At the imperial court they were divided into three classes,—'highest,' 'middle,' and 'lowest,' 上, 中, 下, but the various princes had only the first and third. Of the first order there were properly three, the 卿, or nobles of the state, who were in Loo the chiefs of the 'three families.' Confucius belonged himself to the lower grade. 2. 踧踖, 'the feet moving uneasily,' indicating the respectful anxiety of the mind. 與, low. 1st tone, here appears in the phrase 與與如也, in a new sense.

3. DEMEANOUR OF CONFUCIUS AT THE OFFICIAL RECEPTION OF A VISITOR. 1. The visitor is supposed to be the prince of another state. On the occasion of two princes meeting there was much ceremony. The visitor having arrived, remained outside the front gate, and the host inside his reception room, which was in the ancestral temple. Messages passed between them by means of a number of officers called 介, on the side of the visitor, and 擯, on the side of the host, who formed a zigzag line of communication from the one to the other, and passed their questions and answers along, till an understanding about the visit was thus officially effected. 足躩如 is explained by 盤辟貌, 'the appearance of turning round and inclination.' I suppose I have expressed the idea in the transl. 2. This shows Conf. manner when engaged in the transmission of the messages between the prince and his visitor. The prince's nuncio, in immediate commun.l with himself, was the 上擯, the next was the 承擯, and below were one or more 紹擯. Conf. must have been the *shing pin*, bowing to the right as he transmitted a message to the *shang pin*, who was an officer of the higher grade, and to the left as he commun. one from him to the *shaou pin*. 3. The host having come out to receive his visitor, proceeded in with him, it is said, followed by all their internuncios in a line, and to his manner in this movement this par. is generally referred. But the duty of seeing the guest off, the subj. of next par., belonged to the *shang pin*, and could not be performed by Conf. as merely a *shing pin*. Hence arises a difficulty. Either it is true that Conf. was at one time raised to the rank of the highest dignitaries of the state, or he was temporarily employed, for his knowl. of cerem., after the first act in the reception of visitors, to discharge the duties of one. Assuming this, the 趨進 is to be explained of some of his movements in the reception room. How could he hurry forward when walking in file with the other internuncios? See the 撫餘說, II. 23. 4. 必復命, 'would return the commission,' *i. e.*, he had seen the guest off, according to his duty, and reported it. The ways of China, it appears, were much the same anciently as now. A guest turns round and bows repeatedly in leaving, and the host can't return to his place, till these salutations are ended.

4. DEMEANOUR OF CONFUCIUS IN THE COURT AT AN AUDIENCE. 1. The imperial court consisted of five divisions, each having its peculiar

論語

躬如也、如不容。二節立不中門、行不履閾。三節過位、色勃如也、足躩如也、其言似不足者。四節攝齊升堂、鞠躬如也、屏氣似不息者。五節出、降一等、逞顏色、怡怡如也、沒階、趨進、翼如也、復其位、踧踖如也。

第五章一節執圭、鞠躬如也、如

2. When he was standing, he did not occupy the middle of the gate-way; when he passed in or out, he did not tread upon the threshold.

3. When he was passing the *vacant* place *of the prince*, his countenance appeared to change, and his legs to bend under him, and his words came as if he hardly had breath to utter them.

4. He ascended the dais, holding up his robe with both his hands, and his body bent; holding in his breath also, as if he dared not breathe.

5. When he came out *from the audience*, as soon as he had descended one step, he began to relax his countenance, and had a satisfied look. When he had got to the bottom of the steps, he advanced rapidly to his place, *with his arms* like wings, and on occupying it, his manner *still* showed respectful uneasiness.

CHAPTER V. 1. When he was carrying the sceptre *of his prince*, he seemed to bend his body, as if he were not able to bear its weight. He did not hold it higher than the position of the hands in making

gate. That of a prince of a state consisted only of three, whose gates were named 庫, 雉 and 路. The 公門 is the *foo*, or first of these. The bending his body when passing through, high as the gate was, is supposed to indicate the great reverence which Conf. felt. 2. 不中門=不中於門, 'He did not stand opposite the middle of the gate-way.' Each gate had a post in the centre, called 闑, by which it was divided into two halves, appropriated to ingress and egress. The prince only could stand in the centre of either of them, and he only could tread on the threshold or sill. 3. At the early formal audience at day-break, when the prince came out of the inner apartment, and received the homage of the officers, he occupied a particular spot called 宁. This is the 位, now empty, which Confucius passes in his way to the audience in the inner apartment. 4. 齊 see IX.9. He is now ascending the steps to the 堂, 'the dais,' or raised platform in the inner apartment, where the prince held his council, or gave entertainments, and from which the family rooms of the palace branched off. 5. The audience is now over, and Conf. is returning to his usual place at the formal audience. K'ung Gan-kwŏ makes the 位 to be the 宁 in par. 3, but improperly. 進 after 趨 is an addition that has somehow crept into the ordinary text.

5. DEMEANOUR OF CONFUCIUS WHEN EMPLOYED ON A FRIENDLY EMBASSY. 1. 圭, may be

不勝、上如揖、下如授、勃如戰色、足蹜蹜如有循。○二節享禮、有容色。○三節私覿、愉愉如也。

第六章 一節君子不以紺緅飾。○二節紅紫不以爲褻服。○三節當暑袗絺綌、必表而出之。○四節緇衣羔裘、素衣麑裘、黃衣

a bow, nor lower than their position in giving anything to another. His countenance seemed to change, and look apprehensive, and he dragged his feet along as if they were held by something to the ground.

2. In presenting the presents *with which he was charged*, he wore a placid appearance.

3. At his private audience, he looked highly pleased.

CHAPTER VI. 1. The superior man did not use a deep purple, or a puce colour, in the ornaments of his dress.

2. Even in his undress, he did not wear anything of a red or reddish colour.

3. In warm weather, he had a single garment either of coarse or fine texture, but he wore it displayed over an inner garment.

4. Over lamb's fur he wore a garment of black; over fawn's fur one of white; and over fox's fur one of yellow.

translated 'sceptre,' in the sense simply of 'a badge of authority.' It was a precious stone, conferred by the emperor on the princes, and differed in size and shape, according to their rank. They took it with them when they attended the imper. court, and, acc. to Choo He, and the old interpr., it was carried also by their representatives, as their voucher, on occasions of embassies among themselves. In the 摭餘說, II. 33, however, it is contended, appar. on suff. grounds, that the sceptre then employed was different from the other. 勝, up. 1st tone, 'to be equal to,' 'able for.' 2. The prec. par. describes Conf. manner in the friendly court, at his first interview, showing his credentials, and delivering his message. That done, he had to deliver the various presents with which he was charged. This was called 享,=獻. 3. After all the public presents were delivered, the ambassador had others of his own to give, and his interview for that purpose was called 私覿.—Choo He remarks that there is no record of Confucius ever having been employed on such a mission, and supposes that this ch., and the preced., are simply summaries of the manner in which he used to say duties referred to in them ought to be discharged.

6. RULES OF CONFUCIUS IN REGARD TO HIS DRESS.—The discussions about the colours here mentioned are lengthy and tedious. I am not confident that I have given them all correctly in the transl. 1. 君子 used here to denote Confucius can hardly have come from the hand of a disciple. 紺=深青揚赤色, 'a deep azure flushed with carnation.' 緅=絳色, 'a deep red;' it was dipped thrice in a red dye, and then twice in a black.' 飾, 'for ornament,' *i. e.*, for the edgings of the collar and sleeves. The *kan*, it is said, by Choo He, after K'ung Gan-kwŏ, was worn in fasting, and the *tsow* in mourning, on which account Confucius would not use them. See this and the account of the colours denied in the 摭餘說, *in loc.* 2. There are five colours which go by the name

論語

狐裘。

五節 褻裘長、短右袂。

六節 必有寢衣、長一身有半。

七節 狐貉之厚以居。

八節 去喪、無所不佩。

九節 非帷裳、必殺之。

十節 羔裘玄冠不以弔。

十一節 吉月、必朝服而朝。

5. The fur robe of his undress was long, with the right sleeve short.

6. He required his sleeping dress to be half as long again as his body.

7. When staying at home, he used thick furs of the fox or the badger.

8. When he put off mourning, he wore all the appendages of the girdle.

9. His under-garment, except when it was required to be of the curtain shape, was made of silk cut narrow above and wide below.

10. He did not wear lamb's fur, or a black cap, on a visit of condolence.

11. On the first day of the month, he put on his court robes, and presented himself at court.

of 正, 'correct,' viz., 靑, 黃, 赤, 白, 黑, 'azure, yellow, carnation, white, and black;' others, among which are 紅 and 紫, go by the name of 閒, or 'intermediate.' See the 集證, *in loc.* Conf. would use only the correct colours, and moreover, Choo He adds, red and reddish-blue are liked by women and girls. 褻服, his dress, when in private. 3. 絺 and 綌 were made from the fibres of a creeping plant, the 葛. See the She-king, I. i. 2. 必表而出之, 'he must display and have it outwards.' The interpr. of this, as in the transl., after Choo He, tho' diff. from the old comm., seems to be correct. 4. The lamb's fur belonged to the court dress, the fawn's was worn on embassies, the fox's on occasions of sacrifice, &c. 5. Conf. knew how to blend comfort and convenience. 6. This par., it is supposed, belongs to the next ch., in which case it is not the usual sleeping garment of Conf. that is spoken of, but the one he used in fasting. 長, low. 3d tone, 'over,' 'overplus.' 7. These are the 褻裘 of par. 5. 8. The appendages of the girdle were, the handkerchief, a small knife, a spike for opening knots, &c. 去, up. 2d tone, 'to put away.' 9. The 裳 was the lower garment, reaching below the knees like a kilt or petticoat. For court and sac. dress, it was made curtain like, as wide at top as at bottom. In that worn on other occasions, Conf. saved the cloth in the way described. So, at least, says K'ung Gan-kwo. 殺, read *shae*, up. 3d tone. 10. Lamb's fur was worn black (par. 4), but white is the colour of mourning in China, and Conf. would not visit mourners, but in a sympathizing colour. 11. 吉月, 'the fortunate day of the moon,' *i. e.*, the first of the month. This was Conf. practice, after he had ceased to be in office.

第七章 一節 齊、必有明衣、布。二節 齊、必變食、居必遷坐。

第八章 一節 食不厭精、膾不厭細。二節 食饐而餲、魚餒而肉敗、不食。色惡不食、臭惡不食、失飪不食、不時不食。三節 割不正不食、不得其醬不食。四節 肉雖多、不使勝食氣、惟酒無量、不及亂。五節 沽酒

CHAPTER VII. 1. When fasting, he thought it necessary to have his clothes, brightly clean, and made of linen cloth.

2. When fasting, he thought it necessary to change his food, and also to change the place where he commonly sat in the apartment.

CHAPTER VIII. 1. He did not dislike to have his rice finely cleaned, nor to have his minced meat cut quite small.

2. He did not eat rice which had been injured by heat or damp and turned sour, nor fish or flesh which was gone. He did not eat what was discoloured, or what was of a bad flavour, nor anything which was not in season.

3. He did not eat meat which was not cut properly, nor what was served without its proper sauce.

4. Though there might be a large quantity of meat, he would not allow what he took to exceed the due proportion for the rice. It was only in wine that he laid down no limit for himself, but he did not allow himself to be confused by it.

5. He did not partake of wine and dried meat, bought in the market.

7. RULES OBSERVED BY CONFUCIUS WHEN FASTING. 1. 齊, read *chae*, up 1st tone; see VII. 12. The 6th par. of last ch. should come in as the 2d here. 2. The fasting was not from all food, but only from wine or spirits, and from pot herbs. Observe the diff. between 變 and 遷, the former 'to change,' the lat. 'to change from,' 'to remove.'—The whole ch. may be compared with Matt. VI. 16–18.

8. RULES OF CONFUCIUS ABOUT HIS FOOD. 1. 膾, 'minced meat,' acc. to the comm., was made of beef, mutton, or fish, *uncooked*. 100 *shing* of paddy were reduced to 30, to bring it to the state of 精 rice. 2. 飪, in the dict., is 'overdone,' hence 失飪='wrong in being overdone.' Some, however, make the phrase to mean 'badly cooked,' either, underdone, or overdone. 4. 食 (tsze) 氣, 'the breath of the rice,' or perhaps, 'the life-sustaining power of it,' but 氣 can hardly be translated here. 唯=惟, 'only,' showing, it is said, that in other things he had a limit, but the use of wine being to make glad, he could not beforehand set a limit to the quantity of it. 6. Lit., 'He did not take away ginger in eating.' 8. The prince, anciently (and it is still a custom),

論語

市脯不食。六節不撤薑食。七節不多食。八節祭於公、不宿肉。祭肉不出三日、出三日、不食之矣。九節食不語、寢不言。十節雖疏食菜羹、瓜祭、必齊如也。

第九章席不正不坐。

第十章一節鄉人飲酒、杖者出、斯出矣。二節鄉人儺、朝服而立於阼階。

6. He was never without ginger when he ate.

7. He did not eat much.

8. When he had been *assisting* at the prince's sacrifice, he did not keep the flesh *which he received* over night. The flesh of his *family* sacrifice he did not keep over three days. If kept over three days, people could not eat it.

9. When eating, he did not converse. When in bed, he did not speak.

10 Although his food might be coarse rice and vegetable soup, he would offer *a little of it* in sacrifice with a grave respectful air.

CHAPTER IX. If his mat was not straight, he did not sit on it.

CHAPTER X. 1. When the villagers were drinking together, on those who carried staves going out, he went out immediately after.

2. When the villagers were going through their ceremonies to drive away pestilential influences, he put on his court robes and stood on the eastern steps.

distributed among the assisting ministers the flesh of his sacrifice. Each would only get a little, and so it could be used at once. 10. 瓜 should be changed into 必, according to Choo He. Ho An, however, retains it, and putting a comma after it, joins it with the two preced, specimens of spare diet. The 'sacrificing' refers to a custom something like our saying grace. The master took a few grains of rice, or part of the other provisions, and placed them on the ground, among the sacrificial vessels, a tribute to the worthy or worthies who first taught the art of cooking. The Buddhist priests in their monasteries have a custom of this kind, and on public occasions, as when K'e-ying gave an entertainment in Hongkong in 1845, something like it is sometimes observed, but any such ceremony is unknown among the common habits of the people. However poor might be his fare, Confucius always observed it. 齊, *chae*,=齋, the grave demeanour appropriate to fasting.

9. RULE OF CONFUCIUS ABOUT HIS MAT.

10. OTHER WAYS OF CONFUCIUS IN HIS VILLAGE. 1. At sixty, people carried staves. Conf. here showed his respect for age. 斯 has here an adverbial force,=即. 2. There were three 儺 ceremonies every year, but that in the text was called 'the great *no*,' being observed in the winter season, when the officers led all the people of a village about, searching every house to expel demons, and drive away pestilence. It was conducted with great uproar, and little better than a play, but Conf. saw a good old idea in it, and when the mob was in his house, he stood on the eastern steps (the place of a host receiving guests) in full dress. Some make the steps those of his ancestral temple, and his standing there to be to assure the spirits of his shrine.

〔十一章〕〔一節〕問人於他邦、再拜而送之。〔二節〕康子饋藥、拜而受之、曰、丘未達、不敢嘗。

〔十二章〕廄焚、子退朝、曰、傷人乎、不問馬。

〔十三章〕〔一節〕君賜食、必正席、先嘗之、君賜腥、必熟而薦之、君賜生、必畜之。〔二節〕侍食於君、

CHAPTER XI. 1. When he was sending complimentary inquiries to any one in another state, he bowed twice as he escorted the messenger away.

2. *Ke* K'ang having sent him a present of physic, he bowed and received it, saying, "I do not know it. I dare not taste it."

CHAPTER XII. The stable being burned down, when he was at court, on his return he said, "Has any man been hurt?" He did not ask about the horses.

CHAPTER XIII. 1. When the prince sent him a gift of *cooked* meat, he would adjust his mat, *first* taste it, *and then give it away to others.* When the prince sent him a gift of undressed meat, he would have it cooked, and offer it *to the spirits of his ancestors.* When the prince sent him a gift of a living animal, he would keep it alive.

2. When he was in attendance on the prince and joining in the entertainment, the prince only sacrificed. He first tasted every thing.

11. TRAITS OF CONFUCIUS' INTERCOURSE WITH OTHERS. 1. The two bows were not to the messenger, but intended for the distant friend to whom he was being sent. 2. 康 was the 季康子 of II. 20, *et al.* Conf. accepted the gift, but thought it necessary to let the donor know he could not, for the present at least, avail himself of it.

12. HOW CONFUCIUS VALUED HUMAN LIFE. A 廄 was fitted to accommodate 216 horses. See the 集證, *in loc.* It may be used indeed for a private stable, but it is more natural to take it here for the 國 or state *kew.* This is the view in the 家語.

13. DEMEANOUR OF CONFUCIUS IN RELATION TO HIS PRINCE. 1. He would not offer the cooked meat to the spirits of his ancestors, not knowing but it might previously have been offered by the prince to the spirits of his. But he reverently tasted it, as if he had been in the prince's presence. He 'honoured' the gift of cooked food, 'glorified' the undressed, and 'was kind' to the living animal. 2. The 祭 here is that in ch. 8, 10. Among parties of equal rank, all performed the ceremony, but Conf., with his prince, held that the prince sacrificed for all. He tasted every thing, as if he had been a *cook,* it being the cook's duty to taste every dish, before the prince partook of it. 3. 首, upper 3d tone, 頭向, 'the direction of the head.' The head to the east was the proper position for a person in bed; a sick man might for comfort be lying differently, but Conf. would not see the prince but in the correct position, and also in the court dress, so far as he could accomplish it. 4. He would not wait a moment, but let his carriage follow him.

君祭、先飯。三節疾、君視之、東首、加朝服拖紳。四節君命召、不俟駕、行矣。

十四章入太廟每事問。

十五章一節朋友死、無所歸、曰、於我殯。二節朋友之饋、雖車馬、非祭肉不拜。

十六章一節寢不尸、居不容。二節見齊衰者、雖狎必變、見冕者、與瞽者、雖褻必以貌。三節凶

3. When he was sick and the prince came to visit him, he had his head to the east, made his court robes be spread over him, and drew his girdle across them.

4. When the prince's order called him, without waiting for his carriage to be yoked, he went at once.

CHAPTER XIV. When he entered the ancestral temple of the state, he asked about everything.

CHAPTER XV. 1. When any of his friends died, if he had no relations who could be depended on for the necessary offices, he would say, "I will bury him."

2. When a friend sent him a present, though it might be a carriage and horses, he did not bow.

3. The only present for which he bowed was that of the flesh of sacrifice.

CHAPTER XVI. 1. In bed, he did not lie like a corpse. At home, he did not put on any formal deportment.

2. When he saw any one in a mourning dress, though it might be an acquaintance, he would change countenance; when he saw any one wearing the cap of full dress, or a blind person, though he might be in his undress, he would salute them in a ceremonious manner.

14. A repetition of III. 15. Comp. also ch. 2. These two passages make the explanation, given at III. 15, of the questioning being on his first entrance on office very doubtful.

15. TRAITS OF CONFUCIUS IN THE RELATION OF A FRIEND. 1. 殯, properly, 'the closing up of the coffin,' is here used for all the expenses and services necessary to interment. 2. Between friends there should be a community of goods. 'The flesh of sacrifice,' however, was that which had been offered by his friend to the spirits of his parents or ancestors. That demanded acknowledgment.

16. CONFUCIUS IN BED, AT HOME, HEARING THUNDER, &c. 2. Comp. IX. 9, which is here repeated, with heightening circumstances. 3. 式 is the front bar of a cart or carriage. In fact, the carriage of Confucius' time was

服者式之、式負版者。[四節]有盛饌、必變色而作。[五節]迅雷、風烈、必變。[十七章][一節]升車、必正立、執綏。[二節]車中、不內顧、不疾言、不親指。[十八章][一節]色斯舉矣、翔而後集。[二節]曰、山梁雌雉、時哉時哉。子路共之、三嗅而作。

3. To any person in mourning he bowed forward to the cross-bar of his carriage; he bowed in the same way to any one bearing the tables of population.

4. When he was at an entertainment where there was an abundance of provisions set before him, he would change countenance and rise up.

5. On a sudden clap of thunder, or a violent wind, he would change countenance.

CHAPTER XVII. 1. When he was about to mount his carriage, he would stand straight, holding the cord.

2. When he was in the carriage, he did not turn his head quite round, he did not talk hastily, he did not point with his hands.

CHAPTER XVIII. 1. *Seeing* the countenance, it instantly rises. It flies round, and by and bye settles.

2. *The Master* said, "There is the hen-pheasant on the hill bridge. At its season! At its season!" Tsze-loo made a motion to it. Thrice it smelt him and then rose.

only what we call a cart. In saluting when riding, parties bowed forward to this bar. 4. He showed these signs, with reference to the generosity of the provider.

17. CONFUCIUS AT AND IN HIS CARRIAGE. 1. The 綏 was a strap or cord, attached to the carriage to assist in mounting it. 2. 不內顧, 'He did not look round within,' *i. e.*, turn his head quite round. See the Le Ke, I. i. 5. p. 43.

18. A fragment, which seemingly has no connect. with the rest of the book. Various corrections of characters are proposed, and various views of the meaning given. Ho An's view of the conclusion is this.—'Tsze-loo took it and served it up. The Master thrice smelt it and rose.' 共, up. 2d tone, = 向.

論語

BOOK XI. SEEN TSIN.

先進第十一

第一章 一節 子曰、先進於禮樂、野人也、後進於禮樂、君子也、二節 如用之、則吾從先進。

第二章 一節 子曰、從我於陳蔡者、皆不及門也。二節 德行、顏淵、閔子騫、冉伯牛、仲弓。言語、宰我、子貢。政事、冉

CHAPTER I. 1. The Master said, "The men of former times, in the matters of ceremonies and music, were rustics, *it is said*, while the men of *these* latter times, in ceremonies and music, are accomplished gentlemen.

2. "If I have occasion to use those things, I follow the men of former times."

CHAPTER II. 1. The Master said, "Of those who were with me in Ch'in and Ts'ae, there are none to be found to enter my door."

2. Distinguished for their virtuous principles and practice, there were Yen Yuen, Min Tsze-k'een, Yen Pih-new, and Chung-kung; for their ability in speech, Tsae Go and Tsze-kung; for their adminis-

1. HEADING OF THIS BOOK.—先進第十一, 'The former men—No. XI.' With this Book there commences the second part of the Analects, commonly called the *Hea Lun* (下論). There is, however, no classical authority for this division. It contains 25 chapters, treating mostly of various disciples of the Master, and deciding the point of their worthiness. Min Tsze-K'een appears in it four times, and on this account some attribute the compilation of it to his disciples. There are indications in the style of a peculiar hand.

1. CONFUCIUS' PREFERENCE OF THE SIMPLER WAYS OF FORMER TIMES. 1. 先進, 後進, are said by Choo He to=先輩, 後輩. Literally, the expressions are,—'those who first advanced,' 'those who afterwards advanced,' *i. e.*, on the stage of the world. In Ho An, the chap. is said to speak of the disciples who had first advanced to office, and those who had advanced subsequently,—評其弟子之中仕進先後之輩. But the 2d par. is decidedly against this interpretation. 進 is not to be joined to the succeeding 於禮樂, but 於=*quoad*. It is supposed that the characterizing the 先進 as rustics, and their successors as *keun-tsze*, was a style of his times, which Conf. quotes ironically. We have in it a new instance of the various application of the name *keun-tsze*. In the 備旨, it is said, 'Of the words and actions of men in their mutual intercourse and in the business of government, whatever indicates *respect* is here included in *ceremonies*, and whatever is expressive of *harmony* is here included in *music*.'

2. CONFUCIUS' REGRETFUL MEMORY OF HIS DISCIPLES' FIDELITY. CHARACTERISTICS OF TEN OF THE DISCIPLES. 1. This utterance must have been made towards the close of Conf. life, when

有、季路。文學、子游、子夏。

第三章 子曰、回也、非助我者也、於吾言無所不說。

第四章 子曰、孝哉閔子騫、人不間於其父母昆弟之言。

第五章 南容三復白圭、孔子以其兄之子妻之。

trative talents, Yen Yew and Ke Loo; for their literary acquirements, Tsze-yew and Tsze-hea.

CHAPTER III. The Master said, "Hwuy gives me no assistance. There is nothing that I say in which he does not delight."

CHAPTER IV. The Master said, "Filial indeed is Min Tsze-k'een! Other people say nothing of him different from the report of his parents and brothers."

CHAPTER V. Nan Yung was frequently repeating the *lines about a* white sceptre-stone. Confucius gave him the daughter of his elder brother to wife.

many of his disciples had been removed by death, or separated from him by other causes. In his 62d year or thereabouts, as the accounts go, he was passing, in his wanderings from Ch'in to Ts'ae, when the officers of Ch'in, afraid that he would go on into Tsoo, endeavoured to stop his course, and for several days he and the disciples with him were cut off from food. Both Ch'in and Ts'ae were in the present province of Ho-nan, and are referred to the departments of 陳州 and 汝寧. 2. This par. is to be taken as a note by the compilers of the book, enumerating the principal followers of Conf. on the occasion referred to, with their distinguishing qualities. They are arranged in four classes (四科), and, amounting to ten, are known as the 十哲. The 'four classes' and 'ten wise ones' are often mentioned in connection with the sage's school.

3. HWUY'S SILENT RECEPTION OF THE MASTER'S TEACHINGS. A teacher is sometimes *helped* by the doubts and questions of learners, which lead him to explain himself more fully. Comp. III. 8, 3. 說 for 悅 as in I. 1, 1, but K'ung Gan-kwŏ takes it in its usual pronuncia., =解, 'to explain.'

4. THE FILIAL PIETY OF MIN TSZE-K'EEN. 間, as in VIII. 21, 'could pick out no crevice or flaw in the words, &c.' 陳羣 (about A.D. 200-250) as given in Ho An, explains—'men had no words of disparagement for his conduct in reference to his parents and brothers.' This is the only instance where Conf. calls a disciple by his designation. The use of 子騫 is supposed, in the 合講, to be a mistake of the compilers.

5. CONFUCIUS' APPROBATION OF NAN YUNG. Nan Yung, see V. 1. 三, as in V. 19. I have translated it by 'frequently,' but, in the 'Family Sayings,' it is related that Yung repeated the lines thrice in one day. 白圭, see the She-king, III. iii. 2, st. 5. The lines there are —'A flaw in a white sceptre-stone, may be ground away; but for a flaw in speech, nothing can be done.' In his repeating of these lines, we have, perhaps, the ground-virtue of the char. for which Yung is commended in V. 1. Obs. 孔子, where we might expect 子.

論語

第六章 季康子問弟子孰爲好學。孔子對曰、有顏回者好學、不幸短命死矣、今也則亡。

第七章 顏淵死、顏路請子之車、以爲之椁。子曰、才不才、亦各言其子也、鯉也死、有棺而無椁、吾不徒行以爲之椁、以吾從大夫之後、不可徒行也。

第八章 顏淵死、子曰、噫、天喪子、天喪子。

CHAPTER VI. Ke K'ang asked which of the disciples loved to learn. Confucius replied to him, "There was Yen Hwuy; he loved to learn. Unfortunately his appointed time was short, and he died. Now there is no one *who loves to learn, as he did.*"

CHAPTER VII. 1. When Yen Yuen died, Yen Loo begged the carriage of the Master to get an outer shell for his *son's* coffin.

2. The Master said, "Every one calls his son his son, whether he has talents or has not talents. There was Le; when he died, he had a coffin but no outer shell. I would not walk on foot to get a shell for him, because, following after the great officers, it was not proper that I should walk on foot."

CHAPTER VIII. When Yen Yuen died, the Master said, "Alas! Heaven is destroying me! Heaven is destroying me!"

6. HOW HWUY LOVED TO LEARN. See VI. 2, where the same question is put by the duke Gae, and the same answer is returned, only in a more extended form.

7. HOW CONFUCIUS WOULD NOT SELL HIS CARRIAGE TO BUY A SHELL FOR YEN YUEN. 1. A great chronological difficulty belongs here. Hwuy, according to the 'Family Sayings,' and the 'Historical Records,' must have died several years before Confucius' son, Le. Either the dates in them are false, or this ch. is spurious.—Yen Loo, the father of Hwuy, had himself been a disciple of the sage in former years. 爲之槨 (*i.q.* char. in text),—this is the idiom noticed in V. 7, 3. 爲 would almost seem to be an active verb followed by a double objective. In burying, they used a coffin, called 棺, and an outer shell, without a bottom which was called 槨. 2. 吾從大夫之後, lit., 'I follow in rear of the great officers.' This is said to be an expression of humility. Confucius, retired from office, might still present himself at court, in the robes of his former dignity, and would still be consulted on emergencies. He would no doubt have a foremost place on such occasions.

8. CONFUCIUS FELT HWUY'S DEATH AS IF IT HAD BEEN HIS OWN. The old interpr. make this simply the exclamation of bitter sorrow. The modern, perhaps correctly, make the chief in-

第九章 一節 顏淵死、子哭之慟、從者曰、子慟矣。二節 曰、有慟乎。三節 非夫人之爲慟而誰爲。

第十章 一節 顏淵死、門人欲厚葬之。子曰、不可。二節 門人厚葬之。三節 子曰、回也、視予猶父也、予不得視猶子也、非我也、夫二三子也。

第十一章 季路問事鬼神。子曰、未能事人、焉能事鬼。敢

CHAPTER IX. 1. When Yen Yuen died, the Master bewailed him exceedingly, and the disciples who were with him said, "Sir, your grief is excessive?"

2. "Is it excessive?" said he.

3. "If I am not to mourn bitterly for this man, for whom should I mourn?"

CHAPTER X. 1. When Yen Yuen died, the disciples wished to give him a great funeral, and the Master said, "You may not do so."

2. The disciples did bury him in great style.

3. The Master said, "Hwuy behaved towards me as his father. I have not been able to treat him as my son. The fault is not mine; it belongs to you, O disciples."

CHAPTER XI. Ke Loo asked about serving the spirits *of the dead*. The Master said, "While you are not able to serve men, how can you serve *their* spirits?" *Ke Loo added*, "I venture to ask about death?" He was answered, "While you do not know life, how can you know about death?"

gredient to be grief that the man was gone to whom he looked most for the transmission of his doctrines.

9. CONFUCIUS VINDICATES HIS GREAT GRIEF FOR THE DEATH OF HWUY. 1. 哭 is the loud wail of grief. Moaning with tears is called 泣. 3. 夫人=斯人, 'This man.' The third definition of 夫 in the dict. is 有所指之辭, 'a term of definite indication.'

10. CONFUCIUS' DISSATISFACTION WITH THE GRAND WAY IN WHICH HWUY WAS BURIED. 1. The old interpreters take 門人 as being the disciples of Yen Yuen. This is not natural, and yet we can hardly understand how the disciples of Confucius would act so directly contrary to his express wishes. Conf. objected to a grand funeral as inconsistent with the poverty of the family (see ch. 7). 3. 視, lit., '*regarded* me,' but that term would hardly suit the next clause. 夫, as in the last ch. This pass., indeed, is cited in the dict, in illustration of that use of the term. 二三子, see III. 24.

11. CONFUCIUS AVOIDS ANSWERING QUESTIONS ABOUT SERVING SPIRITS, AND ABOUT DEATH. 鬼神 are here to be taken together, and understood of the spirits of the dead. This appears

問死。曰、未知生、焉知死。

十二 一節 閔子侍側、誾誾如也、子路、行行如也、冉有、子貢、侃侃如也。子樂。二節 若由也、不得其死然。

十三 一節 魯人爲長府。二節 閔子騫曰、仍舊貫、如之何、何必改作。三節 子曰、夫人不言、言必有中。

CHAPTER XII. 1. The disciple Min was standing by his side, looking bland and precise; Tsze-loo, looking bold and soldierly; Yen Yew and Tsze-kung, with a free and straightforward manner. The Master was pleased.

2. He said, "Yew there!—he will not die a natural death."

CHAPTER XIII. 1. Some parties in Loo were going to take down and rebuild the Long treasury.

2. Min Tsze-k'een said, "Suppose it were to be repaired after its old style;—why must it be altered, and made anew?"

3. The Master said, "This man seldom speaks; when he does, he is sure to hit the point."

from Confucius using only 鬼 in his reply, and from the opposition between 人 and 鬼. 人 is man alive, while 鬼 is man dead—a ghost, a spirit. Two views of the replies are found in commentators. The older ones say—'Confucius put off Ke Loo, and gave him no answer, because spirits and death are obscure and unprofitable subjects to talk about.' With this some modern writers agree, as the author of the 翼註, but others, and the majority, say—'Confucius answered the disciple profoundly, and showed him how he should prosecute his inquiries in the proper order. The service of the dead must be in the same spirit as the service of the living. Obedience and sacrifice are equally the expression of the filial heart. Death is only the natural termination of life. We are born with certain gifts and principles, which carry us on to the end of our course.' This is ingenious refining, but, after all, Confucius avoids answering the important questions proposed to him.

12. CONFUCIUS HAPPY WITH HIS DISCIPLES ABOUT HIM. HE WARNS TSZE-LOO. 1. 閔子, like 冉子, VI. 3, 1. 行, read *hang*, low. 3d tone. 2. There wanting here the 子曰 at the commencement, some would change the 樂 at the end of the 1st. par. into 曰, to supply the blank. 若由也,—若 is used with reference to the appearance and manner of Tsze-loo. 然, in the 註疏, is taken as=the final 焉. Some say that it indicates some uncertainty as to the prediction. But it was verified; see on II. 17.

13. WISE ADVICE OF MIN SUN AGAINST USELESS EXPENDITURE. 1. 魯人, not 'the people of Loo,' but as in the transl.,—certain officers, disapprobation of whom is indicated by simply calling them 人. The full meaning of

〔十四章〕一節子曰、由之瑟、奚爲於丘之門。二節門人不敬子路。子曰、由也、升堂矣、未入於室也。

〔十五章〕一節子貢問師與商也孰賢。子曰、師也過、商也不及。二節曰、然則師愈與。三節子曰、過猶不及。

〔十六章〕一節季氏富於周公、而求也爲之聚斂而附

CHAPTER XIV. 1. The Master said, "What has the harpsichord of Yew to do in my door?"

2. The other disciples *began* not to respect Tsze-loo. The Master said, "Yew has ascended to the hall, though he has not yet passed into the inner apartments."

CHAPTER XV 1. Tsze-kung asked which of the two, Sze or Shang, was the superior. The Master said, "Sze goes beyond *the due mean*, and Shang does not come up to it."

2. "Then," said Tsze-kung, "the superiority is with Sze, I suppose."

3. The Master said, "To go beyond is as wrong as to fall short."

CHAPTER XVI. 1. The head of the Ke family was richer than the duke of Chow had been, and yet K'ew collected his imposts for him, and increased his wealth.

爲 is collected from the rest of the chapter. 府 is 'a treasury,' as distinguished from 倉, 'a granary,' and from 庫, 'an arsenal.' 'The Long treasury' was the name of the one in question. 2. The use of 貫 is perplexing. Choo He adopts the explanation of it by the old comm. as=事, 'affair,' but with what propriety I do not see. The character means 'a string of cowries, or cash,' then 'to thread together,' 'to connect.' May not its force be here,—'suppose it were to be carried on—continued—as before'? 3. 夫 as in ch. 9. 中, up. 3d tone, a verb, 'to hit the mark,' as in shooting.

14. CONFUCIUS' ADMONITION AND DEFENCE OF TSZE-LOO. 1. The form of the harpsichord seems to come nearer to that of the *shih* than any other of our instruments. The 瑟 is a kindred instrument with the 琴, commonly called 'the scholar's lute.' See the Chinese Repository, vol. VIII. p. 88. The music made by Yew was more martial in its air than befitted the peace-inculcating school of the sage. 2. This contains a defence of Yew, and an illustration of his real attainments.

15. COMPARISON OF SZE AND SHANG. EXCESS AND DEFECT EQUALLY WRONG. 1. 賢, here=勝, 'to overcome,' 'be superior to,' being interchanged with 愈 in par. 2. We find this meaning of the term also in the dictionary.

16. CONFUCIUS' INDIGNATION AT THE SUPPORT OF USURPATION AND EXTORTION BY ONE OF HIS DISCIPLES. 1. 季氏, see III. 1. Many illustrations might be collected of the encroachments of the Ke family, and its great wealth. 爲之聚斂, 'for him collected and ingathered,' *i. e.*, all his imposts. This clause and the next imply that K'ew was aiding in the matter of laying imposts on the people. 2. 'Beat the

論語

益之。子曰、非吾徒也、小子、鳴鼓而攻之、可也。

十七章 柴也愚。參也魯。師也辟。由也喭。

十八章 子曰、回也其庶乎、屢空。賜不受命、而貨殖焉、億則屢中。

十九章 子張問善人之

2. The Master said, "He is no disciple of mine. My little children, beat the drum and assail him."

CHAPTER XVII. 1. Ch'ae is simple.

2. Sin is dull.

3. Sze is specious.

4. Yew is coarse.

CHAPTER XVIII. 1. The Master said, "There is Hwuy! He has nearly attained *to perfect virtue*. He is often in want."

2. "Tsze does not acquiesce in the appointments *of Heaven*, and his goods are increased by him. Yet his judgments are often correct."

CHAPTER XIX. Tsze-chang asked what were the characteristics of the GOOD man. The Master said, "He does not tread in the footsteps of others, but, moreover, he does not enter the chamber *of the sage*."

drum and assail him,'—this refers to the practice of executing criminals in the market place, and by beat of drum collecting the people to hear their crimes. Comm., however, say that the Master only required the disciples here to tell K'ew of his faults and recover him.

17. CHARACTERS OF THE FOUR DISCIPLES—CH'AE, SIN, SZE, AND YEW. It is supposed a 子曰 is missing from the beginning of this ch. Admitting this, the sentences are to be translated in the present tense, and not in the past which would be required, if the chap. were simply the record of the compilers. 1. Ch'ae, by surname 高, and styled 子羔 (of 羔 there are several *aliases*), has his tablet now the 5th west, in the outer court of the temples. He was small and ugly, but distinguished for his sincerity, filial piety, and justice. Such was the conviction of his impartial justice, that in a time of peril he was saved by a man, whom he had formerly punished with cutting off his feet. 3. 辟, read *p'eih*, is defined in the dict.,—'practising airs with little sincerity.'—Confucius certainly does not here flatter his followers.

18. HWUY AND TSZE CONTRASTED. In Ho An's compilation, this ch. is joined with the preceding as one. 1. 庶, here=近, 'nearly,' 'near to.' It is often found with 乎 following, both terms together being=our 'nearly.' To make out a meaning, the old comm. supply 聖道, 'the way or doctrines of the sages,' and the modern supply 道, 'the truth and right.' 空, up. 3d tone, 'emptied,' *i. e.*, brought to extremity, poor, distressed. Hwuy's being brought often to this state is mentioned merely as an additional circumstance about him, intended to show that he was happy in his deep poverty. Ho An preserves the comment of some one, which is worth giving here, and acc. to which, 空=虛中, 'empty—hearted,' free from all vanities and ambitions. Then 屢=每, 'always.' In this sense 屢空 was the formative element of Hwuy's character. 2. 受, 'to receive,' here='to acquiesce in.' 億=度, 'to form a judgment.'

19. THE GOOD MAN. Comp. VII. 25. By 善人 Choo He understands—質美而未

道。子曰、不踐迹、亦不入於室。

二十 子曰、論篤是與、君子者乎、色莊者乎。

二十一 子路問聞斯行諸。子曰、有父兄在、如之何其聞斯行之。冉有問聞斯行諸。子曰、聞斯行之。公西華曰、由也問聞斯行諸、子曰、有父兄在、求也

CHAPTER XX. The Master said, "If, because a man's discourse appears solid and sincere, we allow him *to be a good man*, is he *really* a superior man? or is his gravity only in appearance?"

CHAPTER XXI. Tsze-loo asked whether he should immediately carry into practice what he heard. The Master said, "There are your father and elder brothers *to be consulted*;—why should you act on that principle of immediately carrying into practice what you hear?" Yen Yew asked the same, whether he should immediately carry into practice what he heard, and the Master answered, "Immediately carry into practice what you hear." Kung-se Hwa said, "Yew asked whether he should carry immediately into practice what he heard, and you said, 'There are your father and elder brothers *to be consulted*.' K'ew asked whether he should immediately carry into practice what he heard, and you said, 'Carry it immediately into practice.' I, Ch'ih, am perplexed, and venture to ask you for an explanation." The Master said, "K'ew is retiring and slow; therefore, I urged him forward. Yew has more than his own share of energy; therefore, I kept him back."

學者, 'one of fine natural capacity, but who has not learned.' Such a man will in many things be a law to himself, and needs not to follow in the wake of others, but after all his progress will be limited. The text is rather enigmatical. 入室, comp. ch. 14, 2.

20. WE MAY NOT HASTILY JUDGE A MAN TO BE GOOD FROM HIS DISCOURSE. 論 is here 'speech,' 'conversation.' In Ho An, this ch. is joined to the preceding one, and is said to give additional characteristics of 'the good man,' mentioned on a diff. occasion.—The construction, however, on that view is all but inextricable.

21. AN INSTANCE IN TSZE-LOO AND YEW OF HOW CONFUCIUS DEALT WITH HIS DISCIPLES ACCORDING TO THEIR CHARACTERS. On Tsze-loo's question, comp. V. 13. 聞斯行諸, 'Hearing *this* (=anything), should I do it *at once* or not?' 行諸=行之乎, like 舍諸, in VI. 4. 兼人,—兼 is explained by Choo He with 勝, 'to overcome,' 'to be superior to.' But we can well take it in its radical signification of 'to unite,' as a hand grasps two sheaves of corn. The phrase is equivalent to our English one in the transl. Similarly, the best pure gold is called 兼金.

論語

問聞斯行諸、子曰、聞斯行之、赤也惑、敢問。子曰、求也退、故進之、由也兼人、故退之。

〔廿二章〕子畏於匡、顏淵後、子曰、吾以女爲死矣。曰、子在、回何敢死。

〔廿三章〕一節 季子然問仲由冉求、可謂大臣與。○二節 子曰、吾以子爲異之問、曾由與求之問。○三節 所謂大臣者、以道事君、不可則止。○四節 今由

CHAPTER XXII. The Master was put in fear in K'wang and Yen Yuen fell behind. The Master, *on his rejoining him*, said, "I thought you had died." *Hwuy* replied, "While you were alive, how should I presume to die?"

CHAPTER XXIII. 1. Ke Tsze-jen asked whether Chung-yew and Yen K'ew could be called great ministers.

2. The Master said, "I thought you would ask about some extraordinary individuals, and you only ask about Yew and K'ew!

3. "What is called a great minister, is one who serves his prince according to what is right, and when he finds he cannot do so, retires.

22. YEN YUEN'S ATTACHMENT TO CONFUCIUS, AND CONFIDENCE IN HIS MISSION. See IX. 5. If Hwuy's answer was anything more than pleasantry, we must pronounce it foolish. The comm., however, expand it thus:—'I knew that you would not perish in this danger, and therefore I would not rashly expose my own life, but preserved it rather, that I might continue to enjoy the benefit of your instructions.' If we inquire how Hwuy knew that Conf. would not perish, we are informed that he shared his master's assurance that he had a divine mission.—See VII. 22, IX. 5.

23. A GREAT MINISTER. CHUNG-YEW AND YEN K'EW ONLY ORDINARY MINISTERS. The paraphrasts sum up the contents thus:—'Conf. represses the boasting of Ke Tsze-jen, and indicates an acquaintance with his traitorous purposes.' 1. Ke Tsze-jen was a younger brother of Ke Hwan, who was the 季氏 of III. 1. Having an ambitious purpose on the dukedom of Loo, he was increasing his officers, and having got the two disciples to enter his service, he boastingly speaks to Conf. about them. 2. 吾以云云, lit., 'I supposed you were making a question of (=about) extraordinary *men*, and lo! it is a question about Yew and K'ew.' 曾=乃; its force is rather diff. from what it has in II. 8, but is much akin to that in III. 6. 4. 具臣 is explained 備臣數而已, 'simply fitted to rank among the number of officers.' 具 often means what is merely 'official.' 具文, 'an official paper.' 具臣, 'mere officials.' 5. 之 supposes an antecedent, such as 主, 'their master.'

與求也、可謂具臣矣。五節曰、然則從之者與。六節子曰、弒父與君、亦不從也。

廿四 一節子路使子羔為費宰。二節子曰、賊夫人之子。三節子路曰、有民人焉、有社稷焉、何必讀書、然後為學。四節子曰、是故惡夫佞者。

廿五 一節子路、曾晳、冉有、公西華、侍坐。二節子曰、以吾一日

4. "Now, as to Yew and K'ew, they may be called ordinary ministers."

5. Tsze-jen said, "Then they will always follow their chief;—will they?"

6. The Master said, "In an act of parricide or regicide, they would not follow him."

CHAPTER XXIV. 1. Tsze-loo got Tsze-kaou appointed governor of Pe.

2. The Master said, "You are injuring a man's son."

3. Tsze-loo said, "There are (there) common people and officers; there are the altars of the spirits of the land and grain. Why must one read books before he can be considered to have learned?"

4. The Master said, "It is on this account that I hate your glib-tongued people."

CHAPTER XXV. 1. Tsze-loo, Tsăng Sih, Yen Yew, and Kung-se Hwa, were sitting by *the Master*.

2. He said to them, "Though I am a day or so older than you, don't think of that.

24. HOW PRELIMINARY STUDY IS NECESSARY TO THE EXERCISE OF GOVERNMENT:—A REPROOF OF TSZE-LOO. 1. 費,—see VI. 7. This commandantship is probably what Min Sun there refused. Tsze-loo had entered into the service of the Ke family (see last ch.), and recommended (使) Tsze-kaou as likely to keep the turbulent Pe in order, thereby withdrawing him from his studies with the Master. 2. 賊, in the sense of 害, 'to injure.' 夫 as in ch. 9, 3. It qualifies the whole phrase 人之子, and is not to be joined only with 人. By denominating Tsze-kaou—'a man's son,' Conf. intimates, I suppose, that the father was injured as well. His son ought not to be so dealt with. 3. The absurd defence of Tsze-loo. It is to this effect:—'The whole duty of man is in treating other men right, and rendering what is due to spiritual beings, and it may be learned practically without the study you require.' 4. 是故, 'on this account,' with reference to Tsze-loo's reply.

25 THE AIMS OF TSZE-LOO, TSANG SIH, YEN YEW, AND KUNG-SE HWA, AND CONFUCIUS' REMARKS ABOUT THEM. Comp. V. 7. 25. 1. The

論語

長乎爾、毋吾以也。三節居則曰、不吾知也、如或知爾、則何以哉。四節子路率爾而對曰、千乘之國、攝乎大國之閒、加之以師旅、因之以饑饉、由也爲之、比及三年、可使有勇、且知方也。夫子哂之。五節求、爾何如。對曰、方六七十、如五六十、求也爲之、比及三年、可使足民、如其禮樂、以

3. "From day to day you are saying, 'We are not known.' If some *prince* were to know you, what would you do?"

4. Tsze-loo hastily and lightly replied, "Suppose the case of a state of ten thousand chariots; let it be straitened between *other* large states; let it be suffering from invading armies; and to this let there be added a famine in corn and in all vegetables:—if I were intrusted with the government of it, in three years' time I could make the people to be bold, and to recognize the rules of righteous conduct." The Master smiled at him.

5. *Turning to Yen Yew, he said,* "K'ew, what are your wishes?" *K'ew* replied, "Suppose a state of sixty or seventy *le* square, or one of fifty or sixty, and let me have the government of it;—in three years' time, I could make plenty to abound among the people. As to *teaching them* the principles of propriety, and music, I must wait for the rise of a superior man *to do that.*"

disciples mentioned here are all familiar to us excepting Tsăng Sih. He was the father of the more celebrated Tsăng Sin, and himself by name Teen (點). The four are mentioned in the order of their age, and Teen would have answered immediately after Tsze-loo, but that Conf. passed him by, as he was occupied with his harpsichord. 2. 長, up 2d tone, 'senior.' Many understand 爾輩, 'ye,' as nom. to the first 以, but it is better with Choo He to take 以=雖, 'although.' 一日, 'one day,' would seem to indicate the importance which the disciples attached to the seniority of their Master, and his wish that they should attach no importance to it. In 勿吾以也 we have a not uncommon inversion. It = 勿以吾爲長, 'don't consider me to be your senior.' 3. 居=平居之時, 'the level, ordinary, course of your lives.' 何以哉=何以爲用哉, 'what would you consider to be your use?' *i. e.*, what course of action would you pursue? 4. 率爾, an adv., ='hastily.' 攝, acc. to Choo He,=管束, acc. to Paou Heen,=迫, 'straitened,' 'urged.'

俟君子。○六節赤、爾何如。對曰、非曰能之、願學焉、宗廟之事、如會同、端章甫、願爲小相焉。○七節點、爾何如。鼓瑟希、鏗爾、舍瑟而作、對曰、異乎三子者之撰。子曰、何傷乎、亦各言其志也。曰、莫春者、春服既成、冠者五六人、童子六七人、浴乎沂、風乎舞雩、詠而歸。夫子喟然歎曰、吾與

6. "What are your wishes, Ch'ih," *said the Master next to Kung-se Hwa. Ch'ih* replied, "I do not say that my ability extends to these things, but I should wish to learn them. At the services of the ancestral temple, and at the audiences of the Princes with the Emperor, I should like, dressed in the dark squaremade robe and the black linen cap, to act as a small assistant."

7. *Last of all, the Master asked T'sang Sih,* "Teen, what are your wishes?" *Teen,* pausing as he was playing on his harpsichord, while it was yet twanging, laid the instrument aside, and rose. "My wishes," he said, "are different from the cherished purposes of these three gentlemen." "What harm is there in that?" said the Master; "do you also, as well as they, speak out your wishes." *Teen* then said, "In *this,* the last month of spring, with the dress of the season all complete, along with five or six young men who have assumed the cap, and six or seven boys, I would wash in the E, enjoy the breeze among the rain-altars, and return home singing." The Master heaved a sigh and said, "I give my approval to Teen."

In the Chow Le, 500 men make a 旅, and 5 旅, or 2,500 men, make a 師. The two terms together have here the meaning given in the transl. 爲之, 'managed it.' 比, lower 3d tone, blends its force with the foll. 及. 方=向, 'towards.' 知方, 'know the quarter to which to turn, the way in which to go.' 5. At the beginning of this paragraph and the two following, we must supply 子曰. 如=或, 'or.' 6. 能之,—之 refers to the 禮樂, in p. 5. 會 is the name for occasional or incidental interviews of the princes with the emperor, what are called 時見. 同 belongs to occasions when they all presented themselves together at court. The 端, (and from its colour called 元端), was a robe of ceremony, so called from its *straight* make, its component parts having no gathers nor slanting cuttings. 章甫 was the name of a cap of

點也。八節三子者出、曾皙後、曾皙曰、夫三子者之言何如。子曰、亦各言其志也已矣。九節曰、夫子何哂由也。十節曰、爲國以禮、其言不讓、是故哂之。十一節唯求則非邦也與、安見方六七十、如五六十、而非邦也者。十二節唯赤則非邦也與。宗廟會同、非諸侯而何、赤也爲之小、孰能爲之大。

8. The three others having gone out, Tsăng Sih remained behind, and said, "What do you think of the words of these three friends?" The Master replied, "They simply told each one his wishes."

9. *Teen* pursued, "Master, why did you smile at Yew?"

10. He was answered, "The management of a state demands the rules of propriety. His words were not humble; therefore I smiled at him."

11. *Teen again said*, "But was it not a state which K'ew proposed for himself?" *The reply was*, "*Yes;* did you ever see a territory of sixty or seventy *le*, or one of fifty or sixty, which was not a state?"

12. *Once more, Teen inquired*, "And was it not a state which Ch'ih proposed for himself?" *The Master again replied*, "*Yes;* who but princes have to do with ancestral temples, and audiences with the Emperor? If Ch'ih were to be a small *assistant* in these *services*, who could be a great one?"

ceremony. It had different names under different dynasties. 甫 means a MAN. The cap was so named, as 'displaying the MAN.' 7. 希=止, 'pausing,' 'stopping.' So, in the dict. 鏗, an adv., expressing the twanging sound of the instrument. 莫, read *moo*, low. 3d tone, the same as 暮, 'sunset,' 'the close of a period of time.' 冠 (up. 3d tone) 者, 'capped men.' Capping was in China a custom similar to the assuming the *toga virilis* among the Romans. It took place at 20. 浴 is not 'to bathe,' but is used with reference to some custom of washing the hands and clothes at some stream in the 3d month, to put away evil influences. 雩 was the name of a sacrifice, accompanied with prayer, for rain. Dancing movements were employed at it, hence the name—舞雩. 11. 曾皙曰 is to be supplied before 唯, and 子曰 before 安. Similar supplements must be made in the next paragraph.—It does not appear whether Teen, even at the last, understood why Conf. had laughed at Tsze-loo, and not at the others. 'It was not,' say the comm., 'because Tsze-loo was extravagant in his aims. They were all thinking of great things, yet not greater than they were able for. Tsze-loo's fault was in the levity with which he had proclaimed his wishes. That was his offence against *propriety*.'

BOOK XII. YEN YUEN.

顏淵第十二

第一章 一節 顏淵問仁。子曰、克己復禮爲仁、一日克己復禮、天下歸仁焉、爲仁由己、而由仁乎哉。二節 顏淵曰、請問其目。子曰、非禮勿視、非禮勿聽、非禮勿言、非禮勿動。顏淵曰、回雖不敏、請事斯語矣。

CHAPTER I. 1. Yen Yuen asked about perfect virtue. The Master said, "To subdue one's-self and return to propriety, is perfect virtue. If a man can for one day subdue himself and return to propriety, all under heaven will ascribe perfect virtue to him. Is the practice of perfect virtue from a man himself, or is it from others?"

2. Yen Yuen said, "I beg to ask the steps of that process." The Master replied, "Look not at what is contrary to propriety; listen not to what is contrary to propriety; speak not what is contrary to propriety; make no movement which is contrary to propriety." Yen Yuen *then* said, "Though I am deficient in intelligence and vigour, I will make it my business to practise this lesson."

HEADING OF THIS BOOK.—顏淵第十二, 'The twelfth Book, beginning with Yen Yuen.' It contains 24 chapters, conveying lessons on perfect virtue, government, and other questions of morality and policy, addressed in conversation by Confucius chiefly to his disciples. The different answers, given about the same subject to different questioners, show well how the sage suited his instructions to the characters and capacities of the parties with whom he had to do.

1. HOW TO ATTAIN TO PERFECT VIRTUE:—A CONVERSATION WITH YEN YUEN. 1. In Ho An, 克己 is explained by 約身, 'to restrain the body.' Choo He defines 克 by 勝, 'to overcome,' and 己 by 身之私欲, 'the selfish desires of the body.' In the 合講, it is said—己非即是私, 但私即附身而存, 故謂私爲己, '己 here is not exactly selfishness, but selfishness is what abides by being attached to the body, and hence it is said that selfishness is 己.' And again, 克己非克去其己, 乃克去己中之私欲也, '克己 is not subduing and putting away the *self*, but subduing and putting away the selfish desires *in the self*.' This 'selfishness in the self' is of a three-fold character:—first, 氣稟, said by Morrison to be 'a person's natural constitution and disposition of mind:' it is, I think, very much the ψυχικὸς ἄνθρωπος or 'animal man;' second, 耳, 目, 口, 鼻之欲, 'the desires of the ears, the eyes, the mouth, the nose;' *i. e.*, the dominating influences of the senses; and third, 爾我, 'Thou and I,' *i. e.*, the lust of superiority. More concisely, the 己 is said, in the

論語

第二章 仲弓問仁。子曰、出門如見大賓、使民如承大祭、己所不欲、勿施於人、在邦無怨、在家無怨。仲弓曰、雍雖不敏、請事斯語矣。

第三章 一節 司馬牛問仁。二節 子曰、仁者其言

CHAPTER II. Chung-kung asked about perfect virtue. The Master said, "*It is*, when you go abroad, *to behave to every one* as if you were receiving a great guest; to employ the people as if you were assisting at a great sacrifice; not to do to others as you would not wish done to yourself; to have no murmuring against you in the country, and none in the family." Chung-kung said, "Though I am deficient in intelligence and vigour, I will make it my business to practise this lesson."

CHAPTER III. 1. Sze-ma New asked about perfect virtue.

2. The Master said, "The man of perfect virtue is cautious and slow in his speech."

翼註, to be the 人心 as opposed to the 道心, 'the mind of man' in opposition to the 'mind of reason.' See the Shoo-king II. ii. 9. This refractory 'mind of man,' it is said, 與生俱生, 'is innate,' or, perhaps, 'connate.' In all these statements, there is an acknowledgment of the fact—the morally abnormal condition of human nature—which underlies the Christian doctrine of original sin. With ref. to the above three-fold classification of selfish desires, the second par. shows that it was the second order of them—the influence of the senses, which Conf. specially intended. 復禮,—see note on 禮, VIII. 2. It is not here *ceremonies*. Choo He defines it—天理之節文, 'the specific divisions and graces of heavenly principle or reason.' This is continually being departed from, on the impulse of selfishness, but there is an ideal of it as *proper* to man, which is to be sought—'returned to'—by overcoming that. 歸 is explained by Choo He by 與, 'to allow.' The gloss of the 備旨 is—稱其仁, 'will praise his perfect virtue.' The whole sentence thus seems to become a mere platitude. Perhaps 天下 is only = our 'every body,' or 'any body.' In Ho An, *kwei* is taken in the sense of 'to return,'—'the empire will return to perfect virtue,' supposing the exemplifier to be a prince. In the next sentence, which is designed to teach that every man may attain to this virtue for himself, 而 = 'or.' 2. 其 refers to 克己復禮. 目 = 條目, 'a list' or 'index.' 事 is used as an active verb;—'I beg to make my business these words.'

2. WHEREIN PERFECT VIRTUE IS REALIZED:—A CONVERSATION WITH CHUNG-KUNG. From this ch., it appears that reverence (敬) and reciprocity (恕), on the largest scale, are perfect virtue. 使民,—'ordering the people,' is apt to be done with haughtiness. This part of the answer may be compared with the apostle's precept—'Honour all men,' only the 'all men' is much more comprehensive there. 己所云云,—comp. V. 11. 在邦, 在家, = 'abroad,' 'at home.' Paou Heen, in Ho An, however, takes the former as denoting the 'prince of a state,' and the lat., 'the chief of a great offcer's establishment.' This is like the interpr. of 歸 in last ch.—The answer, the same as that of Hwuy in last ch., seems to betray the hand of the compiler.

3. CAUTION IN SPEAKING A CHARACTERISTIC OF PERFECT VIRTUE:—A CONVERSATION WITH TSZE-NEW. 1. Tsze-new was the designation of Sze-ma Kang (耕, *alias* 犂), whose tablet is

也訒。三節曰、其言也訒、斯
謂之仁已乎。子曰、爲
之難、言之得無訒乎。
第四章 一節司馬牛問君子。子
曰、君子不憂不懼。二節曰、
不憂不懼、斯爲之君
子矣乎。子曰、內省不
疚、夫何憂何懼。
第五章 一節司馬牛憂曰、人皆
有兄弟、我獨亡。二節子夏

3. "Cautious and slow in his speech!" said New;—"is this what is meant by perfect virtue?" The Master said, "When a man feels the difficulty of doing, can he be other than cautious and slow in speaking?"

CHAPTER IV. 1. Sze-ma New asked about the superior man. The Master said, "The superior man has neither anxiety nor fear."

2. "Being without anxiety or fear!" said New;—"does this constitute what we call the superior man?"

3. The Master said, "When internal examination discovers nothing wrong, what is there to be anxious about, what is there to fear?"

CHAPTER V. 1. Sze-ma New, full of anxiety, said, "*Other* men all have their brothers, I only have not."

2. Tsze-hea said to him, "There is the following saying which I have heard:—

now the 7th east in the outer ranges of the disciples. He belonged to Sung, and was a brother of Hwan T'uy, VII. 22. Their ordinary surname was Heang (向), but that of Hwan could also be used by them, as they were descended from the duke so called. The office of 'Master of the horse' (司馬) had long been in the family, and that title appears here as if it were New's surname. 2. 訒＝言難出, 'the words coming forth with difficulty.' 3. 爲之, 言之,—comp. on 之 in the note on VII. 10, *et al.* —'Doing being difficult, can speaking be without difficulty of utterance.'

4. HOW THE KEUN-TSZE HAS NEITHER ANXIETY NOR FEAR, AND CONSCIOUS RECTITUDE FREES FROM THESE. 1. 憂 is our 'anxiety,' trouble about coming troubles; 懼 is 'fear,' when the troubles have arrived. 2. 疚, is 'a chronic illness;' here it is understood with ref. to the mind, *that* displaying no symptom of disease.

5. CONSOLATION OFFERED BY TSZE-HEA TO TSZE-NEW ANXIOUS ABOUT THE PERIL OF HIS BROTHER. 1. Tsze-new's anxiety was occasioned by the conduct of his eldest brother Hwan T'uy, who, he knew, was contemplating rebellion, which would probably lead to his death. 兄弟, 'elder brothers' and 'younger brothers,' but Tsze-new was himself the youngest of his family. The phrase simply＝'brothers.' 'All have their brothers,'—*i. e.*, all can rest quietly without anxiety in their relation. 2. It is naturally supposed that the author of the observation was Conf. 4. The 翼註 says that the expr:—'all within the four seas are brothers,' 不是通天譜, 'does not mean that all under heaven have the same genealogical register.' Choo He's

曰、商聞之矣。三節 死生有命、富貴在天。四節 君子敬而無失、與人恭而有禮、四海之內、皆兄弟也、君子何患乎無兄弟也。

第六章 子張問明。子曰、浸潤之譖、膚受之愬、不行焉、可謂明也已矣、浸潤之譖、膚受之愬、不行焉、可謂遠也已矣。

3. "'Death and life have their determined appointment; riches and honours depend upon Heaven.'

4. "Let the superior man never fail reverentially to order his own conduct, and let him be respectful to others and observant of propriety:—then all within the four seas will be his brothers. What has the superior man to do with being distressed because he has no brothers?"

CHAPTER VI. Tsze-chang asked what constituted intelligence. The Master said, "He with whom neither slander that gradually soaks *into the mind*, nor statements that startle like a wound in the flesh, are successful, may be called intelligent indeed. Yea, he with whom neither soaking slander, nor startling statements, are successful, may be called far-seeing."

interpr. is that, when a man so acts, other men will love and respect him as a brother. This, no doubt, is the extent of the saying. I have found no satisfactory gloss on the phrase—'the four seas.' It is found in the Shoo-king, the She-king, and the Le-ke. In the 爾雅, a sort of Lexicon, very ancient, which was once reckoned among the *king*, it is explained as a territorial designation, the name of the dwelling-place of all the barbarous tribes. But the great Yu is represented as having made the four seas as four ditches, to which he drained the waters inundating 'the middle kingdom.' Plainly, the ancient conception was of their own country as the great habitable tract, north, south, east, and west of which were four seas or oceans, between whose shores and their own borders the intervening space was not very great, and occupied by wild hordes of inferior races. See the 四書釋地續, II. 24.—Comm. consider Tsze-hea's attempt at consolation altogether wide of the mark.

6. WHAT CONSTITUTES INTELLIGENCE:—ADDRESSED TO TSZE-CHANG. Tsze-chang, it is said, was always seeking to be wise about things lofty and distant, and therefore Conf. brings him back to things near at hand, which it was more necessary for him to attend to. 浸潤之譖, 'soaking, moistening, slander,' which unperceived sinks into the mind. 膚受之愬 (=and interchanged with 訴), 'statements of wrongs which startle like a wound in the flesh,' to which in the surprise credence is given. He with whom these things 不行,—are 'no go,' is intelligent,—yea, far-seeing. 遠=明之至. So, Choo He. The old interpr. differ in their view of 膚受之愬. The 註疏 says—'The skin receives dust which gradually accumulates.' This makes the phrase synonymous with the former.

第七章 一節 子貢問政。子曰、足食、足兵、民信之矣。二節 子貢曰、必不得已而去、於斯三者何先。曰、去兵。三節 子貢曰、必不得已而去、於斯二者何先。曰、去食、自古皆有死、民無信不立。

第八章 一節 棘子成曰、君子質而已矣、何以文爲。二節 子

CHAPTER VII. 1. Tsze-kung asked about government. The Master said, "*The requisites of government are* that there be sufficiency of food, sufficiency of military equipment, and the confidence of the people in their ruler."

2. Tsze-kung said, "If it cannot be helped, and one of these must be dispensed with, which of the three should be foregone first?" "The military equipment," said the Master.

3. Tsze-kung *again* asked, "If it cannot be helped, and one of the remaining two must be dispensed with, which of them should be foregone?" The Master answered, "Part with the food. From of old, death has been the lot of all men; but if the people have no faith *in their rulers*, there is no standing *for the state*."

CHAPTER VIII. 1. Kih Tsze-shing said, "In a superior man it is only the substantial qualities which are wanted;—why should we seek for ornamental accomplishments?"

7. REQUISITES IN GOVERNMENT:—A CONVERSATION WITH TSZE-CHANG. 1. 兵 primarily means 'weapons.' 'A soldier,' the bearer of such weapons, is a secondary meaning. There were no standing armies in Conf. time. The term is to be taken here, as='military equipment,' 'preparation for war.' 信之,—之 refers to 其上, 'their ruler.' 3. The difficulty here is with the concluding clause—無信不立. Transferring the mean. of 信 from par. 1, we naturally render as in the transl., and 不立=國不立, 'the state will not stand.' This is the view, moreover, of the old interpreters. Choo He and his followers, however, seek to make much more of 信. On the 1st par. he comments,—'The granaries being full, and the military preparation complete, then let the influence of instruction proceed. So shall the people have faith in their ruler, and will not leave him or rebel.' On the 3d par. he says,—'If the people be without food, they must die, but death is the inevitable lot of men. If they are without 信, though they live, they have not wherewith to establish themselves. It is better for them in such case to die. Therefore it is better for the ruler to die, not losing faith to his people, so that the people will prefer death rather than lose faith to him.'

8. SUBSTANTIAL QUALITIES AND ACCOMPLISHMENTS IN THE KEUN-TSZE. 1. Tsze-shing was an officer of the state of Wei, and, distressed by the pursuit in the times of what was merely external, made this not sufficiently well-considered remark, to which Tsze-kung replied, in, acc. to Choo He, an equally one-sided manner. 1. 何以文爲 is thus expanded in the 註疏,—何用文章乃爲君子, 'why use accomplishments in order to make a

貢曰、惜乎夫子之說君子也、駟不及舌。（三節）文猶質也、質猶文也、虎豹之鞟、猶犬羊之鞟。

（第九章）（一節）哀公問於有若曰、年饑、用不足、如之何。（二節）有若對曰、盍徹乎。（三節）曰、二、吾猶不足、如之何其徹也。（四節）對曰、百姓足、君孰與不足、百姓不足、君孰與足。

2. Tsze-kung said, "Alas! Your words, sir, show you to be a superior man, but four horses cannot overtake the tongue.

3. "Ornament is as substance; substance is as ornament. The hide of a tiger or leopard stript of its hair, is like the hide of a dog or goat stript of its hair."

CHAPTER IX 1. The duke Gae inquired of Yew Jŏ, saying, "The year is one of scarcity, and *the returns for* expenditure are not sufficient;—what is to be done?"

2. *Yew Jŏ* replied to him, "Why not simply tithe the people."

3. "With two tenths," said the duke, "I find them not enough;—how could I do with that system of one tenth?"

4. Yew Jŏ answered, "If the people have plenty, their prince will not be left to want alone. If the people are in want, their prince cannot enjoy plenty alone."

Keun-tsze?' 2. We may interpret this par., as in the transl., putting a comma after 說. So, Choo He. But the old interpr. seem to have read right on, without any comma, to 也, in which case the par. would be—'alas! sir, for the way in which you speak of the superior man!' And this is the most natural construction. 3. The mod. comm. seem hypercritical in condemning Tsze-kung's language here. He shows the desirableness of the ornamental accomplishments, but does not necessarily put them on the same level with the substantial qualities.

9. LIGHT TAXATION THE BEST WAY TO SECURE THE GOVERNMENT FROM EMBARRASSMENT FOR WANT OF FUNDS. 2. By the statutes of the Chow dynasty, the ground was divided into allotments cultivated in common by the families located upon them, and the produce was divided equally, nine tenths being given to the farmers, and one tenth being reserved as a contribution to the state. This was called the law of 徹, which term=通, 'pervading,' 'general,' with ref., apparently, to the system of *common* labour. 3. A former duke of Loo, Seuen (B. C. 608-590), had imposed an additional tax of another tenth from each family's portion. 4. The meaning of this par. is given in the transl. Literally rendered, it is,—'The people having plenty, the prince—with whom not plenty? The people not having plenty, with whom can the prince have plenty?' Yew Jŏ wished to impress on the duke that a sympathy and common condition should unite him and his people. If he lightened his taxation to the regular tithe, then they would cultivate their allotments with so much vigour, that his receipts would be abundant. They would be able, moreover, to help their kind ruler in any emergency.

第十章 一節 子張問崇德辨惑。子曰、主忠信、徙義、崇德也。二節 愛之欲其生、惡之欲其死、既欲其生、又欲其死、是惑也。三節 誠不以富、亦祇以異。

第十一章 一節 齊景公問政於孔子。二節 孔子對曰、君君、臣臣、父父、子子。三節 公曰、善哉、信如君不君、臣不臣、父不父、子不子、雖有粟、吾得而食諸。

CHAPTER X. 1. Tsze-chang having asked how virtue was to be exalted, and delusions to be discovered, the Master said, "Hold faithfulness and sincerity as first principles, and be moving continually to what is right;—this is the way to exalt one's virtue.

2. "You love a man and wish him to live; you hate him and wish him to die. Having wished him to live, you also wish him to die. This is a case of delusion.

3. "'It may not be on account of her being rich, yet you come to make a difference.'"

CHAPTER XI. 1. The duke King, of Ts'e, asked Confucius about government.

2. Confucius replied, "*There is government*, when the prince is prince, and the minister is minister; when the father is father, and the son is son."

3. "Good!" said the duke; "if, indeed; the prince be not prince, the minister not minister, the father not father, and the son not son, although I have my revenue, can I enjoy it?"

10. HOW TO EXALT VIRTUE AND DISCOVER DELUSIONS. 1. 主忠信,—see I. 8. 2. The Master says nothing about the 辨, 'discriminating,' or 'discovering,' of delusions, but gives an instance of a twofold delusion. Life and death, it is said, are independent of our wishes. To desire for a man either the one or the other, therefore, is one delusion. And on the change of our feelings to change our wishes in reference to the same person, is another. 之,=此人. —But in this Confucius hardly appears to be the sage. 3. See the She-king, II. iv. 4. st. 8. I have translated according to the meaning in the She-king. The quotation may be twisted into some sort of accordance with the preceding par., as a case of delusion, but the comm. Ch'ing (程) is probably correct in supposing that it should be transferred to XVI. 12.

11. GOOD GOVERNMENT OBTAINS ONLY WHEN ALL THE RELATIVE DUTIES ARE MAINTAINED. 1. Conf. went to Ts'e in his 36th year, and finding the reigning duke—styled *King* after his death —overshadowed by his ministers, and thinking of setting aside his eldest son from the succes-

【十二章】一節子曰、片言可以折獄者、其由也與。二節子路無宿諾。

【十三章】子曰、聽訟、吾猶人也、必也、使無訟乎。

【十四章】子張問政。子曰、居之無倦、行之以忠。

【十五章】子曰、博學於文、約之以禮、亦可以弗畔矣夫。

CHAPTER XII. 1. The Master said, "Ah! it is Yew, who could with half a word settle litigations!"

2. Tsze-loo never slept over a promise.

CHAPTER XIII. The Master said, "In hearing litigations, I am like any other body. What is necessary, is to cause *the people* to have no litigations."

CHAPTER XIV. Tsze-chang asked about government. The Master said, "*The art of governing* is to keep *its affairs* before the mind without weariness, and to practise them with undeviating consistency."

CHAPTER XV. The Master said, "By extensively studying all learning, and keeping himself under the restraint of the rules of propriety, *one* may thus likewise not err from what is right."

sion, he shaped his answer to the question about government accordingly. 3 雖有粟, 'although I have the grain,' *i. e.*, my revenue, the tithe of the produce of the country. 吾得而食諸 (食諸, comp. 行諸, XI. 21), 'shall I be able to eat it?'—intimating a sense of the danger he was exposed to from his insubordinate officers.

12. WITH WHAT EASE TSZE-LOO COULD SETTLE LITIGATIONS. 1. We translate here—'could,' and not—'can,' because Conf. is not referring to facts, but simply praising the disciple's character. 片言=半言, 'half a word.' 2. This par. is a note by the compilers, stating a fact about Tsze-loo, to illustrate what the Master said of him. 宿 is explained by Choo He by 留, 'to leave,' 'to let remain.' Its prim. mean. is—'to pass a night.' We have in English, as given in the transl., a corresponding idiom.—In Ho An, 片言 is taken as=偏言, 'one-sided words,' mean. that Tsze-loo could judge rightly on hearing half a case. 宿 again is explained by 豫, 'beforehand.'—'Tsze-loo made no promises beforehand.'

13. TO PREVENT BETTER THAN TO DETERMINE LITIGATIONS. See the 大學傳, IV. 訟, as oppos. to 獄 (prec. ch.) is used of civil causes (爭財曰訟), and the other of criminal (爭罪曰獄). Little stress is to be laid on the 'I.' 吾猶人 simply='One man is as good as another.' Much stress is to be laid on 使, as='to influence to.'

14. THE ART OF GOVERNING. 居, as oppos. to 行, must be an active verb, and is explained by Choo He as in the translation. 之 refers to 政, or, rather, that aspect of government about which Tsze-chang was inquiring. 無倦=始終如一, 'first and last the same;' 以忠=表裏如一, 'externally and internally the same.'

15. HARDLY DIFFERENT FROM VI. 15.

【十六章】子曰、君子成人之美、不成人之惡、小人反是。

【十七章】季康子問政於孔子。孔子對曰、政者正也、子帥以正、孰敢不正。

【十八章】季康子患盜、問於孔子。孔子對曰、苟子之不欲、雖賞之不竊。

【十九章】季康子問政於孔子、曰、如殺無道、以就有道、何如。

CHAPTER XVI. The Master said, "The superior man *seeks to* perfect the admirable qualities of men, and does not *seek to* perfect their bad qualities. The mean man does the opposite of this."

CHAPTER XVII. Ke K'ang asked Confucius about government. Confucius replied, "To govern means to rectify. If you lead on *the people* with correctness, who will dare not to be correct?"

CHAPTER XVIII. Ke K'ang distressed about the number of thieves *in the state*, inquired of Confucius *about how to do away with them*. Confucius said, "If you, sir, were not covetous, although you should reward them to do it, they would not steal."

CHAPTER XIX. Ke K'ang asked Confucius about government, saying, "What do you say to killing the unprincipled for the good of the principled?" Confucius replied, "Sir, in carrying on your government, why should you use killing at all? Let your *evinced*

16. OPPOSITE INFLUENCE UPON OTHERS OF THE SUPERIOR MAN AND THE MEAN MAN.

17. GOVERNMENT MORAL IN ITS END, AND EFFICIENT BY EXAMPLE.

18. THE PEOPLE ARE MADE THIEVES BY THE EXAMPLE OF THEIR RULERS. This is a good instance of Conf. boldness in reproving men in power. Ke K'ang had confirmed himself as head of the Ke family, and entered into all its usurpations, by taking off the infant nephew, who should have been its rightful chief. 不欲=不貪, 'did not covet,' *i. e.*, a position and influence to which you have no right. 苟子之不欲, 'given the fact of your not being ambitious.' 賞之=賞民.

19. KILLING NOT TO BE TALKED OF BY RULERS; THE EFFECT OF THEIR EXAMPLE. In 就有道, 就 is an active verb,=成, or 成就, 'to complete,' 'to perfect.' 德 is used in a vague sense, not positive virtue, but='nature,' 'character.' Some for 上 would read 尙=加, 'to add upon,' but 上 itself must here have substantially that meaning. 草上之風=草加之以風, 'the grass, having the wind upon it.'

論語

孔子對曰、子爲政、焉用殺、子欲善、而民善矣、君子之德風、小人之德草、草上之風、必偃。

〔二十章〕子一節張問士何如、斯可謂之達矣。〇二節子曰、何哉、爾所謂達者。三節子張對曰、在邦必聞、在家必聞。〇四節子曰、是聞也、非達也。〇五節夫達也者、質直而好義、察言而觀色、慮以下人、在邦必達、在家必達。〇六節夫聞也者、色取仁而行

desires be for what is good, and the people will be good. The relation between superiors and inferiors, is like that between the wind and the grass. The grass must bend, when the wind blows across it."

CHAPTER XX. 1. Tsze-chang asked, "What must the officer be, who may be said to be distinguished?"

2. The Master said, "What is it you call being distinguished?"

3. Tsze-chang replied, "It is to be heard of through the state, to be heard of through the family."

4. The Master said, "That is notoriety, not distinction.

5. "Now, the man of distinction is solid and straightforward, and loves righteousness. He examines people's words, and looks at their countenances. He is anxious to humble himself to others. Such a man will be distinguished in the country; he will be distinguished in the family.

6. "As to the man of notoriety, he assumes the appearance of vir-

20. THE MAN OF TRUE DISTINCTION, AND THE MAN OF NOTORIETY. 1. 士 'a scholar,' 'an officer.' The two ideas blend together in China. 達=通達, 'to reach all round.' It includes here the ideas of being influential, and that influence being acknowledged. 3. If 士 be understood of 'an officer,' then 在邦 assumes him to be the minister of a prince of a state, and 在家, that he is only the minister of a great officer, who is the head of a family. If, however, 士 be understood of 'a scholar,' 邦 will=州里, 'the country,' 'people generally,' and 家 will= 族黨, 'the circle of relatives and neighbours.' 5. 也者, see I. 2. 下人,—下 is the verb. The dict. explains it—降也, 自上而下也, 'to descend. From being on high to become low.' But it is here rather more still. 下人, 'to come down below *other* men.'

違、居之不疑、在邦必聞、在家必聞。

廿一章 一節 樊遲從遊於舞雩之下、曰、敢問崇德修慝辨惑。二節 子曰、善哉問。三節 先事後得、非崇德與、攻其惡無攻人之惡、非修慝與、一朝之忿、忘其身以及其親、非惑與。

廿二章 一節 樊遲問仁。子曰、愛人。問

tue, but his actions are opposed to it, and he rests in this character without any doubts *about himself*. Such a man will be heard of in the country; he will be heard of in the family."

CHAPTER XXI. 1. Fan-ch'e rambling with the Master under *the trees* about the rain-altars, said, "I venture to ask how to exalt virtue, to correct cherished evil, and to discover delusions."

2. The Master said, "Truly a good question!

3. "If doing what is to be done be made the first business, and success a secondary consideration;—is not this the way to exalt virtue? To assail one's own wickedness and not assail that of others;—is not this the way to correct cherished evil? For a morning's anger, to disregard one's own life, and involve that of his parents;—is not this a case of delusion?"

CHAPTER XXII. 1. Fan Ch'e asked about benevolence. The Master said, "It is to love *all* men." He asked about knowledge. The Master said, "It is to know *all* men."

2. Fan Ch'e did not immediately understand *these answers*.

21. HOW TO EXALT VIRTUE, CORRECT VICE, AND DISCOVER DELUSIONS. Comp. ch. 10. Here, as there, under the last point of the inquiry, Conf. simply indicates a case of delusion, and perhaps that is the best way to teach how to discover delusions generally. 1. 舞雩, see XI. 25, 11; followed here by 之下, there must be reference to the trees growing about the altars. 慝, formed from 'heart' and 'to conceal,' =secret vice. 3. 先事後得,—comp. with 先難後獲, in VI. 20, which also is the report of a conversation with Fan Ch'e. 其惡,—其=已, 'himself,' 'his own.' 'A morning's anger' must be a small thing, but the consequences of giving way to it are very terrible. The case is one of great delusion.

22. ABOUT BENEVOLENCE AND WISDOM:—HOW KNOWLEDGE SUBSERVES BENEVOLENCE. Fan Ch'e might well deem the Master's replies enigmatical, and, with the help of Tsze-hea's explanations, the student still finds it difficult to

知。子曰、知人。二節樊遲未達。三節子曰、舉直錯諸枉、能使枉者直。四節樊遲退、見子夏、曰、鄉也、吾見於夫子而問知。子曰、舉直錯諸枉、能使枉者直、何謂也。五節子夏曰、富哉、言乎。六節舜有天下、選於衆、舉皐陶、不仁者遠矣。湯有天下、選於衆、舉伊尹、不仁者遠矣。

廿三章子貢問友。子曰、忠告、而善道

3. The Master said, "Employ the upright and put aside all the crooked;—in this way, the crooked can be made to be upright."

4. Fan Ch'e retired, and seeing Tsze-hea, he said to him, "A little ago, I had an interview with our Master, and asked him about knowledge. He said, 'Employ the upright, and put aside all the crooked;—in this way, the crooked can be made to be upright.' What did he mean?"

5. Tsze-hea said, "Truly rich is his saying!

6. "Shun, being in possession of the empire, selected from among all the people and employed Kaou-yaou, on which all who were devoid of virtue disappeared. T'ang being in possession of the empire, selected from among all the people, and employed E-yin, and all who were devoid of virtue disappeared."

CHAPTER XXIII. Tsze-kung asked about friendship. The Master said, "Faithfully admonish *your friend*, and kindly try to lead him. If you find him impracticable, stop. Do not disgrace yourself."

understand the chapter. 1. 仁 here, being opposed to, or distinct from, 知, is to be taken as meaning 'benevolence,' and not as 'perfect virtue.' 2. 未, 'not yet,' *i. e.*, not immediately. 3. See II. 19. 4. 鄉, up. 3d tone, in the dict. explained by 昔, 'formerly.' 6. Kaou-yaou, and E-yin,—see the Shoo-king, II. iii, and III. iv. Shun and T'ang showed their wisdom—their knowledge of men—in the selection of those ministers. That was their employment of the upright, and therefore all devoid of virtue disappeared. That was their making the crooked upright;—and so their love reached to all.

之、不可則止、毋自辱焉。

〔第二十四章〕曾子曰、君子以文會友、以友輔仁。

CHAPTER XXIV. The philosoher Tsăng said, "The superior man on literary grounds meets with his friends, and by their friendship helps his virtue."

23. PRUDENCE IN FRIENDSHIP. 告 read *kuh*, as in III. 7, implying some degree of deference. 道=導, as in II. 3, 1.

24. THE FRIENDSHIP OF THE KEUN-TSZE. 以文, 'by means of letters,' *i. e.*, common literary studies and pursuits.

BOOK XIII. TSZE-LOO.

子路第十三

〔第一章〕子〔一節〕路問政。子曰、先之勞之。請〔二節〕益。曰、無倦。

〔第二章〕仲〔一節〕弓爲季氏

CHAPTER I. 1. Tsze-loo asked about government. The Master said, "Go before the people *with your example*, and be laborious in their affairs."

2. He requested further instruction, and was answered, "Be not weary in these things."

CHAPTER II. 1. Chung-kung, being chief minister to the head of the Ke family, asked about government. The Master said, "Em-

HEADING OF THIS BOOK.—子路第十三, 'Tsze-loo.—Book XIII.' Here, as in the last book, we have a number of subjects touched upon, all bearing more or less directly on the government of the state, and the cultivation of the person. The book extends to thirty chapters.

1. THE SECRET OF SUCCESS IN GOVERNING IS THE UNWEARIED EXAMPLE OF THE RULERS:—A LESSON TO TSZE-LOO. 1. To what understood antecedents do the 之 refer? For the first, we may suppose 民;—先之=率民, or 道民, 'precede the people,' 'lead the people,' that is, do so by the example of your personal conduct. But we cannot in the second clause bring 之(=民) in the same way under the regimen of 勞. 勞之=爲他勤勞, 'to be laborious for them;' that is, to set them the example of diligence in agriculture, &c. It is better, however, according to the idiom I have several times pointed out, to take 之 as giving a sort of neuter and general force to the preceding words, so that the expressions are='example and laboriousness.'—K'ung Gan-kwŏ understands the meaning differently:—'set the people an example, and then you may make them labour.' But this is not so good. 2. 無 in old copies is 毋. The meaning comes to the same.

宰、問政。子曰、先有司、赦小過、舉賢才。二節曰、焉知賢才而舉之。曰、舉爾所知、爾所不知、人其舍諸。

三章 一節子路曰、衞君待子而爲政、子將奚先。二節子曰、必也、正名乎。三節子路曰、有是哉、子之迂也。奚其正。四節子曰、野哉、由也。君子於其所不知、蓋闕如也。五節名不

ploy first the services of your various officers, pardon small faults, and raise to office men of virtue and talents."

2. *Chung-kung* said, "How shall I know the men of virtue and talent, so that I may raise them to office?" He was answered, "Raise to office those whom you know. As to those whom you do not know, will others neglect them?"

CHAPTER III. 1. Tsze-loo said, "The prince of Wei has been waiting for you, in order with you to administer the government. What will you consider the first thing to be done?"

2. The Master replied, "What is necessary is to rectify names."

3. "So, indeed!" said Tsze-loo. "You are wide of the mark. Why must there be such rectification?"

4. The Master said, "How uncultivated you are, Yew! A superior man, in regard to what he does not know, shows a cautious reserve."

2. THE DUTIES CHIEFLY TO BE ATTENDED TO BY A HEAD MINISTER:—A LESSON TO YEN YUNG. 1. 先有司,—comp. VIII. 4, 3. The 有司 are the various smaller officers. A head minister should assign them their duties, and not be interfering in them himself. His business is to examine into the manner in which they discharge them. And in doing so, he should overlook small faults. 2. 人其舍諸,—comp. 山川其舍諸, in VI. 4, though the force of 舍 here is not so great as in that ch. Conf. meaning is, that Chung-kung need not trouble himself about *all* men of worth. Let him advance those he knew. There was no fear that the others would be neglected. Comp. what is said on 'knowing men,' in XII. 22.

3. THE SUPREME IMPORTANCE OF NAMES BEING CORRECT. 1. This conversation is assigned by Choo He to the 11th year of the duke Gae of Loo, when Conf. was 69, and he returned from his wanderings to his native state. Tsze-loo had then been some time in the service of the duke Ch'uh of Wei, who it would appear, had been wishing to get the services of the sage himself, and the disciple did not think that his Master would refuse to accept office, as he had not objected to *his* doing so. 2. 名 must have here a special reference, which Tsze-loo did not apprehend. Nor did the old interpr., for Ma Yung explains the 正名 by 正百事之名, 'to rectify the names of all things.' On this view, the reply would indeed be 'wide of the mark.' The answer is substantially the same as the reply to duke King of Ts'e about

正、則言不順、言不順、則事不成。（六節）事不成、則禮樂不興、禮樂不興、則刑罰不中、刑罰不中、則民無所措手足。（七節）故君子名之必可言也、言之必可行也。君子於其言、無所苟而已矣。

（第四章）（一節）樊遲請學稼。子曰、吾不如老農。請學爲圃。曰、

5. "If names be not correct, language is not in accordance with the truth of things. If language be not in accordance with the truth of things, affairs cannot be carried on to success.

6. "When affairs cannot be carried on to success, proprieties and music will not flourish. When proprieties and music do not flourish, punishments will not be properly awarded. When punishments are not properly awarded, the people do not know how to move hand or foot.

7. "Therefore a superior man considers it necessary that the names he uses may be spoken *appropriately*, and also that what he speaks may be carried out *appropriately*. What the superior man requires, is just that in his words there may be nothing incorrect."

CHAPTER IV 1. Fan Ch'e requested to be taught husbandry. The Master said, "I am not so good for that as an old husbandman." He requested *also* to be taught gardening, and was answered, "I am not so good for that as an old gardener."

govern. in XII. 11, that it obtains when the prince is prince, the father father, &c; that is, when each man in his relations is what the *name* of his relation would require. Now, the duke Ch'uh held the rule of Wei against his father; see VII. 14. Conf., from the necessity of the case and peculiarity of the circumstances, allowed his disciples, notwithstanding that, to take office in Wei; but at the time of this conversation, Ch'uh had been duke for nine years, and ought to have been so established that he could have taken the course of a filial son without subjecting the state to any risks. On this account, Conf. said he would begin with rectifying the name of the duke, that is, with requiring him to resign the dukedom to his father, and be what his name of *son* required him to be. See the 翼註, *in loc.* This view enables us to understand better the climax that follows, tho' its successive steps are still not without difficulty. 正名乎,—乎 may be taken as an exclamation, or as='is it not?' 4. 闕如,—闕 is used in the same sense as in II. 18. The phrase='is putting-aside-like,' *i. e.*, the sup. man reserves and revolves what he is in doubt about, and does not rashly speak. 6. 'Proprieties' here are not ceremonial rules, but ='*order*,' what such rules are designed to display and secure. So, 'music' is equivalent to 'harmony.' 中, 3d tone, is the verb; 不中='do not hit the mark.'

4. A RULER HAS NOT TO OCCUPY HIMSELF WITH WHAT IS PROPERLY THE BUSINESS OF THE PEOPLE. It is to be supposed that Fan Ch'e

吾不如老圃。○二節樊遲出。子曰、小人哉、樊須也。○三節上好禮、則民莫敢不敬、上好義、則民莫敢不服、上好信、則民莫敢不用情、夫如是、則四方之民、襁負其子而至矣、焉用稼。

第五章子曰、誦詩三百、授之以政、不達、使於四方、不能專對、雖多、亦奚以爲。

2. Fan Ch'e having gone out, the Master said, "A small man, indeed, is Fan Seu!"

3. "If a superior love propriety, the people will not dare not to be reverent. If he love righteousness, the people will not dare not to submit *to his example.* If he love good faith, the people will not dare not to be sincere. Now, when these things obtain, the people from all quarters will come to him, bearing their children on their backs. What need has he of a knowledge of husbandry?"

CHAPTER V. The Master said, "Though a man may be able to recite the three hundred odes, yet if, when intrusted with a governmental charge, he knows not how to act, or if, when sent to any quarter on a mission, he cannot give his replies unassisted, notwithstanding the extent *of his learning*, of what practical use is it?"

was at this time in office somewhere, and thinking of the Master, as the villager and high officer did, IX. 2 and 6, that his knowledge embraced almost every subject, he imagined that he might get lessons from him on the two subjects he specifies, which he might use for the benefit of the people. 1. 稼 is properly the 'seed-sowing,' and 圃, 'a kitchen-garden,' but they are used generally, as in the transl. 3. 情, 'the feelings,' 'desires,' but sometimes, as here, in the sense of 'sincerity.' 襁, often joined with 褓, is a cloth with strings by which a child is strapped upon the back of its mother or nurse.—This par. shows what people in office should learn. Conf. intended that it should be repeated to Fan Ch'e.

5. LITERARY ACQUIREMENTS USELESS WITHOUT PRACTICAL ABILITY. 詩三百,—see II. 2 誦, 'to croon over,' as Chinese students do; here,='to have learned.' 專=獨, 'alone,' *i.e.*, unassisted by the individuals of his suite. 多, 'many,' refer. to the 300 odes. 亦, 'also,' here and in other places,=our 'yet,' 'after all.' 奚以爲,—以, it is said,=用, 'use,' and 爲 is a mere expletive,—是語助詞, but each term may have its meaning, as in the translation.

第六章 子曰、其身正、不令而行、其身不正、雖令不從。

第七章 子曰、魯衞之政、兄弟也。

第八章 子謂衞公子荊善居室、始有、曰、苟合矣、少有、曰、苟完矣、富有、曰、苟美矣。

第九章 一節 子適衞、冉有僕。二節 子曰、庶矣哉。三節 冉有曰、既庶矣、

CHAPTER VI. The Master said, "When a prince's personal conduct is correct, his government is effective without the issuing of orders. If his personal conduct is not correct, he may issue orders, but they will not be followed."

CHAPTER VII. The Master said, "The government of Loo and Wei are brothers."

CHAPTER VIII. The Master said of King, a scion of the ducal family of Wei, that he knew the economy of a family well. When he began to have means, he said, "Ha! here is a collection!" when they were a little increased, he said, "Ha! this is complete!" when he had become rich, he said, "Ha! this is admirable!"

CHAPTER IX. 1. When the Master went to Wei, Yen Yew acted as driver of his carriage.

2. The Master observed, "How numerous are the people!"

3. Yew said, "Since they are thus numerous, what more shall be done for them?" "Enrich them," was the reply.

6. HIS PERSONAL CONDUCT ALL IN ALL TO A RULER. A translator finds it impossible here to attain to the terse conciseness of his original.

7. THE SIMILAR CONDITION OF THE STATES OF LOO AND WEI. Comp. VI. 22. Loo's state had been from the influence of Chow-kung, and Wei was the fief of his brother Fung (封), commonly known as K'ang-shuh (康叔). They had, similarly, maintained an equal and brotherly course in their progress, or, as it was in Confucius' time, in their degeneracy. That portion of the present Ho-nan, which runs up and lies between Shan-se and Pih-chih-le, was the bulk of Wei.

8. THE CONTENTMENT OF THE OFFICER KING, AND HIS INDIFFERENCE IN GETTING RICH. King was a great officer of Wei, a scion of its ducal house. 善居室 is a difficult expression. Literally it is—'dwelt well in his house.' 室 implies that he was a married man, the head of a family. The 合講 says the phrase is equivalent to 處家, 'managed his family.' Choo He explains 苟 by 聊且粗畧之意,—'it is significant of indifference and carelessness.' Our word 'ha!' expressing surprise and satisfaction corresponds to it pretty nearly. The 備旨 says that the 曰 is not to be understood as if King really made these utterances, but that Conf. thus vividly represents how he felt.

又何加焉。曰、富之。〔四節〕曰、旣富矣、又何加焉。曰、敎之。

〔第十章〕子曰、苟有用我者、朞月而已可也、三年有成。

〔十一章〕子曰、善人爲邦百年、亦可以勝殘去殺矣、誠哉是言也。

〔十二章〕子曰、如有王者、必世而後仁。

4. "And when they have been enriched, what more shall be done?" The Master said, "Teach them."

CHAPTER X. The Master said, "If there were any of the princes who would employ me, in the course of twelve months, I should have done something considerable. In three years, *the government* would be perfected."

CHAPTER XI. The Master said, "'If good men were to govern a country *in succession* for a hundred years, they would be able to transform the violently bad, and dispense with capital punishments.' True indeed is this saying!"

CHAPTER XII. The Master said, "If a truly royal ruler were to arise, it would *still* require a generation, and then virtue would prevail."

9. A PEOPLE NUMEROUS, WELL-OFF, AND EDUCATED, IS THE GREAT ACHIEVEMENT OF GOVERNMENT. 1. 僕, 'a servant,' but here with the mean. in the translation. That, indeed, is the second meaning of the char. given in the dict.

10. CONFUCIUS' ESTIMATE OF WHAT HE COULD DO, IF EMPLOYED TO ADMINISTER THE GOVERNMENT OF A STATE. 朞, is to be distinguished from 期, and ='a revolution of the year.' There is a comma at 月, and 而已可 are read together. 而已 does not signify, as it often does, 'and nothing more,' but='and have,' 已 being 已經, a sign of the perfect tense. —'Given twelve months, and there would be a passable result. In three years, there would be a completion.'

11. WHAT A HUNDRED YEARS OF GOOD GOVERNMENT COULD EFFECT. Conf. quotes here a saying of his time, and approves of it. 勝, up-per 1st tone, 'to be equal to.' 勝殘, 'would be equal to the violent,' that is, to transform them. 去殺, 'to do away with killing,' that is, with capital punishments, unnecessary with a transformed people.

12. IN WHAT TIME A ROYAL RULER COULD TRANSFORM THE EMPIRE. 王者, 'one who was a king.' The char. 王 is formed by three straight lines representing the three powers of Heaven, Earth, and Man, and a perpendicular line, going through and uniting them, and thus conveys the highest idea of power and influence. See the dict., char. 王. Here it means the highest wisdom and virtue in the highest place.

〔十三〕子曰、苟正其身矣、於從政乎何有、不能正其身、如正人何。

〔十四〕冉子退朝、子曰、何晏也。對曰、有政。子曰、其事也、如有政、雖不吾以、吾其與聞之。

〔十五〕一節 定公問一言而可以興邦、有諸。孔子對曰、言不可以若是其

CHAPTER XIII. The Master said, "If a minister make his own conduct correct, what difficulty will he have in assisting in government? If he cannot rectify himself, what has he to do with rectifying others?"

CHAPTER XIV. The disciple Yen returning from the court, the Master said to him, "How are you so late?" He replied, "We had government business." The Master said, "It must have been *family* affairs. If there had been government business, though I am not *now* in office, I should have been consulted about it."

CHAPTER XV. 1. The duke Ting asked whether there was a single sentence which could make a country prosperous. Confucius replied, "Such an effect cannot be expected from one sentence.

2. "There is a saying, however, which people have—'To be a prince is difficult; to be a minister is not easy.'

世, 'a generation,' or thirty years. See note on II. 23, 1. The old interpr. take 仁 as=仁政, 'virtuous government.'—To save Conf. from the charge of vanity in what he says, in ch. 10, that he could accomplish in three years, it is said, that the perfection which he predicates there would only be the foundation for the virtue here realized.

13. THAT HE BE PERSONALLY CORRECT ESSENTIAL TO AN OFFICER OF GOVERNMENT. Comp. ch. 6. That the subject is here an officer of gov., and not the ruler, appears from the phrase 從政; see note on VI. 6. With reference to the other phraseology of the ch., the 備旨 says that 從政 embraces 正君, 'the rectification of the prince,' and 正民, 'the rectification of the people.'

14 AN IRONICAL ADMONITION TO YEN YEW ON THE USURPING TENDENCIES OF THE KE FAMILY. The point of the ch. turns on the opposition of the phrases 有政 and 其事也;—at the court of the Ke family, that is, they had really been discussing matters of government, affecting the state, and proper only for the prince's court. Conf. affects not to believe it, and says that at the chief's court they could only have been discussing the affairs of his house. 不吾以,—an inversion, and 以=用, 'although I am *now* not employed.' 與, low. 3d tone.—'I should have been present and heard it.' Superannuated officers might go to court on occasions of emergency, and might also be consulted on such, though the gen. rule was to allow them to retire at 70. See the Le Ke, I. i. 28.

15. HOW THE PROSPERITY AND RUIN OF A COUNTRY MAY DEPEND ON THE RULER'S VIEW OF HIS POSITION, HIS FEELING ITS DIFFICULTY, OR ONLY CHERISHING A HEADSTRONG WILL. 1. I should suppose that 一言可以興邦, and

論語

幾也。二節人之言曰、爲君難、爲臣不易。三節如知爲君之難也、不幾乎一言而興邦乎。四節曰、一言而喪邦有諸。孔子對曰、言不可以若是其幾也、人之言曰、予無樂乎爲君、唯其言而莫予違也。五節如其善、而莫之違也、不亦善乎。如不善、而莫之違也、不幾乎一言而喪邦乎。

十六 一節葉公問政。二節子曰、近者說、遠

3. "If *a ruler* knows this,—the difficulty of being a prince,—may there not be expected from this one sentence the prosperity of his country?"

4. *The duke then* said, "Is there a single sentence which can ruin a country?" Confucius replied, "Such an effect as that cannot be expected from one sentence. There is, *however*, the saying which people have—'I have no pleasure in being a prince, only in that no one offer any opposition to what I say!'

5. "If *a ruler's* words be good, is it not also good that no one oppose them? But if they are not good, and no one opposes them, may there not be expected from this one sentence the ruin of his country?"

CHAPTER XVI. 1. The duke of Shĕ asked about government.

2. The Master said, "*Good government obtains, when* those who are near are made happy, and those who are far off are attracted."

the correspond. sent. below were comm. sayings, about which the duke asks, in a way to intimate his disbelief of them—有諸. 幾 is not here in the sense of 'a spring,' or '*primum mobile*,' but=期, in the sense of 'to expect,' 'to be expected from.' 一言=一句, as in II. 2. 2. It is only the first part of the saying on which Conf. dwells. That is called 主, the principal sentence; the other is only 帶說, 'an accessory.' 3. Some put a comma at the first 乎, but it is better to take that 乎 as a preposition;—'May it not be expected that *from* this one word, &c.?' Similarly, par. 4, 乎 is a prep.,=our *in*. 其言,—言 is used specially of the orders, rules, &c., which a ruler may issue.

16. GOOD GOVERNMENT SEEN FROM ITS EFFECTS. 1. 葉, read *shĕ*; see VII. 18. 2. Conf. is supposed to have in view the oppressive and aggressive govt. of Tsoo, to which *Shĕ* belonged.

者來。

十七 子夏爲莒父宰、問政。子曰、無欲速、無見小利、欲速則不達、見小利則大事不成。

十八 葉公語孔子曰、吾黨有直躬者、其父攘羊、而子證之。孔子曰、吾黨之直者異於是、父爲子隱、子爲父隱、直在其中矣。

CHAPTER XVII. Tsze-hea, being governor of Keu-foo, asked about government. The Master said, "Do not be desirous to have things done quickly; do not look at small advantages. Desire to have things done quickly prevents their being done thoroughly. Looking at small advantages prevents great affairs from being accomplished."

CHAPTER XVIII. 1. The duke of Shĕ informed Confucius, saying, "Among us here there are those who may be styled upright in their conduct. If their father have stolen a sheep, they will bear witness to the fact."

2. Confucius said, "Among us, in our part of the country, those who are upright are different from this. The father conceals the misconduct of the son, and the son conceals the misconduct of the father. Uprightness is to be found in this."

17. HASTE AND SMALL ADVANTAGES NOT TO BE DESIRED IN GOVERNING. Keu-foo (*foo*, up. 2d tone) was a small city in the western borders of Loo. 無=毋, the prohibitive particle.

18. NATURAL DUTY AND UPRIGHTNESS IN COLLISION. 1. 吾黨, 'our village,' 'our neighbourhood,' but 黨 must be taken vaguely, as in the transl.; comp. V. 21. We cannot say whether the duke is referring to one or more actual cases, or giving his opinion of what his people would do. Conf. reply would incline us to the latter view. In the 集證, accounts are quoted of such cases, but they are probably founded on this chap. 攘 is 'to steal on occasion,' *i. e.*, on some temptation, as when another person's animal comes into my grounds, and I appropriate it. 證 seems to convey here the idea of accusation, as well as of witnessing. 2. 直在其中,—comp. II. 18, 2. The express. does not absolutely affirm that this is upright, but that in this there is a better principle than in the other conduct.—Any body but a Chinese will say that both the duke's view of the subject and the sage's were incomplete.

論語

〔十九章〕樊遲問仁。子曰、居處恭、執事敬、與人忠、雖之夷狄、不可棄也。

〔二十章〕一節子貢問曰、何如斯可謂之士矣。子曰、行己有恥、使於四方、不辱君命、可謂士矣。二節曰、敢問其次。曰、宗族稱孝焉、鄉黨稱弟焉。三節曰、敢問其次。曰、言必信、行必果、硜硜然、小

CHAPTER XIX. Fan Ch'e asked about perfect virtue. The Master said, "It is, in retirement, to be sedately grave; in the management of business, to be reverently attentive; in intercourse with others, to be strictly sincere. Though a man go among rude uncultivated tribes, these *qualities* may not be neglected."

CHAPTER XX. 1. Tsze-kung asked, saying, "What qualities must a man possess to entitle him to be called an officer?" The Master said, "He who in his conduct of himself maintains a sense of shame, and when sent to any quarter will not disgrace his prince's commission, deserves to be called an officer."

2. *Tsze-kung* pursued, "I venture to ask who may be placed in the next lower rank?" and he was told, "He whom the circle of his relatives pronounce to be filial, whom his fellow-villagers and neighbours pronounce to be fraternal."

3. *Again the disciple* asked, "I venture to ask about the class still next in order." *The Master* said, "They are determined to be sincere in what they say, and to carry out what they do. They are obstinate little men. Yet perhaps they may make the next class."

19. CHARACTERISTICS OF PERFECT VIRTUE. This is the third time that Fan Ch'e is represented as quest. the Master about 仁, and it is supposed by some to have been the first in order. 居處 (up. 2d tone), in oppos. to 執事, = 'dwelling alone,' 'in retirement.' 之 is a verb, as in V. 18, 2, = 往, 'to go to.'

20. DIFFERENT CLASSES OF MEN WHO IN THEIR SEVERAL DEGREES MAY BE STYLED OFFICERS, AND THE INFERIORITY OF THE MASS OF THE OFFICERS OF CONFUCIUS' TIME. 1. 士,—comp. on XII. 20. Here it denotes—not the scholar, but the officer. 有恥, 'has shame,' i. e., will avoid all bad conduct which would subject him to reproach. 2. 宗族, is 'a designation for all who form one body having the same ancestor,' 一是同宗共族之稱. These are also called 九族, 'nine branches of kindred,' being all of the same surname from the great-great-grandfather to the great-great-grandson. 弟 = 悌, not simply 'brotherly,' in the strict sense, but 'submissive,' giving due honour to all older than himself. 3. 硜, 'the sound of stones.'

人哉、抑亦可以爲次矣。四節曰、今之從政者何如。子曰、噫、斗筲之人、何足算也。

廿一章 子曰、不得中行而與之、必也狂狷乎、狂者進取、狷者有所不爲也。

廿二章 一節 子曰、南人有言曰、人而無恆、不可以作巫醫、善夫。二節 不恒其德、或承之

4. *Tsze-kung finally* inquired, "Of what sort are those of the present day, who engage in government?" The Master said, "Pooh! they are so many pecks and hampers, not worth being taken into account."

CHAPTER XXI. The Master said, "Since I cannot get men pursuing the due medium, to whom I might communicate *my instructions*, I must find the ardent and the cautiously-decided. The ardent will advance and lay hold *of truth;* the cautiously-decided will keep themselves from what is wrong."

CHAPTER XXII. 1. The Master said, "The people of the south have a saying—'A man without constancy cannot be either a wizard or a doctor.' Good!

2. "Inconstant in his virtue, he will be visited with disgrace."

硜硜然, 'stone like.' The dict., with ref. to this passage, explains it—小人貌, 'the appearance of a small man.' 4. 斗筲之人 i. e., mere utensils. Comp. on II. 12.

21. CONFUCIUS OBLIGED TO CONTENT HIMSELF WITH THE ARDENT AND CAUTIOUS AS DISCIPLES. Comp. V. 21, and Mencius VII. ii. 37. 與之 is explain. as in the transl.—以道傳之. The 註疏, however, gives simply—與之同處, 'dwell together with them,' and treats the ch. as if it had no reference to the transmission of the sage's doctrines, or to his disciples. 必也, 狂狷乎,—comp. ch. 3, 2. 狷 is explained in the dict. by 褊急, 'contracted and urgent.' Oppos. to 狂, it would seem to denote caution, but yet not a caution which may not be combined with decision. 有所不爲, 'have what they will not do.'

22. THE IMPORTANCE OF FIXITY AND CONSTANCY OF MIND. 1. I translate 巫 by 'wizard,' for want of a better term. In the Chow Le, Bk. XXVI, the *woo* appear sustaining a sort of official status, regularly called in to bring down spiritual beings, obtain showers, &c. They are distinguished as men and women, though 巫 is often feminine, 'a witch,' as opposed to 覡, 'a wizard.' Conf. use of the saying, acc. to Choo He, is this:—'Since such small people must have constancy, how much more ought others to have it!' The ranking of the doctors and wizards together sufficiently shows what was the position of the healing art in those days.—Ching K'ang-shing interprets this par. quite inadmissibly:—'wizards and doctors

論語

羞。三節子曰、不占而已矣。

廿三子曰、君子和而不同、小人同而不和。

廿四子貢問曰、鄉人皆好之、何如。子曰、未可也。鄉人皆惡之、何如。子曰、未可也、不如鄉人之善者好之、其不善者惡之。

廿五子曰、君子易事而難說也、說之不以道、不說也、及

3. The Master said, "This arises simply from not prognosticating."

CHAPTER XXIII. The Master said, "The superior man is affable, but not adulatory; the mean is adulatory, but not affable."

CHAPTER XXIV. Tsze-kung asked saying, "What do you say of a man who is loved by all the people of his village?" The Master replied, "We may not for that accord our approval of him." "And what do you say of him who is hated by all the people of his village?" The Master said, "We may not for that conclude that he is bad. It is better than either of these cases that the good in the village love him, and the bad hate him."

CHAPTER XXV. The Master said, "The superior man is easy to serve and difficult to please. If you try to please him in any way which is not accordant with right, he will not be pleased. But in his employment of men, he uses them according to their capacity. The

cannot manage people who have no constancy.' 2. This is a quotation from the Yih-king, diagram 恆. 3. This is inexplicable to Choo He. Some bring out from it the mean. in the translation.—Ch'ing K'ang-shing says:—'By the Yih we prognosticate good and evil, but in it there is no prognostication of people without constancy.'

23. THE DIFFERENT MANNERS OF THE SUPERIOR AND THE MEAN MAN. Comp. II. 14, but here the parties are contrasted in their more private intercourse with others. 同, 'agreeing with,'=flattering.

24. HOW, TO JUDGE OF A MAN FROM THE LIKINGS AND DISLIKINGS OF OTHERS, WE MUST KNOW THE CHARACTERS OF THOSE OTHERS. 未可,—lit,, 'not yet may,' The general mean. of a Chin. sentence is often plain, and yet we are puzzled to supply exactly the subjects, auxiliaries, &c., which other languages require. In rendering the phrase, I have followed many of the paraphrasts, who complete it thus:—未可信其爲賢也, and 未可信其爲惡也. In the 註疏, however, the second occurrence of it is expanded in the same way as the first.

25. DIFFERENCE BETWEEN THE SUPERIOR AND THE MEAN MAN IN THEIR RELATION TO THOSE EMPLOYED BY THEM. 易事而難說(=悅),—as in the transl., or we may render,—'is easily

其使人也、器之。小人難事而易說也、說之雖不以道、說也、及其使人也、求備焉。

〖二十六〗子曰、君子泰而不驕、小人驕而不泰。

〖二十七〗子曰、剛、毅、木、訥、近仁。

〖二十八〗子路問曰、何如斯可謂之士矣。子曰、切切、偲偲、怡怡如也、可謂士矣、朋友切切偲偲、兄弟怡怡。

mean man is difficult to serve, and easy to please. If you try to please him, though it be in a way which is not accordant with right, he may be pleased. But in his employment of men, he wishes them to be equal to everything."

CHAPTER XXVI. The Master said, "The superior man has a dignified ease without pride. The mean man has pride without a dignified ease."

CHAPTER XXVII. The Master said, "The firm, the enduring, the simple, and the modest, are near to virtue."

CHAPTER XXVIII. Tsze-loo asked saying, "What qualities must a man possess to entitle him to be called a scholar?" The Master said, "He must be thus,—earnest, urgent, and bland:—among his friends, earnest and urgent; among his brethren, bland."

served, but is pleased with difficulty.' 器之,—see II. 12, 器 being here a verb. 求備, is the opposite of 器之, and=以全材責備一人身上, 'he requires all capabilities from a single man.'

26. THE DIFFERENT AIR AND BEARING OF THE SUPERIOR AND THE MEAN MAN.

27. NATURAL QUALITIES WHICH ARE FAVOURABLE TO VIRTUE. 木, 'wood,' here an adj., but not our 'wooden.' It=質樸, 'simple,' 'plain.' 訥, see IV. 24. The gloss on it here is—犀鈍, 'slow and blunt.' 'Modest' seems to be the idea.

28. QUALITIES THAT MARK THE SCHOLAR IN SOCIAL INTERCOURSE. This is the same question as in ch. 20, 1, but 士 is here 'the scholar,' the gentleman of education, without reference to his being in office or not.

論語

【廿九章】子曰、善人教民七年、亦可以卽戎矣。【三十章】子曰、以不教民戰、是謂棄之。

CHAPTER XXIX. The Master said, "Let a good man teach the people seven years, and they may then likewise be employed in war."

CHAPTER XXX. The Master said, "To lead an uninstructed people to war, is to throw them away."

29. HOW THE GOVERNMENT OF A GOOD RULER WILL PREPARE THE PEOPLE FOR WAR. 善人, 'a good man,'—spoken with reference to him as a ruler. The teaching is not to be understood of military training, but of the duties of life and citizenship; a people so taught are morally fitted to fight for their government. What military training may be included in the teaching, would merely be the hunting and drilling in the people's repose from the toils of agriculture. 戎, 'weapons of war.' 可以卽戎,—'they may go to their weapons.'

30. THAT PEOPLE MUST BE TAUGHT, TO PREPARE THEM FOR WAR. Comp. the last ch. The lang. is very strong, and 教 being understood as in last ch., shows how Conf. valued education for all classes.

BOOK XIV. HËEN-WAN.

憲問第十四

【第一章】憲問恥。子曰、邦有道穀、邦無道穀、恥也。

CHAPTER I. Hëen asked what was shameful. The Master said, "When good government prevails in a state, *to be thinking only of his* salary; and, when bad government prevails, *to be thinking, in the same way, only of his* salary;—this is shameful."

HEADING OF THIS BOOK.—憲問第十四, 'Hëen asked—No. XIV.' The glossarist Hing Ping (邢昺) says, 'In this Book we have the characters of the *Three Kings*, and *Two Chiefs*, the courses proper for princes and great officers, the practice of virtue, the knowledge of what is shameful, personal cultivation, and the tranquillizing of the people;—all subjects of great importance in government. They are therefore collected together, and arranged after the last chapter which commences with an inquiry about government.' Some writers are of opinion that the whole book was compiled by Hëen or Yuen Sze, who appears in the first chapter.

1. IT IS SHAMEFUL IN AN OFFICER TO BE CARING ONLY ABOUT HIS EMOLUMENT. Hëen is the Yuen Sze of VI. 3, and if we suppose Conf. answer designed to have a practical application to himself, it is not easily reconcileable with what appears of his character, in that other place. 穀, here=祿, 'emolument,' but its meaning must be pregnant and intensive, as in the transl. If we do not take it so, the sentiment is contradictory to VIII. 13, 3. K'ung Gan-kwŏ, however, takes the following view of the reply:—'When a country is well governed, emolument is right; when a country is ill-governed! to take office and emolument is shameful.' I prefer the construction of Choo He, which appears in the translation.

第二章 克、一節伐、怨、欲、不行焉、可以爲仁矣。二節子曰、可以爲難矣、仁則吾不知也。

第三章 子曰、士而懷居、不足以爲士矣。

第四章 子曰、邦有道、危言危行、邦無道、危行言孫。

第五章 子曰、有德者、必有言、有言者、不必有德、仁者、必有勇、勇者、不必有仁。

CHAPTER II. 1. "When the love of superiority, boasting, resentments, and covetousness are repressed, may this be deemed perfect virtue?"

2. The Master said, "This may be regarded as the achievement of what is difficult. But I do not know that it is to be deemed perfect virtue."

CHAPTER III. The Master said, "The scholar who cherishes the love of comfort, is not fit to be deemed a scholar."

CHAPTER IV. The Master said, "When good government prevails in a state, language may be lofty and bold, and actions the same. When bad government prevails, the actions may be lofty and bold, but the language may be with some reserve."

CHAPTER V. The Master said, "The virtuous will be sure to speak *correctly*, but those whose speech is good may not always be virtuous. Men of principle are sure to be bold, but those who are bold may not always be men of principle."

2. THE PRAISE OF PERFECT VIRTUE IS NOT TO BE ALLOWED FOR THE REPRESSION OF BAD FEELINGS. In Ho An, this ch. is joined to the preceding, and Choo He also takes the first par. to be a question of Yuen Hëen. 1 克, 'overcoming,' *i.e.*, here='the love of superiority.' 伐, as in V. 25, 3. 不行, 'do not go,' *i. e.*, are not allowed to have their way,=are repressed. 2. 難, 'difficult,'—the doing what is difficult. 仁 is *quoad* 仁;—'as to its being perfect virtue, that I do not know.'

3. A SCHOLAR MUST BE AIMING AT WHAT IS HIGHER THAN COMFORT OR PLEASURE. Comp. IV. 11. The 懷居 here is akin to the 懷土 there. Comp. also IV. 9.

4. WHAT ONE DOES MUST ALWAYS BE RIGHT; WHAT ONE FEELS NEED NOT ALWAYS BE SPOKEN:—A LESSON OF PRUDENCE. 孫, for 遜, as in VII. 35. 危, 'terror from being in a high position,' then 'danger,' 'dangerous.' It is used here in a good sense, meaning 'lofty, and what may seem to be, or really be, dangerous,' under a bad government, where good principles do not prevail.

5. WE MAY PREDICATE THE EXTERNAL FROM THE INTERNAL, BUT NOT VICE VERSA. The 有言 must be understood of virtuous speaking

【六章】南宮适問於孔子曰、羿善射、奡盪舟、俱不得其死然、禹稷躬稼、而有天下。夫子不答。南宮适出。子曰、君子哉若人、尚德哉若人。

【七章】子曰、君子而不仁者有矣夫、未有小人而仁者也。

CHAPTER VI. Nan-kung Kwŏh, submitting an inquiry to Confucius, said, "E was skilful at archery, and Ngaou could move a boat along upon the land, but neither of them died a natural death. Yu and Tseih personally wrought at the toils of husbandry, and they became possessors of the empire." The Master made no reply; but when Nan-kung Kwŏh went out, he said, "A superior man indeed is this! An esteemer of virtue indeed is this!"

CHAPTER VII. The Master said, "Superior men, and yet not *always* virtuous, there have been, alas! But there never has been a mean man, and, *at the same time*, virtuous."

and 'virtuously,' or 'correctly,' be supplied to bring out the sense. A translator is puzzled to render 仁者 differently from 有德者. I have said 'men of principle,' the opposition being between moral and animal courage; yet the men of principle may not be without the other, in order to their doing justice to themselves.

6. EMINENT PROWESS CONDUCTING TO RUIN; EMINENT VIRTUE LEADING TO EMPIRE. THE MODESTY OF CONFUCIUS. Nan-kung Kwŏh is said by Choo He to have been the same as Nan Yung in V. 1. But this is doubtful. See on Nan Yung there. Kwŏh, it is said, insinuated in his remark an inquiry, whether Conf. was not like Yu or Tseih, and the great men of the time so many Es and Ngaous; and the sage was modestly silent upon the subject. E and Ngaou carry us back to the 22d century before Christ. The first belonged to a family of princelets, famous, from the time of the emperor 嚳 (B. C. 2432), for their archery, and dethroned the emperor How Seang (后相), B. C. 2145. E was afterwards slain by his minister, Han Tsuh, (寒浞), who then married his wife, and one of their sons (奡, *Keaou*) was the individual here named Ngaou, who was subsequently destroyed by the emperor Shaou-k'ang, the posthumous son of How-seang. Tseih was the son of the emperor 嚳, of whose birth many prodigies are narrated, and appears in the Shoo-king as 后稷, the minister of agriculture to Yaou and Shun, by name 棄. The Chow family traced their descent lineally from him, so that though the empire only came to his descendants more than a thousand years after his time, Nan-kung Kwŏh speaks as if he had got it himself, as Yu did. 君子哉若人,—comp. V. 2.

7. THE HIGHEST VIRTUE NOT EASILY ATTAINED TO, AND INCOMPATIBLE WITH MEANNESS. Comp. IV. 4. We must supply the 'always,' to bring out the meaning.

第八章 子曰、愛之、能勿勞乎、忠焉、能勿誨乎。

第九章 子曰、爲命、裨諶草創之、世叔討論之、行人子羽修飾之、東里子產潤色之。

第十章 一節 或問子產。子曰、惠人也。二節 問子西。曰、彼哉彼哉。三節 問管仲。曰、人也、奪伯氏駢邑三百、飯蔬食、沒齒、

CHAPTER VIII. The Master said, "Can there be love which does not lead to strictness with its object? Can there be loyalty which does not lead to the instruction of its object?"

CHAPTER IX. The Master said, "In preparing the governmental notifications, P'e Shin first made the rough draught; She-shuh examined and discussed its contents; Tsze-yu, the manager of Foreign intercourse, then made additions, or subtractions; and, finally, Tsze-ch'an of Tung-le gave it the proper elegance and finish."

CHAPTER X. 1. Some one asked about Tsze-ch'an. The Master said, "He was a kind man."

2. He asked about Tsze-se. The Master said, "That man! That man!"

3. He asked about Kwan Chung. "For him," said the Master, "the city of P'een, with three hundred families, was taken from the chief of the Pih family, who did not utter a murmuring word, though, till he was toothless, he had only coarse rice to eat."

8. A LESSON FOR PARENTS AND MINISTERS, THAT THEY MUST BE STRICT AND DECIDED. 勞, being ‖ with 誨, is a verb, and conveys the meaning in the translation, diff. from the meaning of the term in XIII. 5. K'ung Gan-kwŏ takes it in the sense of 'to soothe,' 'comfort,' low. 3d tone, but that does not suit the parallelism.

9. THE EXCELLENCE OF THE OFFICIAL NOTIFICATIONS OF CH'ING, OWING TO THE ABILITY OF FOUR OF ITS OFFICERS. The state of Ch'ing, small and surrounded by powerful neighbours, was yet fortunate in having able ministers, through whose mode of conducting its government it enjoyed considerable prosperity. 命, with ref. to this passage, is explained in the dict. by 政令盟會之辭 'the language of government orders, covenants, and conferences.' See the Chow Le, XXV. p. 11. Tsze-ch'an (see V. 15,) was the chief minister of the State, and in preparing such documents first used the services of P'e Shin, who was noted for his wise planning of matters. 'She-shuh' shows the relation of the officer indicated to the ruling family. His name was Yew-keih (游吉). The province of the 行人 was—主國使之禮, 'to superintend the ceremonies of communication with other states.' See the Chow Le, XXXIV. p. 13.

10. THE JUDGMENT OF CONFUCIUS CONCERNING TSZE-CH'AN, TSZE-SE, AND KWAN CHUNG. 1 See V. 15. 2. Tsze-se was the chief minister

無怨言。

十一章 子曰、貧而無怨、難、富而無驕、易。

十二章 子曰、孟公綽、爲趙魏老則優、不可以爲滕薛大夫。

十三章 一節 子路問成人。子曰、若臧武仲之知、公綽之不欲、卞莊子之勇、冉求之藝、文之以禮樂、亦可以爲成人矣。

二節 曰、今之成人者何必然、見

CHAPTER XI. The Master said, "To be poor without murmuring is difficult. To be rich without being proud is easy."

CHAPTER XII. The Master said, "Măng Kung-ch'ŏ is more than fit to be chief officer in the families of Chaou and Wei, but he is not fit to be minister to either of the states T'ăng or Sëĕ."

CHAPTER XIII. 1. Tsze-loo asked what constituted a COMPLETE man. The Master said, "Suppose a man with the knowledge of Tsang Woo-chung, the freedom from covetousness of Kung-ch'ŏ, the bravery of Chwang of Peen, and the varied talents of Yen K'ew; add to these the accomplishments of the rules of propriety and music:—such an one might be reckoned a COMPLETE man."

2. *He then* added, "But what is the necessity for a complete man of the present day to have all these things? The man, who in

of Tsoo. He had refused to accept the nomination to the sovereignty of the state in preference to the rightful heir, but did not oppose the usurping tendencies of the rulers of Tsoo. He had moreover opposed the wish of king Ch'aou to employ the sage. 3. Kwan Chung, —see III. 22. To reward his merits, the duke Hwan conferred on him the domain of the officer mentioned in the text, who had been guilty of some offence. His submitting, as he did, to his changed fortunes was the best tribute to Kwan's excellence.

11. IT IS HARDER TO BEAR POVERTY ARIGHT THAN TO CARRY RICHES. This sentiment may be controverted.

12. THE CAPACITY OF MANG KUNG-CH'Ŏ. Kung-ch'ŏ was the head of the Măng, or Chung-sun family, and, acc. to the 'Historical Records,' was regarded by Conf. more than any other great man of the times in Loo. His estimate of him however, as appears here, was not very high. In the sage's time, the government of the state of Tsin (晉) was in the hands of the three families, Chaou, Wei, and Han (韓), which afterwards divided the territory among themselves, and became, as we shall see in the times of Mencius, three independent principalities. 老,=家臣之長, 'head of the ministers of a family,' often called 家宰. T'ang was a small state, the place of which is seen in the district of the same name in the dep. of Yen-chow. Sëĕ was another small state adjacent to it.

13. OF THE COMPLETE MAN:—A CONVERSATION WITH TSZE-LOO. 1. Tsang Woo-chung had been an officer of Loo in the reign anterior to

利思義、見危授命、久要不忘平生之言、亦可以爲成人矣。

〔十四〕子問公叔文子於公明一節賈曰、信乎、夫子不言、不笑、不取乎。二節公明賈對曰、以告者過也、夫子時然後言、人不厭其言、樂然後笑、人不厭其笑、義然後取、人不厭其取。子曰、其然、豈其然乎。

the view of gain thinks of righteousness; who in the view of danger is prepared to give up his life; and who does not forget an old agreement, however far back it extends:—such a man may be reckoned a COMPLETE man."

CHAPTER XIV. 1. The Master asked Kung-ming Kea about Kung-shuh Wăn, saying, "Is it true that your master speaks not, laughs not, and takes not?"

2. Kung-ming Kea replied, "This has arisen from the reporters going beyond *the truth*.—My master speaks when it is the time to speak, and so men do not get tired of his speaking. He laughs when there is occasion to be joyful, and so men do not get tired of his laughing. He takes when it is consistent with righteousness to do so, and so men do not get tired of his taking." The Master said, "So! But is it so with him?"

that in which Conf. was born. So great was his reputation for wisdom that the people gave him the title of a 聖人, or 'sage.' Woo was his honor. epithet, and 仲 denotes his family place, among his brothers. Chwang, it is said by Choo He, after Chow (周), one of the oldest commentators, whose surname only has come down to us, was 卞邑大夫, 'great officer of the city of Peen.' In the 'Great collection of Surnames,' a secondary branch of a family of the state of Tsaou (曹) having settled in Loo, and being gifted with Peen, its members took their surname thence. For the history of Chwang and of Woo-chung, see the 集證, *in loc.* 亦可云云,—亦 implies that there was a higher style of man still, to whom the epithet *complete* would be more fully applicable. 2. The 曰 is to be understood of Confucius, though some suppose that Tsze-loo is the speaker. 要 up. 1st tone,=約, 'an agreement,' 'a covenant;'—'a long agreement, he does not forget the words of his whole life.' The meaning is what appears in the translation.

14. THE CHARACTER OF KUNG-SHUH WAN, WHO WAS SAID NEITHER TO SPEAK, NOR LAUGH, NOR TAKE. 1. Wăn was the hon. epithet of the individual in question, by name Che (枝), or, as some say, Fă (發), an officer of he state of

論語

〔十五章〕子曰、臧武仲、以防求為後於魯、雖曰不要君、吾不信也。

〔十六章〕子曰、晉文公譎而不正、齊桓公正而不譎。

〔十七章〕一節 子路曰、桓公殺公子糾、召忽死之、管仲不死、

CHAPTER XV. The Master said, "Tsang Woo-chung, keeping possession of Fang, asked of *the duke of* Loo to appoint a successor to him *in his family*. Although it may be said that he was not using force with his sovereign, I believe he was."

CHAPTER XVI. The Master said, "The duke Wǎn of Tsin was crafty and not upright. The duke Hwan of Ts'e was upright and not crafty."

CHAPTER XVII. 1. Tsze-loo said, "The duke Hwan caused his brother Kew to be killed, when Shaou Hwŭh died *with his master*, but Kwan Chung did not die. May not I say that he was wanting in virtue?"

Wei. He was descended from the duke 獻, and was himself the founder of the Kung-shuh family, being so designated, I suppose, because of his relation to the reigning duke. Of Kung-ming Kea nothing seems to be known. 2. 其然,—with reference to Kea's account of Kung-shuh Wǎn. 豈其然乎 intimates Conf. opinion that Kea was himself going beyond the truth.

15. CONDEMNATION OF TSANG WOO-CHUNG FOR FORCING A FAVOUR FROM HIS PRINCE. Woo-chung (see ch. 13) was obliged to fly from Loo, by the animosity of the Măng family, and took refuge in Choo (邾). As the head of the Tsang family, it devolved on him to offer the sacrifices in the ancestral temple, and he wished one of his half-brothers to be made the head of the family, in his room, that those might not be neglected. To strengthen the application for this, which he contrived to get made, he returned himself to the city of Fang, which belonged to his family, and thence sent a message to the court, which was tantamount to a threat that if the application were not granted, he would hold possession of the place. This was what Confucius condemned,—the 以防 in a matter which should have been left to the duke's grace. See all the circumstances in the 左傳, 襄公二十三年. 要, up. 1st tone, as in ch. 13, but with a diff. meaning,=勒, 'to force to do.'

16. THE DIFFERENT CHARACTERS OF THE DUKES WAN OF TSIN AND HWAN OF TS'E. Hwan and Wǎn were the two first of the five leaders of the princes of the empire, who play an important part in Chinese history, during the period of the Chow dynasty known as the Ch'un Ts'ew (春秋). Hwan ruled in Ts'e, B. C. 683–640, and Wǎn in Tsin B. C. 635–627. Of duke Hwan, see the next ch. The attributes mentioned by Conf. are not to be taken absolutely, but as respectively predominating in the two chiefs.

17 THE MERIT OF KWAN CHUNG:—A CONVERSATION WITH TSZE-LOO. 1. 公子糾, 'the duke's son Kew,' but, to avoid the awkwardness of that rendering, I say—'his brother.' Hwan (the hon. ep. His name was 小白.) and Kew had both been refugees in different states, the latter having been carried into Loo, away from the troubles and dangers of Ts'e, by the ministers, Kwan Chung and Shaou Hwuh. On the death of the prince of Ts'e, Hwan anticipated Kew, got to Ts'e, and took possession of the state. Soon after, he required the duke of Loo to put his brother to death, and to deliver up the two ministers, when Shaou (召 here=邵) Hwuh chose to dash his brains out, and die with his master, while Kwan Chung returned gladly to Ts'e, took service with Hwan, became

曰、未仁乎。○二節子曰、桓公九合諸侯、不以兵車、管仲之力也、如其仁、如其仁。

十八 子一節貢曰、管仲非仁者與、桓公殺公子糾、不能死、又相之。○二節子曰、管仲相桓公、霸諸侯、一匡天下、民到于今、受其賜、微管仲、吾其被髮左衽矣。○三節豈若匹夫匹婦之爲諒也、

2. The Master said, "The duke Hwan assembled all the princes together, and that not with weapons of war and chariots:—it was all through the influence of Kwan Chung. Whose beneficence was like his? Whose beneficence was like his?"

CHAPTER XVIII. 1. Tsze-kung said, "Kwan Chung, I apprehend, was wanting in virtue. When the duke Hwan caused his brother Kew to be killed, Kwan Chung was not able to die with him. Moreover, he became prime minister to Hwan."

2. The Master said, "Kwan Chung acted as prime minister to the duke Hwan, made him leader of all the princes, and united and rectified the whole empire. Down to the present day, the people enjoy the gifts which he conferred. But for Kwan Chung, we should now be wearing our hair dishevelled, and the lappets of our coats buttoning on the left side.

his prime minister, and made him supreme arbiter among the various chiefs of the empire. Such conduct was condemned by Tsze-loo. 死之 is a peculiar expression. 2. Conf. defends Kwan Chung, on the ground of the services which he rendered, using 仁 in a different acceptation from that intended by the disciple. 九, upper 1st tone, explained in the dict. by 聚, synonymous with 合, though the 註疏 makes out more than nine assemblages of princes under the presidency of duke Hwan. 如其仁=誰如其仁者, as in the translation.

18. THE MERIT OF KWAN CHUNG:—A CONVERSATION WITH TSZE-KUNG. 1. Tsze-loo's doubts about Kwan Chung arose from his not dying with the prince Kew; Tsze-kung's turned principally on his subsequently becoming premier to Hwan. 2. 匡=正, 'to rectify,' 'reduce to order.' —— blends with 匡 its own verbal force,=' to unite.' 微=無, 'not,' 'if not.' 被 (p'e, low. 1st tone,) 髮,—see the Le-ke, III. iii. 14, where this is mentioned as a characteristic of the eastern barbarians. 左衽—see the Shoo-king, V. xxv. 13. A note in the 集證 says, that anciently the right was the position of honour, and the right hand, moreover, is the more convenient for use, but the practice of the barbarians was contrary to that of China in both points. The sent. of Conf. is, that but for Kwan Chung, his countrymen would have sunk

自經於溝瀆、而莫之知也。

十九章 公叔文子之臣、大夫僎、與文子同升諸公。二節 子聞之曰、可以爲文矣。

二十章 子言衛靈公之無道也、康子曰、夫如是、奚而不喪。二節 孔子曰、仲叔圉治賓客、祝鮀治

3. "Will you require from him the small fidelity of common men and common women, who would commit suicide in a stream or ditch, no one knowing any thing about them?"

CHAPTER XIX. 1. The officer, Sëen, who had been *family*-minister to Kung-shuh Wăn, ascended to the prince's *court* in company with Wăn.

2. The Master, having heard of it, said, "He deserves to be considered WAN."

CHAPTER XX. 1. The Master was speaking about the unprincipled course of the duke Ling of Wei, when *Ke* K'ang said, "Since he is of such a character, how is it he does not lose his throne?"

2. Confucius said, "The Chung-shuh, Yu, has the superinten-

to the state of the rude tribes about them. 3. 匹夫, 匹婦,—see IX. 25. 諒=小信, 'small fidelity,' by which is intended the faithfulness of a married couple of the common people, where the husband takes no concubine in addition to his wife. The argument is this:—'Do you think Kwan Chung should have considered himself bound to Kew, as a common man considers himself bound to his wife? And would you have had him commit suicide, as common people will do on any slight occasion?' Commentators say that there is underlying the vindication this fact:—that Kwan Chung and Shaou Hwuh's adherence to Kew was wrong in the first place, Kew being the younger brother. Chung's conduct therefore was not to be judged as if Kew had been the senior. There is nothing of this, however, in Confucius' words. He vindicates Chung simply on the ground of his subsequent services, and his reference to 'the small fidelity' of husband and wife among the common people is very unhappy. 自經, 'to strangle one's-self,' but in connection with 溝瀆, the phrase must be understood generally,='to commit suicide.'

19. THE MERIT OF KUNG-SHUH WAN IN RECOMMENDING TO OFFICE A MAN OF WORTH. 1. Kung-shuh Wăn,—see ch. 14. The par. is to be understood as intimating that Kung-shuh, seeing the worth and capacity of his minister, had recommended him to his sovereign, and afterwards was not ashamed to appear in the same rank with him at court. 公,=our 'duke's,' *i.e.*, the duke's court. 2. 文, as an honorary epithet, sometimes means—錫民爵位, 'He who confers on a common man rank and office.'

20. THE IMPORTANCE OF GOOD AND ABLE MINISTERS:—SEEN IN THE STATE OF WEI. 1. *Ling* was the hon. epithet of Yuen (元), duke of Wei. B. C. 533-492. He was the husband of Nan-tsze, VI. 26. 2. The Chung-shuh, Yu, is the K'ung Wăn of V. 14. 仲叔 express his family position, according to the degrees of kindred. 'The litanist, T'o,'—see VI. 14. Wang-sun Kea,—see III. 13.

宗廟、王孫賈治軍旅、夫如是、奚其喪。

〔二十一章〕子曰、其言之不怍、則爲之也難。

〔二十二章〕〔一節〕陳成子弒簡公。〔二節〕孔子沐浴而朝、告於哀公曰、陳恆弒其君、請討之。〔三節〕公曰、告夫三子。〔四節〕孔子曰、以吾從大夫之後、不敢不告也、君

dence of his guests and of strangers; the litanist, T'o, has the management of his ancestral temple; and Wang-sun Kea has the direction of the army and forces:—with such officers as these, how should he lose his throne?"

CHAPTER XXI. The Master said, "He who speaks without modesty will find it difficult to make his words good."

CHAPTER XXII. 1. Ch'in Shing murdered the duke Këen *of Ts'e.*

2. Confucius bathed, went to court, and informed the duke Gae, saying, "Ch'in Hăng has slain his sovereign. I beg that you will undertake to punish him."

3. The duke said, "Inform the chiefs of the three families of it."

4. Confucius *retired, and* said, "Following in the rear of the great officers, I did not dare not to represent such a matter, and my prince says, 'Inform the chiefs of the three families of it.'"

21. EXTRAVAGANT SPEECH HARD TO BE MADE GOOD. Comp. IV. 22.

22. HOW CONFUCIUS WISHED TO AVENGE THE MURDER OF THE DUKE OF TS'E:—HIS RIGHTEOUS AND PUBLIC SPIRIT. 1. *Këen*,—'indolent in not a single virtue,' and 'tranquil, not speaking unadvisedly,' are the meanings attached to 簡, as an hon. epithet, while 成 indicates, 'tranquillizer of the people, and establisher of government.' The murder of the duke Këen by his officer, Ch'in Hăng (恆), took place, B. C. 480, barely two years before Conf. death. 2. 沐浴 implies all the fasting and all the solemn preparation, as for a sacrifice or other great occasion. Properly, 沐 is to wash the hair with the water in which rice has been washed, and 浴 is to wash the body with hot water. 請討之,—acc. to the account of this matter in the 左傳, Conf. meant that the duke Gae should himself, with the forces of Loo, undertake the punish. of the regicide. Some mod. comm. cry out against this. The sage's advice, they say, would have been that the duke should report the thing to the emperor, and with his authority associate other princes with himself to do justice on the offender. 3. 告夫三子,—this is the use of 夫 in XI. 24, *et al.* 4. This is taken as the remark of Confucius, or his colloquy with himself, when he had gone out from the duke. 以吾從大夫之後,—see XI. 7. The 者 leaves the sentence incomplete;—'my prince says, Inform the three chiefs of it;—this circumstance.' The paraphrasts complete the sentence by 何耶,—'How is it

曰、告夫三子者。五節之三子告、不可、孔子曰、以吾從大夫之後、不敢不告也。

二十三章 子路問事君。子曰、勿欺也、而犯之。

二十四章 子曰、君子上達、小人下達。

二十五章 子曰、古之學者爲己、今之學者爲人。

二十六章 一節 蘧伯玉使人於孔子。二節 孔子與之坐而問焉、曰、夫子何爲。

5. He went to the chiefs, and informed them, but they would not act. Confucius *then* said, "Following in the rear of the great officers, I did not dare not to represent such a matter."

CHAPTER XXIII. Tsze-loo asked how a sovereign should be served. The Master said, "Do not impose on him, and, moreover, withstand him to his face."

CHAPTER XXIV. The Master said, "The progress of the superior man is upwards; the progress of the mean man is downwards."

CHAPTER XXV. The Master said, "In ancient times, men learned with a view to their own improvement. Now-a-days, men learn with a view to the approbation of others."

CHAPTER XXVI. 1. Keu Pih-yuh sent a messenger *with friendly inquiries* to Confucius.

2. Confucius sat with him, and questioned him. "What," said he, "is your master engaged in?" The messenger replied, "My

that the prince, &c.,?' 5. 之三子,—之 is the verb—'to go to.' 孔子曰,云云,—This was spoken to the chiefs, to reprove them for their disregard of a crime, which concerned every public man.

23. HOW THE MINISTER OF A PRINCE MUST BE SINCERE AND BOLDLY UPRIGHT. 犯之 is well expressed by the phrase in the translation. See the Le-ke, II. i. 12, where it appears that to 犯 was required by the duty of a minister, but not allowed to a son.

24. THE DIFFERENT PROGRESSIVE TENDENCIES OF THE SUPERIOR MAN AND THE MEAN MAN. Ho An takes 達 in the sense of 曉, 'to understand.' The modern view seems better.

25. THE DIFFERENT MOTIVES OF LEARNERS IN OLD TIMES, AND IN THE TIMES OF CONFUCIUS. 爲己, 爲人, 'for themselves, for *other* men.' The meaning is as in the translation.

26. AN ADMIRABLE MESSENGER. 1. Pih-yuh was the designation of Keu Yuen (瑗), an

對曰、夫子欲寡其過、而未能也、使者出、子曰、使乎、使乎。

〔廿七章〕子曰、不在其位、不謀其政。

〔廿八章〕曾子曰、君子思不出其位。

〔廿九章〕子曰、君子恥其言而過其行。

〔三十章〕一節 子曰、君子道者三、我無能焉、仁者不憂、知者不惑、勇者不懼。二節 子貢曰、夫子自道也。

master is anxious to make his faults few, but he has not yet succeeded." He then went out, and the Master said, "A messenger indeed! A messenger indeed!"

CHAPTER XXVII. The Master said, "He who is not in any particular office, has nothing to do with plans for the administration of its duties."

CHAPTER XXVIII. The philosopher Tsăng said, "The superior man, in his thoughts, does not go out of his place."

CHAPTER XXIX. The Master said, "The superior man is modest in his speech, but exceeds in his actions."

CHAPTER XXX. 1. The Master said, "The way of the superior man is threefold, but I am not equal to it. Virtuous, he is free from anxieties; wise, he is free from perplexities; bold, he is free from fear."

2. Tsze-kung said, "Master, that is what you yourself say."

officer of the state of Wei, and a disciple of the sage. His place is now 1st east in the outer court of the temples. Conf. had lodged with him when in Wei, and it was after his return to Loo that Pih-yuh sent to inquire for him.

27. A repetition of VII. 14.

28. THE THOUGHTS OF A SUPERIOR MAN IN HARMONY WITH HIS POSITION. Tsăng here quotes from the 象, or illustration, of the 52d diagram of the Yih-king, but he leaves out one character,—以 before 思, and thereby alters the meaning somewhat. What is said in the Yih, is—'The superior man is thoughtful, and so does not go out of his place.'—The ch., it is said, is inserted here, from its analogy with the preceding.

29. THE SUPERIOR MAN MORE IN DEEDS THAN IN WORDS. 恥其言,—lit., 'is ashamed of his words.' Comp. ch. 21, and IV. 22.

30. CONFUCIUS' HUMBLE ESTIMATE OF HIMSELF, WHICH TSZE-KUNG DENIES. 1. We have the greatest part of this par. in IX. 28, but the translation must be somewhat different, as 仁者, 知者, 勇者, are here in apposition with 君子. 君子道者=君子所以爲道者, 'what the superior man takes to be his path.' 2. 道=言, 'to say.'

〔三十一章〕子貢方人、子曰、賜也賢乎哉、夫我則不暇。〔三十二章〕子曰、不患人之不己知、患其不能也。〔三十三章〕子曰、不逆詐、不億不信、抑亦先覺者、是賢乎。〔三十四章〕〔一節〕微生畝謂孔子曰、丘何爲是栖栖者與、無乃爲佞乎。〔二節〕孔子曰、非敢爲佞也、疾固也。

CHAPTER XXXI. Tsze-kung was *in the habit of* comparing men together. The Master said, "Ts'ze must have reached a high pitch of excellence! Now, I have not leisure *for this*."

CHAPTER XXXII. The Master said, "I will not be concerned at men's not knowing me; I will be concerned at my own want of ability."

CHAPTER XXXIII. The Master said, "He who does not anticipate attempts to deceive him, nor think beforehand of his not being believed, and yet apprehends these things readily when they occur;—is he not a man of superior worth?"

CHAPTER XXXIV. 1. We-shang Mow said to Confucius, "K'ew, how is it that you keep roosting about? Is it not that you are an insinuating talker?"

2. Confucius said, "I do not dare to play the part of such a talker, but I hate obstinacy."

31. ONE'S WORK IS WITH ONE'S-SELF:—AGAINST MAKING COMPARISONS. 賢乎哉= 'Ha! is he not superior?' The remark is ironical.

32. CONCERN SHOULD BE ABOUT OUR PERSONAL ATTAINMENT, AND NOT ABOUT THE ESTIMATION OF OTHERS. See I. 16, *et al.* A critical canon is laid down here by Choo He:—'All passages, the same in meaning and in words, are to be understood as having been spoken only once, and their recurrence is the work of the compilers. Where the meaning is the same and the language a little different, they are to be taken as having been repeated by Confucius himself, with the variations.' According to this rule, the sentiment in this chapter was repeated by the master in four different utterances.

33. QUICK DISCRIMINATION WITHOUT SUSPICIOUSNESS IS HIGHLY MERITORIOUS. 逆, 'to be disobedient,' 'to rebel;' also, 'to meet,' and here 'to anticipate,' *i. e.*, in judgment. 抑亦 see XIII. 19, but the meaning is there 'perhaps,' while here the 抑 is adversative, and='but.' 先覺者 is used in opposition to 後覺者, and='a quick apprehender, one who understands things before others.' So, Choo He. K'ung Gan-kwŏ, however, takes 抑 as conjunctive, and 先覺 in apposition with the two preceding characteristics, and interprets the conclusion—'Is such a man of superior worth?' On Choo He's view, the 乎 is exclamatory.

34. CONFUCIUS NOT SELF-WILLED, AND YET NO GLIB-TONGUED TALKER:—DEFENCE OF HIMSELF FROM THE CHARGE OF AN AGED REPROVER. 1.

三十五 子曰、驥不稱其力、稱其德也。

三十六 或一節曰、以德報怨、何如。二節子曰、何以報德。三節以直報怨、以德報德。

三十七 子一節曰、莫我知也夫。二節子貢曰、何爲其莫知子也。子曰、不怨天、不尤人、下學

CHAPTER XXXV. The Master said, "A horse is called a *k'e*, not because of its strength, but because of its *other* good qualities."

CHAPTER XXXVI. 1. Some one said, "What do you say concerning the principle that injury should be recompensed with kindness?"

2. The Master said, "With what then will you recompense kindness?

3. "Recompense injury with justice, and recompense kindness with kindness."

CHAPTER XXXVII. 1. The Master said, "Alas! there is no one that knows me."

2. Tsze-kung said, "What do you mean by thus saying—that no one knows you?" The Master replied, "I do not murmur against

From We-shang's addressing Conf. by his name, it is presumed that he was an old man. Such a liberty in a young man would have been impudence. It is presumed also, that he was one of those men who kept themselves retired from the world in disgust. 栖 'to perch or roost,' as a bird, used contemptuously with ref. to Conf. going about among the princes and wishing to be called to office. 2. 固=執一不通, 'holding to one idea without intelligence.'

35. VIRTUE, AND NOT STRENGTH, THE FIT SUBJECT OF PRAISE. 驥 was the name of a famous horse of antiquity who could run 1000 *le* in one day. See the dict. *in voc.* It is here used generally for 'a good horse'

36. GOOD IS NOT TO BE RETURNED FOR EVIL; EVIL TO BE MET SIMPLY WITH JUSTICE. 1. 德=恩惠, 'kindness.' 怨, 'resentment,' 'hatred,' here put for what awakens resentment, 'wrong,' 'injury.' The phrase 以德報怨 is found in the 道德經 of Laou-tsze, II. 63, but it is likely that Conf. questioner simply consulted him about it as a saying which he had heard and was inclined to approve himself. 2. 以直, 'with straightness,' *i. e.*, with justice.—How far the ethics of Confucius fall below the Christian standard is evident from this chapter. The same expressions are attributed to Confucius in the Le-ke, XXXII. 11, and it is there added 子曰, 以德報怨, 則寬身之仁 (=人), which is explained,—'He who returns good for evil is a man who is careful of his person,' *i. e.*, will try to avert danger from himself by such a course. The author of the 翼註 says, that the injuries intended by the questioner were only trivial matters, which perhaps might be dealt with in the way he mentioned, but great offences, as those against a sovereign, a father, may not be dealt with by such an inversion of the principles of justice. The Master himself, however, does not fence his deliverance in any way.

37. CONFUCIUS, LAMENTING THAT MEN DID NOT KNOW HIM, RESTS IN THE THOUGHT THAT HEAVEN KNEW HIM. 1. 莫我知,—the inversion for 莫知我, 'does not know me.' He referred, comm. say, to the way in which he pursued his course, simply 爲己, out of his own conviction of duty, and for his own improvement, without regard to success, or the

論語

而上達、知我者其天乎。

〔卅八章〕一節 公伯寮愬子路於季孫、子服景伯以告、曰、夫子固有惑志於公伯寮、吾力猶能肆諸市朝。二節 子曰、道之將行也與、命也、道之將廢也與、命也、公伯寮其如命何。

Heaven. I do not grumble against men. My studies lie low, and my penetration rises high. But there is Heaven;—that knows me!"

CHAPTER XXXVIII. 1. The Kung-pih, Leaou, having slandered Tsze-loo to Ke-sun, Tsze-fuk King-pih informed Confucius of it, saying, "Our master is certainly being led astray by the Kung-pih, Leaou, but I have still power enough left to cut *Leaou* off, and expose his corpse in the market and in the court."

2. The Master said, "If *my* principles are to advance, it is so ordered. If they are to fall to the ground, it is so ordered. What can the Kung-pih, Leaou, do, where such ordering is concerned?"

opinions of others. 2. 何爲其莫知子也, 'what is *that*—no man knows you?' 下學, 上達,—'beneath I learn, above I penetrate;'—the meaning appears to be that he contented himself with the study of men and things, common matters as more ambitious spirits would deem them, but from those he rose to understand the high principles involved in them,—'the appointments of Heaven (天命),' according to one commentator. 知我者, 其天乎,—'He who knows me—is that Heaven?'

38. HOW CONFUCIUS RESTED, AS TO THE PROGRESS OF HIS DOCTRINES, ON THE ORDERING OF HEAVEN:—ON OCCASION OF TSZE-LOO'S BEING SLANDERED. 1. Leaou, called Kung-pih (lit., duke's uncle), probably from an affinity with the ducal house, is said by some to have been a disciple of the sage, but that is not likely, as we find him here slandering Tsze-loo, that he might not be able, in his official connection with the Ke family, to carry the Master's lessons into practice. 景 was the hon. ep. of Tsze-fuh Pih, an officer of Loo. 夫子 refers to Ke-sun. 有惑志,—'is having his will deceived.' Exposing the bodies (陳尸) of criminals, after their execution, was called 肆. The bodies of 'great officers' were so exposed in the court, and those of meaner criminals in the market-place. 市朝 came to be employed together, though the exposure could take place only in one place, just as we have seen 兄弟 used generally for 'brother.' 2. 與 makes the preceding clause conditional, ='if.' 命=天命, 'Heaven's ordering.'

〔三十九章〕子曰、(一節)賢者辟世。(二節)其次辟地。(三節)其次辟色。(四節)其次辟言。

〔四十章〕子曰、作者七人矣。

〔四十一章〕子路宿於石門、晨門曰、奚自。子路曰、自孔氏。曰、是知其不可而爲之者與。

〔四十二章〕(一節)子擊磬於衞、有荷蕢、而過孔氏之門者、

CHAPTER XXXIX. 1. The Master said, "*Some* men of worth retire from the world.

2. "Some retire from *particular* countries.

3. "Some retire because of *disrespectful* looks.

4. "Some retire because of *contradictory* language."

CHAPTER XL. The Master said, "Those who have done this are seven men."

CHAPTER XLI. Tsze-loo happening to pass the night in Shih-mun, the gate-keeper said to him, "Whom do you come from?" Tsze-loo said, "From Mr. K'ung." "It is he,—is it not?"—said the other, "who knows the impracticable nature of the times, and yet will be doing in them."

CHAPTER XLII. 1. The Master was playing, *one day*, on a musical stone in Wei, when a man, carrying a straw basket, passed the door

39. DIFFERENT CAUSES WHY MEN OF WORTH WITHDRAW FROM PUBLIC LIFE, AND DIFFERENT EXTENTS TO WHICH THEY SO WITHDRAW THEMSELVES. 1. 辟, *pe*. low. 3d tone,=避. 2. 其次,—'the next class,' but comm. say that the meaning is no more than 'some,' and that the terms do not indicate any comparison of the parties on the ground of their worthiness. 3. The 'looks,' and 'language' in par. 4, are to be understood of the princes whom the worthies wished to serve.—It is observed in the 日講論語解義, that Conf. could never bear to withdraw himself entirely from the world.

40. THE NUMBER OF MEN OF WORTH WHO HAD WITHDRAWN FROM PUBLIC LIFE IN CONFUCIUS' TIME. This ch. is understood, both by Choo He and the old commentators, in connection with the preceding, as appears in the translation. Choo, however, explains 作 by 起, 'have arisen.' The others explain it by 爲, 'have done this.' They also give the names of the seven men, which, acc. to Choo, is 鑿, 'chiselling,' *i. e.*, forcing out an illustration of the text.

41. CONDEMNATION OF CONFUCIUS' COURSE IN SEEKING TO BE EMPLOYED, BY ONE WHO HAD WITHDRAWN FROM PUBLIC LIFE. The site of Shih-mun is referred to the district of Ch'ang-ts'ing, dep. Ts'e-nan, in Shan-tung. 晨門, 'morning gate,'—a designation of the keeper, as having to open the gate in the morning. He was probably one of the seven worthies, spoken of in the preced. chapter. We might translate 石門 by 'Stony-gate.' It seems to have been one of the frontier passes between Ts'e and Loo. 孔氏, '*the* K'ung,' or Mr. K'ung. Observe the force of the final 與.

42. THE JUDGEMENT OF A RETIRED WORTHY ON CONFUCIUS' COURSE, AND REMARK OF CONFUCIUS THEREON. 1. The *k'ing* was one of the eight musical instruments of the Chinese; see

論語

曰、有心哉、擊磬乎。(二節)既而曰、鄙哉、硜硜乎、莫己知也、斯已而已矣、深則厲、淺則揭。(三節)子曰、果哉、末之難矣。

(四十三章)子張曰、書云、高宗諒陰、三年不言、何謂也。(二節)子曰、何必高宗、古之人皆然、君薨、百官總己、以聽於冢宰三年。

of the house where Confucius was, and said, "His heart is full who *so* beats the musical stone."

2. A little while after, he added, "How contemptible is the one-ideaed obstinacy *those sounds display!* When one is taken no notice of, he has simply at once to give over *his wish for public employment.* 'Deep water must be crossed with the clothes on; shallow water may be crossed with the clothes held up.'"

3. The Master said, "How determined is he in his purpose! *But* this is not difficult."

CHAPTER XLIII. 1. Tsze-chang said, "What is meant when the SHOO says that Kaou-tsung, while observing the usual imperial mourning, was for three years without speaking?"

2. The Master said, "Why must Kaou-tsung *be referred to as an example of this?* The ancients all did so. When the sovereign died, the officers all attended to their several duties, taking instructions from the prime minister for three years."

Medhurst's dict., *in voc.* 過, up. 1st tone, 'to go by.' Meaning 'to go beyond,' 'to exceed,' it is in the 3d tone. 有心哉擊磬乎 is to be read as one sentence, and understood as if there were a 之 after the 哉. 2. 硜硜乎,—see XIII. 24, 3. The 備旨 interprets this clause also, as if a 之 were after the 哉, and 硜硜 had reference to the sounds of the *k'ing*. 深則云云,—see She-king I. iii. 9. st. 1. The quotation was intended to illustrate that we must act according to circumstances. 3. 末=無. 之 seems to be a mere expletive.

43. HOW GOVERNMENT WAS CARRIED ON DURING THE THREE YEARS OF SILENT MOURNING BY THE EMPEROR. 1. 書云,—see the Shoo-king, IV. viii. Sect I. 1, but the passage there is not exactly as in the text. It is there said that Kaou-tsung, after the three years' mourning, still did not speak. 高宗 was the honorary epithet of the emperor Woo-ting (武丁), B. C. 1323–1263. 諒 (*Shoo*, 亮) 陰 (read *gan*), acc. to the dict., means 'the shed where the mourner lived the three years.' Choo He says he does not know the meaning of the terms.—Tsze-chang was perplexed to know how government could be carried on during so long

〔四四章〕子曰、上好禮、則民易使也、

〔四五章〕子路問君子、子曰、脩己以敬。曰、如斯而已乎。曰、脩己以安人、曰、如斯而已乎。曰、脩己以安百姓、脩己以安百姓、堯舜其猶病諸。

〔四六章〕原壤夷俟、子曰、幼

CHAPTER XLIV. The Master said, "When rulers love *to observe* the rules of propriety, the people respond readily to the calls on them for service."

CHAPTER XLV. Tsze-loo asked what constituted the superior man. The Master said, "The cultivation of himself in reverential carefulness." "And is this all?" said *Tsze-loo.* "He cultivates himself so as to give rest to others," was the reply. "And is this all?" *again* asked *Tsze-loo. The Master* said, "He cultivates himself so as to give rest to all the people. He cultivates himself so as to give rest to all the people:—even Yaou and Shun were still solicitous about this."

CHAPTER XLVI. Yuen Jang was squatting on his heels, and so waited *the approach of* the Master, who said to him, "In youth,

a period of silence. 2. 古之人,—the 人 embraces the emperors, and subordinate princes who had their own petty courts. 總已,—in the 備旨 it is said,—總,攝也,不敢放縱意也,'總 is to manage. The meaning is, that they did not dare to allow themselves any license.' The expression is not an easy one. I have followed the paraphrasts.

44. HOW A LOVE OF THE RULES OF PROPRIETY IN RULERS FACILITATES GOVERNMENT.

45. REVERENT SELF-CULTIVATION THE DISTINGUISHING CHARACTERISTIC OF THE KEUN-TSZE. 以敬, it is said, are not to be taken as the *wherewith* of the *Keun-tsze* in his cultivating himself, but as the chief thing which he keeps before him in the process. I translate 以, therefore, by *in*, but in the other sentences, it indicates the realizations, or consequences, of the 修已. 百姓,—'the hundred surnames,' as a designation for the mass of the people, occurs as early as in the *Yaou teen* (堯典). It is=百家姓, 'the surnames of the hundred families, into which number the families of the people were perhaps divided at a very early time. The surnames of the Chinese now amount to several hundreds. The small work—百家姓帖, made in the Sung dynasty, contains nearly 450. In the 集證, *in loc.*, we find a ridiculous reason given for the surnames being a hundred, to the effect that the ancient sages gave a surname for each of the 5 notes of the scale in music, and of the 5 great relations of life and of the 4 seas; consequently, 5 × 5 × 4=100.' It is to be observed, that in the Shoo-king, we find 'a hundred surnames,' interchanged with 萬姓, 'ten thousand surnames,' and it would seem needless, therefore, to seek to attach a definite explanation to the number. 堯舜其猶病諸,—see VI. 28.

46. CONFUCIUS' CONDUCT TO AN UNMANNERLY OLD MAN OF HIS ACQUAINTANCE. Yuen Jang was an old acquaintance of Confucius, but had adopt-

論語

而不孫弟、長而無述焉、老而不死、是爲賊。以杖叩其脛。

四十七章 一節 闕黨童子將命、或問之曰、益者與。

二節 子曰、吾見其居於位也、見其與先生並行也、非求益者也、欲速成者也。

not humble as befits a junior; in manhood, doing nothing worthy of being handed down; and living on to old age:—this is to be a pest." With this he hit him on the shank with his staff.

CHAPTER XLVII. 1. A youth of the village of K'euĕh was employed by *Confucius* to carry the messages between him and his visitors. Some one asked about him, saying, "I suppose he has made great progress."

2. The Master said, "I observe that he is fond of occupying the seat *of a full-grown man;* I observe that he walks shoulder to shoulder with his elders. He is not one who is seeking to make progress *in learning.* He wishes quickly to become a man."

ed the principles of Laou-tsze, and gave himself extraordinary license in his behaviour.—See an instance in the Le-ke, II. Pt. II. iii. 24. 夷俟,—the dict. explains the two words together by 展足箕坐, but that is the meaning of 夷 alone, and 俟=待, 'to wait for.' So, the commentators, old and new. The use of 夷 in this sense is thus explained:—'The 鴟鳥 is fond of squatting, and is therefore called the squatting *ch'e* (蹲鴟), but it is called by some the *ch'e e* (鴟夷), and hence 夷 is used for 蹲, *to squat!*' See the 集證, *in loc.* 孫 for 遜, and 弟 for 悌. 賊,—in the sense of 賊害,=our 'pest,' rather than 'thief.' The address of Conf. might be translated in the 2d person, but it is perhaps better to keep to the 3d, leaving the application to be understood.

47. CONFUCIUS' EMPLOYMENT OF A FORWARD YOUTH. 1. 闕黨,—there is a tradition that Confucius lived and taught in 闕里, but it is much disputed. 將命謂傳賓主之言, '將命 means to convey the messages between visitors and the host.' 益者與,—the inquirer supposed that Conf. employment of the lad was to distinguish him for the progress which he had made. 2. According to the rules of ceremony, a youth must sit in the corner, the body of the room being reserved for fullgrown men. See the Le-ke, II. Pt. I. i. 17. In walking with an elder, a youth was required to keep a little behind him. See the Le-ke, III. v. 15. Confucius' employment of the lad, therefore, was to teach him the courtesies required by his years.

BOOK XV. WEI LING KUNG.

衞靈公第十五

第一章 一節 衞靈公問陳於孔子。孔子對曰、俎豆之事、則嘗聞之矣、軍旅之事、未之學也。明日遂行。二節 在陳絕糧、從者病、莫能興。三節 子路慍見曰、君子亦有窮乎。子曰、君子固窮、小人窮斯濫矣。

CHAPTER I. 1. The duke Ling of Wei asked Confucius about tactics. Confucius replied, "I have heard all about sacrificial vessels, but I have not learned military matters." On this, he took his departure the next day.

2. When he was in Ch'in, their provisions were exhausted, and his followers became so ill that they were unable to rise.

3. Tsze-loo, with evident dissatisfaction, said, "Has the superior man likewise to endure *in this way?*" The Master said, "The superior man may indeed have to endure want, but the mean man, when he is in want, gives way to unbridled license."

HEADING OF THIS BOOK.—衞靈公第十五, 'The duke, Ling, of Wei—Book XV.' The contents of the Book, contained in forty chapters, are as miscellaneous as those of the former. Rather they are more so, some chapters bearing on the public administration of government, several being occupied with the superior man, and others containing lessons of practical wisdom. 'All the subjects,' says Ting Ping, 'illustrate the feeling of the sense of shame and consequent pursuit of the correct course, and therefore the Book immediately follows the preceding one.'

1. CONFUCIUS REFUSES TO TALK ON MILITARY AFFAIRS. IN THE MIDST OF DISTRESS, HE SHOWS THE DISCIPLES HOW THE SUPERIOR MAN IS ABOVE DISTRESS. 1. 陳, read *chin*, low. 3d tone, 'the arrangement of the ranks of an army, here=*tactics*, generally. 俎豆之事,—Comp. 籩豆之事, VIII. 4, 3. The 俎 was a dish, 18 inches long and 8 in. broad, on a stand, 8½ in. high, upon which the flesh of victims was laid, but the meaning is sacrificial vessels generally,=the business of ceremonies. It is said of Conf., in the 'Historical Records,' that when a boy, he was fond of playing at 俎 and 豆. He wished by his reply and departure, to teach the duke that the rules of propriety, and not war, were essential to the government of a state. 2. From Wei, Conf. proceeded to Ch'in, and there met with the distress here mentioned. It is probably the same which is referred to in XI. 2, 1, though there is some chronological difficulty about the subject. (See the note by Choo He in his preface to the Analects.) 3. 固='yes, indeed,' with reference to Tsze-loo's question. Some take it in its sense of 'firm.'—The superior man firmly endures want.'

第二章 一節 子曰、賜也、女以予爲多學而識之者與。對曰、然、非與。 二節 曰、非也、予一以貫之。 三節

第三章 子曰、由、知德者鮮矣。

第四章 子曰、無爲而治者、其舜也與、夫何爲哉、恭己正南面而已矣。

第五章 一節 子張問行。 二節 子曰、言忠信、行篤敬、雖蠻貊之邦、

CHAPTER II. 1. The Master said, "Ts'ze, you think, I suppose, that I am one who learns many things and keeps them in memory?"

2. Tsze-kung replied, "Yes,—but perhaps it is not so?"

3. "No," was the answer; "I *seek* a unity all-pervading."

CHAPTER III. The Master said, "Yew, those who know virtue are few."

CHAPTER IV. The Master said, "May not Shun be instanced as having governed efficiently without exertion? What did he do? He did nothing but gravely and reverently occupy his imperial seat."

CHAPTER V. 1. Tsze-chang asked how a man might conduct himself, *so as to be everywhere appreciated.*

2. The Master said, "Let his words be sincere and truthful, and his actions honorable and careful;—such conduct may be practised among the rude tribes of the South or the North. If his words be

2. HOW CONFUCIUS AIMED AT THE KNOWLEDGE OF AN ALL-PERVADING UNITY. This chapter is to be compared with IV. 15, only, says Choo He, 'that is spoken with reference to practice, and this with reference to knowledge.' But the design of Conf. was probably the same in them both; and I understand the first par. here as meaning—'Ts'ze, do you think that I am aiming, by the exercise of memory, to acquire a varied and extensive knowledge?' Then the 3d paragraph is equivalent to:—'I am not doing this. My aim is to know myself,—the mind which embraces all knowledge, and regulates all practice.' This is the view of the chapter given in the 日講:—此一章書言學貫乎知要, 'This chapter teaches that what is valuable in learning, is the knowledge of that which is important.'

3. FEW REALLY KNOW VIRTUE. This is understood as spoken with reference to the dissatisfaction manifested by Tsze-loo in ch. 1. If he had possessed a right knowledge of virtue, he would not have been so affected by distress.

4. HOW SHUN WAS ABLE TO GOVERN WITHOUT PERSONAL EFFORT. 恭己, 'made himself reverent.' 正南面, 'correctly adjusted his south-wards face;' see VI. 1. Shun succeeding Yaou, there were many ministers o great virtue and ability, to occupy all the offices of the government. All that Shun did, was by his grave and sage example. This is the lesson —the influence of a ruler's personal character.

5. CONDUCT THAT WILL BE APPRECIATED IN ALL PARTS OF THE WORLD. 1. We must supply a good deal to bring out the meaning here. Choo He compares the question with that other of Tsze-chang about the scholar who may be

行矣、言不忠信、行不篤敬、雖州里、行乎哉。三節 立、則見其參於前也、在輿、則見其倚於衡也、夫然後行。四節 子張書諸紳。

第六章 一節 子曰、直哉、史魚、邦有道如矢、邦無道如矢。二節 君子哉、蘧伯玉、邦有道、則仕、邦無道、則可卷而懷之。

not sincere and truthful, and his actions not honorable and careful, will he, with such conduct, be appreciated, even in his neighbourhood?

3. "When he is standing, let him see those two things, as it were fronting him. When he is in a carriage, let him see them attached to the yoke. Then may he subsequently carry them into practice."

4. Tsze-chang wrote these counsels on the end of his sash.

CHAPTER VI. 1. The Master said, "Truly straightforward was the historiographer Yu. When good government prevailed in his state, he was like an arrow. When bad government prevailed, he was like an arrow.

2. "A superior man indeed is Keu Pih-yuh! When good government prevails in his state, he is to be found in office. When bad government prevails, he can roll his principles up, and keeps them in his breast."

called 達; see XII. 20. 2. 貊 is another name for the 北狄, the rude tribes on the north. 2,500 families made up a 州, and 25 made up a 里, but the meaning of the phrase is that given in the translation. 3. 其, 'them,' *i. e.*, such words and actions.—Let him see them 參於前, 'before him, with himself making a trio.' 輿 is properly 'the bottom of a carriage,' planks laid over wheels, a simple 'hackery,' but here it='a carriage.' 4 紳, denotes the ends of the sash that hang down.

6. THE ADMIRABLE CHARACTERS OF TSZE-YU AND KEU PIH-YUH. 1. 子魚 was the designation of 魚子, the historiographer of Wei, on his deathbed, he left a message for his prince, and gave orders that his body should be laid out in a place and manner likely to attract his attention when he paid the visit of condolence. It was so, and the message then delivered had the desired effect. Perhaps it was on hearing this that Confucius made this remark. 如矢, 'as an arrow,' *i. e.*, straight and decided. 2. Keu Pih-yuh,—see XIV. 26. 可=能. 卷而懷之,—之 is to be understood as referring to 'his principles,' or perhaps the clause ='he could roll himself up and keep himself to himself,' *i. e.*, he kept aloof from office.—Comm. say that Tsze-yu's uniform straightforwardness was not equal to Pih-yuh's rightly adapting himself to circumstances.

第七章 子曰、可與言、而不與之言、失人、不可與言、而與之言、失言、知者不失人、亦不失言。

第八章 子曰、志士、仁人、無求生以害仁、有殺身以成仁。

第九章 子貢問爲仁。子曰、工欲善其事、必先利其器、居是邦也、事其大夫之賢者、友其士之仁者。

第十章 一節 顏淵問爲邦。二節 子曰、行夏之

CHAPTER VII. The Master said, "When a man may be spoken with, not to speak to him is to err in reference to the man. When a man may not be spoken with, to speak to him is to err in reference to our words. The wise err neither in regard to their man nor to their words."

CHAPTER VIII. The Master said, "The determined scholar and the man of virtue will not seek to live at the expense of injuring their virtue. They will even sacrifice their lives to preserve their virtue complete."

CHAPTER IX. Tsze-kung asked about the practice of virtue. The Master said, "The mechanic, who wishes to do his work well, must first sharpen his tools. When you are living in any state, take service with the most worthy among its great officers, and make friends of the most virtuous among its scholars."

CHAPTER X. 1. Yen Yuen asked how the government of a country should be administered.

7. THERE ARE MEN WITH WHOM TO SPEAK, AND MEN WITH WHOM TO KEEP SILENCE. THE WISE KNOW THEM. 失言 may be translated, literally and properly,—'to lose our words,' but in English we do not use 'to lose,' in connection with 'men,' in the same way.

8. HIGH NATURES VALUE VIRTUE MORE THAN LIFE. The 志士 and 仁人 are two different classes, the same described IV. 2,—仁者安仁,知者利仁. 有殺身 is naturally translated—'They will kill themselves.' No doubt suicide is included in the expression (See the 疏 to Ho An), and Confucius here justifies that act, as in certain cases expressive of high virtue.

9. HOW INTERCOURSE WITH THE GOOD AIDS THE PRACTICE OF VIRTUE. Comp. Proverbs XXVII. 17, 'Iron sharpeneth iron; so a man sharpeneth the countenance of his friend.'

10. CERTAIN RULES, EXEMPLIFIED IN THE ANCIENT DYNASTIES, TO BE FOLLOWED IN GOVERNING:—A REPLY TO YEN YUEN. 1. The disciple

時。三節乘殷之輅。四節服周之冕。五節樂則韶舞。六節放鄭聲、遠佞人、鄭聲淫、佞人殆。

十一 子曰、人無遠慮、必有近憂。

十二 子曰、已矣乎、吾未見好德如好色者也。

十三 子曰、臧文仲、其竊位者與、知柳下惠之

2. The Master said, "Follow the seasons of Hea.

3. "Ride in the state carriage of Yin.

4. "Wear the ceremonial cap of Chow.

5. "Let the music be the Shaou with its pantomimes.

6. "Banish the songs of Ch'ing, and keep far from specious talkers. The songs of Ch'ing are licentious; specious talkers are dangerous."

CHAPTER XI. The Master said, "If a man take no thought about what is distant, he will find sorrow near at hand."

CHAPTER XII. The Master said, "It is all over! I have not seen one who loves virtue as he loves beauty."

CHAPTER XIII. The Master said, "Was not Tsang Wăn like one who had stolen his situation? He knew the virtue and the talents

modestly put his question with reference to the government of a state (邦), but the Master answers it according to the disciple's ability, as if it had been about the ruling of the empire (治天下). 2. The three great ancient dynasties began the year at different times. According to an ancient tradition, 'Heaven was opened at the time 子; Earth appeared at the time 丑; and Man was born at the time 寅.' 子 commences in our December, at the winter solstice; 丑 a month later; and 寅 a month after 丑. The Chow dynasty began its year with 子; the Shang with 丑; and the Hea with 寅. As human life then commenced, the year, in reference to human labours, naturally proceeds from the spring, and Conf. approved the rule of the Hea dynasty. His decision has been the law of all dynasties since the Ts'in. See the '*Discours Preliminaire, Chap. I*,' in Gaubil's Shoo King. 3. The state carriage of the Yin dynasty was plain and substantial, which Conf. preferred to the more ornamented ones of Chow. 4. Yet he does not object to the more elegant cap of that dynasty, 'the cap,' says Choo He, 'being a small thing, and placed over all the body.' 5. The *shaou* was the music of *Shun*; see III. 25. 舞, —the 'dancers,' or 'pantomimes,' who kept time to the music. See the Shoo-king II. ii. 21. 5. 鄭聲, 'the sounds of Ch'ing,' meaning both the songs of Ch'ing, and the appropriate music to which they were sung. Those songs form the 7th book of the 1st division of the She-king, and are here characterized justly.

11. THE NECESSITY OF FORETHOUGHT AND PRECAUTION.

12. THE RARITY OF A TRUE LOVE OF VIRTUE. 已矣乎,—see V. 26; the rest is a repetition of IX. 17, said to have been spoken by Conf. when he was in Wei, and saw the duke riding out openly in the same carriage with Nan-tsze.

13. AGAINST JEALOUSY OF OTHERS' TALENTS; —THE CASE OF TSANG WAN, AND HWUY OF LEW-HEA. Tsang Wăn-chung,—See V. 17. 竊位 is explained—如盜得而陰據之, 'as if he had got it by theft, and

論語

賢、而不與立也。

十四 子曰、躬自厚而薄責於人、則遠怨矣。

十五 子曰、不曰如之何、如之何者、吾未如之何也已矣。

十六 子曰、群居終日、言不及義、好行小慧、難矣哉。

十七 子曰、君子義以爲質、禮以行之、孫以出之、信

of Hwuy of Lew-hea, and yet did not *procure that he should* stand with him *in court*."

CHAPTER XIV. The Master said, "He who requires much from himself and little from others, will keep himself from *being the object of* resentment."

CHAPTER XV. The Master said, "When a man is not *in the habit of* saying—'What shall I think of this? What shall I think of this?' I can indeed do nothing with him!"

CHAPTER XVI. The Master said, "When a number of people are together, for a whole day, without their conversation turning on righteousness, and when they are fond of carrying out *the suggestions of* a small shrewdness;—theirs is indeed a hard case."

CHAPTER XVII. The Master said, "The superior man *in everything* considers righteousness to be essential. He performs it according to the rules of propriety. He brings it forth in humility. He completes it with sincerity. This is indeed a superior man."

secretly held possession of it.' Tsang Wăn would not recommend Hwuy, because he was an abler and better man than himself. Hwuy is a famous name in China. He was an officer of Loo, so styled after death, whose name was 展獲, and designation 禽. He derived his revenue from a town called Lew-hea, though some say that it was a *lew* or willow tree, overhanging his house, which made him to be known as Lew-hea Hwuy—'Hwuy that lived under the willow tree.' See Mencius, II. i. 9.

14. THE WAY TO WARD OFF RESENTMENTS. 責, it is said, is here 'to require from,' and not 'to reprove,' but the one meaning passes insensibly into the other.

15. NOTHING CAN BE MADE OF PEOPLE WHO TAKE THINGS EASILY, NOT GIVING THEMSELVES THE TROUBLE TO THINK. Comp. VII. 8.

16. AGAINST FRIVOLOUS TALKERS AND SUPERFICIAL SPECULATORS. Choo He explains 難矣哉 by 無以入德而將有患害, 'they have no ground from which to become virtuous, and they will meet with calamity.' Ho An gives Ch'ing K'ang-shing's explanation:—終無成, 'they will never complete any thing.' Our nearly literal translation appears to convey the meaning. 'A hard case,' *i.e.*, they will make nothing out, and nothing can be made of them.

17. THE CONDUCT OF THE SUPERIOR MAN IS RIGHTEOUS, COURTEOUS, HUMBLE, AND SINCERE. 質, is explained by Choo He by 質幹, 'the substance and stem;' and in the 備旨 by

以成之、君子哉。

十八章 子曰、君子病無能焉、不病人之不己知也。

十九章 子曰、君子疾沒世、而名不稱焉。

二十章 子曰、君子求諸己、小人求諸人。

廿一章 子曰、君子矜而不爭、群而不黨。

廿二章 子曰、君子不以言舉人、不以

CHAPTER XVIII. The Master said, "The superior man is distressed by his want of ability. He is not distressed by men's not knowing him."

CHAPTER XIX. The Master said, "The superior man dislikes the thought of his name not being mentioned after his death."

CHAPTER XX. The Master said, "What the superior man seeks, is in himself. What the mean man seeks, is in others.

CHAPTER XXI. The Master said, "The superior man is dignified, but does not wrangle. He is sociable, but not a partizan."

CHAPTER XXII. The Master said, "The superior man does not promote a man *simply* on account of his words, nor does he put aside *good* words because of the man."

基址, 'foundation.' The antecedent to all the 之 is 義, or rather the thing, whatever it be, done righteously.

18. OUR OWN INCOMPETENCY, AND NOT OUR REPUTATION, THE PROPER BUSINESS OF CONCERN TO US. See XIV. 32, *et al.*

19. THE SUPERIOR MAN WISHES TO BE HAD IN REMEMBRANCE. Not, say the commen., that the superior man cares about fame, but fame is the invariable concomitant of merit. He can't have been the superior man, if he be not remembered. 沒世,—see 大學傳, II. In the 備旨, 日講, and many other paraphrases, 沒世 is taken as=終身; 'all his life.'

20. HIS OWN APPROBATION IS THE SUPERIOR MAN'S RULE. THE APPROBATION OF OTHERS IS THE MEAN MAN'S. Comp. XIV. 25.

21. THE SUPERIOR MAN IS DIGNIFIED AND AFFABLE, WITHOUT THE FAULTS TO WHICH THOSE QUALITIES OFTEN LEAD. Comp. II 14, and VII. 30. 矜 is here=莊以持己, 'grave in self-maintenance.'

22. THE SUPERIOR MAN IS DISCRIMINATING, IN HIS EMPLOYMENT OF MEN AND JUDGING OF STATEMENTS.

人廢言。

〔二十三〕子貢問曰、有一言、而可以終身行之者乎。子曰、其恕乎、己所不欲、勿施於人。

〔二十四〕〔一節〕子曰、吾之於人也、誰毀、誰譽、如有所譽者、其有所試矣。〔二節〕斯民也、三代之所以直道而行也。

〔二十五〕子曰、吾猶及史之闕文也、有馬者、借人乘之、今亡已夫。

CHAPTER XXIII. Tsze-kung asked, saying, "Is there one word which may serve as a rule of practice for all one's life?" The Master said, "Is not RECIPROCITY such a word? What you do not want done to yourself, do not do to others."

CHAPTER XXIV. 1. The Master said, "In my dealings with men, whose evil do I blame, whose goodness do I praise, beyond what is proper? If I do sometimes exceed in praise, there must be ground for it in my examination *of the individual.*

2. "This people supplied the ground why the three dynasties pursued the path of straightforwardness."

CHAPTER XXV. The Master said, "Even in my *early* days, a historiographer would leave a blank in his text, and he who had a horse would lend him to another to ride. Now, alas! there are no such things."

23. THE GREAT PRINCIPLE OF RECIPROCITY IS THE RULE OF LIFE. Comp. V. 11. It is singular that Tsze-kung professes there to act on the principle here recommended to him.

24. CONFUCIUS SHOWED HIS RESPECT FOR MEN BY STRICT TRUTHFULNESS IN AWARDING PRAISE OR CENSURE. 1. I have not marked 'beyond what is proper' with italics, because there is really that force in the verbs—毀 and 譽. 'Ground for it in my examination of the individual;'—*i. e.*, from examination of him I believe he will yet verify my words. 2. 斯民也, resumes the 人 of the 1st par., which the 也 indicates. 所以 is to be taken as='the reason why,' and 行 as a neuter verb, of general application. 三代, 'the three dynasties,' with special reference to their great founders, and the principles which they inaugurated.—The truth-approving nature of the people was a rule even to those sages. It was the same to Confucius.

25. INSTANCES OF THE DEGENERACY OF CONFUCIUS' TIMES. Most paraphrasts supply a 見 after 及;—'even in my time I have seen.'

二十六章 子曰、巧言亂德、小不忍、則亂大謀。

二十七章 子曰、眾惡之、必察焉、眾好之、必察焉。

二十八章 子曰、人能弘道、非道弘人。

二十九章 子曰、過而不改、是謂過矣。

三十章 子曰、吾嘗終日

CHAPTER XXVI. The Master said, "Specious words confound virtue. Want of forbearance in small matters confounds great plans."

CHAPTER XXVII. The Master said, "When the multitude hate a man, it is necessary to examine into the case. When the multitude like a man, it is necessary to examine into the case."

CHAPTER XXVIII. The Master said, "A man can enlarge the principles *which he follows;* those principles do not enlarge the man."

CHAPTER XXIX. The Master said, "To have faults and not to reform them,—this, indeed, should be pronounced having faults."

CHAPTER XXX. The Master said, "I have been the whole day

The appointment of the historiographer is referred to Hwang-te, or 'The Yellow emperor,' the inventor of the cycle. The statutes of Chow mention no fewer than five classes of such officers. They were attached also to the feudal courts, and what Confucius says, is that, in his early days, a historiographer, on any point about which he was not sure, would leave a blank; so careful were they to record only truth. 吾猶及 extends on to 有馬云云. This second sentence is explained in Ho An:—'If any one had a horse which he could not tame, he would lend it to another to ride and exercise it!'—The commentator Hoo (胡氏) says well, that the meaning of the chapter must be left in uncertainty.

26. THE DANGER OF SPECIOUS WORDS, AND OF IMPATIENCE. 小不忍 is not 'a little impatience,' but impatience in little things; 'the hastiness,' it is said, 'of women and small people.'

27. IN JUDGING OF A MAN, WE MUST NOT BE GUIDED BY HIS BEING GENERALLY LIKED OR DISLIKED. Comp. XIII. 24.

28. PRINCIPLES OF DUTY AN INSTRUMENT IN THE HAND OF MAN. This sentence is quite mystical in its sententiousness. The 翼註 says:—'道 here is the path of duty, which all men, in their various relations, have to pursue, and man has the three virtues of knowledge, benevolence, and fortitude, wherewith to pursue that path, and so he enlarges it. That virtue remote, occupying an empty place, cannot enlarge man, needs not to be said.' That writer's account of 道 here is probably correct, and 'duty unapprehended,' 'in an empty place,' can have no effect on any man; but this is a mere truism. Duty apprehended is constantly enlarging, elevating, and energizing multitudes, who had previously been uncognizant of it. The first clause of the chapter may be granted, but the second is not in accordance with truth.

29. THE CULPABILITY OF NOT REFORMING KNOWN FAULTS. Comp. I. 8. Choo He's commentary appears to make the meaning somewhat different. He says:—'If one having faults can change them, he comes back to the condition of having no faults. But if he do not change them, then they go on to their completion, and will never come to be changed.'

30. THE FRUITLESSNESS OF THINKING, WITHOUT READING. Comp. II. 15, where the dependence of acquisition and reflection on each other is set forth.—Many comm. say that Conf. merely transfers the things which he here mentions to himself for the sake of others, not that it ever was really thus with himself.

論語

不食、終夜不寢、以思、無益、不如學也。

三十一 子曰、君子謀道不謀食、耕也、餒在其中矣、學也、祿在其中矣、君子憂道、不憂貧。

三十二 子曰、知及之、仁不能守之、雖得之、必失之。二節 知及之、仁能守之、不莊以涖之、則民不敬。三節 知及之、仁能守之、莊以涖之、動之不以禮、未善也。

without eating, and the whole night without sleeping:—occupied with thinking. It was of no use. The better plan is to learn."

CHAPTER XXXI. The Master said, "The object of the superior man is truth. Food is not his object. There is ploughing;—even in that there is *sometimes* want. So with learning;—emolument may be found in it. The superior man is anxious lest he should not get truth; he is not anxious lest poverty should come upon him."

CHAPTER XXXII. 1. The Master said, "When a man's knowledge is sufficient to attain, and his virtue is not sufficient to enable him to hold, whatever he may have gained, he will lose again.

2. "When his knowledge is sufficient to attain, and he has virtue enough to hold fast, if he cannot govern with dignity, the people will not respect him.

3. "When his knowledge is sufficient to attain, and he has virtue enough to hold fast; when he governs also with dignity, yet if he try to move the people contrary to the rules of propriety:—full excellence is not reached."

31. THE SUPERIOR MAN SHOULD NOT BE MERCENARY, BUT HAVE TRUTH FOR HIS OBJECT. Here again we translate 道 by 'truth,' as the best term that offers. 餒, 'hunger,'=want. 'Want may be in the midst of ploughing,'—*i. e.*, husbandry is the way to plenty, and yet despite the labours of the husbandman, a famine or scarcity sometimes occurs. The application of this to the case of learning, however, is not very apt. Is the emolument that sometimes comes with learning a calamity like famine?—Ch'ing K'ang-shing's view is:—'Although' a man may plough, yet, not learning, he will come to hunger. If he learn, he will get emolument, and tho' he do not plough, he will not be in want. This is advising men to learn'!

32. HOW KNOWLEDGE WITHOUT VIRTUE IS NOT LASTING, AND TO KNOWLEDGE AND VIRTUE A RULER SHOULD ADD DIGNITY AND THE RULES OF PROPRIETY. 1. Here the various 之 and the

三十三 子曰、君子不可小知、而可大受也、小人不可大受、而可小知也。

三十四 子曰、民之於仁也、甚於水火、水火吾見蹈而死者矣、未見蹈仁而死者也。

三十五 子曰、當仁、不讓於師。

CHAPTER XXXIII. The Master said, "The superior man cannot be known in little matters; but he may be intrusted with great concerns. The small man may not be intrusted with great concerns, but he may be known in little matters."

CHAPTER XXXIV. The Master said, "Virtue is more to man than either water or fire. I have seen men die from treading on water and fire, but I have never seen a man die from treading the course of virtue."

CHAPTER XXXV. The Master said, "Let every man consider virtue as what devolves on himself. He may not yield the performance of it *even* to his teacher."

two first in the other paragraphs, 指理言, 'have *le*, or principle, for their reference.' In Ho An, however, Paou Heen says:—'A man may have knowledge equal to the management of his office (治其官), but if he have not virtue which can hold it fast, though he get it, he will lose it.' 2. In 涖之, and 動之 below, 之指民言, 'the 之 have 民, or people, for their reference.' 3. The phrase—'to move the people' is analogous to several others, such as 鼓之, 舞之, 興之, 'to drum the people,' 'to dance them,' 'to rouse them.'

33. HOW TO KNOW THE SUPERIOR MAN AND THE MEAN MAN; AND THEIR CAPACITIES. Choo He says—知, 我知之, 'the knowing here is our knowing the individuals.' The 'little matters' are ingenious but trifling arts and accomplishments, in which a really great man may sometimes be deficient, while a small man will be familiar with them. The 'knowing' is not that the parties are *keun-tsze* and *seaou-jin*, but what attainments they have, and for what they are fit. The difficulty, on this view, is with the conclusion—而可小知.—Ho An gives the view of Wang Shuh:—'The way of the *keun-tsze* is profound and far-reaching. He may not let his knowledge be small, and he may receive what is great. The way of the *seaou-jin* is shallow and near. He may let his knowledge be small, and he may not receive what is great.'

34. VIRTUE MORE TO MAN THAN WATER OR FIRE, AND NEVER HURTFUL TO HIM. 民 is here =人, 'man,' as in VI. 20. 民之於仁也—'the people's relation to, or dependence on, virtue.' The case is easily conceivable of men's suffering death on account of their virtue. There have been martyrs for their loyalty and other virtues, as well as for their religious faith. Choo He provides for this diff. in his remarks:—'The want of fire and water is hurtful only to man's body, but to be without virtue is to lose one's mind (the higher nature), and so it is more to him than water or fire.' See on IV. 8.

35. VIRTUE PERSONAL AND OBLIGATORY ON EVERY MAN. The old interpreters take 當 in the sense of 'ought.' Choo He certainly improves on them by taking it in the sense of 擔當, as in the translation. A student at first takes 當 to be in the 2d person, but the 不 following recalls him to the 3d.

論語

三十六章 子曰、君子貞、而不諒。

三十七章 子曰、事君敬其事、而後其食。

三十八章 子曰、有教、無類。

三十九章 子曰、道不同、不相爲謀。

四十章 子曰、辭達而已矣。

四十一章 一節 師冕見、及階、子曰、階也。及席、子曰、席也。

CHAPTER XXXVI. The Master said, "The superior man is correctly firm, and not firm merely."

CHAPTER XXXVII. The Master said, "A minister, in serving his prince, reverently discharges his duties, and makes his emolument a secondary consideration."

CHAPTER XXXVIII. The Master said, "There being instruction, there will be no distinction of classes."

CHAPTER XXXIX. The Master said, "Those whose courses are different cannot lay plans for one another."

CHAPTER XL. The Master said, "In language it is simply required that it convey the meaning."

CHAPTER XLI. 1. The Music-master, Meën, having called upon him, when they came to the steps, the Master said, "Here are the steps." When they came to the mat *for the guest* to sit upon, he

36. THE SUPERIOR MAN'S FIRMNESS IS BASED ON RIGHT. 貞 is used here in the sense which it has throughout the Yih-king. Both it and 諒 imply firmness, but 貞 supposes a moral and intelligent basis which may be absent from 諒; see XIV. 18, 3.

37. THE FAITHFUL MINISTER. The 其 refers not to 君, but to the individual who 事君. We have to supply the subject—'a minister.' 後, as in VI. 20.

38. THE EFFECT OF TEACHING. Choo He says on this:—'The nature of all men is good, but we find among them the different classes of good and bad. This is the effect of physical constitution and of practice. The superior man, in consequence, employs his teaching, and all may be brought back to the state of good, and there is no necessity (The lang. is 不當復論其類之惡) of speaking any more of the badness of some.' This is very extravagant. Teaching is not so omnipotent.—The old interpretation is simply that in teaching there should be no distinction of classes.

39. AGREEMENT IN PRINCIPLE NECESSARY TO CONCORD IN PLANS. 爲 is the 3d tone, but I do not see that there would be any great difference in the meaning, if it were read in its usual 1st tone.

40. PERSPICUITY THE CHIEF VIRTUE OF LANGUAGE. 辭 may be used both of speech and of style.

41. CONSIDERATION OF CONFUCIUS FOR THE BLIND. 1. 師,—*i. q.* 太師, III. 23. Anciently, the blind were employed in the offices of music, partly because their sense of hearing

皆坐、子告之曰、某在斯、某在斯。師冕出。子張問曰、與師言之道與。子曰、然、固相師之道也。

said, "Here is the mat." When all were seated, the Master informed him, saying, "So and so is here; so and so is here."

2. The Music-master, Mëen, having gone out, Tsze-chang asked, saying, "Is it the rule to tell those things to the Music-master?"

3. The Master said, "Yes. This is certainly the rule for those who lead the blind."

was more than ordinarily acute, and partly that they might be made of some use in the world; see the 集證, *in loc.* 見,—low 3d tone. Mëen had come to Conf. house, under the care of a guide, but the sage met him, and undertook the care of him himself. 2. 之 is governed by 言, and refers to the words of Conf. to Mëen in the preceding paragraph.

BOOK XVI. KE SHE.

季氏第十六

第一章 季氏將伐顓臾。冉有季路見於孔子、曰、季氏將有事於顓臾。

CHAPTER I. 1. The head of the Ke family was going to attack Chuen-yu.

2. Yen Yew and Ke Loo had an interview with Confucius, and said, "*Our chief*, Ke, is going to commence operations against Chuen-yu."

HEADING OF THIS BOOK.—季氏第十六. 'The chief of the Ke—No XVI.' Throughout this Book, Confucius is spoken of as 孔子, 'The philosopher K'ung,' and never by the designation 子, or 'The Master.' Then, the style of several of the chapters (IV—XI) is not like the utterances of Confucius to which we have been accustomed. From these circumstances, one commentator, Hung Kwŏh (洪适), supposed that it belonged to the Ts'e (齊) *recensus* of these analects; the other books belonging to the Loo (魯) recensus. This supposition, however, is not otherwise supported.

1. CONFUCIUS EXPOSES THE PRESUMPTUOUS AND IMPOLITIC CONDUCT OF THE CHIEF OF THE KE FAMILY IN PROPOSING TO ATTACK A MINOR STATE, AND REBUKES YEN YEW AND TSZE-LOO FOR ABETTING THE DESIGN. 1. 季氏 and 季孫 below,—see III. 1. Chuen-yu was a

三節 孔子曰、求、無乃爾是過與。四節 夫顓臾、昔者、先王以爲東蒙主、且在邦域之中矣、是社稷之臣也、何以伐爲。五節 冉有曰、夫子欲之、吾二臣者、皆不欲也。六節 孔子曰、求、周任有言曰、陳力就列、不能者止、危而不持、顛而不扶、則將焉用彼相矣。七節 且爾言過矣、虎兕出於柙、龜玉毀於

3. Confucius said, "K'ew, is it not you who are in fault here?

4. "Now, in regard to Chuen-yu, long ago, a former king appointed it to preside over *the sacrifices to* the eastern Mung; moreover, it is in the midst of the territory of our state; and its ruler is a minister in direct connexion with the emperor:—What has *your chief* to do with attacking it?"

5. Yen Yew said, "Our master wishes the thing; neither of us two ministers wishes it."

6. Confucius said, "K'ew, there are the words of Chow Jin,—'When he can put forth his ability, he takes his place in the ranks *of office;* when he finds himself unable to do so, he retires from it. How can he be used as a guide to a blind man, who does not support him when tottering, nor raise him up when fallen?'

7. "And further, you speak wrongly. When a tiger or wild bull escapes from his cage; when a tortoise or gem is injured in its repository:—whose is the fault?"

small territory in Loo, whose ruler was of the 子, or 4th order of nobility. It was one of the states called 附庸, or 'attached,' whose chiefs could not appear in the presence of the emperor, excepting in the train of the prince within whose jurisdiction they were embraced. Their existence was not from a practice like the sub-infeudation, which belonged to the feudal system of Europe. They held of the lord paramount or emperor, but with the restriction which has been mentioned, and with a certain subservience also to their immediate superior. Its particular position is fixed by its proximity to Pe, and to the Mung hill. 伐 is not merely 'to attack,' but 'to attack and punish,' an exercise of judicial authority, which could emanate only from the emperor. The term is used here, to show the nefarious and presumptuous character of the contemplated operations. 2. There is some difficulty here, as, acc. to the 'Historical Records,' the two disciples were not in the service of the Ke family, at the same time. We may suppose, however, that Tsze-loo, returning with the sage from Wei on the invitation of duke Gae, took service a second time, and for a short period, with the Ke family, of which the chief was then Ke K'ang. This brings the time of the

檟中、是誰之過與。○八節冉有曰、今夫顓臾、固、而近於費、今不取、後世必爲子孫憂。○九節孔子曰、求、君子疾夫舍曰欲之、而必爲之辭。○十節丘也、聞有國有家者、不患寡、而患不均、不患貧、而患不安、蓋均無貧、和無寡、安無傾。○十一節夫如

8. Yen Yew said, "But at present, Chuen-yu is strong and near to Pe; if *our chief* do not now take it, it will hereafter be a sorrow to his descendants."

9. Confucius said, "K'ew, the superior man hates that declining to say—'I want such and such a thing,' and framing explanations *for the conduct.*

10. "I have heard that rulers of states and chiefs of families are not troubled lest their people should be few, but are troubled lest they should not keep their several places; that they are not troubled with fears of poverty, but are troubled with fears of a want of contented repose *among the people in their several places.* For when the people keep their several places, there will be no poverty; when harmony prevails, there will be no scarcity of people; and when there is such a *contented* repose, there will be no rebellious upsettings.

transaction to B. C. 483, or 482. 將有事,—lit., 'is going to have an affair.' 3. Conf. addresses himself only to K'ew, as he had been a considerable time, and very active, in the Ke service. 4. It was the prerogative of the princes to sacrifice to the hills and rivers within their jurisdictions;—here was the chief of Chuen-yu, imperially appointed (the 'former king' is probably 成, the second emperor of the Chow dynasty) to be the lord of the Mung mountain, that is, to preside over the sacrifices offered to it. This raised him high above any mere ministers or officers of Loo. The mountain Mung is in the present district of Pe, in the department of E-chow. It was called eastern, to distinguish it from another of the same name in Shen-se, which was the western Mung. 且在邦域之中,—this is mentioned, to show that Chuen-yu was so situated as to give Loo no occasion for apprehension. 社稷之臣, 'a minister of the altars to the spirits of the land and grain.' To those spirits only, the prince had the prerogative of sacrificing. The chief of Chuen-yu having this, how dared an officer of Loo to think of attacking him? The 臣 is used of his relation to the emperor. Choo He makes the phrase=公家之臣, 'a minister of the ducal house,' saying that the three families had usurped all the dominions proper of Loo, leaving only the chiefs of the attached states to appear in the ducal court. I prefer the former interpretation. 何以伐爲 must be understood with reference to the Ke. 爲 appears to be an expletive, unless we conceive it joined with the 何, the two characters together being simply='why' or 'how.' 5. 夫子, our 'master' *i. e.*, the chief of the

是、故遠人不服、則修文德以來之、既來之、則安之。十二節 今由與求也、相夫子、遠人不服、而不能來也、邦分崩離析、而不能守也。十三節 而謀動干戈於邦內、吾恐季孫之憂、不在顓臾、而在蕭牆之內也。

11. "So it is.—Therefore, if remoter people are not submissive, all the influences of civil culture and virtue are to be cultivated to attract them to be so; and when they have been so attracted, they must be made contented and tranquil.

12. "Now, here are you, Yew and K'ew, assisting your chief. Remoter people are not submissive, and, *with your help*, he cannot attract them to him. In his own territory there are divisions and downfalls, leavings and separations, and, *with your help*, he cannot preserve it.

13. "And yet he is planning these hostile movements within our state.—I am afraid that the sorrow of the Ke-sun *family* will not be on account of Chuen-yu, but will be found within the screen of their own court."

Ke family. 6. Chow Jin is by Choo He simply called—'a good historiographer of ancient times.' Some trace him back to the Shang dynasty, and others only to the early times of the Chow. There are other weighty utterances of his in vogue, besides that in the text. 7. Choo He explains 兕 by 野牛, 'a wild bull.' The dict. says it is like an ox, and goes on to describe it as 'one-horned.' The 本草, 獸部, says that 兕 and 犀 are different terms for the same animal, *i. e.*, the rhinoceros. I cannot think that 龜 here is the living tortoise. That would not be kept in a 櫝, or 'coffer,' like a gem. Perhaps the term is, by mistake, for 圭. 9. The regimen of 疾 extends down to the end of the par. 夫,—as in XI. 24. 爲之辭 is the same idiom as 爲之宰, V. 7. 10. Conf. uses the term 患 here, with ref. to the 憂 in p. 8. 均, 'equality,' 謂各得其分, 'means—every one getting his own proper name and place.' From this point, Conf. speaks of the general disorganization of Loo under the management of the three families, and especially of the Ke. By 遠人 we certainly cannot understand the people of Chuen-yu. 11. 來 is to be understood with a hiphil force, 'to make to come,' 'to attract.' 12. 不能來, 不能守, are to be understood of the head of the Ke family, as controlling the government of Loo, and *as being assisted by the two disciples*, so that the reproof falls heavily on them. 13. 在蕭牆之內,—Choo He simply says 蕭牆, 屏也, '*seaou-ts'eang* means a screen.' In the dict., after Ch'ing K'ang-shing, *seaou* in this pass.=肅, 'reverent,' and 牆 alone means 'screen,' and the phrase is thus explained:—'Officers, on reaching the screen, which they had only to pass, to find themselves in the presence of their head, were supposed to become more reverential'; and hence, the expression in the text='among his own immediate officers.'

第二章 一節 孔子曰、天下有道、則禮樂征伐、自天子出、天下無道、則禮樂征伐、自諸侯出、自諸侯出、蓋十世希不失矣、自大夫出、五世希不失矣、陪臣執國命、三世希不失矣。二節 天下有道、則政不在大夫。三節 天下有道、則庶人不議。

CHAPTER II. 1. Confucius said, "When good government prevails in the empire, ceremonies, music, and punitive military expeditions, proceed from the emperor. When bad government prevails in the empire, ceremonies, music, and punitive military expeditions proceed from the princes. When these things proceed from the princes, as a rule, the cases will be few in which they do not lose their power in ten generations. When they proceed from the great officers *of the princes*, *as a rule*, the cases will be few in which they do not lose their power in five generations. When the subsidiary ministers *of the great officers* hold in their grasp the orders of the kingdom, *as a rule*, the cases will be few in which they do not lose their power in three generations.

2. "When right principles prevail in the empire, government will not be in the hands of the great officers.

3. "When right principles prevail in the empire, there will be no discussions among the common people."

2. THE SUPREME AUTHORITY OUGHT EVER TO MAINTAIN ITS POWER. THE VIOLATION OF THIS RULE ALWAYS LEADS TO RUIN, WHICH IS SPEEDIER AS THE RANK OF THE VIOLATOR IS LOWER.—In these utterances, Conf. had reference to the disorganized state of the empire, when 'the son of Heaven' was fast becoming an empty name, the princes of states were in bondage to their great officers, and those again at the mercy of their family ministers. 1. 有道, 無道,—compare XIV. 1. 征伐 are to be taken together, as in the transl. We read of four 征, *i. e.*, expeditions,—east, west, north, and south; and of nine 伐, *i. e.*, nine grounds on which the emperor might order such expeditions. On the imperial prerogatives, see the 中庸, XXVIII. 蓋, is here=大約, 'generally speaking,' 'as a rule.' 陪臣=家臣, 'family-ministers,' 國命 are the same as the previous 禮, 樂, 征, 伐, but having been usurped by the princes, and now again snatched from them by their officers, they can no longer be spoken of as imperial affairs, but only as 國之事, 'state matters.' 3. 議=私議, 'private discussions;' *i. e.*, about the said state of public affairs.

論語

第三章 孔子曰、祿之去公室、五世矣、政逮於大夫、四世矣、故夫三桓之子孫微矣。

第四章 孔子曰、益者三友、損者三友、友直、友諒、友多聞、益矣、友便辟、友善柔、友便佞、損矣。

第五章 孔子曰、益者三樂、損者三樂、樂節禮樂、

CHAPTER III. Confucius said, "The revenue *of the state* has left the ducal house, now for five generations. The government has been in the hands of the great officers for four generations. On this account, the descendants of the three Hwan are much reduced."

CHAPTER IV. Confucius said, "There are three friendships which are advantageous, and three which are injurious. Friendship with the upright; friendship with the sincere; and friendship with the man of much observation:—these are advantageous. Friendship with the man of specious airs; friendship with the insinuatingly soft; and friendship with the glib-tongued:—these are injurious."

CHAPTER V. Confucius said, "There are three things men find enjoyment in which are advantageous, and three things they find enjoyment in which are injurious. To find enjoyment in the discriminating study of ceremonies and music; to find enjoyment in

3. ILLUSTRATION OF THE PRINCIPLES OF THE LAST CHAPTER. In the year B.C. 608, at the death of duke Wăn, his rightful heir was killed, and the son of a concubine raised to the dukedom. He is in the annals as duke Seuen (宣), and after him came Shing, Seang, Ch'aou, and Ting, in whose time this must have been spoken. These dukes were but shadows, pensionaries of their great officers, so that it might be said the revenue had gone from them. Obs. that here and in the prec. ch., 世 is used for 'a reign.' 'The three Hwan' are the three families, as being all descended from duke Hwan; see on II. 5. 故夫,—'therefore,' uttered with a sigh.—Choo He appears to have fallen into a mistake in enumerating the four heads of the Ke family who had administered the government of Loo as Woo, Taou, P'ing, and Hwan, as Taou (悼) died before his father, and would not be said therefore to have the government in his hands. The right enumeration is Wăn (文), Woo (武), P'ing (平), and Hwan (桓). See the 摭餘說, III. XXVI.

4. THREE FRIENDSHIPS ADVANTAGEOUS, AND THREE INJURIOUS. In the 備旨 it is said—三友下各友字俱作交字看, 是我去友人, 'after 三友, the character 友 is always verbal and=交, '*to have intercourse with*.' It is as well to translate the term by 'friendship' throughout. 諒 is here 'sincere,' without the subtractions required in XIV. 18, 3, XV. 36. 便,—here=習熟, 'practised.' 善,柔,—善柔之工, 善 is skilfulness in being bland. 辟, as in XI. 17, 3.

5. THREE SOURCES OF ENJOYMENT ADVANTAGEOUS, AND THREE INJURIOUS. Here we have 樂 with three pronunciations and in three

樂道人之善、樂多賢友、益矣、樂驕樂、樂佚遊、樂宴樂、損矣。

第六章 孔子曰、侍於君子有三愆、言未及之而言、謂之躁、言及之而不言、謂之隱、未見顏色而言、謂之瞽。

第七章 孔子曰、君子有三戒、少之時、血氣未定、戒之

speaking of the goodness of others; to find enjoyment in having many worthy friends:—these are advantageous. To find enjoyment in extravagant pleasures; to find enjoyment in idleness and sauntering; to find enjoyment in the pleasures of feasting:—these are injurious."

CHAPTER VI. Confucius said, "There are three errors to which they who stand in the presence of a man of virtue and station are liable. They may speak when it does not come to them to speak;—this is called rashness. They may not speak when it comes to them to speak;—this is called concealment. They may speak without looking at the countenance *of their superior*;—this is called blindness."

CHAPTER VII. Confucius said, "There are three things which the superior man guards against. In youth, when the physical

different meanings. The leading word is read *ngaou*, low. 3d tone, 'to have enjoyment in,' as in VI. 21. In 禮樂, it is *yŏ*, 'music.' The two others are 樂, *lŏ*, 'joy,' 'to delight in.' 節禮樂,—節=節之, *i. e.*, it is a verb, 'to discriminate;' 'to mark the divisions of.' The idea is that ceremonies and music containing in them the principles of propriety and harmony, the study of them could not but be beneficial to the student himself, as having to exemplify both of those things. 驕, primarily, a 'tall horse,' often used for 'proud'; here,=vain and extravagant self-indulgence. 宴, 'feasting,' including, says a gloss, 'eating, drinking, music, women, &c.'

6. THREE ERRORS IN REGARD TO SPEECH TO BE AVOIDED IN THE PRESENCE OF THE GREAT. 君子, according to Choo He, denotes here 'a man both of rank and virtue.' 'Without looking at the conntenance,'—*i. e.*, to see whether he is paying attention or not.—The general principle is that there is a time to speak. Let that be observed, and these three errors will be avoided.

7. THE VICES WHICH YOUTH, MANHOOD, AND AGE, HAVE TO GUARD AGAINST. 血氣, 'blood and breath.' In the 中庸, XXI, 凡有血氣者='all human beings.' Here the phrase is equivalent to 'the physical powers.' On 未定, 'not yet settled,' the gloss in the

論語

在色、及其壯也、血氣方剛、戒之在鬭、及其老也、血氣既衰、戒之在得。

第八章 一節 孔子曰、君子有三畏、畏天命、畏大人、畏聖人之言。二節 小人不知天命、而不畏也、狎大人、侮聖人之言。

第九章 孔子曰、生而知之者、上也、學而知之者、次也、

powers are not yet settled, he guards against lust. When he is strong, and the physical powers are full of vigour, he guards against quarrelsomeness. When he is old, and the animal powers are decayed, he guards against covetousness."

CHAPTER VIII. 1. Confucius said, "There are three things of which the superior man stands in awe. He stands in awe of the ordinances of Heaven. He stands in awe of great men. He stands in awe of the words of sages.

2. "The mean man does not know the ordinances of Heaven, and *consequently* does not stand in awe of them. He is disrespectful to great men. He makes sport of the words of sages."

CHAPTER IX. Confucius said, "Those who are born with the possession of knowledge are the highest class of men. Those who learn, and so, *readily*, get possession of knowledge, are the next.

備旨 is 一方動之時, 'the time when they are moving most.' As to what causal relation Conf. may have supposed to exist between the state of the physical powers, and the several vices indicated, that is not developed. Hing Ping explains the first caution thus:—'Youth embraces all the period below 29. Then, the physical powers are still weak, and the sinews and bones have not reached their vigour, and indulgence in lust will injure the body."

8. CONTRAST OF THE SUPERIOR AND THE MEAN MAN IN REGARD TO THE THREE THINGS OF WHICH THE FORMER STANDS IN AWE. 天命, according to Choo He, means the moral nature of man, conferred by Heaven. High above the nature of other creatures, it lays him under great responsibility to cherish and cultivate him. The old interpr. take the phrase to indicate Heaven's moral administration by rewards and punishments. The 'great men' are men high in position and great in wisdom and virtue, the royal instructors, who have been raised up by Heaven for the training and ruling of mankind. So, the commentators; but the 狎 suggests at once a more general and a lower view of the phrase.

9. FOUR CLASSES OF MEN IN RELATION TO KNOWLEDGE. On the 1st clause, see on VII. 19, where Conf. disclaims for himself being ranked in the first of the classes here mentioned. The modern commentators say, that men are differenced here by the difference of their 氣質, or 氣稟, on which see Morrison's dict., part, II. vol I. char. 質 困, in the dict., and by commentators, old and new, is explained by 不通, 'not thoroughly understanding.' It

困而學之、又其次也、困而不學、民斯爲下矣。

第十章 孔子曰、君子有九思、視思明、聽思聰、色思溫、貌思恭、言思忠、事思敬、疑思問、忿思難、見得思義。

第十一章 一節 孔子曰、見善如不及、見不善如探湯、吾見其人矣、吾聞其語矣。二節 隱居

Those who are dull and stupid, and yet compass the learning are another class next to these. As to those who are dull and stupid and yet do not learn;—they are the lowest of the people."

CHAPTER X. Confucius said, "The superior man has nine things which are subjects with him of thoughtful consideration. In regard to the use of his eyes, he is anxious to see clearly. In regard to the use of his ears, he is anxious to hear distinctly. In regard to his countenance, he is anxious that it should be benign. In regard to his demeanour, he is anxious that it should be respectful. In regard to his speech, he is anxious that it should be sincere. In regard to his doing of business, he is anxious that it should be reverently careful. In regard to what he doubts about, he is anxious to question others. When he is angry, he thinks of the difficulties his anger may involve him in. When he sees gain to be got, he thinks of righteousness."

CHAPTER XI. 1. Confucius said, "Contemplating good, *and pursuing it*, as if they could not reach it; contemplating evil, *and shrinking from it*, as they would from thrusting the hand into boiling water:—I have seen such men, as I have heard such words.

is not to be joined with 學, as if the meaning were—'they learn with painful effort, although such effort will be required in the case of the 困.

10. NINE SUBJECTS OF THOUGHT TO THE SUPERIOR MAN:—VARIOUS INSTANCES OF THE WAY IN WHICH HE REGULATES HIMSELF. The conciseness of the text contrasts here with the verbosity of the translation, and yet the many words of the latter seem necessary.

11. THE CONTEMPORARIES OF CONFUCIUS COULD ESCHEW EVIL, AND FOLLOW AFTER GOOD, BUT NO ONE OF THE HIGHEST CAPACITY HAD APPEARED AMONG THEM. 1. The two first clauses here and in the next par., also, are quotations of old sayings, current in Confucius' time. Such men were several of the sage's own disciples. 2. 求其志, 'seeking for their aims;' *i. e.*, meditating on them, studying them, fixing them, to be prepared to carry them out, as in the next clause. Such men among the ancients

論語

以求其志、行義以達其道、吾聞其語矣、未見其人也。

〔十二章〕一節 齊景公有馬千駟、死之日、民無德而稱焉、伯夷叔齊、餓于首陽之下、民到于今稱之。二節 其斯之謂與。

〔十三章〕一節 陳亢問於伯魚曰、子亦有異聞乎。二節 對曰、未也。嘗獨立、鯉趨而過庭、曰、學詩乎。對曰、未也。不學詩、無以言。

2. "Living in retirement to study their aims, and practising righteousness to carry out their principles:—I have heard these words, but I have not seen such men."

CHAPTER XII. 1. The duke King of Ts'e had a thousand teams, each of four horses, but on the day of his death, the people did not praise him for a single virtue. P'ih-e and Shuh-ts'e died of hunger at the foot of the Show-yang mountain, and the people, down to the present time, praise them.

2. "Is not that saying illustrated by this?"

CHAPTER XIII. 1. Ch'in K'ang asked Pih-yu, saying, "Have you heard any lessons *from your father* different *from what we have all heard?*"

2. Pih-yu replied, "No. He was standing alone once, when I passed below the hall with hasty steps, and said to me, 'Have you learned the Odes?' On my replying 'Not yet,' *he added*, 'If you do not learn the Odes, you will not be fit to converse with.' I retired and studied the Odes.

were the great ministers E-yem and T'ae-kung. Such might the disciple Yen Hwuy have been, but an early death snatched him away before he could have an opportunity of showing what was in him.

12. WEALTH WITHOUT VIRTUE AND VIRTUE WITHOUT WEALTH;—THEIR DIFFERENT APPRECIATIONS. This chapter is plainly a fragment. As it stands, it would appear to come from the compilers and not from Confucius. Then the 2d par. implies a reference to something which has been lost. Under XII. 10, I have referred to the proposal to transfer to this place the last par. of that chapter which might be explained, so as to harmonize with the sentiment of this. —The duke King of Ts'e,—see XII. 11. Pih-e and Shuh-ts'e,—see VI. 22. The mountain Show-yang is to be found probably in the dep. of 蒲州 in Shan-se.

13. CONFUCIUS' INSTRUCTION OF HIS SON NOT DIFFERENT FROM HIS INSTRUCTION OF THE DISCIPLES GENERALLY. 1. Ch'in K'ang is the Tsze-k'in of I. 10. When Confucius' eldest son was born, the duke of Loo sent the philosopher a present of a carp, on which account he named the child

鯉退而學詩。三節他日又獨立、鯉趨而過庭、曰、學禮乎。對曰、未也。不學禮、無以立。鯉退而學禮。四節聞斯二者。五節陳亢退而喜曰、問一得三、聞詩、聞禮、又聞君子之遠其子也。

十四 邦君之妻、君稱之曰夫人、夫人自稱、曰小童、邦人稱之、曰君夫人、稱

3. "Another day, he was in the same way standing alone, when I passed by below the hall with hasty steps, and said to me, 'Have you learned the rules of Propriety?' On my replying 'Not yet,' *he added*, 'If you do not learn the rules of Propriety, your character cannot be established.' I then retired, and studied the rules of Propriety.

4. "I have heard only these two things from him."

5. Ch'in K'ang retired, and, quite delighted, said, "I asked one thing, and I have got three things. I have heard about the Odes. I have heard about the rules of Propriety. I have also heard that the superior man maintains a distant reserve towards his son."

CHAPTER XIV. The wife of the prince of a State is called by him FOO-JIN. She calls herself SEAOU T'UNG. The people of the State call

鯉, (the carp), and afterwards gave him the designation of 伯魚. 子亦有異聞乎, 'Have you *also* (*i. e.*, as being his son) heard different instructions?' 2. On 詩 here, and 禮, next par., see on VII. 17. Before 不學, here and below, we must supply a 曰. 3. 立, —see VIII. 8. 4. The force of the 者 is to make the whole='what I have heard from him are only these two remarks.' 5. Confucius is, no doubt, intended by 君子, but it is best to translate it generally.

14. APPELLATIONS FOR THE WIFE OF A PRINCE. This chapter may have been spoken by Confucius to rectify some disorder of the times, but there is no intimation to that effect. The different appellations may be thus explained:—妻 is 與己齊者, 'she who is her husband's equal.' The 夫 in 夫人 is taken as =扶, 'to support,' 'to help,' so that that designation is equivalent to 'helpmeet.' 童 means either 'a youth,' or 'a girl.' The wife modestly calls herself 小童, 'the little girl.' The old interpreters take—most naturally—君夫人 as=君之夫人, 'our prince's help-meet,' but the modern comm. take 君 adjectively, as=主, with reference to the office of the wife to 'preside over the internal economy of the palace.' On this view 君夫人 is

諸異邦、曰寡小君、異邦人稱之、亦曰君夫人。

her KEUN FOO-JIN, and, to the people of other States, they call her K'WA SEAOU KEUN. The people of other states also call her KEUN FOO-JIN.

'the domestic help-meet.' The ambassador of a prince spoke of him by the style of 寡君, 'my prince of small virtue.' After that example of modesty, his wife was styled to the people of other States, 'our small prince of small virtue.' The people of other States had no reason to imitate her subjects in that, and so they styled her—'your prince's help-meet,' or 'the domestic help-meet.'

BOOK XVII. YANG HO.

陽貨第十七

第一章 一節 陽貨欲見孔子、孔子不見、歸孔子豚、孔子時其亡也、而往拜之。遇諸塗。二節 謂孔子曰、來、予與爾言、曰、懷其寶、而迷其邦、可謂仁乎。曰、不可。好從

CHAPTER I. 1. Yang Ho wished to see Confucius, but Confucius would not go to see him. *On this*, he sent a present of a pig to Confucius, who, having chosen a time when Ho was not at home, went to pay his respects *for the gift*. He met him, *however*, on the way.

2. *Ho* said to Confucius, "Come, let me speak with you." He then asked, "Can he be called benevolent, who keeps his jewel in his bo-

HEADING OF THIS BOOK.—陽貨第十七, 'Yang Ho, No. XVII.'—As the last Book commenced with the presumption of the Head of the Ke family, who kept his prince in subjection, this begins with an account of an officer, who did for the head of the Ke what he did for the duke of Loo. For this reason—some similarity in the subject matter of the first chapters—this Book, it is said, is placed after the former. It contains 26 chapters.

1. CONFUCIUS' POLITE BUT DIGNIFIED TREATMENT OF A POWERFUL, BUT USURPING AND UNWORTHY, OFFICER. 1. Yang Ho, known also as Yang Hoo (虎), was nominally the principal minister of the Ke family, but its chief was entirely in his hands, and he was scheming to arrogate the whole authority of the state of Loo to himself. He first appears in the Chronicles of Loo about the year B. C. 503, acting against the exiled duke Ch'aou; in B. C. 504, we find

事、而亟失時、可謂知乎。曰、不可。日月逝矣、歲不我與。孔子曰、諾、吾將仕矣。

第二章 子曰、性相近也、習相遠也。

第三章 子曰、唯上知與下愚不移。

som, and leaves his country to confusion?" *Confucius* replied, "No." "Can he be called wise, who is anxious to be engaged in public employment, and yet is constantly losing the opportunity of being so?" *Confucius again* said, "No." "The days and months are passing away; the years do not wait for us." Confucius said, "Right; I will go into office."

CHAPTER II. The Master said, "By nature, men are nearly alike; by practice, they get to be wide apart."

CHAPTER III. The Master said, "There are only the wise of the highest class, and the stupid of the lowest class, who cannot be changed."

him keeping his own chief, Ke Hwan a prisoner, and, in 501, he is driven out, on the failure of his projects, a fugitive into Ts'e. At the time when the incidents in this ch. occurred, Yang Ho was anxious to get, or appear to get, the support of a man of Conf. reputation, and finding that the sage would not call on him, he adopted the expedient of sending him a pig, at a time when Conf. was not at home, the rules of ceremony requiring that when a great officer sent a present to a scholar, and the latter was not in his house on its arrival, he had to go to the officer's house to acknowledge it. See the Le-ke, XIII. iii. 20. 歸 is in the sense of 饋, 'to present food,' properly 'before a superior.' Confucius, however, was not to be entrapped. He also *timed* (時, as a verb) Hoo's being away from home (亡), and went to call on him. 2. 迷其邦, 'deludes, confuses, his country,' but the meaning is only negative, ='leaves his country to confusion.' 亟, read *k'e*, up. 3d tone, 'frequently.' 明—我與,—all this is to be taken as the remark of Yang Ho, and a 日 supplied before 日. 我與; 與, in the dict., and by the old interpreters, is here explained, as in the translation by 待, 'to wait for.'

2. THE DIFFERENCES IN THE CHARACTERS OF MEN ARE CHIEFLY OWING TO HABIT. 性, it is contended, is here not the moral constitution of man, absolutely considered, but his complex, actual nature, with its elements of the material, the animal, and the intellectual, by association with which, the perfectly good moral nature is continually being led astray. The moral nature is the same in all, and though the material organism and disposition do differ in different individuals, they are, at first, more nearly alike than they subsequently become. In the 註疏, we read:—'The nature is the constitution received by man at birth, and is *then* still. While it has not been acted on by external things, men are all like one another; they are 近. After it has been acted on by external things, then practice forms, as it were, a second nature. He who practises what is good, becomes the superior man, and he who practises what is not good, becomes the mean man:—men become 相遠.'—No doubt, it is true that many—perhaps most—of the differences among men are owing to habit.

3. ONLY TWO CLASSES WHOM PRACTICE CANNOT CHANGE. This is a sequel to the last chapter with which it is incorporated in Ho An's edition. The case of the 下愚 would seem to be inconsistent with the doctrine of the perfect goodness of the moral nature of all men. Modern

論語

第四章 一節 子之武城、聞絃歌之聲。○二節 夫子莞爾而笑曰、割雞焉用牛刀。○三節 子游對曰、昔者偃也、聞諸夫子曰、君子學道則愛人、小人學道則易使也。○四節 子曰、二三子、偃之言是也、前言戲之耳。

第五章 一節 公山弗擾以費畔、召、子欲往。○二節 子路不說、曰、末

CHAPTER IV. 1. The Master having come to Woo-hing, heard *there* the sound of stringed instruments and singing.

2. Well-pleased and smiling, he said, "Why use an ox-knife to kill a fowl?"

3. Tsze-yew replied, "Formerly, Master, I heard you say,—'When the man of high station is well instructed, he loves men; when the man of low station is well instructed, he is easily ruled.'"

4. The Master said, "My disciples, Yen's words are right. What I said was only in sport."

CHAPTER V. 1. Kung-shan Fuh-jaou, when he was holding Pe, and in an attitude of rebellion, invited the Master to visit him, who was rather inclined to go.

2. Tsze-loo was displeased, and said, "Indeed you cannot go! Why must you think of going to see Kung-shan?"

commentators, to get over the difficulty, say that they are the 自暴者 and 自棄者 of Mencius, IV. Pt. I. x.

4. HOWEVER SMALL THE SPHERE OF GOVERNMENT, THE HIGHEST INFLUENCES OF PROPRIETIES AND MUSIC SHOULD BE EMPLOYED. 1. Wooshing was in the district of Pe. Tsze-yew appears as the commandant of it, in VI. 12. 弦, 'the silken string of a musical instrument,' used here for stringed instruments generally. In the 備旨 we read, 'The town was named *Woo* (武), from its position, precipitous and favourable to military operations, but Tsze-yew had been able, by his course, to transform the people, and make them change their mail and helmets for stringed instruments and singing. This was what made the Master glad.' 2. 莞 (read *han*, up. 2d tone) 爾, 'smilingly.' 'An ox-knife,' a large instrument, and not necessary for the death of a fowl. Conf. intends by it the high principles of government employed by Tsze-yew. 3. 君子 and 小人 are here indicative of rank, and not of character. 易事 'are easily employed, *i. e.*, 安分從上, 'they rest in their lot, and obey their superiors.' 4. 二三子, as in VII. 23, *et al.* Obs. the force of the final 耳,—'only.'

5. THE LENGTHS TO WHICH CONFUCIUS WAS INCLINED TO GO, TO GET HIS PRINCIPLES CARRIED INTO PRACTICE. Kung-shan Fuh-jaou, called also Kung-shan Fuh-new (狃), by designation 子洩, was a confederate of Yang Ho (ch. I),

之也已、何必公山氏之之也。〔三節〕子曰、夫召我者、而豈徒哉、如有用我者、吾其爲東周乎。

〔第六章〕子張問仁於孔子、孔子曰、能行五者於天下爲仁矣。請問之、曰、恭寬、信、敏、惠。恭則不侮、寬則得衆、信則人任焉、敏則有功、惠則足以使人。

3. The Master said, "Can it be without some reason that he has invited ME? If any one employ me, may I not make an eastern Chow?"

CHAPTER VI. 1. Tsze-chang asked Confucius about perfect virtue. Confucius said, "To be able to practise five things everywhere under heaven constitutes perfect virtue." He begged to ask what they were, and was told, "Gravity, generosity *of soul*, sincerity, earnestness, and kindness. If you are grave, you will not be treated with disrespect. If you are generous, you will win all. If you are sincere, people will repose trust in you. If you are earnest, you will accomplish much. If you are kind, this will enable you to employ the services of others."

and acc. to K'ung Gan-kwŏ, and the 日講, it was after the imprisonment by them, in common, of Ke Hwan, that Fuh-jaou sent this invitation to Conf. Others make the invitation subsequent to Ho's discomfiture and flight to Ts'e. See the 歷代統紀表, B. C. 500. We must conclude, with Tsze-loo, that Conf. ought not to have thought of accepting the invitation of such a man. 2. The first and last 之 are the verb. 末=無. 末之也已,='There is no going there. Indeed there is not.' 何必公山氏之之也, 'why must there be going to (之 here=*to*) *that* (such is the force of 氏) Kung-shan?' 3. 夫召我者,—者 is to be taken here as referring expressly to Fuh-jaou, while its reference below is more general The 我 in 用我, and 吾 are emphatic. The original seat of the Chow dynasty lay west from Loo, and the revival of the principles and government of Wăn and Woo in Loo, or even in Pe, which was but a part of it, might make an eastern Chow; so that Confucius would perform the part of king Wăn.—After all, the sage did not go to Pe.

6. FIVE THINGS THE PRACTICE OF WHICH CONSTITUTES PERFECT VIRTUE. 於天下, 'in under heaven' is simply='any where.' 信則人任,—任, low 3d tone, is explained by Choo He by 倚仗, 'to rely upon,' a meaning of the term not found in the dictionary. See XX. 1, 8.

第七章 一節 佛肸召。子欲往。二節 子路曰、昔者由也、聞諸夫子曰、親於其身、爲不善者、君子不入也。佛肸以中牟畔、子之往也、如之何。三節 子曰、然、有是言也、不曰堅乎、磨而不磷、不曰白乎、涅而不緇。四節 吾豈匏瓜也哉、焉能繫而不食。

CHAPTER VII. 1. Peih Heih inviting him to visit him, the Master was inclined to go.

2. Tsze-loo said, "Master, formerly I have heard you say, 'When a man in his own person is guilty of doing evil, a superior man will not associate with him.' Peih Heih is in rebellion, holding possession of Chung-mow; if you go to him, what shall be said?"

3. The Master said, "Yes, I did use these words. But is it not said, that, if a thing be really hard, it may be ground without being made thin? Is it not said, that, if a thing be really white, it may be steeped in a dark fluid without being made black?

4. "Am I a bitter gourd! How can I be hung up out of the way of being eaten?"

7. CONFUCIUS, INCLINED TO RESPOND TO THE ADVANCES OF AN UNWORTHY MAN, PROTESTS AGAINST HIS CONDUCT BEING JUDGED BY ORDINARY RULES. Comp. ch. V; but the invitation of Peih Heih was subsequent to that of Kung-shan Fuh-jaou, and after Conf. had given up office in Loo. 1. 佛 (read *Peih*) Heih was commandant of Chung-mow, for *the* chief of the Chaou family, in the state of Tsin. 2. 親於其身爲不善者,—'he who himself, in his own person, does what is not good.' 不入,—acc. to K'ung Gan-kwŏ,=不入其國, 'does not enter his state;' acc. to Choo He, it=不入其黨, 'does not enter his party.' There were two places of the name of Chung-mow, one belonging to the state of Ch'ing, and the other to the state of Tsin (晉), which is that intended here, and is referred to the present district of 湯陰, dep. of 彰德, in Ho-nan province. 3. 不曰 is to be taken interrogatively, as in the translation. Ping's paraphrase is—人豈不曰, 'do not men say?' 堅乎云云,—'Is a thing hard, then,' &c. 涅 is explained—'black earth in water, which may be used to dye a black colour.' The application of these strange proverbial sayings is to Conf. himself, as, from his superiority, incapable of being affected by evil communications. 4. This par. is variously explained. By some, 匏瓜 is taken as the name of a star; so that the meaning is—'Am I, like such and such a star, to be hung up, &c?' But we need not depart from the proper meaning of the characters. Choo He, with Ho An, takes 不食 actively:—'A gourd can be hung up, because it does not need to eat. But I must go about, north, south, east, and west, to get food.' This seems to me very unnatural. The expression is taken passively, as in the translation, in the 日講, and other works.

第八章 一節 子曰、由也、女聞六言六蔽矣乎。對曰、未也。二節 居、吾語女。三節 好仁不好學、其蔽也愚、好智不好學、其蔽也蕩、好信不好學、其蔽也賊、好直不好學、其蔽也絞、好勇不好學、其蔽也亂、好剛不好學、其蔽也狂。

CHAPTER VIII. 1. The Master said, "Yew, have you heard the six words to which are attached six becloudings?" Yew replied, "I have not."

2. "Sit down, and I will tell them to you.

3. "There is the love of being benevolent without the love of learning;—the beclouding here leads to a foolish simplicity. There is the love of knowing without the love of learning;—the beclouding here leads to dissipation of mind. There is the love of being sincere without the love of learning;—the beclouding here leads to an injurious disregard of consequences. There is the love of straight-forwardness without the love of learning;—the beclouding here leads to rudeness. There is the love of boldness without the love of learning;—the beclouding here leads to insubordination. There is the love of firmness without the love of learning;—the beclouding here leads to extravagant conduct."

8. KNOWLEDGE, ACQUIRED BY LEARNING, IS NECESSARY TO THE COMPLETION OF VIRTUE, BY PRESERVING THE MIND FROM BEING BECLOUDED. 1. 六言是六字, 'The six 言 are six characters'; see the 備旨. They are, therefore, the benevolence, knowledge, sincerity, straight-forwardness, boldness, and firmness, mentioned below, all virtues, but yet each, when pursued without discrimination, tending to becloud the mind. 蔽=遮掩, 'to cover and screen;' the primary meaning of it is said to be 小草, 'small plants.' 2. 居='sit down.' Tsze-loo had risen, acc. to the rules of propriety, to give his answer; see the Le-ke, I. Pt. I. iii. 21; and Conf. tells him to resume his seat. 3. I give here the paraphrase of the 日講 on the first virtue and its beclouding, which may illustrate the manner in which the whole paragraph is developed:—'In all matters, there is a perfectly right and unchangeable principle, which men ought carefully to study, till they have thoroughly examined and apprehended it. Then their actions will be without error, and their virtue may be perfected. For instance, loving is what rules in benevolence. It is certainly a beautiful virtue, but if you only set yourself to love men, and do not care to study to understand the principle of benevolence, then your mind will be beclouded by that loving, and you will be following a man into a well to save him, so that both he and you will perish. Will not this be foolish simplicity?'

第九章 子曰、小子、何莫學夫詩。詩可以興、可以觀、可以群、可以怨、邇之事父、遠之事君、多識於鳥獸草木之名。

第十章 子謂伯魚曰、女爲周南召南矣乎、人而不爲周南召南、其猶正牆面而立也與。

CHAPTER IX. 1. The Master said, "My children, why do you not study the Book of Poetry?

2. "*The Odes* serve to stimulate the mind.

3. "They may be used for purposes of self-contemplation.

4. "They teach the art of sociability.

5. "They show how to regulate feelings of resentment.

6. "From them you learn the more immediate duty of serving one's father, and the remoter one of serving one's prince.

7. "From them we become largely acquainted with the names of birds, beasts, and plants."

CHAPTER X. The Master said to Pih-yu, "Do you give yourself to the Chow-nan, and the Chaou-nan. The man, who has not studied the Chow-nan and the Chaou-nan, is like one who stands with his face right against a wall. Is he not so?"

9. BENEFITS DERIVED FROM STUDYING THE BOOK OF POETRY. 1. 小子;—see V. 21; VIII. 3. I translate 詩 here by 'the Book of Poetry,' because the lesson is supposed to have been given, after Conf. had completed his compilation of the Odes. The 夫 is *that*, as in XI. 9. 1, *et al.* The descriptions in them of good and evil may have this effect. 3. Their awarding of praise and blame may show a man his own character. 4. Their exhibitions of gravity in the midst of pleasure may have this effect. 羣, as in XV. 21. 5. Their blending of pity and earnest desire with reproofs may teach how to regulate our resentments. 6. 草木, 'grasses and trees,'=plants generally.

10. THE IMPORTANCE OF STUDYING THE CHOW-NAN AND CHAOU-NAN. Chow-nan and Chaou-nan are the titles of the first two Books in the National Songs, or first part of the She-king. For the meaning of the titles, see the She-king, I. i. and I. ii. They are supposed to inculcate important lessons about personal virtue and family-government. Choo He explains 爲 by 學, 'to learn,' 'to study.' It denotes the entire mastery of the studies. 女 (for 汝) 爲云云 is imperative, the 乎 at the end, not being interrogative. 正面牆而立 is for 正面對牆而立. In such a situation, one cannot advance a step, nor see any thing. I have added—'Is he not so?' to bring out the force of the 與.—This chapter in the old editions, is incorporated with the preceding one.

〔十一章〕子曰、禮云禮云、玉帛云乎哉、樂云樂云、鐘鼓云乎哉。

〔十二章〕子曰、色厲而內荏、譬諸小人、其猶穿窬之盜也與。

〔十三章〕子曰、鄉原、德之賊也。

〔十四章〕子曰、道聽而塗說、德之棄也。

CHAPTER XI. The Master said, "'It is according to the rules of propriety,' they say.—'It is according to the rules of propriety,' they say. Are gems and silk all that is meant by propriety? 'It is Music,' they say. 'It is Music,' they say. Are bells and drums all that is meant by Music?"

CHAPTER XII. The Master said, "He who puts on an appearance of stern firmness, while inwardly he is weak, is like one of the small, mean, people;—yea, is he not like the thief who breaks through, or climbs over, a wall?"

CHAPTER XIII. The Master said, "Your good careful people of the villages are the thieves of virtue."

CHAPTER XIV. The Master said, "To tell, as we go along, what we have heard on the way, is to cast away our virtue."

11. IT IS NOT THE EXTERNAL APPURTENANCES WHICH CONSTITUTE PROPRIETY, NOR THE SOUND OF INSTRUMENTS WHICH CONSTITUTES MUSIC. 禮云=所稱爲禮者, 'as to what is called propriety.' The words approach the quotation of a common saying. So 樂云. Having thus given the common views of propriety and music, he refutes them in the questions that follow, 樂 and 禮 being present to the mind as the expressions of respect and harmony.

12. THE MEANNESS OF PRESUMPTION AND PUSILLANIMITY CONJOINED. 色 is here not the countenance merely, but the whole outward appearance. 小人 is explained by 細民, and the latter clause shows emphatically to whom, among the low, mean, people, the individual spoken of is like,—a thief, namely, who is in constant fear of being detected.

13. CONTENTMENT WITH VULGAR WAYS AND VIEWS INJURIOUS TO VIRTUE. See the sentiment of this chapter explained and expanded by Mencius, VII. Pt. II. xxxvii. 7, 8. 原, low. 3d tone, the same as 愿. See the dict., char. 愿. 賊, as in XIV. 46, though it may be translated here, as generally, by the term 'thief.'

14. SWIFTNESS TO SPEAK INCOMPATIBLE WITH THE CULTIVATION OF VIRTUE. It is to be understood that what has been heard contains some good lesson. At once to be talking of it without revolving it, and striving to practise it, shows an indifference to our own improvement. 道 is 'the way' or 'road.' 塗 is the same way, a little farther on.—The glossarist on Ho An's work explains 德之棄 as meaning—'is what the virtuous do not do.' But this is evidently incorrect.

論語

[十五章] [一節] 子曰、鄙夫、可與事君也與哉。[二節] 其未得之也、患得之、既得之、患失之、[三節] 苟患失之、無所不至矣。

[十六章] [一節] 子曰、古者、民有三疾、今也或是之亡也。[二節] 古之狂也肆、今之狂也蕩、古之矜也廉、今之矜也忿戾、古之愚也直、今之愚也詐而已矣。

CHAPTER XV. 1. The Master said, "There are those mean creatures! How impossible it is along with them to serve one's prince!

2. "While they have not got their aims, their anxiety is how to get them. When they have got them, their anxiety is lest they should lose them.

3. "When they are anxious lest such things should be lost, there is nothing to which they will not proceed."

CHAPTER XVI. 1. The Master said, "Anciently, men had three failings, which now perhaps are not to be found.

2. "The high-mindedness of antiquity showed itself in a disregard of small things; the high-mindedness of the present day shows itself in wild license. The stern dignity of antiquity showed itself in grave reserve; the stern dignity of the present day shows itself in quarrelsome perverseness. The stupidity of antiquity showed itself in straightforwardness; the stupidity of the present day shows itself in sheer deceit."

15. THE CASE OF MERCENARY OFFICERS, AND HOW IT IS IMPOSSIBLE TO SERVE ONE'S PRINCE ALONG WITH THEM. 1. 與字作共字看, '與=共,' *i. e.*, 'together with.' 與哉是深慨其不可與意, '與哉=a deep-felt lamentation on the unfitness of such persons to be associated with.' So, the 備旨. But as the remaining paragraphs are all occupied with describing the mercenaries, we must understand Confucius' object as being to condemn the employment of such creatures, rather than to set forth the impossibility of serving with them. 2. The 之 here, and in p. 3, are all to be understood of place and emolument.

16. THE DEFECTS OF FORMER TIMES BECOME VICES IN THE TIME OF CONFUCIUS. 1. 疾, 'bodily sickness,' here used metaphorically for 'errors,' 'vices.' 或是之亡 (*woo*),—'perhaps there is the absence of them.' The next par. shows that worse things had taken their place. 2. That 肆 is only 'a disregard of smaller matters,' or conventionalisms, appears from its opposition to 蕩, which has a more intense signification than in ch. 8. 矜, as in

〔十七章〕子曰、巧言令色鮮矣仁。

〔十八章〕子曰、惡紫之奪朱也、惡鄭聲之亂雅樂也、惡利口之覆邦家者。

〔十九章〕子（一節）曰、予欲無言。（二節）子貢曰、子如不言、則小子何述焉。（三節）子曰、天何言哉、四時行焉、百物生焉、天何言哉。

CHAPTER XVII. The Master said, "Fine words and an insinuating appearance are seldom associated with virtue."

CHAPTER XVIII. The Master said, "I hate the manner in which purple takes away *the lustre of* vermillion. I hate the way in which the songs of Ch'ing confound the music of the Gna. I hate those who with their sharp mouths overthrow kingdoms and families."

CHAPTER XIX. 1. The Master said, "I would prefer not speaking."

2. Tsze-kung said, "If you, Master, do not speak, what shall we, your disciples, have to record?"

3. The Master said, "Does Heaven speak? The four seasons pursue their courses, and all things are *continually* being produced, *but* does Heaven say anything?"

XV. 21, also with an intenser meaning. 廉, 'an angular corner,' which cannot be impinged against without causing pain. It is used for 'purity,' 'modesty,' but the meaning here appears to be that given in the translation.

17. A repetition of I. 3.

18. CONFUCIUS' INDIGNATION AT THE WAY IN WHICH THE WRONG OVERCAME THE RIGHT. 紫之奪朱,—see X. 6, 2. 朱 is here as 'a correct' colour, though it is not among the five such colours mentioned in the note there. 紫 I have here translated—'purple.' 'Black and carnation mixed,' it is said, 'give 紫.' 'The songs or sounds of Ch'ing,'—see XV. 10. 'The nga,'—see on IX. 14. 國家 is a common designation for 'a state,' the 國, or kingdom of the prince, embracing the 家, 'families,' of his great officers.

19. THE ACTIONS OF CONFUCIUS WERE LESSONS AND LAWS, AND NOT HIS WORDS MERELY. Such is the scope of this ch., according to Choo He and his school, The older comm. say that it is a caution to men to pay attention to their conduct rather than to their words. This interpretation is far-fetched, but, on the other hand, it is not easy to defend Conf. from the charge of presumption in comparing himself to Heaven. 3. 天何言哉, 'Does Heaven speak,'—better than 'what does Heaven say?'

論語

二十章 孺悲欲見孔子、孔子辭以疾、將命者出戶、取瑟而歌、使之聞之。

廿一章 一節 宰我問三年之喪、期已久矣。二節 君子三年不爲禮、禮必壞、三年不爲樂、樂必崩。三節 舊穀既沒、新穀既升、鑽燧改火、期可已矣。四節 子曰、食夫稻、衣夫錦、

CHAPTER XX. Joo Pei wished to see Confucius, but Confucius declined, on the ground of being sick, to see him. When the bearer of this message went out at the door, he took his harpsichord, and sang to it, in order that Pei might hear him.

CHAPTER XXI. 1. Tsae Go asked about the three years' mourning *for parents*, *saying* that one year was long enough.

2. "If the superior man," said he, "abstains for three years from the observances of propriety, those observances will be quite lost. If for three years he abstains from music, music will be ruined.

3. "*Within a year*, the old grain is exhausted, and the new grain has sprung up, and, in procuring fire by friction, we go through all the changes of wood for that purpose. After a complete year, the mourning may stop."

4. The Master said, "If you were, *after a year*, to eat good rice, and wear embroidered clothes, would you feel at ease?" "I should," replied Go.

20. HOW CONFUCIUS COULD BE NOT AT HOME, AND YET GIVE INTIMATION TO THE VISITOR OF HIS PRESENCE. Of Joo Pei little is known. He was a man of Loo, and had at one time been in attendance on Confucius to receive his instructions. There must have been some reason—some fault in him—why Conf. would not see him on the occasion in the text, and that he might understand that it was on that account, and not that he was really sick, that he declined his visit, the sage acted as we are told. But what was the necessity for sending a false message in the first place? In the notes to the 儀禮, III. 1, it is said that Joo Pei's fault was in trying to see the master without using the services of an internuncius. 將命者,—see XIV. 47. I translate the last 之 by *him*, but it refers generally to the preceding sentence, and might be left untranslated.

21. THE PERIOD OF THREE YEARS' MOURNING FOR PARENTS; IT MAY NOT ON ANY ACCOUNT BE SHORTENED; THE REASON OF IT. 1. We must understand a 日, either before 三, or, as I prefer, before 期, which is read *ke*, up. 1st tone, the same as 朞, XIII. 10. On the three years' mourning, see the 31st book of the Le-ke. Nominally extending to three years, that period

於女安乎。曰、安。○五節女安、則爲之、夫君子之居喪、食旨不甘、聞樂不樂、居處不安、故不爲也、今女安、則爲之。○六節宰我出。子曰、予之不仁也、子生三年、然後免於父母之懷、夫三年之喪、天下之通喪也、予也、有三年之愛於其父母乎。

5. The Master said, "If you can feel at ease, do it. But a superior man, during the whole period of mourning, does not enjoy pleasant food which he may eat, nor derive pleasure from music which he may hear. He also does not feel at ease, if he is comfortably lodged. Therefore he does not do *what you propose*. But now you feel at ease and may do it."

6. Tsae Go then went out, and the Master said, "This shows Yu's want of virtue. It is not till a child is three years old that it is allowed to leave the arms of its parents. And the three years mourning is universally observed throughout the empire. Did Yu enjoy the three years' affection for his parents?"

comprehended properly but 25 months, and at most 27 months. 2. 此以人事言之,—Tsze-go finds here a reason for his view in the necessity of 'human affairs.' 3. 此以天時言之,—He finds here a reason for his view in 'the seasons of heaven.' 燧 means either 'a piece of metal,'—a speculum,—with which to take fire from the sun, or 'a piece of wood,' with which to get fire by friction or 'boring' (鑽). It has here the latter meaning. Certain woods were assigned to the several seasons, to be employed for this purpose, the elm and willow, for instance to spring, the date and almond trees to summer, &c. 鑽燧改火=鑽燧以取火, 又改乎四時之木, 'In boring with the 燧 to get fire, we have changed from wood to wood through the ones appropriate to the four seasons.' 4. Coarse food and coarse clothing were appropriate, though in varying degree to all the period of mourning. Tsze-go is strangely insensible to the home-put argument of the Master. 稻 is to be understood here as 穀之美者 'the most excellent grain.' The 夫 are demonstrative. 7. 予之不仁也 responds to all that has gone before, and forms a sort of *apodosis*. Conf. added, it is said, the remarks in this par. that they might be reported to Tsae Go, lest he should 'feel at ease' to go and do as he said he could. Still the reason which the Master finds for the statute-period of mourning for parents must be pronounced puerile.

論語

〔二十二章〕子曰、飽食終日、無所用心、難矣哉。不有博奕者乎、爲之、猶賢乎已。

〔二十三章〕子路曰、君子尚勇乎。子曰、君子義以爲上、君子有勇而無義、爲亂、小人有勇而無義、爲盜。

〔二十四章〕一節 子貢曰、君子亦有惡乎。子曰、有惡、惡稱人之惡者、惡居下流而訕上

CHAPTER XXII. The Master said, "Hard is the case of him, who will stuff himself with food the whole day, without applying his mind to anything *good!* Are there not gamesters and chessplayers? To be one of these would still be better than doing nothing at all."

CHAPTER XXIII. Tsze-loo said, "Does the superior man esteem valour?" The Master said, "The superior man holds righteousness to be of highest importance. A man in a superior situation, having valour without righteousness, will be guilty of insubordination; one of the lower people, having valour without righteousness, will commit robbery."

CHAPTER XXIV. 1. Tsze-kung said, "Has the superior man his hatreds also?" The Master said, "He has his hatreds. He hates those who proclaim the evil of others. He hates the man who, being in a low station, slanders his superiors. He hates those who

22. THE HOPELESS CASE OF GLUTTONY AND IDLENESS. 難以哉,—XV. 16. 博 and 弈 are two things. To the former I am unable to give a name; but see some account of it quoted in the 集證 *in loc.* 弈 is 'to play at chess,' of which there are two kinds,—the 圍棋, played with 361 pieces and referred to the emperor Yaou as its inventor, and the 象棋, or ivory chess, played with 32 pieces, and having a great analogy to the European game. Its invention is attributed to the first emperor of the Chow dynasty, though some date its origin a few hundred years later. 爲之,—之 refers to 博弈. 賢, for 勝, as in XI. 15, 1.

23. VALOUR TO BE VALUED ONLY IN SUBORDINATION TO RIGHTEOUSNESS; ITS CONSEQUENCES APART FROM THAT. The first two 君子 are to be understood of the man superior in virtue. The third brings in the idea of rank, with 小人 as its correlate.

24. CHARACTERS DISLIKED BY CONFUCIUS AND TSZE-KUNG. 1. Tsze-kung is understood to have intended Confucius himself by 'the superior man.' 流 is here in the sense of 'class.' 下流=下位之人, 'men of low station.' In 君子亦有惡乎, the force of 亦 is to oppose 惡 to 愛, 'hatreds,' to 'loves.' 2. Hing Ping takes 子貢 as the nominative

者、惡勇而無禮者、惡果敢而窒者。二節曰、賜也、亦有惡乎。惡徼以爲知者、惡不孫以爲勇者、惡訐以爲直者。

〔二十五〕子曰、唯女子與小人、爲難養也、近之則不孫、遠之則怨。

〔二十六〕子曰、年四十而見惡焉、其終也已。

have valour *merely*, and are unobservant of propriety. He hates those who are forward and determined, and, *at the same time*, of contracted understanding."

2. *The Master then* inquired, "Tsze, have you also your hatreds?" *Tsze-kung replied*, "I hate those who pry out matters, and ascribe the knowledge to their wisdom. I hate those who are *only* not modest, and think that they are valorous. I hate those who make known secrets, and think that they are straightforward."

CHAPTER XXV. The Master said, "Of all people, girls and servants are the most difficult to behave to. If you are familiar with them, they lose their humility. If you maintain a reserve towards them, they are discontented."

CHAPTER XXVI. The Master said, "When a man at forty is the object of dislike, he will always continue what he is."

to 曰,—'He went on to say, *I, Tsze, also*,' &c. The modern comm., however, more correctly, understand 子, 'the Master,' as nom. to 曰, and supply another 曰 before 徼,

25. THE DIFFICULTY HOW TO TREAT CONCUBINES AND SERVANTS. 女子 does not mean *women* generally, but girls, *i. e.*, concubines. 小人, in the same way, is here boys, *i. e.*, servants. 養, 'to nourish,' 'to keep,'=to behave to. The force of 唯, 'only,' is as indicated in the translation.

26. THE DIFFICULTY OF IMPROVEMENT IN ADVANCED YEARS. According to Chinese views, at forty a man is at his best in every way. After 惡. we must understand 于君子,—'the object of dislike to the superior man.' 其終=其終于此, 'he will end in this.'—Youth is doubtless the season for improvement, but the sentiment of the chapter is too broadly stated.

BOOK XVIII. WEI TSZE.

微子第十八

第一章 一節 微子去之、箕子為之奴、比干諫而死。二節 孔子曰、殷有三仁焉。

第二章 柳下惠為士師、三黜、人曰、子未可以去乎。曰、直道而事人、焉往而不三黜、枉道而事人、何

CHAPTER I. 1. The viscount of Wei withdrew *from the court.* The viscount of Ke became a slave *to Chow.* Pe-kan remonstrated with him and died.

2. Confucius said, "The Yin dynasty possessed *these* three men of virtue."

CHAPTER II. Hwuy of Lew-hea being chief criminal judge, was thrice dismissed from his office. Some one said to him, "Is it not yet time for you, Sir, to leave this?" He replied, "Serving men in an upright way, where shall I go to, and not experience such a thrice-repeated dismissal? If I choose to serve men in a crooked way, what necessity is there for me to leave the country of my parents?"

HEADING OF THIS BOOK.—微子第十八, 'The viscount of Wei—No. XVIII.' This Book, consisting of only eleven chapters, treats of various individuals famous in Chinese history, as eminent for the way in which they discharged their duties to their sovereign, or for their retirement from public service. It commemorates also some of the worthies of Confucius' days, who lived in retirement rather than be in office in so degenerate times. The object of the whole is to illustrate and vindicate the course of Confucius himself.

1. THE VISCOUNTS OF WEI AND KE, AND PE-KAN:—THREE WORTHIES OF THE YIN DYNASTY. 1. Wei-tsze and Ke-tsze are continually repeated by Chinese, as if they were proper names. But Wei and Ke were the names of two small states, presided over by chiefs of the Tsze, or fourth, degree of nobility, called *viscounts*, for want of a more exact term. They both appear to have been within the limits of the present Shan-se, Wei being referred to the district of 潞城, dep. 潞安, and Ke to 榆社, dep. 遼州. The chief of Wei was an elder brother (by a concubine) of the tyrant Chow, the last emperor of the Yin dynasty, B.C. 1153-1122. The chief of Ke, and Pe-kan, were both uncles of the tyrant. The first, seeing that remonstrances availed nothing, withdrew from court, wishing to preserve the sacrifices of their family, amid the ruin which he saw was impending. The second was thrown into prison, and, to escape death, feigned madness. He was used by Chow as a buffoon. Pe-kan, persisting in his remonstrances, was put barbarously to death, the tyrant having his heart torn out, that he might see, he said, a sage's heart. The 之 in 去之 is explained by 其位, 'his place.' Its reference may also be to 紂, the tyrant himself. On 爲之奴, comp. 爲之宰, V. 7, 3, *et al.*

2. HOW HWUY OF LEW-HEA, THOUGH OFTEN DISMISSED FROM OFFICE, STILL CLAVE TO HIS COUNTRY. Lew-hea Hwuy,—see XV. 13. The office of the 士師 is described in the Chow-

必去父母之邦。

第三章 齊景公待孔子、曰、若季氏、則吾不能、以季孟之閒待之。曰、吾老矣、不能用也。孔子行。

第四章 齊人歸女樂。季桓子受之、三日不朝、孔子行。

第五章 一節 楚狂接輿歌而過

CHAPTER III. The duke King of Ts'e, *with reference to the manner in which* he should treat Confucius, said, "I cannot treat him as I would the chief of the Ke family. I will treat him in a manner between that accorded to the chief of the Ke, and that given to the chief of the Măng family." He *also* said, "I am old; I cannot use *his doctrines.*" Confucius took his departure.

CHAPTER IV. The people of Ts'e sent *to Loo* a present of female musicians, which Ke Hwan received, and for three days no court was held. Confucius took his departure.

CHAPTER V. 1. The madman of Ts'oo, Tsëĕ-yu, passed by Confucius, singing and saying, "Oh FUNG! Oh FUNG! How is your

le, XXXIV. 3. He was under the 司寇, or minister of Crime, but with many subordinate magistrates under him. 三, up. 3d tone, as in V. 19, XI. 5. We may translate 黜, 'was dismissed from office,' or 'retired from office.' 人=或人.—Some remarks akin to that in the text are ascribed to Hwuy's wife. It is observed by the commentator Hoo (胡), that there ought to be another paragraph, giving Conf. judgment upon Hwuy's conduct, but it has been lost.

3. HOW CONFUCIUS LEFT TS'E, WHEN THE DUKE COULD NOT APPRECIATE AND EMPLOY HIM. It was in the year B. C. 516, that Confucius went to Ts'e. The remarks about how he should be treated, &c., are to be understood as having taken place in consultation between the duke and his ministers, and being afterwards reported to the sage. The Măng family (see II. 5) was in the time of Conf., much weaker than the Ke. The chief of it was only the 下卿, lowest noble of Loo, while the Ke was the highest. Yet for the duke of Ts'e to treat Conf. better than the duke of Loo treated the chief of the Măng family, was not dishonouring the sage. We must suppose that Conf. left Ts'e, because of the duke's concluding remarks.

4. HOW CONFUCIUS GAVE UP OFFICIAL SERVICE IN LOO. In the 14th year of the duke Ting, Conf. reached the highest point of his official service. He was minister of crime, and also, acc. to the general opinion, acting premier. He effected in a few months a wonderful renovation of the State, and the neighbouring countries began to fear that under his administration, Loo would overtop and subdue them all. To prevent this, the duke of Ts'e sent a present to Loo of fine horses and of 80 highly accomplished beauties. The duke of Loo was induced to receive these by the advice of the head of the Ke family, Ke Sze (斯), or Ke Hwan. The sage was forgotten; government was neglected. Confucius, indignant and sorrowful, withdrew from office, and for a time, from the country too. 歸 as in XVII. 1, 1. 齊人, 'the people of Ts'e is to be understood of the duke and his ministers.

5. CONFUCIUS AND THE MADMAN OF TS'OO, WHO BLAMES HIS NOT RETIRING FROM THE WORLD. 1. Ts'ëĕ-yu was the designation of one Luh T'ung

論語

孔子、曰、鳳兮鳳兮、何德之衰、往者不可諫、來者猶可追、已而已而、今之從政者殆而。(二節)孔子下、欲與之言。趨而辟之、不得與之言。

(第六章)長沮桀溺耦而耕。孔子過之、使子路問津焉。(二節)長沮曰、夫執輿者爲誰。子路曰、爲孔丘。曰、是魯孔丘與。曰、是也。曰、是知津矣。(三節)問於桀

virtue degenerated! As to the past, reproof is useless; but the future maybe provided against. Give up *your vain pursuit.* Give up *your vain pursuit.* Peril awaits those who now engage in affairs of government."

2. Confucius alighted and wished to converse with him, but *Tsëë-yu* hastened away, so that he could not talk with him.

CHAPTER VI. 1. Ch'ang-tseu and Këë-neih were at work in the field together, when Confucius passed by them, and sent Tsze-loo to enquire for the ford.

2. Ch'ang-tseu said, "Who is he that holds the reins in the carriage there?" Tsze-loo told him, "It is K'ung K'ew." "Is it not K'ung K'ew of Loo?" asked he. "Yes," was the reply, to which the other rejoined, "He knows the ford."

3. *Tsze-loo then* enquired of Këë-neih, who said to him, "Who are you, Sir?" HE answered, "I am Chung Yew." "Are you

(陸通), a native of Ts'oo, who feigned himself mad, to escape being importuned to engage in public service. There are several notices of him in the 集澄, *in loc.* It must have been about the year, B. C. 489, that the incident in the text occurred. By the *fung*, his satirizer or adviser intended Confucius; see IX. 8. The three 而 in the song are simply expletives, pauses for the voice to help out the rhythm. 追, 'to overtake,' generally with reference to the past, but here it has reference to the future. In the dict., with reference to this passage, it is explained by 及, 'to come up to,' and 救, 'to save,'=to provide against.

6. CONFUCIUS AND THE TWO RECLUSES, CH'ANG-TSEU AND KEE-NEIH; WHY HE WOULD NOT WITHDRAW FROM THE WORLD. 1. The surnames and names of these worthies are not known. It is supposed that they belonged to Ts'oo, like the hero of the last chapter, and that the interview with them occurred about the same time. The designations in the text are descriptive of their character and='the long Rester (沮者止而不出),' and 'the firm Recluse (溺者沉而不返).' What kind of field labour is

溺。桀溺曰。子爲誰。曰、爲仲由。曰、是魯孔丘之徒與。對曰、然。曰、滔滔者、天下皆是也、而誰以易之、且而與其從辟人之士也、豈若從辟世之士哉。耰而不輟。四節 子路行以告。夫子憮然曰、鳥獸不可與同群、吾非斯人之徒與而誰與、天下有道、丘不與易也。

not the disciple of K'ung K'ew of Loo?" asked the other. "I am," replied he, and then Keĕ-neih said to him, "Disorder, like a swelling flood, spreads over the whole empire, and who is he that will change it *for you?* Than follow one who merely withdraws from this one and that one, had you not better follow those who have withdrawn from the world altogether?" *With this* he fell to covering up the seed, *and proceeded with his work*, without stopping.

4. Tsze-loo went and reported their remarks, when his master observed with a sigh, "It is impossible to associate with birds and beasts, as if they were the same with us. If I associate not with these people,—with mankind,—with whom shall I associate? If right principles prevailed through the empire, there would be no use for me to change its state."

here denoted by 耕 cannot be determined. 2. 執輿者, 'he who holds the carriage,'=執轡在車者, as in the transl. It is supposed that it was the remarkable appearance of Confucius, which elicited the inquiry. In 是知津, 是='*he*;' *i. e.*, he, going about every where, and seeking to be employed, ought to know the ford. 3. 滔滔者天下,—the speaker here probably pointed to the surging waters before them, for the ford to cross which the travellers were asking. Translating literally, we should say—'swelling and surging, such is all the empire.' 且而,—而=汝, 'you.' 辟人,辟世,—comp. XIV. 39. 耰, 'an implement for drawing the soil over the seed.' It may have been a hoe, or a rake. 4. 徒 is here=類, 'class.' 吾非斯人之徒與而誰與,='If I am not to associate with the class of these men, *i. e.*, with mankind, with whom am I to associate? I cannot associate with birds and beasts.' 丘不與易,—不與, it is said, 作無用,—'there would be no use.' Literally, 'I should not have for whom to change *the state of the empire.*'—The use of 夫子 in this paragraph is remarkable. It must mean 'his Master' and not 'the Master.' The compiler of this chapter can hardly have been a disciple of the sage.

第七章 一節 子路從而後、遇丈人、以杖荷蓧。子路問曰、子見夫子乎。丈人曰、四體不勤、五穀不分、孰爲夫子。植其杖而耘。二節 子路拱而立。三節 止子路宿、殺鷄、爲黍、而食之、見其二子焉。四節 明日、子路行以告。子曰、隱者也、使子路反見之、至、則行矣。五節 子路曰、不仕

CHAPTER VII. 1. Tsze-loo, following the Master, happened to fall behind, when he met an old man, carrying, across his shoulder on a staff, a basket for weeds. Tsze-loo said to him, "Have you seen my master, Sir!" The old man replied, "Your four limbs are unaccustomed to toil; you cannot distinguish the five kinds of grain:—who is your master?" With this, he planted his staff in the ground, and proceeded to weed.

2. Tsze-loo joined his hands across his breast, and stood *before him.*

3. The old man kept Tsze-loo to pass the night in his house, killed a fowl, prepared millet, and feasted him. He also introduced to him his two sons.

4. Next day, Tsze-loo went on his way, and reported *his adventure.* The Master said, "He is a recluse," and sent Tsze-loo back to see him again, but, when he got to the place, the old man was gone.

7. TSZE-LOO'S RENCONTRE WITH AN OLD MAN, A RECLUSE: HIS VINDICATION OF HIS MASTER'S COURSE. This incident in this chapter was probably nearly contemporaneous with those which occupy the two previous ones. Some say that the old man belonged to Shĕ, which was a part of Ts'oo. 1. 後, as in XI. 22, 顔淵後. 丈人 is used for 'an old man,' as early as in the Yih-king, dia. 師. How the phrase comes to have that signification, I have not discovered. 蓧 is simply called by Choo He—竹器, 'a bamboo basket.' The 說文 defines it as in the translation'—芸田器. 四體, 'the four bodies,' *i. e.*, the arms and legs, the four limbs of the body. 'The five grains' are 稻, 黍, 稷, 麥, and 菽, 'rice, millet, panicled millet, wheat, and pulse.' But they are sometimes otherwise enumerated. We have also 'the six kinds,' 'the eight kinds,' 'the nine kinds,' and perhaps other classifications. 2. Tsze-loo, standing with his arms across his breast, indicated his respect, and won upon the old man. 3, 食, *tsze*, low. 3d tone, 'entertained,' 'feasted.' The dict. defines it with this meaning, 以食與人, 'to give food to people.' 5. Tsze-loo is to be understood as here speaking the sentiments of the Master, and vindicating his course. 長幼之節 refers to the manner in which the old man had introduced his sons to him the evening before, and to all the orderly intercourse between old and

無義、長幼之節、不可廢也、君臣之義、如之何其廢之、欲潔其身、而亂大倫、君子之仕也、行其義也、道之不行、已知之矣。

第八章 逸一節民、伯夷、叔齊、虞仲、夷逸、朱張、柳下惠、少連。二節子曰、不降其志、不辱其身、伯夷叔齊與。三節謂柳下惠少連、降志辱身矣、言

5. Tsze-loo then said *to the family*, "Not to take office is not righteous. If the relations between old and young may not be neglected, how is it that he sets aside the duties that should be observed between sovereign and minister? Wishing to maintain his personal purity, he allows that great relation to come to confusion. A superior man takes office, and performs the righteous duties belonging to it. As to the failure of right principles to make progress, he is aware of that."

CHAPTER VIII. 1. The men who have retired to privacy from the world have been Pih-e, Shŭh-ts'e, Yu-chung, E-yih, Choo-chang, Hwuy of Lew-hea, and Shaou-lëen.

2. The Master said, "Refusing to surrender their wills, or to submit to any taint in their persons;—such, I think, were Pih-e and Shuh-ts'e.

young, which he had probably seen in the family. 何其廢之,—其 refers to the old man, but there is an indefiniteness about the Chinese construction, which does not make it so personal as our 'he.' So Confucius is intended by 君子, though that phrase may be taken in its general acceptation. 'He is aware of that;'—but will not therefore shrink from his righteous service.

8. CONFUCIUS' JUDGMENT OF FORMER WORTHIES WHO HAD KEPT FROM THE WORLD. HIS OWN GUIDING PRINCIPLE. 1. 逸民,—'retired people.' 民 is used here just as we sometimes use *people*, without reference to the rank of the individuals spoken of. The 備旨 quotes, upon the phrase, from the 說統, to the following effect:—'逸 here is not the 逸 of seclusion, but is characteristic of men of large souls, who cannot be measured by ordinary rules. They may display their character by retiring from the world. They may display it also in the manner of their discharge of office.' The phrase is guarded in this way, I suppose, because of its application to Hwuy of Lew-hea, who did not obstinately withdraw from the world. Pih-e, and Shuh-ts'e,—see V. 22. Yu-chung should probably be Woo (吳)-chung. He was the brother of T'ae-pih, called Chung-yung (仲雍), and is mentioned in the note on VIII. 1. He retired with T'ae-pih among the barbarous tribes, then occupying the country of Woo, and succeeded to the chieftaincy of them on his brother's death. 'E-yih and Choo-chang,' says Choo He, 'are not found in

中倫、行中慮、其斯而已矣。四節謂虞仲夷逸、隱居放言、身中淸、廢中權。五節我則異於是、無可無不可。

第九章 一節大師摯適齊。二節亞飯干適楚。三飯繚適蔡。四飯缺適秦。三節鼓方叔、

3. "It may be said of Hwuy of Lew-hea, and of Shaou-lëën, that they surrendered their wills, and submitted to taint in their persons, but their words corresponded with reason, and their actions were such as men are anxious to see. This is all that is to be remarked in them.

4. "It may be said of Yu-chung and E-yih, that, while they hid themselves in their seclusion, they gave a license to their words, but, in their persons, they succeeded in preserving their purity, and, in their retirement, they acted according to the exigency of the times.

5. "I am different from all these. I have no course for which I am predetermined, and no course against which I am predetermined."

Chapter IX. 1. The grand music-master, Che, went to Ts'e. Kan, *the master of the band at* the second meal, went to Ts'oo. Leaou, *the band-master at* the third meal, went to Ts'ae. Keuĕh, *the band-master* at the fourth meal, went to Ts'in.

2. Fang-shuh, the drum-master, withdrew to *the north of* the river. Woo, the master of the hand-drum, withdrew to the Han.

the *king* and *chuen* (經傳).' See, however, the 集證, *in loc.* From a passage in the Le-ke, XXI. i. 14, it appears that Shaou-lëën belonged to one of the barbarous tribes on the east, but was well acquainted with, and observant of, the rules of Propriety, particularly those relating to mourning. 3. The 謂, at the beginning of this paragraph and the next, are very perplexing. As there is neither 謂 nor 曰 at the beginning of par. 5, the 子曰 of p. 2 must evidently be carried on to the end of the chapter. Commentators do not seem to have felt the difficulty, and understand 謂 to be in the 3d pers.—'He, *i. e.*, the master, said,' &c. I have made the best of it I could. 倫＝義理之次第, 'the order and series of righteousness and principles.' 慮＝人心之思慮, 'the thoughts and solicitudes of men's hearts.' 4. 'Living in retirement, they gave a license to their words,'—this is intended to show that in this respect they were inferior to Hwuy and Shaou-lëën, who 言中倫. 權,—see note on IX. 29. 5. Confucius' openness to act according to circumstances is to be understood as being always in subordination to right and propriety.

9. The dispersion of the musicians of Loo. The dispersion here narrated is supposed to have taken place in the time of duke Gae. When once Confucius had rectified the music of Loo (IX. 14), the musicians would no longer be assisting in the prostitution of their art, and so, as the disorganization and decay proceeded, the chief among them withdrew to other countries, or from society altogether. 1. 大＝太, as opposed to 少, p. 5, 'grand,' and 'assistant.' 'The music-master, Che,'—see VIII. 15. 2. The princes of China, it would appear, had music at their meals, and a separate band performed at each meal, or, possibly, the band might be the same, but under the superintendence of a separate officer at each meal. The emperor had four meals a day, and the princes of States only three, but it was the prerogative of the duke of Loo to use the ceremonies of

入於河。四節播鼗武、入於漢。五節少師陽、擊磬襄、入於海。

第十章周公謂魯公曰、君子不施其親、不使大臣怨乎不以、故舊無大故、則不棄也、無求備於一人。

第十一章周有八士、伯達、伯适、仲突、仲忽、叔夜、叔夏、季隨、季騧。

Yang, the assistant music-master, and Seang, master of the musical stone, withdrew to *an island in* the sea."

CHAPTER X. The duke of Chow addressed *his son*, the duke of Loo, saying, "The virtuous prince does not neglect his relations. He does not cause the great ministers to repine at his not employing them. Without some great cause, he does not dismiss from their offices the members of old families. He does not seek in one man talents for every employment."

CHAPTER XI. To Chow belonged the eight officers, Pih-tă, Pih-kwŏh, Chung-tŭh, Chung-hwŭh, Shuh-yay, Shuh-hea, Ke-suy, and Ke-kwa.

the imperial household. Nothing is said here of the bandmaster at the first meal, perhaps because he did not leave Loo, or nothing may have been known of him. 3. 'The River' is of course 'the Yellow River.' According to the 四書釋地, art LVI, the expressions 入於河, 入於漢, are to be taken as meaning simply,—'lived on the banks of the Ho, the Han.' The interpr. in the translation is after Choo He, who follows the glossarist Hing Ping. The ancient emperors had their capitals mostly north and east of 'the River, hence, the country north of it was called 河內, and to the south of it was called 河外. I don't see, however, the applicability of this, to the Han, which is a tributary of the Yang-tsze, flowing through Hoo-pih. 5. It was from Sëang that Confucius learned to play on the 琴.

10. INSTRUCTIONS OF CHOW-KUNG TO HIS SON ABOUT GOVERNMENT; A GENEROUS CONSIDERATION OF OTHERS TO BE CHERISHED. 周公,—see VI. 5. The facts of the case seem to be that the duke of Chow was himself appointed to the principality of Loo, but being detained at court by his duties to the young emperor 成, he sent his son 伯禽, here called 'the duke of Loo,' to that state as his representative. 君子 contains here the ideas both of rank and virtue. 施 is read in the up. 2d tone, with the same meaning as 弛. Choo He, indeed, seems to think that 弛 should be in the text, but we have 施 in Ho An, who gives K'ung Gan-kwŏ's interpretation:—施易也, 不以他人之親易已之親, '施 is *to change*. He does not substitute the relatives of other men in the room of his own relatives.' 以,—here=用, 'to use,' 'to employ.' 求備,—see XIII. 25.

11. THE FRUITFULNESS OF THE EARLY TIME OF THE CHOW DYNASTY IN ABLE OFFICERS. The eight individuals mentioned here are said to have been brothers, four pairs of twins by the same mother. This is intimated in their names, the two first being 伯, or *primi*, the next pair 仲, or *secundi*, the third 叔, or *tertii*, and the last two 季. One mother, bearing twins four times in succession, and all proving distinguished men, showed the vigour of the early days of the dynasty in all that was good.—It is disputed to what reign these brothers belonged, nor is their surname ascertained. 達, 适, 突, 忽, seem to be honorary designations.

BOOK XIX. TSZE-CHANG.

子張第十九

〔一〕子張曰、士、見危致命、見得思義、祭思敬、喪思哀、其可已矣。

〔二〕子張曰、執德不弘、信道不篤、焉能爲有、焉能爲亡。

CHAPTER I. Tsze-chang said, "The scholar, *trained for public duty*, seeing threatening danger, is prepared to sacrifice his life. When the opportunity of gain is presented to him, he thinks of righteousness. In sacrificing, his thoughts are reverential. In mourning, his thoughts are about the grief *which he should feel*. Such a man commands our approbation indeed."

CHAPTER II. Tsze-chang said, "When a man holds fast virtue, but without seeking to enlarge it, and believes right principles, but without firm sincerity, what account can be made of his existence or non-existence?"

HEADING OF THIS BOOK.—子張第十九, 'Tsze-chang—No. XIX.' Confucius does not appear personally in this Book at all. Choo He says:—'This Book records the words of the disciples, Tsze-hea being the most frequent speaker, and Tsze-kung next to him. For in the Confucian school, after Yen Yuen there was no one of such discriminating understanding as Tsze-kung, and, after Tsăng Sin no one of such firm sincerity as Tsze-hea.' The disciples deliver their sentiments very much after the manner of their master, and yet we can discern a falling off from him.

1. TSZE-CHANG'S OPINION OF THE CHIEF ATTRIBUTES OF THE TRUE SCHOLAR. 士,—see note on XII. 20, 1. Tsze-chang there asks Confucius about the scholar-officer. 見危,—the danger is to be understood as threatening his country. Hing Ping, indeed, confines the danger to the person of the sovereign, for whom the officer will gladly sacrifice his life. 致命 is the same as 致其身 in I. 7. 已 is not to be explained by 止, as in 而已. The combination 已矣 has occurred before, and=也已 in I. 14. It greatly intensifies the preceding 可.

2. TSZE-CHANG ON NARROW-MINDEDNESS AND A HESITATING FAITH. Hing Ping interprets this chapter in the following way:—'If a man grasp hold of his virtue, and is not widened and

第三章 子夏之門人問交於子張。子張曰、子夏云何。對曰、子夏曰、可者與之、其不可者拒之。子張曰、異乎吾所聞、君子尊賢而容衆、嘉善而矜不能、我之大賢與、於人何所不容、我之不賢與、人將拒我、如之何其拒人也。

第四章 子夏曰、雖小道、必有

CHAPTER III. The disciples of Tsze-hea asked Tsze-chang about the principles of intercourse. Tsze-chang asked, "What does Tsze-hea say on the subject?" They replied, "Tsze-hea says:—'Associate with those who can *advantage you.* Put away from you those who cannot *do so.*' Tsze-chang observed, "This is different from what I have learned. The superior man honours the talented and virtuous, and bears with all. He praises the good, and pities the incompetent. Am I possessed of great talents and virtue?—who is there among men whom I will not bear with? Am I devoid of talents and virtue?—men will put me away from them. What have we to do with the putting away of others?"

CHAPTER IV. Tsze-hea said, "Even in inferior studies and employments there is something worth being looked at, but if it be

enlarged by it, although he may believe good principles, he cannot be sincere and generous.' But it is better to take the clauses as coordinate, and not dependent on each other. With 執德不弘 we may compare XV. 28, which suggests the taking 弘 actively. The two last clauses are perplexing. Choo He, after Gankwŏ apparently, makes them equivalent to—'is of no consideration in the world' (猶言不足輕重).

3. THE DIFFERENT OPINIONS OF TSZE-HEA AND TSZE-CHANG ON THE PRINCIPLES WHICH SHOULD REGULATE OUR INTERCOURSE WITH OTHERS. On the disciples of Tsze-hea, see the 集證, *in loc.* It is strange to me that they should begin their answer to Tsze-chang with the designation 子夏, instead of saying 夫子, 'our Master.' 交,—see V. 16. In 可者不可者, the 可 is taken differently by the old interpreters and the new. Hing Ping expounds:—'If the man be worthy, fit for you to have intercourse with, then have it, but if he be not worthy,' &c. On the other hand, we find:—'If the man will advantage you, he is a fit person (是可者); then maintain intercourse with him,' &c. This seems to be merely carrying out Confucius' rule, I. 8, 3. Choo He, however, approves of Tsze-chang's censure of it, while he thinks also that Tsze-chang's own view is defective.—Paou Heen says.—'Our intercourse with friends should be according to Tsze-hea's rule; general intercourse according to Tsze-chang's.'

4. TSZE-HEA'S OPINION OF THE INAPPLICABILITY OF SMALL PURSUITS TO GREAT OBJECTS. Gardening, husbandry, divining, and the healing art, are all mentioned by Choo He as in-

可觀者焉、致遠恐泥、是以君子不爲也。

第五章 子夏曰、日知其所亡、月無忘其所能、可謂好學也已矣。

第六章 子夏曰、博學而篤志、切問而近思、仁在其中矣。

第七章 子夏曰、百工居肆、以成其事、君子學以致其道。

attempted to carry them out to what is remote, there is a danger of their proving inapplicable. Therefore, the superior man does not practise them."

CHAPTER V. Tsze-hea said, "He, who from day to day recognizes what he has not yet, and from month to month does not forget what he has attained to, may be said indeed to love to learn."

CHAPTER VI. Tsze-hea said, "There are learning extensively, and having a firm and sincere aim; inquiring with earnestness, and reflecting with self-application:—virtue is in such a course."

CHAPTER VII. Tsze-hea said, "Mechanics have their shops to dwell in, in order to accomplish their works. The superior man learns, in order to reach to the utmost of his principles."

stances of the 小道, 'small ways,' here intended, having their own truth in them, but not available for higher purposes, or what is beyond themselves. 致 is imperative and emphatic,=推極, 'push them to an extreme.' What is intended by 遠, is the far-reaching object of the *Keun-tsze*, 'to cultivate himself and regulate others.' 泥, lower 3d tone, explained in the dict. by 滯, 'water impeded.'—Ho An makes the 小道 to be 異端, 'strange principles.'

5. THE INDICATIONS OF A REAL LOVE OF LEARNING:—BY TSZE-HEA.

6. HOW LEARNING SHOULD BE PURSUED TO LEAD TO VIRTUE:—BY TSZE-HEA. K'ung Gan-kwŏ explains 志 as if it were 識, 'to remember.' On 切問而近思, the 備旨 says—所問, 皆切已之事, 所思, 皆身心之要, 'what are inquired about are things essential to one's self; what are thought about are the important personal duties.' Probably it is so, but all this cannot be put in a translation. On 近思, comp. VII. 28, 4. 仁在其中,—comp. VII. 15; XIII. 18.

7. LEARNING IS THE STUDENT'S WORKSHOP:—BY TSZE-HEA. 肆 is here 所以陳貨鬻之物, 'a place for the display and sale of goods.' A certain quarter was assigned anciently in Chinese towns and cities for mecha-

第八章 子夏曰、小人之過也、必文。

第九章 子夏曰、君子有三變、望之儼然、卽之也溫、聽其言也厲。

第十章 子夏曰、君子信而後勞其民、未信、則以爲厲己也、信而後諫、未信、則以爲謗己也。

十一章 子夏曰、大德不踰閑、

CHAPTER VIII. Tsze-hea said, "The mean man is sure to gloss his faults."

CHAPTER IX. Tsze-hea said, "The superior man undergoes three changes. Looked at from a distance, he appears stern; when approached, he is mild; when he is heard to speak, his language is firm and decided."

CHAPTER X. Tsze-hea said, "The superior man, having obtained their confidence, may then impose labours on his people. If he have not gained their confidence, they will think that he is oppressing them. Having obtained the confidence *of his prince*, he may then remonstrate with him. If he have not gained his confidence, *the prince* will think that he is vilifying him."

CHAPTER XI. Tsze-hea said, "When a person does not transgress the boundary-line in the great virtues, he may pass and repass it in the small virtues."

nics, and all of one art were required to have their shops together. A son must follow his father's profession, and, seeing nothing but the exercise of that around him, it was supposed that he would not be led to think of anything else, and become very proficient in it.

8. GLOSSING HIS FAULTS THE PROOF OF THE MEAN MAN:—BY TSZE-HEA. Lit., 'The faults of the mean man, must gloss,' *i. e.*, *he* is sure to gloss. 文, in this sense, a verb, low. 3d tone.

9. CHANGING APPEARANCES OF THE SUPERIOR MAN TO OTHERS:—BY TSZE-HEA. Tsze-hea probably intended Confucius by the *Keun-tsze*, but there is a general applicability in his language and sentiments. 望之, 卽之,—lit., 'look towards him,' 'approach him.'—The description is about equivalent to our '*fortiter in re, suaviter in modo.*'

10. THE IMPORTANCE OF ENJOYING CONFIDENCE TO THE RIGHT SERVING OF SUPERIORS AND ORDERING OF INFERIORS:—BY TSZE-HEA. Choo He gives to 信 here the double meaning of 'being sincere,' and 'being believed in.' The last is the proper force of the term, but it requires the possession of the former quality.

11. THE GREAT VIRTUES DEMAND THE CHIEF ATTENTION, AND THE SMALL ONES MAY BE SOMEWHAT VIOLATED:—BY TSZE-HEA. The sentiment here is very questionable. A different turn however, is given to the chapter in the older interpreters. Hing Ping, expanding K'ung Gan-kwŏ says:—'Men of great virtue never go beyond the boundary-line; it is enough for those who are virtuous in a less degree to keep near to it, going beyond and coming back.' We adopt the more natural interpretation of

小德出入可也。

〔十二章〕一節子游曰、子夏之門人小子、當洒掃、應對、進退、則可矣、抑末也、本之則無、如之何。二節子夏聞之曰、噫、言游過矣、君子之道、孰先傳焉、孰後倦焉、譬諸草木、區以別矣、君子之道、焉可誣也、有始有卒者、其惟聖人乎。

CHAPTER XII. 1. Tsze-yew said, "The disciples and followers of Tsze-hea, in sprinkling and sweeping the ground, in answering and replying, in advancing and receding, are sufficiently accomplished. But these are only the branches *of learning*, and they are left ignorant of what is essential.—How can they be acknowledged as sufficiently taught?"

2. Tsze-hea heard of the remark and said, "Alas! Yen Yew is wrong. According to the way of the superior man *in teaching*, what departments are there which he considers of prime importance, and delivers? what are there which he considers of secondary importance, and allows himself to be idle about? *But* as in the case of plants, which are assorted according to their classes, *so he deals with his disciples.* How can the way of a superior man be such as to make fools of *any of* them? Is it not the sage alone, who can unite in one the beginning and the consummation *of learning?*"

Choo He. 閑, 'a piece of wood, in a doorway, obstructing ingress and egress;' then, 'an inclosure' generally, 'a railing,' whatever limits and confines.

12. TSZE-HEA'S DEFENCE OF HIS OWN GRADUATED METHOD OF TEACHING:—AGAINST TSZE-YEW. 1. 小子 is to be taken in apposition with 門人, being merely, as we have found it previously, an affectionate method of speaking of the disciples. The sprinkling, &c., are the things which boys were supposed anciently to be taught, the rudiments of learning, from which they advanced to all that is inculcated in the 大學. But as Tsze-hea's pupils were not boys, but men, we should understand, I suppose, these specifications as but a contemptuous reference to his instructions, as embracing merely what was external. 洒, read *shae* and *sha*, up. 1st tone, 'to sprinkle the ground before sweeping.' 應, upper 3d tone, 'to answer a call.' 對, 'to answer a question.' 抑='but,' as in VII. 33. 本之 is expanded by the paraphrasts —若本之所在, 'as to that in which the root (or, what is essential) is.' This is, no doubt, the meaning, but the phrase itself is abrupt and enigmatical. 如之何=如之何其可哉, in opposition to the 則可矣 above. 2. The general scope of Tsze-hea's reply is sufficiently plain, but the old interpreters and new differ in explaining the several sentences. After dwelling long on it, I have agreed generally

〔十三章〕子夏曰、仕而優則學、學而優則仕。

〔十四章〕子游曰、喪致乎哀而止。

〔十五章〕子游曰、吾友張也、爲難能也、然而未仁。

〔十六章〕曾子曰、堂堂乎張也、難與並爲仁矣。

〔十七章〕曾子曰、吾聞諸夫子、人未有自致者也、必也親喪乎。

CHAPTER XIII. Tsze-hea said, "The officer, *having discharged all his duties*, should devote his leisure to learning. The student, having completed his learning, should apply himself to be an officer."

CHAPTER XIV. Tsze-hea said, "Mourning, having been carried to the utmost degree of grief, should stop with that."

CHAPTER XV. Tsze-hea said, "My friend Chang can do things which are hard to be done, but yet he is not perfectly virtuous."

CHAPTER XVI. The philosopher Tsăng said, "How imposing is the manner of Chang! It is difficult along with him to practise virtue."

CHAPTER XVII. The philosopher Tsăng said, "I heard this from our Master:—'Men may not have shown what is in them to the full extent, and yet they will be found to do so, on occasion of mourning for their parents.'"

with the new school, and followed Choo He in the translation. 區 is explained in the dict. by 類, 'classes.'

13. THE OFFICER AND THE STUDENT SHOULD ATTEND EACH TO HIS PROPER WORK IN THE FIRST INSTANCE:—BY TSZE-YEW. 優＝有餘力, in I. 6.—The saying needs to be much supplemented in translating, in order to bring out its meaning.

14. THE TRAPPINGS OF MOURNING MAY BE DISPENSED WITH:—BY TSZE-YEW. The sentiment here is perhaps the same as that of Confucius in III. 4, but the sage guards and explains his utterance.—K'ung Gan kwŏ, following an expression in the 孝經, makes the meaning to be that the mourner may not endanger his health or life by excessive grief and abstinence.

15. TSZE-YEW'S OPINION OF TSZE-CHANG, AS MINDING TOO MUCH HIGH THINGS.

16. THE PHILOSOPHER TSANG'S OPINION OF TSZE-CHANG, AS TOO HIGH-PITCHED FOR FRIENDSHIP. 堂堂 is explained in the dict. by 盛也, 正也, 'exuberant,' 'correct.' It is to be understood of Chang's manner and appearance, keeping himself aloof from other men in his high-pitched course.

17. HOW GRIEF FOR THE LOSS OF PARENTS BRINGS OUT THE REAL NATURE OF MAN: BY TSANG SIN. 自 is said to indicate the ideas both of 自已, 'one's self,' and 自然 'naturally.' 自致, 'to put one's self out to the utmost,'

十八章 曾子曰、吾聞諸夫子、孟莊子之孝也、其他可能也、其不改父之臣、與父之政、是難能也。

十九章 孟氏使陽膚爲士師、問於曾子。曾子曰、上失其道、民散久矣、如得其情、則哀矜而勿喜。

二十章 子貢曰、紂之不善、不如是之甚也、是以君子

CHAPTER XVIII. The philosopher Tsăng said, "I have heard this from our Master:—'The filial piety of Măng Chwang, in other matters, was what other men are competent to, but, as seen in his not changing the ministers of his father, nor his father's mode of government, it is difficult to be attained to.'"

CHAPTER XIX. The chief of the Măng family having appointed Yang Foo to be chief criminal judge, the latter consulted the philosopher Tsăng. Tsăng said, "The rulers have failed in their duties, and the people consequently been disorganized, for a long time. When you have found out the truth *of any accusation*, be grieved for and pity them, and do not feel joy *at your own ability*."

CHAPTER XX. Tsze-kung said, "Chow's wickedness was not so great *as that name implies*. Therefore, the superior man hates to

as we should say—'to come out fully,' *i. e.*, in one's proper nature and character. On the construction of 必也,親喪乎, comp. XII. 13. 吾聞諸夫子—諸 seems to=之, *it*, so that 諸 and 夫子 are like two objectives, both governed by 聞.

18. THE FILIAL PIETY OF MANG CHWANG:—BY TSANG SIN. Chwang was the honorary epithet of Suh (速), the head of the Măng family, not long anterior to Confucius. His father, acc. to Choo He, had been a man of great merit, nor was he inferior to him, but his virtue especially appeared in what the text mentions.—Ho An gives the comment of Ma Yung, that though there were bad men among his father's ministers, and defects in his government, yet Chwang made no change in the one or the other, during the three years of mourning, and that it was this which constituted his excellence.

19. HOW A CRIMINAL JUDGE SHOULD CHERISH COMPASSION IN HIS ADMINISTRATION OF JUSTICE:—BY TSANG SIN. Seven disciples of Tsăng Sin are more particularly mentioned, one of them being this Yang Foo. 散 is to be understood of the moral state of the people, and not, physically, of their being scattered from their dwellings. 情 has occurred before in the sense of—'the truth,' which it has here.

20. THE DANGER OF A BAD NAME:—BY TSZE-KUNG. 如是之甚, 'so very bad as this;'—the *this* (是) is understood by Hing Ping as referring to the epithet—紂, which cannot be called honorary in this instance. According to the laws for such terms, it means—殘忍損

惡居下流、天下之惡皆歸焉。

二十一章 子貢曰、君子之過也、如日月之食焉、過也、人皆見之、更也、人皆仰之。

二十二章 一節 衛公孫朝問於子貢曰、仲尼焉學。二節 子貢曰、文武之道、未墜於地、在人、賢者識其大者、不賢者識其小者、莫不有文武之道焉、夫子焉不學、而亦何常師之有、

dwell in a low-lying situation, where all the evil of the world will flow in upon him."

CHAPTER XXI. Tsze-kung said, "The faults of the superior man are like the eclipses of the sun and moon. He has his faults, and all men see them; he changes again, and all men look up to him."

CHAPTER XXII. 1. Kung-sun Ch'aou of Wei asked Tsze-kung, saying, "From whom did Chung-ne get his learning?"

2. Tsze-kung replied, "The doctrines of Wăn and Woo have not yet fallen to the earth. They are to be found among men. Men of talents and virtue remember the greater principles of them, and others, not possessing such talents and virtue, remember the smaller. *Thus*, all possess the doctrines of Wăn and Woo. Where could our Master go that he should not have an opportunity of learning them? And yet what necessity was there for his having a regular master?"

義, 'cruel and unmerciful, injurious to righteousness.' If the 是 does not in this way refer to the name, the remark would seem to have occurred in a conversation about the wickedness of Chow. 下流 is a low-lying situation, to which the streams flow and waters drain, representing here a bad reputation, which gets the credit of every vice.

21. THE SUPERIOR MAN DOES NOT CONCEAL HIS ERRORS, NOR PERSIST IN THEM:—BY TSZE-KUNG. Such is the lesson of this chapter, as expanded in the 日講. The sun and the moon being here spoken of together, the 食 must be confined to 'eclipses,' but the term is also applied to the ordinary waning of the moon.

22. CONFUCIUS' SOURCES OF KNOWLEDGE WERE THE RECOLLECTIONS AND TRADITIONS OF THE PRINCIPLES ON WAN AND WOO:—BY TSZE-KUNG. 1. Of the questioner here we have no other memorial. His surname indicates that he was a descendant of some of the dukes of Wei. Observe how he calls Confucius by his designation of 仲尼 or 'Ne *secundus*.' (There was an elder brother, a concubine's son, who was called 伯

論語

〔二十三〕一節叔孫武叔語大夫於朝曰、子貢賢於仲尼。二節子服景伯以告子貢。子貢曰、譬之宮牆、賜之牆也及肩、窺見室家之好。三節夫子之牆數仞、不得其門而入、不見宗廟之美、百官之富。四節得其門者或寡矣、夫子之云、不亦宜乎。

CHAPTER XXIII. 1. Shuh-sun Woo-shuh observed to the great officers in the court, saying, "Tsze-kung is superior to Chung-ne."

2. Tsze-fuh King-pih reported the observation to Tsze-kung, who said, "Let me use the comparison of a house and its *encompassing* wall. My wall *only* reaches to the shoulders. One may peep over it, and see whatever is valuable in the apartments.

3. "The wall of my master is several fathoms high. If one do not find the door and enter by it, he cannot see the ancestral temple with its beauties, nor all the officers in their rich array.

4. "But I may assume that they are few who find the door. Was not the observation of the chief only what might have been expected?"

尼.) 仲尼焉學, 'How did Chung-ne learn?' but the 'how'='from whom?' The expression below, however,—夫子焉不學, expounded as in the translation, might suggest, from 'what quarter?' rather than 'from what person?' as the proper rendering. The last clause is taken by modern commentators, as asserting Conf. connate knowledge, but Gan-kwŏ finds in it only a repetition of the statement that the sage found teachers everywhere.

23. TSZE-KUNG REPUDIATES BEING THOUGHT SUPERIOR TO CONFUCIUS, AND, BY THE COMPARISON OF A HOUSE AND WALL, SHOWS HOW ORDINARY PEOPLE COULD NOT UNDERSTAND THE MASTER. 1. 武 was the hon. epithet of Chow Kew (州仇), one of the chiefs of the Shuh-sun family. From a mention of him in the 家語, 顏回篇, we may conclude that he was given to envy and detraction. 賢,— used here as in XI. 15, 1. 2. Tsze-fuh King-pih,—see XIV. 38. 譬之宮牆,—宮 is to be taken generally for a house or building, and not in its now common acceptation of 'a palace.' It is a poor house, as representing the disciple, and a ducal mansion as representing his master. Many commen. make the wall to be the sole object in the comparison, and 宮牆=宮之牆. It is better, with the 合講, to take both the house and the wall as members of the comp., and 宮牆=宮與牆. The wall is not a part of the house, but one inclosing it. 3. 仞 means 7 cubits. I have translated it—'fathoms.' 4. The 夫子 here refers to Woo-shuh.

二十四 叔孫武叔毀仲尼。子貢曰、無以爲也、仲尼不可毀也、他人之賢者、丘陵也、猶可踰也、仲尼、日月也、無得而踰焉、人雖欲自絕、其何傷於日月乎、多見其不知量也。

二十五 一節 陳子禽謂子貢曰、子爲恭也、仲尼豈賢於子乎。二節 子貢曰、君子一言以爲知、一言以爲不知、言不可不慎也。三節 夫子之

CHAPTER XXIV. Shuh-sun Woo-shuh having spoken revilingly of Chung-ne, Tsze-kung said, "It is of no use doing so. Chung-ne cannot be reviled. The talents and virtue of other men are hillocks and mounds, which may be stept over. Chung-ne is the sun or moon, which it is not possible to step over. Although a man may wish to cut himself off *from the sage*, what harm can he do to the sun or moon? He only shows that he does not know his own capacity."

CHAPTER XXV. 1. Tsze-k'in, addressing Tsze-kung, said, "You are too modest. How can Chung-ne be said to be superior to you?"

2. Tsze-kung said to him, "For one word a man is *often* deemed to be wise, and for one word he is *often* deemed to be foolish. We ought to be careful indeed in what we say.

3. "Our Master cannot be attained to, just in the same way as the heavens cannot be gone up to by the steps of a stair.

24. CONFUCIUS IS LIKE THE SUN OR MOON, HIGH ABOVE THE REACH OF DEPRECIATION:—BY TSZE-KUNG. 無以爲 is explained by Choo He (and the gloss of Hing Ping is the same) as =無用爲此, 'it is of no use to do this.' 他人之賢者,—他人 is to be understood, acc. to the 備旨, as embracing all other sages. 自絕,—I have supplied '*from the sage*,' after most modern paraphrasts. Hing Ping, however, supplies '*from the sun and moon*.' The meaning comes to the same. Choo He says that 多 here is the same with 祇, 'only.' Hing Ping takes it as=適, 'just.' This meaning of the char. is not given in the dictionary, but it is necessary here; see supplement to Hing Ping's 疏, *in loc.*

25. CONFUCIUS CAN NO MORE BE EQUALLED THAN THE HEAVENS CAN BE CLIMBED:—BY TSZE-KUNG. We find it difficult to conceive of the sage's disciples speaking to one another, as Tsze-k'in does here to Tsze-kung, and Hing

不可及也、猶天之不可階而升也。四節夫子之得邦家者、所謂立之斯立、道之斯行、綏之斯來、動之斯和、其生也榮、其死也哀、如之何其可及也。

4. "Were our Master in the position of the prince of a State or the chief of a Family, we should find verified the description *which has been given of a sage's rule*:—he would plant the people, and forthwith they would be established; he would lead them on, and forthwith they would follow him; he would make them happy, and forthwith *multitudes* would resort to *his dominions;* he would stimulate them, and forthwith they would be harmonious. While he lived, he would be glorious. When he died, he would be bitterly lamented. How is it possible for him to be attained to?"

Ping says that this was not the disciple Tsze-k'in, but another man of the same surname and designation. But this is inadmissible, especially as we find the same parties, in I. 10, talking about the character of their master. 1. 子爲恭, 'you are doing the modest.' 2. 君子 has here its lightest meaning. The 備旨 makes it=學者, 'a student,' but 'a man,' as in the transl., is quite as much as it denotes. Comp. its use in I. 8, *et al.* 3. 夫子之得邦家者 must be understood hypothetically, because he never was in the position here assigned to him. 斯,—as in X. 10, 1. 道 is for 導, as in I. 5. 來,—as in XVI. 1, 11. 動之,—as in XV. 32, 3. 之, *them*, 'the people' being always understood.

BOOK XX. YAOU YUE.

堯曰第二十

〔第一章〕〔一節〕堯曰、咨爾舜、天之曆數在爾躬、允執其中、四海困窮、天祿永終。〔二節〕舜亦以命禹。〔三節〕曰、予小子履、敢用玄牡、敢昭告于皇皇后帝、有罪不敢赦、帝臣不蔽、簡在帝心、朕躬有罪、無以萬方、萬方有罪、

CHAPTER I. 1. Yaou said, "Oh! you, Shun, the Heaven-determined order of succession now rests in your person. Sincerely hold fast the Due Mean. If there shall be distress and want within the four seas, *your* Heavenly revenue will come to a perpetual end."

2. Shun also used the same language in giving charge to Yu.

3. *T'ang* said, "I, the child Le, presume to use a dark-coloured victim, and presume to announce to Thee, O most great and sovereign God, that the sinner I dare not pardon, and thy ministers, O God, I do not keep in obscurity. The examination of them is by thy mind, O God. If, in my person, I commit offences, they are not to beattributed to you, *the people of* the myriad regions. If you in the myriad regions commit offences, these offences must rest on my person."

HEADING OF THIS BOOK.—堯曰第二十, 'Yaou said—No. XX.' Hing Ping says:—'This records the words of the two emperors, the three kings, and of Confucius, throwing light on the excellence of the ordinances of Heaven, and the transforming power of government. Its doctrines are all those of sages, worthy of being transmitted to posterity. On this account, it brings up the rear of all the other books, without any particular relation to the one immediately preceding.'

1. PRINCIPLES AND WAYS OF YAOU, SHUN, YU, T'ANG, AND WOO. The first five paragraphs here are mostly compiled from different parts of the Shoo-king. But there are many variations of language. The compiler may have thought it sufficient, if he gave the substance of the original in his quotations, without seeking to observe a verbal accuracy, or, possibly, the Shoo-king, as it was in his days, may have contained the passages as he gives them, and the variations be owing to the burning of most of the classical books by the founder of the Ts'in dynasty, and their recovery and restoration in a mutilated state. 1. We do not find this address of Yaou to Shun in the Shoo-king, Pt I., but the different sentences may be gathered from Pt II. ii. 14, 15, where we have the charge of Shun to Yu. Yaou's reign commenced B. C. 2356, and after reigning 73 years, he resigned the administration to Shun. He died., B. C. 2256, and, two years after, Shun occupied the throne, in obedience to the will of the people. 天之曆數,

論語

罪在朕躬。○四節周有大賚、善人是富。○五節雖有周親、不如仁人、百姓有過、在予一人。○六節謹權量、審法度、修廢官、四方之政行焉。○七節興滅國、繼絕世、舉逸民、天下之民歸心焉。○八節所重、民、食、喪、祭。○九節寬則得眾、信則民任焉、敏則有功、公則說。

4. Chow conferred great gifts, and the good were enriched.

5. "Although he has his near relatives, they are not equal to *my* virtuous men. The people are throwing blame upon me, the one man."

6. He carefully attended to the weights and measures, examined the body of the laws, restored the discarded officers, and the good government of the empire took its course.

7. He revived states that had been extinguished, restored families whose line of succession had been broken, and called to office those who had retired into obscurity, so that throughout the empire the hearts of the people turned towards him.

8. What he attached chief importance to, were the food of the people, the duties of mourning, and sacrifices.

9. By his generosity, he won all. By his sincerity, he made the people repose trust in him. By his earnest activity, his achievements were great. By his justice, all were delighted.

lit., 'the represented and calculated numbers of heaven,' *i. e.*, the divisions of the year, its terms, months, and days, all described in a calendar, as they succeed one another with determined regularity. Here, ancient and modern interpreters agree in giving to the expression the meaning which appears in the translation. I may observe here, that Choo He differs often from the old interpreters in explaining these passages of the Shoo-king, but I have followed him, leaving the correctness or incorrectness of his views to be considered in the annotations on the Shoo-king. 3. Before 曰 here we must understand 湯, the designation of the founder of the Shang dynasty. The sentences here may in substance be collected from the Shoo-king, Pt IV. iii. 4, 8. Down to 簡在帝心 is a prayer addressed to God by T'ang, on his undertaking the overthrow of the Hea dynasty, which he rehearses to his nobles and people, after the completion of his work. T'ang's name was 履. We do not find in the Shoo-king the remarkable designation of God—皇皇后帝. For the grounds on which I translate 帝 by *God*, see my work on 'The notions of the Chinese concerning God and Spirits.' 后, now generally used for 'empress,' was anciently used for 'sovereign,' and applied to the emperors. Here, it is an adjective, or in apposition with 帝. The sinner is Këĕ (桀), the tyrant,

第二章 一節 子張問於孔子曰、何如、斯可以從政矣。子曰、尊五美、屏四惡、斯可以從政矣。子張曰、何謂五美。子曰、君子惠而不費、勞而不怨、欲而不貪、泰而不驕、威而不猛。二節 子張曰、何謂惠而不費。子曰、因民之所利而利之、

CHAPTER II. 1. Tsze-chang asked Confucius, saying, "In what way should *a person in authority* act in order that he may conduct government properly?" The Master replied, "Let him honour the five excellent, and banish away the four bad, things;—then may he conduct government properly." Tsze-chang said, "What are meant by the five excellent things?" The Master said, "When the person in authority is beneficent without great expenditure; when he lays tasks *on the people* without their repining; when he *pursues what he* desires without being covetous; when he maintains a dignified ease without being proud; when he is majestic without being fierce."

2. Tsze-chang said, "What is meant by being beneficent without great expenditure?" The Master replied, "When *the person in*

and last emperor of the Hea dynasty. 'The ministers of God' are the able and virtuous men, whom T'ang had called, or would call, to office. By 簡在帝心, T'ang indicates that, in his punishing or rewarding, he only wanted to act in harmony with the mind of God. 無以萬方=萬方小民何預焉, as in the transl. In the dict., it is said that 以 and 與 are interchanged. This is a case in point. 4. In the Shoo-king, Pt V. iii. 8, we find king Woo saying 大賚於四海而萬姓悅服, 'I distributed great rewards through the empire, and all the people were pleased and submitted.' 5. See the Shoo-king, Pt V. i. sect. II. 6. 7. The subject in 雖有周親 is 受 or 紂, tyrant of the Yin dynasty. 周,—in the sense of 至. 過 is used in the sense of 咎, 'to blame.'—The people found fault with him, because he did not come to save them from their sufferings, by destroying their oppressor. The remaining paragraphs are descriptive of the policy of king Woo, but cannot, excepting the 8th one, be traced in the present Shoo-king. 任, par. 9, is in the low. 3d tone. See XVII. 6, which chap., generally, resembles this paragraph.

2. HOW GOVERNMENT MAY BE CONDUCTED WITH EFFICIENCY, BY HONOURING FIVE EXCELLENT THINGS, AND PUTTING AWAY FOUR BAD THINGS:—A CONVERSATION WITH TSZE-CHANG. It is understood that this chapter, and the next, give the ideas of Confucius on government, as a sequel to those of the ancient sages and emperors, whose principles are set forth in the last chapter, to show how Confucius was their proper successor. 1. On 從政 see VI. 6, but the gloss of the 備旨 says—從政只泛說行政, 不作爲大夫, '從政 here denotes generally the practice of government. It is not to be taken as indicating a minister.' We may, however, retain the proper meaning of the phrase, Confucius describing principles to be observed by all in authority, and which will find in the highest their noblest

論語

斯不亦惠而不費乎、擇可勞而勞之、又誰怨、欲仁而得仁、又焉貪、君子無衆寡、無小大、無敢慢、斯不亦泰而不驕乎、君子正其衣冠、尊其瞻視、儼然人望而畏之、斯不亦威而不猛乎。〇三節 子張曰、何謂四惡。子曰、不教而殺、謂之虐、不戒視成、謂之暴、慢令致期、謂之賊、猶

authority makes more beneficial to the people the things from which they naturally derive benefit;—is not this being beneficent without *great* expenditure? When he chooses the labours which are proper, and makes them labour on them, who will repine? When his desires are set on benevolent *government*, and he realizes it, who will accuse him of covetousness? Whether he has to do with many people or few, or with things great or small, he does not dare to indicate any disrespect;—is not this to maintain a dignified ease without any pride? He adjusts his clothes and cap, and throws a dignity into his looks, so that, thus dignified, he is looked at with awe;—is not this to be majestic without being fierce?"

3. Tsze-chang then asked, "What are meant by the four bad things?" The Master said, "To put the people to death without having instructed them;—this is called cruelty. To require from them, *suddenly*, the full tale of work, without having given them warning:—this is called oppression. To issue orders as if without urgency, *at first*, and, when the time comes, *to insist on them with*

embodiment. The 日講 favours this view. See its paraphrase *in loc.* I have therefore translated 君子 by—'a person in authority.' 勞而不怨,—see IV. 18, though the application of the terms there is different. 泰而不驕,—see XIII. 26. 威而不猛,—see VII. 37. 2. 因民云云 is instanced by the promotion of agriculture. 擇可勞云云 is instanced by the employment of the people in advantageous public works. 欲仁云云 is explained:—'Desire for what is not proper is covetousness, but if, while the wish to have the empire overshadowed by his benevolence has not reached to universal advantaging, his desire does not cease, then, with a heart impatient of people's evils, he administers a government impatient of those evils. What he desires is benevolence, and what he gets is the same;—how can he be regarded as covetous?' 視

之與人也、出納之吝、謂之有司。

第三章 一節 子曰、不知命、無以爲君子也。二節 不知禮、無以立也。三節 不知言、無以知人也。

severity;—this is called injury. And, generally speaking, to give *pay or rewards* to men, and yet to do it in a stingy way;—this is called acting the part of a mere official."

CHAPTER III. 1. The Master said, "Without recognizing the ordinances *of Heaven*, it is impossible to be a superior man.

2. "Without an acquaintance with the rules of Propriety, it is impossible for the character to be established.

3. "Without knowing *the force of* words, it is impossible to know men."

is explained here by 責, 'to require from.' We may get that meaning out of the char., which='to examine,' 'to look for.' A good deal has to be supplied, here and in the sentences below, to bring out the meaning as in the translation. 猶之 is explained by 均之, and seems to me to be nearly=our 'on the whole.' 出納,—'giving out,' *i. e., from this* and 'presenting,' *i. e., to that*. The whole is understood to refer to rewarding men for their services, and doing it in an unwilling and stingy manner.

3. THE ORDINANCES OF HEAVEN, THE RULES OF PROPRIETY, AND THE FORCE OF WORDS, ALL NECESSARY TO BE KNOWN. 1. 知 here is not only 'knowing,' but 'believing and resting in.' 命 is the will of Heaven regarding right and wrong, of which man has the standard in his own moral nature. If this be not recognized, a man is the slave of passion, or the sport of feeling. 2. Compare VIII. 8, 2. 3. 知 here supposes much thought and examination of principles. Words are the voice of the heart. To know a man, we must attend well to what and how he thinks.

THE GREAT LEARNING.

大學

子程子曰、大學、孔氏之遺書、而初學入德之門也、於今可見古人爲學次第者、獨賴此篇之存、而論孟次之、學者必由是而學焉、則庶乎其不

My master, the philosopher Ch'ing, says:—"The Great Learning is a book left by Confucius, and forms the gate by which first learners enter into virtue. That we can now perceive the order in which the ancients pursued their learning, is solely owing to the preservation of this work, the Analects and Mencius coming after it. Learners must commence their course with this, and then it may be hoped they will be kept from error."

TITLE OF THE WORK.—大學, 'The Great Learning.' I have pointed out, in the prolegomena, the great differences which are found among Chinese commentators on this Work, on almost every point connected with the criticism and interpretation of it. We encounter them here on the very threshold. The name itself is simply the adoption of the two commencing characters of the treatise, according to the custom noticed at the beginning of the Analects; but in explaining those two characters, the old and new schools differ widely. Anciently, 大 was read as 太, and the oldest commentator whose notes on the work are preserved, Ch'ing K'ang-shing, in the last half of the second century, said that the book was called 大學, 以其記博學,可以爲政, 'because it recorded that extensive learning, which was available for the administration of government.' This view is approved by K'ung Ying-tă (孔穎達), whose expansion of K'ang-shing's notes, written in the first half of the 7th century, still remains. He says—大學,至道矣, '大學 means the highest principles.' Choo He's definition, on the contrary, is—大學者大人之學也, '大學 means the Learning of Adults.' One of the paraphrasts who follow him says—大是大人,與小子對, '大 means adults, in opposition to children.' The grounds of Choo He's interpr. are to be found in his very elegant preface to the Book, where he tries to make it out, that we have here the subjects taught in the advanced schools of antiquity. I have contented myself with the title—'The Great Learning,' which is a literal translation of the characters, whether read as 太學, or 大學.

THE INTRODUCTORY NOTE.—I have thought it well to translate this, and all the other notes and supplements appended by Choo He to the original text, because they appear in nearly all the editions of the work, which fall into the hands of students, and his view of the classics is what must be regarded as the orthodox one. The translation, which is here given, is also, for the most part, according to his views, though my own differing opinion will be found freely expressed in the notes. Another version, following the order of the text, before it was transposed by him and his masters, the Ch'ing, and without reference to his interpretations, will be

差矣。大(一節)學之道、在明明德、在親民、在止於至善。(二節)知止、而后有定、定、而后能靜、

THE TEXT OF CONFUCIUS.

1. What the Great Learning teaches, is—to illustrate illustrious virtue; to renovate the people; and to rest in the highest excellence.

2. The point where to rest being known, the object of pursuit is then determined; and, that being determined, a calm unperturbedness may be attained. To that calmness there will succeed a tranquil

found in the translation of the Le-ke.—子程子,—see note to the Ana. I. i. The Ch'ing here, is the second of the two brothers, to whom reference is made in the prolegomena. 孔氏, 'Confucius,' *the* K'ung, as 季氏 is found continually in the Analects for *the* Ke, *i. e.*, the chief of the Ke family. But how can we say that 'The Great Learning' is a work left by Confucius? Even Choo He ascribes only a small portion of it to the Master, and makes the rest to be the production of the disciple Tsăng, and before his time, the whole work was attributed generally to the sage's grandson. I should be glad if I had authority for taking 孔氏 as=孔門, the Confucian school.

CHAPTER I. THE TEXT OF CONFUCIUS. Such Choo He, as will be seen from his concluding note, determines this chapter to be, and it has been divided into two sections (段), the first containing three paragraphs, occupied with the *heads* (綱領) of the Great Learning, and the second containing four paragraphs, occupied with the *particulars* (條目) of those.

Par. 1. The heads of the Great Learning. 大學之道,—'the way of the Great Learning,' 道 being=修爲之方法, 'the methods of cultivating and practising it,'—the Great Learning, that is. 在, 'is in.' The first 明 is a verb; the second is an adjective, qualifying 德. The illustrious virtue is the virtuous nature which man derives from Heaven. This is perverted as man grows up, through defects of the physical constitution, through inward lusts, and through outward seductions; and the great business of life should be, to bring the nature back to its original purity.—'To renovate the people,'—this object of the Great Learning is made out, by changing the character 親 of the old text into 新. The Ch'ing first proposed the alteration, and Choo He approved of it. When a man has entirely illustrated his own illustrious nature, he has to proceed to bring about the same result in every other man, till 'under heaven' there be not an individual, who is not in the same condition as himself.—'The highest excellence' is understood of the two previous matters. It is not a third and different object of pursuit, but indicates a perseverance in the two others, till they are perfectly accomplished.—According to these explanations, the objects contemplated in the Great Learning, are not three, but two. Suppose them realized, and we should have the whole world of mankind perfectly good, every individual what he ought to be!

Against the above interpretation, we have to consider the older and simpler. 德 is there not the *nature*, but simply virtue, or virtuous conduct, and the first object in the Great Learning is the making of one's-self more and more illustrious in virtue, or the practice of benevolence, reverence, filial piety, kindness, and sincerity. See the 故本大學註辨, *in loc.*—There is nothing, of course, of the *renovating of the people*, in this interpretation. The second object of the Great Learning is 親民=親愛於民, 'to love the people.'—The third object is said by Ying-tă to be 'in resting in conduct which is perfectly good (在止處於至善之行),' and here also, there would seem to be only two objects, for what essential distinction can we make between the first and third? There will be occasion below to refer to the reasons for changing 親 into 新, and their unsatisfactoriness. 'To love the people' is, doubtless, the second thing taught by the Great Learning.— Having the heads of the Great Learning now before us, according to both interpretations of it, we feel that the student of it should be an emperor, and not an ordinary man.

Par. 2. The mental process by which the point of rest may be attained. I confess that I do not well understand this par., in the relation of its parts in itself, nor in relation to the rest of the chapter. Choo He says:—'止 is the ground where we ought to rest;'—namely, the highest ex-

大學

靜、而后能安、安、而
后能慮、慮、而后能
得。○三節物有本末、事有
終始、知所先後、則
近道矣。○四節古之欲明
明德於天下者、先
治其國、欲治其國
者、先齊其家、欲齊
其家者、先脩其身、
欲脩其身者、先正

repose. In that repose there may be careful deliberation, and that deliberation will be followed by the attainment *of the desired end.*

3. Things have their root and their completion. Affairs have their end and their beginning. To know what is first and what is last will lead near to what is taught *in the Great Learning.*

4. The ancients who wished to illustrate illustrious virtue throughout the empire, first ordered well their own States. Wishing to order well their States, they first regulated their families. Wishing to regulate their families, they first cultivated their persons. Wishing to cultivate their persons, they first rectified their hearts. Wishing

cellence mentioned above. But if this be known in the outset, where is the necessity for the 慮, or 'careful deliberation,' which issues in its attainment? The paraphrasts make 知止 to embrace even all that is understood by 格物致知 below.—Ying-tâ is perhaps rather more intelligible. He says:—'When it is known that the rest is to be in the perfectly good, then the mind has fixedness. So it is free from concupiscence, and can be still, not engaging in disturbing pursuits. That still leads to a repose and harmony of the feelings. That state of the feelings fits for careful thought about affairs (能思慮於事), and thence it results that what is right in affairs is attained.' Perhaps, the par. just intimates that the objects of the G. L. being so great, a calm, serious, thoughtfulness is required in proceeding to seek their attainment.

Par. 3. The order of things and methods in the two preceding paragraphs. So, acc. to Choo He, does this par. wind up the two preceding. 'The illustration of virtue,' he says, 'is the *root,* and the renovation of the people is the *completion* (lit., *the branches*). Knowing where to rest is the *beginning*, and being able to attain is the end. The root and the beginning are *what is first.* The completion and end are *what is last.*'—The adherents of the old commentators say, on the contrary, that this par. is introductory to the succeeding ones. They contend that the illustration of virtue and renovation of the people are *doings* (事), and not *things* (物). Acc. to them, the *things* are the person, heart, thoughts, &c., mentioned below, which are 'the root,' and the family, kingdom, and empire, which are 'the branches.' The *affairs* are the various processes put forth on those things.—This, it seems to me, is the correct interpretation.

Par. 4. The different steps by which the illustration of illustrious virtue throughout the empire may be brought about. 明明德於天下 is understood by the school of Choo He as embracing the two first objects of the Great Learning, the illustration, namely of virtue, and the renovation of the people. We are not aided in determining the meaning by the synthetic arrangement of the different steps in the next par., for the result arrived at there is simply—天下平, 'the whole empire was made tranquil.'—Ying-tâ's comment is—章明已之明德使偏於天下, 'to display illustriously their own illustrious virtue (or, virtues), making them reach through the whole empire.' But the influence must be very much transformative. Of the several steps described, the central one is 修身, 'the cultivation of the person,' which, indeed, is called 本, 'the root,' in par.

其心、欲正其心者、先誠其意、欲誠其意者、先致其知、致知在格物。○五節 物格、而后知

to rectify their hearts, they first sought to be sincere in their thoughts. Wishing to be sincere in their thoughts, they first extended to the utmost their knowledge. Such extension of knowledge lay in the investigation of things.

5. Things being investigated, knowledge became complete. Their knowledge being complete, their thoughts were sincere. Their

6. This requires 'the heart to be correct,' and that again 'that the thoughts be sincere.' Choo He defines 心 as 身之所主, 'what the body has for its lord,' and 意 as 心之所發, 'what the 心 sends forth.' Ying-tă says: 一總包萬慮謂之心, 'that which comprehends and embraces all considerings is called the 心;' 爲情所意念謂之意, 'the thoughts under emotion are what is called 意.' 心 is then the meta-physical part of our nature, all that we comprehend under the terms of mind or soul, heart, and spirit. This is conceived of as quiescent, and when its activity is aroused, then we have thoughts and purposes relative to what affects it. The 'being sincere' is explained by 實, 'real.' The sincerity of the thoughts is to be obtained by 致知, which means, acc. to Choo He, 'carrying our knowledge to its utmost extent, with the desire that there may be nothing which it shall not embrace.' This knowledge, finally, is realized 在格物. The same authority takes 物, 'things,' as embracing, 事, 'affairs,' as well. 格, sometimes=至, 'to come or extend to,' and assuming that the 'coming to' here is by study, he makes it=窮究 'to examine exhaustively,' so that '格物 means exhausting by examination the principles of things and affairs, with the desire that their uttermost point may be reached.'—We feel that this explanation cannot be correct, or that, if it be correct, the teaching of the Chinese sage is far beyond and above the condition and capacity of men. How can we suppose that, in order to secure sincerity of thought and our self-cultivation, there is necessarily the study of all the phenomena of physics and metaphysics, and of the events of history? Moreover, Choo He's view of the two last clauses is a consequence of the alterations which he adopts in the order of the text. As that exists in the Le-ke, the 7th par. of this chapter is followed by 此爲知本, 此爲知之至也, which he has transferred and made the 5th chapter of annotations. Ying-tă's comment on it is:—'*The root* means *the person*. The person (*i. e.*, personal character) being regarded as the root, if one can know his own person, this is the knowledge of the root; yea, this is the very extremity of knowledge.' If we apply this conclusion to the clauses under notice, it is said that wishing to make our thoughts sincere we must first carry to the utmost our self-knowledge, and this extension of self-knowledge 在格物. Now, the change of the style indicates that the relation of 致知 and 格物 is different from that of the parts in the other clauses. It is not said that to get the one thing we must first do the other. Rather it seems to me that the 格物 is a consequence of 致知, that in it is seen the other. Now, 式, 'a rule or pattern,' and 正, 'to correct,' are accepted meanings of 格, and 物 being taken generally and loosely as=*things*, 在格物 will tell us that, when his self-knowledge is complete, a man is a law to himself, measuring, and measuring correctly, all things with which he has to do, not led astray or beclouded by them. This is the interpretation strongly insisted on by 羅仲藩, the author of the 古本大學註辨. It is the only view into any sympathy with which I can place my mind. In harmony with it, I would print 致至在格物 as a par. by itself, between the analytic and synthetic processes described in parr. 4, 5. Still there are difficulties connected with it, and I leave the vexed questions, regretting my own inability to clear them up.

Par. 5. The synthesis of the preceding processes. Observe the 致 of the preceding par. is changed into 至, and how 治 now becomes 治, low.

大學

至、知至、而后意誠、意誠、而后心正、心正、而后身脩、身脩、而后家齊、家齊、而后國治、國治、而后天下平。○六節 自天子、以至於庶人、壹是、皆以脩身爲本。○七節 其本亂、而末治者否矣、其所厚者薄、而其所薄者厚、未之有也。

thoughts being sincere, their hearts were then rectified. Their hearts being rectified, their persons were cultivated. Their persons being cultivated, their families were regulated. Their families being regulated, their States were rightly governed. Their States being rightly governed, the whole empire was made tranquil and happy.

6. From the emperor down to the mass of the people, all must consider the cultivation of the person the root of *every thing besides*.

7. It cannot be, when the root is neglected, that what should spring from it will be well ordered. It never has been the case that what was of great importance has been slightly cared for, and, at the same time, that what was of slight importance has been greatly cared for.

3d tone. 治 is explained by 攻理, 'the work of ruling,' and 治 by 理效, 'the result.' 后 is used for 後, as in p. 2.

Par. 6. The cultivation of the person is the prime, radical, thing required from all. I have said above that the Great Learning is adapted only to an emperor, but it is intimated here that *the people* also may take part in it in their degree. 天子, 'Son of Heaven,' a designation of the emperor, 以其命于天, 'because he is ordained by Heaven.' 壹是=一切, 'all.' Ch'ing K'ang-shing, however, says:—壹是, 專行是也, '壹是 means that they uniformly do this.'

Par. 7. Reiteration of the importance of attending to the root. Choo He makes the *root* here to be the person, but accord. to the prec. par., it is 'the cultivation of the person' which is intended. By the 末 or 'branches' is intended the proper ordering, of the family, the state, the empire. 厚 薄, 'thick,' and 'thin,'—used here metaphorically. 所厚, acc. to Choo He, means 'the family,' and 所薄, the state and the empire, but that I cannot understand. 所厚 is the same as the *root*. Mencius has a saying which may illustrate the second part of the paragraph.—於所厚者薄, 無所不薄, 'He, who is careless in what is important, will be careless in every thing.'

右經一章、蓋孔子之言、而曾子述之、其傳十章、則曾子之意、而門人記之也、舊本頗有錯簡、今因程子所定、而更考經文、別爲序次如左。

第一章

一節 康誥曰、克明德。

The preceding chapter of classical text is in the words of Confucius, handed down by the philosopher Tsăng. The ten chapters of explanation which follow contain the views of Tsăng, and were recorded by his disciples. In the old copies of the work, there appeared considerable confusion in these, from the disarrangement of the tablets. But now, availing myself of the decisions of the philosopher Ch'ing, and having examined anew the classical text, I have arranged it in order, as follows:—

COMMENTARY OF THE PHILOSOPHER TSANG.

CHAPTER I. 1. In the Announcement to K'ang it is said, "He was able to make his virtue illustrious."

CONCLUDING NOTE. It has been shown in the prolegomena that there is no ground for the distinction made here between so much *king* attributed to Confucius, and so much 傳, or commentary, ascribed to his disciple Tsăng. The invention of paper is ascribed to Ts'ae Lun (蔡倫), an officer of the Han dynasty, in the time of the emperor Hwo (和), A. D. 89—104. Before that time, and long after also, slips of wood and of bamboo (簡), were used to write and engrave upon. We can easily conceive how a collection of them might get disarranged, but whether those containing the Great Learning did do so is a question vehemently disputed. 右經一章, 'the chapter of classic on the right;' 如左, 'on the left;'—these are expressions=our 'preceding,' and 'as follows,' indicating the Chinese method of writing and printing from the right side of a manuscript or book on to the left.

COMMENTARY OF THE PHILOSOPHER TSANG.

1. THE ILLUSTRATION OF ILLUSTRIOUS VIRTUE. The student will do well to refer here to the text of 'The Great Learning,' as it appears in the Le-ke. He will then see how a considerable portion of it has been broken up, and transposed to form this and the five succeeding chapters. It was, no doubt, the occurrence of 明, in the four paragraphs here, and of the phrase 明德, which determined Choo He to form them into one chapter, and refer them to the first head in the classical text. The old commentators connect them with the great business of making the thoughts sincere. 1. See the Shoo-king, V. x. 3. The words are part of the address of King Woo to his brother Fung (封), called also K'ang-shuh (康叔; 康, the hon. ep.) on appointing him to the marquisate of 衞. The subject of 克 is king Wăn, to whose example K'ang-shuh is referred.—We cannot determine, from this par., between the old interpretation of 德, as ='virtues,' and the new which understands by it,—'the heart or nature, all-virtuous.' 2. See the Shoo-king, IV. v. Sect. I. 2. Choo He takes 諟 as=此, 'this,' or 審, 'to judge,' 'to examine.' The old interpr. explain it by 正, 'to correct.' The sentence is part of the address of the premier, E-yin, to T'ae-këă, the 2d emperor of the Shang dynasty, B. C. 1752—1718. The subject of 顧 is T'ae-kea's father,

二節 大甲曰、顧諟天之明命。三節 帝典曰、克明峻德。四節 皆自明也。

右傳之首章、釋明明德。

傳二章 一節 湯之盤銘曰、苟日新、日日新、又日新。二節 康誥曰、作新民。三節 詩曰、周雖舊邦、其命維新。四節 是故君子無所不用其

2. In the T'ae Këă, it is said, "He contemplated and studied the illustrious decrees of Heaven."

3. In the Canon of the emperor Yaou, it is said, "He was able to make illustrious his lofty virtue."

4. These *passages* all *show how those sovereigns* made themselves illustrious.

The above first chapter of commentary explains the illustration of illustrious virtue.

CHAPTER II. 1. On the bathing-tub of T'ang, the following words were engraved:—"If you can one day renovate yourself, do so from day to day. Yea, let there be daily renovation."

2. In the Announcement to K'ang, it is said, "To stir up the new people."

3. In the Book of Poetry, it is said, "Although Chow was an ancient state, the ordinance which lighted on it was new."

4. Therefore, the superior man in every thing uses his utmost endeavours.

the great T'ang. Choo He understands by 明命, the Heaven-given, illustrious nature of man. The other school take the phrase more generally,=the 顯道, 'displayed ways' of Heaven. 3. See the Shoo-king, I. 2. It is of the emperor Yaou that this is said. 4. The 皆 must be referred to the three quotations.

2. THE RENOVATION OF THE PEOPLE. Here the character 新, 'new,' 'to renovate,' occurs five times, and it was to find something corresponding to it at the commencement of the work, which made the Ch'ing change the 親 of 親民, into 新. But the 新 here have nothing to do with the renovation of the people. This is self-evident in the 1st and 3d parr. The heading of the chapter, as above, is a misnomer. 1. This fact about T'ang's bathing tub had come down by tradition. At least, we do not now find the mention of it anywhere but here. It was customary among the ancients, as it is in China at the present day, to engrave, all about them, on the articles of their furniture, such moral aphorisms and lessons. 2. See the *K'ang Kaou*, p. 7, where K'ang-shuh is exhorted to assist the emperor 'to settle the decree of Heaven, and 作新民,' which may mean to make the bad people of Yin into good people, or to stir up the new people, *i. e., new*, as recently subjected to Chow. 3. See the She-king, III. i. Ode I. st. 1. The subject of the

極。

右傳之二章、釋新民。

〔傳三章〕一節 詩云、邦畿千里、惟民所止。二節 詩云、緡蠻黃鳥、止于丘隅。子曰、於止、知其所止、可以人而不如鳥乎。三節 詩云、穆穆文王、於緝熙敬止、爲人君、止於仁、爲人臣、止於敬、爲人子、止於孝、爲人父、止於慈、與國人交、止於信。四節 詩

The above second chapter of commentary explains the renovating of the people.

CHAPTER III. 1. In the Book of Poetry, it is said, "The imperial domain of a thousand le is where the people rest."

2. In the Book of Poetry, it is said, "The twittering yellow bird rests on a corner of the mound." The Master said, "When it rests, it knows where to rest. Is it possible that a man should not be equal to this bird?"

3. In the Book of Poetry, it is said, "Profound was King Wăn. With how bright and unceasing a feeling of reverence did he regard his resting places!" As a sovereign, he rested in benevolence. As a minister, he rested in reverence. As a son, he rested in filial piety. As a father, he rested in kindness. In communication with his subjects, he rested in good faith.

ode is the praise of king Wăn, whose virtue led to the possession of the empire by his house, more than a thousand years after its first rise. 3. 君子 is here the man of rank and office probably, as well as the man of virtue; but I do not, for my own part, see the particular relation of this to the preced. parr., nor the work which it does in relation to the whole chapter.

3. ON RESTING IN THE HIGHEST EXCELLENCE. The frequent occurrence of 止 in these paragraphs, and of 至善, in par. 4, led Choo He to combine them in one chapter, and connect them with the last clause in the opening par. of the work. 1. See the She-king, IV. iii. Ode III. st. 4. The ode celebrates the rise and establishment of the Shang or Yin dynasty. 畿 is the 1000 *le* around the capital, and constituting the imperial demesne. The quotation shows, according to Choo He, that 物各有所當止之處, 'every thing has the place where it ought to rest.' But that surely is a very sweeping conclusion from the words. 2. See the She-king, II. viii. Ode VI. st. 2, where we have the complaint of a down-trodden man, contrasting his position with that of a bird. For 緡 here, we have 綿 in the She-king. 緡蠻 are intended to express the sound of the bird's singing or chattering. 'The yellow bird' is known by a variety of names. A com-

云、瞻彼淇澳、菉竹猗猗、有斐君子、如切如磋、如琢如磨、瑟兮僩兮、赫兮喧兮、有斐君子、終不可諠兮。如切如磋者、道學也、如琢如磨者、自脩也、瑟兮僩兮者、恂慄也、赫兮喧兮者、威儀也、有斐君子、終不可諠兮者、道盛德至善、民之不能忘

4. In the Book of Poetry, it is said, "Look at that winding course of the K'e, with the green bamboos so luxuriant! Here is our elegant and accomplished prince! As we cut and then file; as we chisel and then grind: *so has he cultivated himself.* How grave is he and dignified! How majestic and distinguished! Our elegant and accomplished prince never can be forgotten." *That expression*— "as we cut and then file," indicates the work of learning. "As we chisel, and then grind," indicates that of self culture. "How grave is he and dignified!" indicates the feeling of cautious reverence. "How commanding and distinguished," indicates an awe-inspiring deportment. "Our elegant and accomplished prince never can be forgotten," indicates how, when virtue is complete and excellence extreme, the people cannot forget them.

mon one is 倉庚, or, properly, 鶬鶊 *ts'ang kang.* It is a species of oriole. The 子曰 are worthy of observation. If the first chapter of the classical text, as Choo He calls it, really contains the words of Confucius, we might have expected it to be headed by these characters. 於止, lit., 'in resting.' 3. See the She-king, III. i. Ode I. st. 4. The stress is here all laid upon the final 止, which does not appear to have any force at all in the original, Choo He himself saying there that it is 語詞, 'a mere supplemental particle.' In 於緝, 於 is read *woo*, and is an interjection. 4. See the She-king, I. v. Ode I. st. 1. The ode celebrates the virtue of the duke *Woo* (武) of Wei (衞), in his laborious endeavours to cultivate his person. There are some verbal differences between the ode in the She-king, and as here quoted; namely, 奧 for 澳; 綠 for 菉; 匪 for 斐. 猗, here, *poetice*, read *O.* 道 is used as = 言, 'says,' or 'means.' It is to be understood before 自修, 恂慄, and 威儀.—The transposition of this par. by Choo He to this place does seem unhappy. It ought evidently to come in connection with the work of 脩身. 5. See the She-king, IV. i. Sect. I. Ode IV. st. 3. The former kings are Wăn and Woo, the founders of the Chow dynasty. 於戲 are an interjection, read *woo hoo.* In the She-king we have 於乎. 烏呼 are found with the same meaning. I translate 其賢, 其親, by 'what they deemed worthy,' 'what they loved.' When we try to determine *what* that what was, we are perplexed by the varying views of the

也。五節詩云、於戲前王不忘、君子賢其賢、而親其親、小人樂其樂、而利其利、此以沒世不忘也。

右傳之三章、釋止於至善。

第四章子曰、聽訟吾猶人也、必也使無訟乎。無情者、不得盡其辭、大畏民志、此謂之本。

右傳之四章、釋本末。

5. In the Book of Poetry, it is said, "Ah! the former kings are not forgotten." *Future* princes deem worthy what they deemed worthy, and love what they loved. The common people delight in what they delighted, and are benefited by their beneficial arrangements. It is on this account that the former kings, after they have quitted the world, are not forgotten.

The above third chapter of commentary explains resting in the highest excellence.

CHAPTER IV. The Master said, "In hearing litigations, I am like any other body. What is necessary is to cause the people to have no litigations?" *So*, those who are devoid of principle find it impossible to carry out their speeches, and a great awe would be struck into men's minds;—this is called knowing the root.

The above fourth chapter of commentary explains the root and the issue.

old and new schools. 沒世,—see Analects, XV. xix.—Acc. to Ying-tă, 'this par. illustrates the business of having the thoughts sincere.' Acc. to Choo He, it tells that how the former kings renovated the people, was by their resting in perfect excellence, so as to be able, throughout the empire and to future ages, to effect that there should not be a single thing but got its proper place.

4. EXPLANATION OF THE ROOT AND THE BRANCHES. See the Analects XII. xiii, from which we understand that the words of Conf. terminate at 訟乎, and that what follows is from the compiler. According to the old commentators, this is the conclusion of the chapter on having the thoughts made sincere, and that 誠其意 is the *root*. But acc. to Choo, it is the illustration of illustrious virtue which is the *root*, while the renovation of the people is the *result* therefrom. Looking at the words of Confucius, we must conclude that *sincerity* was the subject in his mind.

第五章

一節 此謂知本。二節 此謂知之至也。

右傳之五章、蓋釋格物致知之義、而今亡矣、閒嘗竊取程子之意、以補之曰、所謂致知在格物者、言欲致吾之知、在卽物而窮其理也、蓋人心之靈、莫不有知、而天下之物、莫不有理、惟於理有未窮、故其知有不盡也、是以大學始教、必使學者卽凡天下之物、莫

CHAPTER V. 1. This is called knowing the root.
2. This is called the perfecting of knowledge.

The above fifth chapter of the commentary explained the meaning of "investigating things and carrying knowledge to the utmost extent," but it is now lost. I have ventured to take the views of the scholar Ch'ing to supply it, as follows:—The meaning of the expression, "The perfecting of knowledge depends on the investigation of things," is this:—If we wish to carry our knowledge to the utmost, we must investigate the principles of all things we come into contact with, for the intelligent mind of man is certainly formed to know, and there is not a single thing in which its principles do not inhere. But so long as all principles are not investigated, man's knowledge is incomplete. On this account, the Learning for Adults, at the outset of its lessons, instructs the learner, in regard to all things in the world, to proceed from what knowledge he has of their principles, and pursue his investiga-

5. ON THE INVESTIGATION OF THINGS, AND CARRYING KNOWLEDGE TO THE UTMOST EXTENT. 1. This is said by one of the Ch'ing to be 衍文, 'superfluous text.' 2. Choo He considers this to be the conclusion of a chapter which is now lost. But we have seen that the two sentences come in, as the work stands in the Le-ke, at the conclusion of what is deemed the classical text. It is not necessary to add anything here to what has been said there, and in the prolegomena, on the new dispositions of the work from the time of the Sung scholars, and the manner in which Choo He has supplied this supposed missing chapter.

不因其已知之理、而益窮之、以求至乎其極、至於用力之久、而一旦豁然貫通焉、則衆物之表裏精粗、無不到、而吾心之全體大用、無不明矣、此謂物格、此謂知之至也。

第六章 一節 所謂誠其意者、毋自欺也、如惡惡臭、如好好色、此之謂自謙、故君子必慎其獨也。二節 小人閒居爲不善、無所不至、見君子、而后

tion of them, till he reaches the extreme point. After exerting himself in this way for a long time, he will suddenly find himself possessed of a wide and far-reaching penetration. Then, the qualities of all things, whether external or internal, the subtle or the coarse, will all be apprehended, and the mind, in its entire substance and its relations to things, will be perfectly intelligent. This is called the investigation of things. This is called the perfection of knowledge

CHAPTER VI. 1. What is meant by "making the thoughts sincere," is the allowing no self-deception, as *when* we hate a bad smell, and as *when* we love what is beautiful. This is called self-enjoyment. Therefore, the superior man must be watchful over himself when he is alone.

2. There is no evil to which the mean man, dwelling retired, will not proceed, but when he sees a superior man, he instantly tries

6. ON HAVING THE THOUGHTS SINCERE. 1. *The sincerity of the thoughts obtains, when they move without effort to what is right and wrong, and, in order to this, a man must be specially on his guard in his solitary moments.* 自謙 is taken as if it were 自慊,=repose or enjoyment in one's-self. 慊, acc. to Choo He, is in the up. 4th tone, but the dict. makes it up. 2d. 2. *An enforcement of the concluding clause in the last paragraph.* 厭, up. 2d tone, the same as 黶, meaning 閉藏貌, 'the appearance of concealing.' 人之視己,—人 refers to the superior man mentioned above,='the other.' 己 =他, 'him,' and not=*himself*, which is its com-

厭然、揜其不善、而著其善、人之視己、如見其肺肝然、則何益矣、此謂誠於中、形於外、故君子必愼其獨也。

三節 曾子曰、十目所視、十手所指、其嚴乎。

四節 富潤屋、德潤身、心廣、體胖、故君子必誠其意。

右傳之六章、釋誠意。

to disguise himself, concealing his evil, and displaying what is good. The other beholds him, as if he saw his heart and reins;—of what use *is his disguise?* This is an instance of the saying—"What truly is within will be manifested without." Therefore, the superior man must be watchful over himself when he is alone.

3. The disciple Tsăng said, "What ten eyes behold, what ten hands point to, is to be regarded with reverence!"

4. Riches adorn a house, and virtue adorns the person. The mind is expanded, and the body is at ease. Therefore, the superior man must make his thoughts sincere.

The above sixth chapter of commentary explains making the thoughts sincere.

mon signification. 肺肝,—lit., 'the lungs and liver,' but with the meaning which we attach to the expression substituted for it in the translation. The Chinese make the lungs the seat of righteousness, and the liver the seat of benevolence. Compare 今予其敷心腹腎腸 in the Shoo-king, IV. vii. Sect. III. 3. 3. The use of 曾子 at the beginning of this paragraph (and extending, perhaps, over to the next) should suffice to show, that the whole work is not his, as assumed by Choo He. 'Ten' is a round number, put for *many*. The recent commentator, Lo Chung-fan, refers Tsăng's expressions to the multitude of spiritual beings, servants of Heaven or God, who dwell in the regions of the air, and are continually beholding men's conduct. But they are probably only an emphatic way of exhibiting what is said in the preceding paragraph. 4. This par. is commonly referred to Tsăng Sin, but whether correctly so or not cannot be positively affirmed. It is of the same purport as the two preceding, showing that hypocrisy is of no use. Compare Mencius, VII. Pt I. xxi. 4. Ch'ing K'ang-shing explains 胖, (read *pwan*) by 大, 'large,' and Choo He by 安舒, as in the transl. The meaning is probably the same.—It is only the first of these parr. from which we can in any way ascertain the views of the writer on making the thoughts sincere. The other parr. contain only illustration or enforcement. Now the gist of the 1st par. seems to be in 毋自欺, 'allowing no self-deception.' After knowledge has been carried to the utmost, this remains to be done, and it is not true that, when knowledge has been completed, the thoughts become sincere. This fact overthrows Choo He's interpretation of the vexed passages in what he calls the text of Confucius. Let the student examine his note appended to this chapter, and he will see that Choo was not unconscious of this pinch of the difficulty.

傳七章 一節 所謂脩身、在正其心者、身有所忿懥、則不得其正、有所恐懼、則不得其正、有所好樂、則不得其正、有所憂患、則不得其正。二節 心不在焉、視而不見、聽而不聞、食而不知其味。三節 此謂脩身、在正其心。

右傳之七章、釋正心脩身。

CHAPTER VII. 1. What is meant by, "The cultivation of the person depends on rectifying the mind," *may be thus illustrated:*—If a man be under the influence of passion, he will be incorrect in his conduct. He will be the same, if he is under the influence of terror, or under the influence of fond regard, or under that of sorrow and distress.

2. When the mind is not present, we look and do not see; we hear and do not understand; we eat and do not know the taste of what we eat.

3. This is what is meant by saying that the cultivation of the person depends on the rectifying of the mind.

The above seventh chapter of commentary explains rectifying the mind and cultivating the person.

7. ON PERSONAL CULTIVATION AS DEPENDENT ON THE RECTIFICATION OF THE MIND. 1. Here Choo He, following his master Ch'ing, would again alter the text, and change the second 身 into 心. But this is unnecessary. The 身 in 修身 is not the mere material body, but the person, the individual man, in contact with things, and intercourse with society, and the 2d par. shows that the evil conduct in the first is a consequence of the mind's not being under control. In 忿懥, 恐懼, 好樂 (*gaou*), 憂患, the 2d term rises on the signification of the first, and intensifies it. Thus, 忿 is called 'a burst of anger,' and 懥, 'persistence in anger,' &c., &c.—I have said above that 身 here is not the material body. Lo Chung-fan, however, says that it is:—身謂肉身, '身 is the body of flesh.' See his reasonings, *in loc.*, but they do not work conviction in the reader. 2. 心不在焉,— this seems to be a case in point, to prove that we cannot tie 心 in this work to any very definite application. Lo Chung-fan insists that it is 'the God-given *moral* nature,' but 心不在焉 is evidently= 'when the thoughts are otherwise engaged.'

第八章 一節 所謂齊其家、在脩其身者、人之其所親愛、而辟焉、之其所賤惡、而辟焉、之其所畏敬、而辟焉、之其所哀矜、而辟焉、之其所敖惰、而辟焉、故好而知其惡、惡而知其美者、天下鮮矣。二節 故諺有之曰、人莫知其子之惡、莫知其苗之碩。三節 此謂身不脩、不可以齊其家。

CHAPTER VIII. 1. What is meant by "The regulation of one's family depends on the cultivation of his person," is this:—Men are partial where they feel affection and love; partial where they despise and dislike; partial where they stand in awe and reverence; partial where they feel sorrow and compassion ; partial where they are arrogant and rude. Thus it is that there are few men in the world, who love, and at the same time know the bad qualities of *the object of their love*, or who hate, and yet know the excellences of *the object of their hatred*.

2. Hence it is said, in the common adage, "A man does not know the wickedness of his son; he does not know the richness of his growing corn."

3. This is what is meant by saying that if the person be not cultivated, a man cannot regulate his family.

8. THE NECESSITY OF CULTIVATING THE PERSON, IN ORDER TO THE REGULATION OF THE FAMILY. The lesson here is evidently, that men are continually falling into error, in consequence of the partiality of their feelings and affections. How this error affects their personal cultivation, and interferes with the regulating of their families, is not specially indicated. 1. The old interpreters seem to go far astray in their interpretation. They take 之 in 之其所親愛, and the other clauses, as=適, 'to go to,' and 辟 as synonymous with 譬, 'to compare.' Ying-tă thus expands K'ang-shing on 人之其所親愛而辟焉:—'Suppose I go to that man. When I see that he is virtuous, I feel affection for, and love him. I ought then to turn round and compare him with myself. Since he is virtuous and I love him, then, if I cultivate myself and be virtuous, I shall so be able in like manner to make all men feel affection for and love me.' In a similar way the other clauses are dealt with. Choo He takes 之 as=於, 'in regard to,' and 辟 (read *p'eih*) as=偏, 'partial,' 'one-sided.' Even his opponent, Lo Chung-fan, interprets here in the same way. 親愛, and the other combinations are to be taken as if there were a 而, 'and,' between them. 敖 is here=傲, 'proud,' 'un-

右傳之八章、釋脩身齊家。

第九章

〔一節〕所謂治國、必先齊其家者、其家不可教、而能教人者、無之、故君子不出家、而成教於國、孝者、所以事君也、弟者、所以事長也、慈者、所以使衆也。〔二節〕康誥曰、如保赤子、心誠求之、雖不中、不遠矣、未有學養子、而后嫁者也。〔三節〕一家仁、一國興仁、一家讓、一國興讓、一人貪

The above eighth chapter of commentary explains cultivating the person and regulating the family.

CHAPTER IX. 1. What is meant by "In order rightly to govern his State, it is necessary first to regulate his family," is this:—It is not possible for one to teach others, while he cannot teach his own family. Therefore, the ruler, without going beyond his family, completes the lessons for the State. There is filial piety:—therewith the sovereign should be served. There is fraternal submission:—therewith elders and superiors should be served. There is kindness:—therewith the multitude should be treated.

2. In the Announcement to K'ang, it is said, "*Act* as if you were watching over an infant." If a mother is really anxious about it, though she may not hit *exactly the wants of her infant*, she will not be far from doing so. There never has been *a girl* who learned to bring up a child, that she might afterwards marry.

3. From the loving *example* of one family, a whole State becomes loving, and from its courtesies, the whole State becomes courteous,

civil.' 2. 碩,—'great,' 'tall;' 苗之碩,—'the tallness (richness, abundance) of his growing crop.' Farmers were noted, it would appear, in China, so long ago, for grumbling about their crops.

9. ON REGULATING THE FAMILY AS THE MEANS TO THE WELL-ORDERING OF THE STATE. 1. *There is here implied the necessity of self-cultivation to the rule, both of the family and of the State, and that being supposed to exist,—which is the force of the* 故,—*it is shown how the virtues that secure the regulation of the family, have their corresponding virtues in the wider sphere of the State.* 君子 has here both the moral and the political meaning; it is 治國之君子, 'the superior man with whom is the government of the state.'

大學

戾、一國作亂、其機如此、此謂一言僨事、一人定國。○四節堯舜帥天下以仁、而民從之、桀紂帥天下以暴、而民從之、其所令反其所好、而民不從、是故君子、有諸己、而后求諸人、無諸己、而后非諸人、所藏乎身不恕、而能喻諸人者、未之有也。○五節故治國、在齊其家。○六節詩云、桃之夭

while, from the ambition and perverseness of the one man, the whole State may be led to rebellious disorder;—such is the nature of the influence. This verifies the saying, "Affairs may be ruined by a single sentence; a kingdom may be settled by its one man."

4. Yaou and Shun led on the empire with benevolence, and the people followed them. Këĕ and Chow led on the empire with violence, and the people followed them. The orders which these issued were contrary to the practices which they loved, and so the people did not follow them. On this account, the ruler must himself be possessed of the *good* qualities, and then he may require them in the people. He must not have *the bad qualities* in himself, and then he may require that they shall not be in the people. Never has there been a man, who, not having reference to his own character and wishes in dealing with others, was able effectually to instruct them.

5. Thus we see how the government of the State depends on the regulation of the family.

It being once suggested to Choo He that 不可教 should be 不能教, he replied—彼之不可教,即我之不能教, 'The *impossibility* of that's being taught is just my *inability* to teach.' 2. See the Shoo-king, V. x. 7. Both in the Shoo-king and here, some verb, like *act*, must be supplied. This par. seems designed to show that *the ruler must be carried on to his object by an inward, unconstrained, feeling, like that of the mother for her infant.* Lo Chung-fan insists on this as harmonizing with 親民, 'to love the people,' as the second object proposed in the Great Learning. 3 *How certainly and rapidly the influence of the family extends to the State.* 一家 is the one family of the ruler, and 一人 is the ruler. 一人,='I, the one man,' is a way in which the emperor speaks of himself; see Ana. XX. i. 5. 一言=一句, as in Ana. II. ii. 一言僨事, 一人定國,—comp. Ana. XIII. xv. 仁 and 讓 have

夭、其葉蓁蓁、之子于歸、宜其家人、宜其家人、而后可以教國人。〇七節 詩云、宜兄宜弟、宜兄宜弟、而后可以教國人。〇八節 詩云、其儀不忒、正是四國、其爲父子兄弟足法、而后民法之也。〇九節 此謂治國、在齊其家。

6. In the Book of Poetry, it is said, "That peach tree, so delicate and elegant! How luxuriant is its foliage! This girl is going to her husband's house. She will rightly order her household." Let the household be rightly ordered, and then the people of the State may be taught.

7. In the Book of Poetry, it is said, "They can discharge their duties to their elder brothers. They can discharge their duties to their younger brothers." Let the ruler discharge his duties to his elder and younger brothers, and then he may teach the people of the State.

8. In the Book of Poetry, it is said, "In his deportment there is nothing wrong; he rectifies all the people of the State." *Yes;* when the ruler, as a father, a son, and a brother, is a model, then the people imitate him.

9. This is what is meant by saying, "The government of his kingdom depends on his regulation of the family."

reference to the 孝, 弟 (=悌), 慈, in par. 1. 4. *An illustration of the last part of the last paragraph.* But from the examples cited, the sphere of influence is extended from the State to the empire, and the family, moreover, does not intervene between the empire and the ruler. In 其所令, 其 must be understood as referring to the tyrants, Këë and Chow. Their orders were good, but unavailing, in consequence of their own contrary example. 諸=於. 所藏乎身, 'what is kept in one's own person,' *i. e.*, his character and mind. 恕,—see Ana. V. xi; XV. iii. Ying-tă seems to take 不恕 as simply=' good.' 6. See the She-king, I. i. Ode VI. st. 3. The ode celebrates the wife of king Wăn, and the happy influence of their family government. 之子=是子. Obs. 子 is feminine, as in Ana. V. i. 歸, 'going home,' a term for marriage, used by women. 7. See the She-king, II. ii. Ode VI. st. 3. The ode was sung at entertainments, when the emperor feasted the princes. It celebrates their virtues. 8. See the She-king, I. xiv. Ode III. st. 3. It celebrates, acc. to Choo He, the praises of some *keun-tsze*, or ruler. 四國,—not 'four states,' but the four quarters of the state, the whole of it.

右傳之九章、釋齊家治國。

第十章 一節 所謂平天下、在治其國者、上老老、而民興孝、上長長、而民興弟、上恤孤、而民不倍、是以君子、有絜矩之道也。○二節 所惡於上、毋以使下、所惡於下、毋以事上、所惡於前、毋以先後、所惡於後、毋以

The above ninth chapter of commentary explains regulating the family and governing the kingdom.

CHAPTER X. 1. What is meant by "The making the whole empire peaceful and happy depends on the government of his State," is this:—When the sovereign behaves to his aged, as the aged should be behaved to, the people become filial; when the sovereign behaves to his elders, as elders should be behaved to, the people learn brotherly submission; when the sovereign treats compassionately the young and helpless, the people do the same. Thus the ruler has a principle with which, as with a measuring square, he may regulate his conduct.

2. What a man dislikes in his superiors, let him not display in the treatment of his inferiors; what he dislikes in inferiors, let him not display in the service of his superiors; what he hates in those who are before him, let him not therewith precede those who are behind him; what he hates in those who are behind him, let him

10. ON THE WELL-ORDERING OF THE STATE, AND MAKING THE WHOLE EMPIRE PEACEFUL AND HAPPY. The key to this chapter is in the phrase 絜矩之道, the principle of reciprocity, the doing to others as we would that they should do to us, though here, as elsewhere, it is put forth negatively. It is implied in the expression of the last ch.—所藏乎身不恕, but it is here discussed at length, and shown in its highest application. The following analysis of the chapter is translated freely from the 四書輯要:—'This ch. explains the well-ordering of the State, and the tranquillization of the empire. The greatest stress is to be laid on the phrase—*the measuring square*. That, and the expression in the general commentary —*loving and hating what the people love and hate, and not thinking only of the profit*, exhaust the teaching of the chap. It is divided into five parts. The *first*, embracing the two first paragraphs, teaches, that the way to make the empire tranquil and happy is in the principle of the measuring square. The *second* part embraces three paragraphs, and teaches that the application of the measuring square is seen in loving, and hating, in common with the people. The consequences of *losing* and *gaining* are mentioned for the first time in the 4th par., to wind up the ch. so far, showing that the decree of Heaven goes or remains, according as the people's hearts are lost or gained. The *third* part embraces

從前、所惡於右、毋以交於左、所惡於左、毋以交於右、此之謂絜矩之道。○三節 詩云、樂只君子、民之父母、民之所好好之、民之所惡惡之、此之謂民之父母。○四節 詩云、節彼南山、維石巖巖、赫赫師尹、民具爾瞻、有國者、不可以不愼、辟、則爲天下僇矣。○五節 詩

not therewith follow those who are before him; what he hates to receive on the right, let him not bestow on the left; what he hates to receive on the left, let him not bestow on the right:—this is what is called "The principle, with which, as with a measuring square, to regulate one's conduct."

3. In the Book of Poetry, it is said, "How much to be rejoiced in are these princes, the parents of the people!" When *a prince* loves what the people love, and hates what the people hate, then is he what is called the parent of the people.

4. In the Book of Poetry, it is said, "Lofty is that southern hill, with its rugged masses of rocks! Greatly distinguished are you, O *grand*-teacher Yin, the people all look up to you." Rulers of kingdoms may not neglect to be careful. If they deviate *to a mean selfishness*, they will be a disgrace in the empire.

eight paragraphs, and teaches that the most important result of loving and hating in common with the people is seen in making the *root* the primary subject, and the *branch* only secondary. Here, in par. 11, mention is again made of *gaining* and *losing*, illustrating the meaning of the quotation in it, and showing that to the collection or dissipation of the people the decree of Heaven is attached. The *fourth* part consists of five paragraphs, and exhibits the extreme results of loving and hating, as shared with the people, or on one's own private feeling, and it has special reference to the sovereign's employment of ministers, because there is nothing in the principle more important than that. The 19th par. speaks of *gaining and losing*, for the third time, showing that from the 4th par. downwards, in reference both to the hearts of the people and the decree of Heaven, the application or non-application of the principle of the *measuring-square* depends on the mind of the sovereign. The *fifth* part embraces the other paragraphs. Because the root of the evil of a sovereign's not applying that principle, lies in his not knowing how wealth is produced, and employs mean men for that object, the distinction between righteousness and profit is here much insisted on, the former bringing with it all advantages, and the latter leading to all evil consequences. Thus the sovereign is admonished, and it is seen how to be careful of his virtue is the root of the principle of the *measuring-square*; and his loving and hating, in common sympathy with the people, is its reality.'

1. There is here no progress of thought, but a repetition of what has been insisted on in the two last chapters. In 老老, 長長, the first characters are verbs, with the meaning which it requires so many words to bring out in the translation. 弟=悌. 孤,—properly, 'fa-

云、殷之未喪師、克配上帝、儀監于殷、峻命不易、道得衆、則得國、失衆、則失國。○六節是故君子先愼乎德、有德、此有人、有人、此有土、有土、此有財、有財、此有用。○七節德者、本也、財者、末也。○八節外本內末、爭

5. In the Book of Poetry, it is said, "Before the sovereigns of the Yin *dynasty* had lost the *hearts of the* people, they could appear before God. Take warning from *the house of* Yin. The great decree is not easily *preserved.*" This shows that, by gaining the people, the kingdom is gained, and, by losing the people, the kingdom is lost.

6. On this account, the ruler will first take pains about *his own* virtue. Possessing virtue will give him the people. Possessing the people will give him the territory. Possessing the territory will give him its wealth. Possessing the wealth, he will have resources for expenditure.

7. Virtue is the root; wealth is the result.

8. If he make the root his secondary object, and the result his primary, he will *only* wrangle with his people, and teach them rapine.

therless;' here,—'the young and helpless.' 倍, read as, and=背, 'to rebel,' 'to act contrary to.' 君子, here and throughout the ch., has reference to office, and specially to the imperial or highest. 絜矩之道,—絜 is a verb, read *hëě*, acc. to Choo He,=度, 'to measure;' 矩,—the mechanical instrument, 'the square.' It having been seen that the ruler's example is so influential, it follows that the minds of all men are the same in sympathy and tendency. He has then only to take his own mind, and measure therewith the minds of others. If he act accordingly, the grand result—the empire tranquil and happy—will ensue. 2. *A lengthened description of the principle of reciprocity.* 先,—up. 3d tone, 'to precede.' 3. See the She-king, II. ii. Ode V. st. 3. The ode is one that was sung at festivals, and celebrates the virtues of the princes present. Choo He makes 只 (read *che*, up. 2d tone) an expletive. Ch'ing's gloss, in 毛詩註疏, takes it as=是, and the whole is—'I gladden these princes, the parents of the people.' 4. See the She-king, II. iv. Ode VII. st. 1. The ode complains of the emperor Yew (幽), for his employing unworthy ministers. 節, read *ts'ëë*, meaning 'rugged and lofty-looking.' 具=俱, 'all.' 辟, read *p'eih*, as in ch. viii. 僇 is explained in the dict. by 辱, 'disgrace.' Choo He seems to take it as =戮, 'to kill,' as did the old commentators. They say:—'he will be put to death by the people, as were the tyrants, Këě and Chow.' 5. See the She-king, III. i. Ode I. st. 6, where we have 宜 for 儀, and 駿 for 峻. The ode is supposed to be addressed to king Shing (成), to stimulate him to imitate the virtues of his grandfather Wăn. 殷,=' the sovereigns of the Yin dynasty.' The capital of the Shang dynasty was changed to Yin by P'wan-kang, B. C.

民施奪。○九節是故財聚、則民散、財散、則民聚。○十節是故言悖而出者、亦悖而入、貨悖而入者、亦悖而出。○十一節康誥曰、惟命不于常、道善則得之、不善則失之矣。○十二節楚書曰、楚國無以爲寶、惟善、以爲寶。○十三舅犯

9. Hence, the accumulation of wealth is the way to scatter the people; and the letting it be scattered among them is the way to collect the people.

10. And hence, the ruler's words going forth contrary to right, will come back to him in the same way, and wealth, gotten by improper ways, will take its departure by the same.

11. In the Announcement to K'ang, it is said, "The decree indeed may not always rest on *us;*" that is, goodness obtains the decree, and the want of goodness loses it.

12. In the Book of Ts'oo, it is said, "The kingdom of Ts'oo does not consider that to be valuable. It values, *instead*, its good men."

1400, after which the dynasty was so denominated. 配上帝, acc. to Choo He, means 'they were the sovereigns of the emperor, and corresponded to (fronted) God.' K'ang-shing says:—'Before they lost their people, from their virtue, they were also able to appear before Heaven; that is, Heaven accepted their sacrifices.' Lo Chung-fan makes it.—'They harmonized with God; that is, in loving the people.' K'ang-shing's interpretation is, I apprehend, the correct one. 道=言, as in ch. iii. 4. 6. 愼乎德,—德 here, accord. to Choo He, is the 'illustrious virtue' at the beginning of the book. His opponents say that it is the exhibition of virtue; that is, of filial piety, brotherly submission, &c. This is more in harmony with the first par. of the chapter. 8. 外 and 内 are used as verbs,=輕, 重, 'to consider slight,' 'to consider important.' 爭民,—'will wrangle the (*i. e.*, with the) people.' The ruler will be trying to take, and the people will be trying to hold. 施奪,—'he will give'—(*i. e.*, lead the people to,=teach them)—'rapine.' The two phrases=he will be against the people, and well set them against himself, and against one another. Ying-tă explains them—'people wrangling for gain will give reins to their rapacious disposition.' 9. 財散, 'wealth being scattered,'—that is, diffused, and allowed to be so by the ruler, among the people. The collecting and scattering of the people are to be understood with reference to their feelings towards their ruler. 10. The 'words' are to be understood of governmental orders and enactments. 悖, read *pei*,=逆, 'to act contrary to,' 'to rebel,' that which is outraged being 理, 'what is right,' or, in the first place, 民心, 'the people's hearts,' and, in the second place, 君心, 'the ruler's heart.' Our proverb—'goods ill-gotten go ill-spent' might be translated by 貨悖而入者, 亦悖而出, but those words have a diff. meaning in the text. 11. See the *K'ang Kaou*, p. 23. The only difficulty is with 于. K'ang-shing and Ying-tă do not take it as an expletive, but say it=於, 'in,' or 'on;'—'The appointment of Heaven may not constantly rest on one family.' Treating 于 in this way, the supplement in the Shoo-king, should be 'us.'

大學

曰、亡人、無以爲寶、仁親以
爲寶。〇十四節 秦誓曰、若有一个臣、
斷斷兮、無他技、其心休休
焉、其如有容焉、人之有技、
若己有之、人之彥聖、其心
好之、不啻若自其口出、實
能容之、以能保我子孫黎
民、尚亦有利哉。人之有技、
媢疾以惡之、人之彥聖、而
違之、俾不通、實不能容、以

13. *Duke Wăn's* uncle, Fan, said, "Our fugitive does not account that to be precious. What he considers precious, is the affection due to his parent."

14. In the Declaration *of the duke of* Ts'in, it is said, "Let me have but one minister, plain and sincere, not *pretending to* other abilities, but with a simple, upright, mind; and possessed of generosity, *regarding* the talents of others as though he himself possessed them, and, where he finds accomplished and perspicacious men, loving them in his heart more than his mouth expresses, and really showing himself able to bear them *and employ them*:—such a minister will be able to preserve my sons and grandsons, and black-haired people, and benefits likewise to the kingdom may well be looked for from him. But if *it be his character*, when he finds men of ability, to be jealous and hate them; and, when he finds accomplished and perspicacious men, to oppose them and not allow their advancement, showing himself really not able to bear them:—such a minister

道, as in p, 5. 12. The Book of Ts'oo is found in the 國語, 'National records,' a collection purporting to be of the Chow dynasty, and, in relation to the other states, what Confucius' 'Spring and Autumn' is to Loo. The exact words of the text do not occur, but they could easily be constructed from the narrative. An officer of Ts'oo being sent on an embassy to Tsin (晉), the minister who received him asked about a famous girdle of Ts'oo, called 白珩, how much it was worth. The officer replied that his country did not look on such things as its treasures, but on its able and virtuous ministers. 13. 舅犯, 'uncle Fan;' that is, uncle to Wăn, the duke of Ts'in. See Ana. XIV. xvi. Wăn is the 亡人, or, 'fugitive.' In the early part of his life, he was a fugitive, and suffered many vicissitudes of fortune. Once, the duke of Ts'in (秦) having offered to help him, when he was in mourning for his father who had expelled him, to recover Tsin, his uncle Fan gave the reply in the text. The *that* in the translation refers to 得國, 'getting the kingdom.' 14. 'The declaration *of the duke of* Ts'in' is the last

不能保我子孫黎民、亦曰殆哉。○十五節唯仁人、放流之、迸諸四夷、不與同中國、此謂唯仁人、爲能愛人、能惡人。○十六節見賢、而不能舉、舉、而不能先、命也、見不善、而不能退、退、而不能遠、過也。○十七節好人之所惡、惡人之所好、是謂拂人之性、菑必逮夫身。○十八節是故君子、有大道、必忠信以得之、

will not be able to protect my sons and grandsons and black-haired people; and may he not also be pronounced dangerous *to the State?*"

15. It is only the truly virtuous man, who can send away such a man and banish him, driving him out among the barbarous tribes around, determined not to dwell along with him in the Middle kingdom. This is in accordance with the saying, "It is only the truly virtuous man who can love or who can hate others."

16. To see men of worth and not be able to raise them to office; to raise them to office, but not to do so quickly:—this is disrespectful. To see bad men and not be able to remove them; to remove them, but not to do so to a distance:—this is weakness.

17. To love those whom men hate, and to hate those whom men love;—this is to outrage the natural feeling of men. Calamities cannot fail to come down on him who does so.

18. Thus *we see that* the sovereign has a great course *to pursue*. He must show entire self-devotion and sincerity to attain it, and by pride and extravagance he will fail of it.

book in the Shoo-king. It was made by one of the dukes of Ts'in to his officers, after he had sustained a great disaster, in consequence of neglecting the advice of his most faithful minister. Between the text here, and that which we find in the Shoo-king, there are some differences, but they are unimportant. 15. 仁人 is here, acc. to Choo He and his followers, the prince who applies the principle of reciprocity, expounded in the second par. Lo Chung-fan contends that it is 親民者, 'the lover of the people.' The par. is closely connected with the preceding. In 放流之, 之 refers to the bad minister, there described. The 四夷, 'four E;' see the Le-ke, III. iii. 14. 不與同中國=不與之同處中國, 'will not dwell together with him in the Middle kingdom.' China is evidently so denominated, from its being thought to be surrounded by barbarous tribes. 惟仁人能云云,—see Ana. IV. iii. 16. I have translated 命 as if it were

驕泰以失之。○十九節 生財有大道、生之者衆、食之者寡、爲之者疾、用之者舒、則財恆足矣。○二十節 仁者以財發身、不仁者以身發財。○廿一節 未有上好仁、而下不好義者也、未有好義、其事不終者也、未有府庫財、非其財者也。○廿二節 孟獻子曰、畜馬乘、不察於雞豚、伐冰

19. There is a great course *also* for the production of wealth. Let the producers be many and the consumers few. Let there be activity in the production, and economy in the expenditure. Then the wealth will always be sufficient.

20. The virtuous *ruler*, by means of his wealth, makes himself more distinguished. The vicious ruler accumulates wealth, at the expense of his life.

21. Never has there been a case of the sovereign loving benevolence, and the people not loving righteousness. Never has there been a case where the people have loved righteousness, and the affairs of the sovereign have not been carried to completion. And never has there been a case where the wealth in such a State, collected in the treasuries and arsenals, did not continue in the sovereign's possession.

22. The officer Măng Heen said, "He who keeps horses and a carriage does not look after fowls and pigs. The family which

慢, which K'ang-shing thinks should be in the text. Ch'ing E (頤) would substitute 怠, 'idle,' instead of 慢, and Choo He does not know which suggestion to prefer. Lo Chung-fan stoutly contends for retaining 命, and interprets it as='fate,' but he is obliged to supply a good deal himself, to make any sense of the passage. See his argument, *in loc.* The paraphrasts all explain 先 by 早, 'early.' 遠, up 3d tone, but with a hiphil force. 退 is referred to 放流 in last par., and 遠 to 不與同中國. 17. This is spoken of the ruler not having respect to the common feelings of the people in his employment of ministers, and the consequences thereof to himself. 夫, low. 1st tone, is used as in Ana. XI. ix. 4, or= the prep. 乎. *This par. speaks generally of the primal cause of gaining and losing, and shows how the principle of the measuring square must have its root in the ruler's mind.* So, in the 日講. The great course is explained by Choo He as—'the art of occupying the throne, and therein cultivating himself and governing others.' Ying-tă says it is—'the course by which he practises filial piety, fraternal duty, benevolence, and righteousness.' 驕 and 泰 are here qualities of the

之家、不畜牛羊、百乘之家、不畜聚歛之臣、與其有聚歛之臣、寧有盜臣、此謂國不以利爲利、以義爲利也。

廿三節 長國家、而務財用者、必自小人矣、彼爲善之、小人之使爲國家、菑害並至、雖有善者、亦無如之何矣、此謂

keeps its stores of ice does not rear cattle or sheep. *So*, the house which possesses a hundred chariots should not keep a minister to look out for imposts that he may lay them on the people. Than to have such a minister, it were better for that house to have one who should rob it *of its revenues*." This is in accordance with the saying:—"In a State, *pecuniary* gain is not to be considered to be prosperity, but its prosperity *will* be found in righteousness."

23. When he who presides over a State or a family makes his revenues his chief business, he must be under the influence of some small, mean, man. He may consider this man to be good; but when such a person is employed in the administration of a State or family, calamities *from Heaven*, and injuries *from men*, will befal it together, and, though a good man may take his place, he will not be able to remedy the evil. This illustrates *again* the saying, "In a State, gain is not to be considered prosperity, but its prosperity will be found in righteousness."

same nature. They are not contrasted as in Ana. XIII. xxvi. 19. This is understood by K'ang-shing as requiring the promotion of agriculture, and that is included, but does not exhaust the meaning. The consumers are the salaried officers of the government. The sentiment of the whole is good;—where there is cheerful industry in the people, and an economical administration of the government, the finances will be flourishing. 20. The sentiment here is substantially the same as in parr. 7, 8. The old interpretation is different:—'The virtuous man uses his wealth so as to make his person distinguished. He who is not virtuous, toils with his body to increase his wealth.' 21. This shows how the people respond to the influence of the ruler, and that benevolence, even to the scattering of his wealth on the part of the latter, is the way to permanent prosperity and wealth. 22. Hëen was the hon. epithet of Chung-sun Mëě (蔑), a worthy minister of Loo, under the two dukes, who ruled before the birth of Confucius. His sayings, quoted here, were preserved by tradition, or recorded in some work which is now lost. 畜 (read *hüh*) 乘馬,—on a scholar's being first called to office, he was gifted by his prince with a carriage, and four horses. He was then supposed to withdraw from petty ways of getting wealth. The 卿, or high officers of a State, kept ice for use in their funeral rites and sacrifices. 伐冰,—with reference to the *cutting* the ice to store it. 聚歛之臣,—see Ana. XI. xvi. 23. 彼爲善之,—善 is used as a verb,=以爲善, 'considers to be good.' 不以利爲利, 以義爲利,—see Mencius. I. Pt. I. i, *et passim*.

大學

國、不以利爲利、以義爲利也。

右傳之十章、釋治國平天下。凡傳十章、前四章、統論綱領指趣、後六章、細論條目工夫、其第五章、乃明善之要、第六章、乃誠身之本、在初學、尤爲當務之急、讀者不可以其近而忽之也。

The above tenth chapter of commentary explains the government of the State, and the making the empire peaceful and happy.

There are thus, in all, ten chapters of commentary, the first four of which discuss, in a general manner, the scope of the principal topic of the Work; while the other six go particularly into an exhibition of the work required in its subordinate branches. The fifth chapter contains the important subject of comprehending true excellence, and the sixth, what is the foundation of the attainment of true sincerity. Those two chapters demand the especial attention of the learner. Let not the reader despise them because of their simplicity.

THE DOCTRINE OF THE MEAN.

中庸

子程子曰、不偏之謂中、不易之謂庸、中者、天下之正道、庸者、天下之定理、此篇乃孔門傳授心法、子思恐其久而差也、故筆之於書、以授孟子、其書始言一理、中散爲萬事、末復合爲一理、放

My master, the philosopher Ch‘ing, says, "Being without inclination to either side is called CHUNG; *admitting of no change is called* YUNG. *By* CHUNG *is denoted the correct course to be pursued by all under heaven; by* YUNG *is denoted the fixed principle regulating all under heaven. This work contains the law of the mind, which was handed down from one to another, in the Confucian school, till Tsze-sze, fearing lest in the course of time errors should arise about it, committed it to writing, and delivered it to Mencius. The book first speaks of one principle; it next spreads this out, and embraces all things; finally, it returns and gathers them all up under the one principle. Unroll it, and it*

THE TITLE OF THE WORK.—中庸, 'The doctrine of the Mean.' I have not attempted to translate the Chinese character 庸, as to the exact force of which there is considerable difference of opinion, both among native commentators, and among previous translators. Ch‘ing K‘ang-shing said:—名曰中庸者, 以其記中和之爲用也, 'The Work is named 中庸, because it records the practice of the non-deviating mind and of harmony.' He takes 庸, in the sense of 用, 'to use,' 'to employ,' which is the first given to it in the dict., and is found in the Shoo-king, I. p. 9. As to the meaning of 中, and 和, see ch. i. p. 4. This appears to have been the accepted meaning of 庸, in this combination, till Ch‘ing E introduced that of 不易, 'unchanging,' as in the introductory note, which, however, the dict. does not acknowledge. Choo He himself says—中者不偏不倚, 無過不及之名, 庸, 平常也, '*Chung* is the name for what is without inclination or deflection, which neither exceeds nor comes short. *Yung* means ordinary, constant.' The dict. gives another meaning of *Yung*, with special reference to the point before us. It is said—又和也, 'It also means harmony;' and then reference is made to K‘ang-shing's words given above, the compilers not having observed that he immediately subjoins—庸, 用也, show-

之、則彌六合、卷之、則退藏於密、其味無窮、皆實學也、善讀者、玩索而有得焉、則終身用之、有不能盡者矣。

第一章 一節 天命之謂性、率性之謂道、修道之謂教。二節 道也者、不可

fills the universe; roll it up, and it retires and lies hid in mysteriousness. The relish of it is inexhaustible. The whole of it is solid learning. When the skilful reader has explored it with delight till he has apprehended it, he may carry it into practice all his life, and will find that it cannot be exhausted.

CHAPTER I. 1. What Heaven has conferred is called THE NATURE; an accordance with this nature is called THE PATH *of duty;* the regulation of this path is called INSTRUCTION.

ing that he takes *Yung*, in the sense of 'to employ,' and not of 'harmony.' Many, however, adopt this meaning of the term in ch. ii, and my own opinion is decidedly in favour of it, here in the title. The work then treats of the human mind:—in its state of *chung*, absolutely correct, as it is in itself; and in its State of *hwo*, or harmony, acting *ad extra*, according to its correct nature.—In the version of the work, given in the collection of '*Memoires concernant l'histoire, les sciences, &c., des Chinois*,' vol. I, it is styled—'*Juste Milieu*.' Remusat calls it '*L'invariable Milieu*,' after Ch'ing E. Intorcetta, and his coadjutors call it—'*Medium constans vel sempiternum*.' The book treats, they say, '*De* MEDIO SEMPITERNO, *sive de aurea mediocritate illa, quæ est, ut ait Cicero, inter nimium et parum, constanter et omnibus in rebus tenenda*,' Morrison, character 庸, says, '*Chung Yung*, the constant (golden) medium.' Collie calls it—'The golden medium.' The objection which I have to all these names is, that from them it would appear as if 中 were a noun, and 庸 a qualifying adjective, whereas they are co-ordinate terms.

INTRODUCTORY NOTE. 子程子,—see on intro. note to the 大學. On Tsze-sze, and his authorship of this work, see the prolegomena. 六合 is a phrase denoting—'heaven, earth, and the four cardinal points,'=the universe. 善讀者,—not our 'good reader,' but as in the translation.—I will not here anticipate the judgment of the reader on the eulogy of the enthusiastic Ch'ing.

1. It has been stated, in the prolegomena, that the current division of the Chung Yung into chapters was made by Choo He, as well as their subdivision into paragraphs. The 33 chapters, which embrace the work, are again arranged by him in five divisions, as will be seen from his supplementary notes. The first and last chapters are complete in themselves, as the introduction and conclusion of the treatise. The second part contains ten chapters; the third, nine, and the fourth, twelve.

Par. 1. *The principles of duty have their root in the evidenced will of Heaven, and their full exhibition in the teaching of sages.* By 性, or 'nature,' is to be understood the nature of man, though Choo He generalizes it so as to embrace that of brutes also; but only *man* can be cognizant of the *taou* and *keaou*. 命 he defines by 令, 'to command,' 'to order.' But we must take it as in a gloss on a pass. from the Yih-king, quoted in the dict.—命者人所稟受, '*Mang* is what men are endowed with.' Choo He also says that 性 is just 理, the 'principle,' characteristic of any particular nature. But this only involves the subject in mystery. His explanation of 道 by 路, 'a path,' seems to be correct, though some modern writers object to it.—What is taught seems to be this:—To man belongs a moral nature, conferred on him by Heaven or God, by which he is constituted a

須臾離也、可離、非道也、是故君子戒慎乎其所不睹、恐懼乎其所不聞、(三節)莫見乎隱、莫顯乎微、故君子慎其獨也。(四節)喜、怒、哀、樂之未發、謂之中、發而皆中節、謂之和、中也者、天下之大本也、和

2. The path may not be left for an instant. If it could be left, it would not be the path. On this account, the superior man does not wait till he sees things, to be cautious, nor till he hears things, to be apprehensive.

3. There is nothing more visible than what is secret, and nothing more manifest than what is minute. Therefore the superior man is watchful over himself, when he is alone.

4. While there are no stirrings of pleasure, anger, sorrow. or joy, the mind may be said to be in the state of EQUILIBRIUM. When those feelings have been stirred, and they act in their due degree, there ensues what may be called the state of HARMONY. This EQUILIBRIUM is the great root *from which grow all the human actings* in the world, and this HARMONY is the universal path *which they all should pursue.*

law to himself. But as he is prone to deviate from the path in which, according to his nature, he should go, wise and good men—sages—have appeared, to explain and regulate this, helping all by their instructions to walk in it.

Par. 2. The path indicated by the nature may never be left, and the superior man—體道之人, *he who would embody all principles of right and duty—exercises a most sedulous care that he may attain thereto.* 須臾 is a name for a short period of time, of which there are 30 in the 24 hours; but the phrase is commonly used for 'a moment,' 'an instant.' K'ung Ying-tă explains 可離非道,—'what may be left, is a wrong way,' which is not admissible. 離, low. 3d tone,=去, 'to be, or go, away from.' If we translate the two last clauses literally,—'is cautious and careful in regard to what he does not see; is fearful and apprehensive in regard to what he does not hear,—they will not be intelligible to an English reader. A question arises, moreover, whether 其所不睹, 其所不聞, ought not to be understood passively,—'where he is not seen,' 'where he is not heard.' They are so understood by Ying-tă, and the 大學傳, ch. vi., is much in favour, by its analogy, of such an interpretation.

Par. 3. Choo He says that 隱 is 'a dark place;' that 細 means 'small matters;' and that 獨 is 'the place which other men do not know, and is known only to one's-self.' There would thus hardly be here any advance from the last par. It seems to me that the secrecy must be in the recesses of one's own heart, and the minute things, the springs of thought and stirrings of purpose there. The full development of what is intended here is probably to be found in all the subsequent passages about 誠, or 'sincerity.' See 西河合集中庸說, *in loc.*

Par. 4. 'This,' says Choo He, 'speaks of the virtue of the nature and passions, to illustrate the meaning of the statement that the path may not be left.' It is difficult to translate the par.,

也者、天下之達道也。○五節致中和、天地位焉、萬物育焉。

右第一章、子思述所傳之意、以立言、首明道之本原出於天、而不可易、其實體備於己、而不可離、次言存養省察之要、終言聖神功化之極、蓋欲學者於此、反求諸身、

5. Let the states of equilibrium and harmony exist in perfection, and a happy order will prevail throughout heaven and earth, and all things will be nourished and flourish.

In the first chapter which is given above, Tsze-sze states the views which had been handed down to him, as the basis of his discourse. First, it shows clearly how the path of duty is to be traced to its origin in Heaven, and is unchangeable, while the substance of it is provided in ourselves, and may not be departed from. Next, it speaks of the importance of preserving and nourishing this, and of exercising a watchful self-scrutiny with reference to it. Finally, it speaks of the meritorious achievements and transforming influence of sage and spiritual men in their highest extent. The wish of Tsze-sze was that hereby the learner should direct his thoughts inwards, and by searching in himself, there find these

because it is difficult to understand it. 謂之 is different from 之謂 in p. 1. That *defines*; this *describes*. What is described in the first clause, seems to be 性, 'the nature,' capable of all feelings, but unacted on, and in equilibrium.

Par. 5. On this Intorcetta and his colleagues observe :—'*Quis non videt eo dumtaxat collimasse philosophum, ut hominis naturam, quam ab origine sua rectam, sed deinde lapsam et depravatam passim Sinenses docent, ad primævum innocentiæ statum reducere? Atque ita reliquas res creatas, homini jam rebelles, et in ejusdem ruinam armatas, ad pristinum obsequium veluti revocaret. Hoc f. I. s. I. libri Ta Heŏ, hoc item hic et alibi non semel indicat. Etsi autem nesciret philosophus nos a prima felicitate propter peccatum primi parentis excidisse, tamen et tot rerum quæ adversantur et infestæ sunt homini, et ipsius naturæ humanæ ad deteriora tam pronæ, longo usu et contemplatione didicisse videtur, non posse hoc universum, quod homo vitiatus quodam modo vitiarat, connaturali suæ integritati et ordini restitui, nisi prius ipse homo per victoriam sui ipsius, eam, quam amiserat, integritatem et ordinem recuperaret.*' I fancied something of the same kind, before reading their note. Acc. to Choo He, the par. describes the work and influence of sage and spiritual men in their highest issues. The subject is developed in the 4th part of the work, in very extravagant and mystical language. The study of it will modify very much our assent to the views in the above passage. There is in this whole chapter a mixture of sense and

而自得之、以去夫外誘之私、而充其本然之善、楊氏所謂一篇之體要是也、其下十章、蓋子思引夫子之言、以終此章之義。

第二章

一節 仲尼曰、君子中庸、小人反中庸。二節 君子之中庸也、君子而時中、小人之中庸也、小人而無忌憚也。

truths, so that he might put aside all outward temptations appealing to his selfishness, and fill up the measure of the goodness which is natural to him. This chapter is what the writer Yang called it,—"The sum of the whole work." In the ten chapters which follow, Tsze-sze quotes the words of the Master to complete the meaning of this.

CHAPTER II. 1. Chung-ne said, "The superior man *embodies* the course of the Mean; the mean man acts contrary to the course of the Mean.

2. "The superior man's embodying the course of the Mean is because he is a superior man, and so always maintains the Mean. The mean man's acting contrary to the course of the Mean is because he is a mean man, and has no caution."

mysticism,—of what may be grasped, and what tantalizes and eludes the mind. 位, acc. to Choo He,=安其位, 'will rest in their positions.' K'ang-shing explained it by 正, —'will be rectified.' 'Heaven and Earth' are here the parent powers of the universe. Thus Ying-tă expounds:—'Heaven and Earth will get their correct place, and the processes of production and completion will go on according to their principles, so that all things will be nourished and fostered.'

CONCLUDING NOTE. The writer Yang, quoted here, was a distinguished scholar and author in the reign of 英宗, A. D. 1064–1085. He was a disciple of Ch'ing Haou, and a friend both of him and his brother, E. 體要, 'the substance and the abstract,'=the sum.

2. ONLY THE SUPERIOR MAN CAN FOLLOW THE MEAN; THE MEAN MAN IS ALWAYS VIOLATING IT. 1. Why Confucius should here be quoted by his designation, or marriage name, is a moot-point. It is said by some that disciples might in this way refer to their teacher, and a grandson to his grandfather, but such a rule is constituted probable on the strength of this instance, and that in ch. xxx. Others say that it is the honorary designation of the sage, and=the 尼父, which duke Gae used in reference to Confucius, in eulogizing him after his death. See the Le-ke, II. Pt. I. iii. 43. Some verb must be understood between 君子 and 中

中庸

第三章 子曰、中庸其至矣乎、民鮮能久矣。

第四章 一節 子曰、道之不行也、我知之矣、知者、過之、愚者、不及也、道之不明也、我知之矣、賢者、過之、不肖者、不及也。二節 人莫不飲食也、鮮能知味也。

CHAPTER III. The Master said, "Perfect is the virtue which is according to the Mean! Rare have they long been among the people, who could practise it!"

CHAPTER IV. 1. The Master said, "I know how it is that the path *of the Mean* is not walked in:—The knowing go beyond it, and the stupid do not come up to it. I know how it is that the path of the Mean is not understood:—The men of talents and virtue go beyond it, and the worthless do not come up to it.

2. "There is no body but eats and drinks. But they are few who can distinguish flavours."

庸, and I have supposed it to be 體, with most of the paraphrasts. Nearly all seem to be agreed that 中庸 here is the same as 中和, in the last chapter. On the change of terms, Choo He quotes from the scholar Yew (遊), to the effect that 中和 is said with the nature and feelings in view, and 中庸, with reference to virtue and conduct. 2. 君子而時中, is explained by Choo:—'Because he has the virtue of a superior man, and moreover is able always to manage the *chung*.' But I rather think that the *keun-tsze* here is specially to be referred to the same as described in i. 2, and 中=正中. Wang Suh, the famons scholar of the Wei (魏) dynasty, in the 1st part of the 3d cent., quotes 小人之中庸, with 反 before 中, of which Choo He approves. If 反 be not introduced into the text, it must certainly be understood. 忌憚 is the opposite of 戒慎, 恐懼, in i. 2.--This, and the ten chapters which follow, all quote the words of Confucius with reference to the 中庸, to explain the meaning of the first ch.; and 'though there is no connection of composition between them,' says Choo He, 'they are all related by their meaning.'

3. THE RARITY, LONG EXISTING IN CONFUCIUS' TIME, OF THE PRACTICE OF THE MEAN. See the Ana. VI. xxvii. K'ang-shing and Ying-tă take the last clause as='few can practise it long.' But the view in the transl. is better. The change from 仲尼曰 to 子曰 is observable.

4. HOW IT WAS THAT FEW WERE ABLE TO PRACTISE THE MEAN. 1. 道 may be referred to the 道 in the first chapter; immediately following 中庸 in the last, I translate it here —'the path of the Mean.' 知者 and 賢者 are not to be understood as meaning the truly wise and the truly worthy, but only those who in the degenerate times of Confucius deemed themselves to be such. The former thought the course of the Mean not worth their study, and the latter thought it not sufficiently exalted for their practice. 肖,—'as,' 'like.' 不肖 following 賢, indicates individuals of a diff. character, not equal to them. 2. We have here not a comparison, but an illustra., which may help to an understanding of the former par., though it does not seem very apt. People don't

第五章 子曰、道其不行矣夫。

第六章 子曰、舜其大知也與、舜好問、而好察邇言、隱惡、而揚善、執其兩端、用其中於民、其斯以爲舜乎。

第七章 子曰、人皆曰予知、驅而納諸罟擭陷阱之中、而莫之知辟也、人皆曰予知、擇乎中庸、而不能

CHAPTER V. The Master said, "Alas! How is the path of the Mean untrodden!"

CHAPTER VI. The Master said, "There was Shun:—He indeed was greatly wise! Shun loved to question *others*, and to study their words, though they might be shallow. He concealed what was bad *in them*, and displayed what was good. He took hold of their two extremes, *determined* the Mean, and employed it in *his government of* the people. It was by this that he was Shun!"

CHAPTER VII. The Master said, "Men all say, 'We are wise;' but being driven forward and taken in a net, a trap, or a pitfall, they know not how to escape. Men all say, 'We are wise;' but happening to choose the course of the Mean, they are not able to keep it for a round month."

know the true flavour of what they eat and drink, but they need not go beyond that to learn it. So, the Mean belongs to all the actions of ordinary life, and might be discerned and practised in them, without looking for it in extraordinary things.

5. Choo He says:—'From not being understood, therefore it is not practised.' Acc. to K'ang-shing, the remark is a lament that there was no intelligent sovereign to teach the path. But the two views are reconcileable.

6. HOW SHUN PURSUED THE COURSE OF THE MEAN. This example of Shun, it seems to me, is adduced in opposition to the knowing of ch. iv. Shun, tho' a sage, invited the opinions of all men, and found truth of the highest value in their simplest sayings, and was able to determine from them the course of the Mean. 執其兩端,—'the two extremes' are understood by K'ang-shing of the two errors of exceeding and coming short of the Mean. Choo He makes them—'the widest differences in the opinions which he received.' I conceive the meaning to be that he examined the answers which he got, in their entirety, from beginning to end. Comp. 扣其兩端, Ana. IX. vii. His concealing what was bad, and displaying what was good, was alike to encourage people to speak freely to him. K'ang-shing makes the last sentence to turn on the meaning of 舜, when applied as an honorary epithet of the dead, =' Full, all-accomplished;' but Shun was so named when he was alive.

7. THEIR CONTRARY CONDUCT SHOWS MEN'S IGNORANCE OF THE COURSE AND NATURE OF THE MEAN. The first 予知 is to be understood with a general reference, —'We are wise,' *i. e.*, we can very well take care of ourselves. Yet the presumption of such a profession is seen in men's not being able to take care of themselves. The applica. of this illustration is then made to

期月守也。

第八章 子曰、回之爲人也、擇乎中庸、得一善、則拳拳服膺、而弗失之矣。

第九章 子曰、天下國家可均也、爵祿可辭也、白刃可蹈也、中庸不可能也。

第十章 一節 子路問强。○二節 子曰、南方之强與、北方之强與、抑而强與。○三節 寬柔以教、不報

CHAPTER VIII. The Master said, "This was the manner of Hwuy:—he made choice of the Mean, and whenever he got hold of what was good, he clasped it firmly, as if wearing it on his breast, and did not lose it."

CHAPTER IX. The Master said, "The empire, its States, and its families, may be perfectly ruled; dignities and emoluments may be declined; naked weapons may be trampled under the feet;—but the course of the Mean cannot be attained to."

CHAPTER X. 1. Tsze-loo asked about forcefulness.

2. The Master said, "Do you mean the forcefulness of the South, the forcefulness of the North, or the forcefulness which you should cultivate yourself?

the subject in hand, the second 予知 being to be specially understood, with reference to the subject of the Mean. The conclusion in both parts is left to be drawn by the reader for himself. 擭, read *hwa*, low. 3d tone, 'a trap for catching animals.' 期, read *ke*, like 朞, in Ana. XIII. x, though it is here applied to a month, and not, as there, to a year.

8. HOW HWUY HELD FAST THE COURSE OF THE MEAN. Here the example of Hwuy is likewise adduced, in oppos. to those mentioned in ch. iv. All the rest is exegetical of the first clause—回之爲人也, 'Hwuy's playing the man.' 一善 is not '*one* good point,' so much as any one. 拳 is 'the closed fist.' 拳拳,—'the appearance of holding firm.'

9. THE DIFFICULTY OF ATTAINING TO THE COURSE OF THE MEAN. 天下,—'the empire;' we should say—'empires,' but the Chinese know only of *one* empire, and hence this name for it. The empire is made up of States, and each State of Families. See the Ana. V. vii; XII. xx. 均, 'level;' here, a verb,=平治, 'to bring to perfect order.' 刃,—'a sharp, strong, weapon,' used of swords, spears, javelins, &c. 不可能,—*lit.*, 'cannot be *canned*.'

10. ON FORCEFULNESS IN ITS RELATION TO THE MEAN. In the Analects we find Tsze-loo, on various occasions, putting forward the subject of his valour (勇), and claiming, on the ground of it, such praise as the Master awarded to Hwuy. We may suppose, with the old interpreters, that hearing Hwuy commended, as in ch. viii., he wanted to know whether Confucius would not allow that he also could, with his forceful character, seize and hold fast the Mean. 1. For 强, I have ventured to coin the term 'forcefulness.' Choo He defines it correctly—力

無道、南方之强也、君子居之。四節衽金革、死而不厭、北方之强也、而强者居之。五節故君子、和而不流、强哉矯、中立而不倚、强哉矯、國有道、不變塞焉、强哉矯、國無道、至死不變、强哉矯。

3. "To show forbearance and gentleness in teaching others; and not to revenge unreasonable conduct:—this is the forcefulness of Southern regions, and the good man makes it his study.

4. "To lie under arms; and meet death without regret:—this is the forcefulness of Northern regions, and the forceful make it their study.

5. "Therefore, the superior man cultivates *a friendly* harmony, without being weak.—How firm is he in his forcefulness! He stands erect in the middle, without inclining to either side.—How firm is he in his forcefulness! When good principles prevail in the government of his country, he does not change from what he was in retirement.—How firm is he in his forcefulness! When bad principles prevail in the country, he maintains his course to death without changing.—How firm is he in his forcefulness!"

足以勝人之名, 'the name of strength, sufficient to overcome others.' 2. 而 (=汝) 强 must be—'the forcefulness which you should cultivate,' not 'which you have.' If the latter be the meaning, no farther notice of it is taken in Confucius' reply, while he would seem, in the three foll. paragraphs, to describe the three kinds of forcefulness which he specifies. K'ang-shing and Ying-tă say that 而强 means the forcefulness of the Middle kingdom, the North being 'the sandy desert,' and the South, 'the country south of the Yang-tsze.' But this is not allowable. 3. That climate and situation have an influence on character is not to be denied, and the Chinese notions on the subject may be seen in the amplification of the 9th of K'ang-he's celebrated maxims (聖諭廣訓). But to speak of their effects, as Confucius here does, is extravagant. The barbarism of the south, acc. to the interpretation mentioned above, could not have been described by him in these terms. The forcefulness of mildness and forbearance, thus described, is held to come short of the Mean; and therefore 君子 is taken with a low and light meaning, far short of what it has in par. 5. This practice of determining the force of phrases from the context, makes the reading of the Ch. classics perplexing to a student. 居之,—see the Ana. XII. xiv. 4. 衽, 'the lappel in front of a coat;' also, 'a mat.' 衽金革, 'to make a mat of the leather dress (革) and weapons (金).' This forcefulness of the north, it is said, is in excess of the Mean, and the 故, at the beginning of p. 5, 'therefore,'='these two kinds of forcefulness being thus respectively in defect and excess.' 矯 is 强貌, 'the appearance of being energetic.' This illustrates the forcefulness which is in exact accord with the Mean, in the individual's treatment of others, in his regulation of himself, and in relation to public affairs. 有道, 無道;—often in the Analects. I have followed Choo He in translating 塞. Ying-tă paraphrases:—守直不變德行充實, 'He holds

〔十一章〕（一節）子曰、素隱行怪、後世有述焉、吾弗爲之矣。（二節）君子遵道而行、半塗而廢、吾弗能已矣。（三節）君子依乎中庸、遯世不見知、而不悔、唯聖者能之。

〔十二章〕（一節）君子之道、費而隱。（二節）夫婦之愚、可以

CHAPTER XI. 1. The Master said, "To live in obscurity, and yet practise wonders, in order to be mentioned with honour in future ages;—this is what I do not do.

2. "The good man tries to proceed according to the right path, but when he has gone halfway, he abandons it;—I am not able *so* to stop.

3. "The superior man accords with the course of the Mean. Though he may be all unknown, unregarded by the world, he feels no regret.—It is only the sage who is able for this."

CHAPTER XII. 1. The way which the superior man pursues, reaches wide and far, and yet is secret.

to what is upright, and does not change, his virtuous conduct being all-complete.' A modern writer makes the meaning:—'He does not change through being puffed up by the fulness of office.' Both of these views go on the interpretation of 塞 as = 實.

11. ONLY THE SAGE CAN COME UP TO THE REQUIREMENTS OF THE MEAN. 1. 素 is found written 索, 'to examine,' 'to study,' in a work of the Han dynasty, and Choo He adopts that character as the true reading, and explains accordingly:—'To study what is obscure and wrong (隱僻).' K'ang-shing took it as = 傃, 'towards,' and both he and Ying-tă explain as in the translation. It is an objection to Choo He's view, that, in the next ch., 隱 is given as one of the characteristics of the Mean. The 遯世云云, in p. 3, moreover, agree well with the older view. 2. 君子 is here the same as in last ch. p. 3. A distinction is made between 遵道 here and 依道 below. The former, it is said, implies endeavour, while the latter is natural and unconstrained accordance. 3. 君子 here has its very highest signification, and = 聖者 in the last clause. 避世 is said to be diff. from 遯世, the latter being applicable to the recluse who withdraws from the world, while the former may describe one who is in the world, but does not act with a reference to its opinion of him. It will be observed how Confucius declines saying that he had himself attained to this highest style.—'With this ch.,' says Choo He, 'the quotations by Tsze-sze of the Master's words, to explain the meaning of the first chapter, stop. The great object of the work is to set forth wisdom, benevolent virtue, and valour, as the three grand virtues whereby entrance is effected into the path of the Mean, and therefore, at its commencement, they are illustrated by reference to Shun Yen Yuen, and Tsze-loo, Shun possessing the wisdom, Yen Yuen the benevolence, and Tsze-loo the valour. If one of these virtues be absent, there is no way of advancing to the path, and perfecting the virtue. This will be found fully treated of in the 20th chapter.' So, Choo He. The student forming a judgment for himself, however, will not see very distinctly any reference to these cardinal virtues. The utterances of the sage illustrate the phrase 中庸, showing that the course of the Mean had fallen out of observance, some overshooting it, and others coming short of it. When we want some

與知焉、及其致也、雖聖人亦有所不知焉、夫婦之不肖、可以能行焉、及其至也、雖聖人亦有所不能焉、天地之大也、人猶有所憾、故君子語大、天下莫能載焉、語小、天下莫能破焉、(二節)詩云、鳶飛戾天、魚躍于淵、言其

2. Common men and women, however ignorant, may intermeddle with the knowledge of it; yet in its utmost reaches, there is that which even the sage does not know. Common men and women, however much below the ordinary standard of character, can carry it into practice; yet in its utmost reaches, there is that which even the sage is not able to carry into practice. Great as heaven and earth are, men still find some things in them with which to be dissatisfied. Thus it is, that were the superior man to speak of his way in all its greatness, nothing in the world would be found able to embrace it, and were he to speak of it in its minuteness, nothing in the world would be found able to split it.

3. It is said in the Book of Poetry, "The hawk flies up to heaven; the fishes leap in the deep." This expresses how this *way* is seen above and below.

precise directions how to attain to it, we come finally to the conclusion that only the sage is capable of doing so. We greatly want teaching, more practical and precise.

12. THE COURSE OF THE MEAN REACHES FAR AND WIDE, BUT YET IS SECRET. With this ch. the third part of the work commences, and the first sentence,—君子之道,費而隱, may be regarded as its text. If we could determine satisfactorily the signification of those two terms, we should have a good clue to the meaning of the whole, but it is not easy to do so. The old view is inadmissible. K'ang-shing takes 費 as=佹, 'doubly involved,' 'perverted,' and both he and Ying-tă explain:—'When right principles are opposed and disallowed, the superior man retires into obscurity, and does not hold office.' On this view of it, the sentence has nothing to do with the succeeding chapters. The two meanings of 費 in the dict. are—'the free expenditure of money,' and 'dissipation,' or 'waste.' Acc. to Choo He, in this passage, 費即用之廣也, '費 indicates the wide range of the *taou* in practice.' Something like this must be its meaning:—the course of the Mean, requiring everywhere to be exhibited. Choo then defines 隱 as 體之微, 'the minuteness of the *taou* in its nature or essence.' The former answers to the *what* of the *taou*, and the latter, to the *why*. But it rather seems to me, that the 隱 here is the same with the 隱 and 微, i. 4, and that the author simply intended to say, that the way of the superior man reaching everywhere,—embracing all duties,—yet had its secret spring and seat in the Heaven-gifted nature, the individual consciousness of duty in every man. 2. 夫婦=匹夫, 匹婦, Ana. XIV. xviii. 3. But I confess to be all at sea in the study of this par. Choo quotes from the scholar How (侯氏), that what the superior man fails to know, was exemplified in Conf. having to ask about ceremonies,

上下察也。四節君子之道、造端乎夫婦、及其至也、察乎天地。

右第十二章、子思之言、蓋以申明首章道不可離之意也、其下八章、雜引孔子之言以明之。

十三章 一節 子曰、道不遠人、人之爲道而遠人、不可以爲道。二節 詩云、伐柯伐柯、其則不遠、執

4. The way of the superior man may be found, in its simple elements, in the intercourse of common men and women; but in its utmost reaches, it shines brightly through heaven and earth.

The twelfth chapter above contains the words of Tsze-sze, and is designed to illustrate what is said in the first chapter, that "The path may not be left." In the eight chapters which follow, he quotes, in a miscellaneous way, the words of Confucius to illustrate it.

CHAPTER XIII. 1. The Master said, "The path is not far from man. When men try to pursue a course, which is far from the common indications of consciousness, this course cannot be considered THE PATH.

2. "In the Book of Poetry, it is said, 'In hewing an axe-handle, in hewing an axe-handle, the pattern is not far off.' We grasp one axe-handle to hew the other, and yet, if we look askance from

and about offices, and what he fails to practise, was exemplified in Conf. not being on the throne, and in Yaou and Shun's being dissatisfied that they could not make every individual enjoy the benefits of their rule. He adds his own opinion, that wherein men complained of Heaven and Earth, was the partiality of their operations in overshadowing and supporting, producing and completing, the heat of summer, the cold of winter, &c. If such things were intended by the writer, we can only regret the vagueness of his language, and the want of coherence in his argument. In translating 君子語大云云, I have followed Maou Se-ho. 3. See the She-king, III. i. Ode V. st. 3. The ode is in praise of the virtue of king Wăn. 察 is in the sense of 昭著, 'brightly displayed.' The application of the words of the ode does appear strange.

13. THE PATH OF THE MEAN IS NOT FAR TO SEEK. EACH MAN HAS THE LAW OF IT IN HIMSELF, AND IT IS TO BE PURSUED WITH EARNEST SINCERITY. 1. 人之爲道而遠人,—'When men practise a course, and *wish to be* far from men.' The meaning is as in the translation. 2. See the She-king I. xv. Ode V. st. 2. The object of the par. seems to be to show that

柯以伐柯、睨而視之、猶以爲遠、故君子以人治人、改而止。○三節忠恕違道不遠、施諸己而不願、亦勿施於人、○四節君子之道四、丘未能一焉、所求乎子、以事父、未能也、所求乎臣、以事君、未能也、所求乎弟、以事兄、未能也、所求乎朋友、先施之、未能也、庸德之行、庸言之謹、有所

the one to the other, we may consider them as apart. Therefore, the superior man governs men, according to their nature, with what is proper to them, and as soon as they change *what is wrong*, he stops.

3. "When one cultivates to the utmost the principles of his nature, and exercises them on the principle of reciprocity, he is not far from the path. What you do not like, when done to yourself, do not do to others.

4. "In the way of the superior man there are four things, to not one of which have I as yet attained.—To serve my father, as I would require my son to serve me: to this I have not attained; to serve my prince, as I would require my minister to serve me: to this I have not attained; to serve my elder brother, as I would require my younger brother to serve me: to this I have not attained; to set the example in behaving to a friend, as I would require him to behave to me: to this I have not attained. Earnest in practising the ordinary virtues, and careful in speaking about them, if, in his practice, he has anything defective, the superior man dares not but

the rule for dealing with men, according to the principles of the Mean, is nearer to us than the axe in the hand is to the one which is to be cut down with, and fashioned after, it. The branch is hewn, and its form altered from its natural one. Not so with man. The change in him only brings him to his proper state. 3. Comp, Ana. IV. xv. 違 is here a neuter verb,='to be distant from.' 4. Comp. Ana. VII. i., ii., xix., *et al.* The admissions made by Conf. here are important to those who find it necessary, in their intercourse with the Chinese, to insist on his having been, like other men, compassed with infirmity. It must be allowed, however, that the cases, as put by him, are in a measure hypothetical, his father having died when he was a child. In the course of the paragraph, he passes from speaking of himself by his name (丘), to speak of the *keun-tsze*, and the change is most naturally made after the last 能也. 庸德之行, 庸言之謹,—'in the prac-

中庸

不足、不敢不勉、有餘不敢盡、言顧行、行顧言、君子胡不慥慥爾。

十四 一節 君子、素其位而行、不願乎其外、○二節 素富貴、行乎富貴、素貧賤、行乎貧賤、素夷狄、行乎夷狄、素患難、行乎患難、君子無入而不自得焉。○三節 在上位、不陵下、在下位、不援上、正

exert himself; and if, in his words, he has any excess, he dares not allow himself such license. Thus his words have respect to his actions, and his actions have respect to his words; is it not just an entire sincerity which marks the superior man?"

CHAPTER XIV. 1. The superior man does what is proper to the station in which he is; he does not desire to go beyond this.

2. In a position of wealth and honour, he does what is proper to a position of wealth and honour. In a poor and low position, he does what is proper to a poor and low position. Situated among barbarous tribes, he does what is proper to a situation among barbarous tribes. In a position of sorrow and difficulty, he does what is proper to a position of sorrow and difficulty. The superior man can find himself in no situation in which he is not himself.

3. In a high situation, he does not treat with contempt his inferiors. In a low situation, he does not court the favour of his

tice of ordinary virtues,' *i. e.*, the duties of a son, minister, &c., mentioned above, and in the carefulness or ordinary speech, *i. e.*, speaking about those virtues. To the practice belong the clauses 有所不足, 不敢不勉, and to the speaking, the two next clauses. 爾, —as a final particle,=耳, 'simply,' 'just.'

14. HOW THE SUPERIOR MAN, IN EVERY VARYING SITUATION, PURSUES THE MEAN, DOING WHAT IS RIGHT, AND FINDING HIS RULE IN HIMSELF. 1. Choo He takes 素 as=見在, 'at present,' 'now;' but that meaning was made to meet the exigency of the present passage. K'ang-shing takes it, as in ch. xi., as=傃, 'towards.' Maou endeavours to establish this view:—素位者, 卽本來故有之位, '素位 is the proper station in which he has been.' The meaning comes to much the same in all these interpretations. 不願乎其外,—comp. Ana. XIV. xxviii. 2. 行乎富貴=行乎富貴所當行之道, 'He pursues the path, which ought to be pursued amid riches and honours.' So, in the other clauses. 自得,—lit.,='self-possessing.' The paraphrasts make it—'happy in conforming himself to his position.' I consider it equivalent to what is said in ch. ii.,—君子之中庸也, 君子而時中. 3. 援 is explained in the

己而不求於人、則無怨、上不怨天、下不尤人、○四節故君子、居易以俟命、小人、行險以徼幸。○五節子曰、射有似乎君子、失諸正鵠、反求諸其身。

〔十五〕○一節君子之道、辟如行遠必自邇、辟如登高必自卑。○二節詩曰、妻子好合、如鼓瑟琴、兄弟既翕、和樂且

superiors. He rectifies himself, and seeks for nothing from others, so that he has no dissatisfactions. He does not murmur against heaven, nor grumble against men.

4. Thus it is that the superior man is quiet and calm, waiting for the appointments *of Heaven*, while the mean man walks in dangerous paths, looking for lucky occurences.

5. The Master said, "In archery we have something like the way of the superior man. When the archer misses the centre of the target, he turns round and seeks for the cause of his failure in himself."

CHAPTER XV. 1. The way of the superior man may be compared to what takes place in travelling, when to go to a distance we must first traverse the space that is near, and in ascending a height, when we must begin from the lower ground.

2. It is said in the Book of Poetry, "Happy union with wife and children, is like the music of lutes and harps. When there

dict., after K'ang-shing, by 牽持, 'to drag and cling to.' The opposition of the two clauses makes the meaning plain. 上不怨天, 下不尤人,—see Ana. XIV. xxxvii. 4. 易, acc. to K'ang-shing, 猶平安, 'is equivalent to peaceful and tranquil.' Choo He says, 易平地也, '易 means level ground.' This is most correct, but we cannot so well express it in the translation. 幸, as used here, is often written 倖. 5. 正, up. 1st tone, and 鵠, are both names of birds, small and alert, and difficult to be hit. On this account, a picture of the former was painted on the middle of the target, and a figure of the latter was attached to it in leather. It is not meant, however, by this, that they were both used in the same target, at the same time. For another illustration of the way of the superior man from the customs of archery, see Ana., III. vii.

15. IN THE PRACTICE OF THE MEAN THERE IS AN ORDERLY ADVANCE FROM STEP TO STEP. 1. 辟 is read as, and=譬. 2. See the She-king, II. i. Ode IV. st. 7, 8. The ode celebrates, in a regretful tone, the dependence of brethren on one another, and the beauty of brotherly harmony. Maou says:—'Although there may be the happy union of wife and children, like the music of lutes and harps, yet there must also be the harmonious concord of brethren, with its exceeding delight, and then may wife and

耽、宜爾室家、樂爾妻帑。三節子曰、父母其順矣乎。

十六章一節子曰、鬼神之爲德、其盛矣乎。二節視之而弗見、聽之而弗聞、體物而不可遺。三節使天下之人、齊明盛服、以承祭祀、洋

is concord among brethren, the harmony is delightful and enduring. *Thus* may you regulate your family, and enjoy the pleasure of your wife and children."

3. The Master said, "In such a state of things, parents have entire complacence!"

CHAPTER XVI. 1. The Master said, "How abundantly do spiritual beings display the powers that belong to them!

2. "We look for them, but do not see them; we listen to, but do not hear them; yet they enter into all things, and there is nothing without them.

3. "They cause all the people in the empire to fast and purify themselves, and array themselves in their richest dresses, in order to attend at their sacrifices. Then, like overflowing water, they seem to be over the heads, and on the right and left *of their worshippers*.

children be regulated and enjoyed. Brothers are near to us, while wife and children are more remote. Thus it is, that from what is near we proceed to what is remote.' He adds that anciently the relationship of husband and wife was not among the five relationships of society, because the union of brothers is from heaven, and that of husband and wife is from man! 3. This is understood to be a remark of Confucius on the ode. From wife, and children, and brothers, parents at last are reached, illustrating how from what is low we ascend to what is high.—But all this is far-fetched and obscure.

16. AN ILLUSTRATION, FROM THE OPERATION AND INFLUENCE OF SPIRITUAL BEINGS, OF THE WAY OF THE MEAN. What is said of the *kwei-shin* in this chapter is only by way of illustration. There is no design, on the part of the sage, to develop his views on those beings or agencies. The key of it is to be found in the last par., where the 夫微之顯 evidently refers to 莫顯乎微 in ch. i. This par., therefore, should be separated from the others, and not interpreted specially of the *kwei-shin*. I think that Dr. Medhurst, in rendering it (Theology of the Chinese, p. 22)—'How great then is the manifestation of *their* abstruseness! Whilst displaying their sincerity, they are not to be concealed,' was wrong, notwithstanding that he may be defended by the example of many Chinese commentators. The second clause of par. 5,—誠之不可揜如此, appears altogether synonymous with the 誠於中必形於外, in the 大學傳, ch. vi. 2, to which chapter we have seen that the whole of ch. i. pp. 2, 3, has a remarkable similarity. However we may be driven to find a recondite, mystical, meaning for 誠, in the 4th part of this work, there is no necessity to do so here. With regard to what is said of the *kwei-shin*, it is only the first two paragraphs which occasion difficulty. In the 3d par., the sage speaks of the spiritual beings that are sacrificed to. 齊,—read *chae;* see Ana. VII. xii. The same is the subject of the 4th par.; or rather, spiritual beings generally, whether sacrificed to or not, invisible themselves and yet able to behold our conduct. See the She-king, III. iii. Ode II. st. 7. The ode is said to have been composed by one of the dukes of Wei, and was repeated daily in his hearing for his admonition. In the context of the quotation, he is warned to be careful of his conduct, when alone as when in company. For in truth we are never alone. 'Millions of spiritual beings walk the earth,' and can take note of us.

洋乎、如在其上、如在其左右。四節詩曰、神之格思、不可度思、矧可射思。五節夫微之顯、誠之不可揜、如此夫。

十七章 子一節曰、舜其大孝也與、德

4. "It is said in the Book of Poetry, 'The approaches of the spirits, you cannot surmise;—and can you treat them with indifference?'

5. "Such is the manifestness of what is minute! Such is the impossibility of repressing the outgoings of sincerity!"

CHAPTER XVII. 1. The Master said, "How greatly filial was Shun! His virtue was that of a sage; his dignity was the imperial

(思 is a final particle here, without meaning. It is often used so in the She-king. 度, read *tŏh*, lower 4th tone, 'to conjecture,' 'to surmise.' 射, read *yih*, low. 4th tone, 'to dislike.') What now are the *kwei-shin* in the first two paragraphs. Are we to understand by them something different from what they are in the 3d par., to which they run on from the first as the nominative or subject of 使? I think not. The precise meaning of what is said of them in 體物而不可遺 cannot be determined. The old interpreters say that 體=生, 'to give birth to;' that 可=所, 'that which;' that 不可遺=不有所遺, 'there is nothing which they neglect;' and that the meaning of the whole is—'that of all things there is not a single thing which is not produced by the breath (or energy; 氣) of the *kwei-shin*.' This is all that we learn from them. The Sung school explain the terms with reference to their physical theory of the universe, derived, as they think, from the *Yih-king*. Choo He's master, Ch'ing, explains:—'The *kwei-shin* are the energetic operations of Heaven and Earth, and the traces of production and transformation.' The scholar Chang (張氏) says:—'The *kwei-shin* are the easily acting powers of the two breaths of nature (二氣).' Choo He's own account is:—'If we speak of two breaths, then by *kwei* is denoted the efficaciousness of the secondary or inferior one, and by *shin*, that of the superior one. If we speak of one breath, then by *shin* is denoted its advancing and developing, and by *kwei*, its returning and reverting. They are really only one thing.' It is difficult—not to say impossible—to conceive to one's-self what is meant by such descriptions. And nowhere else in the Four Books is there an approach to this meaning of the phrase. Maou Se-ho is more comprehensible, though, after all, it may be doubted whether what he says is more than a play upon words. His explanation is:—'But in truth, the *kwei-shin* are 道. In the *Yih-king* the 陰 and 陽 are considered to be the *kwei-shin;* and it is said—*one* 陰 and *one* 陽 *are called* 道. Thus the *kwei-shin* are the 道, embodied in Heaven (體天) for the nourishment of things. But in the text we have the term 德 instead of 道, because the latter is the name of the absolute as embodied in Heaven, and the former denotes the same not only embodied, but operating to the nourishing of things, for Heaven considers the production of things to be 德.' See the 中庸說, *in loc.*

Remusat translates the first par:—'*Que les vertus des esprits sont sublimes!*' His Latin version is:—'*spirituum geniorumque est virtus: ea capax!*' Intorcetta renders:—'*spiritibus inest operativa virtus et efficacitas, et hæc o quam præstans est! quam multiplex! quam sublimis!*' In a note, he and his friends say that the dignitary of the empire who assisted them, rejecting other interpretations, understood by *kwei-shin* here—'those spirits for the veneration of whom and imploring their help, sacrifices were instituted.' 神 signifies 'spirits,' 'a spirit,' 'spirit;' and 鬼, 'a ghost,' or 'demon.' The former is used for the *animus*, or intelligent soul separated from the body, and the latter for the *anima*, or animal, grosser, soul, so separated. In the text, however, they blend together, and are not to be separately translated. They are together equivalent to 神 in par. 4, 'spirits,' or 'spiritual beings.'

爲聖人、尊爲天子、富有四海之內、宗廟饗之、子孫保之。○二節故大德、必得其位、必得其祿、必得其名、必得其壽。○三節故天之生物、必因其材而篤焉、故栽者培之、傾者覆之。○四節詩曰、嘉樂君子、憲憲令

throne; his riches were all within the four seas. He offered his sacrifices in his ancestral temple, and his descendants preserved the sacrifices to himself.

2. "Therefore having such great virtue, it could not but be that he should obtain the throne, that he should obtain those riches, that he should obtain his fame, that he should attain to his long life.

3. "Thus it is that Heaven, in the production of things, is surely bountiful to them, according to their qualities. Hence the tree that is flourishing, it nourishes, while that which is ready to fall, it overthrows.

4. "In the Book of Poetry, it is said, 'The admirable, amiable, prince, displayed couspicuously his excelling virtue, adjusting his people and adjusting his officers. *Therefore*, he received from Hea-

17. THE VIRTUE OF FILIAL PIETY, EXEMPLIFIED IN SHUN AS CARRIED TO THE HIGHEST POINT, AND REWARDED BY HEAVEN. 1. One does not readily see the connection between Shun's great filial piety, and all the other predicates of him that follow. The paraphrasts, however, try to trace it in this way:—'A son without virtue is insufficient to distinguish his parents. But Shun was born with all knowledge and acted without any effort;—in virtue, a sage. How great was the distinction which he thus conferred on his parents!' And so with regard to the other predicate. See the 日講. 四海之內;—on this expression it is said in the encyclopædia called 博物志:—'The four cardinal points of heaven and earth are connected together by the waters of seas, the earth being a small space in the midst of them. Hence, he who rules over the empire (天下) is said to govern all within the four seas.' See also on Ana. XII. v. 4. The characters 宗廟 are thus explained:—'*Tsung* means honourable. *Meaou* means figure. The two together mean the place where the figures of one's ancestors are.' Choo He says nothing on 宗廟饗之, because he had given in to the views of some who thought that Shun sacrificed merely in the ancestral temple of Yaou. But it is capable of proof that he erected one of his own, and ascended to Hwang-te, as his great progenitor. See Maou's 中庸說, *in loc.* 饗,—'to entertain a guest;' and sometimes for 享, 'to enjoy.' So we must take it here,—'enjoyed him;' that is, his sacrifices. As Shun resigned the throne to Yu, and it did not run in the line of his family, we must take 保之 as in the translation. In the time of the Chow dynasty, there were descendants of Shun, possessed of the state of Ch'in (陳), and of course sacrificing to him. 2. The 其 must refer in every case to 大德;—'its place, its emolument,' &c.; that is, what is appropriate to such great virtue. The whole is to be understood with reference to Shun. He died at the age of 100 years. The word 'virtue,' takes here the place of 'filial piety,' in the last par.,

德、宜民宜人、受祿于天、保佑命之、自天申之。○五節故大德者必受命。

【十八章】一節子曰、無憂者、其惟文王乎、以王季爲父、以武王爲子、父作之、子述之。○二節武王纘大王王季文王之緒、壹戎衣、而有天下、身不失天下之顯名、尊爲天

ven the emoluments of dignity. It protected him, assisted him, decreed him the throne; sending from heaven these favours, *as it were* repeatedly.'

5. "*We may say* therefore that he who is greatly virtuous will be sure to receive the appointment of Heaven."

CHAPTER XVIII. 1. The Master said, "It is only king Wăn of whom it can be said that he had no cause for grief! His father was king Ke, and his son was king Woo. His father laid the foundations of his dignity, and his son transmitted it.

2. King Woo continued the enterprise of king T'ae, king Ke, and king Wăn. He once buckled on his armour, and got possession of the empire. He did not lose the distinguished personal reputation which he had throughout the empire. His dignity was the im-

acc. to Maou, because that is the root, the first and chief, of all virtues. 3. 材 and 篤 (acc. to Choo He,=厚, 'thick,' liberal') are explained by most commentators as equally capable of a good and bad application. This may be said of 材, but not of 篤, and the 生 in 天之生物 would seem to determine the meaning of both to be only good. If this be so, then the last clause 傾者覆之 is only an after-thought of the writer, and, indeed, the sentiment of it is out of place in the chapter. 栽 is best taken, with K'ang-ching, as=殖, and not, with Choo He, as merely=植. 4. See the She-king, III. ii. ode V. st. 1, where we have two slight variations of 假 for 嘉 and 顯 for 憲. The prince spoken of is king Wăn, who is thus brought forward to confirm the lesson taken from Shun. That lesson, however, is stated much too broadly in the last par. It is well to say that only virtue is a solid title to eminence, but to hold forth the certain attainment of wealth and position as an inducement to virtue is not favourable to morality. The case of Confucius himself, who attained neither to power nor to long life, may be adduced as inconsistent with these teachings.

18. ON KING WAN, KING WOO, AND THE DUKE OF CHOW. 1. Shun's father was bad, and the fathers of Yaou and Yu were undistinguished. Yaou and Shun's sons were both bad, and Yu's not remarkable. But to Wăn neither father nor son gave occasion but for satisfaction and happiness. King Ke was the duke Ke-lik (季歷), the most distinguished by his virtues, and prowess, of all the princes of his time. He prepared the way for the elevation of his family. In 父作之, 子述之, the 之 is made to refer to 基業, 'the foundation of the empire, but it may as well be referred to Wăn himself. 2. 大王,—this was the duke T'an-foo (亶父), the father of Ke-

子、富有四海之內、宗廟饗之、子孫保之、○三節武王末受命、周公成文武之德、追王大王王季、上祀先公以天子之禮、斯禮也、達乎諸侯大夫、及士庶人、父爲大夫、子爲士、葬以大夫、祭以士、父爲士、子爲大夫、葬以士、祭以大夫、期之喪、達乎大夫、

perial throne. His riches were the possession of all within the four seas. He offered his sacrifices in his ancestral temple, and his descendants maintained the sacrifices to himself.

3. "It was in his old age that king Woo received the appointment *to the throne*, and the duke of Chow completed the virtuous course of Wăn and Woo. He carried up the title of king to T'ae and Ke, and sacrificed to all the former dukes above them with the imperial ceremonies. And this rule he extended to the princes of the empire, the great officers, the scholars, and the common people. Was the father a great officer and the son a scholar, then the burial was that due to a great officer, and the sacrifice that due to a scholar. Was the father a scholar, and the son a great officer, then the burial was that due to a scholar, and the sacrifice that due to a great officer. The one year's mourning was made to extend *only* to the great officers,

lik, a prince of great eminence, and who, in the decline of the Yin dynasty, drew to his family the thoughts of the people. 緒,—'the end of a cocoon.' It is used here for the beginnings of imperial sway, traceable to the various progenitors of king Woo. 壹戎衣 is interpreted by K'ang-shing:—'He destroyed the great Yin;' and recent commentators defend his view. It is not worth while setting forth what may be said for and against it. 'He did not lose his distinguished reputation;' that is, tho' he proceeded against his rightful sovereign, the people did not change their opinion of his virtue. 3. 末=老, 'when old.' Woo was 87 when he became emperor, and he only reigned 7 years. His brother Tan (旦), the duke of Chow (see Ana. VI. xxii: VII. v.) acted as his chief minister. In 追王, 王 is in the 3d tone, in which the character means—'to exercise the sovereign power.' 上祀先公云云,—the house of Chow traced their lineage, up to the emperor 嚳, B. C. 2432. But in various passages of the Shoo-king, king T'ae and king K'e are spoken of, as if the conference of those titles had been by king Woo. On this there are very long discussions. See the 中庸說, *in loc.* The truth seems to be, that Chow-kung, carrying out his brother's wishes by laws of State, confirmed the titles, and made the general rule about burials and sacrifices which is described. From 斯禮也 to the end, we are at first inclined to translate in the present tense, but the past with a reference to

三年之喪、達乎天子、父母之喪、無貴賤、一也。

【十九】子曰、一節武王周公其達孝矣乎。○二節夫孝者、善繼人之志、善述人之事者也。○三節春秋、脩其祖廟、陳其宗器、設其裳衣、薦其時食。○四節宗廟之禮、所以序昭穆也、序

but the three years' mourning extended to the emperor. In the mourning for a father or mother, he allowed no difference between the noble and the mean."

CHAPTER XIX. 1. The Master said, "How far-extending was the filial piety of king Woo and the duke of Chow!

2. "Now filial piety is seen in the skilful carrying out of the wishes of our fore-fathers, and the skilful carrying forward of their undertakings.

3. "In spring and autumn, they repaired and beautified the temple-halls of their fathers, set forth their ancestral vessels, displayed their various robes, and presented the offerings of the several seasons.

4. "By means of the ceremonies of the ancestral temple, they distinguished the imperial kindred according to their order of descent. By ordering the parties present according to their rank, they

Chow-kung is more correct. The 'year's mourning' is that principally for uncles, and it did not extend beyond the great officers, because their uncles were the subjects of the princes and the emperor, and feelings of kindred must not be allowed to come into collision with the relation of governor and governed. On the 'three years' mourning,' see Ana. XVII. xxi.

19. THE FAR-REACHING FILIAL PIETY OF KING WOO, AND OF THE DUKE OF CHOW. 1. 達 is taken by Choo He as meaning—'universally acknowledged;' 'far-extending' is better, and accords with the meaning of the term in other parts of the work. 2. This definition of 孝, or 'filial piety,' is worthy of notice. Its operation ceases not with the lives of parents and parents' parents. 人 = 前人, 'antecedent men;' but English idiom seems to require the addition of *our*. 3. 春秋,—The emperors of China sacrificed, as they still do, to their ancestors every season. Reckoning from the spring, the names of the sacrifices appear to have been—祠, 禴 or 礿, 嘗, and 烝. Others, however, give the names as 礿, 禘, 嘗, 烝, while some affirm that the spring sacrifice was 禘. Though spring and autumn only are mentioned in the text, we are to understand that what is said of the sacrifices in those seasons applies to all the others. 祖廟,—'Halls or temples of ancestors,' of which the emperors had seven (see the next par.), all included in the name of 宗廟. 宗器, 'ancestral,' or 'venerable, vessels.' Choo He understands by them relics, something like our regalia. Ch'ing K'ang-shing makes them, and apparently with more correctness, simply 'the sacrificial vessels.' 裳衣,—'lower and upper garments,' with the latter of which the

爵、所以辨貴賤也、序事、所以辨賢也、旅酬、下爲上、所以逮賤也、燕毛、所以序齒也、(五節)踐其位、行其禮、奏其樂、敬其所尊、愛其所親、事死如事生、事亡如事存、孝之

distinguished the more noble and the less. By the arrangement of the services, they made a distinction of talents and worth. In the ceremony of general pledging, the inferiors presented the cup to their superiors, and thus something was given the lowest to do. At the *concluding* feast, places were given according to the hair, and thus was made the distinction of years.

5. "They occupied the places of their fore-fathers, practised their ceremonies, and performed their music. They reverenced those whom they honoured, and loved those whom they regarded with affection. Thus they served the dead as they would have served them alive; they served the departed as they would have served them had they been continued among them.

parties personating the deceased were invested. 4. It was an old interpretation that the sacrifices and accompanying services, spoken of here, were not the seasonal services of every year, which are the subject of the prec. par., but the great 禘 and 祫 sacrifices, and to that view I would give in my adhesion. The emperor, as mentioned above had seven 廟. One belonged to the remote ancestor to whom the dynasty traced its origin. At the great sacrifices, his spirit-tablet was placed fronting the east, and on each side were ranged, three in a row, the tablets belonging to the six others, those of them which fronted the south being, in the genealogical line, the fathers of those who fronted the north. As fronting the south, the region of *brilliancy*, the former were called 昭; the latter, from the north, the *sombre* region, were called 穆. As the dynasty was prolonged, and successive emperors died, the older tablets were removed, and transferred to what was called the 祧廟, yet so as that one in the 昭 line displaced the topmost 昭, and so with the 穆. At the sacrifices, the imperial kindred arranged themselves as they were descended from a 昭, on the left, and from a 穆, on the right, and thus a genealogical correctness of place was maintained among them. The ceremony of 'general (旅=衆) pledging' occurred towards the end of the sacrifice. Choo He takes 爲 in the low. 3d tone, saying that to have anything to do at those services was accounted honourable, and after the emperor had commenced the ceremony by taking 'a cup of blessing,' all the juniors presented a similar cup to the seniors, and thus were called into employment. Ying-tă takes 爲 in its ordinary tone, 下爲上, 'the inferiors were the superiors,' *i. e.*, the juniors did present a cup to their elders, but had the honour of drinking first themselves. The 燕 was a concluding feast confined to the imperial kindred. 5. 踐其位, acc. to K'ang-shing, is—'ascended their thrones;' acc. to Choo He it is 'trod on—*i. e.*, occupied—their places in the ancestral temple.' On either view, the statement must be taken with allowance. The ancestors of king Woo had not been emperors, and their places in the temples had only been those of princes. The same may be said of the four particulars which follow. By 'those whom they'—*i. e.*, their progenitors—'honoured' are intended their ancestors, and by 'those whom they loved,' their descendants, and indeed all the people of their government. The two concluding sentences are

至也。六節郊社之禮、所以事上帝也、宗廟之禮、所以祀乎其先也、明乎郊社之禮、禘嘗之義、治國其如示諸掌乎。

二十章 一節 哀公問政。

6. "By the ceremonies of the sacrifices to Heaven and Earth they served God, and by the ceremonies of the ancestral temple they sacrificed to their ancestors. He who understands the ceremonies of the sacrifices to Heaven and Earth, and the meaning of the several sacrifices to ancestors, would find the government of a kingdom as easy as to look into his palm.!"

CHAPTER XX. 1. The duke Gae asked about government.

important, as the Jesuits mainly based on them the defence of their practice in permitting their converts to continue the sacrifices to their ancestors. We read in '*Confucius Sinarum philosophus*,'—the work of Intorcetta and others, to which I have made frequent reference :—*Ex plurimis et clarissimis textibus Sinicis probari potest, legitimum prædicti axiomatis sensum esse, quod eadem intentione et formali motivo Sinenses naturalem pietatem et politicum obsequium erga defunctos exerceant, sicuti erga eosdem adhuc superstites exercebant, ex quibus et ex infra dicendis prudens lector facile deducet, hos ritus circa defunctos fuisse mere civiles, institutos dumtaxat in honorem et obsequium parentum, etiam post mortem non intermittendum; nam si quid illic divinum agnovissent, cur diceret Confucius—Priscos servire solitos defunctis, uti iisdem serviebant viventibus.*' This is ingenious reasoning, but it does not meet the fact that sacrifice is an entirely new element introduced into the service of the dead. 6. I do not understand how it is that their sacrifices to God are adduced here as an illustration of the filial piety of king Wăn and king Woo. What is said about them, however, is important, in reference to the views which we should form about the ancient religion of China. K'ang-shing took 郊 to be the sacrifice to Heaven, offered, at the winter solstice, in the southern suburb (郊) of the imperial city; and 社 to be that offered to the Earth, at the summer solstice, in the northern. Choo He agrees with him. Both of them, however, add that after 上帝 we are to understand 后土, 'Sovereign Earth (不言后土者省文).' This view of 社 here is vehemently controverted by Maou and many others. But neither the opinion of the two great commentators that 后土 is suppressed for the sake of brevity, nor the opinion of others that by 社 we are to understand the tutelary deities of the soil, affects the judgment of the sage himself, that the service of one being—even of God—was designed by all those ceremonies. See my 'Notions of the Chinese concerning God and Spirits,' pp. 50–52. The ceremonies of the ancestral temple embrace the great and less frequent services of the 禘 and 祫 (see the Ana., III. x. xi.) and the seasonal sacrifices, of which only the autumnal one (嘗) is specified here. The old commentators take 示 as=寘, with the meaning of 置, 'to place,' and interpret—'the government of the kingdom would be as easy as to place anything in the palm.' This view is defended in the 中庸說. It has the advantage of accounting better for the 諸. We are to understand 'the meaning of the sacrifices to ancestors,' as including all the uses mentioned in par. 4. I said above that I could not understand the connection between the first part of this par. and the general object of the chapter. Taking the par. by itself, it teaches that a proper knowledge and practice of the duties of religion and filial piety would amply equip a ruler for all the duties of his government.

20. ON GOVERNMENT: SHOWING PRINCIPALLY HOW IT DEPENDS ON THE CHARACTER OF THE OFFICERS ADMINISTERING IT, AND HOW THAT DEPENDS ON THE CHARACTER OF THE SOVEREIGN HIMSELF. We have here one of the fullest expositions of Confucius' views on this subject, though he unfolds them only as a description of the government of the kings Wăn and Woo. In the chapter there is the remarkable intermingling, which we have seen in 'The Great Learning,' of what is peculiar to a ruler, and what is of universal application. From the concluding paragraphs, the transition is easy to the next and most difficult part of the Work.

二節 子曰、文武之政、布在方策、其人存、則其政舉、其人亡、則其政息。三節 人道敏政、地道敏樹、夫政也者、蒲盧也。四節 故爲政在人、取人以身、脩身以道、脩道以仁。五節 仁者、人也、親親爲大、義者、宜也、尊賢

2. The Master said, "The government of Wăn and Woo is displayed in *the records*,—the tablets of wood and bamboo. Let there be the men and the government will flourish; but without the men, their government decays and ceases."

3. "With the *right* men the growth of government is rapid, just as vegetation is rapid in the earth; and moreover *their* government *might be called* an easily-growing rush.

4. "Therefore the administration of government lies in *getting proper* men. Such men are to be got by means of *the ruler's own* character. That character is to be cultivated by his treading in the ways *of duty*. And the treading those ways of duty is to be cultivated by the cherishing of benevolence.

5. "Benevolence is *the characteristic element of* humanity, and the great exercise of it is in loving relatives. Righteousness is *the accordance of actions with what is* right, and the great exercise of

This chapter is found also in the 家語, but with considerable additions.

1. 哀公,—See Ana, II. xix, *et al.* 2. The 方 were tablets of wood, one of which might contain up to 100 characters. The 策 were 簡, or ships of bamboo tied together. In 其人, 其=*such, i. e.*, rulers like Wăn and Woo, and ministers such as they had. 3. K'ang-shing and Ying-tă take 敏 as=勉, 'to exert one's-self,' and interpret:—'A ruler ought to exert himself in the practice of government, as the earth exerts itself to produce and to nurture (樹=殖).' Choo He takes 敏 as=速, 'hasty,' 'to make haste.' 人道敏政,—'man's way hastens government;' but the 人 must be taken with special reference to the preceding par., as in the translation. The old comm. took 蒲盧 as the name of an insect, (so it is defined in the 爾訝) a kind of bee, said to take the young of the mulberry caterpillar, and keep them in its hole, where they are transformed into bees. So, they said, does government transform the people. This is in acc. with the paragraph, as we find it in the 家語,—天道敏生, 人道敏政, 地道敏樹, 夫政者猶蒲盧也, 待化以成. This view is maintained also in the 中庸說. But we cannot hesitate in preferring Choo He's, as in the translation. The other is too absurd. He takes 盧, as if it were 蘆,=葦, which, as well as 蒲, is the name of various rushes or sedges. 4. In the 家語, for 在人, we have 在於得人, which is, no doubt, the meaning. By 道 here, says Choo He, are intended 'the duties of universal obligation,' in par. 8, 'which,' adds Maou, 'are the

爲大、親親之殺、尊賢之等、禮所生也。○六節在下位、不獲乎上、民不可得而治矣。○七節故君子、不可以不脩身、思脩身、不可以不事親、思事親、不可以不知人、思知人、不可以不知天。○八節天下之達道五、所以行之者三、曰君臣也、

it is in honouring the worthy. The decreasing measures of the love due to relatives, and the steps in the honour due to the worthy, are produced by *the principle of* propriety.

6. "When those in inferior situations do not possess the confidence of their superiors, they cannot retain the government of the people.

7. "Hence the sovereign may not neglect the cultivation of his own character. Wishing to cultivate his character, he may not neglect to serve his parents. In order to serve his parents, he may not neglect to acquire a knowledge of men. In order to know men, he may not dispense with a knowledge of Heaven.

8. "The duties of universal obligation are five, and the virtues wherewith they are practised are three. The duties are those between sovereign and minister, between father and son, between hus-

ways of the Mean, in accordance with the nature.' 5. 仁者人也, 'Benevolence is man.' We find the same language in Mencius, and in the Le-ke, XXXII. 15. This virtue is called MAN, 'because loving, feeling, and the forbearing nature, belong to man, as he is born. They are that whereby man is man.' See the 中庸說, *in loc.* 殺,—upper 3d tone, read *shae.* It is opposed to 隆, and means 'decreasing,' 'growing less.' For 禮所生 we have, in the 家語, 禮所以生, which would seem to mean—'are that whereby ceremonies are produced.' But there follow the words—禮者政之本也. The 'produced' in the translation can only='distinguished.' Ying-tă explains 生 by 辨明. 6. This has crept into the text here by mistake. It belongs to par. 17, below. We do not find it here in the 家語. 7. 君子 is here the *ruler* or *sovereign.* I fail in trying to trace the connection between the different parts of this par. 'He may not be without knowing men.'—Why? 'Because,' we are told, 'it is by honouring, and being courteous to the worthy, and securing them as friends, that a man perfects his virtue, and is able to serve his relatives.' 'He may not be without knowing Heaven.'—Why? 'Because,' it is said, 'the gradations in the love of relatives and the honouring the worthy, are all heavenly arrangements, and a heavenly order, natural, necessary, principles.' But in this explanation, 知人 has a very different meaning from what it has in the previous clause. 親, too, is here *parents,* its meaning being more restricted than in par. 5. 8. From this down to par. 11, there is brought before us the character of the '*men,*' mentioned in par. 2, on whom depends the flourishing of '*government,*' which government is exhibited in parr. 12—15. 天下之達道,—'the paths proper to be trodden by all under heaven,

中庸

父子也、夫婦也、昆弟也、朋友之交也、五者、天下之達道也、知、仁、勇、三者、天下之達德也、所以行之者一也。九節 或生而知之、或學而知之、或困而知之、及其知之、一也、或安而行之、或利而行之、或勉强而行之、及其成功、一也。十節 子曰、好學近乎知、力行近乎仁、知恥近乎勇。

band and wife, between elder brother and younger, and those belonging to the intercourse of friends. Those five are the duties of universal obligation. Knowledge, magnanimity, and energy, these three, are the virtues universally binding. And the means by which they carry *the duties* into practice is singleness.

9. "Some are born with the knowledge *of those duties;* some know them by study; and some acquire the knowledge after a painful feeling of their ignorance. But the knowledge being possessed, it comes to the same thing. Some practise them with a natural ease; some from a desire for their advantages; and some by strenuous effort. But the achievement being made, it comes to the same thing."

=the path of the Mean. 知=智, is the *knowledge* necessary to choose the detailed course of duty. 仁 (=心之公, 'the unselfishness of the heart') is the *magnanimity* (so I style it for want of a better term) to pursue it. 勇, is the *valiant energy*, which maintains the permanence of the choice and the practice. 所以行之者一也,—this, acc. to Ying-tă, means—'From the various kings (百王) downwards, in the practising these five duties, and three virtues, there has been but one method. There has been no change in modern times and ancient.' This, however, is not satisfactory. We want a substantive meaning, for 一. This Choo He gives us. He says:—一則誠而已, '一 is simply sincerity;' the sincerity, that is, on which the rest of the work dwells with such strange predication. I translate, therefore, 一 here by *singleness*. There seems a reference in the term to 獨, ch. i. p. 3. The singleness is that of the soul in the apprehension and practice of the duties of the Mean, which is attained to by watchfulness over one's-self, when *alone*. 行之 I understand as in the second clause of the paragraph. 9. Compare Ana., XVI. i. 10. 利,—comp. Ana. XV. ii. 强,—up. 2d tone, 'to force,' 'to employ violent efforts. Choo He says:—'The 之 in 知之, and 行之, refers to the duties of universal obligation.' But is there the threefold difference in the *knowledge* of those duties? And who are they

十一節 知斯三者、則知所以脩身、知所以脩身、則知所以治人、知所以治人、則知所以治天下國家矣。十二節 凡爲天下國家有九經、曰、脩身也、尊賢也、親親也、敬大臣也、體群臣也、子庶民也、來百工

10. The Master said, "To be fond of learning is to be near to knowledge. To practise with vigour is to be near to magnanimity. To possess the feeling of shame is to be near to energy.

11. "He who knows these three things, knows how to cultivate his own character. Knowing how to cultivate his own character, he knows how to govern other men. Knowing how to govern other men, he knows how to govern the empire with all its States and families.

12. "All who have the government of the Empire with its States and families have nine standard rules to follow;—viz., the cultivation of their own characters; the honouring of men of virtue and talents; affection towards their relatives; respect towards the great ministers; kind and considerate treatment of the whole body of officers; dealing with the mass of the people as children; encouraging the resort of all classes of artizans; indulgent treatment of men from a distance; and the kindly cherishing of the princes of the States.

who can practise them with entire ease? 10. Choo He observes that 子曰 is here superfluous. In the 家語, however, we find the last par. followed by—'The duke said, Your words are beautiful and perfect, but I am stupid, and unable to accomplish this.' Then comes this par.—'Confucius said,' &c. The 子曰, therefore, prove, that Tsze-sze took this chapter from some existing document, that which we have in the 家語, or some other. Conf. words were intended to encourage and stimulate the duke, telling him that the three grand virtues might be nearly, if not absolutely, attained to. 知恥,—'knowing to be ashamed,' *i. e.*, being ashamed at being below others, leading to the determination not to be so. 11. 'These three things' are the three things in the last paragraph, which make an approximation at least to the three virtues which connect with the discharge of duty attainable by every one. What connects the various steps of the climax is the unlimited confidence in the power of the example of the ruler, which we have had occasion to point out so frequently in 'The Great Learning.' 12. These nine standard rules, it is to be borne in mind, constitute the government of Wăn and Woo, referred to in par. 2. Comm. arrange the 4th and 5th rules, under the second; and the 6th, 7th, 8th, and 9th, under the third, so that after 'the cultivation of the person,' we have here an expansion of 親親 and 尊賢, in par. 5. 凡爲,—爲=治, 'to govern.' The student will do well to understand a 者 after 家. 尊賢,—by the 賢 here are understood specially the officers called 師, 傅, and 保, the 三公 and the 三孤, who, as teachers, and guardians, were not styled 臣, 'ministers,' or 'servants.' See the Shoo-king V. xxi. 5, 6. 敬大臣,—by the 大臣 are understood

中庸

也、柔遠人也、懷諸侯也。○十三節 脩身、則道立、尊賢、則不惑、親親、則諸父昆弟不怨、敬大臣、則不眩、體群臣、則事之報禮重、子庶民、則百姓勸、來百工、則財用足、柔遠人、則四方歸之、懷諸侯、則天

13. "By the ruler's cultivation of his own character, the duties *of universal obligation* are set forth. By honouring men of virtue and talents, he is preserved from errors of judgment. By showing affection to his relatives, there is no grumbling nor resentment among his uncles and brethren. By respecting the great ministers, he is kept from errors in the practice of government. By kind and considerate treatment of the whole body of officers, they are led to make the most grateful return for his courtesies. By dealing with the mass of the people as his children, they are led to exhort one another to what is good. By encouraging the resort of all classes of artizans, his resources for expenditure are rendered ample. By indulgent treatment of men from a distance, they are brought to resort to him from all quarters. And by kindly cherishing the princes of the States, the whole empire is brought to revere him.

the six 卿,—the minister of Instruction, the minister of Religion, &c. See the Shoo-king, V. xxi. 7—13. 體羣臣,—the 羣臣 are the host of subordinate officers after the two prec. classes. K'ang-shing says,—體猶接納, '體=to receive,' to which Ying-tă adds—與之同體, 'being of the same body with them.' Choo He brings out the force of the term in this way:—體謂設以身處其地, 而察其心也, '體 means that he places himself in their place, and so examines their feelings.' 子庶民,—子 is a verb, 'to make children of,' 'to treat kindly as children.' 來百工,—來=招來, 'to call to come,'=' to encourage.' The 百工, or 'various artizans,' were, by the statutes of Chow, under the superintendence of a special officer, and it was his business to draw them out and forth from among the people. See the Chow-le, XXXIX. 1—5. 柔遠人,—Choo He by 遠人 understands 賓旅, 'guests or envoys, and travellers, or travelling merchants,' K'ang-shing understands by them 蕃國之諸侯, 'the princes of surrounding kingdoms,' *i. e.*, of the tribes that lay beyond the six *fuh* (服), or feudal tenures of the Chow rule. But these would hardly be spoken of before the 諸侯. And among *them*, in the 9th rule, would be included the 賓, or guests, the princes themselves at the imperial court, or their envoys. I doubt whether any others beside the 旅, or travelling merchants, are intended by the 遠人. If we may adopt, however, K'ang-shing's view, this is the rule for the treatment of foreigners by the government of China. 13. This par. describes the happy effects of observing the above nine rules. 道立,—by 道 are understood the five duties of universal obligation. We read in the 日講:—'About these nine rules, the only trouble is, that sovereigns

下畏之。○十四節齊明盛服、非禮不動、所以脩身也、去讒、遠色、賤貨、而貴德、所以勸賢也、尊其位、重其祿、同其好惡、所以勸親親也、官盛任使、所以勸大臣也、忠信重祿、所以勸士也、時使薄斂、所以勸百姓也、日省月試、既

14. "Self-adjustment and purification, with careful regulation of his dress, and the not making a movement contrary to the rules of propriety:—this is the way for the ruler to cultivate his person. Discarding slanderers, and keeping himself from *the seductions of* beauty; making light of riches, and giving honour to virtue:—this is the way for him to encourage men of worth and talents. Giving them places *of honour* and large emolument, and sharing with them in their likes and dislikes:—this is the way for him to encourage his relatives to love him. Giving them numerous officers to discharge their orders and commissions:—this is the way for him to encourage the great ministers. According to them a generous confidence, and making their emoluments large:—this is the way to encourage the body of officers. Employing them only at the proper times, and making the imposts light:—this is the way to encourage the people. By daily examinations and monthly trials, and by making their rations in accordance with their labours:—this is the way to encourage the classes of artizans. To escort them on their departure and meet

are not able to practise them strenuously. Let the ruler be really able to cultivate his person, then will the universal duties and universal virtues be all-complete, so that he shall be an example to the whole empire, with its States and families. Those duties will be set up (道立), and men will know what to imitate.' 不惑 means, acc. to Choo He, '不疑於理,' 'he will have no doubts as to principle.' K'ang-shing explains it by 謀者良, 'his counsels will be good.' This latter is the meaning, the worthies being those specified in the note on the preceding par., their sovereign's counsellors and guides. The addition of 諸 determines the 父 to be uncles. See the 爾雅, I. iv. 昆弟 are all the younger branches of the ruler's kindred. 不眩=不惑, but the deception and mistake will be in the affairs in charge of those great ministers. 羣臣 and 士 are the same parties. 勸,—as in Ana. II. xx. Ying-tă explains it here—'They will exhort and stimulate one another to serve their ruler.' On 財用足, Choo He says:—來百工,則通功易事,農末相資,故財用足, 'The resort of all classes of artizans being encouraged, there is an intercommunication of the productions of labour, and an interchange of men's services, and the husbandman and the trafficker,' (it is this class which is designed by 末)

稟稱事、所以勸百工也、送往迎來、嘉善而矜不能、所以柔遠人也、繼絕世、舉廢國、治亂持危、朝聘以時、厚往而薄來、所以懷諸侯也。十五節 凡爲天下國家有九經、所以行之者一也。十六節 凡事、豫則立、不豫則廢、言前定、則不

them on their coming; to commend the good among them, and show compassion to the imcompetent:—this is the way to treat indulgently men from a distance. To restore families whose line of succession has been broken, and to revive States that have been extinguished; to reduce to order States that are in confusion, and support those which are in peril; to have fixed times for their own reception at court, and the reception of their envoys; to send them away after liberal treatment, and welcome their coming with small contributions:—this is the way to cherish the princes of the States.

15. "All who have the government of the empire with its States and families have the above nine standard rules. And the means by which they are carried into practice is singleness.

16. "In all things success depends on previous preparation, and without such previous preparation there is sure to be failure. If what is to be spoken be previously determined, there will be no

'are aiding to one another. Hence the resources for expenditure are sufficient.' I suppose that Choo felt a want of some mention of agriculture in connection with these rules, and thought to find a place for it here. Maou would make 財=材, and 用=器物. See the 中庸說, *in loc.* Comp. also 大學傳, x. 19. K'ang-shing understands 四方 as meaning 蕃國, 'frontier kingdoms,' but the usage of the phrase is against such an interpretation. 14. After 天下畏之, we have in the 家語,—公曰, 爲之奈何, 'The duke said, *How are these rules to be practised?*' and then follows this par., preceded by 孔子曰, 'Confucius said.' 齊明盛服—comp. ch. xvi. 3. The blending together, as equally important, attention to inward purity and to dress, seems strange enough to a western reader. 勸, throughout,=' to encourage,' 'to stimulate in a friendly way.' I have translated 親親 after the 合講, which says 勸親親謂親之親我. The up. 親 is the noun, and the 2d the verb, just the reverse of the phrase in its previous occurrences. The use of 忠 in reference to the prince's treatment of the officers is strange, but the translation gives what appears to be the meaning. K'ang-shing explained:—'Making large the emolument of the loyal and sincere;' but, according to the analogy of all the other clauses, 忠 and 信 must be descriptive of the ruler. 時使,—comp. Ana. I. v. For 既稟 we have in the 家語, 餼廩.

跲、事前定、則不困、行前定、則不疚、道前定、則不窮。〇十七節在下位、不獲乎上、民不可得而治矣、獲乎上有道、不信乎朋友、不獲乎上矣、信乎朋友有道、不順乎親、不信乎朋友矣、順乎親有道、反諸身不誠、不順乎親矣、誠

stumbling. If affairs be previously determined, there will be no difficulty with them. If one's actions have been previously determined, there will be no sorrow in connection with them. If principles of conduct have been previously determined, the practice of them will be inexhaustible.

17. "When those in inferior situations do not obtain the confidence of the sovereign, they cannot succeed in governing the people. There is a way to obtain the confidence of the sovereign;—if one is not trusted by his friends, he will not get the confidence of his sovereign. There is a way to being trusted by one's friends;—if one is not obedient to his parents, he will not be true to friends. There is a way to being obedient to one's parents;—if one, on turning his

which K'ang-shing explains by 稍食, 'rations allowed by government.' See Morrison, char. 稍. Choo He follows K'ang-shing in this, but I agree with Maou, that 槩 and not 餼 is to be substituted here for 旣. 稱, up. 3d tone, 'to weigh,' 'to be according to.' The trials and examinations, with these rations, show that the artizans are not to be understood of such dispersed among the people, but as collected under the superintendence of the government. Ambassadors from foreign countries have been received up to the present century, according to the rules here prescribed, and the two last regulations are quite in harmony with the moral and political superiority that China claims over the countries which they may represent. But in the case of travellers, and travelling merchants, passing from one state to another, there were anciently regulations, which may be adduced to illustrate all the expressions here. See the 中庸說, and the 日講 *in loc.* 繼絶世, 舉廢國,—see Ana. xx. i. 7. 15. We naturally understand 所以行之者一也, as meaning—'the means by which they are carried into practice is one and the same.' Then this means will be the 豫, or 'previous preparation' of the next. par. This is the interpretation of K'ang-shing and Ying-tă, who take the two parr. together. But acc. to Choo He, 'the one thing' is *sincerity*, as in par. 8. 16. The 'all things' is to be understood with reference to the universal duties, the universal virtues, and the nine standard rules. 17. The object of this par. seems to be to show that the singleness, or sincerity, lies at the basis of that previous preparation, which is essential to success in any and every thing. The steps of the climax conduct us to it as the mental state, necessary to all virtues, and this sincerity is again made dependent on the understanding of what is good, upon which point see the next chapter. 不獲乎上,=acc. to Ying-tă, 不得於君上之意, 'do not get the mind—pleased feeling—of the sovereign.' We use 'to gain,' and 'to win,' sometimes, in a similar way. 18. Premare (*Not, Lin, Sin.*, p. 156) says:—'誠者 *est in obstracto, et* 誠之者 *est in con-*

身有道、不明乎善、不誠乎身矣。○十八節 誠者、天之道也、誠之者、人之道也、誠者、不勉而中、不思而得、從容中道、聖人也、誠之者、擇善而固執之者也。○十九節 博學之、審問之、慎思之、明辨之、篤行之。○二十節 有弗學、學之弗能、弗措也、有弗

thoughts in upon himself, finds a want of sincerity, he will not be obedient to his parents. There is a way to the attainment of sincerity in one's-self;—if a man do not understand what is good, he will not attain sincerity in himself.

18. "Sincerity is the way of Heaven. The attainment of sincerity is the way of men. He who possesses sincerity, is he who, without an effort, hits what is right, and apprehends, without the exercise of thought;—he is the sage who naturally and easily embodies the *right* way. He who attains to sincerity, is he who chooses what is good, and firmly holds it fast.

19. "To this attainment there are requisite the extensive study of what is good, accurate inquiry about it, careful reflection on it, the clear discrimination of it, and the earnest practice of it.

20. "The superior man, while there is any thing he has not studied, or while in what he has studied there is any thing he cannot understand, will not intermit his labour. While there is any thing

creto.' This is not quite correct. For 誠者 is in the concrete, as much as the other, and is said, below, to be characteristic of the sage. 誠者 is the quality possessed absolutely. 誠之者 is the same acquired. 'The way of Heaven,'—this, acc. to Ying-tă,—'the way which Heaven pursues.' Choo He explains it 天理之本然, 'the fundamental natural course of heavenly principle.' Maou says:—此猶中庸之率性以爲道者也, 本乎天也, 'this is like the accordance of nature in the Mean, considered to be THE PATH, having its root in Heaven.' We might acquiesce in this, but for the opposition of 人之道, on which Maou says:—此猶中庸之修道以爲道者也, 成乎人也;—'this is like the cultivation of the path in the Mean, considered to be THE PATH, having its completion from man.' But this takes the second and third utterances in the Work as independent sentiments, which they certainly are not. I do not see my way to rest in any but the old interpretation, extravagant as it is.—At this point, the chapter in the 家語 ceases to be the same with that before us, and diverges to another subject. 19. There are here described the different processes which lead to the attainment of sincerity. The gloss in the 備旨 says that 'the five 之 all refer to the *what is good* in the last ch., the five universal duties, and the nine standard rules being included therein.' Rather it seems

問、問之弗知、弗措也、有弗思、思之弗得、弗措也、有弗辨、辨之弗明、弗措也、有弗行、行之弗篤、弗措也、人一能之、己百之、人十能之、己千之。○廿一節 果能此道矣、雖愚必明、雖柔必强。

廿一章 自誠明、謂之性、自

he has not inquired about, or any thing in what he has inquired about which he does not know, he will not intermit his labour. While there is any thing which he has not reflected on, or any thing in what he has reflected on which he does not apprehend, he will not intermit his labour. While there is any thing which he has not discriminated, or his discrimination is not clear, he will not intermit his labour. If there be any thing which he has not practised, or his practice fails in earnestness, he will not intermit his labour. If another man succeed by one effort, he will use a hundred efforts. If another man succeed by ten efforts, he will use a thousand.

21. "Let a man proceed in this way, and, though dull, he will surely become intelligent; though weak, he will surely become strong."

Chapter XXI. When we have intelligence resulting from sincerity, this condition is to be ascribed to nature; when we have sincerity resulting from intelligence, this condition is to be ascribed

to me, that the 之, acc. to the idiom pointed out several times in the Analects, simply intensifies the meaning of the diff. verbs, whose regimen it is. 20. Here we have the determination which is necessary in the prosecution of the above processes, and par. 21 states the result of it. Choo He makes a pause at the end of the first clause in each part of the par., and interprets thus:—'If he do not study, well. But if he do, he will not give over till he understands what he studies,' and so on. But it seems more natural to carry the supposition in 有 over the whole of every part, as in the translation, which moreover substantially agrees with Ying-tă's interpretation.—Here terminates the third part of the Work. It was to illustrate, as Choo He told us, how 'the path of the Mean cannot be left.' The author seems to have kept this point before him in chapters xiii—xvi., but the next three are devoted to the one subject of filial piety, and the 20th, to the general subject of government. Some things are said worthy of being remembered, and others which require a careful sifting; but, on the whole, we do not find ourselves advanced in an understanding of the argument of the Work.

21. The reciprocal connection of sincerity and intelligence. With this chap. commences the fourth part of the Work, which, as Choo observes in his concluding note, is an expansion of the 18th par. of the prec. chapter. It is, in a great measure, a glorification of the sage, finally resting in the person of Confucius, but the high character of the sage, it is maintained, is not unattainable by others. He realizes the ideal of humanity, but by his example and lessons, the same ideal is brought within the reach of many, perhaps of all. The ideal of humanity,—the perfect character belonging to the sage, which ranks him on a level with Hea-

中庸

明誠、謂之教、誠則明矣、明則誠矣。

右第二十一章、子思承上章、夫子天道人道之意、而立言也、自此以下十二章、皆子思之言、以反覆推明此章之意。

二十二 唯天下至誠、爲能

to instruction. But given the sincerity, and there shall be the intelligence; given the intelligence, and there shall be the sincerity.

The above is the twenty-first chapter. Tsze-sze takes up in it, and discourses from, the subjects of "the way of Heaven" and "the way of men," mentioned in the preceding chapter. The twelve chapters that follow are all from Tsze-sze, repeating and illustrating the meaning of this one.

CHAPTER XXII. It is only he who is possessed of the most complete sincerity that can exist under heaven, who can give its full

ven,—is indicated by 誠, and we have no single term in English, which can be considered as the complete equivalent of that character. The Chinese themselves had great difficulty in arriving at that definition of it which is now generally acquiesced in. In the 四書通 (quoted in the 匯參中庸, XVI. 5), we are told that 'the Han scholars were all ignorant of its meaning. Under the Sung dynasty, first came 李邦直 who defined it by 不欺, *freedom from all deception*. After him, 徐仲車 said that it meant 不息, *ceaselessness*. Then, one of the Ch'ing called it 無妄, *freedom from all moral error*; and finally, Choo He added to this the positive element of 眞實, *truth and reality*, on which the definition of 誠 was complete.' Remusat calls it—*la perfection*, and '*la perfection morale*.' Intorcetta and his friends call it—*vera solidaque perfectio*. Simplicity or singleness of soul seems to be what is chiefly intended by the term;—the disposition to, and capacity of, what is good, without any deteriorating element, with no defect of intelligence, or intromission of selfish thoughts. This belongs to Heaven, to Heaven and Earth, and to the sage. Men, not naturally sages, may, by cultivating the intelligence of what is good, raise themselves to this elevation. 性 and 教 carry us back to the first chapter, but the terms have a different force, and the longer I dwell upon it, the more am I satisfied with Choo He's pronouncement in his 語類, that 性 is here 性之, 'possessing from nature,' and 教=學之, 'learning it,' and therefore I have translated 謂之 by—'is to be ascribed to.' When, however, he makes a difference in the connection between the parts of the two clauses—誠則明矣, 明則誠矣, and explains—誠則無不明, 明則可以至誠, 'sincerity is invariably intelligent, and intelligence may arrive at sincerity,' this is not dealing fairly with his text.

Here, at the outset, I may observe that, in this portion of the Work, there are specially the three following dogmas, which are more than questionable:—1st, That there are some men—sages—naturally in a state of moral perfection; 2d, That the same moral perfection is attainable by others, in whom its development is impeded by their material organization, and the influence of

盡其性、能盡其性、則能盡人之性、能盡人之性、則能盡物之性、能盡物之性、則可以贊天地之化育、可以贊天地之化育、則可以與天地參矣。

development to his nature. Able to give its full development to his own nature, he can do the same to the nature of other men. Able to give its full development to the nature of other men, he can give their full development to the natures of animals and things. Able to give their full development to the natures of creatures and things, he can assist the transforming and nourishing powers of Heaven and Earth. Able to assist the transforming and nourishing powers of Heaven and Earth, he may with Heaven and Earth form a ternion.

external things; and 3d, That the understanding of what is good will certainly lead to such moral perfection.

22. THE RESULTS OF SINCERITY; AND HOW THE POSSESSOR OF IT FORMS A TERNION WITH HEAVEN AND EARTH. On 天下至誠, Choo He says that it denotes 'the reality of the virtue of the sage, to which there is nothing in the world that can be added.' This is correct, and if we were to render—'It is only the most sincere man under heaven,' the translation would be wrong. 盡 means simply 'to exhaust,' but, by what processes and in what way, the character tells us nothing about. The 'giving full development to his nature,' however, may be understood with Maou, as='pursuing THE PATH in accordance with his nature, so that what Heaven has conferred on him is displayed without shortcoming or let.' The 'giving its development to the nature of other men' indicates the sage's helping them, by his example and lessons, to perfect themselves. 'His exhausting the nature of things,' *i. e.*, of all other beings, animate and inanimate, is, acc. to Choo He, 'knowing them completely, and dealing with them correctly,' 'so,' add the paraphrasts, 'that he secures their prosperous increase and development according to their nature. Here, however, a Buddhist idea appears in Choo He's commentary. He says: —'The nature of other men and things (=animals) is the same with my nature,' which, it is observed in Maou's work, is the same with the Buddhist sentiment, that 'a dog has the nature of Buddha,' and with that of the philosopher Kaou, that 'a dog's nature is the same as a man's.' Maou himself illustrates the 'exhausting the nature of things,' by reference to the Shoo-king IV. iii. 2, where we are told that under the first sovereigns of the Hea dynasty, 'the mountains and rivers, all enjoyed tranquillity, and the birds and beasts, the fishes and tortoises, all realized the happiness of their nature.' It is thus that the sage 'assists Heaven and Earth.' K'ang-shing, indeed, explains this by saying:—'The sage, receiving Heaven's appointment to the imperial throne, extends every where a happy tranquillity.' Evidently there is a reference in the language to the mystical paragraph in the 1st chapter—致中和, 天地位焉, 萬物育焉. 'Heaven and Earth' take the place here of the single term—'Heaven,' in ch. xx. par. 18. On this Ying-tă observes:—It is said above, *sincerity is the way of Heaven*, and here mention is made also of *Earth*. The reason is, that the reference above, was to the principle of sincerity in its spiritual and mysterious origin, and thence the expression simple,—*The way of Heaven;* but here we have the transformation and nourishing seen in the production of things, and hence *Earth* is associated with *Heaven*.' This is not very intelligible, but it is to bring out the idea of a *ternion*, that the great, supreme, ruling, Power is thus dualized. 參 is 'a file of three,' and I employ 'ternion,' to express the idea, just as we use 'quaternion,' for a file of four. What is it but blasphemy, thus to file man with the supreme Power?

[二十三] 其次致曲、曲能有誠、誠則形、形則著、著則明、明則動、動則變、變則化、唯天下至誠、爲能化。

[二十四] 至誠之道、可以前知、國家將興、必有禎祥、國家將亡、必有妖孼、見乎蓍龜、動乎四體、禍福將至、善、必先

CHAPTER XXIII. Next to the above is he who cultivates to the utmost the shoots *of goodness* in him. From those he can attain to the possession of sincerity. This sincerity becomes apparent. From being apparent, it becomes manifest. From being manifest, it becomes brilliant. Brilliant, it affects others. Affecting others, they are changed by it. Changed by it, they are transformed. It is only he who is possessed of the most complete sincerity that can exist under heaven, who can transform.

CHAPTER XXIV. It is characteristic of the most entire sincerity to be able to foreknow. When a nation or family is about to flourish, there are sure to be happy omens; and when it is about to perish, there are sure to be unlucky omens. *Such events are* seen in the milfoil and tortoise, and affect the movements of the four limbs.

23. THE WAY OF MAN;—THE DEVELOPMENT OF PERFECT SINCERITY IN THOSE NOT NATURALLY POSSESSED OF IT. 其次, 'the next,' or 'his next,' referring to the 自誠明者, of ch. xxi. 曲 is defined by Choo He—偏, 'one half,' 'a part.' K'ang-shing explains it by 小小之事, 'very small matters.' Maou defines it by 隅, 'a corner,' and refers to Ana. VII. viii, 舉一隅不以三隅反, as a sentiment analogous to the one in 致曲. There is difficulty about the term. It properly means 'crooked,' and with a bad application, like 偏, often signifies 'deflection from what is straight and right.' Yet it cannot have a bad meaning here, for if it have, the phrase,—致曲, will be, in the connection, unintelligible. One writer uses this comparison:—'Put a stone on a bamboo shoot, or where the shoot would show itself, and it will travel round the stone, and come out *crookedly* at its side.' So it is with the good nature, whose free development is repressed. It shows itself in shoots, but if they be cultivated and improved, a moral condition and influence may be attained, equal to that of the sage.

24. THAT ENTIRE SINCERITY CAN FOREKNOW. 至誠之道 is the quality in the abstract, while 至誠 at the end, is the entirely sincere individual,—the sage, by nature, or by attainment. 禎祥, 'lucky omens.' In the dict., 祥 is used to define 禎. 祥 may be used also of inauspicious omens, but here it cannot embrace such. Distinguishing between the two terms, Ying-tă says that unusual appearances of things existing in a country are 祥, and appearances of things new are 禎. 妖孼 are 'unlucky omens,' the former being spoken of 'prodigies of plants, and of strangely dressed boys singing ballads,' and the latter of prodi-

知之、不善、必先知之、故至誠如神。

〔二十五〕誠者、自成也、而道、自道也。〔二節〕誠者、物之終始、不誠無物、是故君子誠之爲貴。〔三節〕誠者、非自成己而已也、所以成物

When calamity or happiness is about to come, the good shall certainly be foreknown by him, and the evil also. Therefore the individual possessed of the most complete sincerity is like a spirit.

CHAPTER XXV. 1. Sincerity is that whereby self-completion is effected, and *its* way is that by which man must direct himself.

2. Sincerity is the end and beginning of things; without sincerity there would be nothing. On this account, the superior man regards the attainment of sincerity as the most excellent thing.

3. The possessor of sincerity does not merely accomplish the self-completion of himself. With this quality he completes *other men and* things *also*. The completing himself *shows his* perfect virtue.

gious animals. The subject of the verbs 見 and 動 is the events, not the omens. For the milfoil and tortoise, see the Yih-king, App. I. xi. They are there called 神物, 'spiritual things.' Divination by the milfoil was called 筮; that by the tortoise was called 卜. They were used from the highest antiquity. See the Shoo-king, II. ii. 18; V. iv. 20–30. 四體, 'four limbs,' are by K'ang-shing interpreted of the feet of the tortoise, each foot being peculiarly appropriate to divination in a particular season. Choo He interprets them of the four limbs of the human body. 如神 must be left as indefinite in the translation as it is in the text.—The whole chapter is eminently absurd, and gives a character of ridiculousness to all the magniloquent teaching about 'entire sincerity.' The foreknowledge attributed to the sage,—the mate of Heaven,—is only a guessing by means of augury, sorcery, and other follies.

25. HOW FROM SINCERITY COMES SELF-COMPLETION, AND THE COMPLETION OF OTHERS AND OF THINGS. I have had difficulty in translating this chapter, because it is difficult to understand it. We wish that we had the writer before us to question him; but if we had, it is not likely that he would be able to afford us much satisfaction. Persuaded that what he denominates *sincerity* is a figment, we may not wonder at the extravagance of its predicates. 1. All the commen. of the Sung school say, that 誠 is here 天命之性, 'the Heaven-conferred nature,' and that 道 is 率性之道, 'the path which is in accordance with the nature.' They are probably correct, but the difficulty comes when we go on with this view of 誠 to the next par. 2. I translate the expansion of this in the 日講:—'All that fill up the space between heaven and earth are things (物). They end and they begin again; they begin and proceed to an end; every change being accomplished by sincerity, and every phenomenon having sincerity unceasingly in it. So far as the mind of man (人之心) is concerned, if there be not sincerity, then every movement of it is vain and false. How can an unreal mind accomplish real things? Although it may do something, that is simply equivalent to nothing. Therefore the superior man searches out the source of sincerity, and examines the evil of insincerity, chooses what is good, and firmly holds it fast, so seeking to arrive at the place of truth and reality.' Maou's explanation is:—'Now, since the reason why the sincerity of spiritual beings is so incapable of being repressed, and why they foreknow, is because they enter into things, and there is nothing without them:—shall there be anything which is without the entirely sincere man, who is as a spirit?' I have given these specimens of commentary, that the

也、成己、仁也、成物、知也、性之德也、合內外之道也、故時措之宜也。○

二十六章 一節 故至誠無息。○二節 不息則久、久則徵、○三節 徵則悠遠、悠遠、則博厚、博厚、則高明。四節 博厚、所以載物也、高明、所以覆物也、悠久、所以成物也。○五節 博厚、配地、高明、配天、悠久、無疆。○六節 如此者、

The completing *other men and* things *shows his* knowledge. *Both these are* virtues belonging to the nature, and *this is* the way by which a union is effected of the external and internal. Therefore, whenever he—*the entirely sincere man*—employs them,—*that is, these virtues,*—*their action will be* right.

CHAPTER XXVI. 1. Hence to entire sincerity there belongs ceaselesssness.

2. Not ceasing, it continues long. Continuing long, it evidences itself.

3. Evidencing itself, it reaches far. Reaching far, it becomes large and substantial. Large and substantial, it becomes high and brilliant.

4. Large and substantial;—this is how it contains *all* things. High and brilliant;—this is how it overspreads *all* things. Reaching far and continuing long;—this is how it perfects *all* things.

5. So large and substantial, *the individual possessing it* is the coequal of Earth. So high and brilliant, it makes him the coequal of Heaven. So far-reaching and long-continuing, it makes him infinite.

reader may, if he can, by means of them, gather some apprehensible meaning from the text. 3. I have translated 成物 by—'complete *other men and* things *also*,' with a reference to the account of the achievements of sincerity, in ch. xxii. On 性之德也, 合外內之道也, the 日講 paraphrases:—'Now both this perfect virtue and knowledge are virtues certainly and originally belonging to our nature, to be referred for their bestowment to Heaven;—what distinction is there in them of external and internal?'—All this, so far as I can see, is but veiling ignorance by words without knowledge.

26. A PARALLEL BETWEEN THE SAGE POSSESSED OF ENTIRE SINCERITY, AND HEAVEN AND EARTH, SHOWING THAT THE SAME QUALITIES BELONG TO THEM. The first six parr. show the way of the sage; the next three show the way of Heaven and Earth; and the last brings the two ways together, in their essential nature, in a passage from the She-king. The doctrine of the chapter is liable to the criticisms which have been made on the 22d ch. And, moreover, there is in it a sad confusion of the visible heavens and earth with the immaterial power and reason which govern them; in a word, with God. 1. Because of the 故, 'hence,' or 'therefore,'

不見而章、不動而變、無爲而成。○七節天地之道、可一言而盡也、其爲物不貳、則其生物不測。○八節天地之道、博也、厚也、高也、明也、悠也、久也。○九節今夫天、斯昭昭之多、及其無窮也、日月星辰繫焉、萬物覆焉、今夫地、一撮土之多、

6. Such being its nature, without any display, it becomes manifested; without any movement, it produces changes; and without any effort, it accomplishes its ends.

7. The way of Heaven and Earth may be completely declared in one sentence.—They are without any doubleness, and so they produce things in a manner that is unfathomable.

8. The way of Heaven and Earth is large and substantial, high and brilliant, far-reaching and long-enduring.

9. The heaven now before us is only this bright shining spot; but when viewed in its inexhaustible extent, the sun, moon, stars, and constellations of the zodiac, are suspended in it, and all things are overspread by it. The earth before us is but a handful of soil; but when regarded in its breadth and thickness, it sustains

Choo He is condemned by recent writers for making a new chapter to commence here. Yet the matter is sufficiently distinct from that of the preceding one. Where the 故 takes hold of the text above, however, it is not easy to discover. The gloss in the 備旨 says that it indicates a conclusion from all the preceding predicates about sincerity. 至誠 is to be understood, now in the abstract, and now in the concrete. But the 6th paragraph seems to be the place to bring out the personal idea, as I have done. 無疆, 'without bounds,'=our *infinite*. Surely it is strange—passing strange—to apply that term in the description of any created being. 7. What I said was the prime idea in 誠, viz., 'simplicity,' 'singleness of soul,' is very conspicuous here. 其爲物不貳,—爲 is the subst. verb. It surprises us, however, to find Heaven and Earth called '*things*,' at the same time that they are represented as by their entire sincerity producing all things. 9. This par. is said to illustrate the unfathomableness of Heaven and Earth in producing things, showing how it springs from their sincerity, or freedom from doubleness. I have already observed how it is only the material heavens and earth which are presented to us. And not only so;—we have mountains, seas, and rivers, set forth as acting with the same unfathomableness as those entire bodies and powers. The 備旨 says on this:—'The hills and waters are what Heaven and Earth produce, and that they should yet be able themselves to produce *other* things, shows still more how Heaven and Earth, in the producing of things, are unfathomable.' The confusion and error in such representations are very lamentable. The use of 多 in the several clauses here perplexes the student. On 斯昭昭之多, Choo He says—此指其一處而言之, 'This is speaking of it'—heaven—'as it appears in one point.' In the 中庸說, *in loc.*, there is an attempt to make this

及其廣厚、載華嶽而不重、振河海而不洩、萬物載焉、今夫山、一卷石之多、及其廣大、草木生之、禽獸居之、寶藏興焉、今夫水、一勺之多、及其不測、黿、鼉、蛟、龍、魚、鼈、生焉、貨財殖焉。十節詩云、維天之命、於穆不已、蓋曰、天之所以爲天也、於乎、不顯、文王之德之純、蓋曰、文王之所以爲文也、純亦不已。

mountains like the Hwa and the Yoh, without feeling their weight, and contains the rivers and seas, without their leaking away. The mountain now before us appears only a stone; but when contemplated in all the vastness of its size, we see how the grass and trees are produced on it, and birds and beasts dwell on it, and precious things which men treasure up are found on it. The water now before us appears but a ladleful; yet extending our view to its unfathomable depths, the largest tortoises, iguanas, iguanadons, dragons, fishes, and turtles, are produced in them, articles of value and sources of wealth abound in them.

10. It is said in the Book of Poetry, "The ordinances of Heaven, how profound are they and unceasing!" The meaning is, that it is thus that Heaven is Heaven. *And again*, "How illustrious was it, the singleness of the virtue of king Wăn!" indicating that it was thus that king Wăn was what he was. Singleness likewise is unceasing.

out by a definition of 多:—多餘也, 言少許耳, '多 is overplus, meaning a small overplus.' 日月星辰,—comp. the Shoo-king, I. 3. In that pass., as well as here, many take 星 as meaning the planets, but we need not depart from the meaning of 'stars' generally. 辰 is applied variously, but used along with the other terms, it denotes the conjunctions of the sun and moon, which divide the circumference of the heavens into twelve parts.

華嶽,—there are five peaks, or 嶽, worshipped in China, the western one of which is called 華 (low. 3d tone) 嶽. Here, however, we are to understand by each term a particular mountain. See the 集證 and 中庸說, *in loc.* In the 集證, the Yellow river, and that only, is understood by 河, but both it and 海 must be taken generally. 卷 read *k'euen*, lower 1st tone, is in the dict., with ref. to this

廿七 一節 大哉聖人之道。二節 洋洋乎、發育萬物、峻極于天。三節 優優大哉、禮儀三百、威儀三千。四節 待其人而後行。五節 故曰、苟不至德、至道不凝焉。六節 故君子、尊德性、而道問學、致廣大、

CHAPTER XXVII. 1. How great is the path proper to the sage!

2. Like overflowing water, it sends forth and nourishes all things, and rises up to the height of heaven.

3. All complete is its greatness! It embraces the three hundred rules of ceremony, and the three thousand rules of demeanour.

4. It waits for the proper man, and then it is trodden.

5. Hence it is said, "Only by perfect virtue can the perfect path, in all its courses, be made a fact."

6. Therefore, the superior man honours his virtuous nature, and maintains constant inquiry and study, seeking to carry it out to its

passage, defined by 區, 'a place,' 'a small plot.' In the 中庸說, 黿 is defined as 介蟲之元 'the first-produced of the chelonia;' 龍 as 鱗蟲之長 'the chief of scaly animals;' 鼉 as being a 'kind of 黿;' 蛟 as being 'a kind of 龍,' while the 鼉 'has scales like a fish, feet like a dragon, and is related to the 黿.' By 貨 are intended pearls and valuable shells; by 財, fish, salt, &c. 10. See the She-king, IV. i. Bk. I. Ode. II. st. 1. The attributes of the ordinances of Heaven, and the virtue of king Wăn, are here set forth, as substantially the same. 純='fine and pure,' 'unmixed.' The dict. gives it the distinct meaning of 'ceaselessness,' quoting the last clause here,—純亦不已, as if it were definition, and not description.

27. THE GLORIOUS PATH OF THE SAGE; AND HOW THE SUPERIOR MAN ENDEAVOURS TO ATTAIN TO IT. The chapter thus divides itself into two parts, one containing five parr., descriptive of the 聖人, or SAGE, and the other two, descriptive of the 君子, or *superior man*, which two appellations are to be here distinguished. 1. 'This par.,' says Choo He, 'embraces the two that follow.' They are, indeed, to be taken as exegetical of it. 道, it is said, is here, as every where else in the work (see the 翼注, *in loc.*), '*the path which is in acc. with the nature.*' The student tries to believe so, and goes on to par. 2, when the predicate about *the nourishing of all things* puzzles and confounds him. 2. 極 is not here the adverb, but=至, 'reaching to.' 3. By 禮儀, we are to understand the greater and more general principles of propriety, 'such,' says the 備旨, 'as capping, marriage, mourning, and sacrifice;' and by 威儀 are intended all the minuter observances of those. The former are also 經禮, 禮經, and 正經; the latter, 曲禮, and 動禮. See the 集證, *in loc.* 300 and 3000 are round numbers. Reference is made to these rules and their minutiæ, to show how, in every one of them, as proceeding from the sage, there is a principle, to be referred to the Heaven-given nature. 4. Comp. ch. xx. 2. In '*Confucius Sinarum Philosophus*,' it is suggested that there may be here a prophecy of the Saviour, and that the writer may have been 'under the influence of that spirit, by whose moving the Sibyls formerly prophesied of Christ.' There is nothing in the text to justify such a thought. 5. 凝, 'to congeal;' then,=成, 'to complete,' and 定, 'to

而盡精微、極高明、而道中庸、温故、而知新、敦厚以崇禮。○七節是故居上不驕、爲下不倍、國有道、其言足以興、國無道、其默足以容、詩曰、既明且哲、以保其身、其此之謂與。

二十八章 一節 子曰、愚而好自用、賤而好自專、生乎今之世、反古之道、如此者、烖及

breadth and greatness, so as to omit none of the more exquisite and minute points which it embraces, and to raise it to its greatest height and brilliancy, so as to pursue the course of the Mean. He cherishes his old knowledge, and is continually acquiring new. He exerts an honest, generous, earnestness, in the esteem and practice of all propriety.

7. Thus, when occupying a high situation, he is not proud, and in a low situation, he is not insubordinate. When the kingdom is well-governed, he is sure by his words to rise; and when it is ill-governed, he is sure by his silence to command forbearance to himself. Is not this what we find in the Book of Poetry,—"Intelligent is he and prudent, and so preserves his person?"

CHAPTER XXVIII. 1. The Master said, "Let a man who is ignorant be fond of using his own judgment; let a man without rank be fond of assuming a directing power to himself; let a man who is living in the present age go back to the ways of antiquity;—on the persons of all who act thus calamities will be sure to come."

fix.' The whole par. is merely a repetition of the prec. one, in other words. 6. 道 in both cases here,=由, 'to proceed from,' or 'by.' It is said correctly, that 首句是一節頭腦, 'the first sentence,—尊德性而道問學, is the brains of the whole paragraph.' 温故而知新,—See Ana. II. xi. 7. This describes the superior man, largely successful in pursuing the course indicated in the prec. par. 倍=背. 詩曰,—See the She-king, III. iii. Ode VI. st. 5.

28. AN ILLUSTRATION OF THE SENTENCE IN THE LAST CHAPTER—'IN A LOW SITUATION HE IS NOT INSUBORDINATE.' There does seem to be a connection of the kind thus indicated between this chapter and the last, but the principal object of what is said here, is to prepare the way for the eulogium of Confucius below,—the eulogium of him, a sage without the throne. 1. The different clauses here may be understood generally, but they have a special reference to the general scope of the chapter. Three things are required to give law to the empire: virtue (including intelligence); rank; and the right time. 愚 is he who wants the virtue; 賤 is he who wants the rank; and the last clause describes

其身者也。○二節非天子、不議禮、不制度、不考文。○三節今天下、車同軌、書同文、行同倫。○四節雖有其位、苟無其德、不敢作禮樂焉、雖有其德、苟無其位、亦不敢作禮樂焉。○五節子曰、吾說夏禮、杞不足徵也、吾學殷禮、有宋存焉、吾學周禮、今用之、吾從周。

2. To no one but the emperor does it belong to order ceremonies, to fix the measures, and to determine the characters.

3. Now, over the empire, carriages have all wheels of the same size; all writing is with the same characters; and for conduct there are the same rules.

4. One may occupy the throne, but if he have not the proper virtue, he may not dare to make ceremonies or music. One may have the virtue, but if he do not occupy the throne, he may not presume to make ceremonies or music.

5. The Master said, "I may describe the ceremonies of the Hea dynasty, but Ke cannot sufficiently attest my words. I have learned the ceremonies of the Yin dynasty, and in Sung they still continue. I have learned the ceremonies of Chow, which are now used, and I follow Chow."

the absence of the right time.—In this last clause, there would seem to be a sentiment, which should have given course in China to the doctrine of Progress. 2. This, and the two next parr. are understood to be the words of Tsze-sze, illustrating the prec. declarations of Confucius. We have here the imperial prerogatives, which might not be usurped. 'Ceremonies' are the rules regulating religion and society; 'the measures' are the prescribed forms and dimensions of buildings, carriages, clothes, &c.; 文 is said by Choo He, after K'ang-shing, to be 書名, 'the names of the characters.' But 文 is properly the form of the character, representing, in the original characters of the language, the 形, or figure of the object denoted. The character and name together are styled 字; and 書 is the name appropriate to many characters, written or printed. 文, in the text, must denote both the form and sound of the character. 議, 'to discuss,' and 考; 'to examine,' but implying, in each case, the consequent ordering and settling. There is a long and eulogistic note here, in '*Confucius Sinarum Philosophus*,' on the admirable uniformity secured by these prerogatives throughout the Chinese empire. It was natural for Roman Catholic writers, to regard Chinese uniformity with sympathy. But the value, or, rather, no value, of such a system in its formative influence on the characters and institutions of men may be judged, both in the empire of China, and in the church of Rome. 3. 今, 'now,' is said with reference to the time of Tsze-sze. The par. is intended to account for Confucius' not giving law to the empire. It was not the time.

中庸

〔二十九〕一節 王天下有三重焉、其寡過矣乎。○二節 上焉者、雖善、無徵、無徵、不信、不信、民弗從、下焉者、雖善、不尊、不尊、不信、不信、民弗從。○三節 故君子之道、本諸身、徵諸庶民、考諸三

CHAPTER XXIX. 1. He who attains to the sovereignty of the empire, having *those* three important things, shall be able to effect that there shall be few errors *under his government*.

2. However excellent may have been the regulations of those of former times, they cannot be attested. Not being attested, they cannot command credence, and not being credited, the people would not follow them. However excellent might be the regulations made by one in an inferior situation, he is not in a position to be honoured. Unhonoured, he cannot command credence, and not being credited, the people would not follow his rules.

3. Therefore the institutions of the Ruler are rooted in his own character and conduct, and sufficient attestation of them is given by the masses of the people. He examines them *by comparison* with those of the three kings, and finds them without mistake. He sets

軌, 'the rut of a wheel.' 4. 禮樂;—but we must understand also 'the measures,' and 'characters,' in par. 2. This par. would seem to reduce most emperors to the condition of *rois fainéants*. 5. See the Ana. III. ix., xiv., which chapters are quoted here; but in regard to what is said of Sung, with an important variation. The par. illustrates how Confucius himself 爲下不倍, 'occupied a low station, without being insubordinate.'

29. AN ILLUSTRATION OF THE SENTENCE IN THE XXVIIITH CHAPTER—'WHEN HE OCCUPIES A HIGH SITUATION, HE IS NOT PROUD;' OR RATHER, THE SAGE AND HIS INSTITUTIONS SEEN IN THEIR EFFECT AND ISSUE. 1. Different opinions have obtained as to what is intended by the 三重, 'three important *things*.' K'ang-shing says they are 三王之禮, 'the ceremonies of the three kings,' *i. e.*, the founders of the three dynasties, Hea, Yin, and Chow. This view we may safely reject. Choo He makes them to be the imperial prerogatives, mentioned in the last chapter, par. 2. This view may, possibly, be correct. But I incline to the view of the commentator Luh (陸氏), of the T'ang dynasty, hat they refer to the virtue, station, and time, which we have seen, in the notes on the last ch., to be necessary to one who would give law to the empire. Maou mentions this view, indicating his own approval of it. 寡 is used as a verb, 'to make few.'—'He shall be able to effect that there shall be few errors,' *i. e.*, few errors among his officers and people. 2. By 上焉者 and 下焉者, K'ang-shing understands 'sovereign' and 'minister,' in which, again, we must pronounce him wrong. The translation follows the interpr. of Choo He, it being understood that the subject of the par. is the regulations to be followed by the people. 上焉者 having a reference both to *time* and to *rank*, 下焉者 must have the same. Thus there is in it an allusion to Confucius, and the way is still further prepared for his eulogium. 3. By 君子 is intended the 王天下者 in par. 1,—the emperor-sage. By 道 must be intended all his institutions and regulations. 'Attestation of them is given by the masses of the people;' *i. e.*, the people believe in such a ruler, and follow his regulations, thus attesting their adaptation to the general requirements of humanity. 'The three kings,' as mentioned above,

王而不繆、建諸天地而不悖、質諸鬼神而無疑、百世以俟聖人而不惑。〇四節質鬼神而無疑、知天也、百世以俟聖人而不惑、知人也。〇五節是故君子、動而世爲天下道、行而世爲天下法、言而世爲天下則、遠之則有望、近之則不厭。〇六節詩曰、在彼無惡、在

them up before heaven and earth, and finds nothing in them contrary to their mode of operation. He presents himself with them before spiritual beings, and no doubts about them arise. He is prepared to wait for the rise of a sage, a hundred ages after, and has no misgivings.

4. His presenting himself *with his institutions* before spiritual beings, without any doubts about them arising, shows that he knows Heaven. His being prepared, without any misgivings, to wait for the rise of a sage a hundred ages after, shows that he knows men.

5. Such being the case, the movements of such a ruler, *illustrating his institutions*, constitute an example to the empire for ages. His acts are for ages a law to the empire. His words are for ages a lesson to the empire. Those who are far from him, look longingly for him; and those who are near him, are never wearied with him.

6. It is said in the Book of Poetry,—"Not disliked there, not tired of here, from day to day and night to night, will they per-

are the founders of the three dynasties, viz., the great Yu, T'ang, the Completer, and Wăn and Woo, who are so often joined together, and spoken of as one. 繆=謬, and should be read in the low. 3d tone. I hardly know what to make of 建諸天地. Choo, in his 語類, says:—此天地只是道耳，謂吾建於此，而與道不相悖也, 'Heaven and Earth here simply mean right reason. The meaning is—I set up *my institutions* here, and there is nothing in them contradictory to right reason.' This, of course, is explaining the text away. But who can do anything better with it? I interpret 質諸鬼神, with ref. to sacrificial institutions, or the general trial of a sovereign's institutions by the efficacy of his sacrifice, in being responded to by the various spirits whom he worships. This is the view of a Ho He-chen (何屺瞻), and is preferable to any other I have met with. 百世以俟聖人而不惑,—compare Mencius, II. Pt. I. ii. 17. 6. See the She-king, IV. i. Bk. II. Ode III. st. 2. It is a great descent to quote that ode here, however, for it is only praising the feudal princes of Chow. 在彼, 'there,' means their own States; and 在此, 'here,' is the imperial court of Chow. For 射, the She-king has 斁.

此無射、庶幾夙夜、以永終譽、君子未有不如此、而蚤有譽於天下者也。

【三十章】一節仲尼祖述堯舜、憲章文武、上律天時、下襲水土。二節辟如天地之無不持載、無不覆幬、辟如四時之錯行、如日月之代明。三節萬物並育、而不相害、道並行、而不相悖、小德川

petuate their praise." Never has there been a ruler, who did not realize this description, that obtained an early renown throughout the empire.

CHAPTER XXX. 1. Chung-ne handed down the doctrines of Yaou and Shun, as if they had been his ancestors, and elegantly displayed the regulations of Wăn and Woo, taking them as his model. Above, he harmonized with the times of heaven, and below, he was conformed to the water and land.

2. He may be compared to heaven and earth, in their supporting and containing, their overshadowing and curtaining, all things. He may be compared to the four seasons in their alternating progress, and to the sun and moon in their successive shining.

3. All things are nourished together without their injuring one another. The courses *of the seasons, and of the sun and moon*, are pursued without any collision among them. The smaller energies

30. THE EULOGIUM OF CONFUCIUS, AS THE BEAU-IDEAL OF THE PERFECTLY SINCERE MAN, THE SAGE, MAKING A TERNION WITH HEAVEN AND EARTH. 1. 仲尼—See ch. ii. The various predicates here are explained by K'ang-shing, and Ying-tă, with reference to the 'Spring and Autumn,' making them descriptive of it, but such a view will not stand examination. In translating the two first clauses, I have followed the editor of the 參匯, who says:—祖述者,以爲祖而纘述之,憲章者,奉爲憲而表章之. In the 紹聞編, it is observed that in what he handed down, Confucius began with Yaou and Shun, because the times of Fuh-he and Shin-nung were very remote. Was not the true reason this, that he knew of nothing in China more remote than Yaou and Shun? By 'the times of heaven' are denoted the ceaseless regular movement, which appears to belong to the heavens; and by the 'water and the land,' we are to understand the earth, in contradistinction from heaven, supposed to be fixed and unmoveable. 律, 'a statute,' 'a law;' here used as a verb, 'to take as a law.' 襲=因, 'to follow,' 'to accord with.' The scope of the par. is, that the qualities of former sages, of Heaven, and of Earth, were all concentrated in Confucius. 2. 辟,—read as, and=譬. 錯, read *ts'ŏh*,=迭, 'successively,' 'alternatingly.'

流、大德敦化、此天地之所以爲大也。一節

卅一章 唯天下至聖、爲能聰、明、睿、知、足以有臨也、寬、裕、溫、柔、足以有容也、發、强、剛、毅、足以有執也、齊、莊、中、正、足以有敬也、文、理、密、察、足以有別也。二節 溥博、淵

are like river currents; the greater energies are seen in mighty transformations. It is this which makes heaven and earth so great.

CHAPTER XXXI. 1. It is only he, possessed of all sagely qualities that can exist under heaven, who shows himself quick in apprehension, clear in discernment, of far-reaching intelligence, and all-embracing knowledge, fitted to exercise rule; magnanimous generous, benign, and mild, fitted to exercise forbearance; impulsive, energetic, firm, and enduring, fitted to maintain a firm hold; self-adjusted, grave, never swerving from the Mean, and correct, fitted to command reverence; accomplished, distinctive, concentrative, and searching, fitted to exercise discrimination.

2. All-embracing is he and vast, deep and active as a fountain, sending forth in their due seasons his virtues.

'This describes,' says Choo He, 'the virtue of the sage.' 3. The wonderful and mysterious course of nature, or—as the Chinese conceive,—of the operations of Heaven and Earth, are described to illustrate the previous comparison of Confucius.

31. THE EULOGIUM ON CONFUCIUS CONTINUED. Choo He says that this chapter is an expansion of the clause in the last paragr. of the preceding,—'The smaller energies are like river currents.' Even if it be so, it will still have reference to Confucius, the subject of the preceding chapter. K'ang-shing's account of the first paragraph is:—言德不如此,不可以君天下也,蓋傷孔子有其德而無其命. 'It describes how no one, who has not virtue such as this, can rule the empire, being a lamentation over the fact that while Confucius had the virtue, he did not have the appointment;' that is, of Heaven, to occupy the throne. Maou's account of the whole chapter is:—'Had it been that Chung-ne possessed the empire, then Chung-ne was a perfect sage. Being a perfect sage, he would certainly have been able to put forth the greater energies, and the smaller energies, of his virtue, so as to rule the world, and show himself the coequal of Heaven and Earth, in the manner here described.' Considering the whole chapter to be thus descriptive of Confucius, I was inclined to translate in the past tense,—'It *was* only he, who could,' &c. Still the author has expressed himself so indefinitely, that I have preferred translating the whole, that it may read as the description of the ideal man, who found, or might have found, his realization in Confucius. 1. 唯天下至聖,—see ch. xxi. 聖 here takes the place of 誠. Collie translates:—'It is only the most HOLY man.' Remusat:—'*Il n'y a dans l'univers qu'un* SAINT, *qui*... So the Jesuits:—'*Hic commemorat et commendat summe* SANCTI *virtutes*.' But *holiness* and *sanctity* are terms which indicate the humble and pious conformity of human character and life to the mind and will of God. The Chinese idea of the 聖人 is far enough from this. 臨,—以尊適卑曰臨, 'the approach of the honourable to the mean is called *lin*.' It denotes the high drawing near to the low, to influence and rule. 2. 淵泉, 'an abyss, a spring,' equal, acc. to Choo He, to—靜深而有本, 'still and deep, and having a root.' 時

泉、而時出之。○三節溥博如天、淵泉如淵、見而民莫不敬、言而民莫不信、行而民莫不說。○五節是以聲名洋溢乎中國、施及蠻貊、舟車所至、人力所通、天之所覆、地之所載、日月所照、霜露所隊、凡有血氣者、莫不尊親、故曰、配天。

三十二 一節 唯天下至誠、爲能經綸

3. All-embracing and vast, he is like heaven. Deep and active as a fountain, he is like the abyss. He is seen, and the people all reverence him; he speaks, and the people all believe him; he acts, and the people all are pleased with him. Therefore his fame overspreads the Middle kingdom, and extends to all barbarous tribes. Wherever ships and carriages reach; wherever the strength of man penetrates; wherever the heavens overshadow and the earth sustains; wherever the sun and moon shine; wherever frosts and dews fall:—all who have blood and breath unfeignedly honour and love him. Hence it is said,—"He is the equal of Heaven."

CHAPTER XXXII. 1. It is only the individual possessed of the most entire sincerity that can exist under heaven, who can adjust

出之, 'always,'—or, in season—'puts them forth,' the 之, 'them,' having reference to the qualities described in par. 1. 3. 見, 'he is seen;'—with reference, says the 備旨, to 'the robes and cap,' the visibilities of the ruler. 'He speaks;'—with reference to his 'instructions, declarations, orders.' 'He acts;'—with reference to his ceremonies, music, punishments, and acts of government.' 4. This par. is the glowing expression of grand conceptions. 蠻 the general name for the rude tribes south of the Middle kingdom. 貊 is another name for the 狄, or rude tribes on the north. The two stand here, like 夷狄, Ana. III. v. and like 四夷, in the 大學傳, x. 15, as representatives of all barbarous tribes. 隊, read *chuy*, low. 3d tone,=墜, 'to fall.'

32. THE EULOGIUM OF CONFUCIUS CONCLUDED. 'The chapter,' says Choo He, 'expands the clause in the last par. of ch. xxix., that the greater energies are seen in mighty transformations.' The sage is here not merely equal to Heaven:—he is another Heaven, an independent being, a God. 1. 經 and 綸 are processes in the manipulation of silk, the former denoting the first separating of the threads, and the latter the subsequent bringing of them together, according to their kinds. 天下之大經,—'the great invariabilities of the world;'

中庸

天下之大經、立天下之大本、知天地之化育、夫焉有所倚。一節肫肫其仁、淵淵其淵、浩浩其天。二節苟不固聰明聖知、達天德者、其孰能知之。三節

三十三章 詩曰、衣錦尚

the great invariable relations of mankind, establish the great fundamental virtues of humanity, and know the transforming and nurturing operations of Heaven and Earth;—shall this individual have any being or any thing beyond himself on which he depends?

2. Call him man in his ideal, how earnest is he! Call him an abyss, how deep is he! Call him Heaven, how vast is he!

3. Who can know him, but he who is indeed quick in apprehension, clear in discernment, of far-reaching intelligence, and all-embracing knowledge, possessing all heavenly virtue?

CHAPTER XXXIII. 1. It is said in the Book of Poetry, "Over

explained of the 達道 and 九經, in ch. xx. 8, 12. 天下之大本,—'the great root of the world;' evidently with reference to the same expression in ch. i. 4. 知 is taken as emphatic;—有默契焉,非旦聞見之知而已, 'he has an intuitive apprehension of, and agreement with, them. It is not that he knows them merely by hearing and seeing.' 夫焉有所倚. This is joined by K'ang-shing with the next par., and he interprets it of the Master's virtue, universally affecting all men, and not partially deflected, reaching only to those near him or to few. Choo He more correctly, as it seems to me, takes it as=倚靠, 'to depend on.' I translate the expansion of the clause which is given in '*Confucius Sinarum Philosophus*.'—'The perfectly holy man of this kind therefore, since he is such and so great, how can it in any way be, that there is any thing in the whole universe, on which he leans, or in which he inheres, or on which he behooves to depend, or to be assisted by it in the first place, that he may afterwards operate?' 2. The three clauses refer severally to the three in the prec. paragraph. 仁 is virtuous humanity in all its dimensions and capacities, existing perfectly in the sage. Of 淵 I do not know what to say. The old Comm. interpret the second and third clauses, as if there were a 如 before 淵 and 天, against which Choo He reclaims, and justly. In the 紹聞編 we read:—天人本無二,人只有此形體,與天便隔,視聽思慮,動作,皆曰由我,各我其我,可知其小也,除却形體,便渾是天。形體如何除得,只克去有我之私,便是除也,天這般廣大,吾心亦這般廣大,而造化無間於我,故曰浩浩其天. 'Heaven and man are not originally two, and man is separate from Heaven only by his having this body. Of their seeing and hearing, their thinking and revolving, their moving and acting, men all say—*It is from* ME. Every one thus brings out his SELF, and his smallness becomes known. But let the body be taken away, and all would be Heaven. How can the body be taken away? Simply by subduing and removing that self-having of the *ego*. This is the taking it away. That being done, so wide and great as Heaven is, my mind is also so wide and great, and production and transformation cannot be separated from me. Hence it is said—*How vast is his Heaven*.' Into such wandering mazes of mysterious speculation are Chinese thinkers conducted by the text:—only to be lost in them. As it is said, in par. 3, that only the sage can know the sage, we may be glad to leave him.

絅、惡其文之著也、故君子之道、闇然而日章、小人之道、的然而日亡、君子之道、淡而不厭、簡而文、溫而理、知遠之近、知風之自、知微之顯、可與入德矣。○二節詩云、潛雖伏矣、亦孔之昭、故君子內省不疚、無惡於志、君子

her embroidered robe she puts a plain, single garment," intimating a dislike to the display of the elegance of the former. Just so, it is the way of the superior man to prefer the concealment *of his virtue*, while it daily becomes more illustrious, and it is the way of the mean man to seek notoriety, while he daily goes more and more to ruin. It is characteristic of the superior man, appearing insipid, yet never to produce satiety; while showing a simple negligence, yet to have his accomplishments recognized; while seemingly plain, yet to be discriminating. He knows how what is distant lies in what is near. He knows where the wind proceeds from. He knows how what is minute becomes manifested. Such an one, we may be sure, will enter into virtue.

2. It is said in the Book of Poetry, "Although *the fish* sink and lie at the bottom, it is still quite clearly seen." Therefore the supe-

33. THE COMMENCEMENT AND THE COMPLETION OF A VIRTUOUS COURSE. The chapter is understood to contain a summary of the whole Work, and to have a special relation to the first chapter. There, a commencement is made with Heaven, as the origin of our nature, in which are grounded the laws of virtuous conduct. This ends with Heaven, and exhibits the progress of virtue, advancing step by step in man, till it is equal to that of High Heaven. There are eight citations from the Book of Poetry, but to make the passages suit his purpose, the author allegorizes them, or alters their meaning, at his pleasure. Origen took no more license with the scriptures of the old and new Testament than Tsze-sze and even Confucius himself do with the Book of Poetry. 1. *The first requisite in the pursuit of virtue is, that the learner think of his own improvement, and do not act from a regard to others.* 詩曰,—see the She-king, I. v. Ode III. st. 1., where we read, however, 衣錦褧衣. 褧 and 絅 are synonyms. 惡 (up. 3d tone) 其云云 is a gloss by Tsze-sze, giving the spirit of the passage. The ode is understood to express the condolence of the people, with the wife of the duke of Wei, worthy of, but denied, the affection of her husband. 君子之道, 小人之道,—道 seems here to correspond exactly to our English *way*, as in the translation. 的然,—the primary meaning of 的 is 明, 'bright,' 'displayed.' 的然, 'displayed-like,' in opp. to 闇然, 'concealed-like.' 知遠之近,—what is *distant*, is the nation to be governed, or the family to be regulated; what is *near*, is the person to be cultivated. 知風之自,—the *wind* is the influence exerted upon others, the *source* of which is one's own

之所不可及者、其唯人之所不見乎。三節 詩云、相在爾室、尙不愧於屋漏、故君子、不動而敬、不言而信。四節 詩曰、奏假無言、時靡有爭、是故君子、不賞而民勸、不怒而民威於鈇鉞。五節 詩曰、不顯惟德、

rior man examines his heart, that there may be nothing wrong there, and that he may have no cause for dissatisfaction with himself. That wherein the superior man cannot be equalled is simply this,—his *work* which other men cannot see.

3. It is said in the Book of Poetry, "Looked at in your apartment, be there free from shame, where you are exposed to the light of heaven." Therefore, the superior man, even when he is not moving, has *a feeling of* reverence, and while he speaks not, he has *the feeling of* truthfulness.

4. It is said in the Book of Poetry, "In silence is the offering presented, and *the spirit* approached to; there is not the slightest contention." Therefore the superior man does not use rewards, and the people are stimulated *to virtue.* He does not show anger, and the people are awed more than by hatchets and battle-axes.

5. It is said in the Book of Poetry, "What needs no display is

virtue. 知微之顯,—comp. ch. i. 3. 可與='it may be granted to such an one,' 與 being in the sense of 許. 2. *The superior man going on to virtue, is watchful over himself, when he is alone.* 詩云,—see the She-king, II. iv. Ode VIII. st. 11. The ode appears to have been written by some officer who was bewailing the disorder and misgovernment of his day. This is one of the comparisons which he uses; —the people are like fish in a shallow pond, unable to save themselves by diving to the bottom. The application of this to the superior man, dealing with himself, in the bottom of his soul, so to speak, and thereby realizing what is good and right, is very far-fetched. 志, 'the will,' is here=心, 'the whole mind,' the self. 3. We have here substantially the same subject as in the last par. The ode is the same which is quoted in ch. xvi. 4, and the citation is from the same stanza of it. 屋漏, acc. to Choo He, was the north-west corner of ancient apartments, the spot most secret and retired. The single panes, in the roofs of Chinese houses, go now by the name, the light of heaven leaking in (漏) through them. Looking at the whole stanza of the ode, we must conclude that there is reference to the light of heaven, and the inspection of spiritual beings, as specially connected with the spot intended. 4. *The result of the processes described in the two preced. parr.* 詩曰,—see the She-king, IV. iii. Ode II. st. 2, where for 奏 we have 鬷. 假 read as, and=格. The ode describes the imperial worship of T'ang, the founder of the Shang dynasty. The first clause belongs to the emperor's act and demeanour: the second to the effect of these on his assistants in the service. They were awed to reverence, and had no striving among themselves. The 鈇鉞 were anciently given by the emperor to a prince, as symbolic of his investiture with a plenipotent authority to pun-

中庸

百辟其刑之、是故君子、篤恭而天下平。○六節詩云、予懷明德、不大聲以色。子曰、聲色之於以化民、末也、詩曰、德輶如毛、毛猶有倫、上天之載、無聲無臭、至矣。

右第三十三章、子思因前章極致之言、反求其本、復自下學爲

virtue. All the princes imitate it." Therefore, the superior man being sincere and reverential, the whole world is conducted to a state of happy tranquillity.

6. It is said in the Book of Poetry, "I regard with pleasure your brilliant virtue, making no great display of itself in sounds and appearances." The Master said, "Among the appliances to transform the people, sounds and appearances are but trivial influences. It is said in another ode, 'His virtue is light as a hair.' Still, a hair will admit of comparison *as to its size.* 'The doings of the supreme Heaven have neither sound nor smell.'—That is perfect virtue."

The above is the thirty-third chapter. Tsze-sze having carried his descriptions to the extremest point in the preceding chapters, turns back in this, and examines the source of his subject; and then

ish the rebellious and refractory. The 鉞 is described as a large-handled axe, eight catties in weight. I call it a battle axe, because it was with one that king Woo despatched the tyrant Chow. 5. *The same subject continued.* 詩曰,—see the She-king, IV. i. Bk. I. Ode IV. st. 3. But in the She-king we must translate.—'There is nothing more illustrious than the virtue *of the sovereign,* all the princes will follow it.' Tsze-sze puts another meaning on the words, and makes them introductory to the next par. 君子 must here be the 王天下者 of ch. xxix. Thus it is that a constant shuffle of terms seems to be going on, and the subject before us is all at once raised to a higher, and inaccessible platform. 6. *Virtue in its highest degree and influence.* 詩云,—see the She-king, III. i. Ode VII. st. 7. The '*I*' is God, who announces to king Wăn the reasons why he had called him to execute his judgments. Wăn's virtue, not sounded nor emblazoned, might come near to the 不顯 of last par., but Confucius fixes on the 大 to show its shortcoming. It had *some,* though not *large* exhibition. He therefore quotes again from III. iii. Ode VI. st. 6, though away from the original intention of the words. But it does not satisfy him that virtue should be likened even to a *hair.* He therefore finally quotes III. i. Ode I. st. 7, where the imperceptible working of Heaven (載=事), in producing the overthrow of the Yin dynasty, is set forth as without sound or smell. That is his highest conception of the nature and power of virtue.

己謹獨之事、推而言之、以馴致乎篤恭而天下平之盛、又贊其妙、至於無聲無臭而後已焉、蓋舉一篇之要、而約言之、其反復丁寧示人之意、至深切矣、學者其可不盡心乎。

again from the work of the learner, free from all selfishness, and watchful over himself when he is alone, he carries out his description, till by easy steps he brings it to the consummation of the whole empire tranquillized by simple and sincere reverentialness. He farther eulogizes its mysteriousness, till he speaks of it at last as without sound or smell. He here takes up the sum of his whole Work, and speaks of it in a compendious manner. Most deep and earnest was he in thus going again over his ground, admonishing and instructing men:—shall the learner not do his utmost in the study of the Work?

INDEXES.

INDEX I.

OF SUBJECTS IN THE CONFUCIAN ANALECTS.

D

E

索引

F

G

H

I

J

K

L

M

N

O

P

Q

R

S

T

U

V

W

Y

INDEX II.

OF PROPER NAMES IN THE CONFUCIAN ANALECTS.

☞ *Names in Italics will be found in their own places in this Index with additional references.*

海上絲綢之路文獻集成　科技與文化編

L

M

N

P

S

Y

INDEX III.

OF SUBJECTS IN THE GREAT LEARNING.

索引

INDEX IV.

OF PROPER NAMES IN THE GREAT LEARNING.

INDEX V.

OF SUBJECTS IN THE DOCTRINE OF THE MEAN.

T

V

INDEX VI.

OF PROPER NAMES IN THE DOCTRINE OF THE MEAN.

C

G

H

K

M

S

T

W

Y

INDEX VII.

OF CHINESE CHARACTERS AND PHRASES;

INTENDED ALSO TO HELP TOWARDS THE FORMATION OF A DICTIONARY AND CONCORDANCE FOR THE CLASSICS.

A.* stands for *Analects*; *G.L.t.*, for *The Great Learning, text*; *G.L.c.*, for *The Great Learning, commentary*; *D.M.*, for *The Doctrine of the Mean*. *In the references to the Analects, books are separated by a colon, and chapters of the same book by a semicolon.

THE 1ST RADICAL 一.

一 *yih* yi (1) One, sometimes=a. A., II. i.: IV. vi. 2; xviii. 2: VI. ix.; xxii.: *et alibi, sæpe*. G.L. c., x. 13. D.M., viii.; xiii. 4; xxvi. 7, 9. (2) One and the same. D.M., xvi. 3; xx. 9. (3) Singleness,=sincerity. D.M., xx. 8, 15. (4) A unity. A., IV. xv. 1: XV. ii. . (5) Adverbially,=by one effort. D.M., xx. 20. (6) As a verb,=to unite in one. A., XIV. xviii. 2. (7) 一人, the one man, a designation of the emperor. A., XX. i. 5. G.L.c., ix. 3. (8) 一....一, partly, now...now. A., XIV. xviii. 2.

七 *ts'eih* ch'i Seven. A., II. iv. 6: XI. xxv. 5, 7, 10; XIII. xxix: XIV. xl.

三 *san* (1) Three. A., I. xi: II. ii.; iv. 2: III. ii.: *et alibi, sæpe*. D.M., xviii. 3; xx. 8, 11; xxvii. 3; xxix. 1. (2) Adverbially,=thrice. A., V. xviii. 1: VIII. i.: X. xviii. 2. Into three parts. A., VIII. xx. 4. But 三省, A., I. iv., on three points. (3) 二三子, ye, disciples. A., III. xxiv.: VII. xxiii.: IX. xi. 3: XI. x. 3; XVII. iv. 4. (4) 三王, three kings; *i.e.*, the founders of the three great dynasties. D. M., xxix. 3. (5) 三歸, the name of a tower. A., III. xxii. 2. (6) 三飯, A, XVIII. ix. 2,=the band-master at the third meal.

三 *san* Up. 3d tone. Thrice. A., V. xix.: XI. v.: XVIII. ii.

上 *shang* chang (1) He, she, it, this, that, which is above, with the corresponding plurals. A., I. ii. 1; III. xxvi.: *et sæpius*. G.L.c., x. 1, 2, 20. D.M., xiv. 3; *et al.* (2) Adverbially,=upwards. A., XIV. xxiv.; xxxvii. 2. (In these instances some tone it low. 2d tone). D.M., xviii. 3; xxx. 1. (3) 在....上, in or on the above of..... A., VI. vii.: IX. xvi. D.M., xvi. 3. (4) 上下, above, below, in opposition, applied to heaven and earth. A., VII. xxx. D.M., xii. 3. (5) 草上之風, the grass, when the wind is upon it. A., XII. xix. (6) 上帝, God, the most High God. G.L.c., x. 5. D.M., xix. 6.

上 *shang* chang Up. 2d tone. To ascend; proceeding upwards. 以上, A., VI. xix.; VII. vii.

下 *hea* hsia Anciently, upper 2d tone. He she, it, this, that, which is below, with the corresponding plurals; both positive and superlative. A., IX. iii. 2: X. ii. 1: XVI. ix. G.L.c., x. 2, 20. D.M., xiv. 3; xix. 4; xx. 6, 17; xxix. 2. (2) 上下, see on 上. (3) 於 or 于......下, in or on the beneath of....A., XII. xxii. 1: XVII. xii. 1. (4) 天下, the world, the empire. A., III. xi.; xxiv.: IV. x.: *et al.* G.L.t., 4, 5: c., viii. 1; ix. 4; x. 1, 4. D.M., i. 4; x. i.: *et al.* (5) Occurs in the proper name 柳下惠, A., XV. xiii.: XVIII. ii.; viii. 1, 3.

下 *hea* hsia A verb, low. 3d tone. To descend. A., III. vii.: V. xiv.: *et al.* (2) 以下, downwards. A., VI. xix. (3) 下人, to humble one's-self to others. A., XII. xx. 5.

丈 *chang* 丈人, an old man. A., XVIII. vii. 1.

不 *puh* pu Not. *Passim.*

且 *ts'eay* ch'ieh Moreover; and moreover. A., II. iii. 2; VI. iv.: VII. xv.: VIII. xi.; xiii. 3: IX. xi. 3: XI. xxv. 4: XVI. i. 4, 17: XVIII. vi. 3. D.M., xv. 2; xxvi. 7.

世 *she* shih (1) An age, a generation. A., II. xxiii. 1. 2: VI. xiv.: XIII. xii.: XVI. i. 8; ii. 1; iii. D.M., XI. i.; xxviii. 1; xxix. 3, 4. (2) To all ages. D.M., xxix. 5. (3) 沒世=after death. A., XV. xix. G.L.c., iii. 5. (4) 絕世, interrupted generations; *i.e.*, families

索引

whose line of succession has been broken. A., XX. i. 8. D.M., xx. 14. (5) The world. A., XIV. xxxiv.: XVIII. vi. 3. G.L.c., xi. 3. (6) 世叔, as a proper name. A., XIV. ix.

丘 *k'ëu* ch'iu (1) A hillock. A. XIX. xx. (2) The name of Confucius. Used by himself. A., V. xxviii.: VII. xxiii.; xxx. 3; xxxiv.: *et al.* D.M., xiii. 4. Applied to him contemptuously. A., XIV. xxxiv. 1: XVIII. vi. 2, 3. (3) Part of a double surname. A., V. xxi.

並 *ping* Properly written 竝. Together, alongside. A., XIV. xlvii. 2: XIX. xvi. G. L.c., x. 22. D.M., xxx. 3.

THE 2D RADICAL. 丨.

个 *ko* 一个人, one man. G.L.c., x. 13.

中 *chung* The middle. (1) 中, and 在 or 於.... 中, in, in the midst of. A., II. xviii. 2: V. i. 1: VII. xv.: X. xvii. 2: XV. xxi.: XVI. i. 4, 5. (2) The heart. G.L.c., vi. 2. (3) The Mean. A., VI. xxvii.: XX. i. 1. D.M., i. 4, 5; ii. 1, 2: *et passim.* (4) 中國, the Middle kingdom, China. G.L.c., x. 15. D.M., xxxi. 4. (5) 中道, midway, halfway. A., VI. x. (6) 中人, mediocre men. A., VI. xix. (7) 中門, to stand in the middle of the gateway. A., X. iv. 2. (8) 中行, to walk in the Mean, to act entirely right. A., XIII. xxi. Comp. D.M., xxxi. 1. (9). 中牟, the name of a place. A., XVII. vii. 2.

中 *chung* Up. 3d tone. To hit the mark; hitting the mark; exact. A., XI. xiii. 3; xviii. 2: XIII. iii. 6: XVIII. viii. 3, 4. G.L. c., ix. 2. D.M., i. 4; xx. 18.

THE 3D RADICAL. 丶.

主 *choo* chu (1) To count as chief or principal. A., I. viii. 2: III. xvi.: IX. xxiv.: XII. x. (2) A master, president. A., XVI. i. 4.

THE 4TH RADICAL 丿.

乃 *nae* nai To be. 無乃....乎 or 與, is it not....? A., VI. i. 3: XIV. xxxiv. i.: XVI. i. 3.

久 *kew* chiu Long, for a long time. A., III. xxiv.: IV. ii.: *et al.* D.M. iii.; xxvi. 2, 4, 5, 8. After a long time. A., V. xvi.

乎 *hoo* hu (1) A particle of interrogation. Found alone; preceded by another interrog. part.; prec. by 不亦. A., I. i.; iv.: II. vii.; viii.; xvii.: VI. xxviii.: VII. xiv. i. 2: *et al., sæpe.* G.L.c., iii. 2. (2) A particle of exclamation. A., VI. v.: VIII. xviii. 5; xix. 1, 2: IX. xx.: *et al.* D.M., xvi. 3; xxvii. 2. Foll. by 哉, giving emphasis. A., III. xiv.: VII. xxix.: *et al.* Prec. by 哉. A., XII. xxii. 5: XIV. xlii. 1, 2. (3) Partly interrog., partly exclam. In this usage it is sometimes preceded by 必也; it is often prec. by 其; and by 矣 immed. before it. A., II. xxi. 2: III. vii.; xi.: IV. vi. 2: V. xviii. 1, 2: *et al., sæpe.* G.L.c., iv. 1; vi. 3. D.M., iii.; xv. 2; xvi. 2; xviii. 2; xix. 2: *et al.* (4) As a preposition, after verbs and adjectives,=*in, to,* &c. A., I. x. 2: II. xvi.: VIII. iv. 3: XVIII. x.; *et al., sæpe.* G.L.c., ix. 4; x. 6. D.M., i. 2; vii.; xiv. 1, 2, 5: *et al., sæpe.* (5) Than, in comparison. A., XI. xxv. 2: XVII. xxii.: XIX. xxv. D.M., i. 4, 莫....乎. (6) 惡乎, how. A., IV. v. 2. (7) Observe 焉爾乎, A., VI. xii.; and 其庶乎, XI. xviii. 1.

乎 *wóo* wu Up. 1st tone. Joined with 於. An exclamation. D.M., xxvi. 10.

之 *che* chih (1) Of. A., I. ii. 2; v.; xi. 1: *et passim.* G.L.T., 1, 4; c., iii. 1: *et passim.* D.M. ii. 2; viii.: *et passim.* In the construct state, the regent follows the 之, and the regimen precedes. They may be respectively a noun, a phrase, or a larger clause. (2) Him, her, it, them. A., I. vii.: XIV. xviii. 1; xix. 2: *et passim.* So, in G.L., and D.M. (3) It is often difficult to find the antecedent to 之, and it seems merely to give a substantive force to the verb. A., II. xiii.: III. xxiii.: XVII. ix. 6: XV. 2, 3: *et sæpe.* D.M., xx. 18, 19, 20: *et al.* (4) 有之, G.L.c., viii. 2; x. 13, as in (2), but 有之 and 無之 are more like our use of impersonal verbs. G.L.c., ix. 1. A., IV. vi. 3. (5) Where 之 comes in a sentence with 未, it is generally transposed. G.L.T., 7. A., IV. vi. 3: *et al.* So. 莫之知避 D.M., vii.: *et al.* All negative adverbs seem to exert this attractive force. (6) 之謂, it is called. D.M., i. 1. G.L.c., vi. 1. A., XVI. xii. 2: *et al.* 謂之 is different, and comes under (2). So, 譬之, A., XIX. xxiii. 2. (7) Obs. the idiom in A., VI. iii. 3: XI. vii. 1, 2; xxv. 11; XVIII. i. 1. (8) 如之何, how. A., III. xix.: XI. xix.: *et al.* (9) 死之, died with, or for, him. A., XIV. xvii. 1.

(10) 末之難, A., XIV. xlii. 3. (11) =於, in regard to. G.L.c., viii. 1. (12) =是, this. G.L.c., ix. 6. (13) As a verb. To go, or come, to. A., V. xviii. 2: XIII. xix.: *et al.* (14) Part of a man's name. A., VI. xiii.

乘 *shing* ch'eng To mount, to ride; spoken of horses, carriages, boats. A., V. vi.: VI. iii. 2: XV. x. 3; xxv.

乘 *shing* ch'eng Low. 3d tone. (1) A carriage. A., I. v.: V. vii. 2, 3: *et al.* G.L.c., x. 22. (2) A team of 4 horses. A., V. xviii. 2.

THE 5TH RADICAL. 乙.

九 *kew* chiu Nine. A., VI. iii. 3: VIII. xxi. 3: XVI. x. 九夷, the nine rude tribes on the east. A., IV. xiv. 九經, the nine standard rules of govt. D.M., xx. 12, 15.

九 *kew* chiu Up. 1st tone. To collect. A., XIV. xvii. 2.

乞 *k'eih* ch'i To beg. A., V. xxiii.

也 *ya* yeh (1) A particle used at the end of sentences. Sometimes it might be dispensed with, and at others it is felt to be necessary, not only to the euphony and strength of the style, but also to give clearness and definiteness to the meaning. A., I. ii. 1; viii. 2: X. i.; ii. 1, 2; iii. 1, 2, 3, 4, 5: *et passim.* So also in G.L., and D.M. It closes also the diff. clauses in a long predicate, where we might use the ';' in English. D.M., xxv. 8: *et al.* (2) It is used after proper names, after some adverbs, and after a clause, in the first member of a sentence, and may be construed as=*as to*, the Latin *quoad.* A., I. x. 1, 2; xv. 3: VII. xxv. 1: XI. vi.; xii. 3; xiv. 2; xv.; xvi. 1; xvii. 1, 2, 3, 4: *et passim.* So, in G.L., and D.M. In these cases it is followed at the end of the sentence, by another particle,—itself, 矣, 焉, 乎. (3) As correlate of 者, in explanation of terms. G.L.c., iii. 4; vi. 1; x. 7. D.M., xxv. A., III. viii. 3: XII. xvii.: *et al, sæpe.* (4) At the end of sentences, we find 者也, sometimes preceded by 者, sometimes not. In these cases, 者 may often be explained as imparting a participial or adjective power to other characters, but not so always. A., V. xxvi.: VI. ii.: VII. xix.: *et sæpe.* So, in G.L., and D.M. (5) 也者 in the first member of a sentence, resuming a previous word, and followed by an explanation or account of it. A., I. ii. 2. D.M., i. 2, 4: *et al., sæpe.* (6)=乎, interrog. A., III. xxii. 1: V. xvii.: VI. xxv. (7) As a final, it appears often followed by other particles:—也與; 也已; 也已矣; 也夫; 也哉.

亂 *lwan* luan (1) To confound; unregulated; confusion, insurrection. A., VII. xx.: VIII. ii.; x.; xiii. 2: X. viii. 4: XV. xxvi.: XVII. viii. 3; xviii.; xxiii.: XVIII. vii. 5. 作亂, to raise confusion, or insurrection. A., I. ii. 1. G.L.T., 7: c., ix. 3. D.M., xx. 14. (2) To put in order; able to govern. A., VIII. xx. 2. (3) The name of a certain part in a musical service. A., VIII. xv.

THE 6TH RADICAL. 亅.

予 *yu* yü (1) I, me, my. A., III. viii. 3: VI. xxvi.; viii. 3: *et al.* D.M., vii.; xxxiii. 6. (2) Name of a disciple of Conf. A., V. ix. 1, 2: XVII. xxi. 6.

事 *sze* chih (1) An affair, affairs; business. A., I. v.; xiv.: III. viii. 2; xv.: XV. i. 1: *et al., sæpe.* G.L.T., 3: c., ix. 3; x. 20. D.M., xix. 2; xx. 16. 有事, having troublesome affairs. A. II viii. Having an affair *with.* A., XVI. i. 2. 從事, to pursue business. A., VIII. v.: XVII. i. 2. 執事, to manage business. A., XIII. xvii. (2) Labours; the results of labour. A., XII. xxi. 3: XV. ix.: XIX. vii. D.M., xx. 14. (3) To serve. A. IX. xv. D.M., xix. 4: *et passim.* (4) 何事於仁 is probably=何有於仁, what difficulty has he in practising benevolence? so that it may be classed under (1). A., VI. xxxiii. 1.

THE 7TH RADICAL. 二.

二 *urh* (1) Two. A., III. xiv.; XII. vii. 3; ix. 2: *et al.* (2) 二三子, see 三 (3).

于 *yu* yü In, on, to, from. A., II. iv. 1; xxi. 2: XX. i. 3: *et al.* G.L.c., iii. 2: *et al.* D.M., xvii. 4: *et al.*

云 *yun* yün (1) Says, saying; gen., in quotations. A., II. xxi. 2: IX. vi. 4: XIV. xliii. 1: XIX. iii.; xxiii. 4. 詩云, often in G.L., and D.M. Observe A., XVII. vi. (2) Closing a sentence, and apparently =*so.* A., VII. xviii. 2; xxxiii.

五 *woo* wu Five. D.M., xx 8. A., II. iv. 1, 4: XX. ii. 1: *et al.*

互 *hoo* hu 互鄉, the name of a village. A., VII. xxviii.

井 *tsing* ching A well. A., VI. xxiv. 1.

亟 *k'e* ch'i Up. 3d tone. Frequently. A., XVII. i. 2.

亞 *ya* 亞飯,=the band-master at the second meal. A., XVIII. ix. 2.

THE 8TH RADICAL. 亠.

亡 *wang* (1) The dead. D.M., xix. 5; xx. 2. (2) To perish, to go to ruin. D.M., xxiv.; xxxiii. 1. (3) To cause to perish. A., VI. viii. (4) Not at home. A., XVII. i. 1. 亡人, a fugitive. G.L.c., x. 12.

亡 *woo* wu Used as 無, not having, being without. A., III. v.: VI. ii.: VII. xxv. 3: XI. vi.: XII. v. 1: XV. xxv: XVII. xvi. 1: XIX. ii.; v.

亢 *k'ang* 陳亢, a disciple of Conf. A., XVI. xiii. 1, 5. The same as 子禽.

交 *keaou* chiao (1). Intercourse, to have intercourse with. A., I. iv.; vii.: V. xvi.: XIX. iii. G.L.c., iii. 3. D.M., xx. 8. (2) To give, to bestow. G.L.c., x. 2.

亦 *yih* yi Also; even then. A., I. xii. 2; xiii.: III. xxii. 3: V. xi.; xx.; iv.: *et sæpe.* G.L.c., iv. 9, 13, 22. D.M., xii. 2: *et al.* 不亦...乎, is it not? But the meaning of *also* may often be brought out. A., I. i. 1, 2, 3: XX. ii. 3: *et al.*

享 *heang* hsiang To offer, present. A., X. v. 2.

THE 9TH RADICAL. 人.

人 *jin* jên (1) A man, other men, man,=humanity. A., I. i. 3; iv.; v.; x. 2: *et passim.* So, in G.L., and D.M. (2) As opposed to 民, meaning officers. D.M., xvii. 4. A., XI. xxiv. 3. (3) 爲人, playing the man, the style of man. A., I. ii.: VIII. xviii. 2. Obs. 人君, 人父, 人子, 人臣, G.L.c., iii. 3. (4) 小人, the mean man, opp. to 君子, *passim.* (5) 聖人, the sage. A., VII. xxv: XVI. viii. 1, 2: XIX. xii. 2. D.M., xii. 2; xvii. 1; xx. 18; xxvii. 1; xxix. 3, 4. (6) 門人, disciples. A., IV. xv. 2: VII. xxviii. 1: *et al.* (7) 庶人, all the people, the masses. A., XVI. ii. 3. G.L.T. 6. D.M., xviii. 3. (8) 善人, the good man. A., VII. xxvi. 2: *et al.* (9) 成人, the complete man. A., XIV. xiii. (10) 婦人, a woman. A., VIII. xx. 3. (11) 夫人, the designation of the wife of the prince of a State. A., XVI. xiv. (13) Used in designations of officers, like our word man in huntsman. 封人, the border-warden. A., III. xxiv. 行人, the manager of foreign intercourse. A., XIV. ix.

仁 *jin* jên Is found *passim.* (1) Benevolence. (2) Perfect virtue.

今 *kin* chin (1) Now; the present, modern, time. *Sæpe.* (2) Used logically, by way of inference. A., XI. xxiii. 4: XVI. i, 8, 12. D.M., xxvi. 9.

仍 *jing* jêng According as. A., XI. xiii. 2.

仕 *see* shih To take—to be in—office. A., V. 5; xviii.: XV. vi. 2: XVII. i. 2: XVIII. vii. 5: XIX. xiii.

他 *t'a* Other, another. A., V. xviii. 2: X. xi. 1: XVI. xiii. 3: XIX. xviii.; xxiv. G.L.c., x. 13.

仞 *jin* jên A measure of eight cubits. A., XIX. xxiii. 3.

代 *tae* tai (1) Instead of, alternate. D.M., xxx. 2. (2) A dynasty. 三代, the three dynasties;—Hea, Shang, and Chow. A., III. xiv. 二代. A., XV. xxiv. 2.

令 *ling* (1) To order. A., XIII. v: XX. ii. 3. G.L.c., ix. 4. (2) Excellent. D.M., xvii. 4. (3) Specious, insinuating. A., I. iii.: V. xxiv. (4) 令尹, designa. of the chief minister of Ts'oo. A., V. xviii. 1.

以 *e* i (1). To do. A., II. x. 1. Rarely found in this sense. ? A., XI. xxv. 3. (2) By, with, according to, and perhaps other English prepositions. G.L.c., ix. 5. D.M., xviii. 3; xx. 4. A., I. v.: II. i.; iii. 1, 2; v. 3: *et passim.* To this belong 所以, therefore, that by which; 是以, hence; 何以, whereby;—which are found *passim.* (3) To take. This use is analogous to the preced., but the 以 precedes the verb, and is often followed by it, without an intervening object, as in 以告, 以與, &c. 以爲, to take to be, to consider, to be considered. Examples occur *passim.* We may refer to it the use of 以 sometimes at the beginning of a sentence,=considering, take it that. (4) To; so as to. G.L.т., 6: c., x. 18. D.M., x. 3; xxvii. 6, 7; xxix. 3, 4, 6. A., II. ii; ix: III. xxiii.: VII. 1, 2; *et passim*. Sometimes we might translate in these cases by—*and thereby*. But not so in such cases as 以至, 以上, 以下, &c. (5) It is often found after 可. 可以, may, may be. (6) To use, to be used. A., III. xxi,: X. xvi. 2: XIII. xiv: XVIII. x. (7) The following instances are peculiar. G.L.c., iii. 5. D.M., xxxiii. 6. A., XIV. xiv. 2: XV. xxx.: XIX. xxv. 4: XX. i. 3.

仰 *yàng* To look up to A., IX. x. 1: XIX. xxi.

任 *jin* jên Low. 1st tone. 周任, a man's name. A., XVI. i. 6.

任 *jin* jên (1) An office, a charge. A., VIII. vii. 1, 2. D.M., xx. 14. (2) To repose trust in. A., XVII. vi. 1: XX. i. 9.

伐 *fă* fa (1) To attack by imperial authority. A., XVI. i. 1, 4; ii. 1. (2) To boast. A., V. xxv. 3: VI. xiii.: XIV. ii. 1. (3) To cut down, or out. D.M., xiii. 2. G.L.c., x. 22.

休 *hew* hsiu 休休, simple and upright. G.L.c., x. 15.

伊 *e* i 伊尹, the minister of the great T'ang. A., XII. xxii. 6.

伏 *fŭh* fu To lie at the bottom. D.M., xxxiii. 2.

仲 *chung* The second of three; the second of brothers. Enters very commonly into designations, as in that of Confucius. D.M., ii.; xxx. A., XIX. xxii,; xxiii.; xxiv.; xxv. Of others. VI. i. 2, 3; iv.: XI. ii. 2: XII. ii.: XIII. ii.—III. xxii. 1, 2, 3: XIV. x. 3; xvii. 1, 2: xviii. 1, 2.—V. xvi.—V. xvii.: XV. xiii.—XIV. xiii.; xv.—XIV. xx. 2.—XVIII. viii. 1, 4.—XVIII. xi. A surname. A., VI. vi.: XI. xxiii.: XVIII. vi.

伯 *pih* pi The eldest of brothers. Enters into designations. A., XVI. xiii.: XVII. x.—XIV. xxvi.: XV. vi. 2.—II. vi.: V. vii.—V. xxii.: VII. ix. 2: XVI. xii.: XVIII. viii.—VI. i. 2.—XVIII. xi. *bis*,—XIV. xxxviii.: XIX. xxiii. 2.—VIII. i. 1.—VI. viii.: XI. ii. 2. A surname. A., XIV. x. 3. 公伯, see 公.

似 *sze* szû Like to, as. A., X. i. 1; iv. 3, 4. D.M., xv. 5.

位 *wei* Position, status. A., IV. xiv.: X. iv. 3, 5: *et al.* D.M., XIV. 1, 3; *et al.* 天地位焉, Heaven and Earth get their places. D.M., i. 5.

佚 *yih* yi Idleness. A., XVI. v.

佑 *yéw* yu To aid. D.M., xvii. 4.

何 *hŏ* What, what kind of, how. A., II. v. 3; vii.; xv.; xxii. 1: XVII. v. 2; ix.; xix. 2, 3: *et sæpe*. G.L.c., vi. 2. (2) 如何, generally with 之 between. What, implying difficulty, indignation, or surprise. Other words are found also between the 如 and 何, and then the phrase=what has......to do with......? G.L.c., x. 22. A., III. xviii.: IX. v. 2; xiii. 2; xxiii.: *et sæpe*. (3) 何如, what as?=what do you think of? how can it be said? A., I. xv. 1: V. iii.; xvii. 1, 2: *et sæpe*. (4) 何有, gen., but not always,=will have no difficulty. A., VI. vi.: VII. ii.: XIII. xiii.: *et al.* (5) 何爲, gen.,=why. A., VI. xxiv.: IX. xv.: XIV. xxvi. 2; xxiv.: *et al.*

作 *tsŏh* tso (1) To make, produce. G.L.c., ix. 3. A., I. ii. 2: XI. xiii. 2. To do. A., VII. xxvii. (2) To lay the foundation of, to be a maker or author. A., VII. i. D.M., xviii. 1. (3) To make,=to be. A., XIII. xxii. (4) To be begun. A., III. xxiii. (5) To rise, arise. A., IX. ix.: X. xvi. 4; xviii. 2: XI. xxv. 7: XIV. xl.

佞 *ning* Glib-tongued. A., V. iv. 1, 2: VI. xiv.: XI. xxiv. 4: XIV. xxxiv. 1, 2: XV. x. 6: XVI. iv.

佛 *peih* pi A surname. A., XVII. vii. 1, 2.

佾 *yih* yi A row of pantomimes. A., III. i.

使 *sze* shih Up. 3d tone. To send on a mission; to be commissioned. A., VI. iii. 1: XIII. v.; xx.: XIV. xxvi. 1, 2.

使 *sze* shih Up. 2d tone. (1) To cause. G.L.c., iv. D.M., xvi. 3. A., II. xx.: III. xxi.: XVIII. vi. 1; vii. 4; x.: *et al.* (2) To employ; to be employed. G.L.c., x. 22. D.M., xx. 14. A., V. vii. 2, 3, 4: VI. vi.; vii.: *et al.* (3) To treat, behave to. G.L.c., ix. 1; x. 2. A., II. xix.: V. xv. (4) Supposing that. A., VIII. xi.

依 *e* i To accord with. D.M., xi. 3. A., VII. vi. 3.

來 *laê* lai (1) To come. A., I. i. 2: *et al.* (2) To encourage, induce to come. D.M., xx. 12, 13. A. xvi. i. 11, 12: XIX. xxv. 4. (3) Coming, future. A., IX. xxii.: XVIII. v.: I. xv. 3.

索引

儒 *joo* ju. A scholar. A., VI. xi.

儀 *e* i. (1) Deportment. G.L.c., ix. 8. (2) Example. G.L.c., x. 5. (3) 禮儀, rules of ceremony. 威儀, rules of deportment. D.M., xxvii. 3. G.L.c., iii. 4. (4) The name of a place. A., III. xxiv.

優 *yëu* yu. Abundant, more than adequate. A., XIV. xii.: XIX. xiii. 優優, D.M., xxvii. 3.

儺 *no* no. Certain ceremonies to expel evil influences. A., X. x. 2.

儼 *yen* yen. 儼然, stern., dignified-like. A., XIX. ix.: XX. ii. 2.

THE 10TH RADICAL. 儿.

允 *yun* jun. Sincerely. A. XX. i. 1.

兄 *heung* hsiung. An elder brother. 兄弟, elder and younger brothers. A brother. A., II. xxi. 2: V. i. 2: XII. v. 1, 4: *et al.* Obs. A. XIII. vii. G.L.c., iv. 7, 8. D.M., xiii. 4; xv. 2.

先 *seen* hsien. (1) First, former, before. A., II. xiii.: X. xiii. 1: *et al.* So, in G.L. and D.M. 先王, the ancient kings. A., I. xii. 1. =a former king. A., XVI. i. 4. (2) Ancestors. D.M., xix. 6. Comp. 先進, A., XI. i. (3) 先生, elders. II. viii.: XIV. xlvii. 2. (4) To make first, or chief. A., VI. xx.: XII. xxi. 3: XIII. ii. (5) 先之, A., XIII. i. To give an example to.

先 *sëen* hsien. Up. 3d tone. To precede. Quickly. G.L.c., x. 2, 15.

克 *k'ih* k'o. (1) To be able, to attain to. G.L.c., i. 1, 2; x. 5. (2) To subdue. A., XII. i. 1. (3) The love of superiority. A., XIV. ii.

免 *mëen* mien. (1) To escape, avoid. A., II. iii. 1: V. i. 2: *et al.* (2) To dispense with, have done with. A., XVII. xxi. 6.

兕 *sze* hsi. A rhinoceros. A., XVI. i. 7.

兢 *king* ching. 兢兢, apprehensive and cautious. A., VIII. iii.

THE 11TH RADICAL. 入.

入 *jüh* ju. To enter. G.L.c., x. 1. D.M., xiv 2. A., III. xv.: *et al.* 出, 入, abroad, at home. A., I. vi.: IX. xv. 3. But in A., XIX. xi, 出入=to pass and repass. 入德, to enter into virtue. D.M., xxxiii. 1.

內 *nuy* nei. Within, internal, internally. 四海之內, the within of—that which is within—the four seas; *i.e.*, the empire. D.M., xvii. 1: *et al.* Precedes the verb, =internally. A., IV. xvii.: *et al.* Obs. A., X. xvii. 7. As a verb G.L.c., x. 7, to make the internal, *i.e.*, of primary importance.

兩 *lëang* liang. Two. D.M., vi. A., III. xxii. 3: IX. vii.

THE 12TH RADICAL. 八.

八 *pă* pa. Eight. A., III. i.: XVIII. xi.

公 *kung*. (1) Public. A., VI. vii. (2) Just. A., XX. i. 9. (3) A duke, dukes. D.M., xviii. 3. A., III. ii.: *et al.* It often occurs in connection with the name and country of the noble spoken of. It enters also into double surnames. 公明, A., XIV. xiv. 1, 2:—公山, XVI. v.:—公西, VII. xxxiii.: XI. xxi.; xx. v.:—公冶, A., V. i. 1. Obs. 公子, A., XIII. viii.—XIV. xvii.; xviii.:—公叔, A., XIV. xiv.:—公伯, A., xxxviii.; 公孫 A., XIX. xxii.; 公門, the palace gate. A., X. iv. 1. 於公, in the prince's *temple*. A., X. viii. 8.

六 *luh* lu. Six. A., II. iv. 5: *et al.*

兮 *he* hsi. A particle of exclamation. O! how! Much used in poetry. G.L.c., iii. 4. A., III. viii. 1: XVIII. v. 1. In G.L.c., x. 13, quoted from the Shoo-king, it appears for 猗.

共 *kung*. Together with, sharing with. A., V. xxv. 2: IX. xxix. 1.

共 *kung*. Up. 2d tone. To move towards. A., II. i.: X. xviii. 2.

兵 *ping*. Weapons of war. A., XII. vii. 1, 2: XIV. xvii. 2.

其 *k'e* chi The third personal pronoun, in all genders, numbers, and cases; the; that. *Passim*

具 *keu* chü (1) 具臣, an ordinary minister. A., XI. xxiii. 4. (2)=俱, all. G.L.c., x. 4.

典 *teen* tien A classic, a canon. 帝典, G.L.c., i. 3.

兼 *keen* chien 兼人. A., XI. xxi.,=to have more than one man's ability.

THE 13TH RADICAL. 冂.

冉 *yen* A surname. 冉有, A., III vi.: VII. xiv.: *et al*; the same as 冉求, A., VI. x.: *et al.* 冉伯牛, A., XI. ii. 2. Observe. 冉子, A., VI. iii.: XIII. xiv.

再 *tsae* tsai Repeated, twice. A., XV. xix.: X. xi. 1.

冕 *meen* mien (1) A cap of full dress or ceremony. A., VIII. xxi.: IX. iii. 1; ix.: X. xvi. 2: XV. x. 4. (2) The name of a music-master. A., XV. xli. 1, 2.

THE 14TH RADICAL. 冖.

冠 *kwan* kuan A cap. A., X. vi. 10: XX. ii. 2.

冠 *kwan* kuan Up. 3d tone. Capped, *i.e.*, young men about 20. A., XI. xxv. 7.

冢 *ch'ung* Great, chief. 冢宰, the prime minister. A., XIV. xliii. 2.

THE 15TH RADICAL. 冫.

冰 *ping* Ice. G.L.c., x. 22. A., VIII. iii.

冶 *yay* yeh 公冶, a double surname. A., V. i.

凝 *ying* To congeal; to settle and complete. D.M., xxvii. 5, 道不凝.

THE 16TH RADICAL. 几.

凡 *fan* All;—at commencement of clause. D. M., xx. 12, 15, 16; xxxi. 4.

THE 17TH RADICAL. 凵.

凶 *heung* hsiung 凶服, mourning clothes. A., X. xvi. 3.

出 *ch'uh* ch'u (1) To go, or come, forth. A., III. xxiv.: IV. xv.; xxi.: *et al.* To go beyond. 出家, beyond the family. G.L.c., ix. 1. 出三日, beyond three days. A., X. viii. 8. 出入, see on 入. (2) To put forth. D.M., xxxi. 2. A., VIII. iv. 3: IX. viii.: XV. xvii. 出納, to give. A., XX. ii. 2. 出之, to put outside. A., X. vi. 8.

THE 18TH RADICAL. 刀.

刀 *taou* tao A knife. A., XVII. iv. 2.

刃 *jin* jên A sharp weapon. D.M., ix.

分 *fan* fên (1) To divide; to be divided. A., VIII. xx. 4: XVI. i. 12. (2) To distinguish. A., XVIII. vii. 1.

切 *ts'ëë* ch'ieh (1) To cut. G.L.c., iii. 4. A., I. xv. 2. (2) Earnestly. A., XIX. vi. 切切, earnest. A., XIII. xxviii.

刑 *hing* hsing (1) Punishment. A., II. iii. 1: IV. xi.: V. i. 2: XIII. iii. 6. (2) To imitate. D.M., xxxiii. 5.

列 *lëë* lieh A rank (as of office). A., XVI. i. 6.

利 *le* li (1) To sharpen. A., XV. ix. 利口, sharpness of speech. A., XVII. xviii. (2) Gain, profit;—rather in a mean sense. G.L.c., x. 22, 23. A., IV. xii.: *et al.*, Beneficial arrangements; profitableness; profitable. G.L.c., iii. 5; x. 14, 22, 23. A., IX. i.: XX. ii. 2. (3) To get the benefit of. G.L.c., iii. 5. To benefit. A., XX. ii. 2. To desire. A., iv. ii.

別 *pëë* pieh Up. 4th tone. To discriminate, to difference. D.M., xxxi. 1. A., II. vii.: XIX. xii. 2.

制 *che* chih To determine, fix. D.M., xxviii. 2.

到 *taou* tao Down to. A., XVI. xii.

則 *tsih* tsê (1) Then; denoting either a logical consequence or sequence of time. *Passim.* 然則, so then, well then. A., III. xxii. 3; XI. xv. 3; xxiii. 5. 一則,一則, partly, partly. A., IV. xx. (2) A rule, a pattern. D.M., xiii. 2. (3) To make a pattern of, to correspond to. A., VIII. xix. 1.

索引

喜 *he* hsi Joy, joyful, to be joyful. D.M., i. 4. A., IV. xx.: V. vi.; xviii 1 : XVI. xiii. 5 : XIX. xix.

喟 *wei* 喟然, sighingly. A., IX. x. 1 : XI. xxv. 7.

喪 *sang* To mourn, mourning; mourning clothes. D.M., xviii. 3. A., III. iv. 3; x.: VI. 8: XVII. xxi. 1, 5, 6: *et al.*

喪 *sang* Up. 3d tone. To lose. G.L.c., x. 5. To lose office, a throne. A., III. xxiv.: XIV. xx. 1. 2. (2) To let be lost, to destroy. A., IX. v. 3 : XI. viii.: XIII. xv. 4. 5.

喧 *heuen* hsüan 喧兮, how distinguished! G.L.c., iii. 4.

嘉 *kea* chia Admirable. D.M., xvii. 4. To commend, honour. D.M., xx. 14. A., XIX. iii.

嗚 *woo* wu 嗚呼, alas! A., III. vi.

喭 *ngan* an Coarse, rude. A., XI. xvii. 4.

嘗 *ch'ang* (1) To taste. A., X. xi. 2; xiii. 1. (2) Name of the autumnal sacrifice. D.M., xix. 6. (3) Indicates the present complete and past tenses, being often joined with 未. A., III. xxiv.: VIII. v.: *et al.*

器 *k'e* ch'i (1) A vessel, a tool. D.M., xix. 3. A., XV. ix. Metaphorically. A., II. xii.: V. iii. (2) Capacity, calibre. A., III. xxii. 1. (3) To use according to capacity. A., XIII. xxv.

噫 *e* i An exclamation of grief; of contempt. A., XI. viii.: XIX. xii. 2 : XIII. xx. 4.

嚴 *yên* Severe, dignified. G.L.c., vi. 3.

THE 31st RADICAL. 口.

四 *sze* szû Four. *Sæpe.* Four things. A., VII. xxiv.: IX. iv. 四國, the four parts of the State. G.L.c., ix. 8. 四夷, the barbarians on the four sides of the empire. G.L.c., x. 14. 四體, the four limbs. D.M., xxiv. A., XVIII. vii. 四飯, A., XVIII. ix. 3.

因 *yin* (1) As a preposition. Because of, taking occasion from. D.M., xvii. 8. A., XX. ii. 2. (2) As a verb. To follow, succeed to. A., II. xxiii. 2: XI. xxv. 4. To rely on. A., I. xiii.

回 *hwuy* hui The name of Conf. favourite disciple. *Sæpe.* 顏回, A., VI. ii.: XI. vi

困 *k'wǎn* k'uen (1) Distressed, reduced to straits. D.M., xx. 9. A., XX. i. 1. 酒困, overcome with wine. A., IX. xv. (2) Stupidity and the feeling of it. D.M., xx. 16. A., XVI. ix.

固 *koo* ku (1) Firm, strong. A., I. viii.: XVI. i. 8. ? XV. i. 3. (2) Obstinate, obstinacy. A., IX. iv.: XIV. xxxiv. 2. (3) Mean, niggardly. A., VII. xxxv. (4) Firmly. D.M., xx. 18. (5) Certainly, indeed. D.M., xxxii. 3. A., IX. vi. 2: XIV. xxxviii. 1: XV. i. 3; xli. 3.

圃 *poo* pu A gardener. A., XIII. iv. 1.

圉 *yu* yü The name of an officer. A., XIV. xx. 2.

國 *kwŏ* ~~kuo~~ A State. *Passim.* 中國, the Middle kingdom. D.M., xxvii. 4: *et al.* Only in this phrase is the term used for the empire. 千乘之國, one of the largest States, equipping 1,000 chariots. A., I. v.: *et al.* 爲國, to administer a State. A., IV. xiii.

圖 *t'oo* t'u (1) To think, imagine. A., VII. xiii. (2) A map. A., IX. viii.

THE 32d RADICAL. 土.

土 *t'oo* t'u (1) The ground, ground, earth. D.M., xxvi. 9. A., V. ix. 1. (2) 水土, water and land. D.M., xxx. 1. (3) Comfort. A., IV. xi.

圭 *kwei* kuei A precious stone, differently shaped, used as a badge of authority. A., X. v. 1: XI. v.

地 *te* ti (1) The earth, the ground. D.M., xx. 3. A., IX. xviii.: XIX. xxii. 2. (2) Any particular country. A., XIV. xxxix. 2. (3) Throughout the Doctrine of the Mean, it occurs constantly as the correlative of 天, heaven, the phrase 天地 being now the component parts, and now the great powers, of the universe.

在 *tsae* tsai (1) To be in to consist in, depend on, the where and wherein following. *Passim.* (2) To be present. G.L.c., vii. 2. A., XI. xxi. (3) To be in life. A., I. xi.: IV. xix. 在 is followed not unfrequently by 上, 中, 內, with words intervening. Observe A., XIX. xxii. 2: XX. i. 5.

均 *keun* chün Level. An equally adjusted state of society A., XVI. i. 10. As a verb; to adjust, keep in order. D.M., ix.

坐 *tso* To sit. A., X. vii. 2; ix. 1: *et al.*

坦 *t'an* Broad and level. Satisfied. A., VII. xxxvi.

坫 *teen* tien An earthen stand for cups. 反坫, A., III. xxii. 3.

城 *ch'ing* ch'êng In the name of a place. 武城, A., VI. xii.: XVII. iv.

域 *yih* yü Boundaries, territory. A., XVI. i. 4.

執 *chih* To hold, keep hold of. D.M., vi.; xiii. 2: *et al.* A., VI. viii.: VII. xi: *et al.* 執禮, to maintain the rules of propriety. A., VII. xvii. 執御, to practise charioteering. A., IX. ii. 2. 執事, to manage business. A., XIII. xix. 執國命, to grasp the govt. of a State. A., XVI. ii

培 *pei* To nourish. D.M., xvii. 3.

堂 *t'ang* (1) The hall or principal apartment. ascended to by steps. A., III. ii.: X. iv. 4: XI. xiv. 2. (2) 堂堂, exuberant; an imposing manner. A., XIX. xvi.

堅 *keen* chien Firm, hard. A., IX. x. 1; XVII. vii. 3.

堪 *k'an* To be able, to endure. A., VI. ix.

堯 *yaou* yao The name of an ancient emperor. A., VIII. xix.: XX. i. 1. Coupled with Shun. G.L., ix. 4: *et al.*

報 *paou* pao To revenge, recompense, return. D.M., x. 3; xx. 13. A., XIV. xxxvi. 1, 2, 3.

塗 *t'oo* t'u A road, the way. D.M., xi. 2. A. XVII. i. 1; xiv.

墜 *ch'uy* ch'ui To fall, be fallen. A., XIX. xxii. 2.

塞 *sih* sae (1) To shut up, as a screen. A., III. xxii. 3. (2) An unemployed condition. D.M., x. 5.

壞 *hwae* huai To be ruined. A., XVII. xxi. 2.

壤 *jang* A man's name. A. XIV. xlvi.

THE 33D RADICAL. 士.

士 *sze* shih (1) A scholar. A., IV. ix.: VIII. vii.: *et al.* (2) An officer. D.M., xiii. 3; xx. 13, 14. A., XIII. xx. 1; xxviii.: *et al.* In many cases these two meanings are united. A., XII. xx: XV. viii.: *et al.* (3) A gilly. 執鞭之士, a groom. (4) 士師, Criminal judge. A., XVIII. ii.: XIX. xix.

壯 *chwang* chuang Vigorous, in manhood. A., XVI. vii.

壹 *yih* yi Once. D.M., xviii. 2. 壹是, one and all. G.L.T, 6.

壽 *show* shou Longevity, long-lived. D.M., xvii. 2. A., VI. xxi.

THE 35TH RADICAL. 夊.

夏 *hea* 'hsia (1) Name of an ancient dynasty. D.M., xxviii. 5. A., II. xxiii. 2: *et al.* 夏后氏, the founder of the Hea dynasty. A., III. xxi. 1. (2) Great. 諸夏, a name of China. A., III. v. (3) Used in a man's name. A., XVIII. xi. (4) 子夏, the designation of one of Conf. disciples. A., I. vii.: *et al, sæpe.*

THE 36TH RADICAL. 夕

夕 *seih* hsi The evening. A., IV. vii.

外 *wae* wai (1) Without, beyond, external. G.L.c., vi. 2. D.M., xiv. 1; xxv. 3. (2) As a verb. To make secondary. G.L.c., x. 8.

夙 *suh* su Early ?=from day to day. D.M., xxix. 6.

多 *to* Many, much A., II. xviii. 2: IV. xii.: VII. xxvii.: *et al.* ? XIX. xxiv. 1, where 多=祇, *only;* and D.M.. xxvi. 9, where it=a little.

夜 *yay* yeh (1) Night. A., IX. xvi.: XV. xxx. D. M., xxix. 6. (2) 叔夜, a man's designation. A., XVIII. xi.

夢 *mung* mêng To dream. A., VII. v.

THE 37TH RADICAL. 大.

大 *ta* Great; greatly. *Passim.* 大夫, see 夫.

太 *t'ae* t'ai Up. 3d tone, with aspirate. Excessive. A., VI. i. 3. Used for 太. D.M., xviii.

天 *t'een* t'ien Heaven. (1) The material heaven, or firmament. D.M., xii. 3; xxvi. 5: *et al.* A., XIX. xxv. 3. (2) More commonly, the char. stands for the supreme, governing, Power, the author of man's nature, and orderer of his lot. G.L.c., i. 2. D.M., i. 1; xiv. 3; xvii. 3, 4; xx. 7. 18; xxxii. 1, 2, 3: xxxiii, 6. (上天). A., II. iv. 4: III. xiii. 2; xxiv.: V. xii. 3: VI. xxvi.: VII. xxii.: VIII. xix. 1: IX. v. 3; vi. 2; xi. 2: XI. viii.: XII. v. 3: XIV xxxvii. 2: XVI. viii. 1, 2: XVII. xix. 3: XX. i. 1. (3) In the Doctrine of the Mean (not in the Analects), we find the phrase 天地 of very frequent occurrence. sometimes denoting the material heavens and earth, but more frequently as a dualization of nature, producing, transforming, completing, i. 5; xii. 2, 4: xxii: *et al.* (4) 天子, a designation of the emperor. G.L. т., 6. D.M., xvii. 1: *et al.* A., III. ii.: XVI. ii. (5) 天下, see 下.

太 *t'ae* t'ai (1) 太王, one of the ancestors of the Chow dyn. D.M., xviii. 2, 3. (2) 太宰, title of a high officer. A., IX. vi. 1, 3. (3) 太師, grand Music-master. A., III. xxiii.: VIII. xv.: XVIII. ix. (4) 太甲, the title of a Book of the Shoo-king, G.L.c., ii. 2.

夫 *foo* fu (1) An individual man. 匹夫, a common man. A., IX. xxv.: XIV. xviii. 3. With 鄙,=a fellow. A., XIX. vii.: XVII. xv. 夫婦, husband and wife. D.M., xii. 2, 4; xx. 8. A., XIV. xviii. 3. (2) 大夫, a general name, applicable to all the ministers or officers at a court. D.M., xviii. 3. A., V. xviii. 2: X. ii. 1: *et al, sæpe.* (3) 夫人, title of the wife of the prince of a State. A., XXVI. xiv. (4) 夫子, master, my, our, your, master, applied often to Confucius, but not confined to him. A., I. x. 1, 2: III. xxiv.: IV. xv. 2; *et al, sæpe.*

夫 *foo* fu Low. 1st tone. (1) An initial particle, which may generally be rendered by *now.* D.M., xix. 2; xxxii. 1. A., VI. xxviii. 2: IX. xvi.: *et al., sæpe.* (2) A final particle, with exclamatory force. D.M., v.; xvi. 5. A., VI. viii.; xxv.: VII. x. 1: VIII. iii. 1: *et al., sæpe.* (3) Neither at the begin. nor end of sentences and clauses, as a kind of demonstrative. D. M., xxvi. 9. A., XI. ix. 3; x. 3; xiii. 3; xx. 2, 4: *et al.* (4) After some verbs, as a prep., between them and their regimen. G.L.c., x. 16. A., XVI. i. 9: XVII. ix; xxi. 4.

夭 *yaou* yao 夭夭, exuberant in foliage. G.L.c., ix 6. 夭夭如, pleased-like. A., VII. iv.

失 *shih* To lose, to fail of or in. G.L.c., x. 5, 11, 18. D.M., viii.; xiv. 5; xviii. 2. A., I. xiii.: IV. xxii.: *et al., sæpe.*

夷 *e* i (1) To squat upon the heels. A., XIV. xlvi. (2) A name denoting rude and barbarous tribes, appropriate to those on the East of China, of whom there were nine tribes. A., IX. xiii. 1. It is generally associated with 狄. A., III. v.: XIII. xix. D.M., xiv. 2. 四夷, G.L.c., x. 15. (3) As a posth. title. A., V. xxii.: *et al.* (4) Part of a name. A., XVIII. viii. 1, 4.

奏 *tsow* tsou To perform, as music. D.M., xix. 5. To present, approach (but the mean. is doubtful), D.M., xxxiii. 4.

奔 *pun* pên To run away, flee. A., VI. xii..

奚 *he* hsi Why, how, what. A., II. xxi. 1, 2: III. ii: VII. xviii. 2: XI. xiv.: XIII. iii. 1, 3; v.: XIV. xx. 1, 2. 奚自, from whom. A., XIV. xxi.

奪 *t'ŏ* t'o Rapine; to take away, carry off. G.L.c., x. 8. A., IX. xxv.: XIV. x. 3: XVII. xviii. 不可奪, cannot be carried from his principles. A., VIII. vi.

奢 *ch'ay* ch'ê Wasteful, extravagant. A., III. iv. 3: VII. xxxv.

奧 *gaou* ao The south-west corner of an apartment. A., III. xiii. 1.

THE 38TH RADICAL. 女.

女 *neu* nü 女子, girls,=concubines. A., XVII. xxv. 女樂, female musicians. A., XVIII. iv.

女 *joo* ju For 汝. You, both nom. and obj. A., II. xvii.: *et al.*

奴 *noo* nu A slave. A., XVIII. i.

好 *haou* hao Good, goodness, excellence. G.L.c., vi. 1. A., XIX. xxiii. 2.

好 *haou* hao Up. 3d tone. To love, like, be fond of. *Passim.* 兩君之好, the loving, *i.e.*, the friendly, meeting, of two princes. A., III. xxii. 3.

索引

THE 39TH RADICAL. 子.

xxxviii.: XVI. i. 13.—II. v. 2.—III. xiii.: XIV. xx. 2.—XIX. xxii.

孫 *sun* Up. 3d tone, used for 遜. Complaisant, docile, obedient. A., VII. xxxv.: XIV. iv.: *et al.*

孰 *shuh* shu Who? which? D.M., xxxii. 3. A., III. xv.; xxii. 3: *et al., sæpe.* What? A., III. i.

學 *heŏ* hsio To learn; learned; learning. G.L.T., 1. D.M., xx. 9, 10, 19. 20. A., I. i. 1; vi.; vii.; viii.; xiv.: *et al., sæpe.*

孺 *joo* ju A., surname. A., XVII. xx.

孼 *nëë* nieh Unlucky omens of prodigious animals. D.M, xxiv.

THE 40TH RADICAL. 宀.

守 *show* shou To keep, to maintain, D.M., vii. A., VIII. xiii. 1: XV. xxxii. 1, 2, 3: XVI. i. 12.

安 *gan* an (1) A condition of entire tranquillity. G.L.T., 2. A., XVI. i. 10. (2) Without any effort. D.M., xx. 9. A., III. xxxvii. (3) Comfort, at ease. A., I. xiv.: XVII. xxi. 4, 5. (4) To rest in. A., II. x. 3: IV. ii. (5) To give rest to. A., V. xxv. 4: XIV. xlv.: XVI. i. 11. (9) An interrogative,=how, where. A., XI. xxv. 10.

宋 *sung* The name of a State. D.M., xxviii. 5. A., III. ix.: VI. xiv,

完 *wan* Complete. A., XIII. viii.

宗 *tsung* (1) Honourable, pertaining to one's ancestors. 宗廟, the ancestral temple. D.M., xvii. 1: *et al.* A., X. i. 2: *et al.* 宗器, D.M., xix. 3. 宗族, kindred. A., XIII. xx. 2. (2) To follow as master. A., I. xiii. (3) 高宗, an ancient emperor, A., XIV. xliii.

官 *kwan* kuan An officer of government. D.M., xx. 14. A., III. xxii. 2: XIV. xliii. 2: XIX. xxiii. 3: XX. i. 6.

定 *ting* Determined, settled. G.L.T., 2. D.M., xx. 16. A., XVI. 7. To settle. G.L.c., ix. 3.

宜 *e* i (1) Right, what is right. D.M., xx. 5; xxv. 3. (2) Reasonable, to be expected. A., XIX. xxi.i. 4. (3) As a verb, to regulate, discharge duty to. G.L.c., ix. 6, 7. D.M., xv. 2; xvii. 4.

客 *k'ih* k'o Strangers, guests. 賓客, A., V. vii. 4: XIV. xx. 2.

宮 *kung* A house. A., XIX. xxiii. 2. 宮室, VIII. xxi.

室 *shih* (1) An apartment, the inner rooms of a house. D.M., xxxiii. 3. A., IX. xxx.: XI. xiv. 2; xix. So, 室家, A., XIX. xxiii. 2. (2) A family. A., V. vii. 3: VI. xii., XIII. viii. So 室家, D.M., xv, 2. 公室, the ducal house. A., XVI. iii. (3) 宮室, a house. A., VIII. xxi.

害 *hae* hai Injury, to injure. G.L.c., x. 22. D.M., xxx. 3. A., II. xvi.: XV. viii.

宰 *tsae* tsai (1) Governor or commandant, of a town. A., V. vii. 3: VI. iii. 3; vii.: xii.: XI. xxiv.: XIII. xvii. (2) Head minister to a chief. A., XIII. ii. (3) 冢宰, a premier. A., XIV. xliii. (4) The surname of one of Conf. disciples. A., V. ix.: *et al.*

宴 *yen* Feasting. A., XVI. v.

家 *kea* chia (1) The family. G.L.T., 4, 5: c., viii. 1. 3: ix. 1, 3, 5. 家人, the household, c., ix. 6. 室家, D.M, xv. 2. (2) A family, the name for the possessions of the chiefs in a State. G.L.c, x. 22, 23. D.M., ix.; xx. 11, 12, 15; xxiv. A., III. ii.: V. vii. 3: XII. ii.; xx. 3, 5, 6: XVI. i. 10: XVII. xviii.: XIX. xxv. 4. (3) 室家, apartments. A., XIX. xxiii. 2.

容 *yung* (1) To bear, admit A., X. iv. 1. (2) Forbearance, to forbear. G.L., x. 14. D.M., xxxi. 1. A., XIX. iii. To command forbearance. D.M., xxvii. 7. (3) Deportment. A., VIII. iv. 3: X. vi. 1. 容色, a placid appearance. A., X. v. 2. (4) 從容, easy, unconstrained. (5) A name. A., V. i. 2: XI. v.

宿 *suh* su (1) To stop over night. A., XIV. xli.: XVIII. vii. 3. To keep over night. A., X. viii. 8: XII. xii. 2. (2) Asleep and perching. A., VII. xxvi.

寄 *ke* chi To commit to one's charge. A., VIII. vi.

密 *meih* mi Concentrative. D.M., xxxi. 1.

富 *foo* fu Rich, riches. G.L.c., vi. 4. D.M., xvii. 1; xviii. 2. A., I. xv. 1: *et al.* Metaph., A., XII. xxii. 5. To enrich. A., XIII. ix. 3, 4: XX. i. 4. Often joined with 貴.

寒 *han* Cold, wintry. A., IX. xxvii.

索引

察 *ch'a* ch'a (1) To examine, to study; studious. D.M., vi.; xxxi. 1. A., II. x. 3: *et al.* To look after. G.L.c., x. 22. (2) To be displayed. D.M., xii. 3, 4.

寡 *kwa* kua (1) Few, to make few. G.L.c., x. 19. D.M., xxix. 1. A., II. xviii. 2: VIII. v.: *et al.* (2) 寡小君, a designation of the wife of the prince of a State. A., XVI. xiv.

寧 *ning* After 與 with intervening words, than, so and so it is better to. G.L.c., x. 22. A., III. iv. 3; xiii. 1: *et al.*

寢 *ts'in* ch'in To sleep, be in bed. A., V. ix.: X. viii. 9; xvi. 1: XV. xxx. 寢衣, sleeping dress. A., X. vi. 6.

實 *shih* (1) Full. A., VIII. v. (2) Fruit. A., IX. xx. 1. (3) Really. G.L.c., x. 14.

寬 *k'wan* k'uan Generous, magnanimous. D.M., x. 3; xxxi. 1. A., III. xxvi.: XVII. vi.: XX. i. 9.

審 *shin* shên To examine accurately, discriminate. D.M., xx. 19. A., XX. i. 1.

寮 *leaou* liao A name. A., XIV. xxxviii.

寶 *paou* pao Precious; precious things; a jewel. G.L.c., x. 12, 13. D.M., xxvi. 9. A., XVII. i. 2.

THE 41st RADICAL. 寸.

射 *shay* she Archery. D.M., xiv. 5. A., III. vii.; xvi.: IX. ii. 2: XIV. vi. Read *shih*. A., VII. xxvi, to shoot with an arrow and string.

射 *yih* yi To dislike, be disliked. D.M., xvi. 4; xxix. 6.

將 *tseang* chiang (1) Shall, will, to be going to, to be about to. D.M., xxiv. A., III. xxiv.: XVI. i. 1, 2, 6: *et al.* (2) 將聖, a sage, or thereabouts. A., IX. vi. 2. (3) 將命, to act as *internuncius*. A., XIV. xlvii. 1: XVII. xx.

專 *chuen* chuan (1) Alone, unassisted. A., XIII. v. (2) Assuming, presuming. 自專, D.M., xxviii. 1.

尊 *tsun* (1) Honourable in dignity. D.M., xvii. 2; xviii. 2. (2) To honour. D.M., xix. 5; xx. 5, 8, 13, 14: *et al.* A., XIX. iii.: XX. ii. 1, 2.

對 *tuy* tui To reply to, in reply. Spoken of an inferior answering a superior. *Passim.* The only case where we can conceive of an equality between the parties is A., XVIII. vi. 3.

THE 42d RADICAL. 小.

小 *seaou* hsiao Small, smallness; in small matters, D.M., xii. 2; xxx. 3. A., I. xii. 1: II. xxii.: *et al.* *Sæpe.* 小人, see on 人. 小子, my little children, my disciples. A., V. xxi.: VIII. iii.: XI. xvi. 2: XVII. ix. We, the disciples. A., XVII. xix. 2. The disciples. A., XIX. xii. I, a little child. A., XX. i. 3. 小君, 小童, designations of the wife of the prince of a State. A., XVI. xiv.

少 *shaou* shao (1) A little. A., XIII. viii. (2) 少師, the assistant music-muster. A., XVIII. ix. 5. (3) 少連, A name. A., XVIII. xviii. 1, 8.

少 *shaou* shao Up. 3d tone. Young, youth. A., V. xxv. 4: IX. vi. 3; ix.: XVI. vii.

尚 *shang* (1) To esteem. A., XVI. vi.: XVII. xxiii. To add to, esteem above. A., IV. vi. 1. To place over. D.M., xxxiii. 1. (2) Still, likewise. G.L.c., x. 14. (3) Pray, let it be. D.M., xxxiii. 3.

THE 43d RADICAL. 尢.

尤 *yew* yu 尤人, to blame men. D.M., xiv. 3. A., XIV. xxxvii. 2. Occasions for blame. A., IV. vi.

就 *tsew* chiu (1) To approach to. A., I. xiv.: XVI. i. 6. (2) To complete, for the good of. A., XII. xix.

THE 44th RADICAL. 尸.

尸 *she* shih Corpse-like. A., X. xvi. 1.

尺 *ch'ih* A cubit. A., VIII. vi.

尼 *ne* ni 仲尼, Confucius. D.M., ii. 1; xxx. i. A., XIX. xxii.; xxiii.; xxiv.; xxv.

尹 *yin* (1) To correct. 令尹, good corrector, designation of the chief minister of Ts'oo. A., V. xviii. 1. (2) 伊尹, an ancient minister. A., XII. xxii. 6. (3) 師尹, an ancient minister, grand-teacher. G.L.c., x. 4.

居 *keu* chü (1) To dwell in, to reside. G.L.c., vi. 2. D.M., xxvi. 9. A., II. i.: *et al*, *sæpe.* With a reference to privacy. A., X. vi. 7; vii. 2; xvi. 1: XI. xxv. 3: XIII. viii.: *et al.* (2) Metaphorically, applied to situations, virtues. D.M., x. 3, 4; xxvii. 7. A., III. xxvi.: *et al.*, *sæpe.* (3) To

索引

帛 *pih* pai Silk. A., XVII. xi.

帝 *te* ti (1) God. A., XX. i. 3. 上帝, see 上. (2) An emperor. 帝典, The Canon of the emperor, name of a portion of the Shoo-king. G.L. c., i. 3.

帥 *shwae* shuai A commander, general. A., IX. xxv.

帥 *suh* su To lead on. A., XII. xvii. G.L.c., ix. 4.

師 *sze* szû (1) The multitude, the people. G.L.c., x. 5. (2) A host, properly of 2,500 men. 師旅, A., XI. xxv. 4 (3) A teacher. A., II. xi.: VII. xxi.: XV. xxxv.: XIX. xxii. 2. (4) 士師, the chief criminal judge. A., XVIII. ii.: XIX. xix. (5) 太師樂. 太師, The grand music master. A., III. xxxiii.: VIII. xv.: XVIII. ix. 1. 少師, the assistant do. A., XVIII. ix. 5. 師 alone. A., XV. xli. 1, 2. (6) The grand-teacher, one of the highest officers. G.L.c., x. 4. (7) The name of one of Conf. disciples. A., XI. xv.: XVII. iii.

席 *seih* hsi A mat. A., X. ix.; xiii.: XV. xli. 1.

帶 *tae* tai A sash. A., V. vii. 4.

常 *chang* Constant, regular. G.L.c., X. x. A., XIX. xxii. 2.

帷 *wei* A curtain, curtain-shaped. A., X. vi. 9.

幬 *taou* tao To curtain, overspread. D.M., xxx. 2.

THE 51ST RADICAL. 干.

干 *kan* (1) To seek for, with a view to. A., II. xviii. 1. (2) A shield. 干戈, shields and spears,=war. A., XVI. i. 13. (3) 比干, an uncle of the tyrant Chow, A., XVIII. 1. (4) The name of a band-master of Loo. A., XVIII. ix. 2.

平 *p'ing* (1) A state of perfect tranquillity; to bring to, or be brought to, such a state. G.L.T., 5, c., x. 1. D.M., xxxiii. 5. (2) Level. A., IX. xviii. 平生, the whole life. A., XIV. xiii. 2. (3) An hon. epithet. A., V. xvi.

年 *nëen* nien A year, years, the year. D.M., xviii. 3. A., I. xi.: *et al., sæpe.*

幸 *hing* hsing Luck, fortunate, fortunately. D.M., xiv. 4. A., VI. ii.; xvii.: VII. xxx. 3: XI. vi.

THE 52D RADICAL. 幺.

幼 *yew* yu Young. A., XIV. xlvi.: XVIII. vii. 5.

幾 *ke* chi (1) What is small,=mildly. A., IV. xviii. (2) Influence, what may be expected from. A., XIII. xv. 1, 3, 4, 5. (3) 庶幾, perhaps, peradventure. D.M., xxix. 6.

THE 53D RADICAL. 广.

序 *seu* hsü To arrange in order. D.M., xix. 4.

府 *foo* fu A treasury. G.L.c., 21, A., XI, xiii. 1.

庭 *t'ing* The court of a house. A., III. i.: XVI. xii. 2, 3.

度 *too* tu Measures. D.M., xxviii. 2. 法度, the laws. A., XX. i. 6.

度 *tŏ* to To surmise, conjecture. D.M., xvi. 4.

庫 *k'oo* k'u An arsenal. G.L.c., x. 21.

庶 *shoo* shu (1) Numerous. A., XIII. ix. 2, 3. 庶民, the numerous, the masses of (=the common) people. D.M., xx. 12, 13; xxix. 3. (2) 庶幾, and 庶乎, perhaps, near to. D.M., xxix. 6. A., XI. xviii. 1.

庸 *yung* (1) Ordinary. D.M., xiv. 4. (2) Use, course. In the phrase—中庸. D.M., ii. 1, 2; iii.; vii.; viii.; ix.; xi. 3; xxvii. 6. A., VI. xxvii.

康 *k'ang* (1) The hon. name of one of the chiefs of the Ke family. A., X. xi. 2: XIV. xx.: II. xx.: VI. vii.: XI. vi.: XII. xvii.; xviii.; xix. (2) 康誥, title of a book in the Shoo-king. G.L.c., i. 1; ii. 2; ix. 2; x. 10.

庾 *yu* yü A measure for grain, containing about 120 English pints. A., VI. iii. 1.

海上絲綢之路文獻集成 科技與文化編

往 (1) To go, going. A., IX. xviii.: XVII. i.; v.: VII. 1, 2: XVIII. ii. 1. D.M., xx. 14. 而往, and onwards. A., III. x. (2) The gone, the past. A., I. xv. 3: III. xxi. 2: VII. xxviii. 2: XVIII. v.
wang

征 征伐, punitive military expeditions. A., XVI. ii.
ching
chêng

待 (1) To wait, wait for. A., IX. xii.: XIII. iii. 1. D.M., xxvii. 4. (2) To treat. A., XVIII. iii.
tae
tai

律 To imitate, follow as a model. D.M., xxx. 1.
leüh
lü

後 (1) As a noun. That which is after, the back. *Sæpe.* 在後, A., IX. x. 1. Preceded by 之. A., XIV. xxii. 4. 5: *et al.* A successor. A., XIV. xv. (2) As an adjective. D.M., xi. 1: *et al.* 後死者, A., IX. v. 3. 後生, A., IX. xxii. (3) As an adverb. Afterwards. *Sæpe.* Often follows 然 and 而. (4) As a verb. To come after, fall behind, make an after consideration. A., III. viii. 2: VI. xiii.; xx.: XI. xxii.: xxv. 8: XII. xxi. 3: XV. v. 3; xxvii.: XVIII. vii. 1.
how
hou

徑 A short, cross, path. A., VI. viii.
king
ching

得 (1) To attain to, to be found. G.L.T., 2. D.M., xx. 18, 20. (2) To get, with an objective following. *Sæpe.* Without an objective, getting, anything as gain to be got. A., XVI. vii.; x. 1: XIX. i. (3) The auxiliary *can* often followed by 而. *Sæpe.* (4) Followed by an adjective, and often in the question 焉得 ....can be=can be considered. A., IV. i.: V. x.; xviii. 1, 2: *et al.* (5) 不得已, could not but. A., VII. ii. 3. (6) 自得, to be himself. D.M., xix. 2.
tih
tê

徒 (1) On foot. A., XI. vii. 2. (2) Vainly, without cause. A., XVII. v. 3. (3) Disciple, associate. A., XI. xvi. 2: XVIII. vi. 3, 4.
t'oo
t'u

徙 To move towards. A., VII. iii.: XII. x. 1.
se
hsi

從 To follow; to act according to. G.L.c., ix. 4; x. 2. D.M., xxviii. 5; xxix. 2. A., II. iv. 6; xiii.: *et al.*, *sæpe.* 從政, to be engaged in govt. Generally, in a subordinate capacity,—A., VI. vi.: XIII. xiii.; xx. 4: XVIII. v. 1. But not subordinate in—A., XX. ii. 1. 從事, to be engaged in affairs, to act. A., VIII. v. 1: XVII. i. 2.
ts'ung

從 Up. 3d tone. Proceeding on. A., III. xxiii.
tsung

從 Low. 3d tone. To be in close attendance on. Always 從者 or 從我者. A., III. xxiv.: V. vi.: XI. ii. 1: ii.: XV. i 2.
tsung

從 從容, naturally and easily. D.M., xx. 18.
sung

御 To drive a carriage. A., II. v. 2: IX. ii. 2.
yu
yü

復 (1) To make good. A., I. xiii. (2) To report a commission. A., X. iii. 4. (3) To return to. A., X. iv. 5: XII. i. 1. (4) To repeat. A., XI. v.
fuh
fu

復 Again. A., VI. vii.: VII. v. As a verb. A., VII. viii.
fow
fou

循 (1) 循循然, by orderly method. A., IX. x. 2. (2) Tethered. A., X. v. 1.
seun
sun

微 (1) That which is minute, minute. D. M., i. 3; xvi. 5; xxvi. 6; xxxiii. 1. Reduced. A., XVI. iii. (2) A negative particle, if not. A., XIV. xxviii. 2. (3) 微子, the viscount of the State Wei. A., XVIII. i. (4) 微生, a double surname. A., V. xxiii.—XIV. xxxiv.
we
wei

徵 (1) To be evidenced. D.M., xxvi. 2, 3. (2) To attest, be attested. D.M., xxviii. 5; xxix. 2, 8. A., III. ix.
ching
chêng

德 Virtue, virtuous. *Passim.* Energy, influence. D.M., xvi. 1. A., XII. xix.
tih
tê

徹 (1) To remove. A., III. ii. (2) Pervading, with reference to a law of tithe. A., XII. ix. 2, 3.
ch'ĕ

徼 (1) To seek. D.M., xix. 4. (2) To copy another's and pretend that it is one's own; to pry out. A., XVII. xxiv. 2.
k'eaou
hsiao

THE 61ST RADICAL. 心.

心 The heart, the mind:—denotes the mental constitution generally. Is not found in the Chung Yung. G.L.T., 4, 5: c. vi. 4; vii. 1, 2, 3; ix. 2; x. 14. A., II. iv. 6: VI. v.: XIV. xlii. 1: XVII. xxii.: XX. i. 3, 7.
sin
shin

必 Must, used as an auxiliary; often= will certainly, would certainly. Sometimes also with no verb following. *Passim.* 必也, what must,=what is necessary is........ Sometimes conditionally. G.L.c., iv. 1. A., III. vii.: VI. vii.; xxviii.:
peih
pi

THE 66TH RADICAL. 攴.

改 *kae* kai — To alter, to change. Both active and neuter. D.M., xiii. 2. A., I. viii. 4; xi.: V. ix. 2: VI. ix.; VII. iii.; xxi. (here it simply=to avoid): IX. xxiii; xxiv.: XI. xiii. 2: XV. xxxi.: XVII. xxi. 3. Obs. A., XIX. xviii.

攻 *kung* — To assail,=to reprove. A., XI. xvi. 2: XII. xxi. 3. =to study. A., II. xvi.

放 *fang* — (1) To drive, put, away G.L.c., x. 15: A., XV. x. 6. (2) To indulge, give license to. A., XVIII. viii. 4. (3) A name. A., III. iv.; vi.

放 *fang* — Up. 2d tone. To accord with; having regard to. A., IV. xii.

政 *ching* chêng — Government; the principles of government; a govt. charge. *Passim.* =laws. A., II. iii. 1. 爲政, to administer government, as supreme or subordinate. A., II. i.; xxi. 1: XII. xix. 從政, to be engaged in govt., as subordinate. A., VI. vi.: XIII. xiii. 1; xx. 4: XVIII. v. 1. Except, perhaps, A., XX. ii. 1.

故 *koo* ku — (1) Therefore. *Passim.* We have frequently 是故, with the same meaning, but perhaps a little more emphasis. Obs. A., III. ix. where 故 is at the end of the clause.=because, that's the cause. (2) Old, what is old. A., II. xi.: XVIII. x. D.M., xxvii. 6.

敏 *min* — To be earnest and active, earnest activity. A., I. xiv.: IV. xxiv. 1: V. xiv.: VII. xix.: XVI. vi.: XX. i. 9. Combining the idea of intelligence. A., XII. i. 2; ii. As a verb, to hasten, produce quickly. D.M., xx. 3.

教 *keaou* chiao — To teach, instruct. G.L.c., ix. 1, 6, 7. D.M., x. 3. A. II. xx.: VII. xxiv.: VIII. ix. 4: XIII. ix. 4; xxix.: XV. xxxviii.: XX. ii. 3. 不教, uninstructed. A., XIII. xxx. Instruction. D.M., i. 1; xxi.

救 *kew* chiu — To stop, to save from. A., III. vi.

敖 *gaou* ao — 敖惰, arrogant and rude. G.L.c., viii. 1.

敗 *pae* pai — (1) Gone, spoiled, as meat. A., X. viii. 2. (2) 司敗, minister of crime. A., VII. xxx.

敝 *pe* pi — To spoil; spoiled,—spoken of clothes. A., V. xxv. 2: IX. xxvi.

敢 *kan* — To presume, to dare. D.M., xiii. 4; xxviii. 4. A., V. viii. 2: VI. xiii.: *et al, sæpe.* 豈敢, how dare I?—an expression of humility. A., VII. xxxiii. 1. In the 1st person, often=our 'allow me.' A., XI. xi.; xxi. 1: XII. xxi. 1: XIII. xx. 2, 3. Obs. A., XX. i. 3. 果敢, presumptuous. A., XVII. xxiv. 1.

散 *san* — To scatter, disperse. G.L.c., x. 9. To be scattered, disorganized. A., XIX. xix.

敦 *tun* — Liberal, generous, great. D.M., xxvii. 6; xxx. 3.

敬 *king* ching — (1) To reverence, to respect; to be reverential, cherish the feeling of reverence. *Passim.* To be reverenced. D.M., xxxi. 1. In reference to business. A., I. v.: VI. i. 3: XIII. xix.: XV. xxxvii.: XVI. x. 畏敬, to be filled with awe and reverence. G.L.c., viii. 1. (2) An honorary epithet. A., VIII. iv.

數 *soo* shu — (1) Some, several. A., VII. xvi.: XIX. xxiii. 3. (2) 歷數, the determined time. A., XX. i. 1.

數 *sŏ* so — Frequently. A., IV. xxvi.

斂 *lëen* lien — To ingather. Applied to imposts. G. L.c., x. 21. D.M., xx. 14. A., XI. xvi.

THE 67TH RADICAL. 文.

文 *wăn* wên — (1) The characters of the language. D. M., xxviii. 2, 3. A., XV. xxv. (2) Records, literary monuments. A., III. ix. (3) Literature, polite studies. A., I. vi.: VI. xxv.: VII. xxiv.; xxxii.: IX. x. 2: XI. ii. 2: XII. xv.; xxiv.: XVI. i. 11. (4) Accomplished, accomplishments, elegance. D.M, xxxi. 1; xxxiii 1. A., III. xiv.: V. xiv.: VI. xvi.: XII. viii. 1, 3: XIV. xiii. 1; xix. 2. (5)=The cause of truth. A., IX. v. 2, 3. (6) 文章, elegant manners and discourses; elegant institutions. A., V. xii.: VIII. xix. 2. (7) Used as the honorary epithet, becoming in effect the name. D.M., xviii. 1, 2, 3: *et al.* G.L.c., iii. 3. A., IX. v. 2: XIX. xxii. 2.—A., XIV. xvi.—A., V. xiv. —A., V. xvii.: XV. xiii.—A., V. xviii. 2. —A., V. xix.—A., XIV. xiv.; xix. Used also in the name 子文, A., V. xviii.

文 *wăn* wên — Low. 3d tone. To gloss. A., XIX. viii.

斐 *fe* fei — Accomplished. G.L.c., iii. 4. 斐然, A., V. xx. 1.

THE 68TH RADICAL. 斗.

斗 *tow* tou — A peck. A., XIII. xx. 4.

索引

THE 69TH RADICAL. 斤.

斯 *sze* szû (1) This, these. *Passim.* Its antecedent is often a clause. (2) Forthwith. A., X. x. 1; xviii. 1: XIV. xlii. 2, and perhaps some other places.

新 *sin* hsin To renovate. G.L.c., iii. 1. New, what is new. G.L.c., iii. 2, 3. D.M., xxvii. 6. A., II. xi.: V. xviii.: XVII. xxi. 3.

斷 *twan* tuan Up. 3d tone. 斷斷兮, plain and sincere. G.L.c., x. 14.

THE 70TH RADICAL. 方.

方 *fang* (1) A region, regions. D.M., x. 2, 3, 4. A., I. i. 2; xx. i. 3. 四方, the four quarters,=all parts of the empire, or of a State. D.M., xx. 13. A., XIII. iv. 3: XX. i. 6. =Any quarter. A., XIII. v.; xx. A settled definite place. A., IV. xix. (2) Tablets of wood. D.M., xx. 2. (3) An art, the way. A., VI. xxviii. 3. (4) Right rules. A., XI. xxv. 4. (5) Square. A., XI. xxv. 5. 11. (6) To compare. A., XIV. xxi. (7) Then. A., XVI. vii. (8) Used in a designation. A., XVIII. ix. 3.

於 *yu* yü *Passim.* Its proper meaning is *in, at, on,* in regard to place. But after many verbs and adjectives we must translate by other prepositions, as *from, to,* &c. After the possessive 之, it=*in relation to.* With adjectives it forms the comparative degree, and=*than.* D.M., xxxiii. 4. A., XI. xvi. 1: XIX. xxv. 1. Observe 於我, A., X. xv. 1,=on me, be it mine.

於 *woo* wu An exclamation. G.L.c., iii. 3, 5. D.M., xxvi. 10.

施 *she* shih (1) To give, do, use. D.M., xiii. 3, 4. A., II. xxi. 2: XII. ii.: XV. xxiii. G.L.c., x. 12. (2) To make a display of. A., V. xxv. 3.

施 *she* shih Up. 3d tone. To confer on, so as to reach to. D.M., xxxi. 4: A., VI. xxviii. 1. There is not much appreciable difference between the char. in this tone and the last.

施 *ch'e* ch'ih For 弛, to treat remissly. A., XVIII. x.

旅 *leu* lü (1) A body of 500 solidiers. 師旅, 軍旅, forces. A., XI. xxv. 4: XIV. xx. 2: XV. i. 1. (2) All, general. D.M., xix. 4. (3) The name of a sacrifice. A., III. vi.

族 *tsuh* tsu The circle of relatives. A., XIII. xx. 2.

THE 71ST RADICAL. 无.

旣 *ke* chi (1) A particle of past time,=have, having, having been. D.M., xv. 2; xxvii. 7. A., III. x.; xxi. 2: IX. v. 2; x. 3: *et al., sæpe.* (2) Used adverbially. That done, =then, by-and-by. A., XIV. xlii. 2. (3) Used for 餼, or 槩, *k'e.* Rations. D.M., xx. 14.

THE 72D RADICAL. 日.

日 *jih* (1) The sun. D.M., xxvi. 9; xxx. 2; xxxi. 4. A., XIX. xxi.; xxiv. (2) A day, days. G.L.c., ii. 1. A., II. ix.: IV. vi. 2: VII. ix. 2: *et al., sæpe.* (3) Adverbially. Daily, D.M., xx. 14; xxxiii. 1. A., I. iv. On some days. A., VI. v. 日日, every day. G.L.c., ii. 1.

旨 *che* chih What is pleasant, spoken of food. A., XVII. xxi. 5.

昆 *kwăn* k'uên An elder brother. D.M., xx. 8. 昆弟, brothers; the younger branches of one's relatives, generally. D.M., xx. 13. A., XI. iv.

明 *ming* (1) Clear, illustrious, brilliant; clearly. G.L.T., 1, 4: c., i. 2. D.M., xx. 19, 20; xxiii.; xxvi. 3, 4, 5, 8; xxvii. 6; xxx. 2; xxxiii. 6. A., XVI. x. (2) To illustrate. G.L.T., 1, 4: c., i. 1, 3, 4. (3) Intelligence, intelligent. D.M., xx. 21; xxi.; xxvi. 7; xxxi. 1; xxxii. 3. A., II. vi. (4) To understand. D.M., iv. 1; xix. 6. (5) To purify, purification; clean. D.M., xvi. 3; xx. 14. A., X. vii. 1. (6) 明日, next day. A., XV. i. 1; XVIII. vii. 4. (7) 公明, as a double surname. A., XIV. xiv. In names. A., V. xxiv.—A., VI. xii.

易 *yih* yi (1) To change. A., I. vii.: XVIII. vi. 3, 4. (2) The name of the Yih classic. A., VII. xvi.

易 *e* i Low. 3d tone. (1) Easy, easily. A., VIII. xii.: XIII. xv. 2; xxv.: XIV. xi.; xliv.: XVII. iv. 3. Easily preserved, G.L.c., x. 5. Ease,=calmness, tranquillity. D.M., xiv. 4. (3) Minute attention to observances. A., III. iv. 3.

昔 *seih* hsi Formerly. 昔者, A., VIII. v.: XVI. i. 4: XVII. iv. 3; vii. 2.

星 *sing* hsing A star, stars. A., II. i. D.M., xxvi. 9.

春 *ch'un* The spring. A., XI. xxv. 7. D.M., xix. 3.

昭 *ch'aou* ch'ao (1) Bright; to be clearly seen; clearly. A., XX. i. 3. D.M., xxvi. 4; xxxiii. 2. (2) 昭穆, the tablets in the ancestral temple, acc. to the order of precedence. D.M., xix. 4. (3) Hon. ep. of a duke of Loo. A., VII. xxx.

是 *she* shih (1) This, these. *Passim.* It often resumes a previous clause, and often contains the copula,=this is. 如是, 若是, thus, such. 是故, 是以, therefore. Also 是用, A., V. xxii. (2) To be. A., IX. xxx. 1: XI. xx.: XVI. i. 3, 4, 7: *et al.* (3) Right. A., XVII. iv. 4. (4) 壹是,=all. G.L.T., 6.

時 *she* shih (1) Time, times. A., XVI. vii. D.M., xxx. 1. Opportunity. A., XVII. 1. 2. (2) The seasons. D.M., xxx. 2. A., XIX. iii. Seasonal. D.M., xix. 3. A., X. viii. 2: XVIII. 2. (3) Seasonably, at proper times. D.M., xx. 14; xxxi. 2. A., XIV. xiv. 2. 以時, A., I. v. (4) Always. D.M., ii. 2; xxv. 3. A., I. i. 1. (5) To time, watch. A., XVII. i. 1.

晉 *tsin* chin The name of a State. A., XIV. xvi.

晏 *gan* an (1) Late. A., XIII. xiv. (2) A surname. A., V. xvi.

晝 *chow* chou The daytime; adverbially. A., V. ix. 1: IX. xvi.

晨 *shin* ch'ên The morning. 晨門, style of a gatekeeper. A., XIV. xli.

晳 *seih* hsi Designation of one of Conf. disciples. A., XI. xxv. 1.

暇 *hea* hsia Leisure. A., XIV. xxxi.

暑 *shoo* shu Warm weather. A., X. vi. 3.

景 *king* ching An hon. epithet. A., XII. xi.: XVI. xii.: XVIII. iii. 景伯, an hon. designation. A., XIV. xxxviii.: XIX xxiii. 2.

暴 *paou* pao (1) Violence, oppression. G.L.c., ix. 4. A., VIII. iv. 3: XX. ii. 3. (2) To attack, or strike, unarmed. A., VII. x. 3.

曆 *leih* li Calculated and represented. A., XX. i. 1.

THE 73D RADICAL. 日.

日 *yuĕ* yüeh To speak, to say, saying. *Passim* Generally, the nominative is expressed, but not always, and then 日=it is said. D. M., xxvii. 5; *et al.* Sometimes it=namely. D.M., xx. 8, 12; *et al.* 蓋日, meaning, for it says. D.M., xxvi. 10.

曲 *k'euh* ch'ü (2) Bent. A., VII. xv. (2) Shoots, what is small. D.M., xxiii.

更 *kăng* kêng To change. A., XIX. xxi.

書 *shoo* shu (1) To write. A., XV. v. 4. Writing, writings, books. D.M., xxxviii. 3. A., XI. xxiv. 3: XIV. xliii. 1. (2) The Shoo-king, or classic of History. A., II. xxi. 2: VII. xvii. (3) 楚書, the name of a Book. G.L.c., x. 11.

曾 *tsăng* tsêng The surname of one of Conf. principal disciples, and of his father. G.L.c., vi. 3. A., I. iv.: *et al, sæpe.* A., XI. xxv. 1, 8.

曾 *ts'ang* ts'êng Low. 1st tone. A conjunction,=then, but. A., II. viii.: III. vi.: XI. xxiii. 2.

會 *hwuy* hui (1) To associate with. A., XII. xxiv. (2) Interviews of the princes with the emperor. A., XI. xxv. 6, 12.

THE 74TH RADICAL. 月.

月 *yuĕ* yüeh (1) The moon. D.M., xxvi. 9; xxx. 2; xxxi. 4. A., XIX. xxi.; xxiv. (2) A month, months. D.M., vii. A., VI. v.: VII. xiii.: X. vi. 11: XIII. x.: XVII. i. 2. Monthly, from month to month. D.M., xx. 14. A., XIX. 5.

有 *yew* yu (1) To have, possess. *Passim.* Followed by 者,=he who possesses, they who have. But sometimes the 者 is omitted, as in A., I. xiv.: VIII. iv.: XX. i. 1: *et al.* In this sense it not only governs nouns, but is used as an auxiliary to verbs, both active and passive. (2) The impersonal substantive verb, there is, there was. *Passim.* In very many instances, it is difficult to say whether the character is used thus, or as in 1. 有之, and the negative 未之有 at the end of sentences, are to be observed. G.L.T., A., I. ii. 1: IV. vi. 3: *et al.* 何有=there is no difficulty. A., IV. xiii.: *et al.* But this not always. A., VII. ii.: *et al.* Obs' A., XIX. ii. (3) The surname of one of Conf. disciples. A., I. ii. 1; xii.; xiii.: XII. ix. 1, 2. The name of another. A., III. vi.: VII. xiv.: *et al, sæpe.*

索引

有 *yew* yu Low. 3d tone. And. A., II. iv. 1: X. vi. 6.

朋 *p'ăng* p'êng A fellow-student; a friend, friends. A., I. i. 2. 朋友, see under 友.

服 *fuh* fu (1) To wear. A., II. xix.: XV. x. 4. Metaph. D.M., viii. Clothes. D.M., xvi. 3; xx. 14. A., VIII. xxi.: X. vi. 2, 11: *et al.* (2) To submit. A., XIII. iv. 3: XVI. i. 11, 12. 服事, to serve. A., VIII. xx. 4. 服勞, to undergo the labour. A., II. viii. (3) 子服, appy. a surname. A., XIV. xxxviii. XIX. xxiii. 2.

胡 *hoo* hu How. D.M., xiii. 4.

朕 *ch'in* ch'ên The imperial *I*. A., XX. i. 3.

朔 *sŏ* so The first day of the moon. A., III. xvi. 1.

望 *wang* To look towards, admiring and expecting. D.M., xxix. 5. A., XIX. ix.: XX. ii. 2. =to compare one's-self to. A., V. viii. 2.

朝 *chaou* chao (1) Morning, in the morning. A., IV. viii.: XII. xxi. 3. (2) A name. A., VI. xiv.

朝 *ch'aou* ch'ao (1) The court. A., V. vii. 4: XIV. xxxviii.: XIX. xxiii. 1. (2) To be in court, appear in court. A., X. ii. 1; vi. i.: XIV. xxii. 2. 退朝, to retire from court. A., X. xii.: XIII. xiv. (3) To hold a court, give audience. D.M., xx. 14. A., XVIII. iv. (4) Court, as an adjective. A., X. x. ii.; xiii. 3. (5) A name. A., XIX. xxii.

期 *k'e* ch'i (1) A fixed time. A., XX. ii. 3. (2) A name. A., VII. xxx. 2, 3.

期 *ke* chi A round year. D.M., xviii. 3. A., XVII. xxi. 1, 2. 期月, a round month. D.M., vii.

朞 *ke* chi 朞月, a round year. A., XIII. x.

THE 75TH RADICAL. 木.

木 *muh* mu (1) Trees. D.M., xxvi. 9. A., XVII. ix. 7: XIX. xii. 2. (2) Wood. A., V. ix. 1. (3) Wooden. A., III. xxiv. (4) Simple, plain. A., XIII. xxvii.

未 *we* wei Not yet. *Passim* We may sometimes translate by *not*, but the force of the *yet* is always to be detected. It is joined with 嘗. A., III. xxiv.: VI. xii.: VII. vii.; ix.: IX. xxx. 2. Its power, in common with other negatives, to attract 之 to itself, and make it precede the verb which governs it, is to be noted. G. L.T., 7: c., ix. 4. A., I. ii. 2: V. v. x.; xiii.: *et al.*

末 *mŏ* mo (1) The end, the product, result, in opp. to 本, the root. G.L.T., 3, 7: c., x. 7. (2) Small, trivial. D.M., xxxiii. 6. A., XIX. xii. 1. (3) In old age. D.M., xviii. 3. (4) Not, do not. A., IX. x. 3; xxiii.: XIV. xlii. 3: XV. xv.: XVII. v. 2.

本 *pun* pên The root; what is radical, essential. G. L.T., 3, 6, 7: c., iv.; v.; x. 7. D.M., i. 4; xxxii. 1. A., I. ii. 2: XIX. xii 1. What is first to be attended to. A., III. iv. 1. To be rooted. D.M., xxix. 3.

朱 *choo* chu (1) Vermillion colour. A., XVII. xviii. (2) A surname. A., XVIII. viii.

朽 *hew* hsiu Rotten. A., V. ix. 1.

杇 *woo* wu To plaster. A., V. ix. 1.

杞 *k'e* ch'i The name of a State. A., III. ix. D.M., xxviii. 5.

杖 *chang* chang A staff. A., XIV. xlvi.: XVIII. vii. 1. 杖者, those who carried staves. A., X. x. 1.

束 *shuh* shu (1) To bind, gird. A., V. vii. 4. (2) A bundle of dried flesh. A., VII. vii.

林 *lin* A surname. A., III. iv. 1; vi.

東 *tung* (1) The east, eastern. A., XVII. v. 3. To turn to the east. A., X. xiii. 3. (2) 東蒙, a mountain. A., XVI i. 4. 東里, a place. A., XIV. ix. 1.

某 *mow* mou So-and-so. A., XV. xli. 1.

松 *sung* The pine tree. A., III. xxi. 1: IX. xxvii.

枉 *wang* Crooked, used metaphorically. A., II. xix.: XII. xxii. 3, 4. With verbal force. A., XVIII. ii.

枕 *chin* To use as a pillow. A., VII. xv.

索引

櫝 *tuh* tu — A coffer, a repository. A., XVI. i. 7.

THE 76TH RADICAL. 欠.

次 *ts'ze* tz'ŭ — (1) Next in order or degree. D.M., xxiii. 1; A., VII. xxvii.: XIII. xx. 2, 3: XVI. ix. In A., XIV. xxxix. 2, 3, 4, 其次 only=some. (2) 造次, in moments of haste.

欲 *yuh* yü — (1) To desire, to wish. G.L.T., 4. A., II. ii. 6: III. x.; xvii. 1: *et al., sæpe.* (2) To be covetous,=貪. A., XII. xviii.: XIV. ii.; xiii. In A., XX. i. 1, 2, 欲 is distinguished from 貪.

欺 *k'e* ch'i — To deceive, impose upon; to be deceived. G.L.C., vi. 1. A., VI. xxiv.: IX. xi. 2: XIV. xxiii.

歌 *ko* — To sing. A., VII. v. 2; xxxi.: XVII. iv.; xx.: XVIII. v.

歎 *t'an* — To sigh, with the idea of admiration. A., IX. x. 1: XI. xxv. 7.

THE 77TH RADICAL. 止.

止 *che* chih — (1) To rest; where to rest. G.L.T., 1, 2: C., iii. 1, 2, 3. (2) To stop, desist. D. M., xiii. 2. A., IX. xviii.; xx.: XI. xxiii. 3: XII. xxiii.: XVI. i. 6: XIX. xiv. (3) To detain. A., XVIII. vii. 3.

正 *ching* chêng — (1) To rectify, to adjust; be rectified. G.L.T., 4, 5: C., vii. 1, 3; ix. 8. D.M., xiv. 3. A., I. xiv.: VIII. iv. 3: *et al., sæpe.* (2) Correct, correctness, correctly. G.L. C., vii. 1. D.M., xxxi. 1. A., X. viii. 3; ix.; xiii. 1; xvii. 1: In these examples, correct,=square, straight. A., XIII. iii. 4, 5; vi.: XIV. xvi. (3) Just, exactly. A., VII. xxxiii. Observe A., XVII. x.

正 *ching* chêng — Up. 1st tone. The bull's eye in a target. D.M., xiv. 5.

此 *ts'ze* tz'ŭ — This. *Sæpe.* 如此, thus. G.L.C., ix. 3. D.M., xvi. 5; xxvi. 6; xxviii. 1. 在此, here. D.M., xxix. 6. The character does not occur in the Analects.

武 *woo* wu — (1) The honorary epithet of the first emperor of the Chow dynasty. D.M., xviii. 1, 2, 3. *Et al., sæpe.* The name of his music. A., III. xxv. (2) The hon. ep. of others. A., XIV. xiii.; xv. A., V. xx.—A., II. vi.: V. vii.—A., XIX. xxiii.; xxiv. (3) A name. A., XVIII. ix. 4. (4) 武城, name of a place. A., VI. xii.: XVII. iv.

歲 *suy* sui — The year, years. A., IX. xxvii.: XVII. i. 2.

歸 *kwei* kuei — (1) To return. A., V. xxii.: XI. xxv. 7. (2) To revert to. A., I. ix.: XII. i. 1. (3) To turn to. D.M., xx. 13. To flow to. A., XIX. xx. 歸心, to turn to in heart. A., XX. i. 7. (4) To turn to, depend on. A., X. xv. 1. (5) To present. A., XVII. i. 1: XVIII. iv. (6) =to be married. G.L.C., ix. 6. (7) 三歸, see on 三.

THE 78TH RADICAL. 歹.

死 *sze* szŭ — To die; death; the dead. D.M., x. 4, 5; xix. 5. A., II. v. 3: IV. viii.: XI. vi.; vii. 1, 2; viii.: ix.; x.; xi.; xii. 2; xxii.: *et al, sæpe.* 後死者, a future mortal. A., IX. v. 3.

殆 *t'ae* t'ai — Dangerous;—both what is perilous, and being in peril. G.L.C., x. 3. A, II. xv.; xviii. 2: XV. x. 6: XVIII. v. 1.

殖 *chih* — To be largely produced; to be amassed. D.M., xxvi. 9. A., XI. xviii. 2.

殘 *ts'an* — Vicious, violently bad. A., XIII. xi.

殯 *pin* — To coffin,=to bury. A., X. xv. 1.

THE 79TH RADICAL. 殳.

殺 *shă* sha — To kill. A., XII. xix.: XIV. xvii. 1; xviii. 1: XV. viii.: XVIII. vii. 3: XX. ii. 2. =Capital punishments. XIII. xi.

殺 *shae* shai — Gradually decreasing. D.M., xx. 5. A., X. vi. 9.

殷 *yin* — The name of a dynasty. G.L.C., x. v. D.M, xxviii. 5. A., II. xxiii. 2: *et al.*

殿 *teen* tien — Up. 3d tone. To bring up the rear A., VI. xiii.

毀 *wei* — (1) To blame excessively, revile. A., XV. xxiv.: XIX. xxiv. (2) To be broken. A., XVI. i. 7.

毅 *e* i — Determined and enduring. D.M., xxxi. 1. A., VIII. vii. 1: XIII. xxv.

THE 80TH RADICAL. 毋.

毋 *woo* wu — Do not,=do not do, do not have, &c. G.L.C., vi. 1; x. 2. A., VI. iii. 4: IX. xxiv.: XI. xxv. 2: XII. xxiii. In A., IX. iv.; it is taken as=無, the simple negative, but its ordinary meaning may be retained.

母 *moo* mu — A mother. A., VI. iii. 1. 父母, a parent, parents. G.L.c., x. 3. D.M., xv. 3: xviii. 3. A., I. vii.: II. vi.: IV. xviii.; xix.; xxi.: XI. iv.: XVII. xxi. 6: XVIII. ii.

每 *mei* — Every. A., III. xv.: X. xiv.

THE 81st RADICAL. 比.

比 *pe* pi — To compare, be compared. A., VII. i.

比 *pe* pi — Low. 3d tone. (1) To follow. A., IV. x. (2) Partizanly. A., II. xiv. (3) Joined with 及, within, by the time of. A., XI. xxv. 4, 5.

THE 82d RADICAL. 毛.

毛 *maou* mao — The hair, a hair. D.M., xix. 4; xxxiii. 6.

THE 83d RADICAL. 氏.

氏 *she* shih — A family. Follows surnames, and denotes particular individuals. A., III. i.: *et al.*—A., III. xxi.—A., XIV. x.—A., 3. —A., III. xxii.—A., XIV. xli.; xlii.—A., XIX. xix.

民 *min* — (1) The people, the multitude. *Passim.* (2) = 人, man, men. A., VI. xx.: XV. xxxiv. And perhaps in some other places, as D.M., iii. A., VI. xxvii.: XVI. ix.: XVII. xvi.

THE 84th RADICAL. 气.

氣 *k'e* ch'i — Breath. A., X. iv. 4. 血氣, blood and breath,=the physical powers. A., XVI. vii. 有血氣者, mankind. D.M., xxxi. 4. Observe 辭氣, A., VIII. iv. 3, and 食氣, A., X. viii. 4.

THE 85th RADICAL. 水.

水 *shwuy* shui — Water. D.M., xxvi. 9; xxx. 1. A., VI. xxi.: VII. xv.: XV. xxxiv.

永 *yung* — To perpetuate, perpetual. D.M., xxix. 6. A., XX. i. 1.

汎 *fan* — Universally. A., I. vi.

求 *k'ew* ch'iu — (1) To seek for; also to ask, request. G.L.c., ix. 2, 4. D.M., xiii. 4; xiv. 3, 5. A., I. x. 1, 2; xiv.: IV. xiv.: *et al., sæpe.* (2) The name of one of Conf. disciples. A., V. vii. 3: VI. vi.; x.: *et al., sæpe.*

汶 *wăn* wên — The name of a stream. A., VI. vii.

沂 *e* i — The name of a stream. A., XI. xxv. 7.

沐 *mŭh* mu — 沐浴, to bathe. A., XIV. xxii. 2.

沒 *mŭh* mu — (1) To die, be dead. A., I. xi.: IX. v. 2. 沒世, after death. G.L.c., iii. 5. A., XV. xix. (2) To exhaust, be exhausted. A., XVII. xxi. 3. 沒階, A., X. iv. 5. 沒齒, A., XIV. x. 3.

沛 *p'ei* — 顛沛, in danger, in confusion. A., IV. v. 3.

河 *ho* — Rivers, a river D.M., xxvi. 9. A., VII. x. 3. *The* river, *i.e.*, the Yellow river. A., IX. viii.: XVIII. ix. 3.

治 *ch'e* ch'ih — To regulate, manage, govern. G.L.T., 4: c., ix. 1, 5; x. 1. D.M., xiii. 2; xix. 6, 11, 14, 17. A., V. vii. 2: XIV. xxii. 2.

治 *che* chih — To be regulated, to be well governed. G.L.T., 5, 7. A., VIII. xx. 1: XV. iv.

沮 *tseu* chü — 長沮, the designation of a recluse. A., XVIII. vi. 1, 2,

沽 *koo* ku — To sell. A., IX. xii. Retailed. A., X. viii. 5.

泥 *ne* ni — Low. 3d tone. To be obstructed, inapplicable. A., XIX. iv.

泉 *ts'euen* ch'üan — A fountain, a spring. D.M., xxxi. 2, 3.

法 *fă* fa — (1) A model; to imitate. G.L.c., ix. 8. D.M., xxix. 5. (2) Law-like, =strict; laws. A., IX. xxiii.: XX. i. 6.

泰 *t'ae* t'ai — (1) A dignified ease. A., VII. xxv. 3. Oppos. to 驕, A., XIII. xxvi.: XX. ii. 1, 2. (2) Arrogant. A., IX. iii. 2. Coupled with 驕, G.L.c., x. 18. (3) 泰山, the name of a mountain. A., III. vi. 泰伯, hon. designation of an ancient worthy. A., VIII. i. 泰誓, name of a Book in the Shoo-king. G.L.c., x. 14.

洋 *yang* — 洋溢, to overflow. D.M., xxxi. 4. 洋洋乎, the appearance of vast swelling waters, grandly. D.M., xvi. 3; xxvii. 2. A., VIII. xv.

索引

洒 *shae* shai — To sprinkle. A., XIX. xii. 1.

洫 *heuĕ* hsüeh — A water channel, a ditch. 溝洫, A., VIII. xxi.

津 *tsin* chin — A ford. A., XVIII. xi. 1, 2.

洩 *sëĕ* hsieh — To leak. D.M., xxvi. 9.

流 *lew* liu — (1) Flowing, a current. D.M., xxx. 3. (2) Weak, unstable. D.M., x. 5. (3) To banish. 放流, G.L.c., x. 15. (4) 下流, a low-lying situation. A., XVII. xxiv. 1: XIX. xx.

浩 *haou* hao — 浩浩, vast. D.M., xxxii. 3.

浮 *fow* fou — To float, floating. A., V. vi.: VII. xv.

浴 *yuh* yü — To wash. A., XI. xxv. 7. 沐浴, to bathe. A., XIV. xxii. 2.

海 *hae* hai — The sea, seas. D.M., xxvi. 9. A., V. vi.: XVIII. ix. 5. 四海, a name for the empire, the world. D.M., xvii. 1; xviii. 2. A., XII. v. 4: XX. i. 1.

浸 *tsin* chin — To soak. A., XII. vi.

涖 *le* li — The approach of a superior; to govern, preside over. A., XV. xxxii. 2, 3.

涅 *neĕ* nieh — To steep in muddy water. A., XVII. vii. 3.

淇 *k'e* ch'i — The name of a stream. G.L.c., iii. 4.

淡 *tan* — Insipid. D.M., xxxiii. 1.

淫 *yin* — Licentious. A., III. xx.: XV. x. 6.

深 *shin* shên — Deep. A., VIII. iii.: XIV. xlii. 2.

淸 *ts'ing* ch'ing — Pure, purity. A., V. xviii. 2: XVIII. viii. 4.

淵 *yuen* yüan — (1) A gulf, an abyss; deep, the deep. D.M., xii. 3; xxxi. 2, 3; xxxii. 2. A., VIII. iii. (2) The name of Conf. favourite disciple. A., V. xxv.: VII. xii.: *et al., sæpe.*

淺 *ts'een* ch'ien — Shallow. A., XIV. xlii. 2.

溫 *wăn* wên — (1) Benign, unpretending. A., VII. xxxvii.: XVI. x.: XIX. ix. D.M., xxxi. 1; xxxiii. 1. (2) To cherish, know thoroughly. A., II. xi. D.M., xxvii. 6.

游 *yew* yu — (1) To ramble, to seek recreation. A., VII. vi. 4. (2) 子游, the desig. of one of Conf. disciples. A., II. vii.: IV. xxv.: *et al., sæpe.*

測 *ts'ih* ts'ê — To fathom. 不測, unfathomable. D.M., xxvi. 7, 9.

湯 *t'ang* — (1) Boiling water. A., XVI. xi. (2) Name of the first emperor of the Shang dynasty. G.L.c., ii. 1. A., XII. xxii. 6.

滕 *t'ăng* t'êng — The name of a State. A., XIV. xii.

滔 *t'aou* t'ao — 滔滔, the appearance of an inundation. A., XVIII. v. 3.

漆 *ts'eih* ch'i — 漆雕, a double surname. A., V. v.

溺 *neih* ni — 桀溺, the name of a recluse. A., XVIII. vi.

溢 *yih* yi — 洋溢, to overflow. D.M., xxxi. 4.

溥 *p'oo* p'u — Great, all-embracing. D.M., xxxi. 2, 3.

漏 *low* lou — To leak. 屋漏, the part of a house open to the light of heaven. D.M., xxxiii. 3.

溝 *kow* kou — A ditch. 溝洫, A., VIII. xxi. 溝瀆, A., XIV. xviii. 3.

漢 *han* — The name of a river. A., XVIII. ix. 4.

潔 *këĕ* chieh — To purify, pure. A., VII. xxviii. 2: XVIII. vii. 5.

潤 *jun* — To soak, moisten, enrich, adorn. G.L.c., vi. 4. A., XII. vi.: XIV. ix.

滅 *mëĕ* mieh — (1) To extinguish; be extinguished. A., XX. i. 7. (2) 滅明, a name. A., VI. xii.

潛 *ts'een* ch'ien — To dive, sink. D.M., xxxiii. 2.

澹 *t'an* — 澹臺, a double surname. A., VI. xii.

濟 *tse* chi — To help, benefit. A., VI. xxviii. 1.

瀆 *tuh* tu — A ditch. 溝瀆, A., XIV. xviii. 3.

澳 *yuh* yü — A bank, the winding and curving of a river's banks. G.L.c., iii. 4.

濫 *lan* — To overflow, exceed due bounds. A., XV. i. 3.

灌 *kwan* kuan — To pour out a libation. A., III. x.

THE 86TH RADICAL. 火.

火 *ho* huo — Fire. A, XV. xxxiv. 改火, 'to change the fire,' *i.e.*, to get fire in all the diff't. ways. A., XVII. xxi. 3.

烈 *lëë* lieh — Violent. A., X. xvi. 5.

烖 *tsae* tsai — *I. q.* 災, calamity. D.M., xxviii. 1.

焉 *yen* — A final particle. *Passim.* (1) It is found at the end of clauses, when the mind expects the sequel. G.L.c., vii. 2. D.M., xi. 1; xiii. 4. A., V. xxiii.: VI. vii. *et al., sæpe.* (2) It is found at the end of sentences, and gives a liveliness to the style. D.M., x. 5; xiv. 2. A., I. xiv.: IV. xvii.: *et al., sæpe.* (3) It is found often at the end of correlative clauses and sentences. G.L.c., viii. 1; x 13. D. M, i. 5; xii. 2; xxvi. 9. A., VIII. xiii. 3: XI. xxiv. 3: XIII. xx. 2: *et al.* (4) Observe D.M., xxix. 2. A., V. xii.

焉 *yen* — Up. 1st tone. An interrogative particle, generally best translated by 'how.' It is placed at the beginning of the clause to which it belongs, unless where another particle, or the nominative, immediately precedes. D.M., xxxii. 1. A., II. x. 4: III. xxii. 2: IV. i.: V. ii.; iv. 2; x.; xviii. 1, 2: *et al., sæpe.*

無 *woo* wu — No, not, to be without, not to have. *Passim.* Joined to verbs, adjectives, and nouns. It is often followed by 所. A., III. vii.: IX. ii. 1: *et al.* The 所 must sometimes be understood. A., XX. iii. 1, 2, 3: *et al.* 無....不, a strong affirmation, often with 所 between. G.L.c., ii. 4: vi. 2: *et al.* So 未一無. A., VII. vii. 1. 無乃....乎, 無寧....乎, forms of interrogation. A., IX. vi. 3. VI. i. 3: *et al.* Opposed to 有, standing absolutely,=the state of being without. A., IX. xi. 2: VIII. v. 1. So 無之, there is not it, opposed to 有之. G.L.c., ix. 1. Observe 無以爲, it is of no use doing so. A., XIX. xxiv.

焚 *fun* fên — To be burned. A., X. xii.

然 *jen* jan — (1) So. A., III. xiii. 2: VI. xxiv.: VIII. xx. 3: XIV. xiii. 2. =yes. A., XV. ii. 2; xli. 3: XVII. vii. 3: XVIII. vi. 3. 然則, so then, well then. 然而, so but. A., III. xxii. 3: XI. xiv. 2; xxiii. 5: XIX. xv. (2) To be right. A., VI. i 4. (3) 然後, and afterwards. A., VI. xvi.: IX. xiv.: xxvii.: *et al.* (4) Added to adjectives, forming adverbs. G.L.c., vi. 2. D.M., xxxiii. 1. A., V. xxi.: IX. x. 1, 2: XX. ii. 2: XIX. ix.: *et al.*—Obs. A., VIII. xxi.: XI. xii. 2: XIV. vi. 1. (5) 子然, name of a member of the 季 family. A., XI. xxiii.

煥 *hwan* huan — 煥煥乎, how glorious. A., VIII. xix. 2.

照 *chaou* chao — To enlighten, to shine on. D.M., xxxi. 4.

熙 *he* hsi — Bright. G.L.c., iii. 3.

熟 *shuh* shu — Cooked, to cook. A., X. xiii. 1.

燕 *yen* — (1) A feast. D.M., xix. 4. (2) Easy and unoccupied. A., VII. iv.

燧 *suy* sui — 鑽燧, to obtain fire by boring, or friction. A., XVII. xxi. 3.

THE 87TH RADICAL. 爫.

爭 *tsăng* tsêng — To wrangle, to strive. G.L.c., x. 7. D.M., xxxiii. 4. A., III. vii.: XV. xxi.

爲 *wei* — To do, to make. G.L.c., vi. 2; x. 18. (1) D.M., xi. 1; xiii. 1; xvi. 1. A., III. xxvi.: XIV. xv.: xviii.: XIX. iv.; xv.; xvi.: *et al., sæpe.* =to be in charge of, to administer, to govern. D.M., xx. 12, 15. A., II. i.: IV. xiii.: XI. xxv. 4, 5: XIII. iii. 1; xi.: *et al.* 何爲=why. A., VIII. xxiv.: XIV. xxxiv.; xxxvii. 2. (2) To be. G.L.c., x. 5. D.M., vi.: xvii. 1. A., I. ii. 2; xii.: VI. ii.; iii. 3; vii.; xi.; xii.: *et al., sæpe.* At the beginning of clauses, it may be often translated by who is. D.M., xxii.; xxiii.: *et al* (3) Before nouns of relation, and others, it,=to play, as, to show one's-self to be. G.L.c., iii. 3; ix. 8. D.M., viii. 2. A., I. ii. 1: XIII. xv. 2, 3, 4: *et al.* (4) 以爲, with or without intermediate words. To take to be,=to regard as, to consider, to have to be; to use to make. G.L.T., 6; x. 11, 12, 21, 22. D.M., xviii. 1. A., II. viii.: III. viii.; xviii.; xxiv.: XIV. ii. 1, 2; iii.; xiii. 1, 2; xix. 2: *et al., sæpe.* Sometimes 爲 is found alone, without the 以. A., IX. xi. 2: XIX. ii: XI. xxiv. 3: *et al.* Obs. A., XII. viii.: XIII. v.: XIX. xxiv. Obs. also 爲之奴, A., XVIII. i., and the same idiom in other places.

爲 *wei* Low. 3d tone. For, because of, in behalf of, with a view to, because; to be for. D.M., xix. 4. ? A., I. iv.: III. xvi.: xxii. 2: VI. iii. 1; vii.: VII. xiv. 1, 2: XI. ix. 3; xvi. 1: XIII. xviii. 2: XIV. xxv.: XV. xxxix.

爵 *tsëŏ* chio Rank, dignity. D.M., ix.; xix. 1.

THE 88TH RADICAL. 父.

父 *foo* fu A father. *Sæpe.* 諸父昆弟, uncles and cousins. D.M., xx. 13. So 父兄, A., IX. xv. 父母, parents, a parent. *sæpe.* To be—play—the father. A., XII. xi. 1, 2. 人父, see 人.

父 *foo* fu Up. 2d tone. 莒父, name of a place. A., XIII. xviii.

THE 89TH RADICAL. 爻.

爾 *urh* (1) You, your. G.L.c., x. 4. D.M., xv. 2; xxxiii. 3. A., III. xvii. 2: V. xi., xxv. 1: *et al., sæpe.* (2) After adjectives; making adverbs. A., IX. x. 3: XI. xxv. 4: XVII. iv. 2. (3) A final particle, synonymous with 耳, simply, just. D. M., xiii. 4. A., X. i. 2. 云爾, so, just. A., VII. xviii. 2: xxxiii.

THE 90TH RADICAL. 爿.

牆 *ts'eang* ch'iang A wall. A., V. ix. 1: XVII. x: XIX. xxiii. 2, 3. 蕭牆, a screen in a prince's court. A., XVI. i. 13.

THE 91ST RADICAL. 片.

片 *p'een* p'ien A splinter, a half. A., XII. xii.

版 *pan* Tables of population. A., X. xvi. 3.

牖 *yew* yu A window. A., VI. viii.

THE 93D RADICAL. 牛.

牛 *new* niu (1) A cow, an ox, the cow kind. A., VI. iv.: XVII. iv. 2. G.L.c., x. 21. (2) 伯牛, the designation of one of the disciples. A., VI. viii.: XI. ii. 2. 司馬牛, a disciple of Conf. A., XII. iii.; iv.; v.

牟 *mow* mou 中牟, the name of a place. A., XVII. vii. 2.

牢 *laou* lao Surname of one of Conf. disciples. A., IX. vi. 4.

牡 *mow* mou The male of animals, translated *victim.* A., XX. i. 3.

物 *wuh* wu A thing, things. 萬物, all things. =animals and things. D.M., xxii. =men and things. D.M., xxv. 2, 3.

犁 *le* li 犁牛, a brindled cow. A., VI. iv.

THE 94TH RADICAL. 犬.

犬 *k'euen* ch'üan A dog. A., II. vii.: XII. viii. 3.

犯 *fan* (1) To offend, be offended, against. A., ii. 1: VIII. v. To withstand to the face. A., XIV. xxiii. (2) 舊犯, uncle Fan. G.L.c., x. 13.

狂 *k'wang* k'uang Ardent, ambitious, extravagant, extravagance. A., V. xxi.: VIII. xvi.: XIII. xxi. 1: XVII. viii. 3; xvi 2. A madman. A., XVIII. v. 1.

狄 *teih* ti The name of the northern barbarians. 夷狄, barbarous tribes. D.M., xiv. 2. A., III. v.: XIII. xix.

狎 *heă* hsia (1) To be familiar with. A., X. xvi. 2. (2) To be disrespectful to. A., XVI. viii. 2.

狐 *hoo* hu A fox. A., IX. xxvi. 1: X. vi. 4, 7.

狷 *keuen* chuan Cautious and decided. A., XIII. xxi.

猗 *e* i — 猗猗, the appearance of luxuriance. G.L.c., iii. 4.

猛 *măng* mêng — Fierce. A., VII. xxxvii.: XX. ii. 1, 2.

猶 *yew* yu — (1) As. G.L.c., iv. A., V. xviii. 2: VII. xxxii.: XI. x.; xv.: XII. viii. 3; xiii.: XVII. x.; xii.: XIX. xxv. 3. (2) Still, yet. D.M., xii. 2; xiii. 2; xxxiii. 6. A., VI. xxviii. 1: VIII. xvii.: XII. ix 3: XIV. xxxviii. 1; xlv.: XV. xxv. 1: XVII. xxii.: XVIII. v. 1: XIX. xxv.

獄 *yŏ* yü — Litigations. A., XII. xii.

獨 *tuh* tu — (1) Only. A., XII. xii. (2) Alone. A., XVI. xiii. 2, 3. 其獨, the being alone. G.L.c., vi. 1, 2. D.M., i. 3.

獲 *hwŏ* huo — To obtain; acquisition. A., VI. xx. To obtain the confidence of, to gain. D.M., xx. 6, 17. 獲罪, to sin, offend against. A., III. xiii 2.

獻 *heen* hsien — (1) Used for 賢, wise men. A., III. ix. (2) An honorary epithet. G.L.c., x. 22.

獸 *show* shou — Wild animals. D.M., xxvi. 9. A., XVII. ix, 7: XVIII. vi. 4.

THE 95TH RADICAL. 玄.

玄 *heuen* hsüan — Dark-coloured. A., X. vi. 10: XX. i. 3.

率 *suh* hsü — (1) To follow, accord with. D.M., i. 1. (2) 率爾, hastily. A., XI. xxv. 4.

THE 96TH RADICAL. 玉.

玉 *yuh* yü — (1) A gem, gems. A., IX. xii.: XVI. i. 7: XVII. xi. (2) 伯玉, a designation. A., XIV. xxvi.: XV. xi. 2.

王 *wang* — (1) A king, kings. G.L.c., iii. 5. A., XIII. xii. 先王, the former kings. A., I. xii. 2. A former king. A., XVI. i. 4. (2) 王孫, a double surname. A., III. xiii.: XIV. xx. 2.

王 *wang* — Low. 3d tone. To exercise true, kingly authority. D.M., xviii. 3; xxix. 1. 追王, to carry up the title of king to. D.M., xviii. 3.

理 *le* li — Distinctive, discriminating. D.M., xxxi. 1; xxxiii. 1.

琢 *chŏ* cho — To cut, as jewels or gems. G.L.c., iii. 4. A., I. xv. 2.

琴 *k'in* ch'in — A harp, or lute. D.M., xv. 2.

瑟 *sih* shê — (1) Stern, majestic. G.L.c., iii. 4. (2) The harpsichord. A., XI. xiv. 1; xxv. 7: XVII. xx. 1. 琴瑟, D.M., xv. 2.

璉 *leen* lien — A gemmed vessel, used in sacrifice. 瑚璉, A., V. iii.

瑚 *hoo* hu — Same as the above.

THE 97TH RADICAL. 瓜.

瓜 *kwa* kua — A gourd. 匏瓜, A., XVII. vii. 4. Supposed to be instead of 必. A., X. viii. 10.

瓢 *p'eaou* p'iao — A calabash. A., VI. ix.

THE 99TH RADICAL. 甘.

甘 *kan* — Sweet, to enjoy as sweet or pleasant. A., XVII. xxi. 5.

甚 *shin* shên — Excessive, to an exceeding degree. A., VII. v.; xxviii. 2: VIII. x.: XV. xxxiv. 甚於...., more important than. A., XIX. xx.

THE 100TH RADICAL. 生.

生 *săng* shêng — (1) To produce, to be produced. G.L.c., x. 18. D.M., xvii. 3; xx. 5; xxvi. 7, 9. A., I. ii. 2: VII. xxii.: XVII. xix. 3. (2) To be born. D.M., xx. 9; xxviii. 1. A., VII. xix. 生而知之, born with knowledge. A., XVI. ix.: VI. xvii. (3) To live. A., VI. xvii.: XII. x. 2: XVII. xxi. 6. The living, when living. D.M., xix. 5. A., II. v. 3: X. xiii. 1. Life. A., XI. x.: XII. v. 3: XV. viii.: XIX. xxv. 4. 先生, elders. A., II. viii.: XIV. xlvii. 2. 後生, a youth. A., IX. xxii. 平生, the life-time. A., XIV. xiii. 2. (4) 微生, a double surname. A., XIV. xxxiv.—V. xxiii.

產 *san* ch'an — 子產, the designation of a statesman of Conf. time. A., V. xv.: XIV. ix.; x.

THE 101st RADICAL. 用.

用 *yung* (1) To use; to employ (in office), to expend. G.L.c., ii. 4; x. 18. D.M., vi.; xxviii. 1. 自用, D.M., xxxviii. 5. A., I. v.; xii. 1: VII. x.: XIII. iv. 3: *et al.* 焉用, why use?=of what use is? A., V. iv. 2: XII. xix.: XVI. i. 6: XVII. iv. 2. (2) 是用=是以, thereby. A., V. xxii.

甯 *ning* A surname. A., V. xx.

THE 102d RADICAL. 田.

由 *yew* yu (1) From, proceeding from. A., XII. i. 1. 所由, motives. A., II. x. 2. =by, to proceed by, to follow. A., I. xii. 1: VI. xii.; xv.: VIII. ix.: IX. x. 3. (2) The name of Tsze-loo, one of Conf. disciples. A., II. xvii.: V. vi.; vii.: *et al, sæpe.* 仲由. A., VI. vi.: VI. xxiii.; XVIII. vi. 3.

申 *shin* shên (1) To repeat. D.M., xvii. 4. (2) 申申如, easy-like. A., VII. iv. (3) A surname. A., V. x.

甲 *keă* chia 太甲, the name of a Book in the Shoo-king. G.L.c., i. 2.

畏 *wei* To respect. A., IX. xxii. 畏敬, G.L.c., viii. 1. To reverence. D.M. xx. 13. To stand in awe of. A., XVI. viii. 1, 2: XX. ii. 2. To be put in fear. A., IX. v.: XI. xxii.

畔 *pwan* pan To transgress what is right. A., VI. xxv.: XII. xv. To rebel. A., XVII. v.; vii. 2.

畜 *ch'euh* ch'u To breed, nourish. G.L.c., x. 21. A., X. xiii. 1.

畝 *mow* mou A name. A., XIV. xxxiv.

畫 *hwă* hua To mark off by a line, to limit one's-self. A., VI. x.

異 *e* i (1) Different (follow. by 乎 and 於). A., I. x. 2: XI. xxv. 7: XII. x. 3: *et al.* =Other. A., XVI. xiv. (2) Strange, extraordinary. A., II. xvi.: XI. xxiii. 2.

當 *tang* (1) To undertake, sustain. A., XV. xxxv. (2) As a preposition, in, in regard to. A., X. vi. 3: XIX. xii.

畿 *ke* chi The imperial domains. G.L.c., iii. 1.

疆 *keang* chiang A boundary, a limit. 無疆, boundless. D.M., xxvi. 5.

THE 103d RADICAL. 疋.

疏 *soo* shu (1) Distance—in feeling. A., IV. xxvi. (2) Coarse. A., VII. xv.: X. viii. 10: XIV. x. 3.

疑 *e* i To doubt, doubtful points. D.M., xxix. 3, 4. A., II. xviii. 2: XII. xx. 6: XVI. x.

THE 104th RADICAL. 疒.

疚 *kew* chiu A chronic illness; spoken of the mind, dolorous, dissatisfied. D.M., xx. 16; xxxiii. 2. A., XII. iv. 2.

疾 *tseih* chi (1) Sickness, to be sick, ill. A., II. vi.: VI. viii.: VIII. iii.; iv.: X. xiii. 3: XVII. xx. Spoken of conduct. A., XVII. xvi. 疾病. A., VII. xxxiv.: *et al.* (2) To dislike. A., VIII. x.: XIV. xxxiv. 2: XV. xix.: XVI i. 9. 媢疾, to be jealous. G.L.c., x. 13. (3) Actively, hastily. G.L.c., x. 18. A., X. xvii. 2.

病 *ping* (1) Severe sickness. To become sick. A., IX. xi. 2; XV. i. 2. 疾病, A., VII. xxxiv.: IX. xi. 1. (2) To be solicitous about, distressed about. A., VI. xxviii. 1: XIV. xlv.: XV. xviii.

THE 105th RADICAL. 癶.

登 *tăng* têng To ascend. D.M., xv. 1.

發 *fă* fa To send forth, =to produce. D.M., xxvii. 2. Passive, to be put, to go, forth. D.M., i. 4. Impulsive. D.M., xxxi. 1. So, 發憤, A., VII. xviii. 2. =To help out. A., VII. viii. =To set forth, to illustrate. A., II. ix. To make illustrious. G.L.c., x. 20. To increase. G. L.c., x. 20.

THE 106th RADICAL. 白.

白 *pih* pai White. A., XI. v.: XVII. vii. 3. =naked, applied to weapons. D.M., ix.

百 *pih* pai A hundred. D.M., xxvii. 3; xxix. 3, 4. A., II. ii.: *et al.* =all, used as a round number for the whole of a class. 百工, D.M., xx. 12, 13. A., XIX. vii. 百辟, D.M., xxxiii. 5. 百世, A.,

THE 110TH RADICAL. 矛.

矜 *king* ching To show compassion to. D.M., xx. 14. A., XIX. iii. 哀矜, G.L.c., viii. 1. A., XIX. xix. (2) Dignified, stern dignity. A., XV. xxi.: XVII. xvi. 2.

THE 111TH RADICAL. 矢.

矢 *she* shih (1) An arrow. A., XV. vi. (2) 矢之, to swear, protest. A., VI. xxvi.

矣 *e* i A final particle, found *passim*. It gives definiteness and decision to statements, and is peculiarly appropriate to a terse, conversational style. Where the last clause of a sentence or paragraph commences with 則, 斯, or 亦, the final character is nearly always 矣. It is used also after 已, and 而已, and before the particles of exclamation,—夫, 乎, and 哉.

知 *che* chih To know, to understand. *Passim.* Sometimes=to acknowledge, *i.e.*, to know and approve or employ. A., I. i. 3: IV. xiv.: VIII. xvi.: XI. xxv. 3: *et al, sæpe.* =knowledge. D.M.T., 4, 5.

知 *che* chih Up. 2d tone, used for 智. Wisdom, wise, to be wise. D.M., iv.; vi.; vii.; xx. 8, 10; xxv. 3; xxxi. 1; xxxii. 3. A., IV. i.; ii.: V. xvii.; xx.: XVII. i. 2; iii.; viii. 3; xxiv. 2; xxv. 2: *et al.*

矩 *keu* chü The instrument the square; used metaphorically. G.L.c., x. 1, 2. A., II. iv. 6.

短 *twan* tuan Short. A., VI. ii.: X. vi. 5: XI. vi.

矧 *chin* chên How much more (or less). D.M., xvi. 4.

矯 *keaou* chiao Bold, firm. D.M., x. 5.

THE 112TH RADICAL. 石.

石 *shih* (1) A stone, a rock. D.M., xxvi. G. L.c., x. 4. (2) 石門, the name of a place. A., XIV. xli.

破 *po* To split open. D.M., xii. 2.

硜 *k'ang* k'êng 硜硜, the appearance of a worthless man; with 然, stupid-like. A., XIII. xx. 3: XIV. xlii. 2.

磋 *ts'o* To file, or plane; to polish. G.L.c., iii. 4. A., I. xv. 2.

碩 *shih* Great,—in size. G.L.c., viii. 2.

磨 *mo* To grind. G.L.c. iii. 4. A., I. xv. 2: XVII. vii. 3.

磷 *lin* A thin stone, to become thin. A., XVII. vii. 3.

磬 *k'ing* ch'ing An instrument of music, a ringing stone. 擊磬, A., XIV. xlii. 1.

THE 113TH RADICAL. 示.

示 *she* shih Used synonymously with 視. D.M., xix. 6. A., III. xi.

祀 *sze* szû To sacrifice to. D.M., xviii. 3; xix. 6. 祀祭, sacrifices. D.M., xvi. 9.

社 *shay* shê The altars of the spirits of the land. A., III. xxi.: XI. xxiv. 3. 社稷之臣, a minister in direct connection with the emperor. A., XVI. i. 4. In D.M., xix. 6, 社 is said to be the place of sacrifice to the Earth.

祇 *ke* ch'i The spirit, or spirits of the earth. A., VII. xxxiv. Read *che*. Just, only. A., XII. x. 3.

祖 *tsoo* tsu 祖述, to hand down as if from his ancestors. D.M., xxx. 1.

神 *shin* shên A spirit, spirits. D.M., xvi. 4; xxiv. 1. A., III. xii. 1. 鬼神, spiritual beings, spirits. D.M., xvi. 1; xxix. 3, 4. A., VI. xx: VIII. xxi: XI. xi. 上下神祇, the spirits of the upper and lower worlds, A., VII. xxxiv.

祥 *ts'eang* ch'iang 禎祥, happy omens. D.M., xxiv.

祝 *chuh* chu 祝鮀,=the priest T'o. A., VI. xiv.: XIV. xx. 2.

祭 *tse* chi To sacrifice, to sacrifice to, offered in sacrifice. D.M., xiii. 3. A., II. v. 3; xxiv. 1: III. xiii. 1: X. viii. 8, 10; xiii. 2; xv. 3: XII. i: XIX. 1. A sacrifice, sacrifices. A., III. xii. 1: XX. i. 8. 祭祀, D.M., xvi. 3.

祿 *luh* lu Emolument, revenue. D.M., ix; xvii. 2, 4; xx. 14. A., II. xviii. 1, 2: XV. xxxi: XVI. iii; xx. i. 1.

禍 *ho* huo Calamity, unhappiness. D.M., xxiv.

THE 117TH RADICAL. 立.

立 *lih* li (1) To stand. D.M., x. 5. A., V. vii. 4: X. iii. 2; iv. 2; x. 2; xvii. 1: *et al.* (2) To establish; to be established. D.M., xx. 13, 16; xxxii. 1. A., I. ii. 2: II. iv. 2: IV. xiv.: VII. xxviii. 2: XIX. xxv. 4: *et al.*

章 *chang* (1) To display, be displayed. D.M., xx. 6; xxxi.; xxxiii. 1. (2) 文章, elegant ways and manifestations. A., V. xii.: VIII. xix. 成章, complete and accomplished. A., V. xxi. (3) 章甫, name of a cap of ceremony. A., XI. xxv. 6.

童 *t'ung* 童子, a youth, a lad. A., VII. xxviii. 1: XI. xxv. 7: XIV. xlvii. 1.

竭 *këë* chieh To exert to the utmost. A., I. vii.: IX. x. 3. To exhaust. A., IX. vii.

端 *twan* tuan (1) A beginning or end, extremities. D.M., vi. A., IX. vii. 造端, to make a beginning. D.M. xii. 4. (2) Doctrines. A., II. xvi. (3) The name of a robe of ceremony. A., XI. xxv. 6.

THE 118TH RADICAL. 竹.

笑 *seaou* hsiao To smile, to laugh. A., III. viii. 1: XIV. xiv. 1, 2: XVII. iv. 2.

等 *tăng* têng (1) A class; degrees. D.M., xx. 5. (2) A step of a stair. A., X. iv. 5.

答 *tă* ta To reply. A., XIV. iv.

策 *ts'ih* ts'ê (1) A tablet of bamboo. D.M., xx. 2. (2) To whip. A., VI. xiii.

筲 *shaou* shao A bamboo vessel. 斗筲之人, men who are mere utensils. A., XIII. xx. 4.

筭 *swan* hsüan To reckon, take into account. A., XIII. xx. 4.

節 *tsëë* chieh (1) A division, what is regularly defined. D.M., i. 4. A., XVIII. vii. 5. (2) An emergency, a decisive time. A., VIII. vi. (3) To regulate. A., I. ii. 2. =to economize. A., I. v. To discriminate. A., XVI. v. (4) The capitals of pillars. A., V. xvii.

管 *kwan* kuan A surname. 管氏, A., III. xxii. 2, 3. 管仲, A., III. xxii. 1, 2, 3: XIV. x. 3; xvii. 1, 2; xviii. 2, 3.

箕 *ke* chi The name of a State. A., XVIII. i. 1.

篤 *tŭh* tu Liberal. D.M. xvii. 3. Firm and sincere; firmly and sincerely. D.M., xx. 19, 20; xxxiii. 6. A., VIII. xiii. 1: XI. xx.: XV. v. 2: XIX. ii.; vi.

簞 *tan* A small round bamboo basket. A., VI. ix. What is said of it there, in the note, is wrong.

簣 *kwei* kuei A basket for carrying earth. A., IX. xviii.

簡 *këen* chien (1) Hasty. A., V. xxi. (2) An easy negligence. A., VI. i. 2, 3. D.M., xxxiii. 1. (3) To examine. A., XX. i. 3.

籩 *pëen* pien A sacrificial vessel, for holding fruits and seeds. A., VIII. iv. 2.

THE 119TH RADICAL. 米.

粟 *suh* hsü Rice in the husk. A., VI. iii. 1, 3. =revenue. A., XII. xi. 3.

精 *tsing* ching (1) Rice finely cleaned. A., X. viii. 1. (2) Minute, exact. D.M., xxvii. 6.

糞 *fun* fên Excrement.=dirty. A., V. ix. 1.

糧 *leang* liang Provisions. A., XV. i. 2.

THE 120TH RADICAL. 糸.

糾 *kew* chiu A name. A., XIV. xvii. 1; xviii. 1.

約 *yŏ* yo (1) To bind, to restrain. A., VI. xxv.: IX. x. 2: XII. xv. 以約, to use restraint, be cautious. A., IV. xxii. (2) Straitened. A., VII. xxv. 3. =Poverty, straitened circumstances. A., IV. ii.

紅 *hung* Red. A., X. vi. 2.

紂 *chow* chou Epithet of the last emperor of the Shang dynasty. A., XIV. xx. 桀紂, G.L. c., ix. 10.

純 *shun* ch'un (1) Silken, made of silk. A., IX. iii. 1. (2) Harmonious. A., III. xxiii. (3) Singleness. D.M., xxvi. 10.

納 *nă* na To make to enter. D.M., vii. To present. A., XX. ii. 3.

縕 *wan* wên — Up. 2d tone. Quilted with hemp. A., IX. xxvi. 1.

繼 *ke* che — To connect, continue. D.M., xix. 2; xx. 14. A., II. xxiii. 2: XX. i. 7. 繼富, to make the rich more rich. A., VI. iii. 2.

纘 *tswan* tsuan — To continue. D.M., xviii. 2.

THE 121st RADICAL. 缶.

缺 *keuě* chüeh — A name. A., XVIII, ix. 2.

THE 122d RADICAL. 网.

罔 *wang* — Labour lost. A., II. xv. To lose, be without. A., VI. xvii. To be entrapt, befooled. A., VI. xxiv.

罕 *han* — Seldom. A., IX. i

罟 *koo* ku — A net, for catching fish. D.M., vii.

罪 *tsuy* tsui — A crime; offence. A., V. i. 1: XX. i. 3. 獲罪, to offend against. A., III. xiii. 2.

罰 *fă* fa — To punish. 刑罰, punishments; as distinguished, 罰 is a fine. A., XIII. iii. 6.

罷 *pa* — To cease; to give over. A., IX. x. 3.

THE 123d RADICAL. 羊.

羊 *yang* — A sheep, or goat. G.L.c., x. 22. A., III. xvii. 1, 2: XII. viii. 3: XIII. xviii.

美 *mei* — Goodness, excellence, beauty, excellent quality. G.L.c., viii. 1. A., I. xii. 1: IV. i.: VI. xiv.: VIII. xi.; xxi.: XII. xvi.: XIII. viii.: XIX. xxiii. 3. 五美, the five excellent qualities of government. A., XX. ii. 1. Beautiful, elegant. A., III. viii.; xxv.: IX. xii.

羔 *kaou* kao — (1) A lamb, or kid. A., X. vi. 4, 11. (2) 子羔, the designation of one of Conf. disciples. A., XI. xxiv.

羞 *sow* sou — Shame, disgrace. A., XIII. xxii. 2.

羣 *keun* ch'ün — (1) A flock,=a class; all of a class. D. M., xx. 12, 13. A., XV. xvi.: XVIII. vi. 4. (2) Sociable, to be sociable. A., XV. xxi.: XVII. ix. 4.

義 *e* i — (1) What is right, righteousness. G.L. c., x. 22, 23. D.M., xx. 5. A., I. xiii.: II. xxiv. 2: *et passim*. (2) Meaning. D. M., xix. 6.

羹 *kăng* kêng — Soup. A., X. viii. 4.

THE 124th RADICAL. 羽.

羽 *yu* yü — A surname. A., XIV. ix.

羿 *e* i — A famous archer of antiquity. A., XIV. vi.

習 *seih* hsi — To practise. A., I. i. 1; iv. By practice. A., XVII. ii.

翔 *ts'eang* ch'iang — To fly round, or backwards and forwards. A., X. xviii. 1.

翕 *heih* hsi — To be united, in concord. D.M., xv. 2. 翕如, applied to music. A., III. xxiii.

翼 *yih* yi — Wings. 翼如, wing-like. A. X iii. 3; iv. 5.

THE 125th RADICAL. 老.

老 *laou* lao — (1) Old, to be old; the old. G.L.c. x., 1. A., V. xxv. 4: XIII. iv. 1: XIV. xlvi.: XVI. vii.: XVIII. iii. Old age. A., VII. xviii. 2. To treat as old. G.L.c., x. 1. (2) A chief officer. A., XIV. xii.

考 *k'aou* k'ao — To examine. D.M., xxix. 3. To examine and determine. D.M., xxviii. 2.

者 *chay* chê — (1) He (or they) who; this (or that), these (or those), who (or which). It is put after the words (verbs, adjectives, nouns), and clauses to which it belongs. G.L.t., 4: c., x. 4, 9, 18, 19. 21, 23. A., XIX. iii.; iv.; xii. 2; xxii. 2: *et passim*. (2) It stands at the end of the first member of a clause or sentence, when the next gives a description or explanation of the subject of the other, terminated generally by the particle 也, but not always. G.L.c., vi. 1; vii. 1; ix. 1; x. 7. D.M., xix. 2; xxv. 1, 2. 3. A., XII. xvi. *et al., sæpe*. (3) 也者 together, at the end of the first member of a sentence, resume a previous word, and lead on to an explanation or account of it. D.M., i. 2, 4; xx. 3. A., XII. xx. 5, 6. The case in A., XI. xxv. 10, is different. (4) 者也, often occurs at the end of sentences, preceded, tho' sometimes not, by 者. G.L.c., ix. 2; x. 20. D.M., xxix. 6. A.,

XVIII. vii. 4: XIX. xvii.: *et al., sæpe.*— In all these cases the proper meaning of 者, as in case (1) is apparent. But (5) we find it where that can hardly be traced, and where sometimes we might translate it by *one* or *that*, and at other times by *so*, *such a thing*, with a ——. but there are cases where it cannot be translated. G.L.T., 7: c., ix. 4. A., VI. ii.: xii.: XI. vi.: XII. viii. 2, 3: XVI. i. 5; xiii. 4: XVII. vi.: XIX. xxv. 4. (6) It forms adverbs with 昔 and 古. A., XVII. vii. 2: xvi.: *et al.* Observe A., IX. xvi.: III. x.

THE 126TH RADICAL. 而.

而 *urh* *Passim.* A conjunction. (1) And. G. L.T., 2, 5: c., ix. 2, 4, 6, 7, 8. D.M., i. 4; ii. 2; xx. 6, 9, 14, 17. A., I. i. 1; ii. 2; iv.; v.; vi.; vii.: xii. 2: *et al., sæpissime.* (2) And yet. G.L.T., 7: c., iii. 2; vii. 2; x. 13, 14. D.M., xxxiii. 1, 3, 4: *et al. sæpissime.* The 'and yet' is often nearly, or altogether, =but. A., II. xiv: VII. xxvi.: XIII. xxv.; xxvi.: *et al., sæpe.* It may often be translated by if. A., III. xxii 3: VII. xi.; xxv. 1, 2; xxx. 2; xxxi.: *et al.* (3) It is used idiomatically, or for the rhythm, after adverbs. A., XI. xxv. 4: XIV. xx. 1; xlii. 2: XVII. iv. 2: *et al.* 然而. A., XIX. xv. 1. (4) After 得 and before a verb, it forms the passive of that verb. A., VIII. i.: XIX. xxiv.; xxv. 3: *et al.* (5) =or. A., XII. i. 1. (6) 而今而後, henceforth, both now and hereafter. A., VI. iii. (7) It is often followed by 已, 已也, 已矣. D.M., xxv. 3. A., II. xv. 2: XIV. xlv.: *et al.* (8) Used for 汝, you, D.M., ix. 2. (9) A., IX. xxx. 1, a mere expletive. 已而已而. A., XVIII. v. 1.

THE 127TH RADICAL. 耒.

耕 *kăng* kêng To plough; to do field-work. A., XV. xxxi.: XVIII. vi. 1.

耦 *gow* ou Two together. A., XVIII. vi. 1.

耰 *yew* yu To cover the seed. A., XVIII. vi. 3.

THE 128TH RADICAL. 耳.

耳 *urh* (1) The ear. A., II. iv. 5: VIII. xv. (2) A final particle, =simply. A., XVII. iv. 4. (3) An expletive. A., VI. xii.

耽 *tan* Yielding pleasure. D.M., xv. 2.

聘 *p'ing* The sending of envoys to one another, or to court, by the princes of the empire. D.M., xx. 14.

聖 *shing* shêng Intelligent, perspicacious. G.L.c., x. 11. D.M., xxxii. 3. Sage, possessing the highest knowledge and excellence. 聖者, a sage. D.M., xi. 3; xxxi. 1. A., VI. xxviii. 1: VII. xxxiii.: IX. vi. 1, 2.

聚 *tseu* chü To collect, be collected. G.L.c., x. 9. 聚斂, to collect imposts. G.L.c., x. 22. A., XI. xvi. 1.

聞 *wăn* wên To hear; to become acquainted with by report. *Passim.* 聽而不聞, to hear and not understand. G.L.c., vii. 2. D.M., xvi. 2.

聞 *wăn* wên Low. 3d tone. To be heard of, notoriety. A., XII. xx. 3, 4, 6.

聰 *ts'ung* Quick in apprehension. D.M., xxxi. 1; xxxii. 3. To hear distinctly. A., XVI. x.

聲 *shing* shêng A sound. D.M., xxxiii. 6. A, XVII. iv. 1. =Songs. A., XV. x. 6: XVII. xviii. 聲名, fame. D.M., xxxi. 4.

聽 *t'ing* To hear, to listen to. G.L.c., iv.: vii. 2. D.M., xvi. 2. A., V. ix. 2: XII. i. 2; xiii.: XVI. x.: XVII. xiv. 聽於, to receive instructions from. A., XIV. xliii. 2.

THE 129TH RADICAL. 聿.

肆 *sze* szû (1) To expose a corpse. A., XIV. xxxviii. 1. (2) Unrestrained, a disregard of smaller matters. A., XVII. xvi. 2. (3). A shop, a stall for goods. A., XIX. vii.

THE 130TH RADICAL. 肉.

肉 *juh* jou Flesh, meat. A., VII. xiii.: X. viii. 2, 4, 8; xv. 2.

肖 *seaou* hsiao 不肖, not equal to, degenerate, worthless. D.M., iv.; xii. 2.

肝 *kan* The liver. 其肺肝, his lungs and liver, =his inward thoughts. G.L.c., vi. 2.

肸 *heih* hsi A name. A., XVII. vii. 1, 2.

肺 *fei* The lungs. See above.

THE 131st RADICAL. 臣.

THE 132d RADICAL. 自.

THE 133d RADICAL. 至.

A., XIX. xvii. To be carried to perfection. A., XIX. xiv. Observe 致期. A., XX. ii. 3. (2) 致身, 致命, to devote one's person, life. A., I. vii.: XIX. i.

臺 t'ae t'ai 澹臺, a surname. A., VI. xii.

THE 134TH RADICAL. 臼.

臾 yu yü (1) 須臾, an instant. D.M., i. 2. (2) 顓臾, the name of a small State. A., XVI. i.

與 yu yü Low. 2d tone. (1) With, along with; to be with, to associate with. G.L.c., iii. 3; x. 15. D.M., xxii. 1; xxiii. A., I. iv.; vii.; xv. 3: *et passim.* (2) And. A., IX. i; ix.: XI. xxiii. 2, 4, 6: *et al.* Sometimes it must be translated by *or*. A., XI. xv.: *et al.* (3) Followed by 寧, and by 豈不, than. G.L.c., x. 22. A., IV. iv. 3; xiii. 1: VII. xxxv.: IX. xi. 3.: XVIII. vi. 3. (4) To give to. A., I. x. 1: V. xxiii.: VI. iii. 1, 3, 4. XX. ii. 3. (5) To grant, concede to, allow. A., V. viii. 3: VII. xxviii. 2: XI. xxv. 7. (6) To wait for. A., XVII. i. 2, 歲不我與. (7) Observe 與比, A., IV. x.; 巽與之言; A., IX. xxiii., 丘不與易, A., XVIII. vi. 4.

與 yu yü (1) Low. 1st tone. A final particle, sometimes interogative, sometimes of admiration, and sometimes of doubt or hesitancy. As interrogative, it generally implies that the answer will be in the affirmative. As indicating doubt or hesitancy, we find it preceded by other final particles. It is followed also by other particles of exclamation. D.M., vi.; x. 2; xvii. 1; xxvii. 7. A., I ii. 2; x. 1, 2; xv. 2: *et al., passim.* Observe A., V. ix. 1, 2: XII. xxviii. 2. (2) 與與, the appearance of dignity and satisfaction. A., X. ii. 2.

與 yu yü Low. 3d tone. Sharing in: concerned with. D.M., xii. 2. A., III. xii. 2: VIII. xviii.: IX. v. 3: XIII. xiv.

興 hing hsing (1) To rise. A., XV. i. 2. =to become. G.L.c., ix. 3; x. 1. So, followed by 於. A., VIII. ii. 2. To be produced. D.M., xxvi. 9. To be aroused, stimulated. A., VIII. viii. 1: XVII. ix. 2. (2) To flourish. D.M., xxiv. A., XIII. iii. 6. To make to flourish; to raise. D.M., xxvii. 7. A., XIII. xv. 1, 3: XX. i. 7.

舉 keu chü (1) To raise; employ, promote. G.L.c., x. 1. D.M., xx. 14. A., II. xix.; xx.: XII. xxii. 3, 4, 6: XIII. ii. 1, 2: XV. xxii.: XX. i. 7. To present: set forth (in discourse). A., VII viii Passive, to be established. D.M., xx. 2. (2) To rise. A., X. xviii. 1.

舊 kew chiu Old G.L.c., ii. 3. A., V. xviii. 1; xxii.: XI. xiii. 2: XVII. xxi. 3. 故舊, =old friends or ministers. A., VIII. ii. 2: XVIII. x. 舊犯, see 犯.

THE 135TH RADICAL. 舌.

舌 shě shê The tongue. A., XII. viii. 2.

舍 shay shê Up. 2d tone, for 捨. (1) To reject. A., VI. iv. To neglect. A., XIII. ii. 2. To leave unemployed. A., VII. x. To lay aside. A., XI. xxv. 7. To omit: decline. A., XVI. i. 9. (2) To cease; give over. A., IX. xvi.

舒 shoo shu =economy. G.L.c., x. 19.

THE 136TH RADICAL. 舛.

舜 shun An ancient emperor. D.M., vi.: xvii. 1. A., VIII. xviii.: *et al.* 堯舜, G.L.c., ix. 4. D.M., xxxi. 1. A., VII. xxviii: XVI. xlv.

舞 woo wu (1) Pantomimes. A., III. i.: XV. x. 5. (2) 舞雩, =the rain altars. A., XI. xxv. 7: XII. xxi. 1.

THE 137TH RADICAL. 舟.

舟 chow chou A ship, a boat. D.M., xxxi. 4. A., XIV. vi.

THE 139TH RADICAL. 色.

色 shih shê (1) Colour, appearance, especially as variously seen in the countenance; the countenance. G.L.c., vi. 1. D.M., xxxiii. 6. A., I. iii.: II. viii.: V. xviii.: *et al. sæpe.* 顏色, A., VIII. iv. 3: X. v. 2: XVI. vi. 潤色, to give the proper finish. (2) Beauty, and the desire for its enjoyment. D.M., xx. 14. A., I. vii.: IX. xvii.: XV. xii.: XVI. vii.

THE 140TH RADICAL. 艸.

芸 yun yün In some copies for 耘. To weed. A., XVIII. vii. 1.

索引

索引

THE 145TH RADICAL. 衣.

衣 *e* i — Clothes, a garment. D.M., xviii. 2. A., IV. ix.: X. iii. 2; vi. 4, 6; vii. 1: xxii. 2. 衣服, A., VIII. xxi. 裳衣, where 裳 denotes the clothes for the lower part of the body. D.M., xix. 3. A., IX. ix.

衣 *e* i — Up. 3d tone. To wear. A., V. xxv. 2: VI. iii. 2: IX. xxvi.: XVII. xxi. 4

哀 *gae* ai — Honorary epithet of a duke of Loo. D. M., xx. A., II. xix.: *et al.*

衽 *jin* jên — Also written 袵. (1) The lappel in front of a coat, buttoning on the right breast. A., XIV. xviii. 2. (2) To sleep on, make a mat of. D.M., x. 4.

表 *peaou* piao — To wear outside. A., X. vi. 3.

衰 *shwae* shuai — To decay, decline. A., VII. v.: XVI. vii.: XVIII. v.

衰 *ts'uy* ts'ui — Mourning clothes, with the edges either unhemmed (齊衰), or frayed (斬衰). A., IX. ix.: X. xvi. 5.

袂 *me* mi — Sleeves. A., X. vi. 5.

被 *p'e* p'ei — 被髮, dishevelled hair. A., XIV. xviii. 2.

袍 *p'aou* p'ao — A robe. A., IX. xxvi.

裁 *ts'ae* ts'ai — To cut and shape clothes;—used metaphorically. A., V. xxi.

裕 *yu* yü — Generous. D.M., xxxi. 1.

裘 *k'ew* ch'iu — Fur garments. A., V. xxv. 2: VI. iii. 2: X. vi. 4, 5, 10.

裳 *shang* shang — The lower garments. 裳衣, A, IX. ix.: X. vi. 9.

襁 *k'eang* ch'iang — A cloth in which infants are strapt to the back. 襁負, to carry on the back. A., XIII. iv. 3.

褻 *see* hsieh — Undress. A., X. vi. 2, 5; xvi. 2.

襄 *seang* hsiang — A name. A., XVIII. ix. 5.

襜 *chen* — 襜如, evenly adjusted. A., X iii. 2.

襲 *shih* hsi — To follow, accord with. D.M., xxx. 1.

THE 146TH RADICAL. 西.

西 *se* hsi — 公西, a double surname. A., VII. xxxiii.: XI. xxi.; xxv.

要 *yaou* yao — (1) An agreement. A., XIV. xxiii. 2. (2) To force. A., XIV. xv.

覆 *fuh* fu — To overthrow. D.M., xvii. 3. A., XVII. xviii. To throw down, as earth on the ground. A., IX. xviii.

覆 *fow* fou — Low. 3d tone. To overspread, cover. D.M., xxvi. 4, 9; xxx. 2; xxxi. 4.

THE 147TH RADICAL. 見.

見 *keen* chien — To see. *Passim.* 視而不見 to see and not perceive. G.L.c., vii. 2. D. M., xvi. 2. Before other verbs, forming the passive voice. D.M., xi. 3. A., XVII. xxvi.

見 *heen* hsien — (1) To be manifest. D.M., i. 3; xxiv.; xxvi. 6; xxxi. 3. A., VIII. xiii. 2: XV. i. 3. (2) To have an interview; to introduce. A., III. xxiv.: VII. xxviii. 1. XV. xli.: XVI. i. 2: XVIII. vii. 3.

視 *she* shih — To observe, to look at. G.L.c., vi. 2, 3. D.M., xiii. 2. A., II. x. 1: XII. i. 2: XVI. x. 視而不見, G.L.c., vii. 2 D.M., xvi. 2. 尊其瞻視, to throw a dignity into his looks. A., XX. i. 2. To visit to see. A., X. xiii. 3. To regard, look upon. A., XI. x. 3. To require, look for. A., XX. ii. 3.

親 *ts'in* ch'in — (1) To love, show affection to. G.L.c., iii. 5. D.M., xix. 5; xx. 5, 13, 14; xxxi. 4. (2) To approach to, seek to be intimate with. A., I. vi.; xiii, 其親 = proper persons to be intimate with. (3) Personal, one's-self. A., XVII. vii. 不親指, did not use his fingers. A., X. xvii. 2. (4) Relatives. D.M., xx. 5, 13, 14. A., VIII. ii. 2: XVIII. x.: XX. i. 5. (5) Parents, a parent. G.L.c., x. 13. D. M., xx. 7, 17. A., XII. xxi. 3: XIX. xvii. (6) Said to be used for 新. G.L.T., i.

覿 *teih* ti — To have an interview and audience. A., X. v. 3.

觀 *kwan* kuan To look at; to mark. A., I. xi.: II. x. 2: III. x.; xxvi.: IV. vii.: V. ix. 2: VIII. xi.: XII. xx. 5: XIX. iv. 詩可以觀, the odes may be used for purposes of self-contemplation. A., XVII. ix. 3.

覺 *keŏ* chio To apprehend. 先覺者, one who is of quick apprehension.

THE 148TH RADICAL. 角.

角 *keŏ* chio A horn; horned. A. VI. iv.

觚 *koo* ku A drinking vessel, made with corners. A., VI. xxiii.

THE 149TH RADICAL. 言

言 *yen* (1) A word, words; a saying, a sentence. G.L.c., ix. 3; x. 9. D.M., vi.; xiii. 4; xx. 6; xxvi. 7; xxvii. 7: xxxiii. 4. A., I. iii.; xiii.; xiv.: II. ii.; xiii.: *et al., passim.* To speak; to speak of; to tell. D.M., xxix. 5; xxxi. 3; xxxiii. 3. A., I. vii.; xv. 3: II. ix.; xviii. 2.: *et al., passim.* =meaning. D.M., xii. 3. (2) The surname of 子游, one of Conf. disciples. A., XIV. xii. 2.

訐 *keë* chieh To expose people's secrets. A., XVII. xxiv. 2.

討 *t'aou* t'ao (1) To punish. A., XIV. xxii. 2. (2) 討論, to examine and discuss. A., XIV. ix.

訒 *jin* jên Words spoken slowly and cautiously. A., XII. iii. 2, 3.

訕 *shan* To rail at, slander A., XVII. xxiv.

託 *tŏ* t'o To entrust, be entrusted, with. A., VIII. vi.

訟 *sung* Litigations. G.L.c., iv. A., XII. xiii. =to accuse. A., V. xxvi.

訥 *nuh* nü Slow in speaking. A., IV. xxiv. Modest. A., XIII. xxvii.

設 *shĕ* shê To set forth, display. D.M., xix. 3.

詐 *cha* Deceitful. A., IX. xi. 2. Deceit. A., XVII. xvi. 2. Deception, attempts to deceive. A., XIV. xxxiii.

詠 *yung* To sing. A., XI. xxv. 7.

試 *she* shih (1) To try, examine. D.M., xx. 14. A., XV. xxiv (2) To be used, have official employment. A., IX. vi. 4.

誄 *luy* lei A collection of Prayers of Eulogy. A., VII. xxxiv.

誅 *choo* chu To reprove. A., V. ix. 1.

詩 *she* shih The Book of Poetry; the pieces in the B. of P. A., I. xv. 3: II. ii.: III. viii. 3: VII. xvii.: VIII. viii. 1: XIII. v.: XVI. xiii. 2, 5: XVII. ix. 1, 2. 詩曰, 詩云, *sæpe.*

語 *yü* yü To speak; to speak of. D.M., xii. 2. A., VII. xx.: X. viii. 9. Words, sayings. A., IX. xxiii.: XII. i. 2; ii.: XVI. xi. 1, 2.

語 *yu* yü Low. 3d tone. To speak to; to tell. A., III. xxiii.: VI. xix: IX. xix.: XIII. xviii. 1: XVII. viii. 2: XIX. xxiii.

誠 *shing* ch'êng To make, be made, sincere; sincerely. G.L.T., 4, 5: c., vi. 1, 2, 4. In the Doctrine of the Mean, the term has a mystical significance. D.M., xvi. 5; xx. 17, 18; xxi.; xxii.: xxiii.; xxiv.; xxv. 1, 2, 3; xxvi. 1; xxxii. 1. Really, sincerely. G. L.c., ix. 2 A., XII. x. 3. True. A., XIII. xi.

誦 *sung* To repeat; hum over. A., IX. xxvi. 3. XIII. v.

說 *shwŏ* shuo (1) To speak of; the speaking (what is said). D.M., xxviii. 5. A., III. xxi 2: XII. viii. 2: XVII. xiv. (2) Meaning. A., III. xi,

說 *yüe* yüeh For 悅. To be pleased; pleased with; a matter of pleasure. D.M., xxxi. 3. A., I. i. 1: V. v.: VI. x.; xxvi.: IX. xxiii.: XI iii.: XIII. xvi. 2; xxv.: XVII. v. 2.

誥 *kaou* kao To enjoin upon; instructions. 康誥, the name of a Book in the Shoo-king. G.L.c., i. 1; ii. 2; ix. 2; x. 10.

誨 *hwuy* hui To instruct; teach. A., II. xvii.: VII. ii.; vii.; xxxiii.: XIV. viii.

誓 *she* shih To declare solemnly; an oath. 泰誓, the name of a Book in the Shoo-king. G.L.c., x. 14.

誰 *shwuy* shui Who, whom. A., VI. xv.: VII. x. 2; IX. xi. 2: XI. ix. 3: XV. xxiv.: XVI. i. 7: XVIII. vi. 2, 3, 4: XX. ii. 2.

誾 *yin* ên The appearance of being bland, yet precise. A., X. ii. 2: XI. xii.

諂 *chen* chan To flatter: flattering. A., I. xv. 1: II. xxiv.: III. xviii.

索引

讒 *ch'an* Slander, =slanderers. D.M., xx. 14.

THE 151ST RADICAL. 豆.

豆 *tow* tou A wooden vessel, in common use, and at sacrifices. 籩豆, A., VIII. iv. 3. 俎豆, A., XV. i. 1.

豈 *k'e* ch'i How. A. VII. xxxiii.: IX. xxx.: XIV. xiv. 2; xviii. 3. Followed by 哉, 也哉, and 乎. A., XVII. v. 3; vii. 4: XVIII. vi. 3: XIX. xxv.

THE 152D RADICAL. 豕.

豚 *t'un* A small pig. G.L.c., x. 22. A., XVII. i. 1.

豫 *yu* yü Preparation beforehand. D.M., xx. 16.

THE 153D RADICAL. 豸.

豹 *p'aou* p'ao A leopard. A., XII. viii. 3.

貊 *mih* mai The barbarous tribes of the north. 蠻貊. D.M., xxxi. 4. A., XV. v. 2.

貌 *maou* mao Aspect, demeanour. A., VIII. iv. 3: XVI. x. 以貌, to use a ceremonious manner. A., X. xvi. 2.

貉 *hŏh* hsio The badger, =badger's fur. A., IX. xxvi.: X. vi. 7.

THE 154TH RADICAL. 貝.

貞 *ching* chên Correct and firm. A., XV. xxxvi.

負 *foo* fu To carry on the back. A., X. xvi. 3: XIII. iv. 3.

財 *ts'ae* ts'ai Wealth. G.L.c., x. 6, 7, 9, 20, 21, 23. 財用, means of expenditure. D.M., xx. 13. =sources of wealth. D.M., xxvi. 9.

貢 *kung* 子貢, one of Confucius' disciples. A., I. x. 1, 2; xv. 1, 2: II. xiii.: *et al., sæpe.*

貧 *p'in* Poor, being in a poor condition; poverty. D.M., xiv. 2. A. I. xv. 1: IV. v. 1: VIII. x.: xiii. 3: XIV. xi.: XV. xxxi.: XVI. i. 10.

貨 *ho* huo Goods. G.L.c., x. 10. A., XI. xviii. 2. Riches D.M., xx. 14. Articles of value. D.M., xxvi. 9.

貪 *t'an* To covet, desire. A., XX. ii. 1, 2. To be ambitious. G.L.c., ix. 3.

貫 *kwan* kuan To go through, pervade. A., IV. xv. 1: XV. ii. 3. It is difficult to assign its meaning in XI. xiii. 2.

貳 *urh* To repeat; repeated. A., VI. ii. 1. 不貳, without doubleness. D.M., xxvi. 7.

責 *tsih* tsê To require from. A., XV. xiv.

貴 *kwei* kuei (1) Noble, being in an honourable condition. Associated with 富, D.M., xiv. 2. A., IV. v. 1: VII. xv.: VIII. xiii. 3: XIV. v. 3. Contrasted with 賤. D.M., xviii. 3; xix. 4. Excellent, valuable. A., I. xii. 1: IX. xxiii. (2) To esteem noble. D.M., xx. 14. A., VIII. iv. 3.

費 *fei* (1) Extended, reaching far and wide. D.M., xii. 1. (2) To expend largely. A., XX. ii. 1, 2.

費 *pe* pi The name of a city. A., VI. vii.: XI. xxiv.: XVI. i. 8: XVII. v.

賊 *tsih* tsei To injure; injury. A., XI. xxiv. 2: XX. ii. 3. An injurious disregard of consequences. A., XVII. viii. 3. A pest. A., XIV. xlvi. Thieves or injurers. A., XVII. xiii.

賞 *shang* To reward. D.M., xxxiii. 4. A., XII. xviii.

賈 *kea* chia A price. A., IX. xii. In up. 2d tone. A name. A., III. xiii.: XIV. xx.—A., XIV. xiv.

賢 *hëen* hsien (1) As an adjective, admirable, virtuous and talented. A., VI. ix.: XIII. ii. 1, 2: *et al.* As a noun, 賢 and 賢者, worthies, men of talents and virtue. G.L.c., x. 16. D.M., iv.; xix. 4; xx. 5, 8, 13, 14. A., I. vii.: IV. xvii.: XV. ix.: *et al., sæpe.* As a verb, to treat as a *hëen.* G.L.c., iii. 5. A., I. vii. (2) To surpass, be better than. A., XI. xv. 1: XVII. xxii.: XIX. xxiii. 1: xxv. 1.

賓 *pin* A guest, a visitor. A., X. iii. 4: XII. ii. 賓客, A., V. vii. 4: XIV. xx. 2.

賜 *ts'ze* tz'ŭ (1) To give; bestow. A., X. xiii. 1. Gifts. A., XIV. xviii. 2. (2) The name of 子貢, one of Conf. disciples. A., I. xv. 3: III. xvii. 2: *et al., sæpe.*

賤 *tseen* chien (1) Mean, in a mean condition. D.M., xix. 4; xxviii. 1. A., IX. vi. 3. Associated with 貧. D.M., xiv. 2; A., IV. v.: VIII. xiii. 3. Contrasted with 貴. D.M., xviii. 3; xix. 4. As a verb, to consider mean. G.L.c., viii. 1. D.M., xx. 14. (2) 子賤, one of Conf. disciples. A., V. ii.

賚 *lae* lai To bestow; gifts. A., XX. i. 4.

賦 *foo* fu =military levies. A., V. vii. 2,

質 *chih* (1) Substantial, solid; substantial qualities. A., XII. xx. 5: VI. xvi.: XII. viii. 1. 3. =essential. A., XV. xvii. (2) To appear, present one's-self, before. D.M., xxix. 3, 4.

贊 *tsan* To assist. D.M, xxii.

THE 155TH RADICAL. 赤.

赤 *ch'ih* (1) 赤子, an infant. G.L.c., ix. 2. (2) The name of Tsze-hwa, one of Conf. disciples. A., V. vii. 4: VI. iii. 2: XI. xxi.; xxv. 6, 11.

赦 *shay* shê To pardon; forgive. A., XIII. ii. 1: XX. i. 3.

赫 *hih* hê 赫兮, how distinguished! G.L,c., iii. 4. 赫赫, greatly distinguished. G.L.c., x. 4.

THE 156TH RADICAL. 走.

起 *k'e* ch'i To assist, bring out one's meaning. A., III. viii. 3.

趙 *chaou* chao A great family of the State of Tsin. A., XV. xii.

趨 *ts'eu* ch'ü To walk quickly. A., IX. ix.: X. iii.; iv. 5. A., XVI. xiii. 2, 3: XVIII. v. 2.

THE 157TH RADICAL. 足

足 *tsuh* tsu (1) The feet. A., VIII. iii.: X. iii. 1: iv. 3; v. 1: XIII. iii. 6. (2) Sufficient, to be sufficient; fit. G.L.c., ix. 8; x. 19. D.M., xiii. 4; xx. 14: xxvii. 7; xxviii. 5: xxxi. 1. A., II. ix.: III. ix.: IV. vi. 2; ix.: *et al., sæpe*, 使足民, to secure sufficient for the people. A., XI. xxv. 5.

足 *tseu* chü Up. 3d tone. Excessive. A., V. xxiv.

跲 *këë* chieh To stumble. D,M., xx. 16.

踐 *tseen* chien To tread on. A., XI. xix. =to occupy. D.M., xix. 5.

踖 *tseih* chi 踧踖, to move reverently. A., X. iv. 5; vi. 2.

踧 *tsuh* tsu 踧踖, see 踖.

踰 *yu* yü To step over; transgress. A., II. iv. 6: XIX. xi.; xxiv.

路 *loo* lu (1) 道路, the road. A., IX. xi. 3. (2) 子路, one of Conf. disciples. D.M., x. 1. A., V. vi.; vii.; xiii.; xxv. 2, 4: *et al., sæpe.* 季路, *idem.* A., V. xxv.: XI. ii. 2; xi.: XVI. i. 2. (3) 顏路, the father of Yen Hwuy. A., XI. vii. 1.

蹈 *taou* tao To trample on. D.M., ix. To tread (the path of virtue). A., XV. xxxiv.

躍 *yŏ* yo To leap. D.M., xii. 3.

蹜 *suh* hsü 蹜蹜, the feet dragging along. A., X. v. 1.

躁 *tsaou* tsao Hurried; rashness. A., XVI. vi.

躩 *k'eŏ* ch'io The legs bending under. A., X. iii. 1; iv. 3.

THE 158TH RADICAL. 身.

身 *shin* shên (1) The body. A., X. vi. 6: XV. viii. (2) One's own person, the person. G.L.T., 4, 5, 6; c., *passim.* D.M., xiv. 5; xx. 4, 7, 11, 12, 13, 14, 17; *et al.* A., I. iv.; vii.: *et al.* In some cases, we might translate by *body*. (3) 終身, all one's life, continually. A., IX. xxvi. 3: XV. xxiii.

躬 *kung* (1) The body. A., X. iv. 1, 4; v. 1: XX. i. 1. (2) In one's own person. A., IV. xxi.: VII. xxxii.: XIII. xviii.: XIV. vi.: XV. xiv.: XX. i. 3.

THE 159TH RADICAL. 車.

車 *keu* chü — A carriage. D.M., xxviii. 3; xxxi. 4. A., II. xxii.: V. xxv. 2: X. xv. 2; xvii. 1, 2: XI. vii. 1: XIV. xvii. 2.

軍 *keun* chün — An army. 三軍, the forces of a great State. A., VII. x. 2: IX. xxv. 軍旅, A., XIV. xxii.: XV. i. 1.

軌 *kwei* kuei — The rut of a wheel. =size, standard. D.M., xxviii. 3.

軏 *yuĕ* yüeh — An arrangement for yoking the horses in a light carriage. A., II. xxii.

輅 *loo* lu — A state carriage. A., XV. x. 3.

輶 *yew* yu — Light. D.M., xxxiii. 6.

載 *tsae* tsai — (1) To contain. D.M., xii. 2; xxvi. 4, 9; xxx. 2; xxxi. 4. (2) Business, doings. D.M., xxxiii. 6.

輔 *foo* fu — To assist. A., XII. xxiv.

輕 *k'ing* ch'ing — Light. A., V. xxv. 2: VI. iii. 2.

輗 *e* i — The cross bar for yoking the oxen in a large carriage. A., II. xxii.

輿 *yu* yü — (1) A carriage. A., XV. v. 3: XVIII. vi. 2. (2) 接輿, a name. A., XVIII. v.

輟 *chuĕ* chüeh — To desist, stop. A., XVIII. vi. 8.

THE 160TH RADICAL. 辛.

辟 *p'eih* p'i — (1) Partial, perverse. G.L.c., viii. 1; x. 4. (2) Specious. A., XI. xvii. 3: XVI. iv.

辟 *peih* pi — A sovereign; applicable to the emperor as well as the princes. In the Ana. only of the princes. D.M., xxxiii. 5. A., III. ii.

辟 *pe* pi — *I.q.* 避. To escape; withdraw from. D.M., vii. A., XIV. xxxix. 1, 2, 3, 4: XVIII. v. 2; vi. 3.

辟 *p'e* p'i — *I.q.* 譬. 辟如, may be compared to. D.M., xv. 1; xxx. 2.

辨 *peen* pien — To discriminate; to discover. D.M., xix. 4; xx. 19, 20. A., XII. x. 1; xxi. 1.

辭 *ts'ze* tz'ŭ — (1) Language; speech. G.L.c., iv. A., XV. xl. 辭氣, =words and tones. A., VIII. iv. 3. 爲之辭 to frame excuses for. A., XVI. i. 9. (2) To refuse, decline. D.M., ix. A., VI. iii. 3; vii.: XVII. xx.

THE 161ST RADICAL. 辰.

辰 *shin* ch'ên — The constellations of the zodiac. D.M., xxvi. 9. 北辰, the north pole star. A., II. i.

農 *nung* nûng — A husbandman. A., XIII. iv. 1.

辱 *jüh* ju — Disgrace; to disgrace. A., I. xiii.: IV. xxv.: XII. xxiii.: XIII. xx.: XVIII. viii. 2, 3.

THE 162D RADICAL. 辵.

迅 *sin* hsin — Sudden. A., X. xvi. 5.

迂 *yu* yü — Wide of the mark. A., XIII. iii. 3.

近 *kin* chin — To be near to. G.L.T., 3. D.M., xx. 10; xxix. 5. A., I. xiii.: *et al.* Nearness. D.M., xxxiii. 1. In what is near, *i.e.*, one's self. A., VI. xxviii. 3: XIX. vi.

迎 *ying* — To meet. D.M., xx. 14.

述 *shuh* shu — To transmit; carry forward. D.M., xviii. 1; xix. 2; xxx. 1. A., VII. i.: XVII. xix. 2. To be handed down to posterity. D.M., xi. 1. A., XIV. xl.

迷 *me* mi — To leave to error. A., XVII. i. 2.

适 *kwoh* kuo — A name. A., XIV. vi.—伯适, A., XVIII. xi.

追 *chuy* chui — To go back in thought, and act according to what may be required. D.M., xviii. 3. A., I. ix. To go forward in the same way. A., XVIII. v.

進 *tsin* chin — To advance, go forward. A., VI. xiii.: VII. xxviii. 2: IX. xviii; xx.: X. iii. 3; iv. 5: XIII. xxi.: XIX. xii. Actively, to call, to urge, forward. A., III. xxv. 2: XI. xxi. 先進, 後進=先輩, 後輩, A., XI. i. 1, 2.

迹 *tseih* chi — Footsteps. A., XI. xix.

適 *shih* To go, proceed, to. A., VI. iii. 2: IX. xxix.: XIII. ix. 1: XVIII. ix. 1, 2.

適 *teih* ti To have the mind set on anything. A., IV. x.

遯 *tun* *I.q.* 遁. To withdraw, lie hid, from. D.M., xi. 3.

遷 *ts'ëen* ch'ien To transfer, remove. A., VI. ii.: X. vii. 2.

遲 *ch'e* ch'i 樊遲, the name of one of Confucius' disciples; *i q.* 樊須. A., II. v. 2, 8: VI. xx.: XII. xxi.; xxii.: XIII. iv.; xix.

遺 *wei* To neglect, be neglected. A., VIII. ii. 2. Observe D.M., xvi. 2.

選 *seuen* hsüan To choose, select. A., XII. xxii. 6.

遵 *tsun* To follow, to observe. A., xi. 2.

邇 *urh* Near. What is near. D.M., xv. 1. Observe A., XVII. ix. 6. =shallow. D.M., vi.

THE 163D RADICAL. 邑.

邑 *yih* yi A city or town. A., V. vii. 3: XIV. x. 3. A hamlet. A., V. xxvii. 駢邑, the city or town of P'een. A., XIV. x. 3.

邦 *pang* A country, a State. G.L.c., ii. 3. A., I. x. 1: III. xxii. 3: *et sæpe.* 邦家, a State embracing the families of its high officers. A., XIX. xxv. 4: *et al.* 邦畿, the imperial domain. G.L.c., iii. 1.

郊 *keaou* chiao The imperial sacrifice to Heaven. D. M., xix. 6.

邪 *seay* hsieh Depraved. A., II. ii.

郁 *yuh* yü 郁郁乎, how complete and elegant! A., III. xiv.

鄉 *heang* hsiang (1) A village. A., XVII. xiii. Joined with 黨. A., VI. iii. 4.: X. i. 1: XIII. xx. 2. 鄉人, villagers. A., X. x. 1, 2: XIII. xxiv. (2) 互鄉, the name of a place. A., VII. xxviii.

鄉 *heang* hsiang Up. 3d tone. Formerly. A., XII. xxii. 4.

鄙 *p'e* p'i Mean; lowness. A., VIII. iv. 3: IX. vi. 3: XIV. xlii. 2. 鄙夫, A., IX. vii.: XVII. xv.

鄰 *lin* A neighbour, neighbours. A., IV. xxiv.: V. xxiii. A neighbourhood. A., VI. iii. 4.

邱 *k'ew* ch'iu *I.q.*, 丘. In some editions. G.L.c., iii. 2.

鄭 *ch'ing* ch'êng The name of a State. A., XV. x 6; XVII. xv.

鄹 *tsow* tsou The native city of Confucius. A., xv.

THE 164TH RADICAL. 酉.

配 *p'ei* To appear before. G.L.c., x. 5. To be the co-equal of. D.M., xxvi. 5; xxxi. 4.

酒 *tsew* chiu Wine; spirits. A., II. viii.: IX. xv.: X. viii. 4, 5; x. 1.

酬 *ch'ow* ch'ou To pledge,—in drinking. D.M., xix. 4.

醬 *tseang* chiang Sauce, pickle. A., X. viii. 3.

醫 *e* 作醫, to be a doctor. A., XIII. xxii.

醯 *he* hsi Vinegar. A., V. xxiii.

THE 166TH RADICAL. 里.

里 *le* li (1) A village, or neighbourhood. A., IV. i. 隣里, A., VI. iii. 4. 州里, A., XV. v. 2. (2) A measure of length, of 360 paces. Anciently,=1897½ Eng. feet; now=1826 feet. G.L.c., iii. 1. A., VIII. vi. (3) 東里, the name of a place in Ch'ing. A., XIV. ix.

重 *chung* Heavy, what is heavy. A., VIII. vii. 1, 2. To feel; to be heavy. D.M., xxvi. 9. Grave. A., I. viii. 1. Earnest, great. D.M., xx. 13. To make large. D.M., xx. 14. To attach importance to. A., XX. i. 8.

野 *yay* yeh Rude, uncultivated. A., VI. xvi.: XIII. iii. 4. 野人, A., XI. i. 1.

量 *leang* liang Measures of capacity. A., XX. i. 6. A measure, limit. A., X. viii. 4. 不知量, not to know one's own capacity. A., XIX. xxiv.

索引

THE 167TH RADICAL. 金.

金 *kin* chin — Metal. =arms. D.M., x. 4.

鈇 *foo* fu — An axe, a hatchet. 鈇鉞 D.M., xxxiii. 4.

鉞 *yuĕ* yüeh — A battle-axe. See above.

釜 *foo* fu — A measure containing 64 *shing*. A., VI. iii. 1.

釣 *teaou* tiao — To angle. A., VII. xxvi.

錦 *kin* chin — Embroidered clothes. D.M., xxxiii. 1. A., XVII. xxi. 4.

銘 *ming* — To engrave; be engraved. G.L.c., ii. 1.

錯 *ts'oh* ts'o — Alternatingly. D.M., xxxii.

錯 *ts'oo* ts'u — To set aside. A., II. xix.: XII. xxii. 3, 4.

鏗 *k'ang* k'êng — 鏗爾, while it was yet twanging; spoken of the sound of a harpsichord. A., XI. xxv. 7.

鐸 *toh* to — 木鐸, a bell with a wooden clapper. A., III. xxiv.

鑽 *tswan* tsuan — To bore; to penetrate. A., IX. x. 1. 鑽燧, to bore wood to procure fire. A., XVII. xxi. 3.

鐘 *chung* — A bell. A., XVII. xi.

THE 168TH RADICAL. 長.

長 *ch'ang* — (1) Long. A., X. vi. 5. 長府, the Long treasury. A., XI. xiii. 1. (2) Said of time. A., IX. ii. =always. A., VII. xxxvi. (3) 長沮, a recluse. A., XVIII. vi. 公冶長, a disciple, and son-in-law, of Conf. A., V. i.

長 *chang* — (1) Up. 2d tone. Old. A., XI. xxv. 2. Grown up. A., XIV. xlvi.: XVII. vii. 5. (長幼). Elders. G.L.c., ix. 1: x. 2. To treat as elders should be treated. G. L.c., x. 2. (2) To preside over, high in station. G.L.c., x. 23.

長 *chang* — Low. 3d tone. More than. A., X. vi. 6.

THE 169TH RADICAL. 門.

門 *mun* — (1) A door, a gate. A., II. xxii. 3: VI. xiii.: XII. ii.: XIV. xlii. Spoken by Conf. of his door, *i.e.*, his school. A., XI. ii. 1: XIV. i. 中門, to stand in the middle of the gate way. A., X. ix. 2. 門人, disciples A., IV. xv. 2: VII. xxviii.: IX. xi.: XI. x. 1, 2; xiv. 2: XIX. iii.; xii. So, 門弟子, A., VIII. iii.: IX. ii. 2. (2) 石門, the name of a place, or barrier-pass. A., XIV. xli.

閑 *hëen* hsien — A boundary, or fending line. A., XIX. xi.

閒 *hëen* hsien — At leisure; retired. G.L.c., vi. 2.

閒 *këen* chien — An interval. Used as a preposition, following its regimen, with 之 before it, =between. A., IV. v. 3: XI. xxv. 4; XVIII. iii. 病閒, during an intermission of sickness. A., IX. xi. 2.

間 *këen* chien — Up. 3d tone. To find a crevice or flaw. A., VIII. xxi.: XI. iv.

閾 *yih* yi — The threshold. A., X. iv. 2.

闇 *gan* an — 闇然, secret, concealed. D.M., xxxiii. 1.

闕 *k'euĕ* ch'üeh — (1) To put aside, exercise reserve. A., II. xviii. 2. 闕如. A., XIII. iii. 4. (2) 闕文, a blank left in the writing. A., XV. xxv. (3) The name of a village. A., XIV. xlvii.

關 *kwan* kuan — 關雎, the first ode in the She-king. A., III. xx.: VIII. xv.

開 *k'ae* k'ai — The name of one of Conf. disciples. A., V. v.

閔 *min* — The surname of one of Conf. disciples. A., VI. vii.: XI. ii.; iv.; xii.; xiii.

THE 170TH RADICAL. 阜.

防 *fang* — The name of a city in Loo. A., XIV. xv.

阼 *tsoo* tsu — The steps, or staircase, on the east. 阼階, A., X. x. 2.

索引

THE 182D RADICAL. 風.

風 *fung* fêng The wind. D.M., xxxiii. 1. A., X. xvi. 5: XII. xix. To enjoy the breeze; to take the air. A., XI. xxv. 7.

THE 183D RADICAL. 飛.

飛 *fei* To fly. D.M., xii. 3.

THE 184TH RADICAL. 食.

食 *shih* (1) To eat. G.L.c., vii. 2. D.M., iv. 2. A., I. xiv.: *et al., saepe.* =to consume. G.L.c., x. 19. =to enjoy. A., XI. xi. 3. To be eaten. A., XVII. vii. 4. 終食之間, a meal's time. A., IV. v. 3. = food. D.M., xix. 3. A., IV. ix.: VIII. xxi.: X. vii. 2: *et al.* (2) An eclipse. A., XIX. xxi.

食 *tsze* tzŭ (1) Rice; food generally. A., II. viii.; VI. ix.: VII. xv.: X. viii. 1, 2, 4, 10: XIV. x. 3. (2) To give food to; to feast. A., XVIII. vii. 3.

飲 *yin* To drink. D.M., iv. 3. A., X. x. 1. As a noun. A., VI. ix.: VIII. xxi.

飲 *yin* Up. 3d tone. To give to drink. A., III. vii.

飪 *jin* jên Meat over done. 失飪不食, he did not eat anything that was over-done. A., X. viii. 2. (This clause has slipt out of the translation.)

飯 *fan* (1) to eat. 飯疏食, A., VII. xv.; XIV. x. 3. In those instances, perhaps 飯=for food. To taste. A., X. xiii. 2. (2) 亞飯, 三飯, 四飯, see 亞, 三, 四. A., XVIII. ix.

飾 *shih* To ornament. A., X. vi. 1. Obs. 修飾之. A., XIV. ix. 1.

飽 *paou* pao To eat to the the full: satiety. A., I. xiv.: VII. ix.: XVII. xxii.

養 *yang* To nourish; to bring up. G.L.c., ix. 2. A., V. xv. =to have about one; to manage. A., XVII. xxv.

養 *yang* Low. 3d tone. To nourish, to support a superior. A., II. vii.

餘 *yu* yü That which is over. 其餘, the others. A., II. xviii. 2: VI. v.: VIII. xi. Superabundant. A., I. vi. 有餘, having excess. D.M., xiii. 4.

餒 *nuy* nei (1) Hunger, want. A., XV. xxxi. (2) Rotten, gone. A., X. viii. 2; spoken of fish.

餓 *go* o Hungry. = to die of famine. A., XVI. xii. 1.

餲 *e* i Rice sour, or with a bad odour. A., X. viii. 2.

餼 *he* ch'i 餼羊, the sheep offered at the inauguration of the new moon. A., III. xvii. 1.

饌 *tsuan* chuan Provisions. A., X. xvi. 4. 先生饌. to set before one's elders. A., II. viii.

饐 *e* i 食饐, rice injured by damp. A., X. viii. 2.

饑 *ke* chi A famine;—specifically of the grain crop. A., XII. ix. 饑饉, a famine. A., XI. xxv. 4.

饉 *kin* chin A famine;—specifically of vegetables. See 饑.

饋 *kuei* kuei To present; anything presented. A., X. xi. 2; xv. 2.

饗 *heang* hsiang To enjoy; to accept a sacrifice. D.M., xvii. 1; xviii. 2.

THE 185TH RADICAL. 首.

首 *show* shou 首陽, the name of a mountain. A., XVI. xii. 1.

首 *show* shou Upper 3d tone. The direction of the head. A., X. xiii. 3.

THE 187TH RADICAL. 馬.

馬 *ma* ma (1) A horse, horses. G.L.c., x. 22. A., II. vii.: V. xviii. 2; xxv. 2: VI. iii. 2; xiii.: X. xii.; xv. 2: XV. xxv.: XVI. xii. 1. (2) 司馬, a double surname. A., XII. iii.; iv.; v. 巫馬, also a double surname. A., VII. xxx.

馮 *ping* 馮河, to attempt to cross a river without using a boat. A., VII. x. 3.

駟 *sze* szŭ A team of four horses. A., XII. viii. 2: XVI. xii.

駕 *kea* chia The yoking of a carriage. A., X. xiii. 4.

騂 *sing* hsing Red. Spoken of a calf to be sacrificed. A., VI. iv.

索引

驕 *keaou* chiao — To be proud; pride. G.L.c., x. 18. D.M., xxvii. 7. A., I. xv.: VIII. xi.: XIII. xxvi.: XIV. xi.: XVI. v.: XX. ii. 1, 2.

驅 *k'eu* ch'ü — To drive. D.M., vii.

驥 *k'e* ch'i — A horse that could go 1,000 le in a day, = a good horse. A., XIV. xxxv.

騫 *k'een* ch'ien — 子騫, the designation of one of Conf. disciples. A., VI. vii.: XI. ii.; iv.; xiii.

騧 *kwa* kua — 季騧, the name of an officer of the Chow dynasty. A., XVIII. xi.

駢 *peen* pien — The name of a town. A., XIV. x. 3.

THE 188TH RADICAL. 骨.

體 *t'e* t'i — (1) The body. G.L.c., vi. 4. 四體, the four limbs. D.M., xxiv. A., XVIII. vii. 1. (2) As a verb. To treat with consideration. D.M., xx. 12, 13. To enter into, be incorporate with. D.M., xvi. 2.

THE 189TH RADICAL. 高.

高 *kaou* kao — (1) High. D.M., xvi.; xxvi. 3, 4, 5, 8; xxvii. 6. A., IX. x. 1. (2) 高宗, the hon. epithet of the emperor 武丁. A., XIV. xliii. A name. (3) 微生高, A., V. xxiii.

THE 190TH RADICAL. 髟.

髮 *fă* fa — The hair. A., XIV. xviii. 2.

THE 191ST RADICAL. 鬥.

鬭 *tow* tou — To contend; quarrelsomeness. A., XVI. vii.

THE 194TH RADICAL. 鬼.

鬼 *kwei* kuei — Manes, the spirit or spirits of the departed. A., II. xxiv.: XI. xi. 鬼神, spiritual beings;—sometimes exclusively names. D.M., xvi.; xxix. 3, 4. A., VI. xx.: VIII. xxi.

魏 *wei* — The name of a great family. A., XIV. xii.

魋 *t'uy* t'ui — 桓魋 a high officer of Sung, an enemy of Conf. A., VII. xxii.

THE 195TH RADICAL. 魚

魚 *yu* yü — (1) A fish, fishes, fish. D.M., xii. 3; xxvi. 9. A., X. viii. 2. (2) 魚子, an historiographer. A., XV. vi. (3) 伯魚, the designa. of Conf. son. A., XVI. xiii. 1: XVIII. x.

魯 *loo* lu — (1) Dull, blunt. A., XI. xvii. 2. (2) The name of a State. A., III. xxiii.: V. ii.: VI. xxii.; *et al.* 魯公, A., XVIII. x.

鮮 *seen* hsien — Up. 2d tone. Few, rare; seldom. G.L.c., viii. 1. D.M., iii.; iv. 2. A., I. ii. 1; iii.: IV. xxii.: VI. xxvii.: XV. iii.: XVII. xvii.

鮀 *t'o* — An officer of Wei. A., VI. xiv.: XIV. xxii.

鯉 *le* li — The name of Confucius' son. A., XI. vii. 2: XVI. xiii. 2, 3.

THE 196TH RADICAL. 鳥.

鳥 *neaou* niao — A bird, birds. G.L.c., iii. 2. A., VIII. iv.: IX. viii.: XVII. ix. 7: XVIII. vi. 4.

鳳 *fung* fêng — A fabulous bird, the phœnix. A., IX. viii. Applied to Confucius. A., XVIII. vi. 1.

鳴 *ming* — (1) The cry of a bird. A., VIII. iv. 2. (2) To sound, to beat. A., XI. xvi. 2.

鳶 *yuen* yüan — A kind of hawk. D.M., xii. 3.

鵠 *kuh* ku — Used as = the bull's eye in a target. D.M., xiv. 5.

THE 198TH RADICAL. 鹿.

麑 *ne* ni — A fawn. A., X. vi. 4.

THE 200TH RADICAL. 麻.

麻 *ma* — Hemp; = linen. A., IX. iii. 1.

THE 201ST RADICAL. 黃.

黃 *hwang* huang — Yellow. G.L.c., iii. 2. A., X. vi. 4.

THE 202D RADICAL. 黍.

黎 *le* li — Black. 黎民, the black-haired people, = the people. G.L.c., x. 14.

THE 203D RADICAL. 黑.

默 *mih* mo — To be silent, silence. D.M., xxxvii. 7. A., VII. ii.

黜 *ch'uh* ch'u — To be dismissed from office. A., XVIII. ii.

點 *teen* tien — The name of 曾晢, one of Conf. disciples. A., XI. xxv. 7.

黨 *tang* — (1) A village. A., IX. ii.: XIV. xlvii. 1. 鄉黨, A., VI. iii. 4: X. i. 1. (2) A class. A., VII. i. =school, pupils. A., V. xxi. 吾黨, we, among us. A., XIII. xviii. 1, 2. (3) A partizan, partizanly. A., VII. xxx. 2: XV. xxi.

THE 204TH RADICAL. 黹.

黻 *fŭh* fu — An apron, belonging to the emperor's dress at sacrifices. A., VIII. xxi.

THE 205TH RADICAL. 黽.

黿 *yuen* yüan — A large tortoise. D.M., xxvi. 9.

鼈 *pëë* pieh — A turtle. D.M., xxvi. 9.

鼉 *t'o* — An iguana. D.M., xxvi. 9.

THE 207TH RADICAL. 鼓.

鼓 *koo* ku — (1) A drum, drums. A., XI. xvi. 2: XVII. xi. (2) Drum-master. A., XVIII. ix. 3. (3) To strike: to play on. D.M., xv. 2. A., XI. xxv. 2. Anciently, for the third of these senses the character 皷 was used.

鼗 *t'aou* t'ao — A kind of hand-drum. 播鼗, to shake the hand-drum. A., XVIII. ix. 4.

THE 210TH RADICAL. 齊.

齊 *ts'e* ch'i — (1) To regulate. G.L.T., 4, 5: c., viii. 1, 2; ix. 1, 5. To give uniformity to. A., II. iii. 1, 2. To equal; be equal with. A., IV. xvii. (2) The name of a State. A., V. xviii. 2: VI. iii. 1, 2; xxii.: VII. xiii.; XII. xi.: XVI. xii.: XVIII. iii.; iv.; ix. —XIV. xvi.; xvii.; xviii. (3) In 叔齊, it is the hon. epithet. A., V. xxii.: VIII. xiv. 2: XVI. xii.: XVIII. viii. 1, 2.

齋 *chae* chai — To fast; religious adjustment. D.M., xvi. 3; xx. 14; xxxi. 1. A., VII. xii.: X. vii. 1, 2; viii. 10.

齊 *tsze* tzŭ — The lower edge of a garment. A., X. iv. 4. 齊衰, in mourning. A., IX. ix.: X. xvi. 2.

THE 211TH RADICAL. 齒.

齒 *che* ch'ih — The teeth. A., XIV. x. 3. Used for years, age. D.M., xix. 4.

THE 212TH RADICAL. 龍.

龍 *lung* — A dragon, dragons. D.M., xxvi. 9.

THE 213TH RADICAL. 龜.

龜 *kwei* kuei — A tortoise. D.M., xxiv. A., XVI. i. 7.

END OF VOL. I.

海上絲綢之路文獻集成

總主編　陳支平　陳春聲

科技與文化編

65

主編　王揚宗　葉　農

海峽出版發行集團
THE STRAITS PUBLISHING & DISTRIBUTING GROUP
福建人民出版社

本册目次

諺語叢話

（*A Collection of Chinese Proverbs*）

〔英〕沙修道（William Scarborough）編譯

《諺語叢話》，英國沙修道編譯。沙修道（William Scarborough，一八四〇—一八九四），英國循道會傳教士。一八六五年抵漢口，協助師惟善（Frederick Porter Smith）籌建並管理普愛醫院。曾發表《中國的稱謂模式》（*Chinese Modes of Address*）等文。是書係近代來華西人所編首部系統論述、翻譯中國諺語之著作。書有序言、導論，末附索引，正文凡二十類，涉及使然作用、動物、商業、家庭事務、教育、幽默、命運、喜悲、語言、法律與政府、人、禮儀、醫藥、道德、謹慎、五倫、宗教、時間、旅行、貧富等，漢語注音俱採用威妥瑪式拼音方案。據一八七五年上海版影印。

諺語叢話

A COLLECTION OF

CHINESE PROVERBS

TRANSLATED AND ARRANGED

BY

WILLIAM SCARBOROUGH,

WESLEYAN MISSIONARY, HANKOW.

With an Introduction, Notes, and Copious Index.

SHANGHAI:
AMERICAN PRESBYTERIAN MISSION PRESS.
London: Trübner and Co., 57 and 59 Ludgate Hill.

1875.

CONTENTS.

PROVERBS.

SECTION I.

ON AGENCY.

SECTION II.

ON ANIMALS.

SECTION III.

ON BUSINESS.

SECTION IV.

ON DOMESTIC CONCERNS.

SECTION V.

ON EDUCATION.

SECTION VI.

FACETIÆ.

SECTION VII.

ON FORTUNE.

SECTION VIII.

ON JOYS AND SORROWS.

SECTION IX.

ON LANGUAGE.

SECTION X.

ON LAW AND GOVERNMENT.

SECTION XI.

ON MAN.

SECTION XII.

ON MANNERS.

SECTION XIII.

ON MEDICINE.

SECTION XIV.

ON MORALS.

Page.

SECTION XV.

ON PRUDENCE.

SECTION XVI.

ON THE FIVE RELATIONS.

SECTION XVII.

ON RELIGION.

SECTION XVIII.

ON TIMES.

SECTION XIX.

ON TRAVEL.

SECTION XX.

ON WEALTH AND POVFRTY,

PREFACE.

This Collection of Chinese Proverbs owes its publication to the belief that there is room for a work of the kind, and that such a work can hardly fail to be both useful and interesting. That the ground is almost unoccupied is easily shown. As far as I can learn, the small compilation of "Chinese Moral Maxims" by Sir J. F. Davis, containing only 200 examples, published in 1823, and now for a long time out of print; and the 441 examples contained in the "Proverbes Chinois" by P. Perny M. A., published in 1869, are the only books that have ever appeared on the subject. Add to these a number of scattered lists, and especially those to be found in Mr. Doolittle's "Hand-book of the Chinese Language," and we have all the previous literature of this subject under our notice.

The probable usefulness of such a book as this I gather partly from my own experience, and partly from the observations of many others. A knowledge of their proverbs is of great value to all who are brought into contact with the Chinese; it is especially so to the Missionary in preaching to them; and even to the general reader, a translation, however imperfect, cannot be without its use and interest. In order that the present compilation may prove useful to those who desire to study both the language and the people of this great empire, I have spared no pains in its preparation; and I feel assured that any faults which may be discovered therein, are not the result of over haste, or carelessness.

It would have been easy to have doubled the size of this compilation, but I have deemed it wiser to publish only a part of the proverbs in my possession. In doing so the reader's convenience has been consulted; and it is hoped that this collection will be found large enough for all practical purposes. In writing out the sounds of the Chinese characters I have adopted Mr. Wade's system of orthography and tones, being under the impression that that is the one at present most widely known, and most generally admired.

In regard to the translations, it may be remarked that in a few cases the vulgarity of the proverb has not allowed of a literal rendering; and that in many others I have refrained from translating the Chinese by an equivalent English proverb, thinking that a literal translation must be more interesting, while at the same time it could not fail to call up to the reader's mind English, French, or other equivalents. It will be observed that most of the chapters begin with a number of rhymed translations. As a principle, I think it right that proverbs rhyming in the original should do so in translation; hence I have endeavoured so to translate all such as rhymed to my ear in the Hankow dialect. The task has been anything but easy, and my attempts at versification may be rough and faulty, but I hope they will not be found unendurable.

The Classification of proverbs is, confessedly, a most difficult undertaking; but, considering the care bestowed thereon, I venture to hope that this compilation will be found tolerably convenient and satisfactory as a book of reference. In making this selection of proverbs, it was not thought fair to exclude altogether the vulgar and immoral. A few of these are admitted—veiled under free translations—as the representatives of a class, which, so far as my experience goes, is not a very large one. Classical proverbial sayings are omitted, since they are well known to be quotations from the standard works.

My most sincere thanks are due to Messrs. A. Wylie and W. Warrick, for their kindness in reading the greater part of the proofs. Other gentlemen have aided and encouraged me in different ways, and to them also this expression of my gratitude is due.

W. S.

HANKOW, MAY 8th 1875.

INTRODUCTION.

Proverbial Philosophy, if genuine, commands the suffrages of all nations. By common consent Asia is acknowledged to be the soil in which it grows to most perfection; and of all Asiatic countries, perhaps China above all others supports and justifies the general opinion. Even a slight acquaintance with the language and people of this country is enough to convince any one of its richness in the maxims of proverbial wisdom. And the closer one's acquaintance becomes, the higher grows our estimate of the value of an extensive knowledge of this branch of native literature. By some, mere lists of proverbs may be treated with contempt, and knowledge of proverbial lore esteemed a light thing in comparison with skill in other branches of philology; but the man does not deserve to become proverbial for his philosophy, who can in any way discountenance the study of the folk-lore of an empire like that of China. The proverbs of China deserve a careful and enthusiastic study.

Naturally enough, the Reader will here expect to find some definition of the subject of this essay. Definitions of proverbs in general have not been attended with very great success; certainly they have not been very unanimous. Ray defines a proverb to be,—"a short sentence or phrase in common use, containing some trope, figure, homonymy, rhyme, or other novity of expression." According to Bohn, a proverb is "an instructive sentence, or common and pithy saying." The Imperial Dictionary defines a proverb as "a short and pithy sentence often repeated, expressing a well known truth or common fact, ascertained by experience or observation." There are few who are not familiar with Lord John Russell's definition—"The wisdom of many, and the wit of one." And there are fewer who will not be glad to be reminded of Tennyson's.—

> ...."Jewels five-words long,
> That, on the stretch'd fore-finger of all Time,
> Sparkle for ever."

None of these definitions can be accepted as accurate, or nearly accurate, descriptions of that which the Chinese themselves call 俗話 *Su-'hua*, or a Common Saying. A Chinese proverb is something almost, if not utterly, indefinable. Of course it bears, in several features, a strong likeness to other branches of the family in various countries; but, of "that sententious brevity," which is said to "constitute the principal beauty of a proverb"—of that brevity without obscurity, which is said to be the very soul of a proverb, it is often totally lacking. Other features it has which are peculiarly its own, and which impart to it a terseness, beauty, aud symmetry, inimitable, at least in the English language.

In order that we may discuss the subject of Chinese Proverbs with some degree of completeness, let us direct our attention to their Number, Sources, Form, Qualities, and Uses.

I.—NUMBER.

The number of Chinese proverbs is certainly very great. In proof of this it is only needful to point to the frequent recurrence of them in the conversation of the people. No matter what may be the topic of conversation, a proverb suitable to the occasion is very likely to be forthcoming. Further proof of this is found in the readiness with which almost any educated man can write off long lists of proverbs from memory. And still further proof is afforded by the great number to be found in native books. In his "Curiosities of Literature," Disraeli assigns to the whole of Europe 20,000 proverbs: China could probably furnish an equal number.

Nor should we look upon the great number and frequent recurrence of such maxims as matter of surprise; for, there is some thing in the humorous and cynical nature of proverbs, certain to recommend them strongly to such a people as the Chinese. Besides, they are a people glad to be saved the trouble of thinking for themselves, and therefore predisposed to adopt the maxims of others who have, by common consent, been esteemed wise men. Moreover, the writings of Confucius, *Facile princeps* of China's sages, contain very much of that brevity and sententiousness characteristic of proverbs in general. And there can be little doubt that, of all language, the Chinese is best adapted to such kind of speech.* Its marvellous flexibility enables it to take any mould the whim of man or custom may suggest; its remarkable copiousness affords an almost unlimited scope in the selection of words, its extreme conciseness fits it to express the greatest number of ideas in the fewest possible symbols; whilst the peculiar construction of its written characters gives it a power of playing upon words altogether unparalleled.†

---

* See M. Julien's "Syntaxe nouvelle de la Langue Chinoise," p. 2, Max Müller's "Lectures on the science of language, pp. 120, 322.

† For a good instance of this, see the proverb number 2720—too long for insertion in this place.

II.—SOURCES.

The Foreign sources of Chinese proverbs have been, up to this time, somewhat meagre. The subject could not fail to attract the attention, and to excite the interest, of those Foreign sinologues who have written on China; hence very few books have appeared, either on the language or people, which have not contained some reference to it, and a specimen list of proverbs. Beyond these numerous lists in which the same examples are repeated again and again, there have only, to my knowledge, appeared two small works exclusively on this subject, namely, those of Sir. John. F. Davis and P. Perny. The "Vocabulary and Handbook of the Chinese Language," published in 1872, by the Rev. Justus Doolittle, contains by far the greatest number of proverbs ever before translated into English or any other Western language. They were supplied by various paræmiographers, and printed, unfortunately, with little or no attempt at classification or arrangement.

Turning to Native sources we find almost the same meagreness. The proverbial lore of China remains yet to be written. Of the vast mass of proverbs in existence, only very few, comparatively, have been reduced to writing and printed in books. A few collections are to be found, and many specimens to be met with scattered over various works, but no book of any size has been compiled on this subject. The reason of this is, probably, the low esteem in which the literati are accustomed to hold all such publications. One of the best and most popular books of this class is the *Chien-pên-hsien-wên* (鑑本賢文), 'A Book of Selected Virtuous Lore'—otherwise, and more commonly called the *Tsêng-kuang* (增廣), or 'Great Collection.' Notwithstanding this latter title it is only a small book of 22 pages, containing about 350 proverbs. Its date and authorship are alike unknown. The book itself is known to almost every one, and if we may judge from a proverb which says that—"Who ever has read the *Tsêng-kuang* is able to converse*"—it is duly appreciated.

Another collection of proverbs, or as Sir John Davis calls it, "a dictionary of quotations," is the *Ming-hsin-pao-chien* (明心寶鑑), "A Precious Mirror to throw light on the mind." This work, not nearly so colloquial as the preceding one, is held in higher esteem by native scholars. It contains about 430 proverbs, arranged in 20 chapters; the compiler's name, however, is withheld, and nothing can be learned respecting its origin.

Many proverbs are found scattered throughout the *Yü-hsio* (幼學), or "Youths' Instructor," an encyclopedia in four volumes, divided into 33 chapters, containing much useful and interesting matter. Beginning with a chapter on Creation and Astronomy, it runs through almost every imaginable subject, stopping with a chapter on Flowers and Trees.

A great number of very excellent proverbs may be found in the *Chieh-jên-i* (解人頤), a work in two volumes, divided into eight sections, by *'Hu Tan An*, It has been published some time during the present dynasty, and the latest edition is dated 1859. It is a compilation in prose and verse of many interesting things on domestic duties, morals, and manners.

The *Chia-pao-ch'üan-chi* (家寶全集), or 'Complete Collection of Family Treasures', is a book out of

* See proverb number 507.

which many proverbs may be gathered. It is a work in 32 volumes, divided into four collections: the first collection treats of the fundamentals of Happiness and longevity; the second, of self-government and the government of a family; the third, of stirring men up to intelligence; and the fourth, of harmonious dispositions. The author of this highly esteemed work is *Shih T'ien-chi* (石天基), who published it in the 46*th* year of the reign of Kanghi, A. D. 1707.

The amplification of the *Shêng-yü* (聖諭), or "Sacred Edict," as well as the *Kan-ying p'ien* (感應篇), or "Book of Rewards and Punishments," supplies several useful examples. The same may be said of the well-known tractate of *Chu Pai-lu* (朱柏廬), called *Chu-tzŭ-chia-yen* (朱子家言), or 'The Household Rules of the Philosopher Chu.' But when all the native literature on the subject has been gathered together, it still remains certain that the bulk of the proverbs current in the land, exist only in the memories, and on the lips of the population.

III.—FORM.

Nothing will sooner strike one who examines a number of Chinese proverbs than the fact of their extreme diversity of form. It may seem, at first, as though there were no rules shaping them after any models whatever. But, just as to the eye of a skilful botanist, the promiscuous growths on the sides of a shady stream fall into ranks and classes, so to one who examines these proverbs with a little care, they will be seen to class themselves together, until, out of what seemed a perfect chaos, several orders arise.

The first and greatest law evident in the formation of Chinese proverbs is that of Parallelism. Great numbers of them take the form of Couplets. This may be accounted for by the facts that couplet making is a favourite amusement of the educated classes, and that couplets, when well turned, are objects of their intense admiration.

Of these Couplet-proverbs there are three kinds. The first and most important of these is the *tui-tzŭ* (對子), or Antithetical Couplet. This is formed according to strictly technical rules. A *tui-tzŭ* may contain any number of words, but the most frequent number is seven in each line. It must be so written that the order of the Tones in the first line shall be, *firstly* deflected, *secondly* even, and *thirdly* deflected; in the second line, *firstly* even, *secondly* deflected, and *thirdly* even; or *vice versa*. Should the first, third, or fifth characters violate this rule, it is of no consequence; the second, fourth, and sixth cannot be allowed to do so. It is essential also that the last character in the first line should be in a deflected tone, and the last in the second line in an even tone. The same characters may not be repeated in either line; and it is essential that there be an antithesis, as well in the sense as in the tones, of the words composing the two lines of the couplet. It is also a rule that particles must be placed in antithesis to particles; and nouns, verbs, etc., to nouns, verbs, etc. The following example with be found to illustrate all these particulars.*

天 上 衆 星 皆 拱 北

T'ien^1 shang^4 chung^4 hsing^1 chieh^1 kung^3 pei^3;

世 間 無 水 不 朝 東

Shih^4 chien^1 wu^2 shui^3 pu^4 ch'ao^2 tung.^{1}

---

* That this description may become more intelligible to any reader unacquainted with the Chinese language, I may observe that the *even* tones are those numbered one and two, the *deflected* tones are those numbered three and four.

"All the stars of heaven salute the north; every stream flows towards the east:" i. e. The Emperor is the centre of attraction.

How highly the Chinese themselves prize these *tui-tzŭ* may be gathered from the following story. Formerly an Imperial Examiner from Peking, surnamed *Shê* (snake), seeing the haughty inscription over one of the entrances to the examination hall at Wuchang —"Only the men of *Hu-quang* possess talent,"—resented the statement, declaring that he would issue one line of a *tui-tzŭ* to which no *Hu-quang* man could write a reply. Accordingly he put forth his riddle in the following line:—

七鴨浮江數數三雙一隻

"Seven ducks floating on the *Chiang*; reckon as you will are only three couples and one." On his return to Peking he mentioned this circumstance to *Hsiung Tzŭ-kang* (熊子剛), an officer in the capital, who happened to be a *Hu-quang* man. Said he, "there are no men of talent in *Hu-quang*; I put out a couplet line to which nobody could reply." "Indeed," said *Hsuing Tzŭ-kang*, "what was it you gave them?" On hearing the line given above, he guilefully replied, "I have heard that a response has been written." Thereupon he repeated to the astonished Examiner his own impromptu line, as follows:—

尺蛇出洞量量九寸十分

A "*Snake* a foot long comes out of its hole: measure as you will it is only 11 inches and 8 eighths long." So the *Hu-quang* man got the best of the joke, and at the same time vindicated his fellow provincials from the charge of stupidity.

After the *tui-tzŭ*, the next class of couplet-proverbs to be mentioned is one which the Chinese call *lien-chü* (聯句), or Connected Sentences. The proverbs in this class are exceedingly numerous; they are of various lengths, of different styles of composition, and are informal in all else but the corresponding number of words in each line. There is generally, however, a sharp antithesis* between the first and second lines. One example will suffice for illustration.

窮 莫 與 富 鬬。富 莫 與 官 鬬

Chʻiung^2 mo^4 yü^3 fu^4 tou^4; fu^4 mo^4 yü^3 kuan^1 tou.^{4}

"The poor must not quarrel with the rich; nor the rich with magistrates."

Another class of couplet-proverbs is composed of such as rhyme. Of these there are a great many which do not seem to rhyme to a foreigner; and, on the other hand, he can hear many rhymes where the native can hear none. The explanation of this is, that in order to rhyme to a native ear, the *tones* must correspond; while a foreigner's ear catches the ring of the rhyme through all such artificial distinctions. One example will suffice to show how melodiously some in this class of proverbs can chime.

好 妻 無 好 漢 天 下 一 大 半

ʻHao^3 chʻi^1 wu^2 ʻhao^3 ʻhan,^{4} tʻien^1 hsia^4 i^1 ta^4 pan^3;

好 漢 無 好 妻 天 下 一 大 堆

ʻHao^3 ʻhan^4 wu^2 ʻhao^3 chʻi,^{4} tʻien^1 hsia^4 i^1 ta^4 tui.^{1}

"In the great majority of cases,
Wives have fair and husbands ugly faces;
But there are many, on the other side,
Where the man is bound to an ugly bride."

We have now done with Parallelism and its influence on the formation of proverbs, and must briefly glance at such as are cast in a more irregular and

* See a striking example of this antithesis in proverb No. 1674.

prosaic mould. Among these a small number is discovered possessing a kind of rhythm, which gives to the proverbs in question a very easy and flowing utterance, almost deserving for them a place along with the versified classes. An example of this is found in the following.—

紐 得 過 人. 來, 紐 不 過 天
Niu[3] tê[2] kuo[4] jên[2] lai,[2] niu[3] pu[4] kuo[4] t'ien.[1]
"Man can be bound, but Heaven cannot."

The great bulk of these prose-proverbs are prosaic enough. Many of them consist of one plain sentence; such as—君子言前。不言後 *Chün[1] tzŭ[3] yen[2] ch'ien[2], pu[4] yen[2] hou.[4]* "The superior man speaks beforehand, not when all is over." Many others are most irregular in shape, amply deserving the name given to them by the Chinese of 長短句 *ch'ang-tuan-chü*, or 'Long and Short Sentences.'[1] Enough having now been said on the Form or construction of proverbs, we will proceed to consider the more interesting subject of their qualities.

IV.—QUALITIES.

It will surprise no one to learn that many of the proverbs of China are low, vulgar, and licentious. It could hardly be otherwise, considering the morally depraved condition of the Chinese as a nation. Nevertheless, it is much to the credit of heathen China that, in this respect, her proverbs do not compare unfavourably with those of Christian England.

Nor will any one at all familiar with the Chinese, be surprised to hear that many of their proverbs are expressive of the highest morality. They are not to be excelled in their praise of virtue and denunciation

1 See the proverb No. 2597, too long for quotation, for a striking illustration of this point.

of vice. But, while giving them credit for so many virtuous sayings, the error must be avoided of crediting them with anything like a corresponding amount of virtue or morality. They are not so good as their proverbs; "for they say, and do not." Still it is a matter for congratulation to find so many closely resembling the sayings of Holy Writ.[1] Many of the Proverbs of Solomon have their counterparts in the proverbs of China. And it will be admitted that in the following, selected out of many quite as good, the tone of morality falls little below that of the Christian standard. 'Better not do kindnesses at all than do them in the hope of recompence.'[2] 'Kindness is greater than law.'[2] 'Do good regardless of consequences.'[2] 'It is a little thing to starve to death; it is a serious matter to lose one's virtue.'[2]

Beauty of sentiment and expression are by no means rare in Chinese proverbs. Expressive of the transient character of earthly happiness, we have—'The bright moon is not round for long; the brilliant cloud is easily scattered.'[3] The vanity and emptiness of earthly wealth and fame could hardly be more beautifully expressed than in the following couplet:

'Wealth among men is like dew among plants:
Foam on the waves is the fame which earth grants.'[3]

'Good words are like a string of pearls,'[3] is perhaps less ornate, but certainly it is little less beautiful than Solomon's—"a word fitly spoken is like apples of gold in pictures of silver."[4] And how could the danger of unguarded speech be more beautifully expressed

1 Reference to the Index will give a list of these.
2 See Nos. 1895, 1898, 1655, 1835.
3 See Nos. 830, 962, 1120, 1123.
4 Prov. 25; 11.

than in the following?—'As the light of a single star tinges the mountains of many regions; so a single unguarded expression injures the virtue of a whole life.'[3] Many more such examples might be quoted, but these few will suffice to show that the proverbs of China are not all bald, prosy, and utilitarian.

Great numbers of proverbs might be quoted to illustrate the quality of Shrewdness; and the difficulty is to know which to select. Let the following, taken almost at random, suffice. 'Don't buy everything that's cheap, and you'll escape being greatly taken in.'[1] 'Before you calculate on buying, calculate on selling.'[1] 'It is not so safe to open the mouth as it is to keep it shut.'[1] 'It takes little time to reprove a man; but it takes a long time to forget reproof.'[1]

'He learns less who looks on than he does who makes;
Less by mere doing than by many mistakes.'[1]

The cynical element, said almost always to characterize the true proverb, abounds in those now under discussion. Tried by this test they are proverbs of the first water. 'A dwarf cannot kick up his feet to any great height.'[2] 'Though a dumb man has eaten gentian he keeps his trouble to himself'[2] 'Hoping to lift up his head, he lifts up his feet: i. e. dies.'[2] 'Get the coffin ready and the man won't die.'[2] 'Men mourn for those who leave fortunes behind them.'[2] 'The head may be cut off, but the tongue cannot be restrained.'[2]

Of Wit and Humour abundance can be found in Chinese proverbs; much more of the latter than the former. To the reader it shall be left to classify, ac-

1 See Nos. 220, 233, 1050, 1692, 2022.

2 See Nos. 705, 787, 801, 931, 958, 1042.

cording to his own taste, the following specimens under one or other of these two categories. A not very thriving business is denoted by the saying. 'To sell a couple of cucumbers in three days.'[1] 'When there's aught to do, the more the better; not so when there's aught to eat.'[1] It is against anything but a doting husband that the following shaft of ridicule is shot: 'To flit and forget to take one's wife.'[1] The *Argumentum ad hominem* is somewhat droll in the following example: 'The lion opens his mouth; the elephant shuts his; shut yours.'[1] An individual out of whom no ray of wisdom shines, is spoken of as 'a leather lantern.[1]' In this class Puns may be included. These, however, to be enjoyed, must be read in the original.[2]

Finally, under the head of Qualities, it must be observed, that amongst Chinese proverbs there are many closely resembling those well known in the West. We find "Practice makes perfect,"[3] in words which cannot well be otherwise translated. The same may be said of "Easier said than done;"[3] of "Never too old to learn;"[3] and several others. "Too many cooks spoil the broth," is expressed in Chinese by, 'Seven hands and eight feet.'[4] "Bad workmen quarrel with their tools," appears in Chinese thus; 'All unskilful fools, Quarrel with their tools.'[4] "As the twig is bent the tree's inclined," becomes slightly altered into, 'As the twig is bent the mulberry grows.'[4] Instead of "a pig in a poke," the Chinese buy 'A cat in a bag.'[4] "At Rome do as the Romans

1 See Nos. 209, 604, 614, 1051, 1381. 2 See Nos. 257, 309, 1310, 1890.
3 See Nos. 103, 118, 563.
4 See Nos. 107, 306, 460, 650, 1969, 2313, 2314,—For more illustrations of this point, see Nos. 36, 77, 106, 178, 317, 605, 620, 727, 752, 1066, 1278, 1396, 1434, 2052, 2335, 2457, 2485, 2 715.

do," is varied into, 'Wherever you go talk as the people of the place talk'[1] And "Man proposes, but God disposes," has more than one counterpart in Chinese.[1]

Possibly enough has now been advanced to show that Chinese proverbs furnish indubitable signs of mental power, and to justify the claim, which we make on their behalf, of equality with the proverbs of other nations.

V.—USES.

In connection with these proverbs the most interesting question remains to be considered, namely, Of what use are they?—Of what use are they to the Chinese themselves? to the foreign student of the Chinese language? and finally, to the general reader? Answers to these questions will bring this introductory essay to its close.

The uses to which the Chinese themselves put these proverbs are principally two. At the great festival of the new year the service of some able penman is obtained, who writes out a number of admired sayings, on long strips of red, orange, yellow, green, or blue paper, as the case may be. These are affixed to doors, to the side-posts of doors, to the pillars of houses, to the masts, stems and sterns of ships, and indeed in all directions. In this way the very habitations of the Chinese become eloquent with sage maxims, felicitous sayings, and well-expressed prayers. But the decorative use to which the proverbs are thus put, is of little importance in comparison with

1 Nos. 107, 306, 460, 650, 1969, 2313, 2314. For more illustrations of this point, see Nos 36, 77, 106, 178, 317, 605, 620, 727, 752, 1066, 1278, 1396, 1434, 2052, 2335, 2457, 2485, 2715.

the use made of them in daily conversation. The talk of modern China is highly seasoned with the salt of its ancient wisdom. And he is a stupid "son of *Han*" indeed, who cannot quote aptly some wise old saw on almost any occasion.

Of what use are these proverbs to the foreign student of the Chinese language? Sir John F. Davis has said that Chinese proverbs are of great grammatical value, inasmuch as they illustrate every grammatical law in the language. It may be true that, to some extent, they will supply models on which the student may construct sentences of his own; but, as they are often very concise and formal, the student who should make a point of doing so would run the risk of speaking in a very stilted and uncommon style. Far greater is their value, as supplying him with phrases and sentences which may be used to enrich and embellish his conversation. Used as quotations their value is immense. So used in conversation they add a piquancy and flavour which greatly delights the Chinese, and makes mutual intercourse more easy and agreeable. But it is to the Missionary that the value of an extensive acquaintance with Chinese proverbs is of the highest importance. Personal experience, as well as the repeated testimony of others, makes us bold to assert that even a limited knowledge of Chinese proverbs is to him of daily and inestimable value. A proverb will often serve to rouse the flagging attention of a congregation, or to arrest it at the commencement of a discourse. A proverb will often serve to produce a smile of good nature in an apparently ill-tempered audience, and so to call forth a kindly feeling which did not seem before to exist. And very often a proverb aptly quoted will serve to convey a truth in the most terse and striking manner, so obviating the necessity for detailed and lengthy argument, whilst they fix at a stroke the idea you are wishing to convey.

And now we come to the use which these proverbs are to the general reader. The question to be discussed is this: what light is thrown upon the character and condition of the Chinese by these proverbs? "The maxims of a people may be considered as a medium which reflects with tolerable accuracy the existing state of their manners and ways of thinking."[1]

To begin with the Chinaman himself. He certainly is a being whose character it is by no means easy to describe; and, if left to our unaided imagination, we might easily caricature him in words, as absurdly as he has long been caricatured in pictures. Guided by the evidence of proverbs we should say that the ideal Chinaman is born with a genius for trade. The number and excellence of those maxims which relate to business point to this conclusion.[2] Next to, or rather in connection with, his business-like qualifications, come out his characteristic shrewdness and prudence.[3] He is a keen observer: 'Those who can do a good trade don't wrangle over taxes.'[4] He is a cautious man: 'Do not lace your boot in a melon field, nor adjust your hat under a plum tree.'[5] He is very discreet: 'If you want to be quiet, do not meddle with other people's busines.'[6] He is wonderfully economical: 'Make every cash serve two purposes.'[7] He is not remarkable for honesty: 'If you would not be cheated ask the price at three shops.'[8] Nor is he

1 Sir John Davis. 2 See the section of proverbs on Business. 3 See the section on Prudence. 4 No. 229. 5 No. 1928. 6 No. 1976. 7 No. 2015. 8 No. 175.

distinguished for truthfulness, for sometimes he deserves the appellation, 'A lying machine.'[1] He is very polite: 'Much politeness offends no one.'[2] The numerous proverbs of a jocular description point him out as a lover of fun. That he is a lover of pleasure, we may gather from the maxim, 'All men love wealth, wine, and women.'[3] And he is a proud man: 'He will be honoured who respects himself; but he who holds himself cheap will be lightly esteemed.'[4] There is a good deal of the Mark Tapley element in him: 'If the wind be strong, yield to the wind; if the rain be heavy, yield to the rain.'[5] He is a very sober man, looking upon wine as, 'A poison which perforates the bowels.'[6] He is a loquacious person, or else many proverbs had not been needed to help him to control his tongue. He is hospitable in his way, and feels bound to entertain his guest with generosity; but he expects quite as much in return, and hopes for more. 'He who lacks hospitality to a guest must be a fool.'[7] He is very conservative. The past with its institutions is all in all to him: 'Observe the present, but reflect the past; without the past there had been no present.'[8] Finally, he is a religious man. His religion fails to make him anything like a virtuous man; it leaves him the victim of many gross superstitions, and enchains him in the fetters of a determined fatalism; but it does something to soothe his conscience, and to satisfy his moral wants. Proverbs in support of these points are too numerous to mention.[9]

Next to the man himself comes the family. The

1 No. 1269. 2 No. 1532. 3 No. 1498. 4 No. 2716. 5 No. 1973. 6 No. 1000. 7 No. 1579. 8 No. 2450. 9 See section xvii, On Religion.

social life of the Chinese, however much has been written about it, still remains comparatively a mystery to foreigners. Into the secrets of their home life the outside barbarian is not admitted. Under these circumstances we can obtain no better information as to the actual condition of a Chinese home than the numerous proverbs on this subject supply.

Home is founded on the relation existing between Husband and Wife; and it would seem that in China the importance of this relation is properly appreciated. 'There are Five Relations, but that of Husband and Wife stands first; there are 3000 great rites, but that of marriage is most important.'[1] The obligation to marry is very clearly acknowledged: 'Early marriage is the duty of both sexes.'[2] It is also firmly believed that marriages are fated: 'Wife, wealth, children, pay, are all predestined.'[3] There is a great deal of superstition cherished in regard to match-making, as well as a great deal of manœuvering on the parts both of parents and professional match-makers. 'When doorways match and houses pair, A marriage may be settled there.'[4] 'Those who rear daughters hope for great suitors.'[5] The parties principally concerned in this matrimonial compact have no voice whatever in the matter, the betrothal taking place when they are both very young; and it cannot afterwards be broken, for, while 'You may exhume a coffin, you may not reject a betrothed son-in-law.'[6] It is of course inevitable, on this principle of selection, that many alliances contracted should turn out anything but satisfactory, or mutually pleasing. So it

1 No. 2202. 2 No. 2189. 3 No. 680. 4 No. 2175. 5 No. 2191. 6 No. 2200.

happens that—'Nine out of ten go-betweens being liars'[1]—'Ugly men marry pretty wives;'[2] and 'A talented bridegroom is sometimes matched with a worthless bride; and a clever woman is sometimes married to a dolt.'[3] And sometimes these matches turn out anything but harmonious, as suggested by the proverb, 'A good husband will not beat his wife.'[4] Occasionally however love ensues upon the marriage tie, and then 'The husband sings and the wife accompanies.'[5] But there is no such thing as even approximate equality between them: 'Husbands are as Heaven to their wives; wives are the slaves of their husbands.'[6] Still the wife, placed in this degrading position, makes her influence, both for good and bad, tell upon her lord and master: 'A virtuous wife causes her husband to be honoured; a bad one brings him to shame.'[7] Her weapon of defence is her tongue; and she is skilful enough in the use of it. Hence the advice. 'Take no notice of what you hear said on the pillow.'[8] It would seem that conjugal fidelity is sometimes violated: 'He detests his own wife, but loves other men's.'[9] Divorce seems to be against the rule, for 'When the two have been united they may not be separated.'[10] And when the husband dies the widow is expected to remain a widow till her death: 'A loyal minister will serve but one prince, a virtuous woman but one husband.'[11] Concubinage is allowed and commonly practised; not, as it seems, to the entire satisfaction of the principal wife: 'If your wife is against it, do not get a concubine.'[12]

1 No. 2195. 2 No. 2206. 3 No. 2213. 4 No. 2223. 5 No. 2209. 6 No. 2220. 7 No. 2230. 8 No. 2229. 9 No. 2227. 10 No. 2214. 11 No. 2242. 12 No. 2226.

From these and many more illustrations we are well able to form a tolerably correct idea of the relation of husband and wife in China. It differs from the same relation in the west mainly in the matters of bethrothal, the use of go-betweens, the toleration of polygamy, and the degraded position of the woman. There is certainly less of that true love, which alone can crown the married state with felicity, in the East than in the West; and consequently married life is not with the Chinese so happy a thing as it is with us.

From husband and wife we come in due sequence to the relation of parents and children. The first thing to be remarked here is the silence of the proverbs on one side of the question. Much is said about the duty of children to parents, but nothing of the duty of parents to children. This silence is very expressive; for no one can have observed the Chinese for long without being struck with the prominence and emphasis with which they insist upon "Children obey your parents," while they almost ignore "Train up a child in the way he should go," and "Ye fathers provoke not your children to wrath." There is another silence equally ominous. Daughters are very seldom mentioned. And this silence is eloquent on the shameful disregard in which female offspring are held by the fathers and mothers of China. It suggests the unnatural, brutal, but common crime, of female infanticide. At her birth the female child is insulted by a comparison to her disfavour with male children. She is said to be worth but one-tenth of what a boy would have been worth.'[1] This degrada-

1 See also No. 195.

tion follows her to her grave; it clings to her as a daughter, sister, wife, and is only partly shaken off when she becomes a mother. As a mother she is honoured by her children with a love and reverence equal to that which they give to their father. But, alas! as soon as she becomes the mother of a child of her own sex she begins to display the traditional disrespect for it, under which she has herself groaned.

Having noticed these two unwelcome silences, let us listen awhile to the many voices which describe to us the state of affairs as existing between parents and children in general. The kindness of parents, so much eulogized in Chinese books, is thus spoken of: 'You must rear children to know parental kindness.'[1] Petting seems to form a part of this parental kindness; for 'The parents' pet is the obedient child.'[2] And this notwithstanding the sensible maxim, 'The rod produces obedient, petting and spoiling disobedient children.'[3] Sometimes great severity is resorted to: 'When the father pursues the son with the rod, he must not follow him for a hundred paces.'[4] It is quite evident that parents exact from their children a vast amount of deference while living and of honour after death: 'Whilst the father lives the son dare not put himself forward.'[5] 'Ancestors however remote must be sacrificed to.'[6] The reason of their intense longing for offspring finds expression in the following homely saying: 'If we have none to foul the bed, we shall have none to burn paper at our graves.'[7] Their unworthy perversion of the Biblical law that parents lay up for their children, not children

1 No. 2138. 2 No. 2129. 3 No. 2133. 4 No. 2144. 5 No. 2132. 6 No. 2363. 7 No. 2171.

for parents, is thus illustrated: 'Rear sons for old age; and lay up grain against famine.[1]' The importance of filial piety, and its nature, we find fully set forth. 'Of a myriad virtues filial piety is the first.'[2] 'He is unfilial who loves wife more than mother.'[3] We dare not injure the bodies received from our parents.'[4]

On the whole, it is evident that parents and children, even in the country renowned for filial piety, do not stand to each other in anything like so satisfactory and pleasant relations, as they do in the west. There is on the part of Chinese parents a great deal of what *we* never expect to find in *our* parents, namely, selfishness. They long for male children that, when ill, they may be supported, and when dead, worshipped by them. They despise their female children because the return of personal service to be expected from them in the future is much less than that which is expected from boys. There is also too much of the proprietor in the Chinese father. His children are his chattels, to be dealt with absolutely as such: he can sell them if he likes; and even should he, in punishing, kill them, he would be very likely to escape scotfree. The mother, too, though not entirely ignored, retires into a much more obscure position than that ordained to her by Providence. In short, there is a stiffness, an artificiality, existing between Chinese parents and children, owing to the many ceremonies which intervene upon their relationship, which does much to destroy the beauty, ease, and gracefulness, of the native home.

There is yet another relation, and one which in

1 No. 2047. 2 No. 1877. 3 No. 2121. 4 No. 2150.

China obtains great prominence, on which a few remarks must be offered, namely that of Elder and Younger Brothers. 'Brothers,' we are told, 'resemble hands and feet.'[1] They are often compared with wives to the disadvantage of the latter: 'Is he a superior man who listens to his wife, and turns against his brother?'[2] The same odious comparison is hinted at in the following: 'The most difficult thing on earth to get is a brother.'[3] The importance of harmony amongst brothers—a theme much insisted on in all books on morality—finds repeated proverbial expression: 'Though the left hand conquer the right no advantage is gained.'[4] That, after all the instructions given, Chinese brothers fail to live together like angels, is evident from the saying that, 'Top and bottom teeth sometimes come into awkward collision.'[5] And the general cause of these fraternal quarrels appears to be the stuff: 'Though brothers are so closely akin, it is each for himself in money matters.'[6] Yet the value of a brother's friendship is fully appreciated, even when business is concerned, for we read the advice, 'go into partnership with a brother.'[7] Here, again, one cannot avoid noticing the omission of any mention of the sisterhood. The relation of Brother and Sister, so pleasant in our ideas, never seems to have dawned upon the native mind. And here—in the constantly implied inferiority of the female—we have the secret explaining the failure of family life in China. Mother, wife, sister, must be restored to the high place which they have a right to adorn, before the homes of China can become worthy of the name.

1 No. 2245. 2 No. 2224. 3 No. 2255. 4 No. 2446. 5 No. 2253. 6 No. 2251. 7 No. 2296.

From Homes we come to Shops. The excellence and superabundance of their business proverbs, would justify us in holding the opinion that they are indeed "a nation of shop-keepers." Without doubt the Chinese are in their very element when driving a bargain and making money. It is truly a study to watch two men engaged in this interesting occupation. It is then that one appreciates, fully, the saying, 'Bargaining is as necessary to trade as poling to a vessel.'[1] They have a correct idea of the personal qualifications necessary to a successful tradesman: 'A man without a smiling face must not open a shop.'[2] They are wide awake to the principle of supply and demand: 'Use both such goods and money as suit your market.'[3] The necessity for speculation is fully acknowledged: 'If a little cash does not go, much cash will not come.'[4] The necessity and potency of capital is fully acknowledged: 'You must have a couple of grains of rice in order to catch fowls.'[5] That a very steady eye is kept on the item of profit, we may learn from the following: 'If no profit he espies, where's the man will early rise?'[6] For ready money they have a relish, notwithstanding that credit is the curse and ruin of their trade: 'Better take 800 than give credit for 1000 cash.'[7] Notwithstanding the frequent assertions by native shop-keepers that they 'Really have but one price,' that their's is indeed a 'One word hall,' there are more proverbs than one suggestive of the fact that prices vary according to circumstances. 'When one cheats up to heaven in the price he asks, you come down to earth in the price

1 No. 198. 2 No. 179. 3 No. 187. 4 No. 176. 5 No. 239. 6 No. 161. 7 No. 253.

you offer.'[1] After this it is refreshing to meet with the following; 'Just scales and full measures injure no man.'[2] That is a maxim worthy of a purer morality than, it is to be feared, can be boasted of in connection with Chinese Commerce.

From Shops we come to Schools. In a country so celebrated for learning as China, it will not be surprising to find many excellent maxims on the subject of education. The importance of it is fully, though roughly, expressed in the following:

'Than a lad without learning, you'd better rear an ass:

Better rear a pig than an uneducated lass.'[3]

It should begin early, because 'as the twig is bent the mulberry grows.'[4] It must not, however, proceed at random, for 'Education requires a proper method.'[5] It may be doubted whether the native method of compelling a pupil, for several years, to commit to memory a number of books, before ever a word of them is explained to him, is a proper method or not; yet it may be said in favour of it, that it appears to suit those who use it tolerably well. The curriculum to be studied may be gathered from the following: 'However stupid sons and grandsons may be, they must read the classics.'[6] 'In study fix your mind on the sages.'[7] The necessity for persevering diligence is frequently the subject of a proverbial saying, 'Every character must be chewed to get out its juice.'[8] The pleasures of learning are also often alluded to: 'Learning is far more precious than gold.'[9] All pursuits are mean in comparison with that of learning.'[10] And

1 No. 202. 2 No. 219. 3 No. 458. 4 No. 460. 5 No. 463. 6 No. 536. 7. No 562. 8 No. 548. 9 No. 538. 10 No. 558.

many are the inducements to a literary life which are set before the native pupil. 'No pleasure equals the pleasure of study.'[1] Study will be sure to yield its golden house.'[2] 'Study will provide you with a lady beautiful as jade.'[3] Many more quotations might be made illustrative of the native schools, literature, literati, and of the vast system of competitive examinations now in vogue; sufficient to show that China is not without a system of education for which she deserves great praise. The separateness of the literary caste is a thing to be regretted; so also is the stunted and changeless nature of the curriculum of studies; so also is that systematic and organized corruption, by means of which unworthy men are enabled to steal for themselves the degrees due to others: but, that learning in China stands in so conspicuous and honorable a position that the learning most honoured is within the reach of even the poorest classes; that by means of his learning the poorest boy in the land may rise to the first rank and office under His Imperial Majesty, is indeed much to the praise and glory of the Celestial Empire.

Judging from the paucity of proverbs on the subject of amusements, one might be led to suppose that the Chinese were any thing but a light-hearted and playful people. It would be a mistake to think so; for no people can be fonder of theatres and gambling than the Chinese. And if opium-smoking be taken into the list of amusements, then, beyond a doubt, the Chinese are a pleasure-loving people. Generally speaking proverbs on such subjects are of a condemnatory kind: on theatres, for instance, we read;

1 No. 571. 2 No. 573. 3 No. 574.

'Once in a while you may go to a play,
But they are not the things for every day.'[1]

On gambling we read, 'Money goes to the gambling-house as criminals to execution.'[2] 'If you believe in gambling you will have to sell your house.'[3] There doubtless exist many proverbs on the subject of amusements which have not been met with, and which would fully substantiate what has been said on the pleasure-loving proclivities of the Chinese.

Passing from gay to grave we enquire what the proverbs teach respecting the Religion of the people. To discover what are the real religious sentiments of a people like the Chinese is no easy matter; but it is not unlikely that we may get nearer to the truth by observing what the people say in their common talk, than by reading what authors and sages have said in books but seldom read.

First, we learn from proverbs that the objects of worship are Heaven, Earth, Sun, Moon, Stars, Idols, and Ancestors. This is not a complete list but it will serve our purpose. The religion which makes most show, and which forces itself perpetually on our attention, is that of idol worship. It is the popular worship of the land. On the feasts of the new and full moon our ears are dinned with the explosion of innumerable crackers. Whenever any act of importance is to be performed, there is a great outward show of belief in the power and control of the idols. Everywhere we stumble on costly temples, filled with the expensive gilded images of a numerous hierarchy of deities, and tended by a throng of shaven priests. People and rulers, high and low, unite to do homage

1 No. 759. 2 No. 764. 3 No. 762.

to the gods of the two friendly sects of Buddhism and Taouism. Now the question is, can the proverbs tell us whether all this is sham or reality? From several it would seem that the idols do not command the faith of the people. 'All idolatrous superstitions are man's invention.'[1] In several well-known proverbs the gods are turned to ridicule, which surely could not be done by men who sincerely believed them to be divine. 'Three strokes of the axe are enough to complete an image of the idol *Yang-ssŭ*.'[2] In this saying the god is made the but of raillery as the type of uncouth, unmannerly boors. In the following he is twitted for his youthful appearance. 'A beard should not be put on his worship the god of sailors.'[3] The same raillery and contempt are shown in another proverb—less elegant than caustic—namely, 'The stinking pig's head meets the smell-less idol.'[4] It would not be fair to take these contemptuous proverbs as conclusive proof of general disbelief in idols. They may be evidence of doubt in many minds, and of total disbelief in the minds of a few, but that is all. The Chinese give many proofs, as well in their conduct as in their proverbial sayings, of their faith in idols. Their faith is doubtless a very superstitious thing, and largely mixed with fear; but such as it is, it is strong enough to tinge their whole life and conduct, and to force out of them large sums of money. 'Though you don't believe in other gods, you'll believe in the god of thunder.'[5] You may carry deception into the *Yamên*, you cannot carry it into the temple.'[6] 'Though you neglect to offer

1 No. 2365. 2 No. 2358. 3 No. 2359. 4 No. 2375. 5 No. 2370. 6 No. 2354.

incense when all is well, you will have to fall at Buddha's feet in time of sorrow.'[1]

Should the testimony of proverbs be thought wavering as to the popular faith in idols, it will be admitted that it distinctly proves that the faith of the people firmly centres upon, and clings to, one great supreme being whom they call *T'ien* and we call Heaven. And if this *T'ien* be not the true God, the likeness is very strange. To *T'ien* the people are in the constant habit of ascribing many of the attributes and actions only ascribable to the true God. He is the God of Providence: '*T'ien* never sends a man without providing for him clothes and income.'[2] 'Our daily bread depends on *T'ien*.'[3] The bountifulness of his regime is thus quaintly expressed: 'when *T'ien* rears a man he grows very fat; when men rear one he is nought but skin and bone.'[4] His omniscience is again and again plainly asserted: 'Man only sees the present, *T'ien* sees into the future.'[5] 'Nothing can escape the eye of *T'ien*.'[6] His rule, as the moral governor of men is alluded to in the following: '*T'ien* sees clearly, and rewards quickly.'[7] And that his rule is merciful appears from the following: 'Imperial *T'ien* will never slight men of sorrow.'[8] As the hearer of human prayers, '*T'ien* responds to man as quickly as shadow to form or echo to voice.'[9] Whilst firmly believing that these and many other proverbs point to the highest and truest religious life of the people, it would not be candid on our part not to allude to the fact that the popular faith in *T'ien* is mixed up with much alloy. *T'ien* is very often confounded with the visible

---

1 No. 2362. 2 No. 2316. 3 No. 2320. 4 No. 2341. 5 No. 2330. 6 No. 2324. 7 No. 2325. 8 No. 2312. 9 No. 2315.

heavens; sometimes *T'ien* is stated to be 理 *li*, Reason or Principle; and oftener still the honour is divided between *T'ien* and *Ti*, the Earth. 'Heaven and Earth are great; father and mother are honourable.'[1] The people seem to associate *T'ien* and *Ti* together as the equivalent of our one word Nature, and to offer thereto a sort of pantheistic reverence. Still the truth remains that the Chinese are not altogether without some knowledge of what closely resembles the true God. Him they ignorantly worship, worship with a divided heart, and with many gross superstitions, yet we should not, on that account, fail to recognise the truth which exists, or fail to make the most of it in order to impart a purer knowledge and a truer faith.

The influence of religion on morals is very small. Indeed religion and morality in China might be assumed to belong to totally different categories, they have so little to do with each other. Even the priesthood, who ought to be the best samples of morality China can produce, are certainly not regarded in the light of holy men. Several proverbs refer to them in terms of anything but respect for the purity of their character, the sincerity of their vows, or the usefulness of their lives. The doctrine of a future state, expressed in many of the proverbs on Rewards and Punishments,[2] may be supposed to exercise some influence for good on the lives of the people; and no doubt this is the case. But then, again, the legitimate influence of this doctrine is negatived by the all-prevalent belief in Fate. The philosophy of their sages; the practical, worldly character of all their moral teaching; the contradictions existing between

1 No. 2343. 5 See chapter on Priests and Nuns. 2 See chapter so named.

their Confucianism and the religious systems of Buddha and Lao Tzŭ, together with the want of power to make men good, visible in all their creeds; have driven them, in a great measure, to the resource of the despairing—to a belief in the inevitable.[1] It is true that Confucianism has furnished them with an ideal saint, the creation of Confucius' imagination, called by the Chinese 君子 *Chün-tzŭ*, and by most foreigners, The Superior man.[2] But this is an ideal only, not a model, not a copyable example; and even as an ideal it is very imperfect.[3] So, to sum up the whole matter of religion, it appears that with the Chinese it is neither dark nor light; the darkness is not utter darkness, the light is not clear. They confuse God with idols, mix superstition up with their worship, separate morality from religion, paralyse themselves by believing in fate, admire and extol an ideal which they never try to copy and could not if they did, and, with a faith in a future state more or less vivid and strong, allow themselves to be completely engrossed in the pursuit of the present.

One more subject of importance claims our attention, namely, the government of the country; and with a few remarks thereon, suggested and supported by the proverbs, our task will be finished. To begin with the Emperor. His exalted position is thus acknowledged: 'The light of all the stars is not equal to that of the moon.'[4] His despotic power is hinted at somewhat significantly thus: 'When the prince wants a minister to die, he dies.'[5] And yet it is said that 'If the Son of Heaven breaks the laws, he is

1 See chapter on Fate. 2 See chapter on the Superior and Mean man.
3 See a very good article on the subject in the 3rd Vol. of the Chinese Recorder, page 129, by the Rev William Ashmore. 4 No. 2093. 5 No. 2091.

guilty like one of the people.'[1] Descending from the Emperor to his servants, we find abundance of proverbs very freely criticising them and their doings. The relative importance of civil and military officers is thus shown:

'One dash of a civil magistrate's pen,
Makes the martial magistrate jump again.'[2]

The question of magisterial integrity is apparently settled in the following apologetic saying: 'An honest magistrate cannot get on.'[3] It would seem that the mandarins are notorious for extortion for we read: 'A magistrate will not consider your poverty, nor the devil your leanness.'[4] And that the magistracy pays well is evident if it be only partially true that 'even an honest *Chih-fu* may during a three years' term of office, save ten myriad snow-white taels of silver.'[5] It is quite right that the mandarin be 'A lord among his people'[6], but from what is said below, it appears that he lords it over them too severely: 'Men's hearts are like iron, and the rule of mandarins like a furnace.'[7] After this it is some satisfaction to find that there are three good rules for men in office, namely, 'Be upright, be cautious, be diligent.'[8] If we come from mandarins to their courts of justice, we find nothing but condemnation. Hell only is the fitting emblem of a magistrate's *yamên*.[9] The *yamên* satellites are comparable only to voracious tigers, or blood-sucking flies.[11] It is shrewdly and significantly said,

'With only right to back you,
Be sure the *yamêns* lack you.'[12]

1 No. 2096. 2 No. 1169. 3 No. 1178. 4 No. 1181. 5 No. 1194. 6 No. 1187. 7. No 1183. 8 No. 1196. 9 No. 1160. 11 No. 1212. 11 No. 1216. 12 No. 1145.

Yet in respect of laws and their administration, we find this noble saying; 'In making laws, severity is indispensable; in administering them, clemency.'[1] From the general testimony of the proverbs it appears that the relations between rulers and ruled in China, is anything but satisfactory. Notwithstanding a few notable exceptions in the persons of disinterested officers; notwithstanding many good laws, and the power to execute them; notwithstanding the many excellent precepts exhorting the Officers to do their duty; Justice often cries out for her rights in vain, the people are oppressed, whilst the mandarins and their satellites are enriched.

In the preceding essay we have endeavoured to express the impartial testimony of the proverbs themselves, rather than to advance any opinions of our own; if error has crept into the account, the means of correcting it lies before the reader. And if the sketch drawn of the condition of things in China be blamed for incompleteness or exaggeration, we can only add that, in the collection of proverbs now presented to the reader, he has ample means at his own disposal for the completion or correction of the picture.

1 No. 1137.

PROVERBS.

SECTION I.—ON AGENCY.

CHAPTER I.

CAUSE AND EFFECT.

1

Every effect has its cause. *Lit.:* Rivers have sources, trees have roots.

水有源頭。木有根

Shui^3 yu^3 yüan^2 t'ou,^{2} mu^4 yu^3 kên.^{1}

2

It thunders loudly, but rains very little.

打得雷大。落得雨小

Ta^3 tê^2 lei^2 ta,^{4} lo^4 tê yü^3 hsiao.^{3}

NOTE.—*e. g.* A trade is conducted with great bustle and show, but little profit is made.

3

Every thing must have a cause.

凡事必有因

Fan^2 shih^4 pi^4 yü^3 yin.^{1}

4

Cut up grass by the root, and it will sprout no more.

剪草除根。萌芽不發

Chien^3 ts'ao^3 ch'u^2 kên,^{1} mêng^2 ya^2 pu^4 fa.^{1}

5

No wind, no motion in the trees.

風不來。樹不動

Fêng^1 pu^4 lai,^{2} shu^4 pu^4 tung.^{4}

6

When the tree falls the shade is gone.

樹倒無陰

Shu^4 tao^3 wu^2 yin^1.

7

Putrid flesh breeds maggots ; rotten fish generates grubs.

肉腐出蟲。魚枯出蠹

Jou^4 fu^3 chʻu^1 chʻung,^{2} yü^2 kʻu^1 chʻu^1 tu.^{4}

8

More fuel more fire.

棚柴火燄高

Pʻêng^2 chʻai^2 ʻhuo^3 yen^4 kao.^{1}

9

Though a tree grow never so high, its falling leaves return to the root.

樹高千丈。葉落歸根

Shu^4 kao^1 chʻien^1 chang,^{4} yeh^4 lo^4 kuei^1 kên.^{1}

10

When a wall is cracked and lofty, its fall must be speedy.

牆隙而高。其崩必疾

Chʻiang^2 chʻi^4 êrh^2 kao,^{1} chʻi^2 pêng^1 pi^4 chi.^{3}

11

To foul the spring and expect the stream to be pure.

濁其源而求流之清

Cho^2 chʻi^2 yüan^2 êrh^2 chʻiu^2 liu^2 chih^1 chʻing.^{1}

12

He wishes to hide his footprints, and yet walks upon the snow.

欲滅跡而足雪踪

Yü^4 mieh^4 chi^1 êrh^2 tsu^2 hsüeh^3 tsung.^{1}

13

In digging up a tree you must begin with the root.

挖樹必從兜子起

Wa^1 shu^4 pi^4 tsʻung^2 tou^1 tzŭ^3 chʻi^3

14

Every thing has its lord.

物各有主

Wu^4 ko^4 yu^4 chu.^{3}

CHAPTER II.

THE NECESSITY OF EFFORT.

15

Sharp as a needle to grind a blunt axe,
Your strength to the utmost will surely tax.

鈍斧磨成鍼。只要工夫深

Tun^4 fu^3 mo^2 chʻêng^2 chên,^{1} chih^3 yao^4 kung^1 fu^1 shên.^{1}

16

To make a man of yourself you must toil; if you don't, you won't.

成人不自在。自在不成人

Chʻêng^2 jên^2 pu^4 tzŭ^4 tsai^4; tzŭ^4 tsai^4 pu^4 chʻêng^2 jên.^{2}

17

If you don't scale the mountain, you can't view the plain.

不上高山。不顯平地

Pu^4 shang^4 kao^1 shan,^{1} pu^4 hsien^3 pʻing^2 ti.^{4}

18

Without climbing mountains no one can know the height of heaven; without diving streams no one can know the thickness of the earth.

不登山不知天之高

Pu^4 têng^1 shan^1 pu^4 chih^1 tʻien^1 chih^1 kao^1;

不臨溪不知地之厚

pu^4 lin^2 chʻi^1 pu^4 chih^1 ti^4 chih^1 ʻhou.^{4}

19

Generals and Premiers spring not from seed sown; men must exert themselves.

將相本無種。男兒當自强

Chiang^1 hsiang^4 pên^3 wu^2 chung^4; nan^2 êrh^2 tang^1 tzŭ^4 chʻiang.^{2}

20

Strike a flint, and you'll get fire; strike it not, and you'll not get even smoke.

擊石原有火。不擊乃無烟

Chi^1 shih^2 yüan^2 yu^3 ʻhuo^3; pu^4 chi^1 nai^3 wu^2 yen.^{1}

21

Without going you can get to nowhere; you can complete nothing without doing.

路不行不到。事不爲不成

Lu^{4} pu^{4} hsing^{2} pu^{4} tao^{4}; shih^{4} pu^{4} wei^{2} pu^{4} chʻêng.^{2}

22

He who does nothing but sit and eat, will wear away a mountain (of wealth).

坐食山崩

Tso^{4} shih^{2} shan^{1} pêng.^{1}

23

If you long for pleasure, you must labour hard to get it.

欲求生快活。須下死工夫

Yü^{4} chʻiu^{2} shêng^{1} kʻuai^{4} ʻhuo,^{2} hsü^{1} hsia^{4} ssŭ^{3} kung^{1} fu.^{1}

24

If you do not enter a tiger's den, you cannot get his cubs.

不入虎穴。不得虎子

Pu^{4} ju^{4} ʻhu^{3} hsüeh,^{4} pu^{4} tê^{2} ʻhu^{3} tzŭ.^{3}

25

He is equal to any task who can subsist on cabbage stalks.

咬得菜根百事可做

Yao^{3} tê^{2} tsʻai^{4} kên^{1} pai^{3} shih^{4} kʻo^{3} tso.^{4}

26

You had better return home and make a net, than go down to the river and desire to get the fishes.

臨淵羨魚。不如退而結網

Lin^{2} yüan^{1} hsien^{4} yü^{2}, pu^{4} ju^{2} tʻui^{4} êrh^{2} chieh^{2} wang.^{3}

27

Never was a good work done without much trouble.

從來好事必竟多磨

Tsʻung^{2} lai^{2} hao^{3} shih^{4} pi^{4} ching^{4} to^{1} mo.^{2}

CHAPTER III.

EXAMPLE.

— 28 —

When the upper beam is crooked, the lower must be wry.
When the middle beam is crooked, in a ruin all must lie.

上 梁 不 正 下 梁 歪
Shang^{4} liang^{2} pu^{4} cheng^{4} hsia^{4} liang^{2} wai^{1};
中 梁 不 正 倒 下 來
Chung^{1} liang^{2} pu^{4} ching^{4} tao^{3} hsia^{4} lai.^{2}

— 29 —

Keep company with good men: and good men you'll learn to be;
But you must shoulder false gods if you follow sorcery.

跟 好 人 學 好 人
Kên^{1} ʻhao^{3} jen^{2} hsio^{2} ʻhao^{3} jên^{2};
跟 端 公 扛 假 神
Kên^{1} tuan^{1} kung^{1} kang^{1} chia^{3} shên.^{2}

NOTE.—*Tan kung* or *Ma chiao* (馬脚) are mediums through whom the idols are supposed to grant answers to prayer.

— 30 —

Keep company with good men, and good men you will imitate;
Keep company with beggars, and sleep outside some temple gate.

跟 好 人 學 好 人
Kên^{1} ʻhao^{3} jên^{2} hsio^{2} ʻhao^{3} jên^{2};
跟 討 飯 的 睡 廟 門
Kên^{1} tʻao^{3} fan^{4} ti^{1} shui^{4} miao^{4} mên.^{2}

— 31 —

One takes the colour of one's company. *Lit.:* Near vermilion one gets stained pink; near ink one gets stained black.

近 硃 者 紫。近 墨 者 黑

Chin^4 chu^1 chê^2 tzŭ^3; chin^4 mei^4 chê^2 ʻhei.^{1}

32

One takes the odour of one's company. *Lit.:* Near putrid fish you'll stink; near the epidendrum you'll be fragrant.

近 鮑 者 臭。近 蘭 者 香

Chin^4 pao^4 chê^2 chʻou^4; chin^4 lan^2 chê^2 hsiang.^{1}

33

Never be with a bad man.

人 斷 不 可 和 小 人 在 一 塊

Jên^2 tuan^4 pu^4 kʻo^3 ʻho^2 hsiao^3 jên^2 tsai^4 yi^1 kʻuai.^{4}

34

Imitate *Ssŭ-ma* who laid up much secret merit.

法 司 馬 廣 積 陰 功

Fa^3 Ssŭ^1-ma^3 kuang^3 chi^2 yin^1 kung.^{1}

35

All bad alike. *Lit.:* Putrid flesh is all of a flavour.

臭 肉 同 味

Chʻou^4 jou^4 tʻung^2 wei.^{4}

36

When one sheep leads the way all the rest follow.

一 羊 前 行 衆 羊 後 繼

Yi^1 yang^2 chʻien^2 hsing^2 chung^4 yang^2 ʻhou^4 chi.^{4}

37

Look not at thieves eating flesh, but look at them suffering punishment.

莫 看 强 盜 吃 肉

Mo^4 kʻan^4 chʻiang^2 tao^4 chʻih^1 jou,^{4}

只 看 强 盜 受 罪

Chih^3 kʻan^4 chʻiang^2 tao^4 shou^4 tsui.^{4}

38

Follow the good, and learn to be so.

跟 好 學 好

Kên^1 ʻhao^3 hsio^2 ʻhao.^{3}

海上絲綢之路文獻集成 科技與文化編

39

When white calico has been dipped in the dyeing vat, nobody can tell it from black.

白 布 吊 在 染 缸 皂 白 難 分

Pai^{2} pu^{4} tiao^{4} tsai^{4} jan^{3} kang^{1} tsao^{4} pai^{2} nan^{2} fen.^{1}

40

When old men are not upright, they teach their sons and grandsons to be rogues.

爲 老 不 正 教 壞 子 孫

Wei^{2} lao^{3} pu^{4} chêng^{4} chiao^{4} ʻhuai^{4} tzŭ^{3} sun.^{1}

41

Follow example. *Lit.:* Recite according to the book.

照 本 宣 科

Chao^{4} pên^{3} hsüan^{1} kʻo.^{1}

42

Follow example in drawing your calabash.

照 樣 畫 葫 蘆

Chao^{4} yang^{4} ʻhua^{4} ʻhu^{2} lu.^{2}

43

He who leads an ox to drink must first wet his own feet.

牽 牛 喝 水 先 打 濕 脚

Chʻien^{1} niu^{2} ʻho^{1} shui^{3} hsien^{1} ta^{3} shih^{1} chiao.^{3}

44

Bad men leave their mark wherever they go. *Lit.:* He who carries lime in a basket, leaves traces wherever he stops.

籮 筐 裝 石 灰。在 處 有 跡 窩

Lo^{2} kʻuang^{1} chuang^{1} shih^{2} ʻhui,^{1} tsai^{4} chʻu^{4} yu^{3} chi^{1} wo.^{1}

45

The people follow the example of those above them.

上 之 所 爲 民 之 歸 也

Shang^{4} chih^{1} so^{3} wei^{2} min^{2} chih^{1} kuei^{1} yeh.^{3}

46

When a large vessel has opened a way, it is easy for a small one to follow.

大船拖成漕。小船不用篙
Ta⁴ chʻuan² tʻo¹ chʻêng² tsʻao,² hsiao³ chʻuan² pu⁴ yung⁴ kao.¹

47

They looked on the good as though they were inimitable; on the bad as on plunging the hand into boiling water.

見善如不及。見惡如探湯
Chien⁴ shan⁴ ju² pu⁴ chi²; chien⁴ o⁴ ju² tʻan¹ tʻang.¹

NOTE.—This was an old saying in Confucius' time, and was quoted by him as applicable to several of his own disciples, as well as to others his contemporaries. See Legge, vol. i, page 178.

48

Shoes made by the Elder Brother's wife, are a pattern for the Younger Brother's wife to copy.

嫂嫂做鞋 嬸子有樣
Sao³ sao³ tso⁴ hsieh¹ shên³ tzŭ³ yu³ yang.⁴

49

You have an itching to do whatever you see others doing.

見人屙屎喉嚨癢
Chien⁴ jên² wo¹ niao⁴ ʻhou² lung³ yang.³

NOTE.—This is a very course, but very common saying. I have purposely given it a free translation.

CHAPTER IV.

IMPOSSIBILITIES.

50

Little pillars, it is plain,
Cannot heavy weights sustain.

不大其棟。不能任重

Pu⁴ ta⁴ ch'i² tung,⁴ pu⁴ nêng² jên⁴ chung.⁴

51

No needle has two sharp points.

針無兩頭利

Chên¹ wu² liang³ t'ou² li.⁴

NOTE.—The meaning of this is that it is impossible for a man to do two things at once.

52

To force a hen to hatch chickens.

按倒鷄母飽兒

An⁴ tao³ chi¹ mu³ pao⁴ êrh.²

53

A toad propping a bedpost firmly.

癞蝦蟆墊牀脚硬掙

Lai⁴ 'ha² ma³ tien⁴ ch'uang² chiao³ ying⁴ chêng.⁴

54

To box in the stern of a pair of trowsers.

褲襠裏打拳

K'u⁴ tang¹ li³ ta³ ch'üan.²

55

Ants removing Mount *T'ai.*

螞蟻搬泰山

Ma³ i³ pan¹ T'ai⁴ Shan.¹

56

You cannot shade off the sun's light with one hand.

一把掌遮不住這日頭

Yi¹ pa¹ chang³ chê¹ pu⁴ chu⁴ chê⁴ jih⁴ t'ou.²

57

Throw a tile over a wall and you cannot say on which side it has lighted.

隔牆丟瓦未知仰撲

Ko^{2} chʻiang^{2} tiu^{1} wa^{1}, wei^{4} chih^{1} yang^{3} pʻu.^{1}

58

It is impossible to tell what is in the future. *Lit.* f One may feel but not see the hair on the back o: one's neck.

後頸窩裏毛摸得到看不見

ʻHou^{4} kêng^{3} wo^{1} li^{3} mao^{2} mo^{1} tê^{2} tao^{4} kʻan^{4} pu^{4} chien.^{4}

59

A clever daughter-in-law cannot cook without rice.

巧媳婦難作無米之炊

Chʻiao^{3} hsi^{2} fu^{4} nan^{2} tso^{4} wu^{2} mi^{3} chih^{1} chʻui.^{1}

60

One foot cannot stand on two boats.

一隻脚踏不得兩隻船

Yi^{1} chih^{1} chiao^{3} tao^{4} pu^{4} tê^{2} liang^{3} chih^{1} chʻuan.^{2}

61

If an ox won't drink, you can't make him bend down his head.

牛不吃水。按不住頭

Niu^{2} pu^{4} chʻih^{1} shui^{3}, an^{4} pu^{4} chu^{4} tʻou.^{2}

62

You cannot clap with one palm.

一個巴掌拍不響

Yi^{1} ko^{4} pa^{1} chang^{3} pʻai^{1} pu^{4} hsiang.^{2}

63

A single strand of silk cannot make a thread; a solitary tree cannot make a grove.

單絲不成綫。孤木不成林

Tan^{1} ssŭ^{1} pu^{4} chʻêng^{2} hsien^{4}; ku^{1} mu^{4} pu^{4} chʻêng^{2} lin.^{2}

64

The materials used in building a temple and its anterooms, are not the branches of one tree only.

諺語叢話

廟廊之材非一木之枝
Miao[4] lang[2] chih[1] ts'ai[2] fei[1] yi[1] mu[4] chih[1] chih.[1]

65

One man cannot do two yamen-runners' work.

一身不能當二役
Yi[1] shên[1] pu[4] nêng[2] tang[1] êrh[4] yi[4]

66

One man cannot manage too many affairs. *Lit.*: Like pumpkins in water, one pops up while you press another down.

水裏按葫蘆你起我落
Shui[3] li[3] an[4] 'hu[2] lu[2] ni[3] ch'i[3] wo[3] lo.[4]

67

One bamboo pole cannot reach the bottom.

一根竹篙打不倒启
Yi[1] ken[1] chu[2] kao[1] ta[3] pu[4] tao[3] tu.[2]

68

Beyond one's strength; as *K'ua Fu's* race after the sun's shadow.

事不量力。如夸父追日
Shih[4] pu[4] liang[2] li[4]; ju[2] K'ua[1] Fu[4] chui[1] jih.[4]

NOTE.—*K'ua Fu*, desiring to overtake the sun's shadow, pursued it into the Vale of *Yang* (陽). In this chase he grew thirsty. He found a river; but its waters could not quench his thirst. He then turned his steps northward that he might drink the waters of *T'ai-tsê* (太澤). But before he got there he died of thirst. Dying, he flung down his staff. Thereupon a heavy rain fell and covered it over with mud. From it sprang the bamboo forest of *Têng* (鄧), which overs ten *li* of ground. *Yu-hsio* (幼學). Bk. I. § *T'ien wên* (天文).

69

One actor cannot perform a play.

獨脚戲難唱
Tu[2] chiao[3] hsi[4] nan[4] ch'ang.[4]

70

One louse cannot raise a coverlet.

一個蝨子頂不起被窩
Yi[1] ko[4] shih[1] tzŭ[3] ting[3] pu[4] ch'i[3] pei[4] wo.[1]

71

How can one pole build a great house!

一 木 焉 能 支 大 厦

Yi¹ mu⁴ yen¹ nêng² chih¹ ta⁴ hsia.⁴

72

This cup of strong wine is hard to swallow.

這 一 杯 湧 酒 難 得 吃

Chê⁴ yi¹ pei¹ yung³ chiu³ nan² tê² ch'ih.¹

73

Sandals for the same foot must be worn by different persons.

同 邊 草 鞋 各 穿 一 隻

T'ung² pien¹ ts'ao³ hsieh² ko⁴ ch'uan¹ yi¹ chih.¹

74

Who can secure a thousand-years' scheme?

誰 人 保 得 千 年 計

Shui² jên² pao³ tê² ch'ien¹ nien² chi.⁴

CHAPTER V.

MODUS OPERANDI.

75

Would you yourself a perfect workman find,
To an embroidery needle an iron pestle grind.

若要功夫深

Jo^{4} yao^{4} kung^{1} fu^{1} shên,^{1}

鐵杵磨成綉花針

Tʻieh^{3} kan^{1} mo^{2} chʻêng^{2} hsiu^{4} ʻhua^{1} chen.^{1}

76

Save thoroughly, if you will;
Kill thoroughly, if you kill.

救人救到頭。殺人殺斷喉

Chiu^{4} jên^{2} chiu^{4} tao^{4} tʻou^{2}; sha^{1} jên^{2} sha^{1} tuan^{4} ʻhou.^{2}

77

Practice makes perfect. *Lit.*:—
The boxer's fist must keep to its task;
And the singer's mouth no rest must ask.

拳不離手。曲不離口

Chʻüan^{2} pu^{4} li^{2} shou^{3}; chʻü^{1} pu^{4} li^{2} kʻou.^{3}

78

Do thoroughly aught you set about:
Kill a pig,—kill him out and out.

做事做到頭。殺猪殺到喉

Tso^{4} shih^{4} tso^{4} tao^{4} tʻou^{2}: sha^{1} chu^{1} sha^{1} tao^{4} ʻhou.^{2}

79

Suppose your wish is to excel,
Before an expert practise well.

要得高。人前操

Yao^{4} tê^{2} kao,^{1} jên^{2} chʻien^{2} tsʻao.^{1}

80

The loftiest towers rise from the ground.

萬丈高樓從地起

Wan^{4} chang^{4} kao^{1} lou^{2} tʻsung^{2} ti^{4} chʻi.^{3}

81

Every thing is difficult at first.

萬事起頭難

Wan^4 shih^4 chʻi^3 tʻou^2 nan.^{2}

82

It is easier to know how to do a thing than to do it.

知非難行之爲難

Chih^1 fei^1 nan^2 hsing^2 chih^1 wei^2 nan.^{2}

83

Easy to look at; difficult to imitate.

見者易。學者難

Chien^4 chê^2 yi^4; hsio^2 chê^2 nan.^{2}

84

Whoever undertakes a task cannot repudiate the responsibility.

領其手不能謝其責

Ling^3 chʻi^2 shou^3 pu^4 nêng^2 hsieh^4 chʻi^2 tsê.^{2}

85

What one knows not how to do is difficult; what one knows how to do is not.

難者不會。會者不難

Nan^2 chê^2 pu^4 ʻhui^4; ʻhui^4 chê^2 pu^4 nan.^{2}

86

What is earned with hard labour is eaten with pleasure.

辛苦討得快活吃

Hsin^1 kʻu^3 tʻao^3 tê^2 kʻuai^4 ʻhuo^2 chʻih.^{1}

87

Draw a tiger incompletely and it is only like a dog.

畫虎不成終類犬

ʻHua^4 ʻhu^3 pu^4 chʻêng^2 chung^1 lei^4 chʻüan.^{3}

88

A hundred paths present a hundred difficulties.

百般道路百般難

Pai^3 pan^1 tao^4 lu^4 pai^3 pan^1 nan.^{2}

諺語叢話

89

In hurry is error.

忙 中 有 錯

'Mang² chung¹ yu³ ts'o.⁴

90

Done leisurely, done well.

從 容 幹 好 事

Ts'ung² yung² kan² hao³ shih.⁴

91

Slow work produces fine goods.

慢 功 出 細 貨

Man⁴ kung¹ ch'u¹ hsi⁴ 'huo.⁴

92

Would you have a steady aim, bore through the rock to the fountains of the sea.

若 要 心 腸 堅。鑿 山 通 海 泉

Jo⁴ yao⁴ hsin¹ ch'ang² chien,¹ tso² shan¹ t'ung¹ 'hai² ch'üan.²

93

Nine-storied terraces rise by a gradual accumulation of bricks.

九 層 之 臺 起 於 累 土

Chiu³ ts'êng² chih¹ t'ai² ch'i³ yü² lei³ t'u.³

94

If you ferry at all, ferry right over.

渡 人 渡 上 岸

Tu⁴ jên² tu⁴ shang⁴ an.⁴

95

What is done hastily is not done well.

辦 事 太 忙 就 有 參 差 了

Pan⁴ shih⁴ t'ai⁴ mang² chiu⁴ yu³ ts'ên¹ ch'a¹ liao.³

96

Iron long fired becomes steel.

久 火 鍊 成 鋼

Chiu³ 'huo³ lien⁴ ch'êng² kang.¹

97

Anything beyond one's strength is never done well.

費力不討巧
Fei^4 li^4 pu^4 tʻao^3 chʻiao.^{3}

98

When the arrow is on the string it must go.

箭在弦上不得不發
Chien^4 tsai^4 hsien^2 shang^4 pu^4 tê^2 pu^4 fa.^{1}

99

What is chopped has not the roundness of what is turned.

砍的沒得車的圓
Kʻan^3 ti^1 mu^2 tê^2 chʻê^1 ti^1 yüan.^{2}

100

What you have to do, do without delay. *Lit.:* Wait till the Yellow River becomes clear, and how old will you be?

等得黃河清人壽幾何
Têng^2 tê^2 ʻHuang^2 ʻHo^2 chʻing^1 jên^2 shou^4 chi^3 ʻho^2?

101

To bottom an affair. *Lit.:* To dig up a tree in search for the root.

挖樹尋根
Wa^1 shu^4 hsin^2 kên.^{1}

102

Use careful reflection, and all things grow easy: shrink from considering, and all things grow hard.

用心計較般般易
Yung^4 hsin^1 chi^4 chiao^4 pan^1 pan^1 yi^4:
退步思量事事難
Tʻui^4 pu^4 ssŭ^1 liang^2 shih^4 shih^4 nan.^{2}

103

Practice makes perfect.

習慣成自然
Hsi^2 kuan^4 chʻêng^2 tzŭ^4 jan.^{2}

104

A novice at the first attempt, an adept at the second.

一回生。二回熟
Yi^1 ʻhui^2 shêng,^{1} êrh^4 ʻhui^2 shou.^{2}

105

To do or say anything by instalements!

傘 把 通 屁 眼。一 節 一 節 的 來

San^3 pa^3 t‘ung^1 p‘i^4 yen,^{3} yi^1 chieh^1 yi^1 chieh^1 ti^1 lai.^{2}

NOTE.—The literal translation of this proverb, more expressive than elegant, I leave to readers of Chinese.

106

Too many cooks spoil the broth. *Lit.:* Seven steersmen, eight sailors, one is uniform the other is not.

七 梢 公。八 水 手。你 齊 我 不 齊

Ch‘i^1 shao^1 kung,^{1} pa^1 shui^3 shou,^{3} ni^3 ch‘i^2 wo^3 pu^4 ch‘i.^{2}

107

The Same. *Lit.:* Seven hands and eight feet.

七 手 八 脚

Ch‘i^1 shou^3 pa^1 chiao.^{3}

108

As easy as to seize a tortoise in a jar.

罈 子 裏 捉 烏 龜。手 到 擎 拏

T‘an^2 tzŭ^3 li^3 cho^1 wu^1 kuei,^{1} shou^3 tao^4 ch‘ing^2 na.^{2}

109

It is easier than to blow dust off anything.

不 費 吹 灰 之 力

Pu^4 fei^4 ch‘ui^1 hui^1 chih^1 li.^{4}

110

Too great haste. *Lit.:* The same night that he catches a thief to the yamun he hurries him.

捉 倒 强 盗 連 夜 解

Cho^1 tao^3 ch‘iang^2 tao^4 lien^2 yeh^4 chieh.^{1}

111

To do hurriedly. *Lit.:* He breaks the *ch‘ing* in burning his incense.

燒 香 打 破 磬

Shao^1 hsiang^1 ta^3 p‘o^4 ch‘ing.^{4}

NOTE.—The *ch‘ing* is a musical stone used for ringing on during worship.

112

Congee naturally thickens as it cools.

粥冷自然綢

Chou¹ lêng³ tzŭ⁴ jan² chʻou.²

NOTE.—The design of this proverb is to warn against hurry or anxiety in doing anything.

113

Mistakes occur through haste, never through doing a thing leisurely.

只有急過的。沒有緩過的

Chih³ yu³ chi² kuo⁴ ti,¹ mu² yu³ ʻhuan³ kuo⁴ ti.¹

114

To perfect diligence nothing is difficult.

一勤天下無難事

Yi¹ chʻin⁴ tʻien¹ hsia⁴ wu² nan² shih.⁴

115

He who hurries cannot walk with a stately step.

忙行無好步

Mang² hsing² wu² hao³ pu.⁴

116

There is nothing difficult in the world; the only fear is that men will be lacking in perseverance.

世上無難事。只怕心不堅

Shih⁴ shang⁴ wu² nan² shih⁴; chih³ pʻa⁴ hsin¹ pu⁴ chien.¹

117

A thousand artisans a thousand plans.

千個師傳千個法

Chʻien¹ ko⁴ shih¹ chuan⁴ chʻien¹ ko⁴ fa.³

118

Easier said than done.

說得出來。做不出來

Shuo¹ tê² chʻu¹ lai,² tso⁴ pu⁴ chʻu² lai.²

CHAPTER VI.

RESOLUTION.

— 119 —

Be resolved and the thing is done.

有 志 者 事 竟 成

Yu[3] chih[4] chê[2] shih[4] ching[4] chʻêng.[2]

— 120 —

Resolution is independent of great age; but without it one lives a hundred years in vain.

有 志 不 在 年 高

Yu[3] chih[4] pu[4] tsai[4] nien[2] kao[1];

無 志 空 長 百 歲

wu[2] chih[4] kʻung[1] chang[3] pai[3] sui.[4]

— 121 —

Through all his ranges of spires the murex will force out his head.

螺 螄 彎 彎 就 自 有 出 頭 路

Lo[2] shih[1] wan[1] wan[1] chiu[4] tsŭ[4] yu[3] chʻu[1] tʻou[2] lu.[4]

— 122 —

Every task can be accomplished by a man of resolution.

事 怕 有 心 人

Shih[4] pʻa[4] yu[3] hsin[1] jên.[2]

— 123 —

With ease a man of worth establishes a family: and what is hard to the true superior man when he resolves?

大 丈 夫 起 家 容 易

Ta[4] chang[4] fu[1] chʻi[3] chia[1] yung[2] yi[4]:

眞 君 子 立 志 何 難

Chên[1] chün[1] tzŭ[3] li[4] chih[4] ho[2] nan?[2]

— 124 —

To do a good trade wants nothing but resolution; to do a large one nothing but application.

事業要好只在志氣
Shih4 yeh4 yao4 hao3 chih3 tsai4 chih4 ch'i4;
事業要大只在勤勞
shih4 yeh4 yao4 ta4 chih3 tsai4 ch'in2 lao.2

125

Possessed of resolution a man may make his living thereby; without it a man must earn his bread by the sweat of his brow.

有志吃志。無志吃力
Yu3 chih4 ch'ih1 chih4; wu2 chih4 ch'ih1 li.4

126

One with life-long resolution rivals the loftiness of Heaven.

平生志氣與天高
P'ing2 shêng1 chih4 ch'i4 yü3 t'ien1 kao.1

127

He who refuses to serve either king or prince is possessed of lofty resolution.

不事王侯高尚其志
Pu4 shih4 wang2 'hou2 kao1 shang4 ch'i2 chih.4

128

The first thing a scholar does is to establish resolution.

士先立志
Shih4 hsien1 li4 chih.4

129

He cannot see the river, his heart is so set on leaping the dragon gate.

兩眼並不觀河水
Liang3 yen3 ping4 pu4 kuan1 'ho2 shui,3
一心只望跳龍門
Yi1 hsin1 chih3 wang4 t'iao4 lung2 mên.2

NOTE.—In this figurative way the resolution with which a scholar attempts to gain his degree is set forth.

130

To be possessed of resolution. *Lit.:* To open the hand in order to grasp the moon in the heavens; to plunge into the sea in order to seize leviathan.

舒 手 就 捉 天 上 月
Shu[1] shou[3] chiu[4] cho[1] t'ien[1] shang[4] yüeh[4];
入 水 能 擒 海 中 鰲
ju[4] shui[3] nêng[2] ch'in[2] 'hai[3] chung[1] ao.[2]

NOTE.—The *Ao* is a fabulous sea monster, said to support the mountain *P'êng-lai* (蓬萊山) on its back.

131

Till transformed into a dragon, the glittering-scaled fish never lost his resolution.

錦 鱗 未 變 志 常 存
Chin[3] lin[2] wei[4] pien[4] chih[4] ch'ang[2] ts'un.[2]

SECTION II.—ON ANIMALS.

CHAPTER I.

BEASTS.

132

Although dogs together fight,
They are very soon all right.

狗相咬。易得好

Kou^3 hsiang^1 ao,^{3} yi^4 tê^2 ʻhao.^{3}

133

The dog understands his master's mood.

狗通人性

Kou^3 tʻung^1 jên^2 hsing.^{4}

134

The dog has no aversion to a poor family.

狗不嫌家貧

Kou^3 pu^4 hsien^2 chia^1 pʻin.^{3}

135

Dogs have more good in them than men think they have.

狗有義人不知

Kou^3 yu^3 i^4 jên^2 pu^4 chih.^{1}

136

One dog barks at something, and a hundred bark at him.

一犬吠形。百犬吠聲

Yi^1 chʻüan^3 fei^4 hsing,^{2} pai^3 chʻüan^3 fei^4 shêng.^{1}

137

The dog guards the night, the cock rules the morn.

犬守夜。鷄司晨

Chʻüan^3 shou^3 yeh,^{4} chi^1 ssŭ^1 chʻên.^{2}

138

The cat steals the rice, and the dog comes and eats it.

貓子搬倒甑。替狗子趕倒張

Mao^1 tzŭ^3 pan^1 tao^3 tsêng,^{4} tʻi^4 kou^3 tsŭ^3 kan^2 tao^3 chang.^{1}

139

The horse never turns its back on its master.

馬 不 背 主

Ma^3 pu^4 pei^4 chu.^{3}

140

Cavalry horses delight in battle.

征 馬 戀 鬭 戰

Chêng^1 ma^3 lien^4 tou^4 chan^4.

141

A good horse resembles a superior man.

良 馬 比 君 子

Liang^2 ma^3 pi^3 chün^1 tzŭ.^{3}

142

Men and beasts are all alike.

人 畜 一 般

Jên^2 shou^4 yi^1 pan.^{1}

NOTE.—This proverb, which reminds one of the saying in the Book of Ecclesiastes—"so that a man hath no pre-eminence above a beast"—is used sometimes to prevent cruelty to animals, and sometimes to dissuade from killing them for food.

143

"In a wind horses and cows don't agree."

風 馬 牛 不 相 及

Fêng^1 ma^3 niu^2 pu^4 hsiang^1 chi.^{2}

144

The horse knows his owner.

馬 能 識 主

Ma^3 nêng^2 shih^4 chu.^{3}

NOTE.—"The ox knoweth his owner, and the ass his master's crib." Isa. i: 3.

145

The Stag, Phœnix, Tortoise, and Dragon, are the four chiefs of birds and beasts.

麟 鳳 龜 龍。謂 之 四 靈

Lin^2 fêng^4 kuei^1 lung,^{2} wei^4 chih^1 ssŭ^4 ling.^{2}

146

The impetuous steed won't brook restraint.

迅 馬 遊 韁。不 必 守 防

Hsin^4 ma^3 yu^2 chiang,^{1} pu^4 pi^4 shou^4 fang.^{2}

CHAPTER II.

BIRDS.

147

The swallow's plastering up its nest is labour lost.

燕 子 啣 泥 一 塲 空

Yen^4 tzŭ^3 hsien^2 ni^2 yi^1 chʻang^2 kʻung.^{1}

NOTE.—This saying rests on the migratory character of the bird for its justification.

148

The yellow hawk does not rob nests for food.

黃 鶯 不 打 窩 下 食

ʻHuang^2 ying^1 pu^4 ta^3 wo^1 hsia^4 shih.^{2}

149

A sparrow is a little bird yet it has liver and gall all complete.

麻 鵲 雖 小 肝 膽 俱 全

Ma^2 chʻiao^3 sui^1 hsiao^3 kan^1 tan^3 chü^4 chʻüan.^{2}

NOTE.—This proverb enforces the necessity of careful attention to the smallest details of any work or service.

150

In cold weather cocks crow at midnight.

寒 鷄 半 夜 啼

ʻHan^2 chi^1 pan^4 yeh^4 tʻi.^{2}

151

Crows are black all the world over.

處 處 老 鴉 一 般 黑

Chʻu^4 chʻu^4 lao^3 ya^1 yi^1 pan^1 ʻhei.^{1}

152

The crow does not devour fowls; they are the prey of the eagle.

老 鴉 不 吃 鷄。該 鷹 的

Lao^3 ya^1 pu^4 chʻih^1 chi^1; kai^1 ying^1 ti.^{1}

153

The wild goose brings the beginning of Autumn.

新 秋 鴈 帶 來

Hsin^1 chʻiu^1 yen^4 tai^4 lai.^{2}

154

The heron eats not heron's flesh.

鷺鷥不吃鷺鷥肉

Lu^4 ssŭ^1 pu^4 ch'ih^1 lu^4 ssŭ^1 jou.^{4}

155

Does the swallow know the wild goose's intention ?

燕雀豈知鴻鵠志

Yen^4 ch'iao^3 ch'i^3 chih^1 'hung^2 ku^3 chih.^{4}

SECTION III.—ON BUSINESS.

CHAPTER I.

BUYING AND SELLING.

156

When two partners have one mind,
Clay is into gold refined.

二人同一心。黃土變成金
Erh^4 jên^2 tʻung^2 yi^1 hsin,^{1} ʻhuang^2 tʻu^3 pien^4 chʻêng^2 chin.^{1}

157

At market prices do your trade,
And mutual wrangling you'll evade,

時值估價。不得相罵
Shih^2 chih^2 ku^1 chia,^{4} pu^4 tê^2 hsiang^1 ma.^{4}

158

Where much pushing must be made,
There cannot be a lively trade.

求買求賣。生意不快
Chʻiu^2 mai^3 chʻiu^2 mai,^{4} shêng^1 i^4 pu^4 kʻuai.^{4}

159

Who does not ready money clutch,
Of business talent has not much.

現錢不抓。不是行家
Hsien^4 chʻien^2 pu^4 chua,^{1} pu^4 shih^4 ʻhang^2 chia.^{1}

160

In melon plots, picking and choosing,
As one proceeds, grow more confusing.

園裡選瓜。越選越差
Yüan^2 li^3 hsüan^3 kua,^{1} yüeh^4 hsüan^3 yüeh^4 chʻa.^{1}

161

If no profit he espies,
Where's the man will early rise?

人無利息。誰肯早起
Jên^2 wu^2 li^4 hsi,^{2} shui^2 kʻên^3 tsao^3 chʻi^3?

162

Hurrying along on both one's feet,
Is all for clothes and something to eat.

兩足忙忙走。只爲身合口
Liang^3 tsu^2 mang^2 mang^2 tsou,^{4} chih^3 wei^4 shên^1 ʻho^2 kʻou.^{3}

163

After a heavy fall of snow,
Fuel, rice, oil, and salt, all dearer grow.

大雪紛紛下
Ta^4 hsüeh^3 fên^1 fên^1 hsia,^{4}
柴米油鹽都長價
Chʻai,^{2} mi,^{3} yu,^{2} yen,^{2} tu^1 chang^3 chia.^{4}

164

From small profits and many expenses,
Comes a whole life of sad consequences.

賺錢少用錢多。一身受奔波
Chuan^4 chʻien^2 shao^3 yung^4 chʻien^2 to,^{1} yi^1 shên^1 shou^4 pên^1 po.^{1}

165

Fortunes of thousands, of thousands ten,
Cannot be made but by able men.

成千累萬。要有力賺
Chʻêng^2 chʻien^1 lei^3 wan,^{4} yao^4 yu^3 li^4 chuan.^{4}

166

He plans less for profit than for quick returns, who
Will buy a thing for three cash and sell it for two.

三個錢買。兩個錢賣
San^1 ko^4 chʻien^2 mai,^{3} liang^3 ko^4 chʻien^2 mai,^{4}
不圖賺錢只圖快
Pu^4 tʻu^2 chuan^4 chʻien^2 chih^3 tʻu^2 kʻuai.^{4}

167

Whenever you go abroad to trade;
Of showing your silver be afraid.

出外做客。不要露白
Chʻu^1 wai^4 tso^4 kʻo,^{4} pu^4 yao^4 lou^4 po.^{2}

168

In fine weather he won't go out;
In dull he hawks cold jelly about;
In the sixth month felt hats he'd sell;
And in the first, door gods as well.

天 晴 不 出 門。天 濕 賣 凉 粉
Tʻien1 chʻing2 pu4 chʻu1 mên;2 tʻien1 shih1 mai4 liang2 fên;3
六 月 賣 氈 帽。正 月 賣 門 神
Lu4 yüeh4 mai4 chan1 mao;4 chêng1 yüeh mai4 mên2 shên.2

NOTE.—In the Chinese December a brisk trade is done in all directions in pictures of gods, etc. for the doors; but no sooner does the new year come in than that trade ceases entirely, and he would show a very foolish inattention to the state of the market who should attempt such a trade in January.

169

You skim the oil, with the broth make free,
Without a word of consulting me.

撇 開 油 喝 湯。不 與 我 相 商
Pʻieh1 kʻai1 yu2 ʻho1 tʻang,1 pu4 yü3 wo3 hsiang1 shang.1

170

Pay your cash and take your grog;
Drink it off and on you jog.

先 錢 後 酒。吃 了 就 走
Hsien1 chʻien2 ʻhou4 chiu;3 chʻih1 liao3 chiu4 tsou.3

171

Profits equally share;
Losses equally bear.

賺 錢 公 分。折 本 公 認
Chuan4 chʻien2 kung1 fên;1 chê2 pên3 kung1 jên.4

172

Buyers are esteemed;
Goods mere grass are deemed.

客 是 寶。貨 是 草
Kʻo4 shih4 pao;3 ʻhuo4 shih4 tsʻao.3

173

By entering all that's sold or bought,
You'll escape much anxious after-thought.

隨 筆 登 賬。免 後 思 量
Sui2 pi3 têng1 chang,4 mien3 ʻhou4 ssŭ1 liang.2

174

Though you have money do not spend it in the twelfth month.

有 錢 莫 買 臘 月 貨

Yu^{3} chʻien^{2} mo^{4} mai^{3} la^{4} yüeh^{4} ʻhuo.^{4}

175

If you would not be cheated ask the price at three shops.

貨 買 三 家 不 上 當

ʻHuo^{4} mai^{3} san^{1} chia^{1} pu^{4} shang^{4} tang.^{1}

176

If a little cash does not go, much cash will not come.

小 錢 不 去。大 錢 不 來

Hsiao^{3} chʻien^{2} pu^{4} chʻü,^{4} ta^{4} chʻien^{2} pu^{4} lai.^{2}

NOTE.—If you do not expend a little money in the entertainment of customers, you will get none.

177

Use the little to get the big.

以 小 到 大

I^{3} hsiao^{3} tao^{4} ta.^{4}

178

Throw a brick to allure a gem.

拋 磚 引 玉

Pʻao^{1} chuan^{1} yin^{3} yü.^{4}

179

A man without a smiling face must not open a shop.

人 無 笑 臉 休 開 店

Jên^{2} wu^{2} hsiao^{4} lien^{3} hsiu^{1} kʻai^{1} tien.^{4}

180

Cheap things are not good; good things are not cheap.

便 宜 不 是 貨。是 貨 不 便 宜

Pien^{4} i^{2} pu^{4} shih^{4} ʻhuo;^{4} shih^{4} ʻhuo^{4} pu^{4} pien^{4} i.^{2}

181

The melon seller declares his melons sweet.

賣 瓜 的 說 瓜 甜

Mai^{4} kua^{1} ti^{1} shuo^{1} kua^{1} tʻien.^{2}

182

Seeing a rush don't pursue.

見快莫趕

Chien^4 kʻuai^4 mo^4 kan.^{2}

183

After ten days' waiting above the rapids, you may traverse nine provinces in a day.

十日灘頭坐。一日走九州

Shih^2 jih^4 tʻan^1 tʻou^2 tso,^{4} yi^1 jih^4 tsou^3 chiu^3 chou.^{1}

NOTE.—This and the preceding proverb point out the advantage to be gained by patient perseverance in trade.

184

There is a time to fish, and a time to dry nets.

打網日灑網時

Ta^3 wang^3 jih,^{4} shai^4 wang^3 shih.^{2}

185

Fuel is not sold in a forest, nor fish on a lake.

林中不賣薪。湖上不鬻魚

Lin^2 chung^1 pu^4 mai^4 hsin,^{1} ʻhu^2 shang^4 pu^4 yu^2 yü.^{2}

186

Great profits, great risks.

利大害大

Li^4 ta^4 ʻhai^4 ta.^{4}

187

Use both such goods and money as suit your market.

貨消碼頭。錢用地頭

ʻHuo^4 hsiao^1 ma^3 tʻou,^{2} chʻien^2 yung^4 ti^4 tʻou.^{2}

188

It is easy to open a shop, but hard to keep it open.

開店容易守店難

Kʻai^1 tien^4 yung^2 yi^4 shou^3 tien^4 nan.^{2}

189

Count cash as though it were gold, and so avoid the least mistake.

數錢如看金。不差半毫分

Shu^4 chʻien^2 ju^2 kʻan^4 chin,^{1} pu^4 chʻa^1 pan^4 ʻhao^2 fên.^{1}

190

Better sell for small profits than fail in business.

折本不如賤賣貨

Chê² pên³ pu⁴ ju² chien⁴ mai⁴ ʻhuo.⁴

191

You cannot cheat one in the trade.

內行不上當

Nei⁴ ʻhang² pu⁴ shang⁴ tang.¹

192

When a steelyard hook is beaten into a nail, both its ends are drawn out straight.

秤鈎打釘兩扯直

Chʻêng³ kou¹ ta³ ting¹ liang³ chʻê³ chih.²

NOTE.—The steelyard hook in question is formed by bending one straight piece of iron wire; straightened out again it assumes its former condition. Hence this proverb is applied to one who is neither richer nor poorer for his trading.

193

Wares are good and bad; prices high and low.

貨有好歹。價有高低

ʻHuo⁴ yu³ hao³ tai;³ chia⁴ yu³ kao¹ ti.¹

194

A man may be more vigorous than his luck; or he may be more unbending than his goods.

人强命不强。人硬貨不硬

Jên² chʻiang² ming⁴ pu⁴ chʻiang;² jên² ying⁴ ʻhuo⁴ pu⁴ ying.⁴

195

When there is no fish in the river, shrimps are dear.

河裡無魚。蝦也貴

ʻHo² li³ wu² yü,² hsia¹ yeh³ kuei.⁴

NOTE.—This saying is sometimes applied to children, showing that daughters are precious in the absence of sons.

196

There may be trade to be done, and none able to do it.

生意有路。人無路

Shêng¹ i⁴ yu³ lu,⁴ jên² wu² lu.⁴

197

What the customer dreads is to be taken in.

買貨的客人怕上當

Mai^3 ʻhuo^4 ti^1 kʻo^4 jên^2 pʻa^4 shang^4 tang.^{1}

198

Bargaining is as necessary to trade as poling to a vessel.

嘴要爭。船要撑

Tsui^3 yao^4 chêng,^{1} chʻuan^2 yao^4 chang.^{3}

199

Ready money can buy any thing in stock.

現錢買現貨

Hsien^4 chʻien^2 mai^3 hsien^4 ʻhuo.^{4}

200

Bad silver will only buy old sow's flesh.

銅銀子買母豬肉

Tʻung^2 yin^2 tzŭ^3 mai^3 mu^3 chu^1 jou.^{4}

201

He sings for joy who makes a profit easily.

得了便財唱雅調

Tê^2 liao^3 pien^4 tsʻai^2 chʻang^4 ya^3 tiao.^{4}

202

When one cheats up to heaven in the price he asks; you come down to earth in the price you offer.

瞞天講價。就地還錢

Man^3 tʻien^1 chiang^3 chia,^{4} chiu^4 ti^4 ʻhuan^2 chʻien.^{2}

203

To fatten the mule and starve the horse.

肥了騾子瘦了馬

Fei^2 liao^3 lo^2 tzŭ^3 shou^4 liao^3 ma.^{3}

NOTE.—This refers to what is said to be common enough in China, namely, one partner's fattening himself at the expense of another.

204

Who cannot catch fish must catch shrimps.

不得魚也得蝦

Pu^4 tê^2 yü^2 yeh^3 tê^2 hsia.^{1}

205

In business one must be perfectly affable.

生意中要一團和氣

Shêng^1 i^4 chung^1 yao^4 yi^1 tʻuan^2 ʻho^2 chʻi.^{4}

206

Every trade has its ways.

生意各有道路

Shêng^1 i^4 ko^4 yu^3 tao^4 lu.^{4}

207

He who can turn his hand to anything, has not the mind of a fool; and stock which never lies dead, naturally yields a profit.

人多變化心不蠢

Jên^2 to^1 pien^4 ʻhua^4 hsin^1 pu^4 chʻun;^{3}

貨不停留利自生

ʻhuo^4 pu^4 tʻing^2 liu^2 li^4 tzŭ^4 shêng.^{1}

208

There are customers for all sorts of goods.

百貨中百客

Pai^3 ʻhuo^4 chung^1 pai^3 kʻo.^{4}

209

To sell a couple of cucumbers in three days.

三天賣兩條黃瓜

San^1 tʻien^1 mai^4 liang^3 tʻiao^2 ʻhuang^2 kua.^{1}

210

When water rises vessels rise; so rise market prices.

水長船高。高抬市價

Shui^3 chʻang^2 chʻuan^2 kao;^{1} kao^1 tʻai^2 shih^4 chia.^{4}

211

High prices attract sellers from afar.

價高招遠客

Chia^4 kao^1 chao^1 yüan^3 kʻo.^{4}

212

One word now will settle a bargain, though prices vary from morning to night.

目下一言爲定

Mu^4 hsia^4 yi^1 yen^2 wei^2 ting,^{4}

早晚時價不同

tsao^3 wan^3 shih^2 chia^4 pu^4 tʻung.^{2}

213

Buyers and sellers dispute over a single cash.

買賣爭毫厘
Mai³ mai⁴ chêng¹ ʻhao² li.²

214

Dispute the price, but don't dispute the weight.

爭價不爭平
Chêng¹ chia⁴ pu⁴ chêng¹ pʻing.²

215

Buying fresh fish and vegetables examine them first, then fix the price.

鮮魚小菜提藍着價
Hsien¹ yü² hsiao³ tsʻai⁴ tʻi² lan² cho² chia.⁴

216

Hold back your goods for a thousand days, and you'll be sure to sell at a profit.

放得千日貨。自有賺錢時
Fang⁴ tê² chʻien¹ jih⁴ ʻhuo,⁴ tzŭ⁴ yu³ chuan⁴ chʻien² shih.²

217

Ten thousand per cent is a cargo of wealth and return to one's home.

一本萬利。滿載而歸
Yi¹ pên² wan⁴ li,⁴ man³ tsai³ êrh³ kuei.¹

218

For profits as small as a fly's head, to rush from east to west.

蠅頭小利。奔西走東
Ying¹ tʻou² hsiao³ li,⁴ pên¹ hsi¹ tsou⁴ tung.¹

219

Just scales and full measures injure no man.

秤平斗滿不虧人
Chʻêng³ pʻing² tou³ man³ pu⁴ kʻuei¹ jên.²

220

Don't buy every thing that's cheap, and you'll escape being greatly taken in.

買不盡便易上不盡當
Mai³ pu⁴ chin⁴ pien⁴ yi⁴ shang⁴ pu⁴ chin⁴ tang.¹

221

He who has patience to wait for a shoal of fish, will catch small ones if not large.

耐 煩 等 得 羣 魚 到
Nai^4 fan^2 têng^2 tê^2 ch'ün^2 yü^2 tao.^{4}
大 魚 不 來 小 魚 來
ta^4 yü^2 pu^4 lai^2 hsiao^3 yü^2 lai.^{2}

222

Own brothers keep careful accounts.

親 兄 弟 明 算 賬
Ch'in^1 hsiung^1 ti^4 ming^2 suan^4 chang.^{4}

223

Relations or not relations, my turnips are three hundred cash per picul.

親 家 不 親 家
Ch'in^1 chia^1 pu^4 ch'in^1 chia,^{1}
蘿 蔔 三 百 錢 一 擔
lo^2 po^1 san^1 pai^3 ch'ien^2 yi^1 tan.^{1}

224

Small trades make great profit.

小 生 意 賺 大 錢
Hsiao^3 shêng^1 i^4 chuan^4 ta^4 ch'ien.^{2}

225

Even a dolt will not sell under cost price to favour any one.

癡 僕 不 把 本 饒 人
Ch'ih^2 'han^4 pu^4 pa^3 pên^3 jao^2 jên.^{2}

226

When you buy, buy genuine articles; and if you must lose, lose as little as possible.

買 貨 買 得 眞。折 本 折 得 輕
Mai^3 'huo^4 mai^3 tê^2 chên;^{1} chê^2 pên^3 chê^2 tê^2 ch'ing.^{1}

227

Those who make money make little exertion; those who make much exertion make no money.

賺 錢 不 費 力。費 力 不 賺 錢
Chuan^4 ch'ien^2 pu^4 fei^4 li;^{4} fei^4 li^4 pu^4 chuan^4 ch'ien.^{2}

228

A good customer won't change his shop, or a good shop lose its customer, once in three years.

好 客 三 年 不 換 店
'Hao³ k'o⁴ san¹ nien² pu⁴ 'huan⁴ tien,⁴

好 店 三 年 不 換 客
'hao³ tien⁴ san¹ nien² pu⁴ 'huan⁴ k'o.⁴

229

Those who can do a good trade don't wrangle over taxes.

會 做 買 賣 不 爭 衙 稅
'Hui⁴ tso⁴ mai³ mai⁴ pu⁴ chêng¹ ya² shui.⁴

230

When *Kuan Lao-yeh* sells bean-curd, the man is strông, the goods are weak.

關 老 爺 賣 豆 腐 人 强 貨 弱
Kuan¹ Lao³ yeh² mai⁴ tou⁴ fu³ jên² ch'iang² 'huo⁴ jo.⁴

NOTE.—In the popular idea *Kuan Lao-yeh* or the god of war, was originally nothing but a bean-curd seller. As such he is represented on the stage. And this proverb is employed in telling a man that however fine a salesman he may be, his goods are not up to the mark.

231

Able to buy, don't so buy as to frighten the seller: able to sell, don't so sell as to frighten the buyer.

會 買 莫 買 怕 人
'Hui⁴ mai³ mo⁴ mai³ p'a⁴ jên;²

會 賣 莫 賣 怕 人
'hui⁴ mai⁴ mo⁴ mai⁴ p'a⁴ jên.²

232

When there is no fish in one spot, cast your hook into another.

此 處 無 魚 別 下 鈎
Tz'ŭ³ ch'u⁴ wu² yü² pieh² hsia⁴ kou.¹

233

"Before you calculate on buying, calculate on selling."

未 算 買。先 算 賣
Wei⁴ suan⁴ mai,³ hsien¹ suan⁴ mai.⁴

234

Don't reckon on this year's bamboo, but on next year's bamboo sprouts.

不圖今年竹。也圖來年笋

Pu⁴ t'u² chin¹ nien² chu,² yeh³ t'u² lai² nien² sun.³

235

A string of cash can but reach to the back of one's heel.

一串錢打起脚後跟

Yi¹ ch'uan⁴ ch'ien² ta³ ch'i³ chiao³ 'hou⁴ kên.¹

NOTE.—This proverb says in effect:—The sum is a mere trifle, not worth contending about.

CHAPTER II.

CAPITAL.

236

Two men seeing eye to eye,
Having money gold can buy:
Without money, though he try,
One can but a needle buy.

兩 人 一 般 心。有 錢 堪 買 金

Liang^3 jên^2 yi^1 pan^1 hsin,^{1} yu^3 chʻien^2 kʻan^1 mai^3 chin:^{1}

一 人 一 般 心。無 錢 堪 買 針

Yi^1 jên^2 yi^1 pan^1 hsin,^{1} wu^2 chʻien^2 kʻan^1 mai^3 chên.^{1}

237

Small profits on large capital are after all great; great profits on small capital are after all small.

本 大 利 小 還 是 大

Pên^3 ta^4 li^4 hsiao^3 ʻhuan^2 shih^4 ta:^{4}

本 小 利 大 還 是 小

pên^3 hsiao^3 li^4 ta^4 ʻhuan^2 shih^4 hsiao.^{3}

238

Great capital great profits.

本 大 利 大

Pên^3 ta^4 li^4 ta.^{4}

239

You cannot trade without some capital. *Lit.:* You must have a couple of grains of rice in order to catch fowls.

扠 鷄 也 要 兩 顆 米

Chʻa^4 chi^1 yeh^3 yao^4 liang^3 kʻo^3 mi.^{3}

240

The same. *Lit.:* No one can sew without a needle: no one can row without water.

非 針 不 引 線。無 水 不 渡 船

Fei^1 chên^1 pu^4 yin^3 hsien:^{4} wu^2 shui^3 pu^4 ta^4 chʻuan.^{2}

241

Though boiled to ribbons the meat is still in the pan.

肉爛了在鍋裏

Jou[4] lan[4] liao[3] tsai[4] kuo[1] li.[3]

NOTE.—Applicable to stock in trade, or capital in hand.

242

Union of capital is like union of fate.

同夥本如同命

Tʻung[2] ʻhuo[3] pên[3] ju[2] tʻung[2] ming.[4]

243

Having capital to open an eating house, I dread not the most capacious stomach.

有錢開飯店。不怕你大肚漢

Yu[3] chʻien[2] kʻai[1] fan[4] tien,[4] pu[4] pʻa[4] ni[3] ta[4] tu[3] ʻhan.[4]

244

A dry finger cannot lick up salt.

乾指甲舔不取鹽來

Kan[1] chih[3] chia[3] tʻien[3] pu[4] chʻü[3] yen[2] lai.[2]

245

Without capital. *Lit.:* A farmer without an ox; a merchant without capital.

庄家無牛。客無本

Chuang[1] chia[1] wu[2] niu;[2] kʻo[4] wu[2] pên.[3]

246

To get on without capital. *Lit.:* He picks up grain and opens a mill.

撿倒麥子開磨坊

Chien[3] tao[3] mai[4] tzŭ[3] kʻai[1] mo[2] fang.[1]

247

To attempt great trade without capital. *Lit.:* With never a single hemp thread in his hand, he thinks to make a dozen nets.

手上沒得一根麻線

Shou[3] shang[4] mu[2] tê[2] yi[1] kên[1] ma[2] hsien,[4]

心裡想打十二股網

hsin[1] li[3] hsiang[3] ta[3] shih[2] êrh[4] ku[3] wang.[3]

CHAPTER III.

DEBTS, CREDIT, BORROWING, AND LENDING.

— 248 —

My capital's small and profits slender,
On credit my goods I can't surrender.

本小利窄。賒欠不得

Pên3 hsiao3 li4 tsê,4 shê1 chʻien4 pu4 té.2

— 249 —

Lend the man money if you have it to spare;
And if you have not, to be civil take care.

有錢將錢。無錢將言

Yu3 chʻien2 chiang1 chʻien;2 wu2 chʻien2 chiang1 yen2

— 250 —

It is not considered debt when the interest has been paid;
Nor when the principal's paid back can a charge of fraud be made.

還利不爲欠。還本不爲騙

ʻHuan2 li4 pu4 wei2 chʻien;4 ʻhuan2 pên3 pu4 wei2 pʻien.4

— 251 —

You borrow my umbrella,—to thank me do not try;
But through the night, I'd ask you, please, hang it up to dry.

借傘勿用謝。只要晾過夜

Chieh4 san3 wu4 yung4 hsieh4; chih3 yao4 liang4 ko4 yeh.4

— 252 —

Iron or brass,
Let nothing pass.

是銅是鐵。腰裏一撇

Shih4 tʻung2 shih4 tʻieh,3 yao1 li3 yi1 pʻieh.1

NOTE.—This proverb advises to take whatever can be got of a debt.

— 253 —

Better take eight hundred than give credit for a thousand cash.

千賒不如八百現

Chʻien1 shê1 pu4 ju2 pa1 pai3 hsien.4

254

Credit cuts off customers.

賒賬斷主顧

Shê[1] chang[4] tuan[4] chu[3] ku.[4]

255

We can deal with ready money customers; those who want credit may spare their breath.

現錢照顧。賒者免言

Hsien[2] ch'ien[2] chao[4] ku[4]; shê[1] chê[2] mien[3] yen.[2]

256

Better twenty per cent on ready money, than thirty per cent on credit.

賒三不如現二

Shê[1] san[1] pu[4] ju[2] hsien[2] êrh.[4]

257

Debt oppresses man. *Lit.*: The character *ch'ien* (debt) presses on the head of the character *jên* (man).

欠字壓人頭

Ch'ien[4] tzŭ[4] ya[1] jên[2] t'ou.[2]

NOTE.—This ingenious play on the word *ch'ien*, will be readily appreciated on an inspection of the way in which that word is written.

258

I shall easily get over this year's famine; but in my plenty it will be hard for you to meet me.

荒年易得過。實收難見人

'Huang[1] nien[2] yi[4] tê[2] ko[4]; shih[2] shou[1] nan[2] chien[4] jên.[2]

NOTE.—Said by one in low water, who wishes to borrow money, to one who refuses to lend it.

259

If any one wishes to enjoy the good will of his kind, let him sell on credit and never collect the money.

世上若要人情好

Shih[4] shang[4] jo[4] yao[4] jên[2] ch'ing[2] 'hao,[3]

賒去貨物莫取錢

shê[1] ch'ü[4] 'huo[4] wu[4] mo[4] ch'ü[3] ch'ien.[2]

260

One year borrows another year's food.

寅年支了卯年糧
Yin² nien² chih¹ liao³ mao³ nien² liang.²

261

He will even lend the plinths of his pillars.

躭倒柱頭把磉礅借人
Tan¹ tao³ chiu⁴ tʻou² pa³ sang³ tun¹ chieh⁴ jên.²

262

He who checks his appetite avoids debt.

忍嘴不欠債
Jên³ tsui³ pu⁴ chʻien⁴ chai.⁴

263

To lend without prospect of repayment. *Lit.:* To throw a fleshy bone at a dog.

丟肉骨打狗子
Tiu¹ jou⁴ ku³ ta³ kou³ tzŭ.³

264

The same. *Lit.:* If you pelt dogs with meat dumplings you will lose all and get nothing.

肉餃打狗有去無來
Jou⁴ chiao³ ta³ kou³ yu³ chʻü⁴ wu² lai.²

265

Urged to pay he resembles a tortoise.

逼得像烏龜
Pi¹ tê² hsiang⁴ wu¹ kuei.¹

NOTE.—This very uncomplimentary saying indicates the difficulty (experienced more particularly as the New Year approaches) of meeting with a debtor. Like the tortoise when assailed, he draws in his head, and hides himself.

266

He cannot pay his debts. *Lit.:* If I kill him he has no skin; if I scrape him he has no flesh.

殺他無皮。刮他無肉
Sha¹ tʻa¹ wu² pʻi;² kua¹ tʻa¹ wu² jou.⁴

267

No fear of dishonesty; the only fear is of penury.

不怕奸。只怕沒錢
Pu⁴ pʻa⁴ chien¹; chih³ pʻa⁴ mu² chʻien.²

NOTE.—Payment may be compelled in the one case, not in the other.

268

When the man dies the debt is lost.

人死債爛

Jên² ssŭ³ chai⁴ lan.⁴

NOTE.—That is if he leave no responsible persons behind, such especially as sons.

269

A son pays his father's debts, but a father will not recognise a son's.

父債子還。子債父不知

Fu⁴ chai⁴ tzŭ³ huan,² tzŭ³ chai⁴ fu⁴ pu⁴ chih.¹

270

Rather check your appetite than get into debt; and though penniless be patient.

忍口莫欠債。無錢且耐煩

Jên³ k'ou³ mo⁴ ch'ien⁴ chai⁴; wu² ch'ien² ch'ich³ nai⁴ fan.²

271

As the rivers pour their waters back again into the sea, so what a man has lent is returned to him again.

水流長江歸大海

Shui³ liu² ch'ang² chiang¹ kuei¹ ta⁴ 'hai,³

原物交還舊主人

yuăn² wu⁴ chiao¹ 'huan² chiu⁴ chu³ jên.²

272

Lend to one who won't repay, and you'll provoke his dislike.

借錢不還反招怪

Chieh⁴ ch'ien² pu⁴ 'huan² fan³ chao¹ kuai.⁴

273

For criminals there are prisons; where are there prisons for debtors?

只有犯罪的。那有該債的牢

Chih³ yu³ fan⁴ tsui⁴ ti¹; na³ yu³ kai¹ chai⁴ ti¹ lao.²

274

If you owe a man anything there is nothing like seeing him often.

欠債不如勤見面

Ch'ien⁴ chai⁴ pu⁴ ju² ch'in² chien⁴ mien.⁴

NOTE.—By this means it is supposed you will keep him in good temper.

275

It is easier to capture a tiger on the mountains, than to ask for a loan of money.

上山捉虎易。開口借錢難

Shang⁴ shan¹ cho¹ hu³ yi,⁴ k'ai¹ k'ou³ chieh⁴ ch'ien² nan.²

276

To borrow of one to pay another. *Lit.*: To tear down an eastern to repair a western wall.

拆東墻補西壁

Chê² tung¹ ch'iang² pu³ hsi¹ pi.³

CHAPTER IV.

FRAUDS.

277

Dealing in smuggled wine is very much in vogue;
Who does so undetected is the clever rogue.

家家賣私酒。不犯是好手

Chia¹ chia¹ mai⁴ ssŭ¹ chiu³; pu⁴ fan⁴ shih⁴ hao³ shou.³

278

If you get taken in say nothing about it.

上當莫做聲

Shang⁴ tang¹ mo⁴ tso⁴ shêng.¹

279

With money in your hand don't be taken in.

將錢不買輸

Chiang¹ ch'ien² pu⁴ mai³ shu.¹

280

You may sell a small quantity of an adulterated article; but you cannot buy a picul of the genuine.

賣得三分假。買不得一担眞

Mai⁴ tê² san¹ fên¹ chia³; mai³ pu⁴ tê² yi¹ tan⁴ chên.¹

281

The priest may run away, the temple cannot.

走了和尙。走不了廟

Tsou³ liao³ 'ho² shang,⁴ tsou³ pu⁴ liao³ miao.⁴

NOTE—Said of men, who, trading in their native places, where their shops or houses are situated, are in no danger of running away.

282

I shall only be taken in this once.

吃虧只這一回

Ch'ih¹ k'uei¹ chih³ chê⁴ yi¹ 'hui.²

283

If you try to dye a genuine red with spurious colouring, you must bear the unfavourable criticisms of by-standers.

假 顏 染 就 眞 紅 色
Chia^3 yen^2 jan^3 chiu^4 chên^1 ʻhung^2 sê,^{4}
也 被 旁 人 說 是 非
yeh^3 pei^4 pʻang^2 jên^2 shuo^1 shih^4 fei.^{1}

284

To stand under a tree waiting for wind.

站 得 樹 下 等 風
Chan^4 tê^2 shu^4 hsia^4 têng^2 fêng.^{1}

NOTE.—This proverb is said to be aimed at those who meanly wait for an opportunity to defraud others by specious offers of worthless services.

285

Ignorant of the jetties to pretend to be a porter.

碼 頭 未 找 倒 就 挑 籮
Ma^3 tʻou^2 wei^4 chao^3 tao^3 chiu^4 tʻiao^1 lo.^{2}

286

To pretend that the house leaks in order to defraud the landlord of his rent.

借 屋 漏 騙 店 錢
Chieh^4 wu^1 lou^4 pʻien^4 tien^4 chʻien.^{2}

287

Buy a cheap thing out of another's hand and you'll be taken in.

吃 虧 是 佔 便 宜
Chʻih^1 kʻuei^1 shih^4 chan^4 pien^4 i.^{2}

288

To follow the Dragon Boat shouting its cry.

跟 倒 龍 船 喊 號 子
Kên^1 tao^3 lung^2 chʻuan^2 ʻhan^3 ʻhao^4 tzŭ.^{3}

NOTE.—This is said of or to any one who makes a mere pretence of working.

289

If I have cheated you out of one, may I die a year before my time!

少 一 個。 短 一 歲
Shao^3 yi^1 ko,^{4} tuan^3 yi^1 sui.^{4}

CHAPTER V.

PAWNING AND SURETISHIP.

290

Who consent as middle-men or sureties to behave,
Accept responsibilities which are exceeding grave.

做中做保。就代不小

Tso^4 chung^1 tso^4 pao,^{3} tan^1 tai^4 pu^4 hsiao.^{3}

291

Do not be surety for one in custody, or for another man's debts.

官不保人。私不保債

Kuan^1 pu^4 pao^3 jên,^{2} ssŭ^1 pu^4 pao^3 chai.^{4}

NOTE.—"He that is surety for a stranger shall smart for it: and he that hateth suretiship is sure." Prov. 11 : 15.

292

To be surety for the bow means being surety for the arrow.

招弓如招箭

Chao^1 kung^1 ju^2 chao^1 chien.^{4}

293

Redeem one pledge with another, still that other is in pawn.

當當抵當當還在

Tang^4 tang^4 ti^2 tang^4 tang^4 ʻhuan^2 tsai.^{4}

294

When going to pawn say nothing about it.

當當莫做聲

Tang^4 tang^4 mo^4 tso^4 shêng.^{1}

295

To do nothing else but pawn. *Lit.:* To pawn, and take out of pawn, and pawn again.

當當取當當抵當

Tang^4 tang^4 chʻü^3 tang^4 tang^4 ti^2 tang.^{4}

296

Military offenders open small pawn shops; wealthy men open large ones.

軍 犯 開 小 押。財 主 開 典 當
Chün[1] fan[4] k'ai[1] hsiao[3] ya[1]; ts'ai[2] chu[3] k'ai[1] tien[3] tang.[4]

297

The axe strikes the chisel, and the chisel enters the wood.

斧 打 鑿。鑿 入 木
Fu[3] ta[3] tso,[2] tso[2] ju[4] mu.[4]

NOTE.—The axe represents the creditor, the chisel the surety, and the wood the debtor.

298

All middle-men prompt you to increase your offer: where is the middle-man who will assist you with his money?

只 有 添 錢 中 人
Chih[3] yu[3] t'ien[1] ch'ien[2] chung[1] jên[2];
那 有 貼 錢 中 人
na[3] yu[3] t'ieh[1] ch'ien[2] chung[1] jên[2]?

299

He who can recommend another has great respectability.

薦 主 面 子 大
Chien[4] chu[3] mien[4] tzŭ[3] ta.[4]

300

"A man is better than a pledge."

當 人 不 當 物
Tang[4] jên[2] pu[4] tang[4] wu.[4]

301

"Middle-men bear no responsibilities; and sureties pay no debts."

中 人 不 挑 担。保 人 不 還 錢
Chung[1] jên[2] pu[4] t'iao[1] tan[1]; pao[3] jên[2] pu[4] 'huan[2] ch'ien.[2]

302

The middle-man settles the bargain. *Lit.*: The words drop from the middle-man's mouth.

話 落 中 人 口
'Hua[4] lo[4] chung[1] jên[2] k'ou.[3]

303

A firm-shouldered surety.

硬肩的保

Ying^4 chien^1 ti^1 pao.^{3}

304

You may be surety for a general's going into battle; can you be surety for his coming out?

保得將軍進。保得將軍出

Pao^3 tê^2 chiang^1 chün^1 chin^4; pao^3 tê^2 chiang^1 chün^1 chʻu^1?

NOTE.—This proverb is of general application.

305

Selling land sell the house on it; and invite a middleman to settle your bargain.

賣基賣巢。請中說合

Mai^4 chi^1 mai^4 chʻao^2; chʻing^3 chung^1 shuo^1 ho.^{2}

CHAPTER VI.

TRADERS.

306

All unskilful fools,
Quarrel with their tools.

自巳無能。反推物鈍
Tzŭ^4 chi^3 wu^2 nêng,^{2} fan^3 tʻui^1 wu^4 tun.^{4}

307

Beat your gong, your candies vend;
Each must to his trade attend.

打鑼賣糖。各有一行
Ta^3 lo^2 mai^4 tʻang^2; ko^4 yu^3 yi^1 ʻhang.^{2}

308

Bachelors to talk of books incline;
Pork butchers delight to talk of swine.

秀才談書。屠戶談猪
Hsiu^4 tsʻai^2 tʻan^2 shu^1; tʻu^2 ʻhu^4 tʻan^2 chu.^{1}

309

One, like the letter *kung*, which can never raise its head,
Can only for one mouth alone secure daily bread.

工字不出頭。只能養一口
Kung^1 tzŭ^4 pu^4 chʻu^1 tʻou,^{2} chih^3 nêng^2 yang^3 yi^1 kʻou.^{2}

NOTE.—A slight inspection of the character *kung* (workman) will show the ingenuity of this pun.

310

On new year's day, and on a feast,
Every kind of work has ceased.

逢年遇節。百工都歇
Fêng^2 nien^2 yü^4 chieh,^{2} pai^3 kung^1 tu^1 hsieh.^{1}

311

No men occupy so degraded a position,
As the brothel-keeper, actor, and low musician.

世間只有三般醜
Shih^4 chien^1 chih^3 yu^3 san^1 pan^1 chʻou,^{3}
忘八戲子吹鼓手
Wang^4 pa^1 hsi^4 tzŭ^3 chʻui^1 ku^3 shou.^{3}

312

Porters and chairmen, without delay,
Soon as the job is done, want their pay.

挑籮抬轎歇下就要

T'iao[1] lo[2] t'ai[2] chiao,[4] hsieh[1] hsia[4] chiu[4] yao.[4]

313

When silversmiths decline to steal,
Their families starvation feel;
When tailors cabbage do refuse,
Their wives are minus drawers to use.

銀匠不偷銀。餓死一家人

Yin[2] chiang[4] pu[4] t'ou[1] yin,[2] o[4] ssŭ[3] yi[1] chia[1] jên[2]:

裁縫不偷布。婦人莫得褲

Ts'ai[2] fêng[3] pu[4] t'ou[1] pu,[4] fu[4] jên[2] mo[4] tê[2] k'u.[4]

314

When husbandmen have stored their grain,
They go to law, or build again.

鄉裏老收了穀

Hsiang[2] li[3] lao[3] shou[1] liao[3] ku,[3]

不打官事就蓋屋

Pu[4] ta[3] kuan[1] shih[4] chiu[4] kai[4] wu.[1]

315

To learn to play the fife and drum steadfastly decline,
If you don't want to sit outside, and to sip cold wine.

爲人莫學吹鼓手

Wei[2] jên[2] mo[4] hsiao[2] ch'ui[1] ku[3] shou,[3]

坐階簷喝冷酒

Tso[4] chieh[1] yen[2] 'ho[1] lêng[3] chiu.[3]

316

To his books a teacher must ever adhere:
His pigs, a poor man must continue to rear.

教學不離書。窮人不離猪

Chiao[4] hsiao[2] pu[4] li[2] shu[1]: ch'iung[2] jên[2] pu[4] li[2] chu.[1]

317

Better be master of one than Jack of all trades.

百藝無如一藝精

Pai[3] i[4] wu[2] ju[2] yi[1] i[4] ching.[1]

318

Every man to his calling. *Lit.:* Separate hongs are like separate hills.

隔行如隔山

Ko^{2} ʻhang^{2} ju^{2} ko^{2} shan.^{1}

319

The same. *Lit.:* The river does not overflow the well.

河水不氾井水

ʻHo^{2} shui^{3} pu^{4} fan^{4} ching^{3} shui.^{3}

320

Two of a trade hate one another.

當行厭當行

Tang^{1} ʻhang^{2} yen^{4} tang^{1} ʻhang.^{2}

321

There is mutual love between men of a creed, mutual jealousy between men of a trade.

同道者相愛。同藝者相嫉

Tʻung^{2} tao^{4} chê^{2} hsiang^{1} ai,^{4} tʻung^{2} i^{4} chê^{2} hsiang^{1} chi.^{4}

322

Serve but a day and you are a slave; deal in ever so small a way and you are a merchant.

幫人一日爲奴

Pang^{1} jên^{2} yi^{1} jih^{4} wei^{2} lu^{2};

肩挑四兩爲客

chien^{1} tʻiao^{1} ssŭ^{4} liang^{3} wei^{2} kʻo.^{4}

323

The fisherman must not desert his boat.

打魚的不離船邊

Ta^{3} yü^{2} ti^{1} pu^{4} li^{2} chʻuan^{2} pien.^{1}

324

There is room for all sorts of traders. *Lit.:* Many boats do not stop up a channel; many vehicles do not block up a road.

船多不礙港。車多不礙路

Chʻuan^{2} to^{1} pu^{4} ai^{4} chiang^{3}; chʻê^{1} to^{1} pu^{4} ai^{4} lu.^{4}

325

Every one to his calling. *Lit.:* The priest reverts to his monastery, and the merchant to his shop.

和 尚 歸 寺。客 歸 店

Ho² shang⁴ kuei¹ ssŭ,⁴ k'o⁴ kuei¹ tien.⁴

326

Pork butchers and dog-slayers will come to no good end.

殺 猪 剝 狗 無 有 下 稍

Sha¹ chu¹ po¹ kou³ wu² yu³ hsia⁴ shao.¹

NOTE.—In this saying vegetarians predict the sure punishment of all who indulge themselves in flesh meat.

327

Traders are like priests.

買 賣 如 修 行

Mai³ mai⁴ ju² hsiu¹ hsing.²

NOTE.—"Priests" *i.e.* virtue cultivators. Patience is the virtue needed by both, and the one here inculcated on tradesmen.

328

Trading with petty hucksters, don't banter them down too much.

與 肩 挑 貿 易。勿 佔 便 宜

Yü³ chien¹ t'iao¹ mao⁴ yi,⁴ wu⁴ chan⁴ pien⁴ i.²

329

A cloth huckster fears not your measure, though long as a carrying pole.

賣 布 的 不 怕 扁 担 量

Mai⁴ pu⁴ ti¹ pu⁴ p'a⁴ pien³ tan⁴ liang.²

NOTE.—You cannot outdo the tallyman. If he uses your measure, which is longer than his, he charges you a higher price.

330

An eatinghouse-keeper does not care how large your stomach is.

開 飯 店 的 不 怕 你 肚 子 大

K'ai¹ fan⁴ tien⁴ ti¹ pu⁴ p'a⁴ ni³ tu³ tzŭ³ ta.⁴

331

Three raw hands are unequal to one good hand.

三 生 趕 不 倒 一 熟

San¹ shêng¹ kan³ pu⁴ tao³ yi¹ shou.²

332

Who keeps the hills, burns the wood; who keeps the stream drinks the water.

管山的燒柴。管河的吃水

Kuan^3 shan^1 ti^1 shao^1 chʻai^2; kuan^3 ʻho^2 ti^1 chʻih^1 shui.^{3}

333

Farmers naturally realize enjoyment.

田家自有樂

Tʻien^2 chia^1 tzŭ^4 yu^3 lo.^{4}

334

There is a senior wrangler in every calling.

行行出狀元

ʻHang^2 ʻhang^2 chʻu^1 chuang^4 yüan.^{2}

335

A man of many trades cannot rear a family.

藝多不養家

I^4 to^1 pu^4 yang^3 chia.^{1}

SECTION. IV—ON DOMESTIC CONCERNS.

CHAPTER I.

FOOD AND CLOTHING.

336

Sow-thistles bitter, or oil made hot,
T'is matter of taste to eat or not.

熱 油 苦 菜。各 隨 人 愛

Jê4 yu2 k'u3 ts'ai,4 ko4 sui2 jên2 ai.4

337

Omit to stretch yourself after each meal,
And lumps in your throat you'll certainly feel.

吃 飯 不 撐 腰。必 定 是 喉 包

Ch'ih1 fan4 pu4 ch'êng1 yao,1 pi4 ting4 shih4 'hou2 pao.1

338

The cocks the morning greet—
My stomach is replete:
The cocks sound forth the noon—
I must be eating soon.

鷄 叫 早。肚 子 飽

Chi1 chiao4 tsao,3 tu3 tzŭ3 pao3:

鷄 叫 中。肚 子 空

Chi1 chiao4 chung,1 tu3 tzŭ3 k'ung.1

339

Of things to use and to refresh us,
Money and salt are the most precious.

吃 盡 天 下 鹽 好

Ch'ih1 chin4 t'ien1 hsia4 yen2 hao,3

用 盡 天 下 錢 好

yung4 chin4 t'ien1 hsia4 ch'ien2 hao.3

340

Don't eat the liver or blood of swine;
Shrimps and tortoises also decline.

猪 不 可 吃 肝 血
Chu^{1} pu^{4} kʻo^{3} chʻih^{1} kan^{1} hsieh^{3};
魚 不 可 喫 蝦 鼈
Yü^{2} pu^{4} kʻo^{3} chʻih^{1} hsia^{1} pieh.^{1}

341

On a journey never mind what progress you are making;
At a meal consider not how much food you are taking.
行 不 計 路。食 不 計 數
Hsing^{2} pu^{4} chi^{4} lu^{4}; shih^{2} pu^{4} chi^{4} shu.^{4}

NOTE.—The meaning of this proverb is, that you should, in eating, only consider the satisfying of hunger; and that, in travelling, you should not annoy the skipper or driver with questions about the distances.

342

Three meals will save a man from want;
Freedom from rags three suits will grant.
飯 有 三 餐 不 餓
Fan^{4} yu^{3} san^{1} tsʻan^{1} pu^{4} o^{4};
衣 有 三 件 不 破
I^{1} yu^{3} san^{1} chien^{4} pu^{4} pʻo.^{4}

343

He who cares for his belly much more than his back,
To face friends in his rags is uncommonly slack.
顧 嘴 不 顧 身。衣 破 難 對 人
Ku^{4} tsui^{3} pu^{4} ku^{4} shên,^{1} i^{1} pʻo^{4} nan^{2} tui^{4} jên.^{2}

344

Clothes can't be made an inch too long;
Boots must not be a fraction wrong.
衣 不 長 寸。鞋 不 差 分
I^{1} pu^{4} chʻang^{2} tsʻun^{4}; hsieh^{2} pu^{4} chʻa^{1} fên.^{1}

345

In dress and food do not break rules.
穿 衣 喫 飯 不 犯 條 律
Chʻuan^{1} i^{1} chʻih^{1} fan^{4} pu^{4} fan^{4} tʻiao^{2} lü.^{4}

346

Do not covet for the mouth and belly, and so slay beasts and birds without restraint.
勿 貪 口 腹 而 恣 殺 牲 禽
Wu^{4} tʻan^{1} kʻou^{2} fu^{2} êrh^{2} tzŭ^{4} sha^{1} shêng^{1} chʻin.^{2}

347

First secure food; then secure clothing.

先顧食。後顧衣

Hsien1 ku4 shih2; hou4 ku4 i.1

348

Though breakfast be good, dinner is better.

侵晨飯好。算不得午後飽

Chʻin1 chʻên2 fan4 hao,3 suan4 pu4 tê2 wu3 ʻhou4 pao.3

349

Only eat fresh fish and ripened rice.

魚喫新鮮。米喫熟

Yü2 chʻih1 hsin1 hsien,1 mi3 chʻih1 shu.2

350

Viands have various flavours; what pleases the palate is good.

物無定味。適口者珍

Wu4 wu2 ting4 wei,4 shih4 kʻou2 chê2 chên.1

351

When rice is not well cooked it is because the steam has been unequally distributed.

飯不熟氣不勻

Fan4 pu4 shu2 chʻi4 pu4 yün.2

352

Rustics feast twice a year; after the new year's feast, they look for the harvest-home.

鄉裏人一年兩回暈

Hsiang1 ni3 jên2 yi1 nien2 liang3 ʻhui2 yün1;

喫了年飯望喫新

chʻih1 liao3 nien2 fan4 wang4 chʻih1 hsin.1

353

Our daily bread depends on Heaven.

喫飯靠天

Chʻih1 fan4 kʻao4 tʻien.1

354

Clothes and food are daily mercies.

衣飯逐日生

I1 fan4 sui2 jih4 shêng.1

海上絲綢之路文獻集成　科技與文化編

355

A hungry man is glad to get boiled wheat.

肚餓好喫麥米飯

Tu^{3} chi^{1} hao^{4} chʻih^{1} mai^{4} mi^{4} fan.^{4}

356

Eyes must be closed to swallow maggots in one's food.

閉眼喫毛蟲

Pi^{4} yen^{3} chʻih^{1} mao^{2} chʻung.^{2}

NOTE.—This is used to complain of the dirtiness of any sort of food.

357

Feed moderately on wholesome food; garden herbs surpass rich viands.

飲食約而糧。園蔬愈珍饈

Yin^{3} shih^{2} yo^{1} êrh^{2} ching^{1}; yüan^{2} su^{1} yü^{4} chên^{1} hsiu.^{1}

358

There is dew for every blade of grass.

一根草有一根草的露水養

Yi^{1} kên^{1} tsʻao^{3} yu^{3} yi^{1} kên^{1} tsʻao^{3} ti^{1} lu^{4} shui^{3} yang.^{3}

359

When the wild bird lacks food, all the earth is before him.

野雀無糧天地寬

Yeh^{3} chʻiao^{3} wu^{2} liang^{2} tʻien^{1} ti^{4} kʻuan.^{1}

NOTE.—This beautiful saying reminds one of the Psalmist's words—"He giveth to the beast his food, and to the young ravens which cry." Ps. 147: 9. It reminds one also of our Lord's words—"Behold the fowls of the air: for they sow not, neither do they reap, nor gather into barns; yet your Heavenly Father feedeth them." Matt. 6: 26.

360

Fresh food is fragrant; stale food stinks.

新是香。陳是臭

Hsin^{1} shih^{4} hsiang^{1}; chʻên^{2} shih^{4} chʻou.^{4}

361

The more you eat, the less flavour; the less you eat, the more flavour.

多喫少滋味。少喫多滋味

To^{1} chʻih^{1} shao^{3} tzŭ^{1} wei^{4}; shao^{3} chʻih^{1} to^{1} tzŭ^{1} wei.^{4}

362

Whatever will fill your belly is good food.

物可充腸皆美食

Wu[4] k'o[3] ch'ung[1] ch'ang[2] chieh[1] mei[3] shih.[2]

363

We scheme for three meals per day, and for one sleep by night.

日圖三餐夜圖一宿

Jih[4] t'u[2] san[1] ts'an,[1] yeh[4] t'u[2] yi[1] hsiu.[3]

364

The mouth is an unlimited measure.

口是無量斗

K'ou[2] shih[4] wu[2] liang[2] tou.[3]

365

Dress makes the gentleman or lady.

有衣打扮便成人

Yu[3] i[1] ta[3] pan[4] pien[4] ch'êng[2] jên.[2]

366

To don the hat and sport the girdle is what everybody likes.

頂冠束帶世人愛

Ting[3] kuan[1] su[2] tai[4] shih[4] jên[2] ai.[4]

367

Those who go swinging and strutting are only dressed out for show.

一搖三擺實排場

Yi[1] yao[2] san[1] pai[3] shih[2] p'ai[2] ch'ang.[2]

368

As a house needs man to set it off, so a man needs clothes.

屋要人襯。人要衣襯

Wu[1] yao[4] jên[2] ch'ên,[4] jên[2] yao[4] i[1] ch'ên.[4]

CHAPTER II.

HOUSEHOLD AFFAIRS.

——— 369 ———

To make a family prosper, is like digging with needles in clay:
To bring a family to ruin, is like washing a sand-bank away.

興 家 爲 如 針 挑 土
Hsing^{1} chia^{1} yu^{2} ju^{2} chên^{1} t'iao^{1} t'u^{3}:
敗 家 猶 如 水 推 洲
Pai^{4} chia^{1} yu^{2} ju^{2} shui^{3} t'ui^{1} chou.^{1}

——— 370 ———

A grown tree spreads its branches wide;
A grown-up household must divide.

人 大 分 家。樹 大 分 椏
Jên^{2} ta^{4} fên^{1} chia^{1}; shu^{4} ta^{4} fên^{1} ya.^{2}

——— 371 ———

The hall which no ancient pictures grace,
Is not the home of an ancient race.

堂 前 無 古 畫。不 是 舊 人 家
T'ang^{2} ch'ien^{2} wu^{2} ku^{3} hua,^{4} pu^{4} shih^{4} chiu^{4} jên^{2} chia.^{1}

——— 372 ———

If you want to get along,
Let the old respect the young.

要 得 好。老 敬 小
Yao^{4} tê^{2} hao,^{3} lao^{3} ching^{4} hsiao.^{3}

——— 373 ———

Whene'er one family comes to grief,
A hundred families send relief.

一 家 不 彀。百 家 相 湊
Yi^{1} chia^{1} pu^{4} kou,^{4} pai^{3} chia^{1} hsiang^{1} ts'ou.^{4}

374

By three days' early rising one day's work you gain;
And from asking any favour you can well refrain.

早 起 三 日 當 一 工
Tsao^3 chʻi^3 san^1 jih^4 tang^4 yi^1 kung^1;
免 得 求 人 落 下 封
Mien^3 tê^2 chʻiu^2 jên^2 lo^4 hsia^4 fêng.^{1}

375

Domestic foibles must not be spread abroad.

家 醜 不 可 外 揚
Chia^1 chʻou^3 pu^4 kʻo^3 wai^4 yang.^{2}

376

When families quarrel, outsiders deride.

家 裡 不 和 外 人 欺
Chia^1 li^3 pu^4 ʻho^2 wai^4 jên^2 chʻi.^{1}

377

Better establish a branch, than cut off a line.

寧 可 成 一 房。不 可 敗 一 戶
Ning^2 kʻo^3 chʻêng^2 yi^1 fang,^{2} pu^4 kʻo^3 pai^4 yi^1 ʻhu.^{4}

NOTE.—You must perpetuate yourself in some way or other, either through your own or an adopted child.

378

Perfect harmony in a family removes all restrictions of speech.

一 團 和 氣。百 無 禁 忌
Yi^1 tʻuan^2 ʻho^2 chʻi,^{4} pai^3 wu^2 chin^4 chi.^{4}

379

To bring disgrace and ruin on the door.

做 得 辱 門 敗 戶
Tso^4 tê^2 ju^4 mên^2 pai^4 ʻhu.^{4}

380

Every household knows when salt and rice are dear.

當 家 纔 知 鹽 米 貴
Tang^1 chia^1 tsʻai^2 chih^1 yen^2 mi^3 kuei.^{4}

381

Quarrelling for superiority will gradually destroy the affairs of a family.

相論逞英豪。家計漸漸退
Hsiang¹ lun⁴ ch'êng³ ying¹ 'hao,² chia¹ chi⁴ chien⁴ chien⁴ t'ui.⁴

382

Fair maids and lovely concubines endanger family happiness.

婢美妾嬌非閨房之福
Pi⁴ mei³ ch'ieh⁴ chiao¹ fei¹ kuei¹ fang² chih¹ fu.²

383

Who takes in his son-in-law brings trouble into his house. *Lit.:* He calls in his son-in-law to play the mountebank.

招女婿搬把戲
Chao¹ nü² hsü⁴ pan¹ pa³ hsi.⁴

Note.—The maiden ought, of course, to leave her father's house and go to that of her husband. The opposite course is sure to result in scenes.

384

When any one in a family breaks the law, the sin is laid to the blame of its head.

家人犯法。罪在家主
Chia¹ jên² fan⁴ fa,³ tsui⁴ tsai⁴ chia¹ chu.³

385

Family quarrels. *Lit.:* One domestic demon mocks another domestic sprite.

家鬼弄家神
Chia¹ kuei³ nung⁴ chia¹ shên.²

386

One who can speak, speaks of markets; one who can't, speaks merely of household affairs.

會說說都市。不會說屋裡
'Hui⁴ shuo¹ shuo¹ tu¹ shih⁴; pu⁴ 'hui⁴ shuo¹ wu¹ li.³

387

It is easier to rule a kingdom than to regulate a family.

國易治。家難齊
Kuo² yi⁴ chih,³ chia¹ nan² ch'i.²

388

"The goodness of a house does not consist in its lofty halls, but in its excluding the weather; the fitness of clothes does not consist in their costliness, but in their make and warmth; the use of food does not consist in its rarity, but in its satisfying the appetite; the excellence of a wife consists not in her beauty, but in her virtue."

房屋不在高堂。不漏便好
Fang^{2} wu^{1} pu^{4} tsai^{4} kao^{1} tʻang,^{2} pu^{4} lou^{4} pien^{4} ʻhao^{3}:

衣服不在綾羅。和煖便好
i^{1} fu^{2} pu^{4} tsai^{4} ling^{2} lo,^{2} ʻho^{2} nuan^{3} pien^{4} ʻhao^{3}:

飲食不在珍饈。一飽便好
yin^{3} shih^{2} pu^{4} tsai^{4} chên^{1} hsiu,^{1} yi^{1} pao^{3} pien^{4} ʻhao^{3}:

娶妻不在顏色。賢德便好
chʻü^{3} chʻi^{1} pu^{4} tsai^{4} yen^{2} sê,^{4} hsien^{2} tê^{2} pien^{4} ʻhao.^{3}

389

Stupid wives and disobedient children no man can manage.

蠢妻逆子無法可治
Chʻun^{3} chʻi^{1} ni^{4} tzŭ^{3} wu^{2} fa^{3} kʻo^{3} chih.^{3}

390

When a family is in a fix, out comes the cash.

錢出急家門
Chʻien^{2} chʻu^{1} chi^{2} chia^{1} mên.^{2}

391

Everything prospers in a united family; though events do not happen according to men's calculations.

家和萬事興。事不由人算
Chia^{1} ʻho^{2} wan^{4} shih^{4} hsing,^{1} shih^{4} pu^{4} yu^{2} jên^{2} suan.^{4}

392

In a united family happiness springs up of itself.

家和福自生
Chia^{1} ʻho^{2} fu^{2} tzŭ^{4} shêng.^{1}

393

The family regulations of a self-complacent lazy fellow must be very much out of order.

頽惰自甘家道必索
T'ui[1] to[4] tzŭ[4] kan[1] chia[1] tao[4] pi[4] so.[3]

394

He gets little more time for sleep who refuses to rise with the dawn.

天亮不起。睡不多時
T'ien[1] liang[4] pu[4] ch'i,[3] shui[4] pu[4] to[1] shih.[2]

395

The loss of one night's sleep entails ten days of discomfort.

一夜不眠。十日不安
Yi[1] yeh[4] pu[4] mien,[2] shih[2] jih[4] pu[4] an.[1]

CHAPTER III.

MASTERS AND SERVANTS.

396

If you don't come it's no matter to me;
But if you do, serve obediently.

你不來我不怪
Ni^{3} pu^{4} lai^{2} wo^{3} pu^{4} kuai^{4};
你要來受我戒
Ni^{3} yao^{4} lai^{2} shou^{4} wo^{3} chieh.^{4}

397

Your wood I've no desire to split;
My axe—I want to shelter it.

不願柴頭破。只願斧頭脫
Pu^{4} yüan^{4} chʻai^{2} tʻou^{2} pʻo^{4}; chih^{3} yüan^{4} fu^{3} tʻou^{2} tʻo.^{1}

Note.—This is said by a servant desiring dismissal, as the preceding one is said by a master desiring to engage a servant.

398

When a servant conceives it hard to stay,
He becomes your foe if not sent away.

起心人難留。留下結冤仇
Chʻi^{3} hsin^{1} jên^{2} nan^{2} liu,^{2} liu^{2} hsia^{4} chieh^{2} yüan^{1} chʻou.^{2}

399

To the man submit,
At whose board you sit.

捧他碗。服他管
Pʻêng^{3} tʻa^{1} wan,^{3} fu^{2} ʻhua^{4} kuan.^{3}

400

Had I been of you afraid, had I with you a marriage made!
I have with you a marriage made, am I then of you afraid!

怕你不嫁你。嫁你不怕你
Pʻa^{4} ni^{3} pu^{4} chia^{4} ni^{3}! chia^{4} ni^{3} pu^{4} pʻa^{4} ni!^{3}

Note.—Having engaged to serve in any way, he, or she, shrinks not from the responsibility.

401

A stick's a stick whether short or tall ;
A man's a man whether great or small.

長 短 是 根 棍。大 小 是 個 人

Chʻang^2 tuan^3 shih^4 kên^1 kun^4; ta^4 hsiao^3 shih^4 ko^4 jên.^{2}

Note.—This is the indignant complaint of a slighted employé.

402

He who to be obliging tries,
Is sure of work whereʻer he hies.

人 要 頑 得 活。處 處 用 得 着

Jên^2 yao^4 wan^2 tê^2 ʻhuo,^{2} chʻu^4 chʻu^4 yung^4 tê^2 cho.^{2}

403

To his breast the man he wants he is ready to embrace : He'd throw him he does not want down any dangerous place.

要 人 抱 在 懷 裏

Yao^4 jên^2 pao^4 tsai^4 ʻhuai^2 li^3:

不 要 人 丟 在 崖 裏

Pu^4 yao^4 jên^2 tiu^1 tsai^4 ai^2 li.^{3}

404

Nourish a sick but never an idle servant.

養 病 不 養 閑

Yang^3 ping^4 pu^4 yang^3 hsien.^{2}

405

Hurry men at work, not at meat.

催 工 莫 催 食

Tsʻui^1 kung^1 mo^4 tsʻui^1 shih.^{2}

406

In a family defend it ; in a country defend it.

在 家 衞 家。在 國 衞 國

Tsai^4 chia^1 wei^4 chia^1; tsai^4 kuo^2 wei^4 kuo.^{2}

407

To serve in a very attentive manner. *Lit.:* To prop the head and help the feet.

抽 頭 扶 脚

Chʻou^1 tʻou^2 fu^2 chiao.^{3}

諺語叢話

408

I can find employment elsewhere. *Lit.*: There are temples elsewhere than on Mount *Ni*.

除 了 尼 山 別 有 廟

Ch'u² liao³ Ni² shan¹ pieh² yu³ miao.⁴

409

Do not employ handsome servants.

奴 僕 勿 用 俊 秀

Nu³ pu² wu⁴ yung⁴ chün⁴ hsiu.⁴

410

Where no handsome servant is kept, the family must be virtuous.

堂 中 無 俊 僕。必 是 好 人 家

T'ang² chung¹ wu² chün⁴ pu,² pi⁴ shih⁴ 'hao³ jên² chia.¹

411

A wise man in a fool's service. *Lit.*: A clear pearl thrown into lacquer.

明 珠 投 漆

Ming² chu¹ t'ou² ch'i.¹

412

Under the master's nose to idle away the time.

打 照 面 過 日 子

Ta³ chao⁴ mien⁴ kuo⁴ jih⁴ tzŭ³.

413

Your pay is certain whether you work or play. *Lit.*: Whether you stand or sit you'll get three hundred taels.

站 倒 三 百 兩。坐 倒 三 百 兩

Chan⁴ tao³ san¹ pai³ liang,³ tso⁴ tao³ san¹ pai³ liang.³

414

The dog presumes on his master's power.

狗 仗 人 勢

Kou³ chang⁴ jên² shih.⁴

NOTE.—Said in reproof of saucy servants.

415

Able men are first employed. *Lit.*: Straight trees are first felled, and sweet wells first drained.

直 木 先 伏。甘 井 先 渴
Chih² mu⁴ hsien¹ fa,² kan¹ ching³ hsien¹ k'o.³

416

If one won't employ me another will. *Lit.:* If there be no light in the east there will be in the west.

東 方 不 亮。西 方 亮
Tung¹ fang¹ pu⁴ liang,⁴ hsi¹ fang¹ liang.⁴

417

When the family becomes ruined the slave may despise his master.

家 敗 奴 欺 主
Chia¹ pai⁴ nu³ ch'i¹ chu.³

418

You have turned round in a whirlpool.

在 回 流 窩 裏。打 一 個 轉 身 的
Tsai⁴ 'hui² liu² wo¹ li,³ ta³ yi¹ ko⁴ chuan³ shên¹ ti.¹

NOTE.—Said in censure of a servant whom one suspects, from his great haste, of having left his work undone.

419

Under a Premier's roof are seven ranks of officials.

宰 相 門 下 七 品 官
Tsai⁴ hsiang¹ mên² hsia⁴ ch'i¹ p'in³ kuan.¹

420

If the magistrate be great, so will be his secretaries and underlings.

官 大 書 差 大
Kuan¹ ta⁴ shu¹ ch'ai¹ ta.⁴

NOTE.—This and the preceding proverb are generally said with the intention of extolling the position of servants under noted or wealthy masters.

421

The fewer servants the better served. *Lit.:* One man will carry two buckets of water for his own use; two will carry one for their joint use; but three will carry none for anybody's use.

一 人 挑 水 吃。二 人 抬 水 吃
Yi¹ jên² t'iao¹ shui³ ch'ih¹; êrh⁴ jên² t'ai² shui³ ch'ih¹;

三 人 沒 得 水 吃
san¹ jên² mu² tê² shui³ ch'ih.¹

422

No man will serve for starvation.

餓夫不能當差

O^4 fu^1 pu^4 nêng^2 tang^1 chʻai.^{1}

423

Though the senders be ten thousand times wrong, it is not the messenger's fault.

千錯萬錯。來人不錯

Chʻien^1 tsʻo^4 wan^4 tsʻo,^{4} lai^2 jên^2 pu^4 tsʻo.^{4}

424

I'll come though you beat me, and though you curse me, but not if I am to lose any pay.

打我來。罵我來

Ta^3 wo^3 lai,^{2} ma^3 wo^3 lai,^{2}

要我吃虧就不來

yao^4 wo^3 chʻih^1 kuʻei^1 chiu^4 pu^4 lai.^{2}

425

Cold tea and cold rice are bearable, but cold words and cold speeches are unendurable.

冷茶冷飯吃得

Lêng^3 chʻa^2 lêng^3 fan^4 chʻih^1 tê,^{2}

冷言冷語受不得

Lêng^3 yen^2 lêng^3 yü^3 shou^4 pu^4 tê.^{2}

426

A lean dog shames his master.

狗瘦主人羞

Kou^3 shou^4 chu^3 jên^2 hsiu.^{1}

427

The nose is bigger than the face.

鼻子大過臉

Pi^2 tzŭ^3 ta^4 kuo^4 lien.^{3}

428

A *tou* of rice is not a *pao* of rice.

斗米不成包

Tou^3 mi^3 pu^4 chʻêng^2 pao.^{1}

NOTE.—One *pao* contains five *tou*. This saying is used, for instance, by a servant, when suspected of bringing home less than he ought to do from the market.

429

Though the peony be beautiful, it must be supported by its green leaves.

牡丹雖好。必要綠葉扶持

Mu³ tan¹ sui¹ ʿhao,³ pi⁴ yao⁴ lu⁴ yeh⁴ fu² chʿih.²

430

If he does not quarrel with his cook for his tea, he does for his rice.

茶裡不尋飯裡尋

Chʿa² li³ pu⁴ hsin² fan⁴ li³ hsin.²

431

Whilst the workman may have 3/10ths of his own way, the master has 7/10ths of his.

三分匠人。七分主人

San¹ fên¹ chiang⁴ jên,² chʿi¹ fên¹ chu³ jên.²

432

Great trees are good to shelter under. (Patronage.)

大樹下好歇陰

Ta⁴ shu⁴ hsia⁴ ʿhao³ hsieh¹ yin.¹

433

Though a tiger may not devour men, his dreadful appearance frightens them.

老虎不吃人惡像難看

Lao³ ʿhu³ pu⁴ chʿih¹ jên² o⁴ hsiang⁴ nan² kʿan.⁴

NOTE.—This proverb illustrates the awe-inspiring influence of masters and superiors generally.

434

The affairs of a thousand men are under the control of one.

千人上路。主事一人

Chʿien¹ jên² shang⁴ lu,⁴ chu³ shih⁴ yi¹ jên.²

435

There is no master in the concern. *Lit.*: One state has three rulers.

一國三公

Yi¹ kuo² san¹ kung.¹

436

To employ volunteers only. *Lit.: Chiang T'ai Kung* angling, catches only volunteers.

姜 太 公 釣 魚 願 者 上 鈎

Chiang[1] T'ai[4] Kung[1] kou[1] yü[2] yüan[4] chê[2] shang[3] kou.[1]

NOTE.—*Chiang T'ai Kung*, or *Chiang Tzŭ-ya* (姜子牙), was a remarkable sage in the time of the celebrated *Wên Wang* (文王), who followed, in obscurity, his favourite pursuit of angling up to the age of eighty years. At that age he became counsellor to the king. One often sees the following sentence pasted over the lattice windows of Chinese dwellings: 姜太公在此諸神迴避 *Chiang T'ai Kung* is inside, keep off, all ye gods." Most of the gods are popularly supposed to owe their deification to this powerful individual, to be under his control, and to stand in considerable awe of him.

437

You can treat an inferior any way you please. *Lit.:* Meat on a block can be chopped any way you like.

蒸 板 上 一 塊 肉

Chêng[1] pan[3] shang[4] yi[1] k'uai[4] jou,[4]

隨 你 橫 砍 直 砍

sui[2] ni[3] 'hêng[4] k'an[3] chih[2] k'an.[3]

438

Though I dismiss one butcher, think you I shall be forced to eat undressed pork?

舍 了 屠 戶。難 道 連 毛 吃 猪

Shê[3] liao[3] t'u[2] 'hu,[4] nan[2] tao[4] lien[2] mao[2] ch'ih[1] chu.[1]

439

The master controls his slave as easily as one can feel the stocking in one's boot.

主 子 管 奴 才。靴 子 裏 摸 襪 子

Chu[3] tzŭ[3] kuan[3] nu[3] ts'ai,[2] hsueh[1] tzŭ[3] li[3] mo[1] wa[4] tzŭ.[3]

440

If you suspect a man don't employ him; if you employ him don't suspect him.

疑 人 莫 用 人。用 人 莫 疑 人

I[2] jên[2] mo[4] yung[4] jên[2]; yung[4] jên[2] mo[4] i[2] jên.[2]

CHAPTER IV.

NEIGHBOURS.

441

When relations and neighbours continue sincere,
Then relations and neighbours have nothing to fear.

親 願 親 好。鄰 愿 鄰 好

Chʻin^1 yüan^4 chʻin^1 hao,^{3} lin^2 yüan^4 lin^2 hao.^{3}

442

Examine the neighbourhood before you choose your dwelling.

徧 處 兒 擇 地 方 住

Pien^4 chʻu^4 êrh^2 tsê^2 ti^4 fang^1 chu.^{4}

443

Dwell in harmony with all your neighbours.

居 街 坊 接 鄰 里

Chü^1 chieh^1 fang^1 chieh^1 lin^2 li.^{3}

444

Mencius' mother selected her neighbourhood.

昔 孟 母 擇 鄰 處

Hsi^2 Mêng^4 mu^3 tsê^2 lin^2 chʻu.^{3}

445

A good bird selects its tree.

良 禽 擇 木 而 棲

Liang^2 chʻin^2 tsê^2 mu^4 êrh^2 chʻi^1.

446

Distant water will not quench a fire near; distant relations are not so good as near neighbours.

遠 水 難 救 近 火

Yüan^3 shui^3 nan^2 chiu^4 chin^4 ʻhuo^3;

遠 親 不 如 近 鄰

yüan^3 chʻin^1 pu^4 ju^2 chin^4 lin.^{2}

NOTE.—"Better is a neighbour that is near than a brother far off." Prov. xxvii: 10.

447

Three years after a family has been divided, its members become as neighbours.

分家三年成鄰舍

Fên[1] chia[1] san[1] nien[2] chʻêng[2] lin[2] shê.[4]

448

The bird chooses its tree, not the tree the bird.

鳥則擇木。木豈能擇鳥

Niao[3] tsê[2] tsê[2] mu,[4] mu[4] chʻi[3] nêng[2] tsê[2] niao.[3]

449

Would you discover the real truth about a person, enquire only of his neighbours.

察實莫過鄰里

Chʻa[2] shih[2] mo[4] kuo[4] lin[2] li.[3]

450

On a journey you must have good company; at home you must have good neighbours.

行要好伴。住要好鄰

Hsing[2] yao[4] hao[3] pan[4]; chu[4] yao[4] hao[3] lin.[2]

451

Better good neighbours near, than relations far away.

得好鄉鄰勝遠親

Tê[2] hao[3] hsiang[1] lin[2] shêng[4] yüan[3] chʻin.[1]

452

The emperor has no waste lands: and there are virtuous men among your neighbours.

朝廷無空地。鄰舍有賢人

Chʻao[2] tʻin[2] wa[2] kʻung[1] ti[4]; lin[2] shê[4] yu[3] hsien[2] jên.[2]

453

Near neighbours are not equal to next-door neighbours, and they are not equal to neighbours across the road.

近鄰不如隔壁

Chin[4] lin[2] pu[4] ju[2] ko[2] pi,[3]

隔壁不如對門

ko[2] pi[3] pu[4] ju[2] tui[4] mên.[2]

454

Near neighbours. *Lit.:* If we have not flowers and trees in common, we have the garden in common.

不 同 花 樹 同 花 園

Pu^4 tʻung^2 ʻhua^1 shu^4 tʻung^2 ʻhua^1 yüan.^{2}

455

Fields are divided from each other; but dwellings are joined together.

田 土 相 界。屋 宇 相 連

Tʻien^2 tʻu^3 hsiang^1 chieh^4; wu^1 yü^3 hsiang^1 lien.^{2}

456

Possessed of a neighbour's knowledge. *Lit.:* I know all about the place's customs, soil, and men.

風 土 人 情 我 盡 知

Fêng^1 tʻu^3 jên^2 chʻing^2 wo^3 chin^4 chih.^{1}

SECTION V.—ON EDUCATION.

CHAPTER I.

EDUCATION GENERALLY.

457

Wives' and children's education,
Won't admit procrastination.

訓 子 嬰 孩。教 婦 初 來

Hsün^4 tzŭ^3 ying^1 ʻhai^2, chiao^4 fu^4 chʻu^1 lai.^{2}

458

Than a lad without learning, you'd better rear an ass:
Better rear a pig than an uneducated lass.

養 子 不 教 如 養 驢

Yang^3 tzŭ^3 pu^4 chiao^4 ju^2 yang^3 lü^2:

養 女 不 教 如 養 猪

Yang^3 nü^2 pu^4 chiao^4 ju^2 yang^3 chu.^{1}

459

Fields left untilled—your granʻries will all empty be:
Books left unread—you'll have a stupid progeny.

有 田 不 耕 倉 廩 虛

Yu^3 tʻien^2 pu^4 kêng^1 tsʻang^1 lin^3 hsü^1:

有 書 不 讀 子 孫 愚

Yu^3 shu^1 pu^4 tu^2 tzŭ^3 sun^1 yü.^{2}

460

As the twig is bent the mulberry grows.

桑 條 從 小 揉

Sang^1 tʻiao^2 tsʻung^2 hsiao^3 jou.^{2}

461

Those who reject iron cannot make steel.

恨 鐵 不 成 鋼

ʻHên^4 tʻieh^2 pu^4 chʻêng^2 kang.^{1}

NOTE.—The meaning of this is, that those who despise the effort to educate will not have educated children.

海上絲綢之路文獻集成 科技與文化編

462

Instruction penetrates the hearts of the good, but blows past the ears of the bad.

善 人 聽 說 心 中 刺
Shan^4 jên^2 tʻing^1 shuo^1 hsin^1 chung^1 tzʻŭ,^{4}
惡 人 聽 說 耳 邊 風
o^4 jên^2 tʻing^1 shuo^1 êrh^3 pien^1 fêng.^{1}

463

Education requires a proper method.

教 子 要 有 義 方
Chiao^4 tzŭ^3 yao^4 yu^3 i^4 fang.^{1}

464

Nothing can be done without instruction.

天 下 之 事 非 教 無 成
Tʻien^1 hsia^4 chih^1 shih^4 fei^1 chiao^4 wu^2 chʻêng.^{2}

465

Teach your son in the hall, your wife on the pillow.

堂 前 教 子。枕 邊 教 妻
Tʻang^2 chʻien^2 chiao^4 tzŭ,^{3} chên^3 pien^1 chiao^4 chʻi.^{1}

466

Though an affair be small, it must be attended to, else it will never be done: though a son be talented, without instruction he will still remain ignorant.

事 雖 小 不 作 不 成
Shih^4 sui^1 hsiao^3 pu^4 tso^4 pu^4 chʻêng^2:
子 雖 賢 不 教 不 明
tzŭ^3 sui^1 hsien^2 pu^4 chiao^4 pu^4 ming.^{2}

467

Teach your descendants the two proper roads—literature and farming.

教 子 孫 兩 條 正 路。惟 讀 惟 耕
Chiao^4 tzŭ^3 sun^1 liang^3 tʻiao^2 chêng^4 lu^4—wei^2 tu^2 wei^2 kêng.^{1}

468

Teaching sons and grandsons, mind you teach them a trade: plant the *sang* and the *che*, but not many flowers.

教子教孫須教藝

Chiao^4 tzŭ^3 chiao^4 sun^1 shun^4 chiao^4 i^4:

栽桑栽柘少栽花

tsai^1 sang^1 tsai^1 che^4 shao^3 tsai^1 ʻhua.^{1}

NOTE.—The *sang* is the mulberry; and the *che*, according to Kanghi, a species of the same, the leaves of which are also used in feeding silk-worms.

469

Superior men are good without instruction; medium men are good with it; but low fellows are bad despite of it.

上等之人不教而善

Shang^4 têng^2 chih^1 jên^2 pu^4 chiao^4 êrh^2 shan^4;

中等之人一教而善

chung^1 têng^2 chih^1 jên^2 yi^1 chiao^4 êrh^2 shan^4;

下等之人教亦不善

hsia^4 têng^2 chih^1 jên^2 chiao^4 i^1 pu^4 shan.^{4}

NOTE.—The first of these are called 聖, Sages of the highest order; the second 賢, Sages of the second order; and the third 愚, the stupid or worthless.

470

The youthful student must carve and grind; he must not complain at the amount of instruction his Teacher gives him: for nothing can be made of yellow gold until it is hammered; and the jewelled sword is useless until it is sharpened.

幼小讀書要琢磨

Yu^4 hsiao^2 tu^2 shu^1 yao^4 cho^2 mo^2;

休恨嚴師教訓多

hsiu^1 ʻhên^4 yen^2 shih^1 chiao^4 hsün^4 to^1:

黃金不打難成器

ʻhuang^2 chin^1 pu^4 ta^3 nan^2 chʻêng^2 chʻi^4;

寶劍鈍時也要磨

pao^3 chien^4 tun^4 shih^2 yeh^3 yao^4 mo.^{2}

CHAPTER II.

EXAMINATIONS.

471

The scholar who wishes his M. A. to gain,
From all tiger drawing must henceforth refrain.

讀書望中舉。不可畫老虎

Tu^{2} shu^{1} wang^{4} chung^{4} chü,^{3} pu^{4} kʻo^{3} ʻhua^{4} lao^{3} ʻhu.^{3}

NOTE.—That is, he must refrain from drawing up indictments, a practice by which many B.A.'s extort unlawful gains.

472

At each of the Chancellor's examinations, held twice in three years,
Each literary, military, old, or young, candidate appears.

學憲三年兩考

Hsiao^{1} hsien^{4} san^{1} nien^{2} liang^{3} kʻao,^{3}

科歲文武大小

Kʻo^{1} sui^{4} wên^{2} wu^{3} ta^{4} hsiao.^{3}

NOTE.—"At each," *i.e.* at the 科考, *kʻo kʻao*, or examination for conferring the B.A. degree; and at the 歲考, *sui kʻao*, an intermediate examination, at which all B.A.'s are bound to appear. This examination bestows no degrees, and is only held in order to keep an eye on the studies of the graduates.

473

Yearly examinations scare the B. A.:
Hay time scares the farmer in much the same way.

秀才怕歲考。耕田怕打草

Hsiu^{4} tsʻai^{2} pʻa^{4} sui^{4} kʻao^{3}: kêng^{1} tʻien^{2} pʻa^{4} ta^{3} tsʻao.^{3}

474

When a dull scholar obtains a B.A.,
We know it is not by a dull essay.

只進黑人。不進黑文

Chih^{3} chin^{4} ʻhei^{1} jên,^{2} pu^{4} chin^{4} ʻhei^{1} wên.^{2}

475

Any man who shows ability may leap the dragon gate.

各顯本勢跳龍門

Ko^{4} hsien^{3} pên^{3} shih^{4} tʻiao^{4} lung^{2} mên.^{2}

NOTE.—"To leap the dragon gate" means, in prose, to obtain a degree.

476

Who fears that his essay will surpass all others, and not that the examiners will reject it?

那 怕 文 章 高 天 下
Na³ pʻa⁴ wên² chang¹ kao¹ tʻien¹ hsia,⁴
試 官 不 中 也 枉 然
shih⁴ kuan¹ pu⁴ chung¹ yeh³ wang³ jan.²

477

In three years a master of arts may degenerate into an ordinary plebeian.

舉 子 三 年 成 白 丁
Chü³ tzŭ³ san¹ nien² chʻêng² pai² ting.¹

NOTE.—That is by neglecting to attend the proper examinations in Peking.

478

Come out first on the Dragon-Tiger list, and in ten years you will be at the Phœnix pool.

一 舉 首 登 龍 虎 榜
Yi¹ chü³ shou³ têng¹ lung² ʻhu³ pang,³
十 年 身 到 鳳 凰 池
shih² nien² shên¹ tao⁴ fêng⁴ ʻhuang² chʻih.²

NOTE.—"The dragon-tiger list" is that published after the examinations for conferring the degree of Master of Arts. And "the phœnix pool" is the Imperial College at Peking.

479

To gain a degree. *Lit.:* The river fish *li* ascends the dragon gate.

河 鯉 登 龍 門
ʻHo² li³ têng¹ lung² mên.²

480

To stand alone on the sea-monster's head.

獨 占 鰲 頭
Tu² chan¹ ao² tʻou.²

NOTE.—The apparently unenviable position here indicated, stands for the very enviable one of coming out senior wrangler in any examination.

481

The attainment of literary honours depends on Fate, Fortune, Geomantic influences, the laying up of secret merit, and on study.

一命。二運。三風水
Yi^{1} min,^{4} êrh^{4} yün,^{4} san^{1} fêng^{1} shui,^{3}
四積陰功。五讀書
ssŭ^{4} chi^{2} yin^{1} kung,^{1} wu^{3} tu^{2} shu.^{1}

482

Any essay is good which gives a man his M.A.
中了文章總是好的
Chung^{4} liao^{3} wên^{2} chang^{1} tsung^{3} shih^{4} ʻhao^{3} ti.^{1}

483

Fear the lack of excellence in your production, not the lack of competence in your examiner.
業患不能精
Yeh^{4} ʻhuan^{4} pu^{4} lêng^{2} ching,^{1}
無患有司之不明
wu^{2} ʻhuan^{4} yu^{3} ssŭ^{1} chih^{1} pu^{4} ming.^{2}

484

Fear the lack of perfectness in your conduct, not the lack of honesty in your examiner.
行患不能成
Hsing^{2} ʻhuan^{4} pu^{4} nêng^{2} chʻêng,^{2}
無患有司之不公
wu^{2} ʻhuan^{4} yu^{3} ssŭ^{1} chih^{1} pu^{4} kung.^{1}

485

The candidate hopes to pass; the criminal fears the cell.
進考望入學。犯罪怕坐牢
Chin^{4} kʻao^{3} wang^{4} ju^{4} hsiao^{2}; fan^{4} tsui^{4} pʻa^{4} tso^{4} lao.^{2}

CHAPTER III.

LITERATI.

486

Studious men to growing corn a perfect likeness bear;
Unstudious men to jungle grass we may well compare.

學者如禾如稻

Hsiao^2 chê^2 ju^2 ʻho^2 ju^2 tao^4;

不學者如蒿如草

Pu^4 hsiao^2 chê^2 ju^2 ʻhao^1 ju^2 tsʻao.^{3}

487

A man chock full of learning up to his chin,
Needs stirring up to bring out that which is in.

文章脹齊頸。不提也不醒

Wên^2 chang^1 chang^4 chʻi^2 ching^3, pu^4 tʻi^2 yeh^3 pu^4 hsing.^{3}

488

A pedant. *Lit.:* One whose mouth is full of particles.

滿嘴裏的之乎也者

Man^3 tsui^3 li^3 ti^1 chih^1 ʻhu^1 yeh^3 chê.^{2}

489

He is the true Bachelor of Arts who can clearly distinguish the uses of the seven particles.

之乎者也已焉哉

Chih^1 ʻhu^1 chê^2 yeh^3 i^3 yen^1 tsai,^{1}

七字能分好秀才

chʻi^1 tzŭ^4 nêng^2 fên^1 ʻhao^3 hsiu^4 tsʻai.^{2}

490

Without leaving his study, a Bachelor of Arts may understand the affairs of the empire.

秀才不出屋。能知天下事

Hsiu^4 tsʻai^2 pu^4 chʻu^1 wu,^{1} nêng^2 chih^1 tʻien^1 hsia^4 shih.^{4}

491

He who fails to become a perfect scholar, may still become a magistrate's clerk.

讀書不成方作吏

Tu^2 shu^1 pu^4 chʻêng^2 fang^1 tso^4 li.^{4}

492

Though you cannot obtain office, you are still a Bachelor of Arts.

求不倒官。有秀才在

Ch'iu² pu⁴ tao³ kuan,¹ yu³ hsiu⁴ ts'ai² tsai.⁴

493

He bored through his wall to steal his neighbour's light.

鑿壁偷光

Tso² pi³ t'ou¹ kuang.¹

NOTE.—This indicates a poor but indefatigable student, such as *K'uang 'Hên* (匡衡), who actually did this. He lived during the Han dynasty; and, though exceedingly poor, by his zeal and perseverance in study, he became a very learned man, and finally rose to the office of Prime Minister.

494

Scholars are their country's treasure, and the richest ornaments of a feast.

士者國之寶。儒爲席上珍

Shih⁴ chê² kuo² chih¹ pao,³ ju² wei² hsi² shang⁴ chên.¹

495

A Bachelor of Arts' kindness is but half a sheet of paper.

秀才人情紙半張

Hsiu⁴ ts'ai² jên² ch'ing² chih³ pan⁴ chang.¹

496

Scholars discuss reason; workmen what they are to eat.

讀書人講理。做工人講嘴

Tu² shu¹ jên² chiang³ li³; tso⁴ kung¹ jên² chiang³ tsui.³

497

He whose learning is coarse and shallow, should not hang out the name of a scholar.

學問粗疎。不可掛讀書之名

Hsiao² wên⁴ ts'u¹ su,¹ pu⁴ k'o³ kua⁴ tu² shu¹ chih¹ ming.²

498

A poor scholar accepts no pity.

寒士不受人憐

'Han² shih⁴ pu⁴ shou⁴ jên² lien.²

499

All look up to a famous scholar.

文名共仰

Wên² ming² kung⁴ yang.³

500

All scholars are brethren.

斯文同骨月

Ssŭ¹ wên² tʻung² ku³ jou.⁴

501

Bachelors of Art are not the sons of poverty; nor are Buddhist priests the sons of wealth.

秀才不是窮家子

Hsiu⁴ tsʻai² pu⁴ shih⁴ chʻiung² chia¹ tzŭ³;

和尚不是富家兒

ʻho² shang⁴ pu⁴ shih⁴ fu⁴ chia¹ êrh.²

502

If you are a student of Confucius, you are bound to observe the rules of *Chou-Kung*.

既讀孔子之書

Chi³ tu² Kʻung³ Tzŭ³ chih¹ shu,¹

必達周公之禮

pi⁴ ta² Chou¹ Kung¹ chih¹ li.³

NOTE.—*Chou-Kung*, son of the famous *Wên Wang* (文王), and brother of the famous *Wu Wang* (武王), was himself famous for his wisdom and politics. Confucius longed to bring his *principles* and institutions into practice, and hence made them the subjects of his own teachings.

503

As a student—under one man: in office—over ten thousand.

學在一人之下

Hsiao² tsai⁴ yi¹ jên² chih¹ hsia⁴:

用在萬人之上

yung⁴ tsai⁴ wan⁴ jên² chih¹ shang.⁴

504

A scholar will serve those who appreciate him; and a lady will dress for those who please her.

士爲知己用。女爲悅已容

Shih⁴ wei⁴ chih¹ chi³ yung⁴; nü³ wei⁴ yüeh⁴ chi³ yung.²

505

He who can handle a pen, will nowhere have need to beg.

手拈一管筆。到處不求人

Shou^3 nien^1 yi^1 kuan^3 pi,^{3} tao^4 chʻu^4 pu^4 chʻiu^2 jên.^{2}

506

When the mind is stored with learning, the bearing will be elegant.

腹有詩書氣自華

Fu^2 yu^3 shih^1 shu^1 chʻi^4 tzŭ^4 ʻhua.^{2}

CHAPTER IV.

LITERATURE.

507

Whoever has read the *Tsêng-kuang* is able to converse.

讀 了 增 廣 會 說 話

Tu^{2} liao^{4} Tsêng^{1}-kuang^{3} ʻhui^{4} shuo^{1} ʻhua.^{4}

NOTE.—The *Tsêng-kuang* or *Chien-pên-hsien-wên* (監本賢文), is a very valuable little book of proverbs, the whole of which is incorporated in this collection.

508

He who has read the *Yu-hsiao* well knows how to curse.

讀 了 幼 學 好 設 罵

Tu^{2} liao^{3} Yu^{4}-hsiao^{2} ʻhao^{3} shê^{4} ma.^{3}

NOTE.—The *Yu-hsiao* is an encyclopedia, in four volumes, containing much useful and interesting matter. It begins with creation and astronomy, and runs through almost every imaginable subject, ending with a chapter on flowers and trees. There seems to be no justification whatever in the book itself for this proverb.

509

He who has read the *Chʻun-chʻiu* understands caution and gravity.

讀 春 秋 曉 得 謹 嚴

Tu^{2} Chʻun^{1}-chʻiu^{1} hsiao^{3} tê^{2} chin^{3} yen.^{2}

NOTE.—This proverb is based on the general supposition that the *Chʻun-chʻiu*, or Spring and Autumn Annals, contains authoritative decisions on the conduct of men in high places; and it is taken for granted that the mere reading thereof, by official men, will produce in them a care to avoid such censure, and a desire to deserve such praise. Dr. Legge, however, denies that such decisions are to be found in the book, and says that it contains nothing but the most bare and brief statements of fact, without note or comment.

510

He who has read the *Tso-chuan* knows how to utter frivolous flatteries.

讀 左 傳 曉 得 浮 誇

Tu^{2} Tso^{3}-chuan^{4} hsiao^{3} tê^{2} fou^{2} kʻua.^{1}

NOTE.—"*Tso-chuan,*" i. e. the Commentary on the *Chʻun-chʻiu* written by *Tso Chʻiu-ming* (左邱明). For a full and interesting account of him and his work, see Dr. Legge's Classics, Vol 5, part 1, proligomena. It is difficult to see how this proverb can be appropriately said in reference to his writings.

511

He who has seen the *San-kuo* will be able to use strategy.

看 三 國 會 用 計

K'an⁴ San¹ - kuo² hui⁴ yung⁴ chi.⁴

NOTE.—"The *San-kuŏ-chi* is a history of the period immediately after the After Han dynasty, when China was divided into the three Kingdoms of 魏 *Wei*, 蜀 *Shu*, and 吳 *Wu*." As this history abounds in tales of strategy the reason for this saying is pretty plain.

512

He who has seen the *Sun-tzŭ* will understand military tactics.

看 孫 子 知 用 兵

K'an⁴ Sun¹ - tzŭ³ chih¹ yung⁴ ping.¹

NOTE.—*Sun-tzŭ* "is a treatise on military tactics in 13 sections, by *Sun Wu* (孫武), an officer in the service of the state *Wu*, during the 6th century B.C." See Wylie's "Notes on Chinese Literature," page 72.

513

He who has seen the Histories knows the affairs of the ancients.

看 綱 鑑 可 以 知 古 人 事 籍

K'an⁴ kang¹ chien⁴ k'o³ i³ chih¹ ku³ jên² shih⁴ chi.²

514

Books are alike the Empire over.

天 下 書 同 文

T'ien¹ hsia⁴ shu¹ t'ung² wên.²

515

Husbandry and letters are the two chief professions.

耕 讀 爲 本

Kêng¹ tu² wei² pên.³

516

The tongue weaves for clothes; the pen tills for food.

舌 織 而 衣。筆 耕 而 食

Shê² chih¹ êrh² i¹; pi³ kêng¹ êrh² shih.²

517

There are pictures in poems, and poems in pictures.

詩 中 有 畫。畫 中 有 詩

Shih¹ chung¹ yu³ 'hua,⁴ 'hua¹ chung¹ yu³ shih.¹

諺語叢話

518

In all famous sects there are fields of enjoyment.

名教中自有樂地

Ming[2] chiao[4] chung[1] tzŭ[4] yu[3] lê[4] yeh.[3]

NOTE.—This, though a general saying, is mostly used in reference to the enjoyments reaped in literary pursuits.

519

Poetry and letters do not neglect three generations.

詩書不負三代

Shih[1] shu[1] pu[4] fu[4] san[1] tai.[4]

520

He who has read the works of *Sun* and *Wu*, can understand the art of war.

讀孫吳之書可以知戰

Tu[2] Sun[1] Wu[2] chih[1] shu[1] k'o[3] i[3] chih[1] chan.[4]

NOTE.—*Sun Pin* (孫臏), an officer in the state of *Ch'i* (齊) in the sixth century B.C. *Wu Ch'i* (吳起), an officer in the state of *Wei* (魏) in the fourth century B.C. He wrote a work on military affairs entitled *Wu-tzŭ* (吳子), in which he discourses on "National Resources, Estimate of the hostile force, Control of the military, Discussion regarding Military affairs, and Rousing the troops." See Wylie's "Notes on Chinese Literature," page 72. See also the *Yu-hsiao* (幼學), section *Wu-chih* (武職).

521

He who has seen maps knows the aspect of the empire.

看地理便知天下形勢

K'an[4] ti[4] li[3] pien[4] chih[1] t'ien[1] hsia[4] hsing[2] shih.[4]

CHAPTER V.

SCHOOLS.

522

Undignified teaching proves a lazy master.

教 不 嚴 師 之 惰

Chiao^4 pu^4 yen^2 shih^1 chih^1 to.^{4}

523

If you are a miser do not educate your son; and if you wish to hide his faults pay no heed to his teacher.

惜 錢 莫 教 子。護 短 莫 從 師

Hsi^2 chʻien^2 mo^4 chiao^4 tzŭ^3; ʻhu^4 tuan^2 mo^4 tsʻung^2 shih.^{1}

524

When a teacher is dignified, teaching is respected.

師 嚴 則 道 尊

Shih^1 yen^2 tsê^2 tao^4 tsun.^{1}

525

If there is no oil in the lamp the wick is wasted in vain.

燈 盞 無 油 枉 費 心

Têng^1 chan^3 wu^2 yu^2 wang^3 fei^4 hsin.^{1}

NOTE.—The teacher wastes his strength when pupils will not try to learn.

526

When a rich man becomes poor he becomes a teacher.

財 主 敗 落 便 教 書

Tsʻai^2 chu^3 pai^4 lo^4 pien^4 chiao^4 shu.^{1}

527

If he sets small tasks, his employers think him lazy; if he gives much work, his scholars cannot get through it.

課 少 了 主 人 嫌 懶 惰

Kʻo^4 shao^3 liao^3 chu^3 jên^2 hsien^2 lan^3 to^4;

功 多 了 弟 子 道 難 爲

kung^1 to^1 liao^3 ti^4 tzŭ^3 tao^4 nan^2 wei.^{2}

528

If you employ a teacher, employ one with a name.

請 師 當 請 名 人

Ch'ing[3] shih[1] tang[1] ch'ing[3] ming[2] jên.[2]

529

Who teaches me a day is my father for life.

一 日 之 師 終 身 爲 父

Yi[1] jih[4] chih[1] shih[1] chung[1] shên[1] wei[2] fu.[4]

CHAPTER VI.

STUDY.

530

If he can study, the peasant's son may become a peer;
And a nobleman's son who can't, must come down from his sphere.

能 學 則 庶 民 之 子 爲 公 卿
Nêng^2 hsiao^2 tsê^2 shu^4 min^2 chih^1 tzŭ^3 wei^2 kung^1 chʻing^1;
不 學 則 公 卿 之 子 爲 庶 民
Pu^4 hsiao^2 tsê^2 kung^1 chʻing^1 chih^1 tzŭ^3 wei^2 shu^4 min.^{2}

531

Books of antiquity still a relish yield;
And no year of famine knows the inkstone field.

自 古 書 有 味。硯 田 無 惡 歲
Tzŭ^4 ku^3 shu^1 yu^3 wei^4; yen^4 tʻien^2 wu^2 o^4 sui.^{4}

532

Content in cotton, pleased with homely food,
You'll find the Odes and History always good.

布 衣 煖。菜 根 香。詩 書 滋 味 長
Pu^4 i^1 nuan,^{3} tsʻai^4 kên^1 hsiang,^{1} shih^1 shu^1 tzŭ^1 wei^4 chʻang.^{2}

533

Natural endowments are precious to a man;
But, gain the prize without hard study, no one can.

天 資 高。學 力 到
Tʻien^1 tzŭ^1 kao^1; hsiao^2 li^4 tao.^{4}

534

Where the sound of reading's heard, that house must gain renown;
Where there is but the sound of song, that house must be oʻerthrown.

家 有 書 聲 家 必 興
Chia^1 yu^3 shu^1 shêng^1 chia^1 pi^4 hsing^1;
家 有 歌 聲 家 必 傾
Chia^1 yu^3 ko^1 shêng^1 chia^1 pi^4 chʻing.^{1}

535

If you only apply your mind to the task,
Why trouble about mastering it, I ask?

只要用心讀。何愁書不熟

Chih³ yao⁴ yung⁴ hsin¹ tu², ʻho² chʻou² shu¹ pu⁴ shou²?

536

However stupid sons and grandsons may be, they must read the classics.

子孫雖愚。經書不可不讀

Tzŭ³ sun¹ sui¹ yü,² ching¹ shu¹ pu⁴ kʻo³ pu⁴ tu.²

537

Three years' reading is not so good as to hear the explanation.

三年讀書不如聽講

San¹ nien² tu² shu¹ pu⁴ ju² tʻing¹ chiang.³

NOTE.—This refers to the ordinary native method of first committing the books to memory, and afterwards listening to the explanation of them.

538

Learning is far more precious than gold.

黃金有價。書無價

Huang² chin¹ yu³ chia⁴, shu¹ wu² chia.⁴

539

They are only horses and cows in clothes who neglect the study of the past and present.

人不學古今。馬牛面襟裾

Jên² pu⁴ hsiao² ku³ chin¹, ma³ niu² mien⁴ chin¹ chü¹.

540

If study be neglected in youth, what will you do in old age?

幼不學。老何爲

Yu⁴ pu⁴ hsiao², lao³ ʻho² wei²?

541

He who neglects to study diligently in youth, will, when white-headed, repent that he put it off until too late.

少年不知勤學早

Shao^{3} nien^{2} pu^{4} chih^{1} chʻin^{2} hsiao^{2} tsao,^{3}

白頭方悔讀書遲

pai^{2} tʻou^{2} fang^{1} ʻhui^{3} tu^{2} shu^{1} chʻih.^{2}

—— 542 ——

Study which does not daily advance will daily retrograde.

功夫不日進則日退

Kung^{1} fu^{1} pu^{4} jih^{4} chin^{4} tsê^{2} jih^{4} tʻui.^{4}

—— 543 ——

He who cannot understand the classics had better return to the plough.

學經不明不如歸耕

Hsiao^{2} ching^{1} pu^{4} ming^{2} pu^{4} ju^{2} kuei^{1} kêng.^{1}

—— 544 ——

Most things are easy to learn, but hard to master.

千般易學。一竅難得

Chʻien^{1} pan^{1} yi^{4} hsiao,^{2} yi^{1} chʻiao^{4} nan^{2} tê.^{2}

—— 545 ——

You cannot open a book without learning something.

開卷有益

Kʻai^{1} chüan^{4} yu^{3} i.^{2}

—— 546 ——

Very studious. *Lit.:* To rub away an iron ink-slab.

磨穿鐵硯

Mo^{2} ch'uan^{1} tʻieh^{3} yen.^{4}

—— 547 ——

It is essential to know the meaning of *real* words, and the use of particles.

實字求解。虛字求神

Shih^{2} tzŭ^{4} chʻiu^{2} chieh^{1}, hsü^{1} tzŭ^{4} chʻiu^{2} shên.^{2}

NOTE.—The "particles," called *hsü-tsŭ* or "*empty* words", are such as 之, sign of the genitive case; 乎, an exclamation; 也, a final; 者, a disjunctive; 已, also a final, denoting completion or conclusion; 焉, an initial; and 哉 also an exclamation. All others are *shih-tsŭ* or "real words." This is the principal, if not the only grammatical distinction common amongst the Chinese. Grammar forms no part of a native scholar's education. And, though it may not be correct to say that there is no grammar of the Chinese language, it is certainly correct to say that the Chinese themselves have no grammar of it.

548

Every character must be chewed to get out its juice.

字 字 要 咬 出 汁 漿 來

Tzŭ^{4} tzŭ^{4} yao^{4} yao^{3} chʻu^{1} chih^{1} chiang^{1} lai.^{2}

549

Study thoroughly and think deeply.

熟 讀 深 思

Shou^{2} tu^{2} shên^{1} ssŭ.^{1}

550

Learning cannot be gulped down. *Lit.:* You cannot swallow dates whole.

不 能 囫 圇 吞 棗

Pu^{4} nêng^{2} ʻhu^{2} lün^{2} tʻun^{1} tsao.^{3}

551

The student must not listen to chatter under his window; he must with undivided attention study the Sages.

兩 耳 不 聽 窗 外 事

Liang^{3} êrh^{3} pu^{4} tʻing^{1} chʻuang^{1} wai^{4} shih^{4};

一 心 只 讀 案 前 書

yi^{1} hsin^{1} chih^{3} tu^{2} an^{4} chʻien^{2} shu.^{1}

552

He who burns his lamp till three o'clock, and is up with the cocks at five, is a resolute student indeed.

三 更 燈 火 五 更 鷄

San^{1} kêng^{1} têng^{1} ʻhuo^{3} wu^{3} kêng^{1} chi,^{1}

正 是 男 兒 立 志 時

chêng^{4} shih^{4} nan^{2} êrh^{2} li^{4} chih^{4} shih.^{2}

553

Your study goes on like a flowing stream.

讀 書 如 流 水

Tu^{2} shu^{1} ju^{2} liu^{2} shui.^{3}

554

Good students resemble workers in hard wood.

善 學 者 如 攻 堅 木

Shan^{4} hsiao^{2} chê^{2} ju^{2} kung^{1} chien^{1} mu.^{4}

555

Be diligent in study, for every character is worth thousands of gold.

讀書須用意。一字值千金

Tu² shu¹ hsü¹ yung⁴ i⁴, yi¹ tzŭ⁴ chih² ch'ien¹ chin.¹

556

To amass gold by millions is not like a clear understanding of the classics.

積金千萬兩。不如明解經書

Chi⁴ chin¹ ch'ien¹ wan⁴ liang³, pu⁴ ju² ming² chieh³ ching¹ shu.¹

557

Knowledge comes by study, ignorance follows its neglect.

人學始知道。不學亦枉然

Jên² hsiao² shih³ chih¹ tao⁴, pu⁴ hsiao² i⁴ wang³ jan.²

558

All pursuits are mean in comparison with that of learning.

世間萬般皆下品

Shih⁴ chien¹ wan⁴ pan¹ chieh¹ hsia⁴ p'in³;

思量惟有讀書高

ssŭ¹ liang² wei² yu³ tu² shu¹ kao.¹

559

Some study shows the need of more.

學然後知不足

Hsiao² jan² 'hou⁴ chih¹ pu⁴ tsu.²

560

Three day's neglect of study leaves one's conversation flavourless.

三日不讀書語言無味

San¹ jih⁴ pu⁴ tu² shu¹ yü³ yen² wu² wei.⁴

561

By eating we overcome hunger; and by study ignorance.

以吃愈饑。以學愈愚

I³ ch'ih¹ yü⁴ chi¹; i³ hsiao² yü⁴ yü.²

562

In study—fix your mind on the Sages; in office—on your prince and country.

讀 書 志 在 聖 賢

Tu^{2} shu^{1} chih^{4} tsai^{4} shêng^{4} hsien^{2};

爲 官 心 存 君 國

wei^{2} kuan^{1} hsin^{1} ts'un^{2} chün^{1} kuo.^{2}

563

You may study to old age and yet have things to learn.

做 到 老 學 不 了

Tso^{4} tao^{4} lao^{3} hsiao^{2} pu^{4} liao.^{3}

564

Read ancient essays and know how to compose modern ones.

讀 古 文 曉 得 做 時 文

Tu^{2} ku^{3} wên^{2} hsiao^{3} tê^{2} tso^{4} shih^{2} wên.^{2}

565

Learning dyes a man more than the colour vermilion or black.

學 之 染 人 勝 於 丹 青

Hsiao^{2} chih^{1} jan^{3} jên^{2} shêng^{4} yü^{2} tan^{1} ch'ing.^{1}

566

Learning is a treasure which follows its owner everywhere.

書 乃 隨 身 之 寶

Shu^{1} nai^{3} sui^{2} shên^{1} chih^{1} pao.^{3}

567

In learning there is neither old nor young; the most intelligent takes precedence.

學 無 老 少。達 者 爲 先

Hsiao^{2} wu^{2} lao^{3} shao^{3}; ta^{2} chê^{2} wei^{2} hsien.^{1}

568

In learning length of study goes for nothing; the most intelligent becomes master.

學 無 前 後。達 者 爲 師

Hsiao^{2} wu^{2} ch'ien^{2} 'hou^{4}; ta^{2} chê^{3} wei^{2} shih.^{1}

569

Past and present times supply unlimited stores of knowledge, but a man's capacity is limited.

古今之事理無窮

Ku^3 chin^1 chih^1 shih^4 li^3 wu^2 chʻiung,^{2}

一人之知識有限

yi^1 jên^2 chih^1 chih^1 shih^4 yu^3 hsien.^{4}

570

Having a chance to use one's reading, we regret that it is so meagre; having accomplished a task, we begin to appreciate its difficulty.

書到用時方恨少

Shu^1 tao^4 yung^4 shih^2 fang^1 ʻhên^4 shao^3:

事從經過始知難

shih^4 tsʻung^2 ching^1 kuo^4 shih^3 chih^1 nan.^{2}

571

No pleasure equals the pleasure of study.

最樂莫如讀書爲善

Tsui^4 lê^4 mo^4 ju^2 tu^2 shu^1 wei^2 shan.^{4}

572

Rich families have no necessity to buy fertile fields; and study will be sure to yield its thousand measures of rice.

富家不用買良田

Fu^4 chia^1 pu^4 yung^4 mai^3 liang^2 tʻien^2;

書中自有千鍾粟

shu^1 chung^1 tzŭ^4 yu^3 chʻien^1 chung^1 su.^{2}

573

Who live in peace have no necessity to rear lofty halls; and study will be sure to yield its golden house.

安居不用架高堂

An^1 chü^1 pu^4 yung^4 chia^4 kao^1 tʻang^2;

書中自有黃金屋

shu^1 chung^1 tzŭ^4 yu^3 ʻhuang^2 chin^1 wu.^{1}

574

Don't trouble yourself over the absence of a good go-between to negociate a marriage for you, for study will provide you with a lady beautiful as jade.

娶妻莫恨無良媒
Ch'ü[3] ch'i[1] mo[4] 'hên[4] wu[2] liang[2] mei,[2]
書中有女顏如玉
shu[1] chung[1] yu[3] nü[2] yen[2] ju[2] yü.[4]

NOTE.—What more powerful inducements to study, than those mentioned in the three preceding proverbs, could be set before the mind of the youthful student

575

Extensive reading is a priceless treasure.

讀得書多無價寶
Tu[2] tê[2] shu[1] to[1] wu[2] chia[4] pao.[3]

576

Don't complain of the trouble of having to master so many classics and histories, but fear lest your leisure should be too limited.

莫厭經史煩。只恐工夫少
Mo[4] yen[4] ching[1] shih[3] fan,[2] chih[3] k'ung[3] kung[1] fu[1] shao.[3]

577

Would you know the affairs of the empire, read the works of the ancients.

欲知天下事。須讀古人書
Yü[4] chih[1] t'ien[1] hsia[4] shih,[4] hsü[1] tu[2] ku[3] jên[2] shu.[1]

SECTION VI.—FACETIÆ.

CHAPTER I.

RIDICULOUS CONDUCT.

578

He who acts *Chia Kuan* in a hulling-mortar hat,
Both pounds himself to death, and proves himself a flat.

戴碓臼跳加官。擂死不好看

Tai^4 tui^4 chiu^4 t'iao^4 Chia^1 Kuan,^{1} lei^2 ssŭ^3 pu^4 'hao^3 k'an.^{4}

Note.—Theatrical performances are popularly supposed to have been originated by the second emperor of the *T'ang* Dynasty, *T'ai Tsung* (太宗), whose reign dates from A.D. 627. And *Chia Kuan*, the actor who opens the play by a majestic march across the stage, is supposed to represent *T'ai Tsung's* prime minister *Wei Chêng* (魏徵).

579

The pig for his blackness is mocked by the crow;
Who of his own ugliness nothing doth know.

老鴉笑猪黑。自醜不覺得

Lao^3 ya^1 hsiao^4 chu^1 'hê^1; tzŭ^3 ch'ou^3 pu^4 chiao^4 tê.^{2}

580

Ridiculous ambition. *Lit.:* The sparrow flying after the hawk.

麻雀跟倒鷂子飛

Ma^2 ch'iao^3 kên^1 tao^3 yao^4 tzŭ^3 fei.^{1}

581

The sheep's tail is too small to cover its own rump.

羊尾巴蓋不倒羊屁股

Yang^2 wei^3 pa^1 kai^4 pu^4 tao^3 yang^2 p'i^4 ku.^{3}

Note.—And yet it would try to cover another's therewith!

582

He leaps over the fish basket to feed on bean curd.

跳過魚籃吃豆腐

T'iao^4 kuo^4 yü^2 lan^2 ch'ih^1 tou^4 fu.^{3}

583

To make ridiculous assumptions. *Lit.*: When the monkey puts on the devil's mask, what a big face he has!

猴子戴鬼臉。好大面孔

ʻHou² tzŭ³ tai⁴ kuei³ lien,³ ʻhao³ ta⁴ mien⁴ kʻung.³

584

Foolish presumption. *Lit.*: To wield the axe before *Pan's* door.

班門弄斧

Pan² mên² nung⁴ fu.³

NOTE.—*Pan* or *Lu Pan* (魯班), the present god of carpenters; anciently a very skilful carpenter in the state of *Lu*.

585

He who weeps at a play distresses himself for the ancients.

看戲的流眼淚。替古人躭憂

Kʻan⁴ hsi⁴ ti¹ liu² yen³ lei,⁴ tʻi⁴ ku³ jên² tan¹ yu.¹

586

The fisherman in the water groping for fish, pities the fisherman in a boat fishing with a net.

跴脚坑的憐憫打絲網的

Tsʻai³ chiao³ kʻêng¹ ti¹ lien² min³ ta³ ssŭ¹ wang³ ti.¹

587

To make a vain attempt. *Lit.*: To try to ring a wooden bell.

撞木鐘的

Chuang¹ mu⁴ chung¹ ti.¹

588

The elder brother should not laugh at the second.

大哥莫笑二哥

Ta⁴ ko¹ mo⁴ hsiao⁴ êrh⁴ ko.¹

589

To confouned distinctions. *Lit.*: To comb the beard and hair together.

鬍子頭髮一把梳

ʻHu² tzŭ³ tʻou² fa³ yi¹ pa³ shu.¹

590

To eat greedily. *Lit.*: To take off the top of the skull, and pour the food in there.

揭開頂瓜皮。把飯倒進去

Chieh^1 kʻai^1 ting^3 kua^1 pʻi,^{2} pa^3 fan^4 tao^3 chin^4 chʻü.^{4}

591

To fix up ornamental wild beasts' heads on the roof of a thatched cottage.

茅屋安獸頭

Mao^2 wu^1 an^1 shou^4 tʻou.^{2}

592

She is a silly hen that sits on duck eggs: and she is a silly old grandmother that pets her daughter's child.

癡鷄母[illegible]鴨娃

Chʻih^2 chi^1 mu^3 pao^4 ya^1 wa^1;

癡家婆疼外孫

chʻih^2 chia^1 pʻo^2 tʻêng^2 wai^4 sun.^{1}

593

Vain expectations. *Lit.*: He only hopes that his calabash will grow as large as heaven.

只望葫蘆天樣大

Chih^3 wang^4 ʻhu^2 lu^2 tʻien^1 yang^4 ta.^{4}

594

To act the dog in the manger.

站住毛厮不阿屎

Chan^4 chu^4 mao^2 ssŭ^1 pu^4 o^1 sui.^{1}

NOTE.—The literal meaning of this saying is rather too coarse for translation.

595

Though his boat is in the river he refuses to wash it.

落得河水不洗船

Lo^4 tê^2 ʻho^2 shui^3 pu^4 hsi^3 chʻuan.^{2}

596

Absurdly lazy. *Lit.*: To use the rump to open the door.

用屁股打門

Yung^4 pʻi^4 ku^3 ta^3 mên.^{2}

597

To hold as virtues in one's self what we consider to be vices in others.

別人屁臭。自己屁香

Pieh^{2} jên^{2} pʻi^{4} chʻou,^{4} tzŭ^{4} chi^{3} pʻi^{4} hsiang.^{1}

NOTE.—This proverb, more exprsssive than elegant, strikingly resembles the Greek one, Βδέειν λιβάνωτον, given on page 159 of Bohn's "Hand-book of Proverbs."

598

He dare not swallow for fear of bone; and he dare not spit it out for fear there is flesh.

呑了怕是骨頭。吐了怕是肉

Tʻun^{1} liao^{3} pʻa^{4} shih^{4} ku^{3} tʻou^{2}; tʻu^{3} liao^{3} pʻa^{4} shih^{4} jou.^{4}

599

A blind man going up into a mountain to survey the scenery.

瞎子上山看景緻

Hsia^{2} tzŭ^{3} shang^{4} shan^{1} kʻan^{4} ching^{3} chih.^{4}

600

To dupe one's self. *Lit.*: In blowing the nose to blind the eyes.

揑著鼻子誆眼睛

Nieh^{1} cho^{2} pi^{2} tzŭ^{3} kʻuang^{2} yen^{3} ching.^{1}

601

The carpenter makes a cangue, and cangues himself.

木匠做枷自枷自

Mu^{4} chiang^{1} tso^{4} chia^{1} tzŭ^{4} chia^{1} tzŭ.^{4}

海上絲綢之路文獻集成 科技與文化編

CHAPTER II.

JOKES.

— 602 —

Fans were originally surnamed Shake;
And Shake often tries his escape to make.

扇子本姓搖。搖起就跑

Shan^4 tzŭ^3 pên^3 hsing^4 Yao^2; Yao^2 chʻi^3 chiu^4 pʻao.^{3}

— 603 —

The Little-Drum star rises in the eastern, sets in the western sky:
If you can recite this seven times over in one breath, so can I.

鼓兒星東邊起西邊落

Ku^3 êrh^2 hsing^1 tung^1 pien^1 chʻi^3 hsi^1 pien^1 lo^4;

你念七遍過。我念七遍過

Ni^3 nien^4 chʻi^1 pien^4 kuo^4 wo^3 nien^4 chʻi^1 pien^4 kuo.^{4}

Note.—Besides meaning "what you can do I can," this ditty is used playfully as suggested in the second line, for a test of length of breath, and power of utterance.

— 604 —

When there's aught to do, the more the better; not so when there's aught to eat.

人多好做活。人少好吃喝

Jên^2 to^1 ʻhao^3 tso^4 ʻhuo^2; jên^2 shao^3 hao^3 chʻih^1 ʻho.^{1}

— 605 —

When the cat's away, the rats come out to stretch their loins.

貓兒去老鼠出來伸腰

Mao^1 êrh^2 chʻü^4 lao^3 shu^3 chʻu^1 lai^2 shên^1 yao.^{1}

— 606 —

As easy as for a scabbed-head to kill flies on his pate.

瘌痢頭上打蒼蠅一打一個

La^1 li^2 tʻou^2 shang^4 ta^3 tsʻang^1 ying^1 yi^1 ta^3 yi^1 ko.^{4}

607

As easy as to catch a flea in the stern of a pair of trousers.

褲 襠 裏 捉 狗 蚤 一 定 有 準

Kʻu^4 tang^1 li^3 cho^1 kou^3 tsao^3 yi^1 ting^4 yu^3 chun.^{3}

608

We have eyed each other well; now, are we good-looking or not?

你 看 我 我 看 你。好 看 不 好 看

Ni^3 kʻan^4 wo^3 wo^3 kʻan^4 ni^3; ʻhao^3 kʻan^4 pu^4 ʻhao^3 kʻan^4?

609

Who can bet on the goodness of his own eyesight may eat the largest sugar plum.

賭 眼 色 吃 大 糖

Tu^3 yen^3 sê^4 chʻih^1 ta^4 tʻang.^{2}

NOTE.—Said in joke when requesting one to make choice out of many things that are alike.

610

You can't catch wild beasts without a net.

無 張 打 野

Wu^2 chang^1 ta^3 yeh.^{1}

611

He is a fool who waits for a servant maid.

癡 漢 等 丫 頭

Chʻih^2 ʻhan^4 têng^2 ya^1 tʻou.^{2}

NOTE.—She won't come, and so he will be made a fool of.

612

Lots of bustle for little profit. *Lit.*: A *Hsün Ssŭ* in official lodgings—a very bustling yamen!

巡 司 打 公 館 熱 鬧 衙 門

Hsün^2 ssŭ^1 ta^3 kung^1 kuan^3 jê^4 nao^4 ya^2 mên.^{2}

NOTE.—*Hsün ssŭ* or *Jên I ssŭ* (仁義司), a very small mandarin.

613

If one breaks wind every body starts.

各 人 打 屁 各 人 驚

Ko^4 jên^2 ta^3 pʻi^4 ko^4 jên^2 ching.^{1}

614

To flit and forget to take one's wife.

徙宅忘妻

Hsi³ chai² wang⁴ ch'i.¹

615

Bundle, umbrella, and I.

包袱雨傘我

Pao¹ fu² yü³ san³ wo.³

NOTE.—The case here supposed is that of an absent minded-traveller who, setting out on his journey with three things, namely his bundle, his umbrella, and himself, gets confused, and thinks he has lost something. Says he "here's my bundle, and here's my umbrella, but where am I?" The use of this proverb is to banter men with bad memories.

616

To wear a summer hat when worshipping at the new year—very hot!

戴涼帽出天方。熱得狠

Tai⁴ liang² mao⁴ ch'u¹ t'ien¹ fang¹—jê⁴ tê² 'hên³!

NOTE.—*T'ien-fang* is that quarter of the heavens in which *hsi-shên* (喜神), a god of happiness, is supposed to reside for any current year. This locality is revealed yearly by the Imperial almanac. On the first day of the year the males, supposing that the *tien fang* be in the south, will go out to the south side of their dwelling, and facing the south perform their prostrations. At this time it is too cold, of course, to wear summer hats, and this proverb is used to laugh down any such foolish ardency.

617

To wear fur coats in summer.

六月天穿皮襖

Lu⁴ yüeh⁴ t'ien¹ ch'uan¹ p'i² ao.³

NOTE.—This is used in banter to one refusing to lend a helping hand on the plea of slight sickness and being so clothed. It also designates ignorance of what is proper.

CHAPTER III.

ABSURD MISTAKES.

618

Misunderstanding that which has been said,
He into mistaken curses is led.

聽錯話。嗐錯罵

T'ing[1] ts'o[4] 'hua,[4] shê[1] ts'o[4] ma.[4]

619

To guess a superior man's mind by a mean man's heart.

以小人之心。度君子之腹

I[3] hsiao[3] jên[2] chih[1] hsin,[1] tu[4] chün[1] tzŭ[3] chih[1] fu.[2]

620

To put any thing into *Li-mi's* hand.

投到李密手裏去了

T'ou[2] tao[4] Li[4] Mi[4] shou[3] li[3] ch'ü[4] liao.[4]

NOTE.—*Li Mi*, a rebel leader at the commencement of the *T'ang* dynasty, noted as much for his abilities as feared for his rapacity. This proverb in its meaning and use almost corresponds to ours:—"It is hard to get butter out of a dog's throat."

621

To dam water with sand.

抓沙抵水

Chua[1] sha[1] ti[2] shui.[3]

622

To feed on fancies. *Lit.:* To look up at plums to quench one's thirst; to draw a loaf to satisfy one's hunger.

望梅止渴。畫餅充饑

Wang[4] mei[2] chih[3] k'o[3]; 'hua[4] ping[3] ch'ung[1] chi.[1]

623

To add fuel to put out a fire.

抱薪救火

Pao[4] hsin[1] ch'iu[4] 'huo.[3]

624

To fill up a well with snow.

挑 雪 填 井

T'iao^1 hsüeh^3 t'ien^2 ching.^{3}

625

Embracing the lamp-stand he dazzles himself with the light.

抱 着 燈 臺 鬪 住 亮

Pao^4 cho^2 têng^1 t'ai^2 tou^4 chu^4 liang.^{4}

626

To seek the ass you are riding on.

騎 驢 覓 驢

Ch'i^2 lü^2 mi^4 lü.^{2}

627

To catch a fish and forget to take away the basket.

得 魚 忘 筌

Tê^2 yü^2 wang^4 ch'ien.^{2}

628

To open one's door and bow in a thief.

開 門 揖 盜

K'ai^1 mên^2 i^1 tao.^{4}

629

To fell a tree to catch a blackbird.

砍 倒 樹 捉 八 哥

K'an^3 tao^3 shu^4 cho^1 pa^1 ko.^{1}

630

To buy a dried fish in order to spare its life, is to know no difference between life and death.

買 乾 魚 放 生。不 知 死 活

Mai^3 kan^1 yü^2 fang^4 shêng,^{1} pu^4 chih^1 ssŭ^3 'huo.^{2}

631

He who dresses in leaf-made clothes when going to put out a fire, provokes calamity on himself.

着 蓑 衣 救 火。惹 禍 上 身

Cho^2 so^1 i^1 ch'iu^4 'huo,^{3} jê^3 'huo^4 shang^3 shên.^{1}

632

To be idle at home, diligent abroad.

家懶外勤

Chia^1 lan^3 wai^4 chʻin.^{2}

633

To boil carrots and garlic together is a sad blunder in cooking.

紅蘿蔔炒大蒜亂炒菜

ʽHung^2 lo^2 pʻu^2 chʻao^3 ta^4 shan^4 lan^4 chʻao^3 tsʻai.^{4}

634

To offer the Filial Classic for sale at the door of Confucius.

孔子門前賣孝經

Kʻung^3 tzŭ^3 mên^2 chʻien^2 mai^4 hsiao^4 ching.^{1}

635

To rear a tortoise shut up in a jar.

關得罎子裏養烏龜

Kuan^1 tê^2 tʻan^2 tzŭ^3 li^3 yang^3 wu^1 kuei.^{1}

636

To ask a blind man the way.

問道於盲

Wên^4 tao^4 yü^1 mang.^{2}

637

To ask instruction of a fool.

求教於愚人

Chʻiu^2 chiao^4 yü^1 yü^2 jên.^{2}

638

To carry a guitar into a mill, and play to the oxen.

抱琵琶進磨坊。對牛彈琴

Pao^4 pʻi^2 pʻa^1 chin^4 mo^2 fang,^{1} tui^4 niu^2 tʻan^2 chʻin.^{2}

639

To raise an army when the war is over, and regret one's lateness.

過後興兵。悔太遲

Kuo^4 ʽhou^4 hsing^1 ping,^{1} ʽhui^3 tʻai^4 chʻih.^{2}

640

To drag for the reflected moon in the water.

水 裏 撈 明 月

Shui^3 li^3 lao^1 ming^3 yueh.^{4}

641

To make a pickaxe in a silversmith's shop.

銀 匠 舖 裏 打 鋤 頭

Yin^2 chiang^4 pʻu^4 li^3 ta^3 chʻu^2 tʻou.^{2}

642

To make gold locks, in a blacksmith's shop.

鐵 匠 舖 裏 打 金 鎖

Tʻieh^3 chiang^4 pʻu^4 li^3 ta^3 chin^1 so.^{3}

643

To stir sesamum seeds and beans together.

蔴 子 攪 豆 子

Ma^2 tzŭ^3 chiao^3 tou^4 tzŭ.^{3}

NOTE.—*i. e.* to mix up incongruous things.

644

To look for bones in an egg.

雞 蛋 裏 頭 挑 骨 頭

Chi^1 tan^4 li^3 tʻou^2 tʻao^1 ku^3 tʻou.^{2}

645

To drop into water to grasp the foam.

落 水 擒 水 泡

Lo^4 shui^3 chʻin^2 shui^3 pʻao.^{4}

646

To shoot a sparrow with a large cannon.

大 礮 打 麻 雀

Ta^4 pʻao^4 ta^3 ma^2 chʻiao.^{3}

647

To scratch one's calf through top boots.

隔 靴 子 抓 癢

Ko^2 hsüeh^1 tzŭ^3 chua^1 yang.^{3}

648

To act in ignorance of the head and tail.

不 曉 得 頭 尾 做 事

Pu^4 hsiao^3 tê^2 tʻou^2 wei^3 tso^4 shih.^{4}

649

To leave anything unfinished.

屙屎不揩屁股

O¹ shih³ pu⁴ k'ai¹ p'i⁴ ku.³

Note.—This proverb is rather too coarse for a literal translation.

650

To buy a cat in a bag.

隔口袋買貓

Ko² k'ou³ tai⁴ mai³ mao.¹

651

To fight the wall after the thieves have gone.

强盜過後殺壁子

Ch'iang² tao⁴ kuo⁴ 'hou⁴ sha¹ pi³ tzŭ.³

SECTION VII.—ON FORTUNE.

CHAPTER I.

FATE.

652

Robberies and fires,
Come as fate requires.

賊　刦　火　燒。命　裏　所　招
Tsei^{2} chieh^{2} ʻhuo^{3} shao,^{1} ming^{4} li^{3} so^{3} chao.^{1}

653

Thunderbolts and fires,
Come as fate requires.

雷　打　火　燒。命　裡　所　招
Lei^{2} ta^{3} ʻhuo^{3} shao,^{1} ming^{4} li^{3} so^{3} chao.^{1}

654

Falling walls and fires,
Come as fate requires.

牆　打　火　燒。命　之　所　招
Chʻiang^{2} ta^{3} ʻhuo^{3} shao,^{1} ming^{4} chih^{1} so^{3} chao.^{1}

655

Fated—you must each other greet;
Not so—you won't each other meet.

有　緣　遇　着。無　緣　錯　過
Yu^{3} yüan^{2} yü^{4} cho^{1}; wu^{2} yüan^{2} tsʻo^{4} kuo.^{4}

656

If you're born lucky no scheming is needed;
And if your heart's good leave fasting unheeded.

命　好　不　用　乖。心　好　不　用　齋
Ming^{4} hao^{3} pu^{4} yung^{4} kuai^{1}; hsin^{1} hao^{3} pu^{4} yung^{4} chai.^{1}

657.

Happiness we'll together share;
Misery we'll together bear.

有　福　同　享。有　禍　同　當
Yu^{3} fu^{2} tʻung^{2} hsiang^{3}; yu^{3} ʻhuo^{4} tʻnng^{2} tang.^{1}

諺語叢話

658

Where'er six horoscopic harmonies you see,
That man will get on well wherever he may be.

命 裡 帶 六 合。處 處 合 得 着

Ming^{4} li^{3} tai^{4} lu^{4} ʻho,^{2} chʻu^{4} chʻu^{4} ʻho^{2} tê^{2} cho.^{1}

659

Both riches and honours are settled by fate;
Their time of arrival each man must await.

富 貴 命 裡 排。各 自 等 時 來

Fu^{4} kuei^{4} ming^{4} li^{3} pʻai^{2}; ko^{4} tzŭ^{4} têng^{2} shih^{2} lai.^{2}

660

When both the heart and the fate are right,
He will to old age in wealth delight.
When the heart is right and the fate is wrong,
Shielding him must to the gods belong.
When fate is right and the heart is wrong,
He will fall in his road half way along.
When both the heart and the fate are wrong,
Penury's griefs he'll struggle among.

心 好 命 又 好。富 貴 直 到 老

Hsin^{1} hao^{3} ming^{4} yu^{4} hao,^{3} fu^{4} kuei^{4} chih^{2} tao^{4} lao.^{3}

心 好 命 不 好。天 地 終 須 保

Hsin^{1} hao^{3} ming^{4} pu^{4} hao,^{3} tʻien^{1} ti^{4} chung^{1} hsü^{1} pao.^{3}

命 好 心 不 好。中 途 夭 折 了

Ming^{4} hao^{3} hsin^{1} pu^{4} hao,^{3} chung^{1} tʻu^{2} yao^{1} chê^{2} liao.^{3}

心 命 俱 不 好。貧 賤 受 煩 惱

Hsin^{1} ming^{4} chü^{4} pu^{4} hao,^{3} pʻin^{3} chien^{4} shou^{4} fan^{2} nao.^{3}

NOTE.—"The gods," *lit.:* "heaven and earth." "He will fall" &c: the meaning is that he will be cut off in the midst of his days and so be unable to enjoy his good fortune.

661

Unjust gains cannot enrich those who are fated to be poor.

橫 財 不 富 命 窮 人

ʻHêng^{4} tsʻai^{2} pu^{4} fu^{4} ming^{4} chʻiung^{2} jên.^{2}

662

Disease may be cured, not fate.

醫得病。醫不得命

I[1] tê[2] ping,[4] i[1] pu[4] tê[2] ming.[4]

663

Beautiful women are very ill-fated.

紅顏女子多薄命

'Hung[2] yen[2] nü[2] tzŭ[3] to[1] po[2] ming.[4]

664

No distance can sever those whom fate unites; no nearness can join those whom fate severs.

有緣千里能相會

Yu[3] yüan[2] ch'ien[1] li[3] nêng[2] hsiang[1] 'hui[4];

無緣對面不相逢

wu[2] yüan[2] tui[4] mien[4] pu[4] hsiang[1] fêng.[2]

665

Happiness has its foundation, and misery its womb.

福生有基。禍生有胎

Fu[2] shêng[1] yu[3] chi,[1] 'huo[4] shêng[1] yu[3] t'ai.[1]

666

If a man's fate is to have only eigth-tenths of a pint of rice, though he traverse the country over, he cannot get a full pint.

命裡只有八合米

Ming[4] li[3] chih[3] yu[3] pa[1] 'ho[2] mi,[3]

走盡天下不滿升

tsou[3] chin[4] t'ien[1] hsia[4] pu[4] man[3] shêng.[1]

667

Every event is settled beforehand; so it is vain to fret over this transitory life.

世事皆先定。浮生空自忙

Shih[4] shih[4] chieh[1] hsien[1] ting[4]; fou[2] shêng[1] k'ung[1] tzŭ[4] mang.[2]

668

Everything is fated; and nothing depends on man.

萬般皆由命。半點不由人

Wan[4] pan[1] chieh[1] yu[2] ming[4]; pan[4] tien[3] pu[4] yu[2] jên.[2]

669

On a road dangers may be met with which can hardly be escaped: and affairs will happen beyond our own control.

路 逢 險 處 難 迴 避

Lu^4 fêng^2 hsien^3 chʻu^4 nan^2 ʻhui^2 pi^4:

事 到 頭 來 不 自 由

shih^4 tao^4 tʻou^2 lai^2 pu^4 tzŭ^4 yu.^{2}

670

Nothing follows man's own calculations; his whole life is arranged by fate.

萬 事 不 由 人 計 較

Wan^4 shih^4 pu^4 yu^2 jên^2 chi^4 chiao^4;

一 生 都 是 命 安 排

yi^1 shêng^1 tu^1 shih^4 ming^4 an^1 pʻai.^{2}

671

Our destiny is fixed, without the slightest reference to our own will.

大 家 都 是 命。半 點 不 由 人

Ta^4 chia^1 tu^1 shih^4 ming,^{4} pan^4 tien^3 pu^4 yu^2 jên.^{2}

672

His heart is loftier than his destiny.

心 高 命 不 高

Hsin^1 kao^1 ming^4 pu^4 kao.^{1}

673

Plant flowers with care, and they may never grow: stick willows in carelessly, and they may yield a pleasant shade.

有 意 栽 花 花 不 發

Yu^3 i^4 tsai^1 ʻhua^1 ʻhua^1 pu^4 fa,^{1}

無 心 插 柳 柳 成 陰

wu^2 hsin^1 chʻa^1 liu^3 liu^3 chʻêng^2 yin.^{1}

674

The more I study, the more I miss the mark: what have I to do with fate? The more I miss the mark, the more I study: what has fate to do with me?

越讀越不中。我其如命何
Yueh^4 tu^2 yueh^4 pu^4 chung^4; wo^3 chʻi^2 ju^2 ming^4 ʻho^2?

越不中越要讀。命其如我何
Yueh^4 pu^4 chung^4 yueh^4 yao^4 tu^2: ming^4 chʻi^2 ju^2 wo^3 ʻho^2?

Note.—This saying of the ancients—in flat contradiction of many of the preceding proverbs—means "that the decree of fate does not violate the liberty of the human will, or impose a *necessity* on man to act either in one way or in another." Milne. *Sacred Edict*, 2nd edition, page 125.

675

Men are good or bad according to their conduct; and their misery or happiness depends on themselves.

善惡隨人作。禍福自己招
Shan^4 o^4 sui^2 jên^2 tso^4; ʻhuo^4 fu^2 tzŭ^4 chi^3 chao.^{1}

Note.—This proverb, as well as the preceding one, shows that the Chinese are not, at all events, consistent necessitarians.

676

The man can, but his fate cannot.

人能命不能
Jên^2 nêng^2 ming^4 pu^4 nêng.^{2}

677

Fate. *Lit.*: The abacus in the temple of the city-god.

城隍廟的算盤
Chʻêng^2 ʻhuang^2 miao^4 ti^1 suan^4 pʻan.^{2}

678

"If it be my wealth it won't go; if he be my son he won't die."

係我財不去。係我子不死
Hsi^4 wo^3 tsʻai^2 pu^4 chʻü^4; hsi^4 wo^3 tzŭ^3 pu^4 szŭ.^{3}

Note.—It is said of *Fan Wên Chêng Kung* 范文正公, that he did not believe in devils. One came to him and questioned him; but still he refused to believe. So this devil said he would kill his first-born son. "Well he might do." After he had done so, as he thought, he came again to see if the gentleman believed; but still he did not. So the devil killed a second youth. Still no change appeared in the philosopher's incredulity, and he threatened to kill a third. The devil, however, now grew nervous, and did not or could not kill that one, who was the real son. Hence the saying "if he be my son he will not die."

679

One's every glass of wine and every slice of meat, are predestined.

杯酒塊肉皆前定
Pei^1 chiu^3 kʻuai^4 jou^4 chieh^1 chʻien^2 ting.^{4}

680

Wife, wealth, children, pay, are all predestined.

妻 財 子 祿 皆 前 定

Chʻi[1] tsʻai[2] tzŭ[3] lu[4] chieh[1] chʻien[2] ting.[4]

681

Virtuous children and official emolument who does not desire? Alas! these are not the theme of your luckless horoscope.

誰 人 不 愛 子 孫 賢

Shui[2] jên[2] pu[4] ai[4] tzŭ[3] sun[1] hsien[2]?

誰 人 不 愛 千 鍾 粟

Shui[2] jên[2] pu[4] ai[4] chʻien[1] chung[1] su[2]?

奈 五 行 不 是 這 般 題 目

nai[4] wu[3] hsing[2] pu[4] shih[4] chê[4] pan[1] tʻi[2] mu.[4]

NOTE.—"Official emolument;" *Lit.:* "1000 *chung* of grain." One *chung* is equal to four *tou*[3] or pecks.

682

Don't say that *Wên Wang's* diagrams are powerless, but fear lest the fortune teller has told them wrong.

莫 道 文 王 卦 不 靈

Mo[4] tao[4] Wên[2] Wang[2] kua[4] pu[4] ling,[2]

只 怕 先 生 斷 不 真

chih[3] pʻa[4] hsien[1] shêng[1] tuan[4] pu[4] chên.[1]

CHAPTER II.

LUCK.

683

He hoards to-day, he hoards to-morrow (!), does nothing else but hoard;
At length he has enough a new umbrella to afford;
When all at once he is assailed, a wind arises quick;—
And both his hands grasp nothing but a bare umbrella stick.

今天攢。明天攢
Chin1 t'ien1 ts'uan2; ming2 t'ien1 ts'uan2;
攢來攢去。買了一把傘
Ts'uan2 lai2 ts'uan2 ch'ü4; mai3 liao3 yi1 pa3 san.3
忽然一陣狂風起
'Hu1 jan2 yi1 chên4 k'uang2 fêng1 ch'i3;—
兩手抱住光竹桿
Liang3 shou3 pao4 chu4 kuang1 chu2 kan.2

684

If luck be low,
To Kiangsi go.

時運低。走江西
Shih4 yün4 ti,1 tsou4 Chiang1 Hsi.1

685

A lucky horoscope doth for a whole life prepare;
And if it be not lucky what use is fervent prayer?

命裡有時終須有
Ming li yu shih chung1 hsü1 yu3;
命裡無時莫苦求
Ming4 li3 wu2 shih2 mo4 k'u3 ch'iu.2

686

The sturdiest army may be laid low:
The axe may sever the sturdiest bough.

兵强則滅。木强則折
Ping1 ch'iang2 tsê2 mieh4; mu4 ch'iang2 tsê2 chê.2

687

If a man's in luck he always finds,
Where'er he goes to, favouring winds.

人在時中。行船遇順風

Jên2 tsai4 shih2 chung,1 hsing2 ch'uan2 yü4 shun4 fêng.1

688

In the morning only some farmhouse pride;
At night he stands by the Emperor's side.

朝爲田舍郎。暮登天子堂

Chao1 wei1 t'ien2 shê4 lang2; mu4 têng1 t'ien1 tzŭ3 t'ang.2

689

A lucky man is stout and fair;
And men lend him twice as much as he wants.
A luckless man is burnt and spare;
And he asks for a loan which no one grants.

人在時中又胖又白

Jên2 tsai4 shih2 chung1 yu4 p'ang4 yu4 pai2;

借錢五十答應一百

Chieh4 ch'ien2 wu3 shih2 ta1 ying4 yi1 pai.3

人不在時又瘦又黑

Jên2 pu4 tsai4 shih2 yu4 shou4 yu4 'hê1;

借錢五十答應沒得

Chieh4 ch'ien2 wu3 shih2 ta1 ying4 mu2 tê.2

690

Peaches blossom in the second month;
Chrysanthemums in the ninth are out;
Each must wait till its time comes about.

桃花二月開。菊花九月開

T'ao2 'hua1 êrh4 yueh4 k'ai1; chü2 'hua1 chiu3 yueh4 k'ai1;

各自等時來

Ko4 tzŭ4 têng3 shih2 lai.2

691

Some like thunder rise in haste:
Some like ashes fall to waste.

一發如雷。一敗如灰

Yi1 fa1 ju2 lei2; yi1 pai4 ju2 'hui.1

692

What the actors cannot do.
Gods and fairies carry through.

戲不彀。神仙湊

Hsi^{4} pu^{4} kou,^{4} shên^{2} hsien^{1} tsʻou.^{4}

NOTE.—Said of any in straights who happen to meet with opportune help.

693

In the halls of magistrates long bodied men sit;
Through the streets in a hurry long leggéd men flit.

上身長坐官堂

Shang^{4} shên^{1} chʻang^{2} tso^{4} kuan^{1} tʻang^{2};

下身長走忙忙

Hsia^{4} shên^{1} chʻang^{2} tsou^{4} mang^{2} mang.^{2}

NOTE.—This is said to be a saying of physiognomical fortune-tellers.

694

It you rattle your chopsticks and bason,
You will be poor to the last generation.

敲碗敲筷。窮死萬代

Chʻiao^{1} wan^{3} chʻiao^{1} kʻuai,^{4} chʻiung^{2} ssŭ^{3} wan^{4} tai.^{4}

695

Quiver my eyelids, my heart throbs in my breast;
Neither sitting nor sleeping can I find rest.

眼跳心驚。坐臥不寧

Yen^{3} tʻiao^{4} hsin^{1} ching^{1}; tso^{4} wo^{4} pu^{4} ning.^{2}

NOTE.—The state of affairs, supposed in this and the preceding proverb, is understood to be ominous of ill luck.

696

Don't boast of good fortune. *Lit.:* Don't let yourself say too much about the fineness of Spring; but have a fear of westerly winds and the recurrence of cold.

人情莫道春光好

Jên^{2} chʻing^{2} mo^{4} tao^{4} chʻun^{1} kuang^{1} hao^{3};

只怕西風有冷時

chih^{3} pʻa^{4} hsi^{1} fêng^{1} yu^{3} lêng^{3} shih.^{2}

697

He goes out empty-handed; he returns a wealthy man.

空手出門。抱財歸家

Kʻung^{1} shou^{3} chʻu^{1} mên^{2}; pao^{4} tsʻai^{2} kuei^{1} chia.^{1}

698

One family builds a wall, and two families get the benefit of it.

一家打牆兩家方便

Yi[1] chia[1] ta[3] ch'iang,[2] liang[3] chia[1] fang[1] pien.[4]

699

Having good luck he need only wound his purse; having it not he must himself be wounded.

有福傷財。無福傷己

Yu[3] fu[2] shang[1] ts'ai[2]; wu[2] fu[2] shang[1] chi.[3]

NOTE.—The case here supposed is that of a man who has broken the law: if he can pay a fine he may escape corporeal punishment.

700

The poorer one is the more devils one meets.

越窮越見鬼

Yueh[4] ch'iung[2] yueh[4] chien[4] kuei.[3]

701

If luck comes, who comes not? If luck comes not, who comes?

時來誰不來。時不來誰來

Shih[2] lai[2] shui[3] pu[4] lai[2]? shih[2] pu[4] lai[2] shui[3] lai[2]?

702

Good luck certain sometime. *Lit.*: A day must come for thrashing out the grain.

稻場打穀終有一日

Tao[4] ch'ang[2] ta[3] ku[3] chung[1] yu[3] yi[1] jih.[4]

703

A scabbed-head following the moon enjoys extra light.

瘌瘰跟着月亮走。沾光沾光

La[1] li[2] kên[1] cho[1] yueh[4] liang[4] tsou,[4] chan[1] kuang[1] chan[1] kuang.[1]

NOTE.—*La-li*,—two words not found in Kanghi, but common enough—signify one whose head is not only bald but covered with glistening and offensive scars. *La-li* are very numerous, and they are very commonly made the butts of ridicule. When one is near, a bystander will exclaim 好大亮 *'hao ta liang*, "what a great light!" to the amusement of all around. They are also nicknamed 毛希 *mao hsi* or "scarce-hair," 葫蘆 *'hu lu* or pumpkin, &c. In this proverb also which expresses the good luck any one enjoys in following another, a shaft of ridicule is aimed at the unfortunate La-li.

704

When a dwarf ascends a staircase, he luckly gets higher every step.

矮子扒樓梯。一步高一步

Ai^{3} tzŭ^{3} pa lou^{2} tʻi,^{1} yi^{1} pu^{4} kao^{1} yi^{1} pu.^{4}

705

A dwarf cannot kick up his feet to any very great height.

矮子打二起。純高也總不高

Ai^{3} tzŭ^{3} ta^{3} êrh^{4} chʻi^{3}, shun^{2} kao^{1} yeh^{3} tsung^{3} pu^{4} kao.^{1}

NOTE.—This cynical proverb formed an apt illustration in the fate of the Hankow dwarf who visited Europe some time ago with *Chang* the giant. The dwarf is said to have returned to Hankow with 300 taels in his pocket. That seemed like kicking to a great height. Before long, however, the friends of the unlucky wight managed to filch out all his money from him: so the proverb came true—he did not kick very high after all.

706

To enjoy good luck. *Lit.:* To hoist the sail before a fair wind.

扯起蓬來走順風

Chʻê^{3} chʻi^{3} pʻêng^{2} lai^{2} tsou^{4} shun^{4} fêng.^{1}

707

Who fears that your pen will pierce the sky?

那怕你一筆抒破天

Na^{3} pʻa^{4} ni^{3} yi^{1} pi^{3} hsü^{3} pʻo^{4} tʻien.^{1}

708

Sudden return of luck. *Lit.:* The swept area produces a large melon.

掃塲結大瓜

Sao^{3} chʻang^{2} chieh^{2} ta^{4} kua.^{1}

709

Unluckily born. *Lit.:* You have slept in the wrong cradle, and issued from the wrong womb.

睡錯搖籮。脫錯了胎

Shui^{4} tsʻo^{4} yao^{2} lo,^{2} tʻo^{1} tsʻo^{4} liao^{3} tʻai.^{1}

710

Out of luck, gold becomes iron; in luck iron resembles gold.

運去金成鐵。時來鐵似金

Yün^4 ch'ü^4 chin^1 ch'êng^2 t'ieh^3; shih^2 lai^2 t'ieh^3 ssŭ^4 chin.^{1}

711

Even the Yellow River has its clear days; how can man be altogether without luck?

黃河尚有澄清日

'Huang^2 'ho^2 shang^4 yu^3 têng^4 ch'ing^1 jih^4;

豈有人無得運時

ch'i^3 yu^3 jên^2 wu^2 tê^2 yün^4 shih^2?

NOTE.—Its clear days happen once or twice in a millenium. Encouraging!

712

The poor may have no wise friend to succour them; but the sick generally have some noble friend to tell them of a remedy.

貧無達士持金贈

P'in^3 wu^2 ta^2 shih^1 ch'ih^2 chin^1 tsêng^4;

病有高人說藥方

ping^4 yu^3 kao^1 jên^2 shuo^1 yao^4 fang.^{1}

713

The leaky house must encounter a succession of rainy nights; and the sailing ship must beat against unfavourable winds.

屋漏更遭連夜雨

Wu^1 lou^4 kêng^1 tsao^1 lien^2 yeh^4 yü^3;

行船却被打頭風

hsing^2 ch'uan^2 ch'üeh^4 pei^4 ta^3 t'ou^2 fêng.^{1}

714

Under each man's name is his own fortune.

各人名下一重天

Ko^4 jên^2 ming^2 hsia^4 yi^1 ch'ung^2 t'ien.^{1}

715

Sour, sweet, bitter, pungent, all must be tasted.

酸甜苦辣都嘗過

Suan^1 t'ien^2 k'u^3 la^4 tu^1 ch'ang^2 kuo.^{4}

716

"The fortunes of men are as uncertain as the winds and clouds of Heaven."

天 有 不 測 風 雲
T'ien[1] yu[3] pu[4] ts'ê[4] fêng[1] yün[2];
人 有 旦 夕 禍 福
jên[2] yu[3] tan[4] hsi[1] 'huo[4] fu.[2]

717

Good swimmers are sometimes drowned; and good riders are sometimes thrown.

善 游 者 溺。善 騎 者 墮
Shan[4] yu[2] chê[2] ni[4]; shan[4] ch'i[2] chê[2] to.[4]

718

The lucky man meets a friend; the unlucky man a fair lady.

時 來 逢 好 友。運 去 遇 佳 人
Shih[2] lai[2] fêng[2] hao[3] yu[3]; yün[4] ch'ü[4] yü[4] chia[1] jên.[2]

719

When the floating clouds are dispersed we see a clear sky.

撥 開 浮 雲 見 青 天
Po[1] k'ai[1] fou[2] yün[2] chien[4] ch'ing[4] t'ien.[1]

720

His horoscope is lucky. *Lit.:* The two stems don't disagree.

兩 干 不 雜
Liang[3] kan[1] pu[4] tsa.[2]

721

It is an unlucky sign when the eyelids quiver.

眼 睛 跳 晦 氣 到
Yen[3] ching[1] t'iao[4] 'hui[4] ch'i[4] tao.[4]

722

A horse may have strength to run a thousand miles, but without a rider it knows not where to go: a man may have the ambition to scale the clouds, but without luck he cannot get on.

馬有千里之能
Ma^3 yu^3 ch'ien^1 li^3 chih^1 nêng,^{2}
非人不能自往
fei^1 jên^2 pu^4 nêng^2 tzŭ^4 wang^3:
人有凌雲之志
jên^2 yu^3 ling^2 yün^2 chih^1 chih,^{4}
非運不能亨通
fei^1 yün^4 pu^4 nêng^2 hsiang^3 t'ung.^{1}

723

A raging wind only strikes those who are in it.

狂風單打下風人
K'uang^2 fêng^1 tan^1 ta^3 hsia^4 fêng^1 jên.^{2}

724

Time will come when luck will change, when Heaven will send down wealth and honour.

有遭一日時運轉
Yu^3 tsao^1 yi^1 jih^4 shih^2 yün^4 chuan,^{3}
富貴榮華天降來
fu^4 kuei^4 yung^2 'hua^2 t'ien^1 chiang^4 lai.^{2}

725

A poor fellow in luck's way. *Lit.*: A ragged sail in a fair wind.

破帆遇順風
P'o^4 fan^1 yü^4 shün^4 fêng.^{1}

726

Kan Lo enjoyed the favour of the state of *Ch'in* at the age of twelve; whilst *T'ai Kung* waited till he was eighty for the emoluments of *Tsou*.

甘羅十二受秦恩
Kan^1 Lo^2 shih^2 êrh^4 shou^2 Ch'in^2 ên^1;
太公八十食周祿
T'ai^4 Kung^1 pa^1 shih^2 shih^2 Chou^1 lu.^{4}

NOTE.—The former of these worthies is said to have been made Prime minister at the early age of twelve; while the latter, the famous *Chiang T'ai Kung* (姜太公), did not reach that honour till he was an old man. All luck!

727

To kill two birds with one stone.

一舉兩得 or 一舉兩便

Yi[1] chü[3] liang[3] tê.[2] Yi[1] chü[3] liang[3] pien.[4]

728

To shoot two arrows at once.

一弓搭兩箭

Yi[1] kung[1] ta[2] liang[3] chien.[4]

729

A pearl wrapped up in straw.

稻草包珍珠

Tao[4] ts'ao[3] pao[1] chên[1] chu.[1]

NOTE.—Said of able or learned persons whose ill luck it is to live unnoticed and unknown.

730

A chance day is better than a chosen one.

選日不如撞日

Hsüan[3] jih[4] pu[4] ju[2] chuang[4] jih.[4]

731

Chance luck. *Lit.*: A blind cock chancing on grain.

瞎雞公撞米頭

Hsia[2] chi[1] kung[1] chuang[4] mi[3] t'ou.[2]

732

An auspicious plant growing up before one's private apartments, may prove to be a good omen one had better be without.

庭前生瑞草。好事不如無

T'ing[2] ch'ien[2] shêng[1] shiu[4] ts'ao[3], 'hao[3] shih[4] pu[4] ju[2] wu.[2]

NOTE.—A somewhat interesting legend is told in connection with this proverb and in explanation of it, to the following effect. In former times a young merchant, a few months after his marriage, and just after his wife had communicated to him the fact that she was enceinte, was obliged to leave home on business likely to detain him for an indefinitely long time. Before taking his leave he deposited with her the half of a ring he had been in the habit of wearing, thinking that it might serve to facilitate recognition should the time of his absence prove very long, or anything untimely befall him. He went away and never returned. Whilst staying at an inn in a certain town, with a large sum of money in his possession, he was poisoned and robbed. But, before death transpired, he took an antidote which he had had the precaution always to carry about with him. This antidote did not save his life, but it preserved his body from decay. The murderer secretly buried him in the courtyard of his house, and the dark deed was not discovered. The neighbours, however, marvelled much to see how suddenly the innkeeper's family had grown rich. And the wonderment did not end there, for, soon it became noised abroad that in the courtyard of this inn a prodigy might be daily witnessed in the shape of a beautiful flowering plant, which sprang up in the morning and faded at night. Crowds came to see the wondrous plant, and from them the lucky inn-keeper drew a considerable revenue.

This had been going on for a long time when the merchant's son, now grown up into a young man, in searching for his father came to the very town in which this prodigy was taking place. He visited the courtyard of the inn; and his curiosity led him to touch the marvellous plant, whereupon it instantly decayed. The inn-keeper, seeing that his hopes of gain were destroyed, in a rage took the young man before the magistrate. The magistrate determined if possible to unravel the double mystery by digging for the root of the plant. That led to the discovery of a corpse in perfect preservation, whose features resembled closely those of the youth, and of the half of a ring corresponding to that which he produced; it also led to the discovery of the murder, the punishment of the culprit, and overthrow of his family. And so it came true that the auspicious plant was unlucky after all.

CHAPTER II.

OPPORTUNITY.

733

It ought to be settled,—you settle it not;
In consequence trouble will fall to your lot.

當 斷 不 斷。反 受 其 難

Tang^{1} tuan^{4} pu^{4} tan^{4}; fan^{3} shou^{4} chʻi^{2} nan.^{3}

734

Until times favour you, no luck can you enjoy:
And should you try to sail, head winds will you annoy.

時 不 至 來 運 不 通

Shih^{2} pu^{4} chih^{4} lai^{2} yün^{4} pu^{4} tʻung^{1}:

行 船 又 遇 擋 頭 風

Hsing^{2} chʻuan^{2} yu^{4} yü^{4} tang^{3} tʻou^{2} fêng.^{1}

735

Since the wind blows your fire,
No need yourself to tire.

因 風 吹 火。用 力 不 多

Yin^{1} fêng^{1} chʻui^{1} ʻhuo,^{3} yung^{4} li^{4} pu^{4} to.^{1}

736

Those near a mandarin get honour; those near a kitchen food.

近 官 得 貴。近 厨 得 食

Chin^{4} kuan^{1} tê^{2} kuei^{4}; chin^{4} chʻu^{2} tê^{2} shih.^{2}

737

He who neglects a good opportunity, must not afterwards complain.

當 取 不 取。過 後 莫 悔

Tang^{1} chʻü^{3} pu^{4} chʻü,^{3} kuo^{4} hou^{4} mo^{4} ʻhui.^{3}

738

When your horse is on the brink of a precipice it is too late to pull the reins; when calamity is upon you repentance is too late.

馬 到 臨 崖 收 韁 晚

Ma^{3} tao^{4} lin^{2} ai^{2} shou^{1} chiang^{1} wan^{3};

禍 至 頭 來 悔 不 及

ʻhuo^{4} chih^{4} tʻou^{2} lai^{2} ʻhui^{3} pu^{4} chi.^{2}

739

Opportunity must sometime visit the meanest. *Lit.:* There comes a day when the bits of reed in a ditch turn over.

陽 溝 裡 篾 片 也 有 翻 身 日

Yang^2 kou^1 li^3 mieh^4 pʻien^4 yeh^3 yu^3 fan^1 shên^1 jih.^{4}

740.

Pass no day idly, youth does not return.

白 日 莫 閑 過。青 春 不 再 來

Pai^1 jih^4 mo^4 hsien^2 kuo,^{4} chʻing^1 chʻun^1 pu^4 tsai^4 lai.^{2}

741

A hero without the opportunity of displaying his bravery.

英 雄 無 用 武 之 處

Ying^1 hsiung^2 wu^2 yung^4 wu^3 chih^1 chʻu.^{4}

742

Enjoying good opportunities. *Lit.:* A water-side tower first catches the moon: trees and flowers in the sun earliest meet the spring.

近 水 樓 臺 先 得 月

Chin^4 shui^3 lou^2 tʻai^2 hsien^1 tê^2 yueh^4:

向 陽 花 木 早 逢 春

hsiang^4 yang^2 ʻhua^1 mu^4 tsao^3 fêng^2 chʻun.^{1}

743

Neglected youth brings miserable age.

少 壯 不 努 力。老 大 徒 傷 悲

Shao^3 chuang^4 pu^4 lu^3 li,^{4} lao^3 ta^4 tʻu^2 shang^1 pei.^{1}

744

A year's opportunities depend on Spring; a day's on the dawn; a family's on harmony; and a life's on industry.

一 年 之 計 在 於 春

Yi^1 nien^2 chih^1 chi^4 tsai^4 yü^1 chʻun^1;

一 日 之 計 在 於 寅

yi^1 jih^4 chih^1 chi^4 tsai^4 yü^1 yin^2;

一 家 之 計 在 於 和

yi^1 chia^1 chih^1 chi^4 tsai^4 yü^1 ʻho^2;

一 生 之 計 在 於 勤

yi^1 shêng^1 chih^1 chi^4 tsai^4 yü^1 chʻin.^{2}

745

If you have but a green willow you can tie your horse thereto: there are roads from everywhere to the capital.

但有綠楊堪繫馬

Tan^4 yu^3 lu^4 yang^2 kʻan^1 chi^4 ma^3:

處處有路透長安

Chʻu^4 chʻu^4 yu^3 lu^4 tʻou^4 Chang^3-An.^{1}

NOTE.—*Chang-an*, the capital of China during the *Tsʻin*, *Han*, *Sui*, and *Tʻang* dynasties: the old name of *Si-ngan-fu*.

746

Every high road leads to Peking.

條條大路通北京

Tʻiao^2 tʻiao^2 ta^4 lu^4 tʻung^1 Pei^3-ching.^{1}

747

When a vessel is in the middle of a river it is too late to stop the leak.

船到江心補漏遲

Chʻuan^2 tao^4 chiang^1 hsin^1 pu^3 lou^4 chʻih.^{2}

748

A fair wind fans the flame; the boat glides with the stream.

順風吹火。下水行船

Shun^4 fêng^1 chʻui^1 ʻhuo^3; hsia^4 shui^3 hsing^2 chʻuan.^{2}

749

If you do not kill a man outright he will live to be your enemy.

殺人不死反爲仇

Sha^1 jên^2 pu^4 ssŭ^3 fan^3 wei^2 chʻou.^{2}

750

He borrows the wind to cross the river.

借風過河

Chieh^4 fêng^1 kuo^4 ʻho.^{2}

751

To light a fire in a hot stove.

熱灶裡着把火

Jê^4 tsao^4 li^3 cho^2 ʻpa^3 ʻhuo.^{3}

752

Strike while the iron's hot.

打 鐵 趕 熱

Ta^3 tʻieh^3 kan^2 jê.^{4}

753

When you see an opportunity, act.

見 幾 而 作

Chien^4 chi^3 êrh^2 tso.^{4}

754

Meet an honourable man and you'll be satisfied with food; meet a premier and you'll be clothed in court dress.

遇 貴 人 吃 飽 飯

Yü^4 kuei^4 jên^2 chʻih^1 pao^3 fan^4:

遇 宰 相 穿 朝 衣

yü^4 tsai^4 hsiang^4 chʻuan^1 chʻao^2 i.^{1}

755

When the melon is ripe it will drop of itself.

瓜 熟 自 落

Kua^1 shu^2 tzŭ^4 lo.^{4}

756

One whom opportunity serves to please all parties. *Lit.:* A sharp knife cuts bean curd leaving both sides smooth.

快 刀 打 豆 腐 兩 面 光

Kʻuai^4 tao^1 ta^3 tou^4 fu^3 liang^3 mien^4 kuang.^{1}

757

When a time to drink wine comes, drink it; and when you are in a proper place sing aloud.

遇 飲 酒 時 須 飲 酒

Yü^4 yin^3 chiu^3 shih^2 hsü^1 yin^3 chiu^3;

得 高 歌 處 且 高 歌

tê^2 kao^1 ko^1 chʻu^4 chʻieh^3 kao^1 ko.^{1}

758

Neither leave a spot when there is fish, nor long for a place of shallow rapids.

休 別 有 魚 處。莫 戀 淺 灘 頭

Hsiu^1 pieh^2 yu^3 yü^2 chʻu,^{4} mo^4 lien^4 chʻien^3 tʻan^1 tʻou.^{2}

SECTION VIII.—ON JOYS AND SORROWS.

CHAPTER I.

AMUSEMENTS.

759

Once in a while you may go to a play,
But they are not the things for every day.

逢場作戲。不可專意

Fêng² ch'ang² tso⁴ hsi,⁴ pu⁴ k'o³ chuan¹ i.⁴

760

After dice throwing and card playing,
Disputes must arise about paying.

抹牌擲骰。必有下場白

Mo³ p'ai² chih⁴ shai,³ pi⁴ yu³ hsia⁴ ch'ang² pai.²

761

Losing comes of winning money.

輸錢只爲贏錢起

Shu¹ ch'ien² chih³ wei⁴ ying² ch'ien² ch'i.³

762

If you believe in gambling you will have to sell your house.

信了賭賣了屋

Hsin⁴ liao³ tu³ mai⁴ liao³ wu.¹

763

When four armed men ascend the arena, each tries to kill the other.

上場四把刀

Shang³ ch'ang² ssŭ pa³ tao,¹

你不殺我我殺你

ni³ pu⁴ sha¹ wo³ wo³ sha¹ ni.³

764

Money goes to the gambling house as criminals to execution.

錢到賭場。人到法場

Ch'ien² tao⁴ tu³ ch'ang,² jên² tao⁴ fa³ ch'ang.²

765

When the gambler's wealth is spent, and his purse empty, he must stop.

賭博家財盡囊空自然休

Tu³ po² chia¹ ts'ai² chin⁴ nang² k'ung¹ tzŭ⁴ jan² hsiu.¹

766

To persuade gentlemen not to gamble, is to win for them.

勸君莫賭是贏錢

Ch'üan⁴ chün¹ mo⁴ tu³ shih⁴ ying² ch'ien.²

767

Men in the game are blind to what men looking on see clearly.

當局者迷旁觀者清

Tang⁴ chü² chê² mi² p'ang² kuan¹ chê² ch'ing.¹

CHAPTER II.

CALAMITY AND GRIEF.

768

'Tis not calamity in any shape,
From which it is possible to escape.

躲 脫 不 是 禍。是 禍 躲 不 脫

To^{2} tʻo^{1} pu^{4} shih^{4} ʻhuo,^{4} shih^{4} ʻhuo^{4} to^{2} pu^{4} tʻo.^{1}

769

To have iron made lips, and feet of beancurd made,
Is such a calamity as no one can evade.

鐵 嘴 豆 腐 脚。是 禍 躲 不 脫

Tʻieh^{3} tsui^{3} tou^{4} fu^{3} chio,^{3} shih^{4} ʻhuo^{4} to^{2} pu^{4} tʻo.^{1}

770

If the white tiger star faces your gate,
Some kind of misfortune must be your fate.

白 虎 當 門 坐。無 災 必 有 禍

Pai^{2} ʻhu^{3} tang^{1} mên^{2} tso,^{4} wu^{2} tsai^{1} pi^{4} yu^{3} ʻhuo.^{4}

771

If men eat flesh and do not flourish,
The reason is the grief they nourish.

吃 肉 不 長 肉。只 爲 多 憂 愁

Chʻih^{1} jou^{4} pu^{4} chang^{3} jou,^{4} chih^{3} wei^{4} to^{1} yu^{1} chʻou.^{2}

772

Once in trouble it is hard to get out. *Lit.:*
To the claw of the heron the bloodsucker sticks,
And he can't shake him off though he lustily kicks.

螞 蝗 搭 倒 鷺 鷥 脚

Ma^{3} ʻhuang^{2} ta^{2} tao^{3} lu^{4} ssŭ^{1} chio,^{3}

要 脫 不 得 脫

Yao^{4} tʻo^{1} pu^{4} tê^{2} tʻo.^{1}

773

Severed living and parted dying,
No grief on earth can be so trying.

生 離 死 別。悲 哀 最 切

Shêng^{1} li^{2} ssŭ^{3} pieh,^{2} pei^{1} ai^{1} tsui^{4} chʻieh.^{4}

774

Full of trouble. *Lit.:*
An ox in a mill—a horse bearing mail—
Actors before the *Chʻeng-shou* turning pale.

牛落磨坊馬落驛
Niu^2 lo^4 mo^2 fang^2 ma^3 lo^4 yi^4—
戲子怕的城守裡
Hsi^4 tsŭ^3 pʻa^4 ti^1 chʻêng^2 shou^3 li.^{3}

NOTE.—"*Chʻêng-shou*," a small military officer, or commandant, in charge of a city; a sort of superintendent of police. He is dreaded by actors on account of his well known rapacity; he will force them to perform without remuneration.

775

Out of the mouth calamities fly:
In by the mouth all sicknesses hie.

禍從口出。病從口入
ʻHuo^4 tsʻung^2 kʻou^3 chʻu^1: ping^4 tsʻung^2 kʻou^3 ju.^{4}

776

Whenever the raven flies over one's head,
There must be before us some trouble to dread.

烏鴉當頭過。無災必有禍
Wu^1 ya^1 tang^1 tʻou^2 kuo,^{4} wu^2 tsai^1 pi^4 yu^3 ʻhuo.^{4}

777

Those who know me, can for me feel;
Can those who don't pray for my weal?

知我者爲我心憂
Chih^1 wo^3 chê^2 wei^4 wo^3 hsin^1 yu^1;
不知我者爲我何求
Pu^4 chih^1 wo^3 chê^2 wei^4 wo^3 ʻho^2 chʻiu^2?

778

On Heaven and Earth he loudly cries;
Both Heaven and Earth his prayer despise.

喊天天不應。叫地地不靈
ʻHan^3 tʻien^1 tʻien^1 pu^4 ying^4; chiao^4 ti^4 ti^4 pu^4 ling.^{2}

779

Men may despise me, but if Heaven does not,
Suffering is an agreeable lot.

人欺天勿欺。吃虧就是便宜
Jên^2 chʻi^1 tʻien^1 wu^4 chʻi,^{1} chʻih^1 kʻuei^1 chiu^4 shih^4 pien^4 i.^{2}

780

"Prosperity and misfortune are common to all times and places."

豐熟年年有。災殃各地方

Fêng¹ shu² nien² nien² yu³, tsai¹ yang¹ ko⁴ ti⁴ fang.¹

781

Our pleasures are shallow, our troubles deep.

所樂者淺。所患者深

So³ lê⁴ chê² ch'ien,³ so³ 'huan⁴ chê² shên.¹

782

Grief knits the brows.

愁鎖眉尖

Ch'ou² so³ mei² chien.¹

783

Full of grief. *Lit.:* Your thoughts are confused as uncarded hemp.

心思亂如麻

Hsin¹ ssŭ¹ lan⁴ ju² ma.²

784

A burnt tortoise keeps his pain inside.

火燒烏龜肉裡疼

'Huo³ shao¹ wu¹ kuei¹ nei⁴ li³ t'eng.²

NOTE.—"The heart knoweth his own bitterness". Prov: xiv, 10.

785

In trouble think of your relations; in danger depend on old friends.

遇急思親戚。臨危托故人

Yü⁴ chi² ssŭ¹ ch'in¹ ch'i⁴; lin² wei² t'o¹ ku⁴ jên.²

786

Calamity and happiness come not of themselves, but only at the call of man.

禍福無門。惟人所招

'Huo⁴ fu² wu² mên,² wei² jên² so³ chao.¹

787

Though a dumb man has eaten gentian, he keeps his trouble to himself.

啞巴吃黄連。苦在心裡

Ya³ pa¹ ch'ih¹ 'huang² lien,² k'u³ tsai⁴ hsin¹ li.³

788

Extreme danger. *Lit.*: A bridge of one pole is very bad to cross.

獨木搭橋眞難得過

Tu² mu⁴ ta² ch'iao² chên¹ nan² tê² kuo.⁴

789

What is the use of weeping over broken vessels? Spilt water cannot be gathered up again.

既墮釜甑反顧何益

Chi³ to⁴ fu³ tsêng⁴ fan³ ku⁴ 'ho² i²?

反覆之水收之實難

Fan³ fu² chih¹ shui³ shou¹ chih¹ shih² nan.²

NOTE.—"For we must needs die, and are as water spilt on the ground, which cannot be gathered up again". 2 Sam: xiv, 14.

790

Out of the wolf's nest into the tiger's mouth.

正離狼窩。反逢虎口

Cheng⁴ li² lang² wo,¹ fan³ fêng² 'hu³ k'ou.³

791

Whilst keeping a tiger from the front door, a wolf enters by the back.

前門拒虎。後門進狼

Ch'ien² nên² chü⁴ 'hu,³ 'hou⁴ mên² chin⁴ lang.²

792

When one leaf moves all the branches shake.

一葉既動百枝皆搖

Yi¹ yeh⁴ chi³ tung⁴ pai³ chih¹ chieh¹ yao.²

793

Whilst men sit in their houses, Heaven sends calamity upon them.

人在家裡坐。禍從天上來

Jên² tsai⁴ chai¹ li³ tso,⁴ 'huo⁴ ts'ung² t'ien¹ shang⁴ lai.²

794

The mischief will fall on your own pate. *Lit.*: When are trackers drowned by the upset of a vessel?

翻船的幾時淹死了扯縴的
Fan[1] ch'uan[2] ti[1] chi[3] shih[2] yen[1] ssŭ[3] liao[3] ch'ê[3] ch'ien[1] ti.[1]

795

Calamities may come down from Heaven; but let us seek to be blameless.

禍從天上來。但求心無愧
'Huo[4] ts'ung[2] t'ing[1] shang[4] lai[2]; tan[4] ch'iu[2] hsin[1] wu[2] k'uei.[4]

796

To extract sweetness from what is bitter.

從苦中得甘
Ts'ung[2] k'u[3] chung[1] tê[2] kan.[1]

797

Worse and worse. *Lit.*: "When a rat creeps up the horn of a cow the higher it mounts the narrower the space."

老鼠扒牛角越扒越尖了
Lao[3] shu[3] pa[1] niu[2] chiao[1] yüeh[4] pa[1] yüeh[4] chien[1] liao.[3]

798

Grief is ten times bitterer than gentian.

苦比黃連勝十分
K'u[3] pi[3] huang[2] lien[2] shêng[4] shih[2] fên.[1]

799

Woe! and Alas! Death is hard to guess.

嗚呼哀哉。人死難猜
Wu[1] 'hu[1] ai[1] tsai[1]! jên[2] ssŭ[3] nan[2] ts'ai.[1]

NOTE.—This furnishes a specimen of the Innuendo: for several other examples, and notes thereon, see Index.

800

Calamity cannot raise its head.

苦不出頭
K'u[3] pu[4] ch'u[1] t'ou.[2]

801

Hoping to lift up his head, he lifts up his feet. *i.e.* dies.

望到伸頭。便要伸脚
Wang[4] tao[4] shên[1] t'ou,[2] pien[4] yao[4] shên[1] chiao.[3]

802

If the heart be not wounded the eyes will not weep.

人不傷心淚不流

Jên^2 pu^4 shang^1 hsin^1 lei^4 pu^4 liu.^{2}

803

The three misfortnnes are,—in youth to lose one's father, in middle age to lose one's wife, and in old age to have no son.

三不幸。少年喪父

San^1 pu^4 hsing,^{4}—shao^3 nien^2 sang^1 fu,^{4}

中年死妻。老來無子

chung^4 nien^2 ssŭ^3 chʻi,^{1} lao^3 lai^2 wu^2 tzŭ.^{3}

804

A blind man on a blind horse, coming at midnight upon a deep ditch.

盲人騎瞎馬。夜半臨深池

Mang^2 jên^2 chʻi^2 hsia^2 ma,^{3} yeh^4 pan^4 lin^2 shên^1 chʻih.^{2}

805

For bringing down calamity there is nothing worse than a bad temper; for warding off misfortune there is nothing better than patient concession.

招殃之端莫狠於氣性

Chao^1 yang^1 chih^1 tuan^1 mo^4 ʻhên^3 yü^2 chʻi^4 hsing^4;

避禍之法莫過於忍讓

pi^4 ʻhuo^4 chih^1 fa^3 mo^4 kuo^4 yü^2 jên^3 jang.^{4}

806

Don't raise waves in the world, and you'll keep ice and coal out of your bosom.

不作風波於世上

Pu^4 tso^4 fêng^1 po^1 yü^2 shih^4 shang,^{4}

自無冰炭到胸中

tzŭ^4 wu^2 ping^1 tʻan^4 tao^4 hsiung^1 chung.^{1}

807

No escape from trouble. *Lit.:* There is no road up to heaven, nor door into the earth.

上天無路。入地無門

Shang^3 tʻien^1 wu^2 lu,^{4} ju^4 ti^4 wu^2 mên.^{2}

808

Sympathy. *Lit.:* When your tooth aches you know how to pity another in the same fix.

齒 疼 方 知 齒 疼 人

Chʻih³ tʻêng² fang¹ chih¹ chʻih³ tʻêng² jên.²

809

The sheep drops into the tiger's jaws.

羊 落 虎 口

Yang² lo⁴ ʻhu³ kʻou.³

810

Better a dog in time of peace, than a man in time of rebellion.

寧 作 太 平 犬。莫 作 逆 亂 人

Ning² tso⁴ tʻai⁴ pʻing² chʻüan,³ mo⁴ tso⁴ ni⁴ lan⁴ jên.²

811

Despite all his thousands and myriads of schemes, a gimlet strikes against his skull.

千 算 萬 算 當 頭 一 鑽

Chʻien¹ suan⁴ wan⁴ suan⁴ tang¹ tʻou² yi¹ tsuan.¹

CHAPTER III.

HAPPINESS.

812

The happiness of good men may be looked on as reward:
The happiness of bad men as a snare we must regard.

善人得福爲之賞

Shan^4 jên^2 tê^2 fu^2 wei^2 chih^1 shang^3:

惡人得福爲之殃

O^4 jên^2 tê^2 fu^2 wei^2 chih^1 yang.^{1}

NOTE.—"The prosperity of fools shall destroy them". Prov: 1; 32.

813

The ox ploughs the field while the horse eats the grain;
One rears a son and another gets the gain.

牛耕田。馬喫穀

Niu^2 kêng^1 tʻien,^{2} ma^3 chʻih^1 ku^3;

別人養兒。他享福

Pieh^2 jên^2 yang^3 êrh,^{2} tʻa^1 hsiang^3 fu.^{2}

814

The more mouths to eat,
So much the more meat.

添人進口。越喫越有

Tʻien^1 jên^2 chin^4 kʻou,^{3} yüeh^4 chʻih^1 yüeh^4 yu.^{3}

815

Happiness he has but no powers of enjoyment,
Who, though his sails are set, must give his oars employment.

有福不會享。扯起篷來盪槳

Yu^3 fu^2 pu^4 ʻhui^4 hsiang,^{3} chʻê^3 chʻi^3 pʻêng^2 lai^2 tʻang^4 chiang.^{3}

816

For neighbours to keep up a friendly tone,
Is equal to finding a precious stone.

和得鄉隣好。猶如檢得寶

ʻHo^2 tê^2 hsiang^1 lin^2 ʻhao,^{3} yu^2 ju^2 chien^3 tê^2 pao.^{3}

817

One man in a house, of joy possessed,
Passes it on to all the rest.

一人有福。拖帶滿屋

Yi^1 jên^2 yu^3 fu,^{2} tʻo^1 tai^4 man^3 wu.^{1}

818

To assail a man with a whole day's cursing and strife,
Only adds to his happiness and lengthens his life.

一天一咒 添福添壽

Yi^1 tʻien^1 yi^1 chou,^{4} tʻien^1 fu^2 tʻien^1 shou.^{4}

819

The hair grows luxuriant when the mind is at rest;
And when a man has nothing to do his nails grow best.

心閒蓄頭髮。身閒蓄指甲

Hsin^1 hsien^2 hsiu^2 tʻou^2 fa^3; shên^1 hsien^2 hsiu^2 chih^3 chia.^{3}

820

In the hum of the market there is money; but in seclusion there is rest.

鬧裡有錢。靜處安身

Nao^4 li^3 yu^2 chʻien^2; ching^4 chʻu^4 an^1 shên.^{1}

821

The older you grow the more hale may you be!

越老越康健

Yüeh^4 lao^3 yüeh^4 kʻang^1 chien.^{4}

822

May you live long, your years be plenteous, and your seasons felicitous!

人壽年豐節氣和

Jên^2 shou^4 nien^2 fêng^1 chieh^1 chʻi^4 ʻho.^{2}

823

With a healthy body a thatched cottage in comfortable; with a settled disposition even cabbage roots are fragrant.

身安茅屋穩。性定菜根香

Shên^1 an^1 mao^2 wu^1 wên^3; hsing^4 ting^4 tsʻai^4 kên^1 hsiang.^{1}

824

If you long for pleasure, you must labour hard to get it.

欲求生快活。須下死工夫

Yü^4 chʻiu^2 shêng^1 kʻuai^4 ʻhuo,^{2} hsü^1 hsia^4 ssŭ^3 kung^1 fu.^{1}

825

Sorrow is born of excessive joy.

樂極生悲

Lê^4 chi^2 shêng^1 pei.^{1}

826

Unjustly gotten happiness must be followed by calamity.

無端獲福。禍必隨之

Wu^2 tuan^1 ʻhuo^4 fu,^{2} ʻhuo^4 pi^4 sui^2 chih.^{1}

827

Days of sorrow pass slowly; times of joy very quickly.

苦日難熬。歡時易過

Kʻu^3 jih^4 nan^2 ao^2; ʻhuan^1 shih^3 i^4 kuo.^{4}

828

Earth has no feasts which don't break up.

天下無不散的筵席

Tʻien^1 hsia^4 wu^2 pu^4 san^4 ti^1 yen^2 hsi.^{2}

829

Happinesses never come in pairs; calamities never come single.

福不雙至。禍不單行

Fu^2 pu^4 shuang^1 chih^4; ʻhuo^4 pu^4 tan^1 hsing.^{1}

830

Happiness is transient. *Lit.:* The bright moon is not round for long; the brilliant cloud is easily scattered.

明月不常圓。彩雲容易散

Ming^2 yueh^4 pu^4 chʻang^2 yüan^2; tsʻai^3 yün^2 yung^2 i^4 san.^{4}

831

Happiness stands by the ugly.

福在醜人邊

Fu^2 tsai^4 chʻou^3 jên^2 pien.^{1}

832

One generation plants the trees under whose cool shade another generation rests.

前人栽樹。後人歇涼

Ch'ien[2] jên[2] tsai[1] shu,[4] 'hou[4] jên[2] hsieh[1] liang.[2]

833

One generation opens up the roads on which another generation travels.

前人開路。後人行

Ch'ien[2] jên[2] k'ai[1] lu,[4] 'hou[4] jên[2] hsing.[2]

834

There are only a few days in the year for eating flesh-meat. *Lit.:* for roasting the *Yamên* sacrifices.

燒衙祭的日子一年有幾回

Shao[1] ya[2] chi[4] ti[1] jih[4] tzŭ[3] yi[1] nien[2] yu[3] chi[3] 'hui.[2]

835

Who do their duty are free from trouble all their lives.

但能依本分。終身無煩惱

Tan[4] neng[2] i[1] pên[3] fên,[1] chung[1] shên[1] wu[2] fan[2] nao.[3]

836

Peace and joy are more precious than yellow gold.

黃金未爲貴。安樂值錢多

'Huang[2] chin[1] wei[4] wei[2] kuei,[4] an[1] lê[4] chih[2] ch'ien[2] to.[1]

837

Of the five happinesses long life is the greatest.

五福之中壽爲先

Wu[3] fu[2] chih[1] chung[1] shou[4] wei[2] hsien.[1]

NOTE.—It is remarkable that, though the Five Happinesses are spoken of everywhere, scarcely any one can tell you what they are. The orthodox five, however, must be those mentioned in the Book of History; viz, Long life 壽, Wealth 富, health 康寧, the cultivation of Virtue 修好德, and a natural death 考終命.

838

Happiness, long life, and health, are the common desire of all men.

福壽康寧。人所同欲

Fu[2] shou[4] k'ang[1] ning,[2] jên[2] so[4] t'ung[2] yü.[4]

839

In a country at peace great talent is honoured; in a family grown wealthy children are proud.

國淸大才貴。家富小兒驕

Kuo^2 ch'ing^1 ta^4 ts'ai^2 kuei^4; chia^1 fu^4 hsiao^3 êrh^2 chiao.^{1}

840

To dwell in peace is happiness.

居之安平爲福

Chü^1 chih^1 an^1 p'ing^2 wei^2 fu^2.

841

More comfortable than the gods!

比神仙還舒服

Pi^3 shên^2 hsien^1 'huan^2 shu^1 fu.^{2}

842

It is good to be neither too high nor too low.

高不得低不得就好

Kao^1 pu^4 tê^2 ti^1 pu^4 te^2 chiu^4 hao.^{3}

843

Happiness is Heaven-sent.

福自天來

Fu^2 tzŭ^4 t'ien^1 lai.^{2}

844

Possessed of happiness don't exhaust it.

有福不可享盡

Yu^3 fu^2 pu^4 k'o^3 hsiang^3 chin.^{4}

845

Without a *Wu-t'ung* tree you can't get the phœnix to visit you.

沒有梧桐樹。叫不着鳳凰來

Mu^2 yu^3 wu^2 t'ung^2 shu,^{4} chiao^4 pu^4 cho^2 fêng^4 huang^2 lai.^{2}

Note.—The meaning of this proverb is, that without some inducement certain benefits cannot be attained. The *Wu-t'ung* tree "is much admired by the Chinese, the popular idea being that its branches are the favourite resort of the phœnix". See Stent's *Vocabulary*, page 673.

846

Having harmony in the family, and being in harmony with all men, all your affairs will be harmonious.

家 和 人 和 萬 事 和
Chia¹ 'ho² jên² 'ho² wan⁴ shih⁴ 'ho²

847

The two words Peace and Rest are worth a thousand taels of gold.

平 安 兩 字 值 千 金
P'ing² an¹ liang³ tzŭ⁴ chih² ch'ien¹ chin.¹

848

When all our affairs are in order great is our felicity and profit.

百 事 從 順 大 吉 大 利
Pai³ shih⁴ ts'ung² shun⁴ ta⁴ chi² ta⁴ li.⁴

849

When happiness comes the mind grows more intelligent.

福 至 心 靈
Fu² chih⁴ hsing¹ ling.²

850

"An immoderate use of dainties generally ends in disease; and pleasure when past is converted into pain."

爽 口 食 多 偏 作 病
Shuang¹ k'ou³ shih² to¹ p'ien¹ tso⁴ ping⁴;
快 心 事 過 恐 生 殃
K'uai⁴ hsin¹ shih⁴ kuo⁴ k'ung³ shêng¹ yang.¹

851

To the contented even poverty and obscurity bring happiness; to the discontented even riches and honours bring misery.

知 足 者 貧 賤 亦 樂
Chih⁴ tsu¹ chê² p'in² chien⁴ i⁴ lê⁴;
不 知 足 者 貴 富 亦 憂
pu⁴ chih¹ tsu² chê² fu⁴ kuei⁴ i⁴ yu¹.

852

A happy condition. *Lit.:* No creditor at the door, and nobody sick in the house.

門前無債主。家中無病人
Mên² chʻien² wu² chai⁴ chu,³ chia¹ chung¹ wu² ping⁴ jên.²

853

The happy know not how time flies.

快活不知時日過
Kʻuai⁴ ʻhuo² pu⁴ chih¹ shih² jih⁴ kuo.⁴

854

The two words Pure and Leisure no money can buy.

清閒兩字錢難買
Chʻing¹ hsien² liang³ tzŭ⁴ chʻien² nan² mai.³

855

Be very careful of happiness; and provoke not calamity.

多惜福少惹禍
To¹ hsi² fu² shao³ jê³ ʻhuo.⁴

856

Since life has nothing in it like tranquility, can it be a thing obtained by chance!

人生無似清閒好
Jên² shêng¹ wu² ssŭ⁴ chʻing¹ hsien² hao,³
得到清閒豈偶然
tê² tao⁴ chʻing¹ hsien² chʻi³ ou³ jan.²

857

Whether rich or poor be pleased with your lot; for he is a fool who can't laugh (under all circumstances).

隨富隨貧且隨喜
Sui² fu⁴ sui² pʻin³ chʻieh³ sui² hʻsi³;
不開口笑是癡人
pu⁴ kʻai¹ kʻou³ hsiao⁴ shih⁴ chʻih² jên.²

858

Three meals per day, one sleep per night.

日度三餐。夜眠一宿
Jih⁴ tu⁴ san¹ tsʻan,¹ yeh⁴ mien² yi¹ su.²

859

You must have four ounces of happiness to get one ounce of gold.

壹兩黃金四兩福氣

Yi[1] liang[3] ʻhuang[2] chin[1] ssŭ[4] liang[3] fu[2] chʻi.[4]

860

Few desires—and buoyant spirits: many cares—and feeble health.

寡欲精神爽。思多血氣衰

Kua[3] yü[4] ching[1] shên[2] shuang[1]: ssŭ[1] to[1] hsieh[3] chʻi[4] shuai.[1]

CHAPTER IV.

INJURIES: GIVEN AND SUSTAINED.

861

One stroke one kick,
Ends the thing quick.

一搥一脚。乾淨撆脫

Yi1 chʻui2 yi1 chio,3 kan1 ching4 pʻieh1 tʻo.1

NOTE.—Said of injury done to anything in one's possession.

862

Shrimps are the victims of big fishes' foul play;
And shrimps in their turn too impose on the clay.

大魚欺蝦。蝦欺泥巴

Ta4 yü2 chʻi1 hsia1; hsia1 chʻi1 ni2 pa.1

863

Though suffering wrong,
Keep working along.

吃得虧。在一堆

Chʻih1 tê2 kʻuei,1 tsai4 yi1 tui.1

864

The moth which dashes into the flame
And burns itself, has itself to blame.

飛蛾撲燈。自燒其身

Fei1 o2 pʻu1 têng,1 tzŭ4 shao1 chʻi2 shên.1

865

Whoe'er provokes misfortune and distress,
Deserves to suffer for his foolishness.

惹禍招災。問罪應該

Jê3 ʻhuo4 chao1 tsai,1 wên4 tsui4 ying1 kai1.

866

In shallow water dragons become the joke of shrimps;
And tigers on the plains are the butt of canine imps.

龍遊淺水遭蝦戲

Lung2 yu2 chʻien3 shui3 tsao1 hsia1 hsi4;

虎落平洋被犬欺

ʻHu3 lo4 pʻing2 yang2 pei4 chʻüan3 chʻi.1

867

He who spurts blood at another, first defiles his own mouth.

含 血 噴 人。先 汙 自 己

ʻHan^{2} hsieh^{3} fên^{4} jên,^{2} hsien^{1} wu^{1} tzŭ^{4} chi.^{3}

868

To injure others you must injure yourself.

害 人 終 害 己

ʻHai^{4} jên^{2} chung^{1} ʻhai^{4} chi.^{3}

869

To come into unpleasant contact with hard men. *Lit.:* To run against a nail.

碰 倒 釘 子

Pʻêng^{4} tao^{3} ting^{1} tsŭ.^{3}

870

At the first stroke of an egg against a stone, the yolk runs out.

鷄 蛋 撞 石 頭。一 撞 就 流 黃

Chi^{1} tan^{4} chuang^{4} shih^{2} tʻou,^{2} yi^{1} chuang^{4} chiu^{4} liu^{2} ʻhuang.^{2}

871

It is easy to avoid an arrow shot in one's sight; but hard to escape one aimed in secret.

明 箭 容 易 躲。暗 箭 最 難 防

Ming^{2} chien^{4} yung^{2} i^{4} to^{2}; an^{4} chien^{4} tsui^{4} nan^{2} fang.^{2}

872

To injure secretly. *Lit.:* To hide mailed soldiers.

暗 藏 甲 兵

An^{4} tsʻang^{2} chia^{3} ping.^{1}

873

The same. *Lit.:* To conceal a dagger in one's sleeve.

袖 裏 藏 刀

Hsiu^{4} li^{3} tsʻang^{2} tao.^{1}

874

To murder by means of another's sword.

借 刀 殺 人

Chieh^{4} tao^{1} sha^{1} jên.^{2}

875

To murder without a sword.

殺人不用刀

Sha^{1} jên^{2} pu^{4} yung^{4} tao.^{1}

876

Injury is infectious. *Lit.:* When a city gate is burning, the fishes suffer in the moat.

城門失火。殃及池魚

Ch'êng^{2} mên^{2} shih^{1} 'huo,^{3} yang^{1} chi^{2} ch'ih^{2} yü.^{2}

877

A wise man will sometimes overlook injuries done to his face.

好漢不吃眼前虧

'Hao^{3} 'han^{4} pu^{4} ch'ih^{1} yen^{3} ch'ien^{2} k'uei.^{1}

878

To injure by means of some great person. *Lit.:* To bring a great hat to oppress one.

拿得大帽子來壓

Na^{2} tê^{2} ta^{4} mao^{4} tzŭ^{3} lai^{2} ya.^{1}

879

Never presume on authority or power to injure orphans or widows.

勿恃勢力而凌逼孤寡

Wu^{4} shih^{4} shih^{4} li^{4} êrh^{2} ling^{2} pi^{1} ku^{1} kua.^{3}

880

As the pig's-blood-seller said to the robber—sup my broth but spare my life.

强盜打死賣猪血的

Ch'iang^{3} tao^{4} ta^{3} ssŭ^{3} mai^{4} chu^{1} hsieh^{3} ti^{1}—

饒命喝湯

Jao^{2} ming^{4} 'ho^{1} t'ang.^{1}

881

The locust chases the cicada, ignorant that the yellow bird is after it.

螳螂捕蟬。豈知黃雀在後

T'ang^{1} lang^{2} pu^{3} ch'an,^{2} ch'i^{3} chih^{1} 'huang^{2} ch'iao^{3} tsai^{4} 'hou.^{4}

882

If you miss the tiger, he won't miss you.

打虎不着。反被虎傷

Ta^3 ʻhu^3 pu^4 cho,^{2} fan^3 pei^4 ʻhu^3 shang.^{1}

883

Summer mosquitoes provoke raps with the fan.

六月蚊虫招扇打

Lu^4 yüeh^4 wên^2 chʻung^2 chao^1 shan^4 ta.^{3}

884

When a man takes fire into his bosom, he provokes his own calamity.

解衣抱火。自惹其災

Chieh^3 i^1 pao^4 ʻhuo,^{3} tzŭ^4 jê^3 chʻi^2 tsai.^{1}

885

To drop the bricks one is carrying, on one's own foot.

自己搬磚打自己的脚

Tzŭ^4 chi^3 pan^1 chuan^1 ta^3 tzŭ^4 chi^3 ti^1 chio.^{3}

886

The load a beggar cannot carry he has begged himself.

告化子背不起自討的

Kao^4 ʻhua^4 tzŭ^3 pei^4 pu^4 chʻi^3 tzŭ^4 tʻao^3 ti.^{1}

887

Paper and pen may take a man's life without the use of a sword.

紙筆殺人不用刀

Chih^3 pi^3 sha^1 jên^2 pu^4 yung^4 tao.^{1}

888

It is the beautiful bird which gets encaged.

嬌鳥被籠

Chiao^1 niao^3 pei^4 lung.^{2}

889

One man may obstruct many. *Lit.:* One dragon may obstruct a thousand rivers.

一龍阻住千江水

Yi^1 lung^2 tsʻu^1 chu^4 chʻien^1 chiang^1 shui.^{3}

890

When one horse will not go, a hundred are thrown into trouble.

一 馬 不 行 百 馬 憂

Yi¹ ma³ pu⁴ hsing² pai³ ma³ yu.¹

891

Cold water entering the mouth drops into the heart.

冷 水 入 口 點 點 在 心

Lêng³ shui³ ju⁴ k'ou³ tien³ tien³ tsai⁴ hsin.¹

NOTE.—Said of slights or injuries, which are not soon forgotten.

892

To draw the big net out of a water-butt.

水 缸 裏 搬 罾 寃 網

Shui³ kang¹ li³ pan¹ tsêng¹ yüan¹ wang.³

NOTE.—This is another specimen of the innuendo, so frequent in Chinese proverbs. The meaning is all in the last two words, which, in sound, exactly resemble 寃 枉, to ill-use, to accuse falsely; and this is the meaning of the proverb.

893

Through life do nothing to make men knit their brows, then the world should not contain a man to grind his teeth at you.

平 生 莫 作 皺 眉 事

P'ing² shêng¹ mo⁴ tso⁴ chou⁴ mei² shih,⁴

世 上 應 無 切 齒 人

shih⁴ shang⁴ ying¹ wu² ch'ieh⁴ ch'ih³ jên.²

894

To entice a sheep into a drove of tigers.

牽 羊 入 虎 群

Ch'ien¹ yang² ju⁴ 'hu³ ch'ün.²

895

Strike a man dead and you must forfeit life; not so if you can deceive him to his death.

打 死 人 要 塡 命

Ta³ ssŭ³ jên² yao⁴ t'ien² ming⁴;

哄 死 人 不 塡 命

'Hung³ ssŭ³ jên² pu⁴ t'ien² ming.⁴

896

To mislead. *Lit.:* To give one a chimney to climb.

把 烟 筒 我 鑽

Pa^3 yen^1 tʻung^3 wo^3 tsuan.^{1}

897

A blind man with inflamed eyes, suffers more and more grievous injury.

瞎 子 害 火 眼。又 狠 又 利 害

Hsia^2 tzŭ^3 ʻhai^4 ʻhuo^3 yen,^{3} yu^4 ʻhên^3 yu^4 li^4 ʻhai.^{4}

898

Chase a dog down a passage, and he will turn again and bite you.

直 巷 趕 狗。回 頭 一 口

Chih^2 hsiang^4 kan^2 kou,^{3} ʻhui^2 tʻou^2 yi^1 kʻou.^{3}

899

To throw stones on a man in a well.

落 井 下 石

Lo^4 ching^3 hsia^4 shih.^{2}

900

To help the tyrant *Chieh* to tyrannize.

助 桀 為 虐

Chu^4 Chieh^2 wei^2 nio.^{4}

901

To injure men is misery; to pity men is happiness.

虧 人 是 禍。饒 人 是 福

Kʻwei^1 jên^2 shih^4 ʻhuo^4; jao^2 jên^2 shih^4 fu.^{2}

902

Man cannot injure man as Heaven can.

人 害 人 不 死

Jên^2 ʻhai^4 jên^2 pu^4 ssŭ^3;

天 害 人 纔 害 死 了

tʻien^1 ʻhai^4 jên^2 tsʻai^2 ʻhai^4 ssŭ^3 liao.^{3}

CHAPTER V.

LIFE AND DEATH.

903

Any kind of life above the sod,
Surpasses burial under the clod.

寧在世上挨。不願土裡埋

Ning^2 tsai^4 shih^4 shang^4 ai,^{2} pu^4 yüan^4 tʻu^3 li^3 mai.^{2}

904

When we take off our boots and stockings to-day,
That we shall wear them to-morrow, who can say?

今日脫了鞋合襪

Chin^1 jih^4 tʻo^1 liao^3 hsieh^2 ʻho^2 wa,^{4}

不知明日靸不靸

Pu^4 chih^1 ming^3 jih^4 sa^1 pu^4 sa.^{1}

905

The man lives, but wit lives not; wit lives and the man grows old.
Life and wit both live; but eʻer a man knows it his days are told.

人生智未生。智生人易老

Jên^2 shêng^1 chih^4 wei^4 shêng^1; chih^4 shêng^1 jên^2 i^4 lao^3:

生智一切生。不覺無常到

Shêng^1 chih^4 yi^1 chʻieh^4 shêng^1; pu^4 chiao^4 wu^2 chʻang^2 tao.^{4}

906

The roots of an old tree in the earth you may find;
But a dead man is fully cut off from his kind.

樹老根還在。人死兩丟開

Shu^4 lao^3 kên^1 ʻhuan^2 tsai^4; jên^2 ssŭ^3 liang^3 tiu^1 kʻai.^{1}

907

On the road to hades (or the Yellow spring) no account is taken of old and young.

黃泉路上無老少

ʻHuang^2 chʻien^2 lu^4 shang^4 wu^2 lao^3 shao.^{3}

908

Insects of every kind covet life and fear death.

蟲 蟻 也 貪 生 怕 死

Chʻung² i³ yeh⁴ tʻan¹ shêng¹ pʻa⁴ ssŭ³.

909

Man's life is like a candle in the wind, or hoar-frost on the tiles.

人 生 在 世。如 風 前 燭

Jên² shêng¹ tsai⁴ shih,⁴ ju² fêng¹ chʻien² chu,²

如 瓦 上 霜

ju² wa¹ shang⁴ shuang.¹

910

Man's life on earth resembles a spring dream; when once the soul has fled, all is over.

人 生 在 世 如 春 夢

Jên² shêng¹ tsai⁴ shih⁴ ju² chʻun¹ mêng⁴;

靈 魂 一 走 萬 事 休

ling² ʻhun² yi¹ tsou⁴ wan⁴ shih⁴ hsiu.¹

911

Though a man live a hundred years still he must die; and the sooner we die the sooner we have done with the body.

人 活 百 歲 也 是 死

Jên² ʻhuo² pai³ sui⁴ yeh³ shih⁴ ssŭ³;

早 死 早 些 脫 了 身

tsao³ ssŭ³ tsao³ hsieh¹ tʻo¹ liao³ shên.¹

912

Man's days are numbered.

人 之 修 短 有 數

Jên² chih¹ hsiu¹ tuan³ yu³ shu.⁴

913

Few have ever attained the age of threescore years and ten.

人 生 七 十 古 來 稀

Jên² shêng¹ chʻi¹ shih² ku³ lai² hsi.¹

914

The fish which sports in the pan has but a short time to live.

魚遊釜中雖生不久

Yü² yu² fu³ chung¹ sui¹ shêng¹ pu⁴ chiu.³

915

Man's life is truly a performance.

人生在世無非是戲

Jên² shêng¹ tsai⁴ shih⁴ wu² fei¹ shih⁴ hsi.⁴

NOTE.—"All the world's a stage."

916

Before a man knows it he has grown white-headed.

不覺又是白頭翁

Pu⁴ chiao⁴ yu⁴ shih⁴ pai² t'ou² wêng.¹

917

In the Great River, preceding waves are swallowed up by those which follow; so in the world, new men take the old men's places.

長江後浪催前浪

Ch'ang² chiang¹ 'hou⁴ lang⁴ ts'ui¹ ch'ien² lang⁴:

世上新人換舊人

shih⁴ shang⁴ hsin¹ jên² 'huan⁴ chiu⁴ jên.²

918

The ancients see not the modern moon; but the modern moon shone on the ancients.

古人不見今時月

Ku³ jên² pu⁴ chien⁴ chin¹ shih² yüeh⁴;

今月曾經照古人

chin¹ yüeh⁴ ts'êng² chin¹ chao⁴ ku³ jên.²

919

There are trees on the mountains a thousand years old; but a centenarian amongst men it is hard to find.

山中也有千年樹

Shan¹ chung¹ yeh³ yu³ ch'ien¹ nien² shu⁴;

世上難逢百歲人

shih⁴ shang⁴ nan² fêng² pai³ sui⁴ jên.²

920

Some hate to see a hoary head, I view one with delight; for many young men die, attaining not an old man's death.

人 見 白 頭 嗔。我 見 白 頭 喜
Jên^{2} chien^{4} pai^{2} tʻou^{2} chʻên^{1}; wo^{3} chien^{4} pai^{2} tʻou^{2} ʻhsi^{3}:

多 少 少 年 亡。不 見 白 頭 死
to^{1} shao^{3} shao^{3} nien^{2} wang,^{2} pu^{4} chien^{4} pai^{2} tʻou^{2} ssŭ.^{3}

921

Man lives a generation as plants a spring.

人 生 一 世。草 生 一 春
Jên^{2} shêng^{1} yi^{1} shih,^{4} tsʻao^{3} shêng^{1} yi^{1} chʻun.^{1}

922

After full moon the light diminishes; after middle age man's affairs begin to lessen.

月 過 十 五 光 明 少
Yueh^{4} kuo^{4} shih^{2} wu^{3} kuang^{1} ming^{2} shao^{3};

人 到 中 年 萬 事 休
jên^{2} tao^{4} chung^{1} nien^{2} wan^{4} shih^{4} hsiu.^{1}

923

Though life cannot reach a hundred years, men cherish the troubles of a thousand.

人 生 不 滿 百。常 懷 千 歲 憂
Jên^{2} shêng^{1} pu^{4} man^{3} pai,^{3} chʻang^{2} ʻhuai^{2} chʻien^{1} sui^{4} yu.^{1}

924

Men live like birds in a wood together; but when the set time comes each takes his flight.

人 生 似 鳥 同 林 宿
Jên^{2} shêng^{1} shih^{4} niao^{3} tʻung^{2} lin^{2} su^{2};

大 限 來 時 各 自 飛
ta^{4} hsien^{4} lai^{2} shih^{2} ko^{4} tzŭ^{4} fei.^{1}

925

Whom *Yen wang* dooms to die in the third watch, can never live on to the fifth.

閻 王 註 定 三 更 死
Yen^{2} wang^{2} chu^{4} ting^{4} san^{1} kêng^{1} ssŭ,^{3}

並 不 留 人 到 五 更
ping⁴ pu⁴ liu² jên² tao⁴ wu³ kêng.¹

NOTE.—*Yen wang* is popularly regarded as one person, a sort of Hades or Pluto; really, however, this designation is applicable to the Ten Kings of Hell, who are supposed to have rule over the life and death of men.

926

Sick folks dread a devil's call (*i.e.* to die).

患 病 的 怕 鬼 叫
ʻHuan⁴ ping⁴ ti¹ pʻa⁴ kuei³ chiao.⁴

927

Death has reached the points of his eyebrows.

死 在 眉 毛 尖 上 來 了
Ssŭ³ tsai⁴ mei² mao² chien¹ shang⁴ lai² liao.³

NOTE.—This means that a man is on the point of death.

928

When the oil is exhausted the lamp dies out.

油 乾 燈 息
Yu² kan¹ têng¹ hsi.²

929

He does not close his eyes in dying.

他 死 不 閉 眼
Tʻa¹ ssŭ³ pu⁴ pi⁴ yen.³

NOTE.—That is because he has some trouble on his mind;—some anxiety for the welfare of his survivors.

930

Who knows whether the bonze or his wooden fish will last the longer?

曉 得 是 和 尙 長 木 魚 長
Hsiao³ tê² shih⁴ ʻho² shang⁴ chʻang² mu⁴ yü² chʻang.²

931

Get the coffin ready and the man won't die.

辦 到 棺 材 人 不 死
Pan⁴ tao⁴ kuan¹ tsʻai² jên² pu⁴ ssŭ.³

932

Fitful life is but a dream.

浮 生 若 夢
Fou² shêng¹ jo⁴ mêng⁴

933

Flowers bloom and wither year by year; but how can an old man grow young again?

花開花謝年年有

ʻHua^{1} kʻai^{1} ʻhua^{1} hsieh^{4} nien^{2} nien^{2} yu^{3};

人老何曾轉少年

jên^{2} lao^{3} ʻho^{2} ʻhui^{4} chuan^{3} shao^{3} nien.^{2}

934

There is a day to be born, and a time to die.

生有日死有時

Shêng^{1} yu^{3} jih^{4} ssŭ^{3} yu^{3} shih.^{2}

Note.—"A time to be born, and a time to die." Eccles. 3. 2.

935

No medicine can secure long life, even to a minister of state; no money can buy for any man a virtuous posterity.

無藥可延卿相壽

Wu^{2} yao^{4} kʻo^{3} yen^{2} chʻing^{1} hsiang^{1} shou^{4};

有錢難買子孫賢

yu^{3} chʻien^{2} nan^{2} mai^{3} tzŭ^{3} sun^{1} hsien.^{2}

936

The great wall of a myriad miles still remains, but *Chin Shih ʻHuang*, who built it, is gone.

長城萬里今猶在

Chʻang^{2} chʻêng^{2} wan^{4} li^{3} chin^{1} yu^{2} tsai,^{4}

不見當年秦始皇

pu^{4} chien^{4} tang^{1} nien^{2} Chʻin^{2} Shih^{3} ʻHuang.^{2}

937

What centenarian has 36,000 days of pleasure?

人生百歲

Jên^{2} shêng^{1} pai^{3} sui,^{4}

那有三萬六千日之樂

na^{3} yu^{3} san^{1} wan^{4} lu^{4} chʻien^{1} jih^{4} chih^{1} lê^{4}?

938

Our whitened bones must needs lie buried under the green sod; and yellow gold will hardly buy back the raven locks of youth.

終須白骨埋青塚；
Chung^1 hsü^1 pai^2 ku^3 mai^2 chʻing^1 chung^3;
難把黃金買黑頭
nan^2 pa^3 ʻhuang^2 chin^1 mai^3 ʻhei^1 tʻou.^{2}

939

The Emperor with all his wealth cannot buy myriads of years.

皇帝有錢難買萬萬歲
ʻHuang^2 Ti^4 yu^3 chʻien^2 nan^2 mai^3 wan^4 wan^4 sui.^{4}

940

A beggar will not cross a rotten bridge.

吃丐不過朽木橋
Chʻih^1 kai^4 pu^4 kuo^4 hsiu^3 mu^4 chʻiao.^{2}

941

To-day secures not to-morrow's affairs.

今朝不保明朝事
Chin^1 chao^1 pu^4 pao^3 ming^2 chao^1 shih.^{4}

942

We can't secure on going to bed that we shall get up again.

上床難保下床來
Shang^3 chʻuang^2 nan^2 pao^3 hsia^4 chʻuang^2 lai.^{2}

943

When a man will risk his life, ten thousand cannot stop him.

一人拚命。萬夫難擋
Yi^1 jên^2 pʻan^1 ming,^{4} wan^4 fu^1 nan^2 tang.^{3}

944

If you envy a man's wealth, do not envy his food; if you are dissatisfied with life, do not be so with death.

妒財莫妒食。怨生莫怨死
Tu^4 tsʻai^2 mo^4 tu^4 shih^2; yüan^4 shêng^1 mo^4 yüan^4 ssŭ.^{3}

945

A generation is like a swift horse passing a crevice.

一世如駒過隙
Yi^1 shih^4 ju^2 chü^1 kuo^4 hsi.^{2}

CHAPTER VI.

MOURNING AND BURIAL.

946

Any soil will do to bury in.

處 處 黃 土 好 埋 人

Chʻu^4 chʻu^4 ʻhuang^2 tʻu^3 ʻhao^3 mai^2 jên.^{2}

947

A son's mourning for his mother startles Heaven and moves Earth.

兒 子 哭 娘 驚 天 動 地

Erh^2 tzŭ^3 kʻu^1 niang^2 ching^1 tʻien^1 tung^4 ti.^{4}

948

A daughter's mourning for her mother is true and sincere.

女 兒 哭 娘 眞 心 實 意

Nü^2 érh^2 kʻu^1 niang^2 chên^1 hsin^1 shih^2 i.^{4}

949

A daughter-in-law's mourning for her mother-in-law is purely hypocritical.

媳 婦 哭 婆 婆 假 情 假 意

Hsi^2 fu^4 kʻu^1 pʻo^2 pʻo^2 chia^3 chʻing^2 chia^3 i.^{4}

950

A son-in-law's mourning for his mother-in-law is short and fitful.

女 壻 哭 丈 母 驢 子 放 屁

Nü^2 hsü^4 kʻu^1 chang^4 mu^3 lü^2 tzŭ^3 fang^4 pʻi.^{4}

NOTE.—The latter part of this proverb I have preferred to translate freely, since it contains an illustration less beautiful than striking.

951

The hare dies and the fox mourns.

兎 死 狐 悲

Tʻu^1 ssŭ^3 ʻhu^2 pei.^{1}

952

When puss mourns for the rat it is all sham pity.

貓 兒 哭 老 鼠 假 慈 悲

Mao¹ êrh² kʻu¹ lao³ shu³ chia³ tzʻŭ² pei.¹

953

When his lady dies, hundreds of visitors haste to condole; but when the general himself dies, not a single soldier appears.

夫 人 死 百 客 臨 門

Fu¹ jên² ssŭ³ pai³ kʻo⁴ lin² mên²;

將 軍 亡 一 卒 不 至

Chiang¹ chün¹ wang² yi¹ tsu² pu⁴ chih.⁴

954

Over a husbands's death a wife will truly mourn three years; over a wife's such favour is not shown for more than a hundred days.

夫 死 三 年 妻 大 孝

Fu¹ ssŭ³ san¹ nien² chʻi¹ ta⁴ hsiao⁴;

妻 死 無 過 百 日 思

chʻi¹ ssŭ³ wu² kuo⁴ pai³ jih⁴ ssŭ.¹

955

Vain is the sacrifice of an unfilial son.

在 生 不 孝。死 祭 無 益

Tsai⁴ shêng¹ pu⁴ hsiao,⁴ ssŭ³ chi⁴ wu² i.²

956

Why should he, who does not honour his parents when living, mourn for them when dead?

在 生 不 把 父 母 敬

Tsai⁴ shêng¹ pu⁴ pa³ fu⁴ mu³ ching,⁴

死 後 何 必 哭 靈 魂

ssŭ³ ʻhou⁴ ʻho² pi⁴ kʻu¹ ling² ʻhun.²

957

To offer a bullock at one's parents' grave, is not equal to presenting them while living with fowls or sucking-pigs.

與 其 椎 牛 而 祭 墓

Yü³ chʻi² chʻui² niu² êrh² chi⁴ mu,⁴

不如雞豚之逮存
pu^{4} ju^{2} chi^{1} t'un^{2} chih^{1} tai^{4} ts'un.^{2}

958

Men mourn for those who leave fortunes behind them.

牀頭一倉穀。死了·有人哭
Ch'uang^{2} t'ou^{2} yi^{1} ts'ang^{1} ku,^{3} ssŭ^{3} liao^{3} yu^{3} jên^{2} k'u.^{1}

959

Don't distress yourself for the dead. *Lit.:* Let the dead care for the dead, and the living for the living.

死的顧死的。活的顧活的
Ssŭ^{3} ti^{1} ku^{4} ssŭ^{3} ti^{1}, 'huo^{2} ti^{1} ku^{4} 'huo^{2} ti.^{1}

960

If a mourner, you cannot sing; if you can sing, you cannot mourn.

哭則不歌。歌則不哭
K'u^{1} tsê^{2} pu^{4} ko^{1}; ko^{1} tsê^{2} pu^{4} k'u.^{1}

CHAPTER VII.

REPUTATION.

961

Fragrant perfumes will exhale wherever musk is found:
And wind will not be needed to spread the scent around.

有麝自然香。莫在當風颺
Yu[3] shê[4] tzŭ[4] jan[2] hsiang[1] : mo[4] tsai[4] tang[1] fêng[1] yang.[2]

962

Wealth among men is like dew among plants;
Foam on the waves is the fame which earth grants.

人閒富貴花閒露
Jên[2] hsien[2] fu[4] kuei[4] ʻhua[1] hsien[2] lou[4]:
世上功名水上漚
Shih[4] shang[4] kung[1] ming[2] shui[3] shang[4] ou.[4]

963

Wealth is but dung; a face is worth thousands of gold.

錢財如糞土。臉面值千金
Chʻien[2] tsʻai[2] ju[2] fên[4] tʻu[3]; lien[3] mien[4] chih[2] chʻien[1] chin.[1]

964

A dying leopard leaves his skin; a dying man his name.

豹死留皮。人死留名
Pao[4] ssŭ[3] liu[2] pʻi[2]; jên[2] ssŭ[3] liu[2] ming.[2]

965

As the scream of the eagle is heard when she has passed over; so a man's name remains after his death.

鴈過留聲。人去留名
Ying[1] kuo[4] liu[2] shêng[1]: jên[2] chʻü[4] liu[2] ming.[2]

966

His fame is great, like thunder in one's ear.

聲名大如雷貫耳
Shêng[1] ming[2] ta[4] ju[2] lei[2] kuan[4] êrh.[3]

967

Merit and fame never crown the lazy.

功名不上懶人頭

Kung^1 ming^2 pu^4 shang^3 lan^3 jên^2 t'ou.^{2}

968

The sound of drumming on a lofty hill is heard far and wide.

高山打鼓。聲名在外

Kao^1 shan^1 ta^3 ku,^{3} shêng^1 ming^2 tsai^4 wai.^{4}

969

Whoever gains fame dignifies his parents.

揚名顯親

Yang^2 ming^2 hsien^3 ch'in.^{1}

970

Wide-spread his fame, who comes with waving flags and roaring cannon.

扯旗放砲。聲名浩蕩

Ch'ê^3 ch'i^2 fang^4 p'ao^4, shêng^1 ming^2 'hao^4 tang.^{4}

971

The tiger is terrible even when dead.

虎死雄心在

'Hu^3 ssŭ^3 hsiung^2 hsin^1 tsai.^{4}

972

A great man who fails to leave a good name for a hundred generations, will leave a bad one for a myriad years.

大丈夫既不能流芳百世

Ta^4 chang^4 fu^1 chi^3 pu^4 nêng^2 liu^2 fang^1 pai^3 shih,^{4}

便遺臭萬年

pien^4 i^2 ch'ou^4 wan^4 nien^2

973

To sweep clean at a stroke.

一笤箒掃得乾淨

Yi^1 t'iao^2 chou^3 sao^3 tê^2 kan^1 ching.^{4}

NOTE.—This is said of a reputation suddenly forfeited from any cause.

974

One's good deeds are known only at home; one's bad deeds far away.

好事不出門。惡事傳千里

'Hao³ shih⁴ pu⁴ ch'u¹ mên²; o⁴ shih⁴ chuan⁴ ch'ien¹ li.³

NOTE.—"The evil which men do, lives after them;
The good is oft interred with their bones."

975

In your ten years secluded study no one will know you; but once take your M. A. degree, and your fame will be known through the empire.

十年窓下無人問

Shih² nien² ch'uang¹ hsia⁴ wu² jên² wên⁴;

一舉成名天下知

yi¹ chü³ ch'êng² ming² t'ien¹ hsia⁴ chih.¹

976

When the dragon has returned to his sea caves, the clouds retain their moisture: after the musk-deer has crossed the green hills, the grass and trees retain its perfume.

龍遊海洞雲猶濕

Lung² yu² 'hai³ tung⁴ yün² yu² shih¹:

麝過青山草木香

shê⁴ kuo⁴ ch'ing¹ shan¹ ts'ao³ mu⁴ hsiang.¹

977

One thounder-clap resounds through the empire.

一下雷哄天下響

Yi¹ hsia⁴ lei² 'hung³ t'ien¹ hsia⁴ hsiang.³

NOTE.—This refers to any act or event by which a man acquires sudden notoriety.

978

Once scale the dragon gate, and your fame is tenfold multiplied.

一登龍門。聲價十倍

Yi¹ têng¹ lung² mên,² shêng¹ chia⁴ shih² pei.⁴

NOTE.—To 'scale the dragon gate' is to take the B. A. degree.

979

When the tiger dies he does not lose his dignity.

虎死不倒威

ʻHu³ ssŭ³ pu⁴ tao³ wei.¹

980

At court men contend for fame; in the market for profit.

爭名入朝。爭利入市

Chêng¹ ming² ju⁴ chʻao³; chêng¹ li⁴ ju⁴ shih.⁴

981

Vicious conduct will cause a man's name to stink for ten thousand years.

爲惡則遺臭萬年

Wei² ʻo⁴ tsê² i² chʻou⁴ wan⁴ nien.²

982

The reputation of a thousand years may depend on the character of a single day.

得失一朝。榮辱千載

Tê² shih¹ yi¹ chao,¹ jung² ju⁴ chʻien¹ tsai.³

983

If one man praises you, a thousand will repeat the praise.

一人道好。千人傳實

Yi¹ jên² tao⁴ hao,³ chʻien¹ jên² chuan⁴ shih.²

CHAPTER VIII.

THE PLEASURES, ETC. OF WINE.

984

Old monarch in the eating line;
He will not touch a drop of wine.

點酒不嘗。吃菜老王

Tien^3 chiu^3 pu^4 chʻang^2—chʻih^1 tsʻai^4 lao^3 wang.^{2}

985

In every morning's stroll for him the wine doth flow;
Returning home at eve fair garlands crown his brow.

朝朝出去酒隨後

Chao^1 chao^1 chʻu^1 chʻü^4 chiu^3 sui^2 ʻhou^4;

夜夜歸來花滿頭

Yeh^4 yeh^4 kuei^1 lai^2 ʻhua^1 man^3 tʻou.^{2}

986

When flowers are blooming then pour out the wine;
But don't ascend the tower when there's no bright moon-shine.

有花方酌酒。無月不登樓

Yu^3 ʻhua^1 fang^1 cho^2 chiu^3; wu^2 yueh^4 pu^4 têng^1 lou.^{2}

987

As limpid streams within earthen banks are bound,
So midst wine's victims are hosts of scholars found.

淸淸之水爲土所防

Chʻing^1 chʻing^1 chih^1 shui^3 wei^2 tʻu^3 so^4 fang,^{2}

濟濟之士爲酒所傷

Chi^4 chi^1 chih^1 shih^4 wei^2 chiu^3 so^4 shang.^{1}

988

Don't begin to drink with day's returning light;
Or you'll be very drunk till six o'clock at night.

莫吃卯時酒。昏昏醉到酉

Mo^4 chʻih^1 mao^3 shih^2 chiu,^{3} ʻhun^1 ʻhun^1 tsui^4 tao^4 yu.^{3}

989

Let those who desire to break off drinking habits, when sober, observe a drunken man.

若要斷酒法。醒眼看醉人

Jo⁴ yao⁴ tuan⁴ chiu³ fa,³ hsing³ yen³ k'an⁴ tsui⁴ jên.²

990

A drop to a thirsty man is like refreshing dew; a cup to one already drunk is worse than none at all.

渴時一滴如甘露

K'o³ shih² yi¹ ti¹ ju² kan¹ lu,⁴

醉後添杯不如無

tsui⁴ 'hou⁴ t'ien¹ pei¹ pu⁴ ju² wu.²

991

Medicine may heal imagined sickness, but wine can never dispel real sorrow.

藥能醫假病。酒不解眞愁

Yao⁴ nêng² i¹ chia³ ping,⁴ chiu³ pu⁴ chieh¹ chên¹ ch'ou.²

992

Three glasses help one to understand great doctrines; perfect intoxication scatters a thousand troubles.

三杯通大道。一醉解千愁

San¹ pei¹ t'ung¹ ta⁴ tao⁴; yi¹ tsui⁴ chieh¹ ch'ien¹ ch'ou.²

993

He got into debt for wine wherever he could.

酒債尋常行處有

Chiu³ chai⁴ hsin² ch'ang² hsing² ch'u⁴ yu.³

NOTE.—This is said of *Li T'ai-pai* (李太白) an epicurean LL. D. of the *T'ang* dynasty; who, because he saw that life was short, determined to enjoy in it as much pleasure as possible.

994

To the drunken man heaven and earth are great; to the man of leisure days and months are long.

醉後乾坤大。閑中日月長

Tsui⁴ 'hou⁴ ch'ien² k'un¹ ta⁴; hsien² chung¹ jih⁴ yueh⁴ ch'ang.²

995

Good wine reddens the face; riches excite the mind.

好酒紅人面。財帛動人心

'Hao³ chiu³ 'hung² jên² mien⁴; ts'ai² pai² tung⁴ jên² hsin.¹

996

With a well-known friend, a thousand cups of wine are few; when opinions disagree, even half a sentence is too much.

酒 逢 知 己 千 杯 少

Chiu^3 fêng^2 chih^1 chi^3 chʻien^1 pei^1 shao^3:

話 不 投 機 半 句 多

hua^4 pu^4 tʻou^2 chi^1 pan^1 chü^4 to.^{1}

997

Three glasses of wine can set everything to rights.

三 杯 和 萬 事

San^1 pu^4 ʻho^2 wan^4 shih.^{4}

998

Wine can both help and hinder business.

酒 能 成 事。酒 能 敗 事

Chiu^3 nêng^2 chʻêng^2 shih,^{4} chiu^3 nêng^2 pai^4 shih.^{4}

999

Wine is a discoverer of secrets.

酒 發 心 腹 之 言

Chiu^3 fa^1 hsin^1 fu^2 chih^1 yen.^{2}

1000

Wine is a poison which perforates the bowels; lechery is a sharp knife which scrapes the bones.

酒 是 穿 腸 毒 藥

Chiu^3 shih^4 chʻuan^1 chʻang^2 tu^2 yao^4;

色 乃 刮 骨 鋼 刀

sê^4 nai^3 kua^3 ku^3 kang^1 tao.^{1}

1001

Wine is a proper drink for men, as grains a proper food for pigs.

酒 是 人 喝 的。糟 是 猪 喫 的

Chiu^3 shih^4 jên^2 ʻho^1 ti,^{1} tsao^1 shih^4 chu^1 chʻih^1 ti.^{1}

NOTE.—This is said to deter men from drinking too much.

1002

To be mad with wine.

發 酒 瘋

Fa^1 chiu^3 fêng.^{1}

1003

Your whole face is reddened with the spring wind.

滿 面 春 風

Man³ mien⁴ ch'un¹ fêng.¹

1004

Do not drink more wine than you are able to carry.

莫 飲 過 量 之 酒

Mo⁴ yin³ kuo⁴ liang² chih¹ chiu.³

1005

Intoxication is not the wine's fault, but the man's.

酒 不 醉 人。人 自 醉

Chiu³ pu⁴ tsui⁴ jên,² jên² tzŭ⁴ tsui.⁴

1006

Drunk but still intelligent.

酒 醉 心 明 白

Chiu³ tsui⁴ hsin¹ ming² pai.²

1007

Whether the affair be settled or not, we must have our eighteen bottles of wine.

成 不 成 十 八 瓶

Ch'êng² pu⁴ ch'êng² shih² pa¹ p'ing.²

1008

When drinking wine remember the poverty of your family.

吃 酒 念 家 貧

Ch'ih¹ chiu³ nien⁴ chia¹. p'in.³

1009

No wine, no company; no wine, no conversation.

無 酒 不 會。無 酒 不 議

Wu² chiu³ pu⁴ 'hui⁴: wu² chiu³ pu⁴ i.⁴

1010

Over the wine cup conversation is light.

酒 杯 說 話 輕

Chiu³ pei¹ shuo¹ 'hua⁴ ch'ing.¹

1011

Rich or not it is my country's wine.

美不美鄉中酒

Mei[3] pu[4] mei[3] hsiang[1] chung[1] chiu.[3]

1012

Excessive joy breeds sorrow; excess of wine disorder.

樂極則悲。酒極則亂

Lê[4] chi[2] tsê[2] pei[1]; chiu[3] chi[2] tsê[2] lan.[4]

SECTION IX.—ON LANGUAGE.

CHAPTER I.

CONVERSATION.

1013

With *Wên wang* your manners and music display;
With *Pa wang* let arms be the talk of the day.

遇文王施禮樂
Yü⁴ Wên² wang² shih¹ li³ yo⁴;
會霸王動干戈
'Hui⁴ Pa⁴ wang² tung⁴ kan¹ ko.¹

NOTE.—*Wên wang.* The King Alfred of Chinese history, who reigned about 1150 years B. C., and forms the link between the *Shang* and the *Chou* dynasties. *Pa wang.* There were five chiefs or Kings thus designated; the most poversful of them was *Huan wang* or *'Huan kung* (桓公), whose reign dates from 717 B. C.

1014

If you deal in tittle-tattle,
In your ears will curses rattle.

傳言過話。多討人駡
Chuan⁴ yen² kuo⁴ 'hua,⁴ to¹ t'ao³ jên² ma.⁴

1015

The talk of a person can never be true,
Who has pointed lips and a very long queue.

嘴尖毛長。說話荒唐
Tsui³ chien¹ mao² ch'ang,² shuo¹ 'hua⁴ 'huang¹ t'ang.²

1016

Suit your talk to your man:
Suit your lot to your plan.

看人說話。看事打卦
K'an⁴ jên² shuo¹ 'hua⁴: k'an⁴ shih⁴ ta³ kua.⁴

1017

If one word misses it aim,
A myriad will do the same.

一言不中。萬言無用
Yi^1 yen^2 pu^4 chung,^{4} wan^4 yen^2 wu^2 yung.^{2}

——— 1018 ———

Say what will please; straight-forward words provoke dislike.

順情說好話。幹直惹人嫌
Shun^4 chʻing^2 shuo^1 ʻhao^3 ʻhua^4; kan^4 chih^2 jê^3 jên^2 hsien.^{2}

——— 1019 ———

Many men, many tongues.

人多舌頭多
Jên^2 to^1 shê^2 tʻou^2 to.^{1}

——— 1020 ———

Who know, don't talk; who talk, don't know.

知者不言。言者不知
Chih^1 chê^2 pu^4 yen^2; yen^2 chê^2 pu^4 chih.^{1}

——— 1021 ———

Sitting alone meditate on your own faults; in conversation talk not of other men's.

靜坐常思己過
Ching^4 tso^4 chʻang^2 ssŭ^1 chi^3 kuo^4;
閒談莫論人非
hsien^2 tʻan^2 mo^4 lun^4 jên^2 fei.^{1}

——— 1022 ———

On weddings and burials it is hard to answer clearly.

紅白喜事難答白
ʻHung^2 pai^2 hsi^3 shih^4 nan^2 ta^1 pai.^{2}

NOTE.—This proverb (another specimen of the innuendo) is commonly used in the sense of—Mind your own business; and frequently only the last three characters are spoken, the others being understood.

——— 1023 ———

There are *Chiang-nan* men sitting by, be careful what you say.

座上有江南
Tso^4 shang^4 yu^3 chiang^1 nan.^{1}

NOTE.—In the *Yu-shioh* (幼學), section *Jên shih* (人事), where this proverb occurs, we read that there exists a song called "The Song of the Partridge" (鷓鴣曲), which when heard by a man from the provinces of *Chiang-nan*, causes him earnestly to desire to return. So when sitting with such guests, it is good manners not to sing that song.

1024

A jar's mouth may be stopped; a man's cannot.

罎口封得住。人口封不住

T'an² k'ou³ fêng¹ tê² chu⁴; jên² k'ou³ fêng¹ pu⁴ chu.⁴

1025

It is a waste of words to repeat a thing three times over.

話說三遍是閑言

'Hua⁴ shuo¹ san¹ pien⁴ shih⁴ hsien² yen.²

1026

Do not talk to a man about what he cannot understand.

不是知音不與談

Pu⁴ shih⁴ chih¹ yin¹ pu⁴ yü³ t'an.²

1027

Never mention *Han Liu.*

不提漢劉二字

Pu⁴ t'i² 'Han⁴ Liu² êrh⁴ tzŭ.⁴

NOTE.—*'Han Liu Hsiu* (漢劉秀) or, according to his reigning title, *'Han Kuang Wu* (漢光武), was the enemy of the usurper *Wang Mang* (王莽). Some one happening to mention *'Han Liu* in his presence, *Wang Mang* uttered this trivial remark, which from that circumstance has become proverbial in the sense of—Never mention a man's enemy before his face.

1028

A troublesomely great talker is sure to make mistakes.

說話囉唆。難免無錯

Shuo¹ 'hua⁴ lo² so,¹ nan² mien³ wu² ts'o.⁴

1029

Never joke in the presence of a Prince.

君前無戲言

Chün¹ ch'ien² wu² hsi⁴ yen.²

1030

Neither let tongue nor pen wag as they list.

言不亂發。筆不妄動

Yen² pu⁴ lan⁴ fa,¹ pi³ pu⁴ wang⁴ tung.⁴

1031

The lion opens his mouth; the elephant shuts his; shut yours.

開口獅子。閉口象。不可亂言
K'ai¹ k'ou³ shih¹ tzŭ³; pi⁴ k'ou³ hsiang⁴; pu⁴ k'o³ lan⁴ yen.²

1032

If one compliments everybody, who will be one's enemy?

逢人說好話。那有不對
Fêng² jên² shuo¹ 'hao³ 'hua,⁴ na³ yu³ pu⁴ tui⁴?

1033

You chatter like magpies over a broken egg.

鴉鵲打破蛋
Ya¹ ch'iao³ ta³ p'o⁴ tan.⁴

1034

Speak carefully and be slow to speak.

謹開口。慢開言
Chin³ k'ai¹ k'ou,³ man⁴ k'ai⁴ yen.²

NOTE.—"Let every man be swift to hear, slow to speak." James 1. 19.

1035

Double-tongued. *Lit.*: To beat a gourd in the east, a ladle in the west.

東打葫蘆。西打瓢
Tung¹ ta³ 'hu² lu,² hsi¹ ta³ p'iao.²

1036

No discussion no rousing.

不提不醒
Pu⁴ t'i² pu⁴ hsin.³

1037

A good questioner is like one beating a bell.

善問者如撞鐘
Shan⁴ wên⁴ chê² ju² chuang⁴ chung.¹

1038

Meeting a man speak of '*Hang*.

逢人說項
Fêng² jên² shuo¹ 'Hang.⁴

NOTE.—That is, speak of some one well known. *Hang Ssŭ* (項斯) was a famous scholar and poet, at the beginning of the *T'ang* Dynasty. See *Yu-hsioh* (幼學), section *Jen-shih* (人事).

海上絲綢之路文獻集成 科技與文化編

1039

Meeting any one say but few words; don't set out all that is in your heart.

逢 人 且 說 三 分 話
Fêng^{2} jên^{2} chʻieh^{3} shuo^{1} san^{1} fên^{1} ʻhua^{4};
未 可 全 拋 一 片 心
wei^{4} kʻo^{3} chʻien^{2} pʻao^{1} yi^{1} pʻien^{4} hsin.^{1}

1040

Beware of being overheard. *Lit.:* Partitions have chinks, and walls have ears.

牆 有 縫。壁 有 耳
Chʻiang^{2} yu^{3} fêng,^{3} pi^{3} yu^{3} êrh.^{3}

1041

A stammerer of few words need not be a fool; a glib-tongued man need not be wise.

吶 吶 寡 言 者 未 必 愚
La^{3} la^{3} kua^{3} yen^{2} chê^{2} wei^{4} pi^{4} yü^{2};
喋 喋 利 口 者 未 必 智
tieh^{2} tieh^{2} li^{4} kʻou^{3} chê^{2} wei^{4} pi^{4} chih.^{4}

1042

The head may be cut off, but the tongue cannot be restrained.

頭 可 斬。舌 不 可 禁
Tʻou^{2} kʻo^{3} chan,^{3} shê^{2} pu^{4} kʻo^{3} chin.^{4}

1043

He who talks much must err; he excels who says nothing.

言 多 必 失。不 言 爲 高
Yen^{2} to^{1} pi^{4} shih^{1}; pu^{4} yen^{2} wei^{2} kao.^{1}

1044

If you converse by the way, remember there may be men in the grass.

路 上 說 話。草 裡 有 人
Lu^{4} shang^{4} shuo^{1} ʻhua,^{4} tsʻao^{3} li^{3} yu^{3} jên.^{2}

1045

Meeting men or devils, talk as they do.

遇人說人話。遇鬼說鬼話
Yü4 jên2 shuo1 jên2 ʻhua,4 yü4 kuei3 shou1 kuei3 ʻhua.4

1046

A man may say what he has seen.

見得到說得出
Chien4 tê2 tao4 shuo1 tê2 chʻu.1

1047

One may discourse with a wise man; it is hard to converse with a fool.

可爲知者道。難與俗人言
Kʻo3 wei2 chih1 chê2 tao4; nan2 yü3 su2 jên2 yen.2

1048

Be careful what you say. *Lit.*: That which goes out of your mouth, goes into other people's ears.

出在你口。入在人耳
Chʻu1 tsai4 ne3 kʻou,3 ju4 tsai4 jên2 êrh.2

1049

Never converse on the faults of others; nor presume to speak of your own virtues.

罔談彼短。靡恃己長
Wang3 tʻan3 pi3 tuan3; mi2 shih4 chi3 chʻang.2

1050

It is not so safe to open the mouth, as it is to keep it shut.

開口不如緘口穩
Kʻai1 kʻou3 pu4 ju2 hsien2 kʻou3 wên3.

1051

In conversation you must exercise control over the feelings.

說話要留情
Shuo1 ʻhua4 yao4 liu2 chʻing.2

CHAPTER II.

SIMILES.

1052

Pompous. *Lit.*: Like an Imperial Preceptor.

像 一 個 太 師 皇

Hsiang⁴ yi¹ ko⁴ t'ai⁴ shih¹ 'huang.²

1053

Stupid. *Lit.*: Like a wooden image.

像 一 個 木 偶 人

Hsiang⁴ yi¹ ko⁴ mu⁴ ou³ jên.²

1054

Very lazy. *Lit.*: Like one who has drawn out his muscles.

像 抽 了 一 副 筋

Hsiang⁴ ch'ou¹ liao² yi¹ fu⁴ chin.¹

1055

Containing stores of ill-arranged information. *Lit.*: Like a waste-paper basket.

像 一 個 字 紙 簍

Hsiang⁴ yi¹ ko⁴ tzŭ⁴ chih⁴ lou.³

1056

Depraved. *Lit.*: Like a door all awry.

像 一 個 歪 門 斜 勢

Hsiang⁴ yi¹ ko⁴ wai¹ mên² hsieh² shih.⁴

1057

Useless. *Lit.*: Like a funeral paper god.

像 一 個 顯 道 神

Hsiang⁴ yi¹ ko⁴ hsien³ tao⁴ shên.²

NOTE.—The *hsien tao shên* are huge, light, paper-covered images, carried at the head of an officer's funeral. Doolittle gives a good description of them in his "Social Life," Vol. i, page 203.

1058

Very ugly. *Lit.*: Like *Yang Fan* of *Ts'ou.*

像 楚 國 楊 樊

Hsiang⁴ Ts'ou² kuo² Yang² fan.²

1059

Poor. *Lit.:* Like anything washed by many waters.

像大水洗了

Hsiang⁴ ta⁴ shui³ hsi³ liao³

1060

Like a beaten dog.

像打殃的狗子

Hsiang⁴ ta³ yang¹ ti¹ kou³ tzŭ.³

1061

Wise. *Lit.:* Like an efficacious tortoise.

像一個靈龜

Hsiang⁴ yi¹ ko⁴ ling² kuei.¹

1062

Like a sister-in-law of *Su Ch'in.*

像一個蘇秦的嫂子

Hsiang⁴ yi¹ ko⁴ Su¹ ch'in² ti¹ sao³ tzŭ.³

NOTE.—That is, to cringe and bow to one in prosperity, whom in adversity you have slighted. See note under proverb 2629.

1063

To come Suddenly and go gradually. *Lit.:* As wind and rain it comes, as small dust it goes.

來如風雨。去似微塵

Lai² ju² fêng¹ yü,³ ch'ü⁴ ssŭ⁴ wei¹ ch'ên.²

1064

Uncared for. *Lit.:* Like a dog whose master is dead.

如喪家的狗

Ju² sang¹ chia¹ ti¹ kou.³

1065

Gradually. *Lit.:* As water soaks into wood.

如水浸木

Ju² shui³ tsin⁴ mu.⁴

1066

Without sustenance. *Lit.:* As a fish out of water.

如魚失水

Ju² yü² shih¹ shui.³

1067

As hard as a stone.

跟 石 頭 這 麼 硬

Kên^{1} shih^{2} tʻou^{2} chê^{4} mo^{3} ying.^{4}

1068

As intimate as brothers.

親 如 同 胞

Chʻin^{1} ju^{2} tʻung^{4} pao.^{1}

1069

As like as two claps of thunder.

雷 同

Lei^{2} tʻung.^{2}

1070

As far as heaven from earth.

天 壤 之 分

Tʻien^{1} jang^{2} chih^{1} fên.^{1}

1071

As far as heaven from the abyss of the ocean.

相 去 天 淵

Hsiang^{1} chʻü^{4} tʻien^{1} yüan.^{1}

1072

As thin as a rail.

骨 瘦 如 柴

Ku^{3} shou^{4} ju^{2} chʻai.^{2}

1073

As weak as cotton.

軟 如 綿

Juan^{3} ju^{2} mien.^{2}

1074

As hard as iron.

硬 似 鐵

Ying^{4} ssŭ^{4} tʻieh.^{3}

1075

As clear as the pebbles at the bottom of a brook.

水 底 沙 明

Shui^{3} ti^{3} sha^{1} ming.^{2}

1076

Gradually. *Lit.:* As the silkworm eats its way.

蠶食而進

Ts'an² shih² êrh² chin.⁴

1077

As stupid as black lacquer.

糊塗像漆

'Hu² t'u² hsiang⁴ ch'i.¹

1078

As orderly as printing-blocks.

印板層次

Yin⁴ pan³ ts'êng² tz'ŭ.⁴

1079

Glib-tongued. *Lit.:* Lips sharp as a knife.

嘴似刀

Tsui³ ssŭ⁴ tao.¹

1080

Smooth-tongued. *Lit.:* A pair of oily lips.

一張油嘴

Yi¹ chang¹ yu² tsui.³

1081

Sudden. *Lit.:* Like a clap of thunder in the sky.

好比半天雲裡一雷

Hao³ pi³ pan⁴ t'ien¹ yün² li³ yi¹ lei.²

1082

Quickly. *Lit.:* As ice melts and hoarfrost evaporates

如冰消霧散一般

Ju² ping¹ hsiao¹ wu³ san⁴ yi¹ pan.¹

1083

Pure as water, clear as a mirror.

清如水。明如鏡

Ch'ing¹ ju² shui,³ ming² ju² ching.⁴

1084

Useless. *Lit.:* As the chaff of fine rice.

如細米外的糠皮
Ju^{2} hsi^{4} mi^{3} wai^{4} ti^{1} kʻang^{1} pʻi.^{2}

1085

As easy as to take anything out of a purse.

探囊取物
Tʻan^{1} nang^{2} chʻü^{3} wu.^{4}

CHAPTER III.

WORDS.

1086

If you always remember the words you have spoken,
Then your peace to the end will continue unbroken.

記得從前話。到老不嗜罵

Chi^4 tê^2 tsʻung^2 chʻien^2 ʻhua,^{4} tao^4 lao^3 pu^4 she^1 ma.^{3}

1087

Faithful words do conduct good while they the ear displease;
And good drugs, bitter in the mouth, may cure the disease.

忠言逆耳利於行

Chung^1 yen^2 ni^4 êrh^3 li^4 yü^1 hsing^2;

良藥苦口利於病

Liang^2 yao^4 kʻu^3 kʻou^3 li^4 yü^1 ping.^{4}

1088

All the words which sages said,
Gods respect and devils dread.

聖賢言語。神欽鬼伏

Sheng^4 hsien^2 yen^2 yü,^{3} shên^2 chʻin^1 kuei^3 fu.^{2}

1089

Whilst our words resemble wind.
Writing leaves a trace behind.

口是風。筆是踪

Kʻou^3 shih^4 fêng,^{1} pi^3 shih^4 tsung.^{1}

1090

If your words are not pleasing, hold in half of them.

話不投機留半句

ʻHua^4 pu^4 tʻou^2 chi^1 liu^2 pan^4 chü.^{4}

1091

Words whispered in the ear may be heard for a thousand miles.

附耳之言聞於千里

Fu^4 êrh^3 chih^1 yen^2 wên^2 yü^1 chʻien^1 li.^{3}

1092

Beat your drum inside your house, and outsiders will not hear.

鼓 在 內 打。聲 不 見 外 响

Ku^{3} tsai^{4} nei^{4} ta,^{3} shêng^{1} pu^{4} chien^{4} wai^{4} hsiang.^{3}

1093

Fine words are incredible; credible words are not fine.

美 言 不 信。信 言 不 美

Mei^{3} yen^{2} pu^{4} hsin^{4}; hsin^{4} yen^{2} pu^{4} mei.^{3}

1094

A man of few words escapes slander, of few desires preserves his health.

寡 言 省 謗。寡 慾 保 身

Kua^{3} yen^{2} shêng^{3} pang,^{4} kua^{3} yü^{4} pao^{3} shên.^{1}

1095

A wise man will learn something even from the words of a fool.

狂 夫 之 言 聖 人 擇 焉

K'uang^{2} fu^{1} chih^{1} yen^{2} shêng^{4} jên^{2} tsê^{2} yen.^{1}

1096

One good word can warm three winter months; one bad one can stir up anger.

好 話 一 句 三 冬 煖

'Hao^{3} 'hua^{4} yi^{1} chü^{4} san^{1} t'ung^{1} nuan^{3};

惡 話 一 句 惱 人 心

O^{4} 'hua^{4} yi^{1} chü^{4} nao^{3} jên^{2} hsin.^{1}

NOTE.—In that part of the *Yu hsiao* (幼學) called *Sui shih* (歲時), a story is told of one *Ko Hsien* (葛仙), a wonderful individual, who performed a feat similar to that referred to in the first line of this proverb. During the cold winter weather he invited some guests to his dwelling; and, on their arrival, he emitted such a fire from his mouth (吐火) as made the house warm as in spring time, so that his guests were obliged to put off some of their clothing. The second line of this proverb bears a strong resemblance to Proverbs 15: 1.—"Grievous words stir up anger."

1097

One word of his settles the matter. *Lit.:* By one stroke of the saw he severs the gourd into a couple of ladles.

一鋸兩把瓢
Yi^1 chü^4 liang^2 pa^3 p'iao.^{2}

—— 1098 ——

One word may be better than hundreds or thousands.

一言勝千百
Yi^1 yen^2 shêng^4 ch'ien^1 pai.^{3}

—— 1099 ——

One word may be worth a thousand *taels* of gold.

一諾千金
Yi^1 no^4 ch'ien^1 chin.^{1}

—— 1100 ——

Listen to a man's words if you wish to know his mind.

欲知心腹事。單聽口中言
Yü^4 chih^1 hsin^1 fu^2 shih,^{4} tan^1 t'ing^1 k'ou^3 chung^1 yen.^{2}

—— 1101 ——

A man's meaning becomes visible when he opens his mouth.

開口見人肺腑
K'ai^1 k'ou^3 chien^4 jên^2 fei^4 fu.^{3}

—— 1102 ——

When a man opens his mind his real meaning becomes evident.

開心見誠
K'ai^1 hsin^1 chien^4 ch'êng.^{2}

—— 1103 ——

What you do not understand, say nothing about.

摸不清白。不要亂答白
Mo^1 pu^4 ch'ing^1 pai,^{2} pu^4 yao^4 lan^4 ta^1 pai.^{2}

—— 1104 ——

Stop up your mouth like a bottle neck; guard your thoughts like a city.

守口如瓶。防意如城
Shou^3 k'ou^3 ju^2 p'ing^1; fang^2 i^4 ju^2 ch'êng.^{2}

—— 1105 ——

Do not talk about a thing when it is done; spilt water cannot be gathered up again.

成事莫說。覆水難收

Chʻêng^2 shih^4 mo^4 shuo^1; fu^2 shui^3 nan^2 shou.^{1}

—— 1106 ——

Praise is hard to get; but censure is easy to give.

好言難得。惡語易施

ʻHao^3 yen^2 nan^2 tê^2; o^4 yü^3 i^4 shih.^{1}

—— 1107 ——

When a man is calm he says nothing; when water is level it flows not.

人平不語。水平不流

Jên^2 pʻing^2 pu^4 yü^3; shui^3 pʻing^2 pu^4 liu.^{2}

—— 1108 ——

No single word can be recalled. *Lit.:* One word let out, a swift horse cannot overtake it.

一言旣出。駟馬難追

Yi^1 yen^2 chi^3 chʻu,^{1} shih^4 ma^3 nan^2 chui.^{1}

—— 1109 ——

One hurtful word wounds like a sharp sword.

傷人一語。利如刀割

Shang^1 jên^2 yi^1 yü,^{3} li^4 ju^2 tao^1 ko.^{1}

—— 1110 ——

What one says may be false; what a hundred say must be true.

一人傳虛。百人傳實

Yi^1 jên^2 chuan^4 hsü^1; pai^3 jên^2 chuan^4 shih.^{2}

—— 1111 ——

The wound of a sharp knife will close up; but the hate provoked by evil words will never die.

利刀割體瘡猶合

Li^4 tao^1 ko^1 tʻi^3 chʻuang^1 yu^2 ʻho^2;

言語傷人恨不消

Yen^2 yü^3 shang^1 jên^2 ʻhên^3 pu^4 hsiao.^{1}

諺語叢話

1112

Books do not exhaust words, nor words thoughts.

書不盡言。言不盡意

Shu^{1} pu^{4} chin^{4} yen,^{2} yen^{2} pu^{4} chin^{4} i.^{4}

1113

Always beware of many words; when words are many there must be error.

處世戒多言。言多必失

Ch'ü^{4} shih^{4} chieh^{4} to^{1} yen^{2}; yen^{2} to^{1} pi^{4} shih.^{1}

1114

Neither drum nor bell can sound unstruck; and words unspoken cannot be understood.

鼓不打不响。鐘不撞不鳴

Ku^{3} pu^{4} ta^{3} pu^{4} hsiang^{3}; chung^{1} pu^{4} chuang^{4} pu^{4} ming^{2};

話不說不明

hua^{4} pu^{4} shuo^{1} pu^{4} ming.^{2}

1115

When good words fill the empire, no one's mouth offends.

言滿天下無口過

Yen^{2} man^{3} t'ien^{1} hsia^{4} wu^{2} k'ou^{3} kuo.^{4}

1116

Three boors cannot carry the word Reason.

三個蠻人擡不起一個理字

San^{1} ko^{4} man^{3} jên^{2} t'ai^{2} pu^{4} ch'i^{3} yi^{1} ko^{4} li^{3} tsŭ.^{4}

1117

Bitter words are medicine; sweet words an epidemic.

苦言藥也甘言疾也

K'u^{3} yen^{2} yao^{4} yeh^{3}; kan^{1} yen^{2} chi^{2} yeh.^{3}

1118

Sages have written thousands and myriads of words to rouse up dreaming men.

聖賢千萬語提醒夢中人

Shêng^{4} hsien^{2} ch'ien^{1} wan^{4} yü^{3} t'i^{2} hsing^{3} mêng^{4} chung^{1} jên.^{2}

1119

Having something to say speak plainly, and never conceal it.

有 話 明 說 不 必 隱 瞞
Yu^3 ʻhua^4 ming^2 shuo,^{1} pu^4 pi^4 yin^3 man.^{3}

1120

Good words are like a string of pearls.

好 語 似 珠 串 一 一
ʻHao^3 yü^3 ssŭ^4 chu^1 chʻuan^4 yi^1 yi.^{1}

1121

" Petty distinctions are injurious to rectitude ; quibbling words violate right reason."

小 辯 害 義。小 言 破 道
Hsiao^3 pien^4 ʻhai^4 i^4; hsiao^3 yen^2 pʻo^4 tao.^{4}

1122

Tall talk is followed by no true action.

高 談 闊 論。沒 有 一 點 實 行
Kao^1 tʻan^2 hûo^4 lun,^{4} mu^2 yu^3 yi^1 tien^3 shih^2 hsing.^{2}

1123

" As the light of a single star tinges the mountains of many regions ; so a single unguarded expression injures the virtue of a whole life."

一 星 之 火 能 燒 萬 頃 之 山
Yi^1 hsing^1 chih^1 ʻhuo^3 nêng^2 shao^1 wan^4 chʻing^3 chih^1 shan^1;
半 句 非 言 誤 損 平 生 之 德
pan^4 chü^4 fei^1 yen^2 wu^4 sun^3 pʻing^2 shêng^1 chih^1 tê.^{2}

1124

Plausible talk is not equal to honest speech ; and a clever man needs but few words.

巧 言 不 如 直 道
Chʻiao^3 yen^2 pu^4 ju^2 chih^2 tao^4;
明 人 不 用 細 說
Ming^2 jên^2 pu^4 yung^4 hsi^4 shuo.^{1}

1125

Words may not be foolishly spoken ; what you say must accord with reason.

言 不 妄 發。發 必 當 理
Yen^2 pu^4 wang^4 fa^1; fa^1 pi^4 tang^4 li.^{3}

1126

Who makes his strength cheap obtains men's respect; who makes his mouth cheap obtains their dislike.

力賤得人敬。口賤得人憎

Li^{4} chien^{4} tê^{2} jên^{2} ching^{4}; k'ou^{3} chien^{4} tê^{2} jên^{2} tsêng.^{1}

1127

When you have anything to say, first think and then say it.

有所言必議之而後言

Yu^{3} so^{3} yen^{2} pi^{4} i^{4} chih^{1} êrh^{2} 'hou^{4} yen.^{2}

1128

He who seldom opens his mouth, often shuts his eyes.

少開口。多閉目

Shao^{3} k'ai^{1} k'ou,^{3} to^{1} pi^{4} mu.^{4}

NOTE.—"Shuts his eyes"; *i. e.* meditatively, thinking well before he speaks

1129

When troubles are few dreams are few; when words are scarce faults are scarce.

慮少夢自少。言稀過亦稀

Lü^{4} shao^{3} mêng^{4} tzŭ^{4} shao^{3}; yen^{2} hsi^{1} kuo^{4} i^{4} hsi.^{1}

1130

The pen can convey one's meaning for a thousand miles.

筆情達千里

Pi^{3} ch'ing^{2} ta^{2} ch'ien^{1} li.^{3}

1131

The mouth which boasts of the sea, utters big words.

誇海口說大話

K'ua^{1} 'hai^{3} k'ou^{3} shuo^{1} ta^{4} 'hua.^{4}

SECTION X.—ON LAW AND GOVERNMENT.

CHAPTER I.

LAWS AND PENALTIES.

1132

Never beat if you must fine;
If you do, all fines decline.

罰就不打。打就不罰

Fa^2 chiu^4 pu^4 ta^3; ta^3 chiu^4 pu^4 fa.^{2}

1133

Try you to defraud in customs and revenue;
The mandarins soon will try to be having you.

瞞關漏稅。拿着問罪

man^3 kuan^1 lou^4 shui^4; na^2 cho^2 wên^4 tsui.^{4}

1134

Whether you punish or reward,
To friend or foe show no regard.

賞不論寃仇。罰不論骨肉

Shang^3 pu^4 lun^4 yüan^1 chʻou,^{2} fa^2 pu^4 lun^4 ku^3 jou.^{4}

1135

Decapitation, strangling, banishment, exile, and transportation, are regulations which may not be broken.

斬絞軍流徒法不可犯

Chan^3 chiao^3 chün^1 liu^2 tʻu,^{2} fa^3 pu^4 kʻo^3 fan.^{4}

1136

He who fears the laws will not break them; he who dreads punishment will escape it.

懼法自不犯法

Chü^4 fa^3 tzŭ^4 pu^4 fan^4 fa^3;

畏刑自可免刑

wei^4 hsing^2 tzŭ^4 kʻo^3 mien^3 hsing.^{2}

1137

In making laws, severity is indispensable; in administering them, clemency.

立法不可不嚴
Li⁴ fa³ pu⁴ k'o³ pu⁴ yen²;
行法不可不恕
hsing² fa³ pu⁴ k'o³ pu⁴ shu.⁴

1138

One word settles life or death; so the pen may not carelessly move.

一字定生死。筆莫亂動
Yi¹ tzŭ⁴ ting⁴ shêng¹ ssu³; pi³ mo⁴ lan⁴ tung.⁴

1139

One word from a magistrate's pen may decide for life or death.

黑筆寫白紙。一字定生死
'Hei¹ pi³ hsieh³ pai² chih,³ yi¹ tzŭ⁴ ting⁴ shêng¹ ssŭ.³

1140

He drew a line on the ground for a prison.

畫地爲獄
'Hua⁴ ti⁴ wei² yü.⁴

NOTE.—This proverbial saying, referring to the obedient people of *Wên wang*, s now used as the equivalent of *pu kan tung* (不敢動) 'I dare not move.'

1141

Though the sword of justice be sharp, it will not slay the innocent.

鋼刀雖快。不斬無罪之人
Kang¹ tao¹ sui¹ k'uai,⁴ pu⁴ chan³ wu² tsui⁴ chih¹ jên.²

1142

If gentle means fail, harsh means will not.

善化不足。惡化有餘
Shan⁴ 'hua⁴ pu⁴ tsu,² o⁴ 'hua⁴ yu³ yü².

1143

No punishment on the Bench, no law below it.

案上無刑。案下無法
An⁴ shang⁴ wu² hsing,² an⁴ hsia⁴ wu² fa.³

CHAPTER II.

LITIGATION.

1144

Happy is the man who himself alone arraigns;
With others go to law, you've trouble for your pains.

訟心者祥。訟人者殃

Sung^{4} hsin^{1} chê^{2} hsiang^{2}; sung^{4} jên^{2} chê^{2} yang.^{1}

1145

With only right to back you,
Be sure the yamens lack you.

八字衙門朝南開

Pa^{1} tzŭ^{4} ya^{2} mên^{2} ch'ao^{2} nan^{2} k'ai,^{1}

有理無錢莫進來

yu^{3} li^{3} wu^{2} ch'ien^{2} mo^{4} chin^{4} lai^{2}.

1146

If the warrant omits your name,
Take you no notice of the same.

榜上無名。呌不應

Pang^{3} shang^{4} wu^{2} ming,^{2} chiao^{4} pu^{4} ying.^{4}

1147

If one family has a lawsuit, ten families are involved in calamity.

一家有事。連累十家

Yi^{1} chia^{1} yu^{3} shih,^{4} lien^{2} lei^{3} shih^{2} chia.^{1}

1148

The bite of a thief goes three inches into the bone.

賊咬一口入骨三分

Tsei^{2} yao^{3} yi^{1} k'ou^{3} ju^{4} ku^{3} san^{1} fên.^{1}

NOTE.—This proverb refers to the false statements sometimes made by prisoners at the bar, charging others with complicity in their offences.

1149

Inform against a man once, and three of his generations will become your enemies.

告人一狀三世冤

Kao^4 jên^2 yi^1 chuang^4 san^1 shih^4 yüan.^{1}

1150

An indictment cannot be got up without lies.

無謊不成詞

Wu^2 ʻhuang^3 pu^4 chʻêng^2 ssŭ.^{2}

1151

If but one word of information against a man get into the court, nine bullocks cannot drag it out again.

一字入公門。九牛拖不出

Yi^1 tzŭ^4 ju^4 Kung^1 mên,^{2} chiu^3 niu^2 tʻo^1 pu^4 chʻu.^{1}

1152

Let householders avoid litigation; for once go to law and there is nothing but trouble.

居家戒爭訟。訟則終凶

Chü^1 chia^1 chieh^4 chêng^1 sung^4; sung^4 tsê^2 chung^1 hsiung.^{1}

1153

Win your lawsuit and lose your money.

贏了官事輸了錢

Ying^2 liao^3 kuan^1 shih^4 shu^1 liao^3 chʻien.^{2}

1154

Winning a cat you lose a cow.

贏了貓兒輸了牛

Ying^2 liao^3 mao^1 êrh^2 shu^1 liao^3 niu.^{2}

1155

"Nine lawsuits out of ten are settled by arbitration."

十場官事九場和

Shih^2 chʻang^2 kuan^1 shih^4 chiu^3 chʻang^2 ʻho.^{2}

1156

The plaintiff's charge makes the defendant seem worthy of death; but the defendant's answer shows there is reason on both sides.

原 告 一 張 紙。被 告 就 要 死
Yüan² kao⁴ yi¹ chang¹ chih,³ pei⁴ kao⁴ chiu⁴ yao⁴ ssŭ³;
被 告 一 張 紙。兩 下 都 有 理
pei⁴ kao⁴ yi¹ chang¹ chih,³ liang² hsia⁴ tu¹ yu³ li.³

1157

His pen is as sharp as a sword.

筆 如 刀 利
Pi³ ʻho² tao¹ li.⁴

NOTE.—Said of one who writes indictments.

1158

To retain some feeling in writing an indictment.

筆 下 留 情
Pi³ hsia⁴ liu² chʻing.²

1159

Wishing to criminate, no difficulty will be met in finding a pretext.

欲 加 之 罪。何 患 無 詞
Yü⁴ chia¹ chih¹ tsui,⁴ ʻho² ʻhuan⁴ wu² ssŭ.²

1160

In life beware of yamens; in death beware of hell.

生 不 入 官 門。死 不 入 地 獄
Shêng¹ pu⁴ ju⁴ kuan¹ mên²; ssŭ³ pu⁴ ju⁴ ti⁴ yü.⁴

1161

On the magistrate's table a sheet of paper; at his feet a pair of lips.

堂 上 一 張 紙。堂 下 一 張 嘴
Tʻang² shang⁴ yi¹ chang¹ chih³; tʻang² hsia⁴ yi¹ chang¹ tsui.³

1162

Before you arrest a magistrate, arrest his domestic.

拿 官 先 拿 家 丁
Na² kuan¹ hsien¹ na² chia¹ ting¹.

1163

Three or six hundred cash; two or four hundred cash; cash for runners, and cash for clerks.

三 六 百。二 四 百。差 費 房 禮
San¹ lu⁴ pai³; êrh⁴ ssŭ⁴ pai³; chʻai¹ fei⁴ fang² li.³

NOTE.—"Hundred" in this connection is said always to mean "thousand!"

1164

Though nine times you present an accusation, the last must agree with the first.

九 狀 不 離 原 詞

Chiu^{3} chuang^{4} pu^{4} li^{2} yüan^{2} ssŭ.^{2}

1165

He who can get up a lawsuit will have calls on his cash.

會 打 官 司 也 要 錢

ʻHui^{4} ta^{3} kuan^{1} ssŭ^{1} yeh^{3} yao^{4} chʻien.^{2}

1166

You cannot get at the Emperor, to tell him your wrongs.

不 能 見 天 子 言 情

Pu^{4} nêng^{2} chien^{4} tʻien^{1} tzŭ^{3} yen^{2} chʻing.^{2}

1167

Of ten reasons by which a magistrate may decide a case, nine are unknown to the public.

官 斷 十 條 理 九 條 人 不 知

Kuan^{1} tuan^{4} shih^{2} tʻiao^{2} li^{3} chiu^{3} tʻiao^{2} jên^{2} pu^{4} chih.^{1}

CHAPTER III.

CIVIL OFFICERS.

1168

Whenever a neighbour office takes,
The event a gen'ral gladness makes.

鄰 舍 做 官。大 家 喜 歡

Lin^{2} shê^{4} tso^{4} kuan,^{1} ta^{4} chia^{1} hsi^{3} ʻhuan.^{1}

1169

One dash of a civil magistrate's pen,
Makes the martial magistrate jump again.

文 官 點 一 筆。武 官 扒 不 急

Wên^{2} kuan^{1} tien^{3} yi^{1} pi,^{3} wu^{3} kuan^{1} pa^{1} pu^{4} chi.^{2}

1170

The magistrate sitting to judge in court,
Is helped by underlings of every sort.

官 府 坐 堂 書 差 衙 役 帮 忙

Kuan^{1} fu^{3} tso^{4} tʻang,^{2} shu^{1} chʻai^{1} ya^{2} yi^{4} pang^{1} mang.^{2}

1171

Do you wish to enjoy a peaceful state—
First settle all claims of the magistrate.

若 要 安。先 完 官

Jo^{4} yao^{4} an,^{1} hsien^{1} wan^{2} kuan.^{1}

1172

Civil and martial mandarins must,
One to his seal, one to his flag, trust.

文 憑 印 信。武 憑 號 令

Wên^{2} pʻing^{2} yin^{4} hsin,^{4} wu^{3} pʻing^{2} ʻhao^{4} ling.^{4}

1173

The two Commissioners of salt and grain,
Keep, each of them, to his own domain.

鹽糧兩道。各管一號
Yen[2] liang[2] liang[2] tao,[4] ko[4] kuan[3] yi[1] ʻhao.[4]

——— 1174 ———

With friends at court, it is easy to get into office.

朝中有人好爲官
Chʻao[2] chung[1] yu[3] jên[2] ʻhao[3] wei[2] kuan.[1]

——— 1175 ———

Deceive but don't insult a mandarin.

瞞官莫欺官
Man[3] kuan[1] mo[4] chʻi[1] kuan.[1]

——— 1176 ———

An officer's door is like a market-place; his heart is like pure water.

臣門如市。臣心似水
Chʻên mên[2] ju[2] shih,[4] chʻên[2] hsin[1] ssŭ[4] shui.[3]

——— 1177 ———

High office is necessarily dangerous.

官高必險
Kuan[1] kao[1] pi[4] hsien.[3]

——— 1178 ———

An honest magistrate cannot get on.

淸官不到頭
Chʻing[1] kuan[1] pu[4] tao[4] tʻou.[2]

——— 1179 ———

The civil magistrate takes his pen and pacifies the empire.

文官把筆安天下
Wên[2] kuan[1] pa[3] pi[3] an[1] tʻien[1] hsia.[4]

——— 1180 ———

The dignity of high office is widely known.

官高爵顯
Kuan[1] kao[1] chüeh[2] hsien.[3]

——— 1181 ———

A magistrate will not consider your poverty, nor the devil your leanness.

官不怕你窮。鬼不怕你瘦

Kuan^1 pu^4 pʻa^4 ni^3 chʻiung,^{2} kuei^3 pu^4 pʻa^4 ni^3 shou.^{4}

NOTE.—The meaning of this caustic saying is, that the one will have your money and the other your life.

1182

An honest magistrate can hardly escape dishonest clerks.

淸官難逃滑吏手

Chʻing^1 kuan^1 nan^2 tʻao^2 ʻhua^2 li^4 shou.^{3}

1183

Men's hearts are like iron, and the rule of mandarins like a furnace.

人心似鐵。官法如爐

Jên^2 hsin^1 ssŭ^4 tʻieh^3; kuan^1 fa^3 ju^2 lu.^{2}

1184

If the homes of the people are without learned sons, where are the magistrates to come from?

家無讀書子。官從何處來

Chia^1 wu^2 tu^2 shu^1 tzŭ,^{3} kuan^1 tsʻung^2 ʻho^2 chʻu^4 lai^2?

1185

A mandarin must aim at being Premier, and so must begin early to contend for the first rank.

爲官須作相。及第早爭先

Wei^2 kuan^1 hsü^1 tso^4 hsiang,^{1} chi^2 ti^4 tsao^3 chêng^1 hsien.^{1}

1186

The magistrate has his proper laws; and the people their private agreements.

官有正條。民有私約

Kuan^1 yu^3 chêng^4 tʻiao^2; min^2 yu^3 ssŭ^1 yo.^{1}

1187

A magistrate who is not a lord among his people, has received the Emperor's high distinction and pay in vain.

爲官不與民作主

Wei^2 kuan^1 pu^4 yü^3 min^2 tso^4 chu,^{3}

枉受朝廷爵祿高

Wang^3 shou^4 chʻao^2 tʻing^2 chüeh^2 lu^4 kao.^{1}

諺語叢話

1188

A wise man before a magistrate will be mute for a little while.

好漢見官三聲啞

'Hao³ 'han⁴ chien⁴ kuan¹ san¹ shêng¹ ya.³

1189

A poor mandarin equals a rich merchant.

窮官當富客

Ch'iung² kuan¹ tang⁴ fu⁴ k'o.⁴

1190

He who takes office far from home only does so for a living.

千里做官只爲嘴

Ch'ien¹ li³ tso⁴ kuan¹ chih³ wei² tsui.³

1191

He who in high station is without pride, is exalted without danger.

在上不驕。高而不危

Tsai¹ shang⁴ pu⁴ chiao,¹ kao¹ êrh² pu⁴ wei.²

1192

A man may display great ability in any office high or low; a man without ability receives high rank and pay in vain.

有才不在官大小

Yu³ ts'ai² pu⁴ tsai⁴ kuan¹ ta⁴ hsiao³;

無才枉受爵祿高

wu² ts'ai² wang³ shou⁴ chüeh² lu⁴ kao.¹

1193

The *Chih-fu* can exterminate families; the *Chih-hsien* can confiscate goods.

滅門知府。抄家知縣

Mieh⁴ mên² chih¹ fu³; ch'ao¹ chia¹ chih¹ hsien.⁴

1194

Even an honest *Chih-fu* may, during a three years term of office, save ten myriad snow-white taels of silver.

一任清知府十萬雪花銀
Yi^1 jên^4 ch'ing^1 Chih^1 fu^3 shih^2 wan^4 hsüeh^3 'hua^1 yin.^{2}

——— 1195 ———

Before he comes into office he reproves a thousand faults; after he comes into office he commits the same himself.

未做官說千般
Wei^4 tso^4 kuan^1 shuo^1 ch'ien^1 pan^1;
做了官是一般
tso^4 liao^3 kuan^1 shih^4 yi^1 pan.^{1}

——— 1196 ———

There are three rules for men in office: be upright, be cautious, be diligent.

當官有三事。曰清。曰愼。曰勤
Tang^1 kuan^1 yu^3 san^1 shih^4: yüeh^1 ch'ing,^{1} yüeh^1 shên,^{4} yüeh^1 ch'in.^{2}

——— 1197 ———

Among magistrates there are distinctions of rank; among their assistants, none.

官有大小。吏無尊卑
Kuan^1 yu^3 ta^4 hsiao^3; li^4 wu^2 tsun^1 pei.^{1}

——— 1198 ———

Better awe-inspiring police than awe-inspiring mandarins; for if the police be not so, the mandarins will be lightly esteemed.

官威不如衙役威
Kuan^1 wei^1 pu^4 ju^2 ya^2 yi^4 wei^1;
衙役不威官就低
ya^2 yi^4 pu^4 wei^1 kuan^1 chiu^4 ti.^{1}

——— 1199 ———

Magistrates innumerable beget sons to die of want; whilst many unofficial men bear sons who turn out courtiers.

無限朱門生殍餓
Wu^2 hsien^4 chu^1 mên^2 shêng^1 o^4 p'iao^3;
幾多白屋出朝郎
chi^3 to^1 pai^2 wu^1 ch'u^1 ch'ao^2 lang.^{2}

1200

Neither dogs nor mandarins injure those who give them anything.

狗 不 咬 屙 屎 的

Kou[3] pu[4] yao[3] o[1] sui[1] ti[1];

官 不 打 送 禮 的

kuan[1] pu[4] ta[3] sung[4] li[3] ti.[1]

NOTE.—This common and very suggestive proverb, is too coarse for any more literal translation than the one given above.

CHAPTER IV.

MILITARY OFFICERS.

1201

When against rebels a general does an army bring,
His first endeavour ought to be to seize the rebel king.

將軍上戰場。擒賊先擒王

Chiang^1 chün^1 shang^3 chan^4 ch'ang,^{2} ch'in^2 tsei^2 hsien^1 ch'in^2 wang.^{2}

1202

Nailmakers don't good iron use;
Nor good men to be soldiers choose.

好鐵不打釘。好人不當兵

'Hao^3 t'ieh^3 pu^4 ta^3 ting^1; 'hao^3 jên^2 pu^4 tang^1 ping.^{1}

1203

Under a powerful general there are no feeble soldiers.

强將手下無弱兵

Ch'iang^2 chiang^1 shou^3 hsia^4 wu^2 jo^4 ping.^{1}

1204

The rank of general is opén to the meanest born.

將軍不怕出身低

Chiang^1 chün^1 pu^4 p'a^4 ch'u^1 shên^1 ti^1

1205

Though you kill ten thousand, you will have three thousand killed.

殺人一萬。自損三千

Sha^1 jên^2 yi^1 wan,^{4} tzŭ^4 sun^3 san^1 ch'ien.^{1}

1206

Armies are kept a thousand days to be used on one.

養軍千日用在一朝

Yang^3 chün^1 ch'ien^1 jih^4 yung^4 tsai^4 yi^1 chao.^{1}

1207

To rush on the foe at the point of the spear, is the mark of a truly brave man; and the scholar who can move heaven and earth is wonderfully talented.

衝鋒破敵眞個大膽
Chʻung1 fêng1 pʻo4 ti2 chên1 ko4 ta4 tan.3
掀天揭地方是奇才
hsien1 tʻien1 chieh1 ti4 fang1 shih4 chi1 tsʻai.2

1208

A great general is honoured everywhere.

大將軍八面威風
Ta4 chiang1 chün1 pa1 mien4 wei1 fêng.1

1209

A (defeated) general never dismounts, so each soldier may flee where he pleases.

將軍不下馬。各自奔前程
Chiang1 chün1 pu4 hsia4 ma,3 ko4 tzŭ4 pên1 chʻien2 chʻêng.2

1210

A thousand soldiers are easily obtained; one general is hard to find.

千兵易得；一將難求
Chʻien1 ping1 i4 tê2; yi1 chiang1 nan2 chʻiu.2

1211

The martial magistrate draws his sword and puts down all rebellion.

武官提刀定干戈
Wu3 kuan1 tʻi2 tao1 ting4 kan1 ko.1

CHAPTER V.

YAMENS AND YAMEN-RUNNERS.

— 1212 —

As sheep drop into a tiger's jaw,
Cash drops into an underling's paw.

錢 落 差 手。羊 落 虎 口

Chʻien^{2} lo^{4} chʻai^{1} shou,^{3} yang^{2} lo^{4} ʻhu^{3} kʻou.^{3}

— 1213 —

A police-runner's actions are subject to fate.
Does he fear lest a shower should sprinkle his pate?

官 差 不 自 由。那 怕 雨 淋 頭

Kuan^{1} chʻai^{1} pu^{4} tzŭ^{4} yu,^{2} na^{3} pʻa^{4} yü^{3} lin^{4} tʻou.^{2}

— 1214 —

Though the yamen be small the law is the same.

衙 門 雖 小 法 度 一 例

Ya^{2} mên^{2} sui^{1} hsiao^{3} fa^{3} tu^{4} yi^{1} li.^{4}

— 1215 —

Yamens are deep as the sea, and their corruptions lofty as heaven.

衙 門 深 似 海。弊 病 大 如 天

Ya^{2} mên^{2} shên^{1} ssŭ^{4} ʻhai,^{3} pi^{4} ping^{4} ta^{4} ju^{2} tʻien.^{1}

— 1216 —

Official underlings see money as a fly sees blood.

公 人 見 錢 如 蒼 蠅 見 血

Kung^{1} jên^{2} chien^{4} chʻien^{2} ju^{2} tsʻang^{1} ying^{1} chien^{4} hsieh.^{3}

— 1217 —

Yamen-runners must be very brave who can deceive, frighten, defraud, and extort.

哄 嚇 騙 詐 差 膽 大

Hung^{3} hsia^{4} pʻien^{4} cha^{4} chʻai^{1} tan^{3} ta.^{4}

NOTE.—See next proverb and note.

— 1218 —

What paddy-fields and corn-fields belong to the yamen?

有麼衙門田。有麼衙門地

Yu^3 mo^1 ya^2 mên^2 t'ien,^{2} yu^3 mo^1 ya^2 mên^2 ti^4?

NOTE.—This is the yamên-runner's reply to the charge conveyed in the preceding proverb.

1219

However wrong the magistrate and his assistants may be, their messenger is not to be blamed.

官差吏差來人不差

Kuan^1 ch'a^1 li^4 ch'a^1 lai^2 jên^2 pu^4 ch'a.^{1}

1220

Those who follow mandarins eat mandarins' rice.

跟官人吃官人

Kên^1 kuan^1 jên^2 ch'ih^1 kuan^1 jên.^{2}

1221

Quickly pay your taxes, even should that empty your purse; then you will be most happy.

國課早完。卽囊橐無餘

Kuo^2 k'o^4 tsao^3 wan,^{2} chi^2 nang^2 t'o^4 wu^2 yü,^{2}

自得至樂

tzŭ^4 tê^2 chih^4 lê.^{4}

1222

An inmate of a yamen may easily acquire merit.

公門中好修行

Kung^1 mên^2 chung^1 'hao^3 hsiu^1 hsing.^{2}

SECTION XI.—ON MAN.

CHAPTER I.

MANKIND.

1223

Take a hundred men, and you
Will find all sorts and every hue.

人生一百。種種色色

Jên² shêng¹ yi¹ pai.³ chung⁴ chung⁴ sê⁴ sê.⁴

1224

Man resembles the stump of a tree;—
Completely dependent on clothing is he.

人是樹樁。全靠衣裳

Jên² shih⁴ shu⁴ chuang,¹ ch'ien² k'ao⁴ i¹ shang.¹

NOTE.—Here is an idea worthy of the author of *Sartor Resartus*.

1225

Men are one in heart, and their hearts one in principle.

人同此心。心同此理

Jên² t'ung² tz'ŭ³ hsin,¹ hsin¹ t'ung² tz'ŭ³ li.³

1226

Who but the sages are free from faults?

人非聖賢孰能無過

Jên² fei¹ shêng¹ hsien² shu² nêng² wu² kuo⁴?

1227

Of men there are good and bad, as of goods there are valuable and worthless.

人有好歹。貨有高低

Jên² yu³ 'hao³ tai,³ 'huo⁴ yu³ kao¹ ti.¹

1228

Man is the most intelligent of all creatures.

人 爲 萬 物 之 靈

Jên^2 wei^2 wan^4 wu^4 chih^1 ling.^{2}

1229

So long as no favour is sought, all men are equal; as the place is level where water flows not.

人 不 求 人 一 般 大

Jên^3 pu^4 chʻiu^2 jên^2 yi^1 pan^1 ta^4;

水 不 流 來 一 般 平

Shui^3 pu^4 liu^2 lai^2 yi^1 pan^1 pʻing.^{2}

1230

He who sits in, and they who carry, the sedan, are alike men.

坐 轎 子 也 是 人

Tso^4 chiao^4 tzŭ^3 yeh^3 shih^4 jên^2;

擡 轎 子 也 是 人

tʻai^2 chiao^4 tzŭ^3 yeh^3 shih^4 jên.^{2}

1231

All men have faces, as all trees have bark.

人 人 有 臉。樹 樹 有 皮

Jên^2 jên^2 yu^3 lien,^{3} shu^4 shu^4 yu^3 pʻi.^{2}

1232

Man is heaven and earth in miniature.

人 身 一 小 天 地

Jên^2 shên^1 yi^1 hsiao^3 tʻien^1 ti.^{4}

1233

When in their lives are men satisfied? The aged may steal a little leisure.

人 生 知 足 何 時 足

Jên^2 shêng^1 chih^1 tsu^2 ʻho^2 shih^2 tsu.^{2}

人 老 偸 閑 且 自 閑

Jên^2 lao^3 tʻou^1 hsien^2 chʻieh^3 shih^4 hsien.^{2}

CHAPTER II.

DIFFERENT KINDS OF MEN.

(1) AGED MEN.

1234

An aged man will always be,
The jewel his his family.
家有老是個寶
Chia¹ yu³ lao,³ shih⁴ ko⁴ pao.³

1235

Old trees become half empty at the core:
Old men see all things clearer than before.
樹老半心空 人老事事通
Shu⁴ lao³ pan⁴ hsin¹ k'ung¹: jên² lao³ shih⁴ shih⁴ t'ung.¹

1236

See the old man of eighty cutting dried reeds:
For each day he does not die, fuel he needs.
八十歲老砍黃蒿
Pa¹ shih² sui⁴ lao³ p'o⁴ 'huang² 'hao.¹
一日不死要柴燒
Yi¹ jih⁴ pu⁴ ssŭ³ yao⁴ ch'ai² shao.¹

1237

There is nothing like newness in clothes; nothing like age in man.
衣莫若新。人莫若故
I¹ mo⁴ jo⁴ hsin¹; jên² mo⁴ jo⁴ ku.⁴

1238

Age lacks kindness, as dry weather dew.
人老無人情。天乾無露水
Jên² lao³ wu² jên² ch'ing,² t'ien¹ kan¹ wu² lu⁴ shui.³

1239

Aged men are virtuous.

年高有德
Nien¹ kao¹ yu³ tê.²

1240

Better die ten years sooner, than live those years in poverty.

願短十年壽。不可老來貧
Yüan⁴ tuan³ shih² nien² shou,⁴ pu⁴ k'o² lao³ lai² p'ing.³

1241

An old man ready to depart. *Lit.:* The sun descending the mountain sides.

下山坡日頭
Hsia⁴ shan¹ p'o¹ jih⁴ t'ou.².

1242

White hairs don't all disappear with the old men, for we see them again on young men's heads.

白髮不隨老人去
Pai² fa³ pu⁴ sui² lao³ jên² ch'ü,⁴
看看又上少年頭
k'an⁴ k'an⁴ yu⁴ shang³ shao³ nien² t'ou.²

1243

I won't laugh at another for having grown old; for that will assuredly happen to me.

莫笑他人老。終須還到我
Mo⁴ hsiao⁴ t'a¹ jên² lao³; chung¹ hsü¹ 'huan² tao⁴ wo.³

1244

We remember riding on bamboos as boys, and lo! we are white with age.

記得少年騎竹馬
Chi⁴ tê² shao³ nien² ch'i² chu² ma,³
看看又是白頭翁
k'an⁴ k'an⁴ yu⁴ shih⁴ pai² t'ou² wêng.¹

1245

On earth impartial justice is with the aged; they will not show mercy to noble offenders.

公道世間惟白髮
Kung^{1} tao^{4} shih^{4} chien^{1} wei^{2} pai^{2} fa^{3};
貴人頭上不曾饒
kuei^{4} jên^{2} t'ou^{2} shang^{4} pu^{4} tsêng^{2} jao.^{2}

1246

The older ginger and cinnamon are, the more pungent their flavour.

薑桂之性愈老愈辣
Chiang^{1} kuei^{1} chih^{1} hsing^{4} yü^{4} lao^{3} yü^{4} la.^{4}

1247

If deferential to experienced old men, in perplexity you can rely on them.

屈志老成急則可相倚
Ch'ü^{1} chih^{4} lao^{3} ch'êng,^{2} chi^{2} tsê^{2} k'o^{3} hsiang^{1} i.^{3}

1248

At seventy a man is a candle in the wind.

七十風前燭
Ch'i^{1} shih^{2} fêng^{1} ch'ien^{2} chu.^{2}

1249

At eighty a man is hoar-frost on the tiles.

八十瓦上霜
Pa^{1} shih^{2} wa^{1} shang^{4} shuang.^{1}

1250

He who won't take an old man's advice, will one day become a beggar.

不信老人言。乞兒有得做
Pu^{4} hsin^{4} lao^{3} jên^{2} yen,^{2} ch'i^{3} êrh^{2} yu^{3} tê^{2} tso.^{4}

1251

He must err grievously, who won't listen to aged men.

不聽老人言。必做心慌事
Pu^{4} t'in^{1} lao^{3} jên^{2} yen,^{2} pi^{4} tso^{4} hsin^{1} huang^{3} shih.^{4}

(2) BAD MEN.

1252

A hook attached to a ring:
To him let nobody cling.

鉤打連環。沒得人攙

Kou¹ ta³ lien² 'huan²: mu² te² jên² ch'an.²

NOTE.—This is a specimen also of the innuendo, or as the Chinese call it 歇後語 *hsieh 'hou yü.* Only the first four words are ever spoken; the last four being always understood. The sense of this proverb is—Let nobody be deceived by him; he is one of the lot.

1253

He who dare risk being made a mangled corse,
May drag an emperor down from his horse.

捨得一身剮

Shê³ tê² yi¹ shên¹ kua,³

皇帝老子挪下馬

'Huang² ti⁴ lao³ tzŭ³ lo² hsia⁴ ma.³

1254

His conduct is cruel, and he fights;
In cursing and swearing he delights.

行兇打架。開口就駡

Hsing² hsiung¹ ta³ chia⁴ k'ai¹ k'ou³ chiu⁴ ma.⁴

1255

A barefaced wight, thinks everything right.

臉皃一皮。百事大吉

Lien³ êrh² yi¹ p'i,² pai³ shih⁴ ta⁴ chi.²

1256

Whose teeth are white and visage yellow,
Is an opium-smoking fellow.

面黃牙齒白。必定鴉片客

Mien⁴ 'huang² ya² ch'ih³ po,² pi⁴ ting⁴ ya¹ p'ien⁴ k'o.⁴

1257

Where he has trodden no grass will grow.

走了路不生草
Tsou^4 liao^3 lu^4 pu^4 shêng^1 tsʻao.^{3}

1258

A rogue is soft as cotton; a fool hard as iron.

光棍軟如綿癡漢硬似鐵
Kuang^1 kun^4 yuan^3 ju^2 mien^2; chʻih^2 ʻhan^4 ying^4 ssŭ^4 tʻieh.^{3}

1259

A rogue fears a simpleton; and a simpleton fears importunity.

光棍怕眼子眼子怕綿纏
Kuang^1 kun^4 pʻa^4 yen^3 tzŭ^3; yen^3 tzŭ^3 pʻa^4 mien^2 chʻan.^{2}

NOTE.—The simpleton may spoil a rogue's plan; and importunity is sure to result in the simpleton's being taken in.

1260

One rat may spoil the nest.

一個老鼠打壞一窠洞
Yi^1 ko^4 lao^3 shu^3 ta^3 ʻhuai^4 yi^1 chʻao^2 tung.^{4}

1261

His heart is not upright whose eye looks askance.

眼斜心不正
Yen^3 hsieh^2 hsin^1 pu^4 chêng^4

1262

Amongst bullies there is always one more overbearing than the rest; and bad men must be by bad men ground down.

强中更有强中手
Chʻiang^2 chung^1 kên^1 yu^3 chʻiang^2 chung^1 shou^3;
惡人須用惡人磨
O^4 jên^2 hsü^1 yung^4 o^4 jên^2 mo.^{2}

1263

A tribe of foxes and dogs.

狐羣狗黨
ʻHu^2 chʻün^2 kou^3 tang.^{3}

1264

A vicious blackguard. *Lit.:* One with a black heart and a rotten liver.

黑 心 爛 肝

ʻHei^1 hsin^1 lan^4 kan.^{1}

1265

A shameless man is ready for anything.

人無廉恥。百事可爲

Jên^2 wu^2 lien^2 chʻih,^{3} pai^3 shih^4 kʻo^3 wei.^{2}

1266

A lazy good-for-nothing. *Lit.:* One who goes slipshod in old shoes.

趿 半 頭 鞋

Sa^1 pan^4 tʻou^2 hsieh.^{2}

1267

Bad men are hated by all. *Lit.:* When a rat crosses the street, every one cries "Hit him."

過 街 老 鼠 齊 吽 打

Kuo^4 chieh^1 lao^3 shu^3 chʻi^2 chiao^4 ta.^{3}

1268

An untruthful man is iron without steel; an untruthful woman is rotten grass and tangled hemp.

男 兒 無 信 鈍 鐵 無 鋼

Nan^2 êrh^2 wu^2 hsin^4 tun^4 tʻieh^3 wu^2 kang^1:

女 兒 無 信 爛 草 麻 瓤

nü^2 êrh^2 wu^2 hsin^4 lan^4 tsʻao^3 ma^2 jang.^{2}

1269

A lying machine.

扯 謊 架 子

Chʻê^3 ʻhuang^3 chia^4 tzŭ.^{3}

1270

A lying machine cannot enter a city gate.

扯 謊 架 子 進 不 得 城 門

Chʻê^3 ʻhuang^3 chia^4 tzŭ^3 chin^4 pu^4 tê^2 chʻêng^2 mên.^{2}

1271

The skin of his face is as thick as a city wall.

臉 有 城 牆 厚

Lien^3 yu^3 chʻêng^4 chʻiang^2 ʻhou.^{4}

1272

A bad man will not confront a good man.

邪不敵正

Hsieh^{2} pu^{4} ti^{2} chêng.^{4}

Union of bad men. *Lit.* : Dry fuel rears a blazing fire.

乾柴傍烈火

Kan^{1} chʻai^{2} pʻang^{2} lieh^{4} ʻhuo.^{3}

1273

The disobedient provoke many stripes.

降人多討打

Chiang^{4} jên^{2} to^{1} tʻao^{3} ta.^{3}

1274

You've put your bowels out of shape by swallowing a carrying-pole.

吃了匾担横了腸子

Chʻih^{1} liao^{3} pien^{3} tan^{1} ʻhêng^{4} liao^{3} chʻang^{2} tzŭ.^{3}

NOTE.—This is said to one who has degenerated into a violent and cruel character.

(3) CLEVER MEN.

1275

Wiser than the emperor none can ever be;
Shrewder than the premier you can never be.

聰明莫過於帝王
Ts'ung[1] ming[2] mo[4] kuo[4] yü[1] ti[4] wang:[2]

伶俐莫過於宰相
Ling[2] li[4] mo[4] kuo[4] yü[1] tsai[4] hsiang.[1]

1276

In the wise and strong,
There is nothing wrong.

精明强幹。絲毫不亂
Ching[1] ming[2] ch'iang[2] kan,[2] ssŭ[1] 'hao[2] pu[4] lan.[4]

1277

Half your talents are natural; the other half acquired.

生成一半。學成一半
Shêng[1] ch'êng[2] yi[1] pan[4]; hsiao[3] ch'êng[2] yi[1] pan.[4]

1278

A word is enough to a clever man.

是明白人說得就知
Shih[4] ming[2] pai[2] jên[2] shuo[1] tê[2] chiu[4] chih.[1]

1279

Clever men are often the servants of fools.

聰明人是糊塗人的用人
Ts'ung[1] ming[2] jên[2] shih[4] 'hu[2] t'u[2] jên[2] ti[1] yung[4] jên.[2]

1280

A clever man needs few words; as a drum but to be lightly beaten.

明人不用細講
Ming[2] jên[2] pu[4] yung[4] hsi[4] chiang.[3]

響鼓不用重搥
hsiang[3] ku[3] pu[4] yung[4] chung[4] ch'iu.[2]

1281

Three fools equal one clever man; three clever men equal one District magistrate.

三 個 愚 人 當 個 明 人
San1 ko4 yü2 jên2 tang1 ko4 ming2 jên;2
三 個 明 人 當 個 知 縣
san1 ko4 ming2 jên2 tang1 ko4 chih1 hsien.4

1282

Clever for a lifetime; foolish for a moment.

聰 明 一 生。糊 塗 一 時
Tsʻung1 ming2 yi1 shêng1; ʻhu2 tʻu2 yi1 shih.2

1283

A wise man can fill a thousand mouths; a fool can only protect himself.

有 智 養 千 口。無 智 保 一 人
Yu3 chih4 yang3 chʻien1 kʻou3; wu2 chih4 pao3 yi1 jên.2

1284

The wise are minished by half; and self-scrutinizing men are all gone.

知 者 減 半。省 者 全 無
Chih1 chê2 chien3 pan4; hsing3 chê2 chʻien2 wu.2

1285

The clever have more, the stupid less, than enough.

巧 者 有 餘。拙 者 不 足
Chʻiao3 chê2 yu3 yü;2 chueh2 chê2 pu4 tsu.2

1286

A wise man needs three assistants.

好 漢 要 三 個 帮 手
ʻHao3 ʻhan4 yao4 san1 ko4 pang1 shou.3

1287

The clever man sees, at a nod of the head.

明 人 點 頭 就 知
Ming2 jên2 tien3 tʻou2 chiu4 chih.1

1288

Clever men are sometimes the dupes of their own cleverness.

聰明反被聰明悞
Tsʻung^1 ming^2 fan^3 pei^4 tsʻung^1 ming^2 wu.^{4}

1290

Dust never stains a highly-polished mirror; nor do licentious vices generate in a mind enlightened with wisdom.

鏡明則塵埃不染
Ching^4 ming^2 tsê^2 chʻên^2 ai^2 pu^4 jan^3;
智明則邪惡不生
chih^4 ming^2 tsê^2 hsieh^2 o^4 pu^4 shêng.^{1}

1291

Let him do a thing once, and he will surpass all others.

凡事閱歷過一回
Fan^2 shih^4 yüeh^4 li^4 kuo^4 yi^1 ʻhui,^{2}
見識總不同人
chien^4 shih^4 tsung^3 pu^4 tʻung^2 jên.^{2}

1292

Enlightened men do no dark deeds.

明人不作暗事
Ming^2 jên^2 pu^4 tso^4 an^4 shih.^{4}

1293

A very cunning man. *Lit.:* A murex wearing a pagoda has one point above another.

螺螄頂寶塔尖過頂
Lo^2 shih^1 ting^3 pao^3 tʻa^3 chien^1 kuo^4 ting.^{3}

1294

A good drum does not require hard striking.

好鼓不用勤搥打
Hao^3 ku^3 pu^4 yung^4 chʻin^2 chʻui^2 ta.^{3}

1295

He has met with his match. *Lit.:* The chess-player has met with a sturdy opponent; the general has encountered a worthy foe.

碁 逢 敵 手。將 遇 良 材
Chʻi^2 fêng^2 ti^2 shou^3; chiang^1 yü^4 liang^2 tsʻai.^{2}

—— 1296 ——

Clever men pronounce sentence on themselves.

明 人 自 斷
Ming^2 jên^2 tzŭ^4 tuan.^{4}

---

(4) CONCEITED MEN,

—— 1297 ——

He is little like men, and less like devils.

三 分 不 像 人。七 分 不 像 鬼
San^1 fên^1 pu^4 hsiang^4 jên,^{2} chʻi^1 fên^1 pu^4 hsiang^4 kuei.^{3}

Note.—Said in contempt of a proud pretentious knave.

—— 1298 ——

A self-conceited bad man must have many errors.

乖 僻 自 是。悔 悞 必 多
Kuai^1 pʻi^1 tzŭ^4 shih,^{4} ʻhui^3 wu^4 pi^4 to.^{1}

—— 1299 ——

His eye beholds an empty world; within its range no man appears.

目 空 一 世。眼 內 無 人
Mu^4 kʻung^1 yi^1 shih^4; yen^3 nei^4 wu^2 jên.^{2}

—— 1300 ——

He looks on others as nonentities.

旁 若 無 人
Pʻang^2 jo^4 wu^2 jên.^{2}

—— 1301 ——

Very fond of bragging.

好 耍 牌 子
ʻHao^4 shua^2 pʻai^2 tzŭ.^{3}

諺語叢話

1302

Its a bragging rat that climbs the steelyards.

老鼠扒秤鈎自稱自

Lao³ shu³ pa¹ ch'êng³ kou¹ tzŭ⁴ ch'êng¹ tzŭ.⁴

1303

One fond of wearing a lofty hat.

愛戴高帽子

Ai⁴ tai⁴ kao¹ mao⁴ tzŭ.³

1304

The self-conceited come to grief; the boastful are but fools.

自滿者敗。自矜者愚

Tzŭ⁴ man³ chê² pai⁴; tzŭ⁴ ching¹ chê² yü.²

1305

A boastful fellow. *Lit.:* One fond of wearing an eel basket.

愛戴鱔魚簍子

Ai⁴ tai⁴ shan⁴ yü² lou³ tzŭ.³

1306

In his eye he has no superiors.

目無長上

Mu⁴ wu² chang³ shang.⁴

1307

Proud talk. *Lit.:* When a toad gapes, what a mouth! and what breath!

癩蝦蟆打呵欠大口大氣

Lai⁴ hsia¹ ma¹ ta³ o¹ ch'ien⁴ ta⁴ k'ou³ ta⁴ ch'i⁴!

1308

The humble receive advantage; the self-sufficient provoke loss.

謙受益。滿招損

Ch'ien¹ shou⁴ i⁴; man³ chao¹ sun.³

1309

Heaven, Earth, Men and Spirits, all love the humble, not the proud; to the humble is given happiness, to the proud calamity.

天地人神俱喜謙不喜盈
T'ien^1 ti^4 jên^2 shên^2 chü^4 hsi^3 ch'ien^1 pu^4 hsi^3 ying^2:
謙者賜之福盈者賜之禍
ch'ien^1 chê^2 tz'ŭ^4 chih^1 fu,^{2} ying^2 chê^2 tz'ŭ^4 chih^1 'huo.^{4}

NOTE.—"Though the Lord be high, yet hath he respect unto the lowly: but the proud he knoweth afar off." Ps. 138: 6.

1310

Proud men are disgusting. *Lit.:* The characters for 'self' and 'great' compose the character for 'stinking'.

自大是個臭字
Tzŭ^4 ta^4 shih^4 ko^4 ch'ou^4 tzŭ.^{4}

1311

A lofty lamp-post lights what is distant, not what is near.

一丈八尺高的燈臺
Yi^1 chang^4 pa^1 ch'ih^3 kao^1 ti^1 têng^1 t'ai,^{2}
照遠不照近
chao^4 yuan^3 pu^4 chao^4 chin.^{4}

NOTE.—This is said of one blind to his own, but not to the faults of other people.

1312

The humble reap advantage; the haughty meet misfortune.

自損者益。自益者殃
Tzŭ^4 sun^3 chê^2 i^2; tzŭ^4 i^2 chê^2 yang.^{1}

諺語叢話

(5) DEFORMED MEN.

1313

From a dwarfish dwarf you'll hear,
Nothing but the strange and queer.

矮子矮。一肚怪

Ai³ tzŭ³ ai,³ yi¹ tu³ kuai.⁴

1314

To pry into what's said the deaf aro too prone;
The dumb cannot bear to let talking alone.

聾子愛打剎。啞叭愛說話

Lung² tzŭ³ ai⁴ ta³ ch'a⁴; ya³ pa¹ ai⁴ shuo¹ 'hua.⁴

1315

The thoughts of the blind are like a knife.

瞎子心思像一把刀

Hsia² tzŭ³ hsin¹ ssŭ¹ hsiang⁴ yi¹ pa³ tao.¹

1316

The blind get led, and the lame supported.

瞎子有人牽。跛子有人扶

Hsia² tzŭ³ yu³ jên² ch'ien,¹ p'o³ tzŭ³ yu³ jên² fu.²

1317

When one blind man leads several blind men, before long all will fall into a fire pit.

一盲引衆盲。相將入火坑

Yi¹ mang² yin³ chung⁴ mang,² hsiang¹ chiang¹ ju⁴ 'huo³ k'êng.¹

1318

When the blind lead the blind, they will certainly fall into a ditch.

瞎子攙扶瞎子

Hsia² tzŭ³ ch'an¹ fu² hsia² tzŭ,³

未必不掉下坑處

wei⁴ pi⁴ pu⁴ tiao⁴ hsia⁴ k'êng¹ ch'u.⁴

NOTE.—"If the blind lead the blind, both shall fall into the ditch." Matt. 15: 14.

1319

The blind are quick at hearing, the deaf are quick at sight.

瞽者善聽。聾者善視

Ku[3] chê[2] shan[4] t'ing,[1] lung[2] chê[2] shan[4] shih.[4]

1320

Dumb men are fond of making signs.

啞叭好做顧點

Ya[3] pa[1] 'hao[4] tso[4] ku[4] tien.[3]

1321

When a dumb man sees his mother, he wants to speak but can't.

啞叭見娘有話說不出

Ya[3] pa[1] chien[4] niang[2] yu[3] 'hua[4] shuo[1] pu[4] ch'u.[1]

1322

Couldn't *Wu Ta Lang*, get a living?

武大郎不過日子

Wu[3] Ta[4] Lang[2] pu[4] kuo[4] jih[4] tzŭ[3]?

NOTE.—*Wu Ta-lang*, a notorious dwarf of the *Sung* dynasty, was less than the least of dwarfs, yet seems to have made his way in the world. Hence the proverb, used by dwarfs when repelling banter.

諺語叢話

(6) EXCITABLE AND ANXIOUS MEN.

1323

Men in a flurry from morning to night,
Seldom are seen to continue all right.

朝也忙暮也忙

Chao[1] yeh[3] mang[2] mu[4] yeh[3] mang.[2]

那見忙人得久長

Na[3] chien[4] mang[2] jên[2] tê[2] chiu[3] chʻang.[2]

1324

An excitable, restless man. *Lit.:* One for whom no *ti-chʻi* was burnt in his ante-natal life.

前世未燒地契

Chʻien[2] shih[4] wei[4] shao[1] ti[4] chʻi.[4]

NOTE.—The *ti-chʻi* is the deed of purchase of the grave written for the dead, and burnt at his funeral by a son or relative. It is supposed that one of the three souls (魂) of the departed takes this document to *Yen Wang* (閻王), or Pluto, for his seal; thereupon the grave is secured against violation, and the soul (魂) which is supposed to reside therein, secured in peaceful possession. That such a paper should not have been burnt at the close of a former life, is thought sufficient to account for any amount of giddiness and restlesness, any person so neglected may display in this.

1325

Flurried men lack wisdom.

忙人無智

Mang[2] jên[2] wu[2] chih.[4]

1326

He has the head of a cat, the eyes of a rat.

貓頭鼠眼

Mao[1] tʻou[2] shu[3] yen.[3]

1327

An unsettled person. *Lit.:* One who now wishes to be off to Nankin to buy horses, and anon to Peking to buy office.

想到南京買馬

Hsiang[3] tao[4] Nan[2] ching[1] mai[3] ma,[3]

又想北京買官

yu[4] hsiang[3] Pei[3] ching[1] mai[3] kuan.[1]

1328

He cannot wait till his cake gets heated.

火裡燒把等不得熱

'Huo^3 li^3 shao^1 pa^1 têng^3 pu^4 tê^2 shu.^{2}

1329

He may sit in a tub of cold water, and it will emit no steam.

坐在冷水盆裡不起氣

Tso^4 tsai^4 lêng^3 shui^4 p'ên^2 li^3 pu^4 ch'i^3 ch'i.^{4}

Note.—Said of a sluggish individual; one *not* excitable.

1330

Anxious as the men of *Ch'i* who feared the heavens might fall.

心多過慮。如杞人憂天

Hsin^1 to^1 kuo^4 lü,^{4} ju^2 Ch'i^3 jên^2 yu^1 t'ien.^{1}

1331

An anxious individual. *Lit.:* One who is afraid that his bones should decay before he is dead.

人還未有死。怕爛了骨頭

Jên^2 'huan^2 wei^4 yu^3 ssŭ,^{3} p'a^4 lan^4 liao^3 ku^3 t'ou.^{2}

1332

The same. *Lit.:* One who is afraid that his eyes should decay before he is dead.

人未死。怕先爛眼睛

Jên^2 wei^4 ssŭ,^{3} p'a^4 hsien^1 lan^4 yen^3 ching.^{1}

1333

One who fears the falling leaves will break his head.

樹葉掉了怕打破頭

Shu^4 yeh^4 tiao^4 liao^3 p'a^4 ta^3 p'o^4 t'ou.^{2}

1334

One who fears the falling dust will crack his skull.

揚塵弔下來。怕打破腦殼

Yang^2 ch'ên^2 tiao^4 hsia^4 lai,^{2} p'a^4 ta^3 p'o^4 nao^3 k'o.^{1}

1335

Early risers are in jolly spirits; anxious thinkers have enfeebled health.

早起精神爽。思多血氣衰

Tsao^3 chʻi^3 ching^1 shên^2 shuang^1; ssŭ^1 to^1 hsieh^3 chʻi^4 shuai.^{1}

(7) GOOD MEN.

1336

One good man represses a hundred bad ones.

一正壓百邪

Yi^1 chêng^4 ya^1 pai^3 hsieh.^{2}

1337

Good men suffer much.

好人多磨難

ʻHao^3 jên^2 to^1 mo^2 nan.^{2}

1338

Virtuous men are a kingdom's treasure.

賢爲國家之寶

Hsien^2 wei^2 kuo^2 chia^1 chih^1 pao.^{3}

1339

There are straight trees on the mountains, but no straight men in the world.

山中有直樹。世上無直人

Shan^1 chung^1 yu^3 chih^2 shu,^{4} shih^4 shang^4 wu^2 chih^2 jên.^{2}

1340

Good men get cheated; as good horses get ridden.

人善被人欺馬善被人騎

Jên^2 shan^4 pei^4 jên^2 chʻi,^{1} ma^3 shan^4 pei^4 jên^2 chʻi.^{2}

1341

Pretty things and good men are difficult to make.

好看難做。好漢難做

ʻHao^3 kʻan^4 nan^2 tso,^{4} ʻhao^3 ʻhan^4 nan^2 tso.^{4}

1342

Men join themselves to the good, but separate from the bad.

好人相逢。惡人相離

Hao³ jên² hsiang¹ fêng,² o⁴ jên² hsiang¹ li.²

1343

He is a good fellow who can endure wrong.

吃得虧是好漢

Ch'ih¹ tê² k'uei¹ shih⁴ 'hao³ 'han.⁴

1344

A good fellow will stick to his bargain.

好漢做事好漢當

'Hao³ 'han⁴ tso⁴ shih⁴ 'hao³ 'han⁴ tang.¹

1345

True gold fears no fire.

眞金不怕火

Chên¹ chin¹ pu⁴ p'a⁴ 'huo.³

1346

An honest man. *Lit.:* One who tells true fortunes.

算老實命的人

Suan⁴ lao³ shih² ming⁴ ti¹ jên.²

1347

The same. *Lit.:* An uncoloured man.

本色人

Pên³ sê⁴ jên.²

1348

Good men are one in a hundred.

世上好人百中選一

Shih⁴ shang⁴ 'hao³ jên² pai³ chung¹ hsien³ yi.¹

1349

There are two good men—one dead, the other unborn.

有兩好人。一个死了一个未生

Yu³ liang² 'hao³ jên,²—yi¹ ko⁴ ssŭ³ liao,³ yi¹ ko⁴ wei⁴ shêng.¹

1350

An innocent man fears nothing. *Lit.*: He who is free from fever fears not to eat water-melons.

心裡無冷病。那怕吃西瓜.

Hsin¹ ni³ wu² lêng³ ping,⁴ na³ pʻa⁴ chʻih¹ hsi¹ kua.¹

1351

His goodness will appear by and by. *Lit.*: As the water recedes the stones appear.

水退石出

Shui³ tʻui⁴ shih² chʻu.¹

1352

Filial, disinterested, and upright men, are honored by all.

孝廉方正。人人奉敬

Hsiao⁴ lien² fang¹ chêng,⁴ jên² jên² fêng⁴ ching.⁴

1353

He is one who pursues a pig in a passage, going and coming in a straight course.

巷裡趕猪。直來直去

Hsiang⁴ li³ kan² chu,¹ chih² lai² chih² chʻü.⁴

1354

His words command general assent whose conduct is upright and unwavering.

行得正。坐得穩。出言人皆準

Hsing² tê² chêng,⁴ tso⁴ tê² wên,³ chʻu¹ yen² jên² chieh¹ chun³.

1355

Good men are not to be found amongst bad ones. *Lit.*: Out of an indigo vat you can't draw white calico.

靛缸裡拉不出白布來

Tien⁴ kang¹ li³ la¹ pu⁴ chʻu¹ pai² pu⁴ lai.²

(8) HYPOCRITES.

1356

The man who pretends to be deaf and dumb,
May have no truth, but of lies will have some.

裝聾作啞。無眞有假

Chuang^1 lung^2 tso^4 ya,^{3} wu^2 chên^1 yu^3 chia.^{3}

1357

When a beggar is out o'nights, it is all a pretence of being busy.

告花子走夜路。都是假忙

Kao^4 ʻhua^1 tzŭ^3 tsou^4 yeh^4 lu,^{4} tu^1 shih^4 chia^3 mang.^{2}

1358

He is a mock sportsman who slings a dead rat in his girdle.

腰裡撇一個死老鼠假充打獵的

Yao^1 li^3 pʻieh^1 yi^1 ko^4 ssŭ^3 lao^3 shu,^{3} chia^3 chʻung^1 ta^3 lieh^4 ti.^{1}

1359

His mouth is sweet as honey; his posteriors biting as ginger.

嘴裡甜如蜜。屁股辣似薑

Tsui^3 li^3 tʻien^2 ju^2 mi^4; pʻi^4 ku^3 la^4 ssŭ^4 chiang.^{1}

1360

In the East he eats dog's head, in the West sheep's head.

東邊吃狗頭。西邊吃羊頭

Tung^1 pien^1 chʻih^1 kou^3 tʻou,^{2} hsi^1 pien^1 chʻih^1 yang^2 tʻou.^{2}

1361

Superior man before folk; mean man in secret.

明爲君子。暗爲小人

Ming^2 wei^2 chün^1 tzŭ,^{3} an^4 wei^2 hsiao^3 jên.^{2}

1362

Saint outside, devil inside. *Lit.*: To have the mouth full of Benevolence, Righteousness, Reason, and Virtue; but to be in heart thief or whore.

一口仁義道德

Yi¹ k'ou³ jên² i⁴ tao⁴ tê²;

肚裡男盜女娼

tu³ li³ nan² tao⁴ nü² ch'ang.¹

1363

When you see a cold-eyed man laugh all over his face, he is secretly hiding a murderous sword in his heart.

見人冷眼笑一面

Chien⁴ jên² lêng³ yen³ hsiao⁴ yi¹ mien,⁴

心中暗藏殺人刀

hsin¹ chung¹ an⁴ ts'ang² sha¹ jên² tao.¹

1364

A laughing *Ts'ao-Ts'ao.*

笑面孔曹操

Hsiao⁴ mien⁴ k'ung³ Ts'ao² Ts'ao.¹

NOTE.—A pleasant but crafty fellow, like *Ts'ao Ts'ao* of *San-kuo* notoriety.

1365

A false superior man; but a true mean man.

僞君子眞小人

Wei⁴ chün¹ tzŭ³ chên¹ hsiao³ jên.²

1366

Outside he wears a sheep's skin, inside he hides a wolf's heart.

外披羊皮。內藏狼心

Wai⁴ p'i¹ yang² p'i,² nei⁴ ts'ang² lang² hsin.¹

NOTE.—"Beware of false prophets, which come to you in sheep's clothing, but inwardly they are ravening wolves." Matt. 7 : 15.

1367

His mouth is sweet as honey; his heart as venomous as a snake.

口裏甜如蜜。心裏毒似蛇

K'ou³ li³ t'ien² ju² mi⁴; hsin¹ li³ tu² ssŭ⁴ shê.²

1368

One mouth with two tongues.

一嘴兩舌頭

Yi^{1} tsui^{3} liang^{3} shê^{2} tʻou.^{2}

1369

A fox assuming a tiger's terror.

狐假虎威

ʻHu^{2} chia^{3} ʻhu^{3} wei.^{1}

1670

Sweet-melon lipped ; bitter-melon hearted.

甜瓜兒嘴。苦瓜兒心

Tʻien^{2} kua^{1} êrh^{2} tsui^{3} ; kʻu^{3} kua^{1} êrh^{2} hsin.^{1}

1371

He has the mouth of a Buddha, the heart of a snake.

佛口蛇心

Fu^{2} kʻou^{3} shê^{2} hsin.^{1}

1372

Like a lamp-stand, he lights others but not himself.

屬燈臺的。照別人。不照自己

Shu^{3} têng^{1} tʻai^{2} ti,^{1} chao^{4} pieh^{2} jên,^{2} pu^{4} chao^{4} tzŭ^{4} chi.^{3}

(9) RICH AND POOR MEN. (SEE SECTION ON WEALTH.)

(10) STUPID MEN.

1373

Whilst the dolt is allowed to dine,
The cunning knave is left to pine.

癡癡呆呆討個飽

Chʻih^{2} chʻih^{2} tai^{1} tai^{1} tʻao^{3} ko^{4} pao,^{3}

刁刁掘掘餓得好

Tiao^{1} tiao^{1} chüeh^{2} chüeh^{2} o^{4} tê^{2} ʻhao.^{3}

1374

He, like a camel in his might,
Prefers the heavy to the light.

他是個駱駝形
Tʻa^1 shih^4 ko^4 lo^4 tʻo^2 hsing,^{2}
托重不托輕
tʻo^1 chung^4 pu^4 tʻo^1 chʻing.^{1}

1375

Of wit and wisdom entirely free,
Dog to another man he must be.

才智無有。爲人走狗
Tsʻai^1 chih^4 wu^2 yu,^{3} wei^2 jên^2 tsou^4 kou.^{3}

1376

Stupid fool! he lets one of his water-buckets fall,
And rushes on as if nothing had happened at all.

懵裏懵懂挑擔水桶
Mêng^1 li^3 mêng^1 tung^3 tʻiao^1 tan^1 shui^3 tʻung,^{3}
落了一隻又往前踵
Lo^4 liao^3 yi^1 chih^1 yu^4 wang^3 chʻien^2 chung.^{3}

1377

You're thick enough for a porridge.

糊塗成羹
ʻHu^2 tʻu^2 chʻêng^2 kêng.^{1}

1378

An ignoramus. *Lit.*: You cannot blow up a fire through a solid stick.

桿麪棍吹火一竅不通
Kan^2 mien^4 kun^4 chʻui^1 ʻhuo^3 yi^1 chʻiao^4 pu^4 tʻung.^{1}

1379

Bore as one will, the pricker will not enter.

使鑽子鑽不動
Shih^3 tsuan^1 tzŭ^3 tsuan^1 pu^4 tung.^{4}

NOTE.—This is said to one intensely stupid. Nothing can be got into him.

1380

A stupid bundle of dregs.

糊塗一包渣
ʻHu^2 tu^2 yi^1 pao^1 cha.^{1}

1381

An ox-leather lantern.

牛皮的燈籠

Niu[2] p'i[2] ti[1] têng[1] lung.[2]

1382

A wooden man.

木頭人

Mu[4] t'ou[2] jên.[2]

1383

A fool. *Lit.:* One hundred, sixty, and ninety.

百六九

Pai[3] lu[4] chiu.[3]

1384

The same. *Lit.:* Three eighty-threes.

三个八十三

San[1] ko[4] pa[1] shih[2] san.[1]

1385

The same. *Lit.:* Two hundred and fifty.

二百五

Erh[4] pai[3] wu.[3]

1386

The same. *Lit.:* The fourth of a thousand cash.

一串錢四開

Yi[1] ch'uan[4] ch'ien[2] ssŭ[4] k'ai.[1]

1387

Black as pitch and ink.

烏漆墨黑

Wu[1] ch'i[1] mo[4] 'hei.[1]

NOTE.—This is said as well of a dark night, as of a dark mind.

1388

Having eyes he yet cannot recognize gold inlaid with jewels.

有眼不識金鑲玉

Yu[3] yen[3] pu[4] shih[4] chin[1] hsiang[1] yü.[4]

1389

One who has not yet opened his eyes.

沒有開過眼空來的

Mu[2] yu[3] k'ai[1] kuo[4] yen[3] k'ung[3] lai[2] ti.[1]

NOTE.—Said of a stupid, raw fellow, who wonders at every thing he sees.

1390

One who looks brighter then he is. *Lit.:* A bright-eyed blind man.

光眼瞎子

Kuang[1] yen[3] hsia[2] tzŭ.[3]

1391

One who mistakes a teapot for a chamber-pot.

把茶壺當夜壺

Pa[3] ch'a[2] 'hu[2] tang[4] yeh[4] 'hu.[2]

1392

Who sits in a well to observe the sky does not see very much.

坐井觀天所見不大

Tso[4] ching[3] kuan[1] t'ien[1] so[3] chien[4] pu[4] ta.[4]

NOTE.—Said of an illiterate ignorant man, whose sphere of observation is naturally limited.

1393

He won't buy soy with money for vinegar.

打醋的錢不買醬油

Ta[3] ts'u[4] ti[1] ch'ien[2] pu[4] mai[3] chiang[4] yu.[2]

NOTE.—Said of one who is so stupid as not to see that it does not matter with which particular money he buys anything, so long as he buys it at all.

1394

Fools are unequal to great undertakings. *Lit.:* You cannot serve dog's flesh at a banquet.

狗肉上不得正席

Kou[3] jou[4] shang[3] pu[4] tê[2] chêng[4] hsi.[2]

1395

A good-for-nothing. *Lit.:* He can make nothing out, either in literature or soldiery.

習文不成。習武不就

Hsi[2] wên[2] pu[4] ch'êng,[2] hsi[2] wu[3] pu[4] chiu.[4]

1396

The more stupid the more happy.

越不聰明反快活

Yüeh^4 pu^4 tsʻung^1 ming^2 fan^3 kʻuai^4 ʻhuo.^{2}

1397

If water be too clear it will contain no fish; and if a man be too parsimonious he will not be wise.

水太清則無魚

Shui^3 tʻai^4 chʻing^1 tsê^2 wu^2 yü,^{2}

人太緊則無智

jên^2 tʻai^4 chin^3 tsê^2 wu^2 chih.^{4}

1398

A goose. *Lit.:* One who meeting a bonze cries out 'Brother-in-law.'

逢到和尙喊姊夫

Fêng^2 tao^4 ʻho^2 shang^4 ʻhan^3 chieh^3 fu.^{1}

1399

A merciful man is not stupid; a stupid man cannot show mercy.

饒人不是癡漢

Jao^2 jên^2 pu^4 shih^4 chʻih^2 ʻhan^4;

癡漢不會饒人

chʻih^2 ʻhan^4 pu^4 ʻhui^4 jao^2 jên.^{2}

1400

One unable to distinguish between right and wrong. *Lit.:* A fleshy, pupil-less eye.

肉眼無珠

Jou^4 yen^3 wu^2 chu.^{1}

(11) SUPERIOR AND MEAN MEN.

1401

The friendship of superior men is like water thin and pure;
Without constant interchange of feasts mean men's friendship can't endure.

君子之交淡如水
Chün^1 tzŭ^3 chih^1 chiao^1 tan^4 ju^2 shui^3:

小人之交嘴換嘴
Hsiao^3 jên^2 chih^1 chiao^1 tsui^3 ʻhuan^4 tsui.^{3}

1402

Honour maketh more humble superior men;
But avoidance the mean man resenteth again.

君子敬之則不勝
Chün^1 tzŭ^3 ching^4 chih^1 tsê^2 pu^4 shêng,^{4}

小人遠之則怨
Hsiao^3 jên^2 yüan^3 chih^1 tsê^2 yüan.^{4}

1403

The superior man but one word needs;
One lash is enough for fiery steeds.

君子一言。快馬一鞭
Chün^1 tzŭ^3 yi^1 yen^2; kʻuai^4 ma^3 yi^1 pien.^{1}

1404

The superior man contents himself in poverty's estate;
The intelligent man submits himself to all that is his fate.

君子安貧。達人知命
Chün^1 tzŭ^3 an^1 pʻin^3: ta^2 jên^2 chih^1 ming.^{4}

1405

There are plenty of men, but few superior men.

人多君子稀
Jên^2 to^1 chün^1 tzŭ^3 hsi.^{1}

1406

Though poor the superior man is not fearful.

君子雖寒而不顫
Chün^1 tzŭ^3 sui^1 ʻhan^2 êrh^2 pu^4 chʻan.^{4}

1407

One evening's conversation with a superior man, is better than ten years of study.
共君一夜話。勝讀十年書
Kung^4 chün^1 yi^1 yeh^4 ʻhua,^{4} shêng^4 tu^2 shih^2 nien^2 shu.^{1}

1408

The superior man speaks beforehand, not when all is over.
君子言前不言後
Chün^1 tzŭ^3 yen^2 chʻien^2 pu^4 yen^2 ʻhou.^{4}

1409

The superior man's life is at the service of Heaven.
大丈夫性命交於天
Ta^4 chang^4 fu^1 hsing^4 ming^4 chiao^1 yü^2 tʻien.^{1}

1410

An equal combination of elegance and plainness is the fashion of the superior man.
文質彬彬君子樣
Wên^2 chih^2 pin^1 pin^1 chün^1 tzŭ^3 yang.^{4}

1411

A superior man breaks off a friendship without any unpleasant words.
君子絕交不出惡言
Chün^1 tzŭ^3 chüeh^4 chiao^1 pu^4 chʻu^1 o^4 yen.^{2}

1412

The superior man avoids intoxicated people.
君子避酒客
Chün^1 tzŭ^3 pi^4 chiu^3 kʻo.^{4}

1413

If the superior man desires wealth, he gets it in a proper fashion.
君子愛財取之有道
Chün^1 tzŭ^3 ai^4 tsʻai^2 chʻü^3 chih^1 yu^3 tao.^{4}

1414

In the wide world men are numberless; but where is the superior man?

茫 茫 四 海 人 無 數
Mang^2 mang^2 ssŭ^4 ʻhai^3 jên^2 wu^2 shu^4;
那 個 男 兒 是 丈 夫
na^3 ko^4 nan^2 êrh^2 shih^4 chang^4 fu^1?

1415

In liquor yet not loquacious, marks a true superior man; just, in respect of wealth, proves one of superior virtue.

酒 中 不 語 眞 君 子
Chiu^3 chung^1 pu^4 yü^3 chên^1 chün^1 tzŭ^3:
財 上 分 明 大 丈 夫
tsʻai^2 shang^4 fên^1 ming^2 ta^4 chang^4 fu.^{1}

1416

When a matter is over, men recognise the superior man.

過 後 思 君 子
Kuo^4 ʻhou^4 ssŭ^1 chün^1 tzŭ.^{3}

1417

Right moves the superior man, profit the mean man.

義 動 君 子。利 動 小 人
I^4 tung^4 chün^1 tzŭ,^{3} li^4 tung^4 hsiao^3 jên.^{2}

1418

The superior man's friendship is thin as water; the mean man's sweet as honey.

君 子 之 交 淡 如 水
Chün^1 tzŭ^3 chih^1 chiao^1 tan^4 ju^2 shui^3;
小 人 之 交 甜 如 蜜
hsiao^3 jên^2 chih^1 chiao^1 tʻien^2 ju^2 mi.^{4}

1419

He is a true superior man who gives coals in snowy weather: he is a mean man who adds flowers to embroidery.

雪 裡 送 炭 眞 君 子
Hsüeh^3 li^3 sung^4 tʻan^4 chên^1 chün^1 tzŭ^3:
錦 上 添 花 是 小 人
chin^3 shang^4 tʻien^1 ʻhua^1 shih^4 hsiao^3 jên.^{2}

1420

The superior man is happy in being such; the mean man is mean to no purpose.

君子樂得做君子
Chün[1] tzŭ[3] lê[4] tê[2] tso[4] chün[1] tzŭ[3];
小人枉自做小人
hsiao[3] jên[2] wang[3] tzŭ[4] tso[4] hsiao[4] jên.[2]

1421

A man with a big head is a superior man; one with big feet is a mean man.

頭大是君子。脚大是小人
T'ou[2] ta[4] shih[4] chün[1] tzŭ[3]; chiao[3] ta[4] shih[4] hsiao[3] jên.[2]

1422

The superior man is able to bear with others; the mean man cherishes an envious spirit.

君子有容人之量
Chün[1] tzŭ[3] yu[3] yung[2] jên[2] chih[1] liang[2];
小人存忌妒之心
hsiao[3] jên[2] ts'un[2] chi[4] kou[4] chih[1] hsin.[1]

1423

The superior man eats for the taste; the mean man gorges himself to death and is not satisfied.

君子吃滋味。小人脹死不足
Chün[1] tzŭ[3] ch'ih[1] tzŭ[1] wei[4]; hsiao[3] jên[2] chang[4] ssŭ[3] pu[4] tsu.[2]

1424

Propriety rules the superior man; law rules the mean man.

禮治君子。法治小人
Li[3] chih[3] chün[1] tzŭ[3]; fa[3] chih[3] hsiao[3] jên.[2]

1425

He whose virtues exceed his talents is the superior man; he whose talents exceed his virtues is the mean man.

德勝才爲君子
Tê[2] shêng[4] ts'ai[2] wei[2] chün[1] tzŭ[3];
才勝德爲小人
ts'ai[2] shêng[4] tê[2] wei[2] hsiao[3] jên.[2]

1426

The superior man's heart is liberal and indulgent; the mean man's heart is selfish and mean.

君子之心公而恕

Chün¹ tzŭ³ chih¹ hsin¹ kung¹ êrh² shu⁴;

小人之心私而刻

hsiao³ jên² chih¹ hsin¹ ssŭ¹ êrh² k'o.⁴

1427

A thief is a mean man; a wise man surpasses the superior man.

賊是小人。知過君子

Tsei² shih⁴ hsiao³ jên²; chih¹ kuo⁴ chün¹ tzŭ.³

1428

A mountain stream is easily swollen and easily exhausted; a mean man's heart is easily moved to and fro.

易長易退山溪水

I⁴ chang³ i⁴ t'ui⁴ shan¹ ch'i¹ shui³:

易反易覆小人心

i⁴ fan³ i⁴ fu² hsiao³ jên² hsin.¹

(12) YOUNG MEN.

1429

Who has no hair upon his lips,
In business will have many slips.

嘴裡無毛。做事不牢

Tsui³ li³ wu² mao,² tso⁴ shih⁴ pu⁴ lao.²

1430

In all sorts of affairs, youths are without experience.

年紀幼嫩。事事未經閱歷

Nien² chi³ yu⁴ nên,⁴ shih⁴ shih⁴ wei⁴ ching¹ yüeh⁴ li.⁴

1431

Inferior in youth, useless in old age.

少 壯 倘 不 如 人
Shao³ chuang⁴ shang⁴ pu⁴ ju² jên.²
老 來 更 多 無 用
lao³ lai² kên¹ to¹ wu² yung.⁴

1432

The mark must be made in youth.

必 定 少 年 高 發
Pi⁴ ting⁴ shao³ nien² kao¹ fa.¹

1433

Withered trees, in Spring burst forth afresh; but men cannot twice be young.

枯 木 逢 春 猶 再 發
K'u¹ mu⁴ fêng² ch'un¹ yu² tsai⁴ fa¹;
人 無 兩 度 再 少 年
jên² wu² liang² tu⁴ tsai⁴ shao³ nien.²

1434

The boy is father to the man. *Lit.:* You may see the man in the boy.

從 小 看 大
Ts'ung² hsiao³ k'an⁴ ta.⁴

1435

In judging of what a boy will be, notice what he is in infancy.

細 娃 看 小 時
Hsi⁴ wa¹ k'an⁴ hsiao³ shih.²

1436

He who enters an asylum for the aged at twenty, enjoys that happiness too soon.

二 十 歲 入 孤 老 院。 享 福 太 早
Erh⁴ shih² sui⁴ ju⁴ ku¹ lao³ yüan,⁴ hsiang³ fu² t'ai⁴ tsao.³

1437

When *Pai Chu-i* was seven months old, he knew the two characters *chih* and *wu.*

白 居 易 生 七 月 便 識 之 無 二 字
Pai² chü¹ I⁴ shêng¹ ch'i¹ yüeh,⁴ pien⁴ shih⁴ chih¹ wu² erh⁴ tzŭ.⁴

諺語叢話

1438

When *Li 'Huo* of the *T'ang* dynasty was just seven years old, he composed his poem *Kao-hsüan-kuo.*

唐李賀纔七歲

T'ang[2] Li[4] 'Huo[4] ts'ai[2] ch'i[1] sui,[4]

作高軒過一篇

tso[4] kao[1] hsüan[1] kuo[4] yi[1] p'ien.[1]

NOTE.—For brief accounts of these two celebrities see the *Yu-hsiao* (幼學) section *wên-tsz'* (文字).

(13) WOMEN.

1439

Mandarins, customers, and widow folk,
You must be careful not to provoke.

一等官。二等客

Yi[1] têng[3] kuan,[1] êrh[4] têng[3] k'o,[4]

三等寡婦。惹不得

San[1] têng[3] kua[3] fu,[4] jê[3] pu[4] tê.[2]

1440

Nine women in ten are jealous.

十个婦人九个妒

Shih[2] ko[4] fu[4] jên[2] chiu[3] ko[4] tu.[4]

1441

A maid marries to please her parents; a widow to please herself.

幼嫁從親。再嫁由身

Yu[4] chia[4] ts'ung[2] ch'in[1]; tsai[4] chia[4] yu[2] shên.[1]

1442

Even *Mo's* mother had some beauty, and *Hsi-shih*, some defect.

嫫母有所美。西施有所醜

Mo[2] mu[3] yu[3] so[3] mei,[3] Hsi[1] shih[1] yu[3] so[3] ch'ou.[3]

NOTE.—*Mo* or *Wang Mo* (王嫫), a scholar of the *Han* dynasty, whose mother, though remarkably ugly, had some redeeming feature. *Hsi-shih*, the beautiful concubine of the King of *Wu* (吳). See note under proverb number 1460.

1443

An ugly Mary an ugly Miss.

醜了梅香醜小姐

Chʻou^3 liao^3 Mei^2 hsiang^1 chʻou^3 hsiao^3 Chieh.^{3}

1444

If heaven wants to rain, or your mother to marry again, nothing can prevent them.

天要下。娘要嫁。無法可制

Tʻien^1 yao^4 hsia,^{4} niang^2 yao^4 chia,^{4} wu^2 fa^3 kʻo^3 chih.^{4}

1445

Lazy women will try to carry everything at once.

懶婆娘做事一担挑

Lan^3 pʻo^2 niang^2 tso^4 shih^4 yi^1 tan^1 tʻiao.^{1}

1446

Unmarried, a woman obeys her father; married, her husband.

在家由父。出嫁從夫

Tsai^4 chia^1 yu^2 fu^4; chʻu^1 chia^4 tsʻung^2 fu.^{1}

1447

I guess that a good-looking woman needs no rouge to make her pretty.

大抵還他肌骨好

Ta^4 ti^2 ʻhuan^3 tʻa^1 chi^1 ku^3 hao,^{2}

不搽紅粉也風流

pu^4 tsʻa^1 ʻhung^2 fên^3 yeh^3 fêng^1 liu^2.

1448

When a chaste lady desires pleasure she gets it properly.

貞婦愛色。納之以禮

Chên^1 fu^4 ai^4 sê,^{4} na^4 chih^1 i^3 li.^{3}

1449

Fair maidens are very unlucky, and clever young men have little beauty.

紅顏女子多薄命

ʻHung^2 yen^2 nü^2 tzŭ^3 to^1 po^2 ming,^{4}

聰明子弟少容顏

tsʻung^1 ming^2 tzŭ^3 ti^4 shao^3 yung^2 yen.^{2}

諺語叢話

1450

A maid's virtue is unlimited; a wife's resentment without end.

女德無極。婦怨無終

Nü[2] tê[2] wu[2] chi[2]; fu[4] yüan[4] wu[2] chung.[1]

1451

There is no such poison in the green snake's mouth or the hornet's sting, as in a woman's heart.

青竹蛇兒口。黃蜂尾上針

Ch'ing[1] chu[2] shê[2] êrh[2] k'ou,[3] huang[2] fêng[1] wei[3] shang[4] chên.[1]

兩般不算毒。最毒婦人心

liang[3] pan[1] pu[4] suan[4] tu,[2] tsui[4] tu[2] fu[4] jên[2] hsin.[1]

1452

The three kinds of nuns, and the six kinds of dames, are the go-betweens of adultery and robbery.

三姑六婆實淫盜之媒

San[1] ku[1] lu[4] p'o[2] shih[2] yin[2] tao[4] chih[1] mei.[2]

NOTE.—The three kinds of nuns here referred to are the Buddhist nun (尼姑), the Tauist nun (道姑), and the Sorceress (覡姑). The six kinds of dames are the go-between (媒婆), the seller of flowers (賣花婆), the midwife (收生婆), the singing girl or prostitute (優婆), the sorceress or spiritual medium (師婆), and the doctoress (醫藥婆). See Doolittle's Vocabulary and Handbook. Vol. 2, page 596,599.

1453

The lover's eye sees a *Hsi-shih* in his mistress.

情人眼內出西施

Ch'ing[2] jên[2] yen[3] nei[4] ch'u[1] Hsi[1] shih.[1]

NOTE.—See notes under proverbs, nos. 1442, 1460.

1454

A smile of her's was worth a thousand taels of gold.

一笑值千金

Yi[1] hsiao[4] chih[2] ch'ien[1] chin.[1]

NOTE.—*Yu wang* (幽王) of the *Chou* (周) dynasty had a concubine called *Pao-ssŭ* (褒似), a great beauty, but very sedate. To make her laugh it is said the emperor resorted to very ridiculous expedients. This proverb, however, is applicable to men as well as women.

1455

The rouged beauty repudiates age; the jolly profligate never speaks of poverty.

紅粉佳人休便老

ʻHung^2 fên^3 chia^1 jên^2 hsiu^1 pien^4 lao^3;

風流浪子莫教貧

fêng^1 liu^2 lang^2 tzŭ^3 mo^4 chiao^4 pʻin.^{3}

1456

The rouged beauty cannot come up to the bloom of youth

紅粉佳人不及當初

ʻHung^2 fên^3 chia^1 jên^2 pu^4 chi^2 tang^1 chʻu.^{1}

1457

A good-looking woman in a house, is the foe of all the plain ones.

好女于室。醜女之仇

ʻHao^3 nü^2 yü^2 shih,^{4} chʻou^3 nü^2 chih^1 chʻou.^{2}

1458

Young she's a *Kuan-yin;* old she's a monkey.

少是觀音。老是猴

Shao^3 shih^4 Kuan^1 Yin,^{1} lao^3 shih^4 ʻhou.^{2}

1459

A woman's virtues need not be of the famous or uncommon kind; her face need not be very beautiful; her conversation need not be very eloquent; and her work need not be very exquisite or surpassing.

婦德者不必才名絕異

Fu^4 tê^2 chê^2 pu^4 pi^4 tsʻai^2 ming^2 chüeh^2 i^4;

婦容者不必顏色美麗

fu^4 yung^2 chê^2 pu^4 pi^4 yen^2 sê^4 mei^3 li^4;

婦言者不必利口辯詞

fu^4 yen^2 chê^2 pu^4 pi^4 li^4 kʻou^3 pien^4 tzʻŭ^2;

婦工者不必技巧過人

fu^4 kung^1 chê^2 pu^4 pi^4 chi^1 chʻiao^3 kuo^4 jên.^{2}

1460

With one smile she overthrows a city; with another, a kingdom.

一 笑 傾 人 城。再 笑 傾 人 國

Yi^1 hsiao^4 ch‘un^1 jên^2 ch‘êng^2; tsai^4 hsiao^4 ch‘un^1 jên^2 kuo.^{2}

Note.—The lady to whom this refers is *Hsi-shih* (西 施) the concubine of *Fu-ch'a* (夫 差), King of the ancient state of *Wu* (吳). She was eminently beautiful, and her beauty so captivated her lord that, for her sake, he neglected the affairs of his kingdom, which thereupon fell into disorder and ruin. Now, the proverb serves to warn against the seductive smiles of beauty.

—— 1461 ——

Three-tenths of her good looks are due to nature, seven-tenths to dress.

三 分 人 才。七 分 打 扮

San^1 fên^1 jên^2 ts‘ai,^{2} ch‘i^1 fên^1 ta^3 pan.^{4}

(14) MISCELLANEOUS.

—— 1462 ——

Who rub off corners and round curves wind,
Will everywhere peace and concord find.

轉 彎 摸 角。處 處 合 得 着

Chuan^3 wan^1 mo^3 chiao,^{1} ch‘u^4 ch‘u^4 ho^2 tê^2 cho.^{2}

—— 1463 ——

A greedy fellow. *Lit.:* One whose eyes are bigger than his belly.

眼 大 肚 皮 小

Yen^3 ta^4 tu^3 p‘i^2 hsiao.^{3}

—— 1464 ——

Fellow-countrymen. *Lit.:* We are all of the same country and of one common well.

都 是 同 鄉 共 井 的 人

Tu^1 shih^4 t‘ung^2 hsiang^1 kung^4 ching^3 ti^1 jên.^{2}

—— 1465 ——

No matter whether relation or not, he is my fellow-countryman.

親 不 親 故 鄉 人

Ch‘in^1 pu^4 ch‘in^1 ku^4 hsiang^1 jên.^{2}

1466

A meddlesome person. *Lit.:* An enthroned monkey with hairy hands and feet.

猴 子 坐 天 下 毛 脚 毛 手

ʻHou^{2} tzŭ^{3} tso^{4} tʻien^{1} hsia^{4} mao^{2} chiao^{3} mao^{2} shou.^{3}

1467

A useless fellow. *Lit.:* A clothes frame: a rice bag.

穿 衣 服 的 架 子。吃 飯 的 袋 子

Chʻuan^{1} i^{1} fu^{2} ti^{1} chia^{4} tzŭ^{3}: chʻih^{1} fan^{4} ti^{1} tai^{4} tzŭ.^{3}

1468

The same. *Lit.:* Literary men can't scribble men's fortunes; military men can't carry water.

文 不 能 測 字。武 不 能 挑 水

Wên^{2} pu^{4} nêng^{2} tsʻê^{4} tzŭ^{4}; wu^{3} pu^{4} nêng^{2} tʻiao^{1} shui.^{3}

1469

One brave as Heaven.

胆 大 如 天

Tan^{3} ta^{4} ju^{2} tʻien.^{1}

1470

An ugly fellow. *Lit.:* The *Ho-shou-wu* changed into human shape.

何 首 烏 變 成 人 形

ʻHo^{2} shou^{3} wu^{1} pien^{4} chʻêng^{2} jên^{2} hsing.^{2}

NOTE.—*Ho-shou-wu;* a kind of herb, bearing some resemblance to a child.

1471

A miser. *Lit.:* One very clear in his accounts.

好 清 白 算 盤 呢

ʻHao^{3} chʻing^{1} pai^{2} suan^{4} pʻan^{2} ni.^{1}

1472

An inhospitable man. *Lit.:* One whose door opens on the top of his house.

屋 山 頭 開 門

Wu^{1} shan^{1} tʻou^{2} kʻai^{1} mên.^{2}

1473

An inexperienced man. *Lit.:* One who has not seen the face of the world.

諺語叢話

沒有見世面的人
Mu[2] yu[3] chien[4] shih[4] mien[4] ti[1] jên.[2]

1474

The same. *Lit.:* One who has not tasted of the sour and the sweet, the bitter and the pungent.

沒有受過酸甜苦辣
Mu[2] yu[3] shou[4] kuo[4] suan[1] tʻien[2] kʻu[3] la.[4]

1475

The amiable get on smoothly. *Lit.:* Fair winds raise no waves.

順風不起浪
Shun[4] fêng[1] pu[4] chʻi[3] lang.[4]

1476

There is nothing mean in a generous man.

為人渾厚自無刻薄
Wei[2] jên[2] ʻhun[4] ʻhou[4] tzŭ[4] wu[2] kʻo[1] po.[2]

CHAPTER III.

HUMAN NATURE.

1477

Just so long as you ask nothing, man's nature is bland;
For wine, abstainers care little what price you demand.

無求到處人情好
Wu^2 chʻiu^2 tao^4 chʻu^4 jên^2 chʻing^2 ʻhao^3:

不飲任他酒價高
Pu^4 yin^3 jên^4 tʻa^1 chiu^3 chia^4 kao.^{1}

1478

To judge man from his face is as hard a feat,
As it would be the ocean in pecks to mete.

凡人不可貌相
Fan^2 jên^2 pu^4 kʻo^3 mao^4 hsiang,^{4}

海水不可斗量.
ʻHai^3 shui^3 pu^4 kʻo^3 tou^3 liang.^{2}

1479

Man by right ascends;
Water downward tends.

人望高處走。水望低處流
Jên^2 wang^4 kao^1 chʻu^4 tsou^4; shui^3 wang^4 ti^1 chʻu^4 liu.^{2}

1480

The measure of heaven and earth you may find;
You'll never be able to, that of the mind.

天可度地可量
Tʻien^1 kʻo^3 tu^4 ti^4 kʻo^3 liang.^{2}

惟有人心不可防
Wei^2 yu^3 jên^2 hsin^1 pu^4 kʻo^3 fang.^{2}

1481

Man's heart can ne'er contented grow;
Possessed of *Lung*, he longs for *Shu*.

人心不足。得隴望蜀
Jên^2 hsin^1 pu^4 tsu^2; tê^2 Lung^3 wang^4 Shu.^{3}

諺語叢話

1482

Woe, and alas! the heart of man is like a poisonous snake;
Unknown, like wheels, the eyes of heaven their revolutions make.

堪 嘆 人 心 毒 似 蛇
K'an[1] t'an[4] jên[2] hsin[1] tu[2] ssŭ[4] shê,[2]

誰 知 天 眼 轉 如 車
Shui[2] chih[1] t'ien[1] yen[3] chuan[3] ju[2] ch'ê.[1]

1483

Though the heavens be high and lofty, man's desires yet higher rise;
And though his well yields wine to sell, for the missing grain he cries.

天 高 不 見 高 人 心 第 一 高
T'ien[1] kao[1] pu[4] chien[4] kao[1] jên[2] hsin[1] ti[4] yi[1] kao[1]:

井 水 做 酒 賣 還 說 猪 無 糟
Ching[3] shui[3] tso[4] chiu[3] mai[4] 'huan[2] shuo[1] chu[1] wu[2] tsao.[1]

1484

Nobody on earth is difficult to manage; all that is necessary is three times to examine one's self.

天 下 無 難 處 之 人
T'ien[1] hsia[4] wu[2] nan[2] ch'u[4] chih[1] jên[2];

只 須 三 个 必 自 反
chih[3] hsü[1] san[1] ko[4] pi[4] tzŭ[4] fan.[3]

NOTE.—The phrase "*Tzŭ-fan*" is taken from Mencius. See Legge, vol ii, page 209.

1485

Instinct naturally inhabits man's heart.

公 道 自 在 人 心
Kung[1] tao[4] tzŭ[4] tsai[4] jên[2] hsin.[1]

1486

A man cannot become perfect in a hundred years; he may become corrupt in less than a day.

百 年 成 之 不 足
Pai[3] nien[2] ch'êng[2] chih[1] pu[4] tsu[2];

一 旦 壞 之 有 餘
yi[1] tan[4] 'huai[4] chih[1] yu[3] yü.[2]

1487

In learning what is good, a thousand days are insufficient; in learning what is bad, an hour is too much.

學好千日不足

Hsiao² ʻhao³ chʻien¹ jih⁴ pu⁴ tsu²;

學歹一時有餘

hsiao² tai³ yi¹ shih² yu³ yü.²

1488

Man's heart secret. *Lit.:* Know I what fœtus is in your womb?

我曉得你肚子裡懷的什麼胎

Wo³ hsiao³ tê² ni³ tu³ tzŭ³ li³ ʻhuai² ti¹ shih² mo¹ tʻai¹?

1489

The same. *Lit.:* I know not what sort of medicine he has in his calabash.

不曉得他葫蘆裡裝什麼藥

Pu⁴ hsiao³ tê² tʻa¹ ʻhu² lu² li³ chuang¹ shih² mo¹ yao.⁴

1490

What the eye sees not, the heart does not vex itself over.

眼不見心不怨

Yen³ pu⁴ chien⁴ hsin¹ pu⁴ yüan.⁴

1491

Water can both sustain and upset a ship.

水能載舟亦能覆舟

Shui³ nêng² tsai⁴ chou¹ i⁴ nêng² fu² chou.¹

NOTE.—This proverb points to the power men have either for good or evil.

1492

It is harder to change a man's natural disposition, than to change rivers and mountains.

江山易改。本性難移

Chiang¹ shan¹ i⁴ kai,³ pên³ hsing⁴ nan² i.²

1493

Man's heart is lofty as heaven; his fate is thin as paper.

心有天高。命如紙薄

Hsin¹ yu³ tʻien¹ kao¹; ming⁴ ju² chih³ po.²

1494

Man's heart is never satisfied; the snake would swallow the elephant.

人心不足蛇吞象

Jên^2 hsin^1 pu^4 tsu^2 shê^2 tʻun^1 hsiang.^{4}

1495

Man's heart is hidden in his belly, as the *chʻui-pi* is in a rice boiler.

人心隔肚皮。飯甑隔·炊箄

Jên^2 hsin^1 ko^2 tu^3 pʻi,^{2} fan^4 tsêng^4 ko^2 chʻui^1 pi.^{4}

NOTE.—*Chui-pi* is a small conical plate of wicker work.

1496

It is easier to fill up the bed of a mountain torrent than to satisfy the heart of man.

谿壑易填。人心難滿

Chʻi^1 ʻho^4 i^4 tʻien,^{2} jên^2 hsin^1 nan^2 man.^{3}

1497

The body may be healed, not the mind.

醫得身。醫不得心

I^1 tê^2 shên,^{1} i^1 pu^4 tê^2 hsin.^{1}

1498

All men love wealth, wine, and women.

酒色人人愛。財帛動人心

Chiu^3 sê^4 jên^2 jên^2 ai,^{4} tsʻai^2 pai^2 tung^4 jên^2 hsin.^{1}

1499

In difficulties men are easily tested, and easily saved.

難中好試人。難中好救人

Nan^2 chung^1 ʻhao^3 shih^4 jên,^{2} nan^2 chung^1 ʻhao^3 chiu^4 jên.^{2}

1500

Distance tests a horse's strength; long service reveals a man's character.

路遙知馬力。事久見人心

Lu^4 yao^2 chih^1 ma^3 li^4; shih^4 chiu^3 chien^4 jên^2 hsin.^{1}

NOTE.—For a long and interesting account of the origin of this proverb, see "Notes and Queries on China and Japan," vol iii, page 181.

1501

The human heart is bad to fathom.

人心難測

Jên^2 hsin^1 nan^2 tsʻê.^{4}

NOTE.—"Who can know it?" Jeremiah 17: 9.

1502

You may draw a tiger's skin, you cannot draw his bones; you may know a man's face, you cannot know his heart.

畫虎畫皮難畫骨

ʻHua^4 ʻhu^3 ʻhua^4 pʻi^2 nan^2 ʻhua^4 ku^3;

知人知面不知心

chih^1 jên^2 chih^1 mien^4 pu^4 chih^1 hsin.^{1}

1503

Man's nature is as thin as sheets of tissue paper; the world is like a game of chess, varying at every move.

人情似紙張張薄

Jên^2 chʻing^2 ssŭ^4 chih^3 chang^1 chang^1 po^2;

世事如棋局局新

shih^4 shih^4 ju^2 chʻi^2 chü^2 chü^2 hsin.^{1}

1504

Man naturally, like water, distinguishes between the high and the low; the world is ever changing, like a cloud.

人情似水分高下

Jên^2 chʻing^2 ssŭ^4 shui^3 fên^1 kao^1 hsia^4:

世事如雲任捲舒

Shih^4 shih^4 ju^2 yün^2 jên^4 chüan^3 shu.^{1}

1505

Living, man knows not his soul; dead, he knows not his corpse.

生不認魂。死不認屍

Shêng^1 pu^4 jên^4 ʻhun^2; ssŭ^3 pu^4 jên^4 shih.^{1}

1506

Rather fear the man whose disposition is a two-edged sword, than the savage tiger of the mountains.

入山不怕傷人虎

Ju^4 shan^1 pu^4 pʻa^4 shang^1 jên^2 ʻhu,^{3}

只怕人情兩面刀
chih^3 pʻa^4 jên^2 chʻing^2 liang^2 mien^4 tao.^{1}

1507

One is anxious when another is not; one may seem to be at leisure when his heart is not so.

你急他未急。人閒心未閒
Ni^3 chi^2 tʻa^1 wei^4 chi^2; jên^2 hsien^2 hsin^1 wei^4 hsien.^{2}

1508

An old man may have a youthful heart; and a poor man may have a noble inclination.

人老心未老。人窮志不窮
Jen^2 lao^3 hsin^1 wei^4 lao^3; jen^2 chʻiung^2 chih^4 pu^4 chʻiung.^{2}

1509

No flower can retain its bloom for a hundred, no man his virtue for a thousand, days.

人無千日好。花無百日紅
Jên^2 wu^2 chʻien^1 jih^4 hao,^{3} ʻhua^1 wu^2 pai^3 jih^4 ʻhung.^{2}

1510

Each man has his own mind, and each mind its peculiar intelligence.

人各有心。心各有見
Jên^2 ko^4 yu^3 hsin,^{1} hsin^1 ko^4 yu^3 chien.^{4}

1511

A mind enlightened is like heaven; a mind in darkness is like hell.

心裏光明是天堂
Hsin^1 li^3 kuang^1 ming^2 shih^4 tʻien^1 tʻang^2;

心裏黑暗是地獄
hsin^1 li^3 ʻhei^1 an^4 shih^4 ti^4 yü.^{4}

NOTE.—Over this proverb, Sir John Davis wrote the beautiful lines:—
"The mind is its own place, and in itself
Can make a heaven of hell, a hell of heaven."

1512

Amongst men who is faultless?

為人誰無個錯處
Wei^2 jên^2 shui^3 wu^2 ko^4 tsʻo^4 chʻu^4?

NOTE.—There is none righteous, no, not one." Rom. 3: 10.

1513

What man is not guilty of one error and half a mistake?

一差半錯。那個沒有

Yi^1 chʻa^1 pan^4 tsʻo,^{4} na^3 ko^4 mu^2 yu^3?

1514

Man errs as the horse stumbles.

人有失錯。馬有漏蹄

Jên^2 yu^3 shih^1 tsʻo,^{4} ma^3 yu^3 lou^4 tʻi.^{2}

1515

Though a snake get into a bamboo tube it is hard to change its wriggling disposition.

蛇入竹筒曲性難改

Shê^2 ju^4 chu^2 tʻung^3 chʻu^1 hsing^4 nan^2 kai.^{3}

1516

Though stones should be transformed to gold, men would not be satisfied.

點石化爲金。人心猶未足

Tien^3 shih^2 hua^4 wei^2 chin,^{1} jên^2 hsin^1 yu^2 wei^4 tsu.^{2}

1517

Fire should be hollow hearted; man true hearted.

火要空心。人要實心

ʻHuo^3 yao^4 kʻung^1 hsin,^{1} jên^2 yao^4 shih^2 hsin.^{1}

1518

The mind is the lord of the man.

心爲一身之主

Hsin^1 wei^2 yi^1 shên^1 chih^1 chu.^{3}

1519

Men love gentleness; dogs love food.

人憐溫存。狗憐食

Jên^2 lien^2 wên^1 tsʻun^2; kou^3 lien^2 shih.^{2}

1520

When you see into man's disposition, you perceive that all is false.

看透人情總是空

Kʻan^4 tʻou^4 jên^2 chʻing^2 tsung^3 shih^4 kʻung.^{1}

NOTE.—"The heart is deceitful above all things." Jeremiah 17: 9.

1521

A man's face is the reflex of his states of mind.

相隨心生。相隨心滅

Hsiang⁴ sui² hsin¹ shêng¹; hsiang⁴ sui² hsin¹ mieh.⁴

1522

However stupid a man may be, he grows clever enough when blaming others: however wise, he becomes a dolt when blaming himself.

人雖至愚責人則明

Jên² sui¹ chih⁴ yü² tsê² jên² tsê² ming²:

人雖至明責己則昏

jên² sui¹ chih⁴ ming² tsê² chi³ tsê² ʻhun.¹

1523

Men know not their own faults, as oxen know not the greatness of their strength.

人不知己過。牛不知力大

Jên² pu⁴ chih¹ chi³ kuo,⁴ niu² pu⁴ chih¹ li⁴ ta.⁴

1524

It is easier to seize the tiger in the hills than to appeal to man for support.

入山擒虎易。開口告人難

Ju⁴ shan¹ chʻin² ʻhu³ i⁴; kʻai¹ kʻou³ kao⁴ jên² nan.²

1525

Who knows himself knows others; for heart can be compared with heart.

知己知彼。將心比心

Chih¹ chi³ chih¹ pi³; chiang¹ hsin¹ pi³ hsin.¹

SECTION XII.—ON MANNERS.

CHAPTER I.

BEARING AND POLITENESS.

1526

A man without politeness must perversely talk:
A weak ox in the harrows falters in his walk.

人無禮說横話
Jen² wu² li³ shuo¹ ʽhêng⁴ ʽhua⁴;
牛無力拉横耙
Niu² wu² li⁴ la¹ ʽhêng⁴ pʽa.²

1527

The politeness of rustics is notably great;
After cursing each other, comes friendly debate.

鄉裡人禮行大
Hsiang¹ li³ jên² li³ hsing² ta⁴;
先罵人後說話
Hsien¹ ma⁴ jên² ʽhou⁴ shuo¹ ʽhua.⁴

1528

Encountering a soldier, it is plain,
The graduate is polite in vain.

秀才遇刀兵。有禮講不清
Hsiu⁴ tsʽai² yü⁴ tao⁴ ping,¹ yu³ li³ chiang³ pu⁴ chʽing.¹

1529

When persons meet they greet;
And cows low when they meet.

人見人說話。牛見牛咿呀
Jen² chien⁴ jen² shuo¹ ʽhua,⁴ niu² chien⁴ niu² i¹ ya.¹

1530

On a damsel's boudoir, or teacher's school,
(To intrude one's-self is against all rule.)

先生學堂。女子繡房
Hsien¹ shêng¹ hsiao³ tʽang,² nü² tzŭ³ hsiu⁴ fang.²

— 1531 —

For the father to sit, and the son to stand,
Is the proper politeness through all the land.

父坐子立。禮貌整齊

Fu^4 tso^4 tzŭ^3 li,^{4} li^3 mao^2 chêng^3 chʻi.^{2}

— 1532 —

Much politeness offends no one.

禮多人不怪

Li^3 to^1 jên^2 pu^4 kuai.^{4}

— 1533 —

Excessive politeness must cover deceit.

禮多人必詐

Li^3 to^1 jên^2 pi^4 cha.^{4}

— 1534 —

Politeness wins the confidence of princes.

有禮服得君王道

Yu^3 li^3 fu^2 tê^2 chün^1 wang^2 tao.^{4}

— 1535 —

Keep your offence in your bosom, and you may meet as before.

怪人心在肚。相見又何妨

Kuai^4 jên^2 hsin^1 tsai^4 tu,^{3} hsiang^1 chien^4 yu^4 ʻho^2 fang.^{1}

— 1536 —

He who confounds morals, must confound manners.

不知好歹。豈識高低

Pu^4 chih^1 hao^4 tai,^{3} chʻi^3 shih^4 kao^1 ti.^{1}

— 1537 —

For pleasing superior officers and governing the people, there is nothing so good as politeness.

安上治民。莫善於禮

An^1 shang^4 chih^3 min,^{2} mo^4 shan^4 yü^2 li.^{3}

— 1538 —

Nobody stands on ceremony in hot weather. *Lit.*: In hot weather there is no superior man.

暑天無君子

Shu^3 tʻien^1 wu^2 chün^1 tzŭ.^{3}

1539

Familiar friends may waive etiquette; but with a rich man you must be very polite.

熟不拘禮。富而多文

Shu^2 pu^4 chü^1 li^3; fu^4 êrh^2 to^1 wên.^{2}

1540

Ill-timed politeness. *Lit.:* He makes his bow behind the rider's back.

馬屁股背後打一恭

Ma^3 pʻi^4 ku^3 pei^4 ʻhou^4 ta^3 yi^1 kung.^{1}

1541

The same. *Lit.:* To make one's bow in the dark.

黑地下作揖

ʻHei^1 ti^4 hsia^4 tso^4 i.^{1}

1542

For every foot of honour shown me, I show ten.

人敬我一尺。我敬人一丈

Jên^2 ching^4 wo^3 yi^1 chʻih,^{3} wo^3 ching^4 jên^2 yi^1 chʻang.^{4}

1543

No medicine can cure a vulgar man.

蠻人無藥醫

Man^2 jên^2 wu^2 yao^4 i.^{1}

1544

Old and young, men and women, ought to be in manners respectful, in conversation dignified.

長幼內外。宜法肅詞嚴

Chang^3 yu^4 nei^4 wai,^{4} i^2 fa^3 su^4 tzʻŭ^2 yen.^{2}

1545

Every officer has his etiquette.

做此官行此禮

Tso^4 tzʻŭ^3 kuan^1 hsing^2 tzʻŭ^3 li.^{3}

1546

Before fathers and mothers, uncles and aunts, itch as you may, you may not dare to scratch.

在父母舅姑之所。癢不敢搔

Tsai^4 fu^4 mu^3 chiu^4 ku^1 chih^1 so,^{3} yang^3 pu^4 kan^3 chua.^{1}

1547

Obedience is better than politeness.

恭敬不如從命

Kung[1] ching[4] pu[4] ju[2] ts'ung[2] ming.[4]

1548

The man may be bad whilst his manners are not.

人惡禮不惡

Jên[2] o[4] li[3] pu[4] o.[4]

1549

He who acts for the emperor is emperor; who acts for the viceroy is viceroy.

奉天子卽天子

Fêng[4] t'ien[1] tzŭ[3] chi[2] t'ien[1] tzŭ[3];

奉諸侯卽諸侯

fêng[4] chu[1] 'hou[2] chi[2] chu[1] 'hou.[2]

1550

I am unworthy this favour. *Lit.*: The sweetmeat-seller having lost his gong-stick dare not strike his gong.

賣糖的掉鑼搥不敢當

Mai[4] t'ang[2] ti[1] tiao[4] lo[2] ch'ui[2] pu[4] kan[2] tang.[1]

CHAPTER II.

COMPLIMENTS.

1551

Offering congratulations, allow me to pray,
That your wealth may increase in a wonderful way!

恭 喜 賀 喜 元 寶 LO 起

Kung^1 hsi^3 ʻho^4 hsi,^{3} yüan^2 pao^3 lo^4 chʻi.^{3}

1552

May he easily grow up, and easily make a man of himself!

易 長 易 成

I^4 chang^3 i^4 chʻêng.^{2}

1553

You certainly will outstrip the common herd!

定 出 人 群

Ting^4 chʻu^1 jên^2 chʻün.^{2}

1554

May you beat all others!

出 人 頭 地

Chʻu^1 jen^2 tʻou^2 ti.^{4}

1555

You are the son of a noble sire!

將 門 之 子

Chiang^1 mên^2 chih^1 tsŭ.^{3}

1556

May all your descendants be famous! *Lit.:* May the epidendrum and the cassia put forth extraordinary fragrance!

蘭 桂 騰 芳

Lan^2 kuei^1 tʻêng^2 fang.^{1}

1557

May your brothers together grow famous!

兄 弟 聯 芳

Hsiung^1 ti^4 lien^2 fang.^{1}

1558

The scholar has beaten his master. *Lit.:* The black dye succeeds the blue and is superior to it.

青出於藍。而勝於藍

Chʻing[1] chʻu[1] yü[2] lan,[2] êrh[2] shêng[4] yü[2] lan.[2]

1559

Yours is the pen of a ready writer!

一揮而就

Yi[1] ʻhui[1] êrh[2] chiu.[4]

1560

A wonderful child! *Lit.:* A swift colt!

千里駒

Chʻien[1] li[3] chü.[1]

CHAPTER III.

PRESENTS.

1561

Do not take anything easily obtained, and forthwith make it out to be unimportant.

莫將容易得。便作等閑看

Mo^4 chiang^1 yung^2 i^4 tê,^{2} pien^4 tso^4 têng^3 hsien^2 kʻan.^{4}

1562

When the bearer of a trifling present to one at a distance, be sure you do not lose it.

千里送毫毛。寄物不寄失

Chʻien^1 li^3 sung^4 ʻhao^2 mao,^{2} chi^4 wu^4 pu^4 chi^4 shih.^{1}

1563

Suit presents to receivers. *Lit.:* Present a jewelled sword to a warrior, a box of rouge to a pretty woman.

寶劍贈於烈士

Pao^3 chien^4 tsêng^4 yü^2 lieh^4 shih,^{4}

紅粉贈於佳人

ʻhung^2 fên^3 tsêng^4 yü^2 chia^1 jên.^{2}

1564

Though he has to bolt his door against creditors, he will borrow money to make a present.

關門躲債主。借債感人情

Kuan^1 mên^2 to^2 chai^4 chu,^{3} chieh^4 chai^4 kan^2 jen^2 chʻing.^{2}

1565

To carry an offering of a pig's head in one's hand, and be unable to find a temple.

躭得猪頭。找不到廟門

Tan^1 tê^2 chu^1 tʻou,^{2} chao^3 pu^4 tao^3 miao^4 mên.^{2}

1566

To get a gift,—make a proper return,—and still feel dissatisfied.

得禮還禮。總不過意

Te^2 li^3 ʻhuan^2 li,^{3} tsung^3 pu^4 kuo^4 i.^{4}

1567

When a trifling present is sent a long way, the gift may be light but the intention is weighty.

千里寄毫毛。禮輕人意重

Chʻien[1] li[3] chi[4] ʻhao[2] mao,[2] li[3] chʻing[1] jên[2] i[4] chung.[4]

1568

To a teacher present minced meat, fish, and shrimps.

供先生肉鮓魚蝦

Kung[1] ʻhsien[1] shêng[1] jou[4] cha[3] yü[2] hsia.[1]

1569

Return gift for gift.

以情還情

I[3] chʻing[2] ʻhuan[2] chʻing.[2]

CHAPTER IV.

ETIQUETTE OF VISITING.

— 1570 —

Better add a peck of rice to our lot,
Than another mouth to eat what we've got.

寧 添 一 斗 莫 添 一 口
Ning^{2} tʻien^{1} yi^{1} tou,^{3} mo^{4} tʻien^{1} yi^{1} kʻou.^{3}

— 1571 —

When magpies chatter before your hall,
You will soon from guests receive a call.

鴉 鵲 堂 前 叫。不 久 有 客 到
Ya^{1} chʻiao^{3} tʻang^{2} chʻien^{2} chiao,^{4} pu^{4} chiu^{3} yu^{3} kʻo^{4} tao.^{4}

— 1572 —

Of ladies beware in making a feast,
Since fifty may mean a hundred, at least.

請 客 莫 請 女 客。五 十 當 一 百
Chʻing^{3} kʻo^{4} mo^{4} chʻing^{3} nü^{2} kʻo,^{4} wu^{3} shih^{2} tang^{4} yi^{1} po.^{2}

NOTE.—Each one may bring a child.

— 1573 —

Do not be afraid of too many guests,
One goose will satisfy all their requests.

請 客 不 怕 多。共 吃 一 隻 鵝
Chʻing^{3} kʻo^{4} pu^{4} pʻa^{4} to,^{1} kung^{4} chʻih^{1} yi^{1} chih^{1} o.^{2}

— 1574 —

Better slight a guest than starve him.

寧 可 慢 客。不 可 餓 客
Ning^{2} kʻo^{3} man^{4} kʻo,^{4} pu^{4} kʻo^{3} o^{4} kʻo.^{4}

— 1575 —

If you do not press an invited guest you will offend him.

請 客 不 催 客 反 以 得 罪 客
Chʻing^{3} kʻo^{4} pu^{4} tsʻui^{1} kʻo,^{1} fan^{3} i^{3} tê^{2} tsui^{4} kʻo.^{4}

1576

Wherever you call, give thanks for tobacco and tea.

走 人 家 多 謝 煙 茶

Tsou^4 jên^2 chia^1 to^1 hsieh^4 yen^1 chʻa.^{2}

1577

It is easy to treat a guest well on his first arrival; but if he stays too long it is hard.

相 見 易 得 好。久 住 難 爲 人

Hsiang^1 chien^4 i^4 tê^2 ʻhao^3; chiu^3 chu^4 nan^2 wei^2 jên^2.

1578

He who cannot in his own house entertain a worthy guest, when abroad will find few to entertain him.

在 家 不 會 迎 賓 客

Tsai^4 chia^1 pu^4 ʻhui^4 ying^2 ping^1 kʻo,^{4}

出 外 方 知 少 主 人

chʻu^1 wai^4 fang^1 chih^1 shao^3 chu^3 jên.^{2}

1579

He who lacks hospitality to guests, must be a fool.

客 來 主 不 顧。應 恐 是 癡 人

Kʻo^4 lai^2 chu^3 pu^4 ku,^{4} ying^4 kʻung^3 shih^4 chʻih^2 jên.^{2}

1580

He who is not hospitable to an excellent guest will have none.

良 賓 主 不 顧。自 是 無 良 賓

Liang^2 pin^1 chu^3 pu^4 ku,^{4} tzŭ^4 shih^4 wu^2 liang^2 pin.^{1}

1581

Long visits make hosts uncivil; when a poor man visits his relations they are cool.

久 住 令 人 賤。貧 來 親 也 疎

Chiu^3 chu^4 ling^4 jên^2 chien^4; pʻin^3 lai^2 chʻin^1 yeh^3 su.^{2}

1582

Having fermented your white wine, you can feast a worthy guest; having spent your gold, you can enjoy the odes and histories.

白 酒 釀 成 筵 好 客

Pai^2 chiu^3 niang^4 chʻêng^2 yen^2 ʻhao^3 kʻo,^{4}

黃 金 散 盡 爲 詩 書

ʻhuang^2 chin^1 san^4 chin^4 wei^2 shih^1 shu.^{1}

1583

Taoist monasteries entertain the genii; schools hide future premiers and scholars.

道院迎仙客。書堂隱相儒

Tao^4 yüan^4 ying^2 hsien^1 kʻo,^{4} shu^1 tʻang^2 yin^3 hsiang^4 ju.^{2}

1584

Though we escort a guest a thousand miles, still we must part.

送君千里。終須一別

Sung^4 chün^1 chʻien^1 li,^{3} chung^1 hsü^1 yi^1 pieh.^{2}

1585

Entertain guests but do not detain them.

宴客切勿留連

Yen^4 kʻo^4 chʻieh^4 wu^4 liu^2 lien.^{2}

1586

His house is constantly full of guests; and the wine cup is never empty.

座上客常滿。杯中酒不空

Tso^4 shang^4 kʻo^4 chʻang^2 man^3; pei^1 chung^1 chiu^3 pu^4 kʻung.^{1}

1587

What wind blew you here?

甚麽風吹了你來

Shên^4 mo^1 fêng^1 chʻui^1 liao^3 ni^3 lai^2?

NOTE.—This is said to an infrequent guest.

1588

In ordinary life you must not be otherwise than economical; when inviting a guest not otherwise than lavish.

居家不可不儉

Chü^1 chia^1 pu^4 kʻo^3 pu^4 chien^3;

請客不可不豐

Chʻing^3 kʻo^4 pu^4 kʻo^3 pu^4 fêng.^{1}

1589

Receive all guests that come, making no difference between relations and others.

客無親疎來者當受

Kʻo^4 wu^4 chʻin^1 su^2 lai^2 chê^2 tang^1 shou.^{4}

諺語叢話

1590

I called at the temple but saw not *T'u Ti.*

上廟勿見土地

Shang³ miao⁴ wu⁴ chien⁴ T'u³ Ti.⁴

NOTE.—The *T'u Ti*, *T'u-shên* (土神), or *shê*⁴ (社), are a pair of idols supposed to have all the cultivated land under their joint protection. They are spoken of as 'husband and wife,' and are represented by male and female figures. Their shrines, often situated most picturesquely, stud the country over. Two festivals during the year, are celebrated in their honour; the first occurs on the fiftieth day after the commencement of Spring (about the middle of March), and the second on the fiftieth day after the commencement of Autumn (about the middle of September). See the *Yu-hsiao* (幼學), section *sui-shih* (歲時). Now this proverb is used when one calls upon a person without being able to see him.

1591

Keep back before a mandarin, but not before a host.

見官莫向前。做客莫在後

Chien⁴ kuan¹ mo⁴ hsiang⁴ ch'ien,² tso⁴ k'o⁴ mo⁴ tsai⁴ 'hou.⁴

1592

As you treat guests at home you will be treated abroad. *Lit.:* At home do not beat men, then abroad men will not beat you.

在家不打人。出外無人打

Tsai⁴ chia¹ pu⁴ ta³ jên,² ch'u¹ wai⁴ wu² jên² ta.³

1593

Relations must be seldom visited; kitchen gardens often.

親戚要走得稀菜園要去得勤

Ch'in¹ ch'i⁴ yao⁴ tsou⁴ tê² hsi¹; ts'ai⁴ yüan² yao⁴ ch'ü⁴ tê² ch'in.²

1594

I sting your lips with your own bread.

仰你的饅頭蠆你的嘴

Yang³ ni³ ti¹ man³ t'ou² ch'ai³ ni³ ti¹ tsui.³

NOTE.—This is said, in apology, by a poor host who is obliged to serve up the gift just received for his guest to eat.

1595

Too much politeness. *Lit.:* No sooner are the tables cleared than he invites me to a return feast.

拭棹還席

Shih⁴ cho¹ 'huan² hsi.²

1596

One guest does not trouble two hosts.

一客不擾二主

Yi[1] k'o[4] pu[4] jao[3] êrh[4] chu.[3]

1597

Singing clearly to each other on the border, still the ferry boat will not tarry; I also cannot tarry; go, yea, go I must; after repeated hesitation, delay I cannot.

唱徹陽關上。小舟也難留

Ch'ang[4] chê[4] yang[2] kuan[1] shang,[4] hsiao[3] chou[1] yeh[3] nan[2] liu[2]

我也難留。去也終須去

wo[3] yeh[3] nan[2] liu.[2] ch'ü[4] yeh[4] chung[1] hsü[1] ch'ü[4];

再三留不住

tsai[4] san[1] liu[2] pu[4] chu.[4]

NOTE.—This shapeless proverb is confessedly difficult to understand. Probably the clear singing referred to, indicates some ancient method of taking farewell, or of bewailing the departure of a guest.

SECTION XIII.—ON MEDICINE.

CHAPTER I.

DISEASE.

1598

Still by a lotus fibre the big salt-junk is bound;
And having reached their climax, diseases must turn round.

藕絲繫得鹽船住
Ou^3 ssŭ^1 chi^4 tê^2 yen^2 chʻuan^2 chu^4;
災殃已滿病自愈
Tsai^1 yang^1 i^3 man^3 ping^4 tzŭ^4 yü.^{4}

NOTE.—This proverb indicates a slight possibility of recovery. There is just a chance.

1599

A little food taken again and again,
Will enable the sick new health to attain.

少喫多餐。病好自安
Shao^3 chʻih^1 to^1 tsʻan,^{2} ping^4 ʻhao^3 tzŭ^4 an.^{1}

1600

Phlegm, waste, wind, worms, and stoppage, sure
Nor gods nor fairies e'er can cure.

痰癆氣蠱隔。神仙醫不得
Tʻan,^{2} lao,^{2} chʻi,^{4} ku^3 ko,^{1} shên^2 hsien^1 i^1 pu^4 tê.^{2}

1601

Medicine for healing, soup for nourishment.

服藥因療病。煎湯爲保身
Fu^2 yao^4 yin^1 liao^3 ping,^{4} chien^1 tʻang^1 wei^4 pao^3 shên.^{1}

1602

Your medicines are as effective as divine assistance.

服藥有靈。其效如神
Fu^2 yao^4 yu^3 ling^2; chʻi^2 hsiao^4 ju^2 shên.^{2}

1603

The prescription was good, but the medicine bad.

說的是眞方。賣的是假藥

Shuo[1] ti[1] shih[4] chên[1] fang,[1] mai[4] ti[1] shih[4] chia[3] yao.[4]

1604

Though you drink a bellyful of medicine, avoid the taste in swallowing it.

藥灌滿腸口吞莫嘗

Yao[4] kuan[4] man[3] chʻang[2] kʻou[3] tʻun[1] mo[4] chʻang.[2]

1605

When medicine cures, the patient is under providential care.

藥醫有緣人

Yao[4] i[1] yu[3] yüan[2] jên.[2]

1606

When a disease returns, no medicine can cure it.

反病無藥醫

Fan[3] ping[4] wu[2] yao[4] i.[1]

1607

There is no such thing as spurious gold, or genuine *o-wei.*

黃金無假。阿魏無眞

ʻHuang[2] chin[1] wu[2] chia,[3] o[1] wei[4] wu[2] chên.[1]

NOTE.—*O-wei*, "assafœtida." For some interesting remarks on this medicine, its use etc., by the Chinese, see Dr. Porter Smith's *Contributions towards the Materia Medica and Natural History of China*, page 27.

1608

Give a man a golden pill, and the devil of his disease will depart in a trice.

投以金丹病魔立退

Tʻou[2] i[3] chin[1] tan[1] ping[4] mo[2] li[4] tʻui.[4]

1609

Men's constitutions differ in different localities.

土性不同

Tʻu[3] hsing[4] pu[4] tʻung.[2]

1610

When disease enters the region of the heart, no medicine can effect a cure.

病入膏肓。不可救藥

Ping^4 ju^4 kao^1 mang,^{2} pu^4 kʻo^3 chiu^4 yao.^{4}

1611

Your ears won't go deaf if you don't have them examined; your eyes won't go blind if you refuse to use washes.

耳不看不聾。眼不洗不瞎

Erh^3 pu^4 kʻan^4 pu^4 lung^2; yen^3 pu^4 hsi^3 pu^4 hsia.^{2}

1612

The most wonderful medicine must fail to cure a sickness caused by resentment.

妙藥難醫寃孽病

Miao^4 yao^4 nan^2 i^1 yüan^1 yeh^4 ping.^{4}

NOTE.—If one man oppresses another to death, the ghost of the murdered man is supposed to haunt and afflict the oppressor with a sickness no medicine can cure.

1613

It is a disease which neither needle nor medicine can reach.

攻之不可。達之不能

Kung^1 chih^1 pu^4 kʻo^3; tê^2 chih^1 pu^4 nêng.^{2}

1614

A willow planted before a cook-house door will die, not live.

竈門栽楊柳。有死無生

Tsao^4 mên^2 tsʻai^1 yang^2 liu,^{3} yu^3 ssŭ^3 wu^2 shêng.^{1}

1615

T'is easy to get a thousand prescriptions, but hard to obtain one good result.

千方易得。一效難求

Chʻien^1 fang^1 i^4 tê,^{2} yi^1 hsiao^4 nan^2 chʻui.^{2}

CHAPTER II.

DOCTORS.

1616

After diagnosis, we proceed to treat
All sorts of diseases, in the way most meet.

問 症 發 藥。與 病 相 合

Wên^{4} chêng^{4} fa^{1} yao,^{4} yü^{3} ping^{4} hsiang^{1} ʻho.^{2}

1617

Chair-riding doctors don't call at the door
Of any patient unluckily poor.

醫 生 坐 轎。 窮 家 不 到

I^{1} shêng^{1} tso^{4} chiao,^{4} chʻiung^{2} chia^{1} pu^{4} tao.^{4}

1618

When the doctor's fame is made,
More folks come than he can aid.

醫 生 出 名。家 家 接 不 贏

I^{1} shêng^{1} chʻu^{1} ming,^{2} chia^{1} chia^{1} chieh^{1} pu^{4} ying.^{2}

1619

He boasts that his merits match those of *Pien Chʻio*;
Yet he's *Yen's* fatal net, for ought that we know.

道 他 功 高 扁 鵲

Tao^{4} tʻa^{1} kung^{1} kao^{1} Pien^{3} Chʻio^{3};

誰 知 他 催 命 閻 羅

Shui^{3} chih^{1} tʻa^{1} tsʻui^{1} ming^{4} Yen^{2} lo.^{2}

NOTE.—*Pien Chʻio* was an ancient doctor spoken of in the *Historical Record*. He was surnaned *Chin* (秦), named *Huan* (緩), and bore the polite designation of *Yueh Jên* (越 人). On one occasion he met *Chʻang Sang-chün* (長 桑 君) a geni (?), and received from him medicine and a medical book. He was also instructed to drink the dew from bamboo trees for thirty days, that at the end of that period his knowledge of diseases might become perfect. And so it happened. See the *Yu-hsiao* (幼 學), Book 4, section *chi-i* (技 藝).

1620

All diseases incident to cold weather and hot,
There must be no question if the doctor knows or not.

風 寒 暑 熱。醫 要 曉 得

Fêng^{1} ʻhan^{2} shu^{3} jê,^{4} i^{1} yao^{4} hsiao^{3} tê.^{2}

1621

He'll warrant a cure when his fee is provided;
Men doubt it, however, and are undecided.

包好受謝。人疑莫決

Pao^{1} ‘hao^{3} shou^{4} hsieh^{4}; jen^{2} i^{2} mo^{4} chüeh.^{2}

1622

The profoundest study of *Wang Shu-‘ho*,
Compared with great practice is mere so so.

熟讀王叔和。不如看症多

Shu^{2} tu^{2} Wang^{2} Shu^{2} ‘Ho,^{2} pu^{4} ju^{2} k‘an^{4} chêng^{4} to.^{1}

NOTE.—*Wang Shu-‘ho*, court physician during the Western *Tsin* dynasty, and author of a celebrated treatise on the pulse. See Wylie's *Notes on Chinese Literature*, page 78.

1623

In a dangerous illness call in three doctors.

急病請三師

Chi^{2} ping^{4} ch‘ing^{3} san^{1} shih.^{1}

1624

A clever doctor cannot cure himself.

良醫不自醫

Liang^{2} i^{1} pu^{4} tzŭ^{4} i.^{1}

1625

A teacher will not speak against a teacher, nor a doctor against a doctor.

師不談師。醫不談醫

Shih^{1} pu^{4} t‘an^{2} shih,^{1} i^{1} pu^{4} t‘an^{2} i.^{1}

1626

If you do not remunerate a doctor for curing you once, you will get no one to do so a second time.

病好不謝醫。下次無人醫

Ping^{4} ‘hao^{3} pu^{4} hsieh^{4} i,^{1} hsia^{4} tz‘ŭ^{4} wu^{2} jên^{2} i.^{1}

1627

Only avail yourself of my ten years' luck, and your complaint will soon be better.

趁我十年運。有病早來醫

Ch‘ên^{4} wo^{3} shih^{2} nien^{2} yün,^{4} yu^{3} ping^{4} tsao^{3} lai^{2} i.^{1}

1628

A doctor has the heart to cut flesh off his thigh to give to his patient, but never the mind to deceive him.

醫有割股之心

I^{1} yu^{3} ko^{1} ku^{3} chih^{1} hsin,^{1}

並無虛假之意

ping^{4} wu^{2} hsü^{1} chia^{3} chih^{1} i.^{4}

1629

Quacks puncture and plaster, but only use spurious drugs.

打針貼膏藥。賣藥的用假藥

Ta^{3} chên^{1} tʻieh^{1} kao^{1} yao,^{4} mai^{4} yao^{4} ti^{1} yung^{4} chia^{3} yao.^{4}

1630

An unskilful doctor kills men with a secret dagger.

學醫不明。暗刀殺人

Hsiao^{2} i^{1} pu^{4} ming,^{2} an^{4} tao^{1} sha^{1} jên.^{2}

1631

The unlucky doctor cures the head of a disease; the lucky doctor its tail.

運去先生醫病頭

Yün^{4} chʻü^{4} hsien^{1} shêng^{1} i^{1} ping^{4} tʻou^{2};

時來先生醫病尾

shih^{2} lai^{2} hsien^{1} shêng^{1} i^{1} ping^{4} wei.^{3}

1632

Doctors have a run of ten years' luck.

行醫有十年大運

Hsing^{2} i^{1} yu^{3} shih^{2} nien^{2} ta^{4} yün.^{4}

1633

Doctors knock at no doors; they only come when invited.

醫不叩門有請纔行

I^{1} pu^{4} kʻou^{4} mên^{2} yu^{3} chʻing^{3} tsʻai^{2} hsing.^{2}

1634

A stupid doctor murders without a sword.

庸醫殺人不用刀

Yung^{2} i^{1} sha^{1} jên^{2} pu^{4} yung^{4} tao.^{1}

1635

You are both laying up secret merit, and taking care of yourself.

半積陰功。半藏身

Pan[4] chi[2] yin[1] kung[1] pan[4] ts'ang[2] shên.[1]

1636

Many children of clever sorcerers are killed by devils; and many children of clever doctors die of disease.

良巫之子多死於鬼

Liang[2] wu[1] chih[1] tzŭ[3] to[1] ssŭ[3] yü[2] kuei[3];

良醫之子多死於病

liang[2] i[1] chih[1] tzŭ[3] to[1] ssŭ[3] yü[2] ping.[4]

1637

To take no medicine is as good as a middling doctor.

不吃藥當中醫

Pu[4] ch'ih[1] yao[4] tang[1] chung[1] i.[1]

1638

When medicine restores a man to health, the doctor truly has the ability of *Ch'i* and *'Huang.*

藥到回春。先生眞岐黃手段

Yao[4] tao[4] 'hui[2] ch'un,[1] hsien[1] shêng[1] chên[1] Ch'i[2] 'Huang[2] shou[3] tan.[4]

NOTE.—*Ch'i Pai* (岐伯) was a minister and also Medical instructor of *'Huang Ti* (黃帝), B. C. 2697. See *Yu-hsiao* (幼學), Book 4, section *Ch'i-yi* (技藝).

1639

He who with three fingers on the pulse can restore a man to health, may not be an able minister, but he is an able physician.

三指活人性命

San[1] chih[3] 'hua[4] jên[2] hsing[4] ming,[4]

不爲良相便爲良醫

Pu[4] wei[2] liang[2] hsiang[4] pien[4] wei[2] liang[2] i.[1]

SECTION XIV.—ON MORALS.

CHAPTER I.

CONSCIENCE.

1640

Men who never violate their consciences, are not afraid of a knock at their door at midnight.

爲人不做虧心事
Wei² jên² pu⁴ tso⁴ k'uei¹ hsin¹ shih.⁴
半夜敲門心不驚
pan⁴ yeh⁴ ch'iao¹ mên² hsin¹ pu⁴ ching.¹

1641

A good conscience pays badly.

良心不中吃喝的
Liang² hsin¹ pu⁴ chung⁴ ch'ih¹ 'ho¹ ti.¹

1642

The same. *Lit.*: Talk of conscience and you will have nothing to eat.

講良心沒飯吃
Chiang³ liang² hsin¹ mu² fan⁴ ch'ih.¹

1643

Do not violate conscience.

莫虧良心
Mo⁴ k'uei¹ liang² hsin.¹

1644

Of all important things, the first is not to cheat the conscience.

再三須重事。第一莫欺心
Tsai⁴ san¹ hsü¹ chung⁴ shih,⁴ ti⁴ yi¹ mo⁴ ch'i¹ hsin.¹

1645

Don't put your conscience on your back.

莫把良心放在背上
Mo⁴ pa³ liang² hsin¹ fang⁴ tsai⁴ pei⁴ shang.⁴

1646

Since one cannot please others in everything, let us only seek not to shame one's own conscience.

豈 能 盡 如 人 意

Chʻi^3 nêng^2 chin^4 ju^2 jên^2 i,^{4}

但 求 無 愧 我 心

tan^4 chʻiu^2 wu^2 kʻuei^4 wo^3 hsin.^{1}

1647

Never do what your conscience cannot endure; never desire what is improper to be done.

莫 作 心 上 過 不 去 之 事

Mo^4 tso^4 hsin^1 shang^4 kuo^4 pu^4 chʻü^4 chih^1 shih^4;

莫 起 事 上 行 不 去 之 心

mo^4 chʻi^3 shih^4 shang^4 hsing^2 pu^4 chʻü^4 chih^1 hsin.^{1}

NOTE.—There is here, in the origninal, a beautiful antithetical collocation of words, which one attempts in vain to copy in the English.

1648

If you would train your disposition you must cultivate virtue; if you cheat your conscience don't assume to be an ascetic.

養 性 須 修 善。 欺 心 莫 吃 齋

Yang^3 hsing^4 hsü^1 hsiu^1 shan^4; chʻi^1 hsin^1 mo^4 chʻih^1 chai.^{1}

1649

Cheat your conscience and a whole life's happiness is destroyed; let your conduct be faulty and Heaven will send you a life of poverty.

欺 心 折 盡 平 生 福

Chʻi^1 hsin^1 chê^2 chin^4 pʻing^2 shêng^1 fu^2;

行 短 天 敎 一 世 貧

hsing^2 tuan^3 tʻien^1 chiao^4 yi^1 shih^4 pʻin.^{3}

1650

To destroy one's good conscience by doing some evil deed. *Lit.:* To distend one's bowels by swallowing a carrying-pole.

吃了偏担横了肠子
Ch'ih[1] liao[3] pien[3] tan[1] 'hêng[4] liao[3] ch'ang[2] tzŭ.[3]

— 1651 —

To corrupt the conscience by unfair dealings. *Lit.:* To eat a coal and blacken the heart.

吃了煤炭黑了心
Ch'ih[1] liao[3] mei[2] t'an[4] 'hei[1] liao[3] hsin.[1]

CHAPTER II.

GOOD WORKS.

1652

To light up a pagoda from top to base,
Is unequal to lighting up a dark place.

點塔七層。不如暗處一燈

Tien^3 tʻa^3 chʻi^1 tsêng,^{2} pu^4 ju^2 an^4 chʻu^4 yi^1 têng.^{1}

1653

The odour of virtuous conduct will last for a hundred generations.

爲善則流芳百世

Wei^2 shan^4 tsê^2 liu^2 fang^1 pai^3 shih.^{4}

1654

Good deeds may fill the empire without provoking any one's dislike.

行滿天下無怨惡

Hsing^2 man^3 tʻien^1 hsia^4 wu^2 yüan wu.^{4}

1655

Do good regardless of consequences.

但行好事。莫問前程

Tan^4 hsing^2 ʻhao^3 shih,^{4} mo^4 wên^4 chʻien^2 chʻêng.^{2}

1656

Good deeds may be done; bad deeds may not.

善事可作。惡事莫爲

Shan^4 shih^4 kʻo^3 tso^4; o^4 shih^4 mo^4 wei.^{2}

1657

Do not consider any vice trivial, and so practise it; do not consider any virtue trivial, and so neglect it.

勿以惡小而爲之

Wu^4 i^3 o^4 hsiao^3 êrh^2 wei^2 chih^1;

勿以善小而不爲

wu^4 i^3 shan^4 hsiao^3 êrh^2 pu^4 wei.^{2}

1658

Do good, and devils and gods will do you honour; do evil, and suffer the chastisement of Heaven.

爲善鬼神欽。作惡被天鑑

Wei^{2} shan^{4} kuei^{3} shên^{2} chʻin^{1}; tso^{4} o^{4} pei^{4} tʻien^{1} chien.^{4}

1659

One good deed atones for a thousand bad ones.

一善改千惡

Yi^{1} shan^{4} kai^{3} chʻien^{1} o.^{4}

1660

It is difficult to know how to give alms. *Lit.:* The good door is hard to open.

善門難開

Shan^{4} mên^{2} nan^{2} kʻai.^{1}

1661

Religious books and preachers, influence but do not injure men.

勸世文勸世人

Chʻüan^{4} shih^{4} wên^{2} chʻüan^{4} shih^{4} jên,^{2}

勸動人心不害人

chʻüan^{4} tung^{4} jên^{2} hsin^{1} pu^{4} ʻhai^{4} jên.^{2}

1662

Cultivating right reason, though unseen of men, if persevered in, will be seen of Heaven.

修道雖無人見

Hsin^{1} tao^{4} sui^{1} wu^{2} jên^{2} chien,^{4}

存心自有天知

tsʻun^{2} hsin^{1} tzŭ^{4} yu^{3} tʻien^{1} chih.^{1}

1663

Exhort men not to commit the smallest sin; but the smallest virtue is advantageous to men.

一毫之惡勸人莫作

Yi^{1} ʻhao^{2} chih^{1} o^{4} chʻüan^{4} jên^{2} mo^{4} tso^{4}:

一毫之善與人方便

yi^{1} ʻhao^{2} chih^{1} shan^{4} yu^{3} jên^{2} fang^{1} pien.^{4}

1664

Each has his own good deeds to do; the gentleman his, the lady hers.

公修公德。、婆修婆德。
Kung^1 hsiu^1 kung^1 tê^2; pʻo^2 hsiu^1 pʻo^2 tê,^{2}
各修各德
ko^4 hsiu^1 ko^4 tê.^{2}

1665

To say you have done good is not goodness; but to do good is.

說好不爲好。做好方爲好
Shuo^1 ʻhao^3 pu^4 wei^2 ʻhao^3; tso^4 ʻhao^3 fang^1 wei^2 ʻhao.^{3}

1666

To do good secretly is optional. *Lit.:* Bowing in the dark is according to every man's own fancy.

黑處作揖。各人憑心
ʻHei^1 chʻu^4 tso^4 i,^{1} ko^4 jên^2 pʻing^2 hsin.^{1}

1667

Never go out on the hills to net birds; nor down to the waters to poison fishes and shrimps.

勿登山而網禽鳥
Wu^4 têng^1 shan^1 êrh^2 wang^3 chʻin^2 niao^3;
勿臨水而毒魚蝦
wu^4 lin^2 shui^3 êrh^2 tu^2 yü^2 hsia.^{1}

NOTE.—This does not mean that you may *shoot* the birds, as Sir Jno. F. Davis suggests, but that their lives should be spared.

1668

Never kill the draught ʻox; nor throw away written paper.

勿宰耕牛。勿棄字紙
Wu^4 tsai^4 kêng^1 niu^2; wu^4 chʻi^4 tzŭ^4 chih.^{3}

1669

In the family leave the family; in the world separate from the world.

在家出家。在世出世
Tsai^4 chia^1 chʻu^1 chia^1; tsai^4 shih^4 chʻu^1 shih.^{4}

NOTE.—"I pray not that thou shouldest take them out of the world, but that thou shouldest keep them from the evil." Jno. 17: 15.

"We need not bid, for cloister'd cell,
Our neighbour and our work farewell;
Nor strive to wind ourselves too high
For sinful man beneath the sky."

1670

He does nothing that cannot be told to others.

無事不可對人言

Wu[2] shih[4] pu[4] k'o[3] tui[4] jên[2] yen.[2]

NOTE.—*Ssŭ-ma Wên Kung* (司馬温公) said of himself that, "All his ife long he had done nothing that he could not tell to others."

1671

It is easier to run down a hill than up one.

下坡容易。上坡難

Hsia[4] p'o[1] yung[2] i,[4] shang[3] p'o[1] nan.[2]

1672

Surely those who have in ten lives cultivated virtue, may cross in the same boat; as those who have in a hundred, may sleep in the same bed.

十世修來同船渡

Shih[2] shih[4] hsiu[1] lai[2] t'ung[2] ch'uan[2] tu[4];

百世修來共枕眠

pai[3] shih[4] hsiu[1] lai[2] kung[4] chên[3] mien.[2]

1673

Men will no more be virtuous without exhortation, than a bell will sound without being struck.

人不勸不善。鐘不打不鳴

Jên[2] pu[4] ch'üan[4] pu[4] shan[4]; chung[1] pu[4] ta[3] pu[4] ming.[2]

1674

It is not hard to talk about good works, but to do them.

言善非難。行善爲難

Yen[2] shan[4] fei[1] nan,[2] hsing[2] shan[4] wei[2] nan.[2]

1675

To save one man's life is better than to build a seven-storied pagoda.

救人一命。勝造七級浮屠

Chiu[4] jên[2] yi[1] ming,[4] shêng[4] tsao[4] ch'i[1] chi[2] fou[2] t'u.[2]

1676

His conduct is naturally exalted who will not condescend to beg.

人 到 無 求 品 自 高

Jên² tao⁴ wu² ch'iu² p'in³ tzŭ⁴ kao.¹

1677

To neglect to save life is one of the greatest of crimes.

見 死 不 救。一 行 大 罪

Chien⁴ ssŭ³ pu⁴ chiu,⁴ yi¹ 'hang² ta⁴ tsui.⁴

CHAPTER III.

REPROOF AND GOOD COUNSEL.

1678

If to be right is your desire,
Then of three aged men enquire.

要 得 好。問 三 老

Yao^{4} tê^{2} ʻhao,^{3} wên^{4} san^{1} lao.^{3}

1679

If to have all things right be your desire,
Then of three aged men you must enquire.

凡 事 要 好。須 問 三 老

Fan^{2} shih^{4} yao^{4} ʻhao,^{3} hsü^{1} wên^{4} san^{1} lao.^{3}

1680

Although you may never have tasted of bacon,
You have seen pigs pass and should not be mistaken.

沒 有 吃 肉。也 看 見 猪 走

Mu^{2} yu^{3} chʻih^{1} jou,^{4} yeh^{3} kʻan^{4} chien^{4} chu^{1} tsou.^{4}

NOTE.—Used by a superior to an inferior, this conveys rebuke. Used by one of one's-self, or by one equal to another, it means that, though lacking actual experience, we have a knowledge of whatever is referred to.

1681

To reprove one for another's warning. *Lit.:* To beat the grass to frighten the snake.

打 草 驚 蛇

Ta^{3} tsʻao^{3} ching^{1} shê.^{2}

1682

The same. *Lit.:* To kill the fowl to frighten the monkey.

殺 雞 嚇 猴

Sha^{1} chi^{1} hsia^{4} ʻhou.^{2}

1683

The same. *Lit.:* He points at *Chang Liang* and curses *ʻHan Hsin;* who does he mean?

指張良罵韓信。爲着誰來

Chih³ Chang¹ Liang² ma⁴ 'Han² Hsin,⁴ wei⁴ cho² shui³ lai²?

NOTE.—*Chang Liang* and *'Han Hsin*, two ministers of *Liu Pang* (劉邦) or *Kao Ti* (高帝), first of the *'Han* emperors, whose reign datesfrom 206 B. C.

1684

The same. *Lit.:* He points at the great melon and curses the gourd.

指冬瓜罵葫蘆

Chih³ tung¹ kua¹ ma⁴ hu² lu.²

1685

The same. *Lit.:* He points at the mulberry and curses the ash.

指桑罵槐

Chih³ sang¹ ma⁴ 'huai.²

1686

A wise man will not reprove a fool.

賢不責愚

Hsien² pu⁴ tsê² yü.²

1687

Faults must be corrected by competent persons. *Lit.:* Crooked trees must come under the straightening hand of the carpenter.

彎木頭自必有直木匠

Wan¹ mu⁴ t'ou² tzŭ⁴ pi⁴ yu³ chih² mu⁴ chiang.⁴

1688

You have done it badly *Lit.:* Your work is like a rat trap.

做得像打老鼠的架子

Tso⁴ tê² hsiang⁴ ta³ lao³ shu³ ti¹ chia⁴ tzŭ.³

1689

Buy a fan to cover your face.

買把扇子遮臉

Mai³ pa³ shan⁴ tzŭ³ chê¹ lien.³

NOTE.—Said to another this conveys reproof; said of one's-self, apology.

1690

Your rump is hung with keys, but what gate do you keep?

屁股掛鑰匙。鎖管那一門

P'i⁴ ku³ kua⁴ yao⁴ ch'ih,² so³ kuan³ na³ yi¹ mên?²

NOTE.—This is used to convey reproof of neglect of duty.

1691

Princes have censors,—fathers, sons that reprove them.

君有臣諫。父有子諫

Chün¹ yu³ ch'ên² chien,⁴ fu⁴ yu³ tzŭ³ chien.⁴

1692

It takes little time to reprove a man; but it takes a long time to forget reproof.

說話時短。記話時長

Shuo¹ 'hua⁴ shih² tuan³; chi⁴ 'hua⁴ shih² ch'ang.²

1693

Flattery is sickness; reproof is medicine.

甘言疾也。苦言藥也

Kan¹ yen² chi² yeh³: k'u³ yen² yao⁴ yeh.³

1694

A bitter mouth is good physic.

苦口是良藥

K'u³ k'ou³ shih⁴ liang² yao.⁴

1695

Reprove yourself as though seeking for something to blame; reprove your friends as though seeking to to excuse their faults.

責己者於無過中求有過

Tsê² chi³ chê² yü² wu² kuo⁴ chung¹ ch'iu² yu³ kuo.⁴

責友者於有過中求無過

Tsê² yu³ chê² yü² yu³ kuo⁴ chung¹ ch'iu² wu² kuo.⁴

1696

Stop your mouth, and talk not of the faults and short-comings of others: and why should you speak of yours to them?

守口莫談人過短
Shou³ k'ou³ mo⁴ t'an² jên² kuo⁴ tuan³:
自短何曾說與人
tzŭ⁴ tuan³ 'ho² ts'eng² shuo¹ yü³ jên.²

1697

Before you blame others, submit yourself to blame.

莫說他人。先輸了自己
Mo⁴ shuo¹ t'a¹ jên,² hsien¹ shu¹ liao³ tzŭ⁴ chi.³

1698

Be vexed with yourself that you have neither branch nor leaf; do not accuse the sun of partiality.

自恨無枝葉。莫怨太陽偏
Tzŭ⁴ 'hên⁴ wu² chih¹ yeh⁴; mo⁴ yüan⁴ t'ai⁴ yang² p'ien.¹

1699

Blame yourself as you would blame others; excuse others as you would yourself.

責人之心責己
Tsê² jên² chih¹ hsin¹ tsê² chi³;
恕己之心恕人
yüan⁴ chi³ chih¹ hsin¹ yüan⁴ jên.²

1700

Why do not those who are continually judging of other men's faults, turn about and judge themselves?

平生只會量人短
P'ing² shêng¹ chih³ 'hui⁴ liang² jên² tuan,³
何不回頭把自量
'ho² pu⁴ 'hui² t'ou² pa³ tzŭ⁴ liang.²

NOTE.—"And why beholdest thou the mote that is in thy brother's eye, but considerest not the beam that is in thine own eye? Matt. 7:3.

1701

First put yourself right, then others.

先正自己。後正他人
Hsien¹ chêng⁴ tzŭ⁴ chi,³ 'hou⁴ chêng⁴ t'a¹ jên.²

1702

He who flatters me is my enemy,—who reproves me is my teacher.

道 吾 好 者 是 吾 賊

Tao^{4} wu^{2} ʿhao^{3} chê^{2} shih^{4} wu^{2} tsei^{2};

道 吾 惡 者 是 吾 師

Tao^{4} wu^{2} o^{4} chê^{2} shih^{4} wu^{2} shih.^{1}

1703

To butt against the nose in washing the face.

洗 臉 碍 住 鼻 子

Hsi^{3} lien^{3} ai^{4} chu^{4} pi^{2} tzŭ.^{3}

NOTE.—The meaning here is of encountering unpleasantness or danger in doing what one ought: for instance, of encountering the dislike of any person of whose conduct we have felt bound to make complaint.

1704

He won't listen to my advice. *Lit.:* He won't obey my helm.

不 應 我 的 舵

Pu^{4} ying^{4} wo^{3} ti^{1} to.^{4}

CHAPTER IV.

VICES.—(1) FLATTERY.

1705

Only inferiors flatter superiors. *Lit.:* As to flattery, it is only given by such as captains of thousands, of hundreds, or of fifties.

論把結不過是千百把總

Lün^{2} pa^{1} chieh^{2} pu^{4} kuo^{4} shih^{4} chʻien^{1} pai^{3} pa^{3} tsung.^{3}

1706

On the departure of a high official, to fire a salute of *four* guns, is flattery that will not go.

大老爺出門放四炮

Ta^{4} lao^{3} yeh^{2} chʻu^{1} mên^{2} fang^{4} ssŭ^{4} pʻao,^{4}

奉承不到家

fêng^{4} chêng^{2} pu^{4} tao^{4} chia.^{1}

1707

Only to flatter the rich. *Lit.:* Only to add fuel to a hot stove.

只在熱竈裡着把火

Chih^{3} tsai^{4} jê^{4} tsao^{4} li^{3} cho^{2} pa^{3} ʻhuo.^{3}

1708

To try importunately to flatter. *Lit.:* His flattery fails, so he adds more salt and pours on more vinegar.

呵哄不彀添鹽酌醋

O^{1} ʻhung^{3} pu^{4} kou^{4} tʻien^{1} yen^{2} cho^{2} tsʻu.^{4}

(2) HYPOCRISY AND DECEIT.

1709

He something out of nothing makes;
And painteth feet upon his snakes.

無中生有。畫蛇添足

Wu^{2} chung^{1} shêng^{1} yu^{3}; ʻhua^{4} shê^{2} tʻien^{1} tsu.^{2}

1710

If you deceive the aged, do not deceive the young; the deceitful heart is not bright and clear.

欺 老 莫 欺 幼。欺 人 心 不 明

Chʻi^{1} lao^{3} mo^{4} chʻi^{1} yu^{4}: chʻi^{1} jên^{2} hsin^{1} pu^{4} ming.^{2}

1711

To lacerate one's skull in order to deceive.

掐 破 腦 殼 騙 人

Tʻao^{1} pʻo^{4} nao^{3} chʻio^{4} pʻien^{4} jên.^{2}

NOTE.—This is sometimes done by knavish beggars in order to extort money.

1712

To point a stag out as a horse.

指 鹿 爲 馬

Chih^{3} lu^{4} wei^{2} ma.^{3}

NOTE.—This was done by *Chao Kao* (趙高), a powerful but traitorous minister of the *Chʻin* (秦) dynasty, to his master the emperor *Erh shih* (二世). Now the saying simply means to deceive.

1713

Sun Wu-kʻung can't turn his summersets in Buddha's palm.

孫 悟 空 跟 兜

Sun^{1} Wu^{4} Kʻung^{1} kên^{1} tou,^{1}

打 不 過 佛 爺 巴 掌 心

ta^{3} pu^{4} kuo^{4} Fu^{2} Yeh^{2} pa^{1} chang^{3} hsin.^{1}

NOTE.—*Sun Wu-kʻung*, a deified or canonized monkey, whose summersets are said to extend over 108,000 *li*. His exploits are related in the *Hsi-yu-chi* (西遊記). This proverb is said to mean—you cannot delude me.

1714

It will not do to say yes before a man's face, and no behind his back.

不 可 面 是 背 非

Pu^{4} kʻo^{3} mien^{4} shih^{4} pei^{4} fei.^{1}

1715

It will not do to say one thing and mean another.

不 可 口 是 心 非

Pu^{4} kʻo^{3} kʻou^{3} shih^{4} hsin^{1} fei.^{1}

1716

Never burn false incense before a true god.

眞菩薩面前莫燒假香

Chên¹ pʻu² sa¹ mien⁴ chʻien² mo⁴ shao¹ chia³ hsiang.¹

1717

To deceive the good and fear the bad.

欺善怕惡

Chʻi¹ shan⁴ pʻa⁴ o.⁴

1718

Delude superiors; it is not worth while to delude inferiors.

瞞上不瞞下

Man² shang⁴ pu⁴ man² hsia.⁴

1719

It is not beauty that beguiles men; men beguile themselves.

色不迷人人自迷

Sê⁴ pu⁴ mi² jên² jên² tzŭ⁴ mi.²

(3) INGRATITUDE.

1720

He freezes my warm blood into an icy cold.

一腔熱血化爲氷炭

Yi¹ chʻiang¹ jê⁴ hsieh⁴ ʻhua⁴ wei² ping¹ tʻan.⁴

NOTE.—This proverb refers to unappreciated service or kindness.

1721

If he had not had a fisherman to lead him on, how could he ever have seen the waves?

不因漁父引。怎得見波濤

Pu⁴ yin¹ yü² fu⁴ yin,³ tsên³ tê² chien⁴ po¹ tʻao.²

NOTE.—These are said to be the words of *Tung Kao Kung* (東皐公), who thus complains of the ingratitude of *Wu Tzŭ-hsü* (伍子胥), a high officer in the State of *Tsʻou* (楚), to whom he had rendered signal service, but by whom his service had been forgotten.

1722

To feed and clothe one's-self without ever recognising the trouble our food has cost the ox,—our clothes the weaver.

吃 飯 不 知 牛 辛 苦
Chʻih^{1} fan^{4} pu^{4} chih^{1} niu^{2} hsin^{1} kʻu^{3};
穿 衣 不 知 紡 綿 人
chʻüan^{1} i^{1} pu^{4} chih^{1} fang^{3} mien^{2} jên.^{2}

1723

To return one's friendship with enmity.

不 以 我 爲 德。反 以 我 爲 仇
Pu^{4} i^{3} wo^{3} wei^{2} tê,^{2} fan^{3} i^{3} wo^{3} wei^{2} chʻou.^{2}

(4) MEANNESS.

1724

He wants his donkey to travel away,
But is not willing to give him his hay.

又 要 驢 子 走 得 好
Yu^{4} yao^{4} lü^{2} tzŭ^{3} tsou^{4} tê^{2} ʻhao,^{3}
又 要 驢 子 不 吃 草
yu^{4} yao^{4} lü^{2} tzŭ^{3} pu^{4} chʻih^{1} tsʻao.^{3}

1725

You cannot endure the great melon, and so you would grind down the small long one.

無 奈 冬 瓜。何 捉 得 瓠 子 磨
Wu^{2} nai^{4} tung^{1} kua,^{1} ʻho^{2} cho^{1} tê^{2} ʻhu^{4} tzŭ^{3} mo.^{2}

1726

To promise much and give little.

說 大 話 用 小 錢
Shuo^{1} ta^{4} ʻhua^{4} yung^{4} hsiao^{3} chʻien.^{2}

1727

To show off by making presents with another's property. *Lit.:* To seize another's cap and throw it on the stage.

諺語叢話

抓 別 人 帽 子 去 打 彩
Chua^1 pieh^2 jên^2 mao^4 tzŭ^3 chʻü^4 ta^3 tsʻai.^{3}

1728

To be generous with other people's things, and grasping with what is one's own.

用 別 人 的 大 方 用 自 己 的 手 緊
Yung^4 pieh^2 jên^2 ti^1 ta^4 fang^1; yung^4 tzŭ^4 chi^3 ti^1 shou^3 chin.^{3}

1729

To toady. *Lit.:* To place one's warm cheek along side another's cold one.

熱 臉 挨 冷 臉
Jê^4 lien^3 ai^2 lêng^3 lien.^{3}

1730

Unable either to use or part with. *Lit.:* The monkey seizes a piece of ginger,—fears to eat it, because it is bitter, throw it away,—and yet cannot part with it.

猴 子 撿 到 一 塊 薑
ʻHou^2 tzŭ^3 chien^3 tao^3 yi^1 kʻuai^4 chiang^1;

吃 了 怕 辣 丟 了 又 捨 不 得
chʻih^1 liao^3 pʻa^4 la^4 tiu^1 liao^3 yu^4 shê^3 pu^4 tê.^{2}

1731

To slight. *Lit.:* To throw into a tub of cold water.

丟 在 冷 水 盆 裡 去 了
Tiu^1 tsai^4 lêng^3 shui^3 pʻên^2 li^3 chʻü^4 liao.^{3}

(5) QUARRELLING AND VIOLENCE.

1732

Cat's paw. *Lit.:* Borrowing *Chʻin* soldiers with *Tsʻou's* to fight,
He scatters his bitter resentment outright.

借 秦 伐 楚。悶 氣 出 透
Chieh^4 Chʻin^2 fa^1 Tsʻou,^{3} mên^4 chʻi^4 chʻu^1 tʻou.^{4}

1733

With monkeyish excitement, like a leopard leaping,
He demands with blows to have all that's in our keeping.

猴急豹跳。强打惡要

ʻHou^2 chi^2 pao^4 tʻiao,^{4} chʻiang^2 ta^3 o^4 yao.^{4}

1734

"Man alive's a trifle,—like a blade of grass;
Kill him though, and then see what will come to pass."

在生是一根草

Tsai^4 shêng^1 shih^4 yi^1 kên^1 tsʻao^3;

死了是一個寶

ssŭ^3 liao^3 shih^4 yi^1 ko^4 pao.^{3}

1735

When against any your anger glows,
Be sure you never do come to blows.

與人發怒。切莫爭鬬

Yü^3 jên^2 fa^1 nu,^{4} chʻieh^4 mo^4 chêng^1 tou.^{4}

1736

One thread of the feeling of kindness retain,
And more pleasant will be your meeting again.

人情留一線。久後好相見

Jên^2 chʻing^2 liu^2 yi^1 hsien,^{4} chiu^3 ʻhou^4 ʻhao^3 hsiang^1 chien.^{4}

1737

To excite a quarrel. *Lit.:* To set on a dog to worry a pig.

唆狗咬猪

So^1 kou^3 yao^3 chu.^{1}

1738

They are not good fists which fight, nor good words which curse.

相打無好拳。相駡無好言

Hsiang^1 ta^3 wu^2 ʻhao^3 chʻüan,^{1} hsiang^1 ma^4 wu^2 ʻhao^3 yen.^{2}

1739

A hopeless quarrel. *Lit.:* A cock fighting a rock.

雞子與石子鬬

Chi^1 tzŭ^3 yü^3 shih^2 tzŭ^3 tou.^{4}

1740

When the heron and oyster quarrelled, the fisherman got the benefit.

鷸蚌相持漁人得利

Yü² pang⁴ hsiang¹ ch'ih² yü² jên² tê² li.⁴

1741

When a road is uneven, those who live on each side level it.

路道不平旁人鏟修

Lu⁴ tao⁴ pu⁴ p'ing² p'ang² jên² ch'an³ hsiu.¹

NOTE.—This is said when bystanders take up an ill-used man's quarrel, and punish for him his oppressor.

1742

Never quarrel with a woman.

男不可與女鬬

Nan² pu⁴ k'o³ yü³ nü² tou.⁴

1743

Never fight a knife with an axe.

刀不可以斧鬬

Tao¹ pu⁴ k'o³ i³ fu³ tou.⁴

1744

Intimate with few affairs, you will have but few troubles; acquainted with many men, you will have many quarrels.

知事少事煩惱少

Chih¹ shih⁴ shao³ shih² fan² nao³ shao³:

識人多處是非多

shih⁴ jên² to¹ ch'u⁴ shih⁴ fei¹ to.¹

1745

A quarrelsome family neighbours despise; quarrelsome neighbours slander each other.

家中不和鄰里欺

Chia¹ chung¹ pu⁴ 'ho² lin² li³ ch'i¹;

鄰里不和說是非

lin² li³ pu⁴ 'ho² shuo¹ shih⁴ fei.¹

1746

Convert great quarrels into small ones, and small ones into nothing.

大事化小。小事化無

Ta⁴ shih⁴ hua⁴ hsiao³, hsiao³ shih⁴ hua⁴ wu.²

1747

A fiddling business!

扯胡琴的事

Ch'ê³ hu⁴ ch'in² ti¹ shih.⁴

NOTE.—I don't wonder that this illustration is used to express a vexatious quarrel; for fiddling in China is worse than organ-grinding at home.

1748

One may reconcile enmities, but not produce them.

寃仇可解不可結

Yüan¹ ch'ou² k'o³ chieh,³ pu⁴ k'o³ chieh.²

1749

Whoever curses a *Kiangsi* man, insults the public generally.

罵一聲江西老表。大家有分

Ma⁴ yi¹ shêng¹ Chiang¹ Hsi¹ lao³ piao³ ta⁴ chia¹ yu³ fên.¹

NOTE.—This is essentially a *Hupeh* proverb. About the beginning of the present dynasty, two rebels, *Li Chih-ch'êng* (李至誠) and *Chang Hsien-chung* (張先忠), devastated this province, and left so few of the inhabitants alive that it had to be repopulated with *Kiangsi* men. So that for a *Hupeh* man to curse a *Kiangsi* man, is to curse an old relation, and to offend the public.

1750

To anchor in order to quarrel.

灣倒船啫罵

Wan¹ tao³ ch'uan² shê² ma.⁴

1751

Each half of the riven bamboo smokes.

劈破竹總夾烟

P'i¹ p'o⁴ chu² tsung³ chia¹ yen.¹

NOTE.—Said of men who, when a quarrel is over, retain some remains of caloric.

1752

Draw your bow but do not discharge the arrow; for it is not so effective to strike as to frighten a man.

開弓莫放箭
Kʻai^1 kung^1 mo^4 fang^4 chien,^{4}
打人不如嚇人强
ta^3 jên^2 pu^4 ju^2 hsia^4 jên^2 chʻiang.^{2}

1753

Quarrels cannot escape the verdict of public opinion.

是非難逃衆口
Shih^4 fei^1 nan^2 tʻao^2 chung^2 kʻou.^{3}

1754

Neither beat a man on a wound, nor curse him about a disgrace.

打莫打人痛處
Ta^3 mo^4 ta^3 jên^2 tʻung^4 chʻu^4;
罵莫罵人羞處
ma^4 mo^4 ma^4 jên^2 hsiu^1 chʻu.^{4}

1755

The old man claims to be right, and the old woman to be more so.

公說公有理。婆說理更長
Kung^1 shuo^1 kung^1 yu^3 li,^{3} pʻo^2 shuo^1 li^3 kêng^1 chʻang.^{2}

1756

Lips wound the heart, as when a mosquito provokes a rap from a fan.

蚊蟲遭扇打。嘴傷人心
Wên^2 chʻung^2 tsao^1 shan^4 ta,^{3} tsui^3 shang^1 jên^2 hsin.^{1}

1757

Indiscriminate cursing. *Lit.:* One bamboo pole beats a whole boat-load of people.

一竹篙子打一船人
Yi^1 chu^2 ʻhao^1 tzŭ^3 ta^3 yi^1 chʻuan^2 jên.^{2}

1758

If you are offended with a person, you must tell him what for.

怪人須要俾人知
Kuai^4 jên^2 hsü^1 yao^4 pei^3 jên^2 chih.^{1}

1759

Two scholars fighting for a pencil.

兩 個 學 生 打 架 爲 筆
Liang^3 ko^4 hsiao^2 shêng^1 ta^3 chia^4 wei^4 pi.^{3}

NOTE.—This is another and very well known specimen of the innuendo. The two last words, identical in sound with 未必 'it is impossible,' are used to convey that meaning; the rest of the proverb need not be spoken.

1760

When men come face to face, their differences vanish.

事 怕 當 面
Shih^4 pʻa^4 tang^1 mien.^{4}

(6) SELFISHNESS.

1761

Each for himself doth his hunger satisfy;
Each for himself is obliged to live and die.

各 人 吃 飯 各 人 飽
Ko^4 jên^2 chʻih^1 fan^4 ko^4 jên^2 pao^3:
各 人 生 死 各 人 了
Ko^4 jên^2 shêng^1 ssŭ^3 ko^4 jên^2 liao.^{3}

1762

Coveting another's measure of rice, you lose full six months' keep;
Whilst wrangling over a quarter of pig, you lose a flock of sheep.

貪 他 一 斗 米 失 却 半 年 糧
Tʻan^1 tʻa^1 yi^1 tou^3 mi^3 shih^1 chʻüeh^4 pan^4 nien^2 liang^2;
爭 他 一 脚 豚 反 失 一 羣 羊
Chêng^1 tʻa^1 yi^1 chiao^3 tʻun^2 fan^3 shih^1 yi^1 chʻün^2 yang.^{2}

1763

Fields are vain and lands are vain,
Men so briefly them retain.
Gold is vain, silver is vain,
Dead, you cannot them regain.
Wives are vain, and children vain,
In Hades they ne'er meet again.

田也空地也空
T'ien² yeh³ k'ung¹ ti⁴ yeh³ k'ung,¹
換了多少主人翁
'Huan⁴ liao³ to¹ shao³ chu³ jên² wêng.¹
金也空銀也空
Chin¹ yeh³ k'ung¹ yin² yeh³ k'ung,¹
死後何曾在手中
Ssŭ³ 'hou⁴ 'ho² ts'êng² tsai⁴ shou³ chung.¹
妻也空子也空
Chi¹ yeh³ k'ung¹ tzŭ³ yeh³ k'ung,¹
黃泉路上不相逢
'Huang² ch'ien² lu⁴ shang⁴ pu⁴ hsiang¹ fêng.²

1764

Its every man for himself,
In the common struggle for pelf.

各是各。你顧你。我顧我
Ko⁴ shih⁴ ko,⁴ ni³ ku⁴ ni,³ wo³ ku⁴ wo.³

1765

Go you along your great highway, and I'll get across my one-pole bridge.

你走你的陽關大路
Ni³ tsou⁴ ni³ ti¹ yang² kuan¹ ta⁴ lu,⁴
我過我的獨木橋
wo³ kuo⁴ wo³ ti¹ tu² mu⁴ ch'iao.²

1766

Other men's glaring eyes do not affect your eyes; other men's stupidity does not affect your family.

他人睍睍不涉你目
T'a¹ jên² hsien⁴ hsien⁴ pu⁴ shê⁴ ni³ mu⁴:
他事碌碌不及你屋
t'a¹ shih⁴ lu⁴ lu⁴ pu⁴ shê⁴ ni³ wu.¹

1767

"Do not neglect your own, in order to weed another's field."

勿舍己而芸人之田
Wu⁴ shê⁴ chi³ êrh² yün² jên² chih¹ t'ien.²

1768

Every fisherman with the great net has his own spot.

搬罾的守埠頭

Pan¹ chêng¹ ti¹ shou³ fou⁴ tʻou.²

1769

To act selfishly. *Lit.:* Both feet and hands bend towards the bosom.

脚彎手彎往懷裡彎

Chiao³ wan¹ shou³ wan¹ wang³ ʻhuai² li³ wan.¹

1770

The stag-hunter will not look at the hare.

逐鹿者不顧兎

Chu² lu⁴ chê² pu⁴ ku⁴ tʻu.⁴

1771

To grasp at gain regardless of suffering inflicted on others. *Lit.:* To gouge out another's eye fearless of blinding him.

剮眼睛不怕瞎

Kua³ yen³ ching¹ pu⁴ pʻa⁴ hsia.²

1772

When there is important business to be transacted, he spares himself the trouble; but let him hear of a little profit, and he will risk his life to get it.

幹大事惜身而避

Kan² ta⁴ shih⁴ hsi² shên¹ êrh² pi⁴;

聞小利亡命而來

wên² hsiao³ li⁴ wang² ming⁴ êrh² lai.²

1773

He who covets small gain, well hardly be able to accomplish great transactions.

貪圖小利。大事難成

Tʻan¹ tʻu² hsiao³ li,⁴ ta⁴ shih⁴ nan² chʻêng.²

1774

He only throws that die which brings in the wealth.

打進財卦

Ta³ chin⁴ tsʻai² kua.⁴

1775

Since men live not a hundred years, it is vain to scheme for a thousand.

人無百歲壽。枉作千年計

Jên2 wu2 pai3 sui4 shou,4 wang3 tso4 chʻien1 nien2 chi.4

1776

Naked we come, and naked we go.

赤身而來。赤身而去

Chʻih4 shên1 êrh2 lai,2 chʻih4 shên1 êrh2 chʻü.4

NOTE.—This sentiment, exactly like that expressed by Job (1 : 21.), is intended to act as a check on covetousness.

1777

Man goes empty-handed when his work on earth is done.

世界做完空手去

Shih4 chieh4 tso4 wan2 kʻung1 shou3 chʻü.4

1778

He who fills his boxes and trunks with clothes, only lays them up for others; for how can he live to wear each one of them out?

盈箱滿籠替人藏

Ying2 hsiang1 man3 lung2 tʻi4 jên2 tsʻang2;

何曾件件穿到老

ʻho2 tsʻêng2 chien4 chien4 chʻuan1 tao4 lao.3

1779

Of all the noble houses of the past, one half in ruins lie, overgrown with grass.

從來多少好樓臺

Tsʻung2 lai2 to1 shao3 ʻhao3 lou2 tʻai,2

半成瓦礫生青草

pan4 chʻêng2 wa1 li4 shêng1 chʻing1 tsʻao.3

1780

There is more money on earth than you can gain; and more offices in the palace than you can fill.

世上錢多賺不盡

Shih4 shang4 chʻien2 to1 chuan4 pu4 chin4;

朝裡官多做不了

chʻao2 li3 kuan1 to1 tso4 pu4 liao.3

1781

There is no one to sweep a common hall.

公 衆 堂 屋 無 人 掃

Kung[1] chung[4] tʻang[2] wu[1] wu[2] jên[2] sao.[3]

1782

First yourself, afterwards others.

先 有 自 己。後 有 他 人

Hsien[1] yu[3] tzŭ[4] chi,[3] ʻhou[4] yu[3] tʻa[1] jên.[2]

1783

Don't boast of being first, for others indeed are before you.

莫 道 君 行 早。更 有 早 行 人

Mo[4] tao[4] chün[1] hsing[2] tsao,[3] kêng[1] yu[3] tsao[3] hsing[2] jên.[2]

---

(7) SLANDER.

1784

Slander rises from nothing but a great deal of chatter;
As offence comes from meddling with another man's matter.

是 非 只 爲 多 開 口

Shih[4] fei[1] chih[3] wei[4] to[1] kʻai[1] kʻou[3];

煩 惱 皆 因 强 出 頭

Fan[2] nao[3] chieh[1] yin[1] chʻiang[2] chʻu[1] tʻou.[2]

1785

His winds and waves may rise, I shall still sit secure in my fishing terrace.

任 他 風 浪 起。穩 坐 釣 魚 臺

Jên[4] tʻa[1] fêng[1] lang[4] chʻi,[3] wên[3] tso[4] tiao[4] yü[2] tʻai.[2]

NOTE.—Said by one conscious of innocence amidst slander.

1786

Slander slits pantaloons.

挑 是 剝 非 撕 褲 子

Tʻiao[1] shih[4] po[1] fei[1] ssŭ[1] kʻu[4] tzŭ.[3]

1787

How can be I guilty of crime, since I never stirred out of my house?

坐 在 屋 裡 犯 夜

Tso^4 tsai^4 wu^1 li^3 fan^4 yeh.^{4}

NOTE.—Said in contradiction of slander.

1788

Slander spreads like fire. *Lit.:* Light a fire in seven places, and eight will burn to smoke.

七 處 放 火 八 處 燒 烟

Chʻi^1 chʻu^4 fang^4 ʻhuo^3 pa^1 chʻu^4 shao^1 yen.^{1}

1789

Baseless slander. *Lit.:* To have waves three feet high without wind, and thunder in a level plain.

無 風 三 尺 浪。平 地 一 聲 雷

Wu^2 fêng^1 san^1 chʻih^3 lang,^{4} pʻing^2 ti^4 yi^1 shêng^1 lei.^{2}

1790

Slander may injure any cause.

事 怕 一 句 言

Shih^4 pʻa^4 yi^1 chü^4 yen.^{2}

1791

What man, behind his back, is not spoken against? And who, before others, does not speak against men?

誰 人 背 後 無 人 說

Shui^3 jên^2 pei^4 ʻhou^4 wu^2 jên^2 shuo^1?

那 個 人 前 不 說 人

na^3 ko^4 jên^2 chʻien^2 pu^4 shuo^1 jên^2?

1792

Those who slander, are slanderers.

來 說 是 非 者。便 是 是 非 人

Lai^2 shuo^1 shih^4 fei^1 chê,^{2} pien^4 shih^4 shih^4 fei^1 jên.^{2}

1793

Slander is of daily occurrence, but if nobody would listen to it, it would soon cease.

是 非 終 日 有。不 聽 自 然 無

Shih^4 fei^1 chung^1 jih^4 yu,^{3} pu^4 tʻing^1 tzŭ^4 jan^2 wu.^{2}

1794

Don't wait for slander to enter your ears, lest it turn former love into hatred.

莫待是非來入耳
Mo[4] tai[4] shih[4] fei[1] lai[2] ju[4] êrh,[3]
從前恩愛反爲仇
ts'ung[2] ch'ien[2] ên[1] ai[4] fan[3] wei[2] ch'ou.[2]

1795

One may leap into the Yellow River, and yet not be washed clean.

跳得黃河洗不清
T'iao[4] tê[2] 'Huang[2] 'ho[2] hsi[3] pu[4] ch'ing.[1]

NOTE.—The meaning is that one cannot clear one's-self of slander.

1796

Idle rumours are rife amongst the men of *Ts'ou.*

楚人多謠
Ts'ou[3] jên[2] to[1] yao.[2]

NOTE.—This saying is not so complimentary to the *Hupeh* and *Hunan* men as another, written over the entry to the *Wu-chang* examination Hall; namely 維楚有材 'only the men of *Ts'ou* possess talent.'

1797

What is said to a man's face is not slander.

當面說話不成是非
Tang[1] mien[4] shuo[1] 'hua[4] pu[4] ch'êng[2] shih[4] fei.[1]

1798

Slander may spring up without a cause.

平白地造謠言
P'ing[2] pai[2] ti[4] tsao[4] yao[2] yen.[2]

1799

Idle slanders do not affect wise men.

謠言不動智者
Yao[2] yen[2] pu[4] tung[4] chih[4] chê.[2]

1800

To be fond of talking of female scandals, wounds Heaven and injures Reason in the first degree.

第一傷天害理
Ti^4 yi^1 shang^1 tʻien^1 ʻhai^4 li,^{3}
好講閨門是非
ʻhao^4 chiang^3 kuei^1 mên^2 shih^4 fei.^{1}

— 1801 —

The tawny cur barks behind one's back.

黃犬背後吠
ʻHuang^2 chʻüan^3 pei^4 ʻhou^4 fei.^{4}

— 1802 —

When the ear will not listen, the heart escapes sorrow.

耳不聽肚不煩
Erh^3 pu^4 tʻing^1 tu^3 pu^4 fan.^{2}

— 1803 —

Unheeded slander. *Lit.:* When the root is deep, winds rage unheeded; can slanting moonbeams trouble an upright tree?

根深不怕風搖動
Kên^1 shên^1 pu^4 pʻa^3 fêng^1 yao^2 tung^4:
樹正何愁月影斜
shu^4 chêng^4 ʻho^2 chʻou^2 yüeh^4 ying^3 hsieh^2?

— 1804 —

To throw the blame of one's faults on others. *Lit.:* To drag *Chang* and pull *Li.*

扯張拉李
Chʻê^3 Chang^1 la^1 Li.^{4}

— 1805 —

Don't blame others for your own faults.

自己有錯休怪別人
Tzŭ^4 chi^3 yu^3 tsʻo^4 hsiu^1 kuai^4 pieh^2 jên.^{2}

(8) STEALING.

1806

To break through brass and iron walls,
Only for more exertion calls.

銅墻鐵壁。只要費點力

T'ung[2] ch'iang[2] t'ieh[3] pi,[3] chih[3] yao[4] fei[4] tien[3] li.[4]

1807

Some duck-egg shells have been scattered by the wind;
You've lost a little property, but never mind.

風吹鴨蛋殼。財去人安樂

Fêng[1] ch'ui[1] ya[1] tan[4] k'o[1]; ts'ai[2] ch'ü[4] jên[2] an[1] lo.[4]

1808

With a thief arrest his stolen store;
With a whore arrest her paramour.

拏賊要拏贜。拏姦要拏雙

Na[2] tsei[2] yao[4] na[2] tsang[1]; na[2] chien[1] yao[4] na[2] shuang.[1]

1809

Thieves steal in the rain, but not when it snows;
Not in the moonlight, but when the wind blows.

偷雨不偷雪。偷風不偷月

T'ou[1] yü[3] pu[4] t'ou[1] hsüeh[3]; t'ou[1] fêng[1] pu[4] t'ou[1] yüeh.[4]

1810

Having lost anything do not suspect men of stealing it.

失物難疑人

Shih[1] wu[4] nan[2] i[2] jên.[2]

1811

Everybody has a black pig.

黑毛猪兒家家有

'Hei[1] mao[2] chu[1] êrh[2] chia[1] chia[1] yu.[3]

Note.—This is used to repel a charge of theft.

1812

All the clothes in the box are counted.

箱子裡衣裳有件數

Hsiang^1 tzŭ^3 li^3 i^1 shang^1 yu^3 chien^4 shu.^{4}

Note.—This is a caution against prigging.

1813

He who steals fowls and dogs, will never change his disposition.

偷雞摸狗。總不改性

T'ou^1 chi^1 mo^1 kou,^{3} tsung^3 pu^4 kai^3 hsing.^{4}

1814

Nothing in the end is got by thieving.

偷得利而後有害

T'ou^1 tê^2 li^4 êrh^2 hou^4 yu^3 hai.^{4}

1815

Robbers get plundered by thieves.

强盜遇着賊打刦

Ch'iang^3 tao^4 yü^4 cho^2 tsei^2 ta^3 chieh.^{2}

1816

A thief who is a stranger, must employ an accomplice who is not one.

遠賊必要近脚

Yüan^3 tsei^2 pi^4 yao^4 chin^4 chiao.^{3}

1817

Though thieves infest the streets, if they have no stolen goods, not one of them can be convicted.

强盜沿街走。無贓不定罪

Ch'iang^2 tao^4 yen^2 chieh^1 tsou,^{4} wu^2 tsang^1 pu^4 ting^4 tsui.^{4}

1818

Gambling is the source of robbery.

賭者盜之源

Tu^3 chê^2 tao^4 chih^1 yüan.^{2}

(9) VARIOUS.

1819

Sweet as a biscuit is a damsel of sixteen;
But her loins are girded with a death-dealing blade.
Notwithstanding we see not men's heads dropping off,
Yet, darkly, in the marrow, her havoc is made.

二 八 佳 人 體 似 酥
Erh⁴ pa¹ chia¹ jên² tʻi³ ssŭ⁴ su¹;
腰 間 仗 劍 斬 凡 夫
Yao¹ chien¹ chang⁴ chien⁴ chan³ fan² fu.¹
雖 然 不 見 人 頭 落
Sui¹ jan² pu⁴ chien⁴ jên² tʻou² lo,⁴
暗 裡 催 人 骨 髓 枯
An⁴ li³ tsʻui¹ jên² ku³ sui³ kʻu.¹

NOTE.—I have purposely given a free translation of this proverb; the moral of it is good; even the original is not plainer than many of the proverbs of Solomon, and it closely resembles that one found in Proverbs, 7: 26.

1820

Only dispense with your face,
You'll do all evil with grace.

把 臉 一 劈。百 事 大 吉
Pa³ lien³ yi¹ pʻi,¹ pai³ shih⁴ ta⁴ chi.²

1821

He who whores and gambles till he wastes his fortune,
When his purse is empty must come to a stop.

嫖 賭 家 財 盡。囊 空 自 然 休
Pʻiao² tu³ chia¹ tsʻai² chin,⁴ nang² kʻung¹ tzŭ⁴ jan² hsiu.¹

1822

Leisure breeds lasciviousness.

逸 則 思 淫
I² tsê² ssŭ¹ yin.²

1823

Water once spilt cannot be gathered up again; passions once indulged cannot be restrained.

水一傾則不可覆
Shui³ yi¹ ch'ing¹ tsê² pu⁴ k'o³ fu²;
性一縱則不可反
hsing⁴ yi¹ tsung⁴ tsê² pu⁴ k'o³ fan.³

1824

Vice cannot be concealed. *Lit.:* An ugly daughter-in-law cannot conceal that fact from her mother-in-law.

醜媳婦難免不見公婆的面
Ch'ou³ hsi² fu⁴ nan² mien³ pu⁴ chien⁴ kung¹ p'o² ti¹ mien.⁴

1825

I look indifferently at you, as at a crab, wondering how long you will be able to carry on your perverse practices.

但將冷眼觀螃蟹
Tan⁴ chiang¹ lêng³ yen³ kuan¹ p'ang² 'hai,³
看你橫行到幾時
k'an⁴ ni³ 'hêng⁴ hsing² tao⁴ chi³ shih.²

1826

Depraved conduct. *Lit.:* A wry-mouthed man blows a trumpet with deflected breath.

歪嘴吹喇叭斜氣
Wai¹ tsui³ ch'ui¹ la³ pa¹ hsieh² ch'i.⁴

1827

Accidental transgression is called error; wilful transgression, sin.

偶然犯事叫做過
Ou³ jan² fan⁴ shih⁴ chiao⁴ tso⁴ kuo⁴;
立心犯法叫做惡
li⁴ hsin¹ fan⁴ fa³ chiao⁴ tso⁴ o.⁴

1828

What is done ignorantly is not sin.

不知者不爲罪
Pu⁴ chih¹ chê² pu⁴ wei² tsui.⁴

1829

Men may not be one day without employment.

人不可一日無業

Jên^2 pu^4 k'o^3 yi^1 jih^4 wu^2 yeh.^{4}

1830

He who will not work shall not eat.

停手就停口

T'ing^2 shou^3 chiu^4 t'ing^2 k'ou.^{3}

NOTE.—"This we commanded you, that if any would not work, neither should he eat." 1 Thess. 3: 10.

CHAPTER V.

VIRTUE AND VICE.

1831

Mercy is the root and core;
Opportunity the door.

慈悲爲本。方便爲門

Tzʻŭ2 pei1 wei2 pên3; fang1 pien4 wei2 mên.2

1832

To act upright is the *rôle*,
Of every god, and human soul.

正直爲人。正直爲神

Chêng4 chih2 wei2 jên,2 chêng4 chih2 wei2 shên.2

1833

They prosper who on virtue's aid depend;
Who trust in vice reach an untimely end.

恃德者昌。恃逆者亡

Ssŭ4 tê2 chê2 chʻang1; ssŭ4 ni4 chê2 wang.2

1834

Following virtue is an ascent steep;
Following vice a precipitous leap.

從善如登。從惡如崩

Tsʻung1 shan4 ju2 têng1: tsʻung1 o4 ju2 pêng.1

1835

It is a little thing to starve to death; it is a serious matter to lose one's virtue.

餓死的事小。失節的事大

O4 ssŭ3 ti1 shih4 hsiao3; shih1 chieh2 ti1 shih4 ta.4

1836

Hold benevolence and righteousness important, and death, in comparison, light.

重仁義。輕死亡

Chung4 jên2 i,4 chʻing1 ssŭ3 wang.2

— 1837 —

Better die than turn your back on Reason.

寧死不可背理

Ning^2 ssŭ^3 pu^4 kʻo^3 pei^4 li.^{3}

— 1838 —

Benevolence, Righteousness, Propriety, Wisdom, and Fidelity, are the principles which ought to be followed.

仁義禮智信。理所當遵

Jên^2 i^4 li^3 chih^4 hsin,^{4} li^3 so^3 tang^1 tsun.^{1}

— 1839 —

Let there be plenty of food and clothing, and propriety and righteousness will flourish.

衣食足而後禮義興

I^1 shih^2 tsu^2 êrh^2 ʻhou^4 li^3 i^4 hsing.^{1}

— 1840 —

Accept your destiny ; do your duty ; be satisfied with your position ; and obey the voice of Heaven.

守命。安分。順時。聽天

Shou^3 ming^4 ; an^1 fên^1 ; shun^4 shih^4 ; tʻing^1 tʻien.^{1}

— 1841 —

Men must set their minds on being honest and straightforward.

居身務期質樸

Chu^1 shên^1 wu^4 chʻi^1 chih^2 pʻu.^{1}

— 1842 —

Fear not when men speak evil of you ; fear lest you should do evil.

不怕說壞了。就怕做壞了

Pu^4 pʻa^4 shuo^1 ʻhuai^4 liao^3; chiu^4 pʻa^4 tso^4 ʻhuai^4 liao.^{3}

— 1843 —

In our actions we should accord with the will of Heaven ; in our words we should consult the feelings of men.

作事須循天理
Tso^4 shih^4 hsü^1 hsün^2 tʻien^1 li^3;
出言要順人心
chʻu^1 yen^2 yao^4 shun^4 jên^2 hsin.^{1}

1844

Truth must always be true, and falsehood false.
眞的假不得。假的眞不得
Chên^1 ti^1 chia^3 pu^4 tê,^{2} chia^3 ti^1 chên^1 pu^4 tê.^{2}

1845

Virtue practised to be seen is not real virtue; vice which fears to be seen is real vice.
善欲人見不是眞善
Shan^4 yü^4 jên^2 chien^4 pu^4 shih^4 chên^1 shan^4;
惡恐人知便是大惡
O^4 kʻung^3 jên^2 chih^1 pien^4 shih^4 ta^4 o.^{4}

1846

Better be upright and want, than wicked and have superabundance.
寧可正而不足不可邪而有餘
Ning^2 kʻo^3 chêng^4 êrh^2 pu^4 tsu,^{2} pu^4 kʻo^3 hsieh^2 êrh^2 yu^3 yü.^{2}

1847

Never lose virtue, nor promote vice.
善不可失。惡不可長
Shan^4 pu^4 kʻo^3 shih^1, o^4 pu^4 kʻo^3 chang.^{3}

1848

All vice avoid, all virtue follow.
諸惡莫作。衆善奉行
Chu^1 o^4 mo^4 tso,^{4} chung^4 shan^4 fêng^4 hsing.^{2}

1849

Virtue is the foundation of happiness, vice the presage of misery.
善乃福之基。惡乃禍之兆
Shan^4 nai^3 fu^2 chih^1 chi^1; o^4 nai^3 ʻhuo^4 chih^1 chao.^{4}

CHAPTER VI.

VIRTUES.—(1) CONCESSION AND FORBEARANCE.

1850

Forbearance is a noble word!
Above its head behold a sword.
Whoe'er in this is like *Chang Kung*
Must happy be and never bored.

忍 字 高 忍 字 高
Jên3 tzŭ4 kao1 jên3 tzŭ4 kao1!
忍 字 頭 上 一 把 刀
Jên3 tzŭ4 t'ou2 shang4 yi1 pa3 tao.1
爲 人 能 效 張 公 忍
Wei2 jên2 nêng2 hsiao4 Chang1 Kung1 jên,3
自 然 快 活 無 煩 惱
Tzŭ4 jan2 k'uai4 'huo2 wu2 fan2 nao.3

Note.—*Chang Kung* was a certain superior man noted for writing out one hundred instances of the application of the word "Forbearance," as well as for his own exemplification of its meaning.

1851

Forbear! a snow mountain though ten thousand *chang* high,
Melts into a river soon as the sun's in the sky.

任 他 雪 山 高 萬 丈
Jên4 t'a1 hsüeh3 shan1 kao1 wan4 chang,4
太 陽 一 出 化 長 江
T'ai4 yang2 yi1 ch'u1 'hua4 ch'ang2 chiang.1

Note.—One *Chang* is equal to 10 Chinese feet, or to 11 feet 9 inches English. *Kao wan chang*, however, is a general term for any lofty height. An inscription at the front of the principal peak of the *Wu-tang shan* informs the visitor that it is *Wan chang kao*.

1852

Imitate *Chang Kung*, who wrote so much on Forbearance.

效 張 公 多 書 忍 字
Hsiao4 Chang1 Kung1 to1 shu1 jên3 tzŭ.4

1853

Forbearance under a slight provocation, may save one a hundred days' trouble.

忍得一時之氣
Jên[3] tê[2] yi[1] shih[2] chih[1] ch'i,[4]
免得百日之憂
mien[3] tê[2] pai[3] jih[4] chih[1] yu.[1]

1854

A moment's want of forbearance may prove a life-long regret.

少間弗忍終身之羞
Shao[3] chien[1] fu[2] jên[3] chung[1] shên[1] chih[1] hsiu.[1]

1855

Endure provocation, repress wrath, forgive an offence, and yield a point.

忍一句。息一怒
Jên[3] yi[1] chü,[4] hsi[2] yi[1] nu,[4]
饒一着退一步
jao[2] yi[1] cho,[2] t'ui[4] yi[1] pu.[4]

1856

When it is proper to forbear, forbear.

得忍且忍。得耐且耐
Tê[2] jên[3] ch'ieh[3] jên,[3] tê[2] nai[4] ch'ieh[3] nai.[4]

1857

Want of forbearance causes small offences to become great.

不忍不耐。小事成大
Pu[4] jên[3] pu[4] nai,[4] hsiao[3] shih[4] ch'êng[2] ta.[4]

1858

The very word "Forbearance" is precious in a house.

忍字家中寶
Jên[3] tzŭ[4] chia[1] chung[1] pao.[3]

1859

Without forbearance you will be in trouble at once; think twice and you will have nought to fear for a hundred years.

不忍一時有禍三思百歲無妨
Pu^4 jên^3 yi^1 shih^2 yu^3 ʽhuo^4; san^1 ssŭ^1 pai^3 sui^4 wu^2 fang.^{1}

—— 1860 ——

Throw off restraint, indulge fits of passion,—and suffer loss; have a forbearing thoughtful mind,—and avoid sorrow.

恣意發狂有失有心忍耐無憂
Tzu^1 i^4 fa^1 kʽuang^2 yu^3 shih^1: yu^3 hsin^1 jên^3 nai^4 wu^2 yu.^{1}

—— 1861 ——

Whoever is willing to suffer, covets not another's advantage.

吃虧是不佔便宜
Chʽih^1 kʽuei^1 shih^4 pu^4 chan^4 pien^4 i.^{2}

—— 1862 ——

To show mercy is reckoned man's duty; to win is reckoned man's ingenuity.

饒人算人之本
Jao^2 jên^2 suan^4 jên^2 chih^1 pên^3;
輸人算人之機
Shu^1 jên^2 suan^4 jên^2 chih^1 chi.^{1}

—— 1863 ——

Lifelong concession of road and dyke; neither loses a hundred paces, nor a single plot.

終身讓路不枉百步
Chung^1 shên^1 jang^4 lu^4 pu^4 wang^3 pai^3 pu^4;
終身讓畔不失一段
chung^1 shên^1 jang^4 pan^4 pu^4 shih^1 yi^1 tuan.^{4}

—— 1864 ——

He will neither concede on the road nor at a feast.

行不讓路坐不讓席
Hsing^2 pu^4 jang^4 lu,^{4} tso^4 pu^4 jang^4 hsi.^{2}

—— 1865 ——

You may walk your horse over a general's or a premier's neck; and pole your boat in the belly of a duke or marquis.

將相項頭堪走馬
Chiang[1] hsiang[4] hsiang[4] t'ou[2] k'an[1] tsou[4] ma[3];
公侯肚裡好撐船
Kung[1] 'hou[2] tu[3] li[3] 'hao[3] chang[4] ch'uan.[2]

NOTE.—This strange proverb is intended to express the boundless generosity and forbearance of the gentlemen mentioned.

1866

Affect a little indistinctness, rather than insist upon absolute correctness.

放模糊些不可頂眞
Fang[4] mo[1] 'hu[2] hsieh,[1] pu[4] k'o[3] ting[3] chên.[1]

1867

Here on earth it is noble to yield even one step; and it is happiness to treat men with even a little generosity.

處世讓一步爲高
Ch'u[3] shih[4] jang[4] yi[1] pu[4] wei[2] kao[1];
待人寬一分是福
tai[4] jên[2] k'uan[1] yi[1] fên[1] shih[4] fu.[2]

1868

One may give way to another, and bear with his bluster; not from weakness but for self-control.

讓人非我弱。守己任他强
Jang[4] jên[2] fei[1] wo[3] jo,[4] shou[3] chi[3] jên[4] t'a[1] ch'iang.[2]

1869

I yield not for fear, but because I'm not fool enough to risk imprisonment.

饒人非我弱。癡漢入牢門
Jao[2] jên[2] fei[1] wo[3] jo,[4] ch'ih[2] 'han[4] ju[4] lao[2] mên.[2]

(2) CONTENTMENT.

— 1870 —

With enough to eat three times a day you must always be content;
And down with your sail when a steady wind has long time kept it bent.

飽 餐 三 飯 常 知 足
Pao³ ts'an¹ san¹ fan⁴ ch'ang² chih¹ tsou²;
得 一 帆 風 便 可 收
Tê² yi¹ fan¹ fêng¹ pien⁴ k'o³ shou.¹

— 1871 —

A constantly contented mind
Free from disgrace you'll always find.

知 足 常 足 終 身 不 辱
Chih¹ tsu² ch'ang² tsu,² chung¹ shên¹ pu⁴ ju.⁴

— 1872 —

Having obtained your wish be content.

得 意 不 可 再 往
Tê² i⁴ pu⁴ k'o³ tsai⁴ wang.³

— 8873 —

Be content with what is sufficient to pass over the present time.

人 生 得 過 隨 時 過
Jên² shêng¹ tê² kuo⁴ sui² shih² kuo.⁴

— 1874 —

Compared with superiors I have less, but compared with inferiors I have more.

比 上 不 足。比 下 有 餘
Pi³ shang⁴ pu⁴ tsu,² pi³ hsia⁴ yu³ yü.²

— 1875 —

Be content with whatever you have.

得 過 且 過
Tê² kuo⁴ ch'ieh³ kuo.⁴

(3) FILIAL PIETY.

1876

First of virtues, as all books confess,
Filial piety and righteousness.

千經萬典。孝義爲先

Chʻien^1 chin^1 wan^4 tien,^{3} hsiao^4 i^4 wei^2 hsien.^{1}

1877

Of a myriad virtues filial piety is the first.

萬善孝爲先

Wan^4 shan^4 hsiao^4 wei^2 hsien.^{1}

1878

Of a myriad vices fornication is the chief; of a hundred virtues, filial piety is the first.

萬惡淫爲首。百行孝爲先

Wan^4 o^4 yin^2 wei^2 shou^3; pai^3 hsing^2 hsiao^4 wei^2 hsien.^{1}

1879

Filial piety moves heaven and earth.

孝心感動天合地

Hsiao^4 hsin^1 kan^2 tung^4 tʻien^1 ʻho^2 ti^4.

1880

A filial son is the joy of his father.

子孝父心寬

Tzŭ^3 hsiao^4 fu^4 hsin^1 kuan.^{1}

1881

One unfilial son involves nine others in ruin.

一子不孝九子皆滅

Yi^1 tzŭ^3 pu^4 hsiao^4 chiu^3 tzŭ^3 chieh^1 mieh.^{4}

1882

When the son lacks dutifulness, the daughter-in-law lacks filial piety.

兒不賢媳不孝

Erh^2 pu^4 hsien^2 hsi^2 pu^4 hsiao.^{4}

(4) GENEROSITY AND KINDNESS.

1883

Who constantly gives, does always possess;
His riches and honours never grow less.

常捨常有富貴長久

Chʻang[2] shê[3] chʻang[2] yu[3]; fu[4] kuei[4] chʻang[2] chiu[3]

NOTE.—"There is that scattereth, and yet increaseth." Prov. 11 : 24.

1884

Instruction impart, men's vices to correct:
And give of your money, their good to effect.

垂訓以格人非

Chʻui[2] hsün[4] i[3] ko[2] jên[2] fei[1];

捐資以成人美

Sun[3] tzŭ[1] i[3] chʻêng[2] jên[2] mei.[3]

1885

Always leave some way of escape to the erring.

萬事留一線之路、

Wan[4] shih[4] liu[2] yi[1] hsien[4] chih[1] lu.[4]

1886

To call up a breeze that all may be cooled.

喚起風來大家涼

ʻHuan[4] chʻi[3] fêng[1] lai[2] ta[4] chia[1] liang.[2]

1887

For one good deed to forget a hundred bad ones.

見人一善。忘其百非

Chien[4] jên[2] yi[1] shan,[4] wang[4] chʻi[2] pai[3] fei.[1]

1888

To conduct a blind man over a bridge.

牽瞎子過橋

Chʻien[1] hsia[2] tzŭ[3] kuo[4] chʻiao.[2]

1889

To stint one's-self and treat others generously.

刻苦自己。厚待別人

Kʻo[1] kʻu[3] tzŭ[4] chi,[3] ʻhou[4] tai[4] pieh[2] jên.[2]

1890

A star, however willing, cannot help the moon.

有星不能照月

Yu^3 hsing^1 pu^4 nêng^2 chao^4 yueh.^{4}

NOTE.—In this proverb there is a play on the word 星 *hsing*, 'star,' which is almost identical in sound with 心 *hsin*, 'heart.'

1891

To light one's lantern for another man.

打燈籠照別人

Ta^3 têng^1 lung^2 chao^4 pieh^2 jên.^{2}

1892

Look not on the gilt face, but on Buddha's face.

不看金面看佛面

Pu^4 k'an^4 chin^1 mien^4 k'an^4 Fu^2 mien.^{4}

NOTE.—Here the "gilt face" represents any offender, "Buddha's face" any intercessor; and the request is that for the intercessor's sake the offender may be forgiven.

1893

"Help men in their necessities, and rescue them from danger."

濟人之急救人之危

Chi^4 jên^2 chih^1 chi,^{2} chiu^4 jên^2 chih^1 wei.^{2}

1894

It is only kindness, and not severity, which can impress at the distance of a thousand miles.

只有千里人情

Chih^3 yu^3 ch'ien^1 li^3 jên^2 ch'ing,^{2}

沒有千里威風

mu^2 yu^3 ch'ien^1 li^3 wei^1 fêng.^{1}

1895

Better not do kindnesses at all, than do them in the hope of recompense.

施恩莫望報。望報莫施恩

Shih^1 ên^1 mo^4 wang^4 pao,^{4} wang^4 pao^4 mo^4 shih^1 ên.^{1}

1896

Do continually acts of kindness; perform every sort of secret virtue.

行 時 時 之 方 便
Hsing^2 shih^2 shih^2 chih^1 fang^1 pien^4;
作 種 種 之 陰 功
tso^4 chung^4 chung^4 chih^1 yin^1 kung.^{1}

1897

To row with the stream in doing a favour.

順 氷 推 舟 做 人 情
Shun^4 shui^3 tʻui^1 chou^1 tso^4 jên^2 chʻing.^{2}

Note.—For instance,—to give wine to one who is fond of it, or books to one fond of study.

1898

Kindness is greater than law.

人 情 大 過 王 法
Jên^2 chʻing^2 ta^4 kuo^4 wang^2 fa.^{3}

1899

Men must be treated with great generosity.

待 人 須 當 量 大
Tai^4 jên^2 hsü^1 tang^1 liang^2 ta.^{4}

(5) GRATITUDE.

1900

Fed on the king's soil, recompense the king's favour.

吃 王 水 土 報 王 恩
Chʻih^1 wang^2 shui^3 tʻu^3 pao^4 wang^2 ên.^{1}

1901

Enjoying the king's dignities and emoluments, recompense the king's favour.

食 王 爵 祿 報 王 恩
Shih^2 wang^2 chüeh^2 lu^4 pao^4 wang^2 ên.^{1}

1902

He who is grateful has nothing to blush for.

心 不 負 人 面 無 慚 色
Hsin^1 pu^4 fu^4 jên^2 mien^4 wu^2 tsʻan^2 sê.^{4}

1903

Thankful for small mercies. *Lit.:* For the favour of a drop of water, pay back a gushing fountain.

得人點水之恩

Tê^2 jên^2 tien^3 shui^3 chih^1 ên,^{1}

須當湧泉之報

hsü^1 tang^1 yung^3 chʻien^2 chih^1 pao.^{4}

1904

If you share a man's wealth, try to lessen his misfortunes.

得人錢財。與人消災

Tê^2 jên^2 chʻien^2 tsʻai,^{2} yü^3 jên^2 hsiao^1 tsai.^{1}

1905

Better that others be ungrateful to me, than that I should be so to others.

寧可負我。切莫負人

Ning^2 kʻo^3 fu^4 wo,^{3} chʻieh^4 mo^4 fu^4 jên.^{2}

1906

Lambs have the grace to suck kneeling; and young crows return part of their food to their parents.

羊有跪乳之恩

Yang^2 yu^3 kuei^4 ju^3 chih^1 ên^1;

鴉有反哺之義

ya^1 yu^3 fan^3 fu^1 chih^1 i.^{4}

1907

As your duty is, when the cultivated fields have yielded their increase, and you are fed and warmed, give thanks to Heaven.

隨分耕鋤收地利

Sui^2 fên^1 kêng^1 chʻu^2 shou^1 ti^4 li,^{4}

他時飽煖謝蒼天

tʻa^1 shih^2 pao^3 nuan^3 hsieh^4 tsʻang^1 tʻien.^{1}

1908

Be forgetful of favours given; be mindful of blessings received.

施惠勿念。受恩莫忘

Shih^1 ʻhui^4 wu^4 nien^4; shou^3 ên^1 mo^4 wang.^{4}

1909

It is unmanly to be ungrateful for favours received.

知恩不報。非爲人也

Chih^{1} ên^{1} pu^{4} pao^{4} fei^{1} wei^{2} jên^{2} yeh.^{3}

1610

He is a brute who forgets favours received, and turns his back on righteousness.

忘恩背義。禽獸之徒

Wang^{4} ên^{1} pei^{4} i,^{4} chʻin^{2} shou^{4} chih^{1} tʻu.^{2}

1911

He who eats another's food, and receives another's favour, is tender in speaking of and dealing with him.

吃人的口軟。得人的手軟

Chʻih^{1} jên^{2} ti^{1} kʻou^{3} juan,^{3} tê^{2} jên^{2} ti^{1} shou^{3} juan.^{3}

1912

To return hate for kindness.

恩將仇報

En^{1} chiang^{1} chʻou^{2} pao.^{4}

1913

Over a bowl of congee or rice, one should remember the trouble it has cost to supply it.

一粥一飯當思來處不易

Yi^{1} chou^{1} yi^{1} fan^{4} tang^{1} ssŭ^{1} lai^{2} chʻu^{4} pu^{4} i.^{4}

1914

He who is ungrateful for favours received is no superior man.

受恩不報非君子

Shou^{4} ên^{1} pu^{4} pao^{4} fei^{1} chün^{1} tzŭ.^{3}

1915

When you put on your clothes, remember the weaver's labour;
When you take your daily food, remember the husbandman's trouble.

身披一縷常思織女之勞

Shên^{1} pʻei^{1} yi^{1} lü^{4} chʻang^{2} ssŭ^{1} chih^{1} nü^{2} chih^{1} lao^{2};

日食三餐每念農夫之苦

jih^{4} shih^{2} san^{1} tsʻan^{1} mei^{3} nien^{4} nung^{2} fu^{1} chih^{1} kʻu.^{3}

1916

He who is grateful for favours received, will be filial as a son and loyal as a minister.

受 人 恩 而 不 忍 負 者
Shou⁴ jên² ên¹ êrh² pu⁴ jên³ fu⁴ chê,²
爲 子 必 孝。爲 臣 必 忠
wei² tzŭ³ pi⁴ hsiao⁴ wei² ch'ên² pi⁴ chung.¹

1917

When you drink from the stream, remember the spring.

飲 水 思 源
Yin³ shui³ ssŭ¹ yüan.²

1918

Eating bamboo-sprouts, remember the planter of the bamboos.

食 笋 須 記 栽 竹 人
Shih² sun³ hsü¹ chi⁴ tsai¹ chu² jên.²

SECTION XV.—ON PRUDENCE.

CHAPTER I.

CAUTION.

1919

Who turns him round to reinspect,
Shall nothing lose through his neglect.

回 頭 再 看。不 得 失 散

ʻHui^{2} tʻou^{2} tsai^{4} kʻan,^{4} pu^{4} tê^{2} shih^{1} san.^{4}

1920

Each must take care of his coat and hat;
Caution is needful, be sure of that.

各 照 衣 帽。小 心 爲 要

Ko^{4} chao^{4} i^{1} mao^{4}: hsiao^{3} hsin^{1} wei^{2} yao.^{4}

1921

Who carefully looks both behind and before,
Of food and of clothes will have always good store.

照 前 照 後。衣 食 常 彀

Chao^{4} chʻien^{2} chao^{4} ʻhou,^{4} i^{1} shih^{2} chʻang^{2} kou.^{4}

1922

You must be clever in mind, and clownish outside;
Make too much of your wisdom, woes will you betide.

內 要 伶 俐 外 要 癡 呆

Nei^{4} yao^{4} ling^{2} li^{4} wai^{4} yao^{4} chʻih^{2} tai^{1};

聰 明 逞 盡 惹 禍 招 災

Tsʻung^{1} ming^{2} chʻêng^{3} chin^{4} jê^{3} ʻhuo^{4} chao^{1} tsai.^{1}

1923

For one bad move, if you're to blame,
Be sure that you will lose the game.

下 錯 一 步。滿 盤 都 輸

Hsia^{4} tsʻo^{4} yi^{1} pu,^{4} man^{4} pʻan^{2} tu^{1} shu.^{1}

1924

Neither take poison, nor break law.

毒人的莫吃。犯法的莫做

Tu[2] jên[2] ti[1] mo[4] ch'ih,[1] fan[4] fa[3] ti[1] mo[4] tso.[4]

1925

Never do what you don't want to be known.

若要人不知。除非己莫爲

Jo[4] yao[4] jên[2] pu[4] chih,[1] ch'u[2] fei[1] chi[3] mo[4] wei.[2]

1926

State all conditions first.

醜話說在先

Ch'ou[3] 'hua[4] shuo[1] tsai[4] hsien.[1]

1927

Beware of winds and waves by day, of thieves by night.

日防風浪之險

Jih[4] fang[2] fêng[1] lang[4] chih[1] hsien,[3]

夜防盜賊之憂

yeh[4] fang[2] tao[4] tsei[2] chih[1] yu.[1]

1928

Avoid suspicion. *Lit.:* Do not lace your boots in a melon field, nor adjust your hat under a plum tree.

瓜田不納履。李下不整冠

Kua[1] t'ien[2] pu[4] na[4] li,[3] li[4] hsia[4] pu[4] chêng[3] kuan.[1]

1929

The same. *Lit.:* In a melon field and under a plum tree avoid suspicion.

瓜田李下。各避嫌疑

Kua[1] t'ien[2] li[4] hsia[4] ko[4] pi[4] hsien[2] i.[2]

1930

Be as careful as if you were entering a battle, or crossing a bridge.

念念有如臨敵日

Nien[4] nien[4] yu[3] ju[2] lin[2] ti[2] jih,[4]

心心常似過橋時

hsin[1] hsin[1] ch'ang[2] ssŭ[4] kuo[4] ch'iao[2] shih,[2]

1931

When you know there are tigers on the hills, don't go there.

明知山有虎。莫向虎山行

Ming[2] chih[1] shan[1] yu[3] ʻhu,[3] mo[4] hsiang[4] ʻhu[3] shan[1] hsing.[2]

1932

In a narrow passage be prepared for danger.

路逢狹處須防劍

Lu[4] fêng[2] hsia[2] chʻu[4] hsü[1] fang[2] chien.[4]

1933

Always be provided against danger and rebellion.

安不可忘危。治不可忘亂

An[1] pu[4] kʻo[3] wang[4] wei,[2] chih[3] pu[4] kʻo[3] wang[4] lan.[4]

1934

In eating, avoid choking ; in walking, avoid stumbling.

吃飯防哽。行路防跌

Chʻih[1] fan[4] fang[2] kêng,[3] hsing[2] lu[4] fang[2] tieh.[2]

1935

Proceed cautiously. *Lit.:* Take a step, drive a pile.

走一步打个樁

Tsou[4] yi[1] pu,[4] ta[3] ko[4] chuang.[1]

1936

Look not on temptation, and your mind will be at rest.

不見所欲使心不亂

Pu[4] chien[4] so[3] yü[4] shih[4] hsin[1] pu[4] lan.[4]

1937

One who acts cautiously may go anywhere ; one who does not, will always be suffering.

小心天下去得

Hsiao[3] hsin[1] tʻien[1] hsia[4] chʻü[4] tê[2];

大意百事吃虧

ta[4] i[4] pai[3] shih[4] chʻih[1] kʻuei.[1]

1938

To act the part of one deaf and dumb.

裝聾作啞

Chuang[1] lung[2] tso[4] ya.[3]

NOTE.—That is for fear of becoming involved in danger or crime.

1939

Over cautious. *Lit.:* To wear strings on a felt hat.

戴 毡 帽 安 繩

Tai^4 chan^1 mao^4 an^1 shêng.^{2}

1940

If you use a walking stick you will not fall; if you take counsel you will not err.

有 拐 棍 兒 不 跌 倒

Yu^3 kuai^3 kun^4 êrh^2 pu^4 tieh^2 tao^3;

有 商 量 兒 不 失 錯

yu^3 shang^1 liang^2 êrh^2 pu^4 shih^1 tsʻo.^{4}

1941

A fall hurts not those who fly low.

飛 不 高 跌 不 傷

Fei^1 pu^4 kao^1 tieh^2 pu^4 shang.^{1}

1942

Partition walls have ears; and there are listeners under the window.

隔 墻 須 有 耳。 窻 外 豈 無 人

Ko^2 chʻiang^2 hsü^1 yü^3 êrh^3; chʻuang^1 wai^4 chʻi^3 wu^2 jên.^{2}

1943

When free from trouble be on your guard; when trouble comes don't get excited.

無 事 時 要 提 防

Wu^2 shih^4 shih^2 yao^4 tʻi^2 fang^2;

有 事 時 要 鎮 定

yu^3 shih^4 shih^2 yao^4 chên^4 ting.^{4}

1944

Diligence is an inestimable treasure, and prudence a defensive charm.

勤 爲 無 價 之 寶

Chʻin^2 wei^2 wu^2 chia^4 chih^1 pao,^{3}

愼 是 護 身 之 符

shên^4 shih^4 ʻhu^4 shên^1 chih^1 fu.^{2}

1945

If there is no one at home, don't leave clothes before the fire to dry; and drying clothes be careful lest a sash may catch the flame.

房裡無人莫烘衣
Fang2 li3 wu2 jên2 mo4 ʻhung1 i1;
烘衣猶恐帶頭垂
ʻhung1 i1 yu2 kʻung3 tai4 tʻou2 chʻui.2

1946

Don't carry a candle near inflammable things; and when you've blown a lamp out, watch the flying sparks.

執燭過防光燥物
Chih2 chu2 kuo4 fang2 kuang1 tsao4 wu4;
吹燈要看火星飛
chʻui1 têng1 yao4 kʻan4 ʻhuo3 hsing1 fei.1

1947

Though a thousand things may claim attention in your household, never go to bed without a look at the kitchen.

家中縱有千般事
Chia1 chung1 tsung4 yu3 chʻien1 pan1 shih,4
臨睡廚房走一回
lin2 shui4 chʻu2 fang2 tsou4 yi1 ʻhui.2

1948

He comes publicly, and goes openly.

來得明。去得白
Lai2 tê2 ming,2 chʻü4 tê2 pai.2

1949

When you travel by boat, be prepared for a duck.

行船辦落水之計
Hsing2 chʻuan2 pan4 lo4 shui3 chih1 chi.4

1950

One wrong thought may cause a life-long regret.

一念之差。終身之悔
Yi1 nien4 chih1 chʻa,1 chung1 shên1 chih1 ʻhui.3

1951

Deviate an inch, and lose a thousand miles.

差之毫釐失之千里

Chʻa^1 chih^1 ʻhao^2 li,^{2} shih^1 chih^1 chʻien^1 li.^{3}

1952

Though the wind has fallen the waves have not yet settled.

風平浪未靜

Fêng^1 pʻing^2 lang^4 wei^4 ching.^{4}

1953

"A good memory is not equal to bad ink."

廣記不如淡墨

Kuang^3 chi^4 pu^4 ju^2 tan^4 mo^4;

1954

Men fear a slip of their pens, women a slip of their morals.

男怕輸筆。女怕輸身

Nan^2 pʻa^4 shu^1 pi,^{3} nü^2 pʻa^4 shu^1 shên.^{1}

1955

Rather fear that you should not prove an adept, than that you should lack employment.

不怕人不請。就怕藝不眞

Pu^4 pʻa^4 jên^2 pu^4 chʻing,^{3} chiu^4 pʻa^4 i^4 pu^4 chên.^{1}

CHAPTER II.

DISCRETION.

1956

No sailor by trade,—
Be of boat-hooks afraid.

不是撑船手。休拏竹篙頭

Pu^4 shih^4 chang^4 chʻuan^2 shou,^{3} hsiu^1 na^2 chu^2 kao^1 tʻou.^{2}

1957

Be only to superior men your wants confessed;
And if you succour, succour only the distressed.

求人須求大丈夫

Chʻiu^2 jên^2 hsü^1 chʻiu^2 ta^4 chang^4 fu^1;

濟人須濟急時無

Chi^4 jên^2 hsü^1 chi^4 chi^2 shih^2 wu.^{2}

1958

Hope little from the yet to you unseen;
Care little for what has already been.

未來休指望。過去莫思量

Wei^4 lai^2 hsiu^1 chih^3 wang^4; kuo^4 chʻü^4 mo^4 ssŭ^1 liang.^{2}

1959

Never ask a family whether things are gay or sad;
For all such information from their faces may be had.

入門休問榮枯事

Ju^4 mên^2 hsiu^1 wên^4 yung^2 kʻu^1 shih^4;

觀見容顏便得知

Kuan^1 chien^4 yung^2 yen^2 pien^4 tê^2 chih.^{1}

1960

Never open your lips when to speak is in vain;
Nor let other folk's business embarrass your brain.

無益語言休着口

Wu^2 i^2 yü^3 yen^2 hsiu^1 cho^2 kʻou^3;

不干己事少當頭

Pu^4 kan^1 chi^3 shih^4 shao^3 tang^1 tʻou.^{2}

1961

Talk to those who can understand, and give to those who need.

說話說與知音。送飯送與飢人

Shuo^{1} ʻhua^{4} shuo^{1} yü^{3} chih^{1} yin,^{1} sung^{4} fan^{4} sung^{4} yü^{3} chi^{1} jên.^{2}

1962

Suit self to circumstances.

見景生情

Chien^{4} ching^{3} shêng^{1} chʻing.^{2}

1963

If your strength be small, don't carry heavy burdens; if your words be worthless, don't give advice.

力微休負重。言輕莫勸人

Li^{4} wei^{1} hsiu^{1} fu^{4} chung^{4}; yen^{2} chʻing^{1} mo^{4} chʻüan^{4} jên.^{2}

1964

If you are poor, keep out of the crowd; if unfortunate, don't seek a relation.

無錢休入衆。遭難莫尋親

Wu^{2} chʻien^{2} hsiu^{1} ju^{4} chung^{4}; tsao^{1} nan^{2} mo^{4} hsin^{2} chʻin.^{1}

1965

Avoid fierce men, and strong wine.

人狠不攙。酒狠不吃

Jên^{2} ʻhên^{3} pu^{4} chʻan,^{1} chiu^{3} ʻhên^{3} pu^{4} chʻih.^{1}

1966

Do not trust in an excessive show of honesty; and beware of an excessive show of kindness.

莫信直中直。須防仁不仁

Mo^{4} hsin^{4} chih^{2} chung^{1} chih^{2}; hsü^{1} fang^{2} jên^{2} pu^{4} jên.^{2}

1967

Do not say what you see; do not know what you are asked; do not meddle with other folk's business; and if you have nothing to do, quickly return home.

見事莫說。問事不知

Chien^{4} shih^{4} mo^{4} shuo^{1}; wên^{4} shih^{4} pu^{4} chih^{1};

閒事莫管。無事早歸

hsien^{2} shih^{4} mo^{4} kuan^{3}; wu^{2} shih^{4} tsao^{3} kuei.^{1}

—— 1968 ——

Do not present your verses to any but a clever man.

不是才人莫獻詩

Pu^{4} shih^{4} tsʻai^{2} jên^{2} mo^{4} hsien^{4} shih.^{4}

—— 1969 ——

Wherever you go, talk as the people of the place talk.

到那裡說那裡話

Tao^{4} na^{4} li^{3} shuo^{1} na^{4} li^{3} ʻhua.^{4}

—— 1970 ——

Neither indulge a slave, nor deceive a child.

奴才不可逞。小孩不可哄

Nu^{3} tsʻai^{2} pu^{4} kʻo^{3} chʻêng,^{3} hsiao^{3} ʻhai^{2} pu^{4} kʻo^{3} ʻhung.^{3}

—— 1971 ——

You had better retire when in greatest favour; and break off friendship when it is closest.

受恩深處宜先退

Shou^{4} ên^{1} shên^{1} chʻu^{4} i^{2} hsien^{1} tʻui^{4};

得意濃時便好休

Tê^{2} i^{4} nung^{2} shih^{2} pien^{4} ʻhao^{3} hsiu.^{1}

—— 1972 ——

When the country is in confusion, look out for a good general; when the family is poor, for a virtuous wife.

國亂思良將。家貧思賢妻

Kuo^{2} lan^{2} ssŭ^{1} liang^{2} chiang^{1}; chia^{1} pʻin^{3} ssŭ^{1} hsien^{2} chʻi.^{1}

—— 1973 ——

Yield to circumstances. *Lit.:* If the wind be strong, yield to the wind; if rain be heavy, yield to rain.

風大隨風。雨大隨雨

Fêng^{1} ta^{4} sui^{2} fêng^{1}; yü^{3} ta^{4} sui^{2} yü.^{3}

—— 1974 ——

If you lost your needle in the grass, go and seek it there.

草裡失針。草裡尋

Tsʻao^{3} li^{3} shih^{1} chên,^{1} tsʻao^{3} li^{3} hsin.^{2}

1975

Let every one sweep away the snow from before his own door, and not meddle with the hoar-frost on his neighbour's tiles.

各 人 自 掃 門 前 雪
Ko[4] jên[2] tzŭ[4] sao[3] mên[2] chien[2] hsüeh,[3]
休 管 他 人 瓦 上 霜
hsiu[1] kuan[3] t'a[1] jên[2] wa[1] shang[4] shuang.[1]

1976

If you want to be quiet, do not meddle with other people's business.

要 得 無 事。少 管 閑 事
Yao[4] tê[2] wu[2] shih,[4] shao[3] kuan[3] hsien[2] shih.[4]

1977

Only govern your own door, and don't talk about other men's daughters and wives.

只 管 自 己 門 戶
Chih[3] kuan[3] tzŭ[4] chi[3] mên[2] 'hu,[4]
休 說 別 人 女 妻
hsiu[1] shuo[1] pieh[2] jên[2] nü[2] ch'i.[1]

1978

Neither spend foolishly, nor work fruitlessly.

錢 不 錯 用。工 無 枉 使
Ch'ien[2] pu[4] ts'o[4] yung,[4] kung[1] wu[2] wang[3] shih.[3]

1979

In the transaction of business, in the use of power, in the use of speech, and in the enjoyment of happiness, don't carry the thing too far.

事 不 可 做 盡。勢 不 可 倚 盡
Shih[4] pu[4] k'o[3] tso[4] chin,[4] shih[4] pu[4] k'o[3] i[3] chin,[4]
言 不 可 道 盡。福 不 可 享 盡
yen[2] pu[4] k'o[3] tao[4] chin,[4] fu[2] pu[4] k'o[3] hsiang[3] chin.[4]

1980

Try to oblige others, and you will be obliged yourself.

與 人 方 便。與 己 方 便
Yü[3] jên[2] fang[1] pien,[4] yü[3] chi[3] fang[1] pien.[4]

1981

If you know where to stop and always stop there, you will never be in disgrace.

知止常止。終身不恥

Chih¹ chih³ ch'ang² chih,³ chung¹ shên¹ pu⁴ ch'ih.³

1982

All that accords with Reason may be done ; but never quarrel over petty profits.

合理可作。小利莫爭

'Ho² li³ k'o³ tso⁴ : hsiao³ li⁴ mo⁴ chêng.¹

1983

Better straightforwardly seize a thing, than beg it in an underhand way.

寧向直中取。不可曲中求

Ning² hsiang⁴ chih² chung¹ ch'ü,³ pu⁴ k'o³ ch'ü¹ chung¹ ch'iu.²

1984

Dread law, and daily live in comfort ; scorn justice, and daily live in trouble.

懼法朝朝樂。欺公日日憂

Chü⁴ fa³ chao¹ chao¹ lê⁴ ; ch'i¹ kung¹ jih⁴ jih⁴ yu.¹

1985

Men of a certain height must wear clothes of a certain length.

幾長人穿幾長衣服

Chi³ ch'ang² jên² ch'uan¹ chi³ ch'ang² i¹ fu.²

1986

Whether victorious or beaten never regret.

輸贏無悔

Shu¹ ying² wu² 'hui.³

1987

Treat a prodigy as though it were none, and it will die out of itself.

見怪不怪。其怪自滅

Chien⁴ kuai⁴ pu⁴ kuai,⁴ ch'i² kuai⁴ tzŭ⁴ mieh.⁴

1988

Better go yourself than send; better do it yourself than ask any one to do it for you.

使口不如自走
Shih³ k'ou³ pu⁴ ju² tzŭ⁴ tsou⁴;

求人不如求己
ch'iu² jên² pu⁴ ju² ch'iu² chi.³

1989

If you would control self you must rebuke self; if you would have faith in men do not suspect them.

守己須責己。信人不疑人
Shou³ chi³ hsü¹ tsê² chi³; hsin⁴ jên² pu⁴ i² jên.²

1990

Temperance in drinking, saves the mind from confusion; restraint of passion, preserves fortunes unimpaired.

少飲不亂性。惜氣免傷財
Shao³ yin³ pu⁴ lan⁴ hsing⁴; hsi² ch'i⁴ mien³ shang¹ ts'ai.²

CHAPTER III.

ECONOMY.

1991

Though you be a millionaire,
Mend one half the clothes you wear.

家 有 一 萬。繚 補 一 半

Chia^1 yu^3 yi^1 wan,^{4} liao^2 pu^3 yi^1 pan.^{4}

1992

If you have only ten *taels* don't hanker for dress:
Never seek, on a hundred, a wife to possess.

拾 兩 銀 子 莫 置 衣

Shih^2 liang^3 yin^2 tzŭ^3 mo^4 chih^4 i^1:

百 兩 銀 子 莫 娶 妻

Pai^3 liang^3 yin^2 tzŭ^3 mo^4 chʻü^3 chʻi.^{1}

1993

Cold water and hot, you must learn to waste not;
For both by man's labour alone have been got.

冷 水 要 人 挑。熱 水 要 人 燒

Lêng^3 shui^3 yao^4 jên^2 tʻiao^1; jê^4 shui^3 yao^4 jên^2 shao.^{1}

1994

It will cost you, to flit from upstairs to down,
Three piculs of the finest rice that is grown.

上 屋 搬 下 屋。要 得 三 担 糯 穀

Shang^4 wu^1 pan^1 hsia^4 wu,^{1} yao^4 tê^2 san^1 tan^1 no^4 ku.^{3}

1995

Have every thing you use substantial and clean:
Earthenware is better than gold and jade.

器 具 質 而 潔。瓦 缶 勝 金 玉

Chʻi^4 chü^4 chih^2 êrh^2 chieh^2; wa^1 fou^4 shêng^4 chin^1 yü.^{4}

1996

Neither build fine houses, nor covet rich fields.

勿 營 華 屋。勿 謀 良 田

Wu^4 ying^2 ʻhua^2 wu,^{1} wu^4 mou^2 liang^2 tʻien.^{2}

1997

Never spend a farthing uselessly.

一文錢不落虛空

Yi¹ wên² ch'ien² pu⁴ lo⁴ hsü¹ k'ung.¹

1998

Though living near water do not waste it.

近水不可多用水

Chin⁴ shui³ pu⁴ k'o³ to¹ yung⁴ shui.³

1999

Though living near mountains do not waste firewood.

近山不可枉燒柴

Chin⁴ shan¹ pu⁴ k'o³ wang³ shao¹ ch'ai.²

2000

Be careful of clothes and always have them;—of food and always have it.

惜衣得衣。惜食得食

Hsi² i¹ tê² i,¹ hsi² shih² tê² shih.²

2001

By all means avoid extravagance.

切勿奢侈過度

Ch'ieh⁴ wu⁴ shê¹ ch'ih³ kuo⁴ tu.⁴

2002

Don't fail to make ends meet.

莫令接不到頭

Mo⁴ ling⁴ chieh¹ pu⁴ tao⁴ t'ou.²

2003

The moon may be saved with a broken drum.

破破鼓救救月

P'o⁴ p'o⁴ ku³ chiu⁴ chiu⁴ yüeh.⁴

2004

It is wanton waste to feed a tortoise with barley.

烏龜吃大麥蹧蹋糧食

Wu¹ kuei¹ ch'ih¹ ta⁴ mai⁴ tsao¹ t'a¹ liang² shih.²

2005

Avoid breaking into a string of cash.

一弔錢開不得串

Yi¹ tiao⁴ ch'ien² k'ai¹ pu⁴ tê² ch'uan.⁴

2006

The trappings cost more than the horse.

買 馬 的 錢 沒 得 製 鞍 的 多

Mai^3 ma^3 ti^1 chʻien^2 mu^2 tê^2 chih^4 an^1 ti^1 to.^{1}

2007

Cheapness may not be economy. *Lit.:* If you buy cheap firewood, you burn the bottom of your copper.

得 了 便 宜 柴。燒 了 夾 底 鍋

Tê^2 liao^3 pʻien^2 i^2 chʻai,^{2} shao^1 liao^3 chia^1 ti^1 kuo.^{1}

2008

To leave economy for extravagance is easy; to leave extravagance for economy difficult.

從 儉 入 奢 易。從 奢 入 儉 難

Tsʻung^2 chien^3 ju^4 shê^1 i^4; tsʻung^2 shê^1 ju^4 chien^3 nan.^{2}

2009

Economy makes men independent.

減 用 免 求 人

Chien^3 yung^4 mien^3 chʻiu^2 jên.^{2}

2010

Cut your cloth according to your measure.

量 體 裁 衣

Liang^2 tʻi^3 tsʻai^2 i.^{1}

2011

Let every farthing go to its legitimate use. *Lit.:* One nail goes for one piece of sugar-stick.

一 個 釘 子 打 一 塊 糖

Yi^1 ko^4 ting^1 tzŭ^3 ta^3 yi^1 kʻuai^4 tʻang.^{2}

2012

In providing for self, practise rigid economy.

自 奉 必 須 儉 約

Tzŭ^4 fêng^4 pi^4 hsü^1 chien^3 yo.^{1}

2013

Taxes are fixed, but expenses are not.

錢 糧 有 數。時 用 無 數

Chʻien^1 liang^2 yu^3 shu,^{4} shih^2 yung^4 wu^2 shu.^{4}

2014

An openwork basket cannot for long dam a stream.

花籃提水難存留

ʻHua^{1} lan^{2} tʻi^{2} shui^{3} nan^{2} tsʻun^{2} liu.^{2}

2015

Make every cash serve two purposes.

一個錢把做兩個用

Yi^{1} ko^{4} chʻien^{2} pa^{3} tso^{4} liang^{3} ko^{4} yung.^{4}

2016

The pœony, though large, is a useless thing; while the date blossom, though small, yields fruit.

牡丹花大空入目

Mu^{3} tan^{1} ʻhua^{1} ta^{4} kʻung^{1} ju^{4} mu^{4};

棗花雖小結實成

tsao^{3} ʻhua^{1} sui^{1} hsiao^{3} chieh^{2} shih^{2} chʻêng.^{2}

2017

Reduction of expenditure brings freedom of action. *Lit.:* Remove the turnips and you'll have plenty of room.

去了蘿蔔地土寬

Chʻü^{4} liao^{3} lo^{2} pʻu^{2} ti^{4} tʻu^{3} kuan.^{1}

2018

Who spare men will always have men to use; who spare their clothes will always have clothes to wear.

惜人得人用。惜衣得衣穿

Hsi^{2} jên^{2} tê^{2} jên^{2} yung^{4}; hsi^{2} i^{1} tê^{2} i^{1} chʻuan.^{1}

2019

It is easy to spend, but hard to make money.

用錢容易賺錢難

Yung^{4} chʻien^{2} yung^{3} i,^{4} chuan^{4} chʻien^{2} nan.^{2}

CHAPTER IV.

EXPERIENCE.

— 2020 —

They know the nature of fishes who near to water dwell;
And those who live near hills know the song of each bird full well.

近水知魚性。近山識鳥音

Chin^{4} shui^{3} chih^{1} yü^{2} hsing^{4}; chin^{4} shan^{1} shih^{4} niao^{3} yin.^{1}

— 2021 —

Once bitten by a snake in passing by,
A second time he will of grass be shy.

一回着蛇咬。二回不躦草

Yi^{1} ʻhui^{2} cho^{2} shê^{2} yao,^{3} êrh^{4} ʻhui^{2} pu^{4} tsan^{3} tsʻao.^{3}

— 2022 —

He learns less who looks on, than he does who makes;
Less by mere doing, than by many mistakes.

見過不如做過

Chien^{4} kuo^{4} pu^{4} ju^{2} tso^{4} kuo^{4};

做過不如錯過多

Tso^{4} kuo^{4} pu^{4} ju^{2} tsʻo^{4} kuo^{4} to.^{1}

— 2023 —

Till some one a fool of you has made,
You can't be up to the tricks of trade.

不上當。不成內行

Pu^{4} shang^{4} tang,^{4} pu^{4} chʻêng^{2} nei^{4} ʻhang.^{2}

— 2024 —

They know what wind is who dwell in nests,—what rain is who dwell in caves.

巢居知風。穴居知雨

Chʻao^{2} chü^{1} chih^{1} fêng,^{1} hsüeh^{4} chü^{1} chih^{1} yü.^{3}

— 2025 —

He who eats bread for the first time feels strange over the first three mouthfuls.

初吃饅頭三口生

Chʻu^{1} chʻih^{1} man^{3} tʻou^{2} san^{1} kʻou^{3} shêng.^{1}

2026

If you have not lived in the country, you do not know what hardship means.

不住鄉不知艱難辛苦

Pu^4 chu^4 hsiang^1 pu^4 chih^1 chien^1 nan^2 hsin^1 k'u.^{3}

2027

If you have not lived in town, you do not know what is polite and proper.

不住城不知禮義

Pu^4 chu^4 ch'êng^2 pu^4 chih^1 li^3 i.^{4}

2028

Suppose no one ever ascended the mountain to see, who would believe that the water flowed down eastward from a height as great as the depth of the sea?

當時若不登高望

T'ang^1 shih^2 jo^4 pu^4 têng^2 kao^1 wang,^{4}

誰信東流海樣深

shui^3 hsin^4 tung^1 liu^3 'hai^3 yang^4 shên^1?

2029

If you drink the water you'll know the fountain.

飲水知源

Yin^3 shui^3 chih^1 yüan.^{2}

2030

He has tasted both the sweet and the bitter.

甘苦備嘗

Kan^1 k'u^3 pei^4 ch'ang.^{2}

2031

What the ear hears is not like what the eye sees.

耳聞不如眼見

Erh^3 wên^2 pu^4 ju^2 yen^3 chien.^{4}

2032

What one hears is doubtful; what ones sees is certain.

耳聽是虛。眼見是實

Erh^3 t'ing^1 shih^4 hsü^1; yen^3 chien^4 shih^4 shih.^{2}

2033

No words equal personal observation.

口說不如身逢

K'ou^3 shuo^1 pu^4 ju^2 shên^1 fêng.^{2}

2034

Every one knows his own affairs best. *Lit.:* Rats know the ways of rats.

耗子纔知耗子路

'Hao^4 tzŭ^3 ts'ai^2 chih^1 'hao^4 tzŭ^3 lu.^{4}

2035

The hole of a serpent, a serpent knows.

蛇 tsan 的洞蛇曉得

Shê^2 tsan^1 ti^1 tung^4 shê^2 hsiao^3 tê.^{2}

2336

No one knows how difficult anything is until he has tried to do it.

事非經過不知難

Shih^4 fei^1 ching^1 kuo^4 pu^4 chih^1 nan.^{2}

2037

Though blind the road is familiar to him.

眼瞎路熟

Yen^3 hsia^2 lu^4 shu.^{2}

2038

Until you go to the Yellow River you will not be satisfied.

不到黃河心不死

Pu^4 tao^4 'Huang^2 'ho^2 hsin^1 pu^4 ssŭ.^{3}

CHAPTER V.

FORETHOUGHT.

2039

Grass not dug up by the roots,
Will again send forth its shoots.

草不除根。終當復生

Tsʻao^3 pu^4 chʻu^2 kên,^{1} chung^1 tang^1 fu^2 shêng.^{1}

2040

Possessing a great tree, why be anxious about fuel?

有得大樹何愁柴燒

Yu^3 tê^2 ta^4 shu^4 ʻho^2 chʻou^2 chʻai^2 shao^1?

2041

Treat men from all parts well, and wherever you go you will be well treated. *Lit.:* Make sure of a clear moon in all the five lakes, and you will not suffer the lack of an angling place.

留得五湖明月在

Liu^2 tê^2 wu^3 ʻhu^2 ming^2 yüeh^4 tsai,^{4}

不愁無處下金鈎

pu^4 chʻou^2 wu^2 chʻu^4 hsia^4 chin^1 kou.^{1}

2042

Yearly guard against famine; nightly guard against thieves.

年年防飢。夜夜防盜

Nien^2 nien^2 fang^2 chi^1; yeh^4 yeh^4 fang^2 tao.^{4}

2043

Living securely, remember danger.

居安思危

Chü^1 an^1 ssŭ^1 wei.^{2}

2044

In plenty think of want; in want do not presume on plenty.

常將有日思無日
Chʻang2 chiang1 yu3 jih4 ssŭ1 wu2 jih4;
莫把無時作有時
Mo4 pa3 wu2 shih2 tso4 yu3 shih.2

2045

Keep your ponds full of water, and you will be prepared against drought; cultivate thoroughly your soil, and it will yield enough to support a family.

池塘積水須防旱
Chʻih2 tʻang2 chi2 shui3 hsü1 fang2 ʻhan4;
田土深耕足養家
tʻien2 tʻu3 shên1 kêng1 tsu2 yang3 chia.1

2046

Plant bamboos before your hall, and the phœnix may come and lodge thereon; rear fish in your ponds, for they may become dragons.

庭栽棲鳳竹。池養化龍魚
Tʻing2 tsai1 chʻi1 fêng4 chu2; chʻih2 yang3 ʻhua4 lung2 yü.2

2047

Rear sons for old age, and lay up grain against famine.

養兒防老。積穀防飢
Yang3 êrh2 fang2 lao3; chi2 ku3 fang2 chi.1

2048

Though the weather be fine take your umbrella; though you are not hungry take some provisions.

晴帶雨傘。飽帶飢糧
Chʻing2 tai4 yü3 san4; pao3 tai4 chi1 liang.2

2349

Thatch your roof before rainy weather; and dig your well before you become parched with thirst.

宜未雨而綢繆
I2 wei4 yü3 êrh2 chʻou2 mu4;
勿臨渴而掘井
wu4 lin2 kʻo3 êrh2 chüeh2 ching.3

2050

Better be too credulous than too sceptical.

寧可信其有。不可信其無
Ning² k'o³ hsin⁴ ch'i² yu,³ pu⁴ k'o³ hsin⁴ ch'i² wu.²

2051

Those who prepare for, will escape trouble.

有備無患
Yu³ pei⁴ wu² 'huan.⁴

NOTE.—There is a well-guarded street in Hankow bearing this inscription.

2052

It is better to ward off than to cure disease.

與其病後能求藥
Yü³ ch'i² ping⁴ 'hou⁴ nêng² ch'iu² yao,⁴
不如病前能自防
pu⁴ ju² ping⁴ ch'ien² nêng² tzŭ⁴ fang.²

2053

Better prevent than cure disease; better diminish than add to trouble.

禦病不如却病
Yü⁴ ping⁴ pu⁴ ju² ch'üeh⁴ ping⁴;
多事不如省事
To¹ shih⁴ pu⁴ ju² shêng³ shih.⁴

2054

He who neither hoards up wealth, nor makes an enemy, may sleep in peace and travel in safety.

一不積財。一不結怨
Yi¹ pu⁴ chi² ts'ai,⁴ yi¹ pu⁴ chieh² yüan,⁴
睡也安寧。走也方便
shui⁴ yeh³ an¹ ning,² tsou⁴ yeh³ fang¹ pien.⁴

2055

Let the past be past; and for the future by no means trouble.

過去事已過去了
Kuo⁴ ch'ü⁴ shih⁴ i³ kuo⁴ ch'ü⁴ liao³;
未來不必預思量
wei⁴ lai² pu⁴ pi⁴ yü⁴ ssŭ¹ liang.²

2056

If you wish to know the road before you, ask of those who have travelled it.

欲 知 前 頭 路。須 問 過 來 人
Yü[4] chih[1] ch'ien[2] t'ou[2] lu,[4] hsü[1] wên[4] kuo[4] lai[2] jên.[2]

2057

Equal to all emergencies. *Lit.:* If water comes, soil can dam it; if rebels come, a general can stop them.

水 來 土 掩。兵 來 將 當
Shui[3] lai[2] t'u[3] yen[3]; ping[1] lai[2] chiang[1] tang.[1]

2058

Forethought is easy, repentance hard.

思 前 容 易 悔 後 難
Ssŭ[1] ch'ien[2] yung[2] i[4] 'hui[3] 'hou[4] nan.[2]

CHAPTER VI.

IMPRUDENCE.

2059

When your money is spent you cut off wine; when growing old you turn to the sacred books.

無錢方斷酒。臨老始看經

Wu^2 chien^2 fang^1 tuan^4 chiu^3; lin^2 lao^3 shih^3 kʻan^4 ching.^{1}

2060

You think only of advance, and never of retreat.

只顧前走。不顧後退

Chih^3 ku^4 chien^2 tsou,^{4} pu^4 ku^4 ʻhou^4 tʻui.^{4}

2261

Do nothing to discredit yourself. *Lit.:* Do not thrust your fingers through your own paper lantern.

紙糊燈籠指穿不得

Chih^3 ʻhu^2 têng^1 lung^2 tsʻu^2 chʻuan^1 pu^4 tê.^{2}

2062

To pretend to be very clever and show one's self to be a fool.

弄巧反拙

Nung^4 chʻiao^3 fan^3 cho.^{1}

2063

To overlade a rickety ship.

破船多攬載

Pʻo^4 chʻuan^2 to^1 lan^3 tsai.^{3}

2064

To pour oil on the flames.

火上添油

ʻHuo^3 shang^4 tʻien^1 yu.^{2}

2065

Through credulity to be deceived into selling one's sitting-hens.

信人哄賣了雞婆種

Hsin^4 jên^2 ʻhung^3 mai^4 liao^3 chi^1 pʻo^2 chung.^{4}

2066

If you plant a grove to rear tigers in, when grown the tigers will injure men.

栽林養虎。虎大傷人

Tsai^{1} lin^{2} yang^{3} ‘hu,^{3} ‘hu^{3} ta^{4} shang^{1} jên.^{1}

2067

To pine one's belly, to spare one's face.

惜了臉皮悞了肚皮

Hsi^{2} liao^{3} lien^{3} p‘i^{2} wu^{4} liao^{3} tu^{3} p‘i.^{2}

2068

To be careless for the present and scheming for the future.

舍近而圖遠

Shê^{4} chin^{4} êrh^{2} t‘u^{2} yüan.^{3}

2069

To sail any way with wind and tide.

隨風倒舵。順水推船

Sui^{2} fêng^{1} tao^{4} to,^{4} shun^{4} shui^{3} t‘ui^{1} ch‘uan.^{2}

2070

He who rouses a sleeping tiger, exposes himself to harm.

把臥着的老虎哄起來了

Pa^{3} wo^{4} cho^{2} ti^{1} lao^{3} ‘hu^{3} ‘hung^{3} ch‘i^{3} lai^{2} liao,^{3}

自找吃虧

tzŭ^{4} chao^{3} ch‘ih^{1} k‘uei.^{1}

2071

To lose the great for the small.

因小失大

Yin^{1} hsiao^{3} shih^{1} ta.^{4}

2072

To be careless in great matters and careful in small ones.

大處不算。小處算

Ta^{4} ch‘u^{4} pu^{4} suan,^{4} hsiao^{3} ch‘u^{4} suan.^{4}

2073

To hide the head and leave the rump exposed.

鑽進頭不顧屁股

Tsüan^{1} chin^{4} t‘ou^{2} pu^{4} ku^{4} p‘i^{4} ku.^{3}

2074

To pare off flesh in one place to mend a sore in another.

剮肉補瘡

Kua³ jou⁴ pu³ chʻuang.¹

2075

To present one's head to a shower of stones.

送腦磕接石頭

Sung⁴ nao³ kʻo¹ chieh¹ shih² tʻou.²

2076

To spare a swelling till it becomes ulcerous.

護疱成膿

ʻHu⁴ pʻao² chʻêng² nung.²

2077

He won't go in fair weather, but waits till rain soaks his pate.

晴乾不肯去。直待雨淋頭

Chʻing² kan¹ pu⁴ kʻên³ chʻü,⁴ chih² tai⁴ yü³ lin⁴ tʻou.²

2078

The swallow which builds its nest on a bamboo door screen, will find it difficult to rest.

燕巢幕上棲身難安

Yen⁴ chʻao² mu⁴ shang⁴ chʻi¹ shên¹ nan² an.¹

2079

Build a cottage by the roadside, and you will not get it finished in three years.

作舍道傍三年不成

Tso⁴ shê⁴ tao⁴ pʻang² san¹ nien² pu⁴ chʻêng.²

2080

To allow anything to go in at one ear and out of the other.

這隻耳躲進。那隻耳躲出

Chê⁴ chih¹ êrh³ to² chin,⁴ na⁴ chih¹ êrh³ to² chʻu.¹

2081

To divulge a secret. *Lit.:* To diclose the horse's foot.

露出馬脚來

Lou⁴ chʻu¹ ma³ chiao³ lai.²

2082

He who rides a tiger is afraid to dismount.

騎虎難下背

Chʻi² ʻhu³ nan⁴ hsia⁴ pei.⁴

2083

Though under the flag-staff; he misses his drill.

旗桿磴下倒悞了操

Chʻi² kan² têng¹ hsia⁴ tao⁴ wu⁴ liao³ tsʻao.¹

2084

To try to stand on two boats at once.

脚踏兩邊船

Chiao³ ta⁴ liang³ pien¹ chʻuan.²

SECTION XVI.—ON THE FIVE RELATIONS.

CHAPTER I.

PRINCE AND MINISTER.

2085

A cup is the Prince that o'er us reigns;
We are the water that cup contains;
Round or square as the cup may be,
Just the same shape you'll the water see.

君猶盃也。民猶水也

Chün^{1} yü^{2} pei^{1} yeh,^{3} min^{2} yu^{2} shui^{3} yeh,^{3}

盃方水方。盃圓水圓

Pei^{1} fang^{1} shui^{3} fang,^{1} pei^{1} yüan^{2} shui^{3} yüan.^{2}

2086

In the Emperor's presence to abide,
Is just like sleeping by a tiger's side.

身在皇帝邊。猶如共虎眠

Shên^{1} tsai^{4} ʻhuang^{2} ti^{4} pien,^{1} yu^{2} ju^{2} kung^{4} ʻhu^{3} mien.^{2}

2087

The minister remonstrates with the Prince, not the Prince with the minister.

只有臣諫君

Chih^{3} yu^{3} chʻên^{2} chien^{4} chün,^{1}

沒有君諫臣之禮

mu^{2} tê^{2} chün^{1} chien^{4} chʻên^{2} chih^{1} li.^{3}

2088

When the Prince is not upright, ministers escape to foreign countries.

君不正臣逃外國

Chün^{1} pu^{4} chêng^{4} chʻên^{2} tʻao^{2} wai^{4} kuo.^{2}

2089

All the stars of heaven salute the north; every stream flows towards the east.

天上衆星皆拱北
T'ien[1] shang[4] chung[4] hsing[1] chieh[1] kung[3] pei[3];
世間無水不朝東
shih[4] chien[1] wu[2] shui[3] pu[4] ch'ao[2] tung.[1]

NOTE.—Thus, according to the high-flown notions of the Chinese, do all officers and people combine to magnify the Son of Heaven.

2090

Each dynasty has its Sons of Heaven, and its ministers.
一朝天子一朝臣
Yi[1] ch'ao[2] t'ien[1] tzŭ[3] yi[1] ch'ao[2] ch'ên.[2]

2091

When the Prince wants a minister to die, he dies.
君要臣死臣就死
Chün[1] yao[4] ch'ên[2] ssŭ[3] ch'ên[2] chiu[4] ssŭ.[3]

2092

The Emperor cannot make men be his magistrates.
朝廷無强官之法
Ch'ao[2] t'ing[2] wu[2] ch'iang[2] kuan[1] chih[1] fa.[3]

2093

The light of all the stars is not equal to that of the moon.
衆星朗朗不如孤月獨明
Chung[4] hsing[1] lang[3] lang[3] pu[4] ju[2] ku[1] yüeh[4] tu[2] ming.[2]

2094

An upright royal family is prospered by Heaven; and under pure magistrates the people enjoy peace.
國正天心順。官淸民自安
Kuo[2] chêng[4] t'ien[1] hsin[1] shun[4]; kuan[1] ch'ing[1] min[2] tzŭ[4] an.[1]

2095

All kinds of divine influence will combine to support a sage Son of Heaven.
聖天子百靈相助
Shêng[4] t'ien[1] tzŭ[3] pai[3] ling[2] hsiang[1] chu.[4]

2096

If the Son of Heaven breaks the laws, he is guilty like one of the people.

天子犯法與民同罪
Tʻien^1 tzŭ^3 fan^4 fa^3 yü^3 min^2 tʻung^2 tsui.^{4}

2097

A faithful minister views death unappalled; a virtuous woman faces danger with a smile.

忠臣視死無難色
Chung^1 chʻên^2 shih^4 ssŭ^3 wu^2 nan^2 sê^4;
烈婦臨危有笑容
lieh^4 fu^4 lin^2 wei^2 yu^3 hsiao^4 yung.^{2}

2098

A loyal minister is not afraid of death; he who is, is not a loyal minister.

忠臣不怕死。怕死不忠臣
Chung^1 chʻên^2 pu^4 pʻa^4 ssŭ^2; pʻa^4 ssŭ^3 pu^4 chung^1 chʻên.^{2}

2099

One attends a Prince as a sheep a tiger; the slightest shortcoming is punished.

伴君如同羊伴虎
Pan^4 chün^1 ju^2 tʻung^2 yang^2 pan^4 hu^3;
一點不到有損傷
yi^4 tien^3 pu^4 tao^4 yu^3 sun^3 shang.^{1}

2100

A selfish minister is not loyal; a loyal minister is not selfish.

私臣不忠。忠臣不私
Ssŭ^1 chʻên^2 pu^4 chung^1; chung^1 chʻên^2 pu^4 ssŭ.^{1}

2101

You must look for loyal ministers amongst filial sons.

求忠臣必入孝子之門
Chʻiu^2 chung^1 chʻên^2 pi^4 ju^4 hsiao^4 tzŭ^3 chih^1 mên.^{2}

CHAPTER II.

PARENTS AND CHILDREN.

2102

As the dragon and the phœnix propagate their kind;
The young rat will be able to bore a hole you'll find.

龍 生 龍 鳳 生 鳳
Lung^2 shêng^2 lung^2 fêng^4 shêng^1 fêng^4;

老 鼠 生 兒 會 打 洞
Lao^3 shu^3 shêng^1 êrh^2 ʻhui^4 ta^3 tung.^{4}

2103

The faults of children are to parents all unknown;
And farmers never know how rich their crops have grown.

人 莫 知 其 子 之 惡
Jên^2 mo^4 chih^1 chʻi^2 tzŭ^3 chih^1 o^4;

農 莫 知 其 苗 之 碩
Nung^2 mo^4 chih^1 chʻi^2 miao^2 chih^1 so.^{2}

2104

Would you see your little ones growing up strong,
They must not clothe heavily, nor eat too long.

要 得 小 兒 安
Yao^4 te^2 hsiao^3 êrh^2 an,^{1}

須 帶 三 分 飢 餓 寒
Hsü^1 tai^4 san^1 fên^1 chi^1 o^4 ʻhan.^{2}

2105

As your fields must be by your own hands sown,
Sons are no use unless they're your own.

田 要 親 耕。子 要 親 生
Tʻien^2 yao^4 chʻin^1 kêng,^{1} tzŭ^3 yao^4 chʻin^1 shêng.^{1}

2106

He kept my early years from care;
I'll keep and comfort his grey hair.

他 養 我 小。我 養 他 老
Tʻa^1 yang^3 wo^3 hsiao^3; wo^3 yang^3 tʻa^1 lao.^{3}

2107

One's own parents may be thrown aside neglected;
While foster parents are as Heaven respected.

生 身 父 母 在 一 邊
Shêng[1] shên[1] fu[4] mu[3] tsai[4] yi[1] pien,[1]
養 身 父 母 大 如 天
Yang[3] shên[1] fu[4] mu[3] ta[4] ju[2] t'ien.[1]

2108

Not to sow parental lands, good sons will take care;
Good daughters will not always their wedding dresses wear.

好 兒 不 種 爺 田 地
'Hao[3] êrh[2] pu[4] chung[4] yeh[2] t'ien[2] ti[4];
好 女 不 穿 嫁 時 衣
'Hao[3] nü[2] pu[4] ch'uan[1] chia[4] shih[2] i.[1]

2109

Near the ancestral home the eldest must reside;
Near to his mother's room the youngest must abide.

長 子 不 離 宗 堂
Chang[3] tzŭ[3] pu[4] li[2] tsung[1] t'ang[2];
么 兒 不 離 娘 房
Yao[1] êrh[2] pu[4] li[2] niang[2] fang.[2]

2110

As seed-corn is from former years reserved,
So children are in former lives deserved.

種 子 隔 年 留。女 兒 前 世 修
Chung[4] tzŭ[3] ko[2] nien[2] liu,[2] nü[2] êrh[2] ch'ien[2] shih[4] hsiu.[1]

2111

One may see what a son will be,
From what he is in infancy.

看 兒 歹 好。須 從 幼 小
K'an[4] êrh[2] tai[3] 'hao,[3] hsü[1] ts'ung[2] yu[4] hsiao.[2]

2112

Wise statesmen are the produce of prosperous dynasties;
And children's children bless the home wherever virtue is.

國 朝 盛 出 賢 臣
Kuo² ch'ao² shêng⁴ ch'u¹ hsien² ch'ên²;
家 道 興 看 子 孫
Chia¹ tao⁴ hsing¹ k'an⁴ tzŭ³ sun.¹

2113

The fruit of one tree may be sour and sweet;
The sons of one mother dull and discreet.

一 樹 之 果 有 酸 有 甜
Yi¹ shu⁴ chih¹ kuo³ yu³ suan¹ yu³ t'ien²;
一 母 之 子 有 愚 有 賢
Yi¹ mu³ chih¹ tzŭ³ yu³ yü² yu³ hsien.²

2114

When descendants are in an unhappy condition,
It's the grave, or the house, has a luckless position!

子 孫 無 福。賴 墳 賴 屋
Tzŭ³ sun¹ wu² fu,² lai⁴ fên² lai⁴ wu.¹

2115

Spoilt children are unfilial sinners.
Spoilt dogs will steal their masters' dinners.

嬌 兒 不 孝。嬌 狗 上 竈
Chiao¹ êrh² pu⁴ hsiao⁴; chiao¹ kou³ shang⁴ tsao.⁴

2116

When fathers are unmerciful, sons fly to distant localities.

父 不 仁 子 奔 他 鄉
Fu⁴ pu⁴ jên² tzŭ³ pên¹ t'a¹ hsiang.¹

2117

Kind father—dutiful son; dutiful son—virtuous daughter-in-law.

父 慈 子 孝。子 孝 媳 賢
Fu⁴ tz'ŭ² tzŭ³ hsiao⁴; tzŭ³ hsiao⁴ hsi² hsien.²

2118

The child knows not what trouble it has given its mother.

養 兒 不 知 娘 辛 苦
Yang³ êrh² pu⁴ chih¹ niang² hsin¹ k'u.³

2119

Like father like son. *Lit.:* Dragons give birth to dragons, and phœnixes hatch phœnixes.

龍生龍子。鳳生鳳兒

Lung² shêng¹ lung² tzŭ,³ fêng⁴ shêng¹ fêng⁴ êrh.²

2120

The same. *Lit.:* Water always drops from the eaves into the same old holes.

屋簷溝裡水

Wu¹ yen² kou¹ li³ shui³

點點滴在舊窩裡

tien³ tien³ ti¹ tsai⁴ chiu⁴ wo¹ li.³

2121

He is unfilial who loves wife more than mother; she is unwise who hates for him her son's wife.

寵妻別母子不孝

Ch'ung³ ch'i¹ pieh² mu³ tzŭ³ pu⁴ hsiao⁴;

替兒嫌妻母不賢

t'i⁴ êrh² hsien² ch'i¹ mu³ pu⁴ hsien.²

2122

He is the son who buries his parents; and worn out silks and satins are dress.

送老歸山纔是兒

Sung⁴ lao³ kuei¹ shan¹ ts'ai² shih⁴ êrh²;

穿破綾羅纔是衣

ch'uan¹ p'o⁴ ling² lo² ts'ai² shih⁴ i.¹

2123

At the bedside in cases of chronic sickness, there are no filial children.

久病牀前無孝子

Chiu³ ping⁴ ch'uang² chien² wu³ hsiao⁴ tzŭ.³

2124

When parents die old, dutiful children may be merry.

父母老死。風流孝子

Fu⁴ mu³ lao³ ssŭ,³ fêng¹ liu² hsiao⁴ tzŭ.³

2125

Strict fathers have filial sons.

嚴 父 出 孝 子

Yen^2 fu^4 chʻu^1 hsiao^4 tzŭ.^{3}

2126

When father and son agree, the family will not fail; when brothers agree, the family will not separate.

父 子 和 而 家 不 退

Fu^4 tzŭ^3 ʻho^2 êrh^2 chia^1 pu^4 tʻui^4:

兄 弟 和 而 家 不 分

hsiung^1 ti^4 ʻho^2 êrh^2 chia^1 pu^4 fên.^{1}

2127

In a gambling-house—no father and son.

賭 錢 場 上 無 父 子

Tu^3 chʻien^2 chʻang^2 shang^4 wu^2 fu^4 tzŭ.^{3}

2128

Bad descendants involve ancestors in disgrace.

後 人 不 好 連 累 上 人

ʻHou^4 jên^2 pu^4 ʻhao,^{3} lien^2 lei^3 shang^4 jên^2.

NOTE.—This is a purely Chinese notion, according to which the sins of descendants are charged upon ancestors; *they* must have committed some enormous crime to cause their descendants thus to sin.

2129

The parents' pet is the obedient child.

爹 娘 痛 的 順 心 兒

Tieh^1 niang^2 tʻung^4 ti^1 shun^4 hsin^1 êrh.^{2}

2130

Parents can hardly secure that their descendants will be wise and good.

父 母 難 保 子 孫 賢

Fu^4 mu^3 nan^2 pao^3 tzŭ^3 sun^1 hsien.^{2}

2131

When a father wants his son to die, he dies.

父 要 子 亡 子 不 留

Fu^4 yao^4 tzŭ^3 wang^2 tzŭ^3 pu^4 liu.^{2}

2132

Whilst the father lives the son dare not put himself forward.

父在子不敢自專

Fu^4 tsai^4 tzŭ^3 pu^4 kan^2 tzŭ^4 chuan.^{1}

2133

The rod produces obedient, petting and spoiling disobedient children.

棍棒頭上出好子

Kun^4 pang^4 t'ou^2 shang^4 ch'u^1 'hao^3 tzŭ,^{3}

嬌疼嬌養忤逆兒

chiao^1 t'eng^2 chiao^1 yang^3 wu^3 ni^4 êrh.^{2}

2134

Good parents,—jolly marriages; good children,—decent funerals.

好爹媽好親事

'Hao^3 tieh^1 ma^1 'hao^3 ch'in^1 shih^4;

好兒女好葬事

'hao^3 êrh^2 nü^2 'hao^3 tsang^4 shih.^{4}

2135

"When a tiger has three whelps at a birth, one of them will be a leopard; when a man has three boys at a birth one of them will be noble."

虎生三子必有一豹

'Hu^3 shêng^1 san^1 tzŭ^3 pi^4 yu^3 yi^1 pao^4;

人生三子必有一貴

Jên^2 shêng^1 san^1 tzŭ^3 pi^4 yu^3 yi^1 kuei.^{4}

NOTE.—Curiously enough, it is said that when a man's wife bears him three sons, he is summoned to the *yamên* to receive a congratulatory present from the magistrate. In one instance, known to my informant, the lucky father received a present of Ten Taels. This will remind the reader of the Queen's bounty on the occasion of triple births.

2136

When selling a son don't stroke his head; if you stroke his head your tears will flow.

賣子莫摩頭。摩頭眼淚流

Mai^4 tzŭ^3 mo^4 mo^1 t'ou^2; mo^1 t'ou^2 yen^3 lei^4 liu.^{2}

2137

Dutiful sires beget dutiful sons; undutiful sires beget undutiful children.

孝順還生孝順子
Hsiao⁴ shun⁴ 'huan² shêng¹ hsiao⁴ shun⁴ tzŭ³;

忤逆還生忤逆兒
wu³ ni⁴ 'huan² shêng¹ wu³ ni⁴ êrh.²

2138

You must rear children to know parental goodness.

養兒方知父母恩
Yang³ êrh² fang¹ chih¹ fu⁴ mu³ ên.¹

2139

He who has a son must depend on him; he who has not, must depend on his son-in-law.

有兒靠兒。無兒靠婿
Yu³ êrh² k'ao⁴ êrh²; wu² êrh² k'ao⁴ hsü.⁴

2140

If my descendants surpass me, why should I covet money?
If they be inferior to me, still why should I do so?

子孫勝似我要錢做甚麼
Tsŭ³ sun¹ shêng⁴ ssŭ⁴ wo³ yao⁴ ch'ien² tso⁴ shên⁴ mo¹?

子孫不如我要錢做甚麼
Tzŭ³ sun¹ pu⁴ ju² wo³ yao⁴ ch'ien² tso⁴ shên⁴ mo¹?

2141

Do not spend your honest wit in fruitless scheming; your descendants must get their share of happiness.

莫把眞心空計較
Mo⁴ pa³ chên¹ hsin¹ k'ung¹ chi⁴ chiao⁴;

兒孫自有兒孫福
êrh² sun¹ tzŭ⁴ yu³ êrh² sun¹ fu.²

2142

Reserve the square-inch plot for your descendants to till.

但存方寸地留與子孫耕
Tan⁴ ts'un² fang¹ ts'un⁴ ti⁴ liu² yü³ tzŭ³ sun¹ kêng.¹

NOTE.—The "square-inch plot" is the heart; and the meaning is that parents must leave a good example to be followed by their children.

2143

Would you love your child, then teach him industry and temperance.

若要愛子教他勤儉

Jo⁴ yao⁴ ai⁴ tzŭ³ chiao⁴ t'a¹ ch'in² chien.³

2144

When the father pursues the son with the rod, he must not follow him for a hundred paces.

老子趕兒不上百步

Lao³ tzŭ³ kan² êrh² pu⁴ shang⁴ pai³ pu.⁴

2145

The broken furnace may turn out good tiles.

破窰出好瓦

P'o⁴ yao² ch'u¹ 'hao³ wa.¹

2146

If you love your child don't spare the rod; if you hate your child give him plenty of dainties.

憐兒多與棒。憎兒多與食

Lien² êrh² to¹ yü³ pang⁴; tsêng¹ êrh² to¹ yü³ shih.²

NOTE.—"He that spareth his rod hateth his son: but he that loveth him chasteneth him betimes." Prov. 13: 24.

2147

The pestle produces white rice; and the rod good children.

杵頭出白米。棒頭出好子

Ch'u³ t'ou² ch'u¹ pai² mi³; pang⁴ t'ou² ch'u¹ 'hao³ tzŭ.²

2148

Let parents say what they will, children must curb their tempers and hold their tongues.

父母言語。忍氣吞聲

Fu⁴ mu³ yen² yü,³ jên³ ch'i⁴ t'un¹ shêng.¹

2149

Grown up sons must separate from their mothers; and grown up daughters from their fathers.

男大避母。女大避父

Na² ta⁴ pi⁴ mu³; nü² ta⁴ pi⁴ fu.⁴

2150

We dare not injure the bodies received from our parents.

身體髮膚受之父母不敢毀傷

Shên^1 t'i^3 fa^3 fu^1 shou^4 chih^1 fu^4 mu,^{3} pu^4 kan^2 'hui^3 shang.^{1}

2151

Whomsoever his parents love, the son loves.

父母愛一人焉。子愛一人焉

Fu^4 mu^3 ai^4 yi^1 jên^2 yen,^{1} tzŭ^3 ai^4 yi^1 jên^2 yen.^{1}

2152

Sons and grandsons have their destined pleasures; do not treat them as horses and cows.

兒孫自有兒孫福

Erh^2 sun^1 tzŭ^4 yu^3 êrh^2 sun^1 fu^2;

莫把兒孫作馬牛

Mo^4 pa^3 êrh^2 sun^1 tso^4 ma^3 niu.^{2}

2153

With right on his side even a son may correct a father.

有理打得爺

Yu^3 li^3 ta^3 tê^2 tieh.^{1}

2154

If you honour your parents at home, why go afar to burn incense?

在家敬父母。何必遠燒香

Tsai^4 chia^1 ching^4 fu^4 mu,^{3} 'ho^2 pi^4 yüan^3 shao^1 hsiang^1?

2155

Every man loves his own flesh and blood.

各人皮肉各人疼

Ko^4 jên^2 p'i^2 jou^4 ko^4 jên^2 t'eng.^{2}

2156

Whether a man strike his father and curse his mother or not, depends on his natural disposition.

打爺駡娘。出自本心

Ta^3 tieh^1 ma^4 niang,^{2} ch'u^1 tzŭ^4 pên^3 hsin.^{1}

2157

A prodigal's repentance is a priceless treasure.

浪子回頭。無價之寶

Lang^4 tzŭ^3 ʻhui^2 tʻou,^{2} wu^2 chia^4 chih^1 pao.^{3}

2158

A stupid son is better than a crafty daughter.

癡男勝過巧女

Chʻih^2 nan^2 shêng^4 kuo^4 chʻiao^3 nü.^{2}

2159

Full-grown fledged birds fly away.

長大老乾各自飛

Chang^3 ta^4 lao^3 chʻien^2 ko^4 tzŭ^4 fei.^{1}

2160

If sons are filial you don't want many.

好子不要多

ʻHao^3 tzŭ^3 pu^4 yao^4 to.^{1}

2161

A daughter-in-law is very diligent on her first arrival.

新娶媳婦初來勤

Hsin^1 chʻü^3 hsi^2 fu^4 chʻu^1 lai^2 chʻin.^{2}

2162

A child does not dislike a plain mother; a dog does not despise a poor master.

子不嫌母醜。狗不厭家貧

Tzŭ^3 pu^4 hsien^2 mu^3 chʻou^3; kou^3 pu^4 yen^4 chia^1 pʻin.^{3}

2163

He is no man who thinks much of his wealth, and little of his parents.

重貨財。薄父母。不成人子

Chung^4 ʻhuo^4 tsʻai,^{2} po^2 fu^4 mu,^{3} pu^4 chʻêng^2 jên^2 tzŭ.^{3}

2164

Imbecile sons boast of their ancestors.

無志男兒把祖宗誇

Wu^2 chih^4 nan^2 êrh^2 pa^3 tsu^3 tsung^1 kʻua.^{1}

2165

Wealth excites men; children awaken their affections.

財 帛 動 人 心。兒 女 痛 人 心

Ts'ai² pai² tung⁴ jên² hsin¹; êrh² nü² t'ung⁴ jên² hsin.¹

2166

He who has sons cannot long remain poor; he who has none cannot long remain rich.

有 兒 貧 不 久。無 子 富 不 長

Yu³ êrh² p'in³ pu⁴ chiu³; wu² tzŭ³ fu⁴ pu⁴ ch'ang.²

2167

Empty granaries bring months and years of want; stupid posterity, laxity in manners and uprightness.

倉 廩 虛 兮 歲 月 乏

Ts'ang¹ lin³ hsü¹ hsi¹ sui⁴ yüeh⁴ fa²;

子 孫 愚 兮 禮 義 疎

tzŭ³ sun¹ yü² hsi¹ li³ i⁴ su.²

2168

Better rear a playful than a stupid child.

寧 可 養 頑 子。不 可 養 癡 子

Ning² k'o² yang³ wan² tzŭ,³ pu⁴ k'o³ yang³ ch'ih² tzŭ.³

2169

Children whom the mother nourished three years at the breast,

leave her of their own accord when grown to man's estate.

三 年 乳 哺 長 懷 抱

San¹ nien² ju³ pu³ ch'ang² huai² pao,⁴

長 大 成 人 各 自 開

chang³ ta⁴ ch'êng² jên² ko⁴ tzŭ⁴ k'ai.¹

2170

It is a miserable family where there are boys and girls: it is geni family where there are none.

有 兒 有 女 是 寃 家

Yu³ êrh² yu³ nü² shih⁴ yüan¹ chia¹;

無 兒 無 女 是 仙 家

wu² êrh² wu² nü² shih⁴ hsien¹ chia.¹

NOTE.—This may be said in jocular reply to congratulations, by the father of a large family.

2171

If we have none to foul the bed, we shall have none to burn paper at our graves.

牀上沒有屙屎的
Ch'uang[2] shang[4] mu[2] yu[3] o[1] sui[1] ti,[1]
墳前沒有燒紙的
fên[2] ch'ien[2] mu[2] yu[3] shao[1] chih[3] ti.[1]

2172

Don't fear that your father won't love you; for when children are wise and good, parents are naturally glad.

不患父不慈。子賢親自樂
Pu[4] 'huan[4] fu[4] pu[4] tz'ŭ[2]; tzŭ[3] hsien[2] ch'in[1] tzŭ[4] lê.[4]

2173

If you would pray for dutiful children, first show filial piety to your father and mother.

要求順子。先孝爹娘
Yao[4] ch'iu[2] shun[4] tzŭ,[3] hsien[1] hsiao[4] tieh[1] niang.[2]

CHAPTER III.

HUSBANDS AND WIVES.

2174

For wives your sons are longing, your maids for husbands call;
This is the one arena in which strive one and all.

兒討媳婦女招郎
Erh2 tʻao3 hsi2 fu4 nü2 chao1 lang2;
人在世間鬧一場
Jên2 tsai4 shih4 chien1 nao4 yi1 chʻang.2

2175

Marriages when properly negociated,
Cause neither family to be aggravated.

結親如結義。兩家莫生氣
Chieh2 chʻin2 ju2 chieh2 i,4 liang3 chia1 mo4 shêng1 chʻi.4

2176

When doorways match and houses pair,
A marriage may be settled there.

門當戶對。兩下成婚配
Mên2 tang1 ʻhu4 tui,4 liang3 hsia4 chʻêng2 hun1 pʻei.4

2177

In betrothing a daughter to any young man,
Very careful enquiry's the only safe plan.

女兒說人家。過細訪查
Nü2 êrh2 shuo1 jên2 chia,1 kuo4 hsi4 fang3 chʻa.2

2178

Where true love exists between husbands and wives,
They're happily joined to the end of their lives.

夫妻愛好。同偕到老
Fu1 chʻi1 ai4 ʻhao,3 tʻung2 chieh2 tao4 lao.3

2179

In the great majority of cases,
Wives have fair, and husbands ugly faces;
Yet there are many, on the other side,
Where the man is bound to an ugly bride.

好妻無好漢。天下一大半
ʻHao^3 chʻi^1 wu^2 ʻhao^3 ʻhan,^{4} tʻien^1 hsia^4 yi^1 ta^4 pan^4.;
好漢無好妻。天下一大堆
ʻHao^3 ʻhan^4 wu^2 ʻhao^3 chʻi,^{1} tʻien^1 hsia^4 yi^1 ta^4 tui.^{1}

2180

Nought must divide the married pair;
Its weight the steelyard cannot spare.

公不離婆。秤不離鉈
Kung^1 pu^4 li^2 pʻo^2; chʻêng^3 pu^4 li^2 tʻo.^{4}

2181

People married early, see in plainness nothing wrong:
And clothes, though made of coarsest cloth, are often very strong.

結髮夫妻醜也好
Chieh^2 fa^3 fu^1 chʻi^1 chʻou^3 yeh^3 ʻhao^3:
粗布縫衣衣也牢
Tsʻu^1 pu^4 fêng^3 i^1 i^1 yeh^3 lao.^{2}

NOTE.—"Early"; *chieh^2 fa,^{3}* the knotting up of the hair, at the age of one and a half or two years.

2182

The bride that is linked to a worthless groom,
Is like a man buried in a luckless tomb.

嫁壞人。葬壞墳
Chia^4 ʻhuai^4 jên,^{2} tsang ʻhuai^4 fên.^{2}

2183

Widow marriage must always be,
Consummated immediately.

過婚嫂。連夜討
Kuo^4 hun^1 sao^3 lien^2 yeh^4 tʻao.^{3}

NOTE.—Else the widow will demand a higher price, or accept some one else's higher bid.

2184

Having lost her first husband, again she's a bride;
And so she gets higher at every stride.

死了前夫嫁後夫一步高一步
Ssŭ^3 liao^3 chʻien^2 fu^1 chia^4 ʻhou^4 fu^1; Yi^1 pu^4 kao^1 yi^1 pu.^{4}

2185

For virtue a woman our wife we make;
For her beauty we a concubine take.

娶妻娶德。娶妾娶色

Chʻü³ chʻi¹ chʻü³ tê²; chʻü³ chʻieh⁴ chʻü³ sê.⁴

2186

Long not for the goddess' beauty divine;
Long that the star of your husband may shine.

不要觀音面。只要夫星現

Pu⁴ yao⁴ Kuan¹ Yin¹ mien⁴; chih³ yao⁴ fu¹ hsing¹ hsien.⁴

NOTE.—"Goddess," *i. e. Kuan Yin*, the well-known goddess of mercy. For an interesting and learned account of this divinity, see Eitel's "Handbook of Chinese Buddhism," page 18.

2187

The dislike of her husband's parents she need not mind;
But from her husband's dislike what escape can she find?

公婆嫌還猶可

Kung¹ pʻo² hsien² huan² yu² kʻo³

丈夫嫌無處躲

Chang⁴ fu¹ hsien² wu² chʻu⁴ to.²

2188

The well-to-do maiden is not married into a poverty-stricken family.

有福之女不落無福之家

Yu³ fu² chih¹ nü² pu⁴ lo⁴ wu² fu² chih¹ chia.¹

2189

Early marriage is the duty of adults of both sexes.

男大須婚。女大須嫁

Nan² ta⁴ hsü¹ ʻhun¹; nü² ta⁴ hsü¹ chia.⁴

2190

A clever match-maker can scold both sides; while a stupid match-maker gets scolded by both.

會做媒的罵兩頭

ʻHui⁴ tso⁴ mei² ti¹ ma⁴ liang³ tʻou²;

不會做媒的兩頭罵

pu⁴ ʻhui⁴ tso⁴ mei² ti¹ liang³ tʻou² ma.⁴

2191

Those who rear daughters hope for great suitors.

養女望高門

Yang³ nü² wang⁴ kao¹ mên.²

2192

The upper classes endow their daughters on marriage; the middle classes do nothing but rear and marry them; and the lower classes make money by marrying them.

上等之人陪錢嫁女

Shang⁴ têng³ chih¹ jên² pʻei² chʻien² chia⁴ nü²;

中等之人養女嫁女

chung¹ têng³ chih¹ jên² yang³ nü² chia⁴ nü²;

下等之人賺錢嫁女

hsia⁴ têng³ chih¹ jên² chuan⁴ chʻien² chia⁴ nü.²

2193

Without clouds in the sky it cannot rain; so without go-betweens a match can never be made.

天上無雲不下雨

Tʻien¹ shang⁴ wu² yün² pu⁴ hsia⁴ yü³;

地下無媒不成親

ti⁴ hsia⁴ wu² mei² pu⁴ chʻêng² chʻin.¹

2194

When one family rears a daughter, a hundred families ask her in marriage.

一家養女百家求

Yi¹ chia¹ yang³ nü² pai³ chia¹ chʻiu.²

2195

In marrying a daughter select an excellent son-in-law; and do not extort costly wedding presents.

嫁女擇佳婿。勿索重聘

Chia⁴ nü² tsê² chia¹ hsü,⁴ wu⁴ so³ chung⁴ pʻin.⁴

2196

In marrying a son seek a virtuous maiden, and scheme not for a rich dowry.

娶媳求淑女。勿計厚奩

Chʻü³ hsi² chʻiu² shu² nü,² wu⁴ chi⁴ ʻhou⁴ lien.²

2197

Negligent farming may induce temporary poverty; but a mistake in marrying blights a whole life.

種田不好一時窮
Chung^4 tʻien^2 pu^4 ʻhao^3 yi^1 shih^2 chʻiung^2;
討壞老婆一生窮
tʻao^3 ʻhuai^4 lao^3 pʻo^2 yi^1 shêng^1 chʻiung.^{2}

2198

Nine out of ten go-betweens are liars.

十媒九謊
Shih^2 mei^2 chiu^3 ʻhuang.^{3}

2199

You expect condiments with vegetables; a pretty face with a concubine.

吃菜吃油鹽。娶妾娶容顏
Chʻih^1 tsʻai^4 chʻih^1 yu^2 yen^2; chʻü^3 chʻieh^4 chʻü^3 yung^2 yen.^{2}

2200

You may exhume a coffin; you may not reject a betrothed son-in-law.

葬墳還可取。擇婿不可悔
Tsang^4 fên^2 ʻhuan^2 kʻo^3 chʻü^3; tsê^2 hsü^4 pu^4 kʻo^3 ʻhui.^{3}

2201

Matrimony, exhort men to complete; strifes, exhort men to put away.

婚姻勸攏。禍患勸開
ʻHun^1 yin^1 chʻüan^4 lung^3; kuo^4 ʻhuan^4 chʻüan^4 kʻai.^{1}

2202

There are Five Relations, but that of husband and wife stands first; there are three thousand great Rites, but that of marriage is most important.

人倫有五夫婦爲先
Jên^2 lün^2 yu^3 wu^3 fu^1 fu^4 wei^2 hsien^1;
大禮三千婚姻最重
ta^4 li^3 san^1 chʻien^1 ʻhun^1 yin^1 tsui^4 chung.^{4}

NOTE.—According to the present custom of speaking of the Five Relations, they occur in the following order: Prince and Minister; Parents and children; Husbands and wives; Elder and younger Brothers; and Friends. But in the *Yi-Ching* the relation of Husband and wife stands first; hence this saying.

2203

Marriage results from ante-natal causes.

前世有緣今世結

Ch'ien^2 shih^4 yu^3 yüan^2 chin^1 shih^4 chieh.^{2}

2204

In the husband fidelity is the thing that's good; in the wife obedience is the thing that's proper.

夫以義爲良。婦以順爲正

Fu^1 i^3 i^4 wei^2 liang^2; fu^4 i^1 shun^4 wei^2 chêng.^{4}

2205

Husband and wife are indeed birds of one grove, but at the bourn of death each takes his separate flight.

夫妻本是同林鳥

Fu^1 ch'i^1 pên^3 shih^4 t'ung^2 lin^2 niao,^{3}

大限到來各時飛

ta^4 hsien^4 tao^4 lai^2 ko^4 tzŭ^4 fei.^{1}

2206

Ugly men marry pretty wives. *Lit.:* Scabbed-heads get flowery boughs.

瘌痢討花枝

La^1 li^2 t'ao^3 'hua^1 chih.^{1}

2207

If they match by nature, marry them.

生成一對。紐成一雙

Shêng^1 ch'êng^2 yi^1 tui,^{4} niu^3 ch'êng^2 yi^1 shuang.^{1}

2208

Husband and wife in perfect concord, are like the music of the harp and lute.

夫妻相好合。琴瑟與笙簧

Fu^1 ch'i^1 hsiang^1 'hao^3 'ho,^{2} ch'in^2 sê^2 yü^2 shêng wang.

2209

Conjugal felicity. *Lit.:* The husband sings and the wife accompanies.

夫唱婦隨

Fu^1 ch'ang^4 fu^4 sui.^{2}

2210

Horses will not re-mate; but men and women will re-marry.

馬無再配。人有重婚

Ma^{3} wu^{2} tsai^{4} pʻei^{4}; jên^{2} yu^{3} chʻung^{2} ʻhun.^{1}

2211

When a man's vessel is upset and its masts broken, he is poor for a time; but when a man marries a bad wife he is poor for life.

翻船折桅一時窮；

Fan^{1} chʻuan^{2} chê^{2} wei^{2} yi^{1} shih^{2} chʻiung^{2};

討壞老婆一生窮

tʻao^{3} ʻhuai^{4} lao^{3} pʻo^{2} yi^{1} shêng^{1} chʻiung.^{2}

2212

The fool fears his old woman; but the virtuous wife reverences her husband.

癡漢怕老婆。賢女敬丈夫

Chʻih^{2} ʻhan^{4} pʻa^{4} lao^{3} pʻo^{2}; hsien^{2} nü^{2} ching^{4} chang^{4} fu.^{1}

2213

A talented bridegroom is sometimes matched with a worthless bride; and a clever woman is sometimes married to a dolt.

清秀才郎到配不良之婦；

Chʻing^{1} hsiu^{4} tsʻai^{2} lang^{2} tao^{4} pʻei^{4} pu^{4} liang^{2} chih^{1} fu^{4};

乖巧女子反招愚拙之夫

kuai^{1} chʻiao^{3} nü^{2} tzŭ^{3} fan^{3} chao^{1} yü^{2} chüeh^{2} chih^{1} fu.^{1}

2214

When the two have been united they may not be separated.

伴人合不可伴人開

Pan^{4} jên^{2} ʻho^{2} pu^{4} kʻo^{3} pan^{4} jên^{2} kʻai.^{1}

2215

Loving husbands and wives, enjoy the enduring affection of their sons and daughters.

夫妻恩厚。兒女情長

Fu^{1} chʻi^{1} ên^{1} ʻhou,^{4} érh^{2} nü^{2} chʻing^{2} chʻang.^{2}

2216

A man may be ten years older than his wife; she must not be one year older than he.

只許男大一層
Chih³ hsü³ nan² ta⁴ yi¹ ts'eng²
不可女長一歲
pu⁴ k'o³ nü² ch'ang⁴ yi¹ sui.⁴

2217

A man without a wife has a home without a mistress; a woman without a husband is an unprotected being.

男無妻家無主
Nan² wu² ch'i¹ chia¹ wu² chu³;
女無夫身無主
nü² wu² fu¹ shên¹ wu² chu.³

2218

When husband and wife disagree, they become the dupes of their own female slaves.

夫婦不和奴婢欺
Fu¹ fu⁴ pu⁴ 'ho² nu³ pi⁴ ch'i.¹

2219

In bed,—husband and wife; out of bed,—guests.

上牀夫婦下牀客
Shang⁴ ch'uang² fu¹ fu,⁴ hsia⁴ ch'uang² k'o.⁴

2220

Husbands are as Heaven to their wives; wives are the slaves of their husbands.

夫乃婦之天。妻乃夫之奴
Fu¹ nai³ fu⁴ chih¹ t'ien¹; ch'i¹ nai³ fu¹ chih¹ nu.³

2221

Husband and wife have no enmities which can survive a night.

夫妻無隔夜之仇
Fu¹ ch'i¹ wu² ko² yeh⁴ chih¹ ch'ou.²

2222

If I keep to my wife, others will keep to theirs.

我不淫人婦。人不淫我妻
Wo³ pu⁴ yin² jên² fu,⁴ jên² pu⁴ yin² wo³ ch'i.¹

2223

A good man will not beat his wife; a good dog will not worry a fowl.

好漢不打妻。好狗不咬雞

ʻHao³ ʻhan⁴ pu⁴ ta³ chʻi¹; ʻhao³ kou³ pu⁴ yao³ chi.¹

2224

Is he a superior man who listens to his wife, and turns against his brother?

聽婦言乖骨肉。豈是丈夫

Tʻing¹ fu⁴ yen² kuai¹ ku³ jou,⁴ chʻi³ shih⁴ chang⁴ fu¹?

2225

Do not curse your wife in the evening, or you will have to sleep alone.

莫罵酉時妻。一夜受孤悽

Mo⁴ ma⁴ yu³ shih² chʻi,¹ yi¹ yeh⁴ shou⁴ ku¹ chʻi.¹

2226

If your wife is against it, do not get a concubine.

吃醋不討小

Chʻih¹ tsʻu⁴ pu⁴ tʻao³ hsiao.³

2227

He detests his own wife, but loves other men's. *Lit.:* He lightly esteems the domestic fowl, but loves the wild pheasant.

輕家雞愛野雉

Chʻing¹ chia¹ chi¹ ai⁴ yeh³ chʻih.⁴

2228

Fine houses are man-measuring skeps; and fair wives are ferry boats.

華屋量人斗。嬌妻渡客船

ʻHua² wu¹ liang³ jên² tou³; chiao¹ chʻi¹ tu⁴ kʻo⁴ chʻuan.²

NOTE.—The moral of this proverb is—Neither covet fine houses nor pretty wives; for, out of the one you will be turned by death, and, after your death, the other will marry again.

2229

Take no notice of what you hear said on the pillow.

枕邊之言莫聽

Chên³ pien¹ chih¹ yen³ mo⁴ tʻing.¹

2230

A virtuous wife causes her husband to be honoured; a bad one brings him to shame.

賢婦令夫貴。惡婦令夫賤

Hsien^2 fu^4 ling^4 fu^1 kuei,^{4} o^4 fu^4 ling^4 fu^1 chien.^{4}

NOTE.—"A virtuous woman is a crown to her husband: but she that maketh ashamed is as rottenness in his bones." Prov. 12; 4.

2231

Ugly wives and stupid maids are priceless treasures.

醜婦拙奴無價之寶

Ch'ou^3 ch'i^1 chüeh^2 nu^3 wu^2 chia^4 chih^1 pao.^{3}

2232

Do not marry wives or concubines who are gorgeously fine.

妻妾切忌豔妝

Ch'i^1 ch'ieh^4 ch'ieh^4 chi^4 yen^4 chuang.^{1}

2233

A virtuous wife saves her husband from evil ways.

家有賢妻。男人不遭橫事

Chia^1 yu^3 hsien^2 ch'i,^{1} nan^2 jên^2 pu^4 tsao^1 hun^4 shih.^{4}

2234

Nothing will frighten a wilful wife but a beating.

強婆娘只怕打

Chiang^4 p'o^2 niang^2 chih^3 p'a^4 ta.^{3}

2235

She who is wife to one man cannot eat the rice of two.

一家女兒吃不得兩家飯

Yi^1 chia^1 nü^2 êrh^2 ch'ih^1 pu^4 tê^2 liang^3 chia^1 fan.^{4}

2236

Slanders cluster round a widow's door.

寡婦門前多是非

Kua^3 fu^4 mên^2 ch'ien^2 to^1 shih^4 fei.^{1}

2237

Dress to meet your parents, undress to meet your husband.

穿衣見父母。脫衣見丈夫

Ch'uan^1 i^1 chien^4 fu^4 mu,^{3} t'o^1 i^1 chien^4 chang^4 fu.^{1}

2238

If she rises early she offends her husband ; if late, his father and mother.

起早了得罪丈夫

Chʻi^3 tsao^3 liao^3 tê^2 tsui^4 chang^4 fu^1 ;

起晏了得罪公婆

chʻi^3 yen^4 liao^3 tê^2 tsui^4 kung^1 pʻo.^{2}

2239

Happy the wife who dies before her husband ; unhappy she who dies after him.

有福死夫前。無福死夫後

Yu^3 fu^2 ssŭ^3 fu^1 chʻien^2 ; wu^2 fu^2 szŭ^3 fu^1 ʻhou.^{4}

2240

Good tempered and careful—she's a good wife indeed.

下氣小心。纔是婦女

Hsia^4 chʻi^4 hsiao^3 hsin^1 tsʻai^2 shih^4 fu^4 nü.^{2}

2241

A good horse will not turn back to eat grass ; and a good wife will not marry a second husband.

好馬不吃回頭草

ʻHao^3 ma^3 pu^4 chʻih^1 ʻhui^2 tʻou^2 tsʻao^3 ;

好妻不嫁二丈夫

ʻhao^3 chʻi^1 pu^4 chia^4 êrh^4 chang^4 fu.^{1}

2242

A loyal minister will serve but one Prince ; a virtuous woman but one husband.

忠臣不事二君

Chung^1 chʻên^2 pu^4 shih^4 êrh^4 chün^1 ;

貞婦不事二夫

chên^1 fu^4 pu^4 shih^4 êrh^4 fu.^{1}

2243

A widow. *Lit.:* A rudderless boat.

無舵之舟

Wu^2 to^4 chih^1 chou.^{1}

CHAPTER IV.

ELDER AND YOUNGER BROTHERS.

2244

"In childhood who as brothers are,
When grown up oft are severed far."

小時是兄弟。長大各鄉里

Hsiao^3 shih^2 shih^4 hsiung^1 ti,^{4} chʻang^4 ta^4 ko^4 hsiang^1 li.^{3}

2245

Brothers resemble hands and feet.

兄弟如手足

Hsiung^1 ti^4 ju^2 shou^3 tsu.^{2}

NOTE.—This is the stereotyped illustration which meets one everywhere in Chinese books.

2246

Though the left hand conquer the right, no advantage is gained.

左拳打右手。雖勝不如無

Tso^3 chʻüan^2 ta^3 yu^4 shou,^{3} sui^1 shêng^4 pu^4 ju^2 wu.^{2}

2247

Torn clothes may be mended; but a hand or foot cannot be stuck on again.

衣裳破尙可補

I^1 shang^1 pʻo^4 shang^4 kʻo^3 pu^3;

手足斷難得連

shou^3 tsu^2 tuan^4 nan^2 tê^2 lien.^{2}

2248

When brothers disagree they are imposed on by others.

兄弟不和旁人欺

Hsiung^1 ti^4 pu^4 ʻho^2 pʻang^2 jên^2 chʻi.^{1}

2249

A brother is harder to get than lands.

難得者兄弟。易得者田地

Nan^2 tê^2 chê^2 hsiung^1 ti^4; i^4 tê^2 chê^2 tʻien^2 ti.^{4}

—— 2250 ——

A brother's injuries are soon healed.

兄 弟 殺 一 刀 貫 一 个 疤

Hsiung^{1} ti^{4} sha^{1} yi^{1} tao^{1} kuan^{4} yi^{1} ko^{4} pa.^{1}

—— 2251 ——

Though brothers are so closely akin, it is each for himself in money matters.

兄 弟 雖 親 財 利 各 別

Hsiung^{1} ti^{4} sui^{1} ch'in^{1} ts'ai^{2} li^{4} ko^{4} pieh.^{2}

—— 2252 ——

Though a brother commit murder, it does not involve his brethren.

弟 兄 殺 人 各 分 手 足

Ti^{4} hsiung^{1} sha^{1} jên^{2} ko^{4} fên^{1} shou^{3} tsu.^{2}

—— 2253 ——

Brothers sometimes disagree. *Lit.:* Top and bottom teeth sometimes come into awkward collision.

齒 牙 也 有 相 撞 日 子

Ch'ih^{3} ya^{2} yeh^{3} yu^{3} hsiang^{1} chuang^{4} jih^{4} tzŭ.^{3}

—— 2254 ——

The same. *Lit.:* Dishes and basins will sometimes get smashed together.

碟 碗 也 有 相 撞 的 日 子

Tieh^{2} wan^{3} yeh^{3} yu^{3} hsiang^{1} chuang^{4} ti^{1} jih^{4} tzŭ.^{3}

—— 2255 ——

The most difficult thing on earth to get is a brother.

天 下 最 難 得 者 兄 弟

T'ien^{1} hsia^{4} tsui^{4} nan^{2} tê^{2} chê^{2} hsiung^{1} ti.^{4}

—— 2256 ——

Kind friends are better than unkind brothers.

兄 弟 相 害 不 如 友 生

Hsiung^{1} ti^{4} hsiang^{1} 'hai^{4} pu^{4} ju^{2} yu^{3} shêng.^{1}

—— 2257 ——

Be he never so good he still is a stranger; be he never so bad he still is part of myself.

好 煞 了 是 他 人
'Hao^3 sha^1 liao^3 shih^4 t'a^1 jên^2;
壞 煞 了 是 自 己
'huai^4 sha^1 liao^3 shih^4 tzŭ^4 chi.^{3}

2258

Never allow the slightest consideration of profit, to injure the affection proper between those who are of the same bone and flesh.

勿 以 絲 毫 利。便 傷 骨 肉 情
Wu^4 i^3 ssŭ^1 'hao^2 li,^{4} pien^4 shang^1 ku^3 jou^4 ch'ing.^{2}

CHAPTER V.

FRIENDS.

2259

Unless you will give him some trifling sum,
You can't get rid of a destitute chum.

說得脫。得八合

Shuo^{1} tê^{2} tʻo,^{1} tê^{2} pa^{1} ʻho.^{2}

Note.—The above is the commonest application to which this proverb is put; it can also be applied to any importunate creditor.

2260

Friendship existence to attain,
Must rest on goodness not on gain.

交義不交財。交財兩不來

Chiao^{1} i^{4} pu^{4} chiao^{1} tsʻai^{2}; chiao^{1} tsʻai^{2} liang^{3} pu^{4} lai.^{2}

2261

Mix with mandarins and grow poor;
With merchants and increase your store;
With Bonzes and you soon will find,
Subscription lists not far behind.

交官窮。交客富

Chiao^{1} kuan^{1} chʻiung^{2}; chiao^{1} kʻo^{4} fu^{4};

交和尚。得緣簿

Chiao^{1} ʻho^{2} shang^{4} tê^{2} yüan^{2} pu.^{4}

2262

With every friend and fellow you meet,
You can do nothing but drink and eat:

三朋四友。碗酒筷肉

San^{1} pʻêng^{2} ssŭ^{4} yu,^{3} wan^{3} chiu^{3} kʻuai^{4} jou.^{4}

2263

Friends are at fault when a man is allowed to wear his dress awry.

衣冠不正朋友之過

I^{1} kuan^{1} pu^{4} chêng^{4} pʻêng^{2} yu^{3} chih^{1} kuo.^{4}

2264

Friends in the morning foes at night.

朝兄弟暮仇敵

Chao^{1} hsiung^{1} ti^{4} mu^{4} chʻou^{2} ti.^{2}

2265

Never make friends of ungenial men.

人到無情切莫相交

Jên^{2} tao^{4} wu^{2} chʻing^{2} chʻieh^{4} mu^{4} hsiang^{1} chiao.^{1}

2266

A well-known friend is a treasure.

人熟是寶

Jên^{2} shu^{2} shih^{4} pao.^{3}

2267

Men are friends the world over.

五湖四海都是朋友

Wu^{3} ʻhu^{2} ssŭ^{4} ʻhai^{3} tu^{1} shih^{4} pʻêng^{2} yu.^{3}

2268

Lingering friendship. *Lit.:* The lotus root may be broken and its silken fibres remain united.

藕斷絲不斷

Ou^{3} tuan^{4} ssŭ^{1} pu^{4} tuan.^{4}

2269

When friendship is real men can talk without reserve.

得意忘言無所不談

Tê^{2} i^{4} wang^{4} yen^{2} wu^{2} so^{3} pu^{4} tʻan.^{2}

2270

A miserable friendship. *Lit.:* An opium-smoker's probe scraped by a bit of pot.

鴉片烟籤子。遇着瓷瓦刮

Ya^{1} pʻien^{4} yen^{1} chʻien^{1} tzŭ,^{3} yü^{4} cho^{2} tzʻŭ^{2} wa^{1} kua.^{1}

2271

Impossible alliance. *Lit.:* Friendship between ice and coal.

冰炭之交 or 冰炭相投

Ping^{1} tʻan^{4} chih^{1} chiao.^{1} or, Ping^{1} tʻan^{4} hsiang^{1} tʻou.^{2}

2272

Who are firmly joined can be hardly severed.

固 結 不 可 解

Ku^4 chieh^2 pu^4 k'o^3 chieh.^{3}

2273

Drink only with familiar friends; and recite poetry only with a poet.

酒 逢 知 己 飲。詩 向 會 人 吟

Chiu^3 fêng^2 chih^1 chi^3 yin^3; shih^1 hsiang^4 'hui^4 jên^2 yin.^{2}

2274

One's acquaintances must fill the empire; but one'e familiar friends must be few.

相 識 滿 天 下。知 心 能 幾 人

Hsiang^1 shih^4 man^3 t'ien^1 hsia^4; chih^1 hsin^1 nêng^2 chi^3 jên.^{2}

2275

Let the politeness of first acquaintances characterize all after intercourse, and in the longest friendship nothing disagreeable will arise.

相 逢 好 似 初 相 識

Hsiang^1 fêng^2 'hao^3 ssŭ^4 ch'u^1 hsiang^1 shih,^{4}

到 老 終 無 怨 恨 心

tao^4 lao^3 chung^1 wu^2 yuan^1 'hên^3 hsin.^{1}

2276

If friends meet and part empty, the blooming peach blossom round the grotto will deride them.

相 逢 不 飲 空 歸 去

Hsiang^1 fêng^2 pu^4 yin^3 k'ung^2 kuei^1 ch'ü,^{4}

洞 口 桃 花 也 笑 人

tung^4 k'ou^3 t'ao^2 'hua^1 yeh^3 hsiao^4 jên.^{2}

2277

Having money and wine your friends will be many; but who will visit you when in distress?

有 錢 有 酒 多 兄 弟

Yu^3 ch'ien^2 yu^3 chiu^3 to^1 hsiung^1 ti^4;

急 難 何 曾 見 一 人

chi^2 nan^2 'ho^2 ts'êng^2 chien^4 yi^1 jên^2?

NOTE.—The poor is hated even of his own neighbour; but the rich hath many riends. Prov. 14; 20.

—— 2278 ——

Unless your friend be your superior, you had better have none; and for a few days observe whether his subsequent greetings equal his first.

結 交 須 勝 己。似 我 不 如 無；
Chieh^2 chiao^1 hsü^1 sheng^4 chi,^{3} ssŭ^4 wo^3 pu^4 ju^3 wu^2;
但 看 三 五 日。相 見 不 如 初.
tan^4 kʻan^4 san^1 wu^3 jih,^{4} hsiang^1 chien^4 pu^4 ju^2 chʻu.^{1}

—— 2279 ——

No joy equals that of making a new friend; no sorrow that of being separated from friends.

樂 莫 樂 兮 新 相 知
Lê^4 mo^4 lê^4 hsi^1 hsin^1 hsiang^1 chih^1;
悲 莫 悲 兮 生 別 離
pei^1 mo^4 pei^1 hsi^1 shêng^1 pieh^2 li.^{2}

—— 2280 ——

Tigers and deer do not stroll together.

虎 鹿 不 同 遊
ʻHu^3 lu^4 pu^4 tʻung^2 yu.^{2}

—— 2281 ——

The crow does not roost with the phœnix.

烏 鴉 不 與 鳳 凰 棲
Wu^1 ya^1 pu^4 yü^3 fêng^4 ʻhuang^2 chʻi.^{1}

—— 2282 ——

Though conversing face to face, their hearts have a thousand hills between them.

對 面 與 語。心 隔 千 山
Tui^4 mien^4 yü^3 yü,^{3} hsin^1 ko^2 chʻien^1 shan.^{1}

—— 2283 ——

He who has friends in every place finds every place delicious.

四 海 交 遊。都 成 蘭 味
Ssŭ^4 ʻhai^3 chiao^1 yu,^{2} tu^1 chʻêng^2 lan^2 wei.^{4}

—— 2284 ——

Of all acquaintanceship, that in which each knows the other's heart, is best.

人之相知。貴相知心

Jên^{2} chih^{1} hsiang^{1} chih,^{1} kuei^{4} hsiang^{1} chih^{1} hsin.^{1}

— 2285 —

When men are friendly even water is sweet.

人要好水也甜

Jên^{2} yao^{4} ʻhao^{3} shui^{3} yeh^{4} tien.^{2}

— 2286 —

You can hardly make a friend in a year; but you can easily offend one in an hour.

一年難相與一個人

Yi^{1} nien^{2} nan^{2} hsiang^{1} yü^{3} yi^{1} ko^{4} jên^{2};

一時便得罪一個人

Yi^{1} shih^{2} pien^{4} tê^{2} tsui^{4} yi^{1} ko^{4} jên.^{2}

— 2287 —

Better associate with one well known than with a stranger.

伴生不如伴熟

Pan^{4} shêng^{1} pu^{4} ju^{2} pan^{4} shu.^{2}

— 2288 —

Having wine and good feeding you'll have plenty of friends; but in the day of adversity—none.

有酒有肉多朋友

Yu^{3} chiu^{3} yu^{3} jou^{4} to^{1} pʻêng^{2} yu^{3};

患難之時一個無

ʻhuan^{4} nan^{2} chih^{1} shih^{2} yi^{1} ko^{4} wu.^{2}

— 2289 —

When purposes agree the most hostile grow friendly; when they disagree near relatives become enemies.

意合則吳越相親

I^{4} ʻho^{2} tsê^{2} Wu^{2} Yüeh^{4} hsiang^{1} chʻin^{1};

意不合則骨肉爲仇敵

i^{4} pu^{4} ʻho^{2} tsê^{2} ku^{3} jou^{4} wei^{2} chʻou^{2} ti.^{2}

Note.—"The most hostile," *lit:* "*Wu* and *Yüeh*"; two ancient States that were often at enmity with each other. The *Yüeh* was finally destroyed by the *Wu*. See Dr. Legge's *Chʻun chʻiu*, pages 759, 831.

2290

Without a good mirror no lady can know her true appearance;
Without a true friend no scholar can know his own errors of conduct.

女無明鏡不知面上精粗
Nü² wu² ming² ching⁴ pu⁴ chih¹ mien⁴ shang⁴ ching¹ tsʻu¹;
士無良友不知行步虧踰
shih⁴ wu² liang² yu³ pu⁴ chih¹ hsing² pu⁴ kʻuei¹ yü.⁴

2291

Two are better than one. *Lit.:* One man's plan is short; the plan of two is long.

一人計短。二人計長
Yi¹ jên² chi⁴ tuan³; êrh⁴ jên² chi⁴ chʻang.²

2292

When the world's affairs are calm we can judge of them; when affection is moderate it will endure.

世事靜方見。人情淡始長
Shih⁴ shih⁴ ching⁴ fang⁴ chien⁴; jên⁴ chʻing² tan⁴ shih³ chʻang.²

CHAPTER VI.

VARIOUS.

— 2293 —

Those who violate the Five Relations and the Five Constant Virtues will quickly perish.

倫 常 乖 舛。立 見 消 亡

Lün^2 ch'ang^2 kuai^1 ch'uan,^{3} li^4 chien^4 hsiao^1 wang.^{2}

— 2294 —

Relatives are bound to stand by one another.

兄 弟 叔 姪。須 分 多 潤 寡

Hsiung^1 ti^4 shu^2 chih^2 hsü^1 fên^1 to^1 jun^4 kua.^{3}

— 2295 —

Friends while good dinners last; husband and wife while fuel and food remain.

酒 肉 朋 友。柴 米 夫 妻

Chiu^3 jou^4 p'êng^2 yu^3; ch'ai^2 mi^3 fu^1 ch'i.^{1}

— 2296 —

Go into partnership with a brother; and into battle with father and son.

打 夥 還 是 親 兄 弟

Ta^3 'huo^3 'huan^2 shih^4 ch'in^1 hsiung^1 ti^4;

上 陣 定 要 父 子 兵

shang^4 chên^4 ting^4 yao^4 fu^4 tzŭ^3 ping.^{1}

— 2297 —

Sons receive their fathers' fortune; and wives share their husbands' lot.

子 登 父 業。妻 受 夫 分

Tzŭ^3 têng^1 fu^4 yeh^4; ch'i^1 shou^4 fu^1 fên.^{1}

— 2298 —

Parents notwithstanding their deep love must be parted from their children; husband and wife though most faithful, must also separate.

父 母 恩 深 終 有 別

Fu^4 mu^3 ên^1 shên^1 chung^1 yu^3 pieh^2;

夫 妻 義 重 也 分 離

fu^1 ch'i^1 i^4 chung^4 yeh^4 fên^1 li.^{2}

2299

One, though related, is no relation; another, though not related, is a relation.

是親不是親。非親却是親

Shih⁴ chʻin¹ pu⁴ shih⁴ chʻin¹; fei¹ chʻin¹ chʻüeh⁴ shih⁴ chʻin.¹

2300

His griefs are few whose wife is virtuous; his heart is enlarged whose sons are dutiful.

妻賢夫禍少。子孝父心寬

Chʻi¹ hsien² fu⁴ ʻhuo⁴ shao³; tzŭ³ hsiao⁴ fu⁴ hsien¹ kʻuan.¹

2301

Princes know their Ministers, Fathers their Children, Elder Brothers their Younger Brothers, and Teachers their Scholars, better than any one else.

知臣莫如君。知子莫如父

Chih¹ chʻên² mo⁴ ju² chün,¹ chih¹ tzŭ³ mo⁴ ju² fu,⁴

知弟莫如兄。知弟莫如師

Chih¹ ti⁴ mo⁴ ju² hsiung,¹ chih¹ ti⁴ mo⁴ ju² shih.¹

2302

Would you know the character of a Prince, then first observe his Ministers; would you become acquainted with a man, first look at his Friends; would you know a Father, first consider his Son.

欲知其君。先視其臣

Yü⁴ chih¹ chʻi² chün,¹ hsien¹ shih⁴ chʻi² chʻên²;

欲識其人。先視其友

Yü⁴ shih⁴ chʻi² jên,² hsien¹ shih⁴ chʻi² yu³;

欲知其父。先視其子

Yü⁴ chih¹ chʻi² fu,⁴ hsien¹ shih⁴ chʻi² tzŭ.³

2303

If we were not an injured family, we should have neither sons nor daughters; if we were not at enmity we should never have been husband and wife.

不是寃家不成兒女
Pu⁴ shih⁴ yüan¹ chia¹ pu⁴ chʻêng² êrh² nü ²;
不是對頭不成夫婦
Pu⁴ shih⁴ tui⁴ tʻou² pu⁴ chʻêng² fu¹ fu.⁴

NOTE.—This is used in reply to congratulation, in a jocular and self-depreciatory sense.

2304

Poverty in a family brings out the dutiful Son; and confusion in the state reveals the loyal Minister.
家貧見孝子。國亂顯忠臣
Chia¹ pʻin³ chien⁴ hsiao⁴ tzŭ³; kuo² lan⁴ hsien³ chung¹ chʻên.²

2305

Who honours his Prince, will think lightly of rank and emolument; who honours his Parents, will honour his wife and child less; who honours his Brothers, will think lightly of money and heritage.
視朝廷重則爵祿輕
Shih⁴ chʻao² tʻing² chung⁴ tzê² chüeh² lu⁴ chʻing¹;
視父母重則妻子輕
Shih⁴ fu⁴ mu³ chung⁴ tsê² chʻi¹ tzŭ³ chʻing¹;
視兄弟重則財產輕
Shih⁴ hsiung¹ ti⁴ chung⁴ tsê² tsʻai² chʻan⁴ chʻing.¹

2306

Those who at home are not given up to their wives and children, will serve their Parents filially; those who abroad do not deceive their Friends, will serve their Prince with loyalty.
內不溺於妻子者。事親必孝
Nei⁴ pu⁴ ni⁴ yü² chʻi¹ tzŭ³ chê,² shih⁴ chʻin¹ pi⁴ hsiao⁴;
外不欺於朋友者。事君必忠
Wai⁴ pu⁴ chʻi¹ yu² pʻêng² yu³ chê,² shih⁴ chün¹ pi⁴ chung.¹

2307

The thing important to the Five Relations is Respectfulness; the perfect embodiment of the Ten Virtues is Sincerity.

諺語叢話

五倫之要在敬

Wu^{3} lun^{2} chih^{1} yao^{4} tsai^{4} ching^{4};

十義之全惟誠

Shih^{2} i^{4} chih^{1} chʿien^{2} wei^{2} chʿêng.^{2}

Note.—The Ten Virtues are those which belong to the Ten members of the Five relations.

2308

He has perfect tranquility whose wife is virtuous and sons obedient; and all things are satisfactory when rains are seasonable and winds moderate.

妻賢子孝一身閒

Chʿi^{1} hsien^{2} tzŭ^{3} hsiao^{4} yi^{1} shên^{1} hsien^{2};

雨順風調萬事足

Yü^{3} shun^{4} fêng^{1} tiao^{4} wan^{4} shih^{4} tsu^{2};

2309

If sincerity be wanting between Prince and Minister the nation will have no peace; if between Parents and Children, the family will have no concord; if between Brothers, their affections will be loosened; if between Friends, their intercourse will be distant.

君臣不信國不安

Chün^{1} chʿên^{2} pu^{4} hsin^{4} kuo^{2} pu^{4} an^{1};

父子不信家不睦

fu^{4} tzŭ^{3} pu^{4} hsin^{4} chia^{1} pu^{4} mu^{4};

兄弟不信情不親

hsiung^{1} ti^{4} pu^{4} hsin^{4} chʿing^{2} pu^{4} chʿin^{1};

朋友不信交易疏

pʿêng^{2} yu^{3} pu^{4} hsin^{4} chiao^{1} i^{1} su.^{2}

2310

The honest truth must not be told between Husband and Wife; and lies must not be told between Friend and Friend.

夫妻面前莫說眞

Fu^{1} chʿi^{1} mien^{4} chʿien^{2} mo^{4} shuo^{1} chên^{1};

朋友面前莫說假

pʿêng^{2} yu^{3} mien^{4} chʿien^{2} mo^{4} shuo^{1} chia.^{3}

Note.—This proverb supposes that the truth between husband and wife could not bear to be told, both being immoral.

SECTION XVII.—ON RELIGION.

CHAPTER I.

HEAVEN OR GOD.

2311

Heaven rules o'er all things, don't fret yourself to pray;
Trouble spent in making plans, is but thrown away.

萬事由天莫强求
Wan4 shih4 yu2 tʻien1 mo4 chʻiang2 chʻiu2:
何須苦苦用機謀
ʻHo2 hsü1 kʻu3 kʻu3 yung4 chi1 mou.2

2312

Imperial Heaven will never slight men of sorrow.

皇天不負苦心人
ʻHuang2 tʻien1 pu4 fu4 kʻu3 hsin1 jên.2

2313

Man would have things so and so, but Heaven negatives his plans.

人便如此如此
Jên2 pien4 ju2 tzʻŭ3 ju2 tzʻŭ,3
天理未然未然
tʻien1 li3 wei4 jan2 wei4 jan.2

2314

It is man's to scheme; it is Heaven's to accomplish.

謀事在人。成事在天
Mou2 shih4 tsai4 jên2; chʻêng2 shih4 tsai4 tʻien.1

2315

Heaven responds to man as quickly as shadow to form or echo to voice.

天之應人敏如影響
Tʻien1 chih1 ying4 jên2 min3 ju2 ying3 hsiang.3

2316

Heaven never sends a man without providing for him clothes and income.

天生一人。必有衣祿

T'ien^{1} shêng^{1} yi^{1} jên,^{2} pi^{4} yu^{3} i^{1} lu.^{4}

2317

What man sees not and knows not, Heaven sees and knows.

人眼不見天眼見

Jên^{2} yen^{3} pu^{4} chien^{4} t'ien^{1} yen^{3} chien^{4};

人不知道天知道

jên^{2} pu^{4} chih^{1} tao^{4} t'ien^{1} chih^{1} tao.^{4}

2318

Man can be bound, but Heaven cannot.

扭得過人來。扭不過天

Niu^{3} tê^{2} kuo^{4} jên^{2} lai,^{2} niu^{3} pu^{4} kuo^{4} t'ien.^{1}

2319

Heaven sent never the man but Earth provided a grave for him.

天生一人。地生一穴

T'ien^{1} shêng^{1} yi^{1} jên,^{2} ti^{4} shêng^{4} yi^{1} hsüeh.^{4}

2320

Our daily bread depends on Heaven.

吃飯靠天

Ch'ih^{1} fan^{4} k'ao^{4} t'ien.^{1}

2321

Heaven knows how each man gets his living.

吃飯不瞞天

Ch'ih^{1} fan^{4} pu^{4} man^{2} t'ien.^{1}

2322

Men deceive good men, Heaven does not; men fear bad men, Heaven does not.

人善人欺天不欺

Jên^{2} shan^{4} jên^{2} ch'i^{1} t'ien^{1} pu^{4} ch'i^{1};

人惡人怕天不怕

jên^{2} o^{4} jên^{2} p'a^{4} t'ien^{1} pu^{4} p'a.^{4}

2323

When men have good desires Heaven must further them.

人有善願天必從之

Jên[2] yu[3] shan[4] yüan[4] tʻien[1] pi[4] tsʻung[2] chih.[1]

2324

Nothing can escape the eye of Heaven.

天眼恢恢。疎而不漏

Tʻien[1] yen[3] ʻhui[1] ʻhui,[1] su[2] êrh[2] pu[4] lou.[4]

2325

Heaven sees clearly, and rewards quickly.

天眼昭昭。報應甚速

Tʻien[1] yen[3] chao[1] chao,[1] pao[4] ying[4] shêng[4] su.[2]

2326

Our whispers thunder in the ear of Heaven; our secret evil deeds flash into the eyes of the gods.

人間私語。天聞若雷

Jên[2] hsien[2] ssŭ[1] yü[3] tʻien[1] wên[2] jo[4] lei[2];

暗室虧心。神目如電

an[4] wu[1] kʻuei[1] hsin[1] shên[2] mu[4] ju[2] tien.[4]

2327

Heaven stands by the good man.

吉人天相

Chʻi[3] jên[2] tʻien[1] hsiang.[1]

2328

A thousand human schemes may be thwarted by one scheme of Heaven.

人有千算不如天一算

Jên[2] yu[3] chʻien[1] suan[4] pu[4] ju[2] tʻien[1] yi[1] suan.[4]

2329

Thunder strikes and Heaven repairs.

雷打天補

Lei[2] ta[3] tʻien[1] pu.[3]

2330

Man only sees the present, Heaven sees into the future.

人見目前。天見久遠

Jên[2] chien[4] mu[4] chʻien,[2] tʻien[1] chien[4] chiu[3] yüan.[3]

2331

Man depends on Heaven, as a ship on her pilot.

人 靠 天 工。船 靠 舵 公

Jên^2 kʻao^4 tʻien^1 kung,^{1} chʻuan^2 kʻao^4 to^4 kung.^{1}

2332

Neither repine against Heaven, nor blame men.

不 怨 天。不 尤 人

Pu^4 yüan^4 tʻien,^{1} pu^4 yu^2 jên.^{2}

2333

To enjoy the favour of Heaven.

托 天 之 福

Tʻo^1 tʻien^1 chih^1 fu.^{2}

2334

It is Heaven's to destine, but it is man's to shorten or prolong his days.

命 在 於 天。數 在 於 人

Ming^4 tsai^4 yü^2 tʻien,^{1} shu^4 tsai^4 yü^2 jên.^{2}

2335

The heart of the people is the heart of Heaven.

民 心 卽 天 心

Min^2 hsin^1 chi^2 tʻien^1 hsin.^{1}

2336

It is for me to put forth the utmost effort, it rests with Heaven to succeed my plan.

盡 其 在 我。聽 其 在 天

Chin^4 chʻi^2 tsai^4 wo^3; tʻing^1 chʻi^2 tsai^4 tʻien.^{1}

2337

When you have fully done your duty, abide the will of Heaven.

盡 人 事 而 聽 天 命

Chin^4 jên^2 shih^4 êrh^2 tʻing^1 tʻien^1 ming.^{4}

2338

Would that Heaven would always produce good men; and that men would always do good!

愿 天 常 生 好 人

Yüan^{4} tʻien^{1} chʻang^{2} shêng^{1} ʻhao^{3} jên^{2};

愿 人 常 行 好 事

yüan^{4} jên^{2} chʻang^{2} hsing^{2} ʻhao^{3} shih.^{4}

——— 2339 ———

There is nothing partial in the ways of Heaven.

天 道 無 私

Tʻien^{1} tao^{4} wu^{2} ssŭ.^{1}

——— 2340 ———

Man may not, but Heaven knows.

人 不 知 天 知

Jen^{2} pu^{4} chih^{1} tʻien^{1} chih.^{1}

——— 2341 ———

When Heaven rears a man he grows very fat; when men rear one he is nought but skin and bone.

天 養 人 胖 腯 腯

Tʻien^{1} yang^{3} jên^{2} pʻang^{4} su^{4} su,^{4}

人 養 人 皮 包 骨

jên^{2} yang^{3} jên^{2} pʻi^{2} pao^{1} ku.^{3}

——— 2342 ———

You may deceive men; you can't deceive Heaven.

瞞 得 過 人 來。瞞 不 過 天

Man^{2} tê^{2} kuo^{4} jên^{2} lai^{2}; man^{2} pu^{4} kuo^{4} tʻien.^{1}

——— 2343 ———

Heaven and Earth are great; father and mother are honourable.

天 地 爲 大。父 母 爲 尊

Tʻien^{1} ti^{4} wei^{2} ta^{4}; fu^{4} mu^{3} wei^{2} tsun.^{1}

——— 2344 ———

Heaven knows, Earth knows, you know, and I know.

天 知 地 知 你 知 我 知

Tʻien^{1} chih,^{1} ti^{4} chih,^{1} ni^{3} chih,^{1} wo^{3} chih.^{1}

NOTE.—This was the noble saying of a virtuous mandarin of the ʻ*Han* dynasty, whose name was *Yang Tsen* (楊 震,) when some one brought him a bribe in the night.

海上絲綢之路文獻集成 科技與文化編

2345

Death and life have their determined appointment; riches and honours depend upon Heaven.

死生有命。富貴在天

Ssŭ[3] shêng[1] yu[3] ming[4]; fu[4] kuei[4] tsai[4] t'ien.[1]

2346

Heaven complies with the wishes of good men; joy springs spontaneous in harmonious homes.

人善天從願 家和福自生

Jên[2] shan[4] t'ien[1] ts'ung[2] yüan[4]; chia[1] 'ho[2] fu[2] tzŭ[4] shêng.[1]

CHAPTER II.

IDOLS AND IDOLATRY.

2347

When troubled with sickness, and very bad,
Petition the gods that health may be had.
患 病 不 好。求 神 上 表
ʿHuan^4 ping^4 pu^4 ʿhao,^{3} chʿiu^2 shên^2 shang^4 piao.^{3}

NOTE.—"Is any among you afflicted? let him pray." James 5: 13.

2348

You may deceive a man;
Deceive a God, who can?
瞞 得 過 人。瞞 不 過 神
Man^2 tê^3 kuo^4 jên,^{2} man^3 pu^4 kuo^4 shên.^{2}

2349

Soon as the cymbals clang,
Three taels go with a bang.
鐃 鈸 一 響。紋 銀 三 兩
Nao^2 po^2 yi^1 hsiang,^{3} wên^2 yin^2 san^1 liang.^{3}

NOTE.—This proverb illustrates the expensiveness of idol worship. One tael is worth about six shillings.

2350

Men without gods can never proceed;
Gods without men are useless indeed.
人 無 神 不 行。神 無 人 不 靈
Jên^2 wu^2 shên^2 pu^4 hsing^2; shên^2 wu^2 jên^2 pu^4 ling.^{2}

2351

Light your stick of incense at the break of every day;
To Heaven, Earth, Sun, Moon, and Stars, devout thanksgiving pay.
Pray that in every place crops may ripen in the Sun;
Wish for every man a long career of life to run.

每日清晨一炷香

Mei^3 jih^4 chʻing^1 chʻên^2 yi^1 chu^4 hsiang^1;

謝天謝地謝三光

Hsieh^4 tʻien^1 hsieh^4 ti^4 hsieh^4 san^1 kuang^1;

所求處處田禾熟

So^1 chʻiu^2 chʻu^4 chʻu^4 tʻien^2 ʻho^2 shu^2;

惟願人人壽命長

Wei^2 yüan^4 jên^2 jên^2 shou^4 ming^4 chʻang.^{2}

2352

To cheat their ancestors men constantly pay,
For sham silver nuggets, good money away.

假銀子肚裡空

Chia^3 ying^2 tzŭ^3 tu^3 li^3 kʻung,^{1}

銅錢買哄祖宗

Tʻung^2 chʻien^2 mai^3 ʻhung^4 tsu^3 tsung.^{1}

2353

Man without divine assistance,
Cannot move an inch of distance.

人無神靈。寸步難行

Jên^2 wu^2 shên^2 ling,^{2} tsʻun^4 pu^4 nan^4 hsing.^{2}

2354

Whatever be the affair, exhort men to avoid deceit; for only three feet above our heads the gods are watching.

萬事勸人休瞞昧

Wan^4 shih^4 chʻüan^4 jên^2 hsiu^1 man^2 mei^4;

舉頭三尺有神明

chü^3 tʻou^2 san^1 chʻih^3 yu^3 shên^2 ming.^{2}

2355

You may carry deception into the *yamên*, you cannot carry it into the temple.

橫心進得衙門

ʻHêng^4 hsin^1 chin^4 tê^2 ya^3 mên,^{2}

橫心進不得廟門

ʻhêng^4 hsin^1 chin^4 pu^4 tê^2 miao^4 mên.^{2}

2356

Kneel once, bow your head thrice, and offer incense morning and evening.

一跪三叩首。早晚一爐香
Yi[1] kuei[4] san[1] k'ou[4] shou,[3] tsao[3] wan[3] yi[1] lu[2] hsiang.[1]

2357

Praying for blessings to reward one's parents, we go up the hill to burn incense.

祈恩報本。朝山進香
Ch'i[2] ên[1] pao[4] pên,[3] ch'ao[2] shan[1] chin[4] hsiang.[1]

2358

He who removes an idol to bathe it, puts the god to needless inconvenience.

搬菩薩洗澡枉勞神
Pan[1] p'u[2] sa[1] hsi[3] tsao[3] wang[3] lao[2] shên.[1]

2359

Three strokes of the axe are enough to complete an image of the idol *Yang-ssŭ.*

三斧頭砍定楊泗菩薩的像
San[1] fu[3] t'ou[2] k'an[3] ting[4] Yang[2] ssŭ[4] p'u[2] sa[1] ti[2] hsiang.[4]

NOTE.—*Yang-ssŭ:* the god of sailors, a beardless divinity, with a somewhat rudely carved triangular head.

2360

A beard should not be put on his Worship the God of sailors.

楊泗老爺鬍子。安不上
Yang[2] ssŭ[4] lao[3] yeh[2] 'hu[2] tzŭ,[3] an[1] pu[4] shang.[4]

NOTE.—The meaning of this proverb lies in the last three words, and it is used to condemn any impropriety.

2361

If you pray to a Buddha, pray to one only.

求佛求一尊
Ch'iu[2] fu[2] ch'iu[2] yi[1] tsun.[1]

2362

When the poor are sick they use charms and invoke idols.

窮人害病。求符扛神
Ch'iung[2] jên[2] 'hai[4] ping[4] ch'iu[2] fu[2] kang[1] shên.[2]

NOTE.—This invocation is through a medium: and it cannot be said that the practice referred to is confined to the poor.

2363

Though you neglect to offer incense when all is well, you will have to fall at Buddha's feet in time of sorrow.

閒時不燒香。急時抱佛脚

Hsien[2] shih[2] pu[4] shao[1] hsiang,[1] chi[3] shih[4] pao[4] fu[2] chiao.[3]

2364

Ancestors however remote must be sincerely sacrificed to.

祖宗雖遠。祭祀不可不誠

Tsu[3] tsung[1] sui[1] yüan,[3] chi[4] ssŭ[4] pu[4] k'o[3] pu[4] ch'êng.[2]

2365

You honour idols but not your parents. *Lit.:* The living Buddhas you do not honour; but you honour dead Buddhas.

活佛不敬。敬死佛

'Huo[2] fu[2] pu[4] ching[4]; ching[4] ssŭ[3] fu.[2]

2366

All idolatrous superstitions are man's invention.

世上無神鬼。百般人做起

Shih[4] shang[4] wu[2] shên[2] kuei,[3] pai[3] pan[1] jên[2] tso[4] ch'i.[3]

2367

All the thousands and myriads of gods are but one God.

千神萬神都是一神

Ch'ien[1] shên[2] wan[4] shên[2] tu[1] shih[1] yi[1] shên.[2]

2368

The god on *Wu-tang-shan* hears the prayers of men from a distance, not of men who live near.

武當山菩薩應遠不應近

Wu[3] tang[4] shan[1] p'u[2] sa[1] ying[4] yüan[3] pu[4] ying[4] chin.[4]

NOTE.—The *Wu-tang-shan* is a very famous mountain situated in the north-west of *Hupeh*, a day's journey from the city of *Chün-chou* (均州). It is a noted retreat of Taoists, and is full of their temples and monasteries. The mountain, with its surrounding scenery, is exceedingly beautiful; and it is the favourite resort of pilgrims from far and near. Their ascent is greatly facilitated by means of a fine stone staircase, with heavy ornamented balustrades on each side; and also, in the steepest parts, by massive iron chains suspended from the balustrades.

There are temples and refreshment rooms at various stages of the ascent, and quite a village near the summit of the peak. The very highest point of what is called, "The peak of the heavenly pillar," is crowned by what is generally believed to be a Golden Temple. This is a very small but unique structure built throughout of brass, and floored with marble. It contains one principal idol called *Tsu shih* (祖師), and this is the gentleman referred to in this proverb. He is said to have been a prince, the son of *Fan Wang* (梵王) a king of some western state tributary to China in the days of the *T'ang* dynasty.

2369

Unless you have business never go up to the temple of the Three Precious Ones.

無事不登三寶殿

Wu² shih⁴ pu⁴ têng¹ san¹ pao³ tien.⁴

2370

The gods of the door are one good and one bad.

門神菩薩一善一惡

Mên² shên² p'u² sa¹ yi¹ shan⁴ yi¹ o.⁴

2371

Though you don't believe in other gods, you'll believe in the God of Thunder; though you don't believe in medicine generally, you'll believe in purgatives.

不信神信雷神

Pu⁴ hsin⁴ shên² hsin⁴ lei² shên²;

不信藥信下藥

pu⁴ hsin⁴ yao⁴ hsin⁴ hsia⁴ yao.⁴

2372

Better do a kindness near home, than go far away to burn incense.

遠處燒香不如近地作福

Yüan³ ch'u⁴ shao¹ hsiang¹ pu⁴ ju² chin⁴ ti⁴ tso⁴ fu.²

2373

You have exposed yourself. *Lit.:* You have burst open the temple door and let the idols see your deed.

推開廟門把菩薩看一看

T'ui¹ k'ai¹ miao⁴ mên² pa³ p'u² sa¹ k'an⁴ yi¹ k'an,⁴

2374

An honest magistrate has lean clerks; a powerful god has fat priests.

官清司吏瘦。神靈廟祝肥

Kuan^1 ch'ing^1 ssŭ^1 li^4 shou^4; shên^2 ling^2 miao^4 chu^4 fei.^{2}

2375

Age robs men of strength, and gods of virtue.

人老無能。神老無靈

Jên^2 lao^3 wu^2 nêng,^{2} shên^2 lao^3 wu^2 ling.^{2}

2376

The stinking pig's-head meets the smell-less idol.

臭猪頭撞倒齈鼻子菩薩

Ch'ou^4 chu^1 t'ou^2 chuang^4 tao^3 nung^4 pi^2 tzŭ^3 p'u^2 sa.^{1}

2377

He knows a fierce-eyed *Lohan*, but not the kind-eyed *Kuan-yin.*

只認得怒眼羅漢

Chih^3 jên^4 tê^2 nu^4 yen^3 lo^2 'han,^{4}

不認得低眉觀音

pu^4 jên^4 tê^2 ti^1 mei^2 kuan^1 ying.^{1}

NOTE.—"Kind-eyed:" *lit:* '*Kuan-yin* of the bending eyebrows.'

CHAPTER III.

PRIESTS AND NUNS.

2378

As a Bonze about to marry,
So your promises miscarry.

和 尙·娶 親 說 過 光 陰

'Ho² shang⁴ ch'ü³ ch'in,¹ shuo¹ kuo⁴ kuang¹ yin.¹

2379

He takes the prayer-book in his hands,
And reads, but no one understands.

撿 倒 一 本 經。念 也 念 不 淸

Chien³ tao³ yi¹ pên³ ching,¹ nien⁴ yeh³ nien⁴ pu⁴ ch'ing.¹

2380

When the drum sounds before the dead man's shrine,
Each day you have to pay a three-tael fine.

靈 前 鼓 响。一 日 三 両

Ling² chien² ku³ hsiang,³ yi¹ jih⁴ san¹ liang.³

2381

If you entrust a great recitation to a wry-mouthed priest, he will spoil it.

一 藏 好 經

Yi¹ ts'ang² 'hao³ ching.¹

把 得 歪 嘴 和 尙 念 壞 了

pa³ tê² wai¹ tsui³ 'ho² shang⁴ nien⁴ 'huai² liao.³

2382

A magistrate is never at leisure; a Bonze always is.

居 官 不 自 在。爲 僧 多 淸 閑

Chụü¹ kuan¹ pu⁴ tzŭ⁴ tsai⁴; wei² sêng¹ to¹ ch'ing¹ hsien.²

2383

The monastery faces the nunnery; there's nothing in that—yet there may be.

男 僧 寺 對 着 女 僧 寺

Nan² sêng¹ ssú⁴ tui⁴ cho² nü² sêng¹ ssŭ⁴;

沒 事 也 有 事

mu² shih⁴ yeh³ yu³ shih.⁴

2384

The priest's door faces the nun's: nothing wrong? there is!

僧門對尼門。無情却有獘

Sêng^{1} mêng^{2} tui^{4} ni^{2} mên:^{2} wu^{2} chʻing^{2}? chʻüeh^{4} yu^{3} pi.^{4}

2385

He has not yet cast off the world.

未脫紅塵

Wei^{4} tʻo^{4} ʻhung^{2} ching.^{1}

2386

To recite the breviary carelessly.

念混搪經

Nien^{4} ʻhun^{4} tʻang^{2} ching.^{1}

2387

One poor Bonze is known to a thousand donors.

一千個施主

Yi^{1} chʻien^{1} ko^{4} shih^{1} chu^{3}

認得我一个小和尙

jên^{4} tê^{2} wo^{3} yi^{1} ko^{4} hsiao^{3} ʻho^{2} shang.^{4}

2388

Keep up to the end your first priestly ardour, and it will be more than enough to make you a Buddha.

出家如初。成佛有餘

Chʻu^{1} chia^{1} ju^{2} chʻu,^{1} chʻêng^{2} fu^{2} yu^{3} yü.^{2}

2389

Pleasanter the cottage with its bamboo hedge, than the monasteries of Taoist or Bonze.

竹籬茅舍風光好

Chu^{2} li^{4} mao^{2} shê^{4} fêng^{1} kuang^{1} ʻhao,^{3}

道院僧房總不如

tao^{4} yüan^{4} sêng^{1} fang^{2} tsung^{3} pu^{4} ju.^{2}

2390

Books exhaustively contain the world's good words; and Bonzes have invaded every noted mountain.

世間好語書說盡

Shih^{4} chien^{1} ʻhao^{3} yü^{3} shu^{1} shuo^{1} chin^{4};

天下名山僧占多

tʻien^{1} hsia^{4} ming^{2} shan^{1} sêng^{1} chan^{4} to.^{1}

2391

Destroy all passion while you light Buddha's lamp.

滅却心頭火。剔起佛前燈

Mieh^4 chʻüeh^4 hsin^1 tʻou^2 ʻhuo,^{3} tʻi^1 chʻi^3 fu^2 chʻien^2 têng.^{1}

2392

If you are a Bonze for a day, ring his bell for a day.

做一日和尙。撞一日鐘

Tsou^4 yi^1 jih^4 ʻho^2 shang,^{4} chuang^4 yi^1 jih^4 chung.^{1}

2393

The sun is high in the sky, but the Bonze has not risen; mark how fame and profit are not equal to leisure.

日高三丈僧未醒

Jih^4 kao^4 san^1 chang^4 sêng^1 wei^4 hsing^3;

看來名利不如閑

Kʻan^4 lai^2 ming^2 li^4 pu^4 ju^2 hsien.^{2}

2394

For one son who becomes a priest, nine generations get to heaven.

一子出家。九族昇天

Yi^1 tzŭ^3 chʻu^1 chia,^{1} chiu^3 tsu^2 shêng^1 tʻien.^{1}

2395

A virtuous woman may meet a Bonze without fear.

裙帶緊褲帶緊

Chʻün^2 tai^4 chin^3 kʻu^4 tai^4 chin,^{3}

和尙身上打得滾

ʻho^2 shang^4 shên^1 shang^4 ta^3 tê^2 kun.^{3}

2396

Buddha's precepts are unbounded, open wide his church's door.

佛法無邊。大開法門

Fu^2 fa^3 wu^2 pien,^{1} ta^4 kʻai^1 fa^3 mên.^{2}

2397

The Bonze is queue-less all his life.

和尙一生無辮子

ʻHo^2 shang^4 yi^1 shêng^1 wu^2 pien^4 tzŭ.^{3}

NOTE.—This joke on the shaven pate of the Buddhist priest, is used in advising a person to take things quietly.

諺語叢話

2398

Those who become priests no longer acknowledge their relations.

出 家 不 認 家

Chʻu^{1} chia^{1} pu^{4} jên^{4} chia.^{1}

2399

"If a man be not enlightened within, what lamp shall he light? If his intentions are not upright, what prayers shall he repeat?"

心 不 光 明 點 甚 燈

Hsin^{1} pu^{4} kuang^{1} ming^{2} tien^{3} shên^{4} têng^{1}?

意 不 公 平 誦 甚 經

I^{4} pu^{4} kung^{1} pʻing^{2} sung^{4} shên^{4} ching^{1}?

2400

Bald-heads are (ready-made) Buddhist priests.

禿 子 爲 和 尙

Tʻu^{1} tzŭ^{3} wei^{2} ʻho^{2} shang.^{4}

2401

Only those become Bonzes who can't get a living.

無 結 梢 做 和 尙

Wu chieh shao tso ʻho shang.

2402

If you wish Buddhism to flourish, then let Bonze praise Bonze.

若 要 佛 法 興。還 是 僧 讚 僧

Jo^{4} yao^{4} fu^{2} fa^{3} hsing,^{1} ʻhuan^{2} shih^{4} sêng^{1} tsan^{4} sêng.^{1}

CHAPTER IV.

REWARDS AND PUNISHMENTS.

—— 2403 ——

Who, out of season, laugh and cry,
Must meet misfortune by and by.

哀樂失時。殃咎必至
Ai^{1} lê^{4} shih^{1} shih,^{2} yang^{1} chiu^{1} pi^{4} chih.^{4}

—— 2404 ——

Those who care but for the joys of to-day,
Fling all thoughts of future mis'ry away.

只圖眼前快活
Chih^{3} tʻu^{2} yen^{3} chʻien^{2} kʻuai^{4} ʻhuo,^{2}
不管死後罪惡
Pu^{4} kuan^{3} ssŭ^{3} ʻhou^{4} tsui^{4} o.^{4}

—— 2405 ——

Who lay up goodness have gladness;
Who lay up evil have sadness.

善積者昌。惡積者喪
Shan^{4} chi^{2} chê^{2} chʻang^{1}; o^{4} chi^{2} chê^{2} sang.^{1}

—— 2406 ——

In curing men of evil ways,
Cangue, and expose to public gaze.

懲治兇惡。枷責發落
Chʻêng^{3} chih^{3} hsiung^{1} o,^{4} chia^{1} tsê^{2} fa^{1} lo.^{4}

—— 2407 ——

Whoe'er an idle life will lead,
Must take starvation as his meed.

一生懶惰。忍飢受餓
Yi^{1} shêng^{1} lan^{3} to,^{4} jên^{3} chi^{1} shou^{4} o.^{4}

—— 2408 ——

On account of abounding ancestral merit,
Some miss the destruction they ought to inherit:
Others lose the promotion their virtues might claim,
Through the crimes which adhere to their ancestral
name.

爲惡不滅。祖有餘德

Wei^4 o^4 pu^4 mieh,^{4} tsu^3 yu^3 yü^2 tê^2:

爲善不昌。祖有餘殃

Wei^4 shan^4 pu^4 chʻang,^{1} tsu^3 yu^3 yü^2 yang.^{1}

2409

Do not mistake, though punishment tarry,
When the day comes it cannot miscarry.

不是不報。日子未到

Pu^4 shih^4 pu^4 pao,^{4} jih^4 tzŭ^3 wei^4 tao.^{4}

NOTE.—"Though hand join in hand, the wicked shall not be unpunished." Prov. 11: 21.

2410

Distant punishment falls on a man's descendants; immediate punishment on the man himself.

遠報則在兒孫

Yüan^3 pao^4 tsê^2 tsai^4 êrh^2 sun^1;

近報就在自己

chin^4 pao^4 chiu^4 tsai^4 tzŭ^4 chi.^{3}

2411

Punishment is certain sooner or later; say not there is no such thing.

莫說眼前無報應

Mo^4 shuo^1 yen^3 chʻien^2 wu^2 pao^4 ying^4;

或是來早與來遲

ʻhuo^4 shih^4 lai^1 tsao^3 yü^3 lai^2 chʻih.^{2}

2412

Do good now and be rewarded hereafter.

今生作福。來生消受

Chin^1 shêng^1 tso^4 fu,^{2} lai^2 shêng^1 hsiao^1 shou.^{4}

2413

He who spares himself no pains shall have a place above others.

吃得苦中苦。做得人上人

Chʻih^1 tê^2 kʻu^3 chung^1 kʻu,^{3} tso^4 tê^2 jên^2 shang^4 jên.^{2}

2414

We only see the living punished; who ever saw a ghost wearing a cangue?

只見活人受罪
Chih³ chien⁴ ʻhuo₀ jên₀ shou⁴ tsui⁴;
那見死鬼帶枷
na³ chien⁴ ssŭ³ kuei³ tai⁴ chia.¹

2415

The tablet before *Yen Wang* contains the words 'not according to man's reckoning.'

閻王面前一塊牌
Yen² wang² mien⁴ chʻien² yi¹ kʻuai⁴ pʻai,²
總不由人算
tsung³ pu⁴ yu² jên² suan.⁴

2416

To be thunderstruck is visible punishment.

雷打眼前報
Lei² ta³ yen³ chʻien² pao.⁴

2417

Our good or evil must have its reward; the only question is—shall it come sooner or later?

善惡到頭終有報
Shan⁴ o⁴ tao⁴ tʻou² chung¹ yu³ pao⁴;
只爭來早與來遲
chih³ chêng¹ lai² tsao³ yü³ lai² chʻih.²

2418

He shall reap hemp who sows hemp, and beans who sows beans.

種蔴得蔴。種豆得豆
Chung⁴ ma² tê² ma,² chung⁴ tou⁴ tê² tou.⁴

NOTE.—"Whatsoever a man soweth, that shall he also reap. Gal. 6: 7.

2419

Every man gets what he cultivates.

各人修。各人得
Ko⁴ jên² hsiu,¹ ko⁴ jên² tê.²

2420

Good has its own reward, evil its own punishment.

善有善報。惡有惡報
Shan⁴ yu³ shan⁴ pao,⁴ o⁴ yu³ o⁴ pao.⁴

2421

Those who do good are very happy ; those who do evil cannot escape.

爲善最樂。爲惡難逃

ʻWei^2 shan^4 tsui^4 lê^4; wei^2 o^4 nan^2 tʻao.^{2}

2422

To excuse a murderer is abhorrent to reason.

殺人可恕。情理難容

Sha^1 jên^2 kʻo^3 shu,^{4} chʻing^2 li^3 nan^2 yung.^{2}

2423

The good live long, the bad die early.

善必壽老。惡必早亡

Shan^4 pi^4 shou^4 lao,^{3} o^4 pi^4 tsao^3 wang.^{3}

2424

He is certain of a rich reward who escapes in a hazardous enterprise.

大難不死。必有厚祿

Ta^4 nan^2 pu^4 ssŭ,^{3} pi^4 yu^3 ʻhou^4 lu.^{4}

2425

Rewards are used to stimulate goodness ; punishment to repress evil.

賞以勸善。罰以懲惡

Shang^3 i^3 chʻüan^4 shan^4; fa^2 i^3 chʻêng^2 o.^{4}

2426

He who from secret malice shoots an arrow at another in the dark, brings calamity on his descendants.

匿怨而用暗箭。禍延子孫

Ni^4 yüan^4 êrh^2 yung^4 an^4 chien,^{4} ʻhuo^4 yen^2 tzŭ^3 sun.^{1}

2427

Good or evil deeds are sure to be discovered. *Lit.* One buried in the snow must after a while be discovered.

雪裡埋人。久後自明

Hsüeh^3 li^3 mai^2 jên,^{2} chiu^3 ʻhou^4 tzŭ^4 ming.^{2}

2428

Grievous wrong necessitates signal redress. *Lit.* A great bend must have a great straightening.

大屈必有大伸
Ta⁴ chʻü¹ pi⁴ yu³ ta⁴ shên.¹

2429

There must come a day when the tumour will be punctured.

總有一天穿疱的日子
Tsung³ yu³ yi¹ tʻien¹ chʻuan¹ pao¹ ti¹ jih⁴ tzŭ.³

2430

If you look on beauty till your heart is filled with lust, you will suffer for it in your wife and daughters.

見色而起淫心。報在妻女
Chien⁴ sê⁴ êrh² chʻi³ ying² hsin,¹ pao⁴ tsai⁴ chʻi¹ nü.²

2431

The upright in heart fear no thunderbolts.

心正不怕雷打
Hsin¹ chêng⁴ pu⁴ pʻa⁴ lei² ta.³

2432

Embrace every chance of laying up merit, and your daily wants will be regularly supplied.

功德隨時積。衣飯逐日生
Kung¹ tê² sui² shih² chi,² i¹ fan⁴ sui² jih⁴ shêng.¹

2433

There is happiness in doing good, and secret merit in virtuous deeds.

積福有福在。行善有陰功
Chi¹ fu² yu² fu² tsai,² hsing¹ shan⁴ yu² yin⁴ kung.¹

2434

Would you know what you were, see what you are;
Would you know what you will be, see what you do.

要知前世因。今生受者是
Yao⁴ chih¹ chʻien² shih⁴ yin,¹ chin¹ shêng¹ shou⁴ chê² shih⁴;
要知來世因今生作者是
yao⁴ chih¹ lai² shih⁴ yin,¹ chin¹ shêng¹ tso⁴ chê² shih.⁴

2435

Cultivate virtue in this world, and you'll be happy in the next.

今世便修來世福

Chih[1] shih[4] pien[4] hsiu[1] lai[2] shih[4] fu.[2]

2436

A human body is hard to beg.

難得討人身的

Nan[2] tê[2] t'ao[3] jên[2] shên[1] ti[1]

NOTE.—This is said in warning to wicked men. The idea is that it will be impossible for a bad man to obtain a *human* body in the future life; he will have to put up with the body of some reptile, bird, or beast.

SECTION XVIII.—ON TIMES.

CHAPTER I.

SEASONS.

2437

When spinach is for sale on the eighth of the fourth moon,
Then planting out their crops all the farmers will be soon.

四 月 八 莧 菜 掐
Ssŭ^{4} yüeh^{4} pa^{1} hsien^{4} tsʻai^{4} chʻia,^{1}
四 鄉 人 家 把 秧 插
Ssŭ^{4} hsiang^{1} jên^{2} chia^{1} pa^{3} hsiang^{1} chʻa.^{1}

2438

On the twenty-eighth of the third month year by year,
Sugar-cane is eaten in every household here.

年 年 三 月 二 十 八
Nien^{2} nien^{2} san^{1} yüeh^{4} êrh^{4} shih^{2} pa,^{1}
家 家 戶 戶 吃 甘 蔗
Chia^{1} chia^{1} ʻhu^{4} ʻhu^{4} chʻih^{1} kan^{1} cha.^{4}

NOTE.—The reference is to a custom, principally if not entirely confined to eth city of *Wu-chang* (武 昌), of keeping a feast on the above date, in honour of *Tung yo* (東 嶽) a Taoist deity, whose birthday it is.

2439

As days lengthen more work may be done. *Lit:* After the winter solstice, days lengthen and a thread may be added.

冬 至 日 長 添 線
Tung^{1} chih^{4} jih^{4} chʻang^{2} tʻien^{1} hsien.^{4}

2440

Spring is sooner recognized by plants than men.

人不知春草知春

Jên2 pu4 chih1 chʻun1 tsʻao3 chih1 chʻun.1

2441

It is spring when the gayest colours abound.

萬紫千紅總是春

Wan4 tzŭ3 chʻien1 ʻhung2 tsung3 shih4 chʻun.1

2442

When Autumn comes the hills are covered with beauty; when spring comes every spot is perfumed with flowers.

秋至滿山多秀色

Chʻiu1 chih4 man3 shan1 to1 hsiu4 sê,4

春來無處不花香

chʻun1 lai2 wu2 chʻu4 pu4 ʻhua1 hsiang.1

2443

Nightingales and flowers fear the passing away of Spring; how then can you teach men to spend it carelessly!

鶯花猶怕春光老

Ying1 ʻhua1 yu2 pʻa4 chʻun1 kuang1 lao3;

豈可教人枉度春

chʻi3 kʻo3 chiao4 jên2 wang3 tu4 chʻun.1

2444

Everything in season. *Lit.:* The mandarin orange is over by the feast of lanterns; and turnips by the coming of spring.

柑子看不得燈

Kan1 tzŭ3 kʻan4 pu4 tê2 têng1;

蘿蔔打不得春

lo2 pʻu2 ta3 pu4 tê2 chʻun.1

2445

When a leaf of the *wu-tʻung* falls, every one knows it is Autumn.

梧桐一葉落。天下盡知秋

Wu^2 tʻung^2 yi^1 yeh^4 lo,^{4} tʻien^1 hsia^4 chin^4 chih^1 chʻiu.^{1}

2446

The year fears mid-autumn, as the month the full moon.

年怕中秋月怕半

Nien^2 pʻa^4 chung^1 chʻiu,^{1} yüeh^4 pʻa^4 pan.^{4}

NOTE.—Because after these times both year and month seem to hasten to their close.

CHAPTER II.

TIME.

2447

As in a looking-glass one's likeness may be shown,
So in the ages past the present may be known.

明 鏡 可 以 察 形
Ming^2 ching^4 kʻo^3 i^3 chʻa^2 hsing,^{2}
往 古 可 以 知 今
Wang^3 ku^3 kʻo^3 yi^3 chih^1 chin.^{1}

2448

An inch of time is like an inch of gold;
But time can never be at that price sold.
A lost inch of gold may be sought somewhere;
Where time may be sought for cannot be told.

一 寸 光 陰 一 寸 金
Yi^1 tsʻun^4 kuang^1 ying^1 yi^1 tsʻun^4 chin^1;
寸 金 難 買 寸 光 陰
Tsʻun^4 chin^1 nan^2 mai^3 tsʻun^4 kuang^1 yin,^{1}
失 去 寸 金 有 尋 處
Shih^1 chʻü^4 tsʻun^4 chin^1 yu^3 hsin^2 chʻu^4;
失 去 光 陰 無 處 尋
Shih^1 chʻü^4 kuang^1 yin^1 wu^2 chʻu^4 hsin.^{2}

2449

Time flies like an arrow; days and months like a shuttle.

光 陰 似 箭。日 月 如 梭
Kuang^1 yin^1 ssŭ^4 chien^4; jih^4 yüeh^4 ju^2 so.^{1}

NOTE.—"My days are swifter than a weaver's shuttle." Job, 7: 6.

2450

Past events are clear as a mirror; future events are as dark as lacquer.

過 去 事 明 如 鏡
Kuo^4 chʻü^4 shih^4 ming^2 ju^2 ching^4;
未 來 事 暗 如 漆
wei^4 lai^2 shih^4 an^4 ju^2 chʻi.^{1}

2451

Observe the present, but reflect the past; without the past there had been no present.

觀今宜鑑古。無古不成今

Kuan^1 chin^1 i^2 chien^4 ku^8; wu^2 ku^3 pu^4 chʻêng^2 chin.^{1}

2452

Time passes easily to those fully employed.

工夫容易過

Kung^1 fu^1 yung^2 i^4 kuo.^{4}

2453

From the past you may forecast the future.

驗其前便知其後

Yen^4 chʻi^2 chʻien^2 pien^4 chih^1 chʻi^2 ʻhou.^{4}

2454

To one full of expectation a moment seems a year.

相思之甚。寸陰若歲

Hsiang^1 ssŭ^1 chih^1 shên,^{4} tsʻun^4 yin^1 jo^4 sui.^{4}

2455

Idly spent years or months hinder a man for life.

虛度歲月。躭擱一生

Hsü^1 tu^4 sui^4 yüeh^4 tan^1 ko^1 yi^1 shêng.^{1}

2456

This morning knows not this evening's affairs.

今朝不知今晚事

Chin^1 chao^1 pu^4 chih^1 chin^1 wan^3 shih.^{4}

2457

One quarter of an hour is worth a thousand *taels* of gold.

一刻千金

Yi^1 kʻo^4 chʻien^1 chin.^{1}

2458

Procrastination is the thief of time.

需者事之賊

Hsü^1 chê^2 shih^4 chih^1 tsei.^{2}

2459

In calmness heaven and earth seem greater; in leisure days and months seem longer.

靜裡乾坤大。閑中日月長
Ching^4 li^3 chʻien^2 kʻun^1 ta^4; hsien^2 chung^1 jih^4 yueh^4 chʻang^2

2460

Rosy-faced ladies resemble trees in Spring: the following years are but a throw of the shuttle.

紅顏比春樹。流年一擲梭
ʻHung^3 yen^2 pi^3 chʻun^1 shu^4; liu^2 nien^3 yi^1 chih^4 so.^{1}

2461

Never waste time.

光陰不可錯過
Kang^1 yin^1 pu^4 kʻo^3 tsʻo^4 kuo.^{4}

2462

We work with the rising, rest with the setting sun.

日出而作。日入而息
Jih^4 chʻu^1 êrh^2 tso,^{4} jih^4 ju^4 êrh^2 hsi.^{2}

CHAPTER III.

WEATHER.

— 2463 —

When it rains about the break of day,
The traveller's sorrows pass away.

雨灑五更頭。行人永無憂

Yü^3 sa^3 wu^3 kêng^1 tʻou,^{2} hsing^2 jên^2 yung^3 wu^2 yu.^{1}

— 2464 —

With lightning in the East, the sun will be red;
With lightning in the West, showers you may dread;
With lightning in the South, it will rain more and more;
With lightning in the North, the southern gale will roar.

東閃日頭紅。西閃雨重重

Tung^1 shan^3 jih^4 tʻou^2 ʻhung^3; ʻhsi^1 shan^3 jü^4 chʻung^2 chʻung^2:

南閃長流水。北閃猛南風

Nan^2 shan^3 chʻang^2 liu^2 shui^3; pei^3 shan^3 mêng^3 nan^2 fêng.^{1}

— 2465 —

Our yesterday's plans have all been put to flight,
For an old north wind has risen in the night.

昨日商量大不同

Tso^2 jih^4 shang^1 liang^2 ta^4 pu^4 tʻung,^{2}

半夜起了老北風

Pan^4 yeh^4 chʻi^3 liao^3 lao^3 pei^3 fêng.^{1}

— 2466 —

In the seventh month vertical, in the eighth oblique;
In the ninth and tenth it is far to seek.

七月中八月偏

Chʻi^1 yüeh^4 chung^1 pa^1 yüeh^4 pʻien^1;

九月十月看不見

Chiu^3 yüeh^4 shih^3 yüeh^4 kʻan^4 pu^4 chien.^{4}

NOTE.—This is said of the 七妹星, the Seven star, or Charles' Wain.

— 2467 —

The seven cornered constellation—Charles's wain,
Rises in the East, in the West descends again.

七姑星七支角
Chʻi1 ku1 hsing1 chʻi1 chih1 chio,2
東邊起西邊落
Tung1 pien1 chʻi3 hsi1 pien1 lo.4

2468

When the weather is hot and hard to bear,
We pursue the breeze for a little fresh air.

天熱難當。趕風乘凉
Tʻien1 jê4 nan2 tang,1 kan3 fêng1 chʻêng4 liang.2

2469

Dread the fifth month's rattling rains;
Dread not the height the water gains.

不怕五月長。只怕五月响
Pu4 pʻa4 wu3 yueh4 chang3; chih3 pʻa4 wu3 yueh4 hsiang.3

2470

On the third of the third month travellers may
Don their thin clothes, and put their thick ones away.

三月三。路上行人脫衣單
San1 yüeh4 san,1 lu4 shang4 hsing2 jên2 tʻo1 i1 tan.1

2471

On the ninth of the ninth month, Traveller beware
Of the lakes! (for there will be storms in the air).

九月九。行人莫向湖邊走
Chiu3 yüeh4 chiu,3 hsing2 jên2 mo4 hsiang4 ʻhu2 pien1 tsou.4

2472

When *chʻing-ming* falls in the second month, don't be in a flurry:
When *chʻing-ming* falls in the third, plant your rice in a hurry.

二月清明不要忙
Erh4 yüeh4 chʻing1 ming2 pu4 yao4 mang2:
三月清明早下秧
San1 yüeh4 chʻing1 ming2 tsao3 hsia4 yang.1

NOTE.—*Chʻing-ming*, rendered "Pure Brightness," is one of the twenty-four terms into which the Chinese year is divided. It falls about the 5th of April, and is mild and genial.

2473

On the ninth month's *ch'ung-yang* all desire,
To gather around the household fire.

九月重陽。抱火進房

Chiu³ yüeh⁴ ch'ung² yang,² pao⁴ 'huo³ chin⁴ fang.²

NOTE.—1, 3, 5, 7 and 9, are numbers belonging to *Yang*. The 9th of the 9th month is a Donble *Yang* number, hence *Ch'ung-yang*, the name of the feast then celebrated.

2474

If it rises at night,
T'will fall at daylight.

關門起。開門息

Kuan¹ mên² ch'i,³ k'ai¹ mên² hsi.²

2475

In the sixth month continuous rain,
Covers all the soil with golden grain.

六月下連陰。徧地是黃金

Lu⁴ yüeh⁴ hsia⁴ lien² yin,² pien⁴ ti⁴ shih⁴ 'huang² chin.¹

2476

When half the seventh month is passed,
With iron *Lohans* men may be classed.

過了七月半。方是鐵羅漢

Kuo⁴ liao³ ch'i¹ yüeh⁴ pan,⁴ fang¹ shih⁴ t'ieh³ lo² 'han.⁴

NOTE.—By "iron *Lohans*" is meant the cast-iron images of the 500, and of the 18 disciples of S'akyamuni, common in Buddhist temples. At the time mentioned in this proverb, the festival of burning paper etc. to the dead occurs; and, according to my informant, it is believed that the Gates of Hades are opened for half a month, and ghosts allowed to wander back to their former abodes. It is the supposed presence of these infernal visitors which makes the people afraid, at this particular period, of sickness or death. If they escape unhurt, afterwards they are as sturdy as 'iron *Lohans*."

2477.

If there be one fine day at the coming in of Spring,
the farmer need not labour hard at ploughing.

但得立春晴一日

Tan⁴ tê² li⁴ ch'un¹ ch'ing² yi¹ jih,⁴

農夫不用力耕田

nung² fu¹ pu⁴ yung⁴ li⁴ kêng¹ t'ien.²

2478

The farmer hopes for rain, the traveller for fine weather.

耕田望落雨。做客望天晴

Kêng1 tʻien2 wang4 lo4 yü3; tso4 kʻo4 wang4 tʻien4 chʻing.2

2479

Though it rain ever so hard on the first of the month, it will not last more than a day.

落雨向初一。落雨莫過日

Lo4 yü3 hsiang3 chʻu1 yi,1 lo4 yü3 mo4 kuo4 jih.4

2480

In the morning look toward the South-east; in the evening toward the North-west.

朝看東南。晚看西北

Chao1 kʻan4 tung1 nan2; wan3 kʻan4 hsi1 pei.3

NOTE.—If the eastern sky be bright in the morning, the day will be fine; if the western sky be bright in the evening, the next day will be fine.

2481

A halo round the moon is a sign of wind.

月暈而風

Yüeh4 yün1 êrh2 fêng.1

2482

If it rain on the winter St. Swithin's, cattle and sheep will die of cold;—on the summer St. Swithin's, you may row to market in a boat;—on the autumn St. Swithin's, rice will produce two ears (both useless);—on the spring St. Swithin's, the earth will be red (with drought) for a thousand miles.

冬甲子雨牛羊凍死

Tung1 chia3 tzŭ3 yü3 niu2 yang2 tung4 ssŭ3;

夏甲子雨撐船就市

hsia4 chia3 tzŭ3 yü3 chang4 chʻuan2 chiu4 shih4;

秋甲子雨禾生兩耳

chʻiu1 chia3 tzŭ3 yü3 ʻho2 shêng1 liang3 êrh2;

春甲子雨赤地千里

chʻun1 chia3 tzŭ3 yü3 chʻih4 ti4 chʻien1 li.3

NOTE.—"St. Swithin's:" *lit: chia-tzu.* This is a term of sixty days; and there are six such terms in a year. They do not, however, correspond exactly with the year. The superstition is that if it rain on the first day of any of these terms, it will be unusually wet for sixty days.

2483

The east wind breaks up the frost.

東 風 解 凍

Tung^1 fêng^1 chieh^3 tung.^{4}

2484

Old dame *Han* has crossed the river; and *Ma* the Buddhist priest is gathering sticks.

韓 婆 婆 過 江。 馬 和 尙 撿 柴

ʻHan^2 pʻo^2 pʻo^2 kuo^4 chiang^1; ma^3 ʻho^2 shang^4 chien^3 chʻai.^{2}

NOTE.—This local proverb is much used by the people of Hankow and Wuchang on the 20th of the 9th month. If that day be fine they use this saying as it stands, and conclude that the coming winter will be severe. If the day be wet and windy, the saying is reversed, and a mild winter is expected.

2485

It is so calm and smooth one might write on the water.

平 風 息 浪。水 裏 寫 得 字

Pʻing^2 fêng^1 hsi^2 lang^4, shui^3 li^3 hsieh^3 tê^2 tzŭ.^{4}

2486

A rainbow in the east will be followed by a fine day; in the west by a rainy day.

東 虹 日 頭。 西 虹 雨

Tung^1 ʻhung^4 jih^4 tʻou^2; hsi^1 ʻhung^4 yü.^{3}

2487

On the 8th, 18th, and 28th, of the fifth month it should rain; if it rains not on the 8th, on the 18th it will not; if it rains not on the 28th, sow your green-coloured beans.

五 月 三 八 都 要 雨

Wu^3 yüeh^4 san^1 pa^1 tu^1 yao^4 yü^3:

頭 八 無 雨 二 八 休

tʻou^2 pa^1 wu^2 yü^3 êrh^4 pa^1 hsiu^1;

三 八 無 雨 種 菉 豆

San^1 pa^1 wu^2 yü^3 chung^4 lu^4 tou.^{4}

NOTE.—Beans are to be sown because the season will prove too dry for corn.

2488

Great heat brings wind.

熱 極 生 風

Jê^4 chi^2 shêng^1 fêng.^{1}

2489

When it snows in six-leaved flakes it is a good omen of a prosperous year.

雪花飛六出先兆豐年

Hsüeh^{3} ʻhua^{1} fei^{1} lu^{4} chʻu^{1} hsien^{1} chao^{4} fêng^{1} nien.^{2}

2490

Fair weather offends nobody; incessant rains make men gloomy.

天晴無人怨。久雨令人愁

Tʻien^{1} chʻing^{2} wu^{2} jên^{2} yüan^{4}; chiu^{3} yü^{3} ling^{4} jên^{2} chʻou.^{2}

2491

Five days' rain, ten days' wind, are both good omens.

五風十雨皆爲瑞

Wu^{3} fêng^{1} shih^{2} yü^{3} chieh^{1} wei^{2} jui.^{4}

2492

Like a fruitful shower after a long drought is the meeting of an old acquaintance in a strange land.

久旱逢甘雨。他鄉遇故知

Chʻiu^{3} ʻhan^{4} fêng^{2} kan^{1} yü,^{3} tʻa^{1} hsiang^{1} yü^{4} ku^{4} chih.^{1}

2493

Weather varies every hundred miles.

百里不同天

Pai^{3} li^{3} pu^{4} tʻung^{2} tʻien.^{1}

2494

How to keep cool. *Lit.:* If the mind be calm the body will keep cool.

心定自然涼

Hsin^{1} ting^{4} tzŭ^{4} jan^{2} liang.^{2}

2495

Nobody complains over a hundred fine days in winter.

冬晴百日無怨

Tung^{1} chʻing^{2} pai^{3} jih^{4} wu^{2} yüan.^{4}

2496

When the mid-autumn moon is beclouded, there will be rain on the next Feast of Lanterns.

雲掩中秋月。雨灑上元燈

Yun² yen³ chung¹ ch'iu¹ yueh,⁴ yü³ sa³ shang⁴ yüan² têng.¹

2497

When it is bright all round it will not rain: when it is bright only over-head it will.

無雨四下亮。有雨頂上光

Wu² yü³ ssŭ⁴ hsia⁴ liang⁴; yu³ yü³ ting³ shang⁴ kuang.¹

2498

The moon of mid-autumn is exceedingly bright.

月到中秋分外明

Yueh⁴ tao⁴ chung¹ ch'iu¹ fên¹ wai⁴ ming.²

2499

From the summer solstice days begin to shorten; from the winter solstice they begin to lengthen.

夏至一陰生。冬至一陽生

Hsia⁴ chih⁴ yi¹ yin¹ shêng¹; tung¹ chih⁴ yi¹ yang² shêng.¹

2500

When the plinths of the pillars are damp there will be rain.

磉潤而雨

Sang³ jun⁴ êrh² yü.³

2501

When it rains in the morning, it will be fine at night.

開門雨。關門晴

K'ai¹ mên² yü,³ kuan¹ mên² ch'ing.²

2502

Cold sends us to the fire; heat sends us into the shade.

因寒向火。怕熱乘涼

Yin¹ han² hsiang⁴ huo³; p'a⁴ jê⁴ ch'ing⁴ liang.²

SECTION XIX.—ON TRAVEL.

CHAPTER I.

SCENERY.

2503

Exactly what heaven must be on high,
Are *Suchow* and *Hangchow* below the sky.

上說天堂。下說蘇杭

Shang¹ shuo¹ t'ien¹ t'ang,² hsia⁴ shuo¹ Su¹ Hang.²

NOTE.—This well-known saying is referred to by Marco Polo, in his description "of the noble and magnificent city of *Kinsai*." Bohn's Edition, page 313.

2504

The rapid rushes down without design; and the white cloud rises from the mountain gorge without any will of its own.

流水下灘非有意

Liu² shui³ hsia⁴ t'an¹ fei¹ yu³ i⁴;

白雲出岫本無心

pai² yün² ch'u¹ hsiu⁴ pên³ wu² hsin.¹

2505

The deep mountain gorges must hide the fierce tigers; as the great sea must receive every small river.

深山畢竟藏猛虎

Shên¹ shan¹ pi⁴ ching⁴ ts'ang² mêng³ 'hu³;

大海終須納細流

ta⁴ 'hai³ chung¹ hsü¹ na⁴ si⁴ liu.²

2506

The sea is boundless; the river bottomless.

海無邊。江無底

'Hai³ wu² pien¹; chiang¹ wu² ti.¹

2507

All the rivers flow into the sea, and yet it is not full.

萬川歸海。而海不盈

Wan⁴ ch'uan¹ kuei¹ 'hai,³ êrh² 'hai³ pu⁴ ying.²

NOTE.—"All the rivers run into the sea; yet the sea is not full." Eccles. 1: 7.

2508

Where hills are lofty rivers are deep.

山高水也高

San^{1} kao^{1} shui^{3} yeh^{3} kao.^{1}

2509

Of noted rivers there are three hundred; of branch streams three thousand.

名川三百。支川三千

Ming^{2} chʻuan^{1} san^{1} pai^{1}; chih^{1} chʻuan^{1} san^{1} chʻien.^{1}

2510

The *Yangtsze* and the *Huai*, every flower and every tree, each has its own peculiar name.

江淮草木。亦知爾名

Chiang^{1} Huai^{2} tsʻao^{3} mu,^{4} i^{4} chih^{1} êrh^{3} ming.^{2}

2511

"The distant grove you see is sure to enclose either a house or a grave."

遠望一叢林。不是屋就是墳

Yüan^{3} wang^{4} yi^{1} chʻung^{2} lin,^{2} pu^{4} shih^{4} wu^{1} chiu^{4} shih^{4} fên.^{2}

CHAPTER II.

TRAVELLING.

2512

A thousand strokes, ten thousand shoves, do less avail,
Than the bending loins of a ragged sail.

千槳萬篙。比不得破篷撐腰

Chʻien^1 chiang^3 wan^4 kao,^{1} pi^3 pu^4 tê^2 pʻo^4 pʻêng^2 chang^4 yao.^{1}

2513

Walk along slowly—perhaps you will,
That I fear not, but lest you stand still.

不怕走得慢。只怕路上站

Pu^4 pʻa^4 tsou^4 tê^2 man,^{4} chih^4 pʻa^4 lu^4 shang^4 chan.^{4}

2514

Ah me! this travelling, who can bear it!
One's suit gets torn and who's to repair it?

出門十分苦。衣破無人補

Chʻu^1 mên^2 shih^2 fên^1 kʻu^3! i^1 pʻo^4 wu^2 jên^2 pu.^{3}

2515

He who does not covet, and is from every falsehood clear,
May travel anywhere he likes without the slightest fear.

手穩嘴穩。到處好安身

Shou^3 wên^3 tsui^3 wen,^{3} tao^4 chʻu^4 ʻhao^3 an^1 shên.^{1}

2516

You go to the end of a stage, on land;
By boat, you stop when the jetty's at hand.

路行站口。船灣碼頭

Lu^1 hsing^2 chan^4 kʻou^3; chʻuan^2 wan^1 ma^3 tʻou.^{2}

2517

Rap on a vessel, and have three days' delay:
Rattle your chopsticks, and pine through the third day.

敲船三日坐。敲碗三日餓
Chʻiao^{1} chʻuan^{2} san^{1} jih^{4} tso^{4}: chʻiao^{1} wan^{3} san^{1} jih^{4} o.^{4}

2518

Of three men on a road, the youngest has to suffer.

三人上路小的吃虧
San^{1} jên^{2} shang^{4} lu,^{4} hsiao^{3} ti^{1} chʻih^{1} kʻuei.^{1}

2519

Put up before it is dark; and when the cock crows take a look at the weather.

未晚先投宿。鷄鳴早看天
Wei^{4} wan^{3} hsien^{1} tʻou^{2} su^{2}; chi^{1} ming^{2} tsao^{3} kʻan^{4} tʻien.^{1}

2520

May the star of happiness shine on all your journey!

一路福星
Yi^{1} lu^{4} fu^{2} hsing^{1}!

2521

May all your journey be in peace!

一路平安。or 一路安穩
Yi^{1} lu^{4} pʻing^{2} an^{1}! or yi^{1} lu^{4} an^{1} wên^{1}!

2522

May you have fair wind all the way!

一路順風
Yi^{1} lu^{4} shun^{4} fêng^{1}!

2523

May fair winds attend you!

順風相送
shun^{3} fêng^{1} hsiang^{1} sung^{4}!

2524

To leave home is easier than to return.

別時容易見時難
Pieh^{2} shih^{2} yung^{2} i^{4} chien^{4} shih^{2} nan.^{2}

2525

He who can use his tongue, can find out any road.

路在口裡。一問就知
Lu^{4} tsai^{4} kʻou^{3} li,^{3} yi^{1} wên^{4} chiu^{4} chih.^{1}

— 2526 —

Better at home than a mile from it.

離家一里不如屋裡

Li^2 chia^1 yi^1 li,^{3} pu^4 ju^2 wu^1 li.^{3}

— 2527 —

A thousand days at home, are better than the shortest time abroad.

在家千日好。出外一時難

Tsai^4 chia^1 chʻien^1 jih^4 ʻhao,^{2} chʻu^1 wai^4 yi^1 shih^2 nan.^{2}

— 2528 —

After three years of drought, all who go out for a day hope for fair weather.

天乾三年。出門一日。都望晴

Tʻien^1 kan^1 san^1 nien,^{2} chʻu^1 mên^2 yi^1 jih,^{4} tu^1 wang^4 chʻing.^{2}

— 2259 —

If a man makes himself friendly wherever he goes, where can he go and not find a friend?

男兒五湖四海爲朋友

Nan^2 êrh^2 wu^3 ʻhu^2 ssŭ^4 ʻhai^3 wei^2 pʻêng^2 yü,^{3}

人到何處不相逢

jên^2 tao^4 ʻho^2 chʻu^4 pu^4 hsiang^1 fêng.^{2}

— 2530 —

Mountains do not hinder a journey so much as rivers.

隔山容易走。隔水最難行

Ko^2 shan^1 yung^2 i^4 tsou,^{4} ko^2 shui^3 tsui^4 nan^2 hsing.^{2}

— 2531 —

On shipboard everything is in the captain's care.

一擔金和寶。交與老艄公

Yi^1 tan^1 chin^1 ʻho^2 pao,^{3} chiao^1 yü^3 lao^3 shao^3 kung.^{1}

— 2532 —

On a journey each pursues his way without alighting to greet every one he meets.

相逢不下馬。各自奔前程

Hsiang^1 fêng^2 pu^4 hsia^4 ma,^{3} ko^4 tzŭ^4 pên^1 chʻien^2 chʻêng.^{2}

2533

There is some cause of anxiety, whether one travel by boat or on horseback.

行 船 跑 馬 三 分 憂

Hsing² ch'uan² p'ao³ ma³ san¹ fên¹ yu.¹

2534

Fellow-travellers must not desert each other.

同 路 無 梭 伴

T'ung² lu⁴ wu² so¹ pan.⁴

2535

A youthful son or brother grows old by travel.

少 年 子 弟 江 湖 老

Shao³ nien² tzŭ³ ti⁴ chiang¹ 'hu² lao.³

2536

Whether you hurry on or take it easy, the road before you has only a certain length.

急 行 慢 行。前 程 只 有 許 多 路

Chi² hsing² man⁴ hsing,² ch'ien² ch'êng² chih³ yu³ hsü³ to¹ lu.⁴

2537

When the vehicle in front upsets, the vehicle following takes more heed.

前 車 覆 後 車 戒

Ch'ien² ch'ê¹ fu² 'hou⁴ ch'ê¹ chieh.⁴

2538

There is no place like home. *Lit.: Ch'ang-an* may be a fine city, but it won't do for a permanent home.

長 安 雖 好。不 是 久 留 之 家

Ch'ang³ an¹ sui¹ 'hao,³ pu⁴ shih⁴ chiu³ liu² chih¹ chia.¹

NOTE.—"*Ch'ang-an*, the name of the old capital of *Shensi* province, also the capital of China in the *Ts'in*, *Han*, *Sui*, and *T'ung* periods." See Dr. Porter Smith's. "Vocabulary of Chinese Proper Names," page 3.

2539

The same. *Lit.: Though Lo-yang* be pleasant, it is not like home.

洛 陽 雖 好 不 如 家

Lo^4 Yang^2 sui^1 ʻhao^3 pu^4 ju^2 chia.^{1}

Note.—*Lo-yang*, the capital of China under the Eastern *Han* dynasty, A. D. 25; now a district city in the prefecture of *Honan*.

—— 2540 ——

Remove but an inch, and you must pay porterage; ship goods for a thousand miles, and you must pay freight.

寸 步 脚 錢。 千 里 船 錢

Tsʻun^4 pu^4 chiao^3 chʻien^2; chʻien^1 li^3 chʻuan^2 chʻien.^{2}

—— 2541 ——

If you can get by land do not go by water.

有 路 莫 登 舟

Yu^3 lu^4 mo^4 têng^1 chou.^{1}

—— 2542 ——

The rider on horseback knows nothing of the toil of those who travel on foot.

騎 馬 的 不 知 步 行 的 苦

Chʻi^2 ma^3 ti^1 pu^4 chih^1 pu^4 hsing^2 ti^1 kʻu.^{3}

—— 2543 ——

When on travel provoke not these three—the old, the young, the blind.

出 門 不 惹 三 子

Chʻu^1 men^2 pu^4 jê^3 san^1 tzŭ^3—

老 子 小 子 瞎 子

lao^3 tzŭ^3 hsiao^3 tzŭ^3 hsia^2 tzŭ.^{3}

—— 2544 ——

You may become a master of Arts in the space of three years; you cannot in ten become an accomplished traveller.

三 年 造 出 一 個 舉 子

San^1 nien^2 tsao^4 chʻu^1 yi^1 ko^4 chü^3 tzŭ^3;

十 年 學 不 倒 一 個 江 湖

Shih^2 nien^2 hsiao^2 pu^4 tao^3 yi^1 ko^4 chiang^1 ʻhu.^{2}

2545

Sitting in a boat, or galloping a horse over a track, you never ask about the road.

坐船跑馬不問路

Tso^4 ch'uan^2 p'ao^3 ma^3 pu^4 wên^4 lu.^{4}

2546

Get off your horse to cross a bridge ; and never wrangle at a ferry.

逢橋須下馬。過渡勿爭船

Fêng^2 ch'iao^2 hsü^1 hsia^4 ma^3; kuo^1 tu^4 wu^4 chêng^1 ch'uan.^{2}

SECTION XX.—ON WEALTH AND POVERTY.

CHAPTER I.

POVERTY.

2547

Of eating fond, at working slow,
You'll short of food and clothing grow.

好吃懶做。衣食不彀

ʻHao^4 chʻih^1 lan^3 tsou,^{4} i^1 shih^2 pn^4 kou.^{4}

2548

The man's poor indeed whose clothing is torn;
Yet rags not patches encounter man's scorn.

衣破眞是苦。笑破莫笑補

I^1 pʻo^4 chên^1 shih^4 ku^3; hsiao^4 pʻo^4 mo^4 hsiao^4 pu.^{3}

2549

In great distress, and penniless.

熬苦受難。無錢措辦

Ao^1 kʻu^3 shou^4 nan,^{2} wu^2 chʻien^2 tsʻu^4 pan.^{4}

2550

My name is Joy; But never a cash have I to employ.

小名叫喜

Hsiao^3 ming^2 chiao^4 Hsi^3;

腰裡沒得一個銅皮

yao^1 li^3 mu^2 tê^2 yi^1 ko^4 tʻung^2 pʻi.^{2}

2551

Just one mealtime without food,
Scattereth all the household brood.

一餐無飯妻離子散

Yi^1 tsʻan^1 wu^2 fan,^{4} chi^1 li^2 tzŭ^3 san.^{4}

2552

The craftier you may be the poorer you will grow;
For craftiness is that which Heaven never will allow.

越 奸 越 狡 越 貧 窮
Yüeh^4 chien^1 yüeh^4 chiao^3 yüeh^4 pʻin^3 chʻiung^2;
奸 狡 原 來 天 不 容
Chien^1 chiao^3 yüan^2 lai^2 tʻien^1 pu^4 yung.^{2}

2553

Let the bells on the necks of your horses be broken,
All relations by marriage will flee at that token.

馬 上 銅 鈴 破。親 戚 無 半 個
Ma^3 shang^4 tʻung^2 ling^2 pʻo,^{4} chʻin^1 chʻi^4 wu^4 pan^4 ko.^{4}

NOTE.—The second line is literally—"Not the half of a relation by marriage will be left."

2554

If you don't spend money wherever you stay,
You'll provoke dislike stay wherever you may.

到 處 不 用 錢。到 處 惹 人 嫌
Tao^4 chʻu^4 pu^4 yung^4 chʻien,^{2} tao^4 chʻu^4 jê^3 jên^2 hsien.^{2}

2555

To be poor in old age men cannot abide;
And the growing corn dreads a wind at noon-tide.

人 怕 老 來 窮。 穀 怕 午 時 風
Jên^2 pʻa^4 lao^3 lai^2 chʻiung^2; ku^3 pʻa^4 wu^3 shih^4 fêng.^{1}

2556

Thirsty yet having nothing to drink; hungry yet having nothing to eat.

渴 無 所 飲。餓 無 所 食
Kʻo^3 wu^2 so^3 yin^3; o^4 wu^2 so^3 shih.^{2}

2557

He can't buy enough rice to fill his belly, or enough wine to make him drunk.

買 飯 不 飽。買 酒 不 醉
Mai^3 fan^4 pu^4 pao,^{3} mai^3 chiu^3 pu^4 tsui.^{4}

2558

A brave fellow may be harassed by the want of one cash.

一 文 錢 逼 倒 英 雄 漢
Yi^1 wên^2 chʻien^2 pi^1 tao^3 ying^1 hsiung^2 ʻhan.^{4}

2559

Poverty forces men to commit crime. *Lit.:* One may know the king's law well enough, but starvation is hard to bear.

明知王法。飢餓難當

Ming^2 chih^1 wang^2 fa,^{3} chi^1 o^4 nan^2 tang.^{1}

2560

Poverty cannot change the virtues of the benevolent and disinterested.

仁人廉士窮不改節

Jên^2 jên^2 lien^2 shih^4 chʻiung^2 pu^4 kai^3 chieh.^{2}

2561

In abject poverty. *Lit.:* His lice are too many to itch; his debts too many to trouble him.

虱多不癢。債多不愁

Shih^1 to^1 pu^4 yang^3; chai^4 to^1 pu^4 chʻou.^{2}

2562

The same. *Lit.:* Without as much rice as a fowl could eat in a day, or a rat in a night.

日無鷄抓之米

Jih^4 wu^2 chi^1 chia^1 chih^1 mi,^{3}

夜無鼠耗之糧

yeh^4 wu^2 shü^3 ʻhao^4 chih^1 liang.^{2}

2563

The same. *Lit.:* Rats run away out of his rice boiler.

飯甑裡跑出老鼠來

Fan^4 tsêng^4 li^3 pʻao^3 chʻu^1 lao^3 shü^3 lai.^{2}

2564

The same. *Lit.:* Just able to save the eyebrows from being burnt.

可救燃眉

Kʻo^3 chiu^4 jan^2 mei.^{2}

2565

Often when want is extremest supplies come.

絕處逢生

Chüeh^2 chʻu^4 fêng^2 shêng.^{1}

2566

Tis hard to have to tell one's wants.

開 口 告 人 難

K'ai¹ k'ou³ kao⁴ jên² nan.²

2567

There is poverty for all kinds of rogues.

百 般 奸 狡 百 般 窮

Pai³ pan¹ chien¹ chiao³ pai³ pan¹ ch'iung.²

2568

Reduced circumstances must be submitted to humbly. *Lit.:* Under another's eaves one must bow the head.

打 得 廊 簷 下。誰 敢 不 低 頭

Ta³ tê² lang² yen² hsia,⁴ shui³ kan² pu⁴ ti¹ t'ou.²

2569

Nothing but thinness makes horses go feebly; Only poverty keeps men from being merry.

馬 行 無 力 皆 因 瘦

Ma³ hsing² wu² li⁴ chieh¹ yin¹ shou⁴;

人 不 風 流 只 爲 貧

jên² pu⁴ fêng¹ liu² chih³ wei⁴ p'in.³

2570

Hunger and cold make men glad of any kind of food and clothes.

飢 不 擇 食。寒 不 擇 衣

Chi¹ pu⁴ tsê² shih,² 'han² pu⁴ tsê² i.¹

2571

In great straights. *Lit.:* When the fire singes one's eyebrows, all one can do is to provide for the present.

火 燒 眉 毛 只 顧 眼 前

'Huo³ shao¹ mei² mao² chih³ ku⁴ yen³ ch'ien.²

2572

At one's wits' end—no road up to the sky, no door into the ground.

無法可制。上天無路
Wu^2 fa^3 kʻo^3 chih^4;—shang^4 tʻien^1 wu^2 lu,^{4}
下地無門
hsia^4 ti^4 wu^2 mên.^{2}

— 2573 —

Penniless. *Lit.:* Naked-handed and empty-fisted.

赤手空拳
Chʻih^4 shou^3 kʻung^1 chʻüan.^{2}

— 2574 —

When poor a man's resolution fails; when lean a horse's hair grows shaggy.

人貧志短。馬瘦毛長
Jên^2 pʻin^3 chih^4 tuan^3; ma^3 shou^4 mao^2 chʻang.^{2}

— 2575 —

A man is not beggared by eating or dressing, but by the failure of his plans.

吃不窮穿不窮
Chʻih^1 pu^4 chʻiung$_0$ chʻuan^1 pu^4 chʻiung,$_0$
算計不到一時窮
suan^4 chi^4 pu^4 tao^4 yi^1 shih^2 chʻiung.^{2}

— 2576 —

In poverty be patient.

無錢且耐煩
Wu^2 chʻien^2 chʻieh^3 nai^4 fan.^{2}

— 2577 —

Do not plead poverty when you ought to spend.

錢當用不辭貧
Chʻien^2 tang^1 yung^4 pu^4 tzʻŭ^2 pʻin.^{3}

— 2578 —

A good Chinese is not afraid to confess the poverty from which he rose.

好漢不怕出身低
ʻHao^3 ʻhan^4 pu^4 pʻa^4 chʻu^1 shên^1 ti.^{1}

— 2579 —

Without oil a lamp can give no light; without money a man can hardly exist.

燈臺無油點不光
Têng¹ t'ai² wu² yu² tien³ pu⁴ kuang¹;
世上無錢難爲人
shih⁴ shang⁴ wu² ch'ien² nan² wei² jên.²

2580

When man becomes poor he calls to mind ancient debts due to him.

人窮思古債
Jên² ch'iung² ssŭ¹ ku³ chai.⁴

CHAPTER II.

POOR MEN.

2581

Destitute knaves, The public saves.

光棍光棍。大家帮趁

Kuang^1 kun^4 kuang^1 kun,^{4} ta^4 chia^1 pang^1 tsʻun.^{4}

2582

A cold stove has no smoke;
No money have poor folk.

冷灶無烟。人窮無錢

Lêng^3 tsao^4 wu^2 yen^4; jên^2 chʻiung^2 wü^2 chʻien.^{2}

2583

One so poor that he is glad to get before a chaff fire.

窮得向粗糠火

Chʻiung^2 tê^2 hsiang^4 tsʻu^1 kʻaug^1 ʻhuo.^{3}

2584

Rice straw gives out much smoke; poor men give out much wrath.

稻草煙多。窮人氣多

Tao^4 tsʻao^3 yen^1 to^1; chʻiung^2 jên^2 chʻi^1 to.^{1}

2585

There is many a good under a shabby hat.

破帽底下有人

Pʻo^4 mao^4 ti^1 hsia^4 yu^3 jên.^{2}

2586

A frog in a well can hardly get out.

井裡蛙蟇總難翻身

Ching^3 li^3 hsia^1 ma^3 tsung^3 nan^2 fan^1 shên^1

2587

Meeting poverty-stricken relatives and neighbours, be very genial and kind.

見貧苦親隣須多温恤

Chien^4 pʻin^3 kʻu^3 chʻin^1 lin^2 hsü^1 to^1 wên^1 hsü.^{1}

2588

Scornfully to treat the poor is most dishonourable.

遇貧窮而作驕態者賤莫甚

Yü⁴ pʻin³ chʻiung² êrh² tso⁴ chiao¹ tʻai⁴ chê² chien⁴ mo⁴ shên.⁴

2589

He who has no store at home, must gallop about for a living.

家無積攢爲口奔馳

Chia¹ wu² chi² tsan³ wei⁴ kʻou³ pên¹ chʻih.²

CHAPTER III.

RICH MEN.

2590

Washing his face he wets his paws;
Eating his rice he wets his jaws.

洗臉打濕手。吃飯打濕口

Hsi^3 lien^3 ta^3 shih^1 shou^3; chʻih^1 fan^4 ta^3 shih^1 kʻou.^{3}

NOTE.—All that a rich man does or needs to do.

2591

He can never want a friend,
On whom wealth and wine attend.

有錢有酒。必有朋友

Yu^3 chʻien^2 yu^3 chiu,^{3} pi^4 yu^3 pʻêng^2 yu.^{3}

2592

When a big vessel comes to pieces, there still remain three piculs of nails.

大船破了還有三担釘

Ta^4 chʻuan^2 pʻo^4 liao^3 ʻhuan^2 yu^3 san^1 tan^1 ting.^{1}

2593

The rich are treated with the respect due to those thirty years older than themselves.

有錢長人三十歲

Yu^3 chʻien^2 chang^4 jên^2 san^1 shih^2 sui.^{4}

2594

Heroes walk a dangerous path; the rich are like flowering branches.

英雄行險道。富貴似花枝

Ying^1 hsiung^2 hsing^2 hsien^3 tao^4; fu^4 kuei^4 ssŭ^4 ʻhua^1 chih.^{1}

2595

If a man has money every place is *Yang-chou* to him.

有錢到處是揚州

Yu^3 chʻien^4 tao^4 chʻu^4 shih^4 yang^4 chou.^{1}

2596

A real rich man is careless of his dress.

眞財主不穿衣

Chên^1 ts'ai^2 chu^3 pu^4 ch'uan^1 i.^{1}

2597

Though you have money, you cannot buy what is not to sell.

有錢難買不賣貨

Yu^3 ch'ien^2 nan^2 mai^3 pu^4 mai^4 'huo.^{4}

2598

There is never a poor man under a gauze hat.

紗帽底下無窮人

Sha^1 mao^4 ti^1 hsia^4 wu^2 ch'iung^2 jên.^{2}

NOTE.—The gauze hat namely of the *Ming* mandarins.

2599

His person loses dignity who has no servants under him.

手下無人身不貴

Shou^3 hsia^4 wu^2 jên^2 shên^1 pu^4 kuei.^{4}

2600

However rich you may be, never slight the literati, nor be rude to artisans.

家有萬貫不可輕師慢匠

Chia^1 yu^3 wan^4 kuan^4 pu^4 k'o^3 ch'ing^1 shih^1 man^4 chiang.^{4}

2601

A great tree attracts the wind.

樹大招風

Shu^4 ta^4 chao^1 fêng.^{1}

NOTE.—A rich man is likely to tempt the squeezers.

CHAPTER IV.

RICH AND POOR MEN.

— 2602 —

The wealthy can no more the village clubs suppress,
Than mountains can the plains of sunshine dispossess.

富貴壓不倒鄉黨

Fu^{4} kuei^{4} ya^{1} pu^{4} tao^{3} hsiang^{1} tang,^{3}

山高遮不住太陽

Shan^{1} kao^{1} chê^{1} pu^{4} chu^{4} tʻai^{4} yang.^{2}

— 2603 —

The rich man anticipates years in advance ;
The poor can but think of what's under his glance.

富人思來年。窮人思眼前

Fu^{4} jên^{2} ssŭ^{1} lai^{2} nien^{2}; chʻiung^{2} jên^{2} ssü^{1} yen^{3} chʻien.^{2}

— 2604 —

Better mend old garments as a poor man's wife,
Than as a rich man's concubine pass your life.

寧可與窮人補破衣

Ning^{2} kʻo^{3} yü^{3} chʻiung^{2} jên^{2} pu^{3} pʻo^{4} i,^{1}

不可與富人當妾妻

Pu^{4} kʻo^{3} yü^{3} fu^{4} jên^{2} tang^{4} chʻieh^{4} chʻi.^{1}

— 2605 —

Let not the poor man murmur, nor the rich man boast in pride,
For with whom are either wealth or want certain to abide ?

貧不怨來富不誇

Pʻin^{3} pu^{4} yüan^{4} lai^{2} fu^{4} pu^{4} kʻua,^{1}

那有久富長貧家

Na^{3} yu^{3} chiu^{3} fu^{4} chʻang^{2} pʻin^{3} chia^{1} ?

— 2606 —

Men honour those of wealth possessed ;
Dogs worry those who are ill-dressed.

人敬有的。狗咬醜的

Jên^{2} ching^{4} yu^{3} ti^{1}: kou^{3} yao^{3} chʻou^{3} ti.^{1}

2607

A man is a dragon, with money in store:
He's an insect without it, and nothing more.

有錢一條龍。無錢一條蟲

Yu^3 chʻien^2 yi^1 tʻiao^2 lung^2; wu^2 chʻien^2 yi^1 tʻiao^2 chʻung.^{2}

2608

He who has wealth has cause to weep;
He who has none may soundly sleep.

有銀着銀累。無銀得覺睡

Yu^3 yin^2 cho^1 yin^2 lei^3; wu^2 yin^2 tê^2 chiao^4 shui.^{4}

2609

Rich men spend their time on books;
After pigs a poor man looks.

富人讀書。窮漢餵猪

Fu^4 jên^2 tu^1 shu^1; chʻiung^2 ʻhan^4 wei^4 chu.^{1}

2610

The fragrant epidendrum may beneath the jungle hide;
The future duke or monarch may beneath thatched roofs abide.

蒿草之下或有蘭香

ʻHao^1 tsʻao^3 chih^1 hsia^4 ʻhuo^4 yu^3 lan^2 hsiang^1;

茅茨之屋或有公王

Mao^2 tzʻŭ^2 chih^1 wu^1 ʻhuo^4 yu^3 kung^1 wang.^{2}

2611

The poor enjoy the grace of the rich; the rich the grace of Heaven.

窮沾富恩。富沾天恩

Chʻiung^2 chan^1 fu^4 ên^1; fu^4 chan^1 tʻien^1 ên.^{1}

2612

A poor man associating with a rich man, will soon be too poor to buy even a pair of breeches.

窮的伴富的。伴的沒褲子

Chʻiung^2 ti^1 pan^4 fu^4 ti,^{1} pan^4 ti^1 mu^2 kʻu^4 tzŭ.^{3}

2613

If poor don't lose your self-reliance; if rich don't act like a fool.

窮莫失志。富莫顛狂
Chʻiung^2 mo^4 shih^1 chih^4; fu^4 mo^4 tien^1 kʻuang.^{2}

2614

If poor don't cheat; if rich don't presume.

貧不可欺。富不可恃
Pʻin^3 pu^4 kʻo^3 chʻi^1; fu^4 pu^4 kʻo^3 shih.^{4}

2615

The rich have many learned friends; the poor have none at all.

富貴多士。貧賤寡交
Fu^4 kuei^4 to^1 shih^4; pʻin^3 chien^4 kua^3 chiao.^{1}

2616

The well-fed know nothing of hunger; the rich nothing of the hardships of the poor.

飽人不知餓人飢
Pao^3 jên^2 pu^4 chih^1 o^4 jên^2 chi^1;
富人不知窮寒苦
fu^4 jên^2 pu^4 chih^1 chʻiung^2 ʻhan^2 kʻu.^{3}

2617

A poor man easily turns flatterer; a rich man soon grows very proud.

貧則易諂。富而多驕
Pʻin^3 tsê^2 i^4 chʻan^3; fu^4 êrh^2 to^1 chiao.^{1}

2618

Nobody calls on the poor man though he dwell in the market place; but distant relations visit the rich man in his retired mountain home.

貧居鬧市無人問
Pʻin^3 chu^1 nao^4 shih^4 wu^2 jên^2 wên^4;
富在深山有遠親
fu^4 tsai^4 shên^1 shan^1 yu^3 yüan^3 chʻin.^{1}

2619

The poor cling to the rich, not the rich to the poor. *Lit.:* It is the crust which sticks to the rice, not the rice which sticks to it.

只 有 巴 巴 粘 飯
Chih^3 yu^3 pa^1 pa^1 chan^1 fan,^{4}
沒 有 飯 粘 巴 巴
Mu^2 yu^3 fan^4 chan^1 pa^1 pa.^{1}

—— 2620 ——

If you have money your words are taken for truth; if not, they are taken for lies; you doubt it? see the wine at a feast,—cup after cup is first pressed on the rich.

有 錢 道 眞 語。無 錢 語 不 眞
Yu^3 chʻien^2 tao^4 chên^1 yü^3; wu^2 chʻien^2 yü^3 pu^4 chên^1:
不 信 但 看 筵 中 酒
pu^4 shih^4? tan^4 kʻan^4 yen^2 chung^1 chiu^3—
杯 杯 先 勸 有 錢 人
pei^1 pei^1 hsien^1 chʻüan^4 yu^3 chʻien^2 jên.^{2}

—— 2621 ——

The poor have peace; the rich many troubles.

貧 窮 自 在。富 貴 多 憂
Pʻin^3 chʻiung^2 tzŭ^4 tsai^4; fu^4 kuei^4 to^1 yu.^{1}

—— 2622 ——

The rich must adhere to duty; the poor must not indulge vain thoughts.

富 貴 定 要 依 本 分
Fu^4 kuei^4 ting^4 yao^4 i^1 pên^3 fên^1;
貧 窮 不 必 枉 思 量
pʻin^3 chʻiung^2 pu^4 pi^4 wang^3 ssŭ^1 liang.^{2}

—— 2623 ——

The rich feed on flesh; the poor on herbs.

富 貴 肉 食。貧 賤 藿 食
Fu^4 kuei^4 jou^4 shih^2; pʻin^3 chien^4 ho^4 shih.^{2}

—— 2624 ——

A man's wealth exalts him three degrees; and a man's poverty degrades him three degrees.

有 錢 高 三 輩。無 錢 低 三 輩
Yu^3 chʻien^2 kao^1 san^1 pei^4; wu^2 chʻien^2 ti^1 san^1 pei.^{4}

2625

The poor man must not murmur; and the rich man must not boast.

貧寒休要怨。富貴不須驕

P'in^3 'han^2 hsiu^1 yao^4 yüan^4; fu^4 kuei^4 pu^4 hsü^1 chiao.^{1}

2626

The well-fed and well-warmed indulge lustful thoughts; the pined and starved encourage thoughts of stealing.

飽煖思淫慾飢寒起盜心

Pao^3 nuan^3 ssŭ^1 yin^2 yü^4; chi^1 'han^2 ch'i^3 tao^4 hsin.^{1}

2627

Those who have money can appear in public; those who have no clothes cannot leave their own doors.

有錢堪出衆。無衣懶出門

Yu^3 ch'ien^2 k'an^1 ch'u^1 chung^4; wu^2 i^1 lan^3 ch'u^1 mên.^{2}

2628

Even the Son of Heaven has his poor relations.

天子脚下有貧親

T'ien^2 tzŭ^3 chiao^3 hsia^3 yu^3 p'in^2 ch'in.^{1}

2629

Even the Emperor has straw-sandalled relations.

皇帝亦有草鞋親

'Huang^2 ti^4 i^4 yu^3 ts'ao^3 hsieh^2 ch'in.^{1}

2630

When one is poor, his parents disown him; but when rich, relations revere him.

貧窮則父母不子

P'in^3 ch'iung^2 tsê^2 fu^4 mu^3 pu^4 tzŭ^3;

富貴則親戚畏懼

fu^4 kuei^4 tsê^2 ch'in^1 ch'i^4 wei^4 chü.^{4}

NOTE.—This is the saying of an ancient worthy named *Su Ch'in* (蘇秦), who flourished as Prime Minister of the Six States of *Ch'i* (齊), *Ts'ou* (楚), *Yen* (燕), *Tsao* (趙), *Wei* (魏) and *'Han* (韓), contemporary with the reign of *Shih 'Huang Ti* (始皇帝) of the *Ch'in* (秦), B. C. 246. He found it true in his own experience. Having tried in vain to find employment in the service of *Shih 'Huang Ti*, he returned crest-fallen to his native state of *Tsao*, only to be ill-received by his parents, wife, and all. After this he gave himself most earnestly to study, often piercing his thigh to keep himself awake. By and by he induced the six small States to make a defensive alliance against the *Chʻin* (秦). His success in this diplomacy gained for him very high rank and widely extended fame. On this, returning to his native place, he was met 30 *li* away from the house by parents, wife, relatives, and friends: hence his famous saying. See the *Chien lio* (鑑畧), *Chan kuo chi* (戰國記).

2631

The poor man's rage, and the rich man's eyes, are great.

窮人的氣大。富人的眼大

Chʻiung^2 jên^2 ti^1 chʻi^4 ta^4; fu^4 jên^2 ti^1 yen^3 ta.^{4}

2632

Though you have money you cannot buy a son; though you have none you may beg a wife with some.

有錢難買親生子

Yu^3 chʻien^2 nan^2 mai^3 chʻin^1 shêng^1 tzŭ^3;

無錢可討有錢妻

wu^2 chʻien^2 kʻo^3 tʻao^3 yu^3 chʻien^2 chʻi.^{1}

2633

The rich man expends money; the poor man strength.

富人捨錢。窮人捨力

Fu^4 jên^2 shê^3 chʻien^2; chʻiung^2 jén^2 shê^3 li.^{4}

2634

The poor must not quarrel with the rich; nor the rich with magistrates.

窮莫與富鬬。富莫與官鬬

Chʻiung^2 mo^4 yü^3 fu^4 tou^4; fu^4 mo^4 yü^3 kuan^1 tou.^{4}

CHAPTER V.

RICHES.

— 2635 —

Great possessions depend on fate;
On diligence small possessions wait.

大富由命。小富由勤

Ta4 fu4 yu2 ming4; hsiao3 fu4 yu2 chʻin.2

— 2636 —

That man is well-to-do in whose house we see,
Fuel, rice, oil, salt, sauce, vinegar, and tea.

柴米油鹽醬醋茶

Chʻai2 mi3 yu2 yen2 chiang4 tsʻu4 chʻa,2

七字安排好人家

Chʻi1 tzŭ4 an1 pʻai2 ʻhao3 jên2 chia.1

— 2637 —

When rats run off with gourds we find,
The thick end always comes behind.

老鼠拖葫蘆。大頭在後頭

Lao3 shu3 tʻo1 ʻhu2 lu,2 ta4 tʻou2 tsai4 ʻhou4 tʻou.2

NOTE.—This proverb is applicable in the case of gradual acquisition of wealth.

— 2638 —

Covet wealth,—and want it:
Don't,—and luck will grant it.

貪財不得財。不貪財自來

Tʻan1 tsʻai2 pu4 tê2 tsʻai2; pu4 tʻan1 tsʻai2 tzŭ4 lai.2

— 2639 —

Sweetness followeth bitter fears,
And leaves us rich for a myriad years.

先苦後甜。富貴萬年

Hsien1 kʻu3 ʻhou4 tʻien,2 fu4 kuei4 wan4 nien.2

— 2640 —

Consult a fortune-teller would you a fortune make;
His answer will direct you without the least mistake.

求財點卦。分毫不差
Chʻiu^2 tsʻai^2 tien^3 kua^4; fên^1 ʻhao^2 pu^4 chʻa.^{1}

2641

When the bells on one's horses resound,
All one's relations gather around.

馬上銅鈴响。親戚都來往
Ma^3 shang^4 tʻung^2 ling^2 hsiang,^{3} chʻin^1 chʻi^4 tu^1 lai^2 wang.^{3}

2642

A glimpse of money makes the blind man see;
Makes the Bonze dispose of his breviary.

瞎子見錢眼也開
Hsia^2 tzŭ^3 chien^4 chʻien^2 yen^3 yeh^3 kʻai^1;
和尙見錢經也賣
ʻHo^2 shang^4 chien^4 chʻien^2 ching^1 yeh^3 mai.^{4}

2643

A pig's head grows tender before the fire;
So before money all quarrels expire.

火到猪頭爛。錢到公事辦
ʻHuo^3 tao^4 chu^1 tʻou^2 lan^4; chʻien^2 tao^4 kung^1 shih^4 pan.^{4}

2644

Estates must descend from heir to heir;
Who has one now will have it to spare.

前人田地後人收
Chʻien^2 jên^2 tʻien^2 ti^4 ʻhou^4 jên^2 shou^1;
還有收人在後頭
ʻHuan^2 yu^3 shou^1 jên^2 tsai^4 ʻhou^4 tʻou.^{2}

2645

Wealth serves for heroism; wine for bravery.

財是英雄。酒是胆
Tsʻai^2 shih^4 ying^1 hsiung^2; chiu^3 shih^4 tan.^{3}

2646

Great wealth troubles its owner; too much food breeds discomfort.

財多累己。食飽傷心
Tsʻai^2 to^1 lei^3 chi^3; shih^2 pao^3 shang^1 hsin.^{1}

2647

Who make a fortune meanly will not enjoy it long.

刻薄成家。理無久享

Kʻo4 po2 chʻêng2 chia,1 li3 wu2 chiu3 hsiang.3

2648

Warn men against keen coveting of wealth, for wealth thus coveted provokes the wrath of Heaven.

勸人不必苦貪財

Chʻüan4 jên2 pu4 pi4 kʻu3 tʻan1 tsʻai2;

貪得財來天降災

tʻan1 tê2 tsʻai2 lai2 tʻien1 chiang4 tsai.1

2649

Honour springs from diligence, and riches from economy.

貴自勤中得。富自儉裡來

Kuei4 tzŭ4 chʻin2 chung1 tê,2 fu4 tzŭ4 chien3 li3 lai.2

2650

Wealth and honour have their root, and cleverness its seed.

富貴有根。聰明有種

Fu4 kuei4 yu3 kên,1 tsung1 ming2 yu3 chung.4

2651

When any family has gold, outsiders have money-scales.

家有黃金外有戥秤

Chia1 yu3 ʻhuang2 chin,1 wai4 yu3 têng3 chʻêng.3

2652

Who does not desire riches? *Lit.:* What cat will not worry rats?

那個猫兒不吃老鼠

Na3 ko4 mao1 êrh2 pu4 chʻih1 lao3 shü.3

2653

Shên Wan san killing a man.

沈萬三打死人

Shên3 Wan4 san1 ta3 ssŭ3 jên.2

NOTE.—*Shên Wan san* of *Nankin* was a sort of Chinese Rothschild. If he happened to kill a man, what matter? he had plenty of money to satisfy the relatives and so escape punishment.

2654

Yellow gold is not grown from seed, but only springs up in diligent and economical families.

黃金無種。獨生勤儉人家

ʻHuang² chin¹ wu² chung,⁴ tu² shêng¹ chʻin² chien³ jên² chia.¹

2655

Wealth is but dung; Benevolence and Righteousness are worth thousands of gold.

錢財如糞土。仁義值千金

Chʻien² tsʻai² ju² fên⁴ tʻu³; jên² i⁴ chih² chʻien¹ chin.¹

2656

If you long for wealth and honour, you must work yourself to death for it.

欲求生富貴。須下死工夫

Yü⁴ chʻiu² shêng¹ fu⁴ kuei,⁴ hsü¹ hsia⁴ ssŭ³ kung¹ fu.¹

2657

Men grind a knife because they dislike it blunt; but when they have sharpened it it cuts their fingers; men pray for wealth because they dislike small incomes; but when they get much it is a personal injury to them.

磨刀恨不利。刀利傷人指

Mo² tao¹ ʻhen⁴ pu⁴ li⁴; tao¹ li⁴ shang¹ jên² chih.³

求財恨不多。財多害人己

chʻiu² tsʻai² ʻhen⁴ pu⁴ to¹; tsʻai² to¹ ʻhai⁴ jên² chi.³

2658

A man seldom gets rich without ill-gotten gain; as a horse does not fatten without feeding in the night.

人無混財不富

Jên² wu² ʻhun⁴ tsʻai² pu⁴ fu⁴;

馬無夜草不肥

ma³ wu² yeh⁴ tsʻao³ pu⁴ fei.²

2659

Pray not for gold, jade, and all sorts of expensive things; but desire that each of your descendants may be virtuous.

不求金玉重重貴
Pu⁴ ch'iu² chin¹ yü⁴ ch'ung² ch'ung³ kuei⁴;
但願兒孫個個賢
tan⁴ yüan⁴ êrh² sun¹ ko⁴ ko⁴ hsien.²

2660

Men will die for wealth, as birds for food.

人爲財死。鳥爲食亡
Jên² wei⁴ ts'ai² ssŭ³ niao³ wei⁴ shih⁴ wang.²

2661

Though your fields yield bushels of rice, you can eat but a pint per day; though your house be never so large, you sleep on but eight feet by night.

良田萬頃日食一升
Liang² t'ien² wan⁴ ch'ing³ jih⁴ shih² yi¹ shêng¹;
大厦千間夜眠八尺
ta⁴ hsia⁴ ch'ien¹ chien¹ yeh⁴ mien² pa¹ ch'ih.³

2662

Much money moves the gods.

廣錢通神
Kuang³ ch'ien² t'ung¹ shên.²

2663

Money hides many offences.

有錢蓋百醜
Yu³ ch'ien² kai⁴ pai³ ch'ou.³

2664

Money can buy living beings for the vilest of purposes.

有錢買得活人倒地
Yu³ ch'ien² mai³ tê² huo² jên² tao³ ti.⁴

2665

Wealth infatuates as well as beauty.

不但色迷人。財也能迷人
Pu⁴ tan⁴ sê⁴ mi² jên,² ts'ai² yeh³ nêng² mi² jên.²

2666

Ability to command does not lie in being very rich; elegance and grace do not depend on multitudes of dresses.

會使不在家豪富
ʻHui^4 shih^3 pu^4 tsai^4 chia^1 ʻhao^2 fu^4;
風流不用着衣多
fêng^1 liu^2 pu^4 yung^4 cho^2 i^1 to.^{1}

2667

Getting gain is like digging with a needle; spending it like water soaking into sand.

利錢猶如針挑土
Li^4 chʻien^2 yu^2 ju^2 chên^1 tʻiao^1 tʻu^3;
用錢猶如水冲沙
yung^4 chʻien^2 yu^2 ju^2 shui^3 chʻung^1 sha.^{1}

2668

Wit protects one man, wealth and honour protect a whole family.

聰明保一人。富貴保一家
Tsung^1 ming^2 pao^3 yi^1 jên,^{2} fu^4 kuei^4 pao^3 yi^1 chia.^{1}

2669

The five grains are more precious than pearls and jade.

珠玉非寶。五穀爲寶
Chü^1 yü^4 fei^1 pao,^{3} wu^3 ku^3 wei^2 pao.^{3}

2670

Amiability begets riches.

和氣生財
ʻHo^2 chʻi^4 shêng^1 tsʻai.^{2}

2671

Obstinate men waste wealth, as obstinate oxen strength.

人拗損財。牛拗損力
Jên^2 yao^3 sun^3 tsʻai,^{2} niu^2 yao^3 sun^3 li.^{4}

2672

"If riches can be acquired with propriety, then acquire them; but let not unjust wealth be sought for with violence."

有道之錢方可取
Yu^3 tao^4 chih^1 chʻien^2 fang^1 kʻo^3 chʻü^3;
無道之財莫强求
wu^2 tao^4 chih^1 tsʻai^2 mo^4 chʻiang^2 lai.^{2}

2673

He who gets a large sum by chance, will either be made very happy, or very miserable by it.

無故而得千金
Wu² ku⁴ êrh² tê² ch'ien¹ chin,¹
不有大福必有大禍
pu⁴ yu³ ta⁴ fu² pi⁴ yu³ ta⁴ 'huo.⁴

2674

When a virtuous man has much wealth, it diminishes his knowledge; when a worthless man has much wealth, it increases his faults.

賢人多財則損其志
Hsien² jên² to¹ ts'ai² tsê² sun³ ch'i² chih⁴:
小人多財則益其過
hsiao³ jên² to¹ ts'ai² tsê² i² ch'i² kuo.⁴

2675

Unjustly-gotten wealth is but snow sprinkled with hot water; lands improperly obtained are but sand-banks in a stream.

無義錢財湯潑雪
Wu² i⁴ ch'ien² ts'ai² t'ang¹ p'o¹ hsüeh³;
儻來田地水推沙
t'ang³ lai² t'ien² ti⁴ shui³ t'ui¹ sha.¹

2676

Never desire unjustly-gotten wealth; nor undertake affairs which don't belong to you.

無義錢財休着想
Wu² i⁴ ch'ien² ts'ai² hsiu¹ cho² hsiang³;
不干己事莫當頭
pu⁴ kan¹ chi³ shih⁴ mo⁴ tang¹ t'ou.²

2677

Unjustly-gotten wealth will go unjustly.

寃枉財來寃枉去
Yüan¹ wang³ ts'ai² lai² yüan¹ wang³ ch'ü.⁴

2678

The fields of the *Changs*, and the houses of the *Lis*, to-day belong to the *Chʻiens*, and to-morrow to the *Lus*.

張門田李門屋
Chang^1 mên^2 tʻien^2 Li^4 mên^2 wu.^{1}
今日錢家明日陸
chin^1 jih^4 Chʻien^2 chia^1 ming^2 jih^4 Lu.^{4}

2679

One family with plenty to eat and wear is the envy of a thousand other families; and half a life-time's fame provokes the resentment of a hundred generations.

一家飽煖千家怨
Yi^1 chia^1 pao^3 nuan^3 chʻien^1 chia^1 yüan^4;
半世功名百世冤
pan^4 shih^4 kung^1 ming^2 pai^3 shih^4 yüan.^{1}

2680

Do not covet wealth on which you have no claim.

勿貪意外之財
Wu^4 tʻan^1 i^4 wai^4 chih^1 tsʻai.^{2}

2681

To grow rich by one's own sole endeavours.

白手成家
Pai^2 shou^3 chʻêng^2 chia.^{1}

2682

Whoever can foresee the affairs of three days, will be rich for several thousand years.

能知三日事。富貴幾千年
Nêng^2 chih^1 san^1 jih^4 shih,^{4} fu^4 kuei^4 chi^3 chʻien^1 nien.^{2}

2683

Come easy, go easy.

易得來。易得去
I^4 tê^2 lai,^{2} i^4 tê^2 chʻü.^{4}

NOTE.—Generally said of wealth.

CHAPTER VI.

RICHES AND POVERTY.

—— 2684 ——

"With money you're a brave son of '*Han*;
Without it you cannot play the man."

有錢男兒漢。無錢漢兒難。

Yu^3 chʻien^2 nan^2 êrh^2 ʻhan^4; wu^2 chʻien^2 ʻhan^4 êrh^3 nan.^{2}

—— 2685 ——

Riches spring from small beginnings; poverty is the result of non-calculation.

富從升合起。貧因不算來

Fu^4 tsʻung^2 shêng^1 ʻho^2 chi^3; pʻin^3 yin^1 pu^4 suan^4 lai.^{2}

—— 2686 ——

Politeness and Righteousness are the children of wealth and contentment: Robbery and Rebellion are the offspring of poverty.

禮義生於富足

Li^3 i^4 shêng^1 yü^2 fu^4 tsu^2:

盜賊出於貧窮

tao^4 tsei^2 chʻu^1 yü^2 pʻin^3 chʻiung.^{2}

—— 2687 ——

With money one may command devils; without it one cannot summon a man.

有錢使得鬼動

Yu^3 chʻien^2 shih^3 tê^2 kuei^3 tʻung^2;

無錢喚不得人來

wu^2 chʻien^2 ʻhuan^4 pu^4 tê^2 jên^2 lai.^{2}

—— 2688 ——

Riches and honours are altogether the results of diligence and economy; poverty is altogether occasioned by a slack hand.

富貴皆因勤儉起

Fu^4 kuei^4 chieh^1 yin^1 chʻin^2 chien^3 chʻi^3;

貧窮都爲手頭鬆

pʻin^3 chʻiung^2 tu^1 wei^4 shou^3 tʻou^2 sung.^{1}

2689

Diligence and economy are the root of wealth and honour; whilst idleness is the shoot of poverty and disgrace.

勤 儉 富 貴 之 本
Ch'in² chien³ fu⁴ kuei⁴ chih¹ pên³;
懶 惰 貧 賤 之 苗
lan³ to⁴ p'in³ chien⁴ chih¹ miao.²

2690

He who is patient in poverty, may become rich.

耐 得 貧。守 得 富
Nai⁴ tê² p'in,³ shou³ tê² fu.⁴

2691

A gay life melts away fortune.

頑 得 化 氷 無 形
Wan² tê² 'hua⁴ shui³ wu² hsing.²

2692

A poverty-stricken family is, as it were, washed clean; a well-to-do family puts on the appearance of youth.

家 貧 如 水 洗。家 寬 出 少 年
Chia¹ p'in³ ju² shui³ hsi³; chia¹ k'uan¹ ch'u¹ shao³ nien.²

MISCELLANEOUS.

2693

In the mock-waves of painted water, no fishes dwell;
In your embroidered flowers though fine, there is no smell.

畫水無魚空作浪

ʻHua^4 shui^3 wu^2 yü^2 kʻung^1 tso^4 lang^4;

繡花雖好不聞香

Hsiu^4 ʻhua^1 sui^4 ʻhao^3 pu^4 wên^2 hsiang.^{1}

2694

Get up by yourself should you happen to fall;
And do not depend on another at all.

自己跌倒自己扒

Tzŭ^4 chi^3 tieh^2 tao^3 tzŭ^4 chi^3 pa^1;

不要靠着別人家

Pu^4 yao^4 kʻao^4 cho^2 pieh^2 jên^2 chia.^{1}

2695

A great tree affords a pleasant shade.

大樹好遮陰

Ta^4 shu^4 ʻhao^3 chê^1 yin.^{1}

2696

I only heard a noise upstairs, but saw no one descend.

只聽樓板响。不見人下樓

Chih^3 tʻing^1 lou^2 pan^3 hsiang,^{3} pu^4 chien^4 jên^2 hsia^4 lou.^{2}

2697

Whilst fire remains in your cooking-stove, guests will never cease to arrive.

竈裡不熄火。路上不斷人

Tsao^4 li^3 pu^4 hsi^2 ʻhuo,^{3} lu^4 shang^4 pu^4 tuan^4 jên.^{2}

2698

Necessity of assistance. *Lit.:* However high a city wall may be, it must have guards stationed inside and outside.

城 墻 高 萬 丈。內 外 要 人 輔
Ch'êng² ch'iang² kao¹ wan⁴ chang,⁴ nei⁴ wai⁴ yao⁴ jên² fu.¹

2699

One grain of rats dung will spoil a whole pan of rice.

一 粒 老 鼠 屎 打 壞 一 鍋 飯
Yi¹ li⁴ lao³ shu³ shih³ ta³ 'huai⁴ yi¹ kuo¹ fan.⁴

2700

He who fishes in muddy water cannot distinguish the great from the small.

混 水 捉 魚。大 小 難 分
'Hun⁴ shui³ cho¹ yü,² ta⁴ hsiao³ nan² fen.¹

2701

Cabinet ministers, head clerks, and beggars, have got as far as they can go.

官 到 尙 書 吏 到 都
Kuan¹ tao⁴ shang⁴ shu¹ li⁴ tao⁴ tu,¹
人 到 討 飯 盡 了 頭
jên² tao⁴ t'ao³ fan⁴ chin⁴ liao³ t'ou.²

2702

A clay drumstick makes but one sound.

黃 泥 巴 鼓 搥 一 下 響
'Huang² ni² pa¹ ku³ ch'ui² yi¹ hsia⁴ hsiang.³

NOTE.—This may be said either of men lacking perseverance, or of things lacking durability.

2703

Scraping iron from a needle's point.

針 杪 上 削 鐵
Chên¹ miao³ shang⁴ hsiao¹ t'ieh.³

NOTE.—The opposite of a lucrative employment.

2704

One horse one saddle.

一 馬 一 鞍
Yi¹ ma³ yi¹ an.¹

2705

It is easier to build up a fortune than to retain one.

創業易。守業難
Ch'uang⁴ yeh⁴ i,⁴ shou³ yeh⁴ nan.²

2706

It is easier to gain than to secure the advantages of victory.

戰勝易。守勝難
Chan⁴ shêng⁴ i,⁴ shou³ shêng⁴ nan.²

2707

The well frog is best in the well.

井裡蝦蟆井裡好
Ching³ li³ hsia¹ ma¹ ching³ li³ 'hao.³

2708

Ghosts fear men much more than men fear them.

人有三分怕鬼
Jên² yu³ san¹ fên¹ p'a⁴ kuei³;
鬼有七分怕人
Kuei³ yu³ ch'i¹ fên¹ p'a⁴ jên.²

2709

First come first served. *Lit.:* Who comes first shall be prince; the next shall be minister.

先到爲君。後到爲臣
Hsien¹ tao⁴ wei² chün¹; 'hou⁴ tao⁴ wei² ch'ên.²

2710

Customs vary in every place.

百里不同風。千里不同俗
Pai³ li³ pu⁴ t'ung² fêng,¹ ch'ien¹ li³ pu⁴ t'ung² su.²

2711

Pretence may become reality.

弄假成眞
Nung⁴ chia³ ch'êng² chên.¹

2712

Six of one and half a dozen of the other. *Lit.:* Half a catty and eight ounces.

半斤八兩
Pan⁴ chin¹ pa¹ liang.³

2713

Planting rice and cutting wheat—busy on all hands.

栽秧割麥兩頭忙

Tsai^1 yang^1 ko^1 mai^4 liang^3 tʻou^2 mang.^{2}

2714

Too busy for pleasure. *Lit.:* I have both to beat the drum and row the boat.

獨打鼓獨划船

Tu^2 ta^3 ku^3 tu^2 hua^2 chʻuan.^{2}

2715

Everything has its special use.

一物服一行

Yi^1 wu^4 fu^2 yi^1 ʻhang.^{2}

2716

A cup in the hand is worth all besides.

萬事不如杯在手

Wan^4 shih^4 pu^4 ju^2 pei^1 tsai^4 shou.^{3}

2717

Self-respect. *Lit.:* He will be honoured who respects himself; but he who holds himself cheap will be lightly esteemed.

自尊自貴。自輕自賤

Tzŭ^4 tsun^1 tzŭ^4 kuei^4; tzŭ^4 chʻing^1 tzŭ^4 chien.^{4}

2718

If a countryman of mine gets beaten I am thereby weakened.

輸了鄉親弱了己

Shu^1 liao^3 hsiang^1 chʻin^1 jo^4 liao^3 chi.^{3}

2719

However much you have promised never fail to give it.

許人一物千金不移

Hsü^3 jên^2 yi^1 wu^4 chʻien^1 chin^1 pu^4 i.^{2}

2720

An able man loves to diminish work; and when diminished it proves him able; one lacking ability, loves to get up an affair; and when got up, it proves him unable.

有 本 事 好 省 事
Yu^3 pên^3 shih^4 ʻhao^4 shêng^3 shih^4;
省 得 事 來 有 本 事
Shêng^3 tê^2 shih^4 lai^2 yu^3 pên^3 shih^4:
沒 本 事 好 生 事
mu^2 pên^3 shih^4 ʻhao^4 shêng^1 shih^4;
生 得 事 來 沒 本 事
shêng^1 tê^2 shih^4 lai^2 mu^2 pên^3 shih.^{4}

NOTE.—This is designed to admonish imbecile people not to meddle with things too great for them. If furnishes also a very good example of play upon words.

INDEX.

諺語叢話

ERRATA.

Page	vi	for	"277"	read	"279."
„	vii	„	"310, 339, 389"	„	"311, 338, 388."
„	xiii	„	"2597"	„	"1597."
„	xvi	„	"2457, 2485, 2715"	„	"2458, 2486, 2716."
„	xx	„	"2716, 2450"	„	"2717, 2451."
„	xxiv	„	"2363"	„	"2364."
„	xxix	line 8. Before "sufficient"		read	"but those already quoted are."
„	xxxi	add one to all the references.			
„	xxxii	for "2362" read "2363."			

Proverb	No.	53	for "螞"	read	"蟆 ma.^{2}"
„	„	68	„ "overs"	„	"covers."
„	„	105	„ "instalements"	„	"instalments."
„	„	112	„ "綢"	„	"稠."
„	„	117	„ "傳" chuan^{4}"	„	"傅 fu.^{4}"
„	„	157	„ "佑"	„	"估."
„	„	175	„ "尙"	„	"上."
„	„	184	„ "灑"	„	"曬."
„	„	217	„ "êrh^{3}"	„	"érh.^{2}"
„	„	240	„ "ta^{4}"	„	"tu.^{4}"
„	„	278	„ "生"	„	"聲."
„	„	314	„ "Hiang^{2}"	„	"Hsiang.^{1}"
„	„	369	„ "爲"	„	"猶."
„	„	378	„ "圖"	„	"團."

Proverb	No.	392	for	"主"	read	"生."
,,	,,	399	,,	"化 ʻhua⁴"	,,	"他 tʻa.¹"
,,	,,	437	,,	"蒸 chêng¹"	,,	"砧 chên.¹"
,,	,,	452	,,	"Wa²"	,,	"Wu.²"
,,	,,	472	,,	"Hsiao¹"	,,	"Hsiao.²"
,,	,,	510	,,	"proligomena"	,,	"prolegomena."
,,	,,	513	,,	"籍"	,,	"蹟."
,,	,,	518	,,	"yeh³"	,,	"ti.⁴"
,,	,,	578	,,	"確"	,,	"碓."
,,	,,	594	,,	"毛"	,,	"茅."
,,	,,	601	,,	"chiang¹"	,,	"chiang.⁴"
,,	,,	644	,,	"tʻao¹"	,,	"tʻiao.¹"
,,	,,	688	,,	"wei¹"	,,	"wei.²"
,,	,,	793	,,	"chai¹"	,,	"chia.¹"
,,	,,	795	,,	"tʻing¹"	,,	"tʻien.¹"
,,	,,	812	,,	"差"	,,	"善."
,,	,,	857	,,	"hʻsi³"	,,	"hsi.³"
,,	,,	886	,,	"告"	,,	"呌."
,,	,,	904	,,	"ming³"	,,	"ming.²"
,,	,,	928	,,	"息"	,,	"熄."
,,	,,	940	,,	"吃"	,,	"乞."
,,	,,	962	,,	"閒 hsien²"	,,	"間 chien.¹"
,,	,,	973	,,	"茗"	,,	"筶."
,,	,,	977	,,	"哄 ʻhung³"	,,	"轟 ʻhung.¹"
,,	,,	997	,,	"pu⁴"	,,	"pei.¹"
,,	,,	1017	,,	"yung²"	,,	"yung.⁴"
,,	,,	1023	,,	"nan¹"	,,	"nan.²"
,,	,,	1034	,,	"Kʻai⁴"	,,	"Kʻai.¹"
,,	,,	1039	,,	"set"	,,	"let."
,,	,,	1104	,,	"pʻing¹"	,,	"pʻing.²"
,,	,,	1153 } 1155 }	,,	"事 shih⁴"	,,	"司 ssŭ.¹"
,,	,,	1157	,,	"ho²"	,,	"ju.²"
,,	,,	1199	,,	"殍 餓"	,,	"餓 殍."
,,	,,	1226	,,	"shêng¹"	,,	"sheng.⁴"
,,	,,	1234	,,	"his"	,,	"of."
,,	,,	1272	,,	"rears"	,,	"near."
,,	,,	1357	,,	"告花 Kao⁴ hua¹"	,,	{ "呌 化 chiao⁴ hua.⁴"

Pages	231,	233	for	“Rich and Poor Men,”	read	“Stupid Men.”
Proverb	No.	1374	”	“托 t'o^{1}”	”	“馱 to.^{4}”
”	”	1389	”	“空”	”	“孔.”
”	”	1427	”	“知 chih^{1}”	”	“智 chih.^{4}”
”	”	1491	”	“載 tsai^{4}”	”	“戴 tai.^{4}”
”	”	1613	”	“tê^{2}”	”	“ta.^{2}”
”	”	1619	”	“geni”	”	“genius.”
”	”	1682	”	“雖”	”	“雞.”
”	”	1699	”	“yuan^{4}”	”	“shu.^{4}”
”	”	1763	”	“chi^{1}”	”	“ch'i.^{1}”

Page 339 for “Gratitude,” read “Economy.”
Proverb No. 2007 for “p'ien,^{2}” read “pien.^{4}”
Page 355 for “Discretion,” read “Prince and Minister.”

Proverb	No.	2123	for	“chien^{2}”	read	“ch'ien.^{2}”
”	”	2149	”	“na^{2}”	”	“nan.^{2}”
”	”	2351	”	“so^{1}”	”	“so.^{3}”
”	”	2385	”	“ching^{1}”	”	“ch'ên.^{2}”
”	”	2433	”	“tsai^{2}”	”	“tsai.^{4}”
		”	”	“hsing^{1}”	”	“hsing.^{2}”
		”	”	“yin^{4}”	”	“yin.^{1}”
”	”	2435	”	“chih^{1}”	”	“chin.^{1}”
”	”	2437	”	“hsiang^{1}”	”	“yang.^{1}”
”	”	2460	”	“following”	”	“flowing.”
”	”	2486	”	“hung^{4}”	”	“hung.^{2}” *
”	”	2585	after	“good”	read	“man.”
”	”	2628	”	“T'ien^{2}”	read	“T'ien.^{1}”
”	”	2674	”	“志”	”	“智.”
”	”	2687	”	“t'ung^{2}”	”	“tung.^{4}”

Errors in punctuation, and mere misprints, are not corrected.

* N. B. This character is read “kang.^{4}” at Hankow, as in Peking.

漢文詩解

（*Poeseos Sinicæ Commentarii: The poetry of the Chinese*）

〔英〕德庇時（John Francis Davis）編譯

《漢文詩解》，英國德庇時編譯。德庇時（John Francis Davis，一七九五—一八九〇），英國漢學家。生於英國倫敦，一八一三年至廣州，任職於英國東印度公司，一八一六年隨阿美士德使團赴京覲見嘉慶帝。一八四四至一八四八年，任香港總督兼英國駐華公使。曾將中國文學作品譯爲英文，主要有《三與樓》（*Three Delicated Rooms*）、《賢文書》（*Maxims*）、《好逑傳》（*The Fortunate Union*）、《漢宮愁》（*The Sorrow of Han*）等。是書自兩方面研究中國詩歌：一爲組成詩句、對聯、對偶之特定規則及韻律産生之源泉；二爲中國詩歌之格律與詩魂、詩境與詩情之特點。據一八七〇年倫敦版影印。

THE POETRY OF THE CHINESE.

解詩文漢

POESEOS SINICÆ COMMENTARII.

THE POETRY OF THE CHINESE.

BY

SIR JOHN FRANCIS DAVIS, BART., K.C.B.,
F.R.S., &c.

NEW AND AUGMENTED EDITION.

LONDON:
ASHER AND CO., BEDFORD STREET.
BERLIN: 11, UNTER DEN LINDEN.
1870.

LONDON:

Printed at the Office of

THE FLYING DRAGON REPORTER,

3, George Yard, Lombard Street.

INTRODUCTION.

When this Treatise was first printed (now more than forty years ago), with types brought from China, in the quarto Transactions of the Royal Asiatic Society, the foreign character was so little known in England, that Lord Palmerston, with his usual pleasantry, said he took it "at first sight for a work on *Entomology.*" But the number of Entomologists (in this peculiar sense) has so increased in the last half century, that the eye has become sufficiently familiar with a page of Chinese type; and a newspaper printed in modern Greek has been followed, in our cosmopolitan London, by the *Fei-Loong*, or "Flying Dragon," a Chinese advertiser, in the original character.

Sir James Macintosh, reviewing in the *Edinburgh* a translation of the Chinese Penal Code by Sir George Staunton, made some striking remarks on its "European good sense," which seems to apply more or less to all branches of Chinese literature. "There is nothing of the monstrous *verbiage* of most other Asiatic productions,—none of the superstitious deliration, the miserable incoherence, the tremendous non-sequiturs, and eternal repetitions of those oracular performances. . . . . When we pass from the ravings of the Zendavesta or the Puranas to the tone of sense and business of this Chinese collection, we seem to be passing from darkness to light—from the drivellings of dotage to the exercise of an improved understanding." The late Lord Brougham, no incompetent judge, when dilating on the same subject, declared the following to be an "admirable precept":—*Let a man only correct himself with the severity he displays to others, and excuse others with the indulgence he shows himself.*

Perhaps the poetry of no language contains a more natural expression of feeling and sentiment, or a style less *ampoulé*, than the Tea-picking Ballad at page 68. This appeared in the *Chinese Repository* long after the first printing of the present Treatise, and the contributor then remarked that it confirmed and illustrated what has been herein advanced on the subject. It must be observed, however, that the construction of the verse in the Ballad is of the simplest description, far less artificial than most of the examples which have been herein adduced—in fact, more suitable to the subject and the occasion, that of a young girl singing at her work on a Spring morning, and giving vent to her almost childish feelings in girlish and pleasing language. The intrinsic merits of the piece are considerable, and the English version by Mr. W. T. Mercer, of Oxford University, so well conveys the meaning and spirit of the original, that I have been glad to avail myself of it.

When Mr. John Gibson Lockhart was editor, in 1829, of the *Quarterly Review*, he found a copy of this Treatise in MS. lying on Mr. Murray's table; and in one of our occasional walks from Regent's Park, about three in the afternoon, to Albemarle Street, he proposed that I should adapt it as an article to the *Quarterly*. This was accordingly done, and it appeared (together with other remarks on the Drama and Romance) in Vol. 41, though, of course, without the original character. After the lapse of a generation and a half, and with the present considerable additions, the reader at this remote date can hardly complain,—Δὶς κράμβη θάνατος.

The reproduction of the Essay, now long since out of print, and principally for the use of Chinese scholars, could not have been effected in the original character without the old type preserved in the archives of the Royal Asiatic Society, nor without the ample Chinese fount, and the able supervision of the Rev. Professor SUMMERS, of King's College, London, to whom, in the event of success, the author is bound to say, like Horace, "Quòd placeo (si placeo) tuum est."

漢文詩解

POESEOS SINICÆ COMMENTARII.

On the Poetry of the Chinese

"Quærere cæpit
Quid————utile ferrent:
Tentavit, quoque, rem si dignè vertere posset."
Hor.

———o———

In the arrangement of our subject, it may perhaps be useful to preserve so much regard to method, as to treat of it separately, under the following two heads:—

Part I. Versification, or the particular rules which prevail in the mere construction of lines, couplets, and stanzas; and the sources whence these derive their melody and rhythm.

Part II. A general view of the style and spirit of Chinese poetry, the character of its imagery and sentiment, and the extent to which it seems to admit of a precise classification, relatively to the divisions and nomenclature adopted in European literature.

To such as should find the first portion of our treatise dry and technical in its details, the second may possibly prove more attractive: but the order of discussion could hardly be inverted with propriety.

PART I.

In Chinese versification, the following are the circumstances which seem chiefly to demand our notice:—1. The nature of the sounds of which the spoken language consists, and the fitness of this for metrical composition. 2. The variation of certain tones, or accents, as prescribed by rule. 3. The use of poetical numbers or measure. 4. The observance of a regular cæsural pause, about the middle of each verse. 5. The use of terminal rhymes. 6. The rhythmical effect produced by the *parallelism* of couplets, which will be explained in its proper place. Compare to Hebrew: synonymous, antithetic, synthetic

1. Of the sounds of the spoken language. The attention of curious persons may perhaps be excited to ascertain what power of melody can be possessed by a system of speech, which has been represented to contain merely about four hundred *monosyllabic* sounds. They may naturally enough imagine, that Chinese poetry must, in point of euphony, rank with those defective verses censured by our own great poet:—

> Where ten low words oft creep in one dull line.

Low words, of any length, are certainly out of place in poetry; but that an English verse is much the worse for consisting of ten monosyllables, does not so clearly appear: and Pope's own poems abound in monosyllabic lines, as may be proved by the slightest examination. A few instances occur even of *couplets* so distinguished:—

> "Ah, if she lend not arms, as well as rules,
> What can she more than tell us we are fools!"
>
> "Talk what you will of taste, my friend, you'll find
> Two of a face, as soon as of a mind."
>
> "There are who have not—and, thank heav'n, there are
> Who, if they have not, think not worth their care."

A summary disposal of the question, by assuming, at once, that it is a case in which melody is unattainable, has to be reconciled with the obvious fact, that the Chinese take a passionate delight in their poetry. Is it likely that so large a portion of the human race should have persisted in the enthusiastic cultivation of an art, which is essentially incapable of possessing that very charm, which everywhere else forms a main element of its attractiveness?* It has pretty generally gone abroad, that *all* the Chinese words are strictly monosyllabic—which only proves that opinions, which nobody is particularly concerned in correcting, will sometimes pass current for a surprising length of time.—Perhaps the circumstance of every word filling the same space in the page, has assisted to perpetuate the notion. It is the business of the present treatise, however, to state all that can fairly be said in favour of its subject; and, with the concurrent opinion of Dr. Morrison, we will endeavour to produce facts, and institute comparisons, which may tend to prove that a considerable portion of the Chinese words are not *absolutely* monosyllabic.

Some of these, if expressed by the powers of the English alphabet, are written *heâe*, *keûen*, *heûé*, *leâou*—every vowel being distinctly pronounced,—and others cannot be properly expressed, except with the direct use of the diæresis, as *lëen*, *t'hëen*, *këë*, &c. Now, with respect to the latter of these, if the necessity for using such a mark were not, of itself, sufficient to prove that they are something more than mere monosyllables, the metrical examples of another language might serve to settle the point:—

> Their *flüid* bodies half dissolv'd in light—
>
> Like some gaunt *lïon* in his gloomy lair.

Any person who has been in the habit of hearing the Chinese pronounce their own language, knows that *lëen*, *sëen*, &c., are quite as dissyllabic as *lion*, *fluid*, and such other words, wherein no consonant intervenes between the two syllables. Similar examples, however, are by no means so abundant in our harsh modern languages, especially those of Germanic extraction, as in Latin and Greek, where almost every line of poetry teems with such vowel sounds; and where (at least in the latter) we constantly meet with *three* successive vowels, forming as many separate syllables—the very circumstance which constitutes the ground of its superor melody.

* A writer of the "Mémoires sur les Chinois" asserts, that their poetry is susceptible of even imitative harmony, and this is no doubt true: but the instance which he adduces may perhaps make the reader smile. "On vante," says he, "l'harmonie imitative d'Homère. Elle est très-familière à la poésie Chinoise: au lieu de dire, par exemple, on entend le bruit des tambours, le Chiking dit, 'On entend le *tang-tang* des tambours.' Cette citation n'est pas des plus heureuses. mais c'est la seule qui me vienne."

But let it be objected, and let us admit for a moment (what in fact is not true), that in Chinese every word is pronounced *in the same time*, and therefore the above distinction signifies little. Does it, with reference to a sister art, make no difference in *music* whether two or three notes be struck in the same measured time—or only one? What, but something very similar to this, was the Greek and Roman practice, as far as we can understand it, of making two short syllables exactly equivalent to a long one, and pronouncing them in the same time. That such matters are not totally indifferent, might be proved by the trite example from Virgil—the well known verse, descriptive of an eager and restless horse, which derives its imitative character from the rapid succession of dactyls; and again, by the opposite artifice, used by the same poet in painting the blinded giant, where the heavy spondaic measure of the line, joined to the redundant terminal syllables, is equally expressive in another way. The discussion of this point, however, is rendered somewhat superfluous by the plain fact, that all Chinese words are *not* pronounced in the same time. Of what are called the " four tones," it is the professed business of the *third* to prolong, and of the *fourth* to shorten them.

The truth seems to be, that the language of China abounds in diphthongal at least, if not in triphthongal sounds, which contribute, when found blended with others that are more strictly monosyllabic, to give to its verse a certain share of varied euphony. There is no occasion to incur the charge of attempting to prove too much: at the same time it does not seem very easy to shew, why such words as *keăĕ* and *keăou*, with every vowel clearly pronounced, should not advance nearly as good a claim to the title even of trisyllabic, as those marked in the following examples, each of them consisting of as many metrical *syllables* as it has letters:

'Ατρείδη, νῦν ἄμμε παλιμπλαγχθέντας 'ΟΐΩ—
"ΗΪΕ σὺν τε Μενοιτιάδῃ, καὶ δὶς ἑταροῖσιν.

Not only, however, do *vowel*-sounds so extensively prevail in the language of which we treat, but the few *consonants* that are to be found in it are, almost without exception, free from the reproach of harshness. There is no terminal consonant whatever, except *n* and its nasal *ng*;* and the initials are only *Ch*—*F*—*G* hard—*H* (if it may be called a consonant)—*J*, soft as in French—*K*—*L*—*M*—*N*—*P*—*S*—*Sz*—*Sh*—*T*—*Th*—*Ts*-and *Tsz*. Of these, *Tsz*, and, if you please, *Ts*, are the only sounds which approach to the character of harshness. The Chinese find it no easy matter to pronounce English words; but Englishmen meet with little difficulty in pronouncing theirs—the natural inference from which is, that our own language, though certainly more varied, is the harsher of the two.

We shall presently see that they possess the usual means, employed by other nations, to give harmony and rhythmical effect to their verse: but it may not be unimportant first to show, that the native and original qualities of the language are such, as not to unsuit it altogether to the purposes of melodious composition,—that the raw material is not unfitted for the manufacture. A notion seems to have existed, that the whole merit of Chinese poetry lay in some curious and fanciful selection of the characters, with a reference to their component parts. As a medium for the communication of ideas, the written language certainly differs from alphabetic systems: but, after all, the characters are the *means* only, and not the *end*. The melody of the sound—the harmony of the structure—and the justness of the sentiment, or beauty of the imagery—constitute, as they do everywhere else, the merits of poetical composition.

2. Such being the natural qualifications of the Chinese language, considered in its *oral* capacity, for poetry—it derives cadence and modulation from the artificial use of the tones, or accents; which appear, however, to have been originally adopted for a very different purpose, and to have owed their existence, rather to the necessity of *perspicuity in speech*, than of *melody in verse*. It may easily be imagined, that where a whole spoken language consists of not more than about four hundred different sounds, hence there would be great danger of two interlocutors misunderstanding each other, from the unavoidable occurrence of the *équivoque*; and hence

*It must be kept in mind, that we here treat of the dialect of literature, and of educated persons. In the south of the empire, words end in *k* & *t*; but provincial corruptions and vulgarisms form no part of the subject.

the necessity for the tones, or accents, consisting of what may, in sufficient conformity with the meaning of their original names, be styled the *even* or *natural*, the *acute*, the *grave*, and the *short*. In point of fact, the first is no accent at all, but rather a negative quality—the absence of all marked intonation; and, accordingly, the Chinese themselves call it *p'ing*, 'even or smooth,' while the three others they class together, under the general name of *tsëĕ*, 'deflected,' that is, deflected from the *natural* tone. These last are, in regular poetical composition, used indifferently for each other; they are considered as being opposed to, and required in verse to be alternated with, the even-toned or unaccented words. It would be quite unprofitable to dwell here upon their minute distinctions, or to endeavour to give particular description of them, because nothing but the mouth of a native can illustrate them properly: they are really—*vox et præterea nihil*, and have already been as fully noticed, as such a subject admitted of, by several writers on Chinese grammar. Suffice it then to say, that by their use the original sounds of the language are varied or multiplied about fourfold, and a great accession made to its fitness for metrical composition. Of a species of technicality which admits so ill of illustration on paper, it is enough to observe, that the words (we shall presently see that these are equivalent to *feet* in other languages) which answer to the *even* numbers in each line,—the second, fourth, sixth, according to the length of the verse,—together with the last word of all,—are, in regular poetry, the subjects of attention with regard to the *alternate* position of the tones called "natural," and "deflected." The rule for placing them seems to have variety, or the avoiding of a too frequent recurrence of the same tone, for its principal object. Their attention to this point goes beyond the single lines, and extends to the couplets: for whatever the intonation of the second, fourth, or sixth words in the first line may be,—whether natural or deflected,—that of the corresponding words in the next line is required to be the opposite. M. Freret, in the "Mémoires de l' Académie," fell into a great error, in asserting that "les Chinois n'ont jamais connu la versification cadencée par l'arrangement de ces tons musicaux: leur poésie a seulement été consacrée par le nombre des syllabes, et dans la suite on a y ajouté la rime." Even the most irregular species of Chinese verse, called *Tsze*, is to a certain degree regulated by the tones, though in a different manner from the foregoing.

3. The next source of harmony that we have to notice, is the use of poetical numbers. Every word of Chinese poetry, instead of being regarded as a mere syllable, may more properly be considered as corresponding to a metrical foot in other languages. It has already been shown, that a considerable portion are dissyllabic—and all of them are pronounced, in the recital of verse, with an emphasis and prolongation of the voice, very different from the manner in which we slur over the unaccented portion of our syllables.

To begin with the smallest number of words that form a measured line in Chinese, we sometimes meet with so few as *three*, repeated like a kind of 'refrain' in popular songs. These songs are called 曲 *keo*, and below is an example of what we might call the *chorus*.

枝中水上春併歸
長楊掃地桃花飛
清風吹人光照衣
光照衣
景將夕
擲黃金
留上客

To the woods and streams the Spring returns,
The long willow-twigs sweep the earth, the peach-blossoms fly;
The clear breeze blows on man, the light shines on his vestments:

It shines on his vestments,
Its brightness precedes the setting;
Prepare the expenses of a feast,
Detain our exalted guest!

The custom of the country, as almost universally throughout the world, reserves the principal meal, or *Cœna*, for the evening, when business is over and both mind and body are left free for enjoyment, and digestion; for they agree with us, that

—"He's a most uncomfortable sinner
Who only eats, but can't digest, his dinner."

This short measure also constitutes occasionally a species of chime for the inculcation of moral maxims; and it was, no doubt, for the similar purpose of *assisting the memory*, that it has been adopted in the composition of the *San tsze king*, or "Trimetrical Classic"—a work evincing considerable ingenuity, though intended for the humble purpose of conveying to youth the rudiments of general knowledge. In China, as elsewhere, persons of high attainments occasionally think it worth their while to devote their talents to the promotion of the great business of education. The following lines are taken, as a specimen of this particular kind of verse, from that portion of the above work, in which the regular succession of all the dynasties, and most celebrated emperors, is turned into rhyme; and it may perhaps remind the English reader of a well-known song, called the "Chapter of Kings:"—

TRIMETERS.

Kaou-tsoo hing—Han nĕĕ këen,
Che Heaou-ping—Wang-mang tsuen:
Kwang-woo hing—Wei Tung-Han;
Sze pĭ nëen—Chung yu Hëen:
Wei, Shŭ, Woo—Tseng Han ting,
Haou San-Kwŏ—Heih leang Tsin.

高祖興
至孝平
光武興
四百年
魏蜀吳
號三國

漢業建
王莽篡
為東漢
終於獻
爭漢鼎
迄兩晉

"Kaou-tsoo arose—And the race of Hān was established,
Until the reign of Heaou-ping—When Wang-mang usurped the empire:
Kwang-woo arose—And established the Eastern family of Hān:
After enduring four hundred years—The Han ended with Hëen-tee:
Wei, Shŭ, and Woo—Contended together for the empire of Hān,
They were called the THREE NATIONS—And continued till the rise of the two dynasties Tsin."

The line of *four* words is the shortest that seems ever to have been used in the higher species of composition. It constitutes the chief part of the measure of the sacred book of odes, called *Sheeking*, the oldest poetical work in China.* There, however, the measure of some pieces is altogether irregular, varying from three, to seven or eight words in a line. Poetry, in most countries, begins with being the vehicle of religion and morality, and the first record of historical facts. Venerated at first as the language of wisdom or inspiration, it is at length cultivated as a pleasurable art, and never fails to improve in harmony, however it may degenerate in other points with the progress of time. "Il faut distinguer dans la poësie," says Racine,

* For two of the most regular odes of this collection, vide infra, Part II. The three hundred odes compiled by Confucius are divided into three parts. 1. *Foong*, Customs and ordinary affairs of life. 2. *Ya*, Government and morals. 3. *Soong*, Eulogies or commendations.

C

"ce qui vient de la *nature*, et ce qui est ajoûté par l'*art*: la nature inspire d'abord la rapidité du style, et la hardiesse des figures; l'art vient ensuite, et pour rendre le style poëtique encore plus rapide, et en même tems plus harmonieux, le resserre dans les bornes étroites de la versification. La poësie naissante n'a point du connoître cet esclavage, puisque les règles de l'art ne s'établissent qu'avec le tems et la reflection." The earliest Chinese poetry, as we find it in the *Sheeking*, appears certainly to have made use of the embellishments of both measure and rhyme, but with a degree of irregularity very different from the polish of modern versification. The lines are occasionally of all lengths; and the rhyme seems to be subject to little rule. It will occasionally occur for six or eight consecutive verses, and there will sometimes be none at all. For the same reason that Pope is more harmonious than Chaucer or Donne, Boileau or Racine than Ronsard, Virgil or Tibullus than old Ennius:

——————"Sic horridus ille
Defluxit numerus"——

so the poetry of China, from the T'āng dynasty (when this art attained its highest perfection) down to the present time, is, in point of *mere versification*, a vast improvement on the *Sheeking*. A writer of their own, in his preface to a collection of poems, compares its progress to the natural growth of a tree. The *Sheeking* he likens to the roots; when Soo-le flourished the buds opened: in the time of Këen-gan there were abundance of leaves: but in the T'āng dynasty many reposed under the shade of this tree, and there were rich supplies of flowers and fruit. It would be strange indeed, if this people were an exception to a rule so general; if an art, in which they took so much delight, had not improved by cultivation, or were, at the present day, devoid of so essential a qualification as the harmony of numbers. The old measure of four words, or feet, is now seldom adopted, being from its shortness unsusceptible of much melody. At the same time it does occasionally occur, chiefly for moral and didactic purposes; and the following may be taken as a specimen.—They are some lines of the Buddhists, or quietists:—

TETRAMETERS.

靈哉一點
不擾不驚
無思無慮
至聖至明
天理昭著
善性根成
一雜於偽
五體摧傾

Ling tsai yĭ tëen – Puh jaou, pŭ king;
Woo sz, woo lü—Che shing, che ming:
T'ëen le chaou choo – Shen sing ken ching:
Yĭ tsă yu wei—Woo tee tsuy king.

"When the heart is enlightened by a spark of the æthereal intelligence,
There is neither perturbation, nor alarm;
There is neither thought, nor anxiety:
But all is moral perfection, and the complete radiance of truth;
Where the heavenly principle pours its light,
The root of a virtuous disposition is perfected:
But once mingling with human frailty,
The whole man will be subdued and overturned."

The improved system of versification consists in lines of *five* words or feet, as well as in the longer and still superior measure of *seven*. These now constitute what are properly called *Shee*, or regular poems, and we give an example of each in this place, though many others will appear in the sequel:–

PENTAMETERS.

久客初歸里
追隨到古榕
聊尋行樂境
且憩倦遊踪
僧對空饒舌
山觀不改容
流連忘日暮
回首晚堂鐘

Kew kĕ tsoo kwei le,
Chuy suy taou Koo-yoong;
Leaou tsin hing lŏ king,
Tseay kee keuen yew tsoong.
Seng tuy koong jaou shĕ;
Shan kwan pŭ kae yoong.
Lew lëen wang jĕ moo,
Hwuy show wan t'ang choong.

"When my ancient guest first returns to our neighbourhood,
I accompany him to the monastery Koo-yoong:
We stroll along together, in search of pleasant walks,
And then rest our weary footsteps within:
The priests sit opposite, indulging their tongues in leisure talk,
—We look at the distant hills, and remark the unchanging features of nature.
Carried on by the stream of converse, we forget the day is closing,
But at last, turning our heads homeward, we listen to the vesper bell."

五峰如指翠相連
撐起炎州半壁天
夜盥銀河摘星斗
朝探碧落弄雲烟
雨餘玉筍空中現
月出明珠掌上懸
疑是巨靈伸一臂
遥從海外数中原

HEPTAMETERS.

Woo foong, ju che, tsuy seang lëen,
Chang k'e Yen-chow, pwan pĭ t'ëen:
Yay yu yin ho tsih sing tów,
Chaou tan pĭ lŏ, loong yun yen:

Yŭ yu, joo seun koong choong hëen,
Yuĕ chŭ, ming choo chang shang heuen:
Ee she Kew-ling shin yĭ pĭ,
Yaou tsoong hae wae soo Choong-yuen.

"See the five variegated peaks of yon mountain, connected like the fingers of the hand,
And rising up from the south, as a wall midway to heaven:
At night, it would pluck, from the inverted concave, the stars of the milky way;
During the day, it explores the zenith, and plays with the clouds:
The rain has ceased—and the shining summits are apparent in the void expanse;
The moon is up—and looks like a bright pearl over the expanded palm:
One might imagine that the Great Spirit had stretched forth an arm,
From afar—from beyond the sea—and was numbering the Nations.*

The boldness of the imagery in the last example is somewhat striking, and the concluding two lines may perhaps serve to redeem it from the reproach of the bathos, to which the simile of the hand might otherwise have exposed it.

Verses containing the number of six, or eight, or more words, form no part of regular poetry in modern times; though they are occasionally found alternated with others, in pieces which do not aspire to regularity of structure, but whose figurative style elevates them above the level of mere prose.—Lines of every length are used in those measured couplets, or sentences in pairs, so nicely balanced both in words and sense, which are adopted in the inculcation of ethical precepts, and of which more will be said hereafter, under the head of *parallelism.*

In aid of the effect of metrical quantity, the Chinese possess another rule of versification, well known to Europeans, but which has never yet been noticed with reference to the subject of the present treatise. It may be premised, that no *sentential* pause ever occurs in the middle of a verse; at least none which could be punctuated with anything beyond a comma in English. Every line is complete within itself: there is nothing of what the French call *enjambement.* But while a reference to written poetry easily establishes this point, the writer of the present observations thought he

* China was formerly divided into separate and independent states.

could plainly perceive, in the correct recital of the longer measures by natives, a very marked *cæsural* pause near the middle of the lines, Repeated trial tended to show, that in verses of *seven* words, the cæsura was invariably after the fourth—and in those of *five*, after the second word. With a view to being quite clear on this subject, reference was made to a gentleman, whose profound knowledge of the language renders him a very competent judge in all matters connected with it. He was soon persuaded of the existence of the fact; and a properly qualified native, being summoned into the room, was requested to read out the longer measures of verse in a low and deliberate manner. The result was, that the cæsura fell exactly in the places above-mentioned, being more strongly marked in some lines than in others, but still unchangeable with regard to *position*—and the native himself (who, by the way, was a *Sewtsae*, i. e. had taken his degree) admitted that such was the case. While the long measures admit of, and in some degree require, this pause of the voice, all lines which contain less than five words appear, by reason of their shortness, to be entirely devoid of it. The existence of the cæsural pause in a particular part of each verse might of itself, be considered as deserving of notice in a treatise of this nature; but the farther connection that it has with the structure of the verse makes it still more worthy of attention.

The language of China is in a great measure composed of what, for want of a better expression, we will call "compound terms," consisting of two words or characters, which may be a noun with its adjective, a verb with its adverb, two nouns united—and a great many other grammatical combinations of the kind. These are always pronounced together,—as much so as parts of the same compound word in other languages. In a verse of *seven* words, the cæsural pause being after the *fourth*, the first section of the line generally * consists of two of these compound terms. The *fourth* and *fifth* characters can never be coupled in this manner, because the pause cannot take place in the middle of a compound term

* *Generally*, because it is not meant to be asserted that Chinese verses are *always*, or *entirely* composed of such terms: they frequently contain a number of single characters, or simple terms; but whenever the others are used, their position in the verse is invariably as above stated.

—but it must be the *first* and *second*, the *third* and *fourth*, which are thus related. This being the case with regard to the *first* section of the verse, the *last*, which contains three characters, is commonly a compound term, with the addition of a single word, which may either precede or come after it. But as this is a subject which may best be illustrated by examples, here follow some lines of *seven* words, in which the verbal construction can be observed—together with the places of the cæsural pause after the fourth word, as far as this may be shown without actual recital.

世事忙忙無了期
何須苦苦用心機
尋些樂處酌杯酒
偷個閒時誦首詩

名花不放不生芳
美玉不磨不生光
不是一番寒徹骨
怎得梅花撲鼻香

She sze mang-mang—woo leaou ke,
Ho seu koo-koo—yung sin ke:
Tsin seay lŏ choo—chŏ pei tsew,
Tow ko hëen she—soong show she.

Ming hwa pŭ fang—pŭ seng fāng,
Mei yu pŭ mo—pŭ seng kwāng;
Pŭ she yĭ fan—han chĕ kŭ,
Tseng tĕ mei hwa—pŏ pe heang.

“ The affairs of the world are all hurry and trouble—without end;
Why, then, with bitter anxiety—waste the heart's springs?
Search for some pleasant spot—to pour out a cup of wine,
Steal a leisure hour—to sing the stanzas of an ode!”

"The fine flower unblown—exhales no sweets,
The fair gem unpolished—exhibits no radiance:
Were it not that once—the cold penetrated its stem,
How could the plum blossom—emit such fragrance?"

We next come to the line of *five* words, where the cæsura falls after the *second*. Here the first division of the verse usually constitutes one compound term; and the last three words are subject to the same law as in the longer line. The following are examples:—

人人若共遵
家國賀太平
放之充海宇
廣之塞乾坤

山色無遠近
看山終日行
峰巒隨處改
行客不知名

Jin jin—jŏ koong tsun,
Kea kwŏ—ho t'ae ping:
Fang che—choong hae yu,
Kwang che—sih këen kwen.

Shan sĕ—woo yuen kin,
K'an shan—choong jĕ hing:
Foong lwan—suy choo kae,
Hing kĕ—puh che ming.

"The whole people—unitedly obeying the laws,
The nation, as a family—will rejoice in peace:
Promulge it—to the extremities of the ocean,
Extend it—to the foundations of the world!

"The tints of the hills—are confounded in their distance,
As the traveller views them—to the end of his daily journey:
The shapes of their peaks and ridges—alter with every change of place,
Until the wanderer—ceases to know their names.

Our English verse of ten syllables derives great advantage from the power of varying its effect, without any prejudice to its melody, by occasionally shifting the place of the cæsura,—unlike the Chinese, where it is fixed and immoveable. In this, however, the latter bears some resemblance to the French alexandrine, always divided into hemistiches by the cæsural pause, with which the sentential pause is most commonly coincident *—as well as to that law of the Latin hexameter, which seems to demand, that in a line *perfectly* euphonic, the cæsura should fall after the first syllable of the third foot ‡.

5. Of rhymes, it is chiefly to be observed, that they occur, in regular poetry, at the end of the alternate verses which answer to the even numbers,—that is, at the termination of every *second* verse. The first one of all frequently gives the rhyme to the whole stanza; but the rest of the uneven-numbered lines seem subject to no rule, and end with any sounds indifferently. The length of the stanza is determined by the recurrence of the same rhyme, and, in a poem of any continuity, it is generally of four lines only,—that is, a quatrain, whose second and fourth lines rhyme together; but occasionally it consists of eight verses, of which four have the same ending. Stanzas, however, or rather short pieces of poetry, are very common of twelve, and even sixteen lines, some of which might, with no great impropriety, be assimilated to what we call sonnets. In the stanza of four lines, it cannot be objected that the rhyme is too frequent; and even in that of eight, it should we considered, that only the second line of every couplet possesses the rhyme; while the intermediate ones are blank, and thus afford a relief to the ear. In our own Spenserian stanza, consisting of nine lines, no less than four of them have the same ending,—that is, the second, fourth, fifth, and seventh,—while three others like-

* "Que toujours dans vos vers—le sens coupant les mots,
Suspende l'hemistiche—en marque le repos."
BOIL. *Art Poét.*

‡ "Purpureus veluti—cúm flos, succisus aratro.
Languescit moriens—lassove papavera collo
Demisere caput—pluviâ cum forté gravantur."

D

wise rhyme together,—the sixth, eight, and ninth. The Chinese, however, do not seem to have a very nice ear for the perception of true rhymes; and this inaccuracy may partly arise from their not possessing such precise symbols, or marks of sound, as our alphabetic letters. In the odes of the *Sheeking*, as the lines and stanzas are occasionally extremely irregular in their length and general structure—" numeri lege soluti"—so the rhymes appear to be under no strict regulation. This seeming neglect may partly result from a change of pronunciation: but there can be little doubt that the subjection of rhyme to more rigid laws was, as well as the other improvements in versification, introduced in the general advancement of the art, under the T'āng dynasty.

The following specimen affords an example of the rhymes in two stanzas of eight lines each:—

三冬晴暖久
一雨正相宜
漠漠沉山閣
輕輕點石池
春風搖蕩日
萬物發生時
爲向農人說
西疇事莫遲

柳色未遮徑
桃花已滿林
物猶憐氣候
吾豈忘天心
隱几人空老
乘時力未任
柴門對滴瀝
行坐一沉吟

STANZA I.

San-tung tsing-nwan kew
Yĭ-yü ching seang-ee :
Mo-mo chin shan kŏ,
King-king tëen shĭh-che:
Chun foong yaou tang jĭ,
Wan-wŭ fă-seng she :
Wei heang noong-jin shwŏ,
Se-chow sz mŏ che.

STANZA II.

Lew-sĕ wei chay king,
Taou-hwa ee mwan lin :
Wŭ yew lëen ke how,
Woo he wang t'ëen-sin :
Yin ke jin hoong-laou,
Shing-she lĭ wei jin :
Chai-mun tuy tĭ-lĭ,
Hing tso yĭ chin-yin.

Felicitous Rains.

1.

"The last month of winter was for the most part clear and mild,
And now at length approach the well-timed showers :
The wide-spread mist has involved yon mountain dwelling,
Its dews are slowly filling each rocky hollow :
The vernal winds obscure the clouded sun,
It is the season for all things in nature to germinate :
Let us convey an exhortation to the husbandman,
That he delay not the business of his western fields."

2.

"The green foliage of the willows has not yet shaded the path,
But the peach-blossoms already cover the grove :
Every inanimate thing seems to feel the influence of the season,
Shall I, then, be unmindful of the purposes of heaven?
Like some who lean on their tables, and grow unprofitably old,
Who exert not their strength in the proper time?
— The rain falls in drops before my rude door-way,
As I stroll about, or sit, immersed in such meditations."

Rhymes, however, are by no means confined to regular verse (of which it is our particular business at present to detail the laws), being very apparent in the following citation, a species of composition called *Tsze*, 辭, something between prose and poetry, in which the rhyme is repeated at the end of lines of indeterminate length. The passage is descriptive of a field or bed of chrysanthemums, flowers which the Chinese admire on account of the brilliancy of their colours, and which they display towards winter in large quantities about their houses :—

瘦影滿籬踈香
三徑深深淺淺
黃相映露下集
英飢可飱風有
黃色誰堪並正
談到可憐嬾如
新病厭厭開出
秋情性漫言盡
目只閒閒須知
詩酒陶家興

Sow-ying mwan le, soo-heang san king, *shin-shin tsëen-tsëen hwang seang*-ying; *loo-hea tsĭ* ying; *ke k'o tsan foong; yew hwang sĕ, shuey kan* ping: *ching tan taou k'o-leen lae joo sin* ping; *yen-yen k'ae chŭ tsew tsing* sing: *man yen tsin mŏ chĕ hëen-hëen; seu che she tsew Taou-kea* hing,

"Their slender shadows fill the enclosure, and a scattered perfume pervades the flower-beds, planted in triple rows: their deeper and lighter tints reflect a yellow light, and the leaves shine varied from beneath the drops of dew: each hungry flowret inhales the passing breeze, as it sheds around its incomparable lustre. The gazer sympathizes with the languishing blossoms, bending their heads all faint and delicate: the mournful view awakes in his mind thoughts suitable to autumn. Say not that it is a sight to satiate the eyes of the indifferent beholder—know that such flowers as these once inspired the poet Taou-yuen-ming *, as he indulged his genius amidst verses and wine."

6. The next feature in the construction of Chinese verse is perhaps the most interesting of all, as it presents a striking coincidence with what has been remarked of the poetry of another Asiatic nation. In the preliminary Dissertation on Hebrew Poetry, prefixed to his translation of Isaiah, Bishop Lowth has treated at some length of a peculiar property which he calls *parallelism*. What that is, will be best explained in his own words :—

"The correspondence of one verse or line with another, I call parallelism.

* For some account of *Taou-yuen-ming*, see "Mémoires sur les Chinois," tom. iii.

—When a proposition is delivered, and a second is subjoined to it, or drawn under it, equivalent, or contrasted with it, in sense, or similar to it in the form of grammatical construction, these I call parallel lines; and the words or phrases, answering one to another in the corresponding lines, parallel terms.—Parallel lines may be reduced to three sorts: parallels *synonymous*, parallels *antithetic*, and parallels *synthetic*."

The *first* kind, Dr. Lowth defines to be those "which correspond one to another by expressing the same sense in different, but equivalent terms; when a proposition is delivered, and is immediately repeated, in the whole or in part, the expression being varied, but the sense entirely or nearly the same:"—

EXAMPLES.

Because I called, and ye refused;
I stretched out my hand, and no one regarded:
But ye have defeated all my counsel;
And would not incline to my reproof:
I also will laugh at your calamity;
I will mock when your fear cometh.

Bow thy heavens, O Jehovah, and descend;
Touch the mountains, and they shall smoke:
Dart forth thy lightnings, and scatter them;
Shoot out thine arrows, and consume them.

The reader is furnished below with examples from the Chinese, which will perhaps be considered as answering to the above description of the Hebrew—with this only difference, that the peculiar structure of the language, of which we now treat, generally renders the parallelism much more exact, and therefore much more striking and obvious—as it is usually *word for word*, the one written opposite to the other. The first two lines have a figurative reference to the perfection of a person's moral character:—

Pĕ pĭ, woo hea, ching che paou,
Tsing lëen, pŭ yen, fă k'e heang.
Sin taou lwan she, woo she choo,
Tsing tang koo tse, chĕ sz pei.

Mŏ hëen te tsĕ, yuen ting seaou,
Pŭ yuen kea pin, hwŏ ke wei.

白璧無瑕呈至寶
青蓮不染發奇香

心到亂時無是處
情當苦際只思悲

莫嫌地窄園亭小
不怨家貧活計微

"The white stone, unfractured, ranks as most precious;
The blue lily, unblemished, emits the finest fragrance."

"The heart, when it is harassed, finds no place of rest;
The mind, in the midst of bitterness, thinks only of grief."

"Be not discontented, though your land be narrow, and your garden small;
Be not disturbed, though your family be poor, and your means contracted."

The *second* kind of parallelism is the *antithetic*, "when," according to the definition of Bishop Lowth, "two lines correspond with one another by an opposition of terms and sentiments." He observes, with reference to his own subject, that "the degrees of antithesis are various, from an exact contraposition of word to word through the whole sentence, down to a general disparity, with something of a contrariety in the two propositions." It may be remarked, with regard to the Chinese, that the antithesis is commonly perfect, both in sentiments and terms.

It is farther to be observed, that the learned prelate takes most of his examples, under this head, from the Proverbs of Solomon, "where they abound: for this form is peculiarly adapted to that kind of writing, to adages, aphorisms, and detached sentences:"—

EXAMPLES.

The memory of the just is a blessing;
But the name of the wicked shall rot.

There is that scattereth, and still increaseth;
And that is unreasonably sparing, yet groweth poor.

—As relates to the Chinese, the case is precisely the same, and no doubt for the same reason. In going over, by way of experiment, a collection of Maxims* compiled by himself, the writer of this immediately found that a very large portion answered to the foregoing description. For example:—

慾寡精神爽
思多血氣衰

清貧常樂
濁富多憂

勿以惡小而爲之
勿以善小而不爲

從善如登
從惡如崩

Yŏ kwa, tsing shin shwang;
Sz to, huĕ ke shwai.

Tsing pin chang lŏ;
Chŏ foo to yew.

Wuh e gŏ seaou, urh wei che;
Wuh e shen seaou, urh puh wei.

Tsoong shen joo teng;
Tsoong gŏ joo peng.

"With few cravings of the heart, the health is flourishing;
With many anxious thoughts, the constitution decays."

* 8vo. London. 1823

"Unsullied poverty is always happy;
Impure wealth brings many sorrows."

"Consider not any vice as trivial, and *therefore* practice it:
Regard not any virtue as unimportant, and *therefore* neglect it."

"Prosecuting virtue, is like ascending a steep;
Pursuing vice, like rushing down a precipice."

But the antithetic parallel is used not merely to give a force to aphorisms; it appears occasionally, though perhaps somewhat less often, in the course of poetry; and is found to exist in every degree, from the strong mutual opposition of *all* the corresponding words in a couplet, to that of only *some* of them:—

觀生如客豈能久
信死有期安可逃

心境靜時身亦靜
慾生還是病生時

仰面空長嘆
低首淚雙垂

富貴他人聚
貧寒親子離

Kwan seng joo kih, ke neng kew;
Sin sze yew ke, gan ko taou.

Sin king tsing she, shin yě tsing;
Yo seng hwan she ping seng she.

Yang mëen, koong chang tan,
Te show, luy shwang chuy;

Foo kwei,—t'a jin tsü,
Pin han,—tsin tsz le.

"Look on life as an uncertain guest, that cannot remain;
Believe that death is fixed, and cannot be escaped."

"When the region of the heart * is at rest, the body too enjoys ease;
But the passions being excited, then disorders of the body arise."

"Supinely gazing, now I vent my sighs,
Now bending down, in tears my sorrow flows;
The wealthy alien claims connubial ties,
The needy kinsman no relation knows †!"

The *third* sort of parallel, noticed by Dr. Lowth, is what he denominates the *synthetic*, or constructive, where each word and line does not exactly answer to its fellow as either equivalent or opposite in sense: but where there is a marked correspondence and equality in the construction of the lines—"such as noun answering to noun, verb to verb, member to member, negative to negative, interrogative to interrogative:"—

EXAMPLES.

Is such then the fast which I choose;
That a man should afflict his soul for a day?
Is it, that he should bow down his head like a bulrush;
And spread sackcloth and ashes for his couch?
Shall this be called a fast,
And a day acceptable to Jehovah?

This is by far the most common species of parallelism with the Chinese. Indeed the first two sorts, already described, are generally accompanied by this last—the correspondence of sense, whether it consists in equivalency or opposition, is almost always attended by correspondence of construction: the latter is often found without the former, while the converse seldom takes place. It pervades their poetry universally, forms its chief characteristic feature, and is the source of a great deal of its artificial beauty. In nearly every specimen produced in the course of this treatise, it may be observed to exist in a more or less marked degree, and unless for the sake of regularity, it would seem almost superfluous to adduce particular examples here. In the romance called *Haoukewchuen*, 好逑傳, or "The Fortunate Union," the

* Morally speaking, and meaning the *mind*.
† The 'Heir in Old Age,' page 9.

K

first of the following two quatrains is introduced in application to the hero, who is distinguished at once by his bravery and his abilities: in the second example, it will be observed that the words are very nicely balanced :—

孤行不畏全憑膽
冷臉驕人要有才
膽似子龍重出世
才如李白再生來

百千萬事應難了
五六十年容易來
得一日閒閒一日
遇三杯飲飲三杯

Koo hing pŭ wei, tseuen ping tan,
Leng lëen keaou jin, yaou yew tsai:
Tan, sz Tsz-loong choong chŭ she,
Tsae, joo Le-pĕ tsae seng lai.

Pĕ, tëen, wan sz, ying nan leaou,
Woo, lew, shĕ nëen, yoong e lai:
Tĕ yĭ jĕ hëen, hëen yĭ jĕ,
Yu san pei yin, yin san pei.

"Thus alone and dauntless he walks—all confident in his courage;
Thus proud and reserved—he must needs possess high talents:
Courage—as if *Tsz-loong*, the hero, had re-appeared in the world;
Talents—as though *Le-pĕ*, the poet, had again been born."

"A hundred—a thousand—ten thousand projects are hard to accomplish;
Five times—six times—ten years very soon arrive:
When you have found a day to be idle—be idle for a day;
When you have met with three cups to drink—then drink your three cups!"

The constructional parallelism of sentences extends to prose composition, and is very frequent in what is called *wun-chang*, 文章, or 'fine writing,'—a measured prose, though not written line beside line, like poetry. Indeed all the three kinds may be met with occasionally in every description of writing that soars above the style of mere conversation or narrative. They do not *alone* constitute poetry, which must have the several other qualifiations already mentioned, as measure, rhyme, &c.;—but being allied to art and embellishment, they claim verse as their proper province, and are carried there to a greater degree of refinement than elsewhere. The following three prose sentences, in which there is a parallelism throughout, combined with a sort of anti-climax, are introduced chiefly for the sake of noticing a striking coincidence of sentiment, in a quarter where one is not prepared to meet with it, except in the case of the most obvious, simple, and general truths :—

上品之人
不教而善
中品之人
教而後善
下品之人
教而不善

Shang pin che jin, pŭ keaou urh shen;
Chung pin che jin, keaou urh how shen;
Hea pin che jin, keaou urh pŭ shen.

The highest order of men (called *Shing*, perfect or inspired) are virtuous, or wise, independently of instruction :—the middle class of men (*Hëen*, good or moral) are so after instruction :—the lowest order (*Yu*, stupid or worthless) are vicious in spite of instruction."

These three classes are, strange to say, most exactly defined in four lines of the Works and Days of Hesiod *—the sentiment could scarcely be more nearly rendered :—

* Edit. Robinson : page 146.

Οὗτος μεν ΠΑΝΑΡΙΣΤΟΣ, ὃς αυτος παντα νοήσει,
ΕΣΘΛΟΣ δ'αυ κἀκεινος, ὃς ευ ειπόντι πιθηται,
'Ος δε κε μητ' αυτος νοεῃ, μητ' αλλ‹υ ακούων,
Εν θυμῳ βαλληται, ὃδ' αυτ' ΑΧΡΗΙΟΣ ἀνηρ.

"He indeed is the BEST of all men, who of *himself* is wise in all things;
Though he is GOOD, who follows a good instructor:
But he who is neither wise of himself, nor, in listening to another,
Remains mindful of advice—this is the WORTHLESS man."

Of the different sorts of parallelism it is perhaps needless to observe, that in no other language could they be carried to such a height as they are in Chinese : the exact equality in the number of words, which form each line of a poetical couplet, and the almost total absence of recurring particles that encumber our European languages, admit of their being adopted with peculiar effect. There is something of an antithetic parallel in the first two lines of Horace's well-known apologue :—

" Rusticus urbanum murem mus paupere fertur
Accepisse cavo, veterem vetus hospes amicum."

But to make this resemble the arrangement of a Chinese couplet—to make the antithesis *sentential* as well as *verbal*—it would be necessary to set prosody at defiance, and write the corresponding words opposite to one another, somewhat in the following way :—

" Rusticus mus, vetus hospes, accepisse fertur
Urbanum murem, veterem amicum, cavo paupere." *

Such refinements, though to some they may appear to savour of trifling, certainly contribute to heighten the peculiar rhythmus of the poetry into which they are introduced, at the same time that they tend to increase its difficulties, and enhance the merit of the composition, on the same principle that makes our neighbours the French so tenacious of rhyming tragedies, and the unities of the drama—" L'art en devient plus difficile, et les difficultés vaincues donnent en tout genre du plaisir et de la gloire."

* It is evident that this transposition ruins the peculiar beauty of expression in the Latin, arising from the immediate contiguity of the antithetic, or corresponding words in the same line, which would be impracticable in the Chinese—a language entirely devoid of all inversion.

The Chinese are so fond of their parallelisms, that the most common decorations of rooms, halls, and temples, are ornamental labels hung opposite to each other, or side by side, and called *Tuy-lëen*, 對聯, which has precisely the meaning of the English term. These are sometimes inscribed on coloured paper, sometimes carved in wood, and distinguished by painting and gilding —but always in pairs. They have generally an allusion to the circumstances of the dwelling, or of the inhabitant : and, by way of illustration merely, we might imagine some Chinese, who affected a just mediocrity in his desires and wishes, suspending on one side of his study a sentence which should have the meaning of,

Caret obsoleti sordibus tecti,

and, exactly opposite to it, another sentence in as many words,

Caret invidendâ sobrius aulâ.

The first two of the following examples were supplied by the kindness of Dr. Morrison ‡: they were taken down by him, during our progress with

松柏蒼龍層漢上
梧桐丹鳳五雲邊

練達人情皆學問
洞明世故即經綸

赫赫有時還寂寂
閒閒到底勝勞勞

‡ In conversing with Dr. Morrison on this property of Chinese verse, and remarking that it was common to other languages, he suggested my adding to the present treatise a close comparison (like the one which I have here instituted) with the instances adduced by Bishop Lowth from the Hebrew. For the hint, therefore, I stand indebted to him.

the British embassy, in the interior of China. The last couplet I wrote down myself, on a visit to a native :—

Soong-pĕ tsang Loong tseng han shang ;
Woo-tsung tan Foong woo yün pëen.

Lëen tă jin-tsing kea heŏ-yun ;
Tung ming she-hoo tsëĕ king-lun.

Hĕ-hĕ yew she hwan shŭ-shŭ ;
Hëen-hëen taou te shing laou-laou.

"From the Pine forest, the azure dragon ascends to the milky way ;
From the Dryandra cordata, the crimson phœnis aspires to the borders of the variegated clouds *."

"Experience and discernment of the human passions may both be called learning ;
Deep and clear insight into the ways of the world also constitute subtle genius ‡."

"Fame and ambition themselves must have their intervals of repose ;
Retirement and leisure are, after all, preferable to labour and anxiety."

In a language so differently constituted from every other in the world, it is sufficiently surprising to find so many points in common as those already described ; but it is still more remarkable that they practise the somewhat refined amusement of what the French call *bouts-rimés*. A drawing on silk in the Chinese style, was sent to me in 1860 by the Colonel of the 3rd Buffs, engaged in the campaign against Peking, and I found on examination that it was an instance of this description. The Emperor had given to two or three of his favourite courtiers the *Yuen-yün* or "Original rhymes" which they were to fill up on a prescribed subject. This subject was the *Heang-shan*, or "Fragrant Hills," being the inner and more secluded portion of the park of the Summer palace, burned down by our forces in just, though bloodless, retribution for the murder of English and French prisoners by the Emperor's order. This turned out to be the birthplace of the Emperor himself, and the following account of it was given by an eye-witness: "Another collection of buildings, embosomed in trees, and girt round by a serpentine

* The dragon and phœnix are here typical of the prosperous man rising to high fame and honours.

‡ Intended to show, that true scholarship and genius are not confined to the mere knowledge of letters.

wall, which ran up the face of the hills, took a turn over their tops, and again descended to the plain. This was called the Fragrant Hills, and formed the fourth or innermost park of the Emperor. The arrangement of these *Heang-shan* pleasure grounds was even more complete than that of the three before mentioned. The flights of stone steps leading from palace to palace, with the usual summer-houses, shady bowers, and delightful terraces, made the spot quite unique, and of a perfect loveliness all its own." A view of the place, as above described, forms the subject of the drawing on silk, which is inscribed with the *bouts-rimés*, as filled up and stamped in red with the Emperor's private seal.

On the Poetry of the Chinese.

PART II.

Thus much having been said concerning mere versification, or what may be styled the outward form of Chinese poetry, we have next to consider the spirit that animates it,—and to ascertain, moreover, under what separate classes this department of their literature may be properly arranged, when viewed in relation to the divisions and nomenclature of European criticism.

It is here deemed necessary to premise, that such a mode of treating our subject is not adopted with the desire, or indeed with much prospect, of discovering any great correspondence or resemblence; but the process of comparison, to whatever result it may lead, is always useful on such occasions. It serves to methodize and give clearness to our conceptions of a subject comparatively new, as the artist sometimes introduces into his sketch a few objects of known and determinate dimensions, to assist in conveying juster notions of what he represents besides. On this occasion, too, it has another and a peculiar use: for everything concerning China stands unfortunately so insulated and remote from whatever generally constitutes a source of interest to Englishmen, that the only effectual way of attracting attention to it, is by bringing it in contact with objects nearer home, and thus allowing it to derive, from association, its fair share of advantage.

Unless submitted with some degree of allowance to the touchstone of European taste, the poetry of China might possibly succeed but indifferently. The test, if it be not considerately applied, is not only an illiberal, but an absurd one; and we have no right hastily to condemn the devotion which the ultra-Gangetic muse (however foreign to ourselves may be her features and garb) inspires in her own native haunts; or to be surprised at the number of her exalted admirers, from Confucius down to Kiënlung,—considering that national taste is the most conventional and capricious thing in the world; that it is determined by the infinite varieties of national character, national models, and national associations; and that even with the same old copies to refer to, and with a general similarity of institutions and customs, the different nations of the great European community vary, on such points, not a little among themselves.

Scimus,— et hanc veniam petimusque damusque vicissim.

There seem to be two causes to which Chinese literature, of the lighter or ornamental kind, has owed its indifferent reception in the West—first, a want of choice and selection in the subjects—and, secondly, a considerable absence of taste and judgment in the mode of treating them. It is really too much to expect that people will trouble themselves to look at what is either stupid or good-for-nothing in itself, or so marred in the intermediate process as to have lost all the attraction that it possessed in the original state. Let us only place the Chinese in our own situation on such occasions, and imagine the dismay of some fastidious scholar who should unluckily stumble upon one of our street ballads, *done* into bad Chinese, that is, with a verbal adherence to the original. It would either prove a perfect enigma, which is supposing the most fortunate case,—or he would thank his stars that the broad ocean divided him from such savages, and burn a supernumerary stick of incense before the shrine of his deified patron. The interests and reputation of Chinese literature in Europe therefore seem to demand, that its professors take some pains to render its introduction as attractive as possible, by a careful selection of the best subjects, and by treating these in such a manner as shall interest the greatest number of tasteful and cultivated readers. To weary the attention with a mere list of barbariphonous and uncouth names, to produce some bald and miserably verbal translation, to present the mere *caput mortuum* of something that in its original shape possessed spirit and beauty, is in fact scaring away attention from a new

F

subject, which, with a little discretion, might be rendered sufficiently attractive even to *general* readers. With such considerations in view, we might look to the successful exploring of the Chinese mine, and to the extraction of the ore of genius and sense from the mass of baser matter in which it happened to be imbedded.

Whenever a work of taste meets with universal approval in its own country, we may be assured that its success is in great measure owing to the merits of its style and language; and therefore it seems singularly injudicious to think of transferring the spirit and effect of such a Chinese composition into bad English, which it must inevitably become, by a servile adherence to the letter of the original. Between the greater number of European languages there is a certain connection, which allows literalness of rendering to be carried to a great extent—but a verbal translation from the one concerning which we now treat, must of necessity degenerate into a horrible jargon, which few persons would undergo the disgust of perusing. These observations do not apply in the same manner to works of scientific or doctrinal detail, as to those of mere *taste*, whose end and aim is to convey pleasure, as well as instruction,—though perhaps chiefly the first. A certain distinction, too, must be made between *prose* and *poetry*: the former doubtless both requires and admits of a closer rendering; with regard to the latter, we may adopt the happy illustration used on a similar occasion: " Celui qui prétendrait juger de quelque POEME que ce fût dans une traduction littérale, pourrait aussi raisonnablement espérer de trouver, sur le revers d'une tapisserie, les figures qu'elle représente dans toute leur délicatesse et toute leur splendeur." Verse, then, must be the shape into which Chinese, as well as all other poetry, ought to be converted, in order to do it mere justice; though in the present treatise, where so many different pieces are introduced for such different purposes, it has been thought expedient to adopt by turns a *prose translation*, a faithful *metrical version*, or an *avowed paraphrase*, as might best suit the subject and the occasion. More has been deferred herein, than suited the writer's own judgment and inclinations, to the prejudices of those who are still partial to the literal side of the question.

To take up our subject at its commencement—the earliest poetry of China, like that of all other nations, appears to have consisted in songs and odes, intended occasionally to be accompanied by music. Such is the nature of that curious compilation, made more than two thousand years since, by Confucius, and illustrative of a state of things certainly very different from that which exists at the present day. It is divided into four portions, of which the first, the largest, and most interesting, is called *Kwoh foong*, 國風 'the manners of different states,'—that is, of the states into which a portion of the present empire was then divided. These had all of them a kind of feudal dependence on one sovereign, who, in order to possess himself of the best means of estimating the character and sentiments of the various people more or less under his sway, was furnished with the songs and odes most popular among each of them. This agrees in a singular manner with the following remark of a writer in the Spectator *: "I have heard," says he, "that a minister of state in the reign of Queen Elizabeth had all manner of books and ballads brought to him, of what kind soever, and took great notice how much they took with the people; upon which he would, and certainly might, very well judge of their present dispositions, and of the most proper way of applying them according to his own purposes."

The bulk of these curious vestiges of antiquity in the *Sheeking* do not rise beyond the most primitive simplicity, and their style and language, without the minute commentary that accompanies them, would not be always intelligible at the present day. This commentary, however, explains and elucidates their meaning, and, by means of the historical associations which it serves to convey, renders these songs the favourite study of the better informed at the present remote period. Every well-educated Chinese has the most celebrated pieces by heart, and there are constant allusions to them in modern poetry and writings of all kinds. Each stanza frequently ends with a species of repetition, or 'refrain,' common to such compositions in general; and, in proof of the extreme simplicity of these primitive songs, one of them is presented below. In the paraphrase which follows, it has

* No. 502.

been necessary to embody the full sense of what is only hinted at in the original, and explained at length in the commentary; according to which commentary, the ode has a reference to the success of a rich and powerful suitor, who carries off the bride that had already been contracted to a humbler rival. The *kieu*, 鳩, or 'robber-bird,' is constantly alluded to in modern writing, as the emblem of unjust appropriation:—

維鵲有巢
之子于歸
維鳩居之
百兩御之

維鵲有巢
之子于歸
維鳩方之
百兩將之

維鵲有巢
之子于歸
維鳩盈之
百兩成之

" The nest yon winged artist builds,
The robber-bird shall tear away;
—So yields her hopes th'affianced maid,
Some wealthy lord's reluctant prey.

" The anxious bird prepares a home,
In which the spoiler soon shall dwell;
—Forth goes the weeping bride, constrain'd,
A hundred cars the triumph swell.

" Mourn for the tiny architect,
A stronger bird hath ta'en its nest;
—Mourn for the hapless, stolen bride,
How vain the pomp to soothe her breast!"

The second and third parts of the ancient book of odes, called respectively *Ta-ya* 大雅 and *Seaou-ya* 小雅, are said to have been composed for the purpose of being sung or recited on state occasions: they treat of the great and virtuous actions of heroes and sages, or express their sentiments. The following example, however, which is taken from the *Seaou-ya* 小雅, would seem rather to be of a more private description. It is explained as referring to the pain felt by the poet at the unworthy conduct of some ungrateful friend; and the allusions to the storm, &c., are of course figurative :—

習習谷風
將恐將懼
將安將樂
維風及雨
維予與女
女轉棄予

習習谷風
將恐將懼
將安將樂
維風及頹
寘予于懷
棄予于遺

習習谷風
無草不死
忘我大德
維山崔嵬
無木不萎
思我小怨

" Now scarce is heard the zephyr's sigh
To breathe along the narrow vale :
Now sudden bursts the storm on high,
In mingled rush of rain and hail.
—While adverse fortune louring frown'd
Than our's no tie could closer be ;
But lo ! when ease and joy were found,
Spurn'd was I, ingrate—spurn'd by thee.

"Now scarce is felt the fanning air
Along the valley's sloping side;
Now winds arise, and light'nings glare,
Pours the fell storm its dreadful tide!
—While fears and troubles closely prest,
By thee my love was gladly sought:
But once again with quiet blest,
Thou view'st me as a thing of nought!

"The faithless calm shall shift again,
Another gale the bleak hill rend,
And every blade shall wither then,
And every tree before it bend:
—Then shalt thou wail thy lonesome lot,
Then vainly seek the injur'd man,
Whose virtues thou hadst all forgot,
And only learn'd his faults to scan."

The fourth and last portion of the ancient poetical classic is called *Soong*, 頌—that is, eulogies or panegyrics on the ancestors of the dynasty Chow, then filling the throne, and on the great personages of antiquity. They appear to have been a species of hymn, sung before the emperor when he sacrificed as *pontifex maximus*, (which has always been the particular office of Chinese sovereigns,) in the temples of heaven and earth, or in the hall of his ancestors. Whatever may be the real character of the *Sheeking* on the score of poetical merit, it is at least curious, as having been *compiled* more than twenty centuries prior to our time, and some portions of it *composed* at a still earlier date. A pervading characteristic of the whole, as might be predicated of the early poetry of every country, is the boldness and frequency of the figures which are introduced.*

* One of the most striking examples appears as a quotation in Dr. Morrison's Dictionary, Part I. page 434:—

"The royal legions were numerous and imposing;
Swift, as if they flew upon wings;
Impetuous, as a torrent or a cataract;
Firm, as the base of a mountain;

It may be laid down as a rule, that every species of composition will be studied and perfected in exact proportion to the estimation in which it is held, or the grandeur and interest of the occasions on which it is employed. When lyric compositions, like the odes of Pindar and the Carmen Seculare &c. of Horace, were displayed on great national and religious festivals,—or shone forth the subjects of public or imperial patronage,—they became objects to which the first geniuses of the age directed their efforts; and the perfection which they attained was commensurate with the esteem in which they were held. In modern China, if odes are expressly composed for great court ceremonials, we have not yet met with any. Such ceremonials are frequently accompanied by music, but that there are words to the music has not been so clearly ascertained.

There is a common species of composition called *Ko*, 歌 which cannot be better rendered than by 'Song,' or 'Rhapsody.' Its structure is as wild as the thoughts and imagery which it generally contains, the lines being of every length but distinguished by recurring rhymes at intervals. Here follows a specimen :—

萬里巡行多少凄涼途路
情看雲山重疊處似我亂
愁交併四邊落葉響秋聲
長空孤雁添悲更題起傷
心事淚如傾回望馬嵬坡
下不覺恨塡膺裊裊旌旗
蔽殘日風搖影匹馬崎岐
怎暫停怎暫停只見黃埃
散漫天昏冥峨嵋山下少
人行冷雨斜風撲面迎

" In my wanderings of a thousand leagues, how many mournful thoughts afflict me

Resistless, as the course of a river,
Forming an unbroken line, in matchless order ;
Their motions inscrutable, their prowess invincible,
They proceeded to the conquest of the state Seu."

on the road—I behold yon cloudy mountains piled one upon another,—the emblems of my accumulated sorrows.—Around me the dropping leaves produce an autumnal sound —In the vast expanse, the solitary wild-fowl adds to my silent grief—I brood over my cares, and my tears descend—Looking back towards the base of *Matuy* Hill, an involuntary melancholy fills my breast—I see the waving banners intercept the setting sun—their shadows dancing in the breeze *—My horse has stopped at the precipitous turning.—Wherefore do we linger, wherefore do we linger?—There is nought but yellow sand drifting around—The sky is growing dark and gloomy—Few are the passengers at the foot of yon arched mountain:—the cold rain, urged by the gusty wind, is driving in my face."

Popular songs and ballads hold but a low rank in the literature of the country: and if we should even go so far as to include under this denomination the detached snatches of irregular verse (also called *Keoh* 曲) which are met with in their drama, the truth of the position would not be materially affected. The stage, and everything pertaining to it, enjoys a lower estimation than in any part of Europe: and we may take occasion to notice in this place, that the Chinese cannot strictly be said to possess *dramatic* poetry, in the sense which the term bears among ourselves, who apply it to the whole of a dramatic composition, and chiefly to tragedy, They make no distinction between tragedy and comedy in their stage pieces, the dialogue of which is composed in ordinary *prose;* while the principal performer now and then chaunts fourth, in unison with music, a species of song or 'vaudeville;' and the name of the tune or air is always inserted at the top of the passage to be sung. Here follow a few lines from the drama ‡ called "An Heir in Old

* This alludes to a tragical event in history, which occurred at the above-mentioned place. The emperor Yuen-tsoong (A. D. 702) had a mistress named Yangkuei, who was discovered carrying on an intrigue with a Tartar prince or noble, called Ganloshan. The emperor abstained from punishing the guilty female, which led to remonstrances on the part of his ministers; but instead of attending to them, he complied with the request of Yangkuei, and gave the Tartar a military command within his dominions. No sooner had the latter reached his destination, than he set up the standard of rebellion, and the emperor, hastily assembling a large army, and accompanied by his favourite Yangkuei, proceeded to meet him in Szechuen. When they had reached the base of the mountain *Matuy*, the soldiers mutinied, declaring that Yangkuei was the occasion of the rebellion, and demanding that she should be put to death before they consented to meet the enemy. The emperor was obliged to comply, and ordered her to be strangled on the spot—but his subsequent grief for her fate was the cause of his own death.

‡ London, 1816. French version, Paris, 1819.

Age." The chief character in the piece, an old man who is anxious to obtain an heir before he dies, sets fire to his bonds of debt, hoping that such a sacrifice may induce the accomplishment of his wishes—and, when the papers are consumed, he breaks out thus:—

"Do'st ask me why, by this rash hand,
A treasure to the flames was given?
Why but t'avert, ere yet too late,
The vengeance of offended heaven!

"Full sixty years, by various arts,
For wealth I've toil'd, without an heir:
Who knows but heaven may yet relent,
And listen to a suppliant's prayer!"

While it is true that the Chinese themselves make no distinction between comedy and tragedy, a translator from their language is still at liberty to apply those terms, according to the serious and dignified, or comic and familiar character of the composition which he selects. The writer of this has therefore not scrupled to give the title of tragedy to a rather favourable specimen of the Chinese stage, which he lately put into an English dress. In the unity of the plot, the dignity of the personages, the grandeur and importance of the events, the strict award of what is called poetical justice,—nay, in the division into five principal portions or acts, it might satisfy the most fastidious and strait-laced of the old European critics. Love and war, too, constitute its whole action, and the language of the imperial lover is frequently passionate to a degree one is not prepared for in such a country as China. The nature of its civil institutions, and the degraded state of the female sex, might generally be pronounced unfavourable to the more elevated strains of the erotic muse. The bulk of the people, it might be thought, are too much straitened for the bare means of subsistence, through the pressing demands of an excessive population, to admit of their lounging about and singing after the most approved manner of idle shepherds and shepherdesses; and the well-educated class, which comprehends almost all the higher ranks, or those in the employ of the government, too proud and unfeeling to make love the theme of their compositions, which are doubtless *chiefly* confined to moral and speculative, or descriptive subjects. The Drama in question, however, if it served no better purpose, might teach us not to pronounce too dogmatically on such points by reasonings *a priori*, but to wait patiently for the fruits of actual research and experience.

It has been observed in Part I. that the most flourishing era of modern poetry was under the T'āng dynasty. The most celebrated poet of that age was the renowned Letaepih, born in the province Szechuen, about A.D. 720. He is made to give the following account of himself in a play called "The Golden Token," which the writer of this once thought of putting into English, but abandoned as deficient in plot and incident. "When I was born," says the poet "my mother dreamed that the morning star shone upon her bosom, and hence called me, Taepih, 'surpassing brightness:' when the emperor Yuentsoong commenced his reign, I was admitted to an audience in the imperial hall, and conversed of state affairs: the son of heaven conferred on me a repast, and helped me with his own hand." The poetical character in China has of old been associated with the liberal use of wine. So it has, apparently, everywhere else. The poetical brain has loved the stimulus of alcohol, or tobacco, or opium, from Anacreon down to Burns, Byron, and Coleridge.

Laudibus arguítur vini vinosus Homerus,
Ennius ipse pater nunquam nisi potus ad arma
Prosiluit dicenda.

The inimitable humour of Byron is displayed in his account of the symposium with Sheridan, when the party was "first silent, then talky, then argumentative, then disputatious, then unintelligible, then altogethery, then inarticulate, and then drunk." Next came the carrying Sheridan down the "d—d corkscrew stair-case, which had certainly been constructed before the discovery of fermented liquors, and to which no legs, however crooked, could possibly accommodate themselves." Letaepih's intemperate propensities occasioned, it is said, his banishment from court; but he remained uncured, and at last fell overboard from the boat in which he was travelling, and was drowned. Any one who thought it worth while to know more concerning this person, and some of his cotemporaries, might find their lives (though without their poetry), given at some length by Father Amyot, in the fifth volume of the "Mémoires sur les Chinois." The following is not a bad sample of an Anacreontic, and may be freely rendered as below ;

日日人空老
年年春更歸
相歡在尊酒
不用惜花飛

Old age hastens on, as each fleet hour passes,
  Though spring ev'ry year re-illumines the glade:
So boys let's be jolly, and fill up our glasses,
  Ah, why should we sigh for the flowers that fade!

A number of esteemed collections, called *T'angshee*, or "Poems of the T'āng Dynasty," are regarded, for the most part, as the compositions of Letaepih, and a few more of the better poets of that day. They contain many favourable specimens, evincing both taste and imagination, and the following passage may be considered as tolerable. A person fishing in a boat, upon a lake, is supposed to have been led, by the track of peach blossoms floating on the water, into a narrow creek, which he pursued to a distance, until he reached a place inhabited by beings who, from the primitive simplicity of their manners, seemed to have escaped, in that secluded retreat, the persecution of the celebrated tyrant Tsinchehwang, 秦始皇 and to have had no communication with the rest of the world since. On his return from this little Chinese paradise, the adventurous boatman related what he had seen,—or perchance only dreamed; but on attempting to find the place again, it had vanished. There is a neat allusion to the famous burning of the books by the tyrant's command :—

炊烟落落少人居
風景依稀太古餘
草木盡生無稅地
子孫常讀未燒書
鷄鳴白日來溪洞
犬吠紅雲出草廬
若使扁舟能再返
十年余欲效為漁

The Inlet of Peach Blossoms.

Few were th' inhabitants of that fair dell,—
Remnants their manners were of other days,—
Flourish'd their fields in peace,—no impost fell
Midway check'd labour's fruitful course,—the lays
Their children sung had 'scaped the *general blaze*:
Adown the vale was heard the cock's shrill strain;
The watch-dog's voice welcom'd the morning rays;
Oh, could my bark those happy fields regain,
Long years of toil I'd brave—nor deem my labours vain!

The following specimen is from the same collection with the preceding. The value of timely showers, to which it alludes, can only be duly felt in a hot climate and a thirsty soil like the south of China, where, according to the common saying, "Three days make a short drought—five days a long one:"—

好雨知時節
當春乃發生
隨風潛入夜
潤物細無聲
野徑雲俱黑
江船火獨明
曉看紅濕處
花重錦官城

An Evening Shower in Spring.

See how the gently falling rain
  Its vernal influence sweetly showers,
As through the calm and tepid eve
  It silently bedews the flowers.

Cloudy and dark th' horizon spreads,
  Save where some boat its light is burning:
But soon the landscape's tints shall glow
  All radiant, with the morn returning.

There exist abundant materials of poetry in what may be called the heroic ages of China, when she was divided into independent states, contending against each other for sovereignty. The following lines are supposed to have been written by a certain emperor to his victorious general, of whose successes in the south he had just heard. The third and fourth lines are transposed in our version:—

The South subdued.

Servant, well done—the erring south restor'd,
Bends to the prowess of thy glittering sword;
High as the orbs thy light'ning standard gleams,
Thy drum's loud music shakes the mountain streams,
And heaven's own race alights on earth again,
The foe to scatter to their murky den!
Know, when with pride thy glad return we hail,
Thy sovereign's hand shall loose his hero's mail!

大將南征胆氣豪
腰橫秋水雁翎刀
風吹鼉鼓山河動
電閃旌旗日月高
天上麒麟原有種
穴中螻蟻豈能逃
太平待詔歸来日
朕與先生解戰袍

No composition, however, to which the name of Epic could properly be applied, has ever rewarded European research. Though poetry exists in some shape or other all over the world, the same universality hardly attaches to that modification of it, which we style the Epopee; and, but for the two great prototypes of Homer, there seems to be no absolute necessity for supposing that it must have arisen, or at least been so frequent, in our western literature. It was confessedly in imitation of Homer that Virgil wrote, and all subsequent epics have been more or less, in conception at least, if not in execution, imitations of these two, or of each other. Voltaire himself has informed us, that when he consulted the advice of a friend previous to composing his own Henriade, he met with no better encouragement than this: "You undertake a work which is not suited to us—les Français n'ont pas la tête épique."—But without going farther for reasons, the first part of this treatise may perhaps have served to demonstrate, that the turn and construction of Chinese verse unfits it for such sustained compositions. To be esteemed good, it must be so highly elaborated, that the costliness of the material may place limits to the size of the structure. It would be a tremendous attempt to preserve such nicely-balanced couplets through the slow length of an epic poem; not to mention, that when the task had been completed, it might weary the reader as much as it had disquieted the author, and bestow upon the first all the sleep of which it had deprived the second. The only long metrical narrations of the Chinese are some novels and licentious * pieces, in which the structure of the verse is altogether loose—a sort of "stans pede in uno" measure—and devoid of those characteristics which constitute the chief merit of their poetry. Such compositions, accordingly, do not possess that degree of estimation, nor hold that rank in literature which, as we have before observed, is necessary to the due perfection of every department of the art. †

There is another description of poetry which we should not look for in China,—namely, the Pastoral,—and for every obvious reasons. It has not only been the care of the government, from the earliest ages, to give every direct encouragement to agriculture, and to the production of food for man alone, but there have always existed some absurd prejudices and maxims, not to say positive laws, against an extended consumption of flesh food. ‡ The penal code denounces severe punishments against those who kill *their own* cattle without an express license.§ It is a well known principle, that where tillage exists to a considerable extent, the rent of land reserved for pasture must, in proportion to its goodness, be equal to that of land employed in producing grain; and this, under a rice cultivation, where three crops per annum are said sometimes to be obtained, must have such an obvious effect in raising the comparative price of meat, as must necessarily discourage its consumption among so frugal a people as the Chinese, even without the intervention of any positive law. There is accordingly no people in the

* There never was any assertion more incorrect than this of Martinius, concerning the lighter poetry of China: "Insunt iis quædam de amando, sed castitatem magis quam nostrorum poetarum mollitiem spirantia, *magna decori ubique cura.*"—In translating the excellent prose romance of "The Fortunate Union," otherwise unexceptionable, the writer of this was obliged to exclude two passages in verse, which were distinguished—"*minimâ decori curâ.*" There are whole poems of the same description.

† Those half-mechanical conceits, of which the principal merit consists in the imitation, in tortured verses, of some object in art or nature, as a knot, a circle, a sceptre, &c., are well known to the Chinese: but sound taste and criticism have universally consigned these *difficiles nugæ* to a very low rank in literature, and we therefore abandon them without further notice.

‡ See a long paper, "Sur l'usage de la viande en Chine." *Mémoires*, tom. xi.

§ Book iv., sect. 233.

world (the Hindoos * always excepted), that consumes so little meat, or so much fish and vegetable food—nor, again, is there any country in which fewer cattle are employed for the purpose of draft and burden. Where every institution tends so fatally to keep a population up to the very utmost limits of a bare subsistance, and where neither pride nor prejudice steps in between the labourer and his work, human exertion naturally supplants every other. In the southern parts of the empire, therefore, beasts of carriage and draft, with the exception of a few miserable riding horses, and a few buffaloes for ploughing, are nearly unknown. Towards Peking, and the uncultivated borders of Tartary, the case becomes altered: but the Great Wall may still be considered, generally, as the boundary which separates two people, one of them exclusively pastoral, and the other as exclusively tillers of the earth.

The esteem in which the business of tillage is held, may be expected to have rendered it the subject of poetical celebration: and we find the praises of fertile fields sung in such strains as the following. Years of dearth they term "years of nothingness:"—

Fields that know no Years of Dearth.

Though man's superfluous labour ceas'd to till
The fertile glebe, ne'er would its bounties end:
Though rusting lay the abandon'd ploughshare—still
O'er the fair land would waving harvests bend!

Less happy soils may pine in years of dearth—
Late though we sow, we *early* reap the field;
A thousand roods of richly-teemed earth,
In verdant crops ten thousand measures yield!

Why haunt we then, the sylvans mossy shrine—
Why ask what harvest shall our toils attend?
See the sweet spring with surer presage shine,
And balmy airs, and length'ning days descend!

* Bishop Heber's Journal proves that the Hindoos themselves are not so scrupulous as they have been supposed. They consume milk, too, which the Chinese, strange to say, never think of.

人工雖未及
不任耕耘早
無年皆有穫
膴膴盈千畝
何須祭田祖
況值春臺啟

地力信非常
偏宜黍稷良
後種亦先芳
菁菁保萬箱
詎要祭農祥
和風日又長

We have next to notice a large class of poetry, which may be properly styled Moral or Didactic. The long citation from the philosopher Kwan-foo tsze 關夫子, given by Dr. Morrison at p. 147 of the Third Part of his Dictionary, comes under this head. It commences thus:—

> "Venerate heaven and earth; perform the rites to the gods,
> Worship your ancestors: be dutiful to your parents:
> Observe the laws: revere your teachers and superiors,
> Love your brothers: and be true to your friends, &c."

The whole piece bears some resemblance to the Golden verses of Pythagoras, particularly in the commencement, which may be thus literally rendered:—

H

"First, as the laws ordain, th' immortal gods
Worship: observe your vows: the great of yore
Next, and the manes of the dead revere:
Honour your parents, and your next of kin, &c."

There are innumerable poems, or rather metrical essays, whose object it is to convey the doctrines and precepts of the great national sages and others. The whole of the well-known work called *Shing yu*, 聖諭 Instructions addressed to the People by the second Emperor of the present Tartar Family, has been cast into a short, rhyming verse. The example, given in Part I. at page 11, comes likewise under this head; as do all the similar productions of the Buddhists, and other sects. We must consider these as forming a portion of the national literature in the gross, although they have nothing to do with Confucius or his doctrines, and are commonly held by the privileged learned in as great contempt as the superstitions to which they pertain.

In the course of their lighter works, Chinese writers frequently introduce moral reflections in verse with very good effect. A couplet, a quatrain, or a passage of eight or more lines, agreeably engages the reader's attention in his progress through a romance or novel, and generally accompanies the transition to some other part of the story. They are not altogether unlike the rhymes at the close of the scenes in our older plays, and usually consist, as those did, of some reflection upon what has gone before, or what is immediately to follow; though in a narrative they certainly find a more proper place than in the drama, and are not there subject to the reproach of bad taste, which has very properly excluded such passages from our own modern stage pieces. Here follow examples from "The Fortunate Union:"—

奸狡休誇用智深
誰知敗露出無心
勸君不必遮人目
上有蒼蒼日鑒臨

模糊世事倏多變
直至交情从自深
若問老天顛倒意
大都假此煉人心

"Vain are the crafty villain's wiles, most vain,
Often, when vaunted most—disgrace, defeat,
Rush headlong in from quarters little feared!
Harken to counsel, friend, and when secure
You deem yourself from mortals' purblind eyes,
Think there's a heaven above, that surveys all!

"Human events in quick vicissitude
Succeed each other: but true friendship's ties
Gain strength from time! Ask ye why sovereign heav'n
Thus vexes mortals?—'Tis to try their hearts
Like metal in the fiery crucible."

Satire, viewed as a means of recommending virtue by discrediting vice, cannot be said to exist in any regular form, or to constitute a particular branch of literature. Some of the ancient pieces in the *Sheeking* have been considered as levelled at persons existing when they were composed; but they have no more claim on this account to the name of satires, than Horace's ode "In Mævium." There is no country, at the same time, in which anonymous lampoons, and similar vehicles of invective or ridicule, are more common. They form one of the most ordinary outlets for the ebullitions of public feeling: and must be considered, by every person who has had opportunities of making the observation, as a very important check, under so absolute a despotism, upon the conduct of Chinese rulers. The highest officers of government are not exempt from these covert attacks, which are constantly made, notwithstanding the severest punishments in case of detection :—

> ———" I will ease my heart,
> Although it be with hazard of my head."

The following are specimens of satirical passages introduced in the course of a novel, to ridicule the worthless characters, both male and female :—

只道諛言人所喜
誰知轉變做羞恥
若非天賦老面皮
痛削如何當得起

珠面金髮宮樣粧
朱脣海濶額山長
閻王見慣渾閑事
嚇殺劉郎與阮郎

> " He thought his flattering phrases needs must prove
> Welcome—nor dream'd of foul repulse and shame :
> And had not bounteous heav'n his forehead arm'd
> With impudence unmatch'd, this keen rebuff
> Had stung him ! "

> " In pearls and gold all gorgeously attir'd,
> No arts could deck her native ugliness;
> The demon king might view her as his own—
> She carried terror to a bridegroom's eye !"

We now proceed to consider a very extensive department of Chinese poetry, the Descriptive, which to us strangers must be the most agreeable of all, and which really possesses some attractive features. The whole language abounds in figurative expressions, derived from the most pleasing or most striking objects and circumstances in nature. Thus " Spring dreams and autumnal clouds " mean flitting visions of happiness—unattainable good is represented by " the moon's reflection in the wave "—" floating clouds obscuring the day " express the temporary shade thrown by detraction on illustrious characters—difficulty of acting is figured by " the grass and tangle in one's path "—female beauty by the obvious and common semblance of " a fair flower"—" spring" is the emblem of joy, " autumn" of sorrow—gladness is expressed by the heart's flowers being all full-blown"—the virtue of the female character is pictured under " the white gem, the pure crystal, the cold and transparent ice"—" the season when peach blossoms are in beauty " means that of marriage, as marriages were anciently celebrated in spring—searchers after pleasure are depicted under the figure of " bees and butterflies among flowers"—and so on without end.

There exist a great number of figurative allusions, which contain a particular reference to some event in history or romance ; and as the facts, or fables, at which these only *hint*, cannot sometimes be discovered without the assistance of a well-informed native, this circumstance constitutes a considerable obstacle, in the present state of our knowledge, to the successful study of Chinese poetry, anywhere but in the country itself. The following are examples of such allusions :—" The heart that responds to the lute" means yielding to seductive arts, and refers to the story of a young damsel named *Wun keun*, who, being beloved by a youth called *Sze ma*, was serenaded by him on the lute, with a song called *Foong kew hwang*, 鳳 求 凰 or " the bird *foong* in search of its mate." The story says that *Ke sin toong*, 其 心 動, " her heart was moved," and she eloped with her admirer towards morning, leaving the traces of her flight along the dewy pathway.

A grateful return for benefits is implied under these expressions: "The spirit which knit the grass"—and "the bird that brought the yellow flowers." 1. An emperor of the dynasty called *Chow* 周, enjoined it on his son and successor to bury alive, after the old Scythian or Tartar fashon, one of his favourite mistresses in the same grave with himself. The son, however, refrained from executing this portion of the imperial will, on the ground of its cruelty, and gave away the lady in marriage to a noble. On making war against the state called *Tsin* 秦, the new emperor was opposed by a formidable leader; but he dreamed at night that he saw the deceased father of the lady he had saved from death, who told him, that in return for the life granted to his daughter, he would assist him against the enemy. The result proved the vision to be prophetic—the hostile leader was defeated, and some invisible agent so twisted the long grass which impeded his flight, as to cause his capture. 2. A person who saw a bird fall to the earth, wounded by an arrow, had the humanity to draw out the weapon, and restore the bird to liberty as soon as it recovered. Being soon afterwards sick and in danger of his life, the bird appeared to him, bearing in its bill some yellow flowers, which the patient was advised to try, and which presently restored him to health.

The poetry of China is not unsupplied with mythological aids: every element of nature—with all the phenomena that these exhibit—each hill, stream, and wood, has its presiding spirit. There is *Hwuy loo*, 會羅, "the monarch of fire;" *Luy koong*, 雷公, "the thunder god;" *Luh shin*, 祿神, "the spirit of the autumnal wave;" and others innumerable. An interesting divinity, called *Yuĕ laou*, 月老, "the old man of the moon," deserves some notice. It is his particular business to tie together at their birth, with an invisible silken cord, all youths and maidens who are predestined for each other, after which the most distant separation, and apparently insurmountable obstacles, cannot prevent their ultimate union. This is what is called (*Yew yuen*) 有緣, "having a connection in fate." With such a variety of imaginative resources, and with some of the brightest leaves of the book of nature, displayed to them in an immense tract of country, surpassed by none in natural advantages, this people would be dull indeed, if they could not turn to some account the materials which they possess.

The muse, too, may call to her assistance the smaller race of fairies, or sprites, who are supposed to haunt the recesses of hills and woods, and to exercise either a benign, or a malicious influence over mortals. Possessing but a vague notion of the ideas which the Chinese really entertained of these imaginary persons, the writer of this applied for information to his Sëenseng (or *pundit*, as such a character would be called less far to the east), and the reply was to this effect: "They are mysterious beings who convert themselves at will into the semblance, sometimes of beautiful women, at others of ugly monsters—in infinite variety. They delight most in frustrating the attempts made by the devotees of Fŏ, or Buddha, to reach a superhuman state, and whenever these chance to waver the least in their faith or practice, they become immediately *possessed* ("chŏ leaou moo"), that is, the malicious spirits acquire a dominion over them." Being asked if he believed in their existence, he seemed rather unprepared to answer, but observed that they possessed the greatest influence over the minds of the country-people, and the devotees of the superstition above-mentioned. It may be noticed, that Confucius neither gave the express sanction of his opinion to the existence of unembodied spirits, nor did he expressly deny the same: but transmitted these early traditions of his country exactly as he found them; busying himself chiefly with the more important concerns of political government and morals.

Several of the pieces already given might be arranged under the descriptive class. The following quotation from a novel, called "The Dreams of the Red Chamber," is rather a poetical account of a young Chinese profligate, although it consists of a very irregular species of verse, in six and seven words. The version below is lineatim, and almost verbatim, and pretends to nothing more than a very close adherence to the sense of the original; which, it must be remarked, is not an extract from a long poem, but one of those poetical breaks, with which prose works of taste are generally embellished:

無故尋愁覓恨
有時似傻如狂
縱然生得好皮囊
一膓原來是莽
潦倒不通庶務
愚頑怕讀文章
行為偏僻性乖張
那管人間誹謗

"The paths of trouble heedlessly he braves,
Now shines a wit—and now a madman raves:
His outward form by nature's bounty drest,
Foul weeds usurped the wilderness, his breast;
And bred in tumult, ignorant of rule,
He hated letters—an accomplish'd fool!
In act depraved, contaminate in mind,
Strange! had he fear'd the censures of mankind.

富貴不知樂業
貧窮難耐凄涼
可憐辜負好韶光
于國于家無望
天下無能第一
古今不肖無雙
寄言紈袴與膏粱
莫效此兒形狀

"Titles and wealth to him no joys impart—
By penury pinch'd, he sank beneath the smart:
Oh, wretch! to flee the good thy fate intends,
Oh, hopeless! to thy country and thy friends!
In uselessness, the first beneath the sky,
And curst, in sinning, with supremacy!
Minions of pride and luxury, lend an ear,
And shun his follies, if his fate ye fear!"

The language of descriptive poetry exists in every intermediate gradation, from the perfectly formed couplet and stanza, to those figurative compositions, which differ from prose in little else than the brilliancy of their imagery, or the elevation of their sentiment. Besides the *Tsze*, of which an example has been given in the First Part (page 19), there is a still less fettered species—a kind of impassioned prose, into which the writer of a narrative now and then breaks forth, when inspired by the occasion. The following example is taken from the romance of "The Fortunate Union," and describes the heroine when she is first seen by her future lover. The parallelisms are marked and divided by colons in the translation :—

嬌媚如花而肌膚光艷羞灼灼之浮華輕盈似燕而舉止安詳笑翩翩之失措眉畫春山而淺濃多態覺春山之有愧眼橫秋水而流轉生情怪秋水之無神腰纖欲折立亭亭不怕風吹俊影難描鶴癯癯最宜月照髮光可鑑不假塗膏秀色堪飱何須膩粉慧心悄悄越掩越靈望而知其為仙子中人俠骨冷冷愈柔愈烈察而識其非閨閣之秀蕙性蘭心初只疑美人顏色珠圓玉潤久方知君子風流

"With the delicacy of a flower, her complexion displayed a clear brilliancy which put to shame the floating light of day: with the buoyant lightness of the swallow, her movements were ordered with inimitable grace and propriety. The arches of her brows were like the outlines of the vernal hills in the distance, but in their changeful expression they shamed the varying tints of even the vernal hills: the brightness of her eyes equalled that of the clear wave in autumn, but the living sentiment which flowed from them made you wonder how the autumnal wave had lost its deity.* Her waist, like a thread in fineness, seemed ready to break; yet was it straight and erect, and feared not the fanning breeze: the shadowy graces of her person it was as difficult to delineate, as the form of the white bird, rising from the ground by moonlight. The natural gloss of her hair resembled the bright polish of a mirror, without the false assistance of unguents: her face was perfectly lovely in itself, and needed not paint to adorn it. The native intelligence of her mind seemed to have gathered strength from retirement; and beholding her, you might know she was of a superior order of beings: the cold and rigid strictness of her manners, severe as she herself was soft and delicate, proved her to be no ordinary inhabitant of the female apartments. Her sweet and feminine disposition, comparable to fragrant flowers, might lead one at first to class her with other fair ones: but the perfection of this pearl, the polish of this gem, discoverable on a longer acquaintance, proved that she possessed qualities not inferior to the most spirited of the opposite sex."

Under the descriptive class may be properly introduced a very singular production—a poem on London, composed by a Chinese who visited England about the year 1813. Some notice of it appeared, for the first time, in the Quarterly Review for 1817; but the present opportunity admits of the translation being accompanied by the original. No apology, perhaps, is needed for the insertion of the whole poem, notwithstanding its length, considering that it is a native of the remotest shores of Asia who sings the glories of the British capital—"Præsertim cùm omne studium atque omne ingenium contulerit Archias, ad populi Romani gloriam laudemque celebrandam."—The reviewer made a trivial mistake in stating that it was written by "a common Chinese," for the author was in a respectable station of life, and a person of good acquirements, who accompanied home an English gentleman as his instructor in the language. He was in fact a very *uncommon* Chinese, inasmuch as he appears to have possessed an inclination and capacity

* Called *Lŭhshin.*

for observation, by no means usual among his travelled countrymen, who are generally of a class much inferior to himself. The remarks are, as might be expected, confined exclusively to objects which at once strike the eye, and they do not extend to the remoter points of intelligent investigation, since the author's very limited knowledge of our language, and total inability to comprehend the nature of our institutions, placed such higher objects entirely out of his reach. Being a simple description, the poem contains but few flights of fancy; and as it would be a hopeless attempt, however well they may sound in Chinese, to give dignity in verse to matters so perfectly domestic and familiar to ourselves, it has been judged best to subjoin a literal prose translation :—

LONDON, IN TEN STANZAS.

海遥西北極
有國號英崙
地冷宜親火
樓高可摘星
意誠尊禮拜
心好尚持經
獨恨佛啷嘶
干戈不暫停

1.

Afar in the ocean, towards the extremities of the north-west,
There is a nation, or country, called ENGLAND :
The clime is frigid, and you are compelled to approach the fire ;
The houses are so lofty, that you may pluck the stars :
The pious inhabitants respect the ceremonies of worship,
And the virtuous among them ever read the Sacred books :
They bear a peculiar enmity towards the *French* nation,*
The weapons of war rest not for a moment (between them).

* In 1813.

山澤鍾靈秀
層巒展畫眉
賦人尊女貴
在地應坤滋
少女紅花臉
佳人白玉肌
由來情愛重
夫婦樂相依

2.

Their fertile hills, adorned with the richest luxuriance,
Resemble, in the outline of their summits, the arched eyebrows (of a fair woman).
The inhabitants are inspired with a respect for the female sex,
Who in this land correspond with the perfect features of nature:
Their young maidens have cheeks resembling red blossoms,
And the complexion of their beauties is like the white gem:
Of old has connubial affection been highly esteemed among them,
Husband and wife delight in mutual harmony.

夏月村郊晚
行人不斷遊
草長資牧馬
欄濶任棲牛
拾麥歌宜唱
尋花興未休
相呼早回首
烟霧恐迷留

3.

In the summer evenings, through the hamlets and gardens beyond the town,
Crowds of walkers ramble without number:
The grass is allowed to grow as a provision for horses,
And enclosures of wooden-rails form pastures for cattle.

The harvest is gathered in with the singing of songs:
The loiterers roam in search of flowers without end,
And call to each other to return in good time,
Lest the foggy clouds bewilder and detain them.

戲樓關永晝
燈後綵屏開
生旦姿容美
衣裝錦繡裁
曲歌琴笛和
跳舞皷簫催
最是詠諧趣
人人笑臉迴

4.

Their theatres are closed during the long days;
It is after dark that the painted scenes are displayed:
The faces of the actors are handsome to behold,
And their dresses are composed of silk and satin:
Their voices resound in unison with stringed and wind instruments,
And they dance to the inspiring note of drums and flutes:
It constitutes the perfection of harmonious delight,
Every one retires with a smiling countenance.

兩岸分南北
三橋隔水通
舟船過胯下
人馬步雲中
石磴千層疊
河流九派溶
洛陽天下冠
形勢畧相同

5.

The two banks of the river lie to the north and south,
Three bridges interrupt the stream, and form a communication.
Vessels of every kind pass between the arches,
While men and horses pace among the clouds :
A thousand masses of stone rise one above the other,
And the river flows through nine channels :
The bridge of *Loyang*, which out-tops all in our empire,
Is in shape and size somewhat like these.

富庶烟花地
帝城雙鳳闕
人工鬪物華
雲樹萬人家
公子馳車馬
佳人曳縠紗
六街花柳地
何處種桑蔴

6.

It is a rich, populous, and highly adorned land,
Its workmen vie with each other in the excellence of their manufactures.
Within the circuit of the imperial residence is a splendid palace ;
Lofty trees are immingled with unnumbered dwellings.
The young gentry ride in wheel-carriages and on horseback,
And the fair women clothe themselves in silken garments :
*The space in each street being devoted to ornament,
Where is there room for the mere useful productions of the earth ?

* Literally, "Every street being devoted to flowers and willows, where is there space to plant mulberries and hemp (to produce silk and flax)?"—There are explanatory notes, and a commentary, in the original, which we have not thought it necessary to give here.

高閣層層上
豪華第宅隆
鐵欄傍户密
河水繞牆通
粉壁塗文采
玻牕綴錦紅
最宜街上望
樓宇畫圖中

7.

The towering edifices rise story above story,
In all the stateliness of splendid mansions :
Railings of iron thickly stud the sides of every entrance,
And streams from the river circulate through the walls :
The sides of each apartment are variegated with devices ;
Through the windows of glass appear the scarlet hangings ;
And in the street itself is presented a beautiful scene,
The congregated buildings have all the aspect of a picture.

九月蘭墪裡
人情樂遠遊
移家入村郭
探友落鄉陬
車馬聲寥日
魚鰕價賤秋
樓房多寂寞
破壞及時修

8.

In London, about the period of the ninth moon,
The inhabitants delight in travelling to a distance :
They change their abodes, and betake themselves to the country,
Visiting their friends in their rural retreats :

The prolonged sound of carriages and steeds is heard through the day:
Then in autumn the prices of provisions fall:
And the greater number of dwellings being untenanted,
Such as require it are repaired and adorned.

大路多平坦
條條十字衢
兩傍行士女
中道騁騈車
夜市人喧店
冬寒雪積塗
晚燈懸路際
火燭燦星如

9.

The spacious streets are exceedingly smooth and level,
Each being crossed by others at intervals:
On either side perambulate men and women,
In the centre career along the carriages and horses;
The mingled sound of voices is heard in the shops at evening:
During midwinter the heaped-up snows adhere to the pathway;
Lamps are displayed at night along the street sides,
Whose radiance twinkles like the stars of the sky.

地冷難栽稻
由來不阻饑
濃茶調酪潤
烘麵裹脂肥
美饌盛銀盒
佳醪酌玉卮
土風尊飲食
入席預更衣

10.

The climate is too cold for the cultivation of rice,
But they have for ages been exempt from the evils of famine;
With strong tea they immingle rich cream,
And their baked wheaten bread is involved in unctuous lard.
Here excellent meats are served in covers of silver,
And fine wines are poured into gem-like cups;
The custom of the country pays respect to the ceremony of meals,
Previous to the repast, they make a change in their vestments.

Of a similar description with the stanzas on London is another poem, not concerning the English exclusively, but Europeans in general, composed by a Hong merchant who has been dead some years. This person, notwithstanding his unpoetical profession, was possessed of very respectable literary acquirements, and one of his sons held a high rank in the Imperial College at Peking:—"After an intercourse of thirty years (to use his own expressions), which had made him tolerably familiar with the peculiarities of foreigners, he had retired, stricken in years, into solitude, and amused himself over his cups (like Le-tae-pĭ, of course) in composing a score of stanzas commemorative of some strange customs and opinions prevailing beyond the seas."—The production corresponds with its title, *Se-yang tsa yoong*, 西洋雜詠 "Unconnected Stanzas on Europeans," and after the perusal of the foregoing description from a person who had viewed us at home, may be deemed curious, as depicting the estimation formed of us by one who had never left his own country. With that want of minute discrimination which might be expected under such circumstances, the verses treat chiefly of those leading features which are common to all nations wearing hats and coats, and mingle, together with the rest, the Papist rites and ceremonies of the Portuguese at Macao. Being less interesting to Englishmen than the poem which has already been given at full length, it may suffice to present an abstract of whatever observations it contains most deserving of notice.

The retired Bard commences with lauding the good faith of the foreigners,

K

who "make use of no formality, in their most extensive bargains, more solemn than a mere shake of the hand," and proceeds to hint, in the next verse, that "the simple virtues of barbarians have been the subject of praise from the oldest times." It is quite true that commercial transactions of the largest description are frequently conducted at Canton on the mere faith of promises; and the good poet had never been in the way of seeing our legal stamps and lawyers' bills at home, which might have gone far to make him withdraw his last compliment.

"When a guest arrives, the host helps him with his own hand to the juice of the grape;" and it is added in a note, "they welcome visitors with wine, and not with tea," which is the Chinese fashion. "To touch glasses in drinking is a mark of friendship. In winter evenings they sit by the fire, and pour out *cold* wine, careless of the snows which lie deep beyond the door." In China they always warm their wine. So they sometimes do in England, witness "Oxford Nightcaps."

"They make light of their lives," it is observed, "on occasions of personal contest, and when two of them quarrel, the consequences may be very serious. They stand face to face, and discharge fire-arms at each other on a given signal." In a note it is said, "If one fall, the survivor is not punished: if neither fall, there is an end of the quarrel." "They do this," adds the poet, "to show that they are not afraid—and so forth." An unconscious satire on the absurd custom of duelling, which our successors will rank with the "trial by battle," the *corsned*, and the drowning of witches.

Our author marvels much at the comparatively late period at which Europeans marry, but endeavours to explain it in this way: "Their distant voyages abroad keep them long from home, and it is not until they have accumulated a fortune that they return to take a wife. Many do not marry before fifty years of age; and if the bride be very young on these occasions, it is nothing unusual." The knowledge of the worthy Hong merchant on this subject seems to have been much on a par with that of the St. Helena lady, who asked if London were not thrown into great excitement by the arrival of the Indian fleet.*

* Mentioned as long ago as by Horace Walpole.

"In the regulation of the annual period, they have no intercalary moon, but the new year always commences ten days after the winter solstice. On this occasion they powder their heads with white dust, and all get tipsy." This evidently refers to good old times, and to manners now gone by. The author himself adds in a note: "This habit has of late years worn out." There is a variety of other detached observations, less worthy of notice, and the poem concludes with mentioning, that "the foreigners had been fighting together for some twenty years; but it was to be hoped they would soon make peace with one another, and all have an opportunity of improving themselves by an intercourse with China." Which they have since done, somewhat at China's expense.

In some remarks on the origin and progress of this distant Literature in England,* I observed that there was a favourable specimen of Poetry in the Eighth Volume of the Chinese Repository. The subject is the gathering of Tea-leaves among the hills in Spring. The young girl who sings the ballad describes the scenery, the weather, her own feelings, &c., and displays a natural and half-childish vanity which is at once pleasing and amusing. A very neat English version has since been made by Mr. W. T. MERCER, M.A. Oxon, and this so well conveys both the sense and the style of the original, that it has been printed below, stanza for stanza, page for page with the Chinese. The correspondent of the Repository states that the original was obtained from one of the merchants of the Green-tea country, being prettily printed on a square sheet of paper with a flowered red border. He remarks that it illustrates many points in the construction of Chinese verse, pointed out in the first edition of this present treatise. But the simple and popular nature of the Ballad would have rendered such niceties of construction, as have been explained in Part I., quite out of place. The verse, accordingly, is of that careless, easy and flowing character best suited to the occasion.

* Chinese Miscellanies, p. 70.

采茶詞

TEA-PICKING BALLAD.

一

儂家住萬山中
村北村南盡茗叢
社後雨前忙不了
朝朝早起課茶工

二

曉起臨粧畧整容
提籃出戶霧方濃
小姑大婦同携手
問上松羅第幾峰

三

空濛曉色早山矼
霧葉雲芽未易降
不識爲誰來解渴
教儂辛苦日雙雙

I.

Where thousand hills the vale enclose, our little hut is there,
And on the sloping sides around, the Tea grows everywhere;
And I must rise at early dawn, as busy as can be,
To get my daily labour done, and pluck the leafy tea.

II.

At early dawn I seize my crate, and sighing, oh, for rest,
Through the thick mist I pass the door, with sloven hair half-drest;
The dames and maidens call to me, as hand in hand they go,
"What steep do you, miss, climb to-day, what steep of high Sunglo?"

III.

Dark is the sky, the twilight dim still on the hills is set,
The dewy leaves and cloudy buds may not be gather'd yet;
Oh, who are they, the thirsty ones, for whom this work we do;
For whom we spend our daily toil, in bands of two and two?

四

雙雙相伴采茶枝
細語叮嚀莫要遲
既恐梢頭芽欲老
更防來日雨絲絲

五

采罷枝頭葉自稀
提籃貯滿始言歸
同人笑向池前過
驚起雙鳧兩處飛

六

一池碧水浸芙蕖
葉小如錢半未舒
行向磯頭清淺處
試看儂貌近何如

IV.

Like fellows we each other aid, and to each other say,
As down we pull the yielding twigs, "Sweet sister, don't delay;
E'en now the buds are growing old, all on the boughs atop,
And then to-morrow—who can tell?—the drizzling rain may drop."

V.

We've picked enow, the topmost bough is bare of leaves, and so
We lift our brimming loads, and by the homeward path we go;
In merry laughter by the pool, the lotus pool we hie,
When hark! uprise a Mallard pair, and hence affrighted fly!

VI.

Limpid and clear the pool, and there how rich the lotus grows,
And only half its opening leaves, round as the coins, it shows—
I bend me o'er the jutting brink, and to myself I say,
I marvel in the glassy stream, how looks my face to-day?

七

兩鬢髼鬆貌帶枯
誰家有婦醜如奴
只緣日日將茶采
雨灑風吹失故吾

八

朝來風雨又凄凄
小笠長藍手自提
采得旗鎗歸去後
相看却是半身泥

九

今日窓前天色佳
忙梳鴉鬢緊橫釵
忽忽便向園中去
忘却泥濘未換鞋

VII.

My face is dirty, out of trim my hair is, and awry,
Oh tell me where's the little girl so ugly now as I?
'Tis all because whole weary hours I'm forc'd to pick the tea,
And driving winds and soaking show'rs have made me what you see!

VIII.

With morn again come wind and rain, and though so fierce and strong,
With basket big and little hat I wend my way along;
Then home once more, when all is pick'd, and everybody sees
How muddy all our dresses are, and dabbled to the knees!

IX.

I saw this morning through the door a pleasant day set in,
Be sure I quickly drest my hair, and neatly fix'd my pin;
And featly sped I down the path to gain the wonted spot,
But, never thinking of the mire, my working shoes forgot!

十

園中纔到又聞雷
濕透弓鞋未肯回
遙囑鄰姑傳信去
把儂青笠寄將來

十一

小笠蒙頭不庇身
衣衫半濕像漁人
手中提着青絲籠
只少長竿與細綸

十二

雨過枝頭汎碧紋
樊來香氣便氤氳
高低摘盡黃金縷
染得衣襟處處芬

X.

The garden reach'd, my bow-shap'd shoes are soaking through and through;
And the sky is chang'd—the thunder rolls—I don't know what to do;
I'll call my comrades on the hill to pass the word with speed,
And fetch my green umbrella hat, to help me in my need.

XI.

But my little hat does little good, my plight is very sad!
I stand with clothes all dripping wet, like some poor fisher-lad;
Like him I have a basket, too, of meshes woven fine,
A fisher-lad, if I only had his fishing rod and line.

XII.

The rain is o'er, the outer leaves their branching fibres show,
Shake down the branch, and the fragrant scent about us 'gins to blow;
Gather the yellow golden threads that high and low are found—
Ah, what a precious odour now is wafted all around!

十三

芬芳香氣似蘭蓀
品色休寧勝婺源
采罷新芽施又發
今朝已是第三番

十四

番番辛苦不辭難
鴉髻斜家玉指寒
惟願儂家茶色好
賽他雀舌與龍團

十五

一月何曾一日閒
早時出采暮方還
更深尚在爐前焙
怎不教人損玉顏

XIII.

No sweeter perfume does the wild and fair Aglaia shed,
Throughout Woo-yuen's bounds my tea the choicest will be said;
When all are pick'd we'll leave the shoots to bud again in spring,
But for this morning we have done the third, last gathering.

XIV.

Oh, weary is our picking, yet do I my toil withhold?
My maiden locks are all askew, my pearly fingers cold;
I only wish our tea to be superior over all,
O'er this one's "sparrow-tongue," and o'er the other's "dragon ball."*

XV.

Oh, for a month I weary strive to find a leisure day,
I go to pick at early dawn, and until dusk I stay;
Till midnight at the firing-pan I hold my irksome place;
But may not labour hard as this impair my pretty face?

* Technical terms.

十六

容顏雖瘦志常堅
焙出金芽分外妍
知是何人調玉碗
閒教纖手侍兒煎

十七

活火煎來破寂寥
那知摘取苦多嬌
無端一陣狂風雨
遍體淋淋似水澆

十八

雨橫風狂鳥離巢
雙雙猶自戀花梢
緣何夫壻輕言別
愁上心來手忘捎

XVI.

But if my face be somewhat lank, more firm shall be my mind,
I'll fire my tea that all else shall be my golden buds behind;
But yet the thought arises, who the pretty maid shall be,
To put the leaves in jewell'd cup, from thence to drink my tea?

XVII.

Her griefs all flee as she makes her tea, and she is glad, but oh,
Where shall she learn the toils of us who labour for her so?
And shall she know of the winds that blow, and the rains that pour their wrath,
And drench and soak us through and through, as plunged into a bath.

XVIII.

In driving rains and howling winds the birds forsake the nest,
Yet many a loving pair are seen still on the boughs to rest;
Oh, wherefore, lov'd one, with light look didst thou send me away?
I cannot, grieving as I grieve, go through my work to day.

L

十九

縱使愁腸似桔槔
且安貧苦莫辭勞
只圖焙得新茶好
縷縷旗鎗起白毫

二十

工夫那敢自蹉跎
尚覺儂家事務多
焙出乾茶忙去采
今朝還要上松蘿

二十一

手挽筠藍鬢戴花
松蘿山下采山茶
途中姊妹勞相問
笑指前村是妾家

XIX.

But though my bosom rise and fall, like bucket in a well,
Patient and toiling as I am, 'gainst work I'll near rebel.
My care shall be to have my tea fired to a tender brown,
And let the *flag* and *awl*, well roll'd, display their whitish down.*

XX.

Hah, for my toil, ho, for my steps! aweary tho' I be,
In our poor house, for working folk, there's lots of work, I see;
When the firing and the drying's done, off at the call I go,
And once again this very morn I climb the high Sung-lo!

XXI.

My wicker basket slung on arm, and hair entwined with flowers,
To the slopes I go of the high Sung-lo, and pick the tea for hours;
How laugh we, sisters, on the road—what a merry turn we've got!
I giggle and say, as I point down the way—there, look, there lies our cot.

* The *flag* is the name for the terminal shoots, where they just begin to unroll; the *awl* designates those which are still unrolled, and sharp-pointed. This may be easily observed in the finest black tea, called by us Pekoe, covered with a white down, *Pak-ho*, whence the name.

二十二

妾家樓屋傍垂楊
一帶青陰護草堂
明日若蒙來約伴
到門先覺焙茶香

二十三

乍暖還寒屢變更
焙茶天色最難平
西山日落東山雨
道是多晴却少晴

二十四

今日西山山色青
攜籃候伴坐村亭
小姑更覺嬌覺慣
睡倚欄杆喚不醒

XXII.

Your handmaid 'neath the sweet green shade in shelter'd cot abides,
Where the pendent willow's sweeping bough the thatchy dwelling hides:
To-morrow, if you wish it so, my guests I pray you'll be!
The door you'll know by the fragrant scent, the scent of the firing tea.

XXIII.

Awhile 'tis cold, and then 'tis warm, when I want to fire my tea,
The sky is sure to shift and change—and all to worry me:
When the Sun goes down on the western hills, on the eastern there is rain!
And however fair he promises, he promises in vain.

XXIV.

To-day the tint of the western hills is looking bright and fair,
And I bear my crate to the stile, and wait my fellow toiler there:
A little tender lass is she—she leans upon the rail,
And sleeps—and though I hail her, she answers not my hail.

二十五

直待高呼始應承
半開媚眼若難勝
忽忽便向前頭走
提着籃兒忘着篷

二十六

同行迤邐過南樓
樓畔花開海石榴
欲待折來分插戴
樹高不攀到梢頭

二十七

黃鳥枝頭美好音
可人天氣半晴陰
攀枝各把衷情訴
說到傷心淚不禁

XXV.

And when at length, to my loudest call, she murmurs a reply,
'Tis as if hard to conquer sleep, and with half-opened eye;
Up starts she, and with straggling steps along the path she's gone;
She brings her basket, but forgets to put the cover on!

XXVI.

Together trudge we, and we pass the lodge of the southern bowers,
Where the beautiful sea-pomegranate waves all its yellow flowers;
Fain would we stop and pluck a few to deck our tresses gay,
But the tree is high, and 'tis vain to try to reach the tempting spray.

XXVII.

The pretty birds upon the bough sing songs so sweet to hear,
And the sky is so delicious now, half cloudy and half clear;
While bending o'er her work, each maid will prattle of her woe,
And we talk till our hearts are sorely hurt, and tears unstinted flow.

二十八

破却工夫未滿籃
北枝尋罷又圖南
無端折得同心葉
纖手攀來鬢上簪

二十九

茶品由來苦勝甜
箇中滋味兩般兼
不知却爲誰甜苦
掐破儂家玉指尖

三十

任他飛燕自呢喃
去采新茶換舊衫
却把袖兒高捲起
從教露出手纖纖

XXVIII.

Our time is up, and yet not full our baskets to the mouth,
The twigs anorth are fully search'd, let's seek them in the south;
Just then by chance I snapped a twig whose leaves were all apair;
See, with my taper fingers now I fix it in my hair.

XXIX.

Of all the various kinds of tea, the bitter beats the sweet,
But for whomever either seeks, for him I'll find a treat;
Though who it is shall drink them, as bitter or sweet they be,
I know not, friend—but the pearly end of my finger only see!

XXX.

Ye twittering swallows rise and fall, in your flight around the hill,
But when next I go to the high Sunglo, I'll change my gown—I will;
And I'll roll up the cuff and show arm enough, for my arm is fair to see;
Oh, if ever there were a fair round arm, that arm belongs to me!

M

A retrospect of our subject might tend to show, that the poetry in question most naturally arranges itself under three general heads: 1. Odes and Songs; 2. Moral and Didactic Pieces; 3. Descriptive and Sentimental. These different kinds are, however, so blended together occasionally, and run so much into one another, that it is not always very easy, nor indeed perhaps is it of much consequence, to separate them. It has been remarked before, that as the substance and dialogue of their drama is always in prose, and the musical parts come properly under the definition of songs, the Chinese cannot with strictness be said to possess what *we mean* by dramatic poetry, that is, tragedies or plays of any kind composed mainly in verse.

At the end of this treatise will be found a miscellaneous selection of poetical pieces, extracted at random; and for the satisfaction of those who may prefer such a mode, they are accompanied, not by metrical versions, but by prose translations, as literal as they could be well rendered; although it must always be kept in mind, this is a most disadvantageous dress for the poetry of any language whatever.

In thus coming to a conclusion, the author feels himself bound, as well for the sake of the subject, as his own, to notice the manner in which Professor Rémusat, of Paris, has done him the honour to quote his opinion regarding Chinese poetry. In the preface to his translation of the *Yu-keau-le*, 玉嬌梨 when treating of the passages in verse with which that novel is interspersed, and of their frequent obscurity, M. Rémusat observes, "Le traducteur des Nouvelles dont j'ai précédemment fait mention, assure que les vers dont il s'agit sont principalement destinés à flatter l'oreille, et que le sens y est très souvent sacrifié à l'harmonie." Now the passage to which M. Rémusat alludes is the following, and it confines itself so expressly to the *musical*, or *operatic portions of the drama*, that it would seem impossible to extend its application either to novels, or to any other part of Chinese literature: "A considerable portion of the PLAYS of the Chinese consists of a sort of irregular verse, which is *sung*, or *chanted with music.* This is often very obscure in its import; and as, according to the Chinese themselves, the gratification of the ear is its main object, sense itself appears sometimes to be neglected (not *sacrificed*), for the sake of a pleasing sound." That this is really the case, as regards the songs of the drama alone, is proved, as well by the verbal testimony of natives, as by the following passage from the preface to "The Hundred Plays of Yuen," which refers chiefly to stage rules:—

雖字有差訛不傷音律不爲害也大低先要明腔後要識譜

"Although the words may be wrong, provided that the laws of sound and cadence be not violated, there is no harm done:—generally speaking, the study of the tune, or air, must be the first consideration, and the knowledge of the part (or rôle) the second." This is all extremely possible, and finds a parallel in our own opera and stage songs, some of which are sufficiently insignificant, and intended merely as pegs to hang musical notes upon—but that he should ever have said anything so extravagant regarding poems which are addressed expressly to the *eye* and the *understanding*, and to them only, the writer of this must utterly disclaim. As M. Rémusat could not have intended to misrepresent his meaning, he feels persuaded that the quotation was made from memory.

Since it would appear, then, that Chinese poetry generally *has* a meaning, although this meaning may not always be very easy to arrive at,* some effectual means of increasing our acquaintance with it is perhaps one of the greatest desiderata in eastern literature. It is very easy to "harden ignorance into contempt," and to assume that whatever is unknown is not worth knowing: but the excellent use which has already been made (witness Moore's poems) of oriental thoughts and imagery, derived from languages of Asia more familiar to us, might encourage some extension in the range of our enquiries. Fruits of the highest culture may be improved and varied by foreign-grafts; and as our gardens have already been indebted to China for a few choice flowers, who knows but our poetry may some day lie under a similar obligation? However small the prospect of advantage, every scrap

* "La langue poétique des Chinois est véritablement intraduisible; on pourrait peut-être ajouter qu'elle est souvent *inintelligible*."—M. Rémusat.

of *novelty* may turn out to be a real gain;—the declining age of some of the finest literature the world ever saw having borne witness, that ordinary topics of poetry will at last grow threadbare, and become tiresome through much use:—

> "Nota magis nulli domus est sua, quàm mihi lucus
> Martis, et Æoliis vicinum rupibus antrum
> Vulcani—quid agant venti, quas torqueat umbras
> Æacus—unde alius furtivæ devehat aurum
> Pelliculæ—quantas jaculetur Monychus ornos:
> —Exspectes eadem a summo, minimoque poetâ."

MISCELLANEOUS POETRY.

高瀑三千尺
芙蓉九疊屏
撐天開日月
飛雪走雷霆
我作雲中鶴
凌風控杳冥
囘看吳楚裏
點點暮烟青

On ascending the Highest Peak of the Leushan.*

There falls a precipitous cascade of three thousand feet;
Here the Hibiscus shades every rising summit;
The mountain touches the sky, and separates the orbs;
The drifting snows fly amidst the thunder.
I am like the white bird among the clouds,
I insult the winds, and invade the powerful abyss.
—As I turn and look down on each neighbouring province,
The evening smoke of the dwellings rises in blue specks.

* A mountain near the Po-yang Lake, visited by the Embassy in 1816.

十年不相見
相見即相離
縱有重來約
殊非少壯時
流雲多逐影
落葉不歸枝
又作南來雁
青山何處期

On taking leave of a Friend.

Ten years have elapsed since last we parted,
And no sooner have we met, than we part again :
We may bind ourselves by promises to renew this meeting,
But we shall never be so young as we are now !
The shadows of the passing clouds speedily vanish—
The fallen leaf returns not to its branch :
Should I fly, like the wild bird, to seek you in the south,
In what what part of yon blue mountains shall we meet ?

文彩宜深隱
羅浮是汝鄉
芳菲那可久
雲路好翺翔
露濕丹青重
風清錦翅長
兒童憐復損
珍重此行藏

On giving liberty to a Butterfly.

Those variegated hues should be less rashly exposed,
The recesses of the mountains are thy proper haunts :
The fragrant, but short-lived herbs are there,
And those airy paths will best suit thy flight :
Thy crimson form is heavy with dew,
Thy embroidered wings should expatiate in the clear breeze :
Destruction here awaits thee from the fondness of the boy,
Go then, and hide thy treasures from his reach.

N

惡樹何年值
崔嵬信不材
高花飛不斷
落葉掃難開
影蔽三冬日
陰含萬古苔
恨無柯在手
剪伐實堪哉

*On a worthless Tree.**

In what year wast thou planted, vile tree!
Thy lofty, bare trunk, is truly good for nothing:
Thy blossoms fly aloft incessantly,
Thy falling leaves there is no sweeping away:
Thou hidest the sun during the winter months;
The shady side of thee is overrun with old moss:
Alas, that I had not an axe in my hand,
To cut thee away, as thou well deservest!

作客春將暮
飛飛花亂開
浮雲未北返
孤鴈且南迴
海響先知雨
風多不辨雷
瓊南清絕地
長嘯一徘徊

Written at the Capital of the Island of Haenan.

While here I travel, the Spring is drawing to a close;
The blossoms fly confusedly, and leave their branches:
I am a floating cloud that returns not north,
I am a solitary wildfowl, bewildered in the south:
By the ocean's murmur, the rainy storm is approaching,
The loudness of the winds conceals the thunder's sound:
This *Keungnan* is a land clean divided from my home,
Here I breathe my long sighs, all perplexed and irresolute.

* "Ille et nefasto te posuit die," &c. *Horat. in Arborem*, II. 13.

虹亭橋畔海螺東
蘭芷羅生別作叢
芳氣自盈空谷裏
一枝飛入玉瓶中
蕭蕭孤影如良友
習習虛堂有素風
日夕馨香懷袖裏
不知心賞有誰同

On a Sprig of Epidendrum, in a Porcelain Vase.

By the side of *Hoongting* bridge, to the east of the stream *Haelo*,
There grows thickly the Epidendrum, making a grove of its own :
Its fragrant breath fills the lonely valley,
And a single sprig hath flown hither, to replenish this precious vase :
The solitary flower finds a companion in its own shadow,
Blown by the gentle breeze that pervades my empty hall :
My sleeves are scented with its morning and evening sweets,
I know of none whose delight in it can equal mine.

懨懨低斂淡黃衫
緊抱孤芳未許探
香口倦開檀半掩
苦心欲吐栢猶含
一枝瘦去容儀病
幾瓣攢來影帶慚
不是畏寒疑不放
要留春色占江南

Inscribed under the Drawing of a wax-coloured Calycanthus. (Lămei.)

Tranquilly bending, clothed in its vest of pale yellow,
The flower preserves, in single seclusion, its inviolate sweets:
With faintly opening mouth, its fragrance is but half exhaled,
Like some half-told sorrow, still half undisclosed:
It droops, with slender stalk, in delicate guise,
While its close petals carry all the aspect of modesty:
Deem not, that fear of the chill will prevents it from blowing—
It reserves those vernal hues to compete with the fairest flowers of *Keangnan.*

一梅忽作两重芳
仔細看來覺異常
認作紅顏饒雪色
欲稱白面帶霞光
莫非残醉微添暈
疑是初醒落曉粧
休怪題詩難下筆
枝頭春色費商量

On the Drawing of a blush-coloured Plum Blossom. (Meihwa.)

One flower combines in itself all the merits of two,
While a closer examination only displays its rare charms:
Would you style it a rosy beauty—it is rich, too, in snowy hues;
Would you call it a pale one—it displays the tints of the morning sky:
It resembles some fair complexion, slightly heightened by wine—
It is like some maiden, risen fresh from sleep to her morning toilet:
Cease to wonder at the hesitation of the poet's pencil;
The loveliness of the object has dispersed his powers of thought!"

夜中不能寐
起行無所適
依然扃柴扉
孤燈坐永夕
寒蟲一何悲
唧唧鳴空壁
如將平生心
相與訴孤寂

Midnight Thoughts.

1. 'Tis the depth of night, and I cannot slumber—
I rise up and stroll without object or purpose ;
I return, and again bar my humble door,
And sit by my solitary lamp until the morning—
What is the cause of lament to that cricket,
Whose monotonous note sounds from yon bare wall ?
It would seem to take up the history of its life,
—To tell me of its state of solitary desertion.

孤寂亦可苦
我行當遠役
關山去千里
蒼芒雲水錫
未知他鄉意
安忘故園戚
悠悠百年間
憂傷終難極

2. This solitary desertion !—how bitter do I find it !
Let me then push my rovings to a distance :
Let me visit the passes and mountains a hundred leagues hence,
Like some devotee of Buddha, wandering amidst clouds and torrents.
Ignorant of what is passing elsewhere,
How shall I forget the melancholy of my own home ?
Thus dull and mournful through life's whole course,
My sorrows and pains can never have an end.

披衣起待月
待月月偏遲
倏忽峰坳出
先來樹杪時
金波何蕩漾
銀漢渺參差
直到參橫後
猶然去夢思

On getting up to see the Moon rise.

I throw on my clothes, and wait for the Moon,
—I wait for the Moon, which rises late:
She breaks at length from behind yon hilly summit,
And first illumines the tops of the trees:
How ruffled is the surface of yon golden waves!
The silver stream of the sky* displays a vague and unequal light:
Thus lingering until the stars of Orion (*Tsan*) have set,
I return to sleep, and dream all over again.

長老峰前青帝歸
長老峰下雨聲稀
桃花李花歷亂發
白鳥黃鳥參差飛
忽憶去年臨海寺
正當此日弄春暉
大兄小弟無消息
獨坐空山心緒微

* The milky way.

Written at the Commencement of Spring.

To the front of yon old peaked hill, the sovereign of verdure (Spring) returns;
At the base of yon old peaked hill the rain is gently falling:
The peach and pear blossoms successively open and blend their hues,
The white and the yellow bird fly hither and thither:
I recollect how last year, at the monastery that overlooks the sea,
On this very day I watched the spring displaying its brightness.
No tidings have since reached me of my distant brethren:
I sit solitary in this lonely mountain, and brood over my thoughts.

天氣今年異昔年
紛紛萬物各爭妍
已驚柳絮條條長
又訝辛夷簇簇鮮

五色翩翩雀亂飛
爭喧爭食滿山扉
羅浮洞口應常見
紫玉臺邊到亦稀

At the New Year. (February.)

1. The climate this season excels all seasons past;
   With gaily blended hues, all things in nature vie for beauty.
   Already surprised by the early progress of the pendent willow sprigs,
   I next admire the fresh luxuriance of the purple Magnolias.

2. Birds of every colour fly about in mingled confusion,
   And with the noise of their contentious repasts fill my hilly dwelling:
   The ravines of this *Lofow* mountain are their constant haunts,
   They visit not in such numbers the lofty levels of *Tszeyu.*

村村門戶向山開
吉日都從此地來
山上笑聲山下應
紛紛聚響總如雷

一時鐘板故相喧
總是清齋食客繁
安得皇天能雨粟
與君日日共盤飧

3. The doors of every village are opened towards the hills,
And crowds on this festive day flock thence hither;
The notes of merriment on high are answered by like notes below,
The mingled tumult of sounds is like the distant thunder.

4. Why do the bells and wooden instruments mingle their clamour?
The crowded guests are assembled to partake of the lenten feast:
But sovereign heaven no longer sends its showers of grain
To replenish, worthy friends, your diurnal repasts!*

* The priests of Buddha are assembled by the ringing of bells, &c., to their entertainments of herbs, fruits, and sweetmeats, being forbidden the use of flesh and wine. Their monasteries are in the recesses of hills, wherever hills prevail, and always in the most romantic spots. The two last lines allude to the following tradition. When *Yoong-lŏ*, of the family called *Ming*, usurped the whole empire (A.D. 1400), one of his nephews, the proper heir, shaved his head, and assuming the habit of a priest, retired to the depths of the mountains. The living rock there opened, and poured out a constant supply of grain for the support of the royal refugee. After his death, the miracle still went on, until a covetous priest, not satisfied with the quantity of grain thus obtained, enlarged the hole or fissure in the stone through which it flowed,—when the supply immediately stopped altogether, as the proper reward of his cupidity.

圖書在版編目（CIP）數據

海上絲綢之路文獻集成．科技與文化編．第八輯／王揚宗，葉農主編．-- 福州：福建人民出版社，2024.7. -- ISBN 978-7-211-09500-1

Ⅰ. K203

中國國家版本館CIP數據核字第2024U070P2號

海上絲綢之路文獻集成·科技與文化編（第八輯）

主　　編　王揚宗　葉　農
文化卷主編　葉　農
責任編輯　連天雄
美術編輯　白　玫
出版發行　福建人民出版社
電　　話　0591-87533169（發行部）
電子郵箱　fjpph7221@126.com
地　　址　福建省福州市東水路 76 號
經　　銷　福建新華發行（集團）有限責任公司
印刷裝訂　上海中華印刷有限公司
地　　址　上海市青浦區匯金路 889 號
電　　話　021-69213456
開　　本　787 毫米 ×1092 毫米　1/16
印　　張　281
版　　次　2024 年 7 月第 1 版第 1 次印刷
書　　號　ISBN 978-7-211-09500-1
定　　價　3200.00 元（共 8 册）

国家出版基金项目
NATIONAL PUBLICATION FOUNDATION

海上絲綢之路文獻集成

總主編　陳支平　陳春聲

科技與文化編 59

主編　王揚宗　葉　農

海峽出版發行集團
THE STRAITS PUBLISHING & DISTRIBUTING GROUP
福建人民出版社

本册目次

孟子

（*The Works of Mencius*）

〔英〕理雅各（James Legge）編譯

《孟子》，英國理雅各編譯。理雅各（James Legge，一八一五—一八九七），英國倫敦會傳教士，法國漢學儒蓮獎首位得主。於一八六一至一八七二年相繼出版《中國經典》（*The Chinese Classics*）五卷，於一八七九至一八九一年相繼出版《中國聖書》（*The Sacred Books of China*）六卷。諸種中國經典譯作，被後世奉爲標準譯本。所英譯《孟子》收録於《中國經典》第二卷，一八六一年出版。《孟子》爲「四書」之一，譯注繼承中國經典詮釋傳統，既精準直譯原文主旨，亦以補充、意譯及轉換之法，務使譯文曉暢通達。《孟子》七篇正文前有理雅各撰緒論四章，後附主題詞、專名與漢語字詞索引。據一八九五年牛津版影印。

孟子

THE CHINESE CLASSICS

THE WORKS OF MENCIUS

LEGGE

VOL. II.

London
HENRY FROWDE
OXFORD UNIVERSITY PRESS WAREHOUSE
AMEN CORNER, E.C.

New York
MACMILLAN & CO., 66 FIFTH AVENUE

孟子

THE

CHINESE CLASSICS

WITH

A TRANSLATION, CRITICAL AND EXEGETICAL NOTES, PROLEGOMENA, AND COPIOUS INDEXES

BY

JAMES LEGGE

PROFESSOR OF CHINESE IN THE UNIVERSITY OF OXFORD

FORMERLY OF THE LONDON MISSIONARY SOCIETY

IN SEVEN VOLUMES

SECOND EDITION, REVISED

VOL. II

CONTAINING

THE WORKS OF MENCIUS

Oxford

AT THE CLARENDON PRESS

1895

7

不以文害辭，不以辭害志，以意逆志，是爲得之。

Mencius, V. Pt. I. iv. 2.

ADVERTISEMENT.

THE reader is referred to what is said in the Preface to Volume I as to how the author was led to undertake the translation of the Chinese Classics, and how he was assisted in the preparation and publication of his earlier volumes by the late Hon. Joseph Jardine, Esq., and after his death by his brother, who is now Sir Robert Jardine, Baronet.

When this second volume was ready for the press in 1861, another merchant-prince of China, the late Hon. John Dent, Esq., with a similar generosity, presented a considerable sum to the author, in order that the successive volumes might be sold to missionaries at a much reduced price. And this was done till the amount of his gift was more than exhausted;—to missionaries, without distinction of nationality or creed. The last sale of this kind, it may be stated, was to a missionary in Korea, where at present, we may suppose, all missionary labours are suspended. Of Volume II, as of Volume I, an edition of a thousand copies was printed. Both of these volumes being exhausted, it was necessary to publish new editions of them, which the Delegates of the Clarendon Press undertook to do. The same care has been taken in the printing of this second volume as in that of the former one, and the same alterations adopted in transliterating the pronunciation of Chinese characters.

J. L.

OXFORD, *October*, 1894.

孟子

CONTENTS.

THE PROLEGOMENA.

CHAPTER I.

OF THE WORKS OF MENCIUS.

CHAPTER II.

MENCIUS AND HIS DISCIPLES.

CHAPTER III.

OF YANG CHÛ AND MO TÎ.

CHAPTER IV.

WORKS CONSULTED IN PREPARING THE VOLUME.

THE BODY OF THE VOLUME.

THE WORKS OF MENCIUS.

INDEXES.

PROLEGOMENA.

CHAPTER I.

OF THE WORKS OF MENCIUS.

SECTION I.

THEIR RECOGNITION UNDER THE HAN DYNASTY, AND BEFORE IT.

1. In the third of the catalogues of Liû Hsin[1], containing a list of the Works of Scholars[2] which had been collected up to his time (about A.D. 1), and in the first subdivision, devoted to authors of the classical or orthodox School, we have the entry—'The Works of Mencius, in eleven Books[3].' At that date, therefore, Mencius's writings were known and registered as a part of the literature of China.

2. A hundred years before Hsin, we have the testimony of the historian Sze-mâ Ch'ien. In the seventy-fourth Book of his 'Historical Records,' there is a brief memoir of Mencius[4], where he says that the philosopher, having withdrawn into private life, 'along with the disciples of Wan Chang, prefaced the *Shih* and the *Shû*, unfolded the views of Confucius, and made "The Works of Mencius, in seven Books[5]."'

The discrepancy that appears between these testimonies, in regard to the number of the Books which went by the common name of Mencius, will be considered in the sequel. In the meanwhile it is shown that the writings of Mencius were recognised by scholars a hundred years before the Christian era, which takes us back to little more than a century and a half from the date assigned to his death.

[1] See vol. i. proleg. pp. 4, 5. [2] 諸子略. [3] 孟子十一篇. [4] 史記,七十四,列傳,第十四. [5] 與萬章之徒,序詩書,述仲尼之意,作孟子七篇.

3. Among writers of the Han dynasty earlier than Sze-mâ Ch'ien, there were Han Ying[1] and Tung Chung-shû[2], contemporaries, in the reigns of the emperors Wăn, Ching, and Wû[3] (B.C. 179–87). Portions of their Works remain, and in them are found quotations from Mencius[4].

4. But we find references to Mencius and his Works anterior to the dynasty of Han. In the literary remains of K'ung Fû, to whose concealment of many of the classical Works on the issuing of the edict for their destruction posterity is so much indebted[5], there are accounts of Mencius, and many details of his history[6].

Between Mencius and the rise of the Ch'in dynasty flourished the philosopher Hsün Ch'ing[7], of whose writings enough is still preserved to form a large volume. By many he is regarded as the ablest of all the followers of Confucius. He several times makes mention of Mencius, and one of his most important chapters, 'That Human Nature is Evil[8],' seems to have been written expressly against Mencius's doctrine of its goodness. He quotes his arguments, and endeavours to set them aside.

5. I have used the term *recognition* in the heading of this section, because the scholars of the Han dynasty do not seem to have had any trouble in forming or settling the text of Mencius such as we have seen they had with the Confucian Analects.

And here a statement made by Châo Ch'î, whose labours upon our philosopher I shall notice in the next section, deserves to be considered. He says:—'When Ch'in sought by its fires to destroy the Classical Books, and put the scholars to death in pits, there was an end of the School of Mencius. His Works, however, were included under the common name of "Philosophical," and so the tablets containing them escaped destruction[9].' Mâ Twan-lin does not hesitate to say that the statement is incorrect[10]; and it seems strange that Mencius should have been exempted from the sweep of a measure intended to extinguish the memory of the most ancient and illustrious

[1] 韓嬰. [2] 董仲舒. [3] 太宗孝文皇帝；孝景皇帝；世宗孝武皇帝. [4] See 四書拓餘說, 孟子, art. I, and 焦孝廉孟子正義, notes to Châo Ch'î's preface. [5] See vol. i. proleg. p. 36. [6] I have not been able to refer to the writings of K'ung Fû themselves, but extracts from them are given in the notes to Chû Hsî's preface to Mencius in the 四書經註集證. [7] 荀卿. [8] 荀子, 性惡篇. [9] 其書號爲諸子, 故篇籍得不泯絕; see Châo Ch'î's preface to Mencius. [10] 文獻通考, Bk. clxxxiv, upon Mencius.

孟子

sovereigns of China and of their principles. But the same thing is affirmed in regard to the writings of at least one other author of antiquity, the philosopher Yü[1]; and the frequent quotations of Mencius by Han Ying and Tung Chung-shû, indicating that his Works were a complete collection in their times, give some confirmation to Ch'î's account.

On the whole, the evidence seems rather to preponderate in its favour. Mencius did not obtain his place as 'a classic' till long after the time of the Ch'in dynasty; and though the infuriate emperor would doubtless have given special orders to destroy his writings, if his attention had been called to them, we can easily conceive their being overlooked, and escaping with a mass of others which were not considered dangerous to the new rule.

6. Another statement of Châo Ch'î shows that the Works of Mencius, once recognised under the Han dynasty, were for a time at least kept with a watchful care. He says that, in the reign of the emperor Hsiâo-wăn (B.C. 178–155), 'the Lun-yü, the Hsiâo-ching, Mencius, and the *R*-yâ were all put under the care of a Board of "Great Scholars," which was subsequently done away with, only "The Five Ching" being left under such guardianship[2].' Chû Hsî has observed that the Books of the Han dynasty supply no evidence of such a Board; but its existence may be inferred from a letter of Liû Hsin, complaining of the supineness with which the scholars seconded his quest for the scattered monuments of literature. He says:—'Under the emperor Hsiâo-wăn, the Shû-ching reappeared, and the Shih-ching began to sprout and bud afresh. Throughout the empire, a multitude of books were continually making their appearance, and among them the Records and Sayings of all the Philosophers, which likewise had their place assigned to them in the Courts of Learning, and a Board of Great Scholars appointed to their charge[3].'

As the Board of Great Scholars in charge of the Five Ching was instituted B.C. 135, we may suppose that the previous arrangement hardly lasted half a century. That it did exist for a time, however,

[1] 逢行珪註鬻子叙云,遭秦暴亂,書紀略盡,鬻子不與焚燒; see 焦孝廉孟子正義, notes on Châo Ch'î's preface. [2] 孝文皇帝欲廣遊學之路,論語,孝經,孟子,爾雅,皆置博士,後罷傳記博士,獨立五經而已. [3] See the 文獻通考, Bk. clxxiv. pp. 9, 10.

shows the value set upon the writings of Mencius, and confirms the point which I have sought to set forth in this section,—that there were Works of Mencius current in China before the Han dynasty, and which were eagerly recognised and cherished by the scholars under it, who had it in charge to collect the ancient literary productions of their country.

SECTION II.

CHÂO CH'Î AND HIS LABOURS UPON MENCIUS.

1. It has been shown that the Works of Mencius were sufficiently well known from nearly the beginning of the Han dynasty; but its more distinguished scholars do not seem to have devoted themselves to their study and elucidation. The Classics claimed their first attention. There was much labour to be done in collecting and collating the fragments of them, and to unfold their meaning was the chief duty of every one who thought himself equal to the task. Mencius was but one of the literati, a scholar like themselves. He could wait. We must come down to the second century of the Christian era to find the first commentary on his writings.

In the prolegomena to the Confucian Analects, Section i. 7, I have spoken of Chăng Hsüan or Chăng K'ang-ch'ăng, who died at the age of seventy-four, some time between A.D. 190–220, after having commented on every ancient classical book. It is said by some[1] that he embraced the Works of Mencius in his labours. If he did so, which to me is very doubtful, the result has not come down to posterity. To give to our philosopher such a treatment as he deserved, and compose a commentary that should descend to the latest posterity, was the work of Châo Ch'î, of whom we have a memoir in the fifty-fourth chapter of the Biographies in the Books of the second Han dynasty.

2. Ch'î was born A.D. 108. His father was a censor about the

[1] In the 'Books of the Sûi dynasty' (A.D. 589–617), Bk. xxxix, 經籍志, 三, we find that there were then in the national Repositories three Works on Mencius,—Châo Ch'î's, one by Chăng Hsüan, and one by Liû Hsi (劉熙), also a scholar of Han, but probably not earlier than Châo Ch'î. The same Works were existing under the T'ang dynasty (618 907);—see the 'Books of T'ang,' Bk. xlix, 藝文志, 三. By the rise of the Sung dynasty (A.D. 975 or 960), however, the two last were both lost. The entries in the Records of Sûi and T'ang would seem to prove that Chăng Hsüan had written on Mencius, but in the sketches of his life which I have consulted,—and that in the 'Books of the After Han dynasty,' 列傳第二十五, must be the basis of all the rest,—there is no mention made of his having done so.

court of the emperor Hsiâo-ân[1], and gave him the name of Chiâ, which he afterwards changed into Ch'î for the purpose of concealment, changing also his original designation of T'âi-ch'ing into Pin-ch'ing[2]. It was his boast that he could trace his descent from the ancient sovereign Chwan-hsü[3], B.C. 2510.

In his youth Ch'î was distinguished for his intelligence and diligent study of the Classics. He married a niece of the celebrated scholar and statesman Mâ Yung[4], but bore himself proudly towards him and her other relatives. A stern independence and hatred of the sycophancy of the times were from the first characteristic of him, and proved the source of many troubles.

When he was over thirty, Ch'î was attacked with some severe and lingering illness, in consequence of which he lay upon his bed for seven years. At one time, thinking he was near his end, he addressed a nephew who was with him in the following terms:—'Born a man into the world, in retirement I have not displayed the principles exemplified on Mount Chî[5], nor in office achieved the merit of Î and Lü[6]. Heaven has not granted me such distinction. What more shall I say? Set up a round stone before my grave, and engrave on it the inscription,—"Here lies a recluse of Han, by surname Châo and by name Chiâ. He had the will, but not the opportunity. Such was his fate. Alas!"'

Contrary to expectation, Ch'î recovered, and in A.D. 154 we find him again engaged in public life, but in four years he is flying into obscurity under a feigned name, to escape the resentment of T'ang Hăng[7], one of the principal ministers, and his partisans. He saved his life, but his family and relatives fell victims to the vengeance of his enemies, and for some time he wandered about the country of the Chiang and Hwâi, or among the mountains and by the sea-coast on the north of the present Shan-tung. One day as he was selling cakes in a market-place, his noble presence attracted the attention of Sun Ch'ung[8], a young gentleman of Ân-ch'iû, who was passing by in a carriage, and to him on being questioned he made known his

[1] 孝安皇帝. [2] 趙歧,字邠卿,初名嘉,字臺卿,後避難,故自改名字. [3] 顓頊. [4] 馬融. [5] 箕山之操. It was to Mount Chî that 巢父 and 許由, two ancient worthies, are said to have withdrawn, when Yâo wished to promote them to honour. [6] These are the well-known Î Yin (伊尹) and T'âi-kung Wang (太公望). [7] 唐衡. [8] 安邱,孫崇. The name Ân-ch'iû still remains in the district so called of the department of Ch'ing-châu (青州).

history. This proved a fortunate rencontre for him. Sun Ch'ung took him home, and kept him for several years concealed somewhere 'in the centre of a double wall[1].' And now it was that he solaced his hard lot with literary studies. He wooed the muse in twenty-three poetical compositions, which he called 'Songs of Adversity[2],' and achieved his commentary on Mencius.

On the fall of the T'ang faction, when a political amnesty was proclaimed, Ch'î emerged from his friendly confinement, but only to fall a victim again to the intrigues of the time. The first year of the emperor Ling, A.D. 168, was the commencement of an imprisonment which lasted more than ten years; but nothing could crush his elasticity, or daunt his perseverance. In 185, when he had nearly reached fourscore, he was active as ever in the field of political strife, and wrought loyally to sustain the fortunes of the falling dynasty. He died at last in A.D. 201, when he was over ninety, in Ching-châu, whither he had gone on a mission in behalf of his imperial master. Before his death he had a tomb prepared for himself, which was long shown, or pretended to be shown, in what is now the district city of Chiang-ling in the department of Ching-châu in Hû-pei[3].

3. From the above account of Châo Ch'î, it will be seen that his commentary on Mencius was prepared under great disadvantages. That he, a fugitive and in such close hiding, should have been able to produce a work such as it is, shows the extent of his reading and acquirements in early days. I have said so much about him, because his name should be added to the long roll of illustrious men who have found comfort in sore adversity from the pursuits of literature and philosophy. As to his mode of dealing with his subject, it will be sufficient to give his own account:—

'I wished to set my mind on some literary work, by which I might be assisted to the government of my thoughts, and forget the approach of old age. But the six classics had all been explained and carefully elucidated by previous scholars. Of all the orthodox school there was only Mencius, wide and deep, minute and exquisite, yet obscure at times and hard to see through, who seemed to me to deserve to be properly ordered and digested. Upon this I brought forth whatever I had learned, collected testimonies from the Classics

[1] 複壁中. [2] 戹屯歌,二十三章. [3] 湖北,荆州府,江陵縣.

孟子

and other books, and divided my author into chapters and sentences. My annotations are given along with the original text, and of every chapter I have separately indicated the scope. The Books I have divided into two Parts, the first and second, making in all fourteen sections.

'On the whole, with regard to my labour, I do not venture to think that it speaks the man of mark, but as a gift to the learner, it may dispel some doubts and resolve perplexities. It is not for me, however, to pronounce on its excellencies or defects. Let men of discernment who come after me observe its errors and omissions and correct them;—that will be a good service[1].'

SECTION III.

OTHER COMMENTATORS.

1. All the commentaries on Mencius made prior to the Sung dynasty (A. D. 960[2]) having perished, excepting that of Châo Ch'î, I will not therefore make an attempt to enumerate them particularly. Only three names deserve to be mentioned, as frequent reference is made to them in Critical Introductions to our philosopher. They were all of the T'ang dynasty, extending, if we embrace in it what is called 'The After T'ang,' from A.D. 618 to 936. The first is that of Lû Shan-ching[3], who declined to adopt Châo Ch'î's division of the whole into fourteen sections or parts, and many of whose interpretations, differing from those of the older authority, have been received into the now standard commentary of Chû Hsî. The other two names are those of Chang Yî[4] and Ting Kung-chû[5], whose principal object was to determine the sounds and tones of characters about which there could be dispute. All that we know of their views is from the works of Sun Shih and Chû Hsî, who have many references to them in their notes.

2. During the Sung dynasty, the commentators on Mencius were a multitude, but it is only necessary that I speak of two.

The most distinguished scholar of the early reigns was Sun Shih[6], who is now generally alluded to by his posthumous or honorary epithet of 'The Illustrious Duke[7].' We find him high in favour and

[1] See the 孟子題辭. [2] Some date the commencement of the Sung dynasty in A. D. 960. [3] 陸善經. [4] 張鎰. [5] 丁公著. [6] 孫奭. [7] 宣公.

reputation in the time of T'âi-tsung (976–998), Chăn-tsung (998–1022), and Zăn-tsung (1023–1063)[1]. By imperial command, in association with several other officers, he prepared a work in two Parts, under the title of 'The Sounds and Meaning of Mencius,' and presented it to the court[2]. Occasion was taken from this for a strange imposture. In the edition of 'The Thirteen Ching,' Mencius always appears with 'The Commentary of Châo Ch'î' and 'The Correct Meaning of Shun Shih[3].' Under the Sung dynasty, what were called 'correct meanings' were made for most of the Classics. They are commentaries and annotations on the principal commentator who is considered as the expounder of the Classic, the author not hesitating, however, to indicate any peculiar views of his own. The genuineness of Shih's 'Correct Meaning of Mencius' is questioned by few, but there seems to be no doubt of its being really a forgery, at the same time that it contains the substance of the true work of 'The Illustrious Duke,' so far as that embraced the meaning of Mencius and of Châo Ch'î. The account of it given in the preface to 'An Examination of the Text in the Commentary and Annotations on Mencius,' by Yüan Yüan of the present dynasty, is—'Sun Shih himself made no "Correct Meaning;" but some one—I know not who—supposing that his Work was really of that character, and that there were many things in the commentary which were not explained, and passages also of an unsatisfactory nature, he transcribed the whole of Shih's Work on "The Sounds and Meaning," and having interpolated some words of his own, published it under the title of "The Annotations of Sun Shih." He was the same person who is styled by Chû Hsî "a scholar of Shâo-wû[4]."'

In the twelfth century Chû Hsî appeared upon the stage, and entered into the labours of all his predecessors. He published one Work separately upon Mencius[5], and two upon Mencius and the Confucian Analects[6]. The second of these, 'Collected Comments on the Analects and Mencius,' is now the standard authority on the

[1] 太宗,眞宗,仁宗. [2] 孟子音義,二卷.—In or about the year 1008, a book was found, at one of the palace gates, with the title of 'The Book of Heaven' (天書). The emperor at first was inclined to go in state and accept it, but he thought of consulting Shih. Shih replied according to a sentiment of Mencius (V. Pt. I. v. 3) that 'Heaven does not speak,' and asked how then there could be any Book of Heaven. Was this Book of Heaven, thus rejected on Shih's counsel, a copy of our Sacred Scriptures, which some Nestorian Christian was endeavouring in the manner indicated to bring before the court of China? [3] 漢趙氏註,宋孫奭疏. [4] 阮云孟子註疏校勘記序. [5] 孟子指要. [6] 論孟集義; 論孟集註.

孟子

subject, and has been the test of orthodoxy and scholarship in the literary examinations since A. D. 1315.

3. Under the present dynasty two important contributions have been made to the study of Mencius. They are both published in the 'Explanations of the Classics under the Imperial Dynasty of Ch'ing[1].' The former, bearing the title of 'An Examination of the Text in the Commentary and Annotations of Mencius,' forms the sections from 1039 to 1054. It is by Yüan Yüan, the Governor-General under whose auspices that compilation was published. Its simple aim is to establish the true reading by a collation of the oldest and best manuscripts and editions, and of the remains of a series of stone tablets containing the text of Mencius, which were prepared in the reign of Kâo-tsung (A.D. 1128–1162), and are now existing in the Examination Hall of Hăng-châu. The second Work, which is still more important, is embraced in the sections 1117–1146. Its title is—'The Correct Meaning of Mencius, by Chiâo Hsün, a Chü-zăn of Chiang-tû[2].' It is intended to be such a Work as Sun Shih would have produced, had he really made what has been so long current in the world under his name. I must regret that I was not earlier acquainted with it.

SECTION IV.

INTEGRITY; AUTHORSHIP; AND RECEPTION AMONG THE CLASSICAL BOOKS.

1. We have seen how the Works of Mencius were catalogued by Liû Hsin as being in 'eleven Books,' while a century earlier Sze-mâ Ch'ien referred to them as consisting only of 'seven.' The question has very much vexed Chinese scholars whether there ever really were four additional Books of Mencius which have been lost.

2. Châo Ch'î says in his preface:—'There likewise are four additional Books, entitled "A Discussion of the Goodness of Man's Nature," "An Explanation of Terms," "The Classic of Filial Piety," and "The Practice of Government." But neither breadth nor depth marks their composition. It is not like that of the seven acknowledged Books. It may be judged they are not really the production of Mencius, but have been palmed upon the world by some subsequent imitator of him[3].' As the four Books in question are lost, and only

[1] See vol. i. proleg. p. 133. [2] 孟子正義,江都焦孝廉循著.
[3] 又有外書四篇,性善辯,文說,孝經,爲政,其文不能

a very few quotations from Mencius, that are not found in his Works which we have, can be fished up from ancient authors, our best plan is to acquiesce in the conclusion of Châo Ch'î. The specification of 'Seven Books' by Sze-mâ Ch'ien is an important corroboration of it. In the two centuries preceding our era, we may conceive that the four Books whose titles are given by him were made and published under the name of Mencius, and Hsin would only do his duty in including them in his catalogue, unless their falsehood was generally acknowledged. Ch'î devoting himself to the study of our author, and satisfied from internal evidence that they were not his, only did his duty in rejecting them. There is no evidence that his decision was called in question by any scholar of the Han or the dynasties immediately following, when we may suppose that the Books were still in existence.

The author of 'Supplemental Observations on the Four Books[1],' says upon this subject:—' "It would be better to be without books than to give entire credit to them[2];"—this is the rule for reading ancient books laid down by Mencius himself, and the rule for us after-men in reading about what purport to be lost books of his. The seven Books which we have "comprehend *the doctrine of* heaven and earth, examine and set forth ten thousand topics, discuss the subjects of benevolence and righteousness, reason and virtue, the nature *of man* and the decrees *of Heaven*, misery and happiness[3]." Brilliantly are these things treated of, in a way far beyond what any disciple of Kung-sun Ch'âu or Wan Chang could have attained to. What is the use of disputing about other matters? Ho Sheh has his "Expurgated Mencius[4]," but Mencius cannot be expurgated. Lin Chin-sze has his "Continuation of Mencius," but Mencius needs no continuation. I venture to say—"*Besides the Seven Books there were no other Works of Mencius.*"'

3. I have said, in the note at the end of this volume, that Châo Ch'î gives the total of the characters in Mencius as 34,685, while they are now found actually to amount to 35,226. This difference has been ingeniously accounted for by supposing that the continually recurring

宏深,不與內篇相似,似非孟子本眞,後世依放而託也.

[1] See vol. i. proleg. p. 131. [2] Mencius, VII. Pt. II. iii. [3] This is the language of Châo Ch'î. [4] Mâ Twan-lin mentions two authors who had taken in hand to expurgate Mencius, but neither of them is called 何涉. He mentions Lin Chin-sze, calling him Lin Shăn-sze (林愼思), and his Work.

孟子

'Mencius' and 'Mencius said' were not in his copies. There would be no use for them on his view that the whole was composed by Mencius himself. If they were added subsequently, they would about make up the actual excess of the number of characters above his computation. The point is not one of importance, and I have touched on it simply because it leads us to the question of the *authorship* of the Works.

4. On this point Sze-mâ Ch'ien and Châo Ch'î are agreed. They say that Mencius composed the seven Books himself, and yet that he did so along with certain of his disciples. The words of the latter are:—'He withdrew from public life, collected and digested the conversations which he had had with his distinguished disciples, Kung-sun Ch'âu, Wan Chang, and others, on the difficulties and doubts which they had expressed, and also compiled himself his deliverances as *ex cathedrâ*;—and so published the seven Books of his writings.'

This view of the authorship seems to have been first called in question by Han Yü[1], commonly referred to as 'Han, the duke of Literature[2],' a famous scholar in the eighth and ninth centuries, under the T'ang dynasty, who expressed himself in the following terms:—'The Books of Mencius were not published by himself. After his death, his disciples, Wan Chang and Kung-sun Ch'âu, in communication with each other, recorded the words of Mencius[3].'

5. If we wish to adjudicate in the matter, we find that we have a difficult task in hand. One thing is plain—the book is not the work of many hands like the Confucian Analects. 'If we look at the style of the composition,' says Chû Hsî, 'it is as if the whole were melted together, and not composed by joining piece to piece[4].' This language is too strong, but there is a degree of truth and force in it. No principle of chronology guided the arrangement of the different parts, and a foreigner may be pardoned if now and then the 'pearls' seem to him 'at random strung;' yet the collection is characterised by a uniformity of style, and an endeavour in the separate Books to preserve a unity of matter. This consideration, however, is not

[1] 韓愈,字退之. [2] 韓文公. [3] 孟軻之書,非軻自著,軻既沒,其徒萬章公孫丑,相與記軻所言焉耳; see note by Chû Hsî in his prefatory notice to Mencius. [4] 觀其筆勢,如鎔鑄而成,非綴緝所就者; quoted in 四書拓餘說,孟子, art. I.

enough to decide the question. Such as the work is, we can conceive it proceeding either from Mencius himself, or from the labours of *a few of his disciples engaged on it in concert.*

The author of the 'Topography of the Four Books[1]' has this argument to show that the Works of Mencius are by Mencius himself:—'The Confucian Analects,' he says, 'were made by the disciples, and therefore they record minutely the appearance and manners of the sage. But the seven Books were made by Mencius himself, and therefore we have nothing in them excepting the words and public movements of the philosopher[2].' This peculiarity is certainly consonant with the hypothesis of Mencius's own authorship, and so far may dispose us to adopt it.

On the other hand, as the princes of Mencius's time to whom any reference is made are always mentioned by the honorary epithets conferred on them after their death, it is argued that those at least must have been introduced by his disciples. There are many passages, again, which savour more of a disciple or other narrator than of the philosopher himself. There is, for instance, the commencing sentences of Book III. Pt. I:—'When the duke Wăn of T'ăng was crown-prince, having to go to Ch'û, he went by way of Sung, and visited Mencius (lit. *the philosopher Măng*). Mencius discoursed to him how the nature of man is good, and when speaking, always made laudatory reference to Yâo and Shun. When the crown-prince was returning from Ch'û, he again visited Mencius. Mencius said to him "Prince, do you doubt my words? The path is one, and only one."'

6. Perhaps the truth after all is as the thing is stated by Sze-mâ Ch'ien,—that Mencius, *along with some of his disciples*, compiled and composed the Work. It would be in their hands and under their guardianship after his death, and they may have made some slight alterations, to prepare it, as we should say, for the press. Yet allowing this, there is nothing to prevent us from accepting the sayings and doings as those of Mencius, guaranteed by himself.

7. It now only remains here that I refer to the reception of Mencius's Works among the Classics. We have seen how they were not admitted by Liû Hsin into his catalogue of classical works. Mencius

[1] See vol. i. proleg. p. 131. [2] 論語成于門人之手,故記聖人容貌甚悉,七篇成于已手,故但記言語或出處; see 皇清經解, Sect. xxiv, at the end.

孟子

was then only one of the many scholars or philosophers of the orthodox school. The same classification obtains in the Books of the Sûi and T'ang dynasties; and in fact it was only under the dynasty of Sung that the Works of Mencius and the Confucian Analects were authoritatively ranked together. The first explicitly to proclaim this honour as due to our philosopher was Ch'ăn Chih-châi[1], whose words are—'Since the time when Han, the duke of Literature, delivered his eulogium, "Confucius handed *the scheme of doctrine* to Mencius, on whose death the line of transmission was interrupted[2]," the scholars of the empire have all associated Confucius and Mencius together. The Books of Mencius are certainly superior to those of Hsün and Yang, and others who have followed them. Their productions are not to be spoken of in the same day with his.' Chû Hsî adopted the same estimate of Mencius, and by his 'Collected Comments' on him and the Analects bound the two sages together in a union which the government of China, in the several dynasties which have succeeded, has with one temporary exception approved and confirmed.

[1] 陳直齋. The name and the account I take from the 'Supplemental Observations on the Four Books,' art. I, on Mencius. 直, I apprehend, is a misprint for 止, the individual referred to being probably 陳傅良, a great scholar and officer of the twelfth century, known also by the designations of 君舉 and 止齋. [2] This eulogy of Han Yü is to be found subjoined to the brief introduction in the common editions of Mencius. The whole of the passage there quoted is:—'Yâo handed *the scheme of doctrine* down to Shun; Shun handed it to Yü; Yü to T'ang; T'ang to Wăn, Wû, and the duke of Châu; Wăn, Wû, and the duke of Châu to Confucius; and Confucius to Mencius, on whose death there was no further transmission of it. In Hsün and Yang there are snatches of it, but without a nice discrimination; they talk about it, but without a definite particularity.'

CHAPTER II.

MENCIUS AND HIS DISCIPLES.

SECTION I.

LIFE OF MENCIUS.

Paucity and uncertainty of materials.

1. The materials for a Memoir of Mencius are very scanty. The birth and principal incidents of Confucius's life are duly chronicled in the various annotated editions of the Ch'un Ch'iû, and in Sze-mâ Ch'ien. It is not so in the case of Mencius. Ch'ien's account of him is contained in half a dozen columns which are without a single date. That in the 'Cyclopædia of Surnames' only covers half a page. Châo Ch'î is more particular in regard to the early years of his subject, but he is equally indefinite. Our chief informants are K'ung Fû, and Liû Hsiang in his 'Record of Noteworthy Women[1],' but what we find in them has more the character of legend than history.

It is not till we come to the pages of Mencius himself that we are treading on any certain ground. They give the principal incidents of his public life, extending over about twenty-four years. We learn from them that in the course of that time he was in such and such places, and gave expression to such and such opinions; but where he went first and where he went last, it is next to impossible to determine. I have carefully examined three attempts, made by competent scholars of the present dynasty, to construct a Harmony that shall reconcile the statements of the 'Seven Books' with the current chronologies of the time, and do not see my way to adopt entirely the conclusions of any one of them[2]. The value of the Books lies in the record

[1] 劉向列女傳. [2] The three attempts are—one by the author of 'Supplemental Observations on the Four Books,' an outline of which is given in his Notes on Mencius, art. III; one by the author of the 'Topography of the Four Books,' and forming the twenty-fourth section of the 'Explanations of the Classics under the Ch'ing Dynasty;' and one prefixed to the Works of Mencius, in 'The Four Books, with the Relish of the Radical Meaning' (vol. i. proleg. p. 130). These three critics display much ingenuity and research, but their conclusions are conflicting.—I may be pardoned in saying that their learned labours have affected me just as those of the Harmonisers of the Gospel Narratives used to do in former years,—bewildering more than edifying. Most cordially do I agree with Dean Alford (New Testament, vol. i. proleg. I. vii. 5):—'If the Evangelists have delivered to us truly and faithfully the Apostolic Narratives, and if the Apostles spoke as the Holy Spirit enabled them, and brought events and sayings to their recollection, then we may be sure that *if we knew the real process of the transactions*

孟子

which they furnish of Mencius's sentiments, and the lessons which these supply for the regulation of individual conduct and national policy. It is of little importance that we should be able to lay them down in the strict order of time.

With Mencius's withdrawal from public life, all traces of him disappear. All that is said of him is that he spent his later years along with his disciples in the preparation and publication of his Works.

From this paragraph it will be seen that there is not much to be said in this section. I shall relate, first, what is reported of the early years and training of our philosopher, and then look at him as he comes before us in his own pages, in the full maturity of his character and powers.

His surname; birth-place; parents; the year of his birth, B.C. 371.

2. Mencius is the latinized form of Măng-tsze[1], 'The philosopher Măng.' His surname thus connects him with the Măng or Măng-sun family, one of the three great Houses of Lû, whose usurpations were such an offence to Confucius in his time. Their power was broken in the reign of duke Âi (B.C. 494–468), and they thenceforth dwindle into comparative insignificance. Some branches remained in obscurity in Lû, and others went forth to the neighbouring States.

The branch from which Mencius sprang found a home in the small adjacent principality of Tsâu[2], which in former times had been known by the name of Chû[3]. It was afterwards absorbed by Lû, and its name is said to be still retained in one of the districts of the department of Yen-châu in Shan-tung[4]. There I visited his temple in 1873, saw his image, and drank of a spring which supplied a well of bright, clear water close by. Confucius was a native of a district of Lû having the same name, which many contend was also the birthplace of Mencius, making him a native of Lû and not of the State of Tsâu. To my mind the evidence is decidedly against such a view[5].

themselves, that knowledge would enable us to give an account of the diversities of narration and arrangement which the Gospels now present to us. But *without such knowledge*, all attempts to accomplish this analysis in minute detail must be *merely conjectural*, and must tend to weaken the Evangelic testimony rather than to strengthen it.'

[1] 孟子. [2] 騶 (written also 鄒) 國. [3] 邾. [4] 山東,兗州府,鄒縣. [5] 閻若據 and 曹之升 stoutly maintain the different sides of this question, the latter giving five arguments to show that the Tsâu of Mencius was the Tsâu of Lû. As Mencius went from Ch'î on the death of his mother to bury her in Lû (Bk. II. Pt. II. vii), this appears to prove that he was a native of that State. But the conclusion is not

Mencius's name was K'o[1]. His designation does not appear in his Works, nor is any given to him by Sze-mâ Ch'ien or Châo Ch'î. The latter says that he did not know how he had been styled; but the legends tell that he was called Tsze-chü[2], and Tsze-yü[3]. The same authorities—if we can call them such—say that his father's name was Chî[4], and that he was styled Kung-î[5]. They say also that his mother's maiden surname was Chang[6]. Nothing is related of the former but that he died when his son was quite young, but the latter must have a paragraph to herself. 'The mother of Mencius' is famous in China, and held up to the present time as a model of what a mother should be.

The year of Mencius's birth was probably the fourth of the sovereign Lieh, B.C. 372[7]. He lived to the age of 84, dying in the year B.C. 289, the 26th of the sovereign Nan[8], with whom terminated the long sovereignty of the Châu dynasty. The first twenty-three years of his life thus synchronized with the last twenty-three of Plato's. Aristotle, Zeno, Epicurus, Demosthenes, and other great men of the West, were also his contemporaries. When we place Mencius among them, he can look them in the face. He does not need to hide a diminished head.

Mencius's mother.

3. It was his misfortune, according to Châo Ch'î, 'to lose his father at an early period[9]; but in his youthful years he enjoyed the lessons of his kind mother, who thrice changed her residence on his account.'

necessary. Lû had been for several generations the State of his family, and on that account he might wish to inter his parent there, according to the custom of the Châu dynasty (see the Lî Chî, Bk. II. Sect. I. i. 27). The way in which Tsâu always appears as the residence of Mencius, when he is what we should say 'at home,' appears to me decisive of the question, though neither of the disputants presses it into his service. Compare Bk. III. Pt. I. ii; Bk. VI. Pt. II. i and v. The point is really of no importance, for the States of Tsâu and Lû adjoined. 'The rattle of the watchman in the one was heard in the other.'

[1] 軻. [2] 子車 and 子居, the one character taking the place of the other from the similarity of the sound. [3] 子輿. [4] 激. [5] 公宜. I find 宣 sometimes instead of 宜. [6] 仉氏. [7] 烈王,四年,己酉. [8] 赧王二十六年,壬申.—The 'Genealogical Register of the Măng Family' says that Mencius was born in the year 己酉, the 37th of the sovereign Ting (定), on the 2nd day of the 4th month, and died in the year 壬申, the 26th of the sovereign Nan, on the 15th day of the 1st month. (See 四書拓餘說, 孟子, art. III.) The last of these dates is to be embraced on many grounds, but the first is evidently a mistake. Ting only reigned 28 years, and there is no 己酉 year among them. Reckoning back 84 years from the 26th of Nan, we come to a 己酉 year, the 4th of Lieh, which is now generally acquiesced in as the year of Mencius's birth. [9] Ch'î's words are—夙喪其父. The legend-writers are more

At first they lived near a cemetery, and Mencius amused himself with acting the various scenes which he witnessed at the tombs. 'This,' said the lady, 'is no place for my son;'—and she removed to a house in the market-place. But the change was no improvement. The boy took to playing the part of a salesman, vaunting his wares, and chaffering with customers. His mother sought a new house, and found one at last close by a public school. There her child's attention was taken with the various exercises of politeness which the scholars were taught, and he endeavoured to imitate them. The mother was satisfied. 'This,' she said, 'is the proper place for my son.'

Han Ying relates another story of this period. Near their house was a pig-butcher's. One day Mencius asked his mother what they were killing the pigs for, and was told that it was to feed him. Her conscience immediately reproved her for the answer. She said to herself, 'While I was carrying this boy in my womb, I would not sit down if the mat was not placed square, and I ate no meat which was not cut properly;—so I taught him when he was yet unborn[1]. And now when his intelligence is opening, I am deceiving him;—this is to teach him untruthfulness!' With this she went and bought a piece of pork in order to make good her words.

As Mencius grew up, he was sent to school. When he returned home one day, his mother looked up from the web which she was weaving, and asked him how far he had got on. He answered her with an air of indifference that he was doing well enough, on which she took a knife and cut through the thread of her shuttle. The idler was alarmed, and asked what she meant, when she gave him a long lecture, showing that she had done what he was doing,—that her cutting through her thread was like his neglecting his learning. The admonition, it is said, had its proper effect; the lecture did not need to be repeated.

There are two other narratives in which Chang-shih figures, and though they belong to a later part of Mencius's life, it may be as well to embrace them in the present paragraph.

His wife was squatting down one day in her own room, when

precise, and say that Mencius was only three years old when his father died. This statement, and Ch'î's as well, are difficult to reconcile with what we read in Bk. I. Pt. II. xvi, about the style in which Mencius buried his parents. If we accept the legend, we are reduced there to great straits.

[1] See Chû Hsî's 小學內篇, 立教, 第一, which begins with the educational duties of the mother, while the child is yet unborn.

Mencius went in. He was so much offended at finding her in that position, that he told his mother, and expressed his intention to put her away, because of 'her want of propriety.' 'It is you who have no propriety,' said his mother, 'and not your wife. Do not "The Rules of Propriety" say, "When you are about to ascend a hall, raise your voice; when you enter a door, keep your eyes low?" The reason of the rules is that people may not be taken unprepared; but you entered the door of your private apartment without raising your voice, and so caused your wife to be caught squatting on the ground. The impropriety is with you and not with her.' On this Mencius fell to reproving himself, and did not dare to put away his wife.

One day, when he was living with his mother in Ch'î, she was struck with the sorrowfulness of his aspect as he stood leaning against a pillar, and asked him the cause of it. He replied, 'I have heard that the superior man occupies the place for which he is adapted, accepting no reward to which he does not feel entitled, and not covetous of honour and emolument. Now my doctrines are not practised in Ch'î:—I wish to leave it, but I think of your old age, and am anxious.' His mother said, 'It does not belong to a woman to determine anything of herself, but she is subject to the rule of the three obediences. When young, she has to obey her parents; when married, she has to obey her husband; when a widow, she has to obey her son. You are a man in your full maturity, and I am old. Do you act as your conviction of righteousness tells you you ought to do, and I will act according to the rule which belongs to me. Why should you be anxious about me?'.

Such are the accounts which I have found of the mother of Mencius. Possibly some of them are inventions, but they are devoutly believed by the people of China;—and it must be to their profit. *We* may well believe that she was a woman of very superior character, and that her son's subsequent distinction was in a great degree owing to her influence and training [1].

Mencius's instructors; and early life.

4. From parents we advance to be under tutors and governors. The moulding hand that has wrought upon us in the pliant years of youth always leaves ineffaceable traces upon the character. Can anything be ascertained of the instructor or instructors of Mencius? The reply to this inquiry must be substantially in the negative, though many

[1] All these stories are given in the notes to the preface to Mencius in the 四書經註集證.

孟子

have affirmed that he sat as a pupil at the feet of Tsze-sze, the grandson of Confucius. We are told this by Châo Ch'î, whose words are:—'As he grew up, he studied under Tsze-sze, acquired all the knowledge taught by "The Learned," and became thoroughly acquainted with "The Five Ching," being more especially distinguished for his mastery of the *Shih* and the *Shû*[1].' A reference to dates, however, shows that this must be incorrect. From the death of Confucius to the birth of Mencius there were 108 years, and supposing—what is by no means probable—that Tsze-sze was born in the year his father died, he must have been 112 years old when Mencius was born. The supposition of their having stood to each other in the relation of master and scholar is inconsistent, moreover, with the style in which Mencius refers to Tsze-sze. He mentions him six or seven times, showing an intimate acquaintance with his history, but never once in a manner which indicates that he had personal intercourse with him[2].

Sze-mâ Ch'ien's account is that 'Mencius studied under the disciples of Tsze-sze[3].' This may have been the case. There is nothing on the score of time to make it impossible, or even improbable; but this is all that can be said about it. No famous names out of the school of Tsze-sze have been transmitted to posterity, and Mencius nowhere speaks as if he felt under special obligation to any instructor.

One short sentence contains all that he has said bearing on the point before us:—'Although I could not be a disciple of Confucius myself, I have endeavoured to cultivate *my character and knowledge* by means of others *who were*[4].' The chapter to which this belongs is rather enigmatical. The other member of it says:—'The influence of a sovereign sage terminates with the fifth generation. The influence of an unsceptred sage does the same.' By 'an unsceptred sage' Mencius is understood to mean Confucius; and by extending his influence all over five generations, he shows how it was possible for him to place himself under it by means of others who had been in direct communication with the Master.

We must leave the subject of Mencius's early instructors in the obscurity which rests upon it. The first forty years of his life are

[1] 長師孔子之孫子思,治儒術之道,通五經,尤長於詩書. [2] See the Index of Proper Names. [3] 受業子思之門人.
[4] See Book IV. Pt. II. xxii.

little more than a blank to us. Many of them, we may be sure, were spent in diligent study. He made himself familiar during them with all the literature of his country. Its classics, its histories, its great men, had received his careful attention. Confucius especially became to him the chief of mortal men, the object of his untiring admiration; and in his principles and doctrines he recognised the truth for want of an appreciation of which the bonds of society all round him were being relaxed, and the kingdom hastening to a general anarchy.

How he supported himself in Tsâu, we cannot tell. Perhaps he was possessed of some patrimony; but when he first comes forth from his native State, we find him accompanied by his most eminent disciples. He probably imitated Confucius by assuming the office of a teacher,—not that of a schoolmaster in our acceptation of the word, but that of a professor of morals and learning, encouraging the resort of inquiring minds, in order to resolve their doubts and inform them on the true principles of virtue and society. These disciples would minister to his wants, though we may presume that he sternly maintained his dignity among them, as he afterwards did towards the princes of the time, when he appeared among them as a *lecturer* in another sense of the term. Two instances of this are recorded, though we cannot be sure that they belonged to the earlier period of his life.

'When Kăng of T'ăng made his appearance in your school,' said the disciple Kung-tû, 'it seemed proper that a polite consideration should be paid to him, and yet you did not answer him;—why was that?' Mencius replied, 'I do not answer him who questions me presuming on his ability, nor him who presumes on his talents, nor him who presumes on his age, nor him who presumes on services performed to me, nor him who presumes on old acquaintance. Two of those things were chargeable on Kăng of T'ăng[1].'

The other instance is that of Chiâo of Ts'âo, who said to Mencius, 'I shall be having an interview with the prince of Tsâu, and can ask him to let me have a house to lodge in. I wish to remain here, and receive instruction at your gate.' 'The way of truth,' replied the philosopher, 'is like a great road. It is not difficult to know it. The evil is only that men will not seek it. Do you go home

[1] See Bk. VII. Pt. I. xliii.

孟子

and search for it, and you will have abundance of teachers[1].' This was firmly said, yet not unkindly. It agrees with his observation:—'There are many arts in teaching. I refuse, as inconsistent with my character, to teach a man, but I am only thereby still teaching him[2].'

State of China in Mencius's time.

5. The state of China had waxed worse and worse during the interval that elapsed between Confucius and Mencius. The elements of disorganization which were rife in the times of the earlier sage had gone on to produce their natural results. One feeble sovereign had followed another on the throne, and the dynasty of Châu was ready to vanish away. Men were persuaded of its approaching extinction. The feeling of loyalty to it was no longer a cherished sentiment; and the anxiety and expectation was about what new rule would take its place.

Many of the smaller fiefs or principalities had been reduced to a helpless dependence on, or been absorbed by, the larger ones. Of Lû, Chăng, Wei, Wû, Ch'ăn, and Sung[3], conspicuous in the Analects, we read but little in Mencius. Tsin[4] had been dismembered, and its fragments formed the nuclei of three new and vigorous kingdoms,—Wei, Châo, and Han[5]. Ch'î still maintained its ground, but was barely able to make head against the State of Ch'in[6] in the West, and Ch'û in the South[7]. The struggle for supremacy was between these two; the former, as it was ultimately successful, being the more ambitious and incessant in its aggressions on its neighbours.

The princes were thus at constant warfare with one another. Now two or more would form a league to resist the encroaching Ch'in, and hardly would that object be accomplished before they were at war among themselves. Ambitious statesmen were continually inflaming their quarrels. The recluses of Confucius's days, who withdrew in disgust from the world and its turmoil, had given place to a class of men who came forth from their retirements provided with arts of war or schemes of policy which they recommended to the contending chiefs. They made no scruple of changing their allegiance, as they were moved by whim or interest. Kung-sun Yen and Chang Î may be mentioned as specimens of those characters. 'Are they not really great men?' it was once asked of Mencius.

[1] Bk. VI. Pt. II. ii. 6. [2] Bk. VI. Pt. II. xvi. [3] 魯, 鄭, 衞, 吳, 陳, 宋. [4] 晉. [5] 魏, 趙, 韓. [6] 秦. [7] 楚.

'Let them once be angry, and all the princes are afraid. Let them live quietly, and the flames of trouble are extinguished throughout the kingdom[1].'

It is not wonderful that in such times the minds of men should have doubted of the soundness of the ancient principles of the acknowledged sages of the nation. Doctrines, strange and portentous in the view of Mencius, were openly professed. The authority of Confucius was disowned. The foundations of government were overthrown; the foundations of truth were assailed. Two or three paragraphs from our philosopher will verify and illustrate this representation of the character of his times:—

'A host marches *in attendance on the ruler*, and stores of provisions are consumed. The hungry are deprived of their food, and there is no rest for those who are called to toil. Maledictions are uttered by one to another with eyes askance, and the people proceed to the commission of wickedness. Thus the royal ordinances are violated, and the people are oppressed, and the supplies of food and drink flow away like water. The rulers yield themselves to the *bad* current, or they urge their *evil* way *against a good one;* they are wild; they are utterly lost[2].'

'The five chiefs of the princes were sinners against the three kings. The princes of the present day are sinners against the five chiefs. The great officers of the present day are sinners against the princes. . . . The crime of him who connives at and aids the wickedness of his prince is small, but the crime of him who anticipates and excites that wickedness is great. The officers of the present day all go to meet their sovereigns' wickedness, and therefore I say that they are sinners against them[3].'

'Sage sovereigns cease to arise, and the princes of the States give the reins to their lusts. Unemployed scholars indulge in unreasonable discussions. The words of Yang Chû and Mo Tî fill the kingdom. If you listen to people's discourses, you will find that they have adopted the views either of Yang or of Mo. *Now*, Yang's principle is—"each one for himself," which does not acknowledge *the claims of* the sovereign. Mo's principle is—"to love all equally," which does not acknowledge *the peculiar affection due to* a father. But to acknowledge neither king nor father is to be in the state of a beast. Kung-ming Î said, "In their kitchens there is fat meat. In their

[1] Bk. III. Pt. II. i. [2] Bk. I. Pt. II. iv. 6, 8. [3] Bk. VII. Pt. II. vii. 1, 4.

stables there are fat horses. But their people have the look of hunger, and on the wilds there are those who have died of famine. This is leading on beasts to devour men." If the principles of Yang and Mo are not stopped, and the principles of Confucius not set forth, those perverse speakings will delude the people and stop up *the path of* benevolence and righteousness. When benevolence and righteousness are stopped up, beasts will be led on to devour men, and men will devour one another[1].'

Mencius the first time in Ch'î; some time between B.C. 332 and 323.

6. It is in Ch'î that we first meet with Mencius as a counsellor of the princes[2], and it was in this State that he spent much the greater part of his public life. His residence in it, however, appears to have been divided into two portions, and we know not to which of them to refer many of the chapters which describe his intercourse with the prince (or king, as he claimed to be) and his ministers; but, as I have already observed, this is to us of little moment. Our interest is in what he did and said. It matters little that we cannot assign to each saying and doing its particular date.

That he left Ch'î the first time before B.C. 323 is plausibly inferred from Bk. II. Pt. II. xiv. 3[3]; and assuming that the conversation in the same Book, Pt. I. ii, took place immediately before or after his arrival[4], we can determine that he did not enter the State before B.C. 331, for he speaks of himself as having attained at forty years of age to 'an unperturbed mind.' The two chapters contain the most remarkable expressions indicative of Mencius's estimate of himself. In the first, while he glorifies Confucius as far before all other men who had ever lived, he declines having comparisons drawn between himself and any of the sage's most distinguished disciples. In the

[1] Bk. III. Pt. II. ix. 9. [2] In the 'Annals of the Nation' (vol. i. proleg. p. 134), Mencius's visit to king Hûi of Liang is set down as having occurred in B.C. 335, and under B.C. 318 it is said—'Mencius goes from Liang to Ch'î.' The visit to Liang is placed too early, and that to Ch'î too late. The disasters of king Hûi, mentioned in Bk. I. Pt. I. v. 1, had not all taken place in B.C. 318; and if Mencius remained seventeen years in Liang, it is strange we have only five conversations between him and king Hûi. So far from his not going to Ch'î till B.C. 318, it will be seen from the next note that he was leaving Ch'î before B.C. 323. [3] Mencius's words are—'From the commencement of the Châu dynasty till now more than 700 years have elapsed.' It was to the purpose of his argument to make the time appear as long as possible. Had 800 years elapsed, he would surely have said so. But as the Châu dynasty commenced in B.C. 1121, the year B.C. 322 would be its 800th anniversary, and Mencius's departure from Ch'î did not take place later than the year before B.C. 323. [4] This chapter and the one before it have very much the appearance of having taken place on the way from Tsâu to Ch'î. Mencius has been invited to a powerful court. He is emerging from his obscurity. His disciples expect great things for him. Kung-sun Ch'âu sees him invested with the government of Ch'î, and in the elation of his heart makes his inquiries.

second, when going away sorrowful because he had not wrought the good which he desired, he observes:—'Heaven does not yet wish that the kingdom should enjoy tranquillity and good order. If it wished this, who is there besides me to bring it about?'

We may be certain that Mencius did not go to Ch'î uninvited. His approach was waited for with curious expectation, and the king, spoken of always by his honorary epithet of Hsüan, 'The Illustrious,' sent persons to spy out whether he was like other men[1]. They had their first interview at a place called Ch'ung, which was so little satisfactory to the philosopher that he resolved to make only a short stay in the State. Circumstances occurred to change this resolution, but though he remained, and even accepted office, yet it was only honorary;—he declined receiving any salary[2].

From Ch'ung he appears to have retired to P'ing-lû, where Ch'û, the prime minister, sent him a present, wishing, no doubt, to get into his good graces. I call attention to the circumstance, though trifling in itself, because it illustrates the way in which Mencius carried himself to the great men. He took the gift, but subsequently, when he went to the capital, he did not visit the minister to acknowledge it. His opinion was that Ch'û might have come in person to P'ing-lû to see him. 'There was a gift, but no corresponding respect[3].'

With the governor of P'ing-lû, called K'ung Chü-hsin, Mencius spoke freely, and found him a man open to conviction. 'If one of your spearmen,' said Mencius to him, 'were to lose his place in the ranks three times in one day, would you put him to death or not?' 'I would not wait for three times *to do so*,' replied Chü-hsin. Mencius then charged home upon him the sufferings of the people, saying they were equivalent to his losing his place in the ranks. The governor defended himself on the ground that those sufferings were a consequence of the general policy of the State. To this the other replied, 'Here is a man who receives charge of the sheep and cattle of another, undertaking to feed them for him;—of course he must search for pasture-ground and grass. If, after searching for those, he cannot find them, will he return his charge to the owner? or will he stand by and see them die?' The governor's reply was, 'Herein I am guilty[4].'

When Mencius presented himself at the capital of the State, he

[1] Bk. IV. Pt. II. xxxii. [2] Bk. II. Pt. II. xiv. [3] Bk. II. Pt. II. v. [4] Bk. II. Pt. II. iv.

孟子

was honourably received by the king. Many of the conversations with the sovereign and officers which are scattered through the seven Books, though the first and second are richest in them, must be referred to this period. The one which is first in place[1], and which contains the fullest exposition of the philosopher's views on government, was probably first likewise in time[2]. It sets forth the grand essential to the exercise of royal government,—a heart on the part of the sovereign impatient of the sufferings of the people, and eager to protect them and make them happy; it brings home to king Hsüan the conviction that he was not without such a heart, and presses on him the truth that his not exercising it was from a want of will and not from any lack of ability; it exposes unsparingly the errors of the course he was pursuing; and concludes by an exhibition of the outlines and happy issues of a true royal sway.

Of this nature were all Mencius's communications with the sovereign; but he lays himself open in one thing to severe censure. Afraid apparently of repelling the prince from him by the severity of his lessons, he tries to lead him on by his very passions. 'I am fond of beauty,' says the king, 'and that is in the way of my attaining to the royal government which you celebrate.' 'Not at all,' replies the philosopher. 'Gratify yourself, only do not let your doing so interfere with the people's getting similar enjoyment for themselves[3].' So the love of money, the love of war, and the love of music are dealt with. Mencius thought that if he could only get the good of the people to be recognised by Hsüan as the great aim which he was to pursue, his tone of mind would be so elevated, that the selfish passions and gratifications of which he was the slave would be purified or altogether displaced. And so it would have been. Where he fails, is in putting his points as if benevolence and selfishness, covetousness and generosity might exist together. Chinese moralists rightly find fault with him in this respect, and say that Confucius never condescended to such a style of argument.

Notwithstanding the apparent cordiality of the king's reception of him, and the freedom with which Mencius spoke his mind at their interviews, a certain suspiciousness appears to have been maintained between them. Neither of them would bend to the other.

[1] Bk. I. Pt. I. vii. [2] I judge that this was the first *set* conversation between king Hsüan and Mencius, because of the inquiry with which the king opens it,—'May I be informed by you of the transactions of Hwan of Ch'î, and Wăn of Tsin?' A very brief acquaintance with our philosopher would have taught him that he was the last person to apply to about those characters. [3] Bk. I. Pt. II. i. iii. v; *et al.*

Mencius would not bow to the royal state; Hsüan would not vail bonnet to the philosopher's cloak. We have one amusing instance of the struggles to which this sometimes gave rise. One day Mencius was preparing to go to court of his own free will, when a messenger arrived from the king, saying he had intended to come and see him, but was prevented by a cold, and asking whether Mencius would not appear at the audience next morning. Mencius saw that this was a device on the part of the king to avoid stooping to visit him, and though he had been about to go to court, he replied at once that he was unwell. He did not hesitate to meet the king's falsehood with one of his own.

He did not wish, however, that the king should be ignorant of the truth, and went out next morning to pay a visit of condolence. He supposed that messengers would be sent from the court to inquire about his health, and that, when they took back word that he had gone out visiting, the king would understand how his sickness of the day before was only feigned.

It happened as he expected. The king sent a messenger, and his physician besides. Mencius being out, they were received by Măng Chung, either his son or cousin, who complicated the affair by an invention of his own. 'To-day,' he said, 'he was a little better, and hastened to go to court. I don't know whether he has reached it by this time or not.' No sooner were the visitors gone with this story, than he sent several persons to look for the philosopher, and urge him to go to the court before he returned home.

It was now necessary that a full account of the matter should reach the royal ears; and to accomplish this, Mencius neither went home nor to court, but spent the night at the house of one of the high officers. They had an animated discussion. The officer accused Mencius of showing disrespect to the king. The philosopher replied that no man in Ch'î showed so much respect for the sovereign as he did, for it was only he who brought high and truly royal subjects under his notice.

'That,' said the officer, 'is not my meaning. The rule is—"When the prince's order calls, the carriage must not be waited for." You were going to the court, but when you heard the king's message, you did not do so. This seems not in accordance with that rule.' Mencius explained:—'There are three things universally acknowledged to be honourable,—nobility, age, and virtue. In courts, nobility holds the first place; in villages, age; and for helping one's generation and

孟子

presiding over the people, the other two are not equal to virtue. The possession of one of the three does not authorise the despising of one who has the other two.

'A prince who is to accomplish great deeds will have ministers whom he does not call to go to see him. When he wishes to consult with them, he goes to them. The prince who does not honour the virtuous, and delight in their ways of doing, to this extent, is not worth having to do with.

'There was T'ang with Î Yin:—he first learned of him, and then made him his minister; and so without difficulty he became sovereign. There was the duke Hwan with Kwan Chung:—he first learned of him, and then made him his minister; and so without difficulty he became chief of all the princes.

'So did T'ang behave to Î Yin, and the duke Hwan to Kwan Chung, that they would not venture to call them to go to them. If Kwan Chung might not be called to him by his prince, how much less may I be called, who would not play the part of Kwan Chung[1]!'

We are to suppose that these sentiments were conveyed to the king by the officer with whom Mencius spent the night. It is a pity that the exposition of them could only be effected in such a roundabout manner, and was preceded by such acts of prevarication. But where the two parties were so suspicious of each other, we need not wonder that they separated before long. Mencius resigned his honorary appointment, and prepared to return to Tsâu. On this occasion king Hsüan visited him, and after some complimentary expressions asked whether he might expect to see him again. 'I dare not request permission to visit you *at any particular time*,' replied Mencius, 'but, indeed, it is what I desire[2].'

The king made another attempt to detain him, and sent an officer, called Shih, to propose to him to remain in the State, on the understanding that he should have a house large enough to accommodate his disciples, and an allowance of ten thousand measures of grain to support them. All Mencius's efforts had not sufficed to make king Hsüan and his ministers understand him. They thought he was really actuated like themselves by a desire for wealth. He indignantly rejected the proposal, and pointed out the folly of

[1] Bk. II. Pt. II. ii. [2] Bk. II. Pt. II. x. I consider that this chapter, and others here referred to, belong to Mencius's first departure from Ch'i. I do so because we can hardly suppose that the king and his officers would not have understood him better by the end of his second residence. Moreover, while Mencius retires, his language in x. 2 and xi. 5, 6 is of such a nature that it leaves an opening for him to return again.

it, considering that he had already declined a hundred thousand measures in holding only an honorary appointment[1].

So Mencius turned his back on Ch'î; but he withdrew with a slow and lingering step, stopping three nights in one place, to afford the king an opportunity to recall him on a proper understanding. Some reproached him with his hesitancy, but he sufficiently explained himself. 'The king,' he said, 'is, after all, one who may be made to do good. If he were to use me, would it be for the happiness of Ch'î only? It would be for the happiness of the people of the whole kingdom. I am hoping that the king will change; I am daily hoping for this.

'Am I like one of your little-minded people? They will remonstrate with their prince, and on their remonstrance not being accepted, they get angry, and, with their passion displayed in their countenance, they take their leave, and travel with all their strength for a whole day, before they will rest[2].'

Mencius in T'ăng;—from his leaving Ch'î to B.C. 318.

7. After he left Ch'î, Mencius found a home for some time in the small principality of T'ăng, on the south of Ch'î, in the ruler of which he had a sincere admirer and docile pupil. He did not proceed thither immediately, however, but seems to have taken his way to Sung, which consisted mostly of the present department of Kwei-tei in Ho-nan[3]. There he was visited by the crown-prince of T'ăng, who made a long detour, while on a journey to Ch'û, for the purpose of seeing him. The philosopher discoursed on the goodness of human nature, and the excellent ways of Yâo and Shun. His hearer admired, but doubted. He could not forget, however, and the lessons which he received produced fruit before long.

[1] I have said in a note, Bk. II. Pt. II. x. 5, that 100,000 *chung* was the fixed allowance of a 卿, which Mencius had declined to receive. When we look narrowly into the matter, however, we see that this could hardly be the case. It is known that four measures were used in Ch'î,—the 豆, 區, 釜, and 鍾, and that a *chung* was = ten *fû*, or six 石 and four *tâu*. 10,000 *chung* would thus = 64,000 stone, and Mencius declined 640,000 stone of grain. No officer of Ch'î could have an income so much as that. The measures of the Han dynasty are ascertained to have been only one-fifth the capacity of the present. Assuming that those of Châu and Han agreed, and bringing the above computations to the present standard, Mencius was offered an annual amount of 12,800 stone of grain for his disciples, and he had himself refused in all 128,000 stone. With this reduction, and taking any grain we please as the standard of valuation, the amount is still much beyond what we can suppose to have been a 卿's salary.—閻若璩 supposes that Mencius intends by 100,000 *chung* the sum of the income during all the years he had held his honorary office. [2] Bk. II. Pt. II. xii. [3] This is gathered from Bk. III. Pt. I. i. 1, where the crown-prince of T'ăng visits Mencius, and from Bk. II. Pt. II. iii, where his accepting a gift in Sung appears to have been subsequent to his refusing one in Ch'î.

孟子

From Sung Mencius returned to Tsâu, by way of Hsieh. In both Sung and Hsieh he accepted large gifts from the rulers, which help us in some measure to understand how he could maintain an expenditure which must have been great, and which gave occasion also for an ingenious exposition of the principles on which he guided his course among the princes. 'When you were in Ch'î,' said one of his disciples, 'you refused a hundred *yi* of fine gold, which the king sent, while in Sung you accepted seventy *yi*, and in Hsieh fifty[1]. If you were right in refusing the gift in the first case, you did wrong in accepting it in the other two. If you were right in accepting it in those two cases, you were wrong in refusing it in Ch'î. You must accept one of these alternatives.' 'I did right in all the cases,' replied Mencius. 'When I was in Sung, I was about to undertake a long journey. Travellers must be provided with what is necessary for their expenses. The prince's message was—"a present against travelling expenses;" why should I have declined the gift? In Hsieh I was under apprehensions for my safety, and taking measures for my protection. The message was—"I have heard you are taking measures to protect yourself, and send this to help you in procuring arms." Why should I have declined the gift? But when I was in Ch'î, I had no occasion for money. To send a man a gift when he has no occasion for it is to bribe him. How is it possible that a superior man should be taken with a bribe[2]?'

Before Mencius had been long in Tsâu, the crown-prince of T'ăng succeeded to the rule of the principality, and calling to mind the lessons which he had heard in Sung, sent an officer to consult the philosopher on the manner in which he should perform the funeral and mourning services for his father[3]. Mencius of course advised him to carry out in the strictest manner the ancient regulations. The new prince's relatives and the officers of the State opposed, but

[1] I have supposed in the translation, Bk. II. Pt. II. iii. 1, that the metal of these gifts was silver and not gold. 閻若據, however, seems to make it clear that we ought to understand that it was gold. (See 皇淸經解, 孟子生卒年月考, p. 6.) Pressed with the objection that 2,400 ounces of gold seems too large a sum, he goes on to make it appear that under the Ch'in dynasty, a *yi* or twenty-four ounces of gold was only equal to 15,000 cash, or fifteen taels of silver of the present day! This is a point on which I do not know that we can attain any positive certainty. [2] Bk. II. Pt. II. iii. [3] Bk. III. Pt. I. ii. The note of time which is relied on as enabling us to follow Mencius here is the intimation, Bk. I. Pt. II. xiv, that 'Ch'î was about to fortify Hsieh.' This is referred to B.C. 320, when king Hsüan appointed his brother 田嬰 over the dependency of Hsieh, and took measures to fortify it.

ineffectually. Mencius's counsel was followed, and the effect was great. Duke Wăn became an object of general admiration.

By and by Mencius proceeded himself to T'ăng. We may suppose that he was invited thither by the prince as soon as the rules of mourning would allow his holding free communication with him. The chapters which give an account of their conversations are really interesting. Mencius recommended that attention should be chiefly directed to the encouragement of agriculture and education. He would have nourishment secured both for the body and the mind of every subject[1]. When the duke was lamenting the danger to which he was exposed from his powerful and encroaching neighbours, Mencius told him he might adopt one of two courses;—either leave his State, and like king T'âi go and find a settlement elsewhere, or be prepared to die for his patrimony. 'If you do good,' said he, 'among your descendants in after generations there will be one who shall attain to the royal dignity. But results are with Heaven. What is Ch'î to you, O prince? Be strong to do good. That is all your business[2].'

After all, nothing came of Mencius's residence in T'ăng. We should like to know what made him leave it. Confucius said that, if any of the princes were to employ him, he should achieve something considerable in twelve months, and in the course of three years, the government would be perfected[3]. Mencius taught that, in his time, with half the merit of former days double the result might be accomplished[4]. Here in T'ăng a fair field seemed to be afforded him, but he was not able to make his promise good. Possibly the good purposes and docility of duke Wăn may not have held out, or Mencius may have found that it was easier to theorise about government, than actually to carry it on. Whatever may have been the cause, we find him in B.C. 319 at the court of king Hûi of Liang.

Before he left T'ăng, Mencius had his rencounter with the disciples of the 'shrike-tongued barbarian of the South,' one Hsü Hsing, who came to T'ăng on hearing of the reforms which were being made at Mencius's advice by the duke Wăn. This was one of the dreamy speculators of the time, to whom I have already alluded. He pretended to follow the lessons of Shăn-nâng, one of the reputed founders of the kingdom and the father of husbandry, and came to T'ăng with

[1] Bk. III. Pt. I. iii. [2] Bk. I. Pt. II. xiii. xiv. xv. [3] Confucian Analects, XIII. x.
[4] Bk. II. Pt. I. i. 13.

孟子

his plough upon his shoulder, followed by scores of followers, all wearing the coarsest clothes, and supporting themselves by making mats and sandals. It was one of his maxims that 'the magistrates should be labouring-men.' He would have the sovereign grow his own rice, and cook his own meals. Not a few of 'The Learned' were led away by his doctrines, but Mencius girt up his loins to oppose the heresy, and ably vindicated the propriety of a division of labour, and of a lettered class conducting the government. It is just possible that the appearance of Hsü Hsing, and the countenance shown to him, may have had something to do with Mencius's leaving the State.

Mencius in Liang;—B.C. 319, 318.

8. Liang was another name for Wei, one of the States into which Tsin had been divided. King Hûi, early in his reign, B.C. 364, had made the city of Tâ-liang, in the present department of K'âi-făng, his capital, and given its name to his whole principality. It was the year before his death, when Mencius visited him [1]. A long, stormy, and disastrous rule was about to terminate, but the king was as full of activity and warlike enterprise as ever he had been. At his first interview with Mencius, he addressed him in the well-known words, 'Venerable Sir, since you have not counted it far to come here, a distance of a thousand *lî*, may I presume that you are likewise provided with counsels to profit my kingdom?' Mencius in reply starts from the word *profit*, and expatiates eloquently on the evil consequences that must ensue from making a regard to profit the ground of conduct or the rule of policy. As for himself, his theme must be benevolence and righteousness. On these he would discourse, but on nothing else, and in following them a prince would obtain true and sure advantages.

Only five conversations are related between king Hûi and the philosopher. They are all in the spirit of the first which has just been described, and of those which he had with king Hsüan of Ch'î.

[1] There are various difficulties about the reign of king Hûi of Liang. Sze-mâ Ch'ien makes it commence in 369 and terminate in 334. He is then succeeded by Hsiang (襄), whose reign ends in 318; and he is followed by Âi (哀) till 295. What are called 'The Bamboo Books' (竹書) extend Hûi's reign to B.C. 318, and the next twenty years are assigned to king Âi. 'The Annals of the Nation' (which are compiled from 'The General Mirror of History' [通鑑]) follow the Bamboo Books in the length of king Hûi's reign, but make him followed by Hsiang; and take no note of a king Âi.—From Mencius we may be assured that Hûi was succeeded by Hsiang, and the view of his Life, which I have followed in this sketch, leads to the longer period assigned to his reign.

There is the same freedom of expostulation, or, rather, boldness of reproof, and the same unhesitating assurance of the success that would follow the adoption of his principles. The most remarkable is the third, where we have a sounder doctrine than where he tells king Hsüan that his love of beauty and money and valour need not interfere with his administration of royal government. Hûi is boasting of his diligence in the government of his State, and sympathy with the sufferings of his people, as far beyond those of any of the neighbouring rulers, and wondering how he was not more prosperous than they. Mencius replies, 'Your Majesty is fond of war;—let me take an illustration from it. The drums sound, and the weapons are crossed, when suddenly the soldiers on one side throw away their coats of mail, trail their weapons behind them, and run. Some of them run a hundred paces, and some run only fifty. What would you think if those who run fifty paces were to laugh at those who run a hundred paces?' 'They may not do so,' said the king; 'they only did not run a hundred paces, but they also ran.' 'Since your Majesty knows this,' was the reply, 'you need not hope that your people will become more numerous than those of the neighbouring kingdoms.' The king was thus taught that half-measures would not do. Royal government, to be effectual, must be carried out faithfully and in its spirit.

King Hûi died in B.C. 319, and was succeeded by his son, the king Hsiang. Mencius appears to have had but one interview with him. When he came out from it, he observed to some of his friends:—'When I looked at him from a distance, he did not appear like a sovereign; when I drew near to him, I saw nothing venerable about him[1].'

It was of no use to remain any longer in Liang; he left it, and we meet with him again in Ch'î.

Mencius the second time in Ch'î;—to B.C. 311.

9. Whether he returned immediately to Ch'î we cannot tell, but the probability is that he did, and remained in it till the year B.C. 311[2]. When he left it about seven years before, he had made provision for his return in case of a change of mind in king Hsüan. The philosopher, I

[1] Bk. I. Pt. I. vi. [2] This conclusion is adopted because it was in 311 that Yen rebelled, when the king said that he was very much ashamed when he thought of Mencius, who had strongly condemned his policy towards the State of Yen.—This is another case in which the chronology is differently laid down by the authorities, Sze-mâ Ch'ien saying that Yen was taken by king Min (湣王), the son and successor of Hsüan.

孟子

apprehend, was content with an insufficient assurance of such an alteration. Be that as it may, he went back, and took an appointment again as a high noble.

If he was contented with a smaller reformation on the part of the king than he must have desired, Mencius was not himself different from what he had been. In the court and among the high officers his deportment was equally unbending; he was the same stern mentor.

Among the officers was one Wang Hwan, called also Tsze-âo, a favourite with the king, insolent and presuming. Him Mencius treated with an indifference and even contempt which must have been very provoking. A large party were met one time at the house of an officer who had lost a son, for the purpose of expressing their condolences. Mencius was among them, when suddenly Wang Hwan made his appearance. One and another moved to do him honour and win from him a smile,—all indeed but Mencius, who paid no regard to him. The other complained of the rudeness, but the philosopher could show that his conduct was only in accordance with the rules of Propriety [1].

Another time, Mencius was sent as the chief of a mission of condolence to the court of T'ăng, Wang Hwan being the assistant commissioner. Every morning and evening he waited upon Mencius, who never once exchanged a word with him on the business of their mission [2].

Now and then he became the object of unpleasant remark and censure. At his instigation, an officer, Ch'î Wâ, remonstrated with the king on some abuse, and had in consequence to resign his office. The people were not pleased with Mencius, thus advising others to their harm, and yet continuing to retain his own position undisturbed. 'In the course which he marked out for Ch'î Wâ,' they said, 'he did well, but we do not know as to the course which he pursues for himself.' The philosopher, however, was never at a loss in rendering a reason. He declared that, as his office was honorary, he could act 'freely and without restraint either in going forward or retiring [3].' In this matter we have more sympathy with the condemnation than with the defence.

Some time during these years there occurred the death of Mencius's excellent mother. She had been with him in Ch'î, and

[1] Bk. IV. Pt. II. xxvii. [2] Bk. II. Pt. II. vi. [3] Bk. II. Pt. II. v.

he carried the coffin to Lû, to bury it near the dust of his father and ancestors. The funeral was a splendid one. Mencius perhaps erred in having it so from his dislike to the Mohists, who advocated a spare simplicity in all funeral matters[1]. His arrangements certainly excited the astonishment of some of his own disciples[2], and were the occasion of general remark[3]. He defended himself on the ground that 'the superior man will not for all the world be niggardly to his parents,' and that, as he had the means, there was no reason why he should not give all the expression in his power to his natural feelings.

Having paid this last tribute of filial duty, Mencius returned to Ch'î, but he could not appear at court till the three years of his mourning were accomplished[4]. It could not be long after this when trouble and confusion arose in Yen, a large State to the north-west of Ch'î, in the present Chih-lî. Its prince, who was a poor weakling, wished to go through the sham of resigning his throne to his prime minister, understanding that he would decline it, and that thus he would have the credit of playing the part of the ancient Yâo, while at the same time he retained his kingdom. The minister, however, accepted the tender, and, as he proved a tyrannical ruler, great dissatisfaction arose. Ch'ăn T'ung, an officer of Ch'î, asked Mencius whether Yen might be smitten. He replied that it might, for its prince had no right to resign it to his minister, and the minister no right to receive it. 'Suppose,' said he, 'there were an officer here with whom you were pleased, and that, without informing the king, you were privately to give him your salary and rank; and suppose that this officer, also without the king's orders, were privately to receive them from you:—would such a transaction be allowable? And where is the difference between the case of Yen and this[5]?'

Whether these sentiments were reported to king Hsüan or not, he proceeded to attack Yen, and found it an easy prey. Mencius was charged with having advised the measure, but he ingeniously repudiated the accusation. 'I answered Ch'ăn T'ung that Yen might be smitten. If he had asked me—"Who may smite it?" I would have answered him—"He who is the minister of Heaven may smite it." Suppose the case of a murderer, and that one asks me—"May this man be put to death?" I will answer him—"He may." If he

[1] Bk. III. Pt. I. v. 2. [2] Bk. II. Pt. II. vii. [3] Bk. I. Pt. II. xvi. [4] Some are of opinion that Mencius stopped all the period of mourning in Lû, but the more natural conclusion, Bk. II. Pt. II. vii. 1, seems to me that he returned to Ch'î, and stayed at Ying, without going to court. [5] Bk. II. Pt. II. viii.

孟子

ask me—"Who may put him to death?" I will answer him—"The chief criminal judge may put him to death." But now with one Yen to smite another Yen:—how should I have advised this?' This reference to 'The minister of Heaven' strikingly illustrates what was said about the state of China in Mencius's time. He tells us in one place that hostile States do not correct one another, and that only the supreme authority can punish its subjects by force of arms[1]. But there was now no supreme authority in China. He saw in the sovereign but 'the shadow of an empty name.' His conception of a minister of Heaven was not unworthy. He was one who, by the distinction which he gave to talents and virtue, and by his encouragement of agriculture and commerce, attracted all people to him as a parent. He would have no enemy under heaven, and could not help attaining to the royal dignity[2].

King Hsüan, after conquering and appropriating Yen, tried to get Mencius's sanction of the proceeding, alleging the ease and rapidity with which he had effected the conquest as an evidence of the favour of Heaven. But the philosopher was true to himself. The people of Yen, he said, had submitted, because they expected to find in the king a deliverer from the evils under which they groaned. If they were pleased, he might retain the State, but if he tried to keep it by force, there would simply be another revolution[3].

The king's love of power prevailed. He determined to keep his prey, and ere long a combination was formed among the neighbouring princes to wrest Yen from him. Full of alarm he again consulted Mencius, but got no comfort from him. 'Let him restore his captives and spoils, consult with the people of Yen, and appoint them a ruler;—so he might be able to avert the threatened attack[4].'

The result was as Mencius had predicted. The people of Yen rebelled. The king felt ashamed before the philosopher, whose second residence in Ch'î was thus brought to an unpleasant termination.

10. We do not know that Mencius visited any of the princes after this. On leaving Ch'î, he took his way again to Sung, the duke of which had taken the title of king in B.C. 318. A report also had gone abroad that he was setting about to practise the true royal government, but Mencius soon satisfied himself of its incorrectness[5].

Mencius in Lû; —B.C. 309.

The last court at which we find him is that of Lû, B.C. 309. The

[1] Bk. VII. Pt. II. ii. [2] Bk. II. Pt. I. v. [3] Bk. I. Pt. II. x. [4] Bk. I. Pt. II. xi. [5] See Bk. III. Pt. II. v. vi.

duke P'ing had there called Yo-chăng, one of the philosopher's disciples, to his councils, and indeed committed to him the administration of the government. When Mencius heard of it, he was so overjoyed that he could not sleep[1].

The first appearance (in point of time) of this Yo-chăng in the seven Books is not much to his credit. He comes to Ch'î in the train of Wang Hwan, the favourite who was an offence to the philosopher, and is very sharply reproved for joining himself to such a character 'for the sake of the loaves and fishes[2].' Other references to him are more favourable. Mencius declares him to be 'a good man,' 'a real man[3].' He allows that 'he is not a man of vigour,' nor 'a man wise in council,' nor 'a man of much information,' but he says—'he is a man that loves what is good,' and 'the love of what is good is more than a sufficient qualification for the government of the kingdom;—how much more is it so for the State of Lû[4]?'

Either on his own impulse or by Yo-chăng's invitation, Mencius went himself also to Lû, hoping that the prince who had committed his government to the disciple might be willing to listen to the counsels of the master. The duke was informed of his arrival by Yo-chăng, and also of the deference which he exacted. He resolved to go and visit him and invite him to the court. The horses were put to the carriage, and the duke was ready to start, when the intervention of his favourite, a worthless creature called Tsang Ts'ang, diverted him from his good purpose. When told by the duke that he was going to visit the scholar Măng, Ts'ang said, 'That you demean yourself to pay the honour of the first visit to a common man, is, I apprehend, because you think that he is a man of talents and virtue. From such men the rules of ceremonial proprieties and right proceed; but on the occasion of this Măng's second mourning, his observances exceeded those of the former. Do not go to see him, my prince.' The duke said, 'I will not;'—and carriage and horses were ordered back to their places.

As soon as Yo-chăng had an audience of the duke, he explained the charge of impropriety which had been brought against Mencius; but the evil was done. The duke had taken his course. 'I told him,' said Yo-chăng, 'about you, and he was coming to see you, when Tsang Ts'ang stopped him.' Mencius replied to him, 'A man's

[1] Bk. VI. Pt. II. xiii. [2] Bk. IV. Pt. I. xxv. [3] Bk. VII. Pt. II. xxv. [4] Bk. VI. Pt. II. xiii.

孟子

advancement is effected, it may be, by others, and the stopping him is, it may be, from the efforts of others. But to advance a man or to stop his advance is really beyond the power of other men; my not finding in the prince of Lû a ruler who would confide in me, and put my counsels into practice, is from Heaven. How could that scion of the Tsang family cause me not to find the ruler that would suit me[1]?'

Mencius appears to have accepted this intimation of the will of Heaven as final. He has a remarkable saying, that Heaven controls the development of a man's faculties and affections, but as there is an adaptation in his nature for these, the superior man does not say—'It is the appointment of Heaven[2].' In accordance with this principle he had striven long against the adverse circumstances which threw his hopes of influencing the rulers of his time again and again in the dust. On his first leaving Lû we saw how he said:—'Heaven does not yet wish that the country should enjoy tranquillity and good order.' For about fifteen years, however, he persevered, if peradventure there might be a change in the Heavenly councils. Now at last he bowed in submission. The year after and he would reach his grand climacteric. We lose sight of him. He retired from courts and great officers. We can but think and conjecture of him, according to tradition, passing the last twenty years of his life amid the more congenial society of his disciples, discoursing to them, and compiling the Works which have survived as his memorial to the present day.

11. I have endeavoured in the preceding paragraphs to put together the principal incidents of Mencius's history as they may be gathered from his Writings. There is no other source of information about him, and we must regret that they tell us nothing of his domestic life and habits. In one of the stories about his mother there is an allusion to his wife, from which we may conclude that his marriage was not without its bitternesses. It is probable that the Măng Chung, mentioned in Bk. II. Pt. II. ii, was his son, though this is not easily reconcileable with what we read in Bk. VI. Pt. I. v. of a Măng Ch'î, who was, according to Châo Ch'î, a brother of Măng Chung. We must believe that he left a family, for his descendants form a large clan at the present day. Hsî-wăn, the fifty-sixth in descent from Mencius, was, in the reign of Chiâ-ching (A.D. 1522–

[1] Bk. I. Pt. II. xvi. [2] Bk. III. Pt. II. i. ii.

1566), constituted a member of the Han-lin college, and of the Board in charge of the Five Ching, which honour was to be hereditary in the family, and the holder of it to preside at the sacrifices to his ancestor[1]. China's appreciation of our philosopher could not be more strikingly shown. Honours flow back in this empire. The descendant ennobles his ancestors. But in the case of Mencius, as in that of Confucius, this order is reversed. No excellence of descendants can extend to them; and the nation acknowledges its obligations to them by nobility and distinction conferred through all generations upon their posterity.

SECTION II.

HIS INFLUENCE AND OPINIONS.

1. Confucius had hardly passed off the stage of life before his merits began to be acknowledged. The duke Âi, who had neglected his counsels when he was alive, was the first to pronounce his eulogy, and to order that public sacrifices should be offered to him. His disciples proclaimed their estimation of him as superior to all the sages whom China had ever seen. Before long this view of him took possession of the empire; and since the Han dynasty, he has been the man whom sovereign and people have delighted to honour.

The memory of Mencius was not so distinguished. We have seen that many centuries elapsed before his Writings were received among the Classics of the empire. It was natural that under the same dynasty when this was done the man himself should be admitted to share in the sacrifices presented to Confucius.

Acknowledgement of Mencius's merits by the government.

The emperor Shăn Tsung[2], in A.D. 1083, issued a patent, constituting Mencius 'Duke of the kingdom of Tsâu[3],' and ordering a temple to be built to him in the district of Tsâu, at the spot where the philosopher had been interred. In the following year it was enacted that he should have a place in the temple of Confucius, next to that of Yen Yüan, the favourite disciple of the sage.

In A.D. 1330, the emperor Wăn Tsung[4], of the Yüan dynasty, made an addition to Mencius's title, and styled him 'Duke of the

[1] See Morrison's Dictionary, on Mencius, character 孟. [2] 神宗, A.D. 1068–1085. [3] 鄒國公. [4] 文宗, A.D. 1330–1333.

孟子

State of Tsâu, Inferior Sage[1].' This continued till the rise of the Ming dynasty, the founder of which, Hung-wû, had his indignation excited in 1372 by one of Mencius's conversations with king Hsüan. The philosopher had said:—'When the prince regards his ministers as his hands and feet, the ministers regard their prince as their belly and heart; when he regards them as his dogs and horses, they regard him as any other man; when he regards them as ground or grass, they regard him as a robber and an enemy[2].' To apply such names as *robber* and *enemy* in any case to sovereigns seemed to the imperial reader an unpardonable outrage, and he ordered Mencius to be degraded from his place in the temples of Confucius, declaring also that if any one remonstrated on the proceeding he should be dealt with as guilty of 'Contempt of Majesty.'

The scholars of China have never been slow to vindicate the memory of its sages and worthies. Undeterred by the imperial threat, Ch'ien T'ang[3], a president of the Board of Punishments, appeared with a remonstrance, saying,—'I will die for Mencius, and my death will be crowned with glory.' The emperor was moved by his earnestness, and allowed him to go scathless. In the following year, moreover, examination and reflection produced a change of mind. He issued a second proclamation to the effect that Mencius, by exposing heretical doctrines and overthrowing perverse speakings, had set forth clearly the principles of Confucius, and ought to be restored to his place as one of his assessors[4].

[1] 鄒國亞聖公. The 亞 has been translated 'second-rate,' but it is by no means so depreciating a term as that, simply indicating that Mencius was second to Confucius. The title 亞聖 was first applied to him by Châo Ch'î. [2] Bk. IV. Pt. II. iii. [3] 錢唐.

[4] I have taken this account from 'The Sacrificial Canon of the Sage's Temples' (vol. i. proleg. p. 132). Dr. Morrison in his Dictionary, under the character 孟, adds that the change in the emperor's mind was produced by his reading the remarkable passage in Bk. VI. Pt. II. xv, about trials and hardships as the way by which Heaven prepares men for great services. He thought it was descriptive of himself, and that he could argue from it a good title to the crown;—and so he was mollified to the philosopher. It may be worth while to give here the concluding remarks in 'The Paraphrase for Daily Lessons, Explaining the Meaning of the Four Books' (vol. i. proleg. p. 130), on the chapter of Mencius which was deemed by the imperial reader so objectionable:—'Mencius wished that sovereigns should treat their ministers according to propriety, and nourish them with kindness, and therefore he used these perilous words in order to alarm and rouse them. As to the other side, the part of ministers, though the sovereign regard them as his hands and feet, they ought notwithstanding to discharge most earnestly their duties of loyalty and love. Yea, though he regard them as dogs and horses, or as the ground and grass, they ought still more to perform their part in spite of all difficulties, and oblivious of their persons. They may on no account make the manner in which they are regarded, whether it be of appreciation or contempt, the standard by which they regulate the measure of their grateful service. The words of Confucius, that *the ruler should behave to his ministers according to propriety, and the ministers*

In 1530, the ninth year of the reign of Chiâ-ching, a general revision was made of the sacrificial canon for the sage's temple, and the title of Mencius was changed into—'The philosopher Măng, Inferior Sage.' So it continues to the present day. His place is the second on the west, next to that of the philosopher Tsăng. Originally, we have seen, he followed Yen Hûi, but Hûi, Tsze-sze, Tsăng, and Măng were appointed the sage's four assessors, and had their relative positions fixed, in 1267.

Estimate of Mencius by himself and by scholars.

2. The second edict of Hung-wû, restoring Mencius to his place in the temples of Confucius, states fairly enough the services which he is held to have rendered to his country. The philosopher's own estimate of himself has partly appeared in the sketch of his Life[1]. He seemed to start with astonishment when his disciple Kung-sun Ch'âu was disposed to rank him as a sage[2]; but he also said on one occasion—'When sages shall rise up again, they will not change my words[3].' Evidently, he was of opinion that the mantle of Confucius had fallen upon him. A work was to be done in his generation, and he felt himself able to undertake it. After describing what had been accomplished by the great Yü, by Châu-kung, and Confucius, he adds:—'I also wish to rectify men's hearts, and to put an end to those perverse doctrines, to oppose their one-sided actions, and banish away their licentious expressions; and thus to carry on the work of the three sages[4].'

The place which Mencius occupies in the estimation of the literati of China may be seen by the following testimonies, selected from those appended by Chû Hsî to the prefatory notice of his Life in the 'Collected Comments.'

Han Yü[5] says, 'If we wish to study the doctrines of the sages, we must begin with Mencius.' He also quotes the opinion of Yang Tsze-yün[6], 'Yang and Mo were stopping up the way *of truth*, when Mencius refuted them, and scattered their delusions without difficulty;' and then remarks upon it:—'When Yang and Mo walked abroad, the true doctrine had nearly come to nought. Though

serve their sovereign with faithfulness, contain the unchanging rule for all ages.' The authors of the 'Daily Lessons' did their work by imperial order, and evidently had the fear of the court before their eyes. Their language implies a censure of our philosopher. There will ever be a grudge against him in the minds of despots, and their creatures will be ready to depreciate him.

[1] See above, pp. 23, 24. [2] Bk. II. Pt. I. ii. 18, 19. [3] Bk. III. Pt. II. ix. 10. [4] Bk. III. Pt. II. ix. 13. [5] See above, pp. 11, 12. [6] 揚子雲;—died A. D. 18.

孟子

Mencius possessed talents and virtue, even those of a sage, he did not occupy the throne. He could only speak and not act. With all his earnestness, what could he do? It is owing, however, to his words, that learners now-a-days still know how to revere Confucius, to honour benevolence and righteousness, to esteem the true sovereign and despise the mere pretender. But the grand rules and laws of the sage and sage-sovereigns had been lost beyond the power of redemption; only one in a hundred of them was preserved. Can it be said in those circumstances that Mencius had an easy task? Yet had it not been for him, we should have been buttoning the lappets of our coats on the left side, and our discourse would have been all confused and indistinct;—it is on this account that I have honoured Mencius, and consider his merit not inferior to that of Yü.'

One asked the philosopher Ch'ăng[1] whether Mencius might be pronounced to be a sage. He replied, 'I do not dare to say altogether that he was a sage, but his learning had reached the extremest point.' The same great scholar also said:—'The merit of Mencius in regard to the doctrine of the sages is more than can be told. Confucius only spoke of *benevolence*, but as soon as Mencius opens his mouth, we hear of *benevolence* and *righteousness*. Confucius only spoke of the *will* or *mind*, but Mencius enlarged also on *the nourishment of the passion-nature*. In these two respects his merit was great.' 'Mencius did great service to the world by his teaching the goodness of man's nature.' 'Mencius had a certain amount of the heroical spirit, and to that there always belong some jutting corners, the effect of which is very injurious. Yen Yüan, all round and complete, was different from this. He was but a hair's-breadth removed from a sage, while Mencius must be placed in a lower rank, a great worthy, an inferior sage.' Ch'ăng was asked where what he called the heroical spirit of Mencius could be seen. 'We have only to compare his words with those of Confucius,' he said, 'and we shall perceive it. It is like the comparison of ice or crystal with a precious jade-stone. The ice is bright enough, but the precious stone, without so much brilliancy, has a softness and richness all its own[2].' The scholar

[1] 程子; see vol. i. proleg. p. 24.

[2] This is probably the original of what appears in the 'Mémoires concernant les Chinois,' in the notice of Mencius, vol. iii, and which Thornton (vol. ii. pp. 216, 217) has faithfully translated therefrom in the following terms:—'Confucius, through prudence or modesty, often dissimulated; he did not always say what he might have said: Măng-tsze, on the contrary, was incapable of constraining himself; he spoke what he thought, and without the

Yang[1] says:—'The great object of Mencius in his writings is to rectify men's hearts, teaching them to preserve their heart and nourish their nature, and to recover their lost heart. When he discourses of benevolence, righteousness, propriety, and knowledge, he refers to the principles of these in the heart commiserating, feeling shame and dislike, affected with modesty and complaisance, approving and disapproving. When he speaks of the evils springing from perverted speakings, he says—"Growing first in the mind, they prove injurious to government." When he shows how a prince should be served, he says—"Correct what is wrong in his mind. Once rectify the prince, and the kingdom will be settled." With him the thousand changes and ten thousand operations of men all come from the mind or heart. If a man once rectify his heart, little else will remain for him to do. In "The Great Learning," the cultivation of the person, the regulation of the family, the government of the State, and the tranquillisation of the empire, all have their root in rectifying the heart and making the thoughts sincere. If the heart be rectified, we recognise at once the goodness of the nature. On this account, whenever Mencius came into contact with people, he testified that man's nature is good. When Âu-yang Yung-shû[2] says, that in the lessons of the sages, man's nature does not occupy the first place, he is wrong. There is nothing to be put before this. Yâo and Shun are the models for ten thousand ages simply because they followed their nature. And to follow our nature is just to accord with Heavenly principle. To use plans and arts, away from this, though they may be successful in great achievement, is the selfishness of human desires, and as far removed from the mode of action of the sage, as earth is from heaven.' I shall close these testimonies with a sentence from Chû Hsî himself. He says:—'Mencius, when compared with Confucius, always appears to speak in too lofty a style; but when we hear him proclaiming the goodness of man's

least fear or reserve. He resembles ice of the purest water, through which we can see all its defects as well as its beauties: Confucius, on the other hand, is like a precious gem, which, though not so pellucid as ice, has more strength and solidity.' The former of these sentences is quite alien from the style of Chinese thinking and expression.

[1] 楊氏. This is 楊時, styled 中立, but more commonly referred to as 楊龜山. He was one of the great scholars of the Sung dynasty, a friend of the two Ch'ăng. He has a place in the temples of Confucius. [2] 歐陽永叔. This was one of China's greatest scholars. He has now a place in the temples of Confucius.

nature, and celebrating Yâo and Shun, then we likewise perceive the solidity of his discourses[1].'

Correctness of the above testimonies. Mencius's own peculiarities appear in his expositions of doctrine.

3. The judgment concerning our philosopher contained in the above quotations will approve itself to every one who has carefully perused his Works. The long passage from Yang Kwei-shan is especially valuable, and puts the principal characteristic of Mencius's teachings in a clear light. Whether those teachings have the intrinsic value which is ascribed to them is another question, which I will endeavour to discuss in the present section without prejudice. But Mencius's position with reference to 'the doctrines of the sages' is correctly assigned. We are not to look for new truths in him. And this does not lead his countrymen to think less highly of him. I ventured to lay it down as one grand cause of the position and influence of Confucius, that he was simply the preserver of the monuments of antiquity, and the exemplifier and expounder of the maxims of the golden age of China. In this Mencius must share with him.

But while we are not to look to Mencius for new truths, the peculiarities of his natural character were more striking than those of his master. There was an element of 'the heroical' about him. He was a dialectician, moreover. If he did not like disputing, as he protested that he did not, yet, when forced to it, he showed himself a master of the art. An ingenuity and subtlety, which we cannot but enjoy, often mark his reasonings. We have more sympathy with him than with Confucius. He comes closer to us. He is not so awe-ful, but he is more admirable. The doctrines of the sages take a tinge from his mind in passing through it, and it is with that Mencian character about them that they are now held by the cultivated classes and by readers generally.

I will now call attention to a few passages illustrative of these remarks. Some might prefer to search them out for themselves in the body of the volume, and I am far from intending to exhaust the subject. There will be many readers, however, pleased to have the means of forming an idea of the man for themselves brought within small compass. My next object will be to review his doctrine concerning man's mental constitution and the nourishment of the passion-nature, in which he is said to have rendered special service

[1] See 朱子全書, 卷二十.

to the cause of truth. That done, I will conclude by pointing out what I conceive to be his chief defects as a moral and political teacher. To the opinions of Yang Chû and Mo, which he took credit to himself for assailing and exposing, it will be necessary to devote another chapter.

4. It was pointed out in treating of the opinions of Confucius, that he allowed no 'right divine' to a sovereign, independent of his exercising a benevolent rule. This was one of the topics, however, of which he was shy. With Mencius, on the contrary, it was a favourite theme. The degeneracy of the times and the ardour of his disposition prompted him equally to the free expression of his convictions about it.

Specimens of Mencius's opinions, and manner of advocating them.

'The people,' he said, 'are the most important element *in a nation;* the spirits of the land and grain are the next; the sovereign is the lightest. When a prince endangers the altars of the spirits of the land and grain, he is changed, and another appointed in his place. When the sacrificial victims have been perfect, the millet in its vessels all pure, and the sacrifices offered at their proper seasons, if yet there ensue drought, or the waters overflow, the spirits of the land and grain are changed, and others appointed in their place[1].'

On government.—The people more important than the sovereign.

'*The people are the most important element in a nation, and the sovereign is the lightest;*'—that is certainly a bold and ringing affirmation. Mencius was not afraid to follow it to the conclusion that the sovereign who was exercising an injurious rule should be dethroned. His existence is not to be allowed to interfere with the general good. Killing in such a case is no murder. King Hsüan once asked, 'Was it so that T'ang banished Chieh, and that king Wû smote Châu?' Mencius replied, 'It is so in the records.' The king asked, 'May a minister then put his sovereign to death?' Our philosopher's reply was:—'He who outrages the benevolence proper to his nature is called a robber; he who outrages righteousness is called a ruffian. The robber and ruffian we call a mere fellow. I have heard of the cutting off of the fellow Châu, but I have not heard in his case of the putting a sovereign to death[2].'

An unworthy sovereign may be dethroned or put to death.

With regard to the ground of the relation between ruler and

[1] Bk. VII. Pt. II. xiv. [2] Bk. I. Pt. II. viii.

孟子

people, Mencius refers it very clearly to the will of God. In one place he adapts for his own purpose the language of king Wû in the Shû-ching:—'Heaven having produced the inferior people, appointed for them rulers and teachers, with the purpose that they should be assisting to God, and therefore distinguished them throughout the four quarters of the kingdom[1].' But the question arises—How can this will of Heaven be known? Mencius has endeavoured to answer it. He says:—'Heaven gives the throne, but its appointment is not conferred with specific injunctions. Heaven does not speak. It shows its will by a man's personal conduct and his conduct of affairs.' The conclusion of the whole matter is:—'Heaven sees according as the people see; Heaven hears according as the people hear[2].'

The ground of the relation between ruler and people.

It may not be easy to dispute these principles. I for one have no hesitation in admitting them. Their application, however, must always be attended with difficulty. Here is a sovereign who is the very reverse of a minister of God for good. He ought to be removed, but who is to remove him? Mencius teaches in one passage that the duty is to be performed by his relatives who are also ministers. The king Hsüan asked him about the office of chief ministers. Mencius said, 'Which chief ministers is your Majesty asking about?' 'Are there differences among them,' inquired the king. 'There are,' was the reply; 'there are the chief ministers who are noble and relatives of the prince, and there are those who are of a different surname.' The king said, 'I beg to ask about the chief ministers who are noble and relatives of the prince.' Mencius answered, 'If the prince have great faults, they ought to remonstrate with him, and if he do not listen to them after they have done so again and again, they ought to dethrone him.' The king on this looked moved, and changed countenance. Mencius said, 'Let not your Majesty be offended. You asked me, and I dare not answer but according to truth[3].'

An unworthy ruler may be dethroned by his relatives.

This plan for disposing of an unworthy sovereign has been acted on in China and in other countries. It is the best that can be adopted to secure the throne in the ruling House. But where there are no relatives that have the virtue and power to play such a part, what is to be done? Mencius has two ways of meeting this difficulty. Contrary

Virtuous ministers, and the minister of Heaven, may dethrone a ruler.

[1] Bk. I. Pt. II. iii. 7. [2] Bk. V. Pt. I. v. [3] Bk. V. Pt. II. ix.

to his general rule[1] for the conduct of ministers who are not relatives, he allows that even they may, under certain conditions, take summary measures with their sovereign. His disciple Kung-sun Ch'âu said to him, 'Î Yin said, "I cannot be near and see him so disobedient to reason," and therewith he banished T'âi-chiâ to T'ung. The people were much pleased. When T'âi-chiâ became virtuous, he brought him back, and the people were again much pleased. When worthies are ministers, may they indeed banish their sovereigns in this way when they are not virtuous?' Mencius replied, 'If they have the same purpose as Î Yin, they may. If they have not the same purpose, it would be usurpation[2].' His grand device, however, is what he calls 'the minister of Heaven.' When the sovereign has become worthless and useless, his hope is that Heaven will raise up some one for the help of the people;—some one who shall so occupy in his original subordinate position as to draw all eyes and hearts to himself[3]. Let him then raise the standard, not of rebellion, but of righteousness[4], and he cannot help attaining to the highest dignity. So it was with the great T'ang; so it was with the kings Wăn and Wû. Of the last Mencius says:—'There was one man'—i.e. the tyrant Châu—'pursuing a violent and disorderly course in the kingdom, and king Wû was ashamed of it. By one display of his anger, he gave repose to all the people[5].' He would have been glad if any one of the princes of his own time had been able to vault in a similar way to the sovereign throne, and he went about counselling them to the attempt. 'Let your Majesty,' said he to king Hsüan, 'in like manner, by one burst of anger, give repose to all the people of the nation.' This was in fact advising to rebellion, but the philosopher would have recked little of such a charge. The house of Châu had forfeited in his view its title to the kingdom. Alas! among all the princes he had to do with, he did not find one who could be stirred to so honourable an action.

We need not wonder that Mencius, putting forth the above views so boldly and broadly, should not be a favourite with the rulers of China. His sentiments, professed by the literati, and known and read by all the people, have operated powerfully to compel the good behaviour of 'the powers that be.' It may be said that they encourage the aims of selfish ambition, and the lawlessness of the

[1] Bk. V. Pt. II. ix. 1. [2] Bk. VII. Pt. I. xxxi. [3] Bk. II. Pt. I. v. 6. [4] 起義兵, 'a raising of righteous soldiers;'—this is what all rebel leaders in China profess to do. [5] Bk. I. Pt. II. iii. 7.

孟子

licentious mob. I grant it. They are lessons for the virtuous, and not for the lawless and disobedient, but the government of China would have been more of a grinding despotism, if it had not been for them.

The influence of personal character in a ruler.

On the readiness of the people to be governed Mencius only differs from Confucius in the more vehement style in which he expresses his views. He does not dwell so much on the influence of personal virtue, and I pointed out, in the sketch of his Life, how he all but compromised his character in his communications with king Hsüan, telling him that his love of women, of war, and of wealth might be so regulated as not to interfere with his exercise of true royal government. Still he speaks at times correctly and emphatically on this subject. He quotes Confucius's language on the influence generally of superiors on inferiors, —that 'the relation between them is like that between the wind and grass; the grass must bend when the wind blows upon it[1];' and he says himself:—'It is not enough to remonstrate with a sovereign on account of the mal-employment of ministers, nor to blame errors of government. It is only the great man who can rectify what is wrong in the sovereign's mind. Let the prince be benevolent, and all his acts will be benevolent. Let the prince be righteous, and all his acts will be righteous. Let the prince be correct, and all his acts will be correct. Once rectify the prince, and the kingdom will be firmly settled[2].'

Benevolent government, and its effects.

But the misery which he saw around him, in consequence of the prevailing anarchy and constant wars between State and State, led Mencius to insist on the necessity of what he called 'a benevolent government.' The king Hsiang asked him, 'Who can unite the kingdom under one sway?' and his reply was, 'He who has no pleasure in killing men can so unite it[3].' His being so possessed with the sad condition of his time likewise gave occasion, we may suppose, to the utterance of another sentiment sufficiently remarkable. 'Never,' said he, 'has he who would by his excellence subdue men been able to subdue them. Let a prince seek by his excellence to nourish men, and he will be able to subdue the whole kingdom. It is impossible that any one should become ruler of the kingdom to whom it has not yielded the subjection of the heart[4].' The highest style of excellence will of course

[1] Bk. III. Pt. I. ii. 4. [2] Bk. IV. Pt. I. xx. [3] Bk. I. Pt. I. vi. [4] Bk. IV. Pt. II. xvi.

have its outgoings in benevolence. Apart from that, it will be powerless, as Mencius says. His words are akin to those of Paul:—'Scarcely for a righteous man will one die: yet peradventure for a good man some would even dare to die.'

On the effects of a benevolent rule he says:—'Chieh and Châu's losing the throne arose from their losing the people; and to lose the people means to lose their hearts. There is a way to get the throne:—get the people, and the throne is got. There is a way to get the people:—get their hearts, and the people are got. There is a way to get their hearts:—it is simply to collect for them what they like, and not to lay on them what they dislike. The people turn to a benevolent rule as water flows downwards, and as wild beasts fly to the wilderness. As the otter aids the deep waters, driving the fish into them, and as the hawk aids the thickets, driving the little birds to them, so Chieh and Châu aided T'ang and Wû, driving the people to them. If among the present sovereigns of the kingdom there were one who loved benevolence, all the other princes would aid him by driving the people to him. Although he wished not to become sovereign, he could not avoid becoming so[1].'

Two principal elements of this benevolent rule, much insisted on by Mencius, deserve to be made prominent. They are to be found indicated in the Analects, and in the older Classics also, but it was reserved for our philosopher to set them forth, sharply defined in his own style, and to show the connexion between them. They are:—that the people be made well off, and that they be educated; and the former is necessary in order to the efficiency of the other.

To make the people prosperous, and to educate them, are important elements in a benevolent rule.

Once, when Confucius was passing through Wei in company with Yen Yû, he was struck with the populousness of the State. The disciple said, 'Since the people are thus numerous, what more shall be done for them?' Confucius answered, 'Enrich them.' 'And when they have been enriched, what more shall be done for them?' The reply was—'Teach them[2].' This brief conversation contains the germs of the ideas on which Mencius delighted to dwell.

We read in one place:—'Let it be seen to that their fields of grain and hemp are well cultivated, and make the taxes on them light:—so the people may be made rich.

[1] Bk. IV. Pt. I. ix. [2] Confucian Analects, XIII. ix.

孟子

'Let it be seen to that they use their resources of food seasonably, and expend their wealth only on the prescribed ceremonies:—so their wealth will be more than can be consumed.

'The people cannot live without water and fire; yet if you knock at a man's door in the dusk of the evening, and ask for water and fire, there is no man who will not give them, such is the abundance of these things. A sage governs the kingdom so as to cause pulse and grain to be as abundant as water and fire. When pulse and grain are as abundant as water and fire, how shall the people be other than virtuous[1]?'

Again he says:—'In good years the youth of a country are most of them good, while in bad years they abandon themselves to evil[2].'

It is in his conversations, however, with king Hsüan of Ch'î and duke Wăn of T'ăng, that we find the fullest exposition of the points in hand. 'It is only scholars'—officers, men of a superior order—'who, without a certain livelihood, are able to maintain a fixed heart. As to the people, if they have not a certain livelihood, it follows that they will not have a fixed heart. And if they have not a fixed heart, there is nothing which they will not do in the way of self-abandonment, of moral deflection, of depravity, and of wild license. When they have thus been involved in crime, to follow them up and punish them:—this is to entrap the people. Therefore an intelligent ruler will regulate the livelihood of the people, so as to make sure that, above, they shall have sufficient wherewith to serve their parents, and, below, sufficient wherewith to support their wives and children; that in good years they shall always be abundantly satisfied, and that in bad years they shall escape the danger of perishing. After this he may urge them, and they will proceed to what is good, for in this case the people will follow after that with ease[3].'

It is not necessary to remark here on the measures which Mencius recommends in order to secure a certain livelihood for the people. They embrace the regulation both of agriculture and commerce[4]. And education would be directed simply to illustrate the human relations[5]. What he says on these subjects is not without shrewdness, though many of his recommendations are inappropriate to the present state of society in China itself as well as in other countries. But his principle, that good government should contemplate, and

[1] Bk. VII. Pt. I. xxiii. [2] Bk. VI. Pt. I. vii. [3] Bk. I. Pt. I. vii. 20, 21; Bk. III. Pt. I. iii. 3. [4] Bk. III. Pt. I. iii; Bk. I. Pt. II. iv; Bk. II. Pt. I. v, *et al.* [5] Bk. III. Pt. I. iii. 10.

will be seen in, the material wellbeing of the people, is worthy of all honour. Whether government should interfere to secure the education of the people is questioned by not a few. The religious denomination to which I have the honour to belong has distinguished itself by opposing such a doctrine in England,—more zealously perhaps than wisely. But when Mencius teaches that with the mass of men education will have little success where the life is embittered by a miserable poverty, he shows himself well acquainted with human nature. Educationists now seem generally to recognise it, but I think it is only within a century that it has assumed in Europe the definiteness and importance with which it appeared to Mencius here in China two thousand years ago.

We saw how Mencius, when he was residing in T'ăng, came into contact with a class of enthusiasts, who advocated a return to the primitive state of society,

'When Adam delved and Eve span.'

Necessity for a division of labour, and that government be conducted by a lettered class.

They said that wise and able princes should cultivate the ground equally and along with their people, and eat the fruit of their labour, —that 'to have granaries, arsenals, and treasuries was an oppressing of the people.' Mencius exposed these errors very happily, showing the necessity to society of a division of labour, and that the conduct of government should be in the hands of a lettered class. 'I suppose,' he said to a follower of the strange doctrines, 'that Hsü Hsing sows grain and eats the produce. Is it not so?' 'It is so,' was the answer. 'I suppose that he also weaves cloth, and wears his own manufacture. Is it not so?' 'No; Hsü wears clothes of hair-cloth.' 'Does he wear a cap?' 'He wears a cap.' 'What kind of cap?' 'A plain cap.' 'Is it woven by himself?' 'No; he gets it in exchange for grain.' 'Why does Hsü not weave it himself?' 'That would injure his husbandry.' 'Does Hsü cook his food in boilers and earthenware pans, and does he plough with an iron share?' 'Yes.' 'Does he make those articles himself?' 'No; he gets them in exchange for grain.' On these admissions Mencius proceeds:—'The getting those various articles in exchange for grain is not oppressive to the potter and the founder, and the potter and the founder in their turn, in exchanging their various articles for grain, are not oppressive to the husbandman. How should such a thing be supposed? But why does not Hsü, *on his principles*,

孟子

act the potter and founder, supplying himself with the articles which he uses solely from his own establishment? Why does he go confusedly dealing and exchanging with the handicraftsmen? Why does he not spare himself so much trouble?' His opponent attempted a reply:—'The business of the handicraftsman can by no means be carried on along with the business of husbandry.' Mencius resumed:—'Then, is it the government of the kingdom which alone can be carried on along with the practice of husbandry? Great men have their proper business, and little men have their proper business. Moreover, in the case of any single individual, whatever articles he can require are ready to his hand, being produced by the various handicraftsmen;—if he must first make them for his own use, this way of doing would keep all the people running about upon the roads. Hence there is the saying:—"Some men labour with their minds, and some with their strength. Those who labour with their minds govern others; those who labour with their strength are governed by others. Those who are governed by others support them; those who govern others are supported by them." This is a principle universally recognised[1].'

Sir John Davis has observed that this is exactly Pope's line,

'And those who think still govern those who toil[2].'

Mencius goes on to illustrate it very clearly by referring to the labours of Yâo and Shun. His opponent makes a feeble attempt at the end to say a word in favour of the new doctrines he had embraced:—'If Hsü's doctrines were followed there would not be two prices in the market, nor any deceit in the kingdom. If a boy were sent to the market, no one would impose on him; linen and silk of the same length would be of the same price. So it would be with bundles of hemp and silk, being of the same weight; with the different kinds of grain, being the same in quantity; and with shoes which were the same in size.' Mencius meets this with a decisive reply:—'It is the nature of things to be of unequal quality; some are twice, some five times, some ten times, some a hundred times, some a thousand times, some ten thousand times as valuable as others. If you reduce them all to the same standard, that must throw the world into confusion. If large shoes were of the same price with small shoes, who would make them? For

[1] Bk. III. Pt. I. iv. [2] The Chinese, vol. ii. p. 56.

people to follow the doctrines of Hsü would be for them to lead one another on to practise deceit. How can they avail for the government of a State?'

There is only one other subject which I shall here notice, with Mencius's opinions upon it,—the position, namely, which he occupied himself with reference to the princes of his time. He calls it that of 'a Teacher,' but that term in our language very inadequately represents it. He wished to meet with some ruler who would look to him as 'guide, philosopher, and friend,' regulating himself by his counsels, and thereafter committing to him the entire administration of his government. Such men, he insisted, there had been in China from the earliest ages. Shun had been such to Yâo; Yü and Kâo-yâo had been such to Shun; Î Yin had been such to T'ang; T'âi-kung Wang had been such to king Wăn; Châu-kung had been such to the kings Wû and Ch'ăng; Confucius might have been such to any prince who knew his merit; Tsze-sze was such, in a degree, to the dukes Hûi of Pî and Mû of Lû[1]. The wandering scholars of his own day, who went from court to court, sometimes with good intentions and sometimes with bad, pretended to this character; but Mencius held them in abhorrence. They disgraced the character and prostituted it, and he stood forth as its vindicator and true exemplifier.

Mencius's position as 'a Teacher.'

Never did Christian priest lift up his mitred front, or show his shaven crown, or wear his Geneva gown, more loftily in courts and palaces than Mencius, the Teacher, demeaned himself. We have seen what struggles sometimes arose between him and the princes who would fain have had him bend to their power and place. 'Those,' said he, 'who give counsel to the great should despise them, and not look at their pomp and display. Halls several fathoms high, with beams projecting several cubits:—these, if my wishes were to be realised, I would not have. Food spread before me over ten cubits square, and attendant women to the amount of hundreds:—these, though my wishes were realised, I would not have. Pleasure and wine, and the dash of hunting, with thousands of chariots following after me:—these, though my wishes were realised, I would not have. What they esteem are what I would have nothing to do with; what I esteem are the rules of the ancients.—Why should

[1] See Bk. V. Pt. II. iii. vii, *et al.*

孟子

I stand in awe of them[1]?' Before we bring a charge of pride against Mencius on account of this language and his conduct in accordance with it, we must bear in mind that the literati in China do in reality occupy the place of priests and ministers in Christian kingdoms. Sovereign and people have to seek the law at their lips. The ground on which they stand,—'the rules of the ancients,'—affords but poor footing compared with the Word of God; still it is to them the truth, the unalterable law of right and duty, and, as the expounders of it, they have to maintain a dignity which will not compromise its claims. That 'scholars are the first and head of the four classes of the people' is a maxim universally admitted. I do desiderate in Mencius any approach to humility of soul, but I would not draw my illustrations of the defect from the boldness of his speech and deportment as 'a Teacher.'

But in one respect I am not sure but that our philosopher failed to act worthy of the character which he thus assumed. The great men to whom he was in the habit of referring as his patterns nearly all rose from deep poverty to their subsequent eminence. 'Shun came from among the channelled fields; Fû Yüeh was called to office from the midst of his building-frames; Kâo Ko from his fish and salt[2].' 'Î Yin was a farmer in Hsin. When T'ang sent persons with presents of silk, to entreat him to enter his service, he said, with an air of indifference and self-satisfaction, "What can I do with those silks with which T'ang invites me? Is it not best for me to abide in the channelled fields, and there delight myself with the principles of Yâo and Shun[3]?"' It does not appear that any of those worthies accepted favours while they were not in office, or from men whom they disapproved. With Mencius it was very different: he took largely from the princes whom he lectured and denounced. Possibly he might plead in justification the example of Confucius, but he carried the practice to a greater extent than that sage had ever done,—to an extent which staggered even his own disciples and elicited their frequent inquiries. For instance, 'P'ang Kăng asked him, saying, "Is it not an extravagant procedure to go from one prince to another and live upon them, followed by several tens of carriages, and attended by several hundred men?"' Mencius replied, 'If there be

The charge against him of living on the princes.

[1] Bk. VII. Pt. II. xxxiv. This passage was written on the pillars of a hall in College Street, East, where the gospel was first preached publicly by myself in their own tongue to the people of Canton, in February, 1858. [2] Bk. VI. Pt. II. xv. 1. [3] Bk. V. Pt. I. vii. 2, 3.

not a proper ground for taking it, a single bamboo-cup of rice may not be received from a man. If there be such a proper ground, then Shun's receiving the empire from Yâo is not to be considered excessive. Do you think it was excessive?' 'No,' said the other, 'but for a scholar performing no service to receive his support notwithstanding is improper.' Mencius answered, 'If you do not have an intercommunication of the productions of labour, and an interchange of men's services, so that one from his overplus may supply the deficiency of another, then husbandmen will have a superfluity of grain, and women will have a superfluity of cloth. If you have such an interchange, carpenters and carriage-wrights may all get their food from you. Here now is a man who, at home, is filial, and, abroad, respectful to his elders, and who watches over the principles of the ancient kings, awaiting the rise of future learners,—and yet you will refuse to support him. How is it that you give honour to the carpenter and carriage-wright, and slight him who practises benevolence and righteousness?' P'ang Kăng said, 'The aim of the carpenter and carriage-wright is by their trades to seek for a living. Is it also the aim of the superior man in his practice of principles to seek for a living?' 'What have you to do,' returned Mencius, 'with his purpose? He is of service to you. He deserves to be supported, and should be supported. And let me ask—Do you remunerate a man's intention, or do you remunerate his service?' To this Kăng replied, 'I remunerate his intention.' Mencius said, 'There is a man here who breaks your tiles and draws unsightly figures on your walls;—his purpose may be thereby to seek for his living, but will you indeed remunerate him?' 'No,' said Kăng; and Mencius then concluded, 'That being the case, it is not the purpose which you remunerate, but the work done[1].'

The ingenuity of Mencius in the above conversation will not be questioned. The position from which he starts in his defence, that society is based on a division of labour and an interchange of services, is sound, and he fairly hits and overthrows his disciples on the point that we remunerate a man not for his aim but for his work done. But he does not quite meet the charge against himself. This will better appear from another brief conversation with Kung-sun Ch'âu on the same subject. 'It is said, in the Book of Poetry,' observed Châu,

'"He will not eat the bread of idleness."

[1] Bk. III. Pt. II. iv.

孟子

How is it that we see superior men eating without labouring?' Mencius replied, 'When a superior man resides in a country, if the sovereign employ his counsels, he comes to tranquillity, wealth, honour, and glory; if the young in it follow his instructions, they become filial, obedient to their elders, true-hearted, and faithful.—What greater example can there be than this of not eating the bread of idleness[1]?'

The argument here is based on the supposition that the superior man has free course, is appreciated by the sovereign, and venerated and obeyed by the people. But this never was the case with Mencius. Only once, the short time that he was in T'ăng, did a ruler listen favourably to his counsels. His lessons, it may be granted, were calculated to be of the greatest benefit to the communities where he was, but it is difficult to see the 'work done,' for which he could claim the remuneration. His reasoning might very well be applied to vindicate a government's extending its patronage to literary men, where it recognised in a general way the advantages to be derived from their pursuits. Still more does it accord with that employed in western nations where ecclesiastical establishments form one of the institutions of a country. The members belonging to them must have their maintenance, independently of the personal character of the rulers. But Mencius's position was more that of a reformer. His claims were of those of his personal merit. It seems to me that P'ang Kăng had reason to doubt the propriety of his course, and characterise it as extravagant.

Another disciple, Wan Chang, pressed him very closely with the inconsistency of his taking freely the gifts of the princes on whom he was wont to pass sentence so roundly. Mencius had insisted that, where the donor offered his gift on a ground of reason and in a manner accordant with propriety, even Confucius would have received it. 'Here now,' said Chang, 'is one who stops and robs people outside the city gates. He offers his gift on a ground of reason and in a proper manner;—would it be right to receive it so acquired by robbery?' The philosopher of course said it would not, and the other pursued:—'The princes of the present day take from their people just as a robber despoils his victim. Yet if they put a good face of propriety on their gifts, the superior man receives them. I venture to ask you to explain this.' Mencius answered:—

[1] Bk. VII. Pt. I. xxxii.

'Do you think that, if there should arise a truly imperial sovereign, he would collect the princes of the present day and put them all to death? Or would he admonish them, and then, on their not changing their ways, put them to death? Indeed to call every one who takes what does not properly belong to him a robber, is pushing a point of resemblance to the utmost, and insisting on the most refined idea of righteousness[1].'

Here again we must admire the ingenuity of Mencius; but it amuses us more than it satisfies. It was very well for him to maintain his dignity as 'a Teacher,' and not go to the princes when they called him, but his refusal would have had more weight, if he had kept his hands clean from all their offerings. I have said above that if less awe-ful than Confucius, he is more admirable. Perhaps it would be better to say he is more brilliant. There is some truth in the saying of the scholar Ch'ăng, that the one is the glass that glitters, and the other the jade that is truly valuable.

Without dwelling on other characteristics of Mencius, or culling from him other striking sayings,—of which there are many,—I proceed to exhibit and discuss his doctrine of the goodness of human nature.

Mencius's view of human nature; its identity with that of Bishop Butler.

5. If the remarks which I have just made on the intercourse of Mencius with the princes of his day have lowered him somewhat in the estimation of my readers, his doctrine of human nature, and the force with which he advocates it, will not fail to produce a high appreciation of him as a moralist and thinker. In concluding my exhibition of the opinions of Confucius in the former volume, I have observed that 'he threw no light on any of the questions which have a world-wide interest.' This Mencius did. The constitution of man's nature, and how far it supplies to him a rule of conduct and a law of duty, are inquiries than which there can hardly be any others of more importance. They were largely discussed in the Schools of Greece. A hundred vigorous and acute minds of modern Europe have occupied themselves with them. It will hardly be questioned in England that the palm for clear and just thinking on the subject belongs to Bishop Butler, but it will presently be seen that his views and those of Mencius are, as nearly as possible, identical. There is a difference of nomenclature and a combination

[1] Bk.V. Pt. II. iv.

孟子

of parts, in which the advantage is with the Christian prelate. Felicity of illustration and charm of style belong to the Chinese philosopher. The doctrine in both is the same.

View of Confucius.

The utterances of Confucius on the subject of our nature were few and brief. The most remarkable is where he says:—'Man is born for uprightness. If a man be without uprightness and yet live, his escape *from death* is the effect of mere good fortune[1].' This is in entire accordance with Mencius's view, and as he appeals to the sage in his own support[2], though we cannot elsewhere find the words which he quotes, we may believe that Confucius would have approved of the sentiments of his follower, and frowned on those who have employed some of his sayings in confirmation of other conclusions[3]. I am satisfied in my own mind on this point. His repeated enunciation of 'the golden rule,' though only in a negative form, is sufficient evidence of it.

View of Tsze-sze.

The opening sentence of 'The Doctrine of the Mean,'—'What Heaven has conferred is called THE NATURE; an accordance with this nature is called THE PATH; the regulation of the path is called INSTRUCTION,'—finds a much better illustration from Mencius than from Tsze-sze himself. The germ of his doctrine lies in it. We saw reason to discard the notion that he was a pupil of Tsze-sze; but he was acquainted with his treatise just named, and as he has used some other parts of it, we may be surprised that in his discussions on human nature he has made no reference to the above passage.

Prevalent view of man's nature in Mencius's time.

What gave occasion to his dwelling largely on the theme was the prevalence of wild and injurious speculations about it. In nothing did the disorder of the age more appear. Kung-tû, one of his disciples, once went to him and said, 'The philosopher Kâo says:—"Man's nature is neither good nor bad." Some say:—"Man's nature may be made to practise good, and it may be made to practise evil; and accordingly, under Wăn and Wû, the people loved what was good, while, under Yû and Lî, they loved what was cruel." Others say:—"The nature of some is good, and the nature of others is bad. Hence it was that under such a sovereign as Yâo there yet appeared Hsiang; that with such a father as Kû-sâu there yet appeared Shun; and that

[1] Analects, VI. xvii. [2] Bk. VI. Pt. I. vi. 8; viii. 4. [3] See the annotations of the editor of Yang-tsze's (楊子, the 楊 is often written 揚) Work, 脩身篇, in the 十子全書 (vol. i. proleg. p. 132).

with Châu for their sovereign, and the son of their elder brother besides, there were found Ch'î, the viscount of Wei, and the prince Pî-kan." And now you say :—"The nature is good." Then are all those opinions wrong[1]?'

'The nature of man is good,'—this was Mencius's doctrine. By many writers it has been represented as entirely antagonistic to Christianity; and, as thus broadly and briefly enunciated, it sounds startling enough. As fully explained by himself, however, it is not so very terrible. Butler's scheme has been designated 'the system of Zeno baptised into Christ[2].' That of Mencius, identifying closely with the master of the Porch, is yet more susceptible of a similar transformation.

But before endeavouring to make this statement good, it will be well to make some observations on the opinion of the philosopher

View of the philosopher Kâo.

Kâo. He was a contemporary of Mencius, and they came into argumentative collision. One does not see immediately the difference between his opinion, as stated by Kung-tû, and the next. Might not man's nature, though neither good nor bad, be made to practise the one or the other? Kâo's view went to deny any essential distinction between good and evil,—virtue and vice. A man might be made to act in a way commonly called virtue and in a way commonly called evil, but in the one action there was really nothing more approvable than in the other. 'Life,' he said, 'was what was meant by nature[3].' The phenomena of benevolence and righteousness were akin to those of walking and sleeping, eating and seeing. This extravagance afforded scope for Mencius's favourite mode of argument, the *reductio ad absurdum.* He showed, on Kâo's principles, that 'the nature of a dog was like the nature of an ox, and the nature of an ox like the nature of a man.'

The two first conversations[4] between them are more particularly worthy of attention, because, while they are a confutation of his

Mencius's exposure of Kâo's errors, and statement of his own doctrine.

opponent, they indicate clearly our philosopher's own theory. Kâo compared man's nature to a willow tree, and benevolence and righteousness to the cups and bowls that might be fashioned from its wood. Mencius replied that it was not the nature of the willow to produce cups and bowls; they might be made from it indeed, by bending and

[1] Bk. VI. Pt. I. vi. 1-4. [2] Wardlaw's Christian Ethics, edition of 1833, p. 119.
[3] Bk. VI. Pt. I. iii. [4] Bk. VI. Pt. I. i. ii.

孟子

cutting and otherwise injuring it; but must humanity be done such violence to in order to fashion the virtues from it? Kâo again compared the nature to water whirling round in a corner;—open a passage for it in any direction, and it will flow forth accordingly. 'Man's nature,' said he, 'is indifferent to good and evil, just as the water is indifferent to the east and west.' Mencius answered him:—'Water indeed will flow indifferently to the east or west, but will it flow indifferently up or down? The tendency of man's nature to good is like the tendency of water to flow downwards. There are none but have this tendency to good, just as all water flows downwards. By striking water and causing it to leap up, you may make it go over your forehead, and, by damming and leading it, you may force it up a hill; but are such movements according to the nature of water? It is the force applied which causes them. When men are made to do what is not good, their nature is dealt with in this way.'

Mencius has no stronger language than this, as indeed it would be difficult to find any stronger, to declare his belief in the goodness of human nature. To many Christian readers it proves a stumbling-block and offence. But I venture to think that this is without sufficient reason. He is speaking of our nature in its ideal, and not as it actually is,—as we may ascertain from the study of it that it ought to be, and not as it is made to become. My rendering of the sentences last quoted may be objected to, because of my introduction of the term *tendency;* but I have Mencius's express sanction for the representation I give of his meaning. Replying to Kung-tû's question, whether all the other opinions prevalent about man's nature were wrong, and his own, that it is good, correct, he said:—'From the feelings proper to it, we see that it is constituted for the practice of what is good. *This is what I mean in saying that the nature is good.* If men do what is not good, the blame cannot be imputed to their natural powers[1].' Those who find the most fault with him, will hardly question the truth of this last declaration. When a man does wrong, whose is the blame,—the sin? He might be glad to roll the guilt on his Maker, or upon his nature,—which is only an indirect charging of his Maker with it;—but it is his own burden, which he must bear himself.

The proof by which Mencius supports his view of human nature

[1] Bk. VI. Pt. I. vi. 5, 6.

as formed only for virtue is twofold. First, he maintains that there are in man a natural principle of benevolence, a natural principle of righteousness, a natural principle of propriety, and a natural principle of apprehending moral truth. 'These,' he says, 'are not infused into us from without. We are certainly possessed of them; and a different view is simply from want of reflection[1].' In further illustration of this he argued thus:—'All men have a mind which cannot bear to see the sufferings of others;—my meaning may be illustrated thus;—Even now-a-days,' i.e. in these degenerate times, 'if men suddenly see a child about to fall into a well, they will without exception experience a feeling of alarm and distress. They will feel so, not as a ground on which they may gain the favour of the child's parents, nor as a ground on which they may seek the praise of their neighbours and friends, nor from a dislike to the reputation of having been unmoved by such a thing. From this case we may see that the feeling of commiseration is essential to man, that the feeling of shame and dislike is essential to man, that the feeling of modesty and complaisance is essential to man, and that the feeling of approval and disapproval is essential to man. These feelings are the principles respectively of benevolence, righteousness, propriety, and the knowledge *of good and evil.* Men have these four principles just as they have their four limbs[2].'

Proofs that human nature is formed for virtue —First, from its moral constituents.

Let all this be compared with the language of Butler in his three famous *Sermons upon Human Nature.* He shows in the first of these:—'First, that there is a natural principle of benevolence in man; secondly, that the several *passions* and *affections*, which are distinct both from benevolence and self-love, do in general contribute and lead us to *public* good as really as to private; and thirdly, that there is a principle of reflection in men, by which they distinguish between, approve and disapprove their own actions[3].'

[1] Bk. VI. Pt. I. vi. 7.

[2] Bk. II. Pt. I. vi. 3, 4, 5, 6.

[3] I am indebted to Butler for fully understanding Mencius's fourth feeling, that of approving and disapproving, which he calls 'the principle of knowledge,' or wisdom. In the notes, Bk. II. Pt I. vi. 5, I have said that he gives to this term 'a moral sense.' It is the same with Butler's principle of reflection, by which men distinguish between, and approve or disapprove, their own actions.—I have heard gentlemen speak contemptuously of Mencius's case in point, to prove the existence of a feeling of benevolence in man. 'This,' they have said, 'is Mencius's idea of virtue, to save a child from falling into a well. A mighty display of virtue, truly!' Such language arises from misconceiving Mencius's object in putting the case. 'If there be,' says Butler, 'any affection in human nature, the object and end of which is the good of another, this is itself benevolence. Be it ever so short, be it in ever so low a degree, or ever so unhappily confined, it proves the assertion and points out what we were designed for, as

孟子

Is there anything more in this than was apprehended and expressed by Mencius? Butler says in the conclusion of his first discourse that 'Men follow their nature to a certain degree but not entirely; their actions do not come up to the whole of what their nature leads them to; and they often violate their nature.' This also Mencius declares in his own forceful manner:—'When men having these four principles, yet say of themselves that they cannot develop them, they play the thief with themselves, and he who says of his prince that he cannot develop them, plays the thief with his prince[1].' 'Men differ from one another in regard to the principles of their nature;—some as much again as others, some five times as much, and some to an incalculable amount:—it is because they cannot carry out fully their natural powers[2].'

So much for the first or preliminary view of human nature insisted on by Mencius, that it contains principles which are disinterested and virtuous. But there wants something more to make good the position that virtue ought to be supreme, and that it is for it, in opposition to vice, that our nature is formed. To use some of the 'licentious talk' which Butler puts into the mouth of an opponent:—'Virtue and religion require not only that we do good to others, when we are led this way, by benevolence and reflection happening to be stronger than other principles, passions, or appetites; but likewise that the *whole character* be formed upon thought and reflection; that *every* action be directed by some determinate rule, some other rule than the strength or prevalence of any principle or passion. What sign is there in our nature (for the inquiry is only about what is to be collected from thence) that this was intended by its Author? Or how does so various and fickle a temper as that of man appear adapted thereto? . . . As brutes have various instincts, by which they are carried on to the end the Author of their nature intended them for, is not man in the same condition, with this difference

Second proof that human nature is formed for virtue:—that it is a constitution, where the higher principles should serve the lower.

really as though it were in a higher degree and more extensive.' 'It is sufficient that the seeds of it be implanted in our nature.' The illustration from a child falling into a well must be pronounced a happy one. How much lower Mencius could go may be seen from his conversation with king Hsüan, Bk. I. Pt. I. vii, whom he leads to a consciousness of his commiserating mind from the fact that he had not been able to bear the frightened appearance of an ox which was being led by to be killed, and ordered it to be spared. The kindly heart that was moved by the suffering of an animal had only to be carried out, to suffice for the love and protection of all within the four seas.

[1] Bk. II. Pt. I. vi. 6. [2] Bk. VI. Pt. I. vi. 7.

only, that to his instincts (i.e. appetites and passions) is added the principle of reflection or conscience? And as brutes act agreeably to their nature in following that principle or particular instinct which for the present is strongest in them; does not man likewise act agreeably to his nature, or obey the law of his creation, by following that principle, be it passion or conscience, which for the present happens to be strongest in him? . . . Let every one then quietly follow his nature; as passion, reflection, appetite, the several parts of it, happen to be the strongest; but let not the man of virtue take it upon him to blame the ambitious, the covetous, the dissolute; since these, equally with him, obey and follow their nature[1].'

To all this Butler replies by showing that the principle of reflection or conscience is 'not to be considered merely as a principle in the heart, which is to have some influence as well as others, but as a faculty, in kind and in nature, supreme over all others, and which bears its own authority of being so;' that the difference between this and the other constituents of human nature is not 'a difference in strength or degree,' but 'a difference *in nature* and *in kind;*' that 'it was placed within to be our proper governor; to direct and regulate all under principles, passions, and motives of action:—this is its right and office; thus sacred is its authority.' It follows from the view of human nature thus established, that 'the inward frame of man is *a system or constitution;* whose several parts are united, not by a physical principle of individuation, but by the respects they have to each other, the chief of which is the subjection which the appetites, passions, and particular affections have to the one supreme principle of reflection or conscience[2].'

Now, the *substance* of this reasoning is to be found in Mencius. Human nature—the inward frame of man—is with him *a system or constitution* as much as with Butler. He says, for instance:—'There is no part of himself which a man does not love; and as he loves all, so he must nourish all. There is not an inch of skin which he does not love, and so there is not an inch of skin which he will not nourish. FOR EXAMINING WHETHER HIS WAY OF NOURISHING BE GOOD OR NOT, WHAT OTHER RULE IS THERE BUT THIS, THAT HE DETERMINE BY REFLECTING ON HIMSELF WHERE IT SHOULD BE APPLIED?

'Some parts of the body are noble and some ignoble; some great

[1] See Sermon Second. [2] See note to Sermon Third.

孟子

and some small. The great must not be injured for the small, nor the noble for the ignoble. He who nourishes the little belonging to him is a little man, and he who nourishes the great is a great man [1].'

Again:—'Those who follow that part of themselves which is great are great men; those who follow that part which is little are little men [2].'

The great part of ourselves is the moral elements of our constitution; the lower part is the appetites and passions that centre in self. He says finely:—'There is a nobility of Heaven, and there is a nobility of man. Benevolence, righteousness, self-consecration, and fidelity, with unwearied joy in what is good;—these constitute the nobility of Heaven. To be a duke, a noble, or a great officer;—this constitutes the nobility of man [3].'

There is one passage very striking:—'For the mouth to desire *sweet* tastes, the eye to desire *beautiful* colours, the ear to desire *pleasant* sounds, the nose to desire *fragrant* odours, and the four limbs to desire ease and rest;—these things are natural. But there is the appointment *of Heaven* in connexion with them; and the superior man does not say *of his pursuit of them*, "It is my nature." *The exercise of* love between father and son, *the observance of* righteousness between sovereign and minister, the rules of ceremony between host and guest, *the display of* knowledge in recognising the worthy, and *the fulfilling* the heavenly course by the sage;—these are the appointment *of Heaven*. But there is *an adaptation of our* nature for them; and the superior man does not say, in reference to them, "It is the appointment *of Heaven* [4]."'

From these paragraphs it is quite clear that what Mencius considered as deserving properly to be called the nature of man, was not that by which he is a creature of appetites and passions, but that by which he is lifted up into the higher circle of intelligence and virtue. By the phrase, 'the appointment of Heaven,' most Chinese scholars understand the will of Heaven, limiting in the first case the gratification of the appetites, and in the second the exercise of the virtues. To such limitation Mencius teaches there ought to be a cheerful submission so far as the appetites are concerned, but where the virtues are in question, we are to be striving after them notwithstanding adverse and opposing circumstances. THEY ARE

[1] Bk. VI. Pt. I. xiv. [2] Bk. VI. Pt. I. xv. [3] Bk. VI. Pt. I. xvi. [4] Bk. VII. Pt. II. xxiv.

OUR NATURE, what we were made for, what we have to do. I will refer but to one other specimen of his teaching on this subject. 'The will,' he said, using that term for the higher moral nature in activity,—'the will is the leader of the passion-nature. The passion-nature pervades and animates the body. The will is first and chief, and the passion-nature is subordinate to it[1].'

My readers can now judge for themselves whether I exaggerated at all in saying that Mencius's doctrine of human nature was, as nearly as possible, identical with that of Bishop Butler. Sir James Mackintosh has said of the sermons to which I have made reference, and his other cognate discourses, that in them Butler 'taught truths more capable of being exactly distinguished from the doctrines of his predecessors, more satisfactorily established by him, more comprehensively applied to particulars, more rationally connected with each other, and therefore more worthy of the name of *discovery*, than any with which we are acquainted; if we ought not, with some hesitation, to except the first steps of the Grecian philosophers towards a Theory of Morals[2].' It is to be wished that the attention of this great scholar had been called to the writings of our philosopher. Mencius was senior to Zeno, though a portion of their lives synchronised. Butler certainly was not indebted to him for the views which he advocated; but it seems to me that Mencius had left him nothing to *discover*.

But the question now arises—'Is the view of human nature propounded by Mencius correct?' So far as yet appears, I see not how the question can be answered otherwise than in the affirmative. Man was formed for virtue. Be it that his conduct is very far from being conformed to virtue, that simply fastens on him the shame of guilt. Fallen as he may be,—fallen as I believe and know he is,—his nature still bears its testimony, when properly interrogated, against all unrighteousness. Man, heathen man, *a Gentile without the law, is still a law to himself*. So the apostle Paul affirms; and to no moral teacher of Greece or Rome can we appeal for so grand an illustration of the averment as we find in Mencius. I would ask those whom his sayings offend, whether it would have been better for his countrymen if he had taught a contrary doctrine, and told them that man's nature is bad, and that the more they obeyed all its

The proper use of Mencius's views thus far considered.

[1] Bk. II. Pt. I. ii. 9. [2] Encyclopaedia Britannica (8th edition), Second Preliminary Dissertation; on Butler.

孟子

lusts and passions, the more would they be in accordance with it, and the more pursuing the right path? Such a question does not need a reply. The proper use of Mencius's principles is to reprove the Chinese—and ourselves as well—of the thousand acts of sin of which they and we are guilty, that come within their sweep and under their condemnation.

From the ideal of man to his actualism there is a vast descent. Between what he ought to be and what he is, the contrast is melancholy. '*Benevolence*,' said our philosopher, 'is the characteristic of man[1].' It is 'the wide house in which the world should dwell,' while *propriety* is 'the correct position in which the world should ever be found,' and *righteousness* is 'the great path which men should ever be pursuing[2].' In opposition to this, however, hatred, improprieties, unrighteousness are constant phenomena of human life. We find men hateful and hating one another, quenching the light that is in them, and walking in darkness to perform all deeds of shame. 'There is none that doeth good; no, not one.' Mencius would have denied this last sentence, claiming that the sages should be excepted from it; but he is ready enough to admit the fact that men in general do evil and violate the law of their nature. They sacrifice the noble portion of themselves for the gratification of the ignoble; they follow that part which is little, and not that which is great. He can say nothing further in explanation of the fact. He points out indeed the effect of injurious circumstances, and the power of evil example; and he has said several things on these subjects worthy of notice:—'It is not to be wondered at that the king is not wise! Suppose the case of the most easily growing thing in the world;—if you let it have one day's genial heat, and then expose it for ten days to cold, it will not be able to grow. It is but seldom that I have an audience of the king, and when I retire, there come all those who act upon him like the cold. Though I succeed in bringing out some buds of goodness, of what avail is it[3]?' 'In good years the children of the people are most of them good, while in bad years the most of them abandon themselves to evil. It is not owing to their natural powers conferred on them by Heaven that they are thus different: the abandonment is owing to the circumstances through which they allow their minds to be

How Mencius admitted much actual evil, and how he accounted for it.

[1] Bk. VII. Pt. II. xvi. [2] Bk. III. Pt. II. ii. 3. [3] Bk. VI. Pt. I. ix.

ensnared and drowned in evil. There now is barley: let it be sown and covered up; the ground being the same, and the time of sowing likewise the same, it grows rapidly up, and when the full time is come, it is all found to be ripe. Any inequalities *of produce* will be owing to *the difference of* the soil as rich or poor, the unequal nourishment afforded by the rains and dews, and to the different ways in which man has performed his business[1].'

The inconsistencies in human conduct did not escape his observation. After showing that there is that in human nature which will sometimes make men part with life sooner than with righteousness, he goes on:—'And yet a man will accept ten thousand *chung* without any consideration of propriety and righteousness. What can they add to him? When he takes them, is it not that he may obtain beautiful mansions, that he may secure the services of wives and concubines, or that the poor and needy may be helped by him?' The scalpel is used here with a bold and skilful hand. The lust of the flesh, and the lust of the eyes, and the pride of life are laid bare, nor does our author stop, till he has exposed the subtle workings of the delusion that the end may sanctify the means, that evil may be wrought that good may come. He pursues:—'In the former case the offered bounty was not received, though it would have saved from death, and now the emolument is taken for the sake of beautiful mansions. The bounty that would have preserved from death was not received, and the emolument is taken to get the services of wives and concubines. The bounty that would have saved from death was not received, and the emolument is taken that one's poor and needy acquaintance may be helped. Was it then not possible likewise to decline this? This is a case of what is called—"Losing the proper nature of one's mind[2]."'

To the principle implied in the concluding sentences of this quotation Mencius most pertinaciously adheres. He will not allow

Original badness cannot be predicated from actual evil.

that original badness can be predicated of human nature from any amount of actual wickedness. 'The trees,' said he, 'of the Niû Mountain were once beautiful. Being situated, however, in the borders of a large State, they were hewn down with axes and bills;—and could they retain their beauty? Still, through the activity of the vegetative life day and night, and the nourishing influence of the

[1] Bk. VI. Pt. I. vii.

[2] Bk. VI. Pt. I. x[illegible]. 7, 8.

孟子

rain and dew, they were not without buds and sprouts springing forth;—but then came the cattle and goats, and browsed upon them. To these things is owing the bare and stripped appearance of the mountain, which when people see, they think it was never finely wooded. But is this the proper nature of the mountain? And so also of what properly belongs to man:—shall it be said that the mind of any man was without benevolence and righteousness? The way in which a man loses his proper goodness of mind is like the way in which the trees are denuded by axes and bills. Hewn down day after day, can the mind retain its beauty? But there is a development of its life day and night; and in the calm air of the morning, just between night and day, the mind feels in a degree the desires and aversions which are proper to humanity; but the feeling is not strong, and it is fettered and destroyed by what takes place during the day. This fettering takes place again and again; the restorative influence of the night is not sufficient to preserve *the proper goodness of the mind;* and when this proves insufficient for that purpose, the nature becomes not much different from that of the irrational animals, which when people see, they think that it never had those powers *which I assert.* But does this condition represent the feelings proper to humanity[1]?'

The actual perfection of the sages, and possible perfection of all.

Up to this point I fail to perceive anything in Mencius's view of human nature that is contrary to the teachings of our Christian scriptures, and that may not be employed with advantage by the missionary in preaching the Gospel to the Chinese. It is far from covering what we know to be the whole duty of man, yet it is defective rather than erroneous. Deferring any consideration of this for a brief space, I now inquire whether Mencius, having an ideal of the goodness of human nature, held also that it had been and could be realised? The answer is that he did. The actual realisation he found in the sages, and he contended that it was within the reach of every individual. 'All things which are the same in kind,' he says, 'are like one another;—why should we doubt in regard to man, as if he were a solitary exception to this? The sage and we are the same in kind[2].' The feet, the mouths, the eyes of the sages were not different from those of other people, neither were their minds. 'Is it so,' he was once asked, 'that all men may be Yâos

[1] Bk. VI. Pt. I. viii. 1, 2. [2] Bk. VI. Pt. I. vii. 3.

F 2

and Shuns?' and he answered, 'It is,' adding by way of explanation:—'To walk slowly, keeping behind his elders, is to perform the part of a younger brother, and to walk quickly and precede his elders is to violate that duty. Now, is it what a man cannot do,—to walk slowly? IT IS WHAT HE DOES NOT DO. The course of Yâo and Shun was simply that of filial piety and fraternal duty. Wear the clothes of Yâo, repeat the words of Yâo, and do the actions of Yâo;—and you will just be a Yâo[1].'

Among the sages, however, Mencius made a distinction. Yâo and Shun exceeded all the rest, unless it might be Confucius. Those three never came short of, never went beyond, the law of their nature. The ideal and the actual were in them always one and the same. The others had only attained to perfection by vigorous effort and culture. Twice at least he has told us this. 'Yâo and Shun were what they were by nature; T'ang and Wû were so by returning *to natural virtue*[2].' The actual result, however, was the same, and therefore he could hold them all up as models to his countrymen of the style of man which they all ought to be and might be. What the compass and square were in the hands of the workman, enabling him to form perfect circles and squares, the sages, 'perfectly exhibiting the human relations,' might be to every earnest individual, enabling him to perfect himself as they were perfect[3].

Mencius's doctrine contains no acknowledgment of the universal proneness to evil. His ideal has been realised by sages, and may be realised by all.

Here we feel that the doctrine of Mencius wants an element which Revelation supplies. He knows nothing of the fact that 'by one man sin entered into the world, and death by sin; and so death passed' (passed on, extended, διῆλθεν) 'to all men, because all sinned.' We have our ideal as well as he; but for the living reality of it we must go back to Adam, as he was made by God in His own image, after His likeness. In him the model is soon shattered, and we do not discover it again, till God's own Son appears in the world, made in the likeness of sinful flesh, yet without sin. While He died for our transgressions, He left us also an example, that we should walk in His steps; and as we do so, we are carried on to glory and virtue. At the same time we find a law in our members warring against the law in our minds, and bringing us into captivity to sin. However we may strive after our ideal, we do not succeed in reaching it. The more we grow in the know-

[1] Bk. VI. Pt. II. ii. 1, 4, 5. [2] Bk. VII. Pt. I. xxx. 1; Pt. II. xxxiii. 1. [3] Bk. IV. Pt. I. ii. 1.

孟子

ledge of Christ, and see in Him the glory of humanity in its true estate, the greater do we feel our own distance to be from it, and that of ourselves we cannot attain to it. There is something wrong about us; we need help from without in order to become even what our nature, apart from Revelation, tells us we ought to be.

When Mencius therefore points us to Yâo, Shun, and Confucius, and says that they were perfect, we cannot accept his statement. Understanding that he is speaking of them only in the sphere of human relations, we must yet believe that in many things they came short. One of them, the greatest of the three in Mencius's estimation, Confucius, again and again confesses so of himself. He was seventy years old, he says, before he could follow what his heart desired without transgressing what was right[1]. It might have been possible to convince the sage that he was under a delusion in this important matter even at that advanced age; but what his language allows is sufficient to upset Mencius's appeal to him. The image of sagely perfection is broken by it. It proves to be but a brilliant and unsubstantial phantasm of our philosopher's own imagining.

When he insists again, that every individual may become what he fancies that the sages were,—i. e. perfect, living in love, walking in righteousness, observant of propriety, approving whatsoever is good, and disapproving whatever is evil,—he is pushing his doctrine beyond its proper limits; he is making a use of it of which it is not capable. It supplies a law of conduct, and I have set it forth as entitled to our highest admiration for the manner in which it does so; but law gives only the knowledge of what we are required to do; it does not give the power to do it. We have seen how when it was necessary to explain accurately his statement that the nature of man is good, Mencius defined it as meaning that 'it is constituted for the practice of that which is good.' Because it is so constituted, it follows that every man ought to practise what is good. But some disorganisation may have happened to the nature; some sad change may have come over it. The very fact that man has, in Mencius's own words, to recover his 'lost mind[2],' shows that the object of the constitution of the nature has not been realised. Whether he can recover it or not, therefore, is a question altogether different from that of its proper design.

In one place, indeed, Mencius has said that 'the great man is he

[1] Confucian Analects, II. iv. 6. [2] Bk. VI. Pt. I. xi. 4.

who does not lose his child's-heart[1].' I can only suppose that, by that expression—'the child's-heart,' he intends the ideal goodness which he affirms of our nature. But to attribute that to the child as actually existing in it is absurd. It has neither done good nor evil. It possesses the capacity for either. It will by-and-by awake to the consciousness that it ought to follow after the one and eschew the other; but when it does so,—I should rather say when *he* does so, for the child has now emerged from a mere creature existence, and assumed the functions of a moral being, he will find that he has already given himself to inordinate affection for the objects of sense; and in the pursuit of gratification he is reckless of what must be acknowledged to be the better and nobler part, reckless also of the interest and claims of others, and glows, whenever thwarted, into passion and fury. The youth is more pliant than the man in whom the dominion of self-seeking has become ingrained as a habit; but no sooner does he become a subject of law, than he is aware of the fact that when he would do good, evil is present with him. The boy has to go in search of his 'lost heart,' as truly as the man of fourscore. Even in him there is an 'old man, corrupt according to the deceitful lusts,' which he has to put off.

Butler's advantage over Mencius, and that he does not make the same application of their common principles.

Butler had an immense advantage over Mencius, arising from his knowledge of the truths of Revelation. Many, admiring his sermons, have yet expressed a measure of dissatisfaction, because he does not in them make explicit reference to the condition of man as fallen and depraved. That he fully admitted the fact we know. He says elsewhere:—'Mankind are represented in scripture to be in a state of ruin.' 'If mankind are corrupted and depraved in their moral character, and so are unfit for that state which Christ is gone to prepare for His disciples; and if the assistance of God's Spirit be necessary to renew their nature, in the degree requisite to their being qualified for that state; all which is implied in the express, though figurative declaration, *Except a man be born of the Spirit, he cannot see the kingdom of God*[2].' . . . How is it, then, that there is no mention of this in the sermons? Dissatisfaction, I have said, has been expressed on account of this silence, and it would have taken the form of more pointed utterance, and more decided condemnation, but for the awe of his great

[1] Bk. IV. Pt. II. xii.

[2] The Analogy of Religion, Part II. chap. i.

孟子

name, and the general appreciation of the service he rendered to Christianity in his work on 'The Analogy of Religion.' But, in truth, dissatisfaction at all is out of place. Butler wrote his sermons as he wrote his Analogy, in consequence of the peculiar necessity of his times. More particularly against Hobbes, denying all moral sentiments and social affections, and making a regard to personal advantage the only motive of human action, it was his business to prove that man's nature is of a very different constitution, comprehending disinterested affections, and above all the supreme element of conscience, which, 'had it strength as it has right, would govern the world.' He proves this, and so accomplishes his work. He had merely to do with the ideal of humanity. It did not belong to him to dwell on the actual feebleness of man to perform what is good. He might have added a few paragraphs to this effect; but it was not the character of his mind to go beyond the task which he had set himself. What is of importance to be observed here is, that he does not make the application of their common principles which Mencius does. He knows of no perfect men; he does not tell his readers that they have merely to set about following their nature, and that, without any aid from without, they will surely and easily go on to perfection.

Mencius's lacking in humility, and sympathy with human error.

Mencius is not to be blamed for his ignorance of what is to us the *Doctrine of the Fall*. He had no means of becoming acquainted with it. We have to regret, however, that his study of human nature produced in him no deep *feeling* on account of men's proneness to go astray. He never betrays any consciousness of his own weakness. In this respect he is again inferior to Confucius, and is far from being, as I have said of him in another aspect of his character, 'more admirable' than he. In the former volume I have shown that we may sometimes recognise in what the sage says of himself the expressions of a genuine humility. He acknowledges that he comes short of what he knows he ought to be. We do not meet with this in Mencius. His merit is that of the speculative thinker. His glance is searching and his penetration deep; but there is wanting that moral sensibility which would draw us to him, in our best moments, as a man of like passions with ourselves. The absence of humility is naturally accompanied with a lack of *sympathy*. There is a hardness about his teachings. He is the professor, performing an operation in the class-room, amid a throng of pupils who are admiring his science

and dexterity, and who forgets in the triumph of his skill the suffering of the patient. The transgressors of their nature are to Mencius 'the tyrants of themselves,' or 'the self-abandoned.' The utmost stretch of his commiseration is a contemptuous 'Alas for them[1]!' The radical defect of the orthodox moral school of China, that there only needs a knowledge of duty to insure its performance, is in him exceedingly apparent. Confucius, Tsze-sze, and Mencius, most strangely never thought of calling this principle in question. It is always as in the formula of Tsze-sze:—'Given the sincerity, and there shall be the intelligence; given the intelligence, and there shall be the sincerity.'

Mencius's ideal of human nature does not embrace duty to God.

I said above that Mencius's doctrine of human nature was defective, inasmuch as even his ideal does not cover the whole field of duty. He says very little of what we owe to God. There is no glow of natural piety in his pages. Instead of the name *God*, containing in itself a recognition of the divine personality and supremacy, we hear from him more commonly, as from Confucius, of *Heaven*. Butler has said:—'By the love of God, I would understand all those regards, all those affections of mind, which are due immediately to Him from such a creature as man, and which rest in Him as their end[2].' Of such affections Mencius knows nothing. In one place he speaks of 'delighting in Heaven[3],' but he is speaking, when he does so, of the sovereign who with a great State serves a small one, and the delight is seen in certain condescensions to the weak and unworthy. Never once, where he is treating of the nature of man, does he make mention of any exercise of the mind as due directly to God. The services of religion come in China under the principle of propriety, and are only a cold formalism; but even here, other things come with Mencius before them. We are told:—'The richest fruit of love is this,—the service of one's parents; the richest fruit of righteousness is this,—the obeying one's elder brothers; the richest fruit of wisdom is this,—the knowing those two things, and not departing from them; the richest fruit of propriety is this,—the ordering and adorning those two things[4].' How different is this from the

[1] Bk. IV. Pt. I. x. [2] First Sermon *Upon the Love of God*. [3] Bk. I. Pt. II. ii. 3.

[4] Bk. IV. Pt. I. xxvii. My friend, the Rev. Mr. Moule, (now Bishop) of Ningpo, has supplied me with the following interesting coincidence with the sentiments of Mencius in this passage, from one of the letters of Charles Lamb to Coleridge, dated November 14, 1796:—'Oh, my friend, cultivate the filial feelings; and let no one think himself relieved from the kind charities of

孟子

reiterated declaration of the Scriptures, that 'the fear of the Lord is the beginning of wisdom!' The first and great commandment, 'Thou shalt *love* the Lord thy God, with all thy heart and soul and mind and strength,' was never thought of, much less delivered, by any Chinese philosopher or sage. Had Mencius apprehended this, and seen how all our duties to our fellow-men are to be performed as to God, he could not have thought so highly as he did of man's powers; a suspicion might have grown up that there is a shadow on the light which he has in himself.

This absence from Mencius's ideal of our nature of the recognition of man's highest obligations is itself a striking illustration of man's estrangement from God. His usage of the term Heaven has combined with the similar practice of his Master to prepare the way for the grosser conceptions of the modern literati, who would often seem to deny the divine personality altogether, and substitute for both God and Heaven a mere principle of order or fitness of things. It has done more: it has left the people in the mass to become an easy prey to the idolatrous fooleries of Buddhism. Yea, the *unreligiousness* of the teachers has helped to deprave still more the religion of the nation, such as it is, and has made of its services a miserable pageant of irreverent forms.

It is time to have done with this portion of my theme. It may be thought that I have done Mencius more than justice in the first part of my remarks, and less than justice at the last; but I hope it is not so. A very important use is to be made both of what he succeeds in, and where he fails, in his discoursing upon human nature. His principles may be, and, I conceive, ought to be, turned against himself. They should be pressed to produce the conviction of sin. There is enough in them, if the conscience be but quickened by the Spirit of God, to make the haughtiest scholar cry out, 'O wretched man that I am! who shall deliver me from this body of death?' Then may it be said to him with effect, 'Behold the Lamb of God, who taketh away the sin of the world!' Then may Christ, as a new and true exemplar of all that man should be, be displayed, 'altogether lovely,' to the trembling mind! Then may a *new heart* be received from Him, that shall thrill in the acknowledgment of the claims both of men and God, and girding up the loins of the mind, address itself to walk in all His commandments and ordinances

relationship: these shall give him peace at the last; *these are the best foundation for every species of benevolence.*'

blameless! One thing should be plain. In Mencius's lessons on human duty there is no hope for his countrymen. If they serve as a schoolmaster to bring them to Christ, they will have done their part; but it is from Christ alone that the help of the Chinese can come.

6. Besides giving more explicit expression to the doctrine of the goodness of man's nature than had been done before him, Mencius has the credit also of calling attention to *the nourishment of the passion-nature.* It may be questioned whether I translate his language exactly by this phrase. What I render *the passion-nature,* Julien renders by '*vitalis spiritus.*' The philosopher says himself that it is difficult to describe what he intends. Attempting such a description, he says:—'This is it:—It is exceedingly great and exceedingly strong. Being nourished by rectitude, and sustaining no injury, it fills up all between heaven and earth. This is it:—It is the mate and assistant of righteousness and reason. Without it man is in a state of starvation. It is produced by the accumulation of righteous deeds; it is not to be taken, as by surprise, by incidental acts of righteousness. If the mind does not feel complacency in the conduct, *this* is starved[1].' From such predicates we may be sure that it is not anything merely or entirely *physical* of which he is speaking. 'The righteous,' said Solomon, 'are bold as a lion.' The Hebrew saying is very much in Mencius's style. That boldness is the result of the *nourishment* for which he thought he had a peculiar aptitude. Strong in it and in a knowledge of words, a faculty of discovering the moral aberrations of others from their forms of speech, he was able to boast of possessing 'an unperturbed mind;' he could 'sit in the centre' of his being, 'and enjoy bright day,' whatever clouds and storms gathered around him.

The nourishment, therefore, of 'the passion-nature,' 'the vital spirit,' or whatever name we choose to give to the subject, is only an effect of general good-doing. This is the practical lesson from all Mencius's high-sounding words. He has illustrated it amusingly: —'There was a man of Sung, who was grieved that his growing corn was not longer, and pulled it up. Having done this, he returned home, looking very wearied, and said to his people, "I am tired to-day. I have been helping the corn to grow long." His son ran to look at it, and found the corn all withered. There are few in the

[1] Bk. II. Pt. I. ii. 13-15.

world, who do not assist the corn *of their passion-nature* to grow long. Some consider it of no benefit to them, and let it alone:—they do not weed their corn. Those who assist it to grow long, pull out their corn. What they do is not only of no benefit to the nature, but it also injures it[1].'

This portion of Mencius's teaching need not detain us. He has put a simple truth in a striking way. That is his merit. It hardly seems of sufficient importance to justify the use which has been made of it in vindicating for him a place among the sages of his country.

7. I said I should end the discussion of Mencius's opinions by pointing out what I conceive to be his chief defects as a moral and political teacher. His defects, however, in the former respect have been already not lightly touched on. So far as they were the consequence of his ignorance, without the light which Revelation sheds on the whole field of human duty, and the sanctions which it discloses of a future state of retribution, I do not advance any charge against his character. That he never indicates any wish to penetrate futurity, and ascertain what comes after death; that he never indicates any consciousness of human weakness, nor moves his mind Godward, longing for more light:—these are things which exhibit strongly the contrast between the mind of the East and the West. His self-sufficiency is his great fault. To know ourselves is commonly supposed to be an important step to humility; but it is not so with him. He has spoken remarkably about the effects of calamity and difficulties. He says:—'When Heaven is about to confer a great office on a man, it first exercises his mind with suffering, and his sinews and bones with toil; it exposes his body to hunger, and subjects him to extreme poverty; it confounds his undertakings. By all these methods it stimulates his mind, hardens his nature, and supplies his incompetencies[2].' Such have been the effects of Heaven's exercising some men with calamities; but if the issue has been a fitting for the *highest offices*, there has been a softening of the nature rather than a hardening of it. Mencius was a stranger to the humbling of the lofty looks of man, and the bowing down of his haughtiness, that the Lord alone may be exalted.

His faults as a political teacher are substantially the same as those of Confucius. More than was the case with his sayings of

[1] Bk. II. Pt. I. ii. 16. [2] Bk. VI. Pt. II. xv.

a political character, the utterances of Mencius have reference to the condition and needs of his own age. They were for the time then being, and not for all time. He knew as little as Confucius of any other great and independent nation besides his own; and he has left one maxim which is deeply treasured by the rulers and the people of China at the present day, and feeds the supercilious idea which they are so unwilling to give up of their own superiority to foreigners. 'I have heard,' said he, 'of men using *the doctrines* of our great land to change barbarians, but I have never yet heard of any being changed by barbarians.' 'I have heard of birds leaving dark valleys to remove to lofty trees, but I have not heard of their descending from lofty trees to enter into dark valleys[1].' Mongol and Tartar sway have not broken the charm of this dangerous flattery, because only in warlike energy were the Mongols and Tartars superior to the Chinese, and when they conquered the country they did homage to its sages. During the last five-and-twenty years, Christian Powers have come to ask admission into China, and to claim to be received as her equals. They do not wish to conquer her territory, though they have battered and broken her defences. With fear and trembling their advances are contemplated. The feeling of dislike to them arises from the dread of their power, and suspicion of their faith. It is feared that they come to subdue; it is known that they come to change. The idol of Chinese superiority is about to be broken. Broken it must be ere long, and a new generation of thinkers will arise, to whom Mencius will be a study but not a guide.

SECTION III.

HIS IMMEDIATE DISCIPLES.

The disciples of Mencius were much fewer in number, and of less distinction than those of Confucius. The longest list does not make them amount to twenty-five; and it is only to complete my plan that I devote a page or two here to their names and surnames.

The chief authority in reference to them is Châo Ch'î. In A.D. 1115, the then emperor of the Sung dynasty conferred titles on all mentioned by Ch'î as disciples or pupils of Mencius, and enacted

[1] Bk. III. Pt. I. iv. 12, 15.

that they should share in the sacrifices offered to their master in his temple in the district of Tsâu. Chû Hsî gives his verdict in the 'Collected Comments' against two of them, and no subsequent scholar has ventured to restore them to their place in the Mencian school. Other names, however, have been found by different writers to supply their room. It is not worth our while to take notice of their discussions.

1. Yo-chăng K'o, styled Tsze-âo (樂正克, 字子敖), a native of Lû. He was titled in 1115 as the 'State-advantaging Marquis' (利國侯). Under the present dynasty, in 1724, he had a place assigned him in the temples of Confucius, the 35th on the west, in the outer court, with the common title of 'The Ancient Worthy, the Philosopher Yo-chăng.'

2. Wan Chang (萬章). He was titled in 1115 as the 'Baron of Extensive Arousing' (博興伯). He has now the next place to the preceding in the Confucian temples.

3. Kung-sun Ch'âu (公孫丑), a native of Ch'î. He was also elevated to the temple of Confucius, and has now the place, east, corresponding to that of Wan Chang, on the west. His title conferred in 1115 was—'Baron of Longevity and Glory' (壽光伯).

4. Kung-tû (公都), immediately precedes Kung-sun Ch'âu in the temples. In the temple of Mencius he was the 'Baron of Tranquillity and Shadiness' (平陰伯).

The above four are the only disciples of Mencius who have places assigned to them in the temples of Confucius.

5. Ch'ăn Tsin (陳臻). 6. Ch'ung Yü (充虞). 7. Chî-sun (季孫). 8. Tsze-shû Î (子叔疑).

These two last are held by Chû Hsî not to have been disciples of Mencius.

9. Kâo (高子). This is to be distinguished from another scholar of the same name, referred to in Bk. VI. Pt. II. iii.

10. Hsü Pî (徐辟). 11. Hsien-ch'iû Măng (咸丘蒙).

12. Ch'ăn Tâi (陳代). 13. P'ăng Kăng (彭更). 14. Û-lû Lien (屋廬連). 15. T'âo Ying (桃應).

These fifteen are said by Châo Ch'î to have been disciples of Mencius. The four that follow are said to have studied under him, or to have been his pupils.

16. Măng Chung (孟仲子). 17. Kâo (告子). This Kâo

can hardly be said to have studied under Mencius; he only argued with him. 18. Tăng Kăng, or Kăng of Tăng (滕更). 19. P'ăn-ch'ăng Kwo (盆成括).

These nineteen rest on the authority of Châo Ch'î. Others have added to them—20. Kung-ming Kâo (公明高). 21. K'wang Chang (匡章). 22. Ch'ăn Chung (陳仲). 23. Lî Lâu (離婁).

APPENDIX.

I have thought it would be interesting to many readers to append here the Essays of two distinguished scholars of China on the subject of Human Nature. The one is in direct opposition to Mencius's doctrine; according to the other, his doctrine is insufficient to explain the phenomena. The author of the first, Hsün K'wang (荀 [*al.* 孫] 況), more commonly called Hsün Ch'ing (卿), was not very much posterior to Mencius. He is said to have borne office both in Ch'î and Ch'û, and to have had at one time Lî Sze (李斯), the prime minister of Shih Hwang-tî, as a pupil. His Works which still remain form a considerable volume. The second essay is from the work of Han Yü, mentioned above, Chap. I. Sect. IV. 4. I shall not occupy any space with criticisms on the style or sentiments of the writers. If the translation appear at times to be inelegant or obscure, the fault is perhaps as much in the original as in myself. A comprehensive and able sketch of 'The Ethics of the Chinese, with special reference to the Doctrines of Human Nature and Sin,' by the Rev. Griffith John, was read before the North China Branch of the Royal Asiatic Society, in November, 1859, and has been published separately. The essays of Hsün and Han are both reviewed in it.

I. THAT THE NATURE IS EVIL.—BY THE PHILOSOPHER HSÜN.

The nature of man is evil; the good which it shows is factitious. There belongs to it, even at his birth, the love of gain, and as actions are in accordance with this, contentions and robberies grow up, and self-denial and yielding to others are not to be found; there belong to it envy and dislike, and as actions are in accordance with these, violence and injuries spring up, and self-devotedness and faith are not to be found; there belong to it the desires of the ears and the eyes, leading to the love of sounds and beauty, and as the actions are in accordance with these, lewdness and disorder spring up, and righteousness and propriety, with their various orderly displays, are not to be found. It thus appears, that to follow man's nature and yield obedience to its feelings will assuredly conduct to contentions and robberies, to the violation of the duties belonging to every one's lot, and the confounding of all distinctions, till the issue will be in a state of savagism; and that there must be the influence of teachers and laws, and the guidance of propriety and righteousness, from which will spring self-denial, yielding to others, and an observance of the well-ordered regulations of conduct, till the issue will be a state of good government.—From all this it is plain that the nature of man is evil; the good which it shows is factitious.

To illustrate.—A crooked stick must be submitted to the pressing-frame to soften and bend it, and then it becomes straight; a blunt knife must be submitted to the grindstone and whetstone, and then it becomes sharp: so, the nature of man, being evil, must be submitted to teachers and laws, and then it becomes correct; it must be submitted to propriety and righteousness, and then it comes under government. If men were without teachers and laws, their condition would be one of deflection and insecurity, entirely incorrect; if they were without propriety and righteousness, their condition would be one of rebellious disorder, rejecting all government. The sage kings of antiquity, understanding that the nature of man was thus evil, in a state of hazardous deflection, and incorrect, rebellious and disorderly, and refusing to be governed, set up the principles of righteousness and propriety, and framed laws and regulations to straighten and ornament the feelings of that nature and correct them,

荀子性惡篇

人之性惡、其善者僞也。今人之性、生而有好利焉、順是故爭奪生、而辭讓亡焉。生而有疾惡焉、順是故殘賊生、而忠信亡焉。生而有耳目之欲、有好聲色焉、順是故淫亂生、而禮義文理亡焉。然則從人之性、順人之情、必出於爭奪、合於犯分亂理而歸於暴、故必將有師法之化、禮義之道、然後出於辭讓、合於文理、而歸於治。用此觀之、然則人之性惡明矣、其善者僞也。

故枸木必將待檃栝烝矯、然後直。鈍金必將待礱厲、然後利。今人之性惡、必將待師法、然後正、得禮義、然後治。今人無師法、則偏險而不正、無禮義則悖亂而不治。古者聖王以人之性惡、以爲偏險而不正、悖亂而不治、是以爲之起禮義、制法度、以矯飾人之情性而正之、以擾化人之情性而導之也、使皆出於治、合於道者也。今之人化師法、積文學、道禮義

to tame and change those same feelings and guide them, so that they might all go forth in the way of moral government and in agreement with reason. Now, the man who is transformed by teachers and laws, gathers on himself the ornament of learning, and proceeds in the path of propriety and righteousness is a superior man; and he who gives the reins to his nature and its feelings, indulges its resentments, and walks contrary to propriety and righteousness is a mean man. Looking at the subject in this way, we see clearly that the nature of man is evil; the good which it shows is factitious.

Mencius said, 'Man has only to learn, and his nature appears to be good;' but I reply,—It is not so. To say so shows that he had not attained to the knowledge of man's nature, nor examined into the difference between what is natural in man and what is factitious. The natural is what the constitution spontaneously moves to:—it needs not to be learned, it needs not to be followed hard after; propriety and righteousness are what the sages have given birth to:—it is by learning that men become capable of them, it is by hard practice that they achieve them. That which is in man, not needing to be learned and striven after, is what I call natural; that in man which is attained to by learning, and achieved by hard striving, is what I call factitious. This is the distinction between those two. By the nature of man, the eyes are capable of seeing, and the ears are capable of hearing. But the power of seeing is inseparable from the eyes, and the power of hearing is inseparable from the ears;—it is plain that the faculties of seeing and hearing do not need to be learned. Mencius says, 'The nature of man is good, but all lose and ruin their nature, and therefore it becomes bad;' but I say that this representation is erroneous. Man being born with his nature, when he thereafter departs from its simple constituent elements, he must lose it. From this consideration we may see clearly that man's nature is evil. What might be called the nature's being good, would be if there were no departing from its simplicity to beautify it, no departing from its elementary dispositions to sharpen it. Suppose that those simple elements no more needed beautifying, and the mind's thoughts no more needed to be turned to good, than the power of vision which is inseparable from the eyes, and the power of hearing which is inseparable from the ears, need to be learned, *then we might say that the nature is good, just as* we say that the eyes see and the ears hear. It is the nature of man, when hungry, to desire to be filled; when cold, to desire to be warmed; when tired, to desire rest:—these are the feelings and nature of man. But now, a man is hungry, and in the presence of an elder he does not dare to eat before him:—he is yielding to that elder; he is tired with labour, and he does not dare to ask for rest:—he is working for some one. A son's yielding to his father and a younger

者爲君子、縱性情、安恣睢、而違禮義者爲小人。用此觀之、然則人之性惡明矣、其善者僞也。

孟子曰、人之學者、其性善。曰、是不然、是不及知人之性、而不察乎人之性僞之分者也。凡性者、天之就也、不可學、不可事。禮義者、聖人之所生也、人之所學而能、所事而成者也。不可學、不可事、而在人者、謂之性、可學而能、可事而成之在人者、謂之僞、是性僞之分也。今人之性、目可以見、耳可以聽。夫可以見之明不離目、可以聽之聰不離耳、目明而耳聰、不可學明矣。孟子曰、今人之性善、將皆失喪其性故也。曰、若是則過矣、今人之性、生而離其朴、離其資、必失而喪之、用此觀之、然則人之性惡明矣。所謂性善者、不離其朴而美之、不離其資而利之也、使夫資朴之於美、心意之於善、若夫可以見之明不離目、可以聽之聰不離耳、故曰目明而耳聰也。今人之性、飢而

brother to his elder, a son's labouring for his father and a younger brother for his elder:—these two instances of conduct are contrary to the nature and against the feelings; but they are according to the course laid down for a filial son, and to the refined distinctions of propriety and righteousness. It appears that if there were an accordance with the feelings and the nature, there would be no self-denial and yielding to others. Self-denial and yielding to others are contrary to the feelings and the nature. In this way we come to see how clear it is that the nature of man is evil; the good which it shows is factitious.

An inquirer will ask, 'If man's nature be evil, whence do propriety and righteousness arise?' I reply:—All propriety and righteousness are the artificial production of the sages, and are not to be considered as growing out of the nature of man. It is just as when a potter makes a vessel from the clay;—the vessel is the product of the workman's art, and is not to be considered as growing out of his nature. Or it is as when another workman cuts and hews a vessel out of wood;—it is the product of his art, and is not to be considered as growing out of his nature. The sages pondered long in thought and gave themselves to practice, and so they succeeded in producing propriety and righteousness, and setting up laws and regulations. Thus it is that propriety and righteousness, laws and regulations, are the artificial product of the sages, and are not to be considered as growing properly from the nature of man.

If we speak of the fondness of the eyes for beauty, or of the mouth for *pleasant* flavours, or of the mind for gain, or of the bones and skin for the enjoyment of ease;—all these grow out of the natural feelings of man. The object is presented and the desire is felt; there needs no effort to produce it. But when the object is presented, and the affection does not move till after hard effort, I say that this effect is factitious. Those cases prove the difference between what is produced by nature and what is produced by art.

Thus the sages transformed their nature, and commenced their artificial work. Having commenced this work with their nature, they produced propriety and righteousness. When propriety and righteousness were produced, they proceeded to frame laws and regulations. It appears, therefore, that propriety and righteousness, laws and regulations, are given birth

欲飽、寒而欲煖、勞而欲休、此人之情性也、今人飢、見長而不敢先食者、將有所讓也、勞而不敢求息者、將有所代也。夫子之讓乎父、弟之讓乎兄、子之代乎父、弟之代乎兄、此二行者皆反於性、而悖於情也。然而孝子之道、禮義之文理也、故順情性、則不辭讓矣、辭讓則悖於情性矣。用此觀之、然則人之性惡明矣、其善者僞也。

問者曰、人之性惡、則禮義惡生。應之曰、凡禮義者、是生於聖人之僞、非故生於人之性也。故陶人埏埴而爲器、然則器生於工人之僞、非故生於人之性也、故工人斲木而成器、然則器生於工人之僞、非故生於人之性也、聖人積思慮習僞、故以生禮義、而起法度、然則禮義法度者、是生於聖人之僞、非故生於人之性也。

若夫目好色、耳好聲、口好味、心好利、骨體膚理好愉佚、是皆生於人之情性者也、感而自然、不待事而後生之者也。夫感而不能然、必且待事而後然者、謂之生於僞、是性僞之所生、其不同之徵也。故聖人化性而起僞、僞起於性、而生禮義、禮義生、而制法度、然則禮義法度者、是聖人之所生也、故聖人之所以同於衆、其不異於衆

to by the sages. Wherein they agree with all other men and do not differ from them, is their nature; wherein they differ from and exceed other men, is this artificial work.

Now to love gain and desire to get;—this is the natural feeling of men. Suppose the case that there is an amount of property or money to be divided among brothers, and let this natural feeling to love gain and to desire to get come into play;—why, then the brothers will be opposing, and snatching from, one another. But where the changing influence of propriety and righteousness, with their refined distinctions, has taken effect, a man will give up to any other man. Thus it is that if they act in accordance with their natural feelings, brothers will quarrel together; and if they have come under the transforming influence of propriety and righteousness, men will give up to other men, to say nothing of brothers. *Again*, the fact that men WISH to do what is good, is because their nature is bad. The thin wishes to be thick; the ugly wish to be beautiful; the narrow wishes to be wide; the poor wish to be rich; the mean wish to be noble:—when anything is not possessed in one's self, he seeks for it outside himself. But the rich do not wish for wealth; the noble do not wish for position:—when anything is possessed by one's self, he does not need to go beyond himself for it. When we look at things in this way, we perceive that the fact of men's WISHING to do what is good is because their nature is evil. It is the case indeed, that man's nature is without propriety and benevolence:—he therefore studies them with vigorous effort and seeks to have them. It is the case that by nature he does not know propriety and righteousness:—he therefore thinks and reflects and seeks to know them. Speaking of man, therefore, as he is by birth simply, he is without propriety and righteousness, without the knowledge of propriety and righteousness. Without propriety and righteousness, man must be all confusion and disorder; without the knowledge of propriety and righteousness, there must ensue all the manifestations of disorder. Man, as he is born, therefore, has in him nothing but the elements of disorder, passive and active. It is plain from this view of the subject that the nature of man is evil; the good which it shows is factitious.

When Mencius says that 'Man's nature is good,' I affirm that it is not so. In ancient times and now, throughout the kingdom, what is meant by good is a condition of correctness, regulation, and happy government; and what is meant by evil, is a condition of deflection, insecurity, and refusing to be under government:—in this lies the distinction between being good and being evil. And now, if man's nature be really so correct, regulated, and happily governed in

者性也、所以異而過衆者僞也。夫好利而欲得者、此人之情性也、假之人有弟兄資財而分者、且順情性、好利而欲得、若是則兄弟相拂奪矣。且化禮義之文理、若是則讓乎國人矣、故順情性、則弟兄爭矣、化禮義、則讓乎國人矣、凡人之欲爲善者、爲性惡也。夫薄願厚、惡願美、狹願廣、貧願富、賤願貴、苟無之中者、必求於外、故富而不願財、貴而不願勢、苟有之中者、必不及於外。用此觀之、人之欲爲善者、爲性惡也。今人之性、固無禮義、故彊學而求有之也、性不知禮義、故思慮而求知之也、然則生而已、則人無禮義、不知禮義、人無禮義則亂、不知禮義則悖、然則生而已、則悖亂在已。用此觀之、人之性惡明矣、其善者僞也。

孟子曰、人之性善。曰、是不然。凡古今天下之所謂善者、正理平治也、所謂惡者、偏險悖亂也、是善惡之分也已。今誠以人之性、固正理平治邪、則有惡用聖王、惡用禮義矣哉。雖有聖王、禮義、

孟子

itself, where would be the use for sage kings? where would be the use for propriety and righteousness? Although there were the sage kings, propriety, and righteousness, what could they add to the nature so correct, regulated, and happily ruled in itself? But it is not so; the nature of man is bad. It was on this account, that anciently the sage kings, understanding that man's nature was bad, in a state of deflection and insecurity, instead of being correct; in a state of rebellious disorder, instead of one of happy rule, set up therefore the majesty of princes and governors to awe it; and set forth propriety and righteousness to change it; and framed laws and statutes of correctness to rule it; and devised severe punishments to restrain it: so that its outgoings might be under the dominion of rule, and in accordance with what is good. This is *the true account of* the governance of the sage kings, and the transforming power of propriety and righteousness. Let us suppose a state of things in which there shall be no majesty of rulers and governors, no influence of propriety and righteousness, no rule of laws and statutes, no restraints of punishment:—what would be the relations of men with one another, all under heaven? The strong would be injuring the weak, and spoiling them; the many would be tyrannizing over the few, and hooting them; a universal disorder and mutual destruction would speedily ensue. When we look at the subject in this way, we see clearly that the nature of man is evil; the good which it shows is factitious.

He who would speak well of ancient times must have undoubted references in the present; he who would speak well of Heaven must substantiate what he says from *the state of* man. In discourse and argument it is an excellent quality when the divisions which are made can be brought together like the halves of a token. When it is so, the arguer may sit down, and discourse of his principles; and he has only to rise up, and they may be set forth and displayed and carried into action. When Mencius says that the nature of man is good, there is no bringing together in the above manner of his divisions. He sits down and talks, but there is no getting up to display and set forth his principles, and put them in operation:—is not his error very gross? To say that the nature is good does away with the sage kings, and makes an end of propriety and righteousness; to say that the nature is bad exalts the sage kings, and dignifies propriety and righteousness. As the origin of the pressing-boards is to be found in the crooked wood, and the origin of the carpenter's marking-line is to be found in things not being straight; so the rise of princes and governors, and the illustration of propriety and righteousness, are to be traced to the badness of the nature. It is clear from this view of the subject that the nature of man is bad; the good which it shows is factitious.

將曷加於正理平治也哉、今不然、人之性惡、故古者、聖人以人之性惡、以爲偏險而不正、悖亂而不治、故爲之立君上之勢、以臨之、明禮義以化之、起法正以治之、重刑罰以禁之、使天下皆出於治、合於善也、是聖王之治、而禮義之化也。今當試去君上之勢、無禮義之化、去法正之治、無刑罰之禁、倚而觀天下民人之相與也。若是、則夫彊者害弱而奪之、衆者暴寡而譁之、天下之悖亂而相亡、不待頃矣。用此觀之、然則人之性惡明矣、其善者僞也。

故善言古者、必有節於今、善言天者、必有徵於人。凡論者、貴其有辨、合有符驗、故坐而言之、起而可設張、而可施行。今孟子曰、人之性善、無辨合符驗、坐而言之、起而不可設張、而不可施行、豈不過甚矣哉。故性善、則去聖王、息禮義矣、性惡、則與聖王、貴禮義矣。故檃栝之生、爲枸木也、繩墨之起、爲不直也、立君上、明禮義、爲性惡也。用此觀之、然則人之性惡明矣、其善者僞也。

A straight piece of wood does not need the pressing-boards to make it straight;—it is so by its nature. A crooked piece of wood must be submitted to the pressing-boards to soften and straighten it, and then it is straight; it is not straight by its nature. So it is that the nature of man, being evil, must be submitted to the rule of the sage kings, and to the transforming influence of propriety and righteousness, and then its outgoings are under the dominion of rule, and in accordance with what is good. This shows clearly that the nature of man is bad; the good which it shows is factitious.

An inquirer may say *again*, 'Propriety and righteousness, though seen in an accumulation of factitious deeds, do yet belong to the nature of man; and thus it was that the sages were able to produce them.' I reply:—It is not so. A potter takes a piece of clay, and produces an earthen dish from it; but are that dish and clay the nature of the potter? A carpenter plies his tools upon a piece of wood, and produces a vessel; but are that vessel and wood the nature of the carpenter? So it is with the sages and propriety and righteousness; they produced them, just as the potter works with the clay. It is plain that there is no reason for saying that propriety and righteousness, and the accumulation of their factitious actions, belong to the proper nature of man. Speaking of the nature of man, it is the same in all,—the same in Yâo and Shun and in Chieh and the robber Chih, the same in the superior man and in the mean man. If you say that propriety and righteousness, with the factitious actions accumulated from them, are the nature of man, on what ground do you proceed to ennoble Yâo and Yü, to ennoble *generally* the superior man? The ground on which we ennoble Yâo, Yü, and the superior man, is their ability to change the nature, and to produce factitious conduct. That factitious conduct being produced, out of it there are brought propriety and righteousness. The sages stand indeed in the same relation to propriety and righteousness, and the factitious conduct resulting from them, as the potter does to his clay:—we have a product in either case. This representation makes it clear that propriety and righteousness, with their factitious results, do not properly belong to the nature of man. *On the other hand*, that which we consider mean in Chieh, the robber Chih, and the mean man generally, is that they follow their nature, act in accordance with its feelings, and indulge its resentments, till all its outgoings are a greed of gain, contentions, and rapine.—It is plain that the nature of man is bad; the good which it shows is factitious.

直木不待檃栝而直者、其性直也、枸木必將待檃栝烝矯、然後直者、以其性不直也、今人之性惡、必將待聖王之治、禮義之化、然後皆出於治、合於善也。用此觀之、然則人之性惡明矣、其善者僞也。

問者曰、禮義積僞者、是人之性、故聖人能生之也。應之曰、是不然、夫陶人埏埴而生瓦、然則瓦埴豈陶人之性也哉。工人斲木而生器、然則器木豈工人之性也哉、夫聖人之於禮義也、辟則陶埏而生之也。然則禮義積僞者、豈人之本性也哉、凡人之性者、堯舜之與桀跖、其性一也、君子之與小人、其性一也。今將以禮義積僞、爲人之性邪、然則有曷貴堯禹、曷貴君子矣哉。凡所貴堯禹君子者、能化性、能起僞。僞起而生禮義、然則聖人之於禮義積僞也、亦陶埏而生之也。用此觀之、然則禮義積僞者、豈人之性也哉。所賤於桀跖小人者、從其性、順其情、安恣睢、以出乎貪利爭奪、故人之性惡明矣、其善者僞也。

Heaven did not make favourites of Tsăng *Shăn*, *Min* Tsze-ch'ien, and Hsiâo-chî, and deal unkindly with the rest of men. How then was it that they alone were distinguished by the greatness of their filial deeds, that all which the name of filial piety implies was complete in them? The reason was that they were entirely subject to the restraints of propriety and righteousness.

Heaven did not make favourites of the people of Ch'î and Lû, and deal unkindly with the people of Ch'in. How then was it that the latter were not equal to the former in the rich manifestation of the filial piety belonging to the righteousness of the relation between father and son, and the respectful observance of the proprieties belonging to the separate functions of husband and wife? The reason was that the people of Ch'in followed the feelings of their nature, indulged its resentments, and contemned propriety and righteousness. We are not to suppose that they were different in their nature.

What is the meaning of the saying, that 'Any traveller on the road may become like Yü?' I answer:—All that made Yü what he was, was his practice of benevolence, righteousness, and his observance of laws and rectitude. But benevolence, righteousness, laws, and rectitude are all capable of being known and being practised. Moreover, any traveller on the road has the capacity of knowing these, and the ability to practise them:—it is plain that he may become like Yü. If you say that benevolence, righteousness, laws, and rectitude are not capable of being known and practised, then Yü himself could not have known, could not have practised them. If you will have it that any traveller on the road is really without the capacity of knowing these things, and the ability to practise them, then, in his home, it will not be competent for him to know the righteousness that should rule between father and son, and, abroad, it will not be competent for him to know the rectitude that should rule between sovereign and minister. But it is not so. There is no one who travels along the road, but may know both that righteousness and that rectitude:—it is plain that the capacity to know and the ability to practise belong to every traveller on the way. Let him, therefore, with his capacity of knowing and ability to practise, take his ground on the knowableness and practicableness of benevolence and righteousness;—and it is clear that he may become like Yü. Yea, let any traveller on the way addict himself to the art of learning with all his heart and

天非私曾騫孝已、而外衆人也。然而曾騫孝已、獨厚於孝之實、而全於孝之名者何也、以綦於禮義故也。

天非私齊魯之民、而外秦人也、然而於父子之義、夫婦之別、不如齊魯之孝、具敬父者何也。以秦人之從情性、安恣睢、慢於禮義故也、豈其性異矣哉。

塗之人可以爲禹、曷謂也。曰、凡禹之所以爲禹者、以其爲仁義法正也。然則仁義法正、有可知可能之理、然而塗之人也、皆有可以知仁義法正之質、皆有可以能仁義法正之具、然則其可以爲禹明矣。今以仁義法正、爲固無可知可能之理邪、然則唯禹不知仁義法正、不能仁義法正也。將使塗之人、固無可以知仁義法正之質、而固無可以能仁義法正之具邪、然則塗之人也、且內不可以知父子之義、外不可以知君臣之正、不然、今塗之人者、皆內可以知父子之義、外可以知君臣之正、然則其可以知之質、可以能之具、其在塗之人明矣、今使塗之人者、以其可以知之質、可以能之具、本夫

the entire bent of his will, thinking, searching, and closely examining;—let him do this day after day, through a long space of time, accumulating what is good, and he will penetrate as far as a spiritual Intelligence, he will become a ternion with Heaven and Earth. It follows that *the characters of* the sages were what any man may reach by accumulation.

It may be said:—'To be sage may thus be reached by accumulation;—why is it that all men cannot accumulate *to this extent?*' I reply:—They may do so, but they cannot be made to do so. The mean man might become a superior man, but he is not willing to be a superior man. The superior man might become a mean man, but he is not willing to be a mean man. It is not that the mean man and the superior man may not become the one the other; their not becoming the one the other is because it is a thing which may be, but cannot be made to be. Any traveller on the road may become like Yü:—the case is so; that any traveller on the road can really become like Yü:—this is not a necessary conclusion. Though any one, however, cannot really become like Yü, that is not contrary at all to the truth that he may become so. One's feet might travel all over the world, but there never was one who was really able to travel all over the world. There is nothing to prevent the mechanic, the farmer, and the merchant from practising each the business of the others, but there has never been a case when it has really been done. Looking at the subject in this way, we see that what may be need not really be; and although it shall not really be, that is not contrary to the truth that it might be. It thus appears that the difference is wide between what is really done or not really done, and what may be or may not be. It is plain that these two cases may not become the one the other.

Yâo asked Shun what was the character of the feelings proper to man. Shun replied, 'The feelings proper to man are very unlovely; why need you ask about them? When a man has got a wife and children, his filial piety withers away; under the influence of lust and gratified desires, his good faith to his friends withers away; when he is full of dignities and emoluments, his loyalty to his sovereign withers away. The natural feelings of man! The natural feelings of man! They are very unlovely. Why need you ask about them? It is only in the case of men of the highest worth that it is not so.'

仁義之可知之理、可能之具、然則其可以爲禹明矣、今使塗之人、伏術爲學專心一志、思索孰察、加日縣久、積善而不息、則通於神明、參於天地矣、故聖人者、人之所積而致矣。

曰、聖可積、而致、然而皆不可積、何也。曰、可以而不可使也。故小人可以爲君子、而不肯爲君子、君子可以爲小人、而不肯爲小人、小人君子者、未嘗不可以相爲也、然而不相爲者、可以而不可使也、故塗之人、可以爲禹、然則塗之人、能爲禹、未必然也、雖不能爲禹、無害可以爲禹。足可以偏行天下、然而未嘗有能偏行天下者也。夫工匠農賈、未嘗不可以相爲事也、然而未嘗能相爲事也。用此觀之、然則可以爲未必能也、雖不能、無害可以爲、然則能不能之與可不可、其不同遠矣、其不可以相爲明矣。

堯問於舜曰、人情何如。舜對曰、人情甚不美、又何問焉、妻子具、而孝衰於親、嗜欲得、而信衰於友、爵祿盈、而忠衰於君、人之情乎、人之情乎、甚不美、又何問焉、唯賢者爲不然。

There is a knowledge characteristic of the sage; a knowledge characteristic of the scholar and superior man; a knowledge characteristic of the mean man; and a knowledge characteristic of the mere servant. In much speech to show his cultivation and maintain consistency, and though he may discuss for a whole day the reasons of a subject, to have a unity pervading the ten thousand changes of discourse:—this is the knowledge of the sage. To speak seldom, and in a brief and sparing manner, and to be orderly in his reasoning, as if its parts were connected with a string:—this is the knowledge of the scholar and superior man. Flattering words and disorderly conduct, with undertakings often followed by regrets:—these mark the knowledge of the mean man. Hasty, officious, smart, and swift, but without consistency; versatile, able, of extensive capabilities, but without use; decisive in discourse, rapid, exact, but the subject unimportant; regardless of right and wrong, taking no account of crooked and straight, to get the victory over others the guiding object:—this is the knowledge of the mere servant.

There is bravery of the highest order; bravery of the middle order; bravery of the lowest order. Boldly to take up his position in the place of the universally acknowledged Mean; boldly to carry into practice his views of the doctrines of the ancient kings; in a high situation, not to defer to a bad sovereign, and in a low situation not to follow the current of a bad people; to consider that there is no poverty where there is virtue, and no wealth or honour where virtue is not; when appreciated by the world, to desire to share in all men's joys and sorrows; when unknown by the world, to stand up grandly alone between heaven and earth, and have no fears:—this is the bravery of the highest order. To be reverently observant of propriety, and sober-minded; to attach importance to adherence to fidelity, and set little store by material wealth; to have the boldness to push forward men of worth and exalt them, to hold back undeserving men, and get them deposed:—this is the bravery of the middle order. To be devoid of self-respect and set a great value on wealth; to feel complacent in calamity, and always have plenty to say for himself; saving himself in any way, without regard to right and wrong; whatever be the real state of a case, making it his object to get the victory over others:—this is the bravery of the lowest order.

The *fan-zăo* and the *chü-shû* were the best bows of antiquity; but without their regulators, they could not adjust themselves. The *tsung* of duke Hwan, the *chûeh* of T'âi-kung, the *lû* of

有聖人之知者、有士君子之知者、有小人之知者、有役夫之知者。多言則文而類、終日議其所以言之千擧萬變、其統類一也、是聖人之知也。少言則徑而省、論而法、若佚之以繩、是士君子之知也。其言也謟、其行也悖、其擧事多悔、是小人之知也。齊給便敏而無類、雜能旁魄而無用、析速粹孰、而不急、不恤是非、不論曲直、以期勝人爲意、是役夫之知也。

有上勇者、有中勇者、有下勇者。天下有中、敢直其身、先王有道、敢行其意、上不循於亂世之君、下不俗於亂世之民、仁之所在、無貧窮、仁之所亡、無富貴、天下知之、則欲與天下同苦樂之、天下不知之、則傀然獨立天地之閒、而不畏、是上勇也。禮恭而意儉、大齊信焉、而輕貨財、賢者敢推而向之、不肖者敢援而廢之、是中勇也。輕身而重貨、恬禍而廣解、苟免不恤是非、然不然之情、以期勝人爲意、是下勇也。

繁弱鉅黍、古之良弓也、然而不得排檠、則不能自

king Wăn, the *hû* of prince Chwang, the *kan-tsiang*, *mŏ-yê*, *chü-chüeh* and *p'i-lü* of Ho-lü—these were the best swords of antiquity; but without the grindstone and whetstone they would not have been sharp; without the strength of the arms that wielded them they would not have cut anything.

The *hwâ-liû*, the *lî-ch'i*, the *hsien-lî*, and the *lü*-r—these were the best horses of antiquity; but there were still necessary for them the restraints in front of bit and bridle, the stimulants behind of whip and cane, and the skilful driving of a Tsâo-fû, and then they could accomplish a thousand *lî* in one day.

So it is with man:—granted to him an excellent capacity of nature and the faculty of intellect, he must still seek for good teachers under whom to place himself, and make choice of friends with whom he may be intimate. Having got good masters and placed himself under them, what he will hear will be the doctrines of Yâo, Shun, Yü, and T'ang; having got good friends and become intimate with them, what he will see will be deeds of self-consecration, fidelity, reverence, and complaisance:—he will go on from day to day to benevolence and righteousness, without being conscious of it: a natural following of them will make him do so. On the other hand, if he live with bad men, what he will hear will be the language of deceit, calumny, imposture, and hypocrisy; what he will see will be conduct of filthiness, insolence, lewdness, corruptness, and greed:—he will be going on from day to day to punishment and disgrace, without being conscious of it; a natural following of them will make him do so.

The Record says, 'If you do not know your son, look at his friends; if you do not know your prince, look at his confidants.' All is the influence of association! All is the influence of association!

正。桓公之葱、太公之闕、文王之錄、莊君之曶、闔閭之干將、莫邪、鉅闕、辟閭、此皆古之良劍也。然而不加砥厲、則不能利、不得人力、則不能斷。

驊騮、騹驥、纖離、綠耳、此皆古之良馬也、然而前必有銜轡之制、後有鞭策之威、加之以造父之馭、然後一日而致千里也。

夫人雖有性質美、而心辯知、必將求賢師而事之、擇良友而友之。得賢師而事之、則所聞者、堯舜禹湯之道也、得良友而友之、則所見者、忠信敬讓之行也、身日進於仁義、而不自知也者、靡使然也。今與不善人處、則所聞者、欺誣詐僞也、所見者、汙漫淫邪、貪利之行也、身且加於刑戮、而不自知者、靡使然也。

傳曰、不知其子、視其友、不知其君、視其左右、靡而已矣、靡而已矣。

II. AN EXAMINATION OF THE NATURE OF MAN.—BY HAN WĂN-KUNG.

The NATURE dates from the date of the life; the FEELINGS date from contact with external things. There are three GRADES of the nature, and it has five CHARACTERISTICS. There are also three GRADES of the feelings, and they have seven CHARACTERISTICS. To explain myself:—The three grades of the nature are—the Superior, the Middle, and the Inferior. The superior grade is good, and good only; the middle grade is capable of being led: it may rise to the superior, or sink to the inferior; the inferior is evil, and evil only. The five characteristics of the nature are—Benevolence, Righteousness, Propriety, Sincerity, and Knowledge. In the Superior Grade, the first of these characteristics is supreme, and the other four are practised. In the Middle Grade, the first of these characteristics is not wanting: it exists, but with a little tendency to its opposite; the other four are in an ill-assorted state. In the Inferior Grade there is the opposite of the first characteristic, and constant rebelliousness against the other four. The grade of the nature regulates the manifestation of the feelings in it. *Again:*—The three grades of the feelings are the Superior, the Middle, and the Inferior; and their seven characteristics are—Joy, Anger, Sorrow, Fear, Love, Hatred, and Desire. In the Superior Grade, these seven all move, and each in its due place and degree. In the Middle Grade, some of the characteristics are in excess, and some in defect; but there is a seeking to give them their due place and degree. In the Inferior Grade, whether they are in excess or defect, there is a reckless acting according to the one in immediate predominance. The grade of the feelings regulates the influence of the nature in reference to them.

Speaking of the nature, Mencius said:—'Man's nature is good;' the philosopher Hsün said:—'Man's nature is bad;' the philosopher Yang said:—'In the nature of man good and evil are mixed together.' Now, to say that the nature, good at first, subsequently becomes

韓文公原性篇

性也者、與生俱生也、情也者、接於物而生也。性之品、有三、而其所以爲性者五。情之品、有三、而其所以爲情者七。曰、何也。曰、性之品、有上中下三。上焉者善焉而已矣。中焉者可導而上下也。下焉者惡焉而已矣。其所以爲性者五、曰仁、曰義、曰禮、曰信、曰智。上焉者之於五也、主於一、而行於四。中焉者之於五也、一也不少、有焉、則少反焉。其於四也混。下焉者之於五也、反於一、而悖於四。性之於情、視其品。情之品、有上中下三、其所以爲情者七、曰喜、曰怒、曰哀、曰懼、曰愛、曰惡、曰欲。上焉者之於七也、動而處其中。中焉者之於七也、有所甚、有所亡、然而求合其中者也。下焉者之於七也、亡與甚、直情而行者也。情之於性、視其品。

孟子之言性、曰、人之性善。荀子之言性、曰、人之性惡。揚子之言性、曰、人之性善惡混。夫始

bad ; or that, bad at first, it subsequently becomes good ; or that, mixed at first, it subsequently becomes, it may be, good, it may be, bad :—in each of these cases only the nature of the middle grade is dealt with, and the superior and inferior grades are neglected. Those philosophers are right about one grade, and wrong about the other two.

When Shû-yü was born, his mother knew, as soon as she looked at him, that he would fall a victim to his love of bribes. When Yang Sze-wo was born, the mother of Shû-hsiang knew, as soon as she heard him cry, that he would cause the destruction of all his kindred. When Yüeh-tsiâo was born, Tsze-wǎn considered it was a great calamity, knowing that through him the ghosts of the *Zo-âo* family would all be famished.—With such cases before us, can it be said that the nature of man (i. e. all men) is good ?

When How-chî was born, his mother had no suffering ; and as soon as he began to creep, he displayed all elegance and intelligence. When king Wǎn was in his mother's womb, she experienced no distress ; after his birth, those who tended him had no trouble ; when he began to learn, his teachers had no vexation.—With such cases before us, can it be said that the nature of man (i. e. all men) is evil ?

Chû was the son of Yâo, and Chün the son of Shun ; Kwan and Ts'âi were sons of king Wǎn. They were instructed to practise nothing but what was good, and yet they turned out villains. Shun was the son of Kû-sâu, and Yü the son of K'wǎn. They were instructed to practise nothing but what was bad, and yet they turned out sages.—With such cases before us, can it be said that in the nature of man (i. e. all men) good and evil are blended together ?

Having these things in view, I say that the three philosophers, to whom I have referred, dealt with the middle grade of the nature, and neglected the superior and the inferior ; that they were right about the one grade, and wrong about the other two.

It may be asked, 'Is it so, then, that the superior and inferior grades of the nature can never be changed ?' I reply :—The nature of the superior grade, by application to learning, becomes more intelligent, and the nature of the inferior grade, through awe of power, comes to have few faults. The superior nature, therefore, may be taught, and the inferior nature may be restrained ; but the grades have been pronounced by Confucius to be unchangeable.

善而進惡歟、始惡而進善歟、始也混而今也善惡歟、皆舉其中而遺其上下者也、得其一而失其二者也。

叔魚之生也、其母視之、知其必以賄死。楊食我之生也、叔向之母、聞其號也、知必滅其宗。越椒之生也、子文以爲大戚、知若敖氏之鬼不食也。人之性果善乎。

后稷之生也、其母無災、其始匍匐也、則岐岐然、嶷嶷然。文王之在母也、母不憂、既生也、傅不勤、既學也、師不煩。人之性果惡乎。

堯之朱、舜之均、文王之管蔡、習非不善也、而卒爲姦、瞽叟之舜、鯀之禹、習非不惡也、而卒爲聖人。人之性善惡果混乎。

故曰、三子之言性也、舉其中而遺其上下者也、得其一而失其二者也。

曰、然則性之上下者、其終不可移乎。曰、上之性、就學而愈明、下之性、畏威而寡非、是故、上者可學、而下者可制也、其品、則孔子謂不移也。

孟子

It may be asked, 'How is it that those who nowadays speak about the nature do so differently from this?' I reply:—Those who nowadays speak about the nature blend with their other views those of Buddhism and Lâo-tsze; and doing so, how could they speak otherwise than differently from me?

曰，今之言性者，異於此，何也。曰，今之言性者，雜佛老而言也，雜佛老而言者，奚言而不異。

CHAPTER III.

OF YANG CHÛ AND MO TÎ.

SECTION I.

THE OPINIONS OF YANG CHÛ.

1. 'The words of Yang Chû and Mo Tî,' said Mencius, 'fill the world. If you listen to people's discourses throughout it, you will find that they have adopted the views of the one or of the other. Now, Yang's principle is—"Each one for himself," which does not acknowledge the claims of the sovereign. Mo's principle is—"To love all equally," which does not acknowledge the peculiar affection due to a father. To acknowledge neither king nor father is to be in the state of a beast. If their principles are not stopped, and the principles of Confucius set forth, their perverse speakings will delude the people, and stop up the path of benevolence and righteousness.

'I am alarmed by these things, and address myself to the defence of the doctrines of the former sages, and to oppose Yang and Mo. I drive away their licentious expressions, so that such perverse speakers may not be able to show themselves. When sages shall rise up again, they will not change my words[1].'

His opposition to Yang and Mo was thus one of the great labours of Mencius's life, and what he deemed the success of it one of his great achievements. His countrymen generally accede to the justice of his claim; though there have not been wanting some to say—justly, as I think and will endeavour to show in the next section—that Mo need not have incurred from him such heavy censure. For Yang no one has a word to say. His leading principle as stated by Mencius is certainly detestable, and so far as we can judge from the slight accounts of him that are to be gathered from other quarters, he seems to have been about 'the least erected spirit,' who ever professed to reason concerning the life and duties of man.

2. The generally received opinion is that Yang belonged to the

[1] Bk. III. Pt. II. ix. 9, 10.

period of 'The Warring States,' the same era of Chinese history as Mencius. He was named Chû, and styled Tsze-chü[1]. In a note on Bk. III. Pt. II. ix. 9, I have supposed that he was of the times of Confucius and Lâo-tsze, having then before me a passage of the Tâoist philosopher Chwang, in which he gives an account of an interview between Lâo-tsze and Yang Chû[2]. That interview, however, must be an invention of Chwang. The natural impression which we receive from all the references of Mencius is that Yang must have been posterior to Confucius, and that his opinions had come into vogue only in the times of our philosopher himself. This view would be placed beyond doubt if we could receive as genuine the chapter on Yang, which is contained in the writings of the philosopher Lieh. And so far we may accept it, as to believe that it gives the sentiments which were attributed to him in the first century before our era[3]. The leading principle ascribed to him by Mencius nowhere appears in it in so many words, but the general tenour of his language is entirely in accordance with it. This will appear from the following specimens, which are all to be found in the seventh chapter of the Books of Lieh. The corresponding English and Chinese paragraphs are indicated by the same letters prefixed to them:—

[a] 'Yang Chû said, "A hundred years are the extreme limit of longevity; and not one man in a thousand enjoys such a period of life. Suppose the case of one who does so:—infancy borne in the arms, and doting old age, will nearly occupy the half; what is forgotten in sleep, and what is lost in the waking day, will nearly occupy the half; pain and sickness, sorrow and bitterness, losses, anxieties, and fears, will nearly occupy the half. There may remain ten years or so; but I reckon that not even in them will be found an hour of smiling self-abandonment, without the shadow of solicitude.—What is the life of man then to be made of? What pleasure is in it?

'"*Is it to be prized* for the pleasure of food and dress? or for the enjoyments of music and beauty? But one cannot be always satisfied with those pleasures; one cannot be always toying with beauty and listening to music. And then there are the restraints of punishments and the stimulants of rewards; the urgings and the repressings of fame and laws:—these make one strive restlessly for the vain praise of an hour, and calculate on the residuary glory after death; they keep him, as with body bent, on the watch against what his ears hear and his eyes see, and attending to the right and the wrong of his conduct and thoughts. In this way

[1] 楊朱,字子居. [2] See 莊子,雜篇,第五, the 寓言, at the end.

[3] Dr. Morrison says of Lieh (Dictionary, character 子):—'Lieh-tsze, an eminent writer of the Tâo sect; lived about the same time as Lâo-tsze, the founder of the sect (B.C. 585).' Lieh's Works are published, with the preface of Liû Hsiang written B.C. 13. Hsiang says Lieh was a native of Chăng (鄭), and a contemporary of duke Mû (穆 or 繆). But Mû's reign extended from B.C. 627 to 604. There is evidently an anachronism somewhere. Hsiang goes on to speak of Lieh's writings, specifying the chapter on Yang Chû, in which there are references to Confucius and his acknowledged fame. Another of Lieh's chapters is all devoted to Confucius's sayings and doings.—This is not the place to attempt an adjustment of the difficulties. The chapter about Yang Chû was current in Liû Hsiang's time, and we may cull from it to illustrate the character of the man.

he loses the real pleasure of his years, and cannot allow himself for a moment.—In what does he differ from an individual manacled and fettered in an inner prison? The people of high antiquity knew both the shortness of life, and how suddenly and completely it might be closed by death, and therefore they obeyed the movements of their hearts, refusing not what it was natural for them to like, nor seeking to avoid any pleasure that occurred to them. They paid no heed to the incitements of fame; they enjoyed themselves according to their nature; they did not resist the common tendency of all things to self-enjoyment; they cared not to be famous after death. They managed to keep clear of punishment; as to fame and praise, being first or last, long life or short life,—these things did not come into their calculations."'

[b] 'Yang Chû said, "Wherein people differ is the matter of life; wherein they agree is death. While they are alive, we have the distinctions of intelligence and stupidity, honourableness and meanness; when they are dead, we have so much stinking rottenness decaying away:—this is the common lot. Yet intelligence and stupidity, honourableness and meanness, are not in one's power; neither is that condition of putridity, decay, and utter disappearance. A man's life is not in his own hands, nor is his death; his intelligence is not his own, nor is his stupidity, nor his honourableness, nor his meanness. All are born and all die;—the intelligent and the stupid, the honourable and the mean. At ten years old some die; at a hundred years old some die. The virtuous and the sage die; the ruffian and the fool also die. Alive, they were Yâo and Shun; dead, they were so much rotten bone. Alive, they were Chieh and Châu; dead, they were so much rotten bone. Who could know any difference between their rotten bones? While alive, therefore, let us hasten to make the best of life; what leisure have we to be thinking of anything after death?"'

[a] 楊朱曰百年、壽之大齊、得百年者、千無一焉。設有一者、孩抱以逮昏老、幾居其半矣、夜眠之所弭、晝覺之所遺、又幾居其半矣、痛疾哀苦、亡失憂懼、又幾居其半矣、量十數年之中、迪然而自得、亡介焉之慮者、亦亡一時之中爾、則人之生也奚爲哉、奚樂哉。爲美厚爾、爲聲色爾。而美厚復不可常饜足、聲色不可常翫聞。乃復爲刑賞之所禁勸、名法之所進退、遑遑爾競一時之虛譽、規死後之餘榮、偊偊爾愼耳目之觀聽、惜身意之是非、徒失當年之至樂、不能自肆於一時、重囚纍梏、何以異哉。太古之人、知生之暫來、知死之暫往、故從心而動、不違自然所好、當身之娛非所去也、故不爲名所勸、從性而游、不逆萬物所好、死後之名非所取也、故不爲刑所及、名譽先後、年命多少、非所量也。

[b] 楊朱曰、萬物所異者生也、所同者死也。生則有賢愚貴賤、是所異也、死則有臭腐消滅、是所同也。雖然、賢愚貴賤、非所能也、臭腐消滅、亦非所能也、故生非所生、死非所死、賢非所賢、愚非所愚、貴非所貴、賤非所賤。然而萬物齊生齊死、齊賢齊愚、齊貴齊賤。十年亦死、百年亦死、仁聖亦死、凶愚亦死、生則堯舜、死則腐骨、生則桀紂、死則腐骨、腐骨一矣、孰知其異。且趣當生、奚遑死後。

c 'Măng-sun Yang asked Yang-tsze, saying, "Here is a man who sets a high value on his life, and takes loving care of his body, hoping that he will not die :—does he do right?" "There is no such thing as not dying," was the reply. "But if he does so, hoping for long life, is he right?" Yang-tsze answered, "One cannot be assured of long life. Setting value upon life will not preserve it; taking care of the body will not make it greatly better. And, in fact, why should long life be made much of? There are the five feelings with their likings and dislikings, —now as in old time; there are the four limbs, now at ease, now in danger,—now as in old time; there are the various experiences of joy and sorrow,—now as in old time; there are the various changes from order to disorder, and from disorder to order,—now as in old time :—all these things I have heard of, and seen, and gone through. A hundred years of them would be more than enough, and shall I wish the pain protracted through a longer life?" Măng-sun said, "If it be so, early death is better than long life. Let a man go to trample on the pointed steel, or throw himself into the caldron or flames, to get what he desires." Yang-tsze answered, "No. Being once born, take your life as it comes, and endure it; and seeking to enjoy yourself as you desire, so await the approach of death. When you are about to die, treat the thing with indifference and endure it; and seeking to accomplish your departure, so abandon yourself to annihilation. Both death and life should be treated with indifference; they should both be endured :—why trouble one's self about earliness or lateness in connexion with them?"'

d 'Ch'in-tsze asked Yang Chû, saying, "If you could benefit the world by parting with one hair of your body, would you do it?" "The world is not to be benefited by a hair," replied Yang. The other urged, "But suppose it could be, what would you do?" To this Yang gave no answer, and Ch'in went out, and reported what had passed to Măng-sun Yang. Măng-sun said, "You do not understand our Master's mind :—let me explain it to you. If by enduring a slight wound in the flesh, you could get ten thousand pieces of gold, would you endure it?" "I would." "If by cutting off one of your limbs, you could get a kingdom, would you do it?" Ch'in was silent; and after a little, Măng-sun Yang resumed, "To part with a hair is a slighter matter than to receive a wound in the flesh, and that again is a slighter matter than to lose a limb :—that you can discern. But consider :—A hair may be

c 孟孫陽問楊子曰、有人於此、貴生愛身、以蘄不死、可乎。曰、理無不死。以蘄久生、可乎。曰、理無久生、生非貴之所能存、身非愛之所能厚。且久生奚爲、五情好惡、古猶今也、四體安危、古猶今也、世事苦樂、古猶今也、變易治亂、古猶今也、既聞之矣、既見之矣、既更之矣、百年猶厭其多、況久生之苦也乎。孟孫陽曰、若然速亡、愈於久生、則踐鋒刃、入湯火、得所志矣。楊子曰、不然、既生則廢而任之、究其所欲以俟於死、將死則廢而任之、究其所之以放於盡、無不廢、無不任、何遽遲速於其間乎。

d 禽子問楊朱曰、去子體之一毛、以濟一世、汝爲之乎。楊子曰、世固非一毛之所濟。禽子曰、假濟、爲之乎。楊子弗應。禽子出語孟孫陽。孟孫陽曰、子不達夫子之心、吾請言之、有侵若肌膚獲萬金者、若爲之乎。曰、爲之。孟孫陽曰、有斷若一節、得一國、子爲之乎。禽子默然有間。孟孫陽曰、一毛微於肌膚、肌膚微於一節省矣、然則積一毛以成肌膚、積肌膚以成一節、一毛固一體萬分中之一物、奈何輕

multiplied till it becomes as important as the piece of flesh, and the piece of flesh may be multiplied till it becomes as important as a limb. A single hair is just one of the ten thousand portions of the body;—why should you make light of it?" Ch'in-tsze replied, "I cannot answer you. If I could refer your words to Lâo Tan or Kwan Yin, they would say that you were right; but if I could refer my words to the great Yü or Mo Tî, they would say that I was right." Măng-sun Yang, on this, turned round, and entered into conversation with his disciples on another subject.'

c 'Yang Chû said, "All agree in considering Shun, Yü, Châu-kung, and Confucius to have been the most admirable of men, and in considering Chieh and Châu to have been the most wicked.

'"Now, Shun had to plough the ground on the south of the Ho, and to play the potter by the Lêi lake. His four limbs had not even a temporary rest; for his mouth and belly he could not find pleasant food and warm clothing. No love of his parents rested upon him; no affection of his brothers and sisters. When he was thirty years old, he had not been able to get the permission of his parents to marry. When Yâo at length resigned to him the throne, he was advanced in age; his wisdom was decayed; his son Shang-chün proved without ability; and he had finally to resign the throne to Yü. Sorrowfully came he to his death. Of all mortals never was one whose life was so worn out and empoisoned as his. K'wăn was required to reduce the deluged land to order; and when his labours were ineffectual, he was put to death on mount Yü, and Yü, *his son*, had to undertake the task, and serve his enemy. All his energies were spent on his labours with the land; a child was born to him, but he could not foster it; he passed his door without entering; his body became bent and withered; the skin of his hands and feet became thick and callous. When at length Shun resigned to him the throne, he lived in a low, mean house, while his sacrificial apron and cap were elegant. Sorrowfully came he to his death. Of all mortals never was one whose life was so saddened and embittered as his. On the death of king Wû, *his son*, king Ch'ăng was young and weak. Châu-kung had to undertake all the royal duties. The duke of Shâo was displeased, and evil reports spread through the kingdom. Châu-kung had to reside three years in the east; he slew his elder brother, and banished his younger; scarcely did he escape with his life. Sorrowfully came he to his death. Of all mortals never was one whose life was so full of hazards and terrors as his. Confucius understood the ways of the ancient sovereigns and kings. He responded to the invitations of the princes of his time. The tree was cut down over him in Sung; the traces of his footsteps were removed in Wei; he was reduced to

之乎。禽子曰、吾不能所以荅子。然則、以子之言、問老聃關尹、則子言當矣、以吾言問大禹墨翟、則吾言當矣。孟孫陽因顧與其徒說他事。

c 楊朱曰、天下之美、歸之舜、禹、周、孔、天下之惡、歸之桀、紂。然而舜耕於河陽、陶於雷澤、四體不得蹔安、口腹不得美厚、父母之所不愛、弟妹之所不親、行年三十、不告而娶、及受堯之禪、年巳長、智巳衰。商鈞不才、禪位於禹、戚戚然以至於死、此天人窮毒者也。鯀治水土、績用不就、殛諸羽山、禹纂業事讐、惟荒土功、子產不字、過門不入、身體偏枯、手足胼胝、及受舜禪、卑宮室、美紱冕、戚戚然以至於死、此天人之憂苦者也。武王既終、成王幼弱、周公攝天子之政、邵公不悅、四國流言、居東三年、誅兄放弟、僅免其身、戚戚然以至於死、此天人之危懼者也。孔子明帝王之道、應時君之聘、伐樹於宋、削迹於衞、窮於商周、圍於陳蔡、

extremity in Shang and Châu; he was surrounded in Ch'ăn and Ts'ăi; he had to bend to the head of the Chî family; he was disgraced by Yang Hû. Sorrowfully came he to his death. Of all mortals never was one whose life was so agitated and hurried as his.

'"Those four sages, during their life, had not a single day's joy. Since their death they have had a *grand* fame that will last through myriads of ages. But that fame is what no one who cares for what is real would choose. Celebrate them;—they do not know it. Reward them;—they do not know it. Their fame is no more to them than to the trunk of a tree or a clod of earth.

'"*On the other hand,* Chieh came into the accumulated wealth of many generations; to him belonged the honour of the royal seat; his wisdom was enough to enable him to set at defiance all below; his power was enough to shake the world. He indulged the pleasures to which his eyes and ears prompted him; he carried out whatever it came into his thoughts to do. Brightly came he to his death. Of all mortals never was one whose life was so luxurious and dissipated as his. *Similarly,* Châu came into the accumulated wealth of many generations; to him belonged the honour of the royal seat; his power enabled him to do whatever he would; his will was everywhere obeyed; he indulged his feelings in all his palaces; he gave the reins to his lusts through the long night; he never made himself bitter by the thought of propriety and righteousness. Brightly came he to his destruction. Of all mortals never was one whose life was so abandoned as his.

'"These two villains, during their life, had the joy of gratifying their desires. Since their death, they have had the *evil* fame of folly and tyranny. But the reality *of enjoyment* is what no fame can give. Reproach them;—they do not know it. Praise them;—they do not know it. Their *ill* fame is no more to them than to the trunk of a tree, or to a clod of earth.

'"To the four sages all admiration is given; yet were their lives bitter to the end, and their common lot was death. To the two villains all condemnation is given; yet their lives were pleasant to the last, and their common lot was likewise death."'

3. The above passages are sufficient to show the character of Yang Chû's mind and of his teachings. It would be doing injustice to Epicurus to compare Yang with him, for though the Grecian philosopher made happiness the chief end of human pursuit, he taught also that 'we cannot live pleasurably without living virtuously and justly.' The Epicurean system is, indeed, unequal

受屈於季氏、見辱於陽虎、戚戚然以至於死、此天民之遑遽者也。凡彼四聖者、生無一日之歡、死有萬世之名、名者、固非實之所取也、雖稱之弗知、雖賞之不知、與株塊無以異矣。桀藉累世之資、居南面之尊、智足以距羣下、威足以震海內、恣耳目之所娛、窮意慮之所爲、熙熙然以至於死、此天民之逸蕩者也。紂亦藉累世之資、居南面之尊、威無不行、志無不從、肆情於傾宮、縱欲於長夜、不以禮義自苦、熙熙然以至於誅、此天民之放縱者也。彼二凶也、生有從欲之歡、死被愚暴之名、實者固非名之所與也、雖毀之不知、雖稱之弗知、此與株塊奚以異矣。彼四聖、雖美之所歸、苦以至終、同歸於死矣、彼二凶、雖惡之所歸、樂以至終、亦同歸於死矣。

to the capacity, and far below the highest complacencies of human nature; but it is widely different from the reckless contempt of all which is esteemed good and great that defiles the pages where Yang is made to tell his views.

We are sometimes reminded by him of fragmentary utterances in the Book of Ecclesiastes.—'In much wisdom is much grief; and he that increaseth knowledge increaseth sorrow.' 'As it happeneth to the fool, so it happeneth even to me; and why was I then more wise? Then I said in my heart, that this also is vanity. For there is no remembrance of the wise more than of the fool for ever; seeing that which now is in the days to come shall all be forgotten. And how dieth the wise man? As the fool. Therefore I hated life; because the work that is wrought under the sun is grievous to me: for all is vanity and vexation of spirit.' 'There is a man whose labour is in wisdom, and in knowledge, and in equity....All his days are sorrows, and his travail grief; yea, his heart taketh not rest in the night:—this is also vanity. There is nothing better for a man than that he should eat and drink, and that he should make his soul enjoy good in his labour.' 'That which befalleth the sons of men befalleth beasts; even one thing befalleth them: as the one dieth, so dieth the other; yea, they have all one breath; so that a man hath no pre-eminence above a beast: for all is vanity. All go to one place; all are of the dust, and all turn to dust again.... Wherefore I perceive that there is nothing better than that a man should rejoice in his own works; for that is his portion: for who shall bring him to see what shall be after him?'

But those thoughts were suggestions of evil from which the Hebrew Preacher recoiled in his own mind; and he put them on record only that he might give their antidote along with them. He vanquished them by his faith in God; and so he ends by saying, 'Let us hear the conclusion of the whole matter:—Fear God, and keep His commandments: for this is the whole duty of man. For God shall bring every work into judgment, with every secret thing, whether it be good, or whether it be evil.' Yang Chû has no redeeming qualities. His reasonings contain no elements to counteract the poison that is in them. He never rises to the thought of God. There are, he allows, such ideas as those of propriety and righteousness, but the effect of them is merely to embitter and mar the enjoyment of life. Fame is but a phantom which only the fool will pursue. It is the same with all at death.

There their being ends. After that there is but so much putridity and rottenness. With him therefore the conclusion of the whole matter is:—'Let us eat and drink; let us live in pleasure; gratify the ears and eyes; get servants and maidens, music, beauty, wine; when the day is insufficient, carry it on through the night; EACH ONE FOR HIMSELF.'

Mencius might well say that if such 'licentious talk' were not arrested, the path of benevolence and righteousness would be stopped up. If Yang's principles had been entertained by the nation, every bond of society would have been dissolved. All the foundations of order would have been destroyed. Vice would have become rampant, and virtue would have been named only to be scorned. There would have remained for the entire State only what Yang saw in store for the individual man—'putridity and rottenness.' Doubtless it was owing to Mencius's opposition that the foul and dangerous current was stayed. He raised up against it the bulwark of human nature formed for virtue. He insisted on benevolence, righteousness, propriety, fidelity, as the noblest attributes of man's conduct. More was needed, but more he could not supply. If he had had a living faith in God, and had been in possession of His revealed will, the present state of China might have been very different. He was able to warn his countrymen of the gulf into which Yang Chû would have plunged them; but he could direct them in the way of truth and duty only imperfectly. He sent them into the dark cave of their own souls, and back to the vague lessons and imperfect examples of their sages; and China has staggered on, waxing feebler and feebler, to the present time. Her people need to be directed above themselves and beyond the present. When stars shine out to them in heaven and from eternity, the nation will perhaps renew its youth, and go forward from strength to strength.

SECTION II.

THE OPINIONS OF MO TÎ.

1. Very different from Yang Chû was Mo Tî. They stood at the opposite poles of human thought and sentiment; and we may wonder that Mencius should have offered the same stern opposition to the opinions of each of them. He did well to oppose the doctrine whose watchword was—'Each one for himself;' was he right in denouncing, as equally injurious, that which taught that the root of all social evils is to be traced to the want of mutual love?

It is allowed that Mo was a native and officer of the State of Sung; but the time when he lived is a matter of dispute. Sze-mâ Ch'ien says that some made him to be a contemporary of Confucius, and that others placed him later[1]. He was certainly later than Confucius, to whom he makes many references, not always complimentary, in his writings. In one of his Treatises, moreover, mention is made of Wăn-tsze[2], an acknowledged disciple of Tsze-hsiâ, so that he must have been very little anterior to Mencius. This is the impression also which I receive from the references to him in our philosopher.

In Liû Hsin's third catalogue the Mohist writers form a subdivision. Six of them are mentioned, including Mo himself to whom seventy-one *p'ien*, or Books, are attributed. So many were then current under his name; but eighteen of them have since been lost. He was an original thinker. He exercised a bolder, though not a more correct, judgment on things than Confucius or his followers. Antiquity was not so sacred to him, and he did not hesitate to condemn the literati—the orthodox—for several of their doctrines and practices.

Two of his peculiar views are adverted to by Mencius, and vehemently condemned. The one is about the regulation of funerals, where Mo contended that a spare simplicity should be the rule[3]. On that I need not dwell. The other is the doctrine

[1] 史記，七十四卷；孟子，荀卿，列傳第十四，at the end.
[2] 文子. [3] Bk. III. Pt. I. v.

孟子

of 'Universal Love[1].' A lengthy exposition of this remains in the Writings which go by Mo's name, though it is not from his own pen, but that of a disciple. Such as it is, with all its repetitions, I give a translation of it. My readers will be able, after perusing it, to go on with me to consider the treatment which the doctrine received at the hands of Mencius.

UNIVERSAL LOVE[1]. PART I.

It is the business of the sages to effect the good government of the world. They must know, therefore, whence disorder and confusion arise, for without this knowledge their object cannot be effected. We may compare them to a physician who undertakes to cure men's diseases :—he must ascertain whence a disease has arisen, and then he can assail it with effect, while, without such knowledge, his endeavours will be in vain. Why should we except the case of those who have to regulate disorder from this rule? They must know whence it has arisen, and then they can regulate it.

It is the business of the sages to effect the good government of the world. They must examine therefore into the cause of disorder; and when they do so they will find that it arises from the want of mutual love. When a minister and a son are not filial to their sovereign and their father, this is what is called disorder. A son loves himself, and does not love his father;—he therefore wrongs his father, and seeks his own advantage: a younger brother loves himself, and does not love his elder brother;—he therefore wrongs his elder brother, and seeks his own advantage: a minister loves himself, and does not love his sovereign;—he therefore wrongs his sovereign, and seeks his own advantage:—all these are cases of what is called disorder. Though it be the father who is not kind to his son, or the elder brother who is not kind to his younger brother, or the sovereign who is not gracious to his minister:—the case comes equally under the general name of disorder. The father loves himself, and does not love his son;—he therefore wrongs his son, and seeks his own advantage: the elder brother loves himself, and does not love his

聖人以治天下爲事者也必知亂之所自起焉、能治之。不知亂之所自起、則不能治。譬之如醫之攻人之疾者然、必知疾之所自起焉、能攻之。不知疾之所自起、則弗能攻。治亂者、何獨不然、必知亂之所自起焉、能治之。不知亂之所自起、則弗能治。聖人以治天下爲事者也、不可不察亂之所自起。當察亂何自起、起不相愛。臣子之不孝君父、所謂亂也。子自愛、不愛父、故虧父而自利、弟自愛、不愛兄、故虧兄而自利、臣自愛、不愛君、故虧君而自利、此所謂亂也。雖父之不慈子、兄之不慈弟、君之不慈臣、此亦天下之所謂亂也。父自愛也、不愛子、故虧子而自利、兄

[1] 兼愛,—兼 represents *a hand grasping two stalks of grain.* 兼愛 is 'a love that grasps or unites many in its embrace.' I do not know how to render it better than by 'universal love.' Mencius and the literati generally find the idea of equality in it also, and 兼愛 is with them = 'To love all equally.'

younger brother;—he therefore wrongs his younger brother, and seeks his own advantage: the sovereign loves himself, and does not love his minister;—he therefore wrongs his minister, and seeks his own advantage. How do these things come to pass? They all arise from the want of mutual love. Take the case of any thief or robber:—it is just the same with him. The thief loves his own house, and does not love his neighbour's house;—he therefore steals from his neighbour's house to benefit his own: the robber loves his own person, and does not love his neighbour;—he therefore does violence to his neighbour to benefit himself. How is this? It all arises from the want of mutual love. Come to the case of great officers throwing each other's Families into confusion, and of princes attacking one another's States:—it is just the same with them. The great officer loves his own Family, and does not love his neighbour's;—he therefore throws his neighbour's Family into disorder to benefit his own: the prince loves his own State, and does not love his neighbour's;—he therefore attacks his neighbour's State to benefit his own. All disorder in the kingdom has the same explanation. When we examine into the cause of it, it is found to be the want of mutual love.

Suppose that universal, mutual love prevailed throughout the kingdom;—if men loved others as they love themselves, disliking to exhibit what was unfilial . . . .[1] And moreover would there be those who were unkind? Looking on their sons, younger brothers, and ministers as themselves, and disliking to exhibit what was unkind . . . . the want of filial duty would disappear. And would there be thieves and robbers? When every man regarded his neighbour's house as his own, who would be found to steal? When every one regarded his neighbour's person as his own, who would be found to rob? Thieves and robbers would disappear. And would there be great officers throwing one another's Families into confusion, and princes attacking one another's States? When officers regarded the Families of others as their own, what one would make confusion? When princes regarded other States as their own, what one would begin an attack? Great officers throwing one another's Families into confusion, and princes attacking one another's States, would disappear.

If, indeed, universal, mutual love prevailed throughout the kingdom; one State not attacking another, and one Family not throwing another into confusion; thieves and robbers nowhere existing; rulers and ministers, fathers and sons, all being filial and kind:—in such a condition

自愛也、不愛弟、故虧弟而自利、君自愛也、不愛臣、故虧臣而自利、是何也、皆起不相愛、雖至天下之爲盜賊者、亦然、盜愛其室、不愛其異室、故竊異室以利其室、賊愛其身、不愛人、故賊人以利其身、此何也、皆起不相愛、雖至大夫之相亂家、諸侯之相攻國者、亦然、大夫各愛家、不愛異家、故亂異家以利家、諸侯各愛其國、不愛異國、故攻異國以利其國、天下之亂物、具此而已矣、察此何自起、皆起不相愛、

若使天下兼相愛、愛人若愛其身、惡施不孝、猶有不慈者乎、視子弟與臣若其身、惡施不慈、不孝亡有、猶有盜賊乎、故視人之室若其室、誰竊、視人身若其身、誰賊、故盜賊亡有、猶有大夫之相亂家、諸侯之相攻國者乎、視人家若其家、誰亂、視人國若其國、誰攻、故大夫之相亂家、諸侯之相攻國者、亡有、

若使天下兼相愛、國與國不相攻、家與家不相亂、盜賊無有、君臣父子、皆能孝慈、若此則天下

[1] There are evidently some omissions and confusion here in the Chinese text.

the nation would be well governed. On this account, how may sages, whose business it is to effect the good government of the kingdom, do but prohibit hatred and advise to love? On this account it is affirmed that universal mutual love throughout the country will lead to its happy order, and that mutual hatred leads to confusion. This was what our master, the philosopher Mo, meant, when he said, 'We must above all inculcate the love of others.'

治。故聖人以治天下爲事者、惡得不禁惡而勸愛、故天下兼相愛則治、相惡則亂、故子墨子曰、不可以不勸愛人者此也。

UNIVERSAL LOVE. PART II.

Our Master, the philosopher Mo, said, 'That which benevolent men consider to be incumbent on them as their business, is to stimulate and promote all that will be advantageous to the nation, and to take away all that is injurious to it. This is what they consider to be their business.'

And what are the things advantageous to the nation, and the things injurious to it? Our master said, 'The mutual attacks of State on State; the mutual usurpations of Family on Family; the mutual robberies of man on man; the want of kindness on the part of the ruler and of loyalty on the part of the minister; the want of tenderness and filial duty between father and son and of harmony between brothers:—these, and such as these, are the things injurious to the kingdom.'

And from what do we find, on examination, that these injurious things are produced[1]? Is it not from the want of mutual love?

Our Master said, 'Yes, they are produced by the want of mutual love. Here is a prince who only knows to love his own State, and does not love his neighbour's;—he therefore does not shrink from raising all the power of his State to attack his neighbour. Here is the chief of a Family who only knows to love it, and does not love his neighbour's;—he therefore does not shrink from raising all his powers to seize on that other Family. Here is a man who only knows to love his own person, and does not love his neighbour's;—he therefore does not shrink from using all his resources to rob his neighbour. Thus it happens, that the princes, not loving one another, have their battle-fields; and the chiefs of Families, not loving one another, have their mutual

子墨子言曰、仁人之所以爲事者、必興天下之利、除去天下之害、以此爲事者也。○然則天下之利何也、天下之害何也。○子墨子言曰、今若國之與國之相攻、家之與家之相篡、人之與人之相賊、君臣不惠忠、父子不慈孝、兄弟不和調、此則天下之害也。○然則崇此害、亦何用生哉。以不相愛生耶。○子墨子言以不相愛生、今諸侯獨知愛其國、不愛人之國、是以不憚舉其國以攻人之國。今家主獨知愛其家、而不愛人之家、是以不憚舉其家以篡人之家。今人獨知愛其身、不愛人之身、是以不憚舉其身以賊人之身。是故諸侯不相愛、則必野戰、家主不相愛、則必相篡、人與人不相愛、則必相賊、君臣不相愛、

[1] Here I would read, in the Chinese text, 察 for 崇 and 由 for 用.—然則察此害亦何由生哉. The translation is accordingly.

usurpations; and men, not loving one another, have their mutual robberies; and rulers and ministers, not loving one another, become unkind and disloyal; and fathers and sons, not loving one another, lose their affection and filial duty; and brothers, not loving one another, contract irreconcileable enmities. Yea, men in general not loving one another, the strong make prey of the weak; the rich do despite to the poor; the noble are insolent to the mean; and the deceitful impose upon the stupid. All the miseries, usurpations, enmities, and hatreds in the world, when traced to their origin, will be found to arise from the want of mutual love. On this account, the benevolent condemn it.'

They may condemn it; but how shall they change it?

Our Master said, 'They may change it by the law of universal mutual love and by the interchange of mutual benefits.'

How will this law of universal mutual love and the interchange of mutual benefits accomplish this?

Our Master said, '*It would lead* to the regarding another's kingdom as one's own: another's family as one's own: another's person as one's own. That being the case, the princes, loving one another, would have no battle-fields; the chiefs of families, loving one another, would attempt no usurpations; men, loving one another, would commit no robberies [1]; rulers and ministers, loving one another, would be gracious and loyal; fathers and sons, loving one another, would be kind and filial; brothers, loving one another, would be harmonious and easily reconciled. Yea, men in general loving one another, the strong would not make prey of the weak; the many would not plunder the few; the rich would not insult the poor; the noble would not be insolent to the mean; and the deceitful would not impose upon the simple. The way in which all the miseries,

則不惠忠、父子不相愛、則不慈孝、兄弟不相愛、則不和調、天下之人、皆不相愛、强必執弱、富必侮貧、貴必敖賤、詐必欺愚、凡天下禍篡怨恨、其所以起者、以不相愛生也、是以仁者非之。既以非之、何以易之。○子墨子言曰、以兼相愛交相利之法易之。○然則兼相愛交相利之法、將柰何哉。○子墨子言、視人之國、若視其國、視人之家、若視其家、視人之身、若視其身、是故諸侯相愛、則[1]不野戰、家主相愛、則不相篡、人與人相愛、則不相賊、貴不敖賤、詐不欺愚、凡天下禍篡怨恨、可使毋起者、以仁者譽之、然而今天下之士、君臣相愛則惠忠、父子相愛則慈孝、兄弟相愛則和調、天下之人、皆相愛、强不執弱、衆不劫寡、富不侮貧、子墨子言曰、然乃若兼則善矣、雖然天下之難物於故也。

[1] The Chinese text is here very confused for several sentences. There are evidently transpositions, omissions, and additions. I have ventured to correct and arrange it as follows:—After 不相賊, I read, 君臣相愛、則惠忠、父子相愛、則慈孝、兄弟相愛、則和調、天下之人皆相愛、强不執弱、衆不劫寡、富不侮貧、貴不敖賤、詐不欺愚、凡天下禍篡怨恨、可使毋起者、以兼相愛生也、是以仁者譽之。○然而今天下之士、君子、曰、然乃若兼、則善矣、雖然、天下之難物也。○子墨子言曰、天下之士、君子、特不識其利辯之故也、今若云云。

usurpations, enmities, and hatreds in the world, may be made not to arise, is universal mutual love. On this account, the benevolent value and praise it.'

Yes; but the scholars of the kingdom and superior men say, 'True; if there were this universal love, it would be good. It is, however, the most difficult thing in the world.'

Our Master said, 'This is because the scholars and superior men simply do not understand the advantageousness *of the law*, and to conduct their reasonings upon that. Take the case of assaulting a city, or of a battle-field, or of the sacrificing one's life for the sake of fame:—this is felt by the people everywhere to be a difficult thing. Yet, if the ruler be pleased with it, both officers and people are able to do it:—how much more might they attain to universal mutual love, and the interchange of mutual benefits, which is different from this! When a man loves others, they respond to and love him; when a man benefits others, they respond to and benefit him; when a man injures others, they respond to and injure him; when a man hates others, they respond to and hate him:—what difficulty is there in the matter? It is only that rulers will not carry on the government on this principle, and so officers do not carry it out in their practice.

'Formerly, the duke Wăn of Tsin liked his officers to be coarsely dressed, and, therefore, they all wore rams' furs, a leathern swordbelt, and a cap of bleached cotton. Thus attired, they went in to the prince's levee, and came out and walked through the court. Why did they do this? The sovereign liked it, and therefore the ministers did it. The duke Ling of Ch'û liked his officers to have small waists, and, therefore, they all limited themselves to a single meal. They held in their breath in putting on their belts, and had to help themselves up by means of the wall. In the course of a year, they looked black, and as if they would die of starvation. Why did they do this[1]? The sovereign liked it, and, therefore, the ministers were able to do it. Kâu-chi'en, the king of Yüeh, liked his ministers to be brave, and taught them to be accustomed to be so. At a general assembly of them, he set on fire the ship where they were, and to try them, said, "All the precious things of Yüeh are here." He then with his own hands beat a drum, and urged them on. When they heard the drum thundering, they rushed confusedly about, and trampled in the fire, till more than a hundred of them perished, when he struck the gong, and called them back[2].

子墨子言曰、天下之士君子、特不識其利、辯其故也、今若夫攻城野戰、殺身爲名、此天下百姓之所皆難也、苟君說之、則士衆能爲之、況於兼相愛交相利、則與此異。夫愛人者、人必從而愛之、利人者、人必從而利之、惡人者、人必從而惡之、害人者、人必從而害之、此何難之有、特上弗以爲政、士不以爲行故也。

昔者晉文公好士之惡衣、故文公之臣、皆牂羊之裘、韋以帶劍、練帛之冠、入以見於君、出以踐朝、是其故何也、君說之、故臣爲之也。昔者楚靈王好士細要、靈王之臣、皆以一飯爲節、脇息然後帶、扶牆然後起、比期年、朝有黧黑之危、是其故何也、君說之、故臣能之也。昔越王句踐好士之勇、教馴其臣、和合之、焚舟失火、試其士曰、越

[1] In 是其故是也, the second 是 is plainly a misprint for 何. [2] Here a sentence or two are wanting, to complete the paragraph in harmony with the two which precede. The characters which follow—長故子墨子言曰—should also be expunged. I have omitted them in the translation.

'Now, little food, bad clothes, and the sacrifice of life for the sake of fame;—these are what it is difficult for people to approve of. Yet, when the sovereign was pleased with it, they were all able, *in those cases*, to bring themselves to them. How much more could they attain to universal mutual love, and the interchange of mutual benefits, which is different from such things! When a man loves others, they respond to and love him; when a man benefits others, they respond to and benefit him; when a man hates others, they respond to and hate him; when a man injures others, they respond to and injure him. It is only that rulers will not carry on their government on this principle, and, so, officers do not carry it out in their practice.'

Yes; but now the officers and superior men say, 'Granted; the universal practice of mutual love would be good; but it is an impracticable thing. It is like taking up the T'âi mountain, and leaping with it over the Ho or the Chî.'

Our Master said, 'That is not the proper comparison for it. To take up the T'âi mountain, and leap with it over the Ho or the Chî, may be called an exercise of most extraordinary strength; it is, in fact, what no one, from antiquity to the present time, has ever been able to do. But how widely different from this is the practice of universal mutual love, and the interchange of mutual benefits!

'Anciently, the sage kings practised this. How do we know that they did so? When Yü reduced all the country to order:—in the west, he made the western Ho and the Yü-tâu, to carry off the waters of Ch'ü-sun-wang; in the north, he made the Fang-yüan, the Pâi-chû, Hâu-chih-tî, and the Tâu of Fû-t'o; setting up also the Tî-ch'û, and chiselling out the Lung-măn, to benefit Yen, Tâi, Hû, Mo, and the people of the western Ho; in the east, he drained the waters to Lû-fang and the marsh of Măng-chû, reducing them to nine channels, to limit the waters of the eastern country, and benefit the people of Ch'î-châu; and in the south, he made the Chiang, the Han, the Hwâi, the *Zû*, the course of the eastern current, and the five lakes, to benefit Ching, Ch'û, and Yüeh, the people of the wild south. These were the doings of Yü; and I am now for practising the *same* universal *mutual love*.

'When king Wăn brought the western country to good order, his light spread, like the sun

國之寶、盡在此、越王親自鼓其士而進之、士聞鼓音破碎、亂行蹈火、而死者、左右百人有餘、越王擊金而退之、是故子墨子言曰、乃若夫少食惡衣殺身而爲名、此天下百姓之所皆難也、若苟君說之、則衆能爲之、況兼相愛交相利、與此異矣。夫愛人者、人亦從而愛之、利人者人亦從而利之、惡人者人亦從而惡之、而害人者人亦從而害之、此何難之有焉、特上不以爲政、而士不以爲行故也、

然而今天下之士君子曰、然乃若兼則善矣、雖然、不可行之物也、譬若挈太山越河濟也。○子墨子言、是非其譬也、夫挈太山而越河濟、可謂畢劫有力矣、自古及今、未有能行之者也、況乎兼相愛交相利、則與此異。古者聖王行之。何以知其然。古者禹治天下、西爲西河漁竇、以泄渠孫皇之水、北爲防原派注、后之邸、嘑池之竇、洒爲底柱、鑿爲龍門、以利燕代胡貉與西河之民、東方漏之陸、防孟諸之澤、灑爲九澮、以楗東土之水、以利冀州之民、南爲江漢淮汝、東流之注、五湖之處、以利荊楚于越、南夷之民、此言禹之事、吾

or the moon, over its four quarters. He did not permit great States to insult small ones; he did not permit the multitude to oppress the fatherless and the widow; he did not permit violence and power to take from the husbandmen their millet, pannicled millet, dogs, and swine. Heaven, as if constrained, visited king Wăn with blessing. The old and childless were enabled to complete their years; the solitary and brotherless could yet mingle among the living; the young and parentless found those on whom they could depend, and grew up. These were the doings of king Wăn; and I am now for practising the same universal *mutual love*.

'King Wû tunneled through the T'âi mountain. The Record says, "There is a way through the mountain, made by me, the descendant of the kings of Châu:—I have accomplished this great work. I have got my virtuous men, and rise up full of reverence for Shang, Hsiâ, and the tribes of the south, the east, and the north. Though he has his multitudes of relatives, they are not equal to my virtuous men. If guilt attach to the people anywhere throughout the kingdom, it is to be required of me, the One man."' This describes the doings of king Wû, and I am now for practising the *same* universal mutual love[1].

If, now, the rulers of the kingdom truly and sincerely wish all in it to be rich, and dislike any being poor; if they desire its good government, and dislike disorder; they ought to practise universal mutual love, and the interchange of mutual benefits. This was the law of the sage kings; it is the way to effect the good government of the nation; it may not but be striven after.

今行兼矣。昔者文王之治西土、若日若月、乍光于四方、于西土、不爲大國侮小國、不爲衆庶侮鰥寡、不爲暴勢奪穡人黍稷狗彘、天屑臨文王慈、是以老而無子者、有所得終其壽、連獨無兄弟者、有所雜於生人之閒、少失其父母者、有所放依而長、此文王之事、則吾今行兼矣。昔者武王將事泰山隧、傳曰、泰山、有道、曾孫周王、有事大事、既獲仁人、尚作以祗商夏、蠻夷醜貉、雖有周親、不若仁人、萬方有罪、維予一人、此言武王之事、吾今行兼矣。是故子墨子言曰、今天下之君子、忠實欲天下之富、而惡其貧、欲天下之治、而惡其亂、當兼相愛、交相利、此聖王之法、天下之治道也、不可不務爲也。

[1] I do not recollect to have read elsewhere of king Wû's tunneling through the T'âi mountain. In what Mo quotes from some Record, we have sentences from different parts of the Shû-ching brought together. The account of the labours of Yü contains names also not elsewhere found. There are, no doubt, many errors in the text.—I omit the 是故子墨子言曰, which follow 行兼矣.

UNIVERSAL LOVE. PART III.

Our Master, the philosopher Mo, said, 'The business of benevolent men requires that they should strive to stimulate and promote what is advantageous to the kingdom, and to take away what is injurious to it.'

Speaking, now, of the present time, what are to be accounted the most injurious things to the kingdom [1]? They are such as the attacking of small States by great ones; the inroads on small Families by great ones; the plunder of the weak by the strong; the oppression of the few by the many; the scheming of the crafty against the simple; the insolence of the noble to the mean. To the same class belong the ungraciousness of rulers [2], and the disloyalty of ministers; the unkindness of fathers, and the want of filial duty on the part of sons. Yea, there is to be added to these the conduct of the mean men [3], who employ their edged weapons and poisoned stuff, water and fire, to rob and injure one another.

Pushing on the inquiry now, let us ask whence all these injurious things arise. Is it from loving others and advantaging others? It must be answered 'No;' and it must likewise be said, 'They arise clearly [4] from hating others and doing violence to others.' If *it be further asked* whether those who hate and do violence to others hold the principle of loving all, or that of making distinctions, it must be replied, 'They make distinctions.' So then, it is this principle of making distinctions between man and man, which gives rise to all that is most injurious in the kingdom. On this account we conclude that that principle is wrong.

Our Master said, 'He who condemns others must have whereby to change them.' To condemn men, and have no means of changing them, is like saving them from fire by plunging them in water. A man's language in such a case must be improper. On this account our Master said, 'There is the principle of loving all, to take the place of that which makes distinctions.'

子墨子言曰、仁人之事者、必務求興天下之利、除天下之害。○然當今之時、天下之害孰爲大。○曰、若大國之攻小國也、大家之亂小家也、强之刦弱、衆之暴寡、詐之謀愚、貴之敖賤、此天下之害也。人與爲人君者之不惠也、臣者之不忠也、父者之不慈也、子者之不孝也、此又天下之害也。又與今人之賤人、執其兵刃毒藥水火、以交相虧賊、此又天下之害也。姑嘗本原若衆害之所自、此胡自生、此自愛人利人生與、即必曰非然也、必曰從惡人賊人生分名乎、天下惡人而賊人者、兼與別與、即必曰別也、然即之交別者、果生天下之大害者與、是故別非也。

子墨子曰、非人者必有以易之、若非人、而無以易之、譬之猶以水救火也、其說將必無可焉。○是故子墨子曰、兼以易

[1] I suppose that the compiler—the disciple of Mo—begins to speak here. Throughout this part, however, the changes in the argument are indistinctly marked. [2] 人與 should here be expunged from the Chinese text. [3] 又與 should here be expunged. [4] I translate 分名 by 'clearly.' 名 is probably a misprint for 明.

孟子

If, now, we ask, 'And how is it that universal love can change *the consequences of* that other principle which makes distinctions?' the answer is, 'If princes were as much for the States of others as for their own, what one among them would raise the forces of his State to attack that of another?—he is for that other as much as for himself. If they were for the capitals of others as much as for their own, what one would raise the forces of his capital to attack that of another?—he is for that as much as for his own. If chiefs regarded the Families of others as their own, what one would lead the power of his Family to throw that of another into confusion?—he is for that other as much as for himself. If, now, States did not attack, nor holders of capitals smite, one another, and if Families were guilty of no mutual aggressions, would this be injurious to the kingdom, or its benefit?' It must be replied, 'This would be advantageous to the kingdom.' Pushing on the inquiry, now, let us ask whence all these benefits arise. Is it from hating others and doing violence to others? It must be answered, 'No;' and it must likewise be said, 'They arise clearly from loving others and doing good to others.' *If it be further asked* whether those who love others and do good to others hold the principle of making distinctions between man and man, or that of loving all, it must be replied, 'They love all.' So then it is this principle of universal mutual love which really gives rise to all that is most beneficial to the nation. On this account we conclude that that principle is right[1].

Our Master said, a little while ago, 'The business of benevolent men requires that they should strive to stimulate and promote what is advantageous to the kingdom, and to take away what is injurious to it.' We have now traced the subject up, and found that it is the principle of universal love which produces all that is most beneficial to the kingdom, and the principle of making distinctions which produces all that is injurious to it. On this account what our

別。○然卽兼之可以易別之故、何也。○曰、藉爲人之國、若爲其國、夫誰獨舉其國以攻人之國者哉、爲彼者由爲已也、爲人之都、若爲其都、夫誰獨舉其都以伐人之都者哉、爲彼猶爲已也、爲人之家、若爲其家、夫誰獨舉其家以亂人之家者哉、爲彼猶爲已也、然卽國都不相攻伐、人家不相亂賊、此天下之害與、天下之利與、卽必曰天下之利也、姑嘗本原、若衆利之所自生、此胡自生、此自惡人賊人生與、卽必曰非然也、必曰從愛人利人生、分名乎。天下愛人而利人者、別與兼與、卽必曰兼也、然卽之交兼者、果生天下之大利者與、是故子墨子曰、兼是也。

且鄉吾本言曰、仁人之事者、必務求興天下之利、除天下之害。○今吾本原兼之所生天下之大利者、吾本原別之所

[1] I here transpose 子墨子曰, and put it after 兼是也. This is required by the preceding argument, which ends simply with 是故別非也. With this transposition, however, some other liberties must still be taken with the next paragraph. In 仁人之是者, 是 should evidently be 事. In the concluding phrase—出乎若方—the adoption of an old gloss, that 乎 should be 平, enables us to make sense of it. What follows, from 今吾將 down to 卽若其利, is confused and difficult. 與, in 與天下之利, is a misprint for 興; but there must be other corruptions and omissions as well. One can see the author's drift; and I have tried to translate accordingly.

Master said, 'The principle of making distinctions between man and man is wrong, and the principle of universal love is right,' turns out to be correct as the sides of a square.

If, now, we just desire to promote the benefit of the kingdom, and select for that purpose the principle of universal love, then the acute ears and piercing eyes of people will hear and see for one another; and the strong limbs of people will move and be ruled for one another; and men of principle will instruct one another. It will come about that the old, who have neither wife nor children, will get supporters who will enable them to complete their years; and the young and weak, who have no parents, will yet find helpers that shall bring them up. On the contrary, if this principle of universal love is held not to be correct, what benefits will arise from such a view? What can be the reason that the scholars of the kingdom, whenever they hear of this principle of universal love, go on to condemn it? Plain as the case is, their words in condemnation of this principle do not stop;—they say, 'It may be good, but how can it be carried into practice?'

Our Master said, 'Supposing that it could not be practised, it seems hard to go on likewise to condemn it. But how can it be good, and yet incapable of being put into practice?'

Let us bring forward two instances to test the matter:—Let any one suppose the case of two individuals, the one of whom shall hold the principle of making distinctions, and the other shall hold the principle of universal love. The former of these will say, 'How can I be for the person of my friend as much as for my own person? how can I be for the parents of my friend as much as for my own parents?' Reasoning in this way, he may see his friend hungry, but he will not feed him; cold, but he will not clothe him; sick, but he will not nurse him; dead, but he will not bury him. Such will be the language of the individual holding the principle of distinction, and such will be his conduct. The language of the other, holding the principle of universality, will be different, and also his conduct. He will say, 'I have heard that he who wishes to play a lofty part among men, will be for the person of his friend as much as for his own person, and for the parents of his friend as much as for his own parents. It is only thus that he can attain his distinction?' Reasoning in this way, when he sees his friend hungry, he will feed him; cold, he will clothe him; sick, he will nurse him; dead, he will bury him. Such will be the language of him who holds the principle of universal love, and such will be his conduct.

生、天下之大害者也。是故子墨子曰、別非而兼是者、出乎若方也。今吾將正求興天下之利、而取之以兼爲正、是故以聰耳明目相爲視聽乎、是以股肱畢强、相爲動宰乎、而有道肆相教誨、是以老而無妻子者、有所侍養以終其壽、幼弱孤童之無父母者、有所放依以長其身。今唯毋以兼爲正、即若其利也。不識天下之士、所以皆聞兼而非者、其故何也。〇然而天下之士、非兼者之言猶未止也、曰、即善矣、雖然、豈可用哉。

子墨子曰、用而不可、雖哉、亦將非之、且焉有善而不可用者。〇姑嘗兩而進之、誰以爲二士、使其一士者執別、使其一士者執兼、是故別士之言曰、吾豈能爲吾友之身、若爲吾身、爲吾友之親、若爲吾親、是故退睹其友、飢即不食、寒即不衣、疾病不侍養、死喪不葬埋、別士之言若此、行若此、兼士之言不然、行亦不然、曰、吾聞爲高士於天下者、必爲其友之身、若爲其身、爲其友之親、若爲其親、然後可以爲高士天下、是故退睹其友、飢則食之、寒則衣

The words of the one of these individuals are a condemnation of those of the other, and their conduct is directly contrary. Suppose now that their words are perfectly sincere, and that their conduct will be carried out,—that their words and actions will correspond like the parts of a token, every word being carried into effect; and let us proceed to put the following questions on the case:—Here is a plain in the open country, and an officer, with coat of mail, gorget, and helmet, is about to take part in a battle to be fought in it, where the issue, whether for life or death, cannot be foreknown; or here is an officer about to be dispatched on a distant commission from Pâ to Yüeh, or from Ch'î to Ching, where the issue of the journey, going and coming, is quite uncertain:—on either of these suppositions, to whom will the officer entrust the charge of his house, the support of his parents, and the care of his wife and children?—to one who holds the principle of universal love? or to one who holds that which makes distinctions? I apprehend there is no one under heaven, man or woman, however stupid, though he may condemn the principle of universal love, but would at such a time make one who holds it the subject of his trust. This is in words to condemn the principle, and when there is occasion to choose between it and the opposite, to approve it;—words and conduct are here in contradiction. I do not know how it is that throughout the kingdom scholars condemn the principle of universal love, whenever they hear it[1].

Plain as the case is, their words in condemnation of it do not cease, but they say, 'This principle may suffice perhaps to guide in the choice of an officer, but it will not guide in the choice of a sovereign[2].'

Let us test this by taking two illustrations:—Let any one suppose the case of two sovereigns, the one of whom shall hold the principle of mutual love, and the other shall hold the principle which makes distinctions. In this case, the latter of them will say, 'How can I be as much for the persons of all my people as for my own? This is much opposed to human feelings. The life of man upon the earth is but a very brief space; it may be compared to the rapid

之、疾病侍養之、死喪葬埋之、兼士之言若此、行若此。若之二者、言相非而行相反與、當使若二士者、言必信、行必果、使言行之合猶合符節也、無言而不行也、然即敢問、今有平原廣野於此、被甲嬰冑將往戰、死生之權未可識也。又有君大夫之遠使於巴越齊荆、往來及否未及否、未可識也、然即敢問、不識將惡也家室、奉承親戚、提挈妻子、而寄託之、不識於兼之有是乎、於別之有是乎。哉以爲當其於此也、天下無愚夫愚婦、雖非兼之人、必寄託之於兼之有是也。此言而非兼、擇即取兼、即此言行拂也。不識天下之士所以皆聞兼而非之者、其故何也。〇然而天下之士、非兼者之言、猶未止也、曰、意可以擇士、而不可以擇君。

子姑嘗兩而進之、誰以爲二君、使其一君者執兼、使一君者執別、是故別君之言、吾惡能爲吾萬民之身爲吾身、此泰非天下之情也、

[1] From 子墨子曰、用而不可 down to this, the general meaning is plain enough. But there must be several corruptions in the text. 哉, for instance, after 別之有是乎, is, plainly, for 我. [2] Here there should follow, 'Our Master said,' and some observations introductory to the two illustrations of the sovereigns. This has been lost, however, and all that remains of it is the solitary 子, in 子姑嘗云云.

movement of a team of horses whirling past a small chink.' Reasoning in this way, he may see his people hungry, but he will not feed them; cold, but he will not clothe them; sick, but he will not nurse them; dead, but he will not bury them. Such will be the language of the sovereign who holds the principle of distinctions, and such will be his conduct. Different will be the language and conduct of the other who holds the principle of universal love. He will say, 'I have heard that he who would show himself a *virtuous and* intelligent sovereign, ought to make his people the first consideration, and think of himself only after them.' Reasoning in this way, when he sees any of the people hungry, he will feed them; cold, he will clothe them; sick, he will nurse them; dead, he will bury them. Such will be the language of the sovereign who holds the principle of universal love, and such his conduct. If we compare the two sovereigns, the words of the one are condemnatory of those of the other, and their actions are opposite. Let us suppose that their words are equally sincere, and that their actions will make them good,—that their words and actions will correspond like the parts of a token, every word being carried into effect; and let us proceed to put the following questions on the case:—Here is a year when a pestilence walks abroad among the people; many of them suffer from cold and famine; multitudes die in the ditches and water-channels. If at such a time they might make an election between the two sovereigns whom we have supposed, which would they prefer? I apprehend there is no one under heaven, however stupid, though he may condemn the principle of universal love, but would at such a time prefer to be under the sovereign who holds it. This is in words to condemn the principle, and, when there is occasion to choose between it and the opposite, to approve it;—words and conduct are here in contradiction. I do not know how it is that throughout the kingdom scholars condemn the principle of universal love, whenever they hear it.

Plain as the case is, their words in condemnation of it do not cease; but they say, 'This universal *mutual love* is benevolent and righteous. That we grant, but how can it be practised? The impracticability of it is like that of taking up the T'âi mountain, and leaping with it over the Chiang or the Ho. We do, indeed, desire this universal love, but it is an impracticable thing!'

Our Master said, 'To take up the T'âi mountain, and leap with it over the Chiang or the

人之生乎地上之無幾何也。譬之猶駟馳而過郤也。是故退睹其萬民、飢即不食、寒即不衣、疾病不侍養、死喪不葬埋。別君之言若此、行若此。兼君之言不然、行亦不然。曰、吾聞爲明君於天下者、必先萬民之身、後爲其身、然後可以爲明君於天下。是故退睹其萬民、飢即食之、寒即衣之、疾病侍養之、死喪葬埋之。兼君之言若此、行若此。然即交若之二君者、言相非而行相反與。常使若二君者、言必信、行必果、使言行之合猶合符節也、無言而不行也。然即敢問、今歲有癘疫、萬民多有勤苦凍餒、轉死溝壑中者、既已衆矣。不識將擇之二君者、將何從也。我以爲當其於此也、天下無愚夫愚婦、雖非兼者、必從兼君是也。言而非兼、擇即取兼、此言行拂也。不識天下所以皆聞兼而非之者、其故何也。○然而天下之士、非兼者之言也、猶未止也。曰、兼即仁矣義矣、雖然、豈可爲哉。吾譬兼之不可爲也、猶挈泰山以超江河也。故兼者直願之也、夫豈可爲之物哉。子墨子曰、夫挈泰山以超江河、自古之及今、生民而

孟子

Ho, is a thing which never has been done, from the highest antiquity to the present time, since men were; but the exercise of mutual love and the interchange of mutual benefits,—this was practised by the ancient sages and six kings.'

How do you know that the ancient sages and the six kings practised this?

Our Master said, 'I was not of the same age and time with them, so that I could myself have heard their voices, or seen their faces; but I know what I say from what they have transmitted to posterity, written on bamboo or cloth, cut in metal or stone, or engraven on their vessels.'

'It is said in "The Great Declaration,"—"King Wăn was like the sun or like the moon; suddenly did his brightness shine through the four quarters of the western region[1]."

'According to these words, king Wăn exercised the principle of universal love on a vast scale. He is compared to the sun or moon which shines on all, without partial favour to any spot under the heavens;—such was the universal love of king Wăn.' What our Master insisted on was thus exemplified in him.

'Again, not only does "The Great Declaration" speak thus;—we find the same thing in "The Declaration of Yü." Yü said, "Ye multitudes, listen all to my words. It is not only I who dare to say a word in favour of war;—against this stupid prince of Miâo we must execute the punishment appointed by Heaven. I am therefore leading your hosts, and go before you all to punish the prince of Miâo[2]."

'Thus Yü punished the prince of Miâo, not to increase his own riches and nobility, nor to obtain happiness and emolument, nor to gratify his ears and eyes;—he did it, seeking to promote what was advantageous to the kingdom, and to take away what was injurious to it. It appears from this, that Yü held the principle of universal love.' What our Master insisted on may be found in him.

'And not only may Yü thus be appealed to;—we have "The words of T'ang" to the same effect. T'ang said, "I, the child Lî, presume to use a dark-coloured victim, and announce to Thee, O supreme Heavenly Sovereign:—Now there is a great drought, and it is right I should

來、未嘗有也、今若夫兼相愛、交相利、此自先聖六王者、親行之。○何知先聖六王之親行之也。○子墨子曰、吾非與之並世同時、親聞其聲、見其色也、以其所書於竹帛、鏤於金石、琢於槃盂、傳遺後世子孫者知之。泰誓曰、文王若日若月、乍照光於四方於西土。即此言、文王之兼愛天下之博大也、譬之日月兼照、天下之無有私也。○即此文王兼也、雖子墨子之所謂兼者、於文王取法焉。○且不惟泰誓爲然、雖禹誓即亦猶是也。禹曰、濟濟有衆、咸聽朕言、非惟小子、敢行稱亂、蠢茲有苗、用天之罰、若予既率爾羣對諸羣以征有苗。禹之征有苗也、非以求以重富貴、干福祿、樂耳目也、以求興天下之利、除天下之害。○即此禹兼也、雖子墨子之所謂兼者、於禹求焉。○且不惟禹誓爲然、雖湯說即亦猶是也。湯曰、惟予小子履、敢用元牡、告於上天后、曰、今天大旱、即當朕身履、未知得罪于上下、有善不敢蔽、有罪不敢赦、簡在帝心、萬方有罪、即當朕

[1] See 'The Great Declaration,' III. 6. The language is somewhat different from the citation.

[2] 'The Declaration of Yü' is what is called 'The Counsels of Yü.' In the twentieth paragraph we find the passage here quoted, or rather we find something like it.

be held responsible for it. I do not know but that I have offended against the Powers above and below. But the good I dare not keep in obscurity, and the sinner I dare not pardon. The examination of this is with Thy mind, O God. If the people throughout the kingdom commit offences, it is to be required of me. If I commit offences, it does not concern the people[1]." From these words we perceive that T'ang, possessing the dignity of sovereign, and the wealth of the kingdom, did not shrink from offering himself as a sacrifice which might be acceptable to God and *other* spiritual beings.' It appears from this that T'ang held the principle of universal love. What our Master insisted on was exemplified in T'ang.

And not only may we appeal in this way to the 'Declarations,' 'Charges,' and 'Words of T'ang,'—we find the same thing in 'The Poems of Châu[2].' One of those poems says,

'Wide and long is the Royal way,
Without deflection, without injustice.
The Royal way is plain and level,
Without injustice, without deflection.
It is straight as an arrow,
It is smooth as a whetstone.
The officers tread it;
The lower people see it.'

Is not this speaking of the *Royal* way in accordance with our style[3]? Anciently, Wăn and Wû, acting with exact justice and impartiality, rewarded the worthy and punished the oppressive, allowing no favouritism to influence them towards their own relatives. It appears from this that Wăn and Wû held the principle of universal love. What our Master insisted on was exemplified in them.—How is it that the scholars throughout the kingdom condemn this universal love, whenever they hear of it? Plain as the case is, the words of those who condemn the principle of universal love do not cease. They say, 'It is not advantageous to the entire devotion to parents which is required;—it is injurious to filial piety[4].' Our Master said, 'Let us bring this objection to the test:—A filial son, having *the happiness of* his parents at heart, considers how it is to be secured. Now, does he, so considering, wish men to love and benefit his parents? or does he wish them to hate and injure his parents?' On this view of the question, it must be evident that he wishes men to love and benefit his parents. And what

身、朕身有罪、無及萬方。卽此言、湯貴
爲天子、富有天下、然且不憚以身爲
犧牲、以祠說于上帝鬼神。○卽此、湯
兼也、雖子墨子之所謂兼者、於湯取
法焉。○且不惟誓、命、與湯說、爲然、周
詩卽亦猶是也。周詩曰、王道蕩蕩、不
偏不黨、王道平平、不黨不偏、其直若
矢、其易若底、君子之所履、小人之所
視。若吾言非語道之謂也、古者文武
爲正均分、賞賢罰暴、勿有親戚兄弟
之所阿。○卽此文武兼也、雖子墨子
之所謂兼者、於文武取法焉、不識天
下之人、所以皆聞兼而非之者、其故
何也。然而天下之非兼者之言猶未
止、曰、意不忠親之利而害爲孝乎。○
子墨子曰、姑嘗本原之、孝子之爲親
度者、吾不識孝子之爲親度者、亦欲
人愛利其親與、意欲人之惡賊其親

[1] See 'The Announcement of T'ang' (湯告) in various places. Compare also more particularly the Analects, XX. i. 3. [2] In the quotation which is immediately subjoined, the first four lines are from a rhythmical passage of the Shû-ching, V. iv. 13. The remaining four are in the Shih-ching, II. v. Ode ix. st. 1. [3] Such I suppose to be the meaning of 若吾言非語道之謂也, if it were amended. [4] The sentence is not clear,—意不忠親之利而害爲孝乎. I have done what I could with it. The scope of the whole paragraph is sufficiently plain. The 遇, farther on, is supposed to be for 偶.

孟子

must he himself first do in order to gain this object? If I first address myself to love and benefit men's parents, will they for that return love and benefit to my parents? or if I first address myself to hate men's parents, will they for that return love and benefit to my parents? It is clear that I must first address myself to love and benefit men's parents, and they will return to me love and benefit to my parents. The conclusion is that a filial son has no alternative.—He must address himself in the first place to love and do good to the parents of others. If it be supposed that this is an accidental course, to be followed on emergency by a filial son, and not sufficient to be regarded as a general rule, let us bring it to the test of what we find in the Books of the ancient kings.—It is said in the Tâ Yâ,

> 'Every word finds its answer;
> Every action its recompense.
> He threw me a peach;
> I returned him a plum.'

These words show that he who loves others will be loved, and that he who hates others will be hated. How is it that the scholars throughout the kingdom condemn this principle of universal love, when they hear it?

Is it that they deem it so difficult as to be impracticable? But there have been more difficult things, which yet have been done. *For instance*, king Ling of Ching was fond of small waists. In his time, the officers of Ching restricted themselves to a handful of rice, till they required a stick to raise themselves, and in walking had to hold themselves up by the wall. Now, it is a difficult thing to restrict one's self in food, but they were able to do it, because it would please king Ling.—It needs not more than a generation to change the manners of the people, such is their desire to move after the pattern of their superiors.

Again, Kâu-chien, the king of Yüeh, was fond of bravery. He spent three years in training his officers to be brave; and then, not knowing fully whether they were so, he set fire to the ship where they were, and urged them forward by a drum into the flames. They advanced, one rank over the bodies of another, till an immense number perished in the water or the flames; and it was not till he ceased to beat the drum, that they retired. Those officers of Yüeh might be pronounced to be full of reverence. To sacrifice one's life in the flames is a difficult thing, but they were able to do it, because it would please their king.—It needed not

與。以說觀之、卽欲人之愛利其親也、然卽吾惡先從事卽得此。若我先從事乎愛利人之親、然後人報我愛利吾親乎、意我先從事乎惡人之親、然後人報我以愛利吾親乎、卽必吾先從事乎愛利人之親、然後人報我以愛利吾親也。然卽之交孝子者、果不得已乎、毋先從事愛利人之親者與。意以天下之孝子、爲遇而不足以爲正乎、姑嘗本原先王之所書、大雅之所道曰、無言而不讐、無德而不報、投我以桃、報之以李。卽此言愛人者必見愛也、而惡人者必見惡也、不識天下之士、所以皆聞愛而非之者、其故何也。

意以爲難而不可爲耶。嘗有難此而可爲者。昔荆靈王好小要、當靈王之身、荆國之士、飯不踰乎一固、據而後興、扶垣而後行、故約食爲其難爲也、然後爲而靈王說之、未踰於世而民可移也、卽求以鄉其上也。

昔者越王勾踐好勇、教其士臣三年、以其知爲未足以知之也、焚舟失火、鼓而進之、其士偃前列、伏水火而死、有不可勝數也、當此之時、不鼓而退也、越國之士、可謂顫矣、故焚身爲其難爲也、然後爲之、越王說

more than a generation to change the manners of the people, such is their desire to move after the pattern of their superiors. *Once more*, duke Wăn of Tsin was fond of garments of coarse flax. In his time, the officers of Tsin wore wide clothes of that fabric, with rams' furs, leathern swordbelts, and coarse canvas sandals. Thus attired, they went in to the duke's levee, and went out and walked through the court. It is a difficult thing to wear such clothes, but they were able to do it, because it would please duke Wăn.—It needs but a generation to change the manners of the people, such is their desire to move after the pattern of their superiors.

Now, little food, a burning ship, and coarse clothes,—these are among the most difficult things to endure; but because the sovereign would be pleased with the enduring them, they were able *in those cases* to do it. It needed no more than a generation to change the manners of the people. Why? Because such is their desire to move after the pattern of their superiors. And now, as to universal mutual love[1], it is an advantageous thing and easily practised,—beyond all calculation. The only reason why it is not practised is, in my opinion, because superiors do not take pleasure in it. If superiors were to take pleasure in it, stimulating men to it by rewards and praise, and awing them from opposition to it by punishments and fines, they would, in my opinion, move to it,—the practice of universal mutual love, and the interchange of mutual benefits,—as fire rises upwards, and as water flows downwards:—nothing would be able to check them. This universal love was the way of the sage kings; it is the principle to secure peace for kings, dukes, and great men; it is the means to secure plenty of food and clothes for the myriads of the people. The best course for the superior man is to well understand the principle of universal love, and to exert himself to practise it. It requires the sovereign to be gracious, and the minister to be loyal; the father to be kind, and the son to be filial; the elder brother to be friendly, and the younger to be obedient. Therefore the superior man,—with whom the chief desire is to see gracious sovereigns and loyal ministers; kind fathers and filial sons; friendly elder brothers and obedient younger ones,—ought to insist on the indispensableness of the practice of universal love. It was the way of the sage kings; it would be the most advantageous thing for the myriads of the people.

之、未踰於世、而民可移也、即求以鄉上也。昔者晉文公好苴服、當文公之時、晉國之士、大布之衣、牂羊之裘、練帛之冠、且苴之屨、入見文公、出以踐之朝、故苴服爲其難爲也、然後爲而文公說之、未踰於世而民可移也、即求以鄉其上也。是故約食焚舟苴服、此天下之至難爲也、然後爲而上說之、未踰於世而民可移也。何故也、即求以鄉其上也。今若夫兼相利、此其有利且易爲也、不可勝計也、我以爲則無有上說之者而已矣、苟有上說之者、勸之以賞譽、威之以刑罰、我以爲人之於就兼相愛交相利也、譬之猶火之就上、水之就下也、不可防止於天下。故兼者聖王之道也、王公大人之所以安也、萬民衣食之所以足也、故君子莫若審兼而務行之、爲人君必惠、爲人臣必忠、爲人父必慈、爲人子必孝、爲人兄必友、爲人弟必悌、故君子莫若欲爲惠君、忠臣慈父孝子友兄悌弟、當若兼之不可不行也、此聖王之道而萬民之大利也。

[1] For 兼相利 we should read 兼相愛.

孟子

2. Notwithstanding the mutilations and corruptions in the text of the preceding Essay, its general scope is clearly discernible, and we obtain from it a sufficient account of Mo's doctrine on the subject of 'Universal Love.' We have now to consider the opposition offered to this doctrine by Mencius. He was not the first, however, to be startled and offended by it. The Essay shows that it was resented as an outrage on the system of orthodox belief during all the lifetime of Mo and his immediate disciples. Men of learning did not cease to be clamorous against it. From the allusions made by Mencius to its prevalence in his days, it would appear that it had overcome much of the hostility which it at first encountered. He stepped forward to do battle with it, and though he had no new arguments to ply, such was the effect of his onset, that 'Universal Love' has ever since been considered, save by some eccentric thinkers, as belonging to the Limbo of Chinese vanities, among other things 'abortive, monstrous, or unkindly mixed.'

We may approach the question conveniently by observing that Mo's attempts to defend his principle were in several points far from the best that could be made. His references to the examples of Yü, T'ang, and the kings Wăn and Wû, are of this nature. Those worthies well performed the work of their generation. They punished the oppressor, and delivered the oppressed. Earnest sentiments of justice and benevolence animated their breasts and directed their course. But they never laid down the doctrine of 'Universal Love,' as the rule for themselves or others.

When he insists, again, that the people might easily be brought to appreciate and practise his doctrine, if their rulers would only set them the example, he shows the same overweening idea of the influence of superiors, and the same ignorance of human nature, which I have had occasion to point out in both Confucius and Mencius. His references to duke Wăn of Tsin, duke Ling of Ch'û, and Kâu-chien of Yüeh, and his argument from what they are said to have effected, only move us to smile. And when he teaches that men are to be *awed* to love one another '*by punishments and fines*,' we feel that he is not understanding fully what he says nor whereof he affirms.

Still, he has broadly and distinctly laid it down, that if men would only universally love one another, the evils which disturb and embitter human society would disappear. I do not say that he has taught the *duty* of universal love. His argument is conducted

on the ground *of expediency*[1]. Whether he had in his own mind a truer, nobler foundation for his principle, does not immediately appear. Be that as it may, his doctrine was that men were to be exhorted to love one another,—to love one another as themselves. According to him, 'princes should be as much for the States of others as for their own. One prince should be for every other as for himself.' So it ought to be also with the Heads of clans, with ministers, with parents, and with men generally.

Here it was that Mencius joined issue with him. He affirmed that 'to love all equally did not acknowledge the peculiar affection due to a parent.' It is to be observed that Mo himself nowhere says that his principle was that of loving all EQUALLY. His disciples drew this conclusion from it. In the third Book of Mencius's Works, we find one of them, Î Chih, contending that the expression in the Shû-ching, about the ancient kings acting towards the people, 'as if they were watching over an infant,' sounded to him as if love were to be *without difference of degree*, the manifestation of it simply commencing with our parents[2]. To this Mencius replied conclusively by asking, 'Does Î really think that a man's affection for the child of his brother is merely like his affection for the child of his neighbour?' With still more force might he have asked, 'Is a man's affection for his father merely like his affection for the father of his neighbour?' Such a question, and the necessary reply to it, are implied in his condemnation of Mo's system, as being 'without father,' that is, denying the peculiar affection due to a father. If Mo had really maintained that a man's father was to be no more to him than the father of any other body, or if his system had necessitated such a consequence, Mencius would only have done his duty to his country in denouncing him, and exposing the fallacy of his reasonings. As the case is, he would have done better if he had shown that no such conclusion necessarily flows from the doctrine of 'Universal Love,' or its preceptive form that we are to love our neighbour as ourselves.

Of course it belonged to Mo himself to defend his views from the imputation. But what he has said on the point is not satisfactory. In reply to the charge that his principle was injurious to filial piety, he endeavoured to show, that, by acting on it, a man would best

[1] This and several other points are well put by the Rev. Dr. Edkins, in his Essay, referred to on p. 133. See Journal of the North-China Branch of the Royal Asiatic Society, No. II, May, 1859.

[2] See Bk. III. Pt. I. v. 3.

孟子

secure the happiness of his parents:—as he addressed himself in the first place to love, and do good to, the parents of others, they would recompense to him the love of, and good-doing to, his parents. It might be so, or it might not. The reply exhibits strikingly in what manner Mo was conducted to the inculcation of universal love, and that really it had in his mind no deeper basis than its expediency. This is his weak point; and if Mencius, whose view of the constitution of human nature, and the binding force of the virtues, apart from all consideration of consequences, was more comprehensive and correct than that of Mo, had founded his opposition on this ground, we could in a measure have sympathised with him. But while Mo appeared to lose sight of the other sentiments of the human mind too much, in his exclusive contemplation of the power of love, he did not doubt but his principle would make sons more filial, and ministers more devoted, and subjects more loyal. The passage which I have just referred to, moreover, does not contain the admission that the love was to be *without any difference of degree.* The fact is, that he hardly seems to have realised the objection with which Mencius afterwards pressed the advocacy of it by his followers. If he did do so, he blinked the difficulty, not seeing his way to give a full and precise reply to it.

This seems to be the exact state of the case between the two philosophers. Mo stumbled on a truth, which, based on a right foundation, is one of the noblest which can animate the human breast, and affords the surest remedy for the ills of society. There is that in it, however, which is startling, and liable to misrepresentation and abuse. Mencius saw the difficulty attaching to it, and unable to sympathise with the generosity of it, set himself to meet it with a most vehement opposition. Nothing, certainly, could be more absurd than his classing Yang Chû and Mo Tî together, as equally the enemies of benevolence and righteousness. When he tries to ridicule Mo, and talks contemptuously about him, how, if he could have benefited the kingdom, by toiling till he rubbed off every hair of his body, he would have done it[1],—this only raises up a barrier between himself and us. It reminds us of the *hardness* of nature which I have elsewhere charged against him.

3. Confucius, I think, might have dealt more fairly and generously with Mo. In writing of him, I called attention to his repeated

[1] Bk. VII. Pt. I. xxvi.

enunciation of 'the golden rule' in a negative form,—'What you do not wish done to yourself, do not do to others[1].' In one place, indeed, he rises for a moment to the full apprehension of it, and recognises the duty of taking the initiative,—of behaving to others in the first instance as he would that they should behave to him[2]. Now, what is this but the practical exercise of the principle of universal love? 'All things whatsoever ye would that men should do to you, do ye even so to them:'—this is simply the manifestation of the requirement, 'Thou shalt love thy neighbour as thyself.' Confucius might have conceded, therefore, to Mo, that the rule of conduct which he laid down was the very best that could be propounded. If he had gone on to remove it from the basis of expediency, and place it on a better foundation, he would have done the greatest service to his countrymen, and entitled himself to a place among the sages of the world.

On this matter I am happy to find myself in agreement with the 'Prince of Literature,' Han Yü[3]. 'Our literati,' says he, 'find fault with Mo because of what he has said on "The Estimation to be attached to Concord[4]," on "Universal Love," on "The Estimation to be given to Men of Worth[5]," on "The Acknowledging of Spiritual Beings[6]," and on "The Awe in which Confucius stood of Great Men,

[1] Vol. i. proleg. p. 109. [2] See proleg. on the 'Doctrine of the Mean,' pp. 48, 49, vol. i.

[3] See the Works of Han Wăn-kung, 十一卷, 讀墨子篇.

[4] This is the title of one of Mo's Essays, the 尙同, forming the third Book of his Works. Generalising after his fashion, he traces all evils up to a want of concord, or agreement of opinion; and goes on to assert that the sovereign must be recognised as the 'Infallible Head,' to lay down the rule of truth and right, saying 天子之所是, 皆是之, 天子之所非, 皆非之, 'What the sovereign approves, all must approve; what the sovereign condemns, all must condemn.' It is an unguarded utterance; and taken absolutely, apart from its connexion, may be represented very much to Mo's disadvantage. See 'Supplemental Observations on the Four Books,' on Mencius, Book I. art. lix. The coincidence between this saying and the language of Hobbes is remarkable.—'Quod legislator praeceperit, id pro bono, quod vetuerit, id pro malo habendum esse.' (*De Cive*, cap. xii. 1.)

[5] This is another of Mo's pieces,—尙賢, the second Book of his Works. He finds a cure for the ills of the nation in princes' honouring and employing only men of worth, without paying regard to their relatives. This is contrary to the third of Confucius's nine standard rules for the government of the nation, set forth in his conversation with duke Âi, as related in the 'Doctrine of the Mean,' ch. xx. But Mo would only discountenance *nepotism*, where it ought to be discountenanced.

[6] This is found in the eighth Book of Mo. The first and second parts of the essay, however, are unfortunately lost. In the third he tells several queer ghost stories, and adduces other proofs, to show the real existence of spiritual beings, and that they take account of men's actions to reward or to punish them. He found another panacea for the ills of the kingdom in this truth. His doctrine here, however, is held to be inconsistent with Confucius's reply to

孟子

and, when he resided in any State, did blame its Great Officers[1]." But when the Ch'un Ch'iû finds fault with arrogant ministers, is not this attaching a similar value to concord? When Confucius speaks of "overflowing in love to all, and cultivating the friendship of the good," and of how "the extensive conferring of benefits constitutes a sage," does he not teach universal love? When he advises "the esteem of the worthy;" when he arranged his disciples into "the four classes," so stimulating and commending them; when he says that "the superior man dislikes the thought of his name not being mentioned after death:"—does not this show the estimation he gave to men of worth? When "he sacrificed as if the spiritual beings were present," and condemned "those who sacrificed as if they were not really sacrificing[2];" when he said, "When I sacrifice, I shall receive blessing:"—was not this acknowledging spiritual beings? The literati and Mo equally approve of Yâo and Shun, and equally condemn Chieh and Châu; they equally teach the cultivation of the person, and the rectifying of the heart, reaching on to the good government of the nation, with all its States and Families:—why should they be so hostile to each other? In my opinion, the discussions which we hear are the work of their followers, vaunting on each side the sayings of their Teacher; there is no such contrariety between the real doctrines of the two Teachers. Confucius would have made use of Mo's views; and Mo would have made use of those of Confucius. If they would not have made use of each other's sentiments, they could not have been K'ung and Mo.'

4. It seems proper, in closing this discussion of Mo's views, to notice the manner in which the subject of 'universal love' appears in Christianity. Its whole law is comprehended in the one word—Love; but how wide is the scope of the term compared with all which it ever entered into the mind of Chinese sage or philosopher to conceive!

Fan Ch'ih, Analects, VI. xx, that wisdom consists in respecting spiritual beings, but at the same time keeping aloof from them. But as between Confucius and Mo, on this point we would agree rather with the latter. He holds an important truth, mingled with superstition; the sage would seem to be sceptical.

[1] Han avoids saying anything on this point. The author of 'Supplemental Observations' is equally silent.

[2] Han is here quoting Analects, III. xii. 2, 吾不與祭如不祭, which he points and interprets after a way of his own. He does not read 與 but 與, in the sense of 許, 'to grant to,' 'to approve of.'

It is most authoritative where the teachers of China are altogether silent, and commands:—'Thou shalt love the Lord, thy God, with all thy heart, and with all thy soul, and with all thy strength, and with all thy mind.' For the Divine Being Christianity thus demands from all men supreme love;—the love of all that is majestic, awing the soul; the love of all that is beautiful, wooing the heart; the love of all that is good, possessing and mastering the entire nature. Such a love, existing, would necessitate obedience to every law, natural or revealed. Christianity, however, goes on to specify the duties which every man owes, as the complement of love to God, to his fellow-men:—'Owe no man anything, but to love one another, for he that loveth another hath fulfilled the law. For this—"Thou shalt not commit adultery," "Thou shalt not kill," "Thou shalt not steal," "Thou shalt not bear false witness," "Thou shalt not covet;" and if there be any other commandment:—the whole is briefly comprehended in this saying, "Thou shalt love thy neighbour as thyself."' This commandment is 'like to' the other, differing from it only in not requiring the *supreme* love which is due to God alone. The rule which it prescribes,—such love to others as we feel for ourselves,—is much more definitely and intelligibly expressed than anything we find in Mo, and is not liable to the cavils with which his doctrine was assailed. Such a love to men, existing, would necessitate the performance of every relative and social duty; we could not help doing to others as we would that they should do to us.

Mo's universal love was to find its scope and consummation in the good government of China. He had not the idea of man as man, any more than Confucius or Mencius. How can that idea be fully realised, indeed, where there is not the right knowledge of one living and true God, the creator and common parent of all? The love which Christianity inculcates is a law of humanity; paramount to all selfish, personal feelings; paramount to all relative, local, national attachments; paramount to all distinctions of race or of religion. Apprehended in the spirit of Christ, it will go forth even to the love of enemies; it will energize in a determination to be always increasing the sum of others' happiness, limited only by the means of doing so.

But I stop. These prolegomena are not the place for disquisition; but I deemed it right to say thus much here of that true, universal love, which at once gives glory to God and effects peace on earth.

孟子

CHAPTER IV.

WORKS WHICH HAVE BEEN CONSULTED IN THE PREPARATION OF THIS VOLUME.

The Works which have been consulted are mostly the same as those used in the preparation of the first volume, of which a list is there given. I have only to add to that :—

I.—OF CHINESE WORKS.

墨子十五卷, 目一卷, 'The Philosopher Mo, in fifteen Books, with one Book on the Titles of his Essays.' This Work was edited and annotated in the forty-eighth year of Ch'ien-lung (A.D. 1784), by Pî Yüan (畢沅), lieutenant-governor of Shen-hsî. From the notes appended to Mo's Essay on 'Universal Love' in the last chapter, it will be seen that the task of editing has been very imperfectly executed. I suppose it is vain to express a wish that some foreign scholar would take it in hand.

五百家註音辯韓昌黎先生全集, 'The Collected Writings of Han Ch'ang-lî, with the Verbal and Critical Notes of five hundred Scholars.' Ch'ang-lî is a local designation for Han Yü, styled T'ûi-chih (退之), and canonized as Wăn-kung (文公), or 'Prince of Literature.' I have said, p. 12, that he was a scholar of the eighth century, but he extended on into the ninth, dying A.D. 824. He stands out as perhaps the most distinguished scholar of the long space between the Han and Sung dynasties. The edition of his Works which I have, with such a collation of commentators, was first published by a Hsü Tâo-chî (許道基), in the twenty-eighth year of Ch'ien-lung (A.D. 1761).

II.—OF TRANSLATIONS AND OTHER WORKS.

MENG TSEU, vel MENCIUM, inter Sinenses Philosophos, Ingenio, Doctrina, Nominisque Claritate, CONFUCIO PROXIMUM, edidit, Latina interpretatione, ad interpretationem Tartaricam utramque recensita, instruxit, et perpetuo commentario, e Sinicis deprompto, illustravit Stanislaus Julien. Paris, 1824–1829.

THE WORKS OF MENCIUS.

BOOK I.

KING HÛI OF LIANG. PART I.

孟子

梁惠王

章句上

第一章 一 孟子見梁惠王。二 王曰、叟不遠千里而來、亦將有以利吾國乎。

CHAPTER I. 1. Mencius *went to* see king Hûi of Liang.

2. The king said, 'Venerable sir, since you have not counted it far to come here, a distance of a thousand *lî*, may I presume that you are provided with counsels to profit my kingdom?'

TITLE OF THE WORK.—孟子, 'The philosopher Măng.' The Work thus simply bears the name, or surname rather, of him whose conversations and opinions it relates, and is said to have been compiled in its present form by the author himself. On the use of 子, after the surname, see on Analects, I. i. The surname and this 子 were combined by the Romish missionaries, and latinized into Mencius, which it is well to adopt throughout the translation, and thereby avoid the constant repetition of the word 'philosopher,' Măng not being distinguished, like K'ung (Confucius), by the crowning epithet of 'The Master.'

TITLE OF THIS BOOK.—梁惠王章句上, 'King Hûi of Liang, in chapters and sentences. Part I.' Like the Books of the Confucian Analects, those of this Work are headed by two or three characters at or near their commencement. Each Book is divided into two parts, called 上下, 'Upper and Lower.' This arrangement was made by Châo Ch'î (趙岐), a scholar of the eastern Han dynasty (died A. D. 201), by whom the chapters and sentences were also divided, and the 章句上, 章句下 remain to the present day, a memorial of his work.

1. BENEVOLENCE AND RIGHTEOUSNESS MENCIUS'S ONLY TOPICS WITH THE PRINCES OF HIS TIME; AND THE ONLY PRINCIPLES WHICH CAN MAKE A COUNTRY PROSPEROUS. 1. 'King Hûi of Liang.'—In the time of Confucius, Tsin (晉) was one of the great States of the nation, but the power of it was usurped by six great families. By B.C. 452, three of those were absorbed by the other three, viz. Wei, Châo, and Han (魏, 趙, and 韓), which continued to encroach on the small remaining power of their prince, until at last they extinguished the ruling house, and divided the whole territory among themselves. The sovereign Wei Lieh (威烈), in his 23rd year, B.C. 402, conferred on the chief of each family the title of Marquis (侯). Wei, called likewise, from the name of its capital, Liang, occupied the south-eastern part of Tsin, Han and Châo lying to the west and north-west of it. The Liang, where Mencius visited king Hûi, is said to have been in the present department of K'âi-făng. Hûi, 'The Kindly,' is the posthumous epithet of the king, whose name was Yung (罃). The title of *king* had been usurped by Ying, at some time before Mencius first visited him, which, it is said, he did in the 35th year of his government, B.C. 336. Mencius visited him on invitation, it must be supposed, and the simple 見=被招往見. 2. Mencius was a native of Tsâu (鄒), in Lû, the name of which is still retained in the Tsâu district of the department of Yen-châu (兗州), in Shan-

三節 孟子對曰、王何必曰利、亦有仁義而已矣。四節 王曰、何以利吾國、大夫曰、何以利吾家、士庶人曰、何以利吾身、上下交征利、而國危矣、萬乘之國、弑其君者、必千乘之家、千乘之國、弑其君者、必百乘之家、萬取千焉、千取百焉、不爲不多矣、苟爲

3. Mencius replied, 'Why must your Majesty use that word "profit?" What I am provided with, are *counsels to* benevolence and righteousness, and these are my only topics.

4. 'If your Majesty say, "What is to be done to profit my kingdom?" the great officers will say, "What is to be done to profit our families?" and the inferior officers and the common people will say, "What is to be done to profit our persons?" Superiors and inferiors will try to snatch this profit the one from the other, and the kingdom will be endangered. In the kingdom of ten thousand chariots, the murderer of his sovereign shall be *the chief of* a family of a thousand chariots. In a kingdom of a thousand chariots, the murderer of his prince shall be *the chief of* a family of a hundred chariots. To have a thousand in ten thousand, and a hundred in a thousand, cannot be said not to be a large allotment, but if righteousness be put last, and profit be put first, they will not be satisfied without snatching *all*.

tung. The king, in complimentary style, calls the distance from Tsâu to Liang a thousand *li*. It is difficult to say what was the exact length of the ancient *li*. At present it is a little more than one-third of an English mile. The 亦, 'also,' occasions some difficulty.—With reference to what is it spoken? Some compare the 亦 . . . 乎 with 不亦乎, Analects, I. i. Others say that the king refers to the many scholars who at the time made it their business to wander from country to country, as advisers to the princes :—'You *also*, like other scholars,' &c. Then, when Mencius, in par. 3, replies—亦有仁義, they say that he refers to Yâo, Shun, &c., as his models :—'I, like them,' &c. But this is too far-fetched. Wang Yin-chih inclines to consider 亦 as for the most part merely a helping particle; especially does he regard it so after 不 in an interrogative clause. Observe the force of 將, delicately and suggestively putting the question. 3. 對,—marking the answer of an inferior, used from respect to the king. 曰 is 'to say,' followed directly by the words spoken. It is not 'to speak of.' 而已矣 mark very decidedly Mencius's purpose to converse only of 仁 and 義. 4. 征,—here = 取, 'to take.' 交征, 'mutually

後義而先利、不奪不饜。〇五節未有仁、而遺其親者也、未有義、而後其君者也。〇六節王亦曰、仁義而已矣、何必曰利。

〔第二章〕一節孟子見梁惠王、王立於沼上、顧鴻鴈麋鹿、曰、賢者亦樂此乎。

二節孟子對曰、賢者而後樂此、不賢者、雖有此

5. 'There never has been a benevolent man who neglected his parents. There never has been a righteous man who made his sovereign an after consideration.

6. 'Let your Majesty also say, "Benevolence and righteousness, and let these be your only themes." Why must you use that word—"profit?"'

CHAP. II. 1. Mencius, *another day*, saw king Hûi of Liang. The king *went and* stood *with him* by a pond, and, looking round at the large geese and deer, said, 'Do wise and good *princes* also find pleasure in these things?'

2. Mencius replied, 'Being wise and good, they have pleasure in these things. If they are not wise and good, though they have these things, they do not find pleasure.

to take;' i. e. superiors from inferiors, and inferiors from superiors. 乘, in 4th tone, 'a carriage or chariot.' The sovereign's domain, = 1,000 *lî* square, produced 10,000 war chariots. A kingdom producing 1,000 chariots was that of a *hâu*, or marquis. He is here called 百乘之家, instead of 百乘之君, because the sovereign has just been denominated by that term. 後 and 先 are verbs. See Analects, VI. xx. 5. The 仁 and 義 here are supposed to result from the sovereign's example.

2. RULERS MUST SHARE THEIR PLEASURES WITH THE PEOPLE. THEY CAN ONLY BE HAPPY WHEN THEY RULE OVER HAPPY SUBJECTS. 1. 王立,—'The king stood;' and the meaning is not that Mencius found him by the pond. The king seems to have received him graciously, and to have led him into the park. 於沼上,—compare Analects, VI. vii, but for which passage I should translate here—'over a pond,' i. e. in some building over the water, such as is still very common in China. 鴻 means 'large geese,' and 麋 is the name for a large kind of deer, but they are joined here, as adjectives, to 鴈 and 鹿. 賢者=賢者之君, 'worthy princes.' It does not refer to Mencius, as some make it out. The reply makes this plain. The king's inquiry is prompted by a sudden dissatisfaction with himself, for being occupied so much with such material gratifications, and = 'Amid all their cares of government do these pleasures find a place with good princes?' 3. See the Shih-ching, III. i. Ode VIII. st. 1, 2. The ode tells how his people delighted in king Wăn. For 鶴 the Shih-ching reads 翯. 於 is read *wû*, an interjection. 古之人 referring to king Wăn, but

不樂也。三節詩云、經始靈臺、經之營之、庶民攻之、不日成之、經始勿亟、庶民子來、王在靈囿、麀鹿攸伏、麀鹿濯濯、白鳥鶴鶴、王在靈沼、於牣魚躍、文王以民力爲臺爲沼、而民歡樂之、謂其臺曰靈臺、謂其沼曰靈沼、樂其有麋鹿魚鼈、古之人與民偕樂、故能樂也。四節湯誓曰、時日害喪、予及女偕亡、民

3. 'It is said in the Book of Poetry,

"He measured out and commenced his marvellous tower;
He measured it out and planned it.
The people addressed themselves to it,
And in less than a day completed it.
When he measured and began it, *he said to them*—Be not so earnest:
But the multitudes came as if they had been his children.
The king was in his marvellous park;
The does reposed about,
The does so sleek and fat:
And the white birds shone glistening.
The king was by his marvellous pond;
How full was it of fishes leaping about!"

'King Wăn used the strength of the people to make his tower and his pond, and yet the people rejoiced to do the work, calling the tower "the marvellous tower," calling the pond "the marvellous pond," and rejoicing that he had his large deer, his fishes, and turtles. The ancients caused the people to have pleasure as well as themselves, and therefore they could enjoy it.

4. 'In the Declaration of T'ang it is said, "O sun, when wilt thou

put generally. 4. See the Shû-ching, IV. Bk. I. i. 3;—T'ang's announcement of his reasons for proceeding against the tyrant Chieh. The words quoted are those of the people. Chieh had pointed to the sun, saying that, as surely as the sun was in heaven, so firm was he on his throne. The people took up his words, and pointing to the sun, thus expressed their hatred

孟子

欲與之偕亡、雖有臺池鳥獸、豈能獨樂哉。

三 梁惠王曰、寡人之於國也、盡心焉耳矣、河內凶、則移其民於河東、移其粟於河內、河東凶、亦然、察鄰國之政、無如寡人之用心者、鄰國之民不加少、寡人之民不加多、何也。孟子對曰、王好

expire? We will die together with thee." The people wished *for Chieh's death*, though they should die with him. Although he had towers, ponds, birds, and animals, how could he have pleasure alone?'

CHAP. III. 1. King Hûi of Liang said, 'Small as my virtue is, in the government of my kingdom, I do indeed exert my mind to the utmost. If the year be bad on the inside of the river, I remove *as many of* the people *as I can* to the east of the river, and convey grain to the country in the inside. When the year is bad on the east of the river, I act on the same plan. On examining the government of the neighbouring kingdoms, I do not find that there is any prince who exerts his mind as I do. And yet the people of the neighbouring kingdoms do not decrease, nor do my people increase. How is this?'

2. Mencius replied, 'Your Majesty is fond of war;—let me take

of the tyrant, preferring death with him to life under him. 時 = 是; 害 is read *ho*; 喪, in 4th tone. Châo Ch'î gives quite another turn to the quotation, making the words an address of the people to T'ang:—'This day he (Chieh) must die. We will go with you to kill him.' Chû Hsî's view is to be preferred. I do not think that the last two clauses are to be understood generally:—'When the people wish to die with a prince,' &c. They must specially refer to Chieh.

3. HALF MEASURES ARE OF LITTLE USE. THE GREAT PRINCIPLES OF ROYAL GOVERNMENT MUST BE FAITHFULLY AND IN THEIR SPIRIT CARRIED OUT. 1. The combination of particles—焉耳矣—gives emphasis to the king's profession of his own devotedness to his kingdom. 寡人 was the designation of themselves used by the princes in speaking to their people, = 寡德之人, 'I, the man of small virtue.' I shall hereafter simply render it by 'I.' Liang was on the south of the river, i.e. the *Ho*, or Yellow river, but portions of the Wei territory lay on the other side, or north of the river. This was called the inside of the river, because the ancient royal capitals had mostly been there, in the province of Ch'î (冀州), comprehending the present Shan-hsî; and the country north of the Ho, looked at from them, was of course 'within,' or on this side of it. 粟,—now used commonly for millet and maize, but here for grain generally. 加少, 加多; literally, 'add few, add many.' To explain the 加, it is said the expressions = 分外少,

戰、請以戰喻、填然鼓之、兵刃既接、棄甲曳兵而走、或百步而後止、或五十步而後止、以五十步笑百步、則何如。曰、不可、直不百步耳、是亦走也。曰、王如知此、則無望民之多於鄰國也。三不違農時、穀不可勝食也、數罟不入洿池、魚鼈不可勝食也、斧斤以時入山林、材

an illustration from war.—*The soldiers move forward to* the sound of the drums; and after their weapons have been crossed, *on one side* they throw away their coats of mail, trail their arms behind them, and run. Some run a hundred paces and stop; some run fifty paces and stop. What would you think if those who run fifty paces were to laugh at those who run a hundred paces?' The king said, 'They should not do so. Though they did not run a hundred paces, yet they also ran away.' 'Since your Majesty knows this,' replied Mencius, 'you need not hope that your people will become more numerous than those of the neighbouring kingdoms.

3. 'If the seasons of husbandry be not interfered with, the grain will be more than can be eaten. If close nets are not allowed to enter the pools and ponds, the fishes and turtles will be more than can be consumed. If the axes and bills enter the hills and forests *only* at the proper time, the wood will be more than can be used.

不外多, 'not fewer, nor larger, than they should for such States be.' 2. 填然 is said to express the sound of the drum. In 鼓之, 鼓 is used as a verb, and 之 refers to 戰士, or soldiers. It was the rule of war to advance at the sound of the drum, and retreat at the sound of the gong. 是亦走也,—literally, 'this also,' i.e. the fifty paces, 'was running away.' 3. Here we have an outline of the first principles of royal government, in contrast with the measures on which the king plumes himself in the 1st par. The 不 is not imperative = 'do not.' The first clauses of the various sentences are conditional. In spring there was the sowing; in summer, the weeding; and in autumn, the harvesting:—those were the seasons and works of husbandry, from which the people might not be called off. 勝, 1st tone. The dictionary explains it by 'to bear,' 'to be adequate to.' 穀不可勝食 = 'there is no eating-power adequate to eat the grain.' 數, here read *tsû*, 'close-meshed.' The meshes of a net were anciently required to be large, of the size of four inches. People might only eat fish a foot long. 山 =

木不可勝用也、穀與魚鼈不可勝食、材木不可勝用、是使民養生喪死無憾也、養生喪死無憾、王道之始也。○四節 五畝之宅、樹之以桑、五十者、可以衣帛矣、雞豚狗彘之畜、無失其時、七十者、可以食肉矣、百畝之田、勿奪其時、數口之家、可以無飢矣、謹庠序之教、申之以

When the grain and fish and turtles are more than can be eaten, and there is more wood than can be used, this enables the people to nourish their living and mourn for their dead, without any feeling against any. This condition, in which the people nourish their living and bury their dead without any feeling against any, is the first step of royal government.

4. 'Let mulberry trees be planted about the homesteads with their five *mâu*, and persons of fifty years may be clothed with silk. In keeping fowls, pigs, dogs, and swine, let not their times of *breeding* be neglected, and persons of seventy years may eat flesh. Let there not be taken away the time that is proper for the cultivation of the farm with its hundred *mâu*, and the family of several mouths that is supported by it shall not suffer from hunger. Let careful attention be paid to education in schools, inculcating in it especially the filial and fraternal duties, and grey-haired men will

wooded hills. 林 = forests in the plains. The time to work in the forests was, according to Chû Hsî, in the autumn, when the growth of the trees for the year was stopped. But in the Châu-lî, we find various rules about cutting down trees,—those on the south of the hill, for instance, in midwinter, those on the north, in summer, &c., which may be alluded to. 無憾 I have translated, 'without any feeling against any,' the ruler being specially intended. 4. The higher principles which complete royal government. We can hardly translate 畝 by 'an acre,' it consisting, at present at least, only of 240 square paces, or 1200 square cubits, and anciently it was much smaller, 100 square paces, of six cubits each, making a *mâu*. The ancient theory for allotting the land was to mark it off in squares of 900 *mâu*, the middle square being called the 公田, or 'government fields.' The other eight were assigned to eight husbandmen and their families, who cultivated the public field in common. But from this twenty *mâu* were cut off, and, in portions of two-and-a-half *mâu*, assigned to the farmers to build on, who had also the same amount of ground in their towns or villages, making five *mâu* in all for their houses. And to have the ground all for growing grain, they were required to plant mulberry

孝悌之義、頒白者、不負戴於道路矣、七十者衣帛食肉、黎民不飢不寒、然而不王者、未之有也。○五節狗彘食人食、而不知檢、塗有餓莩、而不知發、人死、則曰、非我也、歲也、是何異於刺人而殺之、曰、非我也、兵也、王無罪歲、斯天下之民至焉。

第四章 一節 梁惠王曰、寡人願安承

not be seen upon the roads, carrying burdens on their backs or on their heads. It never has been that the ruler of a State, where such results were seen,—persons of seventy wearing silk and eating flesh, and the black-haired people suffering neither from hunger nor cold,—did not attain to the royal dignity.

5. 'Your dogs and swine eat the food of men, and you do not make any restrictive arrangements. There are people dying from famine on the roads, and you do not issue the stores *of your granaries* for them. When people die, you say, "It is not owing to me; it is owing to the year." In what does this differ from stabbing a man and killing him, and then saying—"It was not I; it was the weapon?" Let your Majesty cease to lay the blame on the year, and instantly from all the nation the people will come to you.'

CHAP. IV. 1. King Hûi of Liang said, 'I wish quietly to receive your instructions.'

trees about their houses, for the nourishment of silkworms. 雞,豚 (a young pig) 狗 (the grain-fed, or edible dog) 彘 (the sow) 之畜,—literally, 'as to the nourishing of the fowl,' &c. 數口之家—the ground was distinguished into three kinds;—best, medium, and inferior, feeding a varying number of mouths. To this the expression alludes. 庠序. See on Bk. III. Pt. I. iii. 10. 王, 4th tone, 'to come to reign,' 'to become regnant sovereign.' 5. Mencius now boldly applies the subject, and presses home his faults upon the king. 食人食;—the second 食 is read *tsze*, 4th tone. 檢=制, 'to regulate.' The phrase 不知檢 is not easy;—the translation given accords with the views of most of the commentators.

4. A CONTINUATION OF THE FORMER CHAPTER, CARRYING ON THE APPEAL, IN THE LAST PARAGRAPH, ON THE CHARACTER OF KING HÛI'S OWN GOVERNMENT. 1. 安, 'quietly,' i.e. sincerely and

孟子

教。二節孟子對曰、殺人以梃與刃、有以異乎。曰、無以異也。三節以刃與政、有以異乎。曰、無以異也。四節曰、庖有肥肉、廄有肥馬、民有飢色、野有餓莩、此率獸而食人也。五節獸相食、且人惡之、爲民父母行政、不免於率獸而食人、惡在其爲民父母也。六節仲尼曰、始作俑者、其無後乎、爲其象

2. Mencius replied, 'Is there any difference between killing a man with a stick and with a sword?' *The king* said, 'There is no difference.'

3. 'Is there any difference between doing it with a sword and with *the style of* government?' 'There is no difference,' was the reply.

4. *Mencius then* said, 'In your kitchen there is fat meat; in your stables there are fat horses. *But* your people have the look of hunger, and on the wilds there are those who have died of famine. This is leading on beasts to devour men.

5. 'Beasts devour one another, and men hate them *for doing so.* When *a prince,* being the parent of his people, administers his government so as to be chargeable with leading on beasts to devour men, where is his parental relation to the people?'

6. Chung-nî said, 'Was he not without posterity who first made wooden images *to bury with the dead?* *So he said,* because

without constraint. It is said 安對勉强, 看見其出于誠意. 2, 3. 有以異乎 = 有所以異乎,—literally, 'Is there whereby they are different?' 4. 野,—outside a town were the 郊 (*chiâo*), *suburbs*, but without buildings; outside the *chiâo* were the 牧 (*mû*), *pasture-grounds;* and outside the *mû* were the 野 (*yê*), *wilds*. 5. 且 has the force of 'and yet,' i.e. though they are beasts. So that a 'how much more' is carried on, in effect, to the rest of the paragraph. 人惡之,—惡, 4th tone, the verb. 惡在,—惡, 1st tone, = 何. 'Being the parent of the people,' i.e. this is his designation, and what he ought to be. 6. 俑,—in ancient times, bundles of straw were made, to represent men imperfectly, called 芻靈, and carried to the grave, and buried with the dead, as attendants upon them. In middle antiquity, i.e. after the rise of the Châu dynasty, for those bundles of straw, wooden figures of men were used, having springs in them, by which they could move. Hence they were called 俑, as if 俑 = 踊.

人而用之也、如之何其使斯民飢而死也。

第五章 一節 梁惠王曰、晉國天下莫强焉、叟之所知也、及寡人之身、東敗於齊、長子死焉、西喪地於秦七百里、南辱於楚、寡人恥之、願比死者一洒之、如之何則可。二節 孟子對曰、地方

that man made the semblances of men, and used them *for that purpose*:—what shall be thought of him who causes his people to die of hunger?'

CHAP. V. 1. King Hûi of Liang said, 'There was not in the nation a stronger State than Tsin, as you, venerable Sir, know. But since it descended to me, on the east we have been defeated by Ch'î, and then my eldest son perished; on the west we have lost seven hundred *li* of territory to Ch'in; and on the south we have sustained disgrace at the hands of Ch'û. I have brought shame on my departed predecessors, and wish on their account to wipe it away, once for all. What course is to be pursued to accomplish this?'

2. Mencius replied, 'With a territory which is only a hundred *li* square, it is possible to attain to the royal dignity.

By and by, came the practice of burying living persons with the dead, which Confucius thought was an effect of this invention, and therefore he branded the inventor as in the text. 其無後乎,—the 乎 is partly interrogative, and partly an exclamation = *nonne*. 爲, 3rd tone, = *because*. 如之何 is by some taken as = 'what would he (viz. Confucius) have thought,' &c.? I prefer taking it as in the translation. The designation of Confucius by *Chung-ni* is to be observed. See Doctrine of the Mean, ii. 1.

5. HOW A RULER MAY BEST TAKE SATISFACTION FOR LOSSES WHICH HE HAS SUSTAINED. THAT BENEVOLENT GOVERNMENT WILL RAISE HIM HIGH ABOVE HIS ENEMIES. 1. After the partition of the State of Tsin by the three families of Wei, Châo, and Han (note, chap. i), they were known as the three Tsin, but king Hûi would here seem to appropriate to his own principality the name of the whole State. He does not, however, refer to the strength of Tsin before its partition, but under his two predecessors in the State of Wei. It was in the thirtieth year of his reign, and B.C. 340, that the defeat was received from Ch'î, when his eldest son was taken captive, and afterwards died. That from Ch'in was in the year B.C. 361, when the old capital of the State was taken, and afterwards peace had to be secured by various surrenders of territory. The disgrace from Ch'û was also attended with the loss of territory;—some say seven, some say eight, towns or districts. The nominative to the verbs 敗, 喪, and 辱 does not appear to be 寡人 so much as 晉. 寡人恥之 may be translated—'I am ashamed of these things,' but most commentators make 之 refer to 先人, Hûi's predecessors when Tsin was strong; as in the translation. The same reference they also give to 死者, as not said generally of 'the dead,'—those who had died in the various wars. This view is on the whole preferable to the other, and it gives a better antecedent for the 之 in 洒之. 一 = by one blow, one great

百里、而可以王。○三節王如施仁政於民、省刑罰、薄稅斂、深耕易耨、壯者以暇日、脩其孝弟忠信、入以事其父兄、出以事其長上、可使制梃、以撻秦楚之堅甲利兵矣。○四節彼奪其民時、使不得耕耨、

3. 'If your Majesty will *indeed* dispense a benevolent government to the people, being sparing in the use of punishments and fines, and making the taxes and levies light, so causing that the fields shall be ploughed deep, and the weeding of them be carefully attended to, and that the strong-bodied, during their days of leisure, shall cultivate their filial piety, fraternal respectfulness, sincerity, and truthfulness, serving thereby, at home, their fathers and elder brothers, and, abroad, their elders and superiors,—you will then have a people who can be employed, with sticks which they have prepared, to oppose the strong mail and sharp weapons of the troops of Ch'in and Ch'û.

4. 'The *rulers of those States* rob their people of their time, so that they cannot plough and weed their fields, in order to support

movement. 洒＝洗. 比, the 4th tone, = 爲, 'for.' 2. See Part II. ii. 1; but it seems necessary to take the 方 in this and similar cases as in the translation. There is a pause at 地:—'with territory, which is,' &c. This is the reply to the king's wish for counsel to wipe away his disgraces. He may not only avenge himself on Ch'î, Ch'in, and Ch'û, but he may make himself chief of the whole nation. How, is shown in the next paragraph. 3. 省刑罰, 薄稅斂 are the two great elements of benevolent government, out of which grow the other things specified. 刑罰 can hardly be separated. The dictionary says that 刑 is the general name of 罰. If we make a distinction, it must be as in the translation; 罰 is the redemption-fine for certain crimes. So 稅斂 together represent all taxes. Great differences of opinion obtain as to the significance of the individual terms. Some make 稅 to be the proportion of the land-produce paid to the government, and 斂 all other contributions. By some this explanation is just reversed. A third party makes 稅 to be the tax of produce, and 斂 the graduated *collection* thereof. This last view suits the connexion here. 易, read i, the 3rd tone, = 治. 壯者,—at 30, a man is said to be 壯. Translators have rendered it here by 'the young,' but the meaning is the strong-bodied,—those who could be employed to take the field against the enemy. 可使 does not appear to be—'you can make or employ,' but to be passive with special reference to the 壯者 above. 省, read *shăng*. 撻—'to strike,' 'to smite'—here = 'to oppose.' 4. 彼, 'they' or 'those,' i. e. the rulers of Ch'in and Ch'û. 養, the 4th tone. It is so toned in the case of children supporting their parents, and inferiors their superiors. See in Analects, II. vii. 5. 夫, the 2nd tone, here = 則.

以養其父母、父母凍餓、兄弟妻子離散。五節彼陷溺其民、王往而征之、夫誰與王敵。六節故曰、仁者無敵、王請勿疑。

第六章一節孟子見梁襄王。二節出語人曰、望之不似人君、就之而不見所畏焉、卒然問曰、天下惡乎定。吾對曰、定于一。三節孰能一之。四節對曰、不嗜殺人者能一之。五節孰能與之。六節對曰、

their parents. Their parents suffer from cold and hunger. Brothers, wives, and children are separated and scattered abroad.

5. 'Those *rulers, as it were,* drive their people into pit-falls, or drown them. Your Majesty will go to punish them. In such a case, who will oppose your Majesty?

6. 'In accordance with this is the saying,—"The benevolent has no enemy." I beg your Majesty not to doubt *what I say.*'

CHAP. VI. 1. Mencius went to see the king Hsiang of Liang.

2. On coming out *from the interview,* he said to some persons, 'When I looked at him from a distance, he did not appear like a sovereign; when I drew near to him, I saw nothing venerable about him. Abruptly he asked me, "How can the kingdom be settled?" I replied, "It will be settled by being united under one *sway.*"

3. '"Who can so unite it?"

4. 'I replied, "He who has no pleasure in killing men can so unite it."

5. '"Who can give it to him?"

6. 'I replied, "All the people of the nation will unanimously

6. 故, not 'therefore;' it may indicate a *deduction* from what precedes, or be simply an illustration of it. 勿疑, 'Do not doubt.' It is strange that Julien, in his generally accurate version, should translate this by '*ne cuncteris.*' Hesitancy would, indeed, be an effect of doubting Mencius's words, not the proverb just quoted, but specially the affirmation in par. 2. But the words may not be so rendered.

6. DISAPPOINTMENT OF MENCIUS WITH THE KING HSIANG. BY WHOM THE TORN NATION MAY BE UNITED UNDER ONE SWAY. 1. On the death of king Hûi, he was succeeded by his son *Ho* (赫), called here by his honorary epithet, Hsiang, = 'The land-enlarger and virtuous.' The interview here recorded seems to have taken place immediately after Ho's accession, and Mencius, it is said, was so disappointed by it that he soon left the country. 2. 語, the 4th tone. The 人 probably refers to some friends of the philosopher, and is not to be taken gener-

孟子

天下莫不與也、王知夫苗乎、七八月之閒、旱、則苗槁矣、天油然作雲、沛然下雨、則苗浡然興之矣、其如是、孰能禦之、今夫天下之人牧、未有不嗜殺人者也、如有不嗜殺人者、則天下之民、皆引領而望之矣、誠如是也、民歸之、由水之就下、沛然誰能禦之。一節

第七章 齊宣王問曰、齊桓晉文之

give it to him. Does your Majesty understand the way of the growing grain? During the seventh and eighth months, when drought prevails, the plants become dry. Then the clouds collect densely in the heavens, they send down torrents of rain, and the grain erects itself, as if by a shoot. When it does so, who can keep it back? Now among the shepherds of men throughout the nation, there is not one who does not find pleasure in killing men. If there were one who did not find pleasure in killing men, all the people in the nation would look towards him with outstretched necks. Such being indeed the case, the people would flock to him, as water flows downwards with a rush, which no one can repress."'

CHAP. VII. 1. The king Hsüan of Ch'î asked, saying, 'May

ally. 卒, read ts'ü. 卒然,—compare 率爾, Analects, XI. xxiv. 4. On 望之, 就之, compare Analects, XIX. ix. Châo Ch'î makes 定于 — to = 'It will be settled by him who makes benevolent government his one object.' But this is surely going beyond the text. 5. The 與 is here explained, by Chû Hsî and others, as equivalent to 歸, founding, no doubt, on the 民歸之 in the end. But in Bk. V. Pt. I. v, we have a plain instance of 與, used in connexion with the bestowment of the throne, as in the translation which I have ventured to give, which seems to me, moreover, to accord equally well, if not better, with the rest of the chapter.

6. The 7th and 8th months of Châu were the 5th and 6th of the Hsiâ dynasty, with which the months of the present dynasty agree. 今夫, 一夫, the 1st tone, is used as in the Analects, XI. ix. 3. The 之 at the end is to be referred to 水, the whole, from 由 (=猶), being an illustration of the people's turning with resistless energy to a benevolent ruler.

7. LOVING AND PROTECTING THE PEOPLE IS THE CHARACTERISTIC OF ROYAL GOVERNMENT, AND THE SURE PATH TO THE ROYAL DIGNITY. This long and interesting chapter has been arranged in five parts. In the first part, pars. 1-5, Mencius unfolds the principle of royal government, and tells the king of Ch'î that he possesses

事、可得聞乎。○二節孟子對曰、仲尼之徒、無道桓文之事者、是以後世無傳焉、臣未之聞也、無以、則王乎。○三節曰、德何如則可以王矣。曰、保民、而王、莫之能禦也。○四節曰、若寡人

I be informed by you of the transactions of Hwan of Ch'î, and Wăn of Tsin?'

2. Mencius replied, 'There were none of the disciples of Chung-nî who spoke about the affairs of Hwan and Wăn, and therefore they have not been transmitted to these after-ages;—your servant has not heard them. If you will have me speak, let it be about royal government.'

3. The king said, 'What virtue must there be in order to attain to royal sway?' Mencius answered, 'The love and protection of the people; with this there is no power which can prevent a ruler from attaining to it.'

4. *The king* asked again, 'Is such an one as I competent to

it. In the second part, pars. 6-8, he leads the king on to understand his own mind, and apprehend how he might exercise a royal government. In the third, pars. 9-12, he unfolds how the king may and ought to carry out the kindly heart which he possessed. In the fourth part, pars. 13-17, he shows the absurdity of the king's expecting to gain his end by the course he was pursuing, and how rapid would be the response to an opposite one. In the last part, he shows the government that loves and protects the people in full development, and crowned with royal sway. 1. The king Hsüan ('The Distinguished,' 聖善周聞曰宣), the second of his family, who governed in Ch'î, by surname T'ien (田), and named P'î-chiang (辟疆), began his reign B.C. 332. By some the date of this event is placed nine years earlier. The time of Mencius's visit to him is also matter of dispute;—see 'Life of Mencius,' in the Prolegomena. The ruler of Ch'î was properly only a duke (公 in posthumous title), or a marquis (while alive, 侯); the title of *king* was a usurpation. Hwan and Wăn,—see Analects, XIV. xvi. They were the greatest of the five leaders of the princes, who played so conspicuous a part in the middle time of the Châu dynasty, but to whom Confucius and Mencius so positively refused their approval. 2. 道 is a verb, = 'to speak of,' in which sense it had formerly a tone different from its usage as a noun. 無以, 則王乎,—以 is taken by Chû Hsî as = 已, which it is as well to acquiesce in. See Châo Ch'î's commentary for the all but impossibility of making any sense of the passage in any other way. 王, the 4th tone, and so generally throughout the chapter. As the royal title, it is in the 2nd tone, the simple name of dignity; as implying the attainment or exercise of that dignity, it is the 4th tone. By translating it by 'royal government,' 'royal sway,' we come nearer to giving Mencius's meaning than if we were to use any other term. 3. Here the nominatives of 'king' and 'Mencius' are dropped before 曰, as frequently afterwards. The 曰 just serves the purpose of our points of quotation. 保, 'to preserve,' 'to protect.' I translate it, according to Chû Hsî's account, as = 愛護. A pause is to be made at 民, and 而王 joined to the remainder of the sentence. 4. The hall, or *t'ang*, here mentioned, was probably that where the king was giving audience, and attending to the affairs of government. 牛何之,—the 之 is the verb, = 往. 舍,—also a verb, in 3rd tone. 諸 =

者、可以保民乎哉。曰、可。曰、何由知吾可也。曰、臣聞之胡齕曰、王坐於堂上、有牽牛而過堂下者、王見之、曰、牛何之。對曰、將以釁鐘。王曰、舍之、吾不忍其觳觫、若無罪而就死地。對曰、然則廢釁鐘與。曰、何可廢也、以羊易之。不識有諸。

○五節、曰、有之。曰、是心足以王矣、百姓皆以王爲愛也、臣固知

love and protect the people?' *Mencius* said, 'Yes.' 'How do you know that I am competent for that?' 'I heard the following incident from Hû Ho:—"The king," said he, "was sitting aloft in the hall, when a man appeared, leading an ox past the lower part of it. The king saw him, and asked, Where is the ox going? The man replied, We are going to consecrate a bell with its blood. The king said, Let it go. I cannot bear its frightened appearance, as if it were an innocent person going to the place of death. The man answered, Shall we then omit the consecration of the bell? *The king* said, How can that be omitted? Change it for a sheep." I do not know whether this incident really occurred.'

5. *The king* replied, 'It did,' and *then Mencius* said, 'The heart seen in this is sufficient to carry you to the royal sway. The people all supposed that your Majesty grudged *the animal*, but your servant knows surely, that it was your Majesty's not being able to bear *the sight, which made you do as you did*.'

之, and at the same time with an indirect interrogative force. Chû Hsî explains 釁鐘 from the meaning of 釁 as 'a crack,' 'a crevice,' saying:—'After the casting of a bell, they killed an animal, took its blood, and smeared over the crevices.' But the first meaning of 釁 is—'a sacrifice by blood,' and anciently 'almost all things,' connected with their religious worship, were among the Chinese purified with blood;—their temples, and the vessels in them. See the Lî Chî, Bk. XXII. The reference here is to the religious rite. The only thing is that, in using an *ox* to consecrate his bell, the prince of Ch'î was usurping a royal privilege. 5. 愛 may be taken as the finite verb, = 'you loved, i.e. grudged the animal,' or

王之不忍也。六節王曰、然、誠有百姓者、齊國雖褊小、吾何愛一牛、卽不忍其觳觫、若無罪而就死地、故以羊易之也。七節曰、王無異於百姓之以王爲愛也、以小易大、彼惡知之、王若隱其無罪而就死地、則牛羊何擇焉。王笑曰、是誠何心哉、我非愛其財、而易之以羊也、宜乎百姓之謂我愛也。八節曰、無傷也、是乃仁術也、見牛、未見

6. *The king* said, 'You are right. And yet there really was an appearance of what the people condemned. But though Ch'î be a small and narrow State, how should I grudge one ox? Indeed it was because I could not bear its frightened appearance, as if it were an innocent person going to the place of death, that therefore I changed it for a sheep.'

7. *Mencius* pursued, 'Let not your Majesty deem it strange that the people should think you were grudging *the animal*. When you changed a large one for a small, how should they know *the true reason?* If you felt pained by its being led without guilt to the place of death, what was there to choose between an ox and a sheep?' The king laughed and said, 'What really was my mind in the matter? I did not grudge the expense of it, and changed it for a sheep!—There was reason in the people's saying that I grudged it.'

8. 'There is no harm *in their saying so*,' said *Mencius*. 'Your conduct was an artifice of benevolence. You saw the ox, and had not

as = 'to be niggardly,'—'you were parsimonious.' 6. It is better to make a pause after 然, and give the meaning as in the translation. Châo Ch'î runs it on to the next clause. 誠有百姓者 is elliptical, and the particle 者 denotes this, requiring the supplement which I have given. 卽 acknowledges the truth of Mencius's explanation. 7. 隱 = 痛. 是誠何心哉 expresses the king's quandary. He is now quite perplexed by the way in which Mencius has put the case. 8. 仁術,—compare Analects, VI. xxviii. 3, 仁之方.

羊也、君子之於禽獸也、見其生、不忍見其死、聞其聲、不忍食其肉、是以君子遠庖廚也。○九節 王說曰、詩云、他人有心、予忖度之、夫子之謂也、夫我乃行之、反而求之、不得吾心、夫子言之、於我心有戚戚焉、此心之所以合於王者何也。○十節 曰、有復於王者曰、吾力足以舉百鈞、而不足以舉一羽、明足以察秋毫之末、而不見輿薪、

seen the sheep. So is the superior man affected towards animals, that, having seen them alive, he cannot bear to see them die; having heard their dying cries, he cannot bear to eat their flesh. Therefore he keeps away from his slaughter-house and cook-room.'

9. The king was pleased, and said, 'It is said in the Book of Poetry, "The minds of others, I am able by reflection to measure;"—this is verified, my Master, in your discovery of my motive. I indeed did the thing, but when I turned my thoughts inward, and examined into it, I could not discover my own mind. When you, Master, spoke those words, the movements of compassion began to work in my mind. How is it that this heart has in it what is equal to the royal sway?'

10. *Mencius* replied, 'Suppose a man were to make this statement to your Majesty:—"My strength is sufficient to lift three thousand catties, but it is not sufficient to lift one feather;—my eyesight is sharp enough to examine the point of an autumn hair,

We must take the two words 庖廚 together as indicating the kitchen, where the victims were both killed and cooked. 9. 說=悅. For the ode, see the Book of Poetry, II. v. Ode IV st. 4, where the 他人 has a special reference. 夫子之謂也,—literally, '(This was) a speaking about you, my Master.' 10. 復, read *fû*, the 4th tone, often meaning to report the execution of a mission, as in the phrase—復命. Here it is = 'to inform.' 獨可與,—in order to bring out the force of the 獨, 'only,' it is necessary to make two sentences of this in

則王許之乎。曰、否。今恩足以及禽獸、而功不至於百姓者、獨何與、然則一羽之不舉、爲不用力焉、輿薪之不見、爲不用明焉、百姓之不見保、爲不用恩焉、故王之不王、不爲也、非不能也。○十一、曰、不爲者、與不能者之形、何以異。曰、挾太山以超北海、語人曰、我不能、是誠不能也、爲長者折枝、語人曰、

but I do not see a waggon-load of faggots;"—would your Majesty allow what he said?' 'No,' *was the answer, on which Mencius proceeded,* 'Now here is kindness sufficient to reach to animals, and no benefits are extended from it to the people.—How is this? Is an exception to be made here? The truth is, the feather is not lifted, because strength is not used; the waggon-load of firewood is not seen, because the eyesight is not used; and the people are not loved and protected, because kindness is not employed. Therefore your Majesty's not exercising the royal sway, is because you do not do it, not because you are not able to do it.'

11. *The king* asked, 'How may the difference between the not doing a thing, and the not being able to do it, be represented?' *Mencius* replied, 'In such a thing as taking the T'âi mountain under your arm, and leaping over the north sea with it, if you say to people—"I am not able to do it," that is a real case of not being able. In such a matter as breaking off a branch from a tree at the order of a superior, if you say to people—"I am not able to do it," that is a case of not doing it, it is not a case of not being able to do

English. 不爲也, it is said, = 不肯爲, 'not willing to do it,' but it is better to add nothing to the simple text. We have here, indeed, the famous distinction of 'moral' and 'physical' ability. 11. 形,—'the form,' 'or figure;'—literally, 'How may the figure . . . . be differenced?' 語人,—語, in 4th tone, = 告. 12. Châo Ch'î makes the opening here = 'Treat as their age requires your own old (English idiom seems to require the 2nd person), and treat the old of others in the same way,' but there seems to be a kind of *constructio pregnans*, conveying all that appears in the translation.

我不能、是不爲也、非不能也、故王之不王、非挾太山以超北海之類也、王之不王、是折枝之類也。○十二節老吾老、以及人之老、幼吾幼、以及人之幼、天下可運於掌、詩云、刑于寡妻、至于兄弟、以御于家邦、言舉斯心加諸彼而已、故推恩足以保四海、不推恩、無以保妻子、古之人、所以大過人者、無他

it. Therefore your Majesty's not exercising the royal sway, is not such a case as that of taking the T'âi mountain under your arm, and leaping over the north sea with it. Your Majesty's not exercising the royal sway is a case like that of breaking off a branch from a tree.

12. 'Treat with the reverence due to age the elders in your own family, so that the elders in the families of others shall be similarly treated; treat with the kindness due to youth the young in your own family, so that the young in the families of others shall be similarly treated:—do this, and the kingdom may be made to go round in your palm. It is said in the Book of Poetry, "His example affected his wife. It reached to his brothers, and his family of the State was governed by it."—The language shows how *king Wăn* simply took his *kindly* heart, and exercised it towards those parties. Therefore the carrying out his kindness of heart *by a prince* will suffice for the love and protection of all within the four seas, and if he do not carry it out, he will not be able to protect his wife and children. The way in which the ancients came

天下可運於掌 is made by most commentators to mean—'you may pervade the kingdom with your kindness so easily.' But I must believe that it is the *effect*, and not the *means*, which is thus represented. For the ode, see the Shih-ching, III. i. Ode VI. st. 2. The original celebrates the virtue of king Wăn, and we must translate in the third person, and not in the first. 御＝迓, but the meaning is disputed. Here Chû Hsî explains it by 治. The philosopher now introduces a new element into his discourse. It is no longer the 不忍之心, 'the heart that cannot bear,' i. e. the humane heart, which is necessary to raise to

焉、善推其所爲而已矣、今恩足以及禽獸、而功不至於百姓者獨何與。十三權、然後知輕重、度、然後知長短、物皆然、心爲甚、王請度之。十四抑王興甲兵、危士臣、構怨於諸侯、然後快於心與。十五王曰、否、吾何快於是、將以求吾所大欲也。十六曰、王之所大欲、可得聞與。王笑而不言。曰、

greatly to surpass other men, was no other but this:—simply that they knew well how to carry out, so as to affect others, what they themselves did. Now your kindness is sufficient to reach to animals, and no benefits are extended from it to reach the people.—How is this? Is an exception to be made here?

13. 'By weighing, we know what things are light, and what heavy. By measuring, we know what things are long, and what short. The relations of all things may be thus determined, and it is of the greatest importance to estimate *the motions of* the mind. I beg your Majesty to measure it.

14. 'You collect your equipments of war, endanger your soldiers and officers, and excite the resentment of the other princes;—do these things cause you pleasure in your mind?'

15. The king replied, 'No. How should I derive pleasure from these things? My object in them is to seek for what I greatly desire.'

16. *Mencius* said, 'May I hear from you what it is that you greatly desire?' The king laughed and did not speak. *Mencius*

the royal sway, but it is 推此心, 'the *carrying out* of this heart.' All may have the heart, but all may not be gifted, so to carry it out that it shall affect all others. We cannot wonder that the princes whom Mencius lectured should have thought his talk 迂濶, *transcendental*. 13. The first 度 is 4th tone, *tû*, 'a measure,' the instrument for measuring. But both it and 權 are equivalent to active verbs. 心爲甚 means, that the mind, as affected from without, and going forth to affect, may be light or heavy, long or short, i.e. may be right or wrong, and that in different degrees;—and that it is more important to estimate the character of its action, than to weigh or measure other things. 14. Here Mencius helps the king to measure his mind. 抑,—about the same as our 'come now,' or 'well then.' Further on, its equally accepted meaning of 'or' suits the connexion better. 16. The 與 are all interrogative, in the 2nd tone, and the 爲 are all in the

爲肥甘不足於口與、輕煖不足於體與、抑爲采色不足視於目與、聲音不足聽於耳與、便嬖不足使令於前與、王之諸臣、皆足以供之、而王豈爲是哉。曰、否、吾不爲是也。曰、然則王之所大欲、可知已、欲辟土地、朝秦楚、莅中國、而撫四夷也、以若所爲、求若所欲、猶緣木而求魚也。十七 王曰、若是其甚與。曰、殆有甚焉、緣木求

resumed, '*Are you led to desire it*, because you have not enough of rich and sweet food for your mouth? Or because you have not enough of light and warm *clothing* for your body? Or because you have not enough of beautifully coloured objects to delight your eyes? Or because you have not voices and tones enough to please your ears? Or because you have not enough of attendants and favourites to stand before you and receive your orders? Your Majesty's various officers are sufficient to supply you with those things. How can your Majesty be led to entertain such a desire on account of them?' 'No,' said *the king*; 'my desire is not on account of them.' *Mencius* added, 'Then, what your Majesty greatly desires may be known. You wish to enlarge your territories, to have Ch'in and Ch'û wait at your court, to rule the Middle Kingdom, and to attract to you the barbarous tribes that surround it. But doing what you do to seek for what you desire is like climbing a tree to seek for fish.'

17. *The king* said, 'Is it so bad as that?' 'It is even worse,' was the reply. 'If you climb a tree to seek for fish, although you do

4th tone. 便, read *p'ien*, the 2nd tone, joined with the next character. 可知已,—已 gives a positiveness to the assertion. 辟, read as, and = 闢. 緣木, from the use of the phrase here, has come to be used for 'to climb a tree,' but it simply is—'from a tree.'

17. The 殆, an introductory part., = 'yes, and.' 蓋亦反其本 is spoken with reference to the king's object of ambition:—'By the course you are pursuing you cannot succeed, for,

魚、雖不得魚、無後災、以若所爲、求若所欲、盡心力而爲之、後必有災。曰、可得聞與。曰、鄒人與楚人戰、則王以爲孰勝。曰、楚人勝。曰、然則小固不可以敵大、寡固不可以敵衆、弱固不可以敵彊、海內之地、方千里者九、齊集有其一、以一服八、何以異於鄒敵楚哉、蓋亦反其本矣。

十八 今王發政施仁、使天下仕者、皆欲立於王之朝、耕者、皆欲耕於王之

not get the fish, you will not suffer any subsequent calamity. But doing what you do to seek for what you desire, doing it moreover with all your heart, you will assuredly afterwards meet with calamities.' *The king* asked, 'May I hear *from you the proof of* that?' *Mencius* said, 'If the people of Tsâu should fight with the people of Ch'û, which of them does your Majesty think would conquer?' 'The people of Ch'û would conquer.' 'Yes;—and so it is certain that a small country cannot contend with a great, that few cannot contend with many, that the weak cannot contend with the strong. The territory within the *four* seas embraces nine divisions, each of a thousand *lî* square. All Ch'î together is but one of them. If with one part you try to subdue the other eight, what is the difference between that and Tsâu's contending with Ch'û? For, *with such a desire,* you must turn back to the proper course *for its attainment.*

18. 'Now, if your Majesty will institute a government whose action shall be benevolent, this will cause all the officers in the kingdom to wish to stand in your Majesty's court, and all the farmers

if you wish to do so, you must also turn back to the root of success.' 18. 野,—'fields,' here; not 'wilds.' 出於,—'to come forth in,' i.e. to pass from their own States into yours. 欲

野、商賈、皆欲藏於王之市、行旅、皆欲出於王之塗、天下之欲疾其君者、皆欲赴愬於王、其若是、孰能禦之。○十九 王曰、吾惛、不能進於是矣、願夫子輔吾志、明以教我、我雖不敏、請嘗試之。○二十 曰、無恆產而有恆心者、惟士爲能、若民則無恆產、因無恆心、苟無恆心、放辟邪侈、無不爲已、及陷於罪、然後從

to wish to plough in your Majesty's fields, and all the merchants, both travelling and stationary, to wish to store their goods in your Majesty's market-places, and all travelling strangers to wish to make their tours on your Majesty's roads, and all throughout the kingdom who feel aggrieved by their rulers to wish to come and complain to your Majesty. And when they are so bent, who will be able to keep them back?'

19. The king said, 'I am stupid, and not able to advance to this. I wish you, my Master, to assist my intentions. Teach me clearly; although I am deficient in intelligence and vigour, I will essay and try to carry your instructions into effect.'

20. *Mencius* replied, 'They are only men of education, who, without a certain livelihood, are able to maintain a fixed heart. As to the people, if they have not a certain livelihood, it follows that they will not have a fixed heart. And if they have not a fixed heart, there is nothing which they will not do, in the way of self-abandonment, of moral deflection, of depravity, and of wild license. When they thus have been involved in crime, to follow them up and

疾,—'feeling aggrieved, but must restrain their feelings.' 20. 辟, read as, and = 僻. 罔,—'en-net,' i.e. to entrap. 無所不爲已,—已, see on par. 16. 21. 終身, generally means 'the whole life.' Perhaps we should translate, 'If some years be good, they will all their lives have plenty,' i.e. they will in those years lay by a sufficient provision for bad years. This supposes that the people have felt the power of the instruction and moral

而刑之、是罔民也、焉有仁人在位、罔民而可爲也。○廿一節是故明君制民之產、必使仰足以事父母、俯足以畜妻子、樂歲終身飽、凶年免於死亡、然後驅而之善、故民之從之也輕。○廿二節今也制民之產、仰不足以事父母、俯不足以畜妻子、樂歲終身苦、凶年不免於死亡、此惟救死、而恐不贍、奚暇治禮義

punish them;—this is to entrap the people. How can such a thing as entrapping the people be done under the rule of a benevolent man?

21. 'Therefore an intelligent ruler will regulate the livelihood of the people, so as to make sure that, for those above them, they shall have sufficient wherewith to serve their parents, and, for those below them, sufficient wherewith to support their wives and children; that in good years they shall always be abundantly satisfied, and that in bad years they shall escape the danger of perishing. After this he may urge them, and they will proceed to what is good, for in this case the people will follow after it with ease.

22. 'Now, the livelihood of the people is so regulated, that, above, they have not sufficient wherewith to serve their parents, and, below, they have not sufficient wherewith to support their wives and children. *Notwithstanding* good years, their lives are continually embittered, and, in bad years, they do not escape perishing. In such circumstances they only try to save themselves from death, and are afraid they will not succeed. What leisure have they to cultivate propriety and righteousness?

training that is a part of royal government, which, however, is set forth as consequent on the regulation of the livelihood. Similarly, below. 之善,—之 is the verb, = 往. 民之從之也輕,—Julien censures Noel here for rendering 從之 by '*ipsi (principi) obsequentur*,' and rightly. But I am not sure that the error is not rather in the rendering of 從 than in that of 之. The prince is supposed to exemplify, as well as to urge to, the good course, and the well-off people have no difficulty in following him. 23. 反其

哉。○廿三節王欲行之、則盍反其本矣。○廿四節五畝之宅、樹之以桑、五十者、可以衣帛矣、雞豚狗彘之畜、無失其時、七十者可以食肉矣、百畝之田、勿奪其時、八口之家、可以無飢矣、謹庠序之教、申之以孝悌之義、頒白者、不負戴於道路矣、老者衣帛食肉、黎民不飢不寒、然而不王者、未之有也。

23. 'If your Majesty wishes to effect this *regulation of the livelihood of the people*, why not turn to that which is the essential step to it?

24. 'Let mulberry-trees be planted about the homesteads with their five *mâu*, and persons of fifty years may be clothed with silk. In keeping fowls, pigs, dogs, and swine, let not their times of breeding be neglected, and persons of seventy years may eat flesh. Let there not be taken away the time that is proper for the cultivation of the farm with its hundred *mâu*, and the family of eight mouths that is supported by it shall not suffer from hunger. Let careful attention be paid to education in schools,—the inculcation in it especially of the filial and fraternal duties, and grey-haired men will not be seen upon the roads, carrying burdens on their backs or on their heads. It never has been that the ruler of a State where such results were seen,—the old wearing silk and eating flesh, and the black-haired people suffering neither from hunger nor cold,—did not attain to the royal dignity.'

本, as in par. 17, but with reference to the immediate subject. 24. See ch. iii, the only difference being that, for 數口之家 there, we have 八口之家, eight mouths being the number which 100 *mâu* of medium land were computed to feed.

KING HÛI OF LIANG. PART II.

梁惠王章句下

第一章 一節 莊暴見孟子曰、暴見於王、王語暴以好樂、暴未有以對也。曰、好樂何如。孟子曰、王之好樂甚、則齊國其庶幾乎。二節 他日見於王、曰、王嘗語莊子以好樂、有諸。王變乎色、曰、寡人非能好先王之樂也、直好世俗之樂耳。

CHAPTER I. 1. Chwang Pâo, seeing Mencius, said to him, 'I had an interview with the king. His Majesty told me that he loved music, and I was not prepared with anything to reply to him. What do you pronounce about that love of music?' Mencius replied, 'If the king's love of music were very great, the kingdom of Ch'î would be near to *a state of good government!*'

2. Another day, *Mencius*, having an interview with the king, said, 'Your Majesty, *I have heard*, told the officer Chwang, that you love music;—was it so?' The king changed colour, and said, 'I am unable to love the music of the ancient sovereigns; I only love the music that suits the manners of the *present* age.'

1. HOW THE LOVE OF MUSIC MAY BE MADE SUBSERVIENT TO GOOD GOVERNMENT, AND TO A PRINCE'S OWN ADVANCEMENT. The chapter is a good specimen of Mencius's manner,—how he slips from the point in hand to introduce his own notions, and would win princes over to benevolent government by their very vices. He was no stern moralist, and the Chinese have done well in refusing to rank him with Confucius. 1. Chwang Pâo appears to have been a minister at the court of Ch'î. The 曰 preceding 好樂如何 is unnecessary. If we translate it, we must render—'He then said.' But the paraphrasts all neglect it. 庶幾 (the 1st tone) is a phrase signifying 'near to;' sometimes we find 庶 alone, as in Analects XI. xviii. 1. The subject, nearness to which is indicated, is often left to be gathered from the context, as here. The 王之好樂甚 is a platitude. It should be the text of the chapter, but Mencius proceeds to substitute 樂 *lo* for 樂 *yo*, in his own manner. 2. 直, as in last Pt. ch. iii. 2; observe how the final 耳 adds to the force of 'only.' 'Ancient sovereigns' (i.e. Yâo, Shun, Yü, T'ang, Wăn, and Wû) is a better translation of 先王 than 'former kings.' 3. 由—

三曰、王之好樂甚、則齊其庶幾乎、今之樂由古之樂也。四曰、可得聞與。曰、獨樂樂、與人樂樂、孰樂。曰、不若與人。曰、與少樂樂、與衆樂樂、孰樂。曰、不若與衆。五臣請爲王言樂。六今王鼓樂於此、百姓聞王鐘鼓之聲、管籥之音、舉疾首蹙頞而相告曰、吾王之好鼓樂、夫何使我至於此極也、父子不相見、兄

3. *Mencius* said, 'If your Majesty's love of music were very great, Ch'î would be near to *a state of good government!* The music of the present day is just like the music of antiquity, *as regards effecting that.*'

4. *The king* said, 'May I hear from you the proof of that?' *Mencius* asked, 'Which is the more pleasant,—to enjoy music by yourself alone, or to enjoy it with others?' 'To enjoy it with others,' was the reply. 'And which is the more pleasant,—to enjoy music with a few, or to enjoy it with many?' 'To enjoy it with many.'

5. *Mencius proceeded,* 'Your servant begs to explain *what I have said about* music to your Majesty.

6. 'Now, your Majesty is having music here.—The people hear the noise of your bells and drums, and the notes of your fifes and pipes, and they all, with aching heads, knit their brows, and say to one another, "That's how our king likes his music! But why does he reduce us to this extremity *of distress?*—Fathers and sons cannot see one another. Elder brothers and younger brothers, wives and

猶. 4. 可得聞與, as in the preceding chapter. 獨樂樂,—the second 樂 is *lo*, 'joy,' 'delight.' So, in the next clause, and after 孰. 5. 爲 (the 4th tone) 王, 'for the sake of your Majesty.' 6. 鼓樂,—鼓 is a verb = 作. The ancient dictionary, the 說文, makes a difference between this, and the same word for 'drum,' saying this is formed from 攴, named *p'ú*, while the other is formed from 支. The difference of form is not regarded

弟妻子離散、今王田獵於此、百姓聞王車馬之音、見羽旄之美、舉疾首蹙頞而相告曰、吾王之好田獵、夫何使我至於此極也、父子不相見、兄弟妻子離散、此無他、不與民同樂也。○七今王鼓樂於此、百姓聞王鐘鼓之聲、管籥之音、舉欣欣然有喜色而相告曰、吾王庶幾無疾病與、何以能鼓樂也、今王田獵於此、百姓聞

children, are separated and scattered abroad." Now, your Majesty is hunting here.—The people hear the noise of your carriages and horses, and see the beauty of your plumes and streamers, and they all, with aching heads, knit their brows, and say to one another, "That's how our king likes his hunting! But why does he reduce us to this extremity *of distress*?—Fathers and sons cannot see one another. Elder brothers and younger brothers, wives and children, are separated and scattered abroad." Their feeling thus is from no other reason but that you do not allow the people to have pleasure as well as yourself.

7. 'Now, your Majesty is having music here. The people hear the noise of your bells and drums, and the notes of your fifes and pipes, and they all, delighted, and with joyful looks, say to one another, "That sounds as if our king were free from all sickness! If he were not, how could he enjoy this music?" Now, your Majesty is hunting here.—The people hear the noise of your carriages and

now. 於此, 'here,' used as we use *here* in English, putting a case with little local reference. 舉=俱 or 皆, 'all.' 蹙頞 expresses anguish, not anger. 夫 is here the introductory particle, and is better rendered by *but* than *now*. It will be seen that the preceding 吾王之好鼓樂 is incomplete. The paraphrasts add, to complete it, 固然已. 7. 田 is used synonymously with 畋, 'to hunt.' 聲 and 音 are to each other much as our sound or noise and tone or note. 音

孟子

王車馬之音、見羽旄之美、舉欣欣然有喜色而相告曰、吾王庶幾無疾病與、何以能田獵也、此無他、與民同樂也。八節今王與百姓同樂、則王矣。

第二章 一節齊宣王問曰、文王之囿、方七十里、有諸。孟子對曰、於傳有之。二節曰、若是其大乎。曰、民猶以爲小也。曰、寡人

horses, and see the beauty of your plumes and streamers, and they all, delighted, and with joyful looks, say to one another, "That looks as if our king were free from all sickness! If he were not, how could he enjoy this hunting?" Their feeling thus is from no other reason but that you cause them to have their pleasure as you have yours.

8. 'If your Majesty now will make pleasure a thing common to the people and yourself, the royal sway awaits you.'

CHAP. II. 1. The king Hsüan of Ch'î asked, 'Was it so, that the park of king Wăn contained seventy square *li?*' Mencius replied, 'It is so in the records.'

2. 'Was it so large as that?' exclaimed *the king*. 'The people,' said *Mencius*, 'still looked on it as small.' *The king* added, 'My

is applied appropriately to the fifes and pipes, and also to the carriages and horses, having reference to the music of the *bells* with which these were adorned. Of 羽旄 Chû Hsî simply says that they were 旌屬, 'belonging to the banners.' The 羽 were feathers adorning the top of the flag-staff; the 旄, a number of ox-tails suspended on a rope, one after another, from the top. 與民同樂, compare Pt. I. ii. 3.

2. HOW A RULER MUST NOT INDULGE HIS LOVE FOR PARKS AND HUNTING TO THE DISCOMFORT OF THE PEOPLE. 1. 傳, the 4th tone, 'a record,' an historical narration handing down events to futurity (傳於後人). 方七十里 must be understood—'containing seventy square *li*,' not 'seventy *li* square.' In the 日講, the meaning of 方 here (not similarly, however, in Pt. I. v. 2; vii. 17) is given by 四圍, 'in circumference.' The glossarist on Châo Ch'î explains it by 方濶, which, I think, confirms the meaning I have given. The book or books giving account of this park of king Wăn are now lost. 2. 芻者蕘者 are distinguished thus:—'gatherers of grass to feed animals, and gatherers of grass for fuel.' Observe how these nouns, and 雉 and 兔 that follow, get a verbal force from the 者;—the fodderers, the pheasanters, &c. 3. 郊 is

之囿、方四十里、民猶以爲大、何也。曰文王之囿、方七十里、芻蕘者往焉、雉兎者往焉、與民同之、民以爲小、不亦宜乎。三節 臣始至於境、問國之大禁、然後敢入、臣聞郊關之內、有囿方四十里、殺其麋鹿者、如殺人之罪、則是方四十里、爲阱於國中、民以爲大、不亦宜乎。

第三章 一節 齊宣王問曰、交鄰國有道乎、

park contains *only* forty square *lî*, and the people still look on it as large. How is this?' 'The park of king Wăn,' was the reply, 'contained seventy square *lî*, but the grass-cutters and fuel-gatherers had the privilege of entrance into it; so also had the catchers of pheasants and hares. He shared it with the people, and was it not with reason that they looked on it as small?

3. 'When I first arrived at the borders *of your kingdom*, I inquired about the great prohibitory regulations, before I would venture to enter it; and I heard, that inside the barrier-gates there was a park of forty square *lî*, and that he who killed a deer in it, was held guilty of the same crime as if he had killed a man.—Thus those forty square *lî* are a pitfall in the middle of the kingdom. Is it not with reason that the people look upon them as large?'

CHAP. III. 1. The king Hsüan of Ch'î asked, saying, 'Is there any way *to regulate one's maintenance of* intercourse with

used here in the sense simply of 'bordérs,' and on the borders of the various States there were 'passes' or 'gates,' for the taxation of merchandize, the examination of strangers, &c. 麋鹿, see Pt. I. ii. 1. These forest laws of Ch'î were hardly worse than those enacted by the first Norman sovereigns of England, when whoever killed a deer, a boar, or even a hare, was punished with the loss of his eyes, and with death if the statutes were repeatedly violated.

3. HOW FRIENDLY INTERCOURSE WITH NEIGHBOURING KINGDOMS MAY BE MAINTAINED, AND THE LOVE OF VALOUR MADE SUBSERVIENT TO THE GOOD OF THE PEOPLE, AND THE GLORY OF THE PRINCE. 1. The two first 事 differ in meaning considerably from the two last, and they are explained

孟子對曰、有、惟仁者、爲能以大事小、是故湯事葛、文王事昆夷、惟智者、爲能以小事大、故太王事獯鬻、句踐事吳。○二節以大事小者、樂天者也、以小事大者、畏天者也。樂天者、保天下、畏天者、保其國。○三節詩云、畏天之威、于

neighbouring kingdoms?' Mencius replied, 'There is. But it requires a perfectly virtuous *prince* to be able, with a great *country*, to serve a small one,—as, for instance, T'ang served Ko, and king Wăn served the Kwăn barbarians. And it requires a wise *prince* to be able, with a small *country*, to serve a large one,—as the king T'âi served the Hsün-yü, and Kâu-ch'ien served Wû.

2. 'He who with a great *State* serves a small one, delights in Heaven. He who with a small *State* serves a large one, stands in awe of Heaven. He who delights in Heaven, will affect with his love and protection the whole kingdom. He who stands in awe of Heaven, will affect with his love and protection his own kingdom.

3. 'It is said in the Book of Poetry, "I fear the Majesty of Heaven, and will thus preserve its favouring decree."'

by 撫字周恤 and 聽從服役, i.e. 'cherishing,' and 'obeying,' respectively, but the translation need not be varied. For the affairs of T'ang with Ko, see III. Pt. II. v. Of those of king Wăn with the Kwăn tribes we have nowhere an account which satisfies Mencius's reference to them. Both Châo Ch'î and Chû Hsî make reference to the Shih-ching, III. i. Ode III. st. 8; but what is there said would seem to be of things antecedent to king Wăn. Of king T'âi and the Hsün-yü, see below, chap. xv. A very readable, though romanced account of Kâu-ch'ien's service of Wû is in the Lieh Kwo Chih (列國志), Bk. lxxx. 是故 and 故, 'therefore,' introducing illustrations of what has been said, are = our 'as.' 2. 天, says Chû Hsî, 理而已矣, 'Heaven is just principle, and nothing more.' It is a good instance of the way in which he and others often try to expunge the idea of a governing Power and a personal God from their classics. Heaven is here evidently the superintending, loving Power of the universe. Châo Ch'î says on the whole paragraph :—'The sage delights to pursue the way of Heaven, just as Heaven overspreads everything ;—as was evidenced in T'ang and Wăn's protecting the whole kingdom. The wise measure the time and revere Heaven, and so preserve their States ;—as was evidenced in king T'âi and Kâu-ch'ien.' This view gives to 天 a positive, substantial meaning, though the personality of the Power is not sufficiently prominent. The commentator 王觀濤 says :—'The Heaven here is indeed the Supreme Heaven, but after all it is equivalent to principle and nothing more!' 保, as in Pt. I. vii. 3. 3. See the Shih-ching, IV. i. Bk. I. Ode VII. st. 3. 保, 'to preserve,' 'to keep.' 時 is here taken = 是; not so in the ode. The final 之 refers to the decree or favour of Heaven. 5. Observe the verbal meaning of 大. 6. See the Shih-ching, III. i. Ode

時保之。○四節王曰、大哉言矣、寡人有疾、寡人好勇。○五節對曰、王請無好小勇、夫撫劍疾視曰、彼惡敢當我哉、此匹夫之勇、敵一人者也、王請大之。○六節詩云、王赫斯怒、爰整其旅、以遏徂莒、以篤周祜、以對于天下、此文王之勇也、文王一怒、而安天下之民。○七節書曰、天降下民、作之君、作之師、惟曰、其助上帝、寵之四方、有罪無罪、惟我在、天

4. The king said, 'A great saying! But I have an infirmity;—I love valour.'

5. 'I beg your Majesty,' was the reply, 'not to love small valour. If a man brandishes his sword, looks fiercely, and says, "How dare he withstand me?"—this is the valour of a common man, who can be the opponent only of a single individual. I beg your Majesty to greaten it.

6. 'It is said in the Book of Poetry,

"The king blazed with anger,
And he marshalled his hosts,
To stop the march to Chü,
To consolidate the prosperity of Châu,
To meet the expectations of the nation."

This was the valour of king Wăn. King Wăn, in one burst of his anger, gave repose to all the people of the kingdom.

7. 'In the Book of History it is said, "Heaven having produced the inferior people, made for them rulers and teachers, with the purpose that they should be assisting to God, and therefore distinguished them throughout the four quarters of the land. Whoever

VII. st. 5, where we have 按 for 遏, and 旅 for 莒. 莒 is the name of a State or place, the same probably that in the ode is called 共. 以遏徂莒, 'to stop the march to

孟子

下曷敢有越厥志、一人衡行於天下、武王恥之、此武王之勇也、而武王亦一怒、而安天下之民。今王亦一怒、而安天下之民、民惟恐王之不好勇也。

齊宣王見孟子於雪宮、王曰、賢者亦有此樂乎。孟子對曰、有。人不得、則非其上矣。不得而非其上者非

are offenders, and whoever are innocent, here am I *to deal with them*. How dare any under heaven give indulgence to their refractory wills?" There was one man pursuing a violent and disorderly course in the kingdom, and king Wû was ashamed of it. This was the valour of king Wû. He also, by one display of his anger, gave repose to all the people of the kingdom.

8. 'Let now your Majesty also, in one burst of anger, give repose to all the people of the kingdom. The people are only afraid that your Majesty does not love valour.'

CHAP. IV. 1. The king Hsüan of Ch'î had an interview with Mencius in the Snow palace, and said to him, 'Do men of talents and worth likewise find pleasure in these things?' Mencius replied, 'They do; and if people *generally* are not able *to enjoy themselves*, they condemn their superiors.

2. 'For them, when they cannot enjoy themselves, to condemn their superiors is wrong, but when the superiors of the people do

Chû,' unless we take, with some, 徂 also to be the name of a place. 7. See the Shû-ching, V. i. Sect. I. 7, but the passage as quoted by Mencius is rather different from the original text. 惟曰其助上帝,—literally, 'just saying, They shall be aiding to God.' The sentiment is that of Paul, in Rom. xiii. 1-4, 'The powers ordained of God are the ministers of God.' In 天下曷敢有越厥志 there is an allusion to the tyrant Chieh, who is the 一人 in Mencius's subjoined explanation. 8. 惟恐 is, by some, taken—'The people would only be afraid,' the preceding clause being = 'If your Majesty,' &c. I think the present tense is preferable.

4. A RULER'S PROSPERITY DEPENDS ON HIS EXERCISING A RESTRAINT UPON HIMSELF, AND SYMPATHIZING WITH THE PEOPLE IN THEIR JOYS AND SORROWS. 1. 'The Snow palace' was a pleasure-palace of the princes of Ch'î. Most commentators say that the king had lodged Mencius there, and went to see him, but it may not have been so. Perhaps they only had their interview there. 賢者亦有此樂乎 is

也、爲民上、而不與民同樂者、亦非也。○三節 樂民之樂者、民亦樂其樂、憂民之憂者、民亦憂其憂、樂以天下、憂以天下、然而不王者、未之有也。○四節 昔者、齊景公問於晏子曰、吾欲觀於轉附朝儛、遵海而南、放于琅邪、吾何脩、而可以比於先王觀也。○五節 晏子對曰、善哉問也、天子適

not make enjoyment a thing common to the people and themselves, they also do wrong.

3. 'When a ruler rejoices in the joy of his people, they also rejoice in his joy; when he grieves at the sorrow of his people, they also grieve at his sorrow. A sympathy of joy will pervade the kingdom; a sympathy of sorrow will do the same:—in such a state of things, it cannot be but that the ruler attain to the royal dignity.

4. 'Formerly, the duke Ching of Ch'î asked the minister Yen, saying, "I wish to pay a visit of inspection to Chwan-fû, and Châo-wû, and then to bend my course southward along the shore, till I come to Lang-yê. What shall I do that my tour may be fit to be compared with the visits of inspection made by the ancient sovereigns?"

5. 'The minister Yen replied, "An excellent inquiry! When the Son of Heaven visited the princes, it was called a tour of inspec-

different from the question, in nearly the same words, in Pt. I. ii, 賢者 being there 'worthy princes,' and here 'scholars,' men of worth generally, with a reference to Mencius himself. 人不得,—人 is to be taken as = 民, 'the people,' men generally, and 不得, it is said, 是不得安居之樂, 非指雪宮, is = 'do not get the pleasure of quiet living and enjoyment, not referring to the Snow palace.' 非其上,—非 is used as a verb, = 'to blame,' 'to condemn.' So in the next paragraph. 3. I have given the meaning of the phrases 樂以天下, 憂以天下, which sum up the preceding part of the paragraph, and are not to be understood as spoken of the ruler only. The 合講 says:—'These two sentences are to be explained from the four previous sentences. The phrase 天下 is only a forcible way of saying what is said by 民. The 以 is to be explained as if we read—不以一身, 乃以天下耳, 'the joy and sorrow is *not with* (i.e. *from*) *one individual, but from the whole kingdom*.' 王, the 4th tone. 4. 晏子, see Confucian Analects, V. xvi. The duke Ching

諸侯曰巡狩、巡狩者、巡所守也、諸侯朝于天子曰述職、述職者、述所職也、無非事者、春省耕、而補不足、秋省斂、而助不給、夏諺曰、吾王不遊、吾何以休、吾王不豫、吾何以助、一遊一豫、爲諸侯度、○六節今也不然、師行而糧食、飢者弗食、勞者弗息、

tion, that is, he surveyed the *States* under their care. When the princes attended at the court of the Son of Heaven, it was called a report of office, that is, they reported their administration of their offices. Thus, neither of the proceedings was without a purpose. *And moreover*, in the spring they examined the ploughing, and supplied any deficiency *of seed;* in the autumn they examined the reaping, and supplied any deficiency of yield. There is the saying of the Hsiâ dynasty,—If our king do not take his ramble, what will become of our happiness? If our king do not make his excursion, what will become of our help? That ramble, and that excursion, were a pattern to the princes.

6. '"Now, the state of things is different.—A host marches *in attendance on the ruler*, and stores of provisions are consumed. The hungry are deprived of their food, and there is no rest for those who are called to toil. Maledictions are uttered by one to another

occupied the throne for 58 years, from B.C. 546–488. Chwan-fû and Châo-wû were two hills, which must have been in the north of Ch'î, and looking on the waters now called the Gulf of Pei-chih-lî. Lang-yê was the name both of a mountain and an adjacent city, referred to the present department of Chû-shăng, in Ch'ing-châu. 修=作爲, 'to do.' 5. 狩巡, see the Shû-ching, II. i. 8, 9. 狩 is used as=守. It does not seem necessary to repeat the 巡狩 and 述職 in the translation. This tour of inspection appears to have been made, under the Châu dynasty, once in twelve years, while the princes had to present themselves at court (朝, read *ch'âo*) once in six years. From 春, 'in the spring,' the practices appropriate to the various princes, as well as the sovereign, are described, though, as appears from the last clause, with special reference to the latter. 豫 or 預=遊. By 一遊一預 the spring and autumn visitations are intended, each called 一. 6. 師, properly a body of 2,500 men, but here generally =a host, a multitude. 睊睊胥讒, 民乃作慝 are referred to the people, and the next two clauses to the princes. Yet the 乃 after 民 would rather indicate a different subject for the clause before. 諸侯憂,—

睊睊胥讒、民乃作慝、方命虐民、飲食若流、流連荒亡、爲諸侯憂。○七節從流下、而忘反、謂之流、從流上而忘反、謂之連、從獸無厭、謂之荒、樂酒無厭、謂之亡。○八節先王無流連之樂、荒亡之行。○九節惟君所行也。○十節景公說、大戒於國、出舍於郊、於是始興發、補不足、召太師曰、爲我作君臣相說之樂、蓋徵招角招是

with eyes askance, and the people proceed to the commission of wickedness. Thus the *royal* ordinances are violated, and the people are oppressed, and *the supplies of* food and drink flow away like water. *The rulers* yield themselves to the current, or they urge their way against it; they are wild; they are utterly lost:—these things proceed to the grief of the inferior princes.

7. '"Descending along with the current, and forgetting to return, is what I call yielding to it. Pressing up against it, and forgetting to return, is what I call urging their way against it. Pursuing the chase without satiety is what I call being wild. Delighting in wine without satiety is what I call being lost.

8. '"The ancient sovereigns had no pleasures to which they gave themselves as on the flowing stream; no doings which might be so characterized as wild and lost.

9. '"It is for you, my prince, to pursue your course."'

10. 'The duke Ching was pleased. He issued a proclamation throughout his State, and went out and occupied a shed in the borders. From that time he began to open his granaries to supply the wants of the people, and calling the Grand music-master, he said to him—"Make for me music to suit a prince and his minister pleased

諸侯, by Chû Hsî and others, is explained as in the translation, though this view seems rather forced. Châo Ch'î makes them refer to the princes proper; but how can it be said that these things in which they delighted were a 'grief' to them? 10. 太師, see Analects, VIII. xv. 徵 (read *chi*, the 3rd tone) and 角 are the

孟子

也、其詩曰、畜君何尤、畜君者、好君也。

第五章 一節 齊宣王問曰、人皆謂我毀明堂、毀諸、已乎。二節 孟子對曰、夫明堂者、王者之堂也、王欲行王政、則勿毀之矣。三節 王曰、王政可得聞與。對曰、昔者文王之治

with each other." And it was then that the Chî-shâo and Chio-shâo were made, in the words to which it was said, "Is it a fault to restrain one's prince?" He who restrains his prince loves his prince.'

CHAP. V. 1. The king Hsüan of Ch'î said, 'People all tell me to pull down and remove the Hall of Distinction. Shall I pull it down, or stop *the movement for that object?*'

2. Mencius replied, 'The Hall of Distinction is a Hall appropriate to the sovereigns. If your Majesty wishes to practise the true royal government, then do not pull it down.'

3. The king said, 'May I hear from you what the true royal government is?' 'Formerly,' was the reply, 'king Wăn's govern-

names of two of the five notes in the Chinese scale, the fourth and third. 招 is used for 韶, the name given to the music of Shun. This was said to be preserved in Ch'î, and the same name was given to all Ch'î music. The Chî-shâo and Chio-shâo were, I suppose, two tunes or pieces of music, starting with the notes 徵 and 角 respectively.

5. TRUE ROYAL GOVERNMENT WILL ASSUREDLY RAISE TO THE SUPREME DIGNITY, AND NEITHER GREED OF WEALTH, NOR LOVE OF WOMAN, NEED INTERFERE WITH ITS EXERCISE. However his admirers may try to defend him, here, and in other chapters, Mencius, if he does not counsel to, yet suggests, rebellion. In his days, the Châu dynasty was nearly a century distant from its extinction. And then his accepting the princes, with all their confirmed habits of vice and luxury, and telling them those need not interfere with the benevolence of their government, shows very little knowledge of man, or of men's affairs. 1. 明堂,—not 'the *Ming* or Brilliant Hall.' It was the name given to the palaces occupied in different parts of the country by the sovereigns in their tours of inspection mentioned in the last chapter. See the Book of Rites, Bk. XII. The name *Ming* was given to them, because royal government, &c., were 'displayed' by means of them. The one in the text was at the foot of the T'âi mountain in Ch'î, and as the Son of Heaven no longer made use of it, the suggestion on which he consulted Mencius was made to king Hsüan. In 毀諸已乎 we have two questions,—'Shall I destroy it (諸, the interrogative of hesitancy, so common in Mencius), or, Shall I stop?' 2. The first and third 王 here might have the 4th tone; they quite differ from the second, which is merely the style of king Hsüan. I may give here a note from the 集證 (Pt. I. i. 1) on the force of the terms 君 and 王:—'He who is followed by the people till they form *a flock* (羣), is a *chün*. He to whom they turn and go (往之), is a *wang*. Thus the title *wang* expresses the idea of the people's turning and resorting *to* him who holds it, but the possessor of a State can barely be called a *chün*. It is only the possessor of the whole kingdom who can be styled *wang*.' 3. Ch'î was a double-peaked hill, giving its name to the adjoining country, the old State of Châu. Its name is still retained in the district of Ch'î-shan, in Făng-hsiang, the most western department of Shen-hsî, bordering on Kan-sû. 耕者九

岐也、耕者九一、仕者世祿、關市譏而不征、澤梁無禁、罪人不孥、老而無妻曰鰥、老而無夫曰寡、老而無子曰獨、幼而無父曰孤、此四者、天下之窮民而無告者、文王發政施仁、必先斯四者、詩云、哿矣富人、哀此煢獨。四 王曰、善哉言乎。曰、王如善之、則何爲不行。王曰、寡

ment of Ch'î was as follows:—The husbandmen *cultivated for the government* one-ninth of the land; the descendants of officers were salaried; at the passes and in the markets, *strangers* were inspected, but *goods* were not taxed: there were no prohibitions respecting the ponds and weirs; the wives and children of criminals were not involved in their guilt. There were the old and wifeless, or widowers; the old and husbandless, or widows; the old and childless, or solitaries; the young and fatherless, or orphans:—these four classes are the most destitute of the people, and have none to whom they can tell their wants, and king Wăn, in the institution of his government with its benevolent action, made them the first objects of his regard, as it is said in the Book of Poetry,

"The rich may get through *life well;*
But alas! for the miserable and solitary!"'

4. The king said, 'O excellent words!' *Mencius* said, 'Since your Majesty deems them excellent, why do you not practise them?' 'I have an infirmity,' said the king; 'I am fond of wealth.' The

—, a square *li* was divided into nine parts, each containing 100 *mâu;* eight farming families were located upon them, one part being reserved for government, which was cultivated by the joint labours of the husbandmen;—see III. Pt.I. iii. 仕者世祿,—'officers, hereditary emolument;' that is, descendants of meritorious officers, if men of ability, received office, and, even if they were not, they had pensions, in reward of the merit of their fathers. 'Ponds and weirs,'—it is not to be understood that the *ponds* were artificial. 先斯四,—先 is the verb. For the ode, see the Shih-ching, II. iv. Ode VIII. st. 13, where for 煢 we find 惸. 4. 公劉, 'The duke Liû,' was the great grandson of Hâu-chî, the high ancestor of the Châu family. By him the waning fortunes of his house were revived, and he founded a settlement in 豳 (*Pin*), the present Pin-châu (邠州), in Shen-hsî. The account of his doing so is found in the ode quoted, Shih-ching, III. ii.

人有疾、寡人好貨。對曰、昔者、公劉好貨、詩云、乃積乃倉、乃裹餱糧、于槖于囊、思戢用光、弓矢斯張、干戈戚揚、爰方啟行、故居者有積倉、行者有裹糧也、然後可以爰方啟行、王如好貨、與百姓同之、於王何有。○五節 王曰、寡人有疾、寡人好色。對曰、昔者大王好色、愛厥妃、詩云、古公亶父、來朝走馬、率

reply was, 'Formerly, Kung-liû was fond of wealth. It is said in the Book of Poetry,

"He reared his ricks, and filled his granaries,
He tied up dried provisions and grain,
In bottomless bags, and sacks,
That he might gather his people together, and glorify *his State.*
With bows and arrows all-displayed,
With shields, and spears, and battle-axes, large and small,
He commenced his march."

In this way those who remained in their old seat had their ricks and granaries, and those who marched had their bags of provisions. It was not till after this that he thought he could begin his march. If your Majesty loves wealth, give the people power to gratify the same feeling, and what difficulty will there be in your attaining the royal sway?'

5. The king said, 'I have an infirmity; I am fond of beauty.' The reply was, 'Formerly, king T'âi was fond of beauty, and loved his wife. It is said in the Book of Poetry,

"Kû-kung T'an-fû
Came in the morning, galloping his horse,
By the banks of the western waters,

Ode IV. st. 1. For 乃 we have in the Shih-ching 迺, and for 戢, 輯. 積, read *ts'ze*, in 4th tone, 'to store up,' 'stores.' Chû Hsî explains:—'stores in the open air.' 5. The king T'âi (see the Doctrine of the Mean, chap. xviii) was the ninth in descent from Kung Liû, by name T'an-fû (in 3rd tone). He removed from

西水滸、至于岐下、爰及姜女、聿來胥宇、當是時也、內無怨女、外無曠夫、王如好色、與百姓同之、於王何有。

第六章 一節 孟子謂齊宣王曰、王之臣、有託其妻子於其友、而之楚遊者、比其反也、則凍餒其妻子、則如之何。王曰、棄之。二節 曰、士師不能治士、則如之何。王曰、已之。三節 曰、四境

As far as the foot of Ch'î hill,
Along with the lady of Chiang;
They came and together chose the site for their settlement."

At that time, in the seclusion of the house, there were no dissatisfied women, and abroad, there were no unmarried men. If your Majesty loves beauty, let the people be able to gratify the same feeling, and what difficulty will there be in your attaining the royal sway?'

CHAP. VI. 1. Mencius said to the king Hsüan of Ch'î, 'Suppose that one of your Majesty's ministers were to entrust his wife and children to the care of his friend, while he himself went into Ch'û to travel, and that, on his return, *he should find that* the friend had let his wife and children suffer from cold and hunger;—how ought he to deal with him?' The king said, 'He should cast him off.'

2. *Mencius* proceeded, 'Suppose that the chief criminal judge could not regulate the officers *under him*, how would you deal with him?' The king said, 'Dismiss him.'

3. *Mencius again* said, 'If within the four borders *of your*

Pin to Ch'î, as is celebrated in the ode, Shih-ching, III. i. Ode III. st. 2. 古公=先公, 'the ancient duke,' T'an-fû's title, before it was changed into 大王, 'the king, or sovereign, T'âi.'

6. BRINGING HOME HIS BAD GOVERNMENT TO THE KING OF CH'Î. 1. 之楚,—之 is the verb = 往. 比, in 4th tone, = 及, as in Analects, XI. xxv. 4, 5. 凍 and 餒 = active, *hiphil* verbs. It is better to prefix 'suppose that,' or 'if,' to the whole sentence, in the translation, as the cases in the remaining paragraph cannot well be put directly, as this might be. The replies suggest the renderings of 如之何, which I have given. 2. 士師, see on Analects, XVIII. ii. 治 is the 2nd tone. In the next paragraph, it is the 4th. The two instances well illustrate the difference of signification, which the tone makes.

之內不治、則如之何。王顧左右而言他。

第七章 孟子見齊宣王曰、所謂故國者、非謂有喬木之謂也、有世臣之謂也、王無親臣矣、昔者所進、今日不知其亡也。二節 王曰、吾何以識其不才而舍之。三節 曰、國君進賢、如不得已、將使卑踰尊、疏踰戚、可不慎與。四節 左右皆曰

kingdom there is not good government, what is to be done?' The king looked to the right and left, and spoke of other matters.

CHAP. VII. 1. Mencius, having an interview with the king Hsüan of Ch'î, said to him, 'When men speak of "an ancient kingdom," it is not meant thereby that it has lofty trees in it, but that it has ministers *sprung from families which have been noted in it* for generations. Your Majesty has no intimate ministers *even*. Those whom you advanced yesterday are gone to-day, and you do not know it.'

2. The king said, 'How shall I know that they have not ability, and so avoid employing them at all?'

3. The reply was, 'The ruler of a State advances to office men of talents and virtue only as a matter of necessity. Since he will thereby cause the low to overstep the honourable, and distant to overstep his near relatives, ought he to do so but with caution?

4. 'When all those about you say,—"This is a man of talents

7. THE CARE TO BE EMPLOYED BY A PRINCE IN THE EMPLOYMENT OF MINISTERS; AND THEIR RELATION TO HIMSELF AND THE STABILITY OF HIS KINGDOM. 1. On the idiom 之謂, see Prémare, on character 之; but the samples which he adduces are not quite similar to those in this passage. Literally, the opening sentence would be:—'That which is called an ancient kingdom, is not the saying (之謂) of saying it has lofty trees; it is the saying of—it has hereditary ministers.' The 謂 in 非謂 might be omitted, and yet it adds something in the turn of the sentence. As opposed to 今日, 昔者 = 'yesterday.' Châo Ch'î strangely mistakes the meaning of the last clause, which he makes to be:—'Those whom you advanced on the past day, do evil to-day, and you do not know to cut them off!' 2. 舍 = 捨, the 3rd tone, 'to let go,' 'to dismiss.' 3. 如不得已,—literally, 'as a thing in which he cannot stop.'

賢、未可也、諸大夫皆曰賢、未可也、國人皆曰賢、然後察之、見賢焉、然後用之、左右皆曰不可、勿聽、諸大夫皆曰不可、勿聽、國人皆曰不可、然後察之、見不可焉、然後去之。

○五 左右皆曰可殺、勿聽、諸大夫皆曰可殺、勿聽、國人皆曰可殺、然後察之、見可殺焉、然後殺之、故曰國人殺之也。

○六 如此、然後可以爲民父母。

and worth," you may not therefore believe it. When your great officers all say,—"This is a man of talents and virtue," neither may you for that believe it. When all the people say,—"This is a man of talents and virtue," then examine into the case, and when you find that the man is such, employ him. When all those about you say,—"This man won't do," don't listen to them. When all your great officers say,—"This man won't do," don't listen to them. When the people all say,—"This man won't do," then examine into the case, and when you find that the man won't do, send him away.

5. 'When all those about you say,—"This man deserves death," don't listen to them. When all your great officers say,—"This man deserves death," don't listen to them. When the people all say,—"This man deserves death," then inquire into the case, and when you see that the man deserves death, put him to death. In accordance with this we have the saying, "The people killed him."

6. 'You must act in this way in order to be the parent of the people.'

Compare the Chung Yung, xx. 13. 4. 未可, 'you may not *yet* believe that the man is so and so.' See on Analects, XIII. xxiv. 6. Compare the Great Learning, Commentary x. 3. We may use the second person in translating or, more indefinitely, the third.

孟子

第八章 一節 齊宣王問曰、湯放桀、武王伐紂、有諸。孟子對曰、於傳有之。二節 曰、臣弑其君可乎。三節 曰、賊仁者、謂之賊、賊義者、謂之殘、殘賊之人、謂之一夫、聞誅一夫紂矣、未聞弑君也。

第九章 一節 孟子見齊宣王曰、為巨室、則必使工師求大木、工師得大木、則王喜、以為能

CHAP. VIII. 1. The king Hsüan of Ch'î asked, saying, 'Was it so, that T'ang banished Chieh, and that king Wû smote Châu?' Mencius replied, 'It is so in the records.'

2. *The king* said, 'May a minister *then* put his sovereign to death?'

3. *Mencius* said, 'He who outrages the benevolence *proper to his nature*, is called a robber; he who outrages righteousness, is called a ruffian. The robber and ruffian we call a mere fellow. I have heard of the cutting off of the fellow Châu, but I have not heard of the putting a sovereign to death, *in his case*.'

CHAP. IX. 1. Mencius, having an interview with the king Hsüan of Ch'î, said to him, 'If you are going to build a large mansion, you will surely cause the Master of the workmen to look out for large trees, and when he has found such large trees, you will

8. KILLING A SOVEREIGN IS NOT NECESSARILY REBELLION NOR MURDER. 1. Of T'ang's banishment of Chieh, see the Shû-ching, IV. ii, iii; and of the smiting of Châu, see the same, V. i. 2. 弑 is the word appropriated to regicide, which Mencius in his reply exchanges for 誅. 臣,—'a minister,' i.e. here, a subject. 3. 賊, as a verb, = 傷害, 'to hurt and injure,' as in the Analects, several times. 'To outrage' answers well for it here. In the use of 夫, Mencius seems to refer to the expression 獨夫紂, Shû-ching, V. i. Sect. III. 4.

9. THE ABSURDITY OF A RULER'S NOT ACTING ACCORDING TO THE COUNSEL OF THE MEN OF TALENTS AND VIRTUE, WHOM HE CALLS TO AID IN HIS GOVERNMENT, BUT REQUIRING THEM TO FOLLOW HIS WAYS. In one important point Mencius's illustrations fail. A prince is not supposed to understand either house-building or stone-cutting; he must delegate those matters to the men who do. But government he ought to understand, and he may not delegate it to any scholars or officers. 1. The 工師 was a special officer having charge of all the artisans, &c.;—see the Lî Chî, IV. Sect. I. iii. 13, and Sect. IV. i. 17. 勝, the 1st tone,—see Pt. I. iii. 3. 其任 (the 4th tone),—'its use,' i.e. the building of the

勝其任矣、匠人斲而小之、則王怒以爲不勝其任矣、夫人幼而學之、壯而欲行之、王曰、姑舍女所學而從我、則何如。○二節 今有璞玉於此、雖萬鎰、必使玉人彫琢之、至於治國家、則曰、姑舍女所學而從我、則何以異於教玉人彫琢玉哉。

be glad, thinking that they will answer for the intended object. Should the workmen hew them so as to make them too small, then your Majesty will be angry, thinking that they will not answer for the purpose. Now, a man spends his youth in learning *the principles of right government*, and, being grown up to vigour, he wishes to put them in practice;—if your Majesty says to him, "For the present put aside what you have learned, and follow me," what shall we say?

2. 'Here now you have a gem unwrought, *in the stone*. Although it may be worth 240,000 *taels*, you will surely employ a lapidary to cut and polish it. But when you come to the government of the State, then you say,—"For the present put aside what you have learned, and follow me." How is it that you herein act so differently from your conduct in calling in the lapidary to cut the gem?'

house. The 之 after 學 and 行 are to be understood as referring to 仁 and 義, or as in the translation. 壯 denotes the maturity of thirty years, when one was supposed to be fit for office. 2. The 鎰 was twenty-four Chinese ounces or *taels* (of gold). Chû Hsî, after Châo Ch'î, erroneously makes it twenty ounces. The gem in question, worth so much, would be very dear to the king, *and yet* he would certainly confide to another the polishing of it;—why would he not do so with the State? 國家,—the kingdom, embracing the families and possessions of the nobles. 女=汝. 教, the 1st tone, =使 or 令, 'to make,' not 'to teach.' From 至於, however, was explained by Châo Ch'î (and many still follow him) thus:—'But in the matter of the government of your State, you say,—For the present put aside what you have learned, and follow me. In what does this differ from your teaching—i. e. wishing to teach—the lapidary to cut the gem?' This is the interpretation which Julien adopts in his translation. The other upon the whole appears to me the better. The first 則 is a difficulty in Châo Ch'î's view; the second, in the other. But the final 哉 turns the balance in its favour, and accordingly I have adopted it.

第十章 一節 齊人伐燕勝之。二節 宣王問曰、或謂寡人勿取、或謂寡人取之、以萬乘之國、伐萬乘之國、五旬而舉之、人力不至於此、不取、必有天殃、取之何如。三節 孟子對曰、取之而燕民悅、則取之、古之人有行之者、武王是也、取之而燕民不悅、則勿取、古之人有行之者、文王是也。四節 以

CHAP. X. 1. The people of Ch'î attacked Yen, and conquered it.

2. The king Hsüan asked, saying, 'Some tell me not to take possession of it for myself, and some tell me to take possession of it. For a kingdom of ten thousand chariots, attacking another of ten thousand chariots, to complete the conquest of it in fifty days, is an achievement beyond *mere* human strength. If I do not take possession of it, calamities from Heaven will surely come upon me. What do you say to my taking possession of it?'

3. Mencius replied, 'If the people of Yen will be pleased with your taking possession of it, then do so.—Among the ancients there was *one* who acted on this principle, namely king Wû. If the people of Yen will not be pleased with your taking possession of it, then do not do so.—Among the ancients there was *one* who acted on this principle, namely king Wăn.

4. 'When, with *all the strength of* your country of ten thousand

10. THE DISPOSAL OF KINGDOMS RESTS WITH THE MINDS OF THE PEOPLE. VOX POPULI VOX DEI. We shall find this doctrine often put forth very forcibly by Mencius. Here the king of Ch'î insinuates that it was the will of Heaven that he should take Yen, and Mencius sends him to the will of the people, by which only the other could be ascertained. 1. The State of Yen (the 1st tone) lay north-west from Ch'î, forming part of the present province of Chih-li. Its prince, a poor weakling, had resigned his throne to his prime minister, and great confusion ensued, so that the people welcomed the appearance of the troops of Ch'î, and made no resistance to them. 2. 舉之 is explained as = 勝之, 'to conquer it;' but 舉 has not this signification. Literally, we might render 'and *up* with it.' 3. The common saying is that king Wăn 三分天下有其二, 'had possession of two of the three parts of the kingdom.' Still he did not think that the people were prepared for the entire extinction of the Yin dynasty, and left the completion of the fortunes of his house to his son, king Wû. 4. 食, read *tsze*, 4th tone, 'rice.' 漿 is

萬乘之國、伐萬乘之國、簞食壺漿、以迎王師、豈有他哉、避水火也、如水益深、如火益熱、亦運而已矣。

十一章 一節 齊人伐燕取之、諸侯將謀救燕。宣王曰、諸侯多謀伐寡人者、何以待之、孟子對曰、臣聞七十里、爲政於天下者、湯是也、未聞以千里畏人者也。二節 書曰、湯一征、

chariots, you attacked another country of ten thousand chariots, and *the people brought* baskets of rice and vessels of congee, to meet your Majesty's host, was there any other reason for this but that they hoped to escape out of fire and water? If you make the water more deep and the fire more fierce, they will in like manner make *another* revolution.'

CHAP. XI. 1. The people of Ch'î, having smitten Yen, took possession of it, *and upon this,* the princes of the various States deliberated together, and resolved to deliver Yen *from their power.* The king Hsüan said *to Mencius,* 'The princes have formed many plans to attack me:—how shall I prepare myself for them?' Mencius replied, 'I have heard of one who with seventy *lî* exercised all the functions of government throughout the kingdom. That was T'ang. I have never heard of a *prince* with a thousand *lî* standing in fear of others.'

2. 'It is said in the Book of History, As soon as T'ang began

properly congee, but here used generally for beverages; some say wine. 壺, 'a goblet,' 'a jug,' 'a vase,' a vessel for liquids generally.—The first paragraph, it is said, is constructed according to the rules of composition attributed to Confucius in his 'Spring and Autumn,' the 人 refusing honour to the king of Ch'î. 伐 expresses the ill deserts of Yen. And 勝之 intimates that the conquest was from the disinclination of Yen to fight, not from the power of Ch'î.

11. AMBITION AND AVARICE ONLY MAKE ENEMIES AND BRING DISASTERS. SAFETY AND PROSPERITY LIE IN A BENEVOLENT GOVERNMENT. 1. 將 before 謀救 indicates the execution of the plans to be still in the future. 者 in 諸侯…者 makes the clause like one in English beginning with a nominative absolute. 待之,—literally, 'await them.' 2. See the Shû-ching, IV. ii. 6. Mencius has introduced the clause 天

自葛始、天下信之、東面而征、西夷怨、南面而征、北狄怨、曰、奚爲後我、民望之、若大旱之望雲霓也、歸市者不止、耕者不變、誅其君、而弔其民、若時雨降、民大悅、書曰、徯我后、后來其蘇。今燕虐其民、王往而征之、民以爲將拯己於水火之中也、簞食壺漿以迎王師、若

his work of executing justice, he commenced with Ko. The whole kingdom had confidence in him. When he pursued his work in the east, the rude tribes on the west murmured. So did those on the north, when he was engaged in the south. Their cry was—"Why does he put us last?" *Thus*, the people looked to him, as we look in a time of great drought to the clouds and rainbows. The frequenters of the markets stopped not. The husbandmen made no change *in their operations.* While he punished their rulers, he consoled the people. *His progress* was like the falling of opportune rain, and the people were delighted. It is said *again* in the Book of History, "We have waited for our prince *long;* the prince's coming will be our reviving!"

3. 'Now *the ruler of* Yen was tyrannizing over his people, and your Majesty went and punished him. The people supposed that you were going to deliver them out of the water and the fire, and brought baskets of rice and vessels of congee, to meet your Majesty's host. But you have slain their fathers and elder brothers, and put

下信之, and there are some other differences from the original text. Ko was a small territory, which is referred to the present district of Ning-ling (寗陵) in Kwei-teh (歸德), in Honan. 望雲霓,—the modern commentators ingeniously interpret:—'The people look for rain in drought, and murmur at his not coming, as they dread the appearance of a rainbow, on which the rain will stop.' This is perhaps over-refining, and making too much of the 望. Châo Ch'î says:—'The rainbow appears when it rains, so people, in time of drought, long to see it.' The second quotation is from the same paragraph of the Shû-ching, where we have 予 for 我. 3. Compare last chapter. 若, in 若殺云云, is not our 'if,' but rather 'since.' The critics say 是指數之詞, 不作設詞看, 'it is demonstrative, not conditional.' 父兄,—父 is not *fathers* only, but *uncles* as well.

殺其父兄、係累其子弟、毀其宗廟、遷其重器、如之何其可也、天下固畏齊之彊也、今又倍地、而不行仁政、是動天下之兵也、○四節王速出令、反其旄倪、止其重器、謀於燕衆、置君而後去之、則猶可及止也。

十二章 一節 鄒與魯鬨、穆公問曰、吾有司死者、三十三人、而民莫之死也、誅之、則不可勝誅、不誅、

their sons and younger brothers in confinement. You have pulled down the ancestral temple *of the State*, and are removing *to Ch'î* its precious vessels. How can such a course be deemed proper? *The rest of* the kingdom is indeed *jealously* afraid of the strength of Ch'î; and now, when with a doubled territory you do not put in practice a benevolent government;—it is this which sets the arms of the kingdom in motion.

4. 'If your Majesty will make haste to issue an ordinance, restoring *your captives*, old and young, stopping *the removal of* the precious vessels, *and saying that, after* consulting with the people of Yen, you will appoint them a ruler, and withdraw from the country;—in this way you may still be able to stop *the threatened attack*.'

CHAP. XII. 1. There had been a brush between Tsâu and Lû, when the duke Mû asked *Mencius*, saying, 'Of my officers there were killed thirty-three men, and none of the people would die in their defence. Though I sentenced them to death *for their conduct*, it is impossible to put such a multitude to death. If I do not put them

其宗廟, 其宗器,—其 = 'its or his,' i.e. the kingdom's or the prince's, not their, the people's. 4. 旄, 4th tone, used for 耄, 'people of eighty and ninety.' The clauses after the first are to be understood as the substance of the order or ordinance, which Mencius advised the king to issue.

12. THE AFFECTIONS OF THE PEOPLE CAN ONLY BE SECURED THROUGH A BENEVOLENT GOVERNMENT. AS THEY ARE DEALT WITH BY THEIR SUPERIORS, SO WILL THEY DEAL BY THEM. 1. Tsâu, the native State of Mencius, was a small territory, whose name is still retained, in the district of Tsâu-hsien, in Yen-châu of Shan-tung. 鬨 is explained—'the noise of a struggle.' It is a brush, a skirmish. Tsâu could not stand long against the forces of Lû. Mû,—'the Dis-

則疾視其長上之死而不救、如之何則可也。○二節孟子對曰、凶年饑歲、君之民、老弱轉乎溝壑、壯者散而之四方者、幾千人矣、而君之倉廩實、府庫充、有司莫以告、是上慢而殘下也、曾子曰、戒之戒之、出乎爾者、反乎爾者也、夫民今而後得反之也、君無尤焉。○三節君行仁政、

to death, then there is *the crime unpunished of* their looking angrily on at the death of their officers, and not saving them. How is the exigency of the case to be met?'

2. Mencius replied, 'In calamitous years and years of famine, the old and weak of your people, who have been found lying in the ditches and water-channels, and the able-bodied who have been scattered about to the four quarters, have amounted to several thousands. All the while, your granaries, O prince, have been stored with grain, and your treasuries and arsenals have been full, and not one of your officers has told you *of the distress*. Thus negligent have the superiors *in your State* been, and cruel to their inferiors. The philosopher Tsăng said, "Beware, beware. What proceeds from you, will return to you again." Now at length the people have paid back the conduct of their officers to them. Do not you, O prince, blame them.

3. 'If you will put in practice a benevolent government, this

penser of virtue, and Maintainer of righteousness, outwardly showing inward feeling,'—is the posthumous epithet of the duke. 有司 are to be taken together, ='officers;'—see Analects, VIII. iv. 莫之死 is to be completed 莫 (or 莫肯) 爲之死; compare Analects, XIV. xvii. 則疾視云云 is not to be translated,—'they will hereafter look angrily on, &c.;' the reference is to the crime that had taken place. 2. 凶年 = years of pestilence, and other calamities, such as are immediately described. 夫, 1st tone, indicates the application of the saying. 今而後 = 'now at last.'—They had long been wishing to show their feeling, but only now had they found the opportunity. 反之,—之 refers to the 有司. 3. 其上,—embracing the prince and officers generally; 其長 (the 3rd tone), the officers only. 死其長,—to be supplemented, as in par. 1.

斯民親其上、死其長矣。

〔十三〕滕文公問曰、滕、小國也、間於齊楚、事齊乎、事楚乎。孟子對曰、是謀非吾所能及也、無已、則有一焉、鑿斯池也、築斯城也、與民守之、效死而民弗去、則是可爲也。

〔十四〕滕文公問曰、齊人將築薛、吾甚恐、如之何則可。孟子對曰、昔者、大王居邠、狄人侵之、去之岐

people will love you and all above them, and will die for their officers.'

CHAP. XIII. 1. The duke Wăn of T'ăng asked *Mencius*, saying, 'T'ăng is a small kingdom, and lies between Ch'î and Ch'û. Shall I serve Ch'î? Or shall I serve Ch'û?'

2. Mencius replied, 'This plan *which you propose* is beyond me. If you will have me counsel you, there is one thing *I can suggest*. Dig deeper your moats; build higher your walls; guard them as well as your people. *In case of attack*, be prepared to die *in your defence*, and have the people so that they will not leave you;—this is a proper course.'

CHAP. XIV. 1. The duke Wăn of T'ăng asked *Mencius*, saying, 'The people of Ch'î are going to fortify Hsieh. *The movement* occasions me great alarm. What is the proper course for me to take in the case?'

2. Mencius replied, 'Formerly, when king T'âi dwelt in Pin, the barbarians of the north were *continually* making incursions upon it. He *therefore* left it, went to the foot of mount Ch'î, and there took

13. A PRINCE SHOULD DEPEND ON HIMSELF, AND NOT RELY ON, OR TRY TO PROPITIATE, OTHER POWERS. 1. T'ăng still gives its name to a district of Yen-châu in the south of Shan-tung. North of it was Ch'î, and, in the time of Mencius, Ch'û was threatening it from the south. 間, 4th tone, 'to occupy a space between.' 2. 無已, 則有一焉,—compare Pt. I. vii. 2,—無以,

孟子

山之下居焉、非擇而取之、不得已也。二節苟爲善、後世子孫必有王者矣、君子創業垂統、爲可繼也、若夫成功、則天也、君如彼何哉、彊爲善而已矣。

十五章 一節 滕文公問曰、滕、小國也、竭力以事大國、則不得免焉、如之何則可。孟子對曰、昔者、太王居邠、

up his residence. He did not take that situation, as having selected it. It was a matter of necessity with him.

3. 'If you do good, among your descendants, in after generations, there shall be one who will attain to the royal dignity. A prince lays the foundation of the inheritance, and hands down the beginning *which he has made*, doing what may be continued *by his successors*. As to the accomplishment of the great result, that is with Heaven. What is that Ch'î to you, O prince? Be strong to do good. That is all your business.'

CHAP. XV. 1. The duke Wăn of T'ăng asked Mencius, saying, 'T'ăng is a small State. Though I do my utmost to serve those large kingdoms *on either side of it*, we cannot escape *suffering from them*. What course shall I take that we may do so?' Mencius

則王乎. 斯池,—'these,' = your 'moats.' 效死,—效 = 致, as that is used in Analects, I. vii, *et al.* A good deal must be supplied here in the translation, to bring out Mencius's counsel.

14. A PRINCE, THREATENED BY HIS NEIGHBOURS, WILL FIND HIS BEST DEFENCE AND CONSOLATION IN DOING WHAT IS GOOD AND RIGHT. Mencius was at his wit's end, I suppose, to give duke Wăn an answer. It was all very well to tell him to do good, but the promise of a royal descendant would hardly be much comfort to him. The reward to be realized in this world in the person of another, and the reference to Heaven, as to a fate more than to a personal God,—are melancholy. Contrast Psalm xxxvii. 3,—'Trust in the Lord and do good; so shalt thou dwell in the land, and verily thou shalt be fed.' 1. 薛 was the name of an ancient principality, adjoining T'ăng. It had long been incorporated with Ch'î, which now resumed an old design of fortifying it,—that is, I suppose, of repairing the wall of its principal town, as a basis of operations against T'ăng. 2. See chap. iii, and also the next. 去之岐山下,—it is best to take 之 here as the verb, = 往. 3. 君子,—generally, 'a prince.' 垂統,—統, 'the end of a cocoon, or clue,' 'a beginning.' 若夫, the 夫 is not a mere expletive, but is used as in Analects, XI. ix. 3, *et al.*, 'as to this—the accomplishing,' &c. 彊, the 3rd tone, is the verb.

15. TWO COURSES OPEN TO A PRINCE PRESSED BY HIS ENEMIES;—FLIGHT OR DEATH. 1. Compare chap. iii. 屬,—read *chû*, the 4th tone, 'to assemble,' 'meet with.' 耆,—'a sexagenarian.' 二三子,—see Analects, VII. xxiii, *et al.*

狄人侵之、事之以皮幣、不得免焉、事之以犬馬、不得免焉、事之以珠玉、不得免焉、乃屬其耆老而告之曰、狄人之所欲者、吾土地也、吾聞之也、君子不以其所以養人者害人、二三子、何患乎無君、我將去之、去邠、踰梁山、邑於岐山之下居焉、邠人曰、仁人也、不可失也、從之者如歸市。二或曰、世守也、非身之所能爲也、效

replied, 'Formerly, when king T'âi dwelt in Pin, the barbarians of the north were *constantly* making incursions upon it. He served them with skins and silks, and still he suffered from them. He served them with dogs and horses, and still he suffered from them. He served them with pearls and gems, and still he suffered from them. Seeing this, he assembled the old men, and announced to them, saying, "What the barbarians want is my territory. I have heard this,—that a ruler does not injure his people with that wherewith he nourishes them. My children, why should you be troubled about having no prince? I will leave this." *Accordingly*, he left Pin, crossed the mountain Liang, *built* a town at the foot of mount Ch'î, and dwelt there. The people of Pin said, "He is a benevolent man. We must not lose him." Those who followed him looked like crowds hastening to market.

2. '*On the other hand*, some say, "*The kingdom* is a thing to be kept from generation to generation. One individual cannot under-

何患乎無君 seems to mean :—'If I remain here, I am sure to die from the barbarians. I will go and preserve your ruler for you.' So the paraphrast in the 備旨. The 日講, however, says :—'My children, why need you be troubled about having no prince? When I am gone, whoever can secure your repose, will be your prince and chief. I will leave this, and go elsewhere.' 歸市 is different rather from the same phrase in chap. vii. There it means traders, here market-goers generally. 2. This paragraph is to be understood as spoken *to* a ruler, in his own person. Compare

死勿去。三節君請擇於斯二者。

十六章一節魯平公將出、嬖人臧倉者、請曰、他日君出、則必命有司所之、今乘輿已駕矣、有司未知所之、敢請。公曰、將見孟子。曰、何哉、君所爲輕身以先於匹夫者、以爲賢乎、禮義由賢者出、而孟子之後喪踰前喪、君無見焉。公曰諾。

二節樂正子入見曰、

take to dispose of it in his own person. Let him be prepared to die for it. Let him not quit it."

3. 'I ask you, prince, to make your election between these two courses.'

CHAP. XVI. 1. The duke P'ing of Lû was about to leave *his palace*, when his favourite, one Tsang Ts'ang, made a request to him, saying, 'On other days, when you have gone out, you have given instructions to the officers as to where you were going. But now, the horses have been put to the carriage, and the officers do not yet know where you are going. I venture to ask.' The duke said, 'I am going to see the scholar Măng.' 'How is this?' said the other. 'That you demean yourself, prince, in paying the honour of the first visit to a common man, is, I suppose, because you think that he is a man of talents and virtue. By such men the rules of ceremonial proprieties and right are observed. But on the occasion of this Măng's second mourning, his observances exceeded those of the former. Do not go to see him, my prince.' The duke said, 'I will not.'

2. The officer Yo-chăng entered *the court*, and had an audience.

chap. vii. 爲＝專, 'to take the whole disposal of,' to deal with. It is not to be referred to the 守. The paraphrasts make the whole spoken by the ruler;—thus :—'The territory of the State was handed down by my ancestors to their descendants, that they should keep it from generation to generation. It is not what I can assume in my person the disposal of. If calamities and difficulties come, my course is to fight to the death to keep it. I may not abandon it, and go elsewhere.' The meaning comes to the same. But the 勿 is against this construction.

16. A MAN'S WAY IN LIFE IS ORDERED BY HEAVEN. THE INSTRUMENTALITY OF OTHER MEN IS ONLY SUBORDINATE. 1. The duke P'ing (i.e. 'The Pacificator') had been informed of Mencius's worth, it appears, by Yo-chăng, and was

君奚爲不見孟軻也。曰、或告寡人曰、孟子之後喪踰前喪、是以不往見也。曰、何哉、君所謂踰者、前以士、後以大夫、前以三鼎、而後以五鼎與。曰否、謂棺槨衣衾之美也。曰、非所謂踰也、貧富不同也。三樂正子見孟子曰、克告於君、君爲來見也、

He said, 'Prince, why have you not gone to see Măng K'o?' *The duke* said, 'One told me that, on the occasion of the scholar Măng's second mourning, his observances exceeded those of the former. It is on that account that I have not gone to see him.' 'How is this!' answered Yo-chăng. 'By what you call "exceeding," you mean, I suppose, that, on the first occasion, he used the rites appropriate to a scholar, and, on the second, those appropriate to a great officer; that he first used three tripods, and afterwards five tripods.' *The duke* said, 'No; I refer to the greater excellence of the coffin, the shell, the grave-clothes, and the shroud.' Yo-chăng said, 'That cannot be called "exceeding." That was the difference between being poor and being rich.'

3. *After this*, Yo-chăng saw Mencius, and said to him, 'I told

going out, half-ashamed at the same time to do so, to offer the due respect to him as a professor of moral and political science, by visiting him and asking his services. The author of the 四書拓餘說 approves of the view that the incident in this chapter is to be referred to the 4th year of the sovereign 赧, B.C. 311, but the chronology of the duke P'ing is very confused. 所之,—之＝往. 何哉 is an exclamation of surprise, extending back to 前喪. In 以爲賢乎, the 乎 is hardly so much as an interrogation. I have given its force by —'I suppose.' 出 does not indicate the origin of rites and right, but only their exhibition. The first occasion of Mencius's mourning referred to was that, it is said, for his father. But his father died, according to the received accounts, when he was only a child of three years old. We must suppose that the favourite invented the story. I have retained the surname Măng here, as suiting the paragraph better than Mencius. 2. 樂正 is a double surname. This individual, whose name was K'o (克;—see par. 3), was a disciple of Mencius. The surname probably arose from one of his ancestors having been the music-master of some State, and the name of his office passing over to become the designation of his descendants. The tripods contained the offerings of meat used in sacrifice. The sovereign used nine, the prince of a State seven, a great officer five, and a scholar three. To each tripod belonged its appropriate kind of flesh. 3. 君爲來,—爲, 4th tone, ＝'therefore,' i.e. in consequence of what Yo-chăng had said, the duke was going to visit

孟子

嬖人有臧倉者沮君、君是以不果來也。曰、行或使之、止或尼之、行止非人所能也、吾之不遇魯侯、天也、臧氏之子、焉能使予不遇哉。

the prince about you, and he was consequently coming to see you, when one of his favourites, named Tsang Ts'ang, stopped him, and therefore he did not come according to his purpose.' *Mencius* said, 'A man's advancement is effected, it may be, by others, and the stopping him is, it may be, from the efforts of others. *But* to advance a man or to stop his advance is *really* beyond the power of other men. My not finding *in* the prince of Lû *a ruler who would confide in me, and put my counsels into practice,* is from Heaven. How could that scion of the Tsang family cause me not to find *the ruler that would suit me?*'

Mencius. 尼 is read in the 3rd and 4th tones, both with the same meaning, = 止, 'to stop.' 不遇魯君 is not spoken merely with reference to the duke's not coming, as he had purposed, to meet him. The phrase 不遇 really conveys all the meaning in the translation, however periphrastic that may seem. With this reference of Mencius to Heaven, compare the language of Confucius, Analects, VII. xxii; IX. v; XIV. xxxviii.

BOOK II.

KUNG-SUN CH'ÂU. PART I.

公孫丑章句上

第一章 一節 公孫丑問曰、夫子當路於齊、管仲晏子之功、可復許乎。二節 孟子曰、子誠齊人也、知管仲晏子而已矣。三節 或問乎曾西曰、吾子與子路孰賢、曾西蹵然曰、吾先子之所畏也、曰、然則吾子與管仲孰

CHAPTER I. 1. Kung-sun Ch'âu asked *Mencius*, saying, 'Master, if you were to obtain the ordering of the government in Ch'î, could you promise yourself to accomplish anew such results as those realized by Kwan Chung and Yen?'

2. Mencius said, 'You are indeed a *true* man of Ch'î. You know about Kwan Chung and Yen, and nothing more.

3. 'Some one asked Tsăng Hsî, saying, "Sir, to which do you give the superiority,—to yourself or to Tsze-lû?" Tsăng Hsî looked uneasy, and said, "He was an object of veneration to my grandfather."

TITLE OF THIS BOOK.—The name of Kung-sun Ch'âu, a disciple of Mencius, heading the first chapter, the book is named from him accordingly. On 章句上 see note on the title of the first Book.

1. WHILE MENCIUS WISHED TO SEE A TRUE ROYAL GOVERNMENT AND SWAY IN THE KINGDOM, AND COULD EASILY HAVE REALIZED IT, FROM THE PECULIAR CIRCUMSTANCES OF THE TIME, HE WOULD NOT, TO DO SO, HAVE HAD RECOURSE TO ANY WAYS INCONSISTENT WITH ITS IDEA. 1. Kung-sun Ch'âu, one of Mencius's disciples, belonged to Ch'î, and was probably a cadet of the ducal family. The sons of the princes were generally 公子; their sons again, 公孫, 'ducal grandsons,' and those two characters became the surname of *their* descendants, who mingled with the undistinguished classes of the people. 當路, literally, 'in a way.' Châo Ch'î says,—當仕路, 'in an official way,' and Chû Hsî, 居要地, 'to occupy an important position.' The gloss in the 備旨 says:—'當路 is 操政柄, to grasp the handle of government.' The analogous phrase—當道 is used now to describe an officer's appointment. 管仲,—see Confucian Analects, III. xxii; XIV. x, xvii, xviii. 晏子,—see Analects, V. xvi; Mencius, I. Pt. II. iv. 3. Tsăng Hsî was the grandson, according to Châo Ch'î and Chû Hsî, of Tsăng Shăn, the famous disciple of Confucius. Others say he was Shăn's son. It is a moot-point. 孰賢,—compare Analects, XI. xv. 蹵然,

賢、曾西艴然不悅曰、爾何曾比予於管仲、管仲得君、如彼其專也、行乎國政、如彼其久也、功烈如彼其卑也、爾何曾比予於是。○四節曰、管仲、曾西之所不爲也、而子爲我願之乎。○五節曰、管仲以其君霸、晏子以其君顯、管仲晏子、猶不足爲與。○六節曰、以齊王、由反手也。○七節曰、若是、則弟

"Then," pursued the other, "Do you give the superiority to yourself or to Kwan Chung?" Tsăng Hsî, flushed with anger and displeased, said, "How dare you compare me with Kwan Chung? Considering how entirely Kwan Chung possessed *the confidence of* his prince, how long he enjoyed the direction of the government of the State, and how low, *after all*, was what he accomplished,—how is it that you liken me to him?"

4. 'Thus,' concluded *Mencius*, 'Tsăng Hsî would not play Kwan Chung, and is it what you desire for me that I should do so?'

5. *Kung-sun Ch'âu* said, 'Kwan Chung raised his prince to be the leader of all the other princes, and Yen made his prince illustrious, and do you still think it would not be enough for you to do what they did?'

6. *Mencius* answered, 'To raise Ch'î to the royal dignity would be as easy as it is to turn round the hand.'

7. 'So!' returned the other. 'The perplexity of your disciple

according to Chû, is 不安貌, as in the translation. The dictionary gives it, 敬貌, 'the appearance of reverence.' 先子,—we see what a wide application this character 子 has. 何曾,—曾 is not to be taken as if it were the sign of the present complete tense, though in the dictionary this passage is quoted under that signification of the character. It is here = 則 or 乃. For more than forty years Kwan Chung possessed the entire confidence of the duke Hwan. 4. 爲我,—爲, 4th tone, 'on my behalf.' Sun Shih (孫奭), the paraphrast of Châo Ch'î, takes it as = 以爲:—'Do you think that I desire to do so?' This does not appear to be Ch'î's own interpretation. 5. 管仲晏子猶不足爲與,—literally, 'and are Kwan Chung and Yen still not sufficient to be played?' 7. 若是,—'in this case;' but by using our exclamatory *So!* the spirit of the remark is brought out. 且

子之惑滋甚、且以文王之德百年而後崩、猶未洽於天下、武王周公繼之、然後大行、今言王若易然、則文王不足法與。○八節曰、文王何可當也、由湯至於武丁、賢聖之君六七作、天下歸殷久矣、久則難變也、武丁朝諸侯、有天下、猶運之掌也、紂之去武丁、未久也、其故家遺俗、流風善政、猶有存者、

is hereby very much increased. There was king Wăn, moreover, with all the virtue which belonged to him; and who did not die till he had reached a hundred years:—and still *his influence* had not penetrated throughout the kingdom. It required king Wû and the duke of Châu to continue his course, before that influence greatly prevailed. Now you say that the royal dignity might be so easily obtained:—is king Wăn then not a sufficient object for imitation?'

8. *Mencius* said, 'How can king Wăn be matched? From T'ang to Wû-ting there had appeared six or seven worthy and sage sovereigns. The kingdom had been attached to Yin for a long time, and this length of time made a change difficult. Wû-ting had all the princes coming to his court, and possessed the kingdom as if it had been a thing which he moved round in his palm. *Then*, Châu was removed from Wû-ting by no great interval of time. There were still remaining some of the ancient families and of the old manners, of the influence also which had emanated *from the earlier sovereigns*, and of their good government. Moreover, there were the viscount of

introduces a new subject, and a *stronger one* for the point in hand. King Wăn died at 97.—Ch'âu uses the round number. 今言王若易然,—今言王齊若是之易然, 'Now you say that Ch'î might be raised to the royal sway thus easily.' 8. From T'ang to Wû-ting (B.C. 1765-1323) there were altogether eighteen sovereigns, exclusive of themselves, and from Wû-ting to Châu (1323-1153) seven. 朝 (*ch'âo*), 2nd tone, used as in Bk. I. Pt. I. vii. 16, *et al.* 微子, 比干, 箕子,—see Analects, XVIII. i. The latter two are 王子, as being uncles of Châu, 'royal sons.' 微仲

又有微子微仲、王子比干、箕子、膠鬲、皆賢人也、相與輔相之、故久而後失之也、尺地、莫非其有也、一民、莫非其臣也、然而文王猶方百里起、是以難也。○九節齊人有言曰、雖有智慧、不如乘勢、雖有鎡基、不如待時、今時則易然也。○十節夏后殷周之盛、地未有過千里者也、而齊有其地矣、雞鳴狗吠相聞、

Wei and his second son, their Royal Highnesses Pî-kan and the viscount of Ch'î, and Kâo-ko, all men of ability and virtue, who gave their joint assistance to Châu *in his government*. In consequence of these things, it took a long time for him to lose *the throne*. There was not a foot of ground which he did not possess. There was not one of all the people who was not his subject. So it was on *his side*, and king Wăn at his beginning had only a territory of one hundred square *lî*. On all these accounts, it was difficult for him *immediately to attain to the royal dignity*.

9. 'The people of Ch'î have a saying—"A man may have wisdom and discernment, but that is not like embracing the favourable opportunity. A man may have instruments of husbandry, but that is not like waiting for the *farming* seasons." The present time is one in which *the royal dignity* may be easily attained.

10. 'In the flourishing periods of the Hsiâ, Yin, and Châu dynasties, *the royal* domain did not exceed a thousand *lî*, and Ch'î embraces so much territory. Cocks crow and dogs bark to

was the second son (some say brother) of 微子. Kâo-ko was a distinguished man and minister of the time,—whose worth was first discovered by king Wăn, but who continued loyal to the House of Yin. 輔相,—相, 4th tone. 失之,—之 refers to the throne. 文王猶方云云,—猶, the opp. of former cases, takes the place of 由. 9. 鎡基,—written variously, 兹基, 鎡錤,—was the name for a hoe. 10. 夏后, 殷, 周, see Analects, III. xxi. 辟=闢. The last sentence, as in

而達乎四境、而齊有其民矣、地不改辟矣、民不改聚矣、行仁政而王、莫之能禦也。○十一節 且王者之不作、未有疏於此時者也、民之憔悴於虐政、未有甚於此時者也、饑者易爲食、渴者易爲飲。○十二節 孔子曰、德之流行、速於置郵而傳命。○十三節 當今之時、萬乘之國、行仁政、民之悅之、猶解倒懸也、故事半古之人、

one another, all the way to the four borders of the State:—so Ch'î possesses the people. No change is needed for the enlarging of its territory: no change is needed for the collecting of a population. If its ruler will put in practice a benevolent government, no power will be able to prevent his becoming sovereign.

11. 'Moreover, never was there a time farther removed than the present from the rise of a true sovereign: never was there a time when the sufferings of the people from tyrannical government were more intense than the present. The hungry readily partake of any food, and the thirsty of any drink.

12. 'Confucius said, "The flowing progress of virtue is more rapid than the transmission of *royal* orders by stages and couriers."

13. 'At the present time, in a country of ten thousand chariots, let benevolent government be put in practice, and the people will be delighted with it, as if they were relieved from hanging by the heels. With half the merit of the ancients, double their achievements

Bk. I. Pt. I. vii. 3. 11. The 爲 in 易爲食, 易爲飲 is perplexing. We might put it in the 3rd tone, and 食 and 飲 in the same. But in Bk. VII. Pt. I. xxvii, we have the expressions 飢者甘食, 渴者甘飲, where 食 and 飲 must have their ordinary tones. Stress therefore is not to be laid on the 爲. Perhaps the expressions = 'easily do eating, easily do drinking.' 12. The distinction between 置 and 郵 is much disputed. Some make the former a foot-post, but that is unlikely. It denotes the slower conveyance of despatches, and the other the more rapid. So much seems plain. See the 集證, *in loc.* 13. 猶解倒懸,—Chû Hsî simply

功必倍之、惟此時爲然。

第二章 一節 公孫丑問曰、夫子加齊之卿相、得行道焉、雖由此霸王不異矣、如此、則動心否乎。孟子曰、否、我四十不動心。

二節 曰、若是、則夫子過孟賁遠矣。曰、是不

is sure to be realized. It is only at this time that such could be the case.'

CHAP. II. 1. Kung-sun Ch'âu asked *Mencius*, saying, 'Master, if you were to be appointed a high noble and the prime minister of Ch'î, so as to be able to carry *your* principles into practice, though you should thereupon raise the ruler to the headship of all the other princes, or *even* to the royal dignity, it would not be to be wondered at.—In such a position would your mind be perturbed or not?' Mencius replied, 'No. At forty, I attained to an unperturbed mind.'

2. *Ch'âu* said, 'Since it is so with you, my Master, you are far beyond Măng Păn.' 'The *mere* attainment,' said *Mencius*, 'is not

says :—倒懸喩困苦,'倒懸 expresses bitter suffering.' Literally, it is 'as if they were loosed from being turned upside down and suspended.'

2. THAT MENCIUS HAD ATTAINED TO AN UNPERTURBED MIND; THAT THE MEANS BY WHICH HE HAD DONE SO WAS HIS KNOWLEDGE OF WORDS AND THE NOURISHMENT OF HIS PASSION-NATURE; AND THAT IN THIS HE WAS A FOLLOWER OF CONFUCIUS. The chapter is divided into four parts :—the first, pars. 1–8, showing generally that there are various ways to attain an unperturbed mind; the second, pars. 9, 10, exposing the error of the way taken by the philosopher Kâo; the third, pars. 11–17, unfolding Mencius's own way; and the fourth, pars. 18–28, showing that Mencius followed Confucius, and praising that Sage as the first of mortals. It is chiefly owing to what Mencius says in this chapter about the nourishment of the passion-nature, that a place has been accorded to him among the sages of China, or in immediate proximity to them. His views are substantially these :—Man's nature is composite; he possesses moral and intellectual powers (comprehended by Mencius under the term 心 'heart,' 'mind,' interchanged with 志, 'the will'), and active powers (summed up under the term 氣, and embracing generally the emotions, desires, appetites). The moral and intellectual powers ought to be supreme and govern, but there is a close connexion between them and the others which give effect to them. The active powers may not be stunted, for then the whole character will be feeble. But on the other hand, they must not be allowed to take the lead. They must get their tone from the mind, and the way to develop them in all their completeness is to do good. Let them be vigorous, and the mind clear and pure, and we shall have the man, whom nothing external to himself can perturb,—Horace's *justum et tenacem propositi virum*. In brief, if we take the *sanum corpus* of the Roman adage, as not expressing the mere physical *body*, but the emotional and physical nature, what Mencius exhibits here, may be said to be '*mens sana in corpore sano*.' The attentive reader will, I think, find the above thoughts dispersed through this chapter, and be able to separate them from the irrelevant matter (that especially relating to Confucius), with which they are put forth. 1. 加, 'to add,' and generally 'to confer upon,' is here to be taken passively,—'If on you were conferred the dignity of, &c.' 相, 4th tone.

難、告子先我不動心。○三節曰、不動心有道乎。曰、有○四節北宮黝之養勇也、不膚撓、不目逃、思以一毫挫於人、若撻之於市朝、不受於褐寬博、亦不受於萬乘之君、視刺萬乘之君、若刺褐夫、無嚴諸侯、惡聲至、必反之。○五節孟施舍

difficult. The scholar Kâo had attained to an unperturbed mind at an earlier period of life than I did.'

3. *Ch'âu* asked, 'Is there any way to an unperturbed mind?' The answer was, 'Yes.

4. 'Pî-kung Yû had this way of nourishing his valour:—He did not flinch from any strokes at his body. He did not turn his eyes aside from any thrusts at them. He considered that the slightest push from any one was the same as if he were beaten *before the crowds* in the market-place, and that what he would not receive from *a common man* in his loose large garments of hair, neither should he receive from a prince of ten thousand chariots. He viewed stabbing a prince of ten thousand chariots just as stabbing a fellow dressed in cloth of hair. He feared not any of all the princes. A bad word addressed to him he always returned.

5. 'Măng Shih-shê had this way of nourishing his valour:—

卿相 are not to be separated by an *or*, as 霸王 must be; see on 公卿, Analects, IX. xv. Ch'âu's meaning is that, with so great an office and heavy a charge, the mind might well be perturbed:—would it be so with his master? With Mencius's reply, compare Confucius's account of himself, Analects, II. iv. 3. 2. Măng Păn was a celebrated bravo, who could pull the horn from an ox's head, and feared no man. Kâo is the same who gives the name to the 6th Book of Mencius. 是不難 is not to be understood so much with reference to the case of Măng Păn, as to the attainment of an unperturbed mind, without reference to the way of attaining to it. 3. 道 here = 方法, 'way,' or 'method.' 4. Pî-kung Yû was a bravo, belonging probably to Wei (衞), and connected with its ruling family. 不膚撓 (and tone), 不目逃, literally, 'not skin bend, not eye avoid.' The meaning is not that he had first been wounded in those parts, and still was indifferent to the pain, but that he would press forward, careless of all risks. 思 covers down to 視. 一毫挫, = 'the least push,' = disgrace. 市朝 (*ch'âo*, 2nd tone) are not to be separated, and made—'the market-place or the court.' The latter character is used, because anciently the different parties in the markets were arranged in their respective ranks and places, as the officers in the court. But compare Analects, XIV. xxxviii. 1. 褐寬博 = 褐寬博之夫 (or 賤). 5. There is a difficulty with the 施 in 孟施

之所養勇也、曰、視不勝猶勝也、量敵而後進、慮勝而後會、是畏三軍者也、舍豈能爲必勝哉、能無懼而已矣。○六節 孟施舍似曾子、北宮黝似子夏、夫二子之勇、未知其孰賢、然而孟施舍守約也。○七節 昔者、曾子謂子襄曰、子好勇乎、吾嘗聞大勇於夫子矣、自反而不縮、雖褐寬博、吾不惴焉、自反而縮、雖

He said, "I look upon not conquering and conquering in the same way. To measure the enemy and then advance; to calculate the chances of victory and then engage:—this is to stand in awe of the opposing force. How can I make certain of conquering? I can only rise superior to all fear."

6. 'Măng Shih-shê resembled the philosopher Tsăng. Pî-kung Yû resembled Tsze-hsiâ. I do not know to the valour of which of the two the superiority should be ascribed, but yet Măng Shih-shê attended to what was of the greater importance.

7. 'Formerly, the philosopher Tsăng said to Tsze-hsiang, "Do you love valour? I heard an account of great valour from the Master. *It speaks thus*:—'If, on self-examination, I find that I am not upright, shall I not be in fear even of a poor man in his loose garments of hair-cloth? If, on self-examination, I find that I am upright, I will go forward against thousands and tens of thousands.'"

舍, as this gentleman in the end of the paragraph simply calls himself 舍. Hence the 施 is taken like our 'h'm;'—Măng H'm-shê. The use of Á before the name, especially in the south of China, is analogous to this. Notwithstanding the 所 in the first clause of this paragraph, we need not translate differently from the first clause of the preceding. 三軍,—see Analects, VII. x. 2; used here simply for 'the enemy.' 6. 孰賢,—as in last chapter. Pî-kung Yû thought of others,—of conquering; Măng Shih-shê of himself,—of not being afraid. The basis of the reference to the two disciples is the commonly received idea of their several characters. Tsăng Shăn was reflective, and dealt with himself. Tsze-hsiâ was ambitious, and would not willingly be inferior to others. 7. Tsze-hsiang was a disciple of Tsăng. 縮,—properly, the straight seams, from the top to the edge, with which an ancient cap was made, metaphorically used for 'straight,' 'upright.' 吾不惴焉=吾豈不惴

千萬人、吾往矣。八節孟施舍之守氣、又不如曾子之守約也。九節曰、敢問夫子之不動心、與告子之不動心、可得聞與。告子曰、不得於言、勿求於心、不得於心、勿求於氣、不得於心、勿求於氣、可、不得於言、勿求於心、不可、夫志、氣之帥也、氣、體之充也、夫志至焉、氣次焉、故曰、持

8. '*Yet*, what Măng Shih-shê maintained, being *merely* his physical energy, was after all inferior to what the philosopher Tsăng maintained, which was *indeed* of the most importance.'

9. *Kung-sun Ch'âu* said, 'May I venture to ask an explanation from you, Master, of how you maintain an unperturbed mind, and how the philosopher Kâo does the same?' *Mencius answered*, 'Kâo says,—"What is not attained in words is not to be sought for in the mind; what produces dissatisfaction in the mind, is not to be helped by passion-effort." *This last*,—when there is unrest in the mind, not to seek for relief from passion-effort, may be conceded. But not to seek in the mind for what is not attained in words cannot be conceded. The will is the leader of the passion-nature. The passion-nature pervades and animates the body. The will is *first and* chief, and the passion-nature is subordinate to it. Therefore *I* say,—Maintain firm the will, and do no violence to the passion-nature.'

焉, the interrogation being denoted by the tone of the voice. Still the 焉 is the final particle, and not the initial 'how,' with a different tone, as Julien supposes. 8. Here we first meet the character 氣, so important in this chapter. Its different meanings may be seen in Morrison and Medhurst. Originally it was the same as 气, 'cloudy vapour.' With the addition of 米, 'rice,' or 火, 'fire,' which was an old form, it should indicate 'steam of rice,' or 'steam' generally. The sense in which Mencius uses it, is indicated in the translation and in the preliminary note. The sense springs from its being used as correlate to 心, 'the mind,' taken in connexion with the idea of 'energy' inherent in it, from its composition. Thus it signifies the lower portion of man's constitution; and here, that lower part in its lowest sense,—animal vigour or courage. The 又 refers to what had been conceded to Shê in par. 舍 I translate as if there were a comma or pause after the two 守. 9. Kâo's principle seems to have been this,—utter indifference to everything external, and entire passivity of mind. Modern writers say that in his words is to be found the essence of Buddhism,—that

其志、無暴其氣。十節既曰、志至焉、氣次焉、又曰、持其志、無暴其氣者、何也。曰、志壹、則動氣、氣壹、則動志也、今夫蹶者、趨者、是氣也、而反動其心。十一節敢問夫子惡乎長。曰、我知言、我善養吾浩然之氣。十二節敢問何謂浩然之氣。曰

10. *Ch'âu observed,* 'Since you say—"The will is chief, and the passion-nature is subordinate," how do you also say, "Maintain firm the will, and do no violence to the passion-nature?"' *Mencius* replied, 'When it is the will alone which is active, it moves the passion-nature. When it is the passion-nature alone which is active, it moves the will. For instance now, in the case of a man falling or running, that is from the passion-nature, and yet it moves the mind.'

11. 'I venture to ask,' *said Ch'âu again,* 'wherein you, Master, surpass *Kâo.*' *Mencius* told him, 'I understand words. I am skilful in nourishing my vast, flowing passion-nature.'

12. *Ch'âu* pursued, 'I venture to ask what you mean by your vast, flowing passion-nature!' The reply was, 'It is difficult to describe it.

the object of his attainment was the Buddhistic *nirvâna*, and perhaps this helps us to a glimpse of his meaning. Commentators take sides on 不得於言, whether the 'words' are Kâo's own words, or those of others. To me it is hardly doubtful that they must be taken as the words of others. Mencius's account of himself below, as 'knowing words,' seems to require this. At the same time, a reference to Kâo's arguments with Mencius, in Bk. VI, where he changes the form of his assertions, without seeming to be aware of their refutation, gives some plausibility to the other view. Châo Ch'î understands the expression thus:—'If men's words are bad, I will not inquire about their hearts; if their hearts are bad, I will not inquire about their words!' The 可 is not an approval of Kâo's second proposition, but a concession of it simply as not so bad as his first. Mencius goes on to show wherein he considered it as defective. From his language here, and in the next paragraph, we see that he uses 志 and 心 synonymously. 氣=體之充,—'the 氣 is the filling up of the body.' 氣 might seem here to be little more than the 'breath,' but that meaning would come altogether short of the term throughout the chapter.

10. Ch'âu did not understand what his master had said about the relation between the mind and the passion-nature, and as the latter was subordinate, would have had it disregarded altogether:—hence his question. Mencius shows that the passion-nature is really a part of our constitution, acts upon the mind, and is acted on by it, and may not be disregarded. 壹=專一. The 反 meets Châu's disregard of the passion-nature, as not worth attending to.

11. The illustration here is not a very happy one, leading us to think of 氣 in its merely material signification, as in the last paragraph. On 知言, see par. 17. On 浩然之氣 there is much vain babbling in the commentaries, to show how the 氣 of heaven and earth

難言也。〇十三節其爲氣也、至大至剛、以直養而無害、則塞于天地之間。〇十四節其爲氣也、配義與道、無是餒也。〇十五節是集義所生者、非義襲而取之也、行有不慊於心、則餒矣、我故曰、告子未嘗知義、以其外之也。〇十六節必有事焉而勿正、心勿忘、勿助長也、無若宋人然。宋人有閔其苗之不長、

13. 'This is the passion-nature:—It is exceedingly great, and exceedingly strong. Being nourished by rectitude, and sustaining no injury, it fills up all between heaven and earth.

14. 'This is the passion-nature:—It is the mate and assistant of righteousness and reason. Without it, *man* is in a state of starvation.

15. 'It is produced by the accumulation of righteous deeds; it is not to be obtained by incidental acts of righteousness. If the mind does not feel complacency in the conduct, *the nature* becomes starved. I therefore said, "Kâo has never understood righteousness, because he makes it something external."

16. 'There must be the *constant* practice *of this righteousness*, but without the object *of thereby nourishing the passion-nature*. Let not the mind forget *its work*, but let there be no assisting the growth *of that nature*. Let us not be like the man of Sung. There was a man of Sung, who was grieved that his growing corn was not

is the 氣 also of man. Mencius, it seems to me, has before his mind the ideal of a perfect man, complete in all the parts of his constitution. It is this which gives its elevation to his language. 13. 以直養,—as in pars. 7, 15; 無害,—as in the latter part of par. 15. 塞 is here in the sense of 'to fill up,' not 'to stop up.' Still the 塞乎天地之間 is one of those *heroic* expressions, which fill the ear, but do not inform the mind. 14. A pause must be made after the 是, which refers to the 浩然之氣. 餒 refers to 體, in 體之充, in par. 9. It is better, however, in the translation, to supply 'man,' than 'body.' 15. 襲, 'to take an enemy by surprise;' and 義襲 = 'incidental acts of righteousness.' 餒 refers to the passion-nature itself. The analysis of conduct and feeling here is very good. Mencius's sentiment is just, *'Tis conscience makes cowards of us all.* On the latter sentence, see Bk. VI. v. *et al.* 16. I have given the meaning of the text—必有事焉, 而勿正, 心勿忘, 勿助長 after Châo Ch'î, to whom Chû Hsî also inclines. But for their help, we

而揠之者、芒芒然歸、謂其人曰、今日病矣、予助苗長矣、其子趨而往視之、苗則槁矣、天下之不助苗長者寡矣、以爲無益而舍之者、不耘苗者也、助之長者、揠苗者也、非徒無益、而又害之。十七節 何謂知言。曰、詖辭、知其所蔽、淫辭、知其所陷、邪辭、知其所離、遁辭、知其所窮、生於其心、害於其政、發於

longer, and so he pulled it up. *Having done this,* he returned home, looking very stupid, and said to his people, "I am tired to-day. I have been helping the corn to grow long." His son ran to look at it, and found the corn all withered. There are few in the world, *who do not deal with their passion-nature, as if* they were assisting the corn to grow long. Some indeed consider it of no benefit to them, and let it alone:—they do not weed their corn. They who assist it to grow long, pull out their corn. *What they do is* not only of no benefit *to the nature,* but it also injures it.'

17. *Kung-sun Ch'âu further asked,* 'What do you mean by saying that you understand *whatever* words *you hear?' Mencius* replied, 'When words are one-sided, I know how *the mind of the speaker* is clouded over. When words are extravagant, I know how *the mind* is fallen and sunk. When words are all-depraved, I know how *the mind* has departed *from principle.* When words are evasive, I know how *the mind* is at its wit's end. *These evils* growing in the mind,

should hardly know what to make of it. 正 is taken in the sense of 預期, 'to do with anticipation of, or a view to, an ulterior object.' This meaning of the term is supported by an example from the 春秋傳. 病 = 'tired.' 17. Here, as sometimes before, we miss the preliminary 曰, noting a question by Mencius's interlocutor, and the same omission is frequent in all the rest of the chapter. I have supplied the lacunae after Chû Hsî, who himself follows Lin Chih-ch'î (林之奇), a scholar, who died A.D. 1176. Châo Ch'î sometimes errs egregiously in the last part, through not distinguishing the speakers. With regard to the first ground of Mencius's superiority over Kâo, —his 'knowledge of words,' as he is briefer than on the other, so he is still less satisfactory, —to my mind at least. Perhaps he means to

其政、害於其事、聖人復起、必從吾言矣。十八節宰我、子貢、善爲說辭、冉牛、閔子、顏淵、善言德行、孔子兼之、曰、我於辭命、則不能也、然則夫子既聖矣乎。十九節曰、惡、是何言也、昔者子貢問於孔子曰、夫子聖矣乎、孔子曰、聖、則吾不能、我學不厭、而教不倦

do injury to government, and, displayed in the government, are hurtful to the conduct of affairs. When a Sage shall again arise, he will certainly follow my words.'

18. *On this Ch'âu observed,* 'Tsâi Wo and Tsze-kung were skilful in speaking. Zan Niû, the disciple Min, and Yen Yüan, while their words were good, were distinguished for their virtuous conduct. Confucius united the qualities of the disciples in himself, *but still* he said, "In the matter of speeches, I am not competent."—Then, Master, have you attained to be a Sage?'

19. *Mencius* said, 'Oh! what words are these? Formerly Tsze-kung asked Confucius, saying, "Master, are you a Sage?" Confucius answered him, "A Sage is what I cannot rise to. I learn without satiety, and teach without being tired." Tsze-kung said, "You learn without satiety:—that shows your wisdom. You teach without

say, that however great the dignity to which he might be raised, his knowledge of words, and ability in referring incorrect and injurious speeches to the mental defects from which they sprang, would keep him from being deluded, and preserve his mind unperturbed. One of the scholars Ch'ǎng uses this illustration:—'Mencius with his knowledge of words was like a man seated aloft on the dais, who can distinguish all the movements of the people below the hall, which he could not do, if it were necessary for him to descend and mingle with the crowd.' The concluding remark gives rise to the rest of the chapter, it seeming to Ch'âu that Mencius placed himself by it on the platform of sages. 18. Compare Analects, XI. ii. 2, to the enumeration in which of the excellences of several of Confucius's disciples there seems to be here a reference. There, however, it is said that Zan Niû, Min, and Yen Yüan were distinguished for 德行, and here we have the addition of 善言, which give a good deal of trouble. Some take 言 as a verb,—'were skilful to speak of virtuous conduct.' So the Tartar version, according to Julien. Sun Shih makes it a noun, as I do. The references to the disciples are quite inept. The point of Châu's inquiry lies in Confucius's remark, found nowhere else, and obscure enough. He thinks Mencius is taking more to himself than Confucius did. Châo Ch'î, however, takes 我於辭云云 as a remark of Mencius, but it is quite unnatural to do so. Observe the force of the 既,—*you have come to be.* 19. 惡, in 1st tone; an exclamation, not interrogative. This conversation with Tsze-kung is not found in the Analects. Compare

也、子貢曰、學不厭、智也、教不倦、仁也、仁且智、夫子既聖矣、夫聖、孔子不居、是何言也。○廿昔者、竊聞之、子夏、子游、子張、皆有聖人之一體、冉牛、閔子、顔淵、則具體而微、敢問所安。○廿一曰、姑舍是。○廿二曰、伯夷、伊尹何如。曰、不同道、非其君不事、非其民不使、治則進、亂則退、伯夷也、何事非君、何使非民、治亦進、

being tired:—that shows your benevolence. Benevolent and wise:—Master, you ARE a Sage." Now, since Confucius would not allow himself to be regarded as a Sage, what words were those?'

20. *Ch'âu said*, 'Formerly, I once heard this:—Tsze-hsiâ, Tsze-yû, and Tsze-chang had each one member of the Sage. *Zan* Niû, the disciple Min, and Yen Yüan had all the members, but in small proportions. I venture to ask,—With which of these are you pleased to rank yourself?'

21. *Mencius* replied, 'Let us drop speaking about these, if you please.'

22. *Ch'âu then* asked, 'What do you say of Po-î and Î Yin?' 'Their ways were different *from mine*,' said *Mencius*. 'Not to serve a prince whom he did not esteem, nor command a people whom he did not approve; in a time of good government to take office, and on the occurrence of confusion to retire:—this was *the way of* Po-î. *To say*—"Whom may I not serve? My serving him makes him my ruler. What people may I not command? My commanding them

Analects, VII. ii, xxviii, which latter chapter may possibly be another version of what Mencius says here. 20. 竊 is used with other verbs to give a deferential tone to what they say. 21. Compare Bk. I. Pt. II. xxi. Does Mencius here indicate that he thought himself superior to all the worthies referred to—even to Yen Yüan? Hardly so much as that; but that he could not be content with them for his model.

22. Po-î,—see Analects, V. xxii. Î Yin,—see Analects, XII. xxii. 非其君,非其民,—the emphatic *his*, i.e. as paraphrased in the translation. 何事非君何使非民－得君則事,何所事而非我君,得民則使,何所使而

亂亦進、伊尹也、可以仕則仕、可以止則止、可以久則久、可以速則速、孔子也、皆古聖人也、吾未能有行焉、乃所願、則學孔子也。○廿三節 伯夷伊尹於孔子、若是班乎。曰否、自有生民以來、未有孔子也。○廿四節 曰、然則有同與。曰有、得百里之地而君之、皆能以朝諸侯、有天下、行一不義、殺一不辜、而得天下、皆

makes them my people." In a time of good government to take office, and when disorder prevailed, also to take office :—that was *the way of* Î Yin. When it was proper to go into office, then to go into it; when it was proper to keep retired from office, then to keep retired from it; when it was proper to continue in it long, then to continue in it long; when it was proper to withdraw from it quickly, then to withdraw quickly :—that was *the way of* Confucius. These were all sages of antiquity, and I have not attained to do what they did. But what I wish to do is to learn to be like Confucius.'

23. *Ch'âu said*, 'Comparing Po-î and Î Yin with Confucius, are they to be placed in the same rank?' *Mencius* replied, 'No. Since there were living men until now, there never was *another* Confucius.'

24. *Ch'âu* said, 'Then, did they have *any points of* agreement *with him?*' The reply was,—'Yes. If they had been sovereigns over a hundred *lî* of territory, they would, all of them, have brought all the princes to attend in their court, and have obtained the throne. And none of them, in order to obtain the throne, would have committed one act of unrighteousness, or put to death one innocent person. In those things they agreed with him.'

非我民. I have given the meaning, but the conciseness of the text makes it difficult to a learner. The different ways of Po-î, Î Yin, and Confucius are thus expressed :—'The principle of the first was purity—以清爲其道; that of the second was office—以任爲其道; that of the third was what the time required—以時爲其道.' 23. The meaning of this paragraph is expressed rightly in the

不爲也、是則同。○廿五曰、敢問其所以異。曰、宰我、子貢、有若、智足以知聖人、汙不至阿其所好。○廿六節宰我曰、以予觀於夫子、賢於堯舜遠矣。○廿七節子貢曰、見其禮而知其政、聞其樂、而知其德、由百世之後、等百世之王、莫之能違也、自生民以來、未有夫子也。○廿八節有若曰、豈惟民哉、麒麟之於走獸、鳳凰之於飛鳥、泰

25. *Ch'âu* said, 'I venture to ask wherein he differed from them.' *Mencius* replied, 'Tsâi Wo, Tsze-kung, and Yû Zo had wisdom sufficient to know the sage. *Even had they been ranking themselves* low, they would not have demeaned themselves to flatter their favourite.

26. '*Now*, Tsâi Wo said, "According to my view of our Master, he was far superior to Yâo and Shun."

27. 'Tsze-kung said, "By viewing the ceremonial ordinances *of a prince*, we know *the character of* his government. By hearing his music, we know *the character of* his virtue. After the lapse of a hundred ages I can arrange, according to their merits, the kings of a hundred ages;—not one of them can escape me. From the birth of mankind till now, there has never been *another* like our Master."

28. 'Yû Zo said, "Is it only among men that it is so? There is the Ch'î-lin among quadrupeds, the Făng-hwang among birds, the

translation. If we understand a 之 before the 於, then the idiom is like that of 之於, in Bk. I. Pt. I. iii. 1. 25. 汙,—*wû*, or *wâ*, 'low-lying water,' used here simply for 'low,' with reference to the wisdom of Tsâi Wo and Tsze-kung, in their own estimation. 阿 in the sense of 'partial,' = 'to flatter.' 26. With this and the two next paragraphs, compare the eulogium of Confucius, in the *Chung Yung*, chaps. 30–32, and Analects, XIX. xxiii–xxv. 鳳凰, —see Analects, XI. ix. 28. The *ch'î* is properly the male, and the *lin*, the female of the animal referred to;—a monster, with a deer's body, an ox's tail, and a horse's feet, which appears to greet the birth of a sage, or the reign of a sage sovereign. Both in 麒麟 and 鳳凰, the names of the male and female are put together,

山之於丘垤、河海之於行潦、類也、聖人之於民、亦類也、出於其類、拔乎其萃、自生民以來、未有盛於孔子也。

三章 一節 孟子曰、以力假仁者霸、霸必有大國、以德行仁者王、王不待大、湯以七十里、文王以百里。二節 力服人者、非心服也、力

Tâi mountain among mounds and ant-hills, and rivers and seas among rain-pools. *Though different in degree*, they are the same in kind. So the sages among mankind are also the same in kind. But they stand out from their fellows, and rise above the level, and from the birth of mankind till now, there never has been one so complete as Confucius."'

CHAP. III. 1. Mencius said, 'He who, using force, makes a pretence to benevolence is the leader of the princes. A leader *of the* princes requires a large kingdom. He who, using virtue, practises benevolence is the sovereign of the kingdom. To become the sovereign of the kingdom, *a prince* need not wait for a large *kingdom*. T'ang did it with *only* seventy *lî*, and king Wăn with *only* a hundred.

2. 'When one by force subdues men, they do not submit to him in heart. *They submit, because* their strength is not adequate *to resist*.

to indicate one individual of either sex. The image in 拔乎其萃 is that of stalks of grass or grain, shooting high above the level of the waving field. 未有盛於孔子,—'there has not been one more complete than Confucius.' But this would be no more than putting Confucius on a level with other sages. I have therefore translated after the example of Chû Hsî, who says—自古聖人,固皆異於衆人,然未有如孔子之盛者也. That 於=如 is one of the explanations of the character given by 王引之, in his Treatise on the Particles.

3. THE DIFFERENCE BETWEEN A CHIEFTAIN OF THE PRINCES AND A SOVEREIGN OF THE KINGDOM; AND BETWEEN SUBMISSION SECURED BY FORCE AND THAT PRODUCED BY VIRTUE. 1. 霸 and 王 are here the recognised titles and not = 'to acquire the chieftaincy,' 'to acquire the sovereignty.' In the 集證, we find much said on the meaning of the two characters. 王 is from three strokes (三), denoting heaven, earth, and man, with a fourth stroke, — or unity, going through them, grasping and uniting them together, thus affording the highest possible conception of power or ability. 霸 is synonymous with 伯, and of kindred meaning with the words, of nearly the same sound, 把, 'to

不贍也、以德服人者、中心悅而誠服也、如七十子之服孔子也、詩云、自西自東、自南自北、無思不服、此之謂也。

第四章 一節 孟子曰、仁則榮、不仁則辱、今惡辱而居不仁、是猶惡溼而居下也。二節 如惡之、莫如貴德而尊士、賢者在位、能者在職、國

When one subdues men by virtue, in their hearts' core they are pleased, and sincerely submit, as was the case with the seventy disciples in their submission to Confucius. What is said in the Book of Poetry,

"From the west, from the east,
From the south, from the north,
There was not one who thought of refusing submission,"

is an illustration of this.'

CHAP. IV. 1. Mencius said, 'Benevolence brings glory *to a prince*, and the opposite of it brings disgrace. For *the princes of* the present day to hate disgrace and yet to live complacently doing what is not benevolent, is like hating moisture and yet living in a low situation.

2. 'If *a prince* hates disgrace, the best course for him to pursue, is to esteem virtue and honour *virtuous* scholars, giving the worthiest among them places *of dignity*, and the able offices *of trust*. When throughout his kingdom there is leisure and rest *from external*

grasp with the hand,' and 迫, 'to urge,' 'to press.' 2. 力不贍 is translated by Julien,—'*quia nempe vires* (i. e. *vis armorum*) *ad id obtinendum non sufficiunt*.' Possibly some Chinese commentators may have sanctioned such an interpretation, but it has nowhere come under my notice. The 'seventy disciples' is giving a round number, the enumeration of them differing in different works. We find them reckoned at 73, 76, &c. See in the prolegomena to vol. i, p. 112. For the ode see the Shih-ching, III. i. Ode X. st. 6, celebrating the influence of the kings Wăn and Wû. The four quarters are to be viewed from Hâo (鎬), king Wû's capital. 思 is not to be taken as an abstract noun, = 'thought.' 鄒浩, a statesman and scholar of the eleventh century, says on this chapter:—'He who subdues men by force, has the intention of subduing them, and they dare not but submit. He who subdues men by virtue, has no intention to subdue them, and they cannot but submit. From antiquity downwards there have been many dissertations on the leaders of the princes, and the true sovereign, but none so deep, incisive, and perspicuous as this chapter.'

4. GLORY IS THE SURE RESULT OF BENEVOLENT GOVERNMENT. CALAMITY AND HAPPINESS ARE MEN'S OWN SEEKING. 1. 居不仁, literally, 'to dwell in not-benevolence,' i. e. complacently to go on in the practice of what is not benevolent. 2. 莫如 covers as far as to 政刑,

家閒暇、及是時、明其政刑、雖大國、必畏之矣。○三節 詩云、迨天之未陰雨、徹彼桑土、綢繆牖戶、今此下民、或敢侮予、孔子曰、爲此詩者、其知道乎、能治其國家、誰敢侮之。○四節 今國家閒暇、及是時、般樂怠敖、是自求禍也。○五節 禍福無不自己求之者。○六節 詩云、永

troubles, let him, taking advantage of such a season, clearly *digest* the principles of his government with its legal sanctions, and then even great kingdoms will be constrained to stand in awe of him.

3. 'It is said in the Book of Poetry,

"Before the heavens were dark with rain,
I gathered the bark from the roots of the mulberry trees,
And wove it closely to form the window and door *of my nest*;
Now, *I thought*, ye people below,
Perhaps ye will not dare to insult me."

Confucius said, "Did not he who made this ode understand the way *of governing*?" If a prince is able rightly to govern his kingdom, who will dare to insult him?

4. '*But* now *the princes* take advantage of the time when throughout their kingdoms there is leisure and rest *from external troubles*, to abandon themselves to pleasure and indolent indifference;—they in fact seek for calamities for themselves.

5. 'Calamity and happiness in all cases are men's own seeking.

and 賢者在位 and the next clause are to be taken as in apposition simply with the one preceding. See the Doctrine of the Mean, chap. xx. The 賢者在位 here corresponds to the 尊賢 there, and the 能者在職 may embrace both the 敬大臣 and the 體羣臣. 刑,—not punishments, but penal laws. 3. See the Shih-ching, I. xv. Ode II. st. 2, where for 今此下民 we have 今女下民, the difference not affecting the sense. The ode is an appeal by some small bird to an owl not to destroy its nest, which bird, in Mencius's application of the words, is made to represent a wise prince taking all precautionary measures. 4. 般,—read *p'an*, 2nd tone, nearly synonymous with the next character,—樂 (*lo*). 6. For the ode see the Shih-ching, III. i. Ode I.

言配命、自求多福、太甲曰、天作孽、猶可違、自作孽、不可活、此之謂也。六節

五章 孟子曰、尊賢使能、俊傑在位、則天下之士、皆悅而願立於其朝矣。二節 市、廛而不征、法而不廛、則天下之商、皆悅而願藏於其市

6. 'This is illustrated by what is said in the Book of Poetry,—

"Be always studious to be in harmony with the ordinances *of God*,

So you will certainly get for yourself much happiness;"

and by the passage of the Tâi Chiah,—"When Heaven sends down calamities, it is still possible to escape from them; when we occasion the calamities ourselves, it is not possible any longer to live."'

CHAP. V. 1. Mencius said, 'If *a ruler* give honour to men of talents and virtue and employ the able, so that offices shall all be filled by individuals of distinction and mark;—then all the scholars of the kingdom will be pleased, and wish to stand in his court.

2. 'If, in the market-place *of his capital*, he levy a ground-rent on the shops but do not tax the goods, or enforce the proper regulations without levying a ground-rent;—then all the traders of the kingdom will be pleased, and wish to store their goods in his market-place.

st. 6. 言-念, 'to think of.' For the other quotation, see the Shû-ching, IV. v. Sect. II. 3, where we have 逭, 'to escape,' for 活, but the meaning is the same.

5. VARIOUS POINTS OF TRUE ROYAL GOVERNMENT NEGLECTED BY THE PRINCES OF MENCIUS'S TIME, ATTENTION TO WHICH WOULD SURELY CARRY ANY ONE OF THEM TO THE ROYAL THRONE. 1. Compare last chapter, par. 2. The wisest among 1,000 men is called 俊; the wisest among ten is called 傑. Numbers, however, do not enter into the signification of the terms here. 天下之士云云,—compare Bk. I. Pt. I. vii. 18. 2. 廛, 'a shop, or market-stance,' is used here as a verb, 'to levy ground-rent for such a shop.' According to Chû Hsî, in the 語類, we are to understand the market-place here as that in the capital, which was built on the plan of the division of the land, after the figure of the character 井. The middle square behind was the 市; the centre one was occupied by the palace; the front one by the ancestral and other temples, government treasuries, arsenals, &c.; and the three squares on each side were occupied by the people. He adds that, when traders became too many, a ground-rent was levied; when they were few, it was remitted, and only a surveillance was exercised of the markets by the proper officers. That surveillance extended to the inspection of weights and measures, regulation of the price, &c. See its duties detailed

矣。○三節關、譏而不征、則天下之旅、皆悅而願出於其路矣。○四節耕者助而不稅、則天下之農、皆悅而願耕於其野矣。○五節廛、無夫里之布、則天下之民、皆悅而願爲之氓矣。○六節信能行此五者、則鄰國之民、仰之若父母矣、率其子弟、

3. 'If, at his frontier-passes, there be an inspection of persons, but no taxes charged *on goods or other articles*, then all the travellers of the kingdom will be pleased, and wish to make their tours on his roads.

4. 'If he require that the husbandmen give their mutual aid *to cultivate the public field*, and exact no *other* taxes from them;—then all the husbandmen of the kingdom will be pleased, and wish to plough in his fields.

5. 'If from the occupiers of the shops in his market-place he do not exact the fine of the individual idler, or of the hamlet's quota of cloth, then all the people of the kingdom will be pleased, and wish to come and be his people.

6. 'If *a ruler* can truly practise these five things, then the people in the neighbouring kingdoms will look up to him as a parent. From the first birth of mankind till now, never has any one led

in the Châu-lî, XIV. vii. 3. Compare Bk. I. Pt. II. v. 3; Pt. I. vii. 18. All critics refer for the illustration of this rule to the account of the duties of the 司關, in the Châu-lî, XV. xi. But from that it would appear that the levying no duties at the passes was only in bad years, and hence some have argued that Mencius's lesson was only for the emergency of the time. To avoid that conclusion, the author of the 四書拓餘說 contends that the Châu-lî has been interpolated in the place,—rightly, as it seems to me. 4. The rule of 助而不稅 is the same as that of 耕者九一, Bk. I. Pt. II. v. 3. 5. It is acknowledged by commentators that it is only a vague notion which we can obtain of the meaning of this paragraph. Is 廛 to be taken as in the translation, or verbally as in the second paragraph? What was the 夫布? And what the 里布? It appears from the Châu-lî, that there was a fine, exacted from idlers or loafers in the towns, called 夫布, and it is said that the family which did not plant mulberry trees and flax according to the rules, was condemned to pay one hamlet, or twenty-five families', quota of cloth. But 布 may be taken in the sense of money, simply = 錢, which is a signification attaching to it. We must leave the passage in the obscurity which has always rested on it. Mencius is evidently protesting against some injurious exactions of the time. 氓 - 民, but the addition of the character 亡 seems intended to convey the idea of the people of other States coming to put themselves under a new rule. 6. 信 = 實, 'truly.' Observe

攻其父母、自生民以來、未有能濟者也、如此、則無敵於天下、無敵於天下者、天吏也、然而不王者、未之有也。

第六章 孟子曰、人皆有不忍人之心。(二節)先王有不忍人之心、斯有不忍人之政矣、以不忍人之心、行不忍人之政、治天下可運之掌上。(三節)所以

children to attack their parent, and succeeded in his design. Thus, such a ruler will not have an enemy in all the kingdom, and he who has no enemy in the kingdom is the minister of Heaven. Never has there been a ruler in such a case who did not attain to the royal dignity.'

CHAP. VI. 1. Mencius said, 'All men have a mind which cannot bear *to see the sufferings of* others.

2. 'The ancient kings had this commiserating mind, and they, as a matter of course, had likewise a commiserating government. When with a commiserating mind was practised a commiserating government, to rule the kingdom was *as easy a matter* as to make anything go round in the palm.

the reciprocal influence of 其 in 率其子弟 ('sons and younger brothers' = children) and 攻其父母. 天吏,—'The minister or officer of Heaven.' On this designation the commentator 饒氏雙峰 observes:—'An officer is one commissioned by his sovereign; the officer of Heaven is he who is commissioned by Heaven. He who bears his sovereign's commission can punish men and put them to death. He may deal so with all criminals. He who bears the commission of Heaven, can execute judgment on men, and smite them. With all who are oppressing and misgoverning their kingdoms, he can deal so.'

6. THAT BENEVOLENCE, RIGHTEOUSNESS, PROPRIETY, AND KNOWLEDGE BELONG TO MAN AS NATURALLY AS HIS FOUR LIMBS, AND MAY AS EASILY BE EXERCISED. The assertions made in this chapter are universally true, but they are to be understood as spoken here with special reference to the oppressive ways and government of the princes of Mencius's time. 1. 不忍 alone is used in Bk. I. Pt. I. vii. 4, 5, 6. 人 is added here, because the discourse is entirely of a man's feelings, as exercised towards other men. 心,—'the mind,' embracing the whole mental constitution. The 備旨, after Châo Ch'î, says that 不忍人 means—'cannot bear to injure others.' But it is not only cannot bear to inflict suffering, but also cannot bear to see suffering. The examples in Bk. I. Pt. I. vii, make this plain. 2. 斯,—used adverbially, as in Analects, X. x. 1. 運之,—

謂人皆有不忍人之心者、今人乍見孺子、將入於井、皆有怵惕惻隱之心、非所以內交於孺子之父母也、非所以要譽於鄉黨朋友也、非惡其聲而然也。四節由是觀之、無惻隱之心、非人也、無羞惡之心、非人也、無辭讓之心、非人也、無是非之心、非人也。五節惻隱之心、仁之

3. 'When I say that all men have a mind which cannot bear *to see the sufferings of* others, my meaning may be illustrated thus:—even now-a-days, if men suddenly see a child about to fall into a well, they will without exception experience a feeling of alarm and distress. *They will feel so*, not as a ground on which they may gain the favour of the child's parents, nor as a ground on which they may seek the praise of their neighbours and friends, nor from a dislike to the reputation of *having been unmoved by* such a thing.

4. 'From this case we may perceive that the feeling of commiseration is essential to man, that the feeling of shame and dislike is essential to man, that the feeling of modesty and complaisance is essential to man, and that the feeling of approving and disapproving is essential to man.

5. 'The feeling of commiseration is the principle of benevolence.

之 must be taken generally, = 'a thing,' or as giving a passive signification to the verb.—'The government of the kingdom could be made to go round,' &c. Perhaps the latter construction is to be preferred. The whole is to be translated in the past sense, being descriptive of the ancient kings. 3. 孺, 'an infant at the breast,' here = 'a very young child.' 內 read as, and = 納. 內交,—'to form a friendship with,' 'to get the favour of.' 要,—the 1st tone, = 求. 鄉黨,—compare Analects, VI. iii. 4. 今 is to be joined to 人,—'men of the present time,' in opposition 'to the former kings.'

4. The two negatives 無—非 in the different clauses make the strongest possible affirmation. Literally, 'Without the feeling of commiseration there would not be *man*,' &c., or 'If a person be without this, he is not a man,' &c. 惻隱, 'pain and distress,' but as it is in illustration of the 不忍之心, we may render it by 'commiseration.' 'Shame and dislike,'—the *shame* is for one's own want of goodness, and the *dislike* is of the want of it in other men. 'Modesty and complaisance,'—*modesty* is the unloosing and separating from one's self, and *complaisance* is out-giving to others. 'Approving and disapproving,'—*approving* is the knowledge of goodness, and the approbation of it accordingly, and *disapproving* is the knowledge of what

端也、羞惡之心、義之端也、辭讓之心、禮之端也、是非之心、智之端也。○六節人之有是四端也、猶其有四體也、有是四端而自謂不能者、自賊者也、謂其君不能者、賊其君者也。○七節凡有四端於我者、知皆擴而充之矣、若火之始然、泉之始達、苟能充之、足以保四海、苟不充之、

The feeling of shame and dislike is the principle of righteousness. The feeling of modesty and complaisance is the principle of propriety. The feeling of approving and disapproving is the principle of knowledge.

6. 'Men have these four principles just as they have their four limbs. When men, having these four principles, yet say of themselves that they cannot *develop them*, they play the thief with themselves, and he who says of his prince that he cannot *develop them* plays the thief with his prince.

7. 'Since all men have these four principles in themselves, let them know to give them all their development and completion, and the issue will be like that of fire which has begun to burn, or that of a spring which has begun to find vent. Let them have their complete development, and they will suffice to love and protect all

is evil, and disapprobation of it accordingly. Such is the account of the terms in the text, given by Chû Hsî and others. The feelings described make up, he says, the mind of man, and Mencius 'discoursing about commiseration goes on to enumerate them all.' This seems to be the true account of the introduction of the various principles. They lie together, merely in apposition. In the 或問 and 語類, however, Chû Hsî labours to develop the other three from the first.—Observe that 'the feeling of shame and dislike,' &c., in the original, is—'the mind that feels and dislikes,' &c. 5. 端 is explained by 端緒, 'the end of a clue,' that point outside, which may be laid hold of, and will guide us to all within. From the feelings which he has specified, Mencius reasons to the moral elements of our nature. It will be seen how to 智, 'knowledge,' 'wisdom,' he gives a moral sense. Compare Gen. ii. 17, iii. 5, 6; Job xxxviii. 36. 6. 賊,—compare Bk. I. Pt. II. viii. 3, but we can retain its primitive meaning in the translation. 7. 凡有四端於我者, not 'all who have,' &c., but 'all having,' &c., 於我,—*quasi dicat*, 'in their ego-ity.' 知皆,—皆 belongs to the 擴 below, and refers to the 四端.—The 備旨 says:—知字重看, 'the character 知 is

不足以事父母。

第七章 一節 孟子曰、矢人豈不仁於函人哉、矢人惟恐不傷人、函人惟恐傷人、巫匠亦然、故術不可不慎也。二節 孔子曰、里仁爲美、擇不處仁、焉得智、夫仁、天之尊爵也、人之安宅也、莫之禦而不仁、是不智也。三節 不仁不智、無禮無義、

within the four seas. Let them be denied that development, and they will not suffice for a man to serve his parents with.'

CHAP. VII. 1. Mencius said, 'Is the arrow-maker less benevolent than the maker of armour of defence? *And yet*, the arrow-maker's only fear is lest men should not be hurt, and the armour-maker's only fear is lest men should be hurt. So it is with the priest and the coffin-maker. *The choice of* a profession, therefore, is a thing in which great caution is required.

2. 'Confucius said, "It is virtuous manners which constitute the excellence of a neighbourhood. If a man, in selecting a residence, do not fix on one where such prevail, how can he be wise?" Now, benevolence is the most honourable dignity conferred by Heaven, and the quiet home in which man should dwell. Since no one can hinder us from being so, if yet we are not benevolent;—this is being not wise.

3. 'From the want of benevolence and the want of wisdom will

to have weight attached to it.' This is true, Mencius may well say—'Let men know,' or 'If men know.' How is it that after all his analyses of our nature to prove its goodness, the application of his principles must begin with an IF?

7. AN EXHORTATION TO BENEVOLENCE FROM THE DISGRACE WHICH MUST ATTEND THE WANT OF IT, LIKE THE DISGRACE OF A MAN WHO DOES NOT KNOW HIS PROFESSION. 1. 矢人豈不仁於,—the 不 belongs not to the 豈, but to the 仁. If we might construe it with the 豈, we should have an instance parallel to 盛於 in ii. 28,—'benevolent as,' the 於 being = 如. 函 has the meaning of 'all armour of defence.' 巫,—see Analects, XIII. xxii, where I have translated it 'wizard.' As opposed to 匠 (here = 'a coffin-maker'), one who makes provision for the death of men, it indicates one who prays for men's life and prosperity. But Mencius pursues his illustration too far. An arrow-maker need not be inhumane. 2. See Analects, IV. i. The commentators begin to bring in the idea of a profession at 擇不處仁, but the whole quotation must be taken first in its proper sense. The 不智 at the end refer to the same characters in the quotation. 3. 無 succeeding 不 shows that the

人役也、人役而恥爲役、由弓人而恥爲弓、矢人而恥爲矢也。四節如恥之、莫如爲仁。五節仁者如射、射者正己而後發、發而不中、不怨勝己者、反求諸己而已矣。

第八章 一節孟子曰、子路、人告之以有過、則喜。二節禹聞善言則拜。三節大舜有大焉、善與人同、舍己從人、樂取於人以爲善。

ensue the entire absence of propriety and righteousness;—he who is in such a case must be the servant of other men. To be the servant of men and yet ashamed of such servitude, is like a bow-maker's being ashamed to make bows, or an arrow-maker's being ashamed to make arrows.

4. 'If he be ashamed of his case, his best course is to practise benevolence.

5. 'The man who would be benevolent is like the archer. The archer adjusts himself and then shoots. If he misses, he does not murmur against those who surpass himself. He simply turns round and seeks *the cause of his failure* in himself.'

CHAP. VIII. 1. Mencius said, 'When any one told Tsze-lû that he had a fault, he rejoiced.

2. 'When Yü heard good words, he bowed *to the speaker*.

3. 'The great Shun had a still greater *delight in what was good. He regarded* virtue as the common property of himself and others, giving up his own way to follow that of others, and delighting to learn from others to practise what was good.

second clause ensues from the first. 由,—used for 猶. 5. 仁者=欲爲仁之人. Compare Analects, III. vii and xvi.

8. HOW SAGES AND WORTHIES DELIGHTED IN WHAT IS GOOD. 1. Tsze-lû's ardour in pursuing his self-improvement appears in the Analects, V. xiii; XI. xxi. But the particular point mentioned in the text is nowhere else related of him. 2. In the Shû-ching, II. iii. 1, we have an example of this in Yü. It is said,—禹拜昌言, 'Yü bowed at these excellent words.' 3. 善與人同 is explained by Chû Hsi 公天下之善而不爲私也, 'He considered as public—common—the good of the whole world, and did not think it private to any.' Shun's distinction was that he did not think of himself, as Tsze-lû did, nor of others, as Yü did, but only of what was good, and un-

四節 自耕稼陶漁、以至爲帝、無非取於人者。五節 取諸人以爲善、是與人爲善者也、故君子莫大乎與人爲善。

第九章 一節 孟子曰、伯夷非其君不事、非其友不友、不立於惡人之朝、不與惡人言、立於惡人之朝、與惡人言、如以朝衣朝冠、坐於塗炭、推惡惡之心、思與鄉人立、其冠

4. 'From the time when he ploughed and sowed, exercised the potter's art, and was a fisherman, to the time when he became emperor, he was continually learning from others.

5. 'To take example from others to practise virtue, is to help them in the same practice. Therefore, there is no attribute of the superior man greater than his helping men to practise virtue.'

CHAP. IX. 1. Mencius said, 'Po-î would not serve a prince whom he did not approve, nor associate with a friend whom he did not esteem. He would not stand in a bad prince's court, nor speak with a bad man. To stand in a bad prince's court, or to speak with a bad man, would have been to him the same as to sit with his court robes and court cap amid mire and ashes. Pursuing the examination of his dislike to what was evil, *we find* that he *thought it necessary*, if he happened to be standing with a villager whose cap was not

consciously was carried to it, wherever he saw it. 4. Of Shun in his early days it is related in the 'Historical Records,' that 'he ploughed at the Lî (歷) mountain, did potter's work on the banks of the Yellow River, fished in the Lêi lake (雷澤), and made various implements on the Shâu hill (壽丘), and often resided at Fû-hsiâ (負夏).' There will be occasion to consider where these places were, in connexion with some of Mencius's future references to Shun. Dr. Medhurst supposes them to have been in Shan-hsi. See his Translation of the Shû-ching, p. 332. 5. 與 is here in the sense of 助, 'to help.' The meaning is that others, seeing their virtue so imitated, would be stimulated to greater diligence in the doing of it.

9. PICTURES OF PO-Î AND HÛI OF LIÛ-HSIÂ, AND MENCIUS'S JUDGMENT CONCERNING THEM. 1. Compare chap. ii. 22. In 惡人之朝, 人 refers to the preceding 君, and may be translated *prince*, but in 與惡人立, 人 refers to the preceding 友, and must be translated *man*. 塗炭, 'mire and charcoal.' 推惡惡之心,—推 is Mencius's speaking in his

不正、望望然去之、若將浼焉、是故諸侯雖有善其辭命而至者、不受也、不受也者、是亦不屑就已。○二節柳下惠、不羞汙君、不卑小官、進不隱賢、必以其道、遺佚而不怨、阨窮而不憫、故曰、爾爲爾、我爲我、雖袒裼裸裎於我側、爾焉能浼我哉、故由由然與之偕、而不自失焉、援而止之而止、援而止之而止者、是亦不屑去已。○三節孟

rightly adjusted, to leave him with a high air, as if he were going to be defiled. Therefore, although some of the princes made application to him with very proper messages, he would not receive their gifts.—He would not receive their gifts, counting it inconsistent with his purity to go to them.

2. 'Hûi of Liû-hsiâ was not ashamed to *serve* an impure prince, nor did he think it low to be an inferior officer. When advanced to employment, he did not conceal his virtue, but made it a point to carry out his principles. When neglected and left without office, he did not murmur. When straitened by poverty, he did not grieve. Accordingly, he had a saying, "You are you, and I am I. Although you stand by my side with breast and arms bare, or with your body naked, how can you defile me?" Therefore, self-possessed, he companied with men indifferently, at the same time not losing himself. *When he wished to leave,* if pressed to remain in office, he would remain.—He would remain in office, when pressed to do so, not counting it required by his purity to go away.'

own person. 思 is the 'thought' of Po-î. 望望然, according to Chû Hsî, is 'the appearance of going away without looking round.' Châo Ch'î makes it 'the appearance of being ashamed;'—not so well. The final 已 gives positiveness to the affirmation of the preceding clause. 2. Hûi of Liû-hsiâ,—see Analects, XV. xiii; XVIII. ii, viii. 與之偕,—the 之 properly refers to the party addressed, 'you are you.' 3. Compare chap. ii. 22. 君子,—by this

子曰、伯夷隘、柳下惠不恭、隘與不恭、君子不由也。

3. Mencius said, 'Po-î was narrow-minded, and Hûi of Liû-hsiâ was wanting in self-respect. The superior man will not manifest either narrow-mindedness, or the want of self-respect.'

term we must suppose that Mencius makes a tacit reference to himself, as having proposed Confucius as his model. The writer 韓元少 says:—'Elsewhere Mencius advises men to imitate Î and Hûi, but he is there speaking to the weak and the mean. When here he advises not to follow Î and Hûi, he is speaking for those who wish to do the right thing at the right time.'

KUNG-SUN CH'ÂU. PART II.

公孫丑下

章句

第一章 一節 孟子曰、天時不如地利、地利不如人和。二節 三里之城、七里之郭、環而攻之而不勝、夫

CHAPTER I. 1. Mencius said, 'Opportunities of time *vouchsafed by* Heaven are not equal to advantages of situation *afforded by* the Earth, and advantages of situation afforded by the Earth are not equal to *the union arising from* the accord of Men.

2. '*There is a city,* with an inner wall of three *lî* in circumference, and an outer wall of seven.—*The enemy* surround and attack it, but they are not able to take it. Now, to surround and attack it, there

1. NO ADVANTAGES WHICH A RULER CAN OBTAIN TO EXALT HIM OVER OTHERS ARE TO BE COMPARED WITH HIS GETTING THE HEARTS OF MEN. Because of this chapter Mencius has got a place in China among the writers on the art of war, which surely he would not have wished to claim for himself, his design evidently being to supersede the necessity of war and the recourse to arms altogether. 1. In the 天, 地, 人, we have the doctrine of the 三才, or 'Three Powers,' which is brought out so distinctly in the fourth part of the *Chung Yung*, and to show this in a translation requires it to be diffuse. As to what is said at much length in Chinese commentaries about ascertaining the 'time of Heaven' by divination and astrology, it is to be set aside, as foreign to the mind of Mencius in the text, though many examples of the resort to it may be adduced from the records of antiquity. 2. The city here supposed, with its double circle of fortification, is a small one, the better to illustrate the superiority of advantages of situation, just as the next is a large one, to bring out the still greater superiority of the union of men. As to the evidence that a city of the specified dimensions must be the capital of a baronial State (子男之城), see the 集

孟子

環而攻之、必有得天時者矣、然而不勝者、是天時不如地利也。○三節 城、非不高也、池、非不深也、兵革、非不堅利也、米粟、非不多也、委而去之、是地利不如人和也。○四節 故曰、域民、不以封疆之界、固國、不以山谿之險、威天下、不以兵革之利、得道者多

must have been vouchsafed to them by Heaven the opportunity of time, and in such case their not taking it is because opportunities of time vouchsafed by Heaven are not equal to advantages of situation afforded by the Earth.

3. '*There is a city, whose* walls are distinguished for their height, and whose moats are distinguished for their depth, where the arms *of its defenders*, offensive and defensive, are distinguished for their strength and sharpness, and the stores of rice and other grain are very large. *Yet it is obliged to* be given up and abandoned. This is because advantages of situation afforded by the Earth are not equal to the union arising from the accord of Men.

4. 'In accordance with these principles it is said, "A people is bounded in, not by the limits of dykes and borders; a State is secured, not by the strengths of mountains and rivers; the kingdom is overawed, not by the sharpness *and strength* of arms." He who finds the proper course has many to assist him. He who loses the proper course has few to assist him. When this,—the being assisted by few,—reaches its extreme point, his own relations revolt from *the*

證, *in loc.* 3. 非不, the repeated negation, not only affirms, but with emphasis:—城非不高, 'the wall is not but high,' i.e. is high indeed. 兵,—sharp weapons of offence. 革,—'leather,' intending, principally, the buff-coat, but including all other armour of defence. 米,—'rice,' without the husk; 粟,—'grain,' generally, in the husk. 4. 域, 'a boundary,' 'a border,' is used verbally. 域民,—'to bound a people,' i.e. to separate them from other States. 封 is 'a dyke,' or 'mound.' The commentator 金仁山 says:—'Anciently, in every State, they made a dyke of earth to show its boundary (封土爲疆).' 谿,—'a valley with a stream in it;' here, in opposition to 山, = *rivers* or *streams*. The 道, or 'proper course,' intended is that style of govern-

助、失道者寡助、寡助之至、親戚畔之、多助之至、天下順之。五節以天下之所順、攻親戚之所畔、故君子有不戰、戰必勝矣。

第二章 一節 孟子將朝王、王使人來曰、寡人如就見者也、有寒疾、不可以風。朝、將視朝、不識可使寡人得見乎。對曰、不幸而有疾、

prince. When the being assisted by many reaches its highest point, the whole kingdom becomes obedient to *the prince*.

5. 'When one to whom the whole kingdom is prepared to be obedient, attacks those from whom their own relations revolt, *what must be the result?* Therefore, the true ruler will prefer not to fight; but if he do fight, he must overcome.'

CHAP. II. 1. As Mencius was about to go to court *to see* the king, the king sent a person to him *with this message*,—'I was wishing to come and see you. But I have got a cold, and may not expose myself to the wind. In the morning I will hold my court. I do not know whether you will give me the opportunity of seeing you *then*.' *Mencius* replied, 'Unfortunately, I am unwell, and not able to go to the court.'

ment—benevolence and righteousness—which will secure the 'union of men.' 親戚,—relatives by blood and by affinity. 5. The case put in the two first clauses is here left by Mencius to suggest its own result. The *chün-tsze* is the prince intended above, 'who finds the proper course.' Chû Hsî and others complete 有不戰 by 則已, 'If he do not fight, well;' but the translation gives, I think, a better meaning.

2. HOW MENCIUS CONSIDERED THAT IT WAS SLIGHTING HIM FOR A PRINCE TO CALL HIM BY MESSENGERS TO GO TO SEE HIM, AND THE SHIFTS HE WAS PUT TO TO GET THIS UNDERSTOOD. It must be understood that, at the time to which this chapter refers, Mencius was merely an honoured guest in Ch'î, and had no official situation or emolument. It was for him to pay his respects at court, if he felt inclined to do so; but if the king wished his counsel, it was for him to show his sense of his worth by going to him, and asking him for it. 1. The first, third, and fourth 朝 are *ch'âo*, in 2nd tone, = 'to go to, or wait upon, at court.' So in all the other paragraphs. The second is *châo*, in 1st tone, 'the morning.' The morning, as soon as it was light, was the regular time for the sovereign, and princes, to give audience to their nobles and officers, and proceed to the administration of business. The modern practice corresponds with the ancient in this respect. 如 is said to be here = 欲, 'to wish,' which sense seems to be necessary, though we do not find it in the dictionary. 造, read *ts'âo*, the 4th tone, 'to go to.' The king's cold was merely a pretence. He wanted Mencius to wait on him. Mencius's cold was equally a pretence. Compare Con-

不能造朝。二節明日、出弔於東郭氏、公孫丑曰、昔者、辭以病、今日弔、或者不可乎。曰、昔者疾、今日愈、如之何不弔。三節王使人問疾、醫來、孟仲子對曰、昔者、有王命、有采薪之憂、不能造朝、今病小愈、趨造於朝、我不識能至否乎。使數人要於路、曰、請必無歸、而造於朝。四節不得已

2. Next day, he went out to pay a visit of condolence to some one of the Tung-kwŏh family, when Kung-sun Ch'âu said to him, 'Yesterday, you declined *going to the court* on the ground of being unwell, and to-day you are going to pay a visit of condolence. May this not be regarded as improper?' 'Yesterday,' said *Mencius*, 'I was unwell; to-day, I am better:—why should I not pay this visit?'

3. *In the mean time*, the king sent a messenger to inquire about his sickness, and also a physician. Măng Chung replied to them, 'Yesterday, when the king's order came, he was feeling a little unwell, and could not go to the court. To-day he was a little better, and hastened to go to court. I do not know whether he can have reached it *by this time* or not.' *Having said this*, he sent several men to look for *Mencius* on the way, and say to him, 'I beg that, before you return home, you will go to the court.'

4. *On this*, Mencius felt himself compelled to go to Ching Ch'âu's,

fucius's conduct, Analects, XVII. xx. 2. Tung-kwŏh is not exactly a surname. The individual intended was a descendant of the duke Hwan, and so surnamed Chiang (姜), but that branch of Hwan's descendants to which he belonged having their possessions in the 'eastern' part of the State, the style of Tung-kwŏh appears to have been given to them to distinguish them from the other branches. In going to pay the visit of condolence, Mencius's idea was that the king might hear of it, and understand that he had merely feigned sickness, to show his sense of the disrespect done to him in trying to inveigle him to go to court. 3. It is a moot-point, whether Măng Chung was Mencius's son, or merely a relative. The latter is more likely. 采薪之憂,—literally, 'sorrow of gathering firewood,' = a little sickness. See a similar expression in the Lî Chî, I. Sect. II. i. 3. 8,—君使士射，不能，則辭以疾，言曰某有負薪之憂. On this the 正義 says:—'Carrying firewood was the business of the children of the common people. From the lips of an officer, such language was indicative

P 2

而之景丑氏宿焉、景子曰、內則父子、外則君臣、人之大倫也、父子主恩、君臣主敬、丑見王之敬子也、未見所以敬王也。曰、惡是何言也、齊人無以仁義與王言者、豈以仁義爲不美也、其心曰、是何足與言仁義也云爾、則不敬、莫大乎是、我非堯舜之道、不敢以陳於王前、故齊人莫如我敬王

and there stop the night. Mr. Ching said to him, 'In the family, there is *the relation of* father and son; abroad, there is *the relation of* prince and minister. These are the two great relations among men. Between father and son the ruling principle is kindness. Between prince and minister the ruling principle is respect. I have seen the respect of the king to you, Sir, but I have not seen in what way you show respect to him.' *Mencius* replied, 'Oh! what words are these? Among the people of Ch'î there is no one who speaks to the king about benevolence and righteousness. Are they thus silent because they do not think that benevolence and righteousness are admirable? *No, but* in their hearts they say, "This man is not fit to be spoken with about benevolence and righteousness." Thus they manifest a disrespect than which there can be none greater. I do not dare to set forth before the king any but the ways of Yâo and Shun. There is therefore no man of Ch'î who respects the king so much as I do.'

of humility.' 要, the 1st tone, = 求. Măng Chung, having committed himself to a falsehood, in order to make his words good, was anxious that Mencius should go to court. 4. What compelled Mencius to go to Ching Ch'âu's was his earnest wish that the king should know that his sickness was merely feigned, and that he had not gone to court, only because he *would not be* CALLED to do so. As Măng Chung's falsehood interfered with his first plan, he wished that his motive should get to the king through Ching Ch'âu, who was an officer of Ch'î. After 宿焉, Châo Ch'î appends a note,—'when he told him all the previous incidents.' No doubt, he did so. 惡, the 1st tone, 'oh!' as in Pt. I. ii. 19. 齊人 . . . . 者, observe the force of the 者, carrying on the clause to those following for an explanation of it, as if there were a 所以 after 人. 云爾,—

也。○五節景子曰、否、非此之謂也、禮曰、父召無諾、君命召、不俟駕、固將朝也、聞王命而遂不果、宜與夫禮若不相似然。○六節曰、豈謂是與、曾子曰、晉楚之富、不可及也、彼以其富、我以吾仁、彼以其爵、我以吾義、吾何慊乎哉、夫豈不義、而曾子言之、是或一道也、天下有達尊三、爵

5. Mr. Ching said, 'Not so. That was not what I meant. In the *Book of* Rites it is said, "When a father calls, the answer must be without a moment's hesitation. When the prince's order calls, the carriage must not be waited for." You were certainly going to the court, but when you heard the king's order, then you did not carry your purpose out. This does seem as if it were not in accordance with that rule of propriety.'

6. *Mencius* answered him, 'How can you give that meaning to my conduct? The philosopher Tsăng said, "The wealth of Tsin and Ch'û cannot be equalled. Let *their rulers* have their wealth:—I have my benevolence. Let them have their nobility:—I have my righteousness. Wherein should I be dissatisfied *as inferior to them?*" Now shall we say that these sentiments are not right? Seeing that the philosopher Tsăng spoke them, there is in them, I apprehend, a *real* principle.—In the kingdom there are three things universally acknowledged to be honourable. Nobility is one of them; age is

see Analects, VII. xviii. 5. Different passages are here quoted together from the Book of Rites. 父召無諾,—see Bk. I. Sect. I. iii. 3, 14, 'A son must cry 唯 to his father, and not 諾,' which latter is a lingering response. 君命召不俟駕 is found substantially in Bk. XI. Sect. iii. 2. 夫, in 1st tone, = 斯, as in Analects, XI. ix. 3, *et al.* 6. 豈謂是與 (the 2nd tone),—literally, 'how means (it) this?' 慊 has two opposite meanings, either 'dissatisfied,' or 'satisfied,' in which latter sense it is also *hsieh*. Chû Hsî explains this by making it the same as 嗛, 'something held in the mouth,' according to the nature of which will be the internal feeling. In the text, the idea is that of dissatisfaction. 夫豈不義,—義 is here 當然之理, = 'what is proper and right,' the subject being the remarks of Tsăng. 而曾子言之云云 is

一、齒一、德一、朝廷莫如爵、鄉黨莫如齒、輔世長民莫如德、惡得有其一、以慢其二哉。○七節 故將大有爲之君、必有所不召之臣、欲有謀焉、則就之、其尊德樂道、不如是、不足與有爲也。○八節 故湯之於伊尹、學焉而後臣之、故不勞而王、桓公之於管仲、學焉而後臣之、故不勞而

one of them; virtue is one of them. In courts, nobility holds the first place of the three; in villages, age holds the first place; and for helping one's generation and presiding over the people, the other two are not equal to virtue. How can the possession of *only* one of these *be presumed on* to despise one who possesses the other two?

7. 'Therefore a prince who is to accomplish great deeds will certainly have ministers whom he does not call to go to him. When he wishes to consult with them, he goes to them. The prince who does not honour the virtuous, and delight in their ways of doing, to this extent, is not worth having to do with.

8. 'Accordingly, there was the behaviour of T'ang to Î Yin:—he first learned of him, and then employed him as his minister; and so without difficulty he became sovereign. There was the behaviour of the duke Hwan to Kwan Chung:—he first learned of him, and then employed him as his minister; and so without difficulty he became chief of all the princes.

expanded thus in the 備旨:—'And, Tsăng-tsze speaking them, they contain perhaps another principle different from the vulgar view.' 鄉黨, Analects, X. i. 齒, 'teeth,' =age. 7. 不足與有爲 is by some interpreted—'is not fit to have to do with them,' i.e. the virtuous, but I prefer the meaning adopted in the translation. 8. In the 'Historical Records,' 殷本記, one of the accounts of Î Yin's becoming minister to T'ang is, that it was only after being five times solicited by special messengers that he went to the prince's presence;—see the 集證, on Analects, XII. xxii. The confidence reposed by the duke Hwan in Kwan Chung appears in Pt. I. i. 3. Kwan was brought to Ch'î originally as a prisoner to be put to death, but the duke, knowing his ability and worth, had determined to employ him, and therefore, having first caused him to be relieved of his fetters, and otherwise honourably treated, he drove himself out of his capital to meet and receive him with all distinction, listening to a long discourse on government;

霸。九節今天下、地醜德齊、莫能相尙、無他、好臣其所教、而不好臣其所受教。十節湯之於伊尹、桓公之於管仲、則不敢召、管仲且猶不可召、而況不爲管仲者乎。

三章一節陳臻問曰、前日於齊、王餽兼金一百而不受、於宋餽七十鎰而受、於薛餽五十鎰而受、前日之不受是、則今日之

9. 'Now throughout the kingdom, the territories *of the princes* are of equal extent, and in their achievements they are on a level. Not one of them is able to exceed the others. This is from no other reason, but that they love to make ministers of those whom they teach, and do not love to make ministers of those by whom they might be taught.

10. 'So did T'ang behave to Î Yin, and the duke Hwan to Kwan Chung, that they would not venture to call them to go to them. If Kwan Chung might not be called to him by his prince, how much less may he be called, who would not play the part of Kwan Chung!'

CHAP. III. 1. Ch'ăn Tsin asked *Mencius*, saying, 'Formerly, when you were in Ch'î, the king sent you a present of 2,400 taels of fine silver, and you refused to accept it. When you were in Sung, 1,680 taels were sent to you, which you accepted; and when you were in Hsieh, 1,200 taels were sent, which you *likewise* accepted. If your declining to accept the gift in the first case was right, your accepting

see the 集證, on Analects, III. xxii. 9. 臣,—used as a verb. 10. Compare Pt. I. i.

3. BY WHAT PRINCIPLES MENCIUS WAS GUIDED IN DECLINING OR ACCEPTING THE GIFTS OF PRINCES. 1. Ch'ăn Tsin was one of Mencius's disciples, but this is all that is known of him. 餽,—'to present an offering of food;' here, more generally, 'to send a gift,' = 送. 兼金,—'double metal' (I suppose 白金, or silver), called 'double, as being worth twice as much as the ordinary;'—see Analects, XI. xxi. 一百, i. e. 100 *yi* (鎰), which, as in Bk. I. Pt. II. ix. 2, I estimate at 24 taels. Sung,—the present Kwei-teh in Ho-nan. Hsieh,—see Bk. I. Pt. II. xiv. The reference here, however, is inconsistent with what is stated in the note there, that Hsieh had long been incorporated with

受非也、今日之受是、則前日之不受非也、夫子必居一於此矣。○二節孟子曰、皆是也。○三節當在宋也、予將有遠行、行者必以賮、辭曰、餽賮、予何爲不受。○四節當在薛也、予有戒心、辭曰、聞戒、故爲兵餽之、予何爲不受。○五節若於齊、則未有處也、無處而餽之、是貨之也、焉有君子而可以貨

it in the latter cases was wrong. If your accepting it in the latter cases was right, your declining to do so in the first case was wrong. You must accept, Master, one of these alternatives.'

2. Mencius said, 'I did right in all the cases.

3. 'When I was in Sung, I was about to take a long journey. Travellers must be provided with what is necessary for their expenses. The prince's message was, "A present against travelling-expenses." Why should I have declined the gift?

4. 'When I was in Hsieh, I was apprehensive for my safety, and taking measures for my protection. The message was, "I have heard that you are taking measures to protect yourself, and send this to help you in procuring arms." Why should I have declined the gift?

5. 'But when I was in Ch'i, I had no occasion for money. To send a man a gift when he has no occasion for it, is to bribe him. How is it possible that a superior man should be taken with a bribe?'

Ch. 1. 前日, 今日, mark the relation of time between the cases simply. 今日 is not to be taken as = 'to-day.' 必居一於此, literally, 'must occupy (dwell in) one of these (places).' The meaning is that on either of the suppositions he would be judged to have done *wrong*. 3. 賮 or 贐, 'a gift to a traveller against the expenses of his journey.' 必以賮,—it is difficult to assign its precise force to the 以. I consider the whole clause to be written as from the point of view of the prince of Sung:—in regard to travellers, he considered it was requisite to use the ceremony of 賮. 4. We must paraphrase 戒心 considerably to bring out the meaning. 爲, in 4th tone. 兵, 'a weapon of war,' or the character may be taken here for 'a weapon-bearer,' 'a soldier.' 5. 未有處也,—Julien says,—'*sicut nos Gallice; il n'y a pas lieu à*,' but if it were so, 處 would be the noun, in the 4th tone, whereas it

孟子

取乎。〔四章〕孟子之平陸、謂其大夫曰、子之持戟之士、一日而三失伍、則去之、否乎。曰不待三。〔二節〕然則子之失伍也、亦多矣、凶年饑歲、子之民、老羸轉於溝壑、壯者散而之四方者、幾千人矣。曰、此非距心之所得爲也。〔三節〕曰、今有受人之牛羊、而爲之牧之

CHAP. IV. 1. Mencius having gone to P'ing-lû, addressed the governor of it, saying, 'If *one of* your spearmen should lose his place in the ranks three times in one day, would you, Sir, put him to death or not?' 'I would not wait for three times *to do so*,' was the reply.

2. *Mencius* said, 'Well then, you, Sir, have likewise lost your place in the ranks many times. In bad calamitous years, and years of famine, the old and feeble of your people, who have been found lying in the ditches and water-channels, and the able-bodied, who have been scattered about to the four quarters, have amounted to several thousand.' *The* governor replied, 'That is a state of things in which it does not belong to me Chü-hsin to act.'

3. 'Here,' said *Mencius*, 'is a man who receives charge of the cattle and sheep of another, and undertakes to feed them for him;—

is the verb in the 3rd, = 'to manage,' 'to dispose of.' 未有處=未有所處.

4. HOW MENCIUS BROUGHT CONVICTION OF THEIR FAULTS HOME TO THE KING AND AN OFFICER OF CH'Î. 1. 之 is the verb = 往. P'ing-lû was a city on the southern border of Ch'î;—in the present department of Yen-châu in Shan-tung. The officer's name, as we learn from the last paragraph, was K'ung Chü-hsin. 大夫 here = 宰, 'Governor' or 'Commandant.' The 戟 is variously described. Some say it had three points; others that it had a branch or blade on one side. No doubt, its form varied. 去, the 3rd tone, 'to away with.' Commentators concur in the meaning given in the translation. 2. 凶年云云,—compare Bk. I. Pt. II. xii. 2. Julien finds a difficulty in the 'several thousand,' as not applicable to the population of P'ing-lû. But it was Mencius's way to talk roundly. To make 千人 'one thousand,' we must read 幾, in 1st tone, and suppose the preposition 乎 suppressed. The meaning of the officer's reply is—that to provide for such a state of things, by opening the granaries and other measures, devolved on the supreme authority of the State, and not on him. 3. Compare 非身之所能爲, Bk. I. Pt. II. xv. 2.

者、則必爲之求牧與芻矣、求牧與芻而不得、則反諸其人乎、抑亦立而視其死與。曰、此則距心之罪也。四 他日、見於王曰、王之爲都者、臣知五人焉、知其罪者、惟孔距心、爲王誦之。王曰、此則寡人之罪也。

第五章 孟子謂蚳鼃曰、子之辭靈丘、而請士師、似也、爲其

of course he must search for pasture-ground and grass for them. If, after searching for those, he cannot find them, will he return *his charge to* the owner? or will he stand by and see them die?' 'Herein,' said the officer, 'I am guilty.'

4. Another day, *Mencius* had an audience of the king, and said to him, 'Of the governors of your Majesty's cities I am acquainted with five, but the only one of them who knows his faults is K'ung Chü-hsin.' He then repeated the conversation to the king, who said, 'In this matter, I am the guilty one.'

CHAP. V. 1. Mencius said to Ch'î Wâ, 'There seemed to be reason in your declining the governorship of Ling-ch'iû, and requesting to be appointed chief criminal judge, because *the latter office* would afford you the opportunity of speaking *your views*. Now

The first 牧 is the verb; the second a noun, = pasture-grounds. 諸-於. 其人,—'the man,' i.e. their owner. 抑亦,—the force of the 亦 is—'or—here is another supposition—will he, &c.?' Mencius means that Chü-hsin should not hold office in such circumstances. 4. 見 in 4th tone. 爲都者,—爲 has the sense of 'to administer,' 'to govern;' compare Analects, IV. xiii. 都,—properly 'a capital city,' but also used more generally. In the dictionary we find:—(1) Where the sovereign has his palace is called 都. (2) The cities conferred on the sons and younger brothers of the princes were called 都; in fact, every city with an ancestral temple containing the tablets of former rulers. (3) The cities from which nobles and great officers derived their support were called 都. 爲王,—爲 in 4th tone.

5. THE FREEDOM BELONGING TO MENCIUS IN RELATION TO THE MEASURES OF THE KING OF CH'Î FROM HIS PECULIAR POSITION, AS UNSALARIED. 1. Of Ch'î Wâ we only know what is stated here. Ling-ch'iû is supposed to have been a city on the borders of Ch'î, remote from the court, Ch'î Wâ having declined the governorship of it, that he might be near the king. 士師,—see Bk. I. Pt. II. vi. 2. 爲其可以言,—

可以言也、今既數月矣、未可以言與。○二節 蚳鼃諫於王而不用、致爲臣而去。○三節 齊人曰、所以爲蚳鼃則善矣、所以自爲、則吾不知也。○四節 公都子以告。○五節 曰、吾聞之也、有官守者、不得其職則去、有言責者、不得其言則去、我無官守、我無言責也、則吾進退、豈不綽綽然有餘裕哉。○一節

第六章 孟子爲卿於齊、出弔於滕、

several months have elapsed, and have you yet found nothing of which you might speak?'

2. *On this,* Ch'î Wâ remonstrated *on some matter* with the king, and, his counsel not being taken, resigned his office and went away.

3. The people of Ch'î said, 'In the course which he marked out for Ch'î Wâ he did well, but we do not know as to the course which he pursues for himself.'

4. His disciple Kung-tû told him *these remarks.*

5. *Mencius* said, 'I have heard that he who is in charge of an office, when he is prevented from fulfilling its duties, ought to take his departure, and that he on whom is the responsibility of giving his opinion, when he finds his words unattended to, ought to do the same. But I am in charge of no office; on me devolves no duty of speaking out my opinion:—may not I therefore act freely and without any constraint, either in going forward or in retiring?'

CHAP. VI. 1. Mencius, occupying the position of a high dignitary in Ch'î, went on a mission of condolence to T'ăng. The king

literally, 'because of the possibility to speak.' As criminal judge, Ch'î Wâ would be often in communication with the king, and could remonstrate on any failures in the administration of justice that came under his notice. 2. 致, 'to resign,' 'give up,' as in Analects, I. vii, *et al.* 3. 所以爲 (in 3rd tone), literally, 'whereby for,'=所以爲之處, as in the translation. 4. Kung-tû was a disciple of Mencius. See Bk. III. Pt. II. ix. 1; *et al.* 5. We find the phrase 綽綽有裕, with the same meaning as the more enlarged form in the text.

6. MENCIUS'S BEHAVIOUR WITH AN UNWORTHY ASSOCIATE. 1. 'Occupied the position of a high dignitary:'—so I translate here 爲卿. Mencius's situation appears to have been only

王使蓋大夫、王驩爲輔行、王驩朝暮見、反齊滕之路、未嘗與之言行事也。公孫丑曰、齊卿之位、不爲小矣、齊滕之路、不爲近矣、反之、而未嘗與言行事何也。曰、夫既或治之、予何言哉。

七 孟子自齊葬於魯、反於齊、止於嬴、充虞請曰、前日、不知虞之不肖、使虞敦匠

also sent Wang Hwan, the governor of Kâ, as assistant-commissioner. Wang Hwan, morning and evening, waited upon Mencius, who, during all the way to T'ăng and back, never spoke to him about the business of their mission.

2. Kung-sun Ch'âu said to Mencius, 'The position of a high dignitary of Ch'î is not a small one; the road from Ch'î to T'ăng is not short. How was it that during all the way there and back, you never spoke to Hwan about the matters of your mission?' Mencius replied, 'There were the proper officers who attended to them. What occasion had I to speak to him about them?'

CHAP. VII. 1. Mencius *went* from Ch'î to Lû to bury *his mother*. On his return to Ch'î, he stopped at Ying, where Ch'ung Yü begged to put a question to him, and said, 'Formerly, in ignorance of my incompetency, you employed me to superintend the making of the coffin. As *you were then pressed by* the urgency *of the business*,

honorary, without emolument, and the king employed him on this occasion to give weight by his character to the mission. The officer of 蓋 (read *kâ*) was an unworthy favourite of the king. 輔行, not 'to assist him on the journey,' but with reference to what was the business (所行) of it. 見,—4th tone. 反 implies the 往, or 'going,' as well as 'returning.' 2. 齊卿之位 refers to Wang Hwan, who had been temporarily raised to that dignity for the occasion. 夫 (in 2nd tone) 既或,—'Now there were some'—i.e. the proper officers—治之, 'who attended to them.' The glossarist of Châo Ch'î understands this as spoken of Wang:—'He perhaps attended to them,' i.e. he thought that he knew all about them, and never put any questions to me; but the view adopted is more natural, and gives more point to Mencius's explanation of his conduct.

7. THAT ONE OUGHT TO DO HIS UTMOST IN THE BURIAL OF HIS PARENTS;—ILLUSTRATED BY MENCIUS'S BURIAL OF HIS MOTHER. Compare Bk. I. Pt. II. xvi. 1. The tradition is that Mencius had his mother with him in Ch'î, and that he carried her body to the family sepulchre in Lû.

事、嚴、虞不敢請、今願竊有請也、木若以美然。二節曰、古者、棺椁無度、中古棺七寸、椁稱之、自天子達於庶人、非直為觀美也、然後盡於人心。三節不得、不可以為悅、無財、不可以為悅、得之為有財、古之人皆用之、吾何為獨

I did not venture to put any question to you. Now, however, I wish to take the liberty to submit the matter. The wood *of the coffin*, it appeared to me, was too good.'

2. *Mencius* replied, 'Anciently, there was no rule for the size of either the inner or the outer coffin. In middle antiquity, the inner coffin was made seven inches thick, and the outer one the same. This was *done by all*, from the sovereign to the common people, and not simply for the beauty of the appearance, but because they thus satisfied *the natural feelings of* their hearts.

3. 'If prevented *by statutory regulations from making their coffins in this way*, men cannot have the feeling of pleasure. If they have not the money *to make them in this way*, they cannot have the feeling of pleasure. When they were not prevented, and had the money, the ancients all used this style. Why should I alone not do so?

How long he remained in Lû is uncertain;—perhaps the whole three years proper to the mourning for a parent. Whether his stopping at Ying was for a night merely, or a longer period, is also disputed. Ch'ung Yû was one of his disciples. It has appeared strange that Yû should have cherished the matter so long, and submitted it to his master after a lapse of three years. (This is on the supposition that Mencius's return to Ch'î was after the completion of the three years' mourning.) But it is replied in the 四書釋地, that this only illustrates how fond Mencius's disciples were of applying to him for a solution of their doubts, and the instance of Ch'ăn Tsin, chap. iii, is another case in point of the length of time they would keep things in mind. 請,—as in Bk. I. Pt. II. xvi. 1, 'to beg to put a question.' 敦 = 董治, 'to attend to.' 匠, as in Pt. I. vii. 1. 不肖,—see Chung Yung, chap. iv. 嚴 is explained as in the translation. But for the critics, I should render,—'In the gravity of your sorrow.' 竊,—see Pt. I. ii. 20. 2. 'Middle antiquity' commences with the Châu dynasty. 稱, the 4th tone, 'to correspond, or be equal, to.' 盡於人心,—於 is not what they call an 'empty character,' merely completing the rhythm of the sentence. The whole = 'they felt complete (that they had done their utmost) in their human hearts.' Mencius's account of the equal dimensions of the outer and inner coffin does not agree with what we find in the Lî Chî, XIX. ii. 31. It must be borne in mind also, that the seven inches of the Châu dynasty were only = rather more than four inches of the present day. 3. 不得, being opposed to 無財, requires to be supplemented, as in the

不然。四節且比化者、無使土親膚、於人心獨無恔乎。五節吾聞之也、君子不以天下儉其親。

第八章 一節沈同以其私問曰、燕可伐與。孟子曰、可、子噲不得與人燕、子之不得受燕於子噲、有仕於此、而子悅之、不告於王、而私與之吾子之祿爵、夫士也、亦無王命、

4. 'And moreover, is there no satisfaction to the natural feelings of a man, in preventing the earth from getting near to the bodies of his dead?

5. 'I have heard that the superior man will not for all the world be niggardly to his parents.'

CHAP. VIII. 1. Shăn T'ung, on his own impulse, asked *Mencius*, saying, 'May Yen be smitten?' Mencius replied, 'It may. Tsze-k'wâi had no right to give Yen to another man, and Tsze-chih had no right to receive Yen from Tsze-k'wâi. *Suppose* there were an officer here, with whom you, Sir, were pleased, and that, without informing the king, you were privately to give to him your salary and rank; and suppose that this officer, also without the king's orders, were privately to receive them from you:—would *such a transaction* be allowable? And where is the difference between *the case of Yen and* this?'

translation. For 爲有財, some would give 而有財. The 而 reads better, but the meaning is the same. 4. 比 (the 4th tone) 化者,—the same as 比死者 in Bk. I. Pt. I. v. 1. 化 is used appropriately with reference to the dissolution of the bodies of the dead. 膚, 'skin'=the bodies. 恔, the 4th tone, *hsiâo*. 獨無恔乎,—the meaning is —'shall this thing *alone* give no satisfaction to a son's feelings?' 5. 不以天下云云.—Châo Ch'î interprets this:—'will not deny anything in all the world which he can command to his parents.' So, substantially, the modern paraphrasts.

8. DESERVED PUNISHMENT MAY NOT BE INFLICTED BUT BY PROPER AUTHORITY. A STATE OR NATION MAY ONLY BE SMITTEN BY THE MINISTER OF HEAVEN. The incidents in the history of Yen referred to are briefly these:—Tsze-k'wâi, a weak silly man, was wrought upon to resign his throne to his prime minister Tsze-chih, in the expectation that Tsze-chih would decline the honour, and

孟子

而私受之於子、則可乎、何以異於是。○二節齊人伐燕、或問曰、勸齊伐燕、有諸。曰、未也、沈同問燕可伐與、吾應之曰、可、彼然而伐之也、彼如曰、孰可以伐之、則將應之曰、爲天吏、則可以伐之、今有殺人者、或問之曰、人可殺與、則將應之曰、可、彼如曰、孰可以殺之、則將應之曰、爲士師、則可以殺之、今以燕伐燕、何爲勸之哉。

2. The people of Ch'î smote Yen. Some one asked Mencius, saying, 'Is it really the case that you advised Ch'î to smite Yen?' He replied, 'No. Shăn T'ung asked me whether Yen might be smitten, and I answered him, "It may." They accordingly went and smote it. If he had asked me—"Who may smite it?" I would have answered him, "He who is the minister of Heaven may smite it." Suppose the case of a murderer, and that one asks me—"May this man be put to death?" I will answer him—"He may." If he ask me—"Who may put him to death?" I will answer him,—"The chief criminal judge may put him to death." But now with *one* Yen to smite *another* Yen:—how should I have advised this?'

that thus he would be praised as acting the part of the ancient Yâo, while he retained his kingdom. Tsze-chih, however, accepted the tender, and Tsze-k'wâi was laid upon the shelf. By-and-by, his son endeavoured to wrest back the throne, and great confusion and suffering to the people ensued. Compare Bk. I. Pt. II. x, xi. 1. Shăn (so read, as a surname) T'ung appears to have been a high minister of the State. It is difficult to find a word by which to translate 伐, which implies the idea of Yen's deserving to be punished. 吾子,—referring to Shăn T'ung, but we cannot translate it literally in English. 夫士也,夫, in the 2nd tone, =斯; 士 is the same person as 仕 above, 'a scholar seeking official employment.' 2. 應, the 4th tone. 彼然,—彼 refers to the king and people of Ch'î. 彼如曰,—彼 refers only to Sh'ăn T'ung. 天吏, see Pt. I. v. 6. The one Yen is of course Ch'î, as oppressive as Yen itself.

第九章 一節 燕人畔、王曰、吾甚慙於孟子。二節 陳賈曰、王無患焉。王自以爲與周公、孰仁且智。王曰、惡、是何言也。曰、周公使管叔監殷、管叔以殷畔、知而使之、是不仁也、不知而使之、是不智也、仁智、周公未之盡也、而況於王乎、賈請見而解之。三節 見孟子、問曰、周公何人也。曰、古聖人

CHAP. IX. 1. The people of Yen having rebelled, the king *of Ch'î* said, 'I feel very much ashamed *when I think* of Mencius.'

2. Ch'ăn Chiâ said to him, 'Let not your Majesty be grieved. Whether does your Majesty consider yourself or Châu-kung the more benevolent and wise?' The king replied, 'Oh! what words are those?' 'The duke of Châu,' said *Chiâ*, 'appointed Kwan-shû to oversee *the heir of* Yin, but Kwan-shû with the power of the Yin State rebelled. If knowing that this would happen he appointed Kwan-shû, he was deficient in benevolence. If he appointed him, not knowing that it would happen, he was deficient in knowledge. If the duke of Châu was not completely benevolent and wise, how much less can your Majesty be expected to be so! I beg to go and see Mencius, and relieve your Majesty from that feeling.'

3. *Ch'ăn Chiâ* accordingly saw Mencius, and asked him, saying, 'What kind of man was the duke of Châu?' 'An ancient sage,'

9. HOW MENCIUS BEAT DOWN THE ATTEMPT TO ARGUE IN EXCUSE OF ERRORS AND MISCONDUCT. 1. The people of Yen set up the son of Tsze-k'wâi as king, and rebelled against the yoke which Ch'î had attempted to impose on them. 'Ashamed when I think of Mencius,'—i. e. because of the advice of Mencius in regard to Yen which he had neglected. See Bk. I. Pt. II. x, xi. 2. Ch'ăn Chiâ was an officer of Ch'î. Châu-kung,—see Analects, VII. v, *et al.* The case Chiâ refers to was this:—On king Wû's extinction of the Yin dynasty, sparing the life of Châu's son, he conferred on him the small State of Yin from which the dynasty had taken its name, but placed him under the surveillance of his own two brothers, *Hsien* (鮮) and *Tû* (度), one of them older, and the other younger, than his brother Tan (旦), who was Châu-kung. Hsien has come down to us under the title of Kwan-shû, Kwan being the name of the principality which he received for himself. After Wû's death, and the succession of his son, Hsien and Tû rebelled, when Châu-kung took action against them, put the former to death, and banished the other. 監 (the 1st tone) 殷, —the 殷 here is the son of the sovereign Châu. That below is the name of the State. 解之, —I take 解 in the sense of 'to loose,' 'to free

也。曰、使管叔監殷、管叔以殷畔
也、有諸。曰、然。曰、周公知其將畔
而使之與。曰、不知也。然則聖人
且有過與。曰、周公、弟也、管叔、兄
也、周公之過、不亦宜乎。四節且古之
君子、過則改之、今之君子、過則
順之、古之君子、其過也、如日月
之食、民皆見之、及其更也、民皆
仰之、今之君子、豈徒順之、又從
爲之辭。

was the reply. 'Is it the fact, that he appointed Kwan-shû to oversee *the heir* of Yin, and that Kwan-shû with the State of Yin rebelled?' 'It is.' 'Did the duke of Châu know that he would rebel, and *purposely* appoint him to that office?' *Mencius* said, 'He did not know.' 'Then, though a sage, he still fell into error?' 'The duke of Châu,' answered *Mencius*, 'was the younger brother. Kwan-shû was his elder brother. Was not the error of Châu-kung in accordance with what is right?

4. 'Moreover, when the superior men of old had errors, they reformed them. The superior men of the present time, when they have errors, persist in them. The errors of the superior men of old were like eclipses of the sun and moon. All the people witnessed them, and when they had reformed them, all the people looked up to them *with their former admiration*. *But* do the superior men of the present day only persist in their errors? They go on to apologize for them likewise.'

from,' with reference to the feeling of shame, not 'to explain.' 3. Before 然則 there should be a 曰, as it is the retort of Ch'ăn Chiâ. 聖人且有過與,—且 implies a succeeding clause—'how much more may one inferior to him!'—況下于公者乎.

What Mencius means in conclusion is, that brother ought not to be suspicious of brother: that it is better to be deceived than to impute evil. 4. In 今之君子, the 君子 must be taken vaguely. 更, the 1st tone, = 改. Shall we refer it to the sun and moon, or to the ancient worthies? Primarily, its application is

第十章 一節 孟子致爲臣而歸。二節 王就見孟子曰、前日願見而不可得、得侍、同朝甚喜、今又棄寡人而歸、不識可以繼此而得見乎。對曰、不敢請耳、固所願也。三節 他日、王謂時子曰、我欲中國而授孟子室、養弟子以萬鍾、使諸大夫國人皆有所矜式、子盍爲我言之。四節 時子因陳子而

CHAP. X. 1. Mencius gave up his office, and *made arrangements for* returning *to his native State.*

2. The king came to visit him, and said, 'Formerly, I wished to see you, but in vain. Then, I got the opportunity of being by your side, and all my court joyed exceedingly along with me. Now again you abandon me, and are returning home. I do not know if hereafter I may expect to have another opportunity of seeing you.' Mencius replied, 'I dare not request permission to visit you *at any particular time*, but, indeed, it is what I desire.'

3. Another day, the king said to the officer Shih, 'I wish to give Mencius a house, somewhere in the middle of the kingdom, and to support his disciples with *an allowance of* 10,000 *chung*, that all the officers and the people may have *such an example* to reverence and imitate. Had you not better tell him this for me?'

4. Shih took advantage to convey this message by means of the disciple Ch'ăn, who reported his words to Mencius.

to the heavenly bodies. 爲之辭, the double object after 爲. The remark was a severe thrust at Ch'ăn Chiâ's own conduct.

10. MENCIUS IN LEAVING A COUNTRY OR REMAINING IN IT WAS NOT INFLUENCED BY PECUNIARY CONSIDERATIONS, BUT BY THE OPPORTUNITY DENIED OR ACCORDED TO HIM OF CARRYING HIS PRINCIPLES INTO PRACTICE. 1. 致爲臣,—致 as in chap. v. 2, only it is here simply 'resignation,' with little of the idea of sacrifice. 而歸, 'and returned.' —Châo Ch'î says 'to his house,' and in accordance with this, he interprets 不敢請耳 below, 'I do not venture to ask you to come in person to see me,' which is surely absurd enough. The meaning must be what I have given. 2. 前日,—referring to the time before Mencius first came to Ch'î. 同朝 (ch'âo, 2nd tone)=同朝之臣, 'all the officers of the court with himself.' 繼此=繼此見, 'in continuation of this seeing.' Mencius sees that the king with his complimentary expressions is really bidding him adieu, and answers, accordingly, in as complimentary a way, intimating his purpose to be

以告孟子。陳子以時子之言告孟子。○五節 孟子曰、然、夫時子惡知其不可也、如使予欲富、辭十萬而受萬、是爲欲富乎。○六節 季孫曰、異哉子叔疑、使己爲政、不用、則亦已矣、又使其子弟爲卿、人亦孰不欲富貴、而獨於富貴之中、有私龍斷焉。○七節 古之爲市者、以其所有、易其所無

5. Mencius said, 'Yes; but how should the officer Shih know that the thing could not be? Suppose that I wanted to be rich, having formerly declined 100,000 *chung*, would my now accepting 10,000 be the conduct of one desiring riches?

6. 'Chî-sun said, "A strange man was Tsze-shû Î. He pushed himself into the service of government. *His prince* declining to employ him, he had to retire indeed, but he again schemed that his son or younger brother should be made a high officer. Who indeed is there of men but wishes for riches and honour? But he only, among the seekers of these, tried to monopolize the conspicuous mound.

7. '"Of old time, the market-dealers exchanged the articles which they had for others which they had not, and simply had certain officers to keep order among them. It happened that there was

gone. 3. The king after all does not like the idea of Mencius's going, and thinks of this plan to retain him, which was in reality what Mencius, in chap. iii, calls 'bribing' him. 爲, the 4th tone. 4. Ch'ăn here is the Ch'ăn Tsin of chap. iii. 因 is explained by 依託, 'entrusted to.' But it is more, and = 'to take advantage of,' with reference to Ch'ăn's being a disciple of Mencius. 5. Mencius does not find it convenient to state plainly his real reason for going,—that he was not permitted to see his principles carried into practice, and therefore repels simply the idea of his being accessible to pecuniary considerations. 100,000 *chung* was the fixed allowance of a 卿, which Mencius had declined to receive. 6. Of Chî-sun and Tsze-shû Î we know only what is mentioned here. Châo Ch'î says that they were disciples of Mencius, and that Chî-sun made his remark with a view to induce Mencius to push forward his disciples into the employment which he could not get for himself. But such a view is inadmissible. 使己, 使其子弟,—the first 使, it is said, merely refers to the prince's employment of him, and the second to his contriving and bringing about the employment of his son or younger brother; but why should we not give the character the same force in both cases? 龍, the 3rd tone, read as and = 壟, 'a mound.' 斷, 4th tone, 'cut,' 'abrupt,' 'well defined.' 7. 治, 2nd tone. Observe

Q 2

者、有司者治之耳、有賤丈夫焉、必求龍斷而登之、以左右望、而罔市利、人皆以爲賤、故從而征之、征商、自此賤丈夫始矣。

[十一章] 一節 孟子去齊、宿於晝。二節 有欲爲王留行者、坐而言、不應、隱几而臥。三節 客不悅曰、弟子齊宿而後敢言、夫子臥而不聽、請勿復敢見矣。曰、坐、

a mean fellow, who made it a point to look out for a conspicuous mound, and get up upon it. Thence he looked right and left, to catch in his net the whole gain of the market. The people all thought his conduct mean, and therefore they proceeded to lay a tax upon his wares. The taxing of traders took its rise from this mean fellow."'

CHAP. XI. 1. Mencius, having taken his leave of Ch'î, was passing the night in Châu.

2. A person who wished to detain him on behalf of the king, *came and* sat down, and began to speak to him. *Mencius* gave him no answer, but leant upon his stool and slept.

3. The visitor was displeased, and said, 'I passed the night in careful vigil, before I would venture to speak to you, and you, Master, sleep and do not listen to me. Allow me to request that I may not again presume to see you.' *Mencius* replied, 'Sit down,

the force of 耳, 'only,' which also belongs to it in par. 2, weakening the 不敢請. 征之,—the 之 should be referred to the mean individual spoken of.

11. HOW MENCIUS REPELLED A MAN, WHO, OFFICIOUSLY AND ON HIS OWN IMPULSE, TRIED TO DETAIN HIM IN CH'Î. 1. 晝 was a city on the southern border of Ch'î. Some think it should be written 畫, and refer it to a place in the present district of 臨淄, but this would place it north from Lû, whither Mencius was retiring. Mencius withdrew leisurely, hoping that the king would recall him and pledge himself to follow his counsels. 2. 爲 (4th tone) 王,—'for the king,' i.e. knowing it would please the king. 應,—4th tone. 隱,—the 3rd tone, 'to lean upon.' The 几 was a stool or bench, on which individuals might lean forward, or otherwise, as they sat upon their mats. It could be carried in the hand. See the Lî Chî, Bk. I. Sect. I. ii. 1, 一謀於長者, 必操几杖以從之. 3. 齊 (châi), the 1st tone, =齋, 'to keep a vigil,' 'to fast.' 齊宿,—'fasted and passed

孟子

我明語子、昔者魯繆公、無人乎子思之側、則不能安子思、泄柳申詳、無人乎繆公之側、則不能安其身。四節 子爲長者慮、而不及子思、子絕長者乎、長者絕子乎。

十二章 一節 孟子去齊。尹士語人曰、不識王之不可以爲湯武、則是不明也、識其

and I will explain the case clearly to you. Formerly, if the duke Mû had not kept a person by the side of Tsze-sze, he could not have induced Tsze-sze to remain with him. If Hsieh Liû and Shăn Hsiang had not had a *remembrancer* by the side of the duke Mû, he would not have been able to make them feel at home and remain with him.

4. 'You anxiously form plans with reference to me, but you do not treat me as Tsze-sze was treated. Is it you, Sir, who cut me? Or is it I who cut you?'

CHAP. XII. 1. When Mencius had left Ch'î, Yin Shih spoke about him to others, saying, 'If he did not know that the king could not be made a T'ang or a Wû, that showed his want of intelligence. If he knew that he could not be made such, and came

the night.' 請勿復 (in 4th tone) 敢見 is merely the complimentary way of complaining of what the guest considered the rudeness of his reception. 語, the 4th tone, = 告. 繆, here read *Mû*, was the honorary epithet of the duke Hsien (顯), B.C. 409–375. Tsze-sze,—the grandson of Confucius. Shăn Hsiang,—the son of Tsze-chang (子張), one of Confucius's disciples. Hsieh Liû was a native of Lû, a disciple of the Confucian school. See the Lî Chî, Bk. II. Sect. I. ii. 34, and Bk. XVIII. Sect. II. ii. 11. In this last passage Liû should be Hsieh Liû. 乎 = 在 or 在乎. 安 is said to = 留, simply 'to detain,' but its force is more than that, and = 'to make contented, and so induce to remain.' Great respect, it seems, was shown to Tsze-sze, and he had an attendant from the duke to assure him continually of the respect with which he was cherished. Hsieh Liû and Shăn Hsiang had not such attendants, but they knew that there were one or more officers by the duke's side, to admonish him not to forget them and other worthies. The visitor calls himself 弟子, 'your disciple.' 4. 爲, 4th tone. Mencius calls himself 長 (the 3rd tone) 者, 'the elder.' 子爲長者云云,—the stranger was anxious for (慮) Mencius to remain in Ch'î, but the thing was entirely from himself, not from the king; and his thinking that he could detain him by such a visit showed the little store he set by him;—was, in fact, a *cutting* him.

12. HOW MENCIUS EXPLAINED HIS SEEMING TO LINGER IN CH'Î, AFTER HE HAD RESIGNED HIS OFFICE, AND LEFT THE COURT. 1. All that we know of Yin Shih is that he was a man of Ch'î.

不可、然且至、則是干澤也、千里而見王、不遇故去、三宿而後出晝、是何濡滯也、士則茲不悅。○二節高子以告。○三節曰、夫尹士惡知予哉、千里而見王、是予所欲也、不遇故去、豈予所欲哉、予不得已也。○四節予三宿而後出晝、於予心猶以爲速、王庶幾改之、王如改諸、則必反予。○五節夫出

notwithstanding, that shows he was seeking his own benefit. He came a thousand *lî* to wait on the king; because he did not find in him a ruler to suit him, he took his leave, but how dilatory and lingering was his departure, stopping three nights before he quitted Châu! I am dissatisfied on account of this.'

2. The disciple Kâo informed Mencius *of these remarks*.

3. *Mencius* said, 'How should Yin Shih know me! When I came a thousand *lî* to wait on the king, it was what I desired to do. When I went away because I did not find in him a ruler to suit me, was that what I desired to do? I felt myself constrained to do it.

4. 'When I stopped three nights before I quitted Châu, in my own mind I still considered my departure speedy. I was hoping that the king might change. If the king had changed, he would certainly have recalled me.

5. 'When I quitted Châu, and the king had not sent after me,

Julien properly blames Noel for translating 尹士 by '*literatus cognomine Yin*,' as if 士 were here the noun—'a scholar.' But when he adds that it is here to be pronounced *chi*, to mark that it is a name, this is what neither the dictionary nor any commentary mentions. 語, the 4th tone,=告. 干澤, 'to seek for favours,' i. e. his own benefit;—see Analects, II. xviii. 不遇,—see Bk. I. Pt. II. xvi. 3. 茲=此, 'this.' What Shih chiefly means to charge against Mencius is the lingering character of his departure. 3. Mencius was constrained to leave by the conviction forced on him that he could not in Ch'î carry his principles into practice. 王庶幾 (the 1st tone) 改之, literally, 'The king fortunately near to change it.' This was the thought at the time in Mencius's mind, and 庶幾=' I hoped,' 'I was looking for.' 諸=之. 4. 諸=然後, 'then, and not till then.' 浩然,—see Pt. I. ii. 11. 舍=捨, the 3rd tone. 由=猶. 用 is by many taken as simply=以;

孟子

晝、而王不予追也、予然後浩然有歸志、予雖然、豈舍王哉、王由足用爲善、王如用予、則豈徒齊民安、天下之民舉安、王庶幾改之、予日望之。六節予豈若是小丈夫然哉、諫於其君而不受、則怒悻悻然、見於其面、去則窮日之力、而後宿哉。七節尹士聞之曰、士誠小人也。

十三章一節孟子去齊。充虞路問曰、夫子

then, and not till then, was my mind resolutely bent on returning *to Tsâu*. But, notwithstanding that, how can *it be said that* I give up the king? The king, after all, is one who may be made to do what is good. If he were to use me, would it be for the happiness of the people of Ch'î only? It would be for the happiness of the people of the whole kingdom. I am hoping that the king will change. I am daily hoping for this.

6. 'Am I like one of your little-minded people? They will remonstrate with their prince, and on *their remonstrance not* being accepted, they get angry; and, with their passion displayed in their countenance, they take their leave, and travel with all their strength for a whole day, before they will stop for the night.'

7. When Yin Shih heard this explanation, he said, 'I am indeed a small man.'

CHAP. XIII. 1. When Mencius left Ch'î, Ch'ung Yü questioned him upon the way, saying, 'Master, you look like one who carries

—'the king is, after all, competent to do good,' but 用 expresses more than that. 予日望之 conveys in itself no more than the translation, but the king's change of course involved Mencius's recall to Ch'î. Perhaps we have in the words an amplification of Mencius's thoughts before he quitted Châu. 5. Compare with this paragraph Confucius's defence of Kwan Chung, Analects, XIV. xviii.

13. MENCIUS'S GRIEF AT NOT FINDING AN OPPORTUNITY TO DO THE GOOD WHICH HE COULD. 1. Ch'ung Yü,—the same mentioned in chap. vii. Though Ch'ung Yü attributes the maxim 不怨天不尤人 to his master, we find it

若有不豫色然前日虞聞諸夫子曰、君子不怨天、不尤人。○二節曰、彼一時、此一時也。○三節五百年、必有王者興、其間必有名世者。○四節由周而來、七百有餘歲矣、以其數則過矣、以其時考之則可矣。○五節夫天未欲平治天下也、如欲平治天下、當今之世、舍我其誰也、吾何爲不豫哉。

an air of dissatisfaction in his countenance. But formerly I heard you say—"The superior man does not murmur against Heaven, nor grudge against men."'

2. *Mencius* said, 'That was one time, and this is another.

3. 'It is a rule that a true royal sovereign should arise in the course of five hundred years, and that during that time there should be men illustrious in their generation.

4. 'From the commencement of the Châu dynasty till now, more than seven hundred years have elapsed. Judging numerically, the date is past. Examining the *character of the present* time, we might *expect the rise of such individuals in it.*

5. 'But Heaven does not yet wish that the kingdom should enjoy tranquillity and good order. If it wished this, who is there besides me to bring it about? How should I be otherwise than dissatisfied?'

in Confucius, see Analects, XIV. xxxvii. 3. '500 years,'—this is speaking in very round and loose numbers, even if we judge from the history of China prior to Mencius. 其閒, 'during them,' but the meaning is—at the same time with the sovereign shall arise men able to assist him. 名世 = 有 or 著名于世. 4. The Châu dynasty lasted altogether 867 years, and Mencius died, according to some accounts, at the age of 102, in the second year of the last century, little more than fifty years removed from the extinction of the dynasty. 以其時考之則可矣, literally, 'By the time examining it, then may,' i. e. such things may be. 5. 舍我其誰, literally, 'Letting me go, then who?' Compare last chapter, par. 4, and many other places, where Mencius speaks of what he could accomplish. On the reference to the will of Heaven, compare Analects, IX. v. 3.

十四 一 孟子去齊、居休。公孫丑問曰、仕而不受祿、古之道乎。二 曰、非也、於崇、吾得見王、退而有去志、不欲變、故不受也。三 繼而有師命、不可以請、久於齊、非我志也。

CHAP. XIV. 1. When Mencius left Ch'î, he dwelt in Hsiû. *There* Kung-sun Ch'âu asked him, saying, 'Was it the way of the ancients to hold office without receiving salary?'

2. *Mencius replied,* 'No; when I first saw the king in Ch'ung, it was my intention, on retiring from the interview, to go away. Because I did not wish to change this intention, I declined to receive any salary.

3. 'Immediately after, there came orders for the collection of troops, when it would have been improper for me to beg permission to leave. But to remain *so* long in Ch'î was not my purpose.'

14. THE REASON OF MENCIUS'S HOLDING AN HONORARY OFFICE IN CH'Î WITHOUT SALARY, THAT HE WISHED TO BE FREE IN HIS MOVEMENTS. 1. Hsiû was in the present district of T'ăng (滕) in the department of Yen-châu. Kung-sun Châu's inquiry was simply for information. This appears from the 非 with which it is answered. 2. Ch'ung must be the name of a place in Ch'î, which cannot be more exactly determined. It is not to be confounded with the ancient principality or barony of the same name. 得見 is evidently = 始見. 3. 師命 may be as in the translation, or—'the appointment to the position of a Tutor,' i.e. honorary adviser to the king. This is the interpretation of the glossarist of Châo Ch'î, and is perhaps preferable to the former.

BOOK III.

T'ĂNG WĂN KUNG. PART I.

滕文公章句上

第一章 一節 滕文公爲世子、將之楚、過宋而見孟子。○二節 孟子道性善、言必稱堯舜。○三節 世子自楚反、復見孟子。孟子曰、世子疑吾言乎、夫道、一而已矣。○四節 成覸謂齊景公曰、彼丈夫也、我丈

CHAPTER I. 1. When the prince, afterwards duke Wăn of T'ăng, had to go to Ch'û, he went by way of Sung, and visited Mencius.

2. Mencius discoursed to him how the nature *of man* is good, and when speaking, always made laudatory reference to Yâo and Shun.

3. When the prince was returning from Ch'û, he again visited Mencius. Mencius said to him, 'Prince, do you doubt my words? The path is one, and only one.

4. 'Ch'ăng Chi'en said to duke King of Ch'î, "They were men. I am a man. Why should I stand in awe of them?" Yen Yüan said,

TITLE OF THIS BOOK.—滕文公, 'The duke Wăn of T'ăng.' The Book is so named from the duke Wăn, who is prominent in the first three chapters. Châo Ch'î compares this with the title of the Fifteenth Book of the Analects.

1. HOW ALL MEN BY DEVELOPING THEIR NATURAL GOODNESS MAY BECOME EQUAL TO THE ANCIENT SAGES. 1. The duke Wăn of T'ăng,—see Bk. I. Pt. II. xiii. Wăn is the posthumous title. The crown-prince's name appears to have been Hung (宏). Previous to the Han dynasty, the heirs-apparent of the sovereigns and the princes of States were called indifferently 世子 and 太子. Since then, 太子 has been confined to the imperial heir. The title of 世子 was given, it is said, 欲其世世不絶, 'to indicate the wish that the succession should be unbroken *from generation to generation*.' Ch'û and T'ăng bordering on each other, the prince must have gone out of his way to visit Mencius. In the 'Topography of the Four Books, continued,' it is said:—'Since T'ăng and Ch'û adjoined, so that one had only to lift his feet and pass into Ch'û, why must the crown-prince go round about, a distance of more than 350 *li*, to pass by the capital of Sung? The reason was that Mencius was there, and the prince's putting himself to so much trouble, in going and returning, shows his worthiness.' 2. 道=言, a verb, 'to speak or discourse about.' 必, not 'necessarily,' but 'he made it a point.' 稱 is taken by Chû Hsî and others in the sense of 'to appeal to.' This is supported by par. 3, but the word itself has only the meaning in the translation, with which, moreover, Châo Ch'î agrees. 3. 道一而已,—道

夫也、吾何畏彼哉、顏淵曰、舜何人也、予何人也、有爲者亦若是。公明儀曰、文王、我師也、周公豈欺我哉。五節 今滕絶長補短、將五十里也、猶可以爲善國。書曰、若藥不瞑眩、厥疾不瘳。

二章 一節 滕定公薨、世子謂然友曰、昔者孟子嘗與我言於宋、於心終不忘、今也不幸、至於大

"What kind of man was Shun? What kind of man am I? He who exerts himself will also become such as he was." Kung-ming Î said, "King Wăn is my teacher. How should the duke of Châu deceive me *by those words?*"

5. 'Now, T'ăng, taking its length with its breadth, will amount, I suppose, to fifty *lî*. *It is small, but* still sufficient to make a good State. It is said in the Book of History, "If medicine do not raise a commotion in the patient, his disease will not be cured by it."'

CHAP. II. 1. When the duke Ting of T'ăng died, the prince said to Yen Yû, 'Formerly, Mencius spoke with me in Sung, and in my mind I have never forgotten *his words*. Now, alas!

seems here to be used as in the Chung Yung, i. 1,—'an accordance with this nature is called the Path,' but viewed here more in the consummation of high sageship and distinction to which it leads, which may be reached by treading it, and which can be reached in no other way. We have here for the first time the statement of Mencius's doctrine, which he subsequently dwells so much on, that 'the nature of man is good.' 4. Of Ch'ăng Ch'ien we only know what is here said. 彼丈夫,—彼 referring to the sages. 丈夫,—used for 'man' or 'men,' with the idea of vigour and capability. Kung-ming Î was a disciple first of Tsze-chang, and then of Tsăng Shăn. 文王我師 would appear to have been a remark originally of Châu-kung, which Î appropriates and vindicates on that high authority. 5. 絶長補短,—'cutting the long to supplement the short.' Observe the force of 將, as in the translation. 猶 implying—'It is small, but still.' 善國, compare chap. iii :—'a good kingdom' is such an one as is there described. 若藥云云,—see the Shû-ching, IV. viii. Sect. I. 8. 瞑, read *mien*, the 4th tone.

2. HOW MENCIUS ADVISED THE DUKE OF T'ANG TO CONDUCT THE MOURNING FOR HIS FATHER. 1. 薨 is the proper term to express the death of any of the feudal princes of the kingdom. Yen Yû had been the prince's Grand-tutor (太

故、吾欲使子問於孟子、然後行事。○二節然友之鄒問於孟子。孟子曰、不亦善乎、親喪固所自盡也。曾子曰、生事之以禮、死葬之以禮、祭之以禮、可謂孝矣。諸侯之禮、吾未之學也、雖然、吾嘗聞之矣、三年之喪、齊疏之服、飦粥之食、自天子達於庶人、三代共之。○三節然友反命、定

this great duty to my father devolves upon me; I wish to send you to ask the advice of Mencius, and then to proceed to its *various* services.'

2. *Zan* Yû *accordingly* proceeded to Tsâu, and consulted Mencius. Mencius said, 'Is this not good? In discharging the funeral duties to parents, men indeed feel constrained to do their utmost. The philosopher Tsăng said, "When parents are alive, they should be served according to propriety; when they are dead, they should be buried according to propriety; and they should be sacrificed to according to propriety:—this may be called filial piety." The ceremonies to be observed by the princes I have not learned, but I have heard *these points*:—that the three years' mourning, the garment of coarse cloth with its lower edge even, and the eating of congee, were equally prescribed by the three dynasties, and binding on all, from the sovereign to the mass of the people.'

3. *Zan* Yû reported the execution of his commission, and *the*

傅); I suppose that 然 is the surname. 大故 is a phrase applied to the funeral of, and mourning for, parents;—'the great cause, or matter.' 2. 之鄒,—之 is the verb, = 往. 不亦善乎,—spoken with reference to the prince's sending to consult him on such a subject. 親喪固所自盡,—compare Analects, XIX. xvii. The words attributed to Tsăng Shăn were originally spoken by Confucius; see Analects, II. v. Tsăng may have appropriated them, and spoken them, so as to make them be regarded as his own, or, what is more likely, Mencius here makes a slip of memory. 齊, 1st tone, read *tsze*; see Analects, IX. ix. 飦, as used in the text, read like and = 饘, denotes congee, like 粥, but made thicker. 3. 反命, 'returned the commission,' i.e. reported his execution of it and the reply. 世子 must be understood as the subject of 定. 父兄, 'his fathers and brethren,' i.e.

爲三年之喪、父兄百官皆不欲、曰、吾宗國魯先君莫之行、吾先君亦莫之行也、至於子之身而反之、不可、且志曰、喪祭從先祖、曰、吾有所受之也。四謂然友曰、吾他日未嘗學問、好馳馬試劍、今也、父兄百官、不我足也、恐其不能盡於大事、子爲我問孟子。然友復之鄒、

prince determined that the three years' mourning should be observed. His aged relatives, and the body of the officers, did not wish that it should be so, and said, 'The former princes of Lû, that kingdom which we honour, have, none of them, observed this practice, neither have any of our own former princes observed it. For you to act contrary to their example is not proper. Moreover, the History says,—"In the observances of mourning and sacrifice, ancestors are to be followed," meaning that they received those things from a *proper* source *to hand them down.*'

4. *The prince said again* to Zan Yû, 'Hitherto, I have not given myself to the pursuit of learning, but have found my pleasure in horsemanship and sword-exercise, and now I don't come up to the wishes of my aged relatives and the officers. I am afraid I may not be able to discharge my duty in the great business *that I have entered on;* do you *again* consult Mencius for me.' *On this,* Zan Yû

his uncles and elderly ministers of the ducal family. The phrase is commonly applied by Chinese to the elders of their own surname, whatever be the degrees of their relationship. 吾宗國,—the ducal house of T'ang was descended from one of the sons of king Wăn (Shû-hsiû, 叔繡), but by an inferior wife, while Châu-kung, the ancestor of Lû, was in the true-sovereign line, the author of all the civil institutions of the dynasty, and hence all the other States ruled by descendants of king Wăn were supposed to look up to Lû. That Châu-kung and the first rulers of T'ang had not observed the three years' mourning is not to be supposed. The crown-prince's remonstrants are wrong in attributing to them the neglect of later dukes. 志,—what particular 'history' they refer to is not known. 吾有所受之,—吾 is to be understood as spoken in the person of the ancestors, and I have therefore rendered it by 'they.' Châo Ch'î, however, says that some made this a reply of the prince:—'The prince said, *I have one* (i. e. *Mencius*) *from whom I received it.*' 4. 不我足=不以我足滿其意, as in the translation. 恐其不能,—'I am afraid of the not being able, &c.' It is the sentiment of the prince

問孟子。孟子曰、然、不可以他求者也、孔子曰、君薨、聽於冢宰、歠粥、面深墨、卽位而哭、百官有司、莫敢不哀、先之也、上有好者、下必有甚焉者矣、君子之德、風也、小人之德、草也、草尚之風必偃、是在世子。○五節 然友反命。世子曰、然、是誠在我、五月居廬、未有命戒、百官族人、

went again to Tsâu, and consulted Mencius. Mencius said, 'It is so, but he may not seek *a remedy* in others, *but only in himself.* Confucius said, "When a prince dies, his successor entrusts the administration to the prime minister. He sips the congee. His face is of a deep black. He approaches the place *of mourning,* and weeps. Of all the officers and inferior ministers there is not one who will presume not to join in the lamentation, he setting them this example. What the superior loves, his inferiors will be found to love exceedingly. The relation between superiors and inferiors is like that between the wind and grass. The grass must bend when the wind blows upon it." The business depends on the prince.'

5. *Zan Yû* returned with this answer to his commission, and the prince said, 'It is so. The matter does indeed depend on me.' So for five months he dwelt in the shed, without issuing an order or a caution. All the officers and his relatives said, 'He may be said to understand *the ceremonies.*' When the time of interment arrived,

himself, and 恐 must be translated in the first person, and not in the third, as Julien does. In the 其 there is a reference to his antecedents, as occasioning the present difficulty. 不可以他求 is taken by Ch'âo Ch'î, 'You may not seek (to overcome their opposition) by any other way (but carrying out what you have begun).' Chû Hsî's view, as in the translation, is better. In the quotations from Confucius, Mencius has blended different places of the Analects together, and enlarged them to suit his own purpose, or, it may be, the text of the Analects was different in his time. See Analects, XII. xxi, *et al.* 卽位而哭,—the 位 is the place where the coffin lay, during the five months that elapsed between the death and interment. 5. The 廬 was a shed, built of boards and straw, outside the centre door of the palace, against the surrounding wall, which the mourning prince tenanted till the interment; see the Lî Chî, XVIII. Sect. I. i. 7. 可謂曰知 is supposed by Chû Hsî, with reason, to be corrupted or defective.

可謂曰知、及至葬、四方來觀之、顏色之戚、哭泣之哀、弔者大悅。

第三章 一節 滕文公問爲國。二節 孟子曰、民事不可緩也、詩云、晝爾于茅、宵爾索綯、亟其乘屋、其始播百穀。三節 民之爲道也、有恆

they came from all quarters of the State to witness it. Those who had come *from other States* to condole with him, were greatly pleased with the deep dejection of his countenance and the mournfulness of his wailing and weeping.

CHAP. III. 1. The duke Wăn of T'ăng asked *Mencius* about *the proper way of* governing a kingdom.

2. Mencius said, 'The business of the people may not be remissly attended to. It is said in the Book of Poetry,

> "In the day-light go and gather the grass,
> And at night twist your ropes;
> Then get up quickly on the roofs;—
> *Soon* must we begin sowing *again* the grain."

3. 'The way of the people is this:—If they have a certain

I have translated as if it were 曰可謂知.—Chû Hsi introduces here the following remarks from the commentator Lin (林):—'In the time of Mencius, although the rites to the dead had fallen into neglect, yet the three years' mourning, with the sorrowing heart and afflictive grief, being the expression of what really belongs to man's mind, had not quite perished. Only, sunk in the slough of manners becoming more and more corrupt, men were losing all their moral nature without being conscious of it. When duke Wăn saw Mencius, and heard him speak of the goodness of man's nature, and of Yâo and Shun, that was the occasion of moving and bringing forth his better heart, and on this occasion—of the death of his father—he felt sincerely all the stirrings of sorrow and grief. Then, moreover, when his older relatives and his officers wished not to act as he desired, he turned inwards to reprove himself, and lamented his former conduct which made him not be believed in his present course, not presuming to blame his officers and relatives:—although we must concede an extraordinary natural excellence and ability to him, yet his energy in learning may not be impeached. Finally, when we consider how with what decision he finally acted, and how all, near and far, who saw and heard him, were delighted to acknowledge and admire his conduct, we have an instance of how, when that which belongs to all men's minds is in the first place exhibited by one, others are brought, without any previous purpose, to the pleased acknowledgment and approval of it:—is not this a proof that it is indeed true that *the nature of man is good?*'

3. MENCIUS'S COUNSELS TO THE DUKE OF T'ĂNG FOR THE GOVERNMENT OF HIS KINGDOM. AGRICULTURE AND EDUCATION ARE THE CHIEF THINGS TO BE ATTENDED TO, AND THE FIRST AS AN ESSENTIAL PREPARATION FOR THE SECOND. 1. 爲, in the sense of 治, 'to govern.' 2. By 民事, 'the business of the people,' is intended husbandry. For the ode, see the Shih-ching, I. xv. Ode I. st. 7, written, it is said, by Châu-kung, to impress the sovereign Ch'ăng with a sense of the importance and toils of husbandry. 3. Compare Bk. I. Pt. I. vii. 20. In 民之爲道, the 道 is to be taken lightly, as if the expression

產者、有恆心、無恆產者、無恆心、苟無恆心、放辟邪侈、無不爲已、及陷乎罪、然後從而刑之、是罔民也、焉有仁人在位、罔民而可爲也。○四節 是故賢君必恭儉禮下、取於民有制。○五節 陽虎曰、爲富、不仁矣、爲仁、不富矣。○六節 夏后氏五十而貢、殷人七十而助、

livelihood, they will have a fixed heart; if they have not a certain livelihood, they have not a fixed heart. And if they have not a fixed heart, there is nothing which they will not do in the way of self-abandonment, of moral deflection, of depravity, and of wild license. When they have thus been involved in crime, to follow them up and punish them:—this is to entrap the people. How can such a thing as entrapping the people be done under the rule of a benevolent man?

4. 'Therefore, a ruler who is endowed with talents and virtue will be gravely complaisant and economical, showing a respectful politeness to his ministers, and taking from the people only in accordance with regulated limits.

5. 'Yang Hû said, "He who seeks to be rich will not be benevolent. He who wishes to be benevolent will not be rich."

6. 'The sovereign of the Hsiâ dynasty enacted the fifty *mâu* allotment, and the payment of a tax. The founder of the Yin enacted the seventy *mâu* allotment, and the system of mutual aid. The

were 民之爲民也,—'As to the people's being the people,' i.e. the character of the people is as follows. One commentator expounds the passage thus:—民之爲道,道字只如云民之所以爲民. 此節只言恆產所係之重. 4. 必,—not 'must be,' which would be inconsistent with the 賢, but 'will be,' i.e. will be sure to be. The last two clauses are exegetical of 恭 and 儉. 下 must be understood of 臣, 'ministers,' in contradistinction from the 民, 'people,' in the next clause, though all are of course 'beneath' the ruler. 5. This Yang Hû is the Yang Ho of the Analects, XVII. i. To accord with his unworthy character, the observation is taken in a bad sense, as a dissuasive against the practice of benevolence, while Mencius quotes it to show the incompatibility of the two aims. Great stress is laid on the 爲. 爲富, 爲仁,—'He who makes riches—benevolence—his business.' This force of the character would be well brought out by putting it in 3rd tone, but that would give the observation a good meaning. 6. 夏后氏, 殷人, 周人,—see Analects, III. xxi. By

周人百畝而徹、其實、皆什一也、徹者、徹也、助者、藉也。七節龍子曰、治地莫善於助、莫不善於貢、貢者、校數歲之中以爲常、樂歲、粒米狼戾、多取之而不爲虐、則寡取之、凶年、糞其田而不足、則必取盈焉、爲民父母、使民盻盻然、將終歲勤動、不得以養其父母、又稱貸而益

founder of the Châu enacted the hundred *mâu* allotment, and the share system. In reality, *what was paid* in all these was a tithe. The share system means mutual division. The aid system means mutual dependence.

7. 'Lung said, "For regulating the lands, there is no better system than that of mutual aid, and none which is not better than that of taxing. By the tax system, the regular amount was fixed by taking the average of several years. In good years, when the grain lies about in abundance, much might be taken without its being oppressive, and the actual exaction would be small. But in bad years, the produce being not sufficient to repay the manuring of the fields, this system still requires the taking of the full amount. When the parent of the people causes the people to wear looks of distress, and, after the whole year's toil, yet not to be able to nourish their parents, so

the Hsiâ statutes, every husbandman—head of a family—received fifty *mâu*, and paid the produce of five of them to the government. This payment was the 貢. By those of Yin, 630 *mâu* were divided into nine equal allotments of seventy *mâu* each, the central one being reserved for the government, and eight families on the other allotments uniting in its cultivation. By those of Châu, to one family 100 *mâu* were assigned, and ten families cultivated 1,000 acres in common, dividing the produce, and paying a tenth to government. Such is the account here given by Mencius, but it is very general, and not to be taken, especially as relates to the system of the Châu dynasty, as an accurate exposition of it. More in accordance with the accounts in the Châu Lî is his own system recommended below to Pî Chan. 7. Of the Lung quoted here, all that Châo Ch'î and Chû Hsî say, is that he was 'an ancient worthy.' 狼戾 is said to be synonymous with 狼藉, meaning 'abundant.' That this is the signification is plain enough, but how the characters come to indicate it is not clear. 狼 means 'a wolf,' and 藉 is given in connexion with that character as meaning 'the appearance of things scattered about in confusion.' I cannot find any signification of 戾, 'crooked, perverse, &c.,' from which, as joined to 狼, we can well bring out the

之、便老稚轉乎溝壑、惡在其爲民父母也。○八章夫世祿滕固行之矣。○九章詩云、雨我公田、遂及我私、惟助爲有公田、由此觀之、雖周亦助也。○十章設爲庠序學校、以教之、庠者、養也、校者、教也、序者、射也、夏曰校、殷曰序、周曰庠、學則三代共之、皆所以明人

that they proceed to borrowing to increase their means, till the old people and children are found lying in the ditches and water-channels:—where, *in such a case*, is his parental relation to the people?"

8. 'As to the system of hereditary salaries, that is already observed in T'ăng.

9. 'It is said in the Book of Poetry,

"May the rain come down on our public field,
And then upon our private fields!"

It is only in the system of mutual aid that there is a public field, and from this passage we perceive that even in the Châu dynasty this system has been recognised.

10. 'Establish *hsiang*, *hsü*, *hsio*, and *hsiâo*,—*all those educational institutions*,—for the instruction of *the people*. The name *hsiang* indicates nourishing *as its object*; *hsiâo* indicates teaching; and *hsü* indicates archery. By the Hsiâ dynasty the name *hsiâo* was used; by the Yin, that of *hsü*; and by the Châu, that of *hsiang*. As to the *hsio*, they belonged to the three dynasties, *and by that name*. The object of them all is to illustrate the human relations. When

meaning. 盻盻然 is taken by Châo Ch'î as in the translation, and by Chû Hsî as = 'an angry-looking appearance,' which does not suit so well. 稱 = 舉, 'to lift up,' = 'to proceed to.' 惡 (the 1st tone) 在其爲民父母,—see Bk. I. Pt. I. iv. 5. 8. 夫, 2nd tone. 世祿,—see Bk. I. Pt. II. v. 3. 9. See the Shih-ching, II. vi. Ode VIII. st. 3, a description of husbandry under the Châu dynasty. 雨:—the verb, 4th tone. The object of the quotation is to show that the system of mutual aid obtained under the Châu as well as under the Yin dynasty, and the way is prepared for the instructions given to Pî Chan below. 10. After the due regulation of husbandry, and provision for the 'certain livelihood' of the people, must come the business of education. The *hsio* mentioned were schools of a higher order in the capital of the kingdom and other chief cities of the various States. The others (校, *hsiâo*, 4th tone) were schools in the villages and smaller towns. In the Lî Chî, III. Sect. v. 10, we find the *hsiang* mentioned in connexion with

倫也、人倫明於上、小民親於下。○十一節有王者起、必來取法、是爲王者師也。○十二節詩云、周雖舊邦、其命維新、文王之謂也。子力行之、亦以新子之國。○十三節使畢戰、問井地。孟子曰、子之君、將行仁政、選擇而使子、子必勉之。夫仁政、必自經界始。經界不正、井地

those are *thus* illustrated by superiors, kindly feeling will prevail among the inferior people below.

11. 'Should a real sovereign arise, he will certainly come and take an example *from you;* and thus you will be the teacher of the true sovereign.

12. 'It is said in the Book of Poetry,

"Although Châu was an old country,
It received a new destiny."

That is said with reference to king Wăn. Do you practise those things with vigour, and you also will by them make new your kingdom.'

13. *The duke afterwards* sent Pî Chan to consult *Mencius* about the nine-squares system of dividing the land. Mencius said to him, 'Since your prince, wishing to put in practice a benevolent government, has made choice of you and put you into this employment, you must exert yourself to the utmost. Now, the first thing towards a benevolent government must be to lay down the boundaries. If the boundaries be not defined correctly, the division of the land into

the time of Shun; *hsü* in connexion with the Hsiâ dynasty; *hsio* in connexion with the Yin; and *Chiâo* (膠) in connexion with the *Châu*. There is thus some want of harmony between that passage and the account in the text. Entertainments were given to the aged at different times, and in the schools, as an example to the young of the reverence accorded by the government to age. So the schools were selected for the practice of archery, as a trial of virtue and skill. 人論明於上,—this can hardly mean, 'when the human relations have been illustrated by the example of superiors,' but must have reference to the inculcation of those relations by the institution of schools. The pith of Mencius's advice is—'Provide the means of education for all, the poor as well as the rich.' 12. See the Shih-ching, III. i. Ode I. st. 1. 其命, 'the appointment,' i.e. which lighted on it from Heaven. 13. To understand the 'nine-squares division of the land,' the form of the character 井 needs only to be looked at. If we draw lines to enclose it—thus, 田—we have a square portion of ground divided into nine equal and smaller squares. But can

不均、穀祿不平、是故暴君汙吏、必慢其經界、經界既正、分田制祿、可坐而定也。○十四節夫滕壤地褊小、將爲君子焉、將爲野人焉、無君子、莫治野人、無野人、莫養君子。○十五節請野、九一而助、國中、什一使自賦。○十六節卿以下、必有圭田、

squares will not be equal, and the produce *available for* salaries will not be evenly distributed. On this account, oppressive rulers and impure ministers are sure to neglect this defining of the boundaries. When the boundaries have been defined correctly, the division of the fields and the regulation of allowances may be determined by you, sitting at your ease.

14. 'Although the territory of T'ăng is narrow and small, yet there must be in it men of a superior grade, and there must be in it country-men. If there were not men of a superior grade, there would be none to rule the country-men. If there were not country-men, there would be none to support the men of superior grade.

15. 'I would ask you, in the remoter districts, observing the nine-squares division, to reserve one division to be cultivated on the system of mutual aid, and in the more central parts of the kingdom, to make the people pay for themselves a tenth part of their produce.

16. 'From the highest officers down to the lowest, each one must have his holy field, consisting of fifty *mâu*.

we suppose it possible to divide a territory in this way? The natural irregularities of the surface would be one great obstacle. And we find below the 'holy field,' and other assignments, which must continually have been requiring new arrangement of the boundaries. 14. 君子,—here, generally, for officers, men not earning their bread by the sweat of their brow, and the toil of their hands; see next chapter. 野人, 'country-men,'=by their toil self-supporting people generally. 將=殆; 將爲=殆必有. 15. Here the systems of all the three dynasties would seem to be employed, as the nature of the country permitted, or made advisable, their application. 野 as opposed to 國中 must be understood, as in the translation, ='the country,' 'the remoter districts.' The 九 refers to 公田 in par. 13, and the 一 to 制祿. The former would be the best way in such positions of supporting the 野人, and the latter of supporting the 君子. Similarly, the other clause. 16. 圭 is explained by Châo Ch'î by 潔, and Chû Hsî follows him, though we do not find this meaning of the term in the dictionary. The 圭田 then is 'the clean field,' and as its produce was

圭田、五十畝。十七節餘夫、二十五畝。十八節死徙、無出鄉鄉田同井、出入相友、守望相助、疾病相扶持、則百姓親睦。十九節方里而井、井九百畝、其中為公田、八家皆私百畝、同養公田、公事畢、然後敢治私事、所以別野人也。廿節此其大略也、若夫潤澤之、則在君與子矣。

17. 'Let the supernumerary males have their twenty-five *mâu*.

18. 'On occasions of death, or removal from one dwelling to another, there will be no quitting the district. In the fields of a district, those who belong to the same nine squares render all friendly offices to one another in their going out and coming in, aid one another in keeping watch and ward, and sustain one another in sickness. Thus the people are brought to live in affection and harmony.

19. 'A square *lî* covers nine squares of land, which nine squares contain nine hundred *mâu*. The central square is the public field, and eight families, each having its private hundred *mâu*, cultivate in common the public field. And not till the public work is finished, may they presume to attend to their private affairs. This is the way by which the country-men are distinguished *from those of a superior grade.*

20. 'Those are the great outlines of the system. Happily to modify and adapt it depends on the prince and you.'

intended to supply the means of sacrifice, I translate it by 'the holy field.' It was in addition to the hereditary salary mentioned in par. 8. 17. A family was supposed to embrace the grandfather and grandmother, the husband, wife, and children, the husband being the grandparents' eldest son. The extra fields were for other sons whom they might have, and were given to them when they were sixteen. When they married and became heads of families themselves, they received the regular allotment for a family. This is Chû Hsî's account of this paragraph. 18. The social benefits flowing from the nine-squares division of the land. 'On occasions of death,' i.e. in burying. 19. Under the Châu dynasty, a hundred *pû* or 'paces' made a *mâu's* length, but the exact amount of the pace can hardly be ascertained. Many contend that the fifty *mâu* of Hsiâ, the seventy of Yin, and the hundred of Châu, were actually of the same dimensions. 養,—the 4th tone, so spoken always, when the subject is the support of a superior by an inferior. 20. 若夫 (the 2nd tone), = 至於. 潤澤, 'the softening and moistening,' i.e. the modifying and adapting.

四章 一節 有爲神農之言者、許行、自楚之滕、踵門而告文公曰、遠方之人、聞君行仁政、願受一廛而爲氓。文公與之處、其徒數十人、皆衣褐、捆屨、織席、以爲食。二節 陳良之徒陳相、以其弟辛、負耒耜、

CHAP. IV. 1. There came from Ch'û to T'ăng one Hsü Hsing, who gave out that he acted according to the words of Shăn-năng. Coming right to his gate, he addressed the duke Wăn, saying, 'A man of a distant region, I have heard that you, Prince, are practising a benevolent government, and I wish to receive a site for a house, and to become one of your people.' The duke Wăn gave him a dwelling-place. His disciples, amounting to several tens, all wore clothes of haircloth, and made sandals of hemp and wove mats for a living.

2. *At the same time*, Ch'ăn Hsiang, a disciple of Ch'ăn Liang, and his younger brother, Hsin, with their plough-handles and shares on

4. MENCIUS'S REFUTATION OF THE DOCTRINE THAT THE RULER OUGHT TO LABOUR AT HUSBANDRY WITH HIS OWN HANDS. HE VINDICATES THE PROPRIETY OF THE DIVISION OF LABOUR, AND OF A LETTERED CLASS CONDUCTING GOVERNMENT. The first three paragraphs, it is said, relate how Hsing, the heresiarch, and Hsiang, his follower, wished secretly to destroy the arrangements advised by Mencius for the division of the land. The next eight paragraphs expose the great error of Hsing, that the ruler must labour at the toils of husbandry as well as the people. From the twelfth paragraph to the sixteenth, Hsiang is rebuked for forsaking his master, and taking up with Hsing's heresy. In the last two paragraphs, Mencius proceeds, from the evasive replies of Hsiang, to give the *coup de grâce* to the new pernicious teachings. 1. 爲 is explained, by Châo Ch'î, by 治爲, and 言 as = 道, so that 爲 ... 言者 = 'one who cultivated the doctrines.' Most others take 爲 = 假託, 'making a false pretence of.' Shăn-năng, 'Wonderful husbandman,' is the style of the second of the five famous 帝, or early 'sovereigns,' of Chinese history. He is also called Yen (炎) Tî, 'the Blazing Sovereign.' He is placed between Fû-hsî and Hwang Tî, though separated from the latter by an intervention of seven reigns, extending with his own over 515 years. If any faith could be reposed in this chronology, it would place him B.C. 3212. In the appendix to the Yî-ching, he is celebrated as the Father of Husbandry. Other traditions make him the Father of Medicine also. 之滕,—之 is the verb, = 往. 踵, in the dictionary, after Châo Ch'î is explained by 至, 'came to.' Chû Hsî says that 踵門 = 足至門. 廛 and 氓, see Bk. II. Pt. I. v. 5, but the meaning of 廛 here is different, denoting the ground assigned for the dwelling of a husbandman. 衣 (4th tone) 褐,—it would appear from par. 4 that this 'haircloth' was a very inartificial structure, not woven at least with much art. 屨,—'sandals of hemp,' opposed to 屝, which were made of grass, and 履, which were made of leather. 捆 is explained by 扣椓, 'to beat and hammer.' 席 properly denotes single mats made of rushes (莞蒲). This manufacture of sandals and mats is supposed in the 備旨 to have been only a temporary employment of Hsing's followers till lands should be

而自宋之滕、曰、聞君行聖人之政、是亦聖人也、願爲聖人氓。○三節 陳相見許行而大悅、盡棄其學而學焉、陳相見孟子、道許行之言、曰、滕君、則誠賢君也、雖然、未聞道也、賢者、與民並耕而食、饔飧而治、今也滕有倉廩府庫、則是厲民而以自養也、惡得賢。○四節 孟子曰、許子必

their backs, came from Sung to T'ăng, saying, 'We have heard that you, Prince, are putting into practice the government of the *ancient* sages, *showing that* you are likewise a sage. We wish to become the subjects of a sage.'

3. When Ch'ăn Hsiang saw Hsü Hsing, he was greatly pleased with him, and, abandoning entirely whatever he had learned, became his disciple. Having an interview with Mencius, he related to him *with approbation* the words of Hsü Hsing to the following effect:—'The prince of T'ăng is indeed a worthy prince. He has not yet heard, however, the *real* doctrines *of antiquity*. Now, wise and able princes should cultivate the ground equally and along with their people, and eat *the fruit of their labour*. They should prepare their own meals, morning and evening, while at the same time they carry on their government. But now, *the prince of* T'ăng has his granaries, treasuries, and arsenals, which is an oppressing of the people to nourish himself. How can he be deemed a *real* worthy prince?'

4. Mencius said, 'I suppose that Hsü Hsing sows grain and eats

assigned them. 2. Of the individuals mentioned here, we know nothing more than can be gathered from this chapter. The 耜, or share, as originally made by Shăn-năng, was of wood. In Mencius's time, it had come to be made of iron; see par. 4. 之滕,—之 as above. 3. 道許行之言,—道 is the verb, = 稱述. 賢者,—as in Bk. I. Pt. I. ii. 1. 饔飧 denote the morning and evening meals, but must be taken here as verbs, signifying the preparation of those meals. If 倉 and 廩 are to be distinguished, the latter is a granary for rice, the former for other grain. 養, in 4th tone. The object of Hsü Hsing in these remarks would be to invalidate Mencius's doctrine given in the last chapter, par. 14, that the ruler must be supported by the country-men. 4. Observe the force of 必 . . . 乎, as in the

種粟而後食乎。曰、然。許子必織布而後衣乎。曰、否、許子衣褐。曰、許子冠乎。曰、冠。曰、奚冠。曰、冠素。曰、自織之與。曰、否、以粟易之。曰、許子奚爲不自織。曰、害於耕。曰、許子以釜甑爨、以鐵耕乎。曰、然。自爲之與。曰、否、以粟易之。

五節 以粟易械器者、不爲厲陶冶、陶冶亦以其械器易粟者、豈爲厲農夫哉、且

the produce. Is it not so?' 'It is so,' was the answer. 'I suppose *also* he weaves cloth, and wears his own manufacture. Is it not so?' 'No. Hsü wears clothes of haircloth.' 'Does he wear a cap?' 'He wears a cap.' 'What kind of cap?' 'A plain cap.' 'Is it woven by himself?' 'No. He gets it in exchange for grain.' 'Why does Hsü not weave it himself?' 'That would injure his husbandry.' 'Does Hsü cook his food in boilers and earthenware pans, and does he plough with an iron share?' 'Yes.' 'Does he make those articles himself?' 'No. He gets them in exchange for grain.'

5. *Mencius then said,* 'The getting those various articles in exchange for grain, is not oppressive to the potter and the founder, and the potter and the founder in their turn, in exchanging their various articles for grain, are not oppressive to the husbandman. How should

translation. 粟, 'millet,' but here = grain generally. 衣, 4th tone. 冠素, 'His cap is plain,' i.e. undyed and unadorned. The distinction given by Chû Hsî between 釜 and 甑 is, that the former was used for boiling, and the latter for steaming. Their composition indicates that they were made of iron and clay respectively. The 釜 was distinguished from other iron boilers by having no feet. 5. 以...者 = 'he who gets,' or, as in the translation, 'the getting.' 械,—properly 'stocks,' but also used synonymously with 器. I have added a sentence to bring out the force of 豈 in 豈爲厲云云. Chû Hsî puts a point at 冶, and taking 舍 (in 3rd tone) in the sense of 止, 'only,' construes it with what follows. This is better than to join it, in the sense of house or shop, with 陶冶. Hsiang is here forced to make an admission, fatal to his new master's doctrine, that every man should do everything for himself. The only difficulty is with the 且, which here = 'but.' The two

許子何不爲陶冶、舍皆取諸其宮中而用之、何爲紛紛然、與百工交易、何許子之不憚煩。曰、百工之事、固不可耕且爲也。○六節然則治天下、獨可耕且爲與、有大人之事、有小人之事、且一人之身、而百工之所爲備、如必自爲而後用之、是率天下而路也、故曰、或勞心、或勞力、勞心者、治人、勞力者

such a thing be supposed? And moreover, why does not Hsü act the potter and founder, supplying himself with the articles which he uses solely from his own establishment? Why does he go confusedly dealing and exchanging with the handicraftsmen? Why does he not spare himself so much trouble?' *Ch'an Hsiang replied,* 'The business of the handicraftsman can by no means be carried on along with the business of husbandry.'

6. *Mencius resumed,* 'Then, is it the government of the kingdom which alone can be carried on along with the practice of husbandry? Great men have their proper business, and little men have their proper business. Moreover, in the case of any single individual, *whatever articles he can require* are ready to his hand, being produced by the various handicraftsmen:—if he must first make them for his own use, this way of doing would keep all the people running about upon the roads. Hence, there is the saying, "Some labour with their minds, and some labour with their strength. Those who labour with their minds govern others; those who labour with their strength

preceding sentences are Mencius's affirmations, and he proceeds—'But Hsü Hsing denies this. Why then does he not himself play the potter and founder, &c.?' 6. In 一人之身,而百工之所爲備 the construction is not easy. The correct meaning seems to be that given in the translation. Some take 備 in the sense of 'are all required,' which would make the construction simpler:—'for a single person even, all the productions of the handicraftsmen are necessary.' So, in the paraphrase of the 日講:—'Reckoning in the case of a single individual, his clothes, his food, and his dwelling-place, the productions of the various workers must all be completed in suf-

治於人、治於人者、食人、治人者食於人、天下之通義也。七當堯之時、天下猶未平、洪水橫流、氾濫於天下、草木暢茂、禽獸繁殖、五穀不登、禽獸偪人、獸蹄鳥跡之道、交於中國、堯獨憂之、舉舜而敷治焉、舜使益掌火、益烈山澤而焚之、禽獸逃匿、禹疏九河、瀹濟漯而注

are governed by others. Those who are governed by others support them; those who govern others are supported by them." This is a principle universally recognised.

7. 'In the time of Yâo, when the world had not yet been perfectly reduced to order, the vast waters, flowing out of their channels, made a universal inundation. Vegetation was luxuriant, and birds and beasts swarmed. The various kinds of grain could not be grown. The birds and beasts pressed upon men. The paths marked by the feet of beasts and prints of birds crossed one another throughout the Middle Kingdom. To Yâo alone this caused anxious sorrow. He raised Shun to office, and measures to regulate the disorder were set forth. Shun committed to Yî the direction of the fire to be employed, and Yî set fire to, and consumed, *the forests and vegetation on* the mountains and *in* the marshes, so that the birds and beasts fled away to hide themselves. Yü separated the nine streams, cleared the courses of the Tsî and T'â, and led them all to the sea. He opened

ficiency, and then he has abundantly everything for profitable employment, and can without anxiety support his children and parents.' This gives a good enough meaning in the connexion, but the signification attached to 備 is hardly otherwise authorised. 而路, 'and road them,'=奔走道路. 食, 4th tone, *tsze*. 7. 天下猶未平 carries us back to the time antecedent to Yâo, and 天下 is to be taken in the sense of 'world,' or 'earth.' There is the idea of a wild, confused, chaotic state, on which the successive sages had been at work, without any great amount of success. Then in the next paragraph we have Hâu-chî doing over again the work of Shăn-năng and teaching men husbandry. It is difficult to go beyond Yâo for the founding of the Chinese kingdom. The various questions which would arise here, however, will be found discussed in the first part of the Shû-ching. It is only necessary to observe in reference to the calamity here spoken of, that it is not presented as the consequence of a deluge, or sudden accumulation of water, but from the natural river-

諸海、決汝漢、排淮泗、而注之江、然後中國可得而食也、當是時也、禹八年於外、三過其門而不入、雖欲耕、得乎。○八節 后稷教民稼穡、樹藝五穀、五穀熟、而民人育、人之有道也、飽食煖衣、逸居而無教、則近於禽獸、聖人有憂之、使契爲司徒、教以

a vent also for the Zû and Han, and regulated the course of the Hwâi and Sze, so that they all flowed into the Chiang. When this was done, it became possible for the people of the Middle Kingdom to *cultivate the ground and* get food for themselves. During that time, Yü was eight years away from his home, and though he thrice passed the door of it, he did not enter. Although he had wished to cultivate the ground, could he have done so?

8. 'The Minister of Agriculture taught the people to sow and reap, cultivating the five kinds of grain. When the five kinds of grain were brought to maturity, the people all obtained a subsistence. But men possess a moral nature; and if they are well fed, warmly clad, and comfortably lodged, without being taught at the same time, they become almost like the beasts. This was a subject of anxious solicitude to the sage *Shun*, and he appointed Hsieh to be the Minister of Instruction, to teach the relations of humanity:—how, between father and son, there should be affection; between

channels being all broken up and disordered. 橫, in 4th tone, 'disobedient,' 'unreasonable.' 五穀, 'the five kinds of grains,' are 稻, 黍, 稷, 麥, and 菽, 'paddy, millet, pannicled millet, wheat, and pulse,' but each of these terms must be taken as comprehending several varieties under it. 中國, in opposition to 天下, is the portion of country which was first settled, and regarded as a centre to all surrounding territories. 堯獨憂之,—the 獨 seems to refer to Yâo's position as sovereign, in which it belonged to him to feel this anxiety. For the labours of Shun, Yî, and Yü, see the Shû-ching, Parts I, II, III. 濟, in 3rd tone. 漯,—read T'â. The nine streams all belonged to the Ho, or Yellow river. By them Yü led off a portion of its vast surging waters. The Chiang is the Yang-tsze. Chû Hsî observes that of the rivers mentioned as being led into the Chiang only the Han flows into that stream, while the Hwâi receives the Zû and the Sze, and makes a direct course to the sea. He supposes an error on the part of the recorder of Mencius's words. 8. Hâu-chî, now received as a proper name, is properly the official title of Shun's Minister of Agriculture, Ch'î (棄). 契 (read Hsieh) was the name

人倫、父子有親、君臣有義、夫婦有別、長幼有序、朋友有信、放勳曰、勞之、來之、匡之、直之、輔之、翼之、使自得之、又從而振德之、聖人之憂民如此、而暇耕乎。○九節堯以不得舜爲己憂、舜以不得禹皐陶爲己憂、夫以百畝

sovereign and minister, righteousness; between husband and wife, attention to their separate functions; between old and young, a proper order; and between friends, fidelity. The highly meritorious *sovereign* said to him, "Encourage them; lead them on; rectify them; straighten them; help them; give them wings:—thus causing them to become possessors of themselves. Then follow this up by stimulating them, and conferring benefits on them." When the sages were exercising their solicitude for the people in this way, had they leisure to cultivate the ground?

9. 'What Yâo felt giving him anxiety was the not getting Shun. What Shun felt giving him anxiety was the not getting Yü and Kâo Yâo. But he whose anxiety is about his hundred *mâu* not being properly cultivated, is a *mere* husbandman.

of his Minister of Instruction. For these men and their works, see the Shû-ching, Part II. 藝,—used synonymously with 蓺,=種, 'to plant,' or 'sow.' 人之有道也:—foreigners generally try to construe this expression as they do the 民之爲道也 in the preceding chapter, par. 2, not having regard to the difference of 民 and 人, of 爲 and 有, and the five repetitions of 有 farther on in the paragraph. The interpretation which I have adopted is that of Chû Hsî, and every critic of note whom I have consulted. 聖人 is supposed to be plural,—'the sages.' This, however, cannot be, as the 使 immediately following must be understood with reference to Shun only. What has made 聖人 be taken as plural, is that the instructions addressed to Hsieh are said to be from 放 (3rd tone) 勳, which are two of the epithets applied to Yâo in the opening sentence of the Shû-ching, who is therefore supposed to be the speaker. Yet it was Shun who appointed Hsieh, and gave him his instructions, and may not Mencius intend *him* by 'The highly meritorious'? The address itself is not found in the Shû-ching. 勞 and 來 are both in 4th tone. In 夫婦有別, 別=‘separate functions,' according to which the husband is said to preside over all that is external, and the wife over all that is internal, while to the former it belongs to lead, and to the latter to follow. 9. An illustration of the 有大人之事,有小人之事, in par. 6. 易,—read *i*, in 4th tone, in the sense of 治 (in 2nd tone). The Kâo of Kâo Yâo is generally written as in the text, but the proper form of it is 皋. It is difficult to determine whether to unite the two characters as a double surname, or to keep them apart as surname

之不易爲己憂者、農夫也。○十節分人以財、謂之惠、教人以善、謂之忠、爲天下得人者、謂之仁、是故以天下與人易、爲天下得人難。○十一節孔子曰、大哉、堯之爲君、惟天爲大、惟堯則之、蕩蕩乎、民無能名焉、君哉、舜也、巍巍乎、有天下、而不與焉、堯舜之治天下、豈無所用其心哉、亦不用於耕耳。○十二節吾聞用夏變夷者、未聞變於夷者也、陳

10. 'The imparting by a man to others of his wealth, is called "kindness." The teaching others what is good, is called "the exercise of fidelity." The finding a man who shall benefit the kingdom, is called "benevolence." Hence to give the throne to another man would be easy; to find a man who shall benefit the kingdom is difficult.

11. 'Confucius said, "Great indeed was Yâo as a sovereign. It is only Heaven that is great, and only Yâo corresponded to it. How vast was his virtue! The people could find no name for it. Princely indeed was Shun! How majestic was he, having possession of the kingdom, and yet seeming as if it were nothing to him!" In their governing the kingdom, were there no subjects on which Yâo and Shun employed their minds? There were subjects, only they did not employ their minds on the cultivation of the ground.

12. 'I have heard of men using *the doctrines of* our great land to change barbarians, but I have never yet heard of any being changed

and name. 10. 爲, in the 4th tone, 'on behalf of,' = who shall benefit. 易,—read as in the text, and meaning 'easy.' The difficulty spoken of arises from this, that to find the man in question requires the finder to go out of himself, and is beyond what is in his own power. The reader must bear in mind that 仁 is the name for the highest virtue, the combination of all possible virtues. Compare Analects, VI. xxviii. 11. See Analects, VIII. xviii and xix, which two chapters Mencius blends together with omissions and alterations. Observe the force of 亦 in the last clause. It = 'there were subjects on which they employed their minds, but still, &c.' 12. 夏 and 夷,—used as in Analects, III. v. 先,—the verb,

良、楚產也、悅周公仲尼之道、北學於中國、北方之學者、未能或之先也、彼所謂豪傑之士也、子之兄弟、事之數十年、師死、而遂倍之、○十三節昔者、孔子沒、三年之外、門人治任將歸、入揖於子貢、相嚮而哭、皆失聲、然後歸、子貢反、築室於場、獨居三年、然後歸、他日、子夏、子張、子游、以有若似聖人、欲以

by barbarians. Ch'an Liang was a native of Ch'û. Pleased with the doctrines of Châu-kung and Chung-nî, he came northwards to the Middle Kingdom and studied them. Among the scholars of the northern regions, there was perhaps no one who excelled him. He was what you call a scholar of high and distinguished qualities. You and your brother followed him some tens of years, and when your master died, you forthwith turned away from him.

13. 'Formerly, when Confucius died, after three years had elapsed, his disciples collected their baggage, and prepared to return to their several homes. But on entering to take their leave of Tsze-kung, as they looked towards one another, they wailed, till they all lost their voices. After this they returned to their homes, but Tsze-kung went back, and built a house for himself on the altar-ground, where he lived alone *other* three years, before he returned home. On another occasion, Tsze-hsiâ, Tsze-chang, and Tsze-yû, thinking that Yû *Zo* resembled the sage, wished to render to him the same

in 4th tone. 子之兄弟,—not 'your brothers,' but as in the translation; compare par. 2. 倍 = 背:—observe how Ch'û is here excluded from 'the Middle Kingdom' of Mencius's time. 13. On the death of Confucius, his disciples remained by his grave for three years, mourning for him as for a father, but without wearing the mourning dress. 治任,—both 2nd tone, 'looked after their burdens.' Tsze-kung had acted to all his co-disciples as master of the ceremonies. Hence they took a formal leave of him. 場 is a flat place, an area scooped out upon the surface, and used primarily to sacrifice upon. Here it denotes such an area formed upon the sage's grave. There is a small wooden hut still shown in the Confucian cemetery, and said to be the apartment built by Tsze-kung for himself! I saw it in 1873. On Yû *Zo*'s resemblance to Confucius, see the

所事孔子事之、彊曾子、曾子曰、不可、江漢以濯之、秋陽以暴之、皜皜乎、不可尚已。○十四節今也南蠻鴃舌之人、非先王之道、子倍子之師而學之、亦異於曾子矣。○十五節吾聞出於幽谷、遷于喬木者、未聞下喬木而入於幽谷者。○十六節魯頌曰、戎狄是膺、荊舒是懲、周公方且膺之、子是之學、亦為不善變矣。○十七節從

observances which they had rendered to Confucius. They tried to force the disciple Tsăng to join with them, but he said, "This may not be done. What has been washed in the waters of the Chiang and Han, and bleached in the autumn sun:—how glistening is it! Nothing can be added to it."

14. 'Now here is this shrike-tongued barbarian of the south, whose doctrines are not those of the ancient kings. You turn away from your master and become his disciple. Your conduct is different indeed from that of the philosopher Tsăng.

15. 'I have heard of *birds* leaving dark valleys to remove to lofty trees, but I have not heard of their descending from lofty trees to enter into dark valleys.

16. 'In the Praise-songs of Lû it is said,

"He smote the barbarians of the west and the north,
He punished Ching and Shû."

Thus Châu-kung would be sure to smite them, and you become their disciple again; it appears that your change is not good.'

17. *Ch'an Hsiang said*, 'If Hsü's doctrines were followed, then

Book of Rites, Bk. II. Sect. I. iii. 4. 彊,—in 3rd tone. 暴 is in the 4th tone. 皜,—read *hâo*, in 2nd tone, or *kâo*. 尚=加. Compare 無以尚之, Analects, IV. vi. 1. 14. 鴃,—'the shrike, or butcher bird,' a strong epithet of contempt or dislike, as applied to Hsü Hsing. 倍,—as above. 15. 下,—used as a verb, in 4th tone. 16. See the Book of Poetry, IV. ii. Ode IV. st. 6. The two clauses quoted refer to

許子之道、則市賈不貳、國中無僞、雖使五尺之童適市、莫之或欺、布帛長短同、則賈相若、麻縷絲絮輕重同、則賈相若、五穀多寡同、則賈相若、屨大小同、則賈相若。

○十八節 曰、夫物之不齊、物之情也、或相倍蓰、或相什伯、或相千萬、子比而同之、是亂天下也、巨屨小屨同賈、人豈爲之哉、從許子之道、相率而爲僞者也、惡能治

there would not be two prices in the market, nor any deceit in the kingdom. If a boy of five cubits were sent to the market, no one would impose on him; linen and silk of the same length would be of the same price. So it would be with *bundles of* hemp and silk, being of the same weight; with the different kinds of grain, being the same in quantity; and with shoes which were of the same size.'

18. *Mencius* replied, 'It is the nature of things to be of unequal quality. Some are twice, some five times, some ten times, some a hundred times, some a thousand times, some ten thousand times as valuable as others. If you reduce them all to the same standard, that must throw the kingdom into confusion. If large shoes and small shoes were of the same price, who would make them? For people to follow the doctrines of Hsü, would be for them to lead one another on to practise deceit. How can they avail for the government of a State?'

the achievements of the duke Hsî. Mencius uses them as if they expressed the approbation of his ancestor Châu-kung. 17. 賈,—read *chiâ*, 4th tone, = 價. 五尺之童,—see Analects, VIII. vi. 麻縷絲絮 must be joined together, I think, in pairs, in opposition to the 布帛 above, the manufactured articles. 縷 is explained, in the 說文, by 綫, 'threads,' and may be used of silk or flax. 絮 is explained, also in the 說文, by 敝緜, 'spoiled, or bad, floss.' Its general application is to floss of an inferior quality. 18. 倍,—different from that in pars. 12, 15, meaning 'as much again.' 相=相去, 'are separated from each other,' or 'are to each other as.' The size of the shoes is mentioned as a thing more

國家。

第五章 一節 墨者夷之、因徐辟而求見孟子。孟子曰、吾固願見、今吾尚病、病愈、我且往見、夷子不來。二節 他日、又求見孟子、孟子曰、吾今則可以見矣、不直、則道不見、我且直之、吾聞夷子墨者、墨之治喪也、以薄爲其道也、夷子思以易天下、豈以爲非是

CHAP. V. 1. The Mohist, Î Chih, sought, through Hsü Pî, to see Mencius. Mencius said, 'I indeed wish to see him, but at present I am still unwell. When I am better, I will myself go and see him. He need not come here *again*.'

2. Next day, *Î Chih* again sought to see Mencius. Mencius said, 'To-day I am able to see him. But if I do not correct his errors, the *true* principles will not be fully evident. Let me first correct him. I have heard that this Î is a Mohist. Now Mo considers that in the regulation of funeral matters a spare simplicity should be the rule. Î thinks with *Mo's doctrines* to change *the customs of* the kingdom;—how does he regard them as if they were wrong, and not

palpable than their quality, and exposing more easily the absurdity of Hsü's proposition.

5. HOW MENCIUS CONVINCED A MOHIST OF HIS ERROR, THAT ALL MEN WERE TO BE LOVED EQUALLY, WITHOUT DIFFERENCE OF DEGREE. 1. Mo, by name 翟 (read *Ti*), was a heresiarch between the times of Confucius and Mencius. His most distinguishing principle was that of universal and equal love, which he contended would remedy all the evils of society;—see next Part, chap. ix, *et al.* It has been contended, however, by the Rev. Dr. Edkins, that Mencius's account of Mo's views is unfair. See Journal of the North-China Branch of the Royal Asiatic Society, No. II. Some of Mo's writings remain, and some notice of them will be found in the prolegomena. 徐辟 (read *Pi* or *Pî*) was a disciple of Mencius. The philosopher, according to the opinion of Chû Hsî, was well enough, but feigned sickness and told Î Chih that he need not come again to see him,—to try his sincerity. It is to be understood that Chih had intimated that he was dissatisfied with his Mohism, and Mencius would be guided in his judgment of his really being so, by testing his desire to obtain an interview with him. It is difficult to express the force of the particle 且;—'myself' comes near it. 夷子不來 is Mencius's remark, and Châo Ch'î is wrong, when he carries it on to the next paragraph, and construes—'Î in consequence did not then come, but another day, &c.' 2. 他日, 'another day;' probably, 'next day.' The repetition of the application satisfied Mencius that Chih was really anxious to be instructed. 直, Chû Hsî says, = 盡言以相正, 'to expound the truth fully to correct him.' 不見,—見, 4th tone. 我且直之,—

而不貴也、然而夷子葬其親厚、則是以所賤事親也。

三節 徐子以告夷子、夷子曰、儒者之道、古之人若保赤子、此言何謂也、之則以爲愛無差等、施由親始。徐子以告孟子、孟子曰、夫夷子信以爲人之親其兄之子、爲若親其鄰之赤子乎、彼有取爾也、赤子匍匐將入井、

honour them? Notwithstanding his views, Î buried his parents in a sumptuous manner, and so he served them in the way which *his doctrines* discountenance.'

3. The disciple Hsü informed Î of these remarks. Î said, '*Even according to* the principles of the learned, we find that the ancients *acted towards the people* "as if they were watching over an infant." What does this expression mean? To me it sounds that we are to love *all* without difference of degree; but the manifestation *of love* must begin with our parents.' Hsü reported this reply to Mencius, who said, 'Now, does Î really think that a man's affection for the child of his brother is *merely* like his affection for the infant of a neighbour? What is to be approved in that *expression* is simply this:—that if an infant crawling about is likely to fall into a well,

且 is here = 將, 'will.' The 備旨 says that 對未遽見言, 'it is used with reference to the not readily granting Î an interview.' Mencius wanted to put the applicant right, before conversing with him. We are to suppose that, after the acknowledgment in the concluding paragraph, he admitted Î to his presence. This principle about conducting funerals, or mourning generally, in a spare and inexpensive manner, was a subordinate point of Mo's teaching, and Mencius knowing that Î Chih had not observed it, saw how he could lead him on from it to see the error of the chief principle of the sect. 貴 and 賤 are both verbs. 3. Chih attempts to show that the classical doctrine likewise had the principle of equal and universal love. See the 若保赤子, quoted in the 'Great Learning,' Commentary, ix. 2. 之則,—之 is the name of the speaker. 差, read *ts'ze*, 'uneven.' 差等,—'uneven degrees.' Î Chih does not attempt to vindicate the sumptuous interment of his parents;—he says 施由始親, not knowing what to say. 夫,—2nd tone. 彼有取爾(=耳)也, with what follows, requires to be supplemented by the reader:—'The child's falling into the well being thus from no perverse intent, but the consequence of its helplessness, people will all try to save it; and the people, liable to offend in ignorance, are to be dealt with in the same way;—to be instructed and watched over. This is all that we can find

非赤子之罪也、且天之生物也、使之一本、而夷子二本、故也。四節蓋上世、嘗有不葬其親者、其親死、則舉而委之於壑、他日過之、狐狸食之、蠅蚋姑嘬之、其顙有泚、睨而不視、夫泚也、非爲人泚、中心達於面目、蓋歸反

it is no crime in the infant. Moreover, Heaven gives birth to creatures in such a way that they have one root, and Î makes them to have two roots. This is the cause *of his error*.

4. 'And, in the most ancient times, there were some who did not inter their parents. When their parents died, they took them up and threw them into some water-channel. Afterwards, when passing by them, *they saw* foxes and wild-cats devouring them, and flies and gnats biting at them. The perspiration started out upon their foreheads, and they looked away, unable to bear the sight. It was not on account of other people that this perspiration flowed. The emotions

in the words which he quotes.' Châo Ch'î makes 彼 refer to Î Chih:—'he only takes a part of the meaning. He loses the scope of the whole, and clings to the word infant.' This is ingenious, but does not seem sound. The 'one root' is the parents (and the seed in reference to inanimate things, but the subject is all about men, and hence the 備旨 says that 物 is to be taken as = 人), to whom therefore should be given a peculiar affection. Mo saying that other men should be loved as much, and in the same way, as parents, made two roots. The 故 is quite enigmatic, but it is explained as I have done. 4. 蓋, not exactly 'for,' but as a more general continuative. Julien translates the first clause:—'*Porro in superioribus seculis nondum erant qui sepelirent suos parentes*,' and he blames Noel for rendering —'*quidam filii parentes suos tumulo non mandabant*.' Mencius, he says, 'is treating of all men, and not of some only.' I cannot, however, get over the 者, which would seem to require the rendering given by Noel. Reference is made indeed to the highest antiquity (上世), when the sages had not yet delivered their rules for ceremonies, but from the clause 非爲人泚 we may infer that even then all were not equally unobservant of what was proper. 過,—the 1st tone. The passing by is not to be taken as fortuitous. Their natural solicitude brought them to see how it was with the bodies. The 狐 is 'the fox.' 狸 or 貍 is a name given to different animals. We have the 貓狸, or 'wild cat;' the 風狸, which appears to be the 'raccoon;' and others. 姑, says Chû Hsî, has no meaning, but is a drawl between the words before and after it. Some would take it for 蛄, a kind of cricket. 非爲人泚,—compare 非所以要譽云云, Bk. II. Pt. I. vi. 3. 中心, 'their middle heart,' the very centre of their being. 蓋歸,—蓋 = 'and forthwith,' but what follows contains a proof of what is said before—中心云云. 反虆梩, 'overturned baskets and shovels,'

虆梩而掩之，掩之，誠是也，則孝子仁人之掩其親，亦必有道矣。

五節 徐子以告夷子，夷子憮然爲閒曰，命之矣。

of their hearts affected their faces and eyes, and instantly they went home, and came back with baskets and spades and covered the bodies. If *the covering them thus* was indeed right, you may see that the filial son and virtuous man, in interring *in a handsome manner* their parents, act according to a proper rule.'

5. The disciple Hsü informed Î of what Mencius had said. Î was thoughtful for a short time, and then said, 'He has instructed me.'

i. e. of earth. 虆,—read *lo* (not *lêi*, as enjoined in the tonal notes in most editions of Mencius), in 2nd tone. The meaning of 梩 is obscure; that of a spade or shovel (wooden, of course) is given, however, to it. The conclusion of the argument is this, that what affection prompted in the first case, was prompted similarly in its more sumptuous exhibition in the progress of civilisation. If any interment was right, a handsome one must be right also. 5. 憮然, in the dictionary, is explained, as 'the appearance of being surprised.' In Analects, XVIII. vi. 4, Chû Hsî explains the phrase by 悵然, 'vexed-like.' I have there translated—'with a sigh.' 命之,—之 is again the speaker's name. 命 is in the sense of 教, 'to instruct.'

T'ĂNG WĂN KUNG. PART II.

滕文公章句下

第一章 一節 陳代曰、不見諸侯、宜若小然、今一見之、大則以王、小則以霸、且志曰、枉尺而直尋、宜若可爲也。○二節 孟子曰、昔齊景公田、招虞人以旌、不至、將殺之、志士不忘在溝壑、勇

CHAPTER I. 1. Ch'ăn Tâi said *to Mencius*, 'In not *going to* wait upon any of the princes, you seem to me to be standing on a small point. If now you were once to wait upon them, the result might be so great that you would make one of them sovereign, or, if smaller, that you would make one of them chief of all the other princes. Moreover, the History says, "By bending *only* one cubit, you make eight cubits straight." It appears to me like a thing which might be done.'

2. Mencius said, 'Formerly, the duke Ching of Ch'î, once when he was hunting, called his forester to him by a flag. *The forester* would not come, *and the duke* was going to kill him. *With reference to this incident, Confucius said,* "The determined officer never forgets

1. How Mencius defended the dignity of reserve by which he regulated his intercourse with the princes of his time. To understand the chapter, it must be borne in mind, that there were many wandering scholars in the days of Mencius, men who went from court to court, recommending themselves to the various princes, and trying to influence the course of events by their counsels. They would stoop for place and employment. Not so with our philosopher. He required that there should be shown to himself a portion of the respect which was due to the principles of which he was the expounder. 1. Ch'ăn Tâi was one of Mencius's disciples. 不見＝不往見. 宜若小然,—'in reason is as if it were small-like.' 大 is said to be 大用, 'if you were greatly employed,' and 小＝小用. It is better to take these terms as in the translation. The clauses must be expanded—大則以其君王, 小則以其君霸. 王,—4th tone. 志,—see Pt. I. ii. 3. The 'thing that might be done' is Mencius's going to wait on the princes. 2. The 虞人 was an officer as old as the time of Shun, who appoints Yî (益), Shû-ching, II. i. 22, saying that 'he could rightly superintend the birds and beasts of the fields and trees on his hills, and in his forests.' In the Châu Lî, Pt. II. Bk. xvi, we have an account of the office, where it appears, that, on occasion of a great hunting, the forester had to clear the paths, and set up flags for the

士不忘喪其元、孔子奚取焉、取非其招不往也、如不待其招而往、何哉。〇三節且夫枉尺而直尋者、以利言也、如以利、則枉尋直尺而利、亦可爲與。〇四節昔者、趙簡子使王良與嬖奚乘、終日而不獲

that his end may be in a ditch or a stream; the brave officer never forgets that he may lose his head." What was it *in the forester* that Confucius thus approved? He approved his not going *to the duke*, when summoned by the article which was not appropriate to him. If one go *to see the princes* without waiting to be invited, what can be thought of him?

3. 'Moreover, *that sentence*, "By bending *only* one cubit, you make eight cubits straight," is spoken with reference to the gain *that may be got*. If gain be the object, then, if it can be got by bending eight cubits to make one cubit straight, may we likewise do that?

4. 'Formerly, the officer Châo Chien made Wang Liang act as charioteer for his favourite Hsî, when, in the course of a whole day,

hunters to collect around. There the charges are the 'hills' and 'marshes,' and here, according to Châo Ch'î and Chû Hsî, they were the 'preserves and parks.' In those times, the various officers had their several tokens, which the prince's messenger bore when he was sent to call any of them. A forester's token was a fur cap, and the one in the text would not answer to a summons with a flag. See the incident in the 左傳, 昭公, 二十年, where the details, however, and Confucius's judgment on it, are different. It is there said:—'The prince of Ch'î was hunting in P'î and summoned the forester with *a bow*. As the forester did not come, the prince had him seized, when he excused himself, saying, *In the huntings of former princes*, 大夫 *have been summoned with a banner*; 士, *with a bow; and the forester with a fur cap. As I did not see the fur cap, I did not venture to approach.* The duke on this dismissed the man. Chung-nî said, *He observed the law of his office, rather than the ordinary rule of answering the summons. Superior men will approve of his act.*' 田,—used for 畋 or 佃. The observations which must be taken as made by Confucius are found nowhere else. 元,—here = 首, 'the head.' 不忘 is a difficult phrase in the connexion. I have made the best of it I could. The first 其招 is plain enough—the summons appropriate to him, i.e. to a forester. We cannot lay so much stress, however, on the 其 in the same phrase in the last sentence, the subject of the chapter being the question of Mencius's waiting on the princes without being called by them at all. 3. 且夫 (2nd tone) is more forcible and argumentative than 且 alone. 如以利 = 如以計利爲心. The question in 亦可爲與 is an appeal to Tâi's own sense of what was right. Admitting what he asked in par. 1, any amount of evil might be done that good might come. Was he prepared to allow that? 4. The Chien (簡) in Châo Chien is the posthumous epithet. His name was 鞅 (*Yang*), a noble of Tsin, in the time of Confucius, and Wang Liang was his charioteer, famous for his skill. Liang appears in the histories of the time—the 左傳 and 國語—by different

一禽、嬖奚反命曰、天下之賤工也、或以告王良、良曰、請復之、彊而後可、一朝而獲十禽。嬖奚反命曰、天下之良工也。簡子曰、我使掌與女乘、謂王良、良不可、曰、吾爲之範我馳驅、終日不獲一、爲之詭遇、一朝而獲十。詩云、不失其馳、舍矢如破、我不貫與小人乘、請辭。

they did not get a single bird. The favourite Hsî reported this result, saying, "He is the poorest charioteer in the world." Some one told this to Wang Liang, who said, "I beg leave to *try* again." By dint of pressing, this was accorded to him, when in one morning they got ten birds. The favourite, reporting this result, said, "He is the best charioteer in the world." Chien said, "I will make him always drive your chariot for you." When he told Wang Liang so, *however*, Liang refused, saying, "I *drove* for him, strictly observing the proper rules for driving, and in the whole day he did not get one *bird*. I *drove* for him so as deceitfully to intercept *the birds*, and in one morning he got ten. It is said in the Book of Poetry,

'There is no failure in the management of their horses;
The arrows are discharged surely, like the blows of an axe.'

I am not accustomed to drive for a mean man. I beg leave to decline the office."

names. He is called 郵無恤, 郵無正, 郵良, as well as 王良;—see the 四書拓餘說, *in loc.* 與=爲, 'for,' and 乘 (4th tone), 'a chariot,' is used as a verb, 'to drive a chariot.' 反命,—see Pt. I. ii. 3. It is a phrase of form. 工,—'a mechanic,' 'an artist;' here='a charioteer.' 請復(4th tone)之,—'I beg to *again* it.' 彊,—2nd tone. 掌與女(=汝)乘,—'to manage the chariot-driving for you.' It is not common in Chinese to separate, as here, the verb and its object. 良不可, 'Liang might not,' i. e. would not be induced to take the office. 吾爲(4th tone)之範我馳驅, 'I for him *law-ed* my racing my horses and whipping them.' 詩云,—see the Shih-ching, II. iii. Ode V. st. 6. Literally the two lines are, 'They err not in the galloping; they let go the arrows, as if rending.' 舍,—the 3rd tone. 貫,—used for 慣. 5. 比,—4th tone, in the sense

五節 御者、且羞與射者比、比而得禽獸、雖若丘陵、弗爲也、如枉道而從彼、何也、且子過矣、枉己者、未有能直人者也。

第二章 一節 景春曰、公孫衍、張儀、豈不誠大丈夫哉、一怒而諸侯懼、安居而天下熄。二節 孟子曰、是焉得爲大丈夫乎、子未學禮乎、丈夫之冠也、父

5. '*Thus* this charioteer even was ashamed to bend improperly to the will of *such an* archer. Though, by bending to it, they would have caught birds and animals sufficient to form a hill, he would not do so. If I were to bend my principles and follow those *princes*, of what kind would my conduct be? And you are wrong. Never has a man who has bent himself been able to make others straight.'

CHAP. II. 1. Ching Ch'un said *to Mencius*, 'Are not Kung-sun Yen and Chang Î really great men? Let them once be angry, and all the princes are afraid. Let them live quietly, and the flames of trouble are extinguished throughout the kingdom.'

2. Mencius said, 'How can such men be great men? Have you not read the Ritual *Usages?*—"At the capping of a young man, his

of 'to flatter.' 丘陵,—to be taken together, 'a mound,' 'a hill.' The 彼,—'that, or those,' referring to 諸侯 in par. 1. We must supply *I*, as the subject of 枉. The concluding remark is just, but hardly consistent with the allowances for their personal misconduct which Mencius was prepared to make to the princes.

2. MENCIUS'S CONCEPTION OF THE GREAT MAN. 1. Ching Ch'un was a man of Mencius's days, 'a practiser of the art of up-and-across' (爲縱橫之術者), i.e. one who plumed himself on his versatility. Kung-sun Yen and Chang Î were also men of that age, natives of Wei (魏), and among the most celebrated of the ambitious scholars, who went from State to State, seeking employment, and embroiling the princes;—see the 'Historical Records,' Book C, 列傳, chap. x. 丈夫,—see Pt. I. i. 4. The phrase is used, however, in the next paragraph for 'a grown-up youth.' 熄 has, in the Shwo Wăn, the opposite meanings of 'feeding a fire' and 'extinguishing a fire.' The latter is its meaning here. 2. 是,—referring to Yen and Î with what is said about them above. 焉,—the interrogative, in 1st tone. The 'Rites' or 'Book of Rites,' to which Mencius here chiefly refers, is not the compilation now received among the higher classics, under the name of the Lî Chî, but the Î Lî (儀禮). He throws various passages together, and, according to his wont, is not careful to quote correctly. In the Î Lî, not only does her mother admonish the bride, but her father also, and his concubines, and all to the effect

孟子

命之、女子之嫁也、母命之、往送之門、戒之曰、往之女家、必敬必戒、無違夫子、以順爲正者、妾婦之道也。三節居天下之廣居、立天下之正位、行天下之大道、得志、與民由之、不得志、獨行其道、富貴不能淫、貧賤不能移、威武不能屈、此之謂大丈夫。

father admonishes him. At the marrying away of a young woman, her mother admonishes her, accompanying her to the door on her leaving, and cautioning her with these words, 'You are going to your home. You must be respectful; you must be careful. Do not disobey your husband.'" *Thus*, to look upon compliance as their correct course is the rule for women.

3. 'To dwell in the wide house of the world, to stand in the correct seat of the world, and to walk in the great path of the world; when he obtains his desire *for office*, to practise his principles for the good of the people; and when that desire is disappointed, to practise them alone; to be above the power of riches and honours to make dissipated, of poverty and mean condition to make swerve from principle, and of power and force to make bend:—these characteristics constitute the great man.'

that she is to be obedient, though the husband (here called 夫子) is not expressly mentioned. See the 儀禮註疏, Bk. II. pp. 49, 50. For the ceremonies of Capping, see the same, Bk. I. In 送之門 and, more especially, in 往之女(汝)家 the 之 joins the verbs and nouns, and is construed as the verb, = 往. 妾婦 are to be taken together,—'a concubine-woman.' Mencius uses the term 妾 in his contempt for Yen and I, who, with all their bluster, only pandered to the passions of the princes. Obedience is the rule for all women, and specially so for secondary wives. 3. 'The wide house of the world' is *benevolence* or *love*, the chief and home of all the virtues; 'the correct seat' is *propriety*; and 'the great path' is *righteousness*. 與民由之 (the 之 refers to the virtues so metaphorically indicated),—'walks according to them along with the people.' The paraphrase in the 日講 says:—'Getting his desire, and being employed in the world, he comes forth, and carries out these principles of benevolence, propriety, and righteousness towards the people, and pursues them along with them.' 此之謂,—'this is what is called,' = such is the description of, a really 'great man.'

第三章 一節 周霄問曰、古之君子仕乎。孟子曰、仕、傳曰、孔子三月無君、則皇皇如也、出疆、必載質、公明儀曰、古之人、三月無君則弔。二節 三月無君則弔、不以急乎。三節 曰、士之失位也、猶諸侯之失國家也、禮曰、諸侯耕助、以供粢盛、

CHAP. III. 1. Châu Hsiâo asked *Mencius*, saying, 'Did superior men of old time take office?' Mencius replied, 'They did. The Record says, "If Confucius was three months without *being employed by some* ruler, he looked anxious and unhappy. When he passed from the boundary of a State, he was sure to carry with him his proper gift of introduction." Kung-ming Î said, "Among the ancients, if an officer was three months unemployed by a ruler, he was condoled with."'

2. *Hsiâo said*, 'Did not this condoling, on being three months unemployed by a ruler, show a too great urgency?'

3. *Mencius* answered, 'The loss of his place to an officer is like the loss of his State to a prince. It is said in the Book of Rites, "A prince ploughs himself, and is assisted *by the people*, to supply

3. OFFICE IS TO BE EAGERLY DESIRED, AND YET IT MAY NOT BE SOUGHT BUT BY ITS PROPER PATH. It will be seen that the questioner of Mencius in this chapter—a man of Wei, and one of the wandering scholars of the time—wished to condemn the philosopher for the dignity of reserve which he maintained in his intercourse with the various princes. Mencius does not evade any of his questions, and very satisfactorily vindicates himself. 1. 傳,—the 4th tone, the 'Record;' whatever it was, it is now lost. 無君,—'without a ruler,' i. e. without office. 皇皇如 is 'the appearance of one who is seeking for something and cannot find it.' It is appropriate to a mourner in the first stages of grief after bereavement. 質,—read *chi*, in 3rd tone, synonymous with 贄. Every person waiting on another,—a superior,—was supposed to pave his way by some introductory gift, and each official rank had its proper article to be used for that purpose by all belonging to it. See the Lî Chî, Bk. I. Pt. II. iii. 19. Confucius carried this with him, that he might not lose any opportunity of getting to be in office again. Kung-ming Î, we are told by Châo Ch'î, was 'a worthy,' but of what time and what state, we do not know. An individual of the same surname is mentioned, Analects, XIV. xiv. Julien translates 則弔 incorrectly by—'*tunc in luctu erant*.' The paraphrase of the 日講 says:—'Then people all came to condole with and to comfort them.' 2. 以 is to be taken as synonymous with 已; 時不已急乎. 3. 國家,—the State, embracing the families of the nobles. In his quotations from the Lî Chî, Mencius combines and adapts to his purpose, with more, however, than his usual freedom, different passages. See Bk. XXI. Sect. ii. pars. 5-7, and Bk. IV. Sect. I. iii. 12, Sect. II. i. 19. Chû Hsî, to illustrate the text, gives

孟子

夫人蠶繅、以爲衣服、犧牲不成、粢盛不潔、衣服不備、不敢以祭、惟士無田、則亦不祭、牲殺器皿、衣服不備、不敢以祭、則不敢以宴、亦不足弔乎。四節出疆必載質、何也。五節曰、士之仕也、猶農夫之耕也、農夫豈爲出疆、舍其耒

the millet *for sacrifice*. His wife keeps silkworms, and unwinds their cocoons, to make the garments *for sacrifice*." If the victims be not perfect, the millet not pure, and the dress not complete, he does not presume to sacrifice. "And the scholar who, *out of office*, has no *holy* field, in the same way, does not sacrifice. The victims for slaughter, the vessels, and the garments, not being all complete, he does not presume to sacrifice, and then neither may he dare to feel happy." Is there not here sufficient ground also for condolence?'

4. *Hsiâo again asked*, 'What was the meaning of *Confucius's* always carrying his proper gift of introduction with him, when he passed over the boundaries *of the State where he had been*?'

5. 'An officer's being in office,' was the reply, 'is like the ploughing of a husbandman. Does a husbandman part with his plough, because he goes from one State to another?'

another summary of the passages in the Lî Chî, thus:—'It is said in the Book of Rites, The princes had their special field of 100 *mâu*, in which, wearing their crown, with its blue flaps turned up, they held the plough to commence the ploughing, which was afterwards completed with the help of the common people. The produce of this field was reaped and stored in the ducal granary, to supply the vessels of millet in the ancestral temple. They also caused the family women (世婦) of their harem to attend to the silkworms, in the silkworm house attached to the State mulberry trees, and to bring the cocoons to them. These were then presented to their wives, who received them in their sacrificial headdress and robe, soaked them, and thrice drew out a thread. They then distributed the cocoons among the ladies of the three palaces, to prepare the threads for the ornaments on the robes to be worn in sacrificing to the former kings and dukes.' 盛, the 2nd tone, 'the millet placed in the sacrificial vessel.' 犧牲,—牲, the victim, whatever it might be; 犧, the victim, as pure and perfect. The officer's field is the 圭 field, Pt. I. iii. 16. 器皿 together = vessels. Chû Hsî says the 皿 were the covers of the 器. 以宴,—'to feast,' = to feel happy. The argument is that it was not the mere loss of office which was a proper subject for grief and condolence, but the consequences of it, especially in not being able to continue his proper sacrifices, as here set forth. 5. 舍,—the 3rd tone. 耒耜,—see Pt. I. iv. par. 2.

耜哉。六節、曰、晉國、亦仕國也、未嘗聞仕如此其急、仕如此其急也、君子之難仕何也。曰、丈夫生、而願爲之有室、女子生、而願爲之有家、父母之心、人皆有之、不待父母之命、媒妁之言、鑽穴隙相窺、踰牆相從、則父母國人皆賤之、古之人未嘗不欲仕也、又惡不由其道、不由其道而往者、與鑽穴隙之類也。

6. *Hsiâo* pursued, 'The kingdom of Tsin is one, as well as others, of official employments, but I have not heard of anyone being thus earnest about being in office. If there should be this urgency, why does a superior man make any difficulty about taking it?' *Mencius* answered, 'When a son is born, what is desired for him is that he may have a wife; when a daughter is born, what is desired for her is that she may have a husband. This feeling of the parents is possessed by all men. If *the young people*, without waiting for the orders of their parents, and the arrangements of the go-betweens, shall bore holes to steal a sight of each other, or get over the wall to be with each other, then their parents and all other people will despise them. The ancients did indeed always desire to be in office, but they also hated being so by any improper way. *To seek office* by an improper way is of a class with *young people's* boring holes.'

6. 'The kingdom of Tsin,'—see Bk. I. Pt. I. v. 1. 君子之難仕,—by the 君子, Hsiâo evidently intends Mencius himself, who, however, does not notice the insinuation. 丈夫 and 女子,—here simply 'a son,' 'a daughter.' A man marrying is said 有室, 'to have an apartment,' and a woman marrying, 有家, 'to have a family,' or 'home.' On the go-between, see the Châu Lî, Pt. II. Bk. vi. pars. 54–60; the Shih-ching, I. viii. Ode VI. st. 4. The law of marriage here referred to by Mencius still obtains, and seems to have been the rule of the Chinese race from time immemorial. 相從,—從＝就, 而往,—往＝往見諸侯.

【四章】彭更問曰、後車數十乘、（一節）從者數百人、以傳食於諸侯、不以泰乎。孟子曰、非其道、則一簞食不可受於人、如其道、則舜受堯之天下、不以爲泰、子以爲泰乎。曰、（二節）否。士無事而食、不可也。曰、（三節）子不通功易事、以羨補不足、則農有餘粟、女有餘布、子如通之、則梓匠輪輿、皆

CHAP. IV. 1. P'ăng Kăng asked *Mencius*, saying, 'Is it not an extravagant procedure to go from one prince to another and live upon them, followed by several tens of carriages, and attended by several hundred men?' Mencius replied, 'If there be not a proper ground *for taking it*, a single bamboo-cup of rice may not be received from a man. If there be such a proper ground, then Shun's receiving the kingdom from Yâo is not to be considered excessive. Do you think it was excessive?'

2. *Kăng* said, 'No. But for a scholar *performing* no service to receive his support notwithstanding is improper.'

3. *Mencius* answered, 'If you do not have an intercommunication of the productions of labour, and an interchange of *men's* services, so that *one from his* overplus may supply the deficiency *of another*, then husbandmen will have a superfluity of grain, and women will have a superfluity of cloth. If you have such an interchange,

4. THE LABOURER IS WORTHY OF HIS HIRE, AND THERE IS NO LABOURER SO WORTHY AS THE SCHOLAR WHO INSTRUCTS MEN IN VIRTUE. 1. P'ăng Kăng was a disciple of Mencius. His object in addressing him, as in this chapter, seems to have been to stir him up to visit the princes and go into office. 乘,—4th tone, following 車, as a numeral or classifier. 從者,—從, 4th tone, 'an attendant,' 'a follower,' not in a moral sense. 傳,—the 3rd tone, explained in the dictionary by 續, 'to connect,' 'succeed to.' 以傳, 'by succession.'—The phrase is felt to be a difficult one. Sun Shih explains it thus:—'Mencius got his support from the princes, and the chariots and disciples got their support from Mencius. It came to this that the support of all was from the contributions of the princes, and hence it is said that by their mutual connexion they all lived on the princes.' 簞食,—食 (*tsze*), 4th tone, 'rice cooked.' Compare Analects, VI.ix. 堯之天下, 'Yâo's world,' i.e. the kingdom from Yâo. 舜 may be construed very well as the nominative to the first 以爲. 3. 守先王之道以待後之學

得食於子、於此有人焉、入則孝、出則弟、守先王之道、以待後之學者、而不得食於子、子何尊梓匠輪輿而輕爲仁義者哉。四節曰、梓匠輪輿、其志將以求食也、君子之爲道也、其志亦將以求食與。曰、子何以其志爲哉、其有功於子、可食而食之矣、且子食志乎、食功乎。曰、

carpenters and carriage-wrights may all get their food from you. Here now is a man, who, at home, is filial, and abroad, respectful to his elders; who watches over the principles of the ancient kings, awaiting *the rise of* future learners:—and yet you will refuse to support him. How is it that you give honour to the carpenter and carriage-wright, and slight him who practises benevolence and righteousness?'

4. *P'ăng Kăng* said, 'The aim of the carpenter and carriage-wright is *by their trades* to seek for a living. Is it also the aim of the superior man in his practice of principles thereby to seek for a living?' 'What have you to do,' returned *Mencius*, 'with his purpose? He is of service to you. He deserves to be supported, and should be supported. And *let me ask*,—Do you remunerate a man's intention, or do you remunerate his service.' *To this Kăng* replied, 'I remunerate his intention.'

者,—the paraphrase in the 合講 is:—'He firmly guards the principles of benevolence and righteousness transmitted by the ancient kings, so that they do not get obscured or obstructed by perverse discourses, but hereby await future learners, and secure their having matter of instruction and models of imitation, whereby they may enter into truth and right. Thus he continues the past and opens the way for the future, and does service to the world.' 以待, thus, = 'for the benefit of.' The 梓 and 匠 are both workers in wood, the 梓人's work being in smaller things, such as vessels and articles of furniture, and the 匠人's in large, such as building houses, &c. The 輪人 made the wheels and also the cover of a carriage; the 輿人 the other parts. 4. Observe how appropriately 將, expressive of futurity or object, follows 志. 可食而食之,—here 食 and the three that follow, are read as in 一簞食, but with a different meaning, being = 'to feed' (active or passive), 'to give

食志。五節曰、有人於此、毀瓦畫墁、其志將以求食也、則子食之乎。曰、否。曰、然則子非食志也、食功也。

第五章 一節萬章問曰、宋、小國也、今將行王政、齊楚惡而伐之、則如之何。二節孟子曰、湯居亳、與葛爲鄰、葛伯放而不祀。湯使人問之曰、何爲不祀。曰、無以供犧牲也、湯使遺之牛羊、葛伯食

5. *Mencius* said, 'There is a man here, who breaks your tiles, and draws *unsightly* figures on your walls;—his purpose may be thereby to seek for his living, but will you indeed remunerate him?' 'No,' said Kăng; *and Mencius then* concluded, 'That being the case, it is not the purpose which you remunerate, but the work done.'

CHAP. V. 1. Wan Chang asked *Mencius*, saying, 'Sung is a small State. *Its ruler* is now setting about to practise the *true* royal government, and Ch'î and Ch'û hate and attack him. What in this case is to be done?'

2. *Mencius* replied, 'When T'ang dwelt in Po, he adjoined to *the State of* Ko, the chief of which was living in a dissolute state and neglecting *his proper* sacrifices. T'ang sent messengers to inquire why he did not sacrifice. He replied, "I have no means of supplying the *necessary* victims." *On this*, T'ang caused oxen and sheep to be sent to him, but he ate them, and still continued not to sacrifice.

rice to.' 5. 畫 (4th tone) 墁,—墁 means 'ornaments on walls;'—we must therefore take 畫 in a bad sense, to correspond to the 毀. A man wishes to mend the roof, but he only breaks it; to ornament the wall, but he only disfigures it.

5. THE PRINCE WHO WILL SET HIMSELF TO PRACTISE A BENEVOLENT GOVERNMENT ON THE PRINCIPLES OF THE ANCIENT KINGS HAS NONE TO FEAR. 1. Wan Chang was a disciple of Mencius, the fifth book of whose Works is named from him. What he says here may surprise us, because we know that the duke of Sung (its capital was in the present district of Shang-ch'iû [商邱], in the Kwei-teh department of Ho-nan), or king, as he styled himself, was entirely worthless and oppressive; see the 'Historical Records,' Book XXXVIII, 宋微子世家, towards the end. 2. Compare Bk. I. Pt. II. iii. 1, and xi. 2. Po, the capital of T'ang (though there were three places of the same name), is referred to the same department of Ho-nan as the country of Ko, viz. that of

之、又不以祀。湯又使人問之曰、何爲不祀。曰、無以供粢盛也。湯使亳衆往爲之耕、老弱饋食。葛伯率其民、要其有酒食黍稻者奪之、不授者殺之。有童子以黍肉餉、殺而奪之。書曰、葛伯仇餉、此之謂也。○三爲其殺是童子而征之、四海之內、皆曰、非富天下也、爲匹夫匹

T'ang again sent messengers to ask him the same question as before, when he replied, "I have no means of obtaining the *necessary* millet." *On this*, T'ang sent the mass of the people of Po to go and till the ground for him, while the old and feeble carried their food to them. The chief of Ko led his people to intercept those who were thus charged with wine, cooked rice, millet, and paddy, and took their stores from them, while they killed those who refused to give them up. There was a boy who had some millet and flesh for the labourers, who was thus slain and robbed. What is said in the Book of History, "The chief of Ko behaved as an enemy to the provision-carriers," has reference to this.

3. 'Because of his murder of this boy, *T'ang* proceeded to punish him. All within the four seas said, "It is not because he desires the riches of the kingdom, but to avenge a common man and woman."

Kwei-teh. Its site is said to have been distant from the site of the supposed capital of Ko only about 100 *li*, so that T'ang might easily render the services here mentioned to the 伯, chief or baron, of Ko. 無以供,—'no means of supplying,' i. e. of obtaining. 餽, 4th tone, = 饋. 粢盛 (2nd tone),—see last chapter. 爲之,—爲, 4th tone. 饋食,—食 (*tsze*), 4th tone. 要, 1st tone;—we find it defined in the dictionary, by 'to meet with,' 'to extort,' which approximate to the meaning here. 酒食,—食, as above, 4th tone. 書曰,—see the Shû-ching, IV. ii. 6.—In the 四書拓餘說, *in loc.*, 王厚齊 is quoted, to the effect that if Mencius had not been thus particular in explaining what is alluded to in the words of the Shû-ching, the interpretations of them would have been endless. But that in his time there were ancient books which could be appealed to. 3. 爲, 4th tone. 匹夫匹婦,—'common men and women;'—see Analects, XIV. xviii. 3. The phrases are understood here, however, with a special application to the father and mother of the murdered boy.

孟子

婦復讐也。四湯始征、自葛載、十一征、而無敵於天下、東面而征、西夷怨、南面而征、北狄怨、曰、奚爲後我、民之望之、若大旱之望雨也、歸市者弗止、芸者不變、誅其君、弔其民、如時雨降、民大悅、書曰、徯我后、后來其無罰。五有攸不爲臣、東征、綏厥士女、匪厥玄黃、紹我周王見休、惟臣附于大邑周、其

4. 'When T'ang began his work of executing justice, he commenced with Ko, and *though* he made eleven punitive expeditions, he had not an enemy in the kingdom. When he pursued his work in the east, the rude tribes in the west murmured. So did those on the north, when he was engaged in the south. Their cry was—"Why does he make us last." *Thus*, the people's longing for him was like their longing for rain in a time of great drought. The frequenters of the markets stopped not. Those engaged in weeding *in the fields* made no change *in their operations*. While he punished their rulers, he consoled the people. *His progress* was like the falling of opportune rain, and the people were delighted. It is said in the Book of History, "We have waited for our prince. When our prince comes, we may escape from the punishments *under which we suffer*."

5. 'There being some who would not become the subjects *of Châu*, *king Wû* proceeded to punish them on the east. He gave tranquillity to their people, who *welcomed him* with baskets full of their black and yellow silks, *saying*—"From henceforth we shall serve

4. Compare Bk. I. Pt. II. xi. 2. There are, however, some variations in the phrases. 載=始. The quotation in the end is from a different part of the Shû-ching;—see Pt. IV. v. Section II. 5. The eleven punitive expeditions of T'ang cannot all be determined. From the Shih-ching and Shû-ching six only are made out, while by some their number is given as twenty-two, and twenty-seven;—see the 集證, *in loc.* 5. Down to 大邑周,—the substance of this paragraph is found in the Shû-ching;—see Pt. V. iii. 7; but this Book is confessed to require much emendation in its arrangement. 士女=男女. 匪,—used for 篚. 匪厥玄黃,—'basketed their azure and yellow *silks*.' It is said:—'Heaven is azure, and Earth is yellow. King Wû was

君子實玄黃于匪、以迎其君子、其小人簞食壺漿、以迎其小人、救民於水火之中、取其殘而已矣。六太誓曰、我武惟揚、侵于之疆、則取于殘、殺伐用張、于湯有光。七不行王政云爾、苟行王政、四海之內、皆舉首而望之、欲以爲君、齊楚雖大、何畏焉。

the sovereign of *our dynasty of* Châu, that we may be made happy by him." So they joined themselves, as subjects, to the great city of Châu. Thus, the men of station *of Shang* took baskets full of black and yellow *silks* to meet the men of station of *Châu*, and the lower classes of the one met those of the other with baskets of rice and vessels of congee. *Wû* saved the people from the midst of fire and water, seizing only their oppressors, *and destroying them.*'

6. 'In the Great Declaration it is said, "My power shall be put forth, and, invading the territories *of Shang*, I will seize the oppressor. I will put him to death to punish him:—so shall the greatness of my work appear, more glorious than that of T'ang."

7. '*Sung* is not, as you say, practising *true* royal government, and so forth. If it were practising royal government, all within the four seas would be lifting up their heads, and looking for *its prince*, wishing to have him for their sovereign. Great as Ch'î and Ch'û are, what would there be to fear from them?'

able to put away the evils of the Yin rule, and gave the people rest. He might be compared to Heaven and Earth, overshadowing and sustaining all things in order to nourish men.' 紹 (we have 昭 in the Shû-ching),—'to continue.' We must understand a 'saying,' and bring out the meaning of 紹 thus:—'Formerly we served Shang, and now we continue to serve, but our service is to Châu.' 大邑周, literally, 'great city (or citied) Châu,' which is an irregular phrase, perhaps equal to Châu of the Great Capital. The 日講 has 皆心悅誠服,而盡歸附於大邑周焉. From 其君子 onwards, Mencius explains the meaning of the Shû-ching. 6. This quotation from Pt. V. i. Sect. II. 8, is to illustrate the last clause of the preceding paragraph. 7. 云爾,—see Analects, VII. xviii. 云, however, does not here simply act as a particle closing the sentence, but also refers to the whole of Wan Chang's statement at the commencement of the conversation.

章六 一 孟子謂戴不勝曰、子欲子之王之善與、我明告子、有楚大夫於此、欲其子之齊語也、則使齊人傅諸、使楚人傅諸。曰、使齊人傅之。曰、一齊人傅之、衆楚人咻之、雖日撻而求其齊也、不可得矣、引而置之莊嶽之間、數年、雖日撻而求其楚、亦不可得矣。二 子謂薛居州、善士也、使之居於王所、在

CHAP. VI. 1. Mencius said to Tâi Pû-shăng, 'I see that you are desiring your king to be virtuous, and I will plainly tell you *how he may be made so.* Suppose that there is a great officer of Ch'û here, who wishes his son to learn the speech of Ch'î. Will he in that case employ a man of Ch'î as his tutor, or a man of Ch'û?' 'He will employ a man of Ch'î to teach him,' said *Pû-shăng. Mencius* went on, 'If *but* one man of Ch'î be teaching him, and there be a multitude of men of Ch'û continually shouting out about him, although *his father* beat him every day, wishing him to learn the speech of Ch'î, it will be impossible for him to do so. But in the same way, if he were to be taken and placed for several years in Chwang or Yo, though *his father* should beat him, wishing him to speak the language of Ch'û, it would be impossible for him to do so.

2. 'You supposed that Hsieh Chü-châu was a scholar of virtue, and you have got him placed in attendance on the king. Suppose

6. THE INFLUENCE OF EXAMPLE AND ASSOCIATION. THE IMPORTANCE OF HAVING VIRTUOUS MEN ABOUT A SOVEREIGN'S PERSON. 1. Tâi Pû-shăng was a minister of Sung, the descendant of one of its dukes who had received the posthumous epithet of Tâi, which had been adopted as their surname by a branch of his posterity. 子欲 . . . 與,—與, 2nd tone, the interrogative implying an affirmative reply. 欲其子之齊語, 'wishes the Ch'î speech of his son,' i.e. wishes his son to learn Ch'î. 諸,—interrogative, and equal to 之乎. 咻, read *hsiû*, = 讙, 'shouting,' 'clamorous.' Chwang and Yo were two well-known quarters in the capital of Ch'î, the former being the name of a street, and the latter the name of a neighbourhood; see the 四書拓餘說, *in loc.* 2. Hsieh Chü-châu was also a minister of Sung, a descendant of one of the princes of Hsieh, whose family had adopted the name

於王所者、長幼卑尊、皆薛居州也、王誰與爲不善、在王所者、長幼卑尊、皆非薛居州也、王誰與爲善、一薛居州、獨如宋王何。

七 公孫丑問曰、不見諸侯、何義。孟子曰、古者、不爲臣不見。二 段干木、踰垣而辟之、泄柳閉門而不

that all in attendance on the king, old and young, high and low, were Hsieh Chü-châus, whom would the king have to do evil with? And suppose that all in attendance on the king, old and young, high and low, are not Hsieh Chü-châus, whom will the king have to do good with? What can one Hsieh Chü-châu do alone for the king of Sung?'

CHAP. VII. 1. Kung-sun Châu asked *Mencius*, saying, 'What is the point of righteousness involved in your not going to see the princes?' *Mencius* replied, 'Among the ancients, if one had not been a minister *in a State*, he did not go to see *the sovereign*.

2. 'Twan Kan-mû leaped over his wall to avoid the prince. Hsieh Liû shut his door, and would not admit the prince. These

of their original State as their surname. In the 萬姓通譜 we read :—'Tâi Pû-shăng said to Hsieh Chü-châu, "It is only the virtuous scholar (善士) who can set forth what is virtuous, and shut up the way of what is corrupt. You are a scholar of virtue; cannot you make the king virtuous?"' But this and what follows was probably constructed from Mencius's remark, and so I prefer to take 謂 as = 'supposed,' 'believed,' not 'said.' 長,—the 3rd tone. 居於王所,—'to dwell in the king's place,' i.e. to be about him.

7. MENCIUS DEFENDS HIS NOT GOING TO SEE THE PRINCES BY THE EXAMPLE AND MAXIMS OF THE ANCIENTS. 1. 何義 is not simply—'what is the meaning?' but 'what is the rightness?' Mencius, however, does not state distinctly the principle of the thing, but appeals to prescription and precedent. 不爲臣 = 未爲臣, or 未仕於其國. In the Analects, XIV. xxii, we have an example of how Confucius, not then actually in office, but having been so, went to see the duke of Lû. 2. Twan Kan-mû was a scholar of Wei (魏), who refused to see the prince Wăn (文). Wăn was the posthumous title of 斯, B.C. 426-386. In the 'Historical Records,' it is mentioned that he received the writings of Tsze-hsiâ, and never drove past Kan-mû's house without bowing forward to the front bar of his carriage. 辟 = 避, 4th tone. 之 refers to the prince Wăn. Hsieh Liû was a scholar of Lû, who refused to admit (內 = 納) the duke Mû (繆); see Bk. II. Pt. II. xi. 3. The incident referred to here must have been previous to the time spoken of there. 迫斯可以見矣,—literally, 'being urgent, this (or,

內、是皆已甚、迫、斯可以見矣。三節陽貨欲見孔子、而惡無禮、大夫有賜於士、不得受於其家、則往拜其門、陽貨瞰孔子之亡也、而饋孔子蒸豚、孔子亦瞰其亡也、而往拜之、當是時、陽貨先、豈得不見。四節曾子曰、脅肩諂笑、病于夏畦。子路曰、未同而言、觀其色赧赧然、非由之所知也。由是觀之、則君子

two, however, *carried their scrupulosity* to excess. When *a prince* is urgent, it is not improper to see him.

3. 'Yang Ho wished to get Confucius to go to see him, but disliked doing so by any want of propriety. *As it is the rule, therefore, that* when a great officer sends a gift to a scholar, if the latter be not at home to receive it, he must go to the *officer's* to pay his respects, Yang Ho watched when Confucius was out, and sent him a roasted pig. Confucius, in his turn, watched when Ho was out, and went to pay his respects to him. At that time, Yang Ho had taken the initiative;—how could *Confucius* decline *going* to see him?

4. 'Tsăng-tsze said, "They who shrug up their shoulders, and laugh in a flattering way, toil harder than the summer *labourer in the* fields." Tsze-lû said, "There are those who talk with people with whom they have no *great* community *of feeling*. If you look at their countenances, they are full of blushes. I do not *desire to* know such persons." By considering these *remarks*, the *spirit* which the superior man nourishes may be known.'

then) may be seen.' 3. 欲見,—見, it is noted here, should be read in the 4th tone, with a *hiphil* sense. Compare Analects, XVII. i. 惡,—the verb, in 4th tone. 大夫有賜云云,—see the Lî Chî, XI. Sect. iii. 20. Mencius, however, does not quote the exact words. 亡=無, and so read. 4. 脅肩, 'to rib,' i.e. to shrug, 'the shoulders.' 病, as in Bk. II. Pt. I. ii. 16. 夏畦=夏月治畦之人. Chû Hsî makes 君子 to mean 'those two superior men,' referring to Tsăng and Tsze-lû, but this seems to be unnecessary.

之所養、可知已矣。

第八章 一節 戴盈之曰、什一、去關市之征、今茲未能、請輕之、以待來年、然後已、何如。二節 孟子曰、今有人日攘其鄰之雞者、或告之曰、是非君子之道、曰、請損之、月攘一雞、以待來年、然後已。三節 如知其非義、斯速已矣、何待來年。

第九章 一節 公都子曰、外人皆稱夫

CHAP. VIII. 1. Tâi Ying-chih said to *Mencius*, 'I am not able at present and immediately to do with the levying of a tithe *only*, and abolishing the duties charged at the passes and in the markets. With your leave I will lighten, however, both the tax and the duties, until next year, and will then make an end of them. What do you think of such a course?'

2. Mencius said, 'Here is a man, who every day appropriates some of his neighbour's strayed fowls. Some one says to him, "Such is not the way of a good man;" and he replies, "With your leave I will diminish my appropriations, and will take only one fowl a month, until next year, when I will make an end of the practice."

3. 'If you know that the thing is unrighteous, then use all despatch in putting an end to it:—why wait till next year?'

CHAP. IX. 1. The disciple Kung-tû said to *Mencius*, 'Master, the people beyond *our school* all speak of you as being fond of

8. WHAT IS WRONG SHOULD BE PUT AN END TO AT ONCE, WITHOUT RESERVE AND WITHOUT DELAY. 1. Tâi Ying-chih was a great officer of Sung, supposed by some to be the same with Tâi Pû-shăng, chap. vi. Mencius had, no doubt, been talking with him on the points indicated; see Bk. I. Pt. II. v. 3; Bk. II. Pt. I. v. 3; Bk. III. Pt. I. iii. 請, here and below, is simply the speaker's polite way of indicating his resolution. 2. 攘, = here as in Analects, XIII. xviii. 君子,—here, = 'a good man.' 損之, 'diminish it,' i. e. the amount of his captures. 3. 斯 is used adverbially, = 'at once.' 已 in all the paragraphs is the verb = 'have done with it,' 'put an end to it.'

9. MENCIUS DEFENDS HIMSELF AGAINST THE CHARGE OF BEING FOND OF DISPUTING. WHAT LED TO HIS APPEARING TO BE SO WAS THE NECESSITY OF THE TIME. Compare Bk. II. Pt. I. ii. 17. Mencius would appear from this chapter to have believed that the mantle of Confucius had fallen upon him, and that his position was that of a sage, on whom it devolved to live and labour for the world. 1. 外人,—'outside men,' i. e. people in general, all beyond his school, as the representative of orthodoxy in the kingdom. 敢問何, according to the gloss in the 備旨,

子好辯、敢問何也。孟子曰、予豈好辯哉、予不得已也。○二節天下之生久矣、一治一亂。○三節當堯之時、水逆行、氾濫於中國、蛇龍居之、民無所定、下者爲巢、上者爲營窟、書曰、洚水警余、洚水者、洪水也。○四節使禹治之、禹掘地而注之海、驅蛇龍而放之菹、水

disputing. I venture to ask whether it be so.' *Mencius* replied, 'Indeed, I am not fond of disputing; but I am compelled to do it.

2. 'A long time has elapsed since this world *of men* received its being, and there has been *along its history* now a period of good order, and now a period of confusion.

3. 'In the time of Yâo, the waters, flowing out of their channels, inundated the Middle Kingdom. Snakes and dragons occupied it, and the people had no place where they could settle themselves. In the low grounds they made nests for themselves *on the trees or raised platforms*, and in the high grounds they made caves. It is said in the Book of History, "The waters in their wild course warned me." Those "waters in their wild course" were the waters of the great inundation.

4. '*Shun* employed Yü to reduce the waters to order. Yü dug open *their obstructed channels*, and conducted them to the sea. He drove away the snakes and dragons, and forced them into the grassy

='I venture to ask why you are so fond of disputing,' as if Kung-tû admitted the charge of the outside people. But it is better to interpret as in the translation. The spirit of 予豈好辯哉 seems to be better given in English by dropping the interrogation. 2. Commentators are unanimous in understanding 天下之生 not of the material world, and taking 生 as=生民. It is remarkable, then, that Mencius, in his review of the history of mankind, does not go beyond the time of Yâo (compare Pt. I. iv), and that at its commencement he places a period not of good order (治, 4th tone), but of confusion. 3. Mark the variations of phraseology here from Pt. I. iv. 7. 書曰,—see the Shû-ching, II. ii. 14, where for 警 we have 儆. The 'nests' were huts on high-raised platforms. In the Lî Chî, VII. Sect. I. par. 8, these are said to have been the summer habitations of the earliest men, and 營窟, the winter. 營窟='artificial caves,' i.e. caves hollowed out from heaps of earth raised upon the ground. 洚水 is the same as the 水逆行 above. Chû Hsî explains it by 'deep and shoreless.' 4. 掘地, —'dug the earth,' but with the meaning in the translation. 菹 is read by Chû Hsî *tsü*,

由地中行、江淮河漢是也、險阻既遠、鳥獸之害人者消、然後人得平土而居之。

五節 堯舜既沒、聖人之道衰、暴君代作、壞宮室以爲汙池、民無所安息、棄田以爲園囿、使民不得衣食、邪說暴行又作、園囿汙池沛澤多、而禽獸至、及紂之身、天下又大亂。

六節 周公相武王、誅紂

marshes. *On this*, the waters pursued their course through the country, even the waters of the Chiang, the Hwâi, the Ho, and the Han, and the dangers and obstructions which they had occasioned were removed. The birds and beasts which had injured the people *also* disappeared, and after this men found the plains *available for them*, and occupied them.

5. 'After the death of Yâo and Shun, the principles that mark sages fell into decay. Oppressive sovereigns arose one after another, who pulled down houses to make ponds and lakes, so that the people *knew* not where they could rest in quiet; they threw fields out of cultivation to form gardens and parks, so that the people could not get clothes and food. *Afterwards*, corrupt speakings and oppressive deeds became more rife; gardens and parks, ponds and lakes, thickets and marshes became more numerous, and birds and beasts swarmed. By the time of *the tyrant* Châu, the kingdom was again in a state of great confusion.

6. 'Châu-kung assisted king Wû, and destroyed Châu. He

but wrongly. With the meaning in the text, it is read *tsieh*. 水由地中行,—'the waters travelled in the middle or bosom of the earth,' i.e. were no longer spread abroad over its surface. Chû Hsi makes 地中＝兩涯之間, 'between their banks,' but that is not so much the idea, as that the waters pursued a course to the sea, through the land, instead of being spread over its surface. 5. In describing this period of confusion, Mencius seems to ignore the sageship of T'ang, and of the kings Wăn and Wû;—especially that of T'ang. 行,—in 4th tone. 沛, as associated with 澤, means thick marshy jungles, where beasts could find shelter. The 水 in its composition requires that we recognise the marshiness of the thickets or cover. But this account of the country down to the rise of the Châu dynasty implies that it was thinly peopled. 6. The kingdom of Yen is referred to a portion of the present district of Ch'ü-fâu (曲阜) in Yen-

孟子

伐奄、三年討其君、驅飛廉於海隅而戮之、滅國者五十、驅虎豹犀象而遠之、天下大悅、書曰、丕顯哉、文王謨、丕承哉、武王烈、佑啟我後人、咸以正無缺。○七世衰道微、邪說暴行有作、臣弒其君者有之、子弒其父者有之。○八孔子懼、作春秋、春秋、天子之事也、是故孔子曰、知

smote Yen, and after three years put its sovereign to death. He drove Fei-lien to a corner by the sea, and slew him. The States which he extinguished amounted to fifty. He drove far away also the tigers, leopards, rhinoceroses, and elephants;—and all the people was greatly delighted. It is said in the Book of History, "Great and splendid were the plans of king Wăn! Greatly were they carried out by the energy of king Wû! They are for the assistance and instruction of us who are of an after day. They are all in principle correct, and deficient in nothing."

7. '*Again* the world fell into decay, and principles faded away. Perverse speakings and oppressive deeds waxed rife again. There were instances of ministers who murdered their sovereigns, and of sons who murdered their fathers.

8. 'Confucius was afraid, and made the "Spring and Autumn." What the "Spring and Autumn" contains are matters proper to the sovereign. On this account Confucius said, "Yes! It is the Spring

châu, Shan-tung. Châo Ch'î connects 三年討其君 with 誅紂, but it seems to belong more naturally to 伐奄. Fei-lien was a favourite minister of Châu, who aided him in his enormities. In the 'Historical Records,' Bk. IV, 秦本記, at the beginning, he appears as 蜚廉, but without mention of his banishment and death. The place called 'a corner by the sea' cannot be determined. And it would be vain to try to enumerate the 'fifty kingdoms,' which Châu-kung extinguished. The 夷狄, in par. 11, must be supposed to have been among them. The 'tigers, leopards, &c.,' are the animals kept by Châu, not those infesting the country, as in the more ancient periods. 書曰,—see the Shû-ching, V. xxv. 6. 7. 行, 4th tone. 有作,—有 read as, and = 又. 8. 'Spring and Autumn,'—annals of Lû for 242 years (B.C. 721–479), with Confucius's annotations, or rather, as is absurdly contended, adapted by him to express a correct judgment on every event and actor. They are composed as a sovereign

我者、其惟春秋乎、罪我者、其惟春秋乎。(九節)聖王不作、諸侯放恣、處士橫議、楊朱墨翟之言盈天下、天下之言不歸楊、則歸墨、楊氏爲我、是無君也、墨氏兼愛、是無父也、無父無君、是禽獸也、公明儀曰、庖有肥肉、廐有肥馬、民有饑色、野有餓莩、此率獸而食人也、楊墨之

and Autumn which will make men know me, and it is the Spring and Autumn which will make men condemn me."

9. '*Once more*, sage sovereigns cease to arise, and the princes of the States give the reins to their lusts. Unemployed scholars indulge in unreasonable discussions. The words of Yang Chû and Mo Tî fill the country. *If you listen to* people's discourses throughout it, *you will find that* they have adopted the views either of Yang or of Mo. *Now*, Yang's principle is—" each one for himself," which does not acknowledge *the claims of* the sovereign. Mo's principle is—" to love all equally," which does not acknowledge *the peculiar affection due to* a father. But to acknowledge neither king nor father is to be in the state of a beast. Kung-ming Î said, "In their kitchens, there is fat meat. In their stables, there are fat horses. But their people have the look of hunger, and on the wilds there are those who have died of famine. This is leading on beasts to devour men."

would have composed them. As Confucius was a sage without the throne, if one of the sovereign sages had written annals, he would have done so, as Confucius has done. Chû Hsî quotes from the commentator Hû (胡安國):—'Chung-nî made the *Spring and Autumn*, to lodge in it the true royal laws. There are the firm exhibition of the constant duties; the proper use of ceremonial distinctions; the assertion of *Heaven's* decree of *favour* to the virtuous; and the punishment of the guilty:—all these things, of which it may be said in brief that they are the business of the sovereign.' (Compare on Hû's language, the Shû-ching, II. iii. 7.) It was by the study of this book, therefore, that Confucius wished himself to be known, though he knew that he exposed himself to presumption on account of the sovereign's point of view from which he looked at everything in it. This is the meaning of 罪我者其惟春秋乎, and not—'Those who condemn me (i.e. bad ministers and prince) will do so on account of my condemnations of them in it,' which is the view of Châo Ch'î. I have dropped the interrogations in the translation. 9. 處,—the 3rd tone, applied to a virgin dwelling in the seclusion of her apartments, and here to a scholar with-

道不息、孔子之道不著、是邪說誣民、充塞仁義也、仁義充塞、則率獸食人、人將相食。十吾爲此懼、閑先聖之道、距楊墨、放淫辭、邪說者不得作。作於其心、害於其事。作於其事、害於其政。聖人復起、不易吾言矣。十一昔者、禹抑洪水、而天下平。周公兼夷狄、驅猛獸、而百姓寧。

If the principles of Yang and Mo be not stopped, and the principles of Confucius not set forth, then those perverse speakings will delude the people, and stop up *the path* of benevolence and righteousness. When benevolence and righteousness are stopped up, beasts will be led on to devour men, and men will devour one another.

10. 'I am alarmed by these things, and address myself to the defence of the doctrines of the former sages, and to oppose Yang and Mo. I drive away their licentious expressions, so that such perverse speakers may not be able to show themselves. *Their delusions* spring up in men's minds, and do injury to their practice of affairs. Shown in their practice of affairs, they are pernicious to their government. When sages shall rise up again, they will not change my words.

11. 'In former times, Yü repressed the vast waters *of the inundation,* and the country was reduced to order. Châu-kung's achievements extended even to the barbarous tribes of the east and north, and he drove away all ferocious animals, and the people enjoyed repose. Confucius completed the "Spring and Autumn," and rebellious ministers and villainous sons were struck with terror.

out public employment. Yang Chû, called also Yang Shû (戍) and Yang Tsze-chü (子居), was a heresiarch of the times of Confucius and Lâo-tsze, of which last he is said to have been a disciple. In the days of Mencius, his principles appear to have been very rife. We may call his school the *selfish* school of China (爲我,—爲, the 4th tone), as Mo's was the *transcendental.* 庖有肥肉云云,—see Bk. I. Pt. I. iv. 4. 10. 爲,—4th tone. 作於其心云云,—see Bk. II. Pt. I. ii. 17. 11. 兼,—'embraced,' 'comprehended,' i. e. among the fifty States referred to above. 賊子,—

孔子成春秋、而亂臣賊子懼。十二詩云、戎狄是膺、荊舒是懲、則莫我敢承、無父無君、是周公所膺也。十三我亦欲正人心、息邪說、距詖行、放淫辭、以承三聖者。豈好辯哉、予不得已也。十四能言距楊墨者、聖人之徒也。

第十章 一節 匡章曰、陳仲子豈不誠廉士哉、居於陵、三日不食、

12. 'It is said in the Book of Poetry,

"He smote the barbarians of the west and the north;
He punished Ching and Shû;
And no one dared to resist us."

These father-deniers and king-deniers would have been smitten by Châu-kung.

13. 'I also wish to rectify men's hearts, and to put an end to those perverse doctrines, to oppose their one-sided actions and banish away their licentious expressions;—and thus to carry on the work of the three sages. Do I do so because I am fond of disputing? I am compelled to do it.

14. 'Whoever is able to oppose Yang and Mo is a disciple of the sages.'

CHAP. X. 1. K'wang Chang said *to Mencius*, 'Is not Ch'ăn Chung a man of true self-denying purity? He was living in Wû-ling, and for three days was without food, till he could neither hear

the parricides, mentioned in par. 7. 12. See Pt. I. iv. 16. The remark in the note there is equally applicable to the quotation here. 13. 詖行,—行, in 2nd tone. Compare Bk. II. Pt. I. ii. 17. 14. This concluding remark is of a piece with the hesitancy shown by Mencius in Bk. II. Pt. I. ii, to claim boldly his place in the line of sages along with Confucius.

10. THE MAN WHO WILL AVOID ALL ASSOCIATION WITH, AND OBLIGATION TO, THOSE OF WHOM HE DOES NOT APPROVE, MUST NEEDS GO OUT OF THE WORLD. 1. Kw'ang Chang and Ch'ăn Chung, called also Ch'ăn Tsze-chung (子終), were both men of Ch'î, the former high in the employment and confidence of the prince, the latter, as we learn from this chapter, belonging to an old and noble family of the State. His principles appear to have been those of Hsü Hsing (Pt. I. iv), or even more severe. We may compare him with the *recluses* of Confucius's time. Wû-ling (於 read *wû*) appears to have been a poor wild place, to which Chung and his wife, like-minded with himself, had retired. It is referred either to the district of Ch'ang-shan or that of Tsze-

耳無聞、目無見也、井上有李、螬食實者、過半矣。匍匐往將食之、三咽、然後耳有聞、目有見。孟子曰、於齊國之士、吾必以仲子爲巨擘焉。雖然、仲子惡能廉、充仲子之操、則蚓而後可者也。夫蚓、上食槁壤、下飲黃泉。仲子所居之室、伯夷之所築與、抑亦盜跖之所築與。所食之粟、伯夷之所樹與、抑亦盜跖之所樹與、是未

nor see. Over a well there grew a plum-tree, the fruit of which had been more than half eaten by worms. He crawled to it, and tried to eat *some of the fruit*, when, after swallowing three mouthfuls, he recovered his sight and hearing.'

2. Mencius replied, 'Among the scholars of Ch'î, I must regard Chung as the thumb *among the fingers*. But still, where is the self-denying purity *he pretends to?* To carry out the principles which he holds, one must become an earthworm, for so only can it be done.

3. 'Now, an earthworm eats the dry mould above, and drinks the yellow spring below. Was the house in which Chung dwells built by a Po-î? or was it built by a robber like Chih? Was the millet which he eats planted by a Po-î? or was it planted by a robber like Chih? These are things which cannot be known.'

ch'wan in the department of Ts'î-nan. The 螬 is a worm proper to excrementitious matter. The term here is used, I suppose, to heighten our sense of the strait to which Chung was reduced by his self-denial. 咽, read *yen*, 4th tone, = 呑, 'to swallow.' 2. 充 = 推而滿之, 'to carry out fully.' 3. Po-î,—see Analects, V. xxii, *et al.* Chih was a famous robber chief of Confucius's time, a younger brother of Hûi of Liû-hsiâ. There was, however, it is said, in high antiquity in the times of Hwang-tî, a noted robber of the same name, which was given to Hûi's brother, because of the similarity of his course. Tâo Chih (the robber Chih) has come to be like a proper name.—As Chung withdrew from human society, lest he should be defiled by it, Mencius shows that unless he were a worm, he could not be independent of other men. Even the house he lived in, and the millet he ate, might be the result of the labour of a villain like Tâo-chih, or of a worthy like Po-î, for anything he could tell.

可知也。(四)曰、是何傷哉、彼身織屨、妻辟纑、以易之也。(五)曰、仲子、齊之世家也、兄戴、蓋祿萬鍾、以兄之祿、爲不義之祿、而不食也、以兄之室、爲不義之室、而不居也。辟兄離母、處於於陵。他日歸、則有饋其兄生鵝者。己頻顣曰、惡用是鶃鶃者爲哉。他日、其母殺是鵝也、與之食之、其兄自外至、曰、是鶃鶃之肉也、出而哇之。(六)以母

4. 'But,' said *Chang*, 'what does that matter? He himself weaves sandals of hemp, and his wife twists and dresses threads of hemp to sell or exchange them.'

5. Mencius rejoined, 'Chung belongs to an ancient and noble family of Ch'î. His elder brother Tâi received from Kâ a revenue of 10,000 *chung*, but he considered his brother's emolument to be unrighteous, and would not eat of it, and in the same way he considered his brother's house to be unrighteous, and would not dwell in it. Avoiding his brother and leaving his mother, he went and dwelt in Wû-ling. One day afterwards, he returned *to their house*, when it happened that some one sent his brother a present of a live goose. He, knitting his eyebrows, said, "What are you going to use that cackling thing for?" By-and-by his mother killed the goose, and gave him some of it to eat. Just then his brother came into the house, and said, "It is the flesh of that cackling thing," upon which he went out and vomited it.

6. 'Thus, what his mother gave him he would not eat, but what

4. 何傷,—compare 無傷 in Bk. I. Pt. I. vii. 8. 織屨,—see Pt. I. iv. 辟, read *pi*, —纑, 'to twist,' as threads of hemp on the knee. This meaning is not found in the dictionary, but Châo Ch'î explains it by 緝績, and 纑 by 練, 'to prepare for weaving.' 5. 蓋,—in 4th tone, as in Bk. II. Pt. II. vi. 1. 祿萬鍾,—see Bk. II. Pt. II. x. 3. 辟,—

孟子

則不食、以妻則食之。以兄之室、則弗居、以於陵則居之。是尚爲能充其類也乎。若仲子者、蚓而後充其操者也。

his wife gives him he eats. He will not dwell in his brother's house, but he dwells in Wû-ling. How can he in such circumstances complete the style of life which he professes? With such principles as Chung holds, a man must be an earthworm, and then he can carry them out.'

the same as 避. 頻顣, used for 顰蹙. 鶃,—read *ni*, the sound made by a goose. 是鶃鶃者,—'this cackler.' 6. 以母則不食 is expanded by Chû Hsî,—以母之食爲不義而不食, 'he considered what his mother gave him to eat not to be righteous, and would not eat it.' Similarly he brings out the force of the 以 in the other clauses. The glossarist of Châo Ch'î treats it more loosely, as in the translation.

BOOK IV.

LÎ LÂU. PART I.

離婁章句上

第一章 孟子曰、離婁之明、公輸子之巧、不以規矩、不能成方員、師曠之聰、不以六律、不能正五音、堯舜之道、不以仁政、不能平治天下。二節 今有仁心仁

CHAPTER I. 1. Mencius said, 'The power of vision of Lî Lâu, and skill of hand of Kung-shû, without the compass and square, could not form squares and circles. The acute ear of the music-master K'wang, without the pitch-tubes, could not determine correctly the five notes. The principles of Yâo and Shun, without a benevolent government, could not secure the tranquil order of the kingdom.

2. 'There are now *princes* who have benevolent hearts and a

With this Book commences what is commonly called the second or lower part of the works of Mencius, but that division is not recognised in the critical editions. It is named Lî Lâu, from its commencing with those two characters, and contains twenty-eight chapters, which are most of them shorter than those of the preceding Books.

1. THERE IS AN ART OF GOVERNMENT, AS WELL AS A WISH TO GOVERN WELL, TO BE LEARNED FROM THE EXAMPLE AND PRINCIPLES OF THE ANCIENT KINGS, AND WHICH REQUIRES TO BE STUDIED AND PRACTISED BY RULERS AND THEIR MINISTERS. 1. Lî Lâu, called also Lî Chû (朱), carries us back to a very high Chinese antiquity. He was, it is said, of the time of Hwang-tî, and so acute of vision, that, at the distance of 100 paces, he could discern the smallest hair. He is often referred to by the Tâoist writer Chwang (莊). Some say that Lî Lâu was a disciple of Mencius, but this is altogether unlikely. Kung-shû, named Pan (written 班 and 般), was a celebrated mechanist of Lû, of the times of Confucius. He is fabled to have made birds of bamboo, that could continue flying for three days, and horses of wood, moved by springs, which could draw carriages. He is now the god of carpenters, and is worshipped by them; see the Lî Chî, Bk. II. Sect. II. ii. 21. There are some, however, who make two men of the name, an earlier and a later. K'wang, styled Tsze-yê (子野), was music-master and a wise counsellor of Tsin, a little prior to the time of Confucius;—see the 左傳襄公,十四年. 六律, 'six pitch-tubes,' put by *synecdoche* for 十二律, or 'twelve tubes,' invented, it is said, in the earliest times, to determine by their various adjusted lengths the notes of the musical scale. Six of them go by the name of *lü* (呂), which are to be understood as comprehended under the phrase in the text. The five notes are the five full notes of the octave, neglecting the semitones. They are called 宫, 商, 角, 徵 (*chi*), 羽;—see on the Shû-ching, II. i. 24. 堯舜之道,—道 is to be taken 'emptily,' meaning the benevolent wish to govern well, such as animated Yâo and Shun. 仁政 is the same

聞、而民不被其澤、不可法於後世者、不行先王之道也。○三節故曰、徒善、不足以為政、徒法、不能以自行。○四節詩云、不愆不忘、率由舊章、遵先王之法而過者、未之有也。○五節聖人既竭目力焉、繼之以規矩準繩、以為方員平直、不可勝用也、既竭耳力焉、繼

reputation for benevolence, while yet the people do not receive any benefits from them, nor will they leave any example to future ages;—all because they do not put into practice the ways of the ancient kings.

3. 'Hence we have the saying:—"Virtue alone is not sufficient for the exercise of government; laws alone cannot carry themselves into practice."

4. 'It is said in the Book of Poetry,

"Without transgression, without forgetfulness,
Following the ancient statutes."

Never has any one fallen into error, who followed the laws of the ancient kings.

5. 'When the sages had used the vigour of their eyes, they called in to their aid the compass, the square, the level, and the line, to make things square, round, level, and straight:—the use of the *instruments* is inexhaustible. When they had used their power

finding its embodiment,=the right art of government, having the same relation to it as the compass to circles, &c. 2. 聞,—4th tone. Observe the correlation of 者 and 也, the last clause assigning the reason of what is said in the preceding ones. 先王之道,—here, and below, the 道 must be taken differently from its application in the last paragraph, and=the 仁政 of that. The commentator 范 refers to king Hsüan of Ch'i (Bk. I. Pt. I. vii) as an instance of the princes who have a benevolent heart, and to the first emperor of the Liang dynasty (A. D. 502–556), whose Buddhistic scrupulosity about taking life made him have a benevolent reputation. Yet the heart of the one did not advantage the State, nor the reputation of the other the empire. 3. 徒善,—here 'simply being good,' i.e. virtue without laws, and 徒法=laws without virtue, the virtue, however, being understood of the 'benevolent heart.' 4. See the Shih-ching, Pt. III. ii. Ode V. st. 2. 5. 繼之以,—literally, 'continued it with.' The line must be understood of the plumb-line, as well as of the marking-line. 準 is rightly translated,—'the level,' but I have not been able to ascertain its original form in China.

之以六律、正五音、不可勝用也、既竭心思焉、繼之以不忍人之政、而仁覆天下矣。○六節 故曰、爲高、必因丘陵、爲下、必因川澤、爲政、不因先王之道、可謂智乎。○七節 是以惟仁者、宜在高位、不仁而在高位、是播其惡於衆也。○八節 上無道揆也、下無法守也、朝

of hearing to the utmost, they called in the pitch-tubes to their aid to determine the five notes:—the use of those *tubes* is inexhaustible. When they had exerted to the utmost the thoughts of their hearts, they called in to their aid a government that could not endure to witness the sufferings of men:—and their benevolence overspread the kingdom.

6. 'Hence we have the saying:—"To raise a thing high, we must begin from *the top of* a mound or a hill; to dig to a *great* depth, we must commence in *the low ground of* a stream or a marsh." Can he be pronounced wise, who, in the exercise of government, does not proceed according to the ways of the former kings?

7. 'Therefore only the benevolent ought to be in high stations. When a man destitute of benevolence is in a high station, he thereby disseminates his wickedness among all *below him.*

8. 'When the prince has no principles by which he examines *his administration,* and his ministers have no laws by which they

In the 前漢書, 本志, Bk. I, we read:—'From the adjustment of weights and things sprang the *lever* (衡). The lever revolving produced the *circle.* The circle produced the *square.* The square produced the *line.* The line produced the *level.*' On the last sentence 韋昭 says:—'They set up the level to look at the line, using water as the equaliser.' 不可勝 (the 1st tone) 用,—see Bk. I. Pt. I. iii. 3. The subject of 可 is the whole of what precedes from 繼. 不忍人, see Bk. II. Pt. I. vi. 1. 6. 因 = 依, 'to conform to,' i. e., here, to take advantage of. The saying is found in the Lî Chî, VIII. ii. 10. 8. This paragraph is an expansion of the last clause of the preceding, illustrating how the wickedness flows downwards, with its consequences. 上,—'the highest,' i. e. the prince. 下, the next 'below,' his ministers. 朝,—*ch'âo,* the 2nd tone, 'the court,' and 工, as opposed to it, the various officers, as having their 'work' to do. 君子

不信道、工不信度、君子犯義、小人犯刑、國之所存者幸也。九節故曰、城郭不完、兵甲不多、非國之災也、田野不辟、貨財不聚、非國之害也、上無禮、下無學、賊民興、喪無日矣。十節詩曰、天之方蹶、無然泄泄。十一節泄泄、猶沓沓也。十二節事君無義、進退無禮、言則非

keep themselves *in the discharge of their duties*, then in the court obedience is not paid to principle, and in the office obedience is not paid to rule. Superiors violate the laws of righteousness, and inferiors violate the penal laws. It is only by a fortunate chance that a State in such a case is preserved.

9. 'Therefore it is said, "It is not the exterior and interior walls being incomplete, and the supply of weapons offensive and defensive not being large, which constitutes the calamity of a kingdom. It is not the cultivable area not being extended, and stores and wealth not being accumulated, which occasions the ruin of a State." When superiors do not observe the rules of propriety, and inferiors do not learn, then seditious people spring up, and *that State* will perish in no time.

10. 'It is said in the Book of Poetry,

"When such an overthrow *of Châu* is being produced by Heaven,
Be not ye so much at your ease!"

11. '"At your ease;"—that is, dilatory.

12. 'And so dilatory may *those officers* be deemed, who serve their prince without righteousness, who take office and retire from

and 小人,—with reference to station. The 也 at the end of the two clauses shows that they are both equally assertive, though the prince, governed and governing by principles of righteousness, will be a law to his ministers. 9. 城郭,—see Bk. II. Pt. II. i. 2. 辟=闢, as in Bk. I. Pt. I. vii. 16. 田野,—'fields and wilds.' 喪,—4th tone. 10. See the Shih-ching, III. ii. Ode X. 2. 蹶,—read *kwei*, the 4th tone. 泄,—î, 4th tone.—From this paragraph it is the ministers of a prince who are contemplated by Mencius. They have their duty to perform, in order that the benevolent government may be realised. 11. 猶沓沓,—we are to understand that this phrase was commonly used in Mencius's time with this acceptation. 12. 非,—used as a verb, 'to

先王之道者、猶沓沓也。十三故曰、責難於君謂之恭、陳善閉邪謂之敬、吾君不能謂之賊。

二章一孟子曰、規矩、方員之至也、聖人、人倫之至也。二欲爲君、盡君道、欲爲臣、盡臣道、二者、皆法堯舜而已矣、不以舜之所以事堯事君、不敬其君者也、不以堯之所

it without regard to propriety, and who in their words disown the ways of the ancient kings.

13. 'Therefore it is said, "To urge one's sovereign to difficult achievements may be called showing respect for him. To set before him what is good and repress his perversities may be called showing reverence for him. *He who does not do these things, saying to himself,* —My sovereign is incompetent to this, may be said to play the thief with him."'

CHAP. II. 1. Mencius said, 'The compass and square produce perfect circles and squares. By the sages, the human relations are perfectly exhibited.

2. 'He who as a sovereign would perfectly discharge the duties of a sovereign, and he who as a minister would perfectly discharge the duties of a minister, have only to imitate—the one Yâo, and the other Shun. He who does not serve his sovereign as Shun served Yâo, does not respect his sovereign; and he who does not rule his people as Yâo ruled his, injures his people.

slander,' or 'disown.' 13. Compare Bk. II. Pt. II. ii. 4. We are obliged to supply considerably in the translation, to bring out the meaning of the last sentence. 賊 may be taken as a verb —'to injure,' or as I have taken it.

2. A CONTINUATION OF THE LAST CHAPTER;—THAT YÂO AND SHUN ARE THE PERFECT MODELS OF SOVEREIGNS AND MINISTERS, AND THE CONSEQUENCES OF NOT IMITATING THEM. 1. 'The compass and square are the perfection of squares and circles;'—but we must understand the meaning as in the translation. So with the 2nd clause. 人倫,—see Bk. III. Pt. I. iv. 8. 2. 二者='these two' things, putting the above clauses abstractly, but we cannot do that so well in English. The force of 而已, according to the 備旨, is 'to show that there is no other way for the sovereign and minister to pursue.'—Of 'the human relations' only that of sovereign and minister is here adduced, because Mencius was speaking with reference

以治民治民、賊其民者也。〔三節〕孔子曰、道二、仁與不仁而已矣。〔四節〕暴其民甚、則身弒國亡、不甚、則身危國削、名之曰幽厲、雖孝子慈孫、百世不能改也。〔五節〕詩云、殷鑒不遠、在夏后之世、此之謂也。

〔三章〕〔一節〕孟子曰、三代之得天下也、以仁、其失天下也、以不

3. 'Confucius said, "There are but two courses, *which can be pursued*, that of virtue and its opposite."

4. '*A ruler who* carries the oppression of his people to the highest pitch, will himself be slain, and his kingdom will perish. If one stop short of the highest pitch, his life will *notwithstanding* be in danger, and his kingdom will be weakened. He will be styled "The Dark," or "The Cruel," and though he may have filial sons and affectionate grandsons, they will not be able in a hundred generations to change *the designation*.

5. 'This is what is intended in the words of the Book of Poetry,

"The beacon of Yin is not remote,
It is in the time of the (last) sovereign of Hsiâ."'

CHAP. III. 1. Mencius said, 'It was by benevolence that the three dynasties gained the throne, and by not being benevolent that they lost it.

to the rulers of his time. 3. If the remark were Mencius's own, we should translate 仁 by 'benevolence.' The term in Confucius rather denotes 'perfect virtue.' By the course of virtue is intended the imitation of Yâo and Shun; by its opposite, the neglect of them as models. 4. By sovereigns, who carry their oppression to the highest pitch, Mencius intends, as his examples, Chieh and Châu, the last kings of the Hsiâ and Yin dynasties. By 'The Dark' and 'The Cruel,' he intends the twelfth (B.C. 781) and tenth (B.C. 878) kings of the Châu dynasty, who received those posthumous indelible designations. I take 削 in the sense of 'weakened' (dictionary 弱), which it elsewhere has in Mencius. 5. See the Shih-ching, III. iii. Ode I. st. 8, an ode of the time of the monarch Lî (厲), intended for his warning. The sovereign of Hsiâ is the tyrant Chieh, and by Yin is intended the tyrant Châu, by whose fate, though he neglected the lesson furnished him by that of Chieh, it is suggested that Lî should be admonished.

3. THE IMPORTANCE TO ALL, AND SPECIALLY TO RULERS, OF EXERCISING BENEVOLENCE. 1. 'The three dynasties' are the Hsiâ, the Shang, and the Châu. It is a bold utterance, seeing the Châu dynasty was still existing in the time of Mencius, though he regarded it as old and ready to vanish away. He has a reference, according to Chû Hsî, to the sovereigns Lî and Yû, men-

仁。(二節)國之所以廢興存亡者、亦然。(三節)天子不仁、不保四海、諸侯不仁、不保社稷、卿大夫不仁、不保宗廟、士庶人不仁、不保四體。(四節)今惡死亡、而樂不仁、是猶惡醉而强酒。

(第四章)(一節)孟子曰、愛人不親、反其仁、治人不治、反

2. 'It is by the same means that the decaying and flourishing, the preservation and perishing, of States are determined.

3. 'If the sovereign be not benevolent, he cannot preserve the throne *from passing from him.* If the Head of a State be not benevolent, he cannot preserve his rule. If a high noble or great officer be not benevolent, he cannot preserve his ancestral temple. If a scholar or common man be not benevolent, he cannot preserve his four limbs.

4. 'Now they hate death and ruin, and yet delight in being not benevolent;—this is like hating to be drunk, and yet being strong *to drink* wine.'

CHAP. IV. 1. Mencius said, 'If a man love others, and no *responsive* attachment is shown to him, let him turn inwards and examine his own benevolence. If he *is trying to* rule others, and his government is unsuccessful, let him turn inwards and examine his wisdom. If he treats others politely, and they do not return his

tioned in the last chapter. 3. 四海,—'the four seas,' i.e. all with them, as subject to the sovereign's jurisdiction. There is a special reference, however, to the sovereign's right to offer all sacrifices:—those peculiar to himself, and those open to others. 社稷,—'the spirits of the land and the grain,' i.e. the spirits securing the stability and prosperity of a particular State, which it was the prerogative of the ruler to sacrifice to. Hence the expression is here used figuratively. See the Lî Chî, Bk. III. iii. 6. 4. 惡,—the verb, in 4th tone, 'to hate, dislike.' 强 (in 2nd tone) 酒,—like the Hebrew idiom, Isa. v. 22. This is spoken with reference to the princes of Mencius's time.

4. WITH WHAT MEASURE A MAN METES IT WILL BE MEASURED TO HIM AGAIN, AND CONSEQUENTLY BEFORE A MAN DEALS WITH OTHERS, EXPECTING THEM TO BE AFFECTED BY HIM, HE SHOULD FIRST DEAL WITH HIMSELF. The sentiment is expressed quite generally, but a particular reference is to be understood to the princes of Mencius's time. 1. 反 is used in a manner common in Mencius, = 'to turn back from the course being pursued, and then to turn inwards to the work of examination and correction.' In the next paragraph, we have it followed by another verb, 求. In 治人, 治 is in 2nd tone, 'to regulate,' 'to try to rule;' in 不治, 治 is in 4th tone, 'to be regulated,' the government being effective. The clauses—愛人不親, &c., are very concise. The paraphrase in the 備旨 thus expands:—爲治者體仁

其智、禮人不答、反其敬。行有不得者、皆反求諸己、其身正、而天下歸之。詩云、永言配命、自求多福。

孟子曰、人有恆言、皆曰、天下國家、天下之本在國、國之本在家、家之本在身。

孟子曰、為政不難、不

politeness, let him turn inwards and examine his own *feeling of* respect.

2. 'When we do not, by what we do, realise *what we desire,* we must turn inwards, and examine ourselves in every point. When a man's person is correct, the whole kingdom will turn to him *with recognition and submission.*

3. 'It is said in the Book of Poetry,

"Be always studious to be in harmony with the ordinances *of God,*
And you will obtain much happiness."'

CHAP. V. Mencius said, 'People have this common saying,—"The kingdom, the State, the family." The root of the kingdom is in the State. The root of the State is in the family. The root of the family is in the person *of its Head.*'

CHAP. VI. Mencius said, 'The administration of government is not difficult;—it lies in not offending the great families. He whom

以愛人,宜乎人之我親矣,而顧有不親焉,則必反其仁,恐我之愛人有未至也,云云, 'He who administers government embodies benevolence to love men, and it is to be expected men will love him. Should he find however that they do not, he must turn in and examine his benevolence, lest it should be imperfect,' &c. 2. 不得=不得其所欲, 'does not get what he wishes.' 皆,—'all,' with reference to the general form of the preceding clause. 3. See Bk. II. Pt. I. iv. 6.

5. PERSONAL CHARACTER IS NECESSARY TO ALL GOOD INFLUENCE. Compare 'The Superior Learning,' text of Confucius, par. 4. The common saying repeated by all probably means:—the kingdom is made up of its component States, and of their component families;—i.e. the families of the great officers. But Mencius takes its meaning more generally, and carries it out a step farther.

6. THE IMPORTANCE TO A RULER OF SECURING THE ESTEEM AND SUBMISSION OF THE GREAT HOUSES. The 'not offending' is to be taken in a moral sense;—the ruler's doing nothing but what will command the admiring approbation of the old and great families in the State. In illustration of the sentiment, a story is related from Liû Hsiang of the duke Hwan of Ch'î. Lighting, one day in hunting, on an old man

得罪於巨室、巨室之所慕、一國慕之、一國之所慕、天下慕之、故沛然德教溢乎四海。

第七章 一 孟子曰、天下有道、小德役大德、小賢役大賢、天下無道、小役大、弱役强、斯二者、天也、順天者存、逆天者亡。二 齊景公曰、既不能令、又不受命、是

the great families affect, will be affected by the whole State; and he whom *any* one State affects, will be affected by the whole kingdom. When this is the case, such an one's virtue and teachings will spread over all within the four seas like the rush of water.'

CHAP. VII. 1. Mencius said, 'When right government prevails in the kingdom, *princes of* little virtue are submissive to *those of* great, and *those of* little worth to those of great. When bad government prevails in the kingdom, *princes of* small power are submissive to those of great, and the weak to the strong. Both these cases are *the rule of* Heaven. They who accord with Heaven are preserved, and they who rebel against Heaven perish.

2. 'The duke Ching of Ch'î said, "Not to be able to command others, and at the same time to refuse to receive their commands, is to cut one's self off from all intercourse with others." His tears

of eighty-three, the duke sought his blessing, that he might attain a like longevity. The old man then prayed, 'May my ruler enjoy great longevity, despising gems and gold, and making men his jewels!' At the duke's request he prayed a second time, that he might not be ashamed to learn even from his inferiors, and a third time, 'May my ruler not offend against his ministers and the people!' This answer offended the duke. 'A son,' he said, 'may offend against his father, and a minister against his ruler. But how can a ruler offend against his ministers?' The old man replied, 'An offending son may get forgiveness through the intercessions of aunts and uncles. An offending minister may be forgiven by the intercession of the ruler's favourites and attendants. But when Chieh offended against T'ang, and Châu offended against Wû;—those were cases in point. There was no forgiveness for them.' 所慕,—'whom they affect,' not what. Observe the force of 故.

7. HOW THE SUBJECTION OF ONE STATE TO ANOTHER IS DETERMINED AT DIFFERENT TIMES. A PRINCE'S ONLY SECURITY FOR SAFETY AND PROSPERITY IS IN BEING BENEVOLENT. 1. Many commentators say that by 大德 and 大賢 reference is made to the sovereign, but the declarations may as well be taken generally. 斯二者天也,—'Heaven,' it is said, 'embraces here the ideas of what must be in reason, and the different powers of the contrasted States (兼理勢言).' This is true, but why sink the idea of a Providential government which is implied in 'Heaven?' 2. 景公,—see Analects, XII. xi. 絶物,—物

絕物也、涕出而女於吳。○三節今也、小國師大國、而恥受命焉、是猶弟子而恥受命於先師也。○四節如恥之、莫若師文王、師文王、大國五年、小國七年、必爲政於天下矣。○五節詩云、商之孫子、其麗不億、上帝既命、侯于周服、侯服于

flowed forth while he gave his daughter to be married to *the prince of* Wû.

3. 'Now the small States imitate the large, and yet are ashamed to receive their commands. This is like a scholar's being ashamed to receive the commands of his master.

4. 'For a prince who is ashamed of this, the best plan is to imitate king Wăn. Let one imitate king Wăn, and in five years, if his State be large, or in seven years, if it be small, he will be sure to give laws to the kingdom.

5. 'It is said in the Book of Poetry,

"The descendants of *the sovereigns of* the Shang dynasty,
Are in number more than hundreds of thousands,
But, God having passed His decree,
They are all submissive to Châu.
They are submissive to Châu,
Because the decree of Heaven is not unchanging.
The officers of Yin, admirable and alert,
Pour out the libations, and assist in the capital *of Châu.*"

is taken as used for 人, 'men,' but the phrase is a contracted one, and = 與人睽絕, 'separated from other men,' or 絕 may be taken actively, which I prefer, and similarly supplemented. 女,—in 4th tone, 'to give a daughter in marriage.' Wû, corresponding to the northern part of the present Cheh-chiang, and the south of Chiang-sû, was in Confucius's time still reckoned a barbarous territory, and the princes of the Middle Kingdom were ashamed to enter into relations with it. The duke Ching, however, yielded to the force of circumstances and so saved himself. The daughter so married soon died. She pined away for her father and her native Ch'î, and was followed to the grave by her husband. The old king of Wû, barbarian as he was, showed much sympathy for his young daughter-in-law. 3. 師,—'to imitate,' 'to make a master of.' Mencius's meaning is that the smaller States followed the example of the larger ones in what was evil, and yet did not like to submit to them. 弟子,—'a youth,' here, = a pupil. 4. 爲政,—'be exercising government,' = giving law to. 5. See the Shih-ching, III. i. Ode I. stt. 4, 5. 不億 = 不止於億, 'not hundreds of thousands only.' 侯于周服 is an inversion for 侯服于周. 侯 is here an introductory particle,

周、天命靡常、殷士膚敏、祼將于京、孔子曰、仁不可爲衆也、夫國君好仁、天下無敵。六節今也欲無敵於天下、而不以仁、是猶執熱而不以濯也、詩云、誰能執熱、逝不以濯。

第八章孟子曰、一節不仁者、可與言哉、安其危而利其菑、樂其所以亡者、不仁而可與言、則何亡

Confucius said, "*As against so* benevolent *a sovereign*, they could not be deemed a multitude." Thus, if the prince of a State love benevolence, he will have no opponent in all the kingdom.

6. 'Now they wish to have no opponent in all the kingdom, but they *do* not *seek to attain this* by being benevolent. This is like a man laying hold of a heated substance, and not having *first* dipped it in water. It is said in the Book of Poetry,

"Who can take up a heated substance,
Without first dipping it (in water)?"'

CHAP. VIII. 1. Mencius said, 'How is it possible to speak with those *princes* who are not benevolent? Their perils they count safety, their calamities they count profitable, and they have pleasure in the things by which they perish. If it were possible to talk with them who so violate benevolence, how could we have such destruction of States and ruin of Families?

一節. 仁不可爲衆 is to be understood as a remark of Confucius on reading the portion of the Shih-ching just quoted;—'against a benevolent prince, like king Wăn, the myriads of the adherents of Shang ceased to be myriads. They would not act against him.' The expansion in the 日講 = 'numerous as the adherents of Shang were, 以我周之人,是衆不可爲(=以爲)衆.' 6. See the Shih-ching, III. iii. Ode III. st. 5. The ode is referred to the time of the sovereign Lî, when the kingdom was hastening to ruin, and in the lines quoted, the author deplores that there was no resort to proper measures. 逝 is taken as a mere particle of transition.

8. THAT A PRINCE IS THE AGENT OF HIS OWN RUIN BY HIS VICIOUS WAYS AND REFUSING TO BE COUNSELLED. 1. Stress must be laid always on the 不 in 不仁. The expression does not

孟子

國敗家之有。二節有孺子歌曰、滄浪之水淸兮、可以濯我纓、滄浪之水濁兮、可以濯我足。三節孔子曰、小子聽之、淸斯濯纓、濁斯濯足矣、自取之也。四節夫人必自侮、然後人侮之、家必自毀、而後人毀之、國必自伐、而後人伐之。五節太甲曰、天作孽、猶可違、自作孽、不可活、此之謂也。

第九章一節孟子曰、桀紂之失天下也、

2. 'There was a boy singing,
"When the water of the Ts'ang-lang is clear,
It does to wash the strings of my cap;
When the water of the Ts'ang-lang is muddy,
It does to wash my feet."

3. 'Confucius said, "Hear what he sings, my children. When clear, then he will wash his cap-strings; and when muddy, he will wash his feet with it. This *different application* is brought *by the water* on itself."

4. 'A man must first despise himself, and then others will despise him. A family must first destroy itself, and then others will destroy it. A State must first smite itself, and then others will smite it.

5. 'This is illustrated in the passage of the T'âi Chiâ, "When Heaven sends down calamities, it is still possible to escape them. When we occasion the calamities ourselves, it is not possible any longer to live."'

CHAP. IX. 1. Mencius said, 'Chieh and Châu's losing the

denote merely the want of benevolence, but the opposite of it. 言＝忠言, 'to give faithful advice to.' 2. The name Ts'ang-lang (in 2nd tone) is found applied to different streams in different places. That in the text was probably in Shan-tung. 3. 聽之,—之 referring to the words of the song. 斯, = 'this,' intensive, or we may take it adverbially:—'*when* clear, then it serves to wash the cap-strings, &c.' 4, 5. See Bk. II. Pt. I. iv. 4–6.

9. ONLY BY BEING BENEVOLENT CAN A PRINCE RAISE HIMSELF TO BE SOVEREIGN, OR EVEN AVOID RUIN. 1. 與之聚之,—與之＝爲

失其民也、失其民者、失其心也、得天下有道、得其民、斯得天下矣、得其民有道、得其心、斯得民矣、得其心有道、所欲、與之聚之、所惡勿施爾也。○二 民之歸仁也、猶水之就下、獸之走壙也。○三 故爲淵毆魚者獺也、爲叢毆爵者鸇也、爲湯武毆民者、桀與紂也。○四 今天下之君、有好仁者、則諸侯皆爲之毆

throne, arose from their losing the people, and to lose the people means to lose their hearts. There is a way to get the kingdom:—get the people, and the kingdom is got. There is a way to get the people:—get their hearts, and the people are got. There is a way to get their hearts:—it is simply to collect for them what they like, and not to lay on them what they dislike.

2. 'The people turn to a benevolent rule as water flows downwards, and as wild beasts fly to the wilderness.

3. 'Accordingly, *as* the otter aids the deep waters, driving the fish into them, and the hawk aids the thickets, driving the little birds to them, *so* Chieh and Châu aided T'ang and Wû, driving the people to them.

4. 'If among the present rulers of the kingdom, there were one who loved benevolence, all the *other* princes would aid him, by

民. Châo Ch'î interprets it,—聚其所欲而與之, taking 與 in the sense of 'to give,' but this does not appear to be admissible here. To collect for the people what they like, is to govern in such a way that they shall enjoy their lives. One has illustrated the meaning from 鼂 (Châo) 錯, of the Han dynasty, who did service in the recovery of the ancient books, thus:—'Men like long life, and the founders of the three dynasties cherished men's lives and kept them from harm: men love wealth, and those kings enriched them, and kept them from straits, &c. &c.' 2. It is best to take 仁 here in the concrete. 走, as it is marked, is in the 4th tone. The dictionary gives it in the same in Bk. I. Pt. I. iii. 2. 3. 爲,—in 4th tone. 毆-驅. 爲淵毆魚者,—'he or that which drives the fish for the deep waters.' The 獺 is the otter. For a curious particular about it, see the Lî Chî, IV. (月令) Sect. i. I. 8. 爵 is given in the dictionary as 鳥名, 'the name of a bird.' Chû Hsî takes it, how-

矣、雖欲無王、不可得已。五節今之欲王者、猶七年之病、求三年之艾也、苟爲不畜、終身不得、苟不志於仁、終身憂辱、以陷於死亡。六節詩云、其何能淑、載胥及溺、此之謂也。

第十章一節孟子曰、自暴者、不可與有言也、自棄者、不可與有爲也、言非禮義、謂之自暴

driving *the people to him.* Although he wished not to become sovereign, he could not avoid becoming so.

5. 'The case of *one of* the present princes wishing to become sovereign is like the having to seek for mugwort three years old, to cure a seven years' sickness. If it have not been kept in store, the patient may all his life not get it. If the princes do not set their wills on benevolence, all their days will be in sorrow and disgrace, and they will be involved in death and ruin.

6. 'This is illustrated by what is said in the Book of Poetry,

"How *otherwise* can you improve *the kingdom?*
You will only with it go to ruin."'

CHAP. X. 1. Mencius said, 'With those who do violence to themselves, it is impossible to speak. With those who throw themselves away, it is impossible to do anything. To disown in his conversation propriety and righteousness, is what we mean by doing violence to one's self. *To say*—"*I* am not able to dwell in bene-

ever, as = 雀, a general name for small birds. 4. 王,—in 4th tone, and in next paragraph also. 5. 苟爲不畜, 終身不得 is by most commentators interpreted:—'If you now, feeling its want, begin to collect it, it may be available for the cure. You can hold on till it is so. If you do not at once set about it, your case is hopeless.' Perhaps the 爲 and 不 should determine in favour of this view. Châo Ch'î interprets as in the translation. The down of the mugwort, burnt on the skin, is used for purposes of cautery. The older the plant, the better. 6. The quotation from the Shih-ching is of the two lines immediately following the last quotation in chap. vii. 載,—a particle, = 則.

10. A WARNING TO THE VIOLENTLY EVIL, AND THE WEAKLY EVIL. 1. 自暴者, 'those who are cruel to themselves,' i.e. those who deny, and act contrary to their own nature. 非, a verb, 'to disown,' 'to condemn.' 與有言, 有

也、吾身不能居仁由義、謂之自棄也。〔二〕仁、人之安宅也、義、人之正路也。〔三〕曠安宅而不居、舍正路而弗由、哀哉。

〔十一〕孟子曰、道在爾、而求諸遠、事在易而求諸難、人人親其親、長其長、而天下平。

〔十二〕〔一〕孟子曰、居下位而不獲於上、民不可得而治也、獲於上有道、不信於友、弗獲

volence or pursue the path of righteousness," is what we mean by throwing one's self away.

2. 'Benevolence is the tranquil habitation of man, and righteousness is his straight path.

3. 'Alas for them, who leave the tranquil dwelling empty and do not reside in it, and who abandon the right path and do not pursue it?'

CHAP. XI. Mencius said, 'The path *of duty* lies in what is near, and men seek for it in what is remote. The work *of duty* lies in what is easy, and men seek for it in what is difficult. If each man would love his parents and show the due respect to his elders, the whole land would enjoy tranquillity.'

CHAP. XII. 1. Mencius said, 'When those occupying inferior situations do not obtain the confidence of the sovereign, they cannot succeed in governing the people. There is a way to obtain the confidence of the sovereign:—if one is not trusted by his friends, he will not obtain the confidence of his sovereign. There is a way

爲,—'to have conversation (words), to have action (doing) with them.' 3. 舍—for 捨, in 3rd tone. The lamentation is to be understood as for the 自暴者 and the 自棄者. —It is observed that 'this chapter shows that what is right and true (道) do really belong to man, but he extirpates them himself. Profound is the admonition, and learners should give most earnest heed to it.'

11. THE TRANQUIL PROSPERITY OF THE KINGDOM DEPENDS ON THE DISCHARGE OF THE COMMON RELATIONS OF LIFE. 爾=邇, with which it was anciently interchanged. 長, in 3rd tone, comprehends elders and superiors. 道,—as in the Chung Yung, i. 1.

12. THE GREAT WORK OF MEN SHOULD BE TO STRIVE TO ATTAIN PERFECT SINCERITY. See the Chung Yung, xx. pars. 17, 18, which are here substantially quoted. As the twentieth chapter of

於上矣、信於友有道、事親弗悅、弗信於友矣、悅親有道、反身不誠、不悅於親矣、誠身有道、不明乎善、不誠其身矣。○是故誠者、天之道也、思誠者、人之道也。○至誠而不動者、未之有也、不誠、未有能動者也、

[十三]孟子曰、伯夷辟紂、居北海之濱、聞文王作、興曰、盍歸乎來、吾聞西伯善養老者、太公

of being trusted by one's friends:—if one do not serve his parents so as to make them pleased, he will not be trusted by his friends. There is a way to make one's parents pleased:—if one, on turning his thoughts inwards, finds a want of sincerity, he will not give pleasure to his parents. There is a way to the attainment of sincerity in one's self:—if a man do not understand what is good, he will not attain sincerity in himself.

2. 'Therefore, sincerity is the way of Heaven. To think *how* to be sincere is the way of man.

3. 'Never has there been one possessed of complete sincerity, who did not move others. Never has there been one who had not sincerity who was able to move others.'

CHAP. XIII. 1. Mencius said, 'Po-î, that he might avoid Châu, was dwelling on the coast of the northern sea. When he heard of the rise of king Wăn, he roused himself, and said, "Why should I not go and follow him? I have heard that the chief of the West knows well how to nourish the old." T'âi-kung, that he might

the Chung Yung, however, is found also in the 'Family Sayings,' Mencius may have had that, or the fragmentary memorabilia of Confucius, from which it is compiled, before him, and not the Chung Yung.

13. THE INFLUENCE OF GOVERNMENT LIKE THAT OF KING WĂN. 1. Po-î,—see Analects, V. xxii, *et al.* T'âi-kung was Lü Shang (呂尙), a great counsellor of the kings, Wăn and Wû. He was descended from one of Yü's assistants in the regulation of the waters, and on his first rencontre with king Wăn, when he appeared to be only a fisherman, Wăn said 吾太公望子久矣, 'My grandfather looked for you long ago.' This led to his being styled 太公望, or 'Grandfather's Hope.' See the

辟紂、居東海之濱、聞文王作、興曰、盍歸乎來、吾聞西伯善養老者。

二 二老者、天下之大老也、而歸之、是天下之父歸之也、天下之父歸之、其子焉往。

三 諸侯有行文王之政者、七年之內、必為政於天下矣。

十四 一 孟子曰、求也、為季氏宰、無能改於其德、而賦粟倍

avoid Châu, was dwelling on the coast of the eastern sea. When he heard of the rise of king Wăn, he roused himself, and said, "Why should I not go and follow him? I have heard that the chief of the West knows well how to nourish the old."

2. 'Those two old men were the greatest old men of the kingdom. When they came to follow king Wăn, it was the fathers of the kingdom coming to follow him. When the fathers of the kingdom joined him, how could the sons go *to any other?*

3. 'Were any of the princes to practise the government of king Wăn, within seven years he would be sure to be giving laws to the kingdom.'

CHAP. XIV. 1. Mencius said, 'Ch'iû acted as chief officer to the head of the Chî family, whose *evil* ways he was unable to change,

'Historical Records,' Bk. XXXII, 齊太公世家, at the beginning. Though Po-î and T'ai-kung were led in the same way to follow king Wăn, their subsequent courses were very different. 辟-避. Wăn was appointed by Châu chief or baron (伯), his viceroy in the West, to be leader of all the princes in that part of the kingdom. The commentators say this is referred to in 文王作. I should rather interpret 作 of Wăn's 'movements,' style of administration. With 善養老者, compare the account of king Wăn's government in Bk. I. Pt. II. v. 3. 盍歸乎來-盍歸來乎. Still the 來 is somewhat embarrassing. 2. I like the expansion of this paragraph in the 日講:—'Moreover, these two old men were not ordinary men. Distinguished alike by age and virtue, they were the greatest old men of the kingdom. Fit to be so named, the hopes of all looked to them, and the hearts of all were bound to them. All looked up to them as fathers, and felt as their children, so that when they were moved by the government of king Wăn, and came from the coasts of the sea to him, how could the children leave their fathers and go to any others?' 3. 為政,—as in chap. vii. 4. Compare Analects, XIII. x-xii, where Confucius thinks he could have accomplished a similar result in shorter time.

14. AGAINST THE MINISTERS OF HIS TIME WHO

他日、孔子曰、求、非我徒也、小子鳴鼓而攻之可也。〇二節由此觀之、君不行仁政、而富之、皆棄於孔子者也、況於爲之强戰、爭地以戰、殺人盈野、爭城以戰、殺人盈城、此所謂率土地而食人肉、罪不容於死。〇三節故善戰者、服上刑、連諸侯者、次之、辟草

while he exacted from the people double the grain formerly paid. Confucius said, "He is no disciple of mine. Little children, beat the drum and assail him."

2. 'Looking at the subject from this case, *we perceive that* when a prince was not practising benevolent government, all *his ministers* who enriched him were rejected by Confucius:—how much more *would he have rejected* those who are vehement to fight for their *prince!* When contentions about territory are the ground on which they fight, they slaughter men till the fields are filled with them. When some struggle for a city is the ground on which they fight, they slaughter men till the city is filled with them. This is what is called "leading on the land to devour human flesh." Death is not enough for such a crime.

3. 'Therefore, those who are skilful to fight should suffer the highest punishment. Next to them *should be punished* those who unite *some* princes in leagues *against others;* and next to them,

PURSUED THEIR WARLIKE AND OTHER SCHEMES, REGARDLESS OF THE HAPPINESS OF THE PEOPLE. 1. See Analects, XI. xvi. Here is a plain instance of 德 used in a bad sense. 2. 爲之强戰,—爲, in 4th tone. 强 I take as in the 3rd tone, and the phrase 强戰 after the analogy of 强酒, chap. iii. 4. Chû Hsî and others take 强 in the 2nd tone, and make the phrase = 'who fight trusting in the powerfulness of weapons and strength (恃兵力之强而戰).' The proposed interpretation seems much preferable. With the whole phrase compare 爲之聚歛, Analects, XI. xvi. The force of the 爲之, it seems to me, must be to make the whole equal to the rendering of Noel, which Julien condemns—'*qui suum principem ad arma adstimulant.*' To be strong to fight for his prince, is a minister's duty. But to encourage a warlike spirit in him, is injurious to the country. 罪不容於死,—其罪大,死刑不足以容之 'his crime is so great that even capital punishment is not sufficient to contain it.' 3. Here we have three classes of adventurers who were rife in Mencius's time, and who recommended themselves to the

萊任土地者、次之。

〔十五〕一節 孟子曰、存乎人者、莫良於眸子、眸子不能掩其惡、胸中正、則眸子瞭焉、胸中不正、則眸子眊焉。二節 聽其言也、觀其眸子、人焉廋哉。

〔十六〕孟子曰、恭者不侮人、儉者不奪人、侮奪人之君、惟恐不順焉、惡得爲

those who take in grassy commons, imposing the cultivation of the ground *on the people*.'

CHAP. XV. 1. Mencius said, 'Of all the parts of a man's body there is none more excellent than the pupil of the eye. The pupil cannot *be used to* hide a man's wickedness. If within the breast all be correct, the pupil is bright. If within the breast all be not correct, the pupil is dull.

2. 'Listen to a man's words and look at the pupil of his eye. How can a man conceal his character?'

CHAP. XVI. Mencius said, 'The respectful do not despise others. The economical do not plunder others. The prince who treats men with despite and plunders them, is only afraid that they may not prove obedient to him:—how can he be regarded as

prince in the ways described, pursuing their own ends, regardless of the people. Some advanced themselves by their skill in war; some by their talents for intrigue; and some by plans to make the most of the ground, turning every bit of it to account, but for the good of the ruler, not of the people. 辟=闢. 萊,—'a kind of creeper,' 'weeds,'=fields lying fallow or uncultivated. 任土地,—the 土地 is what had been occupied by the 草萊. Chû Hsî expands the phrase thus:—'任土地 means,—to divide this land and give it to the people, making them undertake the charge of cultivating it.'

15. THE PUPIL OF THE EYE THE INDEX OF THE HEART. 1. 存乎人者,—存=在, 'the things that are in man,' i. e. in his body. The excellence of the pupil is from its truthfulness as an index of the heart. The whole is to be understood as spoken by Mencius for the use of those who thought they had only to hear men's words to judge of them. 2. Compare Analects, II. x.

16. DEEDS, NOT WORDS OR MANNERS, NECESSARY TO PROVE MENTAL QUALITIES. 恭者, 儉者, though I have translated them generally, are yet spoken with a reference to the 君 that follows. The princes of Mencius's time made great pretensions, of which their actions proved the insincerity. 侮 and 不奪 are to be understood of the disposition:—'not wish to contemn, &c.' 奪, directly governing 人, is remarkable. 爲恭儉,—爲=以爲 or 名爲, 'to be regarded,' 'to be styled.' The

孟子

恭儉、恭儉、豈可以聲音笑貌爲哉。

十七 淳于髡曰、男女授受不親、禮與。孟子曰、禮也。曰、嫂溺、則援之以手乎。曰、嫂溺不援、是豺狼也、男女授受不親、禮也、嫂溺援之以手者、權也。二節 曰、今天下溺矣、夫子之不援、何也。三節 曰、天下溺、援之以道、嫂溺、援之以手、

respectful or economical? How can respectfulness and economy be made out of tones of the voice, and a smiling manner?'

CHAP. XVII. 1. Shun-yü K'wăn said, 'Is it the rule that males and females shall not allow their hands to touch in giving or receiving anything?' Mencius replied, 'It is the rule.' *K'wăn* asked, 'If a man's sister-in-law be drowning, shall he rescue her with his hand?' Mencius said, 'He who would not so rescue the drowning woman is a wolf. For males and females not to allow their hands to touch in giving and receiving is the *general* rule; when a sister-in-law is drowning, to rescue her with the hand is a peculiar exigency.'

2. *K'wăn* said, 'The whole kingdom is drowning. How strange it is that you will not rescue it!'

3. *Mencius* answered, 'A drowning kingdom must be rescued with right principles, as a drowning sister-in-law has to be rescued with the hand. Do you wish me to rescue the kingdom with my hand?'

final 爲 = 作爲, and in the passive, 'to be made.' 聲音, 'tones' = words.

17. HELP—EFFECTUAL HELP—CAN BE GIVEN TO THE WORLD ONLY IN HARMONY WITH RIGHT AND PROPRIETY. 1. Shun-yü K'wăn was a native of Ch'î, a famous sophist, and otherwise a man of note in his day; see the 'Historical Records,' Bk. CXXVI, 列傳, lxvi. He here tries to entrap Mencius into a confession that he did not well in maintaining his dignity of reserve. For the rule of propriety referred to, see the Lî Chî, I. Sect. I. iii. 31. 不親 = 不以手相親接. 權,—see Analects, IX. xxix; XVIII. viii.—豺狼 may be taken together as = 'a wolf.' The names belong to different animals of the same species. See on Bk. VI. Pt. I. xiv. 4. 2. 夫子 is complimentary, as K'wăn was not a disciple of Mencius. 3. Chû Hsî expands here:—'The drowning kingdom can be rescued only by right principles;—the case is different from that of a drowning sister-in-law who can be rescued by the hand. Now you, wishing to rescue the kingdom, would have me, in violation of right principles, seek alliance with the princes, and so begin by losing the

子欲手援天下乎。

〔十八〕一節公孫丑曰、君子之不教子、何也。二節孟子曰、勢不行也、教者必以正、以正不行、繼之以怒、繼之以怒、則反夷矣、夫子教我以正、夫子未出於正也、則是父子相夷也、父子相夷、則惡矣。三節古者、易子而教之。四節父子之間不責

CHAP. XVIII. 1. Kung-sun Ch'âu said, 'Why is it that the superior man does not *himself* teach his son?'

2. Mencius replied, 'The circumstances of the case forbid its being done. The teacher must inculcate what is correct. When he inculcates what is correct, and his lessons are not practised, he follows them up with being angry. When he follows them up with being angry, then, contrary to what should be, he is offended with his son. *At the same time, the pupil says,* "My master inculcates on me what is correct, and he himself does not proceed in a correct path." The result of this is, that father and son are offended with each other. When father and son come to be offended with each other, the case is evil.

3. 'The ancients exchanged sons, and one taught the son of another.

4. 'Between father and son, there should be no reproving ad-

means wherewith to rescue it. Do you wish to make me save the kingdom with my hand?' I hardly see the point of the last question.

18. HOW A FATHER MAY NOT HIMSELF TEACH HIS SON. 1. This proposition is not to be taken in all its generality. Confucius taught his son, and so did other famous men their sons. We are to understand the first clause of the second paragraph,—勢不行也, as referring to the case of a stupid or perverse child. As to what is said in the third paragraph of the custom of the ancients, I have seen no other proof adduced of it. 2. 反,—'contrary,' i.e. to the affection which should rule between father and son. 夷,—in the sense of 傷, which, however, we must take passively; not 'to wound,' but 'to be wounded,' that is, to be offended. We might take it actively in the first instance; —'contrary to what should be, he wounds—i.e. beats—his son.' But below, in 父子相夷, we cannot give it such an active signification as to suppose that the son will proceed to beat his father. 傷 may well be taken passively, as in the common saying, 眼見心傷. 夫子教我, 云云,—this is to be understood as the resentful murmuring of the son, whose feeling is strongly indicated by the use of 夫子, 'my master,' as applied to his father. 3. The commentators all say, that this only means that the ancients sent out their sons to be taught away from home by masters.

善、責善則離、離則不祥、莫大焉。

〔十九章〕孟子曰、事孰爲大、事親爲大、守孰爲大、守身爲大、不失其身、而能事其親者、吾聞之矣、失其身、而能事其親者、吾未之聞也。〔二節〕孰不爲事、事親、事之本也、孰不爲守、守身、守之本也。〔三節〕曾子養曾晳、必有酒肉、將徹、必請所與、問有餘、必曰、

monitions to what is good. Such reproofs lead to alienation, and than alienation there is nothing more inauspicious.'

CHAP. XIX. 1. Mencius said, 'Of services, which is the greatest? The service of parents is the greatest. Of charges, which is the greatest? The charge of one's self is the greatest. That those who do not fail to keep themselves are able to serve their parents is what I have heard. But I have never heard of any, who, having failed to keep themselves, were able *notwithstanding* to serve their parents.

2. 'There are many services, but the service of parents is the root of all others. There are many charges, but the charge of one's self is the root of all others.

3. 'The philosopher Tsăng, in nourishing Tsăng Hsî, was always sure to have wine and flesh provided. And when they were being

But this is explaining away the 易. 4. 責善-以善責之使行, 'laying what is good on them, and causing them to do it.'

19. THE RIGHT MANNER OF SERVING PARENTS, AND THE IMPORTANCE OF WATCHING OVER ONE'S SELF, IN ORDER TO DO SO. 1. 事孰爲大,—literally, 'of services—i.e. duties of service which a man has to pay to others—which is great?' 守,—charges, what a man has to guard and keep. The keeping one's self from all that is contrary to righteousness. 2. 孰不爲事,—'what is not a service?' i.e. the services a man has to perform are many. 本,—in the sense of 'root,' according to the Chinese way of developing all other services from filial piety; see the Hsiâo-ching (孝經), *passim*. There is more truth in the second part of the paragraph. 3. Hsî was Tsăng Shăn's father; see Analects, XI. xxv. 養,—in 4th tone. 'Nourishing the will,' i.e. gratifying and carrying

有、曾晳死、曾元養曾子、必有酒肉、將徹、不請所與、問有餘、曰、亡矣、將以復進也、此所謂養口體者也、若曾子、則可謂養志也。四節事親若曾子者、可也。

二十章孟子曰、人不足與適也、政不足閒也、惟大人、爲能格君心之非、君仁、

removed, he would ask respectfully to whom he should give *what was left*. If *his father* asked whether there was anything left, he was sure to say, "There is." After the death of Tsăng Hsî, when Tsăng Yüan came to nourish Tsăng-tsze, he was always sure to have wine and flesh provided. But when the things were being removed, he did not ask to whom he should give *what was left*, and if *his father* asked whether there was anything left, he would answer "No;"—intending to bring them in again. This was what is called—"nourishing the mouth and body." We may call Tsăng-tsze's practice—"nourishing the will."

4. 'To serve one's parents as Tsăng-tsze served his, may be accepted *as filial piety*.'

CHAP. XX. Mencius said, 'It is not enough to remonstrate with a *sovereign* on account of *the mal-employment of* ministers, nor to blame *errors of* government. It is only the great man who can rectify what is wrong in the sovereign's mind. Let the prince be

out the father's wishes. 4. The 可也 at the end occasions some difficulty. Chû Hsî quotes from one of the brothers Ch'ăng these words:—'To serve one's parents as Tsăng Shăn did his, may be called the height of filial piety, and yet Mencius only says that it might be accepted as such—可也: did he really think that there was something supererogatory in Tsăng's service?' Possibly, Mencius may have been referring to Tsăng's disclaimer of being deemed a model of filial piety. See the Lî Chî, XXI (祭義), ii. 10, where he says:—'What the superior man calls filial piety, is to anticipate the wishes, and carry out the mind of his parents, always leading them on in what is right and true. I am only one who nourishes his parents. How can I be deemed filial?'

20. A TRULY GREAT MINISTER WILL BE SEEN IN HIS DIRECTING HIS EFFORTS, NOT TO THE CORRECTION OF MATTERS IN DETAIL, BUT OF THE SOVEREIGN'S CHARACTER. 適,—read *chih*, = 謫, 'to reprehend.' 閒,—*chien*, in 4th tone. 人 and 政 are to be taken as in the objective governed by 適 and 閒, and 不足 as used impersonally. 與 = 與君, 'with the sovereign.' Châo Ch'î introduces 與 before 閒 as well. He seems

孟子

莫不仁、君義、莫不義、君正、莫不正、一正君、而國定矣。

二十一 孟子曰、有不虞之譽、有求全之毀。

二十二 孟子曰、人之易其言也、無責耳矣。

二十三 孟子曰、人之患、在好爲人師。

二十四 樂正子從於子敖之

benevolent, and all *his acts* will be benevolent. Let the prince be righteous, and all *his acts* will be righteous. Let the prince be correct, and everything will be correct. Once rectify the ruler, and the kingdom will be firmly settled.'

CHAP. XXI. Mencius said, 'There are cases of praise which could not be expected, and of reproach when the parties have been seeking to be perfect.'

CHAP. XXII. Mencius said, 'Men's being ready with their tongues arises simply from their not having been reproved.'

CHAP. XXIII. Mencius said, 'The evil of men is that they like to be teachers of others.'

CHAP. XXIV. 1. The disciple Yo-chăng went in the train of Tsze-âo to Ch'î.

to interpret differently, from the translation, making 人 (= 小人, 'little men') the subject of 不足:—'little men are not fit to remonstrate with their sovereign.' This is plainly wrong, because we cannot carry it on to the next clause. 格 = 正, 'to correct.'—The sentiment of the chapter is illustrated by an incident related of Mencius by the philosopher 荀 (about B.C. 250):—'As Mencius thrice visited Ch'î, without speaking to the king about the errors of his government, his disciples were surprised, but he simply said, *I must first correct his evil heart.*'

21. PRAISE AND BLAME ARE NOT ALWAYS ACCORDING TO DESERT. 虞,—in the sense of 度, 'to calculate,' 'to measure.' For 毀 in the sense here, 譭 is often used in modern language.

22. THE BENEFIT OF REPROOF. 易,—read *i*, in 4th tone, 'easy.' Chû Hsî supposes that this remark was spoken with some particular reference. This would account for the 耳矣, 'simply.'

23. BE NOT MANY MASTERS. Commentators suppose that Mencius's lesson was that such a liking indicated a self-sufficiency which put an end to self-improvement.

24. HOW MENCIUS REPROVED YO-CHĂNG FOR ASSOCIATING WITH AN UNWORTHY PERSON, AND BEING REMISS IN WAITING ON HIMSELF. 1. Yo-chăng,—see Bk. I. Pt. II. xvi. 2. Tsze-âo was the designation of Wang Hwan, mentioned in Bk. II. Pt. II. vi. From that chapter we may understand that Mencius would not be pleased with one of his disciples associating with such

齊。二節樂正子見孟子。孟子曰、子亦來見我乎。曰、先生何爲出此言也。曰、子來幾日矣。曰、昔者。曰、昔者、則我出此言也、不亦宜乎。曰、舍館未定。曰、子聞之也、舍館定、然後求見長者乎。三節曰、克有罪。

二十五 孟子謂樂正子曰、子之從於子敖來、徒餔啜也。我不意子學古之道、而以餔啜也。

2. He came to see Mencius, who said to him, 'Are you also come to see me?' Yo-chăng replied, 'Master, why do you speak such words?' 'How many days have you been here?' asked Mencius. 'I came yesterday.' 'Yesterday! Is it not with reason then that I thus speak?' 'My lodging-house was not arranged.' 'Have you heard that *a scholar's* lodging-house must be arranged before he visit his elder?'

3. *Yo-chăng* said, 'I have done wrong.'

Chap. XXV. Mencius, addressing the disciple Yo-chăng, said to him, 'Your coming here in the train of Tsze-âo was only because of the food and the drink. I could not have thought that you, having learned the doctrine of the ancients, would have acted with a view to eating and drinking.'

a person. 之,—the verb, = 往. 2. The name is repeated at the beginning of this paragraph, the former being narrative, and introductory merely. 亦來,—the 亦, 'also,' is directed against Tsze-âo. Chû Hsî explains 昔者 by 前日, which, in common parlance, means 'the day before yesterday.' But I do not see that it should have that meaning here. 昔 properly means 'formerly,' and may extend to the remotest antiquity. It is used also for yesterday, the time separated from the present by one rest — 息, as if the same sound of the two characters (昔息) determined the meaning. 長 (in 3rd tone) 者 is used before by Mencius of himself—Bk. II. Pt. II. xi. 4.

25. A further and more direct reproof of Yo-chăng. 餔啜 are both contemptuous terms, = our application of 'the loaves and fishes.' 而以餔啜 = 而以餔啜爲也.

孟子

孟子曰、不孝有三、無後為大。舜不告而娶、為無後也、君子以為猶告也。

孟子曰、仁之實、事親是也、義之實、從兄是也。智之

CHAP. XXVI. 1. Mencius said, 'There are three things which are unfilial, and to have no posterity is the greatest of them.

2. 'Shun married without informing his parents because of this,—*lest he should have* no posterity. Superior men consider that his doing so was the same as if he had informed them.'

CHAP. XXVII. 1. Mencius said, 'The richest fruit of benevolence is this,—the service of one's parents. The richest fruit of righteousness is this,—the obeying one's elder brothers.

2. 'The richest fruit of wisdom is this,—the knowing those two

26. SHUN'S EXTRAORDINARY WAY OF CONTRACTING MARRIAGE JUSTIFIED BY THE MOTIVE. 1. The other two things which are unfilial are, according to Châo Ch'î, first, by a flattering assent to encourage parents in unrighteousness; and secondly, not to succour their poverty and old age by engaging in official service. To be without posterity is greater than those faults, because it is an offence against the whole line of ancestors, and terminates the sacrifices to them.—In Pt. II. xxx, Mencius specifies five things which were commonly deemed unfilial, and not one of these three is among them. It is to be understood that here 不孝有三 is spoken from the point of view of the superior man, and, moreover, that the first paragraph simply lays down the ground for the vindication of Shun. 2. 為無後,—為, in 4th tone. 告 implies getting the parents' permission, as well as informing them. But Shun's parents were so evil, and hated him so much, that they would have prevented his marriage had they been told of it.

27. FILIAL PIETY AND FRATERNAL OBEDIENCE IN THEIR RELATION TO BENEVOLENCE, RIGHTEOUSNESS, WISDOM, PROPRIETY, AND MUSIC. 1. 實 is sometimes opposed to 虛, 'what is solid to what is empty, shadowy;' sometimes to 名, 'what is real to what is nominal;' and sometimes to 華, 'what is substantial to what is ornamental,' 'fruit to flower.' In the text it is used in the last way, and I cannot express it better than by the 'richest fruit.' 是也 is emphatic;—'the fruit of benevolence is the service of parents;—*it is*.' So in the other instances. Benevolence, righteousness, &c., are the principles of those, the capabilities of them in human nature, which may have endless manifestations, but are chiefly and primarily to be seen in the two virtues spoken of.—What strikes us as strange is the subject of music. The difficulty has not escaped native commentators. The author of the 集註本義匯參 says, *in loc.*:—'Benevolence, righteousness, propriety, and knowledge are the four virtues, but this chapter proceeds to speak of music. For the principles of music are really a branch of propriety, and when the ordering and adorning which belong to that are perfect, then harmony and pleasure spring up as a matter of course. In this way we have propriety mentioned first, and then music. Moreover, the fervency of benevolence, the exactness of righteousness, the clearness of knowledge, and the firmness of maintenance, must all have their depth manifested in music. If the chapter had not spoken of music, we should not have seen the whole amount of achievement.' The reader may try to conceive the exact meaning of this writer, who also points out another peculiarity in the chapter, which many have overlooked. Instead of 是也 after 樂, 斯二者, as at the end of the other clauses, we have 樂則生矣, 云云, 'showing,' says he, 'most vividly how his admiration was stirred. It is as if from every sentence there floated up a 是也 upon the paper, so true is it that perfect filial piety and fraternal duty reach to spiritual beings, and shed a light over

實、知斯二者、弗去是也、禮之實、節文斯二者、是也、樂之實、樂斯二者、樂則生矣、生則惡可已也、惡可已、則不知足之蹈之、手之舞之。

二十八 一節 孟子曰、天下大悅而將歸己、視天下悅而歸己、猶草芥也、惟舜爲然、不得乎親、不可以爲人、不順乎親、

things, and not departing from them. The richest fruit of propriety is this,—the ordering and adorning those two things. The richest fruit of music is this,—the rejoicing in those two things. When they are rejoiced in, they grow. Growing, how can they be repressed? When they come to this state that they cannot be repressed, then unconsciously the feet begin to dance and the hands to move.'

CHAP. XXVIII. 1. Mencius said, 'Suppose the case of the whole kingdom turning in great delight to an individual to submit to him.—To regard the whole kingdom *thus* turning to him in great delight but as a bundle of grass;—only Shun was capable of this. *He considered* that if one could not get *the hearts of* his parents he could not be considered *a man*, and that if he could not get to an entire accord with his parents, he could not be considered a son.

the world, and then do we know that in the greatest music there is a harmony with heaven and earth.' 2. Julien translates 去 by *abjicere*. To have that meaning, it must have been in the 3rd tone, which it is not. The first 樂 is *yŏ*, 'music;' the other two are *lŏ*, 'to enjoy.' 不知 is used absolutely, = 'unconsciously,' though we might make 知 personal also,—'we do not know.' 足之蹈之,—'the feet's stamping it.' So the next clause.

28. HOW SHUN VALUED AND EXEMPLIFIED FILIAL PIETY. 1. The first sentence is to be taken generally, and not with reference to Shun simply. It is incomplete. The conclusion would be something like—'this would be accounted the greatest happiness and glory.' 芥 is properly 'the mustard plant,' but it is sometimes, as here, only synonymous with 草. 不得, 云云,—all this is the reasoning of Shun's mind. 不得乎,—like 不獲於, in chap. 12. 不順, 'not to obey,' 'not to accord with,' but Chû Hsî and others labour hard to make it out to mean,—'to bring the parents to accord with what is right, so as to be able then

不可以爲子。二節舜盡事親之道、而瞽瞍厎豫、瞽瞍厎豫、而天下化、瞽瞍厎豫、而天下之爲父子者定、此之謂大孝。

2. 'By Shun's completely fulfilling everything by which a parent could be served, Kû-sâu was brought to find delight *in what was good.* When Kû-sâu was brought to find that delight, the whole kingdom was transformed. When Kû-sâu was brought to find that delight, all fathers and sons in the kingdom were established *in their respective duties.* This is called great filial piety.'

fully to accord with them.' 2. Shun's father is known by the name of Kû-sâu, but both the characters denote 'blind,' and he was so styled, it is said, because of his mental blindness and opposition to all that was good. 豫, in the sense of 'to be pleased,' 'joyful,' understood here with a moral application. 'All fathers and sons, &c.,'—i. e. all sons were made to see, that, whatever might be the characters of their parents, they had only to imitate Shun, and fathers, even though they might be like Kû-sâu, were shamed to reformation.

LÎ LÂU. PART II.

離婁章句下

[一章] [一節] 孟子曰、舜生於諸馮、遷於負夏、卒於鳴條、東夷之人也。[二節] 文王生於岐周、卒於畢郢、西夷之人也。[三節] 地之相去也、千有餘里、世之相後也、千有餘

CHAPTER I. 1. Mencius said, 'Shun was born in Chû-făng, removed to Fû-hsiâ, and died in Ming-t'iâo;—a man near the wild tribes on the east.

2. 'King Wăn was born in Châu by *mount* Ch'î, and died in Pî-ying;—a man near the wild tribes on the west.

3. 'Those regions were distant from one another more than a thousand *lî*, and the age of the one *sage* was posterior to that of the other more than a thousand years. But when they got their wish,

1. THE AGREEMENT OF SAGES NOT AFFECTED BY PLACE OR TIME. 1. The common view derived from the 'Historical Records,' Book I, is, that Shun was a native of Chî-châu, corresponding to the modern Shan-hsî, to which all the places in the text are accordingly referred. Some, however, and especially Tsăng Tsze-kû (曾子固), of the Sung dynasty, find his birth-place in Chî-nan in Shan-tung, and this would seem to be supported by Mencius in this passage. There is considerable difficulty with Ming-t'iâo, as we read in the 'Historical Records,' that in the thirty-ninth year of his reign, Shun died, while on a tour of inspection to the south, in the wilderness of Ts'ang-wû (蒼梧), and was buried on the Chiû-î (九疑) hills in Chiang-nan, which are in Ling-ling (零陵). The discussions on the point are very numerous. See the 集證 and 四書拓餘說, *in loc.*; see also on the Shû-ching, Pt. II. No doubt, Mencius was not speaking without book. 東夷之人, literally, 'a man of the eastern Î, or barbarians,' but the meaning can only be what I have given in the translation. So 西夷之人. 2. Châu, the original seat of the House of Châu, was in the present department of Fung-ts'iang, in Shen-hsî. Pî-ying is to be distinguished from Ying which was the capital of Ch'û, and with which the paraphrast of Châo Ch'î strangely confounds it. Chû Hsî says it was near to Făng (豐) and Hâo (鎬), the successive capitals of king Wû. The former was in Hû-hsien (鄠縣), and the latter in Hsien-yang (咸陽), both in the department of Hsî-an. Pî-ying was in the district of Hsien-ning (咸寧) of the same department, and there the grave of king Wû, or the place of it, is still pointed out. 3. 得志行乎中國,—'when they got their wishes carried out in the Middle Kingdom.' We are to understand that their aim was to carry out their principles, not to get the throne. 符 should be called a tally or token perhaps, rather than 'a seal.' Anciently, the sovereign delivered, as the token of investiture, one half of a tally of wood or some precious stone, reserving the other half in his own keeping. It was cut right

歲、得志行乎中國、若合符節。四先聖後聖、其揆一也。

二 一 子產聽鄭國之政、以其乘輿濟人於溱洧。二 孟子曰、惠而不知爲政。三 歲十一月徒杠成、十二月輿梁成、民未病涉也。四 君子平其

and carried their principles into practice throughout the Middle Kingdom, it was like uniting the two halves of a seal.

4. '*When we examine* those sages, both the earlier and the later, their principles are found to be the same.'

CHAP. II. 1. When Tsze-ch'an was chief minister of the State of Chăng, he would convey people across the Chăn and Wei in his own carriage.

2. Mencius said, 'It was kind, but showed that he did not understand the practice of government.

3. 'When in the eleventh month of the year the foot-bridges are completed, and the carriage-bridges in the twelfth month, the people have not the trouble of wading.

4. 'Let a governor conduct his rule on principles of equal justice,

through a line of characters, indicating the commission, and their halves fitting each other when occasion required, was the test of truth and identity. Originally as we see from the formation of the character (符), the tally must have been of bamboo. 4. 先聖後聖 is to be understood generally, and not of Shun and Wăn merely. 其揆一,—揆 is taken as a verb = 度, 'to reckon,' 'to estimate,' and is understood of the mental exercises of the sages. 其揆,—'their mindings,' the principles which they cherished.

2. GOOD GOVERNMENT LIES IN EQUAL MEASURES FOR THE GENERAL GOOD, NOT IN ACTS OF FAVOUR TO INDIVIDUALS. 1. Tsze-ch'an,—see Analects, V. xv. The Chăn and Wei were two rivers of Chăng, said to have their rise in the Mâ-ling (馬嶺) hills, and to meet at a certain point, after which the common stream seems to have borne the name of both the feeders. They are referred to the department of Ho-nan in Ho-nan province. 聽政,—'was hearing the government,' i. e. was chief minister. 乘, 4th tone. Chû Hsî explains 以其乘輿 by 以其所乘之輿, but 乘 so used is in 2nd tone. He so expands, however, probably from remembering a conversation on Tsze-ch'an between Confucius and Tsze-yû, related in the *Chiâ-yü*, Bk. IV. iv, near the end, and to which Mencius has reference. The sage held that Tsze-ch'an was kind, but only as a mother, loving but not teaching the people, and, in illustration of his view, says that Tsze-ch'an, 以所乘之車濟冬涉, 'used the carriage in which he rode to convey over those who were wading through the water in the winter.' 2. The subject here is the action, not the man. The practice of government is to be seen not in acts of individual kindness and small favours, but in the administration of just and beneficent laws. 3. The eleventh and twelfth months here correspond to the ninth and tenth of the present calendar, which follows

政、行辟人可也、焉得人人而濟之。○五節故爲政者、每人而悅之、日亦不足矣。

第三章 一節 孟子告齊宣王曰、君之視臣如手足、則臣視君如腹心、君之視臣如犬馬、則臣視君如國人、君之視臣如土芥、則臣視君如寇讎。二節 王曰、禮、爲舊君有服、何如、斯可爲服矣。○三節 曰、諫行言聽、

and, when he goes abroad, he may cause people to be removed out of his path. But how can he convey everybody across the rivers?

5. 'It follows that if a governor will *try to* please everybody, he will find the days not sufficient *for his work*.'

CHAP. III. 1. Mencius said to the king Hsüan of Ch'î, 'When the prince regards his ministers as his hands and feet, his ministers regard their prince as their belly and heart; when he regards them as his dogs and horses, they regard him as any other man; when he regards them as the ground or as grass, they regard him as a robber and an enemy.'

2. The king said, 'According to the rules of propriety, a minister wears mourning when he has left the service of a prince. How must *a prince* behave that his *old ministers* may thus go into mourning?'

3. Mencius replied, 'The admonitions *of a minister* having been

the Hsiâ division of the year;—see Analects, XV. x. Mencius refers to a rule for the repair of the bridges, on the termination of agricultural labours. 4. 君子=爲政者, 'a chief minister.' 辟 read as 闢. Removing people from the way, when the prince went forth, was likewise a rule of the Châu dynasty; and not only did it extend to the prince, but to many officers and women. See the Châu-lî, Pt. I. vii. 32. 5. 'The days not sufficient,'—i.e. he will not have time for all he has to do.

3. WHAT TREATMENT SOVEREIGNS GIVE TO THEIR MINISTERS WILL BE RETURNED TO THEM BY A CORRESPONDING BEHAVIOUR. 1. 'As his hands and feet,'—i.e. with kindness and attention. 'As their belly and heart,'—i.e. with watchfulness and honour. 'As his dogs and horses,'—i.e. without respect, but feeding them. 'As any other man,'—literally, 'as a man of the kingdom,' i.e. without any distinction or reverence. 'As ground or as grass,'—i.e. trampling on them, cutting them off. 2. The Lî here referred to is mentioned in the 'Ritual Usages;'—see Bk. XI (卷二十三), 68; *et al.* The passage, however, is obscure. 爲舊君,—'for an old prince,' i.e. a prince whose service he has left. The king falls back on this rule, thinking that Mencius had expressed himself too strongly. 3. 膏澤,—'fat and moistening influences,'

膏澤下於民、有故而去、則君使人導之出疆、又先於其所往、去三年不反、然後收其田里、此之謂三有禮焉、如此、則爲之服矣。四今也爲臣、諫則不行、言則不聽、膏澤不下於民、有故而去、則君搏執之、又極之於其所往、去之日、遂收其田里、此之謂寇讐、寇讐、何服之有。

followed, and his advice listened to, so that blessings have descended on the people, if for some cause he leaves *the country*, the prince sends an escort to conduct him beyond the boundaries. He also anticipates *with recommendatory intimations* his arrival in the country to which he is proceeding. When he has been gone three years and does not return, *only* then at length does he take back his fields and residence. This treatment is what is called a "thrice-repeated display of consideration." When a prince acts thus, mourning will be worn on leaving his service.

4. 'Now-a-days, the remonstrances of a minister are not followed, and his advice is not listened to, so that no blessings descend on the people. When for any cause he leaves the country, the prince tries to seize him and hold him a prisoner. He also pushes him to extremity in the country to which he has gone, and on the very day of his departure, takes back his fields and residence. This treatment shows him to be what we call "a robber and an enemy." What mourning can be worn for a robber and an enemy?'

= blessings. 先於其所往 must be supplemented by 稱揚其賢, 欲其收用之, 'mentions and commends his worth, wishing him to be received and used.' 田,—'fields,' = emoluments. 里,—used for an individual residence. We have not had the character in this sense before. The 'thrice-repeated display of consideration' refers, first, to the escort as a protection from danger; secondly, to the anticipatory recommendations; and thirdly, to the long-continued emoluments, in expectation of the minister's return. 4. Here and above, 有故 is not to be taken as 大故, in Bk. III. Pt. I. ii. 1. We must under-

第四章 孟子曰、無罪而殺士則大夫可以去、無罪而戮民、則士可以徙。

第五章 孟子曰、君仁、莫不仁、君義、莫不義。

第六章 孟子曰、非禮之禮、非義之義、大人弗爲。

第七章 孟子曰、中也養不中、才也養不才、故人樂有賢父兄也、如中也棄不

CHAP. IV. Mencius said, 'When scholars are put to death without any crime, the great officers may leave *the country*. When the people are slaughtered without any crime, the scholars may remove.'

CHAP. V. Mencius said, 'If the sovereign be benevolent, all will be benevolent. If the sovereign be righteous, all will be righteous.'

CHAP. VI. Mencius said, 'Acts of propriety which are not *really* proper, and acts of righteousness which are not *really* righteous, the great man does not do.'

CHAP. VII. Mencius said, 'Those who keep the Mean, train up those who do not, and those who have abilities, train up those who have not, and hence men rejoice in having fathers and elder brothers who are possessed of virtue and talent. If they who keep

stand 'wishes to,' or 'tries to,' before 搏執之, for if the minister were really imprisoned, he could not go to another kingdom.

4. PROMPT ACTION IS NECESSARY AT THE RIGHT TIME. 可以, 'may,' = it is time to. If the opportunity be not taken, while the injustice of the ruler is exercised on those below them, it will soon come to themselves, and it will be too late to escape. The 日講 concludes its paraphrase thus:—'We may see how the ruler should prize virtue, and be slow to punish; and how he should be cautious in execution of the laws, ever trying to practise benevolence. If he can indeed embody the mind of God, who loves all living things, and make the compassion of the ancient sages his rule, then both officers and people will be grateful to him as to Heaven, and long repose and protracted good order will be the result.'

5. THE INFLUENCE OF THE RULER'S EXAMPLE. See Pt. I. xx, where the same words are found, but their application is to stimulate ministers to do their duty in advising, or remonstrating with, their sovereign.

6. THE GREAT MAN MAKES NO MISTAKES IN MATTERS OF PROPRIETY AND RIGHTEOUSNESS. 非禮之禮, 非義之義, expressions in themselves contradictory, must be taken with some latitude. 'Respect,' it is said, 'belongs to propriety, but it may be carried so far as to degenerate into flattery,' &c. &c.

7. WHAT DUTIES ARE DUE FROM, AND MUST BE RENDERED BY, THE VIRTUOUS AND TALENTED TO THE YOUNG AND IGNORANT. 中也, 才也

中、才也棄不才、則賢不肖之相去、其閒不能以寸。

【第八章】孟子曰、人有不爲也、而後可以有爲。

【第九章】孟子曰、言人之不善、當如後患何。

【第十章】孟子曰、仲尼不爲已甚者。

【第十一章】孟子曰、大人者、言不

the Mean spurn those who do not, and they who have abilities spurn those who have not, then the space between them—those so gifted and the ungifted—will not admit an inch.'

CHAP. VIII. Mencius said, 'Men must be decided on what they will NOT do, and then they are able to act with vigour *in what they ought to do.*'

CHAP. IX. Mencius said, 'What future misery have they and ought they to endure, who talk of what is not good in others!'

CHAP. X. Mencius said, 'Chung-nî did not do extraordinary things.'

CHAP. XI. Mencius said, 'The great man does not think before-

= 'given the Mean,' 'given abilities.' 中,—the Mean, the rightly ordered course of conduct. Both it and 才 must be taken here in the concrete. 父兄,—as in Bk. III. Pt. I. ii. 3. 如中也, 云云,—by neglecting their duty, the one class bring themselves to the level of the other. 賢 embraces both the 中 and the 才 above. 不肖,—see the Doctrine of the Mean, iv. 以寸,—'with an inch,' i. e. be measured with an inch.

8. CLEAR DISCRIMINATION OF WHAT IS WRONG AND RIGHT MUST PRECEDE VIGOROUS RIGHT-DOING. Literally, 'men have the not-do, and afterwards they can have the do.' 有爲 implies vigour in the action. Châo Ch'î's commentary is:—'If a man will not condescend to take in any irregular way, he will be found able to yield a thousand chariots.'

9. EVIL SPEAKING IS SURE TO BRING WITH IT EVIL CONSEQUENCES. The 當 here, followed by 如何, creates a difficulty. Chû Hsî supposes the remark was made with some peculiar reference. If we knew that, the difficulty would vanish. The original implies, I think, all that I have expressed in the translation.

10. THAT CONFUCIUS KEPT THE MEAN. 已甚者,—i. e. 'excessive things,' but 'extraordinary' rather approaches the meaning. It may strike the student that the meaning is—'Confucius's inaction (= slowness to act) was excessive,' but in that case we should have had 矣, and not 者, at the end. We may compare with the sentiment the Doctrine of the Mean, xi, xiii; Analects, VII. xx, *et al.*

11. WHAT IS RIGHT IS THE SUPREME PURSUIT OF THE GREAT MAN. Compare Analects, IV. x. 不必,—'does not *must;*' he is beyond the habit of caring for that. 惟義所在,—

必信、行不必果、惟義所在。

十二章 孟子曰、大人者、不失其赤子之心者也。

十三章 孟子曰、養生者、不足以當大事、惟送死可以當大事。

十四章 孟子曰、君子深造之以道、欲其自得之也、自得之、則居之安、

hand of his words that they may be sincere, nor of his actions that they may be resolute;—he simply *speaks and does* what is right.'

CHAP. XII. Mencius said, 'The great man is he who does not lose his child's-heart.'

CHAP. XIII. Mencius said, 'The nourishment of *parents when* living is not sufficient to be accounted the great thing. It is only in the performing their obsequies when dead that we have what can be considered the great thing.'

CHAP. XIV. Mencius said, 'The superior man makes his advances *in what he is learning* with deep earnestness and by the proper course, wishing to get hold of it as in himself. Having got

'only that in which righteousness is;' that only is his concern. In fact he can hardly be said to be *concerned* about this. It is natural to him to pursue the right.

12. A MAN IS GREAT BECAUSE HE IS CHILDLIKE. Châo Ch'î makes 'the great man' to be 'a sovereign,' and 其赤子, 'his children,' i. e. his people, and the sentiment is that the true sovereign is he who does not lose his people's hearts. I mention this interpretation, as showing how learned men have varied and may vary in fixing the meaning of these books. It is sufficiently absurd, and has been entirely displaced by the interpretation which is given in the version. The sentiment may suggest the Saviour's words,—'Except ye be converted, and become as little children, ye shall not enter into the kingdom of heaven.' But Christ speaks of the child's-heart as a thing to be regained; Mencius speaks of it as a thing not to be lost. With Christ, to become as children is to display certain characteristics of children. With Mencius, 'the child's-heart' is the ideal moral condition of humanity. Chû Hsi says:—'The mind of the great man comprehends all changes of phenomena, and the mind of the child is nothing but a pure simplicity, free from all hypocrisy. Yet the great man is the great man, just as he is not led astray by external things, but keeps his original simplicity and freedom from hypocrisy. Carrying this out, he becomes omniscient and omnipotent, great in the highest degree.' We need not suppose that Mencius would himself have expanded his thought in this way.

13. FILIAL PIETY SEEN IN THE OBSEQUIES OF PARENTS. 養生者,—者字指養生之事,—'the character 者 refers to the ways by which the living may be nourished.' It belongs to the phrase 養生, and not to 生 alone. 當=爲,—'to be considered,' 'to constitute.' 送死,—literally, 'to accompany the dead,' but denoting all the last duties to them. It=愼終, Analects, I. ix. The sentiment needs a good deal of explaining and guarding. The obsequies are done, it is said, once for all. If done wrong, the fault cannot be remedied. Probably the remark had a peculiar reference. The 日講 supposes it was spoken against the Mohist practice of burying parents with a spare simplicity;—see III. Pt. I. v.

14. THE VALUE OF LEARNING THOROUGHLY IN-

居之安、則資之深、資之深、則取之左右逢其原、故君子欲其自得之也。

十五 孟子曰、博學而詳說之、將以反說約也。

十六 孟子曰、以善服人者、未有能服人者也、以善養人、然後能服天下、天下不心服、而

hold of it in himself, he abides in it calmly and firmly. Abiding in it calmly and firmly, he reposes a deep reliance on it. Reposing a deep reliance on it, he seizes it on the left and right, meeting everywhere with it as a fountain *from which things flow.* It is on this account that the superior man wishes to get hold of what he is learning as in himself.'

CHAP. XV. Mencius said, 'In learning extensively and discussing minutely what is learned, the object *of the superior man* is that he may be able to go back and set forth in brief what is essential.'

CHAP. XVI. Mencius said, 'Never has he who would by his excellence subdue men been able to subdue them. Let *a prince* seek by his excellence to nourish men, and he will be able to subdue the whole kingdom. It is impossible that any one should become ruler of the people to whom they have not yielded the subjection of the heart.'

WROUGHT INTO THE MIND. 深造之,—造, read *ts'áo*, 4th tone, 'to arrive at;' 之 must refer to the 理, or principles of the subject which is being learnt. 以道 is understood of the proper course or order, the successive steps of study, = 依着次序. 其自得 gives the key to the chapter;—'his self-getting,' i. e. his getting hold of the subject so that his knowledge of it becomes a kind of intuition. 資 = 藉, 'to rely on.' The subject so apprehended in its principles is capable of indefinite application. 'He seizes it on the right and left,'—i. e. he no longer needs his early efforts to apprehend it. It underlies numberless phenomena, in all which he at once detects it, just as water below the earth is found easily and anywhere, on digging the surface.—One may read scores of pages in the Chinese commentators, and yet not get a clear idea in his own mind of the teaching of Mencius in this chapter. Châo Ch'î gives 道 a more substantive meaning than in the translation; thus:—'The reason why the superior man pursues with earnestness to arrive at the depth and mystery of 道, is from a wish to get hold for himself of its source and root, as something belonging to his own nature.' Most critics understand the subject studied to be man's own self, not things external to him. We must leave the subject in its own mist.

15. Chû Hsî says, apparently with reason, that this is a continuation of the last chapter, showing that the object of the superior man in the extensive studies which he pursues, is not vain-glory, but to get to the substance and essence of things. 約 conveys the two ideas of condensation and importance.

16. The object of this chapter, say commentators, is to stimulate rulers to do good in sincerity, with a view, that is, to the good of

王者、未之有也。

十七章 孟子曰、言無實不祥、不祥之實、蔽賢者當之。

十八章 徐子曰、仲尼亟稱於水曰、水哉水哉、何取於水也。一節 孟子曰、原泉混混、不舍晝夜、盈科而後進、放乎四海、有本者如是、是之取

CHAP. XVII. Mencius said, 'Words which are not true are inauspicious, and the words which are most truly obnoxious to the name of inauspicious, are those which throw into the shade men of talents and virtue.'

CHAP. XVIII. 1. The disciple Hsü said, 'Chung-nî often praised water, saying, "O water! O water!" What did he find in water *to praise?*'

2. Mencius replied, 'There is a spring of water; how it gushes out! It rests not day nor night. It fills up every hole, and then advances, flowing on to the four seas. Such is water having a spring! It was this which he found in it to praise.

others. I confess it is to me very enigmatical. Paul's sentiment,—'Scarcely for a righteous man will one die, yet peradventure for a good man some would even dare to die,'—occurs to the mind on reading it, but this is clashed with by its being insisted on that 養人以善 has no reference to the nourishing men's bodies, but is the bringing them to the nourisher's own moral excellence. Châo Ch'î takes the first 善 as meaning 威力, 'majesty and strength.' But this is inadmissible. The point of the chapter is evidently to be found in the contrast of 服 and 養.

17. The translation takes 無實 as an adjective qualifying 言, and there is a play on the term in the use of 實 in the two parts. Chû Hsî mentions another view making 無實 an adverb joined to 不祥, 'there are no words really inauspicious;' i.e. generally speaking, 'only those are obnoxious to be regarded as really inauspicious which throw into,' &c. He says he is unable to decide between the two interpretations, and thinks the text may be mutilated. 者 has reference to 言, and not to 人, to 'words,' not to 'men.'

18. HOW MENCIUS EXPLAINED CONFUCIUS'S PRAISE OF WATER. 1. 亟,—read *chî*, the 2nd tone, 'often.' 稱 (in the sense of 'to praise') 於水,—於 marking the objective case, or = found something to praise in water. See Analects, IX. xvi, though we have not there the exact words of this passage. 2. 科=坎, 'a pit,' i.e. every hollow in its course, 是之取爾, '*it was* just the seizing of this.' One commentator brings out the 是之 in this way—以是之故而取之爾. 3. Here, again, the months are those of Châu, corresponding to the present

孟子

爾。三節苟爲無本、七八月之閒雨集、溝澮皆盈、其涸也、可立而待也、故聲聞過情、君子恥之。

〔十九章〕一節孟子曰、人之所以異於禽獸者、幾希、庶民去之、君子存之。二節舜明於庶物、察於人倫、由仁義

3. 'But suppose that the water has no spring.—In the seventh and eighth months when the rain falls abundantly, the channels in the fields are all filled, but their being dried up again may be expected in a short time. So a superior man is ashamed of a reputation beyond his merits.'

CHAP. XIX. 1. Mencius said, 'That whereby man differs from the lower animals is but small. The mass of people cast it away, while superior men preserve it.

2. 'Shun clearly understood the multitude of things, and closely observed the relations of humanity. He walked along the path of benevolence and righteousness; he did not *need to* pursue benevolence and righteousness.'

third and sixth. 雨集, 'the rains are collected.' 溝澮 were channels belonging to the irrigation of the lands divided on the nine-squares system. 可立而待,—we might translate as = 'one may stand and wait till they are dry,' but 立 is often used = 'quickly.' 情 = 實, as in the Great Learning, Commentary, chap. iv.

19. WHEREBY SAGES ARE DISTINGUISHED FROM OTHER MEN;—ILLUSTRATED IN SHUN. 1. It is to be wished that Mencius had said distinctly what the small (幾, the 1st tone, 希) point distinguishing men from birds and beasts was. According to Chû Hsî, men and creatures have the 理 (intellectual and moral principle) of Heaven and Earth to form their *nature*, and the 氣 (matter) of Heaven and Earth to form their *bodies*, only men's 氣 is more correct than that of beasts, so that they are able to fill up the capacity of their nature. This denies any essential difference between men and animals, and what difference it allows is corporeal or material. Châo Ch'î says:—幾希, 無幾也, 知義與不知義之間耳, '幾希 means not much. It is simply the interval between the knowledge of righteousness, and the want of that knowledge.' This is so far correct, but the difference which it indicates cannot be said to be 'not great.'—But it is not the object of Mencius to indicate the character of that which differences men and animals, and not its amount? 幾希 = is something minute. One commentator refers us to the expression in the Shû-ching,—人心惟危道心惟微 (II. ii. 15), as forming a key to the passage. In that, 人心 is the mind prone to err, in distinction from the 道心, 'the mind of reason,' which it is said is minute. 2. Shun preserving and cultivating this distinctive endowment was led to the character and achievements which are here briefly described. The phrase 庶物, it is said, 該得廣, 凡天地間事物皆是, 'covers a wide extent of meaning, embracing all matters and things in heaven and earth.' The 日講 refers to it all the

行、非行仁義也。

二十章 一節 孟子曰、禹惡旨酒、而好善言。二節 湯執中、立賢無方。三節 文王視民如傷、望道而未之見。四節 武王不泄邇、不忘遠。五節 周公思兼三王、以施四事、其有不合者、仰而思之、夜以繼日、幸而

CHAP. XX. 1. Mencius said, 'Yü hated the pleasant wine, and loved good words.

2. 'T'ang held fast the Mean, and employed men of talents and virtue without regard to where they came from.

3. 'King Wăn looked on the people as *he would on a man who was* wounded, and he looked towards the right path as if he could not see it.

4. 'King Wû did not slight the near, and did not forget the distant.

5. 'The duke of Châu desired to unite in himself *the virtues* of those kings, *those founders of the* three *dynasties*, that he might display in his practice the four things *which they did*. If he saw anything in them not suited *to his time*, he looked up and thought about it, from daytime into the night, and when he was fortunate enough to master the difficulty, he sat waiting for the morning.'

governmental achievements of Shun related in the Shû-ching.

20. THE SAME SUBJECT;—ILLUSTRATED IN YÜ, T'ANG, WĂN, WÛ, AND CHÂU-KUNG. 1. In the Chan Kwo Ts'ê (戰國策), which fills up in a measure the space between the period of the Ch'un Ch'iû and the Han dynasty, Part VI, Article 11, we read that anciently a daughter of the Tî (probably Yâo or Shun) caused Î-tî to make wine (? spirits), and presented it to Yü, who drank some of it, and pronounced it to be pleasant. Then, however, he frowned on Î-tî, and forbade the use of the pleasant liquor, saying, 'In future ages, rulers will through this liquor ruin their States.' Yü's love of good words is commemorated in the Shû-ching, II. ii. 21. 2. 無方 may be understood with reference to class or place;—compare the Shû-ching, IV. ii. 5, 8. 3. 'As he would on one who was wounded,' i.e. he regarded the people with compassionate tenderness. 而 is to be read as 如, with which, according to Chû Hsî, it was anciently interchanged. See the Shû-ching, V. xvi. 11, 12, for illustrations of Wăn's care of the people, and the Shû-ching, III. i. Ode VI, for illustration of the other characteristic. 4. 泄, read *hsieh* (as 洩), and defined by Châo Ch'î as meaning 狎, 'to slight.' The adjectives are to be understood both of persons and things. 5. 三王,—i.e. Yü, T'ang, and the kings Wăn and Wû, who are often classed together as the one founder of the Châu dynasty. 'The four things' are what have been stated in the preceding paragraphs. 其 has 事 for its antecedent. 得之,—'apprehended it,' understood the matter in its principles, so as to be able to bring into his own practice the spirit of those ancient sages.

得之坐以待旦。

【二十一章】一節 孟子曰、王者之迹熄、而詩亡、詩亡、然後春秋作。○二節 晉之乘、楚之檮杌、魯之春秋、一也。○三節 其事、則齊桓晉文、其文則史、孔子曰、其義則丘竊取之矣。

【二十二章】一節 孟子曰、君子之澤、五世而斬、小人之澤、五世

CHAP. XXI. 1. Mencius said, 'The traces of sovereign rule were extinguished, and the *royal* odes ceased to be made. When those odes ceased to be made, then the Ch'un Ch'iû was produced.

2. 'The Shăng of Tsin, the Tâo-wû of Ch'û, and the Ch'un Ch'iû of Lû were books of the same character.

3. 'The subject of *the* Ch'un Ch'iû was the affairs of Hwan of Ch'î and Wăn of Tsin, and its style was the historical. Confucius said, "Its *righteous* decisions I ventured to make."'

CHAP. XXII. 1. Mencius said, 'The influence of a sovereign sage terminates in the fifth generation. The influence of a mere sage does the same.

21. THE SAME SUBJECT;—ILLUSTRATED IN CONFUCIUS. 1. The extinction of the true royal rule of Châu dates from the transference of the capital from Făng and Hâo to Lo by the sovereign P'ing, B.C. 769. From that time, the sovereigns of Châu had the name without the rule. By the 詩 is intended, not the Book of Poems, but the Yâ (雅) portion of them, descriptive of the royal rule of Châu, and to be used on great occasions. 亡 does not mean that the Yâ were lost, but that no additions were made to them, and they degenerated into mere records of the past, and were no longer descriptions of the present. Confucius edited the annals of Lû to supply the place of the Yâ. See Bk. III. Pt. II. ix. 8. 2. Each State had its annals. Those of Tsin were compiled under the name of *Shăng* (4th tone), 'The Carriage;' those of Ch'û under that of *Tâo-wû*, which is explained as the name of a ferocious animal, and more anciently as the denomination of a vile and lawless man. The annals of Lû had the name of 'Spring and Autumn,' two seasons for the whole. 3. 其 refers only to the annals of Lû. They did not contain only the affairs of Hwan and Wăn, but these occupied an early and prominent place in them. 竊,—see Bk. II. Pt. I. ii. 20. 取 makes the expression still more humble, as if Confucius had 'taken' the judgments from the historians, and not made them himself.

22. THE SAME SUBJECT;—ILLUSTRATED IN MENCIUS HIMSELF. 1. Here 君子=聖賢有位者, 'the sage and worthy, who has position,' i. e. who occupies the throne, and 小人=聖賢無位者, 'the sage and worthy, who has no position.' We might suppose that the influence of the former would be more permanent, but Mencius is pleased to say their influence lasts the same time. 澤 is to be taken as = 'influence,' it being understood to

而斬。(二節)予未得爲孔子徒也、予私淑諸人也。

〔廿三章〕孟子曰、可以取、可以無取、取傷廉、可以與、可以無與、與傷惠、可以死、可以無死、死傷勇。

〔廿四章〕逢(一節)蒙學射於羿、盡羿之道、思天下惟羿爲愈己、於是殺羿。孟子曰、是亦羿有罪焉、公明儀曰、

2. 'Although I could not be a disciple of Confucius himself, I have endeavoured to cultivate my virtue by means of others *who were*.'

CHAP. XXIII. Mencius said, 'When it appears proper to take a thing, and *afterwards* not proper, to take it is contrary to moderation. When it appears proper to give a thing and *afterwards* not proper, to give it is contrary to kindness. When it appears proper to sacrifice one's life, and *afterwards* not proper, to sacrifice it is contrary to bravery.'

CHAP. XXIV. 1. P'ang Măng learned archery of Î. When he had acquired completely all the science of Î, he thought that in all the kingdom only Î was superior to himself, and so he slew him. Mencius said, 'In this case Î also was to blame. Kung-ming Î *indeed* said, "It would appear as if he were not to be blamed," but

be of a beneficial character. 2. From the death of Confucius to the birth of Mencius there would be nearly a hundred years, so that, though Mencius could not learn his doctrines from the sage himself, he did so from his grandson Tsze-sze, or some of his disciples. 私 = 竊 in last chapter. 淑 = 善 taken actively. 諸人 = 於人, the 人 referring to Tsze-sze and his school. This and the three preceding chapters should be considered as one, whose purpose is much the same as Bk. III. Pt. II. ix, showing us that Mencius considered himself the successor of Confucius in the line of sages.

23. FIRST JUDGMENTS ARE NOT ALWAYS CORRECT. IMPULSES MUST BE WEIGHED IN THE BALANCE OF REASON, AND WHAT REASON DICTATES MUST BE FOLLOWED. Such is the meaning of this chapter, in translating the separate clauses of which, we must supplement them by introducing 'afterwards.'

24. THE IMPORTANCE OF BEING CAREFUL OF WHOM WE MAKE FRIENDS. The sentiment is good, but Mencius could surely have found better illustrations of it than the second one which he selected. 1. Of Î, see Analects, XIV. xiv. 逢 (P'ang, as formed with 夅, not 夆) 蒙 is said both by Châo Ch'î and Chû Hsî to refer to Î's servants (家衆), but one man is evidently denoted by the name. Î's servants did indeed make themselves parties to his murder, but P'ang Măng is the same, I suppose, with Han Tsû, the principal in it. 云爾,— see Bk. II. Pt. II. ii. 4, and Analects, VII. xviii. 曰薄乎云爾, 'saying, (meaning to say),

孟子

宜若無罪焉、曰、薄乎云爾、惡得無罪。

二 鄭人使子濯孺子侵衞、衞使庾公之斯追之、子濯孺子曰、今日我疾作、不可以執弓、吾死矣夫、問其僕曰、追我者誰也。其僕曰、庾公之斯也。曰、吾生矣。其僕曰、庾公之斯、衞之善射者也、夫子曰、吾生、何謂也。曰、庾公之斯、學射於尹公之他、尹公之他學射於我、夫尹公之他端人也、其取友必端矣。庾公之斯至、曰、夫子何爲不執弓。曰、

he thereby only meant that his blame was slight. How can he be held without *any* blame?'

2. 'The people of Chăng sent Tsze-cho Yü to make a stealthy attack on Wei, which sent Yü-kung Sze to pursue him. Tsze-cho Yü said, "To-day I feel unwell, so that I cannot hold my bow. I am a dead man!" *At the same time* he asked his driver, "Who is it that is pursuing me?" The driver said, "It is Yü-kung Sze," *on which* he exclaimed, "I shall live." The driver said, "Yü-kung Sze is the best archer of Wei, what do you mean by saying 'I shall live?'" *Yü* replied, "Yü-kung Sze learned archery from Yin-kung T'o, who again learned it from me. Now, Yin-kung T'o is an upright man, and the friends of his selection must be upright *also*." When Yü-kung Sze came up, he said, "Master, why are you not holding your bow?"

It was slighter than . . . simply.' 2. 侵, 'to attack stealthily.' An incursion made with music, and the pomp of war, is called 伐, and one without these, 侵. The 之, in the names—庾公之斯 and 尹公之佗, are mere vocal particles. 他,—read t'o. The name is elsewhere found 尹公佗. In the 左傳, under the fourteenth year of duke

今日我疾作、不可以執弓。曰、小人學射於尹公之他、尹公之他學射於夫子、我不忍以夫子之道、反害夫子、雖然、今日之事、君事也、我不敢廢。抽矢扣輪、去其金、發乘矢而後反。

[二十五章] 孟子曰、一節 西子蒙不潔、則人皆掩鼻而過之。二節 雖有惡人、齊戒沐浴、則可以祀上

Yü answered him, "To-day I am feeling unwell, and cannot hold my bow." *On this Sze* said, "I learned archery from Yin-kung T'o, who again learned it from you. I cannot bear to injure you with your own science. The business of to-day, however, is the prince's business, which I dare not neglect." He then took his arrows, knocked off their steel points against the carriage-wheel, discharged four of them, and returned.'

CHAP. XXV. 1. Mencius said, 'If the lady Hsî had been covered with a filthy *head-dress*, all people would have stopped their noses in passing her.

2. 'Though a man may be wicked, yet if he adjust his thoughts, fast, and bathe, he may sacrifice to God.'

襄, we have a narrative bearing some likeness to this account of Mencius, and in which 尹公佗 and 庾公差 figure as famous archers of Wei. It is hardly possible, however, to suppose that the two accounts are of the same thing. 乘, 4th tone, 'a team of four horses,' here used for a set of four arrows.

25. IT IS ONLY MORAL BEAUTY THAT IS TRULY EXCELLENT AND ACCEPTABLE. 1. Hsî-tsze, or 'Western lady,' was a poor girl of Yüeh, named Shih Î (施夷), of surpassing beauty, presented by the king of Yüeh to his enemy the king of Wû, who became devotedly attached to her, and neglected all the duties of his government. She was contemporary with Confucius. The common account is that she was called 'The western lady,' because she lived on the western bank of a certain stream. If we may receive the works of 管子, however, as having really proceeded from that scholar and statesman, there had been a celebrated beauty named Hsî-tsze, two hundred years before the one of Yüeh. In translating 蒙不潔, I have followed Châo Ch'î. 2. 惡, both by Châo Ch'î and Chû Hsî, is taken in the sense of 'ugly,' in opposition to the beauty of the lady Hsî. I cannot but think Mencius intended it in the sense of 'wicked,' and that his object was to encourage men to repentance and well-doing. 齊,—read *châi*. See Analects, VII. xii, *et al.* By the laws of China, it was competent for the sovereign only to sacrifice to God. The language of Mencius, in connexion with this fact, very strikingly shows the virtue he attached to penitent purification.

帝。

二十六章 一節 孟子曰、天下之言性也、則故而已矣、故者以利爲本。二節 所惡於智者、爲其鑿也、如智者若禹之行水也、則無惡於智矣、禹之行水也、行其所無事也、如智者亦行其所無事、則智亦大矣。三節 天之高也、星辰之遠也、苟求

CHAP. XXVI. 1. Mencius said, 'All who speak about the natures *of things*, have in fact only their phenomena *to reason from*, and the value of a phenomenon is in its being natural.

2. 'What I dislike in your wise men is their boring out *their conclusions*. If those wise men would only act as Yü did when he conveyed away the waters, there would be nothing to dislike in their wisdom. The manner in which Yü conveyed away the waters was by doing what gave him no trouble. If your wise men would also do that which gave them no trouble, their knowledge would also be great.

3. 'There is heaven so high; there are the stars so distant. If

26. HOW KNOWLEDGE OUGHT TO BE PURSUED BY THE CAREFUL STUDY OF PHENOMENA. Mencius here points out correctly the path to knowledge. The rule which he lays down is quite in harmony with that of Bacon. It is to be regretted that in China, more perhaps than in any other part of the world, it has been disregarded. 1. 性 is here to be taken quite generally. Julien finds fault with Noel for translating it by *rerum natura*, which appears to be quite correct. Chû Hsî makes it = 人物所得以生之理, than which nothing could be more general. Possibly Mencius may have had in view the disputes about the nature of man which were rife in his time, but the references to Yü's labours with the waters, and to the studies of astronomers, show that the term is used in its most general signification. 故 = our 'phenomenon,' the nature in its development. The character is often used as synonymous with 事, 'facts.' 則 is more than a simple conjunction, and is to be taken in close connexion with the 而已; Châo Ch'î explains—則以故而已, 'can only do so by the 故.' And phenomena, to be valuable, must be natural. 利 = 順, 'following easily,' 'unconstrained.' 2. 智者 is the would-be wise = 'your wise men.' 其鑿, 'their chiselling,' or 'boring,' i.e. their forcing things, instead of 'waiting' for them, which is a 行其所事, 'doing that in which they have *many* affairs, or much to do.' Yü is said 行水, rather than, according to the common phraseology about his labours, 治水, because 行 more appropriately represents the mode of his dealing with the waters, according to their nature, and not by a system of force. 3. 千歲之日至, according to modern scholars, refers to the winter solstice, from the midnight of which, it

其故、千歲之日至、可坐而致也。一節

二十七章 公行子有子之喪、右師往弔、入門、有進而與右師言者、有就右師之位、而與右師言者。二節 孟子不與右師言、右師不悅、曰、諸君子皆與驩言、孟子獨不與驩言、是簡驩也。三節 孟子聞之、曰、禮、朝廷不歷位而相與言、不

we have investigated their phenomena, we may, while sitting *in our places*, go back to the solstice of a thousand years *ago*.'

CHAP. XXVII. 1. The officer Kung-hang having on hand the funeral of one of his sons, the Master of the Right went to condole with him. When *this noble* entered the door, some called him to them and spoke with him, and some went to his place and spoke with him.

2. Mencius did not speak with him, so that he was displeased, and said, 'All the gentlemen have spoken with me. There is only Mencius who does not speak to me, thereby slighting me.'

3. Mencius having heard of this remark, said, 'According to the prescribed rules, in the court, individuals may not change their places to speak with one another, nor may they pass from their ranks to

is supposed, the first calculation of time began; 一致是推致而得之, 'we may calculate up to and get it.' Châo Ch'î, however, makes the meaning to be simply:—'We may sit and determine on what day the solstice occurred a thousand years ago.' See the 四書拓餘說, where this view is approved.

27. HOW MENCIUS WOULD NOT IMITATE OTHERS IN PAYING COURT TO A FAVOURITE. 1. Kung-hang (2nd tone, 'a rank,' 'a row;' various accounts are given of the way in which the term passed along with 公 into a double surname) was an officer of Ch'î, who 'had the funeral of a son.' Neither Châo Ch'î nor Chû Hsî offers any remark on the phrase, but some scholars of the Sung dynasty, subsequent to Chû Hsî, explained it as meaning, 有人子之喪, 'had the funeral duty that devolves on a son,' i. e. was occupied with the funeral of one of his parents, and nearly all commentators have since followed that view. The author of the 四書拓餘說, *in loc.*, shows clearly however, that it is incorrect, and that the true interpretation is the more natural one given in the translation. The Master of the Right here was Wang Hwan (see Bk. II. Pt. II. vi), styled Tsze-âo. At the royal court there were the high nobles, called 太師 and 少師, 'Grand Master' and 'Junior Master.' In the courts of the princes, the corresponding nobles were called 左師 and 右師, 'Master of the Left' and 'Master of

踰階而相揖也、我欲行禮、子敖以我爲簡、不亦異乎。

[二十八]一節 孟子曰、君子所以異於人者、以其存心也、君子以仁存心、以禮存心。○二節 仁者愛人、有禮者敬人。○三節 愛人者、人恆愛之、敬人者、人恆敬之。○四節 有人於此、其待我以橫逆、則君子必自反也、我必不仁也、必無禮也、此物奚宜至哉。○五節 其自反而仁矣、

bow to one another. I was wishing to observe this rule, and Tsze-âo understands it that I was slighting him:—is not this strange?'

CHAP. XXVIII. 1. Mencius said, 'That whereby the superior man is distinguished from other men is what he preserves in his heart;—namely, benevolence and propriety.

2. 'The benevolent man loves others. The man of propriety shows respect to others.

3. 'He who loves others is constantly loved by them. He who respects others is constantly respected by them.

4. 'Here is a man, who treats me in a perverse and unreasonable manner. The superior man in such a case will turn round upon himself—"I must have been wanting in benevolence; I must have been wanting in propriety;—how should this have happened to me?"

5. 'He examines himself, and is *specially* benevolent. He turns

the Right.' 進,—as in Analects, VII. xxx. 2. It is to be understood that all the condolers made their visit by the prince's order, and were consequently to observe the court rules. This is the explanation of Mencius's conduct. 3. 禮 refers to the established usages of the court; see the Châu Lî, Bk. III. v. 65–67; Bk. IV. iv. 3–14; *et al.* 階, 'steps,' or 'stairs,' but here for the ranks of the officers arranged with reference to the steps leading up to the hall.

28. HOW THE SUPERIOR MAN IS DISTINGUISHED BY THE CULTIVATION OF MORAL EXCELLENCE, AND IS PLACED THEREBY BEYOND THE REACH OF CALAMITY. 1. 存心 must not be understood—'he preserves his heart.' The first definition of 存 in K'ang-hsî's dictionary is 在, 'to be in.' It is not so much an active verb, 'to preserve,' as = 'to preserve in.' 4. 橫 (4th tone) 逆 presuppose the exercise of love and respect, which are done despite to. 此物 = 此事. 5. 由 is used for 猶, as often elsewhere. 忠, in

自反而有禮矣、其橫逆由是也、君子必自反也、我必不忠。六節自反而忠矣、其橫逆由是也、君子曰、此亦妄人也已矣、如此、則與禽獸奚擇哉、於禽獸又何難焉。七節是故君子有終身之憂、無一朝之患也。乃若所憂、則有之、舜、人也、我、亦人也、舜爲法於天下、可傳於後世、我由未免爲鄉人也、是則可憂也、憂之如何、如舜而已

round upon himself, and is *specially* observant of propriety. The perversity and unreasonableness of the other, *however*, are still the same. The superior man will *again* turn round on himself—"I must have been failing to do my utmost."

6. 'He turns round upon himself, and proceeds to do his utmost, but still the perversity and unreasonableness of the other are repeated. *On this* the superior man says, "This is a man utterly lost indeed! Since he conducts himself so, what is there to choose between him and a brute? Why should I go to contend with a brute?"

7. 'Thus it is that the superior man has a life-long anxiety and not one morning's calamity. As to what is matter of anxiety to him, that *indeed* he has.—*He says*, "Shun was a man, and I also am a man. *But* Shun became an example to all the kingdom, and *his conduct* was worthy to be handed down to after ages, while I am nothing better than a villager." This indeed is the proper matter of anxiety to him. And in what way is he anxious about it? Just that he may be like

the sense of 盡已, 'doing one's utmost.' 6. 難, 4th tone,=校, 'to compare with.' It is explained in the dictionary, with reference to this passage, by 責, 'to charge,' 'to reprove.' 7. 憂,—proceeding from within; 患,—coming from without. 一朝之患 must be understood from the expressions below:—There may be calamity, but the superior man is superior to it. 乃, 'but.' We must supply,—'He should be without anxiety, *but* he has anxiety.' 若夫,—夫, 2nd tone. 亡=無.

矣、若夫君子所患、則亡矣、非仁無爲也、非禮無行也、如有一朝之患、則君子不患矣。

廿九 一節 禹稷當平世、三過其門而不入、孔子賢之。二節 顏子當亂世、居於陋巷、一簞食、一瓢飲、人不堪其憂、顏子不改其樂、孔子賢之。三節 孟子曰、禹稷顏回同道。四節 禹思天下有溺者、由己溺之也、稷思天下有飢者、由己

Shun:—then only will he stop. As to what the superior man would feel to be a calamity, there is no such thing. He does nothing which is not according to propriety. If there should befall him one morning's calamity, the superior man does not account it a calamity.'

CHAP. XXIX. 1. Yü and Chî, in an age when the world was being brought back to order, thrice passed their doors without entering them. Confucius praised them.

2. The disciple Yen, in an age of disorder, dwelt in a mean narrow lane, having his single bamboo-cup of rice, and his single gourd-dish of water; other men could not have endured the distress, but he did not allow his joy to be affected by it. Confucius praised him.

3. Mencius said, 'Yü, Chî, and Yen Hûi agreed in the principle of their conduct.

4. 'Yü thought that if any one in the kingdom were drowned, it was as if he drowned him. Chî thought that if any one in the kingdom suffered hunger, it was as if he famished him. It was on this account that they were so earnest.

29. A RECONCILING PRINCIPLE WILL BE FOUND TO UNDERLIE THE OUTWARDLY DIFFERENT CONDUCT OF GREAT AND GOOD MEN;—IN HONOUR OF YEN HÛI, WITH A REFERENCE TO MENCIUS HIMSELF. 1. See Bk. III. Pt. I. iv. 6, 7, 8. The thrice passing his door without entering it was proper to Yü, though it is here attributed also to Chî. 賢,—used as a verb, 'to pronounce a worthy,'—'to praise.' 2. See Analects, VI. ix. 平世 and 亂世 are contrasted, but a tranquil age was not a characteristic of Yü and Chî's time. It was an age of tranquillization. 3. 同道,—道 = 理之當然, 'what was proper in principle.' 4. 由,—used for 猶.

飢之也、是以如是其急也。五節禹稷顏子、易地則皆然。六節今有同室之人鬭者、救之、雖被髮纓冠而救之、可也。七節鄉鄰有鬭者、被髮纓冠而往救之、則惑也、雖閉戶、可也。

三十章一節公都子曰、匡章通國皆稱不孝焉、夫子與之遊、又從而禮貌之、敢問

5. 'If Yü and Chî, and Yen-tsze, had exchanged places, each would have done what the other did.

6. 'Here now in the same apartment with you are people fighting:—*you ought to* part them. Though you part them with your cap simply tied over your unbound hair, your conduct will be allowable.

7. 'If the fighting be *only* in the village or neighbourhood, if you go to put an end to it with your cap tied over your hair unbound, you will be in error. Although you should shut your door *in such a case*, your conduct would be allowable.'

CHAP. XXX. 1. The disciple Kung-tû said, 'Throughout the whole kingdom everybody pronounces K'wang Chang unfilial. But you, Master, keep company with him, and moreover treat him with politeness. I venture to ask why you do so.'

5. 則皆然, literally, 'then all so,' the meaning being as in the translation. Yen Hûi, in the circumstances of Yü and Chî, would have been found labouring with as much energy and self-denial for the public good as they showed; and Yü and Chî, in the circumstances of Hûi, would have lived in obscurity, contented as he was, and happy in the pursuit of the truth and in cultivation of themselves. 6. 被,—read *p'i*, 2nd tone. The rules anciently prescribed for dressing were very minute. Much had to be done with the hair before the final act of putting on the cap, and tying its strings (纓) under the chin, could be performed. In the case in the text, all this is neglected. The urgency of the case, and the intimacy of the individual with the parties quarrelling, justify such neglect. 救之,—literally, 'to save them,' i.e. to part them. This was the case of Yü and Chî, in their relation to their times, while that in the next paragraph is supposed to illustrate the case of Yen Hûi in relation to his. But Mencius's illustrations are generally happier than these.

30. HOW MENCIUS EXPLAINED HIS FRIENDLY INTERCOURSE WITH A MAN CHARGED WITH BEING UNFILIAL. 1. K'wang Chang was an officer of Ch'î. His name, according to 顧麟士, was Chang, and designation Chang-tsze, so that Kung-tû calls him by his name, and Mencius by his designation. In opposition to this, 蔡虛齋 says that Kung-tû merely drops a part of the designation, just as when Yen Hûi is called Yen Yüan, instead of Yen Tsze-yüan. But both these explanations are to be rejected. Chang was the name, and the

何也。○二節孟子曰、世俗所謂不孝者五、惰其四支、不顧父母之養、一不孝也、博弈好飲酒、不顧父母之養、二不孝也、好貨財、私妻子、不顧父母之養、三不孝也、從耳目之欲、以爲父母戮、四不孝也、好勇鬬狠、以危父母、五不孝也、章子有一於是乎。○三節夫章子、子父責善、而不相遇也。○四節責善、朋友之道也、

2. Mencius replied, 'There are five things which are pronounced in the common usage of the age to be unfilial. The first is laziness in the use of one's four limbs, without attending to the nourishment of his parents. The second is gambling and chess-playing, and being fond of wine, without attending to the nourishment of his parents. The third is being fond of goods and money, and selfishly attached to his wife and children, without attending to the nourishment of his parents. The fourth is following the desires of one's ears and eyes, so as to bring his parents to disgrace. The fifth is being fond of bravery, fighting and quarrelling so as to endanger his parents. Is Chang guilty of any one of these things?

3. 'Now between Chang and his father there arose disagreement, he, the son, reproving his father, to urge him to what was good.

4. 'To urge one another to what is good by reproofs is the way of friends. But such urging between father and son is the greatest injury to the kindness, *which should prevail between them.*

子 in 章子 is simply equivalent to our Mr. 與之遊, 'ramble with him,' i.e. as commonly understood, 'allow him to come about your gate, your school.' 又從, 'and moreover from that,' i.e. in addition to that. 2. 博弈, may be taken together, simply = 'chess-playing,' or separately, as in the translation; see Analects, XVII. xxii. 私妻子, 'selfishly—i.e. partially putting them out of their due place, above his parents, = loving wife and children.' I cannot see why some should give a sensual meaning to 私 here. The advance of meaning from 戮 to 危 shows that the former is to be taken in the lighter sense of 'disgrace.' 3, 4. Compare Pt. I. xviii. 子父責善,—子 precedes 父 here to show that K'wang Chang had been the aggressor.

父子責善、賊恩之大者。五節夫章子、豈不欲有夫妻子母之屬哉、爲得罪於父、不得近、出妻屏子、終身不養焉、其設心以爲不若是、是則罪之大者、是則章子已矣。一節

〔三十一〕曾子居武城、有越寇、或曰、寇至、盍去諸。曰、無寓人於我室、毀傷其薪木。寇退、則曰、脩我牆屋、我將反。寇退、曾子反、

5. 'Moreover, did not Chang wish to have *in his family* the relationships of husband and wife, child and mother? But because he had offended his father, and was not permitted to approach him, he sent away his wife, and drove forth his son, and all his life receives no cherishing attention from them. He settled it in his mind that if he did not act in this way, his would be one of the greatest of crimes.—Such and nothing more is the case of Chang.'

CHAP. XXXI. 1. When the philosopher Tsăng dwelt in Wû-ch'ăng, there came a band from Yüeh to plunder it. Some one said *to him*, 'The plunderers are coming:—why not leave this?' Tsăng *on this left the city*, saying to *the man in charge of the house*, 'Do not lodge any persons in my house, lest they break and injure the plants and trees.' When the plunderers withdrew, he sent word to him, saying, 'Repair the walls of my house. I am about to return.'

5. 屏, 3rd tone. Readers not Chinese will think that Chang's treatment of his wife and son was more criminal than his conduct to his father. 是則罪之大者,—是, 'this,' embracing the two things, his giving offence to his father, and still continuing to enjoy the comforts of wife and son.

31. HOW MENCIUS EXPLAINED THE DIFFERENT CONDUCT OF TSĂNG-TSZE AND OF TSZE-SZE IN SIMILAR CIRCUMSTANCES. 1. Wû-ch'ăng, as in Analects, VI. xii. It appears below that Tsăng had opened a school or lecture-room in the place. Many understand that he had been invited to do so,—to be a 賓師, 'guest and teacher,'—by the commandant. Wû-ch'ăng is probably to be referred to a place in the district of 嘉祥 in the department of Yen-châu. It was thus in the south of Shan-tung. South from it, and covering the present Chiang-sû and part of Cheh-chiang, were the possessions of Wû (吳) and Yüeh, all in Tsăng-tsze's time subject to Yüeh. See in the 集證, *in loc.*, a somewhat similar incident in Tsăng's life (probably a different version of the same), in

左右曰、待先生如此、其忠且敬也、寇至、則先去以爲民望、寇退、則反、殆於不可。沈猶行曰、是非汝所知也、昔沈猶有負芻之禍、從先生者七十人、未有與焉。○二節子思居於衞、有齊寇、或曰、寇至、盍去諸。子思曰、如伋去、君誰與守。○三節孟子曰、曾子子思同道、曾子師也、父兄也、

When the plunderers retired, the philosopher Tsăng returned *accordingly*. His disciples said, 'Since our master was treated with so much sincerity and respect, for him to be the first to go away on the arrival of the plunderers, so as to be observed by the people, and then to return on their retiring, appears to us to be improper.' Ch'ăn-yû Hsing said, 'You do not understand this matter. Formerly, when Ch'ăn-yû was exposed to the outbreak of the grass-carriers, there were seventy disciples in our master's following, and none of them took part in the matter.'

2. When Tsze-sze was living in Wei, there came a band from Ch'î to plunder. Some one said to him, 'The plunderers are coming;—why not leave this?' Tsze-sze said, 'If I go away, whom will the prince have to guard *the State* with?'

3. Mencius said, 'The philosophers Tsăng and Tsze-sze agreed in

which the plunderers are from Lû. 曰,無寓,云云,—the translation needs to be supplemented here considerably to bring out the meaning. 薪 is explained in the K'ang-hsî Dictionary, with reference to this passage, by 草, 'grass,' or small plants generally. 寇退則曰,—this 曰 must = 'sent word to.' 牆屋,—we should rather expect 屋牆; but 屋 perhaps has to be taken in the sense of 'roof.' The two characters, however, = 'house.' If 待 be translated actively, we must supply as a nominative—'the governor of the city.' Ch'ăn- (沈 is pronounced as 審; so commonly; but the point is doubtful; see the 集證, *in loc.*) yû Hsing is supposed to have been a disciple of Tsăng, and a native of Wû-ch'ăng. The Ch'ăn-yû whom he mentions below was another person of the same surname with whom Tsăng and his disciples (從者 = 左右 above) were living. Perhaps he was the Head of the Ch'ăn-yû Family or Clan. 與, 4th tone. Ch'ăn-yû Hsing adduces this other case, as analogous to Tsăng's leaving Wû-ch'ăng, intimating that he acted on a certain principle which justified his conduct. 2. 伋 was Tsze-sze's name. 'Was living in Wei,'—i.e. was

子思臣也、微也、曾子子思易地則皆然。

【三十二】儲子曰、王使人瞯夫子、果有以異於人乎。孟子曰、何以異於人哉、堯舜與人同耳。

【三十三】一節 齊人有一妻一妾、而處室者、其良人出、則必饜酒肉而後反、其妻問所與飲食者、則盡富貴也。其妻告其妾曰、良人出、則必饜酒肉而後反、問

the principle of their conduct. Tsăng was a teacher ;—in the place of a father or elder brother. Tsze-sze was a minister ;—in a meaner place. If the philosophers Tsăng and Tsze-sze had exchanged places, the one would have done what the other did.'

CHAP. XXXII. The officer Ch'û said *to Mencius*, 'Master, the king sent persons to spy out whether you were really different from other men.' Mencius said, 'How should I be different from other men? Yâo and Shun were just the same as other men.'

CHAP. XXXIII. 1. A man of Ch'î had a wife and a concubine, and lived together with them in his house. When their husband went out, he would get himself well filled with wine and flesh, and then return, and, on his wife's asking him with whom he ate and drank, they were sure to be all wealthy and honourable people. The wife informed the concubine, saying, 'When our good man goes out, he is sure to come back having partaken plentifully of wine and flesh. I asked with whom he ate and drank, and they are all, *it seems*, wealthy and honourable people. And yet no people

living and sustaining office. But the attack of Wei by Ch'î is not easily verified. 3. The reader can judge how far the defence of Tsăng's conduct is satisfactory.

32. SAGES ARE JUST LIKE OTHER MEN. This Ch'û was a minister of Ch'î. We must suppose that it was the private manners and way of living of Mencius, which the king wanted to spy out, unless the thing occurred on Mencius's first arrival in Ch'î, and before he had any interview with the king.

33. THE DISGRACEFUL MEANS WHICH SOME MEN TAKE TO SEEK FOR THEIR LIVING, AND FOR WEALTH. 1. As Chû Hsî observes, there ought to be, at the beginning of the chapter, 孟子曰, 'Mencius said.' The phrase 而處 (3rd tone) 室者 is not easily managed in translating.

其與飲食者、盡富貴也、而未嘗有顯者來、吾將瞯良人之所之也、蚤起、施從良人之所之、徧國中、無與立談者、卒之東郭墦間之祭者、乞其餘、不足、又顧而之他、此其爲饜足之道也。其妻歸告其妾曰、良人者、所仰望而終身也、今若此、與其妾訕其良人、而相泣於中庭、而良人未之知也、施施從外來、驕其妻妾。二 由君子觀之、則人之所以求富

of distinction ever come here. I will spy out where our good man goes.' *Accordingly*, she got up early in the morning, and privately followed wherever her husband went. Throughout the whole city, there was no one who stood or talked with him. At last, he came to those who were sacrificing among the tombs beyond the outer wall on the east, and begged what they had over. Not being satisfied, he looked about, and went to another party;—and this was the way in which he got himself satiated. His wife returned, and informed the concubine, saying, 'It was to our husband that we looked up in hopeful contemplation, with whom our lot is cast for life;—and now these are his ways!' On this, along with the concubine she reviled their husband, and they wept together in the middle hall. In the meantime the husband, knowing nothing of all this, came in with a jaunty air, carrying himself proudly to his wife and concubine.

2. In the view of a superior man, as to the ways by which men

The subject of it is the 'man of Ch'i,' and not 'the wife and concubine.' It is descriptive of him as living with them, and being the head of a family,—有刑家之責, as is said in the 備旨, 'having the duty of setting an example to its members.' 良人,—corresponding to the Scottish term of 'goodman' for husband. 所與飲食者,—not 'who

貴利達者、其妻妾不羞也、而不相泣者幾希矣。

seek for riches, honours, gain, and advancement, there are few of their wives and concubines who would not be ashamed and weep together *on account of them.*

gave him to drink and eat,' as Julien makes it. 所之,—之, the verb, as also below, and in 之東, 之他. 施從,—施, read *i*, either 2nd or 4th tone. 國,—plainly used for 'city.' 郭,—see Bk. II. Pt. II. i. 2. 之他, 'went to another place,' = 'another party.' 2. 幾希, as in chap. xix. 1, but it is here an adjective, 'few.'

BOOK V.

WAN CHANG. PART I.

萬章章句上

第一章 萬章問曰、舜往于田、號泣于旻天、何爲其號泣也。孟子曰、怨慕也。萬章曰、父母愛之、喜而不忘、父母惡之、勞而不怨、然則舜怨乎。曰、長息問

CHAPTER I. 1. Wan Chang asked *Mencius*, saying, '*When* Shun went into the fields, he cried out and wept towards the pitying heavens. Why did he cry out and weep?' Mencius replied, 'He was dissatisfied, and full of earnest desire.'

2. Wan Chang said, 'When his parents love him, a son rejoices and forgets them not. When his parents hate him, though they punish him, he does not murmur. Was Shun then murmuring

This Book is named from the chief interlocutor in it, Wan Chang (see Bk. III. Pt. II. v). The tradition is that it was in company with Wan Chang's disciples, that Mencius, baffled in his hopes of doing public service, and having retired into privacy, composed the seven Books, which constitute his Works. The first part of this Book is occupied with discussions about Shun, and other ancient worthies.

1. SHUN'S GREAT FILIAL PIETY:—HOW IT CARRIED HIM INTO THE FIELDS TO WEEP AND DEPLORE HIS INABILITY TO SECURE THE AFFECTION AND SYMPATHY OF HIS PARENTS. 1. 號, 2nd tone, 'to cry out.' It has another signification in the same tone,—'to wail,' which would answer equally well. See the incident related in the Shû-ching, II. ii. 21, from which we learn that

於公明高曰、舜往于田、則吾既得聞命矣、號泣于旻天、于父母、則吾不知也、公明高曰、是非爾所知也。夫公明高以孝子之心、爲不若是恝、我竭力耕田、共爲子職而已矣、父母之不我愛、於我何哉。三節帝使其子九男二女、百官牛羊、倉廩備、

against his parents?' Mencius answered, 'Ch'ang Hsî asked Kung-ming Kâo, saying, "As to Shun's going into the fields, I have received your instructions, but I do not know about his weeping and crying out to the pitying heavens and to his parents." Kung-ming Kâo answered him, "You do not understand that matter." Now, Kung-ming Kâo supposed that the heart of the filial son could not be so free of sorrow. *Shun would say,* "I exert my strength to cultivate the fields, but I am thereby only discharging my office as a son. What can there be in me that my parents do not love me?"

3. 'The Tî caused his own children, nine sons and two daughters, the various officers, oxen and sheep, storehouses and granaries, *all*

such behaviour was a characteristic of his earlier life, when he was 'ploughing' at the foot of the Li hill. 旻天,—the name given to the autumnal sky or heavens. Two meanings have been assigned to 旻: 'the variegated,' with reference to the beautiful tints (文章) of matured nature; and 'the compassionate,' as if it were 愍, with reference to the decay of nature. This latter is generally acquiesced in. I have translated 于 by 'towards,' but the paraphrase in the 日講 is:—'He cried out and called upon pitying Heaven, that lovingly overshadows and compassionates this lower world, weeping at the same time.' 怨慕,—simply, 'he was murmuring and desiring.' The murmuring was at himself, but this is purposely kept in the background, and Chang supposed that he was murmuring at his parents. 2. 父母...不怨,—see Analects, IV. xviii. Kung-ming Kâo is generally understood to have been a disciple of Tsăng Shăn, and Ch'ang Hsî again to have been a disciple of Kâo. 吾既得聞命, 'I have received your *commands*;'—'commands,' said deferentially for 'instructions,' as in Bk. III. Pt. I. v. 5. 于父母 is also from the Shû-ching, though omitted above in par. 1. In translating we must reverse the order of 號泣, 'he wept and cried out,—to heaven, to his parents.' 是非爾所知也,—see Bk. IV. Pt. II. xxxi. 1. 不若是恝, 'not so without sorrow,' i.e. not so, as common people would have it, and as Ch'ang Hsî thought would have been right, that he could refrain from weeping and crying out. 我竭, 云云 are the thoughts supposed to pass through Shun's mind. 共=拱, the 1st tone. 3. See the Shû-ching, I. par. 12, but the various incidents of the particular honours conferred

以事舜於畎畝之中、天下之士多就之者、帝將胥天下而遷之焉、爲不順於父母、如窮人無所歸。○四節 天下之士悅之、人之所欲也、而不足以解憂、好色、人之所欲、妻帝之二女、而不足以解憂、富、人之所欲、富有天下、而不足以解憂、貴、人之所欲、貴爲天子、而不足以解憂、人悅之、好色、富貴、無足

to be prepared, to serve Shun amid the channelled fields. Of the scholars of the kingdom there were multitudes who flocked to him. The sovereign designed that *Shun* should superintend the kingdom along with him, and then to transfer it to him entirely. But because his parents were not in accord with him, he felt like a poor man who has nowhere to turn to.

4. 'To be delighted in by all the scholars of the kingdom, is what men desire, but it was not sufficient to remove the sorrow *of Shun*. The possession of beauty is what men desire, and *Shun* had for his wives the two daughters of the Tî, but this was not sufficient to remove his sorrow. Riches are what men desire, and the kingdom was the rich property *of Shun*, but this was not sufficient to remove his sorrow. Honours are what men desire, and *Shun* had the dignity of being sovereign, but this was not sufficient to remove his sorrow. The reason why the being the object of men's delight, with the

on Shun, and his influence, are to be collected from the general history of him and Yâo. There is, however, an important discrepancy between Mencius's account of Shun, and that in the Shû-ching. There, when he is first recommended to Yâo by the high officers, they base their recommendation on the fact of his having overcome the evil that was in his parents and brother, and brought them to self-government. The Shû-ching, moreover, mentions only one son of Yâo, Tan Chû (丹朱), and says nothing of the nine who are here said to have been put under the command of Yâo. They are mentioned, however, in the 'Historical Records,' 虞史記. 帝將胥天下-將與之胥(=相)視天下. 而遷之-自移以與之. 不順於父母,—see Bk. IV. Pt. II. xviii. 1. 4. 色,—色 is here = our 'a beauty,' 'beauties.' 妻, in 2nd tone, here as a verb, 'to wive,' 'to have for wife.' Observe the force

以解憂者、惟順於父母可以解憂。○五節人少、則慕父母、知好色、則慕少艾、有妻子、則慕妻子、仕則慕君、不得於君、則熱中、大孝終身慕父母、五十而慕者、予於大舜見之矣。

第二章 萬章一節問曰、詩云、娶妻如之何、必告父母、信斯言也、宜莫如舜、舜之不告而娶、

possession of beauty, riches, and honours were not sufficient to remove his sorrow, was that it could be removed only by his getting his parents to be in accord with him.

5. 'The desire of the child is towards his father and mother. When he becomes conscious of the attractions of beauty, his desire is towards young and beautiful women. When he comes to have a wife and children, his desire is towards them. When he obtains office, his desire is towards his sovereign :—if he cannot get the regard of his sovereign, he burns within. *But* the man of great filial piety, to the end of his life, has his desire towards his parents. In the great Shun I see the case of one whose desire at fifty years was towards them.'

CHAP. II. 1. Wan Chang asked *Mencius*, saying, 'It is said in the Book of Poetry,

"In marrying a wife, how ought a man to proceed?
He must inform his parents."

If the rule be indeed as here expressed, no man ought to have illustrated it so well as Shun. How was it that Shun's marriage took place without his informing *his parents?*' Mencius replied, 'If he had informed them, he would not have been able to marry. That

of 者, leading on to what follows as the explanation of the preceding circumstances. 5. 少, 4th tone, 'young,' 'little.' 好色,—the term has a different acceptation from that in the preceding paragraph, though I have translated it in the same way. 艾,—in the sense of 美, 'beautiful.'

2. DEFENCE OF SHUN AGAINST THE CHARGES OF VIOLATING THE PROPER RULE IN THE WAY OF HIS MARRYING, AND OF HYPOCRISY IN HIS CONDUCT TO HIS BROTHER. 1, 2. Compare IV. Part I. xxvi. 詩云,—see the Shih-ching, I. viii. Ode VI. st. 3. 告, 4th tone, as in Analects, III. xvii. 信=誠, 'if indeed.' 以懟父母,—if

何也。孟子曰、告則不得娶、男女居室、人之大倫也、如告則廢人之大倫、以懟父母、是以不告也。二節萬章曰、舜之不告而娶、則吾既得聞命矣、帝之妻舜、而不告何也。曰、帝亦知告焉、則不得妻也。三節萬章曰、父母使舜完廩、捐階、瞽瞍焚廩、使浚井、出、從而揜之、象曰、謨蓋都君咸我績、牛羊父母、倉廩

male and female should dwell together, is the greatest of human relations. If *Shun* had informed his parents, he must have made void this greatest of human relations, thereby incurring their resentment. On this account, he did not inform them.'

2. Wan Chang said, 'As to Shun's marrying without informing his parents, I have heard your instructions; but how was it that the Tî *Yâo* gave him his daughters as wives without informing *Shun's parents?*' *Mencius* said, 'The Tî also knew that if he informed them, he could not marry his daughters to him.'

3. Wan Chang said, 'His parents set Shun to repair a granary, to which, the ladder having been removed, Kû-sâu set fire. They *also* made him dig a well. He got out, but they, *not knowing that*, proceeded to cover him up. Hsiang said, "Of the scheme to cover up the city-forming prince, the merit is all mine. Let my parents have his oxen and sheep. Let them have his storehouses and granaries.

he had not married, then his parents would have had cause to be angry with him, for allowing the line of the family to terminate. This seems to be the meaning of the phrase. 聞命,—as in the last chapter. 帝 … 而不告,—告 here is understood as = 're-quiring Shun to inform his parents.' 3. Shun's half-brother is understood to have been the instigator in the attempts on his life here mentioned. The incidents, however, are taken from tradition, and not from the Shû-ching. Shun covered himself with two bamboo screens, and made his way through the fire. In the second case, he found a hole or passage in the side of the wall, and got away by means of it. 都君,—it is mentioned in the last chapter, how the scholars of the kingdom flocked to Shun. They say that if he lived in one place for a year, he formed a 聚, or 'assemblage;' in two years, he formed a 邑, or 'town,' and in three, a 都, or 'capital.' With reference to this, Hsiang

父母、干戈朕、琴朕、弤朕、二嫂使治朕棲、象往入舜宮、舜在牀琴、象曰、鬱陶思君爾、忸怩、舜曰、惟諸臣庶、汝其于予治、不識舜不知象之將殺己與。曰、奚而不知也、象憂亦憂、象喜亦喜。四節曰、然則舜僞喜者與。曰、否、昔者、有饋生魚於鄭子產、子產使校人畜之池、校人烹之、反命曰、始舍之、圉圉焉、少則洋洋焉、攸然而逝、子

His shield and spear shall be mine. His lute shall be mine. His bow shall be mine. His two wives I shall make attend for me to my bed." Hsiang then went away into Shun's palace, and there was Shun on his couch playing on his lute. Hsiang said, "I am come simply because I was thinking anxiously about you." *At the same time*, he blushed deeply. Shun said to him, "There are all my officers:—do you undertake the government of them for me." I do not know whether Shun was ignorant of Hsiang's wishing to kill him.' *Mencius* answered, 'How could he be ignorant of that? But when Hsiang was sorrowful, he was also sorrowful; when Hsiang was joyful, he was also joyful.'

4. *Chang* said, 'In that case, then, did not Shun rejoice hypocritically?' Mencius replied, 'No. Formerly, some one sent a present of a live fish to Tsze-ch'an of Chăng. Tsze-ch'an ordered his pond-keeper to keep it in the pond, but that officer cooked it, and reported the execution of his commission, saying, "When

calls him 都君. 朕, now confined to the imperial WE, was anciently used by high and low. 弤, 'a carved bow,' said to have been given to Shun by Yâo, as a token of his associating him with him on the throne. 二嫂,—literally, 'the two sisters-in-law.' 棲＝牀, 'a bed,' or 'couch.' 鬱陶思君爾,—爾＝耳, as a final particle, 'only.' The expression literally is,—'with suppressed anxiety thinking of you only.' 4. 校 (read *hsiâo*, 4th tone) 人 is taken by all the commentators as

產曰、得其所哉、得其所哉、校人出曰、孰謂子產智、予既烹而食之、曰、得其所哉、得其所哉、故君子可欺以其方、難罔以非其道、彼以愛兄之道來、故誠信而喜之、奚僞焉。

第三章 一節 萬章問曰、象日以殺舜爲事、立爲天子、則放之、何也。孟子曰、封之也、或曰放

I first let it go, it appeared embarrassed. In a little while, it seemed to be somewhat at ease, and then it swam away joyfully." Tsze-ch'an observed, "It had got into its element! It had got into its element!" The pond-keeper then went out and said, "Who calls Tsze-ch'an a wise man? After I had cooked and eaten the fish, he says, "It had got into its element! It had got into its element!" Thus a superior man may be imposed on by what seems to be as it ought to be, but he cannot be entrapped by what is contrary to right principle. Hsiang came in the way in which the love of his elder brother would have made him come; therefore *Shun* sincerely believed him, and rejoiced. What hypocrisy was there?'

CHAP. III. 1. Wan Chang said, 'Hsiang made it his daily business to slay Shun. When *Shun* was made sovereign, how was it that he *only* banished him?' Mencius said, 'He raised him to be a prince. Some supposed that it was banishing him?'

主池沼小吏, 'a small officer over the ponds,' but I do not know that this meaning of the phrase is found elsewhere. 反命,—as in Bk. III. Pt. I. ii. 3. 故君子可欺,云云,—compare Analects, VI. xxiv. 以其方, 'by its class,' the meaning being as in the translation.—Chû Hsî says:—'Mencius says that Shun knew well that Hsiang wished to kill him, but when he saw him sorrowful, he was sorrowful, and when he saw him joyful, he was joyful. The case was that his brotherly feeling could not be repressed. Whether the things mentioned by Wan Chang really occurred or not, we do not know. But Mencius was able to know and describe the mind of Shun, and that is the only thing here worth discussing about.'

3. EXPLANATION AND DEFENCE OF SHUN'S CONDUCT IN THE CASE OF HIS WICKED BROTHER HSIANG;—HOW HE BOTH DISTINGUISHED HIM, AND KEPT HIM UNDER RESTRAINT. 1. 放=置, 'to place,' with the idea of keeping in the place, = 'to banish.' Chang's thought was that Hsiang should have been put to death, and not merely banished. 或曰,—it seems best to understand 曰 as meaning 'supposed,' and not 'said.'

焉。二章萬章曰、舜流共工于幽州、放驩兜于崇山、殺三苗于三危、殛鯀于羽山、四罪而天下咸服、誅不仁也、象至不仁、封之有庳、有庳之人奚罪焉、仁人固如是乎、在他人、則誅之、在弟、則封之。曰、仁人之於弟也、不藏怒焉、不宿怨焉、親愛之而已矣、親之、欲其貴也、愛之、欲其富也、封之有庳、富貴

2. Wan Chang said, 'Shun banished the superintendent of works to Yû-châu; he sent away Hwan-tâu to the mountain Ch'ung; he slew *the prince of* San-miâo in San-wei; and he imprisoned K'wăn on the mountain Yü. When the crimes of those four were thus punished, the whole kingdom acquiesced:—it was a cutting off of men who were destitute of benevolence. But Hsiang was *of all men* the most destitute of benevolence, and *Shun* raised him to be the prince of Yû-pî;—of what crimes had the people of Yû-pî been guilty? Does a benevolent man really act thus? In the case of other men, he cut them off; in the case of his brother, he raised him to be a prince.' *Mencius* replied, 'A benevolent man does not lay up anger, nor cherish resentment against his brother, but only regards him with affection and love. Regarding him with affection, he wishes him to be honourable: regarding him with love, he wishes him to be rich. The appointment *of Hsiang* to be the prince of Yû-pî was to enrich and ennoble him. If while *Shun* himself was sovereign, his

2. The different individuals mentioned here are all spoken of in the Shû-ching, Pt. II. i. 12, which see. 共工 is a name of office. The surname or name of the holder of it is not found in the Shû-ching. Hwan-tâu was the name of the 司徒, 'Minister of Instruction.' He appears in the Shû-ching, as the friend of the 共工, recommending him to Yâo; hence Chû Hsi says that these two were confederate in evil. 三苗 is to be understood, in the text, as '*the prince of* San-miâo,' which was the name of a State, near the Tung-t'ing lake, embracing the present department of 岳州, and extending towards Wû-ch'ang. K'wăn was the name of the father of Yü. The places mentioned are difficult of identification. Yû-pî is referred to the present 道州, and the district of Ling-ling, in the department of 永州,

之也、身爲天子、弟爲匹夫、可謂親愛之乎。三節敢問或曰放者、何謂也。曰、象不得有爲於其國、天子使吏治其國、而納其貢稅焉、故謂之放、豈得暴彼民哉、雖然、欲常常而見之、故源源而來、不及貢以政接於有庳、此之謂也。一節

第四章 咸丘蒙問曰語云、盛德

brother had been a common man, could he have been said to regard him with affection and love?'

3. *Wan Chang* said, 'I venture to ask what you mean by saying that some supposed that it was a banishing of Hsiang?' *Mencius* replied, 'Hsiang could do nothing in his State. The Son of Heaven appointed an officer to administer its government, and to pay over its revenues to him. This treatment of him led to its being said that he was banished. How *indeed* could he be allowed the means of oppressing the people? Nevertheless, *Shun* wished to be continually seeing him, and by this arrangement, he came incessantly *to court*, as is signified in that expression—"He did not wait for the rendering of tribute, or affairs of government, to receive the prince of Yû-pî."'

CHAP. IV. 1. Hsien-ch'iû Măng asked *Mencius*, saying, 'There

in Hû-nan. 殛 is said by Chû Hsî to = 誅, 'to cut off,' but that is too strong. 四罪 = 治此四凶之罪, taking 罪 as meaning 'crimes.' 服, 'submitted,' i. e. acknowledged the justice of the punishments inflicted. 在他人…誅之 appears to be incomplete, as if Mencius had not permitted his disciple to finish what he had to say. 宿怨, 'to lodge, as if for a night, resentment;' compare 宿諾, Analects, XII. xii. 2. 3. 不得有爲, 'did not get to have doing,' i. e. was not allowed to act independently. 其貢稅 = 其國所賦 (taking 貢 as a verb) 之稅. 源源, 'the uninterrupted flowing of a stream.' 不及貢…有庳 is a quotation by Mencius from some book that is now lost. There were regular seasons for the princes in general to repair to court, and emergencies of government which required their presence, but Shun did not wish his brother to wait for such occasions, but to be often with him. The 不 extends over the two clauses, which = 不及貢期而見, 不以政事而見.

4. EXPLANATION OF SHUN'S CONDUCT WITH REFERENCE TO THE SOVEREIGN YÂO, AND HIS FATHER

之士、君不得而臣、父不得而子、舜南面而立、堯帥諸侯北面而朝之、瞽瞍亦北面而朝之、舜見瞽瞍、其容有蹙、孔子曰、於斯時也、天下殆哉岌岌乎、不識此語誠然乎哉。孟子曰、否、此非君子之言、齊東野人之語也、堯老而舜攝也、堯典曰、

is the saying, "A scholar of complete virtue may not be employed as a minister by his sovereign, nor treated as a son by his father. Shun stood with his face to the south, and Yâo, at the head of all the princes, appeared before him at court with his face to the north. Kû-sâu also did the same. When Shun saw Kû-sâu, his countenance became discomposed. Confucius said, At this time, in what a perilous condition was the kingdom! Its state was indeed unsettled."—I do not know whether what is here said really took place.' Mencius replied, 'No. These are not the words of a superior man. They are the sayings of an uncultivated person of the east of Ch'î. When Yâo was old, Shun was associated with him in the government. It is said in the Canon of Yâo, "After twenty and eight years, the Highly Meritorious one deceased. The people acted as if

KÛ-SÂU. 1. Hsien-ch'iû Măng was a disciple of Mencius. The surname Hsien-ch'iû was derived from a place of that name where his progenitors had resided. The saying which Măng adduces extends to 岌岌乎. Two entirely contrary interpretations of it have been given. One is that given in the translation. It is the view of Châo Ch'î, and is found in the modern Pî-chih (備旨), or 'Complete Digest of Annotations on the Four Books.' Most modern commentaries, however, take an opposite view:—'The scholar of complete virtue cannot employ his sovereign as a minister, or treat his father as a son.' This view is preferred by Julien, who styles the other very bad. I am satisfied, however, that the other is the correct one. If it were not, why should Mencius condemn the sentiment as that of an uninstructed man. 舜南面, 云云, follows as a direct example of the principle announced. Shun was the scholar of complete virtue, and therefore the sovereign Yâo, and his father, Kû-sâu, both appeared before him as subjects. 舜見, 云云, and the remarks of Confucius are to be taken as a protest against the arrangements described in the preceding paragraphs. 南面, 北面,—see Analects, VI. i. 野 is to be joined as an adjective with 人, and not as a noun with 東. The passage quoted from the Shû-ching is now found in the canon of Shun, and not that of Yâo;—see II. i. 13. 有, 4th tone. 載, 3rd tone, 'a year.' 放 (3rd tone; see Bk. III. Pt. I. iv. 8) 勳 is not in the classic. 徂 (=殂) 落,—Chû Hsî makes

二十有八載、放勳乃徂落、百姓如喪考妣、三年、四海遏密八音、孔子曰、天無二日、民無二王、舜既爲天子矣、又帥天下諸侯、以爲堯三年喪、是二天子矣。○二節咸丘蒙曰、舜之不臣堯、則吾既得聞命矣、詩云、普天之下、莫非王土、率土之濱、莫非王臣、而舜既爲天子矣、敢

they were mourning for a father or mother for three years, and up to *the borders of* the four seas every sound of music was hushed." Confucius said, "There are not two suns in the sky, nor two sovereigns over the people." Shun having been sovereign, and, moreover, leading on all the princes to observe the three years' mourning for Yâo, there would have been in this case two sovereigns.'

2. Hsien-ch'iû Măng said, 'On the point of Shun's not treating Yâo as a minister, I have received your instructions. *But* it is said in the Book of Poetry,

"Under the whole heaven,
Every spot is the sovereign's ground;
To the borders of the land,
Every individual is the sovereign's minister;"

—and Shun had become sovereign. I venture to ask how it was that Kû-sâu was not one of his ministers.' *Mencius* answered,

殂=升, 'to ascend.' The *animus* ascends at death, and the *anima* 落, 'descends;'—hence the combination = 'dissolution,' 'decease.' The dictionary, however, makes 殂 simply = 往, and the phrase = 'vanish away.' 百姓 is the people within the royal domain; the 四海 denotes the rest of the kingdom, beyond that. Some, however, approved by the 日講, make 百姓 = 百官, 'the officers,' and 四海 = 'all the people.' 考妣,—the terms for a deceased father and mother. 三年,—for 年 the classic has 載. The 八音, 'eight sounds,' are all instruments of music, formed of metal, stone, cord, bamboo, calabash, earthenware, leather, or wood.—The meaning is that up to the time of Yâo's decease, Shun was only vice-king, and, therefore, Yâo never could have appeared before him in the position of a subject. 2. 舜之不臣堯 is not to be taken with reference to the phrase 君不得而臣, but to the general scope of the preceding para-

問瞽瞍之非臣如何。曰、是詩也、非是之謂也、勞於王事而不得養父母也、曰、此莫非王事、我獨賢勞也、故說詩者、不以文害辭、不以辭害志、以意逆志、是爲得之、如以辭而已矣、雲漢之詩曰、周餘黎民、靡有孑遺、信斯言也、是周無遺民也。(三節)孝子之至、莫大乎尊親。尊親之至、莫大乎以天下養、

'That ode is not to be understood in that way:—it speaks of being laboriously engaged in the sovereign's business, so as not to be able to nourish one's parents, *as if the author* said, "This is all the sovereign's business, and *how is it that* I alone am supposed to have ability, and am made to toil in it?" Therefore, those who explain the odes, may not insist on one term so as to do violence to a sentence, nor on a sentence so as to do violence to the general scope. They must try with their thoughts to meet that scope, and then we shall apprehend it. If we simply take single sentences, there is that in the ode called "The Milky Way,"—

> "Of the black-haired people of the remnant of Châu,
> There is not half a one left."

If it had been really as thus expressed, then not an individual of the people of Châu was left.

3. 'Of all which a filial son can attain to, there is nothing greater than his honouring his parents. And of what can be attained to

graph, and especially to Mencius's explanation. The restricting it to the former, in opposition to the maxim—不以辭害志, has led to the erroneous view of the whole passage animadverted on above. Măng is now convinced that it was only on Yâo's death that Shun became full sovereign, but after that event there still remained the relation between him and Kû-sâu, and how could he be at once sovereign and son to him? How was it that Kû-sâu would be at once father and subject to him? 詩云,—see the Shih-ching, II. vi. Ode I. st. 2. 雲漢之詩,—see the Shih-ching, III. iii. Ode IV. st. 3. 志, 'the scope,' i.e. the mind or aim of the writer. 3. 詩曰,—see the Shih-ching, III. i. Ode IX. st. 3, celebrating the praises of king Wû.—This paragraph shows that Shun, by his exaltation, honoured his father only the more exceedingly. He was the more

爲天子父、尊之至也、以天下養、養之至也、詩曰、永言孝思、孝思維則、此之謂也。

四節 書曰、祗載見瞽瞍、夔夔齊栗、瞽瞍亦允若、是爲父不得而子也。

第五章 一節 萬章曰、堯以天下與舜、有諸。孟子曰、否、天子不能以天下與人。

二節 然則舜有天下也、孰與之。曰、天與之。

三節 天

in the honouring one's parents, there is nothing greater than the nourishing them with the whole kingdom. Kû-sâu was the father of the sovereign;—this was the height of honour. *Shun* nourished him with the whole kingdom;—this was the height of nourishing. In this was verified the sentiment in the Book of Poetry,

"Ever cherishing filial thoughts,
Those filial thoughts became an example *to after ages*."

4. 'It is said in the Book of History, "Reverently performing his duties, he waited on Kû-sâu, and was full of veneration and awe. Kû-sâu also believed him and conformed to virtue."—This is the *true* case of *the scholar of complete virtue* not being treated as a son by his father.'

CHAP. V. 1. Wan Chang said, 'Was it the case that Yâo gave the throne to Shun?' Mencius said, 'No. The sovereign cannot give the throne to another.'

2. 'Yes;—but Shun had the throne. Who gave it to him?' 'Heaven gave it to him,' was the answer.

'a son' to Kû-sâu. 4. 書曰,—see the Shû-ching, II. ii. 15. 齊 (read *châi*) 栗 (the classic has 慄),—this seems to be a supplement by Mencius, as if he said, 'There is indeed a meaning in that saying that a scholar of complete virtue cannot be treated as a son by his father, for in the case of Shun and Kû-sâu we see that the father was affected by the son, and not the son by the father.'

5. HOW SHUN GOT THE THRONE BY THE GIFT OF HEAVEN. VOX POPULI VOX DEI. 1. 有諸,—see Bk. I. Pt. II. ii, = 有之乎. 2. 天與之,—is it not plain that by 'Heaven' in this chapter we are to understand GOD? Many commentators understand by it 理, 'reason,' or 'the truth and fitness of things,' saving in the expression—故曰天, in par. 7, where they take it as = 數, 'fate.' On this the author of the 四書諸儒輯要, 'A collection of the most important comments of the Learned

與之者、諄諄然命之乎。曰○四節否、天不言、以行與事、示之而已矣。○五節曰、以行與事、示之者、如之何。曰、天子能薦人於天、不能使天與之天下、諸侯能薦人於天子、不能使天子與之諸侯、大夫能薦人於諸侯、不能使諸侯與之大夫、昔者、堯薦舜於天、而天受之、暴之於民、而

3. '"Heaven gave it to him:"—did *Heaven* confer its appointment on him with specific injunctions?'

4. *Mencius* replied, 'No. Heaven does not speak. It simply showed its will by his personal conduct and his conduct of affairs.'

5. '"It showed its will by his personal conduct and his conduct of affairs:"—how was this?' Mencius's answer was, 'The sovereign can present a man to Heaven, but he cannot make Heaven give that man the throne. A prince can present a man to the sovereign, but he cannot cause the sovereign to make that man a prince. A great officer can present a man to his prince, but he cannot cause the prince to make that man a great officer. Yâo presented Shun to Heaven, and Heaven accepted him. He presented him to the people, and the people accepted him. Therefore I say, "Heaven does not

on the Four Books,' says—盧齋獨以此一天字指數言,其餘天字指理言,大謬. 此章天字以上帝之主宰言,理與數皆在其中, 'Hsü-châi supposes that in this one case (故曰天) the word Heaven means fate. But this is a great error. In this chapter "Heaven" signifies the government of God, within which are included both reason and fate.' 3. 天與之者,—者, = 'as to what you say.' 諄 (the 1st tone) 諄然, 'with repetitions.'—The paraphrase in the 日講 is:—'As to what you say, *Heaven gave it to him*, did Heaven indeed express its instructions and commands to him again and again? If it did not do so, where is the ground for what you say?' 4. 行, 4th tone, 'conduct,' as opposed to 事, 'the conduct of affairs.' 示之, 'showed it,' i.e. its will to give him the throne. The character 示 takes here the place of 命, because 命 would require the use of language, whereas 示 is the simple indication of the will. 5. 百神, 'the hundred' (= all the) 'spirits,' is explained as 天地山川之神, 'the spirits of heaven, earth, the mountains, and the rivers,' i.e. all

民受之、故曰、天不言、以行與事示之而已矣。(六)曰、敢問薦之於天、而天受之、暴之於民、而民受之、如何。曰、使之主祭、而百神享之、是天受之、使之主事、而事治、百姓安之、是民受之也、天與之、人與之、故曰、天子不能以天下與人。(七)舜相堯、二十有八載、非人之所能爲也、

speak. It simply indicated its will by his personal conduct and his conduct of affairs."'

6. *Chang* said, 'I presume to ask how it was that *Yâo* presented *Shun* to Heaven, and Heaven accepted him; and that he exhibited him to the people, and the people accepted him.' *Mencius* replied, 'He caused him to preside over the sacrifices, and all the spirits were well pleased with them;—thus Heaven accepted him. He caused him to preside over the conduct of affairs, and affairs were well administered, so that the people reposed under him;—thus the people accepted him. Heaven gave *the throne* to him. The people gave it to him. Therefore I said, "The sovereign cannot give the throne to another."

7. 'Shun assisted Yâo *in the government* for twenty and eight years;—this was more than man could have done, and was from

spiritual beings, real or supposed. In the Shû-ching, II. i. 6, a distinction is made between the 羣神, 'host of spirits,' and 上帝, 六宗, and 山川, but the phrase here is to be taken as inclusive of all. The sovereign is 百神之主, and Shun entered into all the duties of Yâo, even while Yâo was alive. How the spirits signified their approbation of the sacrifices, we are not told.—Modern critics take the 百神 here as exclusive of Heaven and subordinate to it, being equivalent to the 鬼神, 'the energetic operations of Heaven.' But such views were long subsequent to Mencius's time. 6. 諸侯 is very plainly in the singular notwithstanding the 諸; = 'one of the princes.' I leave the 昔者, 'formerly,' out of the translation. 暴,—read pû, 'to manifest,' 'to exhibit.' 7. 相, 4th tone. 載, 2nd tone. 有, 4th tone. In 天地, 天, it is said, 以氣數言, 'Heaven means destiny.' But why suppose a different meaning of the term? Twenty-eight years were, indeed, a long time for Shun to occupy the place of vice-sovereign as he did, and showed wonderful gifts. I consider that this is an additional illus-

天也、堯崩、三年之喪畢、舜避堯之子、於南河之南、天下諸侯朝覲者、不之堯之子、而之舜、訟獄者、不之堯之子、而之舜、謳歌者、不謳歌堯之子、而謳歌舜、故曰、天也、夫然後之中國、踐天子位焉、而居堯之宮、逼堯之子、是篡也、非天與也。八節 泰誓曰、天視自我民視、天聽、自我民聽、此之謂也。

Heaven. After the death of Yâo, when the three years' mourning was completed, Shun withdrew from the son of Yâo to the south of South river. The princes of the kingdom, however, repairing to court, went not to the son of Yâo, but they went to Shun. Litigants went not to the son of Yâo, but they went to Shun. Singers sang not the son of Yâo, but they sang Shun. Therefore I said, "Heaven *gave him the throne*." It was after these things that he went to the Middle Kingdom, and occupied the seat of the Son of Heaven. If he had, *before these things*, taken up his residence in the palace of Yâo, and had applied pressure to the son of Yâo, it would have been an act of usurpation, and not the gift of Heaven.

8. 'This sentiment is expressed in the words of The Great Declaration,—"Heaven sees according as my people see; Heaven hears according as my people hear."'

tration of the 行 above, by which Heaven intimated its will about Shun. The south of the South river (probably the most southern of the nine streams which Yü opened) would be in the present Ho-nan. Thither Shun retired from Chî-châu, the present Shan-hsî, where Yâo's capital was. For the difference between 朝 (*ch'âo*, 2nd tone) and 覲, see the Lî-chî, I. Sect. II. ii. 11, and notes thereon. 之堯, 之舜, 之中國,—之 = 往, the verb. 訟獄,—see Analects, XII. xiii, but Chû Hsî makes no distinction between the terms here, and explains 訟獄謂獄不决而訟之. 謳歌,—these two terms must be taken together. 歌 is the more general name of the two. The 說文 says that 謳 is 齊歌, 'the singing of many together.' The 正字通 makes 謳 to be the several tunes of the singers. 而 = 若, or 使. 8. 泰誓曰,—see the Shû-ching, V. i. Sect. II. 7.

第六章 萬章問曰、人有言至於禹而德衰、不傳於賢、而傳於子、有諸。孟子曰、否、不然也、天與賢、則與賢、天與子、則與子、昔者、舜薦禹於天、十有七年、舜崩、三年之喪畢、禹避舜之子、於陽城、天下之民從之、若堯崩之後、不從堯之子、而從舜也、禹薦益於天、七年、禹崩、三年之喪畢、益避禹之子、於箕山之陰、朝覲訟獄者、不之

CHAP. VI. 1. Wan Chang asked *Mencius*, saying, 'People say, "When *the disposal of the kingdom* came to Yü, his virtue was inferior *to that of Yâo and Shun*, and he transmitted it not to the worthiest but to his son." Was it so?' Mencius replied, 'No; it was not so. When Heaven gave the kingdom to the worthiest, it was given to the worthiest. When Heaven gave it to the son *of the preceding sovereign*, it was given to him. Shun presented Yü to Heaven. Seventeen years elapsed, and Shun died. When the three years' mourning was expired, Yü withdrew from the son of Shun to Yang-ch'ăng. The people of the kingdom followed him just as after the death of Yâo, instead of following his son, they had followed Shun. Yü presented Yî to Heaven. Seven years elapsed, and Yü died. When the three years' mourning was expired, Yî withdrew from the son of Yü to the north of mount Ch'î. The *princes*, repairing to court, went not to Yî, but they went to Ch'î. Litigants did not go

6. HOW THE THRONE DESCENDED FROM YÜ TO HIS SON, AND NOT TO HIS MINISTER YÎ; THAT YÜ WAS NOT TO BE CONSIDERED ON THAT ACCOUNT AS INFERIOR IN VIRTUE TO YÂO AND SHUN. 1. 至於,—'coming to;' we must understand, 'From Yâo and Shun,' or translate somehow as I have done. Some say that 與賢, 與子 are not to be taken with special reference to Shun and Yü, and to Ch'i, but it seems best to do so. A general inference may be drawn as well from the special cases. 有諸, 'was it so?' i.e. was his virtue inferior, and his transmitting the throne to his son a proof that it was so? 昔者,—omitted in translating, as before. Chû Hsî says, 'Yang-ch'ăng and the north of mount Ch'i were both at the foot of the Sung mountains, places fit for retirement, within deep valleys.' By many they are held to have

益而之啟、曰、吾君之子也、謳歌者、不謳歌益、而謳歌啟、曰、吾君之子也。○二節 丹朱之不肖、舜之子亦不肖、舜之相堯、禹之相舜也、歷年多、施澤於民久、啟賢、能敬承繼禹之道、益之相禹也、歷年少、施澤於民未久、舜、禹、益、相去久遠、其子之賢不肖、皆天也、非人之所能爲也、莫之爲而爲者、天也、莫之致而至者、命也。○三節 匹夫而

to Yî, but they went to Ch'î, saying, "He is the son of our sovereign;" the singers did not sing Yî, but they sang Ch'î, saying, "He is the son of our sovereign."

2. 'That Tan-chû was not equal *to his father*, and Shun's son not equal *to his;* that Shun assisted Yâo, and Yü assisted Shun, for many years, conferring benefits on the people for a long time; that *thus* the length of time during which Shun, Yü, and Yî *assisted in the government* was so different; that Ch'î was able, as a man of talents and virtue, reverently to pursue the same course as Yü; that Yî assisted Yü only for a few years, and had not long conferred benefits on the people; that the periods of service of the three were so different; and that the sons were one superior, and the other superior:—all this was from Heaven, and what could not be brought about by man. That which is done without man's doing is from Heaven. That which happens without man's causing is from the ordinance *of Heaven.*

3. 'In the case of a private individual obtaining the throne, there

been the same place, and that 陰 is a mistake for 陽. They were certainly near each other, and are referred to the district of Tăng-făng (登封), in the department of Ho-nan, in Ho-nan. Yî was Yü's great minister, raised to that dignity after the death of Kâo-yâo;—see the Shû-ching, II. iv. Ch'î was Yü's son, who succeeded him on the throne. 2. Tan-chû was the son of Yâo; see the Shû-ching, I. 9. The son of Shun is not mentioned in the classic. His name was Î-chün (義均), and often appears as Shang Chün, he having been appointed to the principality of Shang (商). In 之相,

有天下者、德必若舜禹、而又有天子薦之者、故仲尼不有天下。四節 繼世以有天下、天之所廢、必若桀紂者也、故益、伊尹、周公、不有天下。五節 伊尹相湯以王於天下、湯崩、太丁未立、外丙二年、仲壬四年、太甲顛覆湯之典刑、伊尹放之於桐、三年、太甲悔過、自怨自艾、於桐處

must be in him virtue equal to that of Shun or Yü; and moreover there must be the presenting of him *to Heaven* by the *preceding* sovereign. It was on this account that Confucius did not obtain the throne.

4. 'When the kingdom is possessed by *natural* succession, the sovereign who is displaced by Heaven must be like Chieh or Châu. It was on this account that Yî, Î Yin, and Châu-kung did not obtain the throne.

5. 'Î Yin assisted T'ang so that he became sovereign over the kingdom. After the demise of T'ang, T'âi-ting having died before he could be appointed sovereign, Wâi-ping reigned two years, and Chung-zăn four. T'âi-chiâ was then turning upside down the statutes of T'ang, when Î Yin placed him in T'ung for three years. *There* T'âi-chiâ repented of his errors, was contrite, and reformed himself. In T'ung he came to dwell in benevolence and walk in

the 相 is in 4th tone. In this paragraph we have a longer sentence than is commonly found in Chinese composition, the 皆 in 皆天也 resuming all the previous clauses, which are in apposition with one another:—'Tan Chû's not being like his father, Shun's son's not being like him,' &c. 相去久遠=歷年久遠之相去. 莫之爲而爲=人莫(=不)爲之而爲, the first 爲 is active; implying the purpose of man, the second is passive; so, as is indicated by the terms, with 致 and 至 in the next sentence. 4. Î Yin was the chief minister of T'ang (see Analects, XII. xxii. 6), and Châu-kung or the duke of Châu, the well-known assistant of his brother, king Wû. 5. 相, in 4th tone. 王, in 3rd tone. 太丁...四年,—I have translated here according to Châo Ch'î. One of the Ch'ăngs gives a different view:—'On the death of T'ang, Wâi-ping was only two years old, and Chung-zăn was but four. T'âi was somewhat older, and therefore was put on the throne;' and between this view and the other, Chû Hsî professes himself unable to decide. The first view appears to me much the more natural, and is founded moreover on the account in the 'Historical Records,' though the histories have been arranged according to the other, and T'âi-chiâ appears as the successor of T'ang. This arrange-

仁遷義、三年、以聽伊尹之訓己也、復歸于亳。六節周公之不有天下、猶益之於夏、伊尹之於殷也。七節孔子曰、唐、虞、禪、夏后、殷、周、繼、其義一也。

第七章 一節萬章問曰、人有言、伊尹以割烹要

righteousness, during those three years, listening to the lessons given to him by Î Yin. Then *Î Yin* again returned *with him* to Po.

6. 'Châu-kung's not getting the throne was like the case of Yî and *the throne of* Hsiâ, or like that of Î Yin and *the throne of* Yin.

7. 'Confucius said, "T'ang and Yü resigned the throne *to their worthy ministers*. The sovereign of Hsiâ and *those of* Yin and Châu transmitted it to their sons. The principle of righteousness was the same *in all the cases*."'

CHAP. VII. 1. Wan Chang asked *Mencius*, saying, 'People say that Î Yin sought an introduction to T'ang by his knowledge of cookery. Was it so?'

ment of the chronology seems indeed required by the statements in the Shû-ching, IV. iv, which do not admit of any reign or reigns being interposed between T'ang and T'âi-chiâ. The author of the 四書拓餘說 proposes the following solution:—'Châo Ch'î's view is inadmissible, being inconsistent with the Shû-ching. The scholar Ch'ăng's view is also to be rejected. For how can we suppose that T'ang, dying over a hundred years old, would leave children of two and four years? And, moreover, on this view Chung-zăn was the elder brother, and Mencius would have mentioned him first. But there is a solution which meets all the difficulties of the case. First, we assume, with the old explanation, that Wâi-ping and Chung-zăn were both dead when T'âi-chiâ succeeded to the throne. Then, with Ch'ăng, we take 年 in the sense of 歲, years of life, and not of reign;—and the meaning thus comes out, that T'âi-ting died before his father, and his brothers Wâi-ping and Chung-zăn died also, the one at the age of two, and the other of four years.' 刑,—in the sense of laws. T'ung was the place where T'ang had been buried, and Po the name of his capital. There is some controversy about the time of T'âi-chiâ's detention in T'ung, whether the three years are to be reckoned from his accession, or from the conclusion of the three years of mourning. The 'Historical Records' sanction the latter view, but the former is generally received, as more in accordance with the Shû-ching. 7. We must understand Confucius's saying,—the second clause of it,—as referring to the first sovereigns of the dynasties mentioned, and 繼, opposed to 禪, = 傳, 'to transmit to,' i.e. their sons. 唐 and 虞 are Yâo and Shun; see the Shû-ching, I, II. 夏后,—see Analects, III. xxxi. 1. Yü originally was the 伯, or Baron, of Hsiâ, a district in the present department of K'âi-făng. The one principle of righteousness was accordance with the will of Heaven, as expressed in par. 1, 天與賢,則與賢,天與子,則與子.

7. VINDICATION OF Î YIN FROM THE CHARGE OF INTRODUCING HIMSELF TO THE SERVICE OF T'ANG BY AN UNWORTHY ARTIFICE. 1. 要, the 1st tone, = 求, or 干, 'to seek,' i.e. an introduction to, or the favour of. Î (伊 is the surname) Yin (尹, the 'regulator,' is the designation) was the chief minister of T'ang. The popular account (found also in the 'Historical Records')

湯、有諸。○二 孟子曰、否、不然、伊尹耕於有莘之野、而樂堯舜之道焉、非其義也、非其道也、祿之以天下、弗顧也、繫馬千駟、弗視也、非其義也、非其道也、一介不以與人、一介不以取諸人。○三 湯使人以幣聘之、囂囂然曰、我何以湯之聘幣爲哉、我豈若處畎畝之中、由是以樂堯舜之道哉。○四 湯三使往聘

2. Mencius replied, 'No, it was not so. Î Yin was a farmer in the lands of the prince of Hsin, delighting in the principles of Yâo and Shun. In any matter contrary to the righteousness which they prescribed, or contrary to their principles, though he had been offered the throne, he would not have regarded it; though there had been yoked for him a thousand teams of horses, he would not have looked at them. In any matter contrary to the righteousness which they prescribed, or contrary to their principles, he would neither have given nor taken a single straw.

3. 'T'ang sent persons with presents of silk to entreat him to enter his service. With an air of indifference and self-satisfaction he said, "What can I do with those silks with which T'ang invites me? Is it not best for me to abide in the channelled fields, and so delight myself with the principles of Yâo and Shun?"

4. 'T'ang thrice sent messengers to invite him. After this, with

in the times of Mencius was, that Î Yin came to Po in the train of a daughter of the prince of Hsin, whom T'ang was marrying, carrying his cooking-instruments with him, that by 'cutting and boiling,' he might recommend himself to favour. 2. 有莘之野,—Î Yin was a native of Hsin, the same territory which under the Châu dynasty was called Kwo, the present Shen-châu (陝州) of Ho-nan. It was not far distant from T'ang's original seat of Po, also in the present Ho-nan. 有莘 = 有莘氏, 'the surname, i.e. the prince, holding Hsin.' 非其義也, 非其道也 are in apposition, the one explanatory of the other. 祿之,—literally, 'emolument him.' 駟, 'a team of four horses.' 介 = 芥. 3. 聘, 'to ask,' often used for 'to ask in marriage;' here, 'to ask to be minister.' 4. 改曰 may be 改

之、既而幡然改曰、與我處畎畝之中、由是以樂堯舜之道、吾豈若使是君爲堯舜之君哉、吾豈若使是民爲堯舜之民哉、吾豈若於吾身親見之哉。〇五節 天之生此民也、使先知覺後知、使先覺覺後覺也、予、天民之先覺者也、予將以斯道覺斯民也、非予覺之而誰也。〇六節 思天下之民、匹夫匹婦、有不被堯舜之澤者、若已推而

the change of resolution displayed in his countenance, he spoke in a different style,—"Instead of abiding in the channelled fields and thereby delighting myself with the principles of Yâo and Shun, had I not better make this prince a prince like Yâo or Shun, and this people like the people of Yâo or Shun? Had I not better in my own person see these things for myself?

5. '"Heaven's plan in the production of mankind is this:—that they who are first informed should instruct those who are later in being informed, and they who first apprehend principles should instruct those who are slower to do so. I am one of Heaven's people who have first apprehended;—I will take these principles and instruct this people in them. If I do not instruct them, who will do so?"

6. 'He thought that among all the people of the kingdom, even the private men and women, if there were any who did not enjoy

其計曰, 'changed his plan, and said,' or 改其言曰, 'changed his words, and said.' 堯舜之君, 'a prince of, = like to, Yâo and Shun.' I do not see exactly the force of 於吾身 in the last sentence, and have therefore simply translated the phrase literally. 5. This paragraph is to be understood as spoken by I Yin. The meaning of 覺, 'to apprehend,' 'to understand,' is an advance on that of 知, simply 'to know.' The student will observe also that it is used actively three times, = 'to instruct.' In 生此民, the 此民, 'this people,' = 'mankind.' 6. 內,—read as, and = 納. 說,—read *shwuy*, in 3nd tone, 'to advise,'

內之溝中、其自任以天下之重如此、故就湯而說之、以伐夏救民。○七節吾未聞枉己而正人者也、況辱己以正天下者乎、聖人之行、不同也、或遠或近、或去或不去、歸潔其身而已矣。○八節吾聞其以堯舜之道要湯、未聞以割烹也。○九節伊訓曰、天誅造攻自牧宮、朕載自亳。

such benefits as Yâo and Shun conferred, it was as if he himself pushed them into a ditch. He took upon himself the heavy charge of the kingdom in this way, and therefore he went to T'ang, and pressed upon him the subject of attacking Hsiâ and saving the people.

7. 'I have not heard of one who bent himself, and at the same time made others straight;—how much less could one disgrace himself, and thereby rectify the whole kingdom? The actions of the sages have been different. Some have kept remote *from court*, and some have drawn near *to it;* some have left their offices, and some have not done so:—that to which those different courses all agree is simply the keeping of their persons pure.

8. 'I have heard that Î Yin sought an introduction to T'ang by the doctrines of Yâo and Shun. I have not heard that he did so by his knowledge of cookery.

9. 'In the "Instructions of Î," it is said, "Heaven destroying Chieh commenced attacking him in the palace of Mû. I commenced in Po."'

'to persuade.' 說之以, 'advised him about.' 7. Compare Bk. III. Pt. II. i. 1, 5. 歸 = 要歸, 'if we seek where they came to, where they centered.' 8. 要,—as in paragraph 1. 9. See the Shû-ching, IV. iv. 2, but the classic and this text are so different that many suppose Mencius to quote from some form of the book referred to which Confucius disallowed. The meaning is that Chieh's atrocities in his palace in Mû led Heaven to destroy him, while Î Yin, in accordance with the will of Heaven, advised T'ang in Po to take action against him. 造 and 載, both = 始, 'to begin.'

孟子

第八章 萬章問曰、或謂孔子於衞主癰疽、於齊主侍人瘠環、有諸乎。孟子曰、否、不然也、好事者爲之也。於衞、主顏讐由、彌子之妻、與子路之妻、兄弟也、彌子謂子路曰、孔子主我、衞卿可得也。子路以告、孔子曰、有命、孔子進以禮、退以義、得之不得、曰、有命、而主癰疽與侍

CHAP. VIII. 1. Wan Chang asked *Mencius*, saying, 'Some say that Confucius, when he was in Wei, lived with the ulcer-doctor, and when he was in Ch'î, with the attendant, Ch'î Hwan;—was it so?' Mencius replied, 'No; it was not so. Those are the inventions of men fond of strange things.

2. 'When he was in Wei, he lived with Yen Ch'âu-yû. The wives of the officer Mî and Tsze-lû were sisters, and Mî told Tsze-lû, "If Confucius will lodge with me, he may attain to the dignity of a high noble of Wei." Tsze-lû informed Confucius of this, and he said, "That is as ordered *by Heaven*." Confucius went into office according to propriety, and retired from it according to righteousness. In regard to his obtaining office or not obtaining it, he said, "That is as ordered." But if he had lodged with the attendant

8. VINDICATION OF CONFUCIUS FROM THE CHARGE OF LODGING WITH UNWORTHY CHARACTERS. 1. 癰, 'a swelling,' 'an ulcer,' and 疽 (read *tsü*, in 1st tone), 'a deep-seated ulcer.' Chû Hsî, after Châo Ch'î, takes the two terms as in the translation. Some, however, take the characters as a man's name, called also 雍渠, 雍雎, and 雍鉏. They are probably right. The 'Historical Records' make 雍渠 to have been the eunuch in attendance on the duke of Wei, when he rode through the market-place with the duchess, followed by the sage,—to his great disgust. 侍人=奄人, 'the eunuch.' Eunuchs were employed during the Châu dynasty. Both the men referred to were unworthy favourites of their respective princes. 好 (in 3rd tone) 事者, 'one who is fond of raising trouble,' and in a lighter sense, as here, 'one who is fond of saying, and doing, strange things.' 主=舍於其家, 'lodged in his house,' literally, '*hosted* him.' In par. 4, 以其所爲主, 'by those of whom they are hosts;' 以其所主, 'by those whom they host,' i. e. make their hosts. 2. Yen Ch'âu-yû, called also 顏濁鄒, was a worthy officer of Wei. One account has it, that he was brother to Tsze-lû's wife, but this is probably incorrect. Mî, with the name Hsiâ (瑕), was an unworthy

人瘠環、是無義無命也。三節孔子不悅於魯衛、遭宋桓司馬、將要而殺之、微服而過宋、是時、孔子當阨、主司城貞子、爲陳侯周臣。四節吾聞觀近臣、以其所爲主、觀遠臣、以其所主、若孔子主癰疽、與侍人瘠環、何以爲孔子。

第九章 一節 萬章問曰、或曰、百里奚、自鬻於秦養牲者、五羊之

Chî Hwan, that would neither have been according to righteousness, nor any ordering *of Heaven.*

3. 'When Confucius, being dissatisfied in Lû and Wei, *had left those States*, he met with the attempt of Hwan, the Master of the Horse, of Sung, to intercept and kill him. He assumed, however, the dress of a common man, and passed by Sung. At that time, though he was in circumstances of distress, he lodged with the city-master Ch'ăng, who was *then* a minister of Châu, the marquis of Ch'ăn.

4. 'I have heard that *the characters of* ministers about court may be discerned from those whom they entertain, and those of stranger officers, from those with whom they lodge. If Confucius had lodged with the ulcer-doctor, and with the attendant Chî Hwan, how could he have been Confucius?'

CHAP. IX. 1. Wan Chang asked *Mencius*, 'Some say that Pâi-lî Hsî sold himself to a cattle-keeper of Ch'in for the skins of

favourite of the duke Ling. 3. Compare Analects, VII. xxii; Hwan is the Hwan T'ûi there. 要, in 1st tone, = 攔截, 'to intercept.' 微服, 'small clothes,' i.e. the dress of a common man. 貞, 'the Pure,' is the honorary epithet of the officer who was Confucius's host, and 周 was the proper name of the prince of Ch'ăn, with whom indeed the independence of the State terminated. Chăng, it is said, afterwards became 'city-master' in Sung, and was known as such;—hence he is so styled here at an earlier period of his life. 4. 近遠 here have a different application from what belongs to them in the last chapter, par. 7.

9. VINDICATION OF PÂI-LÎ HSÎ FROM THE CHARGE OF SELLING HIMSELF AS A STEP TO HIS ADVANCEMENT. 1. Pâi-lî Hsî was chief minister to the duke Mû (穆 = 'the diffuser of virtue, and maintainer of integrity'), B.C. 659-620. His history will be found interestingly detailed in the twenty-fifth and some subsequent Books of the 'History of the Several States' (列國志), though the incidents there are, some of them, different from Mencius's statements about him. With regard to that in this paragraph, it is not easy to understand the popular

皮、食牛、以要秦穆公、信乎。孟子曰、否、不然、好事者爲之也。○二節 百里奚、虞人也、晉人以垂棘之璧、與屈產之乘、假道於虞以伐虢、宮之奇諫、百里奚不諫。○三節 知虞公之不可諫、而去之秦、年已七十矣、曾不知以食牛干秦穆公之爲汙也、可謂智乎、不可諫而不諫、可謂不智

five rams, and fed his oxen, in order to find an introduction to the duke Mû of Ch'in;—was this the case?' Mencius said, 'No; it was not so. This story was invented by men fond of strange things.

2. 'Pâi-lî Hsî was a man of Yü. The people of Tsin, by the inducement of a round piece of jade from Ch'ûi-chî, and four horses of the Ch'ü breed, borrowed a passage through Yü to attack Kwo. *On that occasion*, Kung Chih-ch'î remonstrated *against granting their request*, and Pâi-lî Hsî did not remonstrate.

3. 'When he knew that the duke of Yü was not to be remonstrated with, and, leaving that State, went to Ch'in, he had reached the age of seventy. If by that time he did not know that it would be a mean thing to seek an introduction to the duke Mû of Ch'in by feeding oxen, could he be called wise? But not remonstrating where it was of no use to remonstrate, could he be said not to be

account referred to. The account in the 'Historical Records,' 秦本記, is, that, after the subversion of Yü, Hsî followed its captive duke to Tsin, refusing to take service in that State, and was afterwards sent to Ch'in in a menial capacity, in the train of the eldest daughter of the house of Tsin, who was to become the wife of the duke Mû. Disgusted at being in such a position, Hsî absconded on the road, and fleeing to Ch'û, he became noted for his skill in rearing cattle. The duke Mû somehow heard of his great capacity, and sent to Ch'û, to reclaim him as a runaway servant, offering also to pay for his ransom five rams' skins. He was afraid to offer a more valuable ransom, lest he should awaken suspicions in Ch'û that he wanted to get Hsî on account of his ability; and on obtaining him, he at once made him his chief minister. 食,—read *tsze*, 4th tone, = 飼, 'to feed.' 要,—as in chap. 7, the 1st tone. 好事者,—as in last chapter. 2. Ch'ûi-chî and Ch'û were the names of places in Tsin, the one famous for its jade, the other for its horses. 乘, 4th tone, 'a team of four horses.' Kwo and Yü were small States, adjoining each other, and only safe against the attacks of their more powerful neighbour, Tsin, by their mutual union. Both the officers of Yü, Kung Chih-ch'î and Pâi-lî Hsî, saw this, but Hsî saw also that no remonstrances would prevail with the duke of Yü against the bribes of Tsin. 3. 去

乎、知虞公之將亡、而先去之、不可謂不智也、時舉於秦、知穆公之可與有行也、而相之、可謂不智乎、相秦、而顯其君於天下、可傳於後世、不賢而能之乎、自鬻以成其君、鄉黨自好者不爲、而謂賢者爲之乎。

wise? Knowing that the duke of Yü would be ruined, and leaving him before that event, he cannot be said not to have been wise. Being then advanced in Ch'in, he knew that the duke Mû was one with whom he would enjoy a field for action, and became minister to him;—could he, *acting thus*, be said not to be wise? Having become chief minister of Ch'in, he made his prince distinguished throughout the kingdom, and worthy of being handed down to future ages;—could he have done this, if he had not been a man of talents and virtue? As to selling himself in order to accomplish all the aims of his prince, even a villager who had a regard for himself would not do such a thing; and shall we say that a man of talents and virtue did it?'

之秦,—之=往, the verb. 而先去之,—this may have been prudent, but was not honourable. It is contrary to other accounts of Hsi's conduct. He is said to have urged Chih-ch'î to leave Yü after his remonstrance, while he remained himself to be with the duke in the evil day which he saw approaching. 鄉黨 are to be taken together.

WAN CHANG. PART II.

萬章章句下

第一章 孟子曰、伯夷、目不視惡色、耳不聽惡聲、非其君不事、非其民不使、治則進、亂則退、橫政之所出、橫民之所止、不忍居也、思與鄉人處、如以朝衣朝冠、坐於塗炭也、當紂之時、居北海之濱、以待天下之淸也、故聞伯夷之風者、頑夫廉、懦夫

CHAPTER I. 1. Mencius said, 'Po-î would not allow his eyes to look on a bad sight, nor his ears to listen to a bad sound. He would not serve a prince whom he did not approve, nor command a people whom he did not esteem. In a time of good government he took office, and on the occurrence of confusion he retired. He could not bear to dwell either in *a court* from which a lawless government emanated, or among lawless people. He considered his being in the same place with a villager, as if he were to sit amid mud and coals with his court robes and court cap. In the time of Châu he dwelt on the shores of the North sea, waiting the purification of the kingdom. Therefore when men *now* hear the character of Po-î, the corrupt become pure, and the weak acquire determination.

1. HOW CONFUCIUS DIFFERED FROM AND WAS SUPERIOR TO ALL OTHER SAGES. 1. Compare Bk. II. Pt. I. ii. 22, and ix; Bk. IV. Pt. I. xiii. 1. 橫政之所出, 'the place whence perverse government issues,' i.e. a court. 橫民之所止, 'the place where perverse people stop.' 頑 is properly 'stupid,' 'obstinate,' but here as opposed to 廉, we must take it in the sense of 'corrupt.' Julien, indeed, takes 廉 in the sense of '*habere vim discernendi*.' But it is better to retain its proper signification, and to alter that of 頑, with the gloss in the

有立志。二節伊尹曰、何事非君、何使非民、治亦進、亂亦進、曰、天之生斯民也、使先知覺後知、使先覺覺後覺、予、天民之先覺者也、予將以此道覺此民也、思天下之民、匹夫匹婦、有不與被堯舜之澤者、若己推而內之溝中、其自任以天下之重也。三節柳下惠、不羞汙君、不辭小官、進不隱賢、必以其道、遺佚而不怨、阨窮而不憫、

2. 'Î Yin said, "Whom may I not serve? My serving him makes him my sovereign. What people may I not command? My commanding them makes them my people." In a time of good government he took office, and when confusion prevailed, he also took office. He said, "Heaven's plan in the production of mankind is this:—that they who are first informed should instruct those who are later in being informed, and they who first apprehend principles should instruct those who are slower in doing so. I am the one of Heaven's people who has first apprehended;—I will take these principles and instruct the people in them." He thought that among all the people of the kingdom, even the common men and women, if there were any who did not share in the enjoyment of such benefits as Yâo and Shun conferred, it was as if he himself pushed them into a ditch;—for he took upon himself the heavy charge of the kingdom.

3. 'Hûi of Liû-hsiâ was not ashamed to serve an impure prince, nor did he think it low to be an inferior officer. When advanced to employment, he did not conceal his virtue, *but* made it a point to

備旨,—頑夫無知覺,必貪昧嗜利,故與廉反. 2. Compare Bk. II. Pt. I. ii. 22; and Bk. V. Pt. I. vii. 2-6. Observe, that here instead of 有不被…澤者, we have 有不與被…澤者, = 'if there were any who did not have part in the enjoyment,' &c. 3. Compare Bk. II. Pt. I. ix. 2. The clause 與鄉人,云云, which

孟子

與鄉人處、由由然不忍去也、爾爲爾、我爲我、雖袒裼裸裎於我側、爾焉能浼我哉、故聞柳下惠之風者、鄙夫寬、薄夫敦。四節孔子之去齊、接淅而行、去魯、曰、遲遲吾行也、去父母國之道也、可以速而速、可以久而久、可以處而處、可以仕而仕、孔子也。五節孟子曰、伯夷、聖之清者也、伊尹、聖之任者也、柳

carry out his principles. When dismissed and left without office, he did not murmur. When straitened by poverty, he did not grieve. When thrown into the company of village people, he was quite at ease and could not bear to leave them. *He had a saying*, "You are you, and I am I. Although you stand by my side with breast and arms bare, or with your body naked, how can you defile me?" Therefore when men now hear the character of Hûi of Liû-hsiâ, the mean become generous, and the niggardly become liberal.

4. 'When Confucius was leaving Ch'î, he strained off with his hand the water in which his rice was being rinsed, *took the rice*, and went away. When he left Lû, he said, "I will set out by-and-by:"—it was right he should leave the country of his parents in this way. When it was proper to go away quickly, he did so; when it was proper to delay, he did so; when it was proper to keep in retirement, he did so; when it was proper to go into office, he did so:—this was Confucius.'

5. Mencius said, 'Po-î among the sages was the pure one; Î Yin

is wanting there, makes the 故日 of that place more plain. 袒 is 'to have the arms bare,' and 裼, 'to put off all the upper garment.' 裸裎, together, is 'to have the body naked.' Here and in par. 1, 風 is expressed more nearly by 'character,' than by any other English term. 4. 淅, 'to rinse or wash rice,' 'the water in which rice is washed.' The latter is the sense here. 遲遲吾行 was the answer given by Confucius to Tsze-lû, who wished to hurry him away. 5. I have invented the adjective

下惠聖之和者也、孔子、聖之時者也。六孔子之謂集大成、集大成也者、金聲而玉振之也、金聲也者、始條理也、玉振之也者、終條理也、始條理者、智之事也、終條理者、聖之事也。七智、譬則巧也、聖、譬則力也、由射於百步之外也、其至、爾力也、其中、非爾力也。

was the one most inclined to take office; Hûi of Liû-hsiâ was the accommodating one; and Confucius was the timeous one.

6. 'In Confucius we have what is called a complete concert. A complete concert is when the *large* bell proclaims the *commencement of the music*, and the ringing stone proclaims its close. The metal sound commences the blended harmony of all the instruments, and the winding up with the stone terminates that blended harmony. The commencing that harmony is the work of wisdom. The terminating it is the work of sageness.

7. 'As a comparison for wisdom, we may liken it to skill, and as a comparison for sageness, we may liken it to strength;—as in the case of shooting at a mark a hundred paces distant. That you reach it is owing to your strength, but that you hit the mark is not owing to your strength.'

'timeous' to translate the 時 here, meaning that Confucius did at every *time* what the circumstances of it required, possessing the qualities of all other sages, and displaying them, at the proper time and place. 6. The illustration of Confucius here is from a grand performance of music, in which all the eight kinds of musical instruments are united. One instrument would make a 小成, 'small performance.' Joined, they make a 集大成, 'a collected great performance,'='a concert.' 聲, 始, and 終 are all used as verbs. 條理, 'discriminated rules,' indicates the separate music of the various instruments blended together. 金聲 and 振之 are not parts of the concert, but the signals of its commencement and close, the 之 referring to 集大聲. 7. Observe the comma after 智 and 聖. 由=猶. 'The other three worthies,' it is observed, 'carried one point to an extreme, but Confucius was complete in everything. We may compare each of them to one of the seasons, but Con-

第二章 北宮錡問曰、(一節)周室班爵祿也、如之何。孟子曰、(二節)其詳不可得聞也、諸侯惡其害己也、而皆去其籍、然而軻也、嘗聞其畧也。天子一位、(三節)公一位、侯一位、伯一位、子男同一位、凡五等也、君一位、卿一位、大夫一位、上士一位、中士一位、下士一位、

CHAP. II. 1. Pêi-kung Î asked *Mencius*, saying, 'What was the arrangement of dignities and emoluments determined by the House of Châu?'

2. Mencius replied, 'The particulars of that arrangement cannot be learned, for the princes, disliking them as injurious to themselves, have all made away with the records of them. Still I have learned the general outline of them.

3. 'The SON OF HEAVEN constituted one dignity; the KUNG one; the HÂU one; the PÂI one; and the TSZE and the NAN each one of equal rank:—altogether making five degrees of rank. The RULER *again* constituted one dignity; the CHIEF MINISTER one; the GREAT OFFICERS one; the SCHOLARS OF THE FIRST CLASS one; THOSE OF THE MIDDLE CLASS one; and THOSE OF THE LOWEST CLASS one:—altogether making six degrees of dignity.

fucius was the grand, harmonious air of heaven, flowing through all the seasons.'

2. THE ARRANGEMENT OF DIGNITIES AND EMOLUMENTS ACCORDING TO THE DYNASTY OF CHÂU. 1. Pêi-kung Î was an officer of the State of Wei. The double surname, 'Northern-palace,' had probably been given to the founder of the family from his residence. 2. Many passages might be quoted from the Lî Chî, the Châu Lî, and the Shû-ching, illustrating, more or less, the dignities of the kingdom and their emoluments, but it would be of little use to adduce them after Mencius's declaration that only the general outline of them could be ascertained. It is an important fact which he mentions, that the princes had destroyed (c去, 3rd tone) many of the records before his time. The founder of the Ch'in dynasty had had predecessors and patterns. 惡, 4th tone, 'to hate.'

3. 公, 侯, 伯, 子, 男 have been rendered 'duke, marquis, earl, viscount, and baron,' and also 'duke, prince, count, marquis, and baron,' but they by no means severally correspond to those dignities. It is better to retain the Chinese designations, which, no doubt, were originally meant to indicate certain qualities of those bearing them. 公 = 'just, correct, without selfishness.' 侯, 'taking care of,' = 候, in the sense of 'guarding the borders and important places against banditti; possessed of the power to govern.' 伯 conveys the idea of 'elder and intelligent,' 'one capable of presiding over others.' 子 = 孳, 'to nourish,' 'one who genially cherishes the people.' 男 (from 田, 'field,' and 力, 'strength'), 'one adequate to

凡六等。○四節天子之制、地方千里、公侯皆方百里、伯七十里、子男五十里、凡四等。不能五十里、不達於天子、附於諸侯、曰附庸。○五節天子之卿、受地視侯、大夫受地視伯、元士受地視子男。○六節大國地方百里、君十卿祿、卿祿四

4. 'To the Son of Heaven there was allotted a territory of a thousand *li* square. A Kung and a Hâu had each a hundred *li* square. A Pâi had seventy *li*, and a Tsze and a Nan had each fifty *li*. The assignments altogether were of four amounts. Where the territory did not amount to fifty *li*, the chief could not have access himself to the Son of Heaven. His land was attached to some Hâu-ship, and was called a FÛ-YUNG.

5. 'The Chief ministers of the Son of Heaven received an amount of territory equal to that of a Hâu; a Great officer received as much as a Pâi; and a scholar of the first class as much as a Tsze or a Nan.

6. 'In a great State, where the territory was a hundred *li* square, the ruler had ten times as much income as his Chief ministers;

office and labour.' The name of 君, 'ruler,' 'sovereign,' is applicable to all the dignities enumerated, and under each of them are the secondary or ministerial dignities. 卿=彰, 'one who can illustrate what is good and right.' 夫=扶, 'to support,' 'to sustain;'—大夫, 'a great sustainer.' 士, 'a scholar,' 'an officer;'—任事之稱, 'the designation of one entrusted with business.' 4. 地方千里,—this means, according to the commentator 彭絲, 橫千里, 直千里, 共一百萬里也, '1,000 *li* in breadth, and 1,000 *li* in length, making an area of 1,000,000 *li*.' On this, however, the following judgment is given by the editors of the imperial edition of the five *Ching* of the present dynasty:—'Where we find the word *square* (方) we are not to think of an exact square, but simply that, on a calculation, the amount of territory is equal to so many square *li*. For instance, we are told by the minister Tsan that, at the western capital of Châu, the territory was 800 *li* square. The meaning is that there were 8 × 8 squares of 100 *li*. At the eastern capital again, the territory was 600 *li* square, or 6 × 6 squares of 100 *li*. Putting these two together, we get the total of 1,000 *li* square. So in regard to the various States of the princes, we are to understand that, however their form might be varied by the hills and rivers, their area, in round numbers, amounted to so much;'—see in the Lî Chî, III. i, 2, where the text, however, is not at all perspicuous. 附, 'attached;' 庸, 'meritoriousness.' These States were too small to bear the expenses of appearing before the sovereign, and therefore, the names and surnames of their chiefs were sent into court by the great princes to whom they were *attached*, or perhaps they appeared in their train;—see on Analects, XVI. i. 1. 5. 元士, 'Head scholar,' could only be applied to the scholars of the first class in the sovereign's immediate government. 6. 庶人在官 would be runners, clerks, and other subor-

大夫、大夫倍上士、上士倍中士、中士倍下士、下士與庶人在官者同祿、祿足以代其耕也。○七節次國地方七十里、君十卿祿、卿祿三大夫、大夫倍上士、上士倍中士、中士倍下士、下士與庶人在官者同祿、祿足以代其耕也。○八節小國地方五十里、君十卿祿、卿祿二大夫、大夫

a Chief minister four times as much as a Great officer; a Great officer twice as much as a scholar of the first class; a scholar of the first class twice as much as one of the middle; a scholar of the middle class twice as much as one of the lowest; the scholars of the lowest class, and such of the common people as were employed about the government offices, had for their emolument as much as was equal to what they would have made by tilling the fields.

7. 'In a State of the next order, where the territory was seventy *lî* square, the ruler had ten times as much revenue as his Chief minister; a Chief minister three times as much as a Great officer; a Great officer twice as much as a scholar of the first class; a scholar of the first class twice as much as one of the middle; a scholar of the middle class twice as much as one of the lowest; the scholars of the lowest class, and such of the common people as were employed about the government offices, had for their emolument as much as was equal to what they would have made by tilling the fields.

8. 'In a small State, where the territory was fifty *lî* square, the ruler had ten times as much revenue as his Chief minister; a Chief minister had twice as much as a Great officer; a Great officer twice as much as a scholar of the highest class; a scholar of the highest class twice as much as one of the middle; a scholar of

dinates, which appear in the Châu Lî, as 府, 史, 胥, and 徒. Chû Hsî gives his opinion, that, from the sovereign downwards, all who had lands received their incomes from them, as cultivated on the system of mutual aid, while the landless scholars and other subordinates received according to the income

倍上士、上士倍中士、中士倍下士、下士與庶人在官者同祿、祿足以代其耕也。（九）耕者之所獲、一夫百畝、百畝之糞、上農夫食九人、上次食八人、中食七人、中次食六人、下食五人、庶人在官者、其祿以是爲差。

（三章）（一節）萬章問曰、敢問友、孟子曰、不挾長、不挾貴、不挾兄弟而友、友也者、友其德也、不可以有挾也。

the middle class twice as much as one of the lowest; scholars of the lowest class, and such of the common people as were employed about the government offices, had the same emolument;—as much, namely, as was equal to what they would have made by tilling the fields.

9. 'As to those who tilled the fields, each husbandman received a hundred mâu. When those mâu were manured, the best husbandmen of the highest class supported nine individuals, and those ranking next to them supported eight. The best husbandmen of the second class supported seven individuals, and those ranking next to them supported six; while husbandmen of the lowest class only supported five. The salaries of the common people who were employed about the government offices were regulated according to these differences.'

CHAP. III. 1. Wan Chang asked *Mencius*, saying, 'I venture to ask *the principles of* friendship.' Mencius replied, 'Friendship should be maintained without any presumption on the ground of one's superior age, or station, or *the circumstances of his* relatives. Friendship *with a man* is friendship with his virtue, and does not admit of assumptions of superiority.

from the land. 9. 食,—read *tsze*. 差,—read *ts'ze*, 'uneven,' 'different.'

3. FRIENDSHIP MUST HAVE REFERENCE TO THE VIRTUE OF THE FRIEND. THERE MAY BE NO ASSUMPTION ON THE GROUND OF ONE'S OWN ADVANTAGES. 1. 問友,—問交友之道. 長, 3rd tone, having reference to age. 兄弟, 'one's brethren,' in the widest acceptation of that term. Observe how 也者 takes up

孟子

二節 孟獻子百乘之家也、有友五人焉、樂正裘、牧仲、其三人、則予忘之矣、獻子之與此五人者、友也、無獻子之家者也、此五人者、亦有獻子之家、則不與之友矣。三節 非惟百乘之家爲然也、雖小國之君亦有之、費惠公曰、吾於子思、則師之矣、吾於顏般、則友之矣、王順長息、則事我者也。四節 非惟小國之君爲然也、雖大國之君亦

2. 'There was Măng Hsien, *chief of* a family of a hundred chariots. He had five friends, namely, Yŏ-chăng Chiû, Mû Chung, and three others *whose names* I have forgotten. With those five men Hsien maintained a friendship, because they thought nothing about his family. If they had thought about his family, he would not have maintained his friendship with them.

3. 'Not only has the *chief of* a family of a hundred chariots acted thus. The same thing was exemplified by the sovereign of a small State. The duke Hûi of Pî said, "I treat Tsze-sze as my Teacher, and Yen Pan as my Friend. As to Wang Shun and Ch'ang Hsî, they serve me."

4. 'Not only has the sovereign of a small State acted thus. The same thing has been exemplified by the sovereign of a large State.

the preceding 友, and goes on to its explanation. 其 refers to the individual who is the object of the 友; friendship with him as virtuous will tend to help our virtue. 有挾, 'to have presumptions,' with reference of course to the three points mentioned, but as of those the second most readily comes into collision with friendship, it alone is dwelt upon in the sequel. 2. Măng Hsien,—see 'Great Learning,' Comm. x. 22. 3. 費, read Pî,—see Analects, VI. vii. We must suppose that, after the time of Confucius, some chief had held this place and district with the title of Kung. 'The Kind (惠)' is the honorary epithet. Tsze-sze is Confucius's grandson. 般,—read *pan*. Yen Pan appears to have been the son of the sage's favourite disciple. 4. P'ing ('The Pacificator') was the honorary epithet of the duke 彪, B.C. 556-531. Hâi T'ang was a famous worthy of his State. 入云, '*enter* being said.' 疏

有之、晉平公之於亥唐也、入云則入、坐云則坐、食云則食、雖蔬食菜羹、未嘗不飽、蓋不敢不飽也、然終於此而已矣、弗與共天位也、弗與治天職也、弗與食天祿也、士之尊賢者也、非王公之尊賢也。○五節 舜尙見帝、帝館甥于貳室、亦饗舜、迭爲賓主、是天子而友匹夫

There was the duke P'ing of Tsin with Hâi T'ang:—when *T'ang* told him to come into his house, he came; when he told him to be seated, he sat; when he told him to eat, he ate. There might only be coarse rice and soup of vegetables, but he always ate his fill, not daring to do otherwise. Here, however, he stopped, and went no farther. He did not call him to share any of Heaven's places, or to govern any of Heaven's offices, or to partake of any of Heaven's emoluments. His conduct was but a scholar's honouring virtue and talents, not the honouring them proper to a king or a duke.

5. 'Shun went up to *court* and saw the sovereign, who lodged him as his son-in-law in the second palace. The sovereign also enjoyed there Shun's hospitality. Alternately he was host and guest. Here was the sovereign maintaining friendship with a private man.

食,—食, read *tsze*, 4th tone. The 之 after 平公 and 王公 is wanting in many copies. 與其天位, 云云, would seem to be a complaint that the duke did not share with the scholar his own rank, &c., but the meaning in the translation, which is that given by the commentator, is perhaps the correct one. Rank, station, and revenue are said to be Heaven's, as entrusted to the ruler to be conferred on individuals able to occupy in them for the public good. 5. In this paragraph, Mencius advances another step, and exemplifies the highest style of friendship. Chû Hsî, after Châo Ch'î, explains 尙 by 上, as if it were 'to go up to,' i. e. to court. 貳室 = 副宮, 'attached or supplemental palace.' 饗是就舜宮而饗其食, '饗 means that he went to Shun's palace, and partook of his food.' The more common meaning of 饗, however, is 'to entertain.' 迭爲,—the subject is only Yâo. 賓, 'made a guest' of Shun, was the host. 主, 'made a host' of Shun,

也。六節用下敬上、謂之貴貴、用上敬下、謂之尊賢、貴貴尊賢、其義一也。

第四章 一節萬章問曰、敢問交際、何心也。孟子曰、恭也。二節曰、郤之郤之、爲不恭、何哉。曰、尊者賜之。曰、其所取之者義乎、不義乎、而後受之、以是爲不恭、故弗郤也。三節曰、請無以辭郤之、以心郤之、曰、其取

6. 'Respect shown by inferiors to superiors is called giving to the noble the observance due to rank. Respect shown by superiors to inferiors is called giving honour to talents and virtue. The rightness in each case is the same.'

CHAP. IV. 1. Wan Chang asked *Mencius*, saying, 'I venture to ask what *feeling of the* mind is expressed in the presents of friendship?' Mencius replied, '*The feeling of* respect.'

2. 'How is it,' pursued *Chang*, 'that the declining a present is accounted disrespectful?' The answer was, 'When one of honourable rank presents a gift, to say *in the mind*, "Was the way in which he got this righteous or not? I must know this before I can receive it;"—this is deemed disrespectful, and therefore presents are not declined.'

3. *Wan Chang* asked *again*, 'When one does not take on him in so many express words to refuse the gift, but having declined it

was the guest. 6. 用 = 以, 'for.' 義 = 事之宜, 'the rightness or propriety of things.'

4. HOW MENCIUS DEFENDED THE ACCEPTING PRESENTS FROM THE PRINCES, OPPRESSORS OF THE PEOPLE. 1. 際 is explained by 接, but that term is not to be taken in the sense of 'to receive,' but as a synonym of 交. If we distinguish the two words, we may take 交 as = the 友 of the last chapter, and 際 the gift, expressive of the friendship. 2. Chû Hsî says he does not understand the repetition of 郤之. It has probably crept into the text through the oversight of a transcriber, unless we suppose, with the 合講, that the repetition indicates the firmness and decision with which the gift is refused, but the introduction of that element seems out of place. 曰, 其 (referring to 尊者) 所 (所以) 取之, —曰 is the reflection passing in the mind, as in the next paragraph also. We must suppose 人 as the nominative in 以是爲不恭. 3. 請 is not to be understood of Wan Chang, but as indicating the hesitancy and delicacy of the scholar to whom a gift is offered.

諸民之不義也、而以他辭無受、不可乎。曰、其交也以道、其接也以禮、斯孔子受之矣。○四節萬章曰、今有禦人於國門之外者、其交也以道、其餽也以禮、斯可受禦與。曰、不可。康誥曰、殺越人於貨、閔不畏死、凡民罔不譈、是不待教而誅者也、殷受夏、周受殷、所不辭也、於今

in his heart, saying, "It was taken by him unrighteously from the people," and then assigns some other reason for not receiving it;—is not this a proper course?' *Mencius* said, 'When the donor offers it on a ground of reason, and his manner of doing so is according to propriety;—in such a case Confucius would have received it.'

4. Wan Chang said, 'Here now is one who stops and robs people outside the gates of the city. He offers his gift on a ground of reason, and does so in a manner according to propriety;—would the reception of it so acquired by robbery be proper?' Mencius replied, 'It would not be proper. In "The Announcement to K'ang" it is said, "When men kill others, and roll over their bodies to take their property, being reckless and fearless of death, among all the people there are none but detest them:"—thus, such characters are to be put to death, without waiting to give them warning. Yin received *this rule* from Hsiâ, and Châu received it from Yin. It cannot

其交也, 以道,—其 still referring to 尊者, and 道 to the deservingness of the scholar, or something in his circumstances which renders the gift proper and seasonable. Compare Bk. II. Pt. II. iii. 3, 4. The meaning of 接 is determined (contrary to Châo Ch'î) by the 餽, which takes its place in the next paragraph. 4. 國門之外,—國 as in Bk. IV. Pt. II. xxxiii. 1. 斯可受之與,—斯, as in the last paragraph, adverbially, = 'in this case.' 康誥曰, see the Shû-ching, Bk. V. x. 15, though the text is somewhat altered in the quotation, and 閔 and 譈 take the place of 暋 and 憝. 于 = 'for the sake of,' i.e. to take. 殷 . . . 烈 is a passage of which the meaning is much disputed. Chû Hsî supposes it a gloss that has crept into the text. I have given it what seemed the most likely translation. 其受之,—其 is the party to whom the gift is offered, and 之, the fruit

孟子

爲烈、如之何其受之。○五節曰、今之
諸侯、取之於民也、猶禦也、苟
善其禮際矣、斯君子受之、敢
問何說也。曰、子以爲有王者
作、將比今之諸侯而誅之乎、
其教之不改、而後誅之乎、夫
謂非其有而取之者盜也、充
類至義之盡也、孔子之仕於
魯也、魯人獵較、孔子亦獵較、
獵較猶可、而況受其賜乎。○六節曰、

be questioned, and to the present day is clearly acknowledged. How can the gift *of a robber* be received?'

5. *Chang* said, 'The princes of the present day take from their people just as a robber despoils his victim. Yet if they put a good face of propriety on their gifts, then the superior man receives them. I venture to ask how you explain this.' *Mencius* answered, 'Do you think that, if there should arise a truly royal sovereign, he would collect the princes of the present day, and put them all to death? Or would he admonish them, and then, on their not changing their ways, put them to death? Indeed, to call every one who takes what does not properly belong to him a robber, is pushing a point of resemblance to the utmost, and insisting on the most refined idea of righteousness. When Confucius was in office in Lû, the people struggled together for the game taken in hunting, and he also did the same. If that struggling for the captured game was proper, how much more may the gifts of the princes be received!'

6. *Chang* urged, 'Then are we to suppose that when Confucius

of robbery. 5. 斯,—as above. By 君子 Chang alludes to Mencius himself. 比,—4th tone, 'to take together.' 充類至義之盡,—literally, 'filling up a resemblance to the extremity of righteousness;' the meaning is as in the translation. 獵較 (*chio*) is unintelligible to Chû Hsî. I have given the not unlikely explanation of Châo Ch'î. But to get rid of the declaration that Confucius himself joined in the struggling, the critics all say it only means that he allowed the custom.—The introduction of this yielding on the part of Confucius to a vulgar practice is an adroit manœuvre by Mencius. The offence of the people against propriety in struggling for the game,

然則孔子之仕也、非事道與。曰、事道也。事道、奚獵較也。曰、孔子先簿正祭器、不以四方之食供簿正。曰、奚不去也。曰、爲之兆也、兆足以行矣、而不行、而後去、是以未嘗有所終三年淹也。

七節 孔子有見行可之仕、有際可之仕、有公養之仕、於季桓子、見行可之仕也、於衞

held office, it was not with the view to carry his doctrines into practice?' 'It was with that view,' *Mencius* replied, and *Chang rejoined*, 'If the practice of his doctrines was his business, what had he to do with that struggling for the captured game?' *Mencius* said, 'Confucius first rectified his vessels of sacrifice according to the registers, and did not fill them so rectified with food gathered from every quarter.' 'But why did he not go away?' 'He wished to make a trial *of carrying his doctrines into practice*. When that trial was sufficient to show that they could be practised and they were still not practised, then he went away, and thus it was that he never completed in any State a residence of three years.

7. 'Confucius took office when he saw that the practice *of his doctrines* was likely; he took office when his reception was proper; he took office when he was supported by the State. In the case of his relation to Chî Hwan, he took office, seeing that the practice of

and the offence of the princes in robbing their people, were things of a different class. Yet Mencius's defence of himself in the preceding part of the paragraph is ingenious. It shows that he was eminently a practical man, acting in the way of expediency. How far that way may be pursued will always depend on circumstances. 6. 非事道與 (2nd tone, interrogative) = 非以行道爲事與. 事道奚獵較 is evidently a question of Chang. 先簿正祭器 is unintelligible to Chû Hsî. The translation is after the commentator Hsü (徐氏). 'Food gathered from every quarter,'—i. e. gathered without discrimination. It would appear that the practice of 獵較 had some connexion with the offering of sacrifices, and that Confucius thought that if he only rectified the rules for sacrifice, the practice would fall into disuse. But the whole passage and its bearing on the struggling for game is obscure. 兆,—'a prognostic,' 'an omen,' used figuratively. 7. See the 'Life of Confucius,' though it is only here that we have mention of the sage's connexion with the duke Hsiâo. Indeed no duke appears in the annals of Wei with such a posthumous title. Chû Hsî supposes that the duke Ch'û (see Analects, VII. xiv, note) is intended, in which the author of

靈公、際可之仕也、於衞孝公、公養之仕也。〔五章〕○一節孟子曰、仕、非爲貧也、而有時乎爲貧、娶妻、非爲養也、而有時乎爲養。○二節爲貧者、辭尊居卑、辭富居貧。○三節辭尊居卑、辭富居貧、惡乎宜乎、抱關擊柝。○四節孔子嘗爲委吏矣、曰、會計

his doctrines was likely. With the duke Ling of Wei he took office, because his reception was proper. With the duke Hsiâo of Wei he took office, because he was maintained by the State.'

CHAP. V. 1. Mencius said, 'Office is not *sought* on account of poverty, yet there are times when one seeks office on that account. Marriage is not entered into for the sake of being attended to by the wife, yet there are times when one marries on that account.

2. 'He who *takes office* on account of his poverty must decline an honourable situation and occupy a low one; he must decline riches and prefer to be poor.

3. 'What office will be in harmony with this declining an honourable situation and occupying a low one, this declining riches and preferring to be poor? *Such an one as* that of guarding the gates, or beating the watchman's stick.

4. 'Confucius was once keeper of stores, and he then said, "My calculations must be all right. That is all I have to care about."

the 四書拓餘說 acquiesces. The text mentions Chi Hwan, and not duke Ting, because the duke and his government were under the control of that nobleman.

5. HOW OFFICE MAY BE TAKEN ON ACCOUNT OF POVERTY, BUT ONLY ON CERTAIN CONDITIONS. 1. 仕 and 娶妻,—it is as well to translate here abstractly, 'office,' and 'marriage.' 爲, 4th tone, 'for,' 'on account of.' The proper motive for taking office is supposed to be the carrying principles—the truth, and the right—into practice, and the proper motive for marriage is the begetting of children, or rather of a son, to continue one's line. 乎,—not interrogative, but serving as a pause for the voice. 養, 4th tone, 'the being supported,' but we may take it generally, as in the translation. 2. 尊,—i. e. 尊位, 'an honourable situation,' and 富—富祿, 'rich emolument.' 3. 惡, the 1st tone, 'how.' The first 乎 as above, and helping the rhythm of the sentence. 抱關 (going round the barrier-gates, 'embracing' them, as it were) and 擊柝 are to be taken together, and not as two things, or offices; see the Yî-ching, App. III. Sect. II. 18. 4. In Sze-mâ Ch'ien's History of Confucius, for 委 (4th tone) 吏 we have 季氏史, but in a case of this kind the authority of Mencius is to be followed. 會,—read *kwâi*, 3rd tone, 'entries in a book.' Annual calculations of accounts are denomin-

當而已矣、嘗爲乘田矣、曰、牛羊茁壯長而已矣。[五節]位卑而言高、罪也、立乎人之本朝、而道不行、恥也。

[第六章] 萬章曰、士之不託諸侯、何也。孟子曰、不敢也、諸侯失國、而後託於諸侯、禮也、士之託於諸侯、非禮也。[二節]萬

He was once in charge of the public fields, and he then said, "The oxen and sheep must be fat and strong, and superior. That is all I have to care about."

5. 'When one is in a low situation, to speak of high matters is a crime. When a scholar stands in a prince's court, and his principles are not carried into practice, it is a shame to him.'

CHAP. VI. 1. Wan Chang said, 'What is the reason that a scholar does not accept a stated support from a prince?' Mencius replied, 'He does not presume to do so. When a prince loses his State, and then accepts a stated support from another prince, this is in accordance with propriety. But for a scholar to accept such support from any of the princes is not in accordance with propriety.'

2. Wan Chang said, 'If the prince send him a present of grain,

ated 會, and monthly, 計, when a distinction is made between the terms. 當, 4th tone. 乘 (4th tone) 田 = 主苑囿芻牧之吏, but I do not understand the use of 乘 in this sense. Here again the history has 爲司職 (*yi* = 樴) 吏. These were the first offices Confucius took, before the death of his mother, and while they were yet struggling with poverty. 5. 立乎 (= 于) 人之本朝 (*ch'âou*, 2nd tone),—it is difficult to express the force of the 本; 'to stand in a man's proper court,' i.e. the court of the prince who has called him to office, and where he *ought* to develop and carry out his principles. It is said that this paragraph gives the reasons why he who takes office for poverty must be content with a low situation and small emolument, but the connexion is somewhat difficult to trace. The 四書味根錄 says:—'Why did Confucius confine himself to having his calculations exact, and his cattle sleek and fat? Because in his humble position he had nothing to do with business of the State, and he would not incur the crime of usurping a higher office. If, making a pretence of poverty, a man keep long clinging to high office, he stands in his prince's court, but carries not principles into practice:—can he lay his hand on his heart, and not feel the shame of making his office of none effect?' This is true, but it is not necessary that he who takes office because he is poor should continue to occupy it simply with the desire to get rich.

6. HOW A SCHOLAR MAY NOT BECOME A DEPENDENT BY ACCEPTING PAY WITHOUT OFFICE, AND HOW THE REPEATED PRESENTS OF A PRINCE TO A SCHOLAR MUST BE MADE. 1. 士 is here the scholar, the candidate for public office and use, still unemployed. 不託, 'does not depend on,' i.e. assure himself of a regular support by receiving regular pay though not in office. On one prince,

章曰、君餽之粟、則受之乎。曰、受之。受之何義也。曰、君之於氓也、固周之。（三節）曰、周之則受、賜之則不受、何也。曰、不敢也。曰、敢問其不敢、何也。曰、抱關擊柝者、皆有常職、以食於上、無常職而賜於上者、以爲不恭也。（四節）曰、君餽之、則受之、不識可常繼乎。曰、繆公之於子思也、亟

for instance, does he accept it?' 'He accepts it,' answered *Mencius*. 'On what principle of righteousness does he accept it?' 'Why—the prince ought to assist the people in their necessities.'

3. *Chang* pursued, 'Why is it that the scholar will *thus* accept the prince's help, but will not accept his pay?' The answer was, 'He does not presume to do so.' 'I venture to ask why he does not presume to do so.' 'Even the keepers of the gates, with their watchmen's sticks, have their regular offices for which they can take their support from the prince. He who without a regular office should receive the pay of the prince must be deemed disrespectful.'

4. Chang asked, 'If the prince sends a scholar a present, he accepts it;—I do not know whether this present may be constantly repeated.' *Mencius* answered, 'There was the conduct of the duke

driven from his State, finding an assured and regular support with another, see the Lî-chî, IX. Sect. I. i. 13. It is only stated there, however, that a prince did not employ another refugee prince as a minister. We know only from Mencius, so far as I am aware, that a prince driven from his own dominions would find maintenance in another State, according to a sort of law. 2. 何義, 'what is the principle of righteousness?' or simply—'what is the explanation of?' 周=賙, 'to give alms,' and generally to help the needy. 氓,—see Bk. II. Pt. I. v. 5. A scholar not in office is only one of the people. 3. 賜之, 'if he give him,' i. e. 賜之祿 'give him pay.' This brings out all the meaning that is in 託. 賜於上,—賜 is passive, or = 'to receive pay.' 不恭, 'disrespectful,' is to be taken in its implication of a want of humility in the scholar, who is only one of the people having no office, and yet is content to take pay, as if he had. 4. 亟,—read *ch'i*, 4th tone (below, the same), 'frequently.' 鼎肉, 'caldron flesh,' i. e. flesh cooked. 標,—*piâo*, the 1st tone, 'to motion with the hand.' 使者,—使, 4th tone. 伋 was Taze-sze's name. To bow, raising the

問、亟餽鼎肉、子思不悅於卒也、摽使者出諸大門之外、北面稽首再拜而不受、曰、今而後知君之犬馬畜伋、蓋自是臺無餽也、悅賢不能舉、又不能養也、可謂悅賢乎。○五節、曰、敢問國君欲養君子、如何、斯可謂養矣。曰、以君命將之、再拜稽首而受、其後、廩人繼粟、庖人繼

Mû to Tsze-sze—He made frequent inquiries after Tsze-sze's health, and sent him frequent presents of cooked meat. Tsze-sze was displeased; and at length, having motioned to the messenger to go outside the great door, he bowed his head to the ground with his face to the north, did obeisance twice, and declined the gift, saying, "From this time forth I shall know that the prince supports me as a dog or a horse." And so from that time a servant was no more sent with the presents. When a prince professes to be pleased with a man of talents and virtue, and can neither promote him to office, nor support him *in the proper way*, can he be said to be pleased with him?'

5. Chang said, 'I venture to ask how the sovereign of a State, when he wishes to support a superior man, must proceed, that he may be said to do so in the proper way?' Mencius answered, '*At first*, the present must be offered with the prince's commission, and the scholar, making obeisance twice with his head bowed to the ground, will receive it. But after this the storekeeper will continue

hands to the bent forehead, was called 拜手; lowering the hands in the first place to the ground, and then raising them to the forehead, was called 拜; bowing the head to the earth was called 稽首. Tsze-sze appears on this occasion to have first performed the most profound expression of homage, as if in the prince's presence, and then to have bowed twice, with his hands to the ground, in addition. All this he did, outside the gate, which was the appropriate place in the case of declining the gifts. If they were received, the party performed his obeisances inside. To bring out the meaning of 'for,' that properly belongs to 蓋, we must translate it here by 'and so.' 臺,—the designation of an officer or servant of a very low class.

5. 以君命將之,—將=奉 君命, 'a message from the prince,' reminding of course the scholar of his obligation. 僕僕爾,—an adverb, 'the appearance of being troubled.'

肉、不以君命將之、子思以爲鼎肉、使已僕僕爾亟拜也、非養君子之道也。[六節]堯之於舜也、使其子九男事之、二女女焉、百官牛羊倉廩備、以養舜於畎畝之中、後舉而加諸上位、故曰、王公之尊賢者也。

[七章][一節]萬章曰、敢問不見諸侯、何義也。孟子曰、在國曰市井之臣、在野曰草莽之臣、皆謂庶

to send grain, and the master of the kitchen to send meat, presenting it as if without the prince's express commission. Tsze-sze considered that the meat from the prince's caldron, giving him the annoyance of constantly doing obeisance, was not the way to support a superior man.

6. 'There was Yâo's conduct to Shun:—He caused his nine sons to serve him, and gave him his two daughters in marriage; he caused the various officers, oxen and sheep, storehouses and granaries, *all* to be prepared to support Shun amid the channelled fields, and then he raised him to the most exalted situation. From this we have the expression—"The honouring of virtue and talents proper to a king or a duke."'

CHAP. VII. 1. Wan Chang said, 'I venture to ask what principle of righteousness is involved in *a scholar's* not going to see the princes?' Mencius replied, 'A scholar residing in the city is called "a minister of the market-place and well," and one residing in the country is called "a minister of the grass and plants." In both cases he is a common man, and it is the rule of propriety that common

6. See Pt. I. i. 3. 二女女焉,—the second 女 is read *nü*, in 4th tone.

7. WHY A SCHOLAR SHOULD DECLINE GOING TO SEE THE PRINCES, WHEN CALLED BY THEM. Compare Bk. III. Pt. II. i, *et al.* 1. We supply 士 as the subject of 見; and other verbal characters; Wan Chang evidently intends Mencius himself. 國, 'city,' as in chap. iv. par. 4. 莽,—here as a synonym, in apposition with 草. 臣 in 市井, 草莽之臣 is different from the 爲臣 below. Every in-

人、庶人不傳質爲臣、不敢見於諸侯、禮也。二節萬章曰、庶人召之役、則往役、君欲見之、召之、則不往見之、何也。曰、往役、義也、往見、不義也。三節且君之欲見之也、何爲也哉、曰、爲其多聞也、爲其賢也。曰、爲其多聞也、則天子不召師、而況諸侯乎、爲其賢也、則吾未聞欲見賢而召之也。四節繆公亟見於子思、

men, who have not presented the introductory present and become ministers, should not presume to have interviews with the prince.'

2. Wan Chang said, 'If a common man is called to perform any service, he goes and performs it;—how is it that a scholar, when the prince, wishing to see him, calls him to his presence, refuses to go?' Mencius replied, 'It is right to go and perform the service; it would not be right to go and see the prince.'

3. 'And,' *added Mencius*, 'on what account is it that the prince wishes to see *the scholar?*' 'Because of his extensive information, or because of his talents and virtue,' was the reply. 'If because of his extensive information,' said Mencius, 'such a person is a teacher, and the sovereign would not call him;—how much less may any of the princes do so? If because of his talents and virtue, then I have not heard of any one wishing to see a person with those qualities, and calling him to his presence.

4. 'During the frequent interviews of the duke Mû with Tsze-sze,

dividual may be called a 臣, as being a subject, and bound to serve the sovereign, and this is the meaning of the term in those two phrases. In the other case it denotes one who is officially 'a minister.' 傳=通. 質,—*chî*, in 3rd tone; see Bk. III. Pt. II. iii, 1, and notes. There is a force in the 於, in 見於諸侯, which it is difficult to indicate in another language. 2. 'It is right to go and perform the service,' i. e. it is right in the common man, to perform service being his 職, or office. And so with the scholar. He will go when called as a scholar should be called, but only then. 3. The 爲 are all in the 4th tone. It must be borne in mind that the conversation is all about a scholar who is not in office; compare par. 9. 4. 千乘 (in 4th tone) 之國=千乘之君

曰、古千乘之國、以友士、何如。子思不悅、曰、古之人有言曰、事之云乎、豈曰友之云乎。子思之不悅也、豈不曰、以位、則子君也、我臣也、何敢與君友也、以德、則子事我者也、奚可以與我友、千乘之君、求與之友、而不可得也、而況可召與。○五節 齊景公田、招虞人以旌、不至、將殺之、志士不忘在溝壑、勇士不忘喪其元、孔子奚取

he *one day* said to him, "Anciently, princes of a thousand chariots have yet been on terms of friendship with scholars;—what do you think *of such an intercourse?*" Tsze-sze was displeased, and said, "The ancients have said, 'The scholar should be served:' how should they have merely said that *he should be made a friend of?*" When Tsze-sze was thus displeased, did he not say *within himself*,—"With regard to our stations, you are sovereign, and I am subject. How can I presume to be on terms of friendship with my sovereign? With regard to our virtue, you ought to make me your master. How can you be on terms of friendship with me?" *Thus*, when a ruler of a thousand chariots sought to be on terms of friendship with a scholar, he could not obtain his wish:—how much less could he call him to his presence!

5. 'The duke Ching of Ch'î, once, when he was hunting, called his forester to him by a flag. *The forester* would not come, *and the duke* was going to kill him. *With reference to this incident, Confucius said*, "The determined officer never forgets that *his end*

below; 以 = with all his dignity, 'yet.' 云乎 = 云爾, Bk. IV. Pt. II. xxiv. 1, *et al.*, but the second 乎 also responds to 豈. The paraphrase in the 日講 is:—古之人有言, 人君於士, 當師事之, 豈但如君所言友之云乎. 5. See Bk. III. Pt. II. i. 2. 6. The explanation of the various flags here is from Chû Hsî, after

焉、取非其招不往也。○六節曰、敢問招虞人何以。曰、以皮冠、庶人以旃、士以旂、大夫以旌。○七節以大夫之招招虞人、虞人死不敢往、以士之招招庶人、庶人豈敢往哉、況乎以不賢人之招招賢人乎。○八節欲見賢人而不以其道、猶欲其入而閉之門也、夫義、路也、禮、門也、惟君子能由

may be in a ditch or a stream ; the brave officer never forgets that he may lose his head." What was it *in the forester* that Confucius thus approved? He approved his not going *to the duke*, when summoned by the article which was not appropriate to him.'

6. Chang said, 'May I ask with what a forester should be summoned?' Mencius replied, 'With a skin cap. A common man *should be summoned* with a plain banner; a scholar *who has taken office*, with one having dragons embroidered on it; and a Great officer, with one having feathers suspended from the top of the staff.

7. 'When the forester was summoned with the article appropriate to the summoning of a Great officer, he would have died rather than presume to go. If a common man were summoned with the article appropriate to the summoning of a scholar, how could he presume to go? How much more may we expect this refusal to go, when a man of talents and virtue is summoned in a way which is inappropriate to his character!

8. 'When a prince wishes to see a man of talents and virtue, and does not take the proper course *to get his wish*, it is as if he wished him to enter *his palace*, and shut the door against him.

the Châu Lî. The dictionary may be consulted about them. 何以=何用. 7. A man of talents and virtue ought not to be called at all; the prince ought to go to *him*. 8. 閉之門,—this is another case of a verb followed by the pronoun and another objective;—literally, 'shut him the door.' 詩云,—see the Shih-ching, II. v. Ode IX. st. 1. Julien condemns the translating 周道 by 'the way to Châu,' but that is the meaning of the terms in the ode; and, as the royal highway, it is used to indicate figuratively the great way of righteousness. 底,—in the ode 砥 (*chih*), the 3rd tone. The ode is attributed to an officer of one of the

是路、出入是門也、詩云、周道如底、其直如矢、君子所履、小人所視。（九節）萬章曰、孔子君命召、不俟駕而行、然則孔子非與。曰、孔子當仕有官職、而以其官召之也。

（第八章）（一節）孟子謂萬章曰、一鄉之善士、斯友一鄉之善士、一國之善士、斯友一國之善士、天下之善士、斯友天下

Now, righteousness is the way, and propriety is the door, but it is only the superior man who can follow this way, and go out and in by this door. It is said in the Book of Poetry,

"The way to Châu is level like a whetstone,
And straight as an arrow.
The officers tread it,
And the lower people see it."'

9. Wan Chang said, 'When Confucius received the prince's message calling him, he went without waiting for his carriage. Doing so, did Confucius do wrong?' Mencius replied, 'Confucius was in office, and had to observe its appropriate duties. And moreover, he was summoned on the business of his office.'

CHAP. VIII. 1. Mencius said to Wan Chang, 'The scholar whose virtue is most distinguished in a village shall make friends of all the virtuous scholars in the village. The scholar whose virtue is most distinguished throughout a State shall make friends of all the virtuous scholars of that State. The scholar whose virtue is most distinguished throughout the kingdom shall make friends of all the virtuous scholars of the kingdom.

eastern States, mourning over the oppressive and exhausting labours which were required from the people. The 'royal highway' presents itself to him, formerly crowded by officers hastening to and from the capital, and the people hurrying to their labours, but now toiled slowly and painfully along. 9. See Analects, X. xiii. 4.

8. THE REALIZATION OF THE GREATEST ADVANTAGES OF FRIENDSHIP, AND THAT IT IS DEPENDENT ON ONE'S SELF. 1. 'The virtuous scholar of one village,—he shall make friends of the virtuous scholars of (that) one village:'—the first 善 is in the superlative degree, and 友 is not only 'to be friends with,' but also 'to realize the uses of friendship.' The eminence attained by the individual attracts all the others to him,

之善士。二節以友天下之善士、爲未足、又尙論古之人、頌其詩、讀其書、不知其人可乎、是以論其世也、是尙友也。

第九章 一節齊宣王問卿。孟子曰、王何卿之問也。王曰、卿不同乎。曰、不同、有貴戚之卿、有異姓之卿。王曰、請問貴戚之卿。曰、君有大過、則諫、反覆之而不聽、則易位。二節王勃然變乎色。三節曰、王

2. 'When a scholar feels that his friendship with all the virtuous scholars of the kingdom is not sufficient *to satisfy him*, he proceeds to ascend to consider the men of antiquity. He repeats their poems, and reads their books, and as he does not know what they were as men, to ascertain this, he considers their history. This is to ascend and make friends *of the men of antiquity*.'

CHAP. IX. 1. The king Hsüan of Ch'î asked about *the office of* high ministers. Mencius said, 'Which high ministers is your Majesty asking about?' 'Are there differences among them?' inquired the king. 'There are,' was the reply. 'There are the high ministers who are noble and relatives *of the prince*, and there are those who are of a different surname.' The king said, 'I beg to ask about the high ministers who are noble and relatives of the prince.' Mencius answered, 'If the prince have great faults, they ought to remonstrate with him, and if he do not listen to them after they have done so again and again, they ought to dethrone him.'

2. The king on this looked moved, and changed countenance.

and he has thus the opportunity of learning from them, which no inflation because of his own general superiority prevents him from doing. 2. 尙=上. 又尙, 'he proceeds and ascends.' 頌=誦, 'to repeat,' 'croon over.' 可乎=可否, 'proper or not?' 其世, 'their age,' i.e. what they were in their age.—We are hardly to understand the poetry and books here generally. Mencius seems to have had in his eye the Book of Poetry, and the Book of History.

9. THE DUTIES OF THE DIFFERENT CLASSES OF HIGH MINISTERS. 1. 君有大過,—such ministers will overlook small faults. To animadvert on them would be inconsistent with

孟子

勿異也、王問臣、臣不敢不以正對。四 王色定、然後請問異姓之卿。曰、君有過則諫、反覆之而不聽、則去。

3. Mencius said, 'Let not your Majesty be offended. You asked me, and I dare not answer but according to truth.'

4. The king's countenance became composed, and he then begged to ask about high ministers who were of a different surname *from the prince*. Mencius said, 'When the prince has faults, they ought to remonstrate with him; and if he do not listen to them after they have done this again and again, they ought to leave *the State*.'

their consanguinity. No distinction is made of faults, as great or small, when the other class of ministers is spoken of. 'Great faults' are such as endanger the safety of the State. 3. 勿異, 'don't think it strange,' but = 'don't be offended.'—We may not wonder that duke Hsüan should have been moved and surprised by the doctrines of Mencius as announced in this chapter. It is true that the members of the family of which the ruler is the Head have the nearest interest in his ruling well, but to teach them that it belongs to them, in case of his not taking their advice, to proceed to dethrone him, is likely to produce the most disastrous effects. Chû Hsî notices that the able and virtuous relatives of the tyrant Châu (紂) were not able to do their duty as here laid down, while Ho Kwang, a minister of another surname, was able to do it in the case of the king of Ch'ang-yî (昌邑王), whom he placed in B.C. 74, though not the proper heir, on the throne in succession to the emperor Châo. His nominee, however, proved unequal to his position. See the Memoir of Ho Kwang in the Thirty-eighth Book of the Biographies of the first Han dynasty.

BOOK VI.

KÂO TSZE. PART I.

告子章句上

第一章 告子曰、性、猶杞柳也、義、猶桮棬也、以人性爲仁義、猶以杞柳爲桮棬。○孟子曰、子能順杞柳之性、而以爲桮棬乎、將戕賊杞柳、而後以爲桮棬

CHAPTER I. 1. The philosopher Kâo said, '*Man's* nature is like the *ch'î*-willow, and righteousness is like a cup or a bowl. The fashioning benevolence and righteousness out of man's nature is like the making cups and bowls from the *ch'î*-willow.'

2. Mencius replied, 'Can you, leaving untouched the nature of the willow, make with it cups and bowls? You must do violence and injury to the willow, before you can make cups and bowls with

Kâo, from whom this Book is named, is the same who is referred to in Bk. II. Pt. I. ii. His name was Pû-hai (不害), a speculatist of Mencius's day, who is said to have given himself equally to the study of the orthodox doctrines and those of the heresiarch Mo (Bk. III. Pt. I. v; Pt. II. ix). See the 四書拓餘說, on Mencius, Vol. I. Art. xxix. He appears from this Book to have been much perplexed respecting the real character of human nature in its relations to good and evil. This is the principal subject discussed in this Book. For his views of human nature as here developed, Mencius is mainly indebted for his place among the Sages of his country. 'In the first Part,' says the 四書味根錄, 'he treats first of *the nature*, then of *the heart*, and then of *instruction*, the whole being analogous to the lessons in the Doctrine of the Mean. The second Part continues to treat of the same subject, and a resemblance will generally be found between the views of the parties there combated, and those of the scholar Kâo.'

1. THAT BENEVOLENCE AND RIGHTEOUSNESS ARE NO UNNATURAL PRODUCTS OF HUMAN NATURE. There underlies the words of Kâo here, says Chû Hsi, the view of the philosopher Hsün (荀) that human nature is evil (性惡). This is putting the case too strongly. It is an induction from his words, which Kâo would probably have disallowed. Hsün (see the *prolegomena*, and Morrison under the character 子), accounted by many the most distinguished scholar of the Confucian school, appears to have maintained positively that all good was foreign to the nature of man;—人之性惡，其善者僞也, 'man's nature is bad; his good is artificial.' 1. The 杞 and the 柳 are taken by some as two trees, but it is better to take them together, the first character giving the species of the other. It is described as 'growing by the water-side, like a common willow, the leaf coarse and white, with the veins small and reddish.' 2. 順, 'according with,' 'following,' i.e. 'leaving untouched,' 'doing no violence to.' 戕賊人,—人=人性, 'man's nature,' humanity. Kâo had said that man's nature could be *made into* benevolence and righteousness, and Mencius exposes the error

也、如將戕賊杞柳而以爲桮棬、則亦將戕賊人以爲仁義與、率天下之人、而禍仁義者、必子之言夫。

〔二〕告子曰、性、猶湍水也、決諸東方則東流、決諸西方則西流、人性之無分於善不善也、猶水之無分於東西也。〔二〕孟子曰、水信無分於東西、無分於上下乎、人性

it. If you must do violence and injury to the willow in order to make cups and bowls with it, *on your principles* you must in the same way do violence and injury to humanity in order to fashion from it benevolence and righteousness! Your words, alas! would certainly lead all men on to reckon benevolence and righteousness to be calamities.'

CHAP. II. 1. The philosopher Kâo said, '*Man's* nature is like water whirling round *in a corner*. Open a passage for it to the east, and it will flow to the east; open a passage for it to the west, and it will flow to the west. Man's nature is indifferent to good and evil, just as the water is indifferent to the east and west.'

2. Mencius replied, 'Water indeed *will flow* indifferently to the east or west, but will it flow indifferently up or down? The

by here substituting 戕賊 for 爲, in doing which he is justified by the nature of the action that has to be put forth on the wood of the willow. 禍仁義, 'calamitize benevolence and righteousness.' I take the meaning to be as in the translation. If their nature must be hacked and bent to bring those virtues from it, men would certainly account them to be calamities.

2. MAN'S NATURE IS NOT INDIFFERENT TO GOOD AND EVIL. ITS PROPER TENDENCY IS TO GOOD. That man is indifferent to good and evil, or that the tendencies to these are both blended in his nature, was the doctrine of Yang Hsiung (揚雄), a philosopher about the beginning of our era (B.C. 53–A.D. 18). We have the following sentence from him:—'In the nature of man good and evil are mixed. The cultivation of the good in it makes a good man; the cultivation of the evil makes a bad man. The passion-nature in its movements may be called the horse of good or evil.' (十子全書, 楊子, 修身篇.) 人無有不善 is the sum of the chapter on Mencius's part. His opponent's views were wrong, but did he himself have the whole truth? 1. 湍水, as explained in the dictionary, 'water flowing rapidly,' and 'water rippling over the sand.' Châo Ch'î, followed by Chû Hsî, explains it as in the translation, which is certainly better adapted to the passage. 2. 信,—as an adverb, 'truly.' 人性之善,

之善也猶水之就下也、人無有不善、水無有不下。三節今夫水、搏而躍之、可使過顙、激而行之、可使在山、是豈水之性哉、其勢則然也、人之可使爲不善、其性亦猶是也。

第三章 一節告子曰、生之謂性。二節孟子曰、生之謂性也、猶白之謂白與。曰、然。白羽之白也、猶

tendency of man's nature to good is like the tendency of water to flow downwards. There are none but have this tendency to good, *just as* all water flows downwards.

3. 'Now by striking water and causing it to leap up, you may make it go over your forehead, and, by damming and leading it, you may force it up a hill;—but are such movements according to the nature of water? It is the force applied which causes them. When men are made to do what is not good, their nature is dealt with in this way.'

CHAP. III. 1. The philosopher Kâo said, 'Life is what we call nature.'

2. Mencius asked him, 'Do you say that by nature you mean life, just as you say that white is white?' 'Yes, I do,' was the reply. Mencius added, 'Is the whiteness of a white feather like that of

—literally, 'the goodness of man's nature,' but we must take 善 as = 'tendency to good.' 3. 激, to provoke,' 'to fret,' the *consequence of a dam*. 激而行之,—'dam and walk it,' i.e. by gradually leading it from dam to dam. Chû Hsî says:—'This chapter tells us that the nature is properly good, and if we accord with it, we shall do nothing which is not good; that it is properly without evil, and we must violate it therefore, before we can do evil. It shows that the nature is properly not without a decided character, or that it may do good or evil indifferently.'

3. THE NATURE IS NOT TO BE CONFOUNDED WITH THE PHENOMENA OF LIFE. 1. 'By 生,' says Chû Hsî, 'is intended that whereby men and animals perceive and move,' and the sentiment, he adds, is analogous to that of the Buddhists, who make 作用, 'doing and using,' to be the nature. We must understand by the term, I think, the phenomena of life, and Kâo's idea led to the ridiculous conclusion that wherever there were the phenomena of life, the nature of the subjects must be the same. At any rate, Mencius here makes him allow this. 2, 3. The 與, 4th tone, all interrogative, and = 'you allow this, I suppose.'—We find it difficult to place ourselves in sympathy with Kâo in this conversation, or to

孟子

白雪之白、白雪之白、猶白玉之白與。曰、然。三節然則犬之性、猶牛之性、牛之性、猶人之性與。

第四章 一節告子曰、食、色、性也、仁、內也、非外也、義、外也、非內也。二節孟子曰、何以謂仁內義外也。曰、彼長、而我長之、非有長於我也、猶彼白、而我白之、從其白於外也、故謂之

white snow, and the whiteness of white snow like that of white jade?' *Kâo again* said 'Yes.'

3. 'Very well,' *pursued Mencius.* 'Is the nature of a dog like the nature of an ox, and the nature of an ox like the nature of a man?'

CHAP. IV. 1. The philosopher Kâo said, '*To enjoy* food and *delight in* colours is nature. Benevolence is internal and not external; righteousness is external and not internal.'

2. Mencius asked him, 'What is the ground of your saying that benevolence is internal and righteousness external?' He replied, 'There is a man older than I, and I give honour to his age. It is not that there is *first* in me a principle of such reverence to age. It is just as when there is a white man, and I consider him white;— according as he is so externally to me. On this account, I pronounce *of righteousness* that it is external.'

follow Mencius in passing from the second paragraph to the third. His questions in paragraph 2 all refer to qualities, and then he jumps to others about the nature.

4. THAT THE BENEVOLENT AFFECTIONS AND THE DISCRIMINATIONS OF WHAT IS RIGHT ARE EQUALLY INTERNAL. 1. 食色-甘食悅色. We might suppose that 色 here denoted 'the appetite of sex.' But another view is preferred. Thus the commentator 熙周 observes:— 'The infant knows to drink the breast, and to look at fire, which illustrates the text 食色性.' It is important to observe that by 義 is denoted 事物之宜, 'the determining what conduct in reference to them is required by men and things external to us, and giving it to them.' Kâo contends that as we are moved by our own internal impulse to food and colours, so we are also in the exercise of benevolence, but not in that of righteousness. 2. 長,— always 3rd tone. In 彼長 it is the adjective, but in the other cases it is the verb. 非有長於我-非先有長之之心在我. The second 白 is also a verb.

外也。○三節曰、異於白馬之白也、無以異於白人之白也、不識長馬之長也、無以異於長人之長與、且謂長者義乎、長之者義乎。○四節曰、吾弟則愛之、秦人之弟則不愛也、是以我爲悅者也、故謂之內、長楚人之長、亦長吾之長、是以長爲悅者也、故謂

3. *Mencius* said, 'There is no difference between our pronouncing a white horse to be white and our pronouncing a white man to be white. But is there no difference between the regard with which we acknowledge the age of an old horse and that with which we acknowledge the age of an old man? And what is it which is called righteousness?—the fact of a man's being old? or the fact of our giving honour to his age?'

4. *Kâo* said, 'There is my younger brother;—I love him. But the younger brother of a man of Ch'in I do not love: that is, the feeling is determined by myself, and therefore I say that benevolence is internal. *On the other hand*, I give honour to an old man of Ch'û, and I also give honour to an old man of my own *people*: that is, the feeling is determined by the age, and therefore I say that righteousness is external.'

3. 異於, at the commencement, have crept by some oversight into the text. They must be disregarded. 白馬, 白人, 長馬, 長人,—白 and 長 are the verbs, = the 長之 below. 且謂, 云云, 'and do you say? &c.,' but the meaning comes out better by expanding the words a little. The 日講 says:—'The recognition of the whiteness of a horse is not different from the recognition of the whiteness of a man. So indeed it is. But when we acknowledge the age of a horse, we simply with the mouth pronounce that it is old. In acknowledging, however, the age of a man, there is at the same time the feeling of respect in the mind. The case is different from our recognition of the age of a horse.' 4. 秦人, 楚人,= indifferent people, strangers. 以我爲悅, 以長爲悅,—the meaning is, no doubt, as in the translation, but the use of 悅 in both cases occasions some difficulty. Here again I may translate from the 日講, which attempts to bring out the meaning of 悅:—'I love my younger brother and do not love the younger brother of a man of Ch'in; that is, the love depends on me. Him with whom my heart is pleased, I love (悅乎我之心, 則愛之), and him with whom my heart is not pleased, I do not love. But the reverence is in both cases determined by the age. Wherever we meet with age, there we

孟子

之外也。五節 曰、耆秦人之炙、無以異於耆吾炙、夫物、則亦有然者也、然則耆炙、亦有外與。

五章 一節 孟季子問公都子曰、何以謂義內也。二節 曰、行吾敬、故謂之內也。三節 鄉人長於伯兄一歲、則誰敬。曰、敬兄。酌則誰先。曰、先酌鄉人。所敬在此、所長在彼、果在外、非由

5. *Mencius* answered him, 'Our enjoyment of meat roasted by a man of Ch'in does not differ from our enjoyment of meat roasted by ourselves. Thus, *what you insist on* takes place also in the case of such things, and will you say likewise that our enjoyment of a roast is external?'

CHAP. V. 1. The disciple Măng Chî asked Kung-tû, saying, 'On what ground is it said that righteousness is internal?'

2. Kung-tû replied, 'We *therein* act out our feeling of respect, and therefore it is said to be internal.'

3. *The other objected*, 'Suppose the case of a villager older than your elder brother by one year, to which of them would you show the *greater* respect?' 'To my brother,' was the reply. 'But for which of them would you first pour out wine *at a feast?*' 'For the villager.' *Măng Chî argued*, '*Now* your feeling of reverence rests on the one, and *now* the honour due to age is rendered to the other;—this is certainly determined by what is without, and does not proceed from within.'

have the feeling of complacency (凡遇長皆在所悅), and it does not necessarily proceed from our own mind.' After reading all this, a perplexity is still felt to attach to the use of 悅. 5. 耆-嗜.—Mencius silences his opponent by showing that the same difficulty would attach to the principle with which he himself started; namely, that the enjoyment of food was internal, and sprang from the inner springs of our being.

5. THE SAME SUBJECT;—THE DISCRIMINATIONS OF WHAT IS RIGHT ARE FROM WITHIN. 1. Măng Chî was a younger brother of Măng Chung, mentioned in Bk. II. Pt. II. ii. 3. Their relation to each other in point of age is determined by the characters 仲 and 季. Măng Chî had heard the previous conversation with Kâo, or heard of it, and feeling some doubts on the subject he applied to Kung-tû (Bk. II. Pt. II. v. 4) for their solution. 'On what ground is it said?'—i.e. by our master, by Mencius. 3. The questions here are evidently by Măng Chî.

內也。四節公都子不能答、以告孟子。孟子曰、敬叔父乎、敬弟乎。彼將曰、敬叔父。曰、弟爲尸、則誰敬。彼將曰、敬弟。子曰、惡在其敬叔父也。彼將曰、在位故也。子亦曰、在位故也、庸敬在兄、斯須之敬在鄉人。五節季子聞之曰、敬叔父則敬、敬弟則敬、果在外、非由內也。公都子曰、冬日、則飲湯、夏日、則飲水、然

4. Kung-tû was unable to reply, and told the conversation to Mencius. Mencius said, '*You should ask him*, "Which do you respect most,—your uncle, or your younger brother?" He will answer, "My uncle." Ask him *again*, "If your younger brother be personating a dead ancestor, to which do you show the greater respect,—*to him or to your uncle?*" He will say, "To my younger brother." You can go on, "But where is the respect due, as you said, to your uncle?" He will reply to this, "*I show the respect to my younger brother*, because of the position which he occupies," and you can likewise say, "*So my respect to the villager is* because of the position which he occupies. Ordinarily, my respect is rendered to my elder brother; for a brief season, *on occasion*, it is rendered to the villager."'

5. *Măng* Chî heard this and observed, 'When respect is due to my uncle, I respect him, and when respect is due to my younger brother, I respect him;—the thing is certainly determined by what is without, and does not proceed from within.' Kung-tû replied, 'In winter we drink things hot, in summer we drink things cold; and

伯 is in the general sense of 長, 'elder.' 4. The translation needs to be supplemented, to show that Mencius gives his decision in the form of a dialogue between the two disciples. 叔父, 'a father's younger brother,' but used generally for 'an uncle.' 弟爲尸,—in sacrificing to the departed, some one—a certain one of the descendants, if possible—was made the 尸, or 'personator of the dead,' into whom the spirit of the other was supposed to descend to receive the worship. 惡在其敬,—the 其 = 'as you said.' 斯須 = 暫時; compare the 'Doctrine of the Mean,' i. 2. 5. 湯, 水, 'hot

孟子

則飲食亦在外也。

【第六章】一節 公都子曰、告子曰、性無善、無不善也。二節 或曰、性、可以爲善、可以爲不善、是故文武興、則民好善、幽厲興、則民好暴。三節 或曰、有性善、有性不善、是故以堯爲君、而有象、以瞽瞍爲父、而有舜、以紂爲兄之子、且以爲君、而有微子啟、王子比干。四節 今曰、

so, *on your principle*, eating and drinking also depend on what is external!'

CHAP. VI. 1. The disciple Kung-tû said, 'The philosopher Kâo says, "*Man's* nature is neither good nor bad."

2. 'Some say, "*Man's* nature may be made to practise good, and it may be made to practise evil, and accordingly, under Wăn and Wû, the people loved what was good, *while* under Yû and Lî, they loved what was cruel."

3. 'Some say, "The nature of some is good, and the nature of others is bad. Hence it was that under such a sovereign as Yâo there yet appeared Hsiang; that with such a father as Kû-sâu there yet appeared Shun; and that with Châu for their sovereign, and the son of their elder brother besides, there were found Ch'î, the viscount of Wei, and the prince Pî-kan.

4. 'And now you say, "The nature is good." Then are all those wrong?'

water,' or 'soup,' and 'water;' 水 must be taken as 'cold' water. Kung-tû answers after the example of his master in the last paragraph of the preceding chapter.

6. EXPLANATION OF MENCIUS'S OWN DOCTRINE THAT MAN'S NATURE IS GOOD. 1. Chû Hsî says that the view of Kâo, as here affirmed, had been advocated by Sû Tung-p'o (東坡) and Hû, styled Wăn-ting Kung (胡文定公), near to his own times. 2. This is the view propounded by Kâo in the second chapter. 爲 is explained by 習, and 可以爲 = 可以使爲. 3. 啟 was the name of the viscount of Wei; see Analects, XVIII. i. Both he and Pî-kan are here made to be uncles of Châu, while Ch'î, according to the Shû-ching, was his half-brother. Chû Hsî supposes some error to have crept into the text. For convenience in translating, I have changed the order of 爲兄之子, 且以爲君. 王子, —as the sons of the princes of States were called 公子.—This view of human nature found

性善、然則彼皆非與。

五節 孟子曰、乃若其情、則可以爲善矣、乃所謂善也。

六節 若夫爲不善、非才之罪也。

七節 惻隱之心、人皆有之、羞惡之心、人皆有之、恭敬之心、人皆有之、是非之心、人皆有之、惻隱之心、仁也、羞惡之心、義也、恭敬之心、禮也、是非之心、

5. Mencius said, 'From the feelings proper to it, it is constituted for the practice of what is good. This is what I mean in saying that *the nature* is good.

6. 'If men do what is not good, the blame cannot be imputed to their natural powers.

7. 'The feeling of commiseration belongs to all men; so does that of shame and dislike; and that of reverence and respect; and that of approving and disapproving. The feeling of commiseration *implies the principle of* benevolence; that of shame and dislike, the principle of righteousness; that of reverence and respect, the principle of propriety; and that of approving and disapproving, the principle of knowledge. Benevolence, righteousness, propriety, and knowledge are not infused into us from without. We are certainly

an advocate afterwards in the famous Han Wăn-kung (韓文公) of the T'ang dynasty. 4, 5. 乃若, = 'as to,' 'looking at.' Chû Hsî calls them an initial particle. The 其, of course, refers to 性 or 'nature,' which is the subject of the next clause—可以爲善. This being the amount of Mencius's doctrine, that by the study of our nature we may see that it is formed for goodness, there seems nothing to object to in it. By 情 is denoted 性之動, 'the movements of the nature,' i.e. the inward feelings and tendencies, 'stirred up.'—Châo Ch'î takes 若 here in the sense of 順, 'to obey,' 'to accord with,' on which the translation would be—'If it act in accordance with its feelings, or emotional tendencies.' The meaning, however, is the same on the whole. 可以爲善 is not so definite as we could wish. Chû Hsî expands it:—人之情, 本但可以爲善, 而不可以爲惡, 'the feelings of man may properly be used only to do good, and may not be used to do evil.' This seems to be the meaning. 6. 才 = 材質, 人之能也, 'man's ability,' 'his natural powers.' 若夫 (in 2nd tone),—'as to,' 'in the case of.' 7. Compare Bk. II. Pt. I. vi. 4, 5. 恭敬之心, however, takes the place of 辭讓之心 there. 弗思耳 is the *apodosis* of a sentence, and the *protasis* must be supplied as in the translation. 舍

智也、仁、義、禮、智、非由外鑠我也、我固有之也、弗思耳矣、故曰、求則得之、舍則失之、或相倍蓰、而無算者、不能盡其才者也。

八節

詩曰、天生蒸民、有物有則、民之秉夷、好是懿德。孔子曰、爲此詩者、其知道乎。故有物、必有則、民之秉夷也、故好是懿德。

furnished with them. *And a different view* is simply owing to want of reflection. Hence it is said, "Seek and you will find them. Neglect and you will lose them." Men differ from one another in regard to them;—some as much again as others, some five times as much, and some to an incalculable amount:—it is because they cannot carry out fully their *natural* powers.

8. 'It is said in the Book of Poetry,

"Heaven in producing mankind,
Gave them their *various* faculties and relations with *their specific* laws.
These are the invariable rules of nature for all to hold,
And *all* love this admirable virtue."

Confucius said, "The maker of this ode knew indeed the principle *of our nature!*" We may thus see that every faculty and relation must have its law, and since there are invariable rules for all to hold, they consequently love this admirable virtue.'

—捨, 3rd tone. 或相倍云云,—與善相去, 或一倍, 云云, 'they lose them so that they depart from what is good, some as far again as others, &c.' 8. 詩曰, see the Shih-ching, III. Pt. III. Ode VI. st. 1, where we have 烝 for 蒸, and 彝 for 夷. 有物有則,—'have things, have laws,' but the things specially intended are our constitution with reference to the world of sense, and the various circles of relationship. The quotation is designed specially to illustrate par. 5, but the conclusion drawn is stronger than the statement there. It is said the people actually love (好, 4th tone), and are not merely constituted to love, the admirable virtue.

第七章 一節 孟子曰、富歲、子弟多賴、凶歲、子弟多暴、非天之降才爾殊也、其所以陷溺其心者然也、○二節 今夫麰麥、播種而耰之、其地同、樹之時、又同、浡然而生、至於日至之時皆熟矣、雖有不同、則地有肥磽、雨露之養、人事之不齊也、○三節 故凡同類者、舉相

CHAP. VII. 1. Mencius said, 'In good years the children of the people are most of them good, while in bad years the most of them abandon themselves to evil. It is not owing to any difference of their natural powers conferred by Heaven that they are thus different. The abandonment is owing to the circumstances through which they allow their minds to be ensnared and drowned *in evil*.

2. 'There now is barley.—Let it be sown and covered up; the ground being the same, and the time of sowing likewise the same, it grows rapidly up, and, when the full time is come, it is all found to be ripe. Although there may be inequalities *of produce*, that is owing to the *difference of the* soil, as rich or poor, to the *unequal* nourishment afforded by the rains and dews, and to the different ways in which man has performed his business *in reference to it*.

3. 'Thus all things which are the same in kind are like to one

7. ALL MEN ARE THE SAME IN MIND;—SAGES AND OTHERS. IT FOLLOWS THAT THE NATURE OF ALL MEN, LIKE THAT OF THE SAGES, IS GOOD. 1. 富歲, 'rich years,'=豐年, 'plentiful years.' 賴 is given by Châo Ch'î as=善, 'good,' and 暴=惡, 'evil.' But 暴=the Mencian phrase—自暴, 'self-abandonment,' and there is the proper meaning of 賴, 'to depend on,' also in that term. 'In rich years, 子弟 (sons and brothers, i.e. the young whose characters are plastic) *depend on* the plenty and are good.' Temptations do not lead them from their natural bent. 爾殊也,—the use of 爾 here is peculiar. Most take it as=如此, 'thus;'—see Wang Yăn-chih, *in voc.* Some take it in its proper pronominal meaning, as if Mencius in a lively manner turned to the young:—'It is not from the powers conferred by Heaven that you are different.' 然, 'so,' referring specially to the self-abandonment. 2. 麰麥 go together=' barley.' 播種 (3rd tone, the noun), 'sow the seeds.' 耰, properly, 'a kind of harrow.' 日至, not 'the solstice,' but 'the days (i.e. the time, harvest-time) are come.' 3. 舉=

孟子

似也、何獨至於人而疑之、聖人與我同類者。

四節 故龍子曰、不知足而爲屨、我知其不爲蕢也、屨之相似、天下之足同也。

五節 口之於味、有同耆也、易牙、先得我口之所耆者也、如使口之於味也、其性與人殊、若犬馬之與我不同類也、則天下何耆皆從易牙之於味也、至於味、天下期於易牙、是天下

another;—why should we doubt in regard to man, as if he were a solitary exception to this? The sage and we are the same in kind.

4. 'In accordance with this the scholar Lung said, "If a man make hempen sandals without knowing *the size of people's* feet, *yet* I know that he will not make *them like* baskets." Sandals are all like one another, because all men's feet are like one another.

5. '*So* with the mouth and flavours;—all mouths have the same relishes. Yî-yâ *only* apprehended before me what my mouth relishes. Suppose that his mouth in its relish for flavours differed from that of other men, as is the case with dogs or horses which are not the same in kind with us, why should all men be found following Yî-yâ in their relishes? In the matter of tastes all the people model themselves after Yî-yâ; that is, the mouths of all men are like one another.

皆, 'all.' 何獨, 云云, 'why only come to man and doubt it?' 4. 故, illustrating, not inferring. So, below; except perhaps in the last instance of its use. Of the Lung who is quoted nothing seems to be known;—see Bk. III. Pt. I. iii. 7. 屨, see Bk. III. Pt. I. iv. 1. 5. 耆=嗜. 口之於味有同耆也, literally, 'The relation of mouths to tastes is that they have the same relishes.' Yî-yâ was the cook of the famous duke Hwan of Ch'î (B.C. 684–642), a worthless man, but great in his art. 先得, 云云, is better translated 'apprehended before me,' than 'was the first to apprehend,' &c., and *only* is evidently to be supplied. 如使口之於味,—the 口 here is to be understood with reference to Yî-yâ. 其性, 'its nature,' i. e. its likings and dislikings in the matter of tastes. 天下期於易牙,—期, 'to fix a limit,' or 'to aim at.'

之口相似也。○六節惟耳亦然、至於聲、天下期於師曠、是天下之耳相似也。○七節惟目亦然、至於子都、天下莫不知其姣也、不知子都之姣者、無目者也。○八節故曰、口之於味也、有同耆焉、耳之於聲也、有同聽焉、目之於色也、有同美焉、至於心、獨無所同然乎、心之所同然者、何也、謂理也、義也、聖人先得我心

6. 'And so also it is with the ear. In the matter of sounds, the whole people model themselves after the music-master K'wang; that is, the ears of all men are like one another.

7. 'And so also it is with the eye. In the case of Tsze-tû, there is no man but would recognise that he was beautiful. Any one who would not recognise the beauty of Tsze-tû must have no eyes.

8. 'Therefore I say,—*Men's* mouths agree in having the same relishes; their ears agree in enjoying the same sounds; their eyes agree in recognising the same beauty:—shall their minds alone be without that which they similarly approve? What is it then of which they similarly approve? It is, I say, the principles *of our nature*, and the determinations of righteousness. The sages only apprehended before me that of which my mind approves along with other men. Therefore the principles of our nature and the deter-

6. 惟耳亦然,—惟 is here in the sense of our *but*, from *botan*, the connective particle, though it often corresponds to our other *but*, a disjunctive, or exceptive, = 'only.' 師曠, see Bk. IV. Pt. I. i. 1. 7. Tsze-tû was the designation of Kung-sun O (公孫閼), an officer of Chăng about B.C. 700, distinguished for his beauty. See his villainy and death in the seventh chapter of the 'History of the Several States.' 8. 無所同然乎,—然 is to be taken as a verb, 'to approve.' 謂 merely indicates the answers to the preceding question. It is not so much as 'I say' in the translation. 理 = 心之體, 'the mental constitution,' the moral nature, and 義 = 心之用, that constitution or nature, acting outwardly. 芻, 'hay,' 'fodder,' used for 'grass-fed animals,' such as sheep and oxen. 豢 = 'corn or rice-fed animals,' such as dogs and pigs.

之所同然耳、故理義之悅我心、猶芻豢之悅我口。

第八章 一節 孟子曰、牛山之木嘗美矣、以其郊於大國也、斧斤伐之、可以爲美乎、是其日夜之所息、雨露之所潤、非無萌櫱之生焉、牛羊又從而牧之、是以若彼濯濯也、人見其濯濯也、以爲未嘗有材焉、此豈山之性也哉。二節 雖存乎人者、豈無仁義之心哉、其所以放

minations of righteousness are agreeable to my mind, just as the flesh of grass and grain-fed animals is agreeable to my mouth.'

CHAP. VIII. 1. Mencius said, 'The trees of the Niû mountain were once beautiful. Being situated, however, in the borders of a large State, they were hewn down with axes and bills;—and could they retain their beauty? Still through the activity of the vegetative life day and night, and the nourishing influence of the rain and dew, they were not without buds and sprouts springing forth, but then came the cattle and goats and browsed upon them. To these things is owing the bare and stripped appearance *of the mountain*, and when people *now* see it, they think it was never finely wooded. But is this the nature of the mountain?

2. 'And so *also of* what properly belongs to man;—shall it be said that the mind *of any man* was without benevolence and righteous-

8. HOW IT IS THAT THE NATURE PROPERLY GOOD COMES TO APPEAR AS IF IT WERE NOT SO;—FROM NOT RECEIVING ITS PROPER NOURISHMENT. 1. The Niû mountain was in the south-east of Ch'î. It is referred to the present district of Lin-tsze (臨淄) in the department of Ch'ing-châu. 以其郊於大國=以其所生之郊在于大國. 可以爲美乎,—'could they be beautiful?' i.e. 'could they retain their beauty?' 是其日夜之所息,—the 是 is difficult;—'there is what they grow day and night,' the 息 referring to the 氣化生物, what we may call 'vegetative life.' The use of 濯濯 here is peculiar. 材=材木, 'trees of materials,' fine trees. 2. The connexion indicated by 雖,

其良心者、亦猶斧斤之於木也、旦旦而伐之、可以爲美乎、其日夜之所息、平旦之氣、其好惡與人相近也者幾希、則其旦晝之所爲、有梏亡之矣、梏之反覆、則其夜氣不足以存、夜氣不足以存、則其違禽獸不遠矣、人見其禽獸也、而以爲未嘗有才焉者、是豈人

ness? The way in which a man loses his proper goodness of mind is like the way in which the trees are denuded by axes and bills. Hewn down day after day, can it—*the mind*—retain its beauty? But there is a development of its life day and night, and in the *calm* air of the morning, just between night and day, the mind feels in a degree those desires and aversions which are proper to humanity, but the feeling is not strong, and it is fettered and destroyed by what takes place during the day. This fettering taking place again and again, the restorative influence of the night is not sufficient to preserve *the proper goodness of the mind;* and when this proves insufficient for that purpose, the nature becomes not much different from that of the irrational animals, and when people *now* see it, they think that it never had those powers *which I assert.* But does this condition represent the feelings proper to humanity?

'although,' may be thus traced:—'Not only is such the case of the Niû mountain. Although we speak of what properly belongs to man (存=在), we shall find that the same thing obtains.' The next clause is to be translated in the past tense, the question having reference to a mind or nature, which has been allowed to run to waste. 其, 'he,'='a man.' 放=失. 良心,—'the good mental constitution or nature.' 平, 'even,' indicates the time that lies *evenly* between the night and day. It is difficult to catch the exact idea conveyed by 氣, in this clause, and where it occurs below, the calm of the air, the corresponding calm of the spirit, and the moral invigoration from the repose of the night, being blended in it. The next clause is difficult. Chåo Ch'î makes it:—'The mind is not far removed in its likings and dislikings (好, 惡, both in 4th tone) from those which are proper to humanity.' The more common interpretation is that which I have given. 幾希,—see Bk. IV. Pt. II.

之情也哉。○三節 故苟得其養，無物不長，苟失其養，無物不消。○四節 孔子曰，操則存，舍則亡，出入無時，莫知其鄉，惟心之謂與。

第九章 一節 孟子曰，無或乎王之不智也。○二節 雖有天下易生之物也，一日暴之，十日寒之，未有能生者也，吾見亦罕矣，吾退而寒之

3. 'Therefore, if it receive its proper nourishment, there is nothing which will not grow. If it lose its proper nourishment, there is nothing which will not decay away.

4. 'Confucius said, "Hold it fast, and it remains with you. Let it go, and you lose it. Its outgoing and incoming cannot be defined as to time or place." It is the mind of which this is said!'

CHAP. IX. 1. Mencius said, 'It is not to be wondered at that the king is not wise!

2. 'Suppose the case of the most easily growing thing in the world;—if you let it have one day's genial heat, and then expose it for ten days to cold, it will not be able to grow. It is but seldom that I have an audience of the king, and when I retire, there come

xix. 1. 旦晝＝日間. 3. 無物,—物 embraces both things in nature, and the nature of man. 4. This is a remark of Confucius for which we are indebted to Mencius. 舍＝捨. 出入, 云云,—'its outgoings and incomings have no *set* time; no one knows its direction.' 與, 2nd tone, ＝'is it not?' or an exclamation. This paragraph is thus expanded by Chû Hsî:—'Confucius said of the mind, "If you hold it fast, it is here; if you let it go, it is lost and gone: so without determinate time is its outgoing and incoming, and also without determinate place." Mencius quoted his words to illustrate the unfathomableness of the spiritual and intelligent mind, how easy it is to have it or to lose it, and how difficult to preserve and keep it, and how it may not be left unnourished for an instant. Learners ought constantly to be exerting their strength to insure the pureness of its spirit, and the settledness of its passion-nature, as in the calm of the morning, then will the mind always be preserved, and everywhere and in all circumstances its manifestations will be those of benevolence and righteousness.'

9. ILLUSTRATING THE LAST CHAPTER.—HOW THE KING OF CH'I'S WANT OF WISDOM WAS OWING TO NEGLECT AND BAD ASSOCIATIONS. 1. 或 is used for 惑, 'to be perplexed.' 乎 is an exclamation. The king is understood to be the king Hsüan of Ch'î; see I. ii. 2. 暴,—*pû*, often written 曝, 'to dry in the sun,' here＝溫, 'to warm genially.' 未有,云云,—the 未, 'not yet,' 'never,' puts the general truth as an inference from the past. 見,—the 4th tone, *hsien*. Chû Hsî points the last clause—吾,如有萌焉,何哉, 'though there

者至矣、吾如有萌焉、何哉。三節今夫弈之爲數、小數也、不專心致志、則不得也。弈秋、通國之善弈者也、使弈秋誨二人弈、其一人專心致志、惟弈秋之爲聽、一人雖聽之、一心以爲有鴻鵠將至、思援弓繳而射之、雖與之俱學、弗若之矣、爲是其智弗若與、曰、非然也。

all those who act upon him like the cold. Though I succeed in bringing out some buds *of goodness*, of what avail is it?

3. 'Now chess-playing is but a small art, but without his whole mind being given, and his will bent, to it, a man cannot succeed at it. Chess Ch'iû is the best chess-player in all the kingdom. Suppose that he is teaching two men to play.—The one gives to the subject his whole mind and bends to it all his will, doing nothing but listening to Chess Ch'iû. The other, although *he seems to be* listening to him, has his whole mind running on a swan which he thinks is approaching, and wishes to bend his bow, adjust the string to the arrow, and shoot it. Although he is learning along with the other, he does not come up to him. Why?—because his intelligence is not equal? Not so.'

may be sprouts of goodness, what can I do?' In this way, 吾 and 何哉 are connected, and there is the intermediate clause between them, which is an unusual thing in Chinese. Feeling this difficulty, Châo Ch'î makes 吾 the nominative to 有萌 and interprets,—'Although I wish to encourage the sprouting of his goodness, how can I do so?' I have followed this construction, taking the force of the terms, however, differently. 3. 今夫 (2nd tone), 云云,—'now the character of chess-playing as an art, is that it is a small art.' 奕秋,—Ch'iû was the man's name, and he was called *Chess* Ch'iû from his skill at the game. 鴻鵠, 'a great *ku*,' which is also called 'the heavenly goose' = the swan. 繳 (*cho*) 而射 (*shih*) 之;—see Analects, VII. xxvi. 爲 (4th tone) 是其智弗若與 (2nd tone),—'Is it because of this, the inferiority of his (*natural*) intelligence?' 是 and the following words being in apposition.

第十章 一節 孟子曰、魚、我所欲也、熊掌、亦我所欲也、二者、不可得兼、舍魚而取熊掌者也、生、亦我所欲也、義、亦我所欲也、二者、不可得兼、舍生而取義者也。二節 生亦我所欲、所欲、有甚於生者、故不爲苟得也、死亦我所惡、所惡有甚於死者、故患有所不辟也。三節 如使人之所欲、莫甚於生、則凡可以得生者、何

CHAP. X. 1. Mencius said, 'I like fish, and I also like bear's paws. If I cannot have the two together, I will let the fish go, and take the bear's paws. So, I like life, and I also like righteousness. If I cannot keep the two together, I will let life go, and choose righteousness.

2. 'I like life indeed, but there is that which I like more than life, and therefore, I will not seek to possess it by any improper ways. I dislike death indeed, but there is that which I dislike more than death, and therefore there are occasions when I will not avoid danger.

3. 'If among the things which man likes there were nothing which he liked more than life, why should he not use every means

10. THAT IT IS PROPER TO MAN'S NATURE TO LOVE RIGHTEOUSNESS MORE THAN LIFE, AND HOW IT IS THAT MANY ACT AS IF IT WERE NOT SO. 1. 'Bear's palms' have been a delicacy in China from the earliest times. They require a long time, it seems, to cook them thoroughly. The king Ch'ăng of Ch'û, B. C. 625, being besieged in his palace, requested that he might have a dish of bear's palms before he was put to death,—hoping that help would come while they were being cooked. 2. 生亦我所欲,—the 亦 is retained from the preceding paragraph. We may render it by 'indeed.' 所欲, 云云, is to be translated indicatively. It is explanatory of the conclusion of the last paragraph,—舍生而取義. 不爲 (emphatic) 苟得, 'I won't do improper getting,' i. e. of life. The paraphrasts mostly say—不爲苟且以得生, 'I will not act improperly to get life.' 患, 'sorrow,' 'calamity,' = danger of death. 辟 = 避. It seems better to construe as I have done, making 患 governed by 辟, than to make 患 = a clause by itself, and suppose 死 as the object of 辟.

不用也、使人之所惡莫甚於死者、則凡可以辟患者、何不爲也。○四節由是則生、而有不用也、由是則可以辟患、而有不爲也。○五節是故所欲有甚於生者、所惡有甚於死者、非獨賢者有是心也、人皆有之、賢者能勿喪耳。○六節一簞食、一豆羹、得之則生、弗得則死、嘑爾而與之、行道

by which he could preserve it? If among the things which man dislikes there were nothing which he disliked more than death, why should he not do everything by which he could avoid danger?

4. 'There are cases when men by a certain course might preserve life, and they do not employ it; when by certain things they might avoid danger, and they will not do them.

5. 'Therefore, men have that which they like more than life, and that which they dislike more than death. They are not men of distinguished talents and virtue only who have this mental nature. All men have it; what belongs to such men is simply that they do not lose it.

6. 'Here are a small basket of rice and a platter of soup, and the case is one in which the getting them will preserve life, and the want of them will be death;—if they are offered with an insulting

4. I translate here differently both from Châo Ch'î and Chû Hsî. They take 由是 to be = 'From this righteousness-loving nature so displayed,' as if the paragraph were merely an inference from the two preceding. I understand the paragraph to be a repetition of the two preceding, and introductory to the one which follows. 由是則生, 'by this course (any particular course) there is life,' 而有不用, 'and yet in cases it is not used.' This gives a much easier and more legitimate construction. 5. 能勿喪 (4th tone),—stress must not be laid on the 能. 勿 is simply negative, not prohibitive. 6. 嘑, 4th tone. 嘑爾 is explained 咄啐之貌, 'the appearance of reproachful clamour,' but the 蹴爾 shows that more than the idea of 'appearance,' or demonstration is intended. 行道之人=乞人, below, and not simply 'any ordinary man upon the way,' as Chû Hsî makes it. 不屑, see Bk. II. Pt. I. ix. 1.—This paragraph is intended to illustrate the 人皆有之 of the preceding. Even in the poorest and most distressed of men,

之人弗受、蹴爾而與之、乞人不屑也。○七節萬鍾、則不辨禮義而受之、萬鍾於我何加焉、爲宮室之美、妻妾之奉、所識窮乏者得我與。○八節鄉爲身死而不受、今爲宮室之美爲之、鄉爲身死而不受、今爲妻妾之奉爲之、鄉爲身死而不受、今爲所識窮

voice, even a tramper will not receive them, or if you first tread upon them, even a beggar will not stoop to take them.

7. '*And yet* a man will accept of ten thousand chung, without any consideration of propriety or righteousness. What can the ten thousand chung add to him? *When he takes them,* is it not that he may obtain beautiful mansions, that he may secure the services of wives and concubines, or that the poor and needy of his acquaintance may be helped by him?

8. 'In the former case *the offered bounty* was not received, though it would have saved from death, and now *the emolument* is taken for the sake of beautiful mansions. *The bounty* that would have preserved from death was not received, and *the emolument* is taken to get the service of wives and concubines. *The bounty* that would

the 羞惡之心 will show itself. 7. 萬鍾,—see Bk. II. Pt. II. x. 3. 萬鍾於我何加焉,—'what do they add to me?' There is here a contrast with the case in the former paragraph, which was one of life or death. The large emolument was not an absolute necessity. But also there is the lofty, and true, idea, that a man's personality is something independent of, and higher than, all external advantages. The meaning is better brought out in English by changing the person from the first to the third. 爲妻妾之奉, 'because of the services of wives and concubines.' 妻 is plural as well as 妾, though according to the law of China there could be only one *wife*, however many concubines there might be. 所識窮乏者得我=所知識窮乏者感我之惠, 'that the poor of his acquaintance may be grateful for his kindness.' A gloss in the 四書味根錄 says:—'The thinking of the poor would seem to be a thought of kindly feeling, but the true nature of it is shown in the 得我, *may get* ME. The idea is not of benevolence, but selfishness.' 8. 鄉, the 4th tone, = 向. 爲 (4th tone) 身死, 'for the body dying,' i. e. to save from dying. 是亦不可以已乎,—是 is

之者得我而爲之、是亦不可以已乎、此之謂失其本心。

十一章 孟子曰、(一節)仁、人心也、義、人路也。(二節)舍其路而弗由、放其心而不知求、哀哉。(三節)人有雞犬放、則知求之、有放心而不知求。(四節)學問之道無他、求其放心而已矣。

十二章 孟子曰、(一節)今有無名之指、

have saved from death was not received, and *the emolument* is taken that one's poor and needy acquaintance may be helped by him. Was it then not possible likewise to decline this? This is a case of what is called—"Losing the proper nature of one's mind."'

CHAP. XI. 1. Mencius said, 'Benevolence is man's mind, and righteousness is man's path.

2. 'How lamentable is it to neglect the path and not pursue it, to lose this mind and not know to seek it again!

3. 'When men's fowls and dogs are lost, they know to seek for them again, but they lose their mind, and do not know to seek for it.

4. 'The great end of learning is nothing else but to seek for the lost mind.'

CHAP. XII. 1. Mencius said, 'Here is a *man whose* fourth finger is bent and cannot be stretched out straight. It is not painful, nor

emphatic,—this large emolument, taken for such purposes.—For an example in point to illustrate par. 6, see the Lî-chî, II. Sect. II. iii. 17.

11. HOW MEN HAVING LOST THE PROPER QUALITIES OF THEIR NATURE SHOULD SEEK TO RECOVER THEM. 1. 'Benevolence is man's mind, or heart,' i.e. it is the proper and universal characteristic of man's nature, as the 正義 on Châo Ch'î says,—人人有之, 'all men have it.' 'Benevolence' would seem to include here all the other moral qualities of humanity. Chû Hsî says 仁者心之德; yet we have the usual Mencian specification of 'righteousness' along with it. 4. 學問之道,—道=切要, 'that which is most important in.'—The Chinese sages always end with the recovery of 'the old heart;' the idea of 'a new heart' is unknown to them. One of the Ch'ăng says:—'The thousand words and ten thousand sayings of the sages and worthies are simply designed to lead men to get hold of their lost minds, and make them again enter their bodies. This accomplished, they can push their inquiries upwards, and from the lowest studies acquire the highest knowledge.'

12. HOW MEN ARE SENSIBLE OF BODILY, AND NOT OF MENTAL OR MORAL, DEFECTS. 1. 無名之指, 'the nameless finger,' i.e. the fourth, reckoning from the thumb as the first. It is

屈而不信、非疾痛害事也、如有能信之者、則不遠秦楚之路、爲指之不若人也。

二節 指不若人、則知惡之、心不若人、則不知惡、此之謂不知類也。

十三章 孟子曰、拱把之桐梓、人苟欲生之、皆知所以養之者、至於身、而不知所以養之者、豈愛身不若桐梓哉、

does it incommode his business, and yet if there be any one who can make it straight, he will not think the way from Ch'in to Ch'û far *to go to him;* because his finger is not like the finger of other people.

2. 'When a man's finger is not like those of other people, he knows to feel dissatisfied, but if his mind be not like that of other people, he does not know to feel dissatisfaction. This is called—"Ignorance of the relative *importance of things.*"'

CHAP. XIII. Mencius said, 'Anybody who wishes to cultivate the *t'ung* or the *tsze,* which may be grasped with both hands, *perhaps* with one, knows by what means to nourish them. In the case of their own persons, men do not know by what means to nourish them. Is it to be supposed that their regard of their own persons is inferior to their regard for a *t'ung* or *tsze?* Their want of reflection is extreme.'

so styled, as of less use than the others, and less needing a name. 信,—read as, and with the meaning of, 伸 (*shin*). 不遠秦楚之路=雖越秦楚相去之路, 不以爲遠, 'though he should pass over all the way between Ch'in and Ch'û, he will not think it far.' 2. 不知類,—'not knowing kinds,' or degrees. 類=等.

13. MEN'S EXTREME WANT OF THOUGHT IN REGARD TO THE CULTIVATION OF THEMSELVES. The *t'ung* and *tsze* resemble each other. The latter is called by the Chinese 'the king of trees,' and its wood is well adapted for their block-engraving. Of the *t'ung* there are various arrangements, some making three kinds of it, some four, and some seven. The wood of the first kind, or white *t'ung* (白桐), is the best for making musical instruments like the lute. Bretschneider makes the *t'ung* to be the *paulownia;* and the *tsze*, the *rottlera Japonica*, or the *catalpa.* 至於身,—身, 'the body,' but here 'the person,' the whole human being. 豈...哉='is it to be supposed?' A supplementary note in the 備旨 says that 'by

弗思甚也。

十四 一節 孟子曰、人之於身也、兼所愛、兼所愛、則兼所養也、無尺寸之膚不愛焉、則無尺寸之膚不養也、所以考其善不善者、豈有他哉、於己取之而已矣。二節 體有貴賤、有小大、無以小害大、無以賤害貴、養其小者爲小人、養其大者爲大人。三節 今有場師、舍其梧檟、養其樲棘、

CHAP. XIV. 1. Mencius said, 'There is no part of himself which a man does not love, and as he loves all, so he must nourish all. There is not an inch of skin which he does not love, and so there is not an inch of skin which he will not nourish. For examining whether *his way of nourishing* be good or not, what other rule is there but this, that he determine by *reflecting on* himself where it should be applied?

2. 'Some parts of the body are noble, and some ignoble; some great, and some small. The great must not be injured for the small, nor the noble for the ignoble. He who nourishes the little belonging to him is a little man, and he who nourishes the great is a great man.

3. 'Here is a plantation-keeper, who neglects his *wû* and *chiâ*, and cultivates his sour jujube-trees;—he is a poor plantation-keeper.

nourishing the 身 here is intended the ruling of the mind, to nourish our inner man, and paying careful attention to the body, to nourish our outer man.'

14. THE ATTENTION GIVEN BY MEN TO THE NOURISHMENT OF THE DIFFERENT PARTS OF THEIR NATURE MUST BE REGULATED BY THE RELATIVE IMPORTANCE OF THOSE PARTS. 1. 身,—as in the last chapter, but with more special reference to the body. 兼所愛, 'unites what he loves,' i.e. loves all. 尺寸, 'a cubit *or* an inch,' but the meaning is—the least bit of, = our 'an inch.' 所以考, 云云, requires to be supplemented a good deal in translating. The meaning is plain:—A man is to determine for himself, by reflection on his constitution, what parts are more important and should have the greater attention paid to them. Compare the two last paragraphs of Analects, VI. xxviii. 2. 體, 'the members of the body,' but the character, like 身, is to be understood with a tacit reference to the mental part of our constitution as well. 3. The 場人 was an officer under the Châu dynasty, who had the superintendence of the ruler's plantations and orchards;—see the Châu Lî, II. Pt. XVI. xxiii. 1. The *wû* (the *sterculia platanifolia*, according to Bretschneider) and the

則爲賤場師焉。四節養其一指、而失其肩背、而不知也、則爲狼疾人也。五節飲食之人、則人賤之矣、爲其養小以失大也。六節飲食之人、無有失也、則口腹豈適爲尺寸之膚哉。

十五 一節公都子問曰、鈞是人也、或爲大人、或爲小人、何也。孟子曰、從其大體爲大人、從其小體爲小人。二節曰、鈞是人也、或從

4. 'He who nourishes one of his fingers, neglecting his shoulders or his back, without knowing *that he is doing so*, is a man *who resembles* a hurried wolf.

5. 'A man who *only* eats and drinks is counted mean by others;—because he nourishes what is little to the neglect of what is great.

6. 'If a man, *fond of his* eating and drinking, were not to neglect *what is of more importance*, how should his mouth and belly be considered as no more than an inch of skin?'

CHAP. XV. 1. The disciple Kung-tû said, 'All are equally men, but some are great men, and some are little men;—how is this?' Mencius replied, 'Those who follow that part of themselves which is great are great men; those who follow that part which is little are little men.'

2. Kung-tû pursued, 'All are equally men, but some follow

chiâ are used like *t'ung* and *tsze* in the last chapter; or, as some make out, the *sterculia platanifolia* and the *catalpa Japonica*. Two valuable trees are evidently intended by them. 樲棘 go together, 樲 indicating the species. 棘 is generally used with the general meaning of thorns;—but it here indicates a kind of small wild date-tree. The date-tree proper is 棗; this wild tree, 棘; the different forms indicating the *high* tree and the *low bushy* shrub respectively. See the 集證, *in loc.* 4. 失 = 遺. 狼疾, 'a wolf hurried,' i. e. chased, and so unable to exercise the quick sight for which it is famous. 6. The meaning is that the parts considered small and ignoble may have their due share of attention, if the more important parts are first cared for, as they ought to be.

15. HOW SOME ARE GREAT MEN, LORDS OF REASON, AND SOME ARE LITTLE MEN, SLAVES OF SENSE. 1. 鈞 = 均, 'all equally.' 體, 'the members,' but here, more evidently than in the last chapter, it is spoken of our whole constitution, mental as well as physical. 2. 耳目之官, 'the offices of the ears and eyes.' We might

其大體或從其小體、何也。曰、耳目之官不思、而蔽於物、物交物、則引之而已矣、心之官則思、思則得之、不思、則不得也、此天之所與我者、先立乎其大者、則其小者不能奪也、此爲大人而已矣。

〔十六〕一節 孟子曰、有天爵者、有

that part of themselves which is great, and some follow that part which is little;—how is this?' Mencius answered, 'The senses of hearing and seeing do not think, and are obscured by *external* things. When one thing comes into contact with another, as a matter of course it leads it away. To the mind belongs the office of thinking. By thinking, it gets *the right view of things;* by neglecting to think, it fails to do this. These—*the senses and the mind*—are what Heaven has given to us. Let a man first stand fast in *the supremacy of* the nobler part of his constitution, and the inferior part will not be able to take it from him. It is simply this which makes the great man.'

CHAP. XVI. 1. Mencius said, 'There is a nobility of Heaven,

suppose that the senses are so styled, as being conceived to be subject to the control of the ruling mind. We have below, however, the expression 心之官, and 官 is to be taken in both cases as = 'prerogative,' 'business.' Châo Ch'î and his glossarist do not take 耳目之官 as the subject of 思 in 不思, but interpret thus:—'The senses, if there be not the exercise of thought by the mind, are obscured by external things.' But the view of Chû Hsî, as in the translation, is preferable. It is very evident that 心 indicates our whole mental constitution. 物交物,—the first 物 is the external objects, what is heard and seen; the second denotes the senses themselves, which are only things. 引之而已,—而已 = 'as a matter of course.' 得之,—之 = 事物之理, 'the mind apprehends the true nature of the objects of sense,' and of course can guard against their deluding influence. 其大者, 'his what is great,' the nobler part of his constitution, i.e. the mind.—Kung-tû might have gone on to inquire,—'All are equally men. Some stand fast in the nobler part of their constitution, and some allow its supremacy to be snatched away by the inferior part. How is this?' and Mencius would have tried to carry the difficulty a step farther back, and after all have left it where it originally was. His saying that the nature of man is good may be reconciled with the doctrines of evangelical Christianity, but his views of human nature as a whole are open to the three objections stated in the note to the twenty-first chapter of the *Chung Yung*.

16. THERE IS A NOBILITY THAT IS OF HEAVEN, AND A NOBILITY THAT IS OF MAN. THE NEGLECT OF THE FORMER LEADS TO THE LOSS OF THE LATTER. 1. 忠 is the *heart* true in itself, loyal to benevolence and righteousness, and 信 is the *conduct*

人爵者、仁、義、忠、信、樂善不倦、此天爵也、公、卿、大夫、此人爵也。〔二節〕古之人、修其天爵、而人爵從之。〔三節〕今之人、修其天爵、以要人爵、既得人爵、而棄其天爵、則惑之甚者也、終亦必亡而已矣。

〔十七〕〔一節〕孟子曰、欲貴者人之同心也、人人有貴於己

and there is a nobility of man. Benevolence, righteousness, self-consecration, and fidelity, with unwearied joy in *these* virtues;—these constitute the nobility of Heaven. To be a kung, a ch'ing, or a tâ-fû;—this constitutes the nobility of man.

2. 'The men of antiquity cultivated their nobility of Heaven, and the nobility of man came to them in its train.

3. 'The men of the present day cultivate their nobility of Heaven in order to seek for the nobility of man, and when they have obtained that, they throw away the other:—their delusion is extreme. The issue is simply this, that they must lose *that nobility of man* as well.'

CHAP. XVII. 1. Mencius said, 'To desire to be honoured is the common mind of men. And all men have in themselves that which is *truly* honourable. Only they do not think of it.

true to them. 公, 卿, 大夫,—see Bk. V. Pt. II. ii. 3-7. 3. 要, the 1st tone, = 求; 'their delusion is extreme,'—this is well set forth in the 日講:—夫修天爵以要人爵, 是脩之之日, 原先有棄之之心, 已不免於惑矣, 至得人爵而棄天爵, 是得之之後, 並不及要之之時, 則惑之甚者也, 'Now when the nobility of Heaven is cultivated in order to seek for the nobility of man, at the very time it is cultivated, there is a previous mind to throw it away;—showing the existence of delusion. Then when the nobility of man has been got, to throw away the nobility of Heaven, exhibits conduct after attainment not equal to that in the time of search, so that the delusion is extreme.' 終亦必亡而已矣,—亡 has reference to the nobility of man, and is best translated as an active verb, to which the 亦 also points.—Many commentators observe that facts may be referred to, apparently inconsistent with the assertions in this chapter, and then go on to say that such inconsistency is but a lucky accident; the issue *should* always be as Mencius says. Yes; but all moral teachings must be imperfect where the thoughts are bounded by what is seen and temporal.

17. THE TRUE HONOUR WHICH MEN SHOULD DESIRE. 1. 爵 in the last chapter is the material dignity; 貴 in this is the honour,

者、弗思耳、二節人之所貴者、非良貴也、趙孟之所貴、趙孟能賤之。三節詩云、旣醉以酒、旣飽以德、言飽乎仁義也、所以不願人之膏粱之味也、令聞廣譽施於身、所以不願人之文繡也。

十八章一節孟子曰、仁之勝不仁也、猶水勝火、今之爲仁者、猶以一杯水、救一車薪之火

2. 'The honour which men confer is not good honour. Those whom Châo the Great ennobles he can make mean *again*.

3. 'It is said in the Book of Poetry,

"He has filled us with his wine,
He has satiated us with his goodness."

"*Satiated us with his goodness*," that is, satiated us with benevolence and righteousness, and he who is so satiated, consequently, does not wish for the fat meat and fine millet of men. A good reputation and far-reaching praise fall to him, and he does not desire the elegant embroidered garments of men.'

CHAP. XVIII. 1. Mencius said, 'Benevolence subdues its opposite just as water subdues fire. Those, however, who now-a-days practise benevolence *do it* as if with one cup of water they could save a whole waggon-load of fuel which was on fire, and when

such as springs from such dignity. 2. 人之所貴,—人 here and in the next paragraph refers to those who confer dignities. It is not to be understood—'what men consider honour.' 趙孟, 'Châo, the chief.' This title was borne by four ministers of the family of Châo, who at different times held the chief sway in Tsin. They were a sort of 'king-making Warwicks.' In the time of Mencius, the title had become associated with the name of the house. 3. 詩云,—see the Shih-ching, III. ii. Ode III. st. 1. The ode is one responsive from 'his fathers and brethren' to the sovereign who has entertained them. Mencius's application of it is a mere accommodation.

18. IT IS NECESSARY TO PRACTISE BENEVOLENCE WITH ALL ONE'S MIGHT. THIS ONLY WILL PRESERVE IT. 1. 不熄,則謂之,—謂之 = 'were to say of it.' 與 is said by Chû Hsî to = 助, 'to aid.' The 甚 is joined to 與, and not to 不仁. Bad men seeing the ineffectiveness of feeble endeavours to do good are only encouraged in their own course. This meaning of 與 is found elsewhere. Châo Ch'î interprets :—'This also is worse than the case of those who practise what is not benevolent.' But both the sentiment and construction of

也、不熄、則謂之水不勝火、此又與於不仁之甚者也。二節亦終必亡而已矣。

十九章 孟子曰、五穀者、種之美者也、苟爲不熟、不如荑稗、夫仁、亦在乎熟之而已矣。

二十章 一節 孟子曰、羿之教人射、必至於彀、學者亦必志於彀。二節 大匠誨人、必以規矩、學者亦必以規矩。

the flames were not extinguished, were to say that water cannot subdue fire. This conduct, moreover, greatly encourages those who are not benevolent.

2. 'The final issue will simply be this—the loss *of that small amount of benevolence*.'

CHAP. XIX. Mencius said, 'Of all seeds the best are the five kinds of grain, yet if they be not ripe, they are not equal to the *t'î* or the *pâi*. So, the value of benevolence depends entirely on its being brought to maturity.'

CHAP. XX. 1. Mencius said, 'Î, in teaching men to shoot, made it a rule to draw the bow to the full, and his pupils also did the same.

2. 'A master-workman, in teaching others, uses the compass and square, and his pupils do the same.'

this are more difficult than the other. 2. Compare chapter xvi. 3.

19. BENEVOLENCE MUST BE MATURED. 1. 'The five kinds of grain;'—see Bk. III. Pt. I. iv. 7. The *t'î* and *pâi* are two plants closely resembling one another. They are a kind of spurious grain, 'yielding a rice-like seed, but small. They are to be found at all times, in wet situations and dry, and when crushed and roasted, may satisfy the hunger in a time of famine.' Mencius's vivacity of mind and readiness at illustration lead him at times to broad unguarded statements, of which this seems to be one.

20. LEARNING MUST NOT BE BY HALVES. 1. Î,—see Bk. IV. Pt. II. xxiv. 1. 志,—used as 期 in chap. vii. 5. 必志, 'found it necessary to,' or simply the past tense emphatic. So, in the next paragraph. 2. 大匠 = 工師, 'a master-workman.' Chû Hsî says:—'This chapter shows that affairs must be proceeded with according to their laws, and then they can be completed. But if a master neglect these, he cannot teach; and if a pupil neglect these, he cannot learn. In small arts it is so:—how much more with the principles of the sages!'

KÂO TSZE. PART II.

告子章句下

第一章 一節 任人有問屋廬子曰、禮與食孰重。曰、禮重。二節 色與禮孰重。曰、禮重。三節 曰、以禮食、則飢而死、不以禮食、則得食、必以禮乎。親迎、則不得妻、不親迎、則得妻、必親迎乎。四節 屋廬子

CHAPTER I. 1. A man of *Zăn* asked the disciple Wû-lû, saying, 'Is *an observance of* the rules of propriety *in regard to eating*, or eating *merely*, the more important?' The answer was, '*The observance of* the rules of propriety is the more important.'

2. 'Is *the gratifying* the appetite of sex, or *the doing so only* according to the rules of propriety, the more important?' The answer *again* was, '*The observance of* the rules of propriety *in the matter* is the more important.'

3. *The man* pursued, 'If the result of eating only according to the rules of propriety will be death by starvation, while by disregarding those rules we may get food, must they *still* be observed *in such a case?* If according to the rule that he shall go in person to meet his wife a man cannot get married, while by disregarding that rule he may get married, must he *still* observe the rule *in such a case?*'

4. Wû-lû was unable to reply to *these questions*, and the next

1. THE IMPORTANCE OF OBSERVING THE RULES OF PROPRIETY, AND, WHEN THEY MAY BE DISREGARDED, THE EXCEPTION WILL BE FOUND TO PROVE THE RULE. EXTREME CASES MAY NOT BE PRESSED TO INVALIDATE THE PRINCIPLE. 1. 任 (in 2nd tone) was a small State, referred to the present Tsî-ning (濟寧) châu, of the department of Yen-châu, in Shan-tung. It was not far from Mencius's native State of Tsâu, the distance being only between twenty and thirty *lî*. The disciple Wû-lû, who is said to have published books on the doctrines of Lâo-tsze, was a native of the State of Tsin. His name was Lien (連). His questions are not to be understood of propriety in the abstract, but of the rules of propriety understood to regulate the other things which he mentions. 2. 色 is to be understood as in the translation, and this is its common signification in Mencius. I include the 曰, 禮重, in this paragraph. 3. 以禮食,—see the Lî Chî, XXVII. 26, *et al.* 親迎 (4th tone),—see the Lî Chî, XXVII. 38. 4. 之鄒,—之＝往. Châo Ch'î

不能對、明日之鄒、以告孟子。孟子曰、於答是也何有。五節不揣其本、而齊其末、方寸之木、可使高於岑樓。六節金重於羽者、豈謂一鉤金、與一輿羽之謂哉。七節取食之重者、與禮之輕者、而比之、奚翅食重、取色之重者、與禮之輕者、而比之、奚翅色重。八節往應之曰、紾兄之臂、而奪之

day he went to Tsâu, and told them to Mencius. Mencius said, 'What difficulty is there in answering these inquiries?

5. 'If you do not adjust them at their lower extremities, but only put their tops on a level, a piece of wood an inch square may be made to be higher than the pointed peak of a high building.

6. 'Gold is heavier than feathers;—but does that saying have reference, on the one hand, to a single clasp of gold, and, on the other, to a waggon-load of feathers?

7. 'If you take a case where the eating is of the utmost importance and the observing the rules of propriety is of little importance, and compare the things together, why stop with saying merely that the eating is more important? *So*, taking the case where the gratifying the appetite of sex is of the utmost importance and the observing the rules of propriety is of little importance, why stop with merely saying that the gratifying the appetite is the more important?

8. 'Go and answer him thus, "If, by twisting your elder brother's

reads 於 as 烏 (*wû*, 1st tone), making it an exclamation—'oh!' 5. 揣, 'to measure, or feel with the hand.' 本 and 末 are used for 下 and 上. 岑 (*ch'ăn*), 'a high and pointed small hill.' Châo Ch'î takes 岑樓 together as meaning 'a peaked ridge of a hill,' and the dictionary gives this signification to the phrase. The view of Chû Hsî, which I have followed, is better. 6. 金 . . . 者,—者 indicates the clause to be a common saying, and carries us on to some explanation of it. 豈謂 . . . 之謂, 'How does it say (mean) the saying (meaning) of the gold of one hook, and the feathers of one waggon?' Compare Bk. I. Pt. I. vii. 10. 7. 奚翅(-啻)=何但. 8. 紾 (read *ch'ăn*, 3rd tone), both by Châo Ch'î and Chû Hsî, is explained by 戾, 'to bend.' I prefer

食、則得食、不紾、則不得食、則將紾之乎、踰東家牆而摟其處子、則得妻、不摟、則不得妻、則將摟之乎。

第二章

曹交問曰、人皆可以爲堯舜、有諸。孟子曰、然。交聞文王十尺、湯九尺、今交九尺四寸以長、食粟而已、如何則可。曰、奚

arm, and snatching from him what he is eating, you can get food for yourself, while, if you do not do so, you will not get anything to eat, will you so twist his arm? If by getting over your neighbour's wall, and dragging away his virgin daughter, you can get a wife, while if you do not do so, you will not be able to get a wife, will you so drag her away?"'

CHAP. II. 1. Chiâo of Tsâo asked *Mencius*, saying, '*It is said*, "All men may be Yâos and Shuns;"—is it so?' Mencius replied, 'It is.'

2. *Chiâo went on*, 'I have heard that king Wăn was ten cubits *high*, and T'ang nine. Now I am nine cubits four inches in height. *But* I can do nothing but eat *my* millet. What am I to do to realize that saying?'

3. *Mencius* answered him, 'What has this—*the question of size*—

the first meaning of the character given in the dictionary,—that of 轉, 'to turn,' here = 'to twist.' 而奪之食,—here 奪 is followed by two objectives, 之 being = 'from him.' Julien errs strangely in rendering '*Si, rumpens fratris majoris brachium, rapias illud comedendum*.' 東家牆, 'the wall of the house on the east,' i. e. a neighbour's wall. 東家 is a common designation for the master of a house; and I do not know of any instance of its use by a writer earlier than Mencius. 處 (3rd tone) 子, 'a virgin daughter,' one *dwelling* in the harem. 子, as sometimes elsewhere, is feminine.

2. ALL MAY BECOME YÂOS AND SHUNS, AND TO BECOME SO, THEY HAVE ONLY SINCERELY, AND IN THEMSELVES, TO CULTIVATE YÂO AND SHUN'S PRINCIPLES AND WAYS. 1. Châo Ch'i says that Chiâo was a brother of the prince of Ts'âo, but the principality of Ts'âo had been extinguished before the time of Mencius. The descendants of the ruling house had probably taken their surname from their ancient patrimony. Ts'âo is referred to the present district of Ting-t'âo (定陶) in the department of Tsâo-châu, in Shan-tung. 有諸,—compare Bk. I. Pt. II. ii. 1, *et al.* 2. On the heights mentioned here, see Analects, VIII. vi. 以長, 'for my height.' The 以, however, may be taken as simply euphonic. Chiâo's idea is, that physically he was between Wăn and T'ang, who might be considered as having become Yâos or Shuns, and therefore he also might become such, if he

有於是、亦爲之而已矣、有人於此、力不能勝一匹雛、則爲無力人矣、今曰、舉百鈞、則爲有力人矣、然則舉烏獲之任、是亦爲烏獲而已矣、夫人豈以不勝爲患哉、弗爲耳。○四徐行後長者、謂之弟、疾行先長者、謂之不弟、夫徐行者、豈人所不能哉、所不爲也、堯舜之道、孝

to do with the matter? It all lies simply in acting as such. Here is a man, whose strength was not equal to lift a duckling:—he was *then* a man of no strength. But to-day he says, "I can lift 3,000 catties' weight," and he is a man of strength. And so, he who can lift the weight which Wû Hwo lifted is just another Wû Hwo. Why should a man make a want of ability the subject of his grief? It is only that he will not do the thing.

4. 'To walk slowly, keeping behind his elders, is to perform the part of a younger. To walk quickly and precede his elders, is to violate the duty of a younger brother. Now, is it what a man cannot do—to walk slowly? It is what he does not do. The course of Yâo and Shun was simply that of filial piety and fraternal duty.

were shown the right way. 3. 於是,—是 referring to the height, or body generally. 爲之,—之 referring to Yâo and Shun. 匹, is said to be an abbreviation for 鴄 = 鶩, 'a wild duck.' I do not see why it should not be taken simply as a numeral or classifier, and 一匹雛 = 'a chicken.' Wû Hwo was a man noted for his strength. He is mentioned in connexion with the king Wû of Ts'in (B.C. 309–306). Accounts go that he made light of 30,000 catties! 4. 後 and 先 (4th tone) are verbs; 弟 = 悌. Chû Hsi here quotes from the commentator Ch'ăn (陳氏):—'Filial piety and fraternal duty are the natural outgoings of the nature, of which men have an intuitive knowledge, and for which they have an intuitive ability (良知良能). Yâo and Shun showed the perfection of the human relations, but yet they simply acted in accordance with this nature. How could they add a hair's point to it?' He also quotes another (陽氏), who says:—'The way of Yâo and Shun was great, but the pursuit of it lay simply in the rapidity or slowness of their walking and stopping, and not in things that were very high and difficult. It is present to the common people in their daily usages, but they do not

弟而已矣。〇五節 子服堯之服、誦堯之言、行堯之行、是堯而已矣、子服桀之服、誦桀之言、行桀之行、是桀而已矣。〇六節 曰、交得見於鄒君、可以假館、願留而受業於門。〇七節 曰、夫道、若大路然、豈難知哉、人病不求耳、子歸而求之、有餘師。

〔第三章〕一節 公孫丑問曰、高子曰、小弁、小人之詩也、孟子曰、何以言

5. 'Wear the clothes of Yâo, repeat the words of Yâo, and do the actions of Yâo, and you will just be a Yâo. And, if you wear the clothes of Chieh, repeat the words of Chieh, and do the actions of Chieh, you will just be a Chieh.'

6. Chiâo said, 'I shall be having an interview with the prince of Tsâu, and can ask him to let me have a house to lodge in. I wish to remain here, and receive instruction at your gate.'

7. Mencius replied, 'The way of truth is like a great road. It is not difficult to know it. The evil is only that men will not seek it. Do you go home and search for it, and you will have abundance of teachers.'

CHAP. III. 1. Kung-sun Ch'âu asked *about an opinion of the scholar Kâo*, saying, 'Kâo observed, "The Hsiâo P'ân is the ode of a little man."' Mencius asked, 'Why did he say so?' 'Because of the murmuring *which it expresses*,' was the reply.

know it.' 5. The meaning is simply—Imitate the men, do what they did, and you will be such as they were. 6. 交得見 (4th tone),—it is better not to translate this conditionally, as it shows how Chiâo was presuming on his nobility. 7. 夫道, 'Now, the way'—i.e. the way of Yâo and Shun, or generally 'of truth.'

3. EXPLANATION OF THE ODES HSIÂO P'ÂN AND K'ÂI FÂNG. DISSATISFACTION WITH A PARENT IS NOT NECESSARILY UNFILIAL. 1. Kâo appears to have been a disciple of Tsze-hsiâ, and lived to Mencius's time. From the expression 高叟 in par. 2, it is plain, he is not to be confounded with Mencius's own disciple of the same surname, mentioned in Bk. II. Pt. II. xii. 2. 小弁,—see the Shih-ching, II. v. Ode III. 3. The ode is commonly understood to have been written by the master of Î-ch'iû (宜臼), the son and heir-apparent of the sovereign Yû (B.C. 780-770). Led away by the arts of a

之、曰、怨。○二節、曰、固哉、高叟之爲詩也、有人於此、越人關弓而射之、則已談笑而道之、無他、疏之也、其兄關弓而射之、則己垂涕泣而道之、無他、戚之也、小弁之怨、親親也、親親仁也、固矣夫高叟之爲詩也。○三節、曰、凱風何以不怨。○四節、曰、凱風、親之過小者

2. *Mencius* answered, 'How stupid was that old Kâo in dealing with the ode! There is a man here, and a native of Yüeh bends his bow to shoot him. I will advise him *not to do so*, but speaking calmly and smilingly;—for no other reason but that he is not related to me. *But* if my own brother be bending his bow to shoot the man, then I will advise him not to do so, weeping and crying the while;—for no other reason than that he is related to me. The dissatisfaction expressed in the Hsiâo P'ân is the working of relative affection, and that affection shows benevolence. Stupid indeed was old Kâo's criticism on the ode.'

3. *Ch'âu then said*, 'How is it that there is no dissatisfaction expressed in the K'âi Făng?'

4. Mencius replied, 'The parent's fault referred to in the K'âi

mistress, the sovereign degraded Î-ch'iû and his mother, and the ode expresses the sorrow and dissatisfaction which the son could not but feel in such circumstances. Châo Ch'î, however, assigns it another authorship, but on this and other questions, connected with it, see the Shih-ching, *in loc.* 2. 固 is explained by Châo Ch'î by 陋, 'narrow,' and by Chû Hsî by 執滯不通, 'bigoted and not penetrating.' 爲詩 = 治詩. 有人…戚之,— here 已 is to be understood of the speaker or beholder, and 其兄 of his—the speaker's—brother. In 道 (= 言, the verb) 之, 疏之, 戚之, 之 refers to the shooter. 關, read *wan*, = 彎. The paraphrast of Châo Ch'î points, however, and understands differently—'Here is a man of Yüeh, who is about to be shot by another man. I see it and advise the man not to shoot, but coolly and smilingly, because I am not related to the man of Yüeh. But if my brother is about to be shot, &c.' This is ingenious, but not so apt to the subject of the Hsiâo P'ân. When native scholars can construe a passage so differently, we may be sure it is not very definitely expressed. 3. 凱風,—see the Shih-ching, I. iii. Ode VII. The ode is supposed to be the production of seven sons, bewailing the conduct of their widowed mother, who could not live quietly and chastely at home, but they take all the blame to themselves, and express no dissatisfaction with her. 4. We must think there was room enough for dissatisfaction in both cases. And indeed, many commentators say that the received account of the subject of the K'âi Făng must be wrong, or that Mencius's decision on it is

也、小弁、親之過大者也、親之過大、而不怨、是愈疏也、親之過小、而怨、是不可磯也、愈疏、不孝也、不可磯、亦不孝也。五節 孔子曰、舜其至孝矣、五十而慕。

四章 宋牼將之楚、孟子遇於石丘。二節 曰、先生將何之。三節 曰、吾聞秦楚搆兵、我將見楚王、說而罷之、楚王不悅、我將

Făng is small; that referred to in the Hsiâo P'ân is great. Where the parent's fault was great, not to have murmured on account of it would have increased the want of natural affection. Where the parent's fault was small, to have murmured on account of it would have been to act like water which frets and foams about a stone that interrupts its course. To increase the want of natural affection would have been unfilial, and to fret and foam in such a manner would also have been unfilial.

5. 'Confucius said, "Shun was indeed perfectly filial! *And yet*, when he was fifty, he was full of longing desire about his parents."'

CHAP. IV. 1. Sung K'ang being about to go to Ch'û, Mencius met him in Shih-ch'iû.

2. 'Master, where are you going?' asked *Mencius*.

3. *K'ang* replied, 'I have heard that Ch'in and Ch'û are fighting together, and I am going to see the king of Ch'û and persuade him to cease hostilities. If he shall not be pleased *with my advice*,

absurd. But here again, see the Shih-ching, *in loc.* 愈疏, 'mores' (if we had such a verb), 'the distance.' The father's act was unkind; if the son responded to it with indifference, that would increase the distance and alienation between them. 是不可磯也,—the three characters 不可磯 are to be taken together. The mother is compared to a rock or stone in a stream, and the sons to the water fretting about it. But the case in the text is one where the children's affections should flow on undisturbed. 5. Compare Bk. V. Pt. I. i.

4. MENCIUS'S WARNINGS TO SUNG K'ANG ON THE ERROR AND DANGER OF COUNSELLING THE PRINCES FROM THE GROUND OF PROFIT, THE PROPER GROUND BEING THAT OF BENEVOLENCE AND RIGHTEOUSNESS. Compare Bk. I. Pt. I. i, *et al.* 1. K'ang was one of the travelling scholars of the times, who went from State to State, making it their business to counsel (說, *shiu*, 4th tone) the princes, with a view for the most part, though not apparently with him, to exalt themselves. Shih-ch'iû was in the State of Sung. Here, and also in the next paragraph, 之 is the verb. 3. 搆(=戰)兵 = 'battling weapons.' 罷

見秦王、說而罷之、二王、我將有所遇焉。○四節曰、軻也、請無問其詳、願聞其指、說之、將何如。曰、我將言其不利也。曰、先生之志則大矣、先生之號則不可。○五節先生以利、說秦楚之王、秦楚之王、悅於利、以罷三軍之師、是三軍之士、樂罷而悅於利也、爲人臣者、懷利以事其君、爲人子者、懷利以事其父、爲人弟者、懷利以事其兄、是

I shall go to see the king of Ch'in, and persuade him in the same way. Of the two kings I shall *surely* find that I can succeed with one of them.'

4. *Mencius* said, 'I will not venture to ask about the particulars, but I should like to hear the scope of your plan. What course will you take to try to persuade them?' *K'ang* answered, 'I will tell them how unprofitable their course is to them.' 'Master,' said Mencius, 'your aim is great, but your argument is not good.

5. 'If you, starting from the point of profit, offer your persuasive counsels to the kings of Ch'in and Ch'û, and if those kings are pleased with the consideration of profit so as to stop the movements of their armies, then all belonging to those armies will rejoice in the cessation *of war*, and find their pleasure in *the pursuit of* profit. Ministers will serve their sovereign for the profit of which they cherish the thought; sons will serve their fathers, and younger brothers will serve their elder brothers, from the same consideration:—and the issue will be, that, abandoning benevolence and

之, 'make an end of it.' 所遇,—see Bk. I. Pt. II. xv. 3. 4. 請 = our 'if you'll allow me.' Then follows—'not asking the particulars, I should like,' &c. 其不利,—其 refers to the two States. 號,—I take the word 'argument' from Julien. The gloss in the 備旨 is—號是不利之名號, '號 is the name and title of *unprofitable*.' 5. 三軍之

君臣、父子、兄弟、終去仁義、懷利以相接、然而不亡者、未之有也。六節先生以仁義說秦楚之王、秦楚之王、悅於仁義、而罷三軍之師、是三軍之士、樂罷而悅於仁義也、爲人臣者、懷仁義以事其君、爲人子者、懷仁義以事其父、爲人弟者、懷仁義以事其兄、是君臣、父子、兄弟、去利、懷仁義以相接也、然而不王者、未之有也、何

righteousness, sovereign and minister, father and son, younger brother and elder, will carry on all their intercourse with this thought of profit cherished in their breasts. But never has there been such a state *of society*, without ruin being the result of it.

6. 'If you, starting from the ground of benevolence and righteousness, offer your counsels to the kings of Ch'in and Ch'û, and if those kings are pleased with the consideration of benevolence and righteousness so as to stop the operations of their armies, then all belonging to those armies will rejoice in the stopping *from war*, and find their pleasure in benevolence and righteousness. Ministers will serve their sovereign, cherishing the principles of benevolence and righteousness; sons will serve their fathers, and younger brothers will serve their elder brothers, in the same way:—and so, sovereign and minister, father and son, elder brother and younger, abandoning *the thought of* profit, will cherish the principles of benevolence and righteousness, and carry on all their intercourse upon them. But never has there been such a state *of society*, without the State where it prevailed rising to the royal sway. Why must you use that word "profit."'

師, 'the multitudes of the three armies;' see the Analects, VII. x. 士 embraces both 'officers and soldiers.' 6. 然而不王 (4th tone) 者未之有,—here the translation needs to be supplemented considerably.

孟子

必曰利。

〔第五章〕孟子居鄒、季任爲任處守、以幣交、受之而不報、處於平陸、儲子爲相、以幣交、受之而不報。○二節 他日、由鄒之任、見季子、由平陸之齊、不見儲子、屋廬子喜曰、連得閒矣。○三節 問曰、夫子之任見季子、之齊不見儲子、爲其爲相與。○四節 曰、非也、書曰、享多儀、

CHAP. V. 1. When Mencius was residing in Tsâu, the younger brother of the chief of *Z*ăn, who was guardian of *Z*ăn at the time, paid his respects to him by *a present of* silks, which Mencius received, not *going* to acknowledge it. When he was sojourning in P'ing-lû, Ch'û, who was prime minister of the State, sent him a similar present, which he received in the same way.

2. Subsequently, going from Tsâu to *Z*ăn, he visited the guardian; but when he went from P'ing-lû to *the capital of* Ch'î, he did not visit the minister Ch'û. The disciple Wû-lû was glad, and said, 'I have got an opportunity *to obtain some instruction*.'

3. He asked *accordingly*, 'Master, when you went to *Z*ăn, you visited the chief's brother; and when you went to Ch'î, you did not visit Ch'û. Was it not because he is *only* the minister?'

4. *Mencius* replied, 'No. It is said in the Book of History, "In presenting an offering to a superior, most depends on the demonstrations of respect. If those demonstrations are not equal

5. HOW MENCIUS REGULATED HIMSELF IN DIFFERENTLY ACKNOWLEDGING FAVOURS WHICH HE RECEIVED. 1. 季任, and 季子 below, look much as if the former were the surname and name of the individual spoken of, yet Châo Ch'î's explanation of the terms, which is that followed in the translation, is no doubt correct. 任,—see chap. i. 以幣交,—see Bk. V. Pt. II. iv. 不報=不往報. 平陸,—see Bk. II. Pt. II. vi. 1. 2. The two 之 here, and in the next paragraph=往. 之齊, 'went to Ch'î,' i.e. to the capital of the State, as P'ing-lû was in Ch'î. 閒,—*chien*, 3rd tone. 連 (Wû-lû's name) 得閒=連得其閒隙而問, 'I have got an opportunity' (literally, crevice), 'to ask.' 4. 書曰,—see the Shû-ching, V. xii. 12, but in the classic the last clause 惟不役志于享 is not explanatory of the preceding, but is itself the first clause of a new sentence. See the Shû-

儀不及物、曰、不享、惟不役志于享。○五節爲其不成享也。○六節屋廬子悅、或問之、屋廬子曰、季子不得之鄒、儲子得之平陸。

第六章 淳于髡曰、一節先名實者、爲人也、後名實者、自爲也、夫子在三卿之中、名實未加於上下、而去之、仁者、固如此乎。○二節孟子曰、居下位、不以

to the things offered, we say there is no offering, that is, there is no act of the will in presenting the offering."

5. '*This is* because the things so offered do not constitute an offering to a superior.'

6. Wû-lû was pleased, and when some one asked him *what Mencius meant*, he said, 'The younger of Zăn could not go to Tsâu, but the minister Ch'û might have gone to P'ing-lû.'

CHAP. VI. 1. Shun-yü K'wăn said, 'He who makes fame and meritorious services his first objects, acts with a regard to others. He who makes them only secondary objects, acts with a regard to himself. You, master, were ranked among the three chief ministers *of the State*, but before your fame and services had reached either to the prince or the people, you have left your place. Is this indeed the way of the benevolent?'

2. Mencius replied, 'There was Po-î;—he abode in an inferior

ching, *in loc.* 5. This is Mencius's explanation of the passage quoted. 6. The guardian of a State could not leave it to pay a visit in another. There was no reason, however, why Ch'û should not have paid his respects to Mencius in person.

6. HOW MENCIUS REPLIED TO THE INSINUATIONS OF SHUN-YÜ K'WĂN, CONDEMNING HIM FOR LEAVING OFFICE WITHOUT ACCOMPLISHING ANYTHING. 1. Shun-yü K'wăn,—see Bk. IV. Pt. I. xvii. That chapter and the notes should be read along with this. 名 and 實 are not here opposed to each other, as often,—'name' and 'reality.' The 'name' here is the fame of the 'reality.' 爲人, 'with a regard to others,' i.e. such a man's motive in public life is to benefit others. 自爲-爲己, 'with a regard to himself,' i.e. such a man's motive is to cultivate his own good and excellence. 上 refers to the prince; 下 refers to the people. 仁者,—it is assumed that the fact of Mencius's being among the high ministers of State took him out of the category of those who made themselves their aim in life, and the 仁者 therefore is a hit of the questioner. Throughout the chapter, 仁 has perhaps more the idea of perfect virtue, free from all selfishness, than of benevolence. 2. Po-î, &c., see Bk. V. Pt. II. i, with the other references there given. That Î Yin went five

孟子

賢事不肖者、伯夷也、五就湯、五就桀者、伊尹也、不惡汙君、不辭小官者、柳下惠也、三子者、不同道、其趨一也、一者、何也、曰、仁也、君子亦仁而已矣、何必同。○三節、曰、魯繆公之時、公儀子爲政、子柳子思爲臣、魯之削也、滋甚、若是乎、賢者之無益於國也。○四節、曰、虞不用百里奚而亡、秦穆公用之而霸、不用

situation, and would not, with his virtue, serve a degenerate prince. There was Î Yin;—he five times went to T'ang, and five times went to Chieh. There was Hûi of Liû-hsiâ;—he did not disdain to serve a vile prince, nor did he decline a small office. The courses pursued by those three worthies were different, but their aim was one. And what was their one aim? We must answer—"To be perfectly virtuous." And so it is simply after this that superior men strive. Why must they all *pursue* the same *course?*'

3. *K'wăn* pursued, 'In the time of the duke Mû of Lû, the government was in the hands of Kung-î, while Tsze-liû and Tsze-sze were ministers. *And yet*, the dismemberment of Lû then increased exceedingly. Such was the case, a specimen how your men of virtue are of no advantage to a kingdom!'

4. *Mencius* said, '*The prince of* Yü did not use Pâi-lî Hsî, and thereby lost his State. The duke Mû of Chin used him, and became chief of all the princes. Ruin is the consequence of not employing

times to T'ang, and five times to Chieh is only mentioned here, however. He went to T'ang, it is said, in consequence of the pressing urgency of his solicitations, and then T'ang sent him to the tyrant to warn and advise him. Nothing could be farther at first from the wish of them both than to dethrone Chieh. 趨, 'to run,' used figuratively, 4th tone. 3. In this paragraph, K'wăn advances in his condemnation of Mencius. At first he charged him with having left his office before he had accomplished anything. Here he insinuates that though he had remained, he would not have served the State. Tsze-liû is the Hsieh Liû of Bk. II. Pt. II. xi; compare that chapter with this. Kung-î (named 休) was prime minister of Lû, a man of merit and principle. Mencius might have denied the fact alleged by K'wăn, of the increased dismemberment of Lû under duke Mû. 4. Pâi-lî Hsî,—see Bk. V. Pt. I. ix. 用, 不用,—the 'using' means follow-

賢則亡、削、何可得與。○五節曰、昔者、王豹處於淇、而河西善謳、緜駒處於高唐、而齊右善歌、華周杞梁之妻、善哭其夫、而變國俗、有諸內、必形諸外、爲其事、而無其功者、髡未嘗覩之也、是故無賢者也、有、則髡必識之。○六節曰、孔子爲魯司寇、不用、從而祭、燔肉不至、不稅冕而行、

men of virtue and talents;—how can it rest with dismemberment *merely*?'

5. *K'wăn* urged *again*, 'Formerly, when Wang P'âo dwelt on the Ch'î, the people on the west of the *Yellow* River all became skilful at singing in *his* abrupt manner. When Mien Ch'ü lived in Kâo-t'ang, the people in the parts of Ch'î on the west became skilful at singing in *his* prolonged manner. The wives of Hwa Châu and Ch'î Liang bewailed their husbands so skilfully, that they changed the manners of the State. When there is *the gift* within, it manifests itself without. I have never seen the man who could do the deeds *of a worthy*, and did not realize the work of one. Therefore there are *now* no men of talents and virtue. If there were, I should know them.'

6. *Mencius* answered, 'When Confucius was chief minister of Justice in Lû, the prince came not to follow *his counsels*. Soon after there was the *solstitial* sacrifice, and when a part of the flesh presented

ing the minister's counsels and plans. 削, 何可得與 (2nd tone),—before 削, we must understand 求, 'If you seek for dismemberment merely, as the consequence,' &c. 5. The individuals named here all belonged to Ch'î, excepting the first, who was of Wei. 歌 is the general name for singing, and 謳, a particular style, said to be 短聲, 'short,' 'abrupt.' 齊右, it is said, 概指齊西鄙而言, i.e. 'The Right of Ch'î denotes all about the western borders of the State.' Hwa (4th tone) Châu and Ch'î Liang were officers slain in battle, whose wives bewailed their loss in so pitiful a manner as to affect the whole State. Their cries, it is said, even rent the wall of the capital of Ch'î. See the 集證 and the 四書拓餘說, *in loc.*—The object of K'wăn is simply to insinuate that Mencius was a pretender, for that wherever ability was it was sure to come out. 6. Mencius shields himself behind Confucius, implying that he was beyond

不知者、以爲爲肉也、其知者、以爲爲無禮也、乃孔子則欲以微罪行、不欲爲苟去、君子之所爲、衆人固不識也。

第七章 一節 孟子曰、五霸者三王之罪人也、今之諸侯、五霸之罪人也、今之大夫、今之諸侯之罪人也。二節 天子適諸侯、曰巡狩、諸侯

in sacrifice was not sent to him, he went away even without taking off his cap of ceremony. Those who did not know him supposed it was on account of the flesh. Those who knew him supposed that it was on account *of the neglect* of the usual ceremony. The fact was, that Confucius wanted to go away on occasion of some small offence, not wishing to do so without some apparent cause. All men cannot be expected to understand the conduct of a superior man.'

CHAP. VII. 1. Mencius said, 'The five chiefs of the princes were sinners against the three kings. The princes of the present day are sinners against the five chiefs. The Great officers of the present day are sinners against the princes.

2. 'The sovereign visited the princes, which was called "A tour of Inspection." The princes attended at the court of the sovereign,

the knowledge of K'wăn.—The State of Ch'î, afraid of the influence of Confucius, who was acting as prime minister of Lû, sent to the duke a present of beautiful singing-girls and horses. The duke accepted them, and abandoned himself to dissipation. Confucius determined to leave the State, but not wishing to expose the bad conduct of his prince, looked about for some other reason which he might assign for going away, and found it in the matter mentioned. The 祭 is the 郊祭. 稅 is used for 脫. 爲苟去, 'to do a disorderly going away.'

7. THE PROGRESS AND MANNER OF DEGENERACY FROM THE THREE KINGS TO THE FIVE CHIEFS OF THE PRINCES, AND FROM THE FIVE CHIEFS TO THE PRINCES AND OFFICERS OF MENCIUS'S TIME. 1. The 'three kings' are the founders of the three dynasties of Hsiâ, Shang, and Châu. The 'five chiefs of the princes' were the duke Hwan of Ch'î (B.C. 684-642), the duke Wăn of Tsin (636-629), the duke Mû of Ch'in (659-620), the duke Hsiang of Sung (651-636), and the king Chwang of Ch'û (613-591). There are two enumerations of the 'five leading princes,' one called 三代之五伯, or chiefs of the three dynasties, and the other 春秋之五伯, or chiefs of the Ch'un-ch'iû. Only Hwan of Ch'î and Wăn of Tsin are common to the two. But Mencius is speaking only of those included in the second enumeration, and though there is some difference of opinion in regard to some of the individuals in it, the above list is probably that which he held. 'Sinners against,'—i.e. violating their principles and ways. 2. 天子...不給,—see Bk. I. Pt. II. iv. 5. 辟=闢; see

朝於天子、曰述職、春省耕、而補不足、秋省斂、而助不給、入其疆、土地辟、田野治、養老尊賢、俊傑在位、則有慶、慶以地、入其疆、土地荒蕪、遺老失賢、掊克在位、則有讓、一不朝、則貶其爵、再不朝、則削其地、三不朝、則六師移之、是故天子討而不伐、諸侯伐而不討、五霸者、摟諸侯以伐諸侯者也、

which was called "Giving a report of office." It was a custom in the spring to examine the ploughing, and supply any deficiency *of seed;* and in autumn to examine the reaping, and assist where there was a deficiency of the crop. When *the sovereign* entered the boundaries of a State, if the *new* ground was being reclaimed, and the *old* fields well cultivated; if the old were nourished and the worthy honoured; and if men of distinguished talents were placed in office: then *the prince* was rewarded,—rewarded with an addition to his territory. *On the other hand,* if, on entering a State, the ground was found left wild or overrun with weeds; if the old were neglected and the worthy unhonoured; and if the offices were filled with hard tax-gatherers: then *the prince* was reprimanded. If *a prince* once omitted his attendance at court, he was punished by degradation of rank; if he did so a second time, he was deprived of a portion of his territory; if he did so a third time, the royal forces *were set in motion,* and he was removed *from his government.* Thus the sovereign commanded the punishment, but did not himself inflict it, while the princes inflicted the punishment, but did not command it. The five

Bk. I. Pt. I. vii. 16. 俊傑在位,—see Bk. II. Pt. I. v. 1. 慶=賞, 'to reward.' 掊克=聚斂臣, 'impost-collecting ministers;' literally, perhaps, 'grasping and able men.' Down to 讓 is explicatory of 巡狩. What follows belongs to 述職. 六師(=軍),—see Analects, VII. x. 是故='in harmony with these things,' all power being lodged with the sovereign, and the princes being dependent on him. 討=治, 'to super-

故曰、五霸者、三王之罪人也。○三五霸桓公爲盛、葵丘之會諸侯、束牲載書而不歃血、初命曰、誅不孝、無易樹子、無以妾爲妻、再命曰、尊賢育才、以彰有德、三命曰、敬老慈幼、無忘賓旅、四命曰、士無世官、官事無攝、取士必得、無專殺大夫、五命曰、無曲防、無遏糴、無有封

chiefs, *however*, dragged the princes to punish other princes, and hence I say that they were sinners against the three kings.

3. 'Of the five chiefs the most powerful was the duke Hwan. At the assembly of the princes in K'wei-ch'iû, he bound the victim and placed the writing upon it, but did not *slay it to* smear their mouths with the blood. The first injunction in their agreement was,—"Slay the unfilial; change not the son who has been appointed heir; exalt not a concubine to be the wife." The second was,—"Honour the worthy, and maintain the talented, to give distinction to the virtuous." The third was,—"Respect the old, and be kind to the young. Be not forgetful of strangers and travellers." The fourth was,—"Let not offices be hereditary, nor let officers be pluralists. In the selection of officers let the object be to get the proper men. Let not a *ruler* take it on himself to put to death a Great officer." The

intend, or order, punishment;' 伐, 'to inflict the punishment.' 3. The duke Hwan nine times brought together an assembly of the princes, the chief gathering being at K'wei-ch'iû, B.C. 650. At those meetings, the usual custom was first to dig a square pit, over which the victim was slain. Its left ear was cut off, and its blood received in an ornamented vessel. The president then read the articles of agreement, with his face to the north, as in the presence of the spirits of the sun and moon, after which all the members of the meeting took the blood, and smeared the sides of their mouths with it. This was called 歃 (*shâ*) 血. The victim was then placed in the pit, the articles of agreement placed upon it, and the whole covered up. This was called 載書. See the 集證, *in loc.* On the occasion in the text, Hwan dispensed with some of those ceremonies. 命 was the term appropriated to the articles of agreement at such solemn assemblies, indicating that they were enjoined by the sovereign. 樹子, 'the son who has been tree-ed,' i.e. set up. 賓, 'guests,' officers from other States. 士無世官, 'officers no hereditary offices;' see Bk. I. Pt. II. 5. 3. 取士必得=必得其人. 無曲防, 'no crooked embankments.' 曲 has a

而不告、曰、凡我同盟之人、旣盟之後、言歸于好。今之諸侯、皆犯此五禁、故曰、今之諸侯、五霸之罪人也。長四節君之惡、其罪小、逢君之惡、其罪大、今之大夫、皆逢君之惡、故曰、今之大夫、今之諸侯之罪人也。

第八章 魯一節欲使愼子爲將軍。二節孟

fifth was,—"Follow no crooked policy in making embankments. Impose no restrictions on the sale of grain. Let there be no promotions without *first* announcing them *to the sovereign*." It was *then* said, "All we who have united in this agreement shall hereafter maintain amicable relations." The princes of the present day all violate these five prohibitions, and therefore I say that the princes of the present day are sinners against the five chiefs.

4. 'The crime of him who connives at, and aids, the wickedness of his prince is small, but the crime of him who anticipates and excites that wickedness is great. The officers of the present day all go to meet their sovereigns' *wickedness*, and therefore I say that the Great officers of the present day are sinners against the princes.'

CHAP. VIII. 1. *The prince of* Lû wanted to make the minister Shăn commander of his army.

2. Mencius said, 'To employ an uninstructed people *in war* may

moral application. No embankments must be made selfishly to take the water from others, or to inundate them. 無遏糴, 'do not repress the sale of grain,' i.e. to other States in famine or distress. 封, 'appointments,' to territory or to office. 4. 長君之惡, 'to lengthen the wickedness of the ruler,' i.e. to connive at and to aid it. 逢君之惡, 'to meet the wickedness of the ruler,' i.e. to anticipate and excite it.

8. MENCIUS'S OPPOSITION TO THE WARLIKE AMBITION OF THE PRINCE OF LÛ AND HIS MINISTER SHĂN KÛ-LÎ. 1. At this time Lû wanted to take advantage of difficulties in Ch'î, and get possession of Nan-yang. That was the name of the region on the south of mount T'âi, which had originally belonged to Lû. On the north of the mountain was the territory of Ch'î. Between the two States there had been frequent struggles for the district, which the duke P'ing of Lû (平公) now hoped to recover. Shăn, below, calls himself Kû-lî, but some say that that was the name of a Mohist under whom he had studied. His proper name was Tâo (到). He was a native of 趙, and not of Lû, but having a reputation for military skill, the duke of Lû wished to employ his services.

子曰、不教民而用之、謂之殃民、殃民者、不容於堯舜之世。○三節一戰勝齊、遂有南陽、然且不可。○四節愼子勃然不悅曰、此則滑釐所不識也。○五節曰、吾明告子、天子之地方千里、不千里、不足以待諸侯、諸侯之地、方百里、不百里、不足以守宗廟之典籍。○六節周公之封於魯、爲方百里也、地非不足、而儉於百里、太公之封於齊也、亦爲方百

be said to be destroying the people. A destroyer of the people would not have been tolerated in the times of Yâo and Shun.

3. 'Though by a single battle you should subdue Ch'î, and get possession of Nan-yang, the thing ought not to be done.'

4. Shăn changed countenance, and said in displeasure, 'This is what I, Kû-lî, do not understand.'

5. *Mencius* said, 'I will lay the case plainly before you. The territory appropriated to the sovereign is 1,000 *lî* square. Without a thousand *lî*, he would not have sufficient for his entertainment of the princes. The territory appropriated to a Hâu is 100 *lî* square. Without 100 *lî*, he would not have sufficient wherewith to observe the statutes kept in his ancestral temple.

6. 'When Châu-kung was invested with *the principality of* Lû, it was a hundred *lî* square. The territory was indeed enough, but it was not more than 100 *lî*. When T'âi-kung was invested with the principality of Ch'î, it was 100 *lî* square. The territory was indeed enough, but it was not more than 100 *lî*.

將軍, now the common term for general, appears to have come into vogue about Mencius's time. In the text it = 'commander-in-chief.' 2. Compare Analects, XIII. xxx.—We may infer from this paragraph, that Shăn had himself been the adviser of the projected enterprise.

5. 宗廟之典籍, 'the statute-records of the ancestral temple.' Those records prescribed everything to be observed in the public sacrifices, interviews with other princes, &c., and were kept in the temple. 6. Compare

里也、地非不足也、而儉於百里。七節今魯方百里者、五、子以爲有王者作、則魯在所損乎、在所益乎。八節徒取諸彼以與此、然且仁者不爲、況於殺人以求之乎。九節君子之事君也、務引其君以當道、志於仁而已。

第九章孟子曰、一節今之事君者曰、我能爲君辟土地、充府庫、今之所謂良臣、古之所謂民賊也、君不鄉

7. 'Now Lû is five times 100 *lî* square. If a *true* royal ruler were to arise, whether do you think that Lû would be diminished or increased by him?

8. 'If it were merely taking the place from the one *State* to give it to the other, a benevolent man would not do it;—how much less will he do so, when the end is to be sought by the slaughter of men!

9. 'The way in which a superior man serves his prince contemplates simply the leading him in the right path, and directing his mind to benevolence.'

CHAP. IX. 1. Mencius said, 'Those who now-a-days serve their sovereigns say, "We can for our sovereign enlarge the limits of the cultivated ground, and fill his treasuries and arsenals." Such persons are now-a-days called "Good ministers," but anciently they were called "Robbers of the people." If a sovereign follows not

Analects, VI. xxii. 儉, 'sparingly,' = only. 8. 徒, 'merely,' i. e. if there were no struggle and no slaughter in the matter. 9. 當道 here is different from the same phrase, 當路, in Bk. II. Pt. I. i. 1.

9. HOW THE MINISTERS OF MENCIUS'S TIME PANDERED TO THEIR SOVEREIGNS' THIRST FOR WEALTH AND POWER. 1. 辟(=闢)土地,—it is to be understood that this was to be done at the expense of the people, taking their commons from them, and making them labour. Otherwise, it does not seem objectionable.—Châo Ch'î, however, gives the phrase another meaning, making it = 侵小國, 'appropriate small States,' but this is contrary to analogous passages, and confounds this paragraph with

道、不志於仁、而求富之、是富桀也。二節我能爲君約與國、戰必克、今之所謂良臣、古之所謂民賊也、君不鄉道、不志於仁、而求爲之强戰、是輔桀也。三節由今之道、無變今之俗、雖與之天下、不能一朝居也。

第十章 白圭曰、吾欲二十而取一、何如。二節孟子曰、子之道、貉

the right way, nor has his mind bent on benevolence, to seek to enrich him is to enrich a Chieh.

2. '*Or they will say,* "We can for our sovereign form alliances with other States, so that our battles must be successful." Such persons are now-a-days called "Good ministers," but anciently they were called "Robbers of the people." If a sovereign follows not the right way, nor has his mind directed to benevolence, to seek to enrich him is to enrich a Chieh.

3. 'Although a prince, pursuing the path of the present day, and not changing its practices, were to have the throne given to him, he could not retain it for a single morning.'

CHAP. X. 1. Pâi Kwei said, 'I want to take a twentieth *of the produce only as the tax.* What do you think of it?'

2. Mencius said, 'Your way would be that of the Mo.

the next; compare Bk. IV. Pt. I. xiv. 2. 約與國, 'ally with *other* States.' Here Châo Ch'î differs again, making 約=期, 'to determine beforehand,' 'undertake,' and joining 與國戰, 'undertake in fighting with hostile countries to conquer.' This also is an inferior construction. 3. 朝居=朝居其位, 'occupy the position for a morning.'

10. AN ORDERED STATE CAN ONLY SUBSIST WITH A PROPER SYSTEM OF TAXATION, AND THAT ORIGINATING WITH YÂO AND SHUN IS THE PROPER ONE FOR CHINA. 1. Pâi Kwei, styled Tan (see next chapter), was a man of Châu, ascetic in his own habits, and fond of innovations. Hence the suggestion in this chapter.—So, Châo Ch'î, and Chû Hsî has followed him. The author of the 四書拓餘說, however, contends that the Pâi Kwei described as above on the authority of the 'Historical Records,' 列傳, lxix, was not the same here introduced. See that Work, *in loc.* 2. 貉 or 貊 was a common name for the barbarous tribes on the north. They were a pastoral people, and the climate of their country was cold. No doubt their civilization was inferior to that of

道也。三節萬室之國、一人陶、則可乎。曰、不可、器不足用也。四節曰、夫貉五穀不生、惟黍生之、無城郭宮室宗廟祭祀之禮、無諸侯幣帛饔飧、無百官有司、故二十取一而足也。五節今居中國、去人倫、無君子、如之何其可也。六節陶以寡、且不可以爲國、況無君子乎。七節欲輕之於堯舜之道者、大貉小貉也、欲重之於

3. 'In a country of ten thousand families, would it do to have *only* one potter?' *Kwei* replied, 'No. The vessels would not be enough to use.'

4. *Mencius* went on, 'In Mo *all* the five kinds of grain are not grown; it only produces the millet. There are no fortified cities, no edifices, no ancestral temples, no ceremonies of sacrifice; there are no princes requiring presents and entertainments; there is no system of officers with their various subordinates. On these accounts a tax of one-twentieth of the produce is sufficient *there*.

5. 'But now it is the Middle Kingdom that we live in. To banish the relationships of men, and have no superior men;—how can such a state of things be thought of?

6. 'With but few potters a kingdom cannot subsist;—how much less can it subsist without men of a higher rank than others?

7. 'If we wish to make the taxation lighter than the system of Yâo and Shun, we shall just have a great Mo and a small Mo.

China, but Mencius's account of them must be taken with allowance. 4. 城郭,—see Bk. II. Pt. II. i. 2. 宮室 go together as a general designation of edifices, called 宮, as 'four-walled and roofed,' and 室 (實) as 'furnished.' So 祭祀 go together as synonymous, and also 幣帛, 'pieces of silk, given as presents.' 饔, 'the morning meal;' 飧, 'the evening meal;' together = 'entertainments.' 5, 6. 君子,—referring to the 百官, 有司. 7. The meaning is, that, under such systems, China would become in the one case a copy of the Mo, and in the other of its state under the tyrant Chieh.

堯舜之道者、大桀小桀也。

〔十一章〕〔一節〕白圭曰、丹之治水也、愈於禹。〔二節〕孟子曰、子過矣、禹之治水、水之道也。〔三節〕是故禹以四海為壑、今吾子以鄰國為壑。〔四節〕水逆行、謂之洚水、洚水者、洪水也、仁人之所惡也、吾子過矣。

〔十二章〕孟子曰、君子不亮、惡乎執。

〔十三章〕〔一節〕魯欲使樂正子為政、孟子曰、吾聞之、喜而不寐。〔二節〕公孫丑

If we wish to make it heavier, we shall just have the great Chieh and the small Chieh.'

CHAP. XI. 1. Pâi Kwei said, 'My management of the waters is superior to that of Yü.'

2. Mencius replied, 'You are wrong, Sir. Yü's regulation of the waters was according to the laws of water.

3. 'He therefore made the four seas their receptacle, while you make the neighbouring States their receptacle.

4. 'Water flowing out of its channels is called an inundation. Inundating waters are a vast *waste* of water, and what a benevolent man detests. You are wrong, my good Sir.'

CHAP. XII. Mencius said, 'If a scholar have not faith, how shall he take a firm hold *of things*?'

CHAP. XIII. 1. *The prince of* Lû wanting to commit the administration of his government to the disciple Yo-chăng, Mencius said, 'When I heard of it, I was so glad that I could not sleep.'

2. Kung-sun Ch'âu asked, 'Is Yo-chăng a man of vigour?' and

11. PÂI KWEI'S PRESUMPTUOUS IDEA THAT HE COULD REGULATE THE WATERS BETTER THAN YÜ DID. 1. There had been some partial inundations, where the services of Pâi Kwei were called in, and he had reduced them by turning the waters into other States, saving one at the expense of injuring others. 2. 水之道 = 順水之性. 4. See Bk. III. Pt. II. ix. 3, but 洪水 has there a particular application.

12. FAITH IN PRINCIPLES NECESSARY TO FIRMNESS IN ACTION. 亮 used as 諒. Chû Hsî explains it by 信.

13. OF WHAT IMPORTANCE TO A MINISTER—TO GOVERNMENT—IT IS TO LOVE WHAT IS GOOD. 1. 爲政, 'to administer the government,' as in

曰、樂正子强乎。曰、否。有知慮乎。曰、否。多聞識乎。曰、否。〇三然則奚爲喜而不寐。〇四曰、其爲人也、好善。〇五曰、好善足乎。〇六曰、好善優於天下、而況魯國乎。〇七夫苟好善、則四海之內、皆將輕千里而來、告之以善。〇八夫苟不好善、則人將曰、訑訑、予既已知之矣、訑訑之聲音顏色、距人於千里之外、士止於千里之外、則

was answered, 'No.' 'Is he wise in council?' 'No.' 'Is he possessed of much information?' 'No.'

3. 'What then made you so glad that you could not sleep?'

4. 'He is a man who loves what is good.'

5. 'Is the love of what is good sufficient?'

6. 'The love of what is good is more than a sufficient qualification for the government of the kingdom;—how much more is it so for the State of Lû!

7. 'If *a minister* love what is good, all within the four seas will count 1,000 *lî* but a small distance, and will come and lay their good thoughts before him.

8. 'If he do not love what is good, men will say, "How self-conceited he looks? *He is saying to himself*, I know it." The language and looks of that self-conceit will keep men off at a distance of 1,000 *lî*. When good men stop 1,000 *lî* off, calumniators, flatterers, and sycophants will make their appearance. When a minister

chap. vi. 3. 2. 有知慮乎,—知 is in the 3rd tone; 'has he wisdom and deliberation?'—The three gifts mentioned here were those considered most important to government in that age, and Kung-sun Ch'âu knowing Yo-chăng to be deficient in them, put his questions accordingly. 4. On this paragraph it is said in the 日講:—'In the administration of government, the most excellent quality is without prejudice and dispassionately (虛中) to receive what is good. Now in regard to all good words and good actions, Yo-chăng in his heart sincerely loved them.' 5, 6. 足 is what is simply sufficient. 優 is what is sufficient and more. 8. 訑訑, as defined by Chû Hsî, is—自足其智,不嗜善言之

孟子

讒諂面諛之人至矣、與讒諂面諛之人居、國欲治、可得乎。

〔十四章〕一節 陳子曰、古之君子、何如則仕。孟子曰、所就三、所去三。二節 迎之致敬以有禮、言將行其言也、則就之、禮貌未衰、言弗行也、則去之。三節 其次、雖未行其言也、迎之致敬以有禮、則就之、禮貌衰、則

lives among calumniators, flatterers, and sycophants, though he may wish the State to be well governed, is it possible for it to be so?'

Chap. XIV. 1. The disciple Ch'ăn said, 'What were the principles on which superior men of old took office?' Mencius replied, 'There were three cases in which they accepted office, and three in which they left it.

2. 'If received with the utmost respect and all polite observances, and they could say *to themselves* that the prince would carry their words into practice, then they took office with him. *Afterwards*, although there might be no remission in the polite demeanour of the prince, if their words were not carried into practice, they would leave him.

3. 'The second case was that in which, though *the prince could not be expected* at once to carry their words into practice, yet being received by him with the utmost respect, they took office with him. But afterwards, if there was a remission in his polite demeanour, they would leave him.

貌, 'the appearance of being satisfied with one's own knowledge, and having no relish for good words.' 士 = 善人.

14. Grounds of taking and leaving office. Compare Bk. V. Pt. II. iv. 7. The three cases mentioned here are respectively the 行可之仕, the 際可, and the 公養, of that place. 1. This Ch'ăn is the Ch'ăn Tsin, Bk. II. Pt. II. iii. 2. 迎 is simply = 接待, not 'to go out to meet.' 3. 雖未行其言 is to be understood as thought in the scholar's mind, corresponding to 言將行其言 in the preceding paragraph. In the 日講 indeed, the 言 there is made to be the language of the ruler, but see the gloss of the 備旨,

去之。四節其下、朝不食、夕不食、饑餓不能出門戶、君聞之、曰、吾大者、不能行其道、又不能從其言也、使饑餓於我土地、吾恥之、周之、亦可受也、免死而已矣。

〔十五〕一節孟子曰、舜發於畎畝之中、傅說舉於版築之間、膠鬲舉於魚鹽之中、管夷吾、舉於士、孫叔敖、舉於海、百

4. 'The last case was that of *the superior man* who had nothing to eat, either morning or evening, and was so famished that he could not move out of his door. If the prince, on hearing of his state, said, "I must fail in the great point,—that of carrying his doctrines into practice, neither am I able to follow his words, but I am ashamed to allow him to die of want in my country;" the assistance offered in such a case might be received, but not beyond what was sufficient to avert death.'

CHAP. XV. 1. Mencius said, 'Shun rose from among the channelled fields. Fû Yüeh was called to office from the midst of his building frames; Chiâo-ko from his fish and salt; Kwan Î-wû from the hands of his gaoler; Sun-shû Âo from *his hiding by* the sea-shore; and Pâi-lî Hsî from the market-place.

in loc. 4. The assistance is in the shape of employment offered. If not, then 不可受 would not be a case of 就仕.

15. TRIALS AND HARDSHIPS THE WAY IN WHICH HEAVEN PREPARES MEN FOR GREAT SERVICES. 1. With Shun, Kwan Î-wû, and Pâi-lî Hsî, the student must be familiar. Fû Yüeh,—see the Shû-ching, Pt. IV. Bk. VII, where it is related that the sovereign Kâo Tsung having 'dreamt that God gave him a good assistant,' caused a picture of the man he had seen in his dream to be made, and 'search made for him through the kingdom, when he was found dwelling in the wilderness of Fû-yen (傅巖之野).' In the 'Historical Records,' it is said the surname was given in the dream as 傅, and the name as 悅. Chiâo Ko is mentioned in Bk. II. Pt. I. i. 8, where it is said in the notes that his worth, when living in retirement, was discovered by king Wăn. He was then selling fish and salt, and on Wăn's recommendation was raised to office by the last sovereign of Yin, to whose fortunes he continued faithful. Sun-shû Âo was prime minister to Chwang of Ch'û, the last of the five chiefs of the princes. So much is beyond dispute, but the circumstances of his elevation, and the family to which he belonged, are uncertain. See the 四書拓餘說, *in loc.* 版築, 'planks and building.' Many of the houses in China are built of earth and mortar beaten together within a moveable frame, in which the walls are formed.

孟子

里奚、舉於市。○二節故天將降大任於是人也、必先苦其心志、勞其筋骨、餓其體膚、空乏其身、行拂亂其所爲、所以動心忍性、曾益其所不能。○三節人恆過、然後能改、困於心、衡於慮、而後作、徵於色發於聲、而後喻。○四節入則無法家拂士、出則無敵國外患者、國恆亡。○五節然後知生於憂

2. 'Thus, when Heaven is about to confer a great office on any man, it first exercises his mind with suffering, and his sinews and bones with toil. It exposes his body to hunger, and subjects him to extreme poverty. It confounds his undertakings. By all these methods it stimulates his mind, hardens his nature, and supplies his incompetencies.

3. 'Men for the most part err, and are afterwards able to reform. They are distressed in mind and perplexed in their thoughts, and then they arise to vigorous reformation. When things have been evidenced in men's looks, and set forth in their words, then they understand them.

4. 'If a prince have not about his court families attached to the laws and worthy counsellors, and if abroad there are not hostile States or other external calamities, his kingdom will generally come to ruin.

5. 'From these things we see how life springs from sorrow and calamity, and death from ease and pleasure.'

舉士,—士 is the officer who was in charge of him. 2. 餓其體膚, 'hungers his members and skin.' 空乏其身, 'empties his person.' 行佛, 云云, 'as to his doings, confounds what he is doing.' 行 is taken as 行事, and 爲 as 心所謀爲. 曾,—used for 增. 3. The same thing holds true of ordinary men. They are improved by difficulties. 衡,—used for 横. 徵於色, 云云,—the meaning is, that, though most men are not quick of apprehension, yet when things are clearly before them, they can lay hold of them. 4. The same thing is true of a State. 法家, 'law families,' i. e. old families to whom the laws of the State are familiar and dear. 拂 is used for 弼. Such families and officers will stimulate the prince's mind by their lessons and remonstrances, and

患、而死於安樂也。

十六 孟子曰、教亦多術矣、予不屑之教誨也者、是亦教誨之而已矣。

CHAP. XVI. Mencius said, 'There are many arts in teaching. I refuse, as inconsistent with my character, to teach a man, but I am only thereby still teaching him.'

foreign danger will rouse him to carefulness and exertion.

16. HOW A REFUSAL TO TEACH MAY BE TEACHING. The 亦 in 亦教 is not without its force, but we can hardly express it in a translation. 予不屑之教誨-予不屑教誨之. The 者 carries us on to the next clause for an explanation of what has been said.

BOOK VII.

TSIN SIN. PART I.

盡心章句上

第一章 孟子曰、盡其心者、知其性也、知其性、則知天矣。存其

CHAPTER I. 1. Mencius said, 'He who has exhausted all his mental constitution knows his nature. Knowing his nature, he knows Heaven.

TITLE OF THIS BOOK.—Like the previous Books, this is named from the commencing words—盡心, 'The exhausting of all the mental constitution.' It contains many more chapters than any of them, being, for the most part, brief enigmatical sentences, conveying Mencius's views of human nature. It is more abstruse also, and the student will have much difficulty in satisfying himself that he has really hit the exact meaning of the philosopher. The author of the 四書味根錄 says:—'This Book was made by Mencius in his old age. Its style is terse, and its meaning deep, and we cannot discover an order of subjects in its chapters. He had completed the previous six Books, and this grew up under his pencil, as his mind was affected, and he was prompted to give expression to his thoughts. The first chapter may be regarded, however, as a compendium of the whole.'

1. BY THE STUDY OF OURSELVES WE COME TO THE KNOWLEDGE OF HEAVEN, AND HEAVEN IS SERVED BY OUR OBEYING OUR NATURE. 1. 盡其心 is, I conceive, to make one's self acquainted with all his mind, to arrest his consciousness, and ascertain what he is. This of course gives a man the knowledge of his nature, and as he is the creature of Heaven, its attributes must be corresponding. It is much to be wished that instead of the term Heaven, vague and indefinite, Mencius had simply said 'God.' I can get no other meaning from this paragraph. Chû Hsî, however, and all his school say that there

孟子

心、養其性、所以事天也。[三節]殀壽不貳、修身以俟之、所以立命也。

[第二章]孟子曰、[一節]莫非命也、順受其正。

2. 'To preserve one's mental constitution, and nourish one's nature, is the way to serve Heaven.

3. 'When neither a premature death nor long life causes a man any double-mindedness, but he waits in the cultivation of his personal character *for whatever issue;*—this is the way in which he establishes his *Heaven*-ordained being.'

CHAP. II. 1. Mencius said, 'There is an appointment for everything. A man should receive submissively what may be correctly ascribed thereto.

is no work or labour in 盡其心; that it is the 知至 of the Confucian chapter in the 'Superior Learning,' according to their view of it; that all the labour is in 知其性, which is the 物格 of that chapter. If this be correct, we should translate:—'He who completely develops his mental constitution, has known (come to know) his nature,' but I cannot construe the words so. 2. The 'preservation' is the holding fast what we have from Heaven, and the 'nourishing' is the acting in harmony therewith, so that the 'serving Heaven' is just being and doing what It has intimated in our constitution to be Its will concerning us. 3. 命 is our nature, according to the opening words of the *Chung Yung*,—天命之謂性. 立 is to be taken as an active verb. 不貳=不疑, 'causes no doubts,' i.e. no doubts as to what is to be done. 俟之,—之 referring to 殀壽.—It may be well to give the views of Châo Ch'î on this chapter. On the first paragraph he says:—'To the nature there belong the principles of benevolence, righteousness, propriety, and knowledge. The mind is designed to regulate them (心以制之); and having the distinction of being correct, a man can put forth all his mind to think of doing good, and then he may be said to know his nature. When he knows his nature, he knows that the way of Heaven considers what is good to be excellent.' On the second paragraph he says:—'When one is able to preserve his mind, and to nourish his correct nature, he may be called a man of perfect virtue (仁人). The way of Heaven loves life, and the perfect man also loves life. The way of Heaven is without partiality, and only approves of the virtuous. Thus the acting *of the perfect man* agrees with Heaven, and hence it is said,—this is the way by which he serves Heaven.' On the third paragraph he says:—'The perfect man in his conduct is guided by one law. Although he sees that some who have gone before him have been short-lived, and some long-lived, he never has two minds, or changes his way. Let life be short as that of Yen Yüan, or long as that of the duke of Shâo, he refers either case equally to the appointment of Heaven, and cultivates and rectifies his own person to wait for that. It is in this way he establishes the root *of Heaven's* appointments (此所以立命之本).' These explanations do not throw light upon the text, but they show how that may be treated independently of the school of Chû Hsî. And the equal unsatisfactoriness of his interpretation may well lead the student—the foreign student especially—to put forth his strength on the study of the text more than on the commentaries.

2. MAN'S DUTY AS AFFECTED BY THE DECREES OR APPOINTMENTS OF HEAVEN. WHAT MAY BE CORRECTLY ASCRIBED THERETO AND WHAT NOT. Chû Hsî says this is a continuation of the last chapter, developing the meaning of the last paragraph. There is a connexion between the chapters, but 命 is here taken more widely, as extending not only to man's nature, but all the events that befall him. 1. 正命, 'the correct appointment,' i.e. that which is directly the will of Heaven. No consequence flowing from evil or careless conduct is to be understood as being so. Chû Hsî's definition is—莫之致而至者乃爲正命, 'that which comes without being brought on is the correct appointment.'—Châo Ch'î says

二節 是故知命者、不立乎巖牆之下。三節 盡其道而死者、正命也。四節 桎梏死者、非正命也。

第三章 一節 孟子曰、求、則得之、舍、則失之、是求有益於得也、求在我者也。二節 求之有道、得之有命、是求無益於得也、求在外者也。

第四章 一節 孟子曰、萬物皆備於

2. 'Therefore, he who has the true idea of what is *Heaven's* appointment will not stand beneath a precipitous wall.

3. 'Death sustained in the discharge of one's duties may correctly be ascribed to the appointment *of Heaven.*

4. 'Death under handcuffs and fetters cannot correctly be so ascribed.'

CHAP. III. 1. Mencius said, 'When we get by our seeking and lose by our neglecting;—in that case seeking is of use to getting, and the things sought for are those which are in ourselves.

2. 'When the seeking is according to the proper course, and the getting is *only* as appointed;—in that case the seeking is of no use to getting, and the things sought are without ourselves.'

CHAP. IV. 1. Mencius said, 'All things are already complete in us.

there are three ways of speaking about the appointments or decrees of Heaven. Doing good and getting good is called 受命, 'receiving what is appointed.' Doing good and getting evil is called 遭命, 'encountering what is appointed.' Doing evil and getting evil is called 隨命, 'following after what is appointed.' It is only the first of these cases that is spoken of in the text. It must be borne in mind, however, that by 命 here Châo understands death, and that only, and we should acquiesce in this, if there did not seem to be a connexion between this chapter and the preceding. 2. 知命者,—he who knows, or has the true notion of, &c. 巖, 'precipitous' and likely to fall. 4. The fetters are understood to be those of an evil doer. 桎 are fetters for the hands, and 梏 those for the feet.

3. VIRTUE IS SURE TO BE GAINED BY SEEKING IT, BUT RICHES AND OTHER EXTERNAL THINGS NOT. This general sentiment is correct, but the exact truth is sacrificed to the point of the antithesis, when it is said in the second case that seeking is of *no* use to getting. The things 'in ourselves' are benevolence, righteousness, propriety, and knowledge, the endowments proper of our nature. The things 'without ourselves' are riches and dignities. The 'proper course' to seek these is that ascribed to Confucius, 'advancing according to propriety, and retiring according to righteousness,' but yet they are not at our command and control.

4. MAN IS FITTED FOR, AND HAPPY IN, DOING GOOD, AND MAY PERFECT HIMSELF THEREIN. 1. This paragraph is mystical. The all things are taken

我矣。二節反身而誠、樂莫大焉。三節彊恕而行、求仁莫近焉。

第五章孟子曰、行之而不著焉、習矣而不察焉、終身由之而不知其道者、衆也。

第六章孟子曰、人不可以無恥、二節無恥之恥、無恥矣。

第七章孟子曰、恥之於人大

2. 'There is no greater delight than to be conscious of sincerity on self-examination.

3. 'If one acts with a vigorous effort at the law of reciprocity, when he seeks for *the realization of* perfect virtue, nothing can be closer than his approximation to it.'

CHAP. V. Mencius said, 'To act without understanding, and to do so habitually without examination, pursuing the proper path all the life without knowing its nature;—this is the way of multitudes.'

CHAP. VI. Mencius said, 'A man may not be without shame. When one is ashamed of having been without shame, he will *afterwards* not have *occasion* to be ashamed.'

CHAP. VII. 1. Mencius said, 'The sense of shame is to a man of great importance.

as the *principles* of all things, which all things moreover are chiefly the relations of society. When we extend them farther, we get embarrassed. 2. The 誠 here is that so largely treated of in the Chung Yung. 3. 恕 is the judging of others by ourselves, and acting accordingly. Compare the Doctrine of the Mean, xiii. 3.

5. HOW MANY ACT WITHOUT THOUGHT. Compare the Analects, VIII. ix. 行之,由之, —之 is to be understood of 道, but 其道 = 'its nature,' its propriety, which is the object of 著, and its grounds, which is the object of 察. Chû Hsî defines 著 as 知之明, 'knowing clearly,' and 察 as 識之精, 'knowing minutely and exactly.' 'There is much activity,' says the 備旨, 'in the two verbs.' This use of 著 is not common.

6. THE VALUE OF THE FEELING OF SHAME. The last 恥 = shameful conduct.

7. THE SAME SUBJECT. The former chapter, it is said, was by way of exhortation (以勸); this is by way of warning (以戒). The second paragraph is aimed at the wandering scholars of Mencius's time, who were full of plots and schemes to unite and disunite the various princes. 機, 'springs of motion,' 'machinery.' The third paragraph may also be translated, 'If a man be not ashamed at his being not like other men, in what will he be like them?'

矣。二節為機變之巧者、無所用恥焉。三節不恥不若人、何若人有。

第八章孟子曰、古之賢王、好善而忘勢、古之賢士、何獨不然。樂其道、而忘人之勢、故王公不致敬盡禮、則不得亟見之、見、且猶不得亟、而況得而臣之乎。

第九章孟子謂宋句踐曰、一節子好遊

2. 'Those who form contrivances and versatile schemes distinguished for their artfulness, do not allow their sense of shame to come into action.

3. 'When one differs from other men in not having this sense of shame, what will he have in common with them?'

CHAP. VIII. Mencius said, 'The able and virtuous monarchs of antiquity loved virtue and forgot their power. And shall an exception be made of the able and virtuous scholars of antiquity, that they did not do the same? They delighted in their own principles, and were oblivious of the power of princes. Therefore, if kings and dukes did not show the utmost respect, and observe all forms of ceremony, they were not permitted to come frequently and visit them. If they thus found it not in their power to pay them frequent visits, how much less could they get to employ them as ministers?'

CHAP. IX. 1. Mencius said to Sung Kâu-ch'ien, 'Are you fond, Sir, of travelling *to the different courts?* I will tell you about such travelling.

8. HOW THE ANCIENT SCHOLARS MAINTAINED THE DIGNITY OF THEIR CHARACTER AND PRINCIPLES. 善 is not virtue in the abstract, but the good which they saw in others, in the scholars namely. 勢 is their own 'power.' As applied to the scholars, however, these things have to be reversed. They loved their own virtue (其道), and forgot the power of men, i. e. of the princes.

9. HOW A PROFESSIONAL ADVISER OF THE PRINCES MIGHT BE ALWAYS PERFECTLY SATISFIED. THE EXAMPLE OF ANTIQUITY. 1. Some make the party spoken to in this chapter to be Kâu (句 read as 鉤)-ch'ien of Sung. Nothing is known

孟子

乎、吾語子遊。二節人知之、亦囂囂、人不知、亦囂囂。三節曰、何如、斯可以囂囂矣。曰、尊德樂義、則可以囂囂矣。四節故士窮不失義、達不離道。五節窮不失義、故士得己焉、達不離道、故民不失望焉。六節古之人、得志、澤加於民、不得志、修身見於世、窮、則獨善其身、達、則兼善天下。

2. 'If a prince acknowledge you and follow your counsels, be perfectly satisfied. If no one do so, be the same.'

3. *Kâu-ch'ien* said, 'What is to be done to secure this perfect satisfaction?' Mencius replied, 'Honour virtue and delight in righteousness, and so you may *always* be perfectly satisfied.

4. 'Therefore, a scholar, though poor, does not let go *his* righteousness; though prosperous, he does not leave *his own* path.

5. 'Poor and not letting righteousness go;—it is thus that the scholar holds possession of himself. Prosperous and not leaving the *proper* path;—it is thus that the expectations of the people from him are not disappointed.

6. 'When the men of antiquity realized their wishes, benefits were conferred by them on the people. If they did not realize their wishes, they cultivated their personal character, and became illustrious in the world. If poor, they attended to their own virtue in solitude; if advanced to dignity, they made the whole kingdom virtuous as well.'

of him, but that he was one of the adventurers, who travelled about tendering their advice to the different princes. 2. To translate 知之 as I have done here, can hardly be called a paraphrase. Chû Hsi, after Châo Ch'î, explains 囂囂 as 'the appearance of self-possession and freedom from desire.' 'Perfectly satisfied,' conveys the idea of the phrase. 3. It is to be understood that the 'virtue' is that which the scholar has in himself, and the 'righteousness' is the course which he pursues. 4. 窮—人不知之; 達 is the reverse. 5. 'Holds possession of himself,'—i.e. has what he chiefly loves and seeks. 6. 古之人,—人—士.—Chû Hsî observes:—'This chapter shows how the scholar, attaching weight to what is internal, and holding what is external light, will approve himself good in all places and circumstances.'

第十章 孟子曰待文王而後興者、凡民也、若夫豪傑之士、雖無文王猶興。

十一章 孟子曰、附之以韓魏之家、如其自視欿然、則過人遠矣。

十二章 孟子曰、以佚道使民、雖勞不怨、以生道殺民、雖死不怨殺者。

十三章 一節 孟子曰、霸者之民、驩

CHAP. X. Mencius said, 'The mass of men wait for a king Wăn, and then they will receive a rousing impulse. Scholars distinguished *from the mass*, without a king Wăn, rouse themselves.'

CHAP. XI. Mencius said, 'Add to a man the families of Han and Wei. If he then look upon himself without being elated, he is far beyond *the mass of* men.'

CHAP. XII. Mencius said, 'Let the people be employed in the way which is intended to secure their ease, and though they be toiled, they will not murmur. Let them be put to death in the way which is intended to preserve their lives, and though they die, they will not murmur at him who puts them to death.'

CHAP. XIII. 1. Mencius said, 'Under a chief, leading all the princes, the people look brisk and cheerful. Under a true sovereign, they have an air of deep contentment.

10. HOW PEOPLE SHOULD GET THEIR INSPIRATION TO GOOD IN THEMSELVES. 凡民, 'all the people,' i.e. ordinary people. 豪傑=俊傑, in Bk. II. Pt. I. v. 1. When a distinction is made between the characters, he who in wisdom is the first of 10,000 men, is called 英; the first of 1,000 is called 俊; the first of 100 is called 豪; the first of 10 is called 傑.

11. NOT TO BE ELATED BY RICHES IS A PROOF OF SUPERIORITY. Han and Wei,—see Bk. I. Pt. I. i. 1, notes; 'The families of Han and Wei,'—i.e. the wealth and power of those families. 附, used for 益, 'to increase,' indicates the externality of the additions. 欿然 is defined 不自滿足意, 'not being full of and satisfied with one's self.'

12. WHEN A RULER'S AIM IS EVIDENTLY THE PEOPLE'S GOOD, THEY WILL NOT MURMUR AT HIS HARSHEST MEASURES. The first part is explained rightly of toils in agriculture, road-making, bridge-making, &c., and the second of the administration of justice, where I should prefer to think that Mencius had the idea of a just war before him; compare Analects, XX. ii. 2. 佚道, 'a way of ease;' 生道, 'a way of life.'

13. THE DIFFERENT INFLUENCE EXERCISED BY A CHIEF AMONG THE PRINCES, AND BY A TRUE SOVEREIGN. 1. 虞 is explained in the dictionary, with reference to this passage, by 樂. It is the same as 娛 and 驩虞=歡娛. 皞皞 is 廣大自得之貌,

虞如也、王者之民、皞皞如也。二節殺之而不怨、利之而不庸、民日遷善而不知爲之者。三節夫君子所過者化、所存者神、上下與天地同流、豈曰小補之哉。

十四章一節孟子曰、仁言不如仁聲之入人深也。二節善政不如善教之得民也。三節善政、

2. 'Though he slay them, they do not murmur. When he benefits them, they do not think of his merit. From day to day they make progress towards what is good, without knowing who makes them do so.

3. 'Wherever the superior man passes through, transformation follows; wherever he abides, his influence is of a spiritual nature. It flows abroad, above and beneath, like that of Heaven and Earth. How can it be said that he mends society but in a small way!'

CHAP. XIV. 1. Mencius said, 'Kindly words do not enter so deeply into men as a reputation for kindness.

2. 'Good government does not lay hold of the people so much as good instructions.

3. 'Good government is feared by the people, while good instruc-

'the appearance of enlargement and self-possession.' In illustration of the condition of the people under a true sovereign, commentators generally quote a tradition of their state in the golden age of Yâo, when 'entire harmony reigned under heaven, and the lives of the people passed easily away.' Then the old men smote the clods, and sang, 日出而作,日入而息,鑿井而飮,耕田而食,帝力於我何有哉, 'At sunrise we rise, and at sunset we rest. We dig our wells and drink; we cultivate our fields and eat.—What is the strength of the *Tî* to us?' 2. 庸 is used in the sense of 功, 'merit,' or meritorious work, and the analogy of the other clauses determines the meaning of 不庸, as in the translation. 3. 君子 has reference to the 王者, par. 1. It is used here in its highest application, = 'the sage.' 所過,所存,—the latter phrase is interpreted morally, being = 'when he has fixed his mind to produce a result.' This is unnecessary. 神, 'spiritual,' 'mysterious:'—the effects are sure and visible, but the operation is hidden. In the influence of Shun in the time of his obscurity, when the ploughmen yielded the furrow, and the potters made their vessels all sound, we have an example, it is said, of the 所過者化. In what it is presumed would have been the influence of Confucius, had he been in the position of a ruler, as described, Analects XIX. xxv, we have an example of the 所存者神. 補之, as an object for 之, I supply 'society.' It is understood that a leader of the princes only helps the people in a small way.

14. THE VALUE TO A RULER OF REPUTATION AND MORAL INFLUENCES. Kindly words are but brief.

民畏之、善教、民愛之、善政得民財、善教得民心。

【十五】孟子曰、(一節)人之所不學而能者、其良能也、所不慮而知者、其良知也。(二節)孩提之童、無不知愛其親也、及其長也、無不知敬其兄也。(三節)親親、仁也、敬長、義也、無他、達之天下也。

【十六】孟子曰、舜之居深山之

tions are loved by them. Good government gets the people's wealth, while good instructions get their hearts.'

CHAP. XV. 1. Mencius said, 'The ability possessed by men without having been acquired by learning is intuitive ability, and the knowledge possessed by them without the exercise of thought is their intuitive knowledge.

2. 'Children carried in the arms all know to love their parents, and when they are grown *a little*, they all know to love their elder brothers.

3. 'Filial affection for parents is *the working of* benevolence. Respect for elders is *the working of* righteousness. There is no other reason *for those feelings;*—they belong to all under heaven.'

CHAP. XVI. Mencius said, 'When Shun was living amid the deep retired mountains, dwelling with the trees and rocks, and

and on an occasion. A reputation for kindness must be the growth of time and of many evidences. With the whole chapter, compare Analects, II. iii.

15. BENEVOLENCE AND RIGHTEOUSNESS ARE NATURAL TO MAN, PARTS OF HIS CONSTITUTION. 1. I translate 良 by 'intuitive,' but it serves also to denote the 'goodness' of the nature of man. Chû Hsî so defines it:—良者本然之善也. 2. 孩 is defined in the dictionary by 小兒笑, 'an infant smiling.' When an infant has reached to this, then it is 人所提挈, 'taken by people in their arms.' 3. 達之天下 must be supplemented by 無不同, 'extend them (carry the inquiry about them) to all under heaven, and they are the same.' This is just laying down universality as a test that those feelings are intuitive to us. Châo Ch'î, however, explains differently:—'Those who wish to do good, have nothing else to do but to extend these ways of children to all under heaven.'

16. HOW WHAT SHUN WAS DISCOVERED ITSELF IN HIS GREATEST OBSCURITY. 決江河,—the 決 is the water itself bursting its banks; the agency of man in the matter is not to be supposed. So in the 備旨:—決江河謂

中、與木石居、與鹿豕遊、其所以異於深山之野人者幾希、及其聞一善言、見一善行、若決江河、沛然莫之能禦也。

十七　孟子曰、無爲其所不爲、無欲其所不欲、如此而已矣。

十八　一節　孟子曰、人之有德慧術知者、恆存乎疢疾。二節　獨孤臣

wandering among the deer and swine, the difference between him and the rude inhabitants of those remote hills appeared very small. But when he heard a single good word, or saw a single good action, he was like a stream or a river bursting its banks, and flowing out in an irresistible flood.'

CHAP. XVII. Mencius said, 'Let a man not do what *his own sense of righteousness tells him* not to do, and let him not desire what his *sense of righteousness tells him not* to desire;—to act thus is all he has to do.'

CHAP. XVIII. 1. Mencius said, 'Men who are possessed of intelligent virtue and prudence in affairs will generally be found to have been in sickness and troubles.

2. 'They are the friendless minister and concubine's son, who keep their hearts under a sense of peril, and use deep precautions

江之決也,非人決之也. 江河 may be taken generally, or with special reference to the Yang-tsze and Yellow river. I prefer the former.

17. A MAN HAS BUT TO OBEY THE LAW IN HIMSELF. The text is literally—'Not doing what he does not do,' &c. Much must be supplied to make it intelligible in a translation. Châo Ch'î interprets and supplies quite differently:—'Let a man not make another do what he does not do himself,' &c.

18. THE BENEFITS OF TROUBLE AND AFFLICTION. 1. Compare Bk. VI. Pt. II. xv. 德 and 慧, 術 and 知 (4th tone) go together,—'intelligence of virtue, and wisdom of arts.' 存 retains its proper meaning of 在, 'to be in.' 疢 means properly 'fever,' 'any feverish disease,' but here 疢疾 = distresses generally. 2. 惟,—not joined with 孤, but qualifying the whole sentence. 獨 = 孤, 'fatherless,' friendless, not having favour with the sovereign. 孽子 is not the child of one who is a concubine merely, but a concubine in disgrace, or one of a very low rank. 孽 is often taken as if it were 櫱, the shooting forth of a tree after it has been cut down; moreover, the 艹 in it should be 屮.

孽子、其操心也危、其慮患也深、故達。

〔十九章〕一節 孟子曰、有事君人者、事是君、則爲容悅者也。二節 有安社稷臣者、以安社稷爲悅者也。三節 有天民者、達可行於天下、而後行之者也。四節 有大人者、正己而物正者也。

〔二十章〕一節 孟子曰、君子有三樂

against calamity. On this account they become distinguished for their intelligence.'

CHAP. XIX. 1. Mencius said, 'There are persons who serve the prince;—they serve the prince, that is, for the sake of his countenance and favour.

2. 'There are ministers who seek the tranquillity of the State, and find their pleasure in securing that tranquillity.

3. 'There are those who are the people of Heaven. They, *judging that,* if they were in office, they could carry out *their principles,* throughout the kingdom, proceed *so* to carry them out.

4. 'There are those who are great men. They rectify themselves and others are rectified.'

CHAP. XX. 1. Mencius said, 'The superior man has three

19. FOUR DIFFERENT CLASSES OF MINISTERS. 1. 有事君人者, = the 人 is joined with 有, and not to be taken with 君. Mencius speaks of 人, 'persons,' and not 臣, 'ministers,' to indicate his contempt. 爲容悅 is difficult. The common view is what I have given. 容是使君容我, 悅是使君悅我, '*yung* is to cause the prince to bear with—countenance—them;—*yüeh* is to cause the prince to be pleased with them.' In this case, 爲 should be read in 4th tone. It is said, however, to have 專務意, 'the idea of aiming at exclusively.' 2. 社稷臣, see Confucian Analects, XVI. i. 4. 悅, it will be seen, is not used here, as in the last paragraph. 3. 天民, 'Heaven's people,' those who seem dearer to Heaven and more favoured by it;—compare Bk. V. Pt. I. vii. 5. 4. 'The great men' are the sages, the highest style of men. 物 is to be understood of persons = 君民, 'the sovereign and the people.' —The first class of ministers may be styled the mercenary; the second, the loyal; the third have no selfishness, and they embrace the whole kingdom in their regards, but they have their defined aims to be attained by systematic effort, while the fourth, unconsciously but surely, produce the grandest results.

20. THE THINGS WHICH THE SUPERIOR MAN DELIGHTS IN. TO OCCUPY THE THRONE IS NOT AMONG THEM. 1. 王天下 is to be taken as simply = 有天下. The possession of the

而王天下不與存焉。〇二節父母俱存、兄弟無故、一樂也。〇三節仰不愧於天、俯不怍於人、二樂也。〇四節得天下英才而教育之、三樂也。〇五節君子有三樂、而王天下不與存焉。

〔二十一〕一節孟子曰、廣土衆民、君子欲之、所樂不存焉。〇二節中天下而立、定四海之民、君子樂之、所性不存焉。〇三節君子所性、

things in which he delights, and to be ruler over the kingdom is not one of them.

2. 'That his father and mother are both alive, and that the condition of his brothers affords no cause for anxiety;—this is one delight.

3. 'That, when looking up, he has no occasion for shame before Heaven, and, below, he has no occasion to blush before men;—this is a second delight.

4. 'That he can get from the whole kingdom the most talented individuals, and teach and nourish them;—this is the third delight.

5. 'The superior man has three things in which he delights, and to be ruler over the kingdom is not one of them.'

CHAP. XXI. 1. Mencius said, 'Wide territory and a numerous people are desired by the superior man, but what he delights in is not here.

2. 'To stand in the centre of the kingdom, and tranquillize the people within the four seas;—the superior man delights in this, but the highest enjoyment of his nature is not here.

3. 'What belongs by his nature to the superior man cannot be

sovereign sway is indicated, and not the carrying out of the true royal principles. 2. 兄弟無故 may be understood of every painful thing in the condition of his brothers, which would distress him. 3. We cannot but attach a personal meaning to 'Heaven' here.

21. MAN'S OWN NATURE THE MOST IMPORTANT THING TO HIM, AND THE SOURCE OF HIS TRUE ENJOYMENT. 1. This describes the condition of the prince of a large State, who has thereby many opportunities of doing good. 2. This advances on the meaning of the first paragraph. The individual indicated is the sovereign, who by his position can benefit the myriads of the people, and therein he feels delight. 所性—what belongs to him by nature. 3. 君子

雖大行不加焉、雖窮居不損焉、分定故也。四 君子所性、仁、義、禮、智、根於心、其生色也睟然見於面、盎於背、施於四體、四體不言而喻。

二十二 孟子曰、一 伯夷辟紂、居北海之濱、聞文王作、興曰、盍歸乎來、吾聞西伯善養老者、太公辟紂、居

increased by the largeness of his sphere of action, nor diminished by his dwelling in poverty and retirement;—for this reason that it is determinately apportioned to him *by Heaven*.

4. 'What belongs by his nature to the superior man are benevolence, righteousness, propriety, and knowledge. These are rooted in his heart; their growth and manifestation are a mild harmony appearing in the countenance, a rich fullness in the back, and the character imparted to the four limbs. Those limbs understand *to arrange themselves*, without being told.'

CHAP. XXII. 1. Mencius said, 'Po-î, that he might avoid Châu, was dwelling on the coast of the northern sea when he heard of the rise of king Wăn. He roused himself and said, "Why should I not go and follow him? I have heard that the chief of the West knows well how to nourish the old." T'âi-kung, to avoid Châu, was dwelling on the coast of the eastern sea. When he heard of the rise of king

is not to be interpreted only of the prince of a State or the sovereign. Indeed in the two preceding paragraphs, though the individuals indicated are in those positions, the phrase, as well as here, has its moral significancy. 分 (4th tone) 定故也,—the nature is complete as given by Heaven. It can only be developed from within. Nothing can be added to it from without. This seems to be the idea. 4. 其生色也 extend over all the rest of the paragraph. 生 and 色 are in apposition; 色 is not to be taken as under the government of 生. The meaning is simply that moral and intellectual qualities indicate themselves in the general appearance and bearing. 睟然 is explained as 清和潤澤之貌, 'the appearance of what is pure, harmonious, moistening, and rich,' and 盎 as 豐厚盈溢之意, 'meaning what is affluent, generous, full and overflowing.'—The whole description is rather strained.

22. THE GOVERNMENT OF KING WĂN BY WHICH THE AGED WERE NOURISHED. 1. Compare Bk. IV. Pt. I. xiii. 1. 2. This is to be translated historically, as it describes king Wăn's government; compare Bk. I. Pt. I. iii. 4. 匹婦, corresponding to 匹夫, below;—'the private

東海之濱、聞文王作、興曰、盍歸乎來、吾聞西伯善養老者、天下有善養老、則仁人以爲己歸矣。○二節五畝之宅、樹牆下以桑、匹婦蠶之、則老者足以衣帛矣、五母雞、二母彘、無失其時、老者足以無失肉矣、百畝之田、匹夫耕之、八口之家、可以無飢矣。○三節所謂西伯善養老者、制其田里、教之樹畜、導其

Wăn, he said, "Why should I not go and follow him? I have heard that the chief of the West knows well how to nourish the old." If there were a prince in the kingdom, who knew well how to nourish the old, all men of virtue would feel that he was the proper object for them to gather to.

2. 'Around the homestead with its five mâu, the space beneath the walls was planted with mulberry trees, with which the women nourished silkworms, and thus the old were able to have silk to wear. *Each family* had five brood hens and two brood sows, which were kept to their *breeding* seasons, and thus the old were able to have flesh to eat. The husbandmen cultivated their farms of 100 mâu, and thus their families of eight mouths were secured against want.

3. 'The expression, "The chief of the West knows well how to nourish the old," refers to his regulation of the fields and dwellings, his teaching them to plant *the mulberry* and nourish those animals, and his instructing the wives and children, so as to make them nourish

woman,' 'the private man.' 蠶之, 'silk-wormed them,' i.e. nourished silkworms with them. It is observed by 淮南子.—'The silkworm eats and does not drink, going through its transformations in twenty-seven days. The wife of the Yellow Tî (B.C. 2697–2597), whose surname was Hsî-ling (西陵氏), first taught the people to keep silkworms, and to manage their silk, in order to provide clothes. Future ages sacrifice to her as the 先蠶.' Mencius has not mentioned before the number of brood sows and hens apportioned to a family. 3. 此之謂 responds to 所謂 . . . 者, at the beginning. The whole paragraph is the

妻子、使養其老、五十、非帛不煖、七十、非肉不飽、不煖不飽、謂之凍餒、文王之民、無凍餒之老者、此之謂也。

二三 一節 孟子曰、易其田疇、薄其稅斂、民可使富也。二節 食之以時、用之以禮、財不可勝用也。三節 民非水火、不生活、昏暮叩人之門戶、求水火、無弗

their aged. At fifty, warmth cannot be maintained without silks, and at seventy flesh is necessary to satisfy the appetite. Persons not kept warm nor supplied with food are said to be starved and famished, but among the people of king Wăn, there were no aged who were starved or famished. This is the meaning of the expression in question.'

CHAP. XXIII. 1. Mencius said, 'Let it be seen to that their fields of grain and hemp are well cultivated, and make the taxes on them light;—so the people may be made rich.

2. 'Let it be seen to that the people use their resources of food seasonably, and expend their wealth only on the prescribed ceremonies:—so their wealth will be more than can be consumed.

3. 'The people cannot live without water and fire, yet if you knock at a man's door in the dusk of the evening, and ask for water and fire, there is no man who will not give them, such is the

explanation of that expression. 田里,—里 is the dwelling-place, the five *mâu* allotted for buildings.

23. TO PROMOTE THE VIRTUE OF THE PEOPLE, THE FIRST CARE OF A GOVERNMENT SHOULD BE TO CONSULT FOR THEIR BEING WELL OFF. 1. 易, *i*,—4th tone, as in Bk. I. Pt. I. v. 3, *et al.* 田, 'grain fields.' 疇 'flax fields.' 易 and 薄 are both in the imperative, indicating the work of the ruler or government. So 食 and 用 in par. 2, where 之 may be referred to 財, or the resources arising from the government just indicated. 以時 may be best explained from Bk. I. Pt. I. iii. 3, 4. 以禮,—the 禮 are the festive occasions of capping, marriage, &c., excepting on which a strict economy should be enforced. 3. Compare Bk. I. Pt. I. vii. 20-22. 昏 properly denotes half an hour after sunset, or thereabouts. 暮 is 日晚, 'the evening of the day.' The time of the request is inopportune, and the manner of it not according to propriety;—and yet it is granted. 菽 is the

與者、至足矣、聖人治天下、使有菽粟如水火、菽粟如水火、而民焉有不仁者乎。

〔二十四〕一 孟子曰、孔子登東山而小魯、登太山而小天下、故觀於海者、難爲水、遊於聖人之門者、難爲言。二 觀水有術、必觀其瀾、日月有明、容光必照焉。三 流水之爲物也、不盈科不行、君子之志於

abundance of these things. A sage governs the kingdom so as to cause pulse and grain to be as abundant as water and fire. When pulse and grain are as abundant as water and fire, how shall the people be other than virtuous?'

CHAP. XXIV. 1. Mencius said, 'Confucius ascended the eastern hill, and Lû appeared to him small. He ascended the T'âi mountain, and all beneath the heavens appeared to him small. So he who has contemplated the sea, finds it difficult to think anything of *other* waters, and he who has wandered in the gate of the sage, finds it difficult to think anything of the words of *others*.

2. 'There is an art in the contemplation of water.—It is necessary to look at it as foaming in waves. The sun and moon being possessed of brilliancy, their light admitted *even* through an orifice illuminates.

3. 'Flowing water is a thing which does not proceed till it has filled the hollows *in its course*. The student who has set his

general name for all kinds of peas and beans. 粟,—as in Analects, XII. xi. 3.

24. HOW THE GREAT DOCTRINES OF THE SAGES DWARF ALL SMALLER DOCTRINES, AND YET ARE TO BE ADVANCED TO BY SUCCESSIVE STEPS. 1, 2. This paragraph illustrates the greatness of the sage's doctrines. The eastern hill was on the east of the capital of Lû. Some identify it with a small hill, called Fang (防), in the district of Ch'ü-fâu (曲阜), at the foot of which Confucius's parents were buried; others with a hill named Mâng (蒙), in the district of Pi, in the department of Î-châu. The T'âi mountain is the chief of the five great mountains of China. It lay on the extreme east of Ch'î, in the present district of T'âi-an, in the department of the same name. In 難爲水, 爲 is used as in 爲衆, Bk. IV. Pt. I. vii. 5. After seeing the surging ocean, the streams are not worth being taken into account. And light penetrating every cranny assures us of its splendour in the great luminaries. 3. 君子 is here the aspiring student. 章, 'an elegant piece,' here for 'one lesson,' 'one truth.'

道也、不成章不達。

二十五章 一節 孟子曰、鷄鳴而起、孳孳爲善者、舜之徒也。二節 鷄鳴而起、孳孳爲利者、蹠之徒也。三節 欲知舜與蹠之分、無他、利與善之閒也。

二十六章 一節 孟子曰、楊子取爲我、拔一毛而利天下、不爲也。二節 墨子兼愛、摩

mind on the doctrines *of the sage*, does not advance to them but by completing one lesson after another.'

CHAP. XXV. 1. Mencius said, 'He who rises at cock-crowing, and addresses himself earnestly to the practice of virtue, is a disciple of Shun.

2. 'He who rises at cock-crowing, and addresses himself earnestly to the pursuit of gain, is a disciple of Chih.

3. 'If you want to know what separates Shun from Chih, it is simply this,—the interval between *the thought of* gain and *the thought of* virtue.'

CHAP. XXVI. 1. Mencius said, 'The principle of the philosopher Yang was—"Each one for himself." Though he might have benefited the whole kingdom by plucking out a single hair, he would not have done it.

2. 'The philosopher Mo loves all equally. If by rubbing *smooth*

25. THE DIFFERENT RESULTS TO WHICH THE LOVE OF GOOD AND THE LOVE OF GAIN LEAD. 1. 'A disciple of Shun,'—i.e. although such a man may not himself attain to be a sage, he is treading in the steps of one. 2. Chih (蹠 being used for 跖) is the robber Chih; see Bk. III. Pt. II. x. 3. 爲利,—爲 is used here as in chap. xix. 1. I should prefer myself to read it in the 4th tone. It is observed by the scholar Ch'ăng that 'by *good* and *gain* are intended the public mind and the selfish mind (公私而已).' 3. 利與善之閒 is intended to represent the slightness of the separation between them, in its initial principles, and I therefore supply 'the thought of.'

26. THE ERRORS OF YANG, MO, AND TSZE-MO. OBSTINATE ADHERENCE TO A COURSE WHICH WE MAY DEEM ABSTRACTLY RIGHT IS PERILOUS. 1. 'The philosopher Yang,'—see Bk. III. Pt. II. ix. 9, 10, 14. Chû Hsî says:—取者僅足之意, '取 conveys the idea of what is barely sufficient.' This is not correct. 楊子取—楊子所取, 'that which the philosopher Yang chose, was.' . . . . In the writings of the scholar Lieh (列子), Bk. VII, we find Yang Chû speaking of Po-ch'ăng Tsze-kâo (伯成子高) that 'he would not pull out one of his hairs to benefit others,' and when questioned himself 'if he would pull out a hair to help an age,' declining to reply. 2. 'The philosopher Mo,'—see Bk. III. Pt. I. v. 1; Pt. II. ix. 9, 10, 14. We are not to understand the rubbing the body smooth as an isolated act which somehow would benefit the kingdom. The smoothness would arise from labours undergone for the kingdom, like those of the great Yü, who wrought

頂放踵、利天下爲之。三節子莫執中、執中爲近之、執中無權、猶執一也。四節所惡執一者、爲其賊道也、舉一而廢百也。

廿七章 一節 孟子曰、飢者甘食、渴者甘飲、是未得飲食之正也、飢渴害之也、豈惟口腹有飢渴之害、人心亦皆有害。二節人能無以飢

his whole body from the crown to the heel, he could have benefited the kingdom, he would have done it.

3. 'Tsze-mo holds a medium *between these*. By holding that medium, he is nearer the right. But by holding it without leaving room for the exigency of circumstances, it becomes like their holding their one point.

4. 'The reason why I hate that holding to one point is the injury it does to the way *of right principle*. It takes up one point and disregards a hundred others.'

CHAP. XXVII. 1. Mencius said, 'The hungry think any food sweet, and the thirsty think the same of any drink, and thus they do not get the right taste of what they eat and drink. The hunger and thirst, in fact, injure *their palate*. And is it only the mouth and belly which are injured by hunger and thirst? Men's minds are also injured by them.

2. 'If a man can prevent the evils of hunger and thirst from

and waded till he had worn away all the hair on his legs. See the 集證, *in loc.* 3. Of Tsze-mo nothing seems to be known, but that he belonged to Lû. 執中 must be clearly understood as referring to a Mean between the selfishness of Yang Chû and the transcendentalism of Mo Tî. 近之=近道, the 道 mentioned in par. 4. The necessity of attending to the exigency of circumstances is illustrated by saying that a case may be conceived when it would be duty to deny a single hair to save the kingdom, and a case when it would be duty to rub the whole body smooth to do so. The orthodox way (道) of China is to do what is right with reference to the whole circumstances of every case and time.

27. THE IMPORTANCE OF NOT ALLOWING THE MIND TO BE INJURED BY POVERTY AND A MEAN CONDITION. 1. 甘 perhaps is used adverbially, = 'readily;' compare Bk. II. Pt. I. i. 11. The two clauses 是未 and 飢渴 run parallel to each other, the latter being explanatory of the former. 害之,—之=口腹. With reference to the mind, hunger and thirst stand for poverty and a mean condition. 2. 能無以...爲='can prevent being,' 無 being

湯之害、爲心害、則不及人不爲憂矣。

二十八章 孟子曰、柳下惠不以三公易其介。

二十九章 孟子曰、有爲者、辟若掘井、掘井九軔、而不及泉、猶爲棄井也。

三十章 一節 孟子曰、堯舜、性之也、湯武、身之也、五霸、假之也。二節 久假而不歸、

being any evils to his mind, he need not have any sorrow about not being equal to other men.'

CHAP. XXVIII. Mencius said, 'Hûi of Liû-hsiâ would not for the three highest offices of State have changed his firm purpose of life.'

CHAP. XXIX. Mencius said, 'A man with definite aims to be accomplished may be compared to one digging a well. To dig the well to a depth of seventy-two cubits, *and stop* without reaching the spring, is after all throwing away the well.'

CHAP. XXX. 1. Mencius said, '*Benevolence and righteousness* were natural to Yâo and Shun. T'ang and Wû made them their own. The five chiefs of the princes feigned them.

2. 'Having borrowed them long and not returned them, how could it be known they did not own them?'

emphatic. 不及人,—人 refers to great men, sages, and worthies. Such a man has himself really advanced far in the path of greatness.

28. HÛI OF LIÛ-HSIÂ'S FIRMNESS. 'Hûi of Liû-hsiâ,'—see Bk. II. Pt. I. ix. 2, 3; Bk. V. Pt. II. i. 3, 5; Bk. VI. Pt. II. vi. 2. 和, 'mildness,' 'friendly impressibility,' was a characteristic of Hûi, and Mencius, therefore, notices how it was associated with firmness of mind. The 'three *kung*' are the three highest officers about the royal court, each equal in dignity to the highest rank of nobility.

29. ONLY THAT LABOUR IS TO BE PRIZED WHICH ACCOMPLISHES ITS OBJECT. 辟,—used for 譬. 軔 = 仞, 'eight cubits.' In the Analects, XIX. xxiii. 3, it is said, in the note, that the 仞 was seven cubits, while here its length is given as eight. Its exact length is a moot point. See the 集證, *in loc.* 有爲者, 'one who has that which he is doing.' The application may be very wide.

30. THE DIFFERENCE BETWEEN YÂO, SHUN, T'ANG, AND WÛ, ON THE ONE HAND, AND THE FIVE CHIEFS, ON THE OTHER, IN RELATION TO BENEVOLENCE AND RIGHTEOUSNESS. 1. 之 no doubt refers to 仁義, 'benevolence and righteousness,' and a translation can hardly be made without supplying those terms. Though Yâo and Shun stood on a higher platform than T'ang and Wû, they agreed in sincerity, which is the common point of contrast between them and the chiefs. 身之, 'incorporated them' = made them their own. 2. Chû Hsî explains 歸 by 還, 'returned.' Admitting this, the meaning of 假 passes from 'feigning' to 'borrowing.' He seems to prefer viewing 惡知

惡知其非有也。

【卅一章】【一節】公孫丑曰、伊尹曰、予不狎于不順、放太甲于桐、民大悅、太甲賢、又反之、民大悅。【二節】賢者之爲人臣也、其君不賢、則固可放與。【三節】孟子曰、有伊尹之志、則可、無伊尹之志、則簒也。

【卅二章】公孫丑曰、詩曰、不素餐兮、君子之不耕而食、何也、

CHAP. XXXI. 1. Kung-sun Ch'âu said, 'Î Yin said, "I cannot be near *and see him so* disobedient *to reason*," and therewith he banished T'âi-chiâ to T'ung. The people were much pleased. When T'âi-chiâ became virtuous, he brought him back, and the people were *again* much pleased.

2. 'When worthies are ministers, may they indeed banish their sovereigns *in this way* when they are not virtuous?'

3. Mencius replied, 'If they have the same purpose as Î Yin, they may. If they have not the same purpose, it would be usurpation.'

CHAP. XXXII. Kung-sun Ch'âu said, 'It is said, in the Book of Poetry,

"He will not eat the bread of idleness!"

How is it that *we see* superior men eating without labouring?' Mencius replied, 'When a superior man resides in a country, if its

as = 'how could they themselves know?' but I much prefer the view in the translation.

31. THE END MAY JUSTIFY THE MEANS, BUT THE PRINCIPLE SHOULD NOT BE READILY APPLIED. 1. Compare Bk. V. Pt. I. vi. 5. 伊尹曰,—see the Shû-ching, Pt. IV. v. Bk. I. 9. The words are taken somewhat differently in the commentary on the *ching*, but I have followed what seems the most likely meaning of them. 3. 志 is the purpose, not suddenly formed on an emergency, but the determination and object of the whole life. It is said—志以其素定者言.

32. THE SERVICES WHICH A SUPERIOR MAN RENDERS TO A COUNTRY ENTITLE HIM, WITHOUT HIS DOING OFFICIAL DUTY, TO SUPPORT. This is an instance of the oft-repeated insinuation against Mencius, that he was content to be supported by the princes, while he would not take office; compare Bk. III. Pt. II. iv. 詩曰,—see the Shih-ching, I. ix. Ode VI. 素=空, 'empty,' without doing service. The old commentators and the new differ somewhat in their interpretations of the ode, but they agree in understanding its great lesson to be that people should not be receiving emolument, who do not actively serve their country. 耕, 'ploughing,' labouring. This term is suggested from the ode,

孟子曰、君子居是國也、其君用之、則安、富、尊、榮、其子弟從之、則孝、悌、忠、信、不素餐兮、孰大於是。二節

〔三十三〕王子墊問曰、士何事。一節 孟子曰、尚志。二節 曰、何謂尚志。曰、仁義而已矣、殺一無罪、非仁也、非其有而取之、非義也、居惡在、仁是也、路惡在、義是也、居仁由義、大人之事備矣。三節

sovereign employ his counsels, he comes to tranquillity, wealth, honour, and glory. If the young in it follow his instructions, they become filial, obedient to their elders, true-hearted, and faithful.— What greater example can there be than this of not eating the bread of idleness?'

CHAP. XXXIII. 1. The king's son, Tien, asked *Mencius*, saying, 'What is the business of the *unemployed* scholar?'

2. Mencius replied, 'To exalt his aim.'

3. *Tien* asked *again*, 'What do you mean by exalting the aim?' The answer was, '*Setting it* simply on benevolence and righteousness. *He thinks* how to put a single innocent person to death is contrary to benevolence; how to take what one has not *a right to* is contrary to righteousness; that one's dwelling should be benevolence; and one's path should be righteousness. Where else should he dwell? What other path should he pursue? When benevolence is the dwelling-place *of the heart*, and righteousness the path *of the life*, the business of a great man is complete.'

where it occurs, 用之, 'use him,' i.e. his counsels, not as a minister.

33. HOW A SCHOLAR PREPARES HIMSELF FOR THE DUTIES TO WHICH HE ASPIRES. 1. Tien was the son of the king of Ch'i. His question probably had reference to the wandering scholars of the time, whose ways he disliked. They were no favourites with Mencius, but he prefers to reply to the prince according to his ideal of the scholar. 3. 仁 . . . 義是也 represent the scholar's thoughts, his nursing his aim. We can hardly take 大人 as in chap. xix. 4, where it denotes the sages, the very highest style of men. Here it denotes rather the individuals in the various grades of official employment, to which 'the scholar' may attain.

三十四章 孟子曰、仲子、不義、與之齊國而弗受、人皆信之、是舍簞食豆羹之義也、人莫大焉亡親戚君臣上下、以其小者、信其大者、奚可哉。

三十五章 桃應問曰、舜爲天子、皐陶爲士、瞽瞍殺人、則如之何。孟子曰、執之而

CHAP. XXXIV. Mencius said, 'Supposing that the kingdom of Ch'î were offered, contrary to righteousness, to *Ch'ăn* Chung, he would not receive it, and all people believe in him, *as a man of the highest worth*. But this is *only* the righteousness which declines a dish of rice or a plate of soup. A man can have no greater *crimes* than to disown his parents and relatives, and the relations of sovereign and minister, superiors and inferiors. How can it be allowed to give a man credit for the great *excellences* because he possesses a small one?'

CHAP. XXXV. 1. T'âo Ying asked, saying, 'Shun being sovereign, and Kâo-yâo chief minister of justice, if Kû-sâu had murdered a man, what would have been done in the case?'

2. Mencius said, '*Kâo-yâo* would simply have apprehended him.'

34. HOW MEN JUDGE WRONGLY OF CHARACTER, OVERLOOKING, IN THEIR ADMIRATION OF ONE STRIKING EXCELLENCE, GREAT FAILURES AND DEFICIENCIES. 仲子 is the Ch'ăn Chung of Bk. III. Pt. II. x, which see. I substitute the surname to avoid translating 子. In the translation of 人莫大焉, 焉 is taken as used for 乎, and what follows is under the regimen of 大, as if we were to complete the construction in this way:—人之罪莫大乎亡親云云. Châo Ch'î interprets quite differently:—'But what a man should exalt is the greatest virtues, the propriety and righteousness in the great relations of life. He, however, denies them, &c.' Certainly the solecism of taking 焉 for 乎 is better than this. 亡,—used for 無, but as a verb. Wang Yin-chih construes as I do, making the 焉 = 乎, = 於, and construing 大 consequently in the comparative degree.

35. WHAT SHUN AND HIS MINISTER OF CRIME WOULD HAVE DONE, IF SHUN'S FATHER HAD COMMITTED A MURDER. 1. T'âo Ying was a disciple of Mencius. This is all that is known of him. 士 is not to be understood here as merely = 士師, Analects, XVIII. ii; XIX. xix. The 士 of Shun's time was the same as the 大司寇 of the Châu dynasty, the officer of Crime, under whom were the 士師, and others more subordinate. See the 集證, *in loc.* 2. We must understand Kâo-yâo as the

已矣。〔三節〕然則舜不禁與。〔四節〕曰、夫舜惡得而禁之。夫有所受之也。〔五節〕然則舜如之何。〔六節〕曰、舜視棄天下、猶棄敝蹝也。竊負而逃、遵海濱而處、終身訢然樂而忘天下。

〔卅六章〕〔一節〕孟子自范之齊、望見齊王之子、喟然歎曰、居移氣、養移體、大哉居乎。夫非盡人之子與。〔二節〕孟子曰、王子宮

3. 'But would not Shun have forbidden such a thing?'

4. 'Indeed, how could Shun have forbidden it? *Kâo-yâo* had received *the law* from *a proper* source.'

5. 'In that case what would Shun have done?'

6. 'Shun would have regarded abandoning the kingdom as throwing away a worn-out sandal. He would privately have taken *his father* on his back, and retired into concealment, living somewhere along the sea-coast. There he would have been all his life, cheerful and happy, forgetting the kingdom.'

CHAP. XXXVI. 1. Mencius, going from Fan to Ch'î, saw the king of Ch'î's son at a distance, and said with a deep sigh, 'One's position alters the air, *just as* the nurture affects the body. Great is the influence of position! Are *we* not all men's sons *in this respect?*'

2. Mencius said, 'The residence, the carriages and horses, and

nominative to 執. 之 must refer to Kû-sâu, though critics now understand 法 as the antecedent. No doubt the meaning is, 'He would simply have observed the law, and dealt with Kû-sâu accordingly.' 3. 有所受之,—compare Bk. III. Pt. I. ii. 3. It is here implied that the law of death for murder was the will of Heaven, that being the source to which a reference is made. Kâo-yâo again must be understood as the nominative to 有. He, as minister of Crime, had to maintain Heaven's authority superior to the sovereign's will.

36. HOW ONE'S MATERIAL POSITION AFFECTS HIS AIR, AND MUCH MORE MAY MORAL CHARACTER BE EXPECTED TO DO SO. 1. Fan was a city of Ch'î, a considerable distance from the capital, to which we must understand Mencius was proceeding. It still gives its name to a district of Pû-châu (濮州), in the department of Ts'âo-châu (曹州). Châo Ch'î says that Fan was a city of Ch'î, the appanage of the king's sons by his concubines. On this view we should translate 王子 in the plural, but it proceeds from supposing that it was in Fan that Mencius saw the 王子, which the text does not at all necessitate. In 之齊, and 之宋 (p. 3), 之=往. 養=奉養,

室、車馬、衣服、多與人同、而王子若彼者、其居使之然也、況居天下之廣居者乎。三節魯君之宋、呼於垤澤之門、守者曰、此非吾君也、何其聲之似我君也、此無他、居相似也。

三十七章一節孟子曰、食而弗愛、豕交之也、愛而不敬、獸畜之也。二節恭敬者、幣之未將者也。三節恭

the dress of the king's son, are mostly the same as those of other men. That he looks so is occasioned by his position. How much more *should* a *peculiar air distinguish* him whose position is in the wide house of the world!

3. 'When the prince of Lû went to Sung, he called out at the T'ieh-châi gate, and the keeper said, "This is not our prince. How is it that his voice is so like that of our prince?" This was occasioned by nothing but the correspondence of their positions.'

CHAP. XXXVII. 1. Mencius said, 'To feed *a scholar* and not love him, is to treat him as a pig. To love him and not respect him, is to keep him as a domestic animal.

2. 'Honouring and respecting are what exist before any offering of gifts.

3. 'If there be honouring and respecting without the reality

'revenue or income.' 夫非盡人之子與,—some understand 王子 in the phrase between 夫 and 非, 'now, are not all kings' sons,' &c. But I prefer to understand with Châo Ch'î, 凡人與王子, and in English to supply *we* rather than *they*. 2. 孟子曰 seem here to be superfluous. 天下之廣居,—see Bk. III. Pt. II. iii. 2. 垤澤, 'ant-hill marsh,' was simply the name of a gate in the capital of Sung.

37. THAT HE BE RESPECTED IS ESSENTIAL TO A SCHOLAR'S ENGAGING IN THE SERVICE OF A PRINCE. 1. 豕交之, 'having pig intercourse with him.' 交 = 接 or 待. 獸, as distinguished from 豕, leads us to think of dogs or horses, animals to which we entertain a sentiment higher than to those which we keep and fatten merely for our eating. 2. 恭敬者 = 所謂恭敬者. The paragraph is an explanation of what is meant by those terms. 將 = 奉, 'presented,' 'offered.' 3. 拘 = 留.

敬而無實、君子不可虛拘。

〔卅八章〕孟子曰、形色、天性也、惟聖人、然後可以踐形。

〔卅九章〕齊〔一節〕宣王欲短喪、公孫丑曰、爲朞之喪、猶愈於已乎。〔二節〕孟子曰、是猶或紾其兄之臂、子謂之姑徐徐云爾、亦教之孝弟而已矣。〔三節〕王子有其母死者、其傅爲之請數月之喪、公孫丑曰、若此者

of them, a superior man may not be retained by such empty *demonstrations*.'

CHAP. XXXVIII. Mencius said, 'The bodily organs with their functions belong to our Heaven-conferred nature. But a man must be a sage before he can satisfy the design of his bodily organization.'

CHAP. XXXIX. 1. The king Hsüan of Ch'î wanted to shorten the period of mourning. Kung-sun Ch'âu said, 'To have one whole year's mourning is better than doing away with it altogether.'

2. Mencius said, 'That is just as if there were one twisting the arm of his elder brother, and you were merely to say to him—"Gently, gently, if you please." Your only course should be to teach such an one filial piety and fraternal duty.'

3. *At that time*, the mother of one of the king's sons had died, and his tutor asked for him that he might be allowed to observe

38. ONLY WITH A SAGE DOES THE BODY ACT ACCORDING TO ITS DESIGN. This is translated according to the consenting view of the modern commentators, but perhaps not correctly. 形 is taken for the bodily organs,—the ears, eyes, hands, feet, &c.; and 色 for their manifested operations,—hearing, seeing, handling, &c. 踐 is used as in the phrase 踐言, 'to tread upon the words,' that is, to fulfil them, to walk, act, according to them. The use of 色, in chap. xxi. 4, is analogous to this use of it here. One critic says:—形色天性, 言形色皆天性所在, 非指形色爲天性也, 'The bodily organs with their operations belong to our Heaven-conferred nature; the meaning is that in these is our Heavenly nature, not that they are that nature.'

39. REPROOF OF KUNG-SUN CH'ÂU FOR ASSENTING TO THE PROPOSAL TO SHORTEN THE PERIOD OF MOURNING. Compare Analects, XVII. xxi. 1. The mourning is to be understood as that of three years for a parent. 3. The king's son here must have been a son by a concubine. Chû Hsî, after Châo Ch'î, supposes that he was not permitted to mourn the three years, through

何如也。四節曰、是欲終之而不可得也、雖加一日、愈於已。謂夫莫之禁而弗爲者也。

四十章 一節孟子曰、君子之所以教者五。二節有如時雨化之者。三節有成德者、有達財者。四節有答問者。五節有私淑艾者。六節此五者、君子之所以教也。

a few months' mourning. Kung-sun Ch'âu asked, 'What do you say of this?'

4. *Mencius* replied, 'This is a case where the party wishes to complete the whole period, but finds it impossible to do so. The addition of even a single day is better than not mourning at all. I spoke of the case where there was no hindrance, and the party neglected the thing itself.'

CHAP. XL. 1. Mencius said, 'There are five ways in which the superior man effects his teaching.

2. 'There are some on whom his influence descends like seasonable rain.

3. 'There are some whose virtue he perfects, and some of whose talents he assists the development.

4. 'There are some whose inquiries he answers.

5. 'There are some who privately cultivate and correct themselves.

6. 'These five ways are the methods in which the superior man effects his teaching.'

the jealous or other opposition of the full queen. In this case the son was anxious to prolong his mourning as much as he could. This explanation, bringing in the opposition of the full queen or wife, seems to be incorrect. See the 集證, *in loc.* While the father was alive, a son shortened the period of mourning for his mother. 4. 謂夫,—夫 has a pronominal force.

40. HOW THE LESSONS OF THE SAGE REACH TO ALL DIFFERENT CLASSES. 1. The wish of the superior man is in all cases one and the same,—to teach. His methods are modified, however, by the different characters of men. 2. This class only want his influence, like plants which only need the dew of heaven. So was it, it is said, with Confucius and his disciples Yen Yüan and Tsăng Shăn. 3. 成德者=成其德者. So a 其 is to be understood before 財 (=材), and 問. So was it with Confucius and the disciples Yen and Min. 4. So was it with Mencius and Wan Chang. 5. This is a class, who never come into actual contact with their teacher, but hear of his doctrines, and learn them. His teachings, though not delivered by himself in person, do notwithstanding reach to them.

〔四一〕〔一節〕公孫丑曰、道則高矣、美矣、宜若登天然、似不可及也、何不使彼爲可幾及、而日孳孳也。〔二節〕孟子曰、大匠不爲拙工改廢繩墨、羿不爲拙射變其彀率。〔三節〕君子引而不發、躍如也、中道而立、能者從之。

〔四二〕〔一節〕孟子曰、天下有道、以道殉身、天下無道、以身殉道。

CHAP. XLI. 1. Kung-sun Ch'âu said, 'Lofty are your principles and admirable, but *to learn them* may well be likened to ascending the heavens,—something which cannot be reached. Why not *adapt your teaching so as to* cause learners to consider them attainable, and so daily exert themselves!'

2. Mencius said, 'A great artificer does not, for the sake of a stupid workman, alter or do away with the marking-line. Î did not, for the sake of a stupid archer, charge his rule for drawing the bow.

3. 'The superior man draws the bow, but does not discharge the arrow, having seemed to leap *with it to the mark;* and he there stands exactly in the middle of the path. Those who are able, follow him.'

CHAP. XLII. 1. Mencius said, 'When right principles prevail throughout the kingdom, one's principles must appear along with one's person. When right principles disappear from the kingdom, one's person must vanish along with one's principles.

41. THE TEACHER OF TRUTH MAY NOT LOWER HIS LESSONS TO SUIT HIS LEARNERS. 1. 何不使彼,—彼, 'those' refers to learners, which antecedent has been implied in the words, 宜若, 云云, 'it is right they should be considered,' &c. 爲可幾及,—爲-以爲, 'to consider,' 'regard.' 2. 繩墨, 'string and ink,' a carpenter's marking-line. 彀率 (read *lü*), 'the limit to which a bow should be drawn.' 3. The difficulty here is with the words 躍如也, literally, 'leaping-like.' They belong, I think, to the superior man in all the action which is represented. No man can be taught how to hit. That is his own act. He is taught to shoot, and that in so lively a manner that the hitting also is, as it were, set forth before him. So with the teacher and learner of truth. As the learner tries to do as he is taught, he will be found laying hold of what he thought unapproachable.

42. ONE MUST LIVE OR DIE WITH HIS PRINCIPLES, ACTING FROM HIMSELF, NOT WITH REGARD TO OTHER MEN. 殉 means 'to bury along with the dead,' to associate with in death as in life.

二節 未聞以道殉乎人者也。

四三章 一節 公都子曰、滕更之在門也、若在所禮、而不答、何也。二節 孟子曰、挾貴而問、挾賢而問、挾長而問、挾有勳勞而問、挾故而問、皆所不答也。滕更有二焉。

四四章 一節 孟子曰、於不可已而已者、無所不已、於所厚者薄、無所不薄也。二節 其進銳者其退速。

2. 'I have not heard of one's principles being dependent for their manifestation on other men.'

CHAP. XLIII. 1. The disciple Kung-tû said, 'When Kăng of T'ăng made his appearance in your school, it seemed proper that a polite consideration should be paid to him, and yet you did not answer him. Why was that?'

2. Mencius replied, 'I do not answer him who questions me presuming on his nobility, nor him who presumes on his talents, nor him who presumes on his age, nor him who presumes on services performed to me, nor him who presumes on old acquaintance. Two of those things were chargeable on Kăng of T'ăng.'

CHAP. XLIV. 1. Mencius said, 'He who stops short where stopping is acknowledged to be not allowable, will stop short in everything. He who behaves shabbily to those whom he ought to treat well, will behave shabbily to all.

2. 'He who advances with precipitation will retire with speed.'

Another meaning is 以身從物, 'with the person to follow after things,' = to pursue. The first 道 is right principles in general. The other 道 are those principles as held by individual men.

43. HOW MENCIUS REQUIRED THE SIMPLE PURSUIT OF TRUTH IN THOSE WHOM HE TAUGHT. Kăng was a younger brother of the prince of T'ăng. His rank made Kung-tû think that more than ordinary respect should have been shown to him, and yet it was no doubt one of the things which made Mencius jealously watch his spirit. Compare Bk. VI. Pt. II. ii. 6, 7.

44. FAILURES IN EVIDENT DUTY WILL BE ACCOMPANIED BY FAILURE IN ALL DUTY. PRECIPITATE ADVANCES ARE FOLLOWED BY SPEEDY RETREATS. The first paragraph, it is said, has reference to errors of defect (不及者之弊), and the second to those of excess (有過).

〔四五章〕孟子曰、君子之於物也、愛之而弗仁、於民也、仁之而弗親、親親而仁民、仁民而愛物。

〔四六章〕一節 孟子曰、知者無不知也、當務之爲急、仁者無不愛也、急親賢之爲務、堯舜之知、而不徧物、急先務也、堯舜之仁、不徧愛人、急親賢

CHAP. XLV. Mencius said, 'In regard to *inferior* creatures, the superior man is kind to them, but not loving. In regard to people generally, he is loving to them, but not affectionate. He is affectionate to his parents, and lovingly disposed to people *generally*. He is lovingly disposed to people *generally*, and kind to creatures.'

CHAP. XLVI. 1. Mencius said, 'The wise embrace all knowledge, but they are most earnest about what is of the greatest importance. The benevolent embrace all in their love, but what they consider of the greatest importance is to cultivate an earnest affection for the virtuous. Even the wisdom of Yâo and Shun did not extend to everything, but they attended earnestly to what was important. Their benevolence did not show itself in acts of kindness to every man, but they earnestly cultivated an affection for the virtuous.

45. THE SUPERIOR MAN IS KIND TO CREATURES, LOVING TO OTHER MEN, AND AFFECTIONATE TO HIS RELATIVES. This was intended, no doubt, against the Mohist doctrine of loving all equally. 物=animals. The second 親 is not to be understood only of parents. Compare 親親, D.M., XX. 12.

46. AGAINST THE PRINCES OF HIS TIME WHO OCCUPIED THEMSELVES WITH THE KNOWLEDGE OF, AND REGARD FOR, WHAT WAS OF LITTLE IMPORTANCE. 1. 無不知, 無不愛 are not our 'omniscient,' and 'all-loving,' but show the tendency and adaptation of the wise and the benevolent. The clauses that follow,—當務之爲急, 急親賢之爲務, show in what way truly great rulers come to an administration which appears to possess those characters. The use of the 之 in those clauses is idiomatic. To reduce it to the ordinary usages of the particle, we must take the first as=惟當務之事爲急, 'but only are they earnest about the things which it is most important *to know*,' and 惟急于親賢之當務, 'but only are they earnest about what is most important, the cultivating affection for the virtuous.' The teaching of the chapter is substantially the same as that of Confucius, Analects, XII. xxii.

也。(二節)不能三年之喪、而緦小功之察、放飯流歠、而問無齒決、是之謂不知務。

2. 'Not to be able to keep the three years' mourning, and to be very particular about that of three months, or that of five months; to eat immoderately and swill down the soup, and at the same time to inquire about *the precept* not to tear the meat with the teeth;—such things show what I call an ignorance of what is most important.'

2. 緦, 'coarse, unbleached, hempen cloth,' worn in mourning during the period of three months for distant relatives. 小功 is the name applied in the case of mourning which extends for five months. 放飯云云, see the Book of Rites, I. Sect. I. iii. 54, 55. These are cases adduced in illustration of what is insisted on in the previous paragraph;—the folly of attending to what is comparatively trivial, while overlooking what is important.

TSIN SIN. PART II.

盡心章句下

第一章 孟子曰、(一節)不仁哉、梁惠王也、仁者、以其所愛、及其所不愛、不仁者、以其所不愛、及其

CHAPTER I. 1. Mencius said, 'The opposite indeed of benevolent was the king Hûi of Liang! The benevolent, beginning with what they care for, proceed to what they do not care for. Those who are the opposite of benevolent, beginning with what they do not care for, proceed to what they care for.'

1. A STRONG CONDEMNATION OF KING HÛI OF LIANG, FOR SACRIFICING TO HIS AMBITION HIS PEOPLE AND EVEN HIS SON. Compare Bk. I. Pt. I. v, and other conversations with king Hûi. 1. 不仁 is more than 'unbenevolent' would mean, if we had such a term. It is nearly = 'cruel,' 'oppressive.' 仁者, 云云,—compare Pt. I. xlv. Only 愛, being there opposed to 仁, is used with reference to animals, while here it expresses the feeling towards children and people and animals, and I have rendered it by 'to care for.' In the first case in the text, the progress is from one degree of love to another; in the second, from

所愛。二節公孫丑曰、何謂也。梁惠王以土地之故、糜爛其民而戰之、大敗、將復之、恐不能勝、故驅其所愛子弟以殉之、是之謂以其所不愛、及其所愛也。

第二章 一節 孟子曰、春秋、無義戰、彼善於此、則有之矣。二節 征者、上伐下也、敵國、不相征也。

2. Kung-sun Ch'âu said, 'What do you mean?' *Mencius answered*, 'The king Hûi of Liang, for the matter of territory, tore and destroyed his people, leading them to battle. Sustaining a great defeat, he would engage again, and afraid lest they should not be able to secure the victory, urged his son whom he loved till he sacrificed him with them. This is what I call—"beginning with what they do not care for, and proceeding to what they care for."'

CHAP. II. 1. Mencius said, 'In the "Spring and Autumn" there are no righteous wars. Instances indeed there are of one war better than another.

2. '"Correction" is when the supreme authority punishes its subjects by force of arms. Hostile States do not correct one another.'

one degree of infliction to another. 2. 糜, 'to boil rice till it is 糜爛, reduced to a pulpy mass.' So did Hûi seem to deal with the bodies of his subjects. 所愛子弟 refers to Hûi's eldest son (Bk. I. Pt. I. v. 1). He is called a 子弟, as being one of the youth of the kingdom. 殉之,—compare Pt. I. xlii.

2. HOW ALL THE FIGHTINGS RECORDED IN THE CH'UN-CH'IÛ WERE UNRIGHTEOUS:—A WARNING TO THE CONTENDING STATES OF MENCIUS'S TIME. 1. 無義戰,—'no righteous battles.' Both Châo Ch'î and Chû Hsî make 戰 = 戰伐之事, 'the affairs of fighting and smiting,' i.e. all the operations of war detailed in the Ch'un-ch'iû. And rightly; for Mencius himself uses the term 伐 in the second paragraph. In the Ch'un-ch'iû itself there are mentioned of 'fightings' (戰) only 23, while the 'smitings' (伐) amount to 213. There are specified in it also 'invasions' (侵); 'sieges' (圍); 'carryings away' (遷); 'extinguishings' (滅); 'defeats' (敗); 'takings' (取); 'surprises' (襲); 'pursuits' (追); and 'defences' (戍); all of which may be comprehended under the term 戰. 2. Explains the assertion in the former paragraph. In the wars recorded by Confucius, one State or chief was said to 征 another, which could not be according to the meaning of the term. By

三章　一節 孟子曰、盡信書、則不如無書。二節 吾於武城、取二三策而已矣。三節 仁人、無敵於天下、以至仁伐至不仁、而何其血之流杵也、

四章　一節 孟子曰、有人曰、我善爲陳、我善爲戰、大罪也。二節 國君好仁、天下無敵焉。三節 南面而征、北

CHAP. III. 1. Mencius said, 'It would be better to be without the Book of History than to give entire credit to it.

2. 'In the "Completion of the War," I select two or three passages only, which I believe.

3. '"The benevolent man has no enemy under heaven. When *the prince* the most benevolent was engaged against him who was the most the opposite, how could the blood *of the people* have flowed till it floated the pestles of the mortars?"'

CHAP. IV. 1. Mencius said, 'There are men who say—"I am skilful at marshalling troops, I am skilful at conducting a battle!"—They are great criminals.

2. 'If the ruler of a State love benevolence, he will have no enemy in the kingdom.

3. 'When *Tang* was executing his work of correction in the

上 is intended the sovereign; by 下 the princes. Compare Bk. VI. Pt. II. vii. 2.

3. WITH WHAT RESERVATION MENCIUS READ THE SHÛ-CHING. This is a difficult chapter for Chinese commentators. Châo Ch'î takes 書 of the Shû-ching, which is the only fair interpretation. Others understand it of books in general. Thus Julien translates—'*Si omnino fidem adhibeas libris.*' Many say that Mencius had in view only the portion of the Shû-ching to which he refers in the next paragraph, but such a restriction of his language is entirely arbitrary. The strangest view is that of the author of the 四書拓餘說, whose judgments generally are sound and sensible. But he says here that Mencius is anticipating the attempts that would be made in after-ages to corrupt the classics, and testifying against them. We can see how the remarks were directed against the propensity to warfare which characterized his contemporaries. 2. 武成 is the title of the third Book in the fifth Part of the Shû-ching, professing to be an account by king Wû of his enterprise against the tyrant Châu. The words quoted in the next paragraph are found in par. 8. 3. For 杵 there are different readings; see the 集澄, *in loc.* Doubtless there is much exaggeration in the language, but Mencius misinterprets the whole passage. The bloodshed was not done by the troops of king Wû, but by the forces of the tyrant turning against one another.

4. COUNSEL TO PRINCES NOT TO ALLOW THEMSELVES TO BE DECEIVED BY MEN WHO WOULD ADVISE THEM TO WAR. 1. Compare Bk. IV. Pt. I. xiv. 3. 2. Compare Bk. I. Pt. I. v. 6. 3. See Bk. I. Pt. II. xi, *et al.* 4. 革車, 'leathern carriages, or chariots,' said by some to be baggage-waggons, but, more probably, by others, chariots of war, each one of which had seventy-two foot-soldiers attached to it, so that Wû's army would

狄怨，東面而征，西夷怨，曰，奚爲後我。四節 武王之伐殷也，革車三百兩，虎賁三千人。五節 王曰，無畏，寧爾也，非敵百姓也，若崩厥角，稽首。六節 征之爲言正也，各欲正己也，焉用戰。

第五章 孟子曰，梓，匠，輪，輿，能與人規矩，不能使人巧。

第六章 孟子曰，舜之飯糗茹草

south, the rude tribes on the north murmured. When he was executing it in the east, the rude tribes on the west murmured. Their cry was—"Why does he make us last?"

4. 'When king Wû punished Yin, he had *only* three hundred chariots of war, and three thousand life-guards.

5. 'The king said, "Do not fear. Let me give you repose. I am no enemy to the people! *On this*, they bowed their heads to the earth, like the horns of animals falling off."

6. '"Royal correction" is but another word for rectifying. Each State wishing itself to be corrected, what need is there for fighting?'

CHAP. V. Mencius said, 'A carpenter or a carriage-maker may give a man the circle and square, but cannot make him skilful *in the use of them.*'

CHAP. VI. Mencius said, 'Shun's manner of eating *his* parched grain and herbs was as if he were to be doing so all his life. When

number 21,600, few as compared with the forces of his opponent. 兩 used for 輛, the 3rd tone, a numerative for carriages. 虎賁 (*pǎn*)—these appear to have been of the character of life-guards, named from their tiger-like courage and bearing. 5. See the Shû-ching, Pt. V. i. Sect. II. 9. But the text of the Classic is hardly recognisable in Mencius's version of it. The original is:—'Rouse ye, my heroes. Do not think that he is not to be feared, but rather hold that he cannot be withstood. The people are full of awe, as if their horns were falling from their heads.' 6. Perhaps it would be well to retain the sound of 征 in the translation, and say, 'Now *chăng* means to rectify.' 各欲正己, 'each people wishes the *chăng-er* to correct itself.'

5. REAL ATTAINMENT MUST BE MADE BY THE LEARNER FOR HIMSELF. Compare Pt. I. xli. See also in Chwang-tsze, Bk. xiii. par. 10. 梓匠輪輿, see Bk. III. Pt. II. iv. 3.

6. THE EQUANIMITY OF SHUN IN POVERTY AND AS SOVEREIGN. 草 must be taken as=菜. 茹 is a word used for 食, applied to eating

也、若將終身焉、及其爲天子也、被袗衣、鼓琴、二女果、若固有之。

第七章 孟子曰、吾今而後知殺人親之重也、殺人之父、人亦殺其父、殺人之兄、人亦殺其兄、然則非自殺之也、一閒耳。

第八章 孟子曰、古之爲關也、將以禦暴。一節 今之爲關也、將以爲暴。二節

he became sovereign, and had the embroidered robes to wear, the lute to play, and the two daughters *of Yâo* to wait on him, he was as if those things belonged to him as a matter of course.'

CHAP. VII. Mencius said, 'From this time forth I know the heavy consequences of killing a man's near relations. When a man kills another's father, that other will kill his father; when a man kills another's elder brother, that other will kill his elder brother. So he does not himself indeed do the act, but there is only an interval *between him and it*.'

CHAP. VIII. 1. Mencius said, 'Anciently, the establishment of the frontier-gates was to guard against violence.

2. 'Nowadays, it is to exercise violence.'

herbs. 飯=食, 'to eat.' The 'embroidered robes' are the royal dress. On Shun's lute, see Bk. V. Pt. I. ii. 3. 果 used for 婐 (*wo*), 'a female attendant.'

7. How THE THOUGHT OF ITS CONSEQUENCES SHOULD MAKE MEN CAREFUL OF THEIR CONDUCT. Chû Hsî observes that this remark must have been made with some special reference,—吾今而後. It is a maxim of Chinese teaching, that 'a man may not live under the same heaven with the slayer of his father, nor in the same State with the slayer of his elder brother;' but Mencius does not seem to think of that, but rather takes occasion from it to warn rulers to make their government firm in the attachment of their subjects, and not provoke their animosity by oppressive acts. —一閒耳,—'there is only one interval;' that is, the death of a man's father or brother is the retribution for his previous conduct, the slayer or avenger only intervening.

8. THE BENEVOLENCE AND SELFISHNESS OF ANCIENT AND MODERN RULE CONTRASTED. Compare Bk. I. Pt. II. v. 3; Bk. II. Pt. I. vi. 2. But one does not see exactly how the ancient rule of examining the person, and not taking the goods, guarded against violence. Here, as elsewhere at times, Mencius is led away by his fondness for antithesis.

第九章 孟子曰、身不行道、不行於妻子、使人不以道、不能行於妻子。

第十章 孟子曰、周于利者、凶年不能殺、周于德者、邪世不能亂。

十一章 孟子曰、好名之人、能讓千乘之國、苟非其人、簞食豆羹見於色、

十二章 一節 孟子曰、不信仁賢、則國

CHAP. IX. Mencius said, 'If a man himself do not walk in the *right* path, it will not be walked in *even* by his wife and children. If he order men according to what is not the *right* way, he will not be able to get the obedience of *even* his wife and children.'

CHAP. X. Mencius said, 'A bad year cannot prove the cause of death to him whose stores of gain are large; an age of corruption cannot confound him whose equipment of virtue is complete.'

CHAP. XI. Mencius said, 'A man who loves fame may be able to decline a State of a thousand chariots; but if he be not *really* the man *to do such a thing*, it will appear in his countenance, in the matter of a dish of rice or a platter of soup.'

CHAP. XII. 1. Mencius said, 'If men of virtue and ability be not confided in, a State will become empty and void.

9. A MAN'S INFLUENCE DEPENDS ON HIS PERSONAL EXAMPLE AND CONDUCT. To the second 行 we are to suppose 道 as the nominative, while the third is like a verb in the *hiphil* conjugation. The 人 is not so much as 他人, 'other men.' The whole 使人不以道 simply = 出令不當理, 'if his orders are not according to reason.'

10. CORRUPT TIMES ARE PROVIDED AGAINST BY ESTABLISHED VIRTUE. 不能殺, 不能亂, may be taken either actively or passively. 周于利者, 'he who is complete in gain,' i.e. he who has gained much, and laid much by. The 日講 expands this into 家有餘貲, 倉有餘粟.

11. A MAN'S TRUE DISPOSITION WILL OFTEN APPEAR IN SMALL MATTERS, WHEN A LOVE OF FAME MAY HAVE CARRIED HIM OVER GREAT DIFFICULTIES. Chû Hsî here expounds well:—觀人不於其所勉, 而於其所忽, 然後可以見其所安之實, 'A man is seen not so much in things which require an effort, as in things which he might easily despise. By bearing this in mind when we observe him, we can see what he really rests in.'

12. THREE THINGS IMPORTANT IN THE ADMINISTRATION OF A STATE. 1. 不信, 'be not con-

空虛。二節無禮義、則上下亂。三節無政事、則財用不足。

十三章孟子曰、不仁而得國者、有之矣、不仁而得天下、未之有也。

十四章孟子曰、一節民爲貴、社稷次之、君爲輕。二節是故得乎丘民、而

2. 'Without the rules of propriety and distinctions of right, the high and the low will be thrown into confusion.

3. 'Without *the great principles of* government and their various business, there will not be wealth sufficient for the expenditure.'

CHAP. XIII. Mencius said, 'There are instances of individuals without benevolence, who have got possession of a *single* State, but there has been no instance of the throne's being got by one without benevolence.'

CHAP. XIV. 1. Mencius said, 'The people are the most important element *in a nation;* the spirits of the land and grain are the next; the sovereign is the lightest.

2. 'Therefore to gain the peasantry is the way to become sovereign;

fided *to;*' perhaps rather 'confided *in.*' 'Will become empty and void.'—Châo Ch'î supplements thus:—'If the prince do not consort with and confide in the virtuous and able, then they will go away, and a country without such persons is said to be empty and void.' 2, 3. 'The high and the low,'—that is, the distinction of ranks. 禮義 may be considered a hendiadys, and so 政事 in the next paragraph. 義 is the right, or *rightness,* on which the rules of propriety are founded, and 事 is the various business that flows from the right principles of government.

13. ONLY BY BENEVOLENCE CAN THE THRONE BE GOT. Many commentators put 有之 in the potential mood, as if it were 或有之. This is not allowable. Facts may be alleged that seem to be in opposition to the concluding statement. The commentator Tsâu (鄒) says:—'From the dynasty of Ch'in downwards, there have been cases, when the throne was got by men without benevolence, but in such cases it has been lost again after one or two reigns.'

14. THE DIFFERENT ELEMENTS OF A NATION—THE PEOPLE, TUTELARY SPIRITS, AND SOVEREIGN, IN RESPECT OF THEIR IMPORTANCE. 1. 社 is properly the altar, or resting-place of the spirit or spirits of the ground, and then used for the sacrifice to that spirit or those spirits. 稷,—'pannicled millet,' and then generally the spirit or spirits presiding over grain. Together, the characters denote the 'tutelary spirits of a country,' on whom its prosperity depends, and to sacrifice to whom was the prerogative of its sovereign.—It is often said that the 社 was 'to sacrifice to the spirits of the five kinds of ground, and the 稷 to sacrifice to those of the five kinds of grain.' But this is merely one of the numerical fancies of which Chinese writers are fond. The five kinds of ground are mountains and forests (山林), rivers and marshes (川澤), mounds (丘陵), places of tombs (墳衍), and plains (原濕). But it would be easy to make another division, just as we have six, eight, and other ways of speaking about the kinds of grain. The regular sacrifices to these tutelary spirits were three:—one in spring, to pray for a good harvest; one in autumn, to give thanks for the harvest; and a third in the first month of winter. 2. 丘民=田野之民, 'the people of

I i 2

爲天子、得乎天子、爲諸侯、得乎諸侯、爲大夫。三諸侯危社稷、則變置。四犧牲既成、粢盛既潔、祭祀以時、然而旱乾水溢、則變置社稷。

十五 孟子曰、聖人、百世之師也、伯夷、柳下惠是也、故聞伯夷之風者、頑夫廉、懦夫有立志、聞柳下

to gain the sovereign is the way to become a prince of a State; to gain the prince of a State is the way to become a great officer.

3. 'When a prince endangers the altars of the spirits of the land and grain, he is changed, and another appointed in his place.

4. 'When the sacrificial victims have been perfect, the millet in its vessels all pure, and the sacrifices offered at their proper seasons, if yet there ensue drought, or the waters overflow, the spirits of the land and grain are changed, and others appointed in their place.'

CHAP. XV. Mencius said, 'A sage is the teacher of a hundred generations:—this is true of Po-î and Hûi of Liû-hsiâ. Therefore when men now hear the character of Po-î, the corrupt become pure, and the weak acquire determination. When they hear the character of Hûi of Liû-hsiâ, the mean become generous, and the

the fields and wilds,' the peasantry. According to the Châu Lî, nine husbandmen, heads of families, formed a *tsing* (井); four *tsing* formed a *yih* (邑); and four *yih* formed a *k'ew* (丘), which would thus contain 144 families. But the phrase 丘人, signifying the peasantry, is yet equivalent to 'the people.' Mencius uses it, his discourse being of the spirits of the land and grain. 3. The change of the 社稷 is taken by most commentators as merely a destroying of the altars and building others. This is Chû Hsi's interpretation:—土穀之神, 不能爲民禦災捍患, 則毀其壇壝而更置之, 'when the spirits of the ground and grain cannot ward off calamities and evils from the people, then their altars and fences are thrown down and others in different places erected.' Châo Ch'î is more brief. He simply says that in such a case 毀社稷而更置之, which may mean that they destroyed the altars or displaced the spirits themselves. A changing of the altars merely does not supply a parallel to the removal of the princes in the preceding paragraph. And there are traces of deposing the spirits in such a case, and appointing others in their places. See the 四書拓餘說, *in loc.*

15. THAT PO-Î AND HÛI OF LIÛ-HSIÂ WERE SAGES PROVED BY THE PERMANENCE OF THEIR INFLUENCE. Compare Bk. V. Pt. II. i, *et al.* 'A hundred generations' is spoken generally. Between the

惠之風者、薄夫敦、鄙夫寬、奮乎百世之上、百世之下、聞者莫不興起也、非聖人而能若是乎、而況於親炙之者乎。

〔十六章〕孟子曰、仁也者、人也、合而言之、道也。

〔十七章〕孟子曰、孔子之去魯、曰、遲遲吾行也、去父母國之道也、去齊、接淅而行、去他國之道也。

niggardly become liberal. *Those two* made themselves distinguished a hundred generations ago, and after a hundred generations, those who hear of them, are all aroused *in this manner*. Could such effects be produced by them, if they had not been sages? And how much more did they affect those who were in contiguity with them, and felt their inspiring influence!'

CHAP. XVI. Mencius said, 'Benevolence is *the distinguishing characteristic of* man. As embodied in man's conduct, it is called the path *of duty*.'

CHAP. XVII. Mencius said, 'When Confucius was leaving Lû, he said, "I will set out by-and-by;"—this was the way in which to leave the State of his parents. When he was leaving Ch'î, he strained off with his hand the water in which his rice was being rinsed, *took the rice*, and went away;—this was the way in which to leave a strange State.'

two worthies themselves, several hundred years intervened.

16. THE RELATION OF BENEVOLENCE TO MAN. This chapter is quite enigmatic. 合 is taken as = 合仁于人身, 'unite benevolence with man's person,' and 道 as the 率性之道 of the Chung-yung. The glossarist of Châo Ch'î refers to Analects, XV. xxviii, which is very good. Chû Hsi, however, mentions that in an edition of Mencius found in Corea, after 人也, there follow accounts of 'righteousness,' 'propriety,' and 'wisdom;'—義也者宜也, 云云. If that was the original reading, the final clause would be:—'These, all united and named, are the path of reason.'

17. HOW CONFUCIUS'S LEAVING LÛ AND CH'Î WAS DIFFERENT. Compare Bk. V. Pt. II. i. 4.

十八章 孟子曰、君子之戹於陳蔡之間、無上下之交也。

十九章 一節 貉稽曰、稽大不理於口。二節 孟子曰、無傷也、士憎茲多口。三節 詩云、憂心悄悄、慍于群小、孔子也、肆不殄厥慍、亦不隕厥問、文王也。

CHAP. XVIII. Mencius said, 'The reason why the superior man was reduced to straits between Ch'ăn and Ts'âi was because neither the princes *of the time* nor their ministers *sympathized or* communicated with him.'

CHAP. XIX. 1. Mo Ch'î said, 'Greatly am I from anything to depend upon from the mouths *of men*.'

2. Mencius observed, 'There is no harm in that. Scholars are more exposed than others to suffer from the mouths *of men*.

3. 'It is said, in the Book of Poetry,

"My heart is disquieted and grieved,
I am hated by the crowd of mean creatures."

This might have been said by Confucius. And again,

"Though he did not remove their wrath,
He did not let fall his own fame."

This might be said of king Wăn.'

18. THE REASON OF CONFUCIUS'S BEING IN STRAITS BETWEEN CH'ĂN AND TS'ÂI. See Analects, XI. ii. The speaking of Confucius simply by the term 君子 is to be noted;—compare Analects, X. vi. 1, *et al.* Châo Ch'î observes that Confucius, in his exceeding modesty, said that he was not equal to the threefold way of the superior man (Analects, XIV. xxx), and therefore he might be spoken of as a superior man. It is difficult to see the point of this observation, nor does it meet the difficulty which arises from the use of the designation in the text. 上=君, 'the sovereigns,' and 下=臣, 'their ministers.' The princes did not honour him and seek his services. Their ministers did not honour him and recommend him to employment. This is the meaning of 無上下之交. The commentators, in their quest for profound meanings, make out the lesson to be that though a sage may be reduced to straits, the way of truth cannot be so reduced.

19. MENCIUS COMFORTS MO CH'Î UNDER CALUMNY BY THE REFLECTION THAT IT WAS THE ORDINARY LOT OF DISTINGUISHED MEN. 1. Of Mo Ch'î, nothing is known beyond what is here intimated. 理 is used in the sense of 賴, 'to depend on.' This is given to it in the dictionary, with a reference to this passage. The meaning is that not only did he not have a good word from men, but was spoken ill of by them. 2. 憎, it is concluded, from the comment of Châo Ch'î, is a mistake for 增, 'to increase,' and 茲 has substantially the same meaning. Retaining 憎, however, and taking 茲 in its sense of *this* or *these*, we get a tolerable meaning, 'The scholar hates those many mouths.' 3. For the first quotation, see the Shih-ching, I. iii. Ode I. st. 4, a description of her condition by the ill-used wife of one of the dukes of Wei (according to Chû Hsî), and which Mencius somewhat strangely would apply to Confucius. For the second, see III. i. Ode III. st. 8, descrip-

〔二十章〕孟子曰、賢者、以其昭昭、使人昭昭、今以其昏昏、使人昭昭。

〔廿一章〕孟子謂高子曰、山徑之蹊閒、介然用之而成路、爲閒不用、則茅塞之矣、今茅塞子之心矣。

〔廿二章〕一節 高子曰、禹之聲、尚文王之聲。〇二節 孟子曰、何以言之。曰、以追蠡。〇三節 曰、是奚足

CHAP. XX. Mencius said, '*Anciently*, men of virtue and talents by means of their own enlightenment made others enlightened. Nowadays, it is tried, *while they are themselves in darkness*, and by means of that darkness, to make others enlightened.'

CHAP. XXI. Mencius said to the disciple Kâo, 'There are the footpaths along the hills;—if suddenly they be used, they become roads; and if, as suddenly they are not used, the wild grass fills them up. Now, the wild grass fills up your mind.'

CHAP. XXII. 1. The disciple Kâo said, 'The music of Yü was better than that of king Wăn.'

2. Mencius observed, 'On what ground do you say so?' and the other replied, 'Because at the pivot the knob of Yü's bells is nearly worn through.'

3. *Mencius* said, 'How can that be a sufficient proof? Are

tive of the king T'âi, though applied to Wăn. 閒 is in the sense of 聞, 'report,' 'reputation.'

20. HOW THE ANCIENTS LED ON MEN BY THEIR EXAMPLE, WHILE THE RULERS OF MENCIUS'S TIME TRIED TO URGE MEN CONTRARY TO THEIR EXAMPLE. In translating, I supply 古之 before 賢者, in contrast with the 今 below. To the two 使 a very different force is given. The former is the constraining influence of example; the latter is the application of pains and penalties.

21. THAT THE CULTIVATION OF THE MIND MAY NOT BE INTERMITTED. 蹊閒, 'spaces for the foot,'=footpaths; 山徑之蹊閒,—the 'footpaths of the hill-ways.' 介 (read *chiá*, as 戛, according to Chû Hsî, though the dictionary does not give such a sound to the character, nor do we find in it the meaning which suits this passage) 然, 'suddenly;' nearly = 爲閒. The Kâo here must have been a disciple of Mencius, different from the old Kâo, Bk. VI. Pt. II. iii. Châo Ch'î says that after studying with Mencius for some time, and before he fully understood his principles, he went off and addicted himself to some other teacher, and that the remark was made with reference to this course, and its consequences.

22. AN ABSURD REMARK OF THE DISCIPLE KÂO ABOUT THE MUSIC OF YÜ AND KING WĂN. 2. 追,—read *tûi*, 'the knob, or loop, of a bell,' the part by which it is suspended. 蠡, 3rd tone,

哉、城門之軌、兩馬之力與。

〔二十三〕齊饑、一節陳臻曰、國人皆以夫子將復爲發棠、殆不可復。二節孟子曰、是爲馮婦也、晋人有馮婦者、善搏虎、卒爲善士、則之野、有衆逐虎、虎負嵎、莫之敢攖、望見馮婦、趨而迎之、

the ruts at the gate of a city made by a single two-horsed chariot?'

CHAP. XXIII. 1. When Ch'î was suffering from famine, Ch'ăn Tsin said *to Mencius*, 'The people are all thinking that you, Master, will again ask that the granary of T'ang be opened for them. I apprehend you will not do so a second time.'

2. *Mencius* said, 'To do it would be to act like Făng Fû. There was a man of that name in Tsin, famous for his skill in seizing tigers. Afterwards he became a scholar of reputation, and going once out to the wild country, he found the people all in pursuit of a tiger. The tiger took refuge in a corner of a hill, where no one dared to attack him, but when they saw Făng Fû, they ran and met him. Făng Fû *immediately* bared his arms, and descended

an insect that bores through wood; hence, metaphorically, anything having the appearance of being eaten or worn away. 3. The meaning is that what Kâo noticed was only the effect of time or long use, Yü being anterior to king Wăn, and did not necessarily imply any superiority of the music of the one over that of the other. The street contracts at the gate, and all the carriages that have been running over its breadth are obliged to run in the same ruts, which hence are deeper here than elsewhere.—There is much controversy about the phrase 兩馬之力. Châo Ch'î understands 兩馬 as meaning 'two kinds of horses;'—the 國馬, levied from the State, and employed on what we may call the postal service, and the 公馬, or 'public horses,' principally used in military service. On this view the meaning would be that the ruts in question were not made by these two kinds of carriages only. Chû Hsî, after the commentator Făng (豐氏), takes the meaning as I have given it in the translation. Another view takes 兩 in the sense of 車, taking it in the 4th tone, as in chap. iv. 4. See the 四書拓餘說, *in loc.*

23. HOW MENCIUS KNEW WHERE TO STOP AND MAINTAIN HIS OWN DIGNITY IN HIS INTERCOURSE WITH THE PRINCES. 1. At T'ang, whose name is still preserved in the village of Kan-t'ang, in the district of Chî-mo (卽墨), in the department of Lâi-châu, the princes of Ch'î, it would appear, kept grain in store, and on some previous occurrence of famine, Mencius had advised the king to open the granary. In the meantime, however, some difference had occurred between him and the prince. He intended leaving Ch'î, and would not expose himself to a repulse by making an application which might be rejected. 2. 善士, 'a good scholar,' or 'officer,' but 善 is to be taken only as = 'skilful.' 之

馮婦攘臂下車、衆皆悅之、其爲士者笑之。

【二十四章】一節 孟子曰、口之於味也、目之於色也、耳之於聲也、鼻之於臭也、四肢之於安佚也、性也、有命焉、君子不謂性也。二節 仁之於父子也、義之於君臣也、禮之於賓主也、智之於賢者也、聖人之於

from the carriage. The multitude were pleased with him, but those who were scholars laughed at him.'

CHAP. XXIV. 1. Mencius said, 'For the mouth to desire *sweet* tastes, the eye to desire *beautiful* colours, the ear to desire *pleasant* sounds, the nose to desire *fragrant* odours, and the four limbs to desire ease and rest;—these things are natural. But there is the appointment *of Heaven in connexion with them*, and the superior man does not say *of his pursuit of them*, "It is my nature."

2. '*The exercise of* love between father and son, *the observance of* righteousness between sovereign and minister, the rules of ceremony between guest and host, *the display* of knowledge *in* recognising the talented, and *the fulfilling* the heavenly course by the sage;—these are the appointment *of Heaven*. But there is *an adaptation of our*

野,—之=往. It did not belong to Fǎng Fû, now an officer, to be fighting with tigers, playing the part of a bravo.

24. HOW THE SUPERIOR MAN SUBJECTS THE GRATIFICATION OF HIS NATURAL APPETITES TO THE WILL OF HEAVEN, AND PURSUES THE DOING OF GOOD WITHOUT THINKING THAT THE AMOUNT WHICH HE CAN DO MAY BE LIMITED BY THAT WILL. 1. 口之於味, 'the mouth's relation to tastes;' that is, its constitution so as to be pleased with certain tastes. So, all the other clauses. 有命焉, 'there is the appointment *of Heaven*,' i.e. every appetite naturally desires its unlimited gratification, but a limited amount or an entire denial may be the will of Heaven. 2. 智之於賢者 is not 'the possession of knowledge by the talented,' but the exercise of wisdom in reference to them, recognising and appreciating their excellence. The sentiment is well illustrated by the case of Yen Ying, the minister of Ch'i, able and wise, and yet insensible to the superior excellence of Confucius and his principles.—Chû Hsi says well upon this chapter:—'I have heard it observed by my master that the things mentioned in both of these paragraphs are in the constitution of our nature, and likewise ordained by Heaven. Mankind, however, consider that the first five are more especially natural, and, though they may be prevented from obtaining them, still desire them; and that the last five are more especially appointed by Heaven, so that if they do not come to them readily, they do not go on to put forth their strength to reach them. On this account,

天道也、命也、有性焉、君子不謂命也。

〔二十五章〕一節浩生不害問曰、樂正子、何人也、孟子曰、善人也、信人也。二節何謂善、何謂信。三節曰、可欲之謂善。四節有諸己之謂信。五節充實之謂美。六節充實而有光輝之謂大。七節大而化之之謂聖。八節聖而不可知之之謂神。九節樂正

nature *for them*. The superior man does not say, *in reference to them*, "It is the appointment of Heaven."'

CHAP. XXV. 1. Hâo-shăng Pû-hâi asked, saying, 'What sort of man is Yo-chăng?' Mencius replied, 'He is a good man, a real man.'

2. 'What do you mean by "A good man," "A real man?"'

3. The reply was, 'A man who commands our liking is what is called a good man.

4. 'He whose *goodness* is part of himself is what is called a real man.

5. 'He whose *goodness* has been filled up is what is called a beautiful man.

6. 'He whose completed goodness is brightly displayed is what is called a great man.

7. 'When this great man exercises a transforming influence, he is what is called a sage.

8. 'When the sage is beyond our knowledge, he is what is called a spirit-man.

9. 'Yo-chăng is between the two *first* characters, and below the four last.'

Mencius shows what is most important in each case, that he may induce a broader way of thinking in regard to the second class, and repress the way of thinking in regard to the first.'

25. THE CHARACTER OF THE DISCIPLE YO-CHĂNG. DIFFERENT DEGREES OF ATTAINMENT IN CHARACTER, WHICH ARE TO BE AIMED AT. 1. Châo Ch'î tells us that Hâo-shăng is the surname and Pû-hâi the name, and that the individual was a man of Ch'î. This is all we know of him. 3. It is assumed here that the general verdict of mankind will be on the side of goodness. Hence when a man is *desirable*, and commands universal liking, he must be a *good* man. 4. 有諸己, 'having in himself;' i.e. when a man has the goodness, without hypocrisy or pretence. Compare Bk. VI. Pt. II. xiii. Goodness is an attribute entering into all the others, and I have therefore thrice expressed it in the translation. 8. 聖而不可知之之謂神,—with this we may compare what is

子二之中、四之下也。

〔二十六〕孟子曰、逃墨、必歸於楊、逃楊、必歸於儒、歸、斯受之而已矣。○今之與楊墨辯者、如追放豚、既入其苙、又從而招之。

〔二十七〕孟子曰、有布縷之征、粟米之征、力役之征、君子用其一、緩其二、用其二、而民有殍、用其三、而父子離。

CHAP. XXVI. 1. Mencius said, 'Those who are fleeing from *the errors of* Mo naturally turn to Yang, and those who are fleeing from *the errors of* Yang naturally turn to orthodoxy. When they so turn, they should at once and simply be received.

2. 'Those who nowadays dispute with the followers of Yang and Mo do so as if they were pursuing a stray pig, the leg of which, after they have got it to enter the pen, they proceed to tie.'

CHAP. XXVII. Mencius said, 'There are the exactions of hempen-cloth and silk, of grain, and of personal service. The prince requires but one of these *at once*, deferring the other two. If he require two of them *at once*, then the people die of hunger. If he require the three *at once*, then fathers and sons are separated.'

said in the Doctrine of the Mean, 至誠如神, 'the individual possessed of the most complete sincerity is like a spirit.' In the critical remarks in the 四書合講, it is said, indeed, that the expression in the text is stronger than that there, but the two are substantially to the same effect. Some would translate 神 by 'divine,' a rendering which it never can admit of, and yet, in applying to man the term appropriate to the actings and influence of Him whose way is in the sea, and His judgments a great deep, Chinese writers derogate from the prerogatives of God.

26. RECOVERED HERETICS SHOULD BE RECEIVED WITHOUT CASTING THEIR OLD ERRORS IN THEIR TEETH. 1. 歸於儒, 'they turn to the learned.' 'The learned' in Chinese phrase is equivalent to our 'the orthodox.' The name is still claimed in China by the followers of Confucius and other sages, in opposition to the Tâoists and Buddhists. 2. The disputations are with those who *had been* Yangists and Mohists. This sense of 招, 'to tie the legs,' is found in the dictionary with reference to this passage.

27. THE JUST EXACTIONS OF THE GOVERNMENT ARE TO BE MADE DISCRIMINATINGLY AND CONSIDERATELY. 布 is cloth, made from flax. 縷, 'silken fibres not spun;' but here, probably, silk, spun or unspun. 粟, 'grain unthreshed;' 米, the same threshed:—here together, grain generally. The tax of cloth and silk was due in summer, that of grain after harvest, and personal service was for the leisure of winter. 君子=君. The prince might only require them, one at a time, and in their proper seasons.

〔二十八章〕孟子曰、諸侯之寶三、土地、人民、政事、寶珠玉者、殃必及身。

〔二十九章〕盆成括仕於齊、孟子曰、死矣、盆成括。盆成括見殺、門人問曰、夫子何以知其將見殺。曰、其爲人也、小有才、未聞君子之大道也、則足以殺其軀而已矣。

〔三十章〕孟子之滕、館於上宮、有業

CHAP. XXVIII. Mencius said, 'The precious things of a prince are three;—the territory, the people, the government and its business. If one value as most precious pearls and jade, calamity is sure to befall him.'

CHAP. XXIX. P'an-ch'ăng Kwo having obtained an official situation in Ch'î, Mencius said, 'He is a dead man, *that* P'an-ch'ăng Kwo!' P'an-ch'ăng Kwo being put to death, the disciples asked, saying, 'How did you know, Master, that he would meet with death?' Mencius replied, 'He was a man, who had a little ability, but had not learned the great doctrines of the superior man.—He was just qualified to bring death upon himself, but for nothing more.'

CHAP. XXX. 1. When Mencius went to T'ăng, he was lodged in the Upper palace. A sandal in the process of making had been

28. THE PRECIOUS THINGS OF A PRINCE, AND THE DANGER OF OVERLOOKING THEM FOR OTHER THINGS. 土, 'the productive ground,' and 地, 'land generally.' 人 as distinguished from 民 = 'officers,' but the terms are not to be taken separately. So of 政事; see chap. xii.

29. HOW MENCIUS PREDICTED BEFOREHAND THE DEATH OF P'AN-CH'ĂNG KWO. Compare Confucius's prediction of Tsze-lû's death, Analects, XI. xii. Little is known of this Kwo. He is said to have begun learning with Mencius, but to have soon gone away, disappointed by what he heard.

30. THE GENEROUS SPIRIT OF MENCIUS IN DISPENSING HIS INSTRUCTIONS. This, which is the lesson of the chapter, only comes out at the end, and has been commemorated, as being the remark of an individual not of extraordinary character, and at first disposed to find fault with Mencius's disciples. 1. 之滕,—之 = 往. 上宮,—compare 雪宮, Bk. I. Pt. II. iv. This was evidently a palace appropriated by the duke of T'ăng for the lodging of honourable visitors. The first 館

屨於牖上，館人求之弗得。二節或問之曰，若是乎從者之廋也。曰，子以是爲竊屨來與。曰，殆非也。夫子之設科也，往者不追，來者不拒，苟以是心至，斯受之而已矣。

卅一章 一節孟子曰，人皆有所不忍，達之於其所忍，仁也。人皆有所不爲，達之於其所爲，義也。二節人能充無欲害人之

placed there in a window, and when the keeper of the place *came to* look for it, he could not find it.

2. *On this*, some one asked *Mencius*, saying, 'Is it thus that your followers pilfer?' Mencius replied, 'Do you think that they came here to pilfer the sandal?' The man said, 'I apprehend not. But you, Master, having arranged to give lessons, do not go back to inquire into the past, and you do not reject those who come to you. If they come with the mind to learn, you receive them without any more ado.'

CHAP. XXXI. 1. Mencius said, 'All men have some things which they cannot bear;—extend that feeling to what they can bear, and benevolence will be the result. All men have some things which they will not do;—extend that feeling to the things which they do, and righteousness will be the result.

2. 'If a man can give full development to the feeling which

is a verb, 'was lodged.' The second makes a compound noun with 人. 業屨,—the dictionary has, with reference to this passage, 事物已爲而未成曰業, 'things being done, but not completed, are said to be 業.' 2. *Sâu* (=廋), 'to hide,'= to steal and hide. 曰，子以是,—是, 'these,' referring to 'followers.' 夫子之設科云云,—according to Chû Hsî, this is the observation of Mencius's questioner, suddenly awaking to an understanding of the philosopher. Anciently, 夫子 was read 夫予, 'now, I,' and Mencius was supposed to be himself the speaker. Chû Hsî is, no doubt, correct. 設科 is better than 設教, 科 conveying the idea of 'exercises' suited to different capacities. 是心=向道之心.

31. A MAN HAS ONLY TO GIVE DEVELOPMENT TO THE PRINCIPLES OF GOOD WHICH ARE IN HIM, AND SHOW THEMSELVES IN SOME THINGS, TO BE ENTIRELY GOOD AND CORRECT. This is a sentiment which we have found continually occurring in these analects. It supposes that man has more power over himself than he really has. 2. 穿=穿

心、而仁不可勝用也、人能充無穿窬之心、而義不可勝用也。三節 人能充無受爾汝之實、無所往而不爲義也。四節 士未可以言而言、是以言餂之也、可以言而不言、是以不言餂之也、是皆穿窬之類也。

三十二章 一節 孟子曰、言近而指遠者、善言也、守約而施博者、善

makes him shrink from injuring others, his benevolence will be more than can be called into practice. If he can give full development to the feeling which refuses to break through, or jump over, *a wall*, his righteousness will be more than can be called into practice.

3. 'If he can give full development to the real feeling of dislike with which he receives the salutation, "Thou," "Thou," he will act righteously in all places and circumstances.

4. 'When a scholar speaks what he ought not to speak, by *guile of* speech seeking to gain some end; and when he does not speak what he ought to speak, by *guile of* silence seeking to gain some end;—both these cases are of a piece with breaking through *a neighbour's wall.*'

CHAP. XXXII. 1. Mencius said, 'Words which are simple, while their meaning is far-reaching, are good words. Principles which, as held, are compendious, while their application is extensive,

穴, 'to make a hole through.' 窬 = 窬墻 'to jump over a wall.' The two together are equivalent to 'to play the thief.' 3. 'Thou,' 'Thou,' is a style of address greatly at variance with Chinese notions of propriety. It can only be used to the very young and the very mean. A man will revolt from it as used to himself, and 'if he be careful to act so that men will not dare to speak to him in this style, he will go nowhere where he will not do righteousness.'—This is rather far-fetched. 4. 餂, 'to lick with the tongue;' = 'to inveigle.' To find an antecedent to the 之, we must understand the person who is spoken to, or before whom silence is kept; or, perhaps, 之 merely gives effect to the verb in the general sense of 'to gain some end.'

32. AGAINST AIMING AT WHAT IS REMOTE, AND NEGLECTING WHAT IS NEAR. WHAT ARE GOOD WORDS AND GOOD PRINCIPLES. 1. 不下帶,—see the Book of Rites, Bk. I. Sect. II. iii. 15. The ancients did not look at a person below the girdle, so that all above that might be considered as near, beneath the eyes. The phrase 近言 = 'words which are near,' i.e. on

孟子

道也、君子之言也、不下帶、而道存焉。二節君子之守、修其身、而天下平。三節人病舍其田、而芸人之田、所求於人者重、而所以自任者輕。

〔三十三〕一節孟子曰、堯舜、性者也、湯武、反之也。二節動容周旋中禮者、盛德之至也。哭死而哀、非爲生者也。經德不回、非以干祿也。言語必信、非以

are good principles. The words of the superior man do not go below the girdle, but *great* principles are contained in them.

2. 'The principle which the superior man holds is that of personal cultivation, but the kingdom is thereby tranquillized.

3. 'The disease of men is this:—that they neglect their own fields, and go to weed the fields of others, and that what they require from others is great, while what they lay upon themselves is light.'

CHAP. XXXIII. 1. Mencius said, 'Yâo and Shun were what they were by nature; T'ang and Wû were so by returning *to natural virtue*.

2. 'When all the movements, in the countenance and every turn of *the body*, are exactly what is proper, that shows the extreme degree of the complete virtue. Weeping for the dead should be from *real* sorrow, and not because of the living. The regular path of virtue is to be pursued without any bend, and from no view to emolument. The words should all be necessarily sincere, not with any desire to do what is right.

common subjects, simple, plain. So, Chû Hsî; but the passage in the Lî Chî is not so general as his commentary. It gives the rule for looking by the sovereign. He is not to raise his eyes above a minister's collar, nor lower them below the girdle. Châo Ch'î tries to explain the expression without reference to the ancient rule for regulating the looking at men. According to him, 'words not below the girdle are all from near the heart.' 2. This is the explanation of 守約而施博; see Analects, VI. xxv. The paragraph is a good summary of the teaching of The Great Learning.

33. THE PERFECT VIRTUE OF THE HIGHEST SAGES, AND HOW OTHERS FOLLOW AFTER IT. 1. Compare Pt. I. xxx, but 之 has not here a special reference to certain virtues as there. 2. This is an exhibition of the highest style of virtue—that of Yâo and Shun, which does everything right, with no motive beyond the doing so. 'Weeping is from real sorrow, and not because of the living,' i.e. there is nothing of show in it, and no wish to make an impression on

正行也。三節君子行法以俟命而已矣。

三十四章一節孟子曰、說大人則藐之、勿視其巍巍然。二節堂高數仞、榱題數尺、我得志弗爲也、食前方丈、侍妾數百人、我得志弗爲也、般樂飲酒、驅騁田獵、後車千乘、我得志弗爲也、在彼者、皆我所不爲也、在我者、皆古之制也、吾何畏彼哉。

3. 'The superior man performs the law *of right*, and thereby waits simply for what has been appointed.'

CHAP. XXXIV. 1. Mencius said, 'Those who give counsel to the great should despise them, and not look at their pomp and display.

2. 'Halls several times eight cubits high, with beams projecting several cubits;—these, if my wishes were to be realized, I would not have. Food spread before me over ten cubits square, and attendants and concubines to the amount of hundreds;—these, though my wishes were realized, I would not have. Pleasure and wine, and the dash of hunting, with thousands of chariots following after me;—these, though my wishes were realized, I would not have. What they esteem are what I would have nothing to do with; what I esteem are the rules of the ancients.—Why should I stand in awe of them?'

others. 3. Describes the virtue that is next in degree, equally observant of right, but by an intellectual constraint. 法=天理之當然, 'the proper course indicated by Heavenly principles.'

34. HE WHO UNDERTAKES TO COUNSEL THE GREAT, SHOULD BE MORALLY ABOVE THEM. 1. 大人, 'great men.' The phrase is to be understood not of the truly great, as in ch. xxv. 6, *et al.*, but of the socially great, with an especial reference to the princes of the time, dignified by their position, but without corresponding moral qualities. 2. 堂高, 云云, and all the corresponding clauses, are under the government of some words like 彼大人有, 'those great men have,' to which 我弗爲, 'I would not do,' respond. 榱題,—these may be seen in the more important temples and public buildings throughout China, projecting all round, beneath the eaves. 般樂,—see Bk. II. Pt. I. iv. 4. 驅騁田獵, 'spurring and galloping in hunting.' 在彼

【三十五】孟子曰、養心莫善於寡欲、其爲人也寡欲、雖有不存焉者、寡矣、其爲人也多欲、雖有存焉者寡矣。

【三十六】曾晳嗜羊棗、而曾子不忍食羊棗。公孫丑問曰、膾炙與羊棗孰美。孟子曰、膾炙哉。公孫丑曰、然則曾子何爲食膾炙、而不食羊棗。曰、膾炙所同也、羊棗所獨也、諱名不諱姓、

CHAP. XXXV. Mencius said, 'To nourish the mind there is nothing better than to make the desires few. Here is a man whose desires are few:—in some things he may not be able to keep his heart, but they will be few. Here is a man whose desires are many:—in some things he may be able to keep his heart, but they will be few.'

CHAP. XXXVI. 1. Mencius said, 'Tsăng Hsî was fond of sheep-dates, and *his son*, the philosopher Tsăng, could not bear to eat sheep-dates.'

2. Kung-sun Ch'âu asked, saying, 'Which is best,—minced meat and broiled meat, or sheep-dates?' Mencius said, 'Mince and broiled meat, to be sure.' Kung-sun Ch'âu went on, 'Then why did the philosopher Tsăng eat mince and broiled meat, and would not eat sheep-dates?' Mencius answered, 'For mince and broiled meat

者, 'what are in them,' the things which they esteem so. 在我者 = the things which I esteem.

35. THE REGULATION OF THE DESIRES IS ESSENTIAL TO THE NOURISHMENT OF THE MIND. 欲 must be taken in a bad, or at least an inferior sense = the appetites, while 心 is the heart naturally disposed to all virtue. 雖有不存焉, 'although there are'—virtues of the heart, that is—'which are not preserved.'

36. THE FILIAL FEELING OF TSĂNG-TSZE SEEN IN HIS NOT EATING JUJUBES. 1. 羊棗, 'sheep-jujubes,' the small black northern fruit, so called from its resembling sheep's dirt. Such is Chû Hsî's account of the fruit. The writer of the 四書拓餘說, *in loc.*, however, seems to make out a case for 羊棗 being a kind of persimmon. Still, why call it a date, or jujube? See Bretschneider's *Botanicon Sinicum*, p. 118. 2. Hsi must have eaten both the jujubes and the cooked meat, but his liking

姓所同也、名所獨也。

三七 萬章問曰、孔子在陳曰、盍歸乎來、吾黨之士、狂簡、進取、不忘其初、孔子在陳、何思魯之狂士。〇二節 孟子曰、孔子不得中道而與之、必也狂獧乎、狂者進取、獧者有所不爲也、孔子豈不欲中道哉、不可必得、故思其次也。〇三節 敢問何如、斯可謂

there is a common liking, while that for sheep-dates was peculiar. We avoid the name, but do not avoid the surname. The surname is common; the name is peculiar.'

CHAP. XXXVII. 1. Wan Chang asked, saying, 'Confucius, when he was in Ch'ăn, said: "Let me return. The scholars of my school are ambitious, but hasty. They are for advancing and seizing their object, but cannot forget their early ways." Why did Confucius, when he was in Ch'ăn, think of the ambitious scholars of Lû?'

2. Mencius replied, 'Confucius not getting men pursuing the true medium, to whom he might communicate *his instructions*, determined to take the ardent and the cautiously-decided. The ardent would advance to seize their object; the cautiously-decided would keep themselves from certain things. It is not to be thought that Confucius did not wish to get men pursuing the true medium, but being unable to assure himself of finding such, he therefore thought of the next class.'

3. 'I venture to ask what sort of men they were who could be styled "The ambitious?"'

for the jujubes was peculiar, and therefore the sight of them brought him vividly up to his son, and he could not bear to eat them. But such points are not important to illustrate the meaning here.

37. TO CALL TO THE PURSUIT OF THE RIGHT MEDIUM WAS THE OBJECT OF CONFUCIUS AND MENCIUS. VARIOUS CHARACTERS WHO FAIL TO PURSUE THIS, OR ARE OPPOSED TO IT. 1. See Analects, V. xxi. The differences between that text and what we have here will be noted. Perhaps Wan Chang was quoting from memory. 2. See Analects, XIII. xxi. As Mencius quotes that chapter, some think that there should be

狂矣。四節曰、如琴張、曾晳、牧皮者、孔子之所謂狂矣。五節何以謂之狂也。六節曰、其志嘐嘐然、曰、古之人、古之人、夷考其行而不掩焉者也。七節狂者、又不可得、欲得不屑不潔之士而與之、是獧也、是又其次也。八節孔子曰、過我門、而不入我室、我不憾焉者、其惟鄉原乎、鄉原、德之賊也、曰、何如斯可謂之鄉原矣。九節曰、

4. 'Such,' replied Mencius, 'as Ch'in Chang, Tsăng Hsî, and Mû P'ei, were those whom Confucius styled "ambitious?"'

5. 'Why were they styled "ambitious?"'

6. The reply was, 'Their aim led them to talk magniloquently, saying, "The ancients!" "The ancients!" But their actions, where we fairly compare them with *their words, did* not correspond with them.

7. 'When he found also that he could not get such as were *thus* ambitious, he wanted to get scholars who would consider anything impure as beneath them. Those were the cautiously-decided,—a class next to the former.'

8. *Chang pursued his questioning,* 'Confucius said, "They are only your good careful people of the villages at whom I feel no indignation, when they pass my door without entering my house. Your good careful people of the villages are the thieves of virtue." What sort of people were they who could be styled "Your good careful people of the villages?"'

a 曰 in the text after 孔子. 4. Ch'in Chang is the Lâo mentioned, Analects, IX. vi. So, according to Chû Hsi, who quotes an instance from the Tâoist philosopher Chwang, of the waywardness of Lâo, but Chwang's accounts of Confucius and his disciples are not to be trusted. The identification of the individual in the text with Lâo, however, is no doubt correct, though Châo Ch'î makes him to be the Shih of the Analects, referring to XI. xvii. 3, 'Shih is specious,' and adding that he played well on the *ch'in*, and was therefore styled Ch'in. See the 四書拓餘說, *in loc.* Of Mû P'ei nothing is known. 6. 夷,—in the sense of 平, 'even.' 夷考, 'evenly examining.' 掩, 'to cover,' = to make good. 8. The first part of the saying here attributed to Confucius is not found in the Analects. For the second,

何以是嘐嘐也、言不顧行、行不顧言、則曰、古之人、古之人、行何爲踽踽涼涼、生斯世也、爲斯世也、善斯可矣、閹然媚於世也者、是鄉原也。十節萬章曰、一鄉皆稱原人焉、無所往而不爲原人、孔子以爲德之賊、何哉。十一節曰、非之無舉也、刺之無刺也、同乎流俗、合乎汙世、居之似忠信、行之似廉潔、衆皆悅之、自以爲是、而不可與

9. *Mencius* replied, 'They are those who say, "Why are they so magniloquent? Their words have not respect to their actions, and their actions have not respect to their words, but they say,—*The ancients! The ancients!* Why do they act so peculiarly, and are so cold and distant? Born in this age, we should be of this age, to be good is all that is needed." Eunuch-like, flattering their generation;—such are your good careful men of the villages.'

10. Wan Chang said, 'Their whole village styles those men good and careful. In all their conduct they are so. How was it that Confucius considered them the thieves of virtue?'

11. *Mencius* replied, 'If you would blame them, you find nothing to allege. If you would criticise them, you have nothing to criticise. They agree with the current customs. They consent with an impure age. Their principles have a semblance of right-heartedness and truth. Their conduct has a semblance of disinterestedness and purity. All men are pleased with them, and they think themselves right, so that it is impossible to proceed with them to the principles

see XVII. xiii. 9. Before this paragraph we must understand 孟子曰. The 曰 in the text has for its subject 鄉原, or we may take it in the infinitive, making the whole paragraph down to 也者 the antecedent subject to the 是 that follows. 善斯可矣, 'to be good is enough,' i.e. to be accounted good by the age in which they live is enough for them. 踽踽, 'the appearance of walking alone,' i.e. acting peculiarly. 11. 流俗 is literally our

入堯舜之道、故曰、德之賊也。十二節孔子曰、惡似而非者、惡莠、恐其亂苗也、惡佞、恐其亂義也、惡利口、恐其亂信也、惡鄭聲、恐其亂樂也、惡紫、恐其亂朱也、惡鄉原、恐其亂德也。十三節君子反經而已矣、經正、則庶民興、庶民興、斯無邪慝矣。

三十八章 一節孟子曰、由堯舜至於湯、五百有餘歲、若禹、皋陶、則見而

of Yâo and Shun. On this account they are called "The thieves of virtue."

12. 'Confucius said, "I hate a semblance which is not the reality. I hate the darnel, lest it be confounded with the corn. I hate glib-tonguedness, lest it be confounded with righteousness. I hate sharpness of tongue, lest it be confounded with sincerity. I hate the music of Chăng, lest it be confounded with *the true* music. I hate the reddish blue, lest it be confounded with vermilion. I hate your good careful men of the villages, lest they be confounded with the *truly* virtuous."

13. 'The superior man seeks simply to bring back the unchanging standard, and, that being correct, the masses are roused to virtue. When they are so aroused, forthwith perversities and glossed wickedness disappear.'

CHAP. XXXVIII. 1. Mencius said, 'From Yâo and Shun down to T'ang were 500 years and more. As to Yu and Kâo Yâo, they

'current customs,' but 流, at the same time, stigmatizes the customs as bad. 居之＝居之於心者；行之＝行之於身者. 12. These are sayings of Confucius which are only found here. Such a string of them is not in the sage's style. 恐其亂苗, 'lest it confound the corn,'＝be confounded with it. So in the other phrases. 鄭聲,—see Analects, XV. x. 紫,—see Analects, X. vi. 2. 13. This paragraph explains the rest of the chapter. The 經, or 'unchanging standard,' is the 中道, 'the right medium,' which the sage himself pursues, and to which he seeks to recall others.

38. ON THE TRANSMISSION OF THE LINE OF DOCTRINE FROM YÂO TO MENCIUS'S OWN TIME. Compare Bk. II. Pt. II. xiii; Bk. III. Pt. II. x; *et al.* 1. From the commencement of Shun's

知之、若湯、則聞而知之。○二節由湯至於文王、五百有餘歲、若伊尹、萊朱、則見而知之、若文王、則聞而知之。○三節由文王至於孔子、五百有餘歲、若太公望、散宜生、則見而知之、若孔子、則聞而知之。○四節由孔子而來、至於今、百有餘歲、去聖人之世、若此其未遠也、近聖人之居、若此其甚也、然而無有乎爾、則亦無有乎爾。

saw *those earliest sages*, and *so* knew their doctrines, while T'ang heard their doctrines *as transmitted*, and *so* knew them.

2. 'From T'ang to king Wăn were 500 years and more. As to Î Yin, and Lâi Chû, they saw *T'ang* and knew his doctrines, while king Wăn heard them *as transmitted*, and so knew them.

3. 'From king Wăn to Confucius were 500 years and more. As to T'âi-kung Wang and San Î-shăng, they saw *Wăn*, and so knew his doctrines, while Confucius heard them *as transmitted*, and so knew them.

4. 'From Confucius downwards until now, there are *only* 100 years and *somewhat* more. The distance in time from the sage is so far from being remote, and so very near at hand was the sage's residence. In these circumstances, is there no one *to transmit his doctrines?* Yea, is there no one *to do so?*'

reign to that of T'ang's were 489 years, while from T'ang to the rise of the Châu dynasty were 644 years. Here, as before, Bk. II. Pt. II. xiii, Mencius uses 500 as a round number. In 知之, the 之 refers to the doctrines of the sages. 2. Lâi Chû is not exactly identified. Most make him the same with T'ang's minister, Chung-hûi; see the Shû-ching, IV. ii. 3. T'âi-kung Wang,—see Bk. IV. Pt. I. xiii. Of San Î-shăng more can hardly be said to be known than that he was an able minister of king Wăn. Chû Hsî seems to be wrong, however, in making San, instead of San-î, to be the surname. See the 四書拓餘說, *in loc.* 4. The concluding sentences here wonderfully vex commentators. In the 'Supplemental Commentary' (翼註) are found five different interpretations of them. But all agree that Mencius somehow takes upon himself the duty and responsibility of handing down the doctrines of the sage.

孟子

INDEXES.

INDEX I.

OF SUBJECTS.

The references to the Book, Part, Chapter, and Paragraph are marked thus—I. i. 1. 1. *In the first edition, for Parts* i *and* ii *the characters* 上 *and* 下 *were used in all the Indexes.*

孟子

孟子

孟子

INDEX II.

OF PROPER NAMES.

Names in Italics will be found in their own places in this Index, with additional references.

孟子

INDEX III.

OF CHINESE CHARACTERS AND PHRASES;

INTENDED ALSO TO HELP TOWARDS THE FORMATION OF A DICTIONARY AND CONCORDANCE FOR THE CLASSICS.

In the references, Books are separated by a colon; Parts of the same Book, and Chapters, by a semicolon.

THE 1st RADICAL, 一.

一 *yi* (1) One; sometimes = a, I. i. 7. 6, 10, 17; ii. 3. 5; 4. 5, *et alibi, saepe.* 一民, every single individual of all the people, II. i. 1. 8. 一國, any one State, and a whole State, IV. i. 6. 1. 一心, all the heart, VII. ii. 37. 10. 一鄉, VII. ii. 37. 10. 一人, once with a reference to the sovereign, I. ii. 3. 7. 九一, a ninth, 什一, a tenth, 二十一, a twentieth, III. i. 3. 6, 15; ii. 5. 4; 8. 1: VI. ii. 10. 1, 4. 執一, to hold to one point, be obstinate, VII. i. 26. 3, 4. (2) One and the same, exactly similar, VI. i. 14. 4; ii. 9. 3: VII. i. 20. 2, *et al.* (3) To unite, to be united, I. i. 6. 2, 3, 4. (4) As an adverb and conjunction: once, once for all, as soon as, I. i. 5. 1; ii. 3. 6, 8; 11. 2: III. ii. 1. 1; 2. 1: IV. i. 20, *et al.* (5) 一 . . . 一, one . . . another, now . . . now, II. ii. 13. 2: III. ii. 9. 2.

丁 *ting* 太丁, a son of the sovereign T'ang, V. i. 6. 5. 武丁, a sovereign of the Yin dynasty, II. i. 1. 8.

七 *ch'i* Seven, I. i. 3. 4; 7. 24; ii. 2. 1, 2; 11. 1, *et al.* May be used for the seventh, I. i. 6. 6.

丈 *chang* (1) Ten cubits, VII. ii. 34. 2. (2) 丈夫, a man, III. i. 1. 4. 賤(小)丈夫, II. ii. 10. 7; 12. 6. 大丈夫, III. ii. 2. 1, 2, 3. 丈夫 = a son, a man-child, III. ii. 3. 6.

三 *san* (1) Three, I. ii. 12. 1; 16. 2: II. ii. 1. 2; 2. 6: III. i. 2. 2, 3, *et al., saepe.* 三軍, the armies of a great State, II. i. 2. 5, *et al.* 三代, the three dynasties of Hsiâ, Shang, and Châu, III. i. 3. 10, *et al.* 三王, the founders of the three dynasties, IV. ii. 20. 5. 三聖, the three sages, Yü, Châu-kung, and Confucius, III. ii. 9. 13. 三子, the three worthies, Po-î, Î Yin, and Hûi of Liû-hsiâ, VI. ii. 6. 2. 三卿, the three highest officers of a State, VI. ii. 6. 1. 三公, the three highest dignitaries at the sovereign's court, VII. i. 28. 三樂, VII. i. 20. 三寶, VII. ii. 28. May be used for *the third*, VI. ii. 7. 3, *et al.* (2) Adverbially, thrice, II. ii. 4. 1; 12. 1, 4, *et al.* (3) 二三子, my children, I. ii. 15. 1. (4) 三苗, the name of a State, V. ii. 3. 2. 三危, the name of a place, V. ii. 3. 2.

上 *shang* (1) He, she, it, this, that, which is above, with the corresponding plurals,—spoken of place, time, and rank. *Passim.* 上下, constantly appear as correlates, = superiors and inferiors; high and low; above and below. 上者, 下者, on the high grounds, on the low grounds, or they who were above, they who were below, III. ii. 9. 3. 上世, the highest antiquity, III. i. 5. 4. 上刑, the severest punishment, IV. i. 14. 3. 上士, V. ii. 2. 3, 6, 7, 8. 上農, V. ii. 2. 9. 上位, V. ii. 6. 6. (2) A preposition, following the noun, sometimes with 之 between them, and the noun sometimes preceded by 於, and 乎, upon, above, by, I. i. 7. 4: II. i. 6. 2: III. ii. 10. 1: VII. ii. 15; 30. 1. (3) 上帝, God, the most High God, I. ii. 3. 7: IV. i. 7. 5; ii. 25. 2. (4) 上宮, name of a palace, VII. ii. 30. 1.

'上 *shang* The 3rd tone. To ascend, I. ii. 4. 7.

下 *hsiâ* Anciently, the 3rd tone. (1) He, she, it, this, that, which is below, with the corresponding plurals, spoken of place,

time, and rank. *Passim.* On 上下, as correlates, see 上. 其下, the lowest case, VI. ii. 14. 4. Without 其, V. ii. 2. 9. 下士, V. ii. 2. 3, 6, 7, 8. (2) A preposition, used like 上 above. (3) 下帶, to go below the girdle, VII. ii. 32. 1. 爲下, to dig to a great depth, IV. i. 1. 6. (4) 天下, the world, = the kingdom, I. i. 3. 5; 5. 1; 6. 2, 6: V. 1. 3, 4; 3. 2; 4. 1, 3; 5. 1, 2, 5, 6, *et al.*, *saepissime.* 普天之下, V. i. 4. 2. (5) In the name 柳下惠, II. i. 9. 2, 3, *et al.*

下 *hsiâ* A verb, to descend, IV. ii. 3. 3, 4. 下雨, to rain, I. i. 6. 6. 下車, to descend from a carriage, VII. ii. 23. 2. So, 下木, III. i. 4. 15. ? 以下, III. i. 3. 16: and I. ii. 4. 7.

不 *pû* (1) Not. *Passim.* With other negatives,—莫, 無, 非, 罔, it makes a strong affirmative. (2) 不勝, a name, III. ii. 6. 1. 不害, also a name, VII. ii. 25. 1.

丑 *ch'âu* (1) The name of one of Mencius's disciples, Kung-sun Ch'âu, II. i. 1. 1; 2. 1; ii. 2. 2; 6. 2; 14. 1, *et al.* (2) The name of an officer of Ch'î, Ching Ch'âu, II. ii. 2. 4.

丙 *ping* 外丙, a son of the sovereign T'ang, said, according to the interpretation of some, to have reigned two years, V. i. 6. 5.

且 *ch'ieh* (1) And, and moreover, II. i. 1. 11; 2. 19; ii. 7. 4; 9. 2, 4, *et al.*, *saepe.* 且夫, *ib.*, III. ii. 1. 3. (2) And, = and yet, and even if, carrying the mind on to anticipate a reply, which is often given by 況 or 而況 . . . 乎, I. i. 4. 5: II. ii. 9. 3: VI. ii. 10. 6. With this meaning, we find 且猶, II. i. 1. 7; ii. 2. 10: VII. i. 8. 然且, II. ii. 12. 1: VI. ii. 8. 3, 8. Observe 方且, III. i. 4. 16. (3) 且 = will, or let me, III. i. 5. 1, 2.

丕 *p'ei* Great, III. ii. 9. 6.

世 *shih* (1) An age, a generation; ages. May often be translated by—the world, I. i. 7. 2; ii. 14. 3: II. ii. 2. 6: IV. i. 1. 2; ii. 1. 3; 22. 1, *et al.*, *saepe.* 世俗, the manners of the age, I. ii. 1. 2, *et al.* 名世者, famous in their generation, II. ii. 13. 3; compare VII. i. 9. 6. 其世, = their character in their time, V. ii. 8. 2. (2) Hereditary; from age to age, I. ii. 5. 3; 7. 1; 15. 2: III. i. 3. 8; ii. 10. 5. 繼世以有天下, to possess the throne by hereditary succession, V. i. 6. 4.

丘 *ch'iû* (1) A hillock, 丘垤, II. i. 2. 28. 丘陵, III. ii. 1. 5. 丘民, the peasantry (but 丘 is there a territorial designation), VII. ii. 14. 2. (2) The name of Confucius, IV. ii. 21. 3. (3) 咸丘, a double surname, V. i. 4. 1, 2. (4) 靈丘, a city of Ch'î, II. ii. 5. 1. 石丘, a place in Sung, VI. ii. 4. 1, 2. 葵丘, the place of a famous meeting of princes, VI. ii. 7. 3.

竝 *ping* Together, III. i. 4. 3. Also written 並.

THE 2ND RADICAL, 丨.

中 *chung* The middle. (1) Used as a preposition, after the noun, often with 於 or some other preposition before the noun. 之 also is often between the noun and 中, I. ii. 2. 3; 11. 3: II. ii. 10. 6: III. i. 4. 5; ii. 5. 5; 9. 4, *et al.*, *saepe.* (2) 中心, in the heart's core, II. i. 3. 2: III. i. 5. 4. 中國 and 國中, in the middle of the kingdom, II. ii. 10. 3: III. i. 3. 15; 4. 17: IV. ii. 33. 1 (國 here only = city). 其中, the central one, III. i. 3. 19. 熱中, to burn at heart, V. i. 1. 5. 中士, an officer of the middle class, V. ii. 2. In the same chapter, 中 simply, of the middle quality. (3) A mean, average, III. i. 3. 7. (4) The Mean, IV. ii. 20. 2. To keep the Mean, IV. ii. 7. (5) 中天下而立, to stand in the centre of the nation, VII. i. 21. 2; compare 41. 3; 26. 3; ii. 37. 2. (6) 中國, the Middle Kingdom, III. i. 4. 7, 12; ii. 9. 3: VI. ii. 10. 5.

中 *chung* The 4th tone. To hit the mark, II. i. 7. 5: V. ii. 1. 7. 中禮, VII. ii. 33. 2.

THE 3RD RADICAL, 丶.

丹 *tan* (1) 丹朱, the name of Yâo's son, V. i. 6. 2. (2) The name of 白圭, VI. ii. 11. 1.

主 *chû* (1) To count—be counted—as the principal thing, II. ii. 2. 4. (2) To preside over, V. i. 5. 6. (3) Being a host, V. ii. 3. 5: VII. ii. 24. 2. (4) To make one's host, i.e. to lodge with, V. i. 8. 1, 2. Observe pars. 3, 4, 其所爲主 and 其所主.

THE 4TH RADICAL, 丿.

乃 *nâi* (1) To be, I. i. 7. 8, 9; ii. 4. 6: V. i. 4. 1. (2) An initial particle, of varying power,—seeing this, but, now, &c., I. ii. 15. 1: II.

i. 2. 22: IV. ii. 28. 7: VI. i. 6. 5; ii. 6. 6. Observe 乃...乃, VI. i. 6. 5.

久 *chiû* A long time, for a long time; to be a long time, II. i. 1. 3, 8; 2. 22; ii. 14. 3: III. ii. 9. 2: V. i. 6. 2; ii. 1. 4: VII. i. 30. 2.

之 *chih* (1) Of, = the sign of the possessive case. But it would often be very harsh to translate it by *of*, I. i. 1. 4; 3. 1, 3, 4, *et al., saepissime*. The regent follows the 之, and the regimen precedes it. They may be respectively a noun, a phrase, or a larger clause. 之 followed by 於 is very common in Mencius; e.g. VII. ii. 24. (2) Him, her, it, them. *Passim*. (3) It is often difficult to determine the antecedent to 之. It has to be gathered from the context; and sometimes 之 merges in the verb, making it an emphatic neuter, or = a passive; e.g. I. i. 3. 2; 6. 6; 7. 4: IV. ii. 14; 15: VII. i. 8. 1; 5; 13. 3; 30. 1. (4) 有 and 有之, as in (2), but also impersonally, = there is..., I. ii. 3. 1; 8. 1, *et saepe*. So, the negative 未之有, where the 未 attracts the 之 to itself. The same is to be observed of 莫. (5) We have 作之君, I. ii. 3. 7; 爲之辭, II. ii. 9. 4; 與之處, III. i. 4. 1; and other similar expressions, where we may suppose two objectives, the 之 being = to, for, &c., him, it, them. Observe especially 莫之死, I. ii. 12. 1, and 與之, 示之, V. i. 5. (6) 之謂, is called, or is what is called. 此之謂, II. i. 4. 6. We might reduce this to (1), ... is the saying *of* this. But this cannot be done where 謂 is followed by an adjective or other words, e.g. VII. ii. 25. 謂之 comes under (2), compare 名之, IV. i. 2. 4; 何服之有, IV. ii. 3. 4; 何卿之間, V. ii. 9. 1; and 是之取爾, IV. ii. 18. 2. (7) 如之何, how, I. ii. 6. 1; 14. 1, *et saepe*. (8) Observe 草尙之風, III. i. 2. 4. (9) In names, 之奇, V. i. 9. 2; 之師 and 之他, IV. ii. 24. 2; 盈之, III. ii. 8. 1; 子之, II. ii. 8. 1; and 夷之, III. i. 5. 1, 2. (10) As a verb. To go, or come, to, V. i. 5. 7; 6. 1; 9. 3, *et al., saepe*.

乍 *chá* Suddenly, II. i. 6. 3.

乎 *hû* (1) A particle of interrogation. Found alone; preceded by another interrogation, as 焉, 惡, 惡乎, by 不亦, and by 況, I. i. 1. 2; 2. 1: II. ii. 9. 2: III. i. 2. 2: IV. ii. 27. 3: V. i. 7. 7; ii. 5. 3: VI. ii. 1. 3, 8, *et al., saepe*. Also in indirect interrogation, II. ii. 2. 3: IV. ii. 32. 1. (2) A particle of exclamation, I. i. 7. 7; ii. 5. 4: III. i. 4. 11, *et al*. Preceded by 哉, VII. i. 36. 1; followed by 哉, I. i. 8. 4; preceded by 何 and followed by 哉, II. ii. 2. 6. (3) Partly interrogative and partly exclamatory. Alone; preceded by 其, 固, and 必也, I. ii. 1. 1, 3; 2. 2: III. ii. 9. 8: VI. ii. 6. 1: VII. ii. 37. 2, 7, *et al*. Immediately preceded by 矣, II. i. 2. 18, 19. ? by 也, III. ii. 10. 6. (4) A preposition, —after verbs, and adjectives, = in, of, to, from, &c., I. ii. 12. 2; 15. 1: II. i. 3. 10; 2. 28; ii. 11. 3: III. i. 3. 3, 7, *et al., saepe*. Observe 在乎, VI. i. 19. 1. (5) Than, in comparisons, II. ii. 2. 4; i. 8. 5. (6) Observe 有時乎, V. ii. 5. 1; 云乎, V. ii. 7. 4; 盍歸乎來, IV. i. 13. 1; 有乎爾, VII. ii. 38. 4.

乏 *fâ* Needy. 窮乏者, VI. i. 10. 7, 8. 空乏, to impoverish, VI. ii. 15. 2.

乘 *shăng* To mount upon, III. i. 3. 2. To take advantage of, II. i. 1. 9.

乘 *shăng* In 3rd tone. (1) A carriage, I. ii. 16. 1. 萬乘, 千乘, 百乘, 之國, the kingdom, a great State, the possessions of the chief of a large clan, I. i. 1. 4, *et al*. The classifier of carriages, III. ii. 4. 1: IV. ii. 2. 1: VII. ii. 34. 2. (2) To drive a carriage, III. ii. 1. 4. (3) A team of four horses, V. i. 9. 2. (4) A set of four arrows, IV. ii. 24. 2. (5) Name of a Book, IV. ii. 21. 2. (6) 乘田, name of Confucius's office, when in charge of the public fields, V. ii. 5. 4.

THE 5TH RADICAL, 乙.

九 *chiû* Nine, VII. i. 29: VI. ii. 2. 2, *et al*. 九—, a ninth, I. ii. 5. 3. But in III. i. 3. 15, 九— refers to a mode of territorial division.

乞 *ch'i* To beg, IV. ii. 33. 1. 乞人, a beggar, VI. i. 10. 6.

也 *yé* (1) A final particle, used both at the end of sentences, and of clauses, or separate members of a sentence. Sometimes we miss it, where it might be; and sometimes it might be dispensed with, I. i. 2. 2, 3; 3. 1, 2, 3, 4, *et passim*. (2) After the adverb 今; after proper names (though

孟子

rarely in Mencius), and very often after a clause in the first member of a sentence: it = *quoad*, *now*, or may often be left untranslated. In these cases, it is often, but far from always, followed by other particles, I. i. 3. 1; 7. 8, 21, 22: IV. i. 14. 1, *et passim*. (3) As correlate of 者, concluding the explanation of the character or sentiment which precedes 者. The 者, however, is often wanting, I. ii. 4. 2, 3; 10. 2; 11. 1: II. i. 2. 9: III. i. 3. 6, 10, *et saepe*. (4) 者也 is found at the end of sentences, sometimes preceded by 者 and sometimes not. 者, however, may generally be explained independent of the 也, I. i. 1. 5; ii. 3. 2, 5, *et saepe*. (5) 也者 in the first member of a sentence resumes a word or subject, and the explanation or account of it follows, II. i. 9. 1: VII. ii. 37. 9, *et al.* We find 也者, however, at the commencement of a chapter, where no discourse is resumed, VII. ii. 16. Observe VI. i. 8. 2. (6) It is often interrogative, following 何, 惡, 在, &c., I. i. 8. 1; 4. 5; ii. 1. 6, 7; 4. 4, *et saepe*.

乾 *kan* 旱乾, dry, drought, VII. ii. 14. 4.

亂 *lwan* To confound, III. i. 4. 18: VI. ii. 15. 2: VII. ii. 10. 亂 = to be confounded with, VII. ii. 37. 12. Rebellious, III. ii. 9. 11. To be in confusion; a state of confusion, II. i. 2. 22: III. ii. 9. 2, 5: IV. ii. 29. 2: V. ii. 1. 1, 2: VII. ii. 12. 2.

THE 6TH RADICAL, 亅.

予 *yü* I, me, we, my, I. i. 2. 4; 7. 9; ii. 16. 3: II. i. 1. 3; 2. 16, 26; 4. 3, *et al.*, *saepe*.

事 *shih* (1) Affairs; doings, achievements; business, I. i. 7. 1, 2: VII. i. 33. 1, 3; ii. 28. 1, *et al.*, *saepe*. 無非事者, ... were for real business, I. ii. 4. 5. 必有事焉, there must be the practice of ..., II. i. 2. 16. 無事, without doing service, III. ii. 4. 2; without difficulty, IV. ii. 26. 2. 以爲...事, to make—one's business, V. i. 3. 1. 好事者, one who is fond of strange things, V. i. 8. 1; 9. 1. Compare 事 and 功 in III. ii. 4. 3, and VI. ii. 6. 5. (2) To serve—parents, a sovereign, a teacher, a greater State, &c., I. i. 5. 3; 7. 21, 22, *et al.*, *saepe*. 以大事小, I. ii. 3. 1, 2.

THE 7TH RADICAL, 二.

二 *r* (1) Two; the second, III. i. 3. 17; 5. 3, *et al.* (2) 二三子, see 三, (3). But 二三策 = two or three passages, VII. ii. 3. 2.

于 *yü* (1) A preposition = by, to, in, on, for, *saepe*. It occurs commonly in quotations from the older classics. Mencius himself prefers 於, though he does also use 于. (2) In the double surname, 淳于, IV. i. 17. 1: VI. ii. 6. 1, 5.

云 *yün* (1) Says. In a quotation, V. i. 4. 1. Observe V. ii. 3. 4. (2) 云爾, closing a sentence, or the member of a sentence. It is difficult to translate, and Wang Yin-chih regards it simply as a final particle, II. ii. 2. 4: III. ii. 5. 7: IV. ii. 24. 1: VII. i. 39. 2. So 云乎, V. ii. 7. 4.

五 *wû* Five. *Saepe*. 五 = the fifth, IV. ii. 30. 2. Adverbially, = five times, VI. ii. 6. 2.

井 *ching* (1) A well, II. i. 6. 3: III. i. 5. 3: V. i. 2. 3: VII. i. 29. 市井之臣, a scholar living unemployed in a city or market-place, V. ii. 7. 1. (2) A system of dividing the ground on a plan of nine squares, III. i. 3. 13, 18, 19.

亟 *chi* In haste, quickly; to be in haste, I. i. 2. 3: III. i. 3. 2.

亟 *ch'i* The 2nd tone. Frequently, IV. ii. 18. 1: V. ii. 6. 4, 5; 7. 4: VII. i. 8. 1.

THE 8TH RADICAL, 亠.

亡 *wang* (1) To expire, die, I. i. 2. 4: VI. ii. 6. 4. 死亡, I. i. 7. 21, 22: IV. i. 3. 4; 9. 5. To be utterly lost; to perish, I. ii. 4. 6, 7, 8: IV. i. 2. 4; 3. 2; 7. 1; 8. 1; ii. 21. 1: V. i. 9. 3: VI. i. 8. 4; 16. 3; 18. 2; ii. 15. 4. 亡 = not to be found, gone away, I. ii. 7. 1. (2) To cause to die or perish, VI. i. 8. 2. (3) Not at home, III. ii. 7. 3.

亡 *wû* Used for 無, not being, not having, IV. i. 19. 3; ii. 28. 7. Used actively, and = to disown, VII. i. 34.

交 *chiâo* (1) Intercourse; to have intercourse with, I. ii. 3. 1: V. ii. 4. 3, 4: VI. i. 15. 2; ii. 5. 1: VII. ii. 18. 交 = mutually, I. i. 1. 4. 交易, to deal with and exchange, III. i. 4. 5. 交際, intercourse, and its expression by presents, V. ii. 4. 1. To be intermingled, to cross one another, III. i. 4. 7. 內交於..., to seek the favour of ..., II. i. 6. 3. 交 = to treat as, VII. i. 37. 1. (2) A man's name, VI. ii. 2. 1, 2, 6.

亦 *yi* Also. *Saepe.* It is difficult sometimes, and doubtful whether we ought, to bring out the *also* in another language;—as in I. i. 1. 2, 3; 7. 17: II. ii. 10. 6, *et al.* 不亦...乎, 亦...而已 are common phraseologies, I. ii. 2. 2: II. ii. 9. 3: VI. ii. 6. 2: VII. i. 39. 2. Observe 抑亦, II. ii. 4. 3: III. ii. 10. 3. 亦不, where 亦 = still, III. ii. 6. 1: VII. ii. 19. 3; and 則亦 = yea, VII. ii. 38. 4.

亥 *hái* A surname, V. ii. 3. 4.

享 *hsiang* (1) To present an offering; an offering, VI. ii. 5. 4. 5. (2) To accept an offering—as a sacrifice, V. i. 5. 6.

京 *ching* A capital, IV. i. 7. 5.

亮 *liang* To have faith, VI. ii. 12.

亳 *po* The name of T'ang's capital, referred to the present department of Kwei-tĕh in Ho-nan, III. ii. 5. 2: V. i. 6. 5; 7. 9.

亶 *t'an* The name of king T'âi, one of the ancestors of king Wăn, I. ii. 5. 5.

THE 9TH RADICAL, 人.

人 *jĕn* or *zăn* (1) A man, men; other men. *Passim.* 人 = humanity, man's nature, VI. i. 1. 2; 2. 3: VII. ii. 16. 人人, all men, or each man, IV. i. 11; ii. 2. 4, *et al.* (2) It indicates officers and rulers, in distinction from 民, the people, I. i. 2. 3: II. i. 1. 13, *et al.* So, perhaps, VII. ii. 28. —人, with reference to the sovereign, I. ii. 8. 7. (3) Following names of States it = native, natives, people. So 齊人, 魯人, &c. &c. But 殷人 and 周人, III. i. 3. 6, are different, meaning the founders of the Yin and Châu dynasties. So 國人, the people of the State, or merely a common man, I. ii. 7. 4, 5: II. ii. 8. 2; 10. 3: IV. i. 11; ii. 3. 3; 24. 2, *et al.* (4) With other characters, it forms concrete substantives, especially nouns expressing office or profession. We have 匠人 and 玉人, I. ii. 9; 矢人 and 函人, II. i. 7; 廩人, V. ii. 6. 5; 虞人, V. ii. 7. 7; 館人, VII. ii. 30; 校人, V. i. 2. 4. (5) Observe also 罪人; 狄人; 嬖人; 窮人; 鄉人; 族人; 野人, which means both country people, and uncultivated people; 良人 = husband, IV. ii. 33. 1; 侍人, V. i. 8. 1; 聖人, II. i. 2. 17, 20, 22, 25, 28; ii. 9. 3: III. i. 4. 2, 8, 13; ii. 9. 5, 10, 14: IV. i. 1. 5; 2. 1: V. i. 7. 7: VI. i. 7. 3, 8: VII. i. 23. 3; 24; 38; ii. 15; 24. 2; 38. 4; 寡人, the humble 'I' of the prince of a State, I. i. 3. 1; 4. 1; 5. 1; 7. 4, *et al.*; 夫人, the wife of a prince, III. ii. 3. 3; 大人, III. i. 4. 6: IV. i. 20; ii. 6; 11; 12: VII. i. 19. 4; 33. 3; ii. 34. 1; 小人, II. ii. 12. 7: III. i. 2. 4; 4. 6, *et al.*; 庶人, the masses, the people, I. i. 1. 4: II. ii. 7. 2: V. ii. 2. 6, 7, 8, *et al.*; 門人, disciples, III. i. 4. 13: VII. ii. 29; 人牧, 人君, 人臣, 人子, 人弟, but the characters here are possibly not in apposition, but in regimen. (6) 爲人, VII. ii. 35.

什 *shih* 什一, a tenth part, a tithe, III. i. 3. 6, 15; ii. 8. 1.

仁 *zăn* Benevolence, benevolent, to be benevolent. *Passim.* Mencius does not use the term for 'perfect virtue,' as Confucius does, though it may sometimes have that meaning. In VII. ii. 24. 2, *love* seems the proper rendering.

仇 *ch'âu* To show oneself an enemy to, III. ii. 5. 2.

今 *chin* Now, the present, modern time: also, in the same way as our logical use of *now*, in discoursing. *Passim.* We find 今也 and 今夫; 今日, 今時, 當今之時, and 當今之世. 今而後, from this time forth, I. ii. 12. 2, *et al.*

介 *chieh* (1) Firm purpose, VII. i. 28. (2) Used for 芥, a stalk of the mustard plant, a straw, V. i. 7. 2.

介 *chieh* In the 4th tone. 介然, suddenly, VII. i. 21.

仕 *shih* To take—be in—office, II. i. 2. 22; ii. 14. 1: III. ii. 3. 1, 5, 6, *et al.* Observe 當仕, V. ii. 7. 9. 仕者, officers, I. i. 7. 18; ii. 5. 3. So 仕 alone, II. ii. 8. 1.

他 *t'â* (1) Other, another, I. i. 7. 9: V. i. 3. 2; ii. 4. 3: VII. ii. 17. 他日, another day, other days. It may mean formerly, next day, and afterwards, I. ii. 1. 2; 16. 1: II. ii. 4. 4; 10. 3: III. i. 2. 4; 4. 13; 5. 2, 4; ii. 10. 5: IV. i. 14. 1: VI. ii. 5. 2. 無他, nothing else, for no other reason, I. i. 7. 12; ii. 1. 6, 7: II. ii. 2. 9: VI. i. 11. 4; ii. 8. 2: VII. i. 15. 3; 25. 3; 36. 3. So, 豈有

孟子

他哉, I. ii. 10. 4: VI. i. 14. 1. 言他, spoke of something else, I. ii. 6. 3. 之他, went elsewhere, IV. ii. 33. 1. (2) Read *t'o*, a name, IV. ii. 24. 2.

仞 *zăn* A measure of eight cubits, VII. ii. 34. 2.

代 *tâi* (1) Alternate, one after another, III. ii. 9. 5. For, instead of, V. ii. 2. 6, 7, 8. (2) 三代, the three dynasties;—Hsiâ, Shang, and Châu, III. i. 2. 2; 3. 10: IV. i. 3. 1. (3) A name, 陳代, III. ii. 1. 1.

令 *ling* To employ, 使令, to be employed, I. i. 7. 16.

令 *ling* The 4th tone. (1) An order; to order, I. ii. 11. 4: IV. i. 7. 2. (2) Good, VI. i. 17. 3.

以 *î* (1) To take, to use. But our idiom requires, for the most part, that it be translated as a preposition,—*by, at, with, because of, according to*, &c. It precedes the principal verb of the sentence, as in I. i. 2. 3, 文王以民力爲臺, 'king Wăn used the people's strength to make his tower,' or 'made his tower with the people's strength;' or in V. i. 5. 1, 堯以天下與舜, 'Yâo took the kingdom and gave it to Shun;' or simply, 'Yâo gave the kingdom to Shun.' It follows the principal verb, and then its prepositional force is more apparent, e.g. I. i. 4. 2, 殺人以梃, 'to kill a man with a stick.' We might indeed translate, 'to kill a man, using a stick.' Its regimen sometimes precedes it, e.g. V. i. 7. 2, —介不以與人,一介不以取諸人, 'one straw he would not have taken and given to men, or taken and received from men,' or simply, 'he would neither have given nor taken a single straw.' This position of the regimen is for the sake of emphasis. Examples, of the first two usages especially, occur very frequently. Julien argues (see the 'Treatise on Four Chinese Characters,' appended to his Translation of Mencius) that in many cases it is merely = a sign of the accusative case. And it is difficult sometimes to give any other force to the 以, as in II. i. 1. 5: III. i. 4. 10: IV. ii. 28, *et al.*, yet a peculiar significancy may be traced in it. Observe 所以, that by, for, from, which,—a force sometimes sustained by 以 alone; 是以, hence; and 何以, whereby, or wherefore. 以 is found without any regimen, joined to 告, I. ii. 12. 2, *et al., saepe*. 有以 and 無以 are abbreviations for 有所以, 無所以, I. i. 5. 2, 3, *et al.* In a sentence which has no accessory, 以 = to use, to act, according to, &c., e.g. V. ii. 1. 3. 以爲, and often with a regimen of 以 intervening, frequently means to take to be, to consider, to be considered. But by no means always. Sometimes also the 以 is omitted. (2) It often = the conjunction because, II. i. 2. 15, *et al.* (3) To, so as to;—often forming, with a verb following, our infinitive. Sometimes the 以 = 'wherewith to,' 'and thereby,' I. i. 1. 2; 7. 12, 15, 16, 21, 22, *et al., saepe*. To this belong 以來, 以下, and 以至. (4) It is often used after 可, forming our potential mood, and = the *to*, which is suppressed after our auxiliaries. *Passim.* (5) Used as = 已, 'to stop,' I. i. 7. 2. (6) Observe 明以教我, I. i. 7. 19; 樂以天下, I. ii. 4. 3; 以美然, II. ii. 7. 1; 以寸, IV. ii. 7; and some other sporadic cases.

仲 *chung* The second of brothers. It is used in designations, V. i. 6. 5. 仲尼, the designation of Confucius, I. i. 4. 6; 7. 2, *et al.* It follows the surname, or what is equivalent to it, without any other character, and then may be taken as = the name, II. ii. 2. 3:—II. i. 1. 8:—II. i. 1. 1, 2, 3, 4, 5; ii. 2. 8, 10:—V. ii. 3. 2:—III. ii. 10. 1, 2, 3, 5, 6: VII. i. 24.

仰 *yang* To look up to, II. i. 5. 6; ii. 9. 4: IV. ii. 20. 5. 仰望, IV. ii. 33. Used adverbially with the correlate 俯, = above, below, I. i. 7. 21: VII. i. 20. 3.

任 *zăn* (1) A charge, office, VI. ii. 15. 2. 任 = business, purpose, I. ii. 9. 1. A burden, VI. ii. 2. 3. (2) As a verb. To charge, to burden, V. i. 7. 6; ii. 1. 2. Observe IV. i. 14. 3, and 聖之任者, V. ii. 1. 5.

任 *zăn* The 2nd tone. (1) A burden, = baggage, III. i. 4. 13. (2) The name of a small State, VI. ii. 1. 1; 5. 季任, the younger brother of the chief of Zăn, VI. ii. 5. 1.

伊 *î* A surname. 伊尹, the minister of T'ang, II. i. 2. 22, 23; ii. 2. 8, 10, *et al.* 伊訓, the name of a Book in the Shû-ching, V. i. 7. 9.

伋 *ch'i* The name of Confucius's grandson, IV. ii. 31. 2: V. ii. 6. 4.

伍 *wû* Five men in rank or file. 伍 = ranks, II. ii. 4. 1, 2.

伏 *fû* To be lying down, I. i. 2. 3.

伐 *fâ* (1) To smite, to attack; 伐 = to punish, I. ii. 8. 1; 10. 1, 4; 11. 1: II. ii. 8. 1, 2: III. ii. 5. 1, 6; 9. 6: IV. i. 8. 4: V. i. 7. 6; 9. 2: VII. ii. 2. 2; 3. 3; 4. 4. 討而不伐, VI. ii. 7. 2. (2) To hew down, to lop,—applied to trees, and to the mind, VI. i. 8. 1, 2.

休 *hsiû* (1) Happiness; to be happy, I. ii. 4. 5: III. ii. 5. 5. (2) The name of a place, II. ii. 14. 1.

伯 *po* or *pâi* (1) The eldest of brothers, 伯兄, VI. i. 5. 3. (2) A title of nobility, V. ii. 2. 3, 4. So 西伯, IV. i. 13. 1: VII. i. 22. 1, 3. (3) In the designation 伯夷, II. i. 2. 22, 23; 9. 1, 3, *et al.*, *saepe.* (4) Must be used for 佰, a hundred, III. i. 4. 18.

似 *sze* and *shih* As; to be like to, I. i. 6. 2: II. i. 2. 6: VII. i. 26. 3; 41. 1; ii. 37. 11. 相似, like one another, similar, II. ii. 2. 5: VI. i. 7. 3, 4, 5, 6. To be like what is right, II. ii. 5. 1. 似者, a semblance, VII. ii. 37. 12.

位 *wei* (1) Position, status, i. e. of dignity, IV. i. 1. 7; 12. 1: V. i. 5. 7; ii. 2. 3, *et al.*, *saepe.* 在位 is frequent. 正位, the correct place, i. e. propriety, III. ii. 2. 3. 天位, all *legitimate* dignities, V. ii. 3. 4. 易位 = to dethrone, V. ii. 9. 1. (2) Position, place, III. i. 2. 4: IV. ii. 27. 1, 3.

佑 *yû* To assist, III. ii. 9. 6.

何 *ho* (1) What, why, what kind of, I. i. 1. 3, 6, *et al.*, *saepe.* 何也, 何與, 何哉, at the beginning or end of sentences, generally = why is this? how is it? I. i. 3. 1; 7. 10; ii. 16. 1. But sometimes 何也 simply = is or was what? VI. i. 7. 8; ii. 6. 2, *et al.* In VI. i. 9. 2, 何哉 = is of what avail? Other characters sometimes come between 何 and the particles, and with the same difference of usage. 何以, whereby, what to, I. i. 1. 4, *et al.*, *saepe.* 何由, what from? how? I. i. 7. 4. 何爲, what do? why? I. ii. 5. 4: VII. ii. 36. 2. But observe 何爲也哉, V. ii. 7. 3. 何之, where are you going? VI. ii. 4. 2. (2) 如何, generally with 之 between, = what, what is to be done? Difficulty, surprise, or indignation is generally implied, but not always. The phrase 如之何則可, = how is the exigency to be met? is common, I. i. 4. 6; 5. 1; ii. 6. 1, 2, 3: V. ii. 2. 1, *et al.*, *saepe.* Other words are found also between 如 and 何, and then the phrase = what has . . . to do with—? I. ii. 14. 3, *et al.* (3) 何如, what sort of? of what nature? in what manner? At the end of a sentence, 何如 = what do you think of? What shall be said? I. i. 3. 2; 7. 3: VII. ii. 37. 3, 8, *et al.*, *saepe.* (4) 何有, what difficulty is there? I. ii. 5. 5: VI. ii. 1. 4, *et al.*

余 *yü* Me, III. ii. 9. 3.

佚 *yi* (1) Ease, enjoyment, VII. i. 12; ii. 24. (2) To be without office, in obscurity, 遺佚, II. i. 9. 2: V. ii. 1. 3.

作 *tso* (1) To rise up, arise, II. i. 1. 8, 11: III. ii. 9. 5, 7, 9, 10, *et al.* To be aroused, to rise, to act, VI. ii. 15. 3. 我疾作, I have become ill, IV. ii. 24. 2. (2) To make, to form; to cause to be, I. i. 4. 6; ii. 3. 7; 4. 6, 10: II. i. 4. 6: IV. i. 8. 5. To be made, IV. ii. 21. 1.

佞 *ning* Glib-tonguedness, VII. ii. 37. 12.

使 *shih* (1) To cause, to make to; to make to be, I. i. 3. 3; 4. 6; 5. 3, 4; 7. 18, 21, *et al.*, *saepe.* Observe 行或使之, I. ii. 16. 3. 使 = to send (once, we have the addition of 來), II. ii. 2. 1; 6. 1, *et al.*, *saepe.* (2) To employ, to command; no other verb following, II. i. 2. 22; 5. 1, *et al.* (3) 如使 = if, supposing that, II. ii. 10. 5: V. ii. 6. 5: VI. i. 7. 5. Without the 如, VI. i. 9. 3; ii. 14. 4.

使ˋ *shih* The 4th tone. To be commissioned, I. i. 7. 16. 使ˋ者, a messenger, V. ii. 6. 4.

來 *lâi* (1) To come, I. i. 1. 2; 2. 3, *et al.*, *saepe.* 以來 and 而來, downwards, II. i. 2. 23, 27, 28; 5. 6; ii. 13. 4: VII. ii. 38. 4. Observe 盍歸乎來, IV. i. 13. 1, *et al.* (2) The coming, next, III. ii. 8. 1, 2, 3.

來ˋ *lâi* The 4th tone. To lead on, III. i. 4. 8.

侈 *ch'ih* Extravagance, wild license, I. i. 7. 20.

侍 *shih* To be by, in attendance on, II. ii. 10. 2. 侍人, an attendant, with a bad meaning, V. i. 8. 1, 2. 侍妾, attendant girls, concubines, VII. ii. 34. 6.

孟子

供 *kung* To supply, to furnish, I. i. 7. 16: III. ii. 3. 3; 5. 2: V. ii. 4. 6.

侮 *wû* To despise, insult, II. i. 4. 3: IV. i. 8. 4; 16.

侯 *hâu* (1) A title of nobility, V. ii. 2. 3, 4. A prince,—following the name of the State, I. ii. 16. 3: V. i. 8. 3. 諸侯, the princes of the kingdom. *Saepe.* It often = one of the princes, a prince, II. i. 2. 4: III. i. 2, *et al.* Observe I. ii. 4. 6, where the 'Daily Readings' has 小國諸侯. (2) An introductory particle, i.q. 惟, IV. i. 7. 5.

侵 *ch'in* To make incursions on; to attack stealthily, I. ii. 14. 2; 15. 1: III. ii. 5. 6: IV. ii. 24. 2.

使 *p'ien* 便嬖, attendants and favourites, I. i. 7. 16.

係 *hsi* To bind, 係累, I. ii. 11. 3.

俊 *tsun* A man of distinction, 俊傑, II. i. 5. 1: VI. ii. 7. 2.

俑 *yung* Wooden images of the dead, I. i. 4. 6.

俗 *sû* Manners, practices, customs, II. i. 1. 8: VI. ii. 6. 5; 9. 3. 流俗, current customs (with a bad meaning), VII. ii. 37. 11. 世俗, the manners of the age, I. ii. 1. 2: IV. ii. 30. 2.

保 *pâo* (1) To protect and love, I. i. 7. 3, 4, 10, 12; ii. 3. 2, 3: II. i. 6. 7: III. i. 5. 3. (2) To preserve, IV. i. 3. 3.

俟 *sze* To wait for, II. ii. 2. 5: V. ii. 7. 9: VII. i. 1. 3; ii. 33. 3.

信 *hsin* (1) Truthfulness, fidelity, I. i. 5. 3: III. i. 4. 8: VI. i. 16. 1: VII. i. 32; ii. 27. 11, 12. True, real, V. i. 9. 1: VII. ii. 25. 1, 2, 4; 33. 2. (2) To believe; to have confidence in (it may be to obey or follow, as principles; or to employ, as officers), I. ii. 11. 2: IV. i. 1. 8: V. i. 2. 4: VII. i. 34; ii. 3. 1; 12. 1. To be believed; to obtain the confidence of, IV. i. 12. 1; ii. 11. (3) As an adverb, really, truly, II. i. 5. 6: III. i. 5. 3: V. i. 2. 1; 4. 2: VI. i. 2. 2.

信 *shăn* In 1st tone. To stretch out straight, to straighten, VI. i. 12. 1.

修 See 脩.

俯 *fû* To stoop, used adverbially, with the correlate 仰, = below, I. i. 7. 21, 22: VII. i. 20. 3.

俱 *chü* Together; = both, VI. i. 9. 3: VII. i. 20. 2.

倉 *ts'ang* A granary; a storehouse for grain generally. Commonly found along with 廩, a granary for rice, I. ii. 12. 2: III. i. 4. 3: V. i. 1. 3; 2. 3; ii. 6. 6. Used as a verb, I. ii. 5. 4. (2) A name, 臧倉, I. ii. 16. 1, 3.

倍 *pei* (1) To rebel against, revolt from, III. i. 4. 12, 14. (2) Double, as much again as, I. ii. 11. 3: III. i. 4. 18: IV. i. 14. 1: V. ii. 2. 6, 7, 8: VI. ii. 6. 7. In this second sense, the character is aspirated, and in the 2nd tone, in the Canton dialect.

倒 *tâo* Inverted, upside down, II. i. 1. 13.

倦 *chüan* To be tired, weary, II. i. 2. 19: VI. i. 16. 1.

倪 *yi* Children and youths, I. ii. 11. 4.

倫 *lun* Always used with reference to 人倫, the relationships of human society, II. ii. 2. 4: III. i. 3. 10; 4. 8: IV. i. 2. 1; ii. 19. 2: V. i. 2. 1: VI. ii. 10. 5.

偃 *yen* To bend, III. i. 2. 4.

假 *chiâ* (1) To feign, pretend to, II. i. 3. 1: VII. i. 30. 1. (2) To borrow, V. i. 9. 2: VI. ii. 2. 6: VII. i. 30. 1.

偕 *chieh* Together with, I. i. 2. 3, 4. As a verb, II. i. 9. 2.

偪 *pi* To press upon, III. i. 4. 7.

側 *chai* Side, the side, II. i. 9. 2; ii. 9. 3: V. ii. 1. 3.

傑 *chieh* A heroic character, 俊傑, II. i. 5. 1: VI. ii. 7. 2. 豪傑, III. i. 4. 12: VII. i. 10. 1.

傅 *fû* (1) A tutor (an official title), VII. i. 39. 3. To act as tutor, to teach, III. ii. 6. 1. (2) 傅說, an ancient statesman, VI. ii. 15. 1.

備 *pei* All-complete; to be prepared, ready, III. i. 4. 6; ii. 3. 3: V. i. 1. 3; ii. 6. 6: VII. i. 4. 1; 33. 3.

傳 *ch'wan* (1) To transmit, hand down (used both actively and passively), I. i. 7. 2: IV. ii. 28. 7: V. i. 6. 1; 9. 3. (2) To communicate, deliver, as an order, a pledge, II. i. 1. 12: V. ii. 7. 1.

傳 *chwan* The 4th tone. Records, a Record, I. ii. 2. 1; 8. 1: III. ii. 3. 1. Observe 以傳食於諸侯, III. ii. 4. 1. The dictionary defines this use of 傳 by 續.

傷 *shang* To hurt, wound, II. i. 7. 1: IV. ii. 31. 1. Wounded, IV. ii. 20. 3. 傷 = to be contrary to, IV. ii. 23. 無傷, there is no harm, it does not matter, I. i. 7. 8: VII. ii. 19. 2. So, 何傷哉, III. ii. 10. 4.

僕 *p'o* (1) A charioteer, driver, IV. ii. 24. 2. (2) 僕僕爾, an adverb, in a troubled manner, V. ii. 6. 5.

僞 *wei* Deceit; deceitfully, III. i. 4. 17, 18: V. i. 2. 4.

儀 *i* (1) Ceremonies, demonstrations of respect, VI. ii. 5. 4. (2) A name, 張儀, III. ii. 2. 1. 公明儀, III. i. 1. 4; ii. 8. 1; 9. 9: IV. ii. 24. 1. (3) 公儀, a double surname, VI. ii. 6. 3.

億 *yi* A hundred thousand, IV. i. 7. 5.

儉 *chien* Economical, III. i. 3. 4: IV. i. 16. Niggardly to, II. ii. 7. 5. To be limited to, only to amount to, VI. ii. 8. 6.

儛 *wú* 朝儛, the name of a place, I. ii. 4. 4.

儒 *zû* 儒 and 儒者, the learned, the followers of Confucius, the orthodox, III. i. 5. 3: VII. ii. 26. 1.

優 *yû* More than sufficient, VI. ii. 13. 6.

儲 *ch'û* The surname of a minister of Ch'î, IV. ii. 32: VI. ii. 5. 1, 2, 3, 6.

THE 10TH RADICAL, 儿.

元 *yüan* (1) Used for the head, III. ii. 1. 2: V. ii. 7. 5. 元士, head officers, a name appropriate to scholars of the first class in the royal domain, V. ii. 2. 5. (2) A name, 曾元, IV. i. 19. 3.

允 *yün* To believe, accord with, V. i. 4. 4.

兄 *hsiung* An elder brother, II. ii. 9. 3: III. i. 5. 3, *et al., saepe.* 伯兄, the eldest brother, VI. i. 5. 3. 父兄, fathers and elder brothers; elder relatives, I. i. 5. 3; ii. 11. 3, *et al., saepe.* 兄弟, brothers, I. i. 7. 12; ii. 1. 6, *et al., saepe.* Embracing cousins, V. ii. 3. 1. 兄 = sisters, V. i. 8. 2.

充 *ch'ung* (1) To fill; to fill up, develop, carry out, II. i. 6. 7: III. ii. 10. 6: V. ii. 4. 5: VI. ii. 9. 1: VII. ii. 25. 5, 6; 31. 2, 3. 充塞, to stop up, III. ii. 9. 9. Full, I. ii. 12. 2. The filling up, II. i. 2. 9. (2) A surname, II. ii. 7. 1; 13. 1.

兆 *chào* A prognostic, = a trial, V. ii. 4. 6.

先 *hsien* (1) First (adverb and adjective); before (preposition); former, V. i. 9. 3; ii. 4. 6: VI. i. 5. 3; 7. 5, 8; 15. 2; ii. 15. 2: VII. i. 46. 1: II. i. 2. 2. 先君, former princes, III. i. 2. 3. 先王, the former (ancient) sovereigns, I. ii. 1. 2; 4. 4, 8, *et al.* 先生, our master, you, master, IV. i. 24. 2; ii. 31. 1: VI. ii. 4. 2, 4, 5, 6. 先子, my grandfather, II. i. 1. 3. 先知, first knowing; 先覺, first apprehending, V. i. 7. 5; ii. 1. 2. 先聖, the former sages, III. ii. 9. 10. (2) To make first or chief, I. i. 1. 4, *et al.*; 先後 generally appears as correlate. To take the initiative, I. ii. 16. 1: III. ii. 7. 3: IV. ii. 3. 3. (3) 先之, to set the example, III. i. 2. 4. 之先 = to excel him, III. i. 4. 12. Perhaps these examples, and those also under (2), should be read 先, the 4th tone.

先 *hsien* The 4th tone. To precede, VI. ii. 2. 4.

光 *kwang* Light, VII. i. 24. 2. 光 = glory, glorious, III. ii. 5. 6: VII. ii. 25. 6. Observe 用光, I. ii. 5. 4.

克 *k'o* (1) To conquer, VI. ii. 9. 2. 掊克 = grasping able ministers, VI. ii. 7. 2. (2) The name of 樂正子, I. ii. 16. 3: IV. ii. 24. 3.

免 *mien* To escape from, avoid. Followed by 於, I. i. 4. 5; 7. 21, 22. Used absolutely, or actively, I. ii. 15. 1: IV. ii. 28. 7: VI. ii. 14. 4.

兔 *t'û* A rabbit, a hare. 兔者, hare-catchers, I. ii. 2. 2.

兜 *tû* 驩兜, a minister of Shun, banished by him, V. i. 3. 2.

THE 11TH RADICAL, 入.

入 *zû* To enter, I. i. 3. 3; ii. 2. 3; 16. 2, *et al., saepe.* Used metaphorically, 入道, to go in and on to principles, VII. ii. 37. 11. Used in correlation with 出, = at home, at court, and abroad, I. i. 5. 3: III. ii. 4. 3: VI. ii. 15. 4. But in III. i. 3. 18, 出入 = going out and coming in; and in VI. i. 8. 4 they are spoken of the mind.

內 *nêi* (1) Within. A preposition, following the noun, I. i. 3. 1 (河內); 7. 17. When the noun has an adjective joined to it, a 之 precedes 內, I. ii. 2. 3; 6. 3: III. ii. 5. 3, 7, *et al.* (2) With 外, as correlate. The seclusion of the house, the harem, I. ii. 5. 5. The family, generally, II. ii. 2. 4. Internal, what is internal, within, VI. i. 4. 1, 2, 4; 5. 1, 2, 3, 5; ii. 6. 5.

內 *nâ* Used for 納. (1) To receive, III. ii. 7. 2. 內 = to force, V. i. 7. 6; ii. 1. 2.

孟子

(2) 內交, to form a friendship with, gain the favour of, II. i. 6. 3.

全 *ch'üan* To be complete, perfect, IV. i. 21.

兩 *liang* Two, a pair of, VII. ii. 22. 3.

兩 *liang* The 4th tone. A numerative for carriages, VII. ii. 4. 1.

THE 12TH RADICAL, 八.

八 *pâ* Eight, I. i. 7. 17, 24, *et al.*, *saepe.* The eighth, I. i. 6. 6: IV. ii. 18. 3.

公 *kung* (1) Public, III. i. 3. 9. 公養之仕, to take office sustained by the State, V. i. 4. 7. (2) A title of nobility, translated by *duke*, V. ii. 2. 3, 4; 3. 4; 6. 6, *et al.* 三公, the three highest officers at the royal court, VII. i. 28.—It often follows the names of States, and honorary titles of the dukes. 周公, II. i. 1. 7, *et al.*, *saepe.*—齊景公, I. ii. 4. 4, 10, *et al.*—桓公, II. ii. 2. 8, 10, *et al.*—晉平公, V. ii. 3. 4.—秦穆公, V. i. 9. 1, 3, *et al.*—魯繆公, II. ii. 11. 3, *et al.*—魯平公, I. ii. 16. 1.—滕定公, III. i. 2. 1.—滕文公, I. ii. 13. 1, *et al.*—穆公, I. ii. 12. 1.—衞靈公, V. ii. 4. 7.—衞孝公, V. ii. 4. 7.—費惠公, V. ii. 3. 3.—虞公, V. i. 9. 3. (3) Used in double surnames, 公明, V. i. 1. 2.—III. i. 1. 4, *et al.* 公孫, II. i. 1. 1, *et al.* —III. ii. 2. 1. 公都, II. ii. 5. 4: III. ii. 9. 1, *et al.* 公儀, VI. ii. 6. 3. 公輸, IV. i. 1. 1. 公行, IV. ii. 27. 1. Compare 庾公, and 尹公, IV. ii. 24. 2. (4) 公劉, and 古公亶父, ancestors of the Châu family, I. ii. 5. 4, 5. 太公 and 太公望, a minister of the kings Wăn and Wû, IV. i. 13. 1: VI. ii. 8. 6: VII. i. 22. 1; ii. 38. 3.

六 *liû* Six, II. i. 1. 8. 六律, the pitch-tubes, IV. i. 1. 1, 5. 六等, the six degrees of dignity, V. ii. 2. 3. 六師, the royal forces, VI. ii. 7. 2.

兮 *hsi* A particle, much used in poetry, IV. i. 8. 2: VII. i. 32. 1.

共 *kung* To have in common, III. i. 2. 2; 3. 10. To share, V. ii. 3. 4.

共 *kung* The 1st tone. (1) 共爲, to perform, discharge, V. i. 1. 2. (2) 共工, a name of office;—the superintendent of Works, V. i. 3. 2.

兵 *ping* Sharp weapons of war, I. i. 3. 2, 5; 5. 3; 7. 14; ii. 11. 3: II. ii. 1. 3, 4; 3. 4: IV. i. 1. 9: VI. ii. 4. 3.

其 *ch'î* The third personal pronoun; the possessive pronoun of the third person; the, that. Both singular and plural. *Passim.*

具 *chü* Completely provided with, II. i. 2. 20.

典 *tien* (1) A rule, a statute, 典刑, V. i. 6. 5. 典籍, VI. ii. 8. 5. (2) A canon. 堯典, name of a Book of the Shû-ching, V. i. 4. 1.

兼 *chien* To unite, comprehend, embrace together; together, II. i. 2. 18: IV. ii. 20. 5: VI. i. 10. 1; 14. 1; VII. i. 9. 6. Observe III. ii. 9. 11. 兼金, 'fine silver,' II. ii. 3. 1. 兼愛, Mo's principle of loving all equally, III. ii. 9. 9: VII. i. 26. 2.

THE 13TH RADICAL, 冂.

冉 *zan* A surname. 冉牛, a disciple of Confucius, II. i. 2. 18, 20.

再 *tsài* Twice, again, V. ii. 6. 4, 5: VI. ii. 7. 2, 3.

冕 *mien* A cap of full dress or ceremony, VI. ii. 6. 6.

THE 14TH RADICAL, 冖.

冠 *kwan* A cap, a bonnet, II. i. 9. 1: IV. ii. 29. 6, 7: V. ii. 1. 1. To wear a cap, III. i. 4. 4.

冠 *kwan* The 4th tone. To cap; the ceremony of capping, III. ii. 2. 2.

冢 *ch'ung* 冢宰, a prime minister, III. i. 2. 4.

THE 15TH RADICAL, 冫.

冬 *tung* Winter, VI. i. 5. 5.

况 *hwang* More properly 況. How much more,—in the concluding member of a sentence, IV. i. 14. 2. It is generally followed by 乎 at the end of the clause, V. i. 7. 7: VII. i. 36. 2. 况 is sometimes immediately preceded by 而, and in the previous clause we have the particles 且猶, 猶, 然且, and 且, II. ii. 2. 10; 9. 2: V. ii. 4. 5; 7. 3, 4 (與 for 乎), 8 (况乎 . . . 乎): VI. ii. 8. 8; 10. 6: VII. ii. 15.

冶 *yé* To melt, fuse. 冶 = a founder, III. i. 4. 5.

personal service, VII. ii. 27. 1. 竆日之力, to exert one's strength a whole day, II. ii. 12. 6. 兩馬之力, caused by a single two-horsed carriage, VII. ii. 22. 3.

功 *kung* (1) Achievement, work done, I. ii. 14. 3: II. i. 1. 3, 13: VI. ii. 6. 5. 功 = benefits, merit, I. i. 7. 10, 12: III. ii. 4. 4, 5. 通功, an interchange of the productions of labour, III. ii. 4. 3. (2) 小功, a short period of mourning, VII. i. 46. 2.

加 *chiā* To add to; to be added, VI. i. 10. 7: VII. 21. 3; 39. 4. 加少, 加多, to decrease, to increase, I. i. 8. 1. To exercise to, I. i. 7. 12: VI. ii. 6. 1: VII. i. 9. 6. To raise, appoint to; to be raised to, II. i. 2. 1: V. ii. 6. 6.

助 *chú* To help, I. ii. 8. 7; 4. 5: II. i. 2. 16; 5. 4; ii. 1. 4: III. ii. 8. 3 (N.B.)? VI. ii. 7. 2. The system of mutual aid, on which the ground was divided by the Châu dynasty, III. i. 8. 6, 7, 9, 15, 18.

勃 *po* 勃然, the appearance of being moved, or of changing countenance, V. ii. 9. 2: VI. ii. 8. 4.

勇 *yung* Valour, bravery; brave, I. ii. 8. 4, 5, 6, 7, 8: II. i. 2. 4, 5, 6, 7: III. ii. 1. 2: IV. ii. 28. 1; 30. 2: V. ii. 7. 5.

勉 *mien* To urge, 子必勉之, you must exert yourself, III. i. 8. 13.

動 *tung* To move, excite, I. ii. 11. 3. To affect others, IV. i. 12. 3. To stimulate, VI. ii. 15. 2. 動容, movements of the countenance, VII. ii. 33. 2. 動心, 不動心, to be perturbed, unperturbed, in mind, II. i. 2. 1, 2, 3, 9, 10. 勤動, = laborious toil, III. i. 8. 7.

務 *wû* To aim at, attend to chiefly, VI. ii. 8. 9: VII. i. 46. 1, 2.

勝 *shăng* (1) To conquer, be superior to, subdue, I. i. 7. 17; ii. 10. 1: II. i. 2. 5; 7. 5; ii. 1. 2, 5: VI. i. 18. 1; ii. 8. 3: VII. ii. 1. 2. (2) In a name, 戴不勝, III. ii. 6. 1.

勝 *shăng* The 1st tone. To be equal to, to sustain, I. ii. 9. 1. 勝 = to lift, VI. ii. 2. 3. 不可勝, followed by a verb, = more than can be . . ., I. i. 8. 3; ii. 12. 1: IV. i. 1. 5: VII. i. 23. 2; ii. 31. 2.

勞 *lâo* (1) To toil, III. i. 4. 6: V. i. 4. 2. To make to toil, VI. ii. 15. 2. 勞者, the toiled, I. ii. 4. 6. So 勞, in VII. i. 12, but in V. i. 1. 2, 勞 = punished. (2) Services, VII. i. 43. 2.

勞 *lâo* The 4th tone. To encourage, III. i. 4. 8.

勢 *shih* (1) Power, force, VII. i. 8: VI. i. 2. 3. (2) Opportunity, the circumstances of a case, II. i. 1. 9: IV. i. 18. 2.

勤 *ch'in* Laborious, III. i. 8. 7.

勳 *hsün* (1) Meritorious, VII. i. 43. 2. (2) 放勳, the highly Meritorious, an epithet of Yâo, III. i. 4. 8: V. i. 4. 1.

勸 *ch'üan* To advise, encourage, II. ii. 8. 2.

THE 20TH RADICAL, 勹.

勿 *wû* Do not;—prohibitive, I. i. 2. 3; 8. 4; 7. 24; ii. 5. 2; 7. 4, 5; 10. 2, 3; 15. 2: II. i. 2. 9, 16: V. ii. 9. 3: VII. ii. 34. 1. Sometimes the prohibition is indirect, I. i. 5. 6: II. ii. 11. 3: VI. i. 10. 5: ? IV. i. 9. 1.

匍 *p'û* To walk with the hands. 匍匐, to crawl, as an infant, or one unable to walk, III. i. 5. 3; ii. 10. 1.

匐 *pei* Lying on the ground. 匍匐, see above.

THE 21ST RADICAL, 匕.

化 *hwâ* To influence, transform; to be transformed, IV. i. 28. 2: VII. i. 13. 3; 40. 2 (N.B.); ii. 25. 7. 化者, the dead, those whose bodies are in course of decomposition, II. ii. 7. 4.

北 *pei* (1) The north, II. i. 3. 2. In the north, III. i. 4. 12. 北面, the face to the north, the position of ministers in the sovereign's presence, V. i. 4. 1; ii. 6. 4. 北狄, the rude tribes of the north, I. ii. 11. 2: III. ii. 5. 4: VII. ii. 4. 3. 北海, I. i. 7. 11, *et al.* (2) In a double surname, II. i. 2. 4, 6:—V. ii. 2. 1.

THE 22ND RADICAL, 匚.

匠 *chiang* A workman,—properly in wood, III. ii. 4. 3, 4: VII. ii. 5. 1. 匠人, I. ii. 9. 1. 大匠, a master-workman, VI. i. 20. 2: VII. i. 41. 2.

匡 *k'wang* A surname. 匡章, III. ii. 10. 1: IV. ii. 30. 1.

匪 *fei* A basket; to bring in baskets, III. ii. 5. 5.

THE 23RD RADICAL, 匸.

匹 *p'i* 匹夫, a common man, one without any rank, I. ii. 3. 5; 16. 1: V. i. 3. 2; 6. 3; ii. 3. 5. Joined with 匹婦, III. ii. 5. 3: V. i. 7. 6; ii. 1. 2: VII. i. 22. 2. In VI. ii. 2. 3, 匹 should be taken as a numerative for fowls.

匿 *ni* To conceal; to hide themselves, III. i. 4. 7.

18. 2; ii. 24. 2. (6) 反覆, to repeat, again and again, V. ii. 9. 1, 4: VI. i. 7. 2. Observe II. ii. 6. 1, 2.

叔 *shû* (1) 叔父, a father's younger brother, an uncle, VI. i. 5. 4, 5. (2) 管叔, an elder brother of Châu-kung, II. ii. 9. 2, 3. (3) In surnames, VI. ii. 15. 1.—II. ii. 10. 6.

取 *ch'ü* To take, I. ii. 10. 2, 3; 11. 1; 14. 2, *et al.*, *saepe*. To obtain, receive, I. i. 1. 4. To find; choose; approve of, III. i. 5. 3: IV. i. 8. 3; ii. 18. 1, 2; 21. 3; 24. 2, *et al.* To seize, III. ii. 5. 5, 6, *et al.*

受 *shâu* To receive, II. i. 2. 4; 9. 1; ii. 3. 1, 3, 4: V. ii. 4. 2, 3; 6. 4, 5, *et al.*, *saepe*. To accept, V. i. 5. 5, 6. 其所受教, those whose instructions they might receive, II. ii. 2. 9. 有所受之, it was received from a proper source, VII. i. 35. 4.

叟 *sâu* Venerable Sir, I. i. 1. 2; 5. 1. 高叟, that old Kâo, VI. ii. 3. 2.

叢 *ts'ăng* A thicket, IV. i. 9. 2.

THE 30TH RADICAL, 口.

口 *k'âu* (1) The mouth, I. i. 7. 16: VI. i. 7. 5, 8 (口 = the tongue, tongues, VII. ii. 19. 2); 24. 1; 37. 12. 口體, the mouth and body, = the body, IV. i. 19. 3. 口腹, VI. i. 14. 6: VII. i. 27. 1. (2) 口 = individuals, a sort of numerative, I. i. 3. 4; 7. 24: VII. i. 22. 2.

召 *châo* To call, to summon, I. ii. 4. 10: II. ii. 2. 5, 7, 10: V. ii. 7. 2, 3, 4, 9.

叩 *k'âu* To knock at, VII. i. 23. 3.

古 *kû* Antiquity, ancient, I. ii. 1. 3: II. i. 2. 22, *et al.*, *saepe*. 古之人 is of frequent occurrence, sometimes meaning *the ancients* generally, but often the ancient kings and worthies, I. i. 2. 3; 7. 12: II. ii. 1. 13, *et al.* 古者, the ancients, anciently, II. ii. 7. 2: IV. i. 18. 3: III. ii. 7. 1. 古公, the ancient duke, the title of 亶父, an ancestor of the Châu family, I. ii. 5. 5.

可 *k'o* May. *Passim*. Like *may* in English, 可 may represent possibility, liberty, or ability. 可以 is very frequent, = *may*. The 以 may sometimes be explained by *thereby*, *therewith*, but not always. 可 is not always an auxiliary, but often conveys a complete meaning. Observe 可 and 不可 in III. ii. 1. 4, &c. &c.

句 *kau* The 1st tone. In the name 句踐, I. ii. 3. 1.—VII. i. 9. 1.

史 *shih* History; historical, IV. ii. 21. 3.

右 *yû* (1) The right, 左右, to—on—the right and left, I. ii. 6. 3: II. ii. 10. 7: IV. ii. 14. (齊右, the right = the west—of Ch'î, VI. ii. 6. 5.) 右 = attendants, I. ii. 7. 4, 5: ? disciples, IV. ii. 31. 1. (2) 右師, the title of a high officer at the courts of the princes, IV. ii. 27. 1, 2.

司 *sze* To preside over. The phrase 有司 = 'the officers,' generally those of inferior rank, I. ii. 12. 1, 2; 16. 1: III. i. 2. 4: VI. ii. 10. 4. 有司者, II. ii. 10. 7. 司徒, the minister of instruction, III. i. 4. 8. 司寇, the minister of justice, VI. ii. 6. 6. 司城, the city-master, V. i. 8. 3. 司馬, the master of the horse, V. i. 8. 3.

各 *ko* Each, every, VII. i. 4. 6.

合 *ho* (1) To agree with, I. i. 7. 9: IV. ii. 20. 5: VII. ii. 37. 11. (2) To unite, IV. ii. 1. 3. Observe VII. ii. 16. 1.

同 *t'ung* (1) The same, I. ii. 16. 2: II. i. 2. 22: III. i. 4. 17, *et al.*, *saepe*. Often = to be the same, to agree, in or with. 有同與, are there points in which they agree? II. i. 2. 24. To make the same, III. i. 4. 18. To consider as common, II. i. 8. 3. 同乎, agreeing with, VII. ii. 37. 11. 同朝 = all in my court, II. ii. 10. 2. Adverbially,—together, in common, III. i. 3. 19: VII. i. 13. 3. (2) To share, I. ii. 1. 6, 7; 2. 2; 4. 2, *et al.* (3) A name, II. ii. 8. 1, 2.

后 *hâu* (1) A prince, a ruler, I. ii. 11. 2: III. ii. 5. 4. (2) 夏后氏 and 夏后 = the great Yü, the founder of the Hsiâ dynasty. Sometimes = the Hsiâ dynasty, or its founder, II. i. 1. 10: III. i. 3. 6: IV. i. 2. 5: V. i. 6. 7. (3) 后稷, the title of Shun's minister of agriculture, Tsî (Chî), III. i. 4. 8: IV. ii. 29. 1, 2, 3, 4.

名 *ming* (1) The name, VII. ii. 36. 2. To name, III. i. 4. 11: IV. i. 2. 4. 無名之指, the fourth finger, VI. i. 12. 1. (2) Fame, VI. ii. 6. 1: VII. ii. 11. 名世者, illustrious men, II. ii. 13. 3.

吏 *li* An officer, a minister, III. i. 3. 13: V. i. 3. 3. 委吏, the office first held by Confucius, V. ii. 5. 4. 天吏, II. i. 5. 6; ii. 8. 2.

君 *chün* A prince, a ruler. *Passim*. It very often occurs in correlation with 臣, a minister.

be skilful, I. i. 7. 12: II. i. 2. 11, 18, *et al.*, *saepe*. To make good; to cultivate, II. i. 9. 1: V. ii. 4. 5: VII. i. 9. 6.

喜 *hsi* To joy, be glad; joyful, I. ii. 1. 7; 9. 1: II. i. 8. 1; ii. 10. 2: V. i. 1. 2; 2. 3, 4: VI. ii. 5. 2; 13. 1, 3.

喟 *wei* 喟然, the sound of sighing, VII. i. 36. 1.

喩 *yü* (1) To illustrate, I. i. 3. 2. (2) To understand, VIII. ii. 15. 3: VII. i. 21. 4.

喪 *sang* To mourn for, I. i. 3. 3, *et al.* The period of, and all pertaining to, mourning, I. ii. 16. 1, 2: VII. i. 39. 1, 3, *et al.*

喪° *sang* The 4th tone. (1) To die, expire; ruin, I. i. 2. 4: IV. i. 1. 9. (2) To lose, I. i. 5. 1: III. ii. 1. 2: V. ii. 7. 5: VI. i. 10. 5.

喬 *ch'iâo* Lofty. 喬木, I. ii. 7. 1: III. i. 4. 15.

嗜 *shih* To find pleasure in; to relish, I. i. 6. 4, 6: VII. ii. 36. 1.

嘐 *hsiâo* 嘐嘐, magniloquent, VII. ii. 37. 6, 9.

嘑 *hû* 嘑爾, with an insulting voice, VI. i. 10. 6.

嘗 *ch'ang* (1) To try, 嘗試, I. i. 7. 19. (2) Forming the past tense, I. ii. 1. 2: II. i. 2. 7, 15; ii. 6. 1, 2, *et al.*, *saepe*. The combination 未嘗 is frequent.

噲 *k'wâi* In the designation 子噲, II. ii. 8. 1.

嘬 *chwâi* To bite, gnaw, III. i. 5. 4.

器 *ch'i* Vessels; implements, I. ii. 11. 3, 4: V. ii. 4. 6: VI. ii. 10. 3. 械器, III. i. 4. 5. 器皿, III. ii. 3. 3.

嚮 *hsiang* Over against, 相嚮, towards one another, III. i. 4. 13.

嚴 *yen* (1) To dread, II. i. 2. 4. (2) Pressed by urgency of affairs, II. ii. 7. 1.

囂 *hsiâo* 囂囂, indifferent and self-satisfied, V. i. 7. 3: VII. i. 9. 2, 3.

囊 *nang* A sack, I. ii. 5. 4.

THE 31ST RADICAL, 口.

四 *sze* Four. *Saepe*. 四海 and 四海之內, a name for all subject to the royal rule, I. i. 7. 12: III. ii. 5. 3, 7, *et al.*, *saepe*. Observe IV. ii. 18. 2: VI. ii. 11. 3. 四方 and 四境, the four quarters of the kingdom or a State, I. ii. 3. 7; 6. 3: II. i. 1. 10, *et al.* 四體, 四支, and 四肢, the four limbs, II. i. 6. 6: IV. ii. 30. 2: VII. i. 21. 4; ii. 24. 1. 四端, the four virtuous principles of our nature, II. i. 6. 6, 7. 四罪, four criminals, V. i. 3. 2. 四夷, all the barbarous tribes about the Middle Kingdom, I. i. 7. 16.

回 *hûi* The name of Confucius's favourite disciple, IV. ii. 29. 2, 3.

因 *yin* (1) Then, therefore, I. i. 7. 20. (2) By means of, taking advantage of, II. ii. 10. 4: III. i. 5. 1. (3) To accord with, IV. i. 1. 6.

困 *k'wăn* To be distressed, VI. ii. 15. 3.

固 *kû* (1) Firm; to be made strong, II. ii. 1. 4. (2) Stupid, VI. ii. 3. 2. (3) As an adverb, —certainly, indeed, as a matter of course, I. i. 7. 5, 17; ii. 11. 3: VII. ii. 6. 1, *et al.*, *saepe*.

囿 *yû* A park, I. ii. 2. 1, 2, 3: III. ii. 9. 5. 靈囿, the name of king Wăn's park, I. i. 2. 3.

圉 *yü* 圉圉, the appearance of being embarrassed, V. i. 2. 4.

國 *kwo* A State. *Passim*. 萬乘之國, the royal kingdom. 千乘之國, the State of a *hâu*, I. i. 1. 4; but such a State is called 萬乘之國, I. ii. 10. 4: II. i. 1. 13. 國人 = the people, I. ii. 7. 4, 5: VII. ii. 23; but also = a common man, IV. ii. 3. 1. 國家, a State, with its component great families, I. ii. 9. 2, *et al.*, *saepe*. 中國, the Middle Kingdom, I. i. 7. 16, *et al.*; but = in the middle of the State, II. ii. 10. 3. 國 = city, IV. ii. 33. 1: V. ii. 4. 4. Used for 君, V. ii. 7. 4. 爲國, to administer a State, III. i. 3. 1.

園 *yüan* A garden, III. ii. 9. 5.

THE 32ND RADICAL, 土.

土 *t'û* The ground, soil, II. ii. 7. 4: IV. ii. 3. 1: V. i. 4. 2. Territory, VI. ii. 7. 2;—but for this meaning 土地 is commonly used, meaning also newly-cultivated ground, I. i. 7. 16; ii. 15. 1: IV. i. 14. 2, 3: VI. ii. 9. 1; 14. 4, *et al.* 平土, plains, III. ii. 9. 4.

土 *tû* The 4th tone. Bark about the roots of the mulberry tree, II. ii. 4. 3.

在 *tsâi* To be in; to be on; to depend on;—the where, wherein, and whereon following. *Passim*. As a preposition,—in, on, I. i. 7. 20: III. i. 3. 3; in the case of, V. i. 3. 2.

惡在, where is, how is, I. i. 4. 5: III. i. 3. 7: VII. i. 33. 3. Observe 惟我在, I. ii. 3. 7; 惟義所在, IV. ii. 11. 1; also III. ii. 1. 2: VI. i. 2. 3: VII. i. 43. 1.

圭 *kwei* (1) 圭田, the holy field, III. i. 3. 16. (2) A name, VI. ii. 10; 11. 1.

地 *ti* (1) The earth, in correlation with heaven, II. i. 2. 13: VII. i. 13. 3. 地 = position, II. ii. 1. 1, 2, 3: VI. i. 7. 2. (2) The ground; territory, I. i. 5. 1, 2: II. i. 1. 8: V. ii. 2. 4, 5, 6, 7, 8, *et al.*, *saepe*. 地 = lands, III. i. 3. 7. Observe 井地, III. i. 3. 13. 土地 is common in this sense. See 土. 壤地 also occurs, III. i. 3. 14. (3) 地 = place, I. i. 7. 4, 7: IV. ii. 31. 3. 地 = regions, IV. ii. 1. 3.

均 *chün* Equal, III. i. 3. 13.

坐 *tso* To sit, I. i. 7. 4: II. i. 9. 1; ii. 11. 2, 3, *et al.*

垂 *ch'üi* (1) To hand down, I. ii. 14. 3. (2) 垂涕, to shed tears, VI. ii. 3. 2. (3) 垂棘, the name of a place, V. i. 9. 2.

垣 *yüan* A wall, III. ii. 7. 2.

垤 *t'ieh* (1) An anthill, II. i. 2. 28. So Chû Hsî explains it, but in the dictionary its sound with that meaning is *chih*. (2) 垤澤, the name of a gate, VII. i. 36. 3.

城 *ch'ăng* (1) City walls, I. ii. 13. 2: VII. ii. 22. 3. 城郭, inner and outer or suburban walls, II. ii. 1. 2, 3: IV. i. 1. 9: VI. ii. 10. 4. (2) A city, cities, IV. i. 14. 2. 司城, V. i. 8. 3. (3) 武城, the name of a city, IV. ii. 31. 1. 陽城, *id.*, V. i. 6. 1.

域 *yü* A boundary; to bound in, II. ii. 1. 4.

執 *chih* To lay hold of, to hold; to apprehend, IV. i. 7. 6; ii. 3. 4; 20. 2; 24. 2: VI. ii. 12. 1: VII. i. 35. 2. 執中, to hold a medium; 執一, to hold to one point, VII. i. 26. 3, 4.

基 *chi* 鎡基, a hoe, II. i. 1. 9.

堂 *t'ang* The hall or principal apartment in a house, I. i. 7. 4: VII. ii. 34. 2. (2) 明堂, the Brilliant palace, built for the purpose of Audience, I. ii. 5. 1, 2.

堅 *chien* Strong, I. i. 5. 3: II. ii. 1. 3.

堪 *k'an* To endure, IV. ii. 29. 2.

堯 *yâo* The name of the ancient sovereign, II. i. 2. 26; ii. 2. 4, *et al.*, *saepissime*.

報 *pâo* To acknowledge, to reply to, VI. ii. 5. 1.

場 *ch'ang* (1) An open area or arena, III. i. 4. 13. (2) 場師, a plantation keeper, VI. i. 14. 3.

塗 *t'û* (1) Mire, mud, II. i. 9. 1: V. ii. 1. 1 (塗炭). (2) Roads, I. i. 3. 5; 7. 18.

塞 *sâi* To fill up, II. i. 2. 13. 充塞, to fill up and stop, III. ii. 9. 9. So 茅塞, VII. ii. 21. 1.

塡 *t'ien* 塡然, the sound of the drum, I. i. 3. 2.

墁 *man* Ornaments on walls, = to disfigure, III. ii. 4. 5.

境 *ching* A border, a boundary, I. ii. 2. 3. 四境之內, 四境, I. ii. 6. 3: II. i. 1. 10.

墊 *tien* Name of a prince of Ch'î, VII. i. 33. 1.

墨 *mo* (1) Ink. 繩墨, a carpenter's marking line, VII. i. 41. 2. (2) Black, III. i. 2. 4. (3) Surname of a heresiarch. 墨者, a Mohist, III. i. 5. 1, 2: VII. ii. 26. 1, 2. 墨氏, III. ii. 9. 9. 墨翟, III. ii. 9. 10, 14.

墦 *fan* Tombs, IV. ii. 33. 1.

壑 *ho* A channel for water; a ditch, III. i. 5. 4: VI. ii. 11. 3. In other cases, always in combination with 溝, I. ii. 12. 2: II. ii. 4. 2: III. i. 3. 7; ii. 1. 2: V. ii. 7. 5.

壙 *k'wang* A tract beyond cultivation, IV. i. 9. 2.

壤 *zang* (1) Mould, III. ii. 10. 3. (2) 壤地, territory, III. i. 3. 14.

壞 *hwâi* To pull down, III. ii. 9. 5.

THE 33RD RADICAL, 士.

士 *shih* (1) A scholar, a man of education and ability. *Passim*. (2) An officer, I. i. 1. 4, *et saepe*. This and the preceding meaning run into each other. 上士, 中士, 下士, 元士, V. ii. 2. 3, 5, 6, 7, 8.

壬 *zăn* 仲壬, a son of the sovereign T'ang, V. i. 6. 5.

壯 *chwang* Strong, V. ii. 5. 4. 壯 = in vigorous manhood, I. i. 5. 3; ii. 9. 1; 12. 2: II. ii. 4. 2.

壹 *yî* Solely employed, exclusively active, II. i. 2. 1.

壺 *hû* A goblet, or jug; a vessel for liquids, I. ii. 10. 4; 11. 3: III. ii. 5. 5. Always in the phrase 壺漿.

壽 *shâu* Long life, VII. i. 1. 3.

THE 35TH RADICAL, 夊.

夏 *hsiâ* (1) Summer, III. ii. 7. 4: VI. i. 5. 5. (2) Great;—a name for China, III. i. 4. 12. (3) The name of a dynasty, I. ii. 4. 5: III. i. 3. 10: V. i. 6. 6; 7. 6; ii. 4. 4. 夏后氏, the great Yü, the founder of the Hsiâ dynasty, III. i. 3. 6. 夏后, a sovereign, sovereigns, of the Hsiâ, II. i. 1. 10: IV. i. 2. 5 (?): V. i. 6. 7. (4) 子夏, the designation of one of Confucius's disciples, II. i. 2. 6, 20: III. i. 4. 13. (3) 負夏, the name of a place, IV. ii. 1. 1.

夔 *kwei* Repeated, = the appearance of being reverential, V. i. 4. 4.

THE 36TH RADICAL, 夕.

夕 *hsî* The evening, VI. ii. 14. 4.

外 *wâi* The outside; outside; without, III. i. 4. 7; ii. 9. 1; 10. 5: V. ii. 4. 4; 6. 4: VI. i. 6. 7; ii. 6. 5: VII. i. 3. 2. (2) External; what is external, VI. i. 4. 1, 2, 4, 5; 5. 3, 5; ii. 15. 4. To make to be external, II. i. 2. 15. (3) 三年之外, after three years; 於 . . . 外, at a distance of . . ., V. ii. 1. 7; VI. ii. 13. 8. (4) In correlation with 內, abroad, I. ii. 5. 5: II. ii. 2. 4. (5) 外丙, a son of the sovereign Tang, V. i. 6. 5.

夜 *yê* Night, IV. ii. 18. 2; 20. 5: VI. i. 8. 1, 2.

多 *to* Many; much, I. i. 1. 4; iii. 1, 2, *et al.*, *saepe.* To become many, III. ii. 9. 5. In other cases it contains the copula in the same way. Many times, II. ii. 4. 2. Mostly, VII. i. 36. 2. 多聞 and 多聞識, extensive information, V. ii. 7. 3: VI. ii. 13. 2.

THE 37TH RADICAL, 大.

大 *tâ* Great, large; greatly. *Passim.* To make great, I. ii. 3. 5. 大 = if the result were great, III. ii. 1. 1. 大體, the nobler part of our nature, VI. i. 15. 1, 2. 大匠, a master-workman, VI. i. 20. 2: VII. i. 41. 2. 大夫, see 夫. 大人, see 人.

太 *t'âi* 太甲, the name of a Book in the Shû-ching, II. i. 4. 6, *et al.* 太誓, *id.*, III. ii. 5. 6; V. i. 5. 8. 太丁, a son of the sovereign T'ang, V. i. 6. 5. 太王, an ancestor of the House of Châu, I. ii. 3. 1; 5. 5; 14. 2; 15. 1. 太師, the Grand music-master, I. ii. 4. 10. 太公 and 太公望, a minister of Wăn and Wû, IV. i. 13. 1: VI. ii. 8. 6: VII. i. 22. 1; ii. 38. 3. 太山, the T'âi mountain in Shantung, I. i. 7. 11: II. i. 2. 28: VII. i. 24. 1.

天 *t'ien* (1) Heaven;—the material heaven: the heavens, the sky, I. i. 6. 6: II. i. 2. 13; 4. 3: IV. ii. 26. 3: V. i. 4. 1, 2: VII. i. 41. (2) Its more common use is for the supreme, governing Power, with more or less of personality indicated, I. ii. 3. 2, 3, 7; 10. 2; 14. 3; 16. 3: II. i. 4. 6; 5. 6; 7. 2; ii. 1. 1, 2; 8. 2; 13. 1, 5: III. i. 5. 3: IV. i. 1. 10; 7. 1, 5; 8. 5; 12. 2: V. i. 5. 2, 3, 4, 5, 6, 7; 6. 1, 2, 4; 7. 5, 9; ii. 1. 2; 3. 4: VI. i. 6. 8; 7. 1; 15. 2; 16. 1, 2, 3; ii. 15. 2: VII. i. 1. 1, 2; 19. 3; 20. 3; 38. 1; ii. 24. 2: ? V. i. 1. 1, 2. (3) 天子, the highest designation of the sovereign, I. ii. 4. 5: II. ii. 7. 2, *et al.*, *saepe.* 天下, see 下.

夫 *fû* (1) A male, males, I. ii. 5. 5: III. i. 3. 17. A husband, I. ii. 5. 3. 夫 = a fellow, I. ii. 8. 3. So, when joined with 褐, II. i. 2. 4; with 頑, V. ii. 1. 1; with 鄙, V. ii. 1. 3; with 薄, VII. ii. 15. 夫婦, 夫妻, III. i. 4. 8: IV. ii. 30. 5. 匹夫, see 匹. 丈夫, see 丈. 農夫, a husbandman, III. i. 4. 5, 9, *et al.* Observe 夫 . . . 布, II. i. 5. 5. (2) 大夫, a general name for the officers of a court, below the chief minister. *Saepe.* See especially V. ii. 2. 3. (3) 夫子 = our master—used in conversation. Applied to Mencius. *Passim.* Applied to Confucius. *Saepe.* 夫 = your husband, III. ii. 2. 2. Observe IV. i. 18. 2, meaning, my master; and so generally, IV. ii. 24. 3. (4) 夫人, the wife of a prince, III. ii. 3. 3.

夫 *fû* The 2nd tone. (1) An initial particle, which may generally be rendered by *now.* Sometimes, however, we must use *then* or *but:* and sometimes it will hardly admit

of being rendered in English. *Passim.* (2) A final particle, with exclamatory force, IV. ii. 24. 2: VI. i. 1. 2; ii. 7. 2. (3) Intermediate in sentences, with a demonstrative force, I. i. 6. 6: II. ii. 2. 6: VII. i. 39. 4. To this are to be referred 今夫, 若夫, and 且夫, the two former of which are common.

失 *shih* — To lose, II. i. 1. 8; ii. 1. 4; 4. 1, 2, *et al.*, *saepe.* To lose,—not to get, I. i. 3. 4; 7. 24, *et al.* To fail of or in, III. ii. 1. 4: VI. ii. 7. 2, *et al.* 自失, to lose one's self, II. i. 9. 2: compare IV. i. 19. 1.

夷 *i* — (1) Even; evenly. In the phrase 夷考, VII. ii. 37. 6. (2) To wound, = to be offended, IV. i. 18. 2. (3) Used for 彝, the invariable rules of virtue, VI. i. 6. 8. (4) Barbarous tribes;—properly those on the east, as in 夷狄, III. ii. 9. 11. But used generally, III. i. 4. 12. We have also 昆夷, I. ii. 3. 1; 四夷, I. i. 7. 16; 東夷, IV. ii. 1. 1; and 西夷, I. ii. 11. 2, *et al.* (5) A surname, III. i. 5. (6) In the honorary epithet, 伯夷, II. i. 2. 22, 23, *et al.*, *saepe.* Also in the name, 管夷吾, VI. ii. 15. 1.

奄 *yen* — The name of a State, III. ii. 9. 6.

奉 *fung* — Services, VI. i. 10. 7, 8.

奇 *ch'i* — In a name. 宮之奇, V. i. 9. 2.

契 *hsieh* — Shun's minister of Instruction, III. i. 4. 8.

奚 *hsi* — (1) An interrogative particle, = how, why, what, I. i. 7. 22; ii. 11. 2: III. ii. 1. 2; 5. 4: IV. ii. 28. 4, 6: V. i. 2. 3, 4; 3. 2; ii. 4. 6; 7. 4, 5: VI. ii. 1. 7; 2. 3: VII. i. 34; ii. 4. 3; 22. 3. 奚爲, I. ii. 16. 2: VI. ii. 13. 3. In names, 百里奚, V. i. 9. 1, 2: VI. ii. 6. 4; 15. 1.—嬖奚, III. ii. 1. 4.

奪 *t'o* — To snatch, take by force; to rob, I. i. 1. 4; 3. 4; 5. 4; 7. 23: III. ii. 5. 2: IV. i. 16. 1: VI. ii. 1. 8. Observe VI. i. 15. 2.

奮 *fän* — To press forward; to make himself distinguished, VII. ii. 15.

THE 38TH RADICAL, 女.

女 *nü* — A woman, a female; a daughter, I. ii. 5. 5: III. ii. 4. 3; 5. 5: IV. i. 17. 1: V. i. 1. 3, 4; 2. 1; ii. 6. 6: VII. ii. 6. 女子, a daughter, III. ii. 2. 2; 3. 6.

女 *zû* — The 3rd tone. For 汝, you, your, I. i. 2. 4; ii. 9. 1, 2: III. ii. 1. 4; 2. 2.

女 *nü* — The 4th tone. To give a daughter to one in marriage, IV. i. 7. 2: V. ii. 6. 6.

好 *hâo* — The 4th tone. To love, be fond of. *Saepe.* 好事, to be fond of strange things, V. i. 8. 1; 9. 1. 歸于好, to become friendly, VI. ii. 7. 3. Mencius never uses 好 as an adjective in the 3rd tone, 好 = good, fine, unless in V. i. 1. 4.

如 *jû* or *zû* — (1) As. *Saepe.* We often find 如是 and 如此, thus, such, so. (2) As = if, though, since, I. i. 3. 2; 5. 3; ii. 5. 4, 5, *et al.*, *saepe.* So 如使, VI. i. 7. 5; 10. 3, *et al.* (3) 如何, 如之何, 何如, see on 何, but observe the difference between 何如 at the beginning and at the end of a sentence. Observe also I. ii. 14. 3. (4) After adjectives, it = our termination *ly*, VII. i. 13; 12. 2, *et al.* (5) 如 = to wish, II. ii. 2. 1.

妃 *fei* — A consort, a wife. The dictionary says that the most honourable inmate of the harem next to the queen was called 妃, but it seems to have the highest meaning in I. ii. 5. 5.

妄 *wang* — Irregular, utterly lost, IV. ii. 28. 6.

妁 *chiâo* — 媒妁, a go-between, a matchmaker, III. ii. 3. 6.

妣 *pi* — A deceased mother. In 考妣, V. i. 4. 1.

妻 *ch'i* — A wife, I. i. 5. 4, *et al.*, *saepe.* 妻子, wife and child, wives and children. *Saepe.*

妻 *ch'i* — The 4th tone. To give to one to wife, V. i. 2. 2. To have to wife, V. i. 1. 4.

妾 *ch'ieh* — A concubine, IV. ii. 33. 1, 2: VI. i. 10. 7, 8; ii. 7. 3. In VII. ii. 34. 2, 侍妾 = 'attendants and concubines.' 妾婦 = women, III. ii. 2. 2.

始 *shih* — To begin; beginning; first, I. i. 2. 3; 3. 3; 4. 6; ii. 2. 3; 4. 9; 11. 2: II. i. 6. 7; ii. 10. 7: III. i. 3. 2 (*N.B.*), 13; 5. 3; ii. 5. 4: V. i. 2. 4; ii. 1. 6.

姑 *kû* — (1) For the present, if you please, I. ii. 9. 1, 2: II. i. 2. 21: VII. i. 39. 2. (2) In III. i. 5. 4, the meaning is undetermined.

姓 *hsing* — A, or the, surname, V. ii. 9. 1, 4: VII. ii. 36. 2. 百姓, the people, I. i. 7. 5, 6, 7, 10, 12, *et al.*, *saepe.*

委 *wei* — To give up; to cast away, II. ii. 1. 3: III. i. 5. 4.

孟子

委 *wei* The 4th tone. Public stores of grain, &c. 委吏, the first office held by Confucius, V. ii. 5. 4.

姜 *chiang* 姜女, the wife of king T'âi. 姜 is the surname, I. ii. 5. 5.

姣 *chiâo* Beauty, VI. i. 7. 7.

威 *wei* Majesty, dread, I. ii. 3. 3: III. ii. 2. 3. To overawe, II. ii. 1. 4.

娶 *ch'ü* To marry (on the part of the man), IV. i. 26. 2: V. i. 2. 1, 2; ii. 5. 1.

婦 *fû* (1) A married woman, a wife, III. i. 4. 8; ii. 2. 2. 匹婦, III. ii. 5. 3: V. i. 7. 6; ii. 1. 2: VII. i. 22. 2. See 匹. (2) A name, 馮婦, VII. ii. 23. 2.

媒 *mei* 媒妁, a matchmaker, III. ii. 3. 6.

婁 *lâu* A name. 離婁, IV. i. 1. 1.

媚 *mei* To flatter, VII. ii. 37. 9.

嫁 *chiâ* To be married (on the part of the woman), III. ii. 2. 2.

嫂 *sâo* An elder brother's wife, IV. i. 17. 1, 3: V. i. 2. 3.

嬖 *pi* A favourite (in a bad sense), and 嬖人, I. i. 7. 16; ii. 16. 1, 3: III. ii. 1. 4.

嬴 *ying* The name of a place, II. ii. 7. 1.

THE 39TH RADICAL, 子.

子 *tsze* (1) A son. *Passim.* But often it is equivalent to *child, children;*—especially in the frequently recurring phrase 妻子. So, in 赤子, an infant, III. i. 5. 3. 女子, a daughter, III. ii. 3. 6. 處子, a virgin daughter, VI. ii. 1. 8. (2) A general appellation for virtuous men, which may be translated by *gentleman, disciple, philosopher,* &c. *Saepe.* In this sense it is often used in conversation, and is equivalent to *You, Sir.* Observe 吾子, II. ii. 1. 3, and 二三子, my friends, my disciples, I. ii. 15. 1. In this sense it is very common after surnames and honorary epithets. We have 孔子, 孟子, 告子, &c. &c. It is used also after the surname and name or epithet together, as in 孟獻子, *et al.* (3) A title of nobility, V. ii. 2. 3, 4, 5. So, in 微子, II. i. 1. 8: VI. i. 6. 3, and 箕子, II. i. 1. 8. (4) It enters often into designations, as in 子路, 子思, &c. &c. Into names also, as in 西子, IV. ii. 25. 1, and perhaps 孺子, IV. ii. 24. 2. 子叔, II. ii. 10. 6, and 子濯, IV. ii. 24. 2, seem to be equivalent to surnames. (5) Phrases formed with 子 are—天子, the highest name for the sovereign. *Saepe.* 子弟, sons and younger brothers = youths, I. ii. 11. 3: II. i. 5. 6, *et al.;* 弟子, disciples, II. i. 1. 7; ii. 10. 3; 11. 3: IV. i. 7. 3; 子孫, descendants, I. ii. 14. 3, *et al.* Observe IV. i. 7. 3; 先子, see 先: 世子, the crown prince, III. i. 1. 1, *et al.;* 眸子, the pupil of the eye, IV. i. 15. 1, 2; 樹子, the designated heir, VI. ii. 7. 3; 夫子, see 夫; 小子, little children, said to the disciples by Confucius, IV. i. 8. 3; 14. 1; 孺子, a boy, II. i. 6. 3: IV. i. 8. 2; 童子, *id.,* III. ii. 5. 2, 3; and 君子, see 君.

孑 *chieh* Half-an-one, V. i. 4. 2.

孔 *k'ung* A surname. That of Confucius. *Passim.* 孔距心, II. ii. 4. 2, 4.

存 *ts'un* (1) To be in, IV. i. 15. 1, *et al.* 存= to abide, VII. i. 13. 3. (2) To be preserved, II. i. 1. 8, *et al., saepe.* 存= to be alive, VII. i. 20. 2. To preserve, IV. ii. 19. 1, *et al.* Observe 存心, IV. ii. 28.

孝 *hsiâo* (1) Filial piety; filial; to be filial, I. i. 8. 4; 5. 3; 7. 24, *et al., saepe.* (2) The honorary epithet of a duke of Wei, V. ii. 4. 7.

季 *chi* (1) In a name, VI. i. 5. 1, 5. (2) A surname, V. i. 14. 1.—V. ii. 4. 7. 季孫, II. ii. 10. 6. Observe 季子 and 季任, VI. ii. 5.

孟 *măng* (1) The great, chief, 趙孟, VI. i. 17. 2. (2) A surname. That of Mencius. *Passim.* 孟仲子, II. ii. 2. 3.—孟季子, VI. i. 5. 1, 5.—孟獻子, V. ii. 3. 2.—孟施舍 and 孟賁, II. i. 2. 2, 5, 6, 8.

孤 *kû* Young and fatherless, I. ii. 5. 3. 孤 = friendless, VII. i. 18. 2.

孥 *nû* Children. Said by Chû Hsî to mean wives and children, I. ii. 5. 3.

孩 *hâi* An infant, able to smile. 孩提之童, VII. i. 15. 2.

孫 *sun* (1) A grandson, IV. i. 2. 4. 子孫, descendants, I. ii. 14. 3. Observe 孫子, IV. i. 7. 5. (2) In double surnames, II. i. 1. 1, *et al.*—II. ii. 10. 6.—VI. ii. 15. 1.

孰 *shû* Who, which:—interrogative, I. i. 6. 3, 5, 6; 7. 17, 18; ii. 1. 4: IV. i. 19. 1, 2, *et al.*

孳 *tsze* 孳孳, to be earnest and careful in, VII. i. 25. 1, 2; 41. 1.

學 *hsiâo* or *hsio* (1) To learn; learning, I. ii. 9. 1, 2: II. i. 2. 19, 22, *et al.*, *saepe.* 學問, to study, III. i. 2. 4: VI. i. 11. 4. (2) A school, or college, of a higher order, III. i. 3. 10.

孺 *zû* (1) 孺子, a boy, II. i. 6. 3: IV. i. 8. 2. (2) In a name, IV. ii. 24. 2.

孽 *nieh* (1) The sons of concubines, VII. i. 18. 2. (2) 孽 = calamities, II. i. 4. 6: IV. i. 8. 5.

THE 40TH RADICAL, 宀.

宇 *yü* The sides of a house, below the eaves. 宇 = a settlement, I. ii. 5. 5.

宅 *châi* A homestead, a dwelling, I. i. 3. 4; 7. 24: II. i. 7. 2: IV. i. 10. 2, 3: VII. i. 22. 2.

守 *shâu* To guard, have the charge of; to observe, but with the idea of guarding, I. ii. 4. 5; 13. 2; 15. 2: II. i. 2. 6, 8; ii. 5. 5: III. i. 3. 18; ii. 4. 3: IV. i. 8; 19. 1, 2; ii. 31. 2: VI. ii. 5. 1: 7. 5: VII. ii. 32. 1, 2. 守者, a keeper, VII. i. 36. 3.

安 *ân* (1) Ease, quiet, VI. ii. 15. 5: VII. ii. 24. 1. (2) Tranquil; to be in repose; to repose in, II. i. 7. 2; 12. 5: IV. i. 10. 2, 3; 8. 1: V. i. 5. 6: VII. i. 32. 2. (3) To give repose to, I. ii. 3. 6, 7, 8: II. ii. 11. 3: VII. i. 19. 2. (4) Quietly, in tranquillity, I. i. 4. 1: III. ii. 2. 1: IV. ii. 14. 1.

宋 *sung* (1) The name of a State, II. i. 2. 16; ii. 3. 1, 3: III. i. 1. 1; 2. 1; 4. 3, *et al.* (2) A surname, VI. ii. 4. 1.—VII. i. 9. 1.

完 *wan* Complete; to complete, IV. i. 1. 9: V. i. 2. 3.

宗 *tsung* Pertaining to one's ancestors. In the phrase 宗廟, the ancestral temple, I. ii. 11. 3: IV. i. 3. 3: VI. ii. 8. 5; 10. 4. 宗國, the State which we honour, III. i. 2. 3.

官 *kwan* An officer. 百官, all the officers, III. i. 2. 3, 4, 5, *et al.* An office, V. ii. 2. 6, 7, 8, 9, *et al.* In some cases it is hard to say to which of these meanings we should assign the character. Applied to the senses and the mind, VI. i. 15. 2.

定 *ting* (1) To settle, compose; to be settled, I. i. 6. 2: III. i. 2. 3; 3. 13; ii. 9. 3 (*N.B.*): IV. i. 20; 24. 2; 28. 2: V. ii. 9. 4: VII. i. 21. 2, 3. (2) An honorary epithet, III. i. 2. 1.

宜 *î* (1) To be right, reasonable; to seem to be; ought, ought to be, I. i. 7. 7; ii. 2. 2, 3: II. ii. 2. 5; 9. 3: III. ii. 1. 1: IV. i. 1. 7; 24. 2; ii. 24. 1; 28. 4: V. i. 2. 1; ii. 5. 3: VII. i. 41. 1. (2) In a name, VII. ii. 38. 3.

客 *k'o* A visitor, a stranger, II. ii. 11. 3.

室 *shih* (1) A house, I. ii. 9. 1: II. ii. 10. 3, *et al.*, *saepe.* 宮室, houses, edifices, III. ii. 9. 5: VI. i. 10. 7; ii. 10. 4: VII. i. 26. 2. 室 = a palace, V. ii. 3. 5. 室 = a family, a house, IV. i. 6. 1: V. ii. 2. 1: VI. ii. 10. 3. ?處室者, IV. ii. 33. 1. (2) 室 = a wife. 有室, III. ii. 3. 6. 男女居室, male and female dwell together, V. i. 2. 1.

宣 *hsüan* An honorary epithet. 齊宣王, I. i. 7. 1, *et al.*, *saepe.*

宮 *kiung* (1) A palace, V. i. 2. 3; 5. 7; 7. 9. 宮 = a house, an establishment, III. i. 4. 5. 宮室, see 室. (2) A surname, V. i. 9. 2. In the double surname 北宮, II. i. 2. 4, 6.—V. ii. 2. 1. (3) 上宮 and 雪宮 are the names of two palaces, VII. ii. 30. 1: I. ii. 4. 1.

害 *hâi* (1) To injure; to be injured; injury, I. ii. 15. 1: II. i. 2. 13, 16, *et al.*, *saepe.* It is often followed by 於, III. i. 4. 4, *et al.* (2) In a name, 浩生不害, VII. ii. 25. 1.

害 *ho* What, why, I. ii. 2. 4. Chû Hsî, however, explains it here by *when*.

宴 *yen* To be at ease, to feel happy, III. ii. 3. 3.

宵 *hsiâo* At night, III. i. 3. 2.

宰 *ts'âi* (1) A chief officer, IV. i. 14. 1. 冢宰, see 冢. (2) A surname, II. i. 2. 18, 25, 26.

家 *chiâ* (1) A house, a home, III. ii. 2. 2. (2) A family, families, I. i. 3. 4; 7. 24: III. i. 3. 19: VII. i. 22. 2. (3) A family, a clan,—the possessions of a great officer. *Passim.* This is the most common use of the term in Mencius. The combination 國家 is frequent, see 國. Sometimes it = the chief of such a family, I. i. 1. 4: V. ii. 3. 2, 3. (4) A husband, 有家, III. ii. 3. 6. Observe 家邦, I. i. 7. 12; and 東家, VI. ii. 1. 8.

孟子

THE 41ST RADICAL, 寸.

The 42ND RADICAL, 小.

少 *shâo* (1) Few, I. ii. 1. 4: V. i. 6. 2. 加少, to decrease, I. i. 3. 1. (2) In a little, V. i. 2. 4.

少 *shâo* The 4th tone. Young, V. i. 1. 5.

尙 *shang* (1) Still (adv.), III. i. 5. 1; ii. 10. 6. (2) To exalt, VII. i. 33. 2, 3. (3) To surpass, II. ii. 2. 9: VII. ii. 22. 1. (4) 尙 = to go up to court, V. ii. 3. 5. To ascend, V. ii. 8. 2. (5) To add to, be added to. 不可尙已, III. i. 4. 13. Observe 草尙之風, the grass, when the wind is on it . . ., III. i. 2. 4.

THE 43RD RADICAL, 尤.

尤 *yû* (1) A fault, I. ii. 4. 9. (2) To grudge against, to blame, I. ii. 12. 2: II. ii. 13. 1.

就 *chiû* To go to, to approach, I. i. 6. 2, 7; 7. 4, 6, 7, *et al.*, *saepe.*

THE 44TH RADICAL, 尸.

尸 *shih* To personate the dead at sacrifices, being a resting-place for their spirits, VI. i. 5. 4.

尺 *ch'ih* A cubit, II. i. 1. 8: III. i. 4. 17; ii. 1. 1, 3: VI. i. 14. 1, 6; ii. 2. 2: VII. ii. 34. 2.

尼 *nî* The 4th tone. To stop, I. ii. 16. 3.

尼 *nî* 仲尼, the designation of Confucius, I. i. 4. 6; 7. 2, *et al.*

尹 *yin* (1) 伊尹, the chief minister of the sovereign T'ang, II. i. 2. 22, 23, *et al.*, *saepe.* (2) A surname, II. ii. 12. 1, 3, 7. 尹公, apparently a double surname, IV. ii. 24. 2.

居 *chü* (1) To dwell, reside, in,—generally applied to places, but sometimes to official positions; residence, seat. *Passim.* It is applied metaphorically also to virtues, and their opposites, as in II. i. 4. 1: III. ii. 2. 1, 3: III. i. 10. 1, 3: compare II. ii. 2. 19. In VII. ii. 37. 11, 居之 = their principles; compare IV. ii. 14. 居 ——, to choose an alternative, II. ii. 3. 1. In VII. i. 36. 1, 2, 3, 居 = status, position. In VI. ii. 9. 3, = to retain. 居者, those who stayed at home, I. ii. 5. 4. (2) In a name, III. ii. 6. 2.

屋 *wû* (1) A house, III. i. 3. 2: IV. ii. 31. 1 (*N.B.*) (2) 屋廬, a double surname, VI. ii. 1. 1.

屈 *ch'ü* (1) To bend (act.), III. ii. 2. 3. To be bent, VI. i. 12. 1. (2) The name of a place in Tsin, V. i. 9. 2.

屑 *hsieh* Always in the phrase 不屑, = not to consider pure, not to condescend or stoop to, II. i. 9. 1, 2: VI. i. 10. 6; ii. 16. 1: VII. ii. 37. 7.

屏 *ping* The 3rd tone. To drive away, IV. ii. 30. 5.

屨 *chü* Shoes or sandals, made of woven materials, III. i. 4. 1, 17, 18; ii. 10. 4: VI. i. 7. 4: VII. ii. 30. 1, 2.

履 *lü* To tread, V. ii. 7. 8.

屬 *shû* Belongings, = relationships, IV. ii. 30. 5.

屬 *chû* To collect, I. ii. 15. 1.

THE 46TH RADICAL, 山.

山 *shan* Hills, a mountain, II. ii. 1. 4: III. i. 4. 7: VI. i. 2. 3; 8. 1. 山 = wooded hills, I. i. 3. 3. 山徑, hill-paths, VII. ii. 21. 東山, VII. i. 24; 太山, I. i. 7. 11: II. i. 2. 28: VII. i. 24; 梁山, I. ii. 15. 1; 崇山, V. i. 3. 2; 羽山, V. i. 3. 2; 箕山, V. i. 6. 1; 牛山, VI. i. 8. 1; and 岐山, I. ii. 14. 2; 15. 1,—are all names of mountains.

岌 *ko* 岌岌, dangerous, unsettled, V. i. 4. 1.

岐 *ch'i* A mountain, by which was the original seat of the Châu family, giving also its name to the adjacent country, I. ii. 5. 3, 5. 岐周, IV. ii. 1. 2. 岐山, see 山.

岑 *chin* A small high hill. 岑樓, VI. ii. 1. 5.

崇 *ch'ung* (1) The name of a place in Ch'î, II. ii. 14. 2. (2) 崇山, see 山.

崩 *păng* To die,—spoken of a sovereign, II. i. 1. 7: V. i. 5. 7; 6. 1, 5. 崩角, the horns lowered to the ground, as when two bulls are fighting, VII. ii. 4. 5.

嵎 *yü* A corner or bend of a hill, VII. ii. 23. 2.

嶽 *yo* A neighbourhood in the capital of Ch'î, III. ii. 6. 1.

巍 *wei* 巍巍, majestic, III. i. 4. 11: VII. ii. 34. 1.

巖 *yen* Precipitous, VII. i. 2. 2.

THE 47TH RADICAL, 巛.

川 *ch'wan* A stream, IV. i. 1. 1.

巡 *hsün* To perambulate. 巡狩, to make a tour of inspection—spoken of the ancient sovereigns, I. ii. 4. 5: VI. ii. 7. 2.

孟子

巢 *ch'âo* Nests, = shelter-huts, III. ii. 9. 3.

州 *châu* (1) 幽州, the name of a place, V. i. 8. 2. (2) In a name, III. ii. 6. 2.

THE 48TH RADICAL, 工.

工 *kung* (1) A workman, VII. i. 41. 2. 百工, the various workmen, III. i. 4. 5, 6. 工 = a charioteer, III. ii. 1. 4. 工師, the master of the workmen, I. ii. 9. 1. (2) In opposition to 朝, = officers, IV. i. 1. 8. (3) 共工, the title of an ancient high officer, V. i. 3. 3.

左 *tso* The left. 左右, to—on—the left and right, I. ii. 6. 3: II. ii. 10. 7: IV. ii. 14. 1. 左 = attendants, I. ii. 7. 4, 5. ? disciples, IV. ii. 21. 1.

巧 *ch'iâo* Skill; skilful; to be skilful, IV. i. 1. 1: V. ii. 1. 7: VII. i. 7. 2; ii. 5.

巨 *chü* Large, great, I. ii. 9. 1: III. i. 4. 18: IV. i. 6. 巨擘, the thumb, III. ii. 10. 2.

巫 *wû* A witch,—one who prays and makes incantations on behalf of others, II. i. 7. 1.

差 *ts'ze* An order; a difference, III. i. 5. 3: V. ii. 2. 8.

THE 49TH RADICAL, 已.

己 *chî* Self. Myself. Himself, yourself,—and the plurals. *Passim.* 自己, the same, II. i. 4. 5. Observe III. ii. 10. 5: VI. ii. 3. 2: VII. i. 9. 5.

已 *î* (1) To stop, end, I. ii. 5. 1: III. ii. 8. 1, 2, 3, *et al.*, *saepe.* 無已, if I may not stop, I. ii. 18. 2. Its most common use is at the end of sentences in the phrase 而已矣, and there stop, = and nothing more. *Passim.* So 而已, alone, VI. ii. 2. 2. Also without the 而, IV. ii. 30. 5. 不得已, not to be able to stop, what is the result of necessity, is also frequent, I. ii. 7. 3; 14. 2, *et al.*, *saepe.* 已, alone, at the end of clauses and sentences, gives strong emphasis to the previous assertion, I. i. 7. 16, 20: II. i. 9. 1, 2, *et saepe.* (2) 已 = to decline, VI. i. 10. 8; to avoid, IV. i. 9. 4; to dismiss, I. ii. 6. 2. (3) Indicates the past tense. Must be translated sometimes by *was*, *were*, I. ii. 16. 1: IV. ii. 10. 1: VI. ii. 13. 8.

巷 *hsiang* A lane, IV. ii. 29. 2.

THE 50TH RADICAL, 巾.

市 *shih* A market-place, markets, I. i. 7. 18; ii. 5. 3; 11. 2; 15. 1, *et al.* 市井之臣, V. ii. 7. 1. In II. ii. 10. 7, 爲市者 is probably—'those who established markets,' rather than 'market-dealers.' Observe II. i. 5. 2.

布 *pû* Cloth,—of flax, III. i. 4. 17; ii. 4. 3: VII. ii. 27: ? II. i. 5. 5.

希 *hsî* Always in the phrase 幾希, 'little,' few, IV. ii. 19. 1; 33. 2: VI. i. 8. 2: VII. i. 16.

帛 *pâi* Cloth,—of silk, I. i. 3. 4; 7. 24: III. i. 4. 17: VII. i. 22. 2, 3. 幣帛, VI. ii. 10. 4; see 幣.

帝 *tî* (1) A ruler, or sovereign, the ruler;—used of Yâo and Shun, II. i. 8. 9: V. i. 1. 3, 4; 2. 2; ii. 3. 5. (2) 上帝, God, the most High God, I. ii. 3. 7: IV. i. 7. 5; ii. 25. 2.

帥 *shwâi* A leader, II. i. 2. 9.

帥 *shû* Formerly in the entering tone. To lead, V. i. 4. 1.

師 *shih* (1) A military host, I. ii. 4. 6; 10. 4; 11. 3: VI. ii. 4. 5, 6. 六師, the royal armies, VI. ii. 7. 2. (2) A teacher, master, III. i. 1. 4; 3. 11; 4. 12, 14, *et al.* So, 先師, IV. i. 7. 3. (3) To make one's master, to follow, IV. i. 7. 4. (4) 場師, a plantation-keeper, VI. i. 14. 3. 工師, the master of the workmen, I. ii. 9. 1. 太師, the Grand music-master, I. ii. 4. 10. So, 師 alone, IV. i. 1. 1: VI. i. 7. 6. 士師, the chief criminal judge, I. ii. 6. 2: II. ii. 5. 1. 右師, title of a high officer, IV. ii. 27. 1, 2. ? II. ii. 14. 3.

席 *hsî* A mat, mats, III. i. 4. 1.

帶 *tâi* A girdle, a sash, VII. ii. 32. 1.

常 *ch'ang* Regular, V. ii. 6. 2, 4. Constant, unchanging, IV. i. 7. 5. 常 = an average, III. i. 3. 7. 常常, constantly, V. i. 3. 3.

幣 *pî* 幣帛, pieces of silk given as gifts or presents, VI. ii. 10. 4. So, 幣 alone, V. i. 7. 3: VI. ii. 5. 1: VII. i. 37. 2.

幡 *fan* I. q. 翻. 幡然, changing-like, suddenly, V. i. 7. 4.

THE 51st RADICAL, 干.

干 *kan* (1) A shield, I. ii. 5. 4: V. i. 2. 3. (2) To seek for, II. ii. 12. 1: VII. ii. 33. 2. (3) In names. 比干, the uncle of the tyrant Châu, II. i. 1. 8: VI. i. 6. 3. 一段干木, III. ii. 7. 2.

平 *p'ing* (1) To be brought to a state of perfect order. Spoken of the physical condition of the country, III. i. 4. 7; of its government, III. ii. 9. 11: IV. ii. 29. 1: VII. ii. 32. 2. 平治, II. ii. 13. 5: IV. i. 1. 1. 平政, to make government even, to dispense equal justice, IV. ii. 2. 4. Compare III. i. 2. 13. (2) Even, level, IV. i. 1. 5: III. ii. 9. 4. 平旦, the day-break, the time *evenly* between night and day, VI. i. 8. 2. (3) An honorary epithet, V. ii. 3. 5.—I. ii. 16. 1. (4) 平陸, the name of a place, II. ii. 4. 1: VI. ii. 5. 1, 2, 6.

年 *nien* A year, years. *Saepe.*

幸 *hsing* Fortunate, lucky; fortunately, III. i. 2. 1: IV. i. 1. 8. Observe the idiom of 幸 followed by 而, II. ii. 2. 1: IV. ii. 20. 5.

THE 52nd RADICAL, 幺.

幼 *yû* Young, to treat as the young; the young, I. i. 7. 12; ii. 5. 3; 9. 1: III. i. 4. 8; ii. 6. 2: VI. ii. 7. 3.

幽 *yû* (1) Dark, III. i. 4. 15. (2) An honorary or rather dishonouring epithet of a sovereign, IV. i. 2. 4: VI. i. 6. 2. (3) 幽州, the name of a place, V. i. 3. 2.

幾 *chî* The 1st tone. (1) To hope, VII. i. 41. 1. (2) In the phrase 幾希, little, few, IV. ii. 19. 1; 33. 2: VI. i. 8. 2: VII. i. 16. (3) In the phrase 庶幾, near to, or expressive of a wish, I. ii. 1. 1, 3, 7: II. ii. 12, 4, 5.

幾 *chì* Several, I. ii. 12. 2: II. ii. 4. 2. ? how many, IV. i. 24. 2.

THE 53rd RADICAL, 广.

序 *hsü* (1) A kind of school, I. ii. 3. 4; 7. 24: III. i. 3. 10. (2) A due order, III. i. 4. 8.

底 *ti* (1) I. q. 砥, a whetstone, V. ii. 7. 8. (2) 底 = to come to, IV. i. 28. 2.

庖 *p'âo* A kitchen; shambles, I. i. 4. 4; 7. 8: III. ii. 9. 9. 庖, the master of the kitchen, ? purveyor, V. ii. 6. 6.

府 *fû* A treasury. 府庫, I. ii. 12. 2: III. i. 4. 3: VI. ii. 9. 1.

庠 *hsiang* A kind of school, I. i. 3. 4; 7. 24: III. i. 3. 10.

庭 *t'ing* The court below and before the hall or principal apartment of a house, IV. ii. 33. 1.

度 *tû* (1) A measure for determining the length, I. i. 7. 13. (2) A model, rules, I. ii. 4. 5: II. ii. 7. 2: IV. i. 1. 8.

度 *to* To measure, I. i. 7. 9, 13.

庫 *fû* An arsenal, 府庫, see 府.

庳 *pi* 有庳, the name of a State, V. i. 3. 2, 3.

庶 *shû* (1) Numerous, 庶物, the multitude of things, IV. ii. 19. 2. 庶民, the masses of the common people, I. i. 2. 3: IV. ii. 19. 1; VII. ii. 37. 13. 庶人, the common people, I. i. 1. 4: II. ii. 7. 2, *et al., saepe.* (2) In the phrase 庶幾, see 幾.

康 *k'ang* 康誥, the name of a Book in the Shû-ching, V. ii. 4. 4.

庾 *yü* 庾公 appears to be a surname, IV. ii. 24. 2.

廋 *sáu* To pilfer and hide, VII. ii. 30. 3. Not well made; see the dictionary. I. q. 廋 below, and in Analects, II. 10. 4, 5.

庸 *yung* (1) Ordinary, VI. i. 5. 4. (2) Merit; to think of one's merit, VII. i. 13. 3. (3) 附庸, a name of certain small principalities, V. ii. 2. 4.

廉 *lien* Pure, disinterested; purity, moderation, III. ii. 10. 1, 2: IV. ii. 23: V. ii. 1. 1: VII. ii. 15; 37. 11. (2) 飛廉, a supporter of the tyrant Châu, III. ii. 9. 6.

廋 *sáu* To hide, be concealed, IV. i. 15. 2.

廄 *chiû* A stable, I. i. 4. 4: III. ii. 9. 9. But this is a vulgar form of the character in the first text.

廚 *ch'û* A kitchen, I. i. 7. 8.

廛 *ch'an* (1) A house, a dwelling-place, III. i. 4. 1. (2) A stance for a shop or booth, II. i. 5. 5. To levy a ground-rent on such stance, II. i. 5. 2.

廟 *miâo* A shrine or temple. Always in the phrase 宗廟; see 宗.

廢 *fei* To put aside, disregard; to make void, I. i. 7. 4: IV. ii. 24. 2: V. i. 2. 1; 6. 4: VII. i. 26. 4; 41. 2. To decay;—spoken of States, IV. i. 3. 2.

廣 *kwang* Wide, III. ii. 2. 3: VII. i. 21. 1; 36. 2. 廣譽, wide-reaching praise, VI. i. 17. 3.

廩 *lin* A granary. Always in connexion with 倉, I. ii. 12. 2: III. i. 4. 3: V. i. 1. 3; 2. 3; ii. 6. 6. 廩人, the store-keeper, V. ii. 6. 5.

廬 *lû* (1) The shed tenanted by a prince mourning for his father, III. i. 2. 5. (2) 屋廬, see 屋.

THE 54TH RADICAL, 廴.

廷 *t'ing* A courtyard. In the phrase 朝廷, the court, II. ii. 2. 6: IV. ii. 27. 3.

THE 55TH RADICAL, 廾.

弁 *p'an* 小弁, the name of an ode in the Shih-ching, VI. ii. 3. 1, 2, 4.

弈 *yî* Chess-playing, IV. ii. 30. 2: VI. i. 9. 3. 弈秋, a name or nickname, VI. i. 9. 3.

THE 56TH RADICAL, 弋.

式 *shih* To make a model, to imitate, II. ii. 10. 3.

弑 *shih* To murder; to be murdered.—Spoken with reference to killing a sovereign, I. i. 1. 4; ii. 8. 2: III. ii. 9. 7: IV. i. 2. 4.

THE 57TH RADICAL, 弓.

弓 *kung* A bow, I. ii. 5. 4: IV. ii. 24. 2: VI. i. 9. 3; ii. 3. 2. 弓人, a bow-maker, II. i. 7. 3.

弟 *tî* (1) A younger brother, II. ii. 9. 3: III. i. 4. 2, *et al.*, *saepe*. Found often along with 兄. But sometimes 兄弟 = relatives, V. ii. 3. 1; and in V. i. 8. 2, it = sisters. 子之兄弟, you and your brother, III. i. 4. 12. 子弟, sons and younger brothers = youths. *Saepe*. In II. i. 5. 6, it seems to = children; and in VII. ii. 1. 2, a son. (2) Used for 悌, fraternal duty, VII. i. 39. 2. (3) 弟子, disciples, II. i. 1. 7: II. ii. 10. 3; 11. 3 (= I, your disciple): IV. i. 7. 3.

弔 *tiâo* (1) To condole with,—on occasions of death and mourning, II. ii. 2. 2; 6. 1: III. i. 2. 5; ii. 3. 1, 2, 3: IV. ii. 27. 1. (2) To console, I. ii. 11. 2: III. ii. 5. 4.

引 *yin* To draw; to lead on; to lead away, VI. i. 15. 2; ii. 8. 9: VII. i. 41. 3. 引 = to take, III. ii. 6. 1. 引領, to stretch out the neck, I. i. 6. 6.

弗 *fû* Not. *Passim.*

弤 *tî* A bow,—the name of that belonging to Shun, V. i. 2. 3.

弱 *jâo* or *zâo* Weak, the weak, I. i. 7. 17; ii. 12. 2: III. ii. 5. 2: IV. i. 7. 1.

張 *chang* (1) To draw a bow. 張 = to display, to be displayed, I. ii. 5. 4: III. ii. 5. 6. (2) 子張, one of Confucius's disciples, II. i. 2. 20: III. i. 4. 13. 琴張, also one of Confucius's disciples, VII. ii. 37. 4. (3) A surname, 張儀, III. ii. 2. 1.

强 *ch'iang* Strong, vigorous, I. i. 5. 1: IV. i. 7. 1: VI. ii. 13. 2.

强 *ch'iang* The 3rd tone. To make one's self strong to, IV. i. 8. 4; 14. 2: VI. ii. 9. 2.

彊 *ch'iang* Strong; strength, I. i. 7. 17; ii. 11. 3.

彊 *chiang* To act vigorously at, I. ii. 14. 3: VII. i. 4. 3. To force, III. i. 4. 13. 彊 = by dint of pressing, III. ii. 1. 4.

彌 *mi* A surname, V. i. 8. 2.

彀 *kâu* To draw a bow to the full, VI. i. 20. 1: VII. i. 41. 2.

THE 58TH RADICAL, 彐.

彘 *chih* A sow, swine, I. i. 3. 4, 5; 7. 24: VII. i. 22. 2.

THE 59TH RADICAL, 彡.

形 *hsing* (1) The bodily organs, VII. i. 38 (*N. B.*) (2) To manifest, be manifested, VI. i. 6. 5. Appearance, representation, I. i. 7. 11.

彫 *tiâo* To cut, carve, 彫琢, I. ii. 9. 2.

彰 *chang* To display, give distinction to, VI. ii. 7. 3.

彭 *p'ăng* A surname, III. ii. 4. 1.

THE 60TH RADICAL, 彳.

役 *yî* To serve, perform service, IV. i. 7. 1: V. ii. 7. 2. 力役, personal service, VII. ii. 27. A servant, II. ii. 7. 3. 役志, to make the will to serve, VI. ii. 5. 4.

往 *wang* (1) To go to. *Passim.* 無所往而不 . . ., in all places and circumstances . . ., VII. ii. 31. 3; 37. 10. (2) 往者, the past, VII. ii. 30. 2.

征 *chăng* (1) To exact duties; exactions, I. ii. 5. 3: II. i. 5. 2, 3; ii. 10. 7: III. ii. 8. 1: VII. ii. 27. 1. (2) To take, 征利, I. i. 1. 4. (3) To punish, to execute royal justice, I. i. 5. 5; ii. 11. 2, 3: III. ii. 5. 3, 4, 5: VII. ii. 2. 2; 4. 3.

徂 *tsû* (1) To go to; to march, I. ii. 3. 6, but the meaning is doubtful. (2) Seems to be used for 殂, and 徂落, = to decease, V. i. 4. 1.

待 *tài* (1) To wait, to wait for. May sometimes be translated by *until*, II. i. 1. 9; 8. 1; ii. 4. 1, *et al.*, *saepe*. (2) To treat, behave to, entertain, IV. ii. 28. 4; 31. 1: V. ii. 4. 4. In I. ii. 11. 1, the two meanings seem to come together.

很 *han* To be refractory and quarrelsome, IV. ii. 30. 2. Is often written 狠.

律 *lü* Pitch-tubes, for determining the upper musical accords, 六律, IV. i. 1. 1, 5.

後 *hâu* That which is after. (1) As a noun. Posterity, I. i. 4. 6: IV. i. 26. 2. An after period, II. i. 2. 27. Futurity: here 後之 may be considered = an adjective, future, III. ii. 4. 3. (2) As an adjective. Future, coming after, I. ii. 14. 3; 16. 1, *et al.*, *saepe*. (3) As a verb. To make an after consideration, I. i. 1. 4; ii. 11. 2: VII. ii. 4. 3, *et al.* To follow, keep behind, VI. ii. 2. 4. To follow after, succeed to (neuter), IV. ii. 1. 3. (4) As an adverb. Afterwards. *Passim.* Especially when preceded by 然 or 而. 其後, meaning *afterwards*, occurs once. (5) As a conjunction and preposition, after words and clauses, generally preceded by 之 = after, VI. ii. 7. 3, *et al.*

彼 *pi* That, those. *Saepe.* It may be sometimes rendered conveniently by the third personal pronoun.

徐 *hsü* (1) Slowly, VI. ii. 2. 4. 徐徐, gently, VI. i. 39. 2. (2) A surname, III. i. 5. 1, 3, 5: IV. ii. 18. 1.

徑 *ching* A footpath, VII. ii. 21.

徒 *t'û* (1) Foot (adjective), IV. ii. 2. 3. (2) Merely, only, II. i. 2. 16; ii. 9. 4; 13. 5: IV. i. 1. 3; 25: VI. ii. 8. 8. (3) A disciple, disciples, I. i. 7. 2: III. i. 4. 1, 2; ii. 9. 14: IV. ii. 22. 2: VII. i. 25. 1, 2.

得 *tê* (1) To get, to be got; both with and without an objective following. *Passim.* When there is no objective, the sense of the 得 must often be supplied from what precedes. 得乎 and 得於, to gain, to get the regard of, I. ii. 4. 2: IV. i. 28. 1: VII. ii. 14. 2. 必得, must get the proper men, VI. ii. 7. 3. 得我, VI. i. 10. 7, 8. 不得已, see 已. (2) The auxiliary *can*, *could*, 而 comes frequently between 得 and the verb.

徙 *hsi* To remove, III. i. 3. 18: IV. ii. 4. 1.

從 *ts'ung* To follow—both physically, and = to act according to, I. i. 7. 21; ii. 9. 1, 2: IV. ii. 30. 2, *et al.*, *saepe*. 從於, to follow, be in the train of, IV. i. 24. 1; 25. 1. 從 followed by 而 means *to follow up*, = thereupon, thereafter, I. i. 7. 20: II. ii. 10. 2, *et al.*, but each character has its proper meaning. 從 = from, VI. i. 4. 2.

從 *tsung* The 4th tone. 從者, followers in immediate attendance, III. ii. 4. 1: IV. ii. 31. 1: VII. ii. 30. 2.

御 *yü* 御者, a charioteer, III. ii. 1. 5.

御 *yà* I. i. 7. 12. The meaning is doubtful.

徧 *p'ien* All round, the whole of, IV. ii. 33. 1: VII. i. 46. 1.

復 *fû* (1) To report, I. i. 7. 10. (2) To repay, 復讐, to avenge, III. ii. 5. 3.

復 *fâu* The 4th tone. Again, II. i. 1. 1; 2. 17; ii. 11. 3: III. i. 1. 3; 2. 4; ii. 9. 10: IV. i. 19. 3: V. i. 6. 5: VII. ii. 23. 1. As a verb, to repeat, to try again, III. ii. 1. 4: VII. ii. 1. 2.

微 *wei* (1) Small, slight; in small degree, II. i. 2. 20: III. ii. 9. 7: IV. ii. 31. 3: VI. ii. 6. 6. 微服, the dress of a common man, V. i. 8. 3. The sentence to which this belongs has been omitted in the translation.—微服而過宋, 'He assumed, however, a private dress, and passed by Sung.' (2) The name of a State, II. i. 1. 8: VI. i. 6. 3.

徯 *hsi* To wait for, I. ii. 11. 2: III. ii. 5. 4.

徵 *chăng* To be evidenced, VI. ii. 15. 3.

徵 *chih* 徵招, the name of a piece of music, I. ii. 4. 9.

徹 *ch'ch* (1) To put away, II. i. 4. 3. (2) To remove,—as the materials of a meal, IV. i. 19. 3. (3) The share-system on which the Châu dynasty divided the lands, III. i. 3. 6.

德 *tê* Virtue, virtuous. *Passim.* Used for conduct in a bad sense, IV. i. 4. 1. 振德之, to stimulate and do them good, III. i. 4. 8.

THE 61st RADICAL, 心.

心 *hsin* (1) The heart; the mind:—denotes the mental constitution generally. *Saepe.* See note on II. i. 2. (2) In a name, 孔距心, II. ii. 4. 2, 3, 4.

必 *pi* Must, used as an auxiliary, and to assert also what is necessary. Often = what will certainly, would certainly; to be sure to. *Passim.* 必也 only occurs once, VII. ii. 37. 2.

忍 *jăn* or *zăn* (1) To bear, to endure, V. ii. 1. 1, 3, *et al.* 忍人之心, a heart that cannot bear the sufferings of others. So 忍人之政, II. i. 6. 1, 2, 3: IV. ii. 1. 5. (2) To harden, to make enduring, VI. ii. 15. 2.

忖 *ts'un* To reflect, consider. 忖度, to measure by reflection, I. i. 7. 9.

志 *chih* (1) The will; aim, purpose. *Passim.* In II. i. 2. 9, 10, it appears to be used synonymously with 心. In V. i. 4. 2, it = the aim or scope of a writer. 心志, VI. ii. 15. 2. 志於, the will bent on or directed to, is common. We have the phrases—得志, III. ii. 2. 3, *et al.*; 立志, VII. ii. 15, *et al.*; 尙志, VII. i. 33. 2, 3; 役志, VI. ii. 5. 4; 致志, VI. i. 9. 3; 志士, a determined scholar, III. ii. 1. 2: V. ii. 7. 5. (2) A Record, a History, III. i. 2. 3; ii. 1. 1.

忘 *wang* To forget; to be forgetful of, I. ii. 4. 7: II. i. 2. 16: III. i. 2. 1; ii. 1. 2: IV. i. 1. 4; ii. 20. 4: V. i. 1. 2; ii. 3. 2; 7. 5: VI. ii. 7. 3: VII. i. 8. 1; 35. 6; ii. 37. 1.

忠 *chung* True-hearted; true-heartedness, sincerity, I. i. 5. 3: III. i. 4. 10: IV. ii. 28. 5, 6; 31. 1: VI. i. 16. 1: VII. i. 32; ii. 37. 11.

快 *k'wâi* To be cheerful, to find pleasure, I. i. 7. 14, 15.

忸 *no* 忸怩, to be and look ashamed, V. i. 2. 3.

怍 *tso* To blush, VII. i. 20. 3.

怒 *nû* To be angry; anger, I. ii. 3. 6, 7, 8; 9. 1: II. ii. 12. 6: III. ii. 2. 1: IV. i. 18. 2: V. i. 3. 2.

思 *sze* (1) To think; to think of, I. ii. 5. 4: II. i. 2. 4; 3. 2; 9. 1: III. i. 5. 2: IV. i. 12. 2, *et al.*, *saepe.* Thinking, thoughts, IV. i. 1. 5: V. i. 2. 3. (2) 子思, the designation of Confucius's grandson, II. ii. 11. 3, 4: IV. ii. 31. 2, 3: V. ii. 3. 3; 6. 4, 5; 7. 4: VI. ii. 6. 3.

怠 *tâi* 怠敖, indolent and indifferent, II. i. 4. 4.

急 *chî* Urgent, earnest, III. ii. 3. 2, 6: IV. ii. 29. 4: VII. i. 46. 1 (*N.B.*)

性 *hsing* The nature,—generally used of that of man, III. i. 1. 2, and especially in the 6th Book, Part I. Applied generally, or away from man, IV. ii. 26. 1: VI. i. 2. 3; 3. 1. To be natural; to possess, to enjoy by nature, VII. i. 21. 2, 3, 4; 30. 1; ii. 24. 1, 2; 33. 1.

怨 *yüan* To murmur, I. ii. 11. 2: VI. ii. 3. 1, 2, 3, 4, *et al.*, *saepe.* 自怨, to murmur against himself, to become contrite, V. i. 6. 5. 怨天, II. ii. 13. 1; compare II. i. 7. 5. 怨 = to be dissatisfied, V. i. 1. 1; compare I. ii. 5. 5. Resentment, I. i. 7. 14: V. i. 3. 2.

怩 *ni* 忸怩, see 忸.

怵 *ch'ù* 怵惕, to be alarmed, II. i. 6. 3.

恆 *hăng* Constant, fixed; constantly, generally, I. i. 7. 20: III. i. 3. 3: IV. i. 5. 1; ii. 28. 3: VI. ii. 15. 3, 4: VII. i. 18.

恐 *k'ung* To fear, be afraid; sometimes = our *lest*, I. i. 7. 22; ii. 3. 8; 14. 1: II. i. 7. 1: III. i. 2. 4: IV. i. 16. 1: VII. ii. 1. 2; 37. 12.

恔 *hsiâo* The 3rd tone. To feel pleased, II. ii. 7. 4.

恕 *shû* The principle of reciprocity, making our own feelings the rule for our conduct to others, VII. i. 4. 3.

恝 *chieh* The appearance of being without sorrow, V. i. 1. 2.

恣 *tsze* License. 放恣, III. ii. 9. 9.

恥 *ch'ih* The sense of shame; to feel ashamed of; shameful, I. i. 5. 1; ii. 3. 7: II. i. 7. 3, 4: IV. i. 7. 3, 4; ii. 18. 3: V. ii. 5. 5: VI. ii. 14. 4: VII. i. 6; 7. 1, 2, 3.

恩 *ăn* Kindness, I. i. 7. 10, 12: II. ii. 2. 4: IV. ii. 30. 4.

恭 *kung* To respect, honour, IV. i. 1. 13; 16: V. ii. 4. 1; 6. 3. 恭敬, VI. i. 6. 7: VII. i. 37. 2, 3. 恭 = gravely complaisant, III. i. 3. 4. 不恭, wanting in self-respect, II. i. 9. 3.

息 *hsi* (1) To stop (active and neuter), III. ii. 9. 9, 13. To rest from toil, I. ii. 4. 6. 安息, to rest in quiet, III. ii. 9. 5. (2) To grow, applied to trees and to the mind, VI. i. 8. 1, 2. (3) A name, V. i. 1. 2; ii. 3. 3.

悄 *ch'iâo* 悄悄, to be disquieted and grieved, VII. ii. 19. 3.

悌 *ti* Brotherly duty; to be obedient as a younger brother, I. i. 3. 4; 5. 3; 7. 24: III. ii. 4. 3.

悅 *yüeh* (1) To be pleased; to be pleased with, I. ii. 10. 3; 11. 2: II. i. 1. 3, 13; 3. 2; 5. 1, 2, 3, 4, 5, *et al.*, *saepe.* Is sometimes followed by 於, V. i. 8. 3: VI. ii. 4. 5, 6. (2) To please, give pleasure to, IV. i. 12. 1; ii. 2. 5: VI. i. 7. 8.—Observe 爲容悅, VII. i. 19. 1; 以爲悅, II. ii. 7. 3: VII. i. 19. 2; and 以我爲悅, VI. i. 4. 4.

悔 *húi* To repent of, V. i. 6. 5.

患 *hwan* Calamities; what causes sorrow and grief, IV. i. 23; ii. 9. 1; 28. 7: VI. ii. 2. 3; 15. 4, 5: VII. i. 18. 2. What will endanger life, VI. i. 10. 2, 3, 4. To be grieved, I. ii. 15. 1: II. ii. 9. 2.

悴 *sui* 憔悴, famished, to be distressed, II. i. 1. 11.

悻 *hăng* 悻悻然, angry-like, II. ii. 12. 6.

情 *ch'ing* (1) The feelings proper to humanity, VI. i. 6. 5; 8. 2. (2) 情 = the truth, or reality, IV. ii. 18. 3. (3) 情 = the quality or proper nature, III. i. 4. 18.

惑 *hwo* To be deluded, perplexed, II. i. 1. 7: VI. i. 16. 3. To be in error, IV. ii. 29. 7.

惕 *t'i* 怵惕 see 怵.

惟 *wei* A particle, both initial and medial. *Passim.* It almost always means only. Observe its use in quotations from the older classics.

惠 *húi* (1) To be kind; kindness, III. i. 4. 10: IV. ii. 2. 2; 23. (2) An honorary epithet, 梁惠王, I. i. 1. 1; 2. 1, *et al.*—柳下惠, II. i. 9. 2, 3, *et al.*—費惠公, V. ii. 3. 3.

惡 *o* Wicked, bad; wickedness, II. i. 2. 4; 9. 1: IV. i. 1. 7; 15. 1; 18. 2; ii. 25. 2: V. ii. 1. 1: VI. ii. 7. 4.

惡 *wú* To dislike, detest, hate, I. i. 4. 5: II. i. 4. 1, 2; 9. 1, *et al.*, *saepe.* 羞惡之心, II. i. 6. 4, 5: VI. i. 6. 7.

惡 *wû* The 1st tone. (1) How, I. i. 7. 7; ii. 8. 5, *et al.*, *saepe.* It is sometimes followed by 乎, adding an exclamatory force to it, I. i. 6. 2: II. i. 2. 11: V. ii. 5. 3: VI. ii. 12. 1. 惡在, where, how does it consist with, I. i. 4. 5: III. i. 3. 7: VI. i. 5. 4: VII. i. 33. 3. 惡在 is both initial and final. (2) An exclamation, Oh! II. i. 2. 19; ii. 2. 4; 9. 2.

惰 *to* To be lazy, IV. ii. 30. 2.

惴 *chûi* To have mental anxiety, to be afraid, II. i. 2. 7.

惻 *ts'ê* To commiserate, 惻隱之心, II. i. 6. 3, 4, 5: VI. i. 6. 7.

惛 *hwăn* Unintelligent, stupid, I. i. 7. 19.

愆 *ch'ien* Transgression, error, IV. i. 1. 4.

愈 *yü* (1) To be better,—spoken of disease, II. ii. 2. 2, 3: III. i. 5. 1. (2) To surpass, IV. ii. 24. 1. Followed by 於, VI. ii. 11. 1: VII. i. 39. 1, 4. (3) To increase, VI. ii. 8. 4.

意 *i* To think, IV. i. 25. 1. One's own ideas, V. i. 4. 2.

愛 *âi* To love; to care for, I. ii. 5. 5: III. i. 5. 3; ii. 9. 9: IV. i. 4. 1; ii. 28. 2, 3: V. i. 1. 2; 2. 4; 3. 2: VI. i. 4. 4; 13; 14. 1: VII. i. 14. 3; 15. 2; 26. 2; 37. 1; 45; 46. 1; ii. 1. 1, 2. 愛 = to grudge, I. i. 7. 5, 6, 7.

慍 *wăn* To be hated, VII. ii. 19. 3.

愧 *k'wei* To be ashamed, VII. i. 20. 3.

愬 *sû* To complain, announce their wrongs, I. i. 7. 18.

愼 *shăn* (1) To be careful, to be cautious, I. ii. 7. 3: II. i. 7. 1. (2) A surname, VI. ii. 8. 1, 4.

慈 *tsze* To be kind to; affectionate, IV. i. 2. 4: VI. ii. 7. 3.

慊 *ch'ien* (1) To be dissatisfied, II. ii. 2. 4. (2) To be satisfied (also read *ch'ieh*), II. i. 2. 15.

慕 *mû* To desire, to affect, IV. i. 6. 1. To desire with affectionate longing, V. i. 1. 1, 5: VI. ii. 3. 5.

慚 *ts'an* To feel ashamed, II. ii. 9. 1.

慝 *ni* Wickedness; hidden wickedness, I. ii. 4. 6: VII. ii. 37. 13.

慢 *man* To despise; to neglect, I. ii. 12. 2: II. ii. 2. 6: III. i. 3. 13.

慧 *hûi* Intelligence, discernment, II. i. 1. 9: VII. i. 18. 1.

慮 *lü* To think anxiously; to be anxious about, II. i. 2. 5; ii. 11. 4: VII. i. 15. 1; 18. 2. Anxious thoughts, VI. ii. 15. 3. 知慮, VI. ii. 13. 2.

慶 *ch'ing* Congratulation; to be rewarded, VI. ii. 7. 2.

憂 *yü* To be sorrowful; to grieve for; sorrow, cause of distress, I. ii. 4. 6: III. i. 4. 7, 8, 9: IV. i. 9. 5; ii. 28. 7; 29. 2: V. i. 1. 4; ii. 3: VI. ii. 15. 5: VII. i. 27. 2; ii. 19. 3. 采薪之憂, = 'a little sickness,' II. ii. 2. 3. Observe 憂民之憂, I. ii. 4. 3.

憎 *tsăng* To hate. But the text is doubtful, VII. ii. 19. 2.

憔 *ch'iâo* 憔悴, see 悴.

憚 *tan* To dread, to shrink from, III. i. 4. 5.

孟子

憫 *min* To sorrow, II. i. 9. 2: V. ii. 1. 3.

憮 *wû* 憮然, the appearance of being surprised, thoughtful-like, III. i. 5. 5.

憾 *han* To feel indignant, vexed, I. i. 3. 3: VII. ii. 37. 8.

應 *ying* A name, VII. i. 35. 1.

應 *ying* The 4th tone. To answer, II. ii. 8. 2; 11. 2: VI. ii. 1. 8.

懟 *tûi* To incur the resentment of, V. i. 2. 1.

懲 *ch'ăng* To repress; to punish, III. i. 4. 16; ii. 9. 12.

懿 *î* Admirable, VI. i. 6. 8.

懦 *zû* Weak, timid, V. ii. 1. 1: VII. ii. 15.

懷 *hwâi* To cherish in the thoughts, VI. ii. 4. 5, 6.

懸 *hsüan* To be suspended. 倒懸, hung up by the heels, II. i. 1. 13.

懼 *chü* To fear, be alarmed, II. i. 2. 5: III. ii. 2. 1; 9. 8, 10, 11.

THE 62ND RADICAL, 戈.

戈 *ko* A spear, I. ii. 5. 4.

戎 *zung* The wild tribes of the West, III. i. 4. 16; ii. 9. 12.

成 *ch'ăng* (1) To perfect, complete, I. i. 2. 3: IV. i. 1. 1: V. i. 9. 3: VI. ii. 5. 5: VII. i. 40. 3. Observe 成功, I. ii. 14. 3; and 成章, VII. i. 24. 3. To be perfect, III. ii. 3. 3: VII. ii. 14. 4. To become completed, IV. ii. 2. 3: VII. ii. 21. (2) Spoken with reference to music. Confucius is called 集大成, a complete concert, V. ii. 1. 6. (3) A surname, III. i. 1. 4. In a double surname, VII. ii. 29. (4) 武成, the name of a book in the Shû-ching, VII. ii. 3. 2.

我 *wo* (1) I, we, me, us; my, our. *Passim.* Observe 爲我 in III. ii. 9. 9: VII. i. 26. 1; and 於我 and 得我 in VI. i. 4. 4; 10. 7. (2) 宰我, one of Confucius's disciples, II. i. 2. 18, 25, 26.

戒 *chieh* (1) To caution; a caution, III. i. 2. 5; ii. 2. 2. 戒之, beware, I. ii. 12. 2. Cautious, using precautions, II. ii. 3. 4. (2) 齊戒 = to fast, IV. ii. 25. 2. According to the dictionary, this meaning may be reduced to the preceding. (3) To issue a proclamation, I. ii. 4. 9.

戕 *ch'iang* To do violence to, VI. i. 1. 2. This character has several other pronunciations.

或 *hwo* (1) Some (both singular and plural), I. i. 3. 2; ii. 10. 2; 15. 2; 16. 2, *et al., saepe.* (2) Perhaps, II. ii. 2. 6. 或者, II. ii. 2. 2. This meaning and the other are connected, and the dictionary gives them together, saying that 或 is a word of uncertainty. Observe I. ii. 16. 3: II. i. 4. 3; ii. 6. 2: III. i. 4. 12, 17, 18: V. i. 7. 7: VI. i. 6. 7. (3) Used for 惑, VI. i. 9. 1.

戚 *ch'î* (1) A kind of axe, I. ii. 5. 5. (2) Relatives by affinity, I. ii. 7. 3: II. ii. 1. 4, 5: V. ii. 9. 1: VII. i. 34. 1. Used as a verb, 戚之, to consider him as a relative, VI. ii. 3. 2. (3) Sorrow, grief, III. i. 2. 5. 戚戚, the appearance of being sorrowful, I. i. 7. 9.

戟 *chî* A kind of spear, II. ii. 4. 1.

戢 *chî* To collect, I. ii. 5. 4.

戮 *lû* (1) To put to death, to slaughter, III. ii. 9. 6: IV. ii. 4. (2) Disgrace, IV. ii. 30. 2.

戰 *chan* (1) To fight, to conduct battles; fightings, wars, I. i. 3. 2; 7. 17: II. ii. 1. 5: IV. i. 14. 2, 3: VI. ii. 8. 3; 9. 2: VII. ii. 2. 1; 4. 1, 6. 戰之, making them fight, leading them to battle, VII. ii. 1. 2. (2) A name, III. i. 3. 13.

戴 *tâi* (1) To carry on the head, I. i. 3. 4; 7. 24. (2) A surname, III. ii. 6. 1.—III. ii. 8. 1. (3) A name, III. ii. 10. 5.

THE 63RD RADICAL, 戶.

戶 *hû* A door,—properly an inner door, II. i. 4. 3: IV. ii. 29. 7. 門戶, VI. ii. 14. 4: VII. i. 23. 3.

戹 *î* To be distressed, reduced to straits, VII. ii. 18.

所 *so* (1) A place, III. ii. 6. 2: V. i. 2. 4. (2) The compound relative what, = that which, those which. *Passim.* Sometimes it is simply the relative, the antecedent, if we may so call it, being expressed, as in 所居之室. The idea of *place* as the antecedent often enters into the phrase where it is thus used. 無所 and 無所不, 有所 and 有所不 are to be marked, VII. i. 7. 2; ii. 1. 2; 31. 1, 3; 37. 2, 10, *et al., saepe.* 所以, whereby, the whereby, is very common; and 所, alone, has sometimes the same

force. Observe 在所禮, VII. i. 43. 1 (compare IV. ii. 28. 7); 有所受之, III. i. 2. 3: VII. i. 35. 4; 所過, 所存, VII. i. 13. 3; 所就, 所去, VI. ii. 14. 1; 兼所愛, VI. i. 14. 1; 未有所終…, V. ii. 4. 6; 所爲主, 所主, V. i. 8. 4; 惟義所在, IV. ii. 11. 1; 所教, 所受教, II. ii. 2. 9; 所安, II. i. 2. 20; 所之, I. ii. 16. 1; 惟君所行, I. ii. 4. 9.

戾 *li* In the phrase 狼戾, III. i. 3. 7.

THE 64TH RADICAL, 手.

手 *shâu* The hand, hands, II. i. 1. 6: IV. i. 17. 1, 3; 27. 2 (*N.B.*); ii. 3. 1.

才 *ts'âi* The natural powers; abilities, I. ii. 7. 2: VI. i. 6. 6, 7; 7. 1; 8. 2: VII. ii. 29. In the concrete, = men of good talents, IV. ii. 7: VI. ii. 7. 3: VII. i. 20. 4.

扣 *k'âu* To rap, knock against, IV. ii. 24. 2.

扶 *fû* 扶持, to support, sustain, III. i. 3. 18.

承 *ch'ăng* (1) To receive, I. i. 4. 1. (2) To receive and carry out, III. ii. 9. 6, 13. 承繼, V. i. 6. 2. A passage here has been omitted in the text—啟賢, 能敬承繼禹之道, 益之相禹也, 歷年少, 施澤於民未久,—'that Ch'î was a wise and worthy prince, able reverently to receive and carry on the principles of Yü, and that Yih assisted Yü *only* for a few years, conferring benefits on the people for a short time.' (3) To resist, III. ii. 9. 12. This is the meaning assigned by Chû Hsî.

把 *pâ* To grasp,—with one hand. 拱把, VI. i. 13.

抑 *yi* (1) An initial particle, = come now, I. i. 7. 14. (2) Or, I. i. 7. 16. Followed by 亦, II. ii. 4. 3: III. ii. 10. 3. (3) To repress, III. ii. 9. 11.

折 *cheh* To break off, I. i. 7. 11.

抽 *ch'âu* To take out, IV. ii. 24. 2.

拂 *fû* To shake off, 拂亂, to confound, VI. ii. 15. 2. Read *pi*, i.q. 弼, to assist; able, VI. ii. 15. 4.

抱 *pâo* To embrace, encircle, 抱關, to go round the gates, i.e. to guard them, V. ii. 5. 3; 6. 3.

拒 *chü* To resist, to reject, VII. ii. 30. 3.

拔 *pâ* (1) To pull out, VII. i. 26. 1. (2) To rise high, II. i. 2. 28. In this meaning it should probably be read *p'o;* see the dictionary.

拘 *chü* To detain, VII. ii. 35. 3.

拙 *chüeh* Stupid, VII. i. 41. 2.

招 *châo* (1) To call, to summon, III. ii. 1. 2: V. ii. 7. 5, 6, 7. (2) To tie the legs, VII. ii. 26. 2.

招 *shâo* Used for 韶, the name of Shun's music. 徵招, 角招, two pieces of music, I. ii. 4. 9.

拜 *pâi* To make an obeisance; to pay one's respects, II. i. 8. 2: III. ii. 7. 3: V. ii. 6. 4, 5.

拯 *ch'ăng* To deliver, rescue, I. ii. 11. 3.

拱 *kung* To grasp with the two hands, VI. i. 13.

持 *ch'ih* To hold, to grasp, II. ii. 4. 1. Applied to the will,—to maintain, II. i. 2. 9, 10. 扶持, see 扶.

指 *chih* A finger, VI. i. 12. 1, 2; 14. 4. To point out, = meaning, scope, VI. ii. 4. 4: VII. ii. 32. 1.

挫 *ts'o* To push. A push, II. i. 2. 4.

振 *chăn* (1) To stimulate, III. i. 4. 8. (2) To bring to a close, to wind up,—in music, V. ii. 1. 6.

挾 *chiâ* (1) To take under the arm, I. i. 7. 11. (2) To presume on, V. ii. 3. 1: VII. i. 43. 2.

括 *kwo* A name, VII. ii. 29. 1.

捆 *k'wăn* To beat and hammer. 捆屨, to make sandals, III. i. 4. 1.

捐 *chüan* To remove, V. i. 2. 3.

授 *shâu* To give,—properly, with the hand, IV. i. 17. 1. Generally, to give, II. ii. 10. 3. To give up, surrender, III. ii. 5. 2.

掊 *p'âu* To collect imposts. 掊克, = exacting, able ministers, VI. ii. 7. 2.

掌 *chang* (1) The palm, I. i. 7. 12: II. i. 1. 8; 6. 2. 熊掌, bears'-paws, VI. i. 10. 1. (2) To manage, direct, III. i. 4. 7; ii. 1. 4.

排 *p'âi* To arrange, = to regulate the course of, III. i. 4. 7.

掘 *chüeh* To dig, III. ii. 9. 4: VII. i. 29. 1.

接 *chieh* To come into contact; to have intercourse with. (1) To receive, admit to one's presence, V. i. 3. 3. (2) 相接, to have intercourse with, VI. ii. 4. 5, 6. But in I. i. 3. 2, 既接 = being crossed, spoken of weapons. (3) 接淅, to let the water of rice strain off through the hand, V. ii. 1. 4: VII. ii. 17. (4) Used of the manner in which a present is offered, V. ii. 4. 3.

推 *t'ûi* (1) To push, V. i. 7. 6; ii. 1. 2. (2) To push out, carry out, I. i. 7. 12. To consider, prosecute the study of, II. i. 9. 1. In these two cases, we should read the character *ch'ûi*.

掩 *yen* To cover. Applied to the bodies of the dead, III. i. 5. 4; to the nose, IV. ii. 25. 1; to wickedness, IV. i. 15. 1. To cover = to make good, to come up to, VII. ii. 37. 6.

揆 *k'wei* To examine, to calculate, IV. i. 1. 8; ii. 1. 4.

提 *t'i* To lift with the hand, to carry, 孩提之童, children carried in the arms, VII. i. 15. 2.

揖 *yî* To salute, with the hands joined before the breast, = to bow to, III. i. 4. 13: IV. ii. 27. 3.

揚 *yang* (1) To display, be displayed, put forth, III. ii. 5. 6. (2) A kind of battle-axe, I. ii. 5. 4.

揜 *yen* Used for 掩, to cover up, V. i. 2. 3.

揠 *yâ* To pull up, II. i. 2. 16.

揣 *ch'ûi* To feel with the hand, = to adjust, VI. ii. 1. 5.

援 *yüan* (1) To draw,—spoken of a bow, VI. i. 9. 3. 援, to press, to hold fast, II. i. 9. 2. (2) To draw out, to rescue, IV. i. 17. 1, 2, 3.

搆 *kâu* 搆兵, to be fighting together, VI. ii. 4. 3.

損 *sun* To diminish, to be diminished, III. ii. 8. 2: VII. i. 21. 3.

搏 *po* (1) To seize, IV. ii. 3. 4: VII. ii. 23. 2. (2) To strike with the hand, VI. i. 2. 3.

摟 *lâu* To drag, to drag away, VI. ii. 1. 8; 7. 2.

摩 *mo* To rub, i. e. to rub smooth, VII. i. 26. 2.

摽 *piâo* To beckon, to motion to, V. ii. 6. 4.

撓 *nâo* To bend. 膚撓, to flinch from strokes at the body, II. i. 2. 4.

撫 *fû* (1) To tranquillize, = to subdue, I. i. 7. 16. (2) To hold, to grasp, I. ii. 3. 5.

播 *po* To sow; to disseminate, III. i. 3. 2: IV. i. 1. 7: VI. i. 7. 2.

撻 *t'â* To beat, II. i. 2. 4: III. ii. 6. 1. 撻 = to oppose, I. i. 5. 3.

擇 *châi* To choose, I. ii. 14. 2; 15. 2: II. i. 7. 2: III. i. 3. 13: IV. ii. 28. 6. 牛羊何擇, what was there to choose between an ox and a sheep? I. i. 7. 7.

擊 *chî* To beat, strike, 擊柝, V. ii. 5. 3; 6. 3.

操 *ts'âo* To hold fast,—spoken of the mind, VI. i. 8. 4: VII. i. 18. 2. 操 = principles, III. ii. 10. 2, 6. In this meaning it should be the 4th tone, according to the dictionary.

擘 *pi* 巨擘, the thumb, III. ii. 10. 2.

擴 *k'wo* To stretch out and expand, 擴而充之, II. i. 6. 7.

攖 *ying* To encounter, to press near to, VII. ii. 23. 2.

攘 *zang* (1) To steal,—upon occasion offered, III. ii. 8. 2. (2) To bare, VII. ii. 23. 2.

攝 *sheh* To act for, undertake one's duties, V. i. 4. 1. 攝 = a plurality of offices, VI. ii. 7. 3.

THE 65TH RADICAL, 支.

支 *chih* Used for 肢. 四支, the four limbs, IV. ii. 30. 2.

THE 66TH RADICAL, 攴.

收 *shâu* To take back, IV. ii. 3. 3, 4.

攸 *yû* (1) I. q. 所. 有攸, some, III. ii. 5. 5. (2) Appears to be a mere expletive, I. i. 2. 3. (3) 攸然, the appearance of a fish let go in the water, V. i. 2. 4.

改 *kâi* To alter, change (active and neuter); to reform, II. ii. 9. 4: IV. i. 2. 4; 14. 1 (改於); ii. 29. 1: V. ii. 4. 5: VI. ii. 15. 3: VII. i. 41. 2. Observe 改之 and 改諸, II. ii. 12. 4, 5. 改曰, 'spake with an altered mind,' V. i. 7. 4. In II. i. 1. 10, 不改 = does not need more.

攻 *kung* (1) To attack, II. i. 5. 6; ii. 1. 2, 5: V. i. 7. 9. 攻 = to expose one's errors, IV. i. 14. 1. (2) To undertake, to proceed to do, I. i. 2. 3.

放 *fang* (1) To banish,—spoken of men, animals, and doctrines, I. ii. 8. 1: III. ii. 9. 4, 10, 13: V. i. 3. 1, 2, 3; 6. 5: VII. i. 31. 1, 2. (2) To lose, let stray; stray, lost, VI. i. 8. 2; 11. 2, 3, 4: VII. ii. 26. 2. (3) Dissolute, self-abandoned, I. i. 7. 20: III. i. 3. 3; ii. 5. 2. So 放恣, III. ii. 9. 9. (4) 放飯, to eat immoderately; but other meanings are given to the phrase, VII. i. 46. 2.

ʻ放 *fang* The 3rd tone. (1) To, going on to, I. ii. 4. 4: IV. ii. 18. 2: VII. ii. 26. 2. (2) ʻ放勳, a designation of Yâo or (? possibly) of Shun, III. i. 4. 8: V. i. 4. 1.

政 *chăng* Government. *Passim.* 政事, the principles and business of government, VII. ii. 12. 3; 28. So 政刑, II. i. 4. 2. 爲政, the administration of government, is very common; but it = to give law to, in I. ii. 11. 1: IV. i. 7. 4. 聽政, IV. ii. 2. 1. 行政, to practise a government, is common. 施政 is also found. Observe 以政, V. i. 8. 3.

故 *kû* The cause or reason of a thing. (1) 有故, 無故, there being a cause, there being no cause, IV. ii. 3. 3, 4: VII. i. 20. 2 (*N.B.*) Observe 故 alone, III. i. 5. 3. At the end of a clause, 故 = because, VI. i. 5. 4: VII. i. 21. 3. Observe 以...之故, VII. ii. 1. 2. (2) 故 and 是故, in continuation of a subject,—therefore, thus. *Passim.* (3) Facts, phenomena, IV. ii. 26. 1, 3. (4) Ancient, old, I. ii. 7. 1: II. i. 1. 8. 故 = old acquaintance, VII. i. 43. 2.

效 *hsiâo* 效死 = to be prepared to die, to strive to death, I. ii. 13. 2; 15. 2.

教 *chiâo* To teach. *Saepe.* Instructions; lessons, I. i. 3. 4; 7. 24: IV. i. 14. 2, 3. Observe II. i. 2. 19; and V. ii. 4. 4. Pronounced in the 1st tone, it = to call in, to employ, I. ii. 9. 2.

敏 *min* Alert, intelligent, and active, I. i. 7. 19: IV. i. 7. 5.

救 *chiû* To save, I. ii. 11. 1; 12. 1: III. ii. 5. 5: V. i. 7. 6. 救 = to put out, to save from fire, VI. i. 18. 1. 救 = to part, to stop from fighting, IV. ii. 29. 6, 7. 救死, to save themselves from death, I. i. 7. 22.

敖 *âo* (1) 怠敖, indolent indifference, idle sauntering, II. i. 4. 4. (2) A name, VI. ii. 15. 1. (3) 子敖, a designation, IV. i. 24. 1; 25. 1; ii. 27. 3.

敗 *pâi* To ruin, IV. i. 8. 1. To be defeated, I. i. 5. 1: VII. ii. 1. 2.

敝 *pi* Worn-out, VII. i. 35. 6.

敢 *kan* To venture, dare, presume. *Saepe.* 敢問, 'I venture to ask,' is a common way of asking a question. Observe 請勿復敢見, II. ii. 11. 3.

散 *san* (1) To be scattered, I. i. 5. 4; ii. 1. 6; 12. 2: II. ii. 4. 2. (2) A surname, VII. ii. 38. 3.

敦 *tun* (1) Generous, V. ii. 1. 3: VII. ii. 15. (2) To manage; but this meaning is not found in the dictionary, II. ii. 7. 1.

敬 *chăng* To respect, revere; the feeling of reverence; reverential, II. ii. 2. 4: III. ii. 2. 2: IV. i. 2. 2; 4. 1, *et al.*, *saepe.* 恭敬, VI. i. 5. 2, 3, *et al.* On the difference between the terms, see IV. i. 1. 13.

敷 *fû* To set forth, 敷治, III. i. 4. 7.

數 *shû* (1) Number, II. ii. 13. 4. Several, I. i, 3. 4: II. ii. 2. 3; 5. 1, *et al.*, *saepe.* ? a few, VII. i. 39. 3. (2) 數 = an art, VI. i. 9. 3.

數 *ts'û* Close, close-meshed, I. i. 3. 3.

敵 *ti* An enemy, I. i. 5. 5, 6: II. i. 2. 5; 5. 6: III. ii. 5. 4: IV. i. 7. 5, 6: VII. ii. 3. 3; 4. 2. Hostile, VI. ii. 15. 4: VII. ii. 2. 3. To be an enemy to, to oppose, I. i. 7. 17; ii. 3. 5: VII. ii. 4. 5.

敺 *ch'ü* I. q. 驅. To drive, chase, IV. i. 9. 3, 4.

整 *chăng* To marshal, I. ii. 3. 6.

斂 *lien* To ingather. The ingathering,—spoken of the harvest, I. ii. 4. 5: VI. ii. 7. 2. 稅斂, all taxes and imposts, I. i. 5. 3: VII. i. 23. 1.

THE 67TH RADICAL, 文.

文 *wăn* (1) A character, as delineated, = a word, V. i. 4. 2. (2) Style, method of composition, IV. ii. 21. 3. (3) Elegant, adorned, VI. i. 17. 3. To adorn, 節文, IV. i. 27. 2. (4) An honorary epithet, 文王, I. i. 2. 3, *et al.*, *saepissime.*—晋文, II. i. 7. 1, 2: IV. ii. 21. 3.—滕文公, I. ii. 13, *et al.*

THE 69TH RADICAL, 斤.

斤 *chin* A bill,—a general name of all crooked knives, 斧斤, I. i. 3. 3: VI. i. 8. 1, 2.

斧 *fû* An axe. 斧斤, see above.

斬 *chan* To cut in two, = to terminate, IV. ii. 22. 1.

斯 *sze* (1) This, these, I. i. 4. 6; 7. 12; ii. 5. 3, 4, *et al.*, *saepe.* (2) As a conjunction, forthwith, then, thereupon, &c., I. i. 3. 5: II. i. 6. 2: III. ii. 7. 2; 8. 3: VII. ii. 37. 3, 8, 13. In several cases we can hardly tell whether to take the character as a conjunction, or as the demonstrative, following its antecedent, to give emphasis to the sentence. Observe also I. ii. 3. 6, and 5. 4, where it seems a mere expletive. (3) 斯須, i. q. 須臾, an instant, VI. i. 5. 4. (4) In a name, IV. ii. 24. 2.

新 *hsin* New, III. i. 3. 12.

斲 *cho* To cut, hew, I. ii. 9. 1.

斷 *twan* In the phrase, 龍斷, a conspicuous mound, II. ii. 10. 6, 7.

THE 70TH RADICAL, 方.

方 *fang* (1) That which is square, IV. i. 1. 1, 5; 2. 1. Square, the adjective,—followed by the dimension, I. i. 5. 2; 7. 17, *et al.*, *saepe.* Observe the note on V. ii. 2. 4. (2) A quarter, region, direction, III. 4. 1: VI. i. 2. 1. The phrase 四方 is common. 無方, without reference to their where-from, IV. ii. 20. 2. (3) 方 = class, a resemblance, V. i. 2. 4. (4) To neglect, violate, I. ii. 4. 6. (5) As a conjunction, 方且, III. i. 4. 16; 爰方, I. ii. 5. 4.

於 *yü* *Passim.* (1) A preposition, in, at, on. But after many verbs and adjectives we must translate it variously,—by, to, from, &c. &c., and often it need not be translated at all. 至於, down to, coming to, &c., is common. After the possessive 之, 於 = in relation to, and so, sometimes, when not preceded by 之. 於 = compared with, II. i. 2. 23. After 志, it is common, and what may be called composite verbs, such as 得罪, 有功, &c. (2) Than, forming the comparative degree of preceding adjectives. *Saepe.* But observe II. i. 2. 28, at the end.

於 *wû* (1) How! I. i. 2. 3. (2) 於陵, the name of a place, III. ii. 10. 1, 5, 6.

施 *shih* To give, to dispense; to be given to, to be shown, I. i. 5. 3; 7. 18; ii. 5. 3: IV. i. 9. 1: V. i. 6. 2: VI. i. 17. 3: VII. i. 21 (?); ii. 32. 1. (2) In the name, 孟施舍, II. i. 2. 5, 6, 8.

施 *shih* The 1st tone. 施施, complacently, IV. ii. 33. 1.

施 *i* Dodgingly, = secretly, IV. ii. 33. 1.

旂 *ch'i* A flag, with dragons emblazoned, and bells attached, V. ii. 7. 6.

旃 *chan* A flag,—of silk, unemblazoned, V. ii. 7. 6.

旄 *mâo* (1) A white cow's tail,—used to make signals with. 旄 = streamers, I. ii. 1. 6, 7. (2) I.q. 耄, very old persons, I. ii. 11. 4.

旅 *lü* (1) Hosts. Properly, 500 men make a 旅, I. ii. 3. 6. (2) A stranger, a traveller, I. i. 7. 18: II. i. 5. 3: VI. ii. 7. 3.

旋 *hsüan* 周旋, going round, the turnings of the body, VII. ii. 33. 2.

旌 *ching* A flag,—made of feathers suspended from the top of the staff, III. ii. 1. 2: V. ii. 7. 5, 6.

族 *ts'û* The head of an arrow, III. i. 2. 5.

THE 71ST RADICAL, 无.

既 *chi* A particle of past time. May often be translated by have, having, having been, I. i. 3. 2: II. i. 2. 10 (*N.B.*), 18, 19; ii. 5. 1 (*N.B.*); 6. 2 (*N.B.*): III. i. 3. 13; ii. 9. 4, 5, *et al.*, *saepe.* Observe 既而, V. i. 7. 4; 既 . . . 而, VI. i. 16. 3; and 既已, VI. ii. 13. 8. In these and similar instances there should be a comma after 既. It does not form an adverb with the character that follows.

THE 72ND RADICAL, 日.

日 *zăh* (1) The sun, I. i. 2. 4: II. ii. 9. 4: V. i. 4. 1: VII. i. 24. 2. (2) A day, days, the day, II. ii. 4. 1: III. ii. 10. 1: IV. i. 24. 2; ii. 2. 5; 3. 4; 20. 5, *et al.* 他日, see 他. 今日, to-day, II. i. 2. 16, *et al.* 明日, to-morrow, II. ii. 2. 2, *et al.* 前日, formerly, II. ii. 7. 1, *et al.* 終日, all the day, III. ii. 1. 4. 無日, 不日, in no time, I. i. 2. 3: IV. i. 1. 9. 日至, the solstice, IV. ii. 26. 3: but VI. i. 7. 2 is different. 冬日, in winter, VI. i. 5. 5. 暇日, leisure days, I. i. 5. 3. 窮日之力, to exert the strength the whole day, II. ii. 12. 6. 日 alone = daily, from day to day, II. ii. 12. 5: III. ii. 6. 1; 8. 2: V. i. 3. 1, *et al.*

旦 *tan* The morning, IV. ii. 20. 5. 旦旦, from morning to morning, i. q. from day to day, VI. i. 8. 2. 平旦, the day-break, also VI. i. 8. 2.

旨 *chih* Good, pleasant, IV. ii. 20. 1.

旬 *hsün* A decade of days, I. ii. 10. 2.

旱 *han* Drought, season of drought, I. i. 6. 6; ii. 11. 2: III. ii. 5. 4. 旱乾, VII. ii. 14. 4.

旻 *min* 旻天, the name given to the autumnal heavens, = pitying, V. i. 1. 1, 2.

明 *ming* (1) Brightness, VII. i. 24. 2. (2) Intelligent; to be intelligent about, I. i. 7. 21: II. ii. 12. 1: IV. i. 12. 1; ii. 19. 2. (3) To illustrate; to digest clearly, II. i. 4. 2: III. i. 3. 10. (4) Clearly, plainly, II. ii. 11. 3: III. ii. 6. 1: VI. ii. 8. 5. Observe 明以教我, I. i. 7. 19. (5) Power of vision, I. i. 7. 10: IV. i. 1. 1. (6) 明日, to-morrow; see 日. (7) 明堂, see 堂. (8) 公明, a double surname, III. i. 1. 4; ii. 3. 1; 9. 9: IV. ii. 24. 1.—V. i. 1. 2.

易 *yi* (1) To change; to exchange, barter, I. i. 7. 4, 6, 7: II. ii. 10. 7: III. i. 4. 4, 5; 5. 2; ii. 9. 10; 10. 4: IV. i. 18. 3; ii. 29. 5 (*N.B.*); 31. 3: VI. ii. 7. 3: VII. i. 28. 1. 易位 = to dethrone, V. ii. 9. 1. 易事, an interchange of services, III. ii. 4. 3. (2) 易牙, a famous cook of antiquity, VI. i. 7. 5.

易 *i* The 4th tone. (1) Easy; easily, readily; what is easy, III. i. 4. 9, 10: IV. i. 11: VI. i. 9. 2. 易然, II. i. 1. 7, 9; observe also 11, 易爲食云云. 易 = to use readily, IV. i. 22. (2) To cultivate well, I. i. 5. 3: VII. i. 23. 1.

昆 *kwăn* Used for 混. 昆夷, the name of a rude tribe of the West, I. ii. 3. 1.

昔 *hsi* Formerly, III. ii. 1. 2: IV. ii. 31. 1. Instead of 昔 alone, Mencius commonly uses 昔者, I. ii. 4. 4; 5. 3, 4, 5; 14. 2; 15. 1, *et al.*, *saepe*. Sometimes 昔者 = yesterday, I. ii. 7. 1: II. ii. 2. 2, 3: III. ii. 1. 2: IV. i. 24. 2. Sometimes I have left it untranslated.

星 *hsing* A star. 星辰, IV. ii. 26. 3.

春 *ch'un* (1) The spring. 春 = in the spring, I. ii. 4. 5: VI. ii. 7. 2. (2) 春秋, the title of a work by Confucius, III. ii. 9. 8, 11, *et al.* (3) A name, III. ii. 2. 1.

曷 *ho* How? I. ii. 8. 7.

昏 *hun* Dusk, VII. i. 23. 3. Redoubled, = darkness, i. e. ignorance, VII. ii. 20. 1. It is made either with 氏 or with 民.

昭 *châo* 昭昭, brightness,—clear intelligence, VII. ii. 20. 1.

是 *shih* (1) This, these. *Passim.* It often has the whole preceding clause or sentence for its antecedent, = *this is.* It might often be translated also—*in this case.* Observe its peculiar force at the end of a sentence, affirming strongly what has been said in it, I. ii. 10. 3: VII. ii. 15, *et al.* We have 若是, 猶 (and 由) 是, and 如是,—all = thus, such;—observe II. i. 2. 23. 是故 and 是以 = therefore. (2) To be, VI. i. 15. 1, 2, *et al.* (3) Right, III. i. 5. 2, 4: VII. ii. 37. 11. To approve, II. i. 6. 4, 5, *et al.*

時 *shih* (1) Time, times; at—in—the time, I. i. 5. 4; ii. 5. 5: II. i. 1. 9, 11, 13; 4. 2, 4, *et al.*, *saepe*. The proper times or seasons, I. i. 3. 3, 4; 7. 24: VII. i. 22. 2. Seasonable, I. ii. 11. 2: III. ii. 5. 4: VII. i. 40. 2. Timeous,—a characteristic of Confucius, V. ii. 1. 5. 無時, without reference to time, VI. i. 8. 4. 有時, sometimes, V. ii. 5. 1. 天時, opportunities of time afforded by Heaven, II. ii. 1. 1, 2. (2) 時 = 是, this, I. i. 2. 4; ii. 3. 3. (3) A surname, II. ii. 10. 3, 4.

晏 *yen* The surname of a minister of Ch'î, I. ii. 4. 4, 5: II. i. 1. 1, 2, 5.

晉 *tsin* The name of a State, 晉國, I. i. 5. 1, *et al.*—晉人, V. i. 9. 2, *et al.*—晉平公, V. ii. 3. 4.—晉文, I. i. 7. 1, 2, *et al.*

晝 *châu* (1) The day-time, by day, III. i. 3. 2: IV. ii. 18. 2. 旦晝, *id.*, VI. i. 8. 2. (2) The name of a town, II. ii. 11; 12.

普 *p'û* Great, vast. 普天之下, under the whole heaven, V. i. 4. 2.

智 *chih* (1) The principle of, or man's capacity for, knowledge, II. i. 6. 5: IV. i. 27. 2: VI. i. 6. 7; 9. 3: VII. i. 21. 4. (2) Knowledge, wisdom; wise; to be wise, I. ii. 3. 1; II. i. 1. 9; 2. 19, 25, *et al.*, *saepe*.

景 *ching* (1) An honorary epithet, 齊景公, I. ii. 4. 4, 10, *et al.* (2) A surname, 景春, III. ii. 2. 1.—景丑氏, II. ii. 2. 4, 5.

晳 *hsi* The designation of Tsăng Shăn's father, IV. i. 19. 3: VII. ii. 36; 37.

暇 *hsiá* Leisure, I. i. 7. 22: III. i. 4. 8. 閒暇, II. i. 4. 2, 4. 暇日, I. i. 5. 3.

暢 *ch'ang* 暢茂, luxuriant, III. i. 4. 7.

暮 *mû*. The evening, II. ii. 6. 1. 昬暮, the dusk of the evening, VII. i. 23. 3.

暴 *pâo*. (1) Violence, oppression, cruelty, VI. i. 6. 2: VII. ii. 8. 1. Oppressive, III. i. 3. 13; ii. 9. 5, 7. To oppress, IV. i. 2. 4: V. i. 3. 3. Applied to the mind, II. i. 2. 9, 10. 自暴, to do violence to one's nature, IV. i. 10. 1. So 暴 alone, VI. i. 7. 1. (2) A name, I. ii. 1. 1.

暴 *pû*. (1) To dry or bleach in the sun, III. i. 4. 13. 暴 = to warm genially, VI. i. 9. 2. (2) To exhibit, V. i. 5. 5, 6.

曠 *k'wang*. Empty; to leave empty, IV. i. 10. 3. 曠 = unmarried, I. ii. 5. 5.

THE 73RD RADICAL, 曰.

曰 *yüeh*. To say. *Passim*. Often the nominative is not expressed, and must be supplied from the context. In this case, 曰 sometimes = it is said. It is also used in descriptive accounts, and = is called, means.

曲 *ch'ü*. Crooked. Observe 無曲防, VI. ii. 7. 3.

曳 *i*. To trail after one, I. i. 8. 2.

更 *kăng*. (1) To change = to reform, II. ii. 9. 4. It was originally made from 丙 and 攴. (2) A name, III. ii. 4. 1.—VII. i. 43. 1, 2.

書 *shû*. (1) A writing,—of a covenant, VI. ii. 7. 3. Writings, books, V. ii. 8. 2. (2) The Shû-ching, I. ii. 3. 7; 11. 1: III. i. 1. 5; ii. 5. 2, 4; 9. 3, 6: V. i. 4. 4: VI. ii. 5. 4. Observe VII. ii. 3. 1.

曾 *tsăng*. A surname, 曾子, I. ii. 12. 2: II. i. 2. 6, 7, 8, *et al., saepe*. 曾晳, see 晳,—曾元, IV. i. 19. 3.—曾西, II. i. 1. 3, 4.

曾 *ts'ăng*. A particle, indicating the present complete tense, II. i. 1. 3: V. i. 9. 3.

會 *hûi*. To assemble; the assembly of, VI. ii. 7. 3. To meet, = to engage in battle, II. i. 2. 5.

會 *kwei*. To calculate, enter accounts, V. ii. 5. 4.

曹 *ts'ao*. The name of an ancient principality, used as a surname, VI. ii. 2, 1.

THE 74TH RADICAL, 月.

月 *yüeh*. (1) The moon, II. ii. 9. 4: VII. i. 24. 2. (2) A month, months, I. i. 6. 6: II. ii. 5. 1, *et al.* 月 = every month, III. ii. 8. 2.

有 *yû*. (1) To have, possess. *Passim*. (2) The impersonal substantive verb, there is, there was. Also *passim*. It is often difficult to determine to which of these meanings we shall refer particular examples. 有之, and 未之有, at the end of sentences, are to be noted, I. i. 3. 4; 7. 5, 24, *et al., saepe*. 有爲, to have doing, to be capable of achievement, II. ii. 2. 7: III. i. 1. 4: IV. ii. 8. 1: V. i. 8. 3: VII. i. 29. 有餘 = and more, VII. ii. 38. 1, 2, 3, 4, *et al.* 有司, see 司. Observe V. i. 7. 2. (3) The surname of one of Confucius's disciples, II. i. 2. 25, 28: III. i. 4. 13. (4) 有庳, the principality of Shun's brother, V. i. 3. 2, 3.

有 *yû*. The 4th tone. And; again, III. ii. 9. 7: V. i. 4. 1; 5. 7; 6. 1.

朋 *p'ăng*. 朋友, friends, II. i. 6. 3: III. i. 4. 8: IV. ii. 30. 4.

服 *fû*. (1) Clothes, V. i. 8. 3: VI. ii. 2. 5. 衣服, III. ii. 3. 3: VII. i. 36. 2. (2) To wear, V. ii. 2. 5. To wear mourning, IV. ii. 3. 2, 3, 4. (3) To subdue, I. i. 7. 17: II. i. 3. 2: IV. ii. 16. 1. (4) To submit, IV. i. 7. 5: V. i. 3. 2. (5) To be obnoxious to, IV. i. 14. 3.

朕 *chăn*. I (not yet the imperial *we*), V. i. 2. 3 (*N.B.*); 7. 9.

望 *wang*. (1) To look to from a distance; to look for, to hope; expectation, example, what is looked for or to, I. i. 3. 2; 6. 2, 6; ii. 11. 2: II. ii. 12. 5: III. ii. 5. 4, 7: IV. ii. 20. 3; 31. 1: VII. i. 9. 5. 望見, VII. i. 36. 1; ii. 23. 2. 仰望, IV. ii. 33. 1. 守望, III. i. 3. 18. (2) 望望然, = with a high air, II. i. 9. 1. (3) 太公望, a counsellor of Wăn and Wû, VII. ii. 38.

朝 *châo*. The morning; in the morning, I. ii. 5. 5: II. ii. 2. 1; 6. 1: III. ii. 1. 4: IV. ii. 28. 7: VI. ii. 9. 3; 14. 3.

朝 *ch'âo*. (1) A sovereign's court, I. i. 7. 18, *et al.* (2) To appear in court, to do homage to, I. ii. 4. 5: II. ii. 2. 1, 5: V. i. 4. 1: VI. ii. 7. 2. 朝覲, V. i. 5. 7. To make to appear at court, to give audience to, I. i. 7. 16: II. i. 1. 8; 2. 24. (3) Court (adjective), II. i. 9. 1: V. ii. 1. 1. (4) 朝儛, the name of a place, I. ii. 4. 4.

朞 *chi*. A round year, VII. i. 39. 1.

期 *ch'i*. 期 = to model one's self on, VI. i. 7. 5, 6.

THE 75TH RADICAL, 木.

木 *mû*. (1) A tree, trees, I. i. 7. 16, 17; ii. 7. 1; 9. 1, *et al.* Wood, a piece of wood, II. ii. 7. 1: VI. ii. 1. 5. 材木, supplies of wood, I. i. 3. 3. (2) In a name, III. ii. 7. 2.

孟子

THE 76TH RADICAL, 欠.

欺 *ch'i* To impose on; to be imposed on, III. i. 4. 17: V. i. 2. 4.

欿 *k'an* 欿然, without elation, VII. i. 11.

歃 *shâ* 歃血, to smear the sides of the mouth with blood, VI. ii. 7. 3.

歌 *ko* To sing, IV. i. 8. 2: VI. ii. 6. 5 (indicating singing in some peculiar style). Used actively, 謳歌, V. i. 5. 7; 6. 1.

歎 *t'an* To sigh, VII. i. 36. 1.

歠 *ch'üeh* To drink, to sip, III. i. 2. 4. 流歠, to swill down, VII. i. 46. 2.

歡 *hwan* Pleased. 歡樂, to rejoice in, I. i. 2. 3.

THE 77TH RADICAL, 止.

止 *chih* (1) To stop, desist,—spoken of walking, retiring from office, &c., I. i. 3. 2; ii. 16. 3: II. i. 2. 22: III. ii. 5. 4: VI. ii. 13. 8. To stay, reside; to remain, I. ii. 11. 2: II. ii. 7. 1: V. ii. 1. 1. (2) Active, to stop, I. ii. 11. 4: II. i. 9. 2.

正 *chêng* (1) To correct, rectify; to be rectified; correct; what is correct, II. i. 7. 5; 9. 1: III. i. 3. 13; ii. 2. 2, 3; 9. 6, 13, *et al., saepe.* To make straight, V. i. 7. 7. What may be correctly ascribed to, VII. i. 2. 1, 3, 4. (2) To have a purpose in the mind, II. i. 2. 16: VII. ii. 33. 2. (3) 樂正, a double surname;—see 樂.

此 *ts'ze* This, these. *Passim.* 如此, and 若此, thus, so, such, are common.

步 *pû* A pace, I. i. 3. 2: V. ii. 1. 7.

武 *wû* (1) Firmness, martial vigour. 威武, III. ii. 2. 3. (2) 武王, the first sovereign of the Châu dynasty, I. ii. 3. 6; 8. 1; 10. 3, *et al., saepe.* (3) 武丁, a sovereign of the Shang dynasty, II. i. 1. 8. (4) 武城, name of a place, IV. ii. 31. 1. (5) 武成, a Book of the Shû-ching, VII. ii. 3. 2.

歲 *sui* A year, the years; the character of a year as good or bad, I. i. 3. 5: II. ii. 13. 4: VII. ii. 38. 1, 2, 3, 4. 樂歲, I. i. 7. 21, 22: III. i. 3. 7: VI. i. 7. 1 (富歲). 饑歲, I. ii. 12. 2: II. ii. 4. 2.

歷 *li* To pass over, = to change, IV. ii. 27. 3. 歷 = for a period of, V. i. 6. 2.

歸 *kwei* To return, II. i. 2. 16; ii. 10. 1, 2; 12. 5. *et al., saepe.* Used actively, = to repay, VII. i. 30. 2. To turn to, come to, I. i. 6. 6; ii. 11. 2; 15. 1: III. ii. 5. 4; 9. 9, *et al., saepe.*

THE 78TH RADICAL, 歹.

死 *sze* To die; death; the dead, I. i. 3. 5; 4. 6; 7. 4, 6, 7, 8, *et al., saepe.* To die for, I. ii. 12. 3. 死亡, I. i. 7. 21, 22: IV. i. 3. 4; 9. 5.

殀 *yâo* To die at an early age, VII. i. 1. 3.

殃 *yang* Calamities, I. ii. 10. 2: VII. ii. 27. 1. To bring calamities on, to destroy, VI. ii. 8. 2.

殄 *t'ien* To exhaust, extirpate. 殄 = to remove, VII. ii. 19. 3.

殆 *tâi* (1) Perilous, in a dangerous condition, V. i. 4. 1. (2) A particle, I apprehend, is near to, I. i. 7. 17: VII. ii. 23. 1; 30. 2. Followed by 於, IV. ii. 31. 1.

殉 *hsün* To bury along with the dead, to sacrifice, VII. ii. 1. 2. 殉 = to accompany, VII. i. 42. 1, 2.

殊 *shû* To be different, VI. i. 7. 1, 5.

殍 *p'iâo* To die of hunger, VII. ii. 27. 1.

殖 *chih* 繁殖, to swarm, III. i. 4. 7.

殘 *ts'an* To oppress, treat cruelly, I. ii. 12. 2. 殘 = a ruffian, an oppressor, oppressors, I. ii. 8. 3: III. ii. 5. 5, 6.

殛 *chî* According to Chû Hsî, to cut off. ? to imprison, V. i. 3. 2.

THE 79TH RADICAL, 殳.

殷 *yin* The dynasty so called, II. i. 1. 8, 10, *et al., saepe.* 殷人, the founder of the Yin dynasty, III. i. 3. 6.

段 *twan* A surname, III. ii. 7. 2.

殺 *shâ* To kill, put to death, I. i. 3. 5; 4. 2; 6. 4, 6, *et al., saepissime.* Observe III. ii. 3. 3, and VII. ii. 10.

毀 *hui* (1) To pull down; to break, I. ii. 5. 1, 2; 11. 3: III. ii. 4. 5: IV. i. 8. 4; ii. 31. 1. (2) To blame, reproach, IV. i. 21.

THE 80TH RADICAL, 毋.

母 *mû* A mother; 父母, parents, I. i. 5. 4; 7. 21, 22, *et al., saepe.* 民父母, the parent of the people,—spoken of a ruler, I. i. 4. 5; ii. 7. 6: III. i. 3. 7. 母雞, 母彘, brood hens, brood sows, VII. i. 22. 2.

每 *mei* Every, IV. ii. 2. 5.

THE 81ST RADICAL, 比.

比 *pi* (1) To compare, II. i. 1. 3: VI. ii. 1. 7. 比於, to be compared with, I. ii. 4. 4. (2) 比干, an uncle of the tyrant Châu, II. i. 1. 8: VI. i. 6. 3.

比 *pi* The 4th tone. (1) For, on behalf of, I. i. 5. 1: II. ii. 7. 4. (2) And when ..., I. ii. 6. 1. (3) To classify, III. i. 4. 18. (4) To bend to the will of, act as a partizan, III. ii. 1. 5. (5) To join together, to collect, V. ii. 4. 5.

THE 82ND RADICAL, 毛.

毛 *mâo* Hair, VII. i. 26. 1.

毫 *hâo* Fine hair, 秋毫, = what is very small, I. i. 7. 10. 一毫, = the least, one thread of ten filaments of silk being called a 毫, II. i. 2. 4.

THE 83RD RADICAL, 氏.

氏 *shih* Family, I. ii. 16. 3. 夏氏后, the sovereigns of the Hsiâ dynasty, the family, i.e. of the great Yü, the prince of Hsiâ. 季氏, IV. i. 14. 1. 景丑氏, II. ii. 2. 4. 東郭氏, II. ii. 2. 2. 楊氏, 墨氏, III. ii. 9. 9.

民 *min* The people,—usually in distinction from rulers and superior men. *Passim.* Observe the phrases—丘民, VII. ii. 14. 2; 天民, VII. i. 19. 3; 凡民, VII. i. 10. 1: V. ii. 4. 4; 蒸民, VI. i. 6. 8; 庶民, I. i. 2. 3: VII. ii. 37. 13; 黎民, I. i. 3. 4; 7. 24. 民 = mankind, II. i. 2. 23, 27, 28.

氓 *măng* People,—settling in a State from other States, II. i. 5. 5: III. i. 4. 1, 2: V. ii. 6. 2.

THE 84TH RADICAL, 气.

氣 *ch'i* (1) The air, breath, VI. i. 8. 2. (2) Air, = carriage, VII. i. 36. 1. (3) Specially deserving of notice is its use in II. i. 2. 8, 9, 10, 11, 12, 13, 14, = energy, the passion-nature.

THE 85TH RADICAL, 水.

水 *shui* Water, waters, I. ii. 5. 5; 10. 4; 11. 3, *et al., saepe.* 水 = cold water, VI. i. 5. 5.

永 *yung* Perpetually, always, II. i. 4. 6: IV. i. 4. 3: V. i. 4. 3.

氾 *fan* Water overflowing. 氾濫於, to inundate, III. i. 4. 7; ii. 9. 3.

求 *ch'iû* (1) To seek for; to ask for; to seek, I. i. 7. 9, 15, 16, 17; ii. 9. 1, *et al., saepissime.* (2) The name of one of Confucius's disciples, IV. i. 14. 1.

汙 *wû* (1) Impure, vile, mean, II. i. 9. 2: III. i. 3. 13: V. i. 9. 3; ii. 1. 3: VI. ii. 6. 2: VII. ii. 37. 11. (2) A pool, 汙池, III. ii. 9. 5.

汙 *wá* Low. To rank one's self low, II. i. 2. 25. Perhaps some of the instances under 汙, *wû*, should be read as *wá*, particularly III. ii. 9. 5, VII. ii. 37. 11, and one or two others.

汝 *zû* (1) You, thou, IV. ii. 31. 1: V. i. 2. 3: VII. ii. 31. 3. (2) Name of a stream, III. i. 4. 7.

江 *chiang* The river by eminence,—the Yang-tzse, III. i. 4. 7, 13; ii. 9. 4. ? VII. i. 16. 1.

池 *ch'ih* A pond, I. i. 2. 4; 8. 3: III. ii. 9. 5: V. i. 2. 4. A moat, I. ii. 13. 2: II. ii. 1. 3.

決 *chüeh* (1) To lead forth a stream, III. i. 4. 7: VI. i. 2. 1. The waters of a stream overflowing, VII. i. 16. (2) To bite things through with the teeth, VII. i. 46. 2.

沐 *mû* Properly, to wash the hair; 沐浴, to bathe, IV. ii. 25. 2.

沒 *mei* To die, pass away, III. i. 4. 13; ii. 9. 5.

沈 *shăn* A surname, II. ii. 8. 1, 2. 沈猶, a double surname, IV. ii. 31. 1.

沓 *t'â* 沓沓, dilatory, IV. i. 1. 11, 12.

沛 *p'ei* (1) A thick marshy jungle, III. ii. 9. 5. (2) 沛然, vehemently, overwhelmingly, like the sudden fall of rain, or overflow of water, I. i. 6. 6: IV. i. 6. 1: VII. i. 16.

沮 *chü* The 3rd tone. To stop, I. ii. 16. 3.

河 *ho* (1) The Yellow river, III. ii. 9. 4. 河東 and 河內, I. i. 3. 1; 河西, VI. ii. 6. 5. (2) 九河, the nine branches of the 河, which Yü regulated, III. i. 4. 7. 南河, the most southern of these, V. i. 5. 7. (3) May be used for a river generally, II. i. 2. 28: VII. i. 16.

油 *yû* 油然, the appearance of thick clouds, I. i. 6. 6.

沼 *châo* A pond, I. i. 2. 1, 3. 靈沼, the name given to king Wăn's pond, I. i. 2. 3.

治 *ch'i* To govern, regulate; to manage; to attend to, I. i. 7. 22; ii. 5. 3; 6. 2; 9. 2: II. i. 4. 3; 6. 2; ii. 10. 7; 13. 5 (平治), *et al., saepe.*

孟子

瀾 *lan* Large waves, VII. i. 24. 2.

THE 86TH RADICAL, 火.

火 *hwo* Fire, I. ii. 10. 4; 11. 3: II. i. 6. 7: III. i. 4. 7; ii. 5. 5: VI. i. 18. 1: VII. i. 23. 3.

災 *tsâi* Calamity, I. i. 7. 17: IV. i. 1. 9.

炙 *chih* (1) Roast meat, VI. i. 4. 5: VII. ii. 36. (2) To be warmed—immediately affected—by, VII. ii. 15. 1.

炭 *t'an* Charcoal, 塗炭, II. i. 9. 1: V. ii. 1. 1.

烈 *lieh* (1) To set fire to, III. i. 4. 7. (2) Enterprising, energetic, III. ii. 9. (3) 功烈, meritorious achievement, II. i. 1. 3. (4) ? acknowledged, brightly recognised, V. ii. 4. 4.

烏 *wû* A surname, VI. ii. 2. 3.

烹 *p'ăng* To boil, to cook, V. i. 2. 4. 割烹, cookery, V. i. 7. 1, 8.

焚 *făn* To burn, consume with fire, III. i. 4. 7: V. i. 2. 3.

焉 *yen* The 2nd tone. A final particle. *Passim.* (1) At the end of sentences, giving a liveliness to the style, especially where the closing member is brief, perhaps only one word, as in II. ii. 2. 4;—or where it is interrogative, introduced by 何 or some similar character. (2) Correlative clauses are often terminated by 焉, as in VI. i. 7. 8. (3) It is common at the end of clauses, to which we expect a sequel, as in I. i. 7. 12; ii. 7. 4, *et al., saepissime.* (4) Seems to be used for 乎, in VII. i. 34.—焉 often follows adjectives instead of 然, though not in Mencius, unless in V. i. 2. 4; and it certainly partakes of the meaning of that character, and = a lively affirmative *so!*

焉 *yen* The 1st tone. An interrogative particle. How? It stands at the beginning of the clause or member of the sentence to which it belongs, unless where another particle or the nominative immediately precedes, I. i. 7. 20; ii. 16. 3: II. i. 7. 2; 9. 2; ii. 3. 5, *et al., saepe.* 焉 = whither, IV. i. 13. 2.

無 *wû* No, not, without. *Passim.* 無 is the opposite of 有, both in its personal and impersonal usages, = not to have, to be without,—and there is—are—not. As instances of the relation between it and 有, observe I. i. 7. 20, and II. ii. 10. 7. 無所 and 無所不 are common. 無不 make a strong affirmation. So, 無弗, 無非, and 非無. Observe 無時, VI. i. 8. 4, and 無方, IV. ii. 20. 2.

然 *zan* (1) To burn, to flame up, II. i. 6. 7. (2) So; just the same; yes. *Passim.* Observe II. ii. 8. 2, where 然 = accordingly, or they approved. It often occurs at the end of a clause, beginning with 若. We have the combinations—然則, VII. i. 36. 3, 5, *et passim;* 然後, VI. ii. 15. 3, 5, *et saepe;* 然而, VII. ii. 38. 4; 14. 4: VI. ii. 4. 5, 6, *et saepe;* 然且, VI. ii. 8. 8, *et al.;* 雖然, III. i. 2. 2; 4. 3, *et al.* (3) After adjectives, it = *ly* and forms adverbs, or other adjectives, which in English would end in *like*, VII. ii. 37. 6, 9; 34. 1; 21, *et passim.* (4) A surname, III. i. 2.

煖 *hwan* Warm; warmly; to be warm,—spoken with reference to clothing, I. i. 7. 16: III. i. 4. 8: VII. i. 22. 3.

煢 *ch'iung* Solitary; sorrowful, I. ii. 5. 3.

照 *châo* To shine, illuminate, VII. i. 24. 2.

煩 *fan* What is toilsome, trouble, III. i. 4. 5.

熄 *hsî* To be extinguished, VI. i. 18. 1. Metaphorically, III. ii. 2. 1: IV. ii. 21. 1.

熊 *hsiung* A bear, VI. i. 10. 1.

熟 *shû* To be ripe; to be brought to maturity, III. i. 4. 8: VI. i. 7. 2; 19. 1.

熱 *zo* Hot; what is hot, I. ii. 10. 4: IV. i. 7. 6. 熱中, to burn within, V. i. 1. 5.

燔 *fan* I. q. 膰, the flesh of sacrifice, VI. ii. 6. 6.

燕 *yen* The 1st tone. The name of a State, I. ii. 10. 1, 3; 11. 1, 3 (*N.B.*), 4: II. ii. 8. 1, 2. 燕人, II. ii. 9. 1.

營 *ying* To plan,—a building, I. i. 2. 3. 營窟, artificial caves, III. ii. 9. 3.

爛 *lan* 糜爛, to boil to a mass, VII. ii. 1. 2.

爨 *ts'wan* To cook. Chû Hsî says, 'to light a fire,' III. i. 4. 4.

THE 87TH RADICAL, 爪.

爭 *chăng* To strive for, IV. i. 14. 2.

爰 *yüan* A particle, found at the beginning of clauses, and quoted from the Shih-ching. And so, and, I. ii. 3. 6; 5. 4, 5.

爲 *wei* *Passim.* (1) To be, I. i. 1. 4; 7. 20; ii. 2. 3; 3. 1; 4. 5, 6, *et al.*, *saepissime.* At the beginning of clauses, 爲 continuing what precedes, often = *who is, who was.* Before nouns of relation and proper names, it = *to play, to be in the position*, I. ii. 4. 2: II. i. 1. 4; ii. 2. 10, *et al.*, *saepe.* So in the phrase 其爲人也, 以爲, with and without intermediate words, often = to take to be, to regard, to consider, to be considered, I. i. 7. 5, 7; ii. 2. 2; 11. 3, *et saepe.* Often, however, 以爲 simply = to be, or to use to make. (2) To make, to do; to be done, I. i. 2. 3; 7. 10, 11, 12, 13, 16, 17, *et saepissime.* 何爲 and 奚爲 = why, I. ii. 5. 4; 11. 2, *et al.* 有爲, see 有. 爲 = to exercise, to administer, to govern, II. ii. 4. 4: III. i. 3. 1. The phrase 爲政, to administer government, and sometimes to give law to the kingdom, is frequent, I. i. 11. 1: II. ii. 10. 6: IV. i. 1. 3; 6; 7. 4, *et al.* 爲 = to establish, II. ii. 10. 7. So 定爲, III. i. 2. 3; and 設爲, III. i. 3. 10. 爲 = to seek to be, III. i. 3. 5.—Observe 爲食, 爲飲, II. i. 1. 11; 爲陳, 爲戰, VII. ii. 4. 1; 爲說辭, II. i. 2. 18; 民之爲道, III. i. 3. 3, but 人之有道 in 4. 8 is to be understood differently, through the force of the 有; 爲神農之言, III. i. 4. 1; 爲間, III. i. 5. 5: VII. ii. 21; 不可爲衆, IV. i. 7. 5; 我何以...爲哉, V. i. 7. 3; 其所爲主, V. i. 8. 4; 爲詩, VI. ii. 3. 2; 難爲水, 爲言, VII. i. 24. 1; 爲之氓, 爲之辭, 爲之兆, II. i. 5. 5; ii. 9. 4: V. ii. 4. 6.

爲 *wei* The 4th tone. For, in behalf of. Before clauses, it is most conveniently taken as a conjunction, *because*, I. i. 4. 6; 7. 10, 11, 16, *et al.*, *saepissime.* 爲我, for self, the principle of Yang Chû, III. ii. 9. 9: VII. i. 26. 1. Observe 自爲, VI. ii. 6. 1, and 何爲, V. ii. 7. 3. But should not 何爲 and 奚爲 always have the 爲 in the 3rd tone? 爲 = consequently, I. ii. 16. 3.

爵 *chio* (1) Nobility, noble rank, II. i. 7. 2; ii. 2. 6; 8. 1: V. ii. 2. 1 (*N.B.*): VI. i. 16. 1, 2, 3; ii. 7. 2. (2) The name of a bird, or birds in general, IV. i. 9. 3.

THE 88TH RADICAL, 父.

父 *fû* (1) A father. *Passim.* The combinations 父子, 父母, and 父兄 are common. 父母 may denote the ruler, as the parent of the people, I. i. 4. 5; ii. 7. 6. 父兄 may denote all elder relatives, III. i. 2. 3, 4. (2) 亶ᶜ父 (3rd tone), the name of one of the remotest ancestors of the Châu dynasty, I. ii. 5. 5.

THE 89TH RADICAL, 爻.

爾 *r* (1) You, your, I. ii. 12. 2: II. i. 1. 3; 9. 2: V. i. 1. 2; ii. 1. 3, 7: VII. ii. 4. 5; 31. 3. (2) After adjectives, makes adverbs, i.q. 然, VI. i. 10. 6. (3) A final particle, synonymous with 耳, = simply, just so, III. i. 5. 3: IV. i. 9. 1; ii. 18. 2: V. i. 2. 3: VII. ii. 38. 4. 云爾, II. ii. 2. 4: III. ii. 5. 7: IV. ii. 24. 1: VII. i. 39. 2. (4) Thus, VI. i. 7. 1.—? III. i. 3. 2, where perhaps 爾 = you. (5) I.q. 邇, what is near, IV. i. 11.

THE 90TH RADICAL, 爿.

牀 *ch'wang* A couch, V. i. 2. 3.

牆 *ch'iang* A wall, III. ii. 3. 6: IV. ii. 31. 1 (牆屋): VI. ii. 1. 8: VII. i. 2. 2; 22. 2.

THE 91ST RADICAL, 片.

版 *pan* 版築, building-frames, VI. ii. 15. 1.

牖 *yû* A window, VII. ii. 30. 1. 牖戶, spoken of a nest, II. i. 4. 3.

THE 92ND RADICAL, 牙.

牙 *yâ* 易牙, a famous cook of antiquity, VI. i. 7. 5.

THE 93RD RADICAL, 牛.

牛 *niû* (1) A cow, an ox; cattle, I. i. 7. 4, 6, 7, 8: II. ii. 4. 3: III. ii. 5. 2, *et al.* (2) 牛山, the name of a hill, VI. i. 8. 1. (3) 冉牛, one of Confucius's disciples, II. i. 2. 18, 20.

牣 *zăn* Full, II. i. 2. 3.

牧 *mû* (1) To feed, to tend, II. ii. 4. 3. (2) To browse on, VI. i. 8. 1. (3) Pasture, II. ii. 4. 3. (4) 人牧, a shepherd of men, a ruler, I. i. 6. 6. (5) 牧宮, name of a palace, V. i. 7. 9. (6) A surname, V. ii. 3. 2.—VII. ii. 37. 4.

物 *wû* (1) Things, substances, I. i. 7. 13: III. i. 4. 18; 5. 3: IV. ii. 19. 2; 28. 4: VI. i. 4. 5; 8. 3; 9. 2; 15. 2; ii. 5. 4 (articles): VII.

i. 4. 1; 24. 3; 46. 1. (2) The inferior creatures (this meaning is included in some of the above examples), VII. i. 46. 1. (3) 物 = others, IV. i. 7. 2: VII. i. 19. 4.—Observe 有物, 有則, VI. i. 6. 8.

牲 *shăng* (1) Cattle—embracing oxen, sheep, and pigs, and sometimes more kinds, V. i. 9. 1. (2) Cattle set apart for sacrifice, victims, VI. ii. 7. 3. Generally in connexion with 犧, which see.

牼 *k'ăng* A name, VI. ii. 4. 1.

牽 *ch'ien* To lead forward, to drag, I. i. 7. 4.

犀 *hsî* The rhinoceros, III. ii. 9. 6.

犧 *hsi* A victim, called 犧 as being 'spotless,' 犧牲, III. ii. 3. 3; 5. 2: VII. ii. 14. 4.

THE 94TH RADICAL, 犬.

犬 *ch'üan* A dog, dogs, I. ii. 15. 1: IV. ii. 3. 1: V. ii. 6. 4: VI. i. 3. 3; 7. 5; 11. 3.

犯 *fan* To violate, IV. i. 1. 8: VI. ii. 7. 3.

狂 *k'wang* Ambitious, ardent, VII. ii. 37. 1, 2, 3, 4, 5, 7.

狄 *ti* The wild tribes on the North, I. ii. 14. 2; 15. 1: III. i. 4. 16 (戎狄); ii. 9. 11 (夷狄), 12 (戎狄). 北狄, I. ii. 11. 2: III. ii. 5. 4: VII. ii. 4. 3.

狎 *hsiâ* To be near to, VII. i. 31. 1.

狐 *hû* The fox, III. i. 5. 4.

狗 *kàu* A dog, dogs, I. i. 3. 4, 5; 7. 24: II. i. 1. 10.

狩 *shàu* 巡狩, a sovereign's tour of inspection, I. ii. 4. 5: VI. ii. 7. 2. 狩 is explained by 守, and = the fiefs.

狸 *li* Joined with 狐. ? the wild cat, III. i. 5. 4.

狼 *lang* (1) A wolf, IV. i. 17. 1: VI. i. 14. 4. (2) 狼戾 = to lie about in abundance, III. i. 3. 7.

猛 *măng* Fierce, III. ii. 9. 11.

猶 *yû* (1) As; to be as, I. i. 7. 16: II. i. 1. 8, 13; 4. 1; 6. 6, *et al.*, *saepissime*. (2) Still, yet, I. ii. 2. 2; 11. 4: II. i. 1. 5, 7, *et al.*, *saepe*. Observe 且猶 . . . 而況, II. ii. 2. 10; 7. 4. (3) In a double surname, IV. ii. 31. 1.

獄 *yü* 訟獄者, litigants, V. i. 5. 7; 6. 1.

獧 *chüan* Cautiously-decided, VII. ii. 37. 2, 7.

獨 *tû* Only; alone, I. i. 2. 4; 7. 10, 12; ii. 1. 4: II. ii. 7. 3, 4, *et al.*, *saepe*. Old and childless, solitary, I. ii. 5. 3. In solitude, retirement, VII. i. 9. 6, *et al.* Peculiar, VII. ii. 36. 2.

獯 *hsün* 獯鬻, a tribe of northern barbarians, I. ii. 3. 1.

獲 *huo* (1) To get, obtain; catch, III. ii. 1. 4: V. ii. 2. 9. 獲於—to get the confidence of, IV. i. 12. 1. (2) A name, VI. ii. 2. 3.

獵 *lieh* To hunt, 田獵, I. ii. 1. 6, 7: VII. ii. 34. 2. ? 獵較, V. ii. 4. 5, 6.

獸 *shâu* A brute animal; a wild animal, I. i. 4. 5; ii. 4. 7: III. i. 4. 7; ii. 9. 11: IV. i. 9. 2. 獸畜, to nourish as a dog or a horse, VII. i. 37. 1. 禽獸, birds and beasts, irrational animals, is common, I. i. 7. 8, 10, 12: III. i. 4. 7, 8, *et al.* 鳥獸, I. i. 2. 4: III. ii. 9. 4. 走獸, quadrupeds, II. i. 2. 28.

獺 *t'â* An otter, IV. i. 9. 3.

獻 *hsien* An honorary epithet, V. ii. 3. 2.

THE 95TH RADICAL, 玄.

玄 *hsüan* Sky-colour. 玄 = dark silks, III. ii. 5. 5.

率 *hsü* and *shwâi* (1) To follow; following, along, I. ii. 5. 5; IV. i. 1. 4 (率由): V. i. 4. 2. (2) To lead (*shwâi*), I. i. 4. 4, 5: II. i. 5. 6: III. i. 4. 6, 18; ii. 5. 2; 9. 9: IV. ii. 14. 2: VI. i. 1. 2.

率, *lü* 彀率, the limit to which a bow should be drawn, VII. i. 41. 2.

THE 96TH RADICAL, 玉.

玉 *yü* A gem, a precious stone, jade, I. ii. 9. 2; 15. 1: VI. i. 3. 2: VII. ii. 28. 1. Used for the 'musical stone,' V. ii. 1. 6.

王 *wang* (1) A king, kings. *Passim*. 三王, the founders of the three ancient dynasties, VI. ii. 7. 1, 3, *et al.* 王者, one who is a true king, I. ii. 5. 2; 14. 2: II. i. 1. 11, *et al.*, *saepe*. 王政, true royal government, I. ii. 5. 3: III. ii. 5. 7. So, 王道, I. i. 3. 3. On the meaning of 王, see II. i. 3. 1. It follows the names of States and honorary epithets. (2) A surname, V. ii. 3. 3.—III. ii. 1. 4.—VI. ii. 6. 5.—II. ii. 6. 1.

王 *wang* The 4th tone. To exercise the royal authority (active and neuter), I. i. 3. 4; 5. 2; 7. 2, 3, 5, 9, 10, 11, 24; ii. 1. 8; 4. 3; 5. 4, 5: II. i. 1. 6, 7, 10; 2. 1; 5. 6; ii. 2. 8: III. ii. 1. 1: IV. i. 9. 4, 5; ii. 16. 1: V. i. 6. 5: VI. ii. 4. 6: VII. i. 20. 1, 5.

珠 *chû* A pearl, I. ii. 15. 1: VII. ii. 28.

班 *pan* To distribute, arrange, V. ii. 2. 1. Order, rank, II. i. 2. 23.

理 *li* (1) 條理, see 條, V. ii. 1. 6. (2) The mental constitution, VI. i. 7. 8. (3) To depend on, VII. ii. 19. 1.

琢 *cho* To cut and polish a gem, I. ii. 9. 2.

琅 *lang* 琅邪, the name of a place, I. ii. 4. 4.

琴 *ch'in* (1) The harpsichord or lute, V. i. 2. 3: VII. ii. 6. (2) A surname, VII. ii. 37. 4.

璞 *p'o* A gem unwrought, I. ii. 9. 2.

璧 *pi* An auspicious gem, which was fashioned round, V. i. 9. 2.

環 *hwan* (1) To surround, II. ii. 1. 2. (2) A name, V. i. 8. 1, 2, 4.

THE 97TH RADICAL, 瓜.

瓢 *p'iâo* A gourd; a gourd dish, IV. ii. 29. 2.

THE 98TH RADICAL, 瓦.

瓦 *wâ* A tile, III. ii. 4. 5.

甑 *tsăng* An earthenware pot or pan, used for steaming, III. i. 4. 4.

THE 99TH RADICAL, 甘.

甘 *kan* Sweet. 甘 = sweet food, I. i. 7. 16. 甘, to count sweet, or readily, VII. i. 27. 1.

甚 *shăn* Excessive; an exceeding degree; exceedingly, I. i. 7. 17; ii. 1. 1, 3; 14. 1, *et al., saepe*. 甚於 . . . more, in a greater degree, than . . ., II. i. 1. 11: VI. i. 10. 2, 3, 5. 已甚者, extraordinary things, IV. ii. 10. Observe I. i. 7. 13.

THE 100TH RADICAL, 生.

生 *shăng* (1) To produce; to be produced,—spoken of men and things, II. i. 2. 15, 17, 23, 27, 28; 5. 6: III. i. 5. 3; ii. 9. 2, *et al., saepe*. (2) Life; to live; to grow; living, I. i. 3. 3: IV. ii. 24. 2: V. i. 2. 4: VI. i. 3. 1, 2; 10. 1, 2, 3, 4, 5, 6: VII. i. 21. 4; 23. 3, *et al*. 生道, a way of life, i. e. calculated to foster life and happiness, VII. i. 12 1. (3) To be born, to be born in, III. ii. 3. 6: IV. ii. 1. 1, 2: VII. ii. 37. 9. 先生, master, a respectful way of speaking to or of an individual, IV. i. 24. 2; ii. 31. 1: VI. ii. 4. 2, 4, 5, 6. (4) In a double surname, VII. ii. 25. 1. (5) In a name, VII. ii. 38. 3.

產 *ch'ăn* (1) Livelihood, I. i. 7. 20, 21, 22: III. i. 4. 12. (2) A native, III. i. 3. 3. 產 = breed, V. i. 9. 2. (3) 子產, a designation, IV. ii. 2. 1: V. i. 2. 4.

甥 *shăng* A son-in-law, V. ii. 3. 5.

THE 101ST RADICAL, 用.

用 *yung* (1) To use; to be used, I. i. 3. 1, 3; 4. 6; 7. 10, *et al., saepissime*. (2) Used for 以. Initial, = for, on the part of, V. ii. 3. 6; 用 = thereby, I. ii. 5. 4: III. ii. 5. 6.

THE 102ND RADICAL, 田.

田 *t'ien* (1) A field, fields, I. i. 3. 4; 7. 24: III. i. 3 (*N.B.*). 7, 9, 13, 18, 19, *et al., saepe*. 圭田 = the holy field, III. i. 3. 16. 田疇, VII. i. 23. 1. 田野, IV. i. 1. 9: VI. ii. 7. 2. 田里, IV. ii. 3. 3, 4: VII. i. 22. 3. 乘田, the office held by Confucius in charge of the public fields, V. ii. 5. 4. (2) 田 and 田獵, to hunt, I. ii. 1. 6, 7: III. ii. 1. 2: V. ii. 7. 5: VII. ii. 34. 2.

由 *yû* (1) From, proceeding from, I. i. 7. 4; ii. 16. 1: II. i. 1. 8; 2. 1, 27; 6. 4; 9. 3, *et al., saepissime*. (2) By, to proceed by, to walk in, III. ii. 2. 3; 3. 6; 9. 4, *et al., saepe*. (3) Used for 猶, in both its meanings of *as* and *still*, I. i. 6. 6; 7. 3; ii. 1. 3: II. i. 1. 6; ii. 12. 5, *et al*. (4) 由由然, at his ease, II. i. 9. 2: V. ii. 1. 3. (5) The name of 子路, III. ii. 7. 4.—In the name 讎由, V. i. 8. 2.

甲 *chiâ* (1) A coat of mail; = defensive armour, I. i. 3. 2; 5. 3; 7. 14: IV. i. 1. 9. (2) 太甲, the name of a Book in the Shû-ching, II. i. 4. 6: IV. i. 8. 5: V. i. 6. 4: VII. i. 31. 1.

申 *shăn* (1) To inculcate especially, repeatedly, I. i. 3. 4; 7. 24. (2) A surname, II. ii. 11. 3.

男 *nan* (1) A male, IV. i. 17. 1: V. i. 1. 3; 2. 1; ii. 6. 6. (2) A title of nobility, V. ii. 2. 3, 4, 5.

界 *chieh* A border, boundaries, II. ii. 1. 4: III. i. 3. 13.

畏 *wei* To fear, to dread, I. i. 6. 2; ii. 3. 2, 3; 11. 1, 3: II. i. 1. 3; 2. 5; 4. 2: III. i. 1. 4; ii. 5. 7: V. ii. 4. 4: VII. i. 14. 3; ii. 4. 5; 34. 2.

孟子

noun precedes. 衆皆, VII. ii. 23. 2; 37. 11. Observe II. i. 6. 7: III. i. 4. 5.

皜 *hâo* — 皜皜, white and glistening, III. i. 4. 13.

皞 *hâo* — 皞皞如, placid and content-like, VII. i. 13. 1.

THE 107TH RADICAL, 皮.

皮 *p'i* — (1) The hides of animals; the skin with the hair on, I. ii. 15. 1: VI. i. 9. 11; ii. 7. 6. (2) A name, VII. ii. 27. 4.

THE 108TH RADICAL, 皿.

皿 *ming* — A vessel, 器皿, III. ii. 3. 3.

盈 *ying* — (1) To fill; full, III. ii. 9. 9: IV. i. 14. 2; ii. 18. 2, 3: VII. i. 24. 3. The full amount, III. i. 3. 7. (2) In a name, III. ii. 8. 1.

盆 *p'ăn* — 盆成, a double surname, VII. ii. 29. 1.

益 *yi* — (1) To add to; more, I. ii. 10. 4: VI. ii. 8. 7; 15. 2. (2) Of advantage, profitable, II. ii. 2. 16: VI. ii. 6. 3: VII. i. 3. 1, 2. (3) A minister of Shun and Yü, III. i. 4. 7: V. i. 6. 1, 2, 4, 6.

盍 *ho* — Why not; would it not be better to . . ., I. i. 7. 23: II. ii. 10. 3: IV. i. 13. 1; ii. 31. 1, 2: VII. i. 22. 1; ii. 37. 1.

盎 *yang* — An appearance of fullness, VII. i. 21. 4.

盛 *shăng* — Complete, great; flourishing state, II. i. 1. 10; 2. 28: V. i. 4. 1: VI. ii. 7. 3: VII. ii. 33. 2.

盛 *shăng* — The 1st tone. A vesselful, III. ii. 3. 3; 5. 2: VII. ii. 14. 4.

盜 *tâo* — A robber, III. ii. 10. 3: V. ii. 4. 5.

盟 *măng* — To covenant solemnly, VI. ii. 7. 3.

監 *chien* — To oversee, II. ii. 9. 2, 3.

盡 *chin* — (1) To exhaust, to carry out to the utmost degree, in the way of doing or thinking, I. i. 3. 1; 7. 17: II. ii. 9. 2: III. i. 2. 4: V. ii. 4. 5: VI. i. 6. 7: VII. i. 1. 1; 2. 3; 8. Observe 自盡, III. i. 2. 2, and 盡於人心, II. ii. 7. 2. (2) All, IV. ii. 33. 1: VII. i. 36. 1. Entirely, III. i. 4. 3: VII. ii. 3. 1.

THE 109TH RADICAL, 目.

目 *mû* — The eye, I. i. 7. 16: II. i. 2. 4: III. i. 5. 4; ii. 10. 1: IV. i. 1. 5; ii. 30. 2: V. ii. 1. 1: VI. i. 7. 7, 8; 15. 2: VII. ii. 24. 1.

直 *chih* — (1) Straight; to be straight; to make straight, III. ii. 1. 1, 3, 5: IV. i. 1. 6: V. ii. 7. 8. Metaphorically, to correct; rectitude, II. i. 2. 13: III. i. 4. 8; 5. 2. (2) Only, I. i. 3. 2; ii. 1. 2: II. ii. 7. 2.

相 *hsiang* — (1) Mutually; may often be translated by one another, I. i. 4. 5; ii. 1. 6, 7; 4. 10, *et al., saepissime*. (2) A name, III. ii. 4. 2, 3.

相° *hsiang* — To assist, to act as prime minister to; a prime minister, II. i. 1. 8; 2. 1: III. ii. 9. 6: V. i. 5. 7; 6. 2, 5; 9. 3: VI. ii. 5. 1, 3.

盻 *hsi* — 盻盻然, distressed-like, III. i. 3. 7.

省 *hsing* — To inspect, I. ii. 2. 5: VI. ii. 7. 2.

省 *shăng* — To be sparing of, I. i. 5. 3.

眊 *mâo* — Dull, to be dull, IV. i. 15. 1.

眩 *hsüan* — 瞑眩, see 瞑, III. i. 1. 5.

眸 *mău* — 眸子, the pupil of the eye, IV. i. 15. 1, 2.

衆 *chung* — Many, numerous; a multitude; the multitude, I. i. 7. 17; ii. 1. 4; 11. 4, *et al., saepe*.

睟 *sûi* — 睟然, mild-like, VII. i. 21. 4.

睦 *mû* — To be harmonious, III. i. 3. 18.

睨 *i* — To look aside, III. i. 5. 4.

瞑 *ming* — 瞑眩, to throw into a state of confusion,—medicine in its beneficial operation, yet causing distress, III. i. 1. 5.

睊 *chüan* — 睊睊, with eyes askance, I. ii. 4. 6.

瞭 *liâo* — To be clear, IV. i. 15. 1.

瞍 *sâu* — 瞽瞍, the name of Shun's father, IV. i. 28. 2: V. i. 2. 3; 4. 1, 2, 4: VI. i. 6. 3: VII. i. 35.

瞽 *kû* — See above.

瞯 *hsien* — To watch, to spy, IV. ii. 32; 33. 1.

瞰 *k'an* — To watch, III. ii. 7. 3.

THE 110TH RADICAL, 矛.

矜 *ching* — To reverence, 矜式, II. ii. 10. 3.

THE 111TH RADICAL, 矢.

矢 *shih* — An arrow, I. ii. 5. 4: II. i. 7. 1, 3: III. ii. 1. 4: IV. ii. 24. 2: V. ii. 7. 8.

矣 *i* — A final particle, found *passim*. It gives definiteness and decision to statements. Where the last clause of a sentence or paragraph is introduced by 則, 斯, or

亦, it generally ends with 矣. After 而已 it may be looked for. After single adjectives and other words its force is both decisive and exclamatory.

知 *chih* To know, to understand. *Passim.* 知 = to acknowledge, i.e. to know and employ, VII. i. 9. 2.

知 *chih* The 4th tone. Used for 智, to be wise; wise; wisdom. 知者, VII. i. 46. 1. 知慮, VI. ii. 13. 2. 術知, VII. i. 18. 1.

矩 *chü* A square,—the carpenter's instrument so called, IV. i. 1. 1, 5; 2. 1: VI. i. 20. 2: VII. ii. 5.

短 *twan* Short, I. i. 7. 13: III. i. 1. 5 (*N. B.*); 4. 17. To shorten, VII. i. 39. 1.

THE 112TH RADICAL, 石.

石 *shih* (1) A stone, a rock, VII. i. 16. (2) 石丘, the name of a place, VI. ii. 4. 1.

破 *p'o* To break, to split. Used for the blows of an axe, strong and well aimed, III. ii. 1. 4.

磽 *ch'iâo* Stony ground; poor in soil, VI. i. 7. 2.

磯 *chi* Stones in a river, interrupting and fretting the current, VI. ii. 3. 4; there 不可磯 = what will admit of no contradiction.

THE 113TH RADICAL, 示.

示 *shih* To show, indicate, V. i. 5. 4, 5.

社 *shê* The spirits of the land, or their altars. Always in the phrase 社稷, the tutelary spirits of a country, and may be used for the country itself, IV. i. 3. 3: VII. i. 19. 2; ii. 14. 1, 3, 4.

祀 *sze* To sacrifice; to sacrifice to, III. ii. 5. 2: IV. ii. 25. 2. 祭祀, sacrifices, VI. ii. 10. 4: VII. ii. 14. 4.

祜 *hû* Happiness, prosperity, I. ii. 3. 6.

祗 *chih* Reverent, reverently, V. i. 4. 4.

祖 *tsû* 先祖, ancestors, III. i. 2. 3.

神 *shan* (1) A spirit. 百神, all spiritual beings who are sacrificed to, V. i. 5. 6. Spiritual,—mysterious, VII. i. 13. 3; ii. 25. 8. (2) 神農, one of the most ancient sovereigns, III. i. 4. 1.

祥 *hs'iang* Auspicious, IV. i. 18. 4; ii. 17.

祭 *chi* To sacrifice or make offerings to; sacrifices; sacrificial, III. i. 2. 2, 3; ii. 3. 3: IV. ii. 33. 1: V. i. 5. 6; ii. 4. 6: VI. ii. 6. 6 (*N.B.*) 祭祀, see 祀.

祼 *kwan* I. q. 灌. To pour out a libation, IV. i. 7. 5.

祿 *lû* Emolument, revenue, salary, I. ii. 5. 3: II. ii. 8. 1; 14. 1: III. i. 3. 8, 13; ii. 10. 5: V. ii. 2. 1, 6, 7, 8, 9; 3. 5: VII. ii. 33. 2. To grant to, to endow, V. i. 7. 2.

禁 *chin* To forbid, prohibit; prohibitions, I. ii. 2. 3; 5. 3: VI. ii. 7. 3: VII. i. 35. 3, 4; 39. 4.

禍 *hwo* Calamity, II. i. 4. 4, 5. 禍 = an outbreak, attack, IV. ii. 31. 1. Used as a verb, VI. i. 1. 2.

福 *fû* Happiness, II. i. 4. 5, 6: IV. i. 4. 3.

禦 *yü* To withstand, oppose; to hinder; to ward off, I. i. 6. 6; 7. 3, 18: II. i. 1. 10; 7. 2: VII. i. 16; ii. 8. 1. To stop and rob, V. ii. 4. 4, 5.

禪 *shan* To resign, give over to another, V. i. 6. 7.

禮 *li* (1) What is proper; the principle of propriety; the rules of ceremony and politeness in accordance therewith, I. i. 7. 22; ii. 16. 1: II. i. 2. 27; 6. 5; 7. 3, *et al.*, *saepissime.* To be polite to, III. i. 3. 4: VII. i. 43. 1, *et al.* 禮貌, a polite demeanour, VI. ii. 14. 3. The same, used as a verb, IV. ii. 30. 1. (2) The Book of Rites, II. ii. 2. 5: III. ii. 3. 3. The Ritual Usages, III. ii. 2. 2.

THE 114TH RADICAL, 内.

禹 *yü* The great Yü, the founder of the Hsiâ dynasty, II. i. 8. 2: III. i. 4. 7, 9; ii. 9. 4, 11, *et al.*, *saepe.*

禽 *ch'in* Birds, III. ii. 1. 4. In the phrase 禽獸, birds and beasts, irrational animals, sometimes applied metaphorically to men, I. i. 7. 8, 10, 12: III. i. 4. 7, 8; ii. 1. 5; 9. 5, 9: IV. ii. 19. 1; 28. 6: VI. i. 8. 2.

THE 115TH RADICAL, 禾.

私 *sze* Private; privately, III. i. 3. 9, 19: IV. ii. 22. 2 (*N.B.*): VII. i. 40. 5. 以其私, II. ii. 8. 1. As a verb, to be selfishly attached to, to monopolize, II. ii. 10. 6: IV. ii. 30. 2.

秉 *ping* To grasp, maintain. 秉夷, VI. i. 6. 8.

秋 *ch'iû* (1) The autumn; in the autumn; autumnal, I. i. 7. 10; ii. 4. 5: III. i. 4. 13: VI. ii. 7. 2. (2) 春秋, a historical Work, compiled by Confucius, III. ii. 9. 8, 11: IV. ii. 21. 1, 2: VII. ii. 2. 1. (3) A name, VI. i. 9. 3.

科 *k'o* (1) A hollow,—in the bed of a stream, IV. ii. 18. 2: VII. i. 24. 3. (2) 科=lessons, 設科, VII. ii. 30. 2.

秦 *ch'in* The name of a State, I. i. 5. 1, 3; 7. 16: V. i. 9. 1, 3: VI. i. 12. 1; ii. 4. 3, 5, 6. 秦人, VI. i. 4. 4, 5.—V. i. 9. 1, 3: VI. ii. 6. 4.

移 *i* To remove, I. i. 3. 1: III. ii. 2. 3: VI. ii. 7. 2. To alter, VII. i. 36. 1.

稅 *shui* To be taxed, II. i. 5. 4. 稅斂, all taxes, I. i. 5. 3: VII. i. 23. 1. 貢稅 =revenues, V. i. 3. 3.

稅 *t'o* I.q. 脫. To loose, put off, VI. ii. 6. 6.

稗 *pai* A kind of spurious grain, 稗荑, VI. i. 19.

稚 *chih* The young, III. i. 3. 7.

種 *chung* To sow, III. i. 4. 4.

種 *chung* The 3rd tone. Seed, VI. i. 7. 2; 19.

稱 *ch'ăng* (1) To style, to pronounce, to speak of, III. ii. 9. 1: IV. ii. 30. 1: VII. ii. 37. 10. (2) To praise, III. i. 1. 2: IV. ii. 18. 1. (3) To lift up, = to proceed to, III. i. 3. 7.

稱 *ch'ăng* The 4th tone. To correspond, to be equal to, II. ii. 7. 2.

稷 *chi* (1) The spirits presiding over the grain or agriculture of a country. 社稷, see 社. (2) 后稷, the title of Shun's minister of agriculture, III. i. 4. 8. The 后 is dropped, and 稷 becomes a proper name, IV. ii. 29. 1, 2, 3, 4.

稻 *t'ao* Paddy, III. ii. 5. 2.

稼 *chiâ* To sow, II. i. 8. 4: III. i. 4. 8.

稽 *ch'i* (1) To bow down. 稽首, to bow the head to the ground, V. ii. 6. 4, 5: VII. ii. 4. 5. (2) A name, VII. ii. 19. 1.

穀 *kû* A general name for grain, I. i. 3. 3; generally spoken of as 五穀, the five kinds of grain, III. i. 4. 7, 8, 17: VI. i. 19; ii. 10. 4. But we have also 百穀, III. i. 3. 2. 穀祿 the grain available for salaries, III. i. 3. 13.

穆 *mû* An honorary epithet, I. ii. 12. 1.—V. i. 9. 1, 3: VI. ii. 6. 4.

積 *tsze* Stores of straw, grain, &c., in the open air; ricks, I. ii. 5. 4.

穡 *sê* To reap, III. i. 4. 8.

THE 116TH RADICAL, 穴.

穴 *hsüeh* A hole, III. ii. 3. 6.

空 *k'ung* Empty, VII. ii. 12.

空 *k'ung* The 4th tone. 空乏, to impoverish, VI. ii. 15. 2.

穿 *ch'wan* To dig through, VII. ii. 31. 2, 4.

窟 *k'û* A cave artificially excavated, III. ii. 9. 3.

窬 *yü* To leap over,—as if it were 踰, VII. ii. 31. 2, 4. The dictionary explains it differently, however, and makes it = 'an opening in the wall.'

窺 *k'wei* To peep, to steal a sight, III. ii. 3. 6.

窮 *ch'iung* (1) Poor, in poverty and distress, I. ii. 5. 3: V. i. 1. 3: VII. i. 9. 4, 5, 6; 21. 3. 窮乏, VI. i. 10. 7, 8. 阨窮, II. i. 9. 2: V. ii. 1. 3. (2) To exhaust, II. ii. 12. 6. See 力. (3) To be at one's wit's end, II. i. 2. 17.

竊 *ch'ieh* (1) To steal, VII. ii. 30. 2. (2) Privately, VII. i. 35. 6. (3) Joined with other verbs so as to qualify them deferentially, II. i. 2. 20; ii. 7. 1: IV. ii. 21. 3.

THE 117TH RADICAL, 立.

立 *li* (1) To stand; to stand erect, I. i. 2. 1; 7. 18: II. i. 5. 1; 9. 1: III. ii. 2. 3: IV. ii. 33. 1: V. i. 4. 1; ii. 5. 5: VII. i. 2. 2; 21. 2; 41. 3. 立, 而 . . ., = quickly, IV. ii. 18. 3; = with indifference, II. ii. 4. 3. To stand fast, to be established, VI. i. 15. 2. (2) To set up; to appoint, to establish; to be set up, appointed, V. i. 3. 1; 6. 5; ii. 1. 1: VII. i. 1. 3; ii. 15. 1.

章 *chang* (1) Anything definite and complete, a lesson, a piece, VII. i. 24. 3. (2) 章 = rule, canons, IV. i. 1. 4. (3) A name, 萬章, III. ii. 5. 1: V. i. 1. 1, 2, *et al.*, *saepe*.—匡章, III. ii. 10. 1: IV. ii. 30. 1. 章子, IV. ii. 30. 2, 3, 5, is peculiar; see on par. 1.

童 *t'ung* Boys under fifteen. A child, VII. i. 15. 2. A lad, III. i. 4. 17. So 童子, III. ii. 5. 2, 3.

竭 *chieh* To exhaust, to carry to the utmost, I. ii. 15. 1: IV. i. 1. 5: V. i. 1. 2.

端 *twan* (1) A principle, principles, II. i. 6. 5, 6, 7. (2) Correct, upright, IV. ii. 24. 2.

THE 118TH RADICAL, 竹.

笑 *hsiâo* To laugh, to smile; smiling, I. i. 7. 7, 16: III. ii. 7. 4: IV. i. 16. 1: VI. ii. 3. 2. To laugh at, I. i. 3. 2: VII. ii. 23. 2.

符 *fû* A check, or token. 符節, the two halves of such a token, the fitting of which was an evidence of the holder's authority, IV. ii. 1. 3.

等 *tăng* A degree, a class, III. i. 5. 3: V. ii. 2. 2. To graduate, to arrange according to merit, II. i. 2. 27.

筋 *chin* A sinew, a muscle, VI. ii. 15. 2.

答 *tâ* To answer, VI. i. 5. 4; ii. 1. 4: VII. i. 40. 4; 43. 1, 2. To respond to,—in conduct, IV. i. 4. 1.

策 *ts'ê* A slip of bamboo containing writing. 策 = a passage, a piece, VII. ii. 3. 2.

筭 *swan* To reckon. 無筭, incalculable, VI. i. 6. 7.

箕 *chî* (1) The name of a State, 箕子, II. i. 1. 7. (2) 箕山, the name of a hill, V. i. 6. 1.

管 *kwan* (1) A fife or flute, I. ii. 1. 6, 7. (2) An honorary epithet in 管叔, II. ii. 9. 2, 3. A surname in 管仲, and 管夷吾, II. i. 1. 1, 2, 3, 4, 5; ii. 2. 8, 10: VI. ii. 15. 1.

節 *chieh* (1) To regulate, to order according to the proper divisions, IV. i. 27. 2. (2) 符節, see 符.

範 *fan* A law, a rule. Used as a verb, III. ii. 1. 4.

築 *chû* To beat, as in forming mud walls. 築 = to build, I. ii. 13. 2: III. i. 4. 13; ii. 10. 3. 築 = to fortify, I. ii. 14. 1. 板築, see 板.

篡 *ts'wan* To usurp; usurpation, V. i. 5. 7: VII. i. 31. 3.

篤 *tû* To consolidate, I. ii. 3. 6.

簞 *tan* A small basket or dish for holding rice. Always in the phrase 簞食, I. ii. 10. 4; 11. 3: III. ii. 4. 1; 5. 5: IV. ii. 29. 2: VI. i. 10. 6: VII. i. 34; ii. 11.

簡 *chien* (1) To slight, IV. ii. 27. 2, 3. (2) Hasty, VII. ii. 37. 1. (3) An honorary epithet, III. ii. 1. 4.

簿 *pû* A register, V. ii. 4. 6.

籍 *chî* A record, V. ii. 2. 2: VI. ii. 8. 5.

籥 *yo* A musical instrument, pipes, I. ii. 1. 6, 7.

THE 119TH RADICAL, 米.

米 *mî* Rice hulled, II. ii. 1. 3: III. i. 3. 7: VII. ii. 27. 1. See 粟.

粒 *lî* Grains of rice, III. i. 3. 7.

粟 *hsü* Rice in the husk. 米粟, II. ii. 1. 3. 粟米, VII. ii. 27. 1. 粟 alone, I. i. 3. 1: III. i. 4. 4, 5; ii. 4. 3; 10. 3: IV. i. 14. 1: V. ii. 6. 2, 5: VI. ii. 2. 2: VII. i. 23. 3. Medhurst translates it as above, and apparently after K'ang-hsi's dictionary; still the 本草綱目 says that anciently 粟 was the general name for all glumaceous grain. It is now commonly spoken of millet. I have translated it sometimes by 'grain,' and sometimes by 'millet.'

粱 *liang* Barbadoes millet, VI. i. 17. 3.

粢 *tsze* A kind of millet. Always in the phrase 粢盛, III. ii. 3. 3; 5. 2: VII. ii. 14. 4.

粥 *chû* Congee, III. i. 2. 2, 4.

糗 *ch'iû* Parched grain, rice or wheat, VII. ii. 6.

糜 *mî* To boil rice to a mass. 糜爛 = to tear and destroy, VII. ii. 1. 2.

糞 *făn* To manure; the manuring, III. i. 3. 7: V. ii. 2. 9. The rendering of the sentence in the first of these instances is in accordance with the commentaries, but it may be doubted.

糧 *liang* Provisions of grain, I. ii. 4. 6; 5. 4.

糴 *tî* To purchase grain, VI. ii. 7. 3. All the commentaries explain here as if it meant 'to sell grain.' The meaning is—'Do not prevent *our* sale and *their* purchase.'

THE 120TH RADICAL, 糸.

紂 *châu* Epithet of the last sovereign of the Yin dynasty, I. ii. 8. 1, 3: VII. i. 22. 1, *et al.*, *saepe*.

約 *yo* (1) To form alliances, VI. ii. 9. 2. (2) What is most important, II. i. 2. 6, 8. (3) Compendious, VII. ii. 32. 1.—In IV. ii. 15, the term combines the ideas of condensation and importance.

納 *nâ* To pay over, V. i. 8. 3.

紛 *făn* 紛紛然, confusedly, III. i. 4. 5.

素 *sû* (1) Of white, undyed, silk, III. i. 4. 4. (2) For nothing, without doing service, VII. i. 32. 1.

索 *so* Ropes of grass, III. i. 3. 2.

紫 *tsze* Reddish blue, VII. ii. 37. 12.

累 *lêi* I. q. 纍. 係累, to put in confinement, I. ii. 11. 3.

紹 *shâo* — To continue. 紹 = to continue to serve, III. ii. 5. 5.

紾 *chăn* — To twist, VI. ii. 1. 8: VII. i. 39. 2.

終 *chung* — (1) The end. Finally, as the final issue, VI. i. 16. 3; 18. 2; ii. 4. 5. (2) To complete, V. ii. 4. 6: VII. i. 39. 4. To stop, end (active and neuter), V. ii. 1. 6; 3. 4. (3) Perpetual, the whole. 終日, the whole day, III. ii. 1. 4. 終歲, III. i. 3. 7. 終不, never, III. i. 2. 1. 終身, all the life, IV. i. 9. 5; ii. 28. 7; 30. 5. V. i. 1. 5; VII. i. 5; 35. 6; ii. 6. Observe this phrase in I. i. 7. 21, 22, and IV. ii. 33. 1.

絕 *chüeh* — To cut short, III. i. 1. 5. To cut, to stop intercourse with, II. ii. 11. 4: IV. i. 7. 2.

給 *kei* — To supply. 不給, a deficiency in the crop, I. ii. 4. 5: VI. ii. 7. 2.

絮 *hsü* — Rejected floss-silk. 絲絮, III. i. 4. 17.

統 *t'ung* — A thread of connexion. 統 = a beginning, I. ii. 14. 3.

絲 *sze* — Silk from the silkworm. See 絮.

綏 *sui* — To give tranquillity to, III. ii. 5. 5.

經 *ching* — (1) To define, to plan, I. i. 2. 3: III. i. 3. 13. (2) The unchanging standard, VII. ii. 27. 13.

緩 *hwan* — To delay; not to be urgent about, III. i. 3. 2: VII. ii. 27.

綢 *châu* — 綢繆, to intertwine, weave together, II. i. 4. 3.

維 *wei* — A particle,—used as the copula, III. i. 3. 12: V. i. 4. 3.

綯 *t'âo* — To twist. 索綯, III. i. 3. 2.

綽 *ch'o* — 綽綽然, freely, at ease, II. ii. 5. 5.

綿 *mien* — A surname, VI. ii. 6. 5.

緣 *yüan* — From. 緣木 = to climb a tree, or on a tree, I. i. 7. 16, 17.

緦 *sze* — The mourning worn for three months, VII. i. 46. 2.

縮 *hsü* — 縮 = upright, II. i. 2. 7.

縷 *lü* — Threads. 麻縷, III. i. 4. 17. 布縷, VII. ii. 27. 1. Here it probably means cloth of silk.

績 *chi* — Merit, doing, V. i. 2. 3.

繁 *fan* — To abound. 繁殖, III. i. 4. 7.

繅 *sâo* — To unwind a cocoon, III. ii. 3. 3.

繆 *mâu* — (1) 綢繆, see 綢. (2) An honorary epithet, interchanged with 穆, and read *mû*, II. ii. 11. 3: V. ii. 6. 4; 7. 4: VI. ii. 6. 3.

織 *chih* — To weave, III. i. 4. 1, 4; ii. 10. 4.

繡 *hsiû* — Embroidered garments, VI. i. 17. 3.

繩 *shăng* — A line, string,—used with reference to a carpenter's line, IV. i. 1. 5: VII. i. 41. 2.

繫 *chi* — To bind. 繫 = to yoke, V. i. 7. 2.

繳 *cho* — To adjust a string to an arrow, to draw it back after it has been discharged, VI. i. 9. 3.

繼 *chi* — To continue; to be continued, I. ii. 14. 3: II. i. 1. 7: IV. i. 1. 5; 18. 2; ii. 20. 5: V. i. 6. 2, 4 (繼世), 7; ii. 6. 4, 5. 繼此, after this, II. ii. 10. 2. 繼而 . . . , immediately after, II. ii. 14. 3.

纓 *ying* — Strings to tie on a cap, IV. i. 8. 2, 3. To tie on, IV. ii. 29. 6, 7.

纑 *lû* — Hempen threads, III. ii. 10. 4.

THE 121ST RADICAL, 缶.

缺 *ch'üeh* — To be wanting, III. ii. 9. 6.

THE 122ND RADICAL, 网.

罔 *wang* — (1) To catch in a net, II. ii. 10. 7. To entrap, I. i. 7. 20: III. i. 3. 3: V. i. 2. 4. (2) None, not. 罔不, V. ii. 4. 4.

罕 *han* — Seldom, VI. i. 9. 2.

罟 *kû* — A net for catching fish, I. i. 3. 3.

罪 *tsui* — (1) A crime, offence; a fault, I. i. 7. 4, 6, 7, 20; ii. 2. 13: II. ii. 4. 3, 4, *et al.*, *saepe*. 罪人, and sometimes 罪 alone, sinners, criminals, I. ii. 3. 7; 5. 3: V. i. 3. 2: VI. ii. 7. 1, 2, 3, 4. 得罪於 . . . , to offend against, IV. i. 6; ii. 30. 5. (2) To condemn, I. i. 3. 5: III. ii. 9. 8.

置 *chih* — (1) To place, III. ii. 6. 1. To appoint, I. ii. 11. 4. 變置, to displace and appoint others, VII. ii. 14. 3, 4. (2) A stage, a post station, 置郵, II. i. 1. 12.

罰 *fâ* — Punishment, III. ii. 5. 4. 刑罰, I. i. 5. 3; 罰 = penalties, fines.

罷 *pá* To make to cease, to stop, VI. ii. 4. 3, 5, 6.

THE 123RD RADICAL, 羊.

羊 *yang* The sheep or goat, I. i. 7. 4, 6, 7, 8: II. ii. 4. 3: III. ii. 5. 2: V. i. 1. 3; 2. 3; 9. 1; ii. 5. 4; 6. 6: VI. i. 8. 1. 羊棗, sheep-dates, a kind of persimmon, VII. ii. 36. 1, 2.

美 *mei* (1) Good, admirable; beautiful; beauty, I. ii. 1. 6, 7; 16. 2: II. i. 7. 2; ii. 2. 4; 7. 1 (美然, too good), 2: VI. i. 7. 8; 8. 1, 2; 10. 7; 19. 1: VII. i. 41. 1; ii. 25. 5; 36. 2.

羞 *hsiū* To be ashamed; the feeling of shame, II. i. 6. 4, 5; 9. 2: III. ii. 1. 5: IV. ii. 33. 2: V. ii. 1. 3: VI. i. 6. 7.

羣 *ch'ün* A flock, a company, VII. ii. 19. 3.

羨 *hsien* An overplus, III. ii. 4. 3.

義 *i* Righteousness; our consciousness of what is righteous, and the determinations thereof; what is right. *Passim.* The combinations of 仁義, and 禮義, are very common.

羹 *kăng* Soup, V. ii. 3. 4. 豆羹, VI. i. 10. 6: VII. i. 34; ii. 11.

羸 *léi* Meagre, feeble, II. ii. 4. 2.

THE 124TH RADICAL, 羽.

羽 *yü* (1) Feathers, a feather, I. i. 7. 10; ii. 1. 6, 7: VI. i. 3. 2; ii. 1. 6. (2) 羽山, the name of a mountain, V. i. 3. 2.

羿 *i* A famous archer of antiquity, IV. ii. 24. 1: VI. i. 20. 1: VII. i. 41. 2.

翅 *shih* Only, VI. ii. 1. 7.

習 *hsi* To practise, do habitually, VII. i. 5.

翟 *ti* The name of the heresiarch Mo, III. ii. 9. 9, 10, 14.

翼 *yi* Wings. Used as a verb, to give wings to, to assist, III. i. 4. 8.

THE 125TH RADICAL, 老.

老 *lào* To be old; old; the old, I. i. 7. 12, 24; ii. 5. 3; 12. 2; 15. 1: II. ii. 4. 2: III. i. 3. 7; ii. 5. 2: IV. i. 13. 1, 2: V. i. 4. 1: VI. ii. 7. 2, 3: VII. i. 22. 1, 2, 3.

考 *k'ào* (1) A deceased father, V. i. 4. 1. (2) To examine, II. ii. 13. 4: VI. i. 14. 1: VII. ii. 37. 6 (夷考).

者 *chè* *Passim.* (1) He (or they) who; this (or that), these (or those) who (or which). It is put after the words (verbs, adjectives, nouns), and clauses to which it belongs, I. i. 1. 4; 3. 1, 4; 4. 6; 5. 1, 3, 6, *et al.*, *saepissime.* Observe 賢者, I. i. 2. 1, 2; ii. 4. 1; 16. 1, *et al.*; 使者, V. ii. 6. 4; 墨者, III. i. 5. 1, 2, *et similia.* (2) After 若 with intervening words, phrases where a numeral is used, and many other cases, 者 is equivalent to *one*, *this*, *these.* E. g. 若寡人者, 'such an one as I,' I. i. 7. 4; 誠有百姓者, *ibid.* 6; 嬖人有臧倉者, there was one Tsang Ts'ang, I. ii. 16. 3; 三聖者, III. ii. 9. 13; 二者, IV. i. 2. 2.—This seems to be the proper force of the character, so that it is an emphatic demonstrative by which the mind is made to pause on what has just been said. (3) It stands at the end of the first member of a clause or sentence, when the next gives a description or explanation of the subject of the other, terminated generally by the particle 也, but not always, I. i. 7. 9, 12; ii. 4. 2, 3: III. i. 3. 6, 7, *et passim.* (4) 也者, at the end of the first member of a sentence, resume a previous word or statement, and lead on to an explanation or account of it. E. g. II. i. 9. 1. Observe VII. ii. 16.—This case and the preceding may easily be brought under (2). (5) 者也 occur continually at the end of sentences, preceded generally in a previous clause by 者, and for the most part the force of 者 in (1) is apparent, I. i. 1. 5; ii. 3. 2: II. i. 1. 10, 11, *et passim.* (6) It forms adverbs with 昔 and 古, I. ii. 4. 4: II. ii. 7. 2, *et al.*, *saepe.*

耆 *ch'i* Old, aged, I. ii. 15. 1.

耆 *shih* The 4th tone. To relish; a relish, VI. i. 4. 5; 7. 5, 8.

THE 126TH RADICAL, 而.

而 *r* *Passim.* A conjunction, meaning *and*, *and yet*, which latter signification is often nearly or altogether = *but.* Its use, however, is very idiomatic, and it cannot always be literally translated into English. 而已, and 而已矣, are very common. So is 然而, — 'so, and yet.' . . . Observe 繼而, II. ii. 14. 3; 既而, V. i. 7. 4; 從而, VI. i. 8. 1, *et sim.*; also 由 . . . 而來, II. ii. 13. 4, *et al.*; 而誰, V. i. 7. 5. Its use after 得 is to be noted. E. g. IV. ii. 2. 4: V. i. 4. 1, 4.

THE 127TH RADICAL, 耒.

耒 *lêi* A plough-handle, 耒耜, III. i. 4. 2; ii. 3. 5.

耕 *kăng* To plough; to cultivate the ground, I. i. 5. 3, 4; ii. 4. 5: III. i. 4. 3, 4, 5, 6, 7, 8, 11, *et al., saepe.* 耕者 = husbandmen, I. i. 7. 18; ii. 5. 3; 11. 2: II. i. 5. 4. 耕 = to labour, to do work, VII. i. 32. 1.

耘 *yun* To weed, II. i. 2. 16.

耜 *ts'ze* A ploughshare. 耒耜, see 耒.

耨 *nâo* To weed, I. i. 5. 3, 4.

耰 *yû* A harrow. 耰 = to cover the seed, VI. i. 7. 2.

THE 128TH RADICAL, 耳.

耳 *r* (1) The ear, I. i. 7. 16: III. ii. 10. 1: IV. i. 1. 5: V. ii. 1. 1: VI. i. 7. 6, 8; 15. 2: VII. ii. 24. 1. (2) A final particle, simply, only, just, I. i. 3. 2; ii. 1. 2: II. ii. 10. 2, 7: III. i. 4. 11: IV. i. 22; ii. 30. 2: VI. i. 6. 7; 10. 5; 17. 1; ii. 2. 3, 7: VII. ii. 7. 耳 = indeed, I. i. 3. 1 (?).

聘 *p'ing* To invite or call forth men of worth by presents, V. i. 7. 3, 4.

聖 *shăng* Sage (= 'great and capable of transforming'), VII. ii. 25. 7; sageness; a sage, II. i. 1. 8; 2. 18, 19: III. ii. 9. 9, 10, 13: IV. ii. 1. 4: V. ii. 1. 5, 6, 7: VII. ii. 25. 7, 8. 聖人, II. i. 2. 17, 20, 22, 25, 28, *et al., saepe.*

聚 *chü* To collect, to be collected, II. i. 1: IV. i. 1. 9; 9. 1.

聞 *wăn* To hear; to become acquainted with by report, I. i. 7. 1, 2, 4, 8, 16, 17; ii. 1. 4, 6, 7, *et al., saepissime.* 多聞, extensive information, V. ii. 7. 3. 多聞識, *id.*, VI. ii. 13. 2.

聞° *wăn* The 4th tone. Reputation, notoriety, IV. i. 1. 2; ii. 18. 3: VI. i. 17. 3.

聰 *ts'ung* Acuteness of hearing, IV. i. 1. 1.

聲 *shăng* A sound; a voice, I. i. 7. 8; ii. 1. 6, 7: II. i. 2. 4: III. i. 4. 13: V. ii. 1. 6: VI. i. 7. 6, 8; ii. 15. 3: VII. i. 14. 1; 36. 3. 聲音, I. i. 7. 16: VI. ii. 13. 8 (= language). 聲 = music, VII. ii. 22. 1; 37. 12. Reputation, II. i. 6. 3: IV. ii. 18. 3 (聲聞°): VII. i. 14. 1.

職 *chih* An office; the duties of office, I. ii. 4. 5: II. i. 4. 2; ii. 5. 5 (*N.B.*): V. i. 1. 2; ii. 3. 4; 6. 3; 7. 9 (*N.B.*): VI. ii. 7. 2.

聽 *t'ing* To hear, to listen to; to hear and follow, I. i. 7. 16; ii. 7. 4, 5: II. ii. 11. 3: IV. i. 8. 3; 15. 2; ii. 3. 3, 4, *et al.* 聽政, to administer the government, IV. ii. 2. 1. Compare III. i. 2. 4.

THE 129TH RADICAL, 聿.

聿 *yü* So,—a continuative particle, I. ii. 5. 5. The dictionary, however, explains the character here by 自, himself.

肆 *sze* And so, though, VII. ii. 19. 3.

THE 130TH RADICAL, 肉.

肉 *zâu* Flesh, meat, I. i. 3. 4; 4. 4; 7. 8, 24: III. ii. 5. 2; 9. 9; 10. 5: IV. i. 14. 2; 19. 3; ii. 33. 1: V. ii. 6. 4, 5: VI. ii. 6. 6: VII. i. 22. 2, 3.

肖 *hsiâo* 不肖, not equal to, degenerate; incompetency, II. ii. 7. 1: IV. ii. 7. 1: V. i. 6. 2: VI. ii. 6. 2.

肢 *chih* A limb. 四肢, VII. ii. 24. 1.

肥 *fei* Fat (adj.), I. i. 4. 4: III. ii. 9. 9. Rich food, I. i. 7. 16. Rich, spoken of soil, VI. i. 7. 2.

肩 *chien* The shoulders, III. ii. 7. 4: VI. i. 14. 4.

育 *yü* To cherish and train, VI. ii. 7. 3: VII. i. 20. 4. To be maintained and nourished, III. i. 4. 8.

背 *pei* The back, VI. i. 14. 4: VII. i. 21. 4.

胥 *hsü* Mutually, I. ii. 4. 6; 5. 5: IV. i. 9. 6: V. i. 1. 3 (*N. B.*)

胡 *hû* A surname, I. i. 7. 4.

胷 *hsiung* I. q. 胸. The breast, IV. i. 15. 1.

脅 *hsieh* The ribs. 脅 = to shrug up, III. ii. 7. 4.

脩 *hsiû* I. q. 修, to cultivate, improve, I. i. 5. 3: VI. i. 16. 2, 3: VII. i. 1. 3; 9. 6; ii. 32. 1. To repair, IV. ii. 31. 1. 脩 = to do, I. ii. 4. 4.

能 *năng* To be able; can. As the auxiliary, *passim;* but it is often used absolutely, e.g. I. i. 7. 10, 11; ii. 16. 3: V. i. 9. 3, *et al., saepe.* 能 alone, and 能者, men of ability, II. i. 4. 3; 5. 1. Ability, VII. i. 15. 1. 能 = to amount to, V. ii. 2. 4.

腹 *fû* The belly, IV. ii. 3. 1: VI. i. 14. 6: VII. i. 27. 1.

膏 *kâo* 膏 = fat meat, VI. i. 17. 3. 膏澤, rich favours, IV. ii. 3. 3, 4.

膚 *fû* (1) The skin, VI. i. 14. 1, 6. 體膚 and 膚 alone, = the body, II. i. 4; ii. 7. 4: VI. ii. 15. 2. (2) Admirable, IV. i. 7. 5.

膺 *ying* To smite, III. i. 4. 16; ii. 9. 12.

膾 *kwâi* Minced meat, VII. ii. 36. 2.

膠 *chiâo* A surname, II. i. 1. 8: VI. ii. 15. 1.

臂 *pei* The arm, the lower arm, VI. ii. 1. 8: VII. i. 39. 2; ii. 23. 2.

THE 131ST RADICAL, 臣.

臣 *ch'ăn* A minister, an officer of a court, I. i. 7. 14, 16; ii. 4. 10; 6. 1; 7. 1; 8. 2, *et al.*, *saepissime.* 君臣 in correlation often occur. In the first person, 'I, your minister,' I. i. 7. 2, 4, 5, *et al.* In a wider sense, subjects, II. i. 1. 8: III. ii. 5. 5. To employ as a minister, II. ii. 2. 8, 9, *et al.*

臥 *wo* To rest, to sleep, II. ii. 11. 2, 3.

臧 *tsang* A surname, I. ii. 16. 1, 3.

THE 132ND RADICAL, 自.

自 *tsze* (1) From, as a preposition, I. ii. 11. 2: II. i. 2. 23, 27; 3. 2, *et al.*, *saepissime.* According as, V. i. 5. 8. (2) Self, of all persons. Generally joined with verbs in a reflex sense. We have 自反, 自失, 自怨, 自艾, &c. &c., II. i. 2. 7; 4. 4, 5, 6; 6. 6; 9. 2, *et al.*, *saepissime.* Observe 自爲, II. ii. 5. 3: VI. ii. 6. 1.

臭 *ch'âu* Smells, odours, VII. ii. 24. 1.

皐 *kâo* 皐陶, a minister of Shun, III. i. 4. 9, *et al.*

THE 133RD RADICAL, 至.

至 *chih* (1) To come, to arrive at; sometimes = to, till, I. i. 3. 5; 7. 12; ii. 1. 6: II. ii. 2. 4; 9. 1, *et al.*, *saepissime.* 至於, to come to, as to, is very common; e.g. I. ii. 2. 3; 9. 2; 10. 2: VII. ii. 38. 1, 2, 3, 4, *et al.* (2) Most, forming the superlative degree; the utmost degree, II. i. 2. 13: IV. i. 2. 1; 12. 3, *et al.* Chief, II. i. 2. 9. (3) 日至, the solstice, IV. ii. 26. 3.

致 *chih* (1) To carry to the utmost degree, VI. ii. 14. 2, 3: VII. i. 8. 1. 致志, VI. i. 9. 3. (2) To bring about by effort, V. i. 6. 2. 致 = to calculate, IV. ii. 26. 3. (3) To resign, II. ii. 5. 2; 10. 1.

臺 *t'ai* (1) A tower, I. i. 2. 3, 4. 靈臺, the name of king Wan's tower, *ibid.* (2) The designation of a low officer, a servant, V. ii. 6. 4.

臻 *chin* A name, II. ii. 3. 1: VII. ii. 23. 1.

THE 134TH RADICAL, 臼.

與 *yü* (1) With, along with. *Passim.* E.g. I. i. 2. 3; ii. 1. 4, 6, 7, 8: II. i. 9. 1, 2; ii. 2. 4, 5, 7: VII. i. 13. 3; ii. 26. 2. Another preposition, as *from* or *to*, is sometimes required in our idiom. Observe 約與國, VI. ii. 9. 2; and 與禽獸奚擇哉, IV. ii. 28. 6. (2) And, I. i. 3. 3; 4. 2, 3; 7. 11, *et al.*, *saepissime.* Sometimes it is better to translate by *or*, II. i. 1. 3: VI. ii. 1. 1, 2, 6, 7, *et al.* (3) For, III. ii. 1. 4: IV. i. 9. 1. (4) To give, to give to, I. i. 6. 5, 6: V. i. 5. 1, 2, 3, 4, 5, 6, *et al.*, *saepe.* (5) To help, II. i. 7. 5. (6) Than, V. i. 7. 4.

與 *yü* The 4th tone. To share in; to be concerned about, III. i. 4. 11: IV. ii. 31. 1: V. ii. 1. 2: VII. i. 20. 1, 5. VI. i. 18. 1 is marked with this tone, but Chû Hsî explains by 助, 'to assist,' as in (5) above.

與 *yü* The 2nd tone. *Passim.* A final particle, interrogative, and also with exclamatory force. It implies generally that the speaker has a well-formed idea on the subject of the question in his own mind, and that he wishes to express his own surprise, or to involve an opponent in difficulty, I. i. 7. 4, 10, 12, 14, 16, 17; ii. 1. 4, 7; 5. 3; 7. 3; 16. 1, *et al.*, *saepissime.*

興 *hsing* (1) To arise, II. ii. 13. 3: IV. i. 1. 9: VI. i. 6. 2. (2) To rouse one's self, to be aroused, IV. i. 13. 1: VII. i. 10; 22. 1; ii. 15; 37. 13. 興之, to raise itself—spoken of grain, I. i. 6. 6. (3) To raise, I. i. 7. 14. 興發, to open the granaries, I. ii. 4. 9. (4) To flourish, IV. i. 8. 2.

舉 *chü* (1) To lift, to raise, I. i. 7. 10: III. i. 5. 4; ii. 5. 7: VI. ii. 2. 3. 舉 = to promote; to be lifted up, promoted, III. i. 4. 7: V. i. 9. 3; ii. 6. 4, 6: VI. ii. 15. 1. 舉 = to allege, insist on, VII. i. 26. 4; ii. 37. 11. 舉 = to take, I. i. 7. 12. 舉 = to complete, I. ii. 10. 2. (2) All, I. ii. 1. 6, 7: II. ii. 12. 5: VI. i. 7. 3.

舊 *chiû* Old, ancient, III. i. 3. 12: IV. i. 1. 4. 舊 = former, IV. ii. 3. 2.

THE 135TH RADICAL, 舌.

舌 *shé* The tongue, III. i. 4. 14.

舍 *shê* (1) To lodge in a booth, I. ii. 4. 9. 舍館, a lodging-house, IV. i. 24. 2. (2) Only, III. i. 4. 2 (? *N.B.*) (3) A name, II. i. 2. 5, 6, 8.

荒 *hwang* (1) 荒蕪, overgrown with grass and weeds, VI. ii. 7. 2. (2) Wild, ruinously addicted to hunting, I. ii. 4. 6, 7, 8.

莅 *li* To come forth and descend to. 莅 = to govern, I. i. 7. 16.

莊 *chwang* (1) A surname, I. ii. 1. 1, 2. (2) The name of a street in the capital of Ch'i, III. ii. 6. 1.

莒 *chü* The name of an ancient State, I. ii. 3. 6.

莘 *hsin* An ancient name for the territory of 虢 in the time of Châu, V. i. 7. 2.

莠 *yü* A useless plant growing amid corn, and like it. ? Darnel, VII. ii. 37. 12.

莩 *p'iâo* I. q. 殍. To die. 餓莩, I. i. 3. 5; 4. 4: III. ii. 4. 9.

莫 *mo* (1) Not; not to be, not to have, i.q. 無, I. i. 5. 1; ii. 12. 1: II. i. 8. 5; ii. 2. 4, 9, *et al., saepissime*. Often it = no one, and in this case it generally attracts the object of the following verb to itself, I. i. 7. 3; ii. 12. 2: II. i. 1. 10; 2. 27; 7. 2: III. i. 3. 14; 4. 17, *et al., saepe*. 莫不 and 莫非 are strong affirmations, = there is nothing (or none) but . . ., I. i. 6. 6: II. i. 1. 8: IV. i. 20; ii. 5, *et al.* 莫若, see 若. So 莫如, II. i. 4. 2; 7. 4, *et al.* (2) 子莫, a worthy and thinker of Lû, VII. i. 26. 3.

莽 *mang* 莽 = grass, plants, V. ii. 7. 1.

菑 *tsâi* I.q. 災. Calamities, IV. i. 8. 1.

菜 *ts'âi* Vegetables, V. ii. 3. 4.

菹 *tsü* Grassy marshes. ? Bogs, III. ii. 9. 4.

菽 *shû* Pulse, VII. i. 23. 3.

萃 *ts'ûi* A grassy level, II. i. 2. 28.

萊 *lâi* (1) Fields lying fallow; commons, IV. i. 14. 3. (2) A surname, VII. ii. 38. 2.

萌 *măng* Buds; to bud, VI. i. 8. 1; 9. 2.

華 *hwâ* The 4th tone. A surname, VI. ii. 6. 5.

萬 *wan* (1) Ten thousand, I. i. 1. 4; ii. 9. 2; 10. 2, 4: II. i. 1. 13; 2. 4, 7; ii. 10. 3, 5: III. i. 4. 18; ii. 10. 5: VI. i. 10. 7; ii. 10. 3. In several of these examples, the phrase is 萬乘之國, applicable properly only to the royal domain, but used pretentiously of the great fiefs. 萬 = all, VII. i. 4. 1. (2) A surname. 萬章, III. ii. 5. 1: V. i. 1. 1, 2, *et al., saepe*.

落 *lo* To descend, 徂落 = to decease, V. i. 4. 1.

著 *chû* (1) To be manifested, III. ii. 9. 9. (2) To know clearly, VII. i. 5.

葛 *ko* The name of an ancient State. 葛 and 葛伯, I. ii. 3. 1; 11. 2: III. ii. 5. 2, 4.

葵 *k'wei* 葵丘, the name of a place, VI. ii. 7. 3.

葬 *tsang* To bury, inter, II. ii. 7. 1: III. i. 2. 2, 5; 5. 2, 4.

蒙 *măng* (1) To wear on the head, IV. ii. 25. 1. (2) A name. 逢蒙, IV. ii. 24. 1; 咸丘蒙, V. i. 4. 1, 2.

蒸 *chăng* (1) All, 蒸民, VI. i. 6. 8. (2) I.q. 烝, to steam, III. ii. 7. 2.

蓋 *kâi* (1) To cover, V. i. 2. 3. (2) A particle, continuative and sometimes illative, I. i. 7. 17; ii. 4. 9: III. i. 5. 4: V. ii. 3. 4; 6. 4.

蓋 *kô* The name of a place, II. ii. 6. 1: III. ii. 10. 5.

蓰 *hsî* Five times, fivefold, III. i. 4. 18: VI. i. 6. 7.

蔡 *ts'âi* The name of a State, VII. ii. 18.

蔽 *pî* To obscure, cloud over, keep in the shade, II. i. 2. 17: VI. i. 15. 2.

蕘 *zâo* 蕘者, fuel-gatherers, I. ii. 2. 2.

蕢 *kwei* A straw-basket, VI. i. 7. 4.

蕩 *t'ang* Great, 蕩蕩乎, how vast! III. i. 4. 11.

蕪 *wû* Overgrown with weeds. 荒蕪, see 荒.

薄 *po* Thin. 薄 = mean, shabby, V. ii. 1. 3: VII. i. 44. 1; ii. 15. 1. 薄 = slight, IV. ii. 24. 1. 薄 = a spare simplicity, III. i. 5. 2. 薄 = to make light, I. i. 5. 3: VII. i. 23. 1.

薛 *hsieh* (1) The name of a State, I. ii. 14. 1: II. ii. 3. 1, 4. (2) A surname, III. ii. 6. 2.

薦 *chien* To present, to introduce, V. i. 5. 5, 6; 6. 1, 2.

薪 *hsin* (1) Firewood, I. i. 7. 10: VI. i. 18. 1. 采薪之憂 = 'a little sickness,' II. ii. 2. 3. (2) Grass, plants, IV. ii. 31. 1.

薨 *hung* The death of a prince, III. i. 2. 1, 4.

孟子

藉 *tsé* 藉 = mutual dependence, a borrowing of services, III. i. 3. 6.

藏 *ts'ang* To lay up, to deposit, I. i. 7. 18: II. i. 5. 2: V. i. 3. 2.

藐 *miao* To despise, VII. ii. 34. 1.

蓺 *i* I. q. 藝. 樹蓺, to cultivate, III. i. 4. 18.

藥 *yo* Physic, III. i. 1. 5.

蘇 *sû* To revive, I. ii. 11. 2.

虆 *lo* A kind of basket, III. i. 5. 4.

THE 141ST RADICAL, 虍.

虎 *hû* (1) A tiger, III. ii. 9. 6: VII. ii. 23. 2. 虎賁 = life-guards, VII. ii. 4. 4. (2) A name, III. i. 3. 5.

虐 *nio* To oppress, tyrannize over; oppressive, I. ii. 4. 6; 11. 3: II. i. 1. 11: III. i. 3. 7.

處 *ch'û* The 3rd tone, a verb. (1) To reside in, to dwell, III. ii. 10. 5: V. i. 7. 3, 4; ii. 1. 1, 3: VI. ii. 6. 5: VII. i. 35. 6. Observe 處守, VI. ii. 5. 1. 處室, IV. ii. 33. 1. 處仁, to dwell in love, V. i. 6. 5; but the same in II. i. 7. 2 is different. (2) To live in retirement; unemployed, III. ii. 9. 9: V. ii. 1. 4. (3) 處子, an unmarried daughter, VI. ii. 1. 8. (4) To manage as business, an occasion for, II. ii. 3. 5.—In, III. i. 4. 1, 與之處, 'gave him a place to reside in,' perhaps 處 is the 3rd tone.

虛 *hsü* Empty, VII. ii. 12. 1. Used adverbially, VII. i. 37. 3.

虞 *yü* (1) 驩虞如, joyful and pleasant-like, VII. i. 13. 1. (2) To measure, to reckon. 不虞, unexpected, that cannot be reckoned on, IV. i. 21. (3) 虞人, a forester, III. ii. 1. 2: V. ii. 7. 5, 6, 7. (4) 虞 = Shun,—said in the dictionary to be the surname that arose from him, V. i. 6. 7. (5) The name of a State, V. i. 9. 2: VI. ii. 6. 4. 虞公, V. i. 9. 3. (6) A name, II. ii. 7. 1; 13. 1.

號 *hào* A name or mark. 號 = argument, VI. ii. 4. 4.

號 *hâo* The 1st tone. To cry out. 號泣, V. i. 1. 1, 2.

虢 *ko* The name of a State, V. i. 9. 2.

THE 142ND RADICAL, 虫.

蚋 *zùi* 蚋 = 蜹 abbreviated. A gnat, III. i. 5. 4.

蚓 *yin* An earthworm, III. ii. 10. 2, 3, 6.

蚤 *tsào* Interchanged with 早. Early in the morning, IV. ii. 33. 1.

蛇 *shé* A snake, III. ii. 9. 3, 4.

蚳 *ch'ih* A surname, II. ii. 5. 1, 2, 3. But the dictionary does not mention the character as such.

螬 *ts'âo* Dung-worms, III. ii. 10. 1.

蠅 *ying* A fly, III. i. 5. 4.

蠡 *li* An insect that eats through wood. 蠡 = the appearance of being worn away, VII. ii. 22. 2.

蠶 *tsan* The silkworm. To keep silkworms, III. ii. 3. 3. To nourish silkworms on, VII. i. 22. 2.

蠻 *man* The wild tribes of the South, III. i. 4. 14.

THE 143RD RADICAL, 血.

血 *hsieh* Blood, VI. ii. 7. 3: VII. ii. 3. 3.

THE 144TH RADICAL, 行.

行 *hsing* (1) To go; to set out; to proceed, I. ii. 4. 6: II. i. 1. 12, *et al.*, *saepe*. To make to go, to lead, VI. i. 2. 3; ii. 14. 2. To advance, in contrast with 止, 'to stop,' I. ii. 16. 3. 行潦, rain-pools, II. i. 2. 28. 補行, to assist on the journey, or expedition, II. ii. 6. 1. (2) To do, perform; to carry out, to practise; to be practised, carried out, I. i. 4. 5; 7. 9, 23; ii. 5. 2, 4; 9. 1, *et al.*, *saepe*. This meaning is kindred to the above, and derived from it. The *way* regulates the *conduct*. 行道, 'to carry out principles,' often occurs, but 行道之人, VI. i. 10. 6, is literally 'a tramper.' Observe the two meanings in IV. ii. 19. 2.—Observe also 行拂, VI. ii. 15. 2; 行乎, IV. ii. 1. 3, and II. i. 1. 3; 與有行, V. i. 9. 3; 足以行矣, 而不行, and 行可, V. ii. 4. 6, 7. (3) A name, III. i. 4. 1, 3.—IV. ii. 31. 1.

行 *hsìng* The 4th tone. Actions, conduct;—always as a noun, I. ii. 4. 8: II. i. 2. 18: III. ii. 9. 5, 7, 13: IV. ii. 11: V. i. 5. 4, 5; 7. 7: VI. ii. 2. 5: VII. i. 16. 1; ii. 33. 2; 37. 6, 9. Medhurst, Williams, and Wade

give the pronunciation as here represented; but according to K'ang-hsi's dictionary, it should be expressed by *hăng*.

行 *hang* The 2nd tone. 公行, a double surname, IV. ii. 27. 1.

衍 *yen* A name, III. ii. 3. 1.

術 *shû* An art, a contrivance, I. i. 7. 8: VI. ii. 16: VII. i. 18. 1; 24. 2. 術=a profession, II. i. 7. 1.

衛 *wei* The name of a State, IV. ii. 24. 2; 31. 2: V. i. 8. 1, 2, 3. 衛靈公, and 孝公, V. ii. 4. 7.

衡 *hăng* I.q. 横. Crosswise. 衡=disorderly; perplexed, I. ii. 3. 7: VI. ii. 15. 3.

THE 145TH RADICAL, 衣.

衣 *i* Clothes; robes, II. i. 9. 1: III. i. 4. 8; ii. 9. 5: V. ii. 1. 1: VII. ii. 6. 衣服, III. ii. 3. 3: VII. i. 36. 2. 衣=grave-clothes, I. ii. 16. 2.

衣' *i* The 4th tone. To wear, I. i. 3. 4; 7. 24: III. i. 4. 1, 4: VII. i. 22. 2.

衰 *shwâi* To decay, become small and feeble, III. ii. 9. 5, 7: V. i. 6. 1: VI. ii. 14. 2, 3.

衾 *ch'in* A shroud, I. ii. 16. 2.

袒 *t'an* To strip up the sleeve, to bare the arm, 袒裼, II. i. 9. 2: V. ii. 1. 3.

袗 *ch'ăn* Embroidered robes, VII. ii. 6.

被' *p'i* The 4th tone. To be covered with. 被' = to be affected by, to receive, IV. i. 1. 2: V. i. 7. 6; ii. 1. 2. 被'=to wear, to have to wear, VII. ii. 6.

被 *p'i* The 2nd tone. I. q. 披. 被髮, the hair dishevelled, unbound, IV. ii. 29. 5, 6.

裘 *ch'iû* A name, V. ii. 3. 2.

裎 *ch'ăng* Naked. 裸裎, II. i. 9. 2: V. ii. 1. 3.—There must be a difference in the meaning of the two terms, but I have not found it indicated.

裕 *yü* Abundance of clothes; abundance generally. 有餘裕='yea, and more,' II. ii. 5. 5.

補 *pû* To mend clothes. To mend or repair generally; to supply; to assist, I. ii. 4. 5, 10: III. i. 1. 5; ii. 4. 3: VI. ii. 7. 2: VII. i. 13. 3 (*N.B.*)

裸 *lo* Naked. 裸裎, see 裎.

裹 *kwo* To tie or wrap up, I. ii. 5. 4.

裼 *hsi* To put off the upper garment. 袒裼, see 袒.

褊 *pien* Narrow. 褊小, I. i. 7. 6: III. i. 3. 14.

褐 *ho* Cloth of hair; coarse cloth, II. i. 2. 4, 7: III. i. 4. 1, 4.

襄 *hsiang* (1) An honorary epithet. 梁襄王, I. i. 6. 1. (2) 子襄, the designation of a disciple of Tsăng Shăn, II. i. 2. 7.

襲 *hsi* To take by surprise, II. i. 2. 15 (*N.B.*)

THE 146TH RADICAL, 西.

西 *hsi* (1) The west; on the west; western, I. i. 5. 1; ii. 5. 5: II. i. 3. 2: VI. i. 2. 1, 2; ii. 6. 5. 西伯, the chief of the West—king Wăn, IV. i. 13. 1: VII. i. 22. 1, 3. 西夷, I. ii. 11. 2: III. ii. 5. 4: IV. ii. 1. 2: VII. ii. 4. 3. (2) 西子, a famous beauty, IV. ii. 25. 1. (3) Part of the designation of the grandson of Tsăng Shăn, II. i. 1. 3, 4.

要 *yâo* The 1st tone. (1) To seek for, II. ii. 6. 3: VI. i. 16. 3. 要=to seek an introduction to, V. i. 7. 1, 8; 9. 1. (2) 要=to intercept, II. ii. 2. 3: III. ii. 5. 2: V. i. 8. 3.

覆 *fû* (1) 反覆, repeatedly; to repeat, V. ii. 9. 1, 4: VI. i. 8. 2. (2) 顛覆, to overturn, V. i. 6. 5.

覆 *fâu* To cover, overspread, III. i. 1. 5.

THE 147TH RADICAL, 見.

見 *chien* To see. *Passim.* 望見, to see from a distance, VII. i. 36. 1; ii. 23. 2. Very often it = to visit, e.g. I. i. 1. 1: II. ii. 10. 2: III. ii. 7. 1, 2, 3. 見於..., to have an interview with—spoken of a ruler, V. ii. 7. 4. It forms the passive voice, III. ii. 5. 5: VII. ii. 29.

見' *hsien* (1) To appear, to be seen, II. ii. 12. 6: III. i. 5. 2: VII. i. 21. 4; 2. 11. (2) To become illustrious, VII. i. 9. 6. (3) To have an interview with, an audience of..., I. ii. 1. 1, 2; 16. 2: II. ii. 4. 4; 6. 1: V. i. 4. 4 (*N.B.*)

規 *kwei* A compass, the instrument so called, IV. i. 1. 1, 5; 2. 1: VI. i. 20. 2: VII. ii. 5. 1.

視 *shih* To regard, to look at,—often = to consider, II. i. 2. 4, 5: IV. ii. 3. 1; 20. 3, *et al.* To see, I. ii. 3. 5; 12. 1: V. ii. 1. 1; 7. 8, *et al.* 視朝, to hold a court, to give audience, II. ii. 2. 1. 視=equal to, V. ii. 2. 5.

覩 *tû* To see, VI. ii. 6. 5.

孟子

親 *ch'in* (1) To love, show affection to, I. ii. 12. 3: III. i. 5. 3: IV. i. 11. 1, *et al.*, *saepe*. Mutual affection, III. i. 2. 2; 3. 18 (親睦); 4. 8. To be loved, IV. i. 4. 1. (2) To be near, to approach, II. ii. 7. 4: VII. ii. 15. To touch one another, IV. i. 12. 1. Intimate, I. ii. 7. 1. (3) In person, personally, V. i. 7. 4: VI. ii. 1. 3. (4) Relatives. Very often it is used of *parents*, I. i. 1. 5: II. ii. 7. 5: IV. i. 11; 12. 1; 19. 1, 2, 4, *et al.* But it is also used more widely, VII. i. 34; 45; ii. 7. 親戚, II. i. 1. 4, 5.

覲 *chin* To wait on a superior, to appear at court, 朝覲, V. i. 5. 1; 6. 1.

覵 *chien* A name, III. i. 1. 4.

覺 *chüo* To understand, apprehend; to make to understand, to instruct, V. i. 7. 5; ii. 1. 2.

觀 *kwan* To view, contemplate; to discern, II. i. 2. 26; 6. 4; ii. 7. 2: III. i. 2. 5; 3. 9; ii. 7. 4: IV. i. 14. 2; 15. 2; ii. 33. 2: V. i. 8. 4: VII. i. 24. 1, 2. To make a visit of inspection, I. ii. 4. 4.

THE 148TH RADICAL, 角.

角 *chüo* (1) A horn, VII. ii. 4. 5. (2) 角招, the name of a piece of music, I. ii. 4. 10.

解 *chieh* To remove, II. ii. 9. 2 (*N.B.*): V. i. 1. 4. To relieve, to unloose, II. i. 1. 13.

觫 *sü* 觳觫, the appearance of fearing death, I. i. 7. 4, 6.

觳 *hu* See above.

THE 149TH RADICAL, 言.

言 *yen* A word, words; a saying, I. ii. 3. 4; 5. 4, *et passim*. To speak, say; to speak of, I. i. 7. 9, 16; ii. 1. 5; 6. 3, *et saepissime*. 言語, VII. ii. 33. 2. 言 = to mean, meaning, I. i. 7. 12: VI. i. 17. 3. 爲言 = means, VII. ii. 4. 6; but in VII. i. 24. 1 the same phrase = to think anything of the words of others. 言 = to cherish, think of, II. ii. 4. 1, *et al.* This usage is only found in some quotations from the Shih-ching. 有言, to have a saying, or to say, *saepe*. But in IV. i. 10. 1 it = to have speech.

計 *ch'i* To calculate, V. ii. 5. 4.

討 *t'ao* To punish; to order to be punished, VI. ii. 7. 2. To put to death, III. ii. 9. 6.

訑 *i* 訑訑, the appearance of being self-conceited, VI. ii. 13. 8.

訓 *hsün* (1) To instruct, V. i. 6. 5. (2) 伊訓, the name of a Book in the Shû-ching, V. i. 7. 9.

訕 *shan* To revile, IV. ii. 33. 1.

託 *t'o* To entrust, I. ii. 6. 1. 託 = to accept a stated support from, V. ii. 6. 1.

訟 *sung* To contend, wrangle. 訟獄者, litigants, V. i. 5. 7; 6. 1.

訢 *yin* 訢然, cheerfully, VII. i. 35. 6.

設 *shê* To establish, 設爲, III. i. 3. 10. 設科, to institute instruction, VII. ii. 30. 2. 設心, to settle in one's mind, IV. ii. 30. 5.

許 *hsü* (1) To allow, to accede to, I. i. 7. 10. To promise, II. i. 1. 1. (2) A surname, III. i. 4. 1, 3, 4, 5, 17, 18.

詖 *pi* One-sided, only half the truth, II. i. 2. 17: III. ii. 9. 13.

試 *shih* To try. 嘗試, to try to follow, I. i. 7. 19. 試劍, sword-exercise, III. i. 2. 4.

詩 *shih* A piece of poetry; an ode. Generally, with reference to some piece of the Shih-ching, I. ii. 4. 10: II. i. 4. 3: IV. ii. 21. 1: V. i. 4. 2; ii. 8. 2: VI. i. 6. 8; ii. 3. 1, 2. 詩云 and 詩曰 are the forms of quotation from the Shih-ching. *Passim.*

詭 *kwei* Deceitful; deceitfully, III. ii. 1. 4.

詳 *hsiang* (1) Particulars, V. ii. 2. 2: VI. ii. 4. 4. Minutely, IV. ii. 15. 1. (2) A name, II. ii. 11. 3.

誅 *chû* To cut off, to put to death, I. ii. 8. 3; 12. 1: III. ii. 9. 6: V. i. 3. 2; 7. 9; ii. 4. 4, 5: VI. ii. 7. 3.

誓 *shih* 湯誓 and 太誓 are the names of Books in the Shû-ching, I. i. 2. 4.—III. ii. 5. 6: V. i. 5. 8.

語 *yü* 言語, words, VII. ii. 33. 2. A saying, V. i. 4. 1. 語 = speech, language, III. ii. 6. 1.

語 *yü* To tell, speak to about..., I. i. 6. 2; 7. 11; ii. 1. 1, 2: II. ii. 11. 3; 12. 1: VII. i. 9. 1.

誣 *wû* To delude, III. ii. 9. 9.

誦 *sung* To repeat, croon over, VI. ii. 2. 5. To relate, II. ii. 4. 4.

誨 *hui* To instruct, to teach, VI. i. 9. 3; 20. 2; ii. 16 (教誨).

誠 *ch'ăng* (1) To be sincere; sincerity, IV. i. 12. 1, 2 (*N.B.*), 3: VII. i. 4. 2. (2) Really, truly, indeed, I. i. 6. 6; 7. 6, 7, 11: II. i. 1. 2; 3. 2; ii. 12. 7: III. i. 2. 5; 4. 3; 5. 4: V. i. 2. 4; 4. 1.

說 *shwo* To speak of, discuss, III. ii. 9. 10 (說者): IV. ii. 15. 說辭, II. i. 2. 18. To explain, explanation, V. i. 4. 2; ii. 4. 5. Speakings, = doctrines, III. ii. 9. 5, 7, 9, 13.

說 *shüi* To counsel, V. i. 7. 6: VI. ii. 4. 3, 4, 5, 6: VII. ii. 34. 1.

說 *yüeh* I.q. 悅. To be pleased, I. i. 7. 9; ii. 4. 10 (傳說, see 傳).

誰 *shüi* Who, whom, I. i. 5. 5; 6. 6: II. i. 4. 3; ii. 13. 5: III. ii. 6. 2, *et al.*

諂 *ch'an* Abbreviated for 讇. To flatter; flatteringly, III. ii. 7. 4: VI. ii. 13. 8.

諄 *chun* 諄諄然, repeatedly and specifically, V. i. 5. 3.

談 *t'an* To talk with, converse, IV. ii. 33. 1: VI. ii. 3. 2.

論 *lun* To discuss, to consider, V. ii. 8. 2.

請 *ch'ing* To request, to beg; to beg leave. Sometimes, especially in the first person, it is merely a polite way of expressing a purpose, I. i. 3. 2; 5. 6; 7. 13, 19; ii. 1. 5; 3. 5; 15. 3; 16. 1, *et al.*, *saepe*. Observe II. ii. 10. 2; 11. 3: V. ii. 4. 3.

諛 *yü* To flatter, 面諛之人, sycophants, VI. ii. 13. 8.

諫 *chien* To reprove, to remonstrate; admonitions. It is often followed by 於, II. ii. 5. 2; 12. 6: IV. ii. 3. 3, 4: V. i. 9. 2, 3; ii. 9. 1, 4.

諱 *hûi* To avoid, to conceal, VII. ii. 36. 2.

諺 *yen* A common saying, I. ii. 4. 5.

諾 *no* A reply, affirmative and immediate, I. ii. 16. 1: II. ii. 2. 5.

諸 *chû* (1) Not merely one; all, I. i. 7. 16; ii. 7. 4, 5: II. ii. 10. 3. (2) A preposition. In, from, on, to, &c., I. i. 7. 12; ii. 7. 5, *et al.*, *saepissime*. (3) As an interrogative, generally, 諸 = 之乎. Yet once we have the 乎 expressed, V. i. 8. 1; and 諸 remains = 之, which it is in II. ii. 12. 4, where there is no interrogation, I. i. 7. 4; ii. 1. 2; 2. 1; 5. 1 (*N.B.*); 8. 1, *et al.*, *saepissime*. (4) 諸侯, see 侯. (5) 諸馮, the name of a place, IV. ii. 1. 1.

謀 *mâu* To consult, take counsel, I. ii. 11. 1, 4. A counsel, a plan, I. ii. 13. 2. Counselling, II. ii. 2. 7.

謂 *wei* (1) To address, to say to, I. ii. 5. 1; 6. 1; 10. 2: II. i. 2. 7, 16; ii. 4. 1; 5. 1; 10. 3, *et al.*, *saepissime*. To tell to, to inform, III. ii. 1. 4. (2) To say; to speak of, I. i. 6. 17: II. i. 6. 3, 6, *et al.*, *saepe*. 謂 = to suppose, III. ii. 6. 2. (3) To call; to be called, I. i. 2. 3; ii. 4. 7; 8. 3: VII. ii. 37. 3, 4, 5, 8, *et passim*. Observe 之謂, which occurs continually, e.g. I. i. 7. 9: II. i. 3. 2; 4. 6: VII. ii. 25. 2, 3, 4, 5, 6, 7, 8. Sometimes, where 之謂, followed by a particle, terminates the sentence, we can explain the characters without insisting on a peculiar idiom. At other times we can explain them by understanding 所 before 謂; but in a multitude of cases we have simply to accept the idiom. 謂之, which also is frequent, is different. 謂 = to mean, meaning, II. ii. 2. 6: VI. i. 7. 8, *et al.* 何謂, what do you mean, what is meant, II. i. 2. 17: III. i. 5. 3: IV. ii. 24. 2, *et al.*—Observe I. ii. 7. 1: VI. ii. 1. 6.

謨 *mû* To plan; plans, III. ii. 9. 6: V. i. 2. 3.

謳 *âu* To sing,—in some peculiar, abrupt manner, VI. ii. 6. 5. 謳歌, to sing (active and neuter), V. i. 5. 6; 6. 1.

謹 *chin* To give careful attention to, I. i. 3. 4; 7. 24.

譈 *tûi* To detest, V. ii. 4. 4.

譏 *chî* To inspect. 譏而不征, I. ii. 5. 3: II. i. 5. 3.

識 *shih* To know, I. i. 7. 4; ii. 7. 2: II. ii. 2. 1, 3; 10. 2; 12. 1: V. i. 2. 3; 4. 1; ii. 6. 4: VI. i. 4. 3; 10. 7, 8; ii. 6. 5, 6. To understand, VI. ii. 8. 4. 多聞識, of much information, VI. ii. 13. 2.

警 *ching* To warn, III. ii. 9. 3.

譬 *p'i* To compare, 譬則..., V. ii. 1. 7.

議 *i* To discuss, indulge in discussions, III. ii. 9. 9.

譽 *yü* Praise, IV. i. 21: VI. i. 17. 3.

讀 *tû* To read, V. ii. 8. 2.

變 *pien* To change; to be changed, I. ii. 1. 2; 11. 2: II. i. 1. 8; ii. 14. 2: III. i. 4. 12, 16; ii. 5. 4: V. ii. 9. 2: VI. ii. 6. 5; 9. 3: VII. i. 7. 2 (= versatile); 41. 2; ii. 14. 3, 4.

讒 *ch'an* To calumniate, VI. ii. 13. 8. To revile, I. ii. 4. 6.

讎 *ch'âu* (1) An enemy, IV. ii. 3. 1, 4. (2) 復讎, to avenge, III. ii. 5. 3. (3) In a name, V. i. 8. 2.—The character is also written 讐.

讓 *zang* (1) To reprimand; reproof, VI. ii. 7. 2. (2) To yield, to decline, VII. ii. 11. 辭讓, modesty and complaisance, II. i. 6. 4, 5.

THE 150TH RADICAL, 谷.

谷 *kû* A valley, III. i. 4. 15.

谿 *ch'i* A mountain-stream; a river, II. ii. 1. 4.

THE 151ST RADICAL, 豆.

豆 *tâu* A wooden vessel, or dish, 豆羹, VI. i. 10. 6: VII. i. 34; ii. 11.

豈 *ch'i* How. *Passim.* It is generally followed by 哉, at the end of the sentence; e. g. I. i. 2. 4; 6. 16; ii. 10. 4.

THE 152ND RADICAL, 豕.

豕 *shih* The swine, VII. i. 16. 豕交之, to treat one as a pig, VII. i. 37. 1.

豚 *t'un* A young pig, I. i. 3. 4; 7. 24: III. ii. 7. 3: VII. ii. 26. 2.

象 *hsiang* (1) The elephant, III. ii. 9. 6. (2) To resemble, to make to resemble, I. i. 4. 6. (3) The name of Shun's brother, V. i. 2. 3; 3. 1, 2, 3: VI. i. 6. 3.

豢 *hwan* Grain-fed animals, VI. i. 7. 8.

豪 *hâo* The first among a hundred, 豪傑之士, III. i. 4. 12: VII. i. 10.

豫 *yü* (1) To be pleased, satisfied, II. ii. 13. 1, 5: IV. i. 28. 2. (2) To make an excursion, I. ii. 4. 5.

THE 153RD RADICAL, 豸.

豹 *pâo* (1) The leopard, III. ii. 9. 6. (2) A name, VI. ii. 6. 5.

豺 *ch'âi* A kind of wolf, 豺狼, IV. i. 17. 1.

貉 *mâi* (1) A general name for the barbarous tribes of the north, VI. ii. 10. 2, 4, 7. (2) A surname, VII. ii. 19. 1.

貌 *mâo* Aspect, demeanour, IV. i. 16. 禮貌, a polite demeanour, VI. ii. 14. 2, 3; used verbally, IV. ii. 30. 1.

THE 154TH RADICAL, 貝.

貞 *chăng* An honorary epithet, V. i. 8. 3.

負 *fû* (1) To carry on the back, I. i. 3. 4; 7. 24: III. i. 4. 2: IV. ii. 31 (*N.B.*): VII. i. 35. 6. (2) To take refuge in, VII. ii. 23. 2. (3) 負夏, the name of a place, IV. ii. 1. 1.

財 *ts'âi* (1) Wealth, money; expense, I. i. 7. 7: II. ii. 7. 3: III. i. 4. 10, *et al.* 財用, VII. ii. 12. 3. 貨財, IV. i. 1. 9; ii. 30. 2. (2) I. q. 材, talents, VII. i. 40. 3.

貢 *kung* (1) To levy a tax, III. i. 3. 6, 7. 貢稅, revenues, V. i. 3. 3. (2) 子貢, the designation of one of Confucius's disciples, II. i. 2. 18, 19, 25, 27: III. i. 4. 13.

貧 *p'in* Poverty, I. ii. 16. 2: III. ii. 2. 3: V. ii. 5. 1, 2, 3.

貨 *hwo* (1) Goods, property; wealth, I. ii. 5. 4: V. ii. 4. 4. 貨財, see 財. (2) To bribe; a bribe, II. ii. 3. 5. (3) A name, III. ii. 7. 3.

貫 *kwan* I. q. 慣. To be accustomed, III. ii. 1. 4.

責 *tsê* or *châi* To reprove, to be reproved, IV. i. 22. The responsibility of reproving, II. ii. 5. 5. To urge to—implying more or less of reproof, IV. i. 1; 18. 4; ii. 30. 3, 4.

貳 *r* Double, III. i. 4. 17. Double-minded, VII. i. 1. 3. 貳=supplemental, V. ii. 3. 5.

費 *pî* The name of a city and small territory, 費惠公, V. ii. 3. 3.

貴 *kwei* (1) Noble, being in an honourable condition; honour, V. i. 1. 4; 3. 2; ii. 3. 1; 9. 1: VI. i. 17. 1, 2: VII. i. 43. 2; ii. 14. 1 (*N.B.*) 富貴, II. ii. 10. 6: III. ii. 2. 3: IV. ii. 33. 1, 2. 貴賤, VI. i. 14. 2. (2) To esteem noble, to give honour to, II. i. 4. 2: III. i. 5. 2: V. ii. 3. 6, *et al.*

貶 *pien* To diminish, degrade, VI. ii. 7. 2.

貸 *t'âi* To borrow, III. i. 3. 7. The dictionary, however, says that the character, meaning to borrow, should be read *t'i* (old 4th tone), and that, pronounced *t'âi*, it means to lend.

賁 *pun* (1) 虎賁=life-guards, VII. ii. 4. 4. (2) A name, II. i. 2. 2.

資 *tsze* To rely on, IV. ii. 14. 1.

賈 *kû* A stationary trafficker or merchant, I. i. 7. 18.

賈 *chiâ* (1) A price, III. i. 4. 17, 18. (2) A name, II. ii. 9. 2.

賊 *tsêi* To injure, do violence to; to play the thief with, II. i. 6. 6: IV. i. 2. 2; ii. 30. 4: VI. i. 1. 2: VII. i. 26. 4. Seditious; villainous, III. ii. 9. 11: IV. i. 1. 9. An injurer,—may be rendered by 'a thief,' IV. i. 1. 13: VI. ii. 9. 1: VII. ii. 37. 8, 10, 11. 殘賊之人, I. ii. 8. 3.

賓 *pin* A guest, V. ii. 3. 5: VII. ii. 24. 2. 賓旅, VI. ii. 7. 3.

賜 *ts'ze* — To give, present a gift; a gift, III. ii. 7. 3: V. ii. 4. 2, 5. 賜 = to give pay, and 賜於 . . ., to receive pay, V. ii. 6. 3.

賢 *hsien* — (1) Admirable, possessed of talents and virtue; to be talented and virtuous; the possession of talents and virtue. *Passim.* E.g. I. ii. 7. 3, 4; 16. 1: II. i. 4. 2; 5. 1; 9. 2. As a verb, = to praise, IV. ii. 29. 1. (2) To surpass, be superior, II. i. 1. 3; 2. 6, 26.

賤 *chien* — Mean; a mean condition, III. ii. 2. 3 (貧賤): VI. i. 14. 2, 3. 賤 = bad, the worst, III. ii. 1. 4. As a verb, to consider mean; to make mean, II. ii. 10. 7: III. i. 5. 2; ii. 3. 6: VI. i. 14. 5; 17. 2.

賦 *fû* — To exact, IV. i. 14. 1. To pay a tax, III. i. 3. 15.

質 *chi* — A pledge, an introductory present, III. ii. 3. 1, 4: V. ii. 7. 1.

賴 *lâi* — To depend on, = be good, VI. i. 7. 1.

贍 *shan* — To avail for, be adequate to, I. i. 7. 22: II. i. 3. 2.

贐 *chin* — A gift to a traveller for the expenses of his journey, II. ii. 3. 3.

THE 155TH RADICAL, 赤.

赤 *ch'ih* — 赤子, an infant, III. i. 5. 3. 赤子之心, the child-heart, IV. ii. 12.

赧 *nan* — 赧赧然, red and blushingly, III. ii. 7. 4.

赫 *hê* — To blaze with anger, I. ii. 3. 6.

THE 156TH RADICAL, 走.

走 *tsâu* — To run; to run to, I. i. 3. 2: IV. i. 9. 2. To gallop, I. ii. 5. 5. 走獸, quadrupeds, II. i. 2. 28.

赴 *fû* — To come, I. i. 7. 18.

起 *ch'i* — To arise; to rise, II. i. 2. 17: III. i. 3. 11; ii. 9. 10: IV. ii. 33. 1: VII. i. 25. 1, 2. To begin with, II. i. 1. 8. 興起, to be aroused, VII. ii. 15.

超 *ch'âo* — To leap over, I. i. 7. 11.

越 *yüeh* — (1) To go beyond, exceed with, I. ii. 3. 7. (2) 越 = to roll over (顚越), V. ii. 4. 4. (3) The name of a State, IV. ii. 31. 1. 一越人, VI. ii. 3. 2.

趙 *châo* — The name of a part of Tsin, and the clan name of its chief, VI. i. 17. 2. In III. ii. 1. 4, 趙簡子 is, perhaps, 'the officer Chien of Châo.'

趨 *ch'ü* — To run, to hasten, II. i. 2. 10, 16; ii. 2. 3: VII. ii. 23. 2. 其趨, their aim, VI. ii. 6. 2.

THE 157TH RADICAL, 足.

足 *tsû* — (1) The foot, IV. i. 8. 2, 3; ii. 3. 1: VI. i. 7. 4. (2) To be sufficient; enough, I. i. 7. 5, 10, 12, 16, 21, 22; *et passim.* May sometimes be conveniently translated by 'to be able,' e.g. VII. i. 22. 2. 足 = abundant, VII. i. 23. 3. 饜足, to satiate one's self, IV. ii. 33. 1. As a verb, 不我足, do not count me sufficient to . . ., III. i. 2. 4.

跖 *chih* — The name of a famous robber, 盜跖, III. ii. 10. 3.

距 *ch'ü* — To resist, to keep at, or banish to, a distance, III. ii. 9. 10, 13, 14: VI. ii. 13. 8. In a name, II. ii. 4. 2, 4.

跡 *chi* — Foot-prints, III. i. 4. 7.

路 *lû* — (1) A road, a path, I. i. 3. 4; 7. 24: II. i. 5. 3; ii. 2. 3; 6. 1, 2, *et al., saepe.* On the way, II. ii. 13. 1. As a verb, . . . 而路, and run about on the roads, III. i. 4. 6. 當路 = to obtain the management of the government, II. i. 1. 1. (2) 子路, a disciple of Confucius, II. i. 1. 3; 8. 1, *et al.*

踐 *chien* — (1) To tread upon. 踐 = to fulfil, satisfy the design of, VII. i. 38. 1. 踐位, to occupy the throne, V. i. 5. 7. (2) 句踐, the name of a famous prince of Yüeh, I. ii. 3. 1, and of an adventurer of Mencius's time, VII. i. 9. 1.

踰 *yü* — To cross over; to leap over, I. ii. 16. 1: III. ii. 3. 6; 7. 2: IV. ii. 27. 3: VI. ii. 1. 8. To overstep, to exceed, I. ii. 7. 3; 16. 1, 2.

踵 *chung* — (1) The heel, VII. i. 26. 2. (2) To come to, III. i. 4. 1.

踽 *ch'ü* — 踽踽, the appearance of walking alone, i.e. of acting peculiarly; unsociable, VII. ii. 37. 8.

蹄 *t'î* — The foot-prints of animals, III. i. 4. 7.

蹈 *t'âo* — 蹈 = to dance, 足之蹈之, IV. i. 27. 2.

蹊 *hsî* — 蹊間, foot-paths, VII. ii. 21. 1.

蹙 *tsû* — Urged, embarrassed, I. ii. 1. 6: V. i. 4. 1.

蹝 *hsî* — A shoe or sandal of straw, VII. i. 35. 6.

蹠 *chih* — I.q. 跖, VII. i. 25. 2, 3.

孟子

蹴 *tsù* To tread on. 蹴爾 (adverb) = having trampled on, VI. ii. 10. 6.

踧 *tsù* Followed by 然 = uneasy-like, II. i. 1. 3. The uneasiness would be indicated by some motions of the feet.

蹶 *chüeh* (1) To stumble, II. i. 2. 10. (2) To overturn, IV. i. 1. 10. In the tonal notes on this latter passage, we are told to read the character *kwei*; but in the dictionary the meaning, 'to overturn,' is given under the other pronunciation.

躍 *yáo* To leap, I. i. 2. 3: VII. i. 41. 3. To make to leap, VI. i. 2. 3.

THE 158TH RADICAL, 身.

身 *shăn* (1) The body, VI. i. 10. 8; 14. 1; ii. 15. 2. (2) One's person, one's self, I. i. 1. 4; 5. 1; ii. 15. 2; 16. 1: III. i. 2. 3; 4. 6; ii. 9. 5; 10. 4, *et al., saepissime*. 修身, to cultivate one's person; 反身, self-examination; and 守身, to keep one's self; e.g. IV. i. 12. 1; 19. 1, 2: VII. i. 1. 3; 4. 2; 9. 6. 身之 = to acquire by effort, be virtuous by endeavour, VII. i. 30. 1. (3) 終身, all the life. See 終.

軀 *ch'ü* The body, VII. ii. 29. 1.

THE 159TH RADICAL, 車.

車 *chü* or *ch'ê* A carriage, I. ii. 1. 6, 7: III. ii. 4. 1: VII. i. 36. 2; ii. 4. 5 (革車, 'chariots of war'); 34. 2. Read *ch'ê*, with nearly the same meaning. A waggon-load, VI. i. 18. 1.

軌 *kwei* Wheel-ruts, VII. ii. 22. 3.

軍 *chün* (1) A host. 三軍, the armies of a great State, II. i. 2. 5: VI. ii. 4. 5, 6. (2) 將軍, a general, a commander-in-chief, VI. ii. 8. 1.

軔 *zan* I.q. 仞. Eight cubits, VII. i. 29.

軻 *k'o* The name of Mencius, I. ii. 16. 2: V. ii. 2. 1: VI. ii. 4. 4.

較 *chiáo* To struggle. 獵較, V. ii. 4. 5, 6. But the meaning is not well understood.

載 *tsái* (1) To carry with one in the same carriage, III. ii. 3. 1, 4. (2) To begin, III. ii. 5. 4: V. i. 7. 9. (3) A particle, = 則, IV. i. 9. 6. (4) To serve, perform duties to, V. i. 4. 4. (5) 載書, to write articles of agreement, and place them on the victim of the covenant, VI. ii. 7. 3.

載 *tsài* The 3rd tone. A year, V. i. 4. 1; 5. 7.

輔 *fú* To support, to aid, I. i. 7. 19: II. i. 1. 8 (輔相); ii. 2. 6; 6. 1 (*N.B.*): III. i. 4. 8: VI. ii. 9. 2.

輕 *ch'ing* (1) Light, I. i. 7. 13: III. i. 4. 17: VI. ii. 1. 7. 輕 = small, VII. ii. 32. 3. 輕 = least important, VII. ii. 14. 輕 = light clothing, I. i. 7. 16. 輕 = readily, easily, I. i. 7. 21. (2) As a verb. To consider small, VI. ii. 13. 7. To lighten, III. ii. 8. 1: VI. ii. 10. 7. To make light of, to slight, III. ii. 4. 3. 輕身, to undervalue one's self, I. ii. 16. 1.

輝 *húi* Bright. 光輝, brightly displayed, VII. ii. 25. 6.

輪 *lun* (1) The wheel of a carriage, VI. ii. 24. 2. (2) A wheelwright. 輪輿, carriage-wrights, III. ii. 4. 3, 4: VII. ii. 5. 1.

輸 *shū* 公輸, a double surname, IV. i. 1. 1.

輿 *yü* (1) Properly, the bottom or frame of a carriage or waggon. A carriage; a waggon-load, I. i. 7. 10; ii. 16. 1: VI. ii. 1. 6. (2) A carriage-wright; see 輪.

轉 *chwan* (1) To turn over. In the phrase 轉於 (or 乎) 溝壑, I. ii. 12. 2: II. ii. 4. 2: III. i. 3. 7. (2) 轉附, the name of a place, I. ii. 4. 4.

THE 160TH RADICAL, 辛.

辛 *hsin* A name, III. i. 4. 2.

辜 *kû* A transgression. 不辜, innocent, II. i. 2. 24.

辟 *p'i* (1) I.q. 僻. Depraved; moral deflection, I. i. 7. 20: III. i. 3. 3. (2) I.q. 闢. To open up, to bring under cultivation, I. i. 7. 16: II. i. 1. 10: IV. i. 1. 9; 14. 3: VI. ii. 7. 2; 9. 1. (3) To remove from the way, IV. ii. 2. 4. (4) A name, III. i. 5. 1.

辟 *pi* To twist, III. ii. 10. 4. The pronunciation and meaning are taken from the tonal notes and Chû Hsî. The dictionary does not give them.

辟 *pi* I.q. 避. To avoid, III. ii. 7. 2; 10. 5: IV. i. 13. 1: VI. i. 10. 2, 3, 4: VII. i. 22. 1.

辟 *p'i* I.q. 譬. 辟若, may be compared to, VII. i. 29.

辨 *pien* To discriminate, VI. i. 10. 7.

辭 *ts'ze* (1) Language, words, II. i. 2. 17: III. ii. 9. 10, 13. 辭 = a sentence, V. i. 4. 2. 以辭, in express words, V. ii. 4. 3. The

孟子

遊 *yû* To wander; to travel, associate with, I. ii. 6. 1: IV. ii. 30. 1: VII. i. 9. 1; 16. An imperial tour, I. ii. 4. 5. 遊 = to be a student of, VII. i. 24.

運 *yün* To make to go round, = accomplish easily, I. i. 7. 12: II. i. 1. 8; 6. 2. To go round, make a revolution, I. ii. 10. 4.

過 *kwo* The 3rd tone. (1) To go beyond; to exceed; more than, I. i. 7. 12: II. i. 1. 10; 2. 2; ii. 13. 4: III. ii. 10. 1: IV. ii. 18. 3: ? VI. i. 2. 3: VII. i. 11. (2) To err; faults, transgressions, II. i. 8. 1; ii. 9. 3, 4: III. ii. 1. 5: IV. i. 1. 4: V. i. 6. 5; ii. 9. 1, 4: VI. ii. 8. 4; 11. 2, 4; 15. 3.

過 *kwo* The 1st tone. To pass by, I. i. 7. 4: III. i. 1. 1; 4. 7; 5. 4: IV. ii. 25. 1; 29. 1: V. i. 8. 3: VII. i. 13. 3; ii. 38. 7.

遏 *o* To stop, to restrict, I. ii. 8. 6: V. i. 4. 1: VI. ii. 7. 3.

達 *tâ* (1) To reach to, II. i. 1. 10; ii. 7. 2: III. i. 2. 2; 5. 4: V. ii. 2. 4: VII. i. 24. 3. To carry out, to extend, VII. i. 15. 3; 40. 3; ii. 31. (2) To obtain advancement; to be in office, IV. ii. 33. 2: VII. i. 9. 4, 5, 6; 19. 3. To find vent, II. i. 6. 7. (3) To be intelligent, VII. i. 18. 2. (4) Universally acknowledged, II. ii. 2. 6.

道 *tâo* (1) A road, a path, I. i. 3. 4; 7. 24: III. i. 4. 7: IV. i. 8. 5: V. i. 9. 11: VI. i. 8. 2: VII. i. 41. 3. It occurs everywhere with a moral application, meaning the way or course to be pursued, the path of reason, of principle, of truth, &c. E.g. I. ii. 3. 1: II. i. 2. 3, 14; 4. 3; ii. 1. 4; 2. 4, 6, 7; 14. 1. (2) Doctrines, principles, teachings. Also *passim*. E.g. III. i. 4. 3, 12, 14, 18; ii. 1. 5; 2. 3; 4. 4; 9. 5, 7, 9, 10.—This usage and the preceding run into each other. The *principles* underlie the *course*, and the *course* follows from the *principles*. (3) To speak about, discourse, I. i. 7. 2: III. i. 1. 2; 4. 3: VI. ii. 3. 2.

違 *wei* (1) To oppose, go contrary to, I. i. 3. 3: III. ii. 2. 2. (2) To avoid, escape from, II. i. 4. 6: IV. i. 8. 5. To escape notice, II. i. 2. 27. (3) To be distant from, VI. i. 8. 2.

遠 *yüan* To be distant; distant, far, II. i. 2. 2, 26; ii. 3. 3: III. i. 4. 1; ii. 9. 4, *et al.* To keep at a distance, V. i. 7. 7. 遠臣, ministers from a distance, V. i. 8. 4. To consider far, I. i. 1. 2: VI. i. 12. 1.

遠 *yüan* The 4th tone. To put away to a distance; to keep away from, I. i. 7. 8: III. ii. 9. 6.

適 *shih* (1) To go to, I. ii. 4. 5: III. i. 4. 17: VI. ii. 7. 2. (2) Only, merely, VI. i. 14. 6.

適 *chih* I.q. 謫. To blame, remonstrate with, IV. i. 20. 1.

遭 *tsâo* To meet with, V. i. 8. 3.

遲 *ch'ih* 遲遲, slowly, by-and-by, V. ii. 1. 4: VII. ii. 17.

遵 *tsun* To follow, IV. i. 1. 4. To follow the line or course of, I. ii. 4. 4: VII. i. 35. 6.

遷 *ch'ien* To remove, I. ii. 11. 3. To remove to, III. i. 4. 15: IV. ii. 1. 1 (followed by 於). To transfer to, V. i. 1. 3. Applied morally;—to move towards, V. i. 6. 5: VII. i. 13. 2.

選 *hsüan* To choose. 選擇, III. i. 3. 13.

遺 *wei* It is also pronounced î. (1) To neglect, I. i. 1. 5: VII. ii. 7. 2. To be neglected, 遺佚, II. i. 9. 2: V. ii. 1. 3. (2) To be left; remaining, II. i. 1. 8: V. i. 4. 2.

遺 *wèi* The 4th tone. To make a present, to present, III. ii. 5. 2.

避 *pi* To withdraw from, V. i. 5. 7; 6. 1. To avoid, escape from, I. ii. 10. 4.

邇 *r* What is near; the near, IV. ii. 20. 4.

THE 163RD RADICAL, 邑.

邑 *yi* A city or town, III. ii. 5. 5. To build a town, I. ii. 15. 1.

邠 *pin* The name of the ancient seat of the family of Châu, I. ii. 14. 2; 15. 1.

邦 *pang* A State, a country, III. i. 3. 12. Observe 家邦, I. i. 7. 12.

邪 *hsieh* (1) Corrupt, depraved; what is not correct, perversity, I. i. 7. 20: II. i. 2. 17: III. i. 3. 3; ii. 9. 5, 7, 9, 10, 13: IV. i. 1. 13: VII. ii. 10. 1; 37. 13. (2) Read *yé*. 琅邪, the name of a place, I. ii. 4. 4.

郊 *chiâo* The borders of a country; to be situated in the borders, I. ii. 2. 3; 4. 10: VI. i. 8. 1.

郭 *kwo* (1) An outer wall of fortification. 城郭, see 城. 郭 alone, IV. ii. 33. 1. (2) 東郭 = a double surname, II. ii. 2. 2.

郢 *ying* 畢郢, the name of a place, IV. ii. 1. 2.

郵 *yû* A post-station. 置郵, II. i. 1. 12.

都 *tû* (1) A capital, but used for any principal city, II. ii. 4. 4. (2) 都君, a name given to Shun, V. i. 2. 3. (3) 子都, the designation of an ancient officer, distinguished for his beauty, VI. i. 7. 7. (4) 公都, a double surname, belonging to a disciple of Mencius, II. ii. 5. 4: III. ii. 9. 1, *et al.*

鄒 *tsâu* The name of the State of which Mencius was a native, I. i. 7. 17; ii. 12. 1: III. i. 2. 2, 4: VI. ii. 1. 4; 5. 1, 2, 6. 鄒人, I. i. 7. 17. 鄒君, VI. ii. 2. 6.

鄉 *hsiang* A village, a neighbourhood, III. i. 3. 18: IV. ii. 29. 7, *et al.* 鄉人, a villager, II. i. 9. 1: IV. ii. 28. 7: V. ii. 1. 1, 3, *et al.* 鄉黨, II. i. 6. 3; ii. 2. 6, *et al.* 鄉原, your good people of the villages, VII. ii. 37. 12. 鄉=place, VI. i. 8. 4.—In this last instance ought we not to read the character in the 4th tone?

鄕 *hsiang* The 4th tone. I.q. 嚮. (1) Towards; to be directed to, VI. ii. 9. 1, 2. (2) Formerly, in the former case, VI. i. 10. 8.

鄙 *p'i* Mean, niggardly. 鄙夫, V. ii. 1. 3: VII. ii. 15.

鄭 *chăng* The name of a State, IV. ii. 2. 1: V. i. 2. 4: VII. ii. 37. 12. 鄭人, IV. ii. 24. 2.

鄰 *lin* A neighbour, III. i. 3. 3; ii. 8. 2. Neighbouring, III. ii. 5. 2. 鄰國, I. i. 3. 1, 2; ii. 3. 1: II. i. 5. 6: VI. ii. 11. 3. A neighbourhood, 鄉鄰, IV. ii. 29. 7. It is also written 隣.

THE 164TH RADICAL, 酉.

酌 *cho* To pour out wine into the cup, VI. i. 5. 3.

配 *p'ei* To agree, be in harmony, with, II. i. 4. 6: IV. i. 4. 3. To be the mate of, II. i. 2. 14.

酒 *chiû* Wine, spirits, I. ii. 4. 7: III. ii. 5. 2: IV. i. 3. 4 (强酒); 19. 3, *et al.*

醉 *tsûi* To be drunk, IV. i. 3. 4. To be filled, exhilarated, VI. i. 17. 3.

醜 *ch'âu* Fellows. 醜=of equal extent, II. ii. 2. 9.

醫 *i* A physician, II. ii. 2. 3.

釁 *hsin* To consecrate by smearing with blood, I. i. 7. 4.

THE 165TH RADICAL, 釆.

采 *ts'ăi* (1) 采色, variegated colours, I. i. 7. 16. (2) To gather. Observe 采薪之憂, II. ii. 2. 3.

THE 166TH RADICAL, 里.

里 *li* (1) A neighbourhood; a hamlet, II. i. 5. 5; 7. 2. (2) In the phrase 田里, 里=a residence, IV. ii. 3. 3, 4: VII. i. 22. 3. (3) A measure of length. At present it is a little more than one-third of an English mile. 方里 is a square *li*, III. i. 3. 19; but square *lis* are often meant, where the 方 is omitted, I. i. 1. 2; 5. 1, 2; 7. 17; ii. 2. 1, 2, 3; 11. 1, *et al.*, *saepe*. (4) 百里, a double surname, V. i. 9. 1, 2: VI. ii. 6. 4; 15. 1.

重 *chung* Heavy, I. i. 7. 13: III. i. 4. 17: VI. ii. 1. 6. Applied metaphorically;—heavy consequences, VII. ii. 7. Heavy charge, V. i. 7. 6; ii. 1. 2. Great, important; precious, I. ii. 11. 3, 4: VI. ii. 1. 1, 2, 6, 7: VII. ii. 32. 3. As a verb,—to make heavy, VI. ii. 10. 7.

野 *yĕ* Wild country, wilds; the country as opposed to the town, the fields, I. i. 4. 4; 7. 18: II. i. 5. 4: III. ii. 9. 9: IV. i. 14. 2: V. i. 7. 2; ii. 7. 1: VII. ii. 23. 2. 田野, IV. i. 1. 9: VI. ii. 7. 2. 野人, countrymen, men rude and uncultivated, III. i. 3. 14, 19: V. i. 4. 1: VII. i. 16. 1.

量 *liang* To measure, II. i. 2. 5.

釐 *li* In a name, VI. ii. 8. 4.

THE 167TH RADICAL, 金.

金 *chin* Metal, metallic, V. ii. 1. 6. In VI. ii. 1. 6 金=gold. In IV. ii. 24. 2 金=steel. In II. ii. 3. 1 I have translated by silver, but many contend that *gold* is meant.

釜 *fû* An iron boiler, without feet, III. i. 4. 4.

鈞 *chün* (1) A weight of thirty catties, I. i. 7. 10: VI. ii. 2. 3. (2) I.q. 均, all equally, VI. i. 15. 1, 2.

鉤 *kâu* A hook or clasp, VI. ii. 1. 6. In the text it is printed 鈎, which, though used, is not correct.

銳 *zûi* Vigorously, with precipitation, VII. i. 44. 2.

鍾 *chung* The name of a measure, containing sixty-four *tâu* (斗), or nearly seven hundredweight according to present measures, II. ii. 10. 3: III. ii. 10. 5: VI. i. 10. 7.—See a note on the Life of Mencius.

鎡 *tsze* 鎡基, a hoe, II. i. 1. 9.

錡 *i* A name, V. ii. 2. 1.

鎰 *yi* A weight, variously estimated at twenty, twenty-four, and thirty *taels*, or Chinese ounces, I. ii. 9. 2: II. ii. 3. 1.

孟子

鐘 *chung* A bell, I. i. 7. 4; ii. 1. 6, 7.

鐵 *t'ieh* Iron. 鐵 = an iron share, III. i. 4. 4.

鑒 *chien* 鑒 = a mirror; or a beacon, IV. i. 2. 5. It is more commonly written 鑑.

鑠 *shâo* To melt. 鑠 = to infuse, VI. i. 6. 7.

鑽 *tswan* To bore, III. ii. 8. 6.

鑿 *tso* To chisel, or bore. 鑿 = to dig, I. ii. 13. 2. Used metaphorically, IV. ii. 26. 2.

THE 168TH RADICAL, 長.

長 *ch'ang* 2nd tone. (1) Long; length, I. i. 7. 13: III. i. 1. 5; 4. 17. Tall, VI. ii. 2. 2. (2) To excel, II. i. 2. 11. (3) A surname, V. i. 1. 2; ii. 3. 3.

長 *chang* 3rd tone. (1) To be grown up, age; old; elders, III. i. 4. 8; ii. 6. 2: IV. i. 11. 1: V. ii. 3. 1: VI. i. 4. 2, 3, 4; ii. 2. 4: VII. i. 15. 2, 3; 43. 2. Eldest, I. i. 5. 1. 長於, older than, VI. i. 5. 3. As a verb, to give the honour due to age, IV. i. 11: VI. i. 4. 2, 3, 4. 長者, an elder, I. i. 7. 3. It is twice used by Mencius for himself, II. ii. 11. 4: IV. i. 24. 2. (2) To grow, II. i. 2. 16: VI. i. 8. 3. Well grown, superior, V. ii. 5. 4. (3) To preside over, II. ii. 2. 6. Superiors, officers, I. i. 7. 11; ii. 12. 1, 3. (4) To make long. 長 = to connive at and aid, VI. ii. 7. 4.

THE 169TH RADICAL, 門.

門 *măn* A door; a gate, III. i. 4. 1, 7; ii. 2. 2; 7. 2, 3, *et al.*, *saepe*. 門戶, VI. ii. 14. 4. 門 = school, VI. ii. 2. 6: VII. i. 24. 1; 43. 1. 門人, disciples, III. i. 4. 13: VII. ii. 29. 1.

閉 *pi* To shut, III. ii. 7. 2: IV. ii. 29. 7: V. ii. 7. 8. To repress, IV. i. 1. 13.

閔 *min* (1) To be grieved, II. i. 2. 16. (2) Appears in a quotation from the Shû-ching for 暋, violent, reckless, V. ii. 4. 4. (3) The surname of one of Confucius's disciples, II. i. 2. 18, 20.

閑 *hsien* 閑 = to defend, III. ii. 9. 10.

閒 *hsien* 閒暇, to be at leisure, II. i. 4. 2, 4.

閒 *hsien* A space, an interval, II. ii. 13. 3: IV. ii. 7. 1: VII. ii. 21. . . . 之閒, the space between, I. i. 6. 6: III. ii. 6. 1: IV. i. 18. 4; ii. 18. 3: VII. i. 25. 3. So 於 (or 于) . . . 之閒, II. i. 2. 13: VI. ii. 15. 1: VII. i. 18. Among, IV. ii. 33. 1. 爲閒, in a little, III. i. 5. 5: VII. ii. 21. But in some editions, 閒 in these two instances is put in the third tone. The K'ang-hsi dictionary simply says that 間 is the vulgar form of 閒.

閒 *chien* 3rd tone. (1) To occupy the space between, I. ii. 13. 1. (2) To blame, IV. i. 20. (3) 一閒, one interval, VII. ii. 7. (4) 得閒, to find an opportunity, VI. ii. 5. 2.—It is more correct to write 閒, and not 間.

閹 *yen* 閹然, eunuch-like, VII. ii. 37. 8.

關 *kwan* A frontier gate; a pass, I. ii. 2. 3; 5. 3: II. i. 5. 3: III. ii. 8. 1: V. ii. 5. 3; 6. 3: VII. ii. 8. 1.

關 *wan* To bend a bow, VI. ii. 3. 2.

THE 170TH RADICAL, 阜.

阨 *i* Straits; to be in circumstances of distress, V. i. 8. 3. 阨窮, II. i. 9. 2: V. ii. 1. 3.

阱 *ching* A pit-fall, I. ii. 2. 3.

防 *fang* A raised dyke, an embankment, VI. ii. 7. 3.

阻 *chû* An obstruction, a difficult pass. 險阻, III. ii. 9. 4.

阿 *o* To flatter, II. i. 2. 25.

附 *fû* (1) To be attached to. 附庸, the name of certain small principalities, V. ii. 2. 4. To join one's self to, III. ii. 5. 5. To add to, VII. i. 11. (2) 轉附, the name of a place, I. ii. 4. 4.

陋 *lâu* Mean and low, IV. ii. 29. 2.

降 *chiang* (1) To send down, to confer,—spoken of Heaven, VI. i. 7. 1; ii. 15. 2. To produce, I. ii. 3. 7. (2) To descend, come down, I. ii. 11. 2: III. ii. 5. 4.

陰 *yin* (1) To be dark and cloudy, II. i. 4. 3. (2) 陰 = the north side, V. i. 6. 1.

陵 *ling* (1) A high mound, a height, 丘陵, III. ii. 1. 5: IV. i. 1. 6. (2) 於陵, the name of a place, III. ii. 10. 1, 5, 6.

陳 *ch'ăn* (1) To set forth, II. ii. 2. 4: IV. i. 1. 13. (2) A surname, II. ii. 3. 1; 10. 4: VI. ii. 14. 1: VII. ii. 23. 1.—III. ii. 1. 1.—II. ii. 9. 2.—III. ii. 10. 1, 2, 3, 5, 6: VII. i. 34. 1.—III. ii. 4. 2, 3, 12. (3) The name of a State, VII. ii. 18; 37. 1: V. i. 8. 3.

孟子

tions. E.g. I. ii. 4. 5: II. i. 1. 8; 8. 4: VI. ii. 8. 6: VII. i. 2. 1. (2) To be contrary to; what is contrary to. E.g. IV. ii. 6. 1; 28. 7: V. i. 2. 4. (3) To be wrong; what is wrong. E.g. I. ii. 4. 2: II. ii. 3. 1: IV. i. 20. (4) To blame; to disown, I. ii. 4. 1, 2: III. i. 4. 14: IV. i. 1. 12; 10. 1: VII. ii. 37. 11. 是非之心, II. i. 6. 5: VI. i. 6. 7. Observe II. i. 2. 22: V. ii. 1. 2; and VII. ii. 37. 11.

靡 *mi* Not, IV. i. 7. 5: V. i. 4. 2.

THE 176TH RADICAL, 面.

面 *mien* The face, II. ii. 12. 6: III. i. 2. 4; 5. 4, *et al.* 面諛之人, sycophants, VI. ii. 13. 8. 南面, on, or towards, the south, I. ii. 11. 2: III. ii. 5. 4: VII. ii. 4. 3. So 東面; but 南面, in V. i. 4. 1, is the face to the south, the position of a sovereign giving audience. 北面, V. i. 4. 1; ii. 6. 4, is the position of a minister.

THE 177TH RADICAL, 革.

革 *ko* Skins freed from the hair, but not tanned. Still it is used as = leather. 革車, chariots of war, VII. ii. 4. 4. The buff-coat, helmet, and other armour of defence, 兵革, II. ii. 1. 3, 4.

THE 178TH RADICAL, 韋.

韓 *han* The name of a powerful family in Tsin, VII. i. 11.

THE 180TH RADICAL, 音.

音 *yin* A note in music. 五音, IV. i. 1. 1, 5. The sound or notes of musical instruments, I. ii. 1. 6, 7. 八音, V. i. 4. 1. 聲音,—spoken of instruments and the voice, I. i. 7. 16: VI. ii. 13. 8.

THE 181ST RADICAL, 頁.

頂 *ting* The top of the head, VII. i. 26. 2.

順 *shun* (1) To obey; to accord with; obedience; agreeably to reason, submissively, II. ii. 1. 4, 5: III. ii. 2. 2: IV. i. 7. 1; 16: VI. i. 1. 2: VII. i. 2. 1; 31. 1. To persist in, II. ii. 9. 4. Observe IV. i. 28. 1, and V. i. 1. 3, 4. (2) A name, V. ii. 8. 3.

須 *hsü* 斯須, a brief season, VI. i. 5. 4.

頌 *sung* (1) Interchanged with 誦. To repeat, croon over, V. ii. 8. 2. (2) 魯頌, the name of a Book of the Shih-ching, III. i. 4. 16.

頒 *pan* 頒白者, gray-haired people, I. i. 3. 4; 7. 24. See the dictionary on the usage.

頑 *wan* Obstinate. It seems, however, to be used in the sense of *corrupt*, V. ii. 1. 1: VII. ii. 15.

領 *ling* The neck, I. i. 6. 6.

頞 *o* The root of the nose. 蹙頞 = to knit the brows, I. ii. 1. 6.

頻 *p'ăn* Used for 顰. 頻顣 means to turn up the nose, and generally to look dissatisfied, III. ii. 10. 5.

題 *t'i* 榱題, the ornamental wood-work under the eaves of public buildings, VII. ii. 34. 2.

願 *yüan* To wish, desire, I. i. 4. 1; 5. 1; 7. 19: II. i. 1. 4; 2. 22; 5. 1, 2, 3, 4, 5; ii. 7. 1; 10. 2: III. i. 4. 1, 2; 5. 1; ii. 3. 6: VI. i. 17. 3; ii. 2. 6; 4. 4.

顏 *yen* (1) 顏色, the countenance, III. i. 2. 5: VI. ii. 13. 8. (2) A surname, II. i. 2. 18, 20: III. i. 1. 4: IV. ii. 29. 2, 3, 5.—V. i. 8. 2.—V. ii. 3. 3.

顙 *sang* The forehead, III. i. 5. 4: VI. i. 2. 3.

顛 *tien* 顛覆, to overturn, V. i. 6. 5.

類 *lei* A class, sort; kinds, I. i. 7. 11: II. i. 2. 28: III. ii. 3. 6; 10. 6: V. ii. 4. 5: VI. i. 7. 3, 5; 12. 2: VII. ii. 31. 4.

顣 *tsü* I.q. 蹙. 頻顣, see 頻.

顧 *kü* To look round, I. i. 2. 1; ii. 6. 3: IV. ii. 33. 1. To regard, think of, have reference to, IV. ii. 30. 2: V. i. 7. 2: VII. ii. 37. 9.

顯 *hsien* To be distinguished, III. ii. 9. 6: IV. ii. 33. 1. To make illustrious, II. i. 1. 5: V. i. 9. 3.

THE 182ND RADICAL, 風.

風 *făng* (1) The wind, III. i. 2. 4. To expose one's self to the wind, II. ii. 2. 1. (2) Manners; character,—with the idea of influence implied, II. i. 1. 8: V. ii. 1. 1, 3: VII. i. 15. (3) 凱風, the name of an ode in the Shih-ching, VI. ii. 3. 3, 4.

THE 183RD RADICAL, 飛.

飛 *fei* (1) To fly. 飛鳥, birds, II. i. 28. (2) 飛廉, a supporter of the tyrant Châu, III. ii. 9. 6.

THE 184TH RADICAL, 食.

食 *shih* (1) To eat; to consume, devour; to be consumed, I. i. 3. 3, 4, 5; 4. 4, 5; 7. 8, 24, *et passim.* 以爲食, to be a living,

III. i. 4. 1. 食 not unfrequently has this meaning, = to get a living, to support life. (2) Viands, food to eat, III. ii. 4. 4, 5; 9. 5: V. ii. 4. 6 (*N.B.*): VII. ii. 34. 2. (3) An eclipse, II. ii. 9. 4.

食 *tsze* (1) Rice cooked; food generally, I. i. 3. 5; ii. 10. 4; 11. 3, *et al.* (2) To feed, to support; 食於 . . ., to be supported by, III. i. 4. 6; ii. 4. 4, *et al.*, *saepe.* To feed cattle, V. i. 9. 1, 3.

飢 *chi* Interchanged with 饑. To be hungry, to suffer from hunger, I. i. 3. 4; 4. 4, 6; 7. 24; ii. 4. 6, *et al.*, *saepe.*

飦 *chien* A kind of thick congee. 飦粥, III. i. 2. 2.

飧 *sun* The evening meal. 饔飧, III. i. 4. 3: VI. ii. 10. 4. In the first instance the characters have a verbal force.

飲 *yin* To drink; drink, I. ii. 4. 6: II. i. 1. 11: III. ii. 10. 3, *et al.*, *saepe.*

飯 *fàn* To eat, VII. ii. 6. 放飯, to eat immoderately, VII. i. 46. 2.

飽 *pào* To eat to the full, to be filled; to the full, I. i. 7. 21: III. i. 4. 8: V. ii. 3. 4: VII. i. 22. 3. ? Actively, VI. i. 17. 3.

餂 *t'ien* To gain some end with, VII. ii. 31. 4. In the dictionary it is explained by 'to take with a hook,' = to beguile.

餉 *hsiang* To carry provisions to the labourers in the fields; provision-carriers, III. ii. 5. 2.

養 *yang* To nourish,—spoken generally of persons, the body, the mind, &c. *Passim.* To keep cattle, V. i. 9. 1. Nurture, VII. i. 36. 1.

養 *yang* The 4th tone. To support,—used with reference to the support of parents, scholars, and superiors generally, I. i. 5. 4: III. i. 3. 7, 14, 19; 4. 3 (?), *et al.*, *saepe.*

餐 *ts'an* To swallow, to eat and drink. 素餐, to eat the bread of idleness, VII. i. 32. 1.

餒 *nei* To be famished, II. i. 2. 14, 15. 凍餒, I. ii. 6. 1 (used actively): VII. i. 22. 3.

餓 *o* To be hungry, to suffer from hunger, 饑餓, VI. ii. 14. 4. 凍餓, I. i. 5. 4. 餓莩 (or 殍), I. i. 3. 5; 4. 4: III. ii. 9. 9. To expose to hunger, VI. ii. 15. 2.

餔 *pû* To eat. 餔啜, IV. i. 25.

餘 *yü* That which is over; a remnant, the remains, IV. i. 19. 3; ii. 33. 1: V. i. 4. 2. Supernumerary, III. i. 3. 17. 有餘, to have enough and to spare; and more, II. ii. 5. 5; 13. 4: III. ii. 4. 3: VI. ii. 2. 7: VII. ii. 38. 1, 2, 3, 4.

館 *kwan* A lodging-house, IV. i. 24. 2: VI. ii. 2. 6: VII. ii. 30. 1. To lodge (active); to be lodged, IV. i. 24. 2: VII. ii. 30. 1.

餱 *hâu* Dried provisions, I. ii. 5. 4.

餽 *kwei* To present or send as a gift, II. ii. 3. 1, 3, 4, 5: V. ii. 4. 4; 6. 2, 4.

饋 *k'wei* To offer as a gift, i. q. 餽, III. ii. 5. 2; 7. 3; 10. 5: V. i. 2. 4.

饑 *chi* To suffer from famine;—interchanged also with 飢, I. ii. 12. 2: II. ii. 4. 2: VII. i. 22. 2 (飢); ii. 23. 1.

饔 *yung* The morning meal. 饔飧, see 飧.

饗 *hsiang* Generally, to entertain. But = to be entertained by, V. ii. 3. 5.

饜 *yen* To get satiated, to partake plentifully of, IV. ii. 33. 1. To be satisfied, I. i. 1. 4.

THE 185TH RADICAL, 首.

首 *shâu* The head, I. ii. 1. 6: III. ii. 5. 7: V. ii. 6. 4, 5: VII. ii. 4. 5.

THE 187TH RADICAL, 馬.

馬 *mâ* (1) A horse, horses, I. i. 4. 4; ii. 1. 6, 7; 5. 5; 15. 1. 犬馬畜, to nourish as a dog or a horse, V. ii. 6. 4. (2) 司馬, the master of the horse, but used as a sort of surname, V. i. 8. 3.

馮 *fâng* (1) A surname, VII. ii. 23. 2. (2) 諸馮, the name of a place, IV. ii. 1. 1.

馳 *ch'ih* To gallop. 馳馬 = horsemanship, III. i. 2. 4. 馳驅, III. ii. 1. 4.

駟 *sze* A team of four horses, V. i. 7. 2.

駕 *chiâ* The yoking of a carriage, I. ii. 16. 1: II. ii. 2. 5: V. ii. 7. 9.

駒 *chü* A name, VI. ii. 6. 5.

驅 *ch'ü* (1) To drive away, III. ii. 9. 4, 6, 11. (2) To urge, I. i. 7. 21: VII. ii. 1. 2. (3) To urge on a horse, 馳驅, III. ii. 1. 4; 驅騁, VII. ii. 34. 2.

驕 *chiâo* To carry one's self proudly to, IV. ii. 33. 1.

驩 *hwan* (1) I. q. 歡. 驩虞如, cheerful-like, VII. i. 13. 1. (2) 驩兜, a criminal banished by Shun, V. i. 3. 2. (3) A name, II. ii. 6. 1: IV. ii. 27. 2.

騁 *ch'ăng* To gallop. 驅騁, see 驅.

孟子

THE 188TH RADICAL, 骨.

骨 *kû* The bones, VI. ii. 15. 2.

體 *t'i* The body, I. i. 7. 16: II. i. 2. 9: IV. i. 19. 3: VII. i. 36. 1. 四體, the four limbs, II. i. 6. 6: IV. i. 3. 3: VII. i. 21. 4. 大體, 小體, VI. i. 14. 2; 15. 1, 2. 一體, one member; 具體, all the members, II. i. 2. 20.

THE 189TH RADICAL, 高.

高 *kâo* (1) High, lofty, II. ii. 1. 3: IV. i. 1. 6, 7; ii. 26. 3: V. ii. 5. 5: VI. ii. 1. 5: VII. i. 41. 1; ii. 34. 2. (2) A surname, II. ii. 12. 2: VII. ii. 21; 22.—VI. ii. 3. 1, 2. (3) A name, V. i. 1. 2. (4) 高唐, the name of a place, VI. ii. 6. 5.

THE 190TH RADICAL, 髟.

髡 *k'wăn* More correctly written 髡. A name, IV. i. 17. 1: VI. ii. 6. 1, 5.

髮 *fâ* The hair, IV. ii. 29. 6, 7.

THE 191ST RADICAL, 鬥.

鬨 *hung* To fight, to have a brush, I. ii. 12. 1.

鬭 *tâu* To quarrel, IV. ii. 29. 5, 6. 鬭狠, IV. ii. 30. 2.

THE 192ND RADICAL, 鬯.

鬱 *yü* 鬱陶, anxiously, V. i. 2. 3.

THE 193RD RADICAL, 鬲.

鬲 *ko* 膠鬲, a distinguished minister at the close of the Yin dynasty, II. i. 1. 8: VI. ii. 15. 1.

鬻 *yü* (1) To sell, V. i. 9. 1, 3. (2) 獯鬻, the name of a barbarous tribe, I. ii. 3. 1.

THE 194TH RADICAL, 鬼.

魏 *wei* The name of a great family in Tsin, VII. i. 11.

THE 195TH RADICAL, 魚.

魚 *yü* A fish, fish, I. i. 2. 3; 3. 3; 7. 16, 17: IV. i. 9. 3: V. i. 2. 4: VI. i. 10. 1; ii. 15. 1.

魯 *lû* (1) The name of a State, I. ii. 12. 1; 16. 1, 3, *et al.*, *saepe*. 魯人, V. ii. 4. 5. 魯繆公, VI. ii. 6. 3, *et al.* 繆公 occurs in three other places, but without the 魯. 魯平公, I. ii. 16. 1. (2) 魯頌, the name of a Book in the Shih-ching, III. i. 4. 16.

鯀 *kwăn* The father of the great Yü, V. i. 3. 2.

鰥 *kwan* A widower, I. ii. 5. 3.

THE 196TH RADICAL, 鳥.

鳥 *niâo* Birds, I. i. 2. 3, 4: II. i. 2. 28: III. i. 4. 7; ii. 9. 4.

鳳 *fâng* 鳳凰, a sort of Chinese phœnix, II. i. 2. 28.

鳴 *ming* (1) The sound of a bird. 鷄鳴, see 鷄. To beat, cause to sound, IV. i. 14. 1. (2) 鳴條, the name of a place, IV. ii. 1. 1.

鴃 *chüeh* The shrike or butcher-bird, III. i. 4. 14.

鴈 *yen* A wild goose, I. i. 2. 1.

鴻 *hung* Large. Joined with 鴈 and 鵠, I. i. 2. 1: VI. i. 9. 3.

鵝 *o* A goose, III. ii. 10. 5.

鵠 *hû* The swan, VI. i. 9. 3.

鶃 *ni* The cackling of a goose. 鶃鶃者, III. ii. 10. 5.

鶴 *ho* 鶴鶴 = glistening, I. i. 2. 3.

鸇 *chan* A kind of hawk, IV. i. 9. 3.

THE 197TH RADICAL, 鹵.

鹽 *yen* Salt, VI. ii. 15. 1.

THE 198TH RADICAL, 鹿.

鹿 *lû* The deer, I. i. 2. 1, 3; ii. 2. 3: VII. i. 16.

麀 *yû* The female deer, a doe. 麀鹿, I. i. 2. 3.

麋 *mi* A species of deer, distinguished for its size and strength, and that sheds its horns in winter, 麋鹿, I. i. 2. 1; ii. 2. 3.

麒 *ch'i* The male of the Ch'i-lin, a fabulous animal, the chief of all quadrupeds, II. i. 2. 2, 8.

麗 *lî* Number. IV. i. 7. 5.

麟 *lin* — The female of the Ch'î-lin. See 麒.

THE 199TH RADICAL, 麥.

麥 *mâi* — Wheat; all bearded grain. 麰麥, see 麰.

麰 *mâu* — 麰麥, barley, VI. i. 7. 2.

THE 200TH RADICAL, 麻.

麻 *mâ* — Hemp, II. i. 4. 17.

THE 201ST RADICAL, 黃.

黃 *hwang* — Yellow, III. ii. 10. 3. 黃 = yellow silks, III. ii. 5. 5.

THE 202ND RADICAL, 黍.

黍 *shû* — Millet, III. ii. 5. 2: VI. ii. 10. 4.

黎 *lî* — Black. 黎民, the black-haired people, V. i. 4. 2.

THE 203RD RADICAL, 黑.

黝 *yû* — A name, II. i. 2. 4, 6.

黨 *tang* — (1) Properly, a village of 500 families. 鄉黨, a neighbourhood; neighbours, II. i. 6. 3; ii. 2. 6: V. i. 9. 3. (2) A party, a school, VII. ii. 37. 1.

THE 205TH RADICAL, 黽.

鼃 *wâ* — A name, II. ii. 5. 1, 2, 3.

鼈 *pieh* — The turtle, I. i. 2. 3; 8. 3.

THE 206TH RADICAL, 鼎.

鼎 *ting* — A tripod, a boiler with three feet and two ears, I. ii. 16. 2. 鼎肉, flesh from the pot, V. ii. 6. 4, 5.

THE 207TH RADICAL, 鼓.

鼓 *kû* — (1) A drum, I. i. 3. 2; ii. 1. 6, 7: IV. i. 14. 1. (2) To strike, to play on, VII. ii. 6. In this sense the character should have 攴, and not 支, on the right.

THE 209TH RADICAL, 鼻.

鼻 *pî* — The nose, IV. ii. 25. 1: VII. ii. 24. 1.

THE 210TH RADICAL, 齊.

齊 *ch'î* — (1) On a level, equal, II. ii. 2. 9: III. i. 4. 18: VI. i. 7. 2. To adjust evenly, VI. ii. 1. 5. (2) The name of a State, I. i. 5. 1; 7. 6, 17, *et al., saepe*. 齊人, I. ii. 10. 1; 14. 1, *et al.* 齊王, VII. i. 36. 1. 齊宣王, I. i. 7. 1, *et al., saepe*. 齊景公, I. ii. 4. 4, 10, *et al.* 齊桓, I. i. 7. 1, 2: IV. ii. 21. 3.

齊 *châi* — To adjust one's thoughts,—in connexion with fasting, II. ii. 11. 3: IV. ii. 25. 2. 齊栗, the appearance of respect and dread, V. i. 4. 4.

齊 *tsze* — The lower edge of a mourning garment, not hemmed, but even and not frayed, III. i. 2. 2.

THE 211TH RADICAL, 齒.

齒 *ch'ih* — (1) The front teeth. 齒 = with the teeth, VII. i. 46. 2. (2) Age, II. ii. 2. 6.

齕 *kêh* — A name, I. i. 7. 4.

THE 212TH RADICAL, 龍.

龍 *lung* — (1) The dragon, III. ii. 9. 3, 4. (2) A surname, III. i. 3. 7: VI. i. 7. 4.

龍 *lung* — The 3rd tone, used for 壟, a mound. 龍斷, II. ii. 10. 6, 7.

NOTE.

According to the calculation of Châo Ch'î, the Seven Books of Mencius contain in all 261 chapters and 34,685 characters. Tsâo Hsün, a scholar of the present dynasty, gives, as the result of a careful reckoning, 258 chapters and 35,226 characters. (See 焦孝廉孟子正義, on Châo Ch'î's Introduction.)

If there be no omissions in the above Index, the different characters used by Mencius (counting a character for each variation of tone) amount to 2,022, or thereabouts.

In the Analects, the Great Learning, and the Doctrine of the Mean, there are 1,648 different characters.

Altogether the different characters in the Four Books amount to about 2,500, certainly not to 2,600.

END OF VOL. II.

Oxford
PRINTED AT THE CLARENDON PRESS
BY HORACE HART, PRINTER TO THE UNIVERSITY

国家出版基金项目
NATIONAL PUBLICATION FOUNDATION

海上絲綢之路文獻集成

總主編 陳支平 陳春聲

科技與文化編 60

主編 王揚宗 葉 農

海峽出版發行集團
THE STRAITS PUBLISHING & DISTRIBUTING GROUP
福建人民出版社

本册目次

書經［一］

（*The Shoo King, or the Book of Historical Documents*）

〔英〕理雅各（James Legge）編譯

《書經》，英國理雅各（James Legge，一八一五—一八九七），英國倫敦會傳教士，法國漢學儒蓮獎首位得主。於一八六一至一八七二年相繼出版《中國經典》（*The Chinese Classics*）五卷，於一八七九至一八九一年相繼出版《中國聖書》（*The Sacred Books of China*）六卷。諸種中國經典譯作，被後世奉爲標準譯本。所英譯《書經》收録於《中國經典》第三卷，一八六五年出版。正文前有緒論凡六章，其第四章爲今本《竹書紀年》五卷，末附主題詞、專名與漢語字詞索引。據一八六五年香港版影印。

書經

THE CHINESE CLASSICS.

VOL. III.

THE SHOO KING,

OR

THE BOOK OF HISTORICAL DOCUMENTS.

不以文害辭，不以辭害志，以意逆志，是爲得之。

Mencius, V. Pt. I. iv. 2.

書經

THE

CHINESE CLASSICS:

WITH

A TRANSLATION, CRITICAL AND EXEGETICAL NOTES, PROLEGOMENA, AND COPIOUS INDEXES.

BY

JAMES LEGGE, D.D.,

OF THE LONDON MISSIONARY SOCIETY.

IN SEVEN VOLUMES.

VOL. III.—PART I.

CONTAINING

THE FIRST PARTS OF THE SHOO-KING.
OR THE BOOKS OF T'ANG; THE BOOKS OF YU; THE BOOKS OF HEA; THE BOOKS OF SHANG; AND THE PROLEGOMENA.

HONGKONG: AT THE AUTHOR'S.
LONDON: TRÜBNER & Co., 60, PATERNOSTER ROW.
1865.

HONGKONG:

PRINTED AT THE LONDON MISSIONARY SOCIETY'S

PRINTING OFFICE.

PREFACE.

The Author is sorry that so long a time has elapsed between the publication of the Works of Mencius and the appearance of this third volume of his undertaking. He felt it necessary, in 1862, to rest in a great measure from his labours on the Chinese Classics, both to recruit his strength, and to devote himself closely to his directly missionary duties; while certain other tasks were pressed on him by friends, which he could not well decline. In the month of March, 1863, he commenced printing his translation of the Shoo and the accompanying notes; but fresh and unexpected engagements, in connection with his position in Hongkong, interposed many hindrances to the progress of the work; and during the last year he was often laid aside from it by repeated attacks of illness. New views of the text, moreover, and of the various questions considered in the Prolegomena, presented themselves as he proceeded, and in many cases prolonged research and reflection were required before he could make up his mind upon them. He can only hope, now that this portion of his task is done, that the extent and execution of it will be deemed some apology for the delay which has occurred in giving it to the public. He does not anticipate so much delay in the appearance of the volumes that remain. The next will be the *She King*, or the Book of Poetey.

Two translations of the Shoo were already in existence. The older is in French, and was the Work of Father Gaubil, one of the ablest of the many able Jesuit Missionaries of the early part of last century. It was published at Paris in 1,770, under the editorship of M. De Guignes, who interspersed not a few notes of his own among those of the author, besides making other additions to the Work. Gaubil's own manuscript was lost; but the editor had the use of two copies which had been taken of it. He found it necessary, however, he tells us, to review and correct the version by having recourse to the Chinese text; and this is to be deplored. Gaubil may have often paraphrased his original, as M. De Guignes says; but I have no doubt the translation, as written by him, was more correct than as it now appears. The second translation was the work of the late Rev. Dr. Medhurst, and was published by him at Shanghae in 1846. He assigned as his reasons for giving it to the world, that 'Gaubil's translation was too free, and in many respects faulty, and had never been commonly known in England.' It may be doubted, however, whether his version be any improvement on the other. Dr. Medhurst's attainments in Chinese were prodigious. But his work on the Shoo was done hastily. He seems to have consulted no native commentary but that of Ts'ae Ch'in; and his notes are very inferior to those of Gaubil.

The Author ventures to hope that the translation now offered represents the Chinese original much more faithfully than either of those previous ones. When he first wrote it, many years ago, having less confidence in himself than he now has, he made free use both of Gaubil and Medhurst. He wrote it all out again in 1862, seldom, if ever, looking at them; and found it necessary to make many changes in every page. Not a little of it was written out a third time, while the work was going through the press.

The Author has often heard Sinologues speak of the difficulty of understanding the Shoo, and hazard the opinion, that, if we had not the native commentaries, we should not be able to make out the meaning of it at all. He would be far from denying that the book is difficult. His own labour on it has been too toilsome to allow his doing so. At the same time, it is by no means unintelligible. Here and there a passage occurs, which yields no satisfactory result after the most persistent study; but in general, if we had not the native commentaries, we should simply have to study the text as intensely and continuously as the native commentators did. They differ, indeed, very frequently among themselves; but this no more entitles us to say that the meaning of the Shoo cannot be determined than similar discrepancies in the views of interpreters on many texts would justify us in saying that the Bible is unintelligible. In a few places, the Author has been obliged to propound an interpretation quite new. He might have done so in very many more; but he preferred, wherever it was possible, to abide by views that had occurred to some native scholar, rather than start new ones of his own.

The Author is grateful for the kind reception which his two previous volumes have met with from Sinologues both in China and in other countries. One, who of all others has the best right to counsel in such a case, will pardon him for introducing here a suggestion which he offered, and giving his reasons for not attending to it. 'I should have desired,' wrote he, 'that, during the publication of the Four Books, you could have been assisted phrase by phrase, or, so to speak, word by word, by a Chinese scholar perfectly versed in Mandchou. I present this view, that you should not in your following publications deprive yourself of this excellent succour, without which one cannot arrive at an interpretation in conformity with the official (not to say sacramental) sense adopted by the most eminent men of the empire.' Now, before the Author commenced publishing in 1860, the plan thus suggested was considered by him, and he concluded that the advantage to be derived from it would not compensate for the expense and trouble which it would occasion. In the first place, the Manchoos are as dependent as ourselves on the Chinese interpreters. In the second place, the official sense is now very different from what it was before the Sung era; and even in the present dynasty, many of the most distinguished scholars and highest officers do not hesitate to propound and maintain interpretations which are at variance with it. In the third place, the Author hopes, in the course of his labours, to explode not a few of the views about the Classics, which may be pronounced official; believing that, by doing so, he will render the greatest service to the Chinese nation, and facilitate the way for the reception of Christianity by its scholars and people.

Students who read the present volume carefully will find in the annotations little trace of the doubt about the historical genuineness of the first Parts of the Book, and some other points, to which decided expression is given in the Prolegomena. The fact is, that when the earlier notes were written, the doubts in question had not assumed consistency in the Author's mind; and he subsequently thought it the best course to continue his interpretation and criticism of the text on the assumption that the whole was genuine. This would have at least the advantage of enabling the student to understand more readily whatever he might find in native writers.

A great desideratum in the study of the Classics of China is a really good dictionary. The Author is not thinking of the translations or compilations by Morrison, Gonçalves, Medhurst, and others; but the Chinese themselves have no dictionary which gives a satisfactory historical analysis of the characters of the language and traces from the primary meaning of each term its various subsequent applications. When a dictionary shall have been made on true principles, by some one who understands the origin of the characters, and has pursued the history of every one through the various forms which it has assumed, the interpretation of the Classics will be greatly simplified.

The Author's obligations to the Rev. Mr. Chalmers, for the Indexes of Subjects and Proper Names, the Essay on Ancient Chinese Astronomy, printed in the Prolegomena, and for various suggestions and assistance in the progress of the Work, have been great. Nor must he fail to acknowledge gratefully the services rendered to him by Wang T'aou, a graduate of Soo-chow. This scholar, far excelling in classical lore any of his countrymen whom the Author had previously known, came to Hongkong in the end of 1863, and placed at his disposal all the treasures of a large and well-selected library. At the same time, entering with spirit into his labours, now explaining, now arguing, as the case might be, he has not only helped but enlivened many a day of toil.

Mr Frederick Stewart, Head Master of the Government Schools in Hongkong, and Mr. G. M. Bain, of the "China Mail" Office, have very kindly aided in the correction for the press. Few typographical mistakes have escaped their notice. Some errors in Chinese names should have been detected by the Author, but escaped his notice through the pre-occupation of his mind with other matters.

HONGKONG, 12*th July*, 1865.

書經

CONTENTS.

I. THE PROLEGOMENA.

CHAPTER I.

THE HISTORY OF THE SHOO KING.

CHAPTER II.

ON THE CREDIBILITY OF THE RECORDS IN THE SHOO.

CHAPTER III.

ON THE DETERMINATION OF THE PRINCIPAL ERAS IN THE SHOO.

CHAPTER IV.

THE ANNALS OF THE BAMBOO BOOKS.

CHAPTER V.

THE ANCIENT EMPIRE OF CHINA.

CHAPTER VI.

LIST OF THE PRINCIPAL WORKS WHICH HAVE BEEN CONSULTED IN THE PREPARATION OF THIS VOLUME.

II. THE BODY OF THE VOLUME.

III. INDEXES.

書經

ERRATA.

I. IN THE CHINESE TEXT.

Page	Column.		Page	Column.	
71,	2,	for 采 read 釆.	260,	10,	insert 說.
75,	8,	„ 底 „ 厎.	276,	2,	for 出 read 出.
The same alteration elsewhere, except in V., xxii. 16.			313,	4,	„ 祇 „ 祗.
87,	1,	for 戛 read 戞.	In some other cases, the same change.		
141,	8,	„ 刋 „ 刊.	397, *et al.*	8,	for 并 read 幷.
208,	1,	after 變 insert ○	369,	5,	„ 巳 „ 已.
241,	6,	for 愚 read 遇.	558,	6,	„ 王 „ 皇.

PAGE 13,......Col. 6th............................after 命 *dele* Comma.
„ 63,.............4th.............................. for 從 read 從。.
„ 84, Between 2d and 3d Columns,. for 九節 „ 八節.
„ 99,..............7th........................ „ 貞作 „ 貞,作.
„ 168,............2d.......................... „ 罰爾 „ 罰,爾.
„ 218, Between 6th and 7th Columns,......by 嗚 insert 十節.
„ 276,..............9th... ....after 2d 畏 insert a Comma.
„ 390,..............5th.......................... „ 師 insert a Comma.
„ 430,...... ....8th.......................... „ 嚮 *dele* Comma.
„ 454,..............6th............................ for 威。read 威、.
„ 525,..............5th......................... after 曰 insert a Comma.
„ 541,..............2d............................ for 訓。read 訓、.
„ 558,............10th.......................... „ 下。„ 下、.
„ 565,..............5th.......................... „ 功。„ 功、.
„ 592,..............2d............................ by 典 insert 十一節.

II. CHINESE CHARACTERS IN THE NOTES.

Page.	Line.	Column.		Page.	Line.	Column.	
1,	6,	II,	for 徵 read 徵.	87,	2,	II,	for 戛 read 戞.
18,	26,	„	„ 居 „ 宅.	238,	7,	I,	„ 子 „ 于.
20,	10,	„	„ 日 „ 夜.	252,	8,	II,	after 眄) insert 眩.
30,	55,	I,	„ 記 „ 紀.	310,	25,	I,	for 旣 read 哉.
51,	1,	II,	„ 且 „ 乃.	482,	17,	„	„ 天 „ 有.
66,	17,18,	I,	„ 祇 „ 祗.				

III. IN THE PROLEGOMENA.

Page.	Line.		Page.	Line.	
5,.........16,..........................		for 82 read 72.	38,.........21, ...		for Shih read Mih.
7,......... 6, note.............		tables, read tablets.	40,......... 4, ...		„ Sung „ Suy.
11.......... 8,........................		11th „ 12th.	68,......... 8, ...		„ Y'ang „ T'ang.

IV. IN THE TRANSLATION AND NOTES.

Page.	*Line.*	
128,	In title of Book	for II. read I.
289, 294, 301, 306, 320, 343, 350, 362, 376, 381, 399,—		for THE BOOKS OF SHANG read THE BOOKS OF CHOW.
6,	11,	for Hëaou read Gaou.
9,	3,	„ Le „ Leu.
11,	8,	„ Chang „ Chung.
17,	8,	„ Sea „ four Seas.
90,	11,	af. Emperor ins. bowed, and.
128, *et al.*	3,	for Te read Che.
	5,	„ Ta „ T'ae.
137,	3,	af. Këang ins. and went on to Tung-ling.
139,	8,	for Urh read Shoo.
195,	4, 5,	Transpose elders and relations.
223,	11,	af. people *dele* Comma.
335,	4,	„ connection ins. a Comma.
342,	4,	for are like read should examine.
460,	8,	„ te „ to.
481,	3,	„ Hwang „ Hung.
551,	6,	„ screens „ screen.
553,	1,	„ *dele* and.
572,	11,	„ *dele* that of.
630,	7,	„ prosperity read calamity.

Page.	*Line.*	*Column.*	
23,	11,	2,	for 子肖 read 子肖.
	26,		„ Ching „ Suy.
33,	7,	2,	„ -shing „ Shing.
35,	25,	2,	„ 37 „ 27.
46,	21,	1,	„ 6 „ 1.
48,	13,	2,	„ 80 „ 81.
64,	24,	1,	transpose 是 and 時.
85,	14,	2,	for eleven read twelve.
99,	18,	2,	„ 1 „ 12.
141,	14,	2,	af. waters put a full stop.
149,	7,	1,	for Han read Chow.
152,	26,	2,	„ 2d Yu „ Hoo.
162,	14,	1,	„ XXVI., p.10 „ XXII., p.9
223,	11,	1,	„ our „ one.
224,	16,	2,	„ prunasily „ primarily.
317,	30,	2,	„ that „ than.
372,	15,	2,	„ Q „ P.
388,	23,	1,	„ 10 „ 11.

PROLEGOMENA.

CHAPTER I.

THE HISTORY OF THE SHOO KING.

SECTION I.

DOWN TO THE BURNING OF THE BOOKS IN B.C. 212.— THE NAME OF THE SHOO; ITS COMPILATION AND NUMBER OF BOOKS; ITS SOURCES.

Name of the Shoo, and its significancy.

1. I have translated the name Shoo King by 'The Book (or Classic) of Historical Documents.' The term *shoo* shows us by its composition[1] that it denotes 'the pencil speaking;' and hence it is often used as a general designation for the written characters of the language. In the preface to the Shwŏ Wăn, the oldest extant dictionary of the Chinese, we are told that 'when Ts'ang Këĕ first made characters *(shoo)*, they were, according to their classes, resemblances of the objects, and therefore called *wăn* (delineations); that afterwards, when the forms and their sounds (or names) were mutually increased, they were called *tsze* (begetters); and that, as set forth on bamboo or silk, they were called *shoo* (writings).'[2] From this use of the term the transition was easy to the employment of it in the sense of writings or books, applicable to any consecutive compositions; and before the time

1 書=聿曰. 聿 means 'an instrument for writing or describing characters,' and 曰 means 'to speak.' 2 蒼頡之初作書,蓋依類象形,故謂之文,其後形聲相益,即謂之字,字者,孳乳而寖多也,著于竹帛,謂之書,書者如也. The Shwŏ Wăn (說文) was completed A.D. 100, in the 12th year of the 4th emperor of the Eastern Han dynasty (漢和帝永元十二年). The author's name was Heu Shin (許慎). He is often referred to also by his designation of Shuh-chung (叔重).

of Confucius we find it further specially applied to designate the historical remains of antiquity, in distinction from the poems, the accounts of rites, and other monuments of former times.[3] Not that those other documents might not also be called by the general name of *shoo*.[4] The peculiar significancy of the term, however, was well established, and is retained to the present day. *The* SHOO, in the lips of Confucius, denoted documents concerning the history of his country from the most ancient times to his own; as spoken of since the Han dynasty, it has denoted a compilation of such documents, believed (whether correctly or not, we shall presently inquire) to have been made by the sage. In the prolegomena to my first volume, p. 1, I have called it 'The Book of History,' and Medhurst styles it 'The Historical Classic, the most authentic record of the Annals of the Chinese Empire;' but both these designations are calculated to mislead the reader. The Book, even as it is said to have come from the hand of Confucius, never professed to contain a history of China; and much less are we to look in it for the annals of that history. Its several portions furnish important materials to the historian, but he must grope his way through hundreds of years without any assistance from the Shoo. It is simply a collection of historical memorials, extending over a space of about 1,700 years, but on no connected method, and with great gaps between them. This is the character of the Work, and nothing more is indicated by the name Shoo King.

The name Shang Shoo.

2. As to the name 'Shang Shoo,'[1] by which the Classic is very frequently both spoken and written of, it is generally said by scholars that it originated subsequently to the burning of the Books. Thus Maou K'e-ling tells us that 'the Shoo was anciently named simply the Shoo, but that, after the portions of it preserved by Fuh-shang appeared, as they were the Books of highest antiquity, it was named the Shang Shoo.'[2] Maou's statement is

3 See the fourth paragraph. 4 An instance quite in point may be referred to in the third and only existing part of Mih-tsze's treatise on Manes (明鬼篇). On the 6th page, he has two quotations from the Shoo King, and one from the She. The latter is introduced by 周書大雅有之, 'We read in the Ta Ya, *one of the Books of Chow*.'

1 尙書. 2 書舊祇名書, 自伏書出後, 以其爲上古之書, 故名尙, 見孔氏正義. See the 古文尙書寃詞, Bk. I., p. 10. In explanation of the term 尙, Maou adds—若春秋說題辭, 尙者上也, 上世帝王之遺書也, 劉熙釋名 (The 釋名 still remains. Lew He belonged to the closing times of the Han dynasty), 尙者上也, 以堯爲上始, 而書其時事也. A difficulty occurs in receiving this view from the 28th and 30th of the Books of

2]

書經

based on the authority of K'ung Ying-tă, of the T'ang dynasty. It is so far correct,—in saying that the oldest name of the Book was simply the Shoo; but the epithet of *Shang* was in use before the time of Fuh-shang. We find it in the treatise of Mih-tsze referred to above.[3] We may acquiesce in the meaning which is assigned to it. *Shang* may be descriptive of the documents with reference either to their antiquity or to the value set upon them.

Did Confucius compile the classic of the Shoo?

3. In the Analects, Confucius and Tsze-chang quote from the Shoo by the simple formula—'The Shoo says.'[1] In the Great Learning, four different Books, all in the classic as we have it now, are mentioned by name.[2] Mencius sometimes uses the same formula as Confucius,[3] and at other times designates particular Books.[4] It is most natural for us to suppose that Confucius, when he spoke of 'The Shoo,' had in his mind's eye *a collection* of Historical Documents bearing that title,—the same which we still possess in a mutilated condition. But it may not have been so. His language—'The Shoo says'—may mean nothing more than that in one of the ancient documents, come down from former times, well known to many, and open to general research, so and so was to be found written. Such even Chinese critics must allow to have been his meaning, if he used the phrase before he himself made the compilation of the documents which they universally ascribe to him. I propose now to inquire on what authority the sage is believed to have made such a compilation; and, as a specimen of the current tradition on the subject, I may commence by quoting the account in the 'Records of the Suy dynasty' (A.D. 589–617).—'Historical Documents began immediately with the invention of written characters. Confucius inspected the documents in the library of Chow; and having found the records of the four dynasties of Yu, Hea, Shang, and Chow, he preserved the best among them, and rejected the others. Beginning with Yu and

Chow, which belong to the period of what is called the Ch'un-ts'ew; and Maou concludes by saying that as the Books of the Shoo were recovered in the Han dynasty, they then characterised all documents prior to the times of Ts'in as of high antiquity (書出漢代,其視秦以前,皆上古耳). This conclusion of Maou is overthrown by the use of the term by Mih-tsze. 3 See the 明鬼篇,下, p. 7,—故尙書夏書,其次商周之書,語數鬼神之有也.

1 書云. Ana. II. xxi; XIV. xliii. 2 The Great Learning, Comm. i. 1, 2, 3; ii. 2; ix. 2; x. 11, 14. 3 書曰. I. Pt. II. iii. 7; xi. 2: III. Pt. I. i. 4; Pt. II. ix. 6: VI. Pt. II. v. 4. 4 I. Pt. I. ii. 4: II. Pt. I. iv. 6: III. Pt. II. v. 6: IV. Pt. I. viii. 5: V. Pt. I. v. 8: VII. Pt. II. iii.

coming down to Chow, he compiled altogether a hundred Books, and made a preface to them.'[5]

The earliest authority for these statements is that of K'ung Gan-kwŏ, about B.C. 90. When it is said that Confucius compiled the Book of Poetry, substantially as it exists at present, his own language may be adduced in corroboration. He tells us how he reformed the music, and gave the pieces in the Imperial songs and Praise songs all their proper places. He tells us also, in round numbers very nearly approaching the exact calculation, how many the pieces of poetry were.[7] But nowhere does he speak of having laboured in a similar way upon the Shoo, or of the number of documents comprehended in the collection. He spoke of them often with his disciples, as he did of the poems; but neither in the Analects nor in Mencius have we a hint of his having selected a hundred pieces from the mass of early historical memoirs, and composed a preface for them.

Gan-kwŏ's testimony is in the preface to his commentary on the Shoo King, enlarged by the additional Books which had been recovered from the wall of Confucius' house,—of which I will speak at length in the next chapter. Recounting the labours of his 'ancestor, Confucius,' on the Music, Rites, Poems, and other remains of ancient literature, he says that 'he examined and arranged the grand monuments and records, deciding to commence with Yaou and Shun, and to come down to the times of Chow. When there was perplexity and confusion, he mowed them. Expressions frothy and unallowable he cut away. What embraced great principles he retained and developed. What were more minute and yet of importance he carefully selected. Of those deserving to be handed down to other ages and to supply permanent lessons, he made in all one hundred Books, consisting of Canons, Counsels, Instructions, Announcements, Speeches, and Charges.'[8]

5 隋書,志第二十七,經籍一,—書之所興,蓋與文字俱起,孔子觀書周室,得虞,夏,商,周,四代之典,删其善者,上自虞下至周爲百篇,編而序之. 6 Ana. IX. xiv. 7 Ana. II. ii. 8 See the 尙書序 in 'The Thirteen King.'—先君孔子………討論墳典,斷自唐虞以下,訖于周,芟夷煩亂,翦截浮辭,舉其宏綱,撮其機要,足以垂世立教,典,謨,訓,誥,誓,命之文,凡百篇. In an earlier part of the preface Gan-kwŏ has described the 墳 as 'the Books of Fuh-he, Shin-nung, and Hwang-te,' and the 典 as 'the Books of Shaou-haou, Chuen-heuh, Kaou-sin, Yaou, and Shun.' Of these I shall speak farther on; but we must take 墳典 in this paragraph more generally, or its parts will be very inconsequent. Ying-tă expands 討論墳典 into 討整論理此三墳五典,幷三代之書也.

4]

Of Confucius having written a preface to the hundred Books which he thus compiled, Gan-kwŏ does not speak distinctly. His language implies that among the remains which came into his charge there was a preface to the Books, which he broke up into its several parts, prefixing to each Book the portion belonging to it; but he does not say that Confucius was the author of it.[9]

Confucius died B.C. 478, and thus nearly 400 years pass by before we find the compilation of the Shoo ascribed to him. I know that the genuineness of Gan-kwŏ's preface—commonly named 'The Great Preface,'[10]—is called in question, though, as I think, on insufficient grounds; but we find the same testimony which has been adduced from it given about the same time by Sze-ma Ts'een, who was acquainted with Gan-kwŏ, and consulted him specially on the subject of the Shoo.[11] Ts'een's 'Historical Records'[12] must have been completed between B C. 103 and 97, and became current in the reign of the emperor Seuen, B.C. 82—48. In them, in the Life of Confucius, we read that the sage, on his return to Loo in his old age, B.C. 483, 'made a preface to the Records of the Shoo, and compiled and arranged them from the times of Yaou and Shun down to duke Muh of Ts'in.'[13] Ts'een speaks more definitely than Gan-kwŏ on the point of the Preface. The fact of the compilation is equally asserted by both. But they cannot be regarded as independent witnesses. Ts'een's information came to him from Gan-kwŏ; and to them are to be traced all the statements on the subject which we find in the chronicles of the Han and subsequent dynasties. It is possible—it is not improbable—that Confucius did compile a hundred ancient documents, which he wished to be regarded as *the Shoo par eminence.* His doing so would have been in harmony with the character which he gave of himself as 'A transmitter and not a maker, believing in and loving the ancients;'[14] and with his labours on the Classic of poetry and on the Ch'un-ts'ew. The Shoo's beginning with

9 伏生以舜典合於堯典,益稷合於臯陶謨,盤庚三篇合爲一,康王之誥合於顧命,復出此篇幷序,凡五十九篇,爲四十六卷……書序,序所以爲作者之意,昭然義見,宜相附近,故引之各冠其篇首,定五十八篇. 10 大序 11 See the 前漢書,儒林傳,第五十八, p. 9.—安國爲諫大夫,授都尉朝,而司馬遷亦從安國問,故遷書載堯典,禹貢,微子,洪範,金藤,多古文說. 12 史記, 13 序書傳,上紀唐虞之際,下至奏繆,編次其事. See the 史記四十七,孔子,世家第十七, p. 12. 14 Ana. VII. i.

the Canons of Yaou and Shun is also what might have been expected from him of whom it is said in the Doctrine of the Mean that 'He handed down the doctrines of Yaou and Shun as if they had been his ancestors.'[15] But however reasonable in itself may be the belief that he compiled the Shoo as it existed at the time when the ambitious emperor of Ts'in issued his edict that the ancient books should be consigned to the flames, I have thought it right to show that the evidence which we have for it is by no means conclusive. What Gan-kwŏ is supposed to say, and Ts'een says explicitly, about his writing a preface to the compilation, is, it will be presently seen, still more questionable.

4. Whether Confucius determined that so many of the ancient historical documents of his country were worthy of being preserved, and stamped them with his own authority, so fixing the Canon of the Shoo, or not, the evidence is satisfactory enough that after his time there was current under this name an acknowledged and authoritative collection of such documents.

The Shoo after the time of Confucius was a recognized standard collection of ancient documents.

It has been pointed out how he used in his quotations the vague formula—'The Shoo says,' which may mean 'An ancient document says,' or 'One of the Books in the Canon of the Shoo says;' and that Mencius often does the same. The language of the latter philosopher, however, in one place loses much of its force, if we do not understand him to be referring to a definite collection. 'It would be better,' he said, 'to be without the Shoo than to give entire credit to it;' and immediately after, he specifies one of the Books of Chow.—'In the "Completion of the War," I select two or three passages only which I believe.'[1] The natural interpretation of the character *Shoo* as here employed is certainly that which I propose. In my comment upon it, vol. II., p. 355, I have spoken of two or three methods which have been thought of to give it a different meaning. They are all strained, and designed to escape from what we should call *doctrinal* difficulties. Mencius speaks with little reverence for the Shoo, and with little reverence for Confucius, if he believed that the Master had compiled it in the way which K'ung Gan-kwŏ describes. He may have been wrong in doing so,

15 中庸, xxx. 1.

1 Men. VII. Pt. II.—盡信書,則不如無書。吾於武成,取二三策而已矣.

or he may have been right;—what he did say remains in the record of his Works.

The quotation of particular documents by their names in The Great Learning and in Mencius, which has likewise been pointed out, directs us to the same conclusion. The same thing is often found in the Record of Rites.

In the Commentary of Tso-k'ew Ming on the Ch'un-ts'ew, in Mih-tsze, Seun-tsze, and other writers of the two last centuries of the Chow dynasty, a different style of quotation prevails, which is still more decisive on the point in hand. They not only quote the Shoo as Confucius and Mencius do, but they specify the different parts or divisions of it,—the Books of Yu, of Hea, of Shang, of Chow. I need refer the reader only to the quotation from Mih-tsze given in the third note to par. 2 above.

Did the Shoo consist of a hundred Books or Documents?

Whether the Collection of Historical Documents, which was thus current in the closing period of the Chow dynasty, consisted of a hundred different Books, no more and no fewer, is a question on which I find it difficult to give a definite opinion. It was so believed after the Preface to the Shoo was found in the wall of Confucius' house in the reign of the emperor Woo (B.C. 139—86), or earlier.[2] That preface, such as it is, will be seen in this volume, pp. 1—14. Gan-kwŏ assumed that it was complete, and based on it his statement that the Shoo contained the hundred Books mentioned in it. Copies of it were current among the scholars of the Han dynasty, differing a little from that published subsequently as Gan-kwŏ's in the relative order of some of the Books; but we have their testimony as to the entire number in the collection being a hundred.[3]

There are some things, however, which make me hesitate to receive these statements without question. For instance, Sze-ma Ts'een in his Records of the Yin dynasty, when telling us that Woo Heen made the *Heen E*, which is mentioned in the Preface, Not. 22, adds

2 I think it more probable that this event took place in the reign of the emperor King (景帝), B.C. 155–140. It is generally said to have happened in the end of Woo's reign. But king Kung of Loo, to enable whom to enlarge his palace the old house of the sage was being pulled down, died, it is said, B.C. 127, more than 40 years before Woo's reign ended. See Yen Jŏ-keu, as quoted in the 尙書後案辨附, p. 29. The different statements which we find on the subject arise from confounding the date of the discovery of the old tables with that of the completion of Gan-kwŏ's commentary. 3 Thus Ch'ing Heuen or Ch'ing K'ang-shing tells us that the Books of Yu and Hea (or the Yu-hea Books) were 20; those of Shang, 40; and those of Chow, 40:—a hundred in all. See K'ang-shing's brief account of the Shoo, given in the 後案, 卷十三, p. 58.

that he also made the *T'ae-mow*, which has no place in it.[4] In the Commentary of Tso-k'ew, under the 4th year of duke Ting (B.C. 505), mention is made of the Announcement to the prince of K'ang, which is now the 9th of the Books of Chow, and in the same paragraph of a Charge or Announcement to *Pih-k'in*, on which the Preface is silent.[5] In the 21st of the Books of the first dynasty of Han, there is a quotation from 'the *Yuĕ Ts'ae*, one of the Books of the Ancient Text,' and on the same page a Book called *Fung Hing* is spoken of, of neither of which do we read elsewhere.[6]

Further, several writers of the Han dynasty speak of 102, and of 120 Books. It is difficult to explain their language; but it appears inconsistent with the tradition which has since prevailed, that the Canon of the Shoo contained, before the time of Ts'in, only one hundred documents.[7]

Maou K'e-ling endeavours quite unsuccessfully to prove that the phrase, 'A hundred Books,' was older than Gan-kwŏ, and his discovery of the Preface. He refers first to a passage in Mih-tsze, where it is said that 'the duke of Chow read in the morning 100 Books.' This can have nothing to do with the subject. Several of the Books of the Shoo were composed after the time of the duke of Chow. Mih simply means to commend his industry, as is evident from the sentence which follows, that 'in the evening the duke gave audience to 70 officers.'[8] He refers also to a sentence in the writings of Yang Heung, that 'those who in former times spoke of the Shoo, arranged (or prefaced) it in 100 Books';[9] but Yang died A.D. 18, being posterior to Gan-kwŏ by nearly a century; and the sequel of the passage shows that he had in mind critics subsequent to that

4 See the 殷記, p. 3.—巫咸治王家有成, 作咸艾, 作太戊. 5 See the 左傳, 定公四年.—命以伯禽, 而封於少皞之虛...... 命以康誥, 而封於殷虛. 6 See the 律曆志第一, 下.—古文月采篇曰, 云云; 畢命豐刑曰......王命作策豐刑. 7 See the 古文尙書寃詞, 卷二, p 7, and the 經義考, 卷七十三, 書二, p. 1. Maou gives two ways of explaining these expressions. The first is—Add to the acknowledged 100 Books one for the Preface, and one for a different edition of The Great Speech, which somehow was current; thus we have 102. The second refers to the 120.—He adduces a work called 尙書璿璣鈐, where it is said that Confucius found 120 Books; that out of 102 he made the Shang Shoo, and out of 18 the Chung How; and these were the 120 (百兩篇). I do not know how to interpret Chung How (中候). The explanations do not enlighten the darkness of the subject. 8 See Mih-tsze, 卷之十二, 貴義 p. 3, 昔者周公旦朝讀百篇, 夕見漆(=七)十士. 9 See 楊子法言, 卷四, 問神篇, p 4.—昔之說書者序以百.

8]

scholar.—On the one hand, allowing that Gan-kwŏ found the Preface, as it is still current, with the other tablets (which there is no reason to doubt), we cannot be certain that the Canon of the Shoo did not at the end of the Chow dynasty contain more than a hundred Books; nor, on the other hand, can we be certain that the hundred Books mentioned in it were all then existing. Not a few of them may have been lost or cast out before that time. I believe myself that it was so, and will give my reasons for doing so in the next section.

The Preface was not written by Confucius.

That the Preface, whether it be complete or not, was not written by Confucius, is now the prevailing opinion of scholars throughout the empire. I have shown that Gan-kwŏ himself did not ascribe it to the sage. Sze-ma Ts'een did, and was followed by Lew Hin, Pan Koo, Ch'ing Heuen, and other scholars of the Han dynasty. Their doing so proves that they had little of the critical faculty,—unless we are prepared to allow that Confucius was a man of very little discrimination and comprehension of mind. It will be sufficient for me to give here the judgment in the matter of Ts'ae Ch'in, the disciple of Choo He, and whose commentary is now the standard of orthodoxy in the interpretation of the Shoo.—After quoting the opinions of Lew Hin and Pan Koo, he says:—'When we examine the text of the Preface, as it is still preserved, though it is based on the contents of the several Books, the knowledge which it shows is shallow, and the views which it gives are narrow. It sheds light on nothing; and there are things in it at variance with the text of the Classic. On the Books that are lost it is specially servile and brief, affording us not the slightest help. That it is not the work of Confucius is exceedingly plain.'[10]

5. The questions which have thus far been discussed can hardly be regarded as of prime importance. It seemed necessary to give attention to them in a critical introduction to the Shoo; but it matters little to the student that he cannot discern the *imprimatur* of Confucius on the collected Canon;—he has the sage's authority for some Books in it, and he has evidence that after his time there was a Compilation of ancient historical documents acknowledged by the scholars of the empire. And it matters little to him what was the exact number of documents in that Collection;—many of them have been irretrievably lost, and we have to do only with those which are now current as having fortunately escaped the flames of Ts'in. There remains, however, at this part of our in-

10 See the 集傳.書序.

quiries, a question really curious and of great interest.—What were

The sources of the Shoo.

the sources of the Shoo? What proofs have we of the composition in ancient times of such documents as it contains, and of their preservation, so that some of them might be collected in a sort of historical Canon?

To begin with the dynasty of Chow.—We have the Work commonly called 'The Rites of Chow.'[1] It is also and more correctly called 'The Officers of Chow.'[2] Under the several departments into which the administration of the government was divided, it gives the titles of the officers belonging to them, and a description of their duties. I will not vouch for the tradition which ascribes the composition of it to the duke of Chow; but it no doubt contains the institutions and arrangements made by him in completing the establishment of the dynasty.

Under the department of the minister of Religion we find the various officers styled *Sze*,[3] a term which has been translated 'Recorders,'[4] 'Annalists,'[5] 'Historiographers,' and simply 'Clerks.'[6] There are the Grand Recorder, the Assistant Recorder, the Recorder of the Interior, the Recorder of the Exterior, and the Recorder in attendance on the emperor. Arranged under the department of the minister of Religion, they were advisers also of the prime minister of the government, and of Heads of Departments generally, on all subjects which required reference to history and precedent. Among the duties of the Recorder of the Interior were the following:—'In case of any Charge given by the emperor to the prince of a State, to an assistant Grand counsellor, to a minister, or to a great officer, he writes the Charge on tablets;' 'In case of any Memorials on business coming in from the different quarters of the empire, he reads them *to the emperor*;' 'It is his business to write all Charges of the emperor, and to do so in duplicate.'[8] Of the duties of the Re-

1 周禮. Biot names it—'Le Tcheou Li, ou Rites de Tcheou.' 2 周官. This is the name in the grand edition ordered by the emperor K'ëen-lung of the present dynasty,—the 欽定周官義疏. 3 史. 4 This is the definition given in the Shwŏ Wán,—記事者, 'one who records events.' Morrison, Dict., *in voc.*, observes that the character is formed from 'a *hand* seizing the *middle*,' and defines it as 'an impartial narrator of events.' The *hand* holds the pencil, and describes things without swerving to the right or left. 5 Thus Biot renders the term. 6 See my translation of the Analects, VI. xvi. 7 大史, 小史, 內史, 外史, 御史. 8 See the 周官, Ch. xxvi. P. 35, 凡命諸侯, 及孤, 卿, 大夫, 則策命之; p. 36, 凡四方之事書, 內史讀之; p. 38, 內史掌書王命, 遂貳之.

corder of the Exterior it is said:—'He writes all Commands for the exterior domains;' 'He has charge of the Histories of the States in all parts of the empire;' 'He has charge of the Books of the three great sovereigns and the five rulers;' 'It is his business to publish in all parts of the empire the Books and the characters in them.'[9]

These passages show clearly that under the Chow dynasty, from its commencement in the 11th century before our Christian era, there was provision made for the compilation and preservation of imperial charges and ordinances, of records of the operations of the general government, and of histories of the different States; and, moreover, for the preservation and interpretation of documents come down from more ancient times.

The Recorders mentioned in the 'Officers of Chow' belonged of course to the imperial court; but there were similar officers, though not so numerous, at the courts of the various feudal princes. It was of such that Confucius spoke when he said that in his early days a historiographer would leave a blank in his text rather than enter anything of which he had not sufficient evidence.[10] They also were the writers of the Books which Mencius mentions,—'the Shing of Tsin, the Taou-wuh of Ts'oo, and the Ch'un-ts'ew of Loo'[11]

When we ascend from the Chow dynasty to those of Shang and Hea which preceded it, we do not have the same amount of evidence for the existence under them of the class of officers styled Recorders. Chinese critics, indeed, say that it did then exist, and even earlier; my own opinion is, that the institution was in active operation during the dynasties just named:—but the proofs are not adequate. For instance, Ma Twan-lin says, 'The pencil of the recording officers was busy from the time of Hwang-te. Its subsequent operation is clearly seen from what we know of Chung Koo, the Grand Recorder

9 Pp. 39-42. 外史掌書外令;掌四方之志;掌三皇五帝之書;掌達書名於四方. Biot translates this last par.—掌達書名於四方 by 'Ils sort chargés de propager les noms écrits, ou les signes de l'écriture, dans les quatre parties de l'empire.' This was the view of Wang Gan-shih of the Sung dynasty, who says—書名者字也. 書 and 名 are thus taken in apposition, or, at best, as Biot renders, = 'written names,' = characters; which seems to me an unnatural construction. K'ang-shing took 書名 as meaning simply 'the names of the Books,' as 'The Canon of Yaou,' 'The Tribute of Yu;' which names the Recorder of the Exterior made known throughout the empire. So far as the characters 書名 are concerned, this interpretation is the likeliest; but it makes the whole passage so weak and frivolous that it cannot be admitted. K'ang-shing mentions, however, that some took 名 in the sense of 字, 'characters,' and made 書名 = 'the characters in the various Books.' This is nearer to the view which I have taken. 10 Ana. XV. xxv. 11 Men. IV. Pt. II. xxi.

of Hea, and Kaou She, the Grand Recorder of Shang.'[12] But all that we know of the names mentioned is from the Bamboo Books and from the Ch'un-ts'ew of Leu,—both comparatively recent and insufficient authorities.[13] I attach more force to what we find in the 10th of the Books of Chow, par. 13, where Fung is told to warn his 'friends, the Grand Recorder and the Recorder of the Interior,' of the dangers of drunkenness. By the 'Recorder of the Interior' there, it is argued that we must understand the officer who had exercised that function at the imperial court of Shang, and was now living in retirement in the State of Wei after the overthrow of his dynasty.

Independently of the Institution of Recorders, if we may admit the testimony of the Shoo itself, both emperors and ministers were in the habit of committing their ordinances and memorials to writing during the rule of the House of Shang. Woo-ting, B.C. 1321, is described as making a writing to communicate the dream which he had to his ministers;[14] and, more than 400 years earlier, we have E Yin addressing his remonstrances to the young emperor T'ae-këă in a written form.[15] Going back to the dynasty of Hea, we find that the prince of Yin, during the reign of Chung-k'ang, generally believed to have begun B.C. 2158, in addressing his troops, quotes 'The Statutes of Government,' in a manner which makes us conceive of him as referring to some well-known compilation.[16] The grandsons of the great Yu, likewise, make mention, in 'The Songs of the Five Sons,' of his 'Lessons,' doing so in language which suggests to us the formula which Mencius was wont to employ when he was referring to the documents acknowledged to be of authority in his day.[17] There can be no doubt that about 2000 years before our era the art of writing was known in China, and that it was exer-

12 See the 文獻通考, 卷五十一, Art. 史官.—史官筆自黃帝有之, 自後顯著夏太史終古, 高太史商勢. [While this sheet is going through the press, my attention has been called to a Soo-chow edition of Ma Twan-lin's Work, where this passage is read—史官肇自黃帝有之, 自後顯者, 云云. This reading is, no doubt, preferable to that in the copy in my own possession.] 13 See the 竹書紀年, 注箋, 卷之四, p. 12, and 卷之六, p. 28. What Leu says is found, in his Ch'un-ts'ew, 卷第十六, 先識覽第四. The 太平御覽, 卷二百三十五, p. 4, gives the following abstract of his statements:—夏太史令終古, 見夏桀惑亂, 載其圖法而泣, 乃出奔商, 商太史高勢見周, 之迷亂, 載其圖法, 出之周. 14 Pt. IV. Bk. VIII., Pt. i. 2, 15, Bk. V. Pt. i. 2. 16 Part III. Bk. IV. 4. 17 Bk. III. See particularly 訓有之, in par. 6, and compare it with the 於傳有之, in Men. I. Pt. II. ii. 1, *et al.*

書經

cised in the composition of Documents of the nature of those which we read in the Shoo King. Whether an institution like that of the Recorders of Chow existed at so early a date does not appear. We can well believe that, as time went on, all written memorials were produced more numerously and frequently. We can well believe also that, in the revolutions and periods of confusion which occurred, many memorials were lost. Mencius complained that in his time the feudal princes destroyed many of the records of antiquity, that they might the better perpetrate their own usurpations and innovations.[18] The same thing would go on during the dynasties of Shang and Hea. Time is at once a producer and a devourer. Many records of Yu and T'ang and their successors had perished before the Canon of the Shoo was compiled, but sufficient must have remained to supply the materials for a larger collection than was made.

Confucius once expressed himself in a manner which throws light on the point which I am now considering.—'I am able,' said he, 'to describe the ceremonies of the Hea dynasty, but K'e cannot sufficiently attest my words. I am able to describe the ceremonies of the Yin dynasty; but Sung cannot sufficiently attest my words. They cannot do so because of the insufficiency of their records and wise men.'[19] The State of K'e was ruled by the descendants of the great Yu, and that of Sung by those of T'ang. The various institutions of Hea and Shang ought to have been preserved in them, and their scholars should have been careful to watch over the literary monuments that could be appealed to in support of their traditions and ordinances. But the scholars had failed in their duty; the monuments were too mutilated and fragmentary to answer their purpose. The Master would not expose himself to the risk of relating or teaching what he could not substantiate by abundant evidence. Where had he got his own knowledge of the ancient times? Some critics tell us that he was born with it;—an affirmation which no foreigner will admit. He must have obtained it by his diligent research, and his reasoning, satisfactory at least to himself, on what facts he was able to ascertain. His words show us that, while in his time there were still existing documents of a high antiquity, they were not very numerous or complete.

6. Before we pass on to the next chapter, it will be well to say something on 'the Books of the three great sovereigns, and the five

18 V. Pt. II. ii. 2. 19 Ana. III. ix.

rulers,' which 'The Officers of Chow,' as quoted on page 11, mentions as being under the charge of the Recorder of the Exterior. Nothing certain or satisfactory, indeed, has ever been ascertained about them; but the amount of discussion to which they have given rise renders it desirable that I should not leave the passage unnoticed.

The Books of the three Sovereigns and five rulers.

What were those Books? Gan-kwŏ says in his preface, referred to above on page 4, that 'the Books of Fuh-he, Shin-nung, and Hwang-te were called the *Three Fun*, as containing great doctrines; and those of Shaou-haou, Chuen-heuh, Kaou-sin, Yaou, and Shun were called the *five Tëen*, as containing standard doctrines.'[1] He was led to this explanation by a passage in the Tso Chuen, the most valued commentary on the Ch'un-Ts'ew. It is there said, under the 12th year of duke Ch'aou (B.C. 530), that E-Seang, a Recorder of the State of Ts'oo, 'could read the three *Fun*, the five *Tëen*, the eight *Sih*, and the nine *K'ew*.'[2] It would appear from this, that in the time of Confucius there were some books current having the names which are given; but what they were, and whether a portion of them were the same with those mentioned in 'The Officers of Chow,' we cannot tell. Woo Sze-taou,[3] a scholar of the Yuen dynasty, observes:—'The Recorder of the Exterior had charge of the "Books of the three Hwang;" nothing is said of the "three Fun." E-seang could read the "three Fun;" nothing is said in connection with him of the "three Hwang." K'ung Gan-kwŏ thought that the Books of the three Hwang and the three Fun were identical; but there is no good reason to adopt his conclusion.' Too Yu of the Tsin dynasty, the glossarist of the Tso Chuen, contented himself with saying that Fun, Teen, Sih, and K'ew were all 'the names of ancient Books.' Whatever those Books were, we may safely conclude that they were of little worth. According to Gan-kwŏ's own account, Confucius rejected the three *Fun*, and three out of the five *Teen*, when he was compiling the Shoo; and by whomsoever the Shoo was compiled, we are well assured that it never contained any document older than the Canon of Yaou. We should be glad if we could have light thrown on the passage in 'The Officers

1 伏犧、神農、黃帝之書、謂之三墳、言大道也、少昊、顓頊、高辛、唐、虞、之書、謂之五典、言常道也。 2 佐史倚相…其能讀三墳、五典、八索、九丘。 3 吳師道。 He is quoted in the 經義考、書一。

書經

of Chow;' but we must be content, as is so often the case in historical inquiries, to remain in ignorance, and have our curiosity ungratified.[4]

4 I have not thought it worth while to mention in the text a forgery of 'the three Fun,' which was attempted A.D. 1084, when a certain Maou Tsëen (毛漸) pretended to have discovered the ancient Books. The imposition was soon exploded.

SECTION II.

FROM THE BURNING OF THE BOOKS, B.C. 212, TO THE TIME OF CHOO HE, A.D. 1130.

THE RECOVERY OF A PORTION OF THE SHOO BY FUH-SANG, CALLED THE MODERN TEXT; AND OF A SECOND PORTION BY K'UNG GAN-KWO, CALLED THE ANCIENT TEXT. THE GENERAL ACKNOWLEDGMENT OF GAN-KWO'S BOOKS.

1. In the *prolegomena* to vol. I., pp. 6–9, I have given an account of the burning of the books, and of the slaughter of many of the literati, by the first emperor of the Ts'in dynasty. The measures were barbarous and wanton, but the author of them and his advisers adopted them as necessary to the success of the policy which the new dynasty was initiating. The old feudal system of the empire had been abolished; a new order of administration was being introduced; the China of the future, to be ruled for ever by the House of Ts'in, must be dissevered entirely from the China of the past. In order to this the history of former times, it was thought, should be blotted out, and the names which had been held in reverence for hundreds and thousands of years be made to perish from the memory of men. The course taken was like that ascribed to our Edward I., when in A.D. 1284 he assembled all the bards of Wales, and caused them to be put to death. When the premier Le Sze advised that the books should be burned, he made an exception, according to the account of his speech given us by Sze-ma Ts'een, in favour of the copies in keeping of the Board of Great Scholars; but those must have shared the common fate. If they had not done so, the Shoo would not have been far to seek, when the rule of Ts'in came in so short a time to an end.

The burning of the Books.

The founder of that dynasty, which he fondly thought would last for myriads of years, died in B.C. 209. His second son, who succeeded him, was murdered in 204, and the House of Ts'in passed away.

15]

海上絲綢之路文獻集成 科技與文化編

The dynasty of Han dates from B.C. 201, and in the 4th year of its second emperor, B.C. 190, the edict of Ts'in, making it a capital crime to have the ancient books in one's possession, was repealed. Thus, the Shoo and the other classics (with the exception of the Yih-king) were under the ban for less than a quarter of a century.

2. Among the 'Great Scholars' of Ts'in, there had been one named Fuh Shing,[1] but commonly referred to as 'Fuh-săng,[2] which is equivalent to Mr. Fuh, or the scholar Fuh. He belonged to Tse-nan in Shan-tung; and when the order for the burning of the Shoo went forth, he hid the tablets of the copy which he had in a wall. During the struggle which ensued, after the extinction of the Ts'in dynasty, for the possession of the empire, Fuh-săng was a fugitive in various parts; but when the rule of Han was established, he went to look for his hid treasure. Alas! many of the tablets were perished or gone. He recovered only 29 Books (as he thought) of the Classic. Forthwith he commenced teaching, making those Books the basis of his instructions, and from all parts of Shan-tung scholars resorted to him, and sat at his feet.[3]

Fuh-săng

In all this time, no copy of the Shoo had reached the court. The emperor Wăn (B.C. 178--156), after ineffectual attempts to find some scholar who could reproduce it, heard at last of Fuh-săng, and sent to call him. Fuh was then more than 90 years old, and could not travel; and an officer, called Ch'aou Ts'ŏ, belonging to the same department as the Recorders mentioned in the last section, was sent to Tse-nan to receive from him what he had of the Shoo. Whether Ts'ŏ got the very tablets which Fuh had hidden and afterwards found again, or whether he only took a copy of them, we are not told. It is most likely that, being an imperial messenger, he would carry away the originals. However this be, those originals were, and his copy, if he made one, would be, in the new form of the characters introduced under Ts'in,—what was then 'the modern text;' and by this name the portion of the Shoo recovered by Fuh-săng is designated to the present day.

The above account is taken from Sze-ma Ts'een. Gan-kwŏ gives a relation of the circumstances materially different. According to him, 'Fuh-săng of Tse-nan, being more than 90 years of age (when the emperor Wăn was seeking for copies), had lost his originals of the text, and was delivering by

Varying traditions about Fuh-săng.

1 伏勝. 2 伏生. 3 See the 史記, 一百二十一, 儒林, 列傳第六十一.

書經

word of mouth more than twenty Books to disciples.'[4] From another passage we gather that he estimated Fuh-săng's Books, with which he was well acquainted, at 28; but he says nothing of the visit to Fuh of Ch'aou Ts'ŏ. Wei Hwang, of the first century of our era, says that when Ch'aou Ts'ŏ went to him, Fuh-săng, being over 90, was unable to speak plainly, and made use of a (? grand-) daughter to repeat what he said; and that her dialect being different from Ts'ŏ's, he lost 2 or 3 in every ten of her words, supplying them as he best could according to his conception of the meaning.[5] This last account, as being more marvellous, has become the accepted history of the manner in which so many Books of the Shoo were recovered through Fuh-săng. Even Regis follows it, as if he had not been aware of the more trustworthy narrative of Sze-ma Ts'een.[6]

3. The statement of Sze-ma Ts'een, that Fuh-săng found again the tablets containing 29 '*p'ëen*,'—Books, or parts of Books,—of the Shoo, is repeated by Lew Hin in his list of the Books in the imperial library under his charge, of which I have given some account in the *proleg.* to vol. I. pp. 3–5. It is there expressly said, moreover, that there were, in the classical department of the library, '29 portions of the text of the Shang Shoo.'[1] Those Books were:—

The 29 Books of Fuh-săng. 'The Canon of Yaou;' 'The Counsels of Kaou-yaou;' 'The Tribute of Yu;' 'The Speech at Kan;' 'The Speech of T'ang;' 'The Pwan-kăng;' 'The Day of the Supplementary Sacrifice of Kaou-tsung;' 'The Conquest of Le by the Chief of the West;' 'The Viscount of Wei;' 'The Great Speech;' 'The Speech at Muh;' 'The Great Plan;' 'The Metal-bound Coffer;' 'The Great Announcement;' 'The Announcement to K'ang;' 'The Announcement about Drunkenness;' 'The Timber of the Tsze-tree;' 'The Announcement of Shaou;' 'The Announcement about Lŏ;' 'The Numerous Officers;' 'Against Luxurious Ease;' 'Prince Shih;' 'The Numerous Regions;' 'On the Establishment of Government;' 'The Testamentary Charge;' 'Leu on Punishments;' 'The Charge to Prince Wăn;' 'The Speech at Pe;' and 'The Speech of the Duke of Ts'in.'

It was discovered subsequently, that 'The Canon of Shun' was incorporated by Fuh-săng with that of Yaou; the 'Yih and Tseih' with 'The Counsels of Kaou-yaou;' 'The Charge of king K'ang'

4 See Gan-kwŏ's Preface, p. 13. 5 See the 古文尙書宛詞, 卷一, p. 6. 6 See Y-King, vol. I., pp. 104–106.

1 經二十九卷.

with 'The Testamentary Charge;' and that the 'Pwan-kăng,' given by him as one Book, was in reality three Books. Hence it is often said that Fuh-săng's Books amounted to 34,—as was really the case.

But there is a statement very generally accepted,—that Fuh-săng's Books amounted only to 28, which requires some discussion. 'The Great Speech,' as it is now current, forms three Books. In 'the modern text' it formed only one; and it came to be denied, in the time of the Han dynasty, that even that one proceeded from Fuh-săng. Lew Heang says:—'In the end of the reign of the emperor Woo (B.C. 139–86), some one among the people found "The Great Speech" in a wall, and presented it. When it was submitted to the Board of Great Scholars, they were pleased with it, and in a few months all began to teach it.'[2] Ma Yung, Wang Suh, and Ch'ing Heuen, all affirm that 'The Great Speech' was a more recent discovery than the other Books. Wang Ch'ung,[3] towards the end of our first century, wrote:—'In the time of the emperor Seuen (B.C. 72–48), a girl, north of the Ho, among the ruins of an old house, discovered three Books,—one of the Shoo; one of the Le; and one of the Yih. She presented them to the court. The emperor sent them down to the Great Scholars; and from this time the number of the recovered Books of the Shang Shoo came to be fixed at 29.'

Did 'The Great Speech' form one of Fuh-săng's Books?

All these accounts, attributing to 'The Great Speech' a later origin than to the rest of Fuh-săng's Books, must be set aside. Sze-ma Ts'een's testimony is express as to the number of 29; and, what ought to settle the matter, Fuh-săng himself, in the Introduction which he made to the Shoo, used the language of the Book, as the scholars of the eastern Han read it in the text, the preservation of which they ascribed to 'a girl, north of the Ho.'[4] That text was substantially what I have given in this volume in an appendix (pp. 297–299). We cannot wonder that it should have troubled the scholars. Such a piece of wild extravagance, and having in it nothing of the passages of 'The Great Speech,' quoted by Mencius and others!—this to be going abroad as part of the Shoo of Confucius! They would have done right to cast it out of the classic. They were wrong in denying that it was brought to light, after the fires of Ts'in, by Fuh-săng. We are therefore in this position in regard to him. Among his tablets were some containing that farrago,

2 劉向別錄, quoted in the 古文尙書宽詞, 卷一, p. 7. 3 王充. Quoted by Se-ho as above. 4 See as above, pp. 8, 9.

and he must have erred in classing them with the others, which were portions of the true Shoo. I have not been able to think of any other explanation which will unravel, so satisfactorily, the perplexities of the case. Fuh-săng gave to the world 29 Books as of the Shoo, but in regard to one of them he was mistaken. The stories of its being a subsequent discovery, due to a girl, were devised to save his reputation.

Disciples of Fuh-săng; and Schools of the Modern Text.

4. According to what I quoted above, p. 16, from Sze-ma Ts'een, many Scholars resorted to Fuh-săng, and learned from him what he had to teach about the Shoo. His two principal disciples were a Gow-yang Ho-pih,[1] commonly designated Gowyang-săng, and a Chang-săng,[2] to whom he delivered his comments on the Shoo in 41 Books,[3] of which some fragments still remain. Each of these became the founder of a school, the professors and writings of which are distinctly traced by the critics down into the dynasty of Tsin. Ho-pih's successor was a distinguished scholar and officer, called E Hwan.[4] His great-grandson, Gow-yang Kaou,[5] published 'The Shang Shoo in paragraphs and sentences, in 31 Books.'[6] From the same school flowed at least two other Works;[7] 'The meaning of the Shang Shoo explained,' in two Books, and 'Decisions on the Shang Shoo,' by Gow-yang Te-yu and others, in 42 Books.'[8] The reputation of 'The School of Gowyang,' was pre-eminent during the dynasty of the eastern Han.

1 歐陽生，字和伯. 2 張生. 3 傳四十一篇. By the time of the Suy dynasty, this work had dwindled away to three *p'een*. 4 倪寬. 5 歐陽高. 6 尙書章句，三十一卷. See the 前漢藝文志, upon the Shoo. 7 尙書義說，二篇. 8 歐陽氏地餘等尙書議奏. 歐陽學，東京最盛. See the introductory Chapter to Yung-ching's Shoo, 綱領一, pp. 2, 3. The Continuation of Ma Twan-lin's Work (proleg. vol. I., p. 134) gives the following table of the School of Gow-yang.

尙書伏生
|
歐陽和伯
|
倪寬
|
歐陽之子
|
某
|

19]

The school founded by Chang-săng, and which by and by diverged into two branches was not less prolific in Works upon the Shoo. Chang delivered his learning to Hea-how Too-wei a scholar of Loo,[9] from whom it descended to a Hea-how Shing.[10] This Shing was a man of more than ordinary ability and research; and in obedience to an imperial order, he compiled a Work, which appears in Lew Hin's catalogue as 'The Shang Shoo, in paragraphs and sentences, in 29 chapters;'[11] and formed the basis of 'The Greater school of Hea-how.'[12] A nephew of Shing, called Hea-how Këen,[13] published a sequel to Shing's Work, which he called, 'An Explanation of Ancient Views on the Shang Shoo, in 29 Books,' which was also in the imperial library in Lew Hin's time.[14] Këen was looked up to as the founder of 'The Lesser school of Hea-how.'[15] From those two schools proceeded many Works upon the Shoo, the names and authors of which are duly chronicled by Çhow E-tsun, in his 'Examination of the meaning of the King.'[16] But the names are all that remain. Not one of the writings survived, in a complete form, the troubles which prevailed during the reign of Hwae, the third emperor of the dynasty of the Western Ts'in.[17]

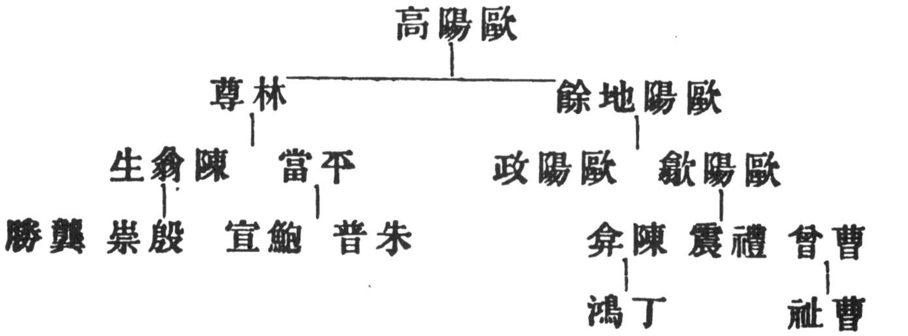

9 夏侯都尉, 魯人. 10 夏侯勝 11 大小夏侯氏章句二十九卷. 12 號爲大夏侯氏學. 13 夏侯建. 14 大小夏侯解故二十九篇. 15 小夏侯氏學. 16 The Hea-how schools are thus exhibited. 17 The reign of the Emperor Hwae (懷) is known by the name of Yang-këa (永嘉). Maou Se-ho says:—及永嘉之亂, 歐陽, 大小夏侯, 尙書並亡.—The Hea-how Schools are thus represented:—

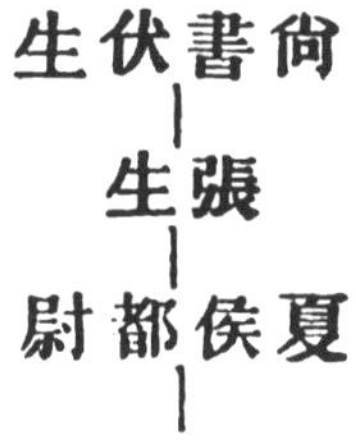

書經

The 'modern text,' therefore, and the views of the scholars who taught it, are now as a whole lost to literature. Under the reign of the emperor Ling, the last but one of the eastern Han, in A.D. 161, Tsae Yung, one of the chief scholars and officers of the time, had 'the modern text' of the Shoo, and the current text of several of the other classics, engraved on stone tablets, and set up with imperial sanction in one of the colleges in Lŏ. Of the tablets of the Shoo there remain only some shattered fragments, containing in all 547 characters.[18] But for the happier fate of the Books discovered about a century after Fuh-săng, of which we have now to speak, there would have remained but a tantalizing record of him, and some sporadic passages of his text gathered from the writings of various scholars. The Shoo had nearly been lost a second time, without any fires of Ts'in, through the natural process of decay, and the convulsions continually occurring in a distracted empire.

5. When the wrath of Ts'in was raging against the Shoo and all who dared to keep it in their possession, there were no doubt several who acted as Fuh-săng did, and hid away their tablets where they hoped to be able to find them and bring them forth at a future time. A descendant of Confucius had done so with the tablets containing the Shoo, the Le, the Classic of Filial Piety, and the Analects, concealing them in a wall of the house where the sage had lived, and which continued to be the home of the K'ung family.[1] But he never reclaimed them. They remained unknown, till towards the latter part of the reign of the emperor Woo. Then, as I have related in the *proleg.*

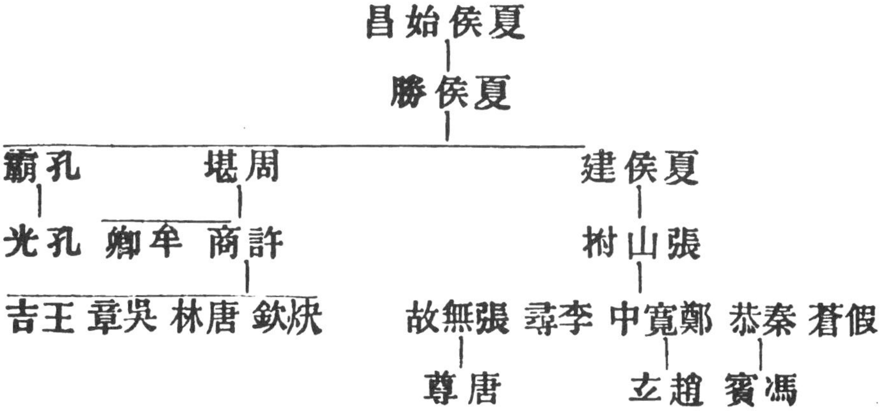

18 See the 隸釋 of 洪适景伯, 卷第十四, 石經尙書殘碑.

1 The name of this individual is not known. Sze-ma Ts'een does not give it. Gan-kwŏ simply says he was one of his forefathers. Some make him a 孔鮒; others a 孔騰 (which is most likely); and the Records of Suy say his name was 孔惠.

21]

to vol. I., pp. 12, 13, the king of Loo, a son of the emperor King, known to posterity by the honorary title of Kung, or 'The Respectful,'[2] was pulling down the house of the K'ung, to enlarge a palace of his own which was adjacent to it. In the wall were found the tablets, or what remained of the tablets, which have just been mentioned; and when the prince went into the hall or principal apartment of the building, he was saluted with strains of music from invisible instruments, which made him give up his purpose of demolition and appropriation. The chronicling of this marvellous circumstance might lead us to look suspiciously on the whole narrative; but the recovery of the tablets, and the delivery of them by the prince to the K'ung family, are things sufficiently attested.[3]

Discovery of the tablets of the Ancient Text.

The chief of the family at that time was K'ung Gan-kwŏ, one of the 'Great Scholars,' and otherwise an officer of distinction. The tablets were committed to his care. He found they were written or engraved in the old form of the characters, which he calls 'tadpole,' and which had long gone into disuse. By the help of Fuh-săng's Books, which were in the modern or current characters of the day, and other resources, he managed, however, to make them out, and found he had got a treasure indeed.—From the tablets of the Shoo he deciphered all the already recovered Books, with the exception of 'The Great Speech,' and of it there was the true copy. In addition he made out other five and twenty Books; and he found a preface containing the names of one hundred Books in all. The additional Books were:—'The Counsels of the great Yu;' 'The Songs of the Five Sons;' 'The Punitive Expedition of Yin;' 'The Announcement of Chung Hwuy;' 'The Announcement of T'ang;' 'The Instructions of E;' 'The T'ae Këă, in 3 Books;' 'Both possessed Pure Virtue;' 'The Charge to Yuĕ, in 3 Books;' 'The Great Speech, in 3 Books;' 'The Completion of the War;' 'The Hounds of Leu;' 'The Charge to the viscount of Wei;' 'The Charge to Chung of Ts'ae;' 'The Officers of Chow;' 'Keun-ch'in;' 'The Charge to *the duke of* Peih;' 'Keun-ya;' and 'the Charge to Keung.' Adding to these the 29 Books of Fuh-săng, and the Books which he had wrongly incorporated with others, and not counting Fuh's 'Great Speech,' we have 58 Books of the Shoo, which were now recovered.

K'ung Gan-kwŏ.

2 魯王共, 景帝子, 共(=恭)其謚也. 3 See 漢藝文志, upon the *Shoo*; Gan-kwŏ's Preface; and a hundred references in the Books of Han and subsequent dynasties. 4 科斗字.

書經

Gan-kwŏ himself reckoned the Preface one Book, and made out the number to be 59. Being all on the tablets in the old 'tadpole' characters, Gan-kwŏ's Books were described, in distinction from Fuh-săng's, as 'the ancient text.'[5]

6. When he had made out to read the tablets in the way which I have described, Gan-kwŏ presented them to the emperor, in B.C. 96, with a transcript in the current characters of the time,[1] keeping a second transcript of them for himself; and he received an order to make a commentary upon the whole.[2] He addressed himself to this work, and accomplished it, and was about to lay before the emperor the result of his studies, when troubles occurred at court, which prevented for a time any attention being paid to literary matters. In B.C. 91, some high officers became victims to a charge of practising magical arts. Next year the emperor fell sick, and a charlatan, named Keang Ch'ung, high in his confidence, and who had a feud with the heir-apparent, declared that the sickness was owing to magical attempts of the prince to compass his father's death. In preparation for this charge, he had contrived to hide a wooden image of the emperor in the prince's palace. An investigation was made. The image was found, and considered by the weak monarch to be proof positive of his son's guilt. The prince, indignant, procured the murder of his accuser, and liberated the felons and others in prison to make head against a force which was sent by the prime minister against him. Being defeated, he fled to the lake region in the south, and there killed himself.[4] The reader will be led by this account to think of the accounts which we have of diablerie and witchcraft in Europe at a later period, and will not wonder that Gan-kwŏ's commentary was neglected amid such scenes, and that the enlarged text which he had deciphered was not officially put in charge of the 'Great Scholars,' to

Gan-kwŏ's Commentary; and how it was not immediately made public.

5 Gan-kwŏ arranged the 58 Books in 46 *Keuen* (卷) or sections, with reference to the notices of them in the preface, where two or more Books are sometimes comprehended under one notice. They are mentioned also in Lew Hin's catalogue as 'the ancient text of the Shang Shoo, in 46 chapters' (尙書古文經, 四十六卷). They are also subsequently designated as 57 *p'ëen*, the 'Canon of Shun' having been supposed to be lost. Other enumerations are adduced and explained in the 1st chapter of Maou Se-ho's 'Wrongs of the Ancient Text.'

1 He tells us in his Preface that 'he wrote them moreover on bamboo tablets.' But he must have made two copies in the current character. If only the 'tadpole' tablets had been deposited in the imperial library, Lew Heang could not have compared them, as we shall find immediately that he did, with Fuh-săng's Books.

2 承詔爲五十九篇作傳.

3 江充.

4 See K'ung Ying-tă's notes on Gan-kwŏ's Preface, towards the conclusion; 通鑑綱目, on the 1st and 2d of the years 征和; and Maou's 'Wrongs of the Shoo,' Ch. II., pp. 5, 6.

whom had been given in the 5th year of Woo (B.C. 135) the care of the five King.[5] Soon after, moreover, Gan-kwŏ himself died, and it was long before his commentary obtained the imperial recognition and sanction.

History of Gan-kwŏ's commentary.

7. Happily, Gan-kwŏ's commentary, though it was not publicly recognised, was not lost. The critics have clearly traced its transmission through the hands of various scholars. The recipient of it from Gan-kwŏ was a Too-wei Chaou,[1] from whom it passed to Yung T'an of Këaou-tung.[2] A Hoo Chang of Ts'ing-ho[3] obtained it from Yung T'an, and passed it on to Seu Gaou of K'wŏ,[4] who delivered it to two disciples,—Wang Hwang,[5] and T'oo Yun.[6] From the latter of these it was received by Shing (or Shwang) K'in of Ho-nan.[7]

The editors of Yung-ching's Shoo, having arrived step by step at Shing K'in, then state that, in the close of the western Han, during the usurpation of Mang (A.D. 9–22), the school of 'the ancient text' was established along with that of Fuh-săng, and that Wang Hwang and T'oo Yun were held in great honour.[8] From this they make a great leap over the dynasties of the Eastern Han, the after Han, and the Western Tsin, to the first reign of the Eastern Tsin (A.D. 317–322), when Mei Tsih of Yu-chang presented to the emperor Yuen a Memorial along with a copy of Gan-kwŏ's commentary. If it really were so, that we could discover no traces of the commentary during those 300 years, there would be ground both for surprise and suspicion on its unexpected re-appearance. But the case does not stand so.

Before taking up the transmission of the commentary on through the later dynasties of Han, and that of Tsin, I must say something more on the testimony which we have from Lew Hin as to the existence of the 'ancient text' in the imperial library, and also call attention to the confirmation which he gives of both text and commentary's being current among scholars outside the official Boards. Not only does he give 'the ancient text of the Shang Shoo, in

5 This neglect of the ancient text is commonly expressed by—未立于學官. The Books peculiar to it are also called in consequence—逸書, and sometimes 外書.

1 都尉朝. 2 膠東庸譚. Yung is commonly referred to as Yung-săng. 3 清河胡常; Chang was styled 少子. He was a 'Great Scholar,' and rose to higher office. 4 虢徐敖. Gaou was also an officer of distinction (右扶風掾). 5 王璜, a native of 琅邪. 6 塗惲, a native of 平陵, and styled 子眞. 7 乘 (al. 桑) 欽, styled 君長. 8 See their 綱領, 一, pp. 4, 5.

46 sections,' at the very top of the list of Books upon the Shoo in his catalogue; but he adds in a note, that his father Heang had compared this with the text of the classic taught by the schools of Gow-yang and of the greater and less Hea-how; that he had found one tablet or slip of the 'Announcement about Drunkenness' wanting, and two of the 'Announcement of Shaou;' that more than 700 characters were different from those in Fuh-săng's Books, and that individual characters were missing here and there to the amount of several tens. Further, in the reign of the emperor Gae (B.C. 5–A.D.), Hin proposed that the ancient text of the Shoo, Tso-k'ew's Ch'un Ts'ew, the She of Maou, and certain unrecognized portions of the Le, should all be publicly acknowledged, and taught and studied in the imperial college. The emperor referred the matter to the classical Board, which opposed Hin's wishes. Indignant, he addressed a letter to the members, which may still be read. It is too long for translation here as a whole; but it contains the following assertions important to my purpose;—that the ancient text of the Shoo, Maou's She and the Tso-chuen, were all in the library; that of the three the Shoo was the most important; *that Yung T'an of Keaou-tung had taught among the people a text corresponding to that in the library;* and that they, the appointed conservators and guardians of the monuments of antiquity, were acting very unworthily in not aiding him to place the texts in the position which was due to them. Hin's remonstrances were bitterly resented, and he would have come to serious damage but for the interference of the emperor in his favour.[9] He was obliged to drop his project; but we may conclude that his efforts were not without effect. It was probably owing to him, that, in the succeeding reign and the usurpation of Mang, with which the Former or Western Han terminated, the claims of the ancient text were acknowledged for a short time.[10]

Having thus strengthened the first links in the chain of evidence for the transmission of Gan-kwŏ's commentary, I go on to the times of the Eastern Han, which are a blank in the account given by the editors of Yung Ching's Shoo.

There was a scholar and officer, named Yin Min,[11] whose life extended over the first two reigns of the dynasty (A.D. 25–74). We

9 See the Memoir of Lew Hin in the 前漢書,楚元王,傳第六. 10 See Maou's Wrongs of the Shoo, III., p. 9. 11 尹敏. See the account of him in the 後漢書,儒林,列傳第六十九,尙.—初習歐陽上書,後受古文,兼善毛詩,穀梁,左氏春秋.

read that in his youth he was a follower of the school of Gow-yang, but afterwards obtained and preferred the ancient texts of the Shang Shoo, the She of Maou, and Tso-k'ew's Ch'un-ts'ew.

About the same time lived Chow Fang,[12] who obtained a copy of the ancient text, and composed 'Miscellaneous Records of the Shang Shoo, in 32 Books.'

In the next reign, and extending on to A.D. 124, we meet with a K'ung He,[13] the then chief of the K'ung family, in which, it is said, 'the ancient text had been handed down from Gan-kwŏ, from father to son, without break.'

Contemporary with He, and carrying the line on to nearly A.D. 150, was Yang Lun,[14] who at first, like Yin Min, was a learner in the Gow-yang School, but afterwards addicted himself to the ancient text, established himself somewhere in an island on a 'great marsh,' and gathered around him more than a thousand disciples.

For more than half a century, the Records seem to be silent on the subject of Gan-kwŏ's ancient text and commentary. We come to the period of the 'After Han,' or, as it is often designated, the period of the 'Three Kingdoms.' In the kingdom of Wei, its first scholar was Wang Suh,[15] whose active life extended from A.D. 221 to 256. He wrote 'Discussions on the Shang Shoo,' and 'a Commentary on the Shang Shoo of the Ancient Text,' portions of both of which were in the imperial library under the dynasty of Suy.[16] Suh is often claimed as having belonged to the school of Gan-kwŏ. The evidence for this is not conclusive. Another 'ancient text,' as we shall see presently, had become public. But the evidence is quite sufficient to show that Suh must have seen Gan-kwŏ's commentary, and had his views moulded by it.

Connecting the 'After Han' and the dynasty of Tsin, we have the name of Hwang-p'oo Meih,[17] whose researches into antiquity remain in the 'Chronicle of Emperors and Kings,'[18] which everywhere quotes the 58 Books of Gan-kwŏ's ancient text. Meih, we are told, was guided in his studies by a cousin of the name of Leang Lew;[19]

12 周防. The account of him follows that of Yin Min.—受古文尚書,撰尚書雜記,三十二篇. 13 孔僖. See the same chapter of the 東漢 Records.—自安國以下,世世傳古文不絕. 14 楊倫. His biography follows that of K'ung He.—師事司徒丁鴻,習古文尚書,講學大澤中,弟子至千餘. 15 魏王肅. 16 尚書駁議;隋志五卷. 古文尚書注;隋志十一卷. 17 皇甫謐. 18 帝王世紀. 19 See the account of Meih, in the Books of Tsin, 列傳,第二十一卷.—謐從姑子外弟梁柳.

and this Lew, we know from another source, possessed Gan-kwŏ's text and commentary. The Records of Tsin are now mutilated. They contain no chapter on Books and Literature like those of Han and other dynasties, and are otherwise defective. It was not always so, however. K'ung Ying-tă quotes a passage, which distinctly traces the ancient text from the time of Wei down to Mei Tsih.[20] 'Ch'ing Ch'ung,'[21] it is said, 'Grand-guardian of Tsin, delivered the Shang Shoo in the ancient text to Soo Yu of Foo-fung;[22] Soo Yu delivered it to Leang Lew of T'een-shwuy [this was the cousin of Hwang-p'oo Meih]; Lëang Lew, who was styled Hung-ke,[23] delivered it to Tsang Ts'aou of Ching-yang, styled Yen-ch'e;[24] Ts'aou delivered it to Mei Tsih of Joo-nan, styled Chung-chin, the chief magistrate of Yu-chang;[25] Tsih presented it to the emperor, and an order was given that it should be made public.'

The records of Suy confirm this account of the coming to light of Gan-kwŏ's text, and the authoritative recognition both of it and his commentary. They tell us that the old tablets (or the copy of them) 'had been preserved in the imperial library of Tsin, but that there was no commentary on them;' that 'in the time of the Eastern Tsin, Mei Tsih, having obtained the commentary of Gan-kwŏ, presented it;' and that 'thereupon the text and commentary had their place assigned them in the national college.'[26]

Having brought down thus far the history of Gan-kwŏ's commentary, I must leave it for a short space, to speak of another ancient text, which made its appearance in the time of the Eastern Han, and gave origin to a school which flourished for several centuries.

8. A scholar and officer, named Too Lin,[1] had been a fugitive, having many wonderful escapes, during the usurpation of Mang. While wandering in Se-chow, he discovered a portion of the Shoo

20 See Ying-tă's long annotation on the title of the Canon of Yaou, on the last page. 21 鄭冲. He attained the dignity of Grand-guardian in A.D. 254. 22 扶風蘇愉. He was styled Hew-yu (休愉), and had high rank in the period Heen-he (咸熙), A. D. 264, 265. 23 梁柳字洪季. 24 城陽臧曹,字彥始. 25 汝南梅賾,字仲眞,眞爲豫章內史,遂于前晉,奏上其書,而施行焉. I have not translated 內史, the name of Tsih's office. I apprehend that at court he was a Recorder of the Interior, and was sent to Yu-chang, the present Keang-se, of which his father appears to have been governor. See the 晉職官志. 26 See 隋志,第二十七,經籍一.—晉世祕府所存,有古文尙書經文,今無有傳者,...至東晉豫章內史,梅賾始得安國之傳奏之,...於是始列國學.

1 杜林. See the account of him in the 後漢書,列傳,第十七卷.

on lacquered tablets in the ancient text,[2] which he so much prized, that he guarded it as his richest treasure, and amid all his dangers always kept it near his person. Afterwards, when the empire was again settled by the first emperor of the Eastern Han, Lin became acquainted with Wei Wang and other scholars. Showing them his discovery, he said, 'In my wanderings and perils I have been afraid that this text would be lost, but now it will be cared for and transmitted by you, and its lessons will not fall to the ground. The ancient text is not, indeed, at present authorised, but I hope you will not repent of what you learn from me.' Wei Wang, we are told, set great store by the Books he was thus made acquainted with, and he composed his 'Explanations of the Meaning of the Shang Shoo,'[3] which were based on them.

Too Lin's lacquered Ancient Text; and the Scholars who commented on it.

Subsequently to Wei Wang, three most eminent scholars published their labours upon Lin's Books. At the close of the Literary Chronicle of the Eastern Han, Pt. I., it is said, 'Kea K'wei produced his "Explanations" of Lin's Books; Ma Yung, his "Commentary;" and Ch'ing Heuen his "Comments and Explanations." From this time the ancient text of the Shang Shoo became distinguished in the world.'[4]

K'wei's work was soon lost. It was in three sections, was undertaken by order of the emperor Chang[5] (A.D. 76–88), and was designed to show wherein Lin's Books agreed with or differed from those of Fuh-săng.[6] Ma Yung's work was existing—a portion of it at least—in the Suy dynasty, in 11 *Keuen*. Heuen published more than one work on the Shoo. The library of Suy contained 'nine *Keuen* of the Shang Shoo,' and three *Keuen* of a 'Great Commentary on the Shang Shoo.'[7] They must have been existing later, for nearly all that we know of them is through quotations made by K'ung Ying-tă and Luh Tih-ming of the T'ang dynasty;—we find them indeed in the Catalogues of T'ang. They are now lost, and have gone, with scores of other works on the Shoo, whose names

2 于西州得漆書古文尙書一卷. There is a difficulty in my mind about Lin's Books being all in one *Keuen*. How are we to understand that term? 3 尙書訓旨. The memoir of Wang, in the 後漢書, says expressly—從杜林受古文尙書,爲作訓旨. 4 杜林得古文尙書,林同郡賈逵爲之作訓,馬融作傳,鄭玄注解,由是古文遂顯於世. 5 肅宗孝章皇帝. 6 Its full title was—尙書古文同異. 7 尙書大傳三卷.

書經

might be picked out in the Han and other chronicles, into the gulf of devouring time.

The 'lacquered' Books, as we learn from Ying-tă,[8] amounted to the same number as Gan-kwŏ's, though they were not all the same as his. They were:—'The Canon of Yaou;' 'The Canon of Shun;' 'The Counsels of the 'Great Yu;' 'The Counsels of Kaou-yaou;' 'The Yih and Tseih;' 'The Tribute of Yu;' 'The Speech at Kan;' 'The Songs of the Five Sons;' 'The Punitive Expedition of Yin;' '*The Kwuh Tsŏ;*' '*The Kew Kung, in nine Books;*' 'The Speech of T'ang;' '*The Teen Paou;*' 'The Announcement of T'ang;' 'Both possessed Pure Virtue;' 'The Instructions of E;' '*The Sze Ming;*' '*The Yuen Ming;*' 'The Pwan-kăng in 3 Books;' 'The Day of the Supplementary Sacrifice of Kaou-tsung;' 'The Conquest of Le by the Chief of the West;' 'The Viscount of Wei;' 'The Great Speech, in 3 Books;' 'The Speech at Muh;' 'The Completion of the War;' 'The Great Plan;' 'The Hounds of Leu;' 'The Metal-bound Coffer;' 'The Great Announcement;' 'The Announcement to K'ang;' 'The Announcement about Drunkenness;' 'The Timber of the Tsze tree;' 'The Announcement of Shaou;' 'The Announcement about Lŏ;' 'The Numerous Officers;' 'Against Luxurious Ease;' 'The Prince Shih;' 'The Numerous Regions;' 'The Establishment of Government;' 'The Testamentary Charge;' 'The Announcement of King K'ang;' 'The Charge to Keung;' 'The Speech at Pe;' 'The Charge to the Prince Wăn;' 'Leu on Punishments;' and 'The Speech of the Duke of Ts'in.'

I have put in italics the Books of Too Lin which were different from those of Gan-kwŏ, amounting to thirteen. An equal number of Gan-kwŏ's were wanting,—'The Announcement,' namely, 'of Chung Hwuy;' 'The T'ae Këă, in 3 Books;' 'The Charge to Yuĕ, in 3 Books;' 'The Charge to the Viscount of Wei;' 'The Charge to Chung of Ts'ae, 'The Officers of Chow;' 'The Keun-ch'in;' 'The Charge to Peih;' and 'The Keun-ya.'

Such were the Books of Too Lin, according to Ying Tă;[8] and on them Kea K'wei, Ma Yung and Ch'ing Heuen commented, according to the Records of Han. The authors of the Records of Suy repeat the latter statement, and immediately add:—'But the Books which they commented on, and handed down, were only 29. They mixed up with them, moreover, the modern text. They did not agree

8 See his notes at the commencement of the Shoo, in his explanation of the title 虞書.

with the ancient copy of K'ung Gan-kwŏ.'[9] There is a perplexity here, which I do not know how to disentangle. We hardly have a comment remaining from this Too-lin School on any Books but those of Fuh-săng! It professed to follow an 'ancient text,' and yet with that it mixed up 'the modern text!' Moreover, Ying-tă has preserved a portion of Ch'ing Heuen's preface to his Shoo, in which he professes himself to be a follower of Gan-kwŏ,[10] and yet his text and Books were different from Gan-kwŏ's! I confess that the 'lacquered' Books of Too Lin are a mystery to me, and as the writings of Kea, Ma, and Ch'ing upon the Shoo have all perished, we can never arrive at satisfactory conclusions about them. I will venture one speculation.—Gan-kwŏ tells us in his Preface, that after he had deciphered his 58 Books, there still remained some fragments of tablets, from which he could make out nothing worth preservation. Others may have attempted to do so, however. We know that a Chang Pa[11] pretended to have made out 100 Books. Now in Lew Hin's Catalogue, the last but one entry on the Shoo is—'Books of Chow, 71 *pëen*.' If we add to Gan-kwŏ's 58 Books, the 13 Too Lin, to which I have called attention above, we obtain the exact number of 71. Is it not a 'concatenation accordingly,' that the lacquered Books were a compilation from this collection? Whatever may be thought of this suggestion, it is plain to me that all which we read about Ch'ing Heuen and others does not affect the validity of the argument for the text and commentary first made public through Mei Tsih as the ancient text deciphered by Gan-kwŏ and the commentary upon it composed by him.

9. I resume the history of Gan-kwŏ's text and commentary, which, it has been seen, were at length publicly acknowledged in the reign of

9 然其—賈逵,馬融,鄭玄—所傳,唯二十九篇,又雜以今文,非孔舊本. 10 The passage is not easy of interpretation.—我先師棘下生子安國,亦好此學,自世祖興,後漢衞,賈,馬,二三君子之業,則雅才好博,既宣之矣,歐陽氏失其本義,今疾此蔽冒,猶疑惑未悛也. The student will see that Ch'ing disowns the schools of the modern text, and claims connection for himself, through Wei Wang, K'wei, and Ma Yung, with Gan-kwŏ. But all these commented on Too Lin's Books. Wang Ming-shing would get out of this difficulty by referring to the account of Kea K'wei in the Records of the Eastern Han, where it is said that 'his father received the ancient text of the Shoo from T'oo Yun,' and that 'K'wei continued to transmit his father's learning.' Thus there is record against record; or it may be that K'wei, like Wei Wang, abandoned his former studies of the Shoo, and addicted himself to Too Lin's Books. 11 張霸. See Maou's 'Wrongs of the Shoo,' Ch. II., p. 7.

書經

the first emperor of the Eastern Tsin (A.D. 317–322). The schools of the modern text had perished during the troubles of the period A.D. 307–312; there were now in the field only those of Ch'ing Heuen and Gan-kwŏ, and for some time they had nearly an equal course. The line of Tsin terminated in A.D. 420, and during 200 years which followed, the supremary of the empire was swayed by six different Houses. We learn from the Records of Suy, that under the dynasty of Ts'e (A.D. 480–502), the followers of Ch'ing greatly predominated;[1] that under those of Leang (A.D. 503–557) and Ch'in, (A.D. 558–588) 'Kung and Ch'ing walked together,[2] and that the same continued under Suy (A.D. 589–617), the school of Ch'ing waxing smaller and smaller.[3]

History of Gan-kwŏ's commentary resumed.

An interregnum of a few years ensued, till the authority of T'ang was acknowledged in A.D. 624, and the empire was united as it had not been since the times of Han. The second emperor of T'ang gave orders for a grand edition of the Shoo, under the superintendence of K'ung Ying-tă, assisted by the principal scholars and officers of the time. They adopted the commentary of Gan-kwŏ, and enriched it with profuse annotations. Their work was ordered to be printed in the 5th year of the third emperor, A.D. 654, and appeared with the title of 'The Correct Meaning of the Shang Shoo, by K'ung Ying-tă and others.'[4] It remains, happily, to the present day. Choo E-tsun gives the titles of about seventy commentaries and other writings upon the Shoo published from the time of Fuh-săng to the T'ang dynasty, of which not one now exists but the commentary of Gan-kwŏ, and it might have disappeared like the rest, if it had not been embodied in the work of Ying-tă. I have indicated my doubts in the former section whether Confucius compiled the Books of the Shoo;—it is certainly to two of his descendants that we are indebted for the recovery and preservation of those of them which are still in our possession.

An important measure with regard to the form of the characters in the text was taken in A.D. 744, by the 6th of the T'ang emperors. Up to that time the text had appeared in the style of the public courts of Han, in which Gan-kwŏ had represented the ancient 'tadpole' characters. The emperor Heaou Ming ordered a Board of Scholars, under the presidency of a Wei Paou,[1] to substitute for

[1] 齊代唯傳鄭義. [2] 梁陳所講,有孔鄭二家. [3] 至隋孔鄭並行,而鄭氏甚微. [4] 孔氏穎達等尚書正義.

[1] 衛包.

this the form which was current in his day, and there appeared 'The Shang Shoo in the Modern Text,' in 13 *keuen*.'[2] The designation of this edition as 'the modern text' is unfortunate, as the student may be led to confound it with the Books of Fuh-săng.[3] But from this time the distinction between the ancient and the modern texts virtually ceased. Fuh-săng's Books, with the exception of his 'Great Speech,' were all comprehended among the 58 Books of Gan-kwŏ, which had now got the field entirely to themselves. All through the T'ang, and on through the period of the 'Five Dynasties' (A.D. 908–974), no scholar doubted but that he had, through the work of Ying-tă, the Books which had been found more than a thousand years before in the wall of Confucius' house.

The sovereignty of the dynasty of Sung dates from A.D. 975, and it lasted for 305 years. It was a period of great mental activity, a protracted Augustan age of Chinese literature. The writers of Sung quoted by the editors of Yung-ching's Shoo amount to 110. The greatest name among them is that of Choo He, who was born in A.D. 1,130. And he is remarkable in connection with the Shoo, for having doubted the authenticity of the Books and commentary ascribed to Gan-kwŏ. In the next section, I shall consider the grounds of his doubts. Up to his time, the authority both of Books and commentary was unchallenged. If some suspicions were entertained, it can hardly be said that they found articulate expression.[4]

While many of the writings on the Shoo in the first half of this period have perished, there still remain sufficient to prove abundantly the learning and ability which were brought to the illustration of the classic. There are the Works of Soo Shih,[5] of Lin Che-k'e,[6]

2 唐孝明皇帝今文尚書,十三卷. 3 Ma Twan-lin clearly explains the change which was thus made:—按漢儒林傳,孔氏有古文尚書,孔安國以今文讀之,唐藝文志有今文尚書十三卷,注言玄宗詔集賢學士,衞包改古文從今文,然則漢之所謂古文者,科斗字今文者隸書也,唐之所謂古文者,隸書,今文者世所通用之俗字也. 4 See last note in the 書經傳說綱領,—where Ch'in Te (陳第), of the Ming dynasty, is quoted, to the effect that Woo Ts'ae-laou (吳才老) anterior to Choo He, was the first to point out the difference between the style of Gan-kwŏ's Books and the others. 5 蘇軾, styled Tung-po (東坡), *al.* Tsze-chen (子瞻), *al.* Mei-shan (眉山). He published 書傳十三卷. 6 林之奇, styled Shaou-ying (少穎), and San-san (三山). His 'Collected Explanations of the Shang-shoo' (尚書集解) was in 58 *keuen*. I can speak of its thoroughness, having read and re-read it.

書經

of Ch'ing Tseaou,[7] of Hea Scen,[8] of Leu Tsoo-heen,[9] and of others not a few.

Of the Books of the Shoo which were never even partially recovered. Had they not perished before the Ts'in dynasty?

10. We found above that, taking together the Books of Gan-kwŏ, and 13 others which were in the catalogue of those of Too Lin, we had in all 71 Books of the Shoo, which were recovered nominally (to say the least) after the fires of Ts'in. There remain 29 Books of the hundred mentioned in the Preface spoken of in the last section. I there suggested (p. 9) that portions might have been cast out or lost from the Collection of Historical Writings before the time of Ts'in. The titles of those 29 were:—'The Kaou Yu;' 'The Le Kuh;' 'The Le Yuh;' 'The Punitive Expeditions of T'ang;' 'The Joo Kew;' 'The Joo Fang;' 'The Hea Shay;' 'The E Che;' 'The Chin Hoo;' 'The Ming Keu;' 'The Tsoo How;' 'The Yuh-ting;' 'The Heen E, in 4 Books;' 'The E Chih;' 'The Chung-ting;' 'The Ho Tan-keă;' 'The Tsoo-yih;' 'The Instructions of Kaou-tsung;' 'The Fun K'e;' 'The Ch'aou Ming;' 'The Kwei Ho;' 'The Kea Ho;' 'The Government of King Ching;' 'The Tsëang Poo-koo;' 'The Charge to Suh-shin, with Presents;' and 'The Pŏ-koo.'

In regard to these titles, it is to be observed, that, where they are not simply names of emperors or ministers, the information given about them in the notices of the preface is so scanty, that there are several of them which we cannot venture to translate. Ts'ae Ch'in, as quoted on p. 9, has called attention to this, saying that on the Books which are lost the Preface is so servile and brief that it does not afford us the slightest assistance. He thence draws the conclusion that the Preface could not be the work of Confucius. Granted; but I draw a further inference, that whensoever and by whomsoever the Preface was made, the author could not have had those Books entire before him. If he had, it is inexplicable that he should not have told us as much about them as he has done generally of the others which still remain. The statement of Gan-kwŏ, that the tablets of the Preface were found with the others in the wall of Confucius' house, is not to be called in question. It was made therefore before the burning of the Books,—and when it was made, there

7 鄭樵, styled Yu-chung (漁仲), and Keă-tse (夾漈). 8 夏僎 styled Yuen-suh (元肅), and K'o-shan (柯山). He produced 'Explanations of the Shang Shoo (尙書解),' in 16 *keuen*. 9 呂祖謙, styled Pih-kung (伯恭) and Tung-lae (東萊). His 'Talkings on the Shoo' (書說) was in 35 chapters.

were existing of many of the *p'een* no more than what now exists—merely the names.

Further, some (seven at least) of the missing Books,—the Heen E, the Kwei Ho, and the Kea Ho—had reference to freaks or prodigies of nature,—'extraordinary things,' of which Confucius did not talk.[1] We may assume that he would not have introduced such Books into a Canon of Historical Documents; and I argue besides, that they had fallen into deserved neglect before the time of Ts'in. The good sense of scholars had seen their incongruity with the other documents of the Shoo, and they had been imperceptibly consigned to oblivion. Add to these considerations, that we have hardly a single sentence in Mencius, the Le, Seun-tsze, or any other writings claiming to be as old as the Chow dynasty, taken from the missing Books, and my conclusion is greatly strengthened, that we have not lost by the fires of Ts'in so much of the Shoo as is commonly supposed.

It is by no means certain that the Canon did not at one time contain more than the hundred Books mentioned in the Preface. It is to me more than probable that it did not contain the whole even of them, when the edict of the Ts'in emperor went forth against it. Of all that appeared for a time to be lost in consequence of the edict much the larger portion was ultimately recovered.

1 Ana. VII. xx.

SECTION III.

From Choo He to the present day.—

Doubts thrown on the Books peculiar to Gan-kwŏ's text and on his Commentary; which, however, are to be received.

1. The editors of Yung-ching's Shoo give the names of 115 scholars of the Yuen (A.D. 1,280–1,367) and Ming (A.D. 1,368–1,644) dynasties, of whose labours they make use in their annotations; and Choo E-tsun, bringing his researches into the last century, enumerates the titles of more than 350 Works upon the classic, from Choo He downwards.

The many Works published on the Shoo, since the time of Choo He.

書經

All these Writings have the whole of the Shoo, or as much as their authors acknowledged to be genuine, for their subject. On particular Books, especially the two Canons, the Tribute of Yu, and the Great Plan, about 200 works have been published during the same time. All this shows how the Shoo continues to hold its place in the minds of the Chinese. Its very difficulties seem to fascinate the scholars, who for the most part repeat one another sadly; but now and then, we find a commentator who endeavours to shake off the trammels of Choo He, and to look on the ancient document with his own eyes.

Choo He did not himself comment on the Shoo.

2. Choo He did not himself publish a complete commentary on the Shoo. He edited, indeed, a copy of the classic, containing the 58 Books of Gan-kwŏ, and the Preface as a separate *p'ëen*.[1] We have also his 'Remarks upon the Shoo,'[2] collected and published by some of his disciples; but they are mostly confined to the Canons, the Counsels of Yu, the Announcement of Shaou, the Announcement about Lŏ, and the Metal-bound Coffer. He had come to entertain very serious doubts as to the authenticity of Gan-kwŏ's commentary, and of the Books additional to Fuh-săng's; and he was painfully impressed with the difficulties of the text even in Fuh-săng's Books,—its errors, transpositions, and deficiencies. He shrank, therefore, from the task of attempting for the Shoo what he had done for the other classics, and in A.D. 1,199, the year before his death, devolved it on Ts'ae Ch'in, one of his favourite disciples, to make 'A Collection of Comments on the Shoo,'[3] instructing him to revive the distinction of 'modern text' and 'ancient text,' and to indicate by those names the relation of each Book to Fuh-săng or to Gan-kwŏ.

The Commentary of Ts'ae.

Ts'ae Ch'in undertook the labour, and completed it in ten years. His commentary appeared in 1,210, and at once attracted general admiration. After K'ung Ying-tă's 'Correct Meaning,' it was certainly the most important work which had been produced upon the Shoo. Nor has it been superseded. It remains to the present day the standard of orthodoxy, and is universally studied throughout the empire. To give only one eulogium of it.—Ho K'eaou-sin,[4] of the Ming dynasty, says:—'From the Han downwards, the works upon the Shoo had been many.

1 尙書古經. E-tsun says he had not seen this work (未見). It was, no doubt, the text adopted by He's disciple, Ts'ae Ch'in. 2 書說. 3 Ts'ae says in his preface:—慶元己未冬,先生文公命沈作書集傳. 4 何喬新. See the 經義考,書十一, p. 4.

But in the comments of Gan-kwŏ there is often much violence done to the text, which the amplifications of Ying-tă labour to sustain. Choo He had a great esteem for the views of Wang Gan-shih,[5] Leu Tsoo-heen, Soo Shih, and Lin Che-k'e; but the first of them errs in forced meanings, the second in excessive ingenuity, the third in summariness, and the fourth in tediousness. When the "Collected Comments" of Ts'ae came forth, distinguishing what Books were peculiar to the modern, and what to the ancient text, and what were common to both, and discussing also the forged prefaces, both the Great one, and the Little, then the grand principles and the grand laws of the two emperors and the three kings were brilliantly displayed to the world.' The scholars of China would deem me but a lukewarm admirer of their model commentator. I have often thought him deficient both in comprehension and discrimination, and prefer to him Lin Che-k'e, tedious as he is said to be. Ts'ae's distinguishing merit is his style, which will often bear comparison, for clearness and grace, with that of Choo He himself.

The Ancient Text and Gan-kwŏ's Commentary still more doubted in the Yuen, Ming, and present dynasties.

3. Choo He's doubts about the authenticity of the Books and commentary ascribed to Gan-kwŏ were plainly enough indicated; but his expression of them was not very decided. The suspicion, once given out by such an authority, went on to grow. Under the Yuen dynasty, about the beginning of the 14th century, Woo Ch'ing published his 'Digest of Remarks on the Shang Shoo.'[1] The Work, so for as it goes, is well worthy of study. Ch'ing was a bold thinker and a daring critic. He handled the text with a freedom which I have not elsewhere seen. But his Work contains none of the Books which were deciphered by Gan-kwŏ. He rejects also the 'Great Speech' which Fuh-săng gave, believing that it was not originally among his Books, and confines himself to the other 28, which he believes are all of the Shoo that we now have.

Under the Ming dynasty, many critics followed in the wake of Woo Ch'ing. Kwei Yew-kwang,[2] and Shih King,[3] may be particularly

5 王安石. He was contemporary with Soo Shih, and, in every respect one of the ablest men of his day. His views were published by his son Wang Fang (王雱). E-tsun gives the work as 王氏安石子雱,新經尙書義. It was in 13 *keuen*, and is unfortunately lost.

1 尙書纂言. Woo Ch'ing (吳澄) is variously styled,—幼淸,草廬, and 臨川. 2 歸有光, styled 熙甫, and 震川. 3 郝敬, styled 仲輿, and 京山.

書經

mentioned. The former tells us that from his youth he had doubted 'all the talk about modern text and ancient text,' and that, afterwards, having met with some dissertations of Woo Ch'ing, he was delighted with the agreement of their views, and tried to obtain the Work of Woo mentioned above. Disappointed in this, he published Fuh-săng's Books with his own commentary, and prefixed the dissertations of Woo.[4] The latter published 'Discussions on and Explanations of the Shang Shoo,'[5] in ten *keuen*. He does not appear to have seen Woo Ch'ing's Writings; but he goes beyond him in his animosity to the ancient text and commentary. In eight of his *keuen*, he explains Fuh-săng's Books; the remaining two are devoted to an exposure (as he thinks) of the falsehood of the ancient text. So strongly had the views of these and other critics taken possession of the scholars of Ming, that in A.D. 1,643 a memorial was presented to the emperor Chwang-lëë,[6] praying that the Books peculiar to the ancient text might be cast out, and the subjects at the competitive examinations be taken only from Fuh-săng's. The dynasty was in its death-throes. The poor emperor had his hands and head more than full with the invading Manchoos; and while the empire passed from his sway, the ancient text was allowed to keep its place.

Under the present dynasty, the current of opinion seems to run, as in the Ming, against the Books, Commentary, and Preface ascribed to Gan-kwŏ. The works of Wang Ming-shing and Keang Shing, of which I have made much use in my notes, speak in almost every page, in the most unmeasured terms, of 'the false K'ung.' The ancient text, however, is not without its defenders. So far as the government is concerned, things remain as they have been since the T'ang dynasty. The editors of Yung-ching's Shoo do not take up the argument. They give prominence, indeed, in their Introduction, to the opinions of Choo He and his followers, but pass no judgment of their own; and they use equal care in unfolding the meaning of the suspected portions, and of those which all acknowledge.

4. I shall conclude this chapter on the history of the Shoo with an exposition of the grounds on which I cherish for myself a confidence in the authenticity of the ancient text and Gan-kwŏ's commentary on it, and some discussion of the principal arguments advanced on the other side. Minor arguments, based on the language

4 The title of his Work is 尙書叙錄. 5 尙書辨解. 6 莊烈愍皇帝, A.D. 1628-1643. 7 See Maou's Wrongs of the Shoo, Ch. I. p. 1.

of particular passages in the Books, have been noticed in the notes upon them in the body of the Work.

[i.] With regard to the Commentary,—the controversy about it has not to a foreigner the interest or importance which it has to a Chinese. Suppose that it really was not the production of Gan-kwŏ, yet there it was, actually existing in the beginning of our 4th century. No one can tell who composed it. Mei Tsih presented it to the emperor Yuen, and it received the authoritative acknowledgment. Tsih did not claim it as his own. He said it was the commentary of K'ung Gan-kwŏ, which had been handed down from one scholar to another for nearly four hundred years. Once made public, it ere long became the standard explanation of the classic; and its authority was unchallenged for more than eight hundred years. We are indebted to the annotations of the T'ang scholars upon it for most of what we know of the views of Ma Yung, Ch'ing Heuen, and other commentators of the Han dynasties. Whether it was written by the true K'ung, or by a false K'ung, it is a work the value of which cannot be over-estimated.

With regard to the Books themselves,—they are supported largely by the quotations from them which occur in the Analects, Mencius, Shih-tsze, Seun-tsze, and other Writings. I have been careful to point out this in the notes upon the several Books. A considerable portion of some of them is in this way guaranteed to us. The Books of the New Testament are not better attested by the citations from them in the works of the early Christian Fathers.

The opponents of the authenticity explain this by asserting that 'the false K'ung' carefully gathered out all the passages of the Shoo which were anywhere quoted, and wove them, along with the other materials of his own devising, so as to form the present Books. But this is only their hypothesis, and a very clumsy and unlikely hypothesis it is. On the one hand, it makes the forger to have been a scholar of very great learning and research; so much so, that we are unwilling to believe that such a man could have stooped to a fraudulent attempt. On the other hand, it makes peculiarities, most natural if we admit the Books, to be silly contrivances to avert the suspicion of forgery. For instance, the text of a passage in the Books and of the same passage as quoted by Mencius has certain verbal differences. An easy explanation presents itself. Mencius was not concerned to be verbally accurate. He was sufficiently so for his purpose. It may even have suited him better to quote according to

書經

the sense than exactly according to the letter. But the hypothesis of which I am speaking requires a different explanation. The 'false K'ung' quoted from Mencius, and purposely altered his text in order to escape detection! This may be said; but it is unlikely in the highest degree. The Books have been subjected to the severest ordeal of unkindly criticism; and to me it is incomparably easier to believe their authenticity than to admit the arguments advanced against them.

[ii.] 'The Books of K'ung first appeared in the time of the Eastern Tsin. No scholars had seen them before that time. This circumstance is a very strong indication of forgery.' So said Choo He; and his assertions are repeated *ad nauseam* to the present time. But the history of the Books and Commentary which I gave in the last section furnishes a sufficient reply to them.

There were at one time, it is admitted on nearly all hands, both the Books and Commentary;—in the reign of the emperor Woo of the first Han. What is alleged, is that these were not the same as those which were made public by means of Mei Tsih. Well:—as to the Books. When Gan-kwŏ had deciphered them, he presented them to the emperor, and they were placed in the imperial library. There they were nearly a hundred years after, when Lew Hin made his catalogues. Hin's father compared their text with that of Fuh-săng's Books, and noted the differences between them. Hin himself endeavoured to have them made the subject of study equally with the smaller collection of Fuh-săng. They continued in the imperial library on to the time of the Eastern Tsin. They were there when Mei Tsih presented both the Books and the Commentary which he had received from Tsang Ts'aou. So the Records of Suy expressly testify. The Books received permanently the authoritative recognition due to them, and were commanded to be studied in the national college, in the time of the Eastern Tsin; but they had been lying on the shelves of the imperial library from the time of Gan-kwŏ downwards. They were not seen or not studied simply because the Government had not required them to be so. Next:—as to the Commentary. That Gan-kwŏ did write a commentary on his 58 Books is allowed, and its transmission is traced from scholar to scholar on into the Eastern Han. When did it perish? There is no intimation that it ever did so. On the contrary, I have shown above, pp. 25–27, that its existence rises as a fact, here and there, at no great intervals of time, on the surface of the literary history of the empire, till we arrive at Mei Tsih. Tsih received 'The Shang Shoo in the ancient text' from Tsang Ts'aou. That Shang Shoo comprehended both Gan-kwŏ's transcript of the text and his commentary. The Records of Sung are decisive on this point.

'But,' the adverse critics persist in alleging,—'but Ch'ing Heuen and Ma Yung, Ch'aou K'e[1] in his comments on Mencius, Wei Ch'aou on the Kwŏ Joo,[2] and Too Yu on the Tso-chuen, when they have to speak of any of the Books peculiar to the ancient text, call them "*Yih Shoo.*"'[3] And they could not otherwise designate them. They had not seen them themselves. They do not call them "*Wang Shoo,*"[4] which would mean *Lost* or *Perished Books.* All that '*Yih Shoo*' denotes, is that the Books were lying concealed, and had no place among the studies in the national college.[5]

It is urged again, 'But if Yin Min, K'ung He, and other scholars, were really in possession of Gan-kwŏ's Books and Commentary, why did they not bring them to the notice of the court, and get them publicly acknowledged before the time of the eastern Tsin?' The argument in this question has been much pressed on me by Wang T'aou, of whom I have spoken in the preface. But there is little weight in it. We know that the attempt of Lew Hin to obtain the recognition both of Books and Commentary was defeated, and he himself obliged, in consequence of it, to retire from court. If we knew all the circumstances of K'ung He and other scholars and of their times, we should probably cease to wonder at their being content to keep their treasures in their own possession. For every event there are in providence the time and the man.

[iii.] 'In the catalogue of Lew Hin, we have the entries:—"Of the Shang Shoo 29 *p'een,*"[6] and "Of Old King 16 *keuen.*"[7] Those old *King* were false Books of the Han times, and were distinguished from the true Books of the Shoo by the carefulness of the Han scholars.' So says Kwei Yew-kwang;—by the strangest misreading of his authority. The words of the catalogue are:—'Of the Shang

1 See the proleg. to vol. II., pp. 4–7. 2 韋昭. Both he and Too Yu were of the Western Tsin. 3 逸書. 4 亡書. 5 See Maou K'e-ling on the meaning of the phrase 逸書 in his 'Wrongs of the Shoo,' Ch. III. p. 4. 6 Wang T'aou writes:—漢書有載，孔僖家有古文尚書，世世相傳，亦載僖子季彥，獨治古義，不在科第之例，而世人莫識，則當肅宗時，何不上進乎，何以謹藏于家，使世不知也. 7 藝文志有尚書二十九篇，古經十六卷. See Yew-kwang's preface, quoted in the 經義考，書十八.

40]

Shoo in the ancient text 46 *keuen*,' and 'Of *King* 29 *keuen*.'[8] Gan-kwŏ's Books and Fuh-săng's are mentioned in the order and manner exactly the opposite of what the critic asserts. If we were to argue from this (which it would be absurd to do) after his fashion, we should say that the Han scholars indicated their confidence in the Books of the ancient text, and their suspicion of Fuh-săng's.

[iv.] 'As compared with Fuh-săng's Books, those peculiar to Gan-kwŏ are much more easily read. The style is so different, that even a tyro is conscious of it. This circumstance is sufficient to awaken suspicions of the latter.' This difference of the texts was first noticed particularly by Woo Ts'ae-laou, who said:—'In the additional Books of Gan-kwŏ, the style flows easily and the characters have their natural significations. It is otherwise with the Books of Fuh-săng, which are so involved and rugged, that it is sometimes not possible to make them out.'[9] Choo He dwelt on the point, and insinuated the conclusion to which it should lead. He had probably spoken more strongly on the subject than he has written, for Ts'ae Ch'in expresses his opinion against the authenticity of Gan-kwŏ's Books very decidedly. 'Fuh-săng,' says he, 'reciting the text, and crooning it over as in the dark, yet strangely managed to give the difficult Books; and Gan-kwŏ examining and deciding among his tadpole tablets, all in confusion and mutilated, only made out those which were easy! This is inexplicable.'[10] Woo Ch'ing and a hundred others follow in a similar strain.

The difference alleged between the texts must be admitted to a considerable extent. There are differences, however, likewise among the Books of Fuh-săng. The difficulty of reading and interpreting the Pwan-kang and the Announcements in the Books of Chow cannot be exaggerated. They have often been to myself an *infandus dolor*. The Canons, on the other hand, are much easier; and some of the other Books are hardly more difficult than the Books of Gan-kwŏ. Nor are *his* Books really easy. They only appear to be so, where we come to one of them, after toiling through some of the more contorted portions common to both texts.

8 尙書古文經,四十六卷;經二十九卷 There is added 傳四十一篇. See above, p. 19. 9 安國所增多之書,皆文從字順,非若伏生之書,詰曲聱牙,至有不可讀者 10 伏生背文暗誦,乃偏得其所難,而安國考定于科斗古書,錯亂磨滅之餘,反專得其所易,則有不可曉者.

Moreover, the style of the Books differs according to their subjects. The Announcements are the hardest to understand of all. The Charges, Speeches, and Instructions are much simpler; and the Books which we owe to Gan-kwŏ consist principally of those. Perhaps he did polish somewhat in his transcription of them. In making out his tadpole tablets, he was in the first place obliged to make use of Fuh-săng's Books. But for them, which had been engraved happily in the newer form of the characters at a time when the knowledge of the ancient form was still possessed, the tablets from the wall of Confucius' house might have been of little use. That Gan-kwŏ did not servilely follow the 'modern text' we conclude from the readings of the schools of Gow-yang and Hea-how, different from his in many passages, which the industry of critics has gathered up; but as he had to learn from it to read the tablets submitted to him, we can understand how he would generally follow it, and take it often on trust, when he could not well tell what his own authority said. When he came, however, to new Books, which were not in Fuh-săng, the case was different. His aids had ceased. He had to make out the text for himself as he best could. I can conceive that, when he had managed to read the greater portion of a paragraph, and yet there were some stubborn characters which defied him, he completed it with characters of his own. That he was faithful and successful in the main is shown by the many passages of his Books that are found in other writings older than his time. But, however we endeavour to account for the smoother style and readier intelligibility of the portions of the Shoo which we owe to him, those characteristics of them are not, to my mind, sufficient to overthrow their claims on other grounds to be regarded as authentic.

[v.] 'The style of Gan-kwŏ's own preface is not like that in other writings of the Western Han. It resembles more the compositions of the Ts'in dynasty. The Little Preface, moreover, was unknown to Fuh-săng; and it savours of the style of the After Han.' Choo He thus expresses himself. The authenticity of the Books does not depend on that of either of the Prefaces; but the great critic certainly fell into a glaring error in ascribing the Little Preface to the time of the After Han. Nearly every sentence of it is found in the Records of Sze-ma Ts'een, a contemporary of Gan-kwŏ, and who, no doubt, had got it from him! Fuh-săng, indeed, was not possessed of it. He may never have had it. If he did have it before the edict against the Shoo, the tablets of it were lost in the same way as

書經

those of all the Shoo which he ever had excepting his 29 Books. 'It savours of the style of the After Han,' and yet we find it in a Work of the First Han, composed fully 300 years before the date which Choo He would assign to it:—this is a striking instance of the little reliance that can be placed on critical judgments, even of the most distinguished scholars, which are based on their taste in the matter of style.

As to the preface of Gan-kwŏ, we must pay the less attention to Choo He's attributing it, on the ground of its style, to the times of Tsin, after finding him so egregiously mistaken in his decision on the same ground about the other. Lew Hin, moreover, in his remarks on the Shoo, prefixed to his list of the Books of it in the imperial library, repeats the most important statements in the Preface, and nearly in its very words.

[vi.] 'Gan-kwŏ says, in his preface, that, when he had finished his commentary, the troubles connected with the practice of magical arts broke out, and he had no opportunity of getting the imperial sanction to his Work. Now all this must be false. We know from the Han Records, that the troubles referred to broke out in B.C. 91.[9] But Sze-ma Ts'een tells us that his Histories came no farther down than the period T'ae-ch'oo (B.C. 103–100).[10] At the conclusion of his account of the K'ung family, he speaks of Gan-kwŏ, saying, "He was one of the Great Scholars under the present reign, and died an early death, after being made guardian of Lin-hwae."[11] It follows that Gan-kwŏ was dead before the year B.C. 100. No troubles, therefore, happening ten years later, could affect him or any of his undertakings.' I do not know who first constructed this argument against the authenticity of Gan-kwŏ's preface, and, by implication, of his commentary; but Maou K'e-ling allows correctly that it displays much ingenuity. And yet there must be a flaw in it.

That the troubles spoken of prevented the recognition of Gan-kwŏ's commentary is asserted repeatedly in the Books of Han. From what source soever it arose, the persuasion that it was so with regard to Gan-kwŏ and his commentary, as his preface represents, has prevailed from the century in which he died down to the present time. If the matter can be decided on the *quod semper, ubique, et ab omnibus*

9 漢武帝紀,征和元年巫蠱起. 10 See the last words of Sze-ma Tseen's Preface, placed at the end of his histories.—大史公曰,余述黃帝以來,至太初而訖. 11 安國爲今皇帝博士,至臨淮大守早卒.

principle, then we must acknowledge the truth of the account given (professedly) by Gan-kwŏ of himself.

With regard to the statement of Sze-ma Ts'een, that his histories were not brought down lower than B.C. 100, there it is, standing out (in a strange way) at the end of the last chapter of his Records, which is a sort of epilogue to the rest. A close study of that chapter, however, has convinced me that he was labouring on his Records for years after B.C. 100, and that his terminating sentence must receive a different interpretation from that commonly put upon it.

In one place, Ts'een tells us that his Records brought the history down from Yaou to the year B.C. 121.[12]

He tells us again, that it was after the defeat sustained by Le Ling at the hands of the Huns, and when he himself endeavoured to appease the anger of the emperor against the unfortunate general, and was therefore put into prison,—that it was then that he addressed himself with redoubled energy to his work of historiography.[13] This date brings us to B.C. 97, three years later than the period *T'ae-ch'oo*.

Further, in the historical Records, there are various narratives and entries of things posterior to B.C. 100,—even narratives of things growing out of the magical delusions which came to a head in B.C. 91.[14] The statement which I have made, therefore, on p. 5, that Ts'een completed his Work in B.C. 96, though many of the critics so affirm, cannot be correct.

The various conflicting statements in Ts'een's Preface, and the later entries in his Records, may be in a measure reconciled in the following way.—At first it was not his intention to bring his history farther down than B.C. 121, in which case he would probably have done little more, in several divisions of the Records, than edit the materials collected by his father. Subsequently, he resolved to bring the history down to the period T'ae-ch'oo, which he did in his account of the emperor Woo. So long as he lived, moreover, he kept adding to his different memoirs, and hence we have the narrative of events which took place later than the year B.C. 91, when the troubles commenced, which prevented the imperial recognition of Gan-kwŏ's

12 於是卒述陶唐以來,至于麟止. See the 太史公自序, p. 6. The emperor Woo fancied that he had found a K'e-lin in B.C. 121, and thereon changed the style of the period from 元朔 to 元狩. 13 七年而大史公遭李陵之禍,幽於縲紲,乃喟然而歎曰,云云. See p. 5. 14 See the Wrongs of the Shoo, pp. 5, 6.

commentary. When he says that Gan-kwŏ died an early death in the reign of the emperor Woo, it does not follow that that event did not take place after the period of *T'ae-ch'oo.*[15]

Whatever may be thought of this suggestion, the statements in the Preface are so directly and repeatedly borne out by the Records of the Han dynasties, that we cannot but admit their verity.

[vii.] 'In the preface to the Shwŏ Wăn, Heu Shin says that his quotations from the Shoo King were taken from K'ung's Books. Yet the passages adduced are all from Fuh-săng's 28 Books, with only one exception. That one is from the Charge to Yuĕ, Pt. i., p. 8; and as it is given in Mencius, the probability is that Shin took it from him. How is it that the lexicographer could be using Gan-kwŏ's Books, and yet we should find in his Work only one doubtful quotation from all the 25 which were recovered by him additional to those of Fuh-săng?' I do not know who was the author of this difficulty; but a difficulty it certainly is. The Books of Gan-kwŏ were 58. Heu Shin says he used them, and yet he quotes only from the little more than one half of them which were common to the 'modern text.' Was there a copy current in Heu Shin's time of Fuh-săng's Books according to Gan-kwŏ's text, *i.e.*, with the different readings which he had preferred from his tablets? This would be one way of solving the difficulty. There is, however, another, which is on the whole to be preferred. Heu Shin undertook his dictionary, after Kea K'wei had declined the task. But in carrying through the work, he made constant reference to that scholar.[16] K'wei, we have seen, had adopted the Books of Too Lin. They were in an 'ancient text,' though different from that of Gan-kwŏ. Shin must have confounded the two, and supposed that, while he was really quoting from Too Lin, he was quoting from Gan-kwŏ. The Books of Too Lin, though not all the same as Gan-kwŏ's, were the same in number. How, even with them before him, Shin's quotations are only from the same Books as Fuh-săng's,—this still leaves the perplexity which I have pointed out above, in connection with the writings of Kea K'wei, Ma Yung, and Ch'ing Heuen.

5. The question of the authenticity of Gan-kwŏ's Books and commentary has now been sufficiently gone into. It had occurred

15 The year of Sze-ma Ts'een's death is disputed. It is often said to have taken place in the end of the emperor Woo's reign. Wang Ming-shing refers it, I think successfully, to the beginning of the next reign,—that of the emperor Ch'aou, B.C. 85–71. See the 十七史商榷, 卷一, p. 4.

16 See Maou's Wrongs of the Shoo, Ch. VII., p. 7-9.

to myself long ago that a complete copy of the Shoo, as it was before the time of the Ts'in dynasty, might possibly be found in Japan. I am pleased to discover that the same idea has been entertained at different times by Chinese scholars. Very decided expression was given to it in the 11th century by Gow-yang Sew,[1] from whom we have a song upon a 'Knife of Japan,' which concludes with :—

May the Shoo complete be yet found in Japan?

'When Seu Fuh went across the sea,
The books had not been burned;
And there the hundred *p'een* remain,
As in the waste inurned.

Strict laws forbid the sending them
Back to our Middle Land;
And thus it is that no one here
The old text has in hand.'[2]

The critics for the most part treat the idea with contempt; and yet in the year 1697, the 36th of K'ang-he, a petition was presented, requesting the emperor to appoint a commission to search for the Shang Shoo, beyond the seas.[3] Japan is now partially opened. By and by, when its language is well known, and access is had to all its literary stores, this matter will be settled.

1 歐陽修, styled 永叔. He died A.D. 1073. 2 All of the song which I have seen runs:—傳聞其國居大海, 土壤沃饒風俗好, 前朝貢獻屢往來, 士人往往工詞藻, 徐福行時書未焚, 逸書百篇今尙存, 令嚴不許傳中國, 舉世無人識古文. See the 經義考書二, p. 6. 3 See Wrongs of the Shoo, Ch. I., pp. 3, 4.

書經

CHAPTER II.

ON THE CREDIBILITY OF THE RECORDS IN THE SHOO.

THE FIRST AND SECOND PARTS ARE LESS RELIABLE THAN THE OTHER THREE, AND HAVE MUCH OF WHAT IS LEGENDARY IN THEM. OF YAOU, SHUN, AND YU, THE LAST IS TO BE REGARDED AS THE FOUNDER OF THE CHINESE EMPIRE. HIS GREAT LABOURS IN REGULATING THE WATERS AND SURVEYING AND DIVIDING THE LAND.

1. The conclusion to which I came in the last Chapter was, that in the 58 Books which now form the *textus receptus* of the Shoo, we have so much of the classic, as it existed in the end of the Chow dynasty. Through Fuh-săng first, and then through K'ung Gan-kwŏ, all this portion—a larger proportion of the whole than is generally supposed—was recovered within little more than a century of the time when the first emperor of Ts'in ordered that the books should be consigned to the flames, and about a century before our Christian era. There were no doubt mutilations and transpositions, as well as alterations of the ancient text, but they were not so great as to affect the substantial integrity of the book. In the subsequent transmission of the Shoo to the present day, the text has undergone the corruptions which are unavoidable to literary documents in their passage over so long a space of time; but the errors which have in this way crept in are not more, nor of more importance, than those which it is the object of critical inquiry to eliminate from our most valuable documents in the West.[1] There is really nothing seriously to shake our confidence in the eight and fifty Books of the Shoo which we have, as being substantially the same with those which were known to Seun-tsze, Mencius, Mih-tsze, Confucius himself, and others.

1 Not a few eminent Chinese critics have laboured to construct an accurate text. There is a large mass of materials in the 古文尚書撰異 of 段玉裁, to which I have made frequent reference; but it would have added too much to my labour, and not have repaid the time to gather up the various readings throughout.

We come now to inquire how far the documents of the Shoo can be relied on as genuine narratives of the events which they profess to relate. And it may be said at once, in reference to the greater number of them, that there is no reasonable ground on which to call them in question. Allowance must be made, indeed, for the colouring with which the founders of one dynasty set forth the misdeeds of the closing reigns of that which they were superseding. I have pointed out, moreover, in the notes on 'The Counsels of the Great Yu,' how the failures of a favourite hero may be glossed over, and actual defeat represented as glorious triumph. But the documents of the Shoo are better entitled, I conceive, to credit than the memorials which are published at the present time in the Peking Gazette.

Whether the documents of the Shoo are reliable or not.

The more recent they are, the more of course are they to be relied on. The Books of Chow were contemporaneous with the events which they describe, and became public property not long after their composition. Provision was made, we have seen, by the statutes of Chow, for the preservation of the monuments of previous dynasties. But those monuments were at no time very numerous, and they could not but be injured, and were not unlikely to be corrupted, in passing from one dynasty to another. From the time of T'ang, the Successful, however, commonly placed in the 18th century before Christ, we seem to be able to tread the field of history with a somewhat confident step.

2. Beyond the time of T'ang we cannot be so sure of our way. Our information is comparatively scanty. It has in itself less of verisimilitude. Legend and narrative are confusedly mixed together. This is more especially apparent in the first and second Parts of the Work.

The oldest documents are not to be relied on so much as the others.

[i.] 'The Book of T'ang,' known as 'The Canon of Yaou,' and all but one portion (which, indeed, must be classed with the others), of 'The Books of Yu' are, professedly, the compilations of a later time. They all commence with the words which I have translated —'On examining into antiquity, we find,'——. If the construction of the paragraphs, which has been generally preferred since the time of Choo He, be adopted, the point on which I am insisting is equally prominent. We should then have to render.—'When we make a study of the ancient emperor Yaou, the ancient emperor Shun, the ancient Yu, the ancient Kaou-yaou, we find,'——. On either version the chronicler separates himself from his subject. He

書經

writes from a modern standpoint. Yaou, Shun, Yu, and Kaou-yaou are in the distant vistas of antiquity.

In my notes on the first paragraph of the Canon of Yaou, I have pointed out the absurdity of the interpretations which the scholars of Han—Gan-kwŏ, Ma Yung, and Ch'ing Heuen—gave of the words in question. Possibly, they had some idea of avoiding the conclusion to which the natural reading of them would lead, and therefore put upon them the forced meanings which they did. Morrison would infer from the first character,[2] that 'a considerable part of the Shoo is merely tradition;' but the character is itself uncertain, and, even if it were not so, no inference from it can be extended beyond the document to which it belongs. The scholars of the Sung and more recent dynasties seem never to have been struck with the uncertainty which either of the admissible interpretations attaches to the whole contents of the first two Parts of the classic. Their critical taste and ability made them reject the strained constructions of earlier times, but it never occurred to them to say to themselves,—'Well; but doing this, and taking the language as it ought to be taken, we cannot claim the authority for the records concerning Yaou, Shun, and Yu, which we are accustomed to do. Who compiled the Canons and the Counsels? When did he or they live? Are we not sapping the foundation of some of the commonly received accounts of the most early period of our national history?' Reflections like these do not appear to have occurred to any of the Chinese critics; but I submit it to my readers, whether they might not have justly done so.

At the same time, it is to be admitted, that the compiler of these Parts was possessed of documents more ancient than his own time,—documents which had probably come down from the age of Yaou and Shun. There are three things which to my mind render this admission necessary. First, there are the titles of the high officers about the courts of the two emperors, which we do not meet at a later age. The principal personage, for instance, was styled 'The Four Mountains;' next to him was 'The General Regulator;' and the minister of Religion was 'The Arranger of the Ancestral Temple.' The peculiarity of these designations indicates that the compiler had received them from tradition or from written records (which is more likely), and that they were not invented by himself. Second, the style of these Parts is distinguished, in several paragraphs, from

1 曰若稽古. 2 曰, See the preface to his dictionary, p. viii.

that of the Books of Hea, Shang and Chow. The exclamations, 'Alas!' 'Ah!' and 'Oh!' in particular, are expressed by characters which we do not find elsewhere used in the same way.[3] Third, the directions of Yaou to his astronomers, to determine the equinoxes and solstices by reference to the stars culminating at those seasons, could not be the inventions of a later age. The equinoxes were then in Taurus (Pleiades) and Scorpio, and the solstices in Leo and Aquarius. We shall find in the next chapter how these statements have been employed to ascertain the era of Yaou. No compiler, ignorant of the precession of the equinoxes, which was not known in China till long after the Christian era, could have framed them with such an adjustment to the time of which he was writing.

The two circumstances which I have pointed out in this paragraph may seem to conflict with each other. In the first place, the compilation of the Books of the first and second Parts of the Shoo, at a date long subsequent to that of which they treat, is calculated to lessen our confidence in them; while the admission, again, of ancient documents among their contents may be thought to establish their authority sufficiently. It is my duty, however, to call attention to both the points. They lie equally upon the face of the Books. It may be impossible to separate what is old from what is more recent, —to distinguish what the compilers added of their own from what was universally received before their time. Perhaps no two critics who make the attempt will come to identical conclusions. For my own part, I have no hesitation in adjudging the first two paragraphs in the Canon of Yaou to the compiler, and generally all the narrative portions in the other Books. I think, likewise, that I can trace his hand in various expressions throughout, which make us think of the dominion of the chieftains Yaou and Shun according to our impressions of the empire when it had been consolidated and extended, many hundreds of years subsequent to them.

Yaou and Shun do not appear as the sage-heroes of history till the time of the Chow dynasty.

[ii.] The references to Yaou and Shun in the succeeding Parts of the Shoo are so very scanty as to excite our surprise, and induce the idea that it was not till the time of the Chow dynasty that they obtained the prominent place in the early history of the empire which is now assigned to them.

In the Books of Hea, Shun is not mentioned at all, and Yaou is mentioned only once. In the third of the 'Songs of the Five Sons,'

3 Consult 吁, 咨, and 都 in Index III.

書經

he appears as 'the prince of T'aou and T'ang, who possessed the country of K'e.' In that description of him we hear the voice of the most early tradition. Yaou is not yet the emperor ruling over 'ten thousand States,' but a prince or chieftain, having his seat north of the Yellow River, and ruling over the land of K'e. We may doubt whether his authority extended over all the territory subsequently known as K'e-chow; but it had not yet reached south of the Ho, and hardly west of it, where it divides the present provinces of Shen-se and Shan-se.

In the Books of Shang, Yaou and Shun are mentioned once, where the language is magniloquent enough; but it is so vague that we can learn nothing from it as to their original position. In the Charge to Yuĕ, (Part. iii., par. 10) E Yin is introduced as having said, 'If I cannot make my sovereign like Yaou and Shun, I shall feel ashamed in my heart as if I were beaten in the market place.' We are then told that Yin, fired with this ambition, so dealt with T'ang the Successful, that he became equal to Great Heaven. By this time Yaou and Shun had become mythical personages, embodying the ideal of a perfect sovereign.

We come to the Books of Chow, and in them we have two references to the ancient heroes. The one is in 'The Officers of Chow,' where Yaou is spoken of under the dynastic name of T'ang, and Shun under that of Yu, and the small number of their officers is contrasted with the multitude of those of Hea and Shang.[4] The second is in 'The Prince of Leu on Punishments,' Ch. II. The passage is very confused; and some critics think that it speaks only of Yaou, while others (with whom I agree) hold that Shun is the subject of it. The traditions of his time (or, it may be, the accounts of them in the Canons) are blended with those of a still earlier date, and we see, as through a mist, the beginnings of the empire, as Shun lays its foundations, now by martial prowess beating down barbarian wickedness, now by humility and benevolence, with the assistance of his chiefs, conciliating the affections of the people.

The above are all the places in the Books of Hea, Shang, and Chow, where Yaou and Shun are referred to. The first of them gives us a simple reminiscence, separated by less than half a century from the year assigned to the death of Shun; and it is very instructive as to the real position which Yaou occupied. From the second we learn nothing valuable; but we find the men growing into larger

4 See Bk. xx., p. 3.—唐虞稽古,建官惟百.

dimensions, as the distance through which they are looked back to lengthens. In the third their original smallness is indicated, though they are said to have secured the repose of the 'ten thousand States.' The fourth is more suggestive, but we know not how to reconcile it with the statements in the Canons of the two first Parts. T'ang is silent about Yaou and Shun, when he is vindicating his overthrow of the Hea dynasty. Woo, in the same way, has nothing to say about them, when he would justify his superseding of the dynasty of Shang. Above all, the duke of Chow, the real establisher of the dynasty of Chow, and the model of Confucius, amid all his appeals to ancient precedents in support of the policy of his House, never mentions them. When we turn to the She King, the book of ancient songs and ballads, no Yaou and Shun are there. It is nearly all, indeed, of the dynasty of Chow, and celebrates the praises of king Wǎn and his ancestors; but it is impossible not to be surprised that no inspiration ever fell upon the 'makers' from the chiefs of K'e. They are mentioned once in the Yih King, but it is in the appendix to that Work, which is ascribed to Confucius, and the authenticity of which is much disputed.

Taking all these things into consideration,—the little that is said about Yaou and Shun in the later Parts of the Shoo itself, and the nature of that little; the absolute silence in reference to them of the She; and the one doubtful mention of them in the Yih,—I am brought to the conclusion, that the compilation of the first two Parts was not made till some time after the commencement of the Chow dynasty. Certain it is, that, during this dynasty, Yaou and Shun received a prominence which they did not previously possess. Confucius in particular adopted them as his favourite heroes, and endowed them with all the virtues, which should render them models to sovereigns in all time. Mencius entered into the spirit of his master, and, according to the bolder character of his own mind, pushed the celebration of them farther, and made them models for all mankind. Then, for the first time, under the hands of these two philosophers, they took their place as the greatest of sages. To the compiler, probably, they owed their designation of '*te*,'[5] emperor or vicegerent of God, as well as all those descriptions which aid the natural illusion of the mind, and set them before us as ruling over a territory equal to that of the kings of Chow.

3. The accounts of Yaou and Shun, and especially of the connec-

5 帝.

書經

tion between them, are so evidently legendary that it seems strange how any one can accept them as materials for history. When Yaou has been on the throne for seventy years, finding the cares of government too great for him, he proposes to resign in favour of his principal minister, the 'Four Mountains.' That worthy declares his virtue unequal to the office. Yaou then asks him whom he can recommend for it; be the worthiest individual a noble or a poor man, he will appoint him to the dignity. This brings Shun upon the stage. All the officers about the court can recommend him,—'Shun of Yu,[1] an unmarried man among the lower people.' His father, a blind man, was also obstinately unprincipled: his mother was insincere: his brother was arrogant; and yet Shun had been able by his filial piety to live harmoniously with them, and to bring them to a considerable measure of self-government and good conduct. Yaou was delighted. He had himself heard something of Shun. He resolved to give him a preliminary trial. And a strange trial it was. He gave him his own two daughters in marriage, and declared that he would test his fitness for the throne by seeing his behaviour with his two wives!

The accounts of Yaou and Shun are evidently legendary.

We are to suppose that Shun stood this test to which he was subjected. We find him next appointed to be 'General Regulator,' the functions of which office he discharged so successfully, that, after three years, Yaou insisted on his consenting to accept the succession to the throne. They then reigned together for about a quarter of a century, till the death of Yaou, who enjoyed the superior dignity, while Shun took all the toils of government.

To the above incidents there are other two to be added from the Shoo. Yaou was not childless. He had at least one son, mentioned as Choo of Tan; but the father did not feel justified in transmitting the empire to him, in consequence of the unworthiness of his character, so much did concern for the public weal transcend Yaou's regard for the distinction of his own family. In regard to Shun, he appears in one place as a farmer, during the early period of his life, in the neighbourhood of mount Leih, which was not far from Yaou's capital.

1 虞舜. Bunsen, calling these characters Yü-shin, supposes that the 虞 is 禹, the name of Yu the Great, and says that they are 'simply a mythical combination of Yü (禹) and Shin (舜), in order to connect the great deliverer [that is, Yu the Great] with the two old emperors, Yaou and Shin.' This is an instance of the errors into which the subtlest reasoners are liable to fall, when they write 'without book.' See 'Egypt's Place in Universal History,' vol. III., p. 399.

In Sze-ma Ts'een and Mencius these scanty notices are largely added to.[2] We have Shun not only as a farmer, but also as a fisherman, and a potter. His 'insincere' mother is his step-mother, and his 'arrogant' brother but a half-brother. Yaou has nine sons, who are sent with his two daughters, and a host of officers, to serve Shun amid the channeled fields. Even after this, his wicked relatives continue to plot against his life; and on one occasion, when they thought they had accomplished their object, the bad brother, after saying that his parents might have the sheep and oxen, storehouses and granaries, proceeds to Shun's house to appropriate his shield and spear, his bow and lute, and his two wives to himself, when lo! there is Shun sitting calmly on a couch, and playing on his lute!

There are other incongruities. Shun's appearing in the Shoo at first merely as a private man was, according to Ts'een, simply through the reduced circumstances of his family. He proves him to have been of the blood royal, and traces his descent from Hwang-te, or the Yellow emperor. But Yaou was also descended from Hwang-te; and thus Shun is made to marry his own cousins,—a heinous crime in Chinese law, and also in the eyes of Chinese moralists. My readers will probably agree with me that we ought not to speak of the *history* of Yaou and Shun, but of legendary tales which we have about them.

The accounts of the connection of Yu with Yaou and Shun are of the same legendary character.

4. Passing on from the connection between Yaou and Shun to that which Yu had with each of them, until he finally succeeded to the latter, we find much that is of the same character. Yaou, in what year of his reign we do not know, appears suddenly startled with the ravages of an inundation. The waters were embracing the mountains, and overtopping the hills, and threatening the heavens with their surging fury. Was there a capable man to whom he could assign the correction of the calamity? All the nobles recommend one K'wăn, to whom Yaou, against his own better judgment, delegates the difficult task; and for nine years K'wăn labours, and the work is still unperformed.

For his want of success, and perhaps for other reasons, K'wăn was put to death; and Yu, who was his son, entered into his labours.[1]

2 See the 史記, 卷一, pp. 6, 7; and Mencius, V. Pt. i. ch. II., *et al.*

1 The subject of the connection between K'wăn and Yu, and between their labours, is invested to me with a good deal of difficulty. It is the universal belief of the Chinese that Yu was the son of K'wăn. The Shoo does not tell us so. The language of 'The Great Plan,' p. 3, does not necessarily imply the fact. Sze-ma Ts'een, Ch. II., p. 1, however, affirms it (禹傷先人

We have nothing definite in the Shoo about the year, or the manner of Yu's designation to the work. Some time after the death of Yaou, when Yu is superintendent of Works, Shun compliments him on the success with which he had regulated the water and the land, and appoints him to be 'General Regulator' under him, as he himself had formerly been under Yaou. The measures of Yu in remedying the disasters of the inundation are detailed at length in the first of the Books of Hea, which I shall consider in the sequel. His appointment to be 'General Regulator' may be considered as preliminary to his being called to occupy the throne. The Shoo does not tell us that Shun had a son; but Mencius assumes that such was the case, and that the son was weak or worthless like Choo of Tan, so that the example of Yaou had again to be copied. Three and thirty years after the death of that sovereign, Shun tells Yu that the laborious duties of the government wearied him, being now between ninety and a hundred years old, and summons him to take the leadership of the people. Yu declined the dignity again and again, till Shun waxed peremptory. They then reigned together for about fifteen years, when Shun died, and Yu was left in sole possession of the empire.

This tale of Yu's accession to the throne is not so marvellous as the story of Shun. It is sufficiently so, however, to bear out what I have suggested of there being a legendary element in it. We cannot but be struck with the way in which the more salient points of the previous narrative re-appear. The empire to the worthiest; the common weal before private and family advantage:—these are the lessons for the enforcement of which the accounts of Yaou, Shun, and Yu, in their relations to one another, were framed to the fashion in which they have descended to us.

Yu is the first historical ruler of China.

5. Yu the Great was the founder of the dynasty of Hea. The throne descended in his line, for a period of about four centuries and a half. This fact sufficiently distinguishes him from Yaou and Shun, and indicates the point of time when the tribe or tribes of the Chinese people passed

父鯀功之不成受誅, 云云), and the language of the Le Ke, 祭法, par. 1, is also very strong in support of it (夏后氏亦禘黃帝而郊鯀,祖顓頊而宗禹). Notwithstanding these testimonies, I still query the point in my own mind. We have no certain data as to when Yu entered on his labours. The statements of Mencius, Bk. III., Pt. i, iv. 7, ascribe his appointment to Shun, while Yaou was still alive; and the notice in 'The Great Plan,' makes it subsequent to K'wăn's death. The language there should, probably, make us take the most emphatic meaning given to the term 殛, applied, in the Canon of Shun, and in Mencius, to Shun's dealing with K'wăn.

from the rule of petty chiefs, and began to assume the form of a nation subject to a sovereign sway. In the time of Mencius there were some who found in the fact merely an evidence of the inferiority of Yu in virtue to the more ancient heroes. 'He made the empire,' it was said, 'a family property, instead of transmitting it, as they did, to the worthiest.' Mencius of course had his reply. It was not Yaou who gave the empire to Shun, but Heaven, of whose providence Yaou was only the instrument. So in the case of Shun and Yu. Shun assisted Yaou in the government 28 years, and Yu assisted Shun 17 years. Yih, Yu's prime minister, however, only assisted him 7 years. Then, moreover, the sons of Yaou and Shun were both bad, while K'e, the son of Yu, was a man of talents and virtue. These differences or contrasts in the situations were all equally from Heaven; which thus brought it about that the people would have K'e to reign over them, and not Yih. Mencius winds up his argument with a dictum of Confucius:—'T'ang [Yaou] and Yu [Shun] resigned the throne to their worthy ministers. The sovereign of Hea [Yu] and the sovereigns of Yin and Chow transmitted it to their sons. The principle of righteousness was the same in all the cases.'[1]

Confucius and Mencius were obliged to resort to this reasoning by the scheme which they had adopted of the ancient history of their country; but they explicitly affirm the fact to which I am calling attention,—that the empire, such as it then was, first became hereditary in the family of Yu. This fact constitutes him a historical personage, and requires that we consider him as the first sovereign of the Chinese nation.

6. Bunsen says:—'Yu the Great is as much an historical king as Charlemagne; and the imperial tribute-roll of his reign in the Shu-king is a contemporary and public document just as certainly as are the capitularies of the king of the Franks.'[1] That Yu is an historical king is freely admitted; but that the tribute-roll of his reign which we have in the Shoo-king was made by him, or is to be accepted as a genuine record of his labours, must be as freely denied.

The account of Yu's labours in the Shoo cannot be received as history.

What Bunsen calls the tribute-roll of Yu's reign is always edited as the first of the Books of Hea, which form in this volune the third Part of the Shoo. But all which it details took place, or is imagined to have taken place, before the death of Yaou, not only before Yu

1 Mencius. V., Pt. I., Chh. v., vi.
1 Place of Egypt in Universal History, vol. III., p. 395.

occupied the throne, but when there was no prospect of his ever doing so. The Book belongs to the period of Yaou and Shun, and appears out of its chronological order. Its proper position would be in the first Part; and it must share in the general uncertainty which I have shown to belong to the documents of the oldest portions of the classic.

In my notes upon the Book, p. 93, I have said that the name,—'The Tribute of Yu'—conveys a very inadequate idea of its contents. It describes generally the labours of Yu in remedying the disasters occasioned by the inundation referred to above, in paragraph 4, as startling Yaou, and his subsequent measures in dividing the land which he had rescued from the waters, and determining and apportioning the revenues to be paid by its different provinces.

To enable us to judge of the credibility of Yu's labours, we must first get before our minds some definite idea of the state of the country when he entered upon them. Mencius thus describes it, giving the picture which he drew to himself from the records of the Shoo:—'In the time of Yaou, when the empire had not yet been reduced to order, the vast waters, flowing out of their channels, made a universal inundation. Vegetation was luxuriant, and birds and beasts swarmed. Grain could not be grown. The birds and beasts pressed upon men. The paths marked by the feet of beasts and prints of birds crossed one another throughout the Middle Kingdom. ......Yu separated the nine different branches of the Ho, cleared the courses of the Tse and T'ă, and led them to the sea. He opened a vent for the Joo and Han, regulated the course of the Hwae and Sze, and led them all to the Keang. When this was done, it was possible for the people of the Middle Kingdom to get food for themselves.'[2] This may seem a sufficiently frightful picture; but it is sketched with colours all too light. Such was the overflow of the waters of the Ho, that Yaou spoke of them, from the point of view in his capital, as embracing the mountains, overtopping the hills, and threatening the heavens. As they proceeded on their eastern course, they separated into a multitude of streams, and formed a delta of part of the present provinces of Chih-le and Shan-tung, where the people were shut up on the elevated grounds. The waters of the Keang required regulating nearly as much. All the affluents of these two mighty rivers, and whatever other streams, like the Hwae, lay between them, were in similar disorder. The mountains where the rivers

2 Mencius, Bk. III., Pt. I. iv. 7.

had their rise, and the chains of which directed their courses, were shaggy with forests, that rose from the marshy jungles which grew around them. If we suppose that when North America began to be colonized from Europe, its rivers, from the St. Lawrence southwards, had all been wildly and destructively flowing abroad, its rolling prairies slimy fens, and its forests pathless, we shall have an unexaggerated idea of what China was, according to the Shoo, in the days of Yu.

Into such a scene of desolation Yu went forth. From beyond the western bounds of the present China proper he is represented as tracking the great rivers, here burning the woods, hewing the rocks, and cutting through the mountains which obstructed their progress, and there deepening their channels, until their waters are brought to flow peacefully into the eastern sea. He forms lakes, and raises mighty embankments, until at length 'the grounds along the waters were everywhere made habitable; the hills were cleared of their superfluous wood; the sources of the streams were cleared; the marshes were well banked; and access to the capital was secured for all within the four seas. A great order was effected in the six magazines *of material wealth;* the different parts of the country were subjected to an exact comparison, so that contribution of revenue could be carefully adjusted according to their resources. The fields were all classified with reference to the three characters of the soil; and the revenues for the Middle Kingdom were established.'

The Shoo does not say what length of time was required to complete so great an achievement; but we can gather from it that it did not extend over very many years. It was *un fait accompli* before the death of Yaou. K'wăn had laboured upon the flooded country for nine years without success; and though it is not expressly said that Yu's appointment was made by Shun after he became co-emperor with Yaou, the presumption is that it was so,—a presumption which might be declared a certainty if we could put confidence in the statements of Mencius. Mencius adds that Yu was eight years away from his home while going backwards and forwards on the work.[3] Sze-ma Ts'een allows Yu thirteen years to put his curb upon the floods; while Ma Yung thought that in three years eight of the provinces were so rectified, that Yaou considered the whole work as good as done, and resigned the administration to Shun.[4]

3 See a portion omitted in the quotation from Mencius above. 4 See the concluding note on p. 150.

書經

I have been careful to point out in my notes the indications which we have that Yu was not left single-handed in the enterprise. He had Yih with him to help to open up the woods with fire. He had Tseih to show the people how to cultivate the ground as it was reclaimed from the waters and the jungles. But if we allow that all the resources of the empire (so to speak) were at his disposal, the work which he is said to have accomplished far exceeds all limits of credibility.

I am glad to be sustained in this opinion by the judgment of the late Edward Biot the younger, and will here introduce some sentences from an able article by him in the 'Journal Asiatique' for August and September, 1842. He says:—'The Yellow river, after its entrance into China, has a further course of 560 leagues; the Këang, taken only from the great lake of Hoo-kwang visited by Yu, has a course of nearly 250 leagues; the Han, from its source to its junction with the Këang, is 150 leagues long. These three rivers present a total length of nearly 1,000 leagues; and adding the other rivers [on which Yu laboured], we must extend the 1,000 to 1,500. ......Chinese antiquity has produced one monument of immense labour,—the great wall, which extends over nearly 300 leagues; but the achievement of this gigantic monument required a great number of years. It was commenced in pieces, in the ancient States of Ts'in, Chaou, and Yen, and was then repaired and lengthened by the first emperor of the Ts'in dynasty. Now such a structure, in masonry, is much easier to make than the embankment of enormous streams along an extent of 1,200 or 1,500 leagues. We know, in effect, how much trouble and time are required to bring such works to perfect solidity. We can judge of it from the repeated overflowings of the Rhone, and the lower Rhone is not a fourth of the size of the Ho and the Këang in the lower part of their course. If we are to believe the commentators, Yu will become a supernatural being, who could lead the immense rivers of China as if he had been engaged in regulating the course of feeble streamlets.'[5]

These illustrations of Biot are sufficiently conclusive. I may put the matter before the reader by one of a different character. I have represented the condition of the surface of China when Yu

5 See the number of the 'Journal Asiatique' referred to, pp. 160, 162. Most of this chapter was written before I had an opportunity of seeing it. A sinologue of very extensive research calling in question, in conversation, the views which I told him I was going to propound about the *Yu Kung*, I was led to make another effort (having made several fruitless ones) to obtain in Hongkong a copy of the 'Journal Asiatique,' that I might find what were Biot's views and was fortunate enough, among a heap of odd numbers, to discover what I wanted.

entered on his labours by supposing the regions of North America, from the St. Lawrence southwards, to have been found in similar disorder and desolation by the early colonists from Europe in the seventeenth century. Those colonists had not the difficulties to cope with which confronted Yu; but we know how slowly they pushed their way into the country. Gradually growing in numbers, receiving constant accessions from Europe, increasing to a great nation, inferior to no other in the world for intelligence and enterprise, in more than two centuries they have not brought their territory more extensively into cultivation and order than Yu did the inundated regions of China in the space of less than twenty years!

The empire, as it appears in 'The Tribute of Yu,' consisted of nine provinces. On the north and west its boundaries were much the same as those of China Proper at the present day. On the east it extended to the sea, and even, according to many, across it, so as to embrace the territory of Corea. Its limits on the south are not very well defined. It certainly did not reach beyond the range of mountains which run along the north of Kwang-tung province, stretching into Kwang-se on the west and Fuh-këen on the east. Even though we do not reckon those three provinces in Yaou's dominion, there still remains an immense empire, about three times as large as France, which we are to suppose was ruled over by him, the chief of K'e, and the different regions of which sent their apportioned contributions of grain, and other articles of tribute, to his capital year by year.

The empire was not so large, nor so organized, in Yu's time as it is represented.

But besides this division of the empire, the Book gives us another into five domains, by which it extended 2,500 *le* from the capital on every side, the whole thus constituting a square of 5,000 *le*. We have Yu's own declaration of his services in completing those domains, and in organizing the regions beyond, as far as the borders of the four seas, and placing them under the government of four presidents.[6] It is impossible for us to put credit in this representation. The five domains cannot be put down on the territory of China, ancient or modern. I have shown in my notes, pp. 148, 149, the difficulties which attend the account that we have of them. With reference to a similar but more minute arrangement of domains given in 'The Rites of Chow,' Biot says that 'it is evident that these symmetrical divisions have nothing of reality.'[7] There is not the

6 See the 'Yih and Tseih,' par. 4. 7 Le Tcheou-li, tome II., p. 169.

same difficulty with the division into nine provinces. Their mountains and rivers are, in the main, the same which have existed since the earth received its present form, and which will continue to the end of the world. The difficulty is in believing that Yu dealt with them as he is said to have done, and that there was in his time an empire exercising sway over such an extent of the country. As we must deny, however, the division into domains, for the making of which we have what purport to be Yu's own words, and which occupies six paragraphs in 'The Tribute of Yu,' it may be deemed less presumptuous to question the division into nine regions, which it is nowhere expressly said in the Shoo that he made,—to question it as not having been in existence at all in his time.

The accounts which we have of the empire subsequent to Yu forbid us to allow that it had attained in his day so great a development. The third sovereign of the Hea dynasty, T'ae-k'ang, grandson of Yu, having crossed the Ho on a hunting expedition, found his return obstructed by the chief of K'eung, and was never able to regain his throne. His five brothers had gone with their mother, and were waiting for his return on the banks of the Lŏ, when they heard of the movement against his authority. They then poured out their sorrow in songs, which are given in the Shoo. One of them refers to Yu as 'The sovereign of the myriad States!' while another speaks of Yaou, 'the prince of T'aou and T'ang, who possessed this country of K'e,'—'this country,' which was then held by the representatives of Yu. Nearly a hundred years elapsed, after the expulsion of T'ae-k'ang, before the House of Hea regained sure possession of the throne. This was done, B.C. 2,078, by Shaou-k'ang, whom we find lurking about, not far from the old capital of Yaou, for nearly the first forty years of his life, now herding the cattle of one chief, and anon acting as cook in the establishment of another, who discovers his worthiness, and gives him his two daughters in marriage. All these events transpire, we may say, on the banks of the Ho, and there is no indication of the country elsewhere being interested in them. It is believed that Yu died at Hwuy-k'e in the present Chĕ-këang; but it was not till the last year of Shaou-k'ang that any chief was appointed in that part of the country in the name of the reigning House.

When we come to the dynasty of Shang, B.C. 1,765–1,122, we find it difficult to admit that even then there was a China at all equal to that which Yu is said to have ruled over. The Shoo tells us of its founder T'ang the Successful; and in him and Këĕ, the last sovereign of the line of Yu, we seem merely to have the chief of Shang warring with the chief of Hea. It next gives us some notices of the minority of T'ae-këă, T'ang's successor; and then there is a blank in the history for three hundred years. When the field is occupied again, we meet with Pwan-kăng, the 17th sovereign, in great trouble, engaged in transferring his capital from the north of the Ho to the present district of Yen-sze in Ho-nan, on the south of it. To reconcile the murmuring people to the trouble of the removal, he reminds them that he was only acting after the example of former kings, and that the capital of the dynasty had already been in five different places. The nation, evidently, had still its seat in the neighbourhood of the Ho, and notwithstanding all that Yu is supposed to have done in regulating the waters of that river, its principal settlement had to be frequently changed in consequence of inundations. The accounts are not those of a great people, but of a tribe which had little difficulty in migrating from one spot to another.

Later still, we find a fact which is more conclusive perhaps on the point in hand than any of the considerations which I have yet adduced. The empire of the Chow dynasty consisted, like that of Yaou, of nine provinces. The old province of K'e formed three of them; Seu was absorbed in Ts'ing; and Lëang had disappeared from the empire altogether. Portions of the more eastern parts of it may have been embraced in the provinces of Yu and Yung, but much the greater part was wild barbarian territory, beyond the limits of the Middle Kingdom.[8] The kings of Chow ruled over a territory less than that of Yaou by the present provinces of Sze-ch'uen and Yun-nan! The dominions of Chow were not under-estimated, but the dimensions of the empire in the days of Yu have been greatly exaggerated. We can no more admit that he ruled over the nine provinces ascribed to him, than that he executed the stupendous labours of which he has the glory.

The view to be taken of the Book *Yu Kung*.

7. What then are we to think of 'The Tribute of Yu,' telling us, as it does, of the nine provinces, and of the labours put forth, and the contributions imposed upon them by Yu? According to Biot, in the article of the 'Journal Asiatique,' already referred to, we are to find in it 'only the progress of a great colony.' He says further:—'Admitting even that Yu really visited all the points mentioned in the chapter, and

8 See the Chow Le, Bk. xxxiii.

so ran over more than the 1,500 leagues of which I have spoken, we should simply have to regard him as the first explorer of the Chinese world. In his general exploration, he established the posts of the colonists or planters on different points of the territory which he occupied by force, or which he obtained by a friendly arrangement with the natives. He caused the wood around those posts to be cut down, and commenced the cultivation of the soil. He may have commenced also, along with his colonists, certain labours on some rivers, carried off some stagnant waters, or embanked some lakes. At every one of his posts, he examined the productions of the ground, and the articles which they could obtain by barter from the natives. He then determined the nature of the contributions which every new colony should send to the mother colony. Such is still, in our days, the method pursued by the leaders of the pioneers who engage in exploring the deserts of America. They establish posts where they may purchase furs from the natives, and may commence at the same time the clearing of the forests. After Yu, the labours of draining the country and clearing the forests continued during some ages, and the result of all was attributed by Chinese tradition to the first chief.'

The reader cannot fail to be struck with the ingenuity of the above view; and I believe that there is an inkling of the truth in it. It is certainly an improvement on the view previously advanced by Father Cibot in his very learned essay on 'The Antiquity of the Chinese,' which appears under the name of 'Ko a Jesuit,' at the beginning of the 'Memoires sur les Chinois.' Himself of opinion that the territory on which Yu laboured was of small extent, Cibot thinks that this chief, remaining at the centre of his government in K'e-chow, might yet have sent expeditions of discovery, and to fix, on the ground of what he had learned of the other provinces, the imposts to be drawn from them, in the same way as has been done under all the succeeding dynasties, when it has been designed to extend the empire by colonies and the opening up of the country. 'Of how many countries of America,' says he, 'have charts and descriptions been given, before they were peopled, or even on the eve of being so? If what has thus been said of their mines, productions, and curiosities, proves the knowledge of Europeans, what we find in the *Yu Kung* will prove the similar knowledge which Yu had of the territory of China.'[1]

1 See Memoires concernant l'Histoire, &c., des Chinois, vol. I., p. 215.

For myself, I cannot admit that Yu really visited all the points which he is said to have done, nor can I find in the order in which his labours are detailed the steps by which the great Chinese colony actually proceeded to occupy the country. We recognize its primitive seat in the southern parts of the present Shan-se, with the Ho on the west and south of it. Across that stream lay the present Shen-se on the one side, and Ho-nan on the other. Into those portions of the country the subjects of Yu would penetrate long before they reached as far south as the Këang. In point of fact we know that they did do so. His son fought a battle with the prince of Hoo, at a place in the present department of Se-ngan in Shen-se; and the usurper E kept his grandson, T'ae-k'ang, a sort of prisoner at large in a part of Ho-nan. But the country of Ho-nan was in the province of Yu, the 7th in order of Yu's operations; and that of Shen-se was in Yung, the last in order. It is plain, therefore, that we are not to look in the *Yu Kung* for indications of the historical course and progress of the great Chinese colony.

'The Tribute of Yu' describes the country of China as its extent came to be ascertained in the course of the dynasties of Hea and Shang, and as its different parts were gradually occupied by the increasing and enterprising multitudes of the Chinese people, and contributed their various proportions of revenue and tribute to the central government which continued to be in K'e-chow. There were memorials of toils which the great Yu had undergone in making good the first foot-hold of his tribe, and of allotments of territory which he had made to the most distinguished among his followers. The nature of the country, in many places covered with forests and inundated, had caused the colonists much trouble in their advances. It occurred to some historiographer to form a theory as to the way in which the whole country might have been brought to order by the founder of the Hea dynasty, and he thereupon proceeded to glorify Yu by ascribing so grand an achievement to him. About the same time the popular stories of Yu's self-denial, in remaining with his wife only four days after their marriage, in passing thrice by his door regardless of the wailings of his infant son K'e, in flying about over the country, here driving his carriage over the level ground, there forcing his way up the rivers in a boat, now toiling through the marshes in a sledge, and anon stalking along the steep and slippery sides of the hills, with spikes to his shoes, with a measuring line in his left hand and a square and pair of compasses in his left, until his

書經

body was wasted to a shadow, and the skin of his hands and feet was callous:—these popular stories found their recognition in the 'Yih and Tseih,' and prompted at once the conception of the romance of the *Yu Kung*, and obtained for it a favourable reception. Then Yu could enter well into association with Yaou and Shun, and form a triad with them at the beginning of the Chinese monarchy. Their wisdom and benevolence appeared in him, combined with a practical devotion to the duties of his position, in which all sovereigns might have a model, that would for ever win them from indolence and self-indulgence, and stimulate them to a painstaking discharge of their responsibilities.

The conclusion to which a careful consideration of 'The Tribute of Yu' has brought me is thus far enough from the opinion of Bunsen, that it was 'a contemporary and public document of his reign.' It is to be regarded on the contrary as *a romance*, of which Yu is the subject, composed long after him,—composed probably after the dynasty which he founded had passed away. Cibot quotes several Chinese authorities, affirming its late composition. Biot seems inclined to attribute the Book, as we now have it, to Confucius. 'It is at least certain,' he says, 'that Confucius brought together in this chapter various *souvenirs* long antecedent to his own epoch;' and he adds, that 'carrying its composition no farther back than this, we should have in it one of the most ancient geographical documents in the world.' But I showed, on pp. 3–6 of these prolegomena, that we have no sufficient reason to believe that Confucius had anything to do with the compilation of the Shoo. We have, moreover, an indication, I think, in the Shoo itself, that the duke of Chow was familiar with this record of Yu's labours. Towards the close of that statesman's counsels to king Ching on the 'Establishment of Government,' we find him saying:—'Have well arranged your military accoutrements and weapons, so that you may go forth beyond the steps of Yu, and be able to travel over all beneath heaven, even to beyond the seas, everywhere meeting with submission.'[2] How was the duke of Chow acquainted with 'the footsteps of Yu?' It must have been either by tradition, or by some written account of them. The latter is the more probable. I have already called attention to the fact, that the large territory included in Yu's province of Lëang did not form a part of the dominions of Chow. It was natural that the duke of Chow, so ambitious and far-reaching as we

2 See Pt. V., Bk. XIX., p. 22.

know him to have been, should be anxious that the sway of his House should not come short of that ascribed to either of the previous dynasties. On another occasion, he summoned the duke of Shaou to go on with him, 'abjuring all idleness, to complete the work of Wăn, till their empire should entirely overspread the land and from the corners of the seas and the sunrising there should not be one disobedient to their rule.'[3] His reference to 'the steps of Yu' does not prove that Yu really travelled and toiled and subdued the face of nature as the *Yu Kung* reports; it only proves that such was the current belief at the commencement of the Chow dynasty, affording at the same time a presumption that that document was then among the archives of the empire. This is my opinion,—that 'The Tribute of Yu' was among the written monuments of ancient times, which passed from the dynasty of Shang, and came under the care of the Recorders of the Exterior under that of Chow. Then subsequently it was very properly incorporated in the collection of Historical documents now known as the Shoo.

8. The opinion of Bunsen, that 'The Tribute of Yu' was a contemporary and public document of Yu's reign, was mainly grounded on the confidence which he reposed in the genuineness of a stone pillar, with an inscription, said to have been erected by Yu on the top of mount Hăng, in the present Hoo-nan. He says:—'We have Yu's own unquestionably genuine account of the labour employed upon the great work by which he saved the country in the inundation. After the Egyptian monuments, there is no extant contemporary testimony more authentic, and none so old as the modest and noble inscription of that extraordinary man. It is true that it has now become illegible, but a copy was made of it about 1200 in the time of the Sung, which has been preserved in the high school of Si-an-fu, and in the imperial archives at Pekin. Hager has given a tracing of it. Only those who are unacquainted with the subject can entertain any doubt as to its originality.'[1] Perhaps, if the learned writer had made himself more fully acquainted with the history of this tablet, he would have expressed himself as strongly against its genuineness.

The casting of tripods or vases and of bells is asserted of Yu by very ancient traditions. Nine vases particularly are ascribed to him, each one having on it a chart of one of the nine provinces. Biot

3 Pt. V., Bk. XVI., p. 21.

1 See 'Egypt's Place,' &c., vol. III., pp. 394, 395.

書經

says of them:—'The existence of these early sculptured or graved charts appears to me entirely admissible;—they represented the nine regions known to the first Chinese, and were not pictures of the empire of Yu. But after the ages which elapsed, without doubt, between this first chief and the dynasty of Chow, and after the extension of the Chinese rule, the respect of the Chinese for their ancestors became transformed into a veritable rite; the personage of Yu increased in their remembrances, and grew into a sort of demigod, who had reduced the world to order. Then the nine regions traced upon the vases of Yu became the nine provinces of his pretended empire.' That there were in the Chow dynasty nine vases, ascribed to Yu, and looked on as palladia of the empire, is sufficiently attested; but it is by no means clear that they had on them a series of charts of his nine provinces. But this is not the place to enter on any discussion of them. The earliest mention of them will be found in a note below.[2] I have introduced them here, merely to contrast the ancient references to them with the comparatively modern era when the stone tablet on mount Hăng began to be spoken of.

History of the tablet of Yu on mount Hăng. It is all a fable.

The first writer whose testimony to the existence of this tablet is adduced is Chaou Yih,[3] a Taouist recluse of the Eastern Han, who lived towards the end of the first century of our era. He has left us a 'History of Woo and Yue;'[4] but the Work so abounds in ridiculous stories, of

2 For Biot's remarks, see the article on the *Yu Kung* in the 'Journal Asiatique,' p. 176. The earliest reference to the tripods of Yu, is, I believe, in the Tso Chuen, under the 3d year of duke Seuen (B.C. 605), where a messenger from the emperor Ting appears in colloquy with a general of the State of Ts'oo. The general wished to know the size and weight of the tripods. The answer was:—'The prosperity of the govt. depends on the sovereign's virtue, and not on the tripods. Anciently, when Hea was distinguished for its virtue, they got plans of distant regions, and *remarkable* objects in them. The nine pastors sent in the metal of their provinces, and tripods were cast, with representations on them of those objects. This was done exhaustively, so that the people could recognize the sprites and evil things; and when they went among the rivers, marshes, hills, and forests, they did not meet with misfortune;—yea, the sprites of the hills and waters did not come in their way. Thus a harmony was secured between the high and the low, and all received the blessing of Heaven. When the virtue of Keĕ was all obscured, the tripods passed over to Shang,—for 600 years. In consequence of the cruel tyranny of Chow of Shang, they passed over to Chow. When the virtue is brilliant, the tripods though light are heavy; when it gives place to darkness and disorder, they become light though heavy. Heaven sustains bright virtue;—where that is, its favour rests. King Ching fixed the tripods in Keă-juh (郟鄏; in the pres. Ho-nan), and divined that the dynasty should last 30 generations, and 700 years. This is Heaven's decree, and though the virtue of Chow is decayed, that decree is not changed. You need not ask about the weight of the tripods.' This account of the tripods is not very clear; but it is as clear in the translation as in the original. We should not infer from it that they had on them charts of the nine provinces. Accounts differ as to what became of them,—whether they came into the possession of Ts'in, or were sunk in a river by the last sovereign of Chow, See the 太平御覽,

which I give a specimen below,[5] that we can put little credit in anything which it relates. Among other things stated in it was this:—that 'the spirit-like Yu had left an inscription on the hill of Keu-leu;'[6]—Keu-leu being the name of one of the 72 peaks given to mount Hăng, and indeed, the principal one of them all, so that the names Keu-leu and Hăng are sometimes used interchangeably. In various topographical Works, written between the Han dynasty and that of Y'ang, mention is made of Yu in connection with mount Hăng; but they only reproduce the fables of Chaou Yih, and say nothing definite of the pillar about which we are inquiring.

Under the T'ang dynasty, accounts of it were abundantly rife; but there is no evidence that they were anything more than stories floating about among the people, or that any person of character had seen the interesting relic. On the contrary, the writer who has given us the fullest description of it, tells us that he had himself been unable to find it on the mountain, after the most diligent search. This was the famous Han Yu, among whose poems is the following, on mount Keu-leu:—

'Upon the peak of Keu-leu, sure there stands,
Yu's pillar, fashioned by most cunning hands;
The stone carnation, characters all green,
Like tadpoles bent, like leeks invert, are seen;

卷第七百五十六, art. 鼎; and the 格致鏡原, 卷四十三, art. 鼎. 3 趙曄. The catalogue of the imperial libraries calls him, 趙煜 See the 四庫全書目錄, 卷六. 4 吳越春秋. 5 Of the accounts of this Book, the reader may take the following specimen:—'K'wăn being thrown into the water, after he was put to death on mount Yu, was changed into a yellow dragon, and became the spirit of abyss of Yu (爲羽淵之神). Yu was then appointed to undertake the task of regulating the waters. For seven years he laboured without effect, and, full of heaviness, ascertained from some books of Hwang-te, that among the pillars of heaven, the south-eastern mountains, there was one called Yuen-wei (宛委), where there was a book concealed, in characters of green gem, on tablets of gold, bound together with silver, which would be of use to him. He then went east, ascended mount Hăng, and sacrificed a white horse. Not finding what he sought, he went to the top of the mountain, looked towards heaven, and whistled. There he fell asleep, and dreamed that a boy, in red embroidered clothes, calling himself the messenger of the azure waters, came to him, and told him that if he ascended the Yuen-wei hill, on such and such a day of the third month, he would find the gold tablets. The boy at the same time indicated that this hill was in the east; and thither Yu went, and on the day appointed dug up the gold tablets, with their gem characters, which told him how to proceed to accomplish his mighty work.' See Chaou's Work, 卷四. 6 神禹有岣嶁山銘. See the 鮚埼亭集, 外編, 卷三十五; and the 曝書亭集, 卷四十七, art. 1. I say in the text that there '*was*' such a statement in Chaou's Work, because that Work is now mutilated, and I have glanced over the copy to which I have access without finding the statement in question.

書經

With pheasants floating here, the phœnix there,
Tigers and dragons make, between, their lair.
A monument so grave is hidden well,
And imps might pry, and nothing find to tell.
A solitary Taouist saw the stone.
'Twas chance him led.—I came, with many a groan,
And, weeping fast, searched round and searched again;
'Twas labour lost, the quest was all in vain.
The monkeys, 'mid the foliage of the wood,
Seemed sadly to bewail my grieving mood.'[7]

Two important points are established by these lines:—the one, that Han Yu himself, though he searched diligently for the pillar, could not find it; the other, that the voucher in his time for its existence was a solitary Taouist, one of a class which deals in things fantastic and prodigious, whose averment we pronounce, with a justifiable foregone conclusion, is more likely to be false than true.

From the T'ang dynasty we come to Sung. For more than three hundred years after Han Yu, we read nothing about the pillar. Still it was talked about; and in the 12th century, two of the ablest men in China purposely visited mount Hăng to put the question as to its existence at rest by their personal examination. They were Choo He, the most distinguished critic and philosopher of his age, and Chang Nan-hëen, also an eminent scholar. Their search for the stone was as fruitless as that of Han Yu had been; and to my mind the judgment of Choo He that it never had any existence but in Taouist dreams is decisive. Chinese writers account for the failure of him and the other intelligent seekers to find it, by attributing to it a personal intelligence. It was 'a spirit-like thing, which could appear and disappear at pleasure.'[8]

Not very long after the search of Choo He, in the period *Kea-ting* (A.D. 1208–1224) of the 13th emperor of the Sung dynasty, there came to the mountain an officer from Sze-ch'uen, called Ho Che, and was

7 See the Works of Han Yu, 卷三.岣嶁山尖神禹碑, 字青石赤形摹奇, 科斗拳身薤倒披. 鸞飄鳳泊拏虎螭, 事嚴迹秘鬼莫窺, 道人獨上偶見之, 我來咨嗟涕漣洏, 千搜萬索何處有, 森森綠樹猿猱悲. Accounts of the pillar, of a similar kind, are found in the 丹鉛總錄, 卷一, quoted from 徐靈期, and 崔融, both, like Han Wăn-kung, of the T'ang dynasty. 8 斯文顯晦, 信有神物. See the 丹鉛總錄, referred to above.

conducted by a woodcutter to the peak of Chuh-yung, where he found the monument and took a copy of it, which he had engraved and set up *in the Taouist monastery* of Kwei-mun.[9] Here then was the monument seen at last, and the inscription on it copied,—more than 3,000 years after its erection. So long time it had endured, standing there on the mountain, exposed to all elemental influences! This alone is sufficient to prove the falsehood of it. I have seen monuments in China a thousand years old, and which had been in a measure sheltered from the weather; but in every case the engraving on them was in some parts illegible. The tablet of Yu could not have stood, where it is said to have done, for such a length of time, and been found in the condition in which Ho Che is said to have found it. What was brought to light in the 13th century was a clumsy forgery. I have called attention by italics to the fact of the copy being set up in a Taouist monastery. A Taouist brain first conceived the idea of the monument, and Taouist hands afterwards fashioned it. An ordinary forger would have left gaps in the inscription to tell their own tale of its ancient date; but it was supposed that posterity would believe that this spirit-like thing had bid defiance to the gnawing tooth and effacing fingers of time.

When the discovery was made public, it was not generally credited. We should have thought that so precious a monument would draw many visitors to it, now that its place was known, and that it would even become an object of the public care. No such thing. Even the copy taken by Ho Che would seem to have had the 'spirit-like' quality, attributed to the monument, of making itself either visible or invisible. Under the Sung dynasty, people refused to receive it; and we have to come to the period Ching-tih[10] of the Ming dynasty, in the early part of the 16th century, before we meet with it again. Then, an officer of the province of Hoo-nan, Chang Ke-wăn,[11] professed to have found the copy engraved by Ho Che, which he transcribed; and since his time it has had its place among the monuments, real or pretended, of Chinese antiquity.

It will occur to the reader to ask whether the stone be still on mount Hăng. In a copy of the inscription, published in 1666, by a Maou Tsăng-këen, which is in the possession of the Rev. Mr. Chalmers, the

9 宋嘉定中,有蜀士,何賢良致,于祝融峰下,樵子導之至碑所,手模其文,刻于夔門觀中. 10 正德. It was under this style that the 11th of the Ming emperors (武宗毅皇帝) reigned, A.D. 1506–1521. 11 張季文.

書經

editor speaks of the difficulty of reaching the top of Keu-leu, how ladders are necessary and hooks, and says that he had himself been to the spot and handled the stone. But he says also, that the characters and stone had both been of an immense size, and are now all in fragments, so that the inscription cannot be made out. Let it be granted that there are some fragments of rock on one of the summits of mount Hăng, with old characters cut on them, how is it known that these were ever any tablet of Yu? or how is any verification obtained from them of the inscription, as we have it? Choo He and Chang Nan-hëen, in the 12th century, might very well have seen the remains described by Tsăng-këen, and decided that Yu had never had anything to do with them. Their character shows certainly that Han Yu and the other writers of the T'ang dynasty were only describing an ideal tablet of Yu,—which, indeed, we might conclude on other grounds. The only voucher for the points involved in the above questions is Ho Che, or rather the story which we have of his discovery of the monument in the 13th century.

The review which I have given of the history of the stone sufficiently shows my own opinion, that it is not entitled to the least credit; and I am supported in this view by the great majority of Chinese archæologists, so little ground is there for Bunsen's affirmation that 'only those who are unacquainted with the subject can entertain any doubt as to its originality.' He based his conclusion on a monograph of the inscription, published at Berlin in 1811 by M. Klaproth, which I have not seen. I have read an account of it, however, in the second volume of Remusat's 'Melanges Asiatiques.' Klaproth, it would appear, having become convinced of the genuineness of the monument, addressed himself particularly to show that the 'tadpole' characters have been correctly identified. This might very well be the case, without the arguments which I have urged against it being at all affected. There was nothing to hinder the maker or makers of it, say in the time of the Sung dynasty, from disguising their fraud, by writing it after the model of the most ancient forms of the characters. My friend, Wang T'aou, in a Chinese monograph of it, observes on this point:—'The maker of it was clever in imitating the ancient form of writing; and it was this ability which enabled him to impose on many.' On the next page the reader will find a copy of the inscription, such as it is, taken from the sheet in the possession of the Rev. Mr. Chalmers. The characters were first reduced by a photograph, and then copied for a wooden block to suit the size of my page. By the side of each tadpole character is the modern form which is supposed to have taken its place. I give it simply as a curiosity. In a note below will be found some remarks on Bunsen's attempt to translate it. More than sufficient space has been allowed to it in the text of these prologomena, as my object, in adverting to it at all, was simply to show that an argument could not be constructed from it to invalidate the opinion which I have advanced as to the late origin of the *Yu Kung*.[12]

12 The identification of a few of the characters in the copy of which Bunsen ventured a translation was different from that in the copy here printed. The 丹鉛總錄 gives the inscription thus:—承帝日嗟, 翼輔佐卿, 洲渚與登, 鳥獸之門, 參身洪流, 而明發爾興, 久旅忘家, 宿嶽麓庭, 智營形折, 心罔弗辰, 往求平定, 華岳泰衡, 宗疏事裒, 勞餘伸禋, 鬱塞昏徙, 南瀆衍亨. 永制食備, 萬國其寧, 竄舞永奔. Now I undertake to say, that of a good deal of this it is not possible to ascertain the meaning with any degree of certainty. Bunsen speaks of a version by Father Amyot, published by Hager, which, he says, is not in the true sense of the word a translation. (This may be seen in Williams' 'Middle Kingdom,' Vol. II., pp. 204, 205.) He acknowledges Klaproth's attempt to be a translation, but not quite accurate in some parts. His own attempt to give an accurate version I will not take the trouble to discuss. He says that those who have any acquaintance with the language will understand, from a literal Latin version of the characters, the philological principle on which his translation is based; but the fact is, that a very moderate acquaintance with the language is sufficient to show that Bunsen knew very little about it. If his interpretation of Egyptian monuments be not better than his interpretation of 'the monument of Yu,' his volumes on 'Egypt's Place in Universal History' are of little value.

If the writer of the inscription knew what he was doing in pencilling his tadpole characters, I do not think they have all been correctly identified. Accepting the identification given in this note, I would propose the following as an approximation to a correct interpretation:—

'I received *the words of* the emperor, saying, "Ah!
Associate helper, aiding noble!
The islands and islets may now be ascended,
That were doors for the birds and beasts.
You devoted your person to the great overflowings,
And with the day-break you rose up.
Long were *you* abroad, forgetting your family;
You lodged at the mountain's foot as in a hall;
Your wisdom schemed; *your* body was broken;
Your heart was all in a tremble.
You went and sought to produce order and settlement.
At Hwa, Yŏ, T'ae, and Hăng.
By adopting the principle of dividing *the waters*, *your* undertakings
were completed.
With the remains of a taper, *you* offered your pure sacrifice.
There were entanglement and obstruction, being swamped, and removals.
The southern river flows on in its course;
For ever is the provision of food made sure;
The myriad States enjoy repose;
The beasts and birds are for ever fled away."'

書經

承帝曰咨翼輔佐卿洲渚與登鳥獸
之門參身洪流而明發爾興以旅忘
家宿嶽麓庭智營形折心罔弗辰往
來平定華嶽泰衡宗疏事裒勞餘伸
種鬱塞昏徙南瀆衍亨衣制食備萬
國其寧竄舞蒸奔

73]

Should the deluge of Yaou be identified with that described in the Book of Genesis?

9. From the view which I have taken of the labours of Yu, the reader will understand that I do not identify the deluge of Yaou with that described by Moses in the Book of Genesis. I am inclined, however, to believe that, in the language of the Shoo-king respecting the terrible nature of the inundation which frightened Yaou and Shun, we have the voice of tradition, affirming the earlier and universal catastrophe,—universal at least in the sense that it involved the destruction of 'all flesh,' all the individuals of our race, excepting those who were preserved with Noah in the ark.

Missionaries,—Protestant missionaries especially,—accepting the labours of Yu as historical, have expressed themselves incautiously on the identity of the two deluges. Dr. Gutzlaff, for instance, wrote:—'We do not doubt but Yaou's was the same flood recorded in sacred history, though we are not able to give the exact date from Chinese history; nor do we hesitate to affirm that China was peopled after the deluge.'[1]

Bunsen has taken occasion from this to express himself with undue severity of 'the confusion and ignorance of the missionaries, believing that Yu's labours referred to the Flood of Noah, which never reached China.'[2] And again:—'The inundation in the reign of Yaou had just as much to do with Noah's flood, as the dams he erected and the canals he dug had to do with the Ark. The learned Jesuit Fathers were well aware of this, but they were prevented by orders from Rome from publishing the truth. The fact of so absurd an idea being accepted by the English and Scotch Missionaries, and even by Morrison himself, is a very melancholy instance of the way in which the sound judgment of learned men may be warped by rabbinical superstition and the intolerant ignorance of their Churches, in the investigation of historical truth.'[3]

Now, Morrison gave his opinion in the matter in very guarded terms; and I do not think that he was farther from the truth than his critic. In the preface to his dictionary, p. xiii., he observes:—'In the Shoo-king mention is made of a great and destructive accumulation of waters upon the face of the earth; whether it be called Inundation or Deluge is immaterial. The removal of the waters, and settling the state of all the various regions then known is understood by the phrase *Yu Kung*. Yu was the person who effected that

1 See 'A Sketch of Chinese History,' &c., vol. I. p. 130. 2 'Place of Egypt,' &c., vol. III. p. 398. 3 See as above, p. 406.

書經

work. This Deluge makes a grand epoch in Chinese History. After a fanciful account of the creation, there follows a period of Chinese civilization, when Fuh-he's successors introduced marriage; government; working in metals; the use of musical instruments; and characters for the division of time. The profligacy and misrule of the monarch Te-chih[4] is noticed, and then follows Yaou's deluge; after which the earth is again represented as overspread by wild uncultivated vegetation, and over-run by savage beasts.....The above is a faithful outline of the picture drawn, by Chinese writers, of the history of the ancient world as known to them. Its similarity to that given by the Jewish Legislator must be observable to every one; and the probability, that both accounts refer to the same remote facts, is not to be overturned by slight anachronisms, or a discordancy in the detail.'

To the same effect are the observations of Dr. Medhurst. He calls the time between Fuh-he and Yaou and Shun the 'traditionary Period' of Chinese history, and adds:—'While we might be unwilling to give full credit to what Chinese writers say of the events of this period, it is not improbable that much of it is drawn by tradition from the correct account of the antediluvian age handed down by Noah to his posterity. The coincidence of ten generations having passed away, the institution of marriage, the invention of music, the rebellion of a portion of the race, and the confused mixture of the divine and human families, closed by the occurrence of the flood in the time of Yaou, might lead us to conclude that in their allusions to this period, the Chinese are merely giving their version of the events that occurred from Adam to Noah. When Yu ascended the throne, the lands were drained, and China became habitable.'[5]

In these representations of two of the most distinguished Protestant missionaries, the traces of 'rabbinical superstition,' and of subjection to 'the intolerant ignorance of their churches,' seem to me hardly discernible. Possibly there may be in the Chinese accounts of Fuh-he and his successors some faint echo of the primitive tradition;—I am not concerned at present to enter upon that subject. What is said in the above quotations about the deluge of Yaou, however, is misleading. The reader is led to suppose that it comes in Chinese history, as caused by the declension and wickedness of the times immediately preceding,—a judgment of Heaven. If it were so,

4 帝摯. 5 China: Its State and Prospects, pp. 5, 6.

the view which they take would be greatly strengthened. But the Shoo is entirely silent on this point. Not a word is said as to the flood's being a punishment of the sins either of ruler or people.

But now, according to the views which I have sought to establish, the labours of Yu are not history, but myth. He did not perform the prodigious achievements on the mountains and rivers which are ascribed to him. That he was the laborious founder of the Chinese empire, and did much within the small space of territory which was then comprehended in its limits, there is no occasion to deny; but the gradual extension of the empire and development of its resources and order, which were the growth and accomplishment of many centuries, have been attributed to him by the Chinese, and their romance has been accepted by missionaries and others. The labours of Yu being denied, no place is left in his time for the deluge of Yaou. The utmost that can be allowed is an inundation of the Ho, destructive enough, no doubt, but altogether unfit to be described in the words put into the mouths of Yaou, Shun and Yu about it. Did the compilers of the first Parts of the Shoo draw upon their fancy for the floods that embraced the mountains and overtopped the hills and assailed the heavens? or did they find them in the tradition of a deluge by which 'all the hills that were under the whole heaven were covered?' I prefer to take the suggestion in the latter question as the fact, and therefore think that in the description of the inundation of Yaou's time we have an imperfect reference to the deluge of Noah.

The population of China in the time of Yu.

10. Before leaving the subject of Yu and his labours, it will be well to say something on another point, the commonly received account of which may be urged as inconsistent with the conclusions I have endeavoured to establish. Can the population of China in Yu's time be ascertained, even approximately?

Two sinologues have touched on this question:—Edward Biot the younger, in articles on 'The Population of China, and its Variations,' in the 'Journal Asiatique' of 1856; and T. Sacharoff, of the Russian Embassy in Peking, in an essay on 'The Rise and Fall of the Chinese Population,' translated into English last year by the Rev. W. Lobscheid.

The articles of Biot were written when his knowledge of Chinese subjects was immature, six years before he published in the same Journal the view of the *Yu Kung*, to which I have had occasion to

書經

make frequent reference. Had they been produced at a later date, he would not have accepted the statement of Ma Twan-lin, that the number of the people, on the conclusion of Yu's labours, amounted to 13,553,923 souls;—a number, which he, on certain hypothetical reasonings of his own, increased to 21,415,198.

Sacharoff would reduce the smaller of these estimates to a single million; but his remarks on the subject betray considerable confusion of thought. He says:—'Two censuses were at the disposal of native authors for ascertaining the amount of the population of China, during the happy reigns of Yaou and Shun, the epochs of the highest civilization. These were:—the division of the country for administrative purposes; and the extent of the really cultivated land. The first would, indeed, be a sufficient ground for arriving at a satisfactory conclusion, if the ancient documents stated the number of the principal provinces. If, *e. g.*, we take the nine provinces, into which Yaou divided the empire in the 23d century, then the population must have been very small, and could hardly exceed 100,000 families, or one million individuals. A calculation based on the extent of arable land proves nothing, because the classics scarcely state how many square rods were counted to a family, whilst nothing is said of the total amount of cultivated land, so that by fixing a certain figure, we are obliged to accept an arbitrarily given number of individuals.'[1]

I have endeavoured to find Ma Twan-lin's authority for the assertion, that, when Yu had reduced the empire to order, the inhabitants amounted to 13,553,923; and the oldest writer in whom I have met with it is Hwang-p'oo Meih, who died A.D. 282.[2] The statement, occurring thus, for the first time, about two thousand five hundred years after the date to which it refers, is of no historical value. As given by Meih, indeed, it is merely the result of certain calculations by him from the extent of the empire ruled by Yaou, and does not profess to be grounded on any certain data. So many absurdities are related, moreover, on the same page about Yu and other ancient worthies, that I am surprised the estimate of the population ever obtained any currency.

For instance, Meih begins by referring to the legends about Shin-nung and Hwang-te,—how the empire of the former extended, from

1 The Numerical Relations of the Population of China, &c., p. 10. Hongkong: A Shortrede & Co., 1864. 2 See Meih's Chronicle of Emperors and Kings, quoted by the editor of the Books of the After Han, 志第十九, p. 1.

east to west, a space of 900,000 *le*, and from north to south, 850,000 *le;* and how the latter, after having invented boats and carriages to traverse this mighty territory, determined the position of the different States in it by astronomical calculations. The author thinks that what is said about Shin-nung exceeds belief; but he goes on to quote the authority of Confucius (taken however from the 'Family Sayings,' an apocryphal Book) for the empire of Chuen-heuh, as extending to the Moving Sands on the west, Cochin-china on the south, the Sea on the east, and Yew-ling (north of Chih-le) on the north; and then, he comes to Yaou and Yu. Yu's nine provinces contained, he estimates, 24,308,024 *k'ing*, or nearly 368 million acres, of which 9,208,024 *k'ing*, or 140 million acres, were cultivable. Then comes in the amount of the population, and the further statement that the empire contained at that time 10,000 States. It is added on the authority of the 'Classic of Hills and Seas,' a book full of all sorts of prodigious stories, that Yu made two of his officers—Ta-chang, and Shoo-hae—walk, the one from the extreme east to the extreme west, and the other from the extreme north to the extreme south, and count their paces. The former traversed 223,300 *le*, and 71 paces; the latter 233,500 *le*, and 75 paces; but we must suppose that Meih was here counting only 100 paces to a *le*.[3] In fact, it is difficult to tell, how he took the terms, for he subjoins that, within the four seas, from east to west were 28,000 *le*, and from north to south 26,000. There were 5,350 famous hills; 467 hills producing copper; and 3,609 producing iron. The writer is evidently writing at random. The estimate of the population is no more to be received than any of all the other notices which he gives.

When Sacharoff says that, if we take the nine provinces, into which Yaou divided the empire, the population could hardly exceed one million individuals, it is difficult to understand what he means. If we could accept 'the nine provinces,' as indeed veritable portions of the empire, and believe that the country was occupied, even thinly, to that extent, we might very well allow a population for them, not of one million, but of twenty millions. But the critical study of the documents of the Shoo forbids us, as I have shown, to think of Yaou and Shun as other than petty chieftains, whose dominions

3 禹使大章步自東極至於西垂,二億三萬三千三百里七十一步,又使竪亥步南極北盡於北垂,二億三萬三千五百里,七十五步. The thing is differently stated in the copy of the 山海經, which I have,—printed in 1818, the 23d year of the reign Këa-k'ing.

書經

hardly extended across the Ho; and though Yu was the founder of a dynasty that lasted for more than four centuries, it is doubtful whether the last of his successors ruled over so much as the nine provinces of Yaou. The arguments on which I have maintained these conclusions might have needed reconsideration, if the estimate of thirteen millions and a half of inhabitants in Yu's time had been supported by a tittle of independent evidence; being merely a rough and random calculation at a period long subsequent, on the assumption of such a territory, those arguments are unaffected by it.

The number of one million which Sacharoff would allow for the Chinese of Yu's time is, it seems to me, abundantly large. The population of the country, in the time of king Ching, when the duke of Chow was administering the government, is given as 13,704,923; that is, according to the current accounts, the population had only increased 151,000 in eleven centuries and a half. If we suppose one million of inhabitants in Yu's time, and that they doubled every two hundred years, they ought to have amounted, in the time of the duke of Chow, to about one hundred millions. And yet we may say that there was no increase at all in all that space of time. About 400 years after, in the 13th year of king Chwang, B.C. 683, the population had decreased below what it was in Yu's days, and is given as only 11,941,923. It is evident from these figures, that the accounts of the population of the empire before our era cannot be regarded as approximations even to the truth;—especially it is evident, that assigning to Yu more than thirteen millions is simply of a piece with the assigning to him the achievements of a demigod on the face of the water and the land.

Ma Twan-lin, after Hwang-p'oo Meih and other early writers, calls attention to the decrease in the number of States, composing the empire, under each of the three early dynasties. At a grand *durbar* held by Yu on mount T'oo, 10,000 princes appeared to do him homage;—there were then 10,000 States. When the dynasty of Shang superseded Hea, those 10,000 were reduced to a little over 3000; and according to Meih, there was a corresponding diminution in the number of the people. In the beginning of the 12th century, B.C., when king Woo established the rule of Chow, his princes were only 1,773; and, again adds Meih, the people had dwindled correspondingly. But the people were more, according to Meih himself, in the beginning of the Chow dynasty than they had been in Yu's days, by 151,000 individuals. I say again, that it is evident the 10,000

States, of more than twenty centuries before our era, never had any existence. The state of the country under the successors of Yu, which I have pointed out on p. 61, is altogether inconsistent with the idea of such an empire. The magniloquent style of speech, however, once introduced, subsequent writers adopted it. Confucius himself and Mencius adhered to it, hiding thereby from themselves, their contemporaries, and posterity the truth about their own times, and the small beginnings of their history in the distant past.

11. I will not attempt to question the credibility of the Books of the Shoo lower down than the time of Yu. Those belonging to his dynasty are only three; and each of them is brief. As I said in the first paragraph, from the beginning of the Shang dynasty, we seem to tread the field of history with a somewhat confident step. The Books of Chow are sufficiently to be depended on, for they must have been made public while the memory of many of the things which they describe was still fresh.

The results which I have endeavoured to bring out in this chapter are:—first, that Yu is a historical personage, and was the founder of the Chinese empire, but that nearly all that the Shoo contains of his labours is fantastical exaggeration; and second, that Yaou and Shun were also real men, chiefs of the earliest Chinese immigrants into the country, but that we must divest them of the grand proportions which they have, as seen through the mists of legend and of philosophical romance. It seems folly to attempt to go beyond the Shoo, and push the history centuries farther back to the time of Fuh-he. We have now to inquire in the next chapter whether it be possible, from the Shoo or other sources, to determine with any satisfaction how long before our era we are to place those worthies.

書經

CHAPTER III.

ON THE DETERMINATION OF THE PRINCIPAL ERAS IN THE SHOO.

THERE IS NO CHRONOLOGY IN THE SHOO; AND IT WAS NOT TILL THE HAN DYNASTY THAT THE CHINESE BEGAN TO ARRANGE THEIR ANCIENT HISTORY WITH REFERENCE TO A COMMON ERA. THE PERIODS OF THE THREE DYNASTIES, AND OF YAOU AND SHUN. CHINESE HISTORY BEGINS ABOUT 2000 YEARS BEFORE CHRIST.

There is no Chronology in the Shoo.

1. On my first conception of this chapter, my idea was to designate it 'The Chronology of the Shoo.' Such is the title of the third chapter of Gaubil's 'Observations on the Shoo-king,' in which he has touched, succinctly and ably, on nearly all the points to which I have to call the attention of the reader. 'The Chronology of the Shoo,' however, would be a misnomer. There is no arrangement or succession of dates in it which can be so described. We learn from it that the dynasty of Chow succeeded to that of Shang, and the dynasty of Shang or Yin to that of Hea; and that prior to Yu, the founder of the Hea, there were the reigns of Shun and Yaou. In its present condition, it contains only scanty notices of a few of the sovereigns in the earlier dynasties, and the length of the reigns of two or three of them is stated; but even when it was complete, it did not embrace a list of all the rulers of China, and of the number of years which they reigned respectively:—and much less did it specify any date as a great era in the distant past, from which the commencement of the successive dynasties, and the accessions of the different monarchs in each of them, should be calculated. As Gaubil has observed, 'If we had only the Shoo-king, we should have but confused ideas of the time comprised in the four [five] Parts of the book.' We need not be surprised at this. The chronology of a nation comes to be cultivated as a science, only after it has long subsisted, and when the necessity is felt of arranging the events of its history in regular series on the course of time.

2. It was in the Han dynasty that it was first attempted to construct a chronological scheme of the history of the empire. For this purpose its scholars employed the well-known cycle of 60 years, in the 2d year of the 76th revolution of which, according to the commonly received views, I am now writing; and which is with the Chinese what the century is with us. It was assumed that this cycle had been made in the reign of Hwang-te by Ta-naou, one of his officers; but I need hardly say that the assumption rests on no satisfactory grounds. Believing the views which I have advocated in the last chapter to be correct, I must pronounce Hwang-te to be a fabulous personage, so far as any connection with the Chinese empire is concerned. If such a man ever lived at all, it was elsewhere than in China; and it is not till we come to the times of Ts'in and Han, more than 2,000 years after the period assigned to him, that we find Ta-naou spoken of at all.[1] And though the invention of the cycle is then generally ascribed to him, there are writers who give the credit of it to Fuh-he long before.[2] What is of more importance to observe is, that the cycle, as it is now universally recited and written, was not employed before the end of the Former Han dynasty, *i.e.*, until after the commencement of our Christian era, to chronicle years at all:—its exclusive use was to chronicle the days. Koo Yen-woo, one of the ablest scholars of the present dynasty, says expressly on this point:—'The 22 cycle characters [*i.e.*, the 10 stem characters from *këă* to *kwei*, and the 12 branch characters from *tsze* to *hae*] were used by the ancients to chronicle the days, and not to chronicle the years. For chronicling the years there were the 10 stem names of *oh-fung*, &c., down to *twan-mung*, and the 12 branch names of *shĕ-t'e-kih*, &c., down to *juy-han*. The way of later times, to say that such a year was *këă-tsze*, and so on, was not the ancient way.'[3] Yen-woo then quotes from the preface to the *Wae-ke*,[4] or 'Additional Records,' a supple-

Chronologising began in the Han dynasty. The cycle of 60 years.

The original use of the *Keă-tsze* cycle was to chronicle days.

1 See the 事物紀原,卷一, art. 甲子. We read:—世本曰,大橈造甲子。呂氏春秋曰,黃帝師大橈。黃帝內傳曰,帝既斬蚩尤,命大橈造甲子,正時。月令章句曰,大橈探五行之情,占斗剛所建,于時始作甲乙以名日,謂之幹,作子丑,以名月,謂之支,支幹相配,以成六旬. 2 See the 通鑑綱目,前編,卷之二.—伏羲氏作甲歷,定歲時. 3 See the 顧炎武日知錄,卷二十, art. 古人不以甲子名歲. 4 劉恕通鑑外紀目錄序.

ment to the 'General Survey' of History by Sze-ma Kwang,[5] with whom Lew Shoo, its author was associate, the following testimony:—'The years of the sovereigns before (!) and after Fuh-he, down to king Le, are, I apprehend, dark and hardly to be ascertained; and we borrow the names of the *kĕă-tsze* cycle to chronicle them;' adding himself:—'When did this practice of borrowing the cycle names to chronicle the years commence? It commenced in the time of the usurper Mang' (A.D. 9—22). The statement of this writer, that the ancients chronicled years by the names oh-fung shĕ-t'e-kih, &c., is very questionable; but I must content myself, for the present, with referring to what is said on the subject in the appendix to this chapter, on the 'Astronomy of the ancient Chinese,' with which the Rev. Mr. Chalmers has favoured me. So far as my reading has gone, there cannot be produced a single unchallengeable example of the naming of any year by any cycle characters whatever, previous to the termination of the Chow dynasty.

In the Shoo itself the current cycle is used to chronicle days, and days only. Years are specified according to their order in the reign of the sovereign to whom they are referred. Such specification of years, however, is in our classic exceedingly rare.

There can be no doubt that before the Han dynasty a list of sovereigns, and of the lengths of their several reigns, was the only method which the Chinese had of determining the duration of their national history. And it would still be a sufficiently satisfactory method, if we had a list of sovereigns and of the years each reigned, that was complete and reliable. We do not have this, however. Even in the early part of the Han dynasty, Sze-ma Ts'een's father and himself were obliged to content themselves with giving simply the names and order of most of the rulers in the dynasties of Shang and Hea. The lengths of the several reigns in

The ancient method of determining the length of Chinese history. The want of documents which could make it available now.

5 Sze-ma Kwang gets the credit of fixing the standard chronology; but let me call the attention of the student to Choo He's account of the matter. He tells us:—'When Kwang first made a Chronological scheme, his earliest date was the 1st year of Wei-lëĕ (B.C. 424). Afterwards, he extended his dates to the time of Kung and Ho (B.C. 840). After this again, he made his "Examination of Antiquity," beginning with the period of "highest antiquity," but he could give no dates of years earlier than that time of Kung and Ho. It was Shaou K'ang-tsëĕ who pushed the calculations up to the 1st year of Yaou (温公初作編年，起于威烈王，後又添至共和，又稽古錄，始自上古，然共和已上之年，已不能推矣，獨邵康節，却推至堯元年，云云). The passage is quoted in Hăng Ch'in-fung's notes on the annals of the Bamboo Books, 卷三, p. 4. Choo He appears to have been fascinated in a measure by the Bamboo Books.

the standard chronology have been determined, mainly, I believe, to make the whole line stretch out to the years which had been fixed on astronomical considerations for the periods of Chung-k'ang of the Hea dynasty and of Yaou. It will be seen in the sequel, and more fully in the next chapter, how the Bamboo Books contrive to shorten many of the reigns, so that those periods shall be less remote than they are commonly placed by about 200 years.

If in the Four Books, or in any other books of the Chow dynasty, we had a statement of the length of the national history from any given era to that of the writer, the notice would be exceedingly valuable. Or, if the lengths of the reigns of the sovereigns of Shang and Hea, cursorily mentioned, were given, we should be in a position to make an approximate computation for ourselves. I do not know, however, of more than two passages in all those books, which are really helpful to us in this point. Both of them are referred to by Gaubil. If the reader will turn to the passage translated from the Tso-chuen, in the note on p. 67 above, he will see it there stated that the dynasty of Shang possessed the empire for 600 years. That is one of the passages. The other is the very last chapter of the Works of Mencius, where that philosopher says that 'from Yaou and Shun to T'ang—a period including all the dynasty of Hea—were 500 years and more; that from T'ang to king Wăn—the period of the Shang dynasty—were 500 years and more; and that from king Wăn to Confucius were 500 years and more.' Now, we know that the birth of Confucius took place in B.C. 551. Adding 551 to the 1500 years 'and more,' given by Mencius, we have the era of Yaou and Shun, at 2,100 years before our Saviour, or thereabouts. The words of Mencius,—'from Yaou and Shun to T'ang,' are, indeed, sadly indefinite. Does he mean the end of Shun's reign, and the beginning of Yu's? or does he mean the beginning of Yaou's reign? I think it was the latter which he intended. But vague as his language is, I do not think that with the most painstaking research we can determine anything more definite and precise concerning the length of Chinese history than it conveys. Mencius knew nothing of rulers before Yaou, nor do I. What we are told of Yaou and Shun, moreover, is little trustworthy. About 2,000 years before the Christian era, China, which has since become so large an empire, rises before us, with small beginnings, in the vista of the past. I do not think that anything more precise than this can be said upon the subject. Let us see.

3. The last of the kings of the Chow dynasty mentioned in the Shoo is P'ing, the 13th of the line, whose 'Charge to Prince Wăn' of Tsin forms the 28th Book of the 5th Part. His place in history is well ascertained. Confucius' Chronicle of the Ch'un Ts'ew commences in B.C. 721. The 1st of the 36 eclipses mentioned in it took place three years after, on the 14th February (N.S.), B.C. 719; and it is recorded that in the month after king P'ing died.[1] Here, therefore, is a point of time about which there can be no dispute. In the words of Gaubil, 'we know the time of the end of the Shoo-king.' An earlier date in the Chow dynasty is known with the same certainty. The She mentions an eclipse which took place on the 29th August, B.C. 775, in the 6th year of king Yew, who preceded P'ing.[2] Yew reigned 11 years, and his predecessor, king Seuen, 46, whose reign consequently commenced B.C. 826. Up to this date Chinese chronologers agree. To the ten reigns before king Seuen, the received chronology assigns 295 years, making the dynasty begin in B.C. 1,121. The Bamboo Books assign to them only 223, making it commence in B.C. 1,049. In the lengths of five of the reigns the two schemes agree; but whether the longer estimate of the other five or the shorter is to be preferred, I do not see that we have sufficient grounds to determine. Gaubil, reasoning from the cycle names of the days, which are given in several of the Books of Chow (as I have pointed out in my notes on the various passages), would fix the commencement of the dynasty in B.C. 1,111 [or 1,110]. If we suppose that Mencius, as is most likely, in saying that 'from king Wăn to Confucius were 500 years and more,' intended by 'king Wăn' the commencement of the Chow dynasty, we have to conclude that this era must be between B.C. 1,051 and 1,161. The date in the Bamboo Books places it too late; that in the common chronology cannot be far from the truth.

The period of the Chow dynasty.

4. In treating of the period of the Shang dynasty, we cannot fix a single reign with certainty by means of astronomical data. The common chronology assigns to it 28 reigns extending over 644 years, so that its commencement was in B.C. 1,765. The Bamboo Books make the sovereigns to be 30, and the aggregate of their reigns only 508, so that the dynasty began in B.C. 1,557. Pan Koo of the Han made the length of the dynasty 529 years.

The period of the Shang dynasty.

1 三年，春王二月，己巳，日有食之。三月，庚戌，天王崩。

2 See the She, Pt. II., Bk. IV., Ode ix.—十月之交，朔日辛卯，日有食之。

The difference of two reigns between the schemes of Sze-ma Kwang and the Bamboo Books is unimportant, and, if they otherwise agreed, could only affect the length of the dynasty by 6 years. Some remarks on those reigns will be found in the note on Mencius, V., Pt. I., v. 5. That the number of reigns is not over-estimated we may infer from the statement of Mencius that between T'ang, the founder of the dynasty, and Woo-ting, the 20th (or 22d) sovereign, 'there had been six or seven worthy and sage rulers.'[1] In the 15th of the Books of Chow, the names of three of the sovereigns are given, and the duration of their reigns, to show how Heaven is likely to crown a good king with length of sway:—T'ae-mow, who reigned 75 years; Woo-ting, who reigned 59; and Tsoo-këă, who reigned 33. The two schemes which I have mentioned agree in the length of those reigns, and of five others. From the statement in the Tso-chuen, that the Shang dynasty lasted 600 years, and that of Mencius, that 'from T'ang to king Wăn were 500 years and more,' we may judge that the 644 years assigned to the Shang by the standard chronology are too many, and the 508 years of the Bamboo Books too few.

The period of the Hea dynasty.

5. According to the common chronology, the dynasty of Hea lasted 439 years; according to the Bamboo Books, it lasted 431. The difference between the two schemes is not great, though they agree exactly in the lengths of three of the reigns only. Mencius' words, that 'from Yaou and Shun to T'ang were 500 years and more,' include the period of Yaou and Shun as well as that of the Hea dynasty; but the years which he assigned to the two early sages, probably, did not differ much, if at all, from the common estimate of the two chronologies.[2] If we add 150 years either to 431 or 439, the sum is under 600 years. The period usually assigned to the Hea dynasty cannot be far from the truth.

In the 4th of the Books of Hea we have the record of an astronomical fact, which we might hope would enable us to determine the time of its occurrence, with as much certainty as the year of the death of king P'ing of the Chow dynasty is determined. In the reign of Chung-k'ang, the 3d of Yu's successors, there was an eclipse of the sun in the sign Fang. Sze-ma Kwang places the event in Chung-k'ang's 1st year,=B.C. 2,158 (or 2,159); the Bamboo Books place it in his 5th year,=, according to them, B.C. 1,947 (or 1,948). Neither

1 See Mencius, II., Pt. I. i. 8.—由湯至於武丁，賢聖之君，六七作.
2 Compare his statements in V. Pt. I., v. and vi.

of these years can be correct. Such an eclipse could not have taken place in them.

Gaubil tells us that the most famous astronomers of the T'ang dynasty, and subsequently those of the Yuen, determined this eclipse for the year B.C. 2,128 (or 2,127) on the 1st day of the 9th month, which year, moreover, they fixed as the 5th of Chung-k'ang; and that other astronomers of the same dynasties determined it for B.C. 2,155 (or 2,154), which would be the 5th of Chung-k'ang in the common chronology. He himself adopted and zealously supported the latter determination; but subsequent and more accurate calculations seem to prove that he was in error. The reader is referred to what I have said on the subject in the body of the Work, pp. 167, 168. The eclipse of B.C. 2,128 may possibly be that mentioned in the Shoo; and yet a different one, or more than one, may be found, within the period of the Hea dynasty, which would satisfy the necessary conditions. The authenticity of the Book in which we have the statement about the eclipse is called in question; but I have pointed out that that particular passage is guaranteed by its being quoted in the Tso-chuen. The history or story in connection with which the statement is given is also put down, by Bunsen [3] and others, as nothing better than 'a popular fable;' and neither am I concerned to deny this:—it may very well consist with the reference to the natural phænomenon which actually occurred. That phænomenon, however, shows that neither of the current chronologies of the time is to be relied on; and it does not by itself enable us to fix the time of the reign of Chung-k'ang.

Period of Yaou and Shun.

6. We come to the earliest period of Chinese history,—that of Yaou and Shun. The Shoo assigns 50 years of independent reigning to Shun: and Sze-ma Kwang and the Bamboo Books adopt the estimate. It says also that he was on the throne along with Yaou 30 years. Mencius says these were only 28; but the two additional years may be made out by supposing that they were years of mourning after the death of Yaou. Yaou had reigned at least 70 years, before he felt the necessity of some one to relieve him of the toils of government.[1] Both Kwang and the Bamboo Books adopt Yaou's 70th year, as the date of Shun's association with him, and so assign to him in all 100 years. Pan Koo gives 70 years to him, and 50 to Shun, thus strangely

3 Egypt's Place in Universal History, vol. III., p. 402.

1 See the Canon of Yaou, p. 12.

allowing the 28 or 30 years of their associate rule to drop altogether out of his chronology.[2] Kwang's standard tables place Yaou's first year in B.C. 2,357, (or 2,356); the Bamboo Books place it in 2,145. There is thus a difference of rather more than 200 years between them. As we found them both wrong in regard to the reign of Chung-k'ang, we must hence conclude that they are wrong also in regard to the period which we are now examining.

It has been generally supposed that Yaou's directions to the astronomers He and Ho, in the first Book of the Shoo, furnished data sufficiently certain to enable us to determine his era. The Shoo does not tell us indeed, in what year of his reign Yaou delivered those instructions, but the chronologers have all assumed that it was in his first year. The remarks of Mr. Chalmers on the point, in the appendix to this chapter, show that the value of Yaou's observations for chronological determinations has been overrated. The emperor tells his officers, that, among other indications which would enable them to fix the exact period of the cardinal points of the year, the vernal equinox might be ascertained by observing the star *neaou;* the summer solstice by observing the star *ho;* the autumnal equinox by observing the star *heu;* and the winter solstice by observing the star *maou.* It was assumed by the scholars of the Han dynasty that by *neaou* was to be understood the constellation or equatorial space then called *sing*,[3] beginning at α Hydra, and including a space of 2°; and that by *ho* was to be understood *fang*,[4] corresponding to π Scorpio, and including 4°. It was assumed also, that, as the result of the observation (of the manner of which the Shoo says nothing), *sing* would be found to pass the meridian at six o'clock in the evening, at the vernal equinox; and that the other stars mentioned would pass it at the same hour at the seasons to which they were referred.

I do not think there is any reason to call these assumptions in question. The scholars of Han, ignorant of the fact of the procession of the equinoxes, could not have arbitrarily fixed the particular stars to suit their chronological views;—their determination of them must have been in accordance with the voice of accredited tradition. Supposing that the stars were all what it is now believed they were, to what conclusions are we led by them as to the era of Yaou?

Bunsen tells us that Ideler, computing the places of the constellations backwards, fixed the accession of Yaou at B.C. 2,163,[5] which is

2 See the 前漢書·律歷下, p. 15. 3 星. 4 房. 5 Place of Egypt, &c., III., p. 100.

only 18 years before the date in the Bamboo Books. On the other hand, J. B. Biot finds in the statements of the Shoo a sufficient confirmation of the date in the received chronology, B.C. 2,357.[6] Freret was of opinion that the observations left an uncertainty to the extent of 3 degrees, leaving a margin of 210 years.[7] It seems to myself that it is better not to insist on pressing what Yaou says about the stars of the equinoxes and solstices into the service of chronology at all. Gaubil, Biot, and the other writers on the subject, all quote Yaou's observations so far as they had astronomical reference; but they take no notice of other and merely popular indications, which he delivered to his officers to help them to ascertain the seasons. They would know the spring, he tells them, by the pairing of birds and beasts, and by the people's beginning to disperse into the country on their agricultural labours. Analogous indications are mentioned for summer and autumn; till in the winter time the people would be found in their cosy corners, and birds and beasts with their coats downy and thick. Taken as a whole, Yaou's instructions to He and Ho are those of a chief speaking popularly, and not after the manner of a philosopher or astronomer. We must not look for exactness in his remarks about the cardinal stars. The mention of them in the earliest portion of the Shoo proves that its compiler, himself, as I showed in the last chapter, of a later date, had traditions or written monuments of a high antiquity at his command; but Yaou was as likely to be speaking of what he had received from his predecessors as of what he had observed for himself; and those predecessors may not have lived in China, but in another region from which the Chinese came. If it were possible to fix the exact century, in which it was first observed that the stars of the equinoxes and solstices were *neaou* and *heu*, *ho* and *maou*, that century may have been anterior to Yaou, and not the one in which he lived.

7. From the review which I have thus taken of the different periods of Chinese history, documents purporting to belong to which are preserved in the Shoo, it will be seen that the year B.C. 775 is the earliest date which can be said to be determined with certainty. The exact year in which the Chow dynasty commenced is not known; and as we ascend the stream of time, the two schemes current among the Chinese themselves diverge more widely from each other, while to neither of them can we accord our credence. The accession of Yu, the first *sovereign* of the nation, was probably at some time in

6 Etudes sur l'Astronomie Indienne et Chinoise. pp. 361 366. 7 Bunsen, as above: p. 101.

the nineteenth century before Christ; and previous to him there were the chiefs Shun and Yaou. Twenty centuries before our era the Chinese nation appears, beginning to be. To attempt to carry its early history to a higher antiquity is without any historical justification. There may have been such men as Chinese writers talk of under the appellations of Chuen-heuh, Hwang-te, Shin-nung, Fuh-he, &c.; but they cannot have been rulers of China. They are children of the mist of tradition, if we should not rather place them in the land of phantasy.

For myself, I had adopted the chronology of the Septuagint as nearer the truth than that of our present Hebrew Bibles, more than five-and-twenty years ago, before it was definitely in my plan of life to come to China as a missionary; but the history of China need not seriously embarrass any one who follows the shortest chronology of Scripture. Writers like Bunsen, who follow the will-o'-the-wisps of their own imagination, may launch their shafts against the intolerance of churches, and narrow-mindedness of missionaries. On Chinese ground we can afford to laugh at *their* intolerance. Each bolt they discharge is mere *brutum fulmen*; each shaft, *imbelle telum*.

APPENDIX

ON THE

ASTRONOMY OF THE ANCIENT CHINESE.

By the Rev. John Chalmers, A.M.

The Earth, the Sun, the Heavens.

1. The Chinese believed the earth to be a plane surface;—"straight, square, and large,"[1] measuring each way about 5,600 *le* (=1,500 miles), and bounded on the four sides by "the four seas."[2] The North sea and the West sea were of course purely imaginary. The earth was motionless, while the sun and the moon and the starry heavens were continually revolving with great rapidity. This is the fixed belief of the Chinese even at the present day. The sun was estimated to be about 15,000 *le* (=4000 miles) from the earth, and it was supposed that the city of Loh was in "the centre of heaven and earth,"—the middle of the Middle Kingdom.[3] In other places the shadow of a perpendicular gnomon was not due north and south at noonday, or else it was too short

1 直, 方, 大, see the Yih-king, 坤卦. 2 Shoo, Pt. II. Bk. I. 13.; Pt. III. Bk. I. Pt. ii. 14—23. 3 Shoo, Pt. V. Bk. XII. 14.

書經

or too long; but here it was not found to deviate in either direction, and its length on midsummer-day was to the length of the gnomon as 15 to 80. The distance assigned to the sun is in fact the earth's radius, and was a natural inference from the plane figure of the earth, taken in connection with the different elevation of the sun in different latitudes. From the same premisses it was also inferred that the shadow would be all awry at noon in places far east or far west of Loh;—those on the east being too near the morning sun, and those on the west too near the evening sun. The following legend [4] may be quoted as illustrative of the supposed nearness of the sun to the earth. "There is a country in the far west, in the place of the setting sun, where every evening the sun goes down with a noise like thunder, and the king of the country leads out a thousand men on the city wall to blow horns and beat gongs and drums, as the only means of keeping little children from being frightened to death by the unearthly roaring of the monster." The writers of the early Han dynasty hesitate not to affirm that the experiment to prove the deviation of the shadow at noon was made with all the necessary apparatus,—clepsydras, gnomons, &c., and found successful. But the clepsydra is not mentioned in any authentic writing of earlier date than the Han; and we may safely conclude that this, as well as some other instruments mentioned by interpreters of the classics, and in the Chow-le, was unknown to the ancient Chinese. The clepsydra is described by Aristotle (B.C. 384—322).

The Chinese have made attempts at various times to calculate the distance of the sidereal heavens. In the History of Tsin [5] the result of a calculation is given with amusing minuteness. It is said:—"By the method of right-angled triangles the distance between heaven and earth was found to be 81,394 *le*, 30 paces, 5 feet, 3 inches, and 6 tenths!" Another calculator [6] gives 216,781½ *le*. The diameter of the sun is given by one writer as 1000 *le*; [7] and he is said to be 7000 *le* below the heavens (the firmament).

The Seasons.

2. "The first calendars of the Greeks were founded on rude observations of the rising and setting of certain stars, as Orion, the Pleiades, Arcturus &c." [1] The same may be said of the calendars of the Chinese. Even after Meton and Callippus the Chinese calendar must have been founded on very "rude" observations indeed. During the two centuries and a half embraced by Confucius' History of the later Chow dynasty, the commencement of the year fell back a whole month. This is demonstrable from the dates of the 36 eclipses, of which a list will be found subjoined, and from a variety of references to months, and days of the cycle of 60, which occur throughout the History. It is probable that an error of another month was committed before the fall of the dynasty in the 3d century B.C. The rapid derangement of the months, and consequently of the seasons during this period, however, most probably arose from the adoption of some erroneous system of intercalation, invented to supersede the troublesome observations of the stars from month to month. And the consequence was, that the knowledge of the stars came to be cultivated only for purposes of astrology,—a science in which accuracy is no object. Hence even at the present day, the signs of the zodiac, or the 28 mansions of the moon, are most frequently represented not as they appear now, but as they appeared to Yaou and Shun. [2] The earliest account, which has any claim to authenticity, of the stars employed to mark the cardinal signs of the zodiac, is in the Canon of Yaou. According to

4 異域志. 5 晉志. 6 張揖. 7 徐整長歷.

1 See Smith's Dictionary of Antiquities, Article *Calendar*. 2 Shoo, Pt. I. Bk. I.

the interpretation of that document, the equinoxes were in Taurus (Pleiades) and Scorpio, and the solstices in Leo and Aquarius in the time of Yaou. No doubt there was a tradition to this effect at the time when the Shoo-king was compiled, for the author knowing nothing of the precession of the equinoxes, could not have adjusted them to the time of which he was writing. His "examination of antiquity"[3] was so far accurate, although the details of his narrative may and even must be mythical. Even Yaou himself may be so. In accordance with Chinese ideas of a sage, Yaou in a few pompous sentences makes it appear that he is perfectly acquainted beforehand with the results of the observations which he orders his astronomers to make:—"You will find the star is in *neaou*," &c. But did they find the stars as Yaou said they would find them? We are supposed to believe that they did, of course; but since we are not told, we claim the liberty to doubt. Suppose, for the sake of argument, that Yaou, before the observations were made, was dependent on tradition for his knowledge, and that his astronomers were capable of making accurate observations, they would in that case have had to report some failure in the verification of his statements. But apart from this, we are prepared to affirm that three of the men sent to the four borders of China could not have seen the stars, which occupied for the time being the equinoctial and solstitial points, culminating on the evenings named. *E.G.*, the first point of Libra could not be seen culminating at nightfall, when the sun is in the first point of Cancer, for it must culminate at 6h. P.M., whereas the sun would not set in any part of China in midsummer much before 7h. P.M., and the stars would not be visible for half an hour after sunset. This last fact would stand equally in the way, at the equinoxes, of the observers' seeing their stars culminating, unless, indeed, the time of observation was several centuries later than the date usually assigned to Yaou (B.C. 2356—2255), so that the stars to be observed had ceased to be exactly in the solstitial colure. The astronomer who went to the *north in winter* is the only one who would have no difficulty of this kind. He might see his star long before it culminated. But unless he had a good clock, he could not tell that it culminated at 6h. P.M. In the course of the long winter evening he would lose his reckoning sadly. The clepsydra also, supposing that he had one, might be ice-bound. The observation could have been made more conveniently in every way at the central station than at the northern border.

The value of the astronomical part of the Canon of Yaou, as a confirmation of the received chronology, has been much overrated. According to the obvious interpretation of the text, Yaou had *reason* to expect the stars he mentioned to be in the equinoctial and solstitial colures. But what his reason was we are left to conjecture. It might be personal observation; or it might be tradition from his great-grandfather, or from Noah himself.

Scorpio, the *Ho* of Yaou, was considered, even to the end of the Chow dynasty, an important guide to the knowledge of the seasons, as is evident from the frequent references to it in the writings of that time.[4] An ode in the Book of Poetry, attributed to Chow-kung, begins with the words,[5] "In the seventh month *Ho* passes on,"—that is to say, passes to the westward of the meridian at nightfall. From which it would follow that in the sixth month it was in the meridian at the same hour. This would have been the case if the seventh month had coincided with ours, or with the end of July and part of August, but not if the year had commenced with our December, as

3 First sentence of Canon of Yaou. 4 左傳．國語 &c. 5 詩．豳風．

書經

the Chinese say the year of the Chow dynasty always did. Here therefore is an argument against the prevailing opinion, which there are other strong reasons for setting aside, that king Woo, when he became emperor, ordered that the year should begin before the winter solstice, while the first month was still absurdly styled the first of spring. The fact is, the months of the year fell into this great disorder afterwards, through neglect, and not on account of an imperial decree. It is probable, however, that even in Chow-kung's time the first month of the year was the last of the winter season, the error of one month passing down from the previous dynasty. As early as B.C. 775, we find the year beginning with our December; and 50 years after, it begins with January again.

The former date, B.C. 775, is very important, as being the earliest which astronomical calculation really confirms. The tenth month of that year commenced on 29th of August (new style)—the 28th day of the cycle of 60—with an eclipse of the sun, which is mentioned in the Book of Poetry.[6] The first month of next year, unless an intercalary month intervened, would begin about the end of November.

The passage in the Tso Chuen,[7] in which Confucius is made to say that in the 12th month of the year, Scorpio was still visible in the west, is not intelligible, for the sun must have passed through Scorpio in October, and the 12th month was certainly not our September.

A very ancient and characteristic method of determining the seasons and months of the year, to which the Chinese are fond of alluding, was by the revolution of Ursa Major. One of its names, of which it has several, is "the Northern Bushel." Under this name it is often confounded with the North Pole, and also with one of the 28 mansions in Sagittarius, which has the same name. Its tail is called the "handle." There is a clear statement of this method of determining the seasons in the writings of Hoh-kwantsze: [8]—"When the tail of the Bear points to the *east* (at nightfall), it is *spring* to all the world. When the tail of the Bear points to the *south*, it is *summer* to all the world. When the tail of the Bear points to the *west*, it is *autumn* to all the world. When the tail of the Bear points to the *north*, it is *winter* to all the world." It is well to keep in mind that the body of the Great Bear was in ancient times considerably nearer to the north pole than it is now, and the tail appeared to move round the pole somewhat like the hand of a clock or watch. The Historical Records say, that the seven stars of the Northern Bushel are spoken of (in the Shoo, Pt. II. Bk. I. p. 5) when it is said, "The pivot and the gem-transverse adjust the seven directors." According to later interpreters, the sun, moon, and five planets are the seven directors, and the pivot, &c., refer to an astronomical instrument. But the ancients knew nothing of the five planets. No reference to them as *five* can be found in the classics. On the contrary, they seem to have supposed, as the Greeks did before Pythagoras, that Lucifer and Hesperus were two stars. Hence in the Book of Poetry we find lines to this effect:—

> "In the east there is Lucifer
> In the west there is Hesper."[9]

And the references to the five planets in the Chow Ritual, and in the three annotated editions of the Chun Ts'ew, are evidence of their later origin. The same may be said of the use of the planet Jupiter for astrological purposes, which belongs to the time of the Contending States, or to the early Han. At that time the period of

6 詩, 小雅. 7 左傳, 哀公十二年. 8 鶡冠子, Sec. V. 9 詩, 小雅.

Jupiter was supposed to be exactly 12 years, so that he gave a year to each sign of the Zodiac, therefore he is always called the *year star.* Considering this exact law of motion in the planet, one Chinese author remarks :—"It must be a spiritual thing without doubt."

The annexed figure will illustrate the use of Ursa Major as a kind of natural clock, whose hand makes one revolution in a year. The earth's surface (square of course) is converted into a dial, and the horizon is divided into 12 parts, making due north the centre of the first division. In theory the time of observation is 6h. P.M. precisely. But it was necessary to wait till the stars were visible. If the tail then pointed due east, it indicated the vernal equinox; but if it pointed due west, as represented in the figure, it was the autumnal equinox.

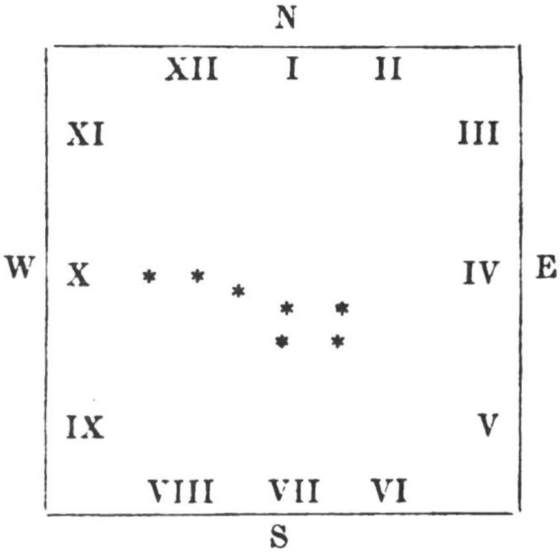

In this instance, the hand of the clock points a little in advance of the sun in the ecliptic, and to the bright stars in Scorpio, for the tail of the Bear always points to Scorpio. So then we have still Scorpio as the sign of mid-autumn.

This symmetrical position of the Great Bear, or "Northern Bushel," with reference to the seasons, is essential to the Chinese creed; and hence to this day, maugre the precession of the equinoxes, it retains its position in the estimation of almost all Chinese, learned and ignorant. The seasons still arrange themselves round the dial in exactly the same way, Winter going to the north, Spring to the east, Summer to the South, and Autumn to the west.

The Zodiac.

3. The most common and the earliest division of the ecliptic is that of the 28 mansions. These are of very unequal extent, and consequently very inconvenient for any purpose but that of astrology. The apportioning of 7 of these mansions to each of the cardinal points is also nothing more than an astrological device; but the Chinese student comes in contact with it so frequently, that some explanation of its origin seems very desirable. We must remember that the hour of midnight at the winter solstice is with the Chinese a grand epoch; a sort of repetition of the T'ae-keih or commencement of all things. Let the circle in the annexed figure represent the position of the ecliptic at midnight in mid-winter, in relation to the Chinese earth, represented by a square space in the centre. At the season and hour in question, in the time of Yaou, Leo would be in the meridian, and south of the zenith in the middle of China; Taurus would be in the west, and Scorpio in the east; and it is correctly inferred that Aquarius, though invisible, would be north of the nadir.

Accordingly, the seven winter mansions of which Aquarius is the centre are assigned to the north, and the seven summer mansions of which Leo is the centre are assigned to the south. Thus far the arrangement agrees with that already described according to the motion of the Great Bear. But the vernal mansions go to the west, and the autumnal ones to the east, reversing the previous direction of these two seasons, and in opposition to the prevailing notion of the Chinese that spring belongs to the east, &c. This discrepancy does not seem however to trouble their minds at all, and we may safely leave it unexplained.

The angular value of the 28 mansions varies from 1° to 30°, and modern books differ materially from the older ones as to the dimensions of each. Even the four great divisions differ more than 30° one from another. The following are their respective lengths as given in the introduction to Yung-ching's Shoo-king. The circle was divided into 365¼ degrees :—

The 7 Northern	Constellations	embrace	98¼ deg.
„ Western	„	„	80 „
„ Southern	„	„	112 „
„ Eastern	„	„	75 „
		Total	365¼ deg.

This division of the ecliptic is, with some slight variations, common to the Arabians, the Hindoos, and the Chinese;—a fact which seems to point to the common origin of these races, or to their inter-communication at a period of which history gives us as yet no information.

Besides this inconvenient system of unequal constellations or mansions, the Chinese have, in common with western nations and the Hindoos, the division of the Zodiac into twelve equal parts or signs. This improvement was probably also introduced in the end of the Chow, or the beginning of the Han dynasty. The Sinologue will see a reference to two of these signs in the Tso Chuen,[1] where they are mentioned for an astrological purpose, in connexion with the planet Jupiter. The following is a list of the Chinese signs, with the constellations to which they correspond. The commencement with Aries is optional, as the Chinese usually write them round a circle.

1 大梁	Aries-Taurus.	7 大火	Libra-Scorpio.
2 實沈	Taurus-Gemini.	8 析木	Scorpio-Sagittarius.
3 鶉首	Gemini-Cancer.	9 星紀	Sagittarius-Capricorn.
4 鶉火	Cancer-Leo.	10 玄枵	Capricorn-Aquarius.
5 鶉尾	Leo-Virgo.	11 娵訾	Aquarius-Pisces.
6 壽星	Virgo-Libra.	12 降婁	Pisces-Aries.

The commencement of the first month of spring between the 20th of January and the 19th of February is said to fall always within the 11th of these signs. This ought therefore to coincide with our Aquarius; and the fact that it includes part of Pisces might be taken as indicative of an earlier date than that of our Zodiacal nomenclature; but it seems rather to be an accommodation to the ancient traditions. We do not find that the ancient Chinese made much practical use of the 12 signs; and even to the present day the 28 mansions of the moon have retained their place in preference to the more scientific division.

1 左傳襄公二十八年

海上絲綢之路文獻集成 科技與文化編

4. Slowly and reluctantly did the Chinese astronomer awake to the recognition of the fact that the position of the equinoxes in the ecliptic was shifting from age to age. With the traditions of 2000 years embodied in the classical literature of his country, and engraven on the tablets of his memory, and with the alteration of a whole sign in the position of the equinoctial points staring him in the face, his mind remained sealed against the entrance of the new idea; and went on in its old ruts by sheer *vis-inertiæ*. Hipparchus (B.C. 160—125) discovered the precession of the equinoxes by comparing his own observations with those of Aristyllus and Timocharis, or others who preceded him by not more than two or three centuries; whereas the first man in China who took notice of the precession lived in the 4th century of the Christion era (Comm. on Canon of Yaou, p. 21). He was separated from Yaou by a period of 2600 years!

Precession of the Equinoxes.

5. The invention of the cycle of 60 is ascribed to Hwang-te (B.C. 2,636), and in particular its application to years is affirmed to have commenced in his reign; but this is a mere fiction. It was not applied to years even in the time of Confucius. The Cycle consists of two sets of characters; one set of 10, and one set of 12,—which are combined in couples, odd to odd and even to even, making in all sixty combinations.

The Cycle of 60; and its Applications.

The "twelve terrestrial branches," as they are called, were first invented, in all probability, to distinguish the twelve spaces into which the horizon is divided, as described above. Their names and order are as-follows:—

Months.

1 子 tsze, 2 丑 ch'ow, 3 寅 yin, 4 卯 maou, 5 辰 shin, 6 巳 sze,
7 午 woo, 8 未 we, 9 申 shin, 10 酉 yew, 11 戌 seuh, 12 亥 hae.

The common mode of expression, 建子, 建丑 &c., "to set up *tsze*," "to set up *ch'ow*," &c., refers to the tail of the Great Bear pointing to *tsze*, *ch'ow*, and the other ten divisions of the dial. *Tsze*, the first character always indicates due north, and the middle of winter.

It was an easy step, from the original application of the 'twelve branches' to the months, to a duodecimal division of the day; but according to native authorities this was not adopted till the time of Han. It does seem strange that the Chinese should have existed so long without any artificial division of the day; and yet in recording eclipses, where the time of the day is a most important item, it is never mentioned.

Hours.

The application of the cycle to days is undoubtedly a very ancient practice. But it would seem from a passage in the Shoo, Pt. II. Bk. IV., par. 8, that the days were originally arranged in tens *only*, by means of the 10 "celestial stems." These are:—

Days.

1 甲 keă, 2 乙 yih, 3 丙 ping, 4 丁 ting, 5 戊 mow,
6 己 ke, 7 庚 kăng, 8 辛 sin, 9 壬 jin, 10 癸 kwei.

Yu is made to say, "I remained with my wife only the days *sin, jin, kwei, keă.*" These are the last three and the first of the above set of characters, and the natural inference from their use here is that they were invented to divide the month into three equal parts (three decades); and that in course of time they were combined with the twelve branches to make the famous Chinese cycle of *sixty*. The first mention of the

1 一日十二時始於漢. See Morrison's View of China, Chron. Tables.

書經

cyclical name of a day is found in the Shoo, Pt. IV. Bk. IV. p. 1. It is said to have been in the 12th month of the first year of the emperor T'ae-këă. The current chronology makes this year to be B.C. 1,752. But the chronology is utterly valueless; and we have no sufficient data by which to verify the day. Moreover, this is the only instance of the use of the cycle which occurs before B.C. 1,121 of the same chronology. In the Books of Chow it is frequently employed.

The state of confusion in which Chinese chronology is found to be, down to the time of the Eastern Chow, and the fact that not a single instance of the application

Years. of the cycle to years can be found till after the classical period, are sufficient to satisfy us that this invaluable method of dating years was never used in ancient times. The first attempt to arrange the years in cycles of sixty is found in Sze-ma Ts'een's Historical Records, in a *table* constructed for the purpose of intercalation, and extending over a period of 76 years, the first year being B.C. 103. But instead of using the Chinese cyclical characters, he employs words of two and three syllables, which, considered from a Chinese point of view, must be pronounced barbarous. We give the names applied to the first thirteen years. Perhaps some one acquainted with the ancient language of the Hindoos may hereafter be able to identify them. The second word in each name has some connexion with the motion of the planet Jupiter; and Sze-ma says that *Sheht'e*, part of the first name, means Jupiter. His commentator adds that Jupiter belongs to the east, and is the essence of wood, the spirit of the Green god, *Ling-wei-jang*. This last word is one of six meaningless trisyllables, applied to the the god of the north pole and to the five elemental gods, during the Han dynasty, for which also we must seek a foreign origin. They are given below :—

Names of Years in Sze-ma Ts'een's History, probably of foreign origin.

B.C.	103	焉逢	攝提格	yenfung	shĕt'ckih.
	102	端蒙	單閼	twanmnug	tangoh.
	101	游兆	執徐	yewchaou	chihseu.
	100	彊梧	大芒落	keangwoo	tamanglŏh.
	99	徒維	敦牂	t'oowei	tuntsang.
	98	祝犂	協洽	chuhle	hĕcheă.
	97	商橫	赤奮若	shanghung	ch'ihfunjŏ.
	96	昭陽	作噩	ch'aouyang	tsŏhgŏh.
	95	橫艾	閹茂	hunggae	yenmow.
	94	尙章	大淵獻	shangchang	tayuenheen.
	93	焉逢	困敦	yenfung	kw'antun.
	92	端蒙	汭漢	twanmung	juyhan.
	91	游兆	攝提格	yewchaou	shĕt'ckih.

Names of gods, probably of foreign origin.

The god of the north pole	北帝	*Yaou pih paou*	耀魄寶.
The Green god (wood)	靑帝	*Ling wei jang*	靈威仰.
The Red god (fire)	赤帝	*Ch'ih p'eaou noo*	赤熛怒.
The Yellow god (earth)	黃帝	*Shay ch'oo new*	含樞紐.

97]

The White god (metal) 白帝 *Pih chaou keu* 白招矩.
The Black god (water) 黑帝 *Heih kwang ke* 叶光紀.

Various attempts have been made to analyse the second word *Sheht'ekih,* (in Cantonese *Shipt'ai kak.* Is *Shipt'ai* intended to represent the Hindoo name of Jupiter,—Vrishaspati; and *kak* the Hindoo chacra, or cycle?) applied to the first year of Sze-ma Ts'een's Table; and to determine which of the 12 branches' it ought to be identified with. Sze-ma himself, besides saying that *sheht'e* is Jupiter, explains the term to mean the place of that planet in the ecliptic; and again, with strange inconsistency, he says elsewhere it is the star or constellation to which the tail of Ursa Major points. In a work called the 'Classic of Stars,'[1] *sheht'e* is said to denote a "spiritual instrument of western nations." Now this confusion of words without knowledge is easily accounted for on the supposition that the cycle of 60 years was introduced from the Hindoos, to whom the Chinese were indebted in the time of Sze-ma Ts'een for other things even more important. In justice to Sze-ma, however, or rather to the compilers of the Work that goes by his name, for it is the work of more than one hand, it ought to be stated that they saw that the motion of Jupiter was in the opposite direction to that in which the "12 branches" are reckoned, and would give them in the reverse order. They therefore had recourse again to the Great Bear; and explained that the character belonging to that month of any year when Jupiter rose before the sun in the east was the cyclical character for that year. They then tell us that, in the year B.C. 103, Jupiter rose in the morning during the first month, which is (寅) *yin,* the third of the 12 branches. This ought therefore to be the cyclical character for 103. But future chronologists made it (丑) *ch'ow,* the second. Probably they did this because the History says that Jupiter was in *ch'ow.* But if this was their reason, they overlooked the fact that on the following year the planet is said to be in (子) *tsze,* and again after another year has elapsed, he is in (亥) *hae,* going backwards over the characters. They evidently lighted upon the wrong expression. The original[2] runs thus:—"In the *sheht'ekih* year, the (陰) *yin* of the year, moving to the left, is in (寅) *yin,* and the star of the year (Jupiter) moving, in the opposite direction, to the right, is in *ch'ow.*" The word (陰) *yin* here is too vague to be translated. It means any thing which is the reverse of the star, or the counter part of the star. Chinese scholars are fond of using this form of expression:—"The year is in *keah-tsze;*"[3] but probably very few ever reflect on the meaning of the phrase, or know that it has its origin in the above passage from the Historical Records, much less could they say for certain whether it is the *yin* of the year, or the *star* of the year, that they intend to say is "in *keah-tsze.*"

The characters before in use for the cycle of 60 days were soon substituted for the longer names: but not without some diversity of opinion as to where the cycle should commence. In the chronological Tables given in the Historical Records the cyclical characters have been supplied by a later hand, from B.C. 840 downwards; but in every case the authority of the scholars of Tsin (A.D. 265-419) is quoted. Seu Kwang[4] seems to be most closely followed; but he was preceded in the same department of labour by Hwangfoo Meih,[5] and perhaps also by the inventor of the so-called Bamboo Books.[6] So then the cycle of 60 years cannot have commenced earlier than the Han,

1 星經. 2 史記,天官書. 3 歲在甲子. 4 徐廣.
5 皇甫謐. 6 竹書紀年.

書經

and owes its present form to the scholars of Tsin; although the Chinese for the most part still glory in the delusion that it was invented by Hwangte, (60 × 75=) 4500 years ago.

6. The Chinese month has always been lunar; and as twelve lunations come short of a solar year by nearly 11 days, it is necessary from time to time to insert an extra month to preserve a general correspondence with the solar year. The statement of Yaou (Shoo, Pt. I. par. 8), that the year consists of 366 days, was made with a view to facilitate the process of intercalation which he ordered his astronomers to conduct. But to reckon the solar year at 366 days would occasion an error of a whole month in 40 years; so that in the course of his long reign of 100 years Yaou might have seen great cause to shorten the solar period. It would seem, however, that neither he nor his successors made any attempt to obtain more accurate numbers, and that in fact their intercalation was regulated by the natural recurrence of the seasons, and rude observations from year to year. During the Chow dynasty, intercalary months were placed at irregular intervals, but most frequently at the end of the year.

Intercalation.

The Chinese seem even then to have had no idea of the proper interval between two intercalations, which is now known to be 32 or 33 months on an average. The amount of error which they actually committed in the commencement of the year has been already referred to; and we now give a few examples gathered from the "Ch'un Ts'ew" of Confucius. According to the theory of later writers, the year ought always to have commenced between November 22 and December 22; but on the contrary we find that the year B.C. 719 commenced .... on January 16;

„ 703	„		„ January 20;
„ 688	„		„ January 4;
„ 685	„		„ January 1;
„ 658	„		„ January 3;
„ 626	„		„ January 8;
„ 605	„	on November 18;	
„ 583	„	„ November 16;	
„ 556	„	„ November 17;	
„ 540	„	„ November 19;	
„ 529	„	„ November 18;	
„ 526	„	„ November 15.	

For an instance of the intercalary month placed at the end of the year on three successive occasions, the reader is referred to Sze-ma Ts'een's Chronological Tables,—Ts'in dynasty, years 207, 204, & 201, B.C. Each of these would be separated from the other by 36 lunations instead of 32; and a proportionate amount of error would be caused in the situation of the months.

In the second century before the Christian era, the Chinese made extraordinary efforts to open communication with the West. They explored due west as far as the borders of Persia. Beyond theno madic tribes of Huns and Scythians, their immediate neighbours, the Chinese travellers found nations comparatively civilised, dwelling in cities and towns. Their horses were far superior to any known in China, and were eagerly coveted by the emperor. They had wine made from grapes, which the rich preserved for many years. Among other objects of interest unknown in Eastern Asia are mentioned single humped camels (C. Arabicus) and ostrich-eggs. At the same time they became acquainted

Reform of the calendar.

with the northern parts of India,—Shindo (Scinde ?), Dahea, &c.[1] Sze-ma Ts'een, who gives a full history of these discoveries, does not indeed tell us that they became acquainted with the cycle of Callippus, either through the Bactrians or the Hindoos; but there is scarcely a shadow of doubt that this was the case. In no other way can we account for the sudden appearance, in Ts'een's History, of a method so far in advance of anything known before in China, and one which had been already employed in the West for more than two centuries. The cycle of Callippus is simply this:—
$4 \times 19 = 76$ years $= 27759$ days $= 940$ lunations. It must have been well known to Alexander, the pupil of Aristotle, and the conqueror of Sogdiana, Bactria, and the Punjab, B.C. 328—325. The reformation of the Chinese calendar by Sze-ma Ts'een and others, with the help of these numbers, dates from the winter solstice of the year 104 B.C. In order to make this epoch appear as perfect as possible, they overlooked minor differences, though amounting to a whole day in the case of the solstice, and declared that new moon, and winter, and midnight, all coincided, at the commencement of the first of the cycle. From this remarkable epoch all dates before and after were to be calculated by the new method. In constructing a calendar for short periods, or even for a century or two, the method was invaluable; but with unlimited faith in its perfection, the Chinese scholars of that day proceeded to solve by means of it all difficult problems of ancient chronology; and here of course it led them astray. We can easily see the amount of error which they committed in reckoning back 16 centuries to the first year of T'ae-keă, or ten centuries to the 13th year of Woo-wang. In round numbers, the error of the Metonic cycle, as modified by Callippus, amounts to one day in the time of new moon for every 300 years, and three days in the time of winter solstice for every 400 years. So then the scholars of Han, in calculating the day of new moon at the commencement of the Chow dynasty, made an error of three days. As Confucius has nowhere told us, and possibly could not tell, how many years the Chow dynasty had lasted up to his own time, the problem the chronologers had to solve was to find a year near the supposed date of Woo-wang, which should commence with the day *sin-maou*. Such a year being found would, according to the Shoo-king, Pt. V. Bk. III. par 1, be the 13th of king Woo. Calculated according to the Metonic cycle from the epoch of Han, the year in question is B.C. 1121. But if we attempt to verify this date by modern methods, we find that the supposed first new moon of 1121 would fall three days later than *sin-maou*, and moreover that the whole lunation would be before the winter solstice, and belong according to the Chinese theory to the preceding year. So then, if we are not prepared to reject all the dates in the Shoo-king as spurious, we have no alternative but to condemn the received chronology. But the chronology of the whole period embraced by the Shoo rests on nothing better than mere conjecture, and imperfect astronomical calculations, made after the reformation of the calendar in the 2nd century B.C. We can have no hesitation therefore in rejecting it.

It may be well to state here one or two additional arguments in favour of the view that the Chinese borrowed their astronomy from the West before the Christian era. It is stated by Sir J. F. Davis, in his work on *The Chinese*, Vol. II. p. 290, that the Hindoo cycle of sixty years "is a cycle of Jupiter, while that of the Chinese is a solar cycle." The learned author does not explain what he understands by "a solar cycle" of 60 years, nor does he give any authority for the statement. We have found, on the

[1] 身毒.大夏.

海上絲綢之路文獻集成 科技與文化编

書經

contrary, that the Chinese cycle, like the Hindoo one, is connected with the period of Jupiter. In the same page of the above work it is said, "Besides the lunar zodiac of twenty-eight mansions, the Hindoos *(unlike the Chinese)* have the solar, including twelve signs." But we have seen that the Chinese have also the twelve signs.

Another proof that the Chinese borrowed from the Hindoos is the use they made of conjunctions of the five planets. The rise of the Han dynasty, it is asserted, was marked by one of those conjunctions. And as the Hindoo era, *cali-yug*, commenced (B.C. 3102) with a conjunction of all the planets, so the Historian of Han places a conjunction of all the planets in the reign of Chuen-heuh (B.C. 2513—2436, mod. chr.), just at the time when that emperor is said to have corrected the calendar, and fixed the commencement of the year in February. The late Baron Bunsen, in his Work on Egypt (Bk. IV. Pt. IV.), has attempted to verify this conjunction of the planets; but this, as well as the credence he gives to the tablet of Yu, only shows his ignorance of the subject; and that he ought to have manifested more of a fellow feeling with the 'ignorant' and 'superstitious' and 'intolerant' missionaries, who mistook the inundation of Yaou for the flood of Noah. These ancient conjunctions of the planets are utterly unworthy of credit. There was a rough approximation to such a conjunction at the commencement of the Han dynasty, in May, 204 B.C. But the only real conjunction of the five on record is that of Sep. 15, 1186 A.D., in the Sung dynasty. The Chinese in this matter seem to have been servile imitators of the Hindoos; and the Hindoos in their turn borrowed from the Greeks. When the expression "ts'eih ching" (七政), "the seven directors," is taken in the sense of sun, moon, and five planets, and applied to days, the idea is obviously and confessedly western.

The Eclipse in the reign of Chung-k'ang.

7. Referring to the Shoo, Pt. III. Bk. IV. parag. 4, we find this sentence:—'On the first day of the last month of autumn the sun and moon did not meet harmoniously in Fang." Upon which there was beating of drums, and a general commotion such as the Chinese usually make on the occasion of an eclipse of the sun. It is evident, from the quotation of the passage in the *Tso-chuen*, that an eclipse of the sun is meant, and also that the record existed in some form or other in the time of *Tso K'ew-ming*. On the other hand, it cannot be denied that the genuineness of this part of the Shoo is open to great suspicion, and in particular, that the phrase 辰弗集于房, *lit.* "The heavenly bodies were not harmonious in the chamber," looks more like a modern form of speech, than a primitive way of denoting an eclipse of the sun. It occurs nowhere else; and although no other eclipse is mentioned in the Shoo, in the other classical writings eclipses of the sun are of common occurrence, and are uniformly denoted by 日有食之 "the sun was eaten." This seems more likely to be the older phrase. And again, with regard to the character 房 *fang*, it is evidently not taken in the Tso-ch'uen for the constellation that now goes by that name, but as equivalent to Shay (舍), any division or mansion of the Zodiac. This interpretation seems also to be favoured by several later writers. The ancient name of the constellation was *Ho* or *Ta-ho*, *i. e.* Scorpio, and it is only called *fang* in the Book of Rites.

But granting that an eclipse within that part of Scorpio which now goes by the name of *Fang* is intended, no such event could have been witnessed during the reign of Chung-k'ang, if we adopt the current chronology. The eclipse of the astronomers of T'ang, although it happens to agree with that of Gaubil, in being on the fifth year of Chung-k'ang, was reckoned according to some other chronology than that which is current now, and was in fact the eclipse of 2127, which has recently come into favour, after Gaubil's has been set aside as invisible (*See Comm. in loc.*) The astronomers of T'ang distinctly state that it was in the year *kwei-tsze*, the 30th of the cycle of years; and on the day *kang-seŭh*, the 47th of the cycle of days. I have found them right even in the day; which implies a high degree of accuracy in their figures, considering that they were calculating an eclipse at the distance of nearly 3000 years. Is it possible that those Chinese astronomers were superior to Gaubil? or was their success in this instance accidental? It was perhaps too late in the day for the scholars of T'ang to fix the uncertain chronology by astronomical calculation, though those of Han practised this method freely with far inferior knowledge.

Those, however, who like the year 2127 as the date of the eclipse may adopt it now without fear of its being hereafter proved invisible. But it is well to keep in mind that eclipses satisfying the conditions are by no means rare. Eclipses of the sun, visible in the northern hemisphere in the sign Scorpio, might be looked for in any of the following years:—

B.C.	2154	2024	1894	1764
	2135	2005	1875	1745
	2127	1997	1867	1737
	2108	1978	1848	1718

ECLIPSES RECORDED BY THE ANCIENT CHINESE.

RECORDED IN THE BOOK OF POETRY.						CALCULATION.				
Emperor's Name.	*Year of Reign.*	*Year of Cycle.*	*Moon.*	*Day of Cycle.*	No.	*Year* B.C.	*Month & day. New style.*	*Chinese Moon.*	*Day of Cycle.*	
幽王	6	2	X	28	I	775	August 29	X	28	Early in the morning, *scarcely visible.*
RECORDED IN THE CH'UN TS'EW.										
平王	51	58	II	6	I	719	February 14	III	6	Visible at sunrise.
桓王	11	9	VII	29 *total.*	II	708	July 8	VIII	29	Total about 3h. P.M.
莊王	2	23	X		III	694	October 3	XI	7	Visible—Afternoon.
惠王	1	42	III		IV	675	April 6	V	49	Sunset.
	8	49	VI.	8	V	668	May 18	VI	8	Morning.
	9	50	XII	60	VI	667	November 3	XII	60	Morning.
	13	54	IX	7	VII	663	August 21	IX	7	Afternoon.
	22	3	IX	45	VIII	654	August 11	IX	45	Afternoon.
襄王	4	10	III	7	IX	647	March 29	V	7	Afternoon.
	7	13	V		X	644	January 28	III	21	*Not visible.*
	26	32	II	60	XI	625	January 26	III	60	Visible at Noon.
匡王	1	46	VI	38	XII	611	April 20	V	38	Sunrise.
定王	6	57	VII	1 *total.*	XIII	600	September 12	X	1	Total about 3h. 30m. P.M.
	8	59	IV	53	XIV	598	February 26	IV	53	Visible at Sunrise.
	15	6	VI	40	XV	591	October 5	XI	8	*Not visible.*
簡王	11	23	VI	3	XVI	574	May 1	VI	3	Visible at Noon.
	12	24	XII	54	XVII	573	October 17	XI	54	Morning.

ECLIPSES RECORDED BY THE ANCIENT CHINESE.—*Continued.*

靈王	13	39	II	32	XVIII	558	January	8	II	32	Noon.
	14	40	VIII	54	XIX	557	May	23	VI *	54	*Scarcely visible* at Sunrise
	19	45	X	53	XX	552	August	25	X	53	Noon.
	20	46	IX	47	XXI	551	August	13	IX	47	Noon.
	20	46	X	17	XXII	551	September		X		*No Eclipse.*
	22	48	II	10	XXIII	550	December	30	II	10	Visible at Sunrise.
	23	49	VII	1 *total.*	XXIV	548	June	12	VII	1	Total about 1h. 15m. P.M.
	23	49	VIII	30	XXV	548	July		VIII		*No Eclipse.*
	26	52	XII	12	XXVI	545	October	7	XI	12	Visible in the Morning.
景王	10	3	IV	41	XXVII	534	March	11	IV	41	Forenoon.
	18	11	VI	54	XXVIII	526	April	10	V	54	Forenoon.
	20	13	VI	11	XXIX	524	August	14	IX	10	Afternoon.
	24	17	VII	19	XXX	520	June	3	VII	19	Forenoon.
	25	18	XII	10	XXXI	519	November	18	XII	10	Afternoon.
敬王	2	20	V	32	XXXII	517	April	1	V	32	Sunrise.
	9	27	XII	48	XXXIII	510	November	7	XII	48	Forenoon.
	15	33	III	48	XXXIV	504	February	10	III	48	Noon.
	22	40	XI	3	XXXV	497	September	15	X	3	Forenoon.
	25	43	VIII	17	XXXVI	494	July	15	VIII	17	Forenoon.

* Intercalary

書經

CHAPTER IV.

THE ANNALS OF THE BAMBOO BOOKS.

THE BAMBOO BOOKS IN GENERAL;—THEIR DISCOVERY AND SUBSEQUENT HISTORY.
THE ANNALS.
HOW FAR THE ANNALS ARE TO BE RELIED ON;—CONCLUSION FROM THEM AS TO THE GENERAL CHARACTER OF THE EARLY RECORDS OF THE SHOO.

1. Having made such frequent reference in the last chapter to the Bamboo Books, I have thought it would be well to devote a chapter specially to them, embodying the text, with a translation, of that portion of them which is most important, and from which the shorter scheme of Chinese chronology is derived. Some Sinologues, like Father De Mailla, have written about them without sufficient discrimination, and have not done them justice; while other students of chronology, like Freret and Bunsen, unable to examine them for themselves, have attached a greater value to them than can be fairly claimed. The student will be glad to have the ancient history of China, as indicated in them, in the same volume with the records of the Shoo; and it will be found that they give important corroboration to some of the views which I have advanced on the older portions of the classic.

What is meant by 'The Bamboo Books.'

'The Bamboo Books' is a comprehensive designation. It is not, indeed, so wide as De Mailla represents, when he says:—'It is the general name given to all ancient Books written on tablets of bamboo, before the manner of making paper was discovered.' Such books might be spoken and written of as 'Bamboo Books.' *The* Bamboo Books is the name appropriate to a large collection of ancient documents, discovered in A.D. 279, embracing nearly twenty different Works, which contained altogether between seventy and eighty chapters or Books.

1 See the first of the P. De Mailla's letters to Freret, prefixed to 'L'Histoire generale de la Chine.

The discovery of those Works is thus related in the history of the emperor Woo, the first of the sovereigns of Tsin, whose supremacy over the empire is acknowledged in chronology:—'In the 5th year of his reign under the title of Hëen-ning[2] [= A.D. 279, the year before the chronological commencement of the Tsin dynasty], some lawless parties in the department of Keih dug open the grave of king Seang of Wei [Died B.C. 295], and found a number of bamboo tablets, written over, in the small seal character, with more than 100,000 words; which were deposited in the imperial library.' But before the tablets were placed in the library, they had sustained various injury and mutilation. The emperor referred them to the principal scholars in the service of the government, to adjust the tablets in order, having first transcribed them in modern characters. The chief among these was one Wei Hăng,[3] famous for his knowledge of the old forms of the characters. He was assisted by Shuh Sih, Ho Këaou, Seun Heuh, and others,—all men of note in their day. In two years their labours were completed, and the tablets were placed in the library in order. De Mailla says that the scholars reported to the emperor unfavourably of the Bamboo Books:—that 'they were filled with reveries, extravagances, and manifest falsities.' I have not found in the Books of Tsin[7] that they gave any such sweeping decision. They made out the names of 15 different Works, the tablets of which, more or less complete, could be arranged together. Some of these Works were, indeed, full of extravagant legends and speculations;—they soon fell into neglect, if they have not entirely perished. There were two among them, however, of a different character:—a copy of the Yih King, in two Books, agreeing with that generally received; and a book of Annals, beginning with the reign of Hwang-te, and coming down to the 16th year of the last emperor of the Chow dynasty, B.C. 298. This was in 12 or 13 chapters.

Manner of their Discovery.

If the scholars of Tsin sent in to the emperor any formal report of their labours, and of their judgment on the different portions of 'the Bamboo Books,' it has not been preserved; but we have the most satisfactory evidence of the points I have just stated, in the appendix or *l'envoi* affixed by Too Yu to his well known edition of the Tso Chuen.[8] He tells us, that on returning, in A.D. 280, from a

2 咸寧,五年. See the Books of Tsin, 帝紀第三, p. 13. 3 衞恒. 4 束晳. 5 和嶠. 6 荀勗. 7 See in particular the history of Shuh Sih, 列傳,第二十一. 8 杜預左傳,後序.

書經

military expedition to Woo, he completed his great Work, when his attention was called to the Bamboo Books which had been recently discovered; that, by the carelessness of the parties who first found them, they had suffered much damage; and that, when he saw them in the library, the portions most complete and distinct were a copy of the Yih King, and certain Annals, relating, in the latter part of them, more particularly, the affairs of the State of Tsin.

The reader will be conscious of a disposition to reject at once the account of the discovery of the Bamboo Books. He has read so much of the recovery of portions of the Shoo from the walls of houses, that he must be tired of this mode of finding lost treasures; and smiles when he is now called on to believe that an old tomb opened, and yielded its literary stores, long after the human remains that had been laid in it had mingled with the dust. From the death of king Sëang to B.C. 279 were 595 years;—so long had these Books been in the bosom of the earth. The speed, moreover, with which the tablets were transcribed and arranged was surprising. It is hard to credit that so much work was done in so brief time. Against the improbabilities in the case, however, we have to place the evidence which is given in support of it. The testimony of Too Yu, especially, a witness entirely competent and disinterested, and which was probably in A.D. 281 or 282, seems to place it beyond a doubt, that there had been a large discovery of ancient Works in a tomb a few years before, of which a most valuable portion was that which is now current under the name of 'The Annals of the Bamboo Books.' How far some of the other portions have been preserved, I am not able to say; but these Annals have held their place in the literature of China. They are mentioned in the catalogues of the Suy and T'ang dynasties.

How the Annals have kept their place in literature.

Shin Yŏ,[9] a scholar and officer of the Lëang dynasty, (A.D. 502—557) published an edition, with a commentary, in the 6th century. Under the Sung dynasty, Choo He made several references to them, not unfavourable. Two scholars of Yuen, Hoo Ying-lin[10] and Yang Shing-gan,[11] laboured upon them; and in the present dynasty five or six different editions and commentaries have been published;—showing that, notwithstanding the generally unfavourable opinion of scholars, the Work has not yet been put out of the court of criticism.

I now subjoin the text and a translation, with a few annotations.

9 沈約,字休文. 10 胡應麟. 11 楊升庵.

107]

竹書紀年卷之一

黃帝軒轅氏

母曰附寶見大電繞北斗樞星光照郊野感而孕二十五月而生帝於壽丘弱而能言龍顏有聖德劾百神朝而使之應龍攻蚩尤戰虎豹熊羆四獸之力以女魃止淫雨天下既定聖德光被羣瑞畢臻有屈軼之草生於庭佞人入朝則草指之是以佞人不敢進

元年、帝即位、居有熊。初制冕服○二十年、景雲見、以雲紀官。有景雲之瑞赤方氣與青方氣相連赤方中有兩星青方中有一星凡三星皆黃色以天清明時見於攝提名曰景星帝黃服齋于中宮坐于玄扈洛水之上有鳳凰集不食生蟲不履生草

2. THE ANNALS OF THE BAMBOO BOOKS.

PART. I.

The reigns of Hwang-te; Che; Chuen-heuh; and Kuh.

I. HWANG-TE; DYNASTIC TITLE HËEN-YUEN.[1]

Note. His mother was called Foo-paou. She witnessed a great flash of lightning, which surrounded the star *ch'oo* (= Dubhe) of the Great Bear with a brightness that lightened all the country about her, and thereupon became pregnant. After 25 months, she gave birth to the emperor in Show-k'ew. When born, he could speak. His countenance was dragon-like; his virtue that of a sage. He could oblige the host of spirits to come to his court, and receive his orders. *He employed* Ying-lung to attack Che-yew, the fight with whom was maintained by the help of tigers, panthers, bears, and grisly bears. By means of the *Heavenly* lady Pă, he stopped the extraordinary rains *caused by the enemy*. When the empire was settled, his sage virtue was brightly extended, and all sorts of auspicious indications appeared. The grass K'euh-yih grew in the court-yard of the palace. When a glib-tongued person was entering the court, this grass pointed to him, so that such men did not dare to present themselves.[2]

1 In his 1st year, when he came to the throne, he dwelt in Yew-hëung.[3] He in-
2 vented the cap with pendents, and the robes to match. In his 20th year, brilliant clouds appeared; and he arranged his officers by names taken from the colours of the clouds.[4]

Note. The auspicious omen of brilliant clouds was in this way:—The vapours of the red quarter [the south] extended so as to join those of the green [the east]. In the red quarter were two stars, and in the green, one;—all of a yellow colour, which appeared, when the heavens were clear and bright, in Shĕ-t'e, and were named the brilliant stars. The emperor in yellow robes fasted in the Middle palace. When he was sitting in *a boat on the* Yuen-hoo, above *its junction with* the Lŏ, there came together phœnixes, male and female. They would not eat any living insect, nor tread on

I. 1 Sze-ma Ts'ëen says that Hwang-te's name was Hëen-yuen; and many others take 氏 here as=名. It seems to me preferable to take it as in the case of Yaou, who was 陶唐氏; and of Shun's 有虞氏. See the Introductory notes to the Canons of Yaou and Shun, Hëen-yuen may have reference to the invention of carriages, which is commonly ascribed to Hwang-te, though these Annals do not mention it; or it may have been the name of a place. There are many methods of accounting for it.

2 This and other notes which follow are supposed by some to be a portion of the text of the Annals. The more likely opinion is, that they are additions to the text by diff't. hands;—several of them, but not all, by Shin Yŏ. As they are not many, I have translated them; but they abound so much in extravagant, monstrous, statements, and besides are so full of errors, that I will rarely occupy space with comments on them.

3 Yew-hëung must be the name of a State. It is referred to what was called 'new Ch'ing' (新鄭), in the pres. Ho-nan. 4 The chiefs

或止帝之東園或巢於阿閣或鳴於庭
其雄自歌其雌自舞麒麟在囿神鳥來
儀有大螻如羊大螾如虹
帝以土氣勝遂以土德王
五十年、秋七月、庚申、鳳鳥至、帝祭于洛水。
庚申天霧三日三夜晝昏帝問天老力
牧容成曰於公何如天老曰臣聞之國
安其主好文則鳳凰居之國亂其主好
武則鳳凰去之今鳳凰翔於東郊而樂
之其鳴音中夷則與天相副以是觀之
天有嚴教以賜帝帝勿犯也召史卜之
龜燋史曰臣不能占也其問之聖人帝
曰已問天老力牧容成矣史北面再拜
曰龜不違聖智故燋霧既除遊于洛水
之上見大魚殺五牲以醮之天乃甚雨
七日七夜魚流於海得圖書焉龍圖出
河龜書出洛赤文篆字以授軒轅接萬
神於明庭今塞
門谷口是也
五十九年、貫胸氏來賓。長股氏來賓〇七
十七年。昌意降居若水。產帝乾荒〇一百

living grass. Some of them abode in the emperor's eastern garden; some built their nests about the corniced galleries *of the palace;* and some sang in the courtyard, the females gambolling to the notes of the males. *K'e-lins also* appeared in the parks; and *other* spirit-like birds came with their measured movements. Four-horned *low* were produced as large as a goat, and the *yin* worms like rainbows. The emperor, considering that the influence of earth was thus predominant, reigned by the virtue of earth.

3 In his 50th year,[5] in the autumn, in the 7th month, on *the day* Kang-shin [57th of cycle], phœnixes, male and female, arrived. The emperor sacrificed at the river Loh.

Note. Beginning with Kăng-shin, the heavens were wrapt in mist for three days and three nights. The emperor asked T'ëen-laou, Leih-muh, and Yung-shing, what they thought of it. T'ëen-laou said, 'I have heard this:—When a kingdom is tranquil, and its ruler is fond of peace, then phœnixes come and dwell in it; when a kingdom is disordered, and its ruler is fond of war, then the phœnixes leave it. Now the phœnixes fly about in your eastern borders rejoicing, the notes of their singing all exactly harmonious, in mutual accord with Heaven. Looking at the thing in this way, Heaven is giving your majesty grave instructions, which you must not disobey.' *The emperor then* called the recorder to divine about the thing, when the tortoise-shell was *only* scorched. The recorder said, 'I cannot divine it; you must ask your sage men.' The emperor replied, 'I have asked T'ëen-laou, Leih-muh, and Yung-shing.' The recorder then did obeisance, twice, with his face to the earth, and said, 'The tortoise will not go against their sage wisdom, and therefore its shell is only scorched.'

When the mists were removed, he made an excursion on the Lŏ, and saw a great fish; and sacrificed to it with five victims, whereupon torrents of rain came down for seven days and seven nights, when the fish floated off the sea, and the emperor obtained the map-writings. The dragon-writing came forth from the Ho, and the tortoise-writing from the Lŏ.

In red lines, and the seal character, they were given to Hëen-yuen. He entertained the myriad spirits in Ming-t'ing, the present valley of Han-mun.

4 In his 59th year, the chief of 'The Perforated Breasts'[6] came to make his sub-
5 mission. So also did the chief of 'The Long Legs.'[6] In his 77th year,
Ch'ang-e[7] left the court, and dwelt by the Jŏ-water; he begat the emperor K'ëen-
6 hwang. In his 100th year, the earth was rent. The emperor went on high.[9]

of the difft. departments were called—'He of the green cloud; he of the white cloud (白雲氏), &c. 5 Some editions read here—'the 57th year,' instead of the 50th.

6 'The Perforated Breasts' and 'The Long Legs' are of course fabulous. We read of them, and other equally monstrous barbarian tribes, in the 'Classic of Mountains and Seas' (山海經). 7 Ch'ang-e was a son (1st or 2d is debated) of Hwang-te, and, not being able for the empire, was sent away to a State near the Jŏ-water, in the pres. Sze-ch'uen. Others have it that he went away himself, in virtuous humility;—all is fabulous. 8 When this son of

年地裂。帝陟。帝王之崩皆曰陟書稱新陟王謂新崩也帝以土德王應地裂而陟葬羣臣有左徹者感思帝德取衣冠几杖而朝之諸侯大夫歲時朝焉

帝摯少昊氏 母曰女節見星如虹下流華渚既而夢接意感生少昊登帝位有鳳凰之瑞或曰名清不居帝位帥鳥師居西方以鳥紀官

帝顓頊高陽氏 母曰女樞見瑤光之星貫月如虹感己於幽房之宮生顓頊於若水首戴干戈有聖德生十年而佐少昊氏二十而登帝位

元年、帝即位、居濮〇十三年、初作歷象〇二十一年、作承雲之樂〇三十年、帝產伯鯀、居天穆之陽〇七十八

Note. The death of emperors and kings is thus spoken of as a going on high. In the Shoo we have 'the recently ascended king,' for the recently deceased [Pt. V. BK. XXIII. 3]. Hwang-te reigned by the virtue of earth;—it was right that his death should be preceded by the rending of the earth. After he was buried, one of his ministers, named Tso-chʻĕ, affected by the thought of the emperor's virtue, took his clothes, cap, bench, and stick, and offered sacrifice to them in a temple. The princes and great officers every year paid their court before them.

II. THE EMPEROR CHE; DYNASTIC TITLE SHAOU-HAOU.[1]

Note. His mother was called Neu-tsëĕ. She witnessed a star like a rainbow come floating down the stream to the islet of Hwá. Thereafter she dreamed she had received it, and was moved in her mind, and bore Shaou-haou. When he ascended the throne, there was the auspicious omen of phœnixes. Some say that his name was Tsʻing, and that he did not occupy the throne. He led an army of birds, and dwelt in the west, where he arranged his officers by *names taken from* birds.

III. THE EMPEROR CHUEN-HEUH; DYNASTIC TITLE KAOU-YANG.[1]

Note. His mother was called Neu-chʻoo. She witnessed the Yaou-kwang star (= Benetnasch) go through the moon like a rainbow, when it moved herself in the palace of Yew-fang, after which she brought forth Chuen-heuh near the Jŏ-water. On his head he bore a shield and spear; and he had the virtue of a sage. When 10 years old, he assisted Shaou-haou; and when 20, he ascended the imperial throne.

1 In his 1st year, when he came to the throne, he dwelt in Puh. In his 13th
2 year, he invented calendaric calculations and delineations *of the heavenly bodies*.
3 In his 21st year, he made the *piece of* music called 'The Answer to the Clouds.'
4 In his 30th year, he begat Pih-kʻwăn, who dwelt in the south of Tʻëen-muh.
5 In his 78th year, he died. Shuh-kʻe made disorder, and was made an end of by the prince of Sin.

Chʻang-e was emperor, we do not know; some identify him with Chuen-heuh; others make that emperor his son. 8 陟. See the last par. of the Canon of Shun.—Many accounts say that Hwang-te did not die, but went up to Heaven on a dragon. Hăng Chʻin-fung gives the following passage, quoted by some writers as from the Bamboo Books:—黃帝既仙去、其臣有左徹者、削木爲黃帝之像、帥諸侯朝奉之, 'Hwang-te having gone away as one of the Immortals, Tso-chʻĕ, one of his ministers, cut an image of him in wood, and led the princes to pay court and reverence to it.' Here was idolatry at a very early time.—This statement was no doubt in one of the Bamboo Books, but not in the Annals. The same may be said of another,—that this 'Tso-chʻĕ raised Chuen-heuh to the throne, 7 years after Hwang-te's death.'

II. 1 Some editions of the Annals give this notice as an addition of Shin Yŏ's. Others separate the name and title from the note, and put them in the text.—Sze-ma Tsʻëen does not give this emperor Che at all. There are many discussions about him, whether he was a son of Hwang-te, or a grandson; or whether he was not rather descended from Fuh-he. His title of Shaou-haou would seem to be in relation with Fuh-he's of Tʻae-haou.

III. 1 Chuen-heuh was a son, or a grandson of Chʻang-e mentioned above. The title of Kaou-

年、帝陟。術器作亂、辛侯滅之。

帝嚳高辛氏

生而駢齒有聖德初封辛侯代高陽氏王天下使瞽人拊鞞鼓擊鐘磬鳳皇鼓翼而舞

元年、帝即位、居亳。〇十六年、帝使重帥師滅有鄶。〇四十五年、帝錫唐侯命。〇六十三年、帝陟。

帝子摯立九年而廢

IV. THE EMPEROR KUH; DYNASTIC TITLE KAOU-SIN.

Note. He was born with double rows of teeth; and had the virtue of a sage. He was at first made prince of Sin, and afterwards succeeded to Kaou-yang as monarch of the empire. He made blind men beat drums, and strike bells and sounding stones, at which phœnixes flapped their wings, and gambolled.

1 In his 1st year, when he came to the throne, he dwelt in Poh. In his 16th year,
2 he made Ch'ung lead an army, and extinguish the State of Yew-kwae. In his
3 45th year, he conferred on the prince of T'ang the appointment to be his successor.
4 In his 63d year, he died.

Note. The emperor's son Che was deposed, after having been appointed nine years.

yang must be derived from some place where he ruled; but two places of this name are assigned to him at different periods of his life:—the 1st in the pres. dis. of Ke, dep. of K'ae-fung, Ho-nan; the 2d in the dep. of Paou-ting, Chih-le.

2 This Puh was probably in the pres. dep. of Tung-ch'ang, Shan-tung. 3 Comp. 歷象, in Can. of Yaou, p. 2. Some editions read 12th instead of 13th. 4 Hăng Ch'in-fung would remove this notice to the 20th year of Hwang-te. 5 This Pih K'wăn, or baron K'wăn, is commonly supposed to be the father of Yu the Great; but in that case K'wăn would be well on to 200 years old, when Yaou calls him to regulate the waters. T'ëen-muh was a mountain, '20,000 feet high,' acc. to the Classic of Mountains and Seas; and on the north of the Jŏ-water, acc. to one of the sporadic passages of the Bamboo Books, found elsewhere (是惟若陽). 術器, 云云, generally appears as a note, but it belongs to the text. Shuh-k'e is said to have been a descendant of Shin-nung, and son of the emp. Kuh.

IV. 1 Kuh was the grandson of Yuen-heaou (元囂), one of Hwang-te's sons. Where the principality of Sin, from which he has his dynastic name, was, seems not to be known. See the dict. *in voc.* 2 This was probably what was afterwards the southern Pŏ. See introd. note to 'The Speech of T'ang.' 3 Yew-kwae was in the pres. dis. of Yung-yang, dep. of K'ae-fung. On who Ch'ung was, see the notes of Hăng Ch'in-fung. 4 The prince of T'ang is Yaou. See on the title of 'The Book of T'ang.' I must translate 錫唐侯命 as I have done. Comp. 錫虞舜命, under the 70th year of Yaou below. The difficulty in the way of the construction is the concluding note about the emperor's son Che; but this may be got over, by transferring it, as an appendix to this par. His appointment was to the succession, and his unworthiness being proved, his father himself deposed him from his place as heir, and gave the succession to his younger brother Yaou. Ch'in-fung argues for this construction, and re-arrangement of the text. I had adopted the construction, however, before reading his remarks.

竹書紀年卷之二

帝堯陶唐氏

母曰慶都生於斗維之野常有黃雲覆其上及長觀于三河常有龍隨之一旦龍負圖而至其文要曰赤受天祐眉八彩鬚髮尺餘長七尺二寸面銳上豐下足履翼宿既而陰風四合赤龍感之孕十四月而生堯於丹陵其狀如圖及長身長十尺有聖德封於唐夢攀天而上高辛氏衰天下歸之

元年丙子、帝即位、居冀。命羲和歷象〇五年、初巡狩四岳〇七年、有麟〇十二年、初治兵〇十六年、渠搜氏來賓〇十九年、命共工治河〇二十九年、春、僬僥氏來朝、貢沒羽〇四十二年、景星見于翼〇五十年、帝游于首山、乘素車玄駒〇五十三年、帝祭于洛〇五十八年、帝使后稷、放帝子朱

PART. II.

The reigns of Yaou and Shun.

I. EMPEROR YAOU; DYNASTIC TITLE, T'AOU AND T'ANG.

Note. His mother was called K'ing-too. She was born in the wild of Tow-wei, and was always overshadowed by a yellow cloud. After she was grown up, whenever she looked into any of the three Ho, there was a dragon following her. One morning the dragon came with a picture and writing. The substance of the writing was:—'The red one has received the favour of Heaven.' The eyebrows *of the figure* were like the character 八, and of vareigated colours. The whiskers were more then a cubit long; and the height was 7 cub. 2 in. The face was sharp above, and broad below. The feet trode on the constellation Yih. After this came darkness and winds on every side; and the red dragon made *K'ing-too* pregnant. Her time lasted 14 months, when she brought forth Yaou in Tan-ling. His appearance was like that in the picture. When he was grown up, his height was ten cubits. He had the virtue of a sage, and was invested with the principality of T'ang. He dreamed that he climbed up to heaven. When Kaou-shin was decaying, the empire turned to him.

1 In his 1st year, which was *ping-tsze* 2 (13th of cycle;=B.C. 2,145), when he came
to the throne, he dwelt in K'e; 3 and commanded He and Ho to make calendaric
2 calculations and delineations *of the heavenly bodies*.4 In his 5th year, he made
3 the first tour of inspection to the four mountains. In his 7th year, there was a
5 *k'e-lin*. In his 12th year, he formed the first standing army. In his
6 15th year, the chief of K'eu-sow came to make his submission. In his 19th year,
7 he ordered the minister of Works 8 to undertake the regulation of the Ho. In
his 29th year, the chief of the Pigmies 9 came to court in token of homage, and offered
8 as tribute their feathers which sank in water. In his 42d year, a brilliant
9 star appeared in Yih [? Crater]. In his 50th year, he travelled for pleasure
about mount Show,10 in a plain carriage drawn by dark-coloured horses.
11 In his 53d year, he sacrificed near the Loh. In his 58th year, he caused

I. 1 See on 'The Songs of the Five Sons,' p. 7. 2 This is the 1st determination of a year by cycle names in the Annals. We fix the year to be B.C. 2,145, by calculating back on the cycle from the 6th year of king Yew of Chow, which (as we have seen) is certainly known. I shall call attention below to the fact that all these cycle names of the years in the Annals were introduced into them after their recovery or discovery. 3 K'e is of course K'e-chow.

書經

於丹水〇六十一年、命崇伯鯀治河〇六十九年、黜崇伯鯀〇七十年、春、正月、帝使四岳錫虞舜命。

帝在位七十年景星出翼鳳凰在庭朱草生嘉禾秀甘露潤醴泉出日月如合璧五星如聯珠廚中自生肉其薄如箑搖動則風生食物寒而不臭名曰箑脯又有草夾階而生月朔始生一莢月半而生十五莢十六日以後日落一莢及晦而盡月小則一莢焦而不落名曰蓂莢一曰歷莢洪水既平歸功於舜將以天下禪之乃潔齋修壇場於河洛擇良日率舜等升首山遵河渚有五老游焉蓋五星之精也相謂曰河圖將來告帝以期知我者重瞳黃姚五老因飛爲流星上入昴二月辛丑昧明禮備至於日昃榮光出河休氣四塞白雲起回風搖乃有龍馬銜甲赤文綠色緣壇而上吐甲圖而去甲似龜背廣九尺其圓以白玉爲檢赤玉爲柙泥以黃金約以青繩檢文曰闓色授帝舜言虞夏當授天命帝乃寫其言藏於東序後二年二月仲辛率羣

12 his son Choo to be sent in banishment by prince Tseih to Tan-shwuy. In his
13 61st year, he ordered the baron K'wan of Ts'ung to regulate the Ho. In his 69th
14 year, he degraded K'wan. In his 70th year, in the spring, in the 1st month, he caused the *chief* of the four mountains to convey to Shun of Yu his charge *to succeed to the throne.*

Note. When the emperor had been on the throne 70 years, a brilliant star issued from the constellation Yih, and phœnixes appeared in the courtyards of the palace; the pearl grass grew, and the admirable grain flourished; sweet dews moistened the ground, and crystal springs issued from the hills; the sun and moon appeared like a pair of gems, and the five planets looked like threaded pearls. In the *imperial* kitchen there appeared of itself a piece of flesh, as thin as a fan, which, when shaken, raised such a wind that all eatables were kept cool and did not spoil. It was called the fan flitch. A kind of grass, moreover, grew on each side of the palace stairs. On the 1st day of the month, it produced one pod, and so on, every day a pod, to the 15th; while on the 16th one pod fell off, and so on, every day a pod, to the last day of the month; and if the month was a short one (of 29 days), one pod shrivelled up, without falling. It was called the felicitous bean, and the calendar bean. When the flooded waters were assuaged, the emperor, attributing the merit of that to Shun, wished to resign in his favour. He thereon purified himself and fasted, built altars near the Ho and the Lŏ, chose a good day, and conducted Shun and others up mount Show. Among the islets of the Ho, there were five old men, walking about, who were the spirits of the five planets. They said to one another, 'The river scheme will come and tell the emperor of the time. He who knows us is the double-pupilled yellow Yaou.' The five old men on this flew away like flowing stars, and ascended into the constellation Maou. On the 2d month, on the sin-chow day, between the dark and light, the ceremonies were all prepared; and when the day began to decline, a glorious light came forth from the Ho, and beautiful vapours filled all the horizon; white clouds rose up, and returning winds blew all about. Then a dragon-horse appeared, bearing in his mouth a scaly cuirass, with red lines on a green ground, ascended the altar, laid down the scheme, and went away. The cuirass was like a tortoise shell, nine cubits broad. The scheme contained a tally of white gem, in a casket of red gem, covered with yellow gold, and bound with a green string. On the tally were the words, 'With pleased countenance given to the emperor Shun'. It said also that Yu and Hëa should receive the appointment of Heaven. The emperor wrote these words, and deposited them in the Eastern college. Two years afterwards, in the 2d month, he led out all his ministers, and dropped a *peih* in the Lŏ. The ceremony over, he retired, and waited for the decline of the day. Then

It is a wide word. 4 See on Can. of Yaou, p. 2. 5 The 'four mountains' are those mentioned in the Can. of Shun, p. 8. 6 兵 is to be taken here in the sense of soldiers, and not merely as weapons of war. 7 See on 'The Tribute of Yu,' Pt. i., p. 83.

8 I should take 共工 as a proper name, but for the Can. of Shun, p. 21. 9 The nation of Pigmies, like the 'Perforated Breasts' and 'Long Legs,' is mentioned in the classic of the Hills and Seas. The 括地志 places it

臣沈璧于洛禮畢退俟至于下昃赤光
起元龜負書而出背甲赤文成字止于
壇其書言當
禪舜遂讓舜
七十一年、帝命二女嬪于舜○七十三年、
春、正月、舜受終于文祖○七十四年、虞舜
初巡狩四岳○七十五年、司空禹治河○
七十六年、司空伐曹魏之戎克之○八十
六年、司空入覲、贄用元圭○八十七年、初
建十有二州○八十九年、作游宮于陶○
九十年、帝游居于陶○九十七年、司空巡
十有二州○一百年、帝陟于陶。
帝子丹朱避舜于房陵舜讓不克朱遂
封于房爲虞賓三年舜即天子之位

帝舜有虞氏

母曰握登見大虹
意感而生舜於姚
墟目重瞳子故名重華龍顏大口黑色
身長六尺一寸舜父母憎舜使其塗廩
自下焚之舜服鳥工衣服飛去又使浚
井自上填之以石舜服龍工衣自旁而

a red light appeared; a tortoise rose from the waters, with a writing in red lines on its back, and rested on the altar. The writing said that he should resign the throne to Shun, which accordingly the emperor did.

15 In his 71st year, he commanded his two daughters to become wives to Shun.
16 In his 73d year, in the spring, in the 1st month, Shun received the resignation of the
17 emperor in *the temple of* the accomplished ancestor. In his 74th year, Shun of
18 Yu made his first tour of inspection to the four mountains. In his 75th year, Yu,
19 the superintendent of Works, regulated the Ho. In his 76th year, the super-
20 intendent of Works smote the hordes of Ts'aou and Wei,[12] and subdued them. In
his 86th year, the superintendent of Works had an audience, using for his article of
21 introduction a dark-coloured mace. In his 87th year, he instituted the division
22 *of the* empire into 12 provinces. In his 89th year, he made a pleasure palace in
23 T'aou. In his 90th year, he took up his residence for relaxation in T'aou.
24 In his 97th year, the superintendent of Works made a tour of survey through the 12
25 provinces. In his 100th year, he died in T'aou.

Note. The emperor's son Choo of Tan kept away from Shun in Fang-ling. Shun tried to yield the throne to him, but in vain. Choo was then invested with T'ang, and became the guest of Yu. After three years, Shun ascended the throne of the son of Heaven.

II. THE EMPEROR SHUN; DYNASTIC TITLE YEW-YU.[1]

Note. His mother was named Uh-tăng. She saw a large rainbow, and her thoughts were so affected by it, that she bore Shun in Yaou-heu. His eyes had double pupils, whence he was named 'Double Brightness.' He had a dragon countenance, a large mouth, and a black body, 6 cubits, 1 inch long. Shun's parents hated him. They made him plaster a granary, and set fire to it beneath:—he had on birds'-work clothes, and flew away. They also made him deepen a well, and filled it with stones from above:—he had on dragons'-work clothes, and got out by the side. He ploughed in Leih. He dreamed that his eyebrows were as long as his hair. Accordingly, he was raised and employed.

on the north of the Roman empire (在大秦國北). 10 Mount Show is the Luy-show of 'The Tribute of Yu,' Pt. ii. 1. 11 Tan-shwuy is referred to the pres. dis. of Nan-yang, dep. Nan-yang, Ho-nan. There was there, no doubt, a stream called Tan.

12 Ts'aou and Wei are two well known States in the time of the Chow;—the former lay in the pres. Shan-tung, the latter in Shen-se. I am not sure that those in the text were the same. They would seem too far apart.

II. 1 See note on the name of Part II. of the Shoo. 2 西王母,—lit., 'the mother

書經

出耕於歷夢眉長於髮遂登庸

元年、己未、帝即位、居冀。作大韶之樂。

帝即位蓂莢生於階鳳凰巢於庭擊石拊石以歌九韶百獸率舞景星出于房地出乘黃之馬

三年、命皐陶作刑。〇九年、西王母來朝。

西王母之來朝獻白環玉玦

十四年、卿雲見、命禹代虞事。

在位十有四年奏鐘石笙管未罷而天大雷雨疾風發屋拔木桴鼓播地鐘磬亂行舞人頓伏樂正狂走舜乃擁璿持衡而笑曰明哉天下非一人之天下也亦乃見于鐘石笙筦乎乃薦禹于天使行天子事也于時和氣普應慶雲興焉若烟非烟若雲非雲郁郁紛紛蕭索輪囷百工相和而歌慶雲帝乃倡之曰慶雲爛兮糺縵縵兮日月光華旦復旦兮羣臣咸進稽首曰明明上天爛然星陳日月光華弘于一人帝乃再歌曰日月有常星辰有行四時從經萬姓允誠於予論樂配天之靈遷于聖賢莫不咸聽鼚乎鼓之軒乎舞之精華以竭褰裳去之於是八風循

1 In his 1st year, which was *ke-wei* (56th of cycle, = B.C. 2,042), when he came to the throne, he dwelt in K'e; and made the music called Ta-shaou.

Note. On his accession, the felicitous bean grew about the stairs, and phœnixes nested in the courts. When they beat and tapped the musical stones, to accompany the nine performances of the Shaou, all the beasts came after one another gambolling. A brilliant star came out in Fang. The earth produced the horse Shing-hwang.

2 In his 3d year, he commanded Kaou-yaou to make *the code of* punishments.

3 In his 9th year, *messengers* from the western Wang-moo [2] came to do homage.

Note. The coming to court from the western Wang-moo was to present white stone rings and archers' thimbles of gem.

4 In his 14th year, auspicious clouds appeared; and he ordered Yu to consult about affairs for him.

Note. In the 14th year of Shun's reign, at a grand performance with bells, musical stones, organs, and flutes, before the service was concluded, there came a great storm of thunder and rain. A violent wind overthrew houses, and tore up trees. The drumsticks and drums were scattered on the ground, and the bells and stones dashed about confusedly. The dancers fell prostrate, and the director of the music ran madly away; but Shun, keeping hold of the frames from which the bells and stones were suspended, laughed and said, 'How clear it is that the empire is not one man's empire! It is signified by these bells, stones, organs, and flutes.' On this he presented Yu to Heaven, and made him perform actions proper to the emperor; whereupon harmonious vapours responded on all sides, and felicitous clouds were seen. They were like smoke, and yet not smoke; like clouds, and yet not clouds; brilliantly confused; twisting and whirling. The officers in mutual harmony sang of those felicitous clouds, the emperor thus leading them on:—'How bright are ye, felicitous clouds! In what order are ye gathered together! The brightness of the sun and moon Is repeated from morn to morn. All the ministers then advanced, and bowing low, said:—'Brilliant are the heavens above, Where the shining stars are arranged. The brightness of the sun and moon Enlarge our one man.' The emperor sang again, 'The sun and moon are constant; The stars and other heavenly bodies have their motions. The four seasons observe their rule. The people are sincere in all their services. When I think of music, The intelligences that respond to Heaven Seem to be transferred to the sages and the worthies. All things listen to it. How do its rolling sounds thrill! How does it inspire the dance!' When the essential brightness was exhausted, the clouds shrivelled up and disappeared. Thereupon

of the king of the west,' or 'the queen-mother of the west.' But the characters are merely the name of a State or kingdom in the distant west. See Hăng's Comm. *in loc.*

3 The prince of Hea is Yu. See the introd. note on the name of the third Part of the Shoo.

通慶雲叢聚蟠龍奮迅於其藏蛟魚踊躍於其淵龜鼈咸出其穴遷虞而事夏舜乃設壇於河依堯故事至于下昃榮光休至黃龍負圖長三十二尺廣九尺出于壇畔赤文綠錯其文言當禪禹

十五年、帝命夏后有事于太室〇十七年、春、二月、入學、初用萬〇二十五年、息慎氏來朝、貢弓矢〇二十九年、帝命子義鈞、封于商〇三十年、葬后育于渭〇三十二年、帝命夏后總師、遂陟方岳〇三十三年、春、正月、夏后受命于神宗、遂復九州〇三十五年、帝命夏后征有苗、有苗氏來朝〇四十二年、玄都氏來朝、貢寶玉〇四十七年、冬、隕霜不殺草木〇四十九年、帝居于鳴條〇五十年、帝陟。

義鈞封于商是謂商均后育娥皇也鳴條有蒼梧之山帝崩遂葬焉今海州

the eight winds all blew genially, and *other* felicitous clouds collected in masses. The crouching dragons came hurriedly out of their dens; iguanadons and fishes leaped up from their deeps; tortoises and turtles came out from their holes,—removing from Yu to serve Hea. Shun then raised an altar at the Ho, as Yaou had done before. When the day declined, there came a fine and glorious light; and a yellow dragon issued and came to the altar, bearing a scheme on his back, 32 cubits long and 9 cubits broad, in lines of red and green intermingled, the words of which were that he should resign in favour of Yu.

5 In his 15th year, he commanded the prince of Hea to conduct the *sacrificial*
6 duties in the Grand apartment. In his 17th year, in the spring, in the 2d month,
when he entered the college, he used for the first time the myriad *dance.* 5
7 In his 25th year, the prince of Seih-shin came to do homage, and paid tribute of
8 bows and arrows. In his 29th year, the emperor invested his son E-keun with
9 *the principality of* Shang. In his 30th year, he buried queen Yuh near the Wei.

Note. Queen Yuh was Ngo-hwang.

10 In his 32d year, he commanded the prince of Hea to take the superintendence
11 of the people, who thereupon visited the mountains of the four quarters.7 In his
33d year, in the spring, in the first month, the prince of Hea received the appointment *to be successor,* in *the temple of* the spiritual ancestor; and restored the division
12 *of the empire* into nine provinces. In his 35th year, he commanded the prince
of Hea to lead a punitive expedition against the Yew-mëaou. The prince of Yew-
13 mëaou came to court and did homage. In his 42d year, the chief of Heuen-too
14 came to court, and paid as tribute precious articles and gems. In his 47th year,
15 the hoar-frosts of winter did not kill the grass or trees. In his 49th year, he
16 dwelt in Ming-t'ëaou.8 In his 50th year, he died.

Note. E-keun had been invested with Shang, and is called Keun of Shang. Queen Yuh was Ngo-hwang. In Ming-t'ëaou was the hill of Ts'ang-woo. There Shun died and was buried. It is now Hae-chow.

4 The classic of Hills and Seas makes 太室 the name of a mountain. The meaning in the transl. is much preferable;—the principal apartment in the ancestral temple.

5 萬 is here the name of a dance (萬, 舞名也). 6 Seih-shin;—elsewhere Suh-shin. 7 Comp. 'The Counsels of Yu,' p. 9. 夏后 is to be understood as the subject of 陟, lit. 'to ascend,' but here='to visit.'

8 See on the last par. of the Can. of Shun.—Some strange passages are gathered from other portions of the Bamboo Books, and supposed to have belonged to 'The Annals,' which give quite a different account of the relations between Yaou and Shun. They make Shun dethrone Yaou, and keep him a prisoner, raise Choo for a time to the throne, and then displace him; and thereafter allow no intercourse between father and son. See Hăng Ch'in-fung's Supplement to the Annals, in the last chapter of his Work.

竹書紀年卷之三

帝禹夏后氏

母曰修已出行見流星貫昴夢接意感既而吞神珠修已背剖而生禹於石紐虎鼻大口兩耳參鏤首戴鉤鈐胸有玉斗足文履已故名文命長有聖德長九尺九寸夢自洗於河取水飲之又有白狐九尾之瑞當堯之世舜舉之禹觀於河有長人白面魚身出曰吾河精也呼禹曰文命治水言訖授禹河圖言治水之事乃退入于淵禹治水既畢天錫玄珪以告成功夏道將興草木暢茂青龍止于郊祝融之神降于崇山乃受舜禪即天子之位洛出龜書是爲洪範、三年喪畢都于陽城

元年、壬子、帝即位、居冀。頒夏時于邦國○二年、咎陶薨○五年、巡狩、會諸侯于塗山。

PART. III.

The dynasty of Hea.

I. THE EMPEROR YU; DYNASTIC TITLE, HEA-HOW.

Note. His mother was called Sew-ke. She saw a falling star, which went through the constellation *Maou*, and in a dream her thoughts were moved till she became pregnant, after which she swallowed a spirits' pearl. Her back opened *in due time*, and she gave birth to Yu in Shih-new. He had a tiger nose and a large mouth. His ears had three orifices. His head bore *the resemblance* of *the stars* Kow and K'een. On his breast seemed a *figure* in gem of the Great Bear, and in the lines of his feet he seemed to tread on the character 已;—hence he was called Wăn-ming. When he grew up, he had the virtue of a sage, and was 9 cub. 6 in. long. He dreamt that he was bathing in the Ho, and drank up the water. He had also the happy omen of a white fox with 9 tails. In the time of Yaou, Shun brought him forward. As he was looking at the Ho, a tall man, with a white face and fish's body, came out and said, 'I am the spirit of the Ho.' He then called Yu, and said, 'Wăn-ming shall regulate the waters.' Having so spoken, he gave Yu a chart of the Ho, containing all about the regulating of the waters; and returned into the deep. When Yu had done regulating the waters, Heaven gave him a dark coloured mace, with which to announce his completed work. When the fortunes of Hea were about to rise, all vegetation was luxuriant, green dragons lay in the borders, and the spirit of Chuh-yung descended on mount Ts'ung:—Shun resigned, and Yu ascended the throne. The Lŏ produced the tortoise Book, called 'The great Plan.' When the three years of mourning were over, he made his capital in Yang-shing.

1 In his 1st year, which was *jin-tsze* (49th of cycle,=B.C. 1,989), when he came to the throne, he dwelt in K'e. He published the seasons of Hea throughout the
3 regions and States. In his 2d year, Kaou-yaou died. In his 5th year, he made a tour of inspection, and assembled the princes at mount T'oo.[1]

I. 1 Mount T'oo,—see on the 'Yih and Tseih', par. 8. 2 The name of Hwuy-k'e remains in the dis. so called, dep. of Shaou-hing, Chĕ-keang. Many wonderful stories are related of the chief of Fang-fung; but all agree that Yu killed him because he came late to the meeting.—Among other notices of Yu, which are not in the Annals, but are elsewhere found, quoted as from them, is this,—that 'from Hwang-te to Yu were 30 generations,' or reigns (黃帝至禹爲世三十世). If this were ever really in the Annals, much of them must be lost.

南巡狩濟江、中流有二黃龍負舟、舟人皆懼、禹笑曰、吾受命于天、屈力以養人、生性也、死命也、奚憂龍哉、龍于是曳尾而逝。

八年、春、會諸侯于會稽、殺防風氏。夏、六月、雨金于夏邑。秋、八月、帝陟于會稽。

禹立四十五年、禹薦益於天、七年禹崩、三年喪畢、天下歸啟。

帝啟

元年、癸亥、帝即位于夏邑、大饗諸侯于鈞臺、諸侯從帝、歸于冀都、大饗諸侯于璿臺。○二年、費侯伯益出就國。王帥師、伐有扈、大戰于甘。○六年、伯益薨、祠之。○八年、帝使孟涂如巴涖訟。○十年、帝巡狩、舞九韶于天穆之野。○十一年、放王季子武觀于西河。○十五年、武觀以西河叛、彭伯壽帥師征西河、武觀來歸。○十六年、陟。

Note. On his way to the south, when crossing the Këang, in the middle of the stream, two yellow dragons took the boat on their backs. The people were all afraid; but Yu laughed and said, 'I received my appointment from Heaven, and labour with all my strength to nourish men. To be born is the course of nature; to die is by *Heaven's* decree. Why be troubled by the dragons?' On this the dragons went away, dragging their tails.

4 In his 8th year, he assembled the princes at Hwuy-k'e,[2] when he put the chief of Fang-fung to death. In the summer, in the 6th month, it rained gold in the *capital* city of Hea. In the autumn, in the 8th month, he died at Hwuy-k'e.

Note. Yu reigned (as associate, or as sovereign) 45 years. He presented Yih to Heaven, and died seven years after. When the three years of mourning were ended, the empire turned to K'e (his son).

II. THE EMPEROR K'E.

1 In his 1st year, which was *kwei-hae*[1] (60th of cycle, = B.C. 1,978), when he came
to the throne in the *capital* city of Hea,[2] he made a great feast to the princes in the
tower of Keun,[3] after which they followed him back to the capital in K'e, when he
2 made a *second* great feast to them in the tower of Seuen. In his 2d year, Pih-
yih, the prince of Pe, left *the court*, and went to his State. The king led his forces
3 to punish the prince of Hoo, when there was a great battle in Kan.[4] In his 6th
4 year, Pih-yih died, and *the emperor* appointed a sacrifice to him.[5] In his 8th
5 year, he sent Mang T'oo to Pa, to preside over litigations. In his 10th year, he
made a tour of inspection, and celebrated a complete service of Shun's music in the
6 wilderness of T'een-muh. In his 11th year, he banished his youngest son,
7 Woo-kwan, beyond the western Ho. In his 15th year, Woo-kwan with the
people about the western Ho rebelled. The baron Show of P'ang led a force to
8 punish them, when Woo-kwan returned to his allegiance. In his 14th year,
the king died.

II. 1 From 壬子, the 1st year of Yu, to this 癸亥, both inclusive, are twelve years; Yu must have died in 己未, leaving 3 complete years, before K'e's accession. This is the rule in these Annals all through the Hea dyn. The years of mourning are left between the deceased emperor and his successor; but this interregnum varies from 2 to 4 years. 2 This is the city in par. 4 of the last reign. Yu had moved his capital, or made a second one. A dis. of Kwei-tih dep. is still so called. Near or in this was the tower of Keun. 諸侯從 may be construed by itself:—'the princes agreed to follow him;' as if the feast had been a political gathering to secure the throne to K'e. 4 See 'The Speech at Kan.' 5 This account does not agree with the account of the death of Yih, which is often attributed to the Annals, and which was no doubt in some of the Bamboo Books; viz. that 'Yih was aiming at the throne, and K'e put him to death' (益干啟立、啟殺之).

帝太康

元年、癸未、帝即位、居斟鄩、畋于洛表、羿入居斟鄩○四年、陟。

帝仲康

元年、己丑、帝即位、居斟鄩○五年、秋九月庚戌、朔日有食之、命胤侯帥師、征羲和○六年、錫昆吾命作伯○七年、陟。世子相出居商邱、依邳侯。

帝相

元年、戊戌、帝即位、居商。征淮夷○二年、征風夷黃夷○七年、于夷來賓○八年、寒浞殺羿、使其子澆居過○九年、相居于斟灌○十五年、商侯相土作乘馬、遂遷于商邱○二十年、寒浞滅戈○二十六年、寒浞使其子澆帥

III. THE EMPEROR T'AE-K'ANG.

1 In his 1st year, which was *kwei-wei* (20th of cycle, = B.C. 1,957), when he came to the throne, he dwelt at Chin-sin. He went hunting beyond the Loh, when E
2 entered and occupied Chin-sin. In his 4th year, he died.

IV. THE EMPEROR CHUNG-K'ANG.

1 In his 1st year, which was *ke-ch'ow* (26th of cycle, = B.C. 1,951), when the em-
2 peror came to the throne, he dwelt in Chin-sin. In his 5th year, in the autumn, in the 9th month, on the day kăng-seuh (47th of cycle), which was the first day of the month, there was an eclipse of the sun, when he ordered the prince of Yin to
3 lead the imperial forces to punish He and Ho.[1] In his 6th year, he conferred
4 on *the prince of* Keun-woo the appointment of leader among the princes.[2] In his 7th year, he died. His son Sëang went away, and dwelt in Shang-k'ew,[3] where he was supported by the prince of P'ei.[4]

V. THE EMPEROR SEANG.

1 In his 1st year, which was *mow-seuh* (35th of cycle, = B.C. 1,942), when he came to the throne, he dwelt in Shang;[1] and led a punitive expedition against the hordes of
2 the Hwae. In his 3d year, he proceeded against the hordes of Fung and Hwang.
4 In his 7th year, the hordes of Yu came to make their submission. In his 8th year, Han-tsuh put E to death, and made his own son Këaou dwell in Ko.[2]
6 In his 9th year, Seang dwelt in Chin-kwan.[3] In his 15th year, Seang-t'oo, the prince of Shang, prepared carriages and horses, and removed to Shang-
8 k'ew. In his 20th year, Han-tsuh extinguished *the House of* Ko.[4] In his 26th year, Han-tsuh made his son Këaou lead an army, and extinguish *the House of*

III. 1 The site of Chin-sin is not well ascertained. The dict. places it in the dis. of Wei (濰縣) dep. of Lae-chow, Shan-tung. Others—more correctly, I think,—refer it to the dis. of Kung, dep. of Ho-nan. 2 See on 'The Songs of the Five Sons.'

IV. 1 See on the 'Punitive Expedition of Yin.' 2 There is repeated mention below of 昆吾氏, and therefore I take the two characters here as in the transl. The country of Keun-woo was the 衞 of subsequent times. 伯 here = 霸, chief or leader among the princes. When the five *pa* are not all referred to the dyn. of Chow, this chief of Keun-woo heads the list. 3 Shang-k'ew is still the name of a dis. in the dep. Kwei-tih. For 依邳侯 some copies read 依同姓諸侯斟灌斟鄩.

V. 1 *I. e.* in Shang-k'ew, the chief city of the Shang family, which now begins to come into prominence. 2 This Ko is ref. to the dis. of

師滅斟灌○二十七年、澆伐斟鄩、大戰于
濰、覆其舟、滅之○二十八年、寒浞使其子
澆、弒帝、后緡歸于有仍、伯靡出奔鬲。
斟灌之墟是爲帝邱后緡方娠逃
出自竇歸于有仍伯靡奔有鬲氏
夏世子少康生、丙寅年○少康自有仍奔虞、
乙酉年○伯靡自鬲帥斟鄩斟灌之師、以伐
浞、世子少康使汝艾伐過、殺澆、甲辰年○伯
子杼、帥師滅戈○伯靡殺寒浞、少康自綸、
歸于夏邑、乙巳年
明年后緡生少康既長爲仍牧正惎澆
能戒之澆使椒求之將至仍少康逃奔
有虞爲之庖正以除其害虞思於是妻
之以二姚而邑諸綸有田一成有衆一
旅能布其德而兆其謀以收夏衆撫其
官職夏之遺臣伯靡自有鬲氏收二斟
之燼以伐浞浞恃澆皆康娛日忘其惡
而不爲備少康使汝艾諜澆初浞娶純

9 Chin-kwan. In his 27th year, Këaou attacked Chin-sin. There was a great battle in Wei, when the boat *of the prince of Chin-sin* was overturned, and he was
10 put to death.5 In his 28th year, Han-tsuh made his son Këaou murder the emperor. The empress Min fled to Yew-jing;6 and Pih-mei made his escape, and fled to Kih.7

Note. The site of Chin-kwan was what was Te-k'ew. The empress Min, who was pregnant, made her escape by a hole, and returned to *her father, the prince of* Jing. Pih-mei fled to the chief of Kih.

11 The heir of the line of Hea, Shaou-k'ang, was born in the year *ping-yin* (=B.C.
12 1,914). He fled from Yew-jing to Yu,9 in the year *yih-yew* (=B.C. 1,895).
13 Pih-mei led the forces of Chin-sin and Chin-kwan from Kih to attack Tsuh; and the heir-son Shaou-k'ang sent Joo-e to attack Ko; and put Këaou to death, in the year *këä-shin* (=B.C. 1,876). His eldest son, Ch'oo, led a force against Ko, and extin-
14 guished it. Pih-mei put Han-tsuh to death, and Shaou-k'ang returned from Lun to the capital of Hea, in the year *yih-ke* (=B.C. 1,875).

Note. In the year after *her flight*, the empress Min gave birth to Shaou-k'ang, who became, when he was grown up, chief herdsman in Jing, and was on the watch against the evil designs of Keaou. Këaou having sent Tsëaou to look for him, Shaou-k'ang fled, before his arrival, to Yu, where he became chief cook. Sze, *the prince* of Yu, gave him his two daughters in marriage, and the city of Lun. There his fields were a *le* square; and his followers amounted to 500. He displayed his virtue, and formed his plans to collect the multitudes of Hea, and raise the hopes of the old officers. An old servant of Hea, called Pih-mei, issuing from Kih, collected all the people that were left of the two Chin, to attack Tsuh. Tsuh trusted in Këaou, and felt quite at ease, giving no thought to his wickedness, and making no preparations. *At the same time*, Shaou-k'ang sent Joo-e to spy out Keaou's condition. Now Tsuh had married a daughter of Shun-woo, by whom he had a son who died early, leaving a widow called Neu-k'e. Këaou obliged *one* Yu to go to her house, and pretend that he had something to ask of her. On this Neu-k'e mended his lower clothes, and they passed the night in the same house. Joo-e sent a party, took them by surprise, and cut off the head of Neu-k'e. Keaou, being very strong and swift, *made his escape;* E then

Yih (掖縣) in Lae-chow. Këaou and a brother are said to have been the sons of Han-tsuh by the wife of E; but they must have been born before E's death. See concluding note in Pt. III. of the Shoo. 3 Chin-kwan is ref.—but not certainly—to the dis. of Show-kwang, dep. Ts'ing-chow, Shan-tung. 4 This Ko lay between the States of Sung and Ch'ing. 5 This Chin-sin would agree with the dis. of Wei. Were there two places of the same name?
6 Yew-jing was in the pres. sub. dep. of Tung-p'ing, dep. of T'ae-ngan, Shan-tung. 7 Kih was in the pres. dis. of P'ing-yuen, dep. Tse-nan.

書經

狐氏有子早死其婦曰女岐寡居澆强圉往至其戶陽有所求女岐爲之縫裳共舍而宿汝艾夜使人襲斷其首乃女岐也澆旣多力又善走艾乃田獵放犬逐獸因嗾澆顚隕乃斬澆以歸于少康於是夏衆滅浞奉少康歸于夏邑諸侯始聞之立爲天子祀夏配天不失舊物

帝少康

元年、丙午、帝卽位、諸侯來朝、賓虞公○二年、方夷來賓○三年、復田稷。

后稷之後不窋失官至是而復

十一年、使商侯冥治河○十八年、遷于原○二十一年、陟。

帝杼

元年、己巳、帝卽位、居原○五年、自原遷于老邱○八年、征于東海、及三壽、得一狐九尾○十三年、商侯冥死于河○十七年、陟。

杼或作帝宁一曰伯杼杼能帥禹者也故夏后氏報焉

hunted him, and let loose a dog, which seized him, so that he fell, when they cut off his head, with which E returned to Shaou-k'ang. After this the multitudes of Hea put Tsuh to death, and carried Shaou-k'ang back to the capital. As soon as the princes heard of it, they raised him to the throne, to sacrifice to his ancestors along with the sacrifices to Heaven; and thus the old possession was not lost.

VI. THE EMPEROR SHAOU-K'ANG.

1 In his 1st year, which was *ping-woo* (43d of cycle, = B.C. 1,874), when he came to
the throne, the princes came to court to do homage. He entertained the duke of Yu
2 as his guest. In his 2d year, the hordes of Fang came to make their submission.
3 In his 3d year, he restored *the descendant of prince* Tseih, the minister of Agriculture.

Note. Puh-fuh, a descendant of prince Tseih, had lost the office, which was now restored.

5 In his 11th year, he caused Ming, the prince of Shang, to regulate the Ho. In
6 his 18th year, he removed to Yuen.[2] In his 21st year, he died.

VII. THE EMPEROR CH'OO.

1 In his 1st year, which was *ke-sze* (6th of cycle, = B.C. 1,851), when he came to
2 the throne, he dwelt in Yuen. In his 5th year, he removed from Yuen to Laou-
3 k'ew. In his 8th year, he went on a punitive expedition towards the eastern
4 sea, as far as San-show, and got a fox with 9 tails. In his 13th year, Ming, the
5 prince of Shang, died, *pursuing his labours* on the Ho. In his 17th year, he died.

Note. The name Ch'oo is written with a difft. character (宁). The emperor is also called Pih-ch'oo. *There was a younger brother*, a worthy descendant of Yu, who was therefore rewarded by the emperor.

Who Mei was is all uncertain. He had been, say many, an adherent of E. This is very unlikely. He appears here a strong partizan of the House of Hea. 9 Yu was in the pres. dis. of Yu-shing, dep. Kwei-tih.
VI. 1 The descendant of Tseih here intended, as restored to the ministry of Agriculture, was probably the famous Kung-lew. 2 Yuen is ref. to the pres. dis. of Tse-yuen, dep. Hwae-k'ing, Ho-nan.
VII. 1 Laou-k'ew is referred to the dis. of Ch'in-lew, dep. of K'ae-fung.

帝芬

元年、戊子、帝即位○三年、九夷來御○十六年、洛伯用、與河伯馮夷鬬○三十三年、封昆吾氏子、于有蘇○三十六年、作圜土○四十四年、陟。

芬或曰芬發

帝芒

元年、壬申、帝即位、以玄珪賓于河○十三年、東狩于海、獲大魚○三十三年、商侯遷于殷○五十八年、陟。

芒或曰帝荒

帝泄

元年、辛未、帝即位○十二年、殷侯子亥、賓于有易、有易殺而放之○十六年、殷侯微、以河伯之師伐有易、殺其君綿臣。

VIII. THE EMPEROR FUN.

1 His 1st year was *mow-tsze* (25th of cycle, = B.C. 1,832), when he came to the
2 throne. In his 2d year, the 9 wild tribes of the east came to perform service.
3 In his 16th year, Yung, the baron of Loh, fought with Fung-e, the baron of Ho.[2]
5 In his 33d year, he appointed the son of the chief of Keun-woo to Soo.[3] In
6 his 36th year, he made a circular enclosure *for a prison*.[4] In his 44th year, he
died.

Note. Fun is by some called Fun-fă.

IX. THE EMPEROR MANG.

1 In his 1st year, which was *jin-shin* (9th of cycle, = B.C. 1,788), when he came to
2 the throne, he *went* with the dark-coloured mace to receive the *baron of* Ho.[1] In
his 13th year, on a tour of inspection to the east as far as the sea, he got a large fish.
4 In his 33d year, the prince of Shang removed to Yin.[2] In his 58th year, he
died.

Note. Mang is in some editions called the emperor Hwang.

X. THE EMPEROR SËEH.

1 His 1st year was *sin-wei* (8th of cycle, = B.C. 1,729), when he came to the throne.
2 In his 12th year, Tsze-hae, prince of Yin, went as guest to Yew-yih, the chief of
3 which put him to death, and sent away *his followers*. In his 16th year, Wei,
prince of Yin, with the forces of the baron of Ho, attacked Yew-yih,[1] and killed its
ruler Mëen-chin.

VIII. 1 夷 is to be taken here in its proper meaning of 'wild tribes of the east.' 御=侍御, 'to wait upon and serve,'—perhaps as warders, guards, &c. 2 Fung-e appears in many writers as a monster or spiritual being. He is evidently in the text merely the chief of the State Ho, or charged with the care of the Ho. 3 Soo was in Tse-yuen, above. 4 All prisons, it is said, in the three dynasties, were circular.

IX. 1 I have translated acc. to the view of Hăng Ch'in-fung:—以元珪往聘河伯耳; but perhaps some service to the Ho is meant. The mace is that of Yu the Great. 2 This Yin is ref. to the dis. of Shang-shwuy, dep. Ch'in-chow.

X. 1 There is a small dep. in Chih-le, called Yih-chow, which may correspond to the ancient Yew-yih.

殷侯子亥賓于有易而淫焉有易之君綿臣殺而放之故殷侯上甲微假師于河伯以伐有易滅之遂殺其君綿臣中葉衰而上甲微復興故殷人報焉

二十一年、命畎夷、白夷、玄夷、風夷、赤夷、黃夷○二十五年、陟。

帝不降

元年、己亥、帝即位○六年、伐九苑○三十五年、殷滅皮氏○五十九年、遜位于弟扃。

帝扃

元年、戊戌、帝即位○十年、帝不降陟。

三代之世內禪惟不降實有聖德

十八年、陟。

帝廑

一名胤甲

元年、己未、帝即位、居西河○四年、作西音。

Note. The prince of of Yin, Tsze-hae, visited Yew-yih, and was guilty of licentious conduct, so that the ruler of Yew-yih, Mëen-chin, slew him, and drove *his followers* away. In consequence of this, Shang-këă-wei of Yin obtained the services of the army of the baron of Ho, attacked and extinguished the State of Yew-yih, putting Mëen-chin to death. For a time Yin had decayed, but when Shang-këă-wei revived its power, the people avenged the wrong that had been done.

4 In his 21st year, he conferred regular dignities on the chiefs of the hordes of
5 K'euen, of the white hordes, the dark hordes, the hordes of Fung, the red hordes, and the yellow hordes. In his 25th year, he died.

XI. THE EMPEROR PUH-KËANG.

1 His 1st year, was *ke-hae* (36th of cycle, = B.C. 1,701), when he came to the
2 throne. In his 6th year, he attacked *the country of* Kew-yuen.[1] In his
4 35th year, Yin made an end of the House of P'e.[2] In his 59th year, he resigned the throne to his younger brother Këung.

XII. THE EMPEROR KËUNG.

1 His 1st year, was *mow-seuh* (35th of cycle, = B.C. 1,642), when he came to the
2 throne. In his 10th year, the emperor Puh-këang died.

Note. In the period of the three dynasties there was only one resignation of the throne,—that by Puh-këang. He must have had the virtue of a sage.

3 In his 18th year, he died.

XIII. THE EMPEROR KIN.

Note. Also called Yin-këă.

1 In his 1st year, which was *ke-wei* (56th of cycle, = B.C. 1,621), when he came
2 to the throne, he dwelt on the west of the Ho.[1] In his 4th year, he made the music of the West. The chief of Keun-woo removed to Heu.[2]

XI. 1 Kew-yuen=the 'nine pasturages,' probably a tract of flat country in the pres. Chih-le. 2 The territory of P'e was in the pres. dis. of Ho-tsin, dep. Keang Chow, Shan-se. It is observed that the extinction of this State was the 1st step of the kind, taken by Shang, to the imperial sway.

XIII. 1 That is, he lived in Shen-se. 'The western Ho' denotes the country west of K'e-chow. 2 Heu corresponded, probably, to the pres. Heu Chow, Ho-nan.

昆吾氏遷于許。巳姓名樊封于衛夏衰爲伯遷于舊許

八年、天有祅孽、十日竝出、其年陟。

帝孔甲

元年、乙巳、帝卽位、居西河。廢豕韋氏、使劉累豢龍○三年、王畋于萯山○五年、作東音○七年、劉累遷于魯陽。王好事鬼神肆行淫亂諸侯化之夏政始衰田于東陽萯山天大風晦盲孔甲迷惑入于民室主人方乳或曰后來見良日也之子必大吉或又曰不勝也之子必有殃孔甲聞之曰以爲余一人子夫誰殃之乃取其子以歸既長爲斧所戕乃作破斧之歌是爲東音劉累所畜龍一雌死潛醢以食夏后夏后饗之既而使求之懼而遷于魯陽其後爲范氏

九年、陟。殷侯復歸于商邱。

帝昊

昊一作皐

Note. The surname *of the founder of Keun-woo* was Ke, and his name Tan. He had been invested with Wei, and when Hea was decaying, *the chief of the House* was Head of the princes, and removed to old Heu.

5 In his 8th year, there was an inauspicious portent in the sky;—ten suns appeared together. In that year the emperor died.

XIV. THE EMPEROR K'UNG-KEA.

1 In his 1st year, which was *yih-sze* (mistake for *ke-sze*, 6th of cycle, = B.C. 1,611), when he came to the throne, he dwelt on the west of the Ho. He displaced the
2 chief of Ch'e-wei, and appointed Lew-luy to feed the dragons.[1] In his 3d year,
3 the king hunted on mount Foo.[2] In his 5th year, he made the music of the East.
4 In his 7th year, Lew Luy removed to Loo-yang.[3]

Note. The king was superstitious, and acted in a disorderly and licentious way. The princes became like him, and the govt. of Hea began to go to decay. He was hunting on mount Foo of Tung-yang, when in a great wind the sky was all overcast. The emperor lost his way, and went into the family of a peasant, whose wife had just been confined. Some said, 'The emperor has come to see you;—it is a good day. This child will have great good fortune.' Some said, 'Not so. This child will be unfortunate.'—When K'ung-këă heard this, he said, 'Let it be the child of me, the emperor; then who can harm it?' Accordingly he took the child with him; but when it was grown up, it was killed by a hatchet, on which he made the song of 'Break the Hatchet;'—what is called 'The music of the East.'

A female dragon of those which Lew Luy had the keeping of died, when he privately made pickle of it, and set it before the emperor, who enjoyed it; and ordered Luy to look for the missing dragon. Luy was afraid, and removed to Loo-yang, where his descendants became the Fan family.

5 In his 9th year, he died. The prince of Yin returned to Shang-k'ew.

XV. THE EMPEROR HAOU.

Note. Also called Kaou.

XIV. 1 The State of Ch'e-wei is ref. to a place in the dep. of Ta-ming, Chih-le. It is hard to say what is meant by feeding the dragons, though there are many legends about it. 2 It is strange how the title of 'king' is here employed for 'emperor.' 3 Or 'to the south of mount Loo;'—in the pres. dis. of Loo-san, dep. Joo-chow, Ho-nan.

元年、庚辰、帝卽位。使豕韋氏復國。

夏衰昆吾豕韋相繼爲伯

三年、陟。

帝發

一名后敬或曰發惠

元年、乙酉、帝卽位。諸夷賓于王門、再保墉會于上池。諸夷入舞○七年、陟。泰山震。

帝癸

一名桀

元年、壬辰、帝卽位、居斟鄩○三年、築傾宮。毀容臺。畎夷入于岐以叛○六年、岐踵戎來賓○十年、五星錯行、夜中星隕如雨。地震。伊洛竭○十一年、會諸侯于仍、有緡氏逃歸、遂滅有緡○十三年、遷于河南。初作輦○十四年、扁帥師伐岷山。

1 His 1st year was *kang-shin* (17th of cycle, = B.C. 1,600), when he came to the throne. He restored the representative of the House of Ch'e-wei to his State.

Note. In the decay of the Hëa, chiefs of Keun-woo and Ch'e-wei succeeded one another as Head of the princes.

2 In his 3d year he died.

XVI. THE EMPEROR FAH.

Note. Also called the emperor King; and Fä-hwuy.

1 In his 1st year, which was *yih-yew* (22d of cycle, = B.C. 1,595), when he came to
the throne, various wild tribes came and made their submission at the king's gate.[1]
He again repaired the walls. There was a meeting on the upper pool, when the wild
2 people came in, and performed their dances. In his 7th year, he died. Mount
T'ae shook.

XVII. THE EMPEROR KWEI.

Note. Called also Këë.

1 In his 1st year, which was *jin-shin* (29th of cycle, = B.C. 1,588), when he came to
2 the throne, he dwelt in Chin-sin. In his 3d year, he built the K'ing palace,
and pulled down the Yung tower.[2] The K'euen hordes penetrated as far as K'e, with
3 the standard of revolt.[3] In his 6th year, the hordes of K'e-chung[4] came to
4 make their submission. In his 10th year, the five planets went out of their
courses. In the night, stars fell like rain. The earth shook. The E and Loh became
5 dry. In his 11th year, he assembled the princes in Jing, when the chief of Yew-min
6 fled home, on which the emperor extinguished Yew-min.[5] In his 13th year, he
removed to the south of the Ho.[6] He made for the first time men-drawn carriages.[7]
7 In his 14th year, Pëen led the imperial forces, and smote Min-san.[8]

XV. 1 王門 should probably be 玉門, 'the gate of gems,'—one of the gates of the palace, so called.

XVI. 1 The meaning of 再保至池 is very much debated. See Hăng Ch'in-fung, *in loc.*

XVII. 1 This, no doubt, was in the dis. of Kung, dep. Ho-nan. 2 For conjectures on the meaning of the names here, see Hăng, *in loc.* 3 Hăng thinks this par. belongs to the reign of king Muh or king E of Chow. 4 The country of K'e-chung, (岐=跂) or 'the people who walked on their toes,' without the heel touching the ground, is placed beyond the Moving sands. 5 See on the time of Shaou-k'ang. The Min *family* occupied the State of Jing. 6. Some city is intended; but commentators are not agreed which. 7 These

癸命扁伐山民山民進女于桀二人
曰琬曰琰后愛二人女無子焉斵其
名于苕華之玉苕是琬華是琰而棄
其元妃于洛曰妹喜於傾宮飾瑤臺
之居

十五年、商侯履遷于亳。○十七年、商使
伊尹來朝。○二十年、伊尹歸于商、及汝
鳩汝方、會于北門。○二十一年、商師征
有洛、克之、遂征荊、荊降。○二十二年、商
侯履來朝、命囚履于夏臺。○二十三年、
釋商侯履。諸侯遂賓于商。○二十六年、
商滅溫。○二十八年、昆吾氏伐商、商會
諸侯于景亳、遂征韋、商師取韋、遂征顧。
太史令終古出奔商。○二十九年、商師
取顧。三日竝出。費伯昌出奔商。冬十月、
鑿山穿陵、以通于河。○三十年、瞿山崩。
殺其大夫關龍逄。商師征昆吾。冬、聆隧
災。○三十一年、商自陑征夏邑、克昆吾、

Note. Some copies read San-min, or hill-people. Kwei ordered Pëen to attack San-min, whose prince presented Këĕ with two ladies, called Yuen and Yen. The emperor loved them, tho' they had no children; and had their names cut on the gems Teaou and Hwa. That on the T'eaou was Yuen; on the Hwa, Yen. He also sent away his first wife Me-he to Lŏ, placing her in the Yaou tower of the K'ing palace.

8 In his 15th year, Le, prince of Shang, removed to Poh.[9]

Note. This was the 1st year of T'ang the Successful.

10 In his 15th year, Shang made E Yin come to court. In his 20th year, E Yin,
11 returning to Shang, met with Joo Kew and Joo Fang at the north gate. In his 21st year, the forces of Shang went on a punitive expedition against the prince of Lŏ, and subdued him. They then went against King,[10] which made submission. In
12 his 22d year, Le, prince of Shang, came to court, when the emperor ordered him to be
13 imprisoned in the tower of Hea.[11] In his 23d year, he set Le at liberty, when the
14 princes went and offered their submission to Shang. In his 26th year, Shang ex-
15 tinguished Wun.[12] In his 28th year, the chief of Keun-woo attacked Shang. Shang assembled the princes in King-poh[13] and proceeded against Wei, which its forces took. They then proceeded against Koo. The Grand recorder Chung Koo left the court
16 and fled to Shang. In his 29th year, the forces of Shang took Koo.[15] Three suns appeared together. The prince of Pe, Ch'ang, left the court and fled to Shang. In the winter, in the 10th month, they chisselled through mountains, and tunnelled hills, to
17 open a communication with the Ho.[16] In his 30th year, there was a fall of mount K'eu.[17] *The emperor* put to death his great officer Kwan Lung-fung. The forces of Shang marched to punish Keun-woo. In the winter, there was a fire in Ling-suy.[18]
18 In his 31st year, Shang proceeded by way of Urh against the capital of Hea; and overcame Keun-woo. Amid great thunder and rain a battle was fought in Ming-

carriages are said to have been made for Me-he, Këĕ's wife. 8 The comm. identify this Min-san with a Mung-san (蒙山);—perhaps corresp. to Mung-san, dep. Ya-chow, in Szechʻuen. 9 This was the 'southern Pŏ.' 10 King;—known afterwards as Ts'oo. 11 This was a State prison;—near Chin-sin. 12 The pres. dis. of Wun, dep. Hwae-k'ing. 13 This is said to have been the 'northern Pŏ.' 14 Probably=Ch'e-wei. 15 Supposed to have been in pres. dis. of Wun-ching, dep. Ts'aou-chow, Shan-tung. 16 This should not have been done in the winter.

大雷雨、戰于鳴條、夏師敗績、桀出奔三朡、商師征三朡、戰于郕、獲桀于焦門、放之于南巢。

自禹至桀十七世有王與無王用歲四百七十一年

t'eaou, when the army of Hea was defeated. Këeh fled away to San-tsung,[19] against which the army of Shang proceeded. A battle was fought at Ching,[20] and Këeh was taken in Tsëaou-mun. He was then banished away to Nan-ch'aou.

Note. From Yu to Këë were 17 reigns. Calculating reigns and interregnums, the dynasty lasted 471 years.

17 K'eu is better known as mount Chin (岑山). 18 See the comment of Sun Che-luh, cited by Hăng. For 聆 some read 聆.

19 San-tsung is ref. to the dis. of Ting-t'aou, dep. Ts'aou-chow. 20 In the sub. dep. of Tung-p'ing, T'ae-ngan.

竹書紀年卷之四

殷商成湯

名履

湯有七名而九征放桀于南巢而還諸侯八譯而來者千八百國奇肱氏以車至乃同尊天乙履爲天子三讓遂即天子之位初高辛氏之世妃曰簡狄以春分玄鳥至之日從帝祀郊禖與其妹浴于玄邱之水有玄鳥銜卵而墜之五色甚好二人競取覆以玉筐簡狄先得而吞之遂孕胸剖而生契長爲堯司徒成功於民受封於商後十三世生主癸主癸之妃曰扶都見白氣貫月意感以乙日生湯號天乙豐下銳上皙而有顊句身而揚聲長九尺臂有四肘是爲成湯湯在亳能修其德伊摯將應湯命夢乘船過日月之旁湯乃東至于洛觀帝堯之壇沈璧退立黃魚雙躍黑鳥隨之止于壇化爲黑玉又有黑龜竝赤文成字

PART. IV.

The Dynasty of Shang.

I. T'ANG THE SUCCESSFUL, OF SHANG OR YIN.

Note. His name was Le. T'ang, *indeed*, had 7 names, and conducted 9 punitive expeditions. When he returned from confining Këĕ in Nan-ch'aou, the princes, having 8 interpreters, came to him, to the number of 1,800. The chief of the 'Wonderful Arms' also came in his chariot. They all wished him, Teen-yih Le, to assume the imperial dignity, to which, after declining thrice, he acceded.

In ancient times, the empress of Kaou-sin, called Këen-teih, at the vernal equinox, when the dark swallow made its appearance, had followed her husband to the suburbs to pray for a son, and was bathing with her sister in the Water of Heuen-k'ew, when a dark swallow dropt from her mouth a beautifully variegated egg. The two sisters strove to cover it with baskets which they had; but Këen-teih succeeded in getting it. She swallowed it, became pregnant, and by-and-by her chest opened, and she gave birth to Sëĕ. When he grew up, he was minister of Instruction to Yaou, who conferred on him the principality of Shang because of his services to the people.

After 13 generations, Sëĕ's descendant, Choo-kwei, was born, whose wife was called Foo-too. She saw a white vapour go through the moon; was moved to pregnancy; and on the day Yih bore T'ang, who was therefore styled T'ëen-yih. The lower part of his face was broad, and it tapered above;—it was white and whiskered. His body was one-sided, and his voice was loud. He was 9 cubits high, and his arms had four joints. He became T'ang the Successful.

T'ang lived in Pŏ, and cultivated his virtue. When E Chi was about to comply with T'ang's invitation, he dreamed that he passed by the sun and moon in a boat.

T'ang came east to Lŏ, to see the altar of Yaou. He dropped a gem in the water, and stood at some distance. Lo! yellow fishes leaped up in pairs; a black bird followed him, and stood on the altar, where it changed into a black gem. There was also a black tortoise, with red lines forming characters, which said that Këĕ of Hea was unprincipled, and that T'ang should supersede him. At the same time, the spirit of T'aou-wuh was seen on mount P'ei. Another spirit, dragging a white wolf, with a hook in his mouth, entered the court of Shang. The virtue of metal waxed powerful;

言夏桀無道湯當代之禱杌之神見于邳山有神牽白狼銜鉤而入商朝金德將盛銀自山溢湯將奉天命放桀夢及天而舐之遂有天下商人後改天下之號曰殷

十八年、癸亥、王即位、居亳。始屋夏社〇十九年、大旱。氐羌來貢〇二十年、大旱。夏桀卒于亭山、禁弦歌舞〇二十一年、大旱。鑄金幣〇二十二年、大旱〇二十三年、大旱〇二十四年、大旱、王禱于桑林、雨〇二十五年、作大濩樂。初巡狩、定獻令〇二十七年、遷九鼎于商邑〇二十九年、陟。

外丙

名勝、

元年、乙亥、王即位、居亳、命卿士伊尹〇二年、陟。

silver overflowed from the hills. When T'ang was about to put Këĕ away, in reverence of the command of Heaven, he dreamed that he went to the sky, and licked it. After this he became possessor of the empire. The people of Shang afterwards changed the title of the dynasty into Yin.

1 In his 18th year, which was *kwei-hae* (60th of cycle, = B.C. 1,557), when he came
to the throne, he dwelt in Poh.[2] He roofed over, for the first time, the altar to the
2 spirits of the land dedicated by the House of Hea.[3] In his 19th year, there was
a great drought. The people of Te-këang came and made their submission.[4]
3 In his 20th year, there was a great drought. Këeh of Hea died at mount T'ing, when
4 it was forbidden to play on stringed instruments, to sing and to dance. In his
6 21st year, there was the great drought. He cast metal money[5] In his 22d and
7 23d years, the drought continued. In his 24th year, the drought still continuing,
8 the king prayed in the mulberry forest, and it rained.[6] In his 25th year, he
made the music of Ta-hoo.[7] He went for the first time on a tour of inspection, and
9 fixed the rules for offerings. In his 27th year, he removed the nine vases to the
10 capital of Shang. In his 29th year, he died.

II. WAE-PING.

Note. Named Shing.

1 In his 1st year, which was *yih-hae* (12th of cycle, = B.C. 1,545), when the king[1]
came to the throne, he dwelt in Poh; and confirmed the appointment of E Yin as
2 prime minister.[2] In his 2d year, he died.

I. 1 The years of T'ang are counted from his accession to the principality of Shang, B.C. 1,574. 2 This was, probably, the western Pŏ,—in the pres. dis. Yen-sze, dep. Ho-nan. 3 T'ang had wished to remove the altars of Hea. Diverted from that purpose, he 'housed' them, or roofed them over,—to remain a monument of the justice of Heaven. 4 See in the She, the 5th of the Praise-songs of Shang. 5 This is understood to have been done for the poor, that they might redeem their children whom they had sold in the famine. 6 See the prayer of T'ang, from Mih-tsze, in the proleg. to Mencius, pp. 116,117. It is singular the Shoo says nothing of this drought. Sze-ma Ts'een says it lasted 7 years; the Ch'un-Ts'ew of Leu, 5 years; these Annals, 6 years. Ts'ëen makes Shwang-lin the name of a wilderness; others say—'the wood of mt. Shwang.' 7 大濩=大護, 'great salvation;'—celebrating T'ang's exploits and prayers.

II. 1 王, 'king,' here replaces 帝, applied in these Annals to the sovereigns of Hea. 2 We must take 命 here in this way. See Hăng, *in loc.*

[129]

仲壬

名庸

元年丁丑、王卽位、居亳、命卿士伊尹○四年、陟。

太甲

名至

元年辛巳、王卽位、居亳、命卿士伊尹、伊尹放太甲于桐、乃自立。約按伊尹自立蓋誤以攝政爲眞爾

七年、王潛出自桐、殺伊尹、天大霧三日、乃立其子伊陟、伊奮、命復其父之田宅、而中分之。約按此文與前後不類蓋後世所益

十年、大饗于太廟、初祀方明○十二年、陟。

沃丁

名絢

III. CHUNG-JIN.

Note. Named Yung.

1 In his 1st year, which was *ting-ch'ow* (14th of cycle, = B.C. 1,543), when he came
2 to the throne, he dwelt in Poh, and confirmed the appointment of E Yin. In his 4th year, he died.

IV. T'AE-KËAH.

Note. Named Che.

1 In his 1st year, which was *sin-sze* (18th of cycle, = B.C. 1,539), when he came to the throne, he dwelt in Poh, and confirmed the appointment of E Yin. E Yin sent T'ae-këah away, and confined him in T'ung, seizing the throne himself.[1]

Note by Yŏ. It is a mistake to say this. The truth is that he only acted as regent.

2 In his 7th year, the king privately escaped from T'ung, and put E Yin to death. The sky was overspread with mists for three days, when he raised to office Yin's sons, E Chih and E Fun, ordered their father's fields and houses to be restored, and equally divided between them.

Note by Yŏ. This par. does not accord with the text before and after it. It is, probably, the addition of an after time.

3 In his 10th year, he celebrated a great service to all his ancestors in the Grand ancestral temple. For the first time he sacrificed to the Intelligences of the *four*
4 quarters.[2] In his 12th year, he died.

V. YUH-TING.

Note. Named Heuen.

IV. 1 This and the next notice are so difft. from the current and classical accounts of E Yin and T'ae-këä, that the friends of these Annals are in great perplexity about them. Hăng Ch'in-fung would refer them to the 'Fragmentary Words' of the Bamboo Books. Seu Wăn-tsing contents himself with saying, after the original commentator, that they are the additions of a later hand.

2 方明=四方之神明. This is the easiest interpretation. Some suppose the 六宗 of Can. of Shun, p. 5, to be meant.

元年、癸巳、王即位、居亳。命卿士咎單。○八年、祠保衡。○十九年、陟。

小庚

名辨、元年、壬子、王即位、居亳。○五年、陟。

小甲

名高、元年、丁巳、王即位、居亳。○十七年、陟。

雍巳

名佃、元年、甲戌、王即位、居亳。○十二年、陟。

太戊

名密、元年、丙戌、王即位、居亳。命卿士伊陟臣扈。○

1 In his 1st year, which was *kwei-sze* (30th of cycle, = B.C. 1,527), when he came to the throne, he dwelt in Poh; and confirmed the appointment of Kaou Shen as prime
3 minister. In his 8th year, he appointed sacrifices to Paou-hang.[1] In his 19th year, he died.

VI. SEAOU-KANG.

Note. Named Pëen.

1 In his 1st year, which was *jin-tsze* (49th of cycle, = B.C. 1,508), when he came to
2 the throne, he dwelt in Poh. In his 5th year, he died.

VII. SEAOU-KEAH.

Note. Named Kaou.

1 In his 1st year, which was *ting-sze* (54th of cycle, = B.C. 1,503), when he came to
2 the throne, he dwelt in Poh. In his 17th year, he died.

VIII. YUNG-KE.

Note. Named Tëen.

1 In his 1st year, which was *këah-seuh* (11th of cycle, = B.C. 1,486), when he came to
2 the throne, he dwelt in Poh. In his 12th year, he died.

IX. T'AE-MOW.

Note. Named Meih.

1 In his 1st year, which was *ping-seuh* (23d of cycle, = B.C. 1,474), when he came to the throne, he dwelt in Poh, and confirmed the appointments[1] of E Chih and Chin

V. 1 This was E Yin. See on the T'ae-këä, Pt. i. p. 1.

IX. 1 From the 15th notice in the preface to the Shoo, Chin-hoo would seem to have been alive in T'ang's time, so that in T'ae-mow's time, acc. to the current chron., he must have been nearly 200 years old. Even acc. to these Annals, he must have been over 100.

七年、有桑穀生于朝○十一年、命巫咸禱于山川○二十六年、西戎來賓。王使王孟聘西戎○三十一年、命費侯中衍爲車正○三十五年、作寅車○四十六年、大有年○五十八年、城蒲姑○六十一年、東九夷來賓○七十五年、陟。

太戊遇祥桑側身修行三年之後遠方慕明德重譯而至者七十六國商道復興廟爲太宗

仲丁

名莊

元年、辛丑、王即位、自亳遷于囂、于河上○六年、征藍夷○九年、陟。

外壬

名發

元年、庚戌、王即位、居囂。邳人姺人叛○十年、陟。

1 Hoo, as his principal ministers. In his 7th year, a mulberry tree and a stalk
2 of grain grew up together in the court. In his 11th year, he commanded Woo
3 Hëen to pray to the hills and rivers. In his 26th year, the hordes of the West
came to make their submission. He sent Wang Măng, as his envoy, with presents
4 to those hordes. In his 31st year, he appointed Chung-yen, prince of Pe, to be
6 master of his carriages. In his 35th year, he made *yin* carriages.[2] In his
7 46th year, there was a very abundant harvest. In his 58th year, he walled
8 P'oo-koo.[3] In his 61st year, the nine hordes of the East came to make their
9 submission. In his 75th year, he died.

Note. After T'ae-mow met with the warning mulberry tree, he inclined himself to the cultivation of his conduct; and after 3 years, there were 76 States from distant regions, which sent messengers, with interpreters, to his court, in admiration of his wise virtue. The fortunes of Shang again revived. His sacrificial title was T'ae-tsung.

X. CHUNG-TING.

Note. Named Chwang.

1 In his 1st year, which was *sin-ch'ow* (38th of cycle, = B.C. 1,399), when he came
2 to the throne, he removed from Poh to Gaou [1] on the Ho. In his 6th year, he
3 went on an expedition against the hordes of Lan.[2] In his 9th year, he died.

XI. WAE-JIN.

Note. Named Fă.

1 In his 1st year, which was *kang-seuh* (47th of cycle, = B.C. 1,390), when he came to the throne, he dwelt in Gaou. The people of P'ei [1] and of Sëen [2] revolted.
2 In his 10th year, he died.

2 Hăng Ch'in-fung says these carriages were of roots of the mulberry tree;—perhaps, referring to their colour.

3 Probably in the pres. dis. of Pŏ-hing, dep. Ts'ing-chow, Shan-tung.

X. 1 Gaou was on a mount Gaou (敖山), in the pres. dis. of Ho-yin, dep. K'ae-fung. Up to this time, the capital had been the western Pŏ. 2 Perhaps in the dis. of Yang-k'euh, dep. T'ae-yuen, Shan-se.

XI. 1 P'ei—the pres. sub. dep. of P'ei Chow, dep. of Seu-chow, Këang-soo. 2 The dis. of Ch'in-lew, dep. K'ae-fung.

河亶甲

名整

元年、庚申、王即位、自囂遷于相○三年、彭伯克邳○四年、征藍夷○五年、姺人入于班方、彭伯、韋伯、伐班方、姺人來賓○九年、陟。

祖乙

名滕

元年、己巳、王即位、自相遷于耿、命彭伯韋伯○二年、圮于耿、自耿遷于庇○三年、命卿士巫賢○八年、城庇○十五年、命邠侯高圉○十九年、陟。

祖乙之世商道復興廟爲中宗

祖辛

名旦

元年、戊子、王即位、居庇○十四年、陟。

XII. HO-TAN-KËAH.

Note. Named Ching.

1 In his 1st year, which was *kang-shin* (57th of cycle, = B.C. 1,380), when he came
2 to the throne, he removed from Gaou to Sëang.[1] In his 3d year, the baron of P'ang
3 subdued P'ei. In his 4th year, he made an expedition against the hordes of Lan.
4 In his 5th year, the people of Sëen entered the region of Pan, when the barons of
P'ang and Wei attacked it, and the people of Sëen came to make their submission.
5 In his 9th year, he died.

XIII. TSOO-YIH.

Note. Named T'ăng.

1 In his 1st year, which was *ke-sze* (6th of cycle, = B.C. 1,371), when he came to the
throne, he removed from Sëang to Kăng.[1] He gave appointments to the barons of
2 P'ang and Wei.[2] In his 2d year, Kăng was inundated, when he removed to
3 Pe.[3] In his 3d year, he confirmed the appointment of Woo Heen as prime
5 minister. In his 8th year, he walled Pe.[3] In his 15th year, he gave an
6 appointment to Kaou-yu, prince of Pin.[4] In his 19th year, he died.

Note. The fortunes of Shang flourished again under Tsoo-yih. His sacrificial title was Chung-tsung.

XIV. TSOO-SIN.

Note. Named Tan.

In his 1st year, which was *mow-tsze* (25th of cycle, = B.C. 1,352), when he came to the throne, he dwelt in Pe. In his 14th year, he died.

XII. 1 In the pres. dis. of Ngan-yang, dep. Chang-tih, Ho-nan.

XIII. 1 In the pres. dis. of Ho-tsin, Këang Chow, Shan-se. 2 What appointments is not said. Many comm. say—'The appoint. of Pa, or chiefs of the princes;' but the text will not bear that construction. 3 Some would go away to the dis. of P'ing-hëang, dep. Shun-tih, Chih-le, for this Pe;—which is very unlikely. 4 In Pin Chow, Shen-se. Kaou-yu was a descendant of Kung-lew. Here was the seat of the Chow family.

開甲名踰、元年壬寅、王即位、居庇○五年、陟。

祖丁名新、元年丁未、王即位、居庇○九年、陟。

南庚名更、元年丙辰、王即位、居庇○三年、遷于奄○六年、陟。

陽甲名和一名和甲、元年壬戌、王即位、居奄○三年、西征丹山戎○四年、陟。

盤庚名旬

XV. K'AE-KËAH.

Note. Named Yu.

1 In his 1st year, which was *jin-yin* (39th of cycle, = B.C. 1,338), when he came to
2 the throne, he dwelt in Pe. In his 5th year, he died.

XVI. TSOO-TING.

Note. Named Sin.

1 In his 1st year, which was *ting-we* (44th of cycle, = B.C. 1,333), when he came to
2 the throne, he dwelt in Pe. In his 9th year, he died.

XVII. NAN-KANG.

Note. Named Kăng.

1 In his 1st year, which was *ping-shin* (53d of cycle, = B.C. 1,324), when he came
3 to the throne, he dwelt in Pe. In his 3d year, he removed to Yen.[1] In his
6th year, he died.

XVIII. YANG-KËAH.

Note. Named Ho. Some style him Ho-këă.

1 In his 1st year, which was *jin-seuh* (59th of cycle, B.C. 1,318), when he came to
2 the throne, he dwelt in Yen. In his 3d year, he made an expedition to the west
3 against the hordes of mount Tan. In his 4th year, he died.

XIX. PWAN-KANG.

Note. Named Seun.

XVII. 1 Yen is no better known than Pe. Some make it out to have been in Shan-tung, in Loo.

XIX. 1 Probably in the dis. of Loo-san, dep. of Joo, Ho-nan. 2 The 'northern Mung'= northern Pŏ, what is called 'King Pŏ,' under

元年、丙寅、王即位、居奄○七年、應侯來朝○十四年、自奄遷于北蒙曰殷○十五年、營殷邑○十九年、命邠侯亞圉○二十八年、陟。

小辛

名頌

元年、甲午、王即位、居殷○三年、陟。

小乙

名斂

元年、丁酉、王即位、居殷○六年、命世子武丁、居于河、學于甘盤○十年、陟。

武丁

名昭

元年、丁未、王即位、居殷、命卿士甘盤○三年、夢求傅說、得之○六年、命卿士傅說、視學養老○十二年、報祀上甲微○二十五年、王子孝已、卒

1 In his 1st year, which was *ping-yin* (3d of cycle, = B.C. 1,314), when he came to
2 the throne, he dwelt in Yen. In his 7th year, the prince of Ying[1] came to do
3 homage. Iu his 14th year, he removed from Yen, to the northern Mung,[2] which
5 was called Yin. In his 15th year, he built the city of Yin. In his 19th year,
6 he confirmed the appointment of A-yu, prince of Pin. In his 28th year, he died.

XX. SEAOU-SIN.

Note. Named Sung.

1 In his 1st year, which was *keah-woo* (31st of cycle, = B.C. 1,286), when he came
2 to the throne, he dwelt in Yin. In his 3d year, he died.

XXI. SEAOU-YIH.

Note. Named Lëen.

1 In his 1st year, which was *ting-yew* (34th of cycle, = B.C. 1,283), when he came
2 to the throne, he dwelt in Yin. In his 6th year, he ordered his heir-son, Woo-ting,
3 to dwell by the Ho, and study under Kan Pwan. In his 11th year, he died.

XXII. WOO-TING.

Note. Named Ch'aou.

1 In his 1st year, which was *ting-we* (44th of cycle, = B.C. 1,273), when he dwelt in
2 Yin, he confirmed the appointment of Kan Pwan as prime minister.[1] In his 3d
3 year, in consequence of a dream, he sought for Foo-yuě, and found him. In his
6th year, he confirmed Foo-yuě in the dignity of prime minister; and inspected the
4 schools where they nourished the aged.[2] In his 12th year, he offered a sacrifice
5 of thanksgiving to Shang-keah Wei.[3] In his 25th year, his son Heaou-e died in

the 28th year of Këë's reign; and Yin under the reign of the emperor Mang.

XXII. 1 See on the Charge to Yuě, Pt. iii., par. 1. 2 These schools were asylums. They were called schools, because the aged who were supported in them would enforce the duties of filial duty and submission. 3 See the note above, on the 16th year of the emp. Mang. 4 To which he had been banished, many say,

于野〇二十九年、肜祭太廟、有雉來〇三十二年、伐鬼方、次于荆〇三十四年、王師克鬼方、氐羌來賓〇四十三年、王師滅大彭〇五十年、征豕韋、克之〇五十九年、陟。

王殷之大仁也力行王道不敢荒寧嘉靖殷邦至于小大無時或怨是時輿地東不過江黃西不過氐羌南不過荆蠻北不過朔方而頌聲作禮廢而復起廟號高宗

祖庚

名曜、

元年丙午、王即位、居殷、作高宗之訓〇十一年、陟。

祖甲

名載、

元年丁巳、王即位、居殷〇十二年、征西戎。冬、王返自西戎〇十三年、西戎來賓、命邠侯組紺〇二十四年、重作湯刑〇二十七年、命王子囂、王子良〇三十三年、陟。

1 a wilderness.[4] In his 29th year, at the supplementary sacrifice in the Grand
2 ancestral temple, a pheasant made its appearance.[5] In his 32d year, he smote the
3 country of the demons,[6] and camped in King. In his 34th year, the king's forces subdued the Demon-region, when the tribes of Te-keang came and made their sub
4 mission. In his 43d year, his forces extinguished the State of Ta-p'ang.
6 In his 50th year, he led an expedition against Ch'e-wei, and subdued it. In his 9th year, he died.

Note. Woo-ting was the great benevolent sovereign of Yin. Vigorously did he carry out the royal principles, not allowing himself in idleness. Admirably did he still the States of Yin, so that, great or small, they never murmured against him. In his time, the empire, on the East, did not extend beyond the Këang and Hwang; on the West, it did not extend beyond Te-këang; on the South, it did not extend beyond King and Man; on the North, it did not extend beyond Sŏ-fang. But Praise-songs were heard again, and ceremonies revived from their decay. He received the sacrificial title of Kaou-tsung.

XXIII. Tsoo-kang.

Note. Named Yaou.

1 In his 1st year, which was *ping-woo* (43d of cycle, = B.C. 1,214), when he came to
2 the throne, he dwelt in Yin; and made 'The Instructions of Kaou-tsung.' In his 11th year, he died.

XXIV. Tsoo-këah.

Note. Named Tsae.

1 In his 1st year, which was *ting-sze* (54th of cycle, = B.C. 1,203), when he came to
2 the throne, he dwelt in Yin. In his 12th year, he led a punitive expedition
3 against the hordes of the West; from which he returned in the winter. In his 13th year, the hordes of the West came to make their submission. He confirmed
4 the appointment of Tsoo-kan, prince of Pin. In his 24th year, he established
5 anew the penal statutes of T'ang. In his 27th year, he gave appointments to his
6 sons, Gaou and Lëang. In his 33d year, he died.

by his father. But this may be an invention of future times. 5 See the ixth of the Books of Shang. 6 See the concluding note to the said Book.

王舊在野及即位知小人之依能保惠庶民不侮鰥寡迨其末也繁刑以攜遠殷道復衰

馮辛

名先、史記作廩辛

元年、庚寅、王即位、居殷○四年、陟。

庚丁

名囂

元年、甲午、王即位、居殷○八年、陟。

武乙

名瞿

元年、壬寅、王即位、居殷、邠遷于岐周○三年、自殷遷于河北。命周公亶父、賜以岐邑○十五年、自河北遷于沬○二十一年、周公亶父薨○二十四年、周師伐程、戰于畢、克之○三十年、周師伐義渠、乃獲其君以歸○三十四年、周公季歷

Note. This king had lived, when young, away from the court, so that, when he came to the throne, he knew the necessities of the inferior people, protected them with kindness, and allowed no contumely to the wifeless and widows. Towards the end of his reign, however, by multiplying punishments, he alienated the people of distant regions; and the fortunes of Yin again decayed.

XXV. FUNG-SIN.

Note. Styled Lin-sin in the Historical Records. His name was Sëen.

1 In his 1st year, which was *kang-yin* (27th of cycle, = B.C. 1,170), when he came
2 to the throne, he dwelt in Yin. In his 4th year, he died.

XXVI. KANG-TING.

Note. Named Gaou.

1 In his 1st year, which was *këah-woo* (31st of cycle, = B.C. 1,166), when he came to
2 the throne, he dwelt in Yin. In his 8th year, he died.

XXVII. WOO-YIH.

Note. Named K'eu.

1 In his 1st year, which was *jin-yin* (39th of cycle, = B.C. 1,158), he dwelt in Yin.
2 *The prince of* Pin removed to Chow near mount K'e.[1] In his 3d year, the king
removed from Yin to the north of the Ho.[2] He confirmed the dignity of T'an-foo as
3 duke of Chow, and conferred on him the city of K'e. In his 15th year, he
4 removed from *the place he then occupied on* the north of the Ho to Mei.[3] In
5 his 21st year, T'an-foo, duke of Chow, died. In his 24th year, the forces of Chow
6 smote Ch'ing. A battle was fought at Peih, which was subdued.[4] In his 30th
year, the forces of Chow attacked E-k'eu,[5] and returned with its ruler as a captive.
7 In his 34th year, Ke-leih, duke of Chow, came and did homage at court, when
the king conferred on him 30 *le* of ground, ten pairs of gems, and ten horses.

XXVII. 1 The prince of Pin, who made this removal, was T'an-foo, or king T'ae, celebrated in the She, and by Mencius. K'e-san is still the name of a dis. in Fung-ts'ëang dep., Shen-se. By this move the House of Chow brought its principal seat nearly 100 miles farther east. 2 I agree with Ch'in-fung that it is better not to try to identify this 'North of the Ho' with any particular site. 3 See on the 'Announcement about Drunkenness,' par. 1. 4 Ch'ing and Peih were in the dis. of Heen-ning, dep. Se-gan. 5 In the pres. dep. of

來朝、王賜地三十里、玉十瑴、馬十匹○三十五年、周公季歷伐西落鬼戎。王畋于河渭、大雷震死。

文丁

史記作太丁非名托

元年、丁丑、王即位、居殷○二年、周公季歷伐燕京之戎、敗績○三年、洹水一日三絕○四年、周公季歷伐余無之戎、克之、命爲牧師○五年、周作程邑○七年、周公季歷伐始呼之戎、克之○十一年、周公季歷伐翳徒之戎、獲其三大夫來獻捷、王殺季歷。

王嘉季歷之功錫之圭瓚秬鬯九命爲伯既而執諸塞庫季歷困而死因謂文丁殺季歷

十二年、有鳳集於岐山○十三年、陟。

8 In his 35th year, Ke-leih, duke of Chow, smote the demon hordes of the Western tribes.[6] The king was hunting between the Ho and the Wei, when he was frightened to death by a great thunderstorm.

XXVIII. WAN-TING.

Note. Wrongly styled T'ae-ting in the Historical Records. His name was T'ŏ.

1 In his 1st year, which was *ting-ch'ow* (14th of cycle, = B.C. 1,123), when he came
2 to the throne, he dwelt in Yin.[1] In his 2d year, Ke-leih, duke of Chow, attacked
3 the hordes of Yen-king,[2] and was defeated. In his 3d year, the Yuen-water
4 thrice ceased to flow in one day. In his 4th year, Ke-leih attacked the hordes of Yu-woo, and subdued them, after which he received the dignity of Pastor and
6 Teacher. In his 5th year, Chow built the city of Ch'ing. In his 7th year,
7 Ke-leih attacked the hordes of Ch'e-hoo, and subdued them. In his 11th year, Ke-leih smote the hordes of E-t'oo, and, having taken their three great chiefs, came with them to court to report his victory. The king put Ke-leih to death.

Note. The king *at first* appreciated the services of Ke-leih, gave him a libation mace, with flavoured spirits of the black millet, and the nine ensigns of distinction as chief of the princes; and after all that, he confined him in the house of restraint, so that Ke-leih died from the trouble, and gave occasion to the saying that Wan-ting killed him.

8 In his 12th year, phœnixes collected on mount K'e.

Note. This was the 1st year of king Wăn of Chow.

9 In his 15th year, the king died.

K'ing-yang, Kan-suh. 6 These 'demon hordes' are diff. from the people of the 'demon region,' subdued by Woo-ting. 落=部落, a tribe.

XXVIII. 1 There is a note here that 'he returned from Mei to Yin.' But Ch'in-fung denies this, and argues that, while his father had moved from the old capital, T'ŏ had continued always in it. 2 The hill of Yen-king was in the pres. dis. of Tsing-lŏ, dep. of Yin, Shan-se. 3 There is nothing improbable in this. The sovereign of the decaying dynasty might, in a sudden fit of jealousy, thus make away with the Head of the rising House. As the fact, however, is not elsewhere mentioned, the friends of the Annals labour to explain away the passage, or to show that it is corrupted.

帝乙

名羨

元年、庚寅、王即位、居殷○三年、王命南仲、西拒昆夷、城朔方。夏、六月、周地震○九年、陟。

帝辛

名受即紂也曰受辛

元年、己亥、王即位、居殷、命九侯周侯邘侯、周侯爲西伯昌○三年、有雀生鸇○四年、大蒐于黎。作炮烙之刑○五年、夏、築南單之臺。雨土于亳○六年、西伯初禴于畢○九年、王師伐有蘇、獲妲已以歸。作瓊室、立玉門○十年、夏、六月、王畋于西郊○十七年、西伯伐翟。冬、王遊於淇○二十一年、春、正月、諸侯朝周。伯夷、叔齊、自孤竹歸于周○二十二年、冬、大蒐于渭

XXIX. TE-YIH.

Note. Named Sëen.

1 In his 1st year, which was *kang-yin* (27th of cycle, = B.C. 1,110), when he came
2 to the throne, he dwelt in Yin. In his 3d year, he ordered Nan Chung to oppose
the hordes of Keun on the west, and to wall *the city of* Soh-fang. In the summer, in
3 the 6th month, there was an earthquake in Chow. In his 9th year, he died.

XXX. TE-SIN.

Note. Named Show. This was Chow. He is also called Show-sin.

1 In his 1st year, which was *ke-hae* (36th of cycle, = B.C. 1,101), when he came to the throne, he dwelt in Yin. He gave appointments to the princes of K'ew, Chow, and Yu.

Note. The prince of Chow was Ch'ang, chief of the West.

3 In his 3d year, a sparrow produced a hawk. In his 4th year, he had a great
4 hunting in Le.[1] He invented the punishment of Roasting.[2] In his 5th year, in
the summer, he built the tower of Nan-tan.[3] There was a shower of earth in Poh.
5 In his 6th year, the chief of the west offered sacrifice for the first time to his an-
6 cestors in Peih.[4] In his 9th year, the royal forces attacked the State of Soo,
and brought away Tan-ke as a captive. *The king* made an apartment for her, with
7 walls of carnation stone, and the doors all-adorned with gems. In his 10th year,
8 in the summer, in the 6th month, he hunted in the western borders. In his 17th
year, the chief of the west smote the Teih.[5] In the winter, the king made a pleasure
9 excursion in K'e.[6] In his 21st year, in the spring, in the 1st month, the princes
went to Chow to do homage. Pih-e and Shuh-ts'e[7] betook themselves to Chow
10 from Koo-chuh. In his 22d year, in the winter, he had a great hunting along

XXX. 1 九 here is read as 仇. It was the name of a State, which was also called 鬼,—probably in the pres. dep. of Chang-tih, Ho-nan. The three princes here seem to have been the three *kung*. 2 See on the ixth of the Books of Shang. 3 What is called in the Shoo 'the Stag tower.' 4 Ke-leih had been buried in Peih. Ch'in-fung supposes this was a sacrifice at his tomb. 5 These were different tribes, occupying the northern regions, west of the Ho. 6 The pres. dis. of K'e, dep. Wei-hwuy. 7 See the Ana., V., xxii., *et al.*

○二十三年、囚西伯于羑里○二十九年、釋西伯、諸侯逆西伯歸于程○三十年、春、三月、西伯率諸侯入貢○三十一年、西伯治兵于畢、得呂尚以爲師○三十二年、五星聚于房。有赤烏集于周社。密人侵阮、西伯帥師伐密○三十三年、密人降于周師、遂遷于程。王錫命西伯、得專征伐。

約按文王受命九年大統未集蓋得專征伐受命自此年始

三十四年、周師取耆及邘、遂伐崇、崇人降。冬、十二月、昆夷侵周○三十五年、周大饑、西伯自程遷于豐○三十六年、春、正月、諸侯朝于周、遂伐昆夷。西伯使世子發營鎬○三十七年、周作辟雍○三十九年、大夫辛甲出奔周○四十年、周作靈臺。王使膠鬲求玉于周○四十一年、春、三月、西伯昌薨。周文王葬畢畢西於豐三十里○四十二年、元年周武王西伯發、受丹書于呂尚。有女子化爲丈夫○

11 the Wei. In his 23d year, he imprisoned the chief of the west in Yew-le.[8]
12 In his 29th year, he liberated the chief of the west, who was met by *many of* the
13 princes, and escorted back to Ch'ing. In his 30th year, in the spring, in the 3d month, the chief of the west led the princes to the court with their tributes. In
14 his 31st year, the chief of the west began to form a regular army in Peih, with Leu
15 Shang as its commander. In his 32d year, there was a conjunction of the five planets in Fang. A red crow lighted on the altar to the spirits of the land in Chow. The people of Meih invaded Yuen, when the chief of the west led a force against
16 Meih.[9] In his 33d year, the people of Meih surrendered to the army of Chow, and were removed to Ch'ing. The king granted power to the chief of the west to punish and attack *offending* States on his own discretion.

Note by Yŏ. King Wăn thus for 9 years received the appointment *of Heaven*; and the empire was not yet all secured by him *at his death.* His plenipotent authority to punish and attack, in which the will of Heaven might be seen, commenced in this year.

17 In his 34th year, the forces of Chow took K'e and Yu; and then attacked Ts'ung, which surrendered. In the winter, in the 12th month, the hordes of Keun overran
18 Chow. In the 35th year, there was a great famine in Chow; when the chief of
19 the west removed from Ch'ing to Fung. In his 36th year, in the spring, in the 1st month, the princes went to court at Chow, and then they smote the hordes of
20 Keun. The chief of the west made his heir-son Fă build Haou. In his 37th
21 year, *the duke of* Chow built an imperial college.[9] In his 39th year, the great
22 officer Sin-këah fled to Chow. In his 40th year, *the duke of* Chow made the
23 spirit-tower. The king sent Kaou-kih to seek for gems in Chow.[10] In his 41st year, in the spring, in the 3d month, Ch'ang, the chief of the west, died.

Note. King Wăn of Chow was buried in Peih;—30 *le* west from Fung.

24 In his 42d year,—(the 1st year of king Woo of Chow)—Fah chief of the west, received the vermilion book from Leu shang.[11] A girl changed into a man. In his

8 In the dis. of T'ang-yin, dep. Chang-tih. 9 Both Meih and Yuen were in the pres. dep. of P'ing-lëang, Kan-suh. 9 The building of a P'eih-yung in Chow was the exercising an imperial prerogative. See on the She, Pt. II, Bk. III., Ode. ii. 10 There is a story of a tablet of gem belonging to the princes of Chow, which Show coveted,

書經

四十三年、春、大閱。嶢山崩（）四十四年、西伯發伐黎○四十七年、內史向摯出奔周（）四十八年、夷羊見。二日並出○五十一年、冬、十一月、戊子、周師渡盟津而還。王囚箕子、殺王子比干。微子出奔○五十二年、庚寅、周始伐殷。秋、周師次于鮮原。冬、十有二月、周師有事于上帝、庸、蜀、羌、髳、微、盧、彭、濮、從周師伐殷。

伐殷至邢邱、更名邢邱曰懷

湯滅夏以至于受二十九王、用歲四百九十六年

25 43d year, in the spring, he had a grand review. *Part of* mount K'aou fell down.
26 In his 44th year, Fah smote Le. In his 47th year, the recorder of the Interior,
27 Hëang Che, fled to Chow. In his 48th year, the E goat[12] was seen. Two suns
28 appeared together. In his 51st year, in the winter, in the 11th month, on the day *mow-tsze* (25th of cycle), the army of Chow crossed the ford of Mang; but returned. The king imprisoned the viscount of K'e; and put his relative, Pe-kan, to
29 death; while the viscount of Wei fled away. In his 52d year, which was *kang-yin* (27th of cycle), Chow made its first attack on Yin. In the autumn, the army of Chow camped in the plain of Sëen. In the winter, in the 12th month, it sacrificed to God. The tribes of Yung, Shuh, Këang, Maou, Wei, Loo, P'ang, and Puh, followed Chow to the attack of Yin.[14]

Note. They marched to Hing-k'ew, the name of which was changed to Hwae.
From the extinction of Hea by T'ang to Show were 29 kings, and 496 years.

and wished thus to get for himself. 11 This was a book of Counsels, containing the principles of Hwang-te, and Chuen-heuh. 12 This was a prodigious thing, 'a spirit-like animal,'—variously described. 13 This was in K'e Chow. 14 See on 'Speech at Muh.'

竹書紀年卷之五

周武王

名發初高辛氏之世妃曰姜嫄助祭郊禖見大人迹履之當時歆如有人道感已遂有身而生男以爲不祥棄之隘巷牛羊避而不踐又送之山林之中會伐林者又取而置寒冰上大鳥以一翼藉覆之姜嫄以爲異乃收養焉名之曰棄枝頤有異相長爲堯稷官有功於民后稷之孫曰公劉有德諸侯皆以天子之禮待之初黃帝之世讖言曰西北爲王期在甲子昌制命發行誅旦行道及公劉之後十三世而生季歷季歷之十年飛龍盈於殷之牧野此蓋聖人在下位將起之符也季歷之妃曰大任夢長人感已溲于豕牢而生昌是爲周文王龍顏虎肩身長十尺胸有四乳大王曰吾世當有興者其在昌乎季歷之兄曰太伯知天命在昌適越終身不反弟仲雍從之故季歷爲嗣以及昌昌爲西伯作邑於豐文王之妃曰太姒夢商庭生棘太子發

PART V.

The dynasty of Chow.

I. KING WOO.

Note. Named Fă. Of old time, Këang Yuen, the wife of the emperor Kaou-sin, was assisting him at a sacrifice in the borders in order to obtain a son, when she saw the footstep of a large man, and trod upon it. At the instant she felt after a certain manner, and, becoming pregnant, by and by gave birth to a son. Thinking the whole thing unlucky, she threw the child away in a narrow lane, but the goats and cattle avoided it, and did not trample on it. She then placed it in a wood, where it was found by a woodcutter. She took it then, and laid it upon the ice, and there a large bird came and covered it with one of his wings. Këang Yuen, surprised by all this, received the child at last, and nursed him, giving him the name of 'Cast-away.'

The lower part of the child's face was largely developed, and his appearance altogether extraordinary. When he was grown up, he became minister of Agriculture to Yaou, and rendered great services to the people. He is known as prince Tseih. His grandson Kung-lew was eminently virtuous, so that the princes behaved to him with the same ceremonies as they did to the emperor.

In the time of Hwang-te, there had been a prophecy, to the effect that 'the chief of the west should become king, in a certain *keă-tsze* year; that Ch'ang should lay the foundations of the dignity, Fă exercise the judgments necessary to it, and Tan develope its principles.' In the 13th generation, accordingly, from Kung-lew, Ke-leih was born; and in his 10th year, a multitude of flying dragons filled the pasture lands of Yin;—an emblem of a sage in an inferior position, who should in course of time rise to his proper distinction.

The wife of Ke-leih was called T'ae-jin, who became pregnant after dreaming that she had been with a tall man. Afterwards, when relieving nature, she gave birth to Ch'ang. This Ch'ang became king Wăn of Chow. He had a dragon's countenance, with a tiger's shoulders; was 10 cubits high; and had 4 nipples on his chest. *His grandfather*, king T'ae, said, 'It will be Ch'ang, in whom our family shall rise to distinction.' Ke-leih's eldest brother was T'ae-pih who, knowing

書經

植梓樹於闕間化爲松栢棫柞以告文王文王幣率羣臣與發竝拜吉夢季秋之甲子赤爵銜書及豐置于昌戶昌拜稽首受其文要曰姬昌蒼帝子亡殷者紂王將畋史編卜之曰將大獲非熊非羆天遺汝師以佐昌臣太祖史疇爲禹卜畋得皐陶其兆類此至于磻溪之水呂尚釣於涯王下趨拜曰望公七年乃今見光景于斯尚立變名答曰望釣得玉璜其文要曰姬受命昌來提撰爾洛鈐報在齊尚出游見赤人自洛出授尚書命曰呂佐昌者子文王夢日月著其身又鸑鷟鳴於岐山孟春六日五緯聚房後有鳳凰銜書游文王之都書文曰殷帝無道虐亂天下皇命已移不得復久靈祇遠離百神吹去五星聚房昭理四海文王既沒太子發代立是爲武王武王駢齒望羊將伐紂至于孟津八百諸侯不期而會咸曰紂可伐矣武王不從及紂殺比干囚箕子微子去之乃伐紂渡孟津中流白魚躍入王舟王俯取魚長三尺目下有赤文成字言紂可伐王寫以世字魚文消燔魚以告天有火自天止於王屋流爲赤烏烏銜穀焉穀者紀后稷之德火者燔魚以告天天

that Heaven's purpose was to be realized in Ch'ang, went away to Yuĕ, and never returned. His next brother, Chung-yung, followed this example; so that Ke-leih remained to be his father's heir, and the succession descended to Ch'ang, who became chief of the West, and made his capital city in Fung.

The wife of king Wăn was called T'ae-sze. She dreamed that in the courtyard of the imperial palace there were thorns growing, while her eldest son Fă planted some *tsze* trees about their own gate, which changed into a fir, a cypress, a *yih*, and a *tsŏ*. This dream she told to king Wăn, who prepared gifts, and led his ministers along with Fă to give thanks for it.

On the kĕă-tsze day, in the last month of autumn, a red bird came to Fung with a writing in its beak, which it put down at the door of Ch'ang. Ch'ang received it with a reverential obeisance, and found the writing to this effect:—'Ke Ch'ang is the son of the God of the empyrean. The destroyer of Yin is Chow.' The king was about to go to hunt, when the recorder Pëen divined the meaning of this writing, and said:—'You will get great spoil; but not a bear nor a grisly bear. Heaven is sending a Grand-tutor to aid you. My ancestor, the recorder Ch'ow, divined once for Yu about hunting; and then he met with Kaou-yaou,—from an omen like that which has now occurred.' The hunting party went on, and at the water of P'wan-k'e, there was Leu Shang, fishing on the bank. The king descended, hastened to him, and said with a bow, 'I have been hoping to meet with you for seven years, and now I find you here.' Shang instantly changed his name at these words, and answered, 'I, Hope (the looked for), fished up a semicircular gem with this inscription:—"Ke has received the appointment of Heaven; Ch'ang will come and take it up. You have fished this up in the Lŏ, and will have your reward in Ts'e."'

Shang went out *one day* rambling, when he saw a red man come out from the Lŏ, who gave him a writing, with the words:—'As a backbone, you must assist Ch'ang.'

King Wăn dreamt that he was clothed with the sun and moon. A phœnix duck sang on mount K'e. In the first month of spring, on the 6th day, the five planets had a conjunction in Fang. Afterwards a male and female phœnix went about Wăn's capital with a writing in their beaks, which said:—'The emperor of Yin has no principle, but oppresses and disorders the empire. The great decree is removed; Yin cannot enjoy it longer. The powerful spirits of the earth have left it; all the spirits are whistled away. The conjunction of the five planets in Fang brightens all within the four seas.'

When king Wan was dead, his eldest son Fă ruled in his stead. His teeth were one piece of bone, and he had a shepherd's eyes. When he was about to attack Chow, and had reached the ford of Măng, 800 princes came together, without any previous understanding, all saying, 'Show may be smitten.' King Woo, however, did not listen to them; but when Show had killed Pe-kan, imprisoned the viscount of K'e, and was abandoned by the viscount of Wei, then he assailed him. When he was crossing the river at the ford of Măng, in the middle of the stream, a white fish leaped into the king's boat. The king stooped down and took it up. It was 3 cubits long, and under its eyes were red lines which formed the characters—'Chow may be smitten.' The king wrote over them the character for 'dynasty,' and the words disappeared. After this he burned the fish in sacrifice, and announced the event to Heaven. Lo! fire came down from heaven, and rested over Wang-uh, gradually floating away into a red bird, with a stalk of grain in its beak. The

火流下應以吉也遂東伐紂勝於牧野兵不血刃而天下歸之乃封呂尚於齊周德既隆草木茂盛蒿堪爲宮室因名蒿室既有天下遂都于鎬

十二年、辛卯、王率西夷諸侯伐殷、敗之于坶野、王親禽受于南單之臺、遂分天之明、立受子祿父、是爲武庚。夏四月、王歸于豐、饗于太廟、命監殷、遂狩於管。作大武樂〇十三年、巢伯來賓。薦殷于太廟、遂大封諸侯。秋大有年〇十四年、王有疾、周文公禱于壇墠、作金縢〇十五年、肅慎氏來賓。初狩方岳、誥于沬邑。冬遷九鼎于洛〇十六年、箕子來朝。秋王師滅蒲姑〇十七年、命王世子誦于東宮。冬十有二月王陟、年五十四。

grain was in commemoration of the virtue of prince Tseih; the fire was an auspicious response from heaven to the burnt-offering of the fish.

Woo then went eastward and attacked Show, whom he vanquished in the wilderness of Muh. His soldiers did not need to stain their swords with blood, *so easily* did the empire turn to him. He invested Leu Shang with the principality of Ts'e. Through the abundance of the virtue of Chow, all vegetation was most luxuriant; even the southernwood could supply materials for building a palace, and hence we have the name—'southernwood house.' When he was possessed of the empire, Woo fixed his capital in Haou.

1 In his 12th year, which was *sin-maou* (28th of cycle, = B.C. 1,049), the king led
the tribes of the west and the princes to attack Yin, and defeated *Show* in the wilder-
ness of Muh. He took with his own hand Show prisoner in the tower of Nan-tan;[2]
and entered into the participation of the bright appointment of Heaven,[3] setting up,
to continue the sacrifices to his ancestors, Luh-foo, the son of Show, known as Woo-
kang.[4] In the summer, in the 4th month, he returned to Fung, and sacrificed in the
ancestral temple. He appointed Inspectors of Yin, and went himself on a tour of
2 inspection to Kwan.[5] He made the music Ta-woo. In his 13th year, the baron
of Ch'aou came to make his submission. He presented *the captives of Yin* in the
Grand ancestral temple;[6] and afterwards granted great investitures to the princes.
3 In the autumn there was a very abundant harvest. In his 14th year, the king
was unwell, when the duke Wan of Chow prayed *for him* on an altar-area, and
4 made 'The Metal-bound Coffer.'[7] In his 15th year, the prince of Suhshin came
to make his submission. He made his first tour of inspection to the mountains of
the four quarters, and made an announcement to the cities of Me.[8] In the winter, he
5 removed the nine tripods to Loh. In his 16th year, the viscount of Ke came to
6 do homage. In the autumn, the royal forces extinguished P'oo-koo. In his
17th year, he appointed his heir-son Sung in the eastern palace to be his successor.
In the winter, in the 12th month, he died, being 94 years old.

I. 1 Reckoning from the 42d year of Show, when Woo succeeded his father, as duke of Chow. 2 禽=擒. See the acct. of Show's death in the note on par. 1 of 'The Successful Completion of the War.' 3 It is diff. to translate 分天之明. I take 明=明命. Some take 分 as by mistake for 受; but I have brought out the same meaning which that would give. The text will not allow the meaning of—'before day-break' (天尙未明), which Wăn-tsing gives. 4 The 立 or 'setting' up of Show's son is to be understood only as I have indicated. There was no participation of the empire with him, as the 分 preceding seems to make Biot suppose. 5 See the note on par. 12 of 'The Metal-bound Coffer.' 6 That is, he presented the left ears which had been cut off. See the She, Pt III., Bk. I. Ode vii., 8. 7 See the Shoo Pt. V., Bk. VI.. 8 This was 'The Announcement about Drunkenness;' but see, in the notes on that Bk. of the Shoo, the controversies about the date and the author. 沬邑=沬邦.

成王

名誦

元年丁酉、春正月、王卽位、命冢宰周文公總百官。庚午、周公誥諸侯于皇門。夏六月、葬武王于畢。秋、王加元服。武庚以殷叛。周文公出居于東。○二年、奄人、徐人及淮夷、入于邶以叛。秋大雷電以風。王逆周文公于郊。遂伐殷。○三年、王師滅殷、殺武庚祿父、遷殷民于衞、遂伐奄、滅蒲姑。姑與四國作亂故周文公伐之○四年、春正月、初朝于廟。夏四月、初嘗麥。王師伐淮夷、遂入奄。○五年、春正月、王在奄、遷其君于蒲姑。夏五月、王至自奄。遷殷民于洛邑、遂營成周。○六年、大蒐于岐陽。○七年、周公復政于王。春二月、王如豐。三月、召康公如洛度邑。甲子、周文公誥多士于成周、遂城東都。王如東都、諸侯來朝。

II. King Ching.

Note. Named Sung.

1 In his 1st year, which was *ting-yew* (34th of cycle, = B.C. 1,043), in the spring, in the 1st month, when he came to the throne, he ordered the prime minister, duke Wăn of Chow, to take the leadership of all the officers. On the day *kang-woo* (7th of cycle), the duke of Chow made an announcement to the princes at the great gate.[1] In the summer, in the 6th month, they buried king Woo in Peih. In the autumn, the king assumed the covering for the head.[2] Woo-kăng with the people of Yin
2 rebelled. Duke Wăn of Chow left the court to reside in the east.[3] In his 2d year, the people of Yen and of Seu, with the hordes of the Hwae, entered Pei[4] with the standard of rebellion. In the autumn, there was a great storm of thunder and lightning, with wind, when the king met the duke of Chow in the borders; and
3 immediately after, they smote Yin. In the 3d year, the king's armies extinguished Yin; Woo-kăng Luh-foo was put to death; the people of Yin were removed to Wei;[5] Yen was forthwith invaded; and P'oo-koo was extinguished.[6]

Note. Koo was aiding in the rebellion of the four kingdoms; and therefore the duke of Chow extinguished it.

4 In his 4th year, in the spring, in the 1st month, he first gave audience *to the princes* in *his father's* temple. In the summer, in the 4th month, he first tasted *the first fruits of* the wheat.[7] The army smote the hordes of the Hwae, and then entered
5 Yen. In his 5th year, in the spring, in the 1st month, the king was in Yen, and removed its ruler to P'oo-koo. In the summer, in the 5th month, he came from Yen, and removed the people of Yin to the city of Loh; and thereon proceeded to build
6 Ching-chow. In his 6th year, he made a grand hunting expedition on the south
7 of mount K'e. In his 7th year, the duke of Chow restored the government to the

II. 2 The 'great gate' was on the left of the 5th or last of the principal gates of the palace. The duke would harangue the nobles in the usual place of 'Audience of govt.' 2 元=首, 'the head.' 'The dress for the head'=the cap. King Ching was now, it is generally said, 14 years old. His capping=the acknowledgement of him as king. 3 See on 'The Metal-bound Coffer,' pp. 12, 13. 4 The portion of Yin, ruled by the king's uncle, Ch'oo. 5 See on the 9th of the Books of Chow. 6 This was said to be done in the last reign. 7 See

冬王歸自東都。立高圉廟。○八年、春正月、王初莅阼親政。命魯侯禽父、齊侯伋、遷庶殷于魯。作象舞。冬十月、王師滅唐、遷其民于杜。○九年、春正月、有事于太廟、初用勺。肅愼氏來朝、王使榮伯錫肅愼氏命○十年、王命唐叔虞爲侯。越裳氏來朝。周文公出居于豐。○十一年、春正月、王如豐。唐叔獻嘉禾、王命唐叔歸禾于周文公。王命周平公治東都。

約按周平公卽君陳周公之子伯禽之弟

十二年、王師燕師城韓。王錫韓侯命。○十三年、王師會齊侯魯侯伐戎。夏六月、魯大禘于周公廟。○十四年、齊師圍曲城、克之。冬、洛邑告成。○十八年、春正月、王如洛邑、定鼎。鳳凰見、遂有事于河。

king. In the spring, in the 2d month, the king went to Fung. In the 3d month, duke K'ang of Shaou went to Loh, to measure *the ground for* the city. On the day *këah-tsze* (1st of cycle), the duke Wăn of Chow made an announcement to the numerous officers in Ching-chow; and thereon they walled the eastern capital. The king then went to it, and the princes came to do him homage. In the winter, he
8 returned from it, and appointed *anew* a shrine to Kaou-yu.[8] In his 8th year, in the spring, in the 1st month, he first took his position as imperial host, and administered the government for himself. He gave orders to K'in-foo, prince of Loo, and K'eih, prince of Ts'e, to remove the multitudes of Yin to Loo. He made the pantomimic dance, called Sëang. In the winter, in the 10th month, his forces extinguished
9 the State of T'ang,[9] and removed its people to Too.[10] In his 9th year, in the spring, in the 1st month, he had a great sacrificial service in the grand ancestral temple, when he first used the *choh*.[11] The chief of Suh-shin came to do homage,
10 when the king employed the baron of Yung to convey his Charge to him.[12] In his 10th year, he appointed his brother Yu of T'ang to be *head of all the* princes.[13] The chief of Yueh-chang [14] appeared to do homage. The duke of Chow left the court,
11 and resided in Fung. In his 11th year, in the spring, in the 1st month, the king went to Fung. His brother of T'ang presented a stalk of fine grain, and was ordered to convey it to the duke Wăn of Chow. The king appointed duke P'ing of Chow to govern the eastern capital.[15]

Note by Yŏ. This duke P'ing of Chow is Keun-ch'in, the son of the duke of Chow, and younger brother of Pih-k'in.

12 In his 12th year, the king's forces and those of Yen walled Han;[16] and the king
13 gave a Charge to the prince of Han. In his 13th year, the king's forces assembled with *those of* the princes of Ts'e and Loo, and smote the hordes of the Jung. In the summer, in the 6th month, *the prince of* Loo offered the grand imperial sacrifice in
14 the temple of the duke of Chow. In his 14th year, the forces of Ts'e invested the city of K'euh,[17] and subdued it. In the winter, the announcement was made of
15 the completion of Loh. In his 18th year, in the spring, in the 1st month, the king went to Loh, and settled *the place of* the tripods there. Phœnixes made their appearance, and a sacrifice was offered near the Ho.

on the Le Ke, Bk. IV., Pt. iii., p. 17. 8 See on the 15th year of Tsoo-yih. 9 Occupied by descendants of Yaou;—in the pres. dis. of Yih-shing, dep. P'ing-yang. 10 In the dis. of Ch'ang-gan, dep. Se-gan. 11 The *chŏ* was a song, with music, made by the duke of Chow, and used at a certain part of the service. 勺=汋=酌. 12 See the Pref. to the Shoo, 56th Notice. 13 There is no end of difficulty in fixing the meaning of this sentence. 14 See the Introductory note to the xxist of the Books of Chow. 15 That is—'appointed him who was subsequently duke P'ing of Chow.' *The* duke of Chow was not yet dead. 16 Prob. in the pres. dis of Koo-ngan, dep. of Shun-t'ëen. Not far from Yen. 17 A place of an eastern tribe, in the pres. dep. of Tung-lae. 18 See on the xxth of the Books of Chow.

武王沒成王少周公旦攝政七年制禮作樂神鳥鳳凰見蓂莢生乃與成王觀于河洛沈璧禮畢王退俟至于日昃榮光竝出幕河青雲浮至青龍臨壇銜玄甲之圖坐之而去禮于洛亦如之玄龜青龍止于壇背甲刻書赤文成字周公援筆以世文寫之書成文消龜墮甲而去其言自周公訖于秦漢盛衰之符麒麟遊苑鳳凰翔庭成王援琴而歌曰鳳凰翔兮於紫庭余何德兮以感靈賴先王兮恩澤臻于胥樂兮民以寧

十九年、王巡狩侯甸方岳、召康公從、歸于宗周。遂正百官、黜豐侯〇二十一年、除治象。周文公薨于豐〇二十二年、葬周文公于畢〇二十四年、於越來賓〇二十五年、王大會諸侯于東都、四夷來賓。冬十月、歸自東都、大事于太廟〇三十年、離戎來賓。

約按離戎驪山之戎也爲林氏所伐告于成王

Note. When king Woo died, king Ching was still young; and Tan, duke of Chow, acted as regent for 7 years. He made the institutions and music of the dynasty. Spirit-like birds and phœnixes appeared; and the mysterious bean grew up. After this he went with king Ching to view the Ho and the Lŏ. Having dropt a gem into the water, and finished all the ceremonies, the king retired and waited till the day declined. Then rays of glory came out, and shrouded all the Ho; and green clouds came floating in the sky. A green dragon came to the altar, carrying in his mouth a dark-coloured shell, with a figure on it, which he placed on the altar, and went away. They did in the same way at the Lŏ, and the same things happened. On the shell in red lines were characters, which the duke of Chow copied in the current forms of the age. When his writing was finished, the tortoise dropped the shell, and went away. The writing was all about the rise and fall in the fortunes of the empire down to the dynasties of Ts'in and Han. K'e-lins wandered in the parks; phœnixes flew about in the courtyards; king Ching took a lute, and sang:—

'The phœnixes fly
All around my hall.
What virtue have I
So spirits to call?

'From the former kings
This influence comes;
Theirs the joy that rings
In the people's homes.'

16 In his 19th year, the king made a tour of inspection to the *how* and *teen* domains, and to the four mountains, the duke K'ang of Shaou being in attendance on him. When he returned to Tsung-chow, he settled the various orders of officers,[18] and
17 degraded the prince of Fung.[19] In his 21st year, he removed the representations
18 of the penal laws.[20] The duke Wan of Chow died in Fung. In his 22d year,
19 he buried duke Wan in Peih. In his 24th year, *the chief of* Yu-yueh came to
20 make his submission.[21] In his 25th year, the king held a great assembly of the princes in the eastern capital, when the wild tribes of the four quarters came to make their submission. In the winter, in the 10th month, he returned from the eastern
21 capital, and performed a great service in the grand ancestral temple. In his 30th year, the hordes of Le came to make their submission.

Note by Yŏ. The hordes of Le belonged to mount Le. They had been smitten by the chief of Lin, who announced the event to king Ching.

19 It is said that when king Woo occupied Haou as his capital, he granted Fung as the appanage of one of his younger brothers, whom Ching degraded for drunkenness. 20 Such representations were hung up before one of the palace gates, and perhaps the gates of public offices generally. Ching thought the people were now so accustomed to the rule of Chow, and acquainted with the laws, that they did not need the lessons of such figures and descriptions. 21 The rulers of Yuĕ, called Yu-yuĕ

三十三年、王遊于卷阿、召康公從、歸于宗周。命王世子釗、如房逆女、房伯祈歸于宗周〇三十四年、雨金于咸陽。

約按咸陽天雨金三年國有大喪

三十七年、夏四月、乙丑、王陟。

康王

名釗

元年、甲戌、春正月、王卽位、命冢宰召康公、總百官。諸侯朝于豐宮〇三年、定樂歌、吉禘于先王、申戒農官、告于廟〇六年、齊太公薨〇九年、唐遷于晉、作宮而美、王使人讓之〇十二年、夏六月、壬申、王如豐、錫畢公命。秋、毛懿公薨〇十六年、錫齊侯伋命。王南巡狩、至九江廬山〇十九年、魯侯禽父薨〇二十一年、魯築茅闕門〇二

22 In his 33d year, the king rambled in Keuen-o,[22] with duke K'ang of Shaou in attendance, and then returned to Tsung-chow. He ordered his heir-son Ch'aou to go to Fang[23] to bring home his bride. K'e, the baron of Fang, escorted her to Tsung-
23 chow. In his 34th year, it rained gold in Hëen-yang.[24]

Note by Yŏ. It rained gold in Hëen-yang; and in 3 years, the empire sustained a great loss.

24 In his 37th year, in the summer, in the 4th month, on the day *yih-ch'ow* (2d of cycle), the king died.

III. KING K'ANG.

Note. Named Ch'aou.

1 In his 1st year, which was *keah-seuh* (11th of cycle,=B.C. 1,006), in the spring, in the 1st month, when he came to the throne, he ordered the prime minister, duke K'ang of Shaou, to take the leadership of all the officers. The princes did homage
2 in the palace of Fung. In his 3d year, he fixed the songs for the different musical performances. The period of mourning being over, he offered the imperial sacrifice to his predecessor.[2] He renewed the admonitions to the officers of agriculture,[3] and
3 announced them in the ancestral temple. In his 6th year, duke T'ae of Ts'e
4 died.[4] In his 9th year, *the prince* of T'ang removed to Tsin,[5] and made a palace
5 in a beautiful style. The king sent and reproved him. In his 12th year, in the summer, in the 6th month, on the *jin-shin* day (9th of cycle), the king went to Fung, and gave his Charge to the duke of Peih.[6] In the autumn, duke E of Maou died.
6 In his 16th year, he give a Charge to K'eih, the duke of Ts'e. He went south
7 on a tour of inspection, as far as mount Loo of Kew-keang. In his 19th year,
8 K'in-foo, prince of Loo, died. In his 21st year, the prince of Loo made *a palace*, with the sentry-lofts above the gates covered with rushes. In his

(于, or 於, 越), were descendants of Yu the Great. The capital was on the north of Hwuy-k'e. 22 See on the She, Pt. III., Bk. II., Ode. viii. 23 The pres. dis. of Fang, dep. Yun-yang, Hoo-pih. Here, it is said, Shun placed Choo, the son of Yaou. 24 A dis. of dep. Se-ngan. Here Ke-leih had at one time his capital.

III. 1 The duke of Chow had made the music; king K'ang now fixed the songs for different pieces. 2 That is, he made all the necessary changes connected with the introduction of his father's shrine into the temple, and sacrificed to him. 3 Supposed to be in 3d of the 2d Bk. of the Praise-songs of Chow. 4 It would appear from 'The Testamentary Charge,' par. 10, that he was dead before this. 5 This change of site was not great. 6 See the xxivth of the Books of Chow. 7 Here the battle about the

十四年、召康公薨○二十六年、秋九月、己未、王陟。

昭王

名瑕、

元年、庚子、春正月、王即位、復設象魏○六年、王錫郇伯命。冬十二月、桃李華○十四年、夏四月、恒星不見。秋七月、魯人弑其君宰○十六年、伐楚涉漢、遇大兕○十九年、春、有星孛于紫微。祭公辛伯、從王伐楚、天大曀、雉兎皆震、喪六師于漢。王陟。

穆王

名滿、

元年、己未、春正月、王即位、作昭宮、命辛伯餘靡。冬十月、築祇宮于南鄭。

自武王至穆王享國百年穆王以下都于西鄭

9 44th year, duke K'ang of Shaou died. In his 26th year, in the autumn, in the
9th month, on the day *ke-wei* (56th of cycle), the king died.

IV. KING CH'AOU.

Note. Named Hëa.

1 In his 1st year, which was *kang-tsze* (37th of cycle, = B.C. 980), in the spring, in
the 1st month, when the king came to the throne, he restored the practice of suspend-
2 ing the representations of the penal laws. In his 6th year, he gave a Charge to
the baron of Seun. In the winter, in the 12th month, peach trees and plum trees
3 were in flower. In his 14th year, in the summer, in the 4th month, the regular
stars were invisible. In the autumn, in the 7th month, the people of Loo killed
4 their ruler Tsae. In his 16th year, *the king* attacked Ts'oo; and, in crossing
5 the Han, met with a large rhinoceros. In his 19th year, in the spring, a comet
appeared in the space Tsze-mei.[2] The duke of Tse[3] and the baron of Sin[4] followed
the king against Ts'oo. The heavens were dark and tempestuous. Pheasants and
hares were terrified. The king's six armies perished in the Han. The king died.

V. KING MUH.

Note. Named Mwan.

1 In his 1st year, which was *ke-wei* (56th of cycle, = B.C. 961), in the spring, in the 1st month, after he came to the throne, he built the palace of Ch'aou, and gave a Charge to Yu-mei, the baron of Sin. In the winter, in the 10th month, he built the palace of Che in Nan-ch'ing.[2]

Note. From king Woo to Muh, the empire was possessed 100 years. From Muh downwards the capital was in Se-ch'ing.

'Nine Keang' is fought over again. See on 'The Tribute of Yu.'

IV. 1 In dis. of E-she, dep. P'oo-chow, Shan-se. 2 Including the stars about the north pole. 3 In Ch'ing Chow, dep. K'ae-fung. Its chiefs were of the family of the duke of Chow. 4 In the dis. Ch'ang-tsze, dep. Loo-ngan, Shan-se.

V. 1 This palace is supposed to have been somehow in commemoration of his father, king Ch'aou. The baron of Sin is represented in some accounts as having rescued him from the Han, though he died in consequence of the fright and injuries received. 2 In Hwa Chow, dep. T'ung-chow, Shen-se. 3 In the

六年、春、徐子誕來朝、錫命爲伯〇八年、春、北唐來賓、獻一驪馬、是生騄耳〇九年、築春宮王所居有鄭宮春宮〇十一年、王命卿士祭公謀父〇十二年、毛公班、共公利、逢公固、帥師從王伐犬戎、冬十月、王北巡狩、遂征犬戎〇十三年、春、祭公帥師、從王西征、次于陽紆、秋七月、西戎來賓、徐戎侵洛、冬十月、造父御王入于宗周〇十四年、王帥楚子伐徐戎、克之、夏四月、王畋于軍邱、五月、作范宮、秋九月、翟人侵畢、冬、蒐于苹澤、作虎牢〇十五年、春正月、留昆氏來賓、作重璧臺、冬、王觀于鹽澤一作王幸安邑觀鹽池非是〇十六年、霍侯舊薨〇王命造父封于趙〇十七年、王西征至昆侖邱、見西王母、其年、

2 In the 6th year, Tan, the viscount of Seu,[3] came to do homage, when the title of
3 baron was conferred on him. In his 8th year, *the chief* of the northern T'ang came to do homage, and presented a very swift mare, which produced *the famous*
4 Luh-urh.[4] In his 9th year, he built the Spring palace.

Note. The king resided in the spring palace, and that of Ch'ing.

5 In his 11th year, he gave additional distinction and a Charge to Mow-foo, duke of
6 Tse, the prime minister. In his 12th year, Pan, duke of Maou, Le, duke of Kung,[5] and Koo, duke of Fung, led their forces, in attendance on the king, against the hordes of the K'euen. In the winter, in the 10th month, the king being on a tour
7 of inspection in the north, punished those hordes. In his 13th year, the duke of Tse attended the king with his forces on an expedition to the west, when they encamped in Yang.[6] In the autumn, in the 7th month, the hordes of the west came to make their submission. The hordes of Seu invaded Loh. In the winter, Ts'aou-foo
8 drove the king *in triumph* into Tsung-chow. In his 14th year, he led the viscount of Ts'oo against the hordes of Seu, and subdued them. In the summer, in the 4th month, he hunted in Keun-k'ew. In the 5th month, he made the palace of Fan. In autumn, in the 9th month, the people of Teih invaded Peih. In the winter, there
9 was a grand hunting in the marsh of P'ing.[8] He built Foo-laou.[9] In his 15th year, in the spring, in the 1st month, the chief of Lew-keun came to make his submission. The king made the tower of Chung-peih. In the winter, he surveyed the Salt marsh.[11]

Note. One copy has here:—'The king went to Ngan-yih, and viewed the Salt pond.' This is wrong.

10 In his 16th year, Kew, prince of Hoh, died. The king gave a Charge to Ts'aou-
11 foo, and invested him with Chaou.[12] In his 17th year, he went on a punitive expedition to mount Keun-lun; and saw the western Wang-moo. That year the chief

pres. dep. of Seu-chow, Keang-soo. 4 King Muh was famous for his horses; he had several,—'Spurn the earth,' 'Mount the clouds,' &c. 5 Should probably be Tsing (井). 6 Undetermined. Some say it was in K'e-chow; others, in Ts'in; others far beyond, 3,000 *le* from Tsung-chow. 7 An ancestor of the House of Ts'in, famous for his skilful and rapid driving. 8 Probably in dis. of Hea-yih, dep. Kwei-tih. It was near the capital of the early kings of Hea. 9 That is 'Tigers' Hold,' in dis. of Ke-shwuy, dep. K'ae-fung. Muh kept tigers here. 10 That is of 'storied *peih* gems.' 11 Supposed to be in the very distant west. Biot says:—'The great lake of the country of Cashgar.' 12 Dis. of Chaou-

西王母來朝、賓于昭宮。秋八月、遷戎于太原。

王北征行流沙千里積羽千里征犬戎取其五王以東西征于青鳥所解山三危西征還履天下億有九萬里

十八年、春正月、王居祇宮、諸侯來朝。〇二十一年、祭文公薨。〇二十四年、王命左史戎夫作記。〇三十五年、荆人入徐、毛伯遷帥師、敗荆人于泲。〇三十七年、大起九師、東至于九江、架黿鼉以爲梁、遂伐越、至于紆。荆人來貢〇三十九年、王會諸侯于塗山。〇四十五年、魯侯濆薨。〇五十一年、作呂刑、命甫侯于豐〇五十五年、王陟于祇宮。

共王

名繄

元年、甲寅、春正月、王即位〇四年、王師滅密〇九年、春正月、丁亥、王使內史良錫毛伯遷命。〇十二年、王陟。

of Wang-moo came to court, and was lodged in the palace of Ch'aou. In the autumn, in the 8th month, *certain* hordes were removed to T'ae-yuen.

Note. The king, in his expeditions to the north, travelled over the country of the Moving Sands, for 1,000 *le*, and that of 'Heaps of Feathers,' for 1,000 *le*. Then he subdued the hordes of the K'euen, and returned to the east, with their five kings as captives. Westwards, he pushed his expeditions to where the green birds cast their feathers (the hill of San-wei). On these expeditions he travelled over 190,000 *le*.

12 In his 18th year, in the spring, in the 1st month, he dwelt in the palace of Che,
13 where the princes came and did homage. In his 21st year, duke Wăn of Tse
14 died. In his 24th year, he ordered Jung-foo, the recorder of the Left, to make a
15 Record.[13] In his 35th year, the people of King entered Seu, when Ts'ëen, baron
16 of Maou, led his forces, and defeated them near the Tse.[14] In his 37th year, the king raised a great force of nine hosts, and proceeded eastward to Këw-keang, where he crossed the water on a bridge of tortoises and iguanadons piled up.[15] After this, he smote the people of Yuĕ as far as Yu. The people of King came with tribute.
18 In his 39th year, he assembled the princes at mount T'oo. In his 45th year,
19 Pe, prince of Loo, died. In his 51st year, he made the code of Leu on Punish-
20 ments, and gave a Charge to the prince of P'oo in Fung.[16] In his 59th year, he died in the palace of Che.

VI. King Kung.

Note. Named E.

1 His 1st year was *këah-yin* (51st of cycle, = B.C. 906), when he came to the
3 throne. In his 4th year, the royal forces extinguished Meih. In his 9th year, in the spring, in the 1st month, on the day *ting-hae* (24th of cycle), the king made Lëang, the recorder of the Interior, convey a Charge to Ts'ëen, baron of Maou.
4 In his 12th year, the king died.

shing, dep. P'ing-yang. 13 It is understood that this Record was a history of the rise and fall of dynasties and States, down to the commencement of the Chow dyn. King Muh had come to himself, and was ashamed of his wars, wanderings, and extravagance. 14 泲—濟. See the Tribute of Yu, Pt. ii. p. 10. 15 Hăng makes this out to be only a bridge of boats 16. See the 27th of the Books of Chow.

懿王

名堅、

元年、丙寅、春正月、王即位、天再旦于鄭○七年、西戎侵鎬○十三年、翟人侵岐○十五年、王自宗周、遷于槐里○十七年、魯厲公擢薨○二十一年、虢公帥師、北伐犬戎、敗逋○二十五年、王陟。

懿王之世興居無節號令不時挈壺氏不能共其職諸侯於是攜德

孝王

名辟方、

元年、辛卯、春正月、王即位、命申侯伐西戎○五年、西戎來獻馬○七年、冬大雨雹、江漢冰、牛馬死、是年厲王生○八年、初牧于汧渭○九年、王陟。

VII. KING E.

Note. Named Këen.

1 In his 1st year, which was *ping-yin* (3d of cycle, = B.C. 894), when he came to
2 the throne, there were two sunrisings in Ch'ing. In his 7th year, the hordes
3 of the west invaded Haou. In his 13th year, the people of Teih invaded K'e.
4 In his 16th year, the king removed from Tsung-chow to Hwae-le.[1] In his
6 17th year, Chih, the duke Le of Loo, died. In his 21st year, the duke of K'woh
led his forces north, against the hordes of the K'euen, by whom he was defeated and
7 put to flight. In his 25th year, the king died.

Note. The movements of king E were without proper regulation; the orders of his government were ill-timed; the holder of the *time*-jar did not attend to his duty:—and the consequence was that the princes began to lose their virtue.

VIII. KING HEAOU.

Note. Named Peih-fang.

1 In his 1st year, which was *sin-maou* (28th of cycle, = B.C. 869), in the spring, in
the 1st month, when he came to the throne, he ordered the prince of Shin[1] to smite the
2 hordes of the west. In his 3d year, the hordes of the west came, and presented
3 horses. In his 7th year, there were great rain and lightnings about the Këang
and the Han; and oxen and horses died.

Note. In this year king Le was born.

4 In his 8th year, they made pasture grounds for the first time of the country about
5 the Keen and the Wei.[2] In his 9th year, the king died.

VII. 1 Given as in the dis. of Hing-p'ing, dep. Se-ngan (Biot). Häng Ch'in-fung contends this was a different place, and that the site is not known. He strongly repudiates the idea that in the movement of king E, or the previous one of Muh to Ch'ing, we are to understand anything like a transference of the capital.

VIII. 1 In dis. of Nan-yang, dep. Nan-yang, Ho-nan. 2 Fei-tsze, of the House of Ts'in, was employed to look after the king's horses here.

書經

夷王

名燮

元年、庚子、春正月、王即位○二年、蜀人呂人、來獻瓊玉。賓于河、用介珪○三年、王致諸侯、烹齊哀公于鼎○六年、王獵于社林、獲犀牛一、以歸○七年、虢公帥師伐太原之戎、至于俞泉、獲馬千匹。冬、雨雹、大如礪。楚子熊渠伐庸、至于鄂○八年、王有疾、諸侯祈于山川。王陟。

厲王

名胡○居彘有汾水焉故又曰汾王

元年、戊申、春正月、王即位、作夷宮、命卿士榮夷公落。楚人來獻龜貝○三年、淮夷侵洛、王命虢公長父、伐之、不克。齊獻公山薨○六年、楚子延卒○八年、初監謗、芮伯良夫戒百官于朝○十一年、西戎入于犬邱

IX. KING E.

Note. Named Sëë.

1 His 1st year was *kang-tsze* (37th of cycle, = B.C. 860), when he came to the
2 throne. In his 2d year, the people of Shuh[1] and the people of Leu[2] came to present carnation and other gems. *The king* performed a service of homage to the Ho,
3 using the large mace.[3] In his 3d year, he assembled the princes, and boiled duke
4 Gae of Ts'e in a tripod.[4] In his 6th year, when hunting in the forest of Shay,[5] he
5 captured a rhinoceros, and carried it home. In his 7th year, the duke of Kwoh led his forces, and smote the hordes of T'ae-yuen as far as Yu-ts'euen, capturing 1,000 horses. In the winter, there was a storm of hail as large as whetstones. Hëung-k'eu,
6 the viscount of Ts'oo, smote the country of Yung[6] as far as Goh.[7] In his 8th year, the king was ill, when the princes prayed to the hills and streams. The king died.

X. KING LE.

Note. Named Hoo. He dwelt at Che, where there is the Fun-water, and hence he is styled also king Fun.

1 In his 1st year, which was *mow-shin* (45th of cycle, = B.C. 852), when he came to the throne, he built the palace of E,[1] and gave a Charge to the prime minister Loh, the duke E of Yung.[2] The people of Ts'oo presented tortoise and other shells. In
2 his 3d year, the hordes of Hwae invaded Loh, when the king ordered Ch'ang-foo, duke of Kwoh, to act against them, which he did without effect. Shan, the duke Hëen
4 of Ts'e, died. In his 6th year, Yen, viscount of Ts'oo, died. In his 8th year, he began the watch for any who reviled him.[3] Lëang-foo, the baron of Juy,[4]
5 cautioned all the officers in the court. In his 11th year, the hordes of the west

IX. 1 Dep. of Ching-too, Sze-ch'uen. 2 In the pres. dis. of Sin-ts'ae, dep. Joo-ning, Ho-nan. 3 See under the 1st year of the emp. Mang of the Hea dynasty. I know not whether this service was connected with the reception of the people of Leu and Shuh, or not. 4 See the history of the House of Ts'e (齊世家), in the Historical Records. 5 Hăng would change 社 into 杜. 6 In dis. Chuh-san, dep. Yun-yang, Hoo-pih. 7 In dis. of Woo-ch'ang.

X. 1 As king Muh built a palace after the name of his father, king Ch'aou. 2 Yung must be the name of a principality. The dict., however, says nothing of this on the character. 3 Acc. to the Chow Joo, the king employed

○十二年、王亡、奔彘。國人圍王宮、執召穆公之子、殺之○十三年、王在彘、共伯和攝行天子事、號曰共和○十四年、玁狁侵宗周西鄙。召穆公帥師追荆蠻、至于洛○十六年、蔡武侯薨。楚子勇卒○十九年、曹夷伯薨○二十二年、大旱。陳幽公薨○二十三年、大旱。宋僖公薨○二十四年、大旱。杞武公薨○二十五年、大旱。楚子嚴卒○二十六年、大旱。王陟于彘。周定公、召穆公、立太子靖爲王、共伯和歸其國、遂大雨。

大旱既久、廬舍俱焚、會汾王崩、卜于太陽、兆曰厲王爲祟、周公召公乃立太子靖、共和遂歸國、和有至德、尊之不喜廢之不怒、逍遙得志于共山之首

宣王

名靖

元年、甲戌、春正月、王即位、周定公召穆公

6 penetrated to K'euen-k'ew. In his 12th year, the king became a fugitive, and fled to Che.[5] The people surrounded the palace; and having seized the son of duke
7 Muh of Shaou, they put him to death.[6] In his 13th year, the king was in Che; and Ho, baron of Kung, administered the imperial duties.[7]

Note. This is styled the period of Kung-ho.

8 In his 14th year, *the hordes of* the Yen-yun[8] overran the western border of Tsung-chow. Duke Muh of Shaou led his forces in pursuit of the southern hordes of King
9 as far as the Loh.[9] In his 16th year, prince Woo of Ts'ae died; and also Yung,
11 the viscount of Ts'oo. In his 19th year, the baron E of Ts'aou died. In
12 his 22d year, there was a great drought; and duke Yew of Ch'in died. In his 23d
13 year, the drought continued; and duke He of Sung died. In his 24th year, the
14 drought continued; and duke Woo of K'e died. In his 25th year, still the
15 drought. Yen, viscount of Ts'oo, died. In his 26th year, there was still the drought, when the king died in Che. The dukes, Ting of Chow and Muh of Shaou, then raised his eldest son Tsing to the throne; Ho, baron of Kung, returned to his State; and there was a great rain.

Note. The great drought had continued so long. that all huts were burned up. When king Fun died, they consulted by the tortoise-shell the *spirit of the* sun, and were answered that Le had been done to death by some monstrous thing. When the dukes of Chow and Shaou had raised his oldest son Tsing to the throne, Ho of Kung returned to his State. He was a man of the greatest virtue. Honours did not make him *overmuch* glad, nor did neglect move him to anger. He afterwards sought his own ease and pleasure in retirement on the top of mount Kung.

XI. KING SEUEN.

Note. Named Tsing.

1 In his 1st year, which was *keah-seuh* (11th of cycle, = B.C. 826), in the spring, in the first month, he came to the throne, when the dukes, Ting of Chow and Muh of

a diviner or magician in this work. 4 In dis. of Chaou-yih, dep. Se-ngan. 5 In dis. of Fun-se, dep. P'ing-yang. 6 The king's son was hidden in the duke of Shaou's house, who gave up his own son instead of him. 7 This is a sure epoch, acknowledged by all Chinese chronologists. Instead of there being only one regent, however, as these Annals say, the more common accounts make out two, Kung and Ho, the dukes of Chow and Shaou. 8 These were afterwards known as the Hëung-noo. 9 If this be the Lŏ river, or the State so called near it, we must suppose that the hordes of Ts'oo had come far north on an invading raid.

輔政。復田賦。作戎車。燕惠侯薨〇二年、錫太師皇父、司馬休父命。魯愼公薨。曹公子蘇弒其君幽伯彊〇三年、王命大夫仲伐西戎。齊武公壽薨〇四年、王命蹶父如韓、韓侯來朝〇五年、夏六月、尹吉甫帥師伐玁狁、至于太原。秋八月、方叔帥師伐荆蠻〇六年、召穆公帥師伐淮夷。王帥師伐徐戎。皇父休父從王伐徐戎、次于淮。王歸自伐徐、錫召穆公命。西戎殺秦仲。楚子霜卒〇七年、王錫申伯命。王命樊侯仲山甫城齊〇八年、初考室。魯武公來朝、錫魯世子戲命〇九年、王會諸侯于東都、遂狩于甫〇十二年、魯武公薨。齊人弒其君厲公無忌、立公子赤〇十五年、衞釐侯薨。王錫虢文公命〇十六年、晉遷于絳〇十八年、蔡夷侯薨〇二十一年、魯公子伯

Shaou, assisted in the government. He restored the field levies.[1] He made chariots
2 of war. Prince Hwuy of Yen died. In his 2d year, he gave a Charge to Hwang-foo, the Grand-tutor; and one to Hew-foo, the Master of the Horse. Duke Shin of Loo died. Soo, a younger son of the House of Ts'aou, murdered his prince, Këang, the
3 baron Yew. In his 3d year, the king ordered the great officer Chung to attack
4 the hordes of the west. Show, the duke Woo of Ts'e, died. In his 4th year, the king ordered Kwei-foo to go to Han, after which the prince of Han came to court.
5 In his 5th year, in the summer, in the 6th month, Yin Keih-foo led his forces, and smote the Yen-yun, as far as T'ae-yuen.[3] In the autumn, in the 8th month, Fang
6 Shuh led his forces, and smote the southern hordes of King.[4] In his 6th year, the duke Muh of Shaou led his forces against the hordes of the Hwae. The king led his forces against the hordes of Seu, having Hwang-foo and Hew-foo in attendance on him, when he camped on the Hwae. When he returned from the expedition, he gave a Charge to duke Muh of Shaou. The hordes of the west killed Chung of
7 Ts'in. Seang, viscount of Ts'oo, died. In his 7th year, the king gave a Charge to the baron of Shin. The king ordered Chung Shan-foo, prince of Fan, to wall
8 Ts'e.[5] In his 8th year, the king first completed the apartments *of one his palaces.* Duke Woo of Loo came to court, when the king appointed his heir-son He to succeed
9 to the principality. In his 9th year, the king assembled the princes in the eastern
10 capital, after which they hunted in Foo.[7] In his 12th year, duke Woo of Loo died. The people of Ts'e murdered their ruler, Woo-ke, known as duke Le, and
11 appointed his son Ch'ih in his room. In his 15th year, prince Le of Wei died.
12 The king gave a Charge to duke Wăn of Kwoh. In his 16th year, Tsin removed
14 its capital to Keang.[8] In his 18th year, prince E of Tse died. In his 21st year, Pih-yu, of the ducal House of Loo, murdered his prince He, known as duke E.

XI. 1 These were charges for military services, regulated by the quality of the lands. They had been neglected during the exile of the last king. 2 This coming of the prince of Han to court is celebrated in the She, Pt. III., Bk. III., Ode vii. Mention is made of Kwei-foo. 3 This expedition is celebrated in the She, Pt. II., Bk. III., Ode iii. 4 See the She, Pt. II., Bk. III., Ode iv. 5 See the She, Pt. III., Bk. III., Ode vi. Fan was in the dis. of Tse-yuen, dep. Hwae-k'ing. We are to understand the metropolis of Tse. 6 考=成 'to finish.' What apartments are intended, it is impossible to say. They may have been, as many suppose, those of a palace in honour of his father. 7 See the She, Pt. II., Bk. III., Ode v. 8 On the north of the dis. of T'ae-p'ing, dep. P'ing-

御、弒其君懿公戲〇二十二年、王錫王子多父命、居洛〇二十四年、齊文公赤薨〇二十五年、大旱、王禱于郊廟、遂雨〇二十七年、宋惠公覸薨〇二十八年、楚子狥卒〇二十九年、初不藉千畝〇三十年、有兎舞於鎬京〇三十二年、王師伐魯、殺伯御、命孝公稱于夷宮。陳僖公孝薨。有馬化爲人〇三十三年、齊成公薨。王師伐太原之戎、不克〇三十七年、有馬化爲狐。燕僖侯卒。楚子鄂卒〇三十八年、王師及晉穆侯、伐條戎奔戎、王師敗逋〇三十九年、王師伐姜戎、戰于千畝、王師敗逋〇四十年、料民于太原。戎人滅姜邑。晉人敗北戎于汾隰〇四十一年、王師敗于申〇四十三年、王殺大夫杜伯、其子隰叔出奔晉。晉穆侯費生薨、弟殤叔自立、世子仇出奔〇四十四年、晉殤叔元年丁巳〇四十六年、王陟。

15 In his 22d year, the king gave his Charge to To-foo, a scion of the royal House,
16 to reside at Loh.[9] In his 24th year, Ch'ih, the duke Wan of Ts'e, died. In
17 his 25th year, there was a great drought, when the king prayed at the border altars
18 and in the ancestral temple; and there was rain. In his 27th year, Këen, the
19 duke Hwuy of Sung, died. In his 28th year, Seun, viscount of Ts'oo, died.
20 In his 29th year, the king for the first time neglected the setting an example of
21 husbandry in his thousand acres field. In his 30th year, hares appeared gam-
22 bolling in the capital Haou. In his 32d year, the royal forces attacked Loo,
and put Pih-yu to death; and the king invested Ch'ing, known as duke Heaou, with
the principality, in the palace of E. Heaou, the duke He of Ch'in, died. A horse
23 changed into a man. In his 33d year, the duke Ching of Ts'e died. The royal
24 forces attacked the hordes of T'ae-yuen without success. In his 37th year, a
horse changed into a fox. The prince He of Yen died. Goh, the viscount of Ts'oo,
25 died. In his 38th year, the royal forces and prince Muh of Tsin proceeded
against the hordes of the T'eaou and the Pun, when they were defeated and put to
26 flight. In his 39th year, the royal forces attacked the Këang hordes, and
27 were defeated, and put to flight in a battle in Ts'ëen-mow.[12] In his 40th year,
he numbered the people in T'ae-yuen.[13] The western hordes destroyed the city of
28 Këang.[14] The people of Tsin defeated some northern hordes in Fun-sih.[15] In
29 his 41st year, his forces were defeated in Shin. In his 43d year, he put to death
the great officer Too Pih, whose son Sih-shuh then fled to Tsin. Fei-sang, the prince
Muh of Tsin, died, when his brother Seang-shuh usurped the principality, and the
30 heir-son K'ew fled. His 44th year was *ting-sze*, the 1st year of Shang-shuh of Tsin.
In his 46th year, the king died.

yang, between it and the small dep. of Këang. The old capital Yih was also in dep. of P'ing-yang. 9 To-foo was a younger son of king Le, and a brother of king Seuen. 10 In a field of 1,000 acres, the emperor turned up a furrow in the spring, to set the people an example of husbandry; the princes did the same in one of 100 acres. From a passage in the Chow Joo, we are led to suppose that Seuen had neglected this practice from the beginning of his reign. The Annals here give us a different impression. The phrase 藉田 is variously explained. 11 Hăng Ch'in-fung thinks that T'eaou and Pun were the surnames of the wild tribes spoken of. Those who make them the names of places entirely fail in identifying Pun. 12 This seems to have been in the dis. of Gŏ-yang, dep. P'ing-yang. The Këang hordes, said to be descended from Yaou's principal minister, 'the Four Mountains,' were numerous and powerful. 13 This T'ae-yuen was in dis. King-yang, dep. Se-ngan. 14 In the dis. Paou-ke, dep. Fung-tsëang. 15 In dis. of K'euh-yuh, dep. P'ing-yang.

幽王

名涅

元年、庚申、春正月、王卽位。晉世子仇、歸
于晉、殺殤叔。晉人立仇、是爲文侯。王錫
太師尹氏皇父命○二年、辛酉晉文侯元年涇
渭洛竭。岐山崩。初增賦。晉文侯同王子
多父伐鄫、克之、乃居鄭父之邱、是爲鄭
桓公○三年、王嬖褒姒。冬、大雷電○四
年、秦人伐西戎。夏六月、隕霜。陳夷公薨
○五年、王世子宜臼出犇申。皇父作都
于向○六年、王命伯士帥師、伐六濟之
戎、王師敗逋。西戎滅蓋。冬十月、辛卯、朔、
日有食之○七年、虢人滅焦○八年、王
錫司徒鄭伯多父命。王立褒姒之子、曰
伯服、爲太子○九年、申侯聘西戎、及鄫
○十年、春、王及諸侯盟于太室。秋九月、
桃杏實。王師伐申○十一年、春正月、日

XII. KING YEW.

Note. Named Nëë.

1 His 1st year was *kang-shin* (57th of cycle, = B.C. 780), when he came to the throne.
K'ew, the heir son of Tsin, returned thither, and slew Shang-shuh. The people
then raised him to the government;—he is known as prince Wan. The king gave a
2 Charge to Yin Hwang-foo, the Grand-tutor. In his 2d year,—*sin-yew*, the 1st year
of prince Wăn of Tsin,—the King, Wei, and Loh, all became dry. *A part* of mount
K'e fell down. *The king* began to increase the taxes, Prince Wan of Tsin, with
To-foo, of the royal House, attacked, Tsang, and subdued it. After this *To-foo* took
3 up his residence on the hill of Ch'ing-foo. He was duke Hwan of Ch'ing.[1] In
his 3d year, the king became enamoured with *his concubine* Paou-sze. In the winter,
4 there was great thunder and lightning. In his 4th year, the people of Ts'in
smote the western hordes. In the summer, in the 6th month, there fell hoar-frost.
5 The duke E of Ch'in died. In his 5th year, his heir-son, E-k'ew, fled from the
6 court to Shin. Hwang-foo prepared *another* capital in Heang.[2] In his 6th year,
the king ordered Pih-sze with the royal forces to attack the hordes of Luh-tse,[3] but
they were defeated and put to flight. The western hordes destroyed K'ae. In the
winter, in the 10th month, on the day *sin-maou*, there was an eclipse of the sun.
8 In his 7th year, the people of Kwoh extinguished Ts'ëaou.[4] In his 8th year,
the king gave an additional dignity to To-foo, baron of Ch'ing, his minister of In-
9 struction. He made Pih-fuh, the son of Paou-sze, his heir apparent. In his 9th
year, the prince of Shin sent an embassy to the western hordes, and to Tsang, and
10 entered *into an engagement with them.* In his 10th year, in the spring,
he made a solemn agreement with the princes in the grand apartment of the ancestral temple.[5] In the autumn, in the 9th month, the peach trees and almond trees
11 were in fruit. The king led his army against Shin. In the 11th year, in the

XII. 1 To-foo, mentioned here, was a younger brother of king Seuen, by whom he had been invested with the principality of Ch'ing. He wished to appropriate the State of Tsăng, which was afterwards done by one of his successors. That State was at this time only subdued. Where Ch'ing-foo was, is not exactly known. 2 As if anticipating the capture, which took place ere long, of the existing capital; but where this Heang was is much debated. 3 These belonged to the Keang tribes. 4 ? In Shen

暈、申人、鄫人、及犬戎、入宗周、弑王、及鄭桓公、犬戎殺王子伯服、執褒姒以歸、申侯、魯侯、許男、鄭子、立宜臼于申、虢公翰立王子余臣于攜、是爲攜王二王竝立

武王滅殷歲在庚寅二十四年歲在甲寅定鼎洛邑至幽王二百五十七年共二百八十一年自武王元年已卯至幽王庚午二百九十二年

平王

名宜臼○自東遷以後始紀晉事王即位皆不書

元年、辛未、王東徙洛邑、錫文侯命。晉侯會衞侯、鄭伯、秦伯、以師從王、入于成周○二年、秦作西畤。魯孝公薨、賜秦晉以邠岐之田、○三年、齊人滅祝。王錫司徒鄭伯命○四年、燕頃侯薨。鄭人滅虢○五年、秦襄公帥師伐戎、卒于師。宋戴公

spring, in the 1st month, the sun and moon had haloes. The people of Shin, of Tsăng, and the hordes of the K'euen, entered Tsung-chow, and murdered the king and duke Hwan of Ch'ing. The *chief of the* K'euen killed the king's son, Pih-fuh, and took Paou-sze as his captive. The princes of Shin and Loo, with the *nan* of Heu and the young lord of Ch'ing, raised E-k'ew, who was in Shin, to the throne; but Han, duke of Kwoh, declared another son of Yew, named Yu-chin, who was in Hwuy, to be king.

Note. This last is known as king Hwuy. There were thus two kings at the same time.—When king Woo made an end of Yin, the year was in *kang-yin*. Twenty-four years after, in the year *këă-yin*, the vases were finally placed in the city of Lŏ. From that time to king Yew, were 257 years;—giving us in all 281 years. From *sin-maou*, the 1st year of Woo, to *kăng-woo*, the last of Yew, were 292 years.

XIII. King P'ing.

Note. Named E-k'ew. From the removal of the capital to the east, the chronicler relates the affairs of Tsin; and the king's coming to the throne is not mentioned.

1 In his 1st year, which was *sin-wei* (8th of cycle, = B.C. 769), the king removed the capital to the east, to the city of Loh. He conferred the dignity *of chief among the princes* on prince Wan.[1] The prince of Tsin united with the prince of Wei, the barons of Ch'ing and Ts'in, and with their troops escorted the king to Ching-chow.[2]
2 In his 2d year, Ts'in made the western altar.[3] Hëaou of Loo died. The king
3 conferred on Ts'in and Tsin the fields of Pin and K'e. In his 3d year, the people of Ts'e extinguished Chuh.[4] The king conferred an additional dignity on the
4 baron of Ch'ing, his minister of Instruction.[5] In his 4th year, the prince king
5 of Yen died. The people of Ch'ing extinguished Kwoh. In his 5th year, the duke Sëang of Ts'in led his forces against the *western* hordes, and died on the ex-

Chow, Ho-nan. 5 太室 is to be taken here as on the occasion of its previous occurrence. This is plain from the She, Pt. II., Book V., Ode iv., which, probably, refers to this meeting of king Yew and the princes.

XIII. 1 See the xxxth of the Books of Chow. 2 Ching-chow is Lŏ. The transference of the capital is the subject of the She, Pt. II., Bk. V., Ode ix. 3 時=神靈之所依止, 'the place where the spirit rests.' Seang, the prince of Ts'in, elated with his new acquisitions in the west, made this altar, where he sacrificed to God. The presumption was somewhat disguised by making the sacrifice be to 'the white god' (白帝). 4 A small State on the north of Ts'e. 5 ? The dignity of duke. The

薨〇六年、燕哀侯薨。鄭遷於溱洧〇七年、楚子儀卒〇八年、鄭殺其大夫關其思〇十年、秦遷于汧渭〇十三年、魏武公薨〇十四年、晉人滅韓〇十八年、秦文公大敗戎師于岐、來歸岐東之田〇二十一年、晉文侯殺王子余臣于攜〇二十三年、宋武公薨〇二十四年、秦作陳寶祠〇二十五年、晉文侯薨。秦初用族刑〇二十六年、丙申晉昭侯元年晉封其弟成師于曲沃〇三十二年、晉潘父弑其君昭侯、納成師、不克、立昭侯之子孝侯、晉人殺潘父〇三十三年、癸卯晉孝侯元年楚人侵申〇三十六年、衛莊公薨。王人戍申〇四十年、齊莊公薨。晉曲沃桓叔成師卒、子鱓立、是爲莊伯、自是晉侯在翼稱翼侯〇四十一年、辛亥莊伯元年春、大雨雪〇四十二

6 pedition. The duke Tae of Sung died. In his 6th year, the prince Gae of Yen
7 died. Ch'ing removed its capital to near the Ts'in and the Hwuy.[6] In his 7th
8 year, E, viscount of Ts'oo, died. In his 8th year, *the baron of* Ch'ing put his
9 great officer, Kwan K'e-sze, to death. In his 10th year, Ts'in removed its capital
10 to near the Këen and the Wei. In his 13th year, the duke Woo of Wei died.
12 In his 14th year, the people of Tsin extinguished Han.[8] In his 18th year,
the duke Wăn of Ts'in inflicted a great defeat on the western hordes in K'e, and
13 came to restore the fields on the east of K'e. In his 21st year, the prince Wăn
14 of Tsin put the king's brother, Yu-chin, to death in Hwuy. In his 23d year,
15 the duke Woo of Sung died. In his 24th year, Ts'in instituted the sacrifices to
16 the Precious ones of Ch'in.[9] In his 25th year, prince Wăn of Tsin died. Ts'in
17 for the first time, used the punishment of destroying criminals' relatives. In his
26th year,—ping-shin, the 1st year of prince Ch'aou of Tsin,—the prince of Tsin invested
18 his younger brother Ching-sze with the city of K'euh-yuh.[10] In his 32d year,
Fan-foo of Tsin murdered his ruler, prince Ch'aou, and called Ching-sze to the
throne;—without success. The people of Tsin then called the son of Ch'aou, who
19 was the prince Heaou, to the sovereignty, and put Fan-foo to death. In his
33d year,—kwei-maou, the 1st year of prince Heaou of Tsin—the people of Ts'oo overran
20 Shin. In his 43d year, the duke Chwang of Wei died. The king's subjects
22 took guard of Shin. In his 40th year, duke Chwang of Ts'e died. Ching-sze,
Hwan-shuh of K'euh-yuh, died; and was succeeded by his son Shen, who is known
as Chwang-pih.

Note. From this time the prince of Tsin dwelt in Yih, and is known as the prince of Yih.

23 In his 41st year,—sin-hae, the 1st year of Chwang-pih,—in the spring, there was a great

10th ode of the She, Bk. V., Pt. II., is referred to this time. 6 The dis. of Hwuy-ch'uen, dep. K'ae-fung. The Ts'in flowed into the Hwuy. See the 13th of the Songs of Ch'ing, in the She, Part I. 7 The Keen is a tributary of the Wei. It gives name to the dis. of Këen-yang, dep. Fung-ts'ëang. 8 A Han, we saw, was walled by Yen in the 12th year of king Ching. That was in dis. of Koo-ngan, dep of Shun-t'ëen. A branch of that House had settled itself in the dis. of Han-shing, dep. T'ung-chow, Shen-se, which was the Han here spoken of. 9 The story is, that two boys, who changed into pheasants, had made their appearance, and it was known, in a wonderful way, that he who got the female would become chief

年、狄人伐翼、至于晉郊。宋襄公薨。魯惠公使宰讓請郊廟之禮、王使史角如魯、諭止之○四十七年、晉曲沃莊伯入翼、弒孝侯、晉人逐之、立孝侯子郄、是爲鄂侯○四十八年、戊午晉鄂侯郄元年無雲而雷。魯惠公薨○四十九年、已未魯隱公元年春秋始此魯隱公、及邾莊公、盟于姑蔑○五十一年、春二月、已巳、日有食之。三月庚戌、王陟。

桓王

名林

元年、壬戌、十月、莊伯以曲沃叛、伐翼、公子萬救翼、荀叔軫追之、至于家谷、翼侯焚曲沃之禾而還、翼侯伐曲沃、大捷、武公請成于翼、至相而還相一作桐○二年、王使虢公伐晉之曲沃、晉鄂侯卒、曲沃莊

24 storm of rain and snow. In his 42d year, the wild tribes of the north attacked Yih,[11] and penetrated to the borders of Tsin. The duke Sëang of Sung died. The duke Hwuy of Loo sent Tsae Jang, to request liberty to use the ceremonies of the imperial border sacrifices and of the ancestral temple. The king sent the recorder
25 Këoh to go to Loo to stop the assumption. In his 47th year, Chwang-pih of K'euh-yuh of Tsin entered Yih, and murdered the prince Heaou. The people of Tsin drove him out, and raised to the sovereignty Keih the son of Heaou, known as
26 prince Goh. In his 48th year,—mow-woo, the 1st year of the prince Goh of Tsin,—
27 there was thunder without any clouds. The duke Hwuy of Loo died. In his 49th year,—ke-wei, the 1st year of duke Yin of Loo. In this year, the Ch'un-Ts'ew begins,—the duke Yin of Loo and the duke Chwang of Choo[12] formed an alliance at Koo-
28 mëë. In his 51st year, in the spring, in the 2d month, on the day *yih-sze* (42d of cycle), there was an eclipse of the sun. In the 3d month, on the day *kang-seuh*, the king died.

XIV. KING HWAN.

Note. Named Lin.

1 His 1st year was *jin-seuh* (59th of cycle, = B.C. 718). In the 10th month, Chwang-pih rebelled in K'euh-yuh, and attacked Yih. Wan, of the ruling House, came to the rescue of Yih, and Chin, the chief of Seun,[1] pursued Chwang-pih as far as the valley of Kea. The prince of Yih then burned the standing grain of K'euh-yuh, and returned. *Afterwards* he attacked the place, and gained a great victory. *Chwang-pih's son, afterwards* duke Woo, solicited peace, came as far as Sëang (or T'ung),
2 and returned. In his 2d year, the king made the duke of Kwoh attack K'ëuh-yuh of Tsin. The prince Goh of Tsin died, when Chwang-pih attacked Tsin. *The*

among the princes, while the possessor of the male would become king. They were called 'The precious ones of Ch'in,' from the place where they appeared. Duke Wăn of Ts'in caught the female, which changed into a stone; and he appointed a sacrifice to them in the pres. dis. of Paou-ke, dep. Fung-ts'ëang. 10 In the dis. so called of dep. P'ing-yang. 11 Mentioned in the note above as the capital of Tsin from the time of prince Heaou. It was in the dis. of Yih-shing, dep. of P'ing-yang. 12 In the dis. of Tsow, dep. Yen-chow. 13 In the dis. of Sze-shwuy, dep. Yen-chow.

XIV. 1 To the west of the river Fun (汾水). 2. That is, could only bring into the

伯復攻晉、晉立鄂侯子光、是爲哀侯〇三年、
甲子、晉哀侯光元年〇四年、曲沃莊伯卒、子稱立、是
爲武公。尚一軍〇五年、曲沃武公元年芮人乘京。荀
人、董伯、皆叛曲沃〇十一年、晉小子侯元年曲沃獲
晉哀侯、晉人立哀侯子爲小子侯。芮伯萬出
奔魏、萬之母逐萬〇十二年、王師秦師圍魏、取芮
伯萬而東之〇十三年、冬、曲沃伯誘晉小子
侯殺之。晉曲沃滅荀、以其地賜大夫原氏黯、
是爲荀叔。戎人逆芮伯萬于郊〇十四年、王
命虢仲伐曲沃、立晉哀侯弟緡于翼、爲晉侯
〇十五年、晉侯緡元年〇十六年、春、滅翼〇十九
年、鄭莊公薨〇二十三年、三月乙未、王陟。

莊王 名佗、

元年乙酉、曲沃尚一軍、異于晉〇六年、五月、
葬桓王〇十五年、王陟。

people of Tsin raised Kwang, the son of prince Goh, to the sovereignty. He is known
4 as prince Gae. His 3d year was *keah-tsze,* the 1st year of prince Gae of Tsin. In
his 4th year, Chwang-pih of K'euh-yuh died, and was succeeded by his son Ch'ing,
5 the duke Woo. *The State* had still only one army.[2] In his 5th year,—the 1st
year of duke Woo of K'euh-yuh,—the people of Juy, Shing-king,[3] the people of Seun,
6 and the baron of Tung,[4] all rebelled against K'euh-yuh. In his 11th year,—1st
year of the prince Seaou-tsze of Tsin,—*the chief of* K'euh-yuh took prince Gae of Tsin
prisoner, when the people of Tsin put Gae's son, known as prince Sëaou-tsze, in his
place. Wan, the baron of Juy, fled to Wei.[5]

Note. Wan was driven out by his mother.

7 In his 12th year, the royal forces and those of Ts'in besieged Wei, took Wan, the
8 baron of Juy, and carried him to the east. In his 13th year, in the winter, the
baron of K'euh-yuh enticed prince Sëaou-tsze of Tsin *to an interview,* and killed
him. He then extinguished *the House of* Seun, and gave its territory to his great
officer Yuen Gan, who became the chief of Seun. Some people of one of the western
9 hordes met Wan, the baron of Juy, in Keaou.[6] In his 14th year, the king ordered
Chung of Kwoh to smite K'euh-yuh, and to raise Min, a younger brother of prince
10 Gae, to be prince of Tsin in Yih. His 15th year was the 1st year of prince Min of Tsin.
11 In his 16th year, in the spring, *K'euh-yuh* extinguished Yih *as the capital of*
12 *Tsin.* In his 19th year, the duke Chwang of Ch'ing died. In his 23d
year, in the 3d month, on the day *yih-wei,* the king died.

XV. KING CHWANG.

Note. Named T'o.

1 In his 1st year, which was *yih-yew* (22d of cycle, = B.C. 695), K'euh-yuh still
2 maintained only one army, different from Tsin. In his 6th year, in the 5th
3 month, he buried king Hwan. In his 15th year, he died.

field 12,500 men. 3 There seems to be something wanting here. 4 In dis. Yung-ho, dep. T'ung-chow. 5 In the small dep. of Keae, Shan-se. 6 This 郊 must be the name of a place. There is the reading of 郊.

161]

釐王 名胡齊

元年、庚子、春、齊桓公會諸侯于北杏、以平宋亂○三年、曲沃武公滅晉侯緡、以寶玉獻王、王命武公以一軍爲晉侯○四年、晉武公三十八年、晉猶不與齊桓公之盟、左傳註晉侯緡是年滅○五年、晉武公卒、子詭諸立、爲獻公○王陟。

惠王 名閬

元年、乙巳、晉獻公元年晉獻公朝。王如成周、周有白兎舞于市○二年、王子頹亂、王居于鄭。鄭人入王府、多取玉、玉化爲蜮、射人○九年、晉城絳○十六年、晉獻公作二軍、滅耿、以賜大夫趙夙、滅魏、以賜大夫畢萬晉滅於大夫趙韓魏萌於此○

XVI. KING LE.

Note. Named Hoo-ts'e.

1 In his 1st year, which was *kang-tsze* (37th of cycle, = B.C. 680), duke Hwan of Ts'e assembled the princes at Pih-hing,[1] to bring to order the troubles of Sung.

2 In his 3d year, duke Woo of K'euh-yuh made an end of prince Min of Tsin, and presented *many of* the precious relics of the State to the king, who appointed him to
3 be prince of Tsin, maintaining only one army. In his 4th year,—the 38th year of duke Woo of Tsin,—Tsin still declined to be present at one of the meetings called by the duke Hwan of Ts'e.

Note. A note in the Tso Chuen says it was in this year prince Min of Tsin was made an end of.

4 In his 5th year, duke Woo of Tsin died, and was succeeded by his son Kwei-choo, known as duke Hëen. The king died.

XVII. KING HWUY.

Note. Named Lëang.

1 In his 1st year, which was *yih-sze* (42d of cycle, = B.C. 675), the 1st year of duke Hëen of Tsin, the duke Hëen of Tsin went to court. The king went to Ching-chow.
2 There a white hare appeared, dancing in the market place. In his 2d year, his son T'uy raised a rebellion, and the king *went and* dwelt in Ch'ing, where the people entered his treasury, and took *many* gems, which changed into *yih* that shot
4 *their venom at* men.[1] In his 9th year, Tsin walled Këang.[2] In his 16th year, the duke Hëen of Tsin formed two armies, and extinguished the State of Kăng,[3] which he gave to his great officer Chaou Suh. He also extinguished Wei, and gave it to his great officer Peih Wan.

Note. This was the germ of the extinction of Tsin by its great officers of Chaou, Han, and Wei.

XVI. 1 In the dis. of Tung-o, dep. T'ae-ngan.

XVII. 1 蜮,—see the She, Pt. II., Bk. V., Ode v., st. 8. It is described as 'a short fox,' which lived in the water, where it filled its mouth with sand, which it shot at the shadows of persons on the bank, who thereon became sick. 3 In the small dep. of Këang, Shanse. This had been one of the capitals of Shang.

十七年、衛懿公及赤狄戰于洞澤洞當作泂○十九年、晉獻公會虞師伐虢、滅下陽、虢公醜奔衛、公命瑕父呂甥邑于虢都○二十五年、春正月狄人伐晉。王陟。

襄王 名鄭

元年、庚午、晉獻公卒、立奚齊、里克殺之、及卓子、立夷吾○二年、辛未晉惠公元年晉殺里克○三年、雨金于晉○七年、秦伯涉河伐晉○十五年、晉惠公卒、子懷公圉立。秦穆公帥師送公子重耳、圍令狐、桑泉、臼衰、皆降于秦師、狐毛與先軫禦秦、至于廬柳、乃謂秦穆公、使公子縶來、與師言、次于郇、盟于軍、公子重耳涉自河曲○十六年、乙酉晉文公元年晉殺子圉○十七年、晉城荀○二十年、周襄王會諸侯于河陽○二十二年、齊師

5 In his 17th year, duke E of Wei fought with the red hordes of the north at the
6 marsh of Tung (or K'eung). In his 19th year, duke Hëen of Tsin united his forces with those of Yu, and, attacking Kwoh, destroyed Hea-yang.[4] Ch'ow, duke of Kwoh, fled to Wei, and *Hëen* ordered Hea-foo Leu-sang[5] to occupy his capital.
7 In his 25th year, in the spring, in the 1st month, some of the northern hordes attacked Tsin. The king died.

XVIII. King Sëang.

Note. Named Ch'ing.

1 In his 1st year, which was *kang-woo* (7th of cycle, = B.C. 650), duke Hëen of Tsin died, and He-ts'e was raised to the sovereignty. Le K'ih, *however,* put him to death, and
2 Ch'oh-tsze *also,* whereon E-woo was chosen. In his 2d year,—*sin-we,* the 1st year
3 of duke Hwuy of Tsin,—*the duke* of Tsin put Le K'ih to death. In his 3d year,
4 it rained gold in Tsin. In his 7th year, the chief of Ts'in crossed the Ho and
5 attacked Tsin. In his 15th year, duke Hwuy of Tsin died, and was succeeded by his son Yu, known as duke Hwae. Duke Muh of Ts'in, with a force, escorted duke Hëen's son, Ch'ung-urh, to the State, and invested Ling-koo,[1] Shwang-ts'euen,[2] and K'ew-shwae,[3] which all surrendered. Koo Wei and Sëen-chin went to Loo-lew[4] to oppose Ts'in, when duke Muh sent his son Chih to speak with them, after which they camped in Seun,[5] and entered into an engagement with Ch'ung-urh in the
6 midst of the army, he having crossed the Ho at Ho-k'euh.[6] In his 16th year,—
7 *yih-yew,* the 1st year of duke Wăn of Tsin,—Tsin put Tsze-yu to death.[7] In his 17th
8 year, Tsin walled Seun.[8] In his 20th year, king Sëang of Chow assembled the
9 princes in Ho-yang.[9] In his 22d year, the army of Ts'e drove out Ch'e, the

4 A city of Kwoh. 5 This name is difficult to explain. Hea, perhaps, was the name of the officer's city, from which he was called Hea-foo. Then Leu would be his name, and Sang would denote his relationship to duke Hëen.

XVIII. 1 In dis. of E-she, dep. P'oo-chow. 2 In Lin-tsin dis., same dep. 3 In Këae Chow. 4 Also in Këae Chow. 5 In north-west of Këae Chow. 6 Or 'the Bend of the Ho,' in dep. of P'oo-chow, where the river bends to the east. 7 Tsze-yu=duke Hwae. 8 Mentioned under the 13th year of king Hwan. 9 Probably in the dis. Măng, dep. Hwae-k'ing. The style of this par. is sufficient-

逐鄭太子齒、奔城張南鄭○二十四年、晉文公卒○二十五年、甲午晉襄公驩元年○三十年、洛絕于泂○三十一年、晉襄公卒○三十二年、辛丑晉靈公夷皐元年○三十三年、王陟。

頃王

名壬臣、

元年、癸卯○六年、彗星入北斗。王陟。

匡王

名班、

元年、己酉○六年、晉靈公爲趙穿所殺、趙盾使穿迎公子黑臀于周、立之。王陟。

定王

名瑜、

元年、乙卯、晉成公元年○六年、晉成公與狄伐秦、獲秦諜、殺之絳市、六日而蘇○七年、晉成公卒于

10 heir-prince of Ch'ing, who fled to Shing-chang Nan-ch'ing.[10] In his 24th
11 year, duke Wan of Tsin died. His 25th year was *këă-woo*, the 1st year of Hwan,
12 the duke Sëang of Tsin. In his 30th year, the Loh was dried up at Hëang.[11]
13 In his 31st year, duke Sëang of Tsin died. His 32d year was *sin-ch'ow*, the 1st
14 year of E-kaou, the duke Ling of Tsin. In his 33d year, the king died.

XIX. KING K'ING.

Note. Named Jin-chin.

2 His 1st year was *kwei-maou* (40th of cycle, = B.C. 617). In his 6th year, a comet entered the Great Bear (Northern Bushel); and the king died.

XX. KING K'WANG.

Note. Named Pan.

2 His 1st year was *ke-yew* (46th of cycle, = B.C. 611). In his 6th year, duke Ling of Tsin was killed by Chaou Ch'uen, who was then sent by Chaou Tun to Chow, to fetch the prince Hih-t'un, and raise him to the dukedom. The king died.

XXI. KING TING.

Note. Named Yu.

1 His 1st year was *yih-maou* (52d of cycle, = B.C. 605), the 1st year of duke Ching of
2 Tsin. In his 6th year, duke Ching of Tsin, with some of the northern hordes, attacked Ts'in, and captured a spy, whom they put to death in the market place of
3 Këang, and who came to life again six days after. In his 7th year, duke Ching

ly remarkable. The king appears on a level with the princes. 10 The text of this par. is evidently corrupt and defective. 11 This name is not elsewhere found. Ch'in-fung guesses that it should be 泂 or 向.

XXI. 1 In dis. Yung-yang, dep. K'ae-fung. 2 See the account of the affair in the Ch'un

書經

扈○八年、壬戌晉景公元年○十八年、齊國佐來獻玉磬紀公之甗○二十一年、王陟。

簡王

名夷、

元年、丙子○五年、晉景公卒○六年、辛巳晉厲公元年○十三年、晉厲公卒。楚共王會宋平公于湖陽○十四年、己丑晉悼公元年王陟。

靈王

名泄、

元年、庚寅○十四年、晉悼公卒○十五年、甲辰晉平公元年○二十七年、王陟。

景王

名貴、

元年、丁巳○十三年、春、有星出婺女。十月、晉平公卒○十四年、庚午晉昭公元年河水赤于龍門三里○十

4 of Tsin died in Hoo.[1] His 8th year was *jin-seuh*, the 1st year of duke King of Tsin.
5 In his 18th year, the Aid of the State of Ts'e came to present some musical stones
6 of gem, and the boiler *which Ts'e had taken* from the duke of Ke.[2] In his 21st
year, the king died.

XXII. KING KËEN.

Note. Named E.

2 His 1st year was *ping-tsze* (13th of cycle, = B.C. 584). In his 5th year, the
3 duke King of Tsin died. His 6th year was *sin-sze*, the 1st year of duke Le of Tsin.
4 In his 13th year, the duke Le of Tsin died. The king Kung of Ts'oo had a
5 meeting with the duke P'ing of Sung in Hoo-yang.[1] In his 14th year, *ke-ch'ow*,
the 1st year of duke Taou of Tsin, the king died.

XXIII. KING LING.

Note. Named Sëe.

2 His 1st year was *kang-yin* (27th of cycle, = B.C. 570). In his 14th year, the
3 duke Taou of Tsin died. His 15th year was *këä-shin*, the 1st year of the duke P'ing
4 of Tsin. In his 27th year, he died.

XXIV. KING KING.

Note. Named Kwei.

2 His 1st year was *ting-sze* (54th of cycle, = B.C. 543). In his 13th year, in the
spring, a star issued from the constellation Woo-neu.[1] In the 10th month, duke P'ing
3 of Tsin died. In his 14th year,—*kăng-woo*, the 1st year of duke Ch'aou of Tsin,—the

Ts'ew and Tso Chuen, under the 2d year of duke Ching.

XXII. 1 Probably in dep. of Keih-gan, Këang-se.

XXIV. 1 'The widow;'—four stars, about the middle of Capricorn.

九年、晉昭公卒。冬、十二月、桃杏花。○二十年、丙子晉頃公元年。○二十五年、晉頃公平王室亂、立敬王。

敬王

名丐

元年、壬午○八年、晉頃公卒○九年、庚寅晉定公元年○十四年、漢不見于天○二十六年、晉青虹見○二十八年、洛絕于周○三十六年、淇絕于舊衞○三十九年、晉城頓丘○四十三年、宋殺其大夫皇瑗于丹水之上、丹水壅不流○四十四年、王陟。

元王

名仁

元年、丙寅、晉定公卒○二年、丁卯晉出公元年○四年、於越滅吳○六年、晉澮絕于梁、丹水三日、

4 waters of the Ho at Lung-mun were red for 3 *le*. In his 19th year, duke Ch'aou of Tsin died. In the winter, in the 12th month, peach trees and almond trees were
5 in flower. His 20th year was the 1st year of the duke K'ing of Tsin. In his
6 25th year, duke K'ing of Tsin pacified the disorders of the royal House, and placed king King on the throne.

XXV. KING KING.

Note. Named K'ae.

2 His 1st year was *jin-woo* (19th of cycle, =B.C. 518). In his 8th year, duke
3 K'ing of Tsin died. His 9th year was *kăng-yin*, the 1st year of duke Ting of Tsin.
5 In his 14th year, the milky way was not visible in the sky. In his 26th year,
6 an azure rainbow was seen in Tsin. In his 28th year, the Loh was dry in Chow.
8 In his 36th year, the K'e was dry in Old Wei.[1] In his 39th year, Tsin walled
9 Tun-k'ew.[2] In his 43d year, *the duke of* Sung killed his great officer Hwang Yuen near the Tan-water, the course of which was stopt, so that it did not flow.[3]
10 In his 44th year, the king died.

XXVI. KING YUEN.

Note. Named Jin.

1 In his 1st year, which was *ping-yin* (3d of cycle, =B.C. 474), the duke Ting of
3 Tsin died. His 2d year was *ting-maou*, the 1st year of duke Ch'uh of Tsin. In his 4th
4 year, *the State of* Yu-yueh extinguished *that of* Woo.[1] In his 6th year, the course of the Kwei[2] of Tsin ceased at Lëang. The course of the Tan[3] water was interrupted,

XXV. 1 'Old Wei;'—*i. e.* Chaou-ko, formerly the capital of Wei, but now belonging to Tsin. 2 In dis. Ts'ing-fung, dep. Ta-ming, Chih-le. 3 There were no fewer than 7 Tan-waters. The one here was also called the P'ëen (派); on which see the dictionary.

XXVI. 1 These two States lay along the seaboard, embracing a considerable portion of Keang-soo and Chĕ-keang. Woo was the more northern of the two. 2 The Kwei took its rise from a mountain in the east of dis. of Këang, in the dep. of the same name, in Shan-se. 3 This took its rise in the dis. Kaou-p'ing, dep. Tsih-chow.

絕不流○七年、齊人鄭人伐衛。王陟。

貞定王

名介

元年、癸酉、於越徙都瑯琊○四年、十一月、於越子句踐卒、是爲菼執、次鹿郢立○六年、晉河絕于扈○七年、晉荀瑤城南梁。一本晉出公二十年

○十年、於越子鹿郢卒、不壽立○十一年、晉出公出奔齊○十二年、河水赤三日。晉荀瑤伐中山、取窮魚之邱○十三年、晉韓龐取盧氏城○十六年、晉出公二十二年○十七年、晉出公薨、乃立昭公之孫、是爲敬公○十八年、庚寅晉敬公元年○二十年、於越子不壽見殺、是爲盲姑、次朱句立○二十二年、楚滅蔡○二十四年、楚滅杞○二十八年、庚子晉敬公十一年。王陟。

5 and stopped for 3 days. In his 7th year, the people of Ts'e and of Ch'ing
attacked Wei. The king died.

XXVII. King Ching-ting.

Note. Named Këae.

1 In his 1st year, which was *kwei-yew* (10th of cycle, = B.C. 467), Yu-yueh removed its
2 capital to Lang-ya.[1] In his 4th year, in the 11th moath, Kow-ts'een, the viscount
of Yu-yueh, known as Tan-chih,[2] died, and was succeeded by *his son,* Luh-ch'ing.
4 In his 6th year, the Ho of Tsin stopt its course at Hoo. In his 7th year,
Seun Yaou of Tsin walled Nan-lëang.[3]

Note. One copy adds:—'In the 20th year of duke Ch'uh of Tsin.'

5 In his 10th year, Luh-ch'ing, the viscount of Yu-yueh died, and was succeeded by
7 Puh-show. In his 11th year, the duke Ch'uh of Tsin fled to Ts'e. In his
12th year, the waters of the Ho were red for three days. Seun Yaou smote Chung-
8 san,[4] and took the hill of K'ëung-yu.[5] In his 13th year, Han P'ang of Tsin
9 took the city of Loo She.[6] His 16th year was the 22d year of the duke Ch'uh of Tsin.
10 In his 17th year, the duke Ch'uh of Tsin died, when a grandson of duke Ch'aou,
11 known as duke King, was raised to the dukedom. His 18th year was the 1st year
12 of duke King of Tsin. In his 20th year, Puh-show, the viscount of Yu-yueh,
13 known as Mang-koo, was put to death, and was succeeded by Choo-kow. In
14 his 22d year, Ts'oo extinguished Ts'ae. In his 24th year, Ts'oo extinguished
15 K'e. In his 28th year, the 11th year of duke King of Tsin, the king died.

XXVII. 1 There was more than one Lang-ya. That here was in the dis. of Choo-shing, dep. Ts'ing-chow, Shan-tung. 2 Kin Le-ts'eang observes that Tan-chih are to be read together as one word, 'after the syllabic way of the west,' being the viscount's name in the speech of Yuĕ. 3 In the dep. of Joo, Ho-nan. 4 In dis. of T'ang, dep. Paou-ting. 5 Supposed to be a place on the river Lae (淶). 6 In the dis. of Loo-she, Shen Chow, Ho-nan.

考王

名嵬

元年、辛丑、敬公十二年、魏文侯立〇十年、楚滅
莒〇十一年、晉敬公卒〇十二年、壬子、晉幽
公柳元年、魯悼公卒〇十四年、魯季孫會晉
幽公于楚邱〇十五年、王陟。

威烈王

名午

元年、丙辰〇三年、晉大旱、地生鹽〇五
年、晉丹水出、反溉〇六年、晉大夫秦嬴、
賊幽公于高寢之上、魏文侯立幽公子
止〇七年、壬戌、晉烈公元年、趙獻子城泫氏、韓
武子都平陽〇八年、趙城平邑〇九年、
楚人伐我南鄙、至于上洛〇十一年、田
公子居思伐邯鄲、圍平邑。於越滅滕〇

XXVIII. KING K'AOU.

Note. Named Wei.

1 In his 1st year, which was *sin-ch'ow* (38th of cycle, =B.C. 439), the 12th year of the duke
2 King, the prince Wan of Wei came to his inheritance. In his 10th year, Ts'oo
4 extinguished Keu.[1] In his 11th year, duke King of Tsin died. In his 12th year,—*jin-tsze*, the 1st year of Lew, the duke Yew of Tsin,—the duke Taou of Loo died.
5 In his 14th year, Ke-sun of Loo had a meeting with the duke Yew of Tsin in
6 Ts'oo-k'ew.[2] In his 15th year, the king died.

XXIX. KING WEI-LËEH.

Note. Named Woo.

2 His 1st year was *ping-shin* (53d of cycle, =B.C. 424). In his 3d year, there
3 was a great drought in Tsin, and the ground produced salt. In his 5th year, the waters of the Tan of Tsin[1] left *their natural course*, and battled in an opposite
4 direction.[2] In his 6th year, Ts'in Ying, a great officer of Tsin, murdered duke Yew in the Lofty chamber, when prince Wan of Wei raised Che, the son of duke
5 Yew, to the dukedom. In his 7th year, which was *jin-seuh*, the 1st year of duke Lëë of Tsin, Hëen-tsze[3] of Chaou walled Heuen-she,[4] and Woo-tsze of Han,[5] made his
6 capital in P'ing-yang. In his 8th year, Chaou walled the city of P'ing.[6] In
7 his 9th year, the people of Ts'oo attacked our south border as far as Shang-loh.[7]
8 In his 11th year, Keu-sze,[8] a son of the ducal Head *of the House* of T'ëen,[9] attacked Han-tan,[10] and besieged the city of P'ing. Yu-yueh extinguished T'ang.[11]

XXVIII. 1 In the dis. of Ngan-k'ew, dep. Ts'ing-chow, Shan-tung. 2 Probably in dis. of Keu-yay, dep. Ts'aou-chow.

XXIX. 1 In dep. of Tsih-chow, Shan-se. 2 溉 here is taken as=擊. 3 The incidents referred to here are not clearly related elsewhere. I am strongly inclined to believe, with some critics, that for 大夫 we should read 夫人; so the meaning is that duke Yew was murdered by his wife, a lady of the House of Ts'in, in his chamber,—his own private and peculiar apartment. 4 The 子 here=officer or chief. 5 In dis. of Ling-ch'uen, dep. Tsih-chow. 6 In dis. of Ch'ang-loh, dep. Ts'ing-chow. 7 In Shang Chow, Shen-se. ——By '*our*' southern border is meant the southern border of Wei. Whereas the Annals have, from the accession of king P'ing, been those more particularly of Tsin, from the 1st year of king K'aou, the 1st also of prince Wan of Wei, they relate to that State. 8 This Keu-sze

十二年、於越子朱句伐郯、以郯子鴣歸○十四年、於越子朱句卒、子翳立○十六年、齊田盻及邯鄲韓舉戰于平邑、邯鄲之師敗逋、遂獲韓舉、取平邑新城○十七年、魏文侯伐秦、至鄭、還築汾陰郃陽。田悼子卒、田布殺其大夫公孫孫、公孫會以廩邱叛于趙、田布圍廩邱、翟角趙孔屑韓師救廩邱、及田布戰于龍澤、田師敗逋○十八年、王命韓景子、趙烈子、及我師伐齊、入長垣○二十三年、王命晉卿魏氏、趙氏、韓氏、爲諸侯○二十四年、王陟。

安王

名驕、

元年、庚辰○九年、晉烈公卒、子桓公立○十年、已丑 晉桓公頎元年 ○十五年、魏

9 In his 12th year, Choo-kow, the viscount of Yu-yueh, attacked T'an,[12] and carried
10 off captive its viscount Koo. In his 14th year, Choo-kow, viscount of Yu-yueh,
11 died, and was succeeded by his son E. In his 16th year, T'een P'an of Ts'e fought near P'ing with Han Keu of Han-tan, when the forces of Han-tan were defeated and put to flight, and *T'een P'an* took Han Keu prisoner, and captured the city of P'ing
12 and Sin-shing.[13] In his 17th year, the prince Wan of Wei invaded Ts'in as far as Ch'ing, and on his return built Fun-yin and Hoh-yang.[14] T'een Taou-tsze died; and T'een Poo put to death his great officer Kung-sun Sun. Kung-sun Hwuy took possession of Lin-k'ëw,[15] and rebelled against Chaou. T'een Poo laid siege to Lin-k'ew, to the rescue of which came Teih Këoh,[16] K'ung Sëë of Chaou, and the army of Han, who fought with Poo near the marsh of Lung, defeated him, and put him to flight.
13 In his 18th year, the king ordered the chiefs King of Han and Lëeh of Chaou, and our forces, to attack Ts'e; when we penetrated within the Long wall.[17] In his 23d year, the king conferred on the nobles of Tsin, each of the Heads of the Houses of
14 Wei, Chaou, and Han, the title of prince.[18] In his 24th year, the king died.

XXX. KING NGAN.

Note. Named Këaou.

1 His 1st year was *kang-shin* (17th of cycle, = B.C. 400). In his 9th year, duke
2 Lëeh of Tsin died, and was succeeded by his son, duke Hwan.[1] His 10th
3 year was *ke-ch'ow*, the 1st year of K'ing, the duke Hwan of Tsin. In his 15th year,

is not read of elsewhere. 9 At this time the family of T'ëen had engrossed the power of Ts'e, over which it asserted ere long sole authority. Still a prince of the House of Leu was nominally ruling, and we can only translate 田公 as I have done. 10 In dis. of Han-tan, dep. Kwang-p'ing, Chih-le. This was the chief city of the House—shortly, the State—of Chaou, one of the dismemberments of Tsin, and we shall find it often used for Chaou. 11 The dis. T'ăng, dep. Yen-chow. 12 Dis. of T'an-shing, dep. E-chow, Shan-tung. 13 Not clearly ascertained. 14 Both these places were in dep. of T'ung-chow, where there is still the dis. of Hŏ-yang. 汾 seems to be a mistake for 洛. 15 In the dis. of Yun-shing, dep. Ts'aou-chow. In most editions of the Annals, Lin-k'ew is said to have been held by Kung-sun Sun, which is evidently wrong. Hăng Ch'in-fung reads 會 instead of 孫. The events indicated in the par. cannot be clearly gathered from other sources. 16 Teih Keoh was of Wei. 17 This appears to have been a wall built by the chiefs of T'een, running from Mt. T'ae to Lang-ya. 18 Here was the imperial sanction to the extinction of the ancient State of Tsin, and the usurpations of the three Houses mentioned. See the note on Mencius, I., Pt. I., i. 1.

文侯卒。在位五十年、大風晝昏。晉太子喜出奔。○十六年、乙未魏武侯擊元年、封公子緩。○二十一年、韓滅鄭、哀侯入于鄭。○二十三年、於越遷于吳。○二十六年、王陟。魏城洛陽、及安邑王垣。七月、於越太子諸咎、弒其君翳。十月越人殺諸咎、越滑、吳人立孚錯枝爲君。

烈王

名喜、

元年丙午、魏公子緩如邯鄲以作難。邯鄲趙地名、於越大夫寺區、定越亂、立初無余、是爲莽安。○二年、秦胡蘇帥師伐韓、韓將韓襄、敗胡蘇于酸水。魏觴諸侯于范臺。晉桓公邑哀侯于鄭。韓山堅、賊其君哀侯。○六年、辛亥梁惠成王元年、韓共侯趙成侯、遷晉桓于屯留。以後更無

the prince Wan of Wei died, having enjoyed his dignity 50 years. There was great wind, and it was dusk at noon. He, the oldest son of the duke of Tsin, fled away. In
4 his 16th year, which was yih-wei, the 1st year of Keih, the prince Woo of Wei, one of the sons of Woo, called Hwan, was appointed to a government *away from the capital*.[2] In
5 his 21st year, Han extinguished *the State of* Ch'ing, and the prince Gae *of Han*
6 took possession of its capital. In his 23d year, Yu-yueh removed its capital to
7 Woo. In his 26th year, the king died. Wei walled Loh-yang,[3] Ngan-yih,[4]
8 and Wang-heuen.[5] In the 7th month, the oldest son of the viscount of Yu-yueh, named Choo-këw, murdered his ruler E.[6] In the 10th month, the people of Yueh put Choo-këw, *also called* Yueh-hwah, to death, and put Foo-ts'oh-che in his place.[7]

XXXI. KING LËEH.

Note. Named He.

1 In his 1st year, which was *ping-woo* (43d of cycle, = B.C. 374), Hwan of the ruling House of Wei went to Han-tan, to produce troubles. Han-tan is the name of a place in Chaou. Sze-k'eu, a great officer of Yu-yueh, settled the disorders of the State, and
2 placed Ts'oo-woo-yu, known as Mang-ngan, at its head. In his 2d year, Hoo Soo of Ts'in led a force against Han, and was defeated by Han Sëang, the general of Han, near the Swan-water.[1] Wei feasted the princes in the tower of Fan.[2] Duke Hwan of Tsin sanctioned the occupation of Ch'ing by prince Gae *of Han* as his
3 capital. Shan Këen of Han slew his ruler, the prince Gae. In his 6th year,—*sin-hae*, the 1st year of king Hwuy-ching of Lëang,—the princes Kung of Han and Ching of Chaou removed the duke Hwan of Tsin to T'wan-lew;[3] —after this, we have nothing more about the affairs of Tsin. Yen, the prince Ching of Chaou, and Joh, the prince E

XXX. 1 These were merely nominal dukes. 2 It is necessary to supplement the text here. The ruler of Wei sent away his son Hwan to avoid future troubles;—which, however, occurred in course of time. 3 Should, probably, be 汾陽, still the name of a dis., dep. Fun-chow. 4 In Këae Chow. 5 In Këang Chow. 6 His ruler was also his father. The thing is related confusedly, here and elsewhere. 7 I have translated here according to the suggestions or conjectures of Hăng Ch'in-fung, who thinks the text is corrupt or mutilated. The capital being now in Woo, 吳人=越人.

XXXI. 1 In the south of the dis. of Yen-tsin, dep. Wei-hwuy. 2 Hăng argues that this passage should come in under the 12th year of king Hëen. 3 In dis. of Ch'ang-tsze, dep. Loo-

書經

晉趙成侯偃、韓懿侯若、伐我葵城事鄭○七年、王陟。我師伐趙圍濁陽。齊田壽帥師伐我、圍觀、觀降。魏大夫王錯出奔韓。

顯王

名扁

元年、癸丑鄭城邢邱。自此韓改稱曰鄭秦子向命爲藍君○二年、河水赤于龍門、三日○三年、公子景賈帥師伐鄭、韓明戰于韓、我師敗逋○四年、夏四月、甲寅、徙都于大梁。王發逢忌之藪、以賜民。於越寺區弟思、弑其君莽安、次無顓立○五年、雨碧于郢、地忽長十丈有餘、高尺半○六年、我師伐邯鄲、取列人、我師伐邯鄲、取肥。雨黍于齊○七年、我與邯鄲榆次陽邑。王會鄭釐侯于巫沙○八年、入河水于圃田、又爲大溝、而引圃水、瑕陽

4 of Han, attacked our city of K'wei.[4] In his 7th year, the king died. Our forces attacked Chaou, and invested Ch'uh-yang.[5] T'ëen Show of Ts'e came with a force against us, and besieged Kwan,[6] which surrendered. Wang Ts'oh, a great officer of Wei, fled to Han.

XXXII. KING HËEN.

Note. Named Peen.

1 In his 1st year, which was *kwei-ch'ow* (50th of cycle, =B.C. 367), Ch'ing walled Hing-k'ew.[1]

Note. From this, the name of Han is exchanged for Ch'ing.

2 Tsze-hëang of Ts'in was appointed ruler of Lan.[2] In his 2d year, the waters
3 of the Ho were red for three days at Lung-mun. In his 3d year, King Këa of
our ruling House led a force against Ch'ing, when Han Ming fought with us in
4 Han,[3] and our forces were defeated and put to flight. In his 4th year, in
the summer, in the 4th month, on the day *këah-yin*, we removed our capital to Ta-
lëang.[4] Our king threw open his preserves in *the marsh of* Fung-ke for the benefit of
the people.[5] Sze, a younger brother of Sze-k'eu of Yu-yueh, murdered him,—Mang-
5 ngan,—his ruler, who was succeeded by Woo-chuen. In his 5th year, it rained *peih*
stones in Ch'ing.[6] Some ground there suddenly became longer by 100 cubits and more,
6 and higher by a cubit and a half. In his 6th year, our forces attacked Han-tan,
and took Lëeh-jin. They attacked it again, and took Fei.[8] It rained millet in Ts'e.
7 In his 7th year, we gave to Han-tan Yu-ts'ze[9] and Yang-yih.[9] Our king had
8 a meeting with the prince Le of Ch'ing at Woo-sha.[10] In his 8th year, we led
the waters of the Ho into *the marsh of* P'oo-t'een,[11] and also made great ditches to

ngan. 4 In dis. of Ho-nuy, dep. of Hwae-k'ing. 5 In dis. of Ch'ang-kŏ, dep. of Heu. It formerly belonged to Han, but had now, perhaps, passed into the possession of Chaou. 6 In dis. of Kwan-shing, dep. Tung-ch'ang.

XXXII. 1 In dis. of Ho-nuy, dep. Hwae-k'ing. 2 In dis. of Lan-t'ëen, dep. Se-ngan. 3 This battle was at a place called Puh-yang (濮陽), on the Puh-water, which had formerly belonged to Wei, but was now held by Han or Ch'ing. 4 Dis. city of Ts'ëang-foo, dep. K'ae-fung;—what is called K'ae-fung. 5 This marsh was not far from the capital. This was one of the measures for which king Hwuy took credit with Mencius. See Mencius, I. Bk. I., iii., 1. 6 In dis. of Këang-ling, dep. King-chow, Hoo-pih. 7 Probably in dis. of Kwang-p'ing, dep. Kwang-p'ing, Chih-le. 8 In dis. Fei-hëang, same dept. 9 Both in dep. T'ae-yuen, where we have still the dis. of Yu-ts'ze. 10 A place upon the river Tse. 11 In dis. of Chung-mow, dep. K'ae-fung. 12 The construction of this passage is not easy.

人自秦導岷山青衣水來歸〇
九年。秦師伐鄭、次于懷、城殷〇
十年、楚師出河水、以水長垣之
外。龍賈帥師築長城于西邊。鄭
取屯留尚子〇十一年、鄭釐侯、
使許息來致地、平邱、戶牖、首垣
諸邑、及鄭馳道、我取枳道、與鄭
鹿。王及鄭釐侯、盟于巫沙、以釋
宅陽之圍、歸釐于鄭〇十二年、
魯恭侯、宋桓侯、衞成侯、鄭釐侯、
來朝。於越子無顓卒、是爲菼蠋
卯、次無疆立〇十三年、邯鄲成
侯、會燕成侯于安邑〇十四年、
秦公孫壯伐鄭、圍焦城、不克。秦
公孫壯、帥師城上枳安陵山民。
邯鄲伐衞、取漆富邱、城之。齊師
及燕、戰于泃水、齊師遁〇十五
年、齊田期伐我東鄙、戰于桂陽、
我師敗逋。東周與鄭高都、鄭釐

lead off the waters of the marsh. The people of Hea-yang led the waters of the
9 Ts'ing-e of mount Min all the way from Ts'in to our State.[12] In his 9th year,
10 the forces of Ts'in attacked Ch'ing, camped in Hwae, and walled Yin.[13] In his
10th year, an army from Ts'oo led out the waters of the Ho to overflow the country outside the Long wall.[14] Lung Këa led a body of troops to build the great wall on
11 our western border.[15] Ch'ing took T'wan-lew and Shang-tsze.[16] In his 11th
year, the prince Le of Ch'ing sent Heu Shih to surrender to us the cities of P'ing-k'ew, Hoo-yew, and Show-yuen, with the country as far as the highway of Ch'ing; while we *ourselves* took Che-taou and Ch'ing-luh.[17] The king had an interview with the prince Le at Woo-sha, where he agreed to raise the siege of Tsih-yang, and
12 to restore *the city of* Le to Ch'ing.[17] In his 12th year, the princes Kung of Loo, Hwan of Sung, Ching of Wei, and Le of Ch'ing, all came to our court, *in acknowledgment of submission*. Woo-chuen, the viscount of Yu-yueh, known as
13 T'an-ch'uh-maou, died, and was succeeded by Woo-këang. In his 13th year, the prince Ching of Han-tan had an interview with the prince Ching of Yen in
14 Ngan-yih. In his 14th year, Kung sun Chwang of Ts'in attacked Ch'ing, and besieged the city of Tsëaou, without being able to take it. He then led his army, and walled Shang-che,[18] Ngan-ling,[19] and San-min. Han-tan attacked Wei, took the hill of Ts'ih-foo,[20] and walled it. The army of Ts'e fought with Yen near the Kow-
15 water,[21] and was put to flight. In his 15th year, T'ëen K'e of Ts'e attacked our eastern border, when a battle was fought at Kwei-yang,[22] in which our forces were

The Ts'ing-e flows from the dis. of Loo-san, dep. Ya-chow, Sze-ch'uen, and ultimately joins the Këang. Seu Tsing-san thinks the meaning is that the people of Hea-yang had performed the service described for Ts'in, and in this year came back to Wei. The meaning in the translation is more natural, and is preferred by Hăng Ch'in-fung. 13 In dis. Ho-nuy, dep. Hwae-k'ing. But the reading is not sure. 14 楚 is here evidently corrupt. Granting that there was in its dominions an erection called 'The Long Wall,' it was too remote from the Ho to allow of our supposing any such attempt on its part as is described. Hăng Ch'in-fung would substitute 韓 for 楚. 15 It is observed that this was the commencement of *the* Great Wall. 16 Shang-tsze is another name for Ch'ang-tsze, pres. name of the district to which T'wan-lew is referred. See above.

17 Wei was at this time pressing Han hard, and the surrenders here mentioned were made to obtain peace. 'The highway of Ch'ing' had formerly been called 'The general Road' (逵路). All the places spoken of are to be looked for in dep. of K'ae-fung. 18 In dis. of Tse-yuen, dep. Hwae-k'ing. 19 In dis. Yen-ling, dep. K'ae-fung. 20 In dis. of Ch'ang-yuen, dep. Ta-ming, Chih-le. 21 Flows thro' the dis. of P'ing-kuh, dep. Shun-t'ëen. 22 Kwei-yang,—prob.=the north of the Kwei river. I have not found any deter-

侯來朝中陽。宋景鼓、衛公孫倉、會齊師圍我襄陵。○十六年、王以韓師敗諸侯師于襄陵。齊侯使楚景舍來求成。邯鄲之師、敗我于桂陵。秦伐韓閼與、惠成王使趙口破之。不知是何年○十七年、燕伐趙、圍濁鹿、趙靈王及代人救濁鹿、敗燕師于勺。晉取玄武濩澤即雷澤舜漁處○十八年、齊築防以爲長城○十九年、王如衛、命公子南爲侯○二十年○二十一年、魏殷臣、趙公孫裒、伐燕、還取夏屋城曲逆○二十二年壬寅、孫何侵楚、入三戶郛。楚伐徐州○二十三年、魏章帥師、及鄭師伐楚、取上蔡。孫何取濦陽。秦孝公會諸侯于逢澤。絳中地坼西絕于汾○二十四年、魏

defeated and put to flight. The eastern Chow,[23] gave Kaou-too,[24] to Ch'ing. The prince Le of Ch'ing came to acknowledge submission *to our king* in Chung-yang. King Koo of Sung and Kung-sun Ts'ang of Wei united their forces with those of
16 Wei, to besiege our Sëang-ling.[25] In his 16th year, our king, with the army of Han, defeated the forces of *those* princes at Sëang-ling, when the prince of Ts'e sent King Shay of Ts'oo to come and ask for peace. The forces of Han-tan defeated us at Kwei-ling.[26] Ts'in attacked *the city* Oh-yu[27] of Han, when our king Hwuy-ching sent Chaou—and defeated Ts'in.

Note. It is not known under what year this last notice should be ranged.

17 In his 17th year, Yen attacked Chaou, and laid siege to Chuh-luh, which was saved by king Ling of Chaou, and the people of Tae, who defeated Yen at Choh.[28] Tsin took Yuen-woo and Hwoh-tsih.[29]

Note. Hwŏ-tsih is the same as Luy-tsih, the marsh of Luy, where Shun fished.

19 In his 18th year, Ts'e built a dyke as a part of its great wall.[30] In his 19th year, our king went to Wei, and commanded that Nan the son of its duke should
21 *only* be prince. His 20th year. In his 21st year, Yin Chin of Wei and Kung-sun Fow of Chaou attacked Yen; and on their return, took Hea-uh,[31] and
22 walled K'euh-yih.[31] In his 22d year, which was *jin-yin*,[32] Sun Ho invaded Ts'oo, and penetrated to the suburbs of San-hoo.[33] Ts'oo attacked Seu-chow.
23 In his 23d year, Chang of Wei, supported by the forces of Ch'ing, led an army against Ts'oo, and took Shang-ts'ae.[34] Sun Ho took Yin-yang.[35] The duke Heaou of Ts'in had an interview with several *of the* princes in Fung-tsih.[36] In Keang
24 there was a rent of the earth, extending west to the *river* Fun. In his 24th year,

mination of the place. 23 This was the emperor, now merely 'the shadow of a great name.' 24 In dis. Lŏ-yang, dept. Ho-nan. 25 In sub. dep. of Shuy, dep. Kwei-tih. 26 In dis. O-tsih, dep. Ts'aou-chow. 27 Dis. of Yu-shay, dep. Lëaou, Shan-se. 28 In dis. Wang-too, dep. Paou-ting. 29 Hwŏ-tsih,—the marsh of Hwŏ, but here the name of a city in the dis. of Yang-shing, dep. Tsih-chow. Yuen-woo must also be the name of a city. But this notice is evidently out of place.—What have we to do at this date with Tsin?

30 This wall of Ts'e has been mentioned before, under the 18th year of king Wei-lëë. It was intended as a protection against Ts'oo. 防, 'a dyke' or embankment against a stream, is used here for a wall, a defence against an enemy. 31 Both in the pres. Ting Chow, Chih-le. 32 Here is evidently a corruption of the text. *Jin-yin* was not the 22d year of king Hëen. Seu Wăn-tsing supposes we should read 王命. 33 Prob. in dis. of Nuy-hëang, dep. Nan-yang. 34 Still the name of a dis., dep. Joo-ning. 35 Belonging to Ts'oo, dis. of Lin-ying, Hëen Chow. 36 The marsh of Fung;—has occurred before.

敗韓馬陵○二十五年、○二十六年、穰疵帥師、及鄭孔夜戰于梁赫、鄭師敗逋、與齊田朌戰于馬陵○二十七年、五月齊田朌及宋人伐我東鄙、圍平陽。九月、秦衞鞅伐我西鄙。十月、邯鄲伐我北鄙。王攻衞鞅、我師敗逋○二十八年、城濟陽。秦封衞鞅于鄔、改名曰商○二十九年、邳遷于薛。三月爲大溝于北郛、以行圃田之水○三十年○三十一年、秦蘇胡帥師伐鄭、韓襄敗秦蘇胡于酸水不知何年附此○三十二年○三十三年、鄭威侯與邯鄲圍襄陵○三十四年、魏惠成王三十六年、改元、稱一年。王與諸侯會于徐州。於越子無疆伐楚○三十五年、楚吾得帥師、及秦伐鄭、圍綸氏不知何年附此○三十六年、楚圍齊於徐州、遂伐於越、殺無疆○三十七年○三十八年、龍賈及秦師、戰於雕陰。我師敗逋。王會鄭威侯于巫沙○三十九年、秦取我汾陰皮氏○四十年、○四十一年、秦歸我焦曲沃○四十二年、九

26 Wei defeated Han at Ma-ling.[37] His 25th year. In his 26th year, *our* Jang Ts'ze led a force, and fought with K'ung Yay of Ch'ing in Lëang-hih,[38] when the army of Ch'ing was defeated and put to flight. *Afterwards*, we fought with T'een
27 P'an at Ma-ling. In his 27th year, in the 5th month, T'een P'an of Ts'e, with the people of Sung, invaded our eastern border, and besieged P'ing-yang. In the 9th month, Yang of Wei, on the part of Ts'in, attacked our western border. In the 10th month, Han-tan attacked our northern border. Our king attacked Yang of Wei, when
28 our troops were defeated and put to flight. In his 28th year, we walled Tse-yang.[39] Ts'in invested Yang of Wei with Woo, the name of which was changed into Shang.[40]
29 In his 29th year, P'ei removed its capital to Sëeh.[41] In the 3rd month, we made
30 a great ditch in our northern suburbs, to carry off the waters of P'oo-t'ëen. His
31 30th year. In his 31st year, Soo Hoo of Ts'in led a force against Ch'ing, and was defeated by Sëang of Han near Swan-water.

Note. It is not known in what year this took place; but it is given here.

33 His 32d year. In his 33d year, the prince Wei of Ch'ing, with Han-tan,
34 besieged Sëang-ling. In his 34th year, Hwuy Ch'ing of Wei, this being his 36th year, changed the style of his reign, and called it his 1st year. The king had a meeting with *several* of the princes in Seu-chow. Woo-këang, the viscount of Yu-
35 yueh, attacked Ts'oo. In his 35th year, Woo-tih of Ts'oo led a force, and in conjunction with Tsin, attacked Ch'ing, and besieged Lun-she.[42]

Note. It is not known in what year this took place; but it is given here.

36 In his 36th year, Ts'oo besieged Ts'e in Seu-chow, and then attacked Yu-yueh, and
38 slew Woo-këang. His 37th year. In his 38th year, *our* Lung Këa fought with an army of Ts'in at Tëaou-yin,[43] when our forces were defeated, and put to flight.
39 Our king had a meeting with the prince Wei of Ch'ing at Woo-sha. In his 39th
41 year, Ts'in took from us Fung-yin[44] and P'e-she.[45] His 40th year. In his 41st year, Ts'in restored to us Tsëaou and K'euh-yuh. In his 42d year, the

37 *I.e.* 'the hill of Ma,' in dep. Ta-ming.
38 Near K'ae-fung. Perhaps we should translate—'fought at night with K'ung of Ch'ing.'
39 Dis. Tse-yang, dep. Tse-nan. 40 Shang Chow of Shen-se. 41 In dep. of T'äng, dep. Yen-chow. 42 In dis. Täng-fung, dep. Ho-nan. 43 In dis. of Kan-ts'euen, dep. Yen-ngan, Shen-se. 44 In dis. Yung-ho, dep.

書經

鼎淪泗沒于淵〇四十三年〇四十四年
〇四十五年、楚敗我襄陵〇四十六年〇
四十七年〇四十八年、王陟。

愼靚王

名定

元年、辛丑、秦取我曲沃平周〇二年。魏惠
成王薨〇三年、癸卯、今王元年〇四年〇
五年〇六年、鄭侯使韓辰歸晉陽、及向。二
月、城陽向、更名陽爲河雍、向爲高平。

隱王

史記作赧王名延
蓋赧隱聲相近

元年、丁未、十月鄭宣王來朝梁。燕子之殺
公子平、不克、齊師殺子之、醢其身〇二年、
齊地景長、長丈餘、高一尺。魏以張儀爲相
〇三年、韓明帥師、伐襄邱。秦王來見于蒲
坂關。四月、越王使公師隅來獻舟三百、箭

43 nine vases were sunk in the Sze, and lost in the deep. His 43d year. His
45 44th year. In his 45th year, Ts'oo defeated us at Seang-ling. His 46th
48 year. His 47th year. In his 48th year, the king died.

XXXIII. King Shin-tsing.

Note. Named Ting.

1 In his 1st year, which was *sin-ch'ow* (38th of cycle, = B.C. 319), Ts'in took from
2 us K'euh-yuh and P'ing-chow.[1] In his 2d year, king Hwuy-ching of Wei died.
4 His 3d year, *kwei-maou*, was the 1st year of our present king. His 4th year.
6 His 5th year. In his 6th year, the prince of Ch'ing sent Han Shin to restore to
us Tsin-yang and Hëang. In the 2d month, we walled Yang and Hëang, changing
the name of the former into Ho-yung,[2] and of the other into Kaou-p'ing.[3]

XXXIV. King Yin.

Note. The Historical Records call this sovereign king Nan, named Yen. This must be owing to the similarity of sound in Nan and Yin.

1 In his 1st year, which was *ting-we* (44th of cycle, = B.C. 313), in the 10th month,
king Seuen of Ch'ing came to acknowledge submission in our court of Lëang. Tsze-che
of Yen attempted to kill his ruler's *eldest* son P'ing, but without success. The army
2 of Ts'e killed Tsze-che, and made pickle of his body. In his 2d year, in the
country of Ts'e, *the ground where they measured* the length of the sun's shadow
lengthened more than ten cubits, and was elevated a cubit.[1] Wei made Chang E its
3 prime minister. In his 3d year, Han Ming led a force against Sëang-k'ew. The
king of Ts'in came, and had an interview with our king at the pass of P'oo-fan.[2] In
the 4th month, the king of Yueh sent Kung-sze Yu to present 300 boats, 5,000,000
arrows, with rhinoceros horns, and elephants' teeth.[3] In the 5th month, Chang E

P'oo-chow. 45 In dis. Ho-tsin, Këang Chow. 46 This statement is much debated. What could have taken the vases to the Sze? XXXIII. 1 In dis Këae-hëw, dep. Fun-chow, Shan-se. 2 In dis. Ho-nuy, dep. Hwae-k'ing. 3 In dis. Tse-yuen, dep. Hwae-k'ing.

XXXIV. 1 I suppose the meaning is what I have given. We had the account of a similar phenomenon before, tho' 景長 here occasions

五百萬、及犀角象齒。五月、張儀卒〇四年、翟章伐衛。魏敗趙將韓舉〇五年、洛入成周、山水大出〇六年、十月大霖雨、疾風、河水溢酸棗。楚庶章帥師來會我、次于襄邱〇七年、翟章救鄭、次于南屈此年末的〇八年、秦公孫爰帥師伐我皮氏、翟章帥師救皮氏、圍疾西風〇九年、城皮氏〇十年、〇十一年、〇十二年、秦拔我蒲坂、晉陽、封谷〇十三年、邯鄲命吏大夫奴遷于九原、將軍大夫適子代吏、皆貂服〇十四年、〇十五年、薛侯來會王于釜邱。楚入雍氏、楚人敗〇十六年、王與齊王會于韓。今王終二十年。

4 died. In his 4th year, Teih Chang attacked Wei. Wei defeated Han Keu, the
5 general of Chaou. In his 5th year, the Loh entered Ching-chow. Waters issued
6 from the hills abundantly. In the 6th year, there were great rains and violent winds. The waters of the Ho overflowed Swan-tsaou.[4] Shoo-chang of Ts'oo came with a force to have a meeting with us, and encamped at Sëang-k'ew. In his
7 7th year, Teih Chang came to the rescue of Ch'ing, and encamped at Nan-këuh.[5]
8 In his 8th year, Kung-sun Yuen of Ts'in led a force against our *city of* P'e-she, the siege of which was raised by the succour of Teih Chang. There was a violent
10 west wind. In his 9th year, we walled P'e-she. His 10th year. His
12 11th year. In his 12th year, Ts'in destroyed our P'oo-fan, Tsin-yang, and Fung-
13 kuh. In his 13th year, Han-tan ordered the Le, the great officers, and their servants, to remove to Këw-yuen.[6] The generals, great officers, sons of the 1st wife,
14 and recorders of Tae, all wore dresses of martens' skins. His 14th year. In
15 his 15th year, the prince of Sëeh came, and had a meeting with our king at Foo-k'ew.
16 The people of Ts'oo penetrated to Yung-she,[7] and were defeated. In his 16th year, our king had a meeting with the king of Ts'e in Han.

This chronicle was finished in the 20th year of our present king.

difficulty. 2 In dis. of Yung-tse, dep. P'oo-chow. 3 This notice must be out of place. Why should Yuĕ have sent these things to Wei, and how could it have sent the boats? 4 Yen-tsin, dep. Wei-hwuy. 5 In Sih Chow, Shan-se. 6 Very remote, north-west of the pres. Yu-lin, Shem-se, more than 700 *le*. The par. is obscure, and the event is not elsewhere clearly related. 7 In sub. dep. of Yu, dep. K'ae-fung.

3. The Reader has now had the opportunity of making himself acquainted with the Annals of the Bamboo Books. As a specimen of the manner in which Chinese scholars deliver their opinion against them, I may quote the language of Wang Ming-shing. He says:—'It may be assumed as certain that they are a compilation which was imposed on the world by Shuh Sih. The forced versions of events in them, with their additions and combinations, are not only not worthy to be believed, but they are not worthy to be discussed. In every age there have been men capable of such mischief and falsehood. What we have to depend on, is that, while the man of knowledge will

General remarks on the Annals.

altogether reject such books, he who may have doubts about so dealing with them will put them on one side. That is the proper way to pursue in studying them.'[1] I cannot by any means agree in so unfavourable a judgment. The sketch of the discovery of *all* the Bamboo books, given in the first paragraph of this chapter, is sufficient to prove that they were not fabricated by Shuh Sih, or by any other, at the beginning of the Tsin dynasty. They had, no doubt, been lying for nearly six centuries in the tomb in which they had been first deposited, when they were then brought anew to light.

Corruptions must be admitted in the Text. The causes of them.

At the same time, the usage to which the tablets were subjected on their discovery, led to the loss of some, the mutilation of others, and a general confusion of their order, which leave abundant room for the exercise of critical ingenuity on the Annals as we now have them. The haste, too, with which the ancient writing was deciphered and transcribed in the current characters of the age, gives occasion to doubt whether that important work could have been executed with the care which its difficulty required. I have called attention in the notes to some of the many transpositions of paragraphs of the present text, which are proposed by Hăng Ch'in-fung, the latest editor of the Annals, and an able and voluminous commentator on them. And there are other paragraphs, which he would cast out altogether, as having been incorporated with them from other portions of the mass of documents found in the tomb of king Sëang. What was called 'Fragmentary Sayings,'[2] or Narratives, of which there were eleven Books, appears to have supplied most of such additions. From the nature of the paragraphs supposed to be derived from this source, and of other fragments collected from various books where they appear as quotations from 'The Bamboo Books' (of which the account of the relations between Yaou and Shun, in note 8, p. 116, may be taken as an example), it appears that, besides the ore of the Annals, the tomb contained a large amount of dross, consisting of the wildest and most ridiculous legends and fables. From this material mainly were composed the long notes which we find interspersed through the Work, the more numerous and the more extravagant and absurd the more distant the times to which they

[1] 必是束晳僞譔………其穿鑿附會，不旦不足信，亦不足辯也，大約妄人何代蔑有，全賴有識者屏黜之，有疑則闕，方爲善讀書. See the 十七史商榷, on the 竹書紀年.

[2] 瑣語，十一篇.

relate. In what must be acknowledged as really belonging to the Annals, there are, moreover, absurdities enow:—entries of prodigious phenomena, showers of gold, monstrous animals, transformations of sex, &c. The reader is often reminded of the marvels in Livy's History. Even if we were sure that we had the chronicle as it was placed in the tomb of king Sëang, we should have to be wary in our treatment of its contents; and much more must we be so, considering that we have it—here with mutilations, and there with additions.

Different characters of different parts of the Annals. Probable date of the compilation of the earliest part.

With the reign of king P'ing, B.C. 769, there is a change in the character of the chronicle. From Hwang-te to that time, the Annals are those of the empire. The sovereigns of the different dynasties are the principal figures, in subordination to whose history the events of the various States are detailed. But from the date mentioned, the princes of Tsin become the principal figures; and they continue to be so, down to B.C. 439, when those of Wei, one of the three States, into which Tsin was dismembered, come into the foreground.[3] From B.C. 769, therefore, the Annals are those of the State of Tsin, composed by its Recorders, and digested subsequently into a more compendious form by one of the officers, bearing that title, of the State of Wei. The earlier chronicle, which is more important and of more general interest, was compiled, probably, about the time that the second portion was commenced, by one of the Recorders of Tsin, and kept in the archives of that State, as an appropriate introduction to its particular affairs.

Conclusion from the Annals against the earlier portions of the Shoo.

This view conducts us to an important conclusion respecting the Shoo. While denying, in the second chapter of these *prolegomena*, that in the older portions of the Shoo we have contemporaneous records of the events which they relate, I have given my opinion, on p. 66, that 'the Tribute of Yu' was, notwithstanding, among the written monuments of the dynasty of Shang, and passed over from its historiographers to those of the dynasty of Chow. I am not going now to retract or modify that opinion; but the fact that these Bamboo Annals contain so little of what the Shoo contains about Shun and Yu, appears to me to have a great significance. The accounts in the Shoo could not have been generally known, or, if known, not generally accepted, when the Annals were made. The character of the two Works is, indeed, different. The Annals give but the skeleton of the history of ancient China; the Shoo gives the flesh

書經

and drapery of the body at particular times. The one tells of events simply, in the fewest possible words; the other describes the scenes and all the attendant circumstances of those events. The numerous appointments, however, of officers by Shun, and the grand labours of Yu, all related in the Shoo, ought, according to the plan of the Work, to have their brief commemoration in the Annals. That they are not so corroborated, proves that they were not accepted as matter of veritable history by the author of our chronicle. I shall dwell somewhat more minutely on this point in the next paragraph. It may suffice here to point it out distinctly. In one respect, the compiler of the documents of the Shoo has shown more discrimination than the compiler of the Annals. He did well in not attempting to go back into the shadowy age before Yaou; but I submit it to my readers, whether the want of corroboration, in the Annals, of the Shoo's accounts of the government of Shun and the labours of Yu, does not bear out my view, that the latter are merely the devices of philosophical romance, intended to present the first beginnings of Chinese history on a grand scale, and under heroes of sagely wisdom and gigantic achievement, who should be a model to sovereigns in all future ages.

Differences between the Annals and the common views of Chinese History.

4. There are two points in which the Annals of the Bamboo Books differ seriously from the generally received views of Chinese history. The one is in the matter of chronology, the years assigned in the Annals to the period between king P'ing of the Chow dynasty and the beginning of Yaou's reign being fewer by 211 than those commonly allowed. The other is that insisted on immediately above,—the contrast between them and the Shoo, in regard to the government of Shun and the labours of Yu.

On the former of these points, something was said in the last chapter. The history of China is certainly shortened in these Annals by the amount just mentioned. The number of sovereigns which they assign is the same as that in the common chronology, excepting in the case of the Shang dynasty, where we have two additional reigns, which, however, would lengthen the period by only 6 years, if the schemes otherwise agreed. The names or titles of the sovereigns, moreover, are for the most part the same, as will be seen in the table subjoined to this chapter. Where the length of the reigns differs, the years assigned in the Annals will generally, though not always, be found to be fewer than in the common tables. We know nothing of the authority on which the duration of the greater number of the reigns is determined in the one scheme or in the other.

Neither the chronology of the Annals, nor that more commonly acknowledged, is supported by sufficient evidence; but it is right that I should point out here the grounds there are for believing that the numbers given in the text of the Annals have been corrupted. This corruption is two-fold.

The chronology of the Annals has been corrupted.

First, from the commencement of Yaou's reign downwards, the 1st year of the reigns is almost always indicated by the ordinary cycle characters. These, I maintain, were added after the discovery of the tablets;—not immediately, indeed, but by a gradual process, which was not completed until the Sung dynasty. In support of this view, I allege the following considerations:—

The cycle denominations of the reigns are spurious.

[i.] It has been shown, on pp. 82, 83, that, before the second Han dynasty, the cycle characters were employed to chronicle days, and not years. In coming to that conclusion, Chinese scholars have not taken these Annals into account. They reach it from a study of all the ancient books known previous to the Han dynasty. The Bamboo Books turn up in the last quarter of our 3d century; and if we are to receive the cycle dates as contemporaneous with the rest of this chronicle, then all the arguments for the conclusion go for nothing. Here was a practice, exceedingly elegant and convenient for marking dates, prevalent when the Annals were composed; and yet no other instance of its use can be adduced from any of the acknowledged early Writings, while Sze-ma Ts'ëen and the other scholars, who first erected chronology in China into a science, knew nothing of it. Only an extreme credulity will admit this.

[ii.] The reader will have observed that a good many dates do not form part of the text of the Annals, but are introduced as notes. Let me refer him particularly to those on p. 120. The inference from this is, that the addition of the cycle dates was not made complete at once, and that subsequent insertions to perfect the system, after the work had become the possession of the public, were thus made in notes;—it was not possible then to enter them in the text.

[iii.] The early citations, under the Tsin dynasty and even later, of passages from the Annals, do not contain these cycle dates. This fact is decisive on the point. Upon the 1st date, that of *ping-tsze*, marking the 1st year of Yaou's reign, Hung E-heuen, a scholar and officer of the present dynasty, in the reigns Këa-k'ing and Taou-kwang, observes:—'The various books which quote the Bamboo

書經

Annals, do so without the cycle dates. It is not till we come to the chapter on chronology in the Books of Suy that we find the 1st year of Yaou quoted as *king-tsze*. Subsequently [in the Sung dynasty], a comment to the "After Chronicle of the Loo Sze" quotes the year as *ping-tsze*,—as we find it in the present copies of the Annals.'[1]

[iv.] If the Annals on their discovery had contained the cycle dates, we could not have had the errors which are found in the concluding notes to the dynasties of Hea and Shang on the length of those periods. This consideration is equally decisive on the matter in hand. Those notes were of early origin. Now, the Hea dynasty began with the year *jin-tsze* and ended with *jin-seuh;* it lasted, therefore, 6 cycles and 11 years,=431, whereas the annotator says its duration was 471 years. The Shang dynasty began with the year *kwei-hae* and ended with *kăng-yin*, comprising 8 cycles and 28 years,=508, whereas the annotator assigns to it 496 years. The error in the one case amounts to 40 years, and in the other only to 12;—if the reigns had been marked at the date of those annotations, as they are now, there could not have been any error at all. We must conclude, on all these grounds, that the cycle names, used to denominate the first years of the reigns throughout the Annals, are an addition made subsequent to the period of their discovery.

The lengths of the reigns have also been altered.

Second, there is ground for thinking that the number of years assigned to the several reigns has also been altered in some cases. There are two considerations which make this probable.

[i.] Apart from the question of the cycle dates, the annotator had only to add together the years assigned to the different sovereigns, to obtain the length of the Shang dynasty. It is difficult to suppose that he should not have executed so simple an operation correctly.

[ii.] With the Hea dynasty the case is different. The addition of all the reigns, taking in the 40 years between Sëang and Shaou-k'ang, gives us only 403 years. About 40 years are dropt, being those of mourning, between the death of one sovereign and the 1st year of his successor. But now in the history of Shuh Sih, referred to on p. 106, it is stated that in the Bamboo Annals 'the years of the Hea dynasty were more than those of Shang.'[2] Attention is

[1] 洪頤煊曰,諸書引竹書紀年.皆無甲子紀年,惟隋書,律歷志,引竹書紀年,堯元年景子,路史後紀註引帝堯元年丙子,與今本同. Quoted by Hăng Ch'in-fung on the 1st year of Yaou.

[2] 夏年多殷.

called to the fact, as one of the peculiarities of the Annals, distinguishing them from the commonly accepted histories of those ancient times. Hăng Ch'in-fung observes upon it:—'When the history of Shuh Sih says that the dynasty of Hea was longer than Shang, whereas in our present copies Shang lasted longer than Hea, I do not know on what ground the statement rested.'[3] He might well say so. But the memoir of Shuh Sih affords us one of the most satisfactory testimonies to the discovery of the Bamboo Books, and the fullest account of the various documents comprehended under the name. The express statement to which I have called attention cannot be got rid of. And it obliges us to conclude, that not only were the cycle characters for years introduced into the Annals after their emergence from the tomb, but that the lengths of the reigns also were altered, so that the value of the chronicle, as a guide in chronology, is altogether taken away.

The Annals are more credible than the Shoo on the period of Yaou, Shun, and Yu.

The second point of difference, mentioned at the beginning of this paragraph, between these Annals and other histories of China, is to my mind of much greater importance. My own researches and reflections having led me to consider most of what we read in the Shoo about the well-ordered government of Shun and the labours of Yu, as the invention of later times, intended to exalt the characters and achievements of those worthies, and place them at the head of Chinese history on a pinnacle of more than human wisdom and greatness, I am pleased with the confirmation which my views receive from the accounts in the Annals. Let the reader compare them carefully with the documents in the Shoo, and I do not think he can fail to be struck with them as I have been. There are points of agreement between the two, as could not but be the case, the authors of them both, whatever they might add of their own, drawing on the same general stock of traditions. But the details of the Annals present the men and their doings in reasonable proportions. We see in them the chiefs of a growing tribe, and not the emperors of a vast and fully organized dominion.

[i.] The labours of Yu are confined in the Annals to the regulation of the Ho. Yaou assigns to him no greater task than Sëaou-k'ang, one of his own successors, has to assign, about 100 years later, to one of the princes of Shang. The same task has often been assigned to officers in subsequent times; might very well be assigned to one in

3 夏年多殷，今本仍殷多夏，不知此傳何所據而云也。

the present reign. Nothing is said of a far-extending, devastating deluge; nothing of Yu's operations on the mountains, or on the general face of the country, or on any river south of the Ho. Had it been in the accepted history of China, when these Annals were compiled, that Yu performed the more than Herculean tasks which the Shoo ascribes to him, it is unaccountable that they should not have mentioned them.

[ii.] The Shoo presents us with a picture of the government of Shun, which makes it appear to have been wonderfully complete. Not only has he Yu as his prime minister, and Kaou-yaou as minister of Crime; but he has his ministers of Instruction, Agriculture, Works, and Religion; his commissioner of Woods and Forests; his director of Music; his minister of Communication. According to the plan of the Annals, the appointment of all those ministers should have been mentioned; but the only names which they contain are those of Yu and Kaou-yaou. It is clear, that of the two-and-twenty great ministers by whom the Shun of the Shoo is surrounded, the greater number were the invention of speculators and dreamers of a later day, who, regardless of the laws of human progress, wished to place at the earliest period of their history a golden age and a magnificent empire, that should be the cynosure of men's eyes in all time.

If the space which I have given in these prolegomena to the Bamboo Annals appear excessive, the use to which I have turned them, to support the conclusions which I had been led on other grounds to form, must be my excuse. Even if it could be substantiated (which it cannot be), that the Annals were fabricated in the Tsin dynasty, the fact would remain, that their fabricator had taken a more reasonable view of the history of his country than any other of its writers has done, and indicated views, which, I venture to think, will be generally adopted by inquirers in the West. Those who come after me will probably assail the hitherto unchallenged accounts of ancient times with a bolder hand and on a more extensive scale than I have done in the present essay.

TABLE OF ANCIENT CHINESE CHRONOLOGY,

According to THE COMMON SCHEME, and to THE BAMBOO ANNALS.

Common Scheme. *Bamboo Annals.*

Emperor's Name.		Years of Reign.	1st Year on Reign.		1st Year of Reign.		Years of Reign.		Emperor's Name.
堯	Yaou,............	100	甲辰	B. C. 2,356	丙子	B. C. 2,145	100	Yaou,............	堯
舜	Shun,............	50	丙戌	„ 2,254	己未	„ 2,042	50	Shun,............	舜
	HEA DYNASTY, WITH TITLE OF 后 OR 王, SOVEREIGN.				HEA DYNASTY, WITH TITLE OF 帝, EMPEROR.				
禹	Yu................	8	丙子	B. C. 2,204	壬子	B. C. 1,989	8	Yu................	禹
啟	K'e..............	9	甲申	„ 2,196	癸亥	„ 1,978	16	K'e.	啟
太康	T'ae-k'ang.......	29	癸巳	„ 2,187	癸未	„ 1,957	4	T'ae-k'ang.......	太康
仲康	Chung-k'ang....	13	壬戌	„ 2,158	己丑	„ 1,951	7	Chung-k'ang....	仲康
相	Sëang............	27	乙亥	„ 2,145	戊戌	„ 1,942	28	Sëang............	相
	Usurpation......	40	壬寅	„ 2,118	丙寅	„ 1,914	40	Usuppation......	
少康	Sh'aou-k'ang....	22	壬午	„ 2,078	丙午	„ 1,874	21	Sh'aou-k'ang....	少康
杼	Ch'oo............	17	甲辰	„ 2,056	己巳	„ 1,851	17	Ch'oo............	杼
槐	Hwae............	26	辛酉	„ 2,039	戊子	„ 1,832	44	Fun..............	芬
芒	Mang............	18	丁亥	„ 2,013	壬申	„ 1,788	58	Mang............	芒
泄	Sëë..............	16	乙巳	„ 1,995	辛未	„ 1,729	25	Sëë..............	泄
不降	Puh-keang.......	59	辛酉	„ 1,979	己亥	„ 1,701	59	Puh-këang.......	不降
扃	Pëen..............	21	庚申	„ 1,920	戊戌	„ 1,642	18	Pëen..............	扃
廑	Kin...............	21	辛巳	„ 1,899	己未	„ 1,621	8	Kin...............	廑

TABLE OF ANCIENT CHINESE CHRONOLOGY.—*Continued.*

孔甲	K'ung-këă........	31	壬寅	B. C. 1,878
臯	Kaou..............	11	癸酉	„ 1,847
發	Fă................	19	甲申	„ 1,836
癸	Kwei..............	52	癸卯	„ 1,817

DYNASTY OF SHANG, WITH TITLE OF 王, OR KING.

湯	T'ang.............	13	乙未	B. C. 1,765
太甲	T'ae-këă..........	33	戊申	„ 1,752
沃丁	Yuh-ting.........	29	辛巳	„ 1,719
太康	T'ae-kang........	25	庚戌	„ 1,690
小甲	Sëaou-këă........	17	乙亥	„ 1,665
雍己	Yung-ke..........	12	壬辰	„ 1,648
太戊	T'ae-mow........	75	甲辰	„ 1,636
仲丁	Chung-ting......	13	己未	„ 1,561
外壬	Wae-jin..........	15	壬申	„ 1,548
河亶甲	Ho-t'an-këă.....	9	丁亥	„ 1,533
祖乙	Tsoo-yih.........	19	丙申	„ 1,524
祖辛	Tsoo-sin.........	16	乙卯	„ 1,505
沃甲	Yuh-këă..........	25	辛未	„ 1,489
祖丁	Tsoo-ting........	32	丙申	„ 1,464
南庚	Nan-kăng........	25	戊辰	„ 1,432

乙巳	B. C. 1,611	9	K'ung-këă........	孔甲
庚辰	„ 1,600	8	Haou.............	昊
乙酉	„ 1,595	7	Fă,...............	發
壬辰	„ 1,588	31	Kwei,............	癸

DYNASTY OF SHANG, WITH TITLE OF 王, OR KING.

癸亥	B. C. 1,557	12	T'ang.............	湯
乙亥	„ 1,545	2	Wae-ping........	外丙
丁丑	„ 1,543	4	Chung-jin........	仲壬
辛巳	„ 1,539	12	T'ae-këă.........	太甲
癸巳	„ 1,527	19	Yuh-ting.........	沃丁
壬子	„ 1,508	5	Sëaou-kăng......	小庚
丁巳	„ 1,503	17	Sëaou-këă.......	小甲
甲戌	„ 1,486	12	Yung-ke..........	雍己
丙戌	„ 1,474	75	T'ae-mow........	太戊
辛丑	„ 1,399	9	Chung-ting......	仲丁
庚戌	„ 1,390	10	Wae-jin..........	外壬
庚申	„ 1,380	9	Ho-t'an-këă.....	河亶甲
己巳	„ 1,371	19	Tsoo-yih.........	祖乙
戊子	„ 1,352	14	Tsoo-sin.........	祖辛
壬寅	„ 1,338	5	K'ae-këă.........	開甲
丁未	„ 1,333	9	Tsoo-ting........	祖丁
丙辰	„ 1,324	6	Nan-kăng........	南庚

TABLE OF ANCIENT CHINESE CHRONOLOGY.—*Continued.*

陽甲	Yang-këä........	7	癸巳	B. C. 1,407	壬戌	B. C. 1,318	4	Yang-këä........	陽甲
盤庚	Pwan-kăng......	28	庚子	„ 1,400	丙寅	„ 1,314	28	Pwan-kăng......	盤庚
小辛	Sëaou-sin.	21	戊辰	„ 1,372	甲午	„ 1,286	3	Sëaou-sin........	小辛
小乙	Sëaou-yih........	28	己丑	„ 1,351	丁酉	„ 1,283	10	Sëaou-yih........	小乙
武丁	Woo-ting.........	59	丁巳	„ 1,323	丁未	„ 1,273	59	Woo-ting..	武丁
祖庚	Tsoo-kăng.......	7	丙辰	„ 1,264	丙午	„ 1,214	11	Tsoo-kăng.	祖庚
祖甲	Tsoo-këä	33	癸亥	„ 1,257	丁巳	„ 1,203	33	Tsoo-këä	祖甲
廩辛	Lin-sin...........	6	丙申	„ 1,224	庚寅	„ 1,170	4	Fung-sin	馮辛
庚丁	Kăng-ting.......	21	壬寅	„ 1,218	甲午	„ 1,166	8	Kăng-ting........	庚丁
武乙	Woo-yih.........	4	癸亥	„ 1,197	壬寅	„ 1,158	35	Woo-yih..........	武乙
太丁	T'ae-ting........	3	丁卯	„ 1,193	丁丑	„ 1,123	18	Wăn-ting.........	文丁
帝乙	Te-yih	37	庚午	„ 1,190	庚寅	„ 1,110	9	Te-yih	帝乙
紂辛	Chow-sin.........	32	丁未	„ 1,153	己亥	„ 1,101	52	Te-sin.............	帝辛

DYNASTY OF CHOW, WITH TITLE OF 王, OR KING. — DYNASTY OF CHOW, WITH TITLE OF 王, OR KING.

武	Woo...............	7	己卯	B. C. 1,121	辛卯	B. C. 1,049	6	Woo...............	武
成	Ching.	37	丙戌	„ 1,114	丁酉	„ 1,043	37	Ching.	成
康	K'ang.	26	癸亥	„ 1,077	甲戌	„ 1,006	26	K'ang.	康
昭	Ch'aou...........	51	己丑	„ 1,051	庚子	„ 980	19	Ch'aou...........	昭
穆	Muh..............	55	庚辰	„ 1,000	己未	„ 961	55	Muh..............	穆
共	Kung.	12	乙亥	„ 945	甲寅	„ 906	12	Kung.............	共
懿	E..................	25	丁亥	„ 933	丙寅	„ 894	25	E..................	懿
孝	Hëaou...........	15	壬子	„ 908	辛卯	„ 869	9	Hëaou	孝

TABLE OF ANCIENT CHINESE CHRONOLOGY.—*Continued.*

夷	E.	16		丁卯	B. C.	893	庚子	B. C.	860		8	E.	夷
厲	Le.	51		癸未	"	877	戊申	"	852		26	Le.	厲
宣	Seuen.	46		甲戌	"	826	甲戌	"	861		46	Seuen.	宣
幽	Yëw	11		庚申	"	780	庚申	"	780		11	Yew	幽
平	P'ing.	51		辛未	"	769	辛未	"	769		51	P'ing.	平
桓	Hwan.	23		壬戌	"	718	壬戌	"	718		23	Hwan.	桓
莊	Chwang.	15		乙酉	"	695	乙酉	"	695		15	Chwang.	莊
僖	He.	5		庚子	"	680	庚子	"	680		5	Le.	釐
惠	Hwuy.	25		乙巳	"	675	乙巳	"	675		25	Hwuy.	惠
襄	Säang.	33		庚午	"	650	庚午	"	650		33	Säang.	襄
頃	K'ing.	6		癸卯	"	617	癸卯	"	617		6	K'ing.	頃
匡	K'wang.	6		己酉	"	611	己酉	"	611		6	K'wang.	匡
定	Ting.	21		乙卯	"	605	乙卯	"	605		21	Ting.	定
簡	Këen.	14		丙子	"	584	丙子	"	584		14	Këen.	簡
靈	Ling.	27		庚寅	"	570	庚寅	"	570		27	Ling.	靈
景	King.	25		丁巳	"	543	丁巳	"	543		25	King.	景
敬	King.	44		壬午	"	518	壬午	"	518		44	King.	敬
元	Yuen.	7		丙寅	"	474	丙寅	"	474		7	Yuen.	元
貞定	Ching-ting.	28		癸酉	"	467	癸酉	"	467		28	Ching-ting.	貞定
考	K'aou.	15		辛丑	"	439	辛丑	"	439		15	K'aou.	考
威烈	Wei-lëĕ.	24		丙辰	"	424	丙辰	"	424		24	Wei-lëĕ.	威烈
安	Ngan.	26		庚辰	"	400	庚辰	"	400		26	Ngan.	安

TABLE OF ANCIENT CHINESE CHRONOLOGY.—*Continued.*

烈	Lëě.	7		丙午	B. C,	374	丙午	B. C.	374		7	Lëě..............	烈
顯	Hëen............	48		癸丑	„	367	癸丑	„	367		48	Hëen............	顯
慎靚	Shin-tsing.	6		辛丑	„	319	辛丑	„	319		6	Shin-tsing.	慎靚
赧	Nan..............	29		丁未	„	313	丁未	„	313			Yin..............	隱

書經

CHAPTER V.

THE ANCIENT EMPIRE OF CHINA.

ENTRANCE OF THE CHINESE INTO CHINA. OTHER EARLY SETTLERS. GROWTH OF THE TRIBE INTO A NATION. RELIGION AND SUPERSTITIONS. FORM AND ISSUES OF THE GOVERNMENT.

First arrival of the Chinese tribe in its future home.

1. About two thousand years before our Christian era, the Chinese tribe first appeared in the country, where it has since increased so greatly. It then occupied a small extent of territory, on the east and north of the Ho,—the more southern portion of the present province of Shan-se. As its course continued to be directed to the east and south (though after it crossed the Ho, it proceeded to extend itself westwards as well), we may conclude that it had come into China from the north-west. Believing that we have in the 10th chapter of the Book of Genesis some hints, not to be called in question, of the way in which the whole earth was overspread by the families of the sons of Noah, I suppose that the family, or collection of families,—the tribe,—which has since grown into the most numerous of the nations, began to move eastwards, from the regions between the Black and Caspian seas, not long after the confusion of tongues. Going on, between the Altaic range of mountains on the north and the Tauric range, with its continuations, on the south, but keeping to the sunny and more attractive south as much as it could, the tribe found itself, at the time I have mentioned, between 40° and 45°, N. L., moving parallel with the Yellow River in the most northern portion of its course. It determined to follow the stream, turned south with it, and moved along its eastern bank, making settlements where the country promised most advantages, till it was stopped by the river ceasing its southward flow, and turning again towards the east. Thus the present Shan-se was the cradle of the Chinese empire. The tribe dwelt there for a brief space, consolidating its

strength under the rule of chieftains, who held their position by their personal qualities more than by any privileges of hereditary descent; and then gradually forced its way, east, west, and south, conflicting with the physical difficulties of the country, and prevailing over the opposition of ruder and less numerous neighbours.

Other early immigrant tribes.

2. Neighbours? Yes. The arrival of the Chinese tribe had been anticipated by others. These may have left the original seat of our infant race in the West earlier than it; or they may have left it at the same time. If they did so, the wave of emigration had broken in its progress. Some portions had separated from the main body, and found their way into the present province of Shen-se; and others, pursuing the same direction with it, but moving with more celerity, had then been pushed forward, by its advance, towards the sea, and subsequently along the sea-board, trying to make good a position for themselves among the mountains and along the streams of the country. We are not to suppose that the land was peopled by these tribes. They were not then living under any settled government, nor were they afterwards able to form a union of their forces, which could cope with the growing power of the larger people. They were scattered here and there over the region north of the Ho, gradually extending southward toward the Këang. Hostilities were constantly breaking out between them and the Chinese, over whom they might gain, once and again, temporary advantages. They increased in their degree, as well as those, and were far from being entirely subdued at the end of the Chow dynasty. Remnants of them still exist in a state of semi-independence in the south-western parts of the empire. Amid the struggles for the supreme power, which arose when one dynasty gave place to another, and the constant contentions, which prevailed among the States into which the empire was divided, the princes readily formed alliances with the chiefs of these wilder tribes. They were of great assistance to king Woo in his conflict with the last sovereign of the dynasty of Shang. In the speech which he delivered to his forces before the decisive battle in the wild of Muh, he addressed the 'men of Yung, Shuh, Këang, Maou, Wei, Loo, P'ang, and Poh,'[1] in addition to his own captains, and the rulers of friendly States. We are told that the wild tribes of the south and north, as well as the people of the great and flowery region, followed and were consenting with him.[2]

1 The Shoo, Pt. V., Bk. III., parr. 2—4. 2 Pt. V., Bk. IV., p. 6.

書經

Edward Biot calls attention to the designation of the early Chinese tribe or colony as 'the black-haired people,' saying that they were doubtless so named in opposition to the different or mixed colour of the hair of the indigenous race.[3] But I cannot admit any 'indigenous race,'—any race that did not come from the same original centre of our world's population as the Chinese themselves. The wild tribes of which we read in the Shoo and Chinese history, were, no doubt, black-haired, as all the remnants of them are at the present day. If we must seek an explanation for the name of 'black-haired people,' as given to the early Chinese, I should say that its origin was anterior to their entrance into China, and that it was employed to distinguish them from other descendants of Noah, from whom they separated, and who, while they journeyed to the east, moved in an opposite and westward direction.

Epithet of black-haired, applied to the early Chinese.

3. It was to their greater civilization, and the various elements of strength flowing from it, that the Chinese owed their superiority over other early settlers in the country. They were able, in virtue of this, to subdue the land and replenish it, while the ruder tribes were gradually pushed into corners, and finally were nearly all absorbed and lost in the prevailing race. The black-haired people brought with them habits of settled labour. Their wealth did not consist, like that of nomads, in their herds and flocks. Shun's governors of provinces in the Shoo are called Pastors or Herdsmen, and Mencius speaks of princes generally as 'Pastors of men;'[1] but pastoral allusions are very few in the literature of China. The people could never have been a tribe of shepherds. They displayed, immediately on their settlement, an acquaintance with the arts of agriculture and weaving. The cultivation of grain to obtain the staff of life, and of flax to supply clothing, at once received their attention. They knew also the value of the silk-worm, and planted the mulberry tree. The exchange of commodities—the practice of commerce on a small scale—was, moreover, early developed among them. It was long, indeed, before they had anything worthy of the name of a city; but fairs were established at convenient places, to which the people resorted from the farms and hamlets about, to barter their various wares.

Characteristics of the early Chinese which made them masters of the country.

In addition to the above endowments, the early Chinese possessed

3 See his Introduction to his translation of the Chow Le, p. 5.
1 Mencius, I., Pt. I., vi. 6.

the elements of intellectual culture. They had some acquaintance with astronomy, knew approximately the length of the year, and recognized the necessity of the practice of intercalation, to prevent the seasons, on a regard to which their processes of agriculture depended, from getting into disorder. They possessed also the elements of their present written characters. The stories current, and which are endorsed by statements in the later semi-classical books, about the invention of the characters by Ts'ang-këë, in the time of Hwang-te, are of no value; and it was not till the Chow dynasty, and the reign particularly of king Seuen (B. C. 825—779), that anything like a dictionary of them was attempted to be compiled;[2] but the original immigrants, I believe, brought with them the art of ideographic writing or engraving. It was rude and imperfect, but it was sufficient for the recording of simple observations of the stars in their courses, and the surface of the earth, and for the orders to be issued by the government of the time. As early as the beginning of the Shang dynasty, we find E Yin presenting a written memorial to his sovereign.[3]

The habits of the other settlers were probably more warlike than those of the Chinese; but their fury would exhaust itself in predatory raids. They were incapable of any united or persistent course of action. We cannot wonder that they were in the long run supplanted and absorbed by a race with the characteristics and advantages which I have pointed out.

4. The reader will understand that what I say in this paragraph on the religion and superstitions of the early Chinese will be based almost entirely on the documents of the Shoo; and that Book has to do with the sayings and doings of the emperors. By and by, we shall have before us all the testimony of all the classical writings, and be prepared to consider these important subjects, as they entered into and affected the life of the people at large. I would willingly have deferred any discussion of them at present; but it was necessary to my design in the present chapter to touch cursorily upon them.

Religion and superstition of the early Chinese.

The chiefs and rulers of the ancient Chinese were not without some considerable knowledge of God; but they were accustomed, on their first appearance in the country, if the earliest portions of the Shoo can be relied on at all, to worship other spiritual Beings as well.

2 See the Introduction to Morrison's Dictionary, and an Essay by Father De Mailla,—, Recherches sur les Characteres Chinois,'—the 7th of the essays, appended to Gaubil's Shoo-king.
3 The Shoo, Pt. IV, Bk. V., Pt. i., par. 1.

書經

There was no sacerdotal or priestly class among them; there were no revelations from Heaven to be studied and expounded. The chieftain was the priest for the tribe; the emperor, for the empire; the prince of a State, for his people; the father, for his family.

Shun had no sooner been designated by Yaou to the active duties of the government as co-emperor with him, than 'he offered a special sacrifice, but with the ordinary forms, to God; sacrificed purely to the six Honoured ones; offered their appropriate sacrifices to the rivers and hills; and extended his worship to the host of spirits.'[1] Subsequently, in the progresses which he is reported to have made to the different mountains where he met the princes of the several quarters of the empire, he always commenced his proceedings with them by 'presenting a burnt-offering to Heaven, and sacrificing in order to the hills and rivers.'[1] I do not refer to these passages as veritable records of what Shun actually did; but they are valuable, as being the ideas of the compilers of the Shoo of what he should have done in his supposed circumstances.

Their idea of God.

The name by which God was designated was *the Ruler*, and *the Supreme Ruler*, denoting emphatically His personality, supremacy, and unity. We find it constantly interchanged with the term *Heaven*, by which the ideas of supremacy and unity are equally conveyed, while that of personality is only indicated vaguely, and by an association of the mind. By God kings were supposed to reign, and princes were required to decree Justice. All were under law to Him, and bound to obey His will. Even on the inferior people He has conferred a moral sense, compliance with which would show their nature invariably right.[2] All powers that be are from Him. He raises one to the throne and puts down another. Obedience is sure to receive His blessing; disobedience, to be visited with His curse.[3] The business of kings is to rule in righteousness and benevolence, so that the people may be happy and good. They are to be an example to all in authority, and to the multitudes under them. Their highest achievement is to cause the people tranquilly to pursue the course which their moral nature would indicate and approve.[4] When they are doing wrong, God admonishes them by judgments,—storms, famine, and other calamities; if they persist in evil, sentence goes forth against them. The dominion is taken from them, and given to others more worthy of it.

1 The Canon of Shun, parr. 6, 8. 2 Pt. IV., Bk. III., par. 2. 3 Pt. IV., Bk. IV., p. 2; *et passim*. 4 Pt. IV., Bk. III., p. 2.

The duke of Chow, in his address on 'The Establishment of Government,'[5] gives a striking summary of the history of the empire down to his own time. Yu the Great, the founder of the Hea dynasty, 'sought for able men, to honour God.' But the way of Këë, the last of his line, was different. He employed cruel men;—and he had no successors. The empire was given to T'ang the Successful, who 'greatly administered the bright ordinances of God.' By and by, T'ang's throne came to Show, who was all violence, so that 'God sovereignly punished him.' The empire was transferred to the House of Chow, whose chiefs showed their fitness for the charge by 'finding out men, who would reverently serve God, and appointing them as presidents and chiefs of the people.'

It was the duty of all men to reverence and honour God, by obeying His law written in their hearts, and seeking His blessing in all their ways; but there was a solemn and national worship of Him, as ruling in nature and providence, which could only be performed by the emperor. It consisted of sacrifices, or offerings rather, and prayers. No image was formed of Him, as indeed the Chinese have never thought of fashioning a likeness of the Supreme.

Their worship of other spiritual Beings.

Who the 'six Honoured ones,' whom Shun sacrificed to next to God, were, is not known. In going on to worship the hills and rivers, and the host of spirits, he must have supposed that there were certain tutelary beings, who presided over the more conspicuous objects of nature, and its various processes. They were under God, and could do nothing, excepting as they were permitted and empowered by Him; but the worship of them was inconsistent with the truth that God demands to be recognized as 'He who worketh all in all,' and will allow no religious homage to be given to any but Himself. It must have always been the parent of many superstitions; and it paved the way for the pantheism which enters largely into the belief of the Chinese at the present day, and of which we find one of the earliest steps in the practice, which commenced with the Chow dynasty, of not only using the term *Heaven* as a synonym for God, but the combination *Heaven and Earth*.[6]

Worship of Ancestors.

There was also among the early Chinese the religious worship of their departed friends, which still continues to be observed by all classes from the emperor downward, and seems of all religious services to have the greatest hold

5 Pt V., Bk., XIX. 6 Pt. V., Bk. I., Pt. i., p. 3.

書經

upon the people. The title given in the Shoo to Shun's minister of Religion is that of 'Arranger of the Ancestral temple.'[7] The rule of Confucius, that 'parents, when dead, should be sacrificed to according to propriety,'[8] was, doubtless, in accordance with a practice which had come down from the earliest times of the nation.

The spirits of the departed were supposed to have a knowledge of the circumstances of their descendants, and to be able to affect them. Events of importance in a family were communicated to them before their shrines; many affairs of government were transacted in the ancestral temple. When Yaou demitted to Shun the business of the government, the ceremony took place in the temple of 'the accomplished ancestor,'[9] the individual to whom Yaou traced his possession of the supreme dignity; and while Yaou lived, Shun, on every return to the capital from his administrative progresses, offered a bullock before the shrine of the same personage.[10] In the same way, when Shun found the toils of government too heavy for him, and called Yu to share them, the ceremony took place in the temple of 'the spiritual ancestor,' the chief in the line of Shun's progenitors. In the remarkable narrative, which we have in the 6th of the Books of Chow, of the duke of Chow's praying for the recovery of his brother, king Woo, from a dangerous illness, and offering to die in his stead, he raises three altars,—to their father, grandfather, and great-grandfather; and prays to them, as having in heaven the charge of watching over their great descendant. When he has ascertained by divination that the king would recover, he declares that he had got Woo's tenure of the throne renewed by the three kings, who had thus consulted for a long futurity of their House.

Ancestors supposed to know the affairs of their descendants, and to be able to affect them.

This case shows us that the spirits of good kings were believed to be in heaven. A more general conclusion is derived from what we read in the 7th of the Books of Shang. The emperor Pwan-kăng, irritated by the opposition of the wealthy and powerful Houses to his measures, and their stirring up the people also to murmur against them, threatens them all with calamities to be sent down by his High ancestor, T'ang the Successful. He tells his ministers, that their ancestors and fathers, who had loyally served his predecessors, were now urgently entreating T'ang, in his spirit-state in heaven, to execute great punishments on their descendants. Not only, therefore,

7 Canon of Shun, p. 23. 8 Ana., II., v. 9 Canon of Shun, p. 4. 10 *Ib.*, p. 8.

did good sovereigns continue to have a happy existence in heaven; but their good ministers shared the happiness with them, and were somehow round about them, as they had been on earth, and took an interest in the progress of the concerns which had occupied them during their lifetime. Modern scholars, following in the wake of Confucius, to whom the future state of the departed was all wrapt in shadows, clouds, and darkness, say that the people of the Shang dynasty were very superstitious.—My object is to bring out the fact, and the nature of their superstition.

There is no hint in the Shoo nor elsewhere, so far as I am aware, of what became of bad emperors and bad ministers after death, nor, indeed, of the future fate of men generally. There is a heaven in the classical books of the Chinese; but there is no hell; and no purgatory. Their oracles are silent as to any doctrine of future rewards and punishments. Their exhortations to well-doing, and their warnings against evil, are all based on a reference to the will of God, and the certainty that in this life virtue will be rewarded and vice punished. 'Of the five happinesses, the first is long life; the second is riches; the third is soundness of body and serenity of mind; the fourth is the love of virtue; and the fifth is doing or receiving to the end the will of Heaven.'[11] There is no promise of rest or comfort beyond the grave. The virtuous man may live and die in suffering and disgrace;—let him be cheered. His posterity will reap the reward of his merits. Some one, sprung from his loins, will become wealthy, or attain to distinction. But if he should have no posterity:—it never occurred to any of the ancient sages to consider such a case.

No hint of the fate of the bad after death; and no inculcation of future rewards and punishments.

I will pass on from this paragraph with a reference to the subject of divination. Although the ancient Chinese can hardly be said to have had the knowledge of a future state, and were not curious to inquire about it, they were anxious to know about the wisdom and issues of their plans for the present life. For this purpose they had recourse to divination. The duke of Chow certainly practised it; and we have a regular staff of diviners among the officers of the Chow dynasty. Pwan-kăng practised it in the dynasty of Shang. And Shun did so also, if we can put faith in 'The Counsels of Yu.' The instruments of divination were the shell of the tortoise and the stalks of a certain grass or reed. By various caustic

Divination.

11 Pt. V., Bk. IV., par. 39.

書經

operations on the former, and by manipulations with the latter, it was supposed possible to ascertain the will of Heaven. I must refer the reader to what I have said about the practice on the seventh section of 'The Great Plan.' It is difficult to understand how the really great men of ancient China could have believed in it. One observation ascribed to Shun is worthy of remark. He tells Yu that 'divination, when fortunate, must not be repeated.'[12] I once saw a father and son divining after one of the fashions of the present day. They tossed the bamboo roots, which came down in the unlucky positions for a dozen times in succession. At last a lucky cast was made. They looked into each other's faces, laughed heartily, and rose up, delighted, from their knees. The divination was now successful, and they dared not repeat it!

Constitution and Issues of the ancient Chinese empire.

5. When the dignity of chief advanced to that of sovereign, and the Chinese tribe grew into a nation, the form which it assumed was that of a feudal empire. It was probably not until the Chow dynasty, that its constitution was fully developed and consolidated; as it is only then that we find in the last part of the Shoo, in the Ch'un Ts'ew, the Rites of Chow, and other Works of the period, materials to give a description of it. King Woo, we are told, after he had overthrown the last sovereign of the line of T'ang, arranged the orders of nobility into five, from duke downwards, and assigned the territories to them on a scale proportioned to their different ranks.[1] But at the beginning of the Hea dynasty, Yu conferred on the chiefs among his followers lands and surnames.[2] The feudal system grew in a great measure out of the necessities of the infant empire. As the ruder tribes were pushed backwards from its growing limits, they would the more fiercely endeavour to resist further encroachment. The measure was sometimes taken of removing them to other distant sites, according to the policy on which the kings of Assyria and Babylon dealt with Israel and Judah. So Shun is reported to have carried away the San-mëaou. But the Chinese empire was too young and insufficiently established itself to pursue this plan generally; and each State therefore was formed with a military constitution of its own, to defend the marches against the irruptions of the barbarians.

12 Pt. II., Bk. II., p. 18.

1 Pt. V., Bk. III., p. 10. 2 See the Tribute of Yu, Pt. ii., p. 16. I seem to see clearly now, that this paragraph and the six that follow should be interpreted of Yu the emperor, and not of him as a minister of Yaou.

What was designed to be the central State of the empire was the appanage of the sovereign himself, and was of the same dimensions as one of the largest of the feudatory States.[3] Over this he ruled like one of the other princes in their several dominions; and he received, likewise, a certain amount of revenue from all the rest of the country, while the nobles were bound to do him military service, whenever called upon. He maintained also a court of great ministers, who superintended the government of the whole empire. The princes were little kings within their own States, and had the power of life and death over the people. They practised the system of sub-infeudation; but their assignments of lands were required to have the imperial sanction.

It was the rule, under the Chow dynasty, that the princes should repair to the court every five years, to give an account of their administration of their governments; and that the emperor should make a general tour through the country every twelve years, to see for himself how they performed their duties. We read in the Canon of Shun, that he made a tour of inspection once in five years, and that the princes appeared at court during the intermediate four.[4] As the empire enlarged, the imperial progresses would naturally become less frequent. By this arrangement, it was endeavoured to maintain a uniformity of administration and customs throughout the States. The various ceremonies to be observed in marriages, funerals and mourning, hospitalities, religious worship, and the conduct of hostilities; the measures of capacity, length, weight, &c.; and the written characters of the language:—these were all determined by imperial prerogative. To innovate in them was a capital offence.[5]

The above is an imperfect outline of the feudal constitution of the ancient empire of China, which was far from enjoying peace and prosperity under it. According to the received accounts, the three dynasties of Hea, Shang, and Chow were established, one after another, by princes of great virtue and force of character, aided in each case by a minister of consummate ability and loyal devotion. Their successors invariably became feeble and worthless. After a few reigns, the imperial rule slackened. Throughout the States there came assumptions and oppressions, each prince doing what was right in his own eyes, without fear of his suzzerain. The wild tribes round

3 Here is the true account of the origin of the names Chung Kwoh (中國), 'Middle State,' and Chung Pang (中邦), 'Middle Region.' 4 Can. of Shun, par. 9. 5 See the Canon of Shun, par. 8; and the Doctrine of the Mean, Ch. XXVIII.

書經

about waxed bold, and kept up a constant excitement and terror by their incursions. Then would come an exceptional reign of more than usual vigour, and a partial order would be established; but the brief prosperity was only like a blink of sunshine in a day of gloom. In the Shoo, the termination of the dynasties of Hea and Shang is attributed to the wickedness of their last emperors. After a long array of feeble princes, there suddenly appear on the throne men of gigantic physical strength, the most daring insolence, and the wildest debaucheries, having neither piety nor ruth; and in contrast with them are princes, whose fathers have for several generations been attracting general notice by their righteousness and benevolence. When Heaven and men can no longer bear the iniquity of the tyrants, the standard of revolt is raised, and the empire speedily comes under a new rule. These accounts are, no doubt, much exaggerated and embellished. Këĕ and Show were not such monsters of vice, nor were T'ang and Woo such prodigies of virtue. More likely is it that the earlier dynasties died out like that of Chow, from sheer exhaustion, and that their last sovereigns were weaklings like king Nan, rather than tyrants.

The practice of polygamy, which was as old as Yaou, was a constant source of disorder. A favourite concubine plays a conspicuous part in the downfall of the dynasties of Shang and Hea, and another signalizes a calamitous epoch in that of Chow. In the various States, this system was ever giving rise to jealousies, factions, usurpations, and abominations which cannot be told. No nation where polygamy exists can long be prosperous or powerful; in a feudal empire its operation must be peculiarly disastrous.

The teachings of Confucius in the Chow dynasty could not arrest the progress of degeneracy and dissolution in a single State. His inculcation of the relations of society and the duties belonging to them had no power. His eulogies of the ancient sages were only the lighting up in the political firmament of so many suns which communicated no heat. Things waxed worse and worse. The pictures which Mencius draws of the misery of his times are frightful. What he auspiced from the doctrines and labours of his master never came to pass. The ancient feudal empire was extinguished, amid universal anarchy, in seas of blood.

The character and achievements of the founder of the Ts'in dynasty have not yet received from historians the attention which they deserve. He destroyed the feudal system of China, and introduced, in its room, the modern despotic empire, which has now lasted rather more than 2,000 years.

The Future.

6. The ancient empire of China passed away, having been weighed in the balances and found wanting. Under the system of rule, which superseded it, the boundaries of the empire have been greatly extended, and the people have grandly increased. Now, however, it would seem to be likewise approaching its end. It would not have endured so long, but for the position of the country at the extremity of the Asiatic continent. Its neighbours were not more powerful than itself, and they were less civilized. Once and again the country has been overrun and subjugated by the descendants of the tribes which disputed the possession of the soil with its earliest colonists; but it has subdued them in its turn by its greater cultivation, and they have become more Chinese than the Chinese themselves. The changes of dynasty since the end of the old empire or classical period have not been revolutions, but only substitutions of one set of rulers for another. In the present century new relations have arisen between China and the rest of the world. Christian nations of the West have come into rude contact with it. In vain did it fall back on the tradition of the 'Middle State,' and proclaim its right to their homage. The prestige of its greatness has vanished before a few ships of war, and the presence of a few thousand soldiers. The despotic empire will shortly pass away as the feudal one did, but with less 'hideous ruin and combustion.' It is needless to speculate on the probabilities of the future. God will be His own interpreter. China, separated from the rest of the world, and without the light of revelation, has played its part, and brought forth its lessons, which will not, I trust, be long without their fitting exposition. Whether it is to be a dependent or independent nation in the future, to be broken up or remain united, the first condition to happiness and prosperity is *humility* on the part of its scholars and rulers. Till they are brought to look at their own history and their sages, falsely so called, according to a true estimate, and to cease from their blind admiration of them, there is no hope for the country.

CHAPTER VI..

LIST OF THE PRINCIPAL WORKS WHICH HAVE BEEN CONSULTED IN THE PREPARATION OF THIS VOLUME.

SECTION I.

CHINESE WORKS.

1 In the 十三經註疏 (see proleg. to vol. I., p. 129) :—

[i.] 尙書註疏, containing the commentary of K'ung Gan-kwŏ, and the expositions made and collected by K'ung Ying-tă and other scholars of the T'ang dynasty (see above, p. 31).

[ii.] 爾雅註疏. This is a sort of dictionary to the classics. The comments are by Kwoh P'oh (郭璞), of the Tsin dynasty, and the exposition, glosses and disquisitions, by Hing Ping (邢昺), of the Sung. 爾雅 may be translated—'The Ready Rectifier.'

3 欽定書經傳說彙纂, 'Compilation and Digest of Comments and Remarks on the Shoo King. By imperial authority.' In 24 Books. I have generally in my notes called this Work—'Yung-ching's Shoo.' It was commanded in 1721, the 60th year of the period K'ang-he, the last year but one of the emperor Benevolent; and appeared with a preface by his son and successor, the emperor Pattern, in 1730, the 8th year of the period Yung-ching. Many great scholars were employed in its preparation and publication. They drew on the writings of 380 scholars,—from the Ts'in dynasty downwards. First, they give the commentary of Ts'ae Ch'in, the disciple of Choo He (see above, pp. 35, 36), interspersed with illustrative glosses. Then follows a collection of passages, confirmatory of Ts'ae's views, taken from their authorities (集說). This is often followed by an appendix of different views of the text, which are conceived to be worthy of examination (附錄). Occasionally, the editors give their own decisions, where they think they have more light than their predecessors had (案). There are maps and illustrations at the beginning, and a critical introduction; while the preface

ascribed to Confucius is given and commented on at the end. This Work may serve the student in lieu of many others. It is a monument of industry and research;—beyond all praise.

4 I have made frequent reference to the other imperial editions of the Classics, mentioned in proleg. to vol. I., p. 131; especially, to the 春秋傳說彙纂, which embodies the *Chuen* of Tso-k'ew, Kung-yang, and Kuh-lëang.

5 欽定周官義疏, 'Discussion of the Meaning of "The Officers of Chow." By imperial authority.' In 48 Books. This Work, with two others on the 'Rites,' was ordered in 1748, the 13th year of the reign K'ëen-lung, by the emperor Pure, to complete the labours of his father, the Benevolent, on the Classics. Edward Biot thus characterises it:—'It is worthy to be compared with the best Works executed in Europe on the different parts of the Bible. I should even say that it is superior to them, if I did not fear being accused of partiality' (Introduction to the Translation of 'The Rites of Chow,' p. xxxv.) The eulogy is deserved, so far as the exhaustive research is concerned. In range of thought and speculation, commentaries on the Chinese Classics and the Bible cannot be compared.

6 御製日講書經解義, 'Daily Lectures, Explaining the Meaning of the Shoo King. By imperial authority.' In 13 Books. It was ordered by the emperor Benevolent in 1,680. I have often quoted it under the name of 'The Daily Explanation.' It has all the qualities which I ascribed to the sister work on the Four Books, 'being full, perspicuous, and elegant.'

7 三山拙齋林先生尚書全解, 'A Complete Explanation of the Shang Shoo, by Lin Chueh-chae of San-shan.' In 40 Books. The author is commonly called Lin Che-k'e; and so I have generally referred to him. His commentary is very voluminous. It is older than Ts'ae Ch'in's, and, in my opinion, superior to it.

8 臨川吳澄今文尚書纂言, 'Digest of Remarks on the Modern Text of the Shang Shoo, by Woo Ching of Lin-ch'uen.' In 4 Books. See above, p. 36. This is *the* commentary of the Yuen dynasty;—terse and original.

9 陳氏師凱書蔡傳旁通, 'The Commentary of Ts'ae on the Shoo Illustrated by Ch'in Sze-k'ae.' Published in 6 Books, in 1,520. It is a commentary on Ts'ae Ch'in's commentary. The author draws his illustrations from 88 different Works.

10 王耕野先生讀書管見, 'Imperfect Views (views through a tube), by Wang Kăng-yay, of passages in the Shoo.' In 2 Books.

書經

This also is a Work of the Yuen dynasty. The views are sometimes very ingenious.

11 王魯齋書疑 'Wang Loo-chae's Doubts about the Shoo.' In 8 chapters. The author was of the Sung dynasty. He is also called Wang Pih (王柏).

12 The 皇清經解 (See proleg. to vol. I., p. 133) contains many Works on the Shoo, or on portions of it. Those which I have made most use of are:—

[i.] 尙書集註音疏 'Comments of himself and others on the Meaning of the Shang Shoo, and on the Pronunciation of the Characters.' The author was a Këang Shing (江聲), of the district of Woo, dep. Soo-chow. It occupies Books 390–403 of the collection;—a Work of vast learning, but dogmatical.

[ii.] 尙書後案, 'Latest Decisions on the Shang Shoo.' By Wang Ming-shing (王鳴盛), an acquaintance of Këang Shing, and of the same district. His main object is to bring out the views of Ch'ing K'ang-shing, as the true exposition of the Classic. The Work occupies Books 404–434, and took the author 34 years to complete it. His research is vast; but his object is one-sided.

[iii.] 尙書今古文註疏, 'The Shang Shoo in the Modern and Ancient Text Commented on and Discussed.' Books 735–773. The Work appeared in 1,815. The author was Sun Sing-yen (孫星衍), an officer of high employments. His 'ancient text' is not that current under this designation, but the variations from Fuh-săng's text, which are found in Ch'ing K'ang-shing and other Han writers.

[iv.] 古文尙書撰異, 'The various Readings of the Ancient Text of the Shang Shoo Collected.' Compiled in the reign of K'ëen-lung, by Twan Yuh-tsae, (段玉裁). The writer uses the designation 'Ancient Text' in the same way as Sun Sing-yen, Këang Shing, and Wang Ming-shing. Books 567–599.

[v.] 禹貢錐指, 'The Needle-touch applied to the Tribute of Yu.' Published in the reign K'ang-he, by Hoo Wei (胡渭). The author had previously been employed, with many other officers, in preparing a statistical account of the present empire. The Work cannot be too highly spoken of. Books 27–47.

17 古文尙書疏證, 'A Discussion of the Evidence for the Ancient Text of the Shang Shoo.' By Yen Jŏ-keu (閻若璩); published in

1,704. The Work is a vehement onset against the genuineness of the commonly received 'Ancient Text,' and was intended to establish, beyond contradiction, the views of Këang Shing, mentioned above. The plan of it extends to 128 Chapters or Arguments; but not a few of them are left blank. It is, no doubt, very able; but, as is said of it in the catalogue of the Imperial Libraries, it is too discursive, and full of repetitions.

18 Of the writings of Maou K'e-ling (proleg. to vol. I., p. 132), bearing on the Shoo, there are:—

[i.] 古文尚書冤詞, 'The Wrongs of the Ancient Text of the Shang Shoo.' In 8 Books. This was intended as an answer to the Work of Yen Jŏ-keu; and it seems to me that Maou has the best of the argument.

[ii.] 尚書廣聽錄, 'New Essays for Readers of the Shang Shoo.' In 5 Books. Throws light on several passages; but the author is too devoted to the commentary of Gan-kwŏ.

[iii.] 舜典補亡, 'The Lost Portions of the Canon of Shun Supplied.' In 1 Book.

21 洪範正論, 'A Correct Discussion of "The Great Plan."' In 5 Books. By Hoo Wei, whose Work on the Tribute of Yu has been noticed above. This is a fit companion to the other.

22 經義考, 'An Examination of the Explanations of the Classics.' In 300 Books. By Choo E-tsun (朱彝尊). It contains a list of all the Works on the Thirteen Classics, lost or preserved, of which the author's industry could ascertain the names, from the earliest time down to the present. Much information is given about many of them; and critical questions connected with them are discussed. The Work was ordered by the emperor Pure (K'ëen-lung), and appears with an Introduction from his pencil.

23 御纂朱子全書, 'A Grand Collection of the Views of Choo He. By imperial authority.' Compiled in 66 Books, in the 52d year of the period K'ang-ke. Books 33 and 34 are on the Shoo.

24 陔餘叢考, 'A Collection of Essays, written at intervals of Filial Duty.' In 43 Books. By Chaou Yih (趙翼). Published in 1,811.

25 Ma Twan-lin's General Examination of Records and Scholars; and its Continuation. See proleg. to vol. I., p. 134.

27 A Cyclopædia of Surnames, or Biographical Dictionary, &c. See proleg. to vol. I., p. 133.

28 The Complete Works of the Ten *Tsze*. See proleg. to vol. I., p. 133.

書經

29 The Philosopher Mih. See proleg. to vol. II., p. 126.

30 The Collected Writings of Han Ch'ang-le. See proleg. to vol. II., p. 126.

31 說文解字, 'Definitions and Explanations of Characters.' This is the dictionary of Heu Shin. See note on p. 1, above. It was not finished A.D. 100, as there stated, but in 121.

32 釋名, 'Explanation of Terms.' In 4 Books. By Lew He (劉熙), a scion of the imperial House of Han.

33 經典釋文, 'An Explanation of the Terms and Phrases in the Classics.' In 30 Books. By Luh Tih-ming (陸德明), of the T'ang dynasty. This is more a dissection of the Classics, excluding Mencius, and including Laou-tsze and Chwang-tsze, giving the sounds of characters, and the meaning of them single and in combination, than a dictionary. It is valuable as a repertory of ancient views.

34 御定康熙字典, 'The Dictionary of K'ang-he. By imperial anthority.' In 42 Books.

35 經韻集字析解
36 四書羣經字詁 } See below, pp. 731, 735.
37 經籍纂詁

38 國語, 'Narratives of the States.' In 21 Books. Belongs to the period of the 'Divided States' (列國); and is commonly ascribed to Tso-k'ew Ming. It is always published with comments by Wei Ch'aou of Woo (吳韋昭), one of the 'Three States.'

39 戰國策注, 'Plans of the Warring States, with Comments.' In 33 Books. Belongs to the closing period of the Chow dynasty. It was compiled in the first instance by a Kaou Yew (高誘), of the Han dynasty; but was subsequently largely supplemented.

40 呂氏春秋, 'The Ch'un Ts'ew of Leu.' In 26 Books. Ascribed to Leu Puh-wei, the prime minister of the founder of the Ts'in dynasty. It is tiresome to read, but is useful in studying the Classics.

41 吳越春秋, 'The Ch'un Ts'ew of Woo and Yuĕ.' See above, pp. 67, 68.

42 昭明文選,李善註, 'Selection of Compositions, by Ch'aou-m'ing, with the Comments of Le Shen.' In 30 Books. Ch'aou-ming is the posthumous title of the compiler, who was heir to the throne during the Lëang dynasty (A.D. 503–557), but died early. The compositions are of various kinds,—poems, letters, epitaphs, &c.; from Tsze-hëa downwards to the first Sung dynasty. The commentator was of the Sung dynasty.

43 二十四史, 'The Historians.' See proleg. to vol. I., p. 134.

44 御批通鑑輯覽,一百十六卷,附明唐桂二王本末三卷, 'Grand Collection of the General Mirror of History, in 116 Books; with a Supplement, containing the History of the two kings, T'ang and K'wei, in the Ming dynasty, in 3 Books. With the imperial views.' A noble work, commanded in the 33d year of K'ëen-lung.

45 資治通鑑綱目, 'General Mirror of History, in Heads and Particulars, for the Assistance of Government.' My copy is an edition of 1,807, in 101 Books, to the end of the Yuen dynasty.

46 綱鑑易知, 'The Mirror of History, made Easy.' In 29 Books. By Woo Sing-k'euen (吳乘權). Published in the 50th year of K'ang-he.

47 竹書紀年, 'The Annals of the Bamboo Books.' In 2 Books. By a Woo Kwan (吳琯), of the Ming dynasty. Contains only the Text, and comments of Shin Yŏ, of the Lëang dynasty.

48 竹書紀年統箋, 'The Bamboo Annals, with a Complete Annotation.' In 12 Books. By Seu Măn-tsing (徐文靖), of the present dynasty. There is also a preliminary Book, carrying the History up to Fuh-he; and one on the Evidences of the Annals. The Geographical notes are most valuable.

49 竹書紀年集證, 'The Bamboo Annals, with Collection of Evidences.' In 50 Books. Published in 1,813, by Ch'in Fung-hăng (陳逢衡). The Work is very carefully executed; by a most able scholar; and seems to exhaust the subject of the Annals.

50 十七史商榷, 'The Seventeen Histories Examined and Displayed.' In 100 Books. By Wang Ming-shing, whose 'Latest Decisions' on the Shoo King have been noticed above. Like that other Work, this also displays amazing research.

51 大清一統志, 'Statistical Account of the Empire under the Great Pure dynasty.' Commanded in the 29th year of the Emperor Pure, A. D. 1,762. In 424 Books.

52 歷代統紀表; and 歷代疆域表. See proleg. to vol. I., pp. 134, 135.

54 日知錄, 'Essays, the Fruit of Daily Acquisitions.' In 32 Books. By Koo Yen-woo (顧炎武). The essays are on a Multitude of subjects, likely to engage the attention of a Chinese Scholar. Published in 1695.

55 太平御覽. A monstrous miscellany, in 1,692 Books, prepared by order of the second emperor of the Sung dynasty, in 977. The

style of his reign at the time was 太平興國; hence the name of the Work.

56 格致鏡原. A miscellany of the present dynasty, inquiring into the origin of the things discussed. In 100 Books. By Ch'in Yuen-lung (陳元龍).

57 事物紀原, 'Record of the Origin of Affairs and Things.' A miscellany of the Sung dynasty. Contains 1,765 articles.

58 丹鉛總錄, 'Miscellaneous Pencillings.' In 27 Books. Originally published under the Ming dynasty in 1,524.

SECTION II.

TRANSLATIONS AND OTHER FOREIGN WORKS.

SEVERAL of the Works, mentioned in the prolegomena to vol. I, pp. 135, 136, have been frequently consulted by me. In addition to them, I have used:—

LE CHOU-KING, un des Livres Sacrés DES CHINOIS, qui renferm les Fondements de leur ancienne Histoire, les Principes des leur Gouvernement et de leur Morale, Traduit et enrichi des notes, par FEU LE P. GAUBIL, Missionaire a la Chine. Revu et corrige, &c., par M. DE GUIGNES, &c. A Paris, 1,770.

THE SHOO KING, or THE HISTORICAL CLASSIC, being the most ancient authentic Record of the Annals of the Chinese Empire, illustrated by LATER COMMENTATORS. Translated by W. H. MEDHURST, Sen. Shanghae, 1,846.

DESCRIPTION Geographique, Historique, Chronologique, Politique, et Physique, DE L'EMPIRE DE LA CHINE, et DE LA TARTARIE CHINOISE, &c., par le P. J. B. DU HALDE, de la Compagnie de JESUS. Tomes quatre; fol. A Paris, 1,735.

JOURNAL ASIATIQUE. Particularly the Numbers for April, May, and July, 1,836; for December, 1841; for May, and August and September, 1842.

LE TCHEOU-LI, ou RITES DES TCHEOU, Traduit pour la premiere fois du Chinois, par FEU EDOUARD BIOT. Tomes deux; 8vo. Paris, 1851.

A SKETCH OF CHINESE HISTORY, Ancient and Modern, &c. By the REV. CHARLES GUTZLAFF. Two volumes; 8vo. London, 1834.

MELANGES ASIATIQUES, &c.; par M. ABEL-REMUSAT. Tomes deux; 8vo. Paris, 1826.

EGYPT'S PLACE IN UNIVERSAL HISTORY. An Historical Investigation in five Books. By C. C. J. BARON BUNSEN, &c. Translated from the German by CHARLES H. COTTRELL, Esq., M.A. London, 1859.

ETUDES SUR L'ASTRONOMIE INDIENNE ET CHINOISE, par J. B. Biot. Paris, 1,862.

THE NUMERICAL RELATIONS OF THE POPULATION OF CHINA, DURING THE 4000 YEARS OF ITS HISTORICAL EXISTENCE, &c. By T. SACHAROFF, Member of the Imperial Russian Embassy in Peking. Translated into English, by the REV. W. LOBSCHEID. Hongkong, 1864.

PREFACE TO THE SHOO KING,

ATTRIBUTED TO CONFUCIUS.

書序

一節 昔在帝堯、聰明文思、光宅天下、將遜于位、讓于虞舜、作堯典。○

1 I. Anciently there was the emperor Yaou, all-informed, intelligent, accomplished, and thoughtful. His glory filled the empire. He wished to retire from the throne, and resign it to Shun of Yu. *Descriptive of all this*, there was made THE CANON OF YAOU.

PREFACE TO THE SHOO KING. This is often called 'The small Preface' (小序), to distinguish it from the larger one (大序 and 尙書序), prefixed by K'ung Gan-kwŏ to his commentary on the Classic. It was among the other monuments recovered from the wall of Confucius' house, which were given to Gan-kwŏ to be deciphered and edited. He incorporated it with the Work itself, breaking it up into its several parts, and prefixing to each Book the portion belonging to it. Other scholars of the Han dynasty edited it in its complete form at the end of the classic. It seems to me better, and to afford more facility of reference to it hereafter, to prefix it here as a whole.

If it were indeed the work of Confucius himself, its value would be inestimable; but its many peculiarities of style, as well as many inanities, forbid us to believe that it is the composition of the Sage. Ch'ing K'ang-shing (鄭康成), Ma Yung (馬融), and Wang Suh (王肅), those great scholars of the Han dynasty, all attribute it to him; and to justify them for doing so, Keang Shing (江聲) appeals to the words of Sze-ma Ts'een (in the 史記孔子世家):—'He prefaced the Records of the Shoo, from the times of T'ang and Yu, down to Muh of Ts'in, arranging their subjects in order (see 江徵君尙書集注音疏, on the 序). This, however, would only be evidence at the most that Confucius had made a preface to the Shoo King; but Ts'een's statement, in which he has been followed by many subsequent chroniclers, was grounded merely on the existence of this document itself, many parts of which he has introduced into his histories (本記), though not all in the order in which they are given by Gan-kwŏ. It is enough to admit with Choo He, that this preface was the production of some writer in the end of the Chow or the beginning of the Ts'in dynasty.—I shall discuss here but sparingly its various statements. That will be done, where necessary, in the introductions to the several Books.

二節 虞舜側微、堯聞之聰明、將使嗣位、歷試諸難、作舜典。〇三節 帝釐下土、方設居方、別生分類、作汨作、九共九篇、

2 II. Shun of Yu was in a low and undistinguished position, when Yaou heard of his comprehensive intelligence, and wishing to make him successor to his throne, made proof of him in many situations of difficulty. *With reference to this*, there was made THE CANON OF SHUN.

3 The emperor regulated the territories, appointing *nobles* to every quarter to reside in them, giving them surnames of distinction, and defining the constituents of each. *Descriptive of this*, there were made the KWUH TSŎ, the KEW KUNG, in nine Books, and the KAOU YU.

I. This paragraph contains, according to the arrangement of the Books which I have adopted, and for which I have elsewhere given the reasons, the notice of only one Book, the first part of the Classic. 'The Canon of Yaou' is edited as the first of 'The Books of Yu,' by those who divide the Work into four parts; and as the first of the Books of Yu-Hea, by those who make only three divisions. 遜 is best explained, with Gan-kwŏ, by 遁, 'to withdraw,' though the 于 following would more readily be translated by 'to' than by 'from.' Both Gan-kwŏ and Ch'ing K'ang-shing understand the 讓 as denoting not the resignation of the throne, but simply of the management of affairs. Yaou was still emperor till his death, and Shun was only his vice. 作堯典,—the 作 is at first referred to 堯 as its subject. The character must be so connected with the principal word in many sentences of the preface. The nominative here, however, is not 堯. In this and many other sentences the 作 is quite vague. We might take it intransitively.—'These subjects *form* the matter of the Canon of Yaou.' The 集傳 says—作者追言作書之意如此,'作 says retrospectively that to relate these matters was the object of the maker of the Book.'

II. This paragraph contains the prefatory notices to the Books of Yu, forming the second part of the classic, though it may be questioned whether another arrangement of some of them would not be more correct. This question has been touched on in the prolegomena. I have thought it sufficient to indicate my own view there, not wishing to make in this volume any further change in the ordinary arrangement of the Books, beyond what I have done in separating the 'Canon of Yaou' from the Books of Yu. Those amounted in Confucius' time, it will be seen, to 15, of which only 4 are now existing, allowing the genuineness of 'The Counsels of the great Yu,' and the right of the 'Canon of Shun' to stand by itself separate from the 'Canon of Yaou,' and of the 'Yih and Tseih' to be separate from the 'Counsels of Kaou Yaou.'

Not. 2. This is a very imperfect account of the Canon of Shun. 'The Book must contain the governmental affairs, first and last, of Shun's reign, and the preface would make it appear that the proof of him in various difficult situations was all the matter treated of!' (See the 集傳.) 3. I have translated after Gan-kwŏ. Keang Shing points differently, and gives quite another view of the meaning. K'ung Ying-tă (孔穎達), Gan-kwŏ's glossarist of the T'ang dynasty (flour. in greater part of the 7th cent.), says—'In such cases, where the text of the classic is lost, we shoot at the meaning in the dark. Gan-kwŏ interpreted according to the words, whether correctly or not cannot be known.' For this reason I have for the most part given the Chinese names of the lost Books, without attempting to translate them. 汨作 may mean 'The Achievements of Government.' 九共 has been translated 'The nine Laws' (共=法); and 'The nine Contributions' (共=給); also 'The nine Hills' (共=邱). All is uncertain. And so also is the meaning of 槀飫. 4. 帝

書經

槀飫。○四節皐陶矢厥謨、禹成厥功、帝舜申之、作大禹皐陶謨、益稷。○五節禹別九州、隨山濬川、任土作貢。○六節啟與有扈戰于甘之野、作甘誓。○七節太康失邦、昆弟五人、須于洛汭、作五子之歌。○八節羲和湎淫、廢時亂日、胤往征之、作胤征。○九節自契至于成

4 Kaou Yaou unfolded his counsels; Yu completed his work; the emperor Shun made him go on to further statements. *With reference to these things*, there were made THE COUNSELS OF THE GREAT YU, and OF KAOU YAOU, and the YIH AND TSEIH.

5 III. Yu marked out the nine provinces; followed the course of the hills, and deepened the rivers; defined the imposts on the land, and the articles of tribute.

6 K'e fought with the prince of Hoo in the wilderness of Kan, when he made THE SPEECH AT KAN.

7 T'ae-k'ang lost his kingdom; and his five brothers waited for him on the north of the Lŏ, and made THE SONGS OF THE FIVE SONS.

8 He and Ho, sunk in wine and excess, neglected the ordering of the seasons, and allowed the days to get into confusion. *The prince of* Yin went to punish them. *Descriptive of this*, there was made THE PUNITIVE EXPEDITION OF YIN.

9 IV. From Sëë to T'ang the Successful, there were eight changes

舜申之,—申之, 'repeated it,' has reference probably to the commencing words of the 'Yih and Tseih'—'The emperor said, Come Yu, you *likewise* must have admirable words.'

III. The four Books in this paragraph constitute the third part of the Shoo. The genuineness of two is questioned; but it is remarkable that Confucius found among the relics of the Hea dynasty, B.C. 2204—1766, only these four documents worthy to be transmitted to posterity. And, indeed, the first of them should belong more properly to the Books of Yu.

Not. 5. 任土作貢,—all the commentators make the 任土 auxiliary to the other characters, ='he assigned the tribute according to the nature and productions of the land.' It seems much simpler to take them as I have done; comp. Mencius, IV. Pt. I. xiv. 3. It will be seen the notice is defective, and wants 作禹貢 at the end. Ch'ing has called attention to this. 6. The style of this notice is considered sufficient evidence that the preface is not the work of Confucius, who would never have represented the emperor and his vassal as if they were fighting on equal terms—與 ... 戰. (See the 集傳.) 7. 須=待. In the text of the Book we have 徯. 8. 胤=胤侯.

IV. This paragraph, containing 23 prefatory notices, enumerates 31 different documents, in

湯、八遷、湯始居亳、從先王居、作帝告、釐沃。○(十節)湯征諸侯。葛伯不祀、湯始征之、作湯征。○(十一節)伊尹去亳適夏、既醜有夏、復歸于亳、入自北門、乃遇汝鳩汝方、作汝鳩、汝方。○(十二節)伊尹相湯伐桀、升自陑、遂與桀戰于鳴條之野、作湯誓。○(十三節)湯既勝夏、欲遷其社、不可、作夏社、疑至、

of the capital. T'ang at first dwelt in Pŏ, choosing the residence of the first sovereign of his House. *Then* were made the TE KUH, and the LE YUH.

10 When T'ang chastised the various princes, the chief of Kŏ was not offering the *appointed* sacrifices. T'ang began his work by chastising him, and *then* was made the T'ANG CHING.

11 E Yin went from Pŏ to Hea. Indignant with the sovereign of Hea, he returned to Pŏ; and as he entered by the north gate, met with Joo Kew and Joo Fang. *With reference to this* were made the JOO KEW, and the JOO FANG.

12 E Yin acted as minister to T'ang, and *advised* him to attack Këĕ. They went up from E, and fought with him in the wilderness of Ming-t'eaou. *Then* was made THE SPEECH OF T'ANG.

13 When T'ang had vanquished Hea, he wished to change its sacrifices to the Spirit of the land, but concluded not to do so. *With*

40 Books or chapters (篇), all belonging to the dynasty of Shang, B.C. 1765—1122. More than half of them are lost,—the first five, classed by some among the Books of the Hea dyn.; the 7th, 8th, 9th, and 10th; the 13th, 15th, and 16th; the 19th to the 25th; and the 29th. Of the remaining 11 documents, there are only 5 whose genuineness is unchallenged. The order in which they stand, moreover, differs somewhat in the preface as edited by Gan-kwŏ, and as approved by Ch'ing and other Han scholars. Not. 9. Sëĕ, from whom the sovereigns of the Shang dyn. traced their descent, was a son of the emp. 嚳, B.C. 2432; whose capital was Pŏ. Kuh must therefore be the 先王, and probably the 帝 in 帝告, 'The Announcement to the Emperor.' 釐沃 may mean 'The Rule of Enrichment.' 10. 湯征, 'The Punitive Expedition of T'ang.' See Men. III. Pt. II. v., and the Announcement of Chung Hwuy. Those who object to the Shoo King of Gan-kwŏ say that the passages of Hwuy's Announcement referred to are a remnant of this Book; see the 尙書後案 of 王鳴盛, *in loc.* 11. Joo Kew and Joo Fang, we may suppose, were two ministers, with whom E Yin discussed the affairs of Hea. 13. 欲遷其社,—

臣扈。○十四節夏師敗績、湯遂從之、遂伐三朡、俘厥寶玉、誼伯仲伯作典寶。○十五節湯歸自夏、至于大坰、仲虺作誥。○十六節湯既黜夏命、復歸于亳、作湯誥。○十七節咎單作明居。○十八節成湯既沒、太甲元年、伊尹作伊訓、肆命、祖后。○十九節太甲既立、不明、伊尹放諸桐、三年、復歸于亳、思庸、伊尹作太

reference to this there were made the HEA SHAY, the E-CHE, and the CHIN-HOO.

14 The army of Hea being entirely defeated, T'ang followed it and smote San-tsung, where he captured the precious relics and gems. *Then* E-pih and Chung-pih made the TEEN PAOU.

15 When T'ang was returning from *the conquest of* Hea, he came to Ta-këung, where Chung Hwuy made his ANNOUNCEMENT.

16 T'ang having made an end of the sovereignty of Hea, returned to Pŏ, and made THE ANNOUNCEMENT OF T'ANG.

17 Kaou Shen made the MING KEU.

18 After the death of T'ang, in the first year of T'ae-këă, E Yin made THE INSTRUCTIONS OF E, the SZE MING, and the TSOO HOW.

19 When T'ae-këă was declared emperor, he proved unintelligent, and E Yin placed him in T'ung. After three years he returned with him to Pŏ, when he had applied his thoughts to the course of duty. *Then* E Yin made the T'AE-KEA in three Books.

see Mencius, VII. Pt. II. xiv.; he says that the spirits of the land and grain might be changed on proof of their powerlessness, and much more might this be done on a change of dynasty as here. But whom was T'ang to place as the 土神, or human assessor of such, in room of 句龍, to whom the Hea dyn. had sacrificed? None was found so worthy. E-che and Chin-hoo were probably two ministers consulted on the subject. 14. The precious relics and gems were those of the Hea emperors. 17. This notice contains no prefatory explanation. There are three others of the same kind. Kaou Shen (so the name is to be read), according to Ma Yung, was minister of Works. 明居 may mean—'Illustration of the way to settle the people.' 18. 肆命,—'A declaration of the way of Heaven,' acc. to Gan-kwŏ; 'of the principles of government,' acc. to Ch'ing. 祖后, 'the past (=deceased) sovereign;' referring to T'ang. 19. 思庸,—王天與 (of the Yuen dyn.) says, 'Gan-kwŏ explains this phrase by *he thought of the constant course of duty;* Soo by *he thought of using the words of E Yin;* Ch'in says, The meaning is expressed by Mencius (V. Pt. I. vi. 5.),—*He repented of his errors, was*

甲三篇。○廿節伊尹作咸有一
德。○廿一節沃丁既葬伊尹于亳、
咎單遂訓伊尹事、作沃丁。
○廿二節伊陟相太戊、亳有祥、桑
穀共生于朝、伊陟贊于巫
咸、作咸乂四篇。○太戊廿三節贊
于伊陟、作伊陟、原命。○仲廿四節
丁遷于囂、作仲丁。○河廿五節亶
甲居相、作河亶甲。○祖廿六節乙
圮于耿、作祖乙。○盤廿七節庚五

20 E Yin made the BOTH POSSESSED PURE VIRTUE.

21 When Yuh-ting had buried E Yin in Pŏ, Kaou Shen then set forth as lessons the doings of E Yin, and there was made the YUH-TING.

22 E Chih was prime minister to T'ae-mow, when ominous appearances showed themselves in Pŏ. A mulberry tree and a stalk of grain grew up in the court. E Chih told Woo Heen, who made the HEEN E in four Books.

23 T'ae-mow spoke on the subject with E Chih, and there were made the E CHIH and the YUEN MING.

24 Chung-ting removed to Heaou, and there was made the CHUNG-TING.

25 Ho-tan-këă lived in Sëang, and there was made the HO-TAN-KEA.

26 Tsoo-yih met with calamity in Kăng, and there was made the TSOO-YIH.

contrite, and reformed himself, &c.' See the 集說, *in loc.*

22. Gan-kwŏ and others refer to 桑穀 as two trees growing together. But how can a stalk of grain be represented as a *tree?* The 說文 dict. explains the char. 楮 by 穀 (? radical 木 and not 禾), a kind of mulberry tree from the bark of which both cloth and paper can be made. We should probably read 穀桑, one tree. Gan-Kwŏ says it attained its size in seven days; Sze-ma Ts'een says one evening! 巫咸,—see the 君奭, par. 7. Ch'ing interprets 'Heen. the Wizard,'—perhaps correctly. Ts'een says that Hëen made the Hëen E, and the T'ae-mow. 23. These last Books are supposed to have been on the subject of the ominous appearances. 原 is the name of a minister. 原命, 'The charge to Yuen.'

25. Ho-tan-këă,—this is always given as the name of the 10th emp. of the Shang dyn. We may suppose that Tan-këă was his name, and that 河 was added, because of some peculiar troubles in his time with that river. See the 通鑑綱目. 26. 圮,—'was overthrown;' *i.e.*, the capital was injured by an

遷、將治亳殷、民咨胥怨、作盤庚三篇。○廿八節高宗夢得說、使百工營求諸野、得諸傅巖、作說命三篇。○廿九節高宗祭成湯、有飛雉升鼎耳而雊、祖己訓諸王、作高宗彤日、高宗之訓。○卅節殷始咎周、周人乘黎、祖伊恐、奔告于受、作西伯戡黎。○卅一節殷既錯天命、微子作誥父師少師。○卅二節惟十有一年、武王伐殷、一

27 Pwan-kang made the fifth change *of capital*, and was about to repair Pŏ, *as the cradle of the* Yin. The people murmured, and expressed themselves resentfully to one another. *With reference to this* there was made the PWAN-KANG, in three Books.

28 Kaou-tsung dreamed that he got Yuĕ, and made all his officers institute a search for him in the wilds. He was found in Foo-yen; and THE CHARGE TO YUE was made in three Books.

29 Kaou-tsung was sacrificing to T'ang the Successful, when a pheasant flew up, and lighted on the ear of a tripod, aud *there* crowed. Tsoo Ke lessoned the king *on the subject*, and made THE DAY OF THE SUPPLEMENTARY SACRIFICE OF KAOU TSUNG, and THE INSTRUCTIONS TO KAOU-TSUNG.

30 Yin's first hatred of Chow was occasioned by its conquest of Le. Tsoo E, full of dread, hurried off to inform Show. *With reference to this* there was made THE CHIEF OF THE WEST'S CONQUEST OF LE.

31 Yin having cast away the sovereignty conferred on it by Heaven, the count of Wei made his announcement to the Grand Tutor and to the Junior Tutor.

32 V. In the eleventh year king Woo smote *the power of* Yin. On the mow-woo day of the first month, his army crossed *the Ho at* Măng-

overflow of the Ho. 31. 錯—廢, as in Ana. II. xix.

V. This paragraph contains notices—such as they are—of 38 different documents in 40 Books, extending from the commencement of the Chow dynasty, B.C. 1121, to 626, within little more than half a century of the birth of Confucius. Eight of the pieces have been lost,—the 5th, 7th, 11th, 12th, 22d, 23d, 27th, and 28th; there are two documents, very different in themselves, each of which claims to be 'The Great Speech;'

月戊午、師渡孟津、作泰誓三篇。○ 卅三節 武王戎車三百兩、虎賁三百人、與受戰于牧野、作牧誓。○ 卅四節 武王伐殷、往伐歸獸、識其政事、作武成。○ 卅五節 武王勝殷、殺受、立武庚、以箕子歸、作洪範。○ 卅六節 武王既勝殷、邦諸侯、班宗彝、作

tsin. *Descriptive of this* there was made THE GREAT SPEECH, in three Books.

33 King Woo, with three hundred chariots of war and three hundred tiger-like officers, fought with Show in the wilderness of Muh. *Then* was made THE SPEECH AT MUH.

34 King Woo smote Yin; and the narrative of his proceeding to the attack, and of his return and sending his animals back to their pastures, with his governmental measures, form THE COMPLETION OF THE WAR.

35 When king Woo conquered Yin, he slew Show, and appointed Woo-kăng *over the original principality of his House.* He got the count of Ke to return to him, and THE GREAT PLAN was made.

36 When king Woo had conquered Yin, he appointed the princes of

of the remaining Books 20 are of unchallenged genuineness, and the claim of the others—the 3d, 6th, 10th, 21st, 26th, 29th, 32d, 33d, and 34th—has been discussed and mainly admitted in the prolegg. These 29 Books form now the fifth and last part of the classic.

Not. 33. 戎車三百兩,虎賁三百人,—see Men. VII. Pt. II. iv. 4, where this sentence appears to be quoted; but with 革 for 戎, and 三千人 for 三百人. Sze-ma Ts'een also has 三千人. Mih Teih, again, says that Woo had 100 chariots, and of 虎賁之卒四百人(明鬼篇下). Another enumeration of 800 is also found. See the 尚書今古文注疏 of 孫星衍, *in loc.* The 虎賁 are said to have been 勇士, 'brave officers,'—centurions, according to Gan-kwŏ (百夫長). 35. 殺受—Show, like another Sardanapalus, burned himself, after being defeated by king Woo. Woo-kăng was Show's son, called also 祿父 (or 甫), was appointed by Woo over the original seat of his House to continue the sacrifices to his forefathers.

箕子—the 大傳, or Introduction to the Shoo, ascribed to 伏生, says, that 'the count of Ke on being delivered from the prison, where he had been put by Show, unwilling to become a servant to the new dynasty, fled to Corea, of which Woo appointed him ruler. This obliged him to come to Woo's court to acknowledge the king's grace, and then it was that the Great Plan was obtained from him.' Others say that his appointment to Corea was a subsequent affair. If so, another explanation of 以箕子歸 has to be sought. 36. 分器, may be translated—'The apportioned vessels.'

邦=封. It was one of the ceremonies of investiture, to give part of the furniture of the ancestral temple of the emperor to the deputed noble. See the 集說. The principles

分器。○西旅獻獒、太保作卅七篇旅獒。○巢伯來朝、芮伯作卅八篇旅巢命。○武王有疾、周公卅九篇作金縢。○武王崩、三監及四十篇淮夷叛、周公相成王、將黜殷、作大誥。○成王既黜殷四十一命、殺武庚、命微子啟代殷後、作微子之命。○唐叔得四十二禾、異畝同穎、獻諸天子、王命唐叔歸周公于東、作歸

the various States, and distributed among them the vessels of the ancestral temple. *With reference to this* there was made the FUN K'E.

37 The western people of Le made an offering of some of their hounds; and the Grand Guardian made THE HOUNDS OF LE.

38 The chief of Ch'aou having come to court, the chief of Juy made and impressed on him the CH'AOU MING.

39 King Woo was sick, which gave occasion to the Book about the duke of Chow's making THE METAL-BOUND CASKET.

40 When king Woo had deceased, the three overseers and the wild tribes of the Hwae rebelled. The duke of Chow acted as prime minister to king Ching; and having purposed to make an end of *the House of* Yin, he made THE GREAT ANNOUNCEMENT.

41 King Ching having made an end of the appointment *in favour of the House* of Yin, and put Woo-kăng to death, he appointed K'e, the count of Wei, to take the place of the descendants of Yin. *Descriptive of this*, there was made THE CHARGE TO THE COUNT OF WEI.

42 The *king's* uncle, the prince of T'ang, found a head of grain, *two stalks* in different plats of ground growing into one ear, and presented it to the king. The king ordered him to send it to the duke of Chow in the east. *Upon this* was made the KWEI HO.

on which the distribution to different ranks was made were probably described in this last Book.

38. There is a difficulty in translating 旅. In not. 43 it = 陳, by which it is explained here; the diff. arises from its following 作. It is said in the 集說,—'The chief of Juy, being in the court and making the royal charge, must have been a minister of the king. 旅 = 陳. He set forth the majesty and virtue of the king to charge Ch'aou.' 42. The prince of T'ang was a younger brother of king Ching's mother; see the 左傳, 昭十五年.

禾。○四十三周公既得命禾、旅天子之命、作嘉禾。○四十四成王既伐管叔蔡叔、以殷餘民封康叔、作康誥、酒誥、梓材。○四十五成王在豐、欲宅洛邑、使召公先相宅、作召誥。○四十六召公既相宅、周公往營成周、使來告卜、作洛誥。○四十七成周既成、遷殷頑民、周公以王命

43 The duke of Chow having got the *king's* charge and the head of grain, set forth the charge of the sovereign, and made the KEA HO.

44 The king Ching having smitten his uncles, the prince of Kwan and the prince of Ts'ae, invested his uncle K'ang with the rule of the remnant of Yin. *With reference to this,* there were made THE ANNOUNCEMENT TO K'ANG, THE ANNOUNCEMENT ABOUT WINE, and THE GOOD MATERIALS.

45 King Ching being in Fung, and wishing to fix his residence at Lŏ, sent the duke of Shaou in the first place to survey the localities. *Then* was made THE ANNOUNCEMENT OF SHAOU.

46 The duke of Shaou having surveyed the localities, the duke of Chow went to build *this capital, called* Ching Chow, and sent a messenger to announce the divinations. With reference to this THE ANNOUNCEMENT ABOUT LO was made.

47 When Ching Chow was completed, the obstinate people of Yin were removed to it. The duke of Chow announced to them the royal will, and THE NUMEROUS OFFICERS was made.

Gan-kwŏ takes 畝=壟, 'a hillock,' 'a mound;' so Choo He elsewhere explains the character. Ch'ing makes it = 苗, 'a stalk of growing grain,' which gives a good meaning, but made for the occasion. 孫星衍 would explain it by 母=拇, 'toes or fingers,' a figurative expression for the grain dividing from the stalk. 歸禾 may be translated 'The Presented Grain.' 43. 得命和,—Ch'ing says, 受王歸己禾之命與其禾, *i.e.*, we must understand an *and* between 命 and 和. Both Keang Shing and Sun Sing-k'een quote here, from 韓詩外傳, what appears to be another legendary account of this head of grain, formed by *three* stalks growing through a mulberry tree into one ear of marvellous size. I have only got the copy of the 外傳, given in the 三代兩漢遺書, which does not contain the legend; and, indeed, Keang Shing quotes from the 外傳五. A similar account is found in 劉向's 說苑, 辨物篇. 嘉禾 = 'The Excellent Grain.' 44. It is disput-

告、作多士。○四十八周公作無逸。○四十九召公爲保、周公爲師、相成王爲左右、召公不悅、周公作君奭。○五十蔡叔既沒、王命蔡仲踐諸侯位、作蔡仲之命。○五十一成王東伐淮夷、遂踐奄、作成王政。○五十二成王既踐奄、將遷其君於蒲姑、周公告召公、作將蒲姑。○五十三成王歸自奄、在宗周誥庶邦、作多方。○五十四周公作立政。○五十五成王既黜殷命、滅淮夷、還

48 The duke of Chow made the Book AGAINST LUXURIOUS EASE.

49 The duke of Shaou acted as guardian and the duke of Chow as tutor, the chief ministers of king Ching, his left and right-hand men. The duke of Shaou was not pleased, and the duke of Chow made the PRINCE SHIH.

50 After the death of the king's uncle, the prince of Ts'ae, the king appointed his son Chung to take his place as a prince *of the empire*. Then was made the CHARGE TO CHANG OF TS'AE.

51 King Ching having smitten the wild tribes of the Hwae on the east, at the same time extinguished the State of Yen. Then was made the CHING WANG CHING.

52 King Ching having extinguished Yen, and wishing to remove its ruler to P'oo-koo, the duke of Chow announced the thing to the duke of Shaou. *Then* there was made the TSEANG P'OO-KOO.

53 King Ching returned from Yen, and in the honoured city of Chow made an announcement to all the States. *Then* was made THE NUMEROUS REGIONS.

54 The duke of Chow made THE ESTABLISHMENT OF GOVERNMENT.

ed whether 康叔 should be translated—'his uncle, K'ang,' or 'his uncle, the prince of K'ang.' See on the 康誥. 51. 踐 is taken by Ch'ing as = 翦, and explained by 滅. Gan-kwŏ agrees with him. 成王政 probably meant 'The Completion of the Royal Government.' See the 集說. 52. 蒲姑 is 薄姑 in the 史記. I don't know

歸在豐、作周官。○五十六成王既伐
東夷、肅愼來賀、王俾榮伯作
賄肅愼之命。○五十七周公在豐將
沒、欲葬成周、公薨、成王葬于
畢、告周公、作亳姑。○五十八周公既
沒、命君陳分正東郊成周、作
君陳。○五十九成王將崩、命召公畢
公率諸侯、相康王、作顧命。○
六十節康王既尸天子、遂誥諸侯作

55 When king Ching had made an end of the House of Yin, and extinguished the wild tribes of the Hwae, he returned to Fung; and there was made THE OFFICERS OF CHOW.

56 When king Ching had smitten the wild tribes of the east, Suh-shin came to congratulate him. The king made the chief of Yung make the CHARGE TO SUH-SHIN, and gave him presents also.

57 The duke of Chow was in Fung and about to die. He wished to be buried in Ching chow; but on his decease king Ching buried him in Peih, making an announcement at his bier. Then was made the PO-KOO.

58 After the death of the duke of Chow, Keun-ch'in was commissioned with the separate charge of regulating Ching Chow in the eastern border, and there was made the KEUN-CH'IN.

59 When king Ching was about to die, he ordered the duke of Shaou and the duke of Peih to take the lead of all the princes to support

what to make of the 將. 56. 肅 (*al.* 息) 愼 was the chief of some wild tribe; but in what quarter is disputed. See the 左傳, 昭九年; and the 國語, 五卷, 魯語, 下. The 集傳 explains 賄 by 賂, and adds that the writer does not understand the meaning of the word as used here. In the passage of the 國語 just referred to, it is said that king Woo made the wild tribes bring the productions and articles of their countries as tribute (以其方賄來貢). Suh-shin, I suppose, had brought such, and the emperor ordered him gifts in return. 57. Sze-ma Ts'een says that Chow-kung on his death-bed said, 'Bury me in Ching-chow, to show that I dare not leave king Ching.' The king, however, buried him in Peih, beside king Wăn, to show that he did not dare to look on Chow-kung as a servant (see the 魯周公世家). 告周公作亳姑. This is very ob-

書經

康王之誥。○六十一康王命作册畢、分居里成周郊、作畢命。○六十二穆王命君牙爲周大司徒、作君牙。○六十三穆王命伯冏爲周大僕正、作冏命。○六十四呂命、穆王訓夏贖刑、作呂刑。○六十五平王錫晉文侯秬鬯圭瓚、作文侯之命。○六十六魯侯伯禽宅曲阜、徐夷並興、東郊

king K'ang. *With reference to this*, there was made THE TESTAMENTARY DECREE.

60 When king K'ang occupied the sovereign place, he made an announcement to all the princes, and there was made THE ANNOUNCEMENT OF KING K'ANG.

61 King K'ang ordered that a document of appointment should be made for the duke of Peih, severally defining the localities in the borders of Ching chow. There was then made the CHARGE TO THE DUKE OF PEIH.

62 King Muh appointed Keun-ya to be the minister of instruction of Chow; and there was made the KEUN-YA.

63 King Muh appointed Pih-keung to be the master of his household; and there was made the CHARGE TO KEUNG.

64 *The prince of* LEU was charged by king Muh to set forth the lessons of Hea on the redemption of punishments; and there was made LEU ON PUNISHMENTS.

65 King P'ing gave to prince Wăn of Tsin spirits of the black millet mixed with odoriferous herbs. *With reference to this*, there was made the CHARGE TO PRINCE WAN.

66 When Pih-k'in, prince of Loo, first dwelt in K'euh-fow, the Seu and other wild tribes rose together in insurrection. The gates on

scure. The announcement must have been to the duke on his bier, or by means of a sacrifice. Some suppose that 亳姑 should be 蒲姑, not 52, and that the subject announced had something to do with the removal of the ruler of Yen, a measure which had originated with Chow-kung. 60. 旣尸天子,—the use of 尸 here is strange. It leads us to 太康尸位 in 'The Songs of the five Sons,' and to 羲和尸厥官 in 'The Punitive Expedition of Yin.' The writer of the preface would seem to have had those passages in view; but the 尸 here simply = 主, and intimates nothing condemnatory of king K'ang.

不開、作費誓。○

六十七 秦穆公伐鄭、晉襄公帥師敗諸殽、還歸、作秦誓。

the eastern frontier were kept shut, and there was made THE SPEECH AT PE.

67 When duke Muh of Ts'in was invading Ch'ing, the duke Sëang of Tsin led an army, and defeated his forces in Heaou. When they returned, he made THE SPEECH OF THE DUKE OF TS'IN

SUMMARY. From this preface it appears that the Shoo-king, as compiled by Confucius, contained 81 Documents in 100 Books. The preface has no division of those into Parts. According to the arrangement made in this volume, Part I., or the Book of T'ang, contained 1 document still existing: Part, II., or the Book of Yu, contained 7 documents in 15 Books, of which 3 in 11 Books are lost; 4 remain, but not all equally allowed: Part III., or the Book of Hea, contained 4 documents in 4 Books, all of which remain, though the genuineness of two of them is questioned: Part IV., or the Book of Shang, contained 31 documents in 40 Books; 20 documents in 23 Books are lost; 11 documents remain, only 5 of which, however, are unquestioned: Part V., or the Book of Chow, contained 38 documents in 40 Books; 8 documents in 8 Books are lost; of 1 there are two very different versions; 20 documents are fully admitted.

書經

THE SHOO KING.

PART I. THE BOOK OF T'ANG.

THE CANON OF YAOU.

尙書

唐書

堯典

曰若稽古、帝堯曰放勳、欽明文思安安、允恭克讓、光被四表、格于上下。○

1 I. Examining into antiquity, *we find that* the emperor Yaou was called Fang-heun. He was reverential, intelligent, accomplished, and thoughtful,—naturally and without effort. He was sincerely courteous, and capable of *all* complaisance. The display *of these qualities* reached to the four extremities *of the empire*, and extended from

TITLE OF THE WHOLE WORK. 尙書.—Anciently, the Work was simply called the Shoo. So Confucius, in the Analects, and Mencius refer to it. See Ana. II. xxi., &c.; Men. I. Pt. II. iii. 7, &c. The addition of 尙,=上, 'High,' is by Ch'ing K'ang-shing attributed to Conf. He says, 'Conf., honouring it, gave it the denomination of 尙書. Honouring and emphasizing it as if it were a Book of Heaven, he therefore called it "The Highest Book,"' (尊而重之若天書然故曰尙書). Gan-kwŏ in his preface ascribes the name to Fuh-shang, who called it, he says, the 尙書 'as being the book of the highest antiquity' (以其上古之書). The use of the name by Mih Teih in his 明鬼篇, however, shows its existence before Fuh's time. With whom and how it originated, we cannot positively say. 書, given by the 說文 as being formed from 聿 and 者 (=著), =what is described or related with a pencil, 'a writing.'

TITLE OF THE PART. 唐書.—In so denominating this portion of the work, I follow the authority of Hea Shin (許愼, of the 2d cent.), who in his dict. (the 說文) quotes part of par. 8 as from the 唐書. Keang Shing and Maou K'e-ling, likewise, both say that this was the arrangement of Fuh-shang himself; see the 集注音疏 of the former *in loc.*, and the 古文尙書寃詞, 卷一,

p. 9, of the latter. Besides, Yaou constituted a dynasty by himself. He and Shun were as distinct from each other as were Shun and Yu. 唐者堯有天下之號, 'T'ang is the dynastic designation of Yaou.' Before he succeeded to the empire, he was prince of T'ang (唐侯). The name is still retained in the district so called of 保定 dep., in Chih-le.

TITLE OF THE BOOK. 堯典, 'The Canon of Yaou.' Yaou is to all readers substantially the name of the emperor. Whether it was so or not, see on par. 1. 典 is found in K'ang-he's dict., under 八, but the 說文 gives it under 丌, 'that which is high and level.' '册 being placed over it, there is thus indicated the exalted nature of the document. The character indicates what is classical, invariable, what may serve as a law, and rule.' The sayings and doings of Yaou and Shun form a pattern for all ages.—With regard to the relative position of the three titles, they are placed here according to modern usage. Under the Han dynasty, the relative position was just the reverse. The title of the Book was put highest, and that of the Work lowest.

CONTENTS OF THE BOOK. Yaou is the subject of the Book; first in his personal character, and the general results of his government; next in his special care for the regulation of the calendar, and the labours of agriculture; and lastly, in his anxiety to find a man to whom in his declining years he could intrust the administration of affairs, and who might succeed him on the throne. He appears before the reader—the sage; the administrator; the patriotic sovereign. There are in all, according to the ordinary, though not unexceptionable arrangement only 12 paragraphs (節), which may be divided into 3 chapters (段 or 大段). Ch. I. contains the parr. 1 and 2; ch. II. contains parr. 3—8; ch. III. contains parr. 9—12.

CH. I. THE SAGELY VIRTUES OF YAOU, AND THE BENEFICENT CHARACTER AND SUCCESSFUL RESULTS OF HIS GOVERNMENT. Par. 1. Choo He gave his decided opinion that the six characters 曰若稽古帝堯 were to be construed together without stop, and were 'the introductory words of the chronicler' (see 朱子全書,卷三十三,堯典);= 'When we make a study of the ancient emperor Yaou.' Anciently, however, a comma was put at 古; 曰 (read also 粵) 若 were taken as a formula of introduction; and 稽古帝堯 were a sentence, of which 帝堯 was the subject, and 稽古 the predicate. K'ang-shing makes 稽=同 and 古=天, and explains, 'Yaou was able to accord with Heaven, and his actions were of equal merit with its' (see any of the comm. of the present dyn.). Support is thought to be given to this view by Conf. words, Ana. VIII. xix. But it is plainly inadmissible. Ma Yung and Gan-kwŏ, taking only 曰 as introductory, make 若=順, and 稽=考. The latter explains, 'He who could accord with and examine ancient principles, and practise them, was the emperor Yaou.' There is not so much violence here to the meaning of terms, as in Ch'ing's interpretation; but Maou K'e-ling points out another and much simpler construction, taking 曰若稽古 as an ancient formula prefixed by chroniclers to their narratives. (Instances may be seen in 孫星衍, *in loc.*) The four characters, then, = 'When we examine into antiquity,' and 堯帝 are the subject of the 曰 which follows; see Maou's 尙書廣聽錄,卷一. 帝堯曰放勳 (*al.* 勛),— The uniform testimony of antiquity is that 放勳 was Yaou's name; 重華 that of Shun; and 文命 that of Yu. So expressly, Sze-ma Ts'een Ch'ing, Ma, and Chaou K'e. Mencius also seems to countenance this, V. Pt. I. iv. 1; though I there, in deference to the Sung scholars, translated the words by 'The Highly Meritorious.' Gan-kwŏ was the first to treat the characters as a descriptive phrase, taking 放 (up. 2d tone)='to learn,' 'to imitate;'—'it may be said of him that he imitated the merit of the highest ages? Choo He's disciple 蔡沈, improved on this, making 放=至, and the phrase='The Highly Meritorious.' But it is better to revert to the ancient view. For the difficulty in its way, arising from Pt II. iii. 1, see *in loc.* But if Fang-heun, &c., were the names of Yaou and the other sages, what account is to be given of the terms 堯, 舜. &c., themselves? This question cannot be settled beyond dispute. They were not 謚, honorary, posthumous titles, as Ma Yung says; for, not to insist on the point that the giving of such titles originated with the Chow dyn., we find both Shun and Yu spoken of and spoken to by those styles;—see, par. 8: Pt. II. i. 3; iv. 1. I must regard them as a kind of 號 or 字, designations. Yaou's reign commenced B.C. 2356. He is the fourth of the "five Te," with whom Sze-ma Ts'een commences his history. After Shun, the sovereigns of China were called by the humbler title of 'Wang' or King, down to the Ts'in dynasty, B.C. 220. 帝 is a synonym of Heaven, and properly denotes 'God.' The 說文 defines it by 諦, 'to judge; and K'ung Ying-tă, expounding the application of it, says that Heaven exercises an impartial rule, judging righteous judgment, and that the name is given to the earthly sovereign, the vicegerent of Heaven, as expected to do the same; see Ying-tă's paraphrase on the first par. of the preface. 欽明文思 (up. 3d tone, exp. by

二節 克明俊德、以親九族、九族既睦、平章百姓、百姓昭明、協和萬邦、黎民於變時雍。

2 earth to heaven. He was able to make the able and virtuous distinguished, and thence proceeded to the love of the nine classes of his kindred, who all became harmonious. He *also* regulated and polished the people *of his domain*, who all became brightly intelligent. *Finally*, he united and harmonized the myriad States *of the empire;* and lo! the black-haired people were transformed. The result was *universal* concord.

Ch'ing—慮深通敏, 'in cogitation profound, in penetration active.') 安安,—欽· 'reverential,'=cherishing a constant feeling of responsibility. This,it is said, is the 'one word' in the Book, indicating the one virtue out of which all Yaou's other qualities grew. Gan-kwŏ takes 安 as a verb—'by these four virtues he gave repose to those to whom repose was due.' Much better to take the phrase as in the translation, with Choo He. Ch'ing read 宴宴.

光被 (3d tone, =及) 四表,—Gan-kwŏ expl. 光 by 充—'those virtues filled up and reached to,' &c. Fuh-shang's text seems to have read 橫 (see the 後案); but in the prefatory notice we read 光. 表=外, 'that which is outside.' Acc. to Ch'ing, 四表=四海之外, 'the remotest limits of the four seas.' 上下=天地, heaven above and earth beneath.

2. 克明俊德,—see the Great Learning, Comm. i. 4, where for 俊 we have 峻. There the 'great virtue' is that of Yaou himself; but the preceding has spoken sufficiently of that. Ch'ing and Gan-kwŏ both take the meaning as in the transl., which moreover agrees with Conf. teaching, Doct. of the Mean, xx. 12, 13, where 親親 follows 尊賢. The commentator in the Great Learning *accommodates* the text of the Classic. 九族=all of the same surname, all the relatives of consanguinity, from the great-great-grandfather to the great-great-grandson. Gow-yang (歐陽), and other interpreters of Fuh-shang's Books, understood the nine classes to be 4 on the father's side, 3 on the mother's, and 2 on the wife's (see Ying-tă *in loc.*). Ch'ing and Gan-kwŏ rightly prefer the former view; but we may say with Ts'ae Ch'in that the relatives by affinity should here be understood as included with the others. 平章百姓,—I have given 百姓, after Ts'ae Ch'in, as meaning 'the people of the imperial domain.' That the phrase must be restricted in signification is plain from the 萬邦 and 黎民 that follow. Gan-kwŏ, however, says that 百姓=百官, 'the various officers.' Ch'ing substantially agrees with him;—百姓=羣臣之父子兄弟. That 'the hundred surnames' was a designation of the great families of the State under the Chow dyn. is shown clearly by Ying-tă, *in loc.* But in the Shoo-king, where the phrase occurs some 14 times, much the more natural interpretation of it is as=民, 'the people.' Part V. x. 10; xvi. 9 are exceptions to this, but the ordinary usage is as I have said. For 平 the 'Historical Records' give 便, and Ch'ing interpreted by 辨, 'to distinguish, to separate.' Hence it has been contended that the original reading was 釆, the old form of which was liable to be mistaken for that cf 平. [I cannot in these notes enter much into the question of various readings, and discuss the correctness of the text. The subject has been treated generally in the prolegg.] 萬邦=萬國 (so it is in the 史記), 'the myriad States,' *i.e.*, the States of all the princes beyond the imperial domain. 黎='black,' *i.e.*, black-haired. Some simply expl. it by 衆, 'all.' 於, an excl., read *woo*. 時=是. Gan-kwŏ brings out the concluding clauses thus:—天下衆民,皆變化從上,是以風俗大和, 'All the people under heaven were transformed, and followed the example of the sovereign, so that their manners became greatly harmonious.'

三節 ○乃命羲和、欽若昊天、曆象日月星辰、敬授人時。○ 四節 分命羲仲、宅嵎夷、日暘谷、

3 II. Thereupon *Yaou* commanded He and Ho, in reverent accordance with *their observation* of the wide heavens, to calculate and delineate *the movements and appearances of* the sun, the moon, the stars, and the zodiacal spaces; and so to deliver respectfully the seasons to the people.

4 He separately commanded the second brother He to reside at Yu-e, in what was called the Bright Valley, and there respectfully to

CH. II. THE MEASURES OF YAOU TO SECURE A CORRECT CALENDAR IN ORDER TO PROMOTE THE BUSINESS OF AGRICULTURE. Par. 3. 乃 being a conjunction, we naturally connect this par. with the preced., as following it in time. Such is not the case, however. Parr. 1 and 2 should be taken as the words of the chronicler whoever he was, and whensoever he wrote, giving his general impressions of Yaou's character and government. Here he begins to make use of documents, yet condensing them in his own language, till we arrive at par. 8. 乃 is equivalent to our 'now.' About the Hes and Hos we need not seek to be wise above what is written here and in Pt. III. iv. It is attempted to connect them with a Ch'ung and Le (重黎) descended from the emp. Shaou-haou, B.C. 2594 (see on Pt. V. xxvii. 6), as hereditary occupants of their offices. They come before us receiving their appointment from Yaou to form a Board of astronomy, and specially to regulate the calendar,—a work so necessary for the purposes of agriculture. Gaubil says they were charged likewise 'to correct the abuses and disorders which had been introduced into manners and religion' (Le Chou-king, p. 6., n. 2); but there is nothing in the text to justify this. It is queried whether those mentioned in par. 3 were elder brothers of the others, heads of their respective families, or merely those brothers, so that we should translate 羲和—'the Hes and the Hos.' Were there three of each surname or only two? The point cannot be settled. I receive the impression that there were three. 欽若(=順)昊天,—'reverently to accord with the vast heaven.' 昊天 is the name specially appropriated to the firmament of summer, when an air of vigour and vastness seems to fill all space. We are not to think of anything beyond the visible expanse and the bodies in it. The 集傳 defines 曆 as 'the writings in which calculations were recorded,' and 象 as 'the instruments with which the heavens were surveyed.' This cannot be. The characters are verbs. 曆 is 'to calendar,' implying calculations and writings; 象, 'a figure,' 'a resemblance,' and, as a verb, 'to imitate,' must here = 'to delineate,' 'to represent.' 星, 'the stars,' generally; both the fixed stars and the planets. 辰, 'the zodiacal spaces.' These, it is said in the 集傳, by the conjunctions of the sun and moon, divide the circumference of heaven into twelve mansions (十二次). For 人時 we should probably read 民時; see 段玉裁's 古文尚書撰異, *in loc.*

Parr. 4-7. It is supposed the work enjoined in the prec. par. has been done. That there may be no mistake in a matter of such importance,—to test the accuracy of the calendar, two members of each of the families He and Ho are appointed to the work of verification at different points. P. 4. The second brother He has his appointment at 嵎夷 (see Pt. III. i. 上. 22), not, as often stated, the present Tăng-chow in Shan-tung, but a place farther to the east in Corea. There was a spot convenient to observe the sun coming up, as from a valley, to enlighten the earth, from which it got its name. The 居 would seem to denote that He's proper residence was at Yu-e, but perhaps it only indicates a sojourn there to make the necessary observations. So in the other parr. This is Choo He's opinion. He was to receive the rising sun, acc. to the 集傳, by carefully noting the length of the shadow cast from a gnomon; but this is not said in the text. The special object of his observation was to ascertain that mid-spring, the vernal equinox, was correctly fixed; and the final end was that the 東作 'labours of the east' might be adjusted. Those labours of the east are the labours of spring; and in the other parr. the south stands for summer, the west for autumn, and the north for winter. On this see the

寅賓出日、平秩東作、日中、星鳥、以殷仲春、厥民析、鳥獸孳尾。○ 五節 申命羲叔、宅南交、平秩南訛、敬致、日永、星

receive as a guest the rising sun, and to adjust and arrange the labours of the spring. "The day," *he said*, "is of the medium length, and the star is in *Neaou*; you may thus exactly determine mid-spring. The people begin to disperse; and birds and beasts breed and copulate."

5 He further commanded the third brother He to reside at Nan-keaou, and arrange the transformations of the summer, and respectfully to observe the extreme limit *of the shadow*. "The day," *said*

易經, 說卦傳, ch. v. The idea underlying the representation seems to be that of an analogy between a day and the year,—the morning, with the sun in the east, corresponding to spring; noon, with the sun in the south, to summer, &c. To guide He in his observations, he is told, 1st, that he would find 日中, 'the day of the average length,' *i.e.*, a mean between its lengths at the solstices, or more probably of the same length as the night, determined by a clepsydra (so, Ma Yung); and 2d, that 'the star was *Neaou*.' But *Neaou* (鳥) is not the name of a star, but of a constellation, or space of the heavens, extending over 112° (see Keang Shing), and embracing 'the seven constellations of the Southern quarter,' called 井, 鬼, 柳, 星, 張, 翼, and 軫. Gan-kwŏ thinks the meaning is that all those seven constellations would be visible on the evening of the vernal equinox. This view cannot be correct, however, because in the next three paragraphs the 星 is the star or 宿, which culminated on each occasion. We have then to adopt as the star indicated here, the central one of the space *Neaou*, which was the view of Ma Yung and K'ang-shing; and it is stated by Ts'ae Ch'in that 張一行, a very learned Buddhist priest of the T'ang dynasty (in the reign of 元宗, A.D. 713–756) calculated this to be the star 鶉火, corresponding to Cor Hydra of the west.

Here Dr. Medhurst in his translation of the Shoo King has made the following note:—'If Cor Hydra culminated at sun-set on the day of the vernal equinox in the time of Yaou, the constellation on the meridian at noon of that day must have been Pleiades in Taurus. Now as by the retrocession of the equinoxes the stars of the zodiac go back a whole sign in 2000 years, it would take 4000 years for the sun to be in Pleiades at the time of the vernal equinox, which is about the time when Yaou is said to have flourished, and affords a strong confirmation of the truth of Chinese chronology. For Pleiades is 56 degrees and one third from the point where the ecliptic crossed the equinoctial A.D. 1800, and as the equinox travels backwards 50 seconds and one tenth per annum, it would take about 4000 years for Pleiades to be in the zenith at noon of the vernal equinox. Referring to Chinese records, we find that Yaou's reign closed 2254 years before Christ, which added to 1800 makes 4054; and a retrocession of 50 seconds and one tenth per annum would give 4050.' See a note to the same effect by the editors of the 書經傳說, *in loc.*

By the equal length of day and night, and the culminating star, He-chung would be able exactly to determine (殷=正, Gan-kwŏ) mid-spring. Two popular characteristics of the season are added. The people would be dispersed, scattered, that is, from their homes and villages where they had been congregated during the winter, and engaged in field work; and animals would be beginning to breed. For 鳥獸孳尾, Sze-ma Ts'een has 鳥獸字微; but the meaning is substantially the same. 5. Another He is sent to Nan-keaou, the border of 安南, Annam, or Cochin-china, called also 交阯. Sze-ma Ts'een says that the sway of the emperor 顓頊 extended 'from 幽陵 on the north to 交阯 on the south.' Ch'ing, supposes that the characters 曰明都, (='in what was called the Bright Capital)' have dropt out of the text after 交. 南訛 (*al.*, 譌 and 爲),- 訛=化 'to transform;' with reference to the changes of things

火、以正仲夏、厥民因、鳥獸希革。○分命和仲、宅西、日昧谷、寅餞納日、平秩西成、宵中、星虛、以殷仲秋、厥民夷、鳥獸毛毨。

六節

he, "is at its longest, and the star is *Ho*; you may thus exactly determine mid-summer. The people are more dispersed; and birds and beasts have their feathers and hair thin, and change their coats."

6 He separately commanded the second brother Ho to reside at the west, in what was called the Dark Valley, and *there* respectfully to convoy the setting sun, and to adjust and arrange the completing labours of the autumn. "The night," *he said*, "is of the medium length, and the star is *Heu*; you may thus exactly determine mid-autumn. The people begin to feel at ease; and birds and beasts have their coats in good condition."

in the productive operations of summer (化育之事, acc. to Gan-kwŏ). 敬致,—I have translated acc. to what is generally supposed to be the meaning, and which can claim the authority of Ch'ing;—see Keang Shing and Sun Sing-yen. A similar measurement was to be practised, it is said, at the other seasons; only Shing will have it, that at the equinoxes it was the shadow cast by the moon which was to be ascertained. Gan-kwŏ, however, may be right when he interprets more simply—敬行其教以致其功, 'reverently carrying out your instructions to give to those productive operations their largest results.' The culminating star at dusk of the summer solstice would be 火 or 'Fire,' the central star of 'the Azure Dragon' (蒼龍), which embraced the seven constellations of the eastern quarter, 角, 亢, 氐, 房, 心, 尾, and 箕, and corresponding to the Heart of Scorpio. The editors of the 書經傳說 say here:—'At the summer solstice in Yaou's time the sun was in 星 (α Hydræ Alphard; Reeves), whereas now it is in 觜 (λ Orion).' This work was ordered in the 8th year of Yung-ching, A.D. 1730. 厥民因,—因='to be going on from,' *i.e.*, 析而又析, 'the people were still more scattered and in the fields than in the spring.'

6. To two younger members of the house of Ho the examination of the times of the autumnal equinox and winter solstice was assigned. The particular place in the west to which Ho-chung had to repair cannot be specified. 餞, 'to convoy;'—by measuring the shadow of the gnomon, acc. to the 集傳; but see on par. 4.

No particular reason but the writer's or the emperor's thought at the time need be sought for the use of 宵 here rather than 日. The culminating star was *Heu*, the centre one of 'The Dark Warrior' (玄武), which embraced the seven constellations of the northern quarter, 斗, 牛, 女, 虛, 危, 室, and 壁, and corresponding to β Aquarius. It is observed here in Yung Ching's Shoo King, 'At the autumnal equinox in Yaou's time the sun was in 房 (β δ π ρ Scorpio); while now it is in 翼 (α Crateris [Alkes]).' 厥民夷,—夷=平. Gan-kwŏ, Ts'ae Ch'in, and Keang, all agree in thus defining 夷, but the meaning they attach to 平 is different. K'ung says that 'the people are still at their labours in the fields, *the same as* in the summer.' Këang says that the people now come down, because of the bleak winds, from the summer heights which they had preferred, and live in the low *level* grounds? The only reasonable interpretation is that of Ts'ae—'The great heats are over, and the people

書經

○申命和叔、宅朔方、曰幽都、平在朔易、日短、星昴、以正仲冬、厥民隩、鳥獸氄毛。○帝曰、咨、汝羲暨和、朞、三

（七節）（八節）

7 He further commanded the third brother Ho to reside in the northern region, in what was called the Sombre Capital, and there to adjust and examine the changes of the winter. "The day," *said he*, "is at its shortest, and the star is *Maou*; thus you may exactly determine mid-winter. The people keep their cosy corners; and the coats of birds and beasts are downy and thick."

8 The emperor said, "Ah! you, He and Ho, a round year consists of three hundred, sixty, and six days. By means of an intercalary

feel at ease.' 7. The 史記 for 朔方 reads 北方. 朔, doubtless, means 'the north.' It is used also for the 'first day of the new month.' Both these are applications of the term, which is explained by 甦, 'to come alive again,' the winter being to the year what its last quarter is to the moon, a season of disappearance and decay, to be succeeded by revival. 平在 (＝察) 朔易,—朔易, 'the changes of the winter:'—the former things pass away; all things become new. The labours of the season are therefore called 'changes.' For 朔易 Ts'een has 伏物, 'the hidden things,' with reference to the energies of nature now working in concealment. 昴, the culminating star, is the centre of the 'White Tiger' (百虎), comprehending the seven constellations of the western quarter, 奎, 婁, 胃, 昴, 畢, 觜, and 參. It is our Pleiades. 'In the time of Yaou, at the winter solstice, the sun was in *heu* (虛, β Aquarius), while now at the same season it is in Ke (箕, γ Sagittarii)'; see the 書經傳說. 厥民隩,—隩 (read *yuh*) is with Ch'ing ＝ 內, 'inside,' and with K'ung ＝ 室, 'house,' 'apartment.' In winter the people keep mostly within, in the warmest places.

Par. 8. The verifications in the four prec. parr. are supposed to have been made; and now the emperor addresses either the two chiefs of the He and Ho families, or all their members whose services had been employed, on the important subject of making the calendar complete by an intercalary month. 咨 ＝ 嗟, an interjection, 'ah!' 暨 ＝ 及, 'and.' 朞三百有六旬 is quoted by Heu Shin, under 稘, which is defined 復其時, 'a revolution of the time.' Gan-kwŏ defines it—匝四時曰朞, 'The circuit of the four seasons is called 朞.' Yaou does not speak scientifically, but says that the round year consists of 366 days. On this Gaubil observes (Le Chou-king, p. 7, n. 4), 'We see that Yaou knew the Julian year of 365¼ days; the fourth year consists of 366 days. We see also that they then intercalated some months to divide the year into four seasons.' But there is nothing in the text to indicate that every fourth year was reckoned 366 days. If it had been so, Yaou's calendar would have been the same as the Julian, and there would have been no necessity for the intercalation of a month at certain regular periods which is indicated. We may well be surprised to find this ancient emperor of China speaking as he does here, in the 24th century before Christ, with so close an approximation to the correct length of the year. On this as gradually ascertained in China with an increasing exactness, I shall quote the following note by the editors of Yung-ching's Shoo:—

'When it is said that the year consists of 366 days, we are to understand that Yaou was speaking in round numbers. The period in question is now called the value of the year. It has been differently estimated by the astronomers of successive dynasties.

'In the Books of the Han dynasty' [ended A.D. 263], 'the circuit of the heavens is divided into 365¼°; and a degree of the heavens is made to correspond to a day of the calendar. At that time it was taken for granted that a circuit of the heavens' [a sidereal year] 'was the same as a circuit of the year' [a tropical year].

'Under the eastern Tsin dynasty' [A.D. 318—420], 'Yu He' [died about the middle of the 4th century. Ts'ae Ch'in says that he was the *first* to distinguish the sidereal year from the tropical, and to bring forward the doctrine of

百有六旬有六日、以閏月定四時成歲、允釐百工、庶

month do you fix the four seasons, and complete the *determination of* the year. *Thereafter*, in exact accordance with this, regulating the various officers, all the works *of the year* will be fully performed."

the precession of the equinoxes, which he estimated at one degree in 50 years] 'reckoned the circuit of the heavens' [= the sidereal year] 'at 365°.26, rather more than 365¼, and the circuit of the year' [= the tropical year] 'at 365.24 days; rather less than 365¼.

'Under the Sung dynasty' [*i.e.*, the northern Sung, which succeeded the Tsin], 'Ho Chingt'een' [about the middle of the 5th century] 'made another alteration in these reckonings, and estimated the circuit of the heavens at 365°.255, and the tropical year at 365.245 days.

'Under the Yuen dynasty, Kwoh Show-king' [died A.D. 1316, at the age of 86], 'on a comparison of ancient and modern observations, fixed the circuit of the heavens at 365°.2575, and the tropical year at 365.2425 days. The accumulation of decimal figures, however, in both of these quantities' [while the degree was made to correspond to a day] 'made all calculations founded upon them difficult.

'But the philosopher Shaou' [邵堯夫; died A.D. 1017; his tablet has a place in the temples of Confucius], 'in his 元會運世, adopted the number 360 as an arbitrary standard, the circumference of the heavens being the basis of his calculations. That being once fixed' [at 360°], 'it became comparatively an easy matter to deal with the other fractional quantities.' [It must be observed that the phrase 天周, circuit or circumference of the heavens, here changes its meaning; and the value assigned to it, in its former sense, of 365.2575, now to be reckoned in days, is as necessary to astronomical calculations as ever.] 'Accordingly, the calendar now published by authority determines the circumference of heaven to be 360° (a degree containing 60 minutes, a minute 60 seconds and all the parts below continuing to be reckoned by 60); and the tropical year consists of 365 days, 5 hours, 48 minutes, 45 seconds (365. 2421875).

'Through successive ages, though the fractional parts have been now a little more and now a little less, the determinations have all been based on the round number in this Canon of Yaou, and have served to illustrate it. As to the conjunctions of the sun and moon, determining the changes and first days of months, and the conjunctions of the sun and' (various fixed stars in) 'the heavens, determining the equinoxes and solstices,—whereas the solar period and the lunations do not correspond, so that there arise what are called the surplus of the former and the deficiency of the latter, there is required the use of intercalation to make the four seasons come each in its proper place. This is the practice indicated in this Canon of Yaou, which constitutes it the model for all ages.'

Yaou certainly commanded his officers to use intercalations;—how they did so we cannot tell. Previous to the Han dynasty, Chinese history does not furnish us with details on the subject of intercalation. In the time of that dyn., however, we find what is called the Metonic cycle well known. It is not mentioned as any discovery of that age. See the 'History of the Former Han' by Pan Koo (班固), finished about A.D. 80, in the 律歷志, 第一, 下, where the whole process is fully described. No doubt it came down to the Han from the Chow, and was probably known in China long before Meton reformed the Athenian calendar according to its principles, B.C. 432. I abstract the following account from Woo Ch'ing (吳澄) of the Yuen dynasty's Work on the Shoo:—A common year of 12 months of 30 days each, or 360 days, is assumed. Not that there ever was such a year in China, as Medhurst says by mistake (Shoo King, p. 8, note); but it is convenient to lay down that as the length of the year in order to exhibit the process of intercalation. Now, the sun makes his circuit of the heavens in 365 days and ¼, or 365 days and 235–940ths (a day being divided into 940 parts). The year as determined by the sun, therefore, is 5 days and 235–940ths over 360, which excess is denominated 氣盈. A synodic revolution of the moon, again, takes place in 29 days and 499–940ths, so that 12 months = 354 days and 348–940ths, short of 360 by 5 days and 592–940ths, which deficiency is denominated 朔虛. Adding the excess and the deficiency, we have 10 days and 827–940ths, the difference of the two from 360 in one year.

In the third year this amounts to 32 days and 601–940ths, when the first intercalation of one synodic period is supposed to be made, leaving 3 days and 102–940ths unabsorbed.

In the sixth year there have accumulated 35 days and 703–940ths, which a second intercalation reduces to 6 days and 204–940ths. A third intercalation in the ninth year would leave 9 days and 306–940ths, which by the eleventh year would amount to 31 days and 80–940ths, reduced by intercalation to 1 day and 521–940ths.

A fifth intercalation in the fourteenth year would leave 4 days and 623–940ths.

A sixth in the seventeenth year would leave 7 days and 725–940ths, which in the nineteenth year would amount to 29 days and 499–940ths, which the last intercalation would exactly absorb.

書經

績咸熙。○九節帝曰、疇咨若時登庸。放齊曰、胤子朱啟明。帝曰、吁、嚚訟、可乎。○十節帝曰、疇咨若予采。驩兜曰、都、共

9 III. The emperor said, "Who will search out for me a man according to the times, whom I may raise and employ?" Fang-ts'e said, "There is your heir-son Choo, who is highly intelligent." The emperor said, "Alas! he is insincere and quarrelsome:—can he do."
10 The emperor said, "Who will search out for me a man equal to the exigency of my affairs?" Hwan-tow said, "Oh! there is the minister of Works, whose merits have just been displayed in various

It is to be observed that the above division of a day into 940 parts was different from that of the Han dynasty, and indeed only began to obtain in the time of the great Sung dyn. Practically, moreover, a month must be estimated by a whole number of days; and hence the Chinese have so many short months in the year of 29 days, while the rest are of 30 days.

允釐百工、庶績咸熙 is very well given by Sze-ma Ts'een—信飭百官、衆功皆興. 百工=百官, 'the hundred' (*i.e.* all, the various) 'officers,' each office having its special department of *work*. It is not said that He and Ho had any further charge of the officers beyond supplying them with a correct calendar.

CH. III. THE ANXIETY OF YAOU TO FIND THE RIGHT MEN FOR THE EXIGENCIES OF THE TIMES, AND ESPECIALLY THE BEST MAN, ON WHOM TO DEVOLVE THE THRONE:—ALL ILLUSTRATING HIS FREEDOM FROM EVERY SELFISH CONSIDERATION. The events described in the prec. 6 parr. are referred by the compilers of Chinese history to the 1st and 2d years of Yaou's reign; but we really cannot say when they took place. Par. 12 belongs to the 70th year of his reign; par. 11 is referred with some probability to the 61st; the 10th must be of about the same date.

P. 9. *Yaou inquires—prob. in open court—for an officer whom he may employ in high affairs.* What the affairs were we cannot know. Ma Yung thinks that by this time the four Hes and Hos were dead, and that one was wanted to enter on their duties as ministers of the four seasons. A meaning is thus found for 時 as =四時; but the view is to be rejected at once. Gan-kwŏ takes 時 as =是, 'these,' and connects the par. with the 8th, making the inquiry to be for a premier to direct all the officers, and all the works of the year, (so also Ts'een); but the only connection between the parr. is of fragments brought together into the present canon. The matter must be left indefinite.

疇=誰, 'who.' 咨 is here not a particle of exclamation, as hitherto, but a verb, =訪問, 'to inquire for.' 若 as in p. 8, 'to accord with.' It is observed that in those times of wise antiquity, forceful control was not the way of sovereigns and ministers, but a cautious accordance with nature and circumstances. 庸=用, 'to use.' Fang-ts'e (Ying-tă makes 放 in the 2d tone) only appears here. He must have been a minister. Sze-ma Ts'een for 胤子 has 嗣子, 胤='to continue, to succeed;' and I have translated accordingly. Gan-kwŏ takes 胤 for the State so called, (see Pt. III. iv.), and 子 for the title of its ruler, = 'count;' and Ying-tă says it seems to him unnatural for the emperor's son to be recommended and spoken of as here. But that only serves to exalt the character of Yaou, who was free from the partialities of common men, that 'do not know the wickedness of their own sons' (Great Learning, Comm. viii. 2). The difficulty would disappear, if we could suppose that Yaou is here proposing to resign his throne. 吁 is a particle of exclamation, intimating the speaker's decided dissent.

P. 10. *Yaou again makes inquiry for a minister who might be equal to the management of his affairs.* Such seems to be the meaning of 采, which is given by Gan-kwŏ as =事. Ma Yung explains it by 官, 'officers,' as if it were a prime minister to be over all the other ministers, who was wanted. Hwan-tow and the K'ung-kung appear in the next Book, p. 12, as two of the four great criminals whom Shun dealt with. 共工 is the name of the one's office. In the next Book, p. 21, Shun calls Ching to the same. It is about = Minister of Works. Ch'ing sup-

工方鳩僝功。帝曰、吁、靜言庸違、象恭、滔天。○帝曰、咨、四岳、湯湯洪水方割、蕩蕩懷山襄陵、浩浩滔天、下民其咨、有能俾乂。僉曰、於、鯀

十一節

ways." The emperor said, "Alas! when unemployed, he can talk; but when employed, his actions turn out differently. He is respectful *only* in appearance. See! the floods assail the heavens."

11 The emperor said, "Oh! *chief of* the four mountains, destructive in their overflow are the waters of the inundation. In their vast extent they embrace the mountains and overtop the hills, threatening the heavens with their floods, so that the inferior people groan and murmur. Is there a capable man, to whom I can assign the correction *of this calamity*? All *in the court* said, "Oh! there is

poses that the Kung-kung here was the 水官, 'officer of the Waters.' He had no doubt, as we shall see, been employed to relieve the distress occasioned by the prevailing floods. 都 is an exclamation, the opposite of 吁, indicating approval and commendation. Choo He says that 方鳩僝功 cannot be understood, but that the old view—as in the transl.—may be allowed to stand. Sze-ma Ts'een gives Hwan-tow's reply:—共工旁聚布功可用. 靜, 'to be still,'=unoccupied. Gan-kwŏ explains it by 謀, 'to plan;' but that meaning only arises from the context here.

滔天 is joined by Gan-kwŏ to the prec. characters:—'He appears to be respectful, but his heart is full of pride as if it would inundate the heavens.' Dissatisfied with this, Ts'ae Ch'in declares the two characters to be unintelligible, and that they dropt into the text here somehow from the next par. In the transl. I have followed an art. on the passage in the 盧學士, 龍城札記, which forms the 388th Book of the 皇清經解. The writer starts from an intimation in the 'Annals of the Bamboo Writings' (竹書紀年), that Yaou in his 19th year appointed the Kung-kung to the management of the Ho. That management had been on the whole unsuccessful. The result was the existing state of inundation, to which Yaou in the text points as evidence of the officer's incompetency.

P. 11. *The appointment of K'wăn to remedy the distress occasioned by an overflowing flood.* This overflow of waters has been called by some western writers 'the deluge of Yaou;' and it has been endeavoured to identify it with the deluge of Noah. The descriptions in the classic, however, will not permit this; see on Pt. III. i. The emperor addresses himself to the 四岳 (or 嶽), literally 'The four Mountains:'—those mentioned in the next Book, par. 8, Tae-tsung or Mount T'ae on the east (in the present Shantung); Mount Hwăng in the south (in Hoonan); Mount Hwa in the west (in Shan-se); and Mount Hăng, in the north. Those were central points in the empire, to which different quarters of it were referred. In the text does Yaou address one great officer styled the chief of the four Mountains, or does he address the body of great officers in charge of the different quarters? Gan-kwŏ held that the four Yŏ were four individuals, the successors of the Hes and Hos, parr. 4–7. K'ang-shing thought that at the time of Yaou's reign to which this par. belongs, the places formerly held by those Hes and Hos were filled by eight chiefs (八伯), who are addressed. Choo He determined that only one man was intended, the president of all the nobles of the empire, regulator of the relations between the court and its feudal retainers. To this opinion I must give in my adhesion. It has its difficulties; but when Yaou proposes to the 四岳, in the next par., to take his place upon the throne, it is impossible to suppose that more than one individual is denoted. 湯 (read *Sëang*) 湯洪水方割,—湯湯=水盛貌, 'the appearance of water in

書經

哉。帝曰、吁、咈哉、方命圮族。岳曰、异哉、試可乃已。帝曰、往欽哉。九載、績用弗成。○ 十二節 帝曰、咨、四岳、朕在位七十載、汝能庸命、巽朕位。岳曰、

K'wăn." The emperor said, "Alas! no, by no means! He is disobedient to orders, and tries to injure his peers." His Eminence said, "Well but——. Try him, and then you can have done with him." The emperor said to K'wăn, "Go; and be reverent!" For nine years he laboured, but the work was unaccomplished.

12 The emperor said, "Oh! you *chief of the* four mountains, I have been on the throne for seventy years. You can carry out my appointments;—I will resign my throne to you." His Eminence said, "I have not the virtue; I should *only* disgrace the imperial seat."

abundance,' a sheet of water; 方, as in prec. par., = 旁, 'on all sides;' 割 'to cut with a knife,' hence generally 'to injure.' 滔 is expl. by 漫, 'great water,' 'water flooding, and destroying things.' 下民其咨,—下民 is exp. by Woo Ch'ing, 居處卑下之民, 'the people who live in the low places'; but the phrase, of not unfrequent occurrence in the mouths of great men in the Shoo, denotes simply the people, in distinction from themselves. Observe the use of 其, completing the rhythm of the clause, and giving the force of a double nominative to the verb.

僉 = 皆, 'all;' *i.e.*, all in the court, not the 四岳 only, but the other nobles with him. Of course it may be said that as the inquiry was addressed only to the Yŏ, and the answer is prefaced by 僉, this character shows that Yŏ was a designation not of one but of many. But tho' there were 4 or 8 Yŏ, I should understand 僉 of others beside them;—so does Yingtă, yet believing that the Yŏ were four.

K'wăn was a minister of Yaou, the father of the great Yu (禹), and chief of the state of Ts'ung (崇伯), corresponding to the present Hoo-heen (鄠縣) in the dep. of Se-ngan in Shen-se.

方命,—方 = 放, 'to disregard, neglect.' Ch'ing and Ma Yung both take the character so, and Ch'ing would also read it as 放, 3d tone. It is merely a conceit, which is given in the 集傳, that 'what is round moves, and what is square (方) stops,' so that 方 comes to mean 'to disregard,' or 'to disobey!' 异哉,—the 說文 defines 异 by 舉, a meaning which I don't see how to understand here. Ts'ae Ch'in says he does not understand the character. The rest of the Yo's reply is given more fully by Sze-ma Ts'een,—試不可用而已. Ch'ing's view is not so good —'Try him. He is fit for this, though not for other duties, in which you need not to employ him.' 載, 'a year. For this, acc. to Yingtă, in the Hea dyn. they subsequently used 歲; in the Shang, 祀; and in the Chow, 年. 績用不成,—we may suppose that the force of 用 merges in that of 績, = 功.

P. 12. *Yaou, having been 70 years on the throne, wishes to resign the administration of affairs to the worthiest, and Shun appears on the stage.*

朕, the imperial We, was anciently simply = I, used both by superiors and inferiors. It was one of the characteristic actions of the founder of the Ts'in dyn. to appropriate it to the sovereign. 庸 (= 用) 命,—'use, carry out my orders.' 巽 = 遜, 'to yield, to resign.' Ch'ing takes it = 入, 'to enter into.' He interprets Yaou's inquiry thus,—'Among all you princes is there

否德、忝帝位。曰、明明揚側陋。師錫帝曰、有鰥在下、曰虞舜。帝曰、俞、予聞、如何。岳曰、瞽子、父頑、母嚚、象傲、克諧以孝、烝烝乂、不格姦。帝曰、我其試哉、女、于時觀厥

The *emperor* said, "Point out some one among the illustrious, or set forth one from among the poor and mean." All *in the court* said to the emperor, "There is an unmarried man among the lower people, called Shun of Yu." The emperor said, "Yes, I have heard of him. What is his character?" His Eminence said, "He is the son of a blind man. His father was obstinately unprincipled; his *step*-mother was insincere; his *half brother* Seang was arrogant. He has been able, however, by his filial piety to live in harmony with them, and to lead them gradually to self-government, so that they no longer proceed to great wickedness." The emperor said, "I will try him!

one, who, acting in harmony with things and obeying the orders of Heaven, can enter in and occupy my throne, discharging the duties that devolve on the emperor?' This is very far-fetched. It is found in a note in the 史記, whose own version of the passage is decisively in favour of what is now the common view:—汝能庸命, 踐朕位. 否德,—Ts'een has 鄙德, with substantially the same meaning. 明 (a verb)＝舉, 'to recommend;' 明 (an adj.)＝高明者, 'those already high and distinguished.' 側陋＝微賤之人, 'men small and mean.' Yaou wants to find the worthiest, in whatever social position. 師＝僉 in the former par., 'all,' and not as Ch'ing thinks, 'the chiefs of the princes.' 錫 is expl. by 與;—'All said to the emperor.' Ts'een has it 衆皆言於堯曰. 虞舜,—see on the title of next Part. 瞽子,—'the son of a blind man.' Gan-kwŏ says that Shun's father was not physically blind, but mentally and morally, so that people spoke of him as if he were really blind, and he received the designation of Koo-sow (瞽瞍). It may have been so, but the general belief of antiquity, and the language of the text are not to be received in other than their natural significancy on mere surmise. 母,—'mother;' not Shun's real mother, but his step-mother. Sze-ma Ts'een says so in express terms. 諧＝和, 'harmony.' It is not easy to say whether we should take it actively—'to bring them to harmony,' or intransitively—'to live in harmony with them.' The usage of the term in the next Book is in favour of the former view. 烝, properly,＝steam.' But steam ascends and moves forward; hence here 烝烝乂＝'to move by gradual progress to self-government.' The account here given of the influence which Shun had produced on his parents and brother is not borne out by the statements in Mencius, Book V. Pt. I., i. and ii. 我其試哉,—'I will test him,' or 'Let me test him.' The 其 has a peculiar force, which neither Premare in his Grammar, nor Morrison, Medhurst, or Williams, in their Dictionaries, has pointed out. The usage is specified in K'ang-he's dictionary, but with no further explanation than that 其 is then 'a particle, helping the sense.' It gives to the whole sentence a half hortatory, half imperative force.

Yaou would test Shun, and a very strange trial it was to which he put him. It impresses my mind with grave doubts as to the trustworthiness of the whole history. As it stands, it shows us one thing,—that polygamy had at this early time obtained among the Chinese.

刑于二女。釐降二女于嬀汭、嬪于虞。帝曰、欽哉。

I will wive him, and then see his behaviour with my two daughters." On this he gave orders, and sent down his two daughters to the north of the Kwei, to be wives in the family of Yu. The emperor said *to them*, "Be reverent!"

From 帝曰 to the end, I have translated according to Choo He's view of the passage:—that down to 刑于二女 we have Yaou's words; from 釐降 to 于虞, what he did; and that the 欽哉 at the end were addressed to his daughters. The construction is not easy; but the interpretation of Gan-kwŏ, and that of Keang Shing in the pres. dyn., make confusion worse confounded. 女 (3d tone),—'to give a daughter to a man to wife.' 刑=法, 'example,' 'behaviour.' The names of Yaou's two daughters are said to have been *Wo-wang* (娥皇) and *Neu-ying* (女英). 'The former,' says Woo Ch'ing, 'became Shun's wife, and the other his concubine.' But this is said, applying the ways of subsequent times to Yaou's age. We cannot acknowledge any inferiority of the one to the other. 嬪 (=婦, 'to be wife to)' applies equally to both. The 嬀 is a small stream in Shan-se, rising where the two depp. of P'ing-yang (平陽) and P'oo-chow (蒲州) border on each other, and flowing southwards to the Ho. 汭 is defined 'the north of a stream;' or it may be, there was a smaller stream so called, which flowed into the Kwei, not far from its junction with the Ho. A note on the 集說 in Yung-ching's Shoo says that there is such a stream so called, but that people may have been led by the text of the Classic to give it that name. Here was the dwelling-place of Shun.

THE SHOO KING.

PART II. THE BOOKS OF YU.

BOOK I. THE CANON OF SHUN.

尚書

虞書

舜典

曰若稽古、帝舜曰重華、協于帝、濬哲文明、温恭允塞、玄德升聞、乃命以位。

1 I. Examining into antiquity, we find that the emperor Shun was called Ch'ung-hwa. He corresponded to the *former* emperor; was profound, wise, accomplished, and intelligent. He was mild and respectful, and entirely sincere. The report of his mysterious virtue was heard on high, and he was appointed to occupy the *imperial* Seat.

Title of the Part. 虞書.—Yu is the dynastic designation of Shun, as T'ang was that of Yaou. It does not appear so clearly, however, how it came to be so. Ts'ae Ch'in, after K'ang-shing, says that 虞 was the 氏 or family name of Shun. Wang Suh said that it was the name of a place or country (地名), held to have been the pres. district of 安邑 in the dep. of 解州 in Shan-se. Some think that Yaou, after marrying his daughters to Shun, appointed him chief of this State (see the 通志 quoted in the 通鑑綱目, on the 70th year of Yaou's reign); but this is inconsistent with the first mention of Shun to Yaou, in the prec. Book. It is commonly held that Shun's ancestors had been lords of the principality of Yu to the time of his father, who somehow lost his patrimony and was reduced to the rank of a private man. It may have been so, and the old title would continue to be cherished, though without the accessories that made it valuable. As to the history of the family of Yu, there is much difficulty in tracing it. Mencius, Book IV. Pt. II. i., tells us that Shun was of the wild tribes of the east, born in Choo-fung. Sze-ma Ts'een makes him descended from Hwang-te through the emp. Chuen-heuh. But as Yaou was also descended from Hwang-te through the emp. K'uh, Yaou and Shun must have had the same surname, and the idea of the one marrying his daughters to the other is so abhorrent to Chinese notions of propriety, that Choo He denounces Ts'een's genealogy as highly injurious to the fame of the sages. As Shun and the ladies would be cousins about ten times removed, a foreigner cannot sympathize with the horror expressed at the thought of their union. From the 國語, 晉語九, and the 左傳, 昭公八年, it appears that there was, or at least that in the time of the Chow dyn. it was believed there was, high up among Shun's ancestors, one of the name of Mŏh (幕), who has no place in Ts'een's genealogy; and some, discrediting entirely the account in the "Historical Records," would fix on this Mŏh as being the progenitor of Shun, chief of the principality of Yu, and not of the lineage of Hwang-te.—I have given these details to illustrate the many uncertainties that attend questions relating to Chinese antiquity.

TITLE OF, AND DISPUTES ABOUT, THE BOOK.—舜典, 'The Canon of Shun.' For the characters themselves, see on the title of the Canon of Yaou, and on par. 1 of that Book. This Canon is all found, with the exception of the first par., both in the texts of Fuh-shang, and of Gan-kwŏ. Fuh-shang, however, taught it as a part of the preceding Canon, and those who now deny the authenticity of the Books additional to his have no Canon of Shun in their editions.

On this question it may be observed:—First, the ancient preface to the Classic shows that there were originally two Canons—that of Yaou, and that of Shun—distinct from each other.

Secondly, about one half of the Book, as we have it, might very well belong to the Canon of Yaou, the parr. 2–12 being all occupied with the trial of Shun and his doings as acting emperor, while Yaou was yet alive. Par. 2, moreover, follows naturally the last par. of the prec. Book.

Thirdly, from par. 14th to the end we have the doings of Shun as emperor, which can with no propriety form a part of the Canon of Yaou.

The natural conclusion from these points is, that in the Canon of Shun we have the whole or a part of what was anciently and properly so called, and another portion which has been improperly separated from the Canon of Yaou. The Shoo has still its two Teen, but the point of division between them has been incorrectly marked.

It accords with this conclusion, that Mencius, Bk. V. Pt. I. iv, quotes par. 13, as from the Canon of Yaou. Other similar quotations of portions of the first part of the Book are adduced. No quotation of any par. of the second part, as belonging to the Canon of Yaou, can be found.

In the 'Historical Records' (五帝本記), immediately after the account of Yaou's death, as in par. 13, there follow various accounts of Shun,—legendary, indeed, in their character, but having the sanction of Mencius, Bk. V. Pt. I. i., *et al.*—which are not now found in the Canon of the Classic. No doubt, the original and less *gossiping* version of those accounts formed, before the dyn. of Ts'in, part of the Shoo; and so much of the Canon of Shun I believe to be lost. See an attempt by Maou K'e-ling to reconstruct the whole, appended to his 尚書廣聽錄.

It is more difficult to come to a conclusion on another question, with which that about the Division of the Canons has been unnecessarily complicated,—the question of the

GENUINENESS OF THE FIRST PARAGRAPH. These twenty-eight characters have a history of their own. Fuh-shang knew nothing of them, nor is it clear that Gan-kwŏ did. Had he found them among the other portions of the Shoo which were recovered from the wall of Confucius' house, the two Canons must have been from the first accurately divided by them.

When the work of Gan-kwŏ was first presented to the Government, as containing the Shoo in larger measure than Fuh-shang's Books, by Mei Tsih (梅賾), sometime in the beginning of the eastern Tsin [unfortunately, the Histories of the Tsin dynasty are some of them lost. The 'Book of Tsin' from which K'ung Ying-tă quotes his account of Tsih does not now exist; and it does not seem possible to ascertain the year when Gan-kwŏ's work was authoritatively recognized], this paragraph was wanting.

During the dyn. of the Southern Ts'e (南齊), in A.D. 497, one Yaou Fang-hing (姚方興) found 'in a large ship' (於大航頭得; so, Ying-tă; in the 'Books of the Suy dynasty [A.D. 589–617], however, it is said that Fang-hing 於大桁市, 'bought it in a large 桁. That character is given in the dict. as used synonymously with 航) a copy of Gan-kwŏ's Canon of Shun with the par. complete. He memorialized the Government on his discovery, and acc. to Maou K'e-ling, divided the Canons as we now have them. Not even yet, however, was the par. publicly recognized. Soon after the presentation of his memorial, Fang-hing was put to death; and the matter continued undecided till the early part of the reign of the first Suy emperor, when another copy was found containing the sentences in question.

This late recognition of the introductory portion of Shun's Canon justifies a suspicion of its genuineness. On the other hand, Ying-tă says that, while Mei Tsih's copy wanted this par., they supplied it from Wang Suh and Fan Ning, the former of whom had written on all the classic, and the latter specially on this Canon. (See the list of Books on the Shoo, in the time of the Suy dyn.) Now Wang Suh died A.D. 259, himself an adherent of the House of Wei (魏), yet before the final extinction of the Han. The industry of critics has also discovered portions of the par. in the remains of writers prior to Suh. Maou K'e-ling quotes especially from Wang Ts'an (王粲), who died A.D. 216, and from Wang Yen-show (王延壽), more than half a century earlier; and contends that the par. must have been with the rest of the Canon deciphered by Gan-kwŏ. Against this conclusion has to be put the fact of the improper division of the Canons, which I have pointed out. My own opinion is that some such par. did originally belong to the Canon of Shun. The fact of the Canon of Yaou, and the Counsels of Kaou Yaou (to say nothing of the Counsels

書經

○慎徽五典、五典克從、納于百揆、百揆時敘、賓于四 二節

2 II. *Shun* carefully set forth the beauty of the five cardinal duties; and they came to be universally observed. Being appointed to be General Regulator, the affairs of each department were arranged in their proper seasons. Having to receive *the princes from* the four

of Yu), being so prefaced, renders it all but certain that this Book had a similar introduction. Portions of this floated about among scholars from one source and another, and gradually coalesced into the par. which we now have. Maou K'e-ling is the best defender of its genuineness, in the second chapter of his 古文尚書寃詞. Against it, see the 60th art. in the 尚書古文疏證 of Yen Jŏ-keu (閻若璩).

Contents of the Book. The meagre and misleading account of the Book given in the prefatory notice of it has been pointed out. Looking at the Canon as it is now edited, we may conveniently divide it into six chapters;—the first, cont. par. 1, describing Shun's virtues and advancement; the second, cont. parr. 2-4, describing Yaou's trial of Shun, and resignation to him of the administration of affairs; the third, cont. parr. 5-11, describing the acts of Shun as Yaou's vicegerent; the fourth, parr. 13 and 14, describing the demise of Yaou, and accession of Shun to the throne; the fifth, parr. 15-27, describing Shun's choice of ministers, and other arrangements; and the sixth, par. 28, recording his death. As Yaou was the subject of the last Book, so is Shun of this.

Ch. I. The sagely virtues of Shun, and his consequent advancement to dignity. On the constr. of 曰若稽古, and on 舜曰重華, see on the last Book, p. 1. When 重華 is taken as descriptive of Shun, and not as his name, the interpretation is—'there was anew a display of virtue in him equal to that of Yaou.' 協于帝,—the 帝 of course is Yaou. 允塞,—塞 'to stop up;' then, 'fill up,' and hence, 'what is solid,' 'solidity.' It is observed by Chin Tih-show (眞德秀, of the Sung dyn.), that in the times of T'ang and Yu they had not yet the character 誠, *sincerity*, and that that is the meaning conveyed here by 允塞 玄德,—玄=幽潛, 'dark and hidden.' An obj. is taken to the genuineness of the whole par. from the phrase, which belongs to the school of Taouism. No doubt it is a common phrase with Taouists, but I do not see why other writers might not use it also to express the idea of 'mysterious virtue.' 升聞, 'ascended and was heard of,' *i.e.*, came to the ears of Yaou. 乃命以位,—acc. to Ts'ae Ch'in, 位 is simply 職位, 'office,' or 'offices,' with reference to the various posts in which Shun was tested. Such an interpr. supposes the par. to be in its proper place; but it has been shown that it should stand after par. 13, and 位 = the throne, the imperial Seat.

Ch. II. Shun fully satisfying Yaou's hopes in various offices, the emperor after three years commits to him the entire administration of affairs. P. 2. It is supposed that Shun, after receiving the emperor's two daughters in marriage, ruled his house well, and Yaou proceeded to try him, first as minister of Instruction. 徽=美, 'to beautify.' Some expl it by 和, 'to harmonize.' 五典, 'the five Canons,'—what are elsewhere called 五教, 'the five lessons,' and 五常, 'the five constant duties,' the virtues belonging to the five social relations of husband and wife, father and son, sovereign and subject, elder and younger brother, and friends. Thereafter Shun 納于百揆, 'was introduced into the office of General Regulator.' 揆, 'to consider,' 'to calculate,'=度. 百揆=揆度百官之事, '百揆 expresses the regulation of the business of all the officers.' The office of General Regulator is not heard of in subseqent dynasties. That of 冢宰 or premier corresponded to it under the Chow. It is said in the 'Historical Records' that in discharging the duties of minister of Instruction, Shun employed the services of 'the eight good men' (八元), descended from Kaou-sin (高辛氏) or the emp. K'uh, whom Yaou had not been able to employ; and in the office of prime minister, that he availed himself of the help of the 'eight triumphant ones' (八愷), descended from Kaou-yang (高陽氏), or the emp. Chuenheüh. The same thing is found in the 左傳. Why may we not suppose that such legends, existing in the ancient documents, were purposely rejected by Confucius himself?

門、四門穆穆、納于大麓、烈風雷雨弗迷。○帝曰、格汝舜、詢事考言、乃言底可績、三載、汝陟帝位。舜讓于德、弗嗣。○正月上日、受終于

quarters of the empire, they all were docilely submissive. Being sent to the great plains at the foot of the mountains, amid violent wind, thunder, and rain, he did not go astray.

3 The emperor said, "Come, you Shun. I have consulted you on *all* affairs, and examined your words, and found that your words can be carried into practice;—*now* for three years. Do you ascend the imperial throne." Shun wished to decline in favour of some

4 one more virtuous, and not to consent to be successor. On the first day, of the first month, *however*, he received Yaou's retirement *from the imperial duties* in the *temple of the* Accomplished ancestor.

Shun was finally tried as the president of the nobles, in the office of the Sze Yŏ (四岳). 賓于四門,—賓, 'a guest,' and also 'to receive a guest,' 'to act the host.' This is its sense here. Ch'ing read it in the 3d tone, as if it had been 儐. 四門,—'to act the host at the four gates,' *i.e.*, to receive the nobles coming from the different quarters. So, Ma Yung. Keang Shing says ingeniously that the four gates were those of the 明堂, or Hall of Audience. The 'Historical Records' have a legend of Shun's banishing away 'the four bad ones' (四凶), in connection with the duties of this office. It is difficult to know what to think of the last part of the par. 麓 is expl. by Ch'ing as 山足, 'the foot of a mountain.' The 'Historical Records' take the account literally as in the transl. Looking at the phrase 納于大麓, following so close upon 納于百揆, it is natural to interpret it in the same way, as indicating Shun's appointment to some office. This Gan-kwŏ has done, and after him Wang Suh. They say—麓, 錄也, 堯納舜于尊顯之官, 使大錄天下萬機之政, '*Luh* means to record. Yaou appointed Shun to an honourable and distinguished office, that he might record the govt. of the empire with its myriad springs.' This might be admitted as a good enough explanation of the phrase, but the sequel about the wind and rain cannot be made to harmonize with it. See in the 集說 various attempts to explain the passage, all unsatisfactory.

P. 3. 詢=咨謀, 'to consult about.' 乃 is in the sense of 汝, 'you.' 底=致, 'to come to, result in.' The paraphrase of the 'Daily Lessons' puts 詢 and 考 in the past complete tense:—'Formerly, when I called you to employment, I consulted you on what you would do, and examined the plans you laid before me.' But why should we suppose that the two had not been in frequent intercourse all along? Ch'ing strangely takes the 'three years' to be three years subsequent to Shun's receiving the nobles of all quarters. The last clause might also be translated—'Shun declined on the ground of his virtue's not being equal to the succession.'

P. 4. This demission of the actual conduct of affairs is referred to the 73d year of Yaou's reign. 正月上日,—see on p. 14. Here 正 (in this sense often, but not necessarily, read in the 1st tone) 月='the first month;' 上日='the first day.' This has been disputed but without reason; see the remarks of Lin Che-k'e (林之奇) in the 集說. Certainly, if this natural interpr. of 上 be rejected, we are altogether at sea as to its meaning. 受終 intimates that 'now Yaou *ended* his imperial administration, and Shun undertook it' (so, Ts'ae Ch'in). 于文祖 must be understood 'in the temple of,' or

文祖。五節 ○在璿璣玉衡、以齊七政。六節 ○肆類于上帝、禋于

5 III. He examined the gem-adorned turning sphere, and the gem transverse *tube*, that he might regulate the seven Directors.
6 Thereafter, he sacrificed specially, but with the ordinary forms, to

'before the shrine of, the accomplished ancestor.' By this ancestor must be intended the individual to whom Yaou traced his possession of the throne,—perhaps Hwang-te. Ma Yung understood by 文祖 Heaven, saying that 'Heaven is the Father (祖) who beautifies all things, and therefore is called 文祖.' This would give a good meaning; but had it been intended, the text would have been different. K'ang-shing thought that Yaou had a Hall of audience and worship, called 五府, corresponding to the 明堂 of the Chow dynasty, the several parts of which were dedicated to 'the five *Tes*,' the Gods or divine powers presiding over nature; and that 文祖 was the name of the hall of the Red Te (赤帝), but is used here, a part for the whole, intending the whole structure. This view comes to be substantially the same with that of Ma Yung. The belief of five Tes was long posterior to the times of Yaou and Shun.

CH. III. LABOURS AND ADMINISTRATION OF SHUN OCCUPYING THE THRONE AS VICEGERENT OF YAOU. P. 5. *Astronomical labours.* 在 = 察, 'to examine,' as in the Canon of Yaou, p. 7. 璿 is the name of some kind of gem; the particular kind can hardly be ascertained. 璣 is given in the dict. as being 器名, 'the name of an instrument,' with a reference to this passage. Ts'ae Ch'in takes the char. as = 機, 'a spring,' 'a contrivance.' We can easily understand that the 玉 was an addition of subsequent times to both characters. Fuh-shang seems to have read 旋機, 'the turning contrivance' (see his 'Preface to the Shoo,' and Keang Shing, *in loc.*). There is no difference about the reading of the next two characters, which mean 'the gem transverse,' and the 玉 there will justify the same in the two previous characters. According to Ts'ae Ch'in, following the ancient interpreters, Gan-kwŏ, Ch'ing, and Ma Yung, the four characters describe a kind of armillary sphere, the 璿璣 representing the revolution of the heavens, and the 'transverse' being a tube made of a precious stone, and placed athwart the sphere, for the purpose of celestial observation. Earlier than Gan-kwŏ, a different view seems to have obtained. Fuh-shang says:—'What was the 旋機? 旋 means to revolve; and 機 means a spring, what is minute. That whose own motion is very small, while the movements which it produces are great, is what is called here 旋機. The words denote the north pole' (尙書大傳). Keang-shing says he approves of this view, but taking the four characters to be a description of the 'Great Bear,' called in Chinese the 'Northern Peck' (北斗). The 'handle' is the 'transverse' of the classic. 天旋 is the name still given to α Dubhe of Ursa Major; 天機 to β Dubhe; and 玉衡 to ε Alioth. This explanation is marked by simplicity, but the text of the classic will not admit of it. The writer must have had some constructed instrument in his mind's eye. De Guignes observes that the details are very singular for the time to which they refer, and asks whether astronomy had then made so much progress (Le Chou King, p. 13, note). But the existence of instruments of the character indicated is in accordance with the astronomical knowledge which we have seen that Yaou possessed. With regard to the form of Shun's sphere, it was no doubt very simple. The figure in Yung Ching's Shoo, said to represent it, is all of modern device.

The object of Shun's labours on the sphere and tube was 'to regulate (齊, "make uniform") the seven Governments.' By these 七政 Ma Yung understood the seven stars of the Great Bear. K'ang-shing said they meant 'spring, autumn, winter, and summer, astronomy, geography, and anthropology' (see Keang Shing, *in loc*). These opinions may be set aside at once. The consent of later times is all but universal to the view of Gan-kwŏ, that the seven governments were the sun, the moon, and the five planets, Mercury, Venus, Mars, Jupiter, and Saturn, each of which had its own rules of government. According to this, we ought to translate 七政, 'the seven regularly governed Bodies.' But we have seen that the study of astronomy in those early times was all for practical purposes. The motions of the heavenly bodies were ascertained, to be a help to the movements of the government on earth. I prefer therefore to render the terms by 'the seven Directors.'

P. 6. *Acts of religious worship.* 肆 = 遂, 'upon this,' 'thereafter.' Gan-kwŏ (especially

六宗、望于山川、徧于群神。○輯五瑞、既月、乃日覲四

God; sacrificed purely to the six Honoured *ones;* offered their appropriate sacrifices to the hills and rivers; and extended his worship to the host of spirits.

7 He called in all the five tokens of gem; and when the month was over, he gave daily audience to the *chief of the* four Mountains, and all the Pastors, *finally* returning the tokens to the several nobles.

as expounded by Ying-tă) makes the char. follow in logical sequence from the prec. par., as if Shun had discovered by his examination of the heavenly bodies, that Yaou's urging him to occupy the throne was from Heaven, and immediately he proceeded to announce his compliance to all superior spiritual powers.

類, 禋, and 望 are the names of different sacrifices. 類 denotes a sacrifice offered to the Highest, on an extraordinary occasion, which characteristic is faintly indicated in the name, 類 being = 'of a sort,' 'a class.' Hence K'ang-shing says that Shun now sacrificed to Shang Te at the round mound, *i.e.*, at the place and with the ceremonies appropriate to the imperial worship of Heaven at the winter solstice. By 上帝 we are to understand God, the supreme Ruler. It is not till we come down to the times of the Chow dyn. that anything can be discovered to lead us to think of Shang Te as other than one and supreme. During the Chow there grew up the doctrine of five Tes, sometimes represented as distinct from Shang Te, and sometimes as different manifestations of Him. It has not, however, maintained itself. K'ang-shing's view of the name here has been indicated above. Ma Yung held that Shang Te was 'The supreme One' (太一); see the Record of Rites, 禮運, Pt. iv. 4. The whole of his comment is:—上帝太一,神在紫微宮,天之最顯者, 'Shang Te is the great One; his spirit occupies the palace of Tsze-wei' [a celestial space about the pole], 'the most distinguished of the heavenly *Powers*.' The blending of astrological fancies with the classical truth appears in it. Wang Suh made Shang Te here simply to be synonymous with Heaven; and Gan-kwŏ himself had defined the name as = 'Heaven and the five Tes' (天及五帝). I cannot doubt but Shang Te is here the name of the true God; but the truth concerning Him and His worship had been perverted even in this early time, as appears from the other clauses of the paragraph.

禋 is supposed by Ch'ing K'ang-shing to be connected with 煙, 'smoke,' and have reference to the burnt sacrifices which were presented; but this view cannot be sustained. The word applies to a sacrifice offered 'with purity and reverence.' Who the 'six Honoured ones' were, it is not possible to ascertain. Fuh-shang and his earlier followers held that, though six were mentioned, only one Being or Power was intended,—a sort of plastic influence, working between heaven and earth and the four cardinal points (see Sun Sing-yen, *in loc.*) Subsequently every interpreter had his own view, as may be seen in Ying-tă. Acc. to Gan-kwŏ, followed by Wang Suh, the six Honoured ones are 'the seasons, cold and heat, the sun, the moon, the stars, and drought.' Of course we must understand that the emp. sacrificed to certain spirits, ruling over these phenomena and things, and residing probably in different stars.

望 is the name of sacrifices offered to the hills and streams. The sacrificer would probably *look towards* the quarter where each mountain or stream was situated. We are to understand that 'the hills and rivers' were all throughout the empire, not the more famous of them only, but all, with their presiding spirits.

Finally, Shun did homage to 'the herd of spirits,'—all spirits of heaven, earth, and men, not included in the above three clauses;—'to mounds, dykes, plains, forests, and the sages and worthies of ancient times.' So says Ying-tă, who points out also how, in thus sacrificing to 'all spirits' (百神), Shun was exercising an imperial prerogative. Such was the solemn worship of Shun, a sage, a perfect man, according to the Chinese ideal. It was offered in the year B.C. 2283, so soon had men departed from the truth of God, and added to His worship of their own inventions.

P. 7. *Shun gives audience to the nobles of the empire, and confirms them in their fiefs.* 五瑞,—'the five gem-signets.'—It is difficult to get a word exactly corresponding to 瑞. Medhurst transl. it by 'sceptre.' The fiefs of the empire were divided into five classes, the chiefs of which were known respectively by the titles of Kung, How, Pih, Tsze, and Nan (see Mencius, Bk. V. Pt. II. ii.); so it was in the Chow dyn., and there was an arrangement, the same or similar, in the earliest times. Each ruler, on obtaining his appointment from the emperor, received a token, differing in size and form according to the rank. This he kept, and brought with him whenever he appeared at

書經

岳群牧、班瑞于群后。○八節歲二月、東巡守、至于岱宗、柴、望秩于山川、肆覲東后、協時月正日、同律度量衡、修

8 In the second month of the year, he made a tour of inspection eastwards, as far as Tae-tsung, where he presented a burnt-offering to Heaven, and sacrificed in order to the hills and rivers. Thereafter he gave audience to the nobles of the East, putting in accord their

court. The separate tokens were so constructed that they fitted into a sort of frame kept in the imperial treasury, by which their genuineness was tested, so that an impostor might in this way be detected. The token held by the *Kung*, or nobles of the highest rank, was called 桓圭; that of the *How*, 信圭; of the *Pih*, 躬圭; of the *Tsze*, 穀璧; and of the *Nan*, 蒲璧 (see the 周禮,春官,大宗伯,二). On Shun's accession to the administration of the empire, it was necessary that all the nobles should have their appointments confirmed by him.

There is a difficulty with the interpretation of 既月. 既 is taken as = 盡, so that the phrase = 'when a month was completed.' That month is understood to be the first month of the year after his accession. The summons had been sent to the nobles, and at the expiry of a month they began to arrive. The 羣牧 were the chiefs of the nobles in the different provinces, the lord-lieutenants, whose official chief again was the 四岳. To them Shun gave daily audience on the subject of the difft. nobles, whom they would introduce, and who were then sent back with their tokens to their various fiefs, to maintain the authority of the vicegerent.

P. 8. *Tours of Inspection.* 巡守 appears in Mencius, I. Pt. II. iv. 5, *et al.*, as 巡狩, = 'perambulated the Charges *of the nobles*.' To what year this first tour is to be referred cannot be determined. Ma Yung held that it was the 5th year after Shun undertook the govt. Gan-kwŏ again makes it the same as that in which he confirmed the nobles. The arranged chronol. places it in the year after, the 74th of Yaou's reign. Perhaps it was so. In making the circuit, Shun first travelled east, as far as 岱宗, called elsewhere and now 泰山, 5 *le* to the north of the district city of T'ae-gan (泰安) in the dep. of the same name in Shan-tung [Lat. 36°30', N., Lon. 1°, E., Med.] This mount. was deemed the first of all the hills of China, and therefore it has the epithet of 宗 or 'Honourable.' When his work was done here, Shun went to the South.

卒乃復,—Gan-kwŏ and Ma Yung take 復 actively:—' he returned the five instruments of gem.' I have followed them. K'ang-shing takes it intrans., and supposes that Shun returned to the capital and sacrificed a single victim at the end of each tour. Choo He, foll. of course by Ts'ae Ch'in and others, also takes it intrans., but without suppos. a return to the cap. Shun simply turns back from his eastward course, and goes in another direction. They also suppose that the text has got transposed, and read 五玉,三帛,二生,一死,贄, immediately after 東后. There is no necessity for such a violent measure, if we take 復 actively, as I have done. From mount T'ae, Shun proceeded to the Southern mountain, generally supposed to have been mount Hwăng (衡), 30 *le* to the north of the dis. city of Hwăng-san (衡山), in Hwăng-chow dep. (衡州), Hoo-nan [Lat. 37°30', N., Lon. 4°15', W., Med.] This has been thought too remote, and other hills not so far south have been fixed on. From mount Hwăng, Shun trav. west to the Western mountain, or mount Hwa (華山), called T'ae-hwa (太華) in the 'Tribute of Yu.' It is 10 *le* south of the dis. city of Hwa-yin (華陰), in Shen-se, dep. of Se-ngan. [Lat. 34°30', N., Lon. 6°30', W., Med.]. From the west, he proc. north, to the Northern mountain. or mount Hăng (恆山), considered, in the sacrificial statutes of the pres. dyn., to be 20 *le* to the south of Hwăn-chow dis. (渾州), dep. of Ta-t'ung (大同), in Shan-se [Lat. 37°30', N., Lon. 2°30', W., Med.] From the north he ret. to the cap., which was at no great distance, in the pres. dep. of P'ing-yang (平陽) in Shan-se; and there he sacrificed a

五禮、五玉、三帛、二生、一死、贄、如五器、卒乃復。五月南巡守、至于南岳、如岱禮。八月西巡守、至于西岳、如初。

seasons and months, and rectifying the days; he made uniform the standard tubes, the measures of length and of capacity, and the steel-yards; he regulated the five *classes of* ceremonies. As to the several articles of introduction,—the five instruments of gem, the three kinds of silk, the two living animals, and the one dead one, when all was over, he returned the five instruments. In the fifth month, he made a similar tour to the south, as far as the southern mountain, observing the same ceremonies as at Tae. In the same way, in

bull (特＝一牛), in the temple of the Cultivated ancestor, announcing the completion of his circuit. 藝祖 is probably the same as 文祖, p. 4. So, Gan-kwŏ and K'ang-shing.

On arriving at each of his halting places, Shun first pres. a burnt-offering to Heaven. 柴, lit., ＝'firewood.' On the altar a pile of wood was reared, on which the victim and other offerings were placed. The practice is the same at the pres. day. The old interp. placed no comma after 宗, but placed one after 柴. Choo He pointed at 宗, and then read on to 川. I put a comma both at 宗 and 柴. 秩, 'in order,'＝如其秩次, 'acc. to their order.' Difft. ranks were assigned to the hills and rivers, and the ceremonies paid to them varied accordingly.

Shun's business at the various points, after giv. audience to the nobles was:—1st, to see that they had the calendar correct—協時 (＝四時) 月 (謂月之大小, *i.e.*, which months were long and which short. So, Gan-kwŏ; and this would imply a process of intercalation like the present) 日 (謂日之甲乙, *i.e.*, the names of the days, their designation by the cycle-characters); 2d, to see that the weights, measures, &c., of the difft. States were uniform. 同律,—'he made uniform the regulation-tubes.' 律 is defined by 分, 'that which divides.' The name was given to twelve tubes, originally made of bamboo, then of some gem, and in the time of the Han dyn. of brass or copper. They were a little more than three tenths of an inch in diameter, and the circumference of the bore was exactly nine tenths. The longest was called 'the yellow cup' (黃鐘), 9 in. long, and the shortest 'the responsive cup' (應鐘), only 4.66 in. The name of 律 more especially belonged to six of them, which gave the sharped notes in music. The others, giving the flat notes, were called 呂. The twelve together about formed, I believe, a chromatic scale. But besides their application to music (see on p. 24), the *hwang chung* was the standard measure of length. The 90th part of it was 1 *fun* (分); 10 *fun* were 1 inch (寸); 10 inches were 1 foot (尺); 10 feet were 1 *chang* (丈); and 10 *chang* were 1 *yin* (引) [It is said that the breadth of a grain of millet (一黍之廣) made a *fun*, and that 90 of them determined the length of the 1st tube. See the 'Commentary of Ts'ae Illustrated' (蔡傳旁通), by Ch'in Sze-k'ae (陳師凱) of the Yuen dyn. (pub. A.D. 1321)]. The same tube was the standard for measures of capacity. 13½ millet grains filled a *fun* of it, and 1200 grains filled the whole. So much made a *yoh* (龠); 2 *yoh* made a *kŏh* (合); 10 *kŏh*, 1 *shing* (升); 10 *shing*, 1 *tow* (斗); 10 *tow*, 1 *hoh* (斛). The tube, again, supplied the standard for weights. 100 grains of millet weighed a *choo* (銖); 24 *choo*; 1 *lëang* (兩) or tael; 16 taels, 1 *kin* (斤), or catty; 30 catties, 1 *keun* (鈞); and 4 *keun*, 1 *shih* (石), or stone. From all these applications of 'the yellow cup' we find it spoken of as 'the root of all human affairs' (黃鐘爲萬事根本).

書經

十有一月朔巡守、至于北岳、如西禮。歸格于藝祖、用特。○（九節）五載一巡守、群后四朝、敷奏以言、明試以功、車

the eighth month, he travelled westwards, as far as the western mountain; and in the eleventh month he travelled northwards, as far as the northern mountain. When he returned *to the capital, he* went to the *temple of the* Cultivated ancestor, and offered a single bullock.

9 In five years there was one tour of inspection, and four appearances of the nobles at court. They set forth a report of their government in words. This was clearly tested by their works. They received chariots and robes according to their services.

Shun would carry with him from the capital standard tubes, measures, steelyards and beams, and weights. There was a 3d subject to occupy him. He had also 'to regulate the five ceremonies.' By these Ch'ing understood the ceremonies to be observed in appearing at court and in their intercourse with one another by the five classes of nobles indicated in the last par. Gan-kwŏ and Ma Yung take the ceremonies to be the same with those recognized under the Chow dyn.,—the various ceremonies of worship (吉禮); the ceremonies appropriate to calamity and mourning (凶禮), the ceremonies appropriate to guests of State (賓禮); the ceremonies appropriate to war (軍禮); and festive ceremonies (嘉禮) appropriate to marriages and other occasions of joy. This latter interpretation is to be preferred.

The nobles in waiting upon Shun brought with them their tokens of investiture,—the 五瑞 of last par., called here 五玉 and 五器; and also various articles which prepared the way for their audience, and are here called 贄. 'A man's gift maketh room for him, and bringeth him before great men.' This obtains in the east more than elsewhere, and obtained from the earliest times. The statutes enacted even in Shun's days recognized it, and endeavoured to regulate it and prevent its abuse. 三帛,—'three fabrics of silk.' Ch'ing says they were red silk (赤繒), on which the descendants of Kaou-sin presented their signets; black silk, on which those of Kaou-yang presented theirs; and white silk, used by the other nobles. Gan-kwŏ and Wang Suh, again, say that they were silks of a deep red, brought by the eldest sons of princes; dark azure silks, brought by 三公之孤; and yellow silks, brought by the chiefs of small attached territories. 二生, 'two living animals,'—lambs or kids, brought by the highest officers in the various States (卿); and geese, brought by inferior officers (大夫). 一死, 'one dead animal,'—pheasants brought by the smaller officers, and scholars expecting employment (士). 如五器, 'as to the five instruments,' *i.e.*, the signets. Those who would transpose this clause (see above) are obliged to expl. 如 by 同, 'to make uniform.'

This year of inspection must have been a busy one to Shun. Many commentators have doubted the possibility of his accomplishing all the work. Some things indicated have been pushed up, I must suppose, from the practices of a subsequent age.

P. 9. *Regular periods of tours of inspection and appearances of the nobles at court, with the results of such appearances.* After the circuit detailed in last par., it was probably enacted by Shun that such a tour should be made every five years. During the intermediate four years, the nobles and princes of the difft. divisions of the empire presented themselves at court. Ma and K'ung suppose that the 'four appearances' were those at the four points of meeting during the year of the imperial circuit. The other view—more in accord with the phrase 四朝—is given by Ch'ing. He says 'the nobles came separately,' intending, we may suppose with Ts'ae Ch'in, that the first year those of the east came, those of the south on the second, &c. 敷奏以言,—敷=陳, 'to lay out, set forth;' 奏=進 'to present,'=to represent. In want of any expressed nominative

服以庸。○十節肇十有二州、封十有二山、濬川。○十一節象以典刑、流宥五刑、鞭作官刑、扑

10 *Shun* instituted the division of the empire into twelve provinces, raising altars upon twelve hills in them. He *likewise* deepened the rivers.

11 He gave delineations of the statutory punishments, enacting banishment as a mitigation of the five *great* inflictions; with the whip to be employed in the magistrates' courts, the stick to be employed in schools, and money to be received for redeemable crimes.

to these verbs, we may take them indefinitely.—'There was setting forth and representation by means of words.' So with the other clauses. 功, 'meritorious service,' is specially applied to 'service to the State' (國); while 庸 is 民功, 'service rendered to the people' like the teaching them agriculture (see the 周禮,夏官,司馬,第四之三). 車服以庸,—see the She King Pt. II., Bk. VII., viii. 以 is here somewhat difft. from its use in the prec. clauses, and = 'according to.'

P. 10 *Division of the empire into twelve provinces, and attendant circumstances.* This division must have taken place several years after Shun's accession to the administration. While Yu was labouring on the flooded provinces, their number was only nine, and the rearrangement of them as twelve must have been subsequent to the conclusion of his work. It is referred by the Annalists to the 81st year of Yaou. Fuh-shang in his Preface assigns it to the first year of Shun's independent reign, which would seem to be more likely. For the provinces, see next Part, Bk. I. Shun divided K'e into the three provinces of Ping (并), K'e (冀) and Yew (幽); and Ts'ing into Ts'ing (青) and Ying (營). See Ying-tă *in loc.* This division into twelve provinces did not last beyond Shun's reign. 封十有二山,—封, 'to raise a mound,' here = 封土爲壇, 'to raise up earth for an altar' (Keang Shing). In every province Shun selected a mountain,—the largest probably,—and made it the 'guardian' of the territory (鎭山). See the 周禮,夏官,司馬,第四之六. 濬, in p. 1, 'profound,' 'deep;' here a verb, = 'to deepen.' The mention of this leads us to refer the whole of this par. to Shun's own reign, some years after the completion of Yu's work.

P. 11. *Punishments.* Comp. p. 20; and Pt. V., Bk. XXVII. 象以典刑,—象, 'to delineate;' as in the Canon of Yaou, p. 3. There is much dispute about the meaning of the char. here. Gan-kwŏ takes it as = 法, 'laws,' and expl.—'according to the laws, he used the regular punishments, not going beyond the laws.' This view may at once be set aside. Ts'ae Ch'in says we are to understand it as in the phrase—'Heaven hangs out its appearances to show to men' (天垂象以示人); which gives us the idea of pictorial representation. 典刑,—'regular punishments,' said to be five in the next clause. Those were branding (on the forehead) (墨); cutting off the nose (劓); cutting off the feet (刖); castration (宮); and death [which might be by various modes of execution] (大辟).

It is maintained by some Chinese scholars that Yaou and Shun did not use those severe punishments. They did not need to do so, it is said. Ma Yung says on the text:—'Kaou Yaou instituted these five punishments, but none made themselves obnoxious to them. There were the representations (其象), but not the criminals' (其人). Fuh-shang speaks of persons liable to these punishments being dressed so as to attract attention, which made a greater impression than the infliction of the penalties would have done. These objections were made at a very early time, and answered by Seun K'ing, in the 3d cent. before Christ. Others allowing that Yaou and Shun had the punishment of death, say that the other four penalties in the flesh (肉刑) originated with the Hea dyn.; but neither is this correct. See Maou K'e-ling's 廣

作教刑、金作贖刑、眚災肆赦、怙終賊刑、欽哉、欽哉、惟刑之恤哉。○十二節 流共工于幽

Inadvertent offences and those which might be caused by misfortune were to be pardoned, but those who offended presumptuously or repeatedly were to be punished with death. "Let me be reverent; let me be reverent," *he said to himself.* "Let compassion rule in punishment."

12 He banished the minister of Works to Yew island; confined Hwantow on mount Tsung; drove the *chief of* San-meaou *and his people*

聽錄,—, *in loc.* Branding and the cutting off of the nose and feet were abolished by the emp. Wăn (文帝) of the Han dynasty (B.C. 178–156). Castration, however, remained on the statute book till the first emperor of the Suy dyn. (A.D. 579–600). From that time to the present the five punishments have been—beating with the bamboo (笞); with the cudgel (杖); the shorter banishment (徒); the longer (流); and (死) death [which may be by decapitation, strangulation, cutting or slicing to pieces, &c.] K'e-ling observes that in this respect the ways of modern times are more humane than the ways of the ancient sages were. 流宥五刑 = 'banishment to mitigate the five severe penalties.' 鞭,—'a whip,' 'a piece of leather tied to a stick.' 扑 *(p'uh)*,—'to beat;'—the Dict. says 'with a stick' (杖); Gan-kwŏ, 'with bramble-twigs, or with branches of the 榎.' The crimes punishable with the whip and stick are supposed to be slighter offences, not only below the penalty of the five inflictions, but also below banishment. The whip was employed against officers in the courts; and the stick against officers in the schools. Medhurst, indeed, translates—'the birch for the flagellation of scholars.' But if the next clause be correctly taken as applying to offences under these two heads, which is the common view of it, a commutation of the birch for a fine in schools becomes absurd,—to say nothing of Shun's condescending to such matters. 金,—'metal,' here = 'copper.' See Sun Sing-yen, *in loc.* 無心之過誤謂之眚, 'offences without intention are called 眚.' 不幸而獲過謂之災, 'offences by mishap are called 災:'—see the 日講. The old interpreters joined the two together—'injuries done without purpose.' 肆 = 縱, 'to let go.' 怙終賊刑,—Ch'ing expands:—怙其姦而終身以爲殘賊則用刑之, 'those who persist in their villainy, and all their lives are criminals, are to be punished.' It is better, with Gan-kwŏ, to take 賊 = 殺, and 怙 as in the translation; 怙 = 有恃, and 終 = 再犯. 欽哉云云,—it is best to take these two sentences as addressed by Shun to himself.

P. 12. *How Shun dealt with the four great criminals of the empire.* We do not know when the transactions here mentioned took place. Sze-ma Ts'een, I mentioned above, has a legend of 'four villains' (四凶), banished by Shun while Yaou was testing him; but he has also incorporated the present par. with his Work, so that he must have considered the 四罪 and the 四凶 to be different individuals.

The minister of Works, Hwan-tow, and K'wăn have all occurred in the Canon of Yaou. 三苗 was the name of a country. This appears clearly from a passage in the 左傳, 昭元年, and especially from the 戰國策, 卷十四, where Woo K'e (吳起) tells one of the princes of Wei (魏) that 'San-meaou had on its left the waves of the P'ang-le (彭蠡), and on its right the waters of the Tung-t'ing (洞庭), Mount Wan (汶山) on the South, and Mount Hwăng (衡) on the north.' This agrees with other accounts of its situation. It possessed the territory now occupied by the depp. of Woo-ch'ang (武昌) in Hoo-pih, Yŏ-chow (岳州) in Hoo-nan, and Kew-keang (九江) in Keang-se. Why it was

洲、放驩兜于崇山、竄三苗于三危、殛鯀于羽山、四罪而天下咸服。○十三節 二十有八載、帝乃殂落、百姓如喪考

into San-wei, and kept them there; held K'wăn till death a prisoner on mount Yu. These four criminals being thus dealt with, universal submission prevailed throughout the empire.

13 IV. After twenty-eight years the emperor demised, when the people mourned for him as for a parent for three years. All within the

called the 'three Meaou,' it is only attempted to account for by foolish legends.

From the 國語, 楚語, 下, we see it was thought in the Chow dyn. that Yaou had been in hostilities with the people of Meaou, and we shall see in the next Book that Yu had likewise to proceed against them. Shun's measure seems to have been to remove their Chief and probably a portion of his people to another part of the country. We must suppose that their chief is specially intended, to make one in the quaternion of four great criminals. 流 = 'to banish.' 放 = 'to put in a place and confine there.' 竄 = 'to drive to, and keep as in prison.' 殛 would seem to mean 'to put to death,' and Ch'ing and Ma Yung expl. it by 誅, 'to take out of the way;' but Gan-kwŏ says that every one of the four criminals was dealt with in the way of 誅. A lighter meaning therefore is given to the term; and indeed, it is not easy to suppose that while Yu was his right hand, and rendering the greatest services to the empire, Shun would put his father to death. Woo Ch'ing says, 殛謂待死于此,以終其身.

幽洲 must originally have been 幽州, the 水 being a subsequent addition. This place was somewhere in the north;—it is said outside Chih-le province, to the north east of Meih-yun (密雲) dis., dep. of Shun-t'een. I am not sure, however, whether it is right to translate 洲, by 'island.' 崇山 was in the south, in the pres. Hoo-nan, in the dis. of Yung-ting (永定) in Le-chow (澧洲). 三危 was a district in the west, deriving its name from a hill of the same name. 'It rises,' says the Statistical Account of the empire under the pres. dyn., 'in the south-east of the dep. of Gan-se (安西) in Kan-suh, with three precipitous summits, which seem threatening to fall' (如危欲墜). 羽山 was in the east, in the pres. Shan-tung, 70 *le* to the north-east of the dis. city of T'an-shing (郯城), in E-chow (沂州).

四罪,—the char. 罪 originally was 辠, for which the founder of the Ts'in dyn. ordered 罪 to be used, disliking its similarity to the char. 皇. After 四罪 we must understand some characters equal to—'being thus discriminatingly dealt with.'

CH. IV. THE DEATH OF YAOU AND ACCESSION OF SHUN TO THE THRONE. P. 13. 二十有八載,—it seems to me that every unprejudiced reader of the classic must understand this as meaning 28 years, reckoning from Shun's accession to the administration of affairs, mentioned p. 4, so that Yaou's death would occur in the 100th year of his reign, B.C. 2257. The matter is complicated, however by what is related in the 'Historical Records,' that Yaou, getting Shun in the 70th year of his reign, employed him for 20 years, and only then resigned to him the administration, dying himself 8 years after. This account would make Yaou's reign extend over 98 years. The conclusion we draw from the classic is all against this view.

殂落 together = 'to decease.' Ts'een has 崩. Choo He says that at death the *animus* goes to heaven, and the *anima* to the earth. In this case, 殂 ought to denote 'to ascend,' but it simply = 往, 'to go away.' 百姓,—as in last Bk., p. 2, the 四海 corresponding to the 萬國 and 黎民 there. Keang Shing remarks that the mourning for three years proves that 百姓 must be confined to officers; but this assumes that 喪 is to be understood in the sense of 'wearing mourning,' and not in that of 'lamenting' generally. Besides, the people of the imperial domain had to

妣。三載。四海遏密八音。○十四節月正元日、舜格于文祖。○十五節詢于四岳、闢四門、明四目、

four seas, the eight instruments of music were stopped and hushed.
14 On the first day of the first month, Shun went to the *temple of the* Accomplished Ancestor.
15 V. He deliberated with the *chief of the* four Mountains, how to throw open all the doors *of communication between the court and the empire*, and sought to see with the eyes and hear with the ears of all.

wear mourning for three months (集傳, *in loc.*); and here they extended of themselves the rule to three years. 考 = a father, deceased; 妣, a mother, deceased. 四海,—'the four seas.' Anciently, the territories occupied by the nine *E* (夷), the eight *Teih* (狄), the seven *Jung* (戎), and the six *Man* (蠻), were called 'the four seas.' All within the four seas was divided into the 'nine provinces.' Within the nine provinces there were arranged the 'five domains,' divided into three,—the imperial, the nobles', the peaceful,—called the 'Middle Kingdom,' and two,—the domain of restraint, and the wild domain,—called the country of the 'four wild tribes;'—see Hoo Ming-king's (胡明經) Introduction to his Work on 'The Tribute of Yu.' According to this view, which is that of the ancient Dictionary, the 爾雅, 'the four seas' is a designation having nothing to do with the seas. The scholars and thinkers of the Sung dyn. did not understand how it could have arisen, and rejected this account of it. The phrase must have had its origin in some idea of the habitable territory as bounded on every side by water (see Con. Ana., XII. v., note). Yen Jŏ-keu, in his 'Topography of the Four Books,' art. 四海, says that the phrase has two meanings; generally it is to be taken in accordance with the ancient view, but sometimes it has a vast and vague signification, and = 天下, 'all under heaven.' Practically, this account is correct, but it says nothing of the origin of the phrase.—In the text, we must take the phrase vaguely, comprehending the empire. Even allowing the account of the 爾雅, 四海 must = 四海之內, or 九州. The writer could not have the barbarous territory beyond the empire in his mind.

八音,—'the eight sounds,' *i.e.*, all musical instruments, made of metal, of stone, of silk, of bamboo, of a gourd, of earth, of leather, or of wood.

P. 14. *Shun's accession to the throne.* This did not take place the year that Yaou died, nor the year after, but when the three years' mourning was expired. Nor did Shun then immediately occupy the throne. He allowed time for the expression of opinion from the nobles and people, and was willing that Yaou's son Choo should succeed to his father. Neither nobles nor people, however, would have any other but Shun to reign over them. See Mencius, Bk. V. Pt. I. v. 7. The date of the accession was B. C. 2254. 月正元日,—comp. p. 4., 正月上日. Gan-kwŏ and Wang Suh supposed the two passages identical, and that 月正 and 元 in the one and 正月 and 上 in the other are only variations of style, which a writer may indulge in without any great reason. Ch'ing on the other hand contends that the changes teach an important fact,—that Shun on his accession to the throne changed the first month of the year, from the month after the winter solstice, to the month beginning with it. It is slender ground on which to build such a conclusion. Suh says that it was only the Yin and Chow dynasties which changed the beginning of the year, and that the Hea dyn. and all previous times made it commence with the third month after the winter solstice; see on Con. Ana. XV. x. An expression in Pt. III. Book. II. p. 3. may be pressed in support of Ching's view. I do not know that there is any other evidence of it, and must here leave the point undetermined. 格于文祖,—文祖, see on p. 4. Shun went now to the temple to announce his accession to the throne; but henceforth he would go to the temple of his own ancestors.

Ch. V. Acts of Shun as emperor. With this par., or the prec., commences what is properly the Canon of Shun, or rather a fragment of that Canon. It wants the beginning, and we may say it wants the end also;—hardly carrying us beyond the events of one year.

P. 15. *Measure of Shun to call forth the good and able to public service, and make himself acquainted with the state of the empire.* 詢 is here more than 'to inquire;' it conveys the idea of plans

達四聰。○十六節咨十有二牧、曰食哉惟時、柔遠能邇、惇德允元、而難任人、蠻夷率服。○十七節舜曰、咨四岳、有能奮庸

16 He consulted with the twelve Pastors, and said, "The food!—it depends on *observing* the seasons. Be kind to the distant, and cultivate the ability of the near. Give honour to the virtuous, and your confidence to the good, while you discountenance the artful:—so shall the barbarous tribes lead on one another to make their submission."

17 Shun said, "Ah! *chief of* the four Mountains, is there any one who can vigorously display his merits, and give wide development

and measures (see the 書經備旨). 闢四門,—'to open the four gates,' *i.e.*, to open the gates of the four quarters, remove every hindrance obstructing the access of worth and ability, wherever situated, to the notice of the sovereign and his service. K'ang-shing supposes an allusion to the audience given by the emperor to his officers 'in the gate.' Keang Shing brings in his favourite idea of 'the four gates of the Hall of Audience.' It is not necessary to be so minute. All agree in the general meaning, that Shun's object was—廣賢路, 'to widen the way of the worthy.' There is more difficulty in apprehending precisely the remaining two phrases—明四目, 達四聰. Gan-kwŏ's expl. of them will suffice:—廣視聽於四方, 使天下無壅塞, 'to enlarge his seeing and hearing throughout the four quarters, that nothing in the empire might be shut up or hid from him.' Good officers, in sympathy with him, would be eyes and ears to him.

P. 16. *Counsels to the twelve pastors of provinces.* 牧, 'pastor,' 'shepherd,' was a name given in the times of Yaou and Shun to the chief or superintendent of all the princes and nobles in a province; indicating that the nourishment of the people should be his chief concern. This is the reason why 'food' is here mentioned first. 食哉惟時,—'Food!—Only the seasons.' This is the second time we find the part. 惟 (see p. 11), which is of very frequent occurrence in the Shoo, and of varied *usus*. As to the sentiment, see Mencius, I. Pt. I. iii. 能邇,—能 is taken by K'ang-shing as = 恣, 'to be indulgent to.' So also the modern comm. Gan-kwŏ and Wang Suh, unwilling to adopt such a meaning, interpreted :—'give repose to the remote, and then you *can* do so to the near.' It does not appear to me that we need to depart from the usual meaning, only giving the term a *hiphil* force. 元=仁厚之人, 'men of benevolence and generosity.' 任人=佞人, 'artful people,' especially in speech. The standard interpretation of 任 is 包藏凶惡之人, 'men who treasure wickedness in their bosoms.' Instead of 任, we have 壬 in Bk. III. 2. [The Dict. gives the 任 of the text in the 3d tone, which must be a mistake.] 蠻夷,—'the wild tribes of the south and the east,' used for such tribes generally. 率=相率, 'lead on one another.'

P. 17. *Appointment of Yu to be General Regulator to Shun, as Shun had formerly been to Yaou.* 舜曰,—the use of 舜 here would seem to be purposely to mark that Shun was now the emperor. Hereafter the phrase is 帝曰. 奮=起, 'to put forward.' It gives the idea of vigour. Ma Yung explains it by 明, 'to illustrate,'—wrongly. 庸=功, 'services,' 'merits.' 熙,—as in the Canon of Yaou, p. 8. 帝之載,—the emp. of course is Yaou; 載, as in Doctr. of the Mean, xxxiii. 6. 百揆,—see par. 2. 亮采,—亮=相, 'to assist,' 'to act as minister to' (see note by Lin Che-k'e in the 集傳); 采=事, as in the Can. of Yaou, p. 10. 惠疇,—惠=順, 'to accord with; 疇=

書經

熙帝之載、使宅百揆、亮采惠疇。僉曰、伯禹作司空。帝曰、俞、咨禹、汝平水土、惟時懋哉。禹拜稽首、讓于稷契暨皐陶。帝曰、俞、汝往哉。○帝十八節曰、棄、黎

to the undertakings of the emperor, whom I may make General Regulator, to aid me in all affairs, and manage each department according to its nature?" All *in the court* said, "There is baron Yu, the superintendent of Works." The emperor said, "Yes. Ah! Yu, you have regulated the water and the land. In this *new office* exert yourself." Yu did obeisance with his head to the ground, and wished to decline in favour of the minister of Agriculture, or Sëĕ, or Kaou-yaou." The emperor said, "Yes; but do you go, *and undertake the duties.*"

18 The emperor said, "K'e, the black-haired people are *still* suffering

類, 'a class.' The meaning of the phrase, so far as it can be ascertained, is given in the transl. Lin Che-k'e says;—謂天下之事,各以其類,無不順也, 'The meaning is, that all the affairs of the empire should be managed naturally, each according to its nature and class.' 僉曰,—as in the Can. of Yaou, p. 11. 伯禹,—Baron Yu. Yu must by this time have superseded, or succeeded to, his father, as chief of Ts'ung; see on Can. of Yaou, p. 11. 司空,—see Pt. V. Bk. XX. 12. The 司空 was one of the great officers of the Chow dyn.; but only here do we find the name in connection with earlier times. In Yaou's time the minister of Works was styled 共工 (Can. of Yaou, p. 10), and we find the same designation continued in this Bk., p. 21. K'ang-shing supposed that 司空 was a special designation given for the time to Yu. It certainly had to do with his labours on the mountains and streams of the flooded empire.

惟時(=是)懋哉,—'now in this exert yourself!' Ma Yung takes 懋=美, 'to beautify;' but the meaning in the transl. is to be preferred. 禹拜稽首,—稽首 is exegetical of the 拜, which signifies 'to do obeisance,' 'to pay one's respects.' In the Chow Le, 春官,宗伯,第三之九, there are specified nine 拜, of which the first is 稽首, 'laying the head to the ground.' 稷 is the name of an office, that of the minister of Agriculture. The individual here mentioned had rendered, it is supposed, such services to the State in his office, that he came to be distinguished by it, and not by his own name which was K'e (棄). He was a son of the emp. K'uh (高辛氏); and to him the emperors of the Chow dyn. referred as their progenitor. See the wonders of his birth and infancy, and the achievements of his life, in the She King, Pt. II. Bk. II. i., *et al.* During Shun's administration of the empire, K'e had been apointed ruler of the state of T'ae (邰), to which his mother had belonged. 契 (*Sëĕ*) was a half-brother of K'e, and had been appointed ruler of Shang (商). From him the emperors of the Shang dyn. were descended. See the accounts of his birth, &c., in the last portion of the She King, the 'Praise-songs of Shang.' 皐陶,—see on Bk. III.

P. 18. *Confirmation of K'e as minister of Agriculture.* This is the confirmation of K'e, not his appointment. As Yu had mentioned him with Sëĕ and Kaou-yaou, the emperor turns to them, and praises them for their services, which they were to continue. All the old interpreters put the verbs in the past tense:—

民阻飢、汝后稷、播時百穀。○十九節帝曰、契、百姓不親、五品不遜、汝作司徒、敬敷五教、在寬。○二十節帝曰、皐陶、蠻夷猾夏、寇賊姦宄、汝作士、五刑

the distress of hunger. It is yours, O prince, the minister of Agriculture, to sow *for them* these various kinds of grain."

19 The emperor said, "Sëë, the people continue unfriendly with one another, and do not observe docilely the five orders *of relationship*. It is yours, as the minister of Instruction, reverently to set forth the lessons of duty belonging to those five orders. Do so with gentleness."

20 The emperor said, "Kaou-yaou, the barbarous tribes disturb our bright great land. There are *also* robbers, murderers, insurgents, and traitors. It is yours, as the minister of Crime, to employ the five

'The people were suffering,' &c. Perhaps we should so translate; but it seems more natural to render as I have done,—after Woo Ch'ing, and the 'Daily Explanation.' 阻＝厄, 'to be straitened.' For 阻 Sze-ma Ts'een has 始, from which some suppose the original reading was 祖, which, indeed, Ma Yung gives. Rather we may suppose that originally there was simply 且. 后稷,—K'e was 后, 'prince,' as being chief of T'ae; as minister of Agriculture he was called 稷, 'millet,' that being considered the best of the five principal grains (Woo Ch'ing.) 時＝是,—'these.' Ch'ing would have it read as 蒔,' 'to transplant.' 百穀,— the hundred grains,' *i.e.*, all the various kinds of grain. Fan Sze-lin (潘士遴, Ming dyn.), indeed, makes out 100 in this way:—under the name of *leaug* (粱), including millet, wheat, &c., 20 kinds; of *taou* (稻), including rice, and all grains that grow in water, 20 kinds; of 菽, *i.e.*, beans, peas, &c., 20 kinds; of vegetables (蔬), 20 kinds; and of fruits (果), 20 kinds.

P. 19. *Confirmation of Sëë as minister of Instruction.* 百姓 is here plainly the people. The common. who have hitherto insisted on the phrase denoting 'the officers,' say nothing about it here. 不親,—I have said '*continue* unfriendly,' to indicate the reference to the past services of Sëë, which is properly supposed. 五品,—品＝'a class,' 'a rank;' 五品, 'the five ranks,' under which human society may be arranged;—parent and child, sovereign and subject, husband and wife, brothers, and friends. 五教, 'the five lessons of duty, belonging to those orders. See Mencius, III. Pt. I. iv. 8, who puts his seal to the meaning of 五品 and 五教. There need be no hesitation, therefore, in rejecting K'ang-shing's view, that the 'five 品' are 'father, mother, elder brother, younger brother, and son,' and the five 教 the duties belonging to those. 在寬,—lit., 'it is in gentleness,' *i.e.*, the people must be drawn, they can't be forced, to those duties.

P. 20. *Confirmation of Kaou-yaou as minister of Crime.* 猾夏,—猾＝亂, 'to throw into confusion.' Ch'ing expl. it by 侵亂, 'to invade and throw into confusion.' 夏, is a name for 'the middle country,' conveying the ideas of 'brightness and greatness.' The character 華 is generally found with it. 姦宄,—在外曰姦, 在內曰宄, 'external troublers are called 姦; internal, 宄.' The latter are *traitors*, members of one's household or State; the former are insurgents.

書經

有服、五服三就、五流有宅、五宅三居、惟明克允。○帝廿一節曰、疇若予工。僉曰、垂哉。帝曰、俞、咨垂、汝共工。垂拜稽

punishments for the treatment of offences, for the infliction of which there are the three appointed places; and the five banishments, with their several places of detention, for which three localities are assigned. Perform your duties with intelligence, and you will secure a sincere submission."

21 The emperor said, "Who is equal to the duty of superintending my workmen?" All *in the court* said, "There is Suy." The emperor said, "Yes. Ah! Suy, you must be minister of Works." Suy did obeisance, with his head to the ground, and wished to decline in

or invaders. 作士,—Ch'ing exp. 士 as 'one who presides over the examination of civil and criminal causes'; Ma says he was 'the chief of such judges.' During the Chow dyn. there was the 士師, or chief criminal judge, but he was only a subordinate to the minister of Crime. Kaou-yaou's office was that of the 大司寇 of the Chow dyn. On the interpr. of 五刑有服,五服三就,五流有宅,五宅三居, opinions are much divided. The five punishments, we may assume, are the branding, castration, &c., mentioned on p. 11. 服, says Woo Ch'ing, 猶衣服之服,謂加其身,'服 indicates the application of the punishment to the body, as a garment is put on'. I do not think we can translate in English more closely than if we say—'There are the five punishments which are to be undergone, and for the undergoing of them there are three places to be resorted to.' What those three places were, cannot be determined.—Ch'ing says—'the open country (原野); the market-place and court (市朝); and the place where the 甸師氏 executed his functions' [more privately, on members of the imperial House]. Ma Yung takes the same view. Gan-kwŏ had determined the three places to be the open country, the market place, and the court,—from misunderstanding a passage in the 國語,魯語,上,大刑用甲兵,云云. Dissatisfied with these explanations, Ts'ae suggested that it may have been that capital sentences were carried into effect in the market place, castration, in some place corresponding to the 'mulberry apartment' (蠶室) of the Han dyn., and the other three punishments, in some other place, screened from the wind.—We must leave the subject undetermined.

The five severe inflictions might be commuted for banishments,—to a greater or less distance. Each banishment was undergone in a certain place (宅); but those five localities were comprehended within three larger divisions of territory. This is the extent of the conclusion to which we can come on this part of the passage. Gan-kwŏ says the lesser banishment was to a distance of a thousand *le*: the second was beyond the limits of the nine provinces; and the third was to the remotest region of barbarism. Ch'ing has a strange view. He would read 宅 as 咤 (*ch'a*), and thinks it means handcuffs, fetters, &c., with which the criminals were secured. 惟明克允,—does this mean, 'Be intelligent and you will secure the acquiescence of the people,' or 'Be intelligent and your sentences will be in accordance with the truth of the cases?' The characters will admit of either meaning. Ts'ae Ch'in joins them together, but a translation can only admit one of them.

P. 21. *Appointment of Suy to be minister of Works.* This office was vacant in consequence of Yu's appointment to be General Regulator. The minister of Works, it would appear, had to look after all the workers, or guilds of workers, in earth, stone, metal, leather, &c. 若予工,—see on 若, in Can. of Yaou, p. 9. 垂 (read *Suy*, like 瑞; see the Dict.),—mention is made of 'the bamboo arrows of Suy,' preserved as precious relics in the times of the Chow dyn.; see Pt. V. Bk. XXII. 19. The Taouist philosopher Chwang also speaks of 'the finger of Suy' (倕); see the 南華外篇,第三). Suy would appear from this to have

首、讓于殳斨暨伯與。帝曰、俞、往哉、汝諧。○帝曰、廿二節疇若予上下草木鳥獸、僉曰、益哉。帝曰、俞、咨益、汝作朕虞。益拜稽首、讓于朱虎熊羆。

favour of Shoo, Ts‘eang, or Pih-yu. The emperor said, "Yes; but do you go and undertake the duties. Effect a harmony *in all the departments.*"

22 The emperor said, "Who is equal to the duty of superintending the grass and trees, with the birds and beasts, on my mountains and in my marshes." All *in the court* said, "There is Yih." The emperor said, "Yes. Ah! Yih, do you be my Forester." Yih did obeisance, with his head to the ground, and wished to decline in favour of Choo, Hoo, Heung, or Pe. The emperor said, "Yes; but do you go, and undertake the duties. You must manage them harmoniously."

been himself a skilful worker. 殳, 斨, 暨伯與 are three men in the 集傳, the two first being supposed to have got their names from their skill in making the weapons which the characters denote. The old interpr. made them two men—殳斨 and 伯與, which Keang Shing would identify with 朱斨 and 伯譽, in the 古今人表 of the Former Han. No doubt it was the object of Pan Koo there to mention the names in this par. 汝諧, is perhaps simply = 'make things go on harmoniously.' Yang Shaou-fang (楊肇芳, Ming dyn.) says:—'Under Suy and Yih there were many departments, which were to be carried on harmoniously.' Some take 諧=偕, 'together with,' and make it refer to Choo, Ts‘eang, and Pih-yu, who were to be Suy's assistants, and in concert with whom he was to manage his duties;—so, Woo Ch‘ing.

P. 22. *Appointment of Yih to be forester.* 上下,—in the Can. of Yaou, p. 6, these characters were equiv. to 'heaven and earth;' here they = 山林, 'hills and forests,' on high ground, and 澤藪, 'marshes and fens,' in low. 益,—Yih had assisted Yu in his labours upon the flooded provinces. We are told that 'Shun then committed to him the direction of the fire to be employed, when he set fire to the forests and vegetation of the mountains and marshes, so that the birds and beasts fled away to hide themselves (Men. III. Bk. I., iv. 7). Some make him a son of Kaou Yaou, but this is not likely (see the 集說, *in loc.*). According to Sze-ma Ts‘een he was descended from Chuen-heuh, and, receiving from Shun the surname of Ying (嬴), became the progenitor of the rulers of Ts‘in (秦). Ts‘een gives his name 伯翳 and not 伯益 (see 秦本紀第五). As Yih had been associated with Yu, this may be the reason why Ch‘ing, Ma, and Wang Suh all read 禹曰益哉 instead of 僉曰益哉. This is considered a flagrant proof of the falsehood of the common text. The 'Historical Records,' however, for 僉曰 read 皆曰. The text from which Sze-ma copied must have had 僉曰. 虞=山澤之官, 'the officer of the hills and marshes.' In the time of the Chow dyn. each department had its superintendent, and the office was of smaller importance. 虞 means 'to consider,' 'to calculate' and the warden of the forests' was so styled, it is said, because he had so much to think about! Some would also make the name of the office to be 朕虞. 朱, 虎, 熊, 羆,—lit., 'the fir,' 'the tiger,' 'the bear,' 'the grisly bear.' These were four officers, brothers, it is said, the sons of Kaou-sin. *Their* names, and those in the last par., might make us compare Shun's court to a council of Red Indians. The Historical Records add that these four men became Yih's assistants. This agrees with the meaning

帝曰、俞、往哉、汝諧。○(廿三節)帝曰、咨四岳、有能典朕三禮。僉曰、伯夷。帝曰、俞、咨伯、汝作秩宗、夙夜惟寅、直哉惟淸。伯拜稽首、讓于夔龍。帝曰、俞、往、欽哉。○(廿四節)帝曰、夔命汝

23 The emperor said, "Ah! *chief of* the four Mountains, is there any one who can direct my three *religious* ceremonies?" All *in the court* said, "There is the baron E." The emperor said, "Yes. Ah! baron, you must be the Arranger of the ancestral temple. Morning and night you must be respectful. Be upright, be pure." The baron did obeisance with his head to the ground, and wished to decline in favour of K'wei or Lung. The emperor said, "Yes; but do you go, and undertake the duties. Be reverential."

24 The emperor said, "K'wei, I appoint you to be Director of music, and to teach our sons, so that the straightforward may yet be mild,

which I said on last par. some give to the diff. word 諧.

P. 23. *Appointment of Pih-e to be minister of Religion.* The 四岳 is specially consulted with reference to the appointment of Yu, p. 17, and the app. here;—showing, it is supposed, the superior importance of the two offices of General Regulator and minister of Religion. 典,—here a verb, = 主, 'to preside over,' 'to direct.' 三禮,—'the three ceremonies.' There is no difference of opinion as to the understanding of these. They are all the observances in the worship of the spirits of heaven (天神), the spirits of earth (地祇), and the spirits of men (人鬼). The ceremonies of the first went by the name of 祀; of the second by that of 祭; of the third by that of 享. The minister of religion under the Chow dyn. was called 大宗伯, and the duties of his office will be found described at length under that name in the 'Rites of Chow' (夏官).

伯夷,—'the baron E, 伯 being his title (爵, Woo Ch'ing). How it is that the emperor addresses him simply by the title, and that the historian describes him simply by it is a difficulty, which has not been solved (see 段玉裁's Work, *in loc.*). The 'Historical Records' do not use 伯 alone, but always say 伯夷. 秩宗,—秩 = 敘次, 'to arrange,' 'to dispose in order'; 宗 = 祖廟, 'the ancestral temple' (this is the proper meaning of the character). That this—Arranger of the ancestral temple—should be the name given to the minister of Religion, shows strikingly the chief place occupied by the worship of their ancestors in the religion of China, from the earliest times. 夙夜惟寅, 直哉惟淸,—Choo He says:—'From reverence there will come uprightness, and from uprightness purity' (惟寅故直, 惟直故淸). I suppose it is so, but it is very difficult to discover in the text the grammatical nexus of the different clauses.

P. 24. *Appointment of K'wei to be minister of Music.* It is singular how great an importance is here attributed to training in music, and that this should have been a special department regulated by imperial statutes from the earliest times. Under the Chow dyn., the minister of Music was styled 大司樂; see the chapter on his duties in the 'Rites of Chow,' 春官, 宗伯, 第二之六. 夔 is the name of a monstrous animal, 'a dragon with one leg.' I can find no other information about the officer thus designated, besides the notice here

典樂、教冑子、直而溫、寬而栗、剛而無虐、簡而無傲、詩言志、歌永言、聲依永、律和聲、八音克諧、無相奪倫、神人以和。夔曰、於、予擊石拊

the gentle may yet be dignified, the strong not tyrannical, and the impetuous not arrogant. Poetry is the expression of earnest thought; singing is the prolonged utterance of that expression. The notes accompany that utterance, and they are harmonized themselves by the pitch pipes. *In this way* the eight different kinds of instruments can all be adjusted so that one shall not take from or interfere with another, and spirits and men will thereby be brought into harmony."

and in Bk. IV., p. 9. 冑 is expl. by Gan-kwŏ by 長, 'eldest,' and he adds—'meaning the eldest son *of the emperor*, and the younger branches of the families of the nobles and officers.' He had before him a passage in the Le Ke,—the 王制, Pt. iv. p. 4, where we are told the minister of Music (樂正) taught 'the poems, ceremonies, and music of the former kings,' and was resorted to by the eldest and other sons of the king, the eldest sons of all the feudal princes, the eldest sons (by their proper wives) of the nobles and officers, and by the promising youth of the kingdom.' 冑, however, denotes descendants generally; and there was at an early time another reading of 育 for 冑, leaving the 子 quite unqualified. In 無虐, 無傲, 無=毋. 詩言志, 歌永言,—志 is defined by 心之所之, 'that to which the mind moves,' and hence it is translated by 'will,' 'aim,' 'purpose.' It denotes thought, but thought earnest and ardent, which seeks display and development. Shun's definition of poetry is not much amiss. 永 is, lit., 'water flowing on long and unbroken.' Ch'ing explains it here by 長, 'to prolong.' Singing is the poetic language 'in linked sweetness long drawn out.' 聲依永, 律和聲,—依 is 'to rely on,' 'to be according to,' 'to keep close to.' Its force is well brought out in the 'Daily Explanation:'—'This singing gives rise to the distinction of notes into high and low, treble and bass,—the five notes of music, indeed, which all come out in connection with the prolonged utterance' (皆依永而出). These five notes (聲) constitute the imperfect scale, common perhaps to all nations in their early attempts to form a musical system, into which no interval of less than a tone is admitted. Their names are *kung* (宮), *shang* (商), *keŏ* (角), *che* (徵, gen. read *ching*, but not in this sense), and *yu* (羽). The tubes (律) which produce and subsequently harmonize (和) these notes, are said to measure, in ninths of an inch, 81, 72, 64, 54, and 48 respectively. The next number in this series, corresponding to the octave to *kung*, should of course be $\frac{1}{2}$ of 80 $= 40\frac{1}{2}$; and we have thus according to our notation G, A, B, D, E, g. The series is constructed, starting from 81 as a basis, by making perfect fifths ascending (3:2), and perfect fourths descending (3:4). Thus from 81 is obtained 54; 54 gives, by the second proportion, 72; 72 again gives 48; and 48 gives 64. Carrying on this process, increasing or decreasing each time, as the case requires, the following set of twelve is obtained:—81, $75\frac{2}{3}$, 72, $67\frac{1}{3}$, 64, $59\frac{2}{3}$, $56\frac{2}{3}$, 54, $50\frac{2}{3}$, 48, $44\frac{2}{3}$, $42\frac{2}{3}$. (The fractions are not very accurate.) Twelve tubes of these several lengths constituted what I have called 'the standard tubes,' whose various application has been pointed out above. As regards the theory of music, could we be sure that the details which have been given, had really been wrought out in Shun's time, we could not refuse them our meed of admiration. The progress of the Chinese in music has not corresponded to such beginnings. A theoretical difficulty and a practical one have hindered them. They have found it impossible in theory for A to hold the same proportion to D as D to g; and in practice they have found that while their calculations might be applied to stringed instruments, the

石、百獸率舞。○ 廿五節 帝曰、龍、朕堲讒說殄行、震驚朕師、命汝作納言、夙夜出納朕命、

[K'wei said, "Oh! I smite the stone; I smite the stone. The various animals lead on one another to dance."].

25 The emperor said, "Lung, I abominate slanderous speakers, and destroyers of *right* ways, who agitate and alarm my people. I appoint you to be the minister of Communication. Early and late give forth my orders and report to me, seeing that every thing is true."

tube g must be made considerably less than half the length of the tube G in order to sound the octave to it. Their division of the tubes into 6 律 and 6 呂, moreover, has complicated the subject, and thrown around it the perplexity of their reasonings about the *yin* and *yang* principles. 八音克諧,—see p. 13. 神人以和,—on this the 'Daily Explanation' says:—'The instruments thus in harmony being played at the sacrifices to Heaven and in the ancestral temple, the spirits are all harmonious; being played in the court, men are all harmonious:—what then must be the power of music in teaching our youth!' 夔曰, 云云,—see Bk. IV. 9. There can be no doubt the reply of K'wei is out of place here,—appears here in fact from some displacement of the ancient tablets.

P. 25. *Appointment of Lung to be minister of Communication.* We are in ignorance of Lung just as we are of K'wei. 堲=疾, 'to detest.' In the 'Historical Records' we have instead of it 畏忌, 'to fear and suspect.' 讒說—'slanderous speeches.' The Taouist Chwang defines 讒 as 'the liking to speak of the evil of others' (漁父篇). 殄=絕, 'to subvert.' 'to make an end of;' 殄行 (3d tone) = 'to subvert the conduct.' The question arises,—Is the conduct subverted that of the individuals themselves? or that of others, so that this clause is an appendix to the former, a description of the object of the slander? Gan-kwŏ and Ma Yung take the latter view, and are followed by the modern interpreters (the 'Daily Explanation' expands—傷絕善人君子所行之事, 'they injure and keep out of view the actions of good and superior men'). Ch'ing takes the former view and explains the two phrases 讒說 and 殄行 by a reference to the words of Ana. XII. xx. 6.—'assuming the appearance of virtue, while opposing it in conduct.' This appears to me the more natural interpretation,—to take the clauses as coordinate. 師=衆, as in Can. of Yaou, p. 12, but does it mean 'all the people,' or 'all those in office'? Ch'ing restricts it to 'ministers' (衆臣); we may take it more generally. 納言 is the name of the office, which may be translated—'Communicator of words.' It is perhaps easier to describe the office, than to translate the terms, or those of the sentence below—出納朕命. Gan-kwŏ says:—'納言 was the officer of the throat and tongue. Hearing the words of those below, he brought them before the sovereign; receiving the words of the sovereign, he proclaimed them to those below:—in either case there was required fidelity' (納言喉舌之官,聽下言,納于上,受上言,宣于下,必以信). Here at the end of Shun's appointment of ministers, Woo Ch'ing has the following note:—'Shun gave nine commissions, of which four were new appointments:—those of Yu, Suy, Yih, and the baron E. On occasion of *their* wish to decline the appointments, he confirmed five ministers in their old offices:—Tseih, Sëĕ, Kaou-yaou, K'wei, and Lung. Some have thought, from the words "I appoint" standing before the designation of these two last, that they likewise were new men. But this is wrong. When the emperor asks advice and then appoints, and the designate makes obeisance and wishes to decline, the appointment is new. When he appoints without asking advice, and the designate does not make obeisance nor wish to decline, there is only a confirmation. Can we suppose that K'wei and Lung would not have made obeisance, on first receiving their appointments? The commentator Wang Yen (王炎) has observed:—"The General Regulator was the head of all the ministers, and therefore Yu first received his appointment. The nourishment of the people is the beginning of royal government, and therefore the minister of agriculture was next appointed. When people are well off, instruction may be given them; hence there followed the appointment of Sëĕ. Punishment

惟允。○帝(廿六節)曰、咨、汝二十有二人、欽哉、惟時亮天功。○(廿七節)三載考績、三考、黜陟幽明、庶績咸熙、分北三苗。○(廿八節)舜

26 The emperor said, "Ah! you, twenty and two men, be reverent, and so shall you aid *me* in performing the service of Heaven."

27 Every three years there was an examination of merits, and after three examinations the undeserving were degraded, and the deserving promoted. By this arrangement the duties of all the departments were fully discharged. The people of San-meaou were discriminated and separated.

is intended to help instruction; hence followed the appointment of Kaou-yaou. Workers make implements and utensils for the benefit of the people:—this is the conclusion of government; hence Suy was appointed, and so far as men are concerned, the organization of the government was pretty well complete. Shun then proceeded to care for the grass and trees, for birds and beasts, appointing Suy. This done, the time came for the cultivation and development of ceremonial observances and music. These two things are the grand consummation of government, by which service is done to Heaven, to earth, and to spirits, and all things are brought to harmony and order; hence there were the appointments of E and K'wei:—of E first and then of K'wei, because music must be a sequel to the ceremonial observances. With music the work of government might be supposed to be ended, but notwithstanding the abundance of able ministers, let slanderous dividers once go abroad, and the men of worth and ability would be made restless, and what had been done would come to nought. On this account the appointment of Lung was made last of all. The design of this was the same with that of Shun's concluding charge to the pastors of the twelve provinces, that they should *make it hard for the artful;* and with Confucius' concluding lesson on the administration of a country—*to keep far from specious talkers.*" (Ana. XV. xx. 6).

P. 26. *General address to all his principal ministers.* 汝二十有二人,—Who were these 22 men? There ought to be but one answer to the question,—that which we find in Ts'ae Ch'in. They were the chief of the four Mountains, the twelve presidents of the provinces, and the nine ministers, whose appointments or confirmations have been related. The old interpreters, thinking that the 四岳 were four individuals, mistook the meaning. Ch'ing is obliged to leave them out altogether, and says the 22 were the 12 presidents of provinces, with Yu, Suy, Yih, Pih-e, K'wei, Lung, Shoo-ts'eang, Pih-yu, Choo-hoo, and Heung-pe; and Wang Ming-shing argues, in his 後案, that this view should not be changed! Gan-kwŏ and Ma Yung leave out Tseih, Sëĕ, and Kaou-yaou, and say the 22 men were Yu, Suy, Yih, Pih-e, K'wei, Lung, the 12 presidents of provinces, and the four ministers called 四岳. This view is followed by Keang Shing. 惟時亮天功,—時=是; 亮 as in p 17. Sze-ma Ts'een has 敬哉惟是相事天.

P. 27. *Institution of examinations; and further discipline of the Meaouites.* 黜陟幽明, *i.e.*, 黜幽陟明; 幽, 'the dark,'=the idle and undeserving; 明 is the opposite of this. 庶績咸熙,—see Can. of Yaou, p. 8. 分北三苗,—北 (read *p'ei*, 3d tone), 'to separate.' Keang Shing would read it *pëĕ*, contending, that the original character was two 八, one over the other, the old form of 別. In what year the Meaou were thus dealt with we cannot tell. Wang Suh thinks that after the discipline of them mentioned p. 12, those who were left in their original seat again proved insubordinate, and another separation and banishment of them had to be made.

CH. VI. SUMMARY OF SHUN'S LIFE; AND DEATH. There is no dispute about the first clause; all allow that Shun, when he was thirty, was called to employment by Yaou, and the testing of him began. The reading of 三十

生三十徵庸、三十在位、五十載、陟方乃死。○

28 VI. In the thirtieth year of his life Shun was called to employment. Thirty years he was on the throne *with Yaou.* Fifty years after, he went on high and died.

在位 is much disputed. Ch'ing read 二十, making Shun's life to have amounted altogether to 100 years. And there *was* a reading of 二十 for 三十. Wang Ming-shing and Twan Yuh-tsae adduce many proofs of it. But on p. 13 we saw that the 28 years there could only be understood of the years during which Shun acted as Yaou's vicegerent. Adding to them the three years of his testing, p. 3, we should have 31 years; but one of those three may naturally be considered the year in which he was called from his obscurity. We shall thus have the 三十 of the text. As to the 50 years on the throne, these must include the two years (three, including the year in which Yaou died) of mourning for Yaou, when opportunity was given for the accession of Yaou's son. Altogether then, Shun was on the throne, with universal recognition, 48 years. his life extended over 110 years; and he died B.C. 2202. Gan-kwŏ, not deducting the two years after Yaou's death, makes Shun's age 112.

陟方乃死,—I have translated this clause after Ts'ae Ch'in, who relies chiefly on the usage of the 'Bamboo Annals,' where 陟 is used of the death of the emperors, and = 崩. The 方 after it is a difficulty, and so is the 且死, for the going on high should be mentioned after the death, and not before it. Gan-kwŏ, to avoid these difficulties, takes 方 in the sense of region, and says 昇道南方巡狩死. 'he went up the way towards the southern region, on a tour of inspection, and died.' Maou K'e-ling argues for this view; but it is inadmissible as an explanation of the text of this paragraph. He builds principally on the account of Shun's life and death in the 'Historical Records.' It is there said:—'When Shun was 20, he was heard of for his filial piety; at 30, he was promoted by Yaou; at 50 he undertook the administration of affairs for Yaou, and when he was 58, Yaou died. At 61, he took his place, and occupied the imperial throne 39 years, after which, being on a tour of inspection in the south, he died in the wilderness of Ts'ang-woo (蒼梧), and was buried at Kew-e (九疑) of Keang-nan, in Ling-ling.' Ling-ling is the name of a district in the pres. dep. of Yung-chow (永州) in Ho-nan, where they still show, or pretend to show, the grave of Shun. Mencius (IV. Pt. II. i.) gives another name to the place of his death.

THE BOOKS OF YU.

BOOK II. THE COUNSELS OF THE GREAT YU.

大禹謨

一節 曰若稽古、大禹曰文命、敷于四海、祗承于帝。○

1 I. On examining into antiquity, we find that the great Yu was called Wăn-ming. Having arranged and divided *the empire*, all to the four seas, in reverent response to the *inquiries of the former* emperor,

Title of the Book.—大禹謨, 'The Counsels of the great Yu.' The Books of the Shoo have been arranged in six classes, according to the nature of their subject-matter. Of those classes the 'Counsels' form the second, containing the wise remarks and suggestions of high officers on the subject of government. In one of the Writings ascribed to K'ung Foo (孔鮒), Confucius is made to say—'In the Counsels of the great Yu, I see the loyalty and diligence, the service and merits of Yu' (孔叢子, 卷一, 論書篇) 謨=謀, 'plans;' but it is implied that the plans are the result of deliberation. Heu Shin defines it 'plans of deliberation;' and his expounder adds:—'The thoughtful consideration of a subject, and the description of a plan in consequence, is what is indicated by 謨.' Yu, it has been seen in the prev. Book, was the son of K'wăn, the chief of Tsung. According to Sze-ma Ts'een, K'wăn was a son of the emp. Chuen-heuh, so that Yu was the great-great-grandson of Hwang-te. He is here called 'the Great,' 'because of the greatness of his merit' (Gan-kwŏ),—the services he rendered on occasion of the great inundations which devastated the empire.

Into the question which is agitated about the Genuineness of the Book I do not here enter; the reader is referred to what has been said on the subject in the *proleg.*, and to the remarks that will be found on particular passages in the annotations. The 'Counsels of Yu' were a portion of the Shoo edited by Confucius. The preface, and many references to it in other books, sufficiently prove this. It was not among the portions recovered and taught by Fuh-shang, but it was among those recovered by K'ung Gan-kwŏ. In the words of Ts'ae Chin:—'The modern text wants it; the ancient text has it' (今文無, 古文有).

Contents. The Book may be divided into three chapters:—the first, embracing 8 parr., and containing various counsels of Yu and Yih on principles and methods of good govt.; the second, parr. 9–19, occupied with Shun's resigning the administration of the govt. to Yu, and cont. many sage observations and maxims; the third, parr. 20, 21, describing Yu's measures against the people of Meaou. The *style* differs from that of the Canons. It is sententious as befits the subject: and we observe in it a tendency to fall into rhythm.

Ch. I. Yu; his counsels and those of Yih on government; compliments between the emperor and those ministers. P. 1. *The achievement of Yu, and occasion of delivering his*

書經

二節曰、后克艱厥后、臣克艱厥臣、政乃乂、黎民敏德。○三節帝曰、俞、允若茲、嘉言罔攸伏、野無遺賢、萬邦咸寧、稽于衆、舍己從人、不虐無告、不廢困窮、惟

2 he said, "If the sovereign can realize the difficulty of his sove-
reignship, and the minister can realize the difficulty of his min-
istry, government will be well ordered, and the people will sedulously
3 seek to be virtuous." The emperor said, "Yes; let this really be the
case, and good words will nowhere lie hidden; no men of virtue and
talents will be neglected away from court; and the myriad States
will all enjoy repose. *But* to ascertain the views of all; to give up
one's own opinion and follow that of others; to refrain from oppress-
ing the helpless; and not to neglect the straitened and poor:—it

counsels. 曰若稽古,大禹曰文命. Gan-kwŏ, followed by Ts'ae Ch'in, takes 文命 as two nouns, the subject of the verb 敷,—'his accomplished virtue and the lessons of his teaching were spread abroad to the four seas,' according to what is said in the last par. of the 'Tribute of Yu.' The commen. Soo Shih (蘇軾), or Soo Tung-po, moreover, asks to what 敷于四海 can be referred, if 文命 be taken as the name of Yu. The first words of the 'Tribute of Yu' enable us to answer the question,—禹敷土, 'Yu divided the land.' To the same effect, in the She-king, Pt. IV., in the 4th of the Praise-songs of Shang, we have 禹敷下土方, where 敷 is explained by 治, 'to regulate.' The meaning therefore may very well be as I have given it in the translation. 四海,—see Bk. I. p. 13. 祇(=敬)承于帝,—'he reverently received—took it up—from the emperor.' Wang K'ang-t'ang (王肯堂, Ming dyn.) says:—'The emp. with his love of questioning and delight in excellence addressed his inquiries to his minister, who reverently responded to his sovereign, laying on him what was difficult and setting forth what was excellent.'

P. 2. *Good govt. depends on sovereign and minister not shrinking from the difficulties of their position.* Comp. Con. Ana., XII. xv. 后=君, 'the sovereign,' 'ruler.' 敏, 'active,' 'alert,' here as a verb, = 'to follow earnestly.' It is better to take the char. thus, than to interpret,—'will quickly be virtuous,' though earnest endeavours will speedily attain their object.

P. 3. *Shun's response to Yu's sentiment, and disclaimer of such merit in himself.* 允,=信, 'truly.' 攸=所; 罔攸, 'nowhere.' 'Good words will nowhere lie hidden,' *i.e.*, all capable of giving lessons of good will find their way to notice. 野, 'the wilds,' 'the fields,'= away from court. 'The myriad States will enjoy 'repose,' being ruled and directed by the wise and good. 舍己從人,—see Men., II. Pt. I. viii. 3. 不虐無告,不廢困窮,—comp. in 莊子,天道篇,—堯曰,吾不敖無告,不廢窮民. It is argued that the text is forged from these passages. I cannot but draw the opposite conclusion. In the chapter of Mencius, especially, he is evidently quoting from various books, in no case specifying their names or sections; the 2d par.,—禹聞善言則拜,—is taken from the Counsels of Kaou-yaou, p. 1;—shall we say that Book of the Shoo is also forged? 惟帝時克,—the emperor is Yaou; 時=是; Ying-tă paraphrases:—

帝時克。○益(四節)曰、都、帝德廣.運、乃聖乃神、乃武乃文、皇天眷命、奄有四海、爲天下君。○禹(五節)曰、惠迪吉、從逆凶、惟影響。○益(六節)曰、吁。戒哉、儆

4 was only the emperor *Yaou* who could attain to this." Yih said, "Oh! your virtue, O emperor, is vast and incessant. It is sagely, spiritual, awe-inspiring, and adorned with all accomplishments. Great Heaven regarded you with its favouring decree, and suddenly you obtained all within the four seas, and became sovereign of the empire."

5 Yu said, "Accordance with the right is good fortune; the following of evil is bad:—the shadow and the echo." Yih said,

6 "Alas! be cautious! Admonish yourself to caution, when there

惟帝堯於是能爲此行, 'it was only Yaou in these matters who could act thus.'

P. 4. *Yih repudiates Shun's disclaimer, and celebrates his virtue.* I can by no means agree with Gan-kwŏ and Ch'in, that the 帝 in 帝德 refers to Yaou. Ch'in observes, indeed, that to take 帝 as some do, as referring to Shun himself, would make the whole plain, and is in harmony with the style of 'The Counsels,' 帝 in the mouth of Shun being Yaou, but 帝 in the mouth of Shun's ministers being Shun. He decides against it, however, because in the simple honesty of those early times Yih would not have praised Shun so to his face! But this is no more than what Kaou-yaou does in this same Book, p 12. 都,—see on Can. of Yaou, p. 8. Choo He here says that 都 meaning the capital, the place where superior men assemble, when used as an exclamation, it conveys the idea of admiration (see the 集說). 運, 'to revolve,' here = 行之不息, 'to move without ceasing.' 乃聖乃神,—see Men. VII. Pt. II. xxv. 7, 8. 乃武乃文.—as the civil (文) always takes precedence in China of the military (武), it is thought necessary to note here that the terms are inverted from the necessity of the rhythm (note in the 集傳). 眷, 'to look round to,'—with the idea of kindly regard. 奄 is taken by Gan-kwŏ as = 同, of which I can't make sense. Ch'in explains it by 盡, 'entirely.' 'the whole of.' The meaning which I have foll. seems more natural; and the rise of Shun might very well be thus described. In the 呂氏春秋, 十三卷 (near the end), we find a portion of this par. quoted from 'the Books of Hea.'—夏書曰, 天子之德廣運, 乃神乃武乃文. Wang Ming-shing argues that the par. of the text was made from this, the maker inserting 乃聖 before 乃神, to complete the rhythm and flow of the whole passage. But is it not more natural to suppose that Leu quotes the Classic incorrectly?

P. 5. *The certain connection between the right and happiness, between the wrong and misery.* 惠 = 順, 'to follow,' 'to accord with,' as in Bk. II. p. 17. 迪, 'to advance,' 'to go forward,' and here opposed to 逆, 'going backwards,' 'rebelliousness,' = 'the right way.' 惟影響 and not 如影響 is an emphatic way of representing the truth of the two prec. statements; so, to say 'is good fortune,' rather than 'leads to good fortune' is not only a literal rendering, but is necessary to give exactly Yu's sentiment. 'We are not to look,' says Ch'in King (陳經, Sung dyn.) 'for good fortune or bad, beyond the complacency or displacency of the mind.' Yu's object by this remark was to deepen the impression of his previous observation.

P. 6. *Exhortation founded on Yu's proposition.* 吁,—see Can. of Yaou, p. 10. 儆

戒無虞、罔失法度、罔遊于逸、罔淫于樂、任賢勿貳、去邪勿疑、疑謀勿成、百志惟熙、罔違道以干百姓之譽、罔咈百姓以從己之欲、無怠無荒、四夷來王。〇七節禹曰、於帝念哉、德惟善政、政在

seems to be no reason for anxiety. Do not fail in due attention to the laws and ordinances. Do not find your enjoyment in indulgent ease. Do not go to excess in pleasure. In your employment of men of worth, let none come between you and them. Put away evil without hesitation. Do not try to carry out doubtful plans. Study that all your purposes may be with the light of reason. Do not go against what is right to get the praise of the people. Do not oppose the people to follow your own desires. *Attend to these things* without idleness or omission, and from the four quarters the barbarous tribes will come and acknowledge your sovereignty."

7 Yu said, "Oh! think *of these things*, O emperor. Virtue is seen in the goodness of the government, and the government is tested

(Choo He says the original read. was 敬) 戒無虞,—'be reverently cautious where there is no calculating,' no forecasting, *i.e.*, no occasion for anxiety. 法度,—not only 'the laws of State and ordinances of govt.,' but all the rules for the regulation of conduct, be it even in eating and drinking (see a note in the 集傳). 淫, 'to go beyond,'—'like water overflowing and not returning.' 貳,—'in employing men of worth, to let mean men come between you and them is called 貳' (集傳). 百志惟熙,—'your hundred movements of mind,—let them be bright.' It is observed by She Lan (時瀾, Sung dyn.):—'The movements of the sages are accordant with reason. Whithersoever their spirits and mental exercises carry them, these are brightly intelligent and great; hence it is said 百志惟熙' (集說). 來王,—the wild tribes outside the provinces did not come regularly to court, but every chieftain of a tribe came once, on his taking the rule, to acknowledge the imperial supremacy; this was called 來王. So it was in the Chow dyn. See a note by Ch'in Sze-k'ae in the 集傳.

In a pass. in the 國策, the clauses 任賢勿貳去邪勿疑 are quoted from the Shoo in an inverted order;—a proof, it is said, that the pres. 'Counsels' is a forged compilation. But such arguments have no force. Irregular quotations from the acknowledged Books are not uncommon. The clause 無怠無荒 is found in the Books of the After Han, 卷五十二, near the end of the sketch of 崔駰 only we have 殆 for 怠. But there are other passages of the classics in the same sketch, without any specific acknowled. See Maou K'e-ling and Wang Ming-shing, *in loc.*

P. 7. *Further exhortations and details by Yu on the subject of government.* Choo He observes that parr. 2—6 were all one conversation, but whether what follows was spoken at the same time cannot be known. P. 7 is gen. connected with the prec. in the manner indicated in the transl., but the 念哉 may = 'think of

養民、水火金木土穀、惟修。正德、利用、厚生、惟和、九功惟敘、九敘惟歌、戒之用休、董之用威、勸之以九歌、俾

by its nourishing of the people. There are water, fire, metal, wood, earth, and grain,—these must be duly regulated; there are the rectification of *the people's* virtue, the conveniences of life, and the securing abundant means of sustentation,—these must be harmoniously attended to. When the nine services *thus indicated* have been orderly accomplished, let that accomplishment be celebrated by songs. Caution the people with gentle words; correct them with the majesty of *law;* stimulate them with the songs on those nine subjects,—in order that your success may never suffer diminution."

what I am now going to say.' 於 (*woo*),—as in Can. of Yaou, p. 2 德惟善政,—惟 connects the two parts of the clause; but I have spoken before of the difficulty in determining exactly the force of the particle. 'Virtue—just *is* good government;'—this is expanded in the Daily Explanations:—'Virtue does not exist ineffectively in one's own mind merely. It should be seen in the conduct of affairs, making the govt. entirely good, and then 'it is real virtue.' Now follows a description of good govt. as consisting in the nourishment of the people,—not the bare support of their bodies, but the sustenance and development of their whole being. We must wish, however, that the description were given in plainer terms.

First, to get food for the people, water, fire, metal, wood, earth [see V. Bk. IV. 5, which purports to be part of Yu's teaching], and grain must be regulated. The grain is the principal thing here, and the result of the whole process of regulation. Fire acting on metal melts it, and metal implements may be fashioned. These act on wood, and wooden implements are made. We have now the plough, &c., to act upon the earth, and by-and-by there will be the grain. But what use of water has been made in this process? Here is a difficulty. Ch'in Sze-k'ae says, 'Water acts on fire—subdues it, makes it subservient—for cookery'!

Second, food being provided, govt. goes on to 正德,—not, as Gan-kwo would make it, the rectification by the ruler of his virtue as an example to the people, but the getting the people to be virtuous—fathers kind, sons filial, &c. To this succeeds 利用, 'the facilitating of things used,' attained by the promotion of arts and commerce; and also 厚生, 'the enrichment of living,' abundant comforts and luxuries. These three great objects, it is said, 惟和, 'are to be harmonious,' to be attained by the measures appropriate to each, without any collision between them.

Third, the aid of song is to be called in, 九功,—'the nine services,' referring to the management of water, of fire, &c., and the other things just detailed. 叙=the 修 and 和 above. 董=督責, 'to urge and reprove.'

In the 左傳, 文七年, we find—夏書曰,戒之用休,董之用威,勸之以九歌,勿使壞,九功之德皆可歌也,謂之九歌,六府三事,謂之九功,水火金木土穀,謂之六府,正德,利用,厚生,謂之三事,義而行之謂之德禮,云云. Here, it is said, are four clauses quoted from the Shoo, and then the author of the Chronicle gives his own explanations of their meaning, which the compiler of the present Book has taken and fashioned into part of the classic. I come to a different conclusion. There is so much quotation, and so much explanation;—and the writer of the 左傳 is fond of such a style. But the explanation would be absurd, if it were not founded on other passages of the Classic. To my mind the 左傳 testifies to the whole of this paragraph and the next.

勿壞。○八節帝曰、俞、地
平天成、六府三事
允治、萬世永賴、時
乃功。○九節帝曰、格汝
禹、朕宅帝位、三十
有三載、耄期、倦于
勤、汝惟不怠、總朕
師。○十節禹曰、朕德罔
克、民不依、皋陶邁
種德、德乃降、黎民

8 The emperor said, "Yes. The earth is *now* reduced to order, and *the influences of* heaven operate with effect; those six magazines and three businesses are all truly regulated, so that a myriad generations may perpetually depend on them:—this is your merit."

9 II. The emperor said, "Come, you, Yu. I have occupied the imperial throne for thirty and three years. I am between ninety and a hundred years old, and the laborious duties weary me. Do

10 you, eschewing all indolence, take the leadership of my people." Yu said, "My virtue is not equal *to the position;* the people will not repose in me. *But there is* Kaou-yaou, with vigorous activity sowing

P. 8. *Complimentary response of Shun.* Yu has urged Shun to a certain style of govt., and Shun responds that the possibility of its realization was all owing to him. 地平,—this refers to Yu's labours on the inundated provinces. 天成,—'Heaven completes.' The meaning is that there could now be seed-time and harvest. Gan-kwŏ foolishly says'—五行序曰成, 'the five elements acting in order is what is called 成'; and Ying-tă more foolishly expands the 'five elements' into the spirits of the five elements' (五行之神). We find this sentence quoted as from the 'Books of Hea' in the 左傳,僖,二十四年. 六府,—'six treasuries' (see Con. Ana. XI. xiii). Those are the water, fire, &c., of the prec. par., the six treasuries' or magazines of nature. 三事,—three businesses,' *i.e.,* the rectification of the people's virtue, &c. 時=是, 'this.' 乃=汝 'you.' This par. prepares the way for the proposal in the next.

Ch. II. Yu is called to act as Shun's vicegerent, and is obliged unwillingly to accept the dignity. P. 9. *Shun on the ground of his age requests Yu to relieve him of the toils of government.* Ninety years of age is called 耄; a century, 期. Shun describing himself by both the terms, we are to understand that he was between 90 and 100, which, indeed, must have been the case after he had been on the throne 33 years. 倦于勤,—Leu Tsoo-hëen (呂祖謙, Sung dyn.) says, 止倦於勤而已,非倦於道. This is exactly our distinction;—'weary *in* the service, not weary *of* it.' 總朕師,—'gather together' (=take the lead of) 'my multitudes' (including both ministers and people). The language differs from that of Yaou to Shun 汝陟帝位, Bk. I. p. 3, because Yaou wished then to resign the throne altogether.

P. 10. *Yu wishes to decline the proposal in favour of Kaou-yaou.* 邁種德.—邁=勵, giving 'the idea of bold movement and strong action;' 種德 is 'to sow virtue,' to exhibit it so as to awaken responsive feeling in others. 念茲在茲,—in transl. these difficult sentences I have followed the view given of them in the 集傳. A difft. view was taken by Gan-kwŏ:—'If you would think of this (=any) man (*i.e.,* to employ him), it must be on the ground of this (=some)

懷之、帝念哉、念茲在茲、釋茲在茲、名言茲在茲、允出茲在茲、惟帝念功、○帝(十一節)曰、皋陶、惟茲臣庶、罔或干予正、汝作士、明于五刑、以弼五教、期于予治、刑期于無

abroad his virtue, which has descended on the black-haired people, till they cherish him in their hearts. O emperor, think of him! When I think of him, my mind rests on him, *as the man for this office;* when I would put him out of my thoughts, they still rest on him; when I name and speak of him, my mind rests on him *for this;* the sincere outgoing of my thoughts about him is that he is the man. O emperor, think of his merits!"

11 The emperor said, "Kaou-yaou, that of these my ministers and people, hardly one is found to offend against the regulations of my government, is owing to your being the minister of Crime, and intelligent in the use of the five punishments to assist the *inculcation of the* five duties, with a view to the perfection of my government, and

merit; if you would not employ him, it must be on the ground of some fault.' As to his expl. of the next clauses, I can really not get hold of it with sufficient definiteness to attempt to describe it. The whole passage from 念茲 to the end is found quoted in the 左傳, 襄, 二十一年, and an explanation of it different both from Gan-kwŏ's and from Ch'in's, but so vague that I cannot adopt it.

The words of the par., 皐陶邁種德, 德乃降, are also found in the 左傳, 莊, 八年, and it is argued that this portion of the pres. 'Counsels of Yu' was evidently plagiarized from that place. We have Too Yu's (杜預, Tsin dyn.) commentary on the 左傳, acc. to which the words of the Shoo King are only 皐陶邁種德, and the 德乃降 are an observation of duke Chwang. Here, it is said, the ignorance of the forger has betrayed him. He found a quotation from the Shoo, and he incorporated it with his compilation, but he incorporated with it what was not a portion of the Shoo. But it may be that it was Too Yu who was in error here. He had not seen the 'old text' of Gan-kwŏ; he had not seen our present Book; and from his own reading of the 左傳 he supposed the quotation from the Shoo terminated at 德, and not at 降. From a study of the 傳, I am persuaded he was in error. Looking at the whole passage where the quotation occurs, I conclude that 德乃降 is a portion of the 'Books of Hea,' whether 降 be read *heang*, or *keang*, about which there is some unnecessary dispute.

Parr. 11—13. *Shun, not listening to Yu's recommendation of Kaou-yaou to be his vicegerent, yet praises the latter for his merits as minister of Crime. Kaou-yaou disclaims the merit, and attributes it to the emperor.* 11. 罔或干予正, —罔或, 'none, perhaps,' = our 'hardly any'; 干 = 犯, 'to offend against,' diff. from its use in p. 6; 正 is by Ying-tă expounded 正道, 'right ways,' but it is better with Ch'in to make it = 政, 'government,' 'regulations of govt.' 期, in both instances, has the force of 'aiming at.' The 集傳 defines well:—期先事取必之謂, 'anticipating the issue beforehand.' Gan-kwŏ

刑、民協于中、時乃功、懋哉。○(十二節)皐陶曰、帝德罔愆、臨下以簡、御衆以寬、罰弗及嗣、賞延于世、宥過無大、刑故無小、罪疑惟輕、功疑惟重、與其殺不辜、寧失不經、好生之德、洽于民心、茲用不犯于有司。○(十三節)帝曰、俾予從

that through punishment there may come to be no punishments, but
the people accord with the *path of the* Mean. *Continue to* be strenu-
12 ous." Kaou-yaou said, "Your virtue, O emperor, is faultless. You
condescend to your ministers with a liberal ease; you preside over
the multitude with a generous forbearance. Punishments do not
extend to the criminal's heirs; while rewards reach to after genera-
tions. You pardon inadvertent faults, however great; and punish
purposed crimes, however small. In cases of doubtful crimes, you
deal with them lightly; in cases of doubtful merit, you prefer the
high estimation. Rather than put to death an innocent person,
you will run the risk of irregularity and error. This life-loving
virtue has penetrated the minds of the people, and this is why
they do not render themselves liable to be punished by your
13 officers." The emperor said, "To enable me to follow after and

badly takes it in the first case as = 當. 期于予治,—'aiming at my govt.' The 治 is in the 3d tone, with an intensive meaning, as in the transl. 民協于中,—Wang Ming-shing quotes from the 韓詩外傳:—聽獄執中者,皐陶也,故曰民協于中. 時乃功,—as in p. 8. 12. 臨 and 御 are both terms of imperial application. 'When a superior visits an inferior, 臨 designates the act'; 'wherever the son of Heaven stops is called 御' (see the Dict.). The diff. between them is indicated by the employment of them in the text. 臨 describ. Shun in his relation to his ministers (下), and 御 in his relation to the people. 嗣 and 世 are here synonyms, = 子孫, 'descendants.' 過 is equal to 眚, Bk. p. 11; 故 is crimes done 'on purpose.' 失不經,—'to fail by being not regular,' not according to the standard. 茲用 = 所以, 'therefore,' 'it is hereby that.' 有司,—'the officers,' 'an official;' see Ana. XX. ii 3, *et al.* I cannot but think that Kaou Yaou intended himself by the phrase, and feel inclined to translate:—'this is why they do not render themselves liable to be punished by *me, who am but* an officer.' In the 左傳, 襄, 二十六年, we find quoted from the 'Books of Hea'—與其殺不辜,寧失不經. 13. Shun reiterates his sense of Kaou-yaou's merits. 惟

欲以治、四方風動、惟乃之休。○帝曰、(十四節)來禹、洚水儆予、成允成功、惟汝賢、克勤于邦、克儉于家、不自滿假、惟汝賢、汝惟不矜、天下莫與汝爭能、汝惟不伐、天下莫與汝爭功、予懋乃德、嘉乃

obtain what I desire in my government, the people everywhere responding as if moved by the wind;—this is your excellence."

14 The emperor said, "Come, Yu. The inundating waters filled me with dread, when you realized all that you represented, and accomplished your task,—thus showing your superiority to other men. Full of toilsome earnestness in the service of the State, and sparing in your expenditure on your family; and this without being full of yourself or elated; you *again* show your superiority to other men. Without any prideful presumption, there is no one in the empire to contest with you the palm of ability; without any boasting, there is no one in the empire to contest with you the claim of me-

乃之休,—乃=汝; 休=美, 'excellence.' In the Works of the philosopher Seun, 大畧篇, we find the first part of this par. with a slight change. He says—舜曰, 維予從欲而治.

Parr. 14–19. *Shun returns to insist on Yu's becoming his vicegerent; delivers various admonitions to him; disallows his repeated attempt to decline the dignity; and finally Yu undertakes the government.* 14. 來禹, 洚水儆予,—see in Men. III. Pt. II. ix. 3, 書曰洚水警余. Ts'ae Ch'in says the old text read 降; and according to that char., Gan-kwŏ explains—'the waters flowing down.' No doubt the text of Mencius has prevailed to change 降 into 洚. 成允成功 is literally—'you accomplished sincerity, you accomplished merit.' I have translated according to the expansion of the meaning in the 集傳. There can be no doubt that by the 'merit' which Yu accomplished is intended his management of the inundating waters. The passage is quoted in the 左傳, 襄六年, and explained in harmony with the case which it is adduced to illustrate:—'when one's good faith is established, he can accomplish his services.' 汝賢=汝賢於人, 'you are superior to, you surpass others;' see this meaning of 賢 in Ana. XI. xv., *et al.* 克勤于邦, 克儉于家,—comp. Ana. VIII. xxi. 假,—in the sense of 大, 'great.' 自假,—'making one's-self great,' being elated. 矜 is defined 自賢, 'making one's-self superior,' and 伐, 自功, 'arrogating to one's-self merit.' There is something like the four clauses beginning 汝惟不矜 in Seun's 君子篇, and also in Laou-tsze's 道德經; but we need not assume that the pres. text was compiled from those passages. 懋 is properly 'to urge,' it may be to urge another, or to exert one's-self, and Ying-tă makes the meaning here—'I urge your virtue.' But this is quite unsuitable, and hence Choo He says that 懋 and 楙 were anciently interchanged, and so understands it in

書經

丕績、天之曆數在汝躬、汝終陟元后。○十五節人心惟危、道心惟微、惟精惟一、允執厥

rit. I see how great is your virtue, how admirable your vast achievements. The determinate appointment of Heaven rests on your person; you must eventually ascend *the throne of* the great sovereign.
15 The mind of man is restless,—prone *to err*; its affinity for the *right* way is small. Be discriminating, be undivided, that you may sin-

the sense of 'great,' 'to consider great.' 天之曆數在汝躬,—see Con. Ana., XX. i. 1, where this and other parts of the pres. parr. are given as having been spoken by Yaou to Shun, though it is added that Shun used the same language in giving charge to Yu. 15. *Warning on the proneness of man to err.* Medhurst translates the first two clauses:—'The carnal mind is treacherous, while the virtuous feeling exists only in a small degree.' Gaubil says:—'The heart of man is full of shoals *(ecueils)*; the heart of Taou is simple and thin *(delie)*'; and adds in a note:—'The heart of man is here opposed to that of Taou. The discourse is of two hearts,—one disengaged (?) from passions, the other simple and very pure. Taou expresses the right reason. It is very natural to think that the idea of a God, pure, simple, and Lord of men, is the source of these words.' Neither translation is good, and the note is altogether fanciful. The first clause does, indeed, suggest to a Christian reader of the classic what is said in the New Testament of the 'carnal mind;' but that phrase is not the correspondency of 人心. 危, moreover, is not 'treacherous,' but 'insecure,' 'tottering,' 'threatening to fall.' When the statement in this clause is taken in connection with that in the next, we have the idea of 'the carnal mind.' 道心 is, indeed, a difft. expression; and we seem to want in 道 some entity or being corresponding to 人. But that cannot be. The 道心 is still the 人心, the mind of man in its relation to the path of duty. The two clauses together tell us very truly that the mind of man, uncertain, unstable in what is good, is ever more likely, without a careful self-government, to fall into the way of evil.

Ying-tă, in paraphrasing Gan-kwŏ, seems to take 人 as = 民, as if Shun were cautioning Yu only about the proclivities of the *people*. But the term is of universal application. Choo He and other philosophers of the Sung dyn. have written much on this text. One of the scholars Ch'ing says:—'The heart of man which is restless denotes the desires of man; the reason to which it has little affinity is heavenly principle' (集說). Choo He says:—'The mouth, the nose, the ears, the eyes, and four limbs all belong to one's own body; they are the things which are of one's self, and are not like the conviction of right and duty (道), which belongs to one with all others. Thus we have at once the root of selfishness, and there is a proneness to it moreover; yet this is not in itself bad;—it is only the root of what is bad.' 'Take what is here called the 人心, and regulate and control (收之) it, and you have the 道心; take the 道心, and leave it uncared for (放之), and you have the 人心.' Putting the question, whether it could be said of the mind of the sages, that it was also restless and prone to err, he replies that the affinity for the right in them completely predominated so as to rule the other. (See the 集說). 惟精惟一,—these denote the exercise of mind and force of will by which the 人心 can be kept from disturbing the 道心, and there will result in practice the strict adherence to the Mean,—the course which neither exceeds nor comes short of what is right.

允執厥中 is found in the Con. Ana., XX. i. 1. The rest of the par., it is said, was made up in the time of the Tsin dyn. by Mei Tsih from Seun K'ing's 解蔽篇. We certainly find there, and quoted as from 道經, the passages 人心之危, 道心之微. There is also much in the context about being 精於道, and 一於道. Seun K'ing has written nothing which he was not likely to do, if he had the Shoo with this passage in his mind. And, on the other hand, it must be allowed that a forger might have compiled the first three clauses of the par. from him. His quoting from the 道經 can hardly be said to be decisive in the question, for as we refer to the Bible often as 'The word of Truth,' 'The book of Truth,' the phrase in question

中。○無(十六節)稽之言勿聽、弗詢之謀勿庸。○可(十七節)愛非君、可畏非民、衆非元后、何戴、后非衆、罔與守邦、欽哉、慎乃有位、敬修其可願、四海困

16 cerely hold fast the Mean. Do not listen to unsubstantiated words;
17 do not follow undeliberated plans. Of all who are to be loved, is not the sovereign the chief? Of all who are to be feared, are not the people the chief? If the multitude were *without* the sovereign, whom should they sustain aloft? If the sovereign had not the multitude, there would be none to guard the country for him. Be reverent. Carefully demean yourself on the throne which you will occupy, respectfully cultivating *the virtues* which are to be desired in you. If within the four seas there be distress and poverty, your Heaven-

may denote the Shoo under a similar designation. One thing is certain,—the sentences were put together before the time of Mei Tsih, for Ma Yung in his 忠經 quoted—惟精惟一、允執厥中 (see the 尙書寃詞, *in loc.*). He who has found reason to accept these 'Counsels' as genuine on other grounds will not have his faith disturbed by the difficulties connected with this passage.

It has been impugned not only on the critical grounds which I have indicated, but as containing heretical doctrine. Wang Ch'ung-yun (王充耘) of the Yuen dyn., and Mei Tsuh (梅鷟) of the Ming, especially, have contended that the idea of human nature which it gives is quite contrary to the orthodox truth; but even Ming-shing condemns them for being carried so far by their detestation of Mei Tsih.

16. *An admonition to prudence and caution in counsel and action.* 稽=考證, 'to examine and attest.' 'Unsubstantiated words' are counsels for which no precedents can be adduced. 'Undeliberated plans' are plans that have not been submitted for general consideration. 庸=用.

The 正名篇 of Seun K'ing concludes with a sentence which would seem to have been suggested by this paragraph:—無稽之言、不見之行、不聞之謀、君子愼之.

17. *Shun intimates his determined purpose that Yu should undertake the duties of the govt., and impresses on him various important considerations.*

The first clause, 可愛非君, and the next are to be taken interrogatively. The 日講 gives them;—民所可愛、豈非君乎、君所可畏、豈非民乎. Comp. a somewhat similar construction in Mencius, II. Pt. I. ii. 22, *et al.* 元后,—as in p. 14; 元=大, 'great.' We find the clauses—衆非元后、何戴、后非衆、無與守邦, quoted from the 'Books of Hea,' in the 國語、周語、上. 戴,—'to carry on the head;' and thence, 'to respect,' 'to honour.' 愼乃有位. I take as—愼汝將有之位, and the next clause also as addressed to Yu in his own person. 可願 is very much the same as 可欲 in Men., VII. Pt. II., xxv. 3. 四海困窮、天祿永終,—see Ana. XX, i. 1. I have adhered to the translation of this sentence which I gave in the Analects. Gan-kwŏ takes quite a different view of it. 'By 困窮,' he says, 'are intended the sufferers of distress through the empire, who have none to appeal to. Let the emperor cultivate the virtues appropriate to him, and care for these, and the possession of the throne will abide for ever in his person' (天之祿籍、長終汝身). Maou K'e-ling shows that previous to the time of the 'Eastern Tsin' this was the

窮、天祿永終、惟口出好興戎、朕言不再。○禹（十八節）曰、枚卜功臣、惟吉之從、帝曰、禹、官占惟先蔽志、昆命于元龜、朕志先定、詢謀僉同、鬼神其依、龜筮協從、卜不習吉。禹拜稽首、固辭。帝曰、毋惟

conferred revenues will come to a perpetual end. It is the mouth which sends forth what is good, and gives rise to war. My words I will not repeat."

18 Yu said, "Submit the meritorious ministers one by one to the trial of divination, and let the fortunate indication be followed." The emperor said, "Yu, the officer of divination, when the mind has been made up on a subject, then refers it to the great tortoise. *Now, in this matter*, my mind was determined in the first place. I consulted and deliberated with all *my ministers and people*, and they were of one accord with me. The spirits signified their assent, the tortoise and grass having both concurred. Divination, when fortunate, may not be repeated." Yu did obeisance, with his head to the ground, and firmly declined the throne. The emperor said, "Do

received interpretation of the language while that which I have followed (and which is much more likely and natural) prevailed from that time; and he argues that if the commentary of Gan-kwŏ were indeed a forgery of Mei Tsih he would not have given the explanation which had by his time gone into disuse. 惟口出好興戎,—see 墨子,尙同,中. Mih quotes the words as from 'The Books of the former Kings,' a usual formula with him when quoting from the Shoo King. It is not easy to trace what connection the truth declared in them has with the other remark of Shun.

18, 19. *Yu, still wishing to decline, and to have his appointment submitted to the trial of divination, is overruled by Shun, and finally enters on the duties of the administration.* 枚卜功臣,—枚, 'the stalk of a plant;' used also for a tally in reckoning things. From this comes its use in the text—枚卜, 'one by one divine about.' 卜,—'to divine;' properly, by means of the tortoise. Here it would seem, to sig. 'to divine generally,' including both the 龜 and 筮 below. 官占,—占, composed of 卜 and 口, indicates the answer supposed to be returned to the divination. 官占 was the officer who determined this. 蔽,—in the sense of 斷, 'to determine.' 昆—in the sense of 後, 'afterwards.' Wang Shih-p'ang (王十朋, Sung dyn.) observes, 'The ancients understood 昆 as the elder brother; he is after the father:—hence the character is explained by 後.' 命于元龜, Ts'ae Ch'in and others explain 命 by 令. He says 令之于龜, 'charges it to the tortoise.' This I do not well understand. Whatever we make of the 命, the general meaning is evidently that given in the transl. We find the whole sentence, with the alteration of one character, quoted from the Books of Hea in the 左傳, 哀十八年,—夏書曰.官占惟能蔽志;昆命于元龜. 朕

汝諧。○（十九節）正月朔旦、受命于神宗、率百官、若帝之初。○（廿節）帝曰、咨禹、惟時有苗弗率、汝徂征。禹乃會群后、誓于師曰、濟濟有衆、咸聽朕命、蠢茲有苗、昏迷不恭、侮慢自賢、反道敗德、君子在野、

19 not do so. It is you who can suitably *occupy my place*." On the
first morning of the first month, *Yu* received the appointment in the *temple of the* spiritual Ancestor, and took the leading of all the officers, as had been done at the commencement of the emperor's *government*.

20 III. The emperor said, "Alas! O Yu, there is only the prince of
the Meaou, who refuses obedience;—do you go and correct him." Yu on this assembled all the princes, and made a speech to the host, saying, "Ye multitudes, listen all to my orders. Stupid is this prince of Meaou, ignorant, erring, and disrespectful. Despiteful and insolent to others, he thinks that all ability and virtue are with himself. A rebel to the right, he destroys *all the obligations*

志先定, 詢謀僉同, 鬼神其依, 龜筮協從, 卜不習志,—see on Pt. V. Bk. IV., pp. 20–31. It is observed by Chin Tih-sew (眞德秀), that we have here the first occurrence in the classics of the phrase 鬼神. 19. 神宗 is explained by Ts'ae Ch'in, as being 'the ancestral temple of Yaou.' But this would be contrary to all analogy. Shun received this appointment in the temple of Yaou's ancestors, and Yu would receive his in the temple of Shun's ancestors. That Shun had established such a temple appears from Confucius' words, Doct. of the Mean, xvii. 1. Ch'in was led into the error by misunderstanding a passage in the 禮記, 祭法, where Shun is spoken of as having 宗 ed Yaou;—see Maou's 尙書廣聽錄, *in loc.*

This accession of Yu to the administration took place B.C. 2222.

CH. III. YU UNDERTAKES AN EXPEDITION AGAINST THE MEAOUITES; ITS CONDUCT AND RESULTS. P. 20. *Yu, being charged to act against the prince of Meaou, assembles his host, and makes a speech to it.* 惟是(=時)有苗弗率,—有苗=有苗之君; such is generally the force of 有 before the name of a country throughout the Shoo. We might render the charr. literally—'the possessor of Meaou.' 率 is here=遵 or 循, 'to honour' 'to be obedient.' It has been said that as Shun had twice dealt with the Meaouites (see Bk. I., pp. 12 and 27), there was nothing left for Yu to do with them. But there is no one chapter, perhaps, in the Shoo King which is so abundantly corroborated by citations from it and references to it in books of the Chow and Han dynn. as the present;—see the 後案, *in loc.* The prince of Meaou against whom he proceeded would not be the one whom Shun banished to San-wei, but some chieftain of the whole or a portion of the tribe who had been left in their native Seat. That Yaou, Shun, and Yu were all obliged to take active measures against them only shows the restlessness of the people, and the difficulty which those sage emperors had in establishing their sway over the country. 誓于師,—'made a speech to the host.' This is the proper meaning of 誓, throughout the Shoo. Formed from 折 and 言, 'to

書經

小人在位、民棄不
保、天降之咎、肆予
以爾衆士、奉辭伐
罪、爾尚一乃心力、
其克有勳。○三旬、 廿一節
苗民逆命、益贊于
禹曰、惟德動天、無
遠弗屆、滿招損、謙
受益、時乃天道、帝

of virtue. Superior men are kept by him in obscurity, and mean men fill all the offices. The people reject and will not protect him. Heaven is sending calamities down upon him. On this account I have assembled you, my multitude of gallant men, and bear the instructions *of the emperor* to punish his crimes. Do you proceed with united heart and strength, so shall our enterprize be crowned with success."

21 At the end of three decades, the people of Meaou continued rebellious against *the emperor's* commands, when Yih came to the help of Yu, saying, " It is virtue which moves Heaven ; there is no distance to which it does not reach. Pride brings loss, and humility receives increase:—this is the way of Heaven. In the early time of the

decide' by 'words,' it often = 'an oath ;' but in the classic its application is to the solemn charge laid upon his soldiers by a general, a speech delivered to a host. It is said in the 禮記, 檀弓, 下, p. 11, that 誓 were first made in the time of the Yin or Shang dyn.; but incorrectly, as the present instance is sufficient to show. The speech of Yu is given by Mih Teih, with some omissions and alterations, in the last part of his chapter on 'Universal Love.' 濟濟 is given in the Dict. as meaning 'the appearance of multitudes' (衆盛之貌), to which Ts'ae Ch'in would add, 'and of marshalled order.' 有衆 simply = 爾衆. This use of 有, in sententious, half rhythmical passages, is not uncommon. 蠢, from 'summer' and 'insects,' signifies 'insects moving about,' brought to all their activity by the summer heat. 'To be insubordinate,' and 'to be stupid,' are secondary significations. It is here a term of contempt, applied to the chief of Meaou, buzzing, heedless, as an insect. 咎 = 災, 'calamities';—this is the meaning given to the character in the 說文. 奉辭 = 奉帝之辭 'bear the words—instructions—of the emperor.' 爾尚一乃 (= 汝) 心力,—尚 is defined in the Dict., and by Ts'ae, as = 庶幾. It has the force of exhortation and entreaty. Hing Ping (邢昺) says, 'it indicates the hope of the mind' (謂心所希望). 其克有勳,—其, 'this,' *i.e.*, such union and energy being realized. 21. 苗民逆命,—Ts'ae explains, 苗頑猶不聽服, 'the *prince of* Meaou obstinately still refused to submit.' The most natural conclusion is that Yu's expedition was unsuccessful, and that the people of Meaou were too strong for him. 益贊,—Yih assisted Yu when labouring to regulate the waters. Here we find him also in Meaou. Afterwards he was his chief minister. There seems to have been a peculiar intimacy between the two. 贊 = 佐 or 助, 'to assist.' 時乃天道,—時 = 是, 'this.'

初于歷山、往于田、日號泣于旻天、于父母、負罪引慝、祗載見瞽瞍、夔夔齊慄、瞽亦允若、至誠感神、矧茲有苗。禹拜昌言曰、俞。班師振旅。帝乃誕敷文德、舞干羽于兩階、七旬、有苗格。○

emperor, when he was living by mount Leih, he went into the fields, and daily cried with tears to compassionate Heaven, and to his parents, taking to himself and bearing all guilt and evil. *At the same time*, with respectful service, he appeared before Koo-sow, looking grave and awe-struck, till Koo also became truly transformed by his example. Entire sincerity moves spiritual beings;—how much more will it move this prince of Meaou!" Yu did homage to the excellent words and said, "Yes." *Thereupon* he led back his army, having drawn off the troops. The emperor *also* set about diffusing his accomplishments and virtue more widely. They danced with shields and feathers between the two staircases *of the court*. In seventy days the prince of Meaou came to make his submission.

帝初于歷山,—the 初 here is always referred to Shun's early life, before he was taken notice of by Yaou. The 日講 here expands it—帝微賤之初,曾耕于歷山, 'early in the emperor's life, when he was in a low and private station, he ploughed upon mount Leih.' In opposition to this, however, Mencius says the weeping and crying to heaven and his parents took place when Shun was 50 years old. See Men. V. Pt. I. i. 5. There is no way of reconciling these representations. Mount Leih is referred to a hill, 30 le south of P'oo-chow (蒲州), dep. of P'ing-yang (平陽), in Shan-se. 號泣于旻天,于父母,—see Men., *loc cit.*, p. 1. 祗載見…允若,—see Men. V. Pt. I. iv. 4. The 日講 expl. 祗載 by 敬修爲子之事, 'he reverently performed the service of a son.' In Men. I translated 允若 by 'believed him and conformed to virtue,' but parag. 3 may satisfy us that 允 is to be taken adverbially. 禹拜昌言,—see Men. II. Pt. I. viii. 2. 班師振旅,—Ts'ae and others take 振 in the sense of 整, 'to adjust,' 'to trim,' and make the whole equal to 'he withdrew his army in good order.' Ts'ae gives also another view, without disapproving of it, according to which 班師 intimates the quitting Meaou, and 振旅 describes what was done on their re-entering the capital. We find the phrase 振旅, however, in the She King, Pt. II., Bk. III., iv., st. 3, where it means 'to draw off the troops.' With reference to that passage, the Dict. explains it by 止, and so I have translated it here.

文德 is explained by Ts'ae Ch'in by 文命德教. I have a persuasion myself that the best translation would be—'the virtues of peace,' 文 being used in opposition to 武. *War* had been tried, and found ineffectual; they would now see what effect would be produced by an exemplification of the blessings of *peace*. 舞干羽于兩階,—see on Ana. III. i. The 舞 was more a posture-making

書經

than what we call *dancing*. 于兩階—于兩階之間, 'between the two staircases,' that appropriated to the sovereign as host, and that employed by his guests. The expression = the 於庭 of the Analects. The shield was a weapon of war appropriate to a war-dance. On this occasion Shun wanted by this exhibition in the court to show how he disliked war. And the consequences, we are told, justified Yih's advice. The prince of Meaou came and made his submission.——From the whole of this 3d. chapter, I conclude that Yu's expedition against Meaou was unsuccessful. He had to retreat. The advice of Yih, with the subsequent measures, and their result, serve merely to gloss over the real fact.

THE BOOKS OF YU.

BOOK III. THE COUNSELS OF KAOU-YAOU.

皐陶謨

曰若稽古、皐陶曰、允迪厥德、謨明弼諧。禹曰、俞、如何。皐

一節

1 I. On examining into antiquity, we find that Kaou-yaou said, "If *a sovereign* sincerely pursue the course of his virtue, the counsels *offered to him* will be intelligent, and the aids *of admonition* will be harmonious." Yu said, "Yes; but explain yourself." Kaou-yaou

TITLE OF THE BOOK.—皐陶 (Yaou) 謨, 'The Counsels of Kaou-yaou.' 'Counsels,'—see on the title of the last Book. Kaou-yaou was minister of Crime to Shun (Bk. I., p. 20). Tsze-hea has recorded his merit, saying, 'Shun, being in possession of the empire, selected from among all *the officers* and employed Kaou-yaou, on which all who were devoid of virtue disappeared' (Ana. XII. xxii. 6). There are few or no reliable details of his history. In the 左傳 he appears with the style of T'ing-këen (字庭堅), one of the 'eight able sons' (才子八人) of the emp. Chuen-heuh; and Wang P'oo-meih (皇甫謐), of the Tsin dyn., says, in his 帝王世紀, that Kaou-yaou was born in K'euh-fow (曲阜, still the name of a district in Yen-chow dep. [兗州], Shan-tung), in the country of Yen (偃), whence he was surnamed Yen. Sze-ma Ts'een in his Record of the sovereigns of Hea (夏本記二), says that Yu, on his accession to the throne, made Kaou-yaou his chief minister, with the view of his ultimately succeeding him, but the design was frustrated by Kaou-yaou's death, and that then his son was appointed to the principality of Ying-luh (英六, in the prov. of Gan-hwuy. We have still the dis. of 英山, in the dep. of 六安), which was extinguished under the Chow dyn., by the power of Ts'oo (楚), and an end was made of the representatives of Kaou-yaou. See a note on Kaou-yaou in the 四書經註集證, Ana. XII. xxii. There is still a clan of the surname Kaou which traces its origin to Kaou-yaou (see the 氏姓譜, 臯氏); but Kaou and yaou are to be taken together as the minister's name.

CONTENTS. The Book is found in the texts both of Fuh-shang and K'ung Gan-kwŏ, so that there is no question of its genuineness. I have divided it into four chapters. The first, pp. 1, 2, enunciates the principle that in govt. the great thing is for the prince to pursue the course of his virtue, which will be seen in his knowledge of men, and giving repose to the people. The second chap., pp. 3—5, is designed

書經

陶曰、都、慎厥身、修思永、惇敍九族、庶明勵翼、邇可遠在茲。禹拜昌言曰、俞。○皐 二節

said, "Oh! let him be careful about his personal cultivation, with thoughts that are far-reaching, and then he will effect a generous kindness and nice observance of distinctions among the nine classes of his kindred; all the intelligent *also* will exert themselves in his service; and from what is near he may reach in this way to what is distant." Yu did reverence to the admirable words, and said,

to illustrate the former of these things,—the knowledge of men; and the third, pp. 6, 7, treats of the repose of the people. In the fourth chap., p. 8, Kaou asserts the reasonableness of his words, and humbly expresses his own desire to be helpful.

CH. I. THE DUTY OF A SOVEREIGN TO BE TRULY VIRTUOUS; ITS HAPPY EFFECTS; ITS NATURE; ITS GRAND EVIDENCES; AND ITS DIFFICULTY. 1. *Kaou-yaou and Yu on the nature and consequences of a sovereign's course of virtue.* 曰若稽古,—see on the 1st par. of the previous Books. Those who would accept K'ang-shing's expl. of 稽古, as applied to Yaou, allow that it is not admissible as applied to the minister; and they say that we must not obstinately think that the same words have always the same meaning in the classics (不可泥于一說, Keang Shing)! When we go on to the next clause—皐陶曰允德云云, however, we cannot explain according to the analogy of the corresponding passages. Tung-po asks—'Will those who take Fang-heun, Ch'ung-hwa, and Wăn-ming, as the names of Yaou, Shun, and Yu, say that Yun-teih (允迪) was the name of Kaou-yaou'? This certainly cannot be said, but we are in no better case if we take Fang-heun and the other expressions as descriptive epithets. *Yun-teih* is neither the name of Kaou-yaou, nor any honourable description of his doings or character. In whatever way we interpret the passages in the other Books, 皐陶 (or, as Keang Shing and others edit, 咎繇) 曰 must be translated, 'Kaou-yaou said.' 允迪厥德, 謨明弼諧,—it is not easy to understand this passage. In the 'Historical Records' it appears as—信其道德, 謀明輔和, 'Believing his path *of duty* and virtue, his plans will be intelligent and his aids harmonious,' 允 being taken as an active verb, =信, and 迪=道, as in the last Book, p. 5. Keang Shing and Sun Yen adopt the same view. But if this were the correct view, we should have read—允厥迪德. All suppose, it will be seen, that Kaou-yaou is speaking of *the sovereign.* Gan-kwŏ takes 迪 as=蹈, 'to tread on,' 'to walk,' so that 迪德='to pursue the course of virtue.' He takes a peculiar view, however, of 厥, which is with him not= 'his,' but 'their,' and 厥德 is 'the virtue of the ancients;' and he expounds the whole:—'A sovereign ought sincerely to tread the path of the virtue of the ancients, planning how to enlarge his intelligence in order to assist and harmonize his govt.' Woo Ch'ing has a view of his own, and takes 允迪厥德 as descriptive of a minister's duty to his sovereign. He defines 迪 by 導, 'to lead forward,' and 明 by 明哲之人, 'intelligent men.' His expos. is:—'The duty of ministers to their sovereign is truly and really to stimulate and promote his virtue. In taking their counsels, he must strive that he have the intelligent to assist him, and must harmonize them.' None of these interpretations is satisfactory, and unable to suggest one more so, I have followed in the transl. the view of Ts'ae Ch'in, who expounds:—'If the sovereign really pursue the course of his virtue, what his ministers counsel will be intelligent, and wherein they would aid him, they will be harmonious.'

This agrees better with what is said in the sequel, though it has its difficulties. An ingenious note by Wang Kăng-t'ang (王肯堂; Ming dyn.) is given in the 集傳;—'謨 indicates the setting forth of counsels and 弼, the exercise of correction. 謨 and 弼 belong to the ministers; 明 and 諧, to the sovereign. When they offer counsels on occasion of occurring affairs, he can understand their mind, without any doubts; when they differ from him and offer admonitions, he can harmonize with their words, and not put himself against them.' This is ingenious, but too refined. While approving of Kaou's words, Yu

陶曰、都、在知人、在安民。禹曰、吁、咸若時、惟帝其難之、知人則哲、能官人、安民則惠、黎民懷之、能哲而惠、何憂乎驩兜、何遷乎有苗、何畏乎巧言令色孔壬。○三節 皋陶曰、都、亦行有九德、亦言

2 "Yes." Kaou-yaou said, "Oh! it lies in knowing men, and in giving repose to the people." Yu said, "Alas! *to attain to* both these things was a difficulty even to the emperor *Yaou*. When *a sovereign* knows men, he is wise, and can put men into their proper offices. When he gives repose to the people, he is kind, and the black-haired people cherish him in their hearts. When *a sovereign* can be *thus* wise and kind, what occasion will he have for anxiety about a Hwan-tow? what to be removing a prince of Meaou? what to fear any one of fair words, insinuating appearance, and great artfulness?"

3 II. Kaou-yaou said, "Oh! there are in all nine virtues to be discovered in conduct; and when we say that a man possesses *any* virtue, that

might well ask—如何, 'what do you mean?' 愼厥身修思永 are to be understood as a sort of explanation of what is intended by 迪厥德. The remaining clauses describe the effects of such a course of virtue. First, there will be 惇敍九族, 'the making generous, and nicely observant of discriminations, the nine classes of his kindred,' equivalent to the regulation of the family or clan, in the Great Learning; second, there will be 庶明勵翼, 'all the intelligent exerting themselves as wings,' equiv. to the govt. of the State: thirdly, there will be the good order of the whole empire, 邇, 'the near,' being the Family and the State, and 遠, 'the distant,' being the empire.—In this way it is attempted to interpret the text,—not very satisfactorily.

2. *Kaou-yaou explains by what processes such effects are realized, and Yu enlarges on their difficulty.* The concluding 'Yes' of the last par. was pronounced, we may suppose, in a tone equiv. to another 如何. 咸若時 (=是),—'all as this,' *i.e.*, to attain to both these things. 惟帝其難之,—Gan-kwŏ, followed by Ts'ae Ch'in, supposes the emp. intended to be Yaou,—correctly, I think. Woo Ch'ing and Keang Shing suppose Shun is referred to. The former gives a hortatory turn to the clause:—'the emperor should feel the difficulty of this.' The latter supposes the force of the 其 is to *insinuate* an advice:—'the emperor—yes, perhaps,—he feels the difficulty of this.' The clause is to me declarative simply. 能官人,—'can *office* men,' *i.e.*, put men into the offices for which they are fit. By 巧言令色孔壬 (壬, comp. 任人, Bk. I., p. 16) it is supposed the 共工 of the Can. of Yaou, p. 10, is intended. This would give three of 'the four criminals' of Yaou's reign, whom Shun punished, leaving only K'wăn, Yu's father, unmentioned, 'Yu,' says K'ang-shing,' purposely concealing *his* name.'

CH. II. ON KNOWING MEN:—THE VIRTUES BY WHICH THEY MAY BE KNOWN; RIGHT MEN IN THE RIGHT PLACES; AND THE IMPORTANCE OF THE EMPEROR'S PERSONAL EXAMPLE. 3. 行有九德,—'Actions (行, 3d tone) have nine virtues.' There is a difficulty with the 亦 before 行. Ts'ae defines it by 總, 'altogether,' 'in all;' and expounds:—'Speaking comprehensively of the virtues which appear in conduct, they are in all nine.' I don't see

其人有德、乃言曰、載采采。禹曰、何。皐陶曰、寬而栗、柔而立、愿而恭、亂而敬、擾而毅、直而溫、簡而廉、剛而塞、彊而義、彰厥有常、吉哉。○四節 日宣三德、夙夜浚明有家、

is as much as to say—he does such and such things." Yu said, "What *are the nine virtues?*" Kaou-yaou said, "Affability combined with dignity; mildness combined with firmness; bluntness combined with respectfulness; aptness for government combined with reverence; docility combined with boldness; straightforwardness combined with gentleness; easiness combined with discrimination; vigour combined with sincerity; and valour combined with righteousness. *When these qualities are* displayed, and that permanently, have we not the good *officer?*

4 When there is a daily display of three *of these* virtues, their possessor could early and late regulate and enlighten the Family, *of*

what else the char. can mean here, but this signification of it is not in the Dict., nor have I seen any other example of it. Keang Shing arguing from the definition of 亦 in the 說文, says that 亦 and 掖 were anciently, interchanged. They were so in the sense of the 'armpit.' 掖 has a secondary mean.—'to uphold,' 'to sustain,' and attributing that also to 亦, he interprets—'supporting the actions of men, there are nine virtues.' I cannot accede to this view. The 亦 which follows has its common meaning of 'and,' 'and moreover.' 載采采,—'He does such and such things.' The Historical Records read, instead of these characters, 始事事; and Woo Ch'ing and Keang Shing both interpret 載 here by 始. It is certainly easier to take it with Gan-kwŏ as = 行. Ying-tă says:—'載 has the signification of transport and movement (運行之義), hence we define it by 行.' 采 = 事, as in Can. of Yaou, p. 10. 載事事 = 其人行某事某事. 寬而栗,—as in Bk. I. p. 24. So also 直而温. 愿而恭,—on 愿 (*al.* 原), see Ana. VIII., xvi; XVII. xiii; and esp., Men. VII. Pt. II. xxxvii. 8, 9. I translate it here by 'bluntness,' acc. to the account of it by Ying-tă—愿者遲鈍·外失於儀. 亂 = 治, 'to govern,' here 治才, an aptness for government, often associated with a spirit of lightness and self-confidence. 簡而廉,—in Bk. I. p. 24, we have 簡而無傲, where I have translated 簡 by 'impetuous.' The impetuous will overlook many things, and in their hot haste not discriminate. The same want of discrimination may result from an easy indifference, which is the force of 簡 here. The pairs of different qualities specified are understood to constitute the unity of the virtue; it is not that the one compensates for the other. 吉 = 善, 'good.'

4. This par. is specially illustrative of 哲, 能官人 in p. 2. It sets forth the knowledge of men turned to the right account by employing them according to their capacity and aptitude. Perhaps as close a translation of the first portion of the par. as can be given (to be intelligible) would be:—'The daily displayer of three virtues *would be* early and late a regulating and brightening holder of a Family.' The 'Daily Explanation' expands it thus:—九德之中·有其三者·能日宣而

日嚴祗敬六德、亮采有邦、翕受敷施、九德咸事、俊乂在官、百僚師師、百工惟時、撫于五辰、庶績其凝。○五節無教逸欲有邦、

which he was made chief. Where there is a daily severe and reverent cultivation of six virtues, their possessor could brilliantly conduct the affairs of the State, *to which he was constituted ruler.* When such men are all received and employed, the possessors of these nine virtues will all have their services. Then men of a thousand and men of a hundred will fill the offices *of the State;* the various ministers will emulate one another; all the officers will accomplish their duties at the proper times, observant of the five *elements-regulated* seasons:—and thus their various duties will be fully accomplished."

5 "Let not *the emperor* set to the rulers of States an example of

克廣之、使之益以著、此三德之有常者也、使之爲大夫而有家、必能夙夜匪懈以治其家、而家之事、無不明治矣、 'When a man has three of these virtues, and can daily display and enlarge them, making them still more conspicuous, he is a man of whom those three virtues are a permanent characteristic. Let him be made a great officer, the head of a Family, and he will be found early and late ruling that Family with all diligence, and its affairs will all be brilliantly regulated.' 浚 is here taken, after Ts'ae, as = 治. The second portion might be similarly translated and expanded. 亮 is here best defined by 明. 翕受敷施,—this is spoken of the supreme authority,—of the emperor. 翕 = 合. 敷施 = 佈而用之. 俊乂在官,—Ma, Wang, and Ch'ing, all describe 俊 as being men in ability and virtue beyond a thousand, and 乂 as men exceeding in the same way a hundred. 百僚師師,—同官曰僚, 'those who are in office together are called 僚;' hence the term is often = 'companions,' 'colleagues.' 師師,—'the one will make the other his model.' 百工惟時,—the 百工 are the same as the 百僚, called 工 with reference to their duties, the work they had to do. 惟時,—comp. the same phrase in Bk. II. p. 16. 撫于五辰,—撫 = 順, 'obedient to,' 'accordant with;' 辰 is defined in the Dict. with ref. to this passage, by 時, and Ch'in says 五辰、四時也, 'the five 辰 are the four seasons.' Of the five elements, wood predominates in the spring; fire in the summer; metal in the autumn; and water in the winter; while earth is to be recognized equally in all the seasons. We read in the Le Ke 禮運, Pt. iii. 2, 播五行於四時, 'the five elements are distributed over the four seasons;' and in the context of that passage much is said on the doctrine of the *Yin* and *Yang*, the five elements, five virtues, five tones, &c., much of which is mystical, and much absurd. In the Historical Records, after 俊乂在官 we have only 百吏肅謹. The rest of the paragraph is wanting;—possibly, because Ts'een and his father did not well understand this phrase. 庶績其凝 (= 成),—comp. in Can. of Yaou, p. 8, 庶績咸熙, which follows after the settlement of the seasons, and the regulation of the officers in accordance with them, which is perhaps all that is meant here by 百官惟時、撫于五辰.

5. *How the emperor must himself set the*

兢兢業業、一日二日萬幾、無曠庶官、天工人其代之。○六節天敘有典、勑我五典五惇哉、天秩有禮、自我五禮有庸哉、同寅協恭、和衷哉、

indolence or dissoluteness. Let him be wary and fearful, *remembering* that in one day or two days there may occur ten thousand springs of things. Let him not have the various officers cumberers of their places. The work is Heaven's;—it is men's to act for it."

6 III. "From Heaven are the *social* arrangements with their several duties; to us it is given to enforce those five duties, and then we have the five courses of generous conduct! From Heaven are the *social* distinctions with their several ceremonies; from us proceed the observances of those five ceremonies, and then do they appear in regular practice! When *sovereign and ministers* show a common *example of careful attention to his duties, and so get all his officers and nobles to give the same.*

無教逸欲有邦—'do not teach idleness and desires to the holders of States.' 無=毋. Gan-kwŏ explains:—不爲逸豫貪欲之教,是有國者之常, 'Do not practise the lessons of idle pleasure and inordinate desires, which is the constant way of the holders of States.' He does not suppose the counsel given to the emperor for his personal benefit, but to concern generally princes and officers; but his interpretation altogether is inadmissible. 教 is the teaching of example;—非必教令,謂上行而下效也 (Ts'ae Ch'in). 幾, 'that which is small and minute,'=機, 'the spring' or motive force, which, indeed, is Keang Shing's text. Gan-kwŏ explains 曠 by 空, 'empty.' The phrase in the transl. gives its force. 天工,人其代之,—Keang Shing says that 人 is the sovereign. So it is, but embracing the officers employed by him;—'the king as supreme, and governors that are sent by him.'

Ch. III. On giving repose to the people:—the accomplishment by means of government of Heaven's purposes for them. 6. 天敘有典,—Keang Shing reads 五典 after Ma Yung; but as we have below—天秩有禮, &c., 有典 is here probably the correct text. And, acc. to the same analogy, 有典 must = a concrete noun, under the govt. of 敘, like 有罪,有德, under the govt. of 討 and 命. We might render therefore:—'Heaven arranges in their orders those who have the cardinal duties.' The orders are of course the constituent relations of society,—sovereign and minister, father and son, brothers, husband and wife, and friends. 勑我五典,—'charges on us the five duties.' 正 is accepted by all the commentators as the explanation of 勑 here. A much better meaning comes from the ordinary signif. of the char. By 我 is intended the sovereign and his ministers and officers,—the sovereign specially, as the head of govt. 五典,—as in Bk. I. p. 2, *et al.* 五惇哉,—perhaps we should give this clause as nearly literally as our language will permit, if we said;—'and to the five there is a large obedience!' 天秩有禮,—'Heaven arranges in their ranks those who have the ceremonies.' The 典 belong to the essential constituents of society; the 禮 have their foundation also in the mind, which seeks for an outward recognition of the different ranks that actually obtain in society. 自我五禮,—'from us'—that is, the sovereign and his ministers—'are the definition and ordering of the five ceremonies.' But what are 'the five ceremonies?' Keang Shing supposes the

天命有德、五服五章哉、天討有罪、五刑五用哉、政事、懋哉懋哉。○ 七節 天聰明、自我民聰明、天明畏、自我民明威、達于上下、敬哉有土。○

reverence and respect for these, do they not harmonize the moral nature *of the people?* Heaven graciously distinguishes the virtuous;—are there not the five habiliments, five decorations of them? Heaven punishes the guilty;—are there not the five punishments to be severally used for that purpose? The business of government!—ought we not to be earnest in it? ought we not to be earnest in it?

7 "Heaven hears and sees as our people hear and see; Heaven brightly approves and displays its terrors, as our people brightly approve and would awe:—such connection there is between the upper and lower worlds. How reverent ought the masters of the earth to be!"

ranks spoken of to be the different orders of nobility, and that the 禮 are the ceremonial distinctions appropriate to each. But this can hardly be correct, though K'ang-shing and Wang Suh both give a partial sanction to it. Down to 衷哉, Kaou-yaou seems to have before him the influence of govt. on the mass of the people. I take myself 五禮 as＝五者之禮, all the ceremonies belonging to the distinctions of rank in connection with the five constituent relations of society. This is the most natural view in the connection. I have hesitated between it and an interpretation in accordance with the use of the phrase in Bk. II. p. 8, which indeed may be harmonized with it. 有庸哉,—here Ma Yung read 五庸哉, which should probably be adopted, on the same ground that 有典 should be sustained,—the analogy, namely, of the other clauses. 同寅協恭和衷哉,—I have followed Choo He and Ts'ae in translating this clause. Keang Shing, in acc. with his view of the prec. one to which I have referred, explains:—'all who advance together to position in the court will be respectful both in body and mind.' He takes 寅 as＝進; 協恭, reverence of the body; and 和衷, reverence of the mind. The view is quite inadmissible. 天命有德,—命＝眷命, 'to regard and appoint,' *i.e.*, to distinguish graciously. 五服五章哉,—see on next Book, p. 4. 五刑五用哉,—see on Bk. I. 11. The commentator She Lan (時瀾) observes:—'In connection with the distinguishing of the virtuous, and punishment of the guilty, there is no reference to anything to be done by us (不云我), to show that reward and punishment are to be simply in harmony with the mind of Heaven. The social arrangements and ceremonial distinctions have indeed their foundation in the mind of Heaven, but man is necessary, with his help and regulations, to complete them. But in the matter of rewards and punishments, man may not introduce one jot or tittle of his own.' This is a good instance of the way in which Chinese critics refine upon the letter of the classical texts.

7. *The sympathy between Heaven and the people.*—A warning to rulers, that they strive to give repose to the people. 天聰明自我民聰明,天明畏自我民明威 (Ma Yung read 威 in both places),—comp. Pt. V. Bk. I. i. p. 11; ii. 7. 達于上下,—'*this* reaches to above and below.' Here 上 refers to heaven, and 下 to the people. 敬哉有土,—on 有土 Ying-tă quotes from K'ang-shing:—'The em-

八節 皋陶曰、朕言惠、可底行。禹曰、俞、乃言底可績。皋陶曰、予未有知、思曰贊贊襄哉。

8 IV. Kaou-yaou said, "My words are reasonable, and may be put in practice." Yu said, "Yes; your words may be put in practice, and crowned with success." Kaou-yaou said, "*As to that* I do not know, but I wish daily to be helpful. May *the government* be perfected!"

peror, the princes, high nobles, and great officers,—all who have their domains—are styled 君; and from the great officer upwards all may be comprehended in the 有土 here, though its chief reference is to the emperor.'

Ch. IV. Kaou-yaou's confidence in his principles; and his humility. 惠=順於理, 'accordant with reason;' comp. the use of 惠 in Bk. I. p. 17; II. p. 5. 底行; 乃言底可績,—comp. Bk. I. p. 3. 思曰贊贊襄哉,—the 'Historical Records' have here simply 思贊道哉. Gan-kwŏ and Ying-tă join the 思 to the upper clause:—'*As to that* I do not know nor think about it.' On the 曰 they make no remark. Keang Shing supposes there may be a transposition of 思曰 for 曰思. and then he would take 曰 as=爰. It is certainly an easier solution of the difficulty to say with Ts'ae Ch'in that 曰 is here a mistake for 日. 贊,—as in the last Book., p. 21. It is repeated, to show that Kaou-yaou would be helpful in any way (所助,非一事). At the second 贊 I put a comma, and read 襄哉 by itself, taking 襄 as=成. For other interpretations, see Keang Shing and Wang Ming-shing.

THE BOOKS OF YU.

BOOK IV. YIH AND TSEIH.

益稷

一節 帝曰、來禹、汝亦昌言。禹拜曰、都、帝、予何言、予思日孜孜。皐陶曰、

1 I. The emperor said, "Come Yu, you also *must* have admirable words *to bring before me.*" Yu did obeisance, and said, "Oh! what can I say *after Kaou-yaou*, O emperor? I can only think of maintaining a daily assiduity." Kaou-yaou said, "Alas! Will you

TITLE OF THE BOOK.—益稷, 'Yih and Tseih.' The names Yih and Tseih occur in the first paragraph, and occasion is thence taken so to entitle the whole Book. But without good reason;—for those worthies do not appear at all as interlocutors in it. Yu is the principal speaker; the Book belongs to the class of 'Counsels.'

Ying-tă says that Ma, Ch'ing, and Wang edited this Book as a portion of the 'Counsels of Kaou-yaou,' and that, in the preface to the Shoo which they made use of, this Book, or, rather, what they considered to be another Book, was called 棄稷, and not 益稷. Keang Shing, acting on this note of Ying-tă's, gives the 4th par. of the preface—咎繇矢厥謨, 禹成厥功, 帝舜申之, 作大禹, 咎繇謨, 棄稷. On first reading there the combination 棄稷, I concluded there was a misprint, on the ground that it was most unnatural to join together the name and the office of the same man in such a way. This is the very point urged by Ying-tă against Ch'ing and the others. He says:—'棄 and 稷 are one man. It is improper to give his name, and then besides to give his office. Those scholars were mistaken' (棄稷一人, 不宜言名, 又言官, 是彼誤耳). As to incorporating the Book with the preceding one, that had been done by Fuh-shang; and the 'modern text' (今文) is always published with this Book as the conclusion of the 'Counsels of Kaou-yaou.'

CONTENTS. These have been divided into three chapters. The first, embracing parr. 1—9, relates a conversation between Yu and the emperor, in the presence of Kaou-yaou. Yu relates his own diligence and achievements as a model to the emp., and administers various advices; and Shun on the other hand insists on what his ministers should be. The second chapter, parr. 9, 10, has no apparent connection with the former. K'wei appears in it as minister of Music. In the third chapter, p. 11, Kaou-yaou and Shun sing to each other on the mutual relations of the sovereign and his ministers.

CH. I. P. 1. *Yu, urged by the emperor to counsel him, describes his own diligence and labours to remedy the calamity of the inundating waters.* 來禹, 汝亦昌言,—the 亦, '*also*,' connects this Book closely with the prec.;—so closely, indeed, that many contend it is only a portion of it, and should not stand by itself as a division of the Shoo. But the expres-

吁、如何。禹曰、洪水滔天、浩浩懷山襄陵、下民昏墊、予乘四載、隨山刊木、暨益奏庶鮮食、予決九川距四海、濬畎澮距川、暨稷播奏庶

describe it?" Yu said, "The inundating waters seemed to assail the heavens, and in their vast extent embraced the mountains and overtopped the hills, so that people were bewildered and overwhelmed. I mounted my four conveyances, and all along the hills hewed down the woods, at the same time along with Yih showing the multitudes how to get flesh to eat. I *also* opened passages for the streams throughout the nine provinces, and conducted them to the sea. I deepened *moreover* the channels and canals, and conducted them to the streams, at the same time along with Tseih

sion in the prefatory notice, 帝舜申之, which is all there is of introduction to the 'Yih and Tseih,' quite agrees with this close connection between it and the other 'Counsels.' 予何言,—'what can I say?' All commen. understand here something equivalent to the '*after Kaou-yaou*' of the translation. 予思日孜孜,—comp. the closing words of last Book. 孜,—the 說文 defines 孜 by 汲汲, 'unceasingly assiduous.' The Historical Records give 孳孳. 皐陶曰, 吁, 如何,—the Historical Records read—皐陶難禹, 曰, 云云, 'Kaou-yaou troubled Yu with the question,' &c. 洪水滔天, 浩浩懷山襄陵,—comp. Can. of Yaou, p. 11, from which Yu would almost seem to be quoting. 下民昏墊—K'ang-shing defines 昏 by 沒, 'to sink in the water,' so that it and the next character have the same meaning. I have followed the better expl. of Gan-kwŏ, who defines 昏 by 瞀. 予乘四載,—the Historical Records give this sentence at much greater length, and Yu is made to say:—'To travel along the dry land, I used a carriage (乘車); to travel along the water, I used a boat (乘舟); to travel through miry places, I used a sledge (泥行乘橇. [*k'eaou*]. To designate this sledge several other characters are used. It is described as being like a sieve, and slid easily over the surface of the soft and marshy ground); to travel on the hills, I used spikes' (乘檋 [*keuh*]. This contrivance is also expressed by various characters. It was only a shoe with a spike, 'like an awl,' under it, to prevent the feet from slipping). 隨山刊木,—隨 is defined by 行. It is better to take it as = 'along,' 刊, written also 栞 and 栞, acc. to older forms, = 'to hew down,' 'to remove.' 暨益奏庶鮮食,—暨 = 與, 'along with;' 奏 = 進, 'to introduce;' 庶 = 衆 or 民, 'the people;' Ma Yung defines 鮮 by 生, meaning, as applied to meat, 'raw,' 'fresh.' 鮮食 is flesh meat, the flesh of birds, beasts, fishes, turtles, &c. But it is not to be supposed that this was eaten raw. Mencius tells us that Shun, in connection with Yu's labours, entrusted to Yih the direction of the fire to be employed, and Yih consumed the trees and tangled vegetation of the forests and marshes, so that the birds and beasts were driven away. In this way the people, unable yet to cultivate their inundated fields, had in the capture of animals a resource against starvation. 奏庶鮮食 = 進衆民于鮮食. Some prefer to expand it—進衆鳥獸魚鼈之肉於民. 決九川距四海,—決, 'to open a passage for a stream;' comp. Men. VI. Pt. I. ii. 九川 is best taken, after Wang Suh,

艱食鮮食、懋遷有無化居、烝民乃粒、萬邦作乂。皐陶曰、俞、師汝昌言。○禹曰、都、帝、愼乃在位。帝曰、俞。禹曰、安汝止、惟幾惟康、其弼直、

二節

sowing *grain*, and showing the multitudes how to procure the food of toil *in addition to* flesh meat. I urged them *further* to exchange what they had for what they had not, and to dispose of their accumulated stores. In this way all the people got grain to eat, and all the States began to come under good rule." Kaou-yaou said, "Yes; *we ought to* model *ourselves* after your excellent words."

2 Yu said, "Oh! be careful, O emperor, of the manner in which you occupy the throne." The emperor said, "Yes." Yu said, "Find your rest in your resting-point. Attend to the springs of things, study stability; and let your assistants be upright:—then

as 九州之川, 'the streams of the nine provinces.' Some have enumerated '*nine* rivers,' as intended by the phrase; but in fact, the rivers on which Yu laboured, as will be seen in the next Book, were many more than nine. 距=至, 'to,' 'to reach to.' 距四海,—'to the four seas.' But what were those 'four seas?' This passage shows to my mind that this phrase, in the mouth of Yu and others, with reference to his labours, has more sound than sense. 濬 (as in Bk. I. p. 10) 畎澮距川,—畎 and 澮 were artificial channels cut in the fields for the purposes of agriculture. The 畎 was the smallest of such channels, a foot deep and a foot wide; the 澮 was the largest, 16 feet wide, and as many deep. Between them there were 遂, 溝, and 洫. So it was at least in the Chow dynasty;—see the Rites of Chow, 考工記之四. 'To the streams' is definite enough, and we ought to have as substantial a meaning in the 'four seas.' 暨稷播,—播, must be taken as = 布種五穀, 'to sow the various kinds of grain.' K'ang-shing, indeed, will have the sowing and cultivating here to be only of vegetables, such as could be grown in marshy ground. 艱食,—'the food of toil,' a good name for the produce of agriculture. Ma Yung read 根食, 'root-grown food.' 懋遷有無化居,—Keang Shing reads 貿, principally on the authority of a passage in Fuh-shang's Introduction to the Shoo, which is now lost. It would give a good enough meaning. 遷,—to remove,' 'as,' says Lin Che-k'e, 'to convey fish and salt to the hilly country, and bring the lumber of the woods to the low grounds.' 居 is defined in the Dict., with reference to this pass., by 積也, 蓄也, 'stores,' 'accumulated materials.' 粒,—米食曰粒, 'rice food is called 粒.' The rice is eaten whole, and not ground. But we should not confine the meaning of 粒 to rice.

P. 2. *Yu admonishes the emperor on the way to secure the blessing and favour of Heaven.* 都帝, 愼乃在位,—comp. 愼乃有位, in Bk. II. p. 17, noting the diff. of 在 and 有. 安汝止,—comp. the Great Learning, T. 2, *et al.* But after this reference, it is difficult to say exactly what Yu means. 惟幾惟康,—惟=思, 'to think of.' Immediately below, however, in 惟動, it is the particle, whose various application is so difficult to determine. 惟動丕應徯志 is expanded in the Daily Explanation thus:—一有動作, 布之政令, 則天下翕然丕應, 若先待我志之發矣, 'on the occasion of any move-

惟動丕應徯志、以昭受上帝、天其申命用休。○帝曰、(三節)吁、臣哉鄰哉、鄰哉臣哉。禹曰、俞。○帝曰、(四節)臣作朕股肱耳目、予欲左右有民、汝翼、

will your every movement be greatly responded to, *as if the people only* waited for your will, and you will brightly receive *gifts from* God. Will not Heaven renew its favouring appointment, and give you blessing?"

3 The emperor said, "Alas! ministers! associates! Associates! ministers!" Yu said, "Yes."

4 The emperor said, "*My* ministers constitute my legs and arms, my ears and eyes. I wish to help and support my people;—you give effect to my wishes. I wish to spread the influence *of my go-*

ment, when you send forth yonr orders about it throughout the empire, they will with one accord greatly respond to them, as if they had first been waiting for the intimating of your will.' 昭受上帝,—'you will brightly receive God.' We must understand 上帝之命, or some similar phrase. 天其申命用休,—the force of the 其=‘will it not be that'—? Woo Ch'ing well expanded the clause:—天亦申重其已然之命而嘉美之. 'Heaven likewise will renew its existing regard, and indicate its favour and esteem.' He interprets the prev. clause, however:—'you will brightly respond to the favour which you have received from God.'

P. 3. *The emperor enlarges on his dependence on his ministers, and the services which they render.*

3. 吁,—'alas'! Shun speaks, it is said, under excitement, unable to receive all that Yu had just said, and with special reference to 其弼直. Ts'ae says:—'臣 indicates the men; 鄰 indicates the office.' Woo Ch'ing makes them two classes, 臣 being the ministers in the administration of business, and 鄰, those in personal attendance on, and intercourse with, the emp. The 臣 and the 隣 must be the same persons, the former term express. their official station, and the latter the personal intimacy of the emp. with them;—see a note by Chang Wang (張綱, Sung dyn.) in the 集說.

4. 臣作朕股肱耳目,—the emp. himself is the head,—元首; see below, p. 11. 左右有民,—左右=助, 'to assist.' Ma Yung says:—左右助, 'to assist on the left hand and the right.' 有民=我所有之民, 'the people which I have,'=my people. 翼,—'wings;' to serve as wings to; then, metaphorically, 'to assist,' 'to give effect to' (成). The literal meaning is lost in the text. 宣力,—'to proclaim my strength.' Gan-kwŏ defines 力 by 治功, 'the services of govt.' 古人之象,—'the ancients.' Gaubil observes:—'It is remarkable that Shun, who is so ancient, speaks of the figures on the dresses of the ancients' (Le Chou-king, p. 36, note). In the first supplement to the Yih King (繫辭下傳, Ch. II. p. 5) we read that Hwang-te, Yaou, and Shun let fall their robes, and the empire was governed (黃帝,堯,舜,垂衣裳而天下治). By 'the ancients,' therefore, we may be conducted to Hwang-te, 'the Yellow emperor,' the inventor of the cycle, B.C. 2637, but not beyond him. There were twelve figures, six painted on the upper garment or robe (衣), and six embroidered on the lower garment (裳). They were called altogether 'the twelve ornaments' (十二章). Those

予欲宣力四方、汝爲、予欲觀古人之象、日、月、星辰、山、龍、華蟲、作會、宗彝、藻、火、粉米、黼、黻、絺繡、以五采彰施

vernment through the four quarters;—you are my agents. I wish to see the emblematic figures of the ancients,—the sun, the moon, the stars, the mountain, the dragon, and the flowery fowl, which are depicted *on the upper garment;* the temple-cup, the aquatic grass, the flames, the grains of rice, the hatchet, and the symbol of distinction, which are embroidered *on the lower garment:—I wish to see* all these displayed with the five colours, so as to form the *official*

on the robe were the sun, the moon, stars (Gan-kwŏ would place a comma in the text after 星, and make the 辰 refer to the three prec. nouns, and be in apposition with them. Ch'in Ts'eang -taou [陳祥道] says the 星 were the five planets, and 辰, the twelve zodiacal spaces. But 星辰 go together, and simply = stars), a mountain, a dragon, and a pheasant (華蟲, 'the variegated animal.' 蟲 is often used not for insects only, but for living creatures generally. These figures—prob. two of each—were painted (作會. 會 is used for 繪). The figures on the lower garment were a cup, used in the services of the ancestral temple (of the temple cups, one had the figure of a tiger on it [虎彝], and another of a kind of monkey [蜼彝]. One or both of these was on the 裳), some kind of water plant, flames, grains of rice, an axe-head (黼. This character denotes a texture of black and white stripes, ornamental. The Dict. says that an axe or hatchet is so called from its white head and black handle. I should rather suppose that 黼 was used for 斧, from their agreement in sound), and what I have called the symbol of distinction (黻. This is defined as a texture of black and azure stripes. As applied to the embroidered ornament, that was made in the form 亞, or two 已 placed back to back). These figures were embroidered (絺繡. Ch'ing takes 絺 to be for 黹, 'to embroider,' syn. with 繡. Gan-kwŏ would take it in its ordinary sense of 'fine cloth made of the fibres of the 葛.' I do not see how it is then to be construed). 以五采彰施于五色,—Ch'ing says that 采 and 色 refer to the same thing, only 采 is the substance of the various colours, unused, and 色 those colours employed in painting and embroidery. The sacrificial robes of the emperor had all these 12 figures painted or embroidered upon them, emblematic of various attributes, which I will not attempt to specify. The 公 or highest nobles were restricted from the use of the sun, moon, and stars; the 侯 and 伯 were further restricted from the mountain and dragon; and, by a constantly decreasing restriction, five sets of official robes were made, indicating the rank of the wearers. See last Book, p. 6,—天命有德, 五服五章哉. [The practice of the earlier times in the use of these ornaments was a good deal altered during the Chow dynasty. The subject is often perplexed, from not bearing this in mind.]

六律, 五聲, 八音,—see Bk. I. p. 24. As to what follows—在治忽以出納五言, I am far from clearly understanding it. 在 is supposed to = 察, 'to examine,' as in Bk. I. p. 5. 忽 is taken as 'the opposite of 治, = misrule. 五言 is made = 五聲. The 'Daily Explanation' paraphrases the passage thus:—音和由政事之修治、音乖、由政事之怠忽、其察之之法、則以朝廷所出之絺綸、民間所納之歌謠、言之叶于五聲、播之樂章者、爲君德民風之驗、

于五色、作服、汝明、予欲聞六律五聲八音、在治忽、以出納五言、汝聽。○予[五節]違、汝弼、汝無面從、退有後言、欽

robes; it is yours to adjust them clearly. I wish to hear the six pitch-tubes, the five notes *determined by them*, and the eight kinds of musical instruments, *regulated again by these*, examining thereby the virtues and defects of my government, according as the *odes* that go from *the court*, and the *ballads* that come in *from the people* are ordered by those five notes:—it is you who hear for me.
5 When I am doing wrong, it is yours to correct me;—do not follow me to my face, and when you have retired, have other remarks to make. Be reverent, ye who stand before and behind and on each side

而我不盡自聽也, 'The harmony of all musical instruments is owing to the happy order of the govt., and their dissonance to its being ill attended to. The method of examining into the matter is to look upon the elegant compositions which proceed from the court, and the songs and ballads which are brought in from the people,—all pieces, in fact, which are put together in harmony with the five notes, and set to music, as evidence of the sovereign's virtue and the people's manners; and I am not able to hear them all for myself.' Gan-kwŏ gives substantially the same view of 在治忽 as the above, but he takes the clause 出納五言 differently, and explains:—'Moreover, the use of music, thus regulated, is to communicate instructions about the five virtues of benevolence, righteousness, propriety, knowledge, and faith, giving them forth to the people to accomplish their transformation.' The reading—在治忽 is by no means certain. The 'Historical Records' give, instead of it, 來治滑, which is unintelligible. Ch'ing read 在治曶, and took 曶 as = 笏, a writing-tablet of gem, ivory, or other material, according to the rank of the bearer. The nobles and officers carried this with them into the court. 'The sovereign also,' says Ch'ing, 'was provided with one, to communicate to the principal officers (五官) the lessons of govt.' But what have those tablets to do with music? Ch'ing's reading does not make the passage any plainer. The reading—采政忽 has had its advocates, but its meaning would not differ from that of the *textus receptus*. In the Books of the 'Former Han' dyn., however, 律曆志上, we have the passage—書曰, 予欲聞六律, 五聲, 八音, 七始, 詠, 以出納五言, 女聽. No doubt this was a current reading in the early times of the Han. It makes the whole clause refer somehow to the subject of music, without introducing the matter of examining about the govt., and so far it is to be preferred. But what are we to understand by the 七始, or 'seven beginnings?' Pan Koo, the historiographer of Han, says they are 'heaven, earth, man, and the four seasons.' So far as I can understand Woo Ch'ing, he understands by them the complete musical scale, containing the five notes (五聲) and two semitones. They are no doubt terms with some musical significance. A sinologue, understanding the theory of music, and having some practical acquaintance with the art, might succeed in elucidating the subject. Pan Koo takes 出納五言 in the same way as Gan-kwŏ. 五言 = 五常之言.—We go on to the next par., wishing that the second part of this were more apprehensible, or that we understood it better.

5. *The duty of ministers freely and openly to correct the sovereign's faults.* 予違,—'I am opposing;' *i.e.*, going contrary to the right (有違戾於道). 汝弼,—with reference to 其弼直 in p. 2. 弼 has the idea of *correction*. 後言 = after and other words. 欽四鄰,—I have translated 四鄰 after Gan-kwŏ, in illustration of whose interpr. Ying-tă refers to 惟予一人無良, 實賴左右前後

四鄰。○庶(六節)頑讒說、若不在時、侯以明之、撻以記之、書用識哉、欲竝生哉、工以納言、時而颺之、格則承之庸

6 of me. As to all the obstinately stupid and calumniating talkers, who are not to be found doing what is right, there is the target to exhibit their true character; the scourge to make them remember; and the book of remembrance! Do we not wish them to live along with us? There are also the masters of music to receive the compositions which they make, and continually to set them forth *in*

有位之士, 匡其不及, in Pt. V., Bk. XXVI., p. 3. Fuh-shang and K'ang-shing after him supposed that there were four ministers attendant on the person of the emp., specially called 鄰,—'a helper on the left, a corrector on the right, a solver of doubts before, and a stimulator of purpose behind.' There is no evidence that there were such officers. 鄰 is here equivalent to 臣, as in p. 3. 6. *That ministers are not only to be strictly faithful to their sovereign, but are to use stringent measures to correct others, and provide a supply of good men for the use of the State.* 庶頑讒說,—these are the 讒說殄行 of Bk. I. p. 25. We are to understand these words not of the people generally, but 'of the sons of officers, and youths of greatest promise of ability, who may be expected to discharge hereafter the functions of the State' (see Woo Ch'ing, *in loc*).

若不在時,—the 時=是. Gan-kwŏ takes it as the 是 emphatic, = 'what is right.' Woo Ch'ing, with ref. to his observation on the prec. clause, says 不在是選者, 'who are not in this selection,' *i.e.*, selection to office. 侯以明之,—'there is the target to show them clearly.' Archery was made much of anciently in China; see the 儀禮, 卷八至十四. Wang Ming-shing, quoting from the 射義, says, 'The archers must advance, retreat, and move round, according to the proper rules. Where the aim of the mind is right, the adjustment of the body will be correct; and thus archery supplies an evidence of character. Unworthy men will not be found hitting frequently. There were three ceremonial trials of archery, belonging to the emperor, the princes, the high ministers and the great officers. First, there was the Great archery, used to select those who should assist at the sacrificial services. Second, there was the Guests' archery, used on occasion of the princes appearing at court, and their visiting among themselves. Third, there was the Festive archery, used at entertainments generally. From the first kind expectant scholars were excluded; but they could take their part in the other trials.' He then goes on to describe the various targets used at those trials. What we call the 'bull's-eye,' was the figure of a small bird (鵠 See Doctr. of the Mean, xiv. 5). Confucius more than once spoke of archery as a discipline of virtue (see Ana. III. xvi., *et al.*). Certain vices will of course unfit men for the successful practice of archery, but to lay down success in archery as a test of moral character is tearing a subject to tatters. The most famous archers of Chinese antiquity were very bad men: see Men. IV., Pt. II., xxiv. 撻以記之,—'there is the scourge to make them remember.' The archery field was, according to this, truly a place of discipline. This illustrates the 扑作教刑 of Bk. I. p. 11.

書用(=以)識 (read *che*) 哉,—'there is the *book*,' not, it must be borne in mind, a book of paper and printing, but a record made on cloth or on a tablet. It does not appear that the record should be confined to the result of the trials in archery;—see the 周禮, 地官, 司徒, 第二之四, where the Heads of districts are all supposed to keep a register of the characters of the people, in reference to the laws generally. 欲竝生哉,—the object of the trial, the punishment, and the record, is to effect a reformation. The characters may be translated—'Oh! we wish them to live together *with us*.' Keang Shing defines 生 by 進, 'to advance;' and explains it by 'to advance to goodness.' This is far-fetched.

工以納言, 時而颺之,—工 is, no doubt, = 樂官, 'an officer of mu-

書經

之、否則威之。○禹曰、俞哉、帝光天之下、至于海隅蒼生、萬邦黎獻、共惟帝臣、惟帝時舉、敷納以言、明庶以功、車服以庸、誰敢不讓、敢

七節

song. If they become reformed, they are to be received and employed; if they do not, let the terrors *of punishment* overtake them."
7 Yu said, "Yes, but let your light, O emperor, shine all through the empire, even to the grassy shores of the seas, and in the myriad States the most worthy of the people will all wish to be your ministers. Then, O emperor, you may advance them to office. They will set forth, and you will receive, their reports; you will make proof of them severally by their merits; you will confer chariots and robes according to their services. Who will then dare

sic.' All commentators agree in this. As to the interpretation of the whole clause, I have followed Ts'ae Ch'in, as in the concluding part of p. 4, without feeling sure of being right. To quote here again from the 'Daily Explanation,' we have there this paraphrase:—然必觀其改過與否、又當命樂官取彼所進納之言、播于樂章、時時而宣颺之、其言和平、是能改過、'But it must be seen whether they really reform or not. The officers of music must also be charged to take the words which they present and send in, and set them to music, continually rehearsing them. If their words are harmonious and mild, it is an evidence of their reformation.' On the other hand, Gan-kwŏ, foll. by Woo Ch'ing and others, thinks the use of the musical officers in the matter was to bring their songs and sentiments to bear on those who had undergone the discipline described, in order to complete their reformation. This is, perhaps, the preferable view. 格則承之,—格, as in Ana. II. iii.

7. *Yu suggests to the emperor that his chief dependence must be on himself, and not on any assistance or correction of his ministers.* 俞哉,—'Yes!' Tung-po says that while this phrase expresses the assent of the mouth, it indicates that the mind does not quite consent. But this is hypercriticism, suggested by the design apparent in the sequel of the paragraph. 海隅蒼生,—隅=角, 'a corner;' 蒼生 is given in the 'Daily Explanation' as equivalent to 黎民, 'all the people;' and this is a meaning now often attached to the phrase. But it is contended that it was not so understood before the Tsin dynasty. 蒼 properly denotes the green colour of grass, and Gan-kwŏ connects the phrase with 海隅 as in the translation (至于海隅蒼蒼然生草木). 黎獻,—獻=賢, 'the worthy,' 'the wise,' as in Ana. III. ix. 黎 may be taken as = 'all;' or in the sense we have hitherto attached to it:—'the wise of the black-haired race.' 時舉,—時=是. The whole clause = 'and your Majesty will simply have to employ them.' 敷納以言,明庶以功,車服以庸,—comp. Bk. I. p. 9. Ying-tă explains the slight difference between the two passages, saying that the first is descriptive of Shun's dealings with the princes, whose standing was recognized, and this speaks of the first selection and employment of officers. Hence we have here 納 and 庶, 納 denoting the receiving and choice of them, and 庶, the distinction of them from their fellows (納謂受取之,庶謂在羣衆). This is ingenious, though the 庶 has to me a suspicious appearance. Choo He would read 試. Keang Shing reads the whole according to a quotation from the 'Books of Hea' (which, however, may possibly be of the passage in the Can. of Shun) in the 左傳,

不敬應、帝不
時、敷同日奏
罔功。○無若 九節
丹朱傲、惟慢
遊是好、傲虐
是作、罔晝夜
頟頟、罔水行
舟、朋淫于家。
用殄厥世、予
創若時、娶于

not to cultivate a humble virtue? Who will dare not to respond to you with reverence? If you, O emperor, do not act thus, all *your ministers* together will daily proceed to a meritless character.

8 "Do not be like the haughty Choo of Tan, who found his pleasure only in indolence and dissipation, and pursued a proud oppression. Day and night, without ceasing, he was thus. He would make boats go where there was no water. He introduced licentious associates into his family. The consequence was that he brought the honours of his House to an end. I took warning from his course. When I

僖,二十七年,—賦納以言,明試以功,車服以庸. 帝不時,敷同日奏罔功,—時=是. 不時=不若是, 'not thus.' 敷同 is taken as =普同, 'all together,' *i.e.*, even the ministers of good character whom you at present employ, to say nothing of the calumniating parties whom you talk about our reforming. We read in the 'Historical Records'—帝即不時,布同善惡,則無功. The compiler of these would seem to have understood 敷同 in the sense of—'if you employ together the good and the bad.' 8. *Yu proceeds to warn Shun by the example of himself. Shun in reply compliments both Yu and Kaou-yaou.* In the 'Historical Records' this par. appears introduced by a 帝曰, while after the equivalent there for 予創若是, we have the addition of 禹曰. Keang Shing follows Ts'een, and edits his text accordingly. He adduces other evidences of the reading, as in the 楚元王傳, in the Books of the Former Han, where we find (in the acct. of 向子政)—帝舜戒伯禹,毋若丹朱敖. There must have been the readings of 帝曰 and 禹曰 in some copies of the Shoo during the Han dyn. But, if we are to judge in the matter by the canon that the more difficult reading is to be preferred, we shall adhere to the *textus receptus*. It is startling to find Yu lecturing Shun, and warning him not to be like Choo of Tan.—Dared a minister to speak so to the sage emperor? This diffi. is somewhat got over by introducing the characters 帝曰, which again necessitate the 禹曰 below. 丹朱,—it is stated, in the 漢書律曆志, that 'Yaou placed his son Choo in 丹淵,' from which it is concluded that Tan was the name of a State to which Yaou appointed his son. 頟頟 is defined 不休息貌 'the appearance of unceasingness.' Ch'ing connects the phrase with the clause below, and says:—'Choo having seen people moving about in boats during the inundation, after the waters were reduced, would still live in a boat, and made men unceasingly push it along.' Wang Ming-shing argues for a metaphorical explanation of 罔水行舟, making it = Mencius 從流忘反 (I. Pt. II. iv. 7),—absurdly, it appears to me. 朋淫家內,—this is illustrated from the orgies of Këĕ, the last emp. of the Hea dyn., who dug a pool, and made a night palace, where men and women lived promiscuously together, and where he once remained himself for a whole month.' 用殄厥世,—殄=絕, 'to extinguish.' Ts'ae Ch'in says 世者世堯之天下也, '世 means making hereditary—handing down to future generations—the empire of Yaou.' 予創若時(=是),—創 (1st tone), 'a wound inflicted by a knife;' here = as in the transl. Gan-kwŏ defines it by 懲, 'to repress,'

塗山、辛壬癸甲、啟呱呱而泣、予弗子、惟荒度土功、弼成五服、至于五千、州十有二師、外薄四海、咸建五長、

married in T'oo-shan, *I remained with my wife only* the days *sin, jin, kwei, and keă*. When *my son* K'e was wailing and weeping, I did not regard him, but kept planning with all my might my labour on the land. *Thus* I assisted in completing the five tenures, extending over 5,000 *le; in appointing* in the provinces twelve Tutors; and in establishing, in the regions beyond, extending to the four seas, five Presidents. These all pursue the right path and are merito-

'to reprove' and Ying-tă says:—'創 and 懲 have both the meaning of seeing wickedness, and stopping one's-self from a similar course.' Ts'een gives, for this clause, 予不能順是, which is quite inane. The clause is natural in the mouth of Yu, unnatural from Shun. I do not see how with this clause we can adopt the reading 帝曰 at the begin. of the par.

娶于塗山,—塗山 was the name of a principality, the daughter of the ruler of which was married by Yu. A hill called 塗, gave its name to the territory, and is identified with one in the pres. prov. of Gan-hwuy, 8 *le* to the south-east of the dis. city of Hwae-yuen (懷遠), dep. of Fung-yang (鳳陽). Ch'ing says that Yu was married on the day 辛, and got the emperor's command to undertake the remedy of the inundation on the day 甲, so that he spent only three nights in his house. But I suppose he was already engaged in his great work, and could only spare four days from it for the business of his marriage. 啟呱呱,—啟 was Yu's son who afterwards succeeded to the throne. The two other characters express the sound of an infant's crying.

弗子, 'did not *son* him,' *i.e.*, did not regard him. Mencius tells us (III. Pt. I. iv. 7) that Yu, when engaged upon the waters, was eight years away from his family, and though he thrice passed the door of his house, did not enter it.

荒=大, 'great,' 'greatly.' 土功, 'the service of the land,' *i.e.*, all the work which he had to perform in regulating the waters.

弼成五服,—see on the next Book, Part ii., parr. 18—22. Yu speaks of himself here, it is said, as only 'assisting,' (弼), because he would attribute the great merit to the emp. Woo Ch'ing, however, considering 弼 to mean, primarily, the effort employed in forming the figure of a bow, explains the text of the figure and formation of the dift. tenures;—a very likely explanation. 州十有二師,—Medhurst has translated this clause:—'In every district I appointed twelve officers,' and then he has a note to the effect that over every province there was established only *one* nobleman, as officer. Gaubil translates the text in the same way as Medhurst:—'Chaque Tcheou eut douze chefs.' It is a vexed question whether in each province there was only one 師, or whether there were eleven. The old interpreters, not without differences among themselves, yet all maintain the larger number. It will be sufficient here to give an abridgment of the views of Ch'ing.—'Inside the tenure of Restriction (要服) were the nine provinces (九州), containing altogether a space of 49,000,000 square *le*. Deducting from these the imperial domain, there remain 48,000,000; or 6,000,000 square *le* to each province. Now, when Yu assembled the princes of the empire at Hwuy-k'e (會稽), they amounted to 10,000. Such was the number of the States of the nine provinces. Over every province was a Pastor (牧), and the worthiest of the princes were selected to be tutors or counsellors (師) to him. For every hundred States there was one 師, and 12 師 would suppose 1200 States. Each province contained of States 100 *le* square, 200; 70 *le* square, 400; 50 *le* square, 800:—altogether 1400. Deduct 200 of these, as an allowance for waste lands, and there remain 1,200 States. Multiply these by 8; we have 9,600, and allowing 400 for States within the imperial domain, we have the 10,000 States forming the empire.' The value of these statements and figures will have to be considered in connection with the next Book. In the meantime, according to these views there were in all

各迪有功、苗頑弗即工、帝其念哉。帝曰、迪朕德、時乃功惟敘、皋陶方祗厥敘、方施象刑惟明。○

rious; but there are *still* the *people of* Meaou, who refuse to acknowledge their duty. Think of this, O emperor." The emperor said, "That my virtue is followed, this is the result of your meritorious services, so orderly displayed. And now Kaou-yaou is respectfully carrying out your arrangements, and employing the represented punishments with entire intelligence."

96 Tutors or Counsellors in the empire. The ancient commentators agree in this view, and many of the moderns follow them,—Ts'ae Ch'in for instance, and the authors of the 'Daily Explanation.' On the other hand, many scholars maintain that, the 12 師 are the same as the 12 牧 of Bk. I., p. 16; and that the appointment of them here is not to be referred to the time when Yu reduced the waters of the inundation, and the provinces were nine in number, but to the subsequent period, when Shun had altered that division, and made twelve provinces (Bk. I. p. 10.) This was the prevailing opinion in the Yuen dyn. Woo Ch'ing advocates it, and so does Wang Kang-yay (王耕野). I may quote the language of the latter:—'Twelve Tutors in provinces were the same officers as those elsewhere denominated pastors. It was their duty to nourish the people, and therefore they were called pastors; it was their duty also to be the instructors of the people, and therefore they were called tutors. Don't let it be supposed that, besides the 12 pastors, there were other 12 princes appointed in every province to be their tutors' (see the 讀書管見, 卷上, *in loc.*) This was the view which occurred to myself on the study of the classic, without reference to commentaries, and I am inclined still to prefer it. I have made the translation so literal that it will admit of either view. 外薄四海, 咸建五長,—it is difficult to know the exact meaning here, as much is in the prec. clause. 外 must be 九州之外, 'beyond the nine provinces.' 薄 (*p'ŏh*)=被, 'reaching to.' 薄四海 is a vague expression, indicating all the territory beyond the nine provinces, which partially acknowledged the imperial sway. Medhurst translates the clause:—'Beyond these districts, even to the four seas, everywhere I established the five elders,' and in a note, translated from Ts'ae, he says:—'Beyond the nine regions, bordering on the four seas, in every part he separately established five elders as superiors, to take the general charge of the country.' The translation of Gaubil is entirely incorrect:—Joining the foll. 各迪有功 closely with the clause immediately preceding, he translates the whole:—'Au dehors je renfermai dans leurs bornes les quatre mers, cinq autres choses furent etablies, et je reussis dans mon entreprise.' This is evidently not the meaning; what the meaning is, it is not so easy to determine. According to my interpretation, it is that there were five chiefs to whom was given the superintendence of all this outlying territory. I do not find this view, however, supported by Chinese authorities. Ch'ing said:—'Outside the nine provinces over five States was appointed a chief, to cause' each of them—*i.e.*, the rulers of each—to observe their duties' (外則五國立長, 使各守其職). This view is supposed to be confirmed by a passage in the Le Ke, 王制, ii. 2, where it is said that 'five States formed a connection, and every connection had a chief' (五國以爲屬, 屬有長). Such an arrangement, however, belonged to the Chow dynasty, and it prevailed all beyond the imperial domain. Woo Ch'ing makes the 五長=五等諸侯, 'the five kinds of princes,' the kung, how, pih, &c. He adds that the 師 were leaders of all princes in a province, the 長 presided each over one State.—Neither of these interpretations appears to me so likely as the one which I suggest. 各迪有功,—I take 迪 as in the last Book p. 1, only that 迪 is here intransitive, unless we take 有功 together, as a noun governed by it. The meaning adopted in the former passage of 迪=導 by Woo Ch'ing would answer here. He of course adheres to it, and Keang Shing here adopts it, making 各迪有功=率道諸侯就功. 弗即工,—即=

書經

九節 夔曰、戛擊鳴球、搏拊琴瑟以詠、祖考來格、虞賓在位、群后德讓、下管鼗鼓、合止

9 II. K'wei said, "When the sounding-stone is tapped or strongly struck; when the lutes are swept or gently touched; to accompany the singing:—the *imperial* progenitors come to the service, the guest of Yu is in his place, and all the nobles show their virtue in giving place to one another. Below there are the flutes and drums and hand-drums, which join in at the sound of the rattle, and cease at the sound of the stopper; with the calabash organs and bells:—all

就; 工=功. 帝曰, 迪朕德, 云云,—in the Historical Records we read for this—道五德乃女功序之也, 皐陶於是敬禹之德, 令民皆則禹, 不如言, 刑從之, 舜德大明. The meaning is substantially the same as that which I have given, with the exception of the view which is taken of the concluding 惟明. It will be seen also that the compiler of the Records supposed Shun's words to terminate with 惟敍, and that what followed was historical. The first 方 is certainly more natural, considered as narrative; as to the second, one would gladly follow Keang Shing, and take it as = 溥.

Ch. II. *K'wei celebrates the power of the music which he superintended.* Ts'ae Ch'in observes that this chapter is to be considered by itself, and has no connection with the previous or subsequent portions of the Book. Shun, he observes, reigned more than 50 years, and must have had many conversations in which Kaou-yaou, K'wei, and Yih took part. The historian has preserved the most remarkable of their remarks, but not in the sequence of their conversations. Ts'ae blames, therefore, the efforts of scholars to force a connection between this and the context. It is as well to admit this view, though the mind naturally likes to think that we have in the various 'Counsels' so many integrals. 戛擊鳴球,—球 is defined as 'the sonorous gem-stone (玉磬), and also as 'a fine gem' (美玉). It is, no doubt, used here in the former application. I have seen a *king*, brought in 1861 from the 'Summer palace,' that had been made for the emp. K'een-lung of jade stone fully an inch thick, and like a ship-builder's' *knee*, the form in which the instrument is commonly represented. When suspended and struck with a piece of metal, it emitted a rich ringing sound.

輕敲曰戛, 重敲曰擊, 'To strike lightly is called 戛; heavily, 擊.' The striking in both ways was applied to the stone, and not, Gan-kwŏ supposes, also to the 柷 and 敔 mentioned below, which he thinks regulated the music in the raised part of the hall, as well as that in the lower. 搏拊琴瑟,—I call the 琴瑟 *lutes*, whithout having for myself definite ideas of the instruments. [I hope to be able to describe them fully and correctly in the next volume, upon the She King]. They were stringed. Ch'ing K'ang-shing says the *k'in* had five strings, and the *shih* twenty-five. There were different sizes and forms of them. A note in the 爾雅 says:—'The *k'in* was 5.66 feet long, with five strings to which other two, called the civil and martial, were subsequently added. The Great *shih* was 8.1 feet long, and 1.8 ft. broad, with 27 strings; the Elegant *shih* of the same size, had 23 strings, and one in common use only 19; the Praise *shih* of the same breadth, but nearly a foot shorter, had 23 strings. Some ascribe the invention of the *k'in* to Fuh-he; some, to Shin-nung: and some to Shun. 搏 is a forcible striking of the strings; and 拊, a slighter. 以詠 is expanded in the 'Daily Explanation' to 以合于人聲之歌, 'to accord with the singing of the human voice.' 祖考,—'grandfather and father,' = ancestors. 祖考來格=祖考之神來至, 'the spirits of ancestors come.' The whole of the service is supposed to take place in the ancestral temple of Shun.

'The guest of Yu' is Choo of Tan, the son of Yaou; comp. are 作賓于王家, Pt. V. Bk. VIII. 1. 下=堂之下, 'in the lower part of the hall.' We understand from this that the sounding-stone and lutes were in

柷敔、笙鏞以閒、鳥獸蹌蹌、簫韶九成、鳳凰來儀。

filling up the intervals; *when* birds and beasts fall moving. When the nine parts of the service according to the emperor's arrangements have all been performed, the male and female phœnix come with their measured gambollings *into the court*."

the higher or raised portion of the hall.

管鼗鼓,—the 管 was a kind of flute, originally made of bamboo. Accounts differ as to its exact form. It is generally figured as double, two tubes, each with a mouth-hole and five other holes. It is difficult to see how the two could be blown together. Other flute instruments were the 籥 and the 篪. 鼗鼓.—鼓 is the general name for drums. The 鼗 was a small drum, held by a handle, with two strings fixed to the sides and terminating in knobs. When twirled by the hand, those knobs struck on the ends, and produced the sound. Pedlars now carry a small instrument of this kind about with them, and by the noise it makes attract the public attention, Ts'ae supposes that the two characters of the text belong to the one instrument, the *t'aou*. Woo Ch'ing, with whom I rather agree, takes them to signify the small hand-drum and the large drum. 合止柷敔,—the 柷, it is said, was a lackered box, a foot deep and 2.4 ft. square (other dimensions are assigned), with a handle going down to the bottom, and moveable so as to strike against the sides when turned round. At the sound of this the other instruments struck up. The 敔 is represented as a couchant tiger of wood, with 27 teeth along the ridge of his back, which when rasped against by a handle gave the signal for the music to stop. This is the common account of these instruments and their use, which however does not go higher than the Han dynasty. Woo Ch'ing calls it in question, and with him agrees Sun Ke-yew (孫繼有; Ming dyn. See the 集說). According to them, the 敔 was made of earth, an instrument similar to the 塤. In this way all the 八音, or eight kinds of musical instruments are mentioned by K'wei. This explanation is not unlikely; but I cannot make out fully what Woo Ch'ing says about 合止 (合止爲二音合作,止則敔止,柷木音,敔當是土音,塤之類,而舊說相傳以爲斵木成伏虎狀,背有鉏鋙,櫟之以爲聲,蓋因敔名而生鉏鋙之義,必不然也). 笙鏞,—the 笙 was made of reeds or tubes (19 in large instruments, and 13 in smaller), placed upright in an emptied calabash, with a cross piece of metal at the mouth of each tube. G. T. Lay, Esq., in his 'The Chinese as they are,' p. 88, has called the *shang* Jubal's organ, and says:—'This seems to be the embryo of our multiform and magnificent organ, and consists of several tubes varying in length, so as to utter sounds at harmonic intervals from each other. These tubes are inserted into a bowl' (were originally placed in a calabash), 'which must be taken as the humble representative of the wind chest, while the office of bellows is of course discharged by the human breath.' The invention of this primitive organ has been ascribed to a fabulous female sovereign (女媧氏), who followed Fuh-he. 鏞=大鐘, 'a large bell.' The invention of the bell is carried up to Koo-yen (鼓延), a grandson of Fuh-he. 以閒 is expanded in the 'Daily Explanation' to 以與堂上衆樂,更迭閒作, 'to strike up at the intervals, in their turns with the instruments in the higher part of the hall.' Ts'ae says:—與詠歌迭奏, 'striking up in their turn with' (after) 'the singing.' The meaning is the same. 蹌蹌 is defined 行動之貌, 'the appearance of moving.' Ts'ae says:—'The music not only moved spirits and men; but even birds and beasts—ignorant creatures—led on one another to gambol to it.' 簫韶九成,—簫韶 are to be taken together as the name of the music of Shun, said to have been made by him in the 5th year of his reign (see the 資治通鑑綱目前編,卷之二). For 簫 we should read 箾, meaning a sort of castanets, held by the dancers as they kept time to the music; but the two characters lose their individual meanings, and represent the music of Shun. 成 is defined by Ying-tă as 樂曲終, 'the completion of the music and song.' He adds that when one song was concluded, another was sung to a different tune; and this was repeated in Shun's music 9 times, with reference to what is said in Bk. II. p. 7,—'when the nine services

書經

十節 夔曰、於、予擊石拊石、百獸率舞、庶尹允諧。○ 十一節 帝庸作歌曰、勅天之命、惟時惟幾、乃歌曰、股肱喜哉、元首起哉、百工熙哉。皐陶拜手稽首、颺言曰、念哉、率作興事、

10 K'wei said, "Oh! when I strike the stone or tap the stone, all kinds of animals lead on one another to gambol, and all the chiefs of the officers become truly harmonious."

11 III. The emperor on this made a song, saying, "Being charged with the favouring appointment of Heaven, we must be careful at every moment, and in the smallest particular." He then sang, saying,

"When the members work joyfully,
The head rises flourishingly;
And the duties of all the officers are fully discharged!"

Kaou-yaou did obeisance, with his head to the ground, and with a loud and rapid voice said, "Oh! think. It is yours to lead on,

have been orderly accomplished, let that accomplishment be celebrated in songs.' 鳳凰來儀,—see Ana., IX. viii. In K'ang-he's dict., char. 鳳, several descriptions of the bird will be found. 來儀＝來舞有容儀, as in the transl. Ch'ing's expl. is different, and to me hardly intelligible. He says, 儀,匹也,來止巢而乘匹. I suppose he means that they came and bred in the court.——K'ung Ying-tă observes that though the descent of the spirits of ancestors is mentioned in connection with the music high up in the hall, and the movements of animals in connection with that below, and the appearance of the phœnix in connection with the whole service, we are not to suppose that the particular effect was owing to the whole or particular part of the service as specified. Ts'ae notices also the opinion of some who explain the statements away, and ask how we can suppose that birds and beasts and phœnixes really came gambolling in the court. He replies that such suspicions merely show ignorance of the power of music, and then he adduces instances duly recorded (見於傳者), quite as marvellous as those in the text. It was the music of Shun, as preserved in Ts'e, which so affected Confucius that for three months he did not know the taste of flesh (Ana. VII. xiii.). P. 10. See Book I. p. 24. I said the passage was out of place there. It would almost seem to be the same here, though the concluding clause,—庶尹允諧, adds a particular point to the effects of music, not mentioned in the prec. par. 尹 is defined, both by Gan-kwŏ and Ch'ing, by 正, which again＝官長, 'the heads of the officers,' *i.e.*, the directors of the various official departments. The 'stone' is here mentioned by K'wei (for particular reasons, which exercise the ingenuity of commentators), by synecdoche,—one of the kinds of musical instruments for all the eight kinds.

Ch. III. Songs of the emperor and Kaou-yaou, on the duties of the emperor and his ministers. This par., if the two prec. did not intervene, might well be taken as a sequel to parr. 4—6 on the part of Shun, and parr. 7, 8, where Yu tells him that his dependence must be on himself, and not on his ministers 庸＝用; but we cannot tell with what reference it is used. It indicates that the reflection and song of Shun were consequent on something previously mentioned, being＝'on this.' There is nothing in the parr. immediately prec. to which the *this* can be referred. 勅天之命,—勅, as in p. 6. of the last Book:—'being charged with the favouring appointment of

愼乃憲、欽哉、屢省乃成、欽哉。乃賡載歌曰、元首明哉、股肱良哉、庶事康哉。又歌曰、元首叢脞哉、股肱惰哉、萬事墮哉。帝拜曰、俞、往欽哉。○

and to originate things, with a careful attention to your laws. Be reverent! Oh! often examine what you have accomplished. Be reverent!" With this he continued the song, saying,

"When the head is intelligent,
The members are good;
And all business will be happily performed!"

He again continued the song, saying,

"When the head is vexatious,
The members are idle;
And all affairs will go to ruin!"

The emperor said, "Yes; go ye, and be reverently *attentive to your duties*!"

Heaven.' 惟時,—comp. 食哉惟時, Bk. I. p. 16. 股肱,—see p. 4. 元首,—the sovereign is evidently intended by this phrase. In Ying-tă's paraphrase (foll. by K'ang-he's dict., char. 元), 元 is taken as =首; but it is rather an adj., with some eulogistic meaning, = 'the great,' 'the superior.' 百工熙哉,—comp in Can. of Yaou, p. 8, 允釐百工,庶績咸熙. 颺言曰,念哉—Gan-kwŏ defines 颺 by 大言而疾, 'with great words and rapid.' 念哉 is evidently addressed to the emp. Ch'ing says that they are a summons to all the ministers to give heed to the warning just uttered by the emperor; and Ming-shing and Keang Shing, in their prejudice, endorse the view. 憲=法, 'the laws.' A careful attention to these on the part of the emp. would be a good example to the officers to attend to their duties. 'Examine what you have accomplished;'—*i.e.*, that you may carry on your undertakings and govt. with the same success. 賡載歌曰,—賡=續, 'to continue.' 載 is taken by Ch'ing as=始, making the meaning,—'he continued and sung his *first* song,' with ref. to 又歌 below. Gan-kwŏ takes it as=成, 'to complete.' making the meaning—'he continued and completed the meaning of the emperor.' 叢脞哉,—Ch'ing explains 叢脞 by 總聚小小之事, 'a general collection of small affairs.' To the same effect, substantially, are the views of Gan-kwŏ and Ma Yung. 'Vexatious,' as in the transl., seems to give the idea, though it is not easy to collect it from the several characters. 墮 (read *to*)=壞, 'to fall in ruins.' 往,欽哉,—see Can. of Yaou, p. 11, *et al.*

THE SHOO KING.

PART III.

THE BOOKS OF HEA.

THE SHOO KING.

PART III. THE BOOKS OF HEA.

BOOK I. THE TRIBUTE OF YU. PART i.

夏書

禹貢上

禹敷土、隨山刊木、奠高山大川。

1 I. Yu divided the land. Following the course of the hills, he hewed down the woods. He determined the high hills and great rivers.

NAME OF THE PART.—夏書, 'The Books of Hea.' 夏 is the dynastic designation under which Yu and his descendants possessed the empire, B.C. 2,204—1,766, a period of 439 years. Hea was a small territory, which still retains the name of Yu (Yu-chow [禹州], dep. of K'ae-fung in Ho-nan), to which he was appointed after the conclusion of his labours on the inundated empire. Hwang-poo Mih (皇甫謐), in his 'Chronicle of Emperors and Kings,' says:—'Yu was constituted Chief of Hea, south of Yu-chow, the present Yang-chih (陽翟) of Ho-nan' (Mih wrote dur. the Tsin dyn.); 'and afterwards, when he succeeded to the throne which Shun resigned in his favour, he took the dynastic designation of Hea.' I have not, indeed, found the appointment of Yu to Hea in the 'Historical Records;' but the tradition of it was current during the Chow dynasty. In the 國語, 周語下, under the year B C. 549, after a long rambling account of Yu's labours, it is said that 'Great Heaven was pleased with him, and gave him the empire, while there was conferred on him' (we must understand by Yaou) 'the surname of Sze (賜姓曰姒), and the clan-name of Holder of Hea (氏曰有夏).' This part of the Shoo King never consisted of more than the four Books, which compose it at present—a fact difficult to be accounted for; and the first of them, much more extensive than all the others together, is descriptive of what took place during the vice-gerency of Shun, before the death of Yaou. Ying-tă says that originally it was among the Books of Yu, but that the historiographers of Hea placed it among those of their dynasty, or perhaps Confucius was the first to assign to it its present place. Whensoever it was first placed among the Books of Hea, there can be no doubt that Ts'ae Ch'in gives the true reason for that arrangement, when he says that the merit here described was the ground of Yu's advancement to the imperial seat.

Name of the Book.—禹貢, 'The Tribute of Yu.' Tribute, however, is not here to be understood in the sense of a contribution *paid by one nation to another* in acknowledgment of subjection and testimony of fealty, but as the contribution paid by subjects to their proper rulers. The barbarous tribes round about the 'Middle Kingdom' bring here, indeed, their 貢, and the attempt by the rulers of the present Manchow dynasty to give the same name to the presents sent to them from Great Britain and other countries was an assumption which needed to be repressed and rebuked; but such offerings occupy a very inferior place, as compared with the 賦 or contribution of revenue, levied from each province. We might rather expect that the Book should be called 禹賦. 貢, however, has the general signification of 'an offering made by inferiors' (下之所供謂之貢), and may embrace the 賦, while that term is more restricted and could not be employed to comprehend the 貢 properly so called. This is the account given by Ying-tă of the name of the Book, and I think correctly. Ts'ae Ch'in endorses a view somewhat different:—'In the Book we have both 貢 and 賦, and yet it is called only by the former. Mencius observes that the sovereign of the Hea dynasty enacted the 50 *mow* allotment, and the payment of a proportion of the produce (夏后氏五十而貢, Bk. III. Pt I. iii. 6). This proportion was determined by taking the average of several years, so that, accord. to this acct., 貢 was the general name for the revenue levied under the Hea dynasty from the land.'

Contents. The name,—'The Tribute of Yu,' gives a very insufficient account of the contents. The determination of the revenue, and of the various articles of tribute was, indeed, very important, but the Book describes generally the labours of Yu in remedying the disasters occasioned by the overflowing waters. Having accomplished that, he went on to define more accurately the boundaries of the different provinces, and to divide the empire into five tenures. It may be regarded as a domesday book of China in the 23d century before Christ: but when we consider that it is contained in the compass of a few pages, we cannot expect very much information from it. Choo He says in several places, that much of what is said about the geography of the country—the mountains and rivers—cannot be understood, in consequence of the changes of names, and the actual changes in nature which have taken place. This is doubtless the case; but when we shall have an accurate and scientific survey of China, and it is known to us in the length and breadth of its provinces as any of the countries of Europe is, this ancient document will be invested with a new interest, and have a light thrown upon it, for want of which we can at present in many places only grope our way. The division of the Book into two parts, which is found in Yung Ching's Shoo, and I have here followed, is convenient, but of modern device. It is still unobserved in many editions, of which I need only mention the 'Daily Explanation.' The first part is conveniently arranged in ten chapters, the first containing only one paragraph; and each of the others containing the account of one province in a good many paragraphs.

On the title of 'The Counsels of the Great Yu' it was observed that the Books of the Shoo have obtained a sixfold classification accord. to their subject-matter. This Book has been referred with reason to the class of the Canons. Chang Kew-ching (張九成, Sung dyn.) has the following observations on the authorship of it:—'Are we to suppose that it was composed by the historiographers? But they could not have known all the minutiæ which we find in it about the regulation of the waters. I venture to give my opinion in this way:—There are the first and last paragraphs, about Yu's dividing the land, &c., and returning his mace;—these are from the historiographers. But all between, from 冀州 down to 訖于四海, is the narrative by Yu himself of his various labours,—his narrative as presented to the emperor, and kept in the bureau of history, whence it was edited by the proper officers with some modifications of the style.'

Ch. I. A summary of Yu's scheme of operations upon the inundated empire. It is the general opinion that this par. lays down the plan on which Yu proceeded to his task; and though there is nothing in the language to determine absolutely in fav. of this interpret., I think it is the most likely. First, he divided the land into nine provinces, and arranged in what order they should be taken in hand. Next, he travelled along the hills, and possessed himself with a general idea of what was to be done to afford a vent for the waters, and conduct them by their natural channels, Lastly, the waters being carried off, he defined the boundaries of the provinces more accurately than had been done before, by reference to the principal mountains and streams. 禹敷土,—敷土, comp. 'Counsels of Yu,' p. 1. Ch'ing defines 敷 by 布, 'to spread out,' 'to arrange,' adding 布治九州之水土, 'he arranged and reduced to order the water and land of the nine provinces.' Ma Yung says that 敷=分; and in Gan-kwŏ we find all these terms together: —洪水汎溢,禹分布治九州之土, 'amid the overflowing of the inundating waters, Yu divided, arranged, and reduced to order the land of the nine provinces.' It may be questioned whether the division of China into nine provinces originated with Yu. The first territorial arrangement of the country is referred to Hwang-te, who, it is said, 'mapped out the country, and divided it into provinces, making in all 10,000 States of 100 *le* each (畫野分州,得百里之國萬區; see the 歷代疆域表, under Hwang-te).

二節 冀州。三節 既載壺口。四節 治梁及岐。五節 既修太原。至于岳陽。六節 覃懷底績。至于衡漳。

2 II. With respect to K'E-CHOW,—he did his work at Hoo-k'ow and
5 took effective measures at Lëang and K'e. Having repaired *the works on* T'ae-yuen, he proceeded on to the south of *mount* Yŏ. He
6 was successful with his labours on Tan-hwae, and went on to the cross-flowing stream of Chang.

In the accounts of Chuen-heuh, the grandson of Hwang-te, we read that he 'established nine provinces,' the names of which are the same as those of Yu. The 'Historical Records' give 傅, instead of 敷, and introduces this par. thus:—'Yu, along with Yih and Tseih, received the emperor's commands, and ordered the princes and people to call forth labourers to divide and arrange the land.' I introduce this passage because it helps us to understand how Yu accomplished his great work. We are too apt to think of him alone in connection with it. He had the merit of suggesting, directing, and superintending; but all the talent and strength of the empire were helping. Yih and Tseih are mentioned by himself as his coadjutors. Passages from the Shoo itself, the 'Historical Records,' &c., indicate that he was also in correspondence with Kaou-yaou, the Sze-yŏ, Pih-e, and the pastors of the provinces, and so had all the resources of the empire at his disposal. This has suggested to Hoo Wei (胡渭) another ingenious view of the meaning of 禹敷土. Taking 敷=傅=賦, 'to give,' 'to assign,' he says:—'What is expressed by 敷 took place before Yu went over his door. K'e-chow was to be assigned to so and so; Yen-chow to so and so; and so on. This was simply the choice and employment of men for the several portions of the work.' 隨山刊木,—see 'Counsels of Yu,' p. 1. Sze-ma Ts'een gives 行山表木, and Keang Shing inclines to interpret 刊 by 表; but we cannot admit this. The woods were hewn down to open up paths for men, and channels for the waters. Mencius tells us that Yih employed fire to destroy the forests and rank vegetation. We may suppose that fire was had recourse to, when peculiar difficulties opposed the use of the axe. 奠高山大川,—奠=定, 'to fix.' He fixed the great rivers and mountains;—but for what purpose? Ts'ae Ch'in answers:—'To distinguish accurately the boundaries of the different provinces.' Yĕh Mung-tih (葉夢得; early in the Sung dyn.) answers:—'As guiding marks to determine the application of the forces necessary to accomplish the work in hand.' Gan-kwŏ and Ma Yung answered:—'To determine their order and degree, with reference to the sacrifices that should be offered to them.' This last view has found a vigorous advocate in Maou K'e-ling, who argues that 奠 denotes the preliminary sacrifices at the commencement of the work, and 旅, those offered at the conclusion of it, so that the 奠高山 here is in correlation with the 九山刊旅 in Part ii., p. 14. But with what is the 奠大川 in correlation? If it be said—with the 九川滌源, there is no notion of sacrifice there. We might accept either the view of Ch'in or that of Mung-tih, but not that advocated by Maou.

CH. II. THE ACCOUNT OF K'E-CHOW. Pp. 2—6. *Engineering labours on the rivers and country.*

P. 2. 冀州. The old interpreters all read on 冀州既載, and placed a comma at 載, making the meaning to be='A description of the work to be done in K'e-chow was first prepared.' No doubt it seemed to them that 既, being generally equivalent to our sign of the perfect tense, presupposed a subject already mentioned. But in p. 5, 既修大原, it introduces a clause in an absolute manner. It is much more in consonance with the analogy of the commencing parr. of the other chapters on the other provinces to put a stop at 州. The only difference is that those others are all defined by certain boundaries, whereas no boundaries are assigned to this. The reason may be, as Ts'ae says, that all the others being defined, the boundaries of this might thence be known; or, as it said by others, it is left undefined, a mark of distinction, as containing the imperial seat, the capital of the empire. Hwang-te is said to have had his capital in Choh-luh (涿鹿); Chuen-heuh, his in Te-k'ew (帝邱); Kaou-sin, his in Poh (亳);

Yaou, his in P'ing-yang; and Shun, his in P'oo-fan (蒲坂);—all of which places were within K'e-chow. As to the actual boundaries of the province, it had the Ho—what is called the Yellow River—on three sides of it, the west south, and east. On the west, between it and Yung-chow, was all that portion of the Ho, which forms the present dividing line of Shen-se and Shan-se, in a course of about 500 miles, according to Williams (The Middle Kingdom, vol. I., p. 15). At the south-western corner of Shan-se, the Ho turns to the east, and first dividing that province from Ho-nan, flows through Ho-nan on to the south-west point of Shan-tung, and afterwards traverses Keang-soo, with a southerly incline, finally disemboguеing itself in about lat. 34°. At any rate, one would have so described its course a few years ago; it is said now to pursue a north-easterly course from somewhere in the border between Shan-tung and Ho-nan. It did this in the time of Yu. It turned north at about the place where Chih-le, Shan-tung, and Ho-nan all touch, and its waters flowed north and east into the present gulph of Pih-chih-le. The southern boundary of K'e-chow, therefore was the Ho in its south-eastern flow, which divided it from Yu-chow; and its eastern boundary was the Ho in its north-eastern flow, which divided it from Yen-chow. [This north-eastern portion is often called the Ho of Yu;—the first change in its direction to a more southerly course took place in the 5th year of the emp. Ting (王定) of the Chow dyn. B.C. 601.] The northern boundary of K'e-chow must be left altogether indefinite.

From this account of the province, it will be seen that Medhurst is in error when he speaks of it as corresponding to the present Shan-se.(Shoo King, p. 83). It was of much larger extent. As stated in 'The Boundaries of the empire in Successive Dynasties,' K'e-chow embraced the present provinces of Chih-le and Shan-se, with the three departments of Chang-tih (彰德), Wei-hwuy (衛輝), and Hwae-k'ing (懷慶) in Ho-nan, and the western portion of Shing-king or Leaou-tung.

Pp. 3, 4. 既載壺口,治梁及岐,—If 既載 be joined, as by the old scholars, with 冀州, it is not possible to construe 壺口. They have said nothing, however, which would indicate that they saw the difficulty.

載 is best taken as = 事, 'to perform service.' Ts'ae and others would combine the meanings of 始 'first,' and 事. He says:—經始治之謂載; but this is not necessary.

壺口 is the name of a hill which we might translate 'Pot's-mouth.' It is 70 *le* to the south-east of the small dep., city of Keih (吉), in Shan-se. Medhurst gives its position as in lat. 36°15', N., long, 6°5', W. of Peking. The Ho passes it in its southward flow, 'seething like a boiling pot' (see a note in the 集傳), and I suppose that in the time of Yu some spur of the mountain encroached upon the stream. South of Hoo-k'ow was the Lung-mun (龍門) or 'Dragon Gate,' an important point of the Ho, so called from a hill of that name; and north of it was the 孟門, or Great Gate,' also an important point. Before Yu's labours, the waters of the Ho not finding free course from Măng-mun downwards, there overflowed, and inundated both K'e-chow and Yung-chow. By what he did on Hoo-k'ow, and his immediately subsequent operations on mount Leang, he achieved one of the most notable of his 'labours,' and 'opened the Dragon-gate.' Leang and K'e are the names of two hills,—belonging, say the scholars of the Sung dyn. to K'e-chow; belonging, said the older interpreters, to Yung-chow. Acc. to Ts'ae, Leang was the Leu-leang (呂梁) hill, corresponding to the present 'Spine hill' (骨脊山), in the north-east of the small dep. of Yung-ning (永寧), belong. to the larger one of Fun-chow (汾州); and K'e was the Hoo-k'e, or 'Fox-peaks,' hill in the same dep. of Fan-chow, in the west of Heaou-e district (孝義縣). Ts'ae says that the waters of the Ho passed at the base of both these hills. But it is objected by Hoo Wei that 'Spine hill' is fully 150 *le* from the Ho, and 'Fox-peaks' more than 330. I must conclude that while it was natural for the Sung scholars to look for Leang and K'e in K'e-chow, they have not been successful in finding them there. Turning to the old interpreters, who refer the hills to Yung-chow, Leang is the pres. mountain of that name, 90 *le* to the north-west of the dis. city of Han-shing (韓城), dep. Se-ngan, in Shen-se; and K'e, called also 'Heaven's pillar' (天柱) is 90 *le* north-east from K'e-san (岐山) dis. city, dep. of Fung-Ts'ëang (鳳翔). The former was not far from the western bank of the Ho, and near to Lung-mun. We can easily see how some operations on it should have been necessary to complete the accomplishment of the object contemplated in beginning at Hoo-k'ow. But why should he have gone westward to mount K'e? Hoo Wei answers :—'By dealing with mount Lëang, a free passage was made for the Ho, and the calamity of inundation was removed from the country on the right and left of this western portion of it. But that country still remained unfit for the purposes of agriculture, covered with pools, undrained, and it was for Yu, acc. to his own words, 'to deepen the channels and canals, and conduct them to the rivers, that Tseih might proceed to his business. But why should he defer proceeding at once to his work on T'ae-yuen and Yŏ-yang, which were near the imperial seat? If he had now gone at once eastward, not a few years must have elapsed before he could come back to this point; and we may conclude also that it was of great importance to the capital itself that this part of the country should be regulated without delay.' These observations seem to give a sufficient explanation of Yu's turning aside a little from K'e-chow to the adjoining prov. on the west. There remains still another point to be touched on, before we proceed to the next par.—We get the impression that Yu's labours commenced at Hoo-k'ow and mount Lëang. But Choo He has questioned this. Referring again to Hoo Wei, he observes:—'Choo in his 語錄 says that he cannot fully credit the common view as to the commencement of Yu's labours, for that if he had opened the passage of the 'Dragon Gate' without previously clearing the channels below, the out-rush of the Ho would only have been more disastrous than before. It was Yu's plan to commence at the lowest point, and therefore in K'e-chow he must have begun at Këĕ-shih, and the nine Ho. These views have been followed, especially by Foo T'ung-shuh (傅同叔); and it is generally concluded that Yu began to deal with the waters in Yen-chow. But let us attend to the aspect of the inundation, as it presented itself to Yaou. He said:—"Destructive is the overflow of the waters. In their vast extent, they embrace the mountains and overtop the hills, threatening the heavens." Mencius' account is:—"In the time of Yaou, the waters flowing out of their channels, inundated the Middle kingdom. Snakes and dragons abounded, and the people had no place where they could settle themselves. In the low grounds they made nests for themselves, and in the high grounds they made caves." This was the aspect of the inundation as it appeared to Yaou, and frightened him; it is described by him accordingly. It was occasioned chiefly by the outburst of the Ho above Mâng-mun, and no other place so urgently required that measures should be taken with it. If Yu could manage the Ho at Lung-mun and mount Leang, he would find no insurmountable difficulties elsewhere; if he could not do this, the capital must have become the home of fishes. But without reference to the capital, here was the spot where it was necessary to take the first measures to remedy the terrible evil.' K'ung Ying-tă reasons in a similar way, and insists that the waters of K'e-chow did not flow through Yen-chow.

P. 5. 既修太原,至于岳陽,—既修, 'having repaired.' This is understood to have reference to the labours of K'wăn, Yu's father, which had not been altogether ineffectual. Choo Hoh-ling (朱鶴齡; of the pres. dyn.) has said:—'On the north of the Ho there are many of K'wăn's dykes. The capital being within the space here indicated, K'wăn had wrought with peculiar energy to defend it from the waters. Yu entered into his labours, availed himself of them and completed them. But there was this difference between the father and the son. Yu went first to the source of the evil, and made a free course for the Ho; whereas K'wăn had confined himself to a branch of it, to the course of the Fun in those parts.' 太原,—lit., 'the great plain;' but the name still exists as that of the principal prefecture of Shan-se, and also of a district of the same. The city of T'ae-yuen is in lat. 37°45', N., lon. 3°55', W. of Peking. 岳陽,—'the south of Yŏ.' Yŏ, called also T'ae-yŏ, was the principal mountain in K'e-chow. It is now the Hoh-t'ae (霍太) hill, 30 *le* to the east of Hoh-chow city, belong. to the dep. of P'ing-yang. It is said to be 200 *le* in circumference, and its southern skirts touch on the two districts of Yoh-yang (岳陽), and Chaou-shing (趙城). Hereabouts Yaou, it is said, had his principal city when marquis of T'ang; but this is doubtful. The 修......至, indicate continuousness of operation, and indeed this paragraph is descriptive of Yu's regulation of the river Fun (汾), which rose in T'ae-yuen, pursued a devious course to Yoh-yang, and afterwards joined the Ho.

P. 6. 覃懷底績,至于衡漳,—Yu is now operating on the borders of the Ho in its eastward course from the south-western corner of the pres. Shan-se. The name of Tan-hwae still partly remains in that of the dep. of Hwae-k'ing (懷慶), in Ho-nan, whose prin. city is in lat. 35°6', N., 3°28', W. of Peking. The territory was low and level, easily inundated therefore, and requiring more toil to be spent on it. The toil and the eventual success are indicated in the phrase 底績;—comp. Can. of Shun, p. 8, and Coun. of Kaou-yaou, p. 8. Having done all that was necessary for the present on the southern portion of the Ho, Yu went on to the junction of the Chang with the Ho; or, as Lin Che-ke says, we may suppose that he crossed over the country, across the mountain ranges of 大行, to the sources of the Chang, and regulated its course, and the country which it drained, all the way to the Ho. 衡 is taken as = 橫, and 衡漳 is 'the cross-flowing Chang,' so called with reference to its course from east to west, or the contrary; a course from north to south or from south to north being described as natural (從);—see the 集說. Ma Yung and Wang Suh were of opinion that 衡 was the name of one river, and 漳 that of another, but there is no evidence to support their view. It appears, however, that the 衡漳 was formed by the union of a 'clear' (清漳) and a 'muddy (濁漳) Chang.' The foll. account of them is taken from the 地理今釋, or 'Modern Geography:'—'The Clear Chang rises 30 *le* to the south-west of the district city of Lŏ-p'ing, (lat. 37°35', N; lon. 2°40', W.), dep. T'ae-yuen. Flowing south-east to the dis. of Shĕ-heen (涉縣), dep. Chang-tih (彰德), Ho-nan, it is there joined by the muddy Chang, at "the Meeting of the Chang." Thence it flows north-east to Chih-le, and in the dis. of Kwang-

[七節] 厥土惟白壤〇[八節] 厥賦惟上上錯、厥田惟中中〇

7, 8 The soil of this province was whitish and mellow. Its contribution of revenue was the first of the highest class, with some proportion of the second. Its fields were the average of the middle class.

p'ing (廣平), in the dep. of the same name, it throws off a branch which joins the Wei, (衞河), while the main stream, skirting the borders of Shan-tung, in the dis. of K'ew-heen (邱縣; dep. Ts'ing-chow) again divides, and sends off a branch northwards to the marsh of Ta-luh (大陸澤), passing on itself through the dep. of Ho-këen (河間) in Chih-le, into dep. of T'een-tsin, where, in the dis. of Ts'ing-hëen (青縣), it unites with the Wei. Thence flowing northwards as far as Se-koo of T'een-tsin, it receives various streams, and holds an eastward course to the sea. At this quarter it is called the Old Chang, to distinguish it from the branch of itself which went off to Ta-luh, and rejoins it at Se-koo, under the name of the New Chang.' (Se-koo, 'the western Koo' [西沽], to distinguish it from Ta-koo (大沽), a name become sufficiently familiar of late years). 'The muddy Chang has its rise in the dis. of Ch'ang-tsze (長子), dep. of Loo-ngan (潞安), Shan-se, and also follows a south-eastern course to the "Meeting of the Chang."' Of course, in Yu's time, the Chang, being absorbed in the Ho, had no subsequent course of its own to the sea. Its junction with the Ho took place in the pres. dep. of Ho-këen, dis. of Fow-shing (阜城; lat. 37°55'. N., lon. about 15', W.).

Pp. 7, 8. *Soil and Revenue.* 7. 土 here denotes the soil or ground, with general reference to the whole province; and it is described by regard both to its colour and nature. Its colour was 'white,' = whitish, and its nature was 壤. This term may be interchanged with 土 in the general sense of soil or ground;—see the 'Rites of Chow,' 地官, 司徒, 第二之二, esp. pp. 23,24. Here, however, where it denotes a particular kind of soil, the word *mellow*, signifying, in this application, 'soft, easily pulverized,' very well represents its meaning. Gan-kwŏ defines it by 無塊, 'without lumps,' and the 說文 by 軟土, 'soft earth.' In the portion of the 'Rites of Chow' just referred to, we have much said about the practical uses to which a knowledge of the different soils should be turned, but the simple statement of the text does not require that I should enter on that subject. 8. Both the revenue and the fields—that is, the cultivable ground—were arranged in three classes (see Part ii., p. 15), and under each class were three divisions. Thus the value of the ground ranged from the 1st to the 9th degree; and the amount of revenue did the same, the general rule, I apprehend, in regard to it being that it should be a tenth of the produce. The amount of revenue would be very much regulated by the character of the ground, but not entirely so. A poor tract of country well cultivated would produce more than a rich one, left to go to waste. The actual produce depended on many other circumstances in addition to the character of the soil, such as the density or sparseness of the population, the system of irrigation, manuring, &c. Here in K'e-chow, the revenue was the highest of the highest class, (厥賦惟上上), with an admixture of the second degree of the same. Such is said to be the force of 錯. Gan-kwŏ and K'ang-shing both define that term in this connection by 雜. Gan-kwŏ says:—雜出第二之賦, 'it mixedly produced the revenue of the second degree.' Ma Yung took a different view (地有上下錯通率第一); but allowing their meaning, we are still unable to say when and where the reduction from the highest amount of revenue was admitted. In the account of the other provinces, the description of the fields always precedes that of the revenue, as is proper, the revenue chiefly depending on the ground; but here the order is reversed. The revenue is mentioned first, and the quality of the fields follows. The most likely explanation, perhaps, of this is that suggested by Lin Che-k'e, that K'e-chow being the imperial domain, its income would be derived not only from the fields, but from a groundrent, and imposts on gardens, orchards, &c., as well. In the other provinces, again, mention is made of 貢, 'articles of tribute,' in addition to the 'revenue.' Those were expressions of their fealty presented by the princes. There was no occasion for them in the imperial domain.

九節 恆衞既從、大陸既作。十節 島夷皮服。十一節 夾右碣石，入于河。○

9 The *waters of the* Hăng and Wei were brought to their proper channels; and Ta-luh was made capable of cultivation.
10 The wild people of the islands brought dresses of skins. Keeping
11 close on the right to the rocks of Këĕ, they entered the Ho.

P. 9. *Other engineering labours.* It is difficult to say why this par. does not immediately follow the 6th. We may reasonably suppose that the country was all rescued from the inundation before measures were taken to fix the revenue. 從＝從其故道, 'to follow their old channels.' 從 has a *hophal* signification. The Hăng river takes its rise from a valley of the hill of the same name, in the pres. dis. of Keuh-yang (曲陽; lat. 38°39′, N.; long. 1°40′, W.), dep. Chin-ting (眞定, called also 定州). Near its source it is called the 'Long Streamlet' (長溪); it pursues an eastern course, to the borders of K'e Chow (祁州), dep Paou-ting (保定), receiving difft. names in its progress. At this point it unites with the Tsze (滋河), and by-and-by flows into the T'ang water (唐水), called also the Kow (滱). The Wei, under the name of Luy-kow (雷溝), rises in the district of Ling-show (靈壽; lat. 38°18′, N., long. 1°57′, W.), and flowing to the south, enters the Hoo-t'o (滹沱). Hoo Wei contends that by the Hang of the text we are to understand the Kow, and by the Wei the Hoo-t'o. The Kow and the Hoo-t'o now unite their streams, and travelling eastwards pass the city of T'een-tsin, and on to the sea. The Hăng and the Wei in Yu's time poured their united waters into the Ho.

大陸既作,—K'ang-shing says that 大陸 is 'the name of a marsh or lake, on the north of Keu-luh' (鉅鹿; lat., 37°17′, N., lon., 1°17′, W.). Modern writers incline to consider it the name of a large tract of flat ground, 'embracing,' says the Daily Explanation, 'the district of Hing-t'ae (邢臺), and the smaller depp. of Chaou (趙州), and Shin (深).' I apprehend the modern view is correct, 陸 having the signification, given in the 爾雅, of 'what is high and level.' As to the lake of Ta-luh, called also Kwang-o (廣阿), it is still very considerable. It touches the dis. of Shuh-luh (束鹿), dep. of Paou-ting (保定); that of Keu-luh, dep. of Shun-tih (順德); those of Lung-p'ing (隆平), and Ning-tsin (寧晉) in Chaou-chow; and Shin-chow:—see a note in the 集傳, and the description of the lake in the 'Statistical Account of the Empire of Ta-ts'ing,' under Shun-tih foo.). The Hăng and the Wei were to the north of Ta-luh, and I suppose that their waters overflowing and running south into the lake made the country difficult of cultivation. Still the repetition of the 既—既從, 既作—implies that a good deal of independent labour had to be expended on Ta-luh.—the country, I suppose, all round the lake, before it was possible to cultivate it, which is the meaning of 作.

Pp. 10, 11. *Tribute brought by barbarous tribes, and their route to the capital.* 10 島夷皮服,—The 'Historical Records' read 鳥夷; as did Ch'ing, Ma, Wang, and others of the Han dynasty. Gan-kwŏ determined that 島 was the proper reading, which was subsequently introduced into the text. He defines the character by 海曲, 'bends of the sea,' *i.e.*, bays, with islands in them that could be inhabited. But the proper definition of 島 is 'an island' (海中可居者曰島). If 鳥 be the proper reading, then 鳥夷, or 'Bird barbarians,' would be the name of a tribe of wild people, for whom we are to look in the islands or mainland, north and east from K'e-chow. Assuming that Gan-kwŏ was right in thinking we should read 島, we are restricted from the mainland. Hoo Wei thinks that only the Japanese and the people of San-han (三韓 (see a long, but extravagant description of this tribe or tribes in the Books of the 'After Han,' 卷七十五) can be intended. But I cannot suppose that, if Japan was then occupied, its people had any intercourse with China, far less acknowledged its sovereignty. The 'skin dresses,' no doubt = furs, rather lead our thoughts to the mainland, to the regions north-east from K'e-chow. 11 夾右碣

十二節 濟河惟兗州。○十三節 九河既道。○十四節 雷夏既澤。○十五節 灉沮會同。○十六節 桑土既蠶。是降丘宅土。○十七節 厥土黑墳。厥草惟繇。厥木惟條。○十八節 厥田惟中下。厥賦貞作。十有三載。乃同。○十九節 厥貢漆絲。厥篚織文。○廿節 浮于濟漯。達于河。○

12 III. *Between* the Tse and the Ho was Yen-chow.
13 The nine branches of the Ho were conducted by their proper
15 channels. Luy-hea was formed into a marsh; *in which the waters of*
16 the Yung and the Tseu were united. The mulberry grounds were
made fit for silkworms, and then *the people* came down from the
heights, and occupied the ground *below*.
17 The soil of this province was blackish and rich; the grass in it
18 became luxuriant, and the trees grew high. Its fields were the
lowest of the middle class. Its revenues just reached what could
be deemed the correct amount; but they were not required from it
as from the other provinces, till after it had been cultivated for
19 thirteen years. Its articles of tribute were varnish and silk; the
baskets from it were filled with woven ornamental *fabrics*.
20 They floated along the Tse and T'ă, and so reached the Ho.

石,—we might translate almost literally—'they *hugged* on the right the rocks of Këĕ.' Evidently these were somewhere on the northern shore of the gulph of Pih-chih-le;—though some have supposed that 碣石 might be the name of a hill, some distance inland, which served as a land-mark to boats—for we can hardly use another term for the craft of those times—entering the Ho. But this view affords no explanation of the expressive phrase 夾右.

In the time of the founder of the Ts'in dynasty, the rock or rocks of Këĕ were well known. He visited them, and had an inscription engraved—we may suppose on the most conspicuous. Subsequently, the emp. Woo (武) visited the place in the year B.C. 109. It is generally referred now to the coast of the dis. of Foo-ning (撫寧; lat. 39°56', lon. 2°52', E.) in the dep. of Yung-p'ing (永平). No traces of such a rock or rocks are now to be found there; but this may be accounted for by encroachments of the sea. See again on Part ii. p. 1. The Ho in Yu's time must have entered the sea in not much less than 40° N. lat.

入于河,—this is evidently descriptive of the route of the wild people with their tribute of furs. The Ho is mentioned as the grand channel by which communication was held with the capital in connection with the tribute of every province. There can be no other meaning here; and when Gan-kwŏ says that it was Yu who returned by the Ho to the capital, to report his labours, and Ch'ing K'ang-shing also interprets the words of Yu, though somewhat differently, we feel that the old interpreters may be very unsafe guides to the understanding of the text.

Ch. III. The Account of Yen-chow.

P. 1. *The boundaries.* Those were the river Tse on the south and east, and the Ho on the north and west. The former separated it from Yu-chow and Ts'ing-chow; the latter, from K'e-chow. The 濟, anciently called also the 泲 had its origin, under the name of the 沇,

in 'King's-house' hill (王屋山), in the pres. Tse-heen (濟縣), dep of Hwae-k'ing, Ho-nan;—see Part ii. p. 10. This would give its rise in about lat. 35°5', N., lon. 4°46', W. Flowing eastwards it now enters the sea, as the 小淸, at about lat. 37°15' N., lon., 1°55', E. Its name appears in its course in that of Tse-nan (濟南), the principal dep. of Shan-tung. Yen-chow did not commence at or near its source. We must place the boundary point between Yen and Yu in the pres. Ts'aou-chow (曹州);—see Hoo Wei, *in loc.* The same critic says on the Ho as the boundary-line of Yen on the west and north:—'At the pres. dis. of Tsoo-shing (lat. 35°20', N.; lon. 2°6', W.), dep. Wei-hwuy of Ho-nan, the Ho proceeded north-east towards the dep. of Ta-ming in Chih-le, and at the hill of Ta-p'ei (大伾), in the dis. of Seun-heen (濬縣; lat. 35°45', N.; lon. 1°38', W.), it made a bend to the west, and flowed northwards past the dep. of Chang-tih in Ho-nan. Then turning eastwards again, it flowed through various depp. of Chih-le—Kwang-p'ing, Shun-tih, Chin-ting, and Ho-kien, on to the sea. This was the old course of the Ho of Yu, the same as the course of the Chang described in the Han dynasty.' According to this account, the Ho of Yu must have disembogued where the Pe-ho (北河, 'the northern Ho') now does. With these boundaries, Yen-chow (兗 is sometimes called 沇) may be said to have contained—of the pres. Shan-tung, the dep. of Tung-ch'ang (東昌), the northern portion of Tse-nan, and western of Yen-chow; and of Chih-le, the dep, of Ta-ming, with portions of those of Ho-keen and T'een tsin:—see the 歷代疆域表. It was not a large province.

Pp. 13—16. *Engineering labours.* 13. 九河旣道-旣道 seems properly explained by Ts'ae—旣順其道, 'were made to follow their courses.' The whole sentence gives the idea that the nine streams or branches were already existing, and that Yu's work was to clear and direct them. K'ang-shing seems rather to have thought that the nine channels were opened by Yu, to diminish the force of the mighty stream (河水自上至此,流盛而地平無岸,故能分爲九,以衰其勢); but such a view cannot be thought of. The truth seems to be that the Ho discharged itself into the sea by many branches, in addition to the main stream described in the last note. These all occupied the northern part of Yen-chow, which formed the delta of the Ho, and Yu, selecting eight or nine of the streams, cleared their course, and by means of them drained the country. It has always been, and still is, a curious inquiry among Chinese scholars, to determine, if possible, the nine Ho. The 爾雅, as if they had all been existing in the Chow dyn., gives their names as T'oo-hae (徒駭); T'ae-she (太史); Ma-këĕ (馬頰); Fuh-foo (覆鬴); Hoo-soo (胡蘇) Këen-këĕ (簡潔); Kow-p'wan (鉤盤); Kih-tsin (鬲津). These are only eight names; and some therefore divide the sixth name into two, making the Këen one stream, and the Këĕ another, while others, more probably, make out the nine by adding to those eight the 'Ho of Yu,' or the main stream, already described. As early as the Han dynasty, it was the opinion of many that it was of no use trying to identify these various streams, the face of the country being so much altered from the time of Yu. Some, indeed, were of opinion even then, that the whole of the delta of the Ho of those early days had been swept away into the sea. Others, however, thought that the Këen-këĕ, the Kow-p'wan, and the Kih-tsin were then determinable; and the researches of the scholars of the T'ang dynasty are said to have determined other three;—but these matters are very doubtful. It is sufficient for us to know that the northern part of Yen-chow, the delta of the Ho, was rescued from the inundating waters by Yu. 14. In the south-east of the small dep. of Puh (濮), sub. to Ts'aou-chow (曹州), is the marsh of Luy, still retaining part of the ancient name. It was in the waters of Luy-hea that Shun fished, according to the 'Historical Records,' and hereabouts also Yaou is said to have rambled (堯作游成陽;成陽 has been the name of Puh-chow under various dynasties). 'Luy-hea was marshed;'—we are not to suppose that Yu now for the first time formed a marsh at this point, but that by draining and embanking he reduced and confined the waters to their proper limits.

Ts'ae quotes a story from the 山海經 about a spirit of thunder with a dragon's body and a man's head, which dwells in the lake and makes a noise like thunder by thumping on its belly. 'Thus,' concludes Ts'ae, 'the lake, originally called the Hea, got its name of Luy-hea, the Thunder-hea.' One Le Che-tsaou (李之藻), of the Ming dyn. ridiculing this story, says that at certain seasons the waters seem to be sucked through some passage at the bottom with a loud noise. 15. I do not think that the Yung and the Tseu have been distinctly identified. They were streams in the neighbourhood of the Luy-hea, and it seems proper to join this par. with the prec., and to read that the two streams were united in the marsh. Yet it may not have been so. Both Gan-kwŏ and K'ang-shing thought so. The latter, indeed, as if he were describing what he had seen, says that the streams first met each other from opposite directions, and then entered the lake in one stream (雝 [so he reads for 灉] 水沮水相觸而合入此澤中). On the other hand, we read in the 'Daily

Explanation:'—'The Yung issuing from the Ho, and the Tseu issuing from the Tse, when the Tse was regulated, the Yung flowed into the Tseu, and they were conducted in one stream to the Ho.'

16 桑土既蠶,—'when the mulberry country was *silkworm-ed;*'—Medhurst translates—'supplied with silkworms;' but the meaning must be rather as I have given. The silkworm dislikes moisture;—as the country was drained, and the waters confined to their proper places, the people could attend to it with success. What particular tract of the country was intended by 桑土 we do not know. The whole of Yen-chow was distinguished for its mulberry trees and silkworms, but especially the region about Puh. K'ang-shing quotes, in illustration, from the 樂記 Bk. I. 6, 桑閒濮上之音. 是(=於是)降(i.e., 民降)丘宅土,—丘 or 邱 is defined by 小陵, 'a small mound' (see the 廣雅); by 土性自然, 'the natural formation of the ground' (孫炎). In Yen-chow the hills were few, but the mounds or rising grounds were many. While the inundation prevailed, the people were driven to these, but now they could descend from the heights, and dwell on the level ground. 宅土=宅平土.

Pp. 17—19. *Soil, revenue, and tribute.* 17. The colour of the soil was the opposite of that of K'e-chow, being 'black,' or blackish. I find it difficult to determine exactly the meaning of 墳 (2d tone). Ma Yung defines it by 膏肥, 'rich and fat;' Gan-kwŏ, by 墳起, as if it meant rising up in mounds or ridges. It is better to abide by Ma's meaning. 厥草惟繇,—繇=茂, 'luxuriant.' The 說文 quotes the passage under 䌛, with the expl. of 草盛皃. 條=長, 'tall.'

Lin Che-k'e observes that the provinces on the north and west were very hilly, and naturally rich in grass and forests, so that there was no occasion to speak of these things in connection with them. The provinces in the south and east, however, were low and wet; they suffered especially from the inundation; all vegetation in them was stunted or unnaturally rank; and therefore the grass and trees of Yen, Seu, and Yang are all made mention of. Hoo Wei observes that this account of the grass and trees of Yen-chow, growing luxuriantly and tall after Yu's labours, would seem to be inconsistent with Mencius' observation that the inundation made all vegetation more luxuriant (Bk. III., Pt. I., iv. 7); and replies that Mencius' idea is that the overflowing waters caused everywhere a rank jungly growth, whereas here the description is of the country under the hand of man, drained of the excessive floods, and responding readily to the toil put forth on it.

18. The fields of this province were ranked in the 6th degree,—the lowest of the middle class. Its revenue was 貞. This char. is defined, both by the ancient and modern interpreters as=正, 'correct,' 'exact,' and further they all agree in saying that the revenue of this province was the lowest of all. Ts'ae brings this meaning out of 正 thus:—'The revenue of Yen was the lightest of all; and the sovereigns of the empire consider that the lightest revenue is the correct thing' (以薄賦爲正). The rest of the par.,—作十有三載乃同, he considers an additional circumstance. Not only was the revenue fixed at the lowest degree, but even that amount was not levied till after 13 years of cultivation, so much more had Yen suffered from the overflow of the waters than the other provinces. This interpretation is upon the whole the best that has been proposed. To take 作 as descriptive of the cultivation of the land is in harmony with its meaning everywhere else in this Book. The old interpreters,—Gan-kwŏ, Ch'ing, and Ma Yung,—all took 作十有三載 as descriptive of the length of time that it took to deliver Yen from the inundating waters, so that it was the very last of the provinces on which the work could be reported as completed. Gan-kwŏ gets a meaning for 貞=正 out of this circumstance:—'Yen was the ninth rescued from the flood, and so its revenue was fixed the ninth or last in degree.' Ch'ing read on 貞=正 with the next characters, with an adverbial meaning,='just,' This may be done, but then there is nothing in the sentence to indicate that the revenue was fixed at the lowest rate. 18, 厥貢,—Choo He says:—'貢 denotes the offerings presented by the princes to the emperor; therefore in all the eight provinces, beyond the imperial domain, we have mention of them.' Under the Chow dyn., those offerings were of nine kinds:—'Offerings available for sacrifice' (祀貢), victims, &c.; 'offerings for the ladies of the harem' (嬪貢), as silk and hemp; 'offerings available for vessels,' (器貢), metal, sounding stones, varnish, &c.; 'offerings available for presents (幣貢), gems, silks, horses, &c.; 'building materials' (材貢); 'offerings of commodities' (貨貢): 'dresses, and materials for dresses' (服貢); 'feathers and hair' (斿貢); 'sundries' (物貢), as fish, fruits, &c.; (see the 'Rites of Chow,' 天官,冢宰第一之二.) The articles from Yen-chow consisted of varnish, the province producing largely the trees which yield it, and silk.

廿一節 海岱惟青州。○廿二節 嵎
夷既畧。○廿三節 濰淄其
道。○廿四節 厥土白墳、海
濱廣斥。○廿五節 厥田惟
上下、厥賦中上。○
廿六節 厥貢鹽絺、海物惟
錯、岱畎絲枲、鉛松
怪石、萊夷作牧、厥
篚檿絲。○廿七節 浮于汶、
達于濟。○

21 IV. The sea and the Tae *mountain* were *the boundaries of* Ts'ING-CHOW.
23 *The territory of* Yu-e was defined; and the Wei and Tsze were conducted by their proper channels.
24 The soil of this province was whitish and rich; near the sea were
25 wide tracts of salt land. Its fields were the lowest of the first class, and its contribution of revenue the highest of the second.
26 Its articles of tribute were salt, fine grass-cloth, and the productions of the sea, of various kinds; with silk, hemp, lead, pine-trees, and strange stones, from the valleys of the Tae. The wild tribes of Lae were taught tillage and pasturage, and brought in their baskets the silk from the mountain mulberry.
27 They floated along the Wăn, and reached the Tse.

厥篚織文,—the 篚 were round bamboo baskets, in which manufactured fabrics were sent to the capital. The 織文 would be various kinds of silks, flowered or ornamented;—but not, some say, woven with various colours.

P. 20. *Course to the Ho, en route for the capital.* To pass from one river into another, without having to take the land and cross the country, is what is denoted by 達. Some think they passed from the Tse into the T'ă, and then into the Ho. It might be so in some cases, but not always. The T'a (in the 說文 we find 濕, and not 漯) had its rise in the pres. dis. of Chaou-shing (朝城; lat. 36° 8', N., lon. 43', W.), dep. Ts'aou-chow, and entered the sea near the pres. dis. city of Lŏ-ngan (樂安; lat. 37° 5', N., lon. 2°10', E.) dep of Ts'ing-chow. Yu is said to have made a junction between one of the branches of the Ho, which he led away from Ta-p'ei, and the T'ă. By this the tribute bearers could reach the Ho; and thence their course to the capital was well defined.

CH. IV. THE ACCOUNT OF TS'ING-CHOW. P. 21. *Its boundaries.* These are given very indefinitely,—the sea and Tae. Tae is the same as Tae-tsung, Can. of Shun, p. 8, the well known T'ae-shan (泰山). In the note on that pass., the district of T'ae-ngan, where the mountain is, is said to belong to the dep. of Tse-nan. So it formerly did; but T'ae-ngan is now constituted itself an independent department. The position of T'ae-ngan city is given from Medhurst in the same place as 36°30', N. lat., 1° E. Lon. According to Biot, the lat. is 36°14', N., and the lon. 45', E. Tae must be understood in the text as defining the boundary of Ts'ing on the west and south. A line drawn in the same lat. would soon reach the Ts'e on the west, and the sea on the east, dividing Ts'ing from Seu-chow. In the time of the Chow dynasty, we find references to a wall (長城) built by princes of Ts'e, to mark this division, and protect themselves from encroachment on the south. See the 禹貢錐指, *in loc.* The sea, again, formed the boundary on the north and east; it would do so on the north so far, to the point where it received the Tse, which would then become the dividing line between Ts'ing and Yen-chow. As to the boundary on the east, the text would never give the idea that it passed beyond the sea which washes the north and east of the

書經

pres. Shan-tung, so that the territory of Ts'ing-chow extended indefinitely into Leaou-tung, and Chaou-seen or Corea. So it would appear, however, to have done. When Shun extended Yu's nine provinces to twelve (Can. of Shun, p, 10), he divided Ts'ing-chow into Ts'ing and Ying (營);—he cut off, that is, from Ts'ing all the indefinitely extended portion lying north and east across the sea, from the present Shan-tung; and constituted it into a new province. In confirmation of this, the 爾雅 may be referred to, where, in the enumeration of the nine provinces, we do not have the name of Ts'ing-chow, but read instead—齊曰營州, 'Ts'e was called Ying-chow.' Now Ts'e embraced nearly all of Ts'ing-chow west of the sea. The calling it 營 proves how Ts'ing and Ying were connected, and is a sufficient answer to the view of some who contend that the Ying-chow of Shun was a section of K'e-chow, and not of Ts'ing-chow. The 'Boundaries of the Empire in successive Dynasties' says:—'Ts'ing-chow embraced the three departments of Ts'ing, Tang, and Lae, with the western portion of Tse-nan, extending also to all the parts of Leaou-tung and Ting-leaou.'

Pp. 22, 23. *Engineering labours.* 22. 嵎夷既略,—Gan-kwŏ defines 略 by 用功小, 'to expend a little labour upon;' but the term—used only here in the description of Yu's operations—has probably a more definite signification. In the first meaning given to 略 in the dict., it is coupled with 經,—經略, meaning 'to define'—or, perhaps to survey—'the boundaries.' Ts'ae adopts this meaning, and adds 爲之封畛, 'to raise dykes and boundaries about it.' Yu-e is the same as the Yu-e, to which Yaou sent the second brother He, to observe the rising sun (Can. of Yaou, p. 4). The name 嵎夷 is writen also 堣夷, 禺銕; 嵎鐵 (evid. a mistake for 銕), and perhaps in other ways. Those who confine Ts'ing-chow within the pres. Shan-tung refer this place to the small dep. of Ning-hae (寧海州; lat. 39°35', N., lon 4°18', E.) in Tăng-chow. But as Yaou would send He to the remotest point eastwards, which was within the limits of the empire, and we have seen that Ts'ing-chow extended to the pres. Corea, it is more natural to conclude that Yu-e was some tract in that region. 23. 潍淄其道,—*lit.*, 'the Wei and the Tsze, their channels,' *i.e.*, were conducted by their proper channels. 其道=既道, p. 8. Ts'ae says, indeed, that 其道 indicates that Yu led the rivers here to their proper channels, while 既道 shows that they were new channels which he made to divide the force of the Ho; but we saw reason to question this view of that portion of Yu's labours. The river Wei rises in the north-east of Keu-chow (lat., 35°35', N.; lon. 2°52', W.), dep. of E-chow (沂州), and flowing east passes by Choo-shing (諸城) in Ts'ing-chow. Thence proceeding north, it enters the sea, 50 *le* to the north-east of Ch'ang-yih (昌邑縣; lat., 36°52', N.; lon., 2°15', E.). The Tsze (淄 is not found in the 說文. Keang-shing edits 甾, with which 菑 was interchanged) rises in the northern slope of Yuen hill (原山), 25 *le* to the West of Poh-san dis. city (博山); thence it flows north-eastwards past the districts of Yih-too (益都), Lin-tsze (臨淄), Loh-ngan (樂安), and Show-kwang (壽光),—all in Ts'ing-chow. Not far from this last city (lat. 36°55', N.; lon., 2°32', E.), it enters the sea by the embouchure of the Ts'ing water (清水泊). With the Wei and Tsze, Yu's labours in Ts'ing-chow terminated;—he had less to do here than in other provinces.

Pp. 24—26. *Soil, revenue, and tribute.* 24. 厥土白墳,—see pp. 7 and 17. 海濱廣斥,—斥謂地鹹鹵 '斥 is descriptive of a country which is salt.' Accord. to the 說文, 斥 and 鹵 are synonyms, salt tracts in the east being described as 斥, and similar tracts in the west as 鹵. The country intended in the text was doubtless the coast of the two departments of Tăng and Lae, where there is an active preparation of salt at the present day. The ancient kingdom of Ts'e was noted for its advantages of salt and fish. 25. The fields of this province were only second in the empire to those of Yung and Seu. 26. 絺,—this char. denotes a fine fabric made of the fibres of the 葛, or *dolichos tuberosus*. A coarser fabric of the same kind was called 綌. Hoo Wei observes that in subsequent ages these fabrics were required only from the southern regions, with the single exception of 15 pieces of 絺葛, which continued to be required from Lin-tsze (臨淄),—a relic of Yu's arrangements. 海物惟錯,—海物, 'things of the sea,' *i.e.*, fishes, crabs, oysters, &c. Gan-kwŏ here defines 錯, as in p. 8, by 雜非一種, 'mixed, not of one kind only.' In opp. to this, Lin Che-k'e says that 海物 sufficiently declares the variety of the articles, without the addition of 惟錯 to convey the same idea. Comparing the sentence with 齒革羽毛惟木, p. 44, he argues that 錯 must be something different

○州。徐惟淮及岱海 廿八節

28 V. The sea, the Tae *mountain*, and the Hwae were the *boundaries of* Ts'EU-CHOW.

from 海物, and = 'grinding stones.' Woo Ch'ing adopts the same view, and argues that 惟 in the middle of a clause is a conjunctive particle, meaning 'and.' The interpretation itself is not unlikely, but the meaning given to 惟 cannot be sustained;—as, *e.g.*, in p. 21. 岱畎,絲,枲,鉛,松,怪石,—畎 here = 谷, 'valleys,' difft. from its use in the 'Yih and Tseih,' p. 1. The 'strange stones' are very perplexing to commentators. Ts'ae gets over the difficulty by supposing they were articles indispensable in the making of certain vessels, and not curiosities, merely to be looked at. 萊夷作牧,—the note of Gan-kwŏ on this is:—萊夷地名,可以放牧, 'Lae-e is the name of a country, adapted for the pasturing of flocks.' This must be a mistake. 萊夷 can only be 'the wild people of Lae.' Yen Sze-koo (顏師古) said they were 'the wild people of mount Lae;' and this mountain is referred to the dis. of Hwang-heen (黃縣) in Tăng-chow. No doubt their name remains in that of the dep. of Lae-chow. We may suppose they were spread over the country embraced now in the two depp. of Tang-chow and Lae-chow. They continued, notwithstanding Yu's discipline and teaching of them, wild and intractable down into the Chow dyn. They figured at the famous interview between the princes of Loo and Ts'e at Keă-kuh, where Confucius distinguished himself (vol. I. proleg. pp. 73, 74). Gan-kwŏ, and Ts'ae after him, make 作牧 one thing, and so did Sze-ma Ts'een who reads 萊夷爲牧. The view in the transl. is more in acc. with the usage of 作 in this Book. Woo Ch'ing and Hoo Wei both approve it. 檿 is the name of a mountain mulberry tree. Silkworms fed on its leaves produced a very tough silk, which made good strings for lutes. We can hardly read the text otherwise than that the baskets of this silk were brought by the wild people of Lae. I make this note because some would extend the 厥 to the whole province, like the 厥貢 at the beginning of the par.

P. 27. *Route of conveyance to the capital.* Arriving at the Tse, the tribute-bearers would go on to the Ho; and thence to the capital. This we readily infer from the former notices of the routes of conveyance. The subject of the Wăn river is a good deal perplexed. There were five streams so called, finally, it would appear, all uniting their waters. The course of the main stream may be thus described. It took its rise in the dis. of Lae-woo (萊蕪; lat., 36°16', N., lon., 1°25', E.), dep. of T'ae-ngan. Flowing past the districts of T'ae-ngan, Fei-shing (肥城), and Ning-yang (寧陽), on to the subordinate dep., of Tung-p'ing (東平; lat., 36°07', N., lon., 03, E.), it entered the Tse. This ancient course of the Wăn cannot now be traced. It was diverted, during the Yuen and Ming dynasties, to feed the Grand Canal.

CH. V. THE ACCOUNT OF SEU-CHOW. P. 28. *Boundaries.* Three boundaries of this province are mentioned, while of the other provinces only two are specified. There was the sea on the east; the Tae mountain on the north; and the river Hwae on the south. For the Hwae see on Part ii., p. 11. It is sufficient here to state that it takes its rise in the dis. of T'ung-pih (桐柏, lat. 32°20', N., lon. 3°10', W.), dep. Nan-yang, of Ho-nan. Flowing east, the main stream of it joins the Yellow river in the dis. of Ts'ing-ho (淸河; lat. 33°35', N., lon. 2°34', E.), dep. Hwae-ngan (淮安), in Keang-soo. In Yu's time it held its own way to the sea, and was the dividing line between Seu-chow and Yang-chow. The Tae mountain is as indefinite a boundary for the north of Seu, as we saw it was for the south of Ts'ing-chow. The north-east dividing-line of the two was where the two depp. of E-chow and Ts'ing-chow now touch. No western boundary is mentioned. In the time of Chow, according to the 爾雅, 'westward from the Tse to the sea was Seu-chow' (濟東曰徐州). We may conclude, therefore, that the Tse was, to some distance at least, the boundary between Seu-chow and Yu-chow. According to the 'Boundaries of Successive Dynasties,' Seu-chow embraced the territory of the pres. dep. of Yen-chow in Shan-tung and all the country south to Seu-chow in Keang-soo; and from the small dep. of Suh-chow (宿州) in Fung-yang, and Sze-chow 泗州, (both in Ngan-hwuy), eastward through Keang-soo, by Seu-chow and the north of Hwae-ngan dep., on to the dep. of Hae-chow (海州). A more detailed account given in a note in the 集傳, from the 'Geography Modernized,' (地理今釋), is to the effect that the present Seu-chow (in Keang-soo); the four districts of Hwae-yuen (懷遠), Woo-ho (五河), Hung-heen (虹

書經

廿九節 淮沂其乂。○ 卅節 蒙羽其藝。○ 卅一節 大野既豬。○ 卅二節 東原底平。○ 卅三節 厥土赤埴墳，草木漸包。○ 卅四節 厥田惟上中，厥賦惟中中。○ 卅五節 厥貢惟土五色，羽畎夏

30 The Hwae and the E *rivers* were regulated. The *hills of* Mung
31 and Yu were brought under cultivation. The *lake of* Ta-yay was
32 confined within its proper limits. The *country of* Tung-yuen was
successfully brought under management.
33 The soil of this province was red, clayey, and rich. The trees and
34 grass became more and more bushy. Its fields were the second of
the highest class; its contribution of revenue was the average of
the second.
35 Its articles of tribute were earth of five different colours; with
the variegated feathers of pheasants from the valleys of the Yu;

縣), and Ling-peih (靈璧), in the dep. of Fung-yang, with the small depp. of Sze and Suh (all in Ngan-hwuy); the six districts of T'aou-yuen (桃源), Ts'ing-ho (清河), Ngan-tung (安東), Suh-ts'ëen (宿遷), Suy-ning (睢寗), and Kan-yu (贛榆), in the dep. of Hwae-ngan, with the small depp. of P'ei-chow (邳州) and Hae-chow (all in Keang-soo); and the whole of Yen-chow, the south of P'ing-yin (平陰) district, and Tung P'ing (東平州), in T'ae-ngan, the dep. of E-chow, and portions of Tse-nam and Ts'ing-chow (all in Shan-tung):—all these were comprehended in the Seu-chow of Yu.

Pp. 29—32. *Engineering labours.* 29. 其乂,—comp. 其道, p. 23. 乂=治, 'to bring to order,' 'to regulate.' On the Hwae, see the prec. note and below, Part ii., p. 11. Ts'ae quotes from Tsăng Yen-ho (曾彥和; like Ts'ae, of the Sung dyn., but earlier) a remark that the Hwae came out of Yu-chow, and when it reached the borders of Seu and Yang, its stream was large, and the injury it did was specially great in Seu, so that the regulation of it is only mentioned in conn. with that prov. It is observed on this, in the 禹貢錐指, that the country of Yang was lower than Seu; the overflow of the Hwae could not be less injurious in the more southern province; and that Yu, no doubt, employed a portion of his assistants at the same time upon the Yang side, and delivered both provinces at once from the evil. Compare what was said on 治梁及岐, p. 4. The E rises in the dis. of E-shwuy (沂水, lat. 35°46′, N., lon. 2°32′, E.; difft. hills 艾山, 沂山, &c., are assigned as its source. Probably difft. streamlets from the same mountain range coalesced in one) of E-chow, and passing through that of T'an-shing (郯城), it enters Këang-soo. There in the sub. dep. of P'ei (邳) in Seu-chow, it unites with the Sze (泗), and proceed. south-east to the dis. of Ts'ing-ho, it enters the Hwae. [There were other rivers called E in Seu-chow. That mentioned Ana., XI. xxv. 7 (浴乎沂) was one of them.] 30. The hill of Mung is 40 *le* to the south of the district city of Mung-yin (蒙陰; lat. 35°50′, N., lon. 1°42′, E.), extending to the borders of the dis. of Pe (費). It is the same with that called by Confucius the eastern Mung (Ana. XVI. i. 4). It is mentioned in the Statistical Account of the present dynasty, that K'ëen-lung, who several times passed the mountain in his visits to Këang-soo and Chĕ-këang, wrote some pieces of poetry on the sight of its snow-covered summits. Mount Yu is 0 *le* to the north of the dis. city of T'an-shing, lat. 34°45′, N., lon. 2°17′, E. This is said to have been the hill where Shun kept K'wăn a prisoner (Can. of Shun, p. 12). The 'Statistical Account' says there can be no doubt on the point, for on the top of the hill there are two springs which unite and form a deep pool (羽潭), and we are told in the 左傳, that the spirit of K'wăn was changed into a yellow bear, which sprang into the gulf of Yu (羽淵)! Hoo Wei, however, and not without apparent reason, would refer the place of K'wăn's banishment to a mount Yu, farther to the east, in the dis. of Fung-lae (蓬萊) in Tăng-chow. 其藝, 'were planted.' Hoo Wei observes: 方耕曰作;既種曰藝, 'Just ploughed is called 作; already planted is called 藝.' When the E was regulated, the country on the west of it to Mung, and on the east of it to Yu, would be so far drained that Yu could proceed to whatever other labours were necessary upon it. 31. 大野既豬,—Sze-ma Ts'een reads:—大野既都. He avoids, as is common with him, the unusual and difficult character. Gan-kwŏ defines:—水所停曰豬, 'where water rests is called 豬.' To the same effect is Wang Suh's definition:—水所停止深者曰豬. The waters overflowed the borders of the lake; by reducing them and by embankments, Yu succeeded in confining them within their proper limits. We can only speak, it will be seen, of the Ta-yay lake or marsh in the past tense. It was in what is now the district of Keu-yay, lat. 35°27', N., lon. 12', W., of the dep. of Ts'aou-chow. In subsequent times it was often called the lake of Keu-yay, 大 and 鉅 having the same signification of 'great.' It had a connection on the south with the Choo (洙) and the Sze, and on the north with the Ts'ing and the Tse, so that it must have been liable to risings of its waters. The country all about it has been liable to inundations of the Ho. A great one happened A.D. 131, which it took more than 20 years to remedy. Repeated inundations from the time of the Han dyn. obliterated all traces of the labours of Yu. In A.D. 1344, the Ho spread over all the districts of Keu-yay, Kea-ts'ëang (嘉祥), Wăn-shang (汶上), and Jin-shing (任城); and when it retired south again, this lake was left quite dry, a tract of level ground;—see the 禹貢錐指, *in loc.* [These notices are interesting They show that the state of the country which called forth Yu's services was not peculiar to his time.] 32. Tung-yuen, 'the eastern plain,' is now the sub. dep. of Tung-p'ing, and some adjacent territory, in the dep. of T'ae-ngan. It was in the north of Seu-chow, but is spoken of as eastern, with reference to its position east of the Tse. 底平,—the 底, as has been observed before, implies the putting forth of effort. The two characters = 'could be levelled;' but we must understand 平 as Gan-kwŏ did. He says:—言可耕, 'the meaning is that it could be cultivated.' Wang Yen (王炎) observes:—'The confining the waters of Ta-yay, and then bringing Tung-yuen under management, were things of which the one was the sequel of the other' (集說).

Pp. 33—35. *Soil, revenue, and tribute.* 33. 土黏曰埴, 'earth adhesive is called clay.' There can be no doubt of the meaning. Ch'ing instead of 埴 read 戠. 草木漸包—the 說文 quotes this sentence as 草木蔪苞. 包 or 苞 has the signification, as applied to trees or shrubs, of 'bushy.' Wang Suh explains:—包相包裹也, '包 means embracing one another,'—showing that he read 包, and an intelligible description of a bushy shrub. 漸 = 'gradually,' 'advancing by degrees.' 34. The cultivable ground of Seu ranked in the second grade, and its revenue was only in the fifth. 35. 土五色,—the soil of Seu-chow was red. Such was its general character, but in different parts earth of different colours must have been found; especially was the country about the pres. districts of Choo-shing (諸城), and T'ung-shan (銅山) in Seu-chow, famed for its coloured earths. The meaning of this tribute is thus expanded by Ying-tă from Gan-kwŏ:—'The emperors raised a mound of earth of the five colours, as an altar to the spirits of the land. On the investiture of any prince, a quantity of earth, of the colour characteristic of the region where his principality lay, was cut away and given to him, which he took home to build an altar with. All the altars thus built, however, were covered with yellow earth. The earth was given to each prince, in bundles covered with white rushes, emblematic of purity.' Ying-tă quotes also from Han Ying's preface to the She King, to the effect that the emperor's altar was five cubits square, green on the east, red on the south, white on the west, black on the north, and all covered with yellow earth. [Comp. Naaman's request to Elisha, 2 Kings, v. 17.] 羽畎夏翟,—羽畎 comp. 岱畎, p. 26. The dict., with reference to this passage, defines 夏 by 五色, 'having the

翟、嶧陽孤桐、泗濱浮磬、淮夷蠙珠暨魚、厥篚玄纖縞。○浮(哥六節)于淮泗、達于河。○

the solitary dryandra from the south of *mount* Yih; and the sounding stones that *seemed to* float near the banks of the Sze. The wild tribes about the Hwae brought oyster-pearls and fish; and their baskets full of deep azure silks, and other silken fabrics, chequered and pure white.

36 They floated along the Hwae and Sze, and so reached the Ho.

five colours,' variegated, and we may accept this meaning, though some would make 夏翟 together the name of a pheasant found about the Yu. 翟 *(teih)* alone means a long-tailed pheasant. The ancient Chinese made great use of feathers on their flags and banners, and for ornament generally. 嶧陽孤桐,—嶧陽, 'the south of Yih.' There were two mountains of this name, one north in the pres. dis. of Tsow (鄒縣) in Yen-chow, and the other south, called 葛嶧, in the sub. dis. of P'ei (邳) in Seu-chow. It is the latter which is intended in the text. The wood of the dryandra is always considered good for making lutes. The older and loftier the tree, the better for the purpose. One that stood solitary on the hill-side or top, having outlived all its compeers, would possess a special value. This is, I suppose, the force of the 孤, or 'solitary.' 泗濱浮磬,—the Sze, which rises in the dis. of Sze-shwuy (泗水; lat. 35°48', N., lon. 1°2', E. The dis. takes its name from the stream, and that again, named from the fact that it is formed by *four* streamlets, each with its separate spring, in Yen-chow, is now one of the feeders of the Grand canal. In Yu's time it flowed into the Hwae in the country of the present Seu-chow. It was after its entrance into the pres. Keang-soo, in the pres. district of T'ung-shan (銅山), that the sounding stones of the text were found. The reason why they are spoken of as 'floating' seems to be that suggested in the translation by the addition of 'seemed to.' At any rate, that is the explanation of the older interpreters. Other views may be seen in the 禹貢錐指, *in loc.* 淮夷蠙珠暨魚,—淮夷 can only mean 'the wild people about the Hwae.' They continued rebellious and intractable long after Yu's time;—see Confucius' Preface, parr. 40, 55. Gan-kwŏ blunders here, as we saw he did upon 萊夷, p. 26. He says that 淮 and 夷 are the names of two rivers. Wang-Suh and Ma Yung agreed with him; but Ch'ing explained as in the translation. 蠙 is another name for 蚌, the common term for the pearl oyster. 厥篚玄纖縞,—here these baskets of silks would seem to have been brought also by the wild tribes of the Hwae, and so the Daily Explanation expressly says (三者亦淮夷所出,命其盛諸篚而貢焉);—comp. on p. 26. Still, 厥篚 may refer to the whole province, like 厥貢 above. 玄, 纖, and 縞, are descriptive of three kinds of silken fabrics:—the first expressing the colour as being 赤黑, 'red and black,' a deep azure; the second indicating a chequered silk, with a black warp and white woof (黑經白緯); and the third, a fabric white and unornamented. Other accounts of these characters may be found in Hoo Wei.

P. 36. *Route of conveyance to the Ho.* 達于河,—Keang Shing edits 達于菏, after the 說文; but the analogy of the corresponding par. in the account of the other provinces is sufficient to justify the reading of the text. We have 河, moreover, in the 'Historical Records.' As to the route itself, it will suffice to give the paraphrase of the 'Daily Explanation:'—'The tribute was conveyed northwards from Seu. First, they floated in boats along the Hwae, and from the Hwae entered the Sze. Proceeding then still north, they went on to the Ho from the Sze, either by the Yung (灉) or by the Tse.'

卅七節 淮海惟揚州。○卅八節 彭蠡既豬。○卅九節 陽鳥攸居。○四十節 三江既入。

37 VI. The Hwae and the sea formed *the boundaries of* YANG-CHOW.
38 *The lake of* P'ang-le was confined to its proper limits; and the sun
40 birds had places to settle on. The three Këang were led to enter
the sea; and it became possible to still the marsh of Chin.

CH. VI. THE ACCOUNT OF YANG-CHOW.

P. 37. *Boundaries.* The Hwae was the boundary on the north, and it is natural to suppose that the other boundary mentioned, the sea, should be referred to the south of the province. This was the view of Gan-kwo (北據淮南距海). If it were really so, Yang-chow must have extended along the coast as far as Cochin-china, and not a few Chinese scholars are ready at the present day to argue that it did so. Others restrict it to more likely dimensions. Hoo Wei contends that the sea which has been specified as a boundary of the provinces of Ts'ing and Seu was that along their east coast, and similarly ought we to think of the sea as a boundary of Yang. K'ang-shing had said, rather indefinitely, that 'the boundaries of Yang-chow were from the Hwae southwards to the sea along the east (揚州界自淮而南至海以東). If I have caught the exact meaning of his words,—至海以東,—I think the amount of his interpretation is all that we can conclude from the text. Yang-chow extended from the Hwae southwards along the coast, but how far is not said. No other province was beyond it in the south, but that it did not extend to the southern shores of the pres. Kwang-tung we may be sure;—where it really did terminate we cannot tell. The articles of tribute and revenue in Yu's time, and the hills and waters mentioned in the account of the empire under the Chow dynasty, lead us to conclude that the imperial dominions did not then extend beyond what is called the 'southern mountain-range,' and the 'five mountains' (南嶺 and 五嶺). Williams in his 'Middle Kingdom,' p. 127, says of this:—'The Nan Ling runs along the north of Kwang-tung, between it and Keang-se and Hoo-nan. The chain takes forty or fifty names in its course from Kwang-se to Fuh-këen, but no part of it is so well-known as the road, twenty four miles in length, which crosses the Mei ling, between Nan-ngan and Nan-heung' [The names of the 'Five ling,' in Hoo Wei's charts, are 越城 on the west, 萌渚, 騎思, 大庾, and 揭陽 on the east.] Of course the territory of China proper gradually extended south and west; but it was the ambition of the founder of the Ts'in dynasty, which first formally incorporated the southern regions with it. Among the forty tracts (郡) into which he divided his empire, we have those of Nan-hae (南海), Kwei-lin (桂林), and Sëang (象), embracing Kwang-tung and Kwang-se on to An-nam or Cochin-china. Hoo Wei, tracing the eastern border of Yang-chow along the coast of Keang-soo, Chĕ-keang, and Fuh-keen, extends it to Ch'aou-yang (潮陽; lat. 23°22', N., lon, 13', E.) dis., of Ch'aou-chow dep., in Can. province. This is certainly bringing it far enough south.

The western boundary of Yang-chow is left quite undefined. Along the greater part of its course it was conterminous with King-chow, and in the north-west with Yu-chow.

The 'Boundaries of Successive Dynasties' speaks within bounds, when it assigns to Yang-chow the present Chĕ-keang, Keang-se, and Fuh-këen (今南直浙江,江西,福建,皆是). To those three provinces the 'Daily Explanation' adds Kwang-tung, of which only a small portion, if any, can be assigned to it. And neither of these accounts carries the province so far west as it went, nor do they give the more northern portion of it. A note in the 集傳, from 'Geography Modernized,' gives the area more in detail. Modernizing its statements a second time, we may say that Yang-chow contained—of Keang-soo, the departments Keang-ning (江寧), Soo-chow (蘇州), Sung-keang (松江), Chang-chow (常州), Chin-keang (鎮江), and Yang-chow (揚州), with the districts of Shan-yang (山陽), and Yen-shing (鹽城), in the dep. of Hwae-ngan (淮安); of Ngan-hwuy, the departments Ngan-k'ing (安慶), Hwuy-chow (徽州), Ning-kwŏ (寧國), Ch'e-chow (池州), T'ae-p'ing (太平), Leu-chow (廬州), with the smaller depp. of Ho Chow (和), Seu Chow (滁), and Kwang-tih (廣德), together with the small dep. of Show Chow (壽), and the districts of Fung-yang (鳳陽), Ting-yuen (定遠),

書經

and Ling-peih (靈壁), in Fung-yang dep., the districts of Hoh-k'ew (霍邱) and T'ae-ho (太和), in dep. of Ying-chow (潁州), and those of Yu-ch'e (盱眙), and T'een-ch'ang (天長), in Sze Chow (泗州); of Ho-nan, the districts of Kwang-shan (光山), and Koo-ch'e (固始) in the small dep. of Kwang (光州); and of Hoo-pih, the small dep. of Ke (蘄州) and the districts of Lo-t'een (羅田), Ke-shwuy (蘄水), Kwang-tse (廣濟), and Hwang-mei (黃梅), in the dep. of Hwang-chow (黃州). The above may be considered the northern portion of the province. Southwards, according to the same detail, were Chĕ-këang, Keang-se, Fuh-keen, and the dep. of Ch'aou-chow in Kwang-tung.

Pp. 38—41. *Engineering labours.* 38. 旣豬,—see p. 31. The P'ang-le is the famous lake well known as the Po-yang, so called from the name of an island in it (鄱陽山). It is in the northern part of Këang-se, and is stated to be 450 *le* in circumference, its waters lapping the coast of 4 diff't. depp.,—Nan-ch'ang (南昌; lat. 28°37', N. lon. 38', W.), whose chief city is dis. from it to the south-west 150 *le;* Jaou-chow on the east (饒州; lat. 28°59', N., lon. 14', E.) distant from it 40 *le;* Nan-k'ang in the north-west (南康; lat. 29° 31', N., lon. 27', W.) distant 5 *le;* and Kew-këang, also on the northwest (九江; lat. 29°51', N., lon. 24', W.), dis. 90 *le.* The P'ang-le marsh or lake received many streams. (Lew Hin, of the Han. dyn., enumerated nine). The services of Yu were required to regulate its banks, and keep the waters within their proper limits. 39. 陽鳥攸居,—one scholar, Lin Che-k'e, supposes that 陽鳥 may be the name of a place. This view might come substantially to the same as the common traditional interpretation, which there is the less reason, therefore, to call in question. 陽=日, 'the sun,' as the great source of energy and brightness. 陽鳥, 'sun birds,' are wild geese, who follow the course of the sun. 'In the winter months they live upon the islets of this lake, in flocks which may be counted by hundreds and thousands. The sun in summer travels south, and in winter north. The geese come south in the 9th month, and in the first month go north again. Thus they avoid the cold and repair to the regions of heat, and are therefore called sun birds' (Woo Ch'ing). The overflowing and disarrangement generally of the lake had driven these birds from their former haunts, to which they could now return after Yu's operations. It does seem a trivial circumstance to mention in such a condensed account of Yu's labours; and it was not unnatural for Lin Che-k'e to cast about for another explanation.

Pp. 40, 41. 三江旣入,—the disputes about the three Keang are endless; and I do not think it is possible to settle them so as to place the meaning of the text beyond dispute. It seems proper to join the par. with the next,—震澤底定; and there is an agreement in the opinion that the 'Shaking Marsh' was what is now called the 'Great Lake,' (太湖), in the south-west of the dep. of Soo-chow, and in the borders between Keang-soo and Chĕ-këang. It would seem that it was owing to the operations on the three Këang that it became possible (底) 'to settle' the disturbed waters of the lake. This would take us away from the great Këang, the Yang-tsze, which flows through Këang-soo to the sea considerably north of Soo-chow. Accordingly, Ts'ae Ch'in follows the authority of Yu Chung-ch'oo (庾仲初; Tsin dynasty. Died about the middle of the 4th century), who made the three Keang to be the Sung-keang (松江), with the two branches into which it separates 70 *le* after issuing from the lake, the L'ow Keang (婁 [in this sense read *low*] 江), flowing north-east into the sea, and the Tung Keang (東江), flowing south-east. The place where the Sung divided, was called the 'Mouth of the three Keang,' (三江口); and we have still the same name, in the north of the dis. of Woo-keang (吳江). This view would seem to satisfy the requirements of the text, but it is objected to it that the existence of the Tung Keang has never been proved;—see Maou K'e-ling, *in loc.* The Sung and the Low might be accepted as one of the three Keang, but cannot be the whole three. When we turn, moreover, to the 國語, we find in the 越語 mention made more than once of the 'three Keang.' It is said paticularly in one place that 'the three Keang surrounded' (= traversed in various directions) 'the States of Woo and Yuĕ' (三江環之民無所移). The three Keang of Chung-ch'oo by no means answer to this description.

The oldest view of the passage—and it is that followed by Soo Tung-po, which Ts'ae mentions, but only to argue against it—considered the 'three Keang' to be only another name for the 'Great Keang,'—the Yang-tsze. It was founded on the expressions 南入于江, 東爲北江, p. 8, Part. ii., and 東爲中江, p. 9. Ch'ing K'ang-shing said:—'On the left uniting with the Han, it became the northern Keang, and after meeting with the P'ang-le it became the southern Keang; between these was the Min Keang, which was the middle Keang;—so at least it was called after issuing

四十一 震澤底定。○ 四十二 篠簜既敷、厥草惟夭、厥木惟喬、厥土惟塗泥。○ 四十三 厥田惟下下、厥賦下上、上錯。○ 四十四 厥貢惟金三

42 The bamboos, small and large, then spread about; the grass grew long and thin, and the trees rose high; the soil was all miry.

43 The fields of this province were the lowest of the lowest class; its contribution of revenue was the highest of the lowest class, with a proportion of the class above.

44 Its articles of tribute were gold, silver, and copper; yaou and

from the P'ang-le. The three Keang separating at the P'ang-le into three openings (or orifices) entered eastwards into the sea';—see the 後案. This account is not very intelligible. One part of it would seem to make the one stream of the Yang-tsze, called by three names in three parts of its course, to be the 'three Keang,' and again this stream would seem to have separated into three at the P'ang-le. As, however, the one or the three entered into the sea, without approaching the 'Shaking Lake,' we do not see how the settlement of that should be connected with the 'three Keang.' Gan-kwŏ thought 'that the three Keang' were the 'Great Keang,' and said, with Ch'ing, that it divided into three after leaving the P'ang-le, but those three branches he conducted all to the 'Shaking Lake,' from which again they proceeded by three courses to the sea. This cannot be the true view. It would oblige us to suppose an alteration from the ancient channel of the grand stream to that which it now pursues of which we have no evidence. As I said, at the beginning of the note, we do not know what rivers the three Keang were. Ch'in Sze-k'ae, in his notes upon Ts'ae's commentary, says at this place:—'If we would interpret the text without reference to views which have been urged, and would look over Yang-chow for the rivers of most advantage or capable of being most injurious to it, we shall find none equal to the Great river,—the Yang-tsze, the Sung Këang, and the Chĕ Keang. Maou K'e-ling, again, makes them out to be the Sung Keang, the Chĕ Keang, and the P'oo-yang (浦陽). The Yang-tsze is too far removed from the others, and too vast in itself. to allow us to couple it with them. The Chĕ Keang, from which Che-keang province takes its name, and the Sung Keang were perhaps two of the three Keang; but I cannot hazard a conjecture about the third.

Pp. 42—44. *Vegetation; soil, revenue, and tribute.* 42. Acc. to the analogy of parr. 17 and 33, we should expect the account of the vegetation to follow, and not to precede, the description of the soil. I have not found a satisfactory explanation of the different order observed here. 篠簜既敷,—篠 is the name of a small-stemmed bamboo. Gan-kwŏ explains it by 竹箭; but we are not to interpret 箭 by 'arrow.' It is merely here a synonym of the term in the text. 簜 is the name of a large species of bamboo, 'the joints of whose stem are a fathom apart';—so said Le Seun (李巡; Han dynasty). 敷=布. Gan-kwŏ expands:—水去已布生, 'when the water was removed, they spread about and grew.' 夭,—comp. the quotation from the She in the Great Learning, comm. ix. 6,—桃之夭夭. Gan-kwŏ explains it here by 少長, the meaning of which I have endeavoured to give in the translation. 喬=高, 'tall.' 厥土惟塗泥,—the 說文 defines 泥 by 黑土在水中者, 'black earth in the midst of water.' We can hardly accept this as a description of the soil of a province so large as we have seen Yang-chow described to be. It shows, however, how greatly the country, where Yu had been, had suffered from the overflow of the rivers.

43. The fields were of the lowest or ninth grade; the revenue was of the seventh, with a proportion of the sixth. 上錯,—see on par. 8. This 上 is in the second tone, meaning 'going up' into the class above. 44. 金三品,—'the three grades of metal.' Those were gold, silver, and copper. In the 'Historical Records,' 卷三十, 平準書, we read:—古者金有三等, 黃金爲上, 白金爲中, 赤金爲下, 'Among

品。瑤琨篠簜、齒革羽毛惟木、島夷卉服、厥篚織貝、厥

keun stones; bamboos small and large; elephants' teeth, hides, feathers, hair, and timber. The wild people of the islands brought garments of grass. The baskets were filled with woven ornamented

the ancients there were three degrees of metal:—the yellow metal, the highest in value; the white metal, the next; and the red metal, the lowest.' I don't know how or where K'ang-shing got his idea that the text meant 'the three colours' (=qualities) 'of copper' (銅三色). Hoo Wei has collected a mass of evidence to show that gold was found in Jaou-chow dep.; that silver also was found there, and in the dep. of Lin-keang (臨江), and that there were copper mines in various parts of Keang-soo. [It is to the western provinces of Yun-nan and Sze-ch'uen that we are now commonly referred for the precious metals.] 瑤琨 are said by Gan-kwŏ to be 'beautiful gems' (美玉). Wang Suh, however, describes them as 'fine stones inferior to gems.' He is supported by the 說文 expressly in his account of the second, and probably also in that of the first;—see the 後案. The 篠 were used for arrow-shafts. One statement says they were solid, which I do not know that any bamboo can be. The 簜 were used,—the larger of them for small packing and other cases, the smaller for flutes and similar instruments. 齒革羽毛惟木,—惟 is here a connective particle, =暨, 'and.' See note on par. 26, upon 惟錯. Lin Che-k'e says that 'by teeth, hides, feathers and hair we are to understand whatever about animals was available for articles of use or for ornament.' More specially, Gan-kwŏ understood by 'teeth' the teeth of elephants, and by 'hides' (革 supposes the hair to be taken off) the hides of the rhinoceros. This view is generally acquiesced in. Are we to suppose then that the rhinoceros and elephant were found in Yang-chow in Yu's time? They may very well have been so. Hoo Wei observes that from the mention or supposed mention of these animals some argue for the extension of the limits of the province beyond the southern mountain-range to Kwang-tung, Kwang-se, and An-nam, and replies that the princes might be required to send articles of value and use purchased from their neighbours, as well as what they could procure in their own territories. 島夷卉服,—Keang Shing here reads 鳥夷, as in p. 10. The Historical Records read as in the text. The occurrence of the name again confirms the ordinary reading. One tribe of wild people, north or south, might have been called the 'Bird barbarians;' but when the name is applied equally to the two extremities of the empire along the sea-board, we must take the phrase as having nothing special in its signification. Hoo Wei would carry us chiefly to Japan for the people here intended; but that is too remote. Possibly the name may include the inhabitants of Formosa, and the Chusan archipelago, as well as of the islands generally along the east coast. 卉草之總名, 卉 is a general name for grasses.' Ts'ae would extend it to 'cotton,' the production of a plant, so that 卉服 should include dresses of cotton; but the cultivation of cotton was first introduced into China during the Sung dynasty. The 卉服 were garments, I apprehend, made of grass or straw, manipulated indeed, but not having undergone any operations of machinery, however rude. 織貝,—Gan-kwŏ takes these for two things,—'fine woven fabrics,' and 'fine shells.' Those shells, it has been supposed, were to serve as pieces of money, for purposes of exchange. But such a use of shells cannot be proved to have existed in the time of Yu. 織貝 would rather seem to be the name of some kind of silken manufacture. So this phrase is generally taken. Ch'ing, on the authority of a passage in the She King, defines 貝 by 錦名, 'the name of variegated silks.' Woo Ch'ing says:—'When the silk was dyed of various colours, and then woven into patterns, the fabric was called 織貝; where the patterns were made with silk not so dyed of various colours, the fabric was called 織文.' The 橘 is a small orange, the *citrus mandarinus*. It grows farther north than the common orange. The 柚 or pummelo seems to grow best in Fuh-këen. 錫命,—Gan-kwŏ says:—錫命乃貢, 言不常也, 'when the order was given, they were sent; this was not a regular tribute.' Wang Suh gives the same explanation, and adds that these fruits were only required from Yang-chow as a supplement to those of King-chow. K'ang-shing took a difft. view, but what he understood exactly by 錫 can hardly be known. He says:—'When there was 錫, it

包橘柚錫貢。○四十五沿于江海、達于淮泗。○四十六荊及衡陽惟

silks. The bundles contained small oranges and pummeloes:—rendered when specially required.

45 They followed the course of the Këang and the sea, and so reached the Hwae and the Sze.

46 VII. The King *mountain* and the South of *the mountain* Hwang were *the boundaries of* KING-CHOW.

was sent; when there was none, it was not sent as tribute. It is with 錫 that we soften metal' (有錫則貢之,或時乏則不貢,錫所以柔金也). 錫 certainly has the meaning of tin; but any mineral article of tribute would not be mentioned here in connection with the fruits. We must adhere to the view of K'ung and Wang.

P. 45. *Route of conveyance to the capital.* 沿 seems to have the meaning of going with the current and keeping along the shore. The tribute-bearers so passed down the Këang to the sea, and then turning north proceeded along the coast to the mouth of the Hwae, which stream they ascended to the place where it received the Sze. By the Sze they would go on to the Ho. This par. would seem to show that there is an error in Mencius' account of Yu's labours, Book III., Part I., iv. 7. He there says that 'Yu opened a vent for the Joo and Han, and regulated the course of the Hwae and Sze, so that they all flowed into the Keang' (決汝漢,排淮泗,而注之江). Now, we know it was not till the Chow dynasty, that a channel or canal was cut across the country to connect the Hwae and the Keang;—see the 左傳哀九年. Mencius does appear to have made a mistake.

CH. VII. THE ACCOUNT OF KING-CHOW. This province was bounded on the north by the mountain King,—the southern King as it is termed (南條之荊山), to distinguish it from the mount King of Yung-chow (p. 76). It is mentioned again, Part ii., par. 3. It is in Hoo-pih, 80 *le* east and north from the dis. city of Nan-chang (南漳; lat. 31°47', N., lon. 4°46', W.), dep. of Sëang-yang (襄陽). East and west from it were other hills, and barrier-passes (關 among them, which separated King from Yu-chow. On the south the prov. was bounded by the south of mount Hăng, which is a very indefinite expression. Hăng (or Hwăng)-shan itself is 30 *le* to the west of the dis. city of Hăng-shan (so called from the mount.; lat. 27°14', N., lon. 3°51', W., Biot), dep. Hăng-chow, Hoo-nan. It is the southern mountain of the Canon of Shun, par. 8. But what is meant by 'the south of Hăng?' Ying-tă replies:—'South of Hăng there was no other famous mountain or large river which could be named as bounding the province. The specification of "the south" shows us that the province extended beyond, southwards from the mountain.' I think it likely that King-chow extended towards the southern range, mentioned in speaking of the boundaries of last province. On the east King-chow and Yang-chow were conterminous, and on the west there was Lëang-chow.

The 'Boundaries of Successive Dynasties' says:—'The present Hoo-kwang' (*i.e.*, Hoo-pih and Hoo-nan); the dep. of Tsun-e (遵義; now belongs to Kwei-chow) in Sze-ch'uen, with the south of Chung-k'ing (重慶) dep; the depp. of Sze-nan (思南), T'ung-jin (銅仁), Yin-chow (恩州) and Shih-ts'ëen (石阡), in Kwei-chow; the whole of Kwang-se; and Leen-chow 連州) dep. in Canton:—all these territories were comprehended in King-chow.' As this authority gave the extent of Yang-chow too limitedly, it thus extends King-chow too much. The 地理今釋 gives the following detail:—'King-chow embraced—of the pres. Hoo-kwang the eleven depp. of Woo-ch'ang (武昌), Han-yang (漢陽), Ngan-luh (安陸), King-chow (荊州), Yŏ-chow (岳州), Ch'ang-sha (長沙), Hăng-chow (衡州), Chang-tih (常德), Shin-chow (辰州), Paou-k'ing (寶慶), and Yung-chow (永州), also the two small depp. of Ch'in (郴) and Tsing (靖), and the wards of Sze-chow (施州衛), together with the dis. of Nan-chang, dep. Seang-yang, the five districts of Ngan-luh (安陸), Yun-mung (雲夢), Heaou-kan (孝感), Ying-shing (應城), and Ying-shan (應山), and the south of the sub. dep. of Suy (隨),—all in dep. of Tih-ngan (德安), the four districts of Hwang-kang

荊州。四十七〇江漢朝宗于海。四十八〇九江孔殷。四十九〇沱潛旣道。

47 The Këang and the Han pursued their common course to the sea,
48 as if they were hastening to court. The nine Këang were brought
49 to complete order. The T'o and Ts'een were conducted by their

(黃岡), Ma-shing (麻城), Hwang-pe (黃陂), and Hwang-ngan (黃安) of the dep. of Hwang-chow; of Sze-ch'uen, the dis. of Këen-ch'e (建始) in K'wei-chow (夔州) dep.; and of Kwang-se, dep. Kwei-lin, the dis. of that name, and the north of Hing-ngan (興安) district.'

Pp. 47-50. *Engineering labours.* 47. The Këang, and the Han,—see on Part ii., parr. 8 and 9. The Këang entered King-chow in the pres. dis. of Pa-tung (巴東; lat. 31°2', N., lon. 6°11', W.), dep. of E-ch'ang (宜昌), and pursuing an eastern course to the dep. city of Han-yang, receives the waters of the Han (lat. 30°34', N., lon. 2°18', W.). The Han flows from Shen-se into Hoo-pih in the dep. of Yun-yang (鄖陽; dep. city, lat. 32°49', N., lon., 5°37', W.), and then holds a south-eastern course to its junction with the Këang. We may suppose that Yu expended no small amount of labour on the two rivers, from their entrance into King-chow on to the point of their junction. Particularly is he said to have operated on a narrow pass in the dis. of Pa-tung (called 巴東峽 and 三峽); but all such achievement is passed over in the text. Wang Ts'ëaou (王樵; Ming dyn.) says:—'The six characters of the par. bring the mighty stream of the united rivers rushing to the sea before our eyes. I have looked at it from Woo-ch'ang, and the vast flood dashing on brought to my mind the idea of a man hurrying with all his speed on some special mission without a thought of anything else.' 朝宗于海,—acc. to Gan-kwŏ and K'ang-shing, 'with the reverence for the sea that is seen in court for the sovereign.' Ts'ae gives the view of them which is seen in the translation. The appearance of the princes at court in the spring, he says, was called 朝; their appearance in summer was called 宗. There is little to choose between the interpretations. The phrase itself, with a similar application, is found in the She King, Part II., Book III., Ode ix. 48. 九江孔殷,—whatever opinion be come to about the 'nine Keang,' I do not see that 孔殷 can with any propriety have a difft. meaning assigned to them from that in the translation, which is after Ts'ae Ch'in, who says that 孔=甚, and 殷=正, adding:—九江水道,甚得其正, 'The channels of the nine Keang were made to be greatly correct.' K'ang-shing took 殷=多 and thought that the par.,—'the nine Këang were very many,' showed simply the difficulty which Yu had in regulating them. Gan-kwŏ, again, took 殷=中, and understood the par. to say that 'the nine Keang occupied all the middle of the land.' On the subject of the nine Keang, a hundred pages would not contain the discussions on one side and another. I will confine myself here to the summary given of them by Maou K'e-ling (向書廣聽錄,二):—

'There are two accounts of the nine Keang. The first is that the Great Keang, on arriving at King-chow, separated into nine streams;—and this is the nine Keang of the "Tribute of Yu,"' (that is, this is the view which Maou himself prefers.) 'The second is that the nine Keang is another name for the P'ang-le lake;—and this is the nine Keang of the Han and Tsin dynasties. As to the view of the Sung scholars, that the lake of T'ung-t'ing is the nine Keang, it is a mere speculation.

'On the first view it may be remarked that the par.—九江孔殷, standing where it does, proves clearly that the nine Keang were within the boundaries of King-chow. Now the comment of Gan-kwŏ is:—"In this province the Great Keang separated into nine channels," which Ying-tă expanded into—"The Great Keang divided and became nine, just as the Great Ho separated itself into the nine Ho." In accordance with this is the statement of Shwang Yin in his work on "The Waters" (桑欽水經;—Shwang Yin belonged to the closing times of the Han dynasty. He is a great authority in geographical matters. His work is always published with the commentary of Le Taou-yuen [酈道元], of the 'After Wei' [後魏] dyn.), that the nine Keang were in the north-west of Hea-sun in Ch'ang-sha" (在長沙下雋西北). Their position must thus have been somewhere to the west of the present King-chow (荊州之西) and the north of Yŏ-chow (岳州之北). To the same effect is the account of Chang Ching (張湞), that they began in Yŏ-ling (鄂陵), and ended at Keang-k'ow (江口), meeting in Shwang-loh (桑落). All these names would not take us far from the pres. dep. of King-chow. And yet, since the time of Yu, these nine branches of the Great Keang have disappeared, leaving only their names. They cannot be traced any more than "the nine Ho." All the earlier scholars agree in this account. The names of the streams, moreover, are given, and though no two enumerations agree in all the nine, about seven will be found the same in all of them.

'As to the second view, that the nine Keang is another name for the P'ang-le lake, it took its origin from an expression of Sze-ma Ts'een in his Historical Records—"I ascended the hill of Leu, and saw where Yu separated the nine Keang" (余登廬山,觀禹疏九江). After him Lew Hin said that the nine streams entered into the P'ang-le; and at last, in Pan Koo's Geography of the Han dynasty, under the district of Sin-yang (尋陽) in Leu-keang dep. (廬江郡), we have the note:—"The nine Keang of the Tribute of Yu were in the south of this. They all united eastwards of this, and became the Great Keang." But this view is easily disposed of. According to the classic, the nine Keang were in King-chow, and the P'ang-le was in Yang-chow;—the two had nothing to do with each other. Moreover, the classic says that the Keang, after passing the nine Keang, went on to Tung-ling, and then flowing gently eastwards united in the north with the P'ang-le (Part. ii., p. 9), so that not only were the nine Keang and the P'ang-le not identical, but Tung-ling and a tract of country lay between them. It is quite clear that Sze-ma Ts'een and all who followed him were in error.

'The divisions of the country got their names very much from those of the waters in them, and mistakes, like that which has been pointed out, came to be stereotyped on the face of the land, giving rise to endless discussions about the original site of places. The tract of Kew-keang (九江郡), as originally established by the Ts'in dynasty, was in King-chow between Se-ling and Ke-chun (在荆州西陵蕲春之間). At the commencement of the Han dynasty, it was taken away and afterwards reappointed, but was placed near to Show-ch'un (壽春), made to approach, that is, to Yang-chow. During the usurpation of Wang-mang (王莽), the Kew-këang of Show-ch'un was changed into the tract of Yen-p'ing (延平郡), and the tract of Yu-chang (豫章) in Keang-nan was changed into Kew-keang; and thus it was that the Kew-keang of King-chow passed into the P'ang-le of Yang-chow.'

Maou goes on to relate other changes in the geographical position assigned to Kew-këang, but that last narrated finally asserted itself; and we have still the dep. of Kew-këang in Keang-se, near the Po-yang lake, the old P'ang-le, as was noticed in the note on par. 38. The demonstration is complete that in the time of Yu the nine Keang and the P'ang-le had no relation together, but were in different provinces, a long way removed from one another.

On the opinion now generally followed, that we are to think of the T'ung-t'ing lake when we read here of the nine Këang, Maou observes that it commenced with Hoo-tan (胡旦, early in the Sung dynasty) He was followed by Chaou Shwŏ-che, (晁說之), Tsăng Yen-ho, and others, especially Choo He, whose advocacy of the view has secured for it its present general acceptance. There are differences of opinion, in the details of it, as to the nine streams having their common receptacle in the T'ung-t'ing. It is difficult also to reconcile it with Part ii. par. 9. I have less difficulty, however, in supposing that the lake is what now corresponds to the nine Keang of Yu than in believing the view of Gan-kwŏ which Maou endorses. If the Great Keang had ever separated its main stream, and become nine streams, history would not be silent as it is as to their disappearance, and traces of their former existence would still be discoverable on a geological survey of the country. Such a survey may yet throw some new light on the meaning of the text.

49. 沱潛既道,—the same words occur again, p. 64, in connection with Leang-chow. There must have been streams with these names in both the provinces. The 爾雅 says:—'Streams issuing from the Keang are called 沱; those issuing from the Han are called 潛.' Gan-kwŏ, says that 'T'o is another name for the Këang.' The likeliest view seems to be that at an island in the middle of the great stream, in the present dis. of Che-këang (枝江, 'the branching of the Këang;' lat. 30°24'. N., lon. 5°6', W.), dep. of King-chow, its waters separated, and flowed for a time in two channels, one north and one south, meeting again near the T'ung-t'ing lake. The northern of these channels was called the T'o. Hoo Wei insists also on another stream called the 'E, water' (夷水), which took its rise in the present dis. of Woo-San (巫山) of K'wei-chow dep. in Sze-ch'uen, and after entering King-chow, joined the Keang in the pres. dis. of E-too (宜都), as also to be accounted one of the 沱, which engaged the labours of Yu. For the Ts'een we are referred to the dep. of Ngan-luh in Hoo-pih, where the name is preserved in that of the dis. of Ts'een-keang (潛江; lat. 30°28', N., lon. 3°40', W.) As the character 潛 also signifies 'to abscond,' 'to lie hidden,' Hoo Wei supposes that the Ts'een of the Han flowed from it under ground in the first place, and then coming to the surface found their way back to the parent stream. Among the branches of the Han now there is one called Leu-fuh (蘆洑), in which name we have a reference to an under-

五十 雲土夢作乂。○五十一 厥土惟塗泥、厥田惟下中、厥賦上下。○五十二 厥貢羽毛齒革、惟金三品、杶榦栝柏、礪砥砮丹、惟箘簵楛、三邦底貢厥名、包

50 proper channels. The land in *the marsh of* Yun *became visible,* and that of Mung was brought under cultivation.

51 The soil of this province was miry; its fields were the average of the lowest class; its contribution of revenue was the lowest of the highest class.

52 Its articles of tribute were feathers, hair, ivory, and hides; gold, silver, and copper; the ch'un tree, wood for bows, cedars and cypresses; grindstones, whetstones, arrow-head stones, and cinnabar. *There were also* the k'wăn and loo bamboos, and the wood of the hoo tree, of which the three regions were able to contribute the best specimens. The three-ribbed rush was put in cases, which *again* were wrapped up.

ground current (宜取伏流之意). This, he supposes, may be the Ts'een of the text. The 'Statistical Account' of the present dyn. confirms this view. 50. The reading of this par. is not certain. In the Han dyn. the prevailing reading was 雲夢土作乂. The founder of the T'ang dynasty issued a proclamation settling the reading to be that now published. The reading depends to my mind on the question of whether there were two marshes, the Yun and the Mung, or only one,—the Yun-mung. Each side of this is very plausibly maintained. On the whole I am inclined to agree with the authors of the 'Daily Explanation,' that the marshes were two, 'the Yun on the north of the Keang, spreading over the country of the present depp. of Ngan-luh and Tih-ngan, and all about the sub. dep. of Meen-yang (沔陽); and the Mung, on the south of the Keang, spreading over the districts of Keang-hea (江夏) and Hwa-yung (華容). We can understand how these might be spoken of sometimes as one lake without reference to the Keang between them, and how it might be called sometimes the Yun, and sometimes the Mung. If, indeed, it was only one, then I can make no meaning of the text. The necessity of the case would make us read 雲夢土. If the two portions were spoken of separately,—about which there is to me no doubt,—then we may interpret as in the translation. The large tract of country covered by the marshes was very much drained by the other labours which have been detailed; north of the Keang the water sank till the ground appeared in places; and south of the Këang, portions of the country were left dry, and could be cultivated.

Pp. 51, 52. *Soil, revenue, and tribute.* 51. The soil of this province was of the same character as that of the last,—'all miry'; which we can well believe of the portion of it, not far removed from the courses of the Keang and Han. Its fields were one degree higher in quality than those of Yang-chow; and its revenue was much higher, owing, we may suppose, to its being more thickly peopled. 52. 羽毛齒革,惟金三品,—comp. p. 44. It is supposed that the articles from the two provinces are mentioned in the order of the quality which distinguished them. Thus, Yang-chow was most noted for its precious metals, and they are therefore mentioned first in p. 44. 杶榦栝柏,—in Yang-chow we have only 惟木. Here various kinds of wood are enumerated. There are four trees, as Gan-kwŏ and Ch'ing unite in saying, and not three only, as we find in the 集傳. Ts'ae joins the two first characters together, and says—'The wood of the Ch'un tree was fit for making bows.' But I have no evidence that it had such a quality. The wood preferred for bows was that of the 柘, by which Gan-kwŏ here defines 榦. Was it the yew tree? I cannot say exactly what tree the *Ch'un* was. It has got the various names of 杶, 櫄, 楯, and 椿, and was good for making musical instruments, and the thills of carriages, and

匭菁茅、厥篚玄纁璣組、九江納錫大龜。○五十三浮于江沱潛漢、逾于洛、至于南河。○

The baskets were filled with deep azure and purple silken fabrics, and with strings of pearls that were not quite round. From the *country of* the nine Këang the great tortoise was presented.

53 They floated along the Keang, the T'o, the Ts'ëen, and the Han; crossed over to the Lŏ, and proceeded to the most southern part of the Ho.

for pillars. Was it the dammar? 柏 is probably the cypress; but I do not know that I am right in calling the 栝 the cedar. It is described as having the leaf of the 柏, and the stem of the 松, or common pine, growing very large, enduring cold, and good for making coffins and boats. 礪砥砮丹,—the *le* and *che* were both stones abounding in the hills of King, adapted for purposes of grinding. The former were of a coarser substance; the latter closer and finer. The *noo* were stones, by their natural shape and quality fitted for being made into arrow-heads. The best are said to be found far north, on the banks of the Hih-lung, where they are called 'water flowers, hard and sharp, approaching to the character of iron (名水花石,堅利,入鐵). 丹=丹砂, 'cinnabar.' 惟箘簵楛,—these were all good for making arrows. The *kwăn* and *loo* grew about the marsh of Yun-mung (Gan-kwŏ). The *hoo* was a tree. We know that it was famed for the arrows made from it, because Confucius, on one occasion, being asked about a bird which lighted on the palace of the prince of Ch'in and died, pierced with a *hoo* arrow, declared that it was transfixed with one of the famous arrows of Suh-sin;—see the references in the note to par. 56 of the Preface. 三邦底貢厥名,—I think it is most natural to connect this clause with the one immediately preceding, and to suppose that it has reference only to the three articles just specified. Many, however, extend it to all the articles of tribute enumerated. What the three countries were, we cannot tell. Tung-po would make the phrase out to mean all the States of King,—'large, small and middling.' Gan-kwŏ, understanding the par. to extend only to the *kwăn*, *loo*, and *hoo*, which he thinks grew about the Yun-mung, naturally takes the three countries to have been three States in the neighbourhood of that marsh. 厥名猶言尤美'厥名='the best of them';—so, Chang Kew-shing (張九成). K'ang-shing very strangely puts a point at 貢, and reads 厥名 as part of the next clause.

包匭菁茅,—the rush here spoken of, described as having 三脊, *i.e.*, three-ribbed, was used for straining the wine at the imperial sacrifices. It was packed in small cases, which again were covered over,—showing the value of the article by the care which was taken of it. This seems to be the meaning of the characters. Gan-kwŏ and Wang Suh put a stop at 包, and understand by it 'bundles' of fruit, as in the case of Yang-chow. The former also takes 菁 and 矛 as being two different articles. K'ang-shang defines 匭 by 纏結, 'to tie or wrap round.' These explanations are all erroneous. I prefer also the meaning which I have given to 包匭 to another which is common, and which='bundles in cases.' 厥篚玄纁璣組,—纁 is another name for 絳. The silk has received three dippings in the dye-fluid. 璣組 are to be taken together. The former character denotes 'pearls that were not round' (珠不圓者, acc. to the 說文); these were strung, and put into the baskets, as I read the text. Some say they were carried by themselves, and not in the baskets. 九江納錫大龜,—'the great tortoise' attained the size, acc. to the 'Historical Records,' (龜策傳) of two cubits and a half. Such a creature would be esteemed very valuable, where divination was much relied on. Gan-kwŏ explains the 錫 as having the same force with the 錫貢 in par. 44. He says;—龜不常用,錫命而納之, 'the tortoise was not a regular article of tribute, but was presented when required by express command.' But the phraseo-

五十四荆河惟豫州。五十五伊洛瀍澗既入于河。五十六滎波既豬。五十七導菏澤被孟豬。五十八厥土惟壤、下土墳壚。五十九厥田惟中上、厥賦錯上中。

54 VIII. The King *mountain* and the Ho were *the boundaries of* YU-CHOW.
55 The E, the Lŏ, the Ch'ëen, and the Këen, were conducted to the
56 Ho. The *marsh of* Yung-po was confined to its proper limits. *The*
57 *waters of the marsh of* Ko were led to that of Măng-choo.
58 The soil of this province was mellow; in the lower parts it was
59 *in some places* rich, *in others* dark and thin. Its fields were the
highest of the middle class; its contribution was the average of the highest class, with a proportion of the very highest.

logy is different, and the nature of the case was different also. The tortoise might not be found, even when specially called for. It is better to take 錫 as a synonym of 納,—a meaning which it often has. The people presented the tor. whenever they met with it. It was always a welcome contribution.

P. 53. *Route of conveyance to the capital.* They floated along the Keang, the T'o, and the Ts'een,—not necessarily from the one of these to the other, but rather, I suppose, according to the place where the various articles were being brought from. It was necessary, however, to reach the Han, which took them to the borders of Yu-chow, where they had to leave their boats, and cross over the country to the Lŏ, by which they might proceed to the southern portion of the Ho, the boundary between Yu-chow and K'e-chow.

CH. VIII. THE ACCOUNT OF YU-CHOW.

P. 54. *Boundaries.* On the south was mount King, which has been spoken of as the northern boundary of King-chow. On the north was the Ho, that is, the southern portion of it which flowed with nearly a direct course from west to east. On the north-west, this prov. touched on the northern slopes of mount Hwa, which is sometimes described as belonging to it. On the east it was conterminous with the provinces of Yen, Seu, and Yang. Yu-chow, indeed, was the central one of Yu's nine divisions of the empire, and was conterminous, for a greater or less distance, with all of them except Ts'ing-chow, which lay off in the east by itself.

The 'Boundaries of Successive Dynasties' says:—'Yu-chow comprehended the present Ho-nan with the department of Yun-yang in Hoo-pih.' The more detailed and exact account of the 'Geography Modernized' is:—'Yu-chow embraced—of the present Ho-nan, the five departments of Ho-nan, K'ae-fung (開封), Kwei-tih (歸德), Nan-yang (南陽), and Joo-ning (汝寧), with the small dep. of Joo (汝州); of Chih-le, the two districts of Tung-ming (東明) and Ch'ang-hwan (長桓), dep. of Ta-ming (大名); of Shan-tung, the four districts of Ting-t'aou (定陶), Shing-woo (城武), Ts'aou (曹), and Tan (單), dep. of Ts'aou-chow (曹州); of Ngan-hwuy, the four districts of Fow-yang (阜陽), Ying-shang (穎上), T'ae-ho (太和), and Mung-shing (蒙城), with the sub. dep. of Pŏ (亳), in the dep. of Ying-chow (潁州); and of Hoo-pih, the five districts of Seang-yang (襄陽), Kwang-hwa (光化), E-shing (宜城), Tsaou-yang (棗陽), and Kuh-shing (穀城); with the sub. dep. of Keun (均州), in the dep. of Seang-yang, the district of Yun (鄖) in the dep. of Yun-yang, and the northern part of the sub. dep. of Suy (隨) in the dep. of Tih-ngan (德安).

Pp. 55—57. *Engineering labours.* 55. Comp. Part ii., par. 13, from which it appears that the four streams or rivers here mentioned, did not separately enter the Ho. The Lŏ received the waters first of the Këen and the

Ch'ëen, and last those of the E. and then proceeded, with them all to the Yellow river. In the text we are told, I suppose, the order in which Yu operated upon them. First, he took in hand the E. and having cleared its course to the Lŏ, continued his labours on that stream on to the Ho, after which he turned to do what was necessary for the Ch'ëen and Këen.

The E-water (伊水) has its source in Bear's-ear hill (熊耳山), in the dis of Looshe (盧氏) lat. 34°01', N. lon. 5°32', W.), in the small dep. of Shen-chow (陜州), Ho-nan. Passing into the dep. of Ho-nan, it flows east, close by the dis. city of Ts'ung (嵩). Bending towards the north, it passes through the districts of E-yang (伊陽) and Lŏ-yang (洛陽), into that of Yen-sze (偃師; lat. 34°45', N., lon. 3°45', W.), 5 *le* to the south-west of whose dis. city it enters the Lŏ. The Lŏ rises in the Ts'in range (秦嶺), 50 *le* to the north of the dis. city of Lŏ-nan (洛 or 雒南; lat. 34°06', N., lon. 6°22', W.), in the small but independent dep. of Shang (商州), in Shen-se. It enters Ho-nan in the dis. of Looshe, and flows north and east through Shenchow, on to Ho-nan dep. Proceeding northeast, through the south of the dis. of Yung-ning (永寧), and the north of E-yang (宜陽), it traverses the dis. of Lŏ-yang, where it receives the Ch'ëen and Këen. Going on eastwards through Yen-sze, where it receives the E, its course is through the north-west of Kung (鞏縣), into the dis. of Fan-shwuy (汜水), dep K'ae-fung, where it enters the Ho. The Ch'ëen and the Këen are both on the north of the Lŏ. The former rises in the west of the dis. of Măng-tsin (孟津); lat. 34°52', N., lon. 3°50'. W.). and flowing south to that of Lŏ-yang, it runs south-east into the Lŏ.

The Këen rises in White-stone hill (白石山), in the north of Min-ch'e district (澠池; lat. 34°46', N., lon. 4°47', W., and flows east, south of Sin-ngan (新安) district city, to the west of Lo-yang dis., where it joins the Ho.

Another Yu has often been wanted since Yu's time to remedy the devastations done by these four streams. In B.C. 184, the E and Lŏ overflowed and carried away nearly 2000 families. In A.D. 223, the same streams occasioned immense loss of life and property. In A.D. 722, a rising of the E destroyed a portion of the city of Tung-too (東都); and another in 800 was equally calamitous. Injuries quite as great are recorded from risings of the Ch'ëen and Këen;—see the 禹貢錐指, *in loc*.

56. Ts'ae Ch'in says that the Yung and the Po were 'two waters,' the former connected with the Tse and the latter with the Lŏ. This view is followed in the 'Daily Explanation;' but it has been satisfactorily refuted by Hoo Wei and others. An older view now commands general acceptance, for it was Yen Sze-koo of the T'ang dynasty, who first advocated the opinion adopted by Ts'ae. Gan-kwŏ, K'angshing, and Ma Yung all hold that the two characters should go together (滎波 or 滎播), as the name of a marsh, that formed by the waters of the Tse, rising up remarkably out of the ground, as described Part ii., par. 10. The name partly remains in those of the districts Yung-tsih (滎澤) and Yung-yang (滎陽) in the dep. of K'ae-fung. The marsh itself in the days of K'ang-shing was dried up, and become so much level ground (今塞爲平地). 57. Following the course of the Tse, Yu proceeded on to the marsh of Ko, taking its name from the hill of Ko, near the pres. dep. city of Ts'aou-chow in Shan-tung, lat. 35°20', N., lon. 52', W. It was also formed by the waters of the Tse, and unable to bring it entirely under management by itself, Yu led off the excess of its waters to the marsh of Măng-choo. This name is variously written,—孟豬, 望諸 in the 'Rites of Chow,' 明都 by Sze-ma Ts'een. A memorial of it remains in the tower of Măng-choo (孟諸臺), 10 *le* to the northeast of the dis. city of Yu-ching (虞城; lat. 34°38', N., lon. 19', W.) dep. of Kwei-tih in Honan. The marsh itself cannot now be traced, and Hoo Wei observes that repeated overflowings of the Ho, which commenced A.D. 1266, and laid the country about Kwei-tih under water, have obliterated all traces of Yu's labours in that quarter. Whether there was a connection between the marsh of Ko and that of Măngchoo which he only cleared, before Yu's time, or whether he opened such a connection in order to carry off the excessive waters of the former, we cannot tell. 被=及, as in Can. of Yaou, par. 1. As the Ho might be considered one of the rivers of Yu-chow and beyond comparison the greatest of them, we may be surprised that nothing is said of any labours performed upon it. We must suppose that when Yu was operating on the northern bank of it, about mount Yoh, and Tan-hwae (pp. 5,6), he had sent detachments over to Yu-chow, and finished at once all that was necessary to be done for the great stream. This left him free to direct his attention first to the Lŏ and its tributary streams in the west of the province, and then to the Tse and the evils it gave rise to in the east.

Pp. 58—60. *Soil, revenue, and tribute.*

58. 壤,—see par. 7. K'e-chow and Yuchow agreed in the general character of their soil, but no colour is assigned to that of Yu-chow, because, we are to suppose, no uniformity characterized it in this respect. 墳壚,—墳, see par. 17, where I adopted Ma Yung's meaning of the term as = 'rich.' This places it in direct opposition to Ts'ae's definition of 壚 as = 疏, 'thin,' 'poor.;' such also was K'ang-shing's ac-

書經

六十 厥貢漆枲絺紵、厥篚纖纊。錫貢磬錯。○六十一 浮于洛、達于河。○六十二 華陽黑水惟梁州。○六十三 岷嶓既藝。○六十四 沱潛既道。○

60 Its articles of tribute were varnish, hemp, a finer hempen cloth, and coarser hempen cloth. The baskets were filled with fine silken fabrics, and fine floss-silk. Stones for polishing sounding-stones were rendered, when required.

61 They floated along the Lŏ, and reached the Ho.

62 IX. The south of *mount* Hwa and the Black-water were *the boundaries* of Leang-chow.

64 The *hills* Min and Po were brought under cultivation. The T'o

count of it. The 說文 defines the char. by 黑剛土, 'black, hard, earth.' I have done the best I could with the two terms. 59. If we look only at the revenue of the province, we should expect its fields to rank much higher than they do; the reason of the disproportion, according to Foo T'ung-shuh (傅同叔), was that the black hard tracts in the lower parts of it were unfit for the cultivation of grain. The student will observe how the place of the 錯 is different from what it occupies in parr. 8 and 43.

60. 漆, 枲, 絺, 紵,—漆, see par. 19; 枲 and 絺, see par. 26; 紵 is a coarse kind of hemp,—a perennial plant, acc. to Luk Ke (陸璣;—紵亦麻也, 宿根在地, 至春自生). A kind of cloth was made from it which was called by the same name. Ts'ae says he cannot tell whether we should understand here the raw material, or the manufactured article. We must suppose, I think, that, as the character follows 絺, we are to understand the cloth. 厥篚纖纊,—纖, see par. 35; 纊—綿絮之細者, as in the translation. 錫貢,—see par. 44. There the phrase *follows* the articles so contributed, they being sufficiently marked off from the other articles by the 厥包 which precede. Here it *precedes* the articles, because, if it followed them, its force might be extended to the others previously mentioned. The 錯 were stones used for polishing other stones and gems, differing from the grinding-stones and whetstones of King-chow, the use of which was to polish articles of metal.

P. 61. *Route of conveyance to the capital.* From the eastern parts of Yu-chow they could at once reach the Ho. From the western, they reached it by means of the Lŏ.

Ch. IX. The account of Leang-chow.

P. 62. *Boundaries.* There is no dispute about the former of the boundaries mentioned. Mount Hwa is 'the western mountain' (西岳) of the Canon of Shun, par. 8, standing 8 *le* on the south of the dis. city of Hwa-yin (華陰; lat. 34°35', N., lon. 6°31', W., Biot), in the dep. of T'ung-chow (同州), acc. to the latest arrangement of Shen-se province. In the small adjacent dep. of Shang (商) is the dep. of Shan-yang (山陽), which is said to be identical with the Hwa-yang of the text. Mount Hwa served as boundary mark to three of Yu's provinces—Leang, Yu, and Yung. On the other boundary,—the Black-water,—there is not the same unanimity of opinion. Gan-kwŏ said:—'On the east this province reached to the south of mount Hwa, and on the west to the Blackwater.' If, indeed, the Blackwater was the boundary of Lëang-chow on the west, we are led to identify it with the river of the same name, also the western boundary of Yung-chow, and described in Part ii., p. 6, as 'flowing into the southern sea.' This view leads to great difficulties, quite as great as those attending the extension of Yang-chow round the sea-coast to Cochin-China. The first distinctly to controvert it appears to have been Sëĕ Sze-lung (薛士龍; Sung dyn.), who took the boundaries mentioned in the text as the northern and southern, and not those on the east and west:—'The northern boundary of Leang-chow was the south of mount Hwa, and on the south it stretched along the Blackwater, the present Loo-water (南距黑水, 黑水今瀘水也).' The name of the Loo had taken the place of the Blackwater in the Han dynasty, and subsequently to the T'ang, the stream has been called the 'river of the Golden Sands' (金沙江); but it is sufficiently proved that this stream, or at least that portion of it from its junction with the Shing-shwuy (繩水) and the Jŏ-shwuy (若水) to their merging in the Min Këang, was called the Blackwater.

Combining the statements of the 'Geography Modernized,' and the 'Statistical Account of the present dynasty,' we have the following description of the southern boundary of Lëang-chow:—'The present Golden Sands of Yun-nan is the Black water of Leang-chow. Its sources are very remote, farther off than those of the Yellow river, in 27°50′, west lon.' (this must surely be an error, as it would take us to about the long. of Calcutta), and between 35° and 36° north lat. Flowing south-east, it enters Yun-nan, near the pass of Tă-shing (塔城), in the border dep. of Le-keang (lat. 26°51′, N., lon. 16°01′, W.). Flowing through the northern part of this province, it enters Sze-ch'uen in the dep. of Ning-yuen (寧遠), and, bending more northwards, enters the Keang in the south of the dep. of Seu-chow' (叙州: lat. 28°38′, N., lon. 11°08′)'.

After the junction of the Loo and the Keang, the latter great stream would continue the southern boundary of Lëang on to King-chow. On the east it was conterminous with Yu-chow and King-chow. Its western boundary cannot, I think, be laid down with any certainty.

It is worthy of remark that neither of the two great dynasties which followed Yu,—neither the Yin nor the Chow, included the province of Leang. Portions of it were embraced in their provinces of Yu and Yung, but the greater part was considered as wild, savage territory, beyond the limits of the Middle Kingdom. We can hardly suppose that the territory of China ever diminished so greatly. It is more reasonable to think that Yu pushed his labours in this direction, not so much because the country was really included in Yaou's empire, as because it was necessary for him to operate upon it for the benefit of the more eastern parts.

The 'Daily Explanation' says:—'Leang-chow embraced the present provinces of Sze-ch'uen, Kwei-chow, and Yun-nan, with the dep. of Han-chung (漢中) in Shen-se, and the small dep. of Këae (階州) in Kan-suh.' This representation is beyond the truth; and that in the 'Boundaries of Successive Dynasties.'—that 'Leang-chow extended over the present Sze-ch'uen, and the dep. of Han-chung in Shen-se,' seems to be too narrow.

The following is the detail in the 'Geography Modernized:'—'Leang-chow embraced—of Shen-se, the dep. of Han-chung, and the small depp. of Hing-ngan (興安) and Shang (商州); of Kan-suh, the small dep. of Keae, and the two districts of Hwuy (徽) and Leang-tang (兩當), in dep. of Ts'in (秦州); of Hoo-pih, the three districts of Fang (房), Chuh-san (竹山) and Chuh-k'e (竹谿), and the west of Yun-se dis. (鄖西), dep. of Yun-yang (鄖陽); and the prov. of Sze-ch'uen.'

Pp. 63—66. *Engineering labours.* 既藝,—see on par. 30. 岷嶓,—see Part ii, parr. 3, 4, 8 and 9. In these mountains were the springs of branches of the great streams of the Keang and Han. Mount Min (the 'Historical Records' read 汶 instead of 岷) is in the most north-western part of Sze-ch'uen, called the T'ing of Sung-p'wan (松潘廳), given by Biot as in lat. 32°38′, N., lon. 12°52′, W. The 'Geography of the Shoo Modernized' says that 'from the small dep. of Min (岷州) in Kung-ch'ang (鞏昌) of Shen-se [now of Kan-suh], a range of lofty mountains with deep valleys stretches westwards to the western borders of the department of Ching-too (成都). The snowy ridges of Mow-chow (茂州) and other famous elevations are to be reckoned to this range. Where Yu began his operations was at the mountain of Lang-kea (浪架) on the very borders on the north-west of Sung-p'wan. Mount Po, called Po-ch'ung in Part ii, p. 3, was not so far west. There were two mountains of the name:—one 90 *le* to the north of the present sub. dep. of Ning-keang (寧羌州; lat. 32°42′, N., lon. 10°, W.), in Han-chung dep. of Shen-se, whence the waters of the eastern Han issued. This was the Po-ch'ung of Part ii. The other was in the pres. small dep. of Ts'in (秦州; lat. 34°36′, N., lon. 10°42′, W.) of Kan-suh; and from it the waters of the western Han issued. The two were distant from each other, north and south, between three and four hundred *le;* but they are to be considered as belonging to the same range. Yu's work on these two mountains is described as 'the clearing the springs of the Keang and the Han' (江漢滌源之事). The text tells us that the country about the foot of the mountains themselves was brought under cultivation. 64. See on par. 46. Gan-kwŏ thought that the T'o and the Ts'een here were the same as those of King-chow, the upper portion of their courses being here referred to. But this view cannot be adopted. Woo Ch'ing says:—'These were the separately flowing branches of the Keang and Han that were in Leang-chow. In the east of the pres. district of P'e, (郫縣 lat. 30°47′, N. lon. 12°32′, W.) dep. of Ching-too was a T'o, which flowed westwards into the Keang. In the south-west of the dis. of Taou-keang (導江) in P'ang-chow' (彭州) [these are names of former territorial divisions; we have now the dis. of P'ang in Ching-too dep., and the dis. of Kwan (灌縣) in the same corresponds to Taou-keang] 'there was another T'o which flowed east into the Keang.

六十五 蔡蒙旅平。○六十六 和夷厎績。○六十七 厥土青黎。○六十八 厥田惟下上、厥賦下中、三錯。○六十九 厥貢璆鐵銀鏤、砮磬、熊羆狐貍織皮。

65 and the Ts'een were conducted by their proper channels. Sacrifices were offered to the hills Ts'ae and Mung, on the regulation of the country about them.

66 *The country of* the wild tribes about the Ho could *now* be successfully operated on.

67 The soil of this province was greenish and light.

68 Its fields were the highest of the lowest class; its contribution of revenue was the average of the lowest class, with proportions of the rates immediately above and below.

69 Its articles of tribute were musical gem-stones, iron, silver, steel, stones for arrowheads, and sounding-stones; with the skins of bears, great bears, foxes, and jackals, and articles woven with their hair.

Again, in the dis. of Chin-foo (眞符) in Yang Chow (洋州) [we have now the dis. of Yang in the dep. of Han-chung, in Shen-se], there was the water of Ts'een-kuh (灊谷), which was a Ts'een. But the branches flowing from the Keang and Han, whether large or small, long or short, all went by the names in the text, and are to be looked for in various places. When the mountains Min and Po were brought under cultivation, the upper parts of the two streams were regulated; and now their courses through all the province were cleared by the measures taken with the various T'o and Ts'een.' 65. The hills of Ts'ae and Mung are both referred to the present dep. of of Ya-chow (雅州; lat. 30°3', N., lon. 13°25', W). Mount Mung seems to be sufficiently well ascertained. The 'Statistical Account' of the pres. dynasty says that it stands on the borders of the three districts of Ya-ngan(雅安), Ming-san (名山), and Loo-san (蘆山), of the above department, and that the best tea of all Sze-ch'uen is grown upon it. Mount Ts'ae is not so well determined. The 'Geography of the Shoo Modernized' identifies it with the hill of Chow-kung (周公山), 5 *le* to the east of Ya-chow city, and the Statistical Account of the Ming dyn., adopting that view, adds that 5 *le* further off there is a place called Leu-p'ing (有地名旅平), where it is probable that Yu offered his sacrifices. But this Leu-p'ing was not heard of till modern times, and, indeed, Yeh Mung-tih (葉夢得), of the Sung dyn., was the first to say that the hill of Chow-kung was the Ts'ae of the Shoo. The Geography of the Han dyn. does not mention the Ts'ae at all. Hoo Wei inclines to the opinion that we are to look for it in one of the famous Ngo-mei hills (峨眉山) in the dis. of the same name (lat. 29°32', N., lon. 12°50', W.), dep of Kea-ting (嘉定). 旅平, —旅 is applied to designate sacrifices offered to mountains;—see Ana. III. vi. The 'Daily Explanation' expands the whole paragraph thus:—'The Mei-water had flowed between the hills of Ts'ae and Mung with a rapid and destructive course, but now all this was remedied, and Yu sacrificed to the mountains, and announced the completion of his work' (蔡蒙二山之間，沫水所經，其勢漂疾爲害，今水土旣平，于是旅祭其山，而告成功焉). 66. Ts'ae gives two views of the meaning of this paragraph, neither of which he accepts as quite satisfactory, though he rather inclines himself to the former of them. It is that propounded by Gan-kwŏ, that the two characters were the name of a tract of country. The other is that Ho and E were the names of two streams. A more natural interpretation is that of K'ang-shing, that 和夷＝和上之夷, 'The wild people upon the Ho,' though, taking the two characters in connection with the rest of the par., we must understand them of the territory occupied by those people.

The 和水 is another name for the 涐水, which came through the pres. Mow Chow (茂州), and, after a long course of about 3,000 *le*, flowed into the Këang in the dep. of Kea-ting. But we can hardly think that the tribes mentioned dwelt along all the stream, even in that portion of it which was in Sze-ch'uen.

Pp. 67—69. *Soil, revenue, and tribute.*
67. In interpreting this par., Ts'ae follows Gan-kwŏ, who gives 黎 as = 黑, 'black,' a meaning which it often has, but which does not seem appropriate here. We should thus be told only the colour of the soil, and nothing about its nature. Gan-kwŏ adds, indeed, to 黑 the charr. 而沃壤 'and rich and mellow;' but this cannot be all indicated by 黎, and the next par. is inconsistent with such a view of the soil of Lëang. The 'Historical Records' read 驪 for 黎, which variation does not assist us at all in determining the meaning. In these circumstances we must look about for another meaning of 黎, and Ma Yung, followed by Wang Suh, has suggested that which I have adopted in the translation. He defined the character by 小疏, 'small and thin.' This suits the passage well enough. The difficulty with it is that we do not find such a meaning of the term elsewhere, and hence it is not given in the Dictionary.
68. Its fields were ranked in the second grade, and the revenue in the 8th, though this sometimes, or perhaps in some places, rose to the 7th, and again fell to the 9th. The 'Daily Explanation' says:—其賦爲下中·三錯,本第八等,或一年而進第七等,又或一年而降第九等,共三等. The revenue of this province was thus only not so low as that of Yen-chow. On this Tsăng Yen-ho has observed that Leang-chow was very mountainous, while the provv. of Yen and Yang had suffered and were still suffering more than others from the overflow of water, and in consequence of these circumstances their revenue was so small. These circumstances would have their influences on the revenue, but still more powerful would be the denseness or sparseness of the population. In the course of time, the States of Woo (吳) Yuĕ (越), Min (閩), and Shuh (蜀),—all belong. to Yang-chow and Lëang-chow, became the most famous for their fertility of all in the empire. 69. 璆鐵銀鏤砮磬,—Ts'ae adopts the meaning of 璆 as 玉磬, 'musical stones of gem,' taking the char. as a synonym of 球. Gan-kwŏ simply defines it by 玉名, 'the name of a gem.' Either of these meanings suits the passage well enough; but K'ang-shing read 鏐, which he defines—黄金之美者, 'the finest gold,' and this, could it be fully established, would suit the passage still better. The regions of Lëang-chow have always been famous for their gold, while the situations and excellence of their gems are unchronicled. By 鐵 we are to understand 'soft iron,' and by 鏤, 'hard iron,' or 'steel.' The latter character is often used for 'to cut and engrave,' with reference to the hardness of the tools necessary for such a purpose. In the time of the Han dynasty, 'Iron-masters' (鐵官) were appointed in several districts of the old Leang-chow to superintend the iron works. Ts'ae refers to two individuals mentioned in the 'Historical Records,' one of the surname Chŏ (卓氏), and the other of the surname Ch'ing (程), both of this part of the empire, who became so wealthy by their smelting that they were deemed equal to princes. 銀 is the 'white metal,' or silver. 砮磬,—see on previous paragraphs. 熊,羆,狐,貍,織皮,—熊 is 'the bear;' the 羆 is described as 'like the bear, of a yellowish white' (爾雅); 'like the bear, with a long neck, and long legs, very fierce and strong, able to pull up trees' (郭璞); 'there are yellow *pe*, and red (赤) *pe*,—it is larger than the 熊, and the grease is coarser.' I do not think we can at present determine exactly the species of the *pe*. The 狐 is 'like a dog, but with a long tail;' the 貍 are 'a small sort of 狐.' Ts'ae, after Soo Tung-po, takes 織皮 as two different things, the former denoting a sort of felt (罽), made from the hair of the animals; the latter denoting furs (以罽者曰織,以裘者曰皮). Other commentators make the two characters to denote only one thing—a fabric woven from the skins tanned, and cut into very small and thin strings (Woo Ch'ing). The view adopted by Ts'ae is to be followed. Quite unnatural is the view of K'ang-shing, who puts a stop at 貍, as if they were the living animals which were sent as tribute, and then takes 織皮 as the name of a barbarous territory:—(西戎之國). There is more reason in the opinion of Woo Ch'ing, Hoo Wei, and others, who instead of stopping at 皮, carry the paragraph on to 來. The furs and hair-cloth are thus the tribute from the wild tribes lying west and north of the province, and the description of the route of conveyance commences in the same way as in the previous provinces.

七十節 西傾、因桓是來、浮于潛、逾于沔、入于渭、亂于河。○ 七十一 黑水西河○惟雍州。○ 七十二 弱水既西。○ 七十三 涇屬渭汭。七十四 漆沮既從。七十五 灃

70 From Se-k'ing they came by the course of the Hwan; floated along the Ts'een; crossed the country to the Mëen; *then* entered the Wei; and ferried over the Ho.
71 X. The Blackwater and the Western Ho were the boundaries of YUNG-CHOW
73 The Weak-water was conducted westwards. The King was led to
74 mingle its waters with those of the Wei. The Tseih and the Ts'eu

P. 70. *Route of conveyance to the capital.* 西傾因桓是來,—see the conclusion of last note. 西傾 is the name of a mountain, which belonged to Yung-chow; its southern slopes, however, passed into Lëang. It is often identified with the mountain of the same name in the district of Chang (漳縣; lat. 34°40', N., lon. 11°50', W.), dep. of Kung-ch'ang in Kan-suh;—see below, Part ii., p. 2. The river Hwan took its rise on the south of the mountain. It is also called the White-water (白水), and flowing into Sze-ch'uen, in the dis. of Ch'aou-hwa (昭化; lat. 32°16', N., lon. 10° 38', W.), dep. Paou-ning, it proceeds to join the western Han. This western Han was the Ts'een, and going up it they should have been able to pass into the Mëen, another branch of the Han, for it flows out of the pres. dis. of Lëŏ-yang (略陽), dep. of Han-chung, and running south-east into the dis. of Mëen, called after it, it there joins the great stream. Perhaps there were shallows in the course of the Ts'een, which rendered it necessary to leave their boats, or it may have been a saving of time and labour to leave the water at some point, and go across the country to the Mëen (see a note in the 集說, by Foo Yin [傅寅]). From the Mëen it was necessary to get to the north, into the Wei, which was in Yung-chow. From the text,—入于渭,—we should conclude that this was accomplished without taking the land again. But this was impossible, their being no water-communication between the Han and the Wei. In the dep. of Fung-ts'eang (鳳翔), however, of Shen-se, and dis. of Mei (郿縣; lat. 34°13', N., lon. 8°38', W.) is the mountain of Ya (衙嶺), from which the stream of Paou (褒水) flows south into the Mëen, while another stream on the north side, the Seäy (斜川), flows into the Wei. Probably, the tribute-bearers ascended the Paou as far as they could, and then went overland to the Seäy. For the Wei, see Part ii., p. 12. It enters the Ho, and of course brought the travellers to that stream, which they ferried across at some suitable point. 絶河而渡曰亂.

CH. X. THE ACCOUNT OF YUNG-CHOW. P. 71. *Boundaries.* The western boundary is here assigned and the eastern. The former—the Black-water—is difft. from the river of the same name, which formed the southern boundary of Lëang-chow;—see on par. 62. It is no doubt the same with the Black-water of Part ii., p. 6, which see. It will be sufficient here to quote from the 禹貢錐指:—'According to Shwang Yin's work on the Waters, with the comment. of Taou-yuen, "The Black-water issued from Fowl-hill in Chang-yih (出自張掖雞山; Chang-yih is now the principal dis. in the dep. of Kan-chow (甘州, lat. 39°, N., lon. 15°32', W.), and flowing south to T'un-hwang (燉煌), the prin. dis., dep. of Ngan-se (安西), passed by the hill of San-wei (三危山), and flowed on to the southern sea." Acc. to the Compilation of Geography (括地志; a work of the T'ang dynasty), "The Black-water rose 120 *le* to the north of E-woo district in E-chow (伊州伊吾縣), and flowing south was lost about the hill of San-wei, in Sha-chow (沙州), 46 *le* to the south-east of the district city of T'un-hwang." We cannot tell which of these accounts is correct. The T'ung-teen (通典; by 杜佑, of the Tsin dynasty) says:—"Accomplished scholars like K'ung and Ch'ing did not know where the Black-water was, because, perhaps, in the lapse of time, it had become dried up."' About the eastern boundary,—the western Ho,—there is no uncertainty. This was the Ho, where it runs from north to south, between the present Shan-se and Shen-se;—called the 'western,' as being the western boundary of K'e-chow, the imperial province. The length of its course from the point in Yu-lin dep. (榆林), where it enters Shen-se, to the district of Hwa-yin, amounts, it is said, to 1,700 *le*.

On the south, Yung-chow was conterminous with Lëang-chow, from mount Hwa westwards, on to Se-k'ing, and again westwards on to Tseih-shih, from which Yu traced the course of the Ho (Part ii., par. 7), and thence again to the Black-water. The northern boundary of the province is not at all intimated in the Shoo, but it must have extended from the position of the pres. city of Yu-lin, lat. 38°18', N., lon., 7°7'. W., westwards along the north of Shen-se and Kan-suh as far as the south boundary did. Hoo Wei says that of Yu's nine provinces this was the largest, and that next to it were K'e and Lëang. 'The extent of Yung, from east to west, was about 3,700 *le*, and from north to south, about 2,500 *le*, while in all this great space there was not much of unoccupied territory.'

Pp. 72—78. *Engineering labours.* 72. The Weak-water,—see Part ii., p. 5. In the 'Statistical Account of the present dynasty,' under the dep. of Kan-chow in Kan-suh, we find the following account of the Jŏ, or Weak-water:—'It rises in the south-west of San-tan district (山丹), and flows north, west of the city, into the district of Ch'ang-yih. Passing that district city on the north, it enters, going on still to the north-west, the borders of Kaou-t'ae (高臺) in Suh-chow (肅州; lat. 39° 45', N., lon. 17°21', W.) This is the Weak-water of the Tribute of Yu.' Some accounts say that it can be crossed in coracles of skin, while yet a piece of straw thrown upon its surface would sink to the bottom. To this feeble sluggishness of its stream its name is ascribed. 既西,—'was conducted westwards.' This was its natural course, and in this it is unique among the rivers mentioned in this Book, all the rest flowing east, with the exception of the Black-water of this province, whose course was south. In the general disorder, which had prevailed, however, we may suppose that it had taken a direction to the south-east, and mingled its waters with those of the Ho. 73. 涇屬渭汭,—屬 is read *chuh*, up. 4th tone,—相連, 'to be connected together.' Gan-kwŏ defined it by 逮—及; and Ma Yung by 入. These meanings are all connected, and it is strange that the dictionary should give Gan-kwo's explanation under the second sound of the character,—*shuh*, low. 4th tone. 渭汭 are to be taken together like 嬀汭 in the Can. of Yaou, par. 12. Ts'ae makes 汭 to be the name of a stream which entered the King, before it joined its waters with those of the Wei. If this had been intended, we may be sure that the text would have been different. 汭 is defined—水北, 'the north of a stream; 水之隈曲, 'the bending bank of a river;' 水中州, 'an island in a river;' and by the 說文, 水相入, 'the meeting of two rivers.' The second and last of these meanings may easily be harmonized. As regards the first meaning, there is no difficulty in the text where the King flows from the north to the Wei. The King, according to the 'Statistical Account of the present dynasty,' makes its appearance in Shen-se in the west of Shun-hwa dis. (淳化; lat. 34°55', N., lon. 7°58', W.), in the small dep. of Pin (邠州); thence it flows past the small dep. of K'een (乾), enters the dep. of Se-ngan, and takes its way, through the districts of Le-ts'euen (醴泉), and King-yang (涇陽), on to that of Kaou-ling (高陵; lat. 34°30', N., lon. 7°24', W., in the south-west of which it joins the Wei. It is said to have its rise in Ke-t'ow hill (笄頭山), 'in the south-west of Ping-lëang dis. (平涼; lat. 35°34', N., lon. 9°48', W.,), dep. of the same name in Kan-suh. The Wei,—see below, Part ii., p. 12. The stream of the King was muddy and that of the Wei clear; and the muddiness of the former became more evident after their junction. There are many poetic allusions to these circumstances;—see the She-king, Part I. Book III., Ode x. 74. 漆沮既從,—we have 恆衞既從 in par. 9, but the 既從 cannot here be taken in the same way. There the phrase indicated that the Hăng and Wei were made to follow their natural channels; here it signifies that the Tseih and Ts'eu were made to join the Wei. Tung-po says:—'The following here is like that with which a youth follows his elder. The Wei was great and the Tseih and the Ts'eu were small; hence it is said that they were made to follow' (note in the 集說). Acc. to the 'Geography of the Shoo Modernized,' the Tseih takes its rise in the pres. dep. of Se-ngan, in the north of the dis. of T'ung-kwan (同官; lat. 35°6', N., lon. 7°25', W.), and flowing past that city on the east, is there joined by the T'ung-kwan river. Proceeding thence south-west to the sub. dep. of Yaou (耀州; lat. 34°56', N., lon. 7°35', W.), it unites with the Ts'eu. The Ts'eu rises in the dis. of Chung-poo (中部; lat. 35°38', N., lon. 7°16', W.), in the small dep. of Luh (鄜州), and after flowing through the dis. of E-keun (宜君), passes into the dep. of Se-ngan, traverses the dis. of T'ung-kwan, on to the south of Yaou Chow, where it unites with the Tseih. Their united waters proceed

書經

水攸同。○荆(七十六)岐既旅、終南惇物、至于鳥鼠。○原(七十七)隰底績、至于豬野。○三(七十八)危既宅、三苗丕敘。○厥(七十九)土惟黃壤。○厥(八十節)田惟上上、○厥賦中下。○

75 were led in a similar way *to the Wei;* and the waters of the Fung found the same receptacle.

76 The mountains King and K'e were sacrificed to, and those of Chung-nan and Shun-wŭh *were also regulated*, and all the way on to
77 that of Neaou-shoo. Successful measures could now be taken with
78 the plains and swamps, even to the marsh of Choo-yay. The *country about* San-wei was made habitable, and the *affairs of the people of* San-meaou were greatly arranged.

79 The soil of the province was yellow and mellow.

80 Its fields were the highest of the highest class; its contribution of revenue was the lowest of the second.

into the district of Foo-p'ing (富平), where they receive the name of Shih-ch'uen (石川河), and holding on in the same direction enter the Wei in the district of Lin-t'ung (臨潼; lat. 34°20', N., lon. 7°28', W.)

75. 灃水攸同,—攸=所. Gan-kwŏ says 灃水所同,同之于渭, 'The waters of the Fung found the same place, *i.e.*, they were conducted in the same way to the Wei.' The Fung has its rise in the hill of Chung-nan, in the south east of the dis. of Hoo (鄠縣東南終南山; the city of Hoo is in lat. 34°8', N., lon. 7°50', W.), of Se-ngan dep., and enters the Wei in the south-east of the district Heen-yang (咸陽). It was on the south of the Wei. Lin Che-k'e observes:—'The territory of Yung-chow bordered on the western Ho, so that before the regulation of that stream, it suffered as well as K'e-chow from the overflow of its waters. After the operations of Yu, however, on Hoo-k'ow, and on the mountains K'e and Lëang, the great stream pursued its way to the east; and when he arrived at Yung-chow he had only to deal with the Weak-water, conducting it to the west, and to lead the waters of the King, the Tseih and the Ts'eu, and the Fung, to the Wei, in which they all went on to the Ho.'

76. 既旅,—see on par 65. The King mountain here is not that of King-chow. We are referred for it to a mountain 10 *le* to the south-west of Foo p'ing (富平; district city, lat. 34°42', N., lon. 7°41'. W.) Mount K'e is the same which I supposed to be meant in par. 4 Chung-nan is 50 *le* to the south of the dis. city of Ch'ang-ngan, the dep. city in fact of Se-ngan; lat. 34°16', N., lon. 7°31', W.) On the east it extends to the dis. of Lan-t'een (藍田; lat 34°5', N., lon. 7°8', W.) and on the west to the district of Mei (郿縣; lat. 34°13', N., lon. 8°38', W.), stretching along altogether an extent of 800 *le*. Shun-wŭh is supposed to be the same with what is now called T'ae-pih hill (太白山) in the south of the district of Mei, called also T'ae-yih (太一 and 太乙). Neaou-shoo, or Bird and Rat mountain, is farther west, and conducts us to the district of Wei-yuen (渭源; 35°8', N., lon. 12°12', W.), dep. of Lan-chow (蘭州) in Kan-suh.

Hoo Wei here makes the following note:—'Ch'in Ta-yew (陳大猷, Sung dyn.) says, "The ancients felt it right to sacrifice on occasion of any great undertaking, and it was specially right to do so in connection with such an undertaking as Yu's. But we have mention of his offering sacrifice only in the provinces of Yung and Leang, because these were the two last provinces where he operated, and his sacrificing in them shows that he had done so in the other provinces as well. Further, Yu's sacrificing is mentioned only in connection with the hills of Ts'ae and Mung in Leang, and those of

King and K'e in Yung, because Ts'ae and Mung were the last hills of Leang, and King and K'e were the first of Yung, so that we may understand he sacrificed to all the others; and thence it is said below that *the hills in all the nine provinces were cleared of their wood and sacrificed to.*" These observations are good, but do not give the proper reason for the use of the term 旅. At Hoo-k'ow the object was the clearing of the Ho: at Lëang and K'e it was the clearing of the Ho and of the country as well;—and hence we have the terms 載 and 治. At Mung, Yu, Min, and Po, the object was the cultivation of the country, and therefore we have the term 藝. At Ts'ae, Mung, King, K'e, Chung-nan, Shun-wŭh, and Neaou-shoo, the object was to clear the streams in the valleys, and had nothing to do with the fields or country, and hence we could not have 藝, but only 旅. At San-wei the object was both to clear the Black-water, and the valley-streams, so that the country might be inhabited, and hence we have the term 宅. The words used in every case have a peculiar appropriateness to the circumstances. They have all a reference to Yu's labours upon the disordered country. We are not to lay stress upon the idea of sacrificing in 旅.'

This is ingenious; but Wei has not told us the peculiar and appropriate meaning in the use of 旅.

77. 'Ground wide and level is called 原; low and wet is called 隰. What we read in the She,—"He measured the plains and marshes," has the same local application as the phrase in the text.' So, Ts'ae Ch'in, following Ch'ing K'ang-shing. The ode referred to is the 6th in the 2nd Book of the 大雅, celebrating the praises of duke Lew, who founded the fortunes of the House of Chow in the territory of Pin (豳). If we thus interpret the text, the region of these operations of Yu was the present Pin-chow (邠州) in Shen-se. Possibly, however, the phrase may have a more extensive reference. Even at present, in a multitude of the districts of Shense and Kan-suh there are one or more not able 原, many of which in Yu's time would be in a marshy condition. For the marsh of Choo-yay we have to go to Kan-suh, 80 *le* east of the district of Chin-fan (鎮番; lat. 38°35', N., lon. 13°20', W.), dep. of Leang-chow (涼州). In the geography of the Han dynasty it is called the marsh of Hew-ch'oo (休屠). To reach this Yu must have crossed the Ho. 78. 三危,—see Can. of Shun, par. 12. The hill identified with this San-wei is in the south-east of the district of T'un-hwang. Thither Shun had removed the most unprincipled and insubordinate of the people of San-mëaou. The banishment had not been without its effect in softening and subduing them, and now when Yu came to ameliorate the condition of their settlement, the moral effect of his kindness is said to have completed the work of their transformation. The Black-water, it was seen on par. 71, passed by the mountain of San-wei. We must suppose that it was by operating on its troubled stream, that Yu effected the change which is intimated in the character of the country around. 三苗丕敍,—Gan-kwŏ explains this:—三苗之族大有次敍, 'the tribe of the San-meaouites had great order and arrangement;' adding—'This is said to set forth the merit of Yu.' I cannot see my way clear to adopt the common modern view that the phrase 丕敍 celebrates the merit of the Meaouites. Ch'ing Heaou, for instance (鄭曉; Ming dyn.), says on 敍:—是遷善改過, 革其凶頑, 'it expresses how they became good, reforming their faults and putting away their malignant stolidity.'

I find two interesting notes on this par. The first is by Leu Tsoo-heen (呂祖謙; of the Sung dynasty), who says:—'The people of San-meaou were driven to San-wei for their evil conduct, and according to the views of after ages they might have been left as banished criminals to themselves, to destroy themselves or to keep themselves alive, without being cared for or pitied. But such was not the mind of those early sages. When they were criminals, it was necessary to banish them; but after that punishment was inflicted, it was thought right to show kindness to them, and to extend to them the influence of good government. Thus it was that Yu having regulated the waters as far as to San-wei, there laid out for the Meaouites the plan of their settlements.'

The other note is by Tsae Ts'in:—'When Shun drove out the people of San-meaou, it was only the worst among them whom he removed to San-wei, while he left the rest in their settlements. But here we find the banished portion displaying great merit, while the others still continued bad and insubordinate. The old settlements of the San-meaouites were amid the strengths of hills and streams, the influence of which fostered such a spirit. Even now-a-days we find the people about the T'ung-t'ing lake ever and anon breaking out and displaying such a spirit; and when they are captured and questioned, most of them are found to have the surname of Meaou.—Are they the descendants of the ancient tribe?'

Ps 79—81. *Soil, revenue, and tribute.*

79. Yellow is considered the proper colour of soil. The soil of Yung-chow was thus the best of all the provinces. 80. The disproportion here between the character of the fields, which were in the first grade, and the amount of the revenue which was only of the sixth grade is very great. It is generally explained by saying that the population was very thin; and I do not see how it can otherwise be accounted for. Hoo Wei having argued for the wide extent of the province, and said

八十一 厥貢惟球琳琅玕。○八十二 浮于積石、至于龍門西河。會于渭汭。○八十三 織皮、崑崙、析支、渠搜、西戎卽敘。○

81 Its articles of tribute were the k'ew and lin *gem-stones*, and the lang-kan *precious stones*.

82 From as far as Tseih-shih they floated on to Lung-mun on the western Ho; they then met, on the north of the Wei, *with the tribute-bearers from other quarters*.

83 Hair-cloth and skins *were brought from* Kwăn-lun, Seih-che, and K'eu-sow;—the wild tribes of the West all coming to submit to *Yu's* arrangements.

there were few empty, uninhabited districts in it, feels the pinch of the difficulty, and tries to get over it by arguing that Yu only levied revenue from the fertile country on either side of the Wei, in which moreover there were many high hills and long valleys. But his reasoning is not satisfactory;—it is tantamount, in fact, to the giving up many of his former statements. 81. Ch'ing defines 球 by 美玉, 'an admirable gem.' The 說文 calls it 玉磬, 'a sounding-stone of gem,' which would agree with the use of the term in Part II., Bk. IV., p. 9. We may conclude that the 球 was a jade suitable for the manufacture of such instruments. The 琳 is called by Ch'ing 美石, 'a beautiful stone.' But in this he stands alone. The 說文 and other authorities agree in referring it also to the class of 玉, or gems. The two characters 琅 and 玕 go together. Gan-kwŏ describes the substance denoted by them as 'a stone, but like a pearl.' Some speak of it as a kind of coral, but we cannot look for coral in the hilly and inland districts of Yung-chow. Possibly it was lazulite, or the *lapis lazuli*.

82. *Route of conveyance to the capital.* Two routes are here indicated. The one—and we may suppose it the principal one—was by the Wei, which would be available for the more southern portion of the province. The other was by the Ho, which was available from the mountain of Tseih-shih (see Part ii., p. 7: it is in the sub. dis. of Ho (河州), lat. 35°44', N., lon. 13°28', W.). Parties living more to the east could of course take the Ho at the most convenient part of its course towards its highest northern latitude when it turned south, and then descend with it as far as the mountain of Lung-mun, on its western bank, in the north-east of Han-shing dis. (韓城; lat. 35°32', N., lon. 5°3', W.). Not far from this, a little south of it, they met with the boats which had come to the Wei, and tracked up from the junction of that stream with the Ho. Here I suppose they all took the shore, and travelled through K'e chow to the capital.

83. *Other articles of tribute. The par. should form part of par.* 81. In this view of the concluding portion of the Part, I agree with Soo Tung-po, to whom Ts'ae Ts'in also inclines. The analogy of 織皮 in par. 69 seems to necessitate it. As the account of all the other provinces, moreover, concludes with the route of conveyance to the capital, we cannot understand why this should not do the same. On par. 69, K'ang-shing took 織皮 as the name of a country; here, with strange inconsistency, he takes them as descriptive of the tribes from K'wăn-lun, Seih-che and K'eu-sow, all 'skin-wearing.' K'wăn-lun, Seih-che, and K'eu-sow are understood to be the names of mountains, giving name to the regions and tribes about them. We have only to conceive of them as representing three tribes of what were called the western barbarians, and those three the greatest of them all, so it is added that all the tribes came and submitted to Yu's arrangements. So says Hoo Wei:—三國皆西戎,而西戎不止於三國,三國乃西戎之大者,皆來入貢,則其餘無不賓服,故曰西戎卽敘. 卽=就, 'to come to.' Gan-kwŏ explains 卽敘 by 皆就次敘, which is equivalent to the 丕敘 in par. 78.

THE BOOKS OF HEA.

BOOK II. THE TRIBUTE OF YU. PART ii.

禹貢下

導岍及岐、至于荆山、逾于河、壺口、雷首、至于太岳、厎柱、析城、至于王屋、太行、恆山、至

1 I. *Yu* surveyed and described the hills, beginning with K'ëen and K'e, and proceeding to mount King; then, crossing the Ho, Hoo-k'ow and Luy-show, going on to T'ae-yŏ. After these came Te-ch'oo and Seih-ching, from which he went to Wang-uh; then there were Ta-hang, and mount Hăng, from which he proceeded to Këĕ-shih, where he reached the sea.

CONTENTS. It has been stated. on page 93, that the division of the Book into two parts is a modern arrangement, and by no means universally followed. It is convenient, however. The first part gives a view of Yu's labours in each particular province. This gives a general view of the mountain ranges of the empire, and of the principal streams, and relates some other labours of Yu, not alluded to before,—his conferring lands and surnames, and dividing the whole territory into five domains. The contents may be divided into five chapters:—the first, parr. 1—4, describing the mountains; the second, parr. 5—13, describing the rivers; the third, parr. 14, 15, containing a summary of all the labours of Yu, hitherto mentioned; the fourth, parr. 16—22, relating his other labours, how he gave lands and surnames, and divided the empire into five domains; and the fifth, par. 23, celebrating Yu's fame, and the completion of his work.

CH. I. THE RANGES OF MOUNTAINS ALONG WHICH YU OPERATED. It is difficult to know how we ought to translate 導 here. We can see how the term, signifying 'to lead,' 'to guide,' may be applied to streams; but there could be no *leading* of the great mountains. Ying-tă says:—'What was done on the hills was for the sake of the waters, and therefore it got the name of 導山.' In the dictionary, 導 is defined by 治, 'to regulate,' with reference to this passage, and on the ground, probably, assigned by Ying-tă. We should understand then, on this view, that Yu went along the mountains indicated, clearing the channels of innumerable small streams, which he conducted to the larger rivers whose names are given. But the question arises—when did he do this? Was it immediately after he divided the land, as mentioned Part i., p. 1? or was it while he was carrying out his operations in each province? It was not while he was operating in each province, for he then proceeded from east to west, and not, as here described, from west to east; and we have no reason to believe that any practical steps were taken till the work was begun at Hoo-k'ow. Part i., p. 3. Following the account of the regulation of the nine provinces, the paragraph here should describe what was done by Yu subsequent to that regulation; and in the first two chapters we seem to have a view of the position of the principal mountains, and the courses of the principal streams, as if Yu had paused to look back upon his work, and take a bird's-eye view of the country. We cannot suppose that he travelled again along the hills or the rivers, for in that case his toil would have been endless, and he must have gone again and again over the same ground. He surveyed mentally the mountains and rivers, and made delineations of them,—their ranges and courses. This is the meaning which I venture to attach to 導,=' to survey and describe.'

Sze-ma Ts'een between 導 and 岍 inserts 九山,—'He surveyed the mountains of the nine provinces.' So we must interpret 九山. Twenty-seven mountains are immediately specified; it is impossible that the mention of them should be preceded by a statement that Yu only dealt with 'nine mountains.' With regard to the order in which the mountains are enumerated, it has given occasion to divide them into different ranges. Ma Yung and Wang Suh considered that there were three;—the northern range (北條), embracing from mount K'een to Keĕ-shih; the middle range (中條), embracing from Se-k'ing to Pei-wei; and the southern range (南條), embracing the rest. Ch'ing K'ang-shing made four ranges of them (四列);—the northern (陰列), from K'een to Keĕ-shih; the next-northern (次陰), from Se-k'ing to Pei-wei; the next-southern (次陽), from Po-ch'ung to Ta-pëĕ; and the southern (正陽), from mount Min to Foo-tseën. His object, we can see, was to make these ranges correspond to the courses of the principal streams,—the Ho, the Hwae, the Han, and the Keang. Since the publication of Ts'ae's commentary, it is customary to speak only of two ranges, a northern and southern. This is only a simplification of K'ang-shing's arrangement.

P. 1. The mountains K'een, K'e, and King were all in Yung-chow,—all in the pres. Shen-se. The 'Statistical Account of the present dynasty' gives mount K'een (Keang Shing edits 岍 and not 岍) as in the west of the sub. dep. of Lung (隴州; lat. 34°48', N. 9°31', W.), dep. Fung-ts'ëang. Others have identified it with a mount Woo (吳山), in the south of the same Lung Chow. The authors of the Statistical Account say the two hills were anciently considered as one. K'e and King,—see Part i., p. 76. The former, like K'een, belongs to the dep. of Fung-ts'ëang. The latter, we saw, was in that of T'ung-chow. Hoo Wei observes that there were anciently three mountains called King:—that in the text, where Yu is said to have cast his nine famous vases (大禹鑄鼎處); that on the borders of the provv. Yu and King, where Pëen Ho found his famous gems. (卞和得玉處; see in the Biographical Dictionary [氏姓譜], surname 卞); the third, not mentioned in the Shoo, in the prov. of Yu, at a place referred to the pres. dep. of Shen (陝州), in Ho-nan, where Hwang-te is said to have cast some vases. 逾于河,—the point at which the Ho was crossed, or supposed to be crossed, is said to have been 35 *le* to the east of the district city of Chaou-yih (朝邑; lat. 34°48', N., lon. 6°26', W.), dep. of T'ung-chow. The phrase certainly reads as if an actual progress of Yu were described; but I must understand it as meaning simply that, had such a progress been made, the Ho must have been crossed here. 壺口,雷首,至于太岳,—壺口, see Part i., p. 4. 雷首 is in the south of the district of Yung-tse (永濟; lat. 34°54', N., lon. 6°13', W.), dep. of P'oo-chow (蒲州). The mountain received in course of time many names. Among them were those of mount Show (首), and Show-yang (首陽), at the foot of which Pih-e and Shuh-ts'e died of hunger (Ana. XVI. xii). 太岳,—see on 岳陽, Part i., p. 5. Yu had come south from Hoo-k'ow to Luy-show, and now again he turns north, in consequence of the urgency with which relief was called for from the capital. The T'ae-yoh is 30 *le* to the east of Hŏh-chow (霍州; lat. 36°34', N., lon. 4°45', W.). 厎柱,析城,至于王屋,—厎 (Sze-ma Ts'een has 砥)柱; Gan-kwŏ says on this, at par. 7, below, that it was the name of a mountain, where the waters of the Ho separated, and passed by, embracing the hill, so that it appeared in the waters like a pillar (山名,河水分流,包山而過,山見水中,若柱然). The place is now referred to the small dep. of Shen in Ho-nan, 40 *le* north-east from the dep. city, lat. 34°45', N., lon. 5°23', W., and is also called by the name of the 'Hill of the three Gates,' or Passages (三門山). The 'Book of the Waters' (水經注) says:—'When Yu was regulating the evils of the inundation, when he found a stream impeded by a mountain, he chiselled through it. So he cut through this hill of Te-choo, perforating it in three places called the "Three Passages."' Chaou

于碣石、入于海。○二節西傾、朱圉、鳥鼠、至于太華、熊耳、外方、桐柏、至于陪尾。○三節導嶓冢、至于荊山、內方、至于大別。○四節岷山之陽、至于衡山、過九江、至于敷淺原。○

2 *South from the Ho, he surveyed* Se-k'ing, Choo-yu, and Neaou-shoo, going on to T'ae-hwa; then Heung-urh, Wae-fang. T'ung-pih, from which he proceeded to Pei-wei.

3 He surveyed and described Po-ch'ung, going on to *the other* mount King; and Nuy-fang, from which he went to Ta-pëĕ.

4 He *did the same with* the south of mount Min, and then went on to mount Hăng. From this he crossed *the lake of* Kew-këang, and went on to the plain of Foo-tsëen.

Tung-he (趙冬曦), a writer of the T'ang dynasty, describes the hill of Te-ch'oo as consisting of six peaks, all rising up in the midst of the stream. On the most northern of them were two pillars, over against each other, standing up near the bank, and forming the passage of the 'Three Gates.' We cannot say what labours Yu performed at this point, nor what was the appearance presented in his time by the hill. Notwithstanding what he did, the Ho has here occasioned incalculable evil to the people, and incalculable trouble to the government. Hoo Wei has made a precis of attempts to overcome the natural difficulties of the passage, from the Han to the Sung dynasty, the result of which appears to have been to aggravate the evil rather than remove it.

The hill of Seih-shing is found in the dep. of Tsih-chow (澤州), in the south-west of the district of Yang-shing (陽城; lat. 35°26', N., lon. 3°52', W.). Wang-uh is in the dep. of Hwae-k'ing, in Ho-nan, 80 *le* to the west of the dis. city of Tse-yuen (濟源; lat. 35°7', N., lon. 3°49', W.). It extends to the borders of Yang-shing district, just mentioned, and presents an appearance as if it consisted of three storeys, like a house. 太行,恆山,至于碣石,入于海,—T'ae-hang is in the south of Fung-t'ae dis. (鳳臺) in Tsih-chow (lat. 35°30', N., 3°39', W.). South of it lies the district of Ho-nuy (河內), dep. of Hwae-k'ing, while, stretching along to the north-east, it touches in its range on the district of Ling-ch'uen (陵川), on the districts of Hoo-kwan (壺關), Loo-shing (潞城), and Le-shing (黎城), dep. of Loo-ngan (潞安), on the dis. of Woo-heang (武鄉) in Pe Chow (沁州), on the dis. of Ho-shun (和順) in Leaou Chow (遼州), and on that of Lŏ-p'ing (樂平) in P'ing-ting dep. It is called by a hundred different names in different parts of its range, but it is really the same mountain of T'ae-hang. 恆山,—see on Can. of Shun, par. 8. It is the northern mountain, the limit of Shun's excursions to the north, and according to the determination of the pres. dyn., is in about lat. 39°41', N., lon. 2°43', W. I don't know where Dr. Medhurst got the latitude which I have assigned to it from him on page 35. According to the geography of the Han dyn., we should look for mount Hăng in Keuh-yang dis. (曲陽; lat. 38°39', N., lon. 1°40', W.), dep. of Chin-ting, in Pih-chih-le. This opinion prevailed through many dynasties. In the Sung dynasty a more northern position began to be claimed for the northern hill, and the Ming dyn. decreed that the proper Hăng was in Shan-se. It did not, however, remove the sacrifices from Keuh-yang. This was done in the 17th year of Shun-che of the present dynasty. We must conclude that the decision of the Ming and the present dynasties is incorrect. The Hăng hill of Shan-se would take us away from the Ho, along which this range of hills is evidently laid down from K'ëen to Këe-shih.

碣石,—see on Part i., p. 11. I must believe that Këĕ-shih was something like Te-ch'oo, only not far from the mouth of the river.

Some would claim for the name the dignity of a mountain like T'ae-hang or Hăng, but this is no more necessary than that Te-ch'oo should have been equal to Seih-shing or Wang-uh. The rocks of Këĕ-shih were existing, it was seen, at the beginning of our era, but they have long disappeared before the encroachments of the sea. It is vain to attempt to lay down their place with nice precision. 入于海,—Ying-tă makes this phrase refer to the range of mountains, which here terminated in the sea. Hoo Wei contends on the other hand that we must understand it of Yu,—that it takes up 逾河, and tells us that Yu here took a boat, and went out some distance to take a survey of the rocks of Këĕ. The view which I have taken of 導 renders it unnecessary to suppose any personal action of Yu; but on the application of the phrase, I choose to agree with Ying-tă rather than with the modern scholar.

P. 2. 西傾,朱圉,鳥鼠,至于太華,—this par. contains the 'second row' of northern hills, according to K'ang-shing's phraseology. Tsăng Yen-ho observes that as no 導 precedes 西傾, we must bring the verb on from the commencement of the prec. par. We must do so, but we can hardly read the two paragraphs together. We have travelled from west to east; and now we return to the west again. 西傾,—see on Part i., p. 70. I have said there that it is often identified with mount Se-k'ing in the dis. of Chang, dep. of Kung-ch'ang. So it is in the Statistical Account of the Ming dyn., but that of the pres. dynasty says this is a mistake. The compilers of that find it rather beyond the extreme west of that dep., within the boundaries of Koko-nor, about 350 *le* to the south-east of the T'ing of T'aou-chow (洮州廳; lat. 34°35', N., lon. 12°57', W.). With them agree Hoo Wei and other scholars. This view is probably the correct one. The mountain has also the names of K'eang-t'ae (强臺), and Se-keang (西彊). 朱圉,—this mountain is 30 *le* to the south-west of the district of Fuh-keang (伏羌; lat 34°38', N., lon. 11°4', W.), in the depart. of Kung-ch'ang. Yen Jŏ-keu says that he visited the mountain, and found it of no very great size, having a reddish appearance; on a rock were the four words engraved—'Choo-yu fixed by Yu' (禹奠朱圉). 鳥鼠,—see on Part i., p. 76, and below, p. 12. The Wei had here its source. Hoo Wei observes at this point:—'Yu in his survey of the hills did not always go forward in a straight course, but went sometimes round about or retraced his steps. Thus instead of going east from Luy-show he went north to T'ae-yŏ, the urgent need of the capital requiring him to do so. As Neaou-shoo was on the east of the T'aou-water (洮水), Yu's most direct and convenient route would have been from Se-k'ing along that stream to Neaou-shoo, instead of which he first went to Choo-yu, and then retraced his way westwards to the other mountain. This is strange, and may lead us to suppose that the names of Choo-yu and Neaou-shoo have somehow changed places in the text.' 太華 is the 'western mountain' of the Canon of Shun, and the mount Hwa of Part i., p. 62. Between Neaou-shoo and T'ae-hwa were the hills of Shun-wuh and Chung-nan (Part i., p. 76), which are not mentioned here. 熊耳,外方,桐柏,至于陪尾,—熊耳 hill is in the south of Loo-she district (盧氏; lat. 34°1', N., lon. 5°32', W.), of Shen-chow, in Honan. There are two peaks, it is said, which rise up covered with verdure, and look like a bear's ears, from which it takes its name. Yu commenced his work on the Lŏ here;—see p. 13. 外方,—this mountain is identified with mount Ts'ung (嵩 or 崇山) in the district of Tăng-fung (登封; lat. 34°30', N., lon. 3°27', W.), dep. Ho-nan in Ho-nan prov. It has received also the names of Ts'ung-kaou (崇高) and T'ae-shih (太室). It came in subsequent times to be considered as the 'Central Mountain' (中嶽), and emperors still make progresses to it. 桐柏,—this mountain has given its name to the district of T'ung-pih (lat. 32°20', N., lon. 3°10', W.) in the dep. of Nan-yang (南陽) of Ho-nan. The Hwae has its source near to it;—see par. 11. Hoo Wei considers that two other hills,—Ta-fuh (大復) 30 *le* east of the dis. city, and T'ae-tsan (胎簪), 30 *le* to the north-west of it, are branches of T'ung-pih, and to be included in the name in the text. 陪尾,—Gan-kwŏ, referring Wae-fang, T'ung-pih, and Pei-wei, all to Yu-chow, sought for the last of them in the hill of Hwang-wei (横尾), 30 *le* to the north of the dis. city of Ngan-luh (安陸), dep. of Tih-ngan (德安), Hoo-pih, which he says the river Hwae passed by. But this was a mistake. Pei-wei is in Shan-tung, dep. of Yen-chow, and the district of Sze-shwuy (lat. 35°48', N., lon. 1°2', E.). The Sze-water (泗水) had here its sources. The 至于 before 陪尾 indicates that there was a considerable distance between it and the last named mountain of T'ung-pih.

P. 3. We return now to the west again, and have to do with the mountains of the southern range. 導嶓冢至于荆山,—嶓冢 see Part i., p 63, and below, p. 8. Ts'ae says that the appearance of the mountain was like a 冢, 'the tumulus of a grave,' and hence it was called Po-ch'ung. Gan-kwŏ on 岷嶓

五節導弱水、至于合黎、餘波入于流沙。○六節導黑水、至于三危、入于南海。○七節導河積石、

5 II. He surveyed the Weak-water as far as Hŏ-le, from which its superfluous waters went away among the Moving sands.

6 He surveyed the Black-water as far as San-wei, from which it went away to enter the southern sea.

旣藝 does not define the situation of mount Po, and Ying-tă, quoting from the Geography of Han, refers it to the tract of Lung-se (隴西郡). This was a mistake, and has occasioned much perplexity in subsequent works on the subject of this mountain, which is in the dep. of Han-chung, in Shen-se. 荊山, —see Part i, p 46. 內方至于大別,—Nuy-fang is identified with mount Chang (章山), in the south-west of the district of Chung-ts'eang,(鍾祥; lat. 31°12', N., lon. 3°57', W.), dep. of Ngan-luh in Hoo-pih. It was in King-chow. The Han passes near it. It is generally laid down in modern maps by the name of Ma-lang hill (馬㫘山). 大別 was also in King-chow. It is close by the dep. city of Han-yang (漢陽; lat. 30°34', N., lon. 2°18', W.), by the junction of the Han and the Këang;—see par. 8. There was also a 小別, 'the small Pëë,' in the district of Han-ch'uen (漢川).

Par. 4. We turn back again, and farther east. 岷 (in the Books of Han, 崏) 山之陽至于衡山,—岷山,—see on Part i., p. 63. Hoo Wei observes that there are four different mountains which are said now to represent the mount Min of the Shoo. The first is in the ward of Sung-p'wan—that described in the note just referred to; the second is in Mow Chow, called often 汶山, which name appears in that of Min-ch'uen district (汶川); the third is in the dis. of Kwan (灌縣), dep of Shing-too; and the fourth is in Min Chow(岷州), dep., of Kung-ch'ang in Kan-suh. Woo Ch'ing's observation is correct, that all the mountains near the sources of the Keang went by the common name of Min. We must bear in mind, however, that what he and others call the sources of the Keang are only sources of branches of it within the limits of China, and flowing from the north to meet the Këang of the 'Golden Sands,' which must be traced westwards to find the true springs of the great river. 衡山, —see on Part i., p. 46. In going on to this, Yu left the Këang five or six hundred *le* to the north. Gan-kwŏ very strangely says that the Këang passed by mount Hăng. 過九江至于敷淺原,—we saw, on Part i., p. 48, how it is all but impossible to come to a definite conclusion about what the Shoo calls the 'Nine Keang.' Whether what is now the T'ung-t'ing lake was intended by the phrase or not, however, the region indicated by it was not far from the site of that. Passing by this region, Yu went on to the plain of Foo-tseen, the place of which is about as difficult of determination. Gan-kwŏ says that this was also called the hill of Foo-yang (傅陽山), and this name conducts us to the district of Po yang in Jaou-chow, Keang-se. How there should be mention of a plain, while the discourse is of hills, it is not easy to see. I suppose that, in travelling north-east from mount Hăng, whatever hills there were up to the termination of the progress at Foo-tseen, were of so little note that it was not thought worth while to mention their names. From the P'ang-le eastwards the hills were so few or small, that here the survey of them was concluded.

Ch. II. The account of the rivers. We must continue here the same meaning which we have attached to 導 in the preceding paragraphs. It is not so absurd in itself, indeed, to speak of leading the waters of the streams as it is to speak of leading the hills; and 導 is used in this sense, as in 導菏澤被孟豬, Part i., p. 57. But we cannot admit that meaning here. In clearing the channels and conducting on the rivers, it was necessary for Yu to begin at the lowest part of their course, and gradually proceed towards their sources; and this he did, as we have seen in the details of his operations in the several provinces. Here, however, he goes from the source to the mouth,—evidently surveying the work that had been accomplished. Hoo Wei says:—'By his personal agency, or by the deputed services of his assistants, Yu had finished his work in the nine provinces, and now he took a boat, and went from the sources of the streams to see whether the work was properly done.' It is not necessary to suppose even this travelling, ac-

書經

cording to the view which I have taken. We have in the paragraphs simply a description of what would have been seen on such a survey.

P. 5. Sze-ma Ts'een, after 導 (with him, 道) has 九川, as we found the addition of 九山 in par. 1; and it so happens that only *nine rivers* are specified. Still the phrase 導九川 must be taken in analogy with 導九山, as speaking not of 'the nine rivers,' but of 'the rivers of the nine provinces.'

The Weak-water,—see on Part i., par. 73. Hŏ-le is the name of a hill rising in the north-west of the dis. of Chang-yih, and stretching along in a north-west direction from the dep. of Kan-chow into the adjoining one of Suh. The 'Statistical Account' gives it in both of the departments. The 'Geography Modernized' says:—'The Moving Sands lie beyond the pass of Kea-kuh' (嘉峪關) in Shen-se [this pass is in the north of Suh Chow, prov. of Kan-suh, at the termination of the great wall], from Soh-ko-ngoh-moo (索科鄂模) northwards, on the east as far as mount Ho-lan (賀蘭山), and on the west as far as the borders of the discontinued Sha-chow (西至廢沙州界; Sha-chow has again been replaced as the Ward of Sha-chow [沙州衛] by the pres. dynasty, in the extreme west of Ngan-se dep.). They extend from north to south more than 1,000 *le*, and from east to west several hundred *le*. The sand rises up and moves or flows along before the wind. Everywhere in the tract indicated this is to be seen.' In the rough map of China and its territories in the 'Universal Geography' (瀛環志略), published by Seu (徐繼畬), the governor of Fuh-këen in 1849, these moving sands are laid down very distinctly. On the east and north they are called Han-hae (瀚海), and on the west the deserts of Gobi (戈壁). The description of the Weak-water in the 'Statistical Account' does not enable us to understand the text, which Hoo Wei has conceived and described in the following way, from a study of all the references to it in older books:—Finding its waters near its source in a troubled condition and flowing eastwards, Yu conducted them from the hill of K'eung-shih (窮石), where they had their origin, north and west to the hill of Hŏ-le. There the main stream took a turn to the north-east, and proceeded to the marsh of Keu-yen (居延澤), which was among the moving sands,—what is called, in the preceding extract from the 'Geography Modernized' Soh-ko-ngoh-moo. But there were times when its waters were so swollen, that instead of all flowing east from the passage in the Hŏ-le hills, a portion overflowed and went westwards. These were the 'superfluous waters' of the text, and they were led away to the west, and lost in the sands of what is now the desert of Gobi. All this is ingeniously conceived and supported; but any distinct traces of this labour of Yu can hardly be expected to be discernible after the lapse of so long a time.

P. 6. The subject of the Blackwater is quite as difficult as that of the Weakwater;—see on Part i., p. 71. There it is given as the western boundary of Yung-chow, corresponding to the western Ho. But on the west of Kan-suh we find no stream answering at all to this description. Black-waters there are, besides that which is given as the boundary of Yung-chow, about ten in number, but not one of them satisfies the requisitions of the text. The last particular stated,—that the Black-water flowed to the southern sea, proves, indeed, that there could have been no such stream in the quarter assigned to the hill of San-wei. In his comments on the 'Book of the Waters,' Le Taou-yuen says:—'The Black-water took its rise in Fowl-hill of Chang-yih, and flowing south to T'un-hwang passed by San-wei, from which it went away still south to the southern sea; but Chang-yih and T'un-hwang were both on the north of the Ho. The way in which the Black-water was able to cross the Ho, and proceed to the southern sea, was that westward from Tseih-shih the course of the Ho is often under ground, so that another stream might flow over it towards the south.' This view is absurd enough. There are no recent observations to support it. After taking the Black-water in this way across the Ho, it would still be necessary to carry it over the main stream of the Këang.

Hoo Wei, seeing that this account could not be adopted, supposes that the stream turned west after passing the hill of San-wei, and after getting beyond the sources of the Ho and the Këang, flowed south again, and entered the southern sea. Of course in thus writing, he knows not what he writes about. Of the rivers flowing south into the sea to the west of China there are the May-këang, or River of Cambodia, the Mei-nam of Siam, the Salween, and the Irawaddy. Many have tried to identify the Black-water with the first of these, which rises in Tibet, and flows through Yun-nan as the Lan-ts'ang (瀾滄江). Here is a river certainly which flows into the southern sea, but the northern part of it can in no ways be made into a boundary of Yung-chow.

Yu's geographical knowledge certainly was at fault in the case of the Black-water. Referring back to Part i., p. 62, where we saw reason to believe that the river of this name there mentioned was the southern boundary of Lëang-chow, and correctly identified with the 'Golden Sands,' or a portion of it, the main stream of the Keang. Now the 'Golden Sands' was known as the Black-water only after it had received the Shing, the Jŏ and the Loo. The Loo, moreover, has itself the name of the Black-water. We can conceive that this was supposed to extend indefinitely to the north, and run along both Lëang-chow and Yung-chow. This would enable us to believe that Yu, or whoever compiled this Book from his memoranda and reports, had the idea, however erroneous, of only one stream in his mind, when speaking of the boundaries of the two provinces. But after this simplification there remains the point of the

至于龍門、南至于華陰、東至于厎柱、又東至于孟津、東過洛汭、至于大伾、北過洚水、至于大陸、又北播為九河、同為逆河、入于海。○

7 He surveyed the Ho from Tseih-shih as far as Lung-mun; and thence, southwards, to the north of mount Hwa; eastward then to Te-ch'oo; eastward again to the ford of Măng; eastwards still he passed the junction of the Lŏ, and went on to Ta-pei. From this the course was northwards, past the Keang-water, on to Ta-luh; north from which the stream was distributed and became the nine Ho, which united again and formed the meeting Ho, when they entered into the sea.

river's flowing to the southern sea. That cannot be got over. There is here a very serious error in the details of the Shoo.

P. 7. *The course of the Ho.* 導河積石至于龍門,—on Tseih-shih, see Part i., p. 82, where its position is given as on the north-west of Ho Chow in the dep. of Lan-chow (蘭州). The compilers of the Statistical Account of the present dynasty, however, place it much farther off, and give it within the boundaries of the territory of Ts'ing-hae (青海) or Koko-nor. The mountain of Ho Chow was indeed, they say, called Tseih-shih as well as the other, but was distinguished from it by the prefix of 'little' (小積石), while the more western one was called the 'great.' Hoo Wei agrees in this view; and if it be correct, then Yu must have proceeded, or at least penetrated by his assistants, a long way west beyond the boundaries of the present China proper. But if he got as far as the 'Snowy Mountain' (雪山),—which I find it difficult to believe, he was still distant from the sources of the Ho. Those are in the extreme west of the Koko-nor. The stream at first and, indeed, through most of its progress in the Koko-nor, is called the river of O-urh-tan (阿爾但河). It is not till it has pursued a tortuous course of more than 2,300 *le* to the fortified post of Kwei-tih (貫德堡), that it receives the name of the 'Yellow River' (黃河). A further progress of between 400 and 500 *le* brings it to the pass of Tseih-shih, flowing past which it enters the boundaries of Ho Chow.

[The Chinese Government cannot be said to have been indifferent to the discovery of the sources of the Ho. The Han, the T'ang, and the Yuen dynasties sent out special officers to trace the stream to its fountain-head. The emperor K'ang-he of the present did the same. We should read the reports of their expeditions with more interest, if it were not for the uncouth form which the names of the mountains and rivers of the Koko-nor assume when represented by Chinese characters. After all that the Chinese themselves have done, much distinction yet awaits the explorer from the west who shall visit the springs of this most fast-rushing and unmanageable of the great rivers of our globe.]

Lung-mun,—see on Part i., p. 82. The Ho, after entering Kan-suh in Ho Chow, flows east and north through the dep. of Lan-chow, and passes into that of Ning-hea (寧夏). This it traverses, now outside, now inside the great wall, going more north than east, and, at length, east of the district of P'ing-lo (平羅; lat. 38°52', N., lon. 4°22', W.), it goes again beyond the great wall into the country of the Ortous Mongols (鄂爾多斯界), which it quite embraces, only entering China proper again in Yu-lin (榆林), the north-eastern department of Shen-se. After this it flows south, sometimes inclining to the west, to the hill of Lung-mun, dep. of T'ung-chow. Hoo-k'ow, we saw, was somewhat to the north of Lung-mun, on the eastern or Shan-se side of the river; and hereabouts Yu commenced his labours. From Tseih-shih to Lung-mun, along the course of the Ho, is a distance of more than 3,000 *le*.

南至于華陰,—華陰 must be translated 'the north of mount Hwa;' see on Part i., p. 62. There is now the district city of Hwa-yin, but there could be no such place in

書經

Yu's time. The north of mount Hwa is specified, as marking the point at which the Ho turned from its southern course to proceed east. Here also we must suppose that Yu had to put forth his skill and resources in its regulation.

東至于厎柱,—see on par. 1. 又東至于孟津,—'the ford of Măng' still gives its name to the district of Măng (孟縣; lat. 34°55′, N., lon. 3°38′, W.), dep. of Hwae-k'ing in Ho-nan. The whole name, indeed, remains in a district of Ho-nan dep., which borders with the dis. of Măng on the north and east, the Ho being between them. The ford is about 20 *le* to the south of the dis. city of Măng. Lin Che-k'e supposes that it was not till he reached this point that Yu found it possible to ford the Ho; but there were during the Chow dynasty other fords between this and Te-ch'oo. Măng was most conveniently situated with reference to the capital. This is the reason why it is specified. 東過洛汭,—see on Part i., p. 55. Here, with reference to the stream of the Ho, we may very well read 洛汭 as in the translation. Elsewhere, as in Book III. par. 3, we must render differently. At the place of junction of the two streams, Yu must have performed some labour. 至于大伾,—the character 伾 is disputed. 岯, 坯, 陫, and 邳, all have their advocates. Connected with the form of the character are the opinions as to whether we should regard 大伾 as the name of a district or place, or of a hill. We may acquiesce in the conclusion of the Statistical Account of the present dynasty that we are to find it in the present Le hill (黎山), 20 *le* to the south-east of the dis. city of Seun (濬縣; lat. 35° 45′, N., lon. 1°38′, W.), in the dep. of Wei-hwuy of Ho-nan. [This is a recent arrangement; this dis. used to be reckoned in the dep. of Ta-ming, Chih-le.] From the ford of Măng to this point, the Ho had been gradually bending northwards. 北過洚水,至于大陸,—the Keang-water [洚 should probably be 降; in the Statistical Account we have 絳] rises in the south-west of the dis. of Chun-lew (屯留), dep. of Loo-ngan in Shan-se, and flowing into the dis. of Loo-shing (潞城), joins the 'Muddy Chang,' (濁漳), which, according to the Geography Modernized, is in consequence also called the Keang-water (降水). This river flowing east entered the Ho of Yu between Ta-pei and Ta-luh. The particular point was probably in the district of Fei-heang (肥鄉), dep. of Kwang-p'ing. Ta-luh,—see on Part i. par. 9. There, however, we have to take 大陸 as the name of a district; here we have to think of some definite place, to be found probably in the district of Ping-heang (平鄉; lat. 37°2′, N., lon. 1°23′, W.), 11 *le* to the north of which we have the site of the old city of Keu-luh. 又北播爲九河,—see on Yen-chow, Part i., par. 13. The successive changes in the course of the main stream of the Ho, and encroachments of the sea since the time of Yu, make it impossible for us now to ascertain those nine streams. The same things also render the rest of the paragraph difficult of elucidation. 同爲逆河,入于海,—it would seem from this that the nine Ho again united their waters, and formed one great river which seemed to contend with the advancing waves of the sea. The union of so many streams in one before entering the sea is difficult to suppose in the circumstances. Can we suppose that by the 逆河 is meant the coast water all along the space included between the Ho and its extreme southern branch, kept in a constant state of agitation by so many channels emptying themselves into it at no great distance from one another? This appears to be what in subsequent times was called the Pŏ-hae (渤海).

[It is clear from the above details that we cannot look for the Ho of Yu on the present face of the country. As it received the Chang river, however, before reaching Ta-luh, which still pursues its course to the sea, and enters it in the dep. of T'een-tsin, we may suppose that the north-eastern part of the Ho's course was not much difft. from the present course of the Chang.
By the time of the famous duke Hwan of Ts'e in the Chow dyn., B.C. 684–642, of the nine Ho all but one had disappeared, and not long after, B.C. 601, in the 5th year of the emp. Ting (定王), 1675 years, acc. to the 'Annals of the various dynn.,' after Yu's labours, the first great change in the course of the stream took place. This, however, did not affect its northern portion. The main stream broke off, not far from Ta-pei, and after running for some time in the T'ă (漯川), broke off from it again, and proceeding east and north, rejoined the Chang, and went on as before to the sea. A second change, more extensive, took place more than 600 years later. In the third year of the usurper Mang (王莽), A.D. 11, the channel from the T'ă northwards disappeared, and the Ho, now in the channel of the Tă and now north of it, flowed east to the sea, which it entered in the pres. district of Le-tsin (利津; lat. 37°32′, N., lon. 1°52′, E.), dep. of Woo-ting (武定), Shantung. For more than 1000 years a struggle was maintained to prevent the stream from going further south, but in A.D. 1194, the main stream broke off in the dep. of Wei-hwuy in Ho-nan, about the district of Sin-heang (新鄉; lat. 35°22′, N., lon. 2°22′, W.), and flowing east and north as far mount Lëang (梁山),

八節

嶓冢導漾、東流爲漢、又東爲滄浪之水、過三澨、至于大別、南入于江、東匯澤爲彭蠡、東爲北江、入于海。○

8 From Po-ch'ung he surveyed the Yang, which, flowing eastwards, became the Han. Farther east, it became the water of Ts'ang-lang; and after passing the three great dykes, went on to Ta-pëe, southwards from which it entered the Keang. Eastward still, and whirling on, it formed the marsh of P'ang-le; and from that its eastern flow was the northern Këang, as which it entered the sea.

in the dis. of Show-chang (壽張), dep. of Yen-chow, it there divided into two branches, one flowing north and east, and entering the sea in the dis. of Le-tsin, the other going east and south till it joined the Hwae, and went on in its channel to the sea. After this, the northern branch gradually became less and less. During the Yuen and Ming dynasties, The Ho finally broke off in the district of Yung-tsih (滎澤), dep. of K'ae-fung, and proceeded east with a very gradual inclination to the south till it joined the Hwae. I have not met with an account of the changes which it has undergone since. Until within a few years it discharged itself into the sea by the old channel of the Hwae.]

P. 8. *The course of the Han.* 嶓冢導漾 (in Sze-ma Ts'een and others, 瀁), 東流爲漢,—see on Part i., p. 63. It is there stated that there were two mountains called Po-ch'ung, one in Kan-suh, in the small dep. of Ts'in (秦州). 60 *le* to the south-east of the dep. city, in which what is called the Western Han (西漢水) takes its rise. Flowing through Ts'in Chow and Keae Chow (階州) into Sze-ch'uen, it is lost in the Kea-ling, which proceeding south through the departments of Paou-ning (保寧), and Shun-k'ing (川慶), enters the Keang, near the dep. city of Chung-k'ing (重慶; lat. 29°42', N., lon. 9°48', W.). The Geography of the Han supposed that this western Han was the Yang of the text, and that we were to look for the Po-ch'ung mountain in the pres. Kan-suh. But there is no connection between the two Hans;—there is none now, nor is it likely that there ever was. The mistake made in the Han dynasty has led to much perplexity and debate on the sentence under notice. The Po-ch'ung of Yu was, no doubt, the mountain in the north of Ning-këang Chow (寧羌州), dep. of Han-chung. Here the Han rises, and for some time after issuing from its springs it was called the Yang. Flowing east along the south of the district of Mëen (沔縣), it passes the dep. city in the dis. of Nan-ch'ing (南鄭), whereabouts the name of Yang ceased, and was superseded by that of Han. From the dep. of Han-chung, the Han passes into that of Hing-ngan, out of which it proceeds from Shen-se into Hoo-pih in the dep. of Yun-yang (鄖陽) Entering from this that of Seang-yang in the sub. dep. of Keun (均州), it took the name of the Water of Ts'ang-lang:—又東爲滄浪之水. There was an island here according to Le Taou-yuen in the middle of the stream, called Ts'ang-lang (漢水中有洲, 曰滄浪洲), which gave occasion to the name which was retained to the junction of its waters with the Keang. It is perhaps a more likely account of the name, that it was given to the stream here from the bluish tinge of its waters. 過三澨至于大別, 南入于江,—this describes the course of the stream from Keun Chow till it mingles its waters with the Heang. On Ta-pëe, see on par. 3. The only difficulty is with 三澨, which Ts'ae says was the name of a stream, or streams. Such also was the view of the older commentators,—Gan-kwŏ, Ch'ing Heuen, Ma Yung, and Wang Suh. The 說文, however, defines 澨 as 'a large dyke on a river's bank where people could dwell' (埤增水邊, 土人所止). This meaning is the better established of the two. Hoo Wei fixes on three points, all in the pres. district of Seang-yang, where he supposes three dykes to have been raised to sustain the impetus of the waters entering the Han, and considers them to be the positions indicated in the text. 東匯澤爲彭蠡, 東爲北江, 入于海,—these clauses present

九節 岷山導江，東別爲沱，又東至于澧，過九江，至于東陵，東迆北會于匯，東爲中江，入于海。○十節 導沇水，東流爲

9 From mount Min he surveyed the Këang, which branching off to the east formed the T'o; eastward again it reached the Le; after this it passed the nine Këang; and flowing eastward and winding to the north, it joined *the Han* in its eddying movements; from that its eastern flow was the middle Këang, as which it entered the sea.

10 He surveyed the Yen water, which flowing eastward became the Tse, and entered the Ho. *Thereafter* it flowed out, and became the

no small difficulties. First, the waters of the Han have now mingled with the Këang;—why should it still be spoken of as if it were a distinct stream? Second, the P'ang-le lake has its own sources and feeders, independent of the Këang, and is moreover a very considerable distance from the river;—it cannot with propriety be represented as being formed by the Han and Këang. Laborious efforts have been made to clear up these points,—with some, but by no means complete, satisfactoriness. I apprehend that the face of the country changed very considerably during the 2,000 years and more that elapsed between Yu and the Han dynasty; whether the changes can still be traced remains to be seen:—see what was said on the nine Keang, pp. 113, 114. The way in which Chinese scholars have dealt with the difficulties of the text will be seen from the two following quotations. First, on the second perplexity which I have indicated, Choo-foo-tsze says:—'The marshing of P'ang-le took place, indeed, to the south of the great Keang. But it did so in consequence of the nature of the ground, which high in the north and low in the south impeded the discharge of the waters from the P'ang-le. Unable to find a sufficient vent, they gathered themselves up, and spread abroad in the form of the lake which we have, several hundred *le* in extent.' Again, on the whole passage Woo Ch'ing has said:—'The Han flowing south enters into the Keang, and then along the northern bank of the Keang, flows eastward, the northern portion of the Keang, and so enters the sea (東行爲江之北，而入于海). But the Han having once entered the Keang, the two became one stream, and yet it is here said—"it flowed eastward as the northern Keang," as if there were still a separate stream;—how is this to be accounted for? Let us bear in mind that the sources of the Han were remote, and its stream great, barely second to the Keang, and all but its peer. Another way of speaking was necessary here than the style usual on the junction of a small stream with a large one; and hence in Part i., p. 47, the Keang and the Han are both mentioned as pursuing their common course to the sea. The Keang is not permitted to absorb both the waters and the name of the Han, but the Han shares in the name of the Këang, becomes in fact "the northern Keang." There are again "the four principal rivers" whose discharge from their basins into the sea is commemorated (記其入海者，著其爲瀆也). Three of them are just one stream, but the fourth is twice commemorated,—as the Keang, and also as the Han. Not that the Ho, for instance, did not carry with it to the sea the waters of many other rivers, but they are all small as compared with it, and might be supposed to be swallowed up in it; but not so with the Han and the Keang. The former must still retain an individuality to the last.'

P. 9. *The course of the Keang.* 岷山導江，東別爲沱，—see on Part i., pp. 49, 63, and 64; and on par. 3 of this Part. At whatever point in the range of hills going by the name of Min, this branch of the Keang takes its rise, it appears in the north-west of Sze-ch'uen, and flows south through the Ward of Sung-p'wan into the small dep. of Mow (茂州). Thence flowing more easterly, it enters the dept. of Ching-too, and in passing through the district of Kwan (灌縣; lat. 30°59', N., lon. 12°46', W.), it throws off the first T'o, often called the river of Pe (郫江), because it immediately passes on the east through the dis. of that name. It goes on south of the small dep. of Mei (眉州); thence through the dep. of Kea-ting (嘉定), to that of Seu-chow (敘州), not far from which (lat. 28°38', N., lon. 11°43', W.) it receives, we are told, the river of Ma-hoo (馬湖). It would be more correct to say that here it joins *the* Keang, the river of the 'Golden Sands' which received the waters of the Ma-hoo not long before. From this point the course of the stream is eastwards, and generally with a gradual inclination to the north. First it traverses the small dep. of Loo (瀘州), on the south-east of the dep. city of which (lat. 28°56′, N., lon. 10°55′, W.) it again receives the T'o, which has collected various streams in its course. From this it proceeds east and north through the depp. of Chung-k'ing (重慶) and K'wei-chow (夔州), and in the Fung-tsëë (奉節) dis. of the latter, it threw off at one time a second T'o. This was the E-water (夷水), which left the Këang at this point, and flowing to the south-east was joined by a stream from the dep. of She-nan (施南) in Hoo-pih, with which it went away east-ward, and rejoined the Këang, which has passed from Sze-ch'uen into Hoo-pih,—rejoined it, after passing the districts of Pa-tung (巴東) and Ch'ang-yang (長陽), dep. of E-ch'ang (宜昌), close by the district city of E-too (宜都), dep. of King-chow. At this point the river from She-nan still flows into the Këang, but the branch which flowed off from the great stream in Fung-tsëë district has long been dried up. I have abridged the above details from the 禹貢錐指. They bring the present course of the Min-keang sufficiently well before us. From the text, however, one gets the impression that, if the main stream was not called by the name of the T'o, it was the branch or branches so styled which engaged the chief attention of Yu.

又東至于澧,過九江,至于東陵,—the former clause left as near the district city of E-too, lat. 30°28′, N., lon. 5°9′, W. This brings us to Pa-ling the chief city and district of the dep. of Yŏ-chow (岳州府巴陵縣), lat. 29°24′, N., lon. 3°33′, W. In Yu's time, 東陵, 'the eastern hill,' would simply be the name of the hill which now occupies the south-western part of the dep. city, called Pa-ling, Pa-k'ew (巴邱), and T'een-yŏ (天岳). Among the old interpreters there is a difference of view, whether 澧 (Sze-ma Ts'een and the Books of Han read 醴) is the name of a hill or of a stream; and Ch'ing lays down a canon, which must be considered arbitrary, to settle the point. He says that in this Book after 過 and 會 we have the names of rivers, but after 至 the names of hills or marshes. Whichever we understand by the term, the name remains in the small dep. of Le, the chief city of which is in lat. 29°37′, N., lon. 4°45′, W. We have also the Le-water, which rising in the dis. of Yung-ting (永定), in the extreme west of the dep., flows eastwards through the whole of it, and passes into Hwa-yung (華容) dis., dep. of Yŏ-chow, where it flows into the T'ung-t'ing lake. Of the 'nine Këang' enough has been already said. This passage certainly assigns the place of them near where the T'ung-t'ing lake is. The great difficulty in my way against acceding to the view of the Sung scholars is that neither here nor elsewhere in the Tribute of Yu are the 'nine Keang' spoken of as a marsh or lake.

東迆北會于匯,—this clause is attended with no little difficulty. Gan-kwŏ took 迆 in the sense of 溢 'to overflow,' and says that 'the stream, overflowing as it went east, divided into separate channels, which all went north and united to form the P'ang-le' (東溢分流,都共北會爲彭蠡). Woo Ch'ing, ingeniously but too violently, removed the clause 東匯澤爲彭蠡, and read it after the text—東迆北會于匯,東匯澤爲彭蠡. 匯 is then a name, in the first place, for the meeting of the Han and Keang, and in the next for the stream of their united waters. These attempts at explanation only show the difficulty of the text. We must suppose that in this par. the Shoo takes no notice of the junction of the Han and the Këang, but the 匯 in it and the prec. par. have the same reference,—are to be understood of the turbulence of the united streams, which caused the formation of the P'ang-le. This turbulence, however, is primarily predicated of the Han, and here the Keang is supposed by an eastward course, winding (迆) to the north, to merge its waters at that point in those of the Han. 東爲中江,入于海,—Gan-kwŏ says:—' We had the northern *Këang*; here we have the middle one; that there was a southern one is plain' (有北,有中,南可知). The Han was called the northern Keang in the last par., after its junction with the great stream. Here the great stream after leaving the P'ang-le, or the point at which the waters which formed it tried to discharge themselves, is called the middle Keang. Possibly, the portion of those waters which did enter may be regarded as the southern Këang, or southern part of the river. Still as the Shoo makes no mention of a southern Këang, we need not trouble ourselves with it. We get the idea certainly of one stream flowing to the sea from this point, and I conclude that the three Keang of Yang-chow (Part i., p. 40) have nothing to do with the Yang-tsze.

P. 10. *The course of the Tse.* What is most remarkable in the account of this river is that it is described as first on the north of the Ho, then crossing that powerful stream, and re-appearing on the south of it. The former part of it is called by Woo Ch'ing 'the northern Tse,' the latter, 'the southern.' The name of the Tse still remains north of the Ho. On the south it has long been lost, but the ancient course of the stream must have been much the same as that of the present Seaou Ts'ing (小清河).

濟、入于河、溢爲滎、東出于陶丘北、又東至于菏、又東北會于汶、又北、東入于海。十一節導淮自桐柏、東會于泗沂、東入于海。○十二節導渭自鳥鼠同穴、東會于灃、又東會于涇、又東過漆沮、入于河。○十三節導洛自熊耳、東北會于澗瀍、又東會于伊、又東北入于河。

Yung *marsh*. Eastward, it issued forth on the north of Taou-k'ew, and flowed further east to the *marsh of* Ko. North-east from this it united with the Wăn, and after flowing north went eastwards on to the sea.

11 He surveyed the Hwae from *the hill of* T'ung-pih. Flowing east, it united with the Sze and the E; and with an eastward course *still* entered the sea.

12 He surveyed the Wei from Neaou-urh-tung-heuĕ. Flowing eastwards it met with the Fung, and eastwards again with the King. Farther east still, it passed the Tseih and the Tseu; and entered the Ho.

13 He surveyed the Lŏ from Heung-urh. Flowing to the north-east, it united with the Këen and the Ch'ëen; eastwards still, it united with the E; and then on the north-east entered the Ho.

導沇水, 東流爲濟, 入于河,—the Statistical Account says of the Tse-water, under the dep. of Hwae-k'ing in Honan:—'It has another name, that of the Yen-water. It rises in the hill of Wang-uh, in the west of the dis. of Tse-yuen, and flowing east along the north of the district, it passes with a south-east course through the north of the district of Măng, and on to the Ho.' There is another stream,—'the Wide Tse' (廣濟),—in the same department, having a longer course very much parallel to this, and more to the east, which some would rather identify with the river of the text. It is not worth the time and space to enter into the discussions of the critics on the subject. For some time after leaving its source the stream was called the Yen, but ere long it was known as the Tse, and soon lost in the Ho. **溢爲滎**,—here Gan-kwŏ says:—'The Tse having entered the Ho flows along with it ten *le* and more, and then shooting across to its south bank, flows along with it again for several *le*, and issues out, as the marsh of Yung, on the south-east of Gaou-ts'ang' (在敖倉東南). All this, about a small stream like the Tse entering a mass of fast-rushing water like the Ho, and yet preserving itself distinct, &c., is absurd. Yung is the same as the marsh of Yung-po, Part i., p. 56;—see the note on that par. **溢** must be understood as flowing out, not from the river but from the ground. The water of the marsh was most likely derived from the Ho, finding its way by some underground communication to the place, but we cannot suppose for a moment that the water of the marsh was that of the Tse, flowing into the Ho from the north and passing through it. 東出于陶丘北,又東至于菏,—陶丘 = 'the small hill of T'aou.' A hill that seems to be composed of two parts, rising like storeys one above the other, is called 陶丘(再成爲陶丘,再成,其形再重也). The name remains in the district of Ting-t'aou (定陶; lat. 35°11', N., lon. 44', W.), dep. of Yen-chow, the hill being 7 *le* to the south-west of the district city. The hill of T'aou was about 500 *le* from the Yung marsh, and here again there bubbled up a spring from the ground, which was strangely supposed to be the waters of the Tse reappearing after so long a subterranean travel. Woo Ch'ing says that the 出 should lead us to think of a well-spring, sending up its waters to the surface from its own bosom. These waters flowed away to the marsh of Ko which they served to augment;—see Part i., p. 57. 又東北會于汶,—the waters of what we may now call the Southern Tse flowed through the marsh of Ko, and on the north-east of it were met by those of the Wăn-water, which is now one of the feeders of the Grand Canal;—see on Part i., p. 27. 又北,東入于海,—the Tse, augmented now by the Wăn, flowed north as far as about the pres. district city of Yang-kuh (陽穀; lat. 36°9', N., lon. 29', W.), and then pursued its way to the sea, very much in the course of the present Seaou-ts'ing (小淸), the name of 淸, 'clear,' having taken its rise from the purity for which the waters of the Tse had always been famous.

P. 11. *The course of the Hwae.* The Hwae rises in the hill of T'ung-pih (see on par. 2), Honan prov., dep. of Nan-yang, dis. of T'ung-pih (lat. 32°20', N,, lon. 3°10', W.). It met with the united streams of the E and the Sze (see on Part i., par. 30) in Keang-soo, dep. of Hwae-ngan, dis. of Ts'ing-ho (lat. 33°35', N., lon. 2°34', E.), and from that point went on east to the sea. The eastern portion of the Hwae's course is now very much changed. From the dis. of T'ung-pih, dep. Nan-yang, it flows east and north through the small dep. of Kwang, where it receives the Joo (汝水), and from the dis. of Koo-ch'e (固始; lat. 32°18', N., lon. 51', W.). it passes into Ngan-hwuy. Entering this prov. in the dep. of Ying-chow (潁州), it traverses it, flowing nearly due east, and collecting many waters, to the small dep. of Sze (泗州; lat. 35°8', lon. 1°52', E.) when it passes through the lake of the 'Great marsh' (洪澤湖), which may be said to be formed by it, into Keang-soo, and from which lake on the north-east it discharges itself again into the Yellow River, in the dis. of Ts'ing-ho, dept. Hwae-ngan. Thenceforth its course is lost in that of the Ho. At the same point the Grand Canal also issues from the Ho, so that we may say there is a connection between the Hwae and the Yang-tsze, which we saw, Part i., p. 45, began to be established in the Chow dynasty. On the northern side of the Ho, the canal now receives the waters of the E and the Sze, which used to flow into the Hwae. In the mention of both the E and the Sze, after their waters had been blended together, Woo Ch'ing finds a case analogous to that of the Han's retaining its individuality after joining the Keang, as in p. 8. The streams, he says, were of about equal size, and therefore the name of each must be preserved. The whole course of the Hwae from T'ung-pih to the sea is about 1,800 *le*.

P. 12. *The course of the Wei.* See on Part i., pp. 73–75. The river rises in the hill of Neaou-shoo-t'ung-heuĕ, in the west of the district of Wei-yuen (渭源), dep. of Lan-chow, Kan-suh. In par. 2, and Part i., p. 76, the mountain is called Neaou-shoo, but here we have its full name, meaning 'Bird and Rat in the Same Hole.' Gan-kwŏ, with his fondness for the marvellous, says that 'a bird and a rat lived in the same holes on this mountain, and paired together as male and female.' The Urh-ya had said that 'a bird called T'oo (鵌), and a rat, called Tuh (鼵), lived here together in the same hole.' This is conceivable; the addition of their pairing is of course absurd. From Lan-chow dep. the river flows into that of Kung-ch'ang, and thence to the small dep. of Ts'in (秦州), from which it passes into Shen-se, the whole of which it traverses till it meets the Ho at the termination of its southward flow. The whole length of its course is now under 1,500 *le*, whereas in the Han dynasty it was given as nearly 1,900. It may have altered its course in some parts.

P. 13. *The course of the Lŏ.* See on Part i., p. 55. 熊耳,—see on par. 2. The Heung-urh hill there mentioned is, no doubt, that of the text, from which Yu began his survey of the Lŏ; but the sources of the stream are more distant, in the small dep. of Shang, in Shen-se, as stated on Part i., p. 55. There is also a Heung-urh hill there, distinguished from this by the prefix of 'Western.' According to the Geography of the Han dynasty, the course of the Lŏ was altogether 1,970 *le*.

十四節 九州攸同、四隩既宅、九山刊旅、九川滌源、九澤既陂、四海會同。○十五節 六府孔修、庶土交正、厎慎財賦、咸則三壤、成賦中邦。○

14 III. *Thus*, throughout the nine provinces a similar order was effected:—the grounds along the waters were everywhere made habitable; the hills were cleared of their superfluous wood and sacrificed to; the sources of the streams were cleared; the marshes were well banked; access to the capital was secured for all within the four seas.

15 A great order was effected in the six magazines *of material wealth;* the different parts of the country were subjected to an exact comparison, so that contribution of revenue could be carefully adjusted according to their resources. The fields were all classified with reference to the three characters of the soil; and the revenues for the Middle region were established.

Ch. III. Pp. 14, 15. A summary of the labours of Yu thus far described. 14. 九州攸同,—this clause is a summary of the whole par.; the other clauses give the particulars of the general order which was established. The phrase 攸同 occurred before, where after Gan-kwŏ, I explained 攸 by 所, its frequent synonym;—see Part i., p. 75. K'ung seems to take the character in the same way here, his comment on the clause being—所同事在下, 'the particulars in which they were made to agree are given below.' This is forced, however. The dict. gives 攸 as sometimes merely 'a helping word' (語助詞), an expletive, and quotes from the She King, Part III., Bk. I., Ode x., stt. 4,5, 四方攸同, which is much akin to the text. We may consider the 攸 therefore as simply supplying the place of the copula. The nine Chow are of course the nine provinces described in Part i. 洲 and 州 were originally interchangeable; and the Urh-ya defines 洲 as 'inhabitable gronnd in the midst of water,' (水中可居者). Now all the habitable ground the ancient Chinese knew was conceived of as surrounded by water, and hence it was called a 州 or continent, and the subdivision was again made of the nine Chow, embracing the empire proper;—see Hoo Wei *in loc.* 四隩既宅,—隩, see Can. of Yaou, p. 7. But we must seek for a different meaning here. That which I have adopted is after Le Seun (李巡), who says:—涯內近水爲隩. Under Yen-chow we are told, Part i., p. 16, that the people could come down from the heights and dwell on the low ground, and under Yung-chow (p. 78), that the country about San-wei was made habitable; the text says that throughout the nine provinces all the low ground near the streams that had formerly been inhabited was recovered from the waters 四隩=四方之隩. This is better than to take it, with Ts'ae and the Daily Explanation, as=四海之隩. 九山刊旅,—九山=九州之山;—see the Introduction to Ch. I. Wang Ts'ëaou (王樵) says:—'刊 and 旅, describing the beginning and end of the work on the hills, embrace all the operations on them. The cutting down the wood was the first step in the regulation of the waters; the sacrificing was the announcement of the completed work.' On 旅, see on Part i., pp. 65,76.

九川滌源,—九川=九州之川; see on par. 5. 滌源, 'had their

錫土姓。（十六節）○祗台德先，不距朕行。（十七節）○五百里甸服，（十八節）百里賦納總，二百里納銍，三百

16 IV. He conferred lands and surnames. *He said*, "Let me go
17 before the empire with reverent attention to my virtue, that none
may act contrary to my conduct."
18 Five hundred *le* constituted THE IMPERIAL DOMAIN. From the first

sources cleared,' is a somewhat difficult expression. Ying-tă says it means that from the source of the rivers to their mouth, Yu cleared all their channel, so that they had no obstruction in their course. This is, no doubt, intended, but the question is as to how it is said by the characters employed. Hoo Wei approves a remark by one of the critics Kin (金氏), that when it is said here that the sources of the rivers were cleared, and not their courses, we must understand by the text the work described by Yu himself—'I deepened the channels, and canals, and conveyed them to the streams.' In this way there were no pools of water about the country to lead to the obstruction of rivers. The remark is well enough, but it leaves the difficulty of the language untouched. We may conclude that if the sources were cleared, the courses would also be attended to;—this is probably the ground of Ying-tă's observation. 九澤既陂,—九澤 must be taken in analogy with 九山 and 九川, as =九州之澤. It does happen, indeed, that we can make out nine marshes mentioned in the first Part,—Luy-hea in Yen-chow; Ta-yay in Ts'eu-chow; P'ang-le and the Shaking marsh in Yang-chow; Yun-mung in King-chow (supposing only *one* marsh intended in p. 50); Yung-po, the marsh of Ko, and Măng-choo in Yu-chow; and Choo-yay in Yung-chow. Notwithstanding this coincidence, we must deal with 九澤 as with 九川. 陂=障, 'a bank or dyke,' used here as a verb. It is synonymous with 隄 in the general signification, but the terms are differently applied, 隄 denoting the high banks on both sides of a river to confine the waters to their channel; 陂, the embankment surrounding a marsh, with sluices to admit water, and others to let it out. 四海會同,—two interpretations have been proposed of this clause. There is that given in the 集傳:—四海之水,無不會同,各有所歸, 'the waters within the four seas all met in a similar way,—each had its place to which it came.' The other, which I have followed in the translation, is that proposed by Gan-kwŏ. Lin Che-k'e explains it by a reference to the conclusion of each chapter on the provinces, which sets forth an account of the route of conveyance to the capital. A commentator Chang (張) observes:—'When the calamity of the inundation was removed, not only could the people of the nine provinces without obstruction, but the barbarous tribes, east, west, north, and south, could likewise all assemble in the capital. We are sent back to the discussions about the meaning of the phrase, 'the four Seas;'—see on the Canon of Shun, p. 13. In this place we must take, I think, the general indefinite signification of the phrase. 會同,—see on Ana. XI., xxv., 6.

P. 15. This is a sort of summary of the portions of Part i., on the soil, fields, revenue, and tribute of the different provinces. 六府孔修,—see on 'The Counsels of Yu,' pp. 7,8. 庶土交正,底慎財賦,—it seems most natural to take 土 here in the sense belonging to it in the first Part,—as meaning the soil, and 庶土, the soil everywhere, with the different characters attaching to it. It will also cover 'the fields,' the account of which always follows it;—to this we are led by the 咸 which follows in the next clause. 底慎 indicates the care and diligence with which Yu proceeded, according to the force that we have seen attaches throughout this Book to 底. The 財 preceding 賦 occasions some perplexity. I have endeavoured to give what I consider is the meaning. 咸則三壤,成賦中邦,—則 is a verb,=法, signifying 'according to,' 'taking as a law;' 三壤, 'the three soils,' *i.e.*, the three grades of quality as 'highest, middle, and lowest,' every grade having also, as we have seen, a threefold subdivision. 中邦 'the middle region,' is held by Hoo Wei to denote the territory in the three first of the domains spoken of in the next chapter.

書經

Ch. IV. Pp. 16—22. Another territorial and political division of the country. The division of the empire into nine provinces was mainly regulated by the natural features of the country,—a reference to the hills and streams. The division here described was of another character and mainly political. Not a few difficult questions arise out of it, which I shall briefly touch on, after discussing exegetically the meaning of the several paragraphs.

P. 16. 錫土姓, 'He conferred lands and surnames,'—this must be understood in close connection with the paragraphs below. The evils occasioned by the overflow of the waters had been in a great measure removed; the lands had everywhere been surveyed; the revenues which they ought to yield had been fixed:—it was necessary that provision should now be made for the government of the multitudes, and the maintenance of the order which had been established. Yu therefore now assigned throughout the province, according to the plan which is subsequently detailed, different portions of territory to those whose birth, or services, or virtue, most entitled them to the distinction. He was himself, indeed, only a minister, a servant, and what he did in this way must have been subject to the approval of Yaou, by whom it was necessary that his acts should be confirmed;—we may well suppose that they were never disallowed. And we may suppose also, that in his conferring lands his first regards were given to the officers who had rendered him the most effectual assistance in his arduous labours.

This assignment of lands was like the action of a conqueror who dispossesses the original possessors of the kingdom which he has subdued, and portions it out among his followers. And there was probably an element of this nature in the action of Yu. The tribes of San-meaou, for instance, were doubtless put under some minister of Yaou. But the strifes of the founders of the Chinese empire with the earlier occupants of the country are barely intimated. Yu's subjugation of it was mainly a reclaiming of it from the wildness of nature, and the disasters brought about by the overflowing of its rivers.

When it is said that Yu conferred surnames as well as names, we cannot but think of his era as that of the real origin of the Chinese empire. Gan-kwŏ's exposition of the par.—it must be borne in mind that he understood Yaou and not Yu as the nominative to 錫—is:—'The emperor, establishing the virtuous, gave them surnames after their places of birth, meaning that such and such a virtuous man was born in such a place, and therefore the name of that place was given to him as a surname to distinguish him, (天子建德,因生以賜姓 [this is a quotation from the 左傳,隱八年], 謂有德之人生此地,以此地名賜之姓,以顯之). The surname, however, was given not only from the birth-place, but after the name of the fief conferred, from the office held by the receiver or one of his ancestors, from any remarkable incident in his life, and from a variety of other circumstances:—the history of surnames among the Chinese is just like the same history in other nations. Subsequent to Yu's time, and especially on the changes of the early dynasties, we have instances of the conferring of lands and surnames; but not at all on the large scale which the text suggests to us as practised by him.

As closely connected with this paragraph and the whole of the chapter, we should keep in mind Yu's own statement in the 'Yih and Tseih,' p. 8:—'I assisted in completing the five tenures, extending over 5,000 *le;* in appointing in the provinces twelve Tutors; and establishing, in the regions beyond, extending to the four seas, five presidents.'

P. 17. I have introduced '*He said*' before this paragraph, understanding it to be a remark made by Yu, related here, amid the account of his achievements, to show how he himself set the chief store by his personal virtue. It seems out of place, indeed, but we cannot help that. Gan-kwŏ rather supposes it to be describing the thought of the emperor, and in an indirect form, from the narrator, and not from the sovereign. 祗=敬. 台=我. 台 and 朕 have the same reference. We have seen how 朕, before the founder of the Ts'in dynasty, was used indifferently by the emperor and by his ministers. Hoo Wei observes:—'From 冀州 (Part. i., p. 2) downwards describes the business of good government and the nourishment of the people; from 錫土姓 describes the business of good instruction and the transformation of the people. 成賦中邦 (par. 25) is what I call good government;—it gets the wealth of the people. 聲教訖于四海 (par. 23) shows what I call the good instruction;—it gets the hearts of the people.'

Pp. 18—22. *The five domains.* 18. 五百里甸服,—I do not see how to translate 服 in this and the other paragraphs otherwise than by 'domain, if, indeed, that word can be called a translation of the Chinese character. The dictionary gives the 五服, and the cognate phrases of 六服, 九服, as a distinct signification of the term, without attempting to deduce it from others that are more common. It is often represented as meaning 'service,' 服事, such and such service being rendered to the emperor here, and such and service being rendered there. So Gan-kwŏ explains 甸服 as denoting 爲天子服治田, 'for the emperor doing service in the cutlivation of the fields.' In whatever way this application of it arose, the character is in effect here simply a designation of territory. 甸 is defined by Ts'ae as =田, 'fields;' and he says:—'Because all the business of this territory was to supply the

里納秸、服、四百里粟、五百里米。○五十九節百里侯服、百里

hundred *le* they brought, as revenue, the whole plant of the grain; from the second, they brought the ears; from the third, they brought *only* the straw, but had to perform other services; from the fourth, *they gave* the grain in the husk; and from the fifth, the grain cleaned.

19 Five hundred *le beyond* constituted THE DOMAIN OF THE NOBLES. The first hundred *le* was occupied by the cities and lands of the

revenue, from the fields, therefore it is called 甸服. Here again the dictionary is very cautious, and defines the term (from the 說文) 'the emperor's 500 *le* of land.' There is, I think a connection between 甸 and 田; but without attempting to indicate what it is, I translate 甸服, 'the imperial domain.' The 500 *le* are understood to extend every way, north, south, east, and west, from the capital, so as to form a square of 1,000 *le*, which may be represented thus:—

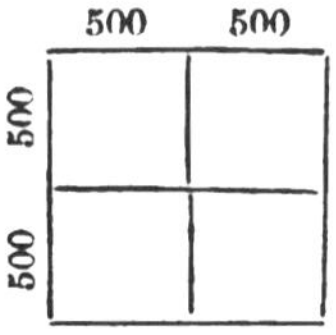

The whole would contain an area of 1,000,000 square *le*.

百里賦納總,—總, meaning 'to collect and bind up,' then = 'all,' 'the whole.' Here applied to the produce of the land it means 'the whole plant.' Ts'ae's definition is very good:—禾本全曰總. 賦—'as revenue;'—not that they brought all the produce to the imperial granaries, but the proportion of it—probably one tenth—as assessed. This was the rule for the first hundred *le* round about the capital. We have no mention of the payment of revenue in the other domains. It was, no doubt, on some arrangement analogous to that made for this *fuh*. The princes occupying the several territories received it, and then paid a tithe of their incomes to the emperor not in kind but in value, in other articles produced in their principalities;—such at least is the account givn by Hoo Wei. 二百里納銍,—銍 primarily means 'a short sickle for reaping grain;' it is then used for the grain reaped with it. Ts'ae says:—刈禾曰銍. He adds, however, 半稾, 'half the stalk.' We are to understand the ear, with a small portion of the stalk, by which the ears could conveniently be bundled together. 三百里納秸,服,—秸 denotes 'the straw,' the plant without the ears or grain. Ts'ae defines it 半稾去皮, which I do not understand. The contribution of revenue from this portion of the domain was thus the least valuable of all, and therefore the inhabitants were called upon to perform other service, which is denoted by 服. Ts'ae would extend this to the first and second hundred *le* as well, and some would extend it to all the other four. But this is quite arbitrary. The service must be confined to the third hundred *le*. What it was we cannot well say, but Kin Keih-p'oo (金吉甫) ingeniously conjectures that it was specially the conveyance of their revenue for the inhabitants of the 4th and 5th hundred *le* beyond. He finds in this an explanation for the omission of 納 in the account of their revenues; he sees also the imperial grace in the arrangement:—those at a moderate distance from the capital paid a small contribution of revenue, and made up for it by their personal service, while those farther off, paying a larger contribution, were spared the labour of conveying it. We can see generally that the contributions from the different hundreds were arranged with reference to their distance from the capital and trouble of conveyance. 四百里粟,五百里米,—粟 and 米 are sometimes used indifferently, with the general signification of 穀 or 'grain.' When a distinction is made between them as here, their meaning is as in the translation:—有殼曰粟,無曰米. [Hoo Wei takes the opportunity to touch here on the burdensome system of transporting the revenue in kind (漕運之法), which has prevailed in China since the time of the Han dynasty. It was a consequence of the change from the feudal system to a centralized government,—an evil in itself, but less than other evils. In times of weakness and confusion like the present it must be found very burdensome.]

P. 19. 五百里侯服,—侯服—侯國之服, 'the domain containing the principalities of the nobles.' By 侯 we must understand all the nobles of the five ranks, (see Mencius, Bk. V. Pt. II., ii.); nor are we to

采、二百里男邦、三百里諸侯。○五廿節百里綏服、三百里揆文教、二百里奮武衞。○

high ministers and great officers; the second, by the principalities of the Nan; the other three hundred were occupied by the various princes.

20 Five hundred *le still beyond* formed the PEACE-SECURING DOMAIN. In the first three hundred *le* they cultivated the lessons of learning and moral duties; in the other three hundred they showed the energies of war and defence.

suppose that they occupied only this domain;—the next was occupied by them as well. Outside the imperial domain, this extended 500 *le* in every direction (Ts'ae). The following figure may be taken as a representation of it:—

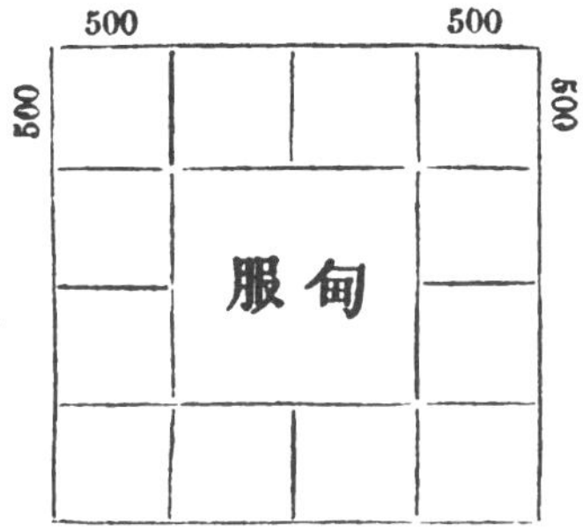

The domain was thus altogether three times the size of the imperial domain, and would contain 3,000,000 square *le*. 百里采,—Ts'ae says:—采,卿大夫邑地,'采 was the cities and lands allotted to the chief ministers and officers.' Those were the nobles and officers in the emperor's immediate service, having their offices within the imperial domain. Outside of it the first hundred *le* was assigned them for their families and support. They took rank in various degrees with the feudal princes. Under the Chow dyn., acc. to Mencius, a chief minister received as much territory as a How, a great officer as much as a Pih, and a scholar of the first class as much as a Tsze or a Nan. Perhaps the arrangement made by Yu was much the same. 二百里爲男邦, —二百里='the second hundred *le*.' The 男 was the lowest of the five ranks of nobility, but the territory assigned to it in the Chow dyn. was the same as that of the Tsze (子). It may have been different under Yaou. The ministers and officers of the emperor took rank, it has been said, with the feudal princes, but from the territories of the Nan being called here 邦, we may conclude that the 采邑 地 were not recognized as principalities. 三百里諸侯,—三百里 is not the third hundred *le* but 'the *remaining* three hundred *le*.' 諸侯 embraces the Kung, How, Pih, and Tsze,—the princes of all the ranks above the Nan. It is conjectured that the smaller principalities were placed next to the imperial domain at once to receive and to afford shelter from the encroachments not unlikely to be attempted by the more powerful lords.

P. 20. 五百里綏服,—this domain was likewise occupied by the princes. 'Being more distant from the imperial seat,' says one of the commentators Chang (張氏), 'the name was changed to 綏, that its occupants might know that the reason why principalities were established was to secure the repose of the royal House.' According to this comment, I have translated 綏 by 'peace-securing.' The domain extended 500 *le* in every direction from that of the nobles in the following way:—

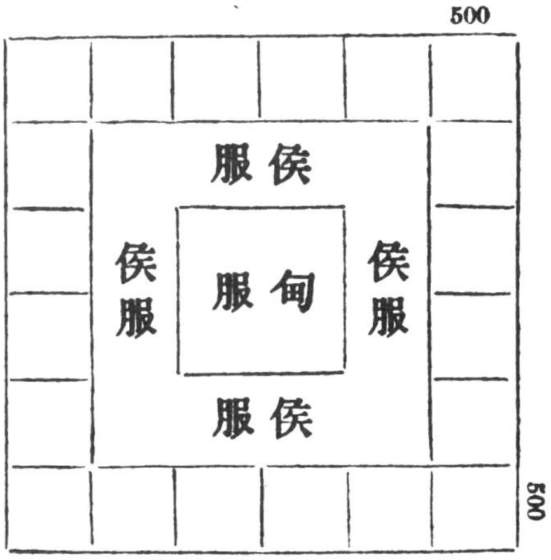

It was thus five times the size of the imperial domain, and contained 5,000,000 square *le*.
三百里揆文教,—'through the first

廿一節 五百里要服、三百里夷、二百里蔡。○

21 Five hundred *le*, *remoter still*, constituted THE DOMAIN OF RESTRAINT. *The first* three hundred *le* were occupied by the tribes of the E; *the next* two hundred by criminals undergoing the lesser banishment.

three hundred *le* of this domain they cultivated lessons of learning and moral duties.' 揆=度, 'to measure,' 'to calculate;'—see on Canon of Shun, p. 2. By its use here we are to understand, it seems to me, that some selection was made in the lessons and instruction which were here given. In all stages of society, especially in the earlier, learning and polite manners must be expected to flourish most in the capital and near it. There will be the higher seminaries and institutions; in distant provinces, schools of no great pretensions, teaching the substance of human duty and the more important acquirements, will be sufficient. 二百里奮武衞,—the principalities in this part of the empire approached the nature of military colonies on the frontiers. They bordered on the wild tribes; it was necessary they should always be prepared to resist aggression. We need not suppose that here they paid no attention to literary and moral training, or that in the inner portion of the domain they altogether neglected the art of war;—the characteristics of the two parts simply were as in the text.

P. 21. 五百里要服,—the dict. deals with 要服 as we saw it did with 服, defining the phrase simply as the name of a territory, without trying to account for its being denominated *Yaou*. In his dictionary, Dr. Medhurst explains 要服, 'the Important Tenure,' in which case we must read 要 in the third tone. This view has the support of Soo Tung-po; but it cannot be admitted. In his translation of the Shoo, Dr. Medhurst renders the phrase—'the Restricted Tenure.' This is more in accordance with the prevailing view. Gan-kwŏ says the domain 要束以文教, *i.e.*, 'was bound and restrained by the instructions of learning.' The idea of restraint seems to be correct; 'the instructions of learning,' as the instrument of that restraint, are foreign to the subject. Many critics assign to 要 the idea of 要約, 'summary,' 'perfunctory.' Thus Leu Tsoo-hëen in the 集說:—'This domain was all occupied by wild tribes, but it was still near the Middle Kingdom, and an easy, summary, jurisdiction was exercised over it;—it was not governed with attention to every particular.' I prefer the view given in the translation, with which indeed this other is not inconsistent. The territory was assigned to the nobles; but with reference to its indigenous inhabitants, they governed them in a 'rough and ready' way, just sufficient to keep them in subjection. It extended in every direction from the Peace-securing domain 500 *le*—thus:—

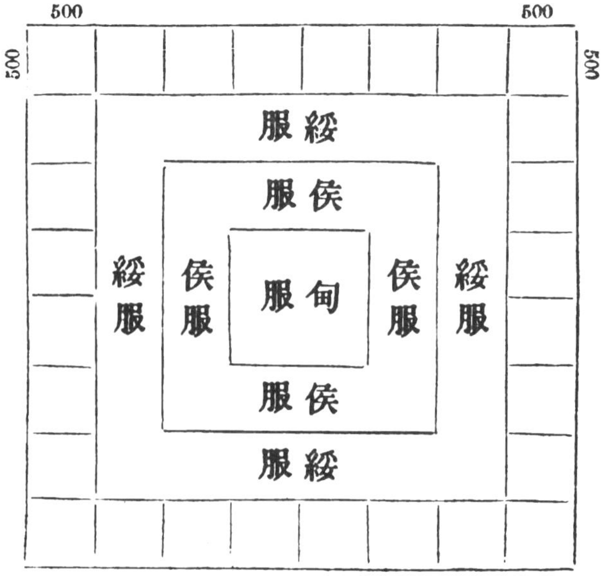

書經

廿二節 五百里荒服、三百里蠻、二百里流。○

22 Five hundred *le*, *the most remote*, constituted THE WILD DOMAIN. Three hundred *le* were occupied by the tribes of the Man; two hundred, by criminals undergoing the greater banishment.

It was thus 7 times the size of the imperial domain, and contained 7,000,000 square *le*.

三百里夷、二里百蔡,—there is nearly a consent on the meaning of 蔡. It is taken as = 放, in Can. of Shun, p. 12, meaning 'to banish and confine.' In the 左傳, 定四年, we read—王於是乎殺管叔而蔡蔡叔. There the opposition of 蔡 and 殺 fixes the meaning of the term. A note, however, says that the, first 蔡 is to be read *shă*, and we find the explanation of this in the character's being given in the 說文 as 𥻦, with the meaning of 'to scatter.' This must have been afterwards mistaken for 蔡. [Here perhaps we have also the explanation of how the 竄三苗, of the Can. of Shun, *loc. cit.*, appears in Mencius, Bk. V. Pt. I., iii. 2, as 殺三苗.] By 蔡, then in the text we must understand banished criminals; and in contrast with the 流 of the next par., that their banishment was of a lighter character, and not to the greatest distance.

The first three hundred *le* were occupied by wild tribes which had not yet been merged in the conquering race, nor driven by it from their original seats. The attempts to explain 夷 as an adjective = 易 or = 平, may be seen in 禹貢錐指. Hoo Wei very pertinently compares with the text the language of Mencius, Bk. IV., Pt. II., i.

P. 22. 五百里荒服,—we have come to the last of the domains. It was called the 荒服 with reference, we may suppose, to the rude character of the inhabitants, and the wildness of the country. It extended 500 *le* in every direction beyond the fourth domain—thus:—

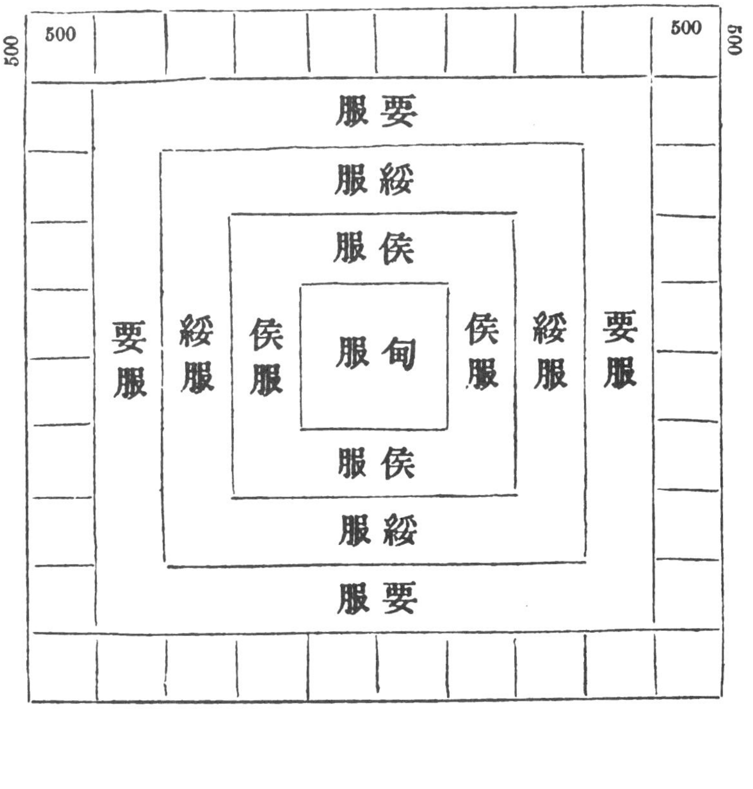

It was thus nine times the size of the imperial domain, and contained 9,000,000 square *le*.

三百里蠻, 二百里流,—蠻 corresponds to the 夷 of the prec. par. The *Man* were considered still more rude and barbarous than the *E*. Properly speaking, 蠻 was the name of the wild tribes on the south; 夷, that of those on the east; 戎, that of those on the west; and 狄, that of those on the north. 蠻夷, however, is used as a designation for *all* the wild tribes, and also 戎狄. Similarly we find the single terms 蠻 and 夷 employed.

流 is used as in Can. of Shun, p 12. It must denote a more distant banishment than 蔡 in the last par. It is not meant that criminals occupied the whole territory, but they had their position assigned to them here among the *Man*.

[The five *Fuh* constituted what we may call the China Proper of Yu's time. Beyond them there was still an outlying territory, over which the ancient emperors claimed authority, and where Yu went on to make political arrangements. 'I assisted,' he says in the Yih and Tseih, p. 8, 'in completing the five domains, extending over 5,000 *le*; in appointing in the provinces twelve Tutors; and in establishing in the regions beyond, extending to the four seas, five presidents.' The nine Chow and the five Fuh covered the same territory, the former being its natural divisions, the latter its artificial and political ones. A subdivision of the five Fuh is insisted on by many, by which the three inner domains constituted the Middle Kingdom,' and the two outer the territory of the 'Four *E*.' On this it is not necessary to dwell. With regard to the five Fuh, certain questions present themselves to the mind.

First, the five domains of Yu formed a square of 5,000 *le*. If the *le* were of the same length as that of the present day, Yu's China must have extended rather more than 1,700 miles from north to south, and from east to west, and contained an area of nearly 3,000,000 square miles. The largest area which can possibly be assigned to the 'Eighteen Provinces' of the present day does not come up to 2,000,000 sq. m.;—see Williams' 'Middle Kingdom,' Vol. I., p. 7. It is not possible that the *le* of Yu could have been equal to the *le* now; but scholars have not been able to determine its measurement. Koo Yen-woo (顧炎武), in the beginning of the present dynasty, contended that the ancient *le* was only 31–50ths of the modern one, but his views do not seem to have obtained general acceptance. If they could be established, Yu's five Fuh would have been rather more than 1,100 miles in each way, which we might admit, so far as the question of extent is concerned.

But second, the five Fuh of Yu surround the imperial domain, which is represented as a square of 1,000 *le* exactly in the centre of them (see in 'Le Chou King,' p. 333, a strange parallel attempted to be drawn by De Guignes between this arrangement and the division of the Holy Land described in the last chapters of Ezekiel). Now the imperial seat of Yaou was in K'e-chow, the most northern of the provinces. His capital was in P'ing-yang, the name of which remains in the dep. P'ing-yang, in Shan-se, lat. 36°6', N., lon. 4°55', W. It could not, therefore, have been in the centre of the domains. This difficulty is clearly seen by Chinese critics. Ts'ae Ch'in observes:—'Though we extend the northern territory of K'e-chow to Yun-chung (雲中; we are to look in the 'Six T'ing of the city of Kwei-hwa' in the extreme north of Shan-se for this. The city of Yun-chung is now the city of T'oh-kih-t'oh [托克托]), to Chŏ (涿; ? dis. of 涿州, dep. of Shun-t'een), and to Yih (易; ? the small dep. of Yih Chow), I am afraid we shall not have 2,500 *le*. Even if we have them, they will consist of a sandy desert without vegetation. On the other hand, in the east and south, whence the greatest revenue now comes, we must put down the domain of Restraint, and the Wild domain. The account of the domains does not seem to harmonize with the nature of the country. Looked at with reference to this, it is unintelligible. I may observe, however, that territories have been very different in ancient and modern times, in regard to their prosperity and the reverse. The country on the north of K'e-chow may not have been the wild and desert tract which we find there in subsequent times; while the regions of Fuh-këen and Chĕ-keang, which were then jungly fens, occupied by barbarous tribes, have now become rich and populous, territory of the highest character. The character of a region cannot be pronounced from its appearance at one era.' This effort of Ts'ae to remove the difficulty cannot be regarded as successful. Barrenness or fertility is one element in it. Even on that point we could not admit Ts'ae's views, unsupported, as regards the north of K'e-chow, by historical evidence; but the main point is that of geographical position. Ch'in Sze-k'ae shows how, on the arrangement described, we must carry the wild domain on the east, into the sea; on the west, beyond Tseih-shih; on the north, 1,200 *le* beyond Yun-chung; while on the south it would not have reached mount Hăng. There is no laying down the five domains on the surface of China. I cannot regard them as anything but an ideal mapping out of the country. This much we may admit,—that Yu placed the smaller principalities next to the imperial, and the larger ones farther off, the indigenous tribes being more strong and numerous according as the distance from the capital increased. In name, the divisions probably existed, and nobles and wild chiefs might be said to belong to one Fuh and another, but there could only be a rough and general approximation to the scheme which Yu had in his mind.

Third, a division of the empire into nine, or more properly ten Fuh, was made under the Chow dynasty. It is twice given in the Chow Le, first in Bk. XXIX., where the domains are called Ke (畿), and again in Bk. XXXIII., where all but the king's Ke are called Fuh. This arrangement may be represented thus:—

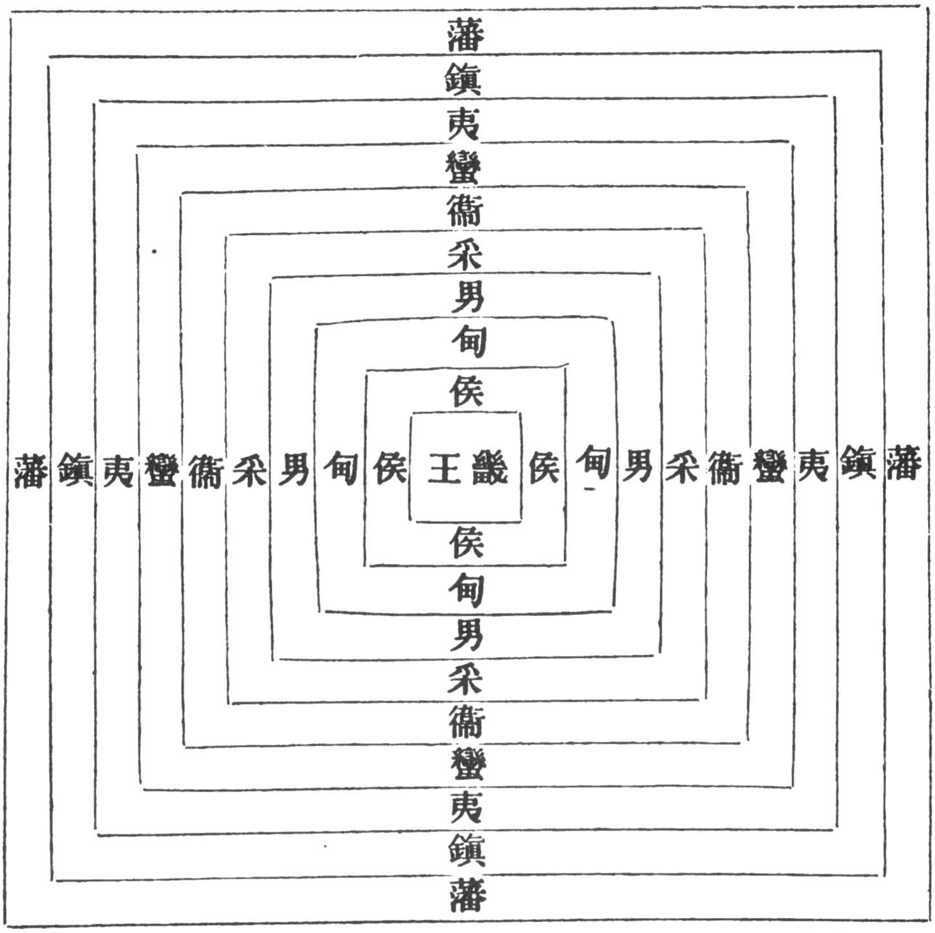

It will be seen that not only are the number of the domains double what Yu made them, but that, where the same names are retained, the order in which they are placed is different. That is a matter, however, to be explained when we come to the 'Chow Le.' The point to be remarked here is that the domains of Han are said to be distant from each other 500 *le*, like those of Yu, and we have the country represented as a square of 10,000 *le*. [The spaces between them in the diagram are smaller than in the prec. diagrams, in order to get the figure upon the page.] How to reconcile the Shoo and the Rites of Chow is a question of much perplexity.

The method adopted by Ch'ing K'ang-shing is the most remarkable. He supposes that the first clause in each of the paragraphs 18—22 gives the Fuh as it had been in the previous part of Yaou's reign, and that the other clauses, always describing 500 *le* in difft. portions, give an addition made by Yu. For instance, the 200 *le* of the Nans' principalities and the 300 of the other princes' were added by him to the second domain, making it altogether 1,000 *le* in each direction from the first. This addition is intended, he contends, by the term 弼 in the Yih and Tseih, p. 8. Making the nine provinces terminate with the Man Fuh of the Chow dynasty, 7,000 *le* from the capital, he gets the 49,000,000 square *le* which I have mentioned in the note on that passage, as the area of the empire proper. The mingled violence and ingenuity of this treatment of the Shoo cannot be contemplated without moving us to smile.

Other methods of reconciling the two accounts have been proposed. Yu's measurements, it is said, were as the bird flies, the Chow dynasty's were as men travel, up and down and winding about. Again, it is urged, the *le* of Yu was double that of Chow, and moreover, the domains of Chow include all the territory beyond Yu's Fuh, which he describes as extending to the four seas. As Ts'ae says, 'To sum the matter up, nothing certain has been said about it' (要之, 皆非的論). The more we extend Yu's domains, the greater difficulty we have to reconcile the classic with the actual face of the ground,—the everlasting hills, the bounding deserts, and the sea embracing the empire on the east and south.]

廿三節 東漸于海、西被于流沙、朔南暨、聲教訖于四海、禹錫玄圭、告厥成功。○

23 V. On the east reaching to the sea; on the west extending to the moving sands; to the utmost limits of the north and south:—his fame and influence filled up all within the four seas. Yu presented a dark coloured gem-stone, and announced the completion of his work.

CH. V. P. 23. THE UNIVERSAL RECOGNITION OF YU'S FAME, AND HIS ANNOUNCEMENT OF HIS COMPLETED WORK. 東漸于海,—漸 (the first tone) is explained by Gan-kwŏ by 入; so also the dict., with ref. to this pass., has 流入. Ts'ae and most recent commentators explain the term by 漬, 'to soak.' As the term is here used along with 被 and 暨, the less emphatic it is made the better. Gan-kwŏ's definition is to be preferred. 西被于流沙,—被, as in Can. of Yaou, p. 1, *et al.* 流沙,—see par. 5. 朔南暨,—朔＝北, the north';—see on Can. of Yaou, par. 7. 暨＝及. The whole ＝'the south and the north being come to.' The extension of Yu's fame in these directions is left thus indefinite, and no place of boundary is specified, because in the Book the termination of the nine provinces north and south is left undefined. 聲教訖于四海,—it does not seem appropriate to bring in 教, 'instructions,' here. Yu has appeared in the whole of the Book as a worker and not as a teacher. The 教 was that given by his doings and character, and not by his works. I have ventured therefore to use 'influence' in the translation, instead of 'instructions.' This is according to the definitions of the term which are the oldest;—see those quoted in the dict. from the 說文 and 釋名. Hoo Wei says that 'the four seas' denote the E on the east, the Jung on the west, the Man on the south, and the Teih on the north. I cannot think so. 訖于四海 is to me a vague phrase, by which the writer would express in the widest admissible terms the extent of Yu's fame. Compare the eulogium of the perfect sage in the Doctrine of the Mean, ch. xxxi. 禹錫玄圭,告厥成功,—錫 as in Can. of Yaou, p. 12. and more particularly, Part i., p. 52—九江納錫大龜,—'to present.' 圭＝瑞玉, 'an auspicious gem.' Of the 'five tokens of gem,' Can. of Shun, p. 7, three were called 圭;—see the note on that passage. The gem-token was conferred by the emperor on the noble,—a delegation to him of his dignity and authority. There seems an incongruity in speaking of one, as in the text, as presented by the minister to the emperor. So strongly has this been felt, that Sze-ma Ts'een produces the passage as—帝錫禹玄圭,以告成功, and Gan-kwŏ takes the same view. The text, however, will not admit of it. The 圭 is called 玄, because, say some, the colour of water is dark, and Yu has regulated the waters; because, say others, the colour of the heavens is of a deep dark, and Yu was engaged on a heavenly work. These sayings are far-fetched; Yu found somewhere such a dark-coloured precious stone, so remarkable that he thought it worthy to be presented to the emperor. The emperor was Yaou, but the stone would be presented in the first place to Shun, as his vice-gerent.

CONCLUDING NOTE. The standard chronology fixes the year in which Yu thus announced the completion of his work as that B. C, 2276, the 80th year of Yaou's reign, and the seventh of Shun's association with him in the government.

According to Mencius (Book III., Pt. I., iv. 7), Yu was eight years employed on the regulation of the waters. There is a different statement in the Historical Records, Bk. XXVII., 河渠書, where it is said, as if from the Books of Hea, that Yu was engaged on the inundating waters for thirteen years (夏書曰,禹抑鴻水,十三年). This estimate of 13 years arose probably from mistaking the meaning of Part i., p. 18.

There was another tradition, that Yu's work extended only over three years. Ma Yung says:—'Yu dealt with the waters for three years, and eight of the provinces were brought to order, on which Yaou considered the work as good as done, and resigned the administration to Shun. All this took place in twelve years after the regulation of the waters had been taken in hand' (*i.e.*, by K'wăn). 'In the year after, the 13th year, Yen-chow was also brought to order, and

Shun publicly accepted the administration.' Ying-tă writes to the same effect. They both include in the thirteen years the nine in which K'wăn laboured in vain.

We may be sure that the work ascribed in this Book to Yu was not done in three or four years. Mencius' assignment of eight years is short enough. Hoo Wei supposes that so much time was occupied with the labour upon the nine provinces, and that the conferring of lands, and arrangement of the five *fuh* occupied so much time more. As to the exact year in which Yu began his labours; when they terminated; and how many years the deluge of Yaou lasted:—these are questions which we cannot determine categorically.

THE BOOKS OF HEA.

BOOK II. THE SPEECH AT KAN.

甘誓

大戰于甘、乃召六卿。○王曰、嗟、六事

1 There was a great battle in Kan. *Previous to it*, the emperor call-
2 ed together the six leaders of his hosts; and said, "Ah! all ye

INTRODUCTORY AND CONNECTING NOTE. It was observed in the first note on the last Book, that though 'The Tribute of Yu' appeared as the first of the Books of Hea, it is descriptive really of what took place during the reign of Yaou. It terminates, accord. to the received chronology, B.C. 2276, 22 years before the accession of Shun to the throne upon Yaou's death. 'The Counsels of the Great Yu' bring us farther down. We have there the accession of Yu to the administration of the empire under Shun, B.C. 2222, and his reduction of the Meaouites, referred to B.C. 2220. The Shoo tells us nothing of Yu's accession to the throne, nor the events of his reign. Shun died B.C. 2207. Yu carried on the government during the years of mourning for his death, and then withdrew, to allow his son, Shang-k'eun (商均), an opportunity of ascending the throne. The people, however, would not have him to be their king;—they preferred Yu (Mencius, Book V., Part I., vi.), whose reign accordingly dates from B.C. 2204. Yaou had given him the surname of Sze (姒). Old and worn out with the fatigues he had undergone, he died after a reign of eight years, short as compared with the reigns of Yaou and Shun. Kaou-yaou whom he had associated with him in the administration died the year after. He then made Yih his prime minister, with the view of his succeeding him. He died on a progress to the south, B.C. 2197, in Hwuy-k'e (會稽), in the pres. dep. of Shaou-hing (紹興), in Chě-këang. He was succeeded by his son K'e (啟), whose reign dates from B.C. 2196, and to whom is attributed the speech recorded in this Book which is assigned to B.C. 2194, the third year of his reign.

[The Chinese chronologists are pleased to lay it down so, and it is hardly worth while quarrelling with the arrangement. Still it is not quite accurate. According to Mencius, Yih administered the govt. during the period of mourning for Yu, and it was not till that was expired, that the people called K'e to occupy his father's place in preference to Yih. His reign therefore should date only from B.C. 2194; should be reckoned only six years instead of nine; and the expedition against the prince of Hoo be referred to his first year instead of his third.]

That the speech at Kan was made by K'e rests on the authority of the Preface to the Shoo, par. 6, which is followed by Sze-ma Ts'een. The Taouist Chwang-tsze, indeed, and Lew Heang, in his 說苑, Bk. VII., 政理篇, say that Yu fought with the prince of Yu; and others speak of the emperor Seang (夏

之人、予誓告汝。○三節有扈氏、威侮五行、怠棄三正、天用勦絶其命、今予惟恭行天之罰。○四節左不攻于左、汝不

who are engaged in my six armies, I have a solemn announcement to make to you.

3 "The prince of Hoo wildly wastes and despises the five elements, and has idly abandoned the three acknowledged commencements of the year. On this account Heaven is about to destroy him, and bring to an end the favour it has shown to him; and I am reverently executing the punishment appointed by Heaven.

4 "If you, left-side men, do not do your work on the left, it will be a disregard of my orders. If you, right-side men, do not do your

后相), three reigns later than K'e, as his antagonist. The statements of Chwang-tsze and Lëw Heang might possibly be reconciled with the Preface, but Mih-tse, (明鬼篇, 三), quotes (with variations) most of the Book, attributing it to Yu. There were evidently two traditions during the Chow dynasty, after the time of Confucius, as to when and by whom the speech at Kan was made.

Title of the Book.—甘誓, 'The Speech at Kan.' 誓,—see on 'The Counsels of the Great Yu', p. 28. The 誓 or 'martial speeches' are given by Ying-tă as the 5th of the component elements of the Shoo. This at Kan is the first of them that forms a distinct Book. We had a speech of Yu to his troops in the passage just referred to. 甘 was the name of the place where the speech was made.

Contents. The emperor, about to engage in battle with a rebellious vassal, assembles his generals and troops, and addresses them. First he declares obscurely the grounds of the expedition which he had undertaken, and concludes by stimulating the soldiers to the display of courage and observance of order by promises of reward and threats of punishment. It is so short that it is not worth while to divide it into chapters.

P. 1. *Occasion of the speech.* 大戰于甘,—the battle is called 'great,' we might suppose, because of the numbers engaged in it, and the obstinacy with which it was contested. Another reason is assigned, however, for the denomination,—that the wickedness of the prince of Hoo, in compelling the emperor to take the field against him, might be more strongly set forth. On the principle of Mencius, VII., Pt. II., ii., the emperor did not fight (戰), but only 'punished;' nor did he take the field till after the means which the constitution of the govt. provided had proved ineffectual. Such came to be the rule, when the feudal system had become fully developed;—we can hardly seek to apply it regularly to the case of K'e at so early a period. 甘 is given by some as the name of a place in the southern border of the principality of Hoo; by others, as the name of a river; by others again, as the name of a marsh; and by others, as the name of a wilderness. There is an agreement, however, as to the locality, and all the representations might be reconciled. We have still the 'Shed of Kan' (甘亭), with the water from the 'valley of Kan' flowing past it, in the dis. of Hoo (鄠縣); lat. 34°8', N., lon. 7°50, W.) dep. of Se-ngan, Shen-se. The Shed or Portico marks, it is said, the place of the battle.

乃召六卿,—we must bring 王 from the next par. as the nominative to 召. The whole Book is only a fragment. This par. must have been the proper sequence originally of a preceding narrative. I introduce '*previous to it*' in the translation, after Sze-ma Ts'een, who has—啟伐之,大戰於甘,將戰作甘誓,乃召六卿申之. 六卿,—'the six high nobles,' here evidently the leaders of the 'six armies' (六軍, and 六師), which composed the military force of the emperor. This is the view of all the commentators.—Ch'ing says:—六卿者六軍之將. We need not trouble ourselves to inquire further what offices these *k'ing* sustained in time of peace. In the Chow dynasty, a 軍 or army consisted of 12,500 men.

Pp. 2, 3. *The grounds of the expedition against Hoo.* The king commences his speech with a sigh,—an Ah! (嗟),—because of the gravity of the matter;—so, Ts'ae. 六事之人,—Ch'ing observes that the change of style from 六卿 to 六事 indicates that the king was addressing not the generals only, but the inferior officers and common soldiers as well. Of course he could not be heard by such a multitude, but his speech would be circulated throughout the host. Gan-kwŏ says:—各有軍事,故曰六事. I have translated accordingly. 3. 有扈氏=the holder of, *i.e.*, the prince invested with, Hoo. This Hoo was the present territory of the district of Hoo in Shen-se. The name in the text was changed in the Ts'in dynasty to the present 鄠. The prince of Hoo, according to Sze-ma Ts'een and the older interpreters, was of the surname Sze, the same as the emperor. I have read of him somewhere as K'e's 庶兄, his elder brother by a secondary wife. Ts'ae does not seem willing to admit so much. The surname is not a point of importance. 威侮五行,怠棄三正,—these two clauses state the crime of Hoo, but in obscure and mystical terms. Ch'ing defines 五行 by 四時, 'the four seasons,' making the phrase analogous with 五辰 in the 'Yih and Tseih,' p. 4;—see the note there. He calls 三正—天地人之正道, 'the correct way of heaven, earth, and man,' meaning probably the same with Ma Yung, that the phrase denotes the commencement of the year in 子 the 11th month, or midwinter, which was called the 天正, the commencement in 丑, the 地正, and the commencement in 寅, the first month of spring, the 人正. This last was the beginning of the year with the Hea dyn.; the Shang began it with the 地正; and the Chow with the 天正. The text would imply, on this view of it, that these diff. commencements had been employed before;—see note on the Canon of Shun, p. 14. If it were so, perhaps the prince of Hoo wanted to begin the year with some other month, as the founder of the Ts'in dyn. afterward adopted the month 亥, the 10th, the first month of winter. Maou K'e-ling's view of the subject is not unreasonable. He considers these two clauses as an obscure intimation from K'e that Hoo refused to acknowledge him as the right successor of Yu. This is an old view. Yaou had been succeeded by Shun, as the worthiest man in the empire, and Shun had been succeeded by Yu. Why should Yu's throne descend to his son? This afforded the pretext for rebellion. Maou further tries to show that by the language used K'e makes the rebellion a crime against Heaven, and not merely an attempt against himself. See the 尙書廣聽錄, *in loc.* We can hardly doubt that the object of the expedition was to put down a dangerous rival. 天用勦絕其命,—勦 is given in the 說文 as 剿 and defined by 絶; 命 is not to be taken as='life,' but the position of the prince of Hoo, as invested with that principality, though, in being deprived of that, we may presume, he would pay the forfeit of his life as well; 用—'on this account,' as in the 'Yih and Tseih,' p. 8, *et al.*

P. 4. *Rules to be observed by the troops.* 左不攻于左,云云,—左=車左, 'the left of the chariot;' 右=車右, 'the right of the chariot.' It appears that in the warfare of those early times, chariots were much used in China, as in other nations in a similar or less advanced stage of civilization,—among the ancient Gauls and Britons, for instance. The ordinary war-chariot for the troops contained only three men,—an archer on the left, a soldier armed with javelins and pike or spear on the right, and the charioteer in the centre. This continued down to the Chow dynasty;—see the 集傳 and 後案, *in loc.* 攻=治,治其事, 'do your work,' *i.e.*, observe the rules laid down for your guidance. So, also, 非其馬之正; comp. Mencius, Bk. III., Pt. II., i. 4. [The pictures of those chariots are not unlike those given of similar war *materiel* on Egyptian and Assyrian monuments.]

P. 5. *The martial law of K'e;—rewards and punishments.* 用命,賞于祖,不用命,戮于社,—祖=遷廟之祖主, 'the spirit-tablets of his ancestors which had been removed from the regular hall of ancestral worship to the special shrine appointed for them;'—see on The Doctrine of the Mean, Ch. xix. So 社=社主, 'the tablets of the spirits of the land.' It would appear from this, that it was the practice of the emperors, when they went on a warlike expedition, to carry with them these two classes of tablets, that they might have with the host, hovering about them, the spirits of their ancestors and the tutelary spirits of the country or dynasty. A variety of passages are adduced to prove the existence of the practice in the Chow dynasty;—it had come from the earlier time. Those tablets were to K'e and his army like the ark of God in the camp of the Israelites. Martial law also was executed before them. And strict law it was. 予則孥戮汝,—孥 is defined by Gan-kwŏ and others by 子, 'children.' But it may

恭命、右不攻于右、汝不恭命、御非其馬之正、汝不恭命。○五節用命、賞于祖、不用命、戮于社、予則孥戮汝。○

work on the right, it will be a disregard of my orders. If you,
charioteers, do not observe the rules for the management of your
5 horses, it will be a disregard of my orders. You who obey my
orders shall be rewarded before my ancestors; and you who dis-
obey my orders shall be put to death before the spirits of the land;
and I will also put your children to death."

include wives as well. The threat='I will also exterminate your families.' Attempts are made to weaken the force of both the terms 戮 and 孥, but without success. A different meaning of 戮 cannot be admitted here from what it has in the preceding clause. Kaou-yaou praised Shun, because with him 'punishments did not extend to the criminal's heirs;'—see 'The Counsels of Yu,' p. 12. The practice of K'e was very different. It may be said that the text is speaking only of military law; and it must be replied that it was the military law of a very cruel and barbarous state of society.

Concluding note. The Pere de Mailla, in his 'Histoire Generale de la Chine,' has wonderfully amplified (? and improved) the account of the battle of Kan. He says (Vol. I., p. 125):—'On the approach of the imperial army, the prince of Hoo drew up his in order of battle. The emperor arranged his troops in this way:—On the two wings he placed his chariots of war which carried 25 men, armed with arrows, pikes, and sabres, and his cavalry in the centre; after which he addressed them as follows:—

"Remember that you are fighting for Heaven. You who are on the wings, be attentive to the orders which will be given you; let it be seen that you are well skilled with your arrows and your pikes. These are my orders; respect them. And you cavaliers, at the first signal which shall be made to you, enter with courage into the ranks, which the arrows will have opened," &c., &c.

The Shoo does not mention the issue of the battle. According to Sze-ma Ts'een, it was the defeat and death of the prince of Hoo (遂滅有扈氏). We find, however, in the 'History made Easy' (綱鑑易知錄) this account:—'Not succeeding, his generals begged to renew the engagement. K'e said, "My present failure is owing to the slenderness of my virtue, and because my instructions are not good." On this he returned with his army to the capital; silenced all his music; sat on a single mat, and confined himself at meals to a single dish. At the same time he was affectionate to his relations, and respectful to his elders; he gave honour to the worthy, and office to the able;—brooding silently over his affairs (隱神; this is an unusual combination, and not found in the Thesaurus. Without other examples, we can only guess at its meaning). After a month, the prince of Hoo submitted and was put to death.'

All this is plainly an imitation of the account of Yu's expedition against the tribe of San-meaou, Pt. II., Bk. II., pp. 19, 20. It is a clumsy imitation of it. Why should the prince of Hoo, thus submitting himself to the emperor's virtue, have been put to death?

We may suppose that K'e was successful at Kan, and put down the rising rebellion. We know nothing of the subsequent events of his reign. He died B.C. 2188, and was succeeded by his son, T'ae-k'ang.

THE BOOKS OF HEA.

BOOK III. THE SONGS OF THE FIVE SONS.

五子之歌

一節太康尸位、以逸豫滅厥德、黎民咸貳、乃盤遊無度、畋于有洛之表、十旬弗反。○

1 I. T'ae-k'ang occupied the throne like a personator of the dead. By idleness and dissipation he extinguished his virtue, till the black-haired people all began to waver in their allegiance. He, however, pursued his pleasure and wanderings without any restraint. He went out to hunt beyond the Lŏ, and a hundred days elapsed with-

TITLE OF THE BOOK.—五子之歌, 'The Songs of the five Sons.' It would have been more correct to name it 'The Songs of the five Brothers.' The singers were the brothers of T'ae-k'ang, bewailing in these strains his evil course and evil fate. The word 'Sons' is probably used with reference to the fact that they were with their mother at the time,—left to her, while he who should have been her chief support had got himself outcast both from her and his kingdom; still there is not a word in the songs having special refeence to her. The Book ranks in that division of the Books of the Shoo, which goes by the name of 'Instructions' (訓). Though the form be poetical, the subject-matter is derived from the lessons left by Yu for the guidance of his posterity.

CONTENTS. After three introductory paragraphs, relating the occasion of the Songs, we have the Songs themselves,—one from each brother. The first deplores how the emperor had lost the affections of the people; the second speaks of his dissipation and extravagance; the third mourns his loss of the imperial seat; the fourth deplores his departure from the principles of Yu, and its disastrous consequences; and the fifth is a wail over their miserable condition. I have divided the whole into two chapters,—the Introduction, and the Songs.

The GENUINENESS of the Book is disputed. It is sufficient to say here that a Book substantially the same as this did form part of Confucius' compilation of the documents of the Shoo.

CH. I Pp. 1—3. HOW T'AE-K'ANG LOST HIS KINGDOM, AND IN WHAT CIRCUMSTANCES HIS BROTHERS COMPOSED THEIR SONGS. I.

二節 有窮后羿。因民弗忍、距于河。○三節 厥弟五人、御其母以從、徯于洛之汭、五子咸怨、述大禹之戒以作歌。○

2 out any sign of his return. *On this*, E, the prince of K'ëung, tak-
ing advantage of the discontent *of the people*, resisted *his return* upon
3 the *north of the* Ho. The emperor's five brothers had attended
their mother in following him, and were waiting for him on the
north of the Lŏ; and, *when they heard of E's movement*, all full of dis-
satisfaction, they related the cautions of the great Yu in the form
of songs.

太康尸位,—T'ae-k'ang was the eldest son of K'e, and succeeded to the empire on his death. His reign dates from B. C. 2187. 尸 is defined by Gan-kwŏ by 主,='to preside over.' The character has that meaning;—see the dict. Its proper signification, however, is 'a corpse,' and it is often used for the personator of the dead in the funeral ceremonies of antiquity;—see the dict., which defines it in this application by 神象, 'the image of the spirit.' Ts'ae has improved on Gan-kwŏ by interpreting the text on this use of the char.—T'ae-k'ang was but a personator on the throne, little better than a sham sovereign. 逸豫,—逸 is 'idleness,' and 豫 is 'pleasure,' 'dissipation.' The meaning of the terms is akin. 貳,—comp Pt. II., p. 5—任賢勿貳. But the usage in the two passages is not identical. Here 咸貳—皆有二心, 'all had two hearts.' 盤遊,—盤=樂, 'pleasure.' We find 般 in Mencius, in the same sense,—e. g., Bk. II., Pt. I., iv. 4, 般樂怠敖. 有洛之表,—for the Lŏ, see the Tribute of Yu, Part i., p. 55, *et al.*; 表—外, 'beyond,' 'the country beyond,'; the 有 is not at all needed for the sense, and I cannot account for its introduction. 2. 有窮后羿—窮 was the name of a principality, referred to the present sub. dep. of Tih (德州), dep. of Tse-nan in Shan-tung. Its holder in the time of T'ae-k'ang was named E. There was a tradition in the Chow dynasty, which made him a descendant of the master of the archers, centuries before, in the time of the emp. Kuh (嚳), whose office was indicated by the character, the name of the office having become hereditary as a personal name in the family. The history of the individual in the text is very obscure, and will be found, so far as it can be ascertained, in the concluding notes to this Book and the next. In the text he appears simply withstanding the return of T'ae-k'ang to his capital. Medhurst translates 距于河 by 'drove him beyond the Yellow river,' but 'drove' is much too strong. T'ae-k'ang had gone beyond the Ho, we know not how far; and E opposed his return. His doing so cannot be defended, but we do not know his motives. He was enabled to do what he did, 因民弗忍, 'because the people could not bear,' *i.e.*, could not bear the indifference and extravagance of T'ae-k'ang. 3. 御其母以從,—御=侍, 'to be in attendance on.' The movement of the mother and brothers had perhaps been previous to the movement of E. The composition of the songs, however, could only have taken place after they had heard of that;—they look on K'e-chow, the peculiar patrimony of their family, as being as good as lost. It is most natural to suppose that while they were waiting for the long delayed return of T'ae-k'ang, they heard of E's action against him. 五子咸怨,—the dissatisfaction is to be supposed to be directed against T'ae-k'ang. See Mencius' defence of such dissatisfaction with a relative, Book VI., Pt. II., iii.

四節其一曰、皇祖有
訓、民可近、不可
下、民惟邦本、本
固邦寧。○五節予視
天下、愚夫愚婦、
一能勝予、一人
三失、怨豈在明、
不見是圖、予臨
兆民、懍乎若朽
索之馭六馬、爲

4 II. The first said,
"It was the lesson of our great ancestor:—
The people should be cherished;
They should not be down-trodden:
The people are the root of a country;
The root firm, the country is tranquil.
5 When I look throughout the empire,
Of the simple men and simple women,
Any one may surpass me.
If I, the one man, err repeatedly;—
Should dissatisfaction be waited for till it appears?
Before it is seen, it should be guarded against.
In my relation to the millions of the people,
I should feel as much anxiety as if I were driving six horses with rotten reins.

CH. II. Pp. 4—9. THE SONGS OF THE BROTHERS.

Pp. 4, 5. *The first brother's song.—How T'ae-k'ang had carelessly lost the affections of the people.* 4 其一＝'the first of them;'—*i.e*, the first in order who spoke, probably the oldest. 皇祖,—Gan-kwŏ takes 皇＝君; Ts'ae makes it＝大. On whichever view, the two characters refer to Yu. 民可近,不可下,—literally, 'the people should be *neared*, they should not be *put down*.' In the 國語,周語,中, we have this passage quoted as 民可近,不可上. Hence it is said that the compiler of this present Book plagiarized the passage from the 國語, changing 上 into 下. I should rather suppose that the speaker in the 國語 changed 下 into 上 from the frequency of that word in his mouth at the time. On this and the next clause, comp. the words of Shun to Yu, Pt. II., Bk. II.,17. 予視天下,—the 予, according to Ts'ae, is the speaker's designation of himself and his brothers. I am not sure of this. Possibly he is still reciting the words of Yu; or he may be speaking in the person of his brother the emperor. This last view is that which I prefer.—It is only in the last two lines, 爲人上者,奈何不敬, that we have the speaker's own reflection. —人三失,怨豈在明,不見是圖,—we find this quoted in the 國語,晉語,三, and also the two last clauses of it in the 左傳,成十六年. If we connect the first clause closely with the other two, the lesson which is taught is of a doubtful character. I have therefore tried to indicate in the translation that the clause which should properly complete the first one is wanting. 予臨兆民,懍乎若朽索之馭六馬,—this passage shows plainly that these words are spoken in the person of the emperor. 兆民—'the millions of the people,' in opposition to 'the one man.' 以尊

書經

人上者、奈何不
敬。○其二曰、訓
有之、內作色荒、
外作禽荒、甘酒
嗜音、峻宇彫牆、
有一于此、未或
不亡。○其三曰、
惟彼陶唐、有此
冀方、今失厥道、
亂其紀綱、乃底

The ruler of men—
How can he be but reverent *of his duty?*"

6 The second said,
"It is in the lessons:—
When the palace is a wild of lust,
And the country a wild for hunting:
When wine is sweet, and music the delight;
When there are lofty roofs and carved walls,—
The existence of any one of these things,
Has never been but the prelude to ruin."

7 The third said,
"There was the prince of T'aou and T'ang,
Who possessed this country of K'e.
Now we have fallen from his ways,
And thrown into confusion his rules and laws;
The consequence is extinction and ruin."

適卑曰臨, 'when the high go to the low, the action is called *lin.*' Ming-shing quotes from Hwae-nan's 說林訓, 君子居民上, 若腐索御奔馬, and from Confucius in the 家語, 致思篇, 懍懍焉若持腐索之扞馬,—passages very like this, but as likely to have been suggested by it as to have suggested it. He also contends that it was not till the Ts'in dynasty that the emperor used *six* horses in his carriage. The point is by no means certain. On the rhymes in this song, see Maou K'e-ling, on 'The Wrongs of the Old Text of the Shoo,' Bk. III.

P. 6. *The song of the second brother.—On the dissipation and extravagance of T'ae-k'ang.* Gan-kwŏ defines 荒 here by 迷亂, 'led astray and disordered.' Such a meaning of the term, however, is not justified by examples. Its proper signification of 'a wild' answers sufficiently. 內外, 'within' and 'without,'= 'the palace' and 'the country.' 禽荒—禽 includes 獸. In the 國語, 越語下, we read—王其且馳騁弋獵, 無至禽荒, 宮中之樂, 無至酒荒. 音—八音, 'the eight kinds of musical instruments; here = 'music' generally. Mencius might seem to have had this passage in view, when he spoke as in VII. Bk. II., xxxiv.

P. 7. *The song of the third brother.—How the imperial patrimony was lost.* 惟彼陶唐, —'there was that T'aou and T'ang.' No doubt it is Yaou who is here intended. He ascended the throne from being prince of T'ang, the name of which remains in the dis. of T'ang, dep. of Paou-ting, Chih-le. [Others, however, will have it that the principality of T'ang was in the pres. district of T'ae-yuen, dep. T'ae-yuen, in Shan-se.] Before he ruled in T'ang, he had been princelet, it is said, in T'aou, referred to the dis. of Ting-t'aou, dep. Ts'aou-chow, Shan-tung. [Others will have it that Yaou lived first in T'ang, and then in T'aou.—So uncertain are such early matters.] Ts'ae says that when raised to the empire, he made T'aou his capital. [In this case T'aou

滅亡。○其八章四曰、明明我祖、萬邦之君、有典有則、貽厥子孫、關石和鈞、王府則有、荒墜厥緒、覆宗九章絕祀。○其

8 The fourth said,
"Brightly intelligent was our ancestor,
Sovereign of the myriad States!
He had canons, he had rules,
Which he transmitted to his posterity.
The standard Stone and the equalizing Quarter
Were in the imperial treasuries.
Wildly have we dropt the clue he gave us,
Overturning our family and extinguishing our sacrifices."

ought to be the same as P'ing-yang.] Setting little store by all these statements, we have the fact that Yaou is often referred to as 陶唐氏. 有此冀方,—Yaou of course possessed the whole empire; but it was in K'e-chow that he had his capital, and it was from it that T'ae-k'ang was now kept. We therefore find it specified in this way. 紀綱,—'rules and laws;'=the lesser regulations and the greater. 紀 properly signifies 'to separate and arrange sorts of silk,' a fine delicate manipulation; 綱 is the large rope of a net, to which the whole is attached. We find the whole of this song with two slight variations, and the addition of one line, in the 左傳. Under the 8th year of duke Gae, Confucius appears quoting from the Books of Hea—惟彼陶唐,帥彼天常,有此冀方,今失其行,亂其紀綱,乃滅而亡.

P. 8. *The fourth brother's song.—How unworthy a successor of Yu T'ae-k'ang had been.* 有典有則,—Gan-kwŏ defines 典 by 經籍, 'standard writings,' or 'books,' and 則 by 法. Ts'ae, much more happily, illustrates the phrases by referring to the second Book of the Rites of Chow, where the six 典, the eight 法, and the eight 則, are all described as in the special charge of the first minister of the crown (冢宰). The *teen* were the general regulations about government, and its several departments of instruction, ceremonies, offices, punishment, and employments. The *tsih* were the special rules about sacrifices, emoluments, the collection of revenue, &c. Yu's canons and rules were more compendious probably than those of a later period; but they would be of the same general nature. 關石和鈞,王府則有,—關 is here explained by 通, and Medhurst translates—'He rendered uniform the weights and harmonized the measures.' But this is wrong. 關 and 和 are two adjectives, qualifying 石 and 鈞, which latter term moreover is not a measure, but the quarter of the 石. Choo He gave it as his opinion that the two phrases were simply the denominations of the weights. We may translate 關 by 'current,' or 'standard,' and 和 by 'equalizing.' By the use of these weights there was an end of petty strifes among the people,—they were made 'harmonious.' The royal treasury contained the standard measures of capacity and length as well; that we must understand:—so widely and carefully had Yu provided for the working of the government. We find this passage quoted in the 國語,周語,下, where the glossarist, Wei Ch'aou (韋昭; of Woo, one of the 'Three Kingdoms'), would make 關='the customs,' a meaning which might be adopted but for the following 和. 覆宗, 'overturning our ancestral temple,'=causing our family to be cast out from the empire.

五曰、嗚呼曷歸、予懷之悲、萬姓仇予、予將疇依、鬱陶乎予心、顏厚有忸怩、弗慎厥德、雖悔可追。

9 The fifth said,
"Oh! whither shall we turn?
The thoughts of our breasts make us sad.
All the people are hostile to us;
On whom can we rely?
Anxieties stand thick in our hearts;
Thick as are our faces, they are covered with blushes.
We have not been careful of our virtue;
And though we repent, we cannot overtake the past."

P. 9. *The song of the fifth brother.—A wail over the sad condition to which they were reduced.* 予懷之悲,—'I dwell on this and am sad;' or, as in the 'Daily Explanation,' 此予懷之所以悲, 'this is why the thoughts of my bosom are sad.' The 予, in this and other places, I have translated in the plural, the brothers in this way taking to themselves the blame attaching to T'ae-k'ang. 鬱陶乎予心,顏厚有忸怩,—comp. Mencius, V., Bk. I., ii 3—鬱陶思君爾,忸怩. Ming-shing contends that the text is plagiarized from that passage. But Mencius must there be quoting from histories of Shun current in his days;—most probably he is quoting from the first part of the Canon of Shun, which is now lost. If this be denied, we may say that Mencius appropriated the language of the text, with quite as much reason as that it was modelled from him. As to the meaning of 鬱陶, it is very much disputed. K'ung explains it by 哀思, 'anxiously, mournfully, thinking.' Others again, as Yen Jŏ-keu, assuming 陶 to mean 'joy,' 'to be joyful,' make the phrase = 'the first emotion of joy not yet finding vent.' This meaning would be quite inappropriate in the text, and they say that this being the proper meaning of the phrase, its use here arose from misunderstanding it in Mencius, and shows the hand of the plagiarist. But the other meaning suits the passage in Mencius much better than this, and is not to be so readily sent out of court. 鬱 properly denotes 'trees growing bushy;' then, 'tangled.' 陶 is 'a potter's furnace;' it is also used for potters' work. The phrase in the text will then signify the 'tangled workings of the mind,' appropriate to its anxious thoughts, rather than its joyful emotions. 顏厚,—'our faces are thick';—this is said to show the strong working of their shame.

CONCLUDING NOTE. Neither from the Shoo nor from the 'Historical Records' do we learn anything about T'ae-k'ang but what is contained in the first three paragraphs of this Book; and from them we cannot say in what year of his reign he undertook his hunting expedition beyond the Lŏ, or what was the result of the movement of E against him. The chronologists, however,—on what authority it is not necessary here to discuss,—refer the expedition to the 19th year of his reign, B.C. 2169: and they say he was never able to recross the Ho. He lived on for ten years in Yang-hea (陽夏), corresponding to the pres. dis. of T'ae-k'ang, dep. of Ch'in-chow, in Ho-nan. His name is there perpetuated. Some writers say that E built a city for him there, and allowed him to occupy it as his capital, and to continue nominally to be emperor. Whatever hand E had in it, chronology recognizes T'ae-k'ang as emperor till his death, B.C. 2159; and the reign of his brother Chung-k'ang, with whom we have to do in the next Book, dates from the year following, B.C. 2158.

THE BOOKS OF HEA.

BOOK IV. THE PUNITIVE EXPEDITION OF YIN.

胤征

一節 惟仲康肇位四海、胤侯命掌六師、羲和廢厥職、酒荒于厥邑、胤后承王命徂征。○二節 告

1 I. When Chung-k'ang commenced his reign over all within the four seas, the prince of Yin was commissioned to take charge of the imperial armies. *At this time* He and Ho had neglected the duties of their office, and were sunk in wine in their *private* cities, and the prince of Yin received the imperial charge to go and punish them.

NAME OF THE BOOK.—胤征, 'The Punitive Expedition of Yin.' 胤 is the name of a State;—where it was situated I have not been able to ascertain. The 胤侯 in par. 1 makes it clear that we must take the first character as the name of a principality. K'ang-shing makes it, in his comment on the 8th par. of the Preface, the name of a minister, which would seem to be a gross blunder. It can be accounted for, however. The Book is one of those whose genuineness is controverted. K'ang-shing had not seen it. To guide him in determining the meaning of 胤, he had only the expression in the Preface, and its occurrence in Pt. V., Bk. XXVI., p. 14. His error is quite excusable. 征, 'punitive expedition,'—the meaning is laid down by Mencius, VII. Pt., II., ii., 2. The Book is rightly assigned to the division of the Shoo, which consists of 誓, 'martial speeches.'

CONTENTS. He and Ho, ministers of the Board of Astronomy, had grossly neglected their duties, and given themselves over to licentious indulgence. The emperor considers them worthy of death, and commissions the prince of Yin to destroy them. The prince on his part assembles his forces, and addresses them on the object of the expedition, setting forth the justice of the punishment to be inflicted, and summoning them to second him with all their energies. This is all that appears on the surface of the Book;—whether we are to understand other ends as contemplated in the expedition will be considered in the notes. I have divided it into two chapters:—the first containing only the first paragraph, and stating generally the grounds of the expedition; the second occupying all the other paragraphs, which contain the speech of the prince of Yin.

Ch. I. P. 1. THE OCCASION OF THE EXPEDITION. 惟仲康肇位四海，胤侯命掌六師,—we can give no meaning to the 惟, standing, as it does here, at the commencement of the Book. In modern style,

于衆、曰嗟、予有衆、聖有謨訓、明徵定保、先王克謹天

2 II. He made an announcement to his hosts saying, "Ah! ye, all my troops, there are the well-counselled instructions of the sage *founder of our dynasty*, clearly verified in their power to give stability and security *to the State*:—'The former kings were carefully

for 肇位四海 we should say 始即位,臨御四海. 命 must be taken passively,—'was charged,' 'was appointed.' 掌六師,—'to handle the six armies.' The prince of Yin was raised to the office of 大司馬, made, in our phraseology, commander-in-chief of the imperial forces. 六師=六軍, 'the six armies,' indicated in Book II., as forming the military force of the emperor;—see on Ana., VII. x. 2. This was the first step of Chung-k'ang on his accession to the throne,—to put his armies in the charge of the prince of Yin. The editors of Yung-ching's Shoo give their opinion that Chung-k'ang succeeded his brother in Yang-hea, and that he was not in possession of Yu's capital called Gan-yih (安邑), and the name of which still remains in the dis. of Gan-yih, in the small dep. of K'eae (解州), separated by the pres. dynasty from P'ing-yang. They suppose that E kept him as well as T'ae-kang from all the country north of the Ho. This is against the view of Gan-kwŏ and Ying-tă, that E called Chung-k'ang to the throne in the room of his brother. Looking at the text, I cannot suppose that Chung-k'ang reigned only over part of the empire. The phrases 四海 and 六師 would seem designed as a protest against such a view. Then he is represented as exercising an authority quite independent in the appointment of the prince of Yin, and sending him subsequently against He and Ho. How it was that Chung-k'ang could possess such an authority, situated as he was between his brother, whom E kept from the best part of the empire, and his son whom E cast out of the whole of it,—this is a historical difficulty which we have not facts enow to enable us to solve. There is much speculation about it among the critics. The wiser course in such a case is to rest contented in our ignorance. 羲和廢厥職,酒荒于厥邑,—this He and Ho would be descendants—sons or grandsons—of the ministers of Yaou; and Ts'ae says that the different offices sustained by them in Yaou's time had now been united in one. We need not think so. He and Ho here may very well be the chiefs of the two families, as they rather seem to be in the Can. of Yaou, p. 3. On Ts'ae's view, 厥邑 will be singular, and Gaubil has accordingly translated 'leur ville.' As they were 卿 or high nobles in the employment of the emperor, their cities would be in the territory next to the imperial domain, the first hundred *le* of the *How fuh*, and probably not far from each other. The phrase 廢厥職, in conn. with the next clause, implies that they had both neglected their duty and abandoned their posts. 酒荒,—comp. 色荒 in the last Book, p. 6. 肖后,—not 肖侯, as above. Ts'ae observes that when the princes of the empire took up their residence at court as high ministers, their style was changed from 侯 to 后.

Some time may have elapsed between the prince of Yin's being appointed commander of the imperial armies and his receiving this commission to punish He and Ho; but we naturally conclude that he led all his powers against them. And was it necessary to do this? They were not living in their own fiefs, surrounded by other nobles yielding a reluctant submission to their suzerain. This circumstance harmonizes with the view that He and Ho were in league with E, and that the main object intended by such a display of force was to overawe that dangerous chief, and to weaken his power by cutting off his confederates.

Ch. II. Pp. 2—7. The speech of the prince of Yin. Pp. 2, 3. *Principles of the State for the guidance of officers and others;—preparatory to the introduction and condemnation of He and Ho.*

2. 嗟,—the speech begins like that at Kan, Bk. II., p. 2. 聖有謨訓,明徵定保,—the 聖 here must refer to Yu. The 'Daily Explanation' paraphrases the passage thus:—我夏聖祖大禹,著有謨訓,其言皆明切徵驗,可以定國保邦. It is quoted in the 左傳, 襄二十一年, with 勳 for 訓,—聖有謨勳,明徵定保. A meaning is there also put upon it not so natural as that which I give to it here. What follows are the counsels of Yu. The 'Daily Explanation' goes on to paraphrase them with a—謨訓有曰. Lin Che-k'e observes that 謨 means the counsels offered by a minister to his sove-

戒、臣人克有常憲、百官修輔、厥后惟明明。○三節 每歲孟春、遒人以木鐸、徇于路、官師相規、工執藝事以諫、其

attentive to the warnings of Heaven, and their ministers observed the regular laws *of their offices*. All the officers, *moreover*, watchfully did their duty to assist *the government*, and the sovereign became
3 entirely intelligent.' Every year in the first *month* of spring, the herald with his wooden-tongued bell goes along the roads, *proclaiming*, 'Ye officers able to direct, be prepared with your admonitions. Ye workmen engaged in mechanical affairs, remonstrate on the

reign, as in the 'Counsels of the great Yu,' 'Counsels of Kaou-yaou,' &c.; but that the rules laid down by a sovereign for the guidance of his descendants are also called by the same name, as in the 'Instructions of E,' p. 8. The usage of 訓 is similar. 先王克謹天戒,—'the former kings,' as spoken of by Yu, must refer to Shun and Yaou, and what others he had heard of before them. Compare the language of Shun in the 'Yih and Tseih,' p. 4,—古人之象. 克謹, 'were able to attend sedulously to;'—克, joined to a verb, often serves to emphasize its meaning. 天戒,—'warnings of Heaven,' such as were supposed to be conveyed by eclipses, and other unusual heavenly phenomena. 臣人,—this is understood to mean the great ministers,—輔弼大臣, while the officers generally, large and small, are spoken of in the phrase 百官 below. The 人 after 臣, however, is peculiar; but it must merge in the 臣. 臣人 corresponds to the 先王 before; we cannot render it 'ministers and people.' 明明 is the redoubled adjective, expressing the meaning intensely. 3. Not only was this general principle laid down in the counsels of Yu, that the ministers and officers should all be earnestly assisting to the sovereign, but there was also a special institution to call forth the experience of all classes for the same object. 遒人 is defined by Gan-kwŏ and in the dictionary by 宣令之官, 'the officer who proclaims the orders.' Ying-tă tries to deduce the meaning from one of the significations of 遒, in which it=聚, 'to collect.' This officer collected the people, and gave them their orders, and hence was derived his name.' We may translate the phrase by 'herald.' 木鐸,—see Ana. III. xxiv. The wooden-tongued bell was used for civil, peaceful objects; in war a metal-tongued bell was used. 徇=徧; 徇于路='all along the roads.' What follows—官師,云云,—is to be understood as the language of the herald's proclamation. So it is taken in the 'Daily Explanation.' This view is established likewise by the account of a similar practice in the Chow dynasty;—see the Chow Le, Bk. III. (天官,小宰), par. 52,—正歲帥治官之屬·而觀治象之法·徇以木鐸·曰,不用法者·國有常刑· 官師相規,—官 and 師 are not two classes, but one. They are called 官 as having office, and 師 as supposed to be men of principle and knowledge, fitted to instruct. So, Ts'ae;—官以職言·師以道言· 規,—'a compass,' then used as=正, 'to correct,' the use of a compass being necessary to make correct circles. There is a difficulty with 相. We naturally interpret 相規 'to correct one another;' but this would give no pertinent meaning. How would the officers' not correcting one another bear on the guilt of He and Ho in not admonishing their sovereign? The object of the 規 must be defects in the emperor's conduct or government. The paraphrase in the 'Daily Explanation' brings out this very clearly:—凡職官有道者·或遇朝廷之德政闕失·卽直言

或不恭、邦有
常刑。○惟時
四節
義和、顛覆厥
德、沈亂于酒、
畔官離次、俶
擾天紀、遐棄
厥司、乃季秋
月朔、辰弗集
于房、瞽奏鼓、
嗇夫馳、庶人

subject of your business! If any of you disrespectfully *neglect this requirement*, the country has regular punishments for you.'

4 "Now here are He and Ho. They have entirely subverted their virtue, and are sunk and lost in wine. They have violated the duties of their office, and left their posts. They have been the first to allow the regulations of heaven to get into disorder, putting far from them their proper business. On the first day of the last month of autumn, the sun and moon did not meet harmoniously in Fang. The blind *musicians* beat their drums; the inferior officers and common people bustled and ran about. He and Ho, however, as if they

以相規正, 'all ye officers, being men of principle, if you see that there are defects in the virtue or government of the court, speak out directly that you may correct them.' This meaning of 相 does not first occur to the reader, but it is admissible;—the emperor is the other party opposite to whom the officers are to suppose themselves placed. 工執藝事以諫,—here we go below the official class; even mechanics might see extravagance in the expenditure of the court on articles of their departments, which they were bound to find some way of remonstrating about,—so earnest was Yu, and such precautions had he taken, that the errors of the sovereign should be brought to his notice.

[Both Gaubil and Medhurst err egregiously in translating these last two clauses. De Mailla hits the meaning of the former, but loses entirely that of the second. Grosier, in a note to De Mailla's version, seems to approve that of Gaubil.]

We find from 遒人 to 以諫 quoted as from the 'Books of Hea' in the 左傳, 襄十四年. 其或不恭,—on this use of 恭, see Mencius, IV., Pt., I., i., 13.

P. 4. *The crimes of He and Ho; and the punishment due to them.* 惟時(=是)羲和, 顛覆厥德, 沈亂于酒,—comp. the She-king, Pt. III., Bk. III., Ode. ii. 3. 畔官離次,—the dict. explains 畔 with ref. to this passage, by 離, 'to leave.' It is better, however, to take it in the sense of 'to disobey,' 'to violate.' 官='the duties of office'; 次='the place,' 'the post' 俶擾天紀,—俶=始, 'the first;' 擾=亂, 'to throw into confusion;' 天紀, 'the heavenly regulators.' See Part V., Bk. IV., p. 8, where those regulators are said to be five,—the seasons of the year, the sun, the moon, the stars, and the calculations of the calendar. The phrase in the text is to be taken generally:—He and Ho had neglected the contemplation of the Heavens, and attention to the calendar, so putting far from them 'their proper business' (厥司=其所司之事). 乃季秋月朔, 辰弗集于房,—here is a specific and flagrant instance of the neglect of duty by those astronomers. On the first day of the last month of autumn it had happened that 辰弗集于房. The year when this took place is not mentioned, but we cannot do other than suppose that it was the same year in which the speech was made, or the one immediately before it. The prince of Yin could not have spoken as he did, if a second autumn had intervened between the phenomenon and the date of his speech. 房—see on the Can. of Yaou, par. 5, where we saw that this was the central constellation of the larger group of constellations in the eastern quarter, called the 'Azure Dragon.' It begins with the star π of Scorpio and ends with σ, and extends over a space of less than $5\frac{1}{2}°$ (see Gaubil's Shoo-king, pp. 68, 69, and

走、羲和尸厥官、罔聞知、昏迷于天象、以干先王之誅、政典曰、先時者、殺無赦、不及時者、殺無赦。五節 ○今予以

were mere personators of the dead in their offices, heard nothing and knew nothing;—so stupidly went they astray *from their duty* in the matter of the heavenly appearances, and rendering themselves liable to the death appointed by the former kings. The statutes of government say, 'When they anticipate the time, let them be put to death without mercy; when they are behind the time, let them be put to death without mercy.'

J. B. Biot's 'Etudes sur l' Astronomie Indienne et Chinoise,' p. 375). The clause 辰弗集于房 has always been understood as describing the fact of an eclipse of the sun, on the day and month indicated, in that portion of the heavens; and there can be no doubt the interpretation is correct. Down to the present day ceremonies substantially the same as those which the prince of Yin goes on to describe are observed on the occurrence of such a phenomenon. The passage is quoted moreover in the 左傳, 昭十七年, corresponding to B.C. 524, and this explanation given of it.—There can be no doubt therefore as to the meaning. As to the characters themselves, Medhurst translates them.—'There was a conjunction of the sun and moon without being fully combined, in the constellation of Fang;' and Gaubil has:—'Le soleil et la lune en conjunction n'ont pas été d'accord dans Fang.' Gaubil's version is a literal translation from the interpretation of Ts'ae Ts'in, who bases it on the fact that in the Books of Han instead of 集 we have 輯, and says that the two characters may be interchanged, adding:—日月會次, 不相和輯. I doubt the interchangeableness of 集 and 輯; but the former has the established significations of 合, [this is Gan-kwŏ's explanation *in loc.*], and 齊, which give the ideas of 'harmonious, regular union.' 辰 must be the conjunction of the sun and moon for the month in question;—see the Canon of Yaou, par. 3. 瞽奏鼓, 嗇夫馳, 庶人走,—these were customs observed on occasion of an eclipse; similar practices were observed under the Chow dynasty; and with some modifications they are prescribed by the Chinese government at the present time. See Biot's Studies above referred to, pp. 357—360. 瞽奏鼓,—by 'the blind' we must understand the musicians who were employed in antiquity because of their blindness, their loss of the sense of sight being supposed to sharpen that of hearing. 奏=伐, 'to strike.' 嗇夫 is explained by Ts'ae—小臣, 'small officers;' according to K'ang-shing, they were *employés* under the Minister of Works. By 庶人 are intended what Mencius, V., Pt. II., ii., 6, calls 庶民在官者, 'such of the common people as were employed about the government offices';—see the note on that passage. Of what these people ran, and the smaller officers galloped about for, we get an idea from the passage of the 左傳 where this text is quoted. We are there told that when an eclipse happened, the emperor fasted, and had the drums beat before the altar of the spirits of the land, while the princes of States presented offerings before that altar and had the drums beat in their court. [It would appear from the same passage, that in the Chow dynasty these things were observed only when eclipses happened on the first day of the first month of the year. In this point the custom of Hea, with which the present usage agrees, differed from that of Chow.] Again, in the Chow Le, Bk. XXXVII. (near the end), we read of the bow and arrows used to deliver the sun, and those used to deliver the moon. On an eclipse of the sun, they shot their arrows into the sky to frighten away the injurious moon, and *vice versa*. See the long note of K'ung Ying-tă on the passage, where immense lore is brought to bear on its illustration. While the phenomenon was occasioning so much excitement, He and Ho were entirely indifferent to it. 尸厥官,—comp. Bk. III., p. 1. 昏迷于天象,—'darkly going astray in regard to the heavenly appearances.' 迷,—comp. Canon of Shun, p. 2.

政典,—see on the last Book, p. 8, 有典有則. 先時者,云云,—there is considerable diversity of view in interpreting this sentence. First, the 'Daily Explanation' paraphrases it thus:—曆官職掌,凡躔度節候,俱要推筭合時,或失于先時,或失于後時,罪當殺無赦, 'They who are intrusted with the office of regulating the calendar must calculate exactly to the time the degrees of motion of the heavenly bodies, with the terms of the year. If they err by being too early or too late, their crime requires that they be put to death without mercy.' This view is approved by Gaubil, who translates:—'Celui qui devance ou qui recule les tems doit être, sans rémission, puni de mort;' and he adds in a note, 'Une loi si severe contre les calculateurs d'éclypses, dans des tems si reculés, denote une ancienne methode pour les éclypses.' Possibly astronomers of this high antiquity in China may have been able to calculate eclipses after a fashion, by means of the cycle of 19 years,—if indeed they were acquainted with that, which is quite uncertain; but I find it difficult to believe they had attained so far. Nor is this interpretation of the text sufficiently evident or attested by tradition to bring us to Gaubil's conclusion.

Second, Gan-kwŏ gives a more general and plausible interpretation. By 時 he understands 'the four seasons, and the four and twenty terms into which they were divided, with the times of new and full moon and the two quarters' (四時節氣,弦望晦朔). On this view the statute was to the effect that the astronomers neglecting their work, and allowing the months and seasons to get into confusion, were to be punished with death. It does not bear directly on the special crime of He and Ho's absence from their posts on the occurrence of the eclipse; but we can conceive of the prince of Yin's thinking it sufficiently to the purpose to appeal to it in addressing his troops.

Third, Lin Che-k'e separated the passage from the par. to which in all editions it is now united, and joined it to the part of the speech which follows. The prince of Yin has done with He and Ho when he has once said that they were liable to the death appointed by the former kings, and then turns to his troops to urge them to do their duty, prefacing his remarks with this reference to the canons of Government on military law, by which neglect of orders, whether in anticipating movements or in delaying them, was punishable with death. This view has been ingeniously supported by Ch'in Leih (陳櫟);—see the 附錄. Choo He condemned Che-k'e's interpretation, on the ground that it was forced, the passage being connected more naturally with the preceding part of the speech than with what follows. The editors of Yung-ching's Shoo, however, profess themselves unable to decide positively between this view and the first. The ordinance is too severe, they say, against the astronomers, who might easily make a mistake in their figures, while it may be acknowledged if it form part of the stern code of martial law. For myself I have hesitated between the second and third views, abiding for the present by the second. The passage, with the slight variation of 逮 for 及, is found in Seun-tsze, 君道篇, but not in a connection which enables us to judge of the meaning he put upon it.

[The eclipse of the sun related in this paragraph has always been a subject of great interest to students of history in China and elsewhere. Could it be satisfactorily verified, a date would be established in Chinese history, which would for ever settle all doubts as to its antiquity and general certainty.

The accession of Chung-k'ang dates, it has been seen, B.C. 2158 (Gaubil says 2159. But there is no real difference between him and me, as I do not reckon the year of our Lord's birth, the dates in my scheme of Chinese chronology running thus:—A.D. 1; A.D.; B.C. 1. Gaubil reckoning—A.D. 1; B.C. 1, my B.C. 2158 is with him B.C. 2159). The Shoo does not say expressly that the eclipse took place in that year, though the ordinary, and perhaps the readiest, inference has been that it did do so. But such an inference may not be correct. The appointment of the prince of Yin may have been one of the first acts of Chung-k'ang, and the expedition against He and Ho may not have been undertaken till some years after. If the eclipse could be verified any time during the reign, i.e., between B.C. 2158 and 2146, there would be a sufficient harmony between the chronology and the astronomy. More than this, in the scantiness of dates and the uncertainties attaching to the particular reigns of the Hea emperors from Yu to Këĕ, one of which uncertainties I pointed out in the concluding note to the last Book, I should almost be prepared to regard with satisfaction a verification of the eclipse in any year of the first half of the 22d century before our era, or even, I will venture to say, between B.C. 2050 and 2158. To be sure, the genuineness of 'The Punitive Expedition of Yin' is called in question; but in regard to this eclipse, we know, on the authority of the 左傳, which I have adduced, that the record of it was in one of the Books of Hea. Whether the Books of the Shoo additional to those derived from Fuh-shang were a compilation of the times of the Tsin dynasty or not, one of them—the real 'Expedition of Yin'—did contain the same passage that we have in the present text.

Now, the year B.C. 2158 must be given up as the date of the eclipse. No such phenomenon could have then occurred. Ts'ae tells us, however, that the astronomers of the T'ang dynasty (by which time they began to have such a knowledge of the precession of the equinoxes as enabled them to attempt these investigations) determined that the eclipse took place in the fifth year of Chung-k'ang. Several of the early Jesuit missionaries applied themselves to solve the point,—none with such devotion to the inquiry

爾有衆、奉將
天罰爾、衆士
同力王室、尙
弼予欽承天
子威命。○火六節
炎崑岡、玉石
俱焚、天吏逸
德、烈于猛火、
殲厥渠魁、脅
從罔治、舊染

5 "Now I, with you all, am entrusted with the execution of the punishment appointed by Heaven. Unite your strength, all of you warriors, for the imperial House. Lend me your help, I pray you, reverently to carry out the dread charge of the son of Heaven."

6 "When the fire blazes over the ridge of Kwăn, gems and stones are burned together; *but* when a minister of Heaven exceeds in doing his duty, the consequences are fiercer than raging fire. I will so

as Father Gaubil, who brought out the result, in harmony with the conclusions of the T'ang scholars, that the eclipse occurred on the 11th October (old style) of the year B.C. 2155 (2154 in my scheme), the 5th year of Chung-k'ang, and that it was visible at Gan-yih at 6h. 49m. in the morning. Here was an important result; the only circumstance to render one dissatisfied with it was that the eclipse must have been very small, extending only over a sixth part of the sun's diameter, so that it was little likely to arrest attention.

Since Gaubil's time the tables used in those calculations have been rendered more accurate, and the conclusions arrived at possess a greater certainty. My friend, the Rev. Mr. Chalmers of Canton, took in hand in the present year to verify the eclipse, and confirmed Gaubil's conclusion so far as regarded the year, the month, and the day, but found that it must have occurred during the night, before the rising of the sun at Gan-yih, and not after it. I have since found that the same result was obtained in France in 1840 by Largeteau, an able astronomer (see Biot's 'Etudes,' p. 377). It would seem then that we must give up the year 2154 as well as 2158. And yet the matter may be considered as still *sub judice*. It is only in the present century that the secular variation of the moon's mean motion, which seriously affects the calculation of eclipses so remote as this of Chung-k'ang, has been determined with an approach to nice exactness. It may yet come out, as the lunar tables are perfected, that the eclipse of 2154 was visible at Gan-yih, and in that case we shall not hesitate to accept it as the one referred to in this Book.

Mr. Chalmers has determined that there were eclipses of the sun, in or near the constellation Fang, in the years B.C. 2135 (or 2136), 2127 (or 2128), and 2108 (or 2109). Of these that B.C. 2127 was visible in China, and very high Chinese authority has contended that it was to it that the prince of Yin referred. For the reasons which I have assigned I could accept either of the dates 2154 or 2127. I can hardly doubt that on one or other of them there was the phenomenon, by their disregard of which He and Ho afforded the ground which is alleged for their punishment. The text on which I have dwelt so long is to be regarded as a strong confirmation of the substantial truth of Chinese history.]

P. 5. *The troops are exhorted to be brave and energetic.* Compare Yu's speech to his army, Pt. II., Bk. II., 20. The 'Daily Explanation' paraphrases 以爾有衆 by 率爾六軍衆士, which is, plainly enough, the meaning, though we cannot give 率 as a synonym of 以. We may say here that 以＝用. 將＝行, 'to execute.' 同力王室＝同心盡力于王室. A preposition like 于, or a verb signifying 'to maintain,' has to be supplied. 承...命,—承 is 'to receive,' but must be taken here with the pregnant meaning of 'executing' as well.

P. 6. *How the imperial charge was to be executed with discrimination, and justice tempered with forbearance.* 火炎崑山,—Ts'ae says that 崑 is 'the name of a mountain, which produces gems.' Gan-kwŏ's account is substantially the same. It is best taken so. The dict. would lead us to say that 崑崙 is meant, which is now referred to the 枯爾坤山, in the west of the Koko-nor, where the Yellow river has its sources. But the text leads us to conceive of the Kwăn as a volcanic mountain, which I have not read that the Kwănlun is. 天吏,—see Mencius, II., Pt. I., v. 6, *et al.* 逸德,—逸＝過, 'to go be-

汙俗、咸與惟新。○嗚呼、威克厥愛、允濟、愛克厥威、允罔功、其爾衆士、懋戒哉。

destroy *only* the chief criminals, and not punish their forced followers, while those who have long been stained by their filthy manners will be allowed to renovate themselves."

7 "Oh! when sternness overcomes compassion, then things are surely conducted to a successful issue. When compassion overcomes sternness, no merit can be achieved. All ye, my warriors, exert yourselves, and be cautious."

yond.' 逸德 is virtue—conduct in the performance of what may be considered duty—carried to its utmost, going beyond. 渠魁,—'the great chiefs.' He and Ho are intended. 脅從,—脅=迫脅, 'pressed.' Those parties had been forced into combination with He and Ho. The expressions here certainly give support to the view that those astronomers were associated with some rebellious movement against the imperial authority.

咸與惟新,—the 'Daily Explanation' has here—皆與赦除,使之改過自新. 與 is to be taken as=許, 'to allow,' 'to grant to.'

P. 7. *The severity of martial law.* We are to understand that the prince of Yin here warns his troops, that if they do not do their duty, they must not expect him to deal with them on any principle of indulgence. As to their duty in the circumstances, the 'Daily Explanation' finds it in the concluding words 懋戒哉, the 懋 referring to p. 4, where they were urged to unite their strength for the imperial House, and the 戒 to p. 6, where it is laid down how their justice was to be tempered. It paraphrases:—懋勉于同力,警戒于逸德,以共濟弼承王命之功哉. This is finding a great deal of meaning in the terms. Yen Jŏ-keu argues strongly that this paragraph is adapted from the 左傳,昭二十三年, where a general of Woo (吳), says:—吾聞之,作事,威克其愛,雖小必濟. It is more likely, however, that the general of Woo was adapting the words from the copies of the Shoo current in his time. His application of them is not happy;—it is enigmatical indeed, but Jŏ-keu's argument is here, as in many other places, too eagerly pursued.

Concluding and connecting note. With this Book terminate Confucius' selections from the monuments of the Hea dynasty subsisting in his time. Seventeen reigns altogether are assigned to it. Chung-k'ang's was the fourth. Of the twelve that follow, the Shoo gives us no intimation; but the name of the last emperor and his wickedness are often mentioned and dwelt upon in the Parts of the classic that follow this.

Sze-ma Ts'een gives us little more than a catalogue of the emperors' reigns, how they came to the throne and how they died. He has not a word on the length of their reigns; and only on K'ung-këă, the 13th from Yu, and Këĕ, the last, does he give a few brief notices of their characters. His whole account is comprised in less than a page. The fragments of the history of those times that have been gathered from other sources, more or less trustworthy, and are found in Choo He's 'General Mirror of History' (通鑑綱目), and in what may be called the 'Standard Annals' (歷代統紀表), may be related in brief space.

Chung-k'ang's reign of 13 years terminated B.C. 2146. We should like to know the relations that existed between him and E, but all we are informed of is that this chief put to death Pih-fung, or the baron Fung (伯封), one of his ministers, a son of K'wei, Shun's minister of Music. We are left in uncertainty as to whether the act was one of justice, the punishment of a criminal, or one of hostility, the cutting off a faithful adherent.

Chung-k'ang was succeeded, B.C. 2145, by his son Seang (后相), who reigned for 27 years. In the first year of his reign he had to withdraw across the Ho to Shang-k'ew (商邱), still the name of the principal district in the dep. of Kwei-tih, Ho-nan. He was driven to this step, we may well believe, by E, who now exercised the supreme authority in K'e-chow. In 2138 E was killed by a minister of his own, or at least on his instigation. The minister's name was Han-tsuh, or perhaps we should rather say Tsuh of the State Han (see the 左傳,襄四年; and comp. Mencius IV. Pt. II. xxiv). He took to himself E's wife, and by her had two sons, Këaou (澆) and He (豷), the former of whom by his father's orders put the emperor to death in Shang-k'ew, B.C. 2118, he himself being only 20 years of age. Various 'punishments' of barbarous tribes are ascribed to Seang in the early years of his reign, which it is difficult to believe he was capable of in his circumstances. We may infer from the accounts, however, that the wild tribes, in and about the empire, took advantge of the weakness and confusion of the government to try and regain their independence or to make plundering incursions.

On the death of Seang, Tsuh claimed the empire, and maintained himself on the throne for 39 years. When the emperor was killed, however, one of his wives, who was pregnant, made her escape to her native State of Jing (仍), of which her father was chief. There she gave birth to a son, known as Shaou-k'ang (少康), who lead a perilous life for nearly 40 years. His existence was known to the usurper, who made various attempts to get him in his power. At one time he was chief herdsman to the chief of Jing; at another he was chief cook to the prince of Yu. The latter chief recognized his worthiness, and gave him his two daughters in marriage, and an establishment in the pres. dis. of Yung-ho, dep. of P'ing-yang. There his capacity and character still more developed themselves. The old adherents of his House took heart. The people remembered Yu. An end was made of the usurping family, and Shaou-k'ang was raised to the throne of his father in B.C. 2078.

Shaou-k'ang's recovery of the throne [we might say K'ang the third; Chung-k'ang was K'ang the second, and T'ae-k'ang K'ang the first] was followed by the reverent acknowledgment of the chiefs of the empire, and the submission of the wild tribes. The only event of his reign which is recorded, however, is his appointment of one of his sons by a secondary wife to be the chief of Yuĕ (越), there to maintain the sacrifices at the tomb of Yu, who died, we saw, at Hwuy-k'e, in the pres. Chĕ-keang. The emperor's son was styled Woo-yu (無餘). He was the first feudal chief established in the regions of Woo and Yuĕ, so slowly did the conquering Chinese firmly establish their rule over the country.

Shaou-k'ang was succeeded, B.C. 2057, by his son Ch'oo, (后杼); and he was followed, after a reign of 17 years, in B.C. 2039, by his son Hwae (后槐).

After Hwae came his son Măng (后芒), B.C. 2013; then Măng's son, Sëĕ (后泄), B.C. 1995; then, Sëĕ's son, Puh-këang (后不降), B.C. 1979; then, Puh-këang's brother, Keung (后扃), B.C. 1920; then, Keung's son, Kin 后廑, B.C. 1899; then, a son of Puh-keang, called K'ung-këă (后孔甲), B.C. 1878.

Sze-ma Ts'een pauses in his list of all but nameless sovereigns to dwell on the character of K'ung-këă, whom he pronounces to have been superstitious and dissipated, so as to alienate from him the hearts of all the princes. In the 27th year of his reign, B.C. 1851, there occurred an event, most important to the fortunes of the Hea dynasty,—the birth of Le (履), son of the chief of Shang, who became in due time T'ang the Successful, the founder of a new line of emperors.

K'ung-këă was succeeded by his son Kaou (后臯), B.C. 1847; and he again by his son Fă (后發), B.C. 1836. Fă died B.C. 1816, leaving the throne to his son Kwei, (癸), with whom the sovereignty of the line of Yu came to an end.

Kwei is better known by his name of Këĕ, 'the Injurer of men and Destroyer of many' (賊人多殺曰桀). The first three and thirty years of his long reign are a blank. Possessing extraordinary strength, able to twist bars of iron about like ropes, he gloried in his vigour, and wearied out the people with expeditions of war. In B.C. 1785, he proceeded to attack the chief of She (有施氏), in the neighbourhood of mount Mung in the present Shan-tung. The chief propitiated his anger by presenting him with his daughter Me-he (妺喜), of surpassing beauty, but more depraved, if possible, than the emperor himself. All thoughts of prudence were lost amid the enjoyment of her charms. He gratified all her caprices. He made her a chamber of carnation-stone, with side apartments of ivory, a splendid tower, and a bed glittering with gems. Around this he heaped up, in their wild dissoluteness, mounds of flesh, hung dried meats on all the trees, filled a pond with wine till they could row a boat on it, while three thousand people would make their appearance at beat of drum and drink up the liquor like so many oxen. All government was neglected. In the mean time the avenger was growing up. T'ang succeeded to his father's principality, B.C. 1783, and soon drew the regards of all thoughtful men to himself. The great officers who felt ashamed of Këë's vices, and mourned the condition of the empire, betook themselves to Shang; the people who groaned beneath the oppression of their lords, too many of whom followed Këë's example, sighed for the gentle rule of T'ang. The emperor was roused to fits of jealousy, and at one time got T'ang in his power, and imprisoned him. He let him go, however; and at last, B.C. 1765, after many misgivings, T'ang took the field against his sovereign. There could be no doubt as to the result. Heaven and earth combined with men to show their detestation of the tyrant. Two suns fought in the sky. The earth shook. Mountains were moved from their strong foundations. Rivers were dried up. Këë was routed, and fled south to Ts'aou, which is still the name of a district in the dep. of Loo-chow (廬州), in Ngan-hwuy, and there he was kept a prisoner till his death three years after. His son and some of his adherents made their way to the wilds of the north, and mingled among the barbarous tribes.

Thus miserably ended the dynasty of Hea, having extended, including the usurpations of E and Tsuh, over 439 years.

THE SHOO KING.

PART IV. THE BOOKS OF SHANG.

BOOK I. THE SPEECH OF T'ANG.

商書

湯誓

王[一節]曰、格爾衆庶、悉聽朕言、非台小子、敢行稱亂、有夏多罪、天命殛之。○今[二節]

1 I. The king said, "Come, ye multitudes of the people, listen all to my words. It is not I, the little child, who dare to undertake *what may seem to be* a rebellious enterprize; but for the many crimes of the sovereign of Hea Heaven has given the charge to destroy him.

NAME OF THE PART.—商書, 'The Books of Shang.' 商 (the reader will distinguish the character from 尙, which is the title given to the whole of the Shoo. A Chinese scholar can discriminate them by their different tones) is the dynastic designation by which T'ang and his descendants possessed the empire, B.C. 1765—1122, a period of 644 years. The family traced their origin up to Hwang-te, through Sëë, (契), a son of the emperor Kuh, and minister of Instruction to Yaou and Shun. For his services at that time he was invested with the principality of Shang, a part or the whole of the territory now forming the small department of Shang in Shen-se, and received the surname of Tsze (子). From Sëë to T'ang were fourteen generations; and we find the latter at a considerable distance from the ancestral fief, and having his capital in the first place, before he dethroned Këë, at the southern Pŏ, which seems correctly referred to the dis. of Shang-k'ew (商邱), dep. of Kwei-tih, in Ho-nan. The title of the dynasty, however, was derived from the original Shang to which Sëë was appointed.

We saw, on the 9th paragraph of the Preface, that more than one half the documents originally composing this Part of the Shoo were lost, while of the 11 Books which still claim to be received in it there are only 5 whose genuineness is not contested.

NAME OF THE BOOK.—湯誓, 'The Speech of T'ang.' We must regard 湯, not as the honorary posthumous title, but as the designation of the emperor during his lifetime;—see in the note on the Canon of Yaou, par. 1. His name, as we have it from himself, was Le (履). Sze-ma Ts'een says it was 天乙, of which I have not met with a satisfactory explanation. 誓,—see on 'The Speech at Kan.'

爾有衆、汝曰、我后不恤我衆、舍我穡事、而割正夏。予惟聞汝衆言、夏氏有罪、予畏上帝、不敢不正。三節 ○今汝

2 "Now, ye multitudes, you are saying, 'Our prince does not compassionate us, but is calling us away from our husbandry to attack and punish *the ruler of* Hea.' I have indeed heard *these* words of you all: *but* the sovereign of Hea is an offender, and, *as* I fear God, I dare not but punish him.

'The Speech of T'ang' is found in both 'the old and modern texts.' It is now the first of the Books of Shang, though it was in the time of Confucius only the sixth. The five that preceded it have been lost;—see on the 'Preface of Confucius.'

CONTENTS. T'ang having summoned his people to take the field with him against Këë, and finding them backward in the enterprise, he addresses them, and sets forth his own reasons for attacking the tyrant, in order to remove their hesitation, and silence their murmurs, while in the end he uses both promises and threats to move them to obey his orders. The whole Book is very short; but I have divided it into two chapters,—the first containing three parr., and giving T'ang's reasons for his course; and the second, in only one par., laying down his martial law. The speech must have been made at Pŏ, and in the year B.C. 1765.

Ch. I. Pp. 1—3. T'ANG'S REASONS FOR ATTACKING KEE, AND THE UNREASONABLENESS OF HIS SUBJECTS' MURMURS. 1. 王曰,—we have no introductory paragraphs as in the 'speech at Kan,' telling us the occasion of the speech. We can, however, supply the want from the preface, p. 12. The use of 王 to denominate T'ang, when he was not yet on the throne, has occasioned a good deal of criticism. Ts'ae says that it is a case of prolepsis by the recorder of the speech. Yet as T'ang was the 天吏, or 'minister of Heaven,' the moment that he took the field, he was the rightful sovereign of the empire, and Këë was only an ordinary man. 非台小子,敢行稱亂,—台 (read *e*)=我, the first personal pronoun. 小子, 'the little child,' is a frequent designation, humbly applied to themselves by the emperors. Ts'ae Peen (蔡卞) says:—'In an announcement to the myriad regions, and in distinction from their multitudes, the emperor calls himself "the one man." Realizing his relation to God, and feeling as in His presence, he calls himself "the little child" (以天子告萬方,故稱予一人,對上帝而言,故稱台小子). 稱=舉, 'to raise up,' 'to undertake.' Keang Shing edits the character with 人 at the side, on the authority of the 說文. T'ang states very distinctly the reason of his movement. Këë, 'the holder of Hea,' was a criminal condemned by Heaven which had given charge to cut him off. But how had Heaven done this? and how was the charge given to T'ang? The answer to both questions is the same:—'By the voice of the people.' 2. Acc. to the view of Gan-kwŏ (and here he is followed by Keang Shing), T'ang addresses in this par. not his own people, but the subjects generally of Këë. 我后, 'our sovereign,' is Këë, and 舍我穡事而割正—'he disregards our husbandry, and exercises a cruel government.' 割 is explained by 剝, with reference to cruel dismemberments inflicted by Këë; and 正 is taken as=政, 'government.' Gan-kwŏ takes no notice of the 夏 after 正. and Keang Shing argues that the character is spurious. With the same critics, moreover, the clause 夏氏有罪 is the language of the people, the words which T'ang had heard from them.

This view has many difficulties,—is inadmissible, indeed. 夏 is here in the text, and we cannot throw it out. Nor can we take 正 in 割正 differently from its mean. in 不敢不正. No similar difficulties attach to the interpretation given by Ts'ae, which I have followed in the translation. 正=治罪, 'to punish,' a well established meaning of the character. 夏氏,—this usage is much akin to our own of calling men by their estates and

書經

其曰、夏罪其如台、夏王率遏衆力、率割夏邑、有衆率怠弗協、曰、時日曷喪、予及汝皆亡、夏德若茲、今朕必往。○四節 爾尙輔予一人、致天之罰、予其大賚汝、爾無不信、朕不食言、爾不從誓言、予則孥戮汝、罔有攸赦。

3 "Now you are saying, 'What are the crimes of Hea to us?' The king of Hea does nothing but exhaust the strength of his people, and exercise oppression in the cities of Hea. His people have all become idle *in his service*, and will not assist him. They are saying, 'When will this sun expire? We will all perish with thee.' Such is the course of *the sovereign of* Hea, and now I must go *and punish him.*

4 II. "Assist, I pray you, me, the one man, to carry out the punishment appointed by Heaven. I will greatly reward you. On no account disbelieve me;—I will not eat my words. If you do not obey the words which I have spoken to you, I will put your children with you to death;—you will find no forgiveness."

possessions. 3. 夏罪其如台,—Gan-kwŏ takes 如台 as=如我所聞之言, 'according to the words which we have heard.' Here Keang Shing rightly declines to follow him, and follows Sze-ma Ts'een, who reads—有罪其奈何, which he interprets as an exclamation of despair. More accordant with the tone of the whole speech, and better warranted by usage is the meaning given in the translation. The two 其 intensify the language;—see on Can. of Yaou, p. 11. 率遏,率割,率怠,—in all these cases 率 is to be taken as=一切, 'in every thing,' 'universally.' Gan-kwŏ is unable to think of any meaning for it but 'to lead,' and labours hard, but unsuccessfully, to explain the passages accordingly. 割夏邑,—here 割 must be explained by 剝. 時(=是)日曷喪,予及汝皆亡,—see on Mencius, I. Pt. II., iv. 4. Ch'ing would seem to make this passage the words of Këĕ himself. He says:—'Këĕ seeing that the people wished to rebel, compared himself to the sun, saying, "Has ever that sun perished? If that sun perish, then I and you will also all perish." He made use of the sun's security from danger, to make the people dread himself;'—see the 後案, *in loc.* Mencius is a safer guide as to the meaning of the text than K'ang-shing. We may well believe, however, that Këĕ had compared himself to the sun. Different traditions say it was in reply to the remonstrances of E Yin that he did so. 夏德若此,—this is a very evident instance of the use of 德 for evil conduct.

Ch. II. P. 4. T'ang's determination to have his orders obeyed.—Promises of reward, and threats of punishment. Comp. Yu's speech in the 'Counsels of Yu,' p 20, and 'The speech at Kan.' 予其大賚爾,—賚=賜, 'to give to,' 'to confer gifts,'='to reward.' Sze-ma Ts'een has 理, which it is difficult to account for. The 其 here is strongly intensive. The usage approaches to that pointed out on Can. of Yaou, p. 12.

汝不從誓言,我則孥戮汝,—the want of such a clause as 汝不從誓言 is felt in 'The speech of Kan,' p. 5. 我則孥戮汝 is there so unconnected that Woo Ch'ing supposes it slipped in by mistake from the present passage.

CONCLUDING NOTE. Though T'ang professed to have it in charge from Heaven to destroy Këĕ, and the charge of Heaven was ascertained from the voice of the people, it is plain from this speech that it cost him some trouble to get the co-operation even of his own subjects. The will of Heaven is not always clearly intimated in providence. Even when it is so, it must be wrought out by those who perceive it amidst and against many conflicting interests and prejudices.

This speech was followed by the battle of Ming-t'eaou (Preface, p. 12), not far from the capital of Hea, and by the defeat and downfall of the tyrant.

THE BOOKS OF SHANG

BOOK II. THE ANNOUNCEMENT OF CHUNG-HWUY.

仲虺之誥

成湯放桀于南巢、惟有慙德、曰、予恐來世以台爲口實。○仲虺乃作誥曰、嗚呼、惟天

1 I. When T'ang, the Successful, was keeping Këë in banishment in Nan-ch'aou, he had a feeling of shame on account of his conduct, and said, "I am afraid that in future ages men will fill their mouths with me."

NAME OF THE BOOK.—仲虺之誥, 'The Announcement of Chung-hwuy.' Chung-hwuy was one of the principal ministers of T'ang, descended from a He-chung (奚仲), Master of the carriages (車正), under the Hea dynasty, and who at first occupied the territory of Sëë (薛), which was in the pres. dis. of T'ăng, (滕), dep. of Yen-chow, Shan-tung. He-chung removed to the pres. sub. department of P'ei (邳) in Këang-soo, but Chung-hwuy appears still in Sëë;—see the 左傳定元年 (near the beginning). The family traced their line up to Hwang-te; their surname was 任;—see the 歷代疆域表. Chaou K'e and many other scholars have made Chung-hwuy the same as Lae-choo (萊朱), a minister of T'ang, mentioned by Mencius, VII., Pt. II., xxxviii. 2; but it is only by inferential reasoning that the point can be made out. 誥=告, 'to tell,' 'to announce to.' 'Announcements' form one of the divisions of the Shoo, and this is the first of them. They are distinguished from the 誓, which are speeches made to an army, as being made in a general assembly for the information of all (誓, 用之于軍旅, 誥, 用之于會同, 以喻衆). From this account of them, we must understand that the 'Announcement of Chung-hwuy' was not addressed to T'ang only, but was spoken or published for the general information.

On a reference to the Preface, it will be seen that there were originally four other Books, which are now lost, between the 'Speech of T'ang' and this. The time that elapsed between the Speech and the Announcement, however, could not have been long; and, indeed, the one follows the other in the arrangement of the Books, which we derive from Ch'ing Heuen and other scholars, who were not acquainted with Gan-kwo's discoveries. According to the Preface, the Announcement was made at a place called Ta-keung, for which in the 'Historical Records' we find T'ae-keuen-t'aou (泰

生民有欲、無主乃亂、惟天生聰明時乂、有夏昏德、民墜塗炭、天乃錫王勇智、表正萬邦、纘禹舊服、茲率厥典、奉若天命。

2 II. On this Chung-hwuy made the following announcement:—"Oh! Heaven gives birth to the people with *such* desires, that without a ruler they must fall into all disorders; and Heaven *again* gives birth to the man of intelligence whose business it is to regulate them. The sovereign of Hea had his virtue all-obscured, and the people were *as if they were* fallen amid mire and charcoal. Heaven hereupon gifted *our* king with valour and wisdom, to serve as a mark and director to the myriad States, and to continue the old ways of Yu. You are now only following the standard course,

卷陶; the 陶 is probably spurious). Ts'een also says that in the interval T'ang, by the advice of E Yin, had proclaimed himself emperor. We are still, therefore, in the year B.C. 1765.

CONTENTS. T'ang is suffering from a feeling of remorse at having dethroned Këĕ, and is afraid that his fame will suffer from his act. Ch'ung-hwuy sets himself to vindicate the course of his chief, and shows first that he was called to the throne by the will of Heaven; next, that he was called to it by the wishes of the people; and finally, he urges on him various wise counsels. The whole naturally falls into 4 chapters:—the first, in one par., giving the occasion of the Announcement; the second, in two parr., showing that T'ang had only obeyed the guidance of Heaven; the third, in three parr., containing how men consented with Heaven in the matter; and the fourth, in three parr., containing Chung-hwuy's own counsels.

CH. I. P. 1. T'ANG'S DOUBT AS TO THE RIGHTEOUSNESS OF HIS COURSE. 成湯,—Gan-kwŏ says:—武功成,故日成湯, 'His military operations were brought to a successful issue, and therefore he was styled 成湯.' Gaubil and De Mailla don't translate 成 at all, but transfer it; Medhurst has 'the accomplished T'ang',—which is not good. 放桀于南巢,—Këĕ had fled to Nan-ch'aou, and T'ang simply took measures that he should remain there. We must not lay much emphasis on the 放. The southern Ch'aou is identified with the pres. dis. of the same name, dep. of Loo-chow in Gan-hwuy.

有慙德.—'He thought,' says the 'Daily Explanation,' 'how Yaou had resigned the throne to Shun, and Shun had resigned it to Yu, and Yu had wished to resign it to Yih, and now he had got it by attacking Këĕ and banishing him, and he was ashamed that his virtue was not equal to that of those ancients' (慙愧其德不如古). It is simpler to take the phrase as in the translation; we may understand 於 after 慙. Comp. Mencius II., Pt. II., ix., 1. 以台爲口實,—lit., 'take me to be a mouth-full.' T'ang's fear evidently was lest future ages should misunderstand his motives, and suppose him to have been actuated by a selfish ambition. The critics refine on the point, and suppose that his anxiety was lest ambitious men should justify their rebellious attempts from his example.

Ch. II. CHUNG-HWUY'S ANNOUNCEMENT. Pp. 2, 3. THAT T'ANG WAS CALLED BY HEAVEN TO DO AS HE HAD DONE. 有欲,—the 'desires' are the senses and the passions, the lusts of men's own hearts. 時乂,—時=是. Gan-kwŏ says:—是治民亂, 'his it is to rule the disorders of the people.' There is a force in the conciseness of the language, which tells us that not only is it the business of the Heaven-appointed to regulate disorders, but that he does do so. 塗炭,—comp. Mencius, II., Pt. I., ix., and V., Pt. II., i. There, sitting in mire and charcoal is used to give the idea of being defiled; and Ming-shing says that as here the phrase gives the idea of misery, it is not rightly employed. The compiler, he argues, borrowed it from Mencius, and misunderstood its meaning. This is very small criticism. To

書經

三節 夏王有罪、矯誣上天、以布命于下、帝用不臧、式商受命、用爽厥師。

四節 簡賢附勢、實繁有徒、肇我邦于有夏、若苗之有莠、若粟之有秕、

3 honouring and obeying the appointment of Heaven. The king of Hea was an offender, falsely pretending to the sanction of supreme Heaven, to spread abroad his commands among the people. On this account God viewed him with disapprobation, caused *our* Shang to receive His appointment, and employed you to enlighten the multitudes of the people.

4 III. "Contemners of the worthy and parasites of the powerful,—many such followers he had indeed, *but* from the first our country was to the sovereign of Hea like weeds among the springing corn,

sit in dust and ashes very strongly conveys the idea of misery. 表正萬國,—表= 'to serve as a signal to,' *i.e.*, by example and all personal ways; 正='to correct,' *i.e.*, by laws and institutions. 纘禹舊服=繼禹舊所服行, 'to continue what Yu of old time practised and did.' 茲率厥典,奉若 (a verb, as in Can. of Yaou, p. 8) 天命,—Gaubil translates—'en suivant ses loix, c'est suivre celles de ciel,' making 厥 refer to Yu, and 厥典='his laws.' Medhurst does the same. They are both wrong. If we are to find an antecedent to 厥, it must be 天 and not 禹. Wang Ts'eaou says well:—上言天意如此,故此言王于此,惟循其常道以順天, 'Above it has been said that such is the mind of Heaven, and hence it is here said, that the king in this course is only pursuing its regular way to be obedient to Heaven. 3. 矯誣上天,—矯 and 誣 are often found together. They both denote, 'falsification,' but the latter has the idea of 'slandering' as well. 帝用不臧,—用, as in the 'Speech at Kan,' p. 3, *et al.*,='on this account;' 臧=善, here taken actively, 'to approve.' 帝, the personal name, the Judge and Ruler, very evidently, takes the place here of the vague phrase—'high Heaven.' 式=用, 'to use,' 'to employ.' The 'Daily Explanation' uses 使, 'to cause,' for it. 用爽厥師,—爽=明, 'to enlighten,' used probably with reference to the 有夏昏德 of last par.

Jŏ-keu calls attention to the manner in which this paragraph appears in Mih-tsze, who has quoted it in every one of his chapters, called 'Against prevailing views of the Decrees or Appointments of Heaven' (非命篇). First we have—於仲虺之告曰,我聞于夏人,矯天命布命于下,帝伐之惡,龔喪厥師. Next it is—我聞有夏人,矯天命布命于下,帝式是惡,用闕師. The third time we have—我聞有夏人,矯天命于下,帝式是增,用爽厥師. It seems absurd to argue from these passages against the genuineness of the present text.

Ch. III. Pp. 4—6. The Announcement continued.—That T'ang was called by men to do as he had done. P. 4. *It was necessary for T'ang to dethrone Keë in order to his own preservation.* 簡賢附勢,實繁有徒,—Medhurst translates:—'*The sovereign of Hea* contemned the wise and attached himself to the mighty, which substantially increased his followers.' Gaubil has the same view. But they are both wrong. The 'Daily Explanation'

小大戰戰、罔不懼于非辜、矧予之德、言足聽聞。○五節惟王不邇聲色、不殖貨利、德懋懋官、功懋懋賞、用人惟己、改過不吝、克寬克仁、彰信兆民。○六節乃葛伯仇餉、初征自葛、東征、西夷怨、南征、

and blasted grains among the good. *Our people*, great and small,
were in constant apprehension, fearful though they were guilty of
no crime. How much more was this the case, when our *prince's*
virtues made them a theme *eagerly* listened to! *Our* king did
5 not approach to *dissolute* music and women; he did not seek to
accumulate property and money. To great virtue he gave great
offices; to great merit he gave great rewards. He employed others
as *if their abilities were* his own; he was not slow to change his errors.
Rightly indulgent and rightly benevolent, from the display *of such
virtue* confidence was reposed in him by the millions of the people.
6 "When the chief of Kŏ showed his enmity to the provision-car-
riers, the work of punishment began with Kŏ. When it went on

paraphrases:—夏王旣已不道、而其所任用者、又皆簡慢賢哲、阿附權勢之人、同惡相濟、徒衆實多。 肇我邦于有夏、云云,—I put a comma after 肇, and take it adverbially,—'from the first.' 我邦 is then in the nominative, the subject of the sentence; and 于有夏='in relation to—or simply to—'the ruler of Hea.' The 'Daily Explanation' makes 于有夏=于有夏之間, 'in the country of Hea.' But 有夏 is 'the holder,' and not the country, 'of Hea.' The whole meaning, moreover, comes out much better on the view I have taken. It sounds strange to have Shang likened to weeds and blasted grains; but it was only Këë who was thus affected by the presence of Shang. The point of comparison is the detestation such things awaken in the mind of the husbandman. 秕 is not 'chaff,' as Medhurst has it, but 穀之不成者, 'the grain that has not ripened.' It is to be distinguished from the 稗 which Mencius mentions, VI., Pt. I., xix. 矧予之德、言足聽聞,—Gan-kwŏ read this passage without a stop.—'How much more when our virtues and words became sufficient to attract attention!' Choo He approved of putting a comma at 德, and making 言足聽聞 a clause by itself. I have followed this view in the translation. 5. *A description of T'ang's virtues.* Medhurst puts all this paragraph in the imperative mood,—'Only let your Majesty not become too familiar with music and women,' &c., &c.;—this is wrong in grammatical construction, and not pertinent to the context. Gaubil translates in the indicative mood, which is correct, but in the present tense, which is wrong. Chung-hwuy is describing the virtues of T'ang, which had attracted universal regard to him, and made the people long that he would dethrone Këë. Wang K'ang-t'ang (王肯堂) says:—此言湯德足人聽聞之實、乃指爲諸侯時言之、'This speaks of the virtues of T'ang when he was one of the princes of the empire.'

6. *A reference to T'ang's former exploits, to show how the people desired him.* See Mencius, I., Pt. I., xi. 2; III., Pt. II., iii., 2—5; and VII., Pt. II. iv. 3. Read also the notes on those

書經

北狄怨、曰、奚獨後予、攸徂之民、室家相慶、曰、徯予后、后來其蘇、民之戴商、厥惟舊哉。○佑七節賢輔德、顯忠遂良、兼弱攻昧、取亂侮亡、推

in the east, the wild tribes of the west murmured; when it went on in the south, those of the north murmured:—they said, 'Why does he make us alone the last?' To whatever people he went, they congratulated one another in their chambers, saying, 'We have waited for our prince;—our prince is come, and we revive.' The people's honouring *our* Shang is a thing of long existence.

7 IV. "Show favour to the able and right-principled *among the princes*, and aid the virtuous; distinguish the loyal, and let the good have free course. Absorb the weak, and punish the wilfully blind; take their States from the disorderly, and deal summarily with those going to ruin. Thus overthrowing the perishing and strengthening what is being preserved, how will the States all flourish!

passages. The Tsin compiler, it is said, made up this passage from Mencius, and Mencius moreover, is quoting from one of the lost Books, the T'ang Ching or 'Punitive Expeditions of T'ang.' Mencius, however, does not particularize any Book, but only quotes generally from the Shoo. I can well believe that he does quote from the T'ang Ching, and also that Chung-hwuy does the same,—if, indeed, we need to suppose any quotation in Chung-hwuy's case. He adduces facts and speeches which were flying about through the mouths of the people at the time.

Ch. IV. The speech concluded.—Counsels to T'ang to help him to preserve the popularity and the throne which he had gained. Ch'in Leih (陳櫟) says:—'The shame of T'ang was the natural feeling of his mind, when he thought of the position which he occupied, as a minister who had effected a revolution and taken the place of his sovereign. Ch'ung-hwuy, in dissipating that feeling, was at first led to praise T'ang, but then he became anxious lest the feeling of shame should give place to one of exultation and pride, and concluded by admonishing him;—such is the way in which a great minister should lead on his sovereign in the right path' (see the 集說 on the first par). 7. 佑賢輔德,—有才德兼備,是謂賢者, 'those who are largely endowed both with talents and virtue are the *heen;* 有積善行仁,是謂有德者, 'those who have accumulated good deeds and shown benevolence are the *tih.*' 'Aid the virtuous,' *i.e.*, reward them, honour them, encourage them to virtue in every way. 遂良,—奉公守法,是謂良者, 'those who seek the common weal and keep the laws, are the *lëang;*' 遂 'to accord with,' 'to make to feel comfortable;' here it denotes every arrangement which could encourage the good in their course.

兼弱,—'the weak' are princes incapable of managing their affairs. They are to be put under a powerful neighbour, or have a 'resident' located with them (after our Indian fashion) from the court. 攻昧,—the 'Daily Explanation' says:—'Punish them, and strip them of a portion of their territory.' 侮亡,—see Mencius, I., Pt. II., iv. 6, 樂酒無厭謂之亡. The 亡 are those who are utterly lost to all virtue, and in the way to certain ruin. 侮 is 'to contemn.' Such princes are to be dealt with summarily and at once.

推亡,—the 亡 here has a slighter meaning than in the clause above, and embraces the 弱, 昧, 亂, and 亡; while the 推 applies to 兼, 攻, 取, and 侮. Similarly 固存 extends to the first four clauses.

亡、固存、邦乃其昌。○八節德日新、萬邦惟懷、志自滿、九族乃離、王懋昭大德、建中于民、以義制事、以禮制心、垂裕後昆、予聞曰、能自得師者王、謂人莫己若者亡、好

8 "When *a sovereign's* virtue is daily being renewed, he is cherished throughout the myriad States; when he is full of his own will, he is abandoned by the nine classes of his kindred. Exert yourself, O king, to make your great virtue illustrious, and set up the *pattern of the* Mean before the people. Order your affairs by righteousness; order your heart by propriety:—so shall you transmit a grand example to posterity. I have heard the saying:—'He who finds instructors for himself, comes to the supreme dominion; he who says that others are not equal to himself, comes to ruin. He who likes to ask becomes enlarged; he who uses *only* himself becomes small.'

This par. is partially and imperfectly quoted in the 左傳 three times. The first is under the 12th year of duke 宣; the second, under the 14th year of 襄; and the third, under the 30th year also of Sëang. See the arguments that have been raised on the first quotation against the genuineness of this Book, in Ming-shing's 後案, and the reply of Maou K'e-ling, in the 'Wrongs of the old Text of the Shoo,' Book. V, upon the 'Announcement of Chung-hwuy.' The quotations certainly prove that we are not to look for verbal accuracy in passages adduced from the classics in the 左傳, and I will add other ancient Books. 8. The above paragraph contained counsels of administration; in this the minister becomes more personal, and tells T'ang what he must do in the government of himself. 德日新……乃離,—these are general propositions, the personal application of which commences with the next clause—王懋昭大德. Ts'ae ingeniously suggests that the inscription about daily renovation on T'ang's bathing-tub, 'Great Learning,' C., ii. 1, may have been in consequence of Chung-hwuy's remark here—德日新. 建中于民,—comp. 允執厥中, in the Counsels of Yu, p. 15. 以義制事, 以禮制心,—'righteousness' is what the judgment of the mind determines to be 'right' in reference to what is beyond ourselves; 'propriety' is the regulation of our own feelings and behaviour, in accordance with all the Heaven-established relations of society. 垂裕後昆,—in the Counsels of Yu, p. 18, we had 昆 in the sense of 'afterwards.' Here, joined with 後, the phrase 後昆 = 'future futurity,' 'future ages.' The 'Daily Explanation' paraphrases the clause:—且非特可建中于民也, 即垂諸後世, 凡子孫之欲制事制心者, 其家法自足相承而有餘裕矣. 予聞, 云云,—all this is intended to inculcate humility on T'ang. 王,—low. 3d tone, 'to exercise, or come to exercise, the imperial authority;'—it often occurs in Mencius. 莫己若者,—莫若己者,—an instance of the negative adverb attracting the pronoun to itself.

In Seun-tsze, 堯問篇, we find 其在仲蘬 (must be for 虺) 之言也, 曰, 諸侯自爲得師者王, 得友者霸, 得疑者存, 自爲謀而莫己若者亡. And in Leu Puh-wei, Lew Hëang, and other later writers, we have

問則裕、自用則小。○九節嗚呼、愼厥終、惟其始、殖有禮、覆昏暴、欽崇天道、永保天命。

9 "Oh! he who would take care for his end must be attentive to his beginning. There is establishment for the observers of propriety, and overthrow for the blinded and wantonly indifferent. To revere and honour the way of Heaven is the way ever to preserve the favouring regard of Heaven."

Chung-hwuy's words, much to the same effect. Of course the impugners of the 'Old Text,' seize on the discrepancy between this and what we read in the Shoo to discredit it. Maou K'e-ling contends that 得友者霸, &c., are Seun-tsze's own addition; and we may suppose have been quoted from him by subsequent writers. But in the text Chung is quoting from a saying common in his time. We need not suppose that he quotes the whole of it, but only so much as suited his purpose. It was easy to enlarge his couplet, and the whole might be ascribed to him. 9. Chung-hwuy concludes with words of warning. T'ang must at once attend to his counsels, and never intermit in the observance of them. 殖有禮, 覆昏暴,—we may take 昏 as = the 自棄者, and 暴 as = the 自暴者, of Mencius, IV., Pt. I., x. The 'Daily Explanation' paraphrases the two clauses thus:—福善禍淫, 上天不易之道, 有禮者, 天必篤厚而培植之, 昏暴者, 天必厭棄而傾覆之. In par. 5 it is said—王不殖貨利, with ref. to which the dict. defines the term by 興生財利; with ref. to its use in this par., it defines it, after Gan-kwŏ, by 封殖, 'to promote.'

THE BOOKS OF SHANG.

BOOK III. THE ANNOUNCEMENT OF T'ANG.

湯誥

一節 王歸自克夏、至于亳、誕告萬方。○二節 王曰、嗟、爾萬方有衆、明聽予

1 I. The king returned from vanquishing Hea, and came to Pŏ. There he made a grand announcement to the myriad regions.

2 II. The king said, "Ah! ye multitudes of the myriad regions, listen clearly to the announcement of me, the one man. The great

THE NAME OF THE BOOK.—湯誥, 'The Announcement of T'ang.' The characters have been already sufficiently explained. There is no difficulty in the use of 誥 here. The Announcement was addressed to the whole empire and delivered, no doubt, in the first place in an assembly of the princes and nobles. The Book is one of those whose genuineness in its present form is controverted.

CONTENTS. The notice in the Preface says that T'ang 'had put an end to the sovereignty of Hea, when he made this Announcement.' We may consider it a coronation speech on the inauguration of the new dynasty. The emperor first shows how he had assumed the dignity in reverent submission to the will of Heaven, and goes on to show the sense he had of the duties devolving on him, and the spirit in which he would discharge them, calling at the same time on the princes and people to co-operate with him. I have divided the whole into three chapters:—the first, in one par., stating the occasion of the Announcement; the second, in 4 parr., referring to the downfall of Hea, and his own elevation to the will of Heaven; and the third, also in 4 parr., announcing the sort of sovereign he meant to be, and asking for sympathy and co-operation.

CH. I. P. 1. THE TIME AND PLACE OF THE ANNOUNCEMENT. We are led to conceive that T'ang was encouraged by the address of Chung-hwuy, and continuing his march from Ta-keung, he arrived at Pŏ his capital. We are still to think here of 'the southern Pŏ,;'—see on the Name of Book I.

CH. II. Pp. 2—5. THE ANNOUNCEMENT.—THAT THE OVERTHROW OF HEA AND HIS OWN ELEVATION WERE BOTH THE WORK OF HEAVEN. 1. HOW THE GREAT GOD HAS MORALLY ENDOWED MEN, AND WHAT IS THE DUTY OF THE SOVEREIGN. 嗟,—as at the commencement of the speech at Kan. 爾萬方有衆, 明聽予一人誥,—On 予一人, see on the 'Speech of T'ang,' p. 1. T'ang summons all the people in all the empire *to hear* his announcement. They might be considered as all present with him by their representatives; and I suppose measures were taken to have his declaration of views made generally known. 惟皇上帝降衷於下民,—we have had the phrase 皇天, 'great Heaven,' in the 'Counsels of Yu,' p. 4, and it often occurs throughout the Shoo; here, and only

一人誥、惟皇上帝、降衷于下民、若有恆性、克綏厥猷

God has conferred *even* on the inferior people a moral sense, compliance with which would show their nature invariably right. *But* to cause them tranquilly to pursue the course which it would indicate, is the work of the sovereign.

here, I think, we have 皇上帝, though once, Part V., Bk. XII., p. 9, we find 皇天上帝. Medhurst translates here—'the great Supreme'; and Gaubil—'L'auguste Chang-ti,' giving the meaning of the characters Chang and Ti in a note as 'Souverain Maître.' The predicate here, and the interchange of the name with 'Heaven,' sufficiently tell us who 'the august sovereign Master,' the 'great supreme Ruler' is. I always translate 上帝 and also 帝, when used with the same application, by 'God,' believing the radical idea in our word to be the same as that in the Chinese,—the idea of supreme rule. Medhurst translates 衷 by 'the due medium,' after Ts'ae, who himself follows his master Choo He. He's language is that '衷 just is 中' (衷只是中). But what is conferred by God is not the due medium as something without man, but the mind that can appreciate such a standard and rule of duty;—see the remarks on the title of The 'Doctrine of the Mean.' vol I., pp. 246, 247. Gaubil translates the term by 'la raison.' 'A moral sense' appears to come nearer to the signification than any other term in English I can think of.

Gan-kwŏ defined it simply by 善, 'good,' which Choo He rightly says gives no appropriate meaning. The word occurs not unfrequently in the 國語 in this sense of 'good'=happiness; and twice we have the phrase 降衷, but only = 'sending down happiness;'—see the 晉語, 二, and the 吳語. 若有恆性, —'according with—obeying—*this*, they have a constant nature.' By the 'constant nature' we are to understand what Mencius calls 'the constant heart;'—see his Works, I., Pt. I., vii., 20, and III., Pt. I., iii. 8. The meaning is as given in the translation. Mencius also enables us to understand why T'ang should specify 'the inferior people,' for he says that 'they are only men of education who, without a certain livelihood, are able to maintain a fixed heart.' T'ang has in his mind's eye the millions of the people, all in contradistinction from 'the one man,' and he says that every one of them has a God-given nature, which, if he obeyed it, would lead him in the path of virtue. 克綏厥猷惟后,—猷=道, 'the path' or 'course'; 厥猷, 'its course,' is that which the nature points to. Chin Tih-sew says, 'When we intend the nature in itself, we speak of 性; when we intend it in action, we speak of 道' (以體言曰性, 以用言曰道). 綏=安, to give tranquillity—security—to.' This is the business of the sovereign.

In explaining this paragraph Gan-kwŏ is more than ordinarily unhappy. His view of 衷 has been adverted to. At 人 he makes a full stop, and then 若有恆性, 克綏厥猷 is all the predicate of 惟后,—describes what is the business of the sovereign,—to accord, namely, with the constant nature which men have, when he can tranquilly set up the lessons for their course' (順人有常之性, 能安立其道教, 則惟爲君之道).

[The editors of Yung-ching's Shoo pause here to enlarge on the wisdom of T'ang, and his services in completing the doctrine of human nature. Yaou had simply told Shun to hold fast the Mean (Con. Ana. XX. i. 1), and Shun, in transferring the lesson to Yu, had said, 'The mind of man is restless, prone to err; its affinity for the *right* way is small. Be discriminating, be undivided, that you may sincerely hold fast the Mean.' The whole doctrine about the endowments of the nature, and those endowments as from Heaven, was contained, it is said, in those sentences, but darkly and enigmatically. It was for T'ang to declare the doctrine clearly, showing a profound thoughtfulness, and an intelligence peculiar to himself, beyond what was to be gained from Yaou and Shun.

I think that T'ang is deserving of this eulogium; the student should not pass lightly from this paragraph to the next. We cannot but admire the distinct recognition of the great God, the Father of man's spirit, the Former of all men for a life of virtue. There is then recognized the proneness of men to go astray, and the sovereign is called on, by the position in which God has placed him, to correct their errors, and keep them right. The whole doctrine of human nature is not here, but there is much of important truth, from which we must start in guiding the Chinese to a knowledge of that doctrine. A hard task is assigned to the sove-

惟后。○三節夏王滅德作威、以敷虐于爾萬方百姓、爾萬方百姓、罹其凶害、弗忍荼毒、並告無辜于上下神祇、天道福善禍淫、降災于夏、

3 "The king of Hea extinguished his virtue and played the tyrant, extending his oppression over you, the people of the myriad regions. Suffering from his cruel injuries, and unable to endure the wormwood and poison, you protested with one accord your innocence to the spirits of heaven and earth. The way of Heaven is to bless the good and to punish the bad. It sent down calamities on *the House of* Hea, to make manifest its crimes.

reign, and no account is taken of the fact that he is as prone to go astray himself as any of the inferior people; but it was not an ordinary mind which could thus conceive of what a sovereign should propose to himself. The lessons of T'ang here are the same which Mencius expounds at length, and vindicates in the first Part of his sixth Book. They have the same excellences and the same deficiencies.]

P. 3. *How the last ruler of Hea had failed to fulfil his duty, and brought on himself the wrath of Heaven.* 滅德,—comp, 敗德, 'Counsels of Yu,' p. 20, and 顚覆厥德. 'Pun. Expedition of Yin,' p. 4; but the phrase in the text is stronger then either of those passages. Këë had cast from him that 'benevolence,' which is the greatest of the virtues, and acc. to Mencius, the grand characteristic of humanity. 萬方百姓,—see on the 'Can. of Yaou,' p. 2, where a distinction is made between 萬方 and 百姓, the former having a more extensive signification than the latter. In the text the phrases are co-extensive. 百姓 must = our 'the people.' We are not to lay stress on the 'hundred.' It is used indefinitely. When a people are surnamed, considerable progress has been made in civilization. 弗忍荼毒,—荼 is the name of a bitter herb; 毒 is used for 'poison.' An old form of 毒 shows it formed from 虫 instead of 毋, so that its original meaning was probably 'venom.' The two terms together denote 'smarting pain,' 'suffering.' 告無辜于上下神祇,—上下=天地. Comp. 'Can. of Yaou,' p. 1, and 'Counsels of Kaou-yaou,' p. 7. 上下神祇=天神地祇;—see the note on 'Can. of Shun,' p. 23. 神 and 祇 may be considered in themselves synonyms. The dict. defines 祇 by 地神; but in usage they denote the spirits of heaven and of earth respectively. In the text, the people appear before us crying out in distress to all superior powers. T'ang himself immediately represents 'Heaven' as responding to their cry. They called on they knew not whom or what Ts'ae refers in illustration to a passage in the 'History of Keuh Yuen' (屈原傳; the 集傳 simply says 屈原曰, which is a mistake. See the 84th Bk. of the 'Historical Records'), which is worth giving at greater length than he does;—天者人之始也,父母者人之本也,人窮則反本,故勞苦倦極,未嘗不呼天也,疾痛慘怛,未嘗不呼父母也, 'From Heaven man derives his beginning; from his parents he grows as his root. When a man is brought to extremity, he turns back to his root, and thus it is that when men are toiled, embittered, and worn out, we hear them always calling upon Heaven, and when they are sick, pained, afflicted, and grieved, we hear them always calling on their parents.' 淫, as opposed here to 善, has the general sense of 'bad,' 'evil;'—see 'Counsels of Yu,' p. 6. 降災,—these 'calamities' are to be understood of the convulsions of nature and various strange phenomena which preceded the fall of Këë.

書經

以彰厥罪。○（四節）肆台小子、將天命明威、不敢赦、敢用玄牡、敢昭告于上天神后、請罪有夏、聿求元聖、與之戮力、以與爾有衆請命。○（五節）上

4 "Therefore, I, the little child, charged with the decree of Heaven and its bright terrors, did not dare to forgive *the criminal.* I presumed to use a dark coloured victim, and making clear announcement to the spiritual Sovereign of the high heavens, requested leave to deal with the ruler of Hea as a criminal. Then I sought for the great sage, with whom I might unite my strength, to request

P. 4. *How T'ang felt himself called on, and prepared himself, to punish the crimes of Këë.* 肆=故, 'therefore.' 將=奉 or 承, 'to bear,' 'to have received.' 奉 and 將 are used together in the 'Punitive Expedition of Yin,' p. 5. 天命明威,—the 'Daily Explanation' paraphrases this by 天命之顯然可畏者, 'the conspicuous terrors of the charge of Heaven.' 玄牡,—under the Hea dynasty they preferred in their victims of sacrifice a dark colour. Under the Shang, it was the reverse; their victims were white. At this time T'ang continued to follow the practice of Hea. K'ang-shing assigns another reason, not so good, for the use of the dark victim;—see the 後案, *in loc.* 上天神后,—Ts'ae by 神后 understands 后土, 'Sovereign Earth.' Lin Che-ke does the same. He says:—神后者后土,皇地祇也, '"The spiritual Sovereign" is the Sovereign Earth, the great spirit of the earth.' In this way the text is equivalent to the 上下神祇 of the last par. I translate upon a different view, having reference to the form in which this passage appears in the Confucian Analects, XX. i. 3, where for 上天神后 we have 皇皇后帝. In Mih-tsze, moreover, who also quotes T'ang's language, we have only 上天后. 聿求元聖, —聿=遂, 'then;' 元聖, 'the great sage,' is to be referred to T'ang's principal adviser and minister, E Yin;—see on the next Book. 戮力=同力. 戮 is here used in the sense of 勠. The two characters are found interchanged. 以與爾有衆請命,—this is paraphrased in the 'Daily Explanation:'—以與爾萬方百姓,請更生之命于天.

A good portion of this paragraph is found in the Con. Ana., as already referred to, but with some considerable variations; and with the addition of p. 8, also with variations. The same portion with the same and other additions is found in the works of Mih-tsze;—see the Prolegomena to Mencius, pp. 116, 117. The rest of the par. is also found with a variation in another part of Mih-tsze. In the second of his chapters 'On Honouring men of Talents and Virtue' (尙賢中), we find 湯誓曰,聿求元聖,與之戮力,同心以治天下. These words, moreover, are given as from 'The Speech of T'ang,' and not from the 'Announcement,' while the rest of the paragraph is quoted by him as 'Words of T'ang,' (湯說), without reference either to 'Speech' or 'Announcement.' To add to the perplexity of the subject, Ho An, quoting K'ung Gan-kwŏ's comment on the passage in the Analects, makes him say that Mih-tsze quotes the 'Speech of T'ang' in the same way as it appears in the text there. I do not see my way clear to an explanation of all these difficulties. The passages of the Shoo quoted in the 20th Bk. of the Analects are brought together in a very loose and irregular manner. As to the comment given by Ho An there from Gan-kwŏ, which speaks of Mih's quoting from the 'Speech of T'ang,' Mih does not say that the passages in the text of the Analects are from that 'Speech,' but only 'Words of T'ang.' Moreover, the additions in Mih would make us refer the language of T'ang not to the time of the 'Speech,' nor to the

天孚佑下民、罪人黜伏、天命弗僭、賁若草木、兆民允殖。(大除) ○ 俾予一人、輯寧爾邦家、兹朕未知獲戾于上下、慄慄危懼、若將隕于深淵。

5 the favour *of Heaven* on behalf of you, my multitudes. High Heaven truly showed its favour to the inferior people, and the criminal has been degraded and subjected. Heaven's appointment is without error;—brilliantly *now* like the blossoming of flowers and trees, the millions of the people show a true reviving.

6 III. "It is given to me, the one man, to give harmony and tranquillity to your States and Families; and now I know not whether I may not offend *the powers* above and below. I am fearful and trembling, as if I should fall into a deep abyss.

time of the 'Announcement' but to a time subsequent to both, towards the close of the seven years of drought which followed his assumption of the empire. If all the discrepancies tell against the genuineness of the 'Announcement,' they tell as much against the 'Speech,' as it is found both in Fuh-shang's text, and in that attributed to Gan-kwŏ. Keang Shing, aware of this, edits the 'Speech of T'ang' with the addition of the par. from the Analects, and of the sentence 聿求元聖,云云, from Mih-tsze. But if he take one part from Mih, why should he not take the whole? We need not wonder that we should meet with such difficulties. Our course seems to be to state them, and where no satisfactory solution of them presents itself, to leave them, without reasoning from them against the modern text or the ancient.

P. 5. *The righteousness of T'ang's dethronement of Këë proved by the issue, and consequent prosperity.* 孚=信, 'truly.' So 允 in the last clause. Hwang Too (黃度) puts the first clause very plainly:—天佑下民,信矣. 罪人, 'the criminal;' this of course is Këë. 天命弗僭,—僭=差, 'in error.' 'The appointment of Heaven' is the withdrawal of its favour from Hea, and the conferring of it on Shang,—the calling T'ang to the throne in the room of Këë. 賁若草木,兆民允殖,—this is a passage which has wonderfully exercised the ingenuity of the interpreters. 賁 (read *pe*)=飾, 'to adorn,' 'to be ornamented.' What is it that the adorning is here predicated of? The two K'ungs, Gan-kwŏ and Ying-tă, say—'the empire.' The language of the former is:—'The evil-doer being cut off from the empire, all is brilliantly adorned, and beautiful as flowers and trees, while the people truly enjoy their life.' Choo He takes the clauses as epexegetical of the preceding 天命弗僭, and the whole ='What Heaven appoints is entirely right;—the world of things and the world of men are made beautiful and happy by it.' The editors of Yung-ching's Shoo give a great variety of views, several preferable, they say, to that of Gan-kwŏ, but none so good as that of Choo He. I prefer to abide by the oldest view.

Ch. III. Pp. 6—9. T'ANG'S FEELINGS AND PURPOSES IN THE POSSESSION OF THE THRONE, AND WISH FOR THE CO-OPERATION OF HIS PRINCES AND PEOPLE. 6. 俾予一人,—this clause and the next would seem to flow on from something preceding, and in some editions it is given as belonging to p. 5, in which case 上天 would be the nominative to 俾. Whether we do so join it, or take the 俾 as I have done in the translation, the 'gift' must be understood as from Heaven. 兹朕未知獲戾于上下,—兹, 'now,' might very well be taken as beginning a new par. 戾=罪. 上下,—as in par. 3. Gan-kwŏ makes the whole to be a humble expression of doubt in T'ang's mind whether he had really been right in dethroning Këë,—'I do not know whether I may not have offended,' &c. But we must suppose T'ang to have now done with Këë. The prec. chapter shows him sufficiently assured on the subject of his dealings with him. Mih-tsze, in the passage referred to on p. 4, has

書經

七節 凡我造邦、無從匪彝、無卽慆淫、各守爾典、以承天休。○八節 爾有善、朕弗敢蔽、罪當朕躬、弗敢自赦、惟簡在上帝之心、其爾萬方有罪、在予一人、予一人有罪、無以

7 "Throughout all the States that enter on a new life under me, do
not, *ye princes*, follow lawless ways; make no approach to insolent
dissoluteness: let every one observe to keep his statutes:—that so
8 we may receive the favour of Heaven. The good in you, I will not
dare to conceal; and for the evil in me, I will not dare to forgive
myself;—I will examine these things in harmony with the mind of
God. When guilt is found anywhere in you who occupy the myriad regions, it must rest on me. When guilt is found in me, the one man, it will not attach to you who occupy the myriad regions.

未知得罪于上下. 7. We are to understand that here T'ang addresses the princes of the different States. This is clear enough from 凡我造邦……各守爾典. 造邦,—the 'Daily Explanation' says that this phrase=新造之邦, 'newly established kingdoms,' adding:—侯邦惟舊,商命惟新,悉與更始,故曰造邦, 'The princes and their States were old, but the rule of Shang was new, and they were all with it making a new beginning,—hence the phrase 造邦.' 卽=就 'to approach to.' In the 國語,周語,二, we have the following passage:—先王之令有之曰,天道賞善而罰淫,故凡我造國,無從非彝,無卽慆淫,各守爾典,以承天休. 8. This par. is closely connected with p. 2. There T'ang gives his very high estimate of the duties of the sovereign; here he says how he would try to come up to it. There he lays it down that the sovereign has to lead the people in the right path, and hence he says here that for all that is wrong among them he must be accountable. 'I will not dare to conceal it,'—the meaning is that virtue and talents will not go with him unrewarded. 惟簡在上帝之心,—Medhurst translates this:—'I shall only submit to the inspection of the supreme mind.' In his 'Dissertation on the Theology of the Chinese,' however, he renders—'The inspection of these things rests with the mind of the Supreme Ruler.' Gaubil construes in the same way:—'Tout est marqué distinctement dans la cœur du Chang-ti.' In the Analects I have translated:—'The examination of them is by Thy mind, O God,' which is not sufficiently definite. But the meaning is not exactly as thus represented; the present translation is more accurate. 惟簡 connects the clause closely with what has preceded, so that we must understand the 簡, or 'examination,' as predicated of T'ang himself, and 在上帝之心 as laying down the rule by which he will be guided in it. Choo He says well:—'Heaven knows all our good and all our crimes. It is as if Heaven noted them down and numbered them up. Your good deeds are all before God, and my evil deeds will also be all before Him.' T'ang declares that he will judge himself and others righteously,—in harmony with the judgment of God. 無以爾萬方=于爾萬方何與焉. On the manner in which this par. appears in quotations, see on par. 4.

爾萬方。○嗚呼、尚克時忱、乃亦有終。

九節

9 "Oh! let us attain to be sincere in these things, and so we shall likewise have a happy consummation."

P. 9. 尚克時忱,—時=是, referring to what has been said in the three prec. paragraphs on the obligations of the sovereign and the princes; 忱=信 or 誠, 'sincere.' 乃亦有終,—有終, 'have an end,' *i.e.*, our dynasty will have a long and happy course.

[In the 'Historical Records,' Sze-ma Ts'een, after giving the 16th paragraph of the Preface, gives a fragment which we should suppose, from his usual practice, was a part of the 'Announcement of T'ang.' Keang Shing, indeed, edits it as being the only portion of the real Announcement that remains. Though not concurring in that view, I have thought it well to append the fragment here:—維三月,王自至於東郊,告諸侯羣后,毋不有功於民,勤力乃事,予乃大罰殛汝,毋予怨,曰,古禹臯陶久勞于外,其有功乎民,民乃有安,東爲江,北爲濟,西爲河,南爲淮,四瀆已修,萬民乃有居,后稷降播農殖百穀,三公咸有功于民,故后有立(?土),昔蚩尤與其大夫作亂百姓,帝乃弗予,有狀,先王言不可不勉,曰,不道毋之在國女毋我怨. This may be translated:—'In the third month, the king came himself to the eastern suburb, and announced to all the princes and the nobles,—'see that you all achieve merit, and vigorously discharge your duties. *If you do not*, I will severely punish you, and put you to death; do not murmur against me.' He said, 'Anciently, Yu and Kaou-yaou laboured long without, and performed meritorious service for the people, who were enabled to dwell in tranquillity. On the east there was the Këang; on the north the Tse; on the west, the Ho; on the south,' the Hwae. These four great streams were brought to order, and the people were able to dwell. *Then* my lord Tseih instructed them how to cultivate the various kinds of grain. These three Kung all achieved merit on behalf of the people and were enfeoffed. Formerly Ch'e-yew and his officers stirred up rebellion among the people, and *Hwang-te* disallowed him, and held him as guilty. The words of the former kings should act as goads to us.' He said, 'Have no unprincipled ways in your kingdoms. *If you have, and I punish you*, do not murmur against me.'

Sze-ma Ts'een adds—'Thus he gave charge to the princes.' It would be a waste of space to make any remarks on such a farrago.]

CONCLUDING NOTE. We here take leave of T'ang, the one, perhaps, of all the ancient princes of China who gets the strongest hold of our sympathies and esteem. Dr. Gutzlaff has said well:—'From his frequent invocations of Shang-te, we might be led to believe that he was a pious prince, who knew something of the true God.' (China Opened, Vol. I., p. 306). His mild but able government of his paternal State drew to him the attention of all the people suffering from the tyranny of Këě. The universal voice called him to do the work of the avenger, and to assume the sovereignty of the empire. He dethroned the oppressor, but not without some misgivings, the natural workings of compassion in a high-toned generous mind. His conception of the imperial duties was high, and he bent himself with hearty earnestness to discharge them. Here the Shoo stops, and none of the lost Books contained anything of his history after his assumption of the throne.

According to the 'Standard Annals,' his reign terminated B.C. 1753, so that his sway over the empire lasted only 13 years. The first 7 of them were a season of trial and calamity. No rain fell. Famine was the consequence of the drought. The sufferings of the people were intense. The issues of the mint were freely distributed among them, but money was of little use when grain was scanty. It was suggested at last, we are told, that some human being should be offered in sacrifice to Heaven, and prayer for rain presented at the same time. 'It is for the people,' said T'ang, 'that rain needs to be sought. If a man must be the victim for such an object, I will be he.' He then fasted, cut off his hair and his nails, and in a plain carriage drawn by white horses, clad in white rushes, in the guise of a sacrificial victim, he proceeded to a grove of mulberry trees, and there prayed, asking whether the calamity was owing to any failure in his government, or misemployment of officers, or extravagance in palaces, or excessive devotion to beauty, or the practice of bribery, or allowance of calumniators. He had not done speaking when a copious rain fell over several thousand *le*.

This account is doubtless much embellished, but through the cloud of exaggeration we can see the generous sovereign sympathizing with the general distress, fasting, and praying for the removal of the calamity.

According to the current chronology, T'ang was succeeded by his grandson, T'ae-këă;—see on the next Book par. 1.

THE BOOKS OF SHANG.

BOOK IV. THE INSTRUCTIONS OF E.

伊訓

惟元祀十有二月乙丑、伊尹祠于先王、奉嗣王祗見厥祖、侯甸群后咸在、百官總己以聽冢宰、伊尹乃明言烈祖之成德、以訓

1 I. In the 12th month of the first year, on *the day* Yuĕ-ch'ow, E Yin sacrificed to the former king, and presented the heir to the throne reverently before his ancestor. All the princes from the domain of the nobles, and the imperial domain, were present; the various officers *also* were in attendance with their several duties to receive orders from the prime minister. E Yin then clearly described the accomplished virtue of the meritorious ancestor for the instruction of the *new* king.

Name of the Book.—伊訓, 'The Instructions of E.' E was the chief minister of T'ang, and was to him almost what Shun had been to Yaou, and Yu to Shun, and Yih to Yu. Mencius gives him his place among sage ministers and counsellors as 'the one most inclined to take office' (V., Pt. II., i). And this was from no facility of temper, or desire for the gains of office. He reasoned:—'Heaven's plan with mankind is that they who are first informed should instruct those who are later in being informed, and they who first apprehend principles should instruct those who are slower in doing so.' 'He thought,' says Mencius, 'that if there were any of the common men and women who did not enjoy such benefits as Yaou and Shun conferred, it was as if he himself pushed them into a ditch.'

Having this character of being so fond of employment, the romancers of the Chow dynasty embellished his history accordingly. He was a native of Sin (莘), the present Shen Chow of Ho-nan, and in Mencius' time the story went that when T'ang was marrying a daughter of the House of Sin, E Yin managed to go to Shang in her train, and got himself taken notice of by T'ang through his skill in cookery. Mencius denies the account, and says that E was a farmer on the lands of Sin, delighting in the principles of Yaou and Shun, and ready to spurn an offer of the empire, if it were made to induce him to do anything contrary to those principles. T'ang heard of his wisdom and ability, and sent messengers with costly presents, inviting him to his court. Twice their visit to him was fruitless, but when they came a third time, being satisfied of T'ang's sincerity, he said, 'Had I not better make this prince a prince like Yaou or Shun, and this people like the people of Yaou or Shun;'—see Men. V., Pt. I., vii. T'ang received him with great deference, and reposed in him entire trust. He sent him to the court of Këë, hoping that his counsels might move the emperor to change his evil course. It was in vain. Five times E went backwards and forwards between Këë and T'ang, till, convinced that the former was incorrigible, he moved T'ang to raise the flag of rebellion, and take the empire for himself. After T'ang's death he continued the watchful guardian of his throne. Of the way in which he dealt with T'ae-këă we shall have to speak in treating of the next Book. The surname of 伊 was derived from the river E, near which he and his parents lived. Leu Puh-wei tells a story of a princess of Sin finding an infant, when she was picking mulberries, in a hollow mulberry tree. This was E. Her father gave him to his cook to bring him up, and on inquiry it was found that his mother had lived on the banks of the E. One night she dreamt, during her pregnancy, that a spirit told her that the sun would discharge a flood of water, and that she must run off to the east. When she rose in the morning, she looked to the sun, and lo! it was as in her dream. Giving the alarm to her neighbours, she fled, and after running ten *le*, she paused to look back, when she saw the town overflowed with water, and was herself changed to a hollow mulberry tree,—the same in which the infant was found! E's name is generally understood to have been Che (摯). Sze-ma Ts'een says it was O-hăng (阿衡);—see next Book, p. 1. Yin (尹) was his 字 or designation. 訓, 'instructions;' this we saw, on the name of Pt. III., Bk. III., was the name of one of the divisions of the Shoo. The 'instructions,' acc. to Lin Che-k'e are of three kinds:—lessons of antiquity transmitted for the guidance of future ages; lessons of ancestors intended specially for the guidance of their posterity; and lessons of faithful ministers like E Yin, addressed to their sovereigns.

According to the Preface, p. 18, in the year that T'ang died, E Yin made three Books, of which these 'Instructions' were one. Of the other two only the names remain; and the genuineness of this is disputed.

CONTENTS. T'ae-këă comes to the throne of his grandfather, young and of unstable character. T'ang's counsellor and friend uses the privilege of his years and station to advise the young monarch,—warns him by the fate of Këë, and stimulates him with the example of T'ang. I have divided the Book into four chapters: the first, in one par., giving the occasion when E Yin delivered his 'lesson;' the second, parr. 2—4, showing how the throne had come down from the great Yu, and was now possessed by T'ae-këă, the scion of another line; the third, parr. 5—7, celebrating the example of T'ang; and the fourth, par. 7., warning T'ae-këă of the fate he would incur if he neglected the advice given to him.

CH. I. P. 1. THE OCCASION OF E'S INSTRUCTIONS. 惟元祀十有二月乙丑,—Hea had used 歲 for 'year;' in the Shang dynasty they preferred the char. 祀. 元祀 must mean the first year of T'ae-këă. The Hea dynasty had begun the year with the month 寅, the first of spring. The Shang removed the commencement of the year a month back, beginning it with 丑. In this way the 12th month of the text is understood to be the 12th month of the Hea year, and the first month of the Shang, so that these instructions of E were delivered in the first month of the year after the death of T'ang. This is the view of Ts'ae and the scholars generally of the Sung dynasty; and Ts'ae goes largely into the proof of what seems a strange thing,—that while the Shang and Chow dynasties differed from Hea as to the commencement of the year, they yet often numbered the months as Hea had done. Maou K'e-ling denies the argument of Ts'ae, and maintains that the 12th month of the text is the 12th month of the Shang year,—the 12th month also of the year in which T'ang died. At the same time, 元祀 is with him the first year of T'ae-këă. According to him, under the Chow dynasty, the new sovereign succeeded of course to the throne immediately on the death of his predecessor, but his first year was reckoned only from the first month of the year which followed. The practice of the Shang sovereigns was different. A month after the death of an emperor, the style of the year was changed, and what remained of it was reckoned to the first year of his successor. This was the view of Gan-kwŏ and Ying-tă. According to it T'ang must have died in the 11th month of the year, and the Instructions of E were delivered in the month after.—I will not undertake at present to decide between these views;—see on the next Book, Pt. ii., 1. What day of the month 乙丑 was we cannot tell. Had it been the first, we should have read 朔, instead of these two characters. 伊尹祠于先王,奉嗣王祗見厥祖,—祠—祭, 'to sacrifice.' The term is used specially for the sacrifices offered in spring in the ancestral temple, but we cannot think of any such ceremony in the text. The 'heir-king' of course is T'ae-këë, and 先王 and 厥祖, are in the singular,—'the former king,' and 'his ancestor,' referring to T'ang.

[This seems to be the place to notice the historical difficulty which there is respecting the succession to T'ang. The Shoo gives no hint of any individual's having interposed between him and T'ae-këă. Indeed the language of the Preface,—'After the death of T'ang, in the first year of T'ae-këă, E Yin made the Instructions of E.' &c., seems to forbid the supposition that T'ae-këă did not immediately follow his grandfather on the throne. The current chronology

于王。○曰、節嗚呼、古有夏先后、方懋厥德、罔有天災、山

2 II. He said, "Oh! of old, the earlier sovereigns of Hea cultivated earnestly their virtue, and then there were no calamities from Heaven. The spirits of the hills and rivers likewise were all in tranquillity;

has been arranged accordingly. T'ang's death is entered B.C. 1753, and the reign of T'ae-këă commences the following year, B.C. 1752.

When we refer to the 'Historical Records,' however, it is said after the mention of the death of T'ang:—'His eldest son, T'ae-ting, died before he could come to the throne, and a younger son, Wae-ping, succeeded. He was the emperor Wae-ping (是爲帝外丙). Wae-ping died after reigning three years, and was succeeded by a younger brother,—a third son of T'ang's,—called Chung-jin. He was the emperor Chung-jin (是爲帝中壬). Chung-jin reigned four years, and on his death E Yin raised to the throne T'ae-këă, son of T'ae-ting, and the eldest grandson of T'ang. He was the emperor T'ae-këă, (是爲帝太甲). Whatever other authority Ts'een may have had for this account, there can be no doubt he took it chiefly from Mencius, V., Pt. I., vi. 5; and the interpretation which he gives of Mencius' words is the most natural, though the passage is not unsusceptible of another interpretation;—see the Works of Mencius, pp. 236, 237. Those who follow the natural reading of Mencius in preference to the natural reading of the Preface to the Shoo, hold, of course, that the mourning of T'ae-këă, which the text supposes, was for Chung-jin and not for T'ang. There is a difficulty;—that must be admitted. For myself, I should follow the Preface, and the standard chronology, holding that T'ae-këă immediately followed T'ang upon the throne.]

What sacrifice E Yin performed to T'ang can hardly be determined. In the Books of the 'Former Han' (律歷志,下), we find the first part of the paragraph, with the addition of 朔 after 丑, and the clause 誕資有牧方明 after 先王. Possibly this clause may be an addition of Pan Koo, the Han chronicler, but the whole passage shows that he understood the sacrifice to be the solemn one to God, offered at the winter solstice. Be this as it may, and I do not think it unlikely, the conducting T'ae-këă to appear before his ancestor was a different ceremony. The appearance was, I suppose, before the coffin of T'ang.

侯甸羣后咸在,—侯甸=侯服甸服;—see 'The Tribute of Yu,' Pt. ii., pp. 18, 19. Perhaps these two domains are mentioned by synecdoche for all the five; or there may not have been time for the nobles who were more remote to reach the court. The mention of the presence of these princes shows us that the occasion was the solemn inauguration of T'ae-këă as successor to T'ang.

百官總已以聽冢宰,—see the Analects, XIV., xiii., 2. I there said that 總已 was a difficult expression, and I do not find it easier now. Gaubil does not try to translate it. Medhurst mistakes the meaning, and has:—'The various officers gave a general account of their affairs, in order to wait for orders from the prime minister.' The 'Daily Explanation' paraphrases:—百官各總攝已職,以聽命于冢宰. Is the phrase simply = 'all and each'? 烈祖,—烈 = 'ardent,' as in Pt. III., Bk. IV., p. 6; here it is defined by 'meritorious' (功), and Ying-tă says, 'T'ang had achieved the lasting service of settling the empire, and was the founder of the dynasty of Shang;—hence he is styled 烈祖.'

[De Mailla's view of this paragraph is seen in the expansion which he gives of it, Vol. I., p. 176.—'Having resolved that T'ae-këă should succeed to T'ang, E Yin, as prime minister and as president of the tribunal of rites, assembled all the princes who were at court, and made them recognize T'ae-këă. It was then the 12th month, and the funeral ceremonies for T'ang were not yet performed. E Yin ordered them with great magnificence, and then brought T'ae-këă, whom he placed on a throne which he had prepared for that purpose in the hall of the ancestors of the Shang dynasty, saluted him emperor, and made him receive in this character the homage of the grandees, the vassal princes, the mandarins and the people. Thereafter, addressing himself to the young emperor, he exhorted him to imitate the virtue of the great prince whom he succeeded, and gave him these advices.'——]

Ch. II. Pp. 2—4. The Instructions of E.—Lessons from the Hea dynasty; from the rise of T'ang; from T'ae-kea's own position at the commencement of his reign. 2. 有夏先后,—'the former emperors possessing Hea.' Lin Che-k'e says that we are to understand all the Hea sovereigns before Këë. That cannot be. K'ung-këă has been singled out for his wickedness; only Yu himself would fully answer to E's description. It suits his purpose to speak of a line of good princes; and many of them would be considered so in com-

川鬼神、亦莫不寧、曁鳥獸魚鼈咸若、于其子孫弗率、皇天降災、假手于我有命、造攻自鳴條、朕哉自亳。○

三節 惟我商王布昭聖武、代虐

and the birds and beasts, the fishes and tortoises, all realized the happiness of their nature. But their descendant did not follow *their example*, and great Heaven sent down calamities, employing the agency of our *ruler*, who had *received* its favouring appointment. The attack *on Hea* may be traced to Ming-t'ëaou, and our *attack on it*
3 began in Pŏ. Our king of Shang had brilliantly displayed his sacred
prowess. When for oppression he substituted his generous gentle-

parison with Këĕ. 方 is an adverb, and stress is to be laid on it. The dict. defines it by 今, 'now.' It = 'then,' 'so long as.' 咸若,—皆順適其性,而得遂其生, 'all quietly followed their nature, and had the enjoyment of their life.' From 山川 down to this describes fancifully, but not without a truth to which the mind responds, the happy condition of the well-governed empire. Ch'in Ta-yew (陳大猷) directs attention to the last par. of the 1st chap. of the 'Doctrine of the Mean,'—致中和,天地位焉,萬物育焉. 于其子孫,—by 子孫 Këĕ is pre-eminently intended. Perhaps E had other earlier and unworthy sovereigns in his mind as well, but Këĕ was the impersonation of all the wickedness of Hea. 于 = 'in the case of.'

皇天降災,—Lin Che-k'e illustrates this by saying that 'the spirits of the hills and rivers could no longer be in tranquillity. Hills fell; rivers were dried up; strange sounds were emitted. Birds and beasts, fishes and tortoises, no longer followed their nature, and many of them were changed into monstrous and prodigious things.' I quote this, as showing how the Chinese share in the feeling of a sympathy between the course of nature and the character and doings of men, so that 'the whole creation groans' and writhes to be delivered from the curse of human wickedness. 假手于我有命,—'borrowed a hand from our having the appointment.' Lin Che-k'e expands the clause well:—假手于我商有天命之成湯,使之伐夏救民,以爲天吏. [Up to this point the paragraph is found, but in a very different form, in the only remaining part of Mih-tsze's Book on 鬼 (明鬼篇,下). He gives it as from the 'Books of Shang:'—嗚呼,古者有夏,方未有禍之時,百獸貞蟲,允及飛鳥,莫不比方,矧在人面,胡敢異心,山川鬼神亦莫敢不寧,若能共允任,天下之合下土之葆. Mih's text is evidently corrupt; yet he could hardly have the 'Instructions of E,' as we now read them.]

造攻,云云,—compare Mencius, V., Pt. I., vii. 9. There we have 'the palace of Muh' (牧宮) instead of Ming-t'eaou. But from the Preface, par. 12, we know that Ming-t'eaou was not far from the cap. of Këĕ. It was there probably that he had the palace of Muh, where his orgies alienated the people from him, and awoke the vengeance of Heaven. [There was another Ming-t'eaou towards the east, where Shun died, according to Mencius, IV., Pt. II., i, 1.] 'Our attack commenced (哉 = 始) in Pŏ,'—the meaning is that the virtues of T'ang, pleasing to both Heaven and men, first displayed in Pŏ, marked him out as the punisher of Këĕ, and the successor to the empire.

P. 3. 聖武,—'his sacred prowess.' 'It is not simply said,' observe the commentators, 'showed his *prowess*, but his *sacred* prowess. The expression intimates that his prowess came from the valour of virtue and righteousness, by

書經

以寬兆民允懷。四節○今王嗣厥德、罔不在初、立愛惟親、立敬惟長、始于家邦、終于四海。五節○嗚呼、先王肇修人紀、從諫弗咈、先民時若、居上克明、爲下克忠、與人不

4 ness, the millions of the people gave him their hearts. Now your Majesty is entering on the inheritance of his virtue;—every thing depends on *how* you commence *your reign*. To set up love, it is for you to love your elders; to set up respect, it is for you to respect your relatives. The commencement is in the family and State; the consummation is in the empire.

5 III. "Oh! the former king began with careful attention to the bonds that hold men together:—he listened to expostulation, and did not seek to resist it; he conformed to *the wisdom of* former people; occupying the highest position, he displayed intelligence; occupying an inferior position, he displayed his loyalty; he allowed *the good qualities* of others, and did not seek that they should have every talent;

which he was able to destroy oppression, deliver the people, and give repose to the empire.'

P. 4. 今王嗣厥德,—T'ae-keă was inheriting the throne. But it was a throne that had been acquired by virtue, and E Yin therefore puts his succession before him in this way. 初=即位之初, 'the beginning of his reign.' The other observations of the paragraph are the same as the lessons set forth at so much length in the concluding chapters of 'The Great Learning.'

Ch. III. Pp. 5—7. The Instructions continued.—The character and regulations of T'ang. 6. 肇修人紀,—Ts'ae says that the 人紀 are 三綱五常, 'the three relations' [prince and minister, husband and wife, father and son] 'and five constant virtues' [benevolence, righteousness, propriety, &c.]. Somewhat differently, Chang Kew-shing tells us:—'Sovereign and minister, father and son, elder and younger brother, husband and wife, elders and juniors, with friends:—all these relationships are held together by propriety and righteousness which are called the "bonds of men"' (有禮義以相維,謂之人紀). We are to understand by 人紀 the fundamental relationships of society, and the moral virtues by which they are securely and happily maintained. Këë had disregarded these virtues and disorganized society; the first work of T'ang was—unconsciously to himself—to exhibit the virtues and reform society. All the rest of the paragraph is an expansion of this clause. 先民時若=先民是順, 'with the former people he was accordant.' By the 'former people' are intended sage men of ancient times, the lessons of whose wisdom had been transmitted. Ying-tă says that 民 is used to indicate that the wisdom was from 'the people.' But the character need not have that force;—compare Pt. V., Bk. XII., p. 11,—相古先民有夏. The sentiment is that T'ang did not consider that all wisdom was with himself, but was ever ready to learn. 爲下克忠,—T'ang's dethroning Këë, and taking the empire to himself, would seem to be contrary to this affirmatiom of his loyalty, but it was not of his own will merely, nor till he had used every method of remonstrance and advice, that he took the field against his sovereign. 與人不求備,—求備,—see Con. Ana., XIII., xxv.; 與人=與人之善, 'he allowed to men their good qualities.' 與=許; the 檢身 in the parallel clause shows that we are to take 與 as a verb. 以至于萬方,—this language well indicates how T'ang was

求備、檢身若不及、以至于有萬邦、茲惟艱哉。○(六節)敷求哲人、俾輔于爾後嗣。○(七節)制官刑、儆于有位、曰、敢有恆舞于宮、酣歌于室、時謂巫風、敢有殉于貨色、恆于遊畋、時謂淫風、敢有侮聖言、

in the government of himself, he seemed to think he could never sufficiently attain.—It was thus he arrived at the possession of the myriad regions. How painstaking was he in these things!
6 He extensively sought out wise men, who should be helpful to you
7 his descendants and heirs. He laid down the punishments for officers, and warned them who were in authority, saying, 'If you dare to have constant dancing in your palaces, and drunken singing in your chambers,—that is called sorcerers' fashion; if you dare to set your hearts on wealth and women, and abandon yourselves to wandering about or to hunting,—that is called the fashion of dissipation; if you dare to contemn the words of sages, to resist the loyal and

carried on, as by the force of circumstances, and not by any ambition of his own, to the supreme dominion. 茲惟艱哉,—the 艱 suggests the idea that the clause does not celebrate T'ang's surmounting all difficulties that opposed his possession of the empire, but his being able to display the virtues which insured his possession of it. Seun-tsze, in his Book on the 'Ways of a Minister' (臣道篇), quotes a passage from the Shoo, which must be another form of the first part of this paragraph. He has:—書曰, 從命而不拂, 微諫而不倦, 爲上則明, 爲下則遜. 6. 敷=廣, 'widely.' Ch'in King (陳經) says:—'T'ang attained the empire with the greatest difficulty, and therefore his anxious thoughts about it went very far forward; it was right he should seek for men of talents and virtue to hand it down to his posterity.' 7. Lin Che-k'e says;—'Although T'ang had sought out wise men to be a help to his descendants, he was still afraid lest the men whom they employed should only think of securing themselves in their offices, and not attend to their duty to remonstrate with and guide their sovereign. He therefore instituted these punishments for officers to admonish them.' E Yin, in calling the young emperor's attention to such ordinances, had regard, no doubt, to the vices and errors into which he saw that T'ae-kĕă was prone to fall.

巫風,—Ying-tă observes that the wizard is called 覡 and the witch 巫, but that 巫 is applicable both to men and women. These persons had intercourse with spiritual beings, and hence the service of spirits is called 巫 (事鬼神曰巫). We have only to think of the frenzied excitement of the ancient sibyls to see how strong and contemptuous is the language of T'ang in reference to the officers of this fashion. 風 is here = 'ways,' 'fashion.' Properly it denotes 'the wind;' thence it is applied to what is exciting and influences others. 殉 is here in the sense of 求, 'to desire,' 'to seek for.' 淫風,—淫=過, 'excess.' 遠耆德比頑童,—遠 (3d tone)=疎遠, 'to be distant to and keep at a distance;' 比=狎比, 'to be familiar

逆忠直、遠耆德、比頑童、時謂亂風。惟茲三風十愆、卿士有一于身、家必喪、邦君一于身、國必亡、臣下不匡、其刑墨、具訓于蒙士。八節 ○嗚

upright, to put far from you the aged and virtuous, and to be familiar with procacious youths,—that is called the fashion of disorder. Now if a high noble or officer be addicted to one of these fashions with their ten evil ways, his Family will surely come to ruin; if the prince of a country be so addicted, his State will surely come to ruin. The minister who does not *try to* correct *those vices in the sovereign* shall be punished with branding.' These rules were minutely enjoined *also* upon cadets in their lessons.

and keep company with.' 頑 is paraphrased by 頑鈍無恥, 'obstinate, stupid, and shameless.' The case of Rehoboam with the counsellors of Solomon and his own young companions will occur to most readers. 三風十愆,—the 'three fashions' are those just mentioned, and the 'ten vices' are the evil ways enumerated in connection with them:—two under the sorcerers' fashion; and four under each of the other two fashions. 家必喪,—家 is here very evidently used for the whole establishment of the noble or officer.

臣下不能匡,其刑墨,—the 'Daily Explanation' paraphrases:—若天子而犯此風愆,則在有位者,皆當盡言直諫,以匡扶其過.若隱忍坐視而不言,是食君之祿,而不忠者也,則必以墨刑加之, to the effect that any officer suffering the emperor to proceed in any of those evil ways without remonstrating with him should be punished with branding. With this the words of T'ang terminate. We are to understand the concluding clause as from E Yin himself. 具訓于蒙士,—the dict., with ref. to this passage, explains 蒙 by 蒙稚卑小之稱, 'the designation of the young and little.' 蒙士 are the sons of officers and nobles being trained in schools to fit them for the duties of mature life. 'They were minutely instructed,' says Ts'ae, 'in these duties, that when they entered on office they might know to administer reproof.'

[Mih-tsze has a passage in his only remaining chapter 'Against Music' (非樂篇,上), where he quotes part of this par. and the next, but evidently his text is very corrupt. He says:—先王之書,湯之官刑有之曰,其恆舞于宮,是謂巫風,其刑,君子出絲二衛,小人否似二伯黃徑乃言曰,嗚呼,舞佯佯,黃言孔章,上帝弗常,九有以亡,上帝不順,降之百殃,其家必壞喪. From this corrupt and mutilated passage we perceive there was a book in Mih's time known as 'The Penal Laws of T'ang.' Of course if such a book was really made by T'ang, we can suppose that E Yin should be quoting from it here. Yen Jŏ-keu contends that such a book was made towards the close of the Shang dynasty, and not by T'ang, and concludes, therefore, that our present 'Instructions of E' bear upon them in this place the manifest stamp of forgery. But he has no direct evidence to show that we should refer 'The Penal Laws of T'ang' to a period several hundred years later than that emperor. All his reasoning on the point is singularly weak.]

呼、嗣王祗厥身、念哉、聖謨洋洋、嘉言孔彰、惟上帝不常、作善降之百祥、作不善降之百殃、爾惟德罔小、萬邦惟慶、爾惟不德、罔大、墜厥宗。

8 IV. "Oh! do you, who *now* succeed to the throne, revere *these instructions* in your person. Think of them!—Sacred counsels of vast importance, admirable words forcibly displayed. *The ways of* God are not invariable;—on the good-doer He sends down all blessings, and on the evil-doer He sends down all miseries. Do you be but virtuous, without consideration of the smallness *of your actions*, and the myriad regions will have cause for congratulation. If you be not virtuous, without consideration of the greatness *of your actions*, *they* will bring the ruin of your ancestral temple."

CH. IV. P. 8. THE INSTRUCTIONS CONCLUDED.—A SOLEMN ADMONITION TO T'AE-KEA TO FOLLOW THE EXAMPLE OF T'ANG, AND TAKE HEED TO HIS WAYS. 祗厥身,—we might translate this—'be reverent of his person,' but the commentators generally prefer to make the lessons of the last par. the object of 祗, and expand the passage by 敬之于身, 'respect them in his person.' 洋洋,—'vast;' comp. 'Doctrine of the Mean,' xvi., 3. 孔=大, 'great,' or 'greatly.' 爾惟德, 云云,—Lin Che-k'e has said on this passage:—K'ung of Han says, "Cultivate your virtue, and not on a small scale; then the whole empire will have cause for congratulation. Do what is not virtuous, and that not on a great scale, and you will overthrow your ancestral temple. These are the instructions of E, showing his true royalty." The meaning of K'ung was that the emperor's virtue must be extremely great, and then he would make the myriad regions happy, while for the overthrow of his ancestral temple it was not necessary that his want of virtue should be great; and this advice showed the true devotion of E Yin. K'ung of T'ang lost this meaning of Gan-kwŏ, and explains it thus:—爲善無小, *i.e.*, all states will rejoice in your little virtue, and how much more will they do so if it be great! 爲惡無大, *i.e.*, a little wickedness will overthrow your ancestral temple, and how much more will great wickedness do so! These two expressions—罔小罔大 are antithetic, but their meaning is the same. Lin then endeavours to show that Gan-kwŏ's interpretation is the only one admissible. The antithetic phrases are certainly somewhat perplexing. I consider that the one of them supposes also the other. 罔小 is equivalent to—'be it small or large,'; and 罔大 to—'be it large or small.' The *tendency* of virtue and vice, without reference to their amount or degree, is as severally represented.

THE BOOKS OF SHANG.

BOOK V. T'AE KEA. PART i.

太甲上

一節 惟嗣王不惠于阿衡。○伊二節尹作書曰、先王顧諟天之明命、以承上下神祇、社稷宗廟、罔不祗肅、天監厥德、用集大命、撫綏萬方、惟尹躬克左右厥辟宅師、肆嗣王丕承基

1 I. The king, on succeeding to the throne, did not follow *the*
2 *advice of* A-hăng. *He, that is,* E Yin, then made the following writing:—'The former king kept his eye continually on the bright requirements of Heaven, and served and obeyed the spirits of heaven and earth, of the land and the grain, and of the ancestral temple;—all with a reverent veneration. Heaven took notice of his virtue, and caused its great appointment to light on him, that he should soothe and tranquillize the myriad regions. I, Yin, then gave my assistance to my sovereign in the settlement of the people. And thus it is that your Majesty, inheriting the crown, have become charged with the line of the great succession.

NAME OF THE BOOK.—太甲, 'T'ae-këă.' This was the name, we saw on the 1st par. of the last Book, of T'ang's grandson and successor. The names of all the Shang emperors after T'ang are made up of the first series of the cyclical characters, called the 'Heavenly Stems' (天幹), with another distinguishing character added. This was the fashion of the dynasty. The Book is divided into three Parts, each of which is called a *p'ëen* (篇). The first Part might stand very well by itself; the second and third have nothing in their contents specially to require a separation of them from each other. Lin Che-k'e observes that the division of several of the Books of the Shoo into Parts arose from their length. Being written or engraved originally on tablets of wood or bamboo, very many of these could not be kept together so as to be read with comfort. A book was therefore tied up in two bundles, marked 上, 下, or in three, marked 上, 中, and 下, as the case might be. The division was made for convenience' sake, rather than from regard to any difference in the matter. This is only partially correct. There are some Books that are not divided, which yet are longer than others that are. Sze-ma Ts'een gives the name as 太甲訓 'The Instructions delivered to T'ae-këă.' It may have been current during the Han dynasty under that title. It does belong to the division of the Shoo which embraces 'Instructions.' The genuineness of the Book is called in question.

CONTENTS. E Yin finds the young sovereign disobedient to his counsels, and insensible to repeated remonstrances. On this the minister takes a high-handed measure, removes the emperor from his palace and companions, and keeps him in a sort of easy confinement, near the grave of his grandfather, all the period of mourning. T'ae-këă becomes penitent and truly reformed. This is the subject of the first Part. Delighted with the change, E Yin brings T'ae-këă back in state to the capital. He congratulates him on his reformation, and the emperor makes a suitable reply; after which E again proceeds to his favourite work of counselling and advising. This first Part is divided into ten parr., which are again arranged in three chapters. The first, containing 3 parr., tells of T'ae-këă's waywardness, and how E Yin called him in a letter to follow the example of his grandfather. The second, in 4 parr., tells of T'ae-këă's continued misconduct, and how E Yin by word of mouth expostulated with him. The third, in 3 parr., shows us the minister's patience worn out, with the bold measure which he took, and its happy effects.

CH. I. Pp. 1—3. T'AE-KEA'S WAYWARDNESS. E YIN REMONSTRATES WITH HIM IN WRITING.

1. 不惠于阿衡,—惠=順, 'to accord,' 'to be obedient.' Compare its use in Pt. II., Bk. I., 17; Bk. II., 5; Bk. III., 8. 阿衡,—this is said by Sze-ma Ts'een to have been the name of E; and it saves the translator considerable trouble to follow this view. The more common opinion, however, and that followed by Ts'ae, is that the characters were the title of an officer—the prime minister in fact—under the Shang dynasty. 阿 is taken as=倚, and the name is then='support and steelyard,' 'buttress and director.' Others make 阿=保, which gives the same result. The name, it is said, was given to E Yin, because of his services to T'ang and to the empire. 2. *E Yin presses in writing the example of T'ang's religious reverence upon T'ae-këă.* 伊尹作書,—this is the first time that we read in the Shoo of any communication addressed otherwise than by word of mouth. Ch'in Leih suggests that perhaps the presenting written or engraved memorials commenced at this time. We are not to think of E Yin as using pencils, ink, and paper. His memorial was on one or more slips of wood or bamboo, lightly engraved, or described perhaps with some colouring matter on the plain surface. Lin Che-k'e observes that down to the Han dynasty the memorials were all upon such slips, and were presented tied up in black bags. 先王顧諟天之明命,—see 'The Great Learning,' C., i., 2. The meaning of 諟 is not well ascertained. It evidently serves to give emphasis to 顧. Choo He and the Sung school generally take 明命, as referring to 'man's nature,' the bright gift conferred on and entrusted to him by Heaven, and the statement is that 'T'ang assiduously cultivated his virtue.' This is twisting the Shoo to support the dogmas of a school. T'ang had regard to the will of Heaven in reference to the whole course of his life and duty. That led him to cultivate his personal virtue, but it took him out of himself also, to do what his circumstances called him to; more especially did he feel it was required of him by Heaven that he should be reverent and devout,—religious, according to his lights. We may believe that T'ae-këă was glaringly neglectful of all religious worship. 承=奉, 'to serve.' 以承, 'so as to serve;' *i.e.*, his regard to the requirements of Heaven did actually make him a regular and reverent worshipper. 天監厥德, 用集大命,—commentators call attention to the manner in which the first of these clauses responds to 顧天之命. T'ang looked up to Heaven, and Heaven looked down on him. 用='and so;'—we have had several instances of this usage. 集, 'to collect;' here='to make to light upon.' Compare the She-king, Pt. III., i., Ode II., 4,—天監在下, 有命既集. 惟尹躬克左右厥辟宅師,—尹躬='Yin's-self,' 'Yin himself.' According to Leu Puh-wei and others, E's name was Che (摯), but he here speaks of himself as Yin. We must suppose that he was styled 尹, because of his services, and better known among the people as 'the Regulator,' 'the Corrector,' than by his name. Here he accepts the designation. 辟 (*peih*),—'a sovereign.' It was applied to the emperor and to princes of States. 師=衆, 'the multitude,' 'the people.' Wang Ts'ëaou says:—'The phrase 宅師 follows from the preceding 撫綏. What is meant by settling—locating—the people, is that after their oppressions were taken away and a gentle rule exercised, they were arranged so that every man was in his proper place' (處之各得其所). 丕承基緒,—緒, comp. III., Bk. III., p 8; 基 is 'a foundation,' that on which any thing rests. Joined with 業, it denotes 'an inheritance,' 'a transmitted property.' The phrase in the text has the same meaning. Ts'ëaou says on the

緒。○惟三節尹躬先見于西邑夏、自周有終、相亦惟終、其後嗣王罔克有終、相亦罔終、嗣王戒哉、祗爾厥辟、辟不辟、忝厥祖。○王惟四節庸罔念聞。○伊五節尹乃言曰、先王

3 "I have seen it myself in Hea with its western capital,—that when its sovereigns went through a prosperous course to the end, their ministers also did the same; but afterwards when their successors could not attain to such a consummation, neither did their ministers. Take warning, O heir-king. Reverently use your sovereignty. The sovereign, if you do not play the sovereign, you will disgrace your ancestor.'

4 II. The king would not think *of these words*, nor listen to them.

5 On this E Yin said, "The former king, before it was light, sought to have large and clear views, and then sat waiting for the morn-

clause that it means that T'ae-këă had come 'to the myriad regions, all established, and to the multitudes of the people, all settled.'

3. *That the minister is more dependent on his sovereign for prosperity than the sovereign on his minister.* T'ae-këă had probably, half in insolence and half in flattery, been saying that he might follow his heart's lusts, while the government was safe in the hands of such a minister as E. 西邑夏,—'Hea of the western city.' The reference must be to Gan-yih, the capital of Hëa, which was farther west then Pŏ, the cap. of Shang. 自周有終,—the 周 here has occasioned much perplexity. On the authority of an expression in the 國語, Gan-kwŏ and others since him have explained it by 忠信, 'loyal and true.' Choo He remarked that to say—以忠信自周, 'by loyalty and faith to perfect one's-self,' would be well enough, but that to define 周 as meaning 'loyal and true' was not allowable; and that the characters 自周 in the text were unintelligible. Wang Pih (王柏), foll. by Kin Le-ts'ëang (金履祥), thought that for 周 we should read 君, the ancient form of which was 㕵, that might easily be mistaken for 周. The editors of Yung-ching's Shoo express their approval of this emendation, and I have translated accordingly. 有終,—comp. Bk. II., 9. 祗爾云云,—爾厥辟=‘your that being sovereign.' Compare 君君, 臣臣, &c., in Con. Ana., XII. xi. In the Book of Rites, 坊記, p. 22, we find the two last clauses,—厥辟不辟, 忝厥祖, quoted from the Shoo, with an interpretation and application, different from their meaning in E's writing.

Ch. II. Pp. 4—7. T'AE-KEA CONTINUES CARELESS, AND E YIN EXPOSTULATES WITH HIM, AND TRIES TO WIN HIM ON TO WHAT WAS RIGHT.

4. Many put a comma at 庸, and explain it by 常.—'T'ae-këă treated E Yin's words as if they were only ordinary and unimportant.' This is Ts'ae's interpretation. Gan-kwŏ, pointing in the same way, explained, —'T'ae-këă kept his ordinary way, and did not change.' Choo He proposed to read the paragraph without a stop at 庸, and to take that character in the sense of 用, so that it simply emphasizes the verbs below;—comp. Bk. VIII., Pt. i., p. 2, —王庸作書以誥. I have translated on this view. 5. 昧爽丕顯,—昧爽, 'the dark and light;'—as we say, 'between the dark and the light,'=‘the grey dawn;'

昧爽丕顯、坐以待旦、旁求俊彥、啓迪後人、無越厥命以自覆。○六節愼乃儉德、惟懷永圖。○七節若虞機張、往省括于度、則釋、欽厥止、率乃祖攸行、惟朕以懌、萬世有辭。

ing. He *also* sought on every side for men of ability and virtue to
instruct and guide his posterity. Do not frustrate his charge *to me*,
6 and bring on yourself your own overthrow. Be careful to strive
7 after the virtue of self-restraint, and cherish far-reaching plans. Be
like the forester, who, when he has adjusted the spring, goes to
examine the end of the arrow, whether it be placed according to
rule, and then lets go;—reverently determine your end, and follow
the ways of your ancestor. Thus I shall be delighted, and be able
to all ages to show that I have discharged my trust.

丕顯, 'was greatly clear.' Kin Le-ts'ëang says well, that the whole clause shows how T'ang kept his eye continually on the requirements of Heaven (此卽先王顧諟之功). 俊,—see on 'Counsels of Kaou-yaou,' p. 4. 彥—美士, 'admirable officers.' The 說文 defines it—美士有文,人所言也. 旁求……後人,—this shows how T'ang's anxieties were not merely for himself and for the time being. 無越厥命,—無=毋; 越 is here not = 踰, 'to transgress,' but 墜, 'to let fall,'— 'to bring to nought;' 厥命 is the charge of T'ae-këä which E supposes to have been specially committed to himself by T'ang. 6. T'ae-këä was losing all self-restraint, plunging into extravagance, and thinking only of the day before him;—hence the two admonitions in this par. 乃—汝. 儉德,—comp. in last Bk., p. 5,—檢身若不及. 7. Gan-kwŏ takes 虞 in the sense of 度, 'to consider,' 'to calculate,' and 若虞機張 = 'as when you calculate the adjusting the spring *of your cross-bow*.' This is admissible; but Choo He prefers, and I think rightly, to take 虞 in the sense of 虞人, or 'forester.' 機, is defined by 弩牙, 'the tooth of the cross-bow.' We are to understand the spring by touching which the instrument was discharged. 括—矢末, 'the end of the arrow,' which was placed against the string, and on the correct placing of which—its being 合於法度—depended the success of the archery. 欽厥止,—compare 'The Great Learning,' C., iii., 3. 萬世有辭,—Ts'ae explains 辭 by 譽, 'praise,' and makes the clause refer to T'ae-këä, = 'all ages will celebrate you.' Lin Che-k'e makes it refer to E Yin, and = 'through all ages be able to say *that I have discharged my trust*,' *i.e.*, be able to give an account of myself. The editors of Yung-ching's Shoo rather approve of this view of Lin's. I have followed it, because it retains the proper signification of 辭. I do not know that the meaning which Ts'ae puts on it can be supported by other examples;—comp. 汝永有辭, Pt. V., Bk. XIII., p. 10.

[In the 'Record of Rites,' and the Book called 緇衣 p. 16, we have quite an array of quotations from the 太甲, more or less agreeing with the received text.—太甲曰,無越厥命,以自覆也,若虞機張,往省括于厥度,則釋。Here par. 6 is omitted. 尹吉曰,惟尹躬天見于西邑夏,自周有終,相亦惟終. Here 吉 is perhaps an error

八節 王未克變。九節 伊尹曰、茲乃不義、習與性成、予弗狎于弗順、營于桐宮、密邇先王其訓、無俾世迷。○十節 王徂桐宮、居憂、克終允德。

8, 9 III. The king was not yet able to change *his course*. E Yin said
to himself, "This is *real* unrighteousness, and is becoming by
practice *a second* nature. I cannot bear to be near *such* a disobe-
dient *fellow*. I will build *a place* in the palace at T'ung, where he
can be quietly near *the remains of* the former king. This will be a les-
10 son which will keep him from going astray all his life." The king went
accordingly to the palace in T'ung, and dwelt during the period of
mourning. In the end he became sincerely virtuous.

for 告, or, more probably, 尹吉 should be 伊尹, and 天 may be for 先.]

Ch. III. Pp. 8—10. T'AE-KEA CONTINUING VICIOUS, E SENDS HIM FROM THE PALACE, AND KEEPS HIM IN CONFINEMENT,—WHICH ENDS IN HIS REFORMATION. 8. 伊尹曰,—曰 is the reflection in E's mind. It is better to take it thus than to expand it with Ying-tă,—'E Yin announced to all the ministers in the court, saying,'—. 茲乃不義習與性成,—Gan-kwŏ explains this:—習行不義將成其性, 'the practice of unrighteousness will become his nature.' This is no doubt the meaning, but it gives us no explanation to account for the use of the 與. Ts'ae avoids the same difficulty by expanding:—伊尹指太甲所爲乃不義之事,習惡而性成者也. If we had 而 in the text instead of 與, the whole would be easy. The 'Daily Explanation' tries to bring out the force of the 與 thus:—習爲不善,若天生性成者然, 'he is practising what is not good as if his nature from his birth were so constituted.' Lin Che-k'e treats it substantially in the same way; and I do not see that anything better can be done. 予弗狎于弗順,—'I will not be near the disobedient.' Such is the natural rendering of the words, and such was the view of them taken by Choo He. Ying-tă, however, and Ts'ae, subsequently, thinking this language would be too harsh in E's mouth, softened it down to—'I will not *allow him to be* near the disobedient.' There is no reason why we should strain the text to avoid the very decided expression of his opinion which E gave, and to maintain in him the Chinese ideal of a hero-sage. He spoke evidently under strong provocation. 營于桐宮,—'T'ung' was the place where T'ang's tomb was. It was, probably, in the pres. dis of Yung-ho (滎河), dep. of P'oo-chow (蒲州), in Shan-se. The site or supposed site of the grave there was washed away by the Fun (汾河), under the Yuen dynasty, when a stone coffin was removed to another position, near which, under the Ming dynasty, an imperial tomb was built. [The sub. dep. of Pŏ (亳), in Gan-hwuy, likewise prefers a claim to include the place of T'ang's grave.] From Mencius, V., Pt. I., vi. 5, we are led to infer that T'ung was the name of a city or district;—nothing is said of it as the place where T'ang had been buried. Ts'ae manipulates the text to 營宮于桐, 'built a palace in T'ung;' and Ying-tă had done the same 營於桐墓立宮. But why should we use such violence with the language, when we are not compelled to do so in order to make any meaning out of it? The text leads us to suppose that there was already a palace in T'ung. E Yin determined to build or fit up some apartment in it, where T'ae-këă might reside,—be confined in fact,—till he gave proof of reformation. 密邇先王其訓,—all the commentators take 密邇 as=親近. We get a better meaning, it seems to me, by taking 密 as='secretly,' 'silently.' We do not know what to do with the 其訓. Lin Che-k'e represents E's idea thus:—'I will make him dwell there, to be near the former king, and think of his instructions.' Ts'ae has:—'I will make him be near the grave of T'ang, where thinking mournfully morning and night, he may rouse up the good that is in him:—thus I will instruct him.' My translation is more after Ts'ae's view.

10. 居憂,—Gan-kwŏ has 居憂位, 'dwelt in the place of sorrow.' There T'ae-këă could not help himself, and had to observe all the established customs of mourning.

CONCLUDING NOTE. [i.] The action of E Yin in dealing with his sovereign has been much canvassed. Mencius was bound on his principles to defend it, and he did not scruple to do so. When Kung-sun Ch'ow asked him whether worthies, being ministers, might indeed banish their vicious sovereigns in this way, he answered, 'If they have the same purpose as E Yin, they may; if they have not the same purpose, it would be usurpation' (VII., Pt. I., xxxi.). This doctrine is startling, but sound. A man in the position of E Yin must be a law to himself, wherever his actions will not clash with the moral laws of God.

[ii.] According to the Shoo, the confinement of T'ae-këă in T'ung took place during the period of mourning, and lasted only to the end of it,—we may say, in round numbers, for three years, as Mencius does. Sze-ma Ts'een gives a different account. We read in the 'Historical Records:'—'When T'ae-këă had been on the throne three years, he proved unintelligent and oppressive, paying no regard to the laws of T'ang, and being guilty of all sorts of disorderly conduct. On this E Yin confined him in the T'ung palace for three years, while he himself administered the government of the empire, and gave audience to the princes. When T'ae-këă had been in T'ung for three years, he became penitent, reproved himself and returned to good, on which E Yin brought him back to the capital, and resigned the government into his hands. The emperor then cultivated his virtue; the princes all signified their allegiance; the people enjoyed tranquillity; and E Yin, in admiration, made the "Instructions to T'ae-këă," in three Parts, in his praise.' We cannot say positively from Mencius that Ts'een's account is incorrect, but we must set it aside, if on no other ground, yet certainly on the authority of the Preface to the Shoo.

THE BOOKS OF SHANG.

BOOK V. T'AE KEA. PART ii.

太甲中

一節 惟三祀、十有二月朔、伊尹以冕服、奉嗣王歸于亳。○二節 作書曰、民

1 I On the first day of the 12th month of the 3d year, E Yin took the imperial cap and robes, and escorted the young king back to

CONTENTS OF THE SECOND PART. The confinement of T'ae-këă in T'ung having produced the desired effect, E Yin brings him back with honour to Pŏ, to undertake the duties of the government, and presents him with a congratulatory address on his reformation. T'ae-këă responds with a proper acknowledgment, and asks the continued assistance and guidance of the minister, who on his part is happy to resume his favourite work of delivering instructions.

The first two parr. form a chapter, describing the emperor's return, and giving the address on his reformation. T'ae Këă's penitent reply, in par. 3, forms a second chapter. The remaining 3 paragraphs, in which E resumes his lessons and counsels, on the example of T'ang, and the duties of T'ae-këă, conclude the part with a third chapter.

Ch. I. THE YOUNG KING IS BROUGHT BACK WITH HONOUR TO PO. E YIN CONGRATULATES HIM AND THE EMPIRE ON HIS REFORMATION.

惟三祀十有二月朔,—this note of time follows from that in the 'Instructions of E,' par. 1. Two years have elapsed from that time. The same question arises.—Is the 12th month the 12th month of the Hea year or of the Shang? I am more inclined to believe that in both passages we have nothing to do with the Hea year. T'ang having died in the eleventh month, T'ae-këă had immediately commenced the formalities of mourning for him,—with no sincerity indeed, but yet nominally. It was now the 26th month since T'ang's death. T'ae-këă was entered into the third year of mourning. At the end of the 24th month it was competent for him to lay aside his sad apparel, array himself in his ordinary robes, and go about all the duties devolving on him. The period of mourning for parents and grandparents is indeed said to be three years; but as the Chinese say that they are three years old, not when they have completed three years of 12 months each, but when they have lived in three years, so T'ae-këă might now, in the 12th month of the 3d year in which he had been on the throne, be considered to have fulfilled the duties of mourning for his grandfather, and take the administration of affairs into his own hands.

Jŏ-keu argues that two years are not enough for all the events that are supposed to have taken place,—the repeated remonstrances with T'ae-këă, his proving himself insensible to advice, his banishment to T'ung, his reformation, and his proving its sincerity. We have not sufficient information to enable us to solve all the difficulties that may be raised; the view of the time which I have followed seems to me more likely then any other;—see the 後案 of Wang Ming-shing, on the one side, and the 尙書廣聽錄, on the other.

冕服,—the distinctive name of the ceremonial bonnet or crown under the Yin or Shang

非后、罔克胥匡以生、后非民、罔以辟四方、皇天眷佑有商、俾嗣王克終厥德、實萬世無疆之休。三節○王拜手稽首曰、予小子不明于德、

2 Pŏ. At the same time, he made the following writing:—"Without the sovereign, the people cannot have that guidance which is necessary to *the comfort of their* lives; without the people, the sovereign could have no sway over the four quarters *of the empire*. Great Heaven has graciously favoured the House of Shang, and granted to you, O young king, at last to become virtuous. This is indeed a blessing that will extend without limit to ten thousand generations."

3 II. The king did obeisance with his face to his hands, and his head to the ground, saying, "I, the little child, was without under-

dynasty was 冔 (see the Record of Rites, 王制, Pt. V., p, 11). Here, however. the general term 冕 is used. Under the Chow dynasty, the emperor had six difft. crowns, with robes appropriate to each. In sacrificing to Heaven, he used one kind of crown and robes, in sacrificing to his ancestors, a different kind; &c., (see the Rites of Chow, 卷二十一, 春官, 司服). Whether the practices under the Shang dyn. were the same, we have no means of knowing. The crown was always in the form of a student's cap, with tassels on which pearls were strung hanging down before and behind, except on the occasion of sacrificing to Heaven, when it is said there were no tassels; on the other occasions the number of pendents and pearls and gems varied, and perhaps the colour. As the text does not say for what particular ceremony T'ae-këă was now arrayed, though I should judge it was either to perform the great solstitial sacrifice to Heaven, or to announce his entering personally on the duties of the government in the ancestral temple, more need not be said on the crown and robes.

2. 民非后...四方, these clauses show how the people and the sovereign are necessary to one another. The only difficulty is with 胥匡以生. Medhurst translates:—'The people have nothing wherewith they may correct each other so as to preserve their lives'; and Gaubil:—'The people cannot live either in peace or in order.' Medhurst's version appears to be the more literal; but we must deal with 胥 here in the same way as with 相 in the clause 官司相規, 'Pun. Expedition of Yin,' par. 3. [In the Record of Rites, 表記, par. 11, we have the passage quoted—太甲曰, 民非后, 無能胥以寧, 后非民無以辟四方.]

皇天......厥德,—the commentators call attention to the way in which it is here taught that T'ae-këă's becoming virtuous was to be ascribed to the influence of Heaven exerted on him. Ts'ae says that 'Heaven secretly drew on his better nature' (陰誘其衷). Shin She-hing (申時行) says:—'In the matter of his thoughts, it was as if Heaven awakened him; in the matter of his actions, it was as if Heaven helped him' (其思也, 若或啟之, 其行也, 若或翼之).

Ch. II. P. 3. T'AE-KEA'S PENITENT REPLY. HE CONFESSES HIS FAULTS IN THE PAST, AND ASKS E YIN TO CONTINUE HIS GUIDANCE TO HIM. 自底不類,—不類=不肖;—see 'Doctrine of the Mean,' iv., 1. The 'Daily Explanation' has:—以自入于不肖, 'and thereby entering among the unworthy.' 欲敗度, 縱敗禮,—these words are quoted in the 左傳, 昭十年. 欲—多欲, 'many desires,' or 'lusts;'

自厎不類、欲敗度、縱敗禮、以速戾于厥躬、天作孽、猶可違、自作孽、不可逭、既往背師保之訓、弗克于厥初、尚賴匡救之德、圖惟厥終。○四節伊尹拜手稽首曰、修厥身、允德協于下、惟明后。○五節先王子惠困窮、民服厥命、

standing of what was virtuous, and was making myself one of the unworthy. By my desires I was setting at nought all rules *of conduct*, and by my self-indulgence I was violating all rules of propriety:—the result must have been speedy ruin to my person. Calamities sent by Heaven may be avoided, but from calamities brought on by one's-self there is no escape. Heretofore I turned my back on the instructions of you, my Tutor and Guardian;—my beginning has been marked by incompetency. May I still rely on your correcting and preserving virtue, keeping this in view that my end may be good!"

4 III. E Yin did obeisance with his face to his hands, and his head to the ground, and said, "To cultivate his person, and by being sincerely virtuous, bring *all* below to harmonious concord with
5 him;—this is the work of the intelligent sovereign. The former king was kind to the distressed and suffering, as if they were his

縱＝縱肆, 'unrestrained indulgence.' Ts'ae says that 度 has reference to the conduct, the ends pursued, and 禮 to the behaviour, the demeanour to others. 天作孽……可逭,—this is twice quoted by Mencius, with 活 instead of 逭;—see Vol. II., p. 15, and p. 175. In the Record of Rites, however, the Bk. 緇衣, par. 16, we find it exactly as in the text. 既往＝已往. It is an adverbial phrase = 'in the past.' 圖惟厥終,—comp. 有終, 罔終, Part i., p. 3.

Ch. III. Pp. 4—6. E Yin resumes his instructions. 4. *Description of an intelligent sovereign.* 伊尹拜手稽首,—see on 'Canon of Shun,' p. 17. This humble obeisance was due from the minister to the sovereign. For the sovereign to pay it to the minister as in the last paragraph, and as we shall see it hereafter often rendered to the duke of Chow, was an act of extreme reverence and condescension. On 修厥身 She-hing has well said that it implies two things:—'the ordering one's affairs by righteousness' (Bk. II., p. 8), in which there will be no 'setting at nought, through lusts, the rules of conduct;' and 'the ordering one's heart by propriety,' in which case there will be no 'violating the rules of demeanour.' 允德協于下, 'and to have sincere virtue harmonizing in *the sphere* beneath.' The 'Daily Explanation,' paraphrases this:—出乎身而加乎民, 將誠實之德, 孚契于人, 自然人心協和, 無不愛戴. 5. *How T'ang by his kindness and sympathy with the distressed drew the hearts of all the people to himself.* 子惠困窮,

罔有不悅、並其
有邦厥鄰、乃曰、
徯我后、后來無
罰。○王懋乃德、
視乃烈祖、無時
豫怠。○奉先思
孝、接下思恭、視
遠惟明、聽德惟
聰、朕承王之休
無斁。

六節 七節

children, and the people submitted to his commands, all with sincere delight. Even in the States of the neighbouring princes the *people* said, 'We are waiting for our sovereign; when our sovereign comes, we shall not suffer the punishments *which we now do*?'

6 "O King, zealously cultivate your virtue. Regard *the example of* your meritorious ancestor. At no time allow yourself in pleasure
7 and idleness. When honouring your ancestors, think how you can prove your filial piety; in receiving your ministers, think how you can show yourself respectful; in looking at what is distant, try to get clear views; have your ears ever open to listen to virtue:—then shall I respond to the excellence of your Majesty with an untiring *devotion to your service*!"

—子 = 'son-ned,' *i.e.*, treated as his children. 並其有邦厥鄰、乃曰、Gan-kwŏ explains this:—湯俱與鄰並有國、鄰國人乃曰、'T'ang and his neighbours were equally possessors of kingdoms, but the people of the neighbouring kingdoms said.' Choo He's representation of the construction is the same:—湯與彼皆有土諸侯、而鄰國之人乃曰、'T'ang and those were all princes possessing States, and yet the people of the neighbouring States said.' They have both caught the meaning. We read 並其有邦厥鄰 without a stop.—'Compeers *with him were* those possessed of States, his neighbours.' Then 乃曰 = 'but it was said,' *i.e.*, it was said in their States by their people. 徯我后、云云,—see the quotation of this by Mencius, III., Pt. II., v., 4. 6, 7. *E Yin exhorts T'ae-këă to cultivate his virtue after the example of T'ang; calls his attention to several important points in which he might make his profiting appear; and promises his own untiring aid.* 朕承王之休無斁,—I will receive the excellence of the king without satiety.' The paraphrase in the 'Daily Explanation' is:—尹承王之休美、益思左右匡救、而不遺其力矣、其何敢厭斁哉、

THE BOOKS OF SHANG.

BOOK V. T'AE-KEA. PART iii.

太甲下

一節 伊尹申誥、于王曰、嗚呼、惟天無親、克敬惟親、民罔常懷、懷于有

1 I. E Yin again made an announcement to the king, saying, "Oh! Heaven has no affections;—only to those who are reverent does it show affection. The people are not constant to those whom they cherish;—they cherish only him who is benevolent. The spirits

CONTENTS OF THE THIRD PART. In the first three paragraphs E Yin dwells on the high and difficult charge to which the emperor is called; points out how good government is to be secured; and concludes by once more exhibiting T'ang as a model. The next five paragraphs contain various counsels and cautions addressed to T'ae-këă. In the last par. a lesson is given at once to sovereigns and ministers.

This portion of the T'ae-këă was perhaps delivered at a later period than the previous one. There is no allusion in it to the emperor's early follies and vices; there is supposed to be an allusion in the close to E's desire to withdraw from public life. In this way we find a reason for its separation from the previous Part. The compiler arranged his documents according to the knowledge which he had of the date of their contents. To the same effect with these remarks are the observations of Ch'in Ta-yew, which we find in the 集說;—'The "Instructions of E" were made before the faults of T'ae-këă had shown themselves, and the minister, wishing to guard against his tendency to self-indulgence, used language stern and severe. The first Part of the "T'ae-këă" was made when the emperor's faults were showing themselves, and then E, not wishing to provoke him, slightly changed his plan, and made his language gentle and insinuating. The second Part was made when T'ae-këă had begun to repent, and E, full of joy and consolation, made his language bland and encouraging. The third Part was made after T'ae-këă had reformed, and then E, anxious lest perhaps the change should not hold out to the last, fashioned his language so as to convey profound and stimulating exhortation. The consummate words of the great minister, now shallow and now deep, are all to be accounted for in this way.'

Ch. I. Pp. 1—3. THE DIFFICULTY OF RIGHTLY OCCUPYING THE IMPERIAL SEAT; THE RULES OF GOOD GOVERNMENT; THE EXAMPLE OF T'ANG.

1. 惟天無親—天無所親, 'Heaven has none whom it loves.' We may supply 常 before 親, after the analogy of the clauses below,—常懷, 常享; and then the meaning will be that 'Heaven is not invariable in its likings;' and we find this idea expressed very many times in the Shoo and other classical books. There must be a reason, however, why we do not have 常 before 親 in the text, and I conceive it is this.—Heaven stands out to the mind of E as the head of all government, the supreme Power and Authority in the world. To rule, as rule, reverence is due from the ruled; from the ruler we look for justice, not love. He has to do with men not simply as men, but as good men or as bad men, to reward the former and to punish the latter. Hence in the text we have it barely and broadly affirmed that 'Heaven has no affections.' This is not the whole truth, which was held by the ancient

仁、鬼神無常享。享于克誠、天位艱哉。○德惟治、否德亂、與治同道罔不興、與亂同事罔不亡、終始慎厥與、惟明明后。○先王惟時懋敬厥德、克配上帝、今王嗣

do not always accept the sacrifices which are offered to them;—
they accept only the sacrifices of the sincere. A place of difficulty
2 is the Heaven-*conferred* seat! Where there are *those* virtues, good
government is realized; where they are not, disorder comes. To
maintain the same principles as those who secured good government
will surely lead to prosperity; to pursue the course of disorder
will surely lead to ruin. He who at last, as at first, is careful as
3 to whom and what he follows is a truly intelligent sovereign.—The
former king was always zealous in the reverent cultivation of his

Chinese, about Heaven, as it is not the whole truth which is held by us about God; yet as it is proper for us to speak of God as 'the Lord of hosts that judgeth righteously,' so the affirmation in the text is properly put forth without any qualification. 鬼神無常享,—享 is 'to enjoy,' *i.e.*, to accept the sacrifices and oblations of the worshipper. We can hardly make a distinction between 鬼 and 神. Medhurst calls them here—'the demons and spirits.' Gaubil simply has—'les esprits.' The spirits of dead ancestors, which might be styled 鬼, and all other spirits from the highest to the lowest, which might be called 神, are embraced in the phrase. E's lesson is that the emperor as the subject of Heaven has to be reverent; as the sovereign of the people, he has to be benevolent; as the head of all religious worship, he has to be sincere. If he be not reverent, Heaven will punish him; if he be not benevolent, men will reject him; if he be not sincere, no spirits will regard him. Well might he add—天位艱哉. Compare on 玆惟艱哉, Bk. III., p. 5.

[Chin Tih-sew observes that here for the first time we have the virtues of reverence, benevolence, and sincerity, announced distinctly and in their connection and references,—a step in the development of the doctrine of Yaou and Shun, Yu and T'ang. The observation is correct. In later times, Confucius, Mencius, and others, made much of E's lessons.]

2. 德惟治,—the 德 is to be taken in close connection with the reverence, benevolence, and sincerity of the prec. par. 治 (3d tone) is good government realized. In 與治 and 與亂 the 與 has a verbal force. This appears from the 慎厥與 which follows. Ts'ae observes that the 道 or principled course of good government is spoken of, because though there may be differences of administrations and ordinances, required by difft. times, a common principle will be found underlying all variations. On the other hand we have only the 事 or courses of disorder, princes who are going to ruin doing so as they are hurried on and away by their several hearts' lusts. 慎厥與,—'be careful of his concurring.' She Lan says ingeniously, but with an over refinement:—'what is intended by 與 is something very subtle;—it is the concurring tendency of the mind.' 惟明明后,—here again is the redoubled adjective, = a superlative. 3. 先王,—this of course is T'ang. 懋敬厥德,—Ts'ae makes this = 'strove to make his virtue reverent,'—with special reference to the reverence towards Heaven mentioned in the first par., and the one of the virtues there specified being adduced here as inclusive of the other two. This seems to be straining the language too much. 克配上帝,—this phrase

有令緒、尚監茲哉。○四節若升高、必自下、若陟遐、必自邇。○五節無輕民事、惟難。無安厥位、惟危。○六節愼終于始。○七節有言逆于汝心、必求諸道、有言遜于汝志、必求諸非道。○八節嗚呼、弗慮胡獲、弗爲胡成。一人元良、萬邦以貞。○

virtue, so that he was the fellow of God. Now, O king, you have entered on the inheritance of his excellent line;—fix your inspection on him!

4 II. "*Your course must be* as when in ascending high you begin
from where 'tis low, and when in travelling far you begin from where
5 'tis near. Do not slight the occupations of the people;—think of
their difficulties; do not yield to a feeling of repose on your throne;—
6, 7 think of its perils. Be careful for the end at the beginning. When
you hear words against which your mind sets itself, you must
inquire whether they be not right; when you hear words which
accord with your own mind, you must inquire whether they be
8 not contrary to what is right. Oh! what attainment can be made
without anxious thought? what achievement can be made without
earnest effort? Let the one man be greatly good, and the myriad
regions will be rectified by him.

has two meanings. It is spoken of the *virtue* of a sovereign, so admirable in the present or the past that he can be described as the mate of God,—as a sovereign upon earth, the one correlate of the Supreme Sovereign above. It is spoken also of the *honours* of a departed sovereign, exalted to association with God in the great sacrificial services rendered to him by the reigning emperor. We are to take the phrase here in the first meaning. 配上帝 occurs again and again in the She King; in the Shoo we have it only in the text, though below we shall meet with 配天, 配皇天, in several places. 令緒,—'the excellent line or clue.' Compare 基緒, Part i. p. 2.

Ch. II. Pp. 4—8. VARIOUS COUNSELS.

4. *How T'ae-këă's progress in virtue should be persistent and progressive.* Comp. in the 'Doctrine of the Mean,' xv. 1, 君子之道辟如行遠必自邇, 云云. 陟 has commonly the signification of 升, 'to ascend.' We must take it here in the general sense of 'to advance.' 5. *The emperor should sympathize with the people's toils, and think of the perils of his own position.* 無—毋. 民事,—'the affairs of the people,' *i.e.*, their toilsome occupations of husbandry, &c. 惟難,—Ts'ae expands this by 而思其難, 'but think of their toilsomeness.' On this use of 惟, compare 惟幾, 惟康, in the 'Yih and Tseih,' p. 2. 6. *To end right the best plan is to begin right.* 7. *T'ae-këă should judge what he hears not by his own likings or dislikings. Palatable advice is probably bad; unpalatable, good.* Wang Ts'ëaou observes well that this is an expansion of 聽德惟聰, in Part ii., p. 7. Compare Con. Ana., IX., xxiii.,

九節 君罔以辯言亂舊政、臣罔以寵利居成功、邦其永孚于休。

9 III. "When the sovereign will not with disputatious words throw the old rules of government into confusion, and the minister will not for favour and gain continue in an office whose work is done;—then the country will lastingly and surely enjoy happiness."

and Mencius, II., Pt. I., ii., 17. 8. *An appeal to T'ae-kĕă from the importance of his influence to be anxiously thoughtful, and earnest in his doings.*

Ch. III. P. 9. E YIN EXPRESSES HIS HOPE THAT THE EMPEROR WILL HOLD ON IN THE IMITATION OF T'ANG, AND INTIMATES HIS OWN INTENTION TO WITHDRAW FROM PUBLIC LIFE. 居成功,—'dwell in accomplished service.' The meaning is as in the translation. Ying-tă says:—'That E Yin addressing his sovereign should turn to speak of the duty of a minister, though his words are general, and announce a great principle, shews that he had himself formed the purpose of retiring.' Soo Tung-po says:—'The disorders of the empire arise from division between the sovereign and his ministers. When the sovereign proceeds disputatiously to change the old rules of government, the minister becomes afraid; and when the minister, for the sake of favour and gain, presumes on the service he has done, the sovereign comes to doubt him. It is thus that disorder begins.' See the 集說.

THE BOOKS OF SHANG.

BOOK VI. BOTH POSSESSED PURE VIRTUE.

咸有一德

一節 伊尹既復政厥辟、將告歸、乃陳戒于德。○

二節 曰、嗚呼、天難諶、命靡常、常厥德、保厥位、厥

I I. E Yin, having returned the government into the hands of his sovereign, and being about to announce his retirement, set forth admonitions on the subject of virtue.

2 II. He said, "Oh! it is difficult to rely on Heaven;—its appointments are not constant. *But if the sovereign see to it that* his virtue

NAME OF THE BOOK.—咸有一德, 'Both possessed pure virtue.' This is part of a sentence in the Book itself; and as the object of the whole is to inculcate the cherishing and maintaining of virtue pure and unchanging, the words are taken to form the name or title.

The author of the Book was E Yin, excepting of course the first paragraph, which is merely a note by the historical compiler. There is a controversy, as will be seen from the next note but one, as to whom E Yin was addressing, but the style is of a piece with that of the last two Books. The Book comes under the head of 'Instructions.'

CONTENTS. E Yin having returned the government into the hands of T'ae-këă, and wishing to withdraw from public life, addresses some cautions to the emperor on the subject of virtue. This is told us in the first par., forming the first chapter In four parr. E shows how the possession or loss of the empire depends on the virtue of the sovereign or his want of it, and illustrates his theme by reference to the downfal of Këë and the rise of T'ang. This forms a second chapter. In the next four parr, forming the third chapter, E dwells on the nature and results of pure virtue, and urges the cultivation of it on T'ae-këă. The two last parr., which form the concluding chapter, tell how this virtue will surely be acknowledged, and how the sovereign may find help to it even among the people.

TO WHOM THE INSTRUCTIONS OF THIS BOOK WERE ADDRESSED. There can be no doubt on this point, if we receive the Book, as we now have it, as genuine. The 'Instructions' in it were delivered to T'ae-këă. And this is confirmed by the position of the note on this Book in the Preface to the Shoo, as printed at the beginning of this volume. It follows immediately the note about the 'T'ae-këă.' In the 'Historical Records,' however, the same note appears in a different place. Ts'een places it immediately after the note of 'The Announcements of T'ang,' and before the death of that emperor. This order is followed by all who impugn the genuineness of the present 'old text.' The 'Both possessed pure virtue' must, they say, have been addressed to T'ang:—that the present copies all make it addressed to T'ae-këă is a clear evidence of their being forged.

The note itself is one of those in the Preface which give no account of the occasion on which the Book or Books that they refer to were

德靡常、九有以亡。○夏王弗克庸德、慢神虐民、皇天弗保、監于萬方、啟迪有命、眷求一德、俾作神主、惟尹

be constant, he will preserve his throne; if his virtue be not con-
3 stant, the nine provinces will be lost by him. The king of Hea
could not maintain the virtue *of his ancestors* unchanged, but
contemned the spirits and oppressed the people. Great Heaven
no *longer* extended its protection to him. It looked out among
the myriad regions to give its guidance to one who might receive
its favour, fondly seeking *a possessor of* pure virtue, whom it might

composed. It says nothing but 'E Yin made the BOTH POSSESSED PURE VIRTUE.' It so happens that there is only one sentence in the present text whose genuineness is beyond dispute. All the rest of the Book may be forged, but this one sentence was in the original 'old text.' It is the part of the 3d par.—惟尹躬暨湯,咸有一德, which is quoted in the 'Record of Rites,' the Bk. 緇衣, par. 10, in the form—尹吉 (see on the last Book, Pt. ii., p. 2) 曰,惟尹躬及湯,咸有壹德. If it were proved that 湯 were the honorary, posthumous title of the founder of the Shang dynasty, this quotation would prove that the lessons of the Book were *not* addressed to him. I have said, however, on the name of 'The Speech of T'ang,' that T'ang ought not to be regarded as an honorary title, but as the designation of the emperor in his life. Still, for the minister thus to introduce his sovereign's designation in an address delivered to that sovereign himself would be an instance of unexampled freedom. It does not appear to be straining the point, to conclude from this passage that the 'Both possessed pure virtue' was not addressed to T'ang. That established, we may believe, without much misgiving, that it was addressed to T'ae-këă.

CH. I. P. 1. OCCASION WHEN THE 'BOTH POSSESSED PURE VIRTUE' WAS SPOKEN. These instructions were delivered when E Yin was about to announce his retirement from public life;—in what year, we cannot tell. The returning of the govt. into the hands of T'ae-këă took place B.C. 1750, and E may very soon after have announced his intention to retire from all toils of administration. So far as the language of this par. is concerned, however, years may have elapsed between the two events. Par. 8 below would rather connect the two things closely together, but in opposition to this is a statement in the 左傳,襄,二十一年, that E Yin, though he had kept T'ae-këă in confinement, yet afterwards acted as prime minister to him (尹伊放太甲而相之). Ying-tă supposes that, though E may have declared his wish to withdraw from the court shortly after the reformation of the emperor, T'ae-këă would not receive his resignation, and prevailed on him to continue at the head of affairs. This is not improbable, and it affords a satisfactory solution of the difficulty. 于德—'on the subject of virtue.' The 'Daily Explanation' says:—以德之當勉,陳戒于君.

CH. II. Pp. 2—5. THE FAVOUR OF HEAVEN IS NOT TO BE RELIED ON;—IT DEPENDS ON THE VIRTUE OF THE SOVEREIGN. THIS TRUTH ILLUSTRATED BY REFERENCE TO THE OVERTHROW OF THE HEA DYNASTY, AND THE RISE OF THE SHANG. 2. Comp. last Book., Pt. iii., pp. 1, 2. 天難諶,—諶=信, 'to be believed,' 'to be trusted.' We have the same phrase in Pt. V., Bk. XVI., p. 4, where the same assertion is made in p. 6, in the words—天不可信. 靡=無. 九有以亡,—九有, 'the nine possessions,'=九州, 'the nine provinces.' This clause is held to prove that the Shang dynasty continued to retain Yu's division of the empire into nine provinces. 3. *The fall of Këĕ and rise of T'ang,—proving the doctrine just affirmed.* 夏王,—this of course is Këĕ. 弗克庸德,—Gan-kwŏ explains this by 不能常其德, 'could not make his virtue constant.' Liu Che-k'e adopts his language, and the 'Daily Explanation' says more explicitly—弗能有此純常之德, 'could not have

躬暨湯、咸有一德、克享天心、受天明命、以有九有之師、爰革夏正。四節 ○非

make lord of *all* the spirits. *Then* there were I, Yin, and T'ang, both possessed of pure virtue, and able to satisfy the mind of Heaven. He received *in consequence* the bright favour of Heaven, and became master of the multitudes of the nine provinces, and

this pure and constant virtue.' The translation shows that I take a different view of the phrase here. There was no virtue at all about Këě; it seems absurd to make E speak of him as if there could have been expected from him virtue of the highest style. 慢神虐民,—comp. last Book, Pt. iii., p. 1. 神 here is equivalent to 鬼神 there. 啟迪有命,—Gan-kwŏ says for this—有天命者開導之, 'to guide on the possessor of the decree of Heaven.' Lin Che-k'e, more correctly and as in the translation, expands—擇其將有天命而開導之. 眷求一德,—一德 is not 'one virtue,' but 'virtue all-one.' Ts'ae says that it means—純一之德,不雜不息之義,即上所謂常德也, 'virtue pure and one, unmixed, unceasing, what is called above "constant virtue."' It is the 誠, 'the singleness or sincerity,' of the 'Doctrine of the Mean,' by which the three virtues of knowledge, magnanimity, and energy are carried into effect.

神主,='lord of the spirits.' Ts'ae says:—神主,百神之主, 'By 神主, is meant lord of the hundred (=all the) spirits.' It is a name for the emperor as chief of the religion of the empire,—in our phrase, 'Head of the Church' of China. Cheang Kew-shing observes:—'The sovereign is lord of all the spirits. Thus we read in the She King (Pt. III., Bk. II., Ode viii., st. 3), "May you be the lord of all the spirits!" Being lord of the spirits, it follows that he is lord of the people. On the other hand we read in the "Many Regions," (Pt. V., Bk. XVIII., p. 6)—"Heaven on this sought a lord of the people." Being lord of the people, it follows that he is lord of the spirits.' This is to the effect that the 'Head of the Church' is the 'Head of the State' as well, and that either of the designations must be understood as inclusive of the other. The term 主, however, cannot be taken with the same force exactly in both the phrases. The 'lord of the people,' is high above them, their ruler; the 'lord of the spirits' is only the president and director in their worship.

[A passage in the Record of Rites, Bk. 祭法, par. 3, makes this modified meaning of the term 'lord,' as applied to the emperor in his relation to 'spirits,' very plain. It is there said—有天下者祭百神,諸侯在其地則拜之, 'The possessor of the empire sacrifices to all the spirits; the princes only sacrifice to those that are within their territories.' As sacrificing to the spirits, the emperor is their host (主人). In this passage of the 'Laws of Sacrifice,' I know that the hundred 神 are the *shin* of the hills, rivers, forests, valleys, &c., and do not embrace the spirits of heaven or those of men. It was probably this prerogative of the emperor to sacrifice to all of these which first originated the designation of him as 百神之主. But the phrase has now a wider application. Gan-kwŏ says that the 神主 in the text=天地神祇之主, 'lord of the spirits of heaven and the spirits of the earth.']

克享天心,—享 is taken here as=當, 'to be suitable to,' 'to correspond to.' Ying-tă says:—'When one's virtue corresponds to the mind of the spirits, then they accept his offerings (德當神意,神乃享之); hence 享 is to be taken as=當.' This is beating about for a meaning. 受天明命,—there can be no doubt as to the meaning of 明命 here. Compare last Book, Pt. i., p. 2. 爰革夏正,—爰=於是, 'and thereupon.' The dict. calls the char. 引詞, 'a connective conjunction.' T'ang made the year commence in 丑, the last month of winter, instead of the beginning of spring, after the practice of the Hea dyn. Lin Che-k'e says that from the language here we may infer that the alteration of the commencement of the year began with T'ang, and was unknown before the Shang dyn. Whether this practice began with T'ang or not is a

天私我有商、惟天佑于一德、非商求于下民、惟民歸于一德。○五節德惟一、動罔不吉、德二三、動罔不凶、惟吉凶不僭在人、惟天降災祥在德。○六節今嗣王新服厥命、惟新厥德、終始惟一、時乃日新。○七節任官惟賢材、左右

4 proceeded to change Hea's commencement of the year. It was not that Heaven had any partiality for the ruler of Shang;—Heaven simply gave its favour to pure virtue. It was not that Shang sought *the allegiance of* the lower people;—the people simply turned
5 to pure virtue. Where the *sovereign's* virtue is pure, his movements are all fortunate; where his virtue is wavering and uncertain, his movements are all unfortunate. Good and evil do not wrongly befall men, because Heaven sends down misery or happiness according to their conduct.
6 III. Now, O young king, you are newly entering on your *great* appointment;—you should be making new your virtue. At last as at first have this as your one object, so shall you make a daily
7 renovation. Let the officers whom you employ be men of virtue and ability, and let the ministers about you be the right men.

disputed point; but Lin infers more than the text will sustain him in doing.

4, 5. *The rise of T'ang was altogether to be ascribed to his pure consistent virtue; and such virtue is ever the sure way to prosperity.* 德二三,—'virtue two and three.' It is said of a man who is unstable, that 朝二,夕三, 'in the morning he is for two, and in the evening for three.' He is 'a double-minded man, unstable in all his ways.' 不僭在人,云云,—compare 天命弗僭, Bk. III., p. 5.

Ch. III. Pp. 6—9. COUNSELS TO T'AE-KEA ON THE DUTY AND THE MEANS OF REALIZING IN HIMSELF THIS PURE AND CONSTANT VIRTUE.

6. *For the maintenance of virtue a daily progress in it is necessary.* 新服厥命,—'newly invested with your appointment.' 惟新厥德,—comp. Bk. II., p. 8. 終始惟一,時 (=是 or 於是) 乃日新,—Choo He explains this by:—'This principle (= way of proceeding) must be connectedly kept up without stopping, and there will be a daily renovation. If there be any intermission, this cannot take place.' Chin Tih-sew says:—'Former scholars have observed, that, if men be not daily going forward in their learning, they will be daily going back. So virtue must be daily renewed.' See the 集說.

7. *Right officers and ministers; and how to make them helpful to the sovereign's virtue.* 賢材,—賢 often embraces 材. The 材 or 'ability' being here expressed, we must confine 賢 to the idea of 'virtue.' 左右=輔弼大臣;—see on the 'Yih and Tseih.' p. 2, 其弼直, and p. 5, 欽四鄰. 其人,—'*the* men,' = 'the right men.' 爲上……爲民,

書經

惟其人、臣爲上爲德、爲下爲民、其難其愼、惟和惟一。(八節)○德無常師、主善爲師、善無常主、協于克一。(九節)○俾萬

The minister, in relation to *his sovereign* above him, has to promote his virtue; and, in relation to the *people* beneath him, has to seek their good. How hard must it be *to find the proper man*! what careful attention must be required! *Thereafter* there must be harmony *cultivated with him*, and a one-ness of confidence placed in him!

8 "Virtue has no invariable model;—a supreme regard to what is good gives the model of it. What is good has no invariable characteristic to be supremely regarded;—it is found where there

—all the 爲 here are in the low. 3d tone, and have a verbal force, = 'to be for.' Ts'ae says that we have 爲德 instead of 爲君, to show that to be virtuous is the course for the sovereign, and, I may add, that to promote his virtue is the great business of the minister with him. 其難,其愼,惟和惟一,—it is not easy to satisfy the mind as to the connection and meaning of these brief, emphatic expressions. Gan-kwŏ made them all refer to the duty of ministers whose business has just been described. Ying-tă thus expounds his view:—'This passage expands the business of ministers. Since what they have to do is so difficult, let them not deem it easy; and since it demands so much care, let them not make light of it. Ministers are thus warned not to slight their duties or consider them easy. Since their duties are not to be deemed light, they ought harmoniously to serve their sovereign;—the whole body of ministers should have one heart in serving him, and so his government will be good. The 一心=一德, so that ministers also are required to have this pure and constant virtue.' In the 語類, Choo He makes 其難其愼 an instruction to the sovereign, while 惟和惟一 are addressed to the ministers. He says:—'The meaning of 其難其愼 is that, since his officers should be thus virtuous and able, and his ministers just the proper men, the sovereign should feel the difficulty in getting them, and the necessity of his being cautiously attentive. The meaning of 惟和惟一 is that, since ministers are charged with such duties, to promote the virtue of their sovereign above them, and the welfare of the people below them, they must be harmonious and united in discharging them.' A third view is that which I have followed in the translation. According to it, each expression contains a counsel to the sovereign in his relation to his officers and ministers. To suppose, with Gan-kwŏ and Ying-tă, that E is speaking here of ministers and for them very much breaks the continuity of his discourse. To suppose, with Choo He, that part is spoken to the sovereign, and part to his ministers, is liable to the same objection, and is like guessing out the meaning rather than reasoning it out. The 'Daily Explanation' thus paraphrases at length the view which I have followed:—人臣之繫于國也、不綦重哉、故其(一人君)方用之也、未能灼知其賢才、則難于任用、而不輕授以官、愼于審察、而必詳核其實、惟恐小人之得伺其間也、及其旣用之也、已灼知其賢才、則和以待之、猜忌可以盡捐、彼此可以相濟、一以任之、毀譽不得雜乘、初終無所疑貳、惟恐君子不得盡其才也。

8. *How to secure a uniformly virtuous course.* 德無常師,—師 is taken in the sense of 法, 'law,' or 'model.' It might be taken as = 'teacher,' as when it is said that 'Confucius had no regular teacher' (何常師之有, Ana. XIX., xxii.). It is better, however, to understand it here as in the translation. 德 or 'virtue' is employed as the general designation

姓咸曰、大哉王言、又曰、一哉王心、克綏先王之祿、永底烝民之生。○嗚呼、七世之廟、可以觀德、萬夫之長、

9 is conformity to the uniform decision *of the mind. Such virtue* will make *the people* with their myriad surnames all say, 'How great are the words of the king!' and also, 'How single and pure is the king's heart!' It will avail to maintain in tranquillity the *great* possession of the former king, and to secure for ever the *happy* life of the multitudes of the people.

10 IV. "Oh! *to retain a place* in the seven-shrined temple of ancestors is a sufficient witness of virtue. To be acknowledged as chief by the myriad heads of families is a sufficient witness of one's government.

of all good actions. By what model shall a man order his conduct that it shall always be virtuous? No invariable model can be supplied to him. But let him have a chief regard to this point,—that his actions be good, and he will not go far wrong. 主,—as in Ana. I., viii., 2. But what is to be the decisive characteristic of what is good? The answer to this question is in the last clause,—協于克一, 'harmony in attaining to the one.' It is not easy to say precisely what is meant. Ts'ae says the idea is not far different from that of Confucius in his famous saying,—吾道一以貫之 (Ana. IV., xv.) The 一 has reference to the 一德, which is in the title of the Book. Man has a monitor in regard to what is good and what is evil in his own breast. Let him only give a uniform obedience to the voice of this monitor, and his whole conduct will be ordered virtuously. 9. *The happy and great results of such a virtuous course.* 俾=使, 'will cause.' A nominative is to be brought on from the last paragraph. 大哉王言,—the 'words of the king' are those published in his ordinances of State. 克綏先王之祿,—the same nominative is to be supplied to 克 as to 俾. 祿 is the 天祿, 'Heaven-conferred revenues,' of the 'Counsels of Yu,' par. 17.

Ch. IV. Pp. 10, 11. THE CHARACTER OF ONE'S GOVERNMENT AND VIRTUE WILL COMMAND ACKNOWLEDGMENT IN THE PRESENT AND THE FUTURE. THE SOVEREIGN SHOULD BE PREPARED TO ACCEPT HELPS TO HIS VIRTUE EVEN FROM THE LOWEST OF THE PEOPLE. 七世之廟,—'the ancestral temple of seven generations.' The emperors had in their ancestral temple the shrines with the spirit-tablets of seven of their ancestors;—see on the 'Doctrine of the Mean,' xix. 4. But in the case of an emperor's possessing great merit, having displayed great virtue and rendered great services to his dynasty, his shrine might remain in addition to the seven regular shrines of the temple. This seems to be the motive presented to T'ae-këă,—that by being greatly virtuous, he might insure to all time a niche—a shrine—in the ancestral temple, and be looked up to by his descendants to the latest period of his dynasty. 萬夫之長,—Lin Che-k'e observes that 萬夫=萬姓 or 萬民, 'the myriad surnames,' or 'the myriads of the people,' and that the whole phrase is equivalent to 天子, or 'emperor.' No doubt this explanation is correct, and I suppose that 夫 is to be taken in the sense of 'husband,' or head of a family. The idea is that when all the people readily submit to the emperor, the excellence of his government may be predicated.

[No little controversy has been raised on this paragraph, and especially on the clause—七世之廟. That the imperial temple of ancestors in the Chow dynasty was fitted up with seven shrines as the rule is acknowledged on all hands; and there is no intimation in the classical books, or in any writings of a high antiquity,—with perhaps one exception, which will be pointed out,—that the practice was different under the dynasties of Shang and Hea. About the middle of the second century of our era, Wei Yuen-shing (韋元成), a great scholar and minister, put forth the view that under the Shang dynasty, the shrines in the imperial temple

可以觀政。○后非民罔使、民非后罔事、無自廣以狹人、匹夫匹婦、不獲自盡、民主罔與成厥功。（十一節）

11 "The sovereign without the people has none whom he can employ; and the people without the sovereign have none whom they can serve. Do not consider yourself so enlarged as to deem others small in comparison. If ordinary men and women do not find the opportunity to give full development to their *virtue*, the people's lord will be without the proper aids to complete his merit."

were only five. Lew Hin and others opposed this opinion; but subsequently it was adopted with some modification by Ch'ing Heuen and Ma Yung; as an opponent to whom Wang Suh put himself forward. The question will not be admitted to be settled yet. The impugners of the present 'old text' hold to the decision of Ch'ing, while Maou K'e-ling has written at great length on the other side in his 廟制折衷.

I have said that there is perhaps one exception to the universal silence in books before our era on there having been any difference in the number of shrines in the early dynasties. That exception is in the 呂氏春秋, in the 13th Bk. of which, and the chapter 諭大, we have the passage—商書日, 五世之廟, 可以觀怪, 萬夫之長, 可以生謀. But I cannot persuade myself that our present text was made by altering this strange quotation.]

11. 后非民......罔事,—comp. last Book, Pt. ii., p. 2. 匹夫匹婦,—comp. Con. Ana., XIV., xviii., 3. 不獲自盡,—'do not obtain to develope themselves to the utmost.' Ts'ae says:—匹夫匹婦, 有一不得自盡於上, 則善不備, 'Let but one common man and woman not be able to display their virtue completely to the sovereign, then there is one instance of what is good not provided,' *i.e.*, not provided to be an example to him. E Yin's idea was that the emperor could and ought to learn good from all, however far they might be beneath him. It must be allowed that there is a falling off in these two concluding paragraphs. They are but an impotent conclusion to the Book.

Concluding note. [i.] *About E Yin.* E Yin had certainly played a most important part in the overthrow of the Hea dynasty, and the establishment of the Shang. Whether he spent his last years in retirement as he wished to do, or was persuaded to continue to be prime minister to his death, we do not know; but he survived T'ae-këă, and died, according to the preface to the Shoo, and to Sze-ma Ts'een, B.C. 1712, more than 100 years old, in the 8th year of Yuh-ting, T'ae-këă's son and successor. He was buried with imperial honours, and a narrative of the transactions of his life was drawn up by another minister called Kaou Shen, which formed one of the documents of the Shoo, but is unfortunately lost. No credit can be given to the statements in the 'Bamboo Books,' that E was keeping T'ae-këă in confinement, while he reigned in his stead, and that T'ae-këă, having escaped in the 7th year of his imprisonment, put him to death, when Heaven put the emperor in such terror by a dense mist of three days' duration that he invested E's son with his honours and possessions.

[ii.] *About T'ae-këă.* History is silent on the events of T'ae-këă's reign after his reformation. He must have held on, however, in the course of virtue, for he earned for himself the shrine in the ancestral temple, and occupied it with the title of 太宗. His reign ended B.C. 1720.

THE BOOKS OF SHANG.

BOOK VII. PWAN-KANG. PART i.

盤庚上

一節 盤庚遷于殷、民不適有居、率籲衆慼、出矢言。

1 I. Pwan-kăng wished to remove to Yin, but the people would not go to dwell there. He therefore appealed to all the discontented, and made the following protestations.

INTRODUCTORY HISTORICAL NOTE. T'ae-këă's reign ended B.C. 1720, and Pwan-kăng's commenced B.C. 1400. More than three centuries of the Shang dynasty is thus a blank in history, so far as the documents of the Shoo are concerned. They were filled up by the reigns of 14 emperors, of whom we know from all other sources little more than the names.

Originally there were 7 other Books between the 'Both possessed pure virtue,' and the 'Pwan-kăng;' but hardly a shred of any of them can now be collected.

The names of the intervening emperors, with all the information that can be brought together about them, are as follow :—

[i.] Yuh-ting (沃丁). He was a son of T'ae-këă; succeeded to his father, B.C. 1719; died, B.C. 1691. We have seen that E Yin died in his reign, and was buried by him magnificently in Pŏ. Soon after this there was made the lost Book, called 'Yuh-ting.'

[ii.] T'ae-kăng (太庚). He was a brother of Yuh-ting. He died, B.C. 1666.

[iii.] Sëaou-këă (小甲). He was a son of T'ae-kăng. He died, B.C. 1649.

[iv.] Yung-ke (雍己). He was a brother of Sëaou-këă. He died, B.C. 1637. During his reign, the government became very weak, and many of the princes did not think it worth their while to appear at court.

[v.] T'ae-mow (太戊). He was a brother of Yung-ke. His prime minister was E Chih, the son of E Yin. In his time there occurred at Pŏ an ominous appearance of a mulberry tree and a stalk of grain growing together. According to Ts'een, T'ae-mow in great alarm consulted his minister about it, when Chih replied, 'I have heard that portents do not overcome virtue. May there not be defects about your government? Let your Majesty cultivate your virtue.' This advice was taken. The emperor became greatly virtuous. The strange growth withered away, and the affair was commemorated in a Book, which is now lost, by a worthy minister called Woo Heen. T'ae-mow reposed great confidence in Chih; the dynasty revived; the princes acknowledged their allegiance; and when the emperor died in B.C. 1562, after reigning 75 years, he received, in the ancestral temple, the title of 中宗. [We might be inclined to doubt the length of this reign. Chow-kung mentions it particularly, in Pt. V., Bk. XV., par. 5.]

[vi.] Chung-ting (仲丁). He was the son of T'ae-mow. He transferred the capital from Pŏ to Gaou (囂; Sze-ma Ts'een writes the name 隞), in the pres. dis. of Ho-yin (河陰), dep. of K'ae-fung, Ho-nan.—There was a Book in the Shoo, giving an account of this

書經

removal; but it is lost. His reign was marked by insurrections and incursions of wild tribes, and by 'internal disorders.' It ended B.C. 1549.

[vii.] Wae-jin (外壬). He was a brother of Chung-ting. His reign ended B.C. 1534, amidst a renewal of 'internal disorders.'

[viii.] Ho-tan-këä (河亶甲). He was a brother of Chung-ting and Wae-jin. An overflow of the Ho made him remove the capital in his first year from Gaou to Sëang, a place in the pres. dep. of Chang-tih (彰德), Ho-nan. His reign was a feeble one, and the fortunes of Shang began again to wane. A Book, which is now lost, commemorated the transference of the seat of govt. The addition of Ho (河) to the emperor's name must have been somehow connected with this. He died B.C. 1525.

[ix.] Tsoo-yih (祖乙). He was a son of Tan-këä. He was obliged to remove the capital from Sëang to Kăng (耿), in the pres. dis. of Ho-tsin (河津), in Këang Chow (絳州), Shan-se. The Book of the Shoo commemorating this is lost. Subsequently he made another charge from Kăng to 邢, in the pres. dis. of Hing-t'ae (邢臺), dep. Shun-tih, Chih-le. [It may be doubted, however, whether 邢 and 耿 were not identical. See Sze-ma Ts'een.] He had for his chief minister Heen (賢), a son of Woo Heen of T'ae-mow's reign, and his govt. displayed a vigour which anew commanded the submission of the princes. He died B.C. 1506.

[x.] Tsoo-sin (祖辛). He was a son of Tsoo-yih. He died B.C. 1490.

[xi.] Yuh-këä (沃甲). He was a brother of Tsoo-sin. He died, B.C. 1465, amid confusion and disorder.

[xii.] Tsoo-ting (祖丁). He was a son of Yuh-këä. He also died in the midst of troubles, B.C. 1433.

[xiii.] Nan-kăng (南庚). He was another son of Yuh-këä. It is the same story;—he died amid troubles, B.C. 1408.

[xiv.] Yang-këä (陽甲). He was a son of Tsoo-ting. The fortunes of the House of Shang seemed to be at a low ebb in his time. He died in B.C. 1401, and was succeeded by his brother Pwan-kăng.

NAME OF THE BOOK.—盤庚, 'Pwan-kăng.' This was the name of the 17th emperor of the Shang dynasty. It is sometimes written 般庚. He is by some reckoned the 19th emp., two reigns—of Wae-ping and Chung-jin—being interposed between T'ang and T'ae-këä. The 左傳 refers to the Book as the 'Announcement of Pwan-kăng;' and it is properly placed in the division of the Shoo which embraces 'Announcements.' The Book is found both in the old text and the modern. There are many passages in it difficult of interpretation. As edited by Confucius, it was in three Parts, which arrangement is retained in the old text, while Fuh-shang had either forgotten, or did not mark it.

CONTENTS. The whole Book centres round the removal of the capital from the north of the Ho to Yin on the south of it. The emperor saw that the removal was necessary, but he was met by the unwillingness of the people and the opposition of the great families. The first Part relates how he endeavoured to justify the measure. It contains two addresses, to the people and to those in high places respectively, designed to secure their cordial co-operation. The second Part brings before us the removal in progress. They have crossed the river, but there continues to be dissatisfaction, which the emperor endeavours to remove by a long and earnest vindication of his policy. The third Part opens with the removal accomplished. The new city has been founded, and the plan of it laid out. The emperor makes a third appeal to the people and chiefs to forget all their heart-burnings, and co-operate with him in building up in the new capital a great destiny for the dynasty.

The first Part has been divided into 17 paragraphs, which may be be divided again into 2 chapters. The former, parr. 1—4, contains, after an introductory reference to the occasion of its delivery, an address, by Pwan-kang, chiefly to the people, vindicating his measure on the authority of precedents, and the advantages it would secure. The other, parr. 5—17, is an address, to those in high places chiefly, complaining of the manner in which they misrepresented him to the people, and consulted only their own selfishness, and threatening them with his high displeasure, if they did not change their ways.

Ch. I. Pp. 1—4. OCCASION OF THE ADDRESSES IN THIS PART. NECESSITY AND DUTY OF REMOVING THE CAPITAL; THE MEASURE VINDICATED BY PRECEDENTS; ADVANTAGES TO BE GAINED BY IT. 1. 盤庚遷于殷,—'Pwan-kăng was removing (the past incomplete tense, = wished to remove) to Yin.' The removal must have been from Kăng, or from 邢, if Tsoo-yih made a second change of his capital; and it was probably necessitated by an overflow of the Ho. The site chosen for the new capital was 殷, called 殷亳 in the prefatory note on the Book, which I have there translated—'Pŏ, *the cradle of the* Yin.' Gankwŏ says here that '殷 is another name of 亳.' Others say that Pŏ was the name of the territory, and Yin that of a particular place in it. The site of Pwan-kăng's new capital was what is called 'the western Pŏ,' in the pres. dis. of Yen-sze (偃師), dep. of Ho-nan, Ho-nan. This was not the Pŏ where T'ang had his capital, when he commenced his work of punishment among the princes with the chief of Kŏ (Bk. II., p. 6). He had, however, probably dwelt previously in this Yin-pŏ, as intimated in the 9th notice of the preface.

二 曰我王來、既爰宅于茲、重我民、無盡劉、不能胥匡以生、卜稽曰其如台。○三 先王有服、恪謹天命、茲猶不常

2 He said, "Our king came, and fixed on this settlement. He did
so from a deep concern for our people, and not because he would
have them all die, where they cannot *now* help each other to preserve
their lives. I have examined the matter by divination, and obtained
3 the reply—'This is no place for us.' When the former kings had
any business, they reverently obeyed the commands of Heaven. In

[After this removal of Pwan-kăng to Yin, the name of the dynasty appears to have been changed from Shang to Yin. Pwan-kăng and his successors all appear in the 'Kang-muh' as kings of Yin, in contradistinction from his predecessors, who are entered as kings of Shang. It is there stated also that he changed the title of the dynasty.]

適有居,—適=往 or 之, 'to go to.' The 'Daily Explanation' has for the whole—往適安居之地, 'go to the place of tranquil dwelling.' 率籲衆慼—率=總; 籲 (the dict. says should be without the 竹)=呼; 慼=憂. Gan-kwŏ took 率 as=領, and 籲 as=和. Ying-tă expands his view:—率領和諧衆憂之人, 'He conducted and *tried to* harmonize all the grieving.' The view given in the translation is much to be preferred. The 說文 quotes the passage with 戚 for 慼, which has unnecessarily made Këang Shing and others insist on 衆戚 as meaning—'all his relatives,'= 'all the high officers.' 出矢言,—矢=誓. Comp. Con. Ana., VI., xxvi.

2. *The necessity and the sanction of a change of capital.* 我王來,—the 王 or king here must be Tsoo-yih. 既爰宅于茲,—既爰='and thereupon.' 爰, however, between 既 and 宅 is perplexing. 于茲=於此, 'here,' referring to Kăng. 重我民. 無盡劉—劉=殺, 'to kill,' or 'to be killed.' Keang Shing gives as the meaning of the passage:—'He governed well, and made the people prosperous. Altho' there were the evils of occurring inundations, they did not hurt the people, and they did not all die.' The view of Gan-kwŏ is better than this:—'Tsoo Yih removed here, because he valued the people, and would not have them all die,' *i.e.*, would not have them all die in Sëang (see the preface, not. 25). The meaning given in the translation is that of Ts'ae, as expanded in the 'Daily Explanation.' It is certainly more germane to the argument of the whole Book. 不能胥匡以生,—comp. Bk. V., Pt. ii., p. 2; but there is not the same difficulty with the 胥 here. [But that that passage of the 'T'ae-këă' is guaranteed by its being expressly quoted in the Le Ke, we should certainly have had Jŏ-keu, and all the impugners of the received 'old text,' referring to this paragraph as the original of it, and insisting that here the plagiarist of Tsin stole from the Pwan-kăng.'] 卜稽之=稽之於卜. 曰其如台,—this is the answer returned to the divination, but expressed in Pwan-kăng's words. 其如台,—comp. Bk. I., p. 3,—夏罪其如台. Ts'ae explains by:—亦曰, 此地無若我何, 言耿不可居, 決當遷.

3. *Precedents of removal in the histories of former reigns.* 服 is to be taken in the sense of 事, 'business,' 'affair.' The 'Daily Explanation' says:—'The former kings, in great governmental emergencies of the empire,' &c. 茲猶不常寧,—茲, 'this,' = in such a matter as this transference of the capital. 猶 is well expressed by 'especially.' The force of it is to connect the clause closely with the preceding.—'If in all matters they obeyed the will of Heaven, how much more did they do so in a matter like this!' 于今五邦,—'by

書經

寧、不常厥邑、于今五邦、今不承于古、罔知天之斷命、矧曰其克從先王之烈。○若顛木之有由蘖、天其永我命于玆新邑、紹復先王之大業、厎綏四方。○盤庚斆于民、由乃在位、以常舊

四節 五節

a case like this especially they did not indulge a constant repose,—they did not abide ever in the same city. Up to this time *the capital has been in* five regions. If we do not now follow the practice of the ancients, we shall be refusing to acknowledge that Heaven is making an end of our dynasty here;—how little can it be said of us that we are following the meritorious course of the former
4 kings! As from the stump of a felled tree there are sprouts and shoots, Heaven will perpetuate its decree in our favour in this new city;—the great possession of the former kings will be continued and renewed; tranquillity will be secured to the four quarters *of the empire*."
5 II. Pwan-kang, in making the people, aware of his views, began with those who were in *high* places, and took the constantly recur-

now,'there have been five regions.' We must understand as in the translation. There is some difficulty in making out the five capitals. They are commonly enumerated as—T'ang's capitals in Shang K'ew and Pŏ, Chung-ting's in Gaou, Ho-tan-këă's in Sëang, Tsoo-yih's in K'ăng. But Shang-k'ew and the Pŏ of T'ang—the Pŏ where he first appears in the Shoo—were identical. If he had previously moved from the 'western Pŏ,' that was anterior to the commencement of the dynasty;—only our capital can be counted to him in the enumeration. Reckoning from T'ang's eastern Pŏ, and including the present change to Yin, or the western Pŏ,—which is the way of many,—we have five capitals; but to include the change which was only in contemplation seems forbidden by the clause which follows—今不承于古. The number of five may be made out by allowing two movements to Tsoo-yih. The point is really of little importance; and to suppose that Pwan-kăng is speaking of five changes which he had made himself, though it is the view of Sze-ma Ts'ëen, is inadmissible.

罔知天之斷命,—the meaning of 斷命 is very much determined by the 永命 in the next par., which is in contrast with it. 矧 corresponds to 猶 above. 猶 = 'how much more'; 矧 = 'how much less.' The commentators all explain 烈 by 業. We get a much better meaning by taking it as = 功,—as in Bk. IV., p. 1.

4. *How a reviving and prosperity would come with a change of capital.* 若顛木之有由蘖,—蘖 (see the dict. on the form of the character) = 斫木餘, 'the remains of a tree that has been cut down.' This justifies—requires, indeed—the translation which I have given of 顛木, which is simply 'a fallen tree.' 由 is defined by 木生條, 'the sprouts and shoots of a tree;'—see the dict. on this use of the character.

Ch. II. Pp. 5—17. PWAN-KANG'S ADDRESS TO THOSE IN HIGH PLACES. HE EXPOSTULATES WITH THEM, AND THREATENS THEM, BECAUSE OF THEIR OPPOSITION TO THE PROPOSED REMOVAL OF THE CAPITAL. 5. Lin Che-k'e and Ts'ae preface this chapter in the following way:—The site of Kăng, being low and liable to inundations, was peculiarly unhappy for the poorer people, who were driven from their homes and

服正、法度、曰、無或敢伏小人之攸箴、王命衆悉至于

ring circumstances of former times to lay down the right law for the *present emergency*, saying, "Let none of you dare to suppress the remonstrances of the poorer people." The king ordered all in common to come to his hall.

scattered about. It had advantages, however, for the large and wealthy families, who were therefore unwilling to leave it, and contrived by unsubstantial statements to bring many of the lower orders to resist the proposed movement along with themselves. They could not blind the minds of all, but they came between those who wished to represent the grievances of their situation and the emperor, preventing the interchange of their views. These were the circumstances, which occasioned Pwan-kăng his difficulties, and to deal with which is his object in this chapter. These observations seem to be correct, and by keeping them in mind, we can better understand the whole of the chapter.

斆于民—斆＝教, 'to teach,' or, better, ＝覺悟, 'to awaken, make aware.'

由乃在位, 以常舊服正法度,—this is a difficult passage, as appears from the difft. views that have been taken of it. Gan-kwŏ, taking 由＝用, and 乃＝汝, supposed the words to be spoken to the people. Ying-tă thus paraphrases his interpretation:—'Pwan-kang instructing the people, said, "You ought to follow the orders of your superiors, and use the constant practice of former times to rectify the law." He wished to charge the people to remove in obedience to the orders of the ministers.' It is added—"He also cautioned the ministers, saying," &c. This is hardly intelligible, and we cannot admit the interposition of a 曰 after the first clause. Keang Shing, Sun Yen, and other interpreters of the present dynasty, take 由 and 乃 in the same way as Lin and Ts'ae, but view the whole differently. Their interpretation is:—'Pwan-kăng, wishing to make the people aware of his views, would do so by means of those in places of authority, and would use the constant practice of former times to lay down the correct way of proceeding. He therefore said to the officers,' &c. On this construction, the constant practice of former times (常舊服,—服＝事, as in par. 3) is not the practice of removing the capital, but that of calling a general assembly of the people to deliberate on such an important measure. 正法度, also, does not mean, as in the translation, to lay down the law of proceeding in what was already determined on, but to consider whether such a proceeding should be taken or not. An insuperable objection to this view is the address which follows, in which no proposition is laid before the assembly, but the ministers and officers simply are sharply spoken to. I append the paraphrase of the 'Daily Explanation':—其(＝盤庚)斆于民也, 自在位者始, 然亦非繩之以法. 動之以威, 惟以先王舊常遷都之事, 以正今日之法度. 見已之順天命者, 取法乎先王, 則人臣之虔職守者, 亦當恪遵乎上命, 其大意若曰云云.

無或敢伏小人之攸箴.—無＝毋; 伏＝藏匿, 'to conceal;' 攸＝所: 箴＝諫, 'to remonstrate.' 箴 prunasily denotes 'a sewing needle,' made of course of bamboo; then a pointed stone used for puncturing the flesh in disease. From this second use of the term comes that in the text. 箴言 are 'pungent words,' that probe the conscience.

王命衆悉至于庭,—王, 'the king.' This of course is Pwan-kang; and it might be well to separate this sentence from the rest of the paragraph, and let it stand by itself, as Lin Che-k'e does. I have said that 'the king of course is Pwan-kăng but Keang Shing and others will have it that we are to understand, after K'ang-shing, that the King was Yang-keă Pwan-kăng's brother and predecessor.' They will have it that, at the time to which this first Part refers, Pwan-kăng was acting as prime minister to him, and was carrying out his wishes in advocating the removal of the capital. They admit at the same time that in the second and third parts Pwan-kăng himself is 'King,' so that we must suppose the transference to have been contemplated and agitated for a considerable time. This theory is altogether gratuitous, and I can find no substantial ground for it in the language of any part of the Book. Sun Yen to support it makes 王命, 云云, to be the words of Pwan-kăng;—'Do not venture to conceal from the people that the King commands all,' &c. But the 攸箴 forbid such a construction. In the 衆悉 we must understand both the people and the officers and ministers. They were

書經

庭。○王若曰、格汝衆、予告汝訓、汝猷黜乃心、無傲從康。○古我先王、亦惟圖任舊人共政、王播告之修、不匿厥指、王用丕欽、罔有逸言、民用丕變、今汝聒聒、起

六節 七節

6 The king spoke to this effect:—"Come, all of you; I will announce to you my instructions. Take counsel how to put away your *selfish* thoughts. Do not with haughty *disregard of me* follow after your own ease.

7 "Of old, our former kings had it as a principal object in their plans to employ the men of old families to share in the government. When they wished to proclaim and announce what was to be attended to, those did not conceal the imperial views, and on this account the kings greatly respected them. They did not exceed the truth *in their communications with the people*, and on this account the

gathered to 'the hall,' congregated, I suppose, all about the royal residence. The meeting, however, was not for deliberation. We may suppose that the people would enjoy the *schooling* of the officers.

[If we will not be satisfied without a reason for the change of style from 'Pwan-kăng' to 'the king,' and think that the inartistical manner in which the compiler did his work does not sufficiently account for it, I see no course but to resort to the theory of different documents, which certain critics make so much use of in accounting for the change from one name of the Supreme Being to another in the Book of Genesis!]•

6. *Reproof of the insolence and selfishness of the officers.* 王若曰,—若曰 intimates that what follows is not all in the exact words of the king, but the substance of what he said. Others will have it that the 若 is appropriate in the mouth of a minister speaking in the name of the sovereign, as we shall find it several times in the next Part; but even there the 若=' substantially thus.' 格爾衆,—the 衆 must be co-extensive with the same term in the last par., embracing officers and people, but the address is at once directed to the officers only. 猷黜乃心,—猷=謀; 黜=去; 乃=汝. 無傲從康,—無=毋; 傲, 'haughty,' 'insolent,' as in the 'Yih and Tseih,' p. 8. The whole is paraphrased:—毋得傲上之命,從已之安.

7. *Degeneracy of Pwan-kăng's ministers and officers as compared with those of former times.* 古我先王,—these 'former Kings' are to be taken generally, as intending all the sovereigns of the dyn. from T'ang downwards. 亦惟圖任舊人共政,—亦, 'also,' *i.e.*, in the same way as Pwan-kăng himself; 惟圖, is not 'only planned,' but 惟 may be taken as the copula, or as amalgamating with the meaning of 圖; 舊人=世臣舊家之人, 'hereditary ministers and men of old families.' Gan-kwŏ takes 舊人 as=老成之人, 'old and experienced men;' but the meaning is clearly indicated in par. 14, and other places. 共政=共治其政. 王播告之修,不匿厥指,—Gan-kwŏ explains this:—王布告人以所修之政,不匿其指, 'when the kings were publishing (=wished to publish) to the people the government which was to be cultivated, they did not conceal their views.' This must be the meaning of the 修, which, standing alone in the text, is enigmatic. The 'Daily Explanation,' finds a

信險膚、予弗知乃所訟。○八節 非予自荒茲德、惟汝含德、不惕予一人、予若觀火、予亦拙謀作乃逸。○九節 若網在綱、有條而不紊、若農服田

people became greatly changed. Now, *however*, you keep clamour-
ing, and get the confidence *of the people* by alarming and shallow
8 speeches. I do not know what you keep wrangling about. In
this movement I am not myself abandoning my proper virtue,
but you conceal the goodness of my intentions, not standing in
awe of me, the one man. I see you as clearly as one sees fire;
but still by my undecided plans I have produced your error.
9 "When the net has its line, there is order and not confusion;
and when the husbandman labours upon the fields, and spends his

great deal of meaning in the clause—不匿厥指, saying it = 'they proclaimed the favour of the sovereign to the people, and reported the remonstrances of the people to the sovereign.' I cannot see more in it than I have expressed in the translation. 罔有逸言,—逸 = 過; 逸言 are 'words going beyond' the truth. 今汝聒聒,—the 說文 quotes this passage not under 聒, but under 䛤, which seems also to have been the reading of Ch'ing K'ang-shing. The meaning of the phrase is given variously. We have—多言之意, 'clamorous' (the 日講 and 集傳); 無知之貌, 'the appearance of stupidity' (Gan-kwŏ); 拒善自用之意, 'self-opinionated, resisting what is good' (Ma Yung and the 說文); 難告之貌 'the appearance of being difficult to be spoken to' (Ch'ing). 起信險膚,—the connection shows that by 險膚 the speeches of the officers are characterized. 險, 'precipitous,' 'hazardous,' = 'alarming.' 膚, 'the skin,' here = 'shallow,' words not more than skin deep. The translation of 起信 is after Lin Che-k'e and Ts'ae. Këang Shing has a different view, and takes 起 = 造, and 信 (1st tone) = 申, the two together = 'you raise and put forth.' 8. *While reproving the perverse opposition of his ministers, Pwan-kăng acknowledges his own weakness.* The meaning of this par. given in the translation is again after the 集傳. 荒 = 廢; comp. its use in Pt. III., Bk. III., p. 8. 茲德,—'this virtue,' *i.e.*, the virtue proper to the sovereign, *to love the people.* 含德,—'conceal the virtue,' *i.e.*, the virtue of the emperor proposing the removal of the capital with a view to the benefit of the people. 予若觀火 = 我視汝情,明若觀火, 'I see your feelings and ways as clearly as if I were looking at fire.' 拙謀,—'stupid plans.' 'Stupid' = undecided, not using force of will and appliances to compel obedience. 作乃逸 = 成汝過失. Gan-kwŏ takes a different view of 惟汝含德, and makes it = 'but you cherish evil thoughts.' Keang Shing agrees with this; but his explanations of 茲德 and 予觀若火 are peculiar. See his comm. *in loc.*

9, 10. *The officers are exhorted to put away their selfishness, and to do real good to the people. The good effects of their doing so are illustrated.*

9. 若網在綱,—'if the net be on the rope.' The rope, going round the mouth or edge of the net, keeps it in order, and affords the means of handling it easily. 有條,—'there are the separate divisions or parts,' = there is order. What the rope is to the net, that the sovereign is to the ministers; and they must allow to him a control over them and

力穡、乃亦有秋。○汝克黜乃心、(十節)施實德于民、至于婚友、丕乃敢大言汝有積德。○乃不畏戎毒(十一節)于遠邇、惰農自安、不昬作勞、不服田畝、越其罔有黍稷。○汝不(十二節)

10 strength in reaping, there is then the *abundant* autumn. If you can
put away your *selfish* thoughts, you will bestow real good upon the
people, reaching to your relatives and friends, and may boldly venture
to make your words great, and say that you have accumulated
11 virtue. You do not fear the great evils which are far and near.
You are like the husbandman who yields himself to ease, and is not
strong to toil and to labour on his acres, and who in such a case
12 cannot have either rice or millet. You do not use friendly and good

guidance of them. This portion of the par. is understood to have reference to the haughty disregard of him shown by Pwan-käng's ministers,—their 傲 (par. 6). 若農,云云,—服田=服勞于田畝; 力穡=盡力于稼穡. The 'reaping' is to be taken as inclusive of the 'sowing.' This portion is understood to be directed against the officers' seeking their ease,—the 從康 of par 6.

10. 實德,—'real, substantial, virtue.' The meaning is that if they would put away their selfishness (see par. 6), and cordially co-operate with the emperor in promoting the removal to Yin, they would be really benefiting the people.
It is not easy to show how the difft. parts of the paragraph depend on one another. No commentator that I have examined has succeeded in doing so. They all, from Gan-kwŏ downwards, have lost the clue to a fair and consistent interpretation, by making the two clauses—汝克黜乃心,施實德于民 run on as if they were connected by an *and*, whereas we should take 施實德,云云, as the results that would flow from their putting away their selfishness. The two first clauses must be joined by a 則, and not by 而, or the 及 of a looser style. 至于婚友,—'reaching—which will reach—to relatives and friends.' 婚 properly denotes 'the kindred of the wife'; here it ='relatives' generally. The great families were opposed to the contemplated movement, as Käng was sufficiently advantageous to them. Pwan-käng here tells them that they likewise, as well as the people generally, would be benefited by it. 丕乃敢大言,—'great(=bold) may be your venturing to magnify yourselves and say,' ———. The straits to which the commentators are put by the language here may be seen in Gan-kwŏ and Keang Shing. The placing of a 則 between the two first clauses makes the interpretation much more easy.

11, 12. *Further reproof of those in high places for their self-seeking and disregard of the emperor's wishes.* 11. 乃不畏戎毒于遠邇,—戎=大, 'great;' 毒=害, 'injuries,' 'evils.' Pwan-käng has reference to the desolation wrought by the overflowing waters, of which the wealthy families hardly seemed to be conscious. Keang Shing says he can get no meaning from the sentence thus construed, and places a stop at 毒, and explains 于遠邇 by 徒計校于遠近, 'you vainly calculate, and compare the distant and the near.' This does not make the meaning more intelligible or the construction more easy. 不昬作勞,—昬=暋, Pt. V. Bk. IX., p. 15, 'to be strong,' 'energetic.' 越 is defined by Ying-tă by 於; but then 於 must be taken as an adverb, =於是, 'thereupon.' Keang Shing gives 卒 for it, ='the result is.' 12. 汝

和吉言于百姓、惟汝自生毒、乃敗禍姦宄以自災于厥身、乃既先惡于民、乃奉其恫、汝悔身何及、相時憸民、猶胥顧于箴言、其發有逸口、矧予制乃短長之命、汝曷弗告朕、而胥動以浮

words to the people, and are only producing suffering for yourselves. As destroyers and calamities, villains and traitors, the punishment shall come on your persons. You set the example of evil, and must feel its smart,—what will it avail you then to repent? Look at the poor people;—they can still consult together about remonstrances *which they wish to address to me*, but when they begin to speak, you are ready with your extravagant talk:—how much more ought you to have me before your eyes, with whom it is to make your lives long or short! Why do you not report their

不……生毒,—吉=善, 'good.' 和吉言, are 'soothing and good words,' by which the officers might have allayed the excitement of the people, and led them to fall in with the emperor's wish to remove to Yin. 惟汝自生毒 must be = the 自災于厥身 below. Pwan-kăng begins to take a higher tone with the officers, and threatens them. Gan-kwŏ supposes the 百姓 here to be the 百官, 'the various officers,' and the lesson to be administered to the 公卿, or 'high nobles' above them. It is a strange and inadmissible interpretation. 乃敗禍……厥身,—the 'Daily Explanation' has for this:—敗禍姦宄之刑,亦且災于汝之身矣. The 乃 may be taken either as = 汝, or as a conjunction. 敗禍 are co-ordinate with 姦宄, and are designations applied to the officers, opposing the emperor as they did. Among all the commentators only Sun Yen has attempted to grapple with the difficulty of these terms, and he only partially and unsuccessfully. 乃既……何及,—乃=汝; 先惡=惡之先, 'the precedents of wickedness;'—so, Ts'ae. 恫=痛. 悔身無及,—the 身 occasions a difficulty here. It is to be joined to 何及. Gan-kwŏ says:—悔之而于身無所及, 'you may repent, but that will not avail your persons.' 相時憸民……之命,—相=視, 'to look at;' 時=是, 'these;' 憸民=小民, 'the lower people.' 憸 (the original form of the char. is disputed) properly means 'sharp-mouthed,'='litigious,' 'flattering.' This meaning is retained in the phrase, in Pt. V., Bk. XIX., p. 20. It would be inappropriate here, and therefore the signif. of 小民 is accepted in its stead. 猶胥顧,云云,—I have translated after the paraphrase of the 'Daily Explanation.' Ts'ae seems to interpret after Lin Che-k'e, who says:—'Look at those poor people;—they can still regard one another in their remonstrances, fearing lest, in the words which they utter, they should transgress with their mouths, and bring misery on themselves. So are the poor people in awe, with reference to the remonstrances which they would speak, and yet you, with regard to me who have the power of life and death over you in my hands, do not stand in awe of me, but haughtily disregard me, and follow your own

言、恐沈于衆、若火之燎于原、不可嚮邇、其猶可撲滅、則惟爾衆自作弗靖、非予有咎。○十三節遲任有言曰、人惟求舊、器非求舊、惟新。○十四節古

words to me, but go about to excite one another by empty speeches, frightening and involving the multitudes in misery? When a fire is blazing in the plains, so that it cannot be approached, can it still be beaten out? Thus for you to cause dispeace in this way:—it is not I who am to blame.

13 "Ch'e Jin has said, 'In men, we seek individuals of old families;

ease.' You are not equal to the poor people.' Gan-kwŏ took the same view of the passage as Lin. The modern view is more in harmony with the tenor of the whole Book.

汝曷弗告……于衆,—恐＝恐動之以禍患, 'frightening and exciting them about the calamity.' 沈＝沈陷之於罪惡, 'plunging and sinking them in wickedness.' 若火……撲滅—in interpreting this sentence, I am obliged to differ from Lin Che-k'e and the 'Daily Explanation.' They understand Pwan-kăng as saying that a blazing fire which could not be approached, might still be beaten out, and he would cause the officers to know that when he arrayed himself in his terrors, they would be consumed before him, and have an end made of all their speeches. But is it true in nature that a fire not approachable can yet be beaten out? There could not be such a thing without appliances of which Pwan-kăng could have no idea. The passage is twice quoted in the 左傳 (隱 六年, and 莊 十四年,) with 惡之易, before 若火之燎, and the meaning is that prolonged wickedness becomes irremediable. It can't be remedied, and must produce its natural result of ruin. So Pwan-kăng threatens his officers, it would be with them. 則惟爾衆自作弗靖, 非予有咎,—the king's anger does not allow him to bring his meaning out fully. He means to say—'In the same way, when you all of yourselves make this dispeace, and will have to take the consequences, you will have only yourselves to blame. You cannot ascribe your suffering to me.' The 'Daily Explanation' says:—此皆汝等不能安靜以奉上命, 自速其禍耳, 豈予樂用威刑以加汝也.

[Lin Che-k'e observes at the close of this paragraph, that the style of the Pwan-kăng is very full of repetitions, the same thought being brought out again and again, and the same illustrations. He compares 予若觀火, 云云, of par. 8, with 若火之燎, 云云, here, and 若農服田, 云云, of par. 9, with 惰農, 云云, of par. 11, adding that however the style may be in *disjecta membra*, there is yet a unity of thought, and though the language be involved and irritating, difficult to understand, yet a man may by repeated exercises of his mind upon it make out the meaning. I think he is correct in saying that the general meaning may be made out; but the style is very rugged. We have to make our way through it, as. [or rare.]
'O'er bog or steep, through straight, rough, dense.

13, 14. *Pwan-kăng seeks to stimulate his officers by reminding them of their fathers, for whose sakes he would deal justly and even kindly with them.*

13. Who Ch'e Jin was is not known. Ch'ing says he was an ancient historiographer. A Chow Jin (周任) is quoted in the same way in the Analects, XVI., i. 人惟求舊,—舊人 must be taken here as in par. 7. Perhaps Ch'e Jin may have intended 'old, experienced men,'—the wiser for the length of their experience,—but Pwan-kăng applies the

我先王、暨乃祖乃父、胥及逸勤、予敢動用非罰、世選爾勞、予不掩爾善、茲予大享于先王、爾祖其從與享之、作福作災、予亦不敢動

14 in vessels, we do not seek old ones, but new.' Formerly, the kings, my predecessors, and your forefathers and fathers, shared together the ease and labours *of the State*;—how should I dare to lay undeserved inflictions on you? For generations the toils of your *families* have been approved, and I will not conceal your goodness. Now when I offer the great sacrifices to my predecessors, your forefathers are present to share in them. *They observe* the happiness I confer and the sufferings I inflict, and I cannot dare to reward virtue that does not exist.

phrase in that other sense. 14. 胥及逸勤,—相與同其勞逸. The 'Daily Explanation' has it—君臣一德,無事則同享其逸,有事則共任其勤, 'sovereigns and ministers possessed a common virtue. In times of quiet, they enjoyed the ease in common; in times of trouble, they shared the burden of the toil together.' 予敢,云云,—we may take this interrogatively, or supply a 不 before 敢, after the analogy of 予亦不敢 in the last clause. 世選爾勞,—'generations have selected your toils.' The meaning is as in the translation. 茲予……享之,—under the Chow dynasty, as we learn from the 'Rites of Chow,' Bk. XXX. (夏官司馬,第四之三), there was a 'Recorder of merits' (司勳), who entered the names of meritorious ministers and officers among the imperial kindred when alive, and regulated the arrangement of their spirit-tablets at the sacrifices in the ancestral temple, when they were dead. The text shows that the practice of giving a place to worthy ministers at imperial sacrifices had descended from the Shang dynasty. The 從 intimates that the spirits of the ministers were supposed not to be present as principals, but as assessors. 作福作災,云云,—the 亦 is to be explained from the relation of the sentence to the preceding. Ts'ae has expressed it:—作福作災,皆簡在先王與祖之心,—'in my rewards and punishments, I seek to be in harmony with the judgment of my predecessors and of your forefathers.' Their judgment is just, and Pwan-kăng wishes that his may *likewise* be so. 動用,—'to move and use;' *i.e.*, he would not of his own motion do anything contrary to what was just.

[Choo He has a note on this passage which is worth referring to. He observes that Pwan-kăng speaks of his predecessors and the forefathers of his ministers, as if they were real existences above them (若有眞物在其上), observing his proceedings from day to day. The meaning, he says, is that Pwan-kăng in his proceedings felt himself, as it were, in the presence of spiritual beings, and no doubts about their justice arose in his mind (質諸鬼神而無疑; see the 'Doct. of the Mean,' xxix. 3). But the common belief of the Yin dynasty venerated spirits (殷俗尙鬼), and therefore he wanted to guide his ministers by what they profoundly believed in. Were there then those beings as real existences after their death? 'The sages,' answers the critical philosopher, 'felt a difficulty in speaking about the spirits of the dead (鬼神之理,聖人蓋難言之). To say that they were really existing, would be wrong, and to say that they were *not* really existing, would also be wrong. The subject, being beyond our *sensible* understanding, may be put on one side.' See the 朱子全書, Bk. xxxiv. Was there

書經

用非德。○十五節予告汝于難、若射之有志、汝無侮老成人、無弱孤有幼、各長于厥居、勉出乃力、聽予一人之作猷。○十六節無有遠邇、用罪伐厥死、用德彰厥善、邦之臧、惟汝衆、邦之不臧、惟予一人有佚罰。○十七節凡爾衆、其惟致告、自今至于後日、各恭爾事、齊乃位、度乃口、罰及爾身弗可悔。

15 "I have announced to you the difficulties *of the present enterprise.*
My will is that of an archer. Do not you despise the old and
experienced, and do not make little of the helpless and young. Seek
every one long continuance in your *new* abode; exert yourselves to
16 listen to the plans of me, the one man. There is *with me* no distinc-
tion of distant and near. The criminal shall die the death; and the
good-doer shall have his virtue displayed. The prosperity of the
country must come from you all. If it fail in prosperity, that must
arise from me, the one man, erring in the application of punish-
17 ment. All of you be sure to make known this announcement. From
this time forward attend respectfully to your business; have *the duties
of* your offices regularly adjusted; bring your mouths under the rule
of law:—lest punishment come upon you, when repentance will be
of no avail."

ever a thinker who more reversed the rule of 'walking by faith and not by sight?']

15. *Pwan-kăng intimates his settled purpose to remove the capital, and summons the officers to co-operate with him.* 予告汝于難,—于難, 'about the difficulties;' i.e., the difficulties of the contemplated movement. 若射之有志,—the archer thinks only of hitting his mark. Everything else is forgotten. So was Pwan-kăng bent to carry out his purpose. 汝無(=毋)侮老成人; 無(=毋)弱孤有幼,—Keang Shing would read the first clause 汝無老侮成人. Such was the reading of K'ang-shing, who says both 老 and 弱 have the meaning of 'despising.' This we might allow, but there is then no proper contrast between 侮 and 孤. 孤有幼=孤與幼, 有 being in the 3d tone, =又 (so, at least Tung-po). There were old people who wished to signify their approbation of the removal, but the officers would not hear them, nor represent their views to the emperor. The young were the greatest

sufferers by remaining at Kăng, but the officers made no account of them. 各長于厥居,—'let every one be long in this abode.' He would have them look forward to a permament abode in Yin, and labour with him to secure it. 16. *How Pwan-kăng would exercise a strict justice. The great responsibility which he felt to be devolving on himself* 遠邇,—'distant and near'; here spoken with reference to kindred and others, and to the various ties by which officers might think they had a claim on the emperor's regard. 用罪=爲惡, 'the doer of evil'; 用德=爲善, 'the doer of good.' The meaning of 伐厥死 is plain enough, but the terms do not severally correspond with the corresponding clause—彰厥善. 善 and 死 don't match each other. 邦之臧, 云云,—佚=失, 'to mistake,' 'to err.' Compare the whole sentiment with T'ang's in Bk. III., p. 8. It is by no means so noble, and yet the first part of it might call forth the sympathy of the higher classes. 17. *Concluding counsels to the officers to co-operate with himself, and avoid the consequences of continuing to oppose him.* 凡爾衆; 其惟致告,—the 其 has here its strongly hortative force, 致告 'carry out the announcement.' Leu Tsoo-heen observes:—'Only those who were in the hall could hear what he said. He charges them therefore to transmit his words, and make them generally known.' If they 'attended respectfully to their business,' there would be no more 'haughty disregard' of their sovereign; if they 'regularly adjusted the duties of their offices,' they would no longer 'follow their own ease'; if they 'brought their mouths under the control of law,' they would no more give utterance to their 'unsubstantial and exaggerated speeches.'

THE BOOKS OF SHANG.

BOOK VII. PWAN-KANG. PART ii.

盤庚中

一 盤庚作、惟涉河、以民遷、乃話民之弗率、誕告用亶其有衆、咸造、勿褻在王庭、盤庚乃

1 I. Pwan-kăng arose, and crossed the river with the people, moving them to *the new capital*. By and by he addressed himself to those of them who were still dissatisfied, and made a full announcement to their multitudes, to induce a sincere *acquiescence in the measure*. They all attended, and *being charged* to take no liberties in the royal

CONTENTS OF THE SECOND PART. Pwan-kăng has commenced the carrying out of his resolution. They have just crossed, or are about to cross, the river on their way to Yin. But dissatisfaction still exists among a portion of the people, and he calls a great assembly to his hall or tent, and argues at length the wisdom of the movement in which they were engaged. First, he insists on his only acting after the example of former kings, and strives to bring the people to see the measure in its proper light as intended for their good, so that they should entirely sympathize with him in it. This brings us to the 10th par., and may form a chapter by itself. Next, he threatens them with the anger of their forefathers, who would punish them for their disobedience to him, as the founder of his House would punish him, if he did not move from a site now all-unfit to be occupied by the people. This subject forms a second chapter, and brings us to par. 14. In the remaining three parr., he calls them to obedience and sympathy, threatening them with severe punishment, if they continued to murmur at the removal or to resist it.

CH. I. OCCASION OF THE ADDRESS. THE REMOVAL OF THE CAPITAL WAS NOT A NEW THING; IT WAS ALTOGETHER INTENDED FOR THE GOOD OF THE STATE; THE DISSATISFACTION OF THE PEOPLE WAS SHORT-SIGHTED AND BLAME-WORTHY. 1. 盤庚作,惟涉河,以民遷,—Gan-kwŏ and Ch'ing read the first six characters here without a stop, and made the meaning—'Pwan-kăng prepared the vessels, or arranged the measures, for crossing the Ho.' The 惟 ought on this view to have a substantive meaning, which Wang Suh has endeavoured to express,—盤庚爲此思南渡河之事, 'Pwan Kăng did this thing,—the thinking on the south to cross the Ho.' All this is very harsh. It is much better to put a stop at 作, and take that character as = 'to arise,' 'to put one's-self in motion,' which is a common use of it. 惟涉河 will then have the meaning in the translation, 惟 having the slightest possible independent signification. The clause taken in this way describes a fact,—the

登進厥民。○二節曰、明聽朕言、無荒失朕命。○三節嗚呼、古我前后、罔不惟民之承、保后胥感、鮮以不浮于天時。○

2 hall, he called them before him, and said, "Listen clearly to my words, and do not disregard my commands.
3 "Oh! of old time my royal predecessors cherished every one and above every thing a respectful care of the people, who again upheld their sovereign with a mutual sympathy. Seldom was it that they were not superior to any *calamitous* time sent by Heaven.

crossing of the river. 乃話民之弗率,—the 說文 defines 話 by 會合善言, 'good words in conference.' Keang Shing accordingly thinks he is justified in taking it in the sense simply of 會合, 'to assemble!' It seems to have been used originally with reference to the speaking of 'good words,' but that force is now lost. We need not even seek to find it in the text. 民之弗率=民之猶弗聽命者. 誕=大, 'great'; 亶=誠 'sincere.' The 'Daily Explanation' puts a stop at 亶, so that 誕告用誠='he made a full announcement with sincerity.' Gan-kwŏ read on to 其有衆, before putting a stop,='he made a great ann., using sincerity with his multitudes.' Keang Shing points in the same way, but takes 誠 actively,='to make sincere;' and I have pointed and translated according to this view. Ma Yung would carry the sentence on to 造, before putting a stop. That character he defines by 爲, 'to make,' so that the meaning is,—'he addressed them that he might bring them all with sincerity to make—get ready—boats to cross the Ho.' This again is too harsh. We must stop at 衆, and then 造 (*ts'aou*, 3d tone)=至. 勿褻在王庭,—this passage has wonderfully exercised the ingenuity of the critics. Keang Shing takes 勿 in the sense of 'flags,' and would change 褻 into 邇, making the meaning 'flags were set up to collect the people in the royal hall.' But this is too violent. Sun Yen makes 勿=未, and 褻=近, and, running the sentence on to what follows, makes out—'Pwan-kang made the people who were not near to the royal hall come forward that he might consult them.' But the meaning he would give to 褻 cannot be sustained. Letting the text stand as it is, we must supply something equivalent to the 'being charged' of the translation before 勿. Leu Tsoo-heen observes that as they had left the old capital, and had not arrived at the new, we can only understand the king's tent by the 'royal hall' (王庭蓋道路行宮). 登進厥民,—登 and 進 combine their meaning together. Ying-tă has well:—延之,使前而告之. Tsoo-heen says that at such a meeting as is indicated, the ministers were in front, and the people behind them, but that here the king called the people—it could only be the chief among them—to the front. I have dropt 厥民 in the translation. 2. 無荒失朕命,—無=毋; 荒失, comp. 荒墜, Pt. III., Bk. III., p. 8.

3. *The kindly sympathy between former emperors and their people, and its happy effects.* 罔不惟民之承='were always and every one the reverent *protectors* of the people.' 承=敬, 'to respect,' 'to have a reverent care of.' The use of the term here is well illustrated by the words of Confucius (Ana. XII., ii.)—使民如承大祭. 保后胥感,—we must understand this as spoken of the people. The 'Daily Explanation' has:—百姓亦莫不保愛其君. Keang Shing and others would join the 保 to 承, which would not be objectionable in itself; but then to take 后胥感 as a clause by itself makes the style too jagged. Shing, however, tries to meet this, as we shall see, by adopting the reading 高 instead of 感. 鮮以

四節 殷降大虐、先王不懷、厥攸作、視民利用遷、汝曷弗念我古后之聞、承汝俾汝、惟喜康共、非汝有咎、比于罰。○五節 予若籲懷茲新邑、亦惟

4 When great calamities were coming down on our empire of
Yin, the former kings did not fondly remain in their place. What
they did was with a view to the people's benefit, and therefore they
moved *their capital*. Why do you not reflect that I, according to
what I have heard of the ancient kings, in my care for you and
actings toward you, am only wishing to rejoice with you in a com-
mon repose? It is not that any guilt attaches to you, so that this
5 movement should be like a punishment. When I call you to cherish
this new city, it is simply on your account, and as an act of great

不浮于天時,—鮮=罕, 'seldom.' Gan-kwŏ takes 浮 in the sense of 行, 'to go,' 'to do.' 'A boat's floating along,' says Ying-tă, 'is its movement on the water, and hence 浮 may be used for "to go."' In this way 浮于天時 is made out to mean—'They acted according to the times of Heaven,' *i.e.*, as we should say, 'the requirements of Providence.' Ts'ae, after Soo Tung-po, takes 浮 as=勝, 'to overcome,' 'get the better of.' It often means 'to overflow,' 'to go beyond,' and hence this signification is evolved. But why need we feel so much difficulty with the term? If we say that 浮于天時='they floated over—tided over—the times of Heaven,' we are brought to an interpretation substantially the same.

I have said above that Keang Shing reads 高 for 感; he also takes 鮮 in the sense of 'great hills in distinction from little ones' (see the dict.), and makes the whole to mean—'The sovereigns ascertained where the high hills were, and removed to them.' The interpretation is so far-fetched, that we can only laugh at it.

4 *The people could not but approve of the measures of the former kings;—why should they disapprove of the present measure, which was conceived in the same spirit as those?* 殷降大虐,—we think at first that 殷 must be the nominative to 降, but that would give no meaning. 殷 stands absolutely,='in our dynasty of Yin.' Then 天 must be understood as the nominative to 降, or that character may be taken passively. The 'Daily Explanation' says:—昔我殷邦,河水爲災,天降大害,云云. 懷=安居, 'to dwell at ease. 汝曷弗念我古后之聞......康共,—the interrogation reaches on to 康共, and 古后之聞 is parenthetical. It might be as well perhaps to end the interrogation at 聞.—'Why do you not think of what you have heard about the former kings, my predecessors?' Then, however, we must understand a 我 as the nominative to 承 and 俾. 承汝,—承 as in last par.; 俾汝,—'give to you,' ='do to you, 'call you to do.' 非汝有過,比于罰,—there is some difficulty here with the 比, which is read with the 3d tone, and ='to be near to,' 'equivalent to.' The 于 following makes it necessary to tone and interpret it thus. The whole='It is not that you have any fault, so that I should be, as it were, punishing you, and banishing you by this removal.' 5. *The movement might be considered as in accordance with the people's wishes.* 予若......汝故,—懷 is here defined by 來, 'to come.' We get a better meaning by taking it in its more common signification of 'to cherish.' Gan-kwŏ, taking 若=順, 籲

汝故、以丕從厥志。○今予將試 六節 以汝遷、安定厥邦、汝不憂朕心之攸困、乃咸大不宣乃心、欽念以忱、動予一人、爾惟自鞠自苦、若乘舟、汝弗濟、臭厥載、爾忱不

6 accordance with your wishes. My present undertaking to remove with you, is to give repose and stability to the State. You *however*, have no sympathy with the anxieties of my mind; but you all keep a great reserve in declaring your minds, *when you might* respectfully think by your sincerity to move me, the one man. You only exhaust and distress yourselves. The case is like that of sailing in a boat;—if you do not cross the stream *at the proper time*, you will destroy all its cargo. Your sincerity does not respond to

一和, and 懷一歸, makes the meaning—'I turn to this new city, in accordance with right principles, and to harmonize you all.' He would then put a stop at 汝, and join the 故 to the last clause,—'I wish to benefit you, and therefore I boldly follow the first impulses of my will, and remove to it.' No one will be found now to advocate such a construction of the text. It is not more objectionable, however, than that proposed by Keang Shing, who would put a stop at 以, reading 亦惟汝故以, as if 以 were 一已, (comp. Mencius, I., Pt. I., vii. 2). He then takes 丕 as 一不, and the meaning is —'I, in accordance with reason, call you to come to this new city, simply and solely for your good. I cannot follow your *wayward* wishes.' The construction of Lin Che-k'e, Ts'ae and others, which I have followed, is much more easy, and the meaning which it gives is in harmony with the whole address. If it be asked how the removal contrary to their wishes could be represented as an act of great accordance with the peo., it may be answered with Yuen Hwang (袁黃), 'To follow the people's temporary wishes would have been a small act of accordance with them; to gratify their desire for the benefit of permanent establishment was an act of great accordance' (從民一時之欲者、其從小;從民永建之利者、其從大、故曰丕從).

6. *The people are reproved for their want of sympathy, and the folly and fruitlessness of their opposition to the movement pointed out.* 今予將試,—'my present experiment,' 'my present undertaking.' 汝不憂朕心之攸困一不憂我憂, 'you do not sorrow with my sorrow,' *i.e.*, you do not enter at all into my trouble of mind about the calamities which threaten us in the old capital. 咸大不宣乃(一汝)心,—'you all greatly do not declare your minds.' 欽念以忱動予一人,—these two clauses are to be read closely together. 欽念一敬想, 'reverently thinking.' 自鞠,一鞠一窮. 汝弗濟,—we must supply 以時 before 濟. 臭厥載,一臭一敗壞, 'to ruin;' comp. Con. Ana., X., viii. 2. The removal from Kăng to Yin was like crossing a stream in a boat. If they delayed, the calamity of inundation would be upon them. 汝忱不屬,一屬 is read *chuh*, 'to be connected with.' It seems most natural to understand the meaning to be as in the translation. From this to the end, the 'Daily Explanation' paraphrases:—汝從上之誠、間斷不屬、則亦焉能有濟乎、惟相與及于沈溺而已、利害昭然如此、爾民皆不稽察、以早決從違、

屬、惟胥以沈、不其或稽、自怒曷瘳。○汝不謀長、以思乃災、汝誕勸憂、今其有今罔後、汝何生在上。○今予命汝一、無起穢以自臭、恐人倚乃身、迂乃心。○予迓

mine, and we are in danger of going together to destruction. You
notwithstanding will not examine the matter:—though you anger
yourselves, what cure will that bring?
7 "You do not consult for a distant day, nor think of the calamity
that must befal you. You greatly encourage one another in what
must prove to your sorrow. Now you have the present, but you
may not have the future. What deliverance can you look for from
8 above? Now I charge you to have but one mind. Do not let wicked
thoughts arise to ruin yourselves. I am afraid that men bend your
persons, and pervert your minds."

但自生怨疾忿怒，亦曷救于沈溺之苦哉，予不能爲汝解已. Gan-kwŏ's interpretation was rather different. He says:—汝忠誠不屬逮古，苟不欲徙，相與沈溺，不考之先王，禍至自怒，何瘳差乎.

Keang Shing reads 迪 (=道) for 稽，and 怨 for 怒, and interprets:—爾衷誠不連屬于我同謀共濟，既臭厥載，惟相與沈水，不其有生道矣 (='you have no way of life'), 雖自怨恚，何瘉乎.

7, 8. *Pwan-kăng reproves the short-sightedness of the people, and warns them against being misled.* 7. 汝不謀長以思乃災—汝不爲長遠之謀，以思不遷之禍, 'you do not adopt any far-reaching counsels to think about the calamity that must result from your not removing.' 勸憂—以憂自勸, 'you advise one another about what will prove to your sorrow.' Ts'ae, after Lin Che-k'e, refers to the case adduced by Mencius (IV., Pt. I., viii.) of those princes who 安其危而利其災，樂其所以亡, as an instance of 勸憂. 今其有今罔後,—this does not mean, as Gan-kwŏ supposed, 'you have no plans for the future,' but 死亡無日, 'your death will soon happen' (see Keang Shing, *in loc.*). 汝何生在上,—for 在上, Gan-kwŏ said 在人上, 'among men.'; Lin Che-k'e, in the same way, 在生民上; Keang Shing says 在地上, 'upon the earth.' Ts'ae alone, and I think correctly, makes 上, 'above,'=天 'heaven,' referring to 予迓續乃命于天, which passage and the text, he says, explain each other (相首尾之辭). 8. 命汝一—命汝專一乃心，從我遷徙, 'I charge you to have but one heart to follow me in the proposed movement.' 無 (=毋) 起穢以自臭,—穢 is explained in the dict., with ref. to this passage, simply by 惡, 'wickedness.' It stands related to 臭, which denotes the fetid odour of articles in a state of decomposition. Pwan-kăng chooses such terms

續乃命于天、予豈汝威、用奉畜汝衆。○十節 予念我先神后之勞爾先、予丕克羞爾、用懷爾然。○十一節 先于政、陳于玆、高后丕乃崇降罪疾、曰

9 "My measures are forecast to prolong your lease of life from
Heaven. Do I force you by my majesty? My object is to support
10 and nourish you all. I think of the toils of my predecessors, *who
are now* the spiritual sovereigns, for your ancestors; I would in the
same way greatly nourish you, and cherish you.
11 II. "Were I to err in my government, and remain long here, my
High sovereign, *the founder of our House*, would send down great
punishment for my crime, and say, 'Why do you oppress my peo-

to show his contempt for the injurious speeches by which the people were led astray. 倚=偏. 迂=曲.

9, 10. *Pwan-kăng, like his predecessors, had but one object in his measures,—the good of the people.* 9. 迓=迎, 'to meet.' 予迓續乃命于天,—'I am going forward to a continuance (prolongation) of your lives from heaven'; *i.e.*, by removing them from Kăng to Yin, he would prolong their lives and prosperity. 用奉畜汝衆,—畜=養, 'to nourish.' 奉畜, 'to bear up and nourish,'= to nourish with all kindly and respectful care. 用 is used with reference to the removal which Pwan-kăng had in his mind, and = 'I am using this—my object in it is—to,' &c. 10. 我先神后,—'my predecessors, the spirit sovereigns.' I think the meaning is as I have given it in the translation. From the last Part, p. 14, and the parr. which follow here, we see how Pwan-kăng thought of his ancestors as still sovereigns, and their ministers as still ministers, in the world of spirits. 我先后之勞爾先,—the 'Daily Explan.' takes 勞 act. = 'to make to toil' (我思我先后之勞爾先人,而先人不以爲勞,而勇于趨利). Lin Che-k'e takes 勞爾先 as = 'toiled with your ancestors' (我先后與爾先祖相與勤勞). I venture to let the view of the meaning, which first occurred to me, stand as in the translation. 羞=養, or the 畜 of the last par. Keang Shing reads 不克 instead of 丕克, and makes the 然 at the close stand by itself, connecting the whole with the next par.—'I think how my predecessors removed their capital, and escaped from the evils threatening them. And I cannot get you to go to this land of enjoyment, where I could give you repose. If indeed it prove so, I shall be failing in my government,' &c.

Ch. II. Pp. 11—14. SPIRITUAL SANCTIONS. HOW FORMER EMPERORS AND THE PEOPLE'S FOREFATHERS WOULD PUNISH FROM HEAVEN BOTH EMPEROR AND PEOPLE, IF THEY DID NOT REMOVE TO YIN. 11. 陳于玆,—陳=久, 'long.' 陳 and 塵, it is said, were anciently interchanged, and as 'dust' accumulated on any thing shows it must have been for some time undisturbed in its place, there grew up the meaning of 'long,' 'long continuance.' However the meaning arose, we must acknowledge it in this passage. 高后,—Lin Che-k'e insists that this phrase here should be taken in the plural, and with the same general reference as 先后 before and after. His reasoning on the subject is not without weight, but I prefer, on the whole, with Ts'ae to understand the 'high sovereign' as being T'ang. 崇=大, 'great,' 'greatly.' 罪疾,—'the pain of—suffering for—crime.' 曷虐朕民,—not that Pwan-kăng oppressed the people; but his sin of *omission* in not removing them from Kăng would be reckoned to him

曷虐朕民。○十二節汝萬民乃不生生、暨予一人猷同心、先后丕降與汝罪疾、曰曷不暨朕幼孫有比、故有爽德、自上其罰汝、汝罔能迪。○十三節古我先后、既勞乃祖乃父、汝共作我畜民、汝有戕則

12 ple?' If you, the myriads of the people, do not attend to the perpetuation of your lives, and cherish one mind with me, the one man, in my plans, my predecessors will send down on you great punishment for your crime, and say, 'Why do you not agree with our young grandson, but so go on to forfeit your virtue?' When they
13 punish you from above, you will have no way of escape. Of old, my royal predecessors toiled for your ancestors and fathers. You are equally the people whom I nourish; but your conduct is in-

as a sin of *commission*. 12. 不生生,—Wang Suh and Gan-kwŏ both explained 生生 by 進進,—'an earnest joyful alacrity,' *i.e.*, in adopting the proposal to transfer the capital. Che-k'e adopted the explanation of Soo Shih as being preferable, in which he was foll. by Ts'ae:—we have in the 集傳;—樂生興事,其生也厚,是謂生生, 'a joyous life, with vigorous enterprises,—a life strong and rich; this is what is meant by 生生.' Much better than either of those views is that in the 'Daily Explanation,' which I have followed;—生生者,生養不窮之意. 暨予一人猷,—hitherto we have had 暨=及, 'and,' a conjunction simply; here and below, it=與. Keang Shing reads 繇 for 猷, and takes it in the sense of 從, but I cannot construe the sentence so. 丕降與爾罪疾,—here the use of 與, where we should expect 于, is strange. 朕幼孫,—'our young grandson.' This of course is Pwan-kăng. 有比,—比,=合 or 同. Keang Shing takes it in the sense of 下順, which also gives a good meaning. 故有爽德,—this clause is joined with the preceding, in the 'Daily Explanation,' which also takes 爽 in the sense of 失. Gan-kwŏ joined the clause with what follows, and took 爽 as=明.—'Therefore he who has the brilliant virtue (*i.e.*, T'ang) from above will punish,' &c. This is inadmissible. Keang Shing, following 賈逵 in an explanation of the same phrase in the 國語, gives it by 貳德, which comes to much the same with 失德. 汝罔能迪,—迪=道. Ts'ae says:—汝無道以自免也, 'you will have no way to make your escape.' 13. 故我先后……畜民,—see on parr. 10 and 9. 汝有戕,則在乃心,—I hardly know what to make of this passage. The 'Daily Explanation' paraphrases it:—汝不法汝祖父而從我以遷,是即戕害生民矣.若有戕害在汝之心,我先王,云云, 'you do not imitate your ancestors by falling into my view of removing. In this you prove yourselves hurtful to the life of the people, and since you have such an injurious object in your hearts, my

在乃心、我先后綏乃祖乃父、乃祖乃父乃斷棄汝、不救乃死。○十四節 茲予有亂政同位、具乃貝玉、乃祖乃父丕乃告我高后曰、作丕刑于朕孫、迪高后丕乃崇降弗祥。○嗚

jurious,—it is cherished in your hearts. Whereas my royal predecessors made happy your ancestors and fathers, your ancestors and fathers will cut you off and abandon you, and not save you
14 from death. Here are those ministers of my government, who share with me the offices *of the State*;—and yet only think of hoarding up cowries and gems! Your ancestors and fathers urgently represent to my High sovereign, saying, 'Execute great punishments on our descendants.' So they intimate to my High sovereign that he should send down great calamities.

predecessors,' &c. Keang Shing would take 在=察, as in the Canon. of Shun, par. 5,= 'What sort of mind does your resistance to my commands betoken? But if you occasion injury to any, my predecessors will examine your hearts. I am afraid they will punish you.'

As much difficulty is found with what follows, —我先后綏乃祖乃父,云云, The 'Daily Explanation' continues the paraphrase which I have just quoted:—'My predecessors, thinking of the great and real toils of your forefathers, will soothe them till there is awakened the thought of punishing you' (必安慰汝祖父,致其用罰之意). Keang Shing takes 綏=妥=止, 'to stop,' and says:—'My predecessors will stop your forefathers, and require them not to save you.' The view which I take will be seen in the translation. Gan-kwŏ interpreted 綏 differently, but his view of the argument, so to speak, was similar. He says:—'My predecessors reposed in the loyalty of your forefathers; and now that you are disloyal, your forefathers will cast away your lives, and not save you from death.' 14. Ts'ae observes on this par. that 'former scholars had taken it as addressed in reproof to Pwan-kăng's ministers, but that, on looking closely at the style, we see that it is a reproof of the ministers indeed, but spoken not directly to them, but of them to the people.' Ts'ae is right in saying that the first portion—茲予有亂政同位,具乃貝玉, is to be understood as spoken about the ministers, but I do not see my way to interpret 乃祖乃父, 'their ancestors and their fathers,' as he does. Here is the difficulty;—why should the ancestors of the people ask their descendants to be punished for the evil conduct of the ministers? A reason can be given, and we may suppose that it was indicated by the tone of voice, though it was not expressed in words. It was that the people by listening to the speeches of such men, and in obedience to them disobeying their sovereign, greatly aggravated their guilt. 亂=治. 同位=共天位. 具=多取而兼有, 'amassing.' 貝玉, —貝=海介蟲, 'a shelled insect of the sea.' Ying-tă says that 'anciently they used the shell as money.' The text is a proof that such a medium of exchange was known in the Shang dynasty. 'Amassing cowries and gems' is a description of the selfish covetousness of the ministers.

十五 呼、今予告汝不易、永敬大恤、無胥絶遠、汝分猷念以相從、各設中于乃心。○十六節 乃有不吉不迪、顚越不恭、暫遇姦宄、我乃劓殄滅之、無遺育、無俾易種于兹新邑。○十七節 往哉生生、今予將試以汝遷、永建乃家。

15 III. "Ah! I have now announced to you my unchangeable purpose:
—do you perpetually respect *my* great anxiety; let us not get alienated
and removed from one another; share in my plans and thoughts,
and be prepared to obey me; let every one of you set up the true
16 rule of conduct in his heart. If there be bad and unprincipled
men, precipitously or carelessly disrespectful *to my orders*, and
taking advantage of this brief season to play the part of villains or
traitors, I will cut off their noses, or utterly exterminate them.
I will leave none of their children. I will not let them perpetuate
their seed in this new city.
17 "Go! preserve and continue your lives. I will now transfer you
to the new capital, and there for ever establish your families."

CH. III. Pp. 15—17. PWAN-KANG ANNOUNCES HIS SETTLED PURPOSE TO PROCEED TO YIN, AND SUMMONS ALL TO SYMPATHIZING CO-OPERATION WITH HIM, WHILE RECUSANTS ARE THREATENED WITH PUNISHMENT AND DEATH.

15 告汝不易,—Wang Suh and Gan-kwŏ read 易 in the 3d tone, and interpreted—'I have announced to you what is not easy,' so that the meaning is the same as that of the first clause, p. 16, Pt. i. Ts'ae adopts this view: but that in the transl., which was originally proposed by K'ang-shing, is followed by Lin Che-k'e and Keang Shing. 大恤=大憂, 'the great sorrow.' Pwan-kang thus characterizes the movement which had occasioned him so much anxiety. 汝分猷念,—Këang Shing reads 比 for 分; but the meaning is the same. 設中于乃心,—'set up the middle in your hearts.' 中=大中至正之則, 'the great exact, and perfectly correct rule.' 16. 乃有不吉不迪,—吉=善; 迪=道; 不吉不迪, are 'men without goodness or principle.' 顚越不恭,—Ts'ae explains these terms by—'overthrowing, transgressing, or not respecting *my commands*;' but we may as well take 越 here as in 無越厥命, V., Pt. i., 5. 暫遇姦宄,—Lin Che-k'e says that the two words 暫遇 are not in harmony with the rest of the sentence, and unintelligible to him; and he will therefore say nothing about them. Ying-tă, giving Gan-kwŏ's view of them, says—'they mean that such persons plundered men whenever they met them; that they did so without intermission' (謂逢人卽刼, 爲之無已). I have done the best with them I could. [Keang Shing puts them out of the text, as an addition by the compiler of the present 'old text.' He reduces the whole par., indeed, to small dimensions,—其有顚越不共, 則劓殄, 云云. His reason

for doing so is that so much is found quoted in the 左傳,哀十一年. But because only so much is quoted, it is absurd to conclude that there never was any more.] 我乃劓云云,—we may compare this with the conclusion of 'The Speech at Kan,' and of 'The Speech of T'ang.' 'Cutting off the nose' was one of the ancient regular punishments;—see on the 'Canon of Shun,' p. 11. 易種,—易=移. 17. 往哉,—comp. 'Can. of Shun,' p. 17, *et al.* 生生,—see p. 12. 今予,云云,—see p. 6.

THE BOOKS OF SHANG.

BOOK VII. PWAN-KANG. PART iii.

盤庚下

盤庚既遷、奠厥攸居、乃正厥位、綏爰有衆。○曰、無戲怠、懋建大

1 1. Pwan-kang having completed the removal, and settled the places of residence, proceeded to adjust their several positions, and then
2 he soothed and comforted the multitudes, saying to them, "Do not play or be idle, but exert yourselves to build here a great destiny *for us*.

CONTENTS OF THE THIRD PART. The removal has been accomplished. Emperor, officers, and people are all at Yin, when he once more addresses them. First, in 7 parr., he goes over much the same ground with the people as he had done before, justifying the measure which he had taken; and then, in the remaining 6 parr. he charges all the chiefs and officers to labour with him in a common sympathy for the good of the people.

Ch. I. Pp. 1—7. OCCASION OF THE ADDRESS. THERE SHOULD BE ENTIRE CONFIDENCE BETWEEN SOVEREIGN AND PEOPLE. THE REMOVAL OF THE CAPITAL WAS IN ACCORDANCE WITH FORMER PRECEDENTS; REQUIRED FOR THE GOOD OF THE PEOPLE; APPROVED BY GOD. 1. *Occasion of the address.* 奠厥攸居, 乃正厥位,—Ch'ing supposed that the former of these clauses described the settlement of *the people*, and the latter the laying out the official residences and public buildings,—such as the ancestral temple, the court, &c. Gan-kwŏ takes the second clause in the same way, and naturally extends the former to the settlement of the officers as well as of the people. Lin Che-k'e argues against this view of the second clause, and says that Pwan-kăng would have had the city laid out, before moving from Kăng, as Chow-kung did afterwards when he wished to make Lŏ the capital of the Chow rule. To my mind the style corroborates this reasoning. The parties interested in 'the dwellings' (攸居) are the same as those concerned in the 'positions' (厥位); but the 乃 intimates an interest of a difft. kind. I am prepared therefore to agree farther with Lin Che-k'e in taking 正厥位 of the arrangements made for the positions of the various classes at a public assembly, where Pwan-kăng gave the address that follows. Woo Ch'ing follows this view. Ts'ae, dissatisfied with that of Gan-kwŏ and Ch'ing, makes the positions to be those of 'sovereign, ministers, high, and low;' but the relations of all these were determined before. 綏爰有衆,—both Gan-kwŏ and Ch'ing again agree in def. 爰 by 于, and explain the clause by 安於有衆, and 安隱于其衆. The construction would be easier, but the symmetry not so good, without the 爰. 2. *The great object to be kept in view by them all at their present crisis.* 無—毋. The comment of Woo Ch'ing on this par. is very good:—

命。○今三節予其敷心腹腎腸、歷告爾百姓于朕志、罔罪爾衆、爾無共怒、協比讒言予一人。○古四節我先王、將多于前功、適于山、用降我凶

3 "Now I have disclosed my heart and belly, my reins and bowels, and have fully declared to you, my people, all my mind. I will not treat any of you as criminals; and do not you *any more* help one another to be angry, and form parties to defame me, the one man.

4 "Of old, my royal predecessor, that his merit might exceed that of those who had gone before him, proceeded to the hill-site. Thereby he removed our evils, and accomplished admirable good for our country.

'When Pwan-kăng tells them "not to play," he requires that they should *reverently* attend to their duties (欲其敬事); when he tells them "not to be idle," he requires them to attend *diligently* to them. By "a great destiny" he intends the destiny of themselves and of the kingdom; and he speaks of "building" this, just as Mencius speaks of "establishing it" (猶孟子言立命; see Men. VII., Pt. I., i., 3). Our destiny depends, indeed, on Heaven, but the establishing it is our own work, by which the people may be made to have the enjoyment of their life, and the fortunes of the kingdom be prolonged. At that time a disregard of the emperor and a seeking of their ease, with an addiction to sport and idleness, were characteristics of the Yin people. Before the removal of the capital, they were afraid of the trouble; after the removal, they thought they had done enough, saying now their lives would be perpetuated, and they need not exert themselves any more. It was to meet all this that the emperor cautioned them as in the text.'

3. *The openness of Pwan-kăng with the people and his kindness should make them respond to him with entire confidence.* 今予其敷,—the 其 is strongly intensive. 敷＝布, or 布露. 歷告＝盡告. I think the verbs here should be translated in the present complete tense, with reference to all that the emp. had said to them. 百姓,—'the people;' including also the 'various officers,' says Ts'ae, 'and their clans.'

[The reading of the first part of this par. adopted by Këang Shing is peculiar, and he is put to great straits to make any sense of it. What he does make is not in harmony with the tenor of the Book. He has:—今我其敷優臤,揚歷告爾,云云.] 罔罪爾衆,—Medhurst translates—'not that I would blame you all;' which is very different from the meaning. Pwan-kăng promises to forget all the past, and goes on to hope that they will not do as they had done. 協比＝合同附和.

4. *What advantages T'ang had secured by fixing his capital in a high situation.* 古我先王,—'the former king' must be T'ang. The characterizing him as 古, 'ancient' is in favour of this view, and from his time the emperors had been obliged to leave one capital after another, in consequence of their low situation exposing them to inundations. We might have expected that it would have been more clearly indicated that the hill-site of T'ang was that to which they were now returned;—but we must take the Book as it is. Those early settlements could not have been built of very permanent materials and structure. 將多于前功,—將＝欲, 'to wish.' 將, as the sign of the future, indicates also the purpose out of which that future grows. One of the definitions of it in the dict. is—將,有其意也. 用降我凶德,—用＝'thereby;' 降＝下. Hwang Too, more intelligibly, defines it here by 減少, 'to diminish.' 我凶德＝'our suffering condition,' referring to the evils of a low situation, exposed to inundation. Lin Che-k'e would make the meaning—'removed our evil habits,' arguing from the Mencian doctrine that want and calamities are the parents of wickedness (see

德嘉績于朕邦。○五節今我民用蕩析離居、罔有定極、爾謂朕曷震動萬民以遷。○六節肆上帝將復我高祖之德、亂越我家、朕及篤敬、恭承民命、用永地于新邑。○七節肆予沖人、非廢厥謀、弔由靈、

5 Now you, my people, were by your position dissipated and separated,
and obliged to leave your dwellings, so that you had no abiding
place. And yet you asked why I was troubling your myriads by
6 removing you here. But God being about to restore the virtue of
my High ancestor, and secure the *good* government of our empire, I
with the sincere and respectful *of my ministers* felt a reverent care for
the lives of the people, and have made a lasting settlement in this
new city.
7 "I, a youth, did not slight your plans;—I *only* used what were

Men. Bk. VI., Pt. I., vii.), where as T'ang removing the people to a location which required industry and rewarded it, greatly improved their moral tone. 嘉績,—another reading is 綏績.

It will be seen that Pwan-kăng throws himself and his people a long way back, to identify themselves with their fathers in the time of T'ang, nearly 400 years before.

5. *How Pwan-kăng had emulated T'ang's proceeding, against the general sentiment, but having the approval of some, and, as he thought, the sanction of God.* 用=以; 以其居處, 'in consequence of their position.' 極=止. 罔有定極, 'had no fixed place of rest.' 爾謂云云,—we must understand, as preliminary to this, something equivalent to —'a removal was urgently called for.' The 'Daily Explanation' has—乃陷于凶德,而宜急圖嘉績之時. [Keang Shing reads 今 before 爾, and 惠 for 謂, making the interpretation still more difficult.] 6. 肆上帝云云,—肆, as 'an introductory particle indicating a change in the thought' (更端辭), is defined in the dict. by 故, 'therefore,' and 今, 'now.' Neither of these terms, however, expresses exactly what seems to be its force here. 'But' comes nearer to it, and Ts'ae indeed explains it by 乃. Pwan-kăng evidently ascribes the movement to an influence exerted by God on the mind of himself and some of his ministers. 亂越我家,—亂=治; 越=及; 家=國家. The meaning of the clause is as in the transl. The only critic who takes a difft. view is Lin Che-k'e, who would retain the common meaning of 亂, 'to confound.' He says:—'God, being about to restore the virtue of T'ang, and make the empire flourish anew under his descendant, brought about the disorder and calamities in Kăng, to lead Pwan-kăng to move to Yin;' and then he goes on to speak of the uses of adversity. This is too ingenious. 朕及篤敬,—we can only understand that the emperor is speaking here of some of his ministers who were of the same mind with himself. Ts'ae says:—我與一二篤敬之臣. Keang Shing would make 及=汲汲, so that the discourse is only of Pwan-kăng, himself.—'I roused to earnest reverence,' &c. 7. *Forgetting their past differences, the emperor is willing to suppose there had been a substantial agreement between the people and himself.* The paragraph is hardly intelligible. Ch'in Leih has said:—'Choo He doubted the

各非敢違卜、用宏兹賁。○八節 嗚呼、邦伯師長、百執事之人、尚皆隱哉。○九節 予其懋簡相爾、念敬我衆。

the best of them. And you did not presumptuously oppose the decision of the tortoise:—so we are *here* to enlarge our great inheritance.
8 II. "Ah! ye chiefs of regions, ye heads of departments, all ye, the hundreds of officers, would that ye were animated by a true
9 sympathy! I will exert myself in the selection and guiding of you;

genuineness of this Part from 多于前功 (in par. 4), and there are passages like 弔由靈, 宏兹賁 here, which are truly difficult to understand. Our best plan is to be content with what the early scholars said about them.' Such a course might be our best plan; but no one whose judgment is worth anything will be content to take it. 予沖人,—幼少在位曰沖, 'a youth on the throne is called 沖.' In the 5th Part of the Shoo we shall find the phrase 沖人 employed several times by the emperors as a humble designation of themselves. This is the first instance of its occurrence. Pwan-kăng was not 'a youth' at this time, but he is pleased to speak as if he were. 弔 (also 迅)=至; 由=用; 靈=善. Ying-tă says:—'On occasion of any great matter, the rule was to consult with all about it. Pwan-kăng did so, and therefore he says, "I did not neglect consulting with you." But in such a case there could not but be different views, and he therefore followed what he considered the best' (故至極用其善者. One hardly knows the exact force of 至極. Perhaps it='in the extremity'). It would appear that the emperor submitted the conclusion to which he came to the decision of the tortoise, and when the divination approved of the transference of the capital, the people ceased their opposition. 用宏兹賁,—宏 and 賁 (read *fun*) have both the meaning of 大 'great;' but the former is a verb, ='to enlarge,' and the latter = a concrete noun,—'great inheritance.' Such is the view of the par. given by the early scholars. Tung-po took another view of the last term, which he read *pe*;—see the 附錄, and a note by the editors of Yung-ching's Shoo. Keang Shing, as usual, strikes out a path here for himself, and with more than his usual ingenuity. I am not sure but it would be well to interpret the par. after him—'I did not slight your plans; but as the best rule felt it right to follow the intelligent tortoise. And you, did not venture to resist the divination,' &c.

Ch. II. Pp. 8—13. CHARGE TO THE NOBLES AND OFFICERS TO SYMPATHIZE WITH HIMSELF, AND SEEK THE GOOD OF THE PEOPLE. 8. By 邦伯 Lin Che-k'e and Ts'ae understand 邦之諸侯, 'the princes of regions;' by 師長,衆官之長, 'the heads of all the officers,' the six high nobles (六卿 and 公卿); and by 百執事之人, 'all the officers,' subordinate to these last. Gan-kwŏ and Ying-tă differed only in their view of 邦伯, by which they understood all the princes of the nine provinces, and two superior princes who exercised a control over them. But the institution of those two princes belonged to the next, or Chow dynasty. And we can hardly suppose that the princes of all the provinces were collected on this occasion. The 邦伯 must be restricted to those within the imperial domain,—the 甸服. Much more must we restrict the 師長, which we should otherwise be inclined to understand according to Yu's use of the terms in the 'Yih and Tseih,' p. 8. 隱=痛, 'to feel pained,'=to look with sympathy upon the condition of the people. [Keang Shing for 隱 read 乘, which he explains by 治職.] 9. 簡=擇, 'to select'; 相=導, 'to lead.' Others take 簡=閱, 'to examine,' and 相=視, 'to see;' giving the meaning,—'I will assiduously examine, and see whether you think reverently of my people.' This meaning is as

書經

十節 朕不肩好貨、敢恭生生、鞠人謀人之保居、敘欽。○十一節 今我既羞告爾于朕志、若否、罔有弗欽。○十二節 無總于貨寶、生生自庸、○十三節 式敷民德、永肩一心。

10 —do ye think reverently of my multitudes. I will not employ those
who are fond of wealth; but those who are rigorously yet reverently
labouring for the lives and increase of the people, nourishing them
and planning for their enduring settlement, I will use and respect.
11 "I have now brought forward and announced to you my mind,
whom I approve and whom I disallow;—let none of you but reve-
12 rence *my will*. Do not seek to accumulate wealth and precious
things; *but* in fostering the life of the people seek to find your merit.
13 Reverently display your virtue in behalf of the people. For ever
maintain *this* one heart."

good as that in the translation. 10. 肩, 'to bear on the shoulder,' is here taken as = 任, 'to employ.' The whole par. is very difficult. Ts'ae acknowledges that he does not understand 鞠人, 謀人, adding that some take 鞠 in the sense of 養, 'to nourish.' Such was the view of K'ang-hing. I have translated after the 'Daily Explanation.' Other views may be seen in Woo Ch'ing and Keang Shing. 敘 = 次敘, 'to arrange,' = to give employment and emolument to according to their qualities. 欽, 'to respect,' = to treat with reverent politeness. 11. 羞 = 進, 'to bring forward.' 若否,—若 = 若者, 'those whom I approve,'—those characterized in the prec. par., as 'labouring for the lives and comfort of the people.' 否 = 否者,—those whom I disallow,'—'those who were fond of wealth.' Keang Shing takes the two characters differently.—'I have shown you my thoughts. Whether you approve of them or disapprove, reverence my will.' 12. 無總于貨寶,—無 = 毋; 總 = 聚; 貨寶 = the 貝玉, of last Part, p. 14. 庸 denotes 民功, 'service done to the people.' Woo Ch'ing, says:—以民之生生爲已實. 13. 式 = 敬, 'to reverence,' 'reverently,' 民德爲民之德. 肩, 'to, bear on the shoulder,' = 'to bear about with one,' 'to maintain.'

Concluding Note. History tells us nothing special of Pwan-kăng after his transference of his capital to Yin. It is only said that he revived the government of T'ang, and the dynasty of Shang prospered again. He reigned 28 years, and died B.C. 1373.

THE BOOKS OF SHANG.

BOOK VIII. THE CHARGE TO YUE. PART i.

說命上

一節 王宅憂、亮陰三祀、既免喪、其惟弗言、群臣咸諫于王曰、嗚呼、知之曰明哲、明哲實作則、天子惟君萬邦、百官承式、王言惟作命、不言、臣下罔攸稟令。

1 I. The king passed the season of sorrow in the mourning shed for three years, and when he had ceased mourning, he still did not speak. The ministers all remonstrated with him, saying, "The man of *quick* knowledge is said to be intelligent; and the intelligent man forms a model. The emperor rules over the myriad regions, and all the officers depend on and reverence him. When the king speaks, *his words* form the commands *for them*; if he do not speak,

INTRODUCTORY HISTORICAL NOTE. Pwan-kăng's reign ended B.C. 1373. Between him and Woo-ting, some events of whose time are commemorated in this and the following Book, there intervened a space of 50 years, occupied by the reigns of Seaou-sin (小辛) and Seaou-yih (小乙), both brothers of Pwan-kăng and Yang-kea, so that we have the remarkable fact of four brothers occupying the throne in succession. Seaou-sin and Seaou-yih are all but nameless sovereigns. Sze-ma Ts'een tells us that the fortunes of the house of T'ang began again to wane under the former, who died B.C. 1352. Of Seaou-yih nothing at all is chronicled, but we are told that in his 26th year Tan-foo (亶父) removed from (豳) to K'e (岐), and gave his settlement the name of Chow. The dynasty which was to supplant that of Shang (or Yin) is already looming in the distance. Seaou-yih died B.C. 1324, and the next year was the first of Woo-ting (武丁), who earned a place for himself in the 'seven-shrined temple,' under the title of 'The High and Venerable' (高宗), and arrested for a time the downfal of his House.

Name of the Book.—說命, 'The Charge to Yuě.' This is the first of the 'Charges' which form one of the divisions of the Shoo. They relate the designation by the emperor of some officer to a particular charge or fief, with the address delivered to him on the occasion. Here the charge is to Yuě on his appointment to be prime minister. The name, however, is not happily chosen. It does very well for the first Part of the Book, but in the other two Parts Yuě is the principal speaker, and not the king. They would be classified properly among the 'Counsels.' Yuě was a recluse, living in obscurity,—on account, we may suppose, of the disorder of the times. Woo-ting's attention was drawn to him in the manner related in the Book, and he was discovered in Foo Yen, or the crags of Foo, from which he was afterwards known as Foo Yuě, as if Foo had been his surname. The Book is only found in the 'old text.' It has been alleged against its genuineness that Sze-ma Ts'een does not say anything about its composition. But this can only be an omission. Ts'een gives several particulars about Yuě; the Preface to the Shoo, and many references in other books, leave no doubt as to the fact of there having originally been a 'Charge to Yuě.'

Contents. The first Part tells us how the emperor was led to meet with Yuě, and appointed him his prime minister, with the charge, which he then delivered to him, and Yue's response to it. In the second Part, Yuě appears counselling the emperor on a variety of points, and the king responds admiringly. In the third Part, the king presents himself first as a pupil at the feet of Yuě, and is lectured on the subject of study, or enlarging his knowledge. Finally, the emperor says he looks to Yuě to be another E Yin, to make him another T'ang.

Contents of the first Part. The whole is edited in 11 paragraphs. The first three form a chapter, relating the peculiar circumstances in which Woo-ting found Yuě. The next 7 parr. relate the elevation of Yuě to the premiership, and the charge which was then given him. The last par. contains Yuě's dutiful reply, and expresses his confidence in the emperor's wisdom.

Ch. I. Pp. 1—3. Occasion of the charge. Woo-ting excites the surprise of his ministers by his protracted silence, which leads them to remonstrate with him. He explains the reason, telling them of a dream in which a sage minister was presented to him, who is found and proves to be Yue. 1. 王宅憂亮陰三祀,—宅憂=居喪, 'to occupy—to abide—during mourning.' 亮陰,—this is a phrase which has occasioned much speculation as to its meaning. The characters are variously written. In Pt. V., Bk. XV., p. 5, they are the same as here. In the Analects, XIV., xiii., we have 諒陰; and in other places we have 諒闇. However we write them, the first should be pronounced in the low. 1st tone, and the second is read *an* or *gan*, up. 1st tone. As to the mean., Choo He, on the Analects, says he does not know it. Gan-kwŏ made it out to be 信默,—'trusting the premier, and silent himself.' In this sense we should have to read 陰 in the usual way; but the explanation is most unlikely. We are indebted to Ch'ing for the view that we are to understand by the phrase the 凶廬, or what is called in the 儀禮, 喪服, Pt. I., 倚廬, the mourning shed which the emperor was supposed to occupy during the period of mourning. Here Woo-ting spent the prescribed period of 'three years,' or 25 months, 'without speaking' (see the pass. in the next Part, Bk. XV.). Not that we are to suppose he preserved an absolute silence; but he abstained from speaking of governmental matters, and left them in the hands of his prime minister.

At the end of this time, he *still* kept silence. We must understand 其惟不言 in this way. The 'Daily Explanation' has:—及大祥後,喪服已除,猶未發號施令,裁決庶務. 知之=有先知之德, 'he who has the ability of earlier apprehension.' There was probably a reference in the minds of the speakers to the language of E Yin about the duty of 'those who are first informed, and first apprehend principles,' to instruct and enlighten others. They compliment the emperor with being such a man, 'knowing,' says Kin Lets'ëang, 'his extraordinary natural gifts' (天資之不凡). 明哲,—Shin She-hing (申時行) explains 'the man of brightness (明者) as one whose large comprehension embraces all principles (方寸虛靈,無一理之不具), and the man of wisdom, (哲者) as one who has examined the minute and knows the displayed, as if a light were thrown on every principle' (察微知著,無一理之不燭). 百官承式,—Ts'ae seems to take 式 as a noun= 'rules,' gov. by 承 'to receive.' It is better to take 承 absolutely. The officers represent themselves as receiving every thing from the emperor. Then 式=敬, 'to respect,' 'to reverence. The 'Daily Explanation' says:—百官之所仰承而欽式者. 稟 (*pin*; 2d tone)=受命, 'to receive commands.' [The question of Tsze-chang in the Analects, in which he quotes the Shoo as saying that 'Kaou-tsung, while mourning in the usual imperial fashion, was for three years without speaking,' was founded probably, not on the text, but on Pt. V., Bk. XV., p. 5.]

二節 王庸作書以誥曰、以台正于四方、台恐德弗類、茲故弗言、恭默思道、夢帝賚予良弼、其代予言。○三節 乃審厥象、俾以形旁求于天下、

2 the ministers have no way to receive their orders." The king on
this made a writing, and informed them, saying, "As it is mine to
secure what is right in the four quarters *of the empire*, I have
been afraid that my virtue is not equal *to that of my predecessors*,
and therefore have not spoken. *But* while I was respectfully
and silently thinking of the *right* way, I dreamt that God gave me
3 a good assistant, who should speak for me." He then minutely
described the appearance of the person, and caused search to be

2. 王庸作書以誥,—庸=用. It emphasizes the 作;—see on Bk. V., Pt. i., p. 4. 正于四方,—comp. 表正萬邦, Bk. II., p. 2. 德弗類,—Gan-kwŏ makes 類=善, 'good.' It is better to take it as in the translation. Ts'ae says:—恐德不類于前人. 思道,—'thinking of the way.' By 道 we are to understand 'the principles and course of good govt.' (治道). 賚=與, 'to give. 弼,—see the 'Yih and Tseih,' parr. 2 and 4. 審厥象,—審, 'to discriminate.' Woo-ting brought back the dream to his mind, till he could distinguish and make out the lineaments and form of the man whom he had seen. The 'Daily Explanation' says:—乃追夢中之所見而諦審其象,繪畫成形. 旁求=遍求, 'to search everywhere,' on all 'sides.' 說 (read *Yuĕ*) 築云云,—Ts'ae takes 築 as=居, 'to dwell,' and is foll. by the 'Daily Explanation;'—I know not upon what authority. We ought not to depart from its common signification, sanctioned as that is by Mencius, who tells us that 'Yuĕ was called to office from the midst of his building frames' (傅說舉於版築之間; Men., VI., Pt. II., xv.). 傅巖之野,—Mih-tsze (尙賢,下篇) speaks of 'the city (? wall) of Foo-yen' (傅巖之城). Gan-kwŏ calls the place—'the crag of the Foo family' (傅氏之巖), and says that the public road went by it, and was injured by a mountain stream. It devolved on a convict in the place to repair it, when Yuĕ, who was living a recluse life in that quarter, and was in great poverty, undertook to do the work, 'in order to get food' (以供食). Sze-ma Ts'een for 傅巖 has 傅險. Whether we call the place Foo-yen, or 'the crag of Foo,' it is agreed that it was 25 *le* north-east from the pres. dis. city of P'ing-luh (平陸; lat. 34° 47', N., lon. 5°25', W.), in Kĕae Chow (解州), Shan-se. Mih-tsze tells us that Yuĕ wore coarse clothes of hair cloth, with a rope for a girdle; and Seun-tsze says that 'his person was like a fish standing up' (傅說之狀,身如植鰭, *lit.*, 'like a perpendicular dorsal fin,' but see the gloss *in loc.* 荀子,非相篇). These are merely the stories floating about in the Chow dynasty.

[As we might expect, this dream of Woo-ting has given rise to no little speculation among Chinese critics. Some have said that the emperor in his wanderings through the empire, to which he alludes at the commencement of Part iii., had become acquainted with the worth and ability of Yuĕ, and knew very well where to find him, so that his telling the courtiers about a dream, and sending through the country to look for Yuĕ, was only an expedient to make them readily acquiesce in his elevation of him to the highest dignity. This view, however, is rejected, as it would subject Woo-ting to a charge of hypocrisa ynd falsehood.

築傅巖之野、惟肖。○[四節]爰立作相、王置諸其左右。[五節]○命

made for him by means of a figure throughout the empire. Yuĕ, a builder in the country of Foo-yen, was found like.

4 II. On this the king raised and made him his prime minister, keeping him also at his side.

Choo He observes that, according to the account in the Shoo, God did really appear to Woo-ting in his dream, and say to him—'I give you a good assistant.' But now people, when they speak of God, intend only the idea of Rule and Government, and say that He has no form, which, it is to be feared, is not a correct mode of expression. If we should say, on the other hand, that the common representations of God as like the 'Great God, Yuh-hwang' are right, this also would be improper. What are we to say in the matter? He leaves this question unanswered. See 朱子全書, Bk. XXXIV.]

[It may be as well here to refer to a passage in the 國語,楚語,上, where we find a great deal of what we have in the 'Charge to Yuĕ.' A minister of king Ling of Ts'oo (靈王, B.C. 539-528), remonstrating with him, says:—昔殷武丁能聳其德,至於神明,以入於河,自河徂亳,於是乎三年默以思道,卿士患之曰,王言以出令也,若不言,是無所稟令也,武丁於是作書曰,以余正四方,余恐德之不類,茲故不言,如是而又使以象夢求四方之賢聖,得傅說以來,升以爲公,而使朝夕規諫,曰,若金用女作礪,若津水用女作舟,若天旱用女作霖雨,啟乃心沃朕心,若藥不瞑眩,厥疾不瘳,若跣不視地,厥足用傷. 若武丁之神明也......使朝夕規誨箴諫,曰,必交修余,無余棄也,云云. The above passage contains most of the 1st Part, and some sentences of the third. It is not quoted as from the Shoo, but there can be no doubt it really was taken from the classic, known both to king Ling and his minister. The historical portions are condensed, and brought together to serve the purpose of the speaker. The whole appears, as it would naturally do, if drawn—not quoted—from our present text. To contend that the text was plagiarized and 'made up' from the 國語 is a strange turning of the tables. Even if it were so, we still have in it so much of the original 'Charge to Yuĕ.']

Ch. II. Pp. 4—10. The elevation of Yuĕ, and the emperor's charge to him. 4. I have translated 相 by 'prime minister,' though I am not sure that the term had, in the Yin dynasty, more than the general meaning of 'assistant.' The proper name for prime minister was then 冢宰;—see Ana., XIV., xliii. It was to this office that Yuĕ was raised—總百官, as it is expressed in Pt. ii., p. 1. Yuĕ became to Woo-ting what E Yin had been to T'ang. 王置諸(=於)左右,—'in these words,' says Ts'ae, 'is intimated Yue's appointment to be "tutor and guardian" as well as prime minister' (以冢宰兼師保也). I do not know, however, that we should find any appointment to offices in the language,—anything more than the emperor's wish that Yuĕ should always act as his most intimate counsellor. We find in Ma Twan-lin (Bk. XXIX., 職官,宰相) that T'ang appointed two 相;—E Yin and Chung Hwuy, the Seang of the right and left respectfully, and that Yuĕ was called to discharge both of their offices. But we cannot pronounce positively, it seems to me, on the offices of so early a time. 爰, at the beginning of the par.,=於是, 'on this,' 'hereupon.' Sze-ma Ts'een says that Woo-ting conferred with Yuĕ, and made proof of him, finding that he was really a sage, before he raised him to these dignities; and Ts'ae says that not to have done so would have been unreasonable. We can well suppose that the emperor entered at once into conference with the strange man, but the Shoo leads us to think only of the dream as the cause of Yuĕ's

之曰、朝夕納誨、以輔
台德。○六節若金、用汝作
礪、若濟巨川、用汝作
舟楫、若歲大旱、用汝
作霖雨。○七節啟乃心、沃
朕心。○八節若藥弗瞑眩、
厥疾弗瘳、若跣弗視
地、厥足用傷。○九節惟暨
乃僚、罔不同心、以匡
乃辟、俾率先王、迪我

5 He charged him, saying, "Morning and evening present your
6 instructions to aid my virtue. Suppose me a weapon of steel;—I
will use you for a whetstone. Suppose me crossing a great stream;
—I will use you for a boat with its oars. Suppose me in a year
7 of great drought;—I will use you as a copious rain. Open your
8 mind, and enrich my mind. *Be you* like medicine, which, if it do
not distress the patient, will not cure his sickness. *Think of me* as
one walking *barefoot*, whose feet are sure to be wounded, if he do
not see the ground.

6 "Do you and your companions cherish all the same mind to assist your Sovereign, that I may follow my royal predecessors, and tread in the steps of my High ancestor, to give repose to the

elevation. 5. 納誨,—納=進, 'to present,' 'to bring forward;' 誨, 'instructions,' —including both teachings and remonstrances. 'The emperor,' says Wang Yen, 'speaks here of instructions and not of remonstrances, in his humility, showing his anxiety to be taught.' 6. *Various illustrations of the advantages of Yuě's teaching.* 若金, and the other commencements of the clauses, are descriptive of the emperor himself. 霖雨,='a copious rain.' 霖 is defined as 'rain continuous for at least three days,' 'rain unceasing.' The three clauses rise, it is said, in intensity of meaning, one above the other. The first shows how Yuě would help the king to accomplish himself (成器); the second has reference to the overcoming of difficulties; the third to the dispensing benefits to the people. 7. 沃朕心,—'to enrich my mind.' The figure of a copious rain is here continued. The 說文 defines 沃 by 灌漑, 'to moisten,' 'to irrigate.' 8. *Illustrations of the advantages of Yuě's remonstrances.* 若藥 and 若跣 are here also descriptive of the emperor;—in the first place as under medical treatment, and in the second place, as walking in a thoughtless and unguarded manner, needing to be warned of his danger. 若藥......瘳,—see Men., III., Pt. I., i., 5. 瞑 (read *mëen*, 3d tone.' Keang Shing edits 眄) are understood to be descriptive of the violent operation of medicine. So decided, and regardless of their immediate effect on himself, would Woo-ting have Yuě's words to be. 跣 is defined in the 說文—足親地, 'the foot close to the ground,' *i.e.*, 'barefoot.' This illustration requires Yuě to point out boldly whatever dangers the emp. might be heedlessly going into. 9. *Yuě must get all under him to have the same mind with himself.* 惟暨乃僚,—we must understand 汝 before 暨, and then the clause = 'you and your associates.' Whether we take 暨 as = 及 or = 與, it stands awkwardly at the beginning of the

書經

高后、以康兆民。○嗚十節呼、欽予時命、其惟有終。○說十一節復于王曰、惟木從繩則正、后從諫則聖、后克聖、臣不命其承、疇敢不祗若王之休命。

10 millions of the people. Oh! respect this charge of mine;—so shall you bring your work to *a good* end."

11 III. Yuĕ replied to the king, saying, "Wood by the use of the line is made straight; and the sovereign who follows reproof becomes sage. When the sovereign can *thus* make himself sage, his ministers, without being charged, anticipate his orders;—who would dare not to act in respectful compliance with this excellent charge of your Majesty?"

clause. 以匡乃辟,—匡 may be taken as in the translation, or as =救 or 正, 'to save,' or 'to correct,' 'to keep right.' The 先王 are all former wise kings of the Shang dyn.; 高后 is specially T'ang. 率 is 循其道, 'to follow their path;' 迪 is 蹈其迹, 'to tread in his footsteps.' 10. 時命=是命. 其惟有終,—有終, see Bk. II., p. 9; Bk. V., Pt. i., p. 3; *et al.* Ts'ae takes 惟 in the sense of 思, 'to think.'—'Respect this charge, thinking from the first upon the issue.'

Ch. III. THE DUTIFUL REPLY OF YUE TO THE ABOVE CHARGE. 說復于王,—復, see on Men., I., Pt. I., vii., 10. 后克聖,—Medhurst translates this—'When the sovereign is a sage;' but we must lay stress on the 克, and connect the clause with the preceding. When ministers see that the sovereign yields himself to be moulded by them,—is like wood in the hands of the carpenter,—they are encouraged to all assiduity in doing their duty. 臣不命其承,—the 'Daily Explanation' expands this:—凡爲臣者,爭欲仰承德意,進獻讜言,雖不命之言,猶且先意承之, 若王之休命,—若='such an'; 'an excellent charge like yours.'

THE BOOKS OF SHANG.

BOOK VIII. THE CHARGE TO YUE. PART ii.

說命中

一 惟說命總百官。○ 二 乃進于王曰、嗚呼、明王奉若天道、建邦設都、樹后王君公、承以大

1 I. Yuĕ having received charge to take the presidency of all the
2 officers, he presented himself before the king, and said, "Oh!
intelligent kings act in reverent accordance with the ways of Heaven.
The founding of States, and setting up of capitals; the appointing
of sovereign kings, of princes and dukes, with their great officers

CONTENTS OF THE SECOND PART. It has already been observed that this Part should be called 'The Counsels of Yuĕ.' In answer to the charge which he had received, Yuĕ presents his advice on various points, all connected with the duty of the sovereign, and the successful conducting of government. In the two last parr., the emperor and the minister give expression to their confidence and complacency in each other.

Ch. I. Pp. 1—11. THE COUNSELS OF YUE. 1, 2. *Occasion of the counsels. All government is not for the gratification and glory of the governing, but for the good of the people.* 1. 總百官,—總一將領, 'to take the lead of.' Lin Che-k'e understands the phrase as denoting that Yuĕ continued to act as the representative of the emperor, doing everything for him, as the prime minister did during the period of mourning. Perhaps it was so. Woo-ting had said that his 'good assistant' should speak for him.

2. 進于王,—進 may be taken as in the translation, or we may we understand 誨 as the object of the verb. With regard to what follows—嗚呼, 明王, 云云, there is considerable difficulty. 明王 would seem to be the subject of all the verbs that follow,—奉若, 建, 設, and 樹. 后王, 'sovereign king,' is understood to be a designation of the emperor (天子), and 君公 to stand for 諸侯 all the feudal princes under him. In this way, 明王 must be taken as singular, and to have reference to the first sovereign, the founder of the Chinese empire. This was the view of Gaubil. He translates:—'Le roi intelligent, qui autrefois se conforma avec respect a la loi du ciel, fonda l'empire et etablit une cour. Il assigna des lieux on devoient resider le roi, les grands vassaux, et les grands officiers. Ce prince intelligent ne s'occupa pas des plaisirs; il n'eut que le gouvernement du peuple en vue.' To this translation he appends the following note:—'Here Yuĕ speaks of the first king of China, but what follows does not give us any light on the time when he reigned. One might still translate, it appears to me, in the plural, and say—the intelligent kings, the

夫師長、不惟逸豫、惟以亂民。○三節惟天聰明、惟聖時憲、惟臣欽若、惟民從乂。○四節惟

and heads of departments:—were not designed to minister to the idleness and the pleasures *of one*, but for the good government of the people.

3 "It is Heaven which is all-intelligent and observing. Let the sage *king* take it as his pattern:—then his ministers will reverently accord with him; and the people will consequently be well governed.

founders of the empire. Yuĕ spoke of the first king as of a known personage. In the commentaries on the Yih-king, Confucius speaks of Fuh-he as the first king; and on this subject the authority of Confucius is preferable to that of others.'

I have not attempted to turn Gaubil's French version of the text into English, that the reader may see it as from his own hand. An intelligent comparison of it with the original will show that it gives the meaning of hardly a single phrase correctly. Several of the renderings are made in order to harmonize the whole with his view that 明王 is in the singular, and denotes the founder of the Chinese empire; but independently of this, the translation is inadmissible. Medhurst takes 明王 indefinitely, and renders it by 'an intelligent king.' His version is better than Gaubil's in the several phrases; but upon the whole it is not satisfactory.

For myself, I must construe the paragraph differently from any critic, native or foreign, that I have read. 明王 cannot be, as Gaubil supposes, 'the intelligent king,'—*the founder of the Chinese State*;—it must be translated—'intelligent kings,' or 'an intelligent king.' 后王 is to be understood, with Ts'ae and other scholars, as denoting 'the emperor,' or 'emperors.' To speak of intelligent kings as appointing emperors (明王樹后王) is absurd, and therefore 明王 cannot be the nominative to 建 and the other verbs. I put a stop at 道; and take 建邦, &c., as clauses in the nominative, the verb of which they are the subject being found in 不惟逸豫. By whom States were founded, and capitals set up, emperors, princes, and dukes, appointed, with all sustaining office under them is indicated in the phrase 天道, and the term 天, with which the next par. commences. It was by Heaven or God, constituting such a social order with a view to the benefit of the people. This construction may appear rather harsh, but it gives a consistent meaning to the whole paragraph, which we fail to get from any other interpretation. It is confirmed in so far by a passage in Mih-tsze (尙同中), where he seems to be partly quoting, and partly commenting on, the text. He says:—先王之書,相年之道,曰,夫建國設都,乃作后王君公,否用泰也,輕 (for 卿) 大夫師長,否用佚也,維辯使治天均,則此語古者上帝鬼神之建設國都,立正長也,非高其爵,厚其祿,富貴佚而錯之也,將以爲萬民興利除害,云云.

3. *The imitation of Heaven by the supreme earthly power is the first step, and surely leads, to good government.* 惟天聰明,—see the 'Counsels of Kaou-yaou.' p. 8. 時憲,—時=是; 憲=法, 'to imitate.' 欽若,—see 'Can. of Yaou,' p. 3. The four clauses of this par. are like pearls, lying side by side. We must take them, and string them together in the manner indicated in the translation. But how is 'the sage king' to imitate Heaven, all-intelligent and observing? The commentators labour to answer this question. The 'Daily Explanation,' for instance, says:—'Heaven aloft on high, without prepossession, entirely just, most spiritual and intelligent, needs not to hearken, and yet hears every thing; needs not to look, and yet sees every thing. The excellences and defects of govt., the happiness and suffering of the people, do not escape its observation. And not only this.—Of all that is done in darkness and in privacy, where there are neither ears nor eyes, nothing escapes its notice. Such is the intelligence and observation of Heaven;—it is for the wise sovereign to take this for his pattern. When his likings and dislikings are free from the becloudings of

口起羞、惟甲冑起戎、惟衣裳在笥、惟干戈省厥躬、王惟戒茲、允茲克明、乃罔不休。○五節惟治亂在庶官、官不及私昵、惟其能、爵罔及惡德、惟其賢。

4 "It is the mouth which gives occasion for shame; they are the coat of mail and helmet which give occasion to war. The upper robes and lower garments *for reward should not be lightly taken from* their chests; before shield and spear are used, one should examine himself. If your Majesty will be cautious in these things, and, believing this about them, attain to their intelligent *use, your government* will in every thing be excellent.

5 "Good government and bad depend upon the various officers. Offices may not be given to men because they are favourites, but only to men of ability. Dignities may not be conferred on men of evil practices, but only on men of worth.

partiality, and his rewards and punishments are all in accordance with right,—like the all-seeing and all-hearing of Heaven; then he can give the law to the empire,' &c. All this is not without truth and force; but Yuĕ's lesson is too vaguely expressed to be of much practical use. Gaubil, however, observes justly that those who have affirmed that the ancient Chinese only understood by Heaven the material heavens have not paid sufficient attention to such passages as the present.

4. *Instances of things in which the endeavour to imitate Heaven will be seen; and the happy effect of doing so.* From the commencement of this par. to 厥躬, is found in the Le Ke, Bk. 緇衣, p. 16, quoted as from the 兌. (evidently for 說)命. Choo He says that the clauses beginning with 惟 are independent of one another. Lin Che-k'e, on the other hand, finds in the third clause the complement of the first, and in the 4th that of the second. It is not worth our while to enter on this question. The tongue is man's glory, but very easily abused; and then it turns out to his shame. The coat of mail and helmet are weapons of defence, but the confidence of strength often leads to insolence and quarrels. The robes in the imperial stores are intended to reward the good and meritorious; but, if distributed carelessly, they are productive of evil effects. Shield and spear are the weapons with which one goes to punish offenders;—but woe to him who undertakes this duty, while his heart condemns himself! The four things are of great importance and easily offended in; and Yuĕ therefore calls the attention of Woo-ting to them. 起戎,—戎＝兵, 'an offensive weapon.' 衣裳,—see the 'Yih and Tseih,' p. 4. 笥 is defined as 'an article of furniture for holding food or clothes' (飯及衣之器). Its figure was square, We may translate it by 'chest.' 戒茲, 允茲,—the former of these 茲 seems to = 'these,' the things, namely which had been spoken of; the latter = 'this,' and indicates what had been said or implied about the mouth, &c.

5. *How the imitation of Heaven should be seen in conferring offices and dignities.* Ying-tă says: 'The performance of duties is called 官; the receiving of rank is called 爵' (治其事謂之官, 受其位謂之爵). We are not to think, however, here of the different dignities among the feudal princes, but of the ranks among the officers in the imperial domain. 私昵,—昵＝近, or 親近, 'near to,' 'familiar with.' 私昵, are the emperor's 'private intimates,' his favourites. 惡德＝包藏凶惡之人, 'men who cherish all evil in their bosoms.'

六節慮善以動、動惟厥時。○七節有其善、喪厥善、矜其能、喪厥功。○八節惟事事、乃其有備、有備無患。○九節無啟寵納侮、無恥過作非。○十節惟厥攸居、政事惟醇。○十一節黷于祭祀、時謂弗

6 "Anxious thought about what will be good should precede your movements. Your movements also should have respect to the time for them.

7 "The indulged consciousness of goodness is the way to lose that goodness. Boasting of ability is the way to lose the merit it might produce.

8 "For all affairs let there be adequate preparation. With preparation there will be no calamities.

9 "Do not open the door for favourites, from whom you will receive contempt. Do not be ashamed of mistakes, and thus make them crimes.

10 "Let your mind rest in its proper objects, and the affairs of your government will be pure.

11 "Officiousness in sacrifices is called irreverence; ceremonies when

The clause—爵罔及惡德 is found, like most of the last par., in the Le Ke, Bk. 緇衣, quoted in the same way from the 兌命.

6. *How the same should be seen in thoughtful and timely action.* 善 is here defined by 當乎理, 'that which is agreeable to right reason or principle.' 7. *And in repressing all prideful thoughts.* 有其善＝自有其善, 'having his goodness to one's-self,' thinking of it, resting in it.

8. *And in preparation for all undertakings, and against emergencies.* On 事事 Gan-kwŏ says 非一事, 'not in one affair merely,' ＝'in all affairs.' Ts'ae seems to take the first char. as a verb—惟事其事, 乃其有備, 'in doing his affairs there should be preparation.' This par. would seem to have been at one time somewhat different. In the 左傳, 襄, 十一年, we find—書曰, 居安思危, 思則有備, 有備則無患. This quotation, however, may be from some other Book of the Shoo, among those that are lost.

9. *And in avoiding favouritism and persistence in mistakes.* 無(＝毋)啟寵,—'do not open favouritism.' The 'contempt,' it is understood, will be from the favourites themselves, bred to it by the familiarity to which they are admitted. 無心失理謂之過, 有心背理謂之非, 'an unintentional failure to do what is right is called *a mistake;* an intentional violation of what is right is called *a crime.*' In the 左傳, 定元年, we read—啟寵納侮, 其此之謂矣. 10. *And in the keeping of the heart.* 惟厥攸(＝所)居,—居＝止. The clause is quite elliptical, and ＝惟居其所止. Comp. 'The Great Learning,' Comm., ch. 3. 醇＝粹清, 'pure and clear,' ＝unmixed. There will be no evil thoughts and bad objects to disturb the govt. 11. *On the service of spirits.* 黷

欽、禮煩則亂、事神則難。○王曰、旨哉、說乃言惟服、乃不良于言、予罔聞于行。○說拜稽首曰、非知之艱、行之惟艱、王忱不艱、允協于先王成德、惟說不言有厥咎。

burdensome lead to disorder. To serve the spirits *in this way* is difficult."

12 II. The king said, "Excellent! Your words, O Yuĕ, should indeed be carried out in the conduct. If you were not so good in counsel,
13 I should not have heard these things for my practice." Yuĕ did obeisance with his head to the ground, and said, "It is not the knowing that is difficult, but the doing. If your Majesty know this, however, there will not be the difficulty, and you will become really equal in complete virtue to the former king. Wherein I, Yuĕ, do not express myself, the blame rests with me."

于祭祀,—黷, means 'to soil,' 'dirty.' The phrase 褻黷 is used, with reference to spiritual beings, in the sense of 'to defile,' 'to profane.' Wherein the profanity which Yuĕ wanted to guard the emperor against consisted, we cannot say precisely. One meaning of 黷, given in the dict., is 數, 'frequently,' 'forwardly.' Now from the next Bk. we shall see that Woo-ting was prone to be officious in the worship of the spirits of the departed, and we have seen how later times charge the Shang dynasty with being superstitious. Officiousness—sacrificing unnecessarily to certain spirits, and at unnecessary times,—and the attempt to please them by the multitude of observances, would seem therefore to be the things here condemned by Yuĕ. 時一是. The last clause—事神則難 would seem to be co-ordinate with the preceding. All the critics, however, understand it as in the translation. [This par., with some alterations and additions, appears in the Le-ke, Bk. 緇衣, p. 25, referred to already under p. 5. We have:—兌命曰,爵無及惡德,民立而正事,純而祭祀,是爲不敬,事煩則亂,事神則難.]

Ch. II. Pp. 12, 13. THE COMPLACENCY OF WOO-TING AND YUĔ IN EACH OTHER. 12. 旨哉,—旨一美, 'admirable.' Ts'ae says that the ancients, in eating and drinking, when any thing particularly pleased their palate, pronounced it 旨; and Woo-ting thus characterizes Yuĕ's words as if they had a flavour. 乃(一汝)言惟服,—服一行, 'to practise.' 13. 王忱不艱—王忱信之,亦不爲難, 'if your Majesty sincerely believes this,—the difficulty of action,—it likewise will not prove to be a difficulty.' In the conclusion of the first Part, Yuĕ says that the sovereign's giving heed to his advisers would encourage them to do their duty. His concluding words here show how the ready ear the emperor yielded to his lessons was spurring him on.

THE BOOKS OF SHANG.

BOOK VIII. THE CHARGE TO YUE. PART iii.

說命下

一節 王曰、來汝說、台小子舊學于甘盤、既乃遯于荒野、入宅于河、自河徂亳、暨厥終罔顯。

1 I. The king said, "Come, O Yuĕ. I, the little one, first learned with Kan Pwan. Afterwards, I lived concealed in the rude country, and then I went to *the inside of* the Ho, and lived there. From the Ho I went to Pŏ;—and the result has been that I am

CONTENTS OF THE THIRD PART. The emperor tells Yuĕ of his early disadvantages, and begs him now to instruct him, enlightening his ignorance, and supplying his deficiencies. To this Yuĕ replies by enlarging on the subjects most important to be learned, and the spirit of the learner. From the 8th paragraph to the end, the emperor praises Yuĕ for what he had already done for him, and expresses his hope that the minister would prove a second E Yin, and frame of him a second T'ang; to which Yuĕ suitably responds.

Ch. I. Pp. 1—7. WOO-TING DEPLORES THE DISADVANTAGES OF HIS EARLY YEARS, AND BEGS YUE TO INSTRUCT HIM. YUE SPEAKS OF THE SUBJECTS OF LEARNING, AND THE SPIRIT REQUIRED IN THE LEARNER. 1. *The early life of Woo-ting.* 台小子舊學于甘盤,—we saw before that 小子, 'the little child,' was appropriately used by the emperor as a humble designation of himself in relation to God. It came, however, to be employed, as in the text, where we can hardly suppose any reference in the mind to that relation. 舊,—'of old;'—we may render it by 'first.' From this clause we should suppose that Kan Pwan had been a learned master, who imparted to Woo-ting the rudiments of learning. From Part V., Bk. XVI., p. 7, however, we learn that he was a great minister. He is there mentioned, indeed, as *the* minister of Woo-ting's time, while nothing is said of Foo Yuĕ. We may suppose that he acted as prime minister on the death of Seaou-yih, and died himself before the period of mourning was expired. What Woo-ting learned with him would be lessons of govt., and such subjects as are treated in 'The Great Learning.' 既乃遯于荒野,云云,—既 stands absolutely,—'afterwards.' 遯—'to withdraw from public life, and live in obscurity.' Chow-kung says, Pt. V., Bk. XV., p. 5, that 'Kaou-tsung toiled, away from the court, among the inferior people.' What was the reason of his doing so, we do not know. Gan-kwŏ says his father sent him for a time to this mode of life, that he might know the hardships of the common people. It is more likely that he was compelled to it by some dire necessity, arising from convulsions of the State with which we are unacquainted. From the fields of the people Woo-ting 'entered the Ho and dwelt,'—resided, acc. to Gan-kwŏ, 'on some island in the Ho.' It is more probable that we should take 入

○爾惟訓于朕志、若作酒醴、爾惟麴糵、若作和羹、爾惟鹽梅、爾交修予、罔予棄、予惟克邁乃訓。○說曰、王、人求多聞、時惟建事、學于古訓、乃有獲、事不師古、以克永世、匪說攸聞。○惟學

2 unenlightened. Do you teach me what should be my aims. Be to me as the yeast and the malt in making sweet spirits; as the salt and the prunes in making agreeable soup. Give your help to cultivate me; do not cast me away:—I shall attain to practise your instructions."

3 Yuĕ said, "O king, men seek to hear much, having in view to establish their affairs. But to learn the lessons of the ancients is the way to attain this. That the affairs of one, not making the ancients his masters, can be perpetuated for generations, is what I have not heard.

宅于河 as=入居于河內, understanding 河內, 'the inside of the Ho' as a designation of K'e-chow generally. From the north of the Ho he removed again to Pŏ,—the capital as re-established by Pwan-kăng;—and the end was (暨厥終) that he was, or thought himself, little versed in the subjects necessary for him to know as emperor. 2. *He asks Yuĕ to instruct him* 爾惟訓于朕志,—'do you instruct me about my aims.' 若作酒醴,爾惟麴糵,—酒 is commonly translated 'wine,' but incorrectly. The term denotes 'spirits, distilled from rice.' 醴 is the product in its earlier stage, before the process of distillation is commenced, after the mashing and fermentation, when 'the juice and the refuse are mixed together,' what is called 'sweet spirits' (醴成而汁滓相將,如今甜酒). 麴=酒母, 'yeast' 糵=牙米, 'the sprouting rice,' 'malt.' 爾交修予,—this clause and the next are found in the long quotation which I made in the first Part from the 國語. In Pt. V., Bk, XXVI., p. 4, we have 交修不逮, where the 交 refers to the united services of many ministers. Here the char. is used with single reference to Yuĕ in his relation to Woo-ting. 邁=行, 'to practise,' indicating the efforts which he would put forth. 3. *Yuĕ replies—first, that the lessons of the ancients are the most important thing to be learned.* 王人求多聞,—Gan-kwŏ joins 王人 together as=王者, 'royal men,' 'kings.' It is better to take 王 in the vocative. Yuĕ addresses Woo-ting—'O king,' as Yu, in the 'Yih and Tseih,' p. 7, addresses Shun, 'O Emperor.' 時惟建事,—時=是, 'thus.' The 'Daily Explanation' says:—是其意惟欲建立修身治天下之事業耳 古訓,—'ancient lessons,' such as are contained in the Canons of Yaou and Shun, and the Counsels of Yu and Kaou-yaou. Ming-shing calls attention to a passage in Ts'een's history of the founder of the Ts'in dynasty—事不師古而能長久者,非所聞也, from which he thinks the last part of the par. was taken. Much more likely

書經

遜志、務時敏、厥修乃來、允懷于茲、道積于厥躬。○五節惟斅學半、念終始典于學、厥德修罔覺。○六節監于先王成憲、其永無愆。○七節惟說式克欽承、旁招俊乂、列于庶位。○八節王曰、嗚呼、說四海之內、

4 "In learning there should be a humble will, and a striving to
maintain a constant earnestness. In such a case *the learner's*
cultivation will surely come. He who sincerely cherishes these
5 things will find all truth accumulating in his person. To teach
is one half of learning. When a man's thoughts from first to last are
constantly fixed on *such* learning, his virtuous cultivation comes
unperceived.
6 "Survey the perfect pattern of the former king;—so may you
7 for ever be preserved from error. Then shall I be able reverently
to meet your views, and on every side to look out for men of eminence to place in the various offices."
8 II. The king said, "Oh! Yuĕ, within the four seas, all look up

is it to have been adopted by the speaker in the passage referred to from the text. 4. *Second, that success in learning depends on docility and persevering earnestness.* 允懷于茲,—'he who sincerely cherishes these things,'—the humility, namely, and persevering earnestness. 道積于厥躬,—道 denotes all the principles of self-cultivation and of govt. taught and practised by the ancients. In the Le Ke, Bk. 學記, par. 9, we read 兌命曰,敬孫,務時敏,厥修乃來. 5. *Third, that learning is perfected by communicating what has been acquired.* 斅學半,—'teaching is the half of learning.' The words are quoted in the 學記, par. 3, and explained.—'When one learns,' it is said, 'he knows his deficiencies. When he teaches, he knows the difficulties *of learning*. A knowledge of his deficiencies leads him to self-inspection; a knowledge of the difficulties leads him to exert himself' (學然後知不足,教然後知困,知不足,然後能自反也,知困,然後能自强也). 念終始典于學,—典=常, 'constant,' 'constantly.' 學 here must be understood to include both the learning and teaching. The clause is found twice in the Le Ke,—once in the 學記, p. 2, and once in the 文王世子, Pt. ii., p. 23. 6, 7. *Finally, that the emperor should adopt T'ang as his model, and Yuĕ would surround the throne with ministers like himself.* 先王成憲,—先王 here is to be taken as referring to T'ang. 憲=法, 'law,' 'pattern.' 惟說式克,—式=用, 'to use;'—taken adverbially as 用 itself often is,= 'hereby.' The emperor's goodness would be to Yuĕ the greatest impulse to do all that devolved on him. 俊乂,—see 'Counsels of Kaou-yaou,' p. 4.

CH. II. Pp. 8—11. THE EMPEROR PRAISES YUE, AND LOOKS FOR STILL GREATER ADVANTAGES FROM HIM. YUE UNDERTAKES TO RESPOND TO THE EMPEROR'S WISHES. 8. *What Yuĕ had done for the emperor.* Comp. Shun's language to Yu, II., Bk. II., p. 8, ending 時乃功,

咸仰朕德、時乃風。○九節股肱惟人、良臣惟聖。○十節昔先正保衡、作我先王、乃曰、予弗克俾厥后惟堯舜、其心愧恥、若撻于市、一夫不獲、則曰時予之辜、佑我烈祖、格于皇天、爾尚明保予、罔俾阿衡、專美有商。○十一節惟后非賢不乂、惟賢非后不食、其爾克紹乃辟于先王、永綏

9 to my virtue:—all through your influence. As his legs and arms form the man, so does a good minister form the sage *king*.

10 "Formerly there was the premier of our dynasty, Paou-hăng, who made my royal predecessor. He said, 'If I cannot make my sovereign like Yaou or Shun, I shall feel ashamed in my heart, as if I were beaten in the market place.' If any one common man did not find *all he should desire*, he said, 'It is my fault.' Thus he assisted my meritorious ancestor, so that he became equal to Great Heaven. Do you give your preserving aid to me, and not let O-hăng engross all the good service to the House of Shang.

11 The sovereign should share his government with none but worthy ministers. The worthy minister should accept his support only from the proper sovereign. May you now succeed in making your prince a successor of my royal ancestor, and in securing the

風 here = 'influence.' 9. *The same subject.* 10. *The emperor wishes Yuĕ to be to him what E Yin had been to T'ang.* 先正保衡,—正 is here explained by 長, 'chief,' 'president.' As applied to E Yin, it denotes his presidency of all the other ministers,—his being premier. On 保衡, see the note on the 'T'ae-këă,' Pt. i., p. 1. 作我先王,—作 exactly corresponds here to our 'made.' Ch'in King (陳經) says:—學于伊尹,湯之爲聖乃尹與起.而作成之. 予弗克,云云,—comp. Men., V., Pt. I., vii.; Pt. II., i., and other places where he speaks of E Yin. 格于皇天,—'he reached to great Heaven.' This is a wild and blasphemous exaggeration, like many of the assertions about the perfectly sincere man and Confucius in the 'Doctrine of the Mean.' The 'Daily Explanation' paraphrases it:—烈祖德業之成,直與天地同流而無間焉. 11. *Woo-ting and Yuĕ both rest complacently in their adaptation to each other, and auspice great things.* 不乂=不與共治, 'does not share the government with.' 不食—不食其祿, 'does not eat his revenue.' 其

民。說拜稽首曰、敢對揚天子之休命。

lasting happiness of the people!" Yuě did obeisance with his head to the ground, and said, "I will venture to respond to, and display abroad, your Majesty's excellent charge."

爾,—we might invert the order of these characters; 其 has its hortatory force. 對—答, 'to answer,' 'to respond to.'

[Choo He observes:—'The lessons of E Yin to T'ae-këă are different from those of Foo Yuĕ to Kaou-tsung. The words of E Yin are repeated again and again, as the small natural comprehension of T'ae-këă required. This was not necessary with Kaou-tsung. His natural ability was good, and he was not chargeable with many faults.']

THE BOOKS OF SHANG.

BOOK IX. THE DAY OF THE SUPPLEMENTARY SACRIFICE OF KAOU-TSUNG.

高宗肜日

一節 高宗肜日、越有雊雉。○二節 祖己曰、惟先格王、正厥事。○三節 乃訓于王曰、惟天監下民、典厥義、降年有永有不永、非天夭民、民中絕命。

1 I. On the day of the supplementary sacrifice of Kaou-tsung, there
2 appeared a crowing pheasant. Tsoo Ke said, "To rectify this affair, the king must first be corrected."
3 Accordingly he lessoned the king, saying, "In its inspection of men below, Heaven's first consideration is of their righteousness; and it bestows on them *accordingly* length of years or the contrary. Heaven does not cut short men's lives;—they bring them to an end

NAME OF THE BOOK.—高宗肜日, 'The day of the Supplementary Sacrifice of Kaou-tsung.' Kaou-tsung, I have already observed, was the title given to Woo-ting in the ancestral temple. Sze-ma Ts'een says that it was conferred on him by his son and successor Tsoo-kăng, with reference to the circumstances commemorated in this Book,—his being taught to be virtuous by the appearance of a pheasant in the manner described. He says also that it was on occasion of this canonization, so to term it, that this Book, and another which is lost,—the 'Instructions to Kaou-tsung' (高宗之訓)—were composed. That the Book was not composed in the reign of Woo-ting is sufficiently proved by the use of the sacrificial title which was given to him; that that title was conferred on him with reference to the occurrence here related is extremely improbable. 肜日,—肜 (Keang Shing has 融. See the note in the 後案 on the history and form of the character) was the name of a supplementary sacrifice, offered on the day following the regular and more solemn service (祭明日又祭). I have not been able to find any precise account of the reason and manner of such an observance. K'ang-shing says it was common to all sacrifices,—'those to Heaven and Earth, to the spirits of the land and the grain, of the hills and rivers, and of ancestors.' It was continued under the Chow dynasty, and was called 繹. Subsequently, it seems to have fallen into disuse.

The words—高宗肜日 may be translated 'The day of the supplementary sacrifice *to*

Kaou-tsung, and this rendering of them has its advocates, who are foll. by De Mailla in his 'Histoire Generale de la Chine.' This view seems to have prevailed in the Yuen dynasty. The editors of Yung-ching's Shoo say that Kin Le-ts'ëang and Tsow Kwei-yew (鄒季友) both thought that the reproof of Tsoo Ke must have been addressed to a young emperor,—to Tsoo-kăng, and that it is not conceivable as addressed to Woo-ting. They say themselves that the words of the 4th par.—乃日其如台 are not to be thought of as addressed to Woo-ting after his character had developed under the counsels of Foo-yuĕ. They therefore suppose the appearance of the pheasant to have taken place in the first year of Woo-ting, and advert to the 11th par. of the second Part of 'The Charge to Yuĕ,' as showing that there was a superstitious element in his character, which might have then given occasion to the remarks of Tsoo Ke. The Preface to the Shoo must be held as conclusive that the sacrificer was Woo-ting, and not Tsoo-kăng. We there read, note 29, 'Kaou-tsung was sacrificing to T'ang the Successful, when a pheasant flew up, and lighted on the ear of a tripod, and there crowed. Tsoo Ke lessoned the king,' &c. The Book is found both in the 'old text and in the modern.' It is classed among the 'Instructions.' Fuh-shang appended it to the 'Pwan-kăng,' so that it was not a separate Book in the 'modern text.'

Contents. A pheasant suddenly makes its appearance and crows, while Kaou-tsung is engaged in the supplementary sacrifice to T'ang. This is understood to be indicative of something wrong in the service, and Tsoo Ke, a worthy minister, proceeds to lecture the emperor on the subject, whose particular fault is intimated in the last par.

Par. 1. *The appearance of a pheasant.* 高宗肜日,—see the note on the name of the Book. 越有雊雉,—we cannot translate 越. The 'Daily Explanation' calls it 發語辭, 'an introductory, or initial particle.' Ying-tă defines it by 於是, 'on this.'

The 說文 says that '雊 is the cry of the male pheasant.' The preface to the Shoo and Sze-ma ts'een, after it, say that the pheasant lighted on the ear—one of the handles—of a tripod. Such an event would of course be understood to be ominous, and the older writers wearied themselves in endeavours to explain the meaning of it, some supposing it a good omen, and some a bad one. Maou K'e-ling ridicules their varying conjectures;—see the 尙書廣聽錄, *in loc.* The only explanation of it I will mention here is that of Fuh-shang (尙書大傳), which is peculiar to himself, and the more strange because it is inconsistent with the tenor of the Book. He says: —'Woo-ting was sacrificing to T'ang, when a pheasant flew up on the handle of a tripod, and crowed. Woo-ting asked Tsoo-ke what it meant, who replied, "The pheasant is a wild bird, and ought not to mount the tripod. Its doing so now shows that it wants to be employed (今升鼎者,欲爲用也). Shall we not have people from distant regions coming to the court?" On this Woo-ting examined himself, and reflected on the ways of the former kings; and in three years envoys, with twisted hair, who needed an interpreter, came to court from six kingdoms (三年編髮重譯來朝者六國). Confucius said, "I have observed how speedily virtue is rewarded in what is related of Woo-ting and the day of his supplementary sacrifice."'

2. *Remark of Tsoo Ke on the subject.* Tsoo Ke was evidently a worthy minister of Woo-ting; but we know nothing of him more than is here related. I suppose 祖 to be the surname. 惟先格王,—王 is here =正, 'to correct,'—see Men., IV., Pt. I., xx., 惟大人爲能格君心之非. Gan-kwŏ takes it as an adj.,=至, and says—'a sovereign of the highest style of principle, when he meets with extraordinary events, corrects his affairs, and the prodigies of themselves pass away.' The 先 before 格 is sufficiently decisive against this view. 正厥事,='to rectify this affair.' I understand the reference to be to the affair or circumstance, which, in Tsoo Ke's opinion, had occasioned the ominous appearance of the pheasant. This remark was not made to the emperor, but to Tsoo Ke's companions, or perhaps we should understand it simply as the thought in his mind.

3, 4. *Tsoo Ke's attempt to rectify the emperor's mind.* 3. *Men's prosperity does not depend on the arbitrary will of Heaven, but on their own conduct.* 下民,—comp. the 'Announcement of T'ang,' p. 2. There, however, I have translated the phrase—'the inferior people,' the people being spoken of in contradistinction from the sovereign. In the text, people and sovereign are all comprehended, and 'men below' seems to give the meaning. 典=主, 'to put first,' 'to make the principal consideration.' 永=長, 'long.' 夭 means 'to die prematurely' (不盡天年謂之夭. 殀 is more common). It is used here actively,='to cause to die prematurely.' Ts'ae observes that it would appear from this language that Woo-ting had been praying in connection with his sacrifice for length of years. The conclusion is not unnatural;—it is more natural than the view of K'ang-shing that shortness of life is here as a specimen of the calamities which men dread, being the one most readily apprehensible by even stupid persons. All calamities are the consequence of men's unrighteousness, and Tsoo Ke would have Woo-ting understand this, by bringing home to his thoughts the one calamity of premature death. Ying-ta follows Ch'ing in this exposition, which

四節 ○民有不若德、不聽罪、天既孚命正厥德、乃曰其如台。○五節 嗚呼、王司敬民、罔非天胤、典祀無豐于昵。

4 in the midst themselves. Some men may not have complied with virtue, and will not acknowledge their crimes, but when Heaven has evidently charged them to correct their conduct, and they still say, 'What is this to us?'—

5 "Oh! Your Majesty's business is to care reverently for the people. And *all* your *ancestors* were the heirs of *the empire favoured by* Heaven;—attend to the sacrifices to *them*, and be not *so* excessive in those to your father."

seems to me very far-fetched. 4. *When men are deaf to the special warnings of Heaven, their case is desperate.* According to the translation, this paragraph is not complete. It was not easy for Tsoo Ke to speak out plainly and fully what was his meaning. He fancied that the emp. was thinking but little of the omen of the pheasant, and wished to warn him against heedlessly pursuing his own course, regardless of the admonitions of Heaven. The transl. is in acc. with the paraphrase of the 'Daily Explanation,' which I subjoin. It will be seen how the meaning is completed in it.—然天未嘗遽絶之也、斯民之中、有不順乎理、而肆意妄爲、不服其罪、而飾非拒諫者、天未嘗不以妖孽爲信驗、以告戒之、夫天旣譴告、欲其順德而聽罪耳、乃謂妖孽特出偶然、無如我何、則重違上天仁愛之心矣、天豈不誅絶之哉. 不聽罪,—'will not hear of their offences,'='will not acknowledge them, and put them away.' 孚, 'sincerely,'=with evidenced sincerity. There is a reference to the appearance of the pheasant as an evident intimation that there was something wrong, needing to be reproved and corrected. Sze-ma Ts'een gives 附 instead of 孚, and Keang Shing reads 付, which he says was anciently interchanged with 附, in the sense of 與, 'to give.' The meaning which he puts on the par. seems to be this:—'Some men do not comply with virtue, and will not acknowledge their crimes. Heaven then gives them charge to correct their conduct, and they say, "What shall we do?"' This interpretation is not by any means so apt to the occasion as that which I have followed. Gan-kwŏ gives still another view of the clause —乃曰其如台;—see the 註疏, in loc.

5. *How Tsoo Ke tried to correct the special error of Woo-ting.* 司 is taken in the sense of 主, having the same meaning as 典, in par. 3. Ts'ae says:—'Your Majesty's office is to reverence the people; to be looking, on a peradventure, for happiness from spirits is not your business' (王之職主於敬民而已、徼福於神、非王之事也). 胤=嗣; 'to inherit,' 'heirs.' 罔非 supposes a subject in the thoughts, which is most naturally expressed by 祖宗, 'your ancestors.' 典=主; 典祀, 'attend to the sacrifices,' *i.e.*, the sacrifices prescribed to all your ancestors. The 'Daily Explanation' has:—吾王承其後、而主其祭、只當一體孝敬, 'your Majesty, succeeding to them, and presiding over the sacrifices to them, should cherish an equal filial reverence for them all.' 昵 (read *ne*, low 2d tone)=禰,—'the shrine appropriated to a father's spirit-tablet in the ancestral temple.' It would appear from this that Woo-ting's fault was the paying some excessive and superstitious reverence to the spirit of his father. This is the one important meaning of the par., and it will be found that the critics, differing in the view they take of the first clauses—王司敬民、罔非天胤、 yet agree in this.

CONCLUDING NOTE. Woo-ting had a very long reign of 59 years, and died B.C. 1265. It is mentioned of him, in the 63rd diagram of the Yih King, that he 'attacked the demon-land, and subdued it in three years' (高宗伐鬼方,三年克之.) This 'demon-region' seems to have been the country of the wild tribes in the north, who never ceased to press upon the more civilized Chinese, till they made themselves masters of the empire, about 2,500 years after Woo-ting's time. A note in the 綱鑑易知 says that in the Hea dynasty they were called 獯鬻; in the Yin, 鬼方; in the Choo 玁狁; under Ts'in and Han, 匈奴; under the T'ang, 突厥; and under the Sung, 契丹.

The last of the Praise-songs of Shang, in the She King, is understood to celebrate the martial prowess of Woo-ting against the wild tribes of King-tsoo, and Choo He supposes that *they* were the people of the 'demon-regions.' In this case we should have to look for those regions on the south of Pŏ, which is not at all likely. If there was a strong effort by the northern hordes against the Chinese supremacy, we may suppose that the half-subdued tribes within the boundaries of the empire took advantage of the opportunity to rise against the government. The movement, however, whether from within or without, was effectually quelled. Woo-ting subdued rebellion, and made peace within all his borders. He arrested the decline of the Shang dynasty, but he could not turn it back. There is duly chronicled in the 41st year of his reign, B.C. 1282, the birth of Leih (季歷), the father of king Wăn, the founder of the dynasty of Chow.

THE BOOKS OF SHANG.

BOOK X. THE CHIEF OF THE WEST'S CONQUEST OF LE.

西伯戡黎

一節 西伯既戡黎、祖伊恐、奔告于王。○二節 曰、天子、天既訖我殷命、格人元龜、罔敢知吉、非先王不相我後人、惟王

1 The chief of the West having subdued Le, Tsoo E was afraid,
2 and hastened to report it to the king. He said, "Son of Heaven,
Heaven is bringing to an end the destiny of our dynasty of Yin; the wisest of men and the great tortoise equally do not venture to know any thing fortunate for it. It is not that the former kings do not aid us, the men of this after time; but by your dissoluteness

INTRODUCTORY HISTORICAL NOTE. Woo-ting's reign terminated in B.C. 1265, and 'the Conquest of Le by the Chief of the West' took place B.C. 1123. Here, therefore, there is again a gap in the history of the Shang dynasty, so far as it might be collected from the documents of the Shoo. Nor is the gap owing to the insensate measure of the founder of the Ts'in dynasty in burning the ancient Books. In the Shoo as it came from the hand of Confucius, the 'Conquest of Le' immediately followed the 'Instructions to Kaou-tsung.'

The conquest of Le took place in the 31st year of Chow-sin, the last emperor of the House of Shang, who succeeded to the throne B.C. 1153. The time between him and Woo-ting was filled up by the reigns of seven sovereigns.

[i.] Woo-ting was succeeded by his son Tsoo-kăng (祖庚). Nothing is related of him. He appears to have been a weak ruler, and died, after a reign of seven years, B.C. 1258.

[ii.] Tsoo-këă (祖甲) followed his brother Tsoo-kăng. One account says that Woo-ting, knowing Tsoo-këă to be worthier and abler than his brother, had wished to leave the empire to him, but that he himself, not to be charged with supplanting Tsoo-kăng, withdrew and kept himself concealed for some time. In B.C. 1257 the people called him to the throne, which he occupied for 33 years.

The standard chronology chronicles no events of his time in which he bore a part. It is noted that in his 28th year, B.C. 1229, Ke-leih the youngest son of Tan-foo, 'the old duke' of Chow, had a son, Ch'ang (昌), by his wife T'ae-jin (太任), whom Choo He delights to celebrate for her many virtues. Ch'ang is known in history as 'king Wăn,' and his father as 'king Ke.' It would appear that Tan-foo died in the same year, but not till he had seen something remarkable about the infant Ch'ang,

書經

which made him say that he would greatly advance the fortunes of their House. In consequence of this, his two eldest sons, T'ae-pih (太伯; see Con. Ana., VIII., i.,) and Chung-yung, (仲雍; *alias*, 虞仲) both declined the dukedom of Chow in favour of Ke-leih, the first year of whose rule, as duke of Chow, dates in B.C. 1228.

Sze-ma Ts'een says that Tsoo-këă was lewd and disorderly (淫亂), and reigned only 16 years.

[iii.] Lin-sin (廩辛) succeeded to his father Tsoo-këă, B.C. 1224, and died after a short reign of six years. That is all history records of him.

[iv.] Lin-sin was followed by his brother Kăng-ting (庚丁), who occupied the throne 21 years.

[v.] Woo-yih (武乙), the son of Kăng-ting, commenced his brief reign of 4 years in B.C. 1197. On this 1st year, or in the year after, he removed the capital from Pŏ once more to the north of the Ho, somewhere in the dep. of Wei-hwuy, Ho-nan. He may have done this to be nearer the eastern part of the empire, which was disturbed in his time by risings of the wild tribes between the Hwae and mount T'ae.

Woo-yih occupies an unenviable place in the annals of China, many attributing to him the first making of idols in China;—see Morrison's 'View of China for Philological purposes,' and De Mailla's History, Vol. I., p. 217. The action on which the charge is based, however, was more that of a madman than of a devotee, a freak of licentious folly, and not the birth of any religious feeling, however perverted. Sze-ma Ts'een simply tells us:—武乙無道,爲偶人,謂之天神,與之博,令人爲行,天神不勝,乃僇辱之,爲革囊盛血,仰而射之,命日射天, 'Woo-yih was without any right principle. He made the image of a man, and called it "the Spirit of Heaven." Then he gamed with it' (博='played dice, or at chess),' causing some one to play for the image. "The spirit of Heaven" was unsuccessful, on which he disgraced it, and made a leather bag which he filled with blood, and then placed aloft and shot at' (the image probably was in the bag as well), 'calling this "shooting at Heaven."' This is all the account we have in the 'Historical Records.' De Mailla, I imagine, *is making for himself* the narrative which he gives, that the emperor 'required all the people to adore the image, and address their vows to it.'

In the 4th year of his reign, while hunting between the Ho and the Wei, Woo-yih suddenly died. Ts'een says that he was struck dead by lightning; and people recognize in that event the just and appropriate vengeance of Heaven which he had insulted.

[vi.] Woo-yih was succeeded by his son T'ae-ting, whose brief reign of three years ended B.C. 1191.

[vii.] Te-yih (帝乙), the son of T'ae-ting, succeeded to his father, and reigned for 37 years, dying in B.C. 1154. During his time the House of Chow greatly increased in power and grew in favour with the people throughout the empire. In the previous reign duke Ke had signalized himself by repelling the incursions of certain wild hordes in the north. Having performed several similar exploits in the first year of Te-yih, the emperor gave him the title, first of 'Master of the Pastors' (命爲牧師), and subsequently invested him with the dignity of 'Chief of all the princes' (侯伯).

In B.C. 1184, duke Ke-leih died, and was succeeded by his son Ch'ang, who thenceforth appears in history under the style of the 'Chief of the West' (西伯). The benevolence which he displayed in the govt. of his own principality made the people everywhere long to be under his rule, and the men of greatest virtue and ability began to collect around him. In B.C. 1168, according to the generally acknowledged chronology, his son Fă (發), afterwards King Woo, the first emperor of the Chow dynasty, was born.

Chow-sin (紂辛) succeeded to the empire, B.C. 1153. He had two brothers older than himself,—K'e, known as the viscount of Wei (微子啟), and Chung-yen (仲衍); but when they were born, their mother had only a secondary place in the harem. Before the birth of Chow-sin, however, she was raised to the dignity of empress, and she and Te-yih were persuaded, against their better judgment, to name him on that account successor to the throne, in preference to K'e. He appears in history with all the attributes of a tyrant. His natural abilities were more than ordinary; his sight and hearing were astonishingly acute; his strength made him a match for the strongest animals; he could make the worse appear to be the better reason, when his ministers attempted to remonstrate with him; he was intemperate, extravagant, and would sacrifice everything to the gratification of his passions. He was the first, we are told, to use ivory chopsticks, which made the viscount of Ke (箕子) sorrowfully remonstrate with him. 'Ivory chopsticks,' said he, 'will be followed by cups of gem; and then you will be wanting to eat bears' paws and leopards' wombs, and proceed to other extravagancies. Your indulgence of your desires may cost you the empire.' Such admonitions were of no use.

In B.C. 1146 in an expedition against the prince of Soo (有蘇氏), he received from him a lady of extraordinary beauty, called Tă-ke (妲已), of whom he became the thrall. It is the story of Këĕ and Me-he over again. Tă-ke was shamelessly lustful and cruel. The most licentious songs were composed for her amusement, and the vilest dances exhibited. The court was at a place in the pres. dis. of K'e (淇縣), dep. of Wei-hwuy, and there a palace was erected for her, with a famous terrace or tower, two *le* wide, and the park around stocked with the rarest animals. This expenditure necessitated heavy exactions, which moved the resentment of the people. At Sha-k'ew (沙丘), in the pres. dis. of P'ing-heang (平鄉), in Chih-le, there was still greater extravagance and dissipation. There was a pond of wine; the trees were hung with flesh; men and women chased each other about, quite naked. In the palace there were nine market-stances, where they drank all night. The princes began to rebel, when Tă-ke said that the majesty of the throne was not sufficiently maintained;—that punishments were too light, and executions too rare. She therefore devised two new instruments of torture. One of them was called 'The Heater,' and consisted of a piece of metal, made hot in a fire, which people were obliged to take up in their hands. The other was a copper pillar, greased all over, and laid above a pit of live charcoal. The culprit had to walk across the pillar, and when his feet slipped, and he fell down into the fire, Tă-ke was greatly delighted. This was called the punishment of 'Roasting' (炮烙之刑). These enormities made the whole empire groan and fume with indignation.

Chow appointed the Chief of the West, the prince of K'ew (九侯), and the prince of Gŏ (鄂侯), his three principal ministers (三公). The two last met a sad fate. The prince of K'ew added his own daughter to the harem, and when she would not enter into its debaucheries, Chow put her to death, and made minced meat of her father. The prince of Gŏ ventured to remonstrate, and was sliced to pieces for his pains. Ch'ang fell at the same time under suspicion and was put in prison (囚于羑里), in a place called Yew-le.

These events are referred to B.C. 1143. Ch'ang, it is said, occupied himself, in prison, with the study of Fuh-he's diagrams, and composed a considerable portion of the present Yih King. In 1141, his sons and subjects propitiated the tyrant with immense gifts; the exigencies of the empire were likewise very pressing, in consequence of risings and incursions of the wild tribes; Ch'ang was released, and invested with greater authority than before. If he had raised the flag of rebellion, he could easily have dethroned the emperor, but he preserved his allegiance, obtained the abolition of the punishment of Roasting, and drew the hearts and thoughts of princes and people more and more to himself and his House. History tells us of his exploits, virtually regent of the empire, till his death in B.C. 1134, when he was succeeded by his son Fă, who inherited his authority and his virtues. Ten years pass on, of the events of which nothing important is related, and we come to B.C. 1123, to which the conquest of Le is referred.

NAME OF THE BOOK.—西伯戡黎, 'The Chief of the West's conquest of Le.' In the details of the preceding note I have followed the account of the closing years of the Shang dynasty, which is now generally received, and acc. to which the chronology in the 歷代統紀表 is arranged; and the Chief of the West who subdued Le is said to have been Fă, the subsequent king Woo. Ts'ae, on the contrary, ascribes the conquest to Ch'ang or king Wăn, agreeing with Fuh-shang, Sze-ma Ts'een, Ch'ing, and all the older critics. The question is discussed at length in the 通鑑綱目, under the 31st year of Chow-sin. It hardly appears to me capable of a clear determination. Choo He was appealed to about it by one of his disciples who said, 'Most of the old interpreters thought that the Chief of the West here was king Wăn; but Ch'in Shaou-nan (陳少南), Leu Pih-kung (呂伯恭), and Sëë Ke-lung (薛季隆), have given their opinion that it was king Woo. Woo Ts'ae-laou (吳才老), also says that the conquest of Le must have closely preceded the attack on Chow himself.' The questioner then proceeded to indicate his own conclusion in favour of the more recent opinion, and asked for the master's decision. Choo He wisely replied, 'We may as well put on one side such questions where the evidence is so scanty' (此等無證據可且闕之).

By the 'West' in the designation 'Chief of the West,' we are to understand the province of Yung on the north, with those of Leang and King on the south,—the western part of the empire in fact.

Sze-ma Ts'een has Ke (飢), for Le, and Fuh-shang had K'e (耆). It is agreed, however, that the country designated extended over what are now the two districts of Le-shing (黎城) and P'ing-shun (平順), dep. of Loo-ngan (潞安) in Shan-se. This was only about 100 miles from Chow's capital, and within the boundaries of the imperial domain. The Chief of the West was no longer confining himself to the west. It was this approach of the army of Chow to the neighbourhood of the emperor which filled with alarm all who continued to cherish any attachment to the House of Shang. What provocation the duke of Chow may have had to attack Le, or by what motives he was actuated, we cannot tell; but it now became plain to all, that however loyally inclined he might be, there was a tide of affairs carrying Chow on to the supremacy of the empire. This is the meaning of the expression in the Preface, that 'Yin's first hatred of Chow was occasioned by the conquest of Le.' The Book is found in both the texts.

It is referred, not very satisfactorily, to the class of 'Announcements.'

CONTENTS. The Chief of the West having overthrown the prince of Le, Tsoo E filled with alarm hurries away to inform the emperor. He sternly sets the truth before him,—that the rule of Yin is hastening to a close through his own evil conduct. The tyrant gives no heed to his

淫戲用自絕。
（三節）○故天棄我、
不有康食、不
虞天性、不迪
率典。○（四節）今我
民罔弗欲喪、
曰、天曷不降
威、大命不摯、
今王其如台。
（五節）○王曰、嗚呼、

3 and sport, O king, you are bringing on the end yourself. On this
account Heaven has cast us off, so that there is distress for want of
food; there is no consideration of our heavenly nature; there is no
4 obedience to the statutes *of the empire*. *Yea*, our people now all
wish *the dynasty* to perish, saying, 'Why does not Heaven send down
its indignation? why does not *some one with* its great decree make
his appearance? what has the present king to do with us?'"
5 The king said, "Oh! is not my life secured by the decree of

remonstrances, but returns an absurd reply; on which Tsoo E withdraws, and sighs over the ruin which he sees cannot now be averted.

P. 1, *Introductory paragraph. The occasion of Tsoo E's address.* 西伯戡黎,—see on the Name of the Book. The 爾雅 defines 戡 by 殺, 'to till;' but the meaning of 勝 or 克, 'to overcome,' 'to subdue,' is to be accepted here. Tsoo E was probably a descendant of Tsoo Ke, the worthy minister of Woo-ting. He hurried away, *i.e.*, from his own city, probably between Le and the capital, to give information to Chow.

Pp. 2—5. *Tsoo E's address.* 2. *That the dynasty of Yin was about to be extinguished,—entirely through the wickedness of Chow.* 天既訖我殷命,—訖=絕, 'to extinguish,' 'to bring to an end.' 我殷命=殷之王命, 'Yin's appointment to the sovereignty' (Gan-kwŏ). 格人元龜,—格=至, 'perfect,' 'of the highest class;' 元=大, 'great.' The tortoise employed for divination at the imperial court was so called by way of eminence, and supposed to measure, length-ways and across, a cubit and two inches. Sze-ma Ts'een has 假人 for 格人, and Keang Shing edits 假爾, reading 假 in the up. 2d tone, = 'to avail of.' He compares the text with the language of the Le Ke, 曲禮, Bk. I., Pt v., p. 24, 假爾泰龜; but the interpretation is intolerably forced and harsh. 惟王淫戲自絕,—Sze-ma Ts'een has 虐, 'oppression,' instead of 戲 'sport.' The meanings are both appropriate. The paraphrasts supply 于天 after 絕,—'you cut yourself off from Heaven.' This does not seem to be necessary. 3. *Evidences of Heaven's abandonment in the miserable and demoralized condition of the people.* 不有康食,—'we have no eating in comfort.' Famine was stalking abroad. 不虞天性,—虞=度, 'to consider,' 'to act upon consideration of.' Demoralization followed upon want. 不迪率典,—典=國家之常典, 'the regular statutes of the empire.'—'We do not tread in and follow the statutes.' Social disorder followed hard on demoralization. Such is the interpretation of this paragraph, and it is the most likely which I have seen. See others in the 註疏, in Keang Shing, and in the 後案. 4. *How the people were openly declaring their longing for the end of the dynasty.* 罔弗欲喪=無不欲王之喪, or 殷之喪, 'the ruin of your Majesty,' or 'the ruin of the dynasty.' 大命不摯,—摯=至, 'to come.' The 'great decree' is the appointment of Heaven to the sovereignty of the empire. Sze-ma Ts'een has—大命胡不至.

P. 5. *The defiant reply of Chow.* 我生,—Chow intends, not only his 'life,' but his 'position' also. The 'Daily Explanation' paraphrases:—爾雖云民心背畔,

我生不有命在天。○ 六節 祖伊反、曰、嗚呼、乃罪多參在上、乃能責命于天。○ 七節 殷之卽喪、指乃功、不無戮于爾邦。

6 Heaven?" Tsoo E returned, and said, "Ah! your crimes which
are many are set above;—and can you speak of your fate as if you
7 give it in charge to Heaven? Yin will very shortly perish. As
to all your deeds, can they but bring ruin on your country?"

將欲亡我·然我尊爲天子,實天生我以主萬民,獨不有命在天乎,小民亦無如我何矣· 6, 7. *Tsoo E's withdrawal and soliloquy on Chow's reply.* 6. 反=還, 'to return.' He left the court, and returned to the place whence he had hurried to bring the news of the conquest of Le. Gan-kwŏ, however, makes the meaning to be—'returned for answer.' 乃(=汝)罪多參在上,—參 is a rank or cluster of 'three, orderly arranged;' hence it has here the meaning of 列, 'arranged in order.' 能責命于天,—'can you charge your fate to Heaven? *i.e.*, can you speak as if you were safe through the decree of Heaven in favour of your House? Only the good-doer can look to Heaven with hope. 7. I have translated here after the 'Daily Explanation' supposing 殷之卽喪 to be a sentence complete, = 殷之喪亡,直在旦夕,不能久延矣. The interpretations of the paragraph, however, are very various. I will only give that of Keang Shing, which = 'When Yin soon comes to ruin, shall not the destroyer declare your deeds, and put you to death in your kingdom?'

[It is remarkable that Tsoo E does not say a word about the growing power of the House of Chow,—makes not a single reference to the Chief of the West. Ts'ae supposes that he knew the loyal feeling of Ch'ing and Fā,—that neither of them was prompted by an ambition to gain the empire, and that even now, if the emperor could only be got to reform, the regent would sustain the dynasty of Shang. We can only note the singularity of the fact;—our hypotheses to account for it may be right or wrong.]

書經

THE BOOKS OF SHANG.

BOOK XI. THE VISCOUNT OF WEI.

微子

微子若曰、父師少師、殷其弗或亂正四方、我祖厎遂陳于上、我用沈酗于酒、用亂敗厥德于下。〇殷罔不

1 I. The viscount of Wei spoke to the following effect:—"Grand Tutor and Junior Tutor, *the House of* Yin, we may conclude, can no longer exercise rule over the four quarters of the empire. The great deeds of our founder were displayed in former ages, but by our being lost and maddened with wine, we have destroyed *the effects*

HISTORICAL NOTE. The conversation recorded in this Book is referred in the chronology to B.C. 1122, the year immediately following the conquest of Le, and that in which the dynasty of Shang perished. The chron. does not make mention, indeed, of this document; but it places in the above year the events mentioned in the 18th Bk. of the Con. Ana., Ch. i,—how the viscount of Wei withdrew from Chow-sin's court, and the viscount of Ke became a slave, while Pe-kan was put to death; and those events are supposed to have followed almost immediately after the conference between the worthies which is here related. Difficulties might be raised against this view; but it is not worth while arguing a point of little importance, and where absolute certainty cannot be attained. The conversation between the viscount of Wei and his friends must have taken place near the time assigned to it,—in one of the closing years of the Shang dynasty.

NAME OF THE BOOK.—微子, 'The Viscount of Wei.' This name seems to have been given after the fashion of the Books of the Confucian Analects. The characters begin the Book and are therefore adopted as its name. The Preface speaks of the viscount of Wei making his *announcement* to the Tutors, and the Book is accordingly placed in the division of 'Announcements.' Like that of the last Book, this arrangement is convenient rather than satisfactory.

Wei (微) was the name of a principality of the 4th order (Men. V., Pt., ii. 3), the holder of which had the title of 子, which some have translated by 'viscount,' others by 'count,' and others again by 'marquis.' It was within the limits of the imperial domain, in the pres. dis. of Loo-shing (潞城), dep. of Loo-gan (潞

安), Shan-se. It has been stated in the introductory note to the last Book, that the viscount of Wei was named K'e (啟), and that he was an elder brother of the emperor, by the same mother, who was, however, only a concubine when K'e was born, and subsequently raised to be empress before the birth of Sin. Such is the account of Sze-ma Ts'een, and other old writers. The authority of Mencius is pleaded in favour of the view that K'e was an uncle of the emperor;—see Men. VI., Pt. I., vi., 3. But Mencius does not allege this himself;—it only appears as an opinion current in his time. As K'e is in this Book addressed as 王子, 'son of the king,' and still more is called 殷王元子, 'the eldest son of the king of Yin,' in the 8th Book of the next Part, par. 1, the account in the 'Historical Records' ought not to be called in question. The Book is found in both the texts.

CONTENTS. Saddened with the thought of the impending ruin of their dynasty, the viscount of Wei seeks the counsel of two other high nobles, and after pourtraying in lively colours the mad dissoluteness of the emperor, and the demoralization of the people, asks them to tell him what was to be done. One of them,—the Grand Tutor—replies to him, describes in still stronger language the sad condition of the empire, and the unavoidable overthrow of the dynasty, and concludes by advising the viscount to make his escape, declaring that he himself would remain at his post and share in the unavoidable ruin. We may make a separate chapter of the language of each of them.

CH. I. Pp. 1—3. THE ADDRESS OF THE VISCOUNT OF WEI TO THE GREAT TUTOR AND THE JUNIOR TUTOR. 1. *How Yin, through the drunkenness of Chow, could no longer sway the empire.* 微子若曰,—compare what is said on 若曰 in the Pwan-kăng, Pt. i., p. 6. 父師, 少師,—父 is here = 太, 'great,' 'grand.' Under the Chow dyn., we find from the next Part, Bk. XXV., there were the 'three *Kung*' (三公) one of whom was styled 太師, and the 'three *Koo*' (三孤), one of whom was the 少師 the highest officers of the empire, and who seem to have formed a sort of privy council to the sovereign. There were inferior officers of the same titles, mentioned by Fuh-shang (大傳),—retired magistrates and scholars who afterwards exercised something like the duties of schoolmasters in the villages, and were called 父師 and 少師. There were also the grand and the assistant music-masters, who were styled 太師 and 少師;—see the Ana., XVIII., ix. The terms in the text must be understood as having the first of these three applications,—as designations of the highest officers about Chow's government. We do not know that there were, in the Shang dyn., the three *Kung* and three *Koo*, as subsequently in the Chow, but the 'grand Tutor' and 'junior Tutor' were of the class of those dignitaries. The individuals thus designated are said to have been 'the viscount of Ke' and 'Pe-kan,' who are both classed with the viscount of Wei in the Analects, XXIII., 1.; all the other commentators say so; and though Sze-ma Ts'een has some expressions both in the 殷本記, and in the 宋微子世家, which seem inconsistent with it, it is hardly worth while to discuss the subject. 殷其弗或亂正四方,—亂 = 治, 'to rule.;' 亂正四方,—comp. 治正于四方, 'Charge to Yue,' Pt. i., p. 2. Woo Ch'ing says that '其 and 或 are both expressions expressive of uncertainty' (皆非必然之辭). This is true of 或, but not true of 其, though it belongs to the peculiar usage of it, which has been more than once pointed out, to *insinuate* the meaning of the speaker. 我祖底遂陳于上,—T'ang is intended by 'our ancestor.' Ts'een gives 敗湯德 instead of 敗厥德 immediately below. We must take 遂 in the sense of 成, 'to accomplish,' and then 底遂 is equivalent to what we call a verbal noun,—'his carrying to the utmost his achieving,' = 'his great deeds.' 陳 = 列, 'to arrange.' 上, and 下 in the end of the par., are used with reference to time. 我用沈酗于酒,—Sze-ma Ts'een has 紂 instead of 我. Chow is no doubt intended, but K'e delicately takes the blame of his vices to all the descendants of T'ang;—compare the use of the pronoun in the 'Songs of the five Sons.' Ts'een also omits the 用, which adds emphasis to the verbs 沈 and 酗. The dict. defines 酗 by 醉怒, 'the anger or fury of drunkenness.' Luk Tih-ming (陸德明) explained the char. by 以酒爲凶, 'the practice of malignant wickedness under the

小大、好草竊姦宄、卿士師師非度、凡有辜罪、乃罔恆獲、小民方興、相爲敵讎、今殷其淪喪、若涉大水、其無津涯、殷遂喪越至于今。c ○

2 *of* his virtue in these after times. The people of Yin, small and great, are given to highway robberies, villainies and treachery. The nobles and officers imitate one another in violating the laws; and for criminals there is no certainty that they will be apprehended. The lesser people *consequently* rise up, and make violent outrages on one another. The dynasty of Yin is now sinking in ruin;—its condition is like that of one crossing a large stream, who can find neither ford nor bank. That Yin should be hurrying to ruin at the present pace!"—

influence of spirits.' 2. *How the people, high and low, were demoralized and lawless, so that there was no hope for the dynasty.* 草竊,—Gan-kwŏ explains this by 草野盜竊, 'steal and rob in the grassy wilds,' making one think of the notoriety in former days of Hounslow heath in England as a place for robberies. Keang Shing takes 草 in the sense of 莠, 'hurtful weeds,' so that it is used adverbially and metaphorically. I prefer the old explanation. 師師非度,—師師＝互相做效, 'imitate one another.' 凡有辜罪,乃罔恆獲,—辜＝罪. The two characters here form a complex term ＝ 'crime,' or 'criminals.' Woo Ch'ing supposes that this clause follows from the prec. He says:—'The nobles and officers are the model of the people, but instead of using the regular laws to apprehend criminals, they forbear with and allow them (卿士爲民師表,凡有辜罪之人,反容縱之,無常法捕獲者). This is the most natural exegesis, and I have followed it. The old interpreters took the passage diff'tly. Gan-kwŏ interprets:—'They are all' (taking 凡＝皆, and referring it to 卿士) 'criminals, and there is not one who can regularly hold fast the due Mean' (皆有辜罪,無秉常得中者). Still more absurd is the view given by K'ang-shing:—'All the ministers are thus criminals, and as to their dignities and emoluments, they do not always get them. The meaning is that the ministers attacked and plundered one another' (羣臣皆有是罪,其爵祿又無常得之者,言屢相攻奪). 相爲敵讎＝相敵相讎, 'fight with one another, revenge themselves on one another.' 今殷其淪喪,—Sze-ma Ts'een has 典喪 instead of 淪喪, so that the meaning is —'The statutes of Yin, every bond of order and govt., are now gone to ruin, and the dyn. is in a condition like that,' &c. This would give a good enough meaning, but we cannot, because we find 典 in Ts'een, conclude that the 淪 in the text is erroneous. One crossing a great stream where there was neither ford nor bank could only sink in the waters. 殷遂喪,越至于今,—越, like the same char. in Bk. IX., p. 1, can hardly be translated. Ma Yung and Gan-kwŏ both try to bring out its meaning as＝於是;—but unsuccessfully. See the 後案, and the 註疏. I consider the clause to be incomplete. The 'Daily Explanation' paraphrases it:—豈意我殷之盛,一旦喪亡相及,至于如此之甚乎, 'How could it have been supposed that on our Yin, once so flourishing, ruin would have suddenly come upon ruin, to such a degree as at the present time?'

三節曰、父師少師、我其發出狂、吾家耄遜于荒、今爾無指、告予顛隮、若之何其。○四節父師若曰、王子、天毒降災荒殷邦、方興沈酗于酒。○五節乃罔畏畏咈其耉長舊有位

3 He added, "Grand Tutor and Junior Tutor, we are manifesting insanity. The venerable of our families have withdrawn to the wilds; and now you indicate nothing, but tell me of the impending ruin;—what is to be done?"

4 II. The Grand Tutor made about the following reply:—"King's son, Heaven in anger is sending down calamities, and wasting the country of Yin. Thence has come about that lost and maddened

5 condition through wine. He has no reverence for things which he ought to reverence, but does despite to the aged elders, the old

P. 3. *K'e represents their sad condition still more vividly, and begs his friends to give him counsel.* 我其發出狂,—Chow is intended here by 我, as in par. 1. 耄,—'a person 90 years old is called 耄;—see Pt., Bk. II., p. 9. 顛隮,—Ying-tă defines and distinguishes these terms, saying that 顛 means 'to fall from a height,' and 隮 'to fall into a ditch.' Nothing can be made of the 其 at the end. we must be content to take it as a mere expletive.' These notes and the translation are all after Ts'ae Ch'in. Gan-kwŏ interprets differently;—thus:—'When I think of this ruin of Yin, I feel as if unwell and become maddened. In my family, my heart is wearied and confused, and I wish to withdraw to the wilds. Now you do not inform me of your views, but tell me of the downfal of the country, and ask what is to be done.' Sza-ma Ts'een's text is a good deal difft.—曰, 太師少師, 我其發出往, 吾家保于喪, 今女無故告, 予顛躋如之何其, 'I will arise and go forth away. My family will be preserved in the ruin. Now you tell me nothing (?). I may fall *into a wrong course*;—what should I do?' Keang Shing's text nearly agrees with Ts'een's, but not quite. I believe the received text is the most correct, and that Ts'ae's interpretation is to be preferred to all the others.

Ch. II. Pp. 4—9. Reply of the Grand Tutor. 4. *He enlarges on what K'e had said about Chow's drunkenness.* 王子,—see the note on the Name of the Book. 毒降,—'is poisonously sending down.' It is difficult to know how to interpret 方興, and connect it with what precedes. We want a nominative expressed to 興, as in par. 2;—to suppose one in 邦, as Gan-kwŏ does is too violent. The meaning given by him, as expanded by Ying-tă, is:—Heaven, sending down cruel and poisonous calamities, gave birth to this insensate and oppressive sovereign, to waste and confound the kingdom of Yin. Chow having proved a drunkard, the people throughout the four quarters are all acted on by him, and addicted to the same vice, so that nothing can be done.' It would appear that the Grand Tutor attributes the ruin of the dynasty to Heaven, and that not in permission or retribution merely. 'He puts it upon Heaven,' says Ts'ae, 'his loyalty and reverence for the emperor not permitting him to put it on him!' If the crimes through which the dynasty was going to ruin were produced by Heaven, that ruin certainly could not be arrested. Ts'een omits altogether the second part of the par., and gives the first—太師曰, 王子, 天篤下災, 亡殷國. 5. *He illustrates what K'e had said on the madness of Chow, and the withdrawal of the old and experienced.* 罔畏畏—不畏其所當畏, as in the

書經

人。○今殷民乃攘竊神祇之犧牷牲、用以容、將食無災。○降監殷民、用乂讎斂、召敵讎不怠、罪合于一、多瘠罔詔。○商今其有災、我

6 official fathers. Now the people of Yin will even steal away the
pure and perfect victims devoted to the spirits of heaven and earth;
and their conduct is connived at, and though they proceed to eat
7 the victims, they suffer no punishment. *On the other hand*, when I
look down and survey the people of Yin, the methods of government
to them are hateful exactions, which call forth outrages and hatred;
—and this without ceasing. Such crime equally belongs to all
in authority, and multitudes are starving with none to whom to
8 appeal. Now is the time of Shang's calamity;—I will arise and
share in its ruin. When ruin overtakes Shang, I will not be the

translation. Comp. Con. Ana., XVI., viii. 耇長=老成之人, 'old, accomplished men.' 耇 denotes 'the appearance of a frosted pear.' Such-like are the faces of old men, and hence the char. is used for 'old.' 6. *He intensifies what had been said of the robberies and villainies of the people of Yin.* The people were guilty not of ordinary robberies only;—they committed sacrilege, and were allowed to do so with impunity. 攘 is 'to steal upon occasion offered,' to appropriate, for instance, a neighbour's sheep trespassing on one's ground; but we cannot here insist on that peculiar meaning of the term. 牲='victim,'—ox, sheep, or pig. 犧 is the victim 'uniform in colour.' 牷 is the same, 'complete,' without blemish. 用以容,—Ts'ae supposes that this clause speaks of 'the officers.'—有司用相容隱. Keang Shing makes Chow himself to be the subject of it. Gan-kwŏ ingeniously joins the 用 to the clause above, and explains it as meaning 'the offerings of fruit and grain.' Maou K'e-ling says that in his earlier years he could not away with this interpretation, but was inclined to adopt it on maturer thought;—see the 尙書廣聽錄, Bk. II., *in loc.* 7. *He describes the outrages and misery of the people in consequence of the oppressions of those in authority.* 降=下, 'down,' 'descending.' 用乂讎斂=凡上所用以治之者,無非讎斂之事, 'all the methods used by their superiors to govern them are only exactions of enemies.' Ma Yung read 稠 for 讎; but the meaning is substantially the same. 召敵讎,—'which call forth outrages and hatred.' This is understood to have reference to 相爲敵讎 in paragraph 2. It would seem to be so; and we may understand the outrages there spoken of as further described here as done in defiant despite to the government. 罪合于一,—'the crimes' are those of the emperor and of the officers generally. 罔詔,—詔=告, 'to tell,' 'to appeal to;'—comp. the use of 告 in the phrase 無告者, Mencius, I., Pt. II., v., 3. 8. *The Grand Tutor declares his own intention to abide all risks at his post, but he advises K'e to withdraw and save himself.* 商今......臣僕,—the reader who has Lin Che-k'e's commentary will be amused by reading his view of this passage. I do not introduce it here, because, though ingenious, it does not show Lin's usual soundness of judgment. 詔王子出迪,—the 'Daily Explanation' paraphrases this:—我告王子,惟出而遠去,乃合于道, 'I tell you, O king's son, that to quit and go far away is the right course for you.' 我舊云刻子=我前

興受其敗、商其淪喪、我罔爲臣僕、詔王子出迪、我舊云刻子、王子弗出、我乃顛隮。○九節 自靖、人自獻于先王、我不顧行遯。

servant *of another dynasty*. *But* I tell you, O king's son, to go away as being the course *for you*. Formerly I injured you by what I said, but if you do not go forth now, our *sacrifices* will entirely perish.
9 Let us rest quietly *in our several parts*, and present ourselves to the former kings. I do not think of making my escape.

日所言,適以害子, 'what I formerly said served to injure you.' It has been mentioned that Te-yih and his empress wished to leave the throne to K'e, and not to Chow-sin, but were dissuaded from the purpose. It is supposed that the text refers to the advocacy at that time by the Grand Tutor of K'e's claims to the throne, which had made him all along an object of jealousy and dislike to Chow. Gan-kwŏ takes 刻 as = 病, 'to be distressed for;'—see the 註疏 *in loc.* Keang Shing, always ready to reject the received text, adopts from Wang Ch'ung (王充) the reading of 孩子; but the meaning which he ingeniously brings out of 舊云孩子 comes in effect to the same thing as that usually followed. 我乃顛隮,—it must be understood that the Grand Tutor speaks here of the sacrifices offered to the founder and all the departed emperors of the House of Shang. He must himself have belonged to the imperial line. If, as is most likely, he was the viscount of Ke, he was an uncle of the emperor;—so the relationship between them is commonly represented. Ts'ae expands the text:—我商家宗祀始隕墜而無所托矣. 9. *They must, each of them, do what they felt to be right.* 自靖,—靖=安, as in Bk. VII., Pt. i., p. 12. Ts'ae says:—各安其義之所當盡, 'let each man rest in the performance of what his circumstances require him to do.' Gan-kwŏ, and here for a wonder Këang Shing is at one with him, takes 靖 in this pass., and in the Pwan-kăng, as = 謀, so that 自靖 = 'take counsel with yourself.' It is difficult to say what is the precise idea in 'presenting themselves to the former kings.' I think it is this,—that if they did what was right, they should have consciences void of offence, as now beheld by their ancestors, or as hereafter to appear before them. 顧 is used as in the T'ae-këä, Pt. i., p. 1, 顧諟天之明命.

[FATES OF THE MEN MENTIONED IN THIS BOOK. The viscount of Wei appears to have acted on the advice given by the Grand Tutor, and to have withdrawn from the court of Yin. The expression in the Ana., XVIII., i.,—微子去之, may be considered as proving this. When and how he withdrew, however, it is not possible to ascertain. According to a description in the 左傳,僖六年, and the account given by Sze-ma Ts'een, after the death of Chow, he went out to meet king Woo at the head of his army, having with him the sacrificial vessel of the House of Shang. He presented himself in miserable plight, almost naked, with his hands bound behind him, and moving forward on his knees, when king Woo received him honourably, and restored him to his former office, whatever that was. This legend has been called in question. In the next Part of the Shoo we shall meet with the viscount again, and see him finally enfeoffed with the principality of Sung, there to continue the representative of the House of Shang.

If the viscount of Ke, whose name was Seu-yu (胥餘), was indeed the Grand Tutor of the text, he did not die with the dynasty, as he seems to have expected. The passage of the Analects referred to says 'he became a slave.' According to Ts'een, he reproved Chow in the first place, and when his friends urged him to make his escape, he refused, and feigned himself to be mad, allowed his hair to hang about uncared for. King Woo found him in prison, and set him free, when he fled away to Corea. We shall meet with him also again in the next Part.

The Junior Tutor is supposed to have been Pe-kan, also a member of the imperial House, though his precise relationship to Chow is uncertain. Mencius calls him 王子, 'king's son' (Book. II., Pt. I., i. 8); Ts'een says no more than that he was 'a relative' (親戚); Ch'ing and others say he was 'an uncle.' He does not appear as a speaker in the text; but the part which he chose was a harder one than the parts of his friends. When he saw how the reproofs of the viscount of Ke were received, he brought the truth before the tyrant with still sterner vehemence. 'I have heard,' said Chow, 'that the heart of a sage has seven apertures;—let us see if it be so.' With this he made Pe-kan be put to death, had his heart cut out, and glutted his eyes with the sight of it.]

[Final overthrow of the Shang dynasty. The dynasty closes, in the chronology, in B.C. 1122, the same year to which the conference between the viscount of Wei and his friends is referred. It was in the year after, however, that Chow-sin died, and for the contest between him and the duke of Chow we must look to the commencing Books of the next Part. The duke of Chow after many delays at last took the field against the tyrant. We are surprised to find that Chow-sin, notwithstanding the general detestation with which he was regarded, was able to bring together an immense host, vastly outnumbering that of the other side. The two armies met in the plain of Muh, in the south of the pres. dis. of Ke, dep. of Wei-hwuy, Ho-nan. Chow-sin's troops failed him in the hour of need. He was totally defeated, and fled to the palace which had been the scene of so many debaucheries with Tă-ke. Arrayed in his most gorgeous robes, and covered with gems, he set fire to the 'Stag Tower,' which he had built for her, and perished in the flames;—yet not so but that his body was found by the duke of Chow, now king Woo, who cut off the head, and had it exhibited on a pole. Tă-ke apparelled herself splendidly, and went out to meet the conqueror, thinking he might be conquered by her charms. She was made prisoner, however, by a detachment of his troops, and put to death by his order, without having the opportunity to present herself before him.]

国家出版基金项目
NATIONAL PUBLICATION FOUNDATION

海上絲綢之路文獻集成

總主編　陳支平　陳春聲

科技與文化編 61

主編　王揚宗　葉　農

海峽出版發行集團
THE STRAITS PUBLISHING & DISTRIBUTING GROUP
福建人民出版社

本册目次

書經［二］

(*The Shoo King, or the Book of Historical Documents*)

〔英〕理雅各（James Legge）編譯

書經

THE CHINESE CLASSICS.

VOL. III.

THE SHOO KING,

OR

THE BOOK OF HISTORICAL DOCUMENTS.

不以文害辭、不以辭害志、以意逆志、是爲得之。

MENCIUS, V. Pt. I. IV. 2.

書經

THE

CHINESE CLASSICS:

WITH

A TRANSLATION, CRITICAL AND EXEGETICAL NOTES,
PROLEGOMENA, AND COPIOUS INDEXES.

BY

JAMES LEGGE, D.D.,

OF THE LONDON MISSIONARY SOCIETY.

IN SEVEN VOLUMES.

VOL. III.—PART II.

CONTAINING

THE FIFTH PART OF THE SHOO KING,
OR THE BOOKS OF CHOW; AND THE INDEXES.

HONGKONG: AT THE AUTHOR'S.
LONDON: TRÜBNER & Co., 60, PATERNOSTER ROW.
1865.

HONGKONG:

PRINTED AT THE LONDON MISSIONARY SOCIETY'S

PRINTING OFFICE.

THE SHOO KING.

PART V. THE BOOKS OF CHOW.

BOOK I. THE GREAT DECLARATION. PART i.

周書

泰誓上

惟十有三年、春、大會于孟津。○王曰、嗟我友邦冢君、越我御事庶士、明聽

1 In the spring of the thirteenth year, there was a great assembly
2 at Măng-tsin. The king said, "Ah! ye hereditary rulers of my
friendly States, and all ye my officers, managers of my affairs, listen
clearly to my declaration.

Name of the Part.—周書, 'The Books of Chow.' Chow is the dynastic designation under which Woo and his descendants possessed the empire from B.C. 1121—255, a period of 867 years. They traced their lineage up to K'e (棄), the minister of Agriculture (后稷) under Shun. K'e is said to have been a son of the emperor K'uh (B.C. 2432). The marvels of his birth and infancy are pleasantly described in the second Part of the She King, and are duly chronicled by Sze-ma Ts'een (周本紀). He was invested with the principality of T'ae (邰), the pres. dis. of Foo-fung (扶風), dep. of Fung-ts'ëang (鳳翔), in Shen-se. In the time of Këĕ, B.C. 1796, the fortunes of the family, which had for some time been waning, revived under Kung-lew (公劉), who established himself in Pin (豳), the pres. small department of 邠. There his descendants remained till B.C. 1326, when Tan-foo, afterwards styled king T'ae in the sacrificial ritual of the dynasty, removed to the foot of mount K'e in the pres. dis. of K'e-san (岐山), dep. of Fung-ts'ëang;—see Men., I., Pt., II., xiv., and xv. The State which he established there was called Chow. King T'ae was succeeded by his son Ke-leih, or king Ke, and he again by his son Ch'ang, or king Wăn, who transmitted his hereditary dominions, greatly increased, and his authority to his son Fă or king Woo. Woo then adopted Chow as the designation of the dynasty which he founded.

The Books of Chow were more numerous, as we might expect, than those of the previous dynasties,—even though they belong only to little more than the first half of its history. Nor did they suffer so much in consequence of the fires of Ts'in as those of the Shang dynasty. Out of 38 documents there remain 20 whose genuineness

is uncontested; and only 8 have been entirely lost. I have said that we might have expected that the Books of Chow would be more numerous than those of Shang; but we could not have expected that so much larger a proportion of them should escape the various dangers to which all were equally exposed.

THE NAME OF THE BOOK.—泰誓, 'The Great Declaration.' 泰=大, 'great.' King Woo, having at last taken the field against Chow, makes three speeches to his officers and men, expounding the grounds of his enterprise, urging them to play the man with him in the cause of humanity and Heaven. Those are brought together, and constitute one grand whole,—'The *great* Declaration.'

THE DIFFERENT TEXTS OF THE BOOK. This subject has been treated of in the prolegomena; and I will content myself here with giving the summary of the discussions that have been raised upon it, which is quoted in the 通鑑綱目 from Kin Le-ts'ëang's 通鑑前編 merely interjecting a remark or two, where his statements can be fairly called in question. The text preferred by Keang Shing and other modern scholars will also be found, with a translation of it, in an appendix to the Book.

Le-ts'ëang says:—'The Shoo of Fuh-shang did not contain the "Great Declaration."' [But see the first Book of Maou K'e-ling's 'Wrongs of the old Text of the Shoo.' The 'Great Declaration' *was* in the Books of Fuh-shang.] 'It was in the "Old Text," found in the wall of Confucius' house; but as the commentary of K'ung Gan-kwŏ was not entered in the imperial college during the Han dynasty, his edition of it did not then become current. Chang Pa (張霸) then fraudulently made a "Great Declaration," in three Parts, which became current, and contained the passage about "a white fish entering king Woo's ship," &c., which is found in Chung-shoo (仲舒) and Sze-ma Ts'een.' [This passage is found in those writers, and also in Fuh-shang's Introduction to the Shoo. There is no necessity to say that the 'Great Declaration,' current during the Han dynasty, was forged by Chang Pa.] 'But in the time of the Eastern Han, Ma Yung and other scholars became aware that this was not the genuine document; and it fell into general discredit, when the "Old Text" made its appearance at the commencement of the Eastern Tsin dynasty. Recently, however, this same Old Text has come to be suspected by the scholar Woo (吳氏). "Its language," he says, "is vehement and arrogant, not to be compared with that of the Declaration of T'ang. As the document appeared so late, we may suppose that the whole of it is not the original text."

'In my opinion, the conduct and language of T'ang and Woo were equally responsive to Heaven and accordant with men. They differed because the circumstances of the men differed. T'ang was the founder of the fortunes of his House; Woo entered into an inheritance which was already flourishing. T'ang's enterprise commenced when men were beginning to look to Shang; Woo's was undertaken when many of the princes had long been followers of the Chiefs of Chow. The battle of Ming-t'eaou was fought by the people of Pŏ, while at Măng-tsin there was a grand assemblage of the princes with their hosts. With such differences of circumstances, we should expect differences of style and manner. As to what is said of Chow's being worse than Këĕ, and the language being more ornate, these things are accounted for by the difference of time. Even allowing that the style was somewhat modified and improved, when the document made its reappearance, we may well believe that it gives us the views of king Woo.'

CONTENTS. These may be stated in the language with which Le-ts'ëang concludes his observations.—'In the first Part, king Woo addresses himself to the princes and others of inferior rank; in the second, to the hosts of the princes; and in the third, to his officers. The ruling idea in the first is the duty of the sovereign,—what he ought to be and do; with this it begins and ends. There is not the same continuity of thought in the second, but the will and purpose of Heaven is the principal thing insisted on. The last Part shows the difference between the good sovereign and the bad, and touches on the consent that there is between Heaven and men. The Book is brilliantly composed, and far transcends the powers of any man of a later age to have made it.'

CONTENTS OF THE FIRST PART. At a great assemblage of the princes, king Woo sets before them the reasons of his proceeding against Chow-sin. Starting from the position that the sovereign is ordained by God for the good of the people, he shows how the king of Shang acted only to the injury of the people. King Wăn would have punished him if he had lived, but now the duty was devolved upon himself, and with their help he would proceed to obey the requirement of Heaven. They need have no fears as to the issue. Favoured by God and men, the expedition could not but be crowned with success. There are eleven paragraphs which are so connected as to form only one chapter.

Par. 1. *The time, place, and occasion of the Declaration.* The time was the spring of the 13th year; but it is hardly possible to place beyond dispute the prior date from which we are to calculate this 13th year. In the first place, the Preface assigns the time to the 11th year (note 32); and there is no way that can be admitted of reconciling the two accounts. The general view is that the 11 in the preface is a mistake for 13, but Lin Che-k'e takes the opposite view, and contends that the 13 in the text should be 11. In the second place, admitting the text to be correct, we find that the standard or common chronology reckons from the 1st year of king Woo's accession to the principality of Chow, which it places in B.C. 1133. This view is ably argued by Ts'ae Ch'in *in loc.* On the other hand, Gan-kwŏ said that the 13th year was to be reckoned from king Wăn's receiving (as indicated by circumstances) the appointment of Heaven to the sovereignty of the empire. He is supposed to have then changed the style of his reign,—to have begun it afresh with a new 'first year.' Nine years then elapsed, and his work was not completed;—the tyrant was still upon the throne, and Wăn

誓。○[三節]惟天地萬物父母、惟人萬物之靈、亶聰明作元后、元后作民父母。

3 "Heaven and Earth is the parent of all creatures; and of all creatures man is the most highly endowed. The sincere, intelligent, and perspicacious *among men* becomes the great sovereign; and

died. Two years more passed by,—the period of mourning for him; and then king Woo took the field, but it was not till the year after, the 4th year of his reign, that the contest between him and Chow-sin was decided. This view is strongly advocated by Maou K'e-ling, against Ts'ae and others, in the third Book of his 尙書廣聽錄. But the various data on which it is endeavoured to decide the question are by no means certain;—see a note in the 歷代統紀表, on the date of king Woo's birth, under B.C. 1168. I must for the present suspend the expression of any opinion of my own on the point.

A controversy, nearly as perplexing, is waged about the time intended by 'the spring,' where we should hardly think there was room for any difference of view. It has been already observed (on 'The Instructions of E' Pt. i., p. 1) that while the Hea dyn. began the year with the 1st month of spring (the month 寅), the Shang began it with the last month of winter (the month 丑). The Chow dynasty removed the commencement of the year farther back still, and made it begin with the second month of winter (the month 子). Ts'ae and a host of followers say that by 'the spring' is intended the months of the Hea year; and this appears reasonable, for however different dynasties might begin their year in different months, they could not change the order of the seasons. The 'spring' of Chow was the same as that of Hea; and if we suppose, as is most natural, that the historian is speaking in the text with reference to the Chow year, then the month intended by 'the spring' must be the first month of that season. Gan-kwŏ, however, understands the month intended to be the *first* of the Chow year, and Maou K'e-ling supports his view. This question will come up again in the course of this and the two next Books.

The place where the declaration was made was Măng-tsin, or at the 'Ford of Măng:'—see the Tribute of Yu, Pt. ii., p. 7. There was there a great assembly of all the princes who already acknowledged the supremacy of Chow, and were confederate with Woo to make an end of the tyrant. Gan-kwŏ says they were the princes of the two thirds of the empire, who had followed the banner of king Wăn (Ana., VIII., xx., 4), and the chiefs of many of the wild tribes;—along with their various hosts.

P. 2. *Opening of the address.* 王曰,—Woo is here styled 'king,' or emperor, by anticipation. Had he been defeated, he would have been 'a rebel;' but as his enterprise was crowned with success, from the moment he began to operate against Chow-sin, he was the sovereign of China, and the other was only 'a solitary fellow' (獨夫; Pt. III., 4). 我友邦冢君,—Ying-tă says—同志爲友, 'they were 友, as having the same mind and aim with him.' 冢君 is literally 'highest rulers,' or 'great rulers.' The 'Daily Explanation' explains the phrase by—各國嗣立之君, which I have followed in the translation. 越我御事庶士,—越=及, 'and;' 御=主 or 治, 'to preside over,' 'to manage.' 御事=治事者, 'managers of affairs.' The 'Daily Explanation' would include the soldiers among the 士 as well as the officers,—衆士卒; but it is better not to extend the meaning of the term so far in this passage. Medhurst strangely and quite erroneously translates 越我御事 by—'it has fallen to me to manage these affairs.' The address begins with 嗟, the exclamation which ordinarily precedes these military speeches.

3. *The sovereign is ordained by Heaven and Earth, because of his virtues, for the good of the people.* Compare the 'Announcement of T'ang,' p. 2. What is to be remarked here is the style of speaking which is new, and places 'Heaven and Earth' in the place of 'Heaven' simply, or 'God.' Woo does not always employ this style. In this same Part he employs both the terms which I have mentioned. There can be no doubt that the deification of 'Heaven and Earth,' which appears in the text, took its rise from the Yih King, of which king Wăn may properly be regarded as the author. No one who reads what Wăn says on the first and second diagrams, and the further explanations of his son Tan (the duke of Chow), can be surprised to find king Woo speaking as he does in the text. 惟人萬物之靈,—'it is man who is the most intelligent of all creatures.' By 萬物 in the first clause we understand

四節 ○今商王受、弗敬上天、降災下民。○五節 沈湎冒色、敢行暴虐、罪人以族、官人以世、惟宮室臺榭陂池侈服、以

4 the great sovereign is the parent of the people. *But* now, Show, the king of Shang, does not reverence Heaven above, and
5 inflicts calamities on the people below. He has been abandoned to drunkenness, and reckless in lust. He has dared to exercise cruel oppression. Along with criminals he has punished all their relatives. He has put men into office on the hereditary principle. He has made it his pursuit to have palaces, towers, pavilions, embankments, ponds, and all other extravagances, to the most painful injury of you,

'all things,' inanimate as well as animate; in the second clause we must confine the meaning to animate creatures. The various tribes of animals have their several measures of intelligence, but all are very inferior to men.

Then, as men are superior to other creatures, there appear among them those who are superior to their fellows;—the sages, who are raised up by Heaven, and become the rulers, teachers,—parents, in fact—of the mass. Ch'in King says on this:—'Man is one among all creatures. Other creatures, however, get but a portion of the energizing element of nature, while he receives it complete:—it is this which makes the nature of man more intelligent and capable than that of other creatures. But though men are endowed with this capacity and intelligence, there are those who are not able to preserve and maintain it, and there must be the quick-apprehending and understanding ruler to be a parent to them. In this way the people are able all to complete their intelligence. The sage possesses before me that of which I have the seeds in common with himself; and among intelligent beings he is the most intelligent' (人者萬物之一也, 物得氣之偏, 人得氣之全, 此人性所以獨靈於物, 然人雖有此靈, 有不能保此靈者, 必得聰明之君以父母之, 斯民始得以各全其靈, 聖人先得我心之所同然, 而爲靈之靈者耳).

Pp. 4, 5. *How Chow had forfeited all his title to the empire, and king Wăn had been charged to punish him.* 4. 商王受,—I have hitherto called the tyrant of Shang by the name of Chow (紂), after Sze-ma Ts'een and Mencius. Here and elsewhere he appears as Show, which Ts'ae says was 'the name of Chow.' Chow is his epithet in history, conferred upon him for his cruelty and wickedness;—see the Dict. on the character (殘忍損義曰紂). Lin Che-k'e says that 紂 was interchanged with 受 from the similarity of the two characters in sound, but he must be wrong, because Show is here used by king Woo before the tyrant's death. 上天下民,—I think these phrases may best be taken as in the translation. 5. 沈湎,—comp. 沈酗于酒, in 'The Viscount of Wei,' p. 1. 冒色,—冒 is 'to go forward with the eyes covered,'='to pursue blindly and recklessly.' 色=女色. 罪人以族,—'he *crimed* men according to their relationships.' The meaning is as in the translation. The 'Daily Explanation' has:—加罪于人, 不但誅其一身, 并其族屬而刑戮之. Mencius points it out as one of the glories of king Wăn's administration of K'e, that 'the wives and children of criminals were not involved in their guilt' (罪人不孥; Bk. I., Pt. II., v. 3,) It was one of the principles of Shun that punishments should not be extended to the offender's children (Counsels of the Great Yu, p. 11.) We have seen Yu's son, (The Speech at Kan, p. 5) and even T'ang, (The Speech of T'ang, p. 4) menacing their troops with the death of their children, if they did not do their duty. That may have been a measure of war; and Chow carried it into all the penal administration of his govt. To what extent the punishment of relations was carried by Chow, we do not learn from the text. Gan-kwŏ supposes that the parents, brothers,

殘害于爾萬姓、焚炙忠良、刳剔孕婦、皇天震怒、命我文考、肅將天威、大勳未集。○肆予小子發、以爾友邦冢君、觀政于商、惟受罔有

the myriad people. He has burned and roasted the loyal and good. He has ripped up pregnant women. Great Heaven was moved with indignation, and charged my deceased father Wăn reverently to display its majesty; but *he died* before the work was completed.

6 "On this account I, Fă, who am but a little child, have by means of you, the hereditary rulers of my friendly States, contemplated the government of Shang; but Show has no repentant

wives and children, (三族) all suffered with the offender. 官人以世,—'he officed men according to their generation, or genealogical connection.' The 'Daily Explanation' makes the meaning to be that Chow put into office all the friends of his favourites. —其用人,則不論賢否,但其心之所喜,即幷其子弟親屬,悉寵任之. But this view of 以世 is unwarrantable. Mencius, in the passage above referred to, says that king Wăn salaried the descendants of meritorious officers. But tho' such men might be salaried, they were called to office only when they had the virtue and ability necessary for its duties. Chow did not look out for able and good men to fill the offices of the State. This is the burden of this part of the indictment against him. 惟宮室……萬姓,—惟—'he only cared for.'—其所務者惟在宮室,云云. The 說文 defines 宮 by 室. The former term is the building as a whole; 室, the apartments in it. Le Seun says:—'臺 is a high terrace of earth, made for the purpose of observation; when a house or houses are built on the top of it, they are called 榭.' 侈服—凡侈靡諸事, 'all extravagances;' 服—事. 焚炙忠良,—this refers to the punishment of Roasting, described in the historical note on the 'Conquest of Le.' 刳剔孕婦,—we saw how Chow caused the heart of Pe-kan to be cut out;—Hwang-poo Meih, of the Tsin dyn., says that he also caused Pe-kan's wife to be ripped up. No earlier account to that effect, however, is known. King Woo is no doubt rehearsing things which were commonly charged upon the tyrant at the time. 皇天,—see on the 'Announcement of T'ang,' p. 2. 命我文考,—考 is the name for a father deceased. King Woo speaks in this way of his father having been charged to punish Chow, to vindicate all the better his own present course. We are not to suppose that any such commission was ever expressly given to Wăn; and Confucius speaks of him as having been faithful to the dyn. of Shang to the last;—see Ana., VIII., xx., 4. 大勳未集—大功未成. We must complete the meaning by adding 而崩, as in the translation.

P. 6. *The task of punishing Chow being now devolved on him, he sets forth the evidence of his hopeless wickedness.* 肆—故, 'therefore.' 以爾……于商,—觀政 is explained by a reference to the same phrase in the 'Both possessed pure Virtue,' p. 10. The princes of the States were to Woo an index of the govt. of Chow. Had they remained loyal to him, that would have shown that his govt. was good. As they were now in the mass revolted from him, and following Woo's banner, it was clear that he was no longer fit to be emperor. Such is the explanation of this passage by Ts'ae, and what is now commonly received; and I see no better course than to acquiesce in it. Gan-kwŏ and the earlier scholars explained it with reference to an assembly, which they imagined, of Woo and the princes at the ford of Tsin, two years before the period of this 'Declaration.' Then he had thoughts of attacking Chow, but on contemplating his govt., concluded that the time was not yet come, and withdrew his troops.

悛心、乃夷居、弗事上帝、神祇、遺厥先宗廟弗祀、犧牲粢盛、既于凶盜、乃曰吾有民有命、罔懲其侮。○天佑下民、(七節)作之君、作之師、惟其克相上帝、寵綏四方、有罪無罪、予曷敢有越厥志。○

heart. He abides squatting on his heels, not serving God or the spirits of heaven and earth, neglecting also the temple of his ancestors, and not sacrificing in it. The victims and the vessels of millet all become the prey of wicked robbers; and still he says, 'The people are mine: the decree is mine,' never trying to correct his
7 contemptuous *mind*. *Now* Heaven, to protect the inferior people, made for them rulers, and made for them instructors, that they might be able to be aiding to God, and secure the tranquillity of the four quarters of the empire. In regard to who are criminals and who are not, how dare I give any allowance to my own wishes?

Such a meeting is not properly substantiated; and the view is otherwise liable to many objections. 夷居,—compare 夷俟, Con. Ana., XIV., xlvi. 弗事上帝神祇,遺厥先宗廟弗祀,—Ts'ae, after Gan-kwŏ, gives for this—廢上帝,百神,宗廟之祀, 'he has discontinued the sacrifices,—to God, the hundred spirits, and the spirits of his ancestors.' Ying-tă observes that the meaning is that Chow had no religion, rendered no service to spiritual beings (不事神祇); God, as the highest of all such beings, being mentioned, to show the enormity of his wickedness. In this way a distinction is made between 上帝 and 神祇, the latter phrase being synonymous with 百神. On the other hand, the 'Daily Explanation,' for 弗事上帝神祇 has—忽慢天地神祇,不知奉事, 'he slights and contemns the spirits of Heaven and Earth, and renders not service to them.' This would confound God with the spirits of Heaven and Earth, which is by no means inconceivable in Woo, when we consider the language of p. 3. Compare also the language of parr. 3 and 4 in the 'Announcement of T'ang.' Upon the whole, however, the gradation of thought in the passage may determine the scale in favour of the former view. 犧牲粢盛,既于凶盜,—犧牲, see the last Book, p. 6; 粢盛, see Men., III., Pt. II., iii., 3; 既—盡, 'are consumed,' or 'are all taken.' The whole corresponds with the words of the Grand Tutor in the par. of the 'Viscount of Wei' just referred to. 有民,有命,—comp. the 'Conquest of Le,' p. 5. 罔懲其侮—無有懲戒其侮慢之意.

P. 7. *He returns to the principles declared in par. 3, and shows that he was constrained by them to attack Chow.* See this par. as it is quoted by Mencius, I., Bk. II., iii., 7. The difference between the text here, and that which he gives is very considerable. We cannot suppose that the present text of the Shoo was forged from Mencius. A plagiarist, attempting such an imposition as is ascribed to 'the false K'ung,' would have taken the language exactly from his copy. We can only believe that Mencius had a copy of the 'Great Declaration' before him, differing not a little from the present, or that he quoted from memory, and allowed himself great license in altering the classic. 寵綏四方,—'to show favour and tranquillize the four quarters *of the empire*.' 予曷敢有越厥志—我何敢

八節 同力度德、同德度義、愛有臣億萬、惟億萬心、予有臣三千、惟一心。○九節 商罪貫盈、天命誅之、予弗順天、厥罪惟鈞。○十節 予小子夙夜祇懼、受命文考、類于上帝、宜于冢土、以爾有衆、底天之罰。

8 "'Where the strength is the same, measure the virtue of the parties; where the virtue is the same, measure their righteousness.' Show has hundreds of thousands and myriads of ministers, but they have hundreds of thousands and myriads of minds; I have three thousand
9 ministers, but they have one mind. The iniquity of Shang is full. Heaven gives command to destroy it. If I did not comply with Heaven, my iniquity would be as great.
10 "I, who am a little child, early and late am filled with apprehensions. I have received charge from my deceased father Wăn; I have offered special sacrifice to God; I have performed the due services to the great Earth;—and I lead the multitude of you to

有過用其心乎, 'how dare I use my own mind too much?' Such is the interpretation of Ts'ae;—越厥志, is 'to go beyond *what is right* with—in accordance with—my own wishes.' The dict. follows Gan-kwŏ in defining 越 here by 遠, 'to put away.'—'My purpose is to destroy the tyrant for the good of the people. Whether he be guilty or not guilty, I will smite him. I will not let go that, my proper purpose.' This is evidently incorrect.

P. 8. *He auspices success from the righteousness of his cause, and the harmony of mind among his followers, though they were comparatively few.* The two first clauses are supposed to be a current saying used against each other by contending parties;—Lin Che-k'e has adduced from the 左傳 two examples of similar couplets. The second clause is not so intelligible as the first. We can understand how when parties were matched in strength, the struggle should be expected to terminate in favour of the more virtuous; but it is difficult to perceive how 'virtue' and 'righteousness' can be set against each other. 受有臣億萬,—Ts'ae says here that 億 denotes 'a hundred myriads,' or a million. This was probably a slip of his pencil. 億,=ten myriads, or 100,000. The subject of Show's more numerous host comes up again in the next Part, p. 6. We may admit it as a fact, and it explains the risings and troubles which disturbed the dynasty of Chow after the death of king Woo. It is difficult, at the same time, to reconcile it with the representations of the general disaffection to the emperor, and of two thirds of the empire having been for years devoted to the House of Chow. See the note on this paragraph in the 後案. It is instructive, though not conclusive in favour of the author's views. 9. *It was woe to Woo himself if he proceeded not to destroy Shang.* Compare the 'Speech of T'ang,' pp. 1, 2; and the 'Announcement of T'ang,' p. 4. 商罪貫盈,—'the crimes of Shang are strung together and full.' 10. *Woo's caution and conscientiousness in proceeding with his enterprise.* 予小子夙夜祇懼,—comp. the 'Announcement of T'ang,' p. 6. 受命文考, 類于上帝, 宜于冢土,—冢=大 'great'; 冢土, 'the great earth,'=大社, 'the altar dedicated to the great spirit of the Earth.' The sacrifice at this altar was called 宜. 類于上帝,

十一節 ○天矜于民、民之所欲、天必從之、爾尚弼予一人、永清四海、時哉弗可失。

11 execute the punishment appointed by Heaven. Heaven compassionates the people. What the people desire, Heaven will be found to give effect to. Do you aid me, the one man, to cleanse for ever *all within* the four seas. Now is the time!—it may not be lost."

—see the 'Canon of Shun,' p. 6. In the Le Ke, Bk. 王制, Pt. ii., 17, we find—天子將出,類乎上帝,宜乎社,造乎禰, 'When the emperor is about to go forth, he offers special sacrifice to God, performs the due services at the altar of the Earth, and goes to the shrine of his father.' Woo had attended to all these observances; and it must have been at the shrine of his father, that he somehow understood himself 'to receive,' as he says here, 'charge' to attack Chow. 底天之罰,—comp. 恭行天之罰, in the 'Speech at Kan,' p. 3. 11. *The enterprise was a proof of the compassion of Heaven for the people, and he summons all the princes and officers to strenuous cooperation with him.* Under the 32nd year of duke Seang, and in another place of the 左傳, we find the passage—民之所欲,天必從之, quoted from the 'Great Declaration.' It is also found in the 國語. 爾尚弼予一人,—see the 'Speech of T'ang,' p. 4.

THE BOOKS OF SHANG.

BOOK I. THE GREAT DECLARATION. PART ii.

泰誓中

惟戊午、王次于河朔、群后以師畢會、王乃徇師而誓。○曰、嗚呼、西土有衆、咸聽朕言。

1 On *the day* mow-woo, the king halted on the north of the River. When all the chiefs with their hosts were assembled, the king re-
2 viewed the hosts, and made the following declaration, saying, "Ah! ye multitudes of the West, listen all to my words.

CONTENTS OF THE SECOND PART. Since the delivery of the first address, the army has crossed the Ho, when Woo reviews it, and makes this speech, which is more especially addressed to the troops. He makes Show and Këë, T'ang and himself, all pass before his men, showing that Show was more wicked than Këë, and that his punishment of him would be more glorious than T'ang's had been of Këë. Heaven will surely crown their enterprise with success; and he therefore in conclusion urges them all to go into battle, not despising the tyrant, but with united hand and heart, to accomplish a work that should last for ages. The whole is divided into 9 paragraphs.

Pp. 1, 2. *The time, place, and occasion of the address; and the parties addressed.* The time was the day *mow-woo*, which we are able to determine, from the 1st par. of the 'Completion of the War,' to have been the 28th day of the 1st month. We are there told that Woo began his march to attack Chow on the day *jin-shin*, which was the 2d of the 1st month. Calculating on to the day *mow-woo*, we ascertain that it was the 28th of the same moon. The controversy, described on the 1st par. of the last Part, on the term 'spring,' however, is not decided by this fixing of the relation between the two dates. Ts'ae will still have the month to be the first of the Hea year,—really the first month of spring; Gan-kwŏ and others will have it to be the first month of the Chow year, the second month of winter. 次于河北,—次=止, 'to stop,' 'to be stationed.' In the interval, therefore, between the two addresses, the army had crossed the Ho. 徇師,—徇 (3d tone)=循, 'to go about.' Hwang Too explains it from the phrase 拊循, 'to cheer and animate.' 'To review' expresses the meaning accurately enough. Perhaps we are to understand that the king first crossed the river and encamped; and then, when all the princes with their troops, had pitched their tents around him, he went through the host and addressed the soldiers. 2. 西土有衆,—Woo and his father had both been 'Chiefs of the West,'—viceroys over that part of the empire.

○我聞吉人爲善、惟日不足、凶人爲不善、亦惟日不足、今商王受、力行無度、播棄犂老、昵比罪人、淫酗肆虐、臣下化之、朋家作仇、脅權相滅、無辜籲天、穢德彰聞。三節

○惟天惠民、惟辟奉天、有夏桀弗克若天、流毒下國、天乃佑命成湯、降黜夏四節

3 "I have heard that the good man, doing good, finds the day insufficient, and that the evil man, doing evil, likewise finds the day insufficient. Now Show, the king of Shang, with strength pursues his lawless way. He has cast away the time-worn sires, and cultivates intimacies with wicked men. Dissolute, intemperate, reckless, oppressive, his ministers have become assimilated to him; and they form parties, and contract animosities, and depend on *the emperor's* power to exterminate one another. The innocent cry to Heaven. The odour of such a state is plainly felt on high.

4 "Heaven loves the people, and the sovereign should reverence *this mind of* Heaven. Këĕ, the sovereign of Hea, could not follow the example of Heaven, but sent forth his poisonous injuries through the States of the empire:—Heaven favoured and charged T'ang, the

P 3. *The dreadful wickedness of Show.* 吉人, 凶人,—comp. the use of 吉 and 凶 in the 'Counsels of Yu,' p 5. Here, however, we are to take the terms in their purely moral signification. This use of them shows the deep conviction that goodness and prosperity, evil and calamity, ought always to be found together. 播棄犂老,—comp. in the 'Viscount of Wei,' p. 3, 耄遜于荒. 播 is here explained by 放, very nearly synonymous with 棄. 犂 is most simply explained by taking it as for 黧, 'black and yellow,' the colour of old men's faces. Mih-tsze says of Chow that he 播棄黎老, where 黎 is probably intended for the character in the text 昵比罪人,—昵 (*neih*), as in the 'charge to Yuĕ p. 5; 比, as in the 'Instructions of E,' p. 7. 朋家作仇—各立朋黨, 互爲仇讐. 脅權,—脅, as in the 'Punitive Expedition of Yin,' p. 6, = 進, 'to press,' 'to force.' The phrase here = 'they make forcible use of—press upon with—the power *of the emperor.*' 籲天 = 告天 or 呼天, 'appeal to Heaven.' 穢德,—'their filthy, fœtid deeds.' See on the 'Pwan-kăng,' Pt. ii., p. 8.

Pp. 4, 5. *Heaven will always overthrow wickedness and tyranny:—illustrated in the case of Këĕ and T'ang, and now in that of Show, who was worse than Këĕ, and himself.* 4. 惠 = 愛 'to love.' 有夏桀 is not = 'there was Këĕ of Hea,' but 有夏之君, 桀,

命。○惟（五節）受罪浮于桀、剝喪元良、賊虐諫輔、謂己有天命、謂敬不足行、謂祭無益、謂暴無傷、厥鑒惟不遠、在彼夏王、天其以予乂民、朕夢協朕卜、襲于休祥、戎商

5 Successful, to make an end of the decree of Hea. But the crimes of Show exceed those of Këĕ. He has stript and degraded the greatly good man; he has behaved with cruel tyranny to his reprover and helper. He says that his is the decree of Heaven; he says that a reverent care of his conduct is not worth observing; he says that sacrifice is of no use; he says that tyranny is no matter. The case for his inspection was not remote;—in that king of Hea. It would seem that Heaven is going by means of me to rule the people. My dreams coincide with my divinations; the auspicious omen is double. My attack on Shang must succeed.

'Këĕ, the ruler who held Hea.' 流毒下國,—流毒于下國, 'flowed out his poison upon the lower States.' Këĕ is conceived of on the throne of the empire, as being raised on high, above his own and all the feudal domains. 降黜夏命,—降黜= 'to bring down and put away.' Comp. the expression in the 55th note of the Preface,—成王既黜殷命. 5. 罪浮于桀,—浮, comp. on the 'Pwan-kang,' Pt. ii., 8. Here it is evidently=勝 or 過, 'to exceed.' 剝喪元良,—剝 'to tear,' 'to peel,'—'to degrade'; 喪 is 失位, 'to lose one's office,' used, here in a *hiphil* sense. It is supposed that this clause has reference to the viscount of Wei, whose withdrawal from court, it would thus appear, was preceded by violence and oppression on the part of Show. The next clause,—賊虐諫輔, is referred to Pe-kan. 謂己有天命,—see the 'Conquest of Le,' p. 5. 敬不足行,—'reverence is not worth being practised.' We had better understand the 'reverence' with reference to his own conduct, and to the business of the State. 祭無益,—this was the cry of the wicked Jews in the time of Malachi,—'It is vain to serve God.' 暴無傷,—無傷,—see Men. I., Pt., vii.' 8. 厥鑒云云,—see the quotation from the She King in Mencius, IV., Pt. I., ii., 5. 天其以予乂民,—observe the force of 其. 朕夢協朕卜,襲于休祥,戎商必克.—We have no other intimation of Woo's being encouraged in a dream to act against Show; his divination may have been before the shrine of his father, referred to in the last Part, p. 10. 襲,=重, 'double,' 'repeated.' 襲于休祥,—'both agree in being auspicious,' 戎, 'a weapon,' here = 'to attack with weapons.' Acc. to the interpretation thus indicated, which is after Ts'ae, the omens were only two, which united in being favourable. In the 國語, however, 周語, 下, the passage is quoted, where the speaker is treating of the agreement of *three* omens, and he adds to the passage—以三襲也. On this view, 襲于休祥 = 'agree with the 休祥,' whatever this was. Lin Che-k'e. adopting this construction, refers to the 24th chap. of the 'Doctrine of the Mean,' where it is said that when a nation or a family is about to flourish, there will be 禎祥, seen in the milfoil and tortoise, &c. There, a substantive meaning may be given to those two

必克。○六節受有
億兆夷人、離
心離德。予有
亂臣十人、同
心同德。雖有
周親、不如仁
人。○七節天視自
我民視、天聽
自我民聽。百
姓有過、在予

6 "Show has hundreds of thousands and millions of ordinary men, divided in heart and divided in practice;—I have of ministers capable of government ten men, one in heart and one in practice. Although he has his nearest relatives with him, they are not like
7 *my* virtuous men. Heaven sees as my people see; Heaven hears as my people hear. The people are blaming me, the one man, *for my*

characters, as to 休祥 here,—namely the occurrence of certain unusual phenomena;—see Ying-tă on the passage of the 中庸. The editors of Yung-ching's Shoo seem on the whole inclined to favour this view.

P. 6. *The greater number of Show's host and adherents was no cause for doubt as to the issue.* See on the 8th par. of last Part. 夷人,—夷—平常, 'common, ordinary men.' 予有亂臣十人,—see Con. Ana., VIII., xx. 周親—周—至, the superlative adverb, 'most.' The phrase 周親, and the whole clause indeed, are difficult. The paraphrase of the 'Daily Explanation' is:—受所親信者,雖有同姓至親,然皆凶人醜類,同惡相濟,我之十臣,雖不盡是我之親戚,然皆是仁厚有德之人,可以經邦濟世, 'Although those in whom Show reposes his most intimate confidence are his nearest relatives of the same surname with himself, yet they are all bad men and detestable, helping him and one another in their common wickedness. My ten ministers, on the other hand, although they are not all my own relatives, are virtuous men, benevolent and generous, fit to rule a country and benefit the age.'

[Confucius said that there was a woman among Woo's ten able ministers;—see the Ana., *loc cit.* She is generally spoken of as 文母, 'mother Wăn,' king Woo's mother, the famous 太姒. Others think Woo's wife, 邑姜, must be intended. It is not easy to believe this.]

P. 7. *The will of Heaven might be seen from the earnest wish of the people that he should destroy Show.* 天視......民聽,—see Men., V., Pt. I., v., 8. It would not be easy to determine the exact meaning of the term 'Heaven' here. The attention of Choo He being called to the applicability of the definition of Heaven as meaning 'Reason,' or 'what is Reasonable' here, replied, 'Heaven certainly means "What is Reasonable"; but it does not mean that only. It means also "the azure vault" (蒼蒼者亦是天); and it means too "the Lord and Ruler who is above" (在上而有主宰者亦是天). The term is to be explained in every place by a consideration of the context. If here you say that it means "what is Reasonable," how can that see and hear? Although the explanations are different, there yet is something common in all the usages. If you know that, you will not be startled by the differences; and if you know them, you will see that they are not inconsistent with the common idea.'—See the passage quoted in the 集說. 百姓有過,在予一人.—Lin Che-k'e takes these words as equivalent to those in the 'Announcement of T'ang,' p. 7, 萬方有罪,在予一人; and most readers will feel inclined at first to agree with him. 過 is to be distinguished, however, from 罪, and the sentiment appropriate to the lips of T'ang, who had vanquished his rival, is not to be expected from Woo, who was only marching to the fight. Gan-kwŏ, as if he had T'ang's words before him, and yet felt the difference between 過 and 罪, interpreted—'It devolves on me, the one man, to teach the people, and correct their

一人、今朕必往。○八節我武惟揚、侵于之疆、取彼凶殘、我伐用張、于湯有光。○九節勗哉夫子、罔或無畏、寧執非敵、百姓懍懍、若崩厥角、嗚呼、乃一德一心、立定厥功、惟克永世。○

8 *delay*;—I must now go forward. My military prowess is displayed,
and I enter his territories, to take the wicked tyrant. My punishment
9 *of evil* will be shown more glorious than that of T'ang. Rouse ye,
my heroes! Do not think that he is not to be feared;—better think
that he cannot be withstood. *His* people stand in trembling awe
of him, as if the horns were falling from their heads. Oh! unite
your energies, unite your hearts;—so shall you forthwith surely
accomplish the work to last for all ages."

errors.' But this idea is foreign to the occasion. Ts'ae's explanation of 過 by 責, 'fault-finding,' 'complaining of,' is very ingenious, and sound. See the Con. Ana., xx., i., 5, where also we have the conclusion of the last paragraph.

P. 8. *The present enterprise was not less but more glorious than that of T'ang.* Compare the paragraph as quoted by Mencius, Bk. III., Pt. II., v., 6. It will be seen to be rhythmical, and this may account for the difficulty which we find in construing it. 侵于之疆 = 侵入受之疆界, 'I invade and enter the boundaries of Show's domain.' 于湯有光,—Ts'ae makes this to = 'and this will reflect light on T'ang,' *i.e.*, will make his mind in attacking Këë more clear. As the editors of Yung-ching's Shoo say, this is too ingenious. Ts'ae wanted to relieve Woo of a portion of the charge of boastfulness, which is urged against the language of this Book; but foreign students of Chinese history do not feel the pressure of such a charge. We are content to take king Woo as we find him, and are not concerned to bring his character either up or down to the Chinese idea of a sage.

P. 9. *He rouses his men to prepare for the fight with stern determination, not undervaluing their enemy, but rather overvaluing him.* A good part of this paragraph is also found in Mencius;—see VII., Pt. II., iv. 5. His variations from the present text are, however, greater, and affect the meaning of the several parts of the par. How to account for the differences is a difficult question. To say that our present 'Old Text' is a forgery, is an absurd solution;—the true solution has yet to be found. 夫子,—'my masters,' here = 'my heroes.' 罔或無畏, 寧執非敵 = 無或以紂為不足畏, 寧執心以為非我所敵也, as in the translation. 百姓懍懍,—the people are understood to be those of Show's domain, and the parts of the empire in the east. The next clause represents them as a flock of cattle, whose horns were being broken. 立定厥功,—the 立 is best taken adverbially, = 'forthwith.'

BOOK I. THE GREAT DECLARATION. PART iii.

泰誓下

時[一節]厥明、王乃大巡六師、明誓衆士。○[二節]王曰、嗚呼、我西土君子、天有顯道、厥類惟彰、今商王受、狎侮五常、荒

1 The time was on the morrow, when the king went round
his six hosts in state, and made a clear declaration to all his
2 officers. He said, "Oh! my valiant men of the west, Heaven has
enjoined the illustrious courses *of duty*, of which the *several* characters
are quite plain. And now Show, the king of Shang treats with con-
temptuous slight the five constant *virtues*, and abandons himself

CONTENTS OF THE THIRD PART. On the day after addressing the troops as in the last Part, Woo had a grand review of all the hosts, and declared his sentiments more particularly to the officers. He sets forth, as before, the crimes of Show against God and men, as sufficiently justifying their enterprise, and urges the officers to support him with all their energies that he might do his work thoroughly, and utterly destroy the tyrant. Having set before them the prospect of rewards and punishments, he concludes with a humble but encouraging reference, to his father Wăn.

P. 1. *The time and occasion of the Declaration, with the parties addressed.* The day was that immediately following that on which the last address was delivered,—the *Ke-wei* day of the calendar. It is supposed that the army was now about to march to meet or seek the enemy. 大巡六師,—大巡, 'went greatly about.' Lew Ying-ts'ew (劉應秋) says that 巡 differs from 循, the latter meaning to go round and cheer, while the former conveys the ideas of marshalling and warning. This is very doubtful. 六師 is used, like 王, throughout the Book, by anticipation. According to the subsequent statutes of the Chow dyn., the imperial forces consisted of six armies or brigades, while those of a great State were only three. In reality the hosts now collected on the banks of the Ho were an imperial force, and so they are denominated the 'six hosts.' 明誓衆士,—衆士, 'all the officers;'—Gan-kwŏ says they were all 'from centurions upwards.'

P. 2. *That Show, violating the laws of Heaven, had set both Heaven and men against him.* 西土君子,—'princely men of the western regions.' 君子 is appropriate as addressed to the officers, though Lin Che-k'e shows that it might be employed also to designate the common soldiers. 天有顯道, 厥類

怠弗敬、自絕于天、結怨于民。○斮朝涉之脛、剖賢人之心、作威殺戮、毒痛四海、崇信姦回、放黜師保、屏棄典刑、囚奴正士、郊社不修、宗廟不享、作奇技淫巧、以悅婦人、上帝弗順、祝降時

to wild idleness and irreverence. He has cut himself off from Heaven, and brought enmity between himself and the people.

3 "He cut through the leg-bones of those who were wading in the morning; he cut out the heart of the worthy man. By the use of his power killing and murdering, he has poisoned and sickened all within the four seas. His honour and confidence are given to the villainous and bad. He has driven from him his instructors and guardians. He has thrown to the winds the statutes and penal laws. He has imprisoned and enslaved the upright officer. He neglects the sacrifices to Heaven and Earth. He has discontinued the offerings in the ancestral temple. He makes contrivances of wonderful device and extraordinary cunning, to please his woman.—God will no longer indulge him, but with a curse is sending down

惟彰,—it seems most proper to explain these clauses by what is said below that Show had violated the 'five virtues.' The 'illustrious ways of Heaven,' therefore, are the various relationships, of society, and 'their characters,' are the duties severally belonging to them. This view is advocated by Ying-tă, who is followed by Ts'ae. Liu Che-k'e, on the other hand, understood by the 'illustrious ways,' Heaven's love of virtue and hatred of vice, and by 'their characters,' the good and evil which severally attend them;—making reference to the use of the phrase 天道 in the 'Counsels of Yu,' p. 21, and in the 'Announcement of T'ang,' p. 3. This interpretation is ingenious and not without merit; but the other is preferable. 狎侮五常,—狎 = 易 or 輕,' 'easily 'lightly;' 狎侮 = 'slights and contemns.' 五常,—see on 五典, 'Can. of Shun,' p. 2.

P. 3. *An enumeration of Show's wickednesses, and summons to the officers to support the king in punishing him.* 斮朝涉之脛,—Gan-kwŏ tells us that Chow, one winter's day, seeing some people wading through a stream, thought their legs had a wondrous power of enduring cold, and had them cut off through the shank-bone, that he might see their marrow. 剖賢人之心,—this refers to the case of Pe-kan. 毒痛四海,—痛 = 病, 'to be sick'; here, 'to make sick.' 姦回,—回 = 邪 or 曲, 'the crooked,' = 'the bad.' 囚奴正士,—this was the case of the count of Ke. 郊社,—see on the 'Doctrine of the Mean,' xix. 6. 婦人,—this refers to Tă-ke. History has not preserved an account of the cunning contrivances referred to. Ts'ae says that since Show contrived 'the punishment of Roasting' to make her laugh, we can well understand that he tasked his ingenuity to the utmost in other things to please her. 祝降時(= 是)喪,—Gan-kwŏ defines 祝 by 斷 (up. 2d tone), 'to cut off,' 'to make an end of.' Ts'ae, misunderstanding 斷 for the same char. in the 3d tone, explains the clause by 斷然降

喪、爾其孜孜奉予一人、恭行天罰。○四節古人有言曰、撫我則后、虐我則讐、獨夫受、洪惟作威、乃汝世讐、樹德務滋、除惡務本、肆予小子、誕以爾衆士殄殲乃讐、爾衆士其尚迪果毅、以登乃辟、功多有厚賞、不迪有顯戮。○五節嗚呼、惟我文考、若日

on him this ruin. Do ye support with untiring zeal me, the one man, reverently to execute the punishment appointed by Heaven.

4 The ancients have said, 'He who soothes us is our sovereign; he who oppresses us is our enemy.' This solitary fellow Show, having exercised great tyranny, is your perpetual enemy. *It is said again*, 'In planting *a man's* virtue, strive to make it great; in putting away *a man's* wickedness, strive to do it from the root.' Here I, who am a little child, by the powerful help of you, all my officers, will utterly exterminate your enemy. Do you, all my officers, march forwards with determined boldness, to sustain your prince. Where there is much merit, there shall be large reward. Where you advance not so, there shall be conspicuous disgrace.

5 "Oh! *the virtue of* my deceased father Wăn was like the shining

是喪亡, 'is determinedly sending down this ruin.' But 祝, like the Hebrew *barak* is a *vox media*, and may be used for 'to curse' as well as 'to bless.' 孜孜—'with unwearied efforts.'

P. 4. *Show had shown himself the enemy of the people, never to be forgiven; and Woo calls his troops to support him in making root and branch work with the tyrant.* 獨夫受,—this was certainly very strong language, applied to Show who was still occupying the throne. See the reference to it by Mencius, I., Pt. II., viii. It is much in his style. Seun-tsze has quoted it as from the 'Great Declaration,' in his 議兵篇. 世讐,—'an hereditary enemy,' one whose memory must be held in detestation in all the future. 樹德……務本,—these clauses are probably sayings of the day like the first two. The former of them appears, slightly varied, as 'an old saying,' in the 左傳,哀元年. 其尙迪果毅,—the union of 其 and 尙, to express earnest exhortation, has occurred more than once. 迪=進, 'to advance.' 果 and 毅 are both defined by 决 and 有决, 'determined.' It is said—致果爲毅, '毅 is the intensest determination.' 登乃辟,—登=成, 'to complete.' The 'Daily Explanation' brings the meaning out by saying:—以成爾君弔民伐罪之功, 'to accomplish the work of your ruler in consoling the people and smiting the criminal.'

Pp. 5, 6. *The virtue of King Wăn, and its effects. Success in the present enterprise would be owing to him; failure, if failure there should be,*

月之照臨、光于四方、顯于西土、惟我有周、誕受多方。○予(六節)克受、非予武、惟朕文考無罪。受克予、非朕文考有罪、惟予小子無良。

and influence of the sun and moon. His brightness extended over the four quarters *of the empire*, and shone signally in the western region. Hence it is that our Chow has received *the allegiance of* many States.
6 If I subdue Show, it will not be my prowess, but the faultless *virtue* of my deceased father Wăn. If Show subdue me, it will not be from any fault of my deceased father Wăn, but because I, who am a little child, am not good."

would all be Woo's own. 5. The greater part of this par. appears in Mih-tsze (兼愛, 下篇), thus:—太誓曰, 文王若日若月, 乍照光于四方于西土. 惟我有周, 誕受多方,—I have translated this in the indicative mood, as historical narrative. Such is the view of Gan-kwŏ who explains;—文王德大, 故受衆方之國, 三分天下, 而有其二, 'The virtue of king Wăn was so great, that he received the allegiance of the States of many quarters, and had two thirds of the empire.' Ts'ae found in the language an auspice of Woo's success in the enterprise in hand. The 'Daily Explanation,' expanding his construction, says:—文考之德, 其所及如此, 是以人心戴之, 天命歸之, 惟我有周, 宜其大受多方而有天下, 'Thus far-reaching was the virtue of my father Wăn:—the hearts of men cherished him, and the decree of Heaven fell to him. Right it is that our House of Chow should receive the allegiance of the many regions, and possess the empire.' I must prefer to construe with the older scholar.

6. The whole of this par. is found with the verbal variation of 紂 for 受, in the Le Ke, Book 坊記, p. 16. In 無罪, 有罪, we must take 罪 lightly, as merely 一過, 'fault,' 'error.'

APPENDIX.

I annex here the "Great Declaration," as it appears in Këang Shing's 尙書集註音疏. He has been at great pains to gather up, and put together, the fragments of the Book, as it was when current in the Han dynasty. Wang Ming-shing, or Wang Kwang-luh (王光祿), gives a much briefer edition of it in his 尙書後案, and arranges many of the sentences, moreover, differently. The fragments give us now in many passages but a farrago of absurdities. We may be sure that a Book containing such things never received the *imprimatur* of Confucius:——

維四月、太子發上祭于畢、下至于孟津之上。○周公曰、都、忞哉、予聞古先哲王之格言。○太子發拜手稽首。○乃告司徒司馬司空、諸凡齊栗、信哉。○予無知、以先祖之有德臣左右小子。予受先公功、畢力賞罰、以定厥功于先祖之遺。○遂興師、師尚父左杖黃戉、右把白旄、以號曰、蒼蒼兕兕、總尒衆庶、與尒舟楫、後至者斬。○太子發升舟中流、白魚入于王舟、王跪取出涘以燎、羣公咸曰休哉。○至于五日、有火自上復于下、至于王屋、流之爲雕、其色赤、其聲魄、五至以穀、俱來。○武王喜、諸大夫皆喜、周公曰、茂哉茂哉、天之見此以勸之也、恐恃之。○正卜古立功立事、可以永年、傳于無窮、丕天之大律。○使上附以周公書、報誥于王、王動色變。○八百諸侯、不召自來、不期同時、不謀同詞、皆曰受可伐矣、王曰尒未知天命、未可伐、維丙午、王還師、前師乃鼓鞞譟、師乃慆、前歌後舞、極于上天下地、咸曰孜孜無怠、天將有立父母、民之有政有居。○

In the fourth month, Fă, the eldest son and successor, went up and sacrificed at [or, to] Peih, and then proceeded to the neighbourhood of Măng-tsin.

The duke of Chow said, "Oh! exert yourself. I have heard the excellent words of the wise and ancient kings." The prince Fă bowed with his face to his hands, and his head to the ground. He then addressed the minister of Instruction, the minister of War, and the minister of Works, with all the other appointed officers,—"Be reverent, firm, and sincere. I am without knowledge, but *I look to* the virtuous ministers of my fathers to help me, who am but a little child. I have received the achieved work of the dukes my predecessors, and will exert my strength in rewards and punishments, to accomplish whatever they have left undone." On this he put the host in motion. The *grand* Tutor, Father Shang, carrying in his right hand an axe yellow with gold, and in his left a white flag, to give out his orders, said, "The hoary wild bull! The hoary wild bull! Lead on all your multitudes. There are your boats and oars. The last come shall be beheaded!"

As the prince Fă had got to the middle of the stream in his boat, a white fish entered it. The king knelt down and took it up. He then went on the bank, and burned it, *in sacrifice to Heaven.* All the dukes said, "This is auspicious!"

On the fifth day there was a *ball of* fire which descended from above, till it came to the king's house, and there dissolved into a crow. Its colour was red; its voice was calm and decided; five times it came bringing a stalk of grain. The king was glad, and all his officers also. The duke of Chow said, "Be strenuous! Be strenuous! Heaven has showed this to encourage us. But let us trust in it with dread." "Examining into antiquity, it is by accomplishing merit and accomplishing business, that one can transmit *his work* to perpetual generations, and magnify the laws of Heaven." They sent up this to be joined to the writing of the duke of Chow, and reported to the king, who was moved, and his countenance changed.

Eight hundred princes came of themselves without being called; they came at the same time without previous agreement; without consultation they all spoke to the same effect, saying, "Show may be attacked." The king said, "You do not know the will of Heaven; it is not yet the time to attack him." On the day ping-woo he accordingly withdrew his army. In front the host beat their drums and shouted. Some of the soldiers lowered their spears, and went through their exercise; with songs in front and dancing behind, they made heaven and earth resound, while they cried out, "Let us never be weary. Heaven is about to raise up a parent for us. The people will have good government and dwell quietly."

司馬在前。○今殷王紂乃用其婦人之言、自絕于天、毀壞其三正。○離逷其王父母弟、乃斷棄其先祖之樂、乃爲淫聲、用變亂正聲、以悅婦人。故今台發、維龔行天罰、勗哉夫子、不可再、不可三。○附下而罔上者死、附上而罔下者刑、與聞國政、而無益于民者退、在上位、而不耐進賢者逐。○紂夷居、不肯事上帝鬼神、棄厥先神祇不祀、乃曰吾有命、毋僇其務、天亦縱之、棄而弗葆。○小人見姦巧、乃聞不言也、發辠鈞。○紂有億兆夷人、亦有離德、余有亂十人、同心同德。○天眡自我民眡、天聽自我民聽。○民之所欲、天必從之。○朕夢協朕卜、襲于休祥、戎商必克。○文王若日若月、照光于四方于西土。○予克紂、非予武、惟朕文考無辠、紂克予、非朕文考有辠、惟予小子無良。○惡乎君子而有顯德、其行甚章、爲鑑不遠、在彼殷王、謂人有命、謂敬不可行、謂祭無益、謂暴無傷、上帝不常、九有以亡、上帝不順、祝降其喪、惟我有周、受之大帝。○獨夫紂。○我武惟揚、侵于之疆、則取于殘、殺伐用張、于湯有光。

The minister of War was in front. "Now, king Chow listens to the words of his woman;—he has cut himself off from Heaven; he has destroyed and ruined *all his hopes* from heaven or earth or men. He has separated himself from his royal uncles and his maternal relatives. He has cast away the music of his forefathers, and by making dissolute melodies he has changed the correct melodies, to please his woman. On this account I, Fă, reverently proceed to execute the punishment determined by Heaven. Rouse ye, my heroes! Don't let us need a second effort, or a third. He who deceives those above him, in the interest of those below, dies; he who deceives those below, in the interest of those above, is punished; he who takes counsel on the government of the kingdom, which is of no use to the people, has to retire; he who is in the highest position, and cannot advance the worthy, must be driven out.

"Chow abides squatting on his heels, and will not serve God or spirits. He has cast away, and will not sacrifice to, the spirits of his fathers. He says on the contrary,—'The decree is mine;' and therefore he will not put forth his strength in the duties to them. Heaven allows him to take this course, having thrown him away, and no more preserving him. A mean man sees villainy and cunning, or hears it, without speaking:—his knowledge makes him as guilty *as the villain.* Chow has hundreds of thousands and millions of ordinary men, but they are divided in their courses; I have ten able men who are one in heart and in course. Heaven sees as my people see, and hears as my people hear. My dreams agree with my divinations; the auspicious omen is double;—my attack on Shang must succeed. King Wăn was like the sun or the moon. He lightened with his shining the four quarters,—the western regions. If I vanquish Chow, it will not be my prowess;—it will be the faultlessness of my father Wăn. If Show vanquishes me, it will not be from any fault of my father Wăn, but because I am not good.

"Oh! when the superior man has illustrious virtue, his conduct is grandly displayed. There is a beacon not distant;—it is in that king of Yin. He says to men that the decree is his; that reverence should not be practised; that sacrifice is of no advantage; that oppression does not matter. God is not constant, and the empire is passing from him. God is not allowing him, but sending down his ruin with a curse. Our House of Chow is receiving *the empire* from the great God. The solitary fellow Chow. Chow has hundreds and tens of thousands of ministers, who have hundreds and tens of thousands of hearts. King Woo has three thousand ministers with one heart. My prowess is displayed; I invade his borders, and will take the tyrant. My punishment *of evil* will be exhibited more glorious than that of T'ang."

THE BOOKS OF SHANG.

BOOK II. THE SPEECH AT MUH.

牧誓

一節 時甲子昧爽、王朝至于商郊牧野、乃誓、王左杖黃鉞、右秉白旄以麾、曰、逖矣西土之

1 I. The time was the grey dawn of the day këă-tsze. On that morning the king came to the open country of Muh in the borders of Shang, and addressed his army. In his left hand he carried a battle-axe, yellow with gold, and in his right he held a white ensign, which he brandished, saying, "Far are ye come, ye

THE NAME OF THE BOOK.—牧誓, 'The Speech at Muh.' Muh [Keang Shing edits 坶 instead of Muh] was in the south of the pres. district of Ke (淇縣), dep. of Wei-hwuy, Ho-nan. It was a tract of open country, stretching into the pres. dis. of Keih (汲), and at no great distance from the capital of Show. King Woo had, no doubt, made choice of it as a favourable field for the decisive battle between him and the tyrant. I return here to the rendering of 誓 by 'Speech,' as in the 'Counsels of the great Yu,' p. 20, and other places. It would have been well if the term 'Declaration' had not been used instead of it in the last Book. The Speech at Muh is found in both texts. There is more of the martial spirit in it than in any other of the speeches of the Shoo.

CONTENTS. It is the morning of the day of battle, for which the king had prepared his host in the three speeches of the last Book. Once more he addresses the confederate princes, his officers, and his men. He sets forth, much as before, but more briefly, the intolerable wickedness of Show, and then instructs and warns the troops on how they should behave themselves in the fight. The speech proper begins with the 5th paragraph. The four parr. that precede may be considered as forming a preliminary chapter.

Ch. I. Pp. 1—4. THE TIME AND CIRCUMSTANCES OF THE SPEECH. 1. *The time; and the appearance of the king.* 時甲子昧爽,—the day 甲子 was six days later than mow-woo ('The Great Speech' Pt. ii., p. 1), which was, we saw, the 28th of the 1st month. The speech at Muh, therefore, is held to have been spoken on the 4th day of the second month. 昧=冥, 'dark;' 爽=明, 'light;' 昧爽, 'the dark and the light,'—the grey dawn. 杖=持, 'to hold in the hand.' Its tone in this sense was diff. at one time from that which it had in its more common signification of 'a staff.' It now seems to be used only with the 3d tone. 秉, (from a *hand* grasping *stalks of grain*) is of similar signification to 杖. The 'axe' is supposed to be called 'yellow,' from its having been ornamented with gold. The 旄 ensign consisted (according to the figures

人。○二節王曰、嗟、我友邦冢君、御事、司徒、司馬、司空、亞旅、師氏、千夫長、百夫長。○三節及庸、蜀、羌、髳、微、盧、彭、濮人。○四節稱爾戈、比爾干、立爾矛、予其誓。○五節王、

2 men of the western regions!" He added, "Ah! ye hereditary rulers of my friendly States; ye managers of affairs, the ministers of instruction, of war, and of public works: the many *officers* subordinate to them: the master of my body-guards: the captains of thousands,
3 and captains of hundreds; and ye, O men of Yung, Shuh, Këang,
4 Maou, Wei, Loo, P'ang, and Pŏ;—lift up your lances, join your shields, raise your spears:—I have a speech to make."

of it, which agree with the component parts of the character) of several ox-tails, suspended as streamers from a staff. By means of this Woo could intimate his wishes as to the order of their position, &c., to the troops, and therefore he carried it in his right hand. Gan-kwŏ says the axe was in the left hand and the flag in the right, to show that Woo considered his work was not so much to kill as to teach. This is being absurdly ingenious. We may be sure that Woo had his axe in his right hand in the battle. 逖=遠, 'far,' 'distant.' The 'Daily Explanation' paraphrases the clause thus:—爾等皆西土之人,我以伐暴救民之故,率爾至此,其行亦已遠矣. Ts'ae observes that he spoke thus to comfort the men under their long travel.

Pp. 2, 3. *The different parties addressed.*

2. 我友邦冢君,御事,—see on the last Book, Pt. i., p. 2. The 'managers of affairs' were the officers immediately after specified, belonging to Woo's own govt.,—to the State of Chow. The 司徒,司馬, and 司空, were three of the 'six ministers' (六卿) under the imperial govt. of Chow, when the dynasty was fully established, and whose duties are described in Bk. XX., parr. 7—13. A great State, such as Chow was before the extinction of the Shang dyn., had only *three* principal ministers, whose names are here given. But we may inquire what the ministers of instruction and works had to do in the camp. Ying-tă says that the former superintended all orders given to the troops, and the latter all the business of intrenchments. Ts'ae seems to have thought that they were there as the generals of the three armies of the State. This is not likely;—see Ch'in Sze-k'ae, *in loc.* We can only form a vague idea on this, as on many other points in the Shoo. 亞旅,—亞=次, 'secondary,' 'of inferior rank'; 旅=衆, 'multitude,' 'many.' I do not find it possible to say whether we are to understand by these characters the 'multitude of inferior officers' generally, or two distinct classes of such. Gan-kwŏ had the former view. He says:—衆大夫,其位次卿, 'The phrase denotes all the great officers, whose posts were inferior to those of the ministers.' Ts'ae on the other hand supposes that the 亞 were the 大夫 or 'great officers,' below, but next in rank to, the ministers, and five of whom filled up the space between each minister and his 士, or 'officers,' of whom there were 27, denoted in the text by the term 旅. 師氏,—'the Instructor.' The functions of an officer thus designated are given at length in the 13th Book of the Chow Le (地官司徒第二之六). He was a ta-foo or great officer of the second grade, and the Tutor of the heir-apparent, at the same time executing various duties about the sovereign, and specially having charge of the guard of foreign—barbarian—mercenaries who kept watch outside the royal gate. In time of war, or when the sovereign went abroad for any other cause, he followed in attendance, with the whole or a portion of that guard. It must have been in this capacity

古人有言曰、牝雞無晨、牝雞之晨、惟家之索。○今^六節^

II. The king said, "The ancients have said, 'The hen does not announce the morning. The crowing of a hen in the morning

that he was present at Muh;—if indeed the 師氏 of the the text was the same officer who is so designated in the Chow Le. Ts'ae follows Gan-kwŏ in saying that the 師氏 were 'the officers who guarded the gates' (以兵守門者). 千夫長, 百夫長,—we can only translate these designations literally as I have done. According to the Chow Le, five men formed a *woo* (伍); five *woo*, or 25 men, formed a *lëang* (兩); four *lëang*, or 100 men, formed a *tsuh* (卒); five *tsuh*, or 500 men, formed a *leu* (旅); five *leu*, or 2,500 men, formed a *sze* (師); and five *sze*, or 12,500 men, formed a *keun* (軍). Gan-kwŏ and Wang Suh both say that the 百夫長, were 'leaders of *tsuh*,' which of course is literally correct; but they say also that the 千夫長 were 'leaders of *sze*,' commanded 2,500 men each. K'ang-shing agrees with them in this, but makes the 百夫長 to have been 'leaders of *leu*' (旅帥),' commanding 500 men each. It seems absurd to insist on such explanations. The arrangements of Woo's army much more probably corresponded with the terms which he employed. 3. The names Yung, Shuh, &c., enumerated here, are said generally to be those of 'eight kingdoms of the rude tribes on the west and south' (西南夷八國名). The first and last are found associated together in the 左傳, 文十六年, in an attack upon the great State of Ts'oo. It is said that 'the people of Yung.... led the hundred *tribes* of the Pŏ to invade Ts'oo;' and from this description of the Pŏ by 'hundreds' it is supposed that they were under no general Head or chieftain, but consisted of many clans, each acknowledging its own chief. The site of the Yung was in the pres. dis. of Chuh-shan (竹山), dep. of Yun-yang (鄖陽), Hoo-pih; that of the Pŏ was in the same prov., dep. of King-chow (荊州), dis. of Shih-show (石首). The country of Shuh was the pres. dep. of Shing-too (成都) in Sze-ch'uen. West and north from this was the country of Këang: while that of Maou and Wei was to the east, radiating from the pres. dis. of Pa (巴縣), dep. of Chung-k'ing, as a centre. Loo is referred to the present dis. of Nan-chang (南漳), dep. of Sëang-yang (襄陽), in Hoo-pih. The name of P'ang remains in P'ang-shan dis., dep. of Mei (眉), Sze-ch'uen. All these tribes, we may suppose, acknowledged the supremacy of the princes of Chow, and had been summoned to assist king Woo in his enterprise against Show. Some critics, like Wang Loo-chae (王魯齋; see his 'Doubts about the Shoo,' on the Speech at Muh), say that they had come to his banner of their own accord, without being called;—which is very unlikely.

[Gaubil says in a note on this par. (Le Chou-king, p. 157), that Yung, Shuh, &c., were the countries on the south-west,—*e.g.*, in Sze-ch'uen and Yun-nan. To this M. de Guignes appends a very bold and sweeping remark:—'I will add,' he says, 'that all the peoples in the text bear the name of 夷, or *barbarians*. Thus, this conquest of China, made by king Woo, was a conquest effected by the foreigners on the west of China.' The remark is unwarranted. So far as we learn from the Shoo, these tribes were only an inferior and auxiliary force on the occasion.]

4. *Attitude in which the troops were required to listen.* 稱=舉, 'to lift up;' apparently ='to bear aloft in the right hand.' 立=立於地, 'to erect on the ground,' *i.e.*, to rest the end on the ground, the points being shown above. There were three weapons of the nature of spears or lances, differing in the forms of their points which would be difficult to describe in brief space, but principally distinguished by their lengths,—the 戈, the 戟 and the 矛. Acc. to Wang Ts'ëaou, the handle of the 戈 was 6 ft. 6 in. long; that of the 戟 16 ft.; and of the 矛, 21 feet. Medhurst translates 戈 by 'javelin;' but I have not seen it anywhere stated that the instrument was thrown from the hand. The 干 or 'shield' was long and comparatively narrow, so as to cover most of the body.

Ch. II. THE SPEECH. Pp. 5, 6. *The crimes of Show.* 5. 晨, 'the morning,' here = 晨鳴報曉, 'crows in the morning to an-

商王受、惟婦言是用、昏棄厥肆祀弗答、昏棄厥遺王父母弟不迪、乃惟四方之多罪逋逃、是崇是長、是信是使、是以爲大夫卿士、俾暴虐于百姓、以姦宄于商邑。○今七節

6 *indicates* the subversion of the family.' Now Show, the king of Shang, follows only the words of his wife. He has blindly thrown away the sacrifices which he should present, and makes no response *for the favours which he has received;* he has blindly thrown away his paternal and maternal relatives, not treating them properly. They are only the vagabonds of the empire, loaded with crimes, whom he honours and exalts, whom he employs and trusts, making them great officers and nobles, so that they can tyrannize over the people, exercising their villainies in the city of Shang.

nounce the day.' 索 is defined by Gan-kwŏ by 盡; and by Keang Shing, after K'ang-shing, by 散. The two definitions are much akin. Woo's language may seem rather undignified; but it was, no doubt, suited to his audience. And we must bear in mind the character and deeds of Tă-ke against whom it was directed.

6. 昬 (*i.q.* 昏) 棄厥肆祀不答,—comp. the last Book, Pt. i., 6; Pt. ii., 5. 肆=陳, 'to set forth;' 厥肆祀=其所當陳之祭祀, 'the sacrifices which he ought to offer.' K'ang-shing understood by 肆祀 'the name of a sacrifice';—but incorrectly. 答, 'to answer,' 'to make an acknowledgment for favours received,' such being the common meaning of sacrifice with the Chinese;—Tung-po says, 祭所以報也, 故謂之答. Here also K'ang-shing incorrectly defines 答 by 問; and 不答=不問, 'without asking any questions, or thinking about them.' 王父母弟,—Gan-kwŏ takes 王父, as=祖 or 'grandfather,' saying that if he thus treated his grand-uncles, we may be sure he did not treat his uncles any better. Woo Ch'ing says that 王父母弟=王之諸父, 諸母, 諸弟, 'the royal uncles, royal aunts, royal cousins.' I think we must join 王父 together, and agree with Wang Ts'eaou that 王父母弟=王父弟與母弟. The general meaning is plain enough,—that Show separated himself from all his relatives, both by blood and by affinity, who would naturally have the interests of the imperial House at heart. 不迪,—迪=道, and 不迪=不以道遇之, as in the translation. Keang Shing takes 迪=進 or 登, and 不迪=不用, 'does not employ them.' The meaning is not unsuitable; but it is not so good as that which I have followed. 逋逃='refugees.' Woo Ch'ing says:—四方多罪之人逃亡而歸紂, 'the great criminals of all quarters make their escape, and betake themselves to Chow.' 商邑,—'the city of Shang,' probably meaning the capital of Show. We might translate 邑, however, in the plural. Keang Shing takes it as=國, 'kingdom' or 'State.'

予發、惟恭行天之罰、今日之事、不愆于六步七步、乃止齊焉、夫子勗哉、○八節不愆于四伐五伐六伐七伐、乃止齊焉、勗哉夫子。○九節尚桓桓、如虎如貔、如熊如羆、于商郊、弗迓克奔、以役西土、勗哉夫子。○十節爾所弗勗、其于爾躬有戮。

7 "Now I, Fă, am simply executing respectfully the punishment
appointed by Heaven. In to-day's business do not advance more
than six or seven steps; and then stop and adjust your ranks:—my
8 brave men, be energetic! Do not exceed four blows, five blows,
six blows, or seven blows; and then stop and adjust your ranks:—
9 my brave men, be energetic! Display a martial bearing. Be like
tigers and panthers, like bears, and grisly bears;—here in the
border of Shang. Do not rush on those who fly *to us in submission,*
but receive them to serve our western land:—my brave men, be
10 energetic! If you are not thus energetic, you will bring destruction
on yourselves."

Pp. 7—10. *Directions about the rules to be observed in the impending battle.* 7. The first part of this par. had better be joined to the one preceding. King Woo speaks in it of himself in contrast with Show;—of himself as engaged on behalf of Heaven to punish one who was an enemy to both Heaven and men. Ts'ae and others, prefixing it to this and the succeeding parr., make a milder spirit breathe in them than the reader will easily perceive. The stopping at every seven steps and seven blows was, they think, that as few of the enemy as possible might be killed. In this way the tyrant would be overthrown and Heaven's justice would be satisfied with the sacrifice of comparatively few lives! The cautions were evidently given that the order of battle might be preserved unbroken. 愆=過, 'to exceed.' 步=進趨, 'to advance hurriedly.', 齊=齊整, 'to adjust and put in order.' The paraphrase of the 'Daily Explanation' is:—其進而迎敵, 不過于六步, 七步, 即便止駐, 以整齊部伍, 然後復從而伐之, 'In advancing to meet the enemy, take no more than six or seven steps. Then stop and adjust your ranks, and go forward again to smite them.' 夫子,—see the last Book, Pt. ii., p. 9.

8. 伐=擊刺, 'to strike and thrust.' They are thus admonished, it is said, lest they should be hurried on in their rage by a desire for slaughter. 9. 桓桓=威武貌 'the appearance of martial prowess.' The 說文 quotes the passage with 狟 instead of 桓. 貔 is described as 豹屬, 'a kind of panther.' 弗迓克奔—'do not meet those who are able to—who really do—run.' The meaning is as in the translation. Këang Shing, however, edits 禦 instead of 迓, after K'ang-shing. Ma Yung also read 禦,

書經

which he explains better than K'ang-shing. Wang Suh read 御, which is susceptible of being taken either for 禦 or 迓. The meaning is substantially the same, whether we adopt 迓 or 禦. 以役西土,—the translation of this is after K'ang-shing. Ma Yung and Wang Suh took the clause as = 'do your best to serve our western land.' Gan-kwŏ understood it differently:—'It is thus you will make them submissively acknowledge the righteousness of our western land.' 10. 爾所不勖,—as 勖哉夫子 has been repeated at the close of the several instructions or admonitions, we must suppose that the warning here belongs to each of them. The 'Daily Explanation' paraphrases the 9th and 10th parr. thus:—過勇，則不免于濫殺，惟當于凶殘者取之，抗拒者誅之，若有奔走來降者，勿迎而擊之，以勞役我西土之人，勉哉爾將士，其武勇是奮而殺降是戒可也，爾將士若于我之命，而有所不勉，或輕進，或貪殺，或無勇而殺降，是違號令，而失紀律也，則軍有常刑，必戮及爾身，罔有攸赦矣，可不戒哉。

THE BOOKS OF SHANG.

BOOK III. THE SUCCESSFUL COMPLETION OF THE WAR.

武成

惟[一節]一月壬辰旁死魄、越翼日癸巳、王朝步自周、于征伐商。○厥[二節]

1 I. In the first month, *the day* jin-shin immediately followed the end of the moon's waning. The next day was kwei-ke, when the king in the morning marched from Chow to attack and punish Shang.

THE NAME OF THE BOOK.—武成, 'The Successful Completion of the War.' The phrase 一武成, meaning, literally, 'military affairs completed,' occurs in the 3d paragraph, and has thence been taken to denominate the Book. It is not objectionable as a designation; though it by no means covers the contents, they all grow up around the accomplishment of Woo's enterprise. The Book is found only in the old Text.

DIFFICULTIES IN THE ARRANGEMENT AND INTERPRETATION. These will fully appear in the course of the exposition; it may be sufficient here to describe them generally, and for that purpose I will use in the first place the words of Ying-tă. He says:—'This Book consists mainly of narrative; the portion composed of the king's words is small. The language of the several parts is without the beginning and the end properly marked, and its composition altogether is different from that of the other Books. From 惟一月 (p. 1) down to 受命于周 (p. 4), the historian relates the march to the attack of Yin, and the return from the enterprise, with the assembling of the princes:—as introductory to the words of the king. From 王若曰 to 大統未集 (both in p. 5), Woo narrates the rise of their House of Chow; from 予小子 (p. 5) to 名山大川 (p. 6), he states how he had inherited the possessions and the duties of king Wăn, and how he declared to the spirits the crimes of Show; from 曰惟有道 (p. 6) to 無作神羞, (p. 8), he repeats his prayer to the spirits. From 既戊午 to the end, the historian again resumes his narrative, and tells of the attack on Show, of his death, of Woo's entrance into the capital of Yin, and of his governmental measures.

The prayer, however, which concludes with 無作神羞, is incomplete. According to the analogy of other prayers, recorded in the 左傳, there ought to be, after those words, some protestation by Woo of his own intentions. And when all the princes and officers were receiving their investitures and commands from the new emperor of the House of Chow, we cannot suppose that he did not address them, in a manner similar to T'ang, in his 'Announcement.' With so many speeches to them before the conflict, we cannot believe that he simply related to them after its close his prayer to the spirits. On these two grounds I must conclude that a portion of the Book, immediately following these words—無作神羞, has been lost.

'Perhaps it was wanting when the tablets were hidden away in the wall; perhaps it was among the confused and broken fragments which Gan-kwŏ says there were in addition to the 58 Books which he recovered. As he found in the tablets of this Book a beginning of it and an end, he did not say anything of the intermediate portion being deficient.'

Ying-tă was thus of opinion that the Book was deficient; but it does not appear that he had any doubts as to the relative order in which the several portions stand. He thought some tablets were lost; but did not suppose that any of those preserved had been displaced. In the Sung dynasty, however, the critics assumed not only that there were portions missing, but that the remaining tablets were all disordered and confused. Ch'ing E-ch'uen (程伊川), Lew Gan-she (劉安世), and others, had their several ways of arranging them so as to produce a consistent narrative; and Ts'ae Ch'in, profiting by the determinations of his master Choo He, produced an edition of the Book, which has superseded the old one in the copies of the Shoo which are now taught in schools. It will be found, with a translation, in an appendix. Scholars of the present dynasty for the most part acquiesce in his views, when they do not discard the old text altogether. There are some, however, who think they can improve on him, and Wang Loo-chae has given a disposition of the paragraphs somewhat different in his edition of 'Doubts about the Shoo.'

Maou K'e-ling will not admit either of disorder or defect in the Book. He has certainly proved by references to the 左傳 and the 國語, that the prayer of Woo to the spirits was a part of his speech or announcement to the princes;—see the 尙書廣聽錄, on the 武成. So far it is established that the disorder in the parts which the Sung critics complained of and tried to remedy,—if indeed we should call it disorder,—existed even during the Chow dynasty. Maou says, 'If the text be not good, we have only to be content with it as it is.' In this he is right. The ingenuity of the critics has not been of service either to history or the classic.

Contents. Those are summarily and correctly stated in the prefatory Notice.—'King Woo smote Yin; and the narrative of his proceeding to the attack, and of his return and sending his animals back to their pastures, with his governmental measures, form '*The Completion of the War*.' The whole is divided in Yung-ching's Shoo into 9 parr., which I have re-arranged in 10, including them also in three chapters. The first chapter, containing 4 parr., consists of brief historical notes of the commencement and close of Woo's expedition. The second also contains 4 parr., and gives the address (or a part of it) delivered by Woo to his nobles and officers on occasion, we may suppose, of their solemn recognition of him as emperor, and of his confirming some of them in their old investitures or appointments, and giving new ones to others. The third, in the two concluding parr., is again historical, and relates several incidents of the battle between Woo and Show, going on to subsequent events, and important governmental measures of the new dynasty.

Ch. I. Pp. 1—4. The march to the attack, and conquest, of Shang. The return, and measures on the conclusion of the war.

1. 惟一月壬辰旁死魄. 一月, 'the first month'; but whether we are to understand the first month of the Hea year,—the first month of spring; or the first month of the Chow year,—the second month of winter, cannot yet be determined. Ts'ae endeavours here to reinforce his view that the month is the first of the Hea year, by calling attention to the language, 一月, and not 正月; but this circumstance is of little weight. 壬辰 is the calendaric name of the day, and it was 旁 (read *p'ang*, 3d tone, = 近, 'near to' 'close by') 死魄, 'next to the *day of the* dead disk.' This expression is generally understood to be descriptive of the first day of the new moon. In p. 4 we find the phrase 生魄, denoting the 15th day or full moon. In p. 2, again, we have 哉生明, 'the beginning of the birth of light,' as denoting the third day, when the moon first becomes visible. It is clear therefore that the term 魄 was applied to the disk of the moon from the the time it began to wane until the new moon reappeared. How it came to be so used, I do not perceive. The 說文 has 霸 instead of 魄, but pronounced in the same way; and in the dict. we find the definition quoted, 一月體黑者謂之霸, 'the body of the moon when dark is called 霸.'

[Fan Sze-lin (潘士遴) observes that after the 1st day of the moon, the light went on to grow, and the darkness of her disk (魄) to disappear; that if the previous month was 'great' (consisted, that is, of 30 days), then on the second day of the month, the 'light' began. He concludes that this was the case here, and that the day denoted by 旁死魄 was not the second but the first day of the month. The editors of Yung-ching's Shoo are inclined to agree with him, saying it is more natural and in rule to find a specification of the first day of the month than of the second. This view does not seem unlikely.]

越翼日癸巳,—越—及; 翼日=明日, 'the morrow:' 癸巳 follows 壬辰 in the calendar. 王朝步自周,—步=行, 'to travel,' 'to march;' 王步 is, literally, 'the king paced *it*.' 周 is understood to stand here for Woo's capital,

四月哉生明、王來自商、至于豐、乃偃武修文、歸馬于華山之陽、放牛于桃林之野、示天下弗服。

2 In the fourth month, at the first appearance of the moon, the king came from Shang to Fung, when he hushed all the movements of war, and attended to the cultivations of peace. He sent back his horses to the south of mount Hwa, and let loose his oxen in the open country of T'aou-lin, showing the empire that he would not use them *again*.

called Haou (鎬), which was 30 *le* south of the pres. dis. city of Ch'ang-gan, dep. of Se-gan, Shen-se. In the next par. it is stated that he returned to Fung, which had been the capital of his father Wan, in the pres. dis. of Hoo (鄠), of the same dep. The two places were only about 8 miles apart; Haou on the east of the river Fung, and Fung on the west of it. The site of Haou was converted into a lake (昆明池) by the emp. Woo (世宗孝武帝, B.C. 139–87) of the Han dyn. 于征伐商,—于=往, 'to go,' 'to proceed.'

[We saw, in the 'Great Speech,' Pt. ii., p. 1, that on the day mow-woo, the 28th day of the 1st month, king Woo halted on the northern bank of the Ho. On that same day he had crossed the river;—see the 9th par. below. The distance from Haou to Măng-tsin is said by Ying-tă to be 1,000 *le*, and I have seen another estimate of it at 900 *le*. Taking the larger number, we have 25 days' marches, of 40 *le* each, or about 14 miles per day, which could be accomplished without difficulty. Five days after (the day 癸亥), Woo drew up his army in the borders of Shang, and waited for the dawn of the next morning, the 4th day of the 2d month, to decide the contest between himself and Show.

After the battle, Show fled to the 'Stag tower,' and burned himself to death. In the mean time, Woo, having received the congratulations of the princes on his victory, pressed on after the tyrant. On arriving at the capital, the people were waiting outside the walls in anxious expectation, which the king relieved by sending his officers among them with the words,—'Supreme Heaven is sending down blessing' (上天降休). The multitudes reverently saluted the king, who bowed to them in return, and hurried on to the place where the dead body of Show was. Having discharged three arrows at it from his chariot, he descended, struck the body with a light sword, and cut the head off with his 'yellow' battle-axe, and made it be suspended from the staff of a large white flag. Much in the same way he dealt with the bodies of two of Show's concubines who had killed themselves; and then returned to his army. These accounts are taken from the 'Historical Records,' and are put down by subsequent writers as lying legends, inconsistent with Woo's character.

Next day he entered the capital of Shang in great state, attended by his brothers and the chiefs of his host, and solemnly accepted the charge of the empire. It was said to him, on behalf of all the nobles, 'The last descendant of the House of Yin having destroyed and disowned the bright virtue of his forefathers, having insolently discontinued the sacrifices to the spirits, and having blindly tyrannized over the people of Shang, the report of his deeds ascended to the great God in heaven' (其章顯聞于天皇上帝). On this, Woo bowed twice, with his head to the ground, and said, 'It is right that I should change the great charge; that I should put away the House of Yin, and receive myself the great appointment of Heaven' He then again bowed twice, with his head to the ground, and went out.

In this way king Woo took on himself the sovereignty of the empire. One of his first steps was to appoint Show's son, Luh-foo (祿父), prince over the domain of Yin; and he appears to have remained in the capital of Shang between two and three months, employed in the measures described in the last two parr. of this Book, and in others requisite to the establishment of the dynasty of his House.]

Pp. 2, 3. *Measures in the 4th month showing that the war was over.* 2. 既四月哉(=始)生明,—this was the 3d day of the month;—see on the last par. But there had been an intercalary month between This is proved in the following manner.—The day 丁未 of par 3 evidently belonged to the 4th

○丁未、祀于周廟、邦甸侯衞、駿奔走、執豆籩、越三日庚戌、柴望、大告武成。○既

3 On the day ting-we he sacrificed in the ancestral temple of Chow, when *the chiefs of* the imperial domain and of the teen, how, and wei domains all hurried about, carrying the dishes. Three days after, he presented a burnt-offering *to Heaven*, and worshipped towards the mountains and rivers, solemnly announcing the successful completion of the war.

month. 甲子, the day of the battle of Muh, was the 4th of the 2d month, which we may suppose had 29 days. This brings us to 庚寅, for the first day of the next month, the 18th of which was a 丁未 day; but it could not be that of the text. We have to count 60 days before we come to the next 丁未 day, which would consequently be in the 5th month, unless there was an intercalary month between the 1st and the 4th. The chronologers are all agreed in supposing that there was a second month intercalary this year; and consequently the ting-we day of the text would be the 18th or 19th of the fourth month. 至于豐,—Fung was the capital of Wăn and here was the ancestral temple of the princes of Chow. That was the reason, as we gather from the next par., why Woo went in the first place to Fung and not to Haou. 偃武修文,—in the rest of the par. we have two instances of the 'hushing of military measures,' (偃 is defined by 臥, 'to sleep,' 'to send to sleep);' what 'the cultivations of peace' were, we are not told. 華山之陽=華山之南, 'the south of mount Hwa.' For mount Hwa, see on 'The Tribute of Yu,' Pt. i., p. 62. The 'wild of T'aou-lin' (Peach forest) is referred to the country about the hill of Muh-new (牧牛), called also the hill of K'wa-foo (夸父), in the south-east of the pres. dep. of T'ung-chow (同州). An objection has been taken to the credibility of the account here on the ground that the horses and oxen belonged to the people,—were only contributed by them for the expedition; and that to appropriate them to himself in this way, instead of returning them to their owners, was an act befitting Show, and not at all to be expected from king Woo. But we may be sure these were Woo's own horses and oxen. If it be granted that the people did supply a portion of the animals used in war, the sovereign himself furnished a larger number;—see K'e-ling's 古文尙書寃詞, Bk. IV., on the point.

[In the Le Ke, the Bk. 樂記, pp. 29-22, there is an expansion of the text, celebrating King Woo. It may be that the author had before him some copy of the 武成, current in the Han dynasty, fuller than that which we now have. In p. 19, it is said—馬散之華山之陽,而弗復乘,牛散之桃林之野,而弗復服,車甲衅而藏之府庫,而弗復用,倒載干戈,包之以虎皮,……然後天下知武王之不復用兵也.]

3. *Various sacrifices, and solemn announcement of the completion of the War.* 丁未祀于周廟,—the fourth month would commence on 己丑 or 庚寅, according as the previous one had 29 or 30 days, and 丁未 must have been the 18th or 19th day. Before setting out on his enterprise, Woo had sacrificed to his father, to God and the earth ('The Great speech,' Pt. i., p. 10); here at its close he sacrifices, and, we may suppose, gives thanks at the same altars. 邦,甸,侯,衞,—see the account and figure on pp. 148, 149, of the divisions of the empire under the Chow dynasty. By the 邦 we must understand, I think, the central division,—the imperial domain (王畿) and 甸,侯,衞, we have three of the divisions which lay beyond it,—a part for the whole of the five domains which constituted the 'middle kingdom.' We cannot account for the irregularity of the order in which they are given. After 衞 we must understand 諸侯, equivalent to '*the chiefs*,' which I have supplied in the translation.

生魄、庶邦冢君暨百工、受命于周。（五節）○王若曰、嗚呼、群

4 After the moon began to wane, the hereditary princes of the various States, and all the officers, received their appointments from Chow.

Gan-kwŏ defines 駿 by 大, 'great,' 'in great state;' it is better to take it with Ts'ae after the 爾雅, as = 速. 豆籩,—see Con. Ana., VIII, iv. 3. It was an honour to the chiefs and princes to assist at the sacrifice. 越三日庚戌,—between ting-we and kăng-seuh there are two days, so the latter was the 21st or 22d day of the month. In Bk. XII., p. 2, we have 丙午越三日戊申, where both ping-woo and mow-shin must be reckoned to make up the three days;—the writers had different methods equally legitimate, of reckoning. 柴,—see on the 'Can. of Shun,' p. 8. 望,—see on the 'Can. of Shun,' p. 6. This sacrifice was offered, I suppose, at the altar of the great earth, mentioned in Bk. I., Pt. i., p. 10. 4. *The princes and officers receive their appointments from Woo, as the first emperor of the dynasty of Chow.* 既生魄, —the moon begins to wane,—the darkness is born—after the full moon. The day indicated in the text is generally supposed to be the 16th; but Ch'in Leih, observes that, if that had been the day, the phrase would have been 哉生魄, corresponding to 既生明 in p. 2. He would lay stress therefore on the 既, as showing that the darkness was not only 'born,' but had made some growth; and fixes the day as the 17th. But here there is a difficulty.—The historian goes backward instead of forward with his narrative; the 17th would precede the day *ting-we*. Ying-tă calls attention to this circumstance, he himself supposing the day to be the 16th; and in the fact of the chiefs assisting at the sacrifice in the ancestral temple he sees a proof that they had previously received their appointments from king Woo. I should myself extend the force of the 既 much more than Ch'in does. Why may not the phrase 既生魄 indicate any between the 15th and the end of the month, when we should come to the 'death' or end of the darkness? The historian has chosen to indicate thus indefinitely the day when the princes and officers received their appointments from Woo. As to their assisting on the day ting-we at his sacrificial service, that might very well be. Things could not be done in order while the revolution was in progress. From the taking the field against Show down to the new commissioning of rulers under the new supremacy, all was irregular and only after this would a new *order* of things take its course.

[In the Books of the early Han dynasty, 律歷志, 第一, 下, compiled by Lew Hin we find three quotations as from the 武成. The first agrees with the 1st par. of the chapter.—惟一月壬辰旁死霸, 若翼日癸巳, 武王乃朝步自周, 于征伐紂. The second is not found in the received text, nor any trace of it; but it agrees sufficiently with the first par. of the 'Speech at Muh,' and the statement in the 9th par. of this Book.—粤若來二 (some editions have 三, incorrectly) 月, 既死霸, 粤五日甲子, 咸劉商王紂. It is then stated that there was a second month intercalary in this year which began with the day 庚寅; that the third month began with 己未, and the fourth month with 己丑. Then comes the third quotation.—惟四月既旁生霸, 粤六日庚戌, 武王燎于周廟, 翼日辛亥祀于天位, 粤五日乙卯, 乃以庶國祀馘于周廟, 'In the fourth month, on the day kăng-seuh, the 6th after the 16th, king Woo made a fire in the ancestral temple of Chow. Next day,—the day sin-hae,—he sacrificed at the altar of Heaven; and five days after,—on the day yih-maou,—attended by the princes of the various States, he sacrificed and presented the heads *of Show and his two concubines* in the ancestral temple.' Here the intimations of time are different from those which we have in parr. 3 and 4 of the text. Possibly the 燎 here = the 柴 of par. 3;—and they are referred to the same day. We cannot trace any other correspondencies.

The question occurs,—Where did Lew Hin find the copy of the 武成, from which he made these quotations? Yen Sze-koo supposed they were taken from some copy of Fuh-shang's Books; see an art. by Choo He in the 集說. But Fuh-shang did not possess the 武成.

后、惟先王建邦啟土、公劉克篤前烈、至于大王、肇基王迹、王季其勤王家、我文考文王、克成厥勳、誕膺天命、以撫方夏、大邦畏其力、小邦懷其德、惟九年、大統

5 II. The king spake to the following effect:—"Oh! ye host of princes, the first of our kings founded the State and commenced our territory. The duke Lew was able to consolidate the merits of his predecessor. But it was the king T'ae who laid the foundations of the imperial inheritance. Then king Ke was diligent for the royal House; and my deceased father, king Wăn, completed his merit, and received the great decree of Heaven to soothe the regions of the great bright land. The great States feared his strength; the small States cherished his virtue. In nine years, however, the whole

Yen Jŏ-ku, Wang, Ming-shing and others think that he took them from the copy of the 'Old Text,' which Gan-kwŏ had transcribed, and which was preserved in one of the imperial repositories. We know that Lew Hin had access to this copy, and it is possible that he might quote from the 武成 in it.

There is, however, another way of accounting for the quotations. There was a copy of the 武成 current in the Han dynasty, as we have seen there was of the 誓泰. K'ang-shing states that it was lost in the reign of the founder of the eastern Han, A.D. 25-57. We do not know whence it was derived. From the last quotation we may suppose that its character was like that of the copy of the 'Great Speech,' which likewise disappeared. It appears to me more likely that the quotations by Lew Hin were made from it than from the 'Old Text' to which he had access. The authority of the received text, such as it is, need not be affected by the differences between it and the passages in the 律歷志.

Ch. II. Pp. 5, 7. ADDRESS OF KING WOO TO THE PRINCES, ON GIVING THEM THEIR INVESTITURES. 5. *Sketch of the history of the House of Chow from its founder to king Woo.* See the introductory note to Book I. on the name of this Part of the Shoo. 先王 'the former king,'='the first of our kings.' Ying-tă says that we know that K'e, Shun's min. of agriculture, must be intended, because he is mentioned before the duke Lew. The predicates—建邦啟土—sufficiently indicate the same. K'e was not a king, but Woo here calls him so. 篤前烈,—篤厚前人功烈. K'e is to be understood as Lew's 'predecessor.' 大王,—by king T'ae is intended Tan-foo. 肇基王迹,—'first founded the traces of imperial sway;' see in the She King, the 'Praise-songs of Loo,' iv. 2, where it is said of T'ae that 'he dwelt on the south of mount K'e, and began to shear the dynasty of Shang' (居岐之陽,實始翦商);—not, say the critics, that he had any intention to do it, but the hearts of the people were so drawn to him, that they became devotedly attached to his House. 文考文王,—'my deceased father Wăn, the king Wăn.' We cannot well repeat the honorary title in the translation. 誕膺,—'greatly received'; 膺=受. 以撫方夏=以撫安四方諸夏. On 夏, see the Can. of Shun, p. 20. 大邦畏其力,小邦懷其德,—this passage is quoted, as from 'the Books of Chow,' in the 左傳,襄三十二年. 大統,—'the great united whole.' 未集=未集於其身, 'was not yet collected in his person.'

未集、予小子其承厥志。○ 六節 底商之罪、告于皇天后土、所過名山大川、曰、惟有道曾孫周王發、將有大正于商、今商王受無道、暴殄天物、害虐烝民、爲天下逋逃

empire was not collected under his rule, and it fell to me, who am but a little child, to carry out his will.

6 Detesting the crimes of Shang, I announced to great Heaven and the sovereign Earth, to the famous hill and the great river, by which I passed, saying, 'I, Fă, the principled, king of Chow, by a long descent, am about to have a great righting with Shang. Show, the king of Shang, is without principle, cruel and destructive to the creatures of Heaven, injurious and tyrannical to the multitudes of the people, chief of the vagabonds of the empire,

[In the 'Doctrine of the Mean,' xviii., 3, it is said that 'the duke of Chow completed the virtuous course of Wăn and Woo,' and that he carried up the title of king to T'ae and Ke, and sacrificed to all the former dukes above them with the imperial ceremonies.' As it was thus the duke of Chow who carried up the title of king to Tan-foo and Ke-leih, completing what Woo had left undone, it has been asked how we find those titles here in the mouth of king Woo. I apprehend that the merit of the duke of Chow was in extending the practice of honouring ancestors, beyond the circle of the imperial family, to 'the princes, the great officers the scholars, and the common people.' King Woo no doubt took counsel on the subject with his brother the duke of Chow. Perhaps it was by his advice that he did it; but there can be no doubt that he had conferred the titles mentioned in the text. The thing is commemorated in the Le Ke, the Bk. 大傳, p. 2. I give the whole paragraph here, because it gives a strong confirmation not only to this par., but also to the two preceding ones.—牧之野,武王之大事也,既事而退,柴於上帝,祈於社,設奠於牧室,遂率天下諸侯執豆籩,逡奔走,追王大王亶父,王季歷,文王昌,不以卑臨尊.]

Pp. 6—8. *He relates the prayer which he addressed to the spirits of Heaven and Earth, of mount Hwa and the Ho, in contemplation of the engagement with Show.* 6. 底商之罪,—there is much difficulty in giving any appropriate meaning to 底. It has been defined by 至, 致, and 極數. The last is given in the 'Daily Explanation;' the 'detesting' in the translation is as allowable, and that is all that can be said for it. 皇天后土,—comp. what was said on the phrase 天地 in Bk. I., Pt. i., p. 8. This is the only place in the Shoo where the combination 后土 occurs. Ying-tă understands, I think correctly, by 名山 mount Hwa, and the Ho by 大川. Critics generally take 山 and 川 in the plural. We must understand, of course, that Woo made his announcement to *the spirits of* Heaven, Earth, the mountain, and the river. 有道曾孫,—I take 有道 and 曾孫 as in apposition. Such is the view of Ying-tă, who observes that Woo, in asking the help of the spirits, and speaking of himself in contrast with Show would not affect a false humility. Ts'ae and others say that by 'the principled' Woo refers to his forefathers, and construe the phrase as under the regimen of 曾孫, which means literally 'great-grandson.' 周王發,—Ts'ae supposes that 周王 is an interpolation,—which seems very likely. 大正,—comp. the use of 正 in the 'Speech of T'ang,' p. 2,—不敢不正. 暴殄天物,

主、萃淵藪、予小子既獲仁人、敢祇承上帝、以遏亂畧、華夏蠻貊、罔不率俾。○恭（七節）天成命、肆予東征、綏厥士

who collect about him as fish in the deep, and beasts in the prairie. I, who am but a little child, having obtained *the help of* virtuous men, presume reverently to comply with *the will of* God, to make an end of his disorderly ways. The great and flowery region, and the wild tribes of the south and north, equally follow and consent
7 with me. Reverently obeying the determinate counsel of Heaven, I pursue my punitive work to the east, to give tranquillity to its

—殄=絕, 'to destroy utterly' 天物, 'the creatures of Heaven;' 'including men,' says Lin Che-k'e, 'but they are further specified,' because of their greater importance.' 爲天下逋逃主, 萃(=聚)淵藪,—the paraphrase of this in the 'Daily Explanation' is:—天下有罪在逃之人, 所當誅鋤之, 以安良善者也, 受反收留之, 與彼爲主, 有司莫之敢捕, 如魚之聚于深淵, 獸之聚于林藪, 'The criminals and vagabonds of the empire ought to be taken off and rooted out, to secure the repose of the good, but Show receives and maintains them, and is their chief, so that the officers do not dare to apprehend them. They are as fish collected in the deep waters, and as beasts gathered together in the forests and thickets.' 予小子既獲仁人,—we have seen the references made by Woo in the 'Great Speech,' Pt. ii., 9, *et al.*, to his 'virtuous men.' We may compare with the sentiment here that of T'ang in his 'Announcement,' p. 4., where he says that before taking his measures against Këë, he 'sought for the great sage, with whom he might unite his strength' (聿求元聖, 與之戮力). 承上帝=承上帝之意, 'to receive or comply with the will of God.' 亂畧,—Gan-kwŏ takes 畧 in the sense of 路, 'ways;' Ts'ae takes it in that of 謀, 'counsels,' 'plans.' Both explanations are allowable. 華夏,—see on the 'Can. of Shun,' p. 20. 蠻貊,—see Ana., XV., v. 2. 率俾,—Ts'ae and others take 俾 here in the sense of 從, 'to follow,' so that the clause = 'all follow one another to follow me.' Gan-kwŏ would put a comma at 率, and taking 俾 in its common signification of 使, join it to the next clause. This has in its favour, that the 肆 in next par. stands more naturally at its commencement than as we read it at present. The rhythm of the style, however, requires that we join 率 and 俾.

[In the 左傳, 昭七年, we find:—昔武王數紂之罪, 以告諸侯, 曰, 紂爲天下逋逃主, 萃淵藪. The quotation is important, not only as guaranteeing so much of the prayer, but also as showing that the prayer was a part of the address which king Woo made to the princes. It is on this that Maou K'e-ling mainly relies in protesting against the way in which Choo He and others propose to break up and re-arrange the paragraphs of this Book.]

7. See the manner in which this paragraph is adduced by Mencius, III., Pt. II., v., 5. There are important alterations in the structure, the philosopher not directly quoting, but using the passage so as to suit his purpose. Gan-kwŏ puts all the verbs in the past tense, saying that the description is of what took place in the 11th year, when there was the first assemblage at Măng-tsin, and Woo returned, without proceeding to the attack of Show. But there is no sufficient evidence of such a meeting. The two clauses, moreover,—恭天成命, 肆予東征, fix the whole par. to the time then being,—the time in which 武 was offering his prayer. 篚厥玄黃,—'basketed their azure and yellow *fabrics*.' See the many descriptions in the 'Tribute of Yu' of the

女、惟其士女、篚厥玄黃、昭我周王、天休震動、用附我大邑周。○(八節)惟爾有神、尚克相予、以濟兆民、無作神羞、○(九節)既戊午、師逾孟津、癸亥、陳于商郊、俟天休命、甲子

men and women. Its men and women bring their baskets full of azure and yellow silks, to show forth *the virtue of* us the kings of Chow. Heaven's favours stir them up, so that they come with
8 their allegiance to our great State of Chow. And now, ye spirits, grant me your aid, that I may relieve the millions of the people, and nothing turn out to your shame!"
9 III. On the day mow-woo the army crossed the ford of Măng; on the day kwei-hae it was drawn up in array in the borders of

offerings brought in baskets. 昭我周王,—'displaying our kings of Chow.' Some say that azure and yellow are the colours of heaven and earth respectively, and that the object of bringing such fabrics was to show that the kings of Chow were as good and beneficent as Heaven and earth. It is not necessary to seek for such a recondite meaning. The bringing of the baskets was an expression of allegiance, and an acknowledgment of the virtues of the House of Chow. 大邑周,—I take 邑 here = 國, as we saw that Këang Shing proposed to do in the last Book, p. 6.

8. 爾有神,—the spirits are those of Heaven and earth, of the mountain and the river. The conclusion is sufficiently bold. Woo must have felt sure that his enterprise was right, and in accordance with the supreme mind and will.

Medhurst (Theology of the Chinese, p. 55) has translated the par.:—'Only may you shins be enabled to assist me in settling the millions of the people, and do not bring disgrace on your shin-ships.' He observes upon it, that 'the form of expression would intimate that there was some power above the shins invoked, and that it was possible they might be unable to grant the needful assistance.' There is no such indication in the form of the expression as he supposes. 尚克相予 is not—'may you *be enabled* to assist me,' but 'grant me, I pray you, your help.' The 克 denotes an efficacy in the spirits themselves, and gives emphasis, as we have often seen to be its force, to the word that follows, so that 克相予 = 'help me indeed.' It is remarkable how, in the course of the prayer, reference is expressly made both to 'God' and to 'Heaven,' as supreme. Why was it not addressed directly to God? There are both imperfect monotheism and polytheism in it. God is recognized as supreme, and at the same time other spirits are recognized, who would give effect to His will, and might be prayed to for that purpose. As Woo addressed his army in the grey dawn of the day at Muh, we may say that he had but the grey dawn of religious knowledge in his mind.

I will not add anything here to what I quoted from Ying-tă in the introductory note on the abruptness and seeming incompleteness with which the prayer terminates. It would have been better if there had been some additional expression of Woo's own feelings and purposes, and some inculcation of duties on the princes. It may be that a portion of the Book has been lost; or it may be that we do have all which Woo was pleased to say.

Ch. III. Pp. 9, 10. THE BATTLE OF MUH, WITH KING WOO'S PROCEEDINGS IMMEDIATELY AFTER; AND SUBSEQUENT MEASURES. 9. 既戊午師逾孟津,—comp. the 'Great Speech,' Pt. i., p. 1. On this same day he delivered the address recorded in that Part. 癸亥陳于商郊,—kwei-hae was the 3rd of the 2d month, five days after mow-woo. From Măng-tsin to Show's capital was 400 *le*, so that Woo must have hurried on his army with great speed. 俟天休命,—'the favourable decree' of Heaven was to be seen in the result of the impending battle, about which Woo felt quite confident. Gan-kwŏ says that this clause has reference to the ceasing of the rains which had fallen all the way from Măng-

昧爽、受率其旅若林、會于牧野、罔有敵于我師、前徒倒戈、攻于後以北、血流漂杵、一戎衣、天下大定、乃反商政、政由舊、釋箕子囚、封比干墓、式商容閭、散鹿臺

Shang, waiting for the gracious decision of Heaven. On the day kĕă-tsze, at early dawn, Show led forward his hosts like a forest, and assembled them in the wilderness of Muh. But they would offer no opposition to our army. Those in the front inverted their spears, and attacked those behind them, till they fled, and the blood flowed till it floated the pestles about. Thus did *king Woo* once don his arms, and the empire was greatly settled. He overthrew the *existing* government of Shang, and made it resume its old course. He delivered the count of Ke from prison, and raised a tumulus over the grave of Pe-kan. He bowed in his carriage at the gate of

tsin, so that they were able during the night to complete the order of battle. This view is at once far-fetched and shallow. 甲子昧爽,—see the 'Speech at Muh,' p. 1. 其旅若林,會于牧野,—see the She King, Pt. III., Bk. I. Ode II., 7, 殷商之旅,其會如林,矢于牧野. Sze-ma Ts'een says that Show's army amounted to 700,000 men, which is doubtless a great exaggeration. 敵于我師,—the historian identifies himself with Woo's army. 以北,—北=奔, 'to flee.' Ts'een gives a difft. account of the battle. At least he makes no mention of Show's troops falling upon one another, but says that 'Woo sent his general Shang-foo, with a hundred of the most daring warriors, to dash forward at the head of a large body. Show's army had no mind to fight, but really wished king Woo to penetrate their host. They therefore inverted their lances, and made way for his men. They in fact all revolted from Show, who fled at once to the "Stag tower."' This account is not reconcileable, however, with the statement which follows about 'the blood flowing till it floated the pestles of the mortars.'

The remarks of Mencius on the passage—血流漂杵 are well known. He attests (VII. Pt. II., iii.) that the 'Completion of the War' contained such a passage, but protests against believing it.—'When the prince the most benevolent was engaged against him who was the most the opposite, how could such a thing be?' It gives, no doubt, an exaggerated description of the slaughter which took place. 杵 means the wooden pestles of the mortars, which the soldiers carried with them to prepare their rice. We need not suppose, as some do (see a note in the 集傳 by 蔡清), that they were the pestles used for pounding the earth in making the intrenchments. Maou K'e-ling prefers the reading of 鹵, 'shields,' for 杵. Mei Tsuh (梅鷟) would save the credit of Mencius at the expense of the classic. If, he argues, it had appeared, as in the present text, that the slaughter was occasioned by Show's troops turning against one another, there would have been no occasion for the philosopher's remark. The forger of Tsin evidently constructed his text that king Woo might not appear chargeable with the bloodshedding, which Mencius supposed might be attributed to him! It is much more natural to believe that Mencius, in the impulse of his ardent nature, spoke as he did,—unadvisedly. 一戎衣,—'once he put on his martial garb.' See in the 'Doctrine of the Mean,' xviii., 2. Comp. also on 殪戎殷, Bk. IX., p. 4. 反商政,—'he turned back the govt. of Shang,' *i.e.*, he took away the oppressive laws of Show, and then—由舊政, 'followed the old govt.' *i.e.*, the

之財、發鉅橋之粟、大賚于四海、而萬姓悅服。○十節列爵惟五、分土惟三、建官惟賢、位事惟能、重民五教、惟食喪祭、惇信明義、崇德報功、垂拱而天下治。

Shang Yung's village. He dispersed the treasures of Luh-t'ae, and distributed the grain of Keu-k'eaou, thus conferring great gifts throughout the empire, and all the people joyfully submitted.

10 He arranged the orders of nobility into five, assigning the territories to them on a threefold scale. He gave offices only to the worthy, and employments only to the able. He attached great importance to the people's being taught the duties of the five relations of society, and to take care for food, for funeral ceremonies, and for sacrifices. He showed the reality of his truthfulness, and proved clearly his righteousness. He honoured virtue, and rewarded merit. Then he had only to let his robes fall down, and fold his hands, and the empire was orderly ruled.

govt. of T'ang and the other good sovereigns who succeeded him. 釋箕子囚,封比干墓,—see the concluding note to the 'Viscount of Wei.' 式商容閭,—式, see Con. Ana.. X., xvi., 3. Shang Yung must have been some worthy in disgrace with Show, and living retired in his village. Ying-tă quotes some account of him from Hwang-p'oo Meih's 帝王世記, but it is the production of a later age. 散鹿臺之財,發鉅橋之粟,—of the 'Stag tower' we have spoken. Keu-k'eaou was in the north east of the pres. dis. of Keuh-chow (曲周), dep. of Kwang-p'ing (廣平). Chih-le, where Show had collected great stores of grain. These two measures were directed to the benefit of the masses of the people, impoverished by the exactions of the tyrant.

P. 10. 列爵惟五,分土惟三,—this agrees with the account of the arrangement of dignities and emoluments determined by the House of Chow, given by Mencius, Book V., Pt. II., ii. The orders of nobility were the Kung, How, Pih, Tsze and Nan, to the two first of which were assigned a hundred *le* square of territory, each, while the Pih had 70, and the Tsze and the Nan only 50 *le* square each. Yen Jŏ-keu absurdly says that this is different from the account of Mencius. It is different, however, from the account which we find in the Chow Le, Bk. IX., (地官,大司徒). There the orders of nobility are five, as in Mencius, but the divisions of territory are also five. To the Kung, it is said, there were assigned 500 *le* square; to the How, 400; to the Pih, 300; to the Tsze, 200; and to the Nan, 100. I don't see how the two accounts are to be reconciled. If it be said that the five-fold territorial division was made by the duke of Chow at a subsequent period, which is the view of K'ang-shing, why did not Mencius advert to it? If it be said, that the larger dimensions arose from the usurpations of the States among themselves, which is the view of Ying-tă, how is it that they have any place in the Chow Le? 建官惟賢,位事惟能,—the historian proceeds to Woo's provisions for the officers about his court. His object was to have none in office but men of talents and virtue, and that each man's duties should be those for which he was specially able. 重民五教,惟食,喪,祭,—Gan-kwŏ explained the former of these clauses by inserting an 與 between 民 and 五教,—'he attached importance to the people, and to the inculcation of the five duties.' This is not so good as to take 民 to be under the regimen

of 五教. The force of 重 extends to the difft. terms in the second clause, and 惟 is used as a connective particle. Lin Che-k'e compares its use here with the same in the 'Tribute of Yu,' Pt. i., pp. 44 and 51. It is said that Woo gave effect to this solicitude for the instruction of the people by establishing schools,—educational institutions of various kinds; and to make good the provision of food, he enacted 'the hundred mow allotment and the share system' (see Mencius, III., Pt. I., iii.). 惇信明義,—惇=厚, 'to make solid, or real.' The 信 or 'truthfulness' belonged, the critics say, to all his governmental orders, and the fidelity with which they were kept, and the 義 or 'righteousness,' to all his actions. We have in the 'Daily Explanation:'—凡出一令,必守之以信,而始終不渝,凡行一事,必裁之以義而動無過舉. 垂拱=垂衣拱手, 'to let the robes hang down, and fold his hands ceremoniously before his breast.' The meaning is, that by the excellence of his institutions and example, there was superseded the necessity of any further laborious measures or efforts. The good order of the government followed as a matter of course.

Concluding Notes. [i]. *On the investitures granted by king Woo.* The 歷代統紀表, under the year B.C. 1121, gives a list of the principal States into which the empire was divided in the dynasty of Chow;—viz. Loo (魯), Wei (衞), Ts'ae (蔡), Tsin (晉), Ts'aou (曹), Ch'ing (鄭), Woo (吳), Yen (燕), Ch'in (陳), Sung (宋), Ts'e (齊), Ts'oo (楚), and Ts'in (秦). I will not here enter into particulars on each of those principalities, as I shall have to speak of most of them in connection with one or other of the following Books. I will now only refer to what is in the Bk. 樂記, of the Le Ke, Part iii., par. 19,—that 'king Woo, on the overthrow of the Shang dynasty, before he descended from his chariot, invested the representative of Hwang-te with the territory of Ke (薊; the pres. dis. of Ta-hing, [大興] in the dep. of Shun-t'een); the representative of Yaou with Chuh (祝; the pres. dis. of Ch'ang-ts'ing [長清], in the dep. of Tse-nan); the representative of Shun with Ch'in (陳; the name remains in that of the dep. Ch'in-chow, Ho-nan); and when he had descended from his chariot,—*i.e.*, subsequently,—he invested the representative of Yu with K'e (杞; this name also remains in that of the dis. of K'e, in the dep. of K'ae-fung); and he sent the representative of the House of Yin to the territory of Sung' (宋; the pres. dis. of Shang-k'ëw (商邱), dep. of Kwei-tih, Ho-nan). These appointments were given, not because of services rendered to the new dynasty, as many others were, but from respect to the memories of the great men represented, that the sacrifices to their spirits might not fall into disuse.

[ii]. *On the specifications of time in this and the two preceding Books.* King Woo proceeded from his capital to the attack of Show on the 3rd day of the 1st month of what is called his 13th year, B.C. 1121 (Gaubil, 1122); and in the 28th day of that month 'in the spring' (according to the 'Great Speech,' Pt. i., p. 1), he crossed the Ho at Măng-ts'in. Ts'ae Ch'in supposes that the year intended was that of Hea, which has been that of all the dynasties of China since the Han. Now the first month of the present Chinese year began on the 18th of our February, and the cycle name of the day was mow-shin (戊申). If we multiply 2984 solar years, which have elapsed since the 13th of Woo's reign, by 365.24224, we obtain the number of days from that time up to the end of last Chinese year, = 1,089,882.84416, or 18164 cycles of days and 42 days more. But it will be found, on calculation, that the first day of new moon in February, 2984 years ago, occurred three days earlier that in the present year. Reckoning back therefore 18,164 cycles and 46 days more from mow-shin of the present year, we come to jin-seuh (壬戌), as the first day of the Hea year in the 13th of Woo's reign; and the view of Ts'ae cannot be sustained.

Reckoning back other 30 days from 壬戌, we come to the day jin-shin (壬辰), as the first day of the first month in the year of Shang; and according to the view of Fan Sze-lin, approved of rather by the editors of Yung-ching's Shoo, this is the day intended in the classic as the first day of the first month spoken of. It is only one day after sin-maou. It would thus appear that not only is Ts'ae in error in saying that we are to understand that the months in the text are the months of the year of Hea, but that the other commentators are equally mistaken in referring them to the year of Chow. They are those of the year of Shang, beginning with the last month of winter. This conclusion lightens somewhat the difficulty occasioned by the mention of "the spring," in the "Great Speech," par. 1. This is spoken with reference to the day mow-woo, which certainly was close upon the spring. If it be thought that the whole of the first month is intended to be described as in 'the spring,' we must believe that in consequence of deficient intercalation, an error of one whole lunation had crept into the calendar by the time of the rise of the Chow dynasty. On suggesting that this might be the case to a very intelligent Chinese scholar, he replied, 'How can you think that the sages could have blundered so?' But it will be found, from what will be seen in the prolegomena on the subject of the astronomy and chronology of the ancient Chinese, that this was probably the case.

蔡沈考定武成

惟一月、壬辰旁死魄、越翼日、癸巳王朝步自周、于征伐商。○底商之罪、告于皇天、后土、所過名山大川、曰、惟有道曾孫周王發、將有大正于商、今商王受無道、暴殄天物、害虐烝民、爲天下逋逃主、萃淵藪、予小子旣獲仁人、敢祗承上帝、以遏亂畧、華夏蠻貊、罔不率俾、惟爾有神、尚克相予、以濟兆民、無作神羞。○旣戊午、師逾孟津、癸亥、陳于商郊、俟天休命、甲子昧爽、受率其旅若林、會于牧野、罔有敵于我師、前徒倒戈、攻于後以北、血流漂杵、一戎衣、天下大定、乃反商政、政由舊、釋箕子囚、封比干墓、式商容閭、散鹿臺之財、發鉅橋之粟、大賚于四海、而萬姓悅服。○厥四月哉生明、王來自商、至于豐、乃偃武修文、歸馬于華山之陽、放牛于桃林之野、示天下弗服。

APPENDIX.

THE COMPLETION OF THE WAR, AS ARRANGED BY TS'AE CH'IN.

In the first month, *the day* jin-shin immediately followed the end of the moon's waning. The next day was kwei-ke, when the king in the morning marched from Chow to attack and punish Shang.

Declaring the crimes of Shang, he announced to great Heaven and the sovereign Earth, to the famous hill and the great river, by which he passed, saying, 'I, Fă, the principled, king of Chow, by a long descent, am about to have a great righting with Shang. Show, the king of Shang, is without principle, cruel and destructive to the creatures of Heaven, injurious and tyrannical to the multitudes of the people, chief of the vagabonds of the empire, who collect about him as fish in the deep, and beasts in the prairie. I, who am but a little child, having obtained *the help of* virtuous men, presume reverently to comply with *the will of* God, to make an end of his disorderly ways. The great and flowery region, and the wild tribes of the south and north, equally follow and consent with me. And now, ye spirits, grant me your aid, that I may relieve the millions of the people, and nothing turn out to your shame!"

On the day mow-woo the army crossed the ford of Măng; on the day kwei-hae it was drawn up in array in the borders of Shang, waiting for the gracious decision of Heaven. On the day këă-tsze, at early dawn, Show led forward his hosts like a forest, and assembled them in the wilerness of Muh. But they would offer no opposition to our army. Those in the front inverted their spears, and attacked those behind them, till they fled, and the blood flowed till it floated the pestles about. Thus did *king Woo* once don his arms, and the empire was greatly settled. He overthrew the *existing* government of Shang, and made it resume its old course. He delivered the count of Ke from prison, and raised a tumulus over the grave of Pe-kan. He bowed in his carriage at the gate of Shang Yung's village. He dispersed the treasures of Luh-t'ae, and distributed the grain of Keu-keaou, thus conferring great gifts throughout the empire; and all the people joyfully submitted.

In the fourth month, at the first appearance of the moon, the king came from Shang to Fung, when he hushed all the movements of war, and attended to the cultivations of peace. He sent back his horses to the south of mount Hwa, and let loose his oxen in the open country of T'aou-lin, showing the empire that he would not use them *again*.

既生魄、庶邦冢君、暨百工、受
命于周。〇丁未、祀于周廟、邦
甸侯衞、駿奔走、執豆籩。越三
日庚戌、柴望、大告武成。〇王
若曰、嗚呼、羣后、惟先王建邦
啓土、公劉克篤前烈、至于太
王、肇基王迹、王季其勤王家、
我文考文王、克成厥勳、誕膺
天命、以撫方夏、大邦畏其力、
小邦懷其德、惟九年、大統未
集、予小子其承厥志。〇恭天
成命、肆予東征、綏厥士女、惟
其士女、篚厥玄黃、昭我周王、
天休震動、用附我大邑周。〇
列爵惟五、分土惟三、建官惟
賢、位事惟能、重民五教、惟食
喪祭、惇信明義、崇德報功、垂
拱而天下治。

After the moon began to wane, the hereditary princes of the various States, and all the officers, received their appointments from Chow.

On the day ting-we he sacrificed in the ancestral temple of Chow, when *the chiefs of* the imperial domain, and of the teen, how, and wei domains, all hurried about, carrying the dishes. Three days after, he presented a burnt-offering *to Heaven*, and worshipped towards the mountains and rivers, solemnly announcing the successful completion of the war.

The king spake to the following effect:—"Oh! ye host of princes, the first of our kings founded the State and commenced our territory. The duke Lew was able to consolidate the merits of his predecessor. But it was the king T'ae who laid the foundations of the imperial inheritance. Then king Ke was diligent for the royal House; and my deceased father, king Wăn, completed his merit, and received the great decree of Heaven to soothe the regions of the great bright land. The great States feared his strength; the small States cherished his virtue. In nine years, however, the whole empire was not collected under his rule, and it fell to me, who am but a little child, to carry out his will. Reverently obeying the determinate counsel of Heaven, I pursued my punitive work to the east, to give tranquillity to its men and women. Its men and women brought their baskets full of azure and yellow silks, to show forth *the virtue of* us the kings of Chow. Heaven's favours stirred them up, so that they came with their allegiance to our great State of Chow.

He arranged the orders of nobility into five, assigning, the territories to them on a threefold scale. He gave offices only to the worthy and employments only to the able. He attached great importance to the people's being taught the duties of the five relations of society, and took care for food, for funeral ceremonies, and for sacrifices. He showed the reality of his truthfulness, and proved clearly his righteousness. He honoured virtue, and rewarded merit. Then he had only to let his robes fall down, and fold his hands and the empire was orderly ruled.

THE BOOKS OF SHANG.

BOOK IV. THE GREAT PLAN.

洪範

惟十有三祀、王訪于箕子。○王乃言曰、嗚呼、箕子、惟天陰隲下民、相協厥居、我不知

1 I. In the thirteenth year, the king went to inquire of the vis-
2 count of Ke, and said to him "Oh! viscount of Ke, Heaven, unseen, has given their constitution to mankind, aiding *also* the harmonious development of it in their various conditions. I do not know how their proper virtues in their various relations should be brought forth in due order."

THE NAME OF THE BOOK.—洪範, 'The Great Plan.' 洪=大, 'great.' 範=法, 'plan.' Other synonyms of 範, given in the dict., are 式 and 模, both conveying the same idea of 'plan,' or 'model.' The name, like that of the last Book, is taken from the Book itself. We read in par. 2, that 'Heaven gave to Yu the Great Plan, with its nine Divisions.' Some would adopt the whole of this,—洪範九疇, as the name; but there would be no advantage gained by departing in such a matter, from the established usage. The Book is found in both the texts.

HISTORY OF THE BOOK, AND MODE OF INTERPRETATION. The viscount of Ke had said that when ruin overtook the House of Shang, he would not be the servant of another dynasty; —see 'The Viscount of Wei,' p. 8. Accordingly, he refused to acknowledge the sovereignty of king Woo, who had delivered him from the prison where Show had put him, and fled—or perhaps only made it known that he would flee —to Corea. King Woo respected and admired his attachment to the fallen dynasty, and invested him with that territory. He now felt constrained to appear at the court of Chow, when the king took the opportunity to consult him on the great principles of government, and the result was that he communicated this 'Great Plan, with its nine Divisions.' Being first made public under the Chow dynasty, it is ranked among the 'Books of Chow.' It is often referred to, however, as one of the 'Books of Shang,' as having emanated from the viscount of Ke, who should properly be adjudged to that dynasty. When we read the Book itself, we see that it originally belonged to the time of Hea, and at least the central portion, or text of it,—par. 4,—should be ascribed to 'the great Yu.' We have therefore a fragment in it of very ancient learning. How this had come into the possession of the viscount of Ke we cannot tell. It does not seem to have occurred to the Chinese critics to make the inquiry. Whether we should ascribe all the paragraphs from the 5th downwards to the viscount, is also a point on which I cannot undertake to pronounce a posi-

tive opinion. Hea Seuen (夏僎; Sung dyn.) says that 'though the words are those of the viscount of Ke, the record of them was made by the historians of Chow.'

That the central portion of the Book, and more or less of the expository part, came down from the times of Hea is not improbable. The use of the number nine, and the naming of the various divisions of the 'Plan,' are in harmony with Yu's style and practice in his 'Counsels,' and in what we may call the 'Domesday Book.'

We are told that 'Heaven—God—gave the plan with its Divisions to Yu.' Upon this Gan-kwŏ says that 'Heaven gave Yu the mysterious tortoise, which made its appearance in the waters of the Lŏ, bearing marks on its back well defined, from 1 to 9; and thereupon Yu determined the meaning of those numbers, and completed the nine divisions of the plan.'

This legend has been fathered on Confucius, as we read in the 'Appendix to the Yih king' (易經, 繫辭), Pt i., p. 38, that 'the Ho gave forth the Scheme, and the Lŏ gave forth the Book (or defined characters), which the sages (or sage) took as their pattern' (河出圖, 洛出書, 聖人則之). If we admit that these words proceeded from Confucius or were edited by him, while it is absurd enough to speak of the two rivers giving forth the Scheme and the Book, he says nothing of the Scheme being on the back of a dragon, which has been the current statement for more than 2,000 years, or of the Book being on the back of a tortoise. Moreover, there is no evidence that he meant to connect the 'Book of Lŏ' with the 'Great Plan' at all. We should rather imagine that he supposed the Scheme and the Book to be equally related to the diagrams of the Yih, and to have been both presented to Fuh-he. I hardly know an interpreter, however, but Lin Che-k'e, who has not adopted the statement of Gan-kwŏ; and the consequence is that the explanations of this Book are overlaid with absurd twaddle about the virtue of numbers as related to Heaven and Earth, to the *Yin* and the *Yang*, the cardinal points, &c., &c.. The following figure has been imagined as that which was exhibited to Yu:—

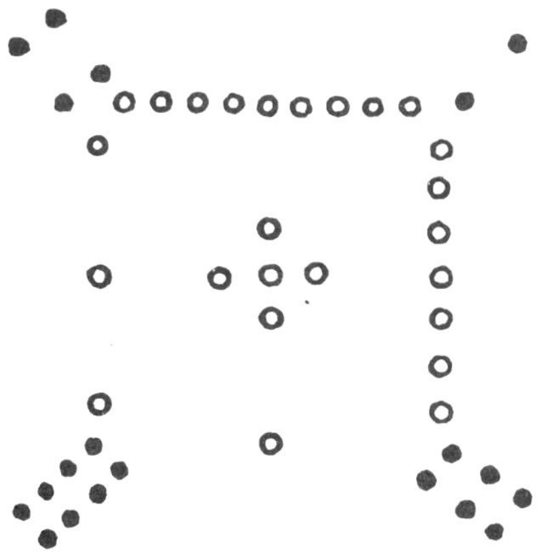

Near the head of the tortoise, it is said, were the nine open marks, and opposite was the one close mark. The two and the four were at the shoulders; the six and the eight were by the feet. Three and seven were on the left and right, and five were in the centre. Out of those numbers, odd and even, heavenly and earthly, now multiplied, now added together, the whole of the Plan and its Divisions is developed, with a glibness of tongue and a leger-de-plume, which only familiarity with the Yih-king, and the applications of it to astrology, geomancy, and other follies can produce. There is of course no 'solid learning' (實學) in all this. We shall have to endeavour to treat seriously of it, when we come to the Yih-king, but it should be exploded from the study of 'The great Plan.' The Book will be found dark enough in itself, but the viscount of Ke says nothing of occult qualities of numbers, from which the ideas in the different divisions of the Plan could be deduced. It will be my object, therefore, simply to elucidate the meaning of the whole as a scheme of government, intended to guide all rulers in the discharge of their duties.

Gaubil says that 'the Book is a treatise at once of Physics, Astrology, Divination, Morals, Politics, and Religion; and that it has a sufficiently close resemblance to the work of Ocellus the Lucanian.' There is a shadowy resemblance between the *Great Plan* and the curious specimen of Pythagorean doctrine which we have in the treatise *On the Universe*. The dissimilarities are still greater and more numerous. More especially are the different characters of the Greek mind, speculative, and the Chinese mind, practical, apparent in the two Works. Where the Chinese writer loses himself in the sheerest follies of his imagining, he would yet grope about for a rule to be of use in the conduct of human affairs. One of the most interesting curiosities which were obtained in 1861 from the 'Summer palace' near Peking, was a scroll, purporting to be in the handwriting of the emperor K'een-lung, dilating on the meaning of 'The great Plan,' and the lessons to be learned by sovereigns from it. There is a general agreement among the critics in assigning its place to the Book either among the 'Counsels' of the Shoo, or among the 'Instructions.'

CONTENTS. I avail myself here, with a little variation, of the account of these given in the 'Complete Digest' of commentaries on the Shoo (書經備旨).—The whole divides itself into three chapters. The first, parr. 1–3, is introductory, and describes how the 'Great Plan with its Divisions' was first made known to Yu, and came at this time to be communicated to king Woo. The second, in p. 4, contains the Plan and its Divisions. The third, parr. 5–40, contains a particular description of the several Divisions. 'The whole,' says the writer, 'exhibits the great model for the govt. of the empire. The fifth or middle division on Royal Perfection is, indeed, the central one of the whole, that about which the Book revolves. The four divisions that precede it show how this royal Perfection is to be accomplished, and the four that follow show how it is to be maintained.'

Ch. I. Pp. 1—3. KING WOO APPLIES TO THE VISCOUNT OF KE FOR INFORMATION ABOUT

HOW THE GOVERNMENT OF THE EMPIRE SHOULD BE CONDUCTED, AND IS TOLD BY HIM OF THE GREAT PLAN WITH NINE DIVISIONS WHICH YU GOT FROM HEAVEN. 1. 十有三祀,—the commentators observe that 祀, the Shang term for 'year,' is here used instead of the Chow 年, the viscount of Ke using the character to which he had been accustomed. 訪, acc. to Ts'ae, =就而問之,='went to and asked him.' It implies 'consultation.' See the note on the History of the Book. 2. 王乃言曰,—'the king thereupon spoke, saying.' The 乃 protracts the style, and indicates the deliberation with which the king made his inquiry. So in the next paragraph,—箕子乃言曰. 箕子,—king Woo, it is observed, addressed the noble by his Shang title, not having yet invested him with the territory of Corea. It may be so; but he might also address him thus, the old designation being familiar to him, even if he had already given him his new appointment. 天陰隲下民,相協厥居,—陰=默, 'secretly,' 'by a hidden influence;' 隲=定, 'to settle.' Sze-ma Ts'een gives the text as 天陰定下民, which shows at least how he understood the term 隲. The meaning then of the first clause is that 'Heaven, working unseen, has made men with certain hidden springs of character.' As Gan-kwŏ says, 天不言而默定下民. This interpretation is much to be preferred to that adopted by Këang Shing and others from Ma Yung, who makes 陰=覆, 'to cover,' 'to overshadow,' and 隲=升=畀=生, 'to produce.' 天陰隲下民 is thus simply ='Heaven that overshadows produced the inferior people.' The next clause is continuative, and is to be referred to Heaven as its subject. 相 (3d. tone)=助, 'to aid.' 協=合, 'to unite,' 'to harmonize.' 厥居,—'their dwelling or abiding.' This expression is difficult. Both the 'Daily Explanation,' and Këang Shing paraphrase it by 其所當居止之理, 'the principles in which they ought to abide.' Gan-kwŏ's language upon it is enigmatical. He says that 'Heaven thus aids and harmonizes their abiding, so that they shall have a provision for prolonged life,' (是助合其居,使有常生之資). Ying-tă in expanding this has some striking things. He says that 'the people have been produced by supreme Heaven (民是上天所生), and both body and soul are Heaven's gift (形神天之所授). Men have thus the material body and the knowing mind, and Heaven further assists them, helping them to harmonize their lives. The right and the wrong of their language, the correctness and errors of their conduct, their enjoyment of clothing and food, the rightness of their various movements:—all these things are to be harmonized by what they are endowed with by Heaven. Accordance with the right way gives life, and error from it leads to death. Thus Heaven has not only given life to men, and conferred upon them a body and mind, but it further assists them to harmonize their conditions of life, so as to have a provision for its continuance' (天非徒賦命於人,授以形體心識,乃復佑助諧合其居業,使有常生之資). The fact is that the obscure text can only be brought out obscurely. We cannot do better than understand 厥居 as meaning 'the principles in which men should rest in their various conditions,' belonging to the complex constitution which God has given them.

I have said that Heaven is the subject spoken of in 相協厥居. The text certainly supplies no other; but Wang Suh supposed a 王者, before 相, thinking the meaning to be that 'Heaven having produced men with their peculiar constitution, and taking an interest in them, it devolves on the sovereign to give effect to the wishes of Heaven for men's virtue and happiness.' Keang Shing follows this view. It cannot be said not to be in harmony with the general teaching of the classics. The text is thereby, indeed, brought into strict accordance with that in the 'Announcement of T'ang,' p. 2. But the language in that passage is sufficiently explicit. I can find no subject in the text for 相協 but 天. The next clause, however, must be understood, I think, with reference to the duty of the sovereign, so that the whole paragraph may be considered as very nearly equivalent to that referred to in the 'Announcement of T'ang.'

我不知其彝倫攸敘,—king Woo, say many critics, knew very well all about the subject, but he thus speaks to bring out the learning of the viscount of Ke. We may rather suppose that he speaks with reference to the Great Plan and its Divisions, of which he had merely heard. 彝=常, 'constant,' regular;' meaning here the nature of man, acting according to the regular laws of its constitution appointed by Heaven. Compare in the She King, Pt. III., Bk. III., Ode vi., st. 1, 天生烝民,有物有則,民之秉彝,好是懿德, 'Heaven, in giving birth to the multitudes of men, to every endowment appointed its appropriate law. The people, holding fast this constant nature, love the virtue which is admirable.' 倫=人倫, 'the relations of human society,' in which are

其彝倫攸敘。○（三節）箕子乃言曰、我聞在昔、鯀陻洪水、汨陳其五行、帝乃震怒、不畀洪範九疇、彝倫攸斁、鯀則殛死、禹乃嗣興、天乃錫禹洪範九疇、彝倫攸敘。○（四節）初

3 The viscount of Ke thereupon replied, "I have heard that of old time K'wăn dammed up the inundating waters, and thereby threw into disorder the arrangement of the five elements. God was thereby roused to anger, and did not give him 'the great Plan with its nine Divisions,' whereby the proper virtues of the various relations were left to go to ruin. K'wăn was then kept a prisoner till his death, and Yu rose up to continue his undertaking. To him Heaven gave 'the great Plan with its nine Divisions,' and thereby the proper virtues of the various relations were brought forth in their order.

seen the virtues of man's nature, intended by 彝. 攸=所; 攸敘=所以敘, 'how they are arranged.'

I have said that this clause is to be understood with reference to the work and duty of the sovereign. Gan-kwŏ, indeed, supposes that Heaven is still the subject (我不知天所以定民之常道理次敘,問何由); but the other view is generally adopted. The explanation of the whole paragraph, given by Ch'in Ya-yen (陳雅言; Ming dyn.) is the best which I have seen:—武王意人君代天理物，必仰承天意以治民，而使其居之順其常，得其正，以無負上天陰隲相協之心者，其道在於敘其秉彝人倫也，我欲敘之，不知所以敘之之道當何如，此間箕子以爲治之道也，箕子於是告以洪範九疇，爲爲治之法，蓋九疇之敘，即彝之所敘也. Gaubil's translation is—'Le ciel a des voies secrettes, par lesquelles il rend le peuple tranquille et fixe. Il s'unit à lui pour l'aider à garder son Etat. Je ne connois point cette regle: quelle est elle?' Medhurst endeavours to keep more close to the text:—'Heaven has secretly settled the lower people, aiding and according with that in which they rest; but I do not know the arrangement of those invariable principles.'

P. 3. 鯀陻洪水,—陻=塞, 'to dam up.' Instead of finding a vent for the accumulated waters, as his son Yu did, K'wăn attempted to remedy the evils of their inundation by damming them up. 汨陳五行,—for the 'five elements,' see the 5th par. 汨=亂, 'to confuse,' 'to throw into disorder.' 陳=列, 'to arrange,' and 陳五行=上帝所陳列之五行, 'the five elements arranged by God.' How K'wăn's damming the waters—dealing wrongly with one element—should derange all the other elements, is a statement which I can make nothing of. 不畀洪範九疇,—畀=與, 'to give to;' 疇=類, 'sorts,' 'classes,' 'divisions.' 彝倫攸斁,—斁 (read *too*) =敗, 'to subvert,' 'to ruin.' How the consequence here stated took place, is likewise a thing which I don't understand. 鯀則殛死,—see the 'Can. of Shun,' p. 12. 天乃錫禹洪範九疇,—we have seen, in the second introductory note, how it is fabled that Yu received the great Plan from

一、曰五行、次二、曰敬用五事、次三、曰農用八政、次四、曰協用五紀、次五、曰建用皇極、次六、曰乂用三德、次七、曰明用稽疑、次八、曰念用庶徵、次九、曰嚮用五福、

4 II. "*Of those divisions*, the first is called 'The five Elements;' the second is called 'The Reverent Practice of the five Businesses'; the third is called 'Earnest Devotion to the eight objects of Government;' the fourth is called 'The Harmonious Use of the five Arrangements'; the fifth is called 'The Establishment and Use of Royal Perfection'; the sixth is called 'The Cultivation and Use of the three Virtues'; the seventh is called 'The Intelligent Use of the Examination of Doubts'; the eighth is called 'The Thoughtful Use of the various Verifications'; the ninth is called 'The Hortatory Use of the five Happinesses, and the Awing Use of the six Extremities.'

Heaven. Lin Che-k'e held that all which is meant by the text is that Heaven gave Yu the mind and the enlightenment to conceive and describe the Plan. Choo He was asked what he thought of this view, and whether it was not contrary to the Yih King, which says that 'the Lŏ gave forth the Book.' He answered, 'Suppose that Heaven had only now given the Book of Lŏ, if it did not also give the mind to interpret it, no man would understand it! Neither the old account, nor Lin Che-k'e's, is to be set aside' (便使而今天錫洛書，若非天啟其心，亦無人理會得，兩說似不可偏廢也). I have said I don't understand how the virtues and relations were left to go to ruin, in consequence of K'wăn's failure: Ch'in Sze-k'ae has tried to explain the difficulty, but with little success. He says:—陶唐之盛，於變時雍之際，又何彝倫之斁哉，此非言朝廷也，蓋五行既汨，九功未敘，獸蹄鳥迹之道，交於中國，堯甚憂之，此彝倫之所以斁也，豈必綱常絕滅，而後謂之斁哉.

Ch. II. P. 4. THE GREAT PLAN AND ITS NINE DIVISIONS. The reader must not suppose that the great Plan was something different from its nine Divisions. It was merely the combination of them.

This paragraph is supposed to be the work of Yu. According to Lew Hin, indeed, the whole 65 characters were upon the back of the tortoise;—see the 前漢書，五行志，上，凡此六十五字，皆洛書本文. Gan-kwŏ says he did not know how many characters were on the back of the tortoise, but that the numbering of the Divisions, 'first,' 'second,' &c., (初一曰，次二曰，云云) was done by Yu. In this way there would be 38 characters left. Some take away the half of these again,—those, namely, which have a verbal or hortatory force,' (敬用，農用，云云), leaving the names of the divisions. The prevailing opinion now, however, is that there were only the 45 small circles, open and close, upon the creature; but even thus much cannot be allowed. The whole story of the tortoise and 'the book of Lŏ' is only fit to be told to children. In the paragraph before us, the characters 五行，五事, &c., had come down from the times of Hea; perhaps the 敬用，農用, &c., had done the same; 初一曰，次二曰, &c., were spoken by the viscount of Ke in the narrative which he gave to Woo.

While discarding the 'book of Lŏ,' it will be a help to the student's memory, and in his reading of the various lore on the Plan, if I append here an outline of the 'Book' with the

書經

威用六極。○一五行、一曰水、二曰火、三曰木、四曰金、五曰土。水曰潤下、火曰炎

5 III. [i.] "First, of the five elements.—The first is named water; the second, fire; the third, wood; the fourth, metal; the fifth, earth. *The nature of* water is to soak and descend; of fire, to blaze and ascend; of wood, to be crooked and to be straight; of metal, to obey and

names of the Divisions added to it. It differs from the common representations of the Plan, by containing the 5th division in the centre, which is ordinarily excluded, from numerical considerations.

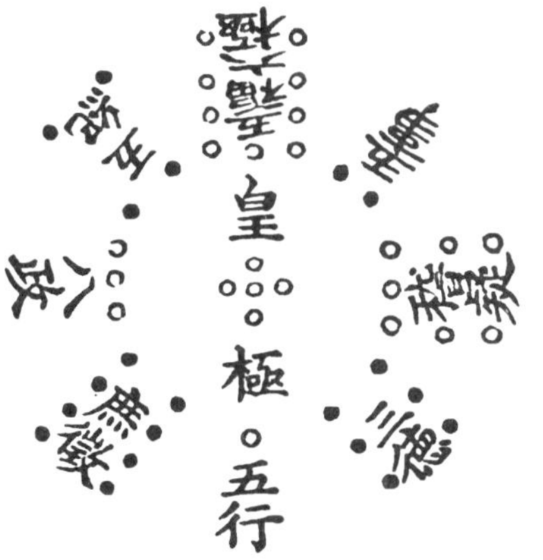

For the names of the subjects of the nine Divisions, see on their several paragraphs that follow. With regard to the 'five 事,' it is said they are to be reverently used. The 事 being personal, belonging to the government of one's self, it is required to be 'reverent' in respect to them. [Keang Shing, after Lew Hin, reads 羞用 for 敬用, but 敬 rests on good authority;—see the 後案, *in loc.*].

The 'eight 政' are to be used 'liberally.' 農 is read as if it were 醲, and defined by 厚. Ma Yung and Wang Suh try to retain the meaning of 農, 'agriculture,'—but ineffectually. The 'five 紀' are to be used 'harmoniously,'—'to bring the works of men into harmony with the times of heaven.' The 'various 徵' are to be used 'thoughtfully.' 念—'with considerate examination.' The 'five 福' are to be used 'encouragingly,'—so as to attract men 'towards' (嚮) what is desired. No numbers, it is observed, are used with reference to the fifth Division, the perfection which it indicates not being capable of measurement.

Ch. III. Pp. 5—40. PARTICULAR DESCRIPTION OF THE NINE DIVISIONS. 5. *Of the five elements.* Gaubil does not translate 行, but gives always—'les cinq *hing*.' We have got into the habit of rendering it in English by 'elements.' But it seems hardly possible to determine what the Chinese mean by the term. By 'elements' we mean 'the first principles or ingredients of which all bodies are composed.' The Pythagoreans, by their four elements of earth, water, air, and fire—a classification first made, apparently, by Ocellus—did not intend so much the nature or essence of material substances, as the forms under which matter is actually presented to us. The term 行, meaning 'to move,' 'to be in action,' shows that the original conception of the Chinese is of a different nature; and it is said, in the dict., that 'the five *hing* move and revolve throughout heaven and earth, without ever ceasing, and hence they are so called (五行運于天地間,未嘗停息,故名). 'Distributed,' say the editors of Yung-ching's Shoo, 'through the four seasons, they make the "five arrangements;" exhibited in prognostications, they give rise to divination by the tortoise and the reeds; having lodgment in the human body, they produce "the five businesses;" moved by good fortune and bad, they produce "the various verifications;" communicated to organisms, they produce the different natures, hard and soft, good and evil; working out their results in the changes of those organisms, they necessitate here benevolence and there meanness, here longevity and there early death:—all these things are from the operation of the five *hing*. But if we speak of them in their simplest and most important character, they are, as here, what man's life depends upon, what the people cannot do without.'

Leaving all this jargon, and turning to the 'counsels of Yu' parr. 7, 8, we find that 'water, fire, metal, wood, and earth' are, along with 'grain,' the 'six magazines,' from which the people are to be provided with what is necessary for their sustenance and comfort. We may content ourselves, therefore, with under-

上、木曰曲直、金曰從革、土爰稼穡、潤下作鹹、炎上作苦、曲直作酸、從革作辛、稼穡作甘。○二 六節 五事、一曰貌、二曰言、三曰視、四曰聽、五曰思、貌曰恭、言曰從、視曰

to change; while the virtue of earth is seen in seed-sowing and ingathering. That which soaks and descends becomes salt; that which blazes and ascends becomes bitter; that which is crooked and straight becomes sour; that which obeys and changes becomes acrid; and from seed-sowing and ingathering comes sweetness.

6 [ii.] "Second, of the five businesses.—The first is called demeanour; the second, speech; the third, seeing; the fourth, hearing; and the fifth, thinking. The *virtue of the* demeanour is called respectfulness; of speech, accordance *with reason;* of seeing, clear-

standing 五行 here as 'the five essentials to human life.' From 水曰潤下 downwards is to be taken as the language of the viscount of Ke, or of the chronicler of Chow, to whom we owe the 'great Plan' of the Shoo; but the language is affected by the study of the Yih-king, which had come into vogue.

水曰潤下,—'water may be described as moistening and descending.' 潤下...... 從革, it is said, 以性言, 'describe the *nature* of the elements.' But *nature* in such a case is only expressive of some *qualities* belonging to them. 稼穡, again, is said to be descriptive of the *virtue* of earth (以德言); and hence we read 土爰稼穡, and not 土曰稼穡. 'Metal obeys and changes'; *i.e.*, it alters its form when acted on by fire.

From 潤下 to the end we have the 五味 or 'five tastes' of the elements;—not, however, the tastes that are proper to them, but those which they are found in course of time to assume. This is denoted by 作, which I have translated 'becomes.' Hea Seuen has said, 'The reason why we find 作 used in connection with the five tastes or flavours of the elements is this.—Water as it issues from the spring is not salt;—but when it flows away to the sea, and is there collected and coagulated together for a long time, the salt taste is produced, and the saltness is made by the soaking and descending. When fire, blazes on without ceasing, charring and scorching for a long time, the bitter taste is produced, and the bitterness is made by the blazing and ascending'; &c., &c. The reader may find a reasonable meaning in all this, if he can. Ts'ae observes that the five elements have their several sounds, colours, and airs, as well as tastes, but the text only speaks of their tastes, those being of greater importance to the people than the others.

P. 6. *Of the five businesses.* To translate 五事 by 'the five businesses' reads awkward and uncouth; but I can do no better with it. Medhurst renders the phrase by 'the five senses,' which is plainly inadmissible. Gaubil gives for it—'les cinq occupations ou affaires.' From the language of p. 4,—敬用五事, we gather that the 'aspect,' 'the speech,' &c., are not themselves the 事, but what give occasion to them. 貌=容儀, 'carriage,' 'demeanour.' 恭, 從, &c., describe the several virtues or desirable characteristics of the 'businesses' (五事之德). 言曰從, 一從=順, 'accordance,' that is, obedience to right and reason. It is strange that the old interpreters, Gan-kwŏ, K'ang-shing, and Ma Yung, all agree in defining 從 by 可從, making the meaning to be—'the virtue of speech is that it move others to follow the speaker.' This is manifestly wrong. 睿=通乎

明、聽曰聰、思曰睿、恭作肅、從作乂、明作哲、聰作謀、睿作聖。○三七節八政、一曰食、二曰貨、三曰祀、四曰司空、五曰司徒、六曰司寇、七曰賓、八曰師。○四八節五紀、一曰歲、

ness; of hearing, distinctness; and of thinking, perspicaciousness. The respectfulness becomes manifest in gravity; accordance *with* reason, in orderliness; the clearness, in wisdom; the distinctness, in deliberation; and the perspicaciousness, in sageness.

7 [iii.] "Third, of the eight objects of government:—the first is called food; the second, commodities; the third, sacrifices; the fourth, the minister of works; the fifth, the minister of instruction; the sixth, the minister of crime; the seventh, *the entertainment of* guests; the eighth, the army.

8 [iv.] "Fourth, of the five arrangements.—The first is called the year; the second, the month; the third, the day; the fourth, the

徹, 'penetrating to what is minute. 肅, 乂, &c., describe the consummation of those virtues (五德之用),—what they come to, as is indicated by the 作.

These businesses are represented as being in the human person what the five elements are in nature. Demeanour is the human correspondency of water, speech that of fire. But again leaving all this, can we tell what the writer would be at? Lin Che-k'e refers to what Mencius says, VII., Pt. I., xxxviii.,—'The bodily organs with their functions belong to our Heaven-conferred nature; but a man must be a sage before he can satisfy the design of his bodily organization;' and then adds that this paragraph contains the science of doing this. Certainly if a man have attained to the results here exhibited, he has made much progress in self-government and personal cultivation.

P. 7. *The eight objects of government.* Medhurst translates 八政 by 'the eight Regulators,' and Gaubil by 'les huit regles du Gouvernement.' It means the eight things to be attended to in government, its objects or departments. They seem to be stated in the order of their importance in the view of the speaker. 'Food' belongs to the department of agriculture, and 'commodities' or 'goods' to that of trade and commerce. These two things being secured, the people would have the essentials of life, and would be able to attend to their duties to spiritual beings and to the dead. Then would come in the minister of works, to secure the comfort of their dwellings; and the minister of instruction to teach them all their moral duties; and the minister of crime to deter them from evil. All festive ceremonies, all the intercourses of society, could then be regulated; and finally the efficiency of the army would be maintained, to secure the general well-being of the State.

It will be seen that the three first and two last are the objects to be attended to in their several departments, while the intermediate three are the names of the ministers. No account can be given of this peculiarity of the style. So the author was pleased to write,—very unsatisfactorily.

P. 8. *The five subjects of arrangement.* Medhurst calls the 五紀, the 'five Arrangers,' and Gaubil, 'les cinq Periodes.' He observes in a note that '紀 is used for chronicles and annals; for a revolution of the stars, of cycles, of years; and that it may express a fixed point for chronology and astronomy.' The term properly denotes 'the sorting of threads of silk,' and thence is applied to the digesting of chronicles and arranging of annals. It is hard to say whether it is intended in the text for the objective work of arranging the measures of the things spoken of, or, for those things as measured and arranged.

歲=天時之一周, 'a complete revolution of the seasons.' 月, 'the moon,' is

二曰月、三曰日、四曰星辰、五曰曆數。○五九疇皇極、皇建其有極、斂時五福、用敷錫厥庶民、惟時厥庶民于汝極、錫汝保極。

stars and planets, and the zodiacal signs; and the fifth, the calendaric calculations.

9 [v.] "Fifth, of royal perfection.—The sovereign having established his highest point of excellence, he concentrates in himself the five happinesses, and then diffuses them so as to give them to his people:—then on their part the multitudes of the people, resting

here = 'month,' the period of a lunation,' including the determination of new and full moon, and the intermediate phases. 日, 'the sun,' is here = 'a day.' 星 辰,—see Can. of Yaou,' p. 8. 歷數,—comp. the use of this phrase in the Canon of Shun, p. 14. It is here used, in its primary meaning, of the computations by which the measures of the year, the month, the day, &c., are determined, and the calendar fixed.

This division of the Plan is substantially the same as Yaou's instructions to his astronomers. The language is too brief to tell us what improvement had been made in the science of astronomy between the time of Yaou, and that of king Woo

Pp. 9--16.. *Royal perfection* Medhurst translates 皇極 by 'the princely perfections;' and Gaubil, by 'le terme du Souverain, on le milieu du Souverain.' Gan-kwŏ had defined the terms by 大中, 'the great Mean,' and his explanation seems to have been unquestioned till the time of the Sung dynasty. Then Choo He insisted that 皇 must be taken here in the sense of 君, 'prince,' 'sovereign,' referring to the way in which it is interchanged with 王 in par. 14 (皇有訓大處,惟皇極之皇不可訓大,皇只當作君,所以說遵王之義,遵王之路,直到後面以爲天下王,其意可見,蓋皇字下從王). Choo's criticism is correct.—He is correct also in rejecting the definition of 極 by 中. 極 is 'the utmost point,'—the extreme of excellence, realized in the person of the sovereign, and serving as an example and attractive influence to all below, both ministers and people. It is supposed to be *in* the centre, the exact middle, but it should not be called the centre or Mean. Take its primary application to 'the beam forming the ridge of a house:'—that is the highest point of the roof, on which the other parts rest, and it is in the centre of it; but it is called 極 and not 中. By 'royal perfection' we are to understand the sovereign, all that he ought to be. Ts'ae dwells upon it in its relation to his personal character, exhibiting all the virtues. Others say it is the accumulation of the personal and governmental excellences described in the previous divisions of the Plan. Our best way is to leave it in its own vagueness.

I have already observed that no place is found for this in the numerical scheme of the 'Great Plan,' arranged according to the principles of the Yih King. There are only 8 diagrams, not 9. This might have shown the critics that this Book was not to be treated on those principles. 9. 斂時(=是)五福,—'collects these five happinesses,' that is, collects, concentrates them in his own person (斂集是五福于皇躬; see the 日講). Happiness, it is supposed, invariably follows virtue;—compare in the 'Counsels of Yu,' p. 5, 惠迪吉,從逆凶,惟影響. The 'five happinesses' must be those of the last Division, and we are surprised to find them mentioned here, with the definitive 時=是 before them. It is not to be wondered at that Hung Mae (洪邁) should have proposed to remove from this down to 錫之福 in p, 11, to the ninth division. The difficulty is a little lightened by taking 時 = 於

書經

○凡十節厥庶民、無有淫朋、人無有比德、惟皇作極。○凡十一節厥庶民、有猷、有爲、有守、汝則念之、不協于極、不罹于咎、皇則受之、而康而色、曰、

10 in your perfection, will give to you the preservation of it. That the multitudes of the people have no lawless confederacies, and that men *in office* have no selfish combinations, will be an effect of the
11 sovereign's establishing his highest point of excellence. Among all the multitudes of the people, when any have counsel, and conduct, and keep themselves from evil, do you bear them in mind; those who do not come up to the highest excellence, and *yet* do not involve themselves in crime, let the sovereign receive; and when a placid

是, 'thereon' or 'thereby,' as in the translation. 用敷錫厥庶民,—'uses them, diffusing and giving them to his multitudinous people.' The king, not able to be happy himself only, seeks to make his people happy;—it is not said by what methods. 惟時, 云云,—Ts'ae expands this:—當時之民亦皆於君之極與之保守,不敢失墜所謂錫保也,言皇極君民所以相與者如此, 'the people, after that, guard and preserve the perfection of the sovereign for him, not daring to lose it or let it drop. This is what is shown by 錫保. The whole tells us what a mutual interest the ruler and the people have in this royal perfection.' It is really difficult to say what the whole tells us. The student will not fail to observe how the viscount of Ke begins here to address himself to king Woo.—汝極. 10. *Royal perfection will banish from the empire all selfish confederacies.* 淫朋=邪黨, 'bad, corrupt parties.' 淫 has here its frequent meaning of 過, 'beyond bounds.' Comp. 朋淫于家 in the 'Yih and Tseih,' p. 8. 人無有比德,—the 人 here, in opp. to the 庶民 above, is understood to mean 有位之人, 'men having office.' 德 is used in a bad sense. 比德=私相比附, 'selfish combining.' 作極 is about *i. q.* 建極 of the last par. Perhaps 作 indicates the various efforts and steps of progress by which 建, the point of establishment, is attained.

11. *How royal perfection will be seen in dealing with superior men, and with inferior men also, bringing the latter to approve and attain to the highest excellence.* 有猷有爲 are men 'mighty in words and deeds.' They are supposed further to be 有守, to have that firm and resolved nature, which will sustain them against temptation. 念之, 'think of them,' 'bear them in mind.' This is = 'give to such your confidence. You may repose trust in them.' 不協于極,—'do not harmonize with—have not yet attained to—the highest excellence.' 不罹于咎=不陷於惡. The 不=而不, with the adversative force of 而, 'and yet.' These are a class of mediocre individuals, different from and inferior to the former. 而康而色,—Gan-kwŏ, taking 而=汝, took this as addressed to king Woo: 汝當安汝顏色以謙下人, 'you ought to compose your countenance, and condescend to those inferior men.' But he is then obliged to understand another 人 as the nominative to 曰,—'when men say,' &c,. It is better to take, with Choo He, 而康而色, as referring to the class of men just described, and = 'when they are pleased, and look so, saying,' &c.. Ts'ae says:—見於

予攸好德、汝則錫之福、時人斯其惟皇之極。○無虐煢十二節獨、而畏高明。○人十三節之有能有為、使羞其行、而邦其昌、凡厥正人、既富方穀、汝弗能使有好于而家、時人斯其辜、于其無好德、汝雖

satisfaction appears in their countenances, and they say—'Our love
is fixed on virtue,' do you then confer favour on them. Those men
12 will in this way advance to the perfection of the sovereign. Do not
oppress the friendless and childless; do not fear the high and
13 illustrious. When men have ability and administrative power, cause
them still more to cultivate their conduct, and the prosperity of the
country will be promoted. All right men, having a competency,
will go on to be good. If you cannot make men have what they
love in their families, they will only proceed to be guilty of crime;

外而有安和之色、發於中而有好德之言、云云. 錫之福,—福 here = 祿, one of the 'five happinesses.' 時(=是)人其惟皇之極,—the 'Daily Explanation' paraphrases this:—將見惟是庶民、感發于念愛之已深、鼓舞于錫福而不倦、斯同歸惟皇之極、而信能以保極矣.

12. Ts'ae says this par. completes the meaning of the one which precedes, and serves to introduce that which follows. To me it interrupts the train of thought, fugitive as that is. Gan-kwŏ says that 煢=單無兄弟, 'solitary, without brothers,' and that 獨 is 無子, 'childless.'

13. Ts'ae says that this paragraph speaks of 'men who are in office' (此言有位者也.) This is in accordance with the distinction made between 庶民 and 人 in par. 10. This is the general view of the critics. I do not think it can be altogether sustained. The 'men' may not be in office, but only aspirants for it. They are inferior to those first mentioned in par. 11, having the ability, and the practical capacity, but being without the conservative (有守) element. If they can be led on to this—使羞(=進)其行—they may be employed, and their employment will conduce to the prosperity of the country. 凡厥正人,—Gan-kwŏ takes 正人 in a moral sense as = 正直之人, 'correct men.' I think his view is right. Ts'ae understands the phrase in an official sense, and says it = 在官之人, 'men who are in official employment.' The phrase may be so taken; but the other view suits the whole paragraph better. 既富,—'being enriched,' having remunerative office conferred on them. 穀=善, 'good.' 方穀,—'then they will be good.' Ts'ae makes this = 'then you may require them to be good.' The idea is the same with that which Mencius often insists on,—that men, when raised above the pressure of want, are likely, may be expected, to cultivate the moral virtues. Though I have followed Gan-kwŏ in his view of 正人, I cannot accept his explanation of this 方穀;—see the 註疏. 汝弗能……其辜,—the principal difficulty here is with 有好于而家. I take 好 in the 3d tone,

錫之福、其作汝用咎。○十四節 無偏無陂、遵王之義、無有作好、遵王之道、無有作惡、遵王之路、無偏無黨、王道蕩蕩、無黨無偏、王道平平、無

while they do not love virtue, though you confer favour on them, they will involve you in the guilt of employing them *thus* evil.

14 "Without deflection, without unevenness,
Pursue the Royal righteousness;
Without any selfish likings,
Pursue the Royal way;
Without any selfish dislikings,
Pursue the Royal path;
Without deflection, without partiality,
Broad and long is the Royal path.
Without partiality, without deflection,
The Royal path is level and easy;

and 有好 as = 有所好, 'to have what they love,' meaning the means of comfortable living. 而家 = 其所有家, 'their families;'—the 而 being taken as merely a pause or rest of the voice. Possibly it may = 汝, 'your,' and 家 may be, by synecdoche, for 國家, so that 而家 = 'your country.' I prefer the other construction however. 時人斯其辜 = 是人則將陷於罪. The whole is in opposition to the preceding clause.—'Let the sovereign employ and remunerate those able and well-meaning men, and they will go on to be really good. If on the contrary they are neglected, and left to suffer penury, they will lose their self-respect, and proceed to become evil.' Hoo Yih-chung (胡一中; Yuen dyn.) explains the passage very much in the same way. He says:—好者自愛重也, 家謂有家者, 凡正長之官, 汝當厚祿而使之富足, 方能爲善, 汝若不先祿之使富, 彼且不自愛重于其有家, 無所顧藉, 則是人將陷於罪. 于其無......用咎,—such men, falling off into crime, may afterwards be put in remunerating offices; but the opportunity has been lost by the sovereign. He will only now reap the fruit of his want of wisdom in dealing with them in the past.

P. 14. *An ancient Song, descriptive of the royal perfection, and stimulating men to imitate it.* We may compare with it the songs of Shun and Kaou-yaou in the 'Yih and Tseih.' The lines are composed of four characters, and every two lines rhyme together after a fashion. The general opinion is that the song was not composed by the viscount of Ke, but that it was a well-known piece, which had come down from the Hea times, and which he recites to king Woo. 無偏無陂, 遵王之義,—Sze-ma Ts'een gives 頗 for 陂, and there can be no doubt this was the reading till the reign of the emperor Heuen-tsung (玄宗) of the T'ang dynasty. A proclamation of his, in the year 744, is still extant, ordering the change from 頗 to 陂, that there might be a rhyme with 義, and referring to the language of the Yih in the diagram 泰,—無平不陂, as suggesting the latter character, which is in meaning much the same as the other. But we might still retain 頗, and read 義 as *go*, to rhyme with it. 儀, which is a derivative from it, is allowed to be sometimes pro-

反無側、王道正直。會其有極、歸其有極。○〔十五〕曰皇極之敷言、是彝是訓、于帝其訓。○〔十六節〕凡厥庶民、極之敷言、是

Without perversity, without one-sidedness,
The Royal path is right and straight.
Seeing this perfect excellence,
Turn to this perfect excellence."

15 He went on to say, "This amplification of the Royal perfection contains the unchanging *rule*, and is the *great* lesson;—yea, it is the
16 lesson of God. All the multitudes, instructed in this amplification of the perfect excellence, and carrying it into practice, will approxi-

nounced so; and, in fact, 我 is the phonetic element in 義 itself. Këang Shing edits—無偏無頗遵王之誼. The dict. also says that 誼 was the reading of the old text. I have not found any authority for this. Ts'ae observes that 偏, 陂, 好 and 惡, in the first three couplets, are descriptive of risings of selfishness in one's own mind, and 偏, 黨, 反, and 側, in the next three, are descriptive of the manifestations of selfishness in one's conduct. A distinction is made between 道 and 路 in this way:—道 is the ideal character of the Royal course, always right (以其爲事物之當然曰道); 路 is that course, as it is to be actually trodden by all (以其爲天下之共由曰路). 王道平平,—平 is read *p'een*, to rhyme with 偏. The phrase is explained by 平易. 會其有極, 歸其有極,—Lin Che-k'e says on this:—建極者如北辰之居所, 而會其極, 歸其極者, 則如衆星之拱北辰也, 'The perfection, set up, is like the north pole-star occupying its place. Meeting with the perfection and turning to it, is like all the other stars moving towards—doing homage to—the pole star.'

Pp. 15, 16. *The viscount of Ke celebrates the description which he has given of the Royal perfection, and the glorious issue to which it leads.*

15. The 曰, at the beginning, must have 箕子 for its subject. Ts'ae calls it 起語辭, 'a term of introduction'; Hea Seuen, 更端辭, 'a term indicating a change in the discourse or argument.' 皇極之敷言,—'the diffuse discourse of Royal perfection.' We must understand all the amplification which the viscount had given of the phrase 皇極. 是彝—彝=常;—'it is constant, invariable.' 是訓,—'it is the lesson' for all. 于帝其訓,—'from God is its lesson.' We must wish that the language of this par. had been more explicit. I will here again make use of the words of Ch'in Ya-yen, while confessing my own want of appreciation of what awakens so much enthusiasm in him, and other Chinese critics:—聖人在上,
既建極而以身教于天下,
復敷言而以言教于天下,
蓋身教者,示以躬行踐履
之實,言教者,使其歌誦吟
詠而得,二者不可偏廢也.
天下惟理爲至常,惟理爲
至大,皇極之敷言,純乎一
理,故謂之常理,故謂之大
訓,是理也,本之於天,惟皇
上帝降衷之理也,言而可
異於降衷之理,是豈天之
君之訓,視之哉,乃天之人,
也,天者其不言之聖人,一
人者,其能言之天,一
二,二而一者也. 16. 極

訓是行、以近天子之光、曰、天子作民父母、以為天下王。○六[十七節]三德、一曰正直、二曰剛克、三曰柔克、平康正直、彊弗友剛克、燮友柔克、沈潛剛克、高明柔克。○[十八節]惟

mate to the glory of the son of Heaven, and say, 'The son of Heaven is the parent of the people, and so becomes the sovereign of the empire.'

17 [vi.] "Sixth, of the three virtues.—The first is called correctness and straightforwardness; the second, strong government; and the third, mild government. In peace and tranquillity, correctness and straightforwardness *must sway;* in violence and disorder, strong government *must sway;* in harmony and order, mild government *must sway.* For the reserved and retiring there is the strong rule; for the lofty and intelligent there is the mild rule.

之敷言 is of course 皇極之敷言. Medhurst erroneously translates the clause—'carry out these wide-spread instructions.' The people are supposed to repeat and croon over the amplification,—especially the song, teaching themselves and one another, and to be aroused to carry the lessons into practice, till they attain to a perfection in their degree equal to that of the sovereign in this. 曰天子·云云,—the people are the subject of the 曰 here. Hea Seuen would refer it to 箕子, like the 曰 in the last par., but he must be wrong. 天子,—'the Son of Heaven;'—see Part III., Bk. IV., 5.

Pp. 17—19. *Of the three virtues.* The three virtues are characteristics of the imperial rule;—they are not personal attributes of the sovereign, but the manifestations of the perfection which is supposed to have been described in the last Division. Their names are 正直, 剛克, and 柔克. Ts'ae makes the names 正直, 剛, and 柔; but the omission of the 克 in the case of the second and third gives them too much the appearance of personal attributes. The second and third are chiefly dwelt on, this division being supplementary to the last,—to show how the Royal perfection will deal with times and cases of an abnormal character. 17. 正直,—see in p. 14, 王道正直. This is the course that the perfect sovereign will naturally and usually take. 剛克,—'strong subduing.' This is the course of the perfect sovereign, when it is necessary for him to put on his terrors. 柔克, 'mild subduing.' This is his course, when it is proper for him to condescend to weaker natures. 彊弗友,—友, 'friendly,' 'disposed to be friendly,' must here be taken as = 順, 'compliant,' 'obedient.' 燮=和, 'harmonious,' 'mild.' 沈潛,—the former of these characters signifies 'to sink beneath the water,' and the second, 'to dive.' 'Disappearance,' 'being hidden,' belongs to both these things, and hence the combination is used in the text to denote individuals who are reserved and retiring, wanting in force of character. In 高明, 'the high and intelligent,' we have the opposite of them, those in whom the forward element predominates. The 'strong rule' must be applied to the former class,—to encourage them, and the 'mild rule' to the latter,—to repress them. The use of the 'virtues' is thus different from what it appears to be in the clauses that precede. Chinese critics do not venture to find fault with this;—to me it makes the text perplexing and enigmatical.

辟作福、惟辟作威、惟辟玉食、臣無有作福作威玉食。○十九節臣之有作福作威玉食、其害于而家、凶于而國、人用側頗僻、民用僭忒。○二十節七稽疑、擇建

18 "It belongs only to the prince to confer favours, to display the
19 terrors of majesty, and to receive the revenues of the empire. There should be no such thing as a minister conferring favours, displaying the terrors *of justice*, or receiving the revenues of the country. Such a thing is injurious to the families, and fatal to the States of the empire;—small officers become one-sided and perverse, and the people commit assumptions and excesses.
20 [vii.] "Seventh, of the examination of doubts.—Having chosen and

18, 19. *The prerogatives of the ruler must be strictly maintained.* Some critics would remove these paragraphs to the last Division. One certainly does not readily perceive what connection they have with the three virtues that have just been spoken of. We can hardly venture on the step of removing them, however, and putting them in another place;—we must be content with them where they are, acknowledging the vexation which their inconsequence occasions us. Only the prince 作福, 'rouses up, employs, the various happinesses;' *i.e.*, he is the source of all favours and dignities. In the same way he only 作威,—is the source of all punishments and degradations. 惟辟玉食,—'only the prince the gemmeous food.' 玉食=珍食, 'the pearly or precious food,' each grain of rice or other corn being spoken of as a gem or pearl. There is no 作, it will be seen, between 辟 and 玉食, and we must therefore supply another verb, and one, it seems to me, of a different meaning. Liu Che-k'e, without repeating the 作, or supplying any other verb, yet understands the clause according to the analogy of the two preceding ones, and takes the 玉食 as meaning all the badges of distinction and favour conferred by the sovereign on his princes and ministers. There is thus no intelligible difference between the first clause, 惟辟作福, and this. Ts'ae says that the 玉食, 'the precious grain,' is what the people contribute to their rulers (下之所以奉上). He must be right. 玉食='the revenues' of the State; and we must understand the verb, 享, 'to enjoy,' 'to receive,' before the phrase. According to this view, 辟 is to be interpreted not of the emperor only, but of all the princes, large and small, in their several States as well. K'ang-shing, Ma Yung, and Wang Suh all insist on this. Ma Yung's words are—辟,君也,玉食,美食,不言王者,關諸侯也. Gan-kwŏ does not speak distinctly on the point; but Ying-tă, in his gloss on the other's annotation, refers to Wang Suh's view, observing that, as the princes, in their several States, had the power of rewards and punishments, and, he might have added, the right to the revenue, this interpretation is perhaps correct. It does seem strange thus to pass from the person and govt. of the emperor; but so it is. 其害于而家,凶于而國,—see on 好于而家, in par. 13. There is the same difficulty in determining the meaning. The two last clauses show how the injury and ruin will arise. There will be a general disorganization of social order, each lower rank trying to usurp the privileges of that above it;—comp. Mencius I., Bk. I., i., 4. 人 and 民 are again opposed to each other, as in the 10th and other paragraphs.

Pp. 20—31. *Of the examination of doubts.* The course proposed for the satisfaction of doubts shows us at how early an age the Chinese had come under the power of absurd supersti-

立卜筮人、乃命卜筮。○廿一節曰雨、曰霽、曰蒙、曰驛、曰克。○廿二節曰貞、曰悔。○廿三節凡七、卜五、占用二、衍忒。○廿四節立時人作卜筮、三人占、則從二人之言。

appointed officers for divining by the tortoise and by the milfoil,
21 they are to be charged *on occasion* to perform their duties. *In doing*
this, they will find *the appearances* of rain, clearing up, cloudiness,
22 want of connection and crossing; and *the symbols*, solidity, and re-
23 pentance. In all *the indications* are seven;—five given by the tortoise,
and two by the milfoil, by which the errors *of affairs* may be
24 traced out. These officers having been appointed, when the opera-
tions with the tortoise and milfoil are proceeded with, three men are
to obtain and interpret the indications and symbols, and the *consent-*
ing words of two of them are to be followed.

tions. In the 'Counsels of Yu,' p. 18, that sage proposes to Shun to submit the question of who should be his successor on the throne to divination, and the emperor replies that he had already done so. There is no reason to doubt, therefore, the genuineness of the great Plan, as a relic of the Hea times, from the nature of this part of it. As soon as the curtain lifts from China, and we get a glimpse of its greatest men about four thousand years ago, we find them trying to build up a science of the will of Heaven and issues of events, from various indications given by the shell of a tortoise and the stalks of the milfoil! Gaubil observes that according to the text the tortoise and milfoil were consulted only in doubtful cases. But we may be sure that if such was the practice of the sages, superstitious observances entered largely as a depraving and disturbing element into the life of the people. They do so at the present day. The old methods of divination have fallen into disuse, and I cannot say how far other methods are sanctioned by the government, but the diviners and soothsayers, of many kinds, form a considerable and influential class of society.

Pp. 20—24 contain some hints as to the manner in which divination was practised. The same subject is treated in the Chow Le, Bk. XXIV; but it is hardly possible to get the two accounts into one's mind so as to understand and be able distinctly to describe the subject.

20. *Two kinds of divination and the appointment of officers to superintend them.* The two kinds of divination were—first, that by means of the tortoise, or tortoise-shell rather, called 卜; and that by means of the stalks of the 蓍 plant, called 筮. 'The tortoise,' says Choo He, 'after great length of years becomes intelligent; and the 蓍 plant will yield, when a hundred years old, a hundred stalks from one root, and is also a spiritual and intelligent thing. The two divinations were in reality a questioning of spiritual beings, the plant and the tortoise being employed, because of their mysterious intelligence, to indicate their intimations. The way of divination by the tortoise was by the application of fire to scorch the tortoise-shell till the indications appeared on it; and that by the stalks of the plant was to manipulate in the prescribed ways forty-nine of them, eighteen different times, till the diagrams were formed' (龜歲久則靈、蓍生百歲、一本百莖、亦物之神靈者、卜筮實問鬼神、以蓍龜神靈之物、故假之以其卦兆、爲卜法以明火爇柴、灼龜爲兆、筮法以四十九蓍、分、掛、揲、扐、凡十有八變、而成卦). See the Chapter on Divination in the 'Historical Records' (龜策、列傳、第六十八). Medhurst says the 蓍 was one of the class of plants called *Achillea millefolium.* Williams calls it 'a sort of labiate plant, like verbena,' thereby leading us to think of the 'holy herb' of Dioscorides, the *verbena officinalis.* The correctness, however, of both these accounts may be doubted. There is a figure of the plant in the 本草綱目(草部隰草類上);

but I have not yet been able to obtain a specimen to have its botanical name and place exactly determined.

We cannot tell how many were the officers of divination in the earlier dynasties, nor what were their several duties. In the Book of the Chow Le, referred to above, we have the 太卜, or 'grand diviner;' the 卜師, or 'master of divination;' the 龜人, or 'keeper of the tortoises;' the 菙氏, or 'preparer of the wood;' and the 占人, or 'the observers and interpreters of the prognostics.' They were all, observe the critics, required to be men far removed from the disturbing influence of passion and prejudice. Only such could be associated with the methods of communication between higher intelligences and men.

Pp. 21—23. *The various indications.* 21. The appearances here described were those made on the shell of the tortoise. The way in which they were obtained seems to have been this.—The outer shell of the tortoise was taken off, leaving the inner portion on which were the marks of the lines of the muscles of the creature, &c. A part of this was selected for operation, and smeared with ink. The fire was then applied beneath, and the ink, when it was examined, according as it had been variously dried by the heat, gave the appearances mentioned. 霽 is defined as 雨止, 'rain stopping,'='the weather clearing up.' 蒙=蒙昧不明, 'cloudiness, obscurity.' 驛, for which K'ung-shing and others have 圛, is understood to mean certain marks scattered about, without connection or relation;—see the remarks, by the editors of Yung-ching's Shoo, on Gan-kwo's definition of the term by 落驛不屬, and Ts'ae's by 絡驛不屬. 克=交錯, meaning lines or cracks in the ink crossing each other. Ts'ae says these appearances belonged severally to the different elements.—that of rain to water, of cloudiness to wood, &c. The whole operation was a piece of absurdity, and we have too little information to say anything certain about it. 22. 貞 and 悔 were the names given to the diagrams formed by the manipulation of the stalks of the *she*. In a complete diagram, composed of two of the eight primary ones, the lower figure is called 'the inner diagram' (內卦), and was styled 貞; the upper figure is called 'the outer diagram' (外卦), and was styled 悔. There were also other conditions according to which these names of 貞 and 悔 were applied to the different figures. How far, however, they obtained in the Hea and Shang dynasties we cannot tell. Our present Yih King is entirely a book of the Chow dynasty; but the text shows that the manipulation of Fuh-he's lines, and the derivation of meanings from the combination of them were practised, at least to some extent, in the earlier times. The meaning of the names 貞 and 悔 is very much debated; and instead of entering on the discussion here, I will content myself with the words of Heang Gan-she (項安世; Sung dyn.), one of the most voluminous writers on the Yih,—'We only know that the inner diagram was 貞 and the outer 悔; we do not know what was intended by those designations.'

23. We have here a *resumé* of the two last parr. with the addition of the enigmatical phrase 衍忒 at the end. 卜五, 占用二,—we must understand a first 用 between 卜 and 五. The 卜占 here is equivalent to 卜筮 in p. 20, so that 筮 is exchanged for 占. 衍忒,—衍=推, 'to infer,' 'to push or carry out;' 忒 may be taken as either=差, 'error,' or=變. Ts'ae adopts the former meaning, and interprets—'By this means the errors of human affairs may be traced out,' that is, may be indicated before they occur, and so be avoided. The 'Daily Explanation,' expanding this view, says—所謂推衍者,推衍于未有過差之先,非遅廻顧慮于已然之後. Choo He adopted the former meaning, and interpreted—'every changing form of indication and symbol being traced out and determined.' See the quotation from him in the 集說; still, when the operations, thus many times varied, had been concluded, the object would be to obtain the guidance of their results in the conduct of affairs. Woo Ch'ing and many others prefer to say that they do not understand the phrase at all.

24. *Care to be taken in performing the divination.* 立時人作卜筮,—時=是, and the whole=既立是所擇之人,以作卜筮之官, 'Having appointed the men thus selected to be the officers of divination.' 三人占,—we are to suppose that they have been charged to perform their duties (乃命卜筮, p. 20), and then three men divine in each way. 占 in the last par. was=筮; here it is used both for 卜 and 筮, including not only the various manipulations, but also the interpreting the results obtained. It is supposed that each man went through his operation further on a different method.

○廿五節汝則有大疑、謀及乃心、
謀及卿士、謀及庶人、謀及
卜筮。○廿六節汝則從、龜從、筮從、
卿士從、庶民從、是之謂大
同。身其康彊、子孫其逢吉。
○廿七節汝則從、龜從、筮從、卿士
逆、庶民逆、吉。○廿八節卿士從、龜
從、筮從、汝則逆、庶民逆、吉。
○廿九節庶民從、龜從、筮從、汝則
逆、卿士逆、吉。○三十節汝則從、龜

25 "If you have doubts about any great matter, consult with your
own heart; consult with your nobles and officers; consult with the
26 masses of the people; consult the tortoise and milfoil. If you, the
tortoise, the milfoil, the nobles and officers, and the common people
all consent to a course, this is what is called a great concord, and
the result will be the welfare of your person, and good fortune to
27 your descendants. If you, the tortoise, and the milfoil all agree,
while the nobles and common people oppose, the result will be
28 fortunate. If the nobles and officers, the tortoise, and the milfoil
all agree, while you oppose and the common people oppose, the
29 result will be fortunate. If the common people, the tortoise and
the milfoil all agree, while you and the nobles and officers oppose,
30 the result will be fortunate. If you and the tortoise agree, while

Pp. 25—31. *Rules for the application of the results of divination, and the varying conclusions of men, to the solution of doubts.* 25. 大疑 is not 'great doubts,' but 'doubts on a great matter.' The 'Daily Explanation' says,—國家大事,有行止可疑而未決者,云云. It is not to be supposed that the emperor would on every little matter or private occasion consult both men and spirits in the way proposed. We must keep in mind that 'the Great Plan' is a scheme of government. There are five parties whose opinions were to be weighed:—first, the emperor himself; next, his high nobles and officers generally (卿士); third, the common people; fourth, the tortoise; and fifth, the stalks of the *she*. The student will remember how the emperor in the Pwan-kăng complains that the opinions of the people were kept from him. Compare also, pp. 2 and 3 in 'The punitive Expedition of Yin.' Choo He observes that the opinions of men were first taken into consideration, but as they are liable to be affected by ignorance, and selfish considerations, the views of the spirits, above such disturbing influences, and intimated by the divinations, were to have the greater weight in the final determination. 26. *The case of a great concord, all the five parties agreeing.*

27. *The emperor, the tortoise-shell, and the milfoil, all agreeing, carry it over the nobles and officers, and the people.* 28. *The nobles and officers, with the tortoise and milfoil, carry it over the sovereign and people.* 29. *The people, with the tortoise and milfoil, carry it over the sovereign, and the nobles and officers.* 30. *When the sovereign and the tortoise were opposed to all the other parties.* In this case, not only are the

從、筮逆、卿士逆、庶民逆、作內、吉、作外、凶。卅一節 ○龜筮共違于人、用靜、吉。用作、凶。卅二節 ○八

the milfoil, the nobles and officers, and the common people oppose, internal operations will be fortunate, and external operations will
31 be unlucky. When the tortoise and milfoil are both opposed to the views of men, there will be good fortune in stillness, and active operations will be unlucky.

opinions of men divided, but the spirits also give different intimations. The doubt therefore remained, and the difficulty was settled by a compromise! 'Internal affairs,' acc. to Gan-kwŏ, were cases of marriages, capping, and sacrifices, within the State; 'external affairs' were military expeditions undertaken beyond it. Choo He says:—'In this case, the tortoise opposing and the milfoil consenting, nothing, it would seem, should be undertaken. But the tortoise-shell was supposed to give surer indications than the plant, and as all the human opinions agreed, it was inferred that internal affairs might be proceeded with and would be fortunate!' It is needless to point out the inconsistency of this. 31. *Where the divinations gave results contrary to all the human opinions.* In this case the spirits carried it over men. 用靜,吉,—'using stillness, there will be good fortune.' By 'stillness' is meant refraining from the undertaking doubted of.

[Many Chinese critics of more recent times seem to have an uneasy feeling of dissatisfaction on the subject of the ancient divinations; but hardly one has the courage boldly and fairly to disown them. To do so would be inconsistent with the proper veneration for the sages.

Ts'ae Ch'in said:—義之所當爲而不爲者、非數之所能知也、義之所不當爲而爲者、亦非數之所能知也、非義不占、非疑不占、非疑而占、謂之侮、非義而占、謂之欺、'Not to do what in right ought to be done:—no rule for this can be obtained from numbers; and no rule can be obtained from them to do what in right ought not to be done. There should be no divination in reference to what would not be right, and no divination where there are no doubts. To divine where there are no doubts is pronounced "a piece of folly;" to do so in reference to what would not be right is pronounced "a piece of deception."'

Woo Ch'ing observed:—天下之事、卿士庶民、皆不可而猶有吉者、蓋自古未之有也、使箕子之說行、後世人君將有棄卿士、忽庶民、而惟龜筮之從、邪說異議、得以乘間而入、天下自此多事矣、此蓋商俗尚鬼、習聞其說、遂信不移、雖箕子之賢、不能拔於流俗也、'From the oldest time never has anything turned out fortunate which the nobles and officers, with the common people, all disapproved of. Were the statements of the viscount of Ke to obtain currency and credence, the sovereigns of future ages would be found casting away their high ministers and officers, and slighting their people, attending only to the intimations of the tortoise-shell and the *she.* Perverted talk and strange principles would find their way to influence, and there would be no end to the troubles of the empire. These passages belong to the fondness for superstition which was characteristic of the Shang dynasty; accustomed to hear such things said, people believed them, and even a man of worth, like the viscount of Ke, could not keep himself from going with the current of the prevailing custom.' These observations are unusually free and sound, as coming from a Chinese scholar. The man who expressed himself thus should have gone on to bolder conclusions, affecting the reputation for sageness of Yu and Shun, and even of Confucius himself. I am sorry to find a writer, so sensible in general as Hoo Wei, trying to beat down the remarks of Ch'ing with the authority of the great sage:—草廬說經、往往有賢智之過、而此說尤爲紕繆、夫子之贊易也、曰、探賾索隱、鉤深致遠、以定天下之吉凶、成天下之亹亹者、莫大乎蓍龜、又曰、人謀、鬼謀、百姓與能、謂其可以斷天下之疑也、大禹之稽疑、豈別有所指、而箕子以卜筮附會

書經

庶徵、曰雨、曰暘、曰燠、曰寒、曰風、曰時、五者來備、各以其敘、庶草蕃廡。○

32 [viii]. "Eighth, of the various verifications.—They are rain; sunshine; heat; cold; wind; and seasonableness. When the five come all complete, and each is in its proper order, *even* the various

之邪使箕子而溺於流俗何以爲箕子, 'Ts'aou-loo' [this is a designation by which Woo Ch'ing is known], 'in his remarks upon the Classics, often speaks about the errors of the worthy and wise; but here he errs and commits himself more than usual. The Master, in his observations on the Yih, has said, "To unravel what is confused, and search out what is mysterious; to hook up what is deep, and reach to what is distant,—thus determining whatever will be fortunate or unlucky, and rousing all men to continuous effort: there is nothing better than the use of the *she* and the tortoise-shell" (see the 繫辭上傳, p. 37. 'The Master' of course is Confucius]. He also says, "Men are consulted; the spirits are consulted; the common people *also* contribute their ability" (繫辭下傳, p. 69), meaning that thus all things doubted of may be determined. Did the great Yu mean anything else than this by his "Examination of Doubts"? and did the viscount of Ke accommodate to that what he said about divination by the tortoise and the milfoil? Had he been sunk in the current of prevailing custom merely, how could he have been the viscount of Ke?']

Pp. 32—38. *Of the various verifications.* Medhurst translates 庶徵 by 'the general verifications;'—rightly, as regards 徵, but wrong, as regards 庶, which = 非一—'not one merely,' 'many,' 'various.' Gaubil renders the phrase by' 'les apparences,'—unhappily. In a note he says:—'I render the Chinese character 徵 by '*apparences*,' not having found any word which would cover the whole extent of its meaning. In the present case, it signifies *meteors, phenomena, appearances*, but in such a sort that those have relation to some other things with which they are connected;—the meteor or phenomenon indicates some good or some evil. It is a kind of correspondence which is supposed, it appears, to exist between the ordinary events of the life of men, and the constitution of the air, according to the different seasons;—what is here said supposes I know not what physical speculation of those times. It is needless to bring to bear on the text the interpretations of the later Chinese, for they are full of false ideas on the subject of physics. It may be also that the viscount of Ke wanted to play the physicist on points which he did not know.'

Gaubil describes correctly the way in which the character 徵 is here applied, but the translator should not render it from what it is applied to, but according to its proper signification. In the dict. it is defined by 證, 'to bear witness,' 'to attest,' and by 明, 'to illustrate;' and then there is quoted from par. 4 of this Book, 念用庶徵. 'Verifications' is probably as good a term as can be found in our language. The giving the name to the various phenomena in the text, and making them indicators of the character of men's conduct, is of a piece with the divinations of the last division. It is another form of superstition. If there underlie the words of the viscount of Ke some feeling of the harmony between the natural and spiritual worlds, which occurs to most men at times, and which strongly affects minds under deep religious thought or on the wings of poetic rapture, his endeavour to give the subject a practical application is so shallow that it only strikes us as grotesque and absurd.

The Division falls into two parts. In the first parr. 32—34, we have a description of the verifying phenomena, and the interpretation of them.

P. 32. 暘 = 日出, 'the sun coming forth,' or = 明, 'brightness,' 'sunshine.' 燠—熱在中, 'warmth diffused,' or = 煖. 'heat.' The meaning of 暘 and 燠 is sufficiently shown by their opposition to 雨 and 寒, 'rain and cold.' 曰時,—I have translated this by 'seasonablenss,' and would extend its meaning to all the preceding verifications, so that there are only five and not six phenomena. The specification of 'five' immediately after (五者來備), and the way in which the phenomena are mentioned in the next par. with the adjunct of 時, seem to require this interpretation. This was the view also of Gan-kwŏ, and is adopted by Choo He and most other critics. Gaubil however, translates 曰時 by '6. Les saisons.' And this view is contend-

卅三節 一極備、凶、一極無、凶。○卅四節 曰休徵、曰肅、時雨若、曰乂、時暘若、曰哲、時燠若、曰謀、時寒若、曰聖、時風若、曰咎徵、曰狂、恆雨若、曰僭、恆暘若、曰豫、恆燠若、曰急、恆寒若、

33 plants will be abundantly luxuriant. Should any one of them be either excessively abundant, or excessively deficient, there is evil.
34 "There are the favourable verifications:—namely, of gravity, which is emblemed by seasonable rain; of orderliness, emblemed by seasonable sunshine; of wisdom, emblemed by seasonable heat; of deliberation, emblemed by seasonable cold; and of sageness, emblemed by seasonable wind. There are also the unfavourable verifications:—namely, of wildness, emblemed by constant rain; of assumption, emblemed by constant sunshine; of indolence, emblemed

ed for by Lin Che-k'e, who understands 時 of 'the round year, the months, and the days,' of which we have the account in the 35th and foll. paragraphs. He took the view from Ts'ae Yuen-too (蔡元度), a critic also of the Sung dyn., earlier than himself. It supposes a more artificial structure of the text than the study of the whole Book authorizes. 各以其敘,—敘=序, 'order,' 'series.' The order of time and the degree of quantity, are both included, (各得其多寡先後之序). 庶草蕃廡,—廡=豐茂, 'abundant,' 'luxuriant.' This is a very simple truth. It is supposed to be mentioned as one of the least consequences of the seasonableness of the various phenomena, from which all others, however great, may be inferred.

33. Gan-kwŏ's expansion of this is—者備極過甚,則凶,一者極無,不至,亦凶,謂不時失敘.

34. *The favourable or good, and the unfavourable or bad, verifications.* The student will see that this par. and the 6th are closely connected. The successful achievement of each of the 'five businesses' has its verification in the character of the phenomena which have been described, and failure in, or the neglect, of them, has also its corresponding outward manifestation. On the 若, with which each clause terminates, Ying-tă observes:—此休咎,皆曰若者,其所致者,皆順其所行,故言若也, 'In every case, good and bad, the issue is in accordance with the course of the conduct, and therefore we find the character 若.' Opposed to 'gravity,' we have 狂,—妄, 'incoherence,' 'wildness.' Opposed to 'orderliness,' we have 僭=差, 'error,' 'presumptuous error.' Opposed to 'wisdom,' there is 豫, 'idleness,' 'indecision' (Wang Suh read 舒, with the same meaning). Opposed to 'deliberation,' there is 急, 'urgency,' 'haste;' and opposed to 'sageness' there is 蒙, 'stupidity.' The various phenomena, by which these qualities good and bad are responded to in nature and providence, are of course all fanciful. Since the Han dynasty, the critics have nearly all abandoned themselves to vain jangling in speculations on the operation of the five elements, and their distributions through the seasons of the year, *en rapport* with the virtues and failings of men. And yet, as we saw on the last Division, many of them do not endorse the statements of the text without misgivings. Ts'ae observes that 'to say on occasion of such and such a 'business' being successfully achieved, there will be the favourable verification corresponding to it, or that on occasion of such and such a 'business' being failed in, there will be the corresponding unfavourable verification, would betray a pertinacious obtuseness,—would show that the speaker was not a man to be talked with on the mysterious opera-

曰蒙、恆風若。○卅五曰、王省惟歲、卿士惟月、師尹惟日。○卅六節歲月日、時無易、百穀用成、乂用明、俊民用章、家用平康。○卅七節日月歲、時既易、百穀

by constant heat; of haste, emblemed by constant cold; and of stupidity, emblemed by constant wind."

35 He went on to say, "The sovereign is to examine the character of the whole year; nobles and officers, that of the months; and
36 the inferior officers, that of the day. If throughout the year, the month, the day, there be an unchanging seasonableness, all the kinds of grain are matured; the operations of government are wise; heroic men stand forth eminent; and in the families *of the people*
37 there are peace and prosperity. If throughout the year, the month, the day, the seasonableness is interrupted, the various kinds of grain

tions of nature. It is not easy to describe the reciprocal meeting of Heaven and men. The hidden springs touched by failure and success, and the minute influences that respond to them:—who can know these but the man who has apprehended all truth (必曰某事得,則某休徵應,某事失,則某咎徵應,則亦膠固不通,而不足與語造化之妙矣,天人之際未易言也,失得之幾,應感之微,非知道者,孰能識之哉)?' This is in effect admitting that the statements of the text can be of no practical use.

Pp. 35—38. We have here apparently an endeavour to show how the 'various verifications are to be thoughtfully made use of,' according to the language of p. 4. By 師尹 we are to understand all the 有司 or inferior officers. See on 庶尹 in the 'Yih and Tseih' p. 10. We may take 師 here as = 庶 or 衆; with regard to the rank of the 尹 which the text mentions, the whole scope of the passage shows it could only be of a lower grade. The sovereign stands to his nobles and great officers as the year to months, including and leading on them all; and they again stand to their inferior *employés* as the month to the days. Must the sovereign then, by the rule here laid down, wait till the year's end before examining his character and ways? I suppose, as he comprehends all dignities in himself, he must be every month doing on himself the examination work of a high officer, and every day that of an inferior. The editors of Yung-ching's Shoo say on this point:—'The sovereign, the high officers, and the inferior officers, it is said here, must examine severally the year, the month, and the day; but this is spoken in a general and vague way, with reference to the different rank of their offices:—we must not stick to a phrase. For instance, a violent wind shall in a day do injury to the grain fields. The wind lasts for a single day only, but its injurious effects extend to the months and the year. Shall we make it relate to the inferior officers? or to the high officers and the sovereign? Whenever any unfavourable verification happens, no one should put the thing off himself. Every one should examine himself, and do so with regard to every matter.' Experience and their own sense have made many in China wiser in many things than their classics, but they will not give up the national idols.

36, 37. 時無易,—'if the times do not change.' But we must take 時 in the same way as in p. 34, meaning 'seasonableness.' The meaning is that if rain and sunshine, heat and cold, and wind all occur seasonably, the various effects enumerated will follow. There is a grain of truth in the assertions, and a bushel of nonsense. Hoo Wei says that 乂 is used with reference to the government of the court (以朝政言之), and 俊民 of individuals who have no office (以無位者言之), while 家 refers to those who are in

用不成、乂用昏不明、俊民用微、家用不寧。○卅八節庶民惟星、星有好風、星有好雨、日月之行、則有冬有夏、月之從星、則以風雨。○卅九節九五福、

do not become matured; the operations of government are dark and unwise; heroic men are reduced to obscurity; and in the families *of the people* there is no repose.

38 "The common people are like the stars. Some stars love the wind, and some love the rain. The course of the sun and moon give winter and summer. The course of the moon among the stars gives wind and rain.

office. In regard to the last clause, I prefer the view which is given in the translation.

[Gaubil has here the following note:—'There is supposed here a mutual correspondence between the ordinary events of the life of men, especially of kings and grandees, and the constitution of the air; but instead of adopting the false ideas which the viscount of Ke may have had on that subject we may reflect on what has been thought about it in Europe, and on what many people still think and say of a culpable and dangerous character. It appears that the Chinese have admitted a homogeneous matter in all bodies; that they have admitted a soul subsisting after the destruction of the body; that they have admitted spirits, and one spiritual Being, Master of heaven, of earth, and of men. But they have been bad physicists, and have troubled themselves little with metaphysics or with logic. They have not thought too much (?) of examining the grounds of their reasoning on the nature of beings; and they have in no way fathomed the question of the union of the soul with the body, nor that of the operations of the soul.'

There is no danger of our adopting the notions of the viscount of Ke on the correspondence between the weather and the characters of men. A great service would be done by the Sinologue, who should take up 'the Great Plan,' and produce a commentary on it for Chinese readers, clearly and minutely unfolding the errors on the constitution of nature and the course of providence of which it is full. From this ground we might go on to shake the stronghold of their confidence in all the ancient teachings and the wisdom of their so-called sages.]

P. 38. *The people should examine the stars.* 庶民惟星,—Medhurst translates this—'The common people are like the stars,' and Gaubil, in the same way,—'Les étoiles représentent les peuples.' This also is the view of Ts'ae, who says:—民之麗乎土,猶星之麗乎天也. But this would make the paragraph of a different character entirely from those immediately preceding. The text is evidently analogous with the clauses of par. 35, and the 省 which we must understand there of the 卿士 and 師尹, we must understand here also after 庶民. 'The people should examine the stars.' But nothing is said of 'verifications' in connection with the stars and the people;—what was to result from the examination of the stars? 'The people,' says Woo Ch'ing, 'would know when it was summer, and when it was winter, when they might expect wind, and when they might expect rain. Knowing these things they could carry on their labours and take their precautionary measures accordingly.' We thus find a meaning in the paragraph, though of a different kind from what the preceding paragraphs would lead us to look for. On the view of the first clause, taken by Ts'ae and the commentators generally, the whole paragraph appears equally out of place, and no reasonable meaning can be given to it. The constellation 箕—the hand of Sagittarius—is said to bring wind, and 畢, or Hyades, to bring rain. Ts'ae goes at great length into the courses of the sun and moon, but all according to the accounts of the astronomers of the Han dynasty. The text specifies no stars from which we might determine the place of the sun in the heavens at the solstices or equinoxes, when the Book was made.

書經

一曰壽、二曰富、三曰康寧、四曰攸好德、五曰考終命。○六（四十節）極、一曰凶短折、二曰疾、三曰憂、四曰貧、五曰惡、六曰弱。

39 [ix]. "Ninth, of the five happinesses.—The first is long life; the second is riches; the third is soundness of body and serenity of mind; the fourth is the love of virtue; the fifth is an end crowning the life.
40 As to the six extremities again, the first is misfortune, shortening the life; the second is sickness; the third is sorrow; the fourth is poverty; the fifth is wickedness; the sixth is weakness."

Pp. 39, 40. *Of the five happinesses and six extremities.* It is said, in p. 4, that 'a hortatory use is to be made of the five happinesses,' and 'an awing use of the six extremities.' It is not easy to see how this division enters into the scheme of the Great Plan. Tsăng Kung (曾鞏) says:—'The nine divisions all describe the course of the sovereign. The happinesses and extremities are conditions by which the sovereign examines his own attainments and defects in reference to the people. That these happinesses should be among the people, is what the sovereign should aim after; and the extremities' being among them is what he should be standing in awe of;'—see the 集說. Hoo Wei, on the other hand, says:—'The five conditions of happiness and six conditions of suffering, are by the doing of Heaven, and not from any arrangements of men. We have it said in the division on Royal Perfection, "He concentrates in himself the five happinesses, and then diffuses them so as to give them to his people;"—we have therefore in this place only the names of the happinesses and their opposites, and nothing about their use' (五福六極,皆天之所爲,非人之所設也,其斂時敷錫之道,具在皇極章中,故此但列其目,而不言其用).

39. 壽,—'longevity;' without specifying any number of years. Gan-kwŏ says it means 120 years; but this is absurd. A man dying over 50 is spoken of by the Chinese as not having a short life. 60 and upwards is reckoned longevity. Ts'ae says that with long life all the other happinesses can be enjoyed, and therefore it occupies the first place among them. 富,—'riches;' probably meaning a competency according to the rank and station. Lin Che-k'e says, 'a sufficiency for food and clothing is 富.' 康寧='freedom from sickness,' *i.e.*, good health,—according to Gan-kwŏ. Modern critics extend the meaning, as in the translation.—形康而心寧. 攸好德=所好者德, 'when virtue is what is loved.' The meaning, says Lin Che-k'e, is a natural disposition tending to the love of virtue rather than of pleasures and other lower things. 考終命,—Ts'ae explains this by the words of Mencius, VII., Pt. I., ii. 1, 順受其正, 'submissively receiving all the will of Heaven.' 考 is generally explained here by 成, 'to accomplish,' and the happiness is that of 'accomplishing to the end the will of Heaven.' This does not differ materially from the view of the translation, which has the advantage of making more evident the proper meaning of 考.

40. 六極,—極=窮='exhaustion,' 'being brought to extremity.' It denotes the opposite of 福. 凶短折 is literally 'disastrous short breaking.' The meaning is —the life coming to an untimely and disastrous close. 疾 and 憂 are the opposite of 康寧. 惡,—Gan-kwŏ explained this by 醜陋, 'ugliness,' and the last extremity—弱, by 尩劣, 'feebleness;'—perhaps in both cases with some reference to the mind as well as the body. 惡 means probably boldness in what is evil, and 弱, weakness in what is good. The viscount of Ke was not so successfnl in enumerating the 'extremities,' as with the 'happinesses.'

[Gaubil, in a concluding note, thinks it not unlikely that the viscount of Ke wished to speak of the 'Book of Lŏ,' and under pretence of explaining this enigma, 'has given very excellent instructions on the duties which princes and subjects ought to observe.' I am unable to agree with the learned Jesuit. The Great Plan is little less of an enigma than the Book of Lŏ. It is full of perplexities and absurdities. There are some right principles of morals and government in it, but after hearing it all, king Woo must have been more in the dark than when he went to the viscont at first with the remark that he did not know how the virtues in men's various relations should be brought forth in their proper order.]

I append here a scheme of the whole Plan, modified from that which is given among the cuts in Yung-ching's Shoo :—

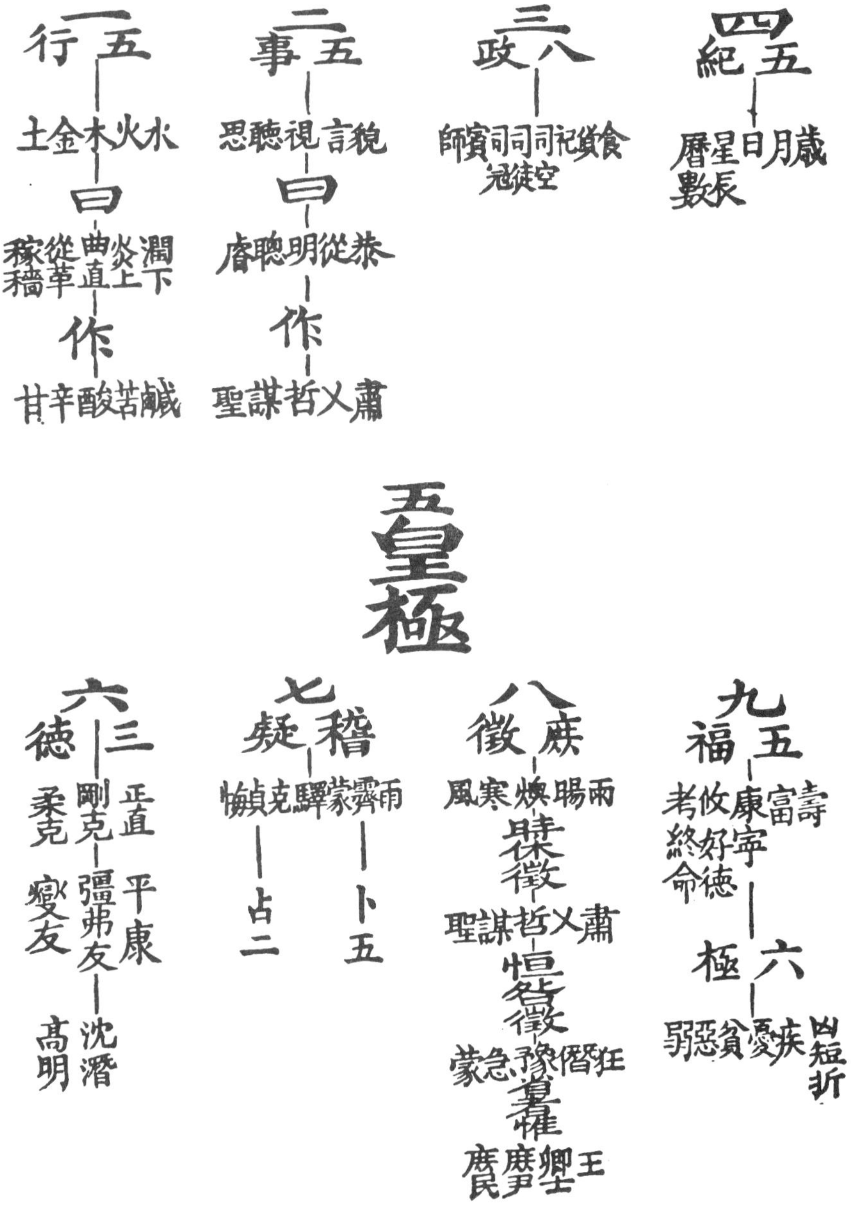

THE BOOKS OF SHANG.

BOOK V. THE HOUNDS OF LEU.

旅獒

(一節) 惟克商、遂通道于九夷八蠻、西旅厎貢厥獒、太保乃作旅獒、用

1 After the conquest of Shang, the way being open to the nine wild and the eight savage tribes, the people of the western tribe of Leu sent in as tribute some of their hounds, on which the Great-guardian made "The Hounds of Leu," by way of instruction to the king.

The Name of the Book.—旅獒, 'The Hounds of Leu.' The 37th note of the Preface, on the subject of this Book, says that the 'western Leu' made an offering of some of their hounds' (西旅獻獒). Leu, therefore, is to be looked for in the west. It was the name of one of the rude tribes, lying in that quarter, beyond the 'nine provinces' of the empire. 獒 is the name of a kind of hound. It was, acc. to the 爾雅, '4 feet—ancient feet, that is—high.' The 說文 describes it as 'knowing the mind of man, and capable of being employed' (知人心可使者). From an instance of its use, quoted in the 集傳 from Kung-yang, it was evidently a blood-hound. The critics generally understand the term in the text in the singular;—I know not why. There is nothing in the Book, and no ancient references to it, which should make us do so. We more naturally take it in the plural, and it seems to me more likely that several hounds, and not one only, would be sent to king Woo.

This is one of the Books found only in Gan-kwŏ's text. K'ang-shing and Ma Yung had not seen it, and they have strangely mistaken the meaning of the prefatory note. '獒,' says K'ang-shing, 'is read like 豪. The rude tribes of the west had no princes, but gave the title of 酋豪 to the strong among them, who governed them for the time. The people of the tribe sent at this time the principal man of their chiefs, to present himself at the court of Chow;'—see the 後案, *in loc.* But this view carries its own refutation on the face of it. The words of the prefatory note are that 'the western Leu presented—as an offering, expressive of their subjection—their 獒.' To suppose that their chief was thus made an article of tribute is absurd. Ch'ing's paraphrase of 獻獒 by 遣來獻見于周 is quite inadmissible. The signification of 獒 as ='hound' is not to be disturbed. The Book belongs to the division of 'Instructions.'

Contents. The Leu people having sent some of their hounds to king Woo, and he having received them, or intimated that he would do so, the Great-guardian remonstrated with him, showing that to receive such animals would be contrary to precedent, would be dangerous to the virtue of the sovereign, and was not the way to deal with outlying tribes and nations.

The reader will think that the Book is much ado about a very small matter, and in truth it is so. It receives an interest, however, when

訓于王。○曰、二節嗚呼、明王愼德、四夷咸賓、無有遠邇、畢獻方物、惟服食器用。○王三節

2 He said, "Oh! the intelligent kings have paid careful attention to their virtue, and the wild tribes on every side have willingly acknowledged subjection to them. The nearer and the more remote have all made offerings of the productions of their countries;—

we see in it a specimen of the feeling and procedure by which the rulers of China have all along sought to regulate their intercourse with foreign nations. 'When the sovereign does not look on foreign things as precious, foreigners will come to him:'—this language is a good exponent of the normal Chinese policy. A self-complacent assumption of superiority—superiority both in wisdom and in power—has always been displayed. I have read references to the steam-engine with its various applications, from men versed in all the learning of China, as if it were nothing more than a toy, to be thought of just as the duke of Shaou thought of the hounds of Leu. Statesmen and people are now, in this nineteenth century, having a rude awakening from their dream.

P. 1. *The occasion on which the Book was made.* This par. might have had a place in the Preface, and Ts'ae calls it 'the proper preface of the Hounds of Leu' (此旅獒之本序). 惟克商,—'on the conquest of Shang.' The 'Daily Explanation' expands the clause:—惟我周武王旣克商而有天下. The 'General History' refers the tribute of the hounds to the 14th year of king Woo, B.C. 1,120. 遂通道于九夷八蠻,—by the 'nine E and eight Man,' we are to understand the barbarous tribes generally,—expressed in the Can. of Shun, p. 16, by the phrase 蠻夷, and by 蠻貊 in the 'Completion of the War,' p. 6. See also on the 'Tribute of Yu,' Pt. ii., p. 22. The diff. rude tribes round about the nine provinces of the empire are variously enumerated. Here we have the '9 夷 and 8 蠻;' in the Le Ke, Bk. XIV., 明堂位, p. 3, we have the '9 夷, 8 蠻, 6 戎, and 5 狄;' in the Chow Le, Bk. XXXIII., 夏官, 司馬, 第四之六, 職方氏, p. 1, we have the 4 夷, 8 蠻, 7 閩, 9 貉, 5 戎, and 6 狄;' in the 國語, 楚語, 下, we have 'the '9 夷 and 100 蠻.'

The numbers are not to be pressed, and we must be content with finding a statement in the text, that the wild tribes all around came or sent to the court of king Woo;—acknowledging his supremacy. Ts'ae says that we are not to understand from 通道, that king Woo used any efforts to open roads to the barbarous regions beyond the limits of the empire proper;—it was his virtue and fame which drew them, and they came, 'climbing the hills as if they had been ladders, and in boats across the sea.' It certainly would not have been discreditable to king Woo to have good roads made throughout all his dominions; and in the passage of the 國語, referred to above, evidently modelled on this part of the Shoo, the opening of the thoroughfares is described as his work:—仲尼曰,昔武王克商,通道於九夷百蠻,使各以其方賄來貢,使無忘職業. 底貢,—the same phrase occurs in the Tribute of Yu, Pt. i., p. 52. The force of 底 passes on to the next character, and indicates that what *it* says took effect. 太保,—it is not said anywhere in the Book who the Great-guardian was; but since the commentary of Gan-kwŏ, the prevailing opinion has been that he was Shih, the duke of Shaou. See on the name of Bk. XII. He was Great-guardian under Woo's successor; and it is supposed—with probability—that he held the office also under Woo.

Pp. 2—10. THE ADDRESS OF THE GREAT-GUARDIAN TO KING WOO AGAINST RECEIVING THE HOUNDS. Pp. 2, 3. *The precedent of former wise kings in receiving articles of tribute, and the use which they made of them.* 2. 明王愼德,—the language here is to be taken historically. Medhurst and Gaubil both miss this point, and render—'When an intelligent prince is careful in the cultivation of his virtue,' &c. The guardian is giving not merely the lesson of duty, but of duty illustrated by example. The 'Daily Explanation' has it:—自古明哲之王,所以保邦安民者,要在謹修其德,云云. 愼德, 'the careful cultivation of virtue,' is said to be the hinge on which the whole of the address moves. 咸

乃昭德之致于異姓之邦、無替厥服、分寶玉于伯叔之國、時庸展親、人不易物、惟德其物。

3 clothes, food, and vessels for use. The kings have then displayed the things thus produced by their virtue, and *distributed them* to *the princes of* the States of different surnames, *to encourage them* not to neglect their duties. The precious things and gems they have distributed among their uncles in charge of States, thereby increasing their attachment *to the throne*. The recipients have *thus* not despised the things, but have seen in them the power of virtue.

賓,—賓 is not merely = 客, 'strangers,' 'guests,' but = 賓服;—see in the dict. on the character. 畢獻方物·惟服食器用,—方物 = 其方所生之物, 'the articles produced by their country,' and we may understand also articles manufactured there. The last clause gives a summary of those articles, and the meaning is that the contributions were restricted to these:—不敢於此外有以奇玩異物進獻者· 3. 異姓之邦,伯叔之國,—the empire being divided into many States or principalities, the emperors of each dynasty apportioned these among their relatives and adherents. 'The States of their uncles' were 同姓之邦, 'regions of the same surname,' *i.e.*, their rulers had the same surname as the emperors. The 'regions of different surnames' were the States ruled by Chiefs, attached to the reigning dynasty, but of a different lineage. To these the emperors 昭德之致, 'displayed what their virtue *thus* produced,'—the productions of remote territories, the tribute from distant tribes. The transitive meaning of 昭 is very much determined by its correlation with 分 in the next part of the par. The things were sent about as imperial gifts among the States; so they were 'displayed,' and served to warn and encourage the chiefs to loyal service and duty. 無替厥服 = 無廢其服事之職· 時庸展親,—Gan-kwŏ explains this by 是用誠信其親親之道, 'thereby verifying the sincerity with which they held the principle of attachment to their relatives,' taking 展 as = 信· Lin Che-k'e supports this interpretation, and quotes with approval the words of Wang Gan-shih,—'Though they loved them, yet if they had not shared their precious things with them, who could have known the sincerity of their love (親之矣而不以所寶分之,則人孰知親親之信也)?' But the clause is evidently related to the preceding 無替厥服, and must describe —not the feeling of the emperors from which the gifts proceeded, but the feeling which they wished to increase in the princes, their relatives. The explanation of 展 by 信 is therefore inadmissible. The meaning in the transl. is given by Ts'ae and in the dictionary:—使之益厚其親·

[In the passage of the 國語 from which I quoted, on the 1st par., the words of Confucius, the sage goes on to say:—於是肅慎氏貢楛矢石砮,其長尺有咫,先王欲昭其令德之致遠也,以示後人,使永監焉,故銘其栝,曰肅慎氏之貢矢,以分太姬配虞胡公,而封諸陳,古者分同姓以珍玉,展親也,分異姓以遠方之職貢,使無忘服也,云云.]

人不易物,惟德其物,—by 人 is intended the various princes, receiving the imperial gifts; 易 = 輕 'to slight.' 不易物,—'have not slighted the things,' have not dared to think lightly of them, however little valuable they might be; 德其物,—'they have virtue-ed the things;' *i.e.*, they have looked at the things in the light of the virtue which

惟德其物。○[四節]德盛不狎侮。狎侮君子、罔以盡人心、狎侮小人、罔以盡其力。○[五節]不役耳目、百度惟貞。○[六節]玩人

4 "Complete virtue allows no contemptuous familiarity. When *a prince* treats superior men with such familiarity, he cannot get them to give him all their hearts; when he so treats inferior men, he cannot
5 get them to put forth for him all their strength. If he be not in bondage to his ears and eyes, all his conduct will be ruled by correctness.
6 By trifling with men he ruins his virtue; by finding his amusement in things he ruins his aims.

produced them, and as monitions to the virtue they themselves ought to cultivate. Gaubil's rendering of this part is sententious, but can be of no help to a student:—'Ainsi les choses qui viennent de la vertu retournent à la vertu.'

[This passage appears in the 左傳, 僖五年, along with two other sentences from 'the Books of Chow,' in the following form:—民不易物, 惟德繄物. The use which is made of it there is to show that virtue is the only sure defence of a State.]

Pp. 4—6. *How the sovereign's careful attention to his virtue will appear in his guarding against improper familiarity with men, and foolish cherishing of useless creatures and things.* This is the meaning that is put upon these paragraphs. The interpretation of them, it will be seen, is perplexing and difficult. 4. 德盛不狎侮,—comp. 狎侮五行, in 'the Great Speech,' Pt. iii., 2. Koo Seih-ch'ow (顧錫疇; Ming dyn.) says upon the terms here:—狎者與之暱也, 侮者禮之倨也, 一是視爲私人, 一是忽爲易與, '狎 is being familiar with them; 侮 is a haughty disregard of the rules of propriety. The former indicates the looking upon them as mere favourites; the latter expresses the treatment of them as easily consorted with.' For the two terms, however, we have the one term 玩, 'to make sport with' in p. 6. The 'Daily Explanation' says, on that par., that the first 玩 is the 玩 of contempt, and the second the 玩 of fondness' (上玩字, 玩忽之意, 下玩字玩好之意). But we must find a common idea expressed by the two applications of 狎侮 here, and of 玩 in p. 6. Such an idea is that of contemptuous familiarity. Directed to creatures like the hounds of Leu, it will have more of the character of trifling sport; directed to men, there will be in the ruler who practises it a want both of self-respect, and of the respect which he owes to them. 君子 is descriptive of men in office, who are to be supposed to have a degree of elevated character. They have their minds—their virtues and acquirements—to serve the sovereign with; but when treated with contemptuous familiarity, they will despise him and go away. 小人 are the people, in whom the familiarity of their superiors is sure to breed contempt, so that they will not be careful to labour for them, as they ought to do, with their strength. Ying-tă, aptly enough, quotes, in illustration of 侮狎君子, the words of E Yin, 接下思恭 (太甲, Pt. ii., p. 7); and the words of Confucius, 使民如承大祭 (Ana., XII., ii.), in illustration of 狎侮小人. 5. 不役耳目—不爲耳目所役, *i.e.*, if he be superior to the external fascinations that assail him through the senses,—what are called 物 in the next paragraph. 百度, 'the hundred measures,'=百爲之度, 'the measures of all his conduct.' A certain rule—of 'correctness' (貞=正)—is supposed, by which the ruler, free from the bondage of his senses, will endeavour to regulate all his conduct. 'His words and actions,' it is said in the 'Daily Explanation,' 'will all be conformed to the measure of perfection, and he will not dare to transgress it an inch.' 6. 玩,—see on par. 4. Contemptuous familiarity with men destroys that self-

喪德、玩物喪志。○志七節以道寧、言以道接。○不八節作無益害有益、功乃成、不貴異物賤用物、民乃足、犬馬非其土性不畜、珍禽奇獸、不育于國、不寶遠物、則遠人格、所寶惟賢、則邇人安。○九節嗚呼、夙夜罔或不勤、不矜細

7 "The aims should repose in what is right; words should be listened to according to their relation to right.

8 "*A prince* should not do what is unprofitable to the injury of what is profitable, and then his merit may be completed. He should not value strange things to the contemning things that are useful, and then his people will be able to supply *all his needs. Even* dogs and horses which are not native to his country he will not keep; fine birds and strange animals he will not nourish in his kingdom. When he does not look on foreign things as precious, foreigners will come to him; when it is worth which is precious to him, *his own* people near at hand will enjoy repose.

9 "Oh! early and late never be but earnest. If you do not attend jealously to your small actions, the result will be to affect your virtue

respect and reverence for right which is at the foundation of all virtue. A fondness for, and fondling of, creatures like the hounds of Leu brings the whole mind down to the level of little things.

P. 7. *The rule for a prince's aims, and his intercourse with others.* 道一所當由之理, 'the principles according to which we ought to proceed.' 言以道接一人之言以道而接. The first clause is illustrated by Mencius' 持其志 (II., Pt. I., ii. 9), and the second by his 我知言 (*ib.*, p. 11); also by Shun's language in 'The Counsels of Yu,' pp. 14—16. The two sayings are good enough in their way, but the object which they serve in the guardian's address is not very evident;—see the remark of Wang Pih at the conclusion of his 'Doubts' about this Book.

P. 8. *What things a sovereign should abstain from cherishing and pursuing, and what things he should prefer and seek.* In this par. the Guardian comes at last to the subject of the hounds of Leu, though he does not expressly mention them. 不作至民乃足,—these two clauses are of a general character, and may be applied to an endless variety of subjects. 民乃足,—'the people will be sufficient.' Chin Tih-sew says:—貴異物,則征求多,而民不足, 'If he set a value on strange things, his exactions and requirements will be so many that the people will not be able to meet them.' 犬馬至不畜,—these dogs and horses might be useful, but being foreign, the virtuous sovereign will have nothing to do with them! 珍禽,—珍 is here an adjective, =珍美之禽. 不寶至人安,—see the remarks on this in the note on the Contents of the Book.

Pp. 9, 10. *How the sovereign is to cultivate his virtue by an untiring attention even to the smallest matters, and what grand results will flow from such*

行、終累大德、爲山九仞、功虧一簣。○允〔十節〕迪茲、生民保厥居、惟乃世王。

in great matters;—as when, in raising a mound of nine fathoms the
10
work is unfinished for want of one basket *of earth*. If you really follow this course, the people will preserve their possessions, and the throne will descend from generation to generation.

a course. 不矜細行,—矜 is used here much with the same meaning as in the Con. Ana. XV., xxi., 君子矜而不爭. Choo He was asked whether the term were not used in the same way in the two passages, and replied, 'Much about it. The idea is that of pitiful consideration, and firm conservation.' (相似,是個矜惜持守之意. 爲山,云云,—see the Con. Ana., IX., xviii. 仞=八尺, 'eight cubits.' I call it 'a fathom,' as being the nearest approximation to it which we have in our designations of measures. The paraphrase in the 'Daily Explanation' is:—譬如爲山者,積累工夫,已至九仞,所少一簣之土,乃心生玩弛,不肯加益九仞之功,到底虧缺山豈可得而成也哉.

10. 允迪茲,—comp. 允迪厥德. Pt., II., Bk. III., p. 1. 生民保厥居,—生民, 'the living people,' is merely an equivalent of 庶民. The phrase is found also in the 孝經. For 保厥居 Medhurst has well—'may protect their hearths.' 惟乃世王=王業可永, 'the imperial inheritance may be perpetuated.' I append Lin Che-k'e's observations on this:—凡後厥王,訓是以既保太如一,受所國中,獻所夷四矢楛氏慎肅觀,訓之保太迪允謂所,矣見以可,類之三世卜,孫子之周,也者茲王世其乎信,百七年卜,十事細亦,獻之獒一卻夫,也則此於見兆之王世而,耳永天祈以所之君大夫知者,休之疆無稷社爲以,命蓋不在大也。

THE BOOKS OF SHANG.

BOOK VI. THE METAL-BOUND *COFFER.*

金縢

既克商二年、王有疾、弗豫。○二公曰、我其爲王穆卜。○周公曰、未可以戚我先王。○

1 I. Two years after the conquest of the Shang dynasty, the king
2 fell ill, and was quite disconsolate. The two dukes said, "Let us
3 reverently consult the tortoise concerning the king"; but the duke
of Chow said, "You may not so distress our former kings."

THE NAME OF THE BOOK.—金縢, 'The Metal-bound.' 縢 is defined by 緘, 'to tie or shut up,' 'to seal or fasten.' A certain chest or coffer, which was fastened with bands of metal, plays an important part among the incidents of the Book. It is called, p. 11, 金縢之匱; and from this the name is taken. The Book is found in both the texts.

CONTENTS. King Woo is very ill, and his death seems imminent. His brother, the duke of Chow, apprehensive of the disasters which such an event would occasion to their infant dynasty, conceives the idea of dying in his stead, and prays to 'the three kings,' their immediate progenitors, that he might be taken and king Woo left. Having done so, and divined that he was heard, he deposits the prayer in the metal-bound coffer, where important archives were kept. The king gets well, and the duke is also spared; but five years after, Woo really dies, and is succeeded by his son, a boy only thirteen years old. Rumours are spread abroad that the duke has designs upon the throne, and he withdraws for a time from the court. At length in the third year of the young king, Heaven interposes. He has occasion to open the metal-bound coffer, and the prayer of the duke is found. His devotion to his brother and the interests of his family is brought to light. The boy monarch weeps because of the unjust suspicions he had harboured, and welcomes the duke back to court, amid unmistakeable demonstrations of the approval of Heaven.

The whole narrative is a very pleasing episode in the history of the times, and is more interesting to the foreign reader than most other portions of the Shoo. It divides itself naturally into two chapters:—the first, parr. 1—11, ending with the depositing the prayer in the coffer; and the second, detailing how it was brought to light, and the duke cleared by means of it from the suspicions which had been cherished of him.

CH. I. Pp. 1—11. THE PRAYER OF THE DUKE OF CHOW; ITS OCCASION; HIS SUBSEQUENT DIVINATION, AND DEPOSITING THE PRAYER IN THE COFFER. 1. *The illness of king Woo.* 既克商二年,—the current chronology refers this to the 14th year of king Woo, the year after the death of Show, B.C. 1,120. K'ang-shing thought that the year of the conquest of Shang should not be included in the two years, and the critics of the present dynasty generally concur with him. Ming-shing says that if the historian had meant to say that the year was that succeeding the change of dynasties, as Gan-kwŏ, Sze-ma Ts'een, and Wang Suh

四節 公乃自以爲功、爲三壇同墠、爲壇于南方北面、周公立焉、植璧秉珪、乃告太王

4 He then took the business on himself, and made three altars of earth, on the same cleared space; and having made another altar on the south, facing the north, he there took his own position. The convex symbols were put *on their altars* and he himself held his mace, while he addressed the kings T'ae, Ke, and Wăn.

think, he would have used 惟 and not 既, and we should have read 惟克商二年. I cannot undertake to settle this trivial point. 弗豫 (so in Sze-ma Ts'een. Këang Shing, after the 說文, gives 不愈)=不悅豫, 'was not happy.' We may suppose that he was distressed, thinking of the troubles that might arise on his death. The other reading—不愈, 'did not get well,' would give a simpler meaning.

2. *Proposal of the two dukes to divine respecting the issue of the king's illness.* The 二公, 'two dukes,' are understood to be 太公 and 召公. The latter is the duke of Shaou spoken of on p. 1 of the last Book. T'ae-kung, —see on Mencius, IV., Pt. I., xiii. He played a very important part in the establishment of the Chow dynasty, as counsellor to Wăn and Woo, and was invested by Woo with the principality of Ts'e, which his descendants held for nearly 640 years. He is the 尙父 in the apocryphal edition of the 'Great Speech.' 穆卜,—穆 (Ts'een has 繆) is defined by Gan-kwŏ, after the 爾雅, by 敬, 'reverently.' Ts'ae gives its meaning—誠一而和, 'with entire sincerity and in common,' saying that on great emergencies all the officers, great and small, united in the ceremony of divination, so that 穆—卜 is equivalent to 共卜, according to the view of an older interpreter whom he cites. This interpretation would give more emphasis to the 戚 in the next par., but I do not see that we can insist on extending the meaning of the term beyond the 敬 of Gan-kwŏ.

3. *The duke of Chow declines the proposal.* 周公,—this is the first time that we meet in the Shoo with this famous name, though we shall find him hereafter playing a most important part. But for him, indeed, the dynasty of Chow would probably not have taken root. He was equally mighty in words and in deeds,—a man of counsel and of action. Confucius regarded his memory with reverence, and spoke of it as an evidence of his own failing powers and disappointed hopes, that the duke of Chow no longer appeared to him in his dreams. He was the 4th son of king Wăn, by his queen T'ae-sze. The eldest was Pih-yih-k'aou (伯邑考); the second was king Woo; and the third was Sëen (鮮), the Kwan Shuh (管叔), mentioned in p. 12. There were six other younger brothers, but of all Wăn's sons, only king Woo and the duke of Chow were representatives of their father's virtue and wisdom. Chow was the name of the city where king T'ae fixed the central seat of his House;—see page 281, on the name of this part of the Shoo. It became the appanage of Wăn's 4th son, Tan (旦), and hence, he is known as the 'duke of Chow.' 戚=憂 'to trouble,' 'to distress.' It would appear that the two dukes proposed to have a solemn service of divination in the ancestral temple of the imperial House, and the duke of Chow negatives their proposal on the ground that there was no necessity for troubling the spirits of the departed kings by so much ado merely to divine the issue of the king's illness. He had himself determined what *he* would do. K'ang-shing says that he negatived their proposal, because he knew that the king would not die at this time. This view is grounded in a passage in the Bk. 文王世子, Pt. i., p. 2., of the Le Ke, where king Wăn is made to interpret a dream of his son so as to assure him of a certain number of years. But there is much in that Book which we cannot receive. If the duke knew that his brother would recover, the prayer which follows, and his offer to die in his room, lose all their meaning and value.

P. 4. *The duke's preparations for his prayer.* 公乃自以爲功,—功=事 'business or duty.' Gan-kwŏ paraphrases:—周公乃自以請命爲已事. 三壇同墠,—築土日壇, 除地日墠, 'the rearing up of earth is called 壇; the clearing away of the ground is called

王季文王。○史（五節）乃册祝曰、惟爾元孫某、遘厲虐疾、若爾三王、是有丕子之責于

5 The *grand* historian *by his order wrote* on tablets his prayer to the following effect:—"A. B., your chief descendant, is suffering from a severe and dangerous sickness;—if you three kings have in heaven the charge of *watching over* him, *Heaven's* great son, let me

墠: The duke cleared and levelled a space of ground, and there he built three altars facing the south, one for each of the kings to whom he intended to pray,—his father, his grandfather, and his great-grandfather, by whose wisdom and virtues the fortunes of their House had culminated in the possession of the empire. On the same area he raised another altar facing the north, where he himself took his place. K'ang-shing says that the altars were at Fung (Bk. III., p. 2.), and that the area remained to his day. 植璧秉珪,—璧 and 珪 (=圭) were two of the 'five tokens of gem,' mentioned in the Can. of Shun, p. 7, conferred by the emperor upon the various princes in connection with their investitures. There were two *peih*, belonging to the *tsze* and the *nan* respectively, and three *kwei*, that appropriate to the duke of Chow being the 桓圭. But we can hardly understand the terms here of the badges of nobility, or tokens of imperial appointment. Gan-kwŏ says the *peih* were brought and laid upon the altars of the three kings in reverence to them, and the *kwei* was the duke's proper *hwan kwei*, which he held in his hands as the evidence of his person and rank in appearing before them. But from p. 8, we should rather conclude that all the articles were proper to the worship of the three kings. The 璧 is described as resting on a square base, while outwards it was round like the arch of heaven.

Pp. 5—8. *The prayer*. 5. 史乃册祝,—史=太史, 'the grand historiographer.' His services were called in to record the prayer. I take 祝 as=祝詞, 'the language of the prayer.' Gan-kwŏ explains the clause:—史爲册書祝辭, 'The historian wrote for him on a tablet (or tablets) the words of the prayer.' This is the view now given in the 'Daily Explanation':—周公告三王之神,命太史書祝詞于册,若曰,云云. This, it seems to me, must be the meaning of the text. K'ang-shing, however, says:—策,周公所作,謂簡書也,祝者讀此簡書以告三王, 'The tablet, *i.e.*, the writing, was made by the duke of Chow; the priest read this writing to inform the three kings.' In this way the 史 is altogether unaccounted for. Woo Ch'ing would put a comma at 册, and explains—'The historiographer wrote the tablet, and the priest (祝) read it.' But who does not get the impression that the duke of Chow was himself the only priest on the occasion? 爾元孫某, —'Your great-grandson, such an one.' The duke, no doubt, used the name of king Woo. But in the Chow dynasty, the practice of 'concealing the name,' as it is called (諱名), came into vogue. K'ang-shing supposes that it was king Ching, who first dropt the name, and substituted 某 for it, when he found the prayer, as related in p. 16. 遘=遇 'to meet with,' Wang K'ăng-t'ang says:—'A sage has nothing about him which could bring on sickness, but he may happen to meet with evil malaria in the air:—hence the use of 遘;'—see a note in the 集傳. We need not lay so much stress on the character. 若爾三王至某之身,—this passage has wonderfully vexed the critics, and the editors of Yung-ching's Shoo say that no one interpretation of it which has been given should be pertinaciously held to. The view in the translation is substantially that of Ts'ae, who says:—武王爲天元子,三王當任其保護之責于天,不可令其死,如欲其死,則請以旦代武王之身, 'King Woo is the great son of Heaven; you three kings ought to have the charge of protecting him in heaven, and should not let him die. If you wish that he should die, pray let me Tan be a substitute for his person.' Feeling that the 于天 lay loosely on this view in the sentence, he supposed that some characters following 天 have been lost. The interpretations of K'ang-shing and Ying-tă

天、以旦代某之身。○予[六節]仁若考、能多材多藝、能事鬼神、乃元孫不若旦多材多藝、不能事神鬼。○乃[七節]命于

6 Tan be a substitute for his person. I have been lovingly obedient to my father; I am possessed of many abilities and arts which fit me to serve spiritual beings. Your chief descendant on the other hand has not so many abilities and arts as I, and is not so
7 capable of serving spiritual beings. And moreover he was appointed in the hall of God to extend his aid to the four quarters *of the empire*, so that he might establish your descendants in this lower world.

may be seen in the 後案 and the 註疏. Choo He preferred the view of a Chaou E-taou (晁以道), that 責 = 'to require the service of,' and the meaning is—'If God require the services of your eldest son in heaven, let me be a substitute for him.' Maou K'e-ling prefers the view of a Seu Chung-san (徐中山):—惟爾元孫某,遘疾若此,儻三王以爲此雖我元孫,實天之大子也,其責甚重,不可死,則旦請代耳. Ts'ae's construction of the sentence is not more objectionable than either of these two. Thus much is plain:—first, that the duke of Chow offered himself to die in the room of his brother king Woo; and second, that he thought his offer might somehow be accepted through the intervention of the great kings, their progenitors, to whom he addressed himself.

P. 6. *Reason why the duke should be taken instead of the king.* 予仁若考,—考 = 父; 若 = 順. Gan-kwŏ gives the meaning as 我仁能順父, 'I could affectionately obey my father.' Ts'ae takes the same view, only extending the meaning of 考 to 祖父, 'forefathers' generally. Medhurst translates the clause by—'my benevolence is equal to that of my forefathers,' which the language will admit of. Woo Ch'ing, indeed, gives for it—我之仁德如父. Still the other view is to be preferred. The duke would probably have declined to say that he was more virtuous than king Woo, though he was conscious of possessing certain qualities which might render him the better addition of the two to the spirit-world. Sze-ma Ts'een has only 旦巧能, and on his authority Keang Shing would cast 仁若 out of the text; but though the 'Historical Records' show us the interpretation which their compiler put upon the Shoo, their authority cannot always be pleaded in favour of this or that reading.

We should be glad if we could ascertain from this paragraph what ideas the duke of Chow had about the other world, but his language is too vague to afford us satisfaction. He says he was better able than his brother to serve spirits;—did he then expect that some such service would have to be performed by him after death? and who was the spirit, or who were the spirits, to whom the service was to have been rendered? These questions are suggested by his words; and yet it may be, that all which he meant to say was that he was more religious,—more acquainted with ceremonies, and fonder of sacrificial services,—and therefore was somehow better fitted for admission to the spirit circle. I suppose he did not know his own meaning very clearly.

Chinese critics are concerned to free the duke of Chow from the charge of boasting which may be fixed on him from the paragraph. Tsëang Te-shăng (蔣悌生; Ming dyn.) says:—'The duke of Chow did not boast of his services, but was the humblest of men;—how is it that here he boasts of himself in such a way to the spirits of the three kings? On this occasion, so important to his family and the kingdom, his love for his brother prevailed over every other consideration. He had not leisure to consider whether he was boasting or modest. The case is one of those instances in which the virtue of sagely men moves Heaven. Let it not be lightly thought of or spoken about;'—see the 集說.

P. 7. *Reason why king Woo should be spared.* 乃命于帝庭,—the 帝 here is 上帝 or God. Ma Yung says:—武王受命于天帝之庭,—'king Woo received appointment in the hall of the God of heaven.' Medhurst has translated:—'He has

帝庭、敷佑四方、用能定爾子孫于下地、四方之民、罔不祇畏、嗚呼、無墜天之降寶命、我先王亦永有依歸。○八節今我卽命于元龜、爾之許我、我其以璧與珪、歸俟爾命、爾不許我、我乃屏璧與珪。○九節乃卜三龜、一習吉、

The people of the four quarters stand in reverent awe of him. Oh! do not let that precious Heaven-conferred appointment fall to the ground, and *all* our former kings will also have a perpetual
8 reliance and resort. I will now seek for your orders from the great tortoise. If you grant *what I request*, I will take these symbols and this mace, and return and wait for the issue. If you do not grant it, I will put them by."
9 The duke then divined with the three tortoises, and all were favourable. He took a key, opened and looked at the *oracular*

received the decree in the imperial hall,' which is a great weakening of the duke's argument, and without the sanction of any critic. 四方至祇畏,—the critics generally connect this with the preceding clause, and extend the force of the 用能 to it. It seems rather to be a description of the success of Woo's govt.,—exaggerated, indeed, but justifiable in the circumstances. 天之降寶命=天所降之寶命,—as in the translation. 我先王,云云,—'our former kings' are all the princes of the House of Chow, from Shun's minister of Agriculture downward. The saying that they would have 'a perpetual reliance and resort' is to the effect that the sacrifices to them would ever be continued.

P. 8. *The duke proposes to divine for the answer of the kings, and tells them what will be the consequence of their refusing his request.* 今我卽命=今我就受三王之命, 'I will now go at once and receive the command—the decision—of you three kings.' 元龜,—see on 大龜, in the 'Tribute of Yu,' Pt. i., 52. The shells of the tortoise employed for imperial divinations were larger than those employed by the princes. 歸俟爾命,—'will return and wait for your orders,' which would be seen in the recovery of king Woo, and the duke's death. Ma says:—待爾命,武王當愈,我當死. 屏璧與珪,—屏 (2d tone)=去 or 藏. The meaning is, that he would put those instruments of worship aside;—the dynasty would fall, and the House of Chow would have no more imperial sacrifices to offer.

Pp. 9, 10. *The divination is favourable, and the duke deposits his prayer in the coffer.* 9. 卜三龜,—'He divined with the three tortoises.' I suppose that the divination took place before the altars, and that a different shell was used to ascertain the mind of each king. Choo He says:—或曰三王前,各一龜卜之. Lin Che-k'e, however, says:—以龜之三兆卜之, 'He divined according to the three prognostics given by the tortoise.' This is in accordance with the language of the Chow Le, Bk. XXIV., p. 1, 太卜掌三兆之法,一曰玉兆,二曰瓦兆,三曰原兆, which Biot

啟籥見書、乃并是吉。○十節公曰、體、王其罔害、予小子新命于三王、惟永終是圖、茲攸俟、能念予一人。○十一節公歸、乃納冊于金縢之匱中、王翼日、乃瘳。

10 responses which also were favourable. He said, "According to the form *of the prognostic*, the king will take no injury. I, who am but a child, have got his appointment renewed by the three kings, by whom a long futurity has been consulted for. I have to wait
11 the issue. They can provide for our one man." *Having said this*, he returned, and placed the tablets in the metal-bound coffer; and next day the king got better.

translates:—'Grand Augure. Il est préposé aux trois methodes pour l'observation des fissures sur l'ecaille de la tortue. La première est appelée fissure de jade; la seconde, fissure de poterie; la troisième, fissure de plaine.' 一習吉,—習=重, or 襲; see the 'Great Speech,' Pt. ii., 5. 啟籥見書,—by 書 we are to understand 占書, 'written oracles.' The par. of the Chow Le, following that quoted above, is—其經兆之體皆百有二十,其頌皆千有二百, 'The forms of the regular prognostications were in all 120, the explanations of which amounted to 1,200.' Those explanations, no doubt, consisting of a few oracular lines; were the 書 of the text. They were kept by themselves, and consulted on occasion, according to certain rules which have not come down. The duke of Chow at this time had recourse to them. The meaning of 籥 in this place is very uncertain. Properly speaking, it denotes a kind of flute. Here it seems to denote a sort of key with which the apartment or chest, or whatever it might be, in which those oracles were kept, was opened. K'ang-shing, Ma Yung, and Wang Suh define it nearly in the same way, as 開藏之管;藏卜兆書管; and 開藏占兆書管. 10. 體=兆之體, 'the form of the prognostic,' appearing on the shell of the tortoise. 惟永終是圖,—Woo Ch'ing understands this to be spoken by the duke of himself, so that he not only understood from the divination that the king would not die, but also that he would get better without himself being taken as a substitute. The words do not convey that impression to my mind. In the 'Daily Explanation,' they are referred to the three kings as in the translation. —我小子新受命于三王,惟以久後子孫爲計,而許我以保佑元子孫矣. 茲攸俟,能念予一人,—茲攸俟= the 歸俟爾命 of par. 8, the only difference being that the words here are those of soliloquy, and not addressed to the kings. The 一人 is king Woo. The duke would seem to be resigning himself to the thought of his own death. He must be taken, but he can confidently leave the king and the dynasty in the care of the three kings.

11. 金縢之匱,—'the metal-bound coffer.' Ts'ae says that it was this coffer which contained the oracles of divination, the same which is alluded to in p. 9. It may have been so; but I should rather suppose it to have been different,—a special chest in which important archives of the dynasty, to be referred to on great emergencies, were kept. The duke gave orders to all whose services he had employed in the ceremony to say nothing about it (see p. 17), but it was right that the record of the prayer should be preserved in this repository. He therefore placed it there, not thinking that it would be—hoping that it would not be—brought to light in his time.

[The prayer of the duke of Chow is addressed to the three kings, and I have said above, that it is addressed to them in the character of mediators or intercessors with Heaven or God,

○十二節武王既喪、管叔及其群弟、乃流言於國曰、公將不利於孺子。○十三節周公

12 II. *Afterwards*, upon the death of king Woo, *the duke's* elder brother, he of Kwan, and his younger brothers, spread a baseless rumour through the kingdom, saying, "The duke will do no good to the

The analogy of the circle of religious notions among the Chinese obliges us to adopt this conclusion, and, in par. 7, we have an express reference to the supreme disposing of God in human affairs. Still it must be allowed that the doctrine of the former kings being only intercessors is not indicated in the text so clearly as it might have been. In illustration of this I shall quote the words of Ts'aou Heŏ-tseuen (曹學佺; Ming dyn). He says:—'The earlier scholars were led, by the words—"I have received a new appointment for him from the three kings," to doubt whether the duke's language (in p. 6)—"I have many abilities and arts which fit me to serve spiritual beings," really referred to Heaven. They rather thought it did not; but we must not thus pertinaciously insist upon particular expressions. Anciently, when sovereigns sacrificed to Heaven and Earth, they associated their ancestors as assessors and sharers at the ceremony; when they prayed for anything to Heaven and Earth, they depended on the efficacious spirituality of their ancestors to present and second their request. Heaven was the most honourable, and they did not dare to approach it abruptly; their ancestors were the nearest to them, and they could, through the kindness between them, make their thoughts known to them. There is no reason why we should not say that the words, "I have received a new appointment from the three kings," are equivalent to "I have received a new appointment for him from Heaven"' (先儒因新命于三王、即疑上文能多材多藝以服事鬼神、非指天言、亦不必如此拘泥、古者人君祀天地、必以祖考配享、其有所禱于天地、亦必藉祖宗之靈、以爲之請、蓋天至尊、不敢唐突、而祖宗至親、殆可以情告也、謂新命于三王、即新受命于天、可也。)

Ch. II. Pp. 12—19. AFTER THE DEATH OF KING WOO THE DUKE OF CHOW FALLS UNDER SUSPICION OF NOT BEING LOYAL TO THE THRONE. TWO YEARS PASS BY, AND THEN HEAVEN INTERPOSES TO BRING HIS INNOCENCE TO LIGHT; THE PRAYER IN THE COFFER IS DISCOVERED, AND THE YOUNG KING ACKNOWLEDGES WITH HIS TEARS THE INJUSTICE OF HIS THOUGHTS, AND RECEIVES THE DUKE BACK, WHILE HEAVEN ACCORDS EVIDENT TOKENS OF ITS APPROVAL.

12. *The manner in which the duke of Chow was brought into suspicion.* The last par. closes with the statement that the king suddenly recovered the day after the duke's prayer. This opens with a reference to his death. Five years have elapsed. Woo died B.C., 1,115, and was succeeded by his son Sung (誦), whose reign dates from B.C. 1,114, and who is known in history by the title of Ching (成), 'the Completer.' Ching was only 13 years old, and the duke of Chow acted as regent of the empire. It was natural he should do so, for he was the ablest of all the sons of Wăn, and had been devotedly attached to his brother Woo, whose chief adviser he had been, and was without the shadow of disloyal feeling. The accession of dignity and influence which he now received, however, moved his elder brother Sëen, and some of his other brothers to envy, and they had come to be engaged in a treasonable conspiracy against the throne. We have seen how Woo, after the death of the tyrant Show, pardoned his son, generally known by the name of Woo-kăng (武庚), and continued him in Yin to maintain the sacrifices to the kings of his line. To guard against the very probable contingency of his rebellion, however, he placed three of his own brothers in the State along with him, with the title of 'Inspectors' or 'Overseers' (三監), who should overawe both him and the old ministers of Show. Those overseers were Sëen, known as Kwan Shuh, older than the duke of Chow; Too (度), known as Ts'ae Shuh (蔡叔), immediately younger than the duke; and Ch'oo (處), known as Hoh Shuh (霍叔), the eighth of Wăn's sons. Perhaps Sëen thought that on the death of Woo the regency, if not the throne, should have devolved upon himself. Mencius ascribes the appointment of him as overseer of Yin to the duke of Chow (see Men., II., Pt. II., ix.), as, no doubt, it was made by Woo on his advice. This may have exasperated him the more against Tan who had thus *shelved* him, he would think, away from the court. However it was induced, soon after the death of Woo, those three brothers entered into a conspiracy with Woo-kăng to throw off the yoke of the

乃告二公曰、我之弗辟、我無以告我先王。○十四節周公居東二年、則罪人斯得。○十五節于

13 *king's* young son." Upon this the duke of Chow represented to the two dukes, saying, "If I do not take the law *to these men*, I shall not be able to make my report to our former kings."

14 He resided accordingly in the east for two years, when the

new dynasty, and as a preliminary step, they endeavoured, in the manner indicated in the text, to stir up division between the regent and his nephew.

管叔,—Kwan was the name of a city and territory,—the pres. sub. dep. of Ch'ing (鄭州), in the dep. of K'ae-fung, Ho-nan. It formed the appanage of Sëen, the third of Wăn's sons. I suppose that 叔 was originally merely indicative of Sëen's place in the line of his brothers (see on Con. Ana., XVIII., xi.); but it has come to be joined with 管, so that Kwan-shuh is now in effect simply a historical name. 羣弟,—'the younger brothers' were Too and Ch'oo, as has been detailed above. 流言,—'set words flowing,' = spread a baseless rumour. 不利於孺子,—'will not be advantageous to the child.' By 孺子, of course, the young emperor is meant. 13. *The resolution of the duke.* 我之弗辟,—ever since the Han dynasty the meaning of 辟 here has been debated. Gan-kwŏ, reading the term *peih*, according to its proper enunciation, defined it by 法, and explained the text by 我不以法法三叔,則我無以成周道,告我先王,—as in the translation. K'ang-shing, on the other hand read 辟 as 避, and with the meaning of that term, so that the text = 'If I do not get out of the way,—leave my dignities, and retire from court,—I shall not be able,' &c., &c. The editors of Yung-ching's Shoo do not give a decided opinion on either side. Ts'ae has followed K'ang-shing, but his master Choo He wavered between the two views, approving now the one, and now the other. Maou K'e-ling has a long note on the subject, in his 尙書廣聽錄, Bk. III., recanting his early opinion in favour of K'ang-shing's view, and giving eight reasons for adopting in preference that of Gan-kwŏ. Some of them are sufficiently forcible. I have no hesitation in differing on this point from the generally approved interpretation sanctioned by Ts'ae.

The duke of Chow, on being aware of the insinuations circulated against him, resolved to meet them with promptitude. He owed a duty to the former kings and to the dynasty, and whatever the young king might think, he would act at once against the rebellious and the disloyal.

14. *Justice done on the criminals.* The different views that are taken of the last paragraph necessarily affect the interpretation of this. Acc. to Gan-kwŏ, the duke spent two years in the east, operating against Woo-kăng and the false brothers, and at the end of that time he had got them into his hands, and dealt with them according to his views of their several guilt. Ying-tă says:—'居東 (this has already been explained by 東征之) 二年,則罪人於此皆得,謂獲三叔及諸叛逆者. K'ang-shing on the other hand says:—居東者,出處東國,待罪以須君之察已, "He resided in the east" means that he left the court and dwelt in an eastern State, allowing the charge of guilt till the king should have examined into it.' The language so far will certainly admit of this interpretation, but what he says on the next clause is too ridiculous. It is:—罪人周公之屬黨與知居攝者,周公出皆奔,今二年盡爲成王所得,謂之罪人,史書成王意也, 'The criminals are the partizans of the duke of Chow and his acquaintances while he held the regency. When he withdrew from the court, they fled; but now in the two years they were all apprehended by king Ching. The historian calls them criminals, writing from the king's point of view.' Even Keang Shing does not venture to adopt this interpretation, but supposes the meaning to be that the duke, while in the east, came to know who the criminals were that had slandered him.

I have said that the phrase 居東 will itself admit of the interpretation put on it by K'ang-shing; but Maou K'e-ling has shown, that if we do not understand it as Gan-kwŏ does, of the duke's operating in the east against his rebellious brothers, there is no other place in that direction from the court, to which his sojourn-

後、公乃爲詩以貽王、名之曰鴟鴞、王亦未敢誚公。○秋、十六大熟、未穫、天大雷電以風、禾盡偃、大木斯拔、邦人大恐、王與大夫盡弁、以啓金縢之書、乃得周公所自以爲功、代武王之說。十七節二公

15 criminals were got *and brought to justice.* Afterwards he made a poem to present to the king, and called it "The Owl." The king on his part did not dare to blame the duke.

16 In the autumn, when the grain was abundant and ripe, but before it was reaped, Heaven sent a great storm of thunder and lightning, along with wind, by which the grain was all beaten down, and great trees torn up. The people were greatly terrified; and the king and great officers, all in their caps of state, proceeded to open the metal-bound coffer, and examine the writings, when they found the words of the duke of Chow when he took on himself the business of taking

ing for so long a time can be assigned with any degree of probability. 15. *The duke sends a poem to the king to clear himself, but is only partially successful.* The poem here referred to is in the She King, Part I., Bk. XV., Ode ii. It begins:—

'O owl, O owl,
You have taken my young ones:
Do not also destroy my nest.
I loved them; I laboured for them;
I nourished them.—How am I to be pitied.'

The received interpretation of it is that it was composed by the duke after he had crushed the insurrectionary movements in Yin, and put to death Woo-kăng and Kwan-shuh. By the 'owl' is intended Woo-kăng; and by the 'nest,' the dynasty of Chow. The writer meant that king Ching should understand by it the devotion which he felt to the imperial House, and the sorrow which the stern justice he had been obliged to execute upon his brother occasioned him. K'ang-shing took a difft. view of it, in accordance with his interpretation of 罪人斯得 in the last par., and supposed that the duke intended by it to expostulate with the king on the persecution of his friends which he had instituted. But we cannot believe that he would have thus addressed the king as an 'Owl.' There is nothing in the poem or ode, which readily suggests the interpretation to be put upon it; but there is perhaps something in what Choo He says, that readers at the time, all-excited by the circumstances to which it had reference, would not find the difficulty in understanding it which we do. 王亦未敢誚公,—誚 is now superseded by 譙; it means 'to reprove,' 'to blame.' The clause is understood to intimate that though the king now partially understood the motives of the duke's conduct, and could not blame him for the way in which he had dealt with his other uncles, he still looked on him with some degree of suspicion.

Pp. 16—18. *Heaven interposes to bring the duke's innocence to light by means of the prayer in the metal-bound coffer.* 16. 秋,—we may suppose this was the autumn of the the third year of Ching,—B.C. 1,112. 雷電以風,—Lin Che-k'e brings out the 以風 by expanding:—天忽雷電大作,又繼之以風, as in the translation. The paraphrase of the 'Daily Explanation' is similar. 王與至之書,—the 弁 was a 'skin cap,' worn in court at audiences. It is generally said that the king was going to divine that he might discover the reason of the unusual storm, and therefore opened the coffer which contained the oracles of divination. But we saw, on p. 11, that it is not certain those oracles were kept in that coffer. Possibly it was a repository of important archives, which

及王乃問諸史與百執事。對曰、信、噫、公命、我勿敢言。○十八節王執書以泣曰、其勿穆卜、昔公勤勞王家、惟予沖人弗及知、今天動威以彰周公之德、惟朕小子其新逆、我國家禮亦宜之。○十九節王出郊、天乃雨、反風禾則盡起、二公命邦人、凡大木所偃、盡起而築之、歲則大熟。

17 the place of king Woo. The king and the two dukes asked the
grand historian and all the other officers about the thing. They re-
plied, "Ah! it was really thus; but the duke charged us that we should
18 not presume to speak about it." The king held the writing, and
wept, saying, "We need not *now* go on reverently to divine.
Formerly the duke was thus earnest for the royal House, but I,
being a child, did not know it. Now Heaven has moved its terrors
to display the virtue of the duke of Chow. That I meet him a new
man, is what the rules of propriety of our empire require."
19 The king then went out to the borders, when Heaven sent down
rain; and by virtue of a contrary wind, the grain all rose up. The
two dukes gave orders to the people to take up all the large trees
which had fallen, and replace them. The year then turned out
very fruitful.

were consulted on great emergencies of the State.

17. 史與百執事,—these were all the officers who had assisted the duke when he made his prayer, &c. 信噫云云,—Ying-tă says:—噫,心不平之聲,'噫 is a sound expressive of dissatisfaction of mind.' Gan-kwŏ calls it 恨辭 They were vexed at being thus obliged to tell what the duke had charged them to keep secret. Keang Shing reads 意, which he explains in a similar way.

18. 其勿穆卜—今觀公書,可知天變之所由,我君臣不必更穆卜矣;—see the 日講. 予沖人,—see on 'The Pwan-kăng,' Pt. iii., p. 7. Here king Ching was really a youth. 惟朕小子其新逆,—逆=迎, 'to meet.' Ma Yung read 親 instead of 新, so that the meaning is—'That I go out and meet him in person,' &c. This certainly gives a good meaning; and Ts'ae and Këang Shing both adopt it. Gan-kwŏ and K'ang-shing, however, both understand 新 as in the translation. The language of the latter is:—新迎,改先時之心,更自新以迎周公. This is rather harsh, but it is more difficult to get a tolerable meaning out of many other passages of the Shoo.

書經

P. 19. *The duke is received back, and Heaven signifies its approbation.* 王出郊,—it is most natural to understand this going forth to the suburbs with reference to the king's purpose indicated in the 朕小子其新逆 of the last par. Gan-kwŏ, however, takes 郊 of the place, outside the city, where the great sacrifice to Heaven was offered, and thought that the going forth was to offer a sacrifice of thanksgiving to Heaven for his deliverance from the unjust suspicions which he had harboured.

Ts'ae says that after reading this paragraph it is impossible to doubt the doctrine of 'verifications,' laid down in the 'Plan!'

[I may here, in the vacant space of this page, introduce Wang Pih's chapter on the 金縢 in his 'Doubts about the Shoo.' His views are questionable, but the student will be glad to have a complete specimen of the style and manner of his Work.—此書敘事體也，與武成同，武成是敘伐商一事始末，此篇是東征前後事，歷六七年始末，詳略之中，有筆力焉，納册啟書，此金縢之首尾也，其敘事不可不詳，其敘流言居東，止五十餘字，簡潔詳明，於曲折抑揚間，事情隱然可判，後來大誥等事，盡含誥於此，武成先列四誓，而總敘武事之終，金縢是敘東征始終，而後列諸誥，法當然也，其餘小小文義，諸家有末一者，因論丕子之責，竊意責字，如責望之責，是責望其事我於天，則繼以願代，中間無鉠文意，若曰，三王有任保護丕子之責于天，則後面能不能事鬼神之語，全無意味矣，如乃命于帝廷，郤脫元孫二字，合復舉乃元孫於此，乃幷是吉者，謂三卜皆吉，此卜者之言，啟篇而參以龜卜之書，乃是證三卜之果吉也，于小子新命于三王者，公欲以身代王，王瘳則公當代命也，惟永終是圖者，我但爲考終之計，玆所待者三王必不忘於一人之言，以代王也，王瘳而公不死，亦天監公之心，而俟從公之代也，在公則當只命以代而已，我之弗辟，天是作入•聲讀，周公以公得下爲心，征誅之事，固不之以私恩而姑息，曰公避卜而居東，非知公者，二穆不只一義，於敬字，爲近，初不祗牾也].

THE BOOKS OF SHANG.

BOOK VII. THE GREAT ANNOUNCEMENT.

大誥

王若曰、猷大誥爾多邦、越爾御事、弗弔、天降割于我家、不少延、洪惟我幼沖人、嗣無疆大歷服、弗造哲、迪民康、矧曰其有能格（一節）

1 I. "The king speaks to the following effect:—'Ho! I make a great announcement to you, *the princes of* the many States, and to you, the managers of my affairs.—Unpitied am I, and Heaven sends down calamities on my House, without exercising the least delay. It greatly occupies my thoughts, that I, so very young. have inherited this illimitable patrimony, with its destinies and domains. I have not displayed wisdom, and led the people to tranquillity, and how much less should I be able to reach the knowledge of the decree of Heaven!

THE NAME OF THE BOOK.—大誥, 'The Great Announcement,' At the commencement of the first paragraph, these two characters,—大誥,—occur, and they are thence taken and made the name of the Book. Gan-kwŏ, indeed, says that the Book sets forth great doctrines for the information of the empire, and thence it received its name (陳大道以誥天下,故以名篇). But we look in vain for any 'great doctrines' in the Book. The emergency which called the announcement forth was sufficiently important to justify the duke of Chow in calling it 'great.' We need not look for any higher or deeper meaning in the title. The Book is found in both the texts.

CONTENTS; DATE; AND STYLE. The prefatory note says, 'When king Woo had deceased, the three overseers and the wild tribes of the Hwae rebelled. The duke of Chow acted as prime minister to king Ching; and having purposed to make an end of the House of Yin, he made "The Great Announcement."' This sets forth the occasion on which the address was composed, but when we come to look at the contents, we find very little appropriate, according to our views, to the circumstances. The young emperor speaks of the

responsibility lying on him to maintain the empire gained by the virtues and prowess of his father, and of the senseless movements of the House of Yin to regain its supremacy: he complains of the reluctance of many of the princes and high officers to second him in putting down the revolt; and proclaims with painful reiteration the support and assurances of success which he has received from the divining tortoise-shells. The three overseers are not mentioned, though we may find an allusion or two to them. The whole tone is feeble. I have divided, it will be seen, the 15 paragraphs in which it is now generally edited into five chapters.

The date of the announcement is generally referred to the third year of Ching B.C., 1,112. But such an arrangement of events supposes the duke of Chow's residence in the east, spoken of in the last Book, to have been a voluntary exile, and that this expedition against Yin was undertaken after he returned in the manner described. But I saw reason to understand the sojourning in the east as a description of this very expedition, and that the return mentioned was on its successful termination. On this view the announcement was made in the first or second year of Ching, and the expedition was finished in the third year. On that point,—the date of the extinction of Woo-kăng and his revolt, there is an agreement.

The style of the Book is about as difficult as that of 'the Pwan-kăng.' 'We may doubt,' says Wang Gan-shih, 'whether parts have not been lost, and other parts have not fallen out of their proper place. Our plan is to let alone what we cannot understand, and to explain what we find ourselves able to do.' 'It is difficult,' says Choo He, 'to point the Book. The sentences are very long, and students generally try to break them up into shorter ones, which makes the interpretation more difficult still.'

Ch. I. Pp. 1, 2. Notwithstanding his youth and incompetencies, the king feels bound, by his duty to his fathers and to Heaven, to do his utmost to put down the revolt which was threatening the recently acquired empire. 1. 王若曰,—these are the words of the duke of Chow, spoken by him as regent of the empire, and in the name of the young king. We are not to suppose indeed that Ching had anything to do with the announcement. Doubting the duke's loyalty, he would not have sent him to attack his other uncles; but the duke acted as the great duties of his position required him to do, and would not allow the safety of the dynasty to be perilled by weak scruples. At the same time it was right that his address should appear as in the name of the king. There was no other king but Ching, and no other is intended by 王 throughout the Book. K'ang-shing, however, says that by 王 we should understand the duke himself. His words are:—王,周公也,周公居攝,命大事,則權稱王, 'The king is the duke of Chow. He was regent of the empire, and in giving charge about such great affairs, in the exigency of the circumstances, he called himself the king.' Keang-shing, Ming-shing, and other opponents of 'the false K'ung,' adopt this view, and the ingenuity with which they argue for it is amusing; but it is too absurd to justify our entering into an examination of their arguments. Comp. the 王若曰 in the Pwan-kăng, Pt. i., 16; and often in several of the Books of Chow that follow. 猷大誥爾多邦,—猷 appears to have come into use, under the Chow dynasty, as an exclamation, like the 咨 of the 'Canon of Yaou.' I do not see what other meaning can be given to it here, or in the next Bk., p. 1; *et al.* Here Ma Yung and others in the Han dynasty read it after 誥,—大誥猷爾,云云,—and explained it by 道. Gan-kwŏ even attempted to give it the same meaning in its place at the beginning of the sentence:—周公稱王命,順大道,以誥天下,云云. But this is exceedingly harsh and unnatural. Lin Che-k'e was the first, so far as I have ascertained, who explained the term as an exclamation. It is a pity that this meaning of it does not appear in the dictionary. 爾多邦=爾在外多邦之諸侯, 越爾御事,—see the 'Great Speech,' Pt. i., p. 2. 弗弔,—弔 (read *teaou*)=恤 'to pity,' as in the She King, Pt. III., Bk. III., Ode x., st. 5. In the 'Pwan-kang,' Pt. iii., 7, it was read *teih*, with the meaning of 至; 'to come to,' *i.e.*, to reach the mark of goodness; and so Gan-kwŏ took it, and Keang Shing takes it, but with different relations to the rest of the sentence;—see the 註疏 and the 尙書集註音疏. Ts'ae expands the phrase as in the translation:—我不爲天所恤. 天降割于我家,不少延,—割=害, 'injuries,' 'calamities.' 'Heaven sends down calamities on my House,'—this has reference especially to the early death of king Woo; and we may include also the present troubles occasioned by the revolt in Yin. 不少延,—'without a little delay.' Blow was following on blow in quick succession. Gan-kwŏ put a stop at 少, and carried 延 to the next sentence. Of this construction I shall speak on the next clause. K'ang-shing pointed as in the text and interpreted 不少延 as='not few and prolonged.' 延 may certainly be thus taken as=長; but the whole phrase 不小延 is more naturally construed as I have done in the translation, following Ts'ae and other Sung critics. 洪惟=大思, 'I greatly think.' Gan-kwŏ, I have just said, began this

知天命。○已[二節]予惟小子、若涉淵水、予惟往求朕攸濟、敷賁、敷前人受命、茲不忘大功、予不敢閉于天降威。

2 'Yes, I who am but a little child am in the position of one who has to cross a deep water;—it must be mine to go and seek how to cross over. *I must* diffuse the elegant institutions of my predecessor, and augment the appointment which he received *from Heaven*;—so shall I be not forgetful of his great work. Nor shall I dare to restrain the majesty of Heaven seen in the inflictions it sends down.

clause with 延, and his comment on 延惟我幼沖人 is—凶害延大,惟累我幼童人,成王言其不可不誅之意, 'The calamities are so protracted and great that they involve me who am so young;—the king's meaning is that there was nothing for him but to cut off the criminals.' This is very far-fetched, and must be rejected. 嗣無疆大歷服,—歷 is defined as=數, 'fate,' destiny.' Woo Ch'ing says:—歷=天之歷數. 服='domains.' Ts'ae says—五服, 'the five domains;' but they were more than 'five' under the Chow dynasty. Nearly all the critics define 服 by 事, and then expand it into something like 服王事; but Ts'ae's meaning is much simpler. 弗造哲,迪民康,—on this Gan-kwŏ has—不能爲造智道以安人, 'I cannot practise the ways of wisdom to repose the people.' Këang Shing has—弗遭逢明哲之人以道于安, 'I have not met with (=found), intelligent men to lead the people to repose.' Better than either, Woo Ch'ing read 造 with an aspirate,='to go to,' 'to arrive at;' and says:—弗能造於明哲以導民於安, 'I have not attained to wisdom, so as to conduct the people to tranquillity.' So I take the words. 矧曰,云云,—I take 格 here with Gan-kwŏ as=至, 'to reach to.' I do not know what the young king, or rather the duke of Chow, had in view by 天命, 'the decree or appointment of Heaven,' nor can I discern the bearing of the whole clause on the rest of the announcement. Perhaps a glimpse of light is afforded by Kin Le-ts'ëang, who says:—此言成王以幼沖嗣位,流言展轉,而事變如此,未能上測天意如何,以起下文求濟卜筮之意, 'This speaks of how king Ching, inheriting the throne at so early an age, with the baseless rumours going about, and such changes of events occurring, was unable to fathom what might be the mind of Heaven, in order to introduce what is said below about his seeking how to cross over his difficulties, and the intimations afforded by divination;'—see the 集說. 2. 已 is used, acc. to Ts'ae, as a continuative particle, indicating that though the speaker had come to a pause, yet he must go on expressing his sentiments (已,承上語辭已而有不能已之意). Our 'Yes' corresponds to it. 予惟往求朕攸濟,—'this,' says Gan-kwŏ, 'expresses the king's awe' (言祇懼). He might have said—'awe and perplexity.' 敷賁,敷前人受命,—the former clause expresses the young king's apprehensive perplexity; this seems to express what under all circumstances he felt it incumbent upon him to do. The language however, is difficult to construe and interpret. Lin Che-k'e says:—'Gan-kwŏ read 賁 *fun*, as in the "Pwan-kăng," Pt. iii., 7, and with the same signif. of *great*, and gave the meaning—'I will spread and practise great principles, so spreading and displaying the appointment received by Wăn and Woo.' But the text only says 敷賁, and to make that='I will display great principles' is wide of the mark and forced. Soo and Lin Tsze-hwuy (林子晦) read the character *pe*, with the meaning of 'to adorn' (飾; as in the 'Announcement of T'ang,' p. 5). Soo then in-

書經

用。○寧王遺我大寶龜、紹天明、卽命曰、有大艱于西土、西土人亦不靜、越茲蠢。三節

3 II. 'The Tranquillizing king left to me the great precious tortoise, to bring into connection with me the intelligence of Heaven. I consulted it, and it told me that there would be great trouble in the region of the west, and that the western people would not be still. Accordingly we have the present senseless movements.

terpreted—"What I diffuse must be to adorn and extend the appointment received by my predecessors, and not forget their merit," while Lin Tsze-hwuy says, "The meaning is—I will cultivate and illustrate the institutions, to impart ornament to the empire." The character 賁 is thus both pronounced and interpreted by them differently from Gan-kwŏ; but the meanings they bring out are as far from being clear as his. Wang Gan-shih says, better than any of them, that the text is maimed, and we need not weary ourselves to fix its meaning. The translation simply follows the view of Ts'ae, which is that of Soo Tung-po. 予不敢, 云云,—in this clause the king intimates how it was his duty to punish Woo-kăng and all aiding him in his revolt. He would let the justice of Heaven take its course; he would not restrain it, but execute it rather against them. 于, following 閉, is rather perplexing; but we have met with it before, similarly following transitive verbs.

Wang Gan-shih put a stop at 威, and read 用 with what follows—寧王, 云云, and Choo He approved of this construction;—see the 附錄. In this point Ts'ae chose to follow the two K'ung, rather than his master. Woo Ch'ing, however, points with Gan-shih, and gives this view of the clause preceding, having closed a paragraph with 大功:—'When Heaven was sending down its terrors on me, I did not dare to conceal them, but used the tortoise,' &c., &c.

Ch. II. Pp. 3—6. THE DIVINATIONS HAD INFORMED THE KING OF THE COMING TROUBLES, AND THEY NOW ASSURED HIM ON THE PRESENT EXPEDITION. MANY OF THE BEST AND ABLEST OF THE PEOPLE WERE SUPPORTING HIM. THEY MIGHT THEREFORE GO FORWARD WITH CONFIDENCE. 3. 寧王,—'the Tranquillizing king.' Gan-kwŏ says that king Wăn is intended; but the phrase 寧考 in par. 8 determines that we interpret the epithet of king Woo, Ching's father. 紹天明,—紹 = 繼, 'to continue and transmit.' At a grand reception of visitors at court there were the attendants and officers who received them, and went between them and the prince. They and their function were called 介紹. Similarly we are told here that the tortoise-shell was a connecting medium between the mind of man and the mind of Heaven. And this was the belief of the duke of Chow! 卽命 is used like the same phrase in the last Book, p. 8. 曰有大至不靜,—this is to be taken as the reply of the tortoise, or the result obtained from the divination. Gan-kwŏ indeed makes the 曰 commence a new paragraph. 卽命 is with him = 'I have consulted it, and received its instruction;' and then for a time all reference to the tortoise ceases, and 曰 = 'The king also says.' This construction is to me intolerably harsh. 曰 follows immediately on the divination by the tortoise-shell, and introduces the reply which was received. That reply is sufficiently enigmatical. The troubles arose in the east, and the oracle was that the west would be troubled. This difficulty is solved by saying that the troubles arose indeed in the east, but they necessarily went on to trouble the west. The 'Daily Explanation' paraphrases the text as if the oracle had been thus explicit:—龜卽命曰,異日東方諸侯起而叛亂,將有大艱難之事于西土,使西土之人,疲于奔命,不得安靜,是西土憂然之時,龜兆已豫告矣. This was, it will be seen, a prophecy, rather than the solution of a doubt, and the oracle was like those of the west. We may compare it with the 'Aio te, Æacida, Romanos vincere posse.' 越茲蠢,—these are again the words of the king. 蠢 = 蟲動, 'insects moving, wriggling about,' in the spring. It is often used in

○四節殷小腆、誕敢紀其敘、天降威、知我國有疵、民不康、曰予復反鄙我周邦。○五節今蠢、今翼日、民獻有十夫、予

4 'Little as the *present* prosperity of Yin is, *its prince* greatly dares to take in hand its *broken* line. Though Heaven sent down its terrors *on his House*, *yet* knowing of the evils in our kingdom, and that the people are not tranquil, he says—"I will recover *my patrimony*"; and so *he wishes* to make our State of Chow a border territory again.

5 'One day there was a senseless movement, and the day after, ten men of worth among the people appeared to help me to go forward

the sense of 'silly,' 'impertinent.' 4. *The guilt of Woo-kăng.* 殷小腆,—this 腆 has marvellously vexed the critics. Gan-kwŏ took it as=小, and K'ang-shing did the same. Ma Yung made it=至, meaning probably 'Yin, who has but little attained.' Wang Suh made it=主 so that 殷小腆='this small princelet of Yin.' The 說文 defines it by 多, 'many or much;' and Ming-shing says this justifies the 小 of Kang-shing, like *lucus a non lucendo!* Ts'ae gives 厚, 'prosperous,' 'flourishing' for it, which is no doubt the correct meaning here. Compare 自洗腆致用酒 in the 'Announcement about Wine,' p. 6. Tung-po was the first to bring this meaning of the term to the interpretation of the text. 敘,—'to arrange,' 'to place in order;' then, 'a series' 'a rank.' Here, being under the govt. of 紀, it is taken as=緒, 'the end of a cocoon, or of a ball of thread;' then 'a thread,' 'a line,' and with the same metaphorical applications as our word 'line.' The clause, as expanded by Ts'ae, is—乃敢大紀其既亡之緒. All the old interpreters understood 天降威 of the troubles of the imperial House, with special reference to the rumours about the duke of Chow set on float by his brothers, following so quickly on the death of king Woo. The same view is taken also by Woo Ch'ing and Këang Shing. If the 知 had been before the 天 we must have construed in this way. The meaning which appears in the translation is given by Ts'ae, who follows his expansion of the previous clause, quoted above, by—是雖天降威于殷,然亦武庚知我國有三叔疵隙,民心不安,故敢,云云. 予復反鄙我周邦,—we must put a stop at 復, and then supply 而欲, as in the translation. 予 is Woo-kăng himself speaking, but we cannot refer the 我 also to him. 予復=我將復殷業. 鄙 is used for 'a border,' 'a border town.' It has here the force of a verb. 5. 今蠢至以于,—獻=賢 (comp. the 'Yih and Tseih,' p. 7. Këang Shing reads 義, but with the same meaning); 于=往, 'to go.' Who the 'ten men of worth' were, we do not know. Gan-kwŏ supposed they belonged to Yin, 'loyal and far-seeing men in the rebellious territory.' This is not likely. I suppose they were men of the imperial domain who had been forward to express their attachment to the dynasty of Chow. The 今蠢,今翼日, indicate the promptitude with which they had come forward. Ts'ae expands the clause:—今武庚蠢動,今之明日,民之賢者十夫,輔我以往,云云. 敉寧武圖功,—敉=撫, 'to soothe,' 'to tranquillize;' 敉寧 go together,=撫定商邦, 'to soothe and settle the country of Shang. 武=繼, 'to continue.' [武 is used for 'military prowess or achievement,' and also for 迹, 'footsteps,' 'traces,' from which the

翼以于、敉寧武圖功、我有大事休朕卜幷吉。○六節肆予告我友邦君、越尹氏庶士御事、曰、予得吉卜、予惟以爾庶邦、于伐殷逋播臣。○七節爾庶邦君、越庶士御事、罔

to restore tranquillity and to perpetuate the plans *of my father*. The great business I am engaging in will have a successful issue, *for* I have divined and always got a favourable intimation. 'There-
6 fore I tell you, the princes of my friendly States, and you, the directors of departments, my officers, and the managers of my affairs,—I have obtained a favourable reply to my divinations. I will now go forward with you from all the States, and punish those vagabond and transported ministers of Yin.
7 III. '*And now*, you the princes of the various States, and you the various officers and managers of my affairs, all retort on me, saying,

signification given to it in the text is derived. How the same character comes to have significations so different is one of the mysteries which a Lexicographer may solve by tracing its history, and showing how forms originally distinct have coalesced in one.] 武圖功＝繼嗣武王所圖之功. This construction of the clause is given by Ts'ae, and Keang Shing concurs in it. Other views may be seen in the 註疏, and in Woo Ch'ing's commentary.

我有,云云,—大事, 'great affair,' referring to the warlike expedition about to be proceeded with. It is said in the 左傳 that 'the "great affairs" of a State are sacrifice and war,' (國之大事,在祀與戎). 幷吉,—'all together are lucky.' The king had divined; and the 'three men' who had operated with the three shells, or interpreted the threefold intimation of the one shell, all foretold a happy result;—see the 'Great Plan,' p. 24. Ts'ae gives the connection of the two parts of the clause thus:—知我有戎事休美者,以朕卜三龜而幷吉也. We are not to suppose that this divining was the same as that mentioned in par. 2. That was earlier, before the rebellion had revealed itself; this was with reference to the expedition which was in progress. 6. 肆予至御事,—肆＝故, 'therefore.' 尹氏, 'the governors or directors,'＝庶官之正, 'the heads of the various magisterial departments.' Gan-kwŏ says they were the 卿大夫, 'nobles and great officers. Compare the 百尹 of Bk. XXII., p. 3. We might bring out the meaning of the 氏 by saying—'the directors, of the several surnames.'

予得吉卜,云云,—于, as in the last par.,＝往. 逋播臣,—'the absconded scattered ministers.' Woo-kăng and the old adherents of his House, who continued with him, are intended by this contemptuous language. There was enough in the circumstances of their condition to afford a ground for so describing them.

Ch. III. Pp. 7—9. THE KING COMPLAINS OF THE RELUCTANCE OF THE PRINCES AND OFFICERS TO GO FORWARD WITH HIM TO THE EXPEDITION, AND REPLIES TO THEIR PROPOSAL TO GO CONTRARY TO THE DIVINATIONS. 7. *The proposal of the princes and officers to go contrary to the oracles, and abandon the expedition.* 罔不反,—'there is not one who does not retort.' K'ang-shing says—無不反我之意, 'all oppose my views.' Keang Shing would take 反 as simply＝復, 'to reply.' The two ideas are here combined in the term. All the rest of the par. is to be taken as the language of the malcontents. Gan-kwŏ, indeed, takes only 艱大,

不反曰艱大、民不靜、亦惟在王宮邦君室、越予小子、考翼不可征、王害不違卜。○肆（八節）予沖人、永思艱、曰、嗚呼、允蠢鰥寡、哀哉、予造天役、遺大投艱于朕身、越予

"The hardships will be great, and that the people are not still has its source really in the king's palace, and in the mansions of those princes of the *troubled* State. We, little ones, and the old reverent men as well, think the expedition ill-advised. Why does your majesty not go contrary to the divination?

8 'I, in my youth, think also continually of the hardships, and say, Alas! these senseless movements will deplorably afflict widowers and widows! But I am the servant of Heaven, which has assigned

'the difficulties will be great,' as their words, and makes out all the rest to be a portion of the king's reply. But, to my mind, the text is altogether unmanageable on this view. The exegesis which I have followed, and which appears in the translation, is not unattended with difficulties; but it gives an interpretation of the passage in harmony with the general tenour of the Announcement, and not harsher, as regards particular expressions, than we are obliged to admit in many other places 民不靜至君室,—this is an allusion, as plain as the duke of Chow could permit himself to make, to the dissatisfaction of his three brothers charged with the oversight of Yin, the rumours which they had spread against himself, and the suspicions which those had awakened in the king's mind. The 邦君 are Sëen, Too, and Ch'oo. 室, as opposed to 宮, I translate by 'mansion.' 越予小子,考翼,不可征,云云,—this passage presents several difficulties, and no construction of it has been proposed, against which objections cannot be urged. 予小子 is taken by Gan-kwŏ of the king speaking of himself, and this is the one strong point in his construction mentioned above. In the translation the phrase is taken in the plural:—so the princes and officers, opposed to the expedition, describe themselves. 考 is taken as=老, 'old,' 'fathers.' 翼=敬, 'to be reverent,' *i.e*, in the conduct of business. The character is thus used in the She King, as may be seen in the dict. 考翼=父老之敬事者. 害 (read in the 4th tone)=曷, 'why.' The paraphrase of the whole in the 'Daily Explanation' is:—予等小子,固無所知識,至于敬事之父老,乃老成練達之人,皆以爲不可,人謀未協,龜兆難憑,曷不違卜,而聽人乎.

Pp. 8, 9. *How the king replies to the princes and officers, complaining of their want of sympathy with him, and urging again the authority of the oracles.* 8. 允蠢鰥寡,哀哉,—'indeed the senseless movements; widowers and widows, alas:' Gan-kwŏ brings out the meaning thus:—信蠢動天下,使無妻無夫者受其害,可哀哉. Woo Ch'ing observes that the young and strong would be carried off to the expedition, and so the widowers and widows would be left in their solitude without those whose duty it was to care for them. 予造天役=予所爲之事,皆天所役使, 'the things which I do are all services required from me by Heaven.' Keang Shing takes 造=遭, as in p. 1, which would give here a good enough meaning. 遺大,投大于我身—Heaven is the nominative to the verbs 遺 and 投. The 'Daily Explanation has:—天

沖人、不卭自恤、義爾邦君、越爾多士、尹氏御事、綏予曰、無毖于恤、不可不成乃寧考圖功。○已予惟小子、九節不敢替上帝命、天休于寧王、興我小邦周、寧王惟卜用、克綏受茲命、今天其相民、矧亦惟卜用、嗚呼、天明

me this great task, and laid this hard duty on my person. I therefore, the young one, do not pity myself, and it would be right in you, the princes of the States, and in you, the many officers, the directors of departments, and the managers of my affairs, to soothe me, saying, "Do not be distressed with sorrow. We shall surely complete the plans of your Tranquillizing father."

9 'Yes, I, the little one, dare not disregard the charge of God. Heaven, favourable to the Tranquillizing king, gave such prosperity to our small State of Chow. The Tranquillizing king divined and acted accordingly, and so he calmly received his *great* appointment. Now Heaven is helping the people;—how much more must I follow the divinations! Oh! the clearly-intimated will of Heaven is to be feared:—it is to help my great inheritance.'"

實以甚大者遺于吾之身, 甚艱者投于吾之身. 不卭自恤,—卭=我 or 身, 'I,' 'myself.' The meaning is that the king would do his duty, without considering the risks and troubles to which it would expose him. 義爾至圖功,—義=以義言之, 'speaking of the case with reference to what is right.' 毖=勞, 'to labour,' 'to distress one's-self.' 無(=毋)毖于恤=君毋勞于憂, 'Let not your Majesty distress yourself about this matter of sorrow.' The princes and officers are then supposed to say that they would dispose of the revolt for him.—凡我爲臣者, 不可不共矢其力, 聲罪致討, 成乃寧考所圖之功.

9. 已,—as in p. 2. 不敢替上帝命,—替=廢, 'to disregard,' 'to make of none effect.' 'The charge of God' is that implied in p. 5, when the divinations were all favourable, and the king was thus instructed to go forward with the expedition against Woo-kăng and his associates. 天休至茲命,—the divinations of king Woo referred to are those mentioned in 'The Great Speech,' Pt. ii., p. 5, 朕夢協朕卜, 襲于休祥. 今天其相民,—How was Heaven now helping the people? Gan-kwŏ replies—'By the coming forward of the ten men of worth to support the king.' Possibly the king, or the duke rather, may have had this in mind. 矧亦惟卜用=況我亦惟卜是用. 天明, 云云—the translation here follows Ts'ae. The 天明, 'intelligence of Heaven,' is that mentioned in p. 3, as conveyed by the 'great tortoise.' Thus clearly intimated, it was to be reverenced. Opposition to it could only entail disaster. How much

畏、弼我丕丕基。○

王曰、爾惟舊人、爾丕克遠省、爾知寧王若勤哉、天閟毖我成功所、予不敢不極卒寧王圖事、肆予大化誘我友邦君、天棐忱辭、其考我民、予曷其不于前寧人圖功攸

10 IV. "The king says, 'You, who are the old ministers, are fully able to examine the long-distant affairs;—you know how great was the toil of the Tranquillizing king. Now where Heaven shuts up and distresses us is the place where I must accomplish my work;—I dare not but do my utmost to complete the plans of the Tranquillizing king. It is on this account that I use such efforts to remove the doubts and carry forward the inclinations of the princes of my friendly States. Heaven *also* assists me with sincere expressions *of attachment*, which I have ascertained among the people;—how dare I but aim at the completion of the work formerly begun by the

more should they be forward to obey it, when it was to establish the dynasty! Këang Shing takes 畏＝威, and the whole＝'The brilliant majesty of Heaven is aiding me to enlarge this great inheritance.'

Ch. IV. Pp. 10—12. THE KING ADDRESSES HIMSELF MORE PARTICULARLY TO THE OLD MINISTERS OF HIS HOUSE; SETS FORTH HIS OWN WISH TO DO HIS DUTY AS A SON AND A SOVEREIGN, AND COMPLAINS OF THEIR WANT OF SYMPATHY WITH HIM. 10. 王曰,—see on 王若曰, p. 1. It is one of the peculiarities of the Announcements in the Books of Chow, that they are broken up into many parts by the recurrence of these phrases. 爾惟至勤哉,—by 舊人 we are to understand the old ministers of king Woo, (武王之舊臣),—the 考翼 of p. 7, who are there quoted as opposed to the expedition. 遠省,—'to examine the remote,' *i.e.*, the affairs of past days. 天閟至圖事,—this is an instance of what Choo He calls the 'long sentences' of the 'Great Announcement.' 閟者否塞不通之意, '閟 means shut up, without thoroughfare.' 毖者艱難不易之意, '毖 means difficult and not easy.' These are the definitions given by Ts'ae, who adds—天之所以否閉艱難國家多難者,乃我成功之所在. The above definition of 閟 is not given in the dictionary, tho' it may be very reasonably derived from the explanation of the term in the 說文 as＝閉門. The dict. makes it＝慎, after Gan-kwŏ, and with reference to this passage. Këang Shing defines it by 勞, which makes it simply a synonym of 毖. Ts'ae took his definition from Lin Che-k'e. 'The place where king Ching had to accomplish his work,' was the east, where the revolt was going on; but the 所 does not indicate the locality simply, but all the circumstances of the case. 肆予至邦君,—化者,化其固滯, 'by 化 is meant dissolving their obstinate obstructions;' 誘者,誘其順從, 'by 誘 is meant inducing them to follow him with accordance.' These again are the definitions of Ts'ae,—very good. 天棐至攸終,—棐 is taken by Gan-kwŏ and most other

書經

終、天亦惟用勤毖我民、若有疾、予曷敢不于前寧人攸受休畢。○王曰、若昔朕(十二節)其逝、朕言艱日思、若考作室、既厎法、厥子乃弗肯堂、矧肯構、厥父菑、厥子乃弗

Tranquillizer? Heaven moreover is thus toiling and distressing my people, so that it is as if they were suffering from disease;—how dare I allow the appointment which the Tranquillizer, my predecessor, received, to be without its happy fulfilment?'"

11 "The king says, 'Formerly, at the initiation of this expedition, I spoke of its difficulties, and revolved them daily. *But* when a *deceased* father,*wishing to* build a house, had laid out the plan, if his son be unwilling to raise up the hall, how much less will he be willing to complete the roof! Or if the father had broken up the ground, and his son is unwilling to sow the seed, how much less

critics as=輔,' 'to aid.' 忱=誠信, 'sincere.' Heaven does not speak;—where were the 'expressions' of its regard? The ten men of worth, who had come forward to encourage the king, might be considered as giving utterance to the 'voice of the people,'=the 'voice of God.' Choo He was dissatisfied with this interpretation of 棐. He said that 'though all the elder scholars concurred in it, it made the passage unintelligible.' He himself, on the authority chiefly of Yen Sze-koo, made the character synonymous with 匪, 'not,' so that the meaning is—'Heaven really does not utter words, but its mind may be ascertained from the mind of the people.' This brings out substantially the same meaning as the other view of 棐. By 寧人 I understand king Woo. It is only a variation of the phrase 寧王. Ts'ae takes it as=寧臣, 'the tranquillizing ministers,' meaning those who had co-operated with king Woo in his great work, and adds that this description of them would cover with shame those of them who were dissuading king Ching from the expedition. See a note from Ch'in Leih on this point in the 附錄. 天亦云云,—here is another consideration, which determined the king's resolution. His father's object was to give repose and happiness to all the people. This revolt was distressing them,—a fever, a serious disease in the State. He must secure the realization of his father's purpose by putting the revolt down. 11. *How his sense of filial duty impelled the king to the expedition.* 若昔日朕其逝=初欲東征之時, 'when I first wished to undertake this expedition to the east.' So, Ts'ae and Woo Ch'ing. Then the 言 and 思 of the next clause are to be taken in the past tense. Woo, indeed, is half disposed to take 言 simply as an expletive or exclamation, but there is no necessity for having recourse to such a construction. Thinking of the difficulties which the expedition was pressed with, the king might have wished to abandon it; but to prevent his doing so, there came in the considerations of his duty to his father which are set forth in the rest of the paragraph. In this way we get a consistent meaning from the whole. Gan-kwŏ and Këang Shing, instead of taking 若昔 as=昔日, or 昔者, give 若 a full verbal force,=順, 'to accord with.' The former then interprets—'In accordance with ancient principles, I must proceed with this expedition to the east (順古道,我其往東征矣). I have spoken quite enough about the difficulties and hardships of the empire, and I daily think of them.' The latter says:—'In accordance with the example of the king my predecessor, I ought to go and punish

肯播、矧肯穫、厥考翼其肯曰、予有後、弗棄基、肆予曷敢不越卬、敉寧王大命。○ 若（十二節）兄考、乃有友伐厥子、民養其勸弗救。

will he be willing to reap the grain! In such a case will the father, *who had himself* been so reverently attentive *to his objects*, be willing to say, "I have an heir who will not abandon the patrimony?"—How dare I, therefore, but use all my powers to give a happy settlement to the great charge entrusted to the Tranquillizing king?

12 'If a father have those among his friends who attack his child, will the elders of his people encourage *the attack*, and not *come to the* rescue?'

these revolters (順昔前王之事，則我其當往征). Of the hardships connected with the expedition I have spoken, and I daily think of them.' The view which I have followed seems to me much preferable to either of these. 若考作室，旣底法，—考 is 'a father deceased.' We must take it so here, king Woo being intended, while Ching is the son on whom it devolves to carry out and finish his father's undertakings. 旣底法，—'has settled the plan,' *i.e.*, has laid out the foundation, and defined all the dimensions,—the length, breadth and height. For 堂 Woo Ch'ing says 築基, 'to build up *on* the foundation.' The meaning evidently is to proceed with the building, according to the plan. 構=蓋, 'to cover;' here,='to construct the roof.'

[Immediately after 構, K'ang-shing read 厥考翼其肯曰，予有後弗棄基, which thus occurred with him twice in the paragraph.] 菑，—反土去草曰菑, 'turning over the earth and removing the grass is called 菑.' It denotes the first steps taken to bring waste land or virgin soil into cultivation. 考翼至棄基—Are we to take 考翼 in the singular, referring to the 考 and 父 in the preceding clauses, or in the plural, like the same phrase in p. 7? Gan-kwŏ and Ts'ae take it in the singular.

Ts'ae says—'The spirit of king Woo in heaven would not be willing to say that he had a son and successor who would not let his inheritance fall to the ground.' The paraphrase in the 'Daily Explanation' takes the phrase in the plural,=其家敬事之父老, 'the old and reverent elders of the family.' This is the view also of Woo Ch'ing, who has:—其父之輔翼者, 'the assistants of his father.' I must understand the phrase in the singular. 肆予云云，—越卬=於我身, 'in my person.' It is a strange and unsatisfactory expression; but all the critics explain it thus.

Q. 12. *The king reproaches the princes and officers who would let the revolt take its course.* A short paragraph, and all but unintelligible. The view which Gan-kwŏ gives may be seen in the 註疏. I cannot make it out, even with the help of Ying-tă. Ts'ae says that he does not understand what is meant by the phrase 民養. He takes it, however, after Soo Tung-po as=人之臣僕, or 民長, as in the translation. 'By 兄考,' he says, 'is intended king Woo; by 友, Woo-kăng and his confederates, the king's uncles; by 子, 'the people; and by 民養, the princes of the States, and the officers.' I would only differ from him in taking 子 not of the people, but of king Ching himself.

○王曰、嗚呼、肆哉、爾庶邦君、越爾御事、爽邦由哲、亦惟十人迪知上帝命、越天棐忱、爾時罔敢易法、矧今天降戾于周邦、惟大艱人、誕鄰胥伐于厥室、爾亦不知天命不易。○予永念曰、

13 V. "The king says, 'Oh! Take heart, ye princes of the various States, and ye managers of my affairs. The enlightening of the country was from the wise, even from the ten men who obeyed and knew the decree of God, and the sincere assistance given by Heaven. At that time none of you presumed to change the *royal* appointments. And now, when Heaven is sending down calamity on the State of Chow, and the authors of these great distresses *appear as if* the inmates of a house were mutually to attack one another, you are without any knowledge that the decree of Heaven is not to be changed!

Ch. V. Pp. 13—15. THE KING CONTRASTS THE PRESENT CONDUCT OF THE PRINCES AND OFFICERS WITH THE PAST, AND TRIES TO STIMULATE THEM TO CARRY OUT THE WISH OF HEAVEN. HE THEN STATES HIS OWN DETERMINATION, AND CONCLUDES BY VINDICATING HIS FOLLOWING THE ORACLES OF DIVINATION. 13. Ts'ae Ch'in, in interpreting this par., struck out a new path for himself, in which I have followed him. The par. mentions 'ten men who obeyed and knew the mind of God.' Were they the 'ten men of worth, mentioned in par. 5, who came forward to support king Ching against the revolt of Yin? All the old interpreters say so, and Woo Ch'ing and Këang Shing, still hold to that view. This is to be said for it, that in the compass of a short Book, we can hardly expect two references to 'ten men,' of the same purport, and yet that they should be difft. men. I would willingly accept Gan-kwŏ's view, if it did not make all attempts to explain the context not only troublesome but to my mind vain. Ts'ae decided that the ten men here were not the ten men of par. 5, but king Woo's 'virtuous men,' his 'ten ministers capable of govt.,' celebrated in 'The Great Speech.' He contends that the predicates of the 'ten men' here are too great for the ten men of the people who came forward to encourage king Ching, and tries to fortify his view by referring to the duke of Chow's language in Bk. XVI., p. 14, where he is speaking of king Wăn's able ministers, as he speaks of the ten men here. The editors of Yung-ching's Shoo accept his view, but with some misgivings, and think it necessary to preserve the other also. 肆=放心, 'put your hearts at ease.' 爽邦由哲,—爽=明, as in 爽厥師, Pt. IV., Bk. II., p. 3. King Woo put an end to the 'dark ways' (昏德) of Show, and displayed the mind of Heaven to the empire, 'by means of the wise men' (由哲), who were his counsellors and helpers,—'the ten men who walked in (迪) and knew the commands of God.' 越天棐忱,—棐=輔, as in p. 10. This clause is collateral with 上帝命, and under the regimen of 迪知. 爾時=爾於是時, 'you at that time.' Among those who followed Woo to the conquest of Shang, there were many of the princes and officers who were now shrinking from the expedition against Woo-kăng. 矧今,云云,—it is difficult to render 矧 here by 'how much more,' in the usual way; yet its force extends to the end of the par., and may be indicated by a point of exclamation. The allusion in 天降戾于周邦 is to the death of king Woo. By 惟大艱人 we

天惟喪殷、若穡夫、予曷敢不終朕畝、天亦惟休于前寧人。○予_{十五節}曷其極卜、敢弗于從、率寧人有指疆土、矧今卜幷吉、肆朕誕以爾東征、天命不僭、卜陳惟若茲。

14 'I ever think and say, Heaven in destroying Yin is doing husbandman's work;—how dare I but complete the business of my fields! Heaven will thereby show its favour to the former Tranquillizer.

15 'How should I be all for the oracle of divination, and presume not to follow your advice? I am following the Tranquillizer, whose purpose embraced all the limits of the land. How much more must I proceed, when the divinations are all favourable! It is on these accounts that I make this expedition in force to the east. There is no mistake about the decree of Heaven. The indications of the divinations are all to the same effect.'"

are to understand the king's uncles, confederate with Woo-käng. For 誕鄰胥伐 Ts'ae gives 大近相伐, and the 'Daily Explanation' has 相逼相攻. 厥室 is taken by Woo Ch'ing of 其邦君之室, and he supposes the meaning of the whole to be that the rebel-uncles were endeavouring to force others of their brothers in their neighbourhoods to join them in the revolt. The meaning I have given is preferable, though the 誕鄰 is difficult to manage. Gan-kwŏ says that when the king's uncles took arms against him, it was truly like the inmates of one house fighting with each other. If king Woo had been commissioned to destroy Show for his wickedness, much more must it be Heaven's will that this revolt should be suppressed; and yet the princes and officers were telling the king not to proceed with the expedition.

Wang Ts'ëaou traces the course of thought in the par. on Ts'ae's view very clearly:—迪知上帝命者、心與天通、自然合理者也、知天命不易者、未能眞知而不敢不信者也、在武王時、商罪貫盈、不可不討、天命如此眷佑有周、夢卜協吉、天之棐忱又如此、在今日武庚作亂、不可不討、天命亦如此、民獻予翼、朕卜幷吉、天之棐忱、亦又如此、是今昔之事、理一也、然在昔有十人之輔、而爾舊人亦不敢易武王之法、今考翼不可征、則不惟易我之法、而言害不違卜、則亦不知天命不可易矣、以昔時奉法之心、爲今日順天之義、則與迪知者惟有間、而與爽邦者實同功矣.

P. 14. 穡夫 is 'a reaper,' but the phrase is here used for a husbandman generally. A husbandman's work is thoroughly to clear his ground of weeds;—he must not let their roots remain. King Woo had spared Show's son, but it was plain that he must now be made an end of. So would king Ching complete the business of his fields. And when hehad done so, the favour of Heaven to king Woo would be more fully displayed;—the empire would be made sure to his posterity. 15. 予曷其極卜,

敢弗于從,—予何敢盡欲用卜,而不從爾勿征之言乎. The answer to this is given in the next clause. It was not merely a question between the oracles and the contrary opinions of many of the princes and officers. There was the example of king Woo and his ministers; and there was the duty of Ching to accomplish the work which his father had begun. These were potent considerations to go into the scale. They would determine in favour of the expedition, even if the oracles were not so decided. As the oracles were so entirely in favour of it, however, there could be—there ought at least to be—no hesitation in going forward. 率寧人有指疆土—循文王有指意,以安疆土. This is Gan-kwŏ's explanation of the words, and I have not met with any other so satisfactory. His only error is in referring 寧人 to king Wăn, instead of king Woo. 天命不僭,—comp. 天命弗僭, in the 'Announcement of T'ang,' p. 5.

[We have thus got to the end of 'The Great Announcement,' the style of which is at least as rugged and difficult as that of 'The Pwan-kăng.' Notwithstanding the uncertainty which attaches to the interpretation of particular passages, however, I cannot but believe that the translation gives, with tolerable correctness, the general meaning of the Book. In the year B.C. 7, when Mang, the duke of Han (漢公莽), was acting as regent of the empire, and designed to usurp the throne, he published an announcement modelled upon that of the duke of Chow. He incorporated the text of the Show with his own statements in a very remarkable way. Këang Shing and some others undertake to correct the text of the Shoo from Mang's Announcement, which ought not, however, to be appealed to for that purpose. It answers very well to show the general view which Mang and the scholars about him took of our Book. Mang's Announcement is preserved in the 前漢書,第五十四卷,翟方進傳.]

THE BOOKS OF SHANG.

BOOK. VIII. THE CHARGE TO THE VISCOUNT OF WEI.

微子之命

王一節若曰、猷殷王元子、惟稽古崇德象賢、統承先王、修其禮物、作賓于王家、與國咸休、永世無窮。○嗚二節呼、乃

1 "The king speaks to the following effect:—"Ho! eldest son of the king of Yin, in accordance with *the statutes of* antiquity, that the honouring of the virtuous belongs to *their descendants* who resemble them in worth, do you continue the line of the kings your ancestors, cultivating their ceremonies and taking care of their various relics. Be a guest *also* in our royal house, enjoying the prosperity of our kingdom, for ever and ever without end.

THE NAME OF THE BOOK.—微子之命, 'The charge to the viscount of Wei.' 微子,—see on the name of the 11th Book of the preceding Part. 命,—see on the name of the 8th Book of the same part.

The prefatory note says:—'King Ching having made an end of the appointment *in favour of the House* of Yin, and put Woo-kăng to death, he appointed K'e, the viscount of Wei, to take the place of the descendants of Yin. Descriptive of this there was made 'The charge to the viscount of Wei.' This no doubt states correctly the time and occasion when the 'Charge' was made. We saw on 'The viscount of Wei,' how K'e was advised by his friends to withdraw from the court of Show and save himself from the destruction which was impending over the tyrant and his House; we saw also the account given by Sze-ma Ts'een of the guise in which K'e presented himself with the sacrificial vessels of his family before king Woo. Some points in that account may be called in question, but there can be no doubt that K'e was honourably received and treated. When it is said that Woo restored him to his former office, I understand that he confirmed him in his appanage of Wei, so that he continued to be 'the viscount of Wei,' up to the date of this Charge, when he was appointed to be the duke of Sung (宋公), there to continue the sacrifices to T'ang, his ancestor and the founder of the dynasty of Shang.

In the first of the concluding notes to the 'Completion of the War,' I have quoted a passage from the Bk. 樂記 of the Le Ke, in which it is said that king Woo, after his victory over Show, 'when he had descended from his chariot, sent the representative of the House of Yin to Sung.' From this statement, some have contended that K'e's investiture with the

dukedom of Sung was from Woo and not from Ching, and was before the revolt which ended in the death of Woo-kăng and not after it. But the editors of Yung-ching's Shoo have given good reasons why the authority of Sze-ma Ts'een, and the preface to the Shoo, should be preferred in this matter to that of the 樂記. If the merits of the men had been the sole ground for Woo's arrangements, he would have at once appointed either of the viscounts of Wei or Ke to continue the sacrifices to T'ang and the other sovereigns of his line, but there were, we can easily conceive, reasons of state, which determined him to make trial, in the first place, of Woo-kăng, as being the son of Show.

The Book is only found in the text of Gan-kwŏ.

CONTENTS. The duke of Chow, as regent of the empire, and in the name of king Ching, tells the viscount that in accordance with the statutes of antiquity, and because of his own worth, he is selected to continue the line of the sovereigns, his ancestors. The virtues of T'ang and of the viscount are then celebrated, and he is charged to go and be prosperous, taking care so to conduct his administration that the new dynasty of Chow might never have occasion to be weary of him. The Book is very short, consisting only of five paragraphs.

P. 1. *The grounds on which the viscount of Wei was called to be the representative of the kings of his line, with some of his duties and privileges.*

王若曰, 猷,—see on the last Book, p. 1. 殷王元子,—元子=首子, or 長子, 'eldest son.' 'The king of Yin' is Te-yih (帝乙), the father both of K'e and Show. How K'e, though older than Show, did not succeed to the throne, has been explained on page 274. Some critics, supposing that 元子 is equivalent to 太子, ='heir-apparent,' and cannot be otherwise applied, have contended on that ground against the authenticity of this Book, but to my mind there is no force in the objection. The 元子 is simply 'the eldest son;'—he may be the heir-apparent, but not necessarily. That idea does not form a part of the significance of the phrase. 稽古崇德象賢,—稽古, see on the 'Canon of Yaou,' p. 1; 崇德謂先聖王之有德者, 則尊崇而奉祀之也, '崇德 means that the virtuous of the ancient sage sovereigns were honoured and sacrificed to;' 象賢謂其後子孫, 有象先聖王之賢者, 則命之以主祀也, '象賢 means that he among the descendants of those ancient sage kings who resembled them in talents and virtue was appointed to preside over the sacrifices to them.' These are the explanations of Ts'ae, similar to those of Gan-kwŏ. He adds:—言古制, 尊崇成湯之德, 以微子象賢而奉其祀也 The text is very concise, and it takes many characters to bring forth its meaning; but the explanation is, no doubt, correct. To the ancient statutes, which prescribed the honouring and sacrificing to the founders of former dynasties, we have a reference in the Le Ke, Bk. 郊特牲, Pt. i, p. 12, where it is said, 天子存二代之後, 猶尊賢也, 尊賢不過二代, 'The emperor preserves *representative* descendants of two dynasties, still honouring the worth of their founders. This honouring of *ancient* worth does not go beyond two dynasties.' In what the honouring was displayed, is partly indicated in the remainder of the paragraph. 統承先王,—the empire gathered under one rule is called 一統. Here the sovereigns of Shang are conceived of as all gathered up or collected in the person of K'e, who should henceforth, in himself and his descendants in the dukedom of Sung, stand forth as their representative. 修其禮物,—by 禮 we are to understand 典禮, 'the canons and ceremonies,' the institutions of Shang which had distinguished it from other dynasties; and by 物 we are to understand 文物, 'the literary monuments and other precious relics of the dynasty,'—carriages, flags, dresses, &c. The descendants of K'e held the dukedom of Sung till nearly the end of the Chow dynasty, but by the time of Confucius many of the ceremonies and relics which it was their business to preserve were lost. The sage bewailed this, and said, 'I am able to describe the ceremonies of the Yin dynasty, but Sung cannot sufficiently attest my words. It cannot do so because of the insufficiency of its records and wise men' (Con. Ana., III. ix.). See the introductory note on the 'Praise-songs of Shang,' in the third Part of the She King. 作賓至無窮,—the representatives of the two previous dynasties were distinguished above the other princes of the empire by being denominated 'guests' of the emperor of the dynasty then existing, as meeting him more on a footing of equality. See the She-king, Part. III., the 'Praise-songs of Chow," Bk, III., Song ii., 振鷺于飛, 于彼西雝, 我客戾止, 亦有斯容. See also in the 左傳, 僖二十四年,—宋, 先代之後也, 於周爲客, 天子有事, 膰焉, 有喪, 拜焉. On this part Ts'ae gives some observations of Leu Taoo-heen, which deserve a place in any commentary:—先王之心公平廣大, 非若後世滅人之國, 惟恐苗裔之存, 爲子孫害, 成王命微子, 方且撫

祖成湯、克齊聖廣淵、皇天眷佑、誕受厥命、撫民以寬、除其邪虐、功加于時、德垂後裔。○爾惟踐（三節）修厥猷、舊有令聞、恪慎克孝、肅恭神人、予嘉乃德、曰篤不忘、上

2 'Oh! your ancestor, T'ang the Successful, was reverent and sage, vast and deep *in his virtue*. The favour and help of Great Heaven lighted upon him, and he received the great appointment, to soothe the people by his gentleness, and to remove their wicked oppressions. His achievements affected all his age, and his virtue was
3 transmitted to his posterity. And you are the one who pursue and cultivate his plans;—this praise belongs to you of old. Reverently and carefully you discharge your filial duties; gravely and respectfully you behave to spirits and to men. I admire your virtue, and pronounce it great, and not to be forgotten. God will always

助愛養、欲其與國咸休、永世無窮、公平廣大氣象、於此可見、'The minds of the ancient kings were just, generous, and enlarged, not like those of the sovereigns of future times, who on the extinction of a kingdom would extirpate all the members of its royal House, fearing that the preservation of them might be injurious to their own posterity. King Ching not only appoints the viscount of Wei duke of Sung, but goes on to soothe and cherish him, wishing him for ever and ever to share in the prosperity of the empire.—Admirably was the just and enlarged spirit displayed in this.' An objection has been taken to the genuineness of the Bk. on the ground of the phrase 與國咸休, it being supposed that the empire would not be denominated 國 merely; but the objection is as futile as that taken from the use of 元子, which has been already pointed out. Compare the language of the last Bk., p. 4, and of 'The Metal-bound Coffer,' p. 18.

P. 2. *The virtue of T'ang, the founder of the Shang dynasty, which made him worthy to be honoured.* 齊=莊 or 肅, 'reverent,' *i.e.*, gravely and reverently attending to all his duties. 皇天眷佑誕受厥命,—comp. in the 'T'ae-këä,' Pt. i. p. 2, 天監厥德用集大命. 撫民以寬, 除其邪虐,—comp. in 'The Instructions of E,' p. 3, 代虐以寬兆民允懷. 功加于時,—時=當時, 'that time,' his own age. 後裔,—'his posterity.' Choo He observes that 裔 properly denotes the bottom of the skirt of a garment (衣裾之末),—the superfluity of it, and from this is applied to express a man's posterity.

P. 3. *The worthiness of K'e, which made him fit to be selected to render the honour due to T'ang.* 踐修厥猷,—猷=道, 'ways' or 'plans; 踐=履其後, 'to tread in the steps of T'ang's ways.' 修 expresses the earnestness with which he sought to carry the plans into practice. 令聞,—'a good reputation.' 恪慎至神人,—Lin Che-k'e joins these two clauses together, and supposes that they refer to K'e's taking care of the sacrificial vessels of his House during the overthrow of the dynasty, and his carrying them with him to the army of Chow. It seems more natural to me, however, to take them as in the translation. 篤不忘=篤厚而不可忘. 上帝時歆,—歆 is 'to enjoy the savour of offerings.' K'e, being the representative of the sovereigns of Shang, had the privilege of offering

帝時歆、下民祗協、庸建爾于上公、尹茲東夏。○四節欽哉、往敷乃訓、愼乃服命、率由典常、以蕃王室、弘乃烈祖、律乃有民、永綏厥位、毗予一人、世世享德、萬邦作式、俾我有周無斁。○五節嗚呼、往哉惟休、無替朕命。

enjoy your offerings; the people will be reverently harmonious *under your sway*. I raise you, therefore, to the rank of High Duke, to rule this eastern part of our great land.

4 'Be reverent. Go and diffuse abroad your instructions; be carefully observant of your robes and various *other* symbols of your appointment; follow and observe the proper statutes!—so as to prove a bulwark to the royal House. Enlarge *the fame of* your meritorious ancestor; be a law to your people!—so as for ever to preserve your dignity. So also shall you be a help to me the one man; future ages will enjoy *the benefit of* your virtue; all the States will take you for a pattern!—and thus you will make our dynasty of Chow never weary of you.

5 Oh! go, and be prosperous. Do not disregard my charge."

the great solstitial sacrifice to God. It is with reference to this that it is said God would always, or at the appointed season of sacrifice, accept his offerings. 庸=用,=所以, 'therefore,' according to the frequent usage of 用 in the Shoo. 尹茲東夏,—尹=治, 'to rule.' Sung, the pres. dep. of Kwei-tih in Ho-nan, lay east from Fung and Haou, the capitals of Wăn and Woo, which were in the pres. dep. of Se-gan, Shen-se.

[In the 左傳, 僖, 十二年, we have an address to the famous Kwan Chung, evidently modelled on the text of this par. and the next:—王曰, 舅氏, 余嘉乃勳, 應乃懿德, 謂督不忘, 往踐乃職, 無逆朕命.]

Pp. 4, 5. *Charges, Cautions, and Encouragements addressed to K'e* 4. 愼乃服命,—as a High duke, K'e had the robes and cap, the carriage, flag, &c., appropriate to his rank, and which were the accompaniments of his investiture:—see the Le-ke, Bk. 王制 Pt. ii., p. 7. He is charged to be carefully—cautiously—observant of them, not transgressing the proper statutes. He must not indulge the ambitious thoughts which had brought ruin on Woo-kăng. 以蕃王室,—蕃=屏衞, 'to screen and defend.' 藩 is more common in this sense. 律乃有民,—Gan-kwŏ says:—以法度齊汝所有之民, 'with laws regulate your people.' But this does not give all the emphasis of the text. The 'Daily Explanation' has better:—儀型爾宋之有民, 而作之師. 毗—輔, 'to assist.' 5. 往哉惟休,—Gan-kwŏ and all the critics after him make 惟休=務休美爾政, 'make your government prosperous and good.' I do not see the necessity for this.

[Wang Yen, Chin Tih-sëw, and other scholars remark on the fact that nothing is said in this Book of the wickedness of Show or of Woo-kăng;—how it shows the consideration of the duke of Chow for the feelings of the viscount of Wei, and the estimation in which his worth was held.]

[Here again there is space to introduce another Chapter from Wang Pih:—

讀而釋商子得不曉武武失衰之者商其吾殺之熏啟徽則今以好所議不公啟間
每然首式箕以粟可聞封之之商子存子年於封者有封庚乎付自其謀爾周謀乘
喟政墓於所發不無乃周湯作微也微八乃後庚其子武祀而稍矣所人幼姦以
卷商干道皆財所然而祀夫七於知非位在而武聞微封足邦時右之故沖外可
廢反比訪此散耳寂既商者六過共家在何後彼未於湯猶宅是左夕之子在謂
不之封復書若服子哉奉此君有所王王者之哉德過祀受於當之朝德嗣叔自
嘗王囚而之心悅微之以於之未之賓武子父晚惡有以受庚土爲處酒崩管行
未武之既範之人於忘父大聖孫下作與微祿其之得可祀武故不遊于王而計
篇昔子閭洪子小獨豈祿有賢子天祀可知庚何紂爲則以封之必共酗武政凶
此嘆箕容得君過者王庚末也賢此之誰不武宋染行子可不紂者與惟幸攝而
十羣蠱以能叛此其其之則義非果身先復果武至之世是必以子詞乃懲有矣
境至敢無不敢於封使庚愚者子之修顧豈叛曰矣命後爲也當微之律非而尊
之必孰言則不甚父可武知父其子艾不者必或久公於謬封不命封曰豈綏命
紂所庚流庚則有其則叛後其也其悔苟叛之知也上感而始祀不始也位不之
復勢武非武言未殺也必而殺仁使痛祀於庚後宋封亦傳之湯而皆詞厥律臣
以叛非叛非流失曰人則者也者叛飲先輕武而於加此之子奉庚書之綏不史
掌之言之弟非之乃非也智非子必必保而若者子乃祀璧微必武此封永之乎
抵庚流庚羣庚周氏子人待說其則則以祀哉智微誅商銜若公命觀加曰庚戒
亂武之武之武曰蘇其果不此封也也行之也待封庚奉周也上禮今非民武告矣]
倡矣弟之發叛故者子子叛曰也人人敀王人不王武以歸說加是也也有創此巖

THE BOOKS OF SHANG.

BOOK. IX. THE ANNOUNCEMENT TO *THE PRINCE OF* K'ANG.

康誥

一節 惟三月哉生魄、周公初基、作新大邑于東國洛、四方民大和會、侯甸男邦采衞、百工播民和、見士于周、周公咸勤、乃洪大誥治。

1 [In the third month, when the moon began to wane, the duke of Chow commenced the foundations and proceeded to build the new great city at Lŏ of the eastern States. The people from every quarter assembled in great harmony. From the How, Teen, Nan, Ts'ae, and Wei domains, the various officers stimulated this harmony of the people, and introduced them to the business there was for Chow. The duke of Chow encouraged all to diligence, and made a great announcement about the performance *of the works.*]

THE NAME OF THE BOOK.—康誥, 'The Announcement to *the prince of* K'ang.' Of the ten sons of king Wăn, the ninth was called Fung (封), generally spoken of as K'ang Shuh (康叔). According to the analogy of the titles of the other brothers,—Kwan Shuh, Ts'ae Shuh, &c., we must conclude that K'ang was the name of Fung's appanage, somewhere within the imperial domain. Ma Yung and Wang Suh expressly affirm this. The only ancient scholar who expressed a different opinion was K'ang-shing, who thought that K'ang was the honorary posthumous title of Fung (康爲號謚). Be this as it may, the Book is the Charge addressed to K'ang, or to the prince of K'ang, on his appointment to the principality of Wei (命爲衞侯), the chief city of which was Chaou-ko, which had been the capital of Show. Wei extended westward from the pres. sub. dep. of K'ae (開州), dep. of Taming in Chih-le, to the borders of the pres. depp. of Wei-hwuy and Hwae-k'ing, in Ho-nan.

That the Book should be called an 'Announcement,' and not a 'Charge' (like the preceding), has occasioned various doubts about it,—and with reason. The title is no doubt taken from the occurrence of the word announcement in the last clause of what stands as the first paragraph (乃洪大誥治); but it will be

seen immediately that there are strong grounds for believing that that paragraph is out of its place, and should be removed to the beginning of Bk. XIII., 'The Announcement concerning Lŏ.'

Wang Pih observes that the Book might very well be named 康叔之命, or 孟侯之命 (from the occurrence of 孟侯, in the 2d par). Its name, however, is 康誥, and that has the sanction of Mencius, who makes express reference to it, in Bk. V., Pt. II., iv., 4. We have it even so designated thrice in 'The Great Learning:'—Comm. i., 1; ii., 2; ix., 2. This carries up very nearly to Confucius himself. If we affirm, as I think we must do, the opinion of the scholars of Sung, that the 1st paragraph does not belong to this Book but to Bk. XIII., we must say what they have not done,—what they would not have ventured to say, even if they had seen to what their argument would lead,—that the great sage here made a mistake in compiling and arranging the tablets of the Shoo.

The Book is found in both the texts.

THE DATE OF THE ANNOUNCEMENT; AND ITS AUTHOR. The one of these points depends very much upon the other. The prefatory note says:—'King Ching, having smitten his uncles, the prince of Kwan and the prince of Ts'ae, invested his uncle of K'ang with the rule of the remnant of Yin. *With reference to this*, there were made "The Announcement to K'ang," "The Announcement about Wine," and "The Good Materials." According to this account, then, the appointment of the prince of K'ang, in connection with which this Charge was delivered to him, was made by king Ching, or rather by the duke of Chow, acting in the king's name. And it was not till the time of the Sung dynasty that this view was called in question. Sze-ma Ts'een repeatedly affirms it. He says:—'Tan, the duke of Chow, having received the commands of king Ching, attacked and slew Woo-kăng, and then divided the territory of Yin into two parts, appointing the viscount of Wei to one of them, over the principality of Sung, and the prince of K'ang to the other, over Wei' (周公旦承成王命,伐誅武庚,分殷地爲二,一封微子啟于宋,一封康叔于衛. See Maou K'e-ling, 尙書廣聽錄; and also the 史記,衛康叔世家, and 宋微子世家). More important still is the testimony given in the 左傳, under the 4th year of duke Ting (定公四年;—B.C. 505), where it is said that after king Woo had overthrown the dynasty of Shang, king Ching settled the empire by means of the regent, the duke of Chow, and that the duke appointed his brother the prince of K'ang over seven of the clans of the domain of Yin, with his seat of government in its capital (封於殷墟).

This view, I have said, was current and uncontradicted for many centuries. Under the dynasty of Sung, Soo Tung-po was the first to throw out the idea that the first paragraph had erroneously found its way into this Book from among the tablets of the 'Announcement about Lŏ.' About the same time, Woo Yih (吳棫; he is also called 才老) and other scholars came to the conclusion that the speaker in the Book was king Woo, and not the duke of Chow. Choo He adopted their views, and was followed by his disciple Ts'ae Ch'in, who sets forth the grounds of them in the following way:—

First, the prince of K'ang was king Ching's uncle (叔父), and could not be called by him 'younger brother,' as is the case in the par. 1. To the reply to this that the duke of Chow was really the speaker, and might so address Fung, he responds that the duke of Chow prefaced all the Charge with 'The king says,' and the words therefore should only be those appropriate to the lips of the king.

Second, if the Charge were given by the duke of Chow, how do we account for the fact that while there are many references in the Book to king Wăn, there is not one to king Woo? And the same question may be asked with reference to the two Books which follow. The words of par. 4,—寡兄勗, have indeed been explained of king Woo, the duke of Chow so speaking of him. But if we suppose that Woo was the speaker, he might very well so describe himself. On the supposition that the duke of Chow was the speaker, the language is contrary to all rule and propriety.

Third, it has been urged that at the time of the overthrow of Shang, Fung was still young, and unfit to be entrusted with an important govt.; and hence that his appointment took place subsequently, under king Ching. But when king Woo obtained the empire, he was about 90 years old. The ten sons of king Wăn, so often referred to, were all by the same mother; Woo was the second of them:—could there be one among them, when Woo was ninety, too young to be entrusted with an important administration? This point is too clear to need to be fortified by other considerations which Ts'ae has adduced.

It cannot be denied that there is much force in the two first of these points. We must assent also to Ts'ae's view of the age of the prince of K'ang. He was no doubt old enough to have received an appointment on the conquest of Shang. But other reasons might have prevented his being invested with a principality which would take him from the imperial court. One such reason, quite sufficient, is suggested in the passage of the 左傳 which has been referred to. It is there said, that, while the duke of Chow was prime minister under the new dynasty, the prince of K'ang was minister of Crime;—and this agrees with the prominent place which the subject of punishments occupies in our Book. The two other points, however, remain;—the general style of the Announcement, and particular expressions in it. For many years, when reading the Shoo without thinking of such critical matters as are now in hand, and without regard to commentators, I got the

○王若曰、二節 孟侯、朕其弟、小子封。○惟三節 乃丕顯考文王、克明四節 德慎罰。○不敢侮鰥寡、庸庸、祗祗、威威、顯民、用肇造我區夏、越我一二邦

2 I. "The king speaks to this effect:—'Head of the princes,
3 my younger brother, little one, Fung.' It was your greatly dis-
tinguished father, the king Wăn, who was able to illustrate his
4 virtue and be careful in the use of punishments. He did not dare
to show any contempt to the widower and widows. He employed
the employable, and revered the reverend; he was terrible to those
who needed to be awed:—*so* getting distinction among the people.
It was thus he laid the first beginnings of *the sway of* our small portion
of the Empire, and the one or two *neighbouring* countries were

impression that the speaker in the text must be king Woo;—see the note in 'The Great Learning,' Comm., Ch. i. But I now give in my adhesion to the older view. The authority of the 左傳, as old as the time of Confucius, and of the Preface, is not to be set aside. The 王若曰 at the beginning, and the 王曰 throughout the paragraphs, assimilate the Book closely to the others in which the duke of Chow is undoubtedly the speaker. It will be seen in the notes that some explanation can be given of the most difficult expressions; and it is hardly competent for us to try the language of a man like the duke of Chow by our ideas of the way in which he ought to have spoken. Maou applies here, with considerable force, the saying of Mencius, that 'it is not every ordinary man who can understand the conduct of superior men' (君子所爲,衆人不識).

It still remains to make a remark or two on THE FIRST PARAGRAPH. It speaks of the founding and completion of the city of Lŏ, which was one of the later labours of the duke of Chow, and is commonly referred to the 7th year of king Ching. As the scholars of Sung wished to make out that the Charge to the prince of K'ang was delivered by king Woo, it was necessary they should remove from it this paragraph;—as was done by Soo Tung-po in the manner which I have related above. But while dissenting from their view of the early origin of the Charge, and not hampered therefore in that respect by the par., I must still maintain the correctness of Shih's decision regarding it.

First, it is appropriate at the commencement of the 'Announcement concerning Lŏ;' while here it is altogether out of place. What had the building of Lŏ to do with the investiture of Fung with the principality of Wei? In the body of the Charge, moreover, there is not a word having reference to Lŏ, or the reasons which had led the duke of Chow to project the establishment of that new city. Second, the appointment of Fung was to Wei, and must have been contemporaneous with the appointment of the viscount of Wei to the government of Sung. It must have taken place in the 3d or 4th year of king Ching, some years before the building of Lŏ.

Gan-kwŏ felt these difficulties, and tried to meet them by supposing that some other noble or nobles had been appointed to rule 'the remnant of Yin,' during the years that elapsed between the suppression of Woo-kăng's rebellion and the building of Lŏ; and that the result having proved unsatisfactory, the prince of K'ang was then called to the task. This supposition is without any historical ground of support; and Lin Che-k'e prefers the view of a scholar Wang, (王博士), who supposed that Fung had been appointed to Wei immediately after the suppression of the rebellion, but that the Charge in this Book was not given to him till the time when Lŏ was built. But this solution is to the full as unsatisfactory as that of Gan-kwŏ. The knot cannot be loosed, it seems to me;—why should we hesitate to cut it, by removing the first par. from this Bk. to the 13th? We have seen, indeed, that but for the occurrence of the word 'announcement' in this par., the Book would hardly have been called by its present name; and yet that name was current in the time of Confucius. The sage himself perhaps misplaced the paragraph, or more probably left it, as he found it, in the wrong place. A Chinese critic would not allow this;—a foreign student may say it, when the weight of evidence seems to require him to do so.

CONTENTS. The key-note of the whole Book is in the clause 明德慎罰,—'the illustration of virtue and the careful use of punishments,' in the 3d paragraph. It has been divided into five chapters. The first three parr. (not including par. 1) celebrate the exhibition of those two things, which was given by king Wăn, whereby he laid the foundations of the imperial sway of his House, and afforded an example for all his descendants. Parr. 5—7 inculcate on Fung how he should illustrate *his* virtue, as the basis of his good govt. of the people intrusted to him. Parr. 8—19, inculcate on him how he should be careful in the use of punishments, and set forth the happy effects that would ensue from his being so. Parr. 20—22 insist on the influence of virtue, as being superior in govt. to that of punishments, and how punishments should all be regulated by the ruler's virtue. The last chapter, parr. 23, 24, winds the subject up with a reference to the uncertainty of the appointments of Heaven, and their dependance for permanence on the discharge of the duties they require from those, on whom they have lighted.

P. 1. See on the 'Announcement concerning Lŏ.'

Ch. I. Pp. 2—4. THE DUKE OF CHOW, ADDRESSING FUNG AS HIS YOUNGER BROTHER, SETS FORTH TO HIM THE ADMIRABLE QUALITIES OF THEIR FATHER WAN. 2. 王若曰,—see on the 1st par. of the 7th Book. The 'king' is king Ching. 孟=長, 'the eldest,' 'the first.' It is here = 'chief;' and 孟侯=諸侯之長, 'Head of the princes.' Acc. to the Le Ke, Bk. 王制, Pt. ii., p. 2, every 州 or province of the empire, embracing 210 國 or States, was under the authority of a chief or 伯. We may conclude therefore that Fung had been invested with that dignity. Fuh-shang has said, indeed, that the son of the emperor when 18 years old, was styled 孟侯 (天子之子,年十八,稱孟侯); and K'ang-shing supposes that it is king Ching who is thus addressed in the text. This is one of the extravagances which we are surprised to find men like Kĕang Shing and Wang Mingshing adopting and defending at the present day. 朕其弟=朕之弟. King Woo might thus have addressed Fung; king Ching could not thus address him. We must believe that, while the duke of Chow spoke as the representative of the young emperor, his nephew, he addressed Fung from the stand-point of his own relation to him. 小子,封,—小子 is often used in the Shoo by emperors, whether old or young, in mock humility, as a depreciatory designation of themselves. In the Great Announcement,' p. 7, we found it interpreted of the princes of States. Here it is spoken to Fung and not by him; and we must take it as the language of kindly, brotherly feeling. Fung was younger than either king Woo, or the duke of Chow; but we cannot suppose that he was under 70 when he was appointed to Wei. 3. 明德慎罰,—these words form the text of the whole Charge. Ts'ae, in illustration of them, quotes from the 左傳, 成二年,—明德愼罰,文王所以造周也,明德,務崇之之謂也,愼罰,務去之之謂. With 克明德 we may compare the 克明俊德, Canon of Yaou, p. 2. The whole tenor of this Book, however, makes it more natural to understand the 德 here of king Wăn's own virtue as seen in his administration of government. 4. 鰥寡,—see 'The Great Announcement,' p. 7; *et al.* 不敢侮鰥寡=the 不虐無告, 'Counsels of Yu,' p. 3. 庸=用, 'to employ.' 祇=敬, 'to reverence.' 庸庸,祇祇,威威=用其所當用,敬其所當敬,威其所當威. 顯民 is a consequence flowing from the virtues just described,=故德著於民; and all that follows, down to 時敘, sets forth the further results of Wăn's conduct thus acknowledged by the people. 肇造我區夏=始造我區域於中夏. 區者小室之名,'區 is the name of a small house.' Here it is employed to denote the original seat of the House of Chow, as but a small territory in the great empire. 惟時怙冒,—the old interpreters put a stop at 怙, and read 冒 along with the clause that follows. I have followed Ts'ae in joining 冒 with 怙. He says:—髣西土之人,怙之如父,冒之如天, 'the people of all the west relied on him as a father, and looked up to him as to Heaven.' I think the rhythm of the clauses is thus preserved better, and there is no more difficulty in interpreting 冒 than there is if we join it to 聞. It is used for 'a covering for the head;' and generally as = 'to cover.' Wăn's influence was like the gracious overshadowing of the firmament. 聞于上帝,—we must understand the virtue or the fame of Wăn as the subject of the verb 聞. 帝休,—'God approved.' The simple 帝 takes the place of 上帝; and

以修、我西土惟時怙冒、聞于上帝、帝休、天乃大命文王、殪戎殷、誕受厥命、越厥邦厥民惟時敘。乃寡兄勖、肆汝小子封、在茲東土。○王五節曰、嗚呼、封、汝念哉、今民

brought under his improving influence, until throughout our western regions all placed in him their reliance. The fame of him ascended up to the High God, and God approved. Heaven gave a great charge to king Wăn, to exterminate the great dynasty of Yin, and receive its great appointment, so that the various States belonging to it and their peoples were brought to an orderly condition. Then your unworthy elder brother exerted himself;—and so it is that you, Fung, the little one, are here in this eastern region.'"

5 II. "The king says, 'Oh! Fung, bear these things in mind. Now *your management of* the people will depend on your reverently

both those names are immediately exchanged for the vague designation of 'Heaven.' 殪=滅, 'to exterminate.' 戎=大, 'great.' 厥邦厥民惟時敘=萬邦萬民各得其理,莫不時敘. It is an exaggeration to speak of Wăn's influence as having thus extended over all the empire; but we cannot find much fault with it in the circumstances. 乃寡兄勖,—those who understand the speaker to be king Woo find no difficulty in his thus speaking of himself as 寡德之兄, 'your brother of slender virtue.' See the use of 寡人 as a designation of themselves by the princes of States in Mencius, I., Pt. I., iii., 1; *et al.* The language has been a stumblingblock, however, to those who maintain that it is employed of king Woo and not by him. Gan-kwŏ made 寡兄 to=寡有之兄, 'our brother whose match is rarely to be found.' But this is a very unlikely expansion of the phrase, and devised to get over the difficulty so strongly felt by a Chinese. I do not see any serious obstacle to our understanding it as in the translation. Why might not the duke of Chow, once at least in his life, speak thus of one brother to another? He had taken himself 'a great part' in all the exploits of Woo; to speak of him was much the same as to speak of himself. We like him all the better for eschewing the flattering tongue. 在茲東土=得以享爵位,在此東方. Wei was not only east from Ching's capital, but it was the eastern part of the territory of which Woo-kăng had been permitted to retain the sway.

Ch. II. Pp. 5—7. How the prince of K'ang should cultivate his virtue, and manifest it in the administration of his government. 5. *Fung should follow the example of king Wăn; gather up lessons from the former kings and wise men of Yin; and from the sage monarchs of remote antiquity.* 今民將在祗遹乃文考,紹聞衣德言,—it will be seen, from the translation, that I understand a 治 before 民, by which 民 is governed. This is after the example of Gan-kwŏ, Lin Che-k'e, Ts'ae, and others. Then, 遹=述, 'to transmit;' 衣=服, 'to put on,'='to carry into practice,'—as in 'The Charge to Yuĕ,' Pt. ii., p. 12, 說乃言惟服. The 'Daily Explanation' has:—今汝治民,將敬述文考之緒,務取所聞之德言,繼紹而服行之,如衣之被身,遵循勿替,可也. Këang Shing takes 民 in the nominative, and supposes that 在 is a verb=視,

將在祗遹乃文考、紹聞衣德言、往敷求于殷先哲王、用保乂民、汝丕遠惟商耈成人、宅心知訓、別求聞由古先哲王、用康保民、弘于天、若德裕乃身、不廢在王

following your father Wăn;—do you carry out his virtuous words which you have heard, and clothe yourself with them. *Moreover*, where you go, seek out extensively *among the traces* of the former wise kings of Yin what you may use in protecting and regulating their people. *Again*, you must more remotely study the old accomplished men of Shang, that you may establish your heart, and know how to instruct the people. *Further still*, you must seek out besides what is to be learned of the wise kings of antiquity, and employ it in the tranquillizing and protecting of the people. *Finally*, enlarge *your thoughts* to the *comprehension of all* Heavenly *principles*, and virtue will be richly displayed in your person, so that you will not render nugatory the king's charge.'"

'to regard,' 'to look at;'—compare its use in the 'Canon of Shun,' p. 5. He also takes 衣 as = 殷, the name of the dynasty. In this way he makes the whole = 今民將視汝之敬述乃文考,紹文考所聞殷之德言,汝當以民爲念. This view is certainly no improvement on the other. 往敷至乂民,—往 = 之國, 'when you go to your State;' 敷求 = 廣求, 'seek out extensively.' 汝丕至知訓,—耈成人, comp. in the 'Viscount of Wei,' p. 5, 咈其耈長,舊有位之人. The course of thought in the paragraph, however, leads us to think of the old accomplished men of a former time, such as E Yin and Foo Yuĕ, by whom the best monarchs of the Shang dynasty had been directed. 惟 is used as a verb, = 思, 'to think of,' 'to study.' 宅心 = 處心, 'to settle your heart,'—to bring it to its proper resting place. 知訓 = 知所以訓民,—'know how to instruct the people.'

別求至保民,—Fung is here sent to the earliest sages and monarchs of the empire,—Yaou, Shun, and Yu. 別求聞由,—'you must elsewhere enquire, that you may learn from and follow.' 由 = 行. 弘于天,云云,—it is not easy to say what is the meaning of 弘于天. Lin Che-k'e says:—'To the other injunctions is still subjoined this 弘于天. Now 弘 means to widen and enlarge. The critic Sëĕ says, "Every man has his heavenly nature, which is in him as a fire that has just been kindled, or a spring which is just issuing forth. What is required is the widening and enlarging of it." This explanation is correct. Step by step the prince of K'ang is carried on to take his rule and pattern from Heaven, after which there is nothing to be added.' I suppose this is the correct view. 'Heaven' is used as the comprehensive designation of all true right principles. The translation has taken its form from the words of Woo Ch'ing,—又當擴充其德,與天爲一,若德足乎已,則王之命汝者,永不廢矣. 6. *With*

命。○王曰、嗚呼、小子封、恫瘝乃身、敬哉、天畏棐忱、民情大可見、小人難保、往盡乃心、無康好逸豫、乃其乂民、我聞曰、怨不在大、亦不在小、惠不惠、懋不懋。○已汝惟小子、乃服惟弘王、應

6 "The king says, 'Oh! Fung, the little one, it is as if some disease were in your person; be respectfully careful. Heaven in its awfulness yet helps the sincere. The feelings of the people can for the most part be discerned, but it is difficult to calculate on the *attachment of the* lower classes. Where you go, employ all your heart. Do not seek repose, nor be fond of idleness and pleasure;—so may you regulate the people. I have heard the saying—"Dissatisfaction is caused not so much by great things or by small things, as by *a ruler's* observance of principle or the reverse, and by his energy of conduct or the reverse."

7 'Yes, it is yours, O little one,—it is your business to enlarge the royal *influence*, and harmoniously to protect this people of Yin.

what awe and cautious diligence Fung should go about the duties of his government. 恫=痛, 'pain.' 瘝=病, 'sickness.' 恫瘝乃身=疾痛在汝身, 'sickness and pain are in your person.' The meaning is that Fung's appointment was not one of ease, but one of labour, in which he should feel the sufferings of the people as if they were wounds in his own person. 天畏棐忱 is equivalent to 天命不常, 雖甚可畏, 然誠則輔之, 'The appointments of Heaven are not unchanging; and though they are to be thought of with awe, yet it helps the sincere.' 民情大可見, 小民難保=至民情, 好惡, 雖大畧可見, 然小民之心, 最爲難保, as in the translation. The uncertainty of the will of Heaven, and the changing of the minds of the people,—these are *two* considerations, which should stimulate Fung to caution and diligence that he might hold fast what he had received. Some would connect 民情大可見 with what precedes, so that the meaning is—'Heaven in its awfulness yet helps the sincere, and this is greatly seen in the feelings of the people.' But this construction of the text is not so good as the other. 無康=毋自安, 'do not give yourself to repose.' 我聞, 云云,—I have followed in the translation here the interpretation which is given by Ts'ae and in the 'Daily Explanation.' I am not sure, however, but it would have been better to adopt the view of Gan-kwŏ which is to this effect:—'The dissatisfaction of the people may be occasioned by things which are great in themselves, and by things which are small. It shows itself unexpectedly, and it is this which makes the people so difficult to be calculated on. A ruler, therefore, ought always to be bringing his conduct, which may have been defective, into conformity with what is right, and to be acting energetically wherever he may have been remiss.' 7. *The great duties of Fung, and how the happy results of his virtue would appear.* 乃服惟弘王,—服=事; 乃服=汝之事, 'your business.' 弘王,—'enlarge the king.' It would seem that the meaning must be as in the translation.

保殷民、亦惟助王宅天命、作新民。○王八節曰、嗚呼、封、敬明乃罰、人有小罪非眚、乃惟終、自作不典、式爾、有厥罪小、乃不可不殺、乃有大罪非終、乃惟眚災、適爾、既道極厥辜、時乃不可殺。○

Thus also shall you assist the king, consolidating the appointment of Heaven, and renovating this people.'"

8 III. "The king says, 'Oh! Fung, deal reverently and understandingly in your infliction of punishments. When men commit small crimes, which are not mischances, but purposed, themselves doing what is contrary to the laws, intentionally, though their crimes be but small, you may not but put them to death. But in the case of great crimes, which are not purposed, but from mischance and misfortune, accidental, if the offenders confess unreservedly their guilt, you may not put them to death.'"

應 is explained by 和, 'harmony,' and here used adverbially. This definition does not occur in the dictionary, but it may be deduced from that of 物相應, 'things answering, responding, to one another.' The people of Yin were not in harmonious accord with the dynasty of Chow. It would be the business of Fung to bring them to be so. The view of Gan-kwŏ is different. He says:—汝惟小子,乃當服行德政,惟弘大王道,上以應天,下以安我所受殷之民衆. 宅=定, 'to settle,' 'to consolidate.' 作新民,—see on 'The Great Learning,' Comm. ii., 2. The 作 and 新 must be taken, however, both as verbs, blending their meaning together. Perhaps a good version would be—'and make a renovated people.'

Ch. III., Pp. 8—19. How Fung should be careful in the use of punishments.

8.) *Modifying circumstances in judging of small and great offences.* 人有小罪,至不可不殺,—comp. the 'Canon of Shun,' p. 10, 式爾—式=用;式爾=用意如此, 'purposely thus.' The meaning of the phrase is determined by its correlation with 適爾=偶爾, 'accidentally,' below. 乃有大罪,云云,—comp. in the 'Canon of Shun,' 眚災肆赦. 既道極厥辜=既自稱道,盡輸其情,不敢隱匿, 'When they have themselves confessed, presenting fully all the circumstances, not daring to conceal anything.' This must be the meaning, though Gan-kwŏ supposes Fung himself, or the judge, to be the subject of the clause, explaining it by—汝盡聽訟之理,以極其罪, 'after you have employed every resource in hearing the case, so as thoroughly to investigate the offence.'

[Soo Shih contended that the 小罪 and 大罪 here were not to be taken absolutely in the sense of small and great offences, but relatively to each other, as less and greater. The less offence is a capital crime as well as the greater one; but the final decision of the judge might find a way of pardon for what seemed at first unpardonable, and would let the sentence of the law take its course, where there might seem at first to be room for forgiveness. I do not see in the text any ground for this criticism. A small offence, purposed and persevered in, becomes a capital crime;—

九節 王曰、嗚呼、封、有敘、時乃大明服、惟民其勅懋和、若有疾、惟民其畢棄咎、若保赤子、惟民其康乂。○十節 非汝封刑人殺人、無或刑人殺人、

9 "The king says, 'Oh! Fung, there must be the right regulation *in this matter*. When you show a great discrimination, subduing *men's hearts*, the people will admonish one another, and strive to be obedient. *Deal with evil*, as if it were a sickness in your person, and the people will entirely put away their faults. *Deal with them*, as if you were guarding your infants, and the people will be tranquil
10 and orderly. It is not you, Fung, who inflict a severe punishment or death upon a man; you may not of yourself so punish a man or

the transgressor is not fit to live. A great offence, not purposed, repented of, and confessed may be pardoned. This is what the paragraph inculcates.]

9. *The influence of the careful use of punishments in transforming the people and making them happy.* 有敘＝刑罰有次序, 'in the use of punishments there is an order.' Këang Shing explains 敘 by 順, and connects with the preceding.—'If you conform to this method of judging in the case of small and great crimes,' &c. But the interposition of 王曰, 嗚呼, 封, forbids any such constructive connection between the paragraphs. 時(＝是)乃大明服,—明者明其罰, '明 refers to the intelligent use of punishments'; 服者服其民, '服 refers to the subjecting the people thereby.' 民其勅懋和＝民其戒勅而勉於和順, 'the people will warn one another, and exert themselves to be harmonious and obedient.' 若有疾,—this clause is evidently to be referred to the person of Fung, like the 若保赤子 below. Let him deal with the crimes of the people, as he would with sickness in his own person, not suffering it, but treating it with tender hand, and the people would be both awed and won to put away their faults. The meaning of 若保赤子 appears clearly from the use which Mencius makes of it, III., Pt. I., v., 3. He says—'If an infant crawling about, is about to fall into a well, it is no crime in the infant.' No man would be roused to anger by the sight of such an infant, and every one would do his utmost to rescue it. Let Fung thus look upon the people, to save them from crime as he would save an infant from falling into a well, and they would be tranquil and orderly.

[Këang Shing joins 若有疾 with the previous clause, taking 疾 in the sense of 速, 'quickly.'—'The people will exert themselves to be harmonious and obedient with the greatest rapidity.' The structure of the paragraph is opposed to such a construction, as I have pointed out above. Shing, however, could plead the authority of Seun K'ing, who says in his 富國篇, 三德者誠乎上, 則下應之, 如景響, 雖欲無明達, 得乎哉, 書曰, 乃大明服, 惟民其力懋和而有疾, 此之謂也. But neither this text nor interpretation of Seun is correct. The same may be said of the way in which he quotes and applies the difficult clause—弘于天 of p. 5, which appears in the same 富國篇 as 弘覆乎天.]

10. *Punishments were to be employed according to the laws. Fung ought not to allow any feeling of his own in the use of them.* I have translated 刑 by 'to inflict a severe punishment;' because 刑人殺人 are opposed to 劓人刵人, the severer punishments to the lighter. What particular punishment or punishments

非汝封、又曰、劓刵人、無或劓刵人。○(十一節)王曰、外事、汝陳時臬、司師茲殷罰有倫。○(十二節)又曰、要囚、服念五六日、至于旬時、丕蔽

put him to death.' Moreover, he says, 'It is not you, Fung, who cut off a man's nose or ears; you may not of yourself cut off a man's nose or ears.'"

11 "The king says, 'In things beyond *your immediate jurisdiction*, have laws set forth which the officers may observe; and those should be the penal laws of Yin, which were right-ordered.'"

12 "He also says, 'In examining the evidence in criminal cases, reflect upon it for five or six days, yea for ten days, or three months. You may then boldly carry your decision into effect in such cases.'"

are intended by it, it is not easy to see. 'Cutting off the nose' was one of the regular five punishments, but not 'cutting off the ears,' though mention is made of this in Bk. XXVII., p. 2. The 又曰 should probably be before the 非汝封 which precedes it in the text,—as in the translation.

11. *In things not falling immediately under his own jurisdiction, he should let the old laws of Yin take their course.* The meaning of this par. is very uncertain. Ts'ae says that he does not understand what is meant by 外事, 'outside affairs.' The common view is that it means 有司之事, 'the affairs of the officers,' matters which it was not necessary the prince himself should take the management of. Then 臬, anciently 'a small post in front of a gate' (門橛), marking a limit, is used for laws. 師=法, 'to follow as the law.' The 'Daily Paraphrase' says:—凡外而有司訟獄之事,必欲一一躬親綜理,勢有所不能,若不示之,昭然是預取法令,而詳定之,昭示出之,使曉然創立屬僚,則有司將有任意一 …

Actually: 凡外而有司訟獄之事,必欲一一躬親綜理,勢有所不能,若不預取法令,而詳定之,昭示屬僚,則有司將有任意出入者矣,汝務講求畫一之規,陳列而頒布之,使曉然確有所守,易以爲治,然是法也,不必別出意見,創立條欵也,但取殷罰以治殷民可矣,云云.

Gan-kwŏ adopted a different exegesis, understanding by 外事=外土諸侯奉王事. But his interpretation is quite unsatisfactory;—see the 註疏. Ts'ae quotes the view of one of the critics Leu (呂氏), that by 外事 are to be understood the affairs of Wei (衛國事) in opposition to the affairs which would come under Fung's notice as the minister of Crime at the imperial court. But the whole tenor of the Book sufficiently proves that the charges in it were delivered with exclusive reference to the govt. of Wei. Këang Shing gives still a difft. view in the foll. words:—外事,聽獄之事也,聽獄在外朝,故曰外事.

P. 12. *How Fung should exercise a cautious deliberation before deciding on criminal cases.* 要囚,—Ts'ae defines this as=獄辭之要者, 'the summary of the pleas in criminal cases.' Medhurst renders it by 'important criminal cases;' and Gaubil by 'S'il s'agit de fautes considerables.' They both err by taking 要 in the 3d tone,='important.' The dict. gives one meaning of 囚, with reference to the text, as 獄辭, 'the evidence in a criminal case;' and, with the same reference it defines 要 as=察, 'to examine.' These meanings

要囚。○十三節王曰、汝陳時臬事、罰蔽殷彝、用其義刑義殺、勿庸以次汝封、乃汝盡遜、曰時敘、惟曰未有遜事。○十四節已、汝惟小子、未其有若汝封之心、朕心朕德、惟乃知。

13 "The king says, 'In setting forth the business of the laws the punishments will be determined by the regular laws of Yin. But you must see that those punishments, as well as the penalty of death, be righteous. And you must not let them be warped to agree with your own inclinations, O Fung. Then shall you be entirely accordant with right, and may say, "These are properly ordered;" yet you must say at the same time, "Perhaps they are
14 not yet entirely accordant with right." Yes, you are the little one;—who has a heart like you, O Fung? My heart and my virtue *also* are known to you.

of the terms are applicable to the phrase when it occurs again in Bk. XV., and I have followed them here. Fung is told that in deciding on evidence, he should do so cautiously, and not hastily. It is supposed to be in a case where guilt would involve death, and when the accused was once executed, there could be no remedying a wrong decision. 服念=服膺而念之. 旬=十日. 時=三月. 蔽=斷, 'to decide.'

P. 13. *Summary of the five preceding paragraphs.* 汝陳時(=是)臬事,—the difficulty here is with the 事. Ts'ae connects it with 臬 by means of an 與,='In setting forth these laws and other matters' (敷陳是法與事). Ying-tă and Këang Shing both give it a verbal force. The latter explains:—汝陳是法以從事于罰. Simpler than either of those methods is the construction of Woo Ch'ing, who makes 事 the object of the verb 陳, and puts 臬 under its regimen;—汝陳列用法之事. 罰蔽殷彝,—蔽, as in the last par.; 彝=常, 'what is regular;'—in this case, 'the ordinary laws' of the former dynasty. Still Fung was not blindly to adopt all the laws of Yin. He must be satisfied that they were righteous,—appropriate to the crime, and suited to the altered times;' 義=宜. 勿庸以次汝封,—庸=用; 次=即 or 就. The whole=刑殺不可以就汝封之意. This is plainly the meaning; but the usage of 次 is peculiar. Ts'ae says that it is the 次 of 次舍, 'a mansion,' 'a dwelling.' 乃汝, 云云,—遜=順 meaning 'accordant with right.' 時叙=是有次叙, having reference to the 有叙 of par. 9. The gist of the whole is, that Fung should never allow a feeling of elation, as if all his affairs were arranged as well as they possibly could be. [Këang Shing, following a quotation by Seun K'ing, in his 致仕篇, of a portion of this paragraph, reduces the whole to—王曰女陳時臬事, 罰蔽殷彝, 誼刑誼殺, 勿庸以即女, 惟曰未有順事. But only prejudice can, in my opinion, make any of Seun's quotations carry it over the authority of the *textus receptus*. Shing interprets the last clause—'But say, "There are still instances of disobedience among the people."' This is far-fetched.

P. 14. *The confidence and affection subsisting between Fung and the duke of Chow.* See on par. 2. Why these expressions of attachment should be interjected here, it is not easy to understand.

○十五節凡民自得罪、寇攘姦宄、殺越人于貨、暋不畏死、罔弗憝。○十六節王曰、封、元惡大憝、矧惟不孝不友、子弗祗服厥父事、大傷厥考心、于父不能字厥子、乃疾厥子、于弟弗念天顯、乃弗克恭厥

15 'All people who of themselves commit crimes, robbing, stealing, practising villainy and treason, and who kill men or violently assault them to take their property, being violent and fearless of death:—those are abhorred by all.'"

16 "The king says, 'Fung, such chief criminals are greatly abhorred, and how much more detestable are the unfilial and unbrotherly!—as the son who does not reverently discharge his duty to his father, but greatly wounds his father's heart; and the father who can no longer love his son, but hates him; and the younger brother who does not think of the manifest will of Heaven, and refuses to respect his elder brother, so that the elder brother does not think of the

Pp. 15—17. *Cases in which severe punishment may be inflicted without hesitation.* 15. *Robbers, murderers, &c.* 自得罪,—'of themselves,' *i.e.*, without being tempted or involved by others, 'offending.' 寇攘姦宄,—comp. the Canon of Shun, p. 26; *et al.* 殺越人于貨,—from this the par. is quoted by Mencius, V. Pt. II., iv. 4, which see. Ts'ae illustrates the meaning of 越 here by a reference to 顚越不恭, in the 'Pwan-kăng,' Pt. ii., 16; but it is not apt. The character must have in the text the meaning of, 'to throw down,' = 'to assault violently.' 暋=强. 憝=惡, 'to hate,' 'to detest.' Justice executed on such parties would meet with general sympathy and approbation. 16. *The case of the unfilial and unbrotherly.* 元惡大憝,—this takes up the case of the parties in the last par. The next clause must be completed as in the translation. Ts'ae gives for it:—況不孝不友之人,而尤爲可惡者. 不孝 is the crime of the son, and 不友 is that of the elder brother. But as the par. goes on to speak of the father's failure in duty as well as the son's, and of the younger brother's as well as his senior's, we must understand by 不孝 all offences between father and son, and by 不友 all between elder brother and younger. 厥考心,—考 is evidently used of the father when alive. 于父,至厥子,—this must be, I think, a fresh case, and is not to be connected with the preceding, as if the 于 were equivalent to 以致, 'so that,' which is the paraphrase of the 'Daily Explanation.' We cannot connect 于弟, which immediately follows, with any clause which precedes. 于父 and 于弟='in the case of the father—the younger brother—who,' &c. 字=愛, 'to love;' 疾=惡, 'to hate.' 天顯 is 'the manifest will of Heaven;' requiring that the younger should serve the elder. 不念鞠子哀,—Gan-kwŏ takes 鞠 in the sense of 穉, 'child,' 'junior,' and explains the clause—不念穉子之可哀, 'does not think of the pity he should cherish for his younger brother.' Lin Che-k'e, foll. by Ts'ae, took 鞠=養,

書經

兄、兄亦不念鞠子哀、大不友于弟、惟弔。茲、不于我政人得罪、天惟與我民彝大泯亂、曰、乃其速由文王作罰、刑茲無赦。○不(十七節)率大戛、矧惟外庶子訓人、惟厥正

toil of their parents in bringing them up, and is very unbrotherly to his junior. If we who are charged with government do not treat parties who proceed to such wickedness as offenders, the laws *of our nature* given by Heaven to our people will be thrown into great disorder or destroyed. You must deal speedily with such parties according to the penal laws of king Wăn, punishing them severely and not pardoning.

17 'These, who are disobedient *to natural principles*, are to be thus severely subjected to the laws;—how much more the officers employed in your State as the instructors of the youth, the heads

and interpreted as in the translation. 惟弔茲至泯亂,—all this must be taken together as one sentence, and interpreted as in the translation. The paraphrase of the 'Daily Explanation' is:—夫廢棄人倫,滅絕天理,至于如此,較之寇攘姦宄,其惡尤甚,使我爲政之人,視爲固然,不加之以罪,則人心無從勸懲,風俗何由丕變,將天所與我民之常性,不大泯滅而紊亂乎. Lin Che-k'e takes quite a diff't. view of the scope of the passage. 弔 is read by him *teaou*, 'to pity,' and not *teih*, = 'to come to.' His interpretation is:—'The criminals I have mentioned above are detested by all, and to be put to death. But these parties are to be pitied. Their offences must be owing to the failures in duty of us who are charged with govt.,' &c. Lin argues ingeniously, but not satisfactorily, in support of his view. We feel that he *ought* to be right. Robbers and murderers must be summarily dealt with for the preservation of society; but unkind fathers and undutiful children, and divided brothers, cannot be taken cognizance of in the same way by the law. The duke of Chow, however, makes them—and here he is correct—in advance of the others in point of guilt, and goes on to say that they are to be punished accordingly, without interposing anything about pitying and teaching them in the first place. 曰乃,云云,—Woo Ch'ing brings out the force of the 曰 very well:—然則如之何哉,汝其曰速由,云云,'What then is to be done? You must say, "I will quickly punish them."' What the law of king Wăn regarding such cases was, we do not know. There is a difficulty in applying here what is said about 不孝之刑, and 不弟之刑, in the Chow Le, Bk. IX., 地官,大司徒.

P. 17. *The case of unworthy and factious officers.* 不率大戛,—this corresponds to the first clause of the last par., and must be construed accordingly. 不率 is descriptive of the 不孝,不友, and 大戛 of the punishment which such received. The difficulty is with the interpretation of 戛. The 爾雅 defines it by 禮, 'propriety,' which is taken to = 常法, 'a constant law.' Gan-kwŏ, adopting this account of the term, makes 不率大戛 all descriptive of the unfilial and unbrotherly, as those who do not comply with the invariable laws of human duty. This is contrary to the analogy of the last clause, which I have pointed out, and it must be rejected.

人、越小臣諸節、乃別播敷、造民大譽、弗念弗庸、瘝厥君、時乃引惡、惟朕憝、已、汝乃其速由茲義率殺。○十八節 亦惟君惟長、不能厥家人、越

of the various official departments, and the petty officers, charged with their several commissions; when they propagate and spread abroad other lessons, seeking the praise of the people, not thinking *of the sovereign* nor using *the rules for their duties*, but distressing him! These lead on to wickedness and are an abomination to me. Shall they be let alone? Do you quickly, according to what is recognized as right, put them to death.

18 'And you are here prince and president;—if you cannot manage your own household, with your petty officers, the instructors, and

Ts'ae makes the word —法, 'laws,' and with verbal force, — 寘之法, 'to subject to the laws.' I have followed this view. Woo Ch'ing gets substantially to the same conclusion by taking it as — 擊, 'to smite,' after the analogy of the 'Yih and Tseih,' p. 9. 外諸子訓人=外諸子以訓人爲職. Medhurst translates the clause by—'the outside princes, whose business it is to instruct the people.' Gaubil has—'Ceux qui, par etat, doivent enseigner les autres;'—more correctly than Medhurst, but he takes no account of the 外. In the Chow Le, Bk. XXXI., p. 16, we have an account of the 諸子, as the various officers charged with the training of the youth of the kingdom, sons of nobles, high officers, and others of the best promise. It is said—諸子掌國子之倅,掌其戒令,與其教治,辨其等,正其位, which Biot translates—'L' attaché aux fils *de dignitaires* est chargé de conduire les supplèants des fils de l' Etat. Il s'occupe de leur règlement special; il dirige leurs etudes; il distingue leurs rangs, et determine leurs positions *dans les ceremonies*.' This was the function of those officers in the imperial domain, at the court:—there were similar officers in the various states, who as distinguished from these were the 外諸子. 厥正人=庶官之長. 越小臣諸節—in the 31st Bk. of the Chow Le, referred to above, we have an account of the office of the 小臣, or 'Minor ministers' (petits serviteurs;—Biot), parr. 53—55. They were charged with the minor orders of the emperor and, in the States, of the princes, conveying them to the parties to whom they were addressed, and as symbols of their authority they carried the 節, tallies, or credentials appropriate to the mission with which they were charged. 乃別播敷=乃別爲條教而頒布之,取悅時俗,要求衆譽,將君上委任之意,全不體念,并國家官守之法,咸廢格不用,徒知違道干譽,以病其君. 時(=是)乃引惡,—'these are leaders of wickedness,' *i.e.*, they set an example of wickedness and led others on to it as well. 由茲義,—'according to this righteousness,' *i.e.*, what is recognized and has been enacted as right to be done in such cases. Gan-kwŏ takes a diff. view of the par. from 乃別播敷, considering it as addressed to Fung himself. Such a construction is most unnatural, and breaks entirely the train of thought.

Pp. 18, 19. *Advice to Fung to be himself an example of what he required in others, and by gentleness make the people rich and happy, and fulfil the hopes which were entertained of him.* Such is the view of these parr. taken by Ts'ae and Woo Ch'ing. Këang Shing supposes that par. 18 speaks of the princes of the various States to which Fung stood in the relation of president (孟侯). The view is ingenious, but it necessitates more wresting and supple-

厥小臣外正、惟威惟虐、大放王命、乃非德用乂。○十九節汝亦罔不克敬典、乃由裕民、惟文王之敬忌、乃裕民曰、我惟有及、則予一人以懌。○二十節王曰、封、爽惟民、迪吉康、我時其惟殷先哲王德、用

heads of departments, but use only terror and violence, you greatly set aside the royal charge, and try to regulate your State contrary to virtue.
19 Do you also in every thing reverence the constant statutes, and so proceed to the happy rule of the people. There are the reverence of king Wăn and his caution;—in proceeding by them to the happy rule of the people, say, "If I can only attain to them." So will you make me the one man to rejoice.'"
20 IV. "The king says, 'Fung, when I think clearly of the people, I see they are to be led to happiness and tranquillity. I think of the virtue of the former wise kings of Yin, whereby they tranquil-

menting of the text than the other. 18. The two preceding parr. had stimulated Fung to be bold in punishing the unfilial and unbrotherly, and refractory officers; but there was a more excellent way,—the way of example. If he could bring all the family virtues into action in his own household, they would flourish also throughout the State. He might so deal with his petty officers, the instructors, and heads of departments also, that they would be glad to perform their duties, instead of having to be punished for the neglect of them. If he could not thus accomplish much by example and influence, his administration would be bad. 小臣外正 = the 外諸子, 正人, and 小臣諸節 of the last par. Choo He took the 惟威惟虐 to be descriptive of the 小臣外正, and supposed the design of the whole to be to warn against being lenient in his government;—see the 集說. I am surprised to find him advocating such an exegesis. 19. 乃由裕民 = 由是求裕民之道, 'by this method seek the proper way of enriching the people,' *i.e.*, of making them good and happy. 'The reverence of king Wăn and his caution' indicate at once his attention to the duties of govt., and the caution of his measures,—particularly those of a penal character. 我惟有及 = 我

惟求能及文王之裕民, 斯已矣.

Ch. IV. Pp. 20—22. How THE VIRTUE OF THE SOVEREIGN IS THE MOST IMPORTANT THING IN THE GOVERNMENT OF THE PEOPLE, AND RULERS SHOULD SEEK BY VIRTUE TO SUPERSEDE THE NECESSITY OF USING PUNISHMENTS. 20. *By the example of the good kings of Yin, and his own wish to copy them, the king seeks to make Fung zealous to govern by virtue.* 爽惟民, 迪吉康,—Gan-kwŏ put a comma at 迪, which character he took in the sense of 道, explaining the whole by 明惟治民之道, 而善安之. Ying-tă expands this into—'O Fung, a ruler ought clearly to think of the proper way to govern the people, and thereby secure for them a happy tranquillity.' It is much better to put the comma at 民, and take 迪 in the sense of 導, 'to lead,' 'to conduct,' *i.e.*, by means of virtuous influence. We thus bring out the meaning in the translation, 爽 being = 明, and 惟 = 思. Woo Ch'ing says, clearly and concisely:—明知斯民, 導迪之, 則吉康. 我時至作求,—時

康乂民、作求、矧今民罔迪不適、不迪、則罔政在厥邦。○王曰、封、予惟不可不監、告汝德之說、于罰之行、今惟民不靜、未戾厥心、迪屢未同、爽惟天其罰殛我、我其不怨、惟厥罪、無在大、亦

(廿一節)

lized and regulated the people, and rouse myself to realize it. Moreover, the people now are sure to follow a leader. If one do not lead them, he cannot be said to exercise a government in their State.'"

21 "The king says, 'Fung, I cannot dispense with the inspection *of the ancients*, and I make this declaration to you about virtue in the use of punishments. Now the people are not quiet; they have not stilled their minds; notwithstanding my frequent leading of them, they have not come to accord *with my government*. I reflect on Heaven's severe punishments, but I do not murmur. The crimes *of the people* whether they are great or many, *are all*

—是, here equivalent to 是以, 'therefore.' 惟=思. The two characters 作求 have been much disputed. The older scholars and Ts'ae took 求=等, 'a mate,' 'a match,' so that 作求=爲等於商先王, 'to be a mate of, equal to, the former kings of Shang.' It seems to me more natural and simple to take the terms as in the translation, —as Lin Che-k'e and Woo Ch'ing do. 今民罔迪不適,—adhering to the meaning of 迪 as =導, these words are susceptible of two meanings. They may be translated —'The people are sure to follow as they are led' (民無導之而不從者), which is the view of Ts'ae; or—'If the people have none to lead them, they will not go on to *the desired condition*' (民無以迪之,則不能自適於吉康之地), which is the view of Woo Ch'ing. The former interpretation is that which the whole of the paragraph requires. The sentiment is too broadly stated, and the issue did not justify it in the case of the people of Yin; but it is not the correctness of the sentiments that a translator has to do with. 不迪則罔政在厥邦,—this expresses very strongly the feeling of the duke of Chow, that a govt. maintained by force did not deserve to be called a government.

P. 21. *By the failure of his own repeated efforts to secure the good govt. of the people of Yin, the king still further stimulates Fung to strive to realize the sway of virtue.* The mention of the repeated efforts to bring the people of Yin to a state of good order is not appropriate in the mouth of king Woo, supposed to give this charge to the prince of K'ang immediately after the conquest of the dynasty. 予惟不可不監,—we may take the 惟 either as =思, 'to think,' or as a particle, ='indeed.' 告汝德之說于罰之行=告汝以德行罰之說, 'I declare to you this saying, that virtue is to preside over the use of punishments.' 未戾厥心,—戾=止, 'to stop.' The people's minds did not acquiesce in the existing state of things, and hence their turbulent movements. 迪屢未同=雖屢經開導,究未能同歸于治. 惟厥罪至在多,—I cannot find any better way of explain-

無在多、矧曰、其尚顯聞于天。○廿二節王曰、嗚呼、封、敬哉、無作怨、勿用非謀非彝、蔽時忱、丕則敏德、用康乃心、顧乃德、遠乃猷、裕乃以民寧、不汝瑕殄。○廿三節王曰、嗚呼、肆汝小子封、惟命不于常、汝

chargeable on me, and how much more shall this be said, when the report of them goes up so manifestly to Heaven!'"

22 "The king says, 'Oh! Fung, be reverent. Do not what will create murmurings; do not use bad counsels, and uncommon ways. Decidedly and with sincerity, give yourself to imitate the active virtue *of the ancients*. Hereby give repose to your mind, examine your virtue, send far forward your plans, and thus by your generous forbearance you will conduct the people to repose *in what is good*:—so shall I not have to blame you or cast you off.'"

23 V. "The king says, 'Oh! you, Fung, the little one, *Heaven's* appointments are not constant. Do you think of this, and do not

ing this than that given in the translation. The 'Daily Explanation' has:—萬方有罪,在予一人,惟厥小民,無知而陷于罪,不在於大,亦不在於多,即至微至纖,皆上人失教之所致也. 其尚顯聞於天,—尚=上. The cry of the crimes of the people of Yin ascended, and was clearly heard in heaven;—it was not merely with a few and slight offences that the king had to charge himself. 22. *Various advices to Fung, winding up the chapter.* 無作怨,—汝愼毋作可怨之事, 'Do not do things that will create murmurings.' This is a dissuasive from the use of punishments. They will be followed by the resentment of the people; govt. carried on by them is not on a good plan; punishments may be occasionally resorted to, but they are not the regular method of procedure. 蔽時忱,—蔽=斷; 時=是; 忱=誠. The clause has an adverbial force, and is carried on to the clauses that follow;—'with the determination of sincerity.' 丕則,—則 is a verb,—'to imitate.'

顧='to have the eyes constantly on,' 'to regard and examine.' 裕乃以民寧,—this will be the result of obedience to the advice just set forth,=由是寬裕不迫,使民日漸月摩,相安於善而不自知,此德化之至耳.

Ch. V. Pp. 23, 24. A CONSIDERATION OF THE UNCERTAINTY OF THE APPOINTMENTS OF HEAVEN SHOULD DEEPEN THE IMPRESSION OF THE WHOLE CHARGE. 23. 肆,—Ts'ae confesses that he does not know the meaning of 肆 here. There does not seem much difficulty in it. We may take it as='therefore,' or 'now.' 命不于常,—命 is of course 天命. For the sentiment, compare 'The Instructions of E,' p. 8; *et al.* See also the expansion of it in 'The Great Learning,' Comm. x. 11. 命不于常,—'the appointments of Heaven are not in—i.e., are not characterized by—constancy.' 無我殄享,—毋或不念,使自我而殄絕所享之國

念哉、無我殄享、明乃服命、高乃聽、用康乂民。○廿四節王若曰、往哉封、勿替敬典、聽朕告汝、乃以殷民世享。

make me deprive you of your dignity. Reflect clearly on the charges you have received. Think highly of what you have heard, and tranquillize and regulate the people accordingly.'"

24 "The king thus says, 'Go, Fung. Do not disregard the statutes you should reverence; hearken to what I have told you:—so with the people of Yin you will enjoy *your dignity*, and hand it down to your posterity.'"

也. Këang Shing makes the meaning to be —'Do not make me deprive you of the privilege of sacrificing to the spirits within your jurisdiction.' The issue is the same; but this meaning of 享 is far-fetched. 明乃服命,—comp. 愼乃服命 in the last Bk., p. 4. 服命 may be taken here as there, 服 being 七章之服, and 命 the 七命 of a prince of Fung's rank. So, Këang Shing; but it seems to me better to take the clause as in the translation,—命汝所受于我之誥命. 高乃聽—we must take 高 in the sense of 'to think highly of.' Ts'ae says:—高其聽, 不可卑忽我言. 24. Ts'ae observes that the 世享 here responds to the 殄享 of the last par. It does so, and shows that 享 is to be taken of the enjoyment of the princely dignity. Gan-kwŏ gives for the clause: —即汝乃以殷民世世享國, 福傳後世.

THE BOOKS OF SHANG.

BOOK X. THE ANNOUNCEMENT ABOUT DRUNKENNESS.

酒誥

王若曰、明大命
于妹邦。○乃穆
考文王、肇國在
西土、厥誥毖庶
邦庶士、越少正
御事、朝夕曰、祀
茲酒、惟天降命、
肇我民惟元祀。

1 "The king speaks to this effect:—'Do you clearly make known my great commands in the country of Mei.

2 'When your reverent father, the king Wăn, laid the foundations of our kingdom in the western region, he delivered announcements and cautions to *the princes of* the various States, all the *high* officers, with their assistants, and the managers of affairs, saying, morning and evening, "For sacrifices spirits should be employed." When Heaven was sending down its *favouring* decree, and laying the foundations of *the eminence of* our people, *spirits* were used only in

THE NAME OF THE BOOK.—酒誥, 'The Announcement about Drunkenness.' I have spoken of the proper meaning of the term 酒 on Part IV., Bk. VIII., Pt. iii., 2. In the 'Songs of the five Sons,' and the 'Punitive Expedition of Yin,' I was unwilling to depart from the common usage of translators, and rendered 酒 by 'wine;' but there can be no doubt that the term in the ancient Books signifies 'spirits distilled from rice,'—our 'ardent spirits.' The French term 'vin' seems to be capable of a wider application than our 'wine.' Gaubil says:—'Le titre de ce chapitre signifie avis ou ordres sur l'usage du vin. Il s'agit ici du vin de riz, qui fut decouvert, suivant la plûpart des auteurs, du tems de Yu, fondateur de la premiere dynastie. Le raisin n'est à la Chine que depuis les premiers Han.' The title therefore might be correctly translated 'The Announcement about Spirits,' but the cursory reader would most readily suppose that the discourse was about spiritual Beings. I have preferred in consequence to render it by—'The Announcement about Drunkenness.'

The Book is found in both the texts. There are the same questions about the date of it, and the speaker in it, which have been discussed with reference to 'The Announcement to the prince of K'ang;' and it is not necessary to enter on them again here. I suppose the speaker to be the duke of Chow, addressing his brother Fung in the name of the young king Ching.

CONTENTS. The Announcement, as has just been said, is, like the last, addressed to Fung as invested with the govt. of Wei. We have seen how the drunken debauchery of Këĕ was the chief cause of the downfal of the Hea dynasty, and how that of Shang was brought to an end mainly by the same vice in Show. The people of Yin had followed the example of their sovereign, and the vice of drunkenness, with its attendant immoralities, extensively characterized the highest and the lowest classes of society. One of Fung's most difficult tasks in his administration would be to correct this evil habit, and he is in this Book summoned to the undertaking. He is instructed on the proper use, and the allowable uses of spirits; the disastrous consequences of drunkenness are strikingly set forth; he is called to roll back the flood of its desolation from his officers and people.

The scholar Woo Ts'ae-laou, earlier than Choo He, thought that there was in the Book sufficient evidence of its being composed of two announcements originally distinct:—the first, embracing parr. 1—7, being addressed by king Woo—[Ts'ae-laou is one of the most earnest advocates of the early date of the Book]—directly to the people of Yin; and the second, parr. 8—17, being addressed to Fung. Ts'ae has examined this hypothesis, in his introductory observations on the Book, and adduced sufficient reasons for rejecting it. The whole, as we now have it, was, no doubt, addressed to Fung; but in the 6th and 7th parr. the king seems to forget that he is speaking to him, and appeals to the people and officers of Yin, for whose sakes the announcement was made. There is nothing unnatural or much out of the way in this.

The criticism of Woo suggests, however, a natural division of the Book into two chapters:—the first preliminary, parr. 1—7, chiefly on the original use and the permissible uses of ardent spirits; the other, addressed directly to Fung, and showing how drunkenness had proved the ruin of the Shang dynasty, and how they of Chow, and particularly Fung in Wei, should turn the lesson to account.

In the 'Complete digest of Commentaries on the Shoo,' the following summary of the contents is given:—The whole is to be looked at from the stand-point of the first par., after which the contents might be divided into 4 chapters. Parr. 2—8 would form the first. The speaker relates the instructions of king Wăn on the subject of spirits, to introduce his own commands to the country of Mei, and concludes by relating how their dynasty of Chow rose by obedience to Wăn's lessons. Parr. 9—12 would form the second. They describe the rise and fall of the Shang dynasty, and how they should look into it as a glass, where they would see their present duty.

The 13th par. strictly charges Fung with the duty of imposing the lessons he received upon his people and officers, and on other princes, and of rendering a personal obedience to them himself. The other parr., 14—17, would form the fourth chapter, and state how obedience to the commands on the use of spirits should be enforced

Ch. I. Pp. 1—7. FUNG IS ORDERED TO MAKE THE KING'S COMMANDS KNOWN THROUGH MEI. THE PRINCIPLES INCULCATED BY KING WAN IN REGARD TO THE USE OF ARDENT SPIRITS ARE STATED; AND THE SPEAKER DECLARES HIS OWN COMMANDS IN HARMONY WITH THEM. 1. In the north of the pres. dis. of K'e (淇縣), in the dep. of Wei-hwuy, Honan, there is a place called 妹鄉,—a relic of the ancient name of the whole territory. It was in Mei that Show had his capital;—the imperial domain north from Chaou-ko, was all called Mei acc. to Gan-kwŏ. In the She king, Pt. I., Bk.' IV., Ode iv., 'the villages of Mei,' 'the north of it,' and 'the east of it,' are all mentioned. The character in use for the name there is 沬, but the country intended is the same which is here called 妹. Fung's principality of Wei must have embraced the greater part of it.

明大命,—明 is in the imperative mood. The whole=封,今汝往治妹地,當以我誥誡之辭敷布于妹邦之臣民.

Pp. 2—6. *The lessons of king Wăn on the use of ardent spirits.* 2, 3. *Spirits should be used only in sacrifices. So it is in times of prosperity; when calamities come upon a State, the cause will be found to be drunkenness.* 乃穆考,—the old interpreters all took 穆 as simply denoting the place of king Wăn's shrine or spirit-tablet in the temple of ancestors;—see on the 'Doctrine of the Mean,' xix., 4. Many still follow this view, as Këang Shing, for instance, who says:—周家世次文王第當穆故稱穆考. I cannot think that this is the meaning, and much prefer to take 穆=敬, as in the translation,—an epithet descriptive of king Wăn, who is celebrated in the She King as the 穆穆文王. It is observed, by those who understand the character in this way, that king Wăn in the last Bk. p. 13, is called 顯考, because the subject there is the manner in which he displayed his virtue (明德), while here he is called 穆考, being spoken of as instructing and cautioning his people. 肇國在西土,—'founded our kingdom in the western regions.' But Wăn was not the *founder* of the House of Chow, whose fortunes had been gradually growing in the west. We must make allowance for the duke of Chow's language in speaking of his father. See, moreover, the statements of king Woo's about Wăn's receiving the command of Heaven, 'to soothe the regions of the empire,' Bk. III., p. 5; *et al.* 厥誥毖至朝夕曰,—'in his announcements &c., he said.' 毖=慎=戒謹, 'to caution,' 'to warn;'—difft. from the meaning of the character in Bk. VII., p. 8. 庶邦 is taken by Lin Che-k'e as=諸侯, 'the princes of the various States,' *i.e.*, of the States within his jurisdiction

書經

三節 ○天降威、我民用大亂喪德、亦罔非酒惟行、越小大邦用喪、亦罔非酒惟辜。○

3 the great sacrifices. When Heaven has sent down its terrors, and our people have thereby been greatly disorganized and lost their virtue, this might also be invariably traced to their indulgence in spirits; yea, the ruin of States, small and great, *by these terrors*, may be also traced invariably to their crime in the use of spirits.

as chief of the west' (西伯). This seems the simplest view of the phrase. 庶士,—'all the officers.' These, acc. to Ying-tă, were the 朝臣, 'ministers of the court.' It is better to understand them as the 正, or 官之長, 'Heads of the various magisterial departments;'—so, the 'Daily Explanation.' Then the 少正 are the assistants of those Heads of departments; and the 御事, all who held any office, however low it might be. 祀茲酒—惟祭祀, 則用此酒, 'only in sacrifices should these ardent spirits be used.' 惟天降命, 肇我民, 惟元祀,—Medhurst translates this:—'And Heaven sent down the decree in the first instance to our people (to make it) that they might use it principally in sacrificing.' Gaubil has:—'Cet ordre, ajoûtoit-il, est venu du ciel; quand pour la première fois il donna le vin aux peuples, il voulut que ce ne fut que pour les cérémonies religieuses.' These versions are erroneous or defective in several points, but they agree in the view they give of the general scope of the passage. It is substantially that propounded by Gan-kwŏ, whose commentary is:—惟天下教命, 始令我民, 知作酒者, 惟爲祭祀. This interpretation has been generally received by the critics. In the 'Daily Explanation' we have:—天令我民始作此酒者, 止爲郊社宗廟之大祭饗而設, 此外無可用酒之時矣. This construction uses too much freedom with the text, which says nothing about Heaven's having given the command to make wine. 肇我民, standing as the characters do here, must be under the government of 降命, and = 'to found our people.' Woo Ch'ing and Këang Shing do not follow the usual view, but their own explanations are not more admissible. Ch'ing says:—如今我民作酒, 惟用之於大祭祀, 是天以此教人也, letting the 肇 slip quietly out of sight. Shing says:—惟天之下教命, 始開導我民者, 惟始于祀也. Here 肇我民 is better dealt with, but I know not whence he derives the 始 in his last clause (始于祀), and I cannot admit the 命 of 降命 to stand here for 教命. The view of the meaning which appears in the translation does not seem to have occurred to any commentator. I am led to it chiefly by considering the relation in which 天降命 here, and 天降威 at the beginning of the next par. evidently stand to each other. I have had occasion before to translate 命 by 'favouring decree' (See IV., Bk. VII, Pt. i., 4; *et al.*) This indeed is its common signification. Heaven only confers its appointments where its approbation has gone before. Compare also the contrast between 威 and 命 in the 'Conquest of Le,' p. 4, *et al.*, exactly corresponding to what appears here. It does not matter whether we understand the speaker to be king Wăn, or, as I rather think, king Ching, commenting on Wăn's 祀茲酒. He goes back to the days of early simplicity and virtue, when that character was being formed in the chiefs and people of Chow, in virtue of which they went on to attain the supremacy of the empire; and then they made no use of spirits excepting at the great sacrifices. In 元祀 the 元=大, and we may take the 'great sacrifices' as those to Heaven, the earth, and ancestors. Sacrifices were not so numerous then as they afterwards became.

In the third par. two causes are assigned for the ruin of virtue and prosperity,—the terrors of Heaven and indulgence in spirits. The 用 expressly asserts the agency of Heaven, and the 亦, as clearly, that of intemperance. We must understand that the terrors of Heaven

are its justice manifested in the punishment of men's guilt. Men first wrest spirits from their proper use to feed their own lusts, and there is a natural issue of evil consequences. Then Heaven, seeing men obstinate in their wicked course, righteously accelerates their overthrow and ruin. Ts'ae says:—酒之禍人也，而以爲天降威者，禍亂之成，是亦天罰. Ts'ae, it will be seen, takes 我民 as simply = 人. So, Gan-kwŏ and others. This avoids the necessity of supposing any special references to events in the history of the House of Chow; but the 我民 is special. We cannot take it here otherwise than in the prec. par. The translation I have given involves such references, tho' we cannot say what events they were which the speaker had in his mind. Indeed, we might translate in the future tense, instead of the present complete as I have done; and in the last portion of the par., 一越小大，云云,—the speaker passes from his own people to speak of the subject with relation to all States great and small. 酒惟行，酒惟辜,—'intemperance is their conduct, intemperance is their guilt.'

[Choo He gives a view of the meaning of 天降命 and 天降威, in which I am not able to concur, but it is worthy to be preserved, and made current beyond the sphere of China. He says:—'Nan-heen (張南軒; a critic of the Sung dynasty, contemporary with Choo He), in his treatise upon this Book, has brought out the meaning of the two phrases 天降命，天降威, much better than any of the critics in the many centuries before him; and here I transcribe the whole of his remarks:—"Strong drink is a thing intended to be used in offering sacrifices and in entertaining guests:—such employment of it is what Heaven has prescribed. But men by their abuse of such drink come to lose their virtue and destroy their persons:—such employment of it is what Heaven has annexed its terrors to. The Buddhists, hating the use of things where Heaven sends down its terrors, put away as well the use of them which Heaven has prescribed. It is not so with us of the Learned (*i.e.*, the Orthodox) school;—we only put away the use of things to which Heaven has annexed its terrors, and the use of them of which it approves remains as a matter of course.

"For instance, in the use of meats and drinks, there is such a thing as wildly abusing and destroying the creatures of Heaven. The Buddhists, disliking this, confine themselves to a vegetable diet, while we only abjure the wild abuse and destruction. In the use of clothes, again, there is such a thing as wasteful extravagance. The Buddhists, disliking this, will have no clothes but those of a dark and sad colour, while we only condemn the extravagance. They, further, through dislike of criminal connection between the sexes, would abolish the relation between husband and wife, while we only denounce the criminal connection.

"The Buddhists, disliking *the excesses to which* the *evil* desires of men *lead*, would put away, along with them, the actions which are in accordance with the justice of Heavenly principles, while we, the orthodox, put away the *evil* desires of men, and what are called Heavenly principles are *the more* brightly seen. Suppose the case of a stream of water.—The Buddhists, through dislike of its being foul with mud, proceed to dam it up with earth. They do not consider that when the earth has dammed up the stream, the supply of water will all be cut off. It is not so with us, the orthodox. We seek only to cleanse away the mud and sand, so that the pure clear water may be available for use. This is the difference between the Buddhists and the Learned school."' (南軒酒誥一段，解天降命天降威處，誠千百年儒者所不及，今備載其說曰，酒之爲物，本以奉祭祀，供賓客，此卽天之降命也，而人以酒之故，至於失德喪身，卽天之降威也，釋氏本惡天之降威者，乃併與天之降命者去之，吾儒則不然，去其降威者而已，降威者去，而降命者自在，如飲食而至於暴殄天物，釋氏惡之，必欲食蔬茹，吾儒則不至於暴殄而已，衣服而至於窮極奢侈，釋氏惡之，必欲衣壞色之衣，吾儒則去其奢侈而已，至於惡淫厭而絶夫婦，吾儒則去其淫厭而已，釋氏本惡人欲，併與天理之公者去之，吾儒去人欲，所謂天理者昭然矣，譬如水焉，釋氏惡其泥沙之濁，而窒之以土，不知土既窒，則無水可飲矣，吾儒不然，澄其泥沙，而水之清者可酌，此儒釋之分也。)

Apart from the interpretation of the disputed phrases in the text, the contrast here drawn between Buddhism and Chinese orthodoxy is interesting. It will, perhaps, suggest to the reader the words of the apostle Paul, about 'forbidding to marry, and commanding to abstain from meats, which God hath created to be received with thanksgiving.' It may remind him also of the controversies in the West about the subjects of vegetarianism, and total abstinence from all spirituous liquors.]

四節 文王誥教小子、有正有事、無彝酒、越庶國飲惟祀、德將無醉。○五節 惟曰、我民迪小子惟土物愛、厥心臧、聰聽祖考之彝訓、越小大德、小

4 'King Wăn admonished and instructed the young and all who were charged with office and in employment, that they should not ordinarily use spirits. Throughout all his States, he required that they should be drunk only on occasion of sacrifices, and then that virtue should preside so that there might be no drunkenness. He said,
5 "Let my people teach their young men that they are to love only the productions of the ground, for so will their hearts be good. Let *the youth also* hearken diligently to the constant lessons of their fathers. Let them look at virtuous actions whether great or small in the same light."

Pp. 4, 5. *Further instructions of king Wăn on the use of spirits, showing his anxiety especially that the young should be kept from the habit of drinking them, and trained to virtuous industry.* In par. 2 we have the opinion of Wăn that spirits were intended to be used only at sacrifices, their strong and fragrant odour being acceptable to the spirits worshipped (蓋藉以薦馨香;—see the 日講, *in loc.*); here it would appear that he also permitted the use of them by the worshippers *after the sacrifices*, only requiring that they should not go to excess.

4. 小子,有正,有事,—小子=少子之稱,'小子 is the appellation of young people.' Ts'ae observes that such are more readily swayed by impulses and led away by strong drink, and therefore king Wăn addressed himself specially to them. But does this paragraph speak of the young only? Kʻang Shing thinks so, and explains 有正有事 as descriptive of 小子:—'the young who have their superiors and their duties.' His language is:—正,長也,小子有長上之人,有服勞之事,常酒則必慢上,而廢事,故戒令毋然. It would simplify this par., if we could consider it all occupied with the duty of the young, but Shing's explanation of 有正,有事 is too forced, and contrary moreover to the analogy of other passages in the Book;—see particularly 有正 in par. 7. I must take 有正, therefore, with Ts'ae, as=有官可守者, and 有事 as=有職業者. 無彝酒=毋常於酒, 'that they should not be always (ordinarily) at wine.' 飲惟祀=其飲惟於祭祀之時, 'their drinking should only be at times of sacrificing.' Compare 祀茲酒 in par. 2. The text is a relaxation or extension of the rule in regard to the use of spirits, which would flow from the former statement. 德將無醉,—將 is here=節, 'to regulate,' 'to keep in order.' We do not find this meaning of the character in the dictionary.

5. 惟曰,—we must suppose 文王 as the subject of 曰. Some think differently. Woo Chʻing, for instance, says that here king Woo delivers to K'ang-shuh the words which he should go and announce to the people of Mei, = 'When you now proceed to your State, you ought to say,' &c. (今汝之往,惟當言,曰). But this is inadmissible. 迪=訓導, 'to instruct and lead,' 'to train.' 厥心臧,—臧=善, 'good.' Ts'ae says:—'When they toil at their sowing and reaping, and labour on their fields, desiring nothing beyond, then what they keep in their minds will be correct, and their goodness will grow from day to day.'

Wăn's idea was that if the young were trained to industrious habits, they would not be likely

子惟一。○妹土、(六節)嗣爾股肱、純其藝黍稷、奔走事厥考厥長、肇牽車牛遠服賈、用孝養厥父母、厥父母慶、自洗腆致用酒。○庶士(七節)有正、越庶伯君子、其爾典聽朕

6 '*Ye people of* the land of Mei, if you can employ your limbs, largely cultivating your millet, and hastening about in the service of your fathers and elders; and if with your carts and oxen you traffic to a distance, that you may thereby filially minister to your parents:—then, when your parents are happy, you may set forth your spirits clear and strong, and use them.

7 'Hearken constantly to my instructions, all ye *high* officers, ye assistants, and all ye noble chiefs:—when you have largely done

to fall a prey to intemperance. The fact sung by our children in the words,

'Satan finds some mischief still
For idle hands to do,'

was held in substance by him. 聰聽—'to give a ready ear to.' 小大德小子惟一,—不可以謹酒爲小德,小德大德,小子惟一視之,可也, 'Let them not look on watchfulness in the use of spirits as a small virtue. The young should look in the same way on what are called great virtues and small virtues, equally observing them.' Gan-kwŏ takes the clause difftly, but not so well. Këang Shing takes it as declarative that the young of king Wăn's States became equally observant of great virtues and small;—but neither can I agree with him.

Pp. 6, 7. *The duke of Chow, in the name of king Ching, addresses the people and officers of Mei directly, and warns them against using spirits excepting in certain specified cases.* P. 6 is addressed to the people. They might drink spirits after having toiled for their parents and done all their duty for them. Both this par. and the next must be taken as addressed directly by the speaker to the people of Mei. Woo Ch'ing and others try to put them into the mouth of Fung, following the 惟曰 of the last par.; but such a construction is forced on the text. 嗣爾股肱,—'connect your arms and legs;' *i.e.*, employ your limbs, one after the other; let none of them be idle. 純其藝黍稷,—純—大; 純藝—'largely, or diligently, cultivate.' 黍 and 稷 are two species of millet, put by synecdoche for 五穀, 'the five kinds of grain;'—intimating perhaps that millet was cultivated more than the others in Mei. 肇牽車牛遠服賈,—肇—敏, 'to be diligent,' 'urgent.' 服—事; 服賈—'doing the business of traffic.' The whole—'if you are diligent in leading about your carts and oxen, pursuing to a distance the business of traffic.' 厥父母慶,—慶—喜慶, 'to be happy and complacent.' This is better than to take the term, with Gan-kwŏ and others, in the sense of 善, 'to approve,' as if the meaning were—'when your parents approve of your conduct.' 自洗腆致用酒,—洗 (*sëen*) and 腆 are both verbs, intimating operations to be performed upon the spirits, to make them fit for use, the effect of the former being to make them clear; of the latter, to make them strong. The 自—自此 the 'then' of the translation. Gaubil cannot be said to translate the clause at all. Medhurst has for it:—'then you may bathe and enjoy your abundance, and after that make use of wine.' The meaning of the whole par. is—that spirits might be used at family feasts. The 'Daily Explanation' expresses this clearly enough in its paraphrase of this clause:—自此,則洗以致其潔,腆以致其豐,以用

教、爾大克羞耇惟君、爾乃飲食醉飽、丕惟曰、爾克永觀省、作稽中德、爾尚克羞饋祀、爾乃自介用逸、兹乃允惟王正事之臣、兹亦惟天若元德、永不忘在王家。

your duty in ministering to your aged and serving your sovereign, you may eat and drink freely and to satiety. And to speak of greater things:—when you can maintain a constant watchful examination of yourselves, and your conduct is in accordance with correct virtue, then may you minister the offerings of sacrifice, and at the same time indulge yourselves in festivity. In such case you will indeed be ministers doing right service to your king, and Heaven likewise will approve your great virtue, so that you shall never be forgotten in the royal House.'"

酒於父母之前,而燕樂於家庭之內,其亦可矣. P. 7 is addressed to the ministers and officers of Mei. I suppose the 庶士,有正 and 庶伯君子 to correspond to the 庶士, 少正, and 御事 of par. 2. The 御事 are here styled 庶伯君子 by way of compliment. 爾大克至醉飽,—Gan-kwŏ supposed that this was addressed to Fung himself, and explains it by—汝大能進老成人之道,則爲君矣,如此,汝乃飲食醉飽之道,先戒羣吏以聽教,次戒康叔以君義. Ming-shing may well set this view aside as 'wide of the mark,' but it is not easy to arrive at the true meaning. The 惟君 is really unmanageable, and Ts'ae honestly confesses that he does not understand it. He explains 羞 by 養 and 羞耇 by 養老, which is a more likely interpretation than any other that I have seen. The translation is after the paraphrase in the 日講:—爾能盡誠致敬,大修養老奉君之禮,則勸酬之間,無非禮節,雖飲食醉飽,亦不爲過矣. 丕惟曰至用逸,—here again Gan-kwŏ strangely supposes that Fung is addressed, and 丕惟曰=我大惟教汝,曰. Kēang Shing supposes that the subject of 曰 is 君;—'when you can 羞耇,惟君, then your prince will say,' &c. This view also is unsatisfactory.

I have taken, with Ts'ae, 丕惟曰 as=以事之大者而言. 作稽中德,—稽=合, 'accordant with;' 中德 is 'virtue exactly correct, without inclination or deflection.' 爾尙克羞饋祀,—尙=庶幾, 'perhaps;' but more is meant than meets the ear. The king politely indicates by the character his full conviction that the officers, being such as he described, would be acceptable worshippers. 羞 is here =進. 爾乃自介用逸,—介=助, 'to assist.' The sacrifice to the spirits is represented as the great or chief ceremony; the subsequent festive indulgence by those who have taken part in it is a subsidiary ceremony (享神爲正,而我後飲,是副之也;—this is the very pithy gloss of a 朱養醇, one of the five critics at the end of the long list of authorities quoted in Yung-ching's

○[八節]王曰、封、我西土棐徂邦君御事小子、尚克用文王教、不腆于酒、故我至于今、克受殷之命。○[九節]王曰、封、我聞惟曰、在昔殷先哲王、迪畏天顯小民、經德秉哲、自成湯咸至于帝乙、成王畏

8 II. "The king says, 'O Fung, in our western regions, the princes of States, the managers of affairs, and the youths, who in former days assisted *our ancestor*, were able to obey the lessons of king Wăn, and indulge in no excess of spirits; and so it is that I have now received the appointment which belonged to Yin.'"

9 "The king says, 'O Fung, I have heard it said that formerly the first wise sovereign of Yin manifested a reverential awe of the bright principles of Heaven, and of the lower people, steadfast in his virtue, and holding fast his wisdom. From him, T'ang the Successful, down to the emperor Yih, the sovereigns all completed

Shoo, whose age the editors say they have been unable to ascertain). 正事之臣,—Woo Ch'ing takes this as = 有正有事之臣, with reference to par. 4; but the context makes it more natural to take the phrase as = 'ministers doing right service.' 天若元德,—若 = 順, 'to accord with,' equivalent to 'to approve.' The critics all call attention to the various relaxations of Wăn's original rule, that spirits should be used only for sacrifices. They say that we have in them an instance of prohibition by permission (不禁之禁). Soo Tung-po says:—'Spirits are what men will not do without. To prohibit them and secure a total abstinence from them is beyond the power even of the sages. Here, therefore, we have warnings on the evils of drunkenness in the abuse of them, and the joy that is found in the virtuous use of them is set forth;—such is the way in which the sages lay their prohibitions upon men' (see the 集說).

Ch. II. Pp. 8—17. THE KING, ADDRESSING FUNG DIRECTLY, SHOWS HIM THE CONSEQUENCES OF TEMPERANCE AND INTEMPERANCE RESPECTIVELY, IN THE FORTUNES OF THEIR OWN HOUSE, AND OF THE DYNASTY OF YIN; AND REQUIRES HIM TO ILLUSTRATE, INCULCATE, AND ENFORCE HIS LESSONS IN MEI. 8. *How the fortunes of Chow had risen by obedience to the lessons of king Wăn.* 我西土至小子,—the 棐徂 make this passage very perplexing. 棐 is taken as = 輔, 'to assist,' and 徂 = 往, 'gone by,' 'of the time past.' The two characters are best joined as descriptive of the parties immediately enumerated,—as in the translation. Gan-kwŏ and Lin Che-k'e suppose that 文王 is the nominative to 棐, which then governs 邦君, &c—我文王在西土, 輔訓往日國君, 云云. This is very unnatural. 尚 = 庶幾, as in the last par. The peculiarity of its use here is that it is all historical. 9, 10. *The example of various virtue, and especially of temperance, afforded in the prosperous times of the Yin dynasty.* 我聞惟曰,—Ying-tă gives for this—我聞於古,所聞惟曰. 迪畏天顯小民,—'walked in the fear of Heaven and of the people.' Compare the 'T'ae-këă,' Pt. iii., p. 1. 自成王咸至于帝乙,—咸, as it now stands, = 徧, 'throughout.' Some would place it after 乙, in which position it would = 'all.' Yih was the father

書經

相、惟御事厥棐有恭、不敢自暇自逸、矧曰其敢崇飲。○越^{十節}在外服、侯甸男衛邦伯、越在內服、百僚庶尹、惟亞惟服宗工、越百姓里居、罔敢湎于酒、不惟不敢、亦不暇、惟助成王德顯、越尹

their royal virtues, and revered their chief ministers, so that their managers of affairs respectfully discharged their helping duties, and dared not to allow themselves in idleness and pleasure;—how much
10 less would they dare to indulge in drinking! Moreover, in the exterior domains, the princes of the States of the How, Teen, Nan and Wei, with their chiefs; and in the interior domain, all the various officers, the directors of the several departments, the inferior officers and employés, and the Heads of great Houses, with the men of honoured name living in retirement, all eschewed indulgence in spirits. Not only did they not dare to indulge in them, but they had not leisure, being occupied with helping to complete their king's virtue and make it more distinguished, and helping the directors of affairs reverently to attend to the service of the sovereign.

of the tyrant Show, himself the 27th emperor of the dynasty. We may admit with Mencius, II., Pt. I., i., 8, that between T'ang and Woo-ting, the 20th of the line, there were six or seven good sovereigns;—the statement in the text is a grand exaggeration. 成王畏相＝成就君德、而無隕越之憂、敬畏賢相、而無驕肆之失. 厥棐有恭,—'in their helping had reverence.' The 有恭 is best understood by reference to Mencius, IV., i. 13,—責難於君謂之恭. 崇飲,—崇＝尙, 'to value,'＝'to indulge in.' 10. 外服, 內服,—by the 內服 we are to understand, of course, the 王畿, or 'imperial domain.' It would appear that an arrangement of the 'domains,' akin to that which obtained under the Chow dynasty, had come, during the dynasty of Yin to supersede the older one introduced by Yu;—see the figure on page 149. By 侯, 甸, 男, 衞, we are to understand the princes of those domains; and by 邦伯 the presidents of those princes (諸侯之長伯). 百僚＝百官之僚屬,—'all the officers belonging to the various departments.' 庶尹＝庶官之長 what are elsewhere called the 正 'the Heads of the various departments.' 惟亞,—亞＝次大夫, 'officers of the second degree.' 惟服,—服＝奔走服事之人, 'petty officers who had to run about discharging their duties.' 宗工＝尊官, 'honoured officers.' Woo Ch'ing describes them as 王朝公卿大夫, 及王子弟食采邑, 爲大宗者. This is probably correct, and I have translated—'Heads of great Houses.' I take 百姓里居 together, and understand 百官 by

人祇辟。○我聞亦惟曰、在今後嗣王酣身、厥命罔顯于民、祇保越怨不易、誕惟厥縱淫泆于非彝、用燕喪威儀、民罔不衋傷心、惟荒腆于酒、不惟自息乃逸、厥心疾狠、不克畏死、辜在商邑、越

11 'I have heard it said likewise, that in these times the last successor of those kings was addicted to drink, so that no charges came from him brightly before the people, and he was reverently and unchangingly bent on doing and cherishing what provoked resentment. Greatly abandoned to extraordinary lewdness and dissipation, for pleasure's sake he ruined all his majesty. The people were all sorely grieved and wounded in heart, but he gave himself wildly up to spirits, not thinking of ceasing, but continuing his excess, till his mind was frenzied, and he had no fear of death. His crimes accumulated in the city of Shang, and though the extinction of the dynasty

百姓. Officers of distinguished name, who had retired because of age from the public service, are intended. 助成王德顯=助成人君之德, 而使之益顯. The 助 extends also to the next clause, so that it=亦助尹人, 使之祇敬君事, 而不少怠. Other explanations of this clause have been proposed, but it does not seem worth while to discuss them. 尹人=御事, above.

11. *The drunkennness of Show, and its issues.* The 在今後嗣王, of course, is Show. 酣 is defined by 樂酒, 'being fond of strong drink.' It is often used to denote a state short of gross intoxication, but we are not to think of that modified signification here. Woo Ch'ing explains 酣身 by 酣酒於身. We might translate it literally—'was a drunken body.' 厥命至不易,—the translation of this part is after Gan-kwŏ and Ts'ae, the latter of whom explains:—昏迷於政, 命令不著於民, 其所祇保者, 惟在於作怨之事, 不肯悛改. Woo Ch'ing construes difftly, but it seems to me with more constraint of the text:—其命令之出, 無能明於民之當祇保, 及民怨之不易弭, 'When he issued his commands, he showed that he did not understand how he ought to reverence and cherish the people, and when they resented his conduct, he would not change or stop it.' 誕惟至威儀,—于非彝=于非法, our 'extraordinary.' Ts'ae refers in illustration to 作奇技淫巧, 以悅婦人, in the 'Great Speech,' Pt. iii., p. 3;—see the account of Show's debaucheries on pp. 269,270. 民罔至畏死,—衋=痛, 'to be grieved,' 'to feel sad and sore.' The 惟 in 不惟自息=思, 'to think of;' and the 乃, which follows,=仍. Keang Shing says well:—不思自止息, 仍

書經

殷國滅無罹、弗惟德馨香祀、登聞于天、誕惟民怨、庶群自酒、腥聞在上、故天降喪于殷、罔愛于殷、惟逸、天非虐、惟民自速辜。○王曰、封、予不惟若茲多誥、古人有言曰、人無於水監、當於 十二節

of Yin *was imminent*, this gave him no concern, and he wrought not that any sacrifices of fragrant virtue might ascend to heaven. The rank odour of the people's resentments, and the drunkenness of his herds of creatures, went loudly up on high, so that Heaven sent down ruin on Yin and showed no love for Yin,—because of such excesses. There is not any cruel oppression of Heaven; people themselves accelerate their guilt, *and its punishment*.'"

12 "The king says, 'O Fung, I have no pleasure in making you this long announcement; but the ancients have said, "Let not men look *only* into water; let them look into the glass of *other* people."

然淫泆,乃之言仍也. 疾狠='angrily wrangled.' 辜在至于天,—商邑 probably means the capital of Show, and 殷國='the dynasty of Yin.' 罹=憂, 'sorrowful.' In 弗惟, 惟=思,—as in 不惟, above. 誕惟至在上,—the 誕惟, like the same characters in the previous part of the par., indicate that what follows was attributable to Show. 自酒='abandoning themselves to drink.' 惟逸=以紂淫泆故, 'because of these excesses of Show.' There is a difficulty with the concluding clauses. All through the par., the speaker has been dilating on the wickedness of Show, and suddenly it seems to be said, at the end, that the ruin of the dynasty was the work of 'the people.' Ts'ae would interpret 民 of Show and his ministers, according to the analogy of 先民 in 'The Instructions of E,' p. 5. Këang Shing takes 民, as=冥, and says—大降喪亡,天非虐也,惟冥冥昏亂,自召辜爾. Other methods to lighten the difficulty have been tried. In the translation, I take 民 as=人, 'men,' 'people' generally.

12. *How the House of Chow should see its duty in the history of Yin.* The meaning of 予不惟若此多誥 is probably what appears in the translation. Ts'ae and Këang Shing bring it out by taking 惟=徒, 'vainly,' *i.e.*, merely for the sake of talking. The 'Daily Explanation' puts it—予豈好爲是多誥哉. 古人有言,云云,—in illustration of this saying, Këang Shing quotes, aptly enough, a fragment of the lost Book of Shang which was called 'The Punitive Expeditions of T'ang' (湯征):—湯曰,人視水見形,視民知治不. 我其可不大監撫于時,—this is to be understood interrogatively. Gan-kwŏ took 撫=撫安, in which he is correctly followed by Ts'ae, whose expansion of the whole is very lucid:—我其可不以殷民之失爲大監戒,以撫安斯時乎. This is much better than, with Këang Shing, to take 撫=循, 'to follow,' 'to accord

民監、今惟殷墜厥命、我其可不大監撫于時。○ 十三節 予惟曰、汝劼毖殷獻臣、侯甸男衞、矧太史友、內史友、越獻臣百宗工、矧惟爾事、服休、

Now that Yin has lost its appointment, ought we not to look much to it as our glass, *and learn* how to secure the repose of our time?

13 'I say to you,—Strenuously warn the worthy ministers of Yin, and *the princes in* the How, the Teen, the Nan, and Wei domains; and still more, your friends, the great Recorder and the Recorder of the interior, and all your worthy ministers, the Heads of great Houses; and still more, those whom you serve—with whom you calmly converse, and who carry out your measures; and still more, those

with,' and 時一是, referring to the good ways of the sovereigns of Yin before Show. His words are:—我其可不監于是, 撫于是乎, 監, 監紂也, 撫, 循也, 謂循商先王之道也, 時是也, 指謂殷.

P. 13. *Fung is required to take home to himself the lessons about temperance, and to enjoin them on the princes and officers in his jurisdiction.* 汝劼至男衞—劼—用力, 'strenuously.' 獻臣—賢臣. These were good ministers of the former dynasty, who were still retained in their former offices under Fung. As 孟侯, or 'Head of the princes,' his authority extended also over the princes of the portions of the domains that were under his jurisdiction. He should strenuously warn them,—on the subject, of course, of abstaining from intemperance. 太史友, 內史友,—the duties of the 太史 and 內史, with other officers of the same department, are described in the Chow Le, Bk. XXVI., 春官, 宗伯, 第三之十. They were very honourable and extensive, and such as brought them into frequent contact and consultation with the 太宰 or prime minister ('grand administrateur general.' Biot). It is said in general that the 太史 had the management of what Biot calls 'the six constitutions (六典), the eight regulations (八法), and the eight statutes (八則).' Those six constitutions were the various departments of the administration,—of rule, of instruction, of ceremonies, of prescripts, of punishments, and of business; the regulations and statutes embraced all connected with the working of those departments. The 內史 again had the management of 'the eight powers or prerogatives' of the emperor (掌八柄之法). These duties branched off into a great variety of minor functions. The 史 kept all the records which were to be appealed to in connection with them, so that we may consider them as having been confidential secretaries and advisers of the prime minister. Biot calls the 太史, 'le grand annaliste,' and 內史, 'l'annaliste de l'interieur.' I prefer to call them 'recorders,' as being a more general term. The various princes had their 'grand Recorder,' but the 'Recorder of the interior' belonged, it is maintained, only to the imperial court; and the individual mentioned in the text is supposed, therefore, to have been the old minister of the court of Shang, now superseded under the new dynasty and living in Wei. However this may be, it is said that the two Recorders were 'friends' of Fung. As men of research and ability and general good character, he would so cherish them.

獻(=賢)臣, 百宗工,—we must suppose these, in distinction from the 獻臣 above, to be those appointed under the existing dynasty. Or, acc. to the view of Woo Ch'ing, we may suppose that they were good men, Heads of influential families, who were not in office, and are called 臣, in the same way as

書經

服采、矧惟若疇、圻父薄違、農父若保、宏父定辟、矧汝剛制于酒。○厥(十四節)或誥曰、群飲、汝勿佚、盡執拘以歸于

who are, as it were, your mates,—your minister of War, who deals with the rebellious, your minister of Agriculture, who is like a protector *to the people*, and your minister of Works, who settles the boundaries; and above all, do you sternly keep yourself from drink.

14 'If you are told that there are companies who drink together, do not fail to apprehend them all, and send them here to Chow, where I may put them to death.

every individual in the empire is supposed to be a 臣 of the sovereign. 爾事, 服休, 服采,—the translation here follows the view of Ts'ae. He supports his explanation of 事 by 'to serve,' from the passage of Mencius, V., Pt. II., vii., 4, where Tsze-sze is introduced as saying, 古之人有言曰, 事之云乎, 豈曰友之云乎, 'The ancients have said, "The scholar (or virtuous officer) should be served;"—how should they have merely said, "He should be made a friend of?"' This view of 事 being adopted, 服休=坐而論道之臣, 'ministers who sit (by their prince) and discourse to him about principles,' and 服采=起而作事之臣, 'ministers who rise and perform the business (of their prince).' 服休 is 'to serve in *hours of* ease;' 服采, 'to serve in active business.' I have hesitated between this view, and that given by Woo Ch'ing:—爾事=服事於爾者, 大夫也, 'those who serve you,—your great officers;' 服休=職之優閑者, 'those whose offices were comparatively easy, and allowed of leisure;' 服采=職之繁劇者, 'those whose offices were more bustling and troublesome.' Gan-kwŏ took a difft. view which is quite inadmissible. He says:—汝身事, 服行美道, 服事治民, making Fung himself, in the discharge of his duties, the subject. This cannot be right. K'ang-shing had still another view, in which he is followed by Këang Shing, acc. to which the whole = 'the employés,—those who are near to you in festivals and leisure, and those who are near at audiences and sacrifices' (汝之執事, 服職于燕息, 及朝祭之臣.) This diversity of opinion serves to show how uncertain the meaning is. 圻父, 'the controller of boundaries,'=司馬, 'the minister of War.' This meaning is determined by the 1st ode in the 4th Book of the She King, Part ii., where it is said—祈(=圻)父, 予王之爪牙. This being determined, it follows that 農父=司徒, 'the minister of Instruction;' and 宏父=司空, 'the minister of Works.' These were the 'three high nobles' (三卿), belonging to the court of one of the princes. They were the highest in authority, and might be considered as their prince's 'mates' (疇匹). 薄 (read *pŏh*)=迫. 薄違=迫逐違命者. The minister of Instruction is called 若保, 'the harmonious preserver.' The promotion of agriculture, which supplies the staff of life, being within his province, he is thus denominated. The minister of Works is called 定辟, 'the settler of rules,' *i.e.*, the decider of all questions about the settlements and tenements of the people. Këang Shing would take 辟 in the sense of 君, which does not seem at all applicable here. 剛制于酒=剛果用力自制酒.

Pp. 14—16. *By what rules obedience to the king's injunctions against the use of spirits were to be enforced.* 14. 汝勿佚,—佚=失, 'to fail.' The punishment here threatened is so far beyond the crime, that the critics fall upon various devices to explain it, or to mitigate the

周、予其殺。○又十五節惟殷之迪諸臣惟工、乃湎于酒、勿庸殺之、姑惟教之。○有十六節斯明享、乃不用我教辭、惟我一人弗恤、弗蠲乃事、時同于殺。○王十七節曰、封、汝典聽朕毖、勿辯乃司、民湎于酒。

15 'As to the ministers and officers of Yin, who have been led to
it, and been addicted to drink, it is not necessary to put them to death;
16 —let them be taught for a time. If they keep these *lessons*, I will
give them bright distinction. If you disregard my lessons, then
I, the one man, will show you no pity. As you cannot cleanse your
way, you shall be classed with those who are to be put to death.'"
17 "The king says, 'O Fung, give constant heed to my admonitions. If you do not manage right your officers, the people will continue lost in drink.'"

force of the language. First, the coming together in companies to drink is supposed to carry with it the design of their assembling, as being not merely to drink, but, under the cloak of that, to plot against the govt. Second, the 其 in 予其殺 is taken to indicate uncertainty. The king would examine for himself into their guilt, and according as he found they had treasonable designs would put them to death. If they really only met to drink, he would inflict on them some lighter penalty. I have allowed the second remark by using the '*may*' in the translation. The former remark may also be correct. If it be not so, we cannot account for the difference of spirit between this and the two next paragraphs. 15. 又惟殷之迪諸臣惟工=今殷之諸百工,其素爲商紂導引爲惡者. Këang Shing says that 惟 in 惟工 is superfluous. We hardly know what to do with it. 16. 有斯明享=商之諸臣果能遵我教訓之辭,存之于心而不忘,我則顯揚之,而享之以爵位,—as in the translation. This is forcing a meaning out of the words. The most that can be said for it is, that it is more likely than any other construction which has been proposed. K'ang-shing took 斯 as=析, which Këang Shing adopts. He has:—又分析其明用我教者,獻之,古者諸侯有獻士于天子之制. 乃不用,云云,—the king here turns to the officers of Yin who should persist obstinately in their drunkenness and other evil ways, and addresses them directly. 弗蠲乃事,=不能潔汝舊染之汙. 時=是 or 於是.

P. 17. *Concluding admonition to Fung.* 勿=不; it is not imperative. 辯=治, 'to rule.' Fung was specially to direct his efforts to discountenance drunkenness in the officers,—the higher classes. If he could not succeed with them, his efforts with the lower classes would be vain.

THE BOOKS OF CHOW.

BOOK XI. THE TIMBER OF THE TSZE TREE.

梓材

王曰、一節 封、以厥庶民暨厥臣、達大家、以厥臣達王、惟邦君。

1 I. "The king says, 'O Fung, to have a good understanding with the multitudes of his people, and his ministers *on the one hand*, and with the great families *on the other*; and *again* to have the same with all the subjects *under his charge* and with the sovereign:—is the part of the prince of a State.

THE NAME OF THE BOOK.—梓材, 'The Timber of the Tsze tree.' Though it does not affect our understanding of the Book, I am sorry that I cannot give the proper botanical name of the Tsze. It is described as allied to the Ts'ew (楸), which has 'the leaves of a cypress and the trunk of a fir' (柏葉, 松身). It was esteemed as the most valuable for making articles of furniture, and for the carver's art. The phrase,—'the timber, or materials, of the Tsze,' occurs in par. 4, and was thence assumed to designate the Book, intimating apparently that the administrator of government ought to give himself to his duties skilfully and thoroughly, as the cabinet-maker deals with his materials. The cultivation of a field and the building of a house are spoken of in the same paragraph; and either of these things might have been used as the name instead of the phrase which it pleased the fancy of the compiler to adopt. The Book is found in both the texts.

CONTENTS. The Book is sadly wanting in unity. The 1st par. is directly addressed to Fung, and we may suppose that the three which follow were so also. He is admonished of his duty to promote a good understanding between the various classes in his State, and between them all and the sovereign; and that, in order to this, his rule must be gentle, eschewing the use of punishments. The interpretation, however, is anything but certain. The remaining paragraphs are of a difft. character. They are not the charges of the emperor, insisting with a prince upon his duties, but the admonitions of a minister loyally and affectionately cautioning his sovereign, and praying for the prosperity of his reign. They would be appropriate as addressed to king Ching by the duke of Chow, or the duke of Shaou. We might also suppose them the response of Fung; but the text gives no intimation of a new speaker being introduced. The whole Book is very unsatisfactory, and it is a translator's greatest comfort that it is short.

Ch. I. Pp. 1—4. *How the prince of a State is a connecting link between all the classes of his people, and between his people and the emperor.* 達=通, 'to reach to,' 'to effect an intercommunication.' By 大家 we are to understand what Mencius, IV., Bk. I., vi., calls 巨室, 'the great Houses,' saying that 'the administration of govt. is not difficult, but lies in not offending the great Families, for whom they affect will be affected by all the State.' It is observed in the 'Complete Digest,' that the force of the 達 is to show how the conduct of the ruler draws forth the approval of all parties, so that there is an uninterrupted flow of their good feeling towards him, and we are not to

○汝若恆越曰、我有師師、司徒、司馬、司空、尹旅、曰、予罔厲殺人、亦厥君先敬勞、肆徂厥敬勞、肆往姦宄殺 二節

2 'If you regularly in giving out your orders say, "My instructors whom I am to follow, my minister of Instruction, my minister of War, and my minister of Works; my Heads of departments, and all ye, my officers, I will on no account with oppressions put men to death;"———. Let the prince also set the example of respecting and encouraging the people, and these will proceed to respect and encourage them. Let him go on in dealing with those who have been traitors and villains, murderers and harbourers of criminals,

take it as intimating that the ruler brings the higher and lower classes into intimacy and good feeling with one another' (達者吾之行事與其情兩相通徹,而無暌阻,非使上下相通之謂). The first 厥臣 is descriptive of the ministers and officers of the State, and those not filling the highest offices, which would for the most part be occupied by the Heads or scions of the great families. The second 厥臣 is descriptive of all the people of the State, the official classes and the unofficial, as being equally the subjects of the sovereign (王) or emperor.

Such is the view of the par. that appears to be given by Ts'ae. Lin Che-k'e took the same, only understanding the 達 of bringing the various classes mentioned into good and harmonious relation with one another. Gan-kwŏ's view was different. He paraphrases:—言當用其衆人之賢者,與其小臣之良者,以通達卿大夫及都家之政於國,信用其臣以通王教於民,言通民事於國,通王教於民,惟乃國君之道. Of this I can make little or nothing. Ch'ing K'ang-shing had still another view which deserves to be noticed only for its singularity. He seems to have read the last clause—以厥臣達王暨邦君; and then by 王 he understood 二王之後, 'the descendants of the emperors of the two previous dynasties;' and by 邦君, the princes of the various States within Fung's jurisdiction, as 孟侯. Adopting this strange view, Këang Shing says—以臣民達大家,則聯上下之情,以臣達王與邦君,則聯邦交之誼.

P. 2. *The prince of a State must inculcate on his ministers, and exemplify himself, leniency in dealing with criminals.* Ts'ae honestly acknowledges that the most of this par. is unintelligible to him, and he does not attempt any paraphrase of it. In the translation, I have followed the 'Daily Explanation.' The meaning given is more likely than any other which it has been attempted to put upon the text;—this is the most that can be said for it. 汝若至殺人,—越 is taken in the sense of 發 or 發令, 'to give forth orders.' This meaning of the term is given in the Dict. (=揚), and supported by examples from the 國語. 師師—相師爲善之意, 'instructors whom I am to make my model:'—comp. the same phrase in Pt. IV., Bk. XI., p. 2; *et al.* The three ministers immediately mentioned are the instructors intended. 尹=正官之長, 'the Heads of the various official departments;' and 旅=衆,—that is, 衆士, 'the whole body of officers.' The 曰 which follows is superfluous, and the sentence is left incomplete. The 'Daily Explanation' supplements it by—'and you all ought to cherish the same regard for the lives of the people' (汝咸當仰體吾好生之心). The older interpreters, followed by Këang Shing and many others, connect 汝若恆越曰,我有

人歷人宥、肆亦見厥君事、戕敗人宥。○王(三節)啟監、厥亂爲民、曰無胥戕、無胥虐、至于敬寡、至于屬婦、合由以

to exercise pardon, and these, when they observe the prince's conduct, will likewise pardon those who have assaulted others
3 and injured their property. When sovereigns appointed inspectors, they did so in order to the government of the people, and said to them, "Do not give way to violence or oppression; and go on to show reverence for the weak, and find connexions for *destitute* women. Your protection of the people must proceed in this way to cherish

師師 with the prec. par., giving it substantially this meaning,—'Do you accord (若=順) with this regular rule for your duty, and (越=于是) then say to yourself, "I have this law which I am to observe."' Then commences with them a new par., and 司徒, &c., form the subject of the second 曰. On this construction the two 曰 are accounted for; but to put 予罔厲殺人 in the mouths of all the officers is inadmissible. 亦厥君先敬勞, 肆徂厥敬勞,—勞, in the 3d tone, is taken in the sense of 慰, 'to comfort,' 'to encourage.' The 'respecting' the people (we must understand 民 or 其民 under the govt. of 敬勞) is to be taken with reference to the ruler's eschewing the use of punishments rather than run the risk of putting any to death unjustly, 'with oppressions.' 肆=遂, 'then,' 'thereupon. 徂=往, 'to go.' The subject of this verb is the ministers and officers above. Gan-kwŏ supposes the 君 to be the subject of 徂, as well as of the previous verbs:—'It is also the way of a ruler to take the initiative in respecting and encouraging the people; do you therefore, in going to rule this people, be careful to respect and encourage them.' Këang Shing takes 亦 as=掖=助, 'to assist,' and connects the clause with the preceding, thus:—'The ministers will say, "We will be cautious with you of putting men to death unjustly." Then they will help their prince to reverence and encourage the people as the thing of greatest importance.' 肆往姦, 至宄—the first of these clauses—肆往, 云云,—is descriptive of the ruler; and the second—肆亦見, 云云,—of his ministers. The former of the two 肆 is in the way, indeed, of this construction. The character introducing, immediately above, the subject of the ministers as distinguished from the ruler, and doing the same here in the second instance, we might have expected 亦往 instead of 肆往. This is a serious difficulty; but the view upon the whole harmonizes with the general scope of the paragraph, and enables us to explain the 亦見君事, to which both Gan-kwŏ and Këang Shing do great violence. 肆往姦宄殺人歷人宥=遂與往日爲姦宄殺人者, 罪人所經歷者, 今皆寬宥, 與之爲新. Ts'ae explains 歷人 by 罪人所過, 'those through whom offenders have passed,' meaning individuals who have connived at crime, and more or less aided and abetted it. 戕敗人 are individuals guilty of lighter offences than those mentioned above, whose cases should be summarily dealt with by his ministers and officers, without their being appealed to the ruler himself. We cannot suppose that this charge to Fung to pardon offenders—even murderers, was to be taken without qualification. He could only be required to note and act upon all mitigating circumstances in his punishment of crime.

P. 3. *The object of the emperors in delegating authority to princes and officers is the kindly and benevolent rule of the people.* 王啟監,—Ts'ae says that 監 has reference to the 'three Inspectors' appointed by king Woo to oversee Wookăng in his govt., and that the same title is given to Fung, as being appointed to a portion of the

容、王其效邦君越御事、厥命曷以、引養引恬、自古王若兹、監罔攸辟。○

them." And when the sovereigns gave their injunctions to the princes of States, and their managers of affairs, what was the charge? It was that they should lead *the people* to the enjoyment of plenty and peace. Such was the way of the kings from of old. An inspector is to eschew the use of punishments.'

same territory. It is very strange that he did not perceive that this view was inconsistent with his other view, that the speaker in this and the two preceding Books was king Woo and not the duke of Chow. Woo could not have spoken thus of what he had done himself. It is better, however, to take 監 as a general title, applicable to all princes—the 公, 侯, 伯, 子 and 男.—Such a use of it is found in the Chow Le, Bk. II., p. 94 (天官太宰),—乃施典于邦國, 而建其牧, 立其監, 云云. 厥亂爲民,—亂 = 治. The whole = 其治本爲民而已. 曰無胥至以容,—we must understand all this as the imperial charge to the princes invested with inspection and rule. The 胥 = 相, indeed, occasions some difficulty, which is best got over by understanding it of those princes and their ministers and people. This is the solution adopted by Lin Che-k'e from Wang Gan-shih (胥者謂君臣上下, 並爲戕虐之政也). Gan-kwŏ took the subject of 曰 to be the 'inspectors.'—Appointed for such a purpose, they ought to teach their people saying, 'Do not among yourselves,' &c. This is plainly inadmissible. 敬寡,—'respect the few,' *i.e.*, those who have few to help them. 屬 *(chuh)* 婦,—婦之窮獨者, 當使之有所歸, 而聯屬之, 'in the case of women reduced to straits and solitary, you ought to bring it about that they shall have those to whom they may turn, and find connexions for them.' This is forcing a meaning out of the 屬; but I do not see what better can be done while the text stands as it does. We must interpret one clause by the analogy of another, and 敬 being a verb in 敬寡, 屬 must be one here. The dict., with reference to this passage, defines 屬 by 恤, 'to pity;'—after Gan-kwŏ, who gives for the clause—存恤妾婦. I do not think, however, that Gan-kwŏ understood 屬 to mean 'to pity.' The sense in which he took this term appears in 妾婦, 'concubines,' = women attached to the proper wife, and inferior to her. He supplied the 存恤, as necessary to make sense of the clause. The 說文 quotes it as—至于嫡婦, 嫡 meaning 妊, 'pregnant.' The critics who adopt this reading suppose that the preceding 敬 ought to be 矜, to which they give the meaning of 鰥, 'widowers;'—but this is mere conjecture. 合由以容,—Ts'ae takes 合 as = 保合 and 容 as = 容蓄, understanding the whole as in the translation (又推而保合一國之民, 率由此道, 以相爲容蓄, 使各得其所焉). It would be hard to say that this is really the meaning; but it is preferable to Gan-kwŏ's exposition,—和合其教, 用大道以容之, 無令見冤枉. 王其效至末,—效 = 責效, 'to give charge to and require service from.' This is akin to the meaning of the character which the dict. defines by 勉. 厥命曷以 = 其命何以哉. 引養引恬,—this is the answer to the question. Ts'ae expands it by—亦惟欲其引掖斯民於生養安全之地而已. 監罔攸辟 = 監其無所用乎刑辟, 'an inspector should have nothing to do with the using of punishments.'

四節 惟曰、若稽田、旣勤敷菑、惟其陳修、爲厥疆畎、若作室家、旣勤垣墉、惟其塗塈茨、若作梓材、旣勤樸斲、惟其塗丹雘。五節 ○今王惟曰、先王旣勤用明德、懷爲夾、庶邦享、作兄弟方來、亦旣用明

4 "He says moreover, 'As in the management of a field, when the soil has all been laboriously turned up, they must proceed by orderly arrangement to make its boundaries and water-courses; as in building a house, after all the toil on its walls, they have to plaster and thatch it; as in working with the wood of the *tsze*, when the toil of the coarser and finer operations has been performed, they have to apply the paint of red and other colours'":——.

5 II. "Now let your Majesty say, 'The former kings diligently employed their illustrious virtue, and produced such attachment by their cherishing *of the princes*, that from all the States they brought offerings, and with brotherly affection they came from all quarters, and likewise showed their virtue illustrious.' Do you, O sovereign,

P. 4. *Fung is required to complete the good work which had been begun.* It will be seen that this paragraph is imperfect. We have the protasis of the sentence thrice repeated in various form, the apodosis being left to be supplied, in some such way as—'so must you, O Fung, proceed in raising in your State the superstructure of govt., of which the foundations have been laid.' 惟曰,—we may understand 王 as the subject of 曰. 稽田,—稽=治, 'to manage,' *i.e.*, to perform all the necessary operations on. 勤敷菑,—comp. Bk. VII., p. 11. 勤敷='toilfully and widely.' 若作室家,—these two characters—室家—are simply equivalent to the 室 in Bk. VII., p. 11, and = our 'house.' Ma Yung says that 'a low wall is called 垣, and a high one, 墉' (牆卑曰垣,高曰墉). 惟其塗塈茨,—'there have to be the clay, the facing plaster, and the thatch grass.' 梓材,—see on the name of the Book. 樸斲,—the first of these characters denotes the rough fashioning of the work, and the second the fine finish given to it (具粗曰樸,致巧曰斲). 雘 is a name given to the various colours used in painting articles of furniture. (采色之名). Wang Kăng-yay observes that 塗, 丹, and 雘 are all verbs, and that we are to understand them—塗之, 丹之, and 雘之, as in the case of 塗, 塈, 茨 above. It would seem that we should construe so, but it is difficult to determine the independent meaning of 塗. See the 讀書管見, *in loc.*

Ch. 5—8. These four paragraphs are evidently addressed not to a subject, but to the sovereign. Gan-kwŏ takes no notice of the difference in style between them and the preceding ones, and Ying-tă says expressly that the king goes on in them to complete his charges to Fung. This view now finds no advocates. The speaker was evidently some loyal minister of Chow. Këang Shing thinks that we have here the response of Fung to the various lessons which he had received. Ming-shing says that, having done with Fung, the duke of Chow now

德后式典集、庶邦丕享。○［六節］皇天既付中國民、越厥疆土于先王。○［七節］肆王惟德用、和懌先後迷民、用懌先王受命。○［八節］已若

use their statutes to attach *the princes*, and all the States will largely come with offerings.

6 "Great Heaven having given this Middle kingdom with its people
7 and territories to the former kings, do you, our present sovereign, employ your virtue, effecting a gentle harmony among the deluded people, leading and urging them on;—so *also* will you please the former kings, who received the appointment *from Heaven*.

turns to king Shing, and speaks some words of warning to him. We need not trouble ourselves with speculation on so uncertain and unimportant a matter.

P. 5. *How Wăn and Woo ruled the princes by the influence of their virtue, and future sovereigns must imitate their example.* 先王,—these 'former kings' can only be Wăn and Woo. What is said of the effects of their sway is much exaggerated. Had it been as the speaker says, there would not have been the troubles which disturbed the reign of king Ching. 懷爲來,—for this Gan-kwŏ gives—懷遠爲近, 'cherished the distant and made them near.' The meaning seems to be that by their kindly cherishing of the princes of States, Wăn and Woo gained them and made them a strength and defence to their govt. (以成來輔之勢). The last of Confucius' 'nine standard rules' for the govt. of the empire,—'the king's cherishing the princes of the States' (懷諸侯),—is traced to this expression. 作兄弟方來,—by 兄弟 Gan-kwŏ understood the princes who were of the imperial House, the uncles and brothers, &c., of the sovereign, in contradistinction from the princes of other surnames. Këang Shing adopts the same view, and extends it to princes related to the imperial House by affinity. It seems to me preferable to take 兄弟 as in the translation, like the 子來 in the quotation from the She King, Mencius, I., Pt. I., ii., 3. 后式典集,—后=君. We are to understand by the term king Ching, as the successor of Wăn and Woo. 式=用, 'to employ.' Another meaning of the term—'to imitate,'—would suit equally well. 典, 'statutes,' has reference to the ruling by virtue, whose influence has just been described. 集, 'to collect,'=to bring around, to attach.

Pp. 6, 7. *How the sovereign must attach the people by a mild rule.* These parr. are held to be the origin of Confucius' sixth standard rule of government,—'to treat the mass of the people kindly as children' (子庶民). 6. The whole of this is one sentence, and Choo He calls attention to it as an instance of the *long* sentences of the Shoo. 中國,—compare 中邦, 'Tribute of Yu,' Pt. ii., p. 15. 7. 肆 is taken as=今, 'now.' In the 附錄 there is an ingenious note by Ch'in Leih, contending that its proper meaning in such cases as this, at the commencement of clauses, is 故, 'therefore,' or 遂, 'and,' 'thereupon,' and not 今. 和懌先後迷民,—迷民, 'the deluded people;' meaning the people of the imperial domain of Yin chiefly, but also of other parts of the empire, who were reluctant to acknowledge the authority of the dynasty of Chow. 先,—'go before;' 後—'come after.' The meaning is that Ching should beset the people 'before and behind' with his virtue and kindness, so leading and urging them on. 用懌先王受命,—this implies that Wăn and Woo could take cognizance of the character and doings of their successor.

書經

茲監、惟曰、欲至于萬年、惟王子子孫孫永保民。

8 "Yes! make these things your study. I can but express my desire that for myriads of years your descendants may be ever the protectors of this people."

P. 8. *A loyal prayer for the permanency and prosperity of the dynasty.* 若茲監,—the 監 here is different from that in par. 8. Ts'ae conjectures that it was from the occurrence of the characters 若茲監 in that par. and this, that the compiler of this Book, not observing the differences of meaning and connection in the two passages, was led to edit the first and last portions as belonging to the same document.

THE BOOKS OF CHOW.

BOOK XII. THE ANNOUNCEMENT OF *THE DUKE OF* SHAOU.

召誥

惟二月既望、越六日乙未、王朝步自周、則至于豐。○惟

1 I. In the second month, on the day Yih-we, six days after the full moon, the king early in the morning proceeded from Chow, and

THE NAME OF THE BOOK.—召誥, 'The Announcement of *the duke of* Shaou.' Shaou was the name of a place within the imperial domain, corresponding to the present district of Hwan-k'euh (垣曲), in the small dep. of Këang (絳州), Shan-se. It was the appanage of Shih (奭), one of the ablest of the men who lent their aid to the establishment of the dynasty of Chow. He appears here as the 'Great-guardian' (太保) of king Ching; and we have met with him before in 'The Hounds of Leu,' and 'The Metal-bound Coffer.' He was one of 'the three dukes,' (三公), or highest officers of the dynasty, and is frequently styled 召公, the 'duke of Shaou.' He appears here in connection with one of the most important enterprizes of the duke of Chow, the building of the city of Lŏh (洛邑), as a new and central capital of the empire. King Woo had conceived the idea of such a city, but it was not carried fully into effect till the reign of his son;—see on the second paragraph below. In Lŏh the duke of Shaou composed the 'Announcement' which forms the subject-matter of this Book, and sent it by the hands of the duke of Chow to the young emperor. It might, perhaps, with more than equal propriety, have been styled 'The Instructions of *the duke of* Shaou' (召訓).

According to Sze-ma Ts'een, Shih belonged to the imperial House of Chow, and consequently had the surname Ke (姬). The historian, Hwang-p'oo Meih, says he was a son of king Wăn by a concubine (文王之庶子);—on what authority I cannot tell. King Woo appointed him to the principality of 'The Northern Yen' (北燕), corresponding to the pres. dep. of Shun-t'een (順天), Chih-le, which was held by his descendants fully nine hundred years. He remained himself, however, at the imperial court. We find him often styled the 'Chief of Shaou' (召伯); and Ts'een says that all the country west of Shen (陝) was under him, as all east of it was under the duke of Chow. See the 史記, 三十四, 燕召公, 世家第四. His posthumous title was K'ang (康), and hence he is sometimes referred to as 召康公奭. As to the date of the Announcement, see on par. 1. It is found in both texts.

CONTENTS. The first seven paragraphs are introductory to the body of the Book, which is composed of the Announcement of Shih. They contain various information about the surveying and planning and building of Lŏh. We may consider them as forming a first or preliminary chapter. Parr. 8—22, contain the Announce-

太保先周公相宅、越若來三月、惟丙午朏、越三日戊申、太保朝至于洛、卜宅、厥

2 came to Fung. Thence the Grand-guardian went before the duke of Chow to inspect the localities, and in the third month, on the day Mow-shin, the third day after the first appearance of the new moon on Ping-woo, came in the morning to Lŏ. He consulted the tortoise about the localities, and having obtained favourable indications, he

ment, which, however, commences properly with par. 9. The 'Complete Digest' says it may be divided into three parts. In the first, parr. 9—12, Shih sets forth the uncertainty of the favour of Heaven, and urges the young king to cultivate 'the virtue of reverence' in order to secure its permanence, concluding with a recommendation to him not to neglect his aged and experienced advisers. The second, parr. 13—18, speaks of the importance and difficulty of the imperial duties, and enforces the same virtue of reverence by reference to the rise and fall of the previous dynasties. In the last part, parr. 19—23, Shih insists on the importance of the king, at this early period of his reign, and on his personal undertaking of the duties of govt., at once setting about the reverence which was required to attach the people to himself and his House, and insure the lasting favour of Heaven. In the last par. the duke of Shaou gives expression to his personal feelings for the king, in the peculiar situation in which he was placed at Lŏ. The burden of the announcement all turns on 'the virtue of reverence.' Let the king only feel how much depends on his reverently attending to his duties, and govern for the people and not for himself:—let him do this, and all will be well. The people will love and support the dynasty of Chow, and Heaven will smile upon and sustain it.

Ch. I. Pp. 1—7. Proceedings of the king, the duke of Shaou, and the duke of Chow, in connection with the building of Lŏh. 1. 惟二月至乙未,—according to this statement, the day Yih-we must have been the 21st of the second month, and, as Gaubil observes, we may, from the data here supplied, determine the year to which the Announcement of Shaou should be referred. It was, he says correctly, the year b.c. 1,098. 乙未 being the 21st day of the second month, 乙亥 must have been the 1st, and the 1st day of that year of Chow must have been Ping-woo (丙午), the 43d day of the cycle. But that was the day of the new moon preceding the winter solstice, from which under this dynasty they calculated the year, in b.c. 1,098, or 1,097 (not reckoning a.d.). This result is not accordant with the current chronology of king Ching's reign, nor with the date assigned to it from the 'Bamboo Books.' The building of Lŏ is assigned to his 7th year, which was, on the received system, b.c. 1,109 (or 1,108), and acc. to the Bamboo Books b.c. 1038. It is enough to call attention to this point here, without going into further discussion about it. Ch'ing K'ang-shing proposed to change 二月 into 一月, in which case the year would have begun with 乙亥, the 11th cycle day; and he assigned the building of Lŏ, after Fuh-shang, to Ching's 5th year instead of the 7th. Even if we were to follow him in these points, we should be equally unable to reconcile the note of time given in the text with the arrangements of the chronologers. 王步至豐,—comp. Bk. III., p. 1. The temple of king Wăn was in Fung, and we may suppose had been left standing when Woo transferred the capital to Haou. Now when such an important thing as the establishing of a new capital, which should rank with Haou, if it did not supersede it, was in progress, it was proper that the king should solemnly announce it in the temples of his father and grandfather. That he might do so to the spirit of king Wăn, he went from Chow or Haou to Fung. 2. To Shih the Grand-guardian, and to the duke of Chow, was assigned the duty of making all the arrangements for carrying out the plans of king Woo about establishing a new capital at Lŏ. In fact, Woo had himself taken some measures towards the accomplishment of his views. We are told in the 左傳, under the year b.c. 708 (桓公,二年), that 'he removed the nine tripods or vases to the city of Lŏ' (武王克商,遷九鼎於洛邑). Those vases might be considered a sort of regalia of the empire. Originally cast by Yu, they had passed from the Hea dynasty to Shang, and were now the property of the House of Chow. See a detailed account of them in the 左傳, under the year b.c. 605 (宣公,三年). Sze-ma Ts'een also gives, in his 'Records of the Chow dynasty,' and probably from some of the lost Books of the Shoo, a conversation between the duke of Chow and Woo, in which the latter says, 'On the south I look to San-t'oo [there is still the mountain of San-t'oo, to the south-west of the district

既得卜、則經營。○越三日庚戌、太保乃以庶殷攻位于洛汭。越五日甲寅、位成。

3 set about laying out the plans. On Kăng-suh, the third day after, he led the people of Yin to prepare the *various* sites on the north of the Lŏ; and this work was completed on the fifth day, Këă-yin.

city of Sung(嵩縣)]; on the north I look, and see the towns near the Yŏh [this is supposed to be the T'ae-hang mountain, north of the Ho, on the border between Shan-se and Ho-nan; see the 'Tribute of Yu,' Part ii., par. 1]; when I look round, I see the Ho; and again I behold the Lŏ and the E' (我南望三途,北望嶽鄙,顧瞻有河,粤瞻洛伊). Ts'een adds that Woo laid out or built a settlement for Chow on the spot, and went away (營周居於洛邑而後去). These passages make it plain that Woo had fixed on Lŏ, at the time of his conquest of Shang, as the proper capital for his dynasty, and had taken measures to make it so. There was already, it is likely, some settlement at the place, which he enlarged. His locating at it the vases of Yu was a sufficient declaration to all the empire of his purpose. And that purpose had not been forgotten by the duke of Chow. When we bring together all the passages referring to Lŏ, the natural conclusion is that he had been gradually enlarging the place, and had even removed to it the more dangerous among the old adherents of Yin who still continued disaffected to the new rule. Up to the time when the action of this Book commences, however, nothing had been done towards the building of the palace and other structures which were the necessary appendages to it, and the planning of all these was, I think, the special mission entrusted to the duke of Shaou.

In the statistical account of the empire under the present dynasty, it is stated that the remains of the ancient city of Lŏ,—what was called 成周城, 'the capital of the completed or established Chow,' are 30 *le* on the north-east of the pres. city of Lŏh-yang (lat. 34° 43', N.; lon. 4°, W.); and those of the old city of Ho-nan, what was the 'imperial city' (王城) and 'the eastern Capital' of Chow—are 5 *le* on the west of it. The imperial city got the name of Ho-nan (河南) about the year B.C. 509, when the emperor King (敬王) left it, and took up his residence in the 成周城. I may add to these notices of Lŏ, that notwithstanding the wishes of king Woo and his labours, king Ching continued to reside at Haou; it was not till the reign of P'ing (平王) that the court was removed to the east, B.C. 769.

惟太保先周公相宅,—that the Grand-guardian (see Bk. XX., p. 5) was the duke of Shaou is nowhere said in the Book itself, but the title and the prefatory note (see page 10) are sufficient evidence on the point. 先 may be construed in the 1st tone or the 3d. 相=視, 'to survey.' 宅,—Këang Shing gives for this, very aptly,—可定居處, 'the places which might be fixed for residence.' The character does not denote so much 'a dwelling,' as the site of a dwelling. 越若至于洛,—Ts'ae takes 越若來 as simply a conjunction (古語辭),=our 'thereupon.' Attempts have been made to translate the characters. Medhurst renders them—'proceeding leisurely on his journey,' which might be taken as a translation of Gan-kwŏ's 於順來, but he wrongly joins them to the preceding clause. Others (see Lin Che-k'e *in loc.*) take them as='so, in obedience to the charge, he came.' Our best plan is to follow the view of Ts'ae. 朏, formed from 月 and 出, 'the moon come forth,' denotes the third day of the month. As this was Ping-woo, the second month must have been 'small,' consisting only of 29 days; and Mow-shin was the 5th of the 3d month. From Fung to Lŏ was 300 *le.*, so that if Shih commenced his journey, as the critics suppose, on the day Yih-we of the month before, he must have travelled leisurely enough. 卜宅=用龜卜宅都之地, 'he used the tortoise to divine where the capital should be built.' Wang K'ang-t'ang observes on 經營, that we are not to understand those terms of any actual work in building, but only of the determination of the dimensions of the wall, the palace or court, the ancestral temple, &c.;—see the 集說. 3. 越三日庚戌,—it may be observed that in these three days both Kăng-suh and Mow-shin are included. So, in the case of the 'three days' in the last par. 以庶殷攻位于洛汭,—庶殷=殷之衆民.

○若（四節）翼日乙卯。周公朝至于洛、則達觀于新邑營。○越（五節）三日丁巳、用牲于郊、牛二、越翼日戊午、乃社于新邑、牛一、羊一、豕一。○越（六節）七

4 The day following, being the day Yih-maou, the duke of Chow came in the morning to Lŏ, and thoroughly surveyed the plans for the new
5 city. On Ting-sze, the third day after, he offered two bulls as victims in the suburbs; and on the morrow, Mow-woo, at the altar to the spirit of the land in the new city, he sacrificed a bull, a goat,

'all the people of Yin.' This confirms what I have said above about the population of the imperial domain of Yin having already been in part removed to Lŏ,—the city commenced by king Woo. 攻位 describes the marking out on the ground of the foundations of the various structures from the plans of Shih. 洛汭,—see 'The Songs of the five Sons,' p. 3. 五日甲寅,—the five days include Kăng-suh and Këă-yin. The latter was the 11th of the 3d month.

Pp. 4—7. *The measures of the duke of Chow.* 4. 達觀于新邑營,—達=徧, 'all over.' The duke made a thorough survey of all the Guardian's plans and arrangements for the building of the new city; and, as we conclude from the next two parr., approved of them. 5. 用牲于郊牛二,—the disputes about the sacrifice or sacrifices here intended are very warm and lengthy. Ts'ae says that by 郊 are intended the sacrifice or sacrifices to Heaven and Earth (郊祭天地也). Whether he meant that the duke of Chow offered two sacrifices,—one to Heaven and one to Earth; or only one sacrifice to Heaven and Earth together, offering the two bulls at the same altar, does not appear. Maou K'e-ling, supposing that the latter was his view, shows that to sacrifice to Heaven and Earth together was an uncanonical practice. But I should rather think that Ts'ae meant that two sacrifices were offered, one to Heaven in the southern suburb, and one to Earth in the northern, a single bull being used at each. These sacrifices of course would be on occasion of the marking out the spots for the respective altars. Maou himself thinks that only one sacrifice—that to Heaven—is spoken of, and that two victims are mentioned, because How-tseih (后稷), as the great ancestor of the House of Chow, was associated with Heaven at the sacrifices to it. So far he is correct in saying that How-tseih participated in the usual sacrifices under the Chow dynasty to Heaven, and that there was special provision for a victim-bull to him, and one to the supernal Power. This was the view, moreover, of Gan-kwŏ. If the text were that 'the duke of Chow sacrificed, to Heaven, using two bulls,' I should adopt it. As the text stands, however, I prefer the view given above, and which I have said was probably that of Ts'ae. 社于新邑,牛一,羊一,豕一,—社='he offered the sacrifice at the altar to the spirit of the land.' Maou contends that this was the sacrifice to Earth, corresponding to the previous one to Heaven. But the text shows clearly that he is wrong, This sacrifice was offered 于新邑, 'in—*i.e.*, within—the new city,' whereas the sacrifices to Heaven and Earth were both celebrated in the suburbs, outside the city. We are to understand here, beyond doubt, the sacrifice to the spirit of the land, with which there was always associated that to the spirit of the grain. The altars were and still are within the wall of the imperial city. Who the spirits thus sacrificed to were, is a question not easy to determine. It seems to me probable that they were not spirits distinct from God, who was served in the sacrifices to Heaven and Earth. Compare the dictum of Confucius in 'The Doctrine of the Mean,' xix., 6. Whatever opinion may be held on this point, the human worthy associated at the sacrifice to the spirit of the land was Kow-lung (勾龍), minister of Works to the very ancient emperor Chuen-heuh, whose place on the list of Chinese sovereigns is immediately after Hwang-te. The human associate with the spirit of the grain was How-tseih. These same names appear in the ritual of the present dynasty (see the 大清通禮,卷之七). A long note on this paragraph by the editors of Yung-ching's Shoo is well worth the attention of the student.

日甲子、周公乃朝用書、命庶殷、侯甸男邦伯。○七節厥既命殷庶、庶殷丕作。○八節太保乃以庶邦冢君出取幣、乃復入、錫周公、曰、拜手稽首

6 and a pig. After seven days, on Këă-tsze, in the morning, from his written *specifications* he gave their several charges to the people of Yin, and to the chiefs of the States from the How, Teen, and Nan
7 tenures. When the people of Yin had thus received their orders, they arose with vigour to do their work.
8 II. The Great-guardian then went out with the hereditary princes of the various States to bring their offerings; and when he entered again, he gave them to the duke of Chow, saying, "With my head in my hands and bowed to the ground, I present these before the

6. 用書,—I have translated 書 by 'written specifications.' The duke had employed the six days after Ting-sze (that day is not included in the 七日) in writing out the work which was to be done in executing the Guardian's plans, with all the necessary specifications, and especially of the parties to whom the different parts of it should be assigned. The Chiefs of countries (邦伯) in the tenures specified must have been the pastors of the provinces (州牧). They would give their instructions to the princes belonging to their respective jurisdictions, who again would issue the necessary commands to the companies of their people whom they had brought with them to labour on the work in hand. 7. Lin Che-k'e observes on this:—'The duke of Shaou completed all his plans for Lŏ in 7 days, from Mow-shin to Këă-yin inclusive; then came the duke of Chow, and in ten days he was ready with all his specifications, and the work was grandly in hand:—so earnest and prompt were they with their measures. All together, from the day Yih-we, when king Ching came to Fung, to the day Këă-sze, there elapsed but one month. The foundation of 10,000 years' possession and prosperity was laid in one month! Future ages could not show such an achievement!' The observation must be accepted with due allowance for its grandiloquence.

Ch. II. Pp. 8—23. THE ANNOUNCEMENT. 8. The old interpreters all thought that king Ching was present in Lŏ when this announcement was made. It may be well to give the exposition of Gan-kwŏ. On 太保至復入 he says:—諸侯公卿竝覲于王,王與周公俱至,文不見者,王無事也,召公與諸侯出取幣,欲因大會顯周公, 'The various princes, the dukes and high nobles appeared together before the king. The king and the duke of Chow had both come to Lŏ. The text is silent about the king's coming, because there was nothing to be done by him *at that time*. The duke of Shaou and all the princes went out to fetch the ceremonial offerings, wishing to take occasion of the great assembly to glorify the duke of Chow.' On 錫周公至若公 he says:—召公以幣入,稱成王命,賜周公曰,敢拜手稽首,陳王所宜順周公之事, 'The duke of Shaou then entered with the offerings, and, proclaiming the command of king Ching, gave them to the duke of Chow, saying, "I venture, with my face to my hands and my head to the ground, to set forth the things in which the king ought to act in accordance with the duke of Chow."' On the last clause he says:—召公指戒成王,而以衆殷諸侯於自乃御治事,爲辭,謙也,諸侯在故托焉, 'The duke of Shaou's aim was to admonish king Ching, and that he addressed himself to the multitudes of Yin and the princes, down to the managers of affairs [see Ying-tă's paraphrase], was the language of modesty. The princes were present, and he took the opportunity to address himself to the king through them.'

K'ang-shing's view of the passage was substantially the same as that of Gan-kwŏ. That the king was present, and that the design of

旅王若公、誥告庶殷、越自乃御事。○嗚九節呼、皇天上帝、改厥元子、茲大國殷之命、惟王受命、無疆惟休、亦無疆惟恤、嗚呼、曷其奈何弗

king and your Grace. Announcements for the instruction of the multitudes of Yin must come from you with whom is the management of affairs.

9 "Oh! God dwelling in the great heavens has changed his decree in favour of his eldest son, and this great dynasty of Yin. Our king has received that decree. Unbounded is the happiness connected with it, and unbounded is the anxiety:—Oh! how can he be other than reverent?

Shih was to glorify the duke of Chow for the services he had performed:—these are assumptions, for which I can find no support in the tenour of the Book itself. That the offerings were presented to the duke of Chow for himself is broadly contrary to the last paragraph. The interpretation, moreover, of 旅王若公, and of 越自乃御事, is intolerably harsh and forced. In the translation I have preferred to follow the views of Ts'ae, who himself followed Choo He. There is a great assembly of the two dukes and the princes who were with them at Lŏ. The duke of Chow is about to return, or at least to send a communication, to king Ching in Haou. The duke of Shaou, revering the king's majesty in the regent, takes the opportunity to send by him the loyal presents of the princes, and his own loyal wishes and advices to the court. And there was the greater propriety in his doing so now, as it was understood that the duke of Chow was about to withdraw from the duties of the regency, and the king might be expected to take the administration of affairs into his own hands. 以庶邦冢君,—以=與; see the dict. *in voc.* 冢君,—comp. Bk I., Pt i., p. 2. 旅王若公—旅=陳, 'to set forth,' 'to exhibit;' with reference to the offerings, which would be set down and displayed in the court below the hall where they were assembled. The 若 is very perplexing. We have seen how the old interpreters tried to manage it. Ts'ae takes it as simply = 與, 'and.' This gives a good enough sense, but I must confess that I cannot think of a similar use of the term elsewhere. 誥告至末,—this is an indirect call to the king to come before the people in his own person, pointing out to them the course of their duty, and leading in the way of it. The duke delicately avoids any direct mention of the king, but he really intends him as 'the manager of affairs.' In this way we see the force of the 自, which the old interpreters could not manage.

Pp. 9—12. *With the favour shown by God to the king there was connected much anxiety. He must reverently cherish the thought of his responsibilities and duties; learn from the experience of the former dynasties; and listen to the advice of his wise and aged ministers.* 9. 皇天上帝,—see on 皇上帝, in 'The Announcement of T'ang,' p. 2. 元子,—see on Bk., VIII., p. 1. Here and in par. 13, it is a designation equivalent to 'the emperor.' When he is called Heaven's eldest son, the mind thinks of the favour which must rest upon him, and may well deem his state secure. K'ang-shing says here:—凡人皆云天之子,天子爲之首耳, 'All men may be called the sons of Heaven; the emperor is the head or the eldest of them.' 惟王受命,—'the king here is king Ching,' = *our* king, who was now become God's eldest son. 曷其奈何不敬,—this puts the duty of being reverent in the strongest way. On the meaning of this 'being reverent' Ts'ae says, that 'it is being sincere and without guile, the eyes, ears, words, and movements all being accordant with reason; the likings and dislikings, the usings and refusings never contrary to *the will of* Heaven. When one's virtue thus agrees with that of Heaven, he will surely be able to receive the bright favouring decree of Heaven' (敬則

敬。○天既遐終大邦殷之命、茲殷多先哲王在天、越厥後王後民、茲服厥命、厥終智藏瘝在、夫知保抱攜持厥婦子、以哀籲天、徂厥亡出執、嗚呼、天亦哀于四方民、其眷命用懋、王其疾 (十節)

10 "When Heaven rejected and made an end of the decree in favour of the great State of Yin, there were many of the former intelligent kings of Yin in heaven. The king, however, who had succeeded to them, the last of their race, from the time of his entering into their appointment, proceeded in such a way as at last to keep the wise in obscurity and the vicious in office. The poor people in such a case, carrying their children and leading their wives, made their moan to Heaven. They even fled away, but were apprehended again. Oh! Heaven had compassion on the people of the four quarters; its favouring decree lighted on our earnest founders. Let the king sedulously cultivate the virtue of reverence.

誠實無妄、視聽言動、一循乎理、好惡用捨、不違乎天、與天同德、固能受天明命也). 10. Much of the language of this paragraph, it is observed by Ts'ae, is difficult of explanation; but there is a general agreement as to the meaning of most of it. King Ching is reminded of the fall of the dyn. of Yin through the misgovernment and wickedness of Show, and how it was because of the earnest virtue of his own predecessors that they had been called to the sovereignty of the empire.—Let it be his to imitate them. 天既至在天,—遐=遠, 'far,' 'distant;' here, as I understand it, = 'to reject.' 終=絕, 'to make an end of.' It is difficult to give the force of the 茲. Perhaps we should join it emphatically to 殷.—'Of *this* Yin, thus rejected, many of the former kings, &c.' The speaker believed that the good kings were in heaven, and he intimates that it might therefore have been expected that they would have been able to preserve their dynasty; but that could not be. 越厥至瘝在,—越 is here = 'but,' 'however.'

後王後民,—both these phrases seem to be best taken of Show, who is the subject of all this portion. Gan-kwŏ, however, understood 厥後王後民, 茲服厥命 of good sovereigns and their people, who worthily continued the sway of their predecessors. It is only at 厥終, 'the last of them,' that the tyrant comes with him upon the stage. 瘝=病, 'to distress.' 瘝在=病民之人在位. 夫知至籲天,—on 夫知 Wang Suh says:—匹夫知欲安其室, 'the ordinary people, who knew enough to wish to secure the comfort of their families.' Compare 匹夫 in Ana., IX., xxv. This is as satisfactory as anything which can be said about the 夫知 here. 夫 should be read in the upper first tone. 徂厥亡出執=往而逃亡, 出見拘執, 無地自容, as in the translation. 其眷命用懋=' it looked round and gave its appointment to those who were employing themselves earnestly *on virtue*.' Comp. 眷命 in 'The Counsels of Yu,' p. 4.

敬德。○十一節相古先民有夏、天迪從子保、面稽天若、今時既墜厥命、今相有殷、天迪格保、面稽天若、今時既墜厥命。○十二節今沖子嗣、則無遺壽耇、曰其稽我古人之德、矧曰其有能稽謀自天。○十三節嗚呼、有王雖小、元子哉、其

11 "Examining the men of antiquity, there was *the founder of* the Hea dynasty. Heaven guided his mind, allowed his descendants to succeed him, and protected them. He acquainted himself with Heaven, and was obedient.—But in process of time the decree in his favour fell to the ground. So also when we examine the case of Yin. Heaven guided *its founder*, so that he corrected *the errors of Shang*, and it protected his descendants. He *also* acquainted himself with Heaven, and was obedient.—But now the decree in favour of him has fallen to
12 the ground. Our king has now come to the throne in his youth:—let him not slight the aged and experienced, for it may be said of them that they have studied the virtuous conduct of our ancient worthies, and still more, that they have matured their plans in the light of Heaven.
13 "Oh! although the king is young, yet is he the eldest son of Heaven. Let him but effect a great harmony with the people, and

Ying-tă gives for the clause:—其眷顧天下、選擇賢聖、命用勉力行敬者、以爲民主. 11. By 有夏, 'the holder of Hea,' we are to understand Yu, as the founder of the Hea dynasty. So by 有殷 T'ang is meant. 先民=古人, 'the ancients.' To 相古 the 今相 afterwards responds. 天迪從子保=天啟迪之、又從其子而保佑之, as in the translation. In the case of T'ang, it was not necessary to take notice of the transmission of the throne to his descendants. The hereditary principle had long been established. 面(=鄉)稽天若=仰考天心、敬順不違, 'he looked up and examined the mind of Heaven, reverently obedient and not opposing it.' The first 今時 must be understood as in the translation. 12. 無遺壽耇,—無=毋, imperative. 耇,—see Bk. IX., p. 5. The 曰 may be taken as in the translation (and it is better taken so), or we may understand it, with Këang Shing, as=當曰, 'he—our young king—ought to say.' On the 稽古人之德, it is said that they could thus give precedents and authorities in every case they were consulted on, and on the 稽謀自天, that in their advice there would thus be nothing contrary to what was right.

Pp. 13—18. *The importance of the king's position, and duties to which he must address himself, especially now on his personally undertaking the*

丕能誠于小民、今休、王不敢後、用顧畏于民碞。○十四節王來紹上帝、自服于土中、旦曰、其作大邑、其自時配皇天、毖祀于上下、其自時中乂、王厥有成命、治民今休。

that will be the blessing of the present time. Let not the king presume to be remiss in this, but continually regard and stand in awe of the perilousness of the people.

14 "Let the king come here as the vicegerent of God, and undertake himself *the duties of government* in the centre of the land. Tan said, 'Now that this great city has been built, from henceforth he may be the mate of great Heaven; from henceforth he may reverently sacrifice to the upper and lower *spirits;* from henceforth he may in this central spot administer successful government.' Thus shall the king enjoy the favouring regard *of Heaven* all complete, and the government of the people will now be prosperous.

responsibilities of the govt. The whole is enforced by a second reference to the previous dynasties.

13. 元子哉,—see on par. 9. 其丕能誠于小民,今休,—the 其 is strongly hortative. 誠=和, 'harmony,' 'to be harmonious.' We had the char. before in 'The Counsels of Yu,' p. 21, where the meaning was different. The 'Daily Explanation' thus paraphrases:—王其大能誠和小民,使之歡欣鼓舞,....,則民情安而天命固,豈不爲今日之休美乎. 王不敢後,—'let the king not postpone'—what? His effecting a great harmony with the people. And that was to be accomplished by means of 'the virtue of reverence.' Gan-kwŏ put a comma at 用, and interpreted—當不敢後能用之士,必任之爲先, 'let the king not leave in the background capable officers, but make employment of them a primary consideration.' This is far-fetched; and so is his explanation of 碞, the erroneousness of which is pointed out in the dict. The character=險, 'precipitous,' 'perilous.' 14. 王來紹上帝,自服于上中,—紹上帝, 'to continue God.' We often find it said of emperors, and especially of the founders of dynasties that they 繼天立極, 'carried on *the work of* Heaven, and set up the perfect *model.*' There underlies such language the view that Heaven delegates its sway to the Powers ordained by it. Compare, for the general sentiment, Bk. I., Pt. i., p. 7; and for the use of 紹, Bk. VII., p. 8. 自服于土中=labour himself in the midst of the land. The 'himself' must have reference to the young king, now undertaking the responsibilities of govt. 服=行事, 'to labour.' Lŏ is said to be 'in the middle of the land' from its central position. It must have been, in the time of Chow, about the central spot of the empire, and was therefore well fitted to be the seat of administration. The commentators speak of it as not only in the middle of the land, but as 'in the centre of heaven and earth,' and they undertake to show how this was determined by means of a dial! See the whole geodesy of the duke of Chow, in the Chow Le, Bk. IX., pp. 26—31.

Lin Che-k'e takes these two clauses as historical, and considers them to be decisive on the point of the king's being at this time in Lŏ. It seems to me much more natural to read them in the imperative mood. 旦曰至中乂,—the duke of Shaou supports his advice by using the similar language of the duke of Chow, whom he names 旦, in accordance with the rule that 'ministers should be called by their

○王先服殷御事、比介于我有周御事、節性、惟日其邁。○王敬作所、不可不敬德。○我不可不監于有夏、亦不可不監于有殷、我不敢知曰、有夏服天命、惟有

15 "Let the king first bring under his influence the managers of affairs of Yin, associating them with the managers of affairs of our dynasty of Chow. This will regulate their *perverted* natures, and they will make daily advancement.

16 "Let the King make reverence the resting-place *of his mind.* He may not but maintain the virtue of reverence.

17 "We should by all means survey the dynasties of Hea and Yin. I do not presume to know and say, 'The dynasty of Hea was to enjoy the favouring decree of Heaven for *so many* years,' nor do I

names in the presence of the emperor.' 配皇天—see on Pt. IV., Bk. V., Pt. iii., p. 3. 毖祀于上下,—compare 上下神祇 in the 'Announcement of T'ang,' p. 3. On 中乂 Wang Ts'eaou says that it denotes that 'from the centre the king would diffuse his rule throughout the four quarters of the empire'(自中而布治於四方). Here the words of Tan seem to terminate. 成命,—'the completed appointment.' The will of Heaven in favour of the House of Chow would now be put beyond doubt and beyond the risk of being assailed.

Pp. 15, 16. The king would have in the first place to attach to his House the disaffected officers of the previous dynasty; but let him bear in mind that he must always set the example of the virtue of reverence in himself. 15. 服 is here a transitive verb. The 'Daily Explanation' defines it by 化, 'to transform.' 比介于我有周御事,—比—親, 'to be near to.' 介—助, 'to assist,' to co-operate with. This extension of confidence to the officers of Yin would be the way to win their confidence and attachment, and the associating them with the friends of the present dynasty would lead them to change their views. 節性,惟日其邁,—Ts'ae gives for this—以節其驕淫之性,則日進於善而不已;—as in the translation. Lin Che-k'e contends that by 性 we should not understand the *perverted* nature, but the *good* nature, which was still in the officers of Yin, and had only to be properly directed. His words are:—節之者,非強其所無也,以其所固有之性,還以治之,去其不善,而反之善也,有以節之,則臣民將遷善遠罪而不自知,惟日其進於善也. The difference of view is more in words than in reality. 16. After all, the *primum mobile* of govt. must be the personal character and example of the king. 王敬作所—王當以敬爲居心之所. The 所 is used like 止 in the 知止 of 'The Great Learning.'

Pp. 17, 18. *The lessons to be learned from the two previous dynasties; and the emphasis which they should have now at the commencement of the present dynasty, and of the king's personal entrance on his responsibilities.* 17. Compare p. 11. The 有夏 and 有殷 here, however, are to be extended to all the sovereigns of the two dynasties. Moreover, what was said above had reference more especially to the establishment of those dynasties by the blessing of Heaven; here the subject is their fall, for want of 'the

歷年、我不敢知曰、不其延、惟不敬厥德、乃早墜厥命、我不敢知曰、有殷受天命、惟有歷年、我不敢知曰、不其延、惟不敬厥德、乃早墜厥命。○（十八節）今王嗣受厥命、我亦惟茲二國命、嗣若功、王乃初服。○（十九節）嗚呼、若生子、罔不在厥初生、自貽哲命、今

presume to know and say, 'It could not continue longer.' The fact was simply that, for want of the virtue of reverence, the decree in its favour prematurely fell to the ground. *Similarly*, I do not presume to know and say, 'The dynasty of Yin was to enjoy the favouring decree of Heaven for *so many* years,' nor do I presume to say, 'It could not continue longer.' The fact simply was that, for want of the virtue of reverence, the decree in its favour pre-
18 maturely fell to the ground. The king has now inherited the decree,—the same decree, I consider, which belonged to those two dynasties. Let him seek to inherit *the virtues of* their meritorious *sovereigns*;—especially at this commencement *of* his duties.
19 "Oh! it is as on the birth of a son, when all depends on *the training of* his early life, through which he may secure his wisdom in the future, as if it were decreed to him. Now Heaven may

virtue of reverence' in their rulers. The 'Daily Explanation' says that the first 我 is to be understood of the king, and the others of the duke of Shaou himself. It is much better to take the character always in the plural. 有夏服天命惟有歷年,—服天命 is more than 受天命, which most of the paraphrases give for it. It indicates not only that Hea received the favouring decree of Heaven, but that it was *under* that decree. The guardian will not venture to say that Heaven had only decreed so many years to its rule.

18. 厥命,—the 厥 is to be understood of 天, 'Heaven.' The next clause is in apposition with this, 惟 being=思. Gan-kwŏ takes it differently, and explains down to 功 where he ends the paragraph thus:—其,夏殷也,繼受其王命,亦惟當以此夏殷長短之命爲監戒,繼順其功德者,而法則之. He overlooks the 我 before 亦惟. 嗣若功,王乃初服=當嗣(=繼)其有功者,况王乃新邑初政,服行教化之始乎. This must be the meaning, but the language is very elliptical

Pp. 19—23. *The great issues depending on the king's now, on his assuming the government, taking the right course; and the Guardian's anxiety that by his virtuous reverence and gentle sway he should lay the foundations of permanent prosperity.*

19. 嗚呼至哲命,—by 初生 we

天其命哲、命吉凶、命歷年、知今我初服。○宅(二十節)新邑、肆惟王其疾敬德、王其德之用、祈天永命。○其(廿一節)惟王勿以小民淫用非彝、亦敢殄戮用乂、民若有功。○其(廿二節)惟王位在

have decreed wisdom *to our king*; it may have decreed good fortune or bad; it may have decreed a *long* course of years:—we only know that now is with him the commencement of his duties.

20 "Dwelling in the new city, let the king now sedulously cultivate the virtue of reverence. When he is all-devoted to this virtue, he may pray to Heaven for a long-abiding decree in his favour.

21 "In the position of king, let him not, because of the excesses of the people in violation of the laws, presume also to rule by the violent infliction of death. When the people are regulated gently, the merit of government is seen.

must understand not the infancy, but the early years, when the child becomes the proper subject of education. Then such a foundation of goodness may be laid, that the youth shall 'himself hand down an appointment of wisdom.' He shall appear to be, shall really be, wise through this training, as much as if Heaven had previously decreed him to be so. 命歷年—或命歷年長久. After this we must understand 皆不可預知, 'all these things we cannot know beforehand.' 20. The Guardian evidently supposes that the king will make the new city which was founded the seat of his government. The meaning of 今, 'now,' for 肆 seems to suit the connection here better than that of 故 or 遂. The 其 in 王其德之用 gives to the second part of the par. a slightly hortative force. Chin Tih-sew observes upon the sentiment, 'The favour of Heaven is entirely just, and is not to be obtained by praying for it. The text tells the king to pray, because to be all-devoted to the practice of virtue is prayer without praying, (天命至公,不可以求而得也,曰祈者,蓋一於用德,乃不祈之祈). Compare with this the words of Confucius about himself, Ana., VII., xxxiv. 21. From 其惟王 to 殄戮用 is one sentence, and a good instance of the long sentences of the Shoo. Gan-kwŏ and Këang Shing, indeed, break it up into two, and understand the first part as meaning—'Let not the king go to excess in employing the people, beyond the regular periods when he may call them out in the public service.' By doing so, he would, as Mencius phrases it, rob the people of their time, and take them away from their necessary labours in agriculture (see Mencius, page 11). But the introduction of such a topic seems foreign to the style of the Announcement. It involves, moreover, taking the 亦敢 which follow as=亦勿敢, which is very harsh. The subject of avoiding punishments in the administration in govt. was a favourite one with king Ching and his ministers. See many passages in Bks. IX., and X. 民若有功, —'when the people accord there is merit. They must be ruled,' 'in harmony with their feelings, and the true laws of their nature.' Ts'ae observes that the people may be compared to the water of a stream when it is overflowing and spreading abroad; it is acting contrary to its nature. But if you dam it up, you only make the evil worse. Lead it into its proper course, and you accom-

德元、小民乃惟刑用于天下、越王顯。○上下勤恤、其曰我受天命、丕若有夏歷年、式勿替有殷歷年、欲王以小民受天永命。○拜手稽首曰、予小臣、敢以王之讐民百君子、越友民、保受

22 "It is for him who is in the position of king to overtop all with his virtue. In this case the people will imitate him throughout the whole empire, and the king will become more illustrious.

23 "Let the king and his ministers labour with a common anxiety, saying, 'We have received the decree of Heaven, and it shall be great as the long-continued years of Hea,—it shall not fail of the long-continued years of Yin.' I wish the king through the inferior people to receive the long-abiding decree of Heaven."

24 III. *The duke of Shaou* then did obeisance with his head to his hands and bowed to the ground, and said, "I, a small minister, presume with the king's *heretofore* hostile people, with all his officers, and his *loyal* friendly people, to maintain and receive his majesty's dread

plish the purpose. 22. 其惟王位在德元,—'He being king, his position is at the head of *all* virtue.' It is simpler to take 元 as = 首, than to give it the substantial meaning which it has in the first diagram of the Yih King, as that quality in Heaven which corresponds to 仁, 'benevolence,' 'goodness complete' in man. 小民乃惟刑 (=法) 用于天下,—'the inferior people on their part will be found imitating him and employing virtue throughout the empire.' 越王顯,—'and the king will be illustrious,' *i.e.*, the virtue of the king will thereby be more widely and brilliantly displayed. 23. 上下勤恤,—by 上下 we are to understand 君臣, 'the sovereign and his ministers.' 恤,—as in p. 9, = 憂, 'to be anxious.' Then the 其 in 其曰 is strongly hortative. 式勿替云云,—both Gan-kwŏ and Ts'ae define 式 by 用, but it is difficult to find a place for any other meaning of it here than as a conjunction = 'and.' The 'Daily Explanation,' after defining it by 用, is obliged in the paraphrase to substitute 又 for it. 勿替 = 'we are determined that it shall not fail of.' At 欲 the duke of Shaou speaks again in his own person. The 'people,' ruled over as he desired, would wish the rule to be perpetual, and the wish of the people would be the wish of Heaven.

Ch. III. Pt. 24. We must understand 召公 before 拜手稽首. The Guardian here winds up his address. He will do his duty with the people under his charge. It remains for the king to secure the permanence of the dynasty. In the meantime he presents the offerings of the princes, to aid at the sacrifices to be offered, on the inauguration of the new capital. 王之讐民,—these are the people of Yin that had been removed to Lŏ, and could still not be spoken of as other than disaffected and hostile. 百君子,—compare the same phrase in Bk. X., p. 7. It is used here

王威命明德、王末有成命、王亦顯、我非敢勤、惟恭奉幣、用供王能祈天永命。

command and brilliant virtue. That the king should finally obtain the decree all complete, and that he should become illustrious,—this I dare not to labour about. I only respectfully bring these offerings to present to his Majesty, to assist in his prayers to Heaven for its long-abiding decree.'"

as complimentary to the ministers and officers of Yin, in whom loyal feelings might arise when they were thus spoken of. The 'friendly people' are the adherents of the House of Chow. 威命 must be the king's charge for the building of Lŏ. 明德 has more sound than sense. 王末至亦顯,—this describes the king's consolidation of the dynasty, and transmitting the crown to his descendants. That must be the king's own work. The Guardian would not presume to think that his labours could effect it. 惟恭,云云,—the king would be coming to Lŏ, and by solemn sacrifices inaugurate the new city, and then the offerings would be useful. This is a delicate way of conveying to him those expressions of the princes' fealty.

Wang Pih's 'Doubts' about this Book and the next are the following:—洛誥之篇,三山林氏說之所終,東萊先生說之所始,文公又於召誥洛誥亦各有說,學者可以釋疑矣,然猶未也,洛誥自周公日之下,朱子以為自此漸不可曉,蓋不知是何時所言,又取葉氏之言,以此篇與召誥參看,又取王氏曰,此誥有不可知者,當缺文,朱子尚謂有疑而後學敢謂無疑者,妄人也,愚竊謂諸誥之中,辭語之不可曉者固多矣,而一篇之體統大槩亦可見,惟召誥洛誥,破碎龐雜,體統不明,此誥未易梳理者也,蓋其中有周公召公相洛卜洛之詞焉,有遷殷民攻位丕作之詞焉,有營洛之詞焉,有成王來洛之詞焉,有祀文武記功宗之詞焉,有周公復辟之詞焉,有成王即辟之詞焉,有成王冊命周公之詞焉,此所以不可以一事觀也,召誥前雖載相洛之事,後止是以成王新政致戒之詞而已,曰王乃初服,若生子,罔不在厥初生,則以疾敬德,為王新政第一義,此則頗自明白,若洛誥恐當作兩節看,相洛卜洛營洛遷頑民,是一節,明禋烝禮,周公欲成王治洛,復政於王,成王止欲歸周即辟,命周公治洛,此是一節,如冊周公之首詞,反殿於篇末,而冊中之詞,反殺雜於前,此皆未易就條理也,第一是復辟之事,程子以來諸儒,只欲作荅王解,以為未嘗失位,安得有復,此義誠精矣,然成王固未嘗失位也,蓋成王前此未嘗親政也,成王幼,周公代王為政,成王長,周公歸政於王,正如伊尹復政厥辟之復,蘇氏所謂歸政初何害義,然亦何所嫌而避此名乎,此愚之所以不能無疑也.

THE BOOKS OF CHOW.

BOOK XIII. THE ANNOUNCEMENT CONCERNING LŎ.

洛誥

周公拜手稽首曰、朕復子明辟。○王

[In the third month when the moon began to wane, the duke of Chow commenced the foundations and proceeded to build the new city at Lŏ of the eastern States. The people from every quarter assembled in great harmony. From the How, Teen, Nan, Ts'ae, and Wei domains the various officers stimulated this harmony of the people, and introduced them to the business there was for Chow. The duke of Chow encouraged them all to diligence, and made a great announcement about the execution *of the works.*]

1 I. The duke of Chow bowed his head to his hands and then to the ground, saying, "Herewith I report the *execution of my commission*

The Name of the Book.—洛誥, 'The Announcement about Lŏ.' The prefatory note (see page 10) says:—'The duke of Shaou having surveyed the localities, the duke of Chow went to build this capital, called Ching Chow, and sent a messenger to announce the divinations. With reference to this, the Announcement about Lŏ was made.' As will be seen from the next note, however, the action of the Book goes many months beyond the report about the survey and divinations; but it all has reference, more or less, to the city of Lŏ. It may well be said to be about Lŏ. The use of the term 'Announcement' has its difficulties, and must be taken more vaguely than in the account of the Announcements of the Shoo which I have given on page 177. The Book is found in both texts.

Contents. Ts'ae says:—'The arrangements for the building of Lŏ having been made, the duke of Chow sent a messenger to inform the king of the result of his divinations. The historian recorded this as the announcement about Lŏ, and at the same time recorded a dialogue between the king and his minister, and how the king charged the duke to remain at Lŏ and conduct the government of it.' He goes on to say more particularly:—'Parr. 1—3 contain the duke's message about his divinations; and par. 4 gives the king's reply. Parr. 5—13 are occupied with instructions from the duke to the king on the measures which he should pursue on taking up his residence at Lŏ. In parr. 14—21, the king charges the duke to remain at Lŏ, and undertake its government. In parr. 22—24, the duke responds, accepting the charge, and dwells on the duties which the king and himself would have to discharge. Parr. 25—28 relate the action of the duke on a certain message and gift from the king, intended for his special honour. In parr. 29—31, the historian relates to sacrifices offered in Lŏ by the king, and the proclamation which he issued, and adds how long the duke continued in his government;—showing how the duke began the city and completed it, and how king Ching, after offering the sacrifices and inaugurating the government, returned to Haou, and did not after all make his capital at Lŏ.'

The Seven divisions thus indicated, present themselves to any careful student of the Book. Maou K'e-ling, differing widely from Ts'ae in his view of the general tenour, and of particular

passages and terms, gives the same, only including parr. 22—28 in one. Many critics make more to do than is necessary about the want of historical order in the Book, and suppose that portions have been lost, and other portions transposed. I have already given my opinion that the first paragraph in 'The Announcement to *the Prince of* K'ang' should be the first par. here. As to other portions being lost, the Book may be explained without resorting to so violent a supposition. It is not by any means so plain as it might be, but I am inclined to think that it is as plain as it ever was.

The first paragraph from the Announcement to the Prince of K'ang. For the reasons why this par. should be edited here and not as a portion of Bk. IX., see page 383. 三月哉生魄,—see on Bk. III., pp. 1 and 4. This would be the 16th day of the month. In the last Book, pp. 4—6, we saw that on the 12th day of the 3d month, the duke of Chow arrived at Lŏ; on the 14th and 15th, he sacrificed to Heaven and Earth, and to the spirit of the land, while on the 21st he was ready with specifications of all the works which were to be executed. It would appear from this par. that on the 16th he made a commencement with the foundations of some of the works. 作新大邑于東國洛,—the 'Daily Explanation' gives for this—作新大邑于成周之東,洛邑之地,而有王城下都之建焉, 'he made the new great city on the east of Ching Chow, in the territory of the city of Lŏ, and there was the building both of the imperial city and of the lower capital.' This may be understood by referring to the note on p. 2 of the last Book; but the text does not so clearly indicate that the building of the two cities is spoken of. The 成周城 went also by the name of 下都, 'the lower capital.' 侯,甸,男邦,采,衞,—see the figure of the domains of Chow on p. 149. The five of them which constituted, with the imperial domain, the 'Middle Kingdom' are here enumerated in their proper order, though why the 邦 should be introduced between 男 and 采 I cannot explain. 百工播民和,—百工=百官, 'all the officers,' including, probably, from the princes downwards; 播民和=宣揚民心之和,—'spread abroad the harmony of the people.' 見士于周,—士 is taken as=事, 'business,' the work to be done. Ch'in Leih explains 見士 by 覲見而趨事, 'presented themselves as if at court, and hastened to the works.' We do not know well what to make of the phrase. 周公咸勤,—the 'Daily Explanation' takes this as='The duke of Chow himself and all with him laboured diligently.' Gan-kwŏ explains it as in the translation. I understand 誥治 as meaning that the duke now announced in a general way the works which were to be executed, preparatory to the specifications which were issued five days after.

Ch. I. Pp. 1—3. THE DUKE'S MESSAGE TO THE KING, INFORMING HIM WHAT HE HAD DONE, AND LAYING BEFORE HIM MAPS, PLANS, AND THE RESULT OF HIS DIVINATIONS. 1. There is a controversy which it is not easy to settle on the meaning of 復 in this par., and the view to be taken of the whole Book depends very much upon it. Gan-kwŏ took 復 as=還政, 'to restore the government.' He explains the whole par. thus:—周公盡禮致敬,言我復還明君之政於子,成王,年二十成人,故必歸政而退老, 'The duke of Chow, in the most ceremonious way and with the utmost reverence, said, "I return the government of the intelligent sovereign to you, my son." By his son he meant king Ching, who was now 20, and full grown. It was requisite that the duke should return the govt. to him, and withdraw into retirement in his old age.' This interpretation, which is still held by many, was not doubted till the Sung dynasty, when the critic Wang (? Wang Gan-shih) was the first to suggest that 復 should be taken as meaning 'to report,' 'to announce the fulfilment of a commission,' referring to the phrase 反命, which is common in Mencius, and to the use of 復 alone by him, Bk. I., Pt. I., vii., 10,—有復於王者. The duke, he contended, had never been anything but regent; he could not speak of himself as *restoring* the govt. This view was adopted by Ts'ae, and became current through his commentary.

Maou K'e-ling refers to the 1st words of Pt. IV., Bk. VI.,—伊尹既復政厥辟, as decisive in favour of the older view; but the use of the 政 there after 復 makes the passages by no means parallel, nor was the position of the duke of Chow to king Ching the same as that of E Yin to T'ae-këă. It must be allowed at the same time that Mencius' 復於王 is different from the simple 復子 of the text.

On the whole, I must incline to the view adopted by Ts'ae. In the answer of the king to the duke's message there is not a word about his accepting the restoration or resignation of the govt. It was understood between them, and throughout the empire, that the time was come for the king to undertake the duties of the administration himself, and we shall see hereafter in this Book that the duke expresses his purpose to go into retirement, now that the building of Lŏ was in a state of forwardness;

如弗敢及天基命定命、予乃胥保大相東土、其基作民明辟。○予三節惟乙卯朝至于洛師、我卜河朔黎水、我乃卜澗水東、瀍水西、惟洛

2 to my son, my intelligent prince. The king appeared as if he would not presume to determine the founding and the fixing of our appointment by Heaven, whereupon I followed the *Grand*-Guardian, and made a great survey of this eastern region, with a view to found the place where he might become the intelligent sovereign of the people.
3 On the day Yih-maou, in the morning, I came to the city of Lŏ. I *first* divined concerning the *country about the* Le water on the north of the Ho. I then divined concerning the east of the Këen water and the west of the Ch'en water, when the *ground near the* Lŏ was

but the most natural interpretation of the text is as in the translation.

The duke's bowing and putting his head to the ground was intended for the king, but performed in the presence of the messenger, who was to carry the report to court. The duke was now in Lŏ, and the king was probably at Haou. The duke calls the king his 'son,' expressing his affection for him, and he calls him his 'intelligent prince,' giving him honour.

P. 2. The view taken of the former par. affects the meaning which is given to this. Gan-kwŏ took 如＝往, 'formerly;' 天基命定命＝天始命周家安定天下之命, 'Heaven's favouring decree when first it charged our House of Chow to tranquillize and settle the empire;' and 予乃胥保＝我乃繼文武安天下之道, 'I therefore continued the ways of Wăn and Woo to tranquillize the empire.' Këang Shing, again, taking 復 in the same way, keeps the natural interpretation of 如 as ＝若, but by 基命 he understands king Wăn, 'the first commissioned,' and by 定命, king Woo 'settler or completer of the commission,' and his view of 胥保 he agrees with Gan-kwŏ, and says that the 基 in 其基＝謀, 'to plan.' The advocates of the other interpretation of 復 understand by 基命, 'the laying the foundations of the appointment to the empire,' and by 成命, 'the securing permanently that appointment'—results which were both to be realized be making Lŏ the capital of the empire.—Then by 保 is intended the duke of Shaou, the 'Grand-guardian' (太保); and 其基作民明辟＝其庶幾爲王始作民明辟之地, as in the translation, the 其 having, as often, the signification of 期, 'to expect,' 'to aim at.' In this way the par. has a unity and consistency in itself, which we do not find in the other interpretations. I cannot but understand it thus, and doing so I cannot but take the previous 復 as Ts'ae does.

P. 3. 予惟至洛師,—see the last Book, p. 4. Lŏ is called 師 as being intended to be the capital, where the emperor should reside. See in the dict.—天子所居曰京師. It is needlessly embarrassing the interpretation to make, with Gan-kwŏ and K'ang-shing, 洛師＝洛之衆. 卜河朔黎水,—I have been strongly inclined to translate this in the past complete tense,—'I had previously divined,' &c. The Le water was a name given to the united stream of the Wei (衞河) and the K'e (淇河), on its reaching a place which was afterwards called Le-yang (黎陽), in the north-east of the pres. dis. of Seun (濬), dep. of Wei-hwuy. This was not far from the old capital of Show,

食、我又卜瀍水東、亦惟洛食、伻來、以圖及獻卜。○王四節拜手稽首曰、公不敢不敬天之休、來相宅、其作周匹休、公既定宅、伻來、來視予

indicated. Again I divined concerning the east of the Ch'en water, and the *ground near the* Lŏ was likewise indicated. I *now* send a messenger with a map, and to present the divinations."

4 II. The king bowed his face to his hands and his head to the ground, saying, "The duke has not dared but to acknowledge reverently the favour of Heaven, and has surveyed the locality to find where our Chow may respond to that favour. Having settled the locality, he has sent his messenger to come and show me the divinations,

and the duke would seem to have thought that it might be sufficient to remove the disaffected people of Yin to it, instead of transporting them so far as Lŏ. The text appears to say that he had divined about this site, after reaching Lŏ; but I think it must have been a previous measure, and intended merely to satisfy the people of Yin. The duke himself could never have seriously contemplated settling the capital of the dynasty there. Whensoever and wheresoever he divined about this place, we must understand that the result was unfavourable. 我乃至洛食,—for the Këen and Ch'en rivers, see the 'Tribute of Yu.' Pt. i., p. 55. The east of the Këen and west of the Ch'en was the site fixed for the imperial city (王城); and the east of the Ch'en was that of 'the lower capital' (下都), to which the people of Yin were removed. But both sites were near the Lŏ, and the divination was favourable in each case. To understand the phrase 洛食, we must refer to the method of divining by the tortoise shell, described on page 336. If the ink, smeared on the back of the shell, was dried up—eaten, licked up—by the fire, the trial was favourable; if it was not so dried up, the result was considered to be unfavourable. Këang Shing, following K'ang-shing, gives another meaning of 食, which I hardly understand. K'ang-shing's words are:—我以乙卯日於洛之衆,觀召公所卜處皆可長久居民,使服田相食. In the last Book nothing is said about the duke of Chow's divining about the sites. This the duke of Shaou had done previous to the arrival of the other. Many say that we are only to understand from the text that the regent adopted the Guardian's divination. But then he had himself divined about the site near the Le water, nor have we reason to suppose that the duke of Shaou had divined for the site of 'the lower capital.' There is a perplexity here which the scantiness of our information does not enable us to unravel. 伻 (perhaps the character should be 抨) 來以圖及獻卜,—伻=使, 'to send;' 圖=洛之地圖, 'a plan or map of the country about the Lŏ.'

Ch. II. P. 4. The King's reply to the message. 王拜手稽首,—see on the 'T'ae-këă,' Pt. ii., pp. 3 and 4. 公不敢至匹休,—by 天之休 we are to understand 天之休命, 'the favouring decree of Heaven,' calling the House of Chow to the sovereignty of the empire; then 其作周匹(=配)休=其意欲所定之宅.爲我周配答天休之地, as in the translation. The passage is obscure, but this seems to be the meaning. 伻來至恆吉,—K'ang-shing thought that by the repetition of 來 it was indicated that two messengers were sent by the duke; but there is no necessity to understand the terms so. 視=示, 'to show to.' 卜休恆吉=卜兆之休美而常吉者. This is better than to take it

卜休恆吉、我二人共貞、公其以予萬億年敬天之休、拜手稽首誨言。○周(五節)公曰、王肇稱殷禮、祀于新邑、咸

favourable and always auspicious. Let us two sustain *the responsibilities* in common. The duke has reverently acknowledged the favour of Heaven, making provision for me for myriads and tens of myriads of years. With my face to my hands and my head to the ground, *I receive* his instructive words."

5 III. The duke of Chow said, "Let the king at first employ the ceremonies of Yin, and sacrifice in the new city, doing everything in

with Gan-kwŏ as—所卜之美常吉之居, 'the admirable sites which he divined, and which will always be fortunate.' 二人共貞,—by the 'two men' are meant the king and the duke of Chow. I don't know what to make of the 貞. Gan-kwŏ has—我與公共正其美, from which I get no meaning apt in the place. Ma Yung explained the term by 當, 'to bear,' 'to sustain,' which is preferable to the other. Hea Sëen says:—王欲與公共當此吉卜, 'The king wishes along with the duke to sustain the duties arising from the auspicious divinations.' 公其至之休,—the meaning of this is that as Heaven had shown its favour to the House of Chow in calling it to the sovereignty, so the duke by all his care in founding the new capital had fixed upon a central seat where that sovereignty could be maintained for ever. Before 誨言 we must understand 以誨, or some words of similar import. I do not think we are to suppose that the king made a second prostration.

Ch. III. Pp. 5—13. ADVICES BY THE DUKE ON THE SACRIFICES WHICH THE KING SHOULD OFFER ON COMMENCING HIS ADMINISTRATION IN THE NEW CITY, AND ABOUT HIS SUBSEQUENT GOVERNMENT. HE ALSO INTIMATES HIS OWN PURPOSE NOW TO RETIRE FROM PUBLIC LIFE.

We must suppose that these advices were given in Haou. The duke had returned there some time after receiving the king's reply to the message which he sent. It is most likely that he had left Lŏ immediately after the duke of Shaou had made what is called his announcement, and set forth before him the various offerings which were presented by the princes, to be used, it is said, at the sacrifices which would be offered,—we may suppose on the solemn inauguration by the king in person of the new city as the capital of the empire. However this may be, it is plain that the duke, in the first instance at least, is speaking to the king in some other place from which he is urging him to go to Lŏ.

P. 5. *The sacrifices which the king should offer in the first place.* 王肇稱殷禮,—both Gan-kwŏ and K'ang-shing take this clause as in the translation, understanding by 殷禮 'the ceremonies of the Yin dynasty.' K'ang-shing says that the ceremonies for the services of the present dynasty had not yet been settled, or if settled, had not yet been made publicly known. That would be done next year, which would be the first of the king's independent reign. In the meantime he should employ the ceremonies of Yin. Ying-tă, on the other hand, in his gloss on Gan-kwŏ's commentary, says that the ceremonies had been settled, but from their general agreement with those of the previous dynasty, they are still called here 殷禮. This remark is very unsatisfactory. We cannot tell why the duke gave this particular advice, but I do not see that the phrase can be rendered otherwise than I have done. Ts'ae, indeed, after Wang Gan-shih and Lin Che-k'e, proposes to take 殷 in the sense of 盛, so that the meaning would be—'Let the king employ the fullest ceremonies.' To justify such a meaning of the term, they refer to an expresion in Kung-yang's commentary on the Ch'un Ts'ew, under the 2d year of duke Wăn (文公二年), where it is said—五年而再殷祭; but 殷 there means 'great,' and not 'full.' The reference is to the 'great sacrifices,' called 祫 and 禘 (see Ana., III., x.). As Maou K'e-ling observes, we may speak of 殷祭, but not of 殷禮. The text is silent on the sacrifice or sacrifices, which the duke wished the king to offer as his first act in the new city. Gan-shih

秩無文。○六節予齊百工、伻從王于周、惟曰、庶有事。○七節今王卽命曰、記功宗、以功作元祀、惟命曰、汝受命篤

6 an orderly way, but without any display. I will marshal all the officers to attend your majesty from Chow, merely saying that probably there will be business to be done.

7 "Let the king instantly give orders, saying, 'Let those distinguished by merit be recorded; the most meritorious shall be the first in the sacrifices.' Let him also command, saying, 'You in whose behalf this order is given must give me your assistance with sincere ear-

supposed it was that mentioned in par. 29;—which is not likely. I should rather suppose it was a series of sacrifices like those offered by Suin on his undertaking the duties of government for Yaou; see the 'Canon of Shun,' p. 6. The occasion was a grand one,—the inauguration of Lŏ as the capital, and of Ching's becoming of age and taking the government in his own hands. 咸秩無文,—秩=序, 'order,' 'to arrange orderly;' 無文,—'without ornament.' Simplicity was a characteristic of the ceremonies of Yin as compared with those of Chow;—see Con. Ana., III., xiv. Gan-kwŏ took 無文 differently, and Ts'ae agrees with him. The latter's exposition of the whole par. is:—王始舉盛禮,祀之于洛邑,皆序其所當祭者,雖祀典不載,而義當祀者,亦序而祭之也, 'Let the king begin by employing the fullest ceremonies in his sacrifices at Lŏ, offering in order to all *the spirits* to which he ought to sacrifice. There may be some to which in right he ought to sacrifice that are not contained in the sacrificial canons; let him likewise sacrifice to them, having arranged them in their proper order.'

P. 6. *In what way the duke would instruct the officers to attend the king to Lŏ.* 齊百工=整齊百官; meaning probably nothing more than what appears in the translation, though some of the critics (see the 集說) dwell on the 齊, as if it included all moral adjustment. 從王于周,—this can only mean—'follow the king from Chow to Lŏ;' as the 'Daily Explanation' has it—從王自周以適洛. 庶有事,—this is not so indefinite as Gan-kwŏ has it,—庶幾有善政事, 'probably there will be some business of good government.' Indeed, he appears to have thought it a remark of the duke to himself, = 'I may consider the govt. will now go on well.' From the usage of the phrase 有事, it would be understood that he intimated that sacrifices were to be offered.

P. 7. *How the king should stimulate the officers to loyal exertions by promising them a place in the sacrificial canon according to their merit.* Compare 'The Pwan-kăng,' Pt. i, p. 16,—茲予大享于先王,爾祖其從與享之, and the note where it is said that under the Chow dynasty there was a 'Recorder of Merits,' who entered the names of meritorious ministers among the imperial kindred when alive, and regulated the arrangement of their spirit tablets at the sacrifices in the ancestral temple, when they were dead. It is to this custom, which the dyn. of Chow took from Yin, that the duke refers. 記功宗=記功之尊顯者, as in the translation. Këang Shing, after Gan-kwŏ, makes 宗 a verb.—'Record the meritorious and honour them.' How they should be honoured is shown in the next clause, so that the general meaning is not affected by the way in which we construe 宗. In the Le Ke, Bk. XXIII., called 祭法, or 'The Laws of Sacrifice,' p. 9, there is a list given of various services to the state which would entitle their performers to be sacrificed to (夫聖王之制祀也,法施於民,則祀之,以死勤事,則祀之,以勞定國,則祀之,能禦大災,則祀之,能捍大患,則祀之). 惟

弼。○八節丕視功載、乃汝其悉自教工。○九節孺子其朋、孺子其朋、其往、無若火、始燄燄、厥攸灼、敘弗其絕。○十節厥若彝、及撫事、如予、惟以在周工、往新邑、伻嚮、即有僚、明作有功、惇大成裕、汝永有

8 nestness.' Freely display the record of merits, for it is you who must yourself in everything train the officers. My young son, can
9 you indulge partiality? If you do so, the consequences hereafter will be like a fire, which, a spark at first, blazes up, and by-and-by cannot be extinguished.
10 "Let your observance of the constant rules of right and your soothing measures be like mine. Take only the officers that are in Chow to go to the new city; and make them there join their *old* associates. With intelligent vigour establish your merit, with a generous largeness richly completing *the public manners*:—so shall you obtain an endless fame."

命云云,—this is evidently to be addressed by the king to the officers, = 王又惟勉勵之曰,汝等既受此褒獎之命,宜感激殊恩,厚輔王室 (see the 日講). Gan-kwŏ strangely takes it as addressed to the king.—惟天命我周邦,汝受天命厚矣,當輔大天命.

Pp. 8, 9. *Publicity should be given to the record of merits, and entire impartiality maintained in it.* 8. 丕視功載,—Gan-kwŏ makes this = 'Observe the services of all the officers, and record the meritorious, omitting none.' It is better to take 視 = 示, as in p. 4. 功載 = 記功之載籍. This record should be displayed where all could see it. The evidences afforded by it of the king's impartiality would powerfully influence the officers to the cultivation of a public spirit. This is the import of the second clause.

9. 朋 = 比 'to be partial;' comp. Ana., II. xiv. 孺子其朋 must be taken interrogatively, = 孺子其可少狥比黨之私乎. 其往 = 自是而往, 'from this forward.' 無 (= 毋) 若火,云云,—'do not be like fire;' &c. It is difficult in translating to keep to the style of the text. 燄燄,—the 說文 defines this by 火行微. 敘 = 'by degrees.' Ts'ae says:—將次第延爇不可得而撲滅矣.

P. 10. *How the king should make the duke his model.* 厥若彝 = 其順常道, 'his (= your) following the constant path.' 惟以在周工往新邑 = 惟用見在周官,勿參以私人往新邑,—'use the officers of Chow that now exist, not mixing with them other men of mercenary views, to proceed to the new city.' The meaning is that the king at first should only surround himself with the men whom the duke had tried and proved. 伻嚮即有僚,—Ts'ae put a comma at 嚮, and interpret-

書經

辭。○公(十一節)曰、已、汝惟沖子、惟終。○汝(十二節)其敬、識百辟享、亦識其有不享、享多儀、儀不及物、惟曰不享、惟不役志于享、凡民惟曰不享、惟事其爽侮。○

11 The duke said, "Yes, young as you are, be it yours to complete
12 *the work of your predecessors.* Cultivate *the spirit of* reverence, and you will know who among the princes *sincerely* present their offerings to you, and who do not. In those offerings there are many observances. If the observances are not equal to the articles, it must be said there is no offering. When there is no service of the will in the offerings *of the princes,* all the people will then say, 'We need not *be troubled about* our offerings,' and affairs will be disturbed by errors and usurpations.

ed 伻嚮 by 使百工知上意嚮, 'cause all the officers to know the views of the sovereign.' But this is too great a supplement to the text, nor is there any necessity for it. 嚮 and 即 may very well be joined together. The duke tells the king to take the officers now in Chow to Lŏ, and there make them join their companions, *i.e.*, labour in their old departments at their old duties. Lin Che-k'e has it:—使之向就舊僚以趨事. It is difficult to say whether we should understand 明作有功, 惇大成裕, as descriptive of the king's measures, or of the conduct of the officers. I have taken it with the former reference. 汝永有辭,—comp. the 'T'ae-këă,' Pt. i., p 7. I did not accept the meaning of 'praise' there, but we may as well admit it here, where the words are addressed to the king, and he is not himself the speaker.

Pp. 11—13. The counsels here are of a wider import, and relate to how the king should deal with the princes of the empire, and attach the masses of the people to himself. The duke also plainly intimates his own purpose to retire from public life. The 公曰 in p. 11 might seem to intimate that they were delivered at a different time and place from those which preceded; but it is better to leave that point as incapable of any very definite settlement. 11. *The greatness of the work devolving on the king.* 已 indicates that the duke felt constrained to go on with what he had to say. 惟終—終文武之業, 'finish the work of Wăn and Woo,' *i.e.*, secure the establishment of the dynasty of Chow. 12. *The importance of sincerity in the offerings and in all expressions of loyalty of the princes; and how the king might know whether they were sincere or not.* Ts'ae puts a stop at 敬, so that 汝其敬 is equivalent to the duke of Shaou's repeated admonition that the king should cultivate the virtue of reverence. It is supposed that Ching, reverent himself and sincere, would, as if intuitively, know whether the princes were sincere or not in their expressions of loyalty. 享多儀,—'in the presenting of offerings, there are many ceremonial usages.' 禮=儀. See the use of this passage made by Mencius, VI., Pt. II., v., 4. The 'Complete Digest,' on that passage, says that 多=厚, and paraphrases—享上貴厚乎禮意. 惟不役志于享=諸侯惟不役志于享, as in the translation. 惟事其爽侮,—爽侮=差爽僭侮. 13. *How*

十三節 乃惟孺子、頒朕不暇、聽朕教汝于棐民彝、汝乃是不蘉、乃時惟不永哉、篤敘乃正父、罔不若予、不敢廢乃命、汝往敬哉、茲予其明農哉、彼裕我民、無遠用戾。○

13 "Do you, my young son, manifest everywhere my unwearied diligence, and listen to my instructions to you how to help the people to observe the constant rules of right. If you do not bestir yourself in these things, you will not be of long continuance. If you sincerely and fully carry out the course of your correct father, and follow exactly my example, there will be no venturing to disregard your orders. Go and be reverent. Henceforth I will study husbandry. There do you generously rule our people, and there is no distance from which they will not come to you."

the king should address himself generally to the government of the people with diligence and reverence. The duke will withdraw to his fields. 乃惟孺子,頒朕不暇,—Ts'ae says he does not understand 頒朕不暇, but thinks the meaning may be—成王當頒布我汲汲不暇者,—as in the translation. This appears to have been the view likewise of Gan-kwŏ. Këang Shing reads on to 聽 before putting a comma, and takes 頒 (the 說文 quotes the passage with 攽)=分, 'to separate,' 'to divide,' alleging for this the authority of K'ang-shing. He has:—政事繁多,孺子分其任,我有所不暇聽, 'The business of government is burdensome. Divide, my son, the duties. *Even* I had not time to listen to everything.' 棐民彝=輔民常性之道, 'to help the course of the people's constant nature.' The meaning seems to be what I have given in the translation. If the people be thus ruled,—influenced, not forced,—it may be hoped they will be forward to obey the guidance. 蘉=勉, 'to use effort,' 'exert one's-self.' There are disputes as to the form of the character, but none as to the meaning. 乃時惟不永哉=汝是惟不可長哉. 篤敘乃正父,—敘, 'to arrange orderly.' Here the meaning is that king Ching's measures should all be ordered after those of his father. We cannot suppose that any other than king Woo is meant by 正父, though Keang Shing explains the phrase by 'those whom your father honoured,' referring to the great captains and ministers who assisted in the overthrow of Show. 予其明農哉,—all the critics understand that the duke of Chow here intimates his purpose to withdraw from public life. Gan-kwŏ, however, would interpret—'I will retire as old, and teach the husbandmen about righteousness;' and in illustration of this, Ying-tă quotes a passage from Fuh-shang's 'Introduction to the Shoo' (尙書大傳), that it was the rule for retired officers to occupy themselves in the villages with teaching the young (禮,致仕之臣,教於州里,大夫爲父師,士爲少師,朝夕坐於門塾而教出入之子弟). But we cannot suppose that the duke of Chow would come under any such rule. 彼裕至末—彼=在彼, 'there,' *i.e.*, in Lŏ; 戾=至, 'to come.' The whole=汝若于彼洛邑,果能盡心教養,寬裕其民,則四方之人,皆愛戴歸往,無遠而不至矣 (see the 日講).

十四節王若曰、公、明保予沖子、公稱丕顯德、以予小子揚文武烈、奉答天命、和恆四方民、居師。○十五節惇宗將禮、稱秩元祀、咸秩無文。○十六節惟公德明光于上下、勤施于四方、

14 IV. The king spoke to this effect:—"O duke, you are the enlightener and sustainer of my youth. You have set forth great and illustrious virtues, that I, notwithstanding my youth, may display a brilliant merit like that of Wăn and Woo; reverently respond to the favour of Heaven; harmonize and long preserve the people of all
15 the regions, and settle their multitudes here; and that I may give due honour to the great ceremony *of recording* the most distinguished, regulating the order for the first places at the sacrifices, and doing everything in an orderly manner without display.
16 "But your virtue, O duke, shines brightly above and below, and is displayed actively throughout the four quarters. On every

Ch. IV. Pp. 14—21. The king, with many compliments, responds to the counsels of the duke, and promises to act accordingly. At the same time he intreats him not to carry out his purpose of retiring, and charges him to remain at Lŏ. Ch'in Leih observes that after the 13th par. there ought to be some mention of the king's having gone with the duke from Haou to Lŏ, and he supposes that a portion of the Book is here lost. The natural inference from parr. 18—21 certainly is that the king, when he spoke them, was in Lŏ; but we need not suppose that any tablets were lost. The Book may never have been longer or less confused than it now is.

Pp. 14, 15. *The king, with mention of his obligations to the duke for his counsels, promises to take his advice about the sacrifices to be offered and the record of merits to be made.* 14. 公明保予沖子,—it is much more natural to construe this historically, in the indicative mood, than to take it with Gan-kwŏ in the imperative. He says the meaning is:—'You ought, O duke, to enlighten and sustain me. You must not leave me' (言公當明安我童子,不可去之). 稱—舉 or 揚, 'to speak of,' 'to display.' The 'great and illustrious virtues' which the duke had celebrated are those implied in the counsels which he had just given. If the king could 揚文武烈, he would display the virtue required in p. 11. If he could 奉答天命, he would escape the evil menaced in the 乃時惟不永 of p. 13. If he could 和恆四方民居師, he would realize the 彼裕我民,無遠用戾, also of p. 13. Choo He says that 居師—營洛邑,定民(—衆民之)居, 'to build the city of Lŏ, and settle the dwelling of the people there.' 15. This par. must be construed in close connection with the preceding. It has reference to the counsel given in p. 7. 惇宗將禮,—將—大, 'great; 宗 is evidently employed from the 記功之宗; 惇—'to deem important,' 'to give the due importance to.' 稱秩元祀,—this also must be interpreted from p. 7. Of the last clause it is not necessary to treat again.

P. 16. *The great services of the duke in the business of the govt., which left the king nothing to do but to attend to the sacrifices.* We must understand all this as said by the king to prepare the way for pressing the request that the duke would not carry out his purpose of withdrawing from public life. 旁作穆穆迓衡,—旁—'on every side' as in the

旁作穆穆、迓衡、不迷文武勤教、予沖子夙夜毖祀。○十七節王曰、公功棐迪篤、罔不若時。○十八節王曰、公、予小子其退、

hand appears your deep reverence to secure the establishment of order, so that you fail in nothing of the earnest lessons of Wăn and Woo. It is for me the youth *only* to attend reverently early and late to the sacrifices."

17 The king said, "Great, O duke, has been your merit in helping and guiding me;—let it ever continue so."

18 The king said, "O duke, it is for me, the little child, to return to my throne in Chow, and I charge you, O duke, to remain behind.

'T'ae-këă,' Pt. i., p. 5,—旁求俊彥. 衡, 'a steelyard,' here = 'to balance,' 'to make even.' When it is said 迓衡, we see the duke calmly and reverently 'meeting' all difficulties and emergencies, and adjusting them with the balance of his wisdom and measures. Gan-kwŏ is evidently wrong, when he takes this clause not as descriptive of the character of the duke's government but of its results, and interprets:—四方旁來,爲敬敬之道,以迎太平之政. 不迷文武勤教,—Këang Shing ingeniously takes this as = 'you make no error; with civil capacity and with military you teach the empire.' I prefer, however, to construe as in the translation. 予沖子,云云,—'What have I to do? I should not do so well as you in the administration of affairs. I have only to perform the sacrifices which devolve upon me.'

P. 17. *The king briefly recapitulates the duke's services, and asks him to continue them, and not withdraw from public life.* 迪=啟, 'to teach,' 'to direct.' Ts'ae says:—公之所以輔我啟我者厚矣,當常如是,未可以言去也. Gan-kwŏ's explanation of 罔不若時, though wrong, is yet amusingly ingenious:—天下無不順,而是公之功, 'the whole empire accords, and affirms by its approval the merit of your services!'

Pp. 18—20. *The king declares his own purpose to return to Haou, and charges the duke to continue in public life, remaining at Lŏ, and completing the measures of government which he had initiated.*

18 On the interpretation of this par. there is as much diversity of opinion as on par. 1. The view in the translation is that of Ts'ae, adopted from Lin Che-k'e and other early scholars of the Sung dyn. The old interpreters, followed by many in the present dynasty, understand that the king is here acceding to the duke's request that he would proceed to Lŏ, and promises that he would there appoint the duke's son, Pih-k'in (伯禽), to the principality of Loo.

Where were the king and the duke when the par. was spoken? The old interpreters say—'In Haou;' and Gan-kwŏ supposes that the king is on his throne, at a solemn audience where the duke has resigned the regency, so that 予其退,卽辟于周 = 'I will when I have retired from this audience, go and be king in Lŏ.' I cannot read the Book without getting the impression that the speakers were now in Lŏ. And without referring to any passages, which might require a lengthy and minute discussion of them, the *fact* that king Ching did not take up his residence at Lŏ, and that this city did not till after many reigns become the real capital of Chow, is sufficient to show that the king is not here promising to go to Lŏ, but saying that he will retire from it. On this view 卽辟于周 has its natural meaning. Chow is Haou, as in the first par. of last Book. I should say that this clause ought to be decisive on the point of the dialogue's taking place in Lŏ, were it not for the 從王于周 of par. 6. And allowing all the weight we can to the interpretation of 于周 necessarily adopted there, I must still think that 卽辟于周 is strongly confirmatory of the view of the Book taken by the Sung scholars.

With regard to 命公後, 'it indicates,' says Këang Shing, 'the appointment of Pih-k'in. The king's idea was that if he conferred the investiture on his son, he might retain the

朕辟于周、命公後。○[十九節]四方迪亂、未定于宗禮、亦未克敉公功。○[二十節]迪將其後、監我士師工、誕保文武受民、亂

19 Order has been initiated throughout the four quarters of the empire; but the ceremonies to be honoured *by general observance* have not yet been settled, and I cannot look on your merit as completed.
20 Commence on a great scale what is to be done by your remaining here, being an example to my officers, and greatly preserving the people whom Wăn and Woo received:—by your good government you will prove the help of the whole empire."

duke at court as the prime minister of the govt.' Nothing can be argued conclusively on either side of the question from the words of the text. 命公後 may be taken as in the translation; and when I look at them without reference to the controversy agitated about them, I must understand them thus. They may, however, likewise be taken as Gan-kwŏ and the other early interpreters did.

Referring to Sze-ma Ts'een, he tells us that king Woo, immediately after the overthrow of Show, invested his brother Tan with the principality of Loo, and that Tan did not proceed to take the charge of it, but remained at court to assist the king, (封周公旦於少昊之虛,曲阜,是爲魯公,周公不就封,留佐武王; See the 魯周公世家第三). He tells us also, that after the death of Woo, when the duke of Chow had resolved, notwithstanding the injurious suspicions afloat about him, to remain as regent of the empire during the minority of Ching, he invested his son Pih-k'in with Loo, and gave him this charge:—'A son of king Wăn, brother of king Woo, and uncle of king Ching, I am not of mean position in the empire. But I have sometimes thrice left my bath unfinished, and thrice left a meal, to receive officers, fearing lest I might fail to secure a man of virtue and ability for the service of the govt. When you go to Loo, be careful lest your being a prince make you arrogant to others.' According to this account, Pih-k'in had been invested with Loo several years before the building of Lŏ. Ts'ae argues the same thing from passages of Bk. XXIX; but I do not insist on them, because Maou K'e-ling has shown that they need not be taken as decisive on the question. Still Ts'een's statements carry in themselves evidence of their correctness. Of all his brothers and adherents, the duke of Chow was the one whom king Woo was bound to reward. No doubt he did confer on him the country of Loo; and as the duke was detained from it all his reign and during so many years of his son's reign, there must have been some one to supply his place. I believe that Pih-k'in went to Loo at once, and that subsequently, in the 3d or 4th year of Ching, his father resigned the dukedom entirely to him. This being the case, there is no room left for the understanding the text—命公後—as the old interpreters did.

19, 20. *The king could not look on the duke's work as done, and he calls his attention to various points which were yet to be settled.* 19. 四方迪亂—四方開治, taking it 迪=啟 or 開. Këang Shing takes it = 進, and says:—四方雖進於治. The meaning is substantially the same. 未定宗禮,—Ts'ae takes 宗禮 as referring to the 功宗 of p. 8, and 惇宗將禮 of p. 15. It may be so, but I rather understand the king to be speaking here of the ceremonies in general, by which their dyn. was to be distinguished from those which preceded it. Këang Shing says they are called 宗禮, 'being honoured by all the empire' (宗禮者言禮爲天下所宗). 亦未克敉公功,—敉, has occurred twice before, in Bk. VII., pp. 5 and 11, joined with 寧, and in the sense of 撫 or 安, 'to soothe' 'to settle.' 'It means,' says Woo Ch'ing, 'to honour and reward.' I do not see how to translate the term faithfully, and bring out a meaning appropriate to the contents. 20. 迪將其後 means, acc. to Ts'ae, 啟大其後, as in the translation. Woo Ch'ing takes 迪將 as 'an introductory phrase,' but says he

爲四輔。○王廿一節曰、公定、予往已、公功肅將祗歡、公無困哉、我惟無斁其康事、公勿替刑、四方其世享。○周廿二節公拜手稽首曰、王命予來承

21 The king said, "Remain, O duke. I will certainly go. Your meritorious deeds are devoutly acknowledged and reverently rejoiced in. Do not, O duke, occasion me this difficulty. I on my part will not be idle or tired in seeking the tranquillity of the people; and let not the example which you have afforded be intermitted. So shall the whole empire enjoy for generations *the benefits of your virtue.*"

22 V. The duke of Chow bowed his face to his hands and his head to the ground, saying, "You have charged me, O king, to come here.

does not understand the meaning of it. The 其後 would certainly seem to have reference to the 命公後 of p. 18. I do not see how Gan-kwŏ makes out of 迪將 his 公留教道,將助我. 監我士師工,—士師工 is equivalent to 百官. Among the officers there were those called 士, and others called 師. 監 may be taken, with Ts'ae, 'to afford an example to,' or, with Gan-kwŏ, 'to inspect,' 'to oversee.' 亂爲四輔,—I do not think that this means more than—'effecting good government, and being a help to me on every side.' Compare with 四輔 the 四鄰 in the 'Yih and Tseih,' p. 5. Ts'ae takes the phrase as a name of the new city, or the two new cities of 成周 and 王城, taken in connection with Haou and Fung, as the *points d' appui* of the empire,—which is far-fetched, and intended to strengthen his view of 後 as meaning to remain at Lŏ, sufficiently strong without such support. In a passage in the Le Ke, Bk. VIII., (文王世子), p. 17, mention is made of the appointment of 四輔 and 三公, from which it would appear that 'four' men were denoted by the former phrase. If so, and we are to interpret the text in acc. with that passage, we must suppose that the king wishes the duke alone to be to him all that those four highest and trusted ministers could be.

P. 21. *The king finally announces his determination not to remain himself at Lŏ, and requires the duke to do so.* Of course the old interpreters make 予往已 mean, 'I will go to Lŏ.' Këang Shing puts no comma at 已, but reads on from 予往 to 祗歡, making 往—往日, 'formerly.' All agree in taking 定—止, only with the old interpreters and their modern adherents it means, 'remain to assist me as my premier,' while with Ts'ae it = 'remain here' at Lŏ. The 'Daily Explanation' paraphrases from 公功 to 困哉 (哉 perhaps should be 我) thus:—我公逕衡迪亂之功,人皆肅敬而奉行之,無敢違逆于外,且祗畏而歡悅之,無有拂戾于中. This is acc. to the views of Ts'ae, and I must think that the other interpretations of this par. are non-natural. 斁—厭, 'to dislike,' 'to turn away from.' 公勿替刑—公勿替所以監我士師工者, taking 刑—儀刑. Këang Shing takes 斁—解, but the meaning comes to the same. He would point the whole differently, however.—我惟無斁,其康事公勿替,刑四方其世享.

Ch. V. Pp. 22—24. THE DUKE ACCEPTS THE CHARGE LAID UPON HIM; SETS FORTH HOW

保乃文祖受命民、越乃光烈考武王、弘朕恭。○孺子(廿三節)來相宅、其大惇典殷獻民、亂爲四方新辟、作周恭先、

I undertake *the charge*, and will protect the people whom your grandfather Wăn received by decree, and *whom* your glorious and meritorious father Woo *also so received*. I will enlarge the reverence which I cherish for you.

23 "*But*, my son, come *frequently* and inspect this settlement. Pay great honour to *old* statutes, and to the good and wise men of Yin. Good government here will make you indeed the new chief of the empire, and an example of *royal* respectfulness to all your

HE WILL FULFIL ITS DUTIES; AND TELLS THE CO-OPERATION WHICH HE EXPECTS FROM HIM.

22. 王命予來,—this has reference evidently to the 命公後 of par. 18. Naturally and legitimately we understand 來 of coming to a place; and that place can be no other than Lŏ. The old interpreters holding that the duke only agrees to remain in public life, without any reference to his undertaking the govt. of the new city, say that his returning might have been called a 去 or 'going away,' so his continuing may be called a 來 or 'coming' (see the gloss of Ying-tă *in loc.*). This is very forced. 承保至武王,—this responds to the king's 誕保文武受民 in p. 20. Woo Ch'ing correctly observes that we are to understand 受命民 after 武王, being omitted in the text for the sake of brevity (省文). 越=及. Gan-kwŏ and Këang Shing take it as =于, with which I cannot make sense. They also take 承 and all the other verbs as in the infinitive mood under the govt. of 命. But it is much better to suppose that in 承 the duke speaks in his own person. To me the 朕 in the last clause necessitates this construction. 弘朕恭,—'I will enlarge my reverence.' 恭 is to be taken according to the account of it by Mencius, IV., Bk. I, i., 13, 責難於君謂之恭. The duke would do his duty; he will not allow the king to be remiss in performing *his*. Wang Ts'eaou says ingeniously:—王於文王武王,皆欲令周公奉其道,安其民,周公分言之,辭繁而不殺者,見其所承之重也,弘朕恭,欲展其事上之敬,意在下文,下兩節,一,以治洛之效望之成王,即所謂弘朕恭也,一,以治洛之事自效,即所謂承保也.

23. 孺子來相宅,—I must translate this in the imperative, according to the view which has been taken of the last. The paraphrase in the 'Complete Digest' is:—王雖歸周,而此洛邑,王當來省視以治之, 'although your majesty is returning, you ought to come and examine and see this city of Lŏ, to govern it.' Though the duke gives up the hope which he had cherished, that the king would take up his residence in the new city, he endeavours to make the best of his disappointment, and hopes that the advantages to be derived from Lŏ will in part at least be secured by frequent and regular visits to it from the king. 典=典章, 'statutes,' *i.e.*, we may suppose, the rules and principles of govt. approved or established by Wăn and Woo. 殷獻(=賢民,) 'the good able people (=men) of Yin,' are, we may again suppose, men belonging to old official families of Yin, who had kept themselves from the degrading vices which had occasioned the downfall of the dynasty. Both 典 and 民 are governed by 惇, and a conjunction is understood between its two objects. This is forcing a meaning out of the text, but the meaning thus obtained is more likely than any other which

曰、其自時中乂、萬邦咸休、惟王有成績。○予(廿四節)旦以多子越御事、篤前人成烈、答其師、作周孚先、考朕昭子刑、乃單文祖

successors of Chow." "From this time," said *the duke*, "by the government administered in this central spot, all parts of the empire will be conducted to repose, and this will be the completion of your merit, O king.

24 "I, Tan, with the numerous officers and managers of affairs, will consolidate the achievements of our predecessors, in response to the *hopes of the* people. I will afford an example of sincerity to future ministers of Chow, seeking to render complete the pattern intended for the enlightenment of you, my son, and thus to carry fully out the virtue of your grandfather Wăn."

has been put upon it. Comp. the view of Gan-kwŏ:—大其厚行典常于殷賢人, and that of Këang Shing:—其大厚取典于殷之賢民. 亂(=治)爲四方新辟,—comp. the 作民明辟 of par. 2. 作周恭先,—Ts'ae expands this by 人君恭以接下,以恭而倡後王, 'as the sovereign shows respectfulness towards your ministers, and by such respectfulness leads the way for future kings.' Gan-kwŏ's view is the same:—爲周家見恭敬之王,後世所推先. Këang Shing brings out nearly the same meaning by another construction of the characters:—作立周邦,以恭敬爲先務. The 曰 is perplexing. The simplest way is to suppose 公 as the nominative to it. I understand 自時 as in the 'Complete Digest'=今而後. With 中乂 compare the 自服土中, and 自時中乂 in the last Book, p. 14. 24. The duke here speaks fully and bravely of what he himself will do. We have had instances before of his superiority to the mock humility with which Chinese statesmen generally veil appreciation of themselves and their services. 多子越御事,—see on the Con. Ana., I., i., for the meaning of 子. 多子 is 'the many gentlemen;' and from the 御事 which follows, we conclude that the gentlemen intended the officers of the superior classes,—as the critics say, 卿大夫. 答其師(=衆)—'in answer to the multitudes.' The meaning must be as in the translation. 作周孚先,—孚=信, 'faithfulness,' 'loyalty.' The expression is correlate to the 作周恭君 of the last par.; and they throw light on each other. As the king would show to future kings an example of respectfulness in dealing with his ministers, so the duke would show to future ministers an example of loyal devotedness in serving his sovereign. 考朕昭子刑,—考=成, 'to complete.' Ts'ae takes 昭子 as=the 明辟 of par. 1, so that the meaning of the clause is—'I will render complete the pattern afforded by you, my illustrious son.' The editors of Yung-ching's Show observe that everywhere else he takes 昭 or=明, 'to enlighten,' and that there is no reason to depart from that signification here; so that the meaning of the whole is as in the translation.

單=盡, 'to complete,' 'to carry fully out.' Everything necessary to consolidate the dynasty might be considered as carrying out—completing—the virtue of king Wăn, its proper founder.

德。○^廿五節^伻來毖殷、乃命寧予、以秬鬯二卣、曰明禋、拜手稽首休享。○^廿六節^予不敢宿、則禋于文王武王。○^廿七節^惠篤敘、

25 VI. *Afterwards, the duke of Chow took occasion to say,* "*The king* has sent messengers to admonish *the people of* Yin, and with a soothing charge to me, along with two flagons of the black millet herb-flavoured spirit, saying, 'Here is a pure sacrificial gift, which with my hands to my face and my head to the ground I offer for you to enjoy its excel-
26 lence.' I dare not keep this, and offer it in sacrifice to king Wăn and
27 king Woo." *In doing so, he prayed,* "Let him be obedient to and

Ch. VI. Pp. 25—28. THE CONDUCT OF THE DUKE IN DECLINING SOME EXTRAORDINARY GIFTS FROM THE KING, AND TAKING OCCASION FROM THEM TO OFFER A PRAYER TO WAN AND WOO, EXPRESSIVE OF HIS LOYALTY.

I cannot say that I am satisfied with the meaning of these parr. as it appears in the translation; but no interpretation of them has been proposed which can be fully acquiesced in by a cautious student. I have mainly followed the view of them given by Ts'ae, who himself followed Soo Shih. The action of them is referred to some time subsequent to that in which the previous parr. were spoken. The king is supposed to have returned to Haou, and thence he sends messages and gifts, doing honour to the duke as if he had been a departed spirit, and were continuing in heaven the guardianship of the dynasty which he had so efficiently discharged during his life. This was improper, and may be deemed improbable; but if we remember how the boy had given ear to the rumours that the duke had designs upon the throne, and consider that even now he was not really following his advice, and fixing his residence at Lŏ, we may believe that the young emperor had more awe of the powerful minister than love for him, and that he wished to propitiate him by such an extraordinary offering.

伻來毖殷,乃命寧予=王遣使誥誡殷民,因念周公之功,而來慰寧之,錫以秩典, 'The king sent messengers with admonitory lessons for the people of Yin, and being impressed with the merits of the duke, at the same time to soothe his mind, by the gift of an extraordinary mark of his regard.' 秬鬯二卣,—秬 is a species of black millet, used in the distillation of spirits. 鬯 is a species of fragrant grass employed to flavour the spirits. The two characters are used here as a name of the spirit which was made from them. 卣 is the name of a cup or bowl of medium size, in which such spirit was usually kept. A larger vessel used for that purpose was called 彝, and a smaller, 罍; the size of the 卣 was between the others. 曰明至末,—this is supposed to be the message of the king which accompanied the offering. 明=潔, 'pure;' 禋=敬, 'to revere,' 'reverent.' The 'Daily Explanation' gives for this clause:—此秬鬯之酒,所以明潔禋敬,以奉神而格帝者也,我敢拜手稽首,以此美物,而致享于公焉. 26. 予不敢宿,—Ts'ae says that 宿 here has the same meaning as the phrase 三宿 in Bk. XXII., p. 26, where the character is explained by 進爵, 'to advance the cup;' making the meaning to be—'I do not dare to drink this spirit.' But it will be seen on that passage, that if we must so define 宿 there, we cannot admit the signification in this text. And why should there be any difficulty in understanding here as I have done. There is an instance of the same usage, quite in point, in the Ana., X., viii., 8. The duke was so far from using for himself the king's gift, that he could not even allow it to remain by him, but presented it at once in a sacrifice to Wăn and Woo. 27. This par. is to be taken as a prayer for the king, offered when the duke sacrificed to Wăn and Woo with the spirit which

無有遘自疾、萬年厭于乃德、殷乃引考。王伻(廿八節)○殷乃承敘萬年、其永觀朕子懷

observant of your course. Let him meet with no evil or sickness. Let him satisfy his descendants for myriads of years with your virtue. Let the people of Yin enjoy protracted prosperity." *He also said to*
28 *the messengers*, "The king has sent you to Yin, which has received his charges well ordered for myriads of years; but let the people ever have to observe the virtue cherished by my son."

had been sent to himself. 惠篤敘,—惠=順, 'to accord with,' 'accordantly;' for 篤敘 comp. the 篤敘乃正父 of p. 13. The clause=願使王順承先業,篤之而不遺,敘之而不紊,憲章是守,無有愆忘,而後可焉, (see the 日講). 無(=毋)有遘自疾,—'let him not bring on (遘=遇, 'to meet with;' but with more of an active signification) himself any sickness.' 萬年厭于乃德,—厭 is in the 3d tone, 'to be full,' 'satiated.' We must suppose that the king is prayed for in his descendants for ten thousand years;—as Ts'ae has it, 子孫萬年厭飽乃德. 殷乃引考,—Ts'ae takes 引考=長壽, 'protracted longevity;' and the 'Daily Explanation' gives for the passage,—願使殷餘之亡民,長享有幹有年之樂, 'make the poor remnant of Yin long enjoy the happiness of prosperity and plenty.' 28. We are to suppose that the duke now addresses the messengers who had come from the king, and sends the counsel here contained to Haou, to the effect that though he would do his duty to carry out the admonitions which had been sent to the people of Yin, yet the government of them could only be effected by the personal virtue of the king.

I am well aware, in thus interpreting these four paragraphs, that serious objections may be taken to the way in which the whole is supplemented, and many of the clauses explained. All that can be said is that the interpretation seems to me more likely than any other that has been proposed. It will suffice if I subjoin here that proposed by Gan-kwŏ. He first reads 伻來毖殷乃命寧 (putting a stop at 寧) along with 考朕昭子刑,乃單文祖德, interpreting—'"The method by which I will complete the enlightenment of you, my son, is to complete the virtue of your grandfather Wăn." This he says with reference to the ceremonies which he would establish. "The reason why you must dwell here in the middle of the land, is that Wăn and Woo have sent you to come and carefully teach the people of Yin, recognising their charge, and giving them repose"' (我所成明子法,乃盡文祖之德,謂典禮也,所以居土中,是文武使已來慎教殷民,乃見命而安之). He then begins a new par. with 予, and on 予以至休享 says:—'The duke of Chow had been regent for seven years; and having produced a happy tranquillity throughout the empire, he took two bowls of black millet wine, and with purity and the utmost reverence had presented it to Wan and Woo that they might enjoy it, and announced to them the happy state of the empire. Having done this, he had resigned the government, but king Ching had induced him to remain as his chief minister. He therefore recounts those things here (周公攝政七年致太平,以黑黍酒二器,明潔致敬,告文武以美享,旣告而致政,成王留之,本(? 故)說之). On from 予不至武王 he says:—'The duke says, "Seeing this happy tranquillity of the empire, I made a pure announcement to Wăn and Woo not delaying over it"' (言我見天下太平,則潔告文武,不經宿). Par. 27 is then taken as addressed to the king, and expounded:—"Do you, in administering the govt., observe the regular constitutions, and carry them fully into execution, with an orderly discrimination. Allow none to follow courses which would be productive of calamity and distress. So will the empire for myriads of years be satiated with your virtue, and *the dynasty of* Yin will for ever become that of Chow" (汝爲政當順典常厚行之;

德。○戊(廿九節)辰、王在新邑烝祭歲、文王騂牛一、武王騂牛一、王命作冊、逸祝冊、惟告

29 VII. On the day Mow-shin, the king in the new city performed the annual winter sacrifice, offering a red bull to king Wăn, and the same to king Woo. He then commanded a declaration to be prepared, which was done by Yih in the form of a prayer, and it simply announced the remaining behind of the duke of Chow. The king's

使有次序、無有遘用患疾之道者、則天下萬年厭於汝德、殷乃長成爲周). On the 28th par. he says:—'"When the king causes the people of Yin, high and low, to have such orderly relations with one another, then will be seen *the course of govt.* for myriads of years, and the people will for ever look to our descendants and turn to their virtue." Thus he stimulates the king to complete the work *begun by Wăn and Woo*' (王使殷民、上下相承有次序、則萬年之道、民其長觀我子孫而歸其德矣、勉使終之).

It would be easy to fill pages with smaller variations of view that have been proposed on this difficult passage; but the student will probably think that it has been dwelt upon at sufficient length. I will, however, here subjoin the version of Gaubil, and a note which he gives on the character 醴. His version is:—'Vous avez envoyé un exprès pour faire instruire les peuples de Yin, et vous lui avez ordonné de me demander en quel état étoit ma santé; outre cela vous m'avez envoyé en present deux vases remplis du vin Ku-tchang, et vous avez ainsi parlé: il faut avoir le cœur pur et respectueux. Je me prosterne à terre, et je me sers de ces deux heureux vases pour marquer mon respect.

'Je n'oserois boire de ce vin; mais je m'en suis déja servi pour honorer avec respect Ven-vang. et Vou-vang.

'Je souhaite que le Roi soit exact à imiter ses ancêtres, qu'il vive long tems sans fâcheux accident, que jusqu'à dix mille ans il ait des imitateurs de sa vertu, que les nouveaux sujets de la dynastie Yin jouissent d'une longue et heureuse suite d'années.

'Je souhaite que jusqu'à dix mille ans vous gouverniez hereusement les peuples de Yin. Dans tout ce qui les regarde, faites ensorte qu'ils se plaisent à suivre vos exemples.'

I need not speak of the character of this version. His note is to the following effect:—'The characters 秬鬯 express a wine made from black millet or 秬, and an odoriferous herb called 鬯. Acc. to the thought of king Ching, this required in him who used it a heart pure and full of respect. It was set apart therefore for the ceremonies performed to Heaven, or spirits, or to ancestors. It was employed perhaps in all the three ceremonies. Now the character which expresses the respect to be shown in the use of this wine is 醴, which is composed of three other characters:—示, meaning *to show to;* 西, *the west;* and 土, *country.* Could the ancient Chinese have had in view, in the use of this character, the country of the west from which they had come forth? Do we have in it, applied to these ceremonies, the vestiges of some ancient ceremony, in which they regarded the west, when they honoured Heaven, the Spirits, or their first ancestors? The Chinese characters are composed of several other characters, and the whole has regard to the thing expressed by the composite character; the several characters are the simple ideas which make the composite one. The analysis which I make here of the character 醴 is but a conjecture. I only give it as such, and I do not care to engage to find proofs of it in the ancient monuments and traditions of China. I know that several Europeans have abused the analysis of Chinese characters; but the Chinese themselves make sometimes such analyses.'

Gaubil was at home when he brought his knowledge of mathematical and astronomical science to bear on the illustration of Chinese chronology; but this conjecture about the meaning of the term 醴 cannot be called happy. 示 suggests the idea of some *religious* meaning, as belonging to the whole character; but the other half of it—垔—is entirely *phonetic,* and suggests merely its name or sound. It enters in the same way into more than 30 other characters. The character is used in the 'Canon of Shun,' p. 6, where I do not know that the idea of the objects sacrificed to being the fathers of the nation who had their seats in the west ever occurred to any one.

Ch. VII. Pp. 29—31. Historical notices of the public announcement of the duke's appointment to remain at Lŏ; and of his subsequent government. 29. 戊辰,

周公其後、王賓殺禋咸格、王入太室祼。○三十節王命周公後、作冊逸誥、在十有二月。○卅一節惟周公誕保文武受命、惟七年。

guests, on occasion *of* the killing the victims and offering the sacrifice, all made their appearance. The king entered the grand apartment, and poured out the libation.

30 The king charged the duke of Chow to remain, and Yih, the preparer of the document, made the declaration;—*all* in the 12th month.

31 *Then* the duke of Chow greatly sustained the decree which Wăn aud Woo had received, through the space of seven years.

—we may conclude from the next par. that this was in the 12th month. The king was then in Lŏ. We may believe that he had come to it expressly for the service which is here described. Gan-kwŏ supposed that he had arrived on the day Mow-shin; but in that case we should have read 王到新邑, and not 王在新邑. 烝 is the name given to the winter sacrifice in the temple of ancestors. Ts'ae read the three characters 烝祭歲 together, with the meaning which I have given in the translation;—whether correctly or not I cannot undertake to say. The 歲, occurring where it does, is a great difficulty. Këang Shing puts a comma at 烝, and then takes 祭歲 as another sacrifice, offered on the first day of the first month of the next year. This was the view of K'ang Shing, who also supposed that after the usual service of the day there was still the special sacrifice to Wăn and Woo, which follows. Lin Che-k'e says the best plan is to allow that the 歲 is inexplicable, and so pass over it. I believe he is right. 騂,—see Ana., VI., iv. 王命作册,—comp. on Bk. VI., p. 5. 逸祝册,—逸 was the name of the 史, or 'Recorder,' who officiated on the occasion;—see again Bk. VI., p. 5, and also Bk. X., p. 13. Over 惟告周公其後 there is fought again the battle as to the meaning of 後, which has been gone into on par. 18. 王賓殺禋咸格,—'the king's guests' denotes all the princes present and assisting at the ceremonies, and specially those representing the previous dynasties. 殺—殺牲, 'killing the victims.' 禋 is descriptive of the whole service as 'a pure sacrifice presented in the temple of ancestors.' 王入太室祼—王乃入太室,祼地以降神, 'the king entered into the great apartment (*i.e.*, the middle hall of the temple), and poured the fragrant spirits on the ground to invite the descent of the spirits.' 30. I understand this par. as a *resumé* of the preceding, with an additional note of time. 31. According to the translation which I have given, the 'seven years' mentioned are to be calculated from the 7th year of king Ching. As Ch'in Sze-k'ae says:—'The duke of Chow acted as regent for seven years, and then wished to retire from public life; but king Ching detained him in the govt. of Lŏ, where he spent other seven years, making in all fourteen years from the death of king Woo' (see the 集說). This view of course is contrary to the old interpreters and those who adhere to their views. They think that the 'seven years' here are simply the seven years of the duke's regency.

THE BOOKS OF CHOW.

BOOK XIV. THE NUMEROUS OFFICERS.

多士

惟(一節)三月、周公初于新邑洛、用告商王士。○

1 I. In the third month, at the commencement of *the government of* the duke of Chow in the new city of Lŏ, he announced *the royal will*

THE NAME OF THE BOOK.—多士, 'The numerous Officers.' By the 'numerous officers' are intended the officers of the previous dynasty, who had been removed along with the people to the new city of Lŏ. The phrase occurs several times, and is taken to designate the Book, which indeed was addressed to those officers. It is found in both the texts, and has its place among the 'Announcements' of the Shoo.

The prefatory note about the Book (see page 10) says that when the new city of Ching-chow was completed, the obstinate people of Yin were removed to it; and that it was then that the duke of Chow announced to them the royal will, as it is here set forth. This statement has given rise to some discussion. We have met with various passages in the two last Books, which make it appear that many of the people of Yin had been removed to the country about the Lŏ before the dukes of Shaou and Chow received their mission to proceed thither. The same thing may be argued from passages in this Book itself as well. Hence Ts'ae follows in the wake of Woo Ts'ae-laou, and says we have here an instance of how little the notices in the so-called Confucian preface are to be depended on. Maou K'e-ling has endeavoured to weaken the force of their observations, but with little success.

It is just possible that king Ching, on returning to Haou after the sacrifice described in the end of last Book, ordered another migration of the people of Yin to Lŏ, and on a large scale; and that their arrival at the new settlement gave occasion to this address. This would reconcile the statement in the preface and the intimations which are found of previous removals of the people; but it can be given only as a supposition.

CONTENTS. The object of the announcement is to reconcile the minds of the people of Yin, and especially of the higher classes among them, to their lot. The day of Yin had gone by. The House of Chow was in the ascendant. They had been dealt with kindly and generously. They had better acquiesce in their condition, and by loyalty deserve well of their new masters. If they did not do so, a worse thing would come upon them.

The address or announcement, much broken up, occupies the whole of the Book after the introductory paragraph. It has been divided into four chapters. The first, parr. 2—4, vindicates the justice of the sovereigns of Chow in taking the empire to themselves. The second parr. 5—15, unfolds the causes why the dynasty of Yin had been set aside. The third, parr. 16—23, shows how it had been necessary to remove the people to Lŏ, and with what good intention the new city had been built. The fourth, parr. 24—26, shows that comfort and prosperity are here at Lŏ open to their attainment, while by perseverance in disaffection they will only bring misery and ruin on themselves.

Ch, I. Pp. 1—4. WHEN THE ADDRESS WAS DELIVERED. THE HOUSE OF CHOW HAD OVERTHROWN THE DYNASTY OF YIN, NOT FROM AMBITION, BUT IN EXECUTION OF THE WILL OF GOD.

1. *Introductory.* 惟三月,—this third month is most naturally reckoned from the sacrifice described in the concluding parr. of the last Book. Some call the year the first of Ching's reign, *i.e.*, after he attained his majority. Others call it the first of the duke of Chow's government of Lŏ. Woo Ching

二節 王若曰、爾殷遺多士、弗弔、旻天大降喪于殷、我有周佑命、將天明威、致王罰、勅殷命、終于帝。○三節 肆爾多士、非我小國敢弋殷命、惟天

2 to the officers of the Shang dynasty, *saying*, "The king speaks to this effect:—'Ye numerous officers who remain from the dynasty of Yin, great ruin came down on Yin from the want of pity in compassionate Heaven, and we, the princes of Chow, received its favouring decree. We accordingly felt charged with its bright terrors; carried out the punishments which kings inflict; rightly disposed of the appointment of Yin; and finished *the work* of God.
3 Now, ye numerous officers, it was not that our small country dared to aim at the appointment of Yin. But Heaven was not with

would identify this month, indeed, with the third of the previous year, and the address here with what I have called the 'written specifications' delivered then to the people of Yin and the chiefs of the various States; but it is sufficient to have referred to his view. 初于新邑洛,—始行治洛之事, 'when he commenced discharging the business of the govt. of Lŏ.' 用告商王士,—we might take 用 as simply = 'thereupon.' The critics, however, all complete its meaning as in the translation,—用成王之命. The officers are said to be those of 'the king of Shang,' meaning Show; or perhaps we should take 王 in the plural, and then 商王, = 'the Shang dynasty.'

Pp. 2—4. *Chow only executed justice in overthrowing Yin,—was but the instrument in the hands of God.* 2. 弗弔旻天大降喪于殷,—for the meaning of 弗弔 comp. Bk. VII., p. 1, and XVI., p. 2. On 旻天, see Pt. II., Bk. II., p., 21, and on Men. v., Pt. I., i., 1. In addition to the two explanations of the meaning of 旻 which are cited in the notes on Mencius, I find a third, given here by Ma Yung,—that the autumnal sky is called 旻, because 'the autumn air is killing' (秋氣殺也); and he argues that what is said immediately after of ruin inflicted by Heaven confirms this acct. of the character. Kēang Shing approves this view; but there is more force in the language, when we take 旻 as = 'compassionate.' With sorrow was the ruin sent down, but Yin could not be spared, so great was its wickedness. —'Without pity, pitying Heaven sent down great ruin on Yin.' 我有周佑命 = 我周受眷佑之命, as in the translation. This requires a considerable supplement. Kēang Shing, without such sup., makes the text = 我周佑助天命, 'our Chow lent its aid to the charge of Heaven;'—with which the student will probably be still less satisfied. 將天明威,—comp. in 'The Announcement of T'ang,' p. 4, 將天命明威. 致王罰,—in 'The Speech of T'ang,' p. 4, we have 致天之罰, 'carry out the punishment appointed by Heaven.' The 'punishment' here is the same, but described with reference to the agents employed by Heaven to execute it. 勅殷命,—it is not easy to catch the exact force of 勅 here and in p. 14. We must accept the definition of it by 正, 'to correct,' 'to rectify.' But in the rectification of the decree of Yin, there was involved the overthrow of the dynasty. 終于帝 = 終上帝之事, 'to complete the work or business of God.' 3. 弋殷命,—弋, 'to shoot at.' See Ana. VII., xxvi. K'ang-shing and Wang Suh read 翼, but they must have written, we may almost say, that

不畀、允罔固亂、弼我、我其敢求位。○四節惟帝不畀、惟我下民秉爲、惟天明畏。○五節我聞曰、上帝引逸、有夏不適逸、則惟帝降格、嚮于時夏、

Yin, for indeed it would not strengthen its misrule. It *therefore*
4 helped us;—did we dare to seek the throne of ourselves? God was not for *Yin*, as appeared from the conduct of our inferior people, in which there is the brilliant dreadfulness of Heaven.
5 II. 'I have heard the saying—"God leads men to tranquil security;" but the sovereign of Hea would not move to such security, whereupon God sent down *corrections*, indicating His mind to

character by mistake for 弋. They define it by 取, 'to take,' and by 驅, 'to drive out.' 天不畀,—'Heaven did not give,' *i.e.*, did not any longer give its favour to Yin. Gan-kwŏ read this on with the next clause, and has 天不與信無堅固治者, 'Heaven did not—or does not—give its favour to those who are not sincerely strengthening their govt.' Këang Shing and Ming-shing, pointing in the same way, but dissatisfied with Gan-kwŏ's explanation, take 罔 = 誣, and change 固 into 怙, on the slenderest ground,—in fact, without any ground at all,—making the whole = 天不與信誣罔而怙亂者, which is to me more unsatisfactory than the view which they condemn. The view given in the translation was first proposed by Soo Shih. 我其敢求位 is to be taken interrogatively. 4. How was the mind of Heaven known to be averted from Yin? This par. supplies the answer:—'By the disaffection of the people.' We have here again the doctrine of *vox populi vox Dei*. 惟帝不畀,—the change of style from the indefinite term 'Heaven' to the personal 'God' is to be remarked. We have met with it before. 惟我下民秉爲 = 惟我下民之所秉爲, 'was what our people held fast and did.' The expression 秉爲 is peculiar, but this explanation of it is much preferable to that of Gan-kwŏ, who reads 爲 in the 3d tone, and says: —惟我周家下民秉心爲我, 'the lower people of our House of Chow maintained their *right* hearts, and were for us.' A peculiar force of the 惟, common in the Shoo, is very marked here. It serves to link the various propositions together, indicating that they form a series, each one being a sequence of what has preceded.

Ch. II. Pp. 5—15. The reasons for the overthrow of Yin; illustrated by reference to Yin's own overthrow of the dynasty of Hea. 5, 6. *The fall of Hea and rise of Shang.* 5. 上帝至適逸,—the meaning of these clauses has been very variously explained. The whole par. seems to me to speak about Këë, and the ruin of the Hea dynasty brought about by him; and in acc. with this, these two preliminary clauses are best understood as in the translation. 上帝引逸 = 上帝引人至於安逸之地, 'God leads men to a condition of tranquil ease.' How does he lead men to this? By the inward satisfaction and outward prosperity which belong to a course marked by obedience to His will. It is added that 'the sovereign of Hea—Këë, that is—would not move to this security.' 有夏不適逸 = 桀乃不適於逸, 自趨於危, 'Këë would not go to security, but hurried himself on to peril' (see 陳大猷 in the 集說). Gan-kwŏ's view makes the passage have reference to Këë, but is more superficial. It is thus paraphrased by Ying-tă:—'The feeling of supreme Heaven is a wish that the people should always enjoy a tranquil happiness; but Këë, the king of Hëa, rebellious to Heaven and injurious to the people, would not allow them to move towards this tranquil happiness.' Këang Shing likewise understood Këë by 有夏, but he takes in 則 as belonging to the second clause. He then says that 引佚 (he reads 佚 for 逸) = 引

弗克庸帝、大淫泆有辭、惟時天罔念聞、厥惟廢元命、降致罰。○乃命爾先祖成湯革夏、俊民甸四方。○自成湯至于帝乙、罔不明德

him. *Këë*, however, would not be warned by God, but proceeded to greater dissoluteness and sloth and excuses for himself. Then Heaven no longer regarded nor heard him, but disallowed his
6 great appointment, and inflicted extreme punishment. Hereupon it charged your founder, T'ang the Successful, to set Hea aside, and by
7 means of able men to rule the empire. From T'ang the Successful down to the emperor Yih, every sovereign sought to make his virtue

進遺佚之賢, 言天欲人君任賢, 'to lead or bring forward worthies left in obscurity, meaning that Heaven wishes sovereigns to employ the worthy.' The second clause = 'but Këë would not conform to this rule of employing the worthy.' Woo Ch'ing struck out a new path for himself, supposing that down to 格 it is the great Yu and other good kings of Hea who are spoken of.—'When sovereigns love idleness and pleasure, God leads and puts them away. But the kings of Hea, like Yu, K'e, and Shaou-k'äng, by their anxious diligence accorded with this mind of Heaven, and went not on to any idle ways, so that God sent down to them his favour and protection (上帝於人君之好逸樂者, 引而去之, 有夏之君, 若禹若啟若少康, 皆以憂勤合天意, 而不適於逸, 則上帝降格眷佑之). This variety of opinion shows that the meaning of the text is uncertain; but that which I have given seems to be decidedly the preferable view of it.

則惟帝降格, 嚮于時夏,—here also, both the meaning and the pointing are far from being agreed upon. Woo Ch'ing's view of the whole par., which has been given above, makes him pass after 格 to Këë, to that 嚮于時夏 = 向至于是夏桀, 'But when it came to this sovereign of Hea, Këë.' Këang Shing, after Ma Yung, puts a comma at 時, and reads 夏 with the next clause. The scope of the whole, however, is pretty clear. In consequence of Këë's character and course, Heaven sent down various premonitory warnings, to arouse him to a recognition of its will. Ts'ae says:—帝猶未遽絶也, 乃降格災異, 以示意嚮於桀. Gan-kwŏ takes the 嚮, 'towards,' as not expressing the *will* of Heaven but its *favour* towards the House of Hea, so that the visitations intimated in 降格 were expressions of its kindly regard, which regard was only extinguished by the subsequent recklessness of Këë. But this is finding too much in the character. 弗克庸帝 = 不能用帝命 (or 戒), 'could not use the warnings given him by God.' 有辭,—comp. 夏王有罪矯誣上天, in the 'Announcement of Chung-hwuy,' p. 3. It is better to understand the phrase as I have done, with such a reference, than to take it, with Woo Ch'ing and others, as simply = 有可罪之辭. 惟時 may be 'then;' or 'thereupon,' 時 = 是. 元命 = 大命, 'great appointment,' *i.e.*, to be sovereign of the empire. This is better than to take 大命 = 始時之命, as Këang Shing does. 降致罰,—'sent down and carried punishment to the uttermost.' 6. 俊民甸四方,—comp. the 'T'ae-këă,' Pt. i. 5, 旁求俊彥. 甸 = 治 'to rule.' Lin Che-k'e joins 俊民 to the preceding 革夏, which is very unlikely.

Pp. 7—12. *How the dynasty of Yin long continued, and how it finally perished.* 7. Com-

恤祀。○八節亦惟天丕建、
保乂有殷、殷王亦罔
敢失帝、罔不配天其
澤。○九節在今後嗣王、誕
罔顯于天、矧曰其有
聽念于先王勤家、誕
淫厥泆、罔顧于天顯
民祗。○十節惟時上帝不
保、降若茲大喪。○十一節惟
天不畀、不明厥德。○

8 illustrious, and duly attended to the sacrifices. And thus it was that while Heaven exerted a great establishing influence, preserving and regulating the house of Yin, its sovereigns on their part were humbly careful not to lose the favour of God, and strove to manifest a good-
9 doing corresponding to that of Heaven. But in these times, their successor showed himself greatly ignorant of *the ways of* Heaven, and much less could it be expected of him that he would be regardful of the earnest labours of his fathers for the country. Greatly abandoned to dissolute idleness, he paid no regard to the bright principles
10 of Heaven, nor the awfulness of the people. On this account God no longer protected him, but sent down the great ruin which we have
11 witnessed. Heaven was not with him because he did not seek to illus-

p. Bk. X., p. 9, 成湯咸至于帝乙, 成王畏相, 云云. 恤祀,—'were anxious about the sacrifices,' *i.e.*, diligently attended to them. The account of T'ang in the 'T'ae-këă,' Pt. i., 2, gives a good illustration both of the 明德 and the 恤祀. 8. Observe how the 亦 in the two parts of the par. correspond to each other. 罔敢失帝,—'did not dare to lose God,' *i.e.*, the favour of God. The critics all say 無敢失上帝之則 or 上帝之意, 'did not dare to neglect the pattern set them by God, or to fail of the wish of God.' 罔不配天其澤 = 使德澤之及民者有以配天之廣大, 'caused their virtuous beneficial influence to reach the people in a manner corresponding to the vastness and greatness of Heaven.' Këang Shing most unwarrantably changes and enervates the sentiment, making the text merely = 無不配天, 享其福澤, 'all stood before Heaven and enjoyed its blessing.' 9. 在今後嗣王,—comp. Bk. X., p. 11. It is Show, of course, who is spoken of. 罔顯于天 = 不明於天道, 'unintelligent of the ways of Heaven.' The meaning given to 罔顯于民 in the par. of the 10th Bk. just referred to might suggest another version of the text; but it will be found that we must take 顯 actively here, whereas it was passive in the other passage. 矧曰,—comp. the same phrase in Bk. X., p. 13; *et al.* 先王勤家 = 先王之勤勞於國家, 'the earnest toil of the former kings for the country.' 罔顧, 云云,—comp. 迪畏天顯小民, Bk. X., p. 9. 10. 惟時 = 惟是之故, 'on this account.' 11. Gan-kwŏ and Këang Shing take this par. as one long clause, assigning the reason of the ruin just men-

十二節凡四方小大邦喪、罔非有辭于罰。○十三節王若曰、爾殷多士、今惟我周王、丕靈承帝事。○十四節有命曰割殷、告勅于帝。○十五節惟我事不貳適、惟爾王家我適。

12 trate his virtue. *Indeed*, with regard to the overthrow of all States,
great and small, throughout the four quarters of the empire, in
every case there are reasons to be alleged for their punishment.'"
13 "The king speaks to this effect:—'Ye numerous officers of Yin,
the case now is this, that the sovereigns of our Chow, from their
14 great goodness were charged with the work of God. There was the
charge to them, "Cut off Yin." *They proceeded to perform it*, and an-
15 nounced the correcting work to God. In our affairs we have followed
no double aims:—ye of the royal house *of Yin* must follow us.

tioned.—大喪之所以降、惟天不與不明其德者故也. It is better to take it as in the translation.—天之所不與紂者、以紂不明其德故耳. 12. A general proposition is here laid down embracing the case of Show. Comp. Bk. X., p. 3.

Pp. 13—15. *The sovereigns of Chow in overthrowing Yin had merely performed the will of God.* 13. 我周王,—'the sovereigns of Chow' were kings Wăn and Woo. 丕靈承帝事,—we must take both 丕 and 靈 as adverbs joined to the verb 承. The kings undertook the work, and they did so with a great and almost more than human efficiency. Le-ts'ëang says:—周之靈承、蓋得於不言之表者矣. With 承帝事 comp. 祗承上帝、以遏亂略, Bk. III., p. 6. 14. 告勅于帝,—we may suppose this announcement to have been made, either while the operations against Show were in progress, as related in Bk. III., pp. 6—8, or after they were completed, as in the same Bk., p. 3. 15. The translation of this par. is after Ts'ae, who succeeds better with it than any other of the critics. He says:—周不貳于帝、殷其能貳於周乎, 'As Chow had not been double to God, dare Yin be double to Chow?' 王家—商王士, p. 1. Lin Che-k'e goes round about the passage in a strange way:—我于割殷之事、應天順人、一舉而定、不待再適殷都、爾乃不明天命所歸、旣亡復叛、乃使我之用兵、遂至于再、乃惟爾商王之家、召我適爾殷都也, 'In the business of cutting off Yin, we were acting in obedience to Heaven and in accordance with men. One movement accomplished the work. We did not need to go twice to the capital of Yin. But you would not discern to whom the favour of Heaven had fallen. After your overthrow you rebelled, and caused us a second time to put our forces in motion. It was you, belonging to the House of the kings of Shang, who called us to go to your capital of Yin.' As far-fetched is the interpretation of Këang Shing, who takes 適=敵, 'enemies.'—惟我事順天下、不有貳心而爲敵者、惟爾王家作難、與我爲敵、謂武庚叛也.

書經

○予(十六節)其曰、惟爾洪無度、我不爾動、自乃邑。○予(十七節)亦念天即于殷大戾、肆不正。○王(十八節)曰、猷、告爾多士、予惟時其遷居西爾、非我一人奉德不康寧、時惟天命、無違、

16 III. 'May I not say that you were very lawless? I did not *want*
17 *to* remove you. The thing came from your own city. When I
consider also how Heaven has drawn near to Yin with *so* great
tribulations, it must be that there was *there* what was not right.'"
18 "The king says, 'Ho! I declare to you, ye numerous officers, it
is simply on account of these things that I have removed and
settled you in the west;—it was not that I, the one man, considered
it a part of my virtue to make you untranquil. The thing was from

Ch. III. Pp. 16—23. They had obliged the king by continued disaffection to remove them to Lŏ. He had dealt kindly with them, and was prepared to do so still more. Their removal to Lŏ was intended for their good. 16, 17. *It was the lawless and continued disaffection of Yin which had necessitated their removal.* 16. 予其曰,云云,—the emphatic force of the 其 is brought out in English by using the negative interrogation. 無度=無法, 'lawless,' 'unregulated.' The reference is to the rebellion of Woo-kăng and his people, with the king's uncles who had been set over them. 不爾動,—動, 'to move,' 'to excite;' in this case = 'to remove.' 自乃邑,—comp. 造攻, 自鳴條 in the 'Instructions of E,' p. 2. 17. Here, as in p. 11, I have translated according to the view of Ts'ae, whose exposition of the whole is—予亦念天就殷邦, 屢降大戾, 紂既死, 武庚又死, 故邪慝不正, 言當遷徙也. Gan-kwŏ expounds it:—我亦念天, 就於殷大罪而加誅者, 故以紂不能正身念法, 'I also thought of Heaven; and having reference to the great crimes of Yin, inflicted the punishment of death, because Show would not correct himself and think of the laws.' This is absurd enough, but not so much so as it may at first appear, Gan-kwŏ understanding the 爾洪無度 of the last par. to have reference to Show. Këang Shing takes a view of the par. quite as wide of the mark, making 正=殺, 'to put to death,' and interpreting:—我亦念武庚之叛, 是天就于殷而大拂戾之, 非爾多士之由, 故不正爾多士, 釋所以不誅而遷之之意.

P. 18. *The king reiterates his assertion that in removing them to Lŏ he was merely obeying the will of Heaven. There was no reason why they should murmur against him.* 猷,—see on Bk. VII., p. 1. 惟時=惟是之故, 'on account of these things,' the facts, mentioned in the two prec. parr. 遷居西爾,—'have transferred your dwelling and *wested* you,' *i.e.*, have removed and settled you here in the west. Lŏ lay south and west from Show's old capital, though it was to the east of Haou, Woo's capital. Këang Shing strangely argues for the meaning of 西 as being 止息, 'to give rest to,' so that the meaning is—'I have changed the place of your dwelling in order to give you rest' (遷所居以西息汝). 非我奉德不康寧=非我奉持其德, 好勞動爾, 不安寧爾. The expres-

朕不敢有後、無我怨。○惟[十九節]爾知、惟殷先人、有冊有典、殷革夏命。○[二十節]今爾又曰、夏迪簡在王庭、有服在百僚、予一人惟聽用德、肆予敢求爾于天邑商、予惟率肆矜爾、非予罪、時惟天命。○

the decree of Heaven; do not resist me; I dare not have any further
19 *change for you.* Do not murmur against me. Ye know that your fathers of the Yin dynasty had their archives and narratives *showing*
20 how Yin superseded the appointment of Hea. Ye now indeed say further, "*The officers of* Hea were chosen and promoted to the imperial court, or had their places among the mass of officers." I, the one man, listen only to the virtuous and employ them; and it was with this view that I presumed te seek you out in *your* heavenly city of Shang. I thereby follow the ancient *example*, and have pity on you. *Your present non-employment* is no fault of mine; it is by the decree of Heaven."

sion 奉德 is here difficult. Këang Shing gives for the whole—非我所秉之德性不靜安, 'was not because my disposition is restless.' 時=是. 無違, 朕不敢有後,—I have translated this after Ts'ae, and Gan-kwŏ took substantially the same meaning:—汝無違命, 我亦不敢有後誅. The editors of Yung-ching's Shoo say this interpretation is suitable enough; but they also mention with approbation another, proposed by Lin Che-k'e:—'The thing was from the decree of Heaven. That was not to be resisted, and I did not dare to make any delay in obeying it. Do not murmur against me, as if the transference of you here proceeded from me.' It is difficult to decide between the two. On the whole, I think the first is preferable.

Pp. 19, 20. *Yin's overthrow of Hea sufficiently justified Chow's overthrow of Yin; and if the officers of Yin were not now treated so well as those of Hea had been, they had only themselves to blame.* 19. 殷先人=殷之先世, 'the prior—early—ages of Yin.' 有冊有典,—Koo Seih-ch'ow says that by 冊 we are to understand the engraved tablets kept in the depositories, and by 典, the same circulated through the empire (藏府曰冊, 頒行曰典). 20. 夏迪至百僚,—迪=進, 'to bring forward;' 簡=拔, 'to make choice of,' 'to promote.' By 夏 we are evidently to understand 夏之士, 'the officers of the Hea dynasty.' The officers of Yin urge that they were not treated as those of Hea had been. 天邑商,—all agree that the capital of the Yin dynasty and country about it are here intended. But why is it called 'the heavenly city?' K'ang-shing says, 'Because it had been originally established by Heaven.' Leu Tsoo-heen and others say, 'Because there the emperors of Yin—the sons of Heaven—had dwelt.' Wang Suh says:—'The king means to say, "Shang, which is now my heavenly city."' I think it may be spoken ironically—'*your* heavenly city.' Këang Shing takes the language from 予一人 to 商 to be spoken of the appointment of the viscount of Wei.—'I also had regard to and employed the virtuous, and I therefore ventured to seek out the descendant of your kings in the city,' &c. This is amusingly ingenious, but few will be found to adopt the

廿一節 王曰、多士、昔朕來自奄、予大降爾四國民命、我乃明致天罰、移爾遐逖、比事臣我宗多遜。○ 廿二節 王

21 "The king says, 'Ye numerous officers, formerly, when I came from Yen, I greatly mitigated the penalty in favour of the lives of the people of your four countries. At the same time I made evident the punishment appointed by Heaven, and removed you to this distant abode, that you might be near the ministers who had served in our honoured *capital*, and *learn* their much obedience.'"

view. The king is evidently speaking of what he had done to those whom he was addressing. 予惟率肆矜爾＝予惟循商故事,矜恤爾而已. The meaning is that the king hoped their removal to Lŏ would lead them to virtue and loyalty, so that it was really an act of kindness to them. While they were vicious and disaffected, it would be contrary to the will of Heaven to confer dignities and offices on them.

P. 21. *The officers and people of Yin had really been dealt with very leniently.* This par. refers to the time three or four years back, when the rebellion of Woo-kăng, supported by the king's uncles, had been disposed of. The wild tribe of the Yen—a district corresponding to the pres. dis. of K'ëuh-fow, dep. of Yen-chow, Shan-tung—had joined with the insurgents. We hear of them again in Bk. XVIII., as in arms a second time against the new dynasty. The crushing of the Yen had been the last act in the suppression of the rebellion. When that was accomplished, the duke of Chow—for he was the agent, though the thing is here ascribed to the king, after the manner of 'The Great Announcement'—had time to deal with the people of Yin. Our natural conclusion from this par. is certainly that many of the people of Yin were then removed to Lŏ. 降爾四國民命,—降 is here used in the sense of 減, 'to diminish,' 'to mitigate.' Their lives were all forfeited; but the king spared their lives, and only banished them. We have not met with this usage of the character before; but it is now quite common in legal language. Gan-kwŏ took 民命 as equivalent to 君. Ying-tă says:—民以君爲命,故民命謂君也, 'The people consider their sovereign to be their life, and hence the sovereign is designated "the life of the people."' The meaning then is—'I made an end of the rulers of your four kingdoms, thereby executing on them the punishment appointed by Heaven.' But this is very far-fetched, and unwarranted. Nor is the view given by Këang Shing more likely.—'I sent down lessons and commands for you, the people of the four kingdoms, and carried clearly out the punishment appointed by Heaven upon their rulers.' By the 'four kingdoms' we are to understand the 'imperial domain of Yin,' which had been portioned out to Woo-kăng, and three of the king's uncles;—see the note on Bk. VI., p. 12. 移爾遐逖＝移爾遠居于洛. Both 遐 and 逖 are defined by 遠 'far,' 'distant.' 比事臣我宗,多遜,—宗 is here taken as＝宗周, 'the honoured Chow,' a name given to Haou, the old capital of Chow, in distinction from the new capital of 成周 at Lŏ. It was in the duke's mind, in prospect of the new capital, that the old trusted ministers of Chow should remove to it, when the influence of their character and principles would affect beneficially the adherents of the old dynasty brought there into contact with them. The translation is after the 'Daily Explanation:'—移爾遠居於洛,使爾得密邇王室,親比臣事我宗周之臣子,遠離頑梗之俗,漸摩遜順之風. There is little to choose between this and the following ingenious exposition by Choo He:—以親我,事我,臣我,宗法我周濟濟多遜之盛, 'that ye might be near us, serve us, and be ministers to us, honouring and imitating the rich and full obedience of our Chow.'

曰、告爾殷多士、今予惟不爾殺、予惟時命有申、今朕作大邑于茲洛、予惟四方罔攸賓、亦惟爾多士、攸服奔走、臣我多遜。○爾(廿三節)乃尚有爾土、爾乃尚寧幹止。○爾(廿四節)克敬、天惟畀矜爾、爾不克敬、爾不啻不有爾土、予

22 "The king says, 'I declare to you, ye numerous officers of Yin, —now I have not put you to death, and therefore I repeat to you my charge again. I have built this great city here in Lŏ, considering that there was no other place in which to receive my guests from the four quarters, and also that you, ye numerous officers, might here with zealous activity, perform the part of ministers to us with
23 much obedience. You have still here I may say your grounds, and here you may still rest in your duties and dwellings.
24 If you can reverently obey, Heaven will favour and compassionate you. If you cannot reverently obey, you will not only not have

Pp. 22, 23. *The king again repeats his objects in building Lŏ, and impresses on the officers of Yin the kindness with which he was treating them.* 22. 予惟不至有申,—申=重, 'to repeat.' They had received one charge on their first removal; the present address might be considered a repetition of it. 今朕作大邑于茲洛,—possibly the 'great city' here may be the 王城, or imperial city, in connection with the building of which we have seen that the duke of Shaou was specially despatched. Though 'the lower capital,' where the officers of Yin were located may have been previously built, at least in part, the design intended by it could not be realized, until the other was likewise prepared. 四方罔攸賓=四方諸侯罔有賓禮之所. The king's 'guests' were the princes coming to court from all the States. 攸服奔走,—'where ye might serve, hasting and running.' 23. Gan-kwŏ took this par. as a promise.—'If you learn obedience to us, and become loyal subjects, then you will still have here your grounds,' &c. But it is better to take the language as historical, and showing how generously they *had been* treated. 尚=庶幾, here=our 'I may say.' 幹=事, 'business,' 'duties.' 止=居, 'dwellings,' 'settlements.'

Ch. IV. Pp. 24—26. LET THE OFFICERS OF YIN ACQUIESCE IN THEIR LOT, AND THEY MAY HAVE A HAPPY AND PROSPEROUS FUTURE IN LŎ. IF THEY REFUSE TO DO SO, THEY WILL BRING ON THEMSELVES UTTER RUIN. 24. 爾克敬,—'If you can reverence.' We are not to find in 敬 here all that is denoted by 'the virtue of reverence' in Bk. XIII., but a standing in awe and submission to what had happened to them. 畀矜爾,—each of these verbs 畀 and 矜 has a meaning of its own. We are not to think that they run into each other. As Lin Che-k'e has it, 天必有以畀予之,矜憐之. 啻=但, 'only.' 致天之罰于爾躬,—compare 致天罰 in p. 21. The

亦致天之罰于爾躬。○廿五節今爾惟時宅爾邑、繼爾居、爾厥有幹有年于茲洛、爾小子乃興、從爾遷。○廿六節王曰、又曰、時予乃或言、爾攸居。

your lands, but I will also carry to the utmost Heaven's inflictions
25 on your persons. Now you may here dwell in your villages, and perpetuate your families; you may pursue your occupations and enjoy your years in this Lŏ; your children also will prosper:—*all* from your being removed here.'"
26 "The king says,—; and again he says, 'Whatsoever I have spoken, is all on account of *my anxiety about* your residence *here*.'"

punishment of Heaven there spoken of had only deprived them of their grounds in Yin; this would deprive them of their lives. 25. 今爾惟時(=是)宅爾邑,—the 爾, prefixed to 邑, indicates, I think, that we are not to suppose that Lŏ is intended by 邑,—which, however, is the view of Lin Che-k'e. Ts'ae says that we are to understand the 'villages' formed by the families around every four 井, or space of 3,600 *mow*. Every family, in connection with such a settlement, had its five *mow*, for houses and private garden,—2½ in the field, and 2½ in the associate village; see Mencius, I., Pt. I., iii., 4. Taking this view, we must understand that the king is not addressing here the *officers* of Yin merely, but the body of the people who had been removed from their old settlements. 居 will then signify the homes of the several families belonging to each village. 幹,—as in p. 23. 從爾遷,—Gan-kwŏ takes this, as an additional predicate about their descendants, and makes 興從爾遷=起從汝化而遷善, 'will arise, and following your transformation also become good.' It is much better to take the clause as I have done,—a view first proposed by Soo Shih.

P. 26. After the 王曰 there must be something wanting. Compare the two last paragraphs of Book XVIII. There is probably something lost also after the 又曰. We cannot take 時 as meaning 'now;' it must be =是, and would hardly commence a sentence. 爾攸居 is also elliptical. Ts'ae brings out the meaning thus:—時我或有所言,皆以爾之所居止爲念也. Kēang Shing makes the clause hortatory:—今我乃有言告汝,汝其安所居哉. This is not so likely.

THE BOOKS OF CHOW.

BOOK. XV. AGAINST LUXURIOUS EASE.

無逸

周公曰、嗚呼、君子所其無逸。○先知稼穡之艱難、乃逸、則知小

1 I. The duke of Chow said, "Oh! the superior man rests in this,
2 —that he will have no luxurious ease. He first understands the
painful toil of sowing and reaping, how it conducts to ease, and thus

THE NAME OF THE BOOK.—無逸, 'Avoiding Luxurious Ease.' These words are taken from the first paragraph. They are the keynote to the whole Book, and hence are rightly taken to designate it. Gaubil says the characters mean—'*Il ne faut pas se livrer au plaisir.*' Medhurst entitles the Book—'On avoiding luxurious ease.' 逸 and 佚 are used interchangeably. Their primary signification is that of 'idleness;' compare Mencius, VII., Pt. II., xxiv. 1, and IV., Pt. II., xxx. 2. But as the character is used in the Shoo, it does not denote a mere passive idleness, but one in which, while the proper duties are neglected, improper lusts and gratifications may be eagerly sought; see the 'Counsels of Yu,' p. 14; *et al.* Still the idea of the term here is that of 'luxurious or indulgent ease.' 無 is used as the imperative 毋. The Book is found in both the texts. It comes under the division of 訓 or 'Instructions.'

CONTENTS. The prefatory note is simply to the effect that 'the duke of Chow made the *Woo Yih;*' without a word about the time or occasion of it. The general view, which there is no reason to dispute, is that the duke of Chow addressed it to king Ching, soon after he had resigned the government into his hands. That the minister thought it necessary thus to admonish the young sovereign confirms what I have several times urged, that there was between them a measure of dissatisfaction on the one side and of suspicion on the other. There are six pauses in the course of the address, which is resumed always with a 周公曰嗚呼, 'The duke of Chow said, "Oh!"' A division into seven chapters is thus suggested.

In parr. 1—3, the duke leads the king to find a rule for himself in the laborious toils which devolve on the husbandman. In parr. 4—7, he refers to the long reigns of three of the sovereigns of the Yin dynasty, and the short reigns of others, as illustrating how the blessing of Heaven rests on the diligent sovereign. In parr. 6—11, the example of their own kings, T'ae, Ke, and Wăn is adduced with the same object. In parr. 12, 13, the duke addresses the king personally, and urges him to follow the example of king Wăn and flee from that of Show. In 14, 15, he stimulates him by reference to ancient precedents to adopt his counsels, and shows the evil effects that will follow if he refuse to do so. In parr. 16—18, he shows him by the examples of the good kings of Yin and of king Wăn how he ought to have regard to the opinions of the common people, and gird himself to diligence. The last par. is a single admonition that the king should lay what had been said to heart.

Ch. I. Pp. 1—3. THE GREAT PRINCIPLE, THAT THERE SHOULD BE NO INDULGENT EASE. IT IS ENFORCED BY A REFERENCE TO THE TOILS OF HUSBANDRY, AND THE FREQUENT DEGENERACY OF THE SONS OF THOSE WHO HAVE TOILED

人之依。○相（三節）小人、厥父母勤勞稼穡、厥子乃不知稼穡之艱難、乃逸、乃諺、既誕、否則侮厥父母、曰、昔之人無聞知。○周（四節）公曰、嗚呼、我

3 he understands *the law of* the support of the inferior people. I have observed among the inferior people, that where the parents have diligently laboured in sowing and reaping, their sons *often* do not understand this painful toil, and abandon themselves to ease, and to village slang, and become quite disorderly. Or where they do not do so, they throw contempt on their parents, saying, 'Those old people have heard nothing and know nothing.'"

4 II. The duke of Chow said, "Oh! I have heard that aforetime the emperor of Yin, Chung-tsung, was grave, humble, reverential, and

HARD. 1. 君子所其無逸,—K'ang-shing thought that 君子 here was spoken simply of the ruler (君子止謂在官長者), without any implication of the virtuous character which is commonly denoted by the expression. He must be wrong. The designation is to be taken of 'the man of virtue,' with an application of it implied to such a man in authority. I take 所 as a verb =止. The usage is akin to that in Bk. XIII., p. 16,—王敬作所. 其無(=毋)逸 is then under the govt. of 所. Ts'ae, after Leu Tsoo-hëen, gives for the par.—君子以無逸爲所, which brings out the meaning very well. Ch'ing and Gan-kwŏ both put a comma at 所,—which is very harsh. The former says:—君子處位爲政,其無自逸豫也; and the latter:—君子之道,所在念德,其無逸豫. 2. It is as well to take 君子 as the subject of the two 知 here. The meaning would be substantially the same if we supposed the language directly addressed to king Ching, when 先知 would ='when you first understand.' The only difficulty is with the 乃逸. The characters simply show that ease and plenty are a result of the toils of husbandry. Gan-kwŏ attributed a sort of hortatory force to them, and interpreted:—稼穡,農夫之艱難事,先知之乃謀逸豫, 'sowing and reaping are the toilsome business of the husbandman. This must first be known, and then plans for ease may be laid.' Soo Shih objected to this that the object of the duke of Chow was to get the king to put away the thought of ease, and it was not likely he would begin to suggest to him the idea of 'planning for ease.' The criticism is subtle, but correct. 'What the inferior people depend on' is their hard toil in the fields. That is the law of their support. Ease comes from it as a matter of course. Ease finds them; they do not seek it. 3. 相小人,—compare 相古先民, Bk. XII., p. 11. 小人,—as in the last par.,=小民. 乃逸乃諺,既誕=乃縱逸自恣,乃習俚巷鄙語,既又誕妄,無所不至, as in the translation. 諺 is 'a proverb,' 'a saying.' Gan-kwŏ understands by it 'coarse language,' taking it=喭;—see Ana. XI., xvi., 4. Këang Shing reads—乃佚,乃憲,既誕不則, 'they become idle, and indulge in pleasure, behave rudely, and are lawless.' I prefer the received text and interpretation. 昔之人=古老之人, as I have translated it; or it may mean—'our predecessors.'

Ch. II. Pp. 4—7. THE ADVANTAGES OF AVOIDING SELF-INDULGENT EASE SHOWN BY THE HISTORY OF SEVERAL OF THE SOVEREIGNS

聞曰、昔在殷王中宗、嚴恭寅畏、天命自度、治民祗懼、不敢荒寧、肆中宗之享國、七十有五年。○五節 其在高宗時、舊勞于外、爰暨小人、作其卽位、乃或亮陰、三年不言、其惟不言、言乃雍、不敢荒寧、嘉靖殷邦、至于小大、

fearful. He measured himself with reference to the appointment of Heaven, and cherished a reverent apprehension in governing the people, not daring to indulge in useless ease. It was thus that Chung-tsung enjoyed the throne for seventy and five years.

5 "If we come to the time of Kaou-tsung, he toiled at first away from the court, and was among the inferior people. When he came to the throne, it may be said that, while he was in the mourning shed, for three years he did not speak. *Afterwards* he was *still inclined* not to speak; but when he did speak, his words were full of harmonious *wisdom*. He did not dare to indulge in useless and easy

OF THE YIN DYNASTY. 4. *The case of Chung-tsung.* 昔在殷王中，宗,—the 在 here and the following parr. = 'in the case of.' 中宗 was the sacrificial title (廟號) of the emperor described. See the note on T'ae-mow, p. 220. 嚴 and 恭 are said to express the king's reverence as shown externally, while 寅 and 畏 describe his inward feeling of it. 天命自度,—by 天命 Ts'ae and many others understand 天理, 'Heavenly principles,' so that the meaning of the clause is, 'He measured (= defined the rules of life for) himself in accordance with heavenly principles.' But this is needless refining. The meaning rather is that Kaou-tsung felt that 'the appointment of Heaven,' which placed him upon the throne, brought with it certain duties and responsibilities, on his discharge of which depended his retaining Heaven's favour; he therefore measured himself to know whether his course was what it ought to be. Woo Ch'ing brings this meaning out very clearly:—天命在躬，易失難保，故反躬自省，謹循法則，惟恐不能永保天命也. I have said on p. 220 that we might doubt the length of Chung-tsung's reign, if it were not thus guaranteed by the duke of Chow. Two brothers are said to have preceded him on the throne;—first Yung-ke, who reigned 12 years, and before him Sëaou-këä, who reigned 17 years. If Chung-tsung were born in the same year that their father died, B.C. 1664, he must have been 30 when he succeeded to the empire.

5. *The case of Kaou-tsung.* See Book. VIII., of the last Part. 其在高宗時,—the 時 should evidently be read with the first clause, but it is difficult to explain it, or to account for it. 舊勞于外，爰暨小人,—comp. 'The Charge to Yuĕ,' Pt. iii., p. 1. The old interpreters took 舊 = 久, 'long.' It is better to take it as = 'at first,' *i.e.*, while his father was alive (當其爲太子之時). 爰 = 於是; and 暨 = 與, 'with.' The text must be supplemented:—於是與小人同其事. It is perplexing to find 暨 used as a preposition, and not simply a conjunction. 作其卽位,—in order

無時或怨、肆高
宗之享國、五十
有九年。○六節其在
祖甲、不義惟王、
舊爲小人、作其
卽位、爰知小人
之依、能保惠于
庶民、不敢侮鰥
寡、肆祖甲之享
國、三十有三年。

ways, but admirably and tranquilly presided over the empire of Yin, till in all its States, great and small, there was not a single murmur. It was thus that Kaou-tsung enjoyed the throne for fifty and nine years.

6 "In the case of Tsoo-këă, he would not unrighteously be emperor, and was at first one of the inferior people. When he came to the throne, he understood *the law of* the support of the inferior people, and was able to exercise a protecting kindness towards their masses, and did not dare to treat with contempt the widower and widows. Thus it was that Tsoo-këă enjoyed the throne for thirty and three years.

to bring out the meaning of 作, Woo Ch'ing says:—起自民間, 卽天子位, 'He arose from among the people, and ascended the imperial seat.' But in trying to account for the 作, he overlooks the 其. 作 has here merely a conjunctive force, = 及. 乃或亮陰, 三年不言,—see 'The Charge to Yuĕ,' Pt. i., p. 1. I have said there that we are not to suppose that the emperor during the years of mourning maintained a total silence, but only kept from speaking on governmental matters. This is perhaps indicated by the 或. 其惟不言, 言乃雍,—I have translated this according to the account which we have in the beginning of 'The Charge to Yue.' K'ang-shing supposed that the duke is still speaking of Kaou-tsung during the time of mourning; but that is very unlikely. The history is evidently being carried on and forward. 嘉靖殷邦,—'he made the States—the empire—of Yin admirable and tranquil,' *i.e.*, he hushed all jarrings, and produced great prosperity.

6. *The case of Tsoo-këă.* Tsoo-këă was the son of Kaou-tsung. I have mentioned on p. 269 that Sze-ma Ts'een says that Tsoo-këă was lewd and disorderly. Similar testimony is found in the 國語. Having respect to these statements, Gan-kwŏ could not admit that the emperor spoken of here was the son of Kaou-tsung, and maintained that we were to find him in T'ae-këă, the grandson of T'ang. But from Chung-tsung the duke comes on to Kaou-tsung, approaching to the rise of their own dynasty of Chow;—how unnatural the address would be if he were now to go back to the beginning of the times of Yin! Moreover, the son of Kaou-tsung was styled Tsoo-këă, while the grandson of T'ang was called T'ae-këă. Nor does the confinement of T'ae-këă for a season by E Yin for his misdeeds sufficiently answer the requirements of the text,—不義惟王, 舊爲小人, 知小人之依. Gan-kwŏ says:—湯孫太甲, 爲王不義, 久爲小人之行, 伊尹放之桐, 'Tae-kea, being king, proved unrighteous. He had long displayed the conduct of an unworthy person, and E Yin confined him in T'ung.' But the meaning thus given to 小人, which has already occurred three times in the address, and always with the signification of 'the inferior people,' without any implication of unworthiness, must be rejected. On every ground we must conclude that the sovereign spoken of was not the grandson of T'ang. He was the son of Kaou-tsung. K'ang-shing has a story that Woo-ting wanted to disinherit Tsoo-këă's elder brother in favour of him, and that Tsoo-këă, thinking such a proceeding would be unrighteous, withdrew and lived for a time among

○七節自時厥後立王、生則逸、生則逸、不知稼穡之艱難、不聞小人之勞、惟耽樂之從、自時厥後、亦罔或克壽、或十年、或七八年、或五六年、或四三年。○八節周公曰、嗚呼、厥亦惟我周太王王季、

7 "The emperors which arose after these all their life-time enjoyed ease. From their birth enjoying ease, they did not understand the painful toil of sowing and reaping, nor hear of the hard labours of the inferior people. They only sought after excessive pleasures, and so not one of them enjoyed the throne for a long period. They continued for ten years, for seven or eight, for five or six, or *perhaps only* for three or four."

8 III. The duke of Chow said, "Oh! there likewise were king T'ae and king Ke of our own Chow, who attained to humility and reverential

the common people (祖甲以爲不義,逃於民間). Ts'ae adduces this as the ground of the language in the text,—不義惟王,舊爲小人. Ying-tă and Maou K'e-ling after him object to this account, that no authority can be adduced for it, and that there is no evidence of Këă's elder brother being unworthy, while it is defaming a good king like Woo-ting to say that he wanted to disinherit his eldest son in favour of a younger brother. K'e-ling, therefore, supposes that Tsoo-këă, in his youth, had been dissolute, and consorted with unworthy associates (不義惟王,舊爲小人,言祖甲少行不義,爰及非類). But here is the meaning of 小人 to which I have objected above. His explanation is as much an hypothesis as that of K'ang-shing, whom he vehemently condemns. The truth is,—while it is plain that it is the son of Kaou-tsung of whom the duke of Chow speaks, we do not know enough of that emperor to explain all his language. Gan-kwŏ for 保惠于庶民 gives 安順於庶民. It is better to take 惠=愛, as in the translation.

7. *The other emperors of Yin.* 生則逸,—'being born, they had ease.' The 'Daily Explanation' says:—身爲帝王之裔,長于宮禁之中,生則止見安逸耳. Këang Shing says ingeniously that the repetition of 生則逸 indicates that thus it was with one emperor and another. It is as well, however, to construe as I have done. 惟耽樂之從—another reading for this is 惟湛樂是從; but the meaning is the same. 克壽—'could come to old age;' but the sequel shows that he is speaking of the occupancy of the throne. A long life and a long reign, however, would generally go together. It is to be observed that the reigns of the other sovereigns of Yin were not so short as the text says. There were six emperors after Tsoo-keă, of whom one reigned 21 years; a second, 23; and the tyrant Show himself, 28. Between Kaou-tsung and Chung-tsung, again, there were 12 reigns, of which only 2 were under ten years.

Ch. III. Pp. 8—11. THE DUKE DIRECTS THE KING'S ATTENTION TO THE PRINCES OF THEIR OWN DYNASTY,—TO KINGS T'AE AND KE, AND ESPECIALLY TO KING WAN. 8. 厥亦云云,—the 厥 corresponds to the 其 with which pp. 5 and 6 begin. 太王,王季,—see Bk. III., p. 5; and the notes in pp. 268, 269.

書經

克自抑畏。○文(九節)王卑服，即康功田功。○徽(十節)柔懿恭，懷保小民，惠鮮鰥寡，自朝至于日中昃，不遑暇食，用咸和萬民。○文(十一節)王不敢盤于遊田，以庶邦惟正之供。文

9 awe. King Wăn dressed meanly, and gave himself to the work of
10 tranquillization, and to that of husbandry. Admirably mild and beautifully humble, he cherished and protected the inferior people, and showed a fostering kindness to the widower and widows. From morning to midday, and from midday to sundown, he did not allow himself time to eat;—thus seeking to secure the happy harmony
11 of the myriads of the people. King Wăn did not dare to go to any excess in his excursions or his hunting, and from the various States he received only the correct amount of contribution. He received

克自抑畏,—抑 means 'to press hard,' and 'to repress.' Hence 自抑='to be humble.' 9. 文王卑服,—comp. what Confucius says about Yu, Ana, VIII., xxi. 即=就, 'to approach to;' here='to apply to.' 康功=安民之功, 'services giving repose to the people.' 田功=養民之功, 'services giving nourishment to the people.' See Mencius, I., Pt. II., v., 3. Këang Shing takes 服=事, so that the par. would have a very unworthy meaning,—'king Wăn occupied himself with mean affairs,' &c.

10. 徽柔懿恭,—徽 and 懿 are both defined by 美, 'admirable,' 'excellent.' If Wăn's mildness, it is said, had not been 徽, it would have been weakness; and if his respectfulness had not been 懿, it would have been hypocrisy (足恭之恭; see Ana. V., xxi.). 惠鮮鰥寡,—惠鮮 is a difficult expression, and Këang Shing reads 惠于鰥寡, which is much simpler. Ts'ae, adhering to the meaning of 鮮 as 'fresh, with no taint of corruption,' says that 'widowers and widows hang their heads down, all out of spirits; and when you give them an alms, you make them as it were become alive.' This is very strained. We must take 鮮=善, a meaning which it sometimes has. Gan-kwŏ seems to miss the meaning altogether, and construes absurdly. 昃 is the sun declining in the west. 自朝至于日中昃=自朝至于日之中,自中至于日之昃. 不遑暇食,—both 遑 and 暇 signify 'leisure.' Ying-tă observes that in their conjunction we have an instance of the duplicated expressions (複語) of the ancients.

11. 盤于遊田,—we met with 盤遊無度 in Pt. III., Bk. III., p. 1, where 盤 has the sense of 樂, 'pleasure.' Here, followed by 于, however, the meaning of 盤桓不止, 'incessant movement,' is to be preferred. On the 遊 see Mencius, I., Pt. II., iv., 5. There were the proper seasons both for tours of inspection and hunting expeditions. Wăn made them both at those seasons, and did not protract them beyond the regulated length of time. 田=畋, 'to hunt.' 以庶邦惟正之供,—Ts'ae, after earlier critics of the Sung dynasty, takes this as=於常貢正數之外,無橫斂也, 'beyond the correct amount of the regular tribute, he made no oppressive exactions;' and he adds that if Wăn dealt in

王受命惟中身、厥享國五十年。○周公曰、嗚呼、繼自今、嗣王則其無淫于觀于逸于遊于田、以萬民、惟正之供。○無皇曰、今日耽樂、乃非民攸訓、非天攸若、時人丕則有愆、無若殷王受

the appointment *of Heaven* in the middle of his life, and enjoyed the throne for fifty years."

12 IV. The duke of Chow said, "Oh! from this time forward, do you who have succeeded to the throne imitate his avoiding of excess in his sights, his ease, his excursions, his hunting; and from the myriads
13 of the people receive only the correct amount of contribution. Do not allow yourself the leisure to say, 'To-day I will indulge in pleasure.' This is not holding out a lesson to the people, nor the way to secure the favour of Heaven. Men will on the contrary

this way with the States which acknowledged his authority as chief of the West, it is easy to see how gentle was his taxation of his own people. Gan-kwŏ interpreted the clause quite differently:—以衆國所取法則,當以正道供待之, which Ying-tă expounds, 'He considered that it was from him that all the States had to take their pattern, so that his proper business was to regulate himself with a right heart, to minister the treatment to them.' This is hardly intelligible; and Këang Shing would gladly reduce the whole clause to 唯政之恭, 'and reverently attended to the business of the govt.,' from a passage in the 國語,楚語上, which even Yuh-tsae says ought not to be credited in the case;—see 段大令古文尚書撰異, *in loc.*

受命惟中身,—Wăn's 'receiving the appointment' here can only be understood of his succeeding to his father as one of the princes of the empire. Gan-kwŏ observes that Wăn died at the age of 97, and as he was 47 when he came to the principality of Chow, the expression 中身, 'middle of his life,' must not be pressed.

Ch. IV. Pp. 12, 13. THE DUKE URGES KING CHING TO MAKE THE MAXIM OF 'NO DAY FOR IDLENESS' THE RULE OF HIS LIFE, AND TO ESCHEW THE EXAMPLE OF SHOW. 12. Gan-kwŏ points 繼自今嗣王,云云, and understands the duke to have in view all future sovereigns of the House of Chow (繼從今已往嗣世之王,皆戒之), so that the 則 that follows is merely a particle. I prefer, however, the construction of Ts'ae, which appears in the translation. Acc. to it, the words are addressed to king Ching, though there is of course a lesson in them for future kings as well; 則 is a verb, = 法, 'to imitate,' and the 其 which follows it refers to king Wăn. 觀 = our 'sight-seeing.' 以萬民 takes here the place of 以庶邦, being appropriate to the case of the emperor, whereas the other expression was descriptive of Wăn as the 'Chief of the West,' the Head of a portion of the States.

Këang Shing gives for the par.—嗚呼繼自今嗣王其毋淫于酒,毋佚于游田,維正之共, which appears in one of the chapters of 'The Books of Han,' and was perhaps the reading of Fuh-shang. 13. 皇 must be taken as = the 遑 of par. 10. 非民攸訓 = 非民之所以爲教, 'is not what the people should take as their lesson. 天攸若—

之迷亂、酗于酒德哉。○周公曰、嗚呼、我聞曰、古之人、猶胥訓告、胥保惠、胥教誨、民無或胥譸張爲幻。○此厥不聽、人乃訓之、乃變亂

十四節 十五節

greatly imitate you, and practise evil. Become not like Show, the king of Yin, who went quite astray, and was abandoned to the practice of drunkenness."

14 V. The duke of Chow said, "Oh! I have heard it said that, in the case of the ancients, *their ministers discharged their functions* in warning and admonishing them, in protecting and *loving* them, in teaching and instructing them; and among their people there was hardly one who would impose on them by extravagant language or deceiv-

15 ing tricks. If you will not listen to this *and profit by it*, your ministers will imitate you, and so the correct laws of the former

天之所順, 'what Heaven will accord with.' 時=是, corresponding to the 乃 above. 時人丕則有愆=是人大則效之,斯有愆尤矣. 酗于酒德,—comp. 'The Viscount of Wei,' p. 1. It is very evident that 德 may be spoken of *vice* as well as of *virtue*.

Ch. V. Pp. 14, 15. The duke urges the king to receive good advice, referring to the case of ancient sovereigns who had done so, and pointing out the evil consequences of a contrary course. 14. By 古之人 we are probably to understand the three sovereigns of Yin celebrated in the second chapter, and king Wăn. 猶胥至教誨,—we have to understand 其臣, 'their ministers,' as the subject of the verbs 訓告, &c. The force of the 猶, 'still,' is thus brought out:—'The virtue of those ancient sovereigns was complete. It seemed as if they needed no assistance; but *still* their ministers did not cease to instruct them,' &c. 胥=相. It indicates the mutual intercourse of sovereigns and ministers, while we must restrict the action of the verbs to the latter. 民無或,云云,—this shows the result throughout the empire, when those good sovereigns were guided and supported in such a way by their ministers. The dict. explains 譸張 together by 誑, 'to lie,' 'to deceive.' This is plainly the meaning, but I do not know that 張 by itself is ever found with this signification. 幻 is defined by 變名易實以眩觀, 'changing names and transposing realities, to deceive the sight.' In Fuh-shang's text this clause appears to have wanted the commencing 民, and the 胥 after 或. 15. An application of the statements in the prec. par. is here made to king Ching. If he will not listen to them, 人乃訓之(=人乃法則之), 'men will learn of him.' The 'men' intended are his ministers. 正刑=正法, 'correct laws.' Ts'ae instances the light punishments and light taxation, which were the rule with ancient good sovereigns, and which would be superseded by severe penalties, and heavy exactions. 至于小大 is to be joined with 正刑. 民否,—'the people disapproving.' The disallowing and changing the laws which were favourable to them will awaken their disaffection and displeasure. Hostile feelings will be cherished in their hearts, and turn to curses on their tongues. 詛祝,—these two terms together=our 'to curse.' Ying-tă says that 'to ask the spirits to make miserable is called 詛; and to announce one's thoughts to the spirits by words is called 祝' (請神加殃謂之詛,以言告神謂之祝). Ts'ae and many others explain the par. in

先王之正刑、至于小
大、民否則厥心違怨、
否則厥口詛祝。○周十六節
公曰、嗚呼、自殷王中
宗、及高宗、及祖甲、及
我周文王、茲四人迪
哲。○十七節厥或告之曰、小
人怨汝詈汝、則皇自
敬德、厥愆、曰朕之愆、
允若時、不啻不敢含

kings, both small and great, will be changed and disordered. The people blaming you will disobey and rebel in their hearts;—yea, they will curse you with their mouths."
16 VI. The duke of Chow said, "Oh! those kings of Yin, Chung-
tsung, Kaou-tsung, and Tsoo-këă, with king Wăn of our Chow,—these
17 four men carried their knowledge into practice. If it was told
them—'The inferior people murmur against you, and revile you,'
then they paid great and reverent attention to their conduct; and
with reference to the faults imputed to them they said, 'Our faults
are really so.' *They acted thus*, not simply not daring to cherish

the way thus exhibited; and I don't think we can do better with it. Woo Ch'ing, taking 此厥不聽 as Ts'ae does, gives for the rest a construction of his own, and makes the meaning—'If you will not hearken to this and profit by it, then men will persuade you to change and confuse the correct laws of the former kings. Those laws were very favourable to the people; and when they are so changed, the people, small and great, will cherish, some of them, a rebellious resentment in their hearts, while others will proceed to curse you with their mouths' (成王于此古人……不聽信，則人乃道說之，以變亂先王之正法，先王之法甚便于民，一變亂之，則至于或小或大，或有違怨于心者矣，或有詛祝于口者矣). Këang Shing reads 此厥不聖，人乃訓變亂正刑云云,—'When the ancient sovereigns were not sage, then men led them away to change,' &c., according to the view of Woo Ch'ing. He is compelled, however, to doubt the genuineness of the 民; and indeed, if 民 be genuine here (and there is no evidence to the contrary), the same character in the prec. par. cannot be assailed. The reading of 聖, moreover, and consequent making this chapter terminate without any application to king Ching, takes from its connection with the rest of the Book.

Ch. VI. Pp. 16—18. THE DUKE PRESSES ON THE KING THE DUTY OF LISTENING TO ADVICE BY THE EXAMPLE OF THE GOOD SOVEREIGNS WHOM HE HAS MENTIONED, AND POINTS OUT AGAIN THE EVIL CONSEQUENCES OF A CONTRARY COURSE. 16. 迪哲,—'trod in the way of their knowledge.' Ts'ae says this is what Mencius calls 'the richest fruit of wisdom,—the knowing, and not putting the knowledge away' (智之實，知而弗去是也; see IV., Pt. I., xxvii. 2.). 17. 皇自敬德,—皇=大, 'great,' 'greatly.' We may take 敬德 as in Bk. XII., or more generally, as I have done in the translation. Ying-tă makes the clause=增修善政, 'they increasingly cultivated good government.'

怒。○此(十八節)厥不聽人乃或譸張爲幻、曰小人怨汝詈汝、則信之、則若時、不永念厥辟、不寬綽厥心、亂罰無罪、殺無辜、怨有同、是叢于厥身。○(十九節)周公曰、嗚呼、嗣王其監于茲。

18 anger. If you will not listen to this *and profit by it*, when men with extravagant language and deceptive tricks say to you, 'The inferior people are murmuring against you and reviling you,' you will believe them. Doing this, you will not be always thinking of your princely duties, and will not cultivate a large and generous heart. You will confusedly punish the crimeless, and put the innocent to death. There will be a general murmuring, which will be concentrated upon your person."

19 VII. The duke of Chow said, "Oh! you king, who have succeeded to the throne, make a study of these things."

厥愆 = 于其所誣毀之愆, 'in the case of the faults which were wrongly imputed to them.' 18. This is the application of the prec. two parr., as par. 15 was an application of 14. Këang Shing cannot adopt 聖 here in the first clause as in p. 15, not having the precedent which he there had. Still he says we ought to read 聖; but I cannot think so. The duke of Chow would not have put the case that the worthies he celebrated could have behaved themselves so unworthily. At 則若是 the transition is abrupt, but the meaning is plain. 不永念厥辟 = 不能永念其爲君之道, as in the translation. This is much better than, with Këang Shing, to read 辟 as *p'eih*, and understand the expression as = 不能引咎自責也, 'they could not have acknowledged the blame, and reproved themselves.' 怨有同,—'resentments will be the same,' *i.e.*, people may receive injuries of different kinds, but all will agree in the feeling of injury and resentment.

Ch. VII. P. 19. *Concluding exhortation, that the king should think of all that had been said to him, and use the address as a light to guide him to safety and excellence,—as a beacon to warn him from what was evil and dangerous.*

THE BOOKS OF CHOW.

BOOK XVI. PRINCE SHIH.

君奭

周公若曰、君奭。弗弔、天降喪于殷、殷既墜厥命、我有周既受、

1 I. The duke of Chow spake to the following effect, "Prince Shih,
2 Heaven, unpitying, sent down ruin on Yin; Yin has lost its appoint-
ment, and the princes of our Chow have received it. I do not dare,
however, to say, as if I knew it, 'The foundation will ever truly

THE NAME OF THE BOOK.—君奭, 'Prince Shih.' With these words the Book begins, and they are taken to be its designation. Shih was the name of the duke of Shaou; see on the title of Book XII. It was to him that the address or announcement here preserved was delivered, so that his name is not an inappropriate designation for it. The Book is found in both the texts.

CONTENTS. Ts'ae says that the duke of Shaou had announced his purpose to retire from office on account of his age, when the duke of Chow persuaded him to remain at his post; and the reasons which he set before him were recorded to form this Book. If this was the design of the duke of Chow, he was a master of the art of veiling his thoughts with a cloud of words. There are expressions which may be taken, indeed, as intimating a wish that the prince Shih should continue at court, but some violence has to be put upon them.

The prefatory notice is to the effect that, when the two dukes were acting as chief ministers to king Ching, the duke of Chow was 'not pleased' (不悅; see p. 11), and the duke of Chow made the 'Prince Shih.' This expression—'not pleased'—has wonderfully vexed the ingenuity of the critics. It is of no use adducing their various explanations of it, for there is nothing in the Book to indicate the existence of such a feeling in Shih's mind. If he was really entertaining such a feeling from any cause, and had in consequence sought leave to withdraw from public life, the duke of Chow thought it his best plan to make no open reference to those delicate points.

The two principal ideas in the address are—that the favour of Heaven can only be permanently secured for a dynasty by the virtue of its sovereigns; and that that virtue is secured mainly by the counsels and help of virtuous ministers. The ablest sovereigns of Shang are mentioned, and the ministers by whose aid it was, in a great measure, that they became what they were. The cases of Wăn and Woo of their own dynasty, similarly aided by able men, are adduced in the same way; and the speaker adverts to the services which they—the two dukes—had already rendered to their House and their sovereign, and insists that they must go on to the end, and accomplish still greater things. It may be that he is all the while combating some suspicion of himself in the mind of prince Shih, and rebuking some purpose which Shih had formed to abandon his post at the helm of the State; but this is only matter of inference, and does not by any means clearly appear. It will be seen that I have, for convenience' sake, arranged the three and twenty paragraphs in four chapters.

Ch. I. Pp. 1—6. CHOW IS FOR THE PRESENT RAISED BY THE FAVOUR OF HEAVEN TO THE SOVEREIGNTY OF THE EMPIRE. BUT THAT FA-

我不敢知曰、厥基永孚于休、若天棐忱、我亦不敢知曰、其終出于不祥。〇嗚呼、君已曰、時我、我亦不敢寧于上帝命、弗永遠念天威越我民罔尤違、惟人、在我

三節

abide in prosperity. [If Heaven aid sincerity,—]' Nor do I dare to say, as if I knew it, 'The final end will issue in our misfor-
3 tunes.' Oh! you have said, O prince, 'It depends on ourselves.' I also do not dare to rest in the favour of God, never forecasting at a distance the terrors of Heaven in the present time when there is no murmuring or disobedience among the people;—*the issue* is with men. Should our present successor to his fathers

YOUR MAY NOT BE PERMANENT. THE DUKE OF CHOW IS ANXIOUS, AND PRINCE SHIH SHOULD BE THE SAME, TO SECURE IT BY CULTIVATING THE VIRTUE OF THE KING. 1. 君奭,—in the plainness of ancient manners, it is said, when people were talking together they called each other by their names. Shih, however, is honoured with the title of 'prince,' which might be given to him, as he had been invested with the principality of Yen. See on the name of Bk. XII. 2. *Chow had superseded Yin in the possession of the empire, but it could not be known beforehand how long it would continue.* 弗弔,云云,—see Bk. XIV., p. 2. The 旣 in the next two clauses has no conjunctive force, but marks the perfect tense. 我不敢知至末,—compare Bk. XII., p. 17. That passage seems to have misled the old interpreters, and still to mislead many of the present day, as to the meaning of the text. They make the speaker to have the fate of the past-away dynasty of Yin before him, and not that of their existing Chow.—'I do not dare to know and say, "The House of Yin at its beginning might have long accorded with prosperous ways,"' &c. It is plain to me that the speaker has before him the destiny of Chow, which they of the dynasty must fashion for themselves. Whether it would be long or short must depend on their conduct. 厥基永孚于休,—'its foundation will for ever be sincerely established in prosperity.' I do not understand the next clause,—若天棐忱, 'if Heaven assist the sincere.' Whether we suppose the speaker to have reference to the past Yin or the present Chow, these words seem equally out of place. To say that either dynasty might be sincerely virtuous, and so be aided by Heaven, and yet not abide in security, is contrary to reason, and to the most strongly cherished principles of Chinese doctrine. Medhurst reads the words with the next part of the par.—'And should Heaven aid us in very deed, still I would not dare positively to affirm that our end would be entirely the result of misfortune.' But such a construction is inadmissible. I have put the clause in the translation as incomplete, and also within brackets, to intimate that I think it out of place. 其終出于不祥,—Këang Shing reads 其祟出于不詳; but he explains 祟 by 終, and 詳 by 善 (=祥). Another reading, evidently false, was—道出于不詳.

Pp. 3—5. *The duty of the ministers of Chow was to do what they could in the present to secure the permanence of the dynasty.* 3. 嗚呼,君已曰,時我,—the simplest way of explaining these words, is by taking 時我=是在我而已, 'it—the permanence of the dyn.—depends on us,' and supposing that the duke refers to a remark to that effect made at some former period by Shih. Lin Che-k'e and others adduce his language in many parts of his Announcement, *e.g.* pp. 19, 20, which they think the duke has in view. This is very likely. Other methods to try to get a meaning from the passage are harsh and violent. Gan-kwŏ, for instance, took the meaning to be—'Oh! prince, what shall I say? I will say, "You should approve of my remaining in the govt."' It is strange that Maou K'e-ling should still approve of such a construction. Woo Ch'ing

後嗣子孫、大弗克恭上下、遏佚前人光、在家不知。○四節天命不易、天難諶、乃其墜命、弗克經歷嗣前人恭明

prove greatly unable to reverence Heaven and the people, and so bring to an end their glory, could we in our families be ignorant of it?
4 The favour of Heaven is not easily preserved. Heaven is hard to be depended on. Men lose its favouring appointment because they cannot pursue and carry out the reverence and brilliant virtue

takes 君已 in the same way, and then makes 日時我 = 'But it is my duty to do my utmost to preserve the favour of Heaven.' 我亦至惟人,—the 惟人 with which this part ends corresponds to the 時我 at the beginning, and = 實惟在人而已. 弗永遠念天威越我民罔尤違 is all one clause, and to be read together,—another instance of Choo He's long sentences in the Announcements of the Shoo. Ts'ae explains it by 不永遠念天之威於我民無尤怨背違之時. Këang Shing puts a stop at 威, understanding the duke as giving one reason for his remaining in the govt. that he could not rest in the present favour of Heaven, but must forecast a change in the aspects of Providence. For the same resolution he finds another reason in the words that follow—越我民罔尤違,惟人在 (so he points), = 'That our people may be kept from murmurs and disaffection depends on the right men being there.' To make the language in any way bear this interpretation he is obliged to suppose that 越 is a mistake for 曰. Gan-kwŏ paused at 命, and made 弗永遠念天威越我民罔尤違 an address to Shih, = 'Why do you not think of the terrors of Heaven, and set about affecting and transforming our people, that they may not commit errors and fall into opposition.' Interpretation could hardly be more unlicensed. Nor does he succeed better in what remains of the par. K'e-ling labours in vain to impart some likelihood to his views. 在我後至末,—the 在 is used as in the last Book, pp. 5 and 6. By 我後嗣子孫 we must understand king Ching. The same interpretation must be given of the reading—我嗣事子孫, adopted by Këang Shing from a passage in the 'Books of the Early Han;'—see the 王莽傳,上. 恭上下,—Ts'ae understands 'Heaven' to be meant by 上, and 'the people' by 下, so that the expression = 敬天敬民. Others understand 'Heaven and Earth' to be intended. 遏佚前人光 = 遏絶佚墜文武光顯. 在家不知 is to be taken interrogatively, = 可得謂在家不知乎. Ts'ae, holding that the object of the address was to induce the duke of Shaou to abandon his purpose of retirement, takes the question as addressed to him,—'Could you be ignorant of it?' The old interpreters, holding that the speaker is much occupied with vindicating his own remaining in the government, take it in the first person, —'Could I be ignorant.' The best plan seems to be to put it as in the translation. It may thus be applied to either of the dukes; and I believe that the duke of Chow intended it both for himself and his friend. 4, 5. 天命不易,天難諶—comp. the 'Both possessed Pure Virtue,' p. 2; *et al.* Këang Shing, on the authority mentioned above, reads—命不易,天應棐諶, which may safely be rejected on internal grounds. In interpreting the rest of the par. there is much difference of view. Acc. to that followed in the translation, 前人恭明德 = 前人之恭德與明德, 'the reverent virtue and the brilliant virtue of their forefathers; the former referring to the 恭上下 of the last par., and the latter to the 前人光. This 恭明德 is governed by the

德。○五節在今予小子旦、非克有正、迪惟前人光、施于我沖子。○六節又曰、天不可信、我道惟寧王德延、天不庸釋于文王受命。○七節公曰、君奭、我聞在昔、成湯既受命、時則有若伊尹、格于皇天、在

5 of their forefathers. Now I, Tan, being but as a little child, am not able to correct *our king*. I would simply conduct him to the glory of his forefathers, and make his youth partaker of that."

6 He also said, "Heaven is not to be trusted. Our course is simply to seek the prolongation of the virtue of the Tranquillizing king, and Heaven will not find occasion to remove its favouring decree which king Wan received."

7 II. The duke said, "Prince Shih, I have heard that of ancient time, when T'ang the Successful had received the favouring decree, he had with him E Yin, making his virtue like that of great Heaven.

verbs 經歷 and 嗣. Gan-kwŏ, instead of construing the passage thus, put a stop at 歷, and read on the conclusion with the first part of the 5th par.—嗣前人恭明德在今予小子旦 'To continue the reverent and brilliant virtue of our forefathers rests now with me the little child Tan.' Këang Shing has nearly the same punctuation. After all this, no two agree in explaining the former portion—乃其 (K. S. omits this 其) 墜命弗克經歷. It will suffice to mention the view of K'e-ling:—夫天之墜命者, 以其不能有經歷人, 'now Heaven lets its favouring decree fall to the ground, because they cannot have men of experience!' For 非克有正, 云云, the 'Daily Explanation' gives:—我非真有格心之術, 可以匡正吾君也, 所孜孜啟迪者, 惟以前人光大之德, 付與我沖子, 使其上而事天, 下而治民, 知所經歷繼嗣, 不至于遏佚前人之光耳.

P. 6. *The favour of Heaven being so uncertain, the way to secure it is by perpetuating the virtue of king Woo.* We are to understand king Woo by 'The Tranquillizing king,'—see on Bk. VII., p. 3. Ts'ae expands the text very clearly:—天固不可信, 然在我之道, 惟以延長武王之德, 使天不容捨文王所受之命也.

Ch. II. Pp. 7—10. WHAT BENEFITS WERE DERIVED DURING THE TIME OF YIN FROM THE GREAT AND ABLE MINISTERS WHO LIVED IN DIFFERENT REIGNS. IT WAS FOR PRINCE SHIH IN HIS TIME TO SERVE IN THE SAME WAY THE DYNASTY OF CHOW. 7. *The most distinguished ministers of Yin, and the emperors under whom they flourished.* 我聞至皇天,—the 若 prefixed to all the names = 'a man like,' yet not implying any other besides the minister thus pointed out. 伊尹,—see the first introductory note on 'The Instructions of E.' 格于皇天,—see 'The Charge to Yuĕ,' Pt. iii., p. 10. 在太甲至保衡,—see on 'The T'ae-këă,' Pt. i. p. 1, and 'The Charge to Yuĕ,' Pt. iii., p. 10. The duke of Chow here calls E Yin by his name or title, with evident reference to the beginning of the 'T'ae-këă.' 太戊至王家

太甲、時則有若保衡、在太戊、時則有若伊陟臣扈格于上帝、巫咸乂王家、在祖乙時則有若巫賢、在武丁、時則有若甘盤。○（八節）率惟茲有陳、保乂有殷、故殷禮陟

T'ae-këă, *again*, had Paou-hăng. T'ae-mow had E Chih and Chin Hoo, through whom his virtue was made to affect God; he had *also* Woo Heen, who regulated the royal House. Tsoo-yih had Woo
8 Heen. Woo-ting had Kan Pwan. These *ministers* carried out their principles, and effected their arrangements, preserving and regulating the empire of Yin, so that, while its ceremonies lasted, *those sove-*

—see the notices 22 and 23 in the Confucian preface. We may assume that in this passage the duke of Chow had before him the Books of Shang mentioned in those notices, which are now lost. If we had them, we should find the expression 格于上帝, as we find 格于皇天 in 'The Charge to Yuĕ.' From the 13th notice in the preface we learn that T'ang had a minister called Chin Hoo. He would be an ancestor probably of the Chin Hoo mentioned here in connection with T'ae-mow. 祖乙至巫賢,—if we had the lost Book Tsoo-yih (see Pref., n. 26), we should probably find this Woo Heen mentioned in it. 甘盤,—see 'The Charge to Yuĕ,' Pt. iii., p. 1. We cannot but be surprised that the duke does not make any mention of Foo Yuĕ. Keang Shing throws out the hint that Kan Pwan and Foo Yuĕ may have been the same man,—which is absurd. Gan-shih says that as Pwan was the earliest instructor of Woo-ting, the wisdom which guided that emperor to get Yuĕ for his minister was owing to him; but this does not account for the omission of Yuĕ in the duke's list. Perhaps something like a reason for it is suggested by the next par. 8. *The happy result of the services of those ministers.* 率惟茲有陳,—this must be spoken of the six great ministers just enumerated.—'In accordance with this,'—*i.e.*, their course of action so described—'they had an arrangement.' The meaning is very obscure. The critics, however, all expand it much as Ts'ae does:—六臣循惟此道,有陳列之功. 殷禮陟配天,—Gan-kwŏ takes 殷禮, 'the ceremonies of Yin,' as = 'the govt. of Yin' (安上治民之禮), and the whole clause as meaning that the govt. of Yin was so good that its sovereigns were on earth the representatives of God above, and occupied the imperial seat (殷得此安上治民之禮,能升配上天,天在人上,故謂之升,爲天之子是配也). This is ingenious, but it imposes too great violence on the language. 禮 cannot be taken as the nominative to 陟 and 配. 殷禮 are most naturally taken adverbially, = 'according to the ceremonial usages of Yin,' or as in the translation. Then 陟 and 配天 are predicates of the emperors of Yin, probably of those who are specially mentioned in the preceding par., the former char. describing them as 'deceased' (see 'The Canon of Shun,' p. 28), and 配天 declaring the fact of their being associated with Heaven in the sacrifices to it. In the present dyn. all its departed emperors are so honoured at the great sacrificial services. Under the Chow dyn. only How-tseih and king Wăn enjoyed the distinction. The rule of the Yin dyn. seems to have been to associate the five emperors of whom the duke has been speaking. [We have perhaps in this custom a reason for the omission of Foo Yuĕ in the prec. par. From the Pwan-kang, Pt. i., 14, we learn that their ministers shared in the sacrifices to the sovereigns of Yin. Each emperor would have one minister as his assessor, and so Woo-ting could not have both Kan Pwan and Foo Yuĕ. Though the latter may have been the greater man of the two, the sacrificial honour was given to the other as having been the earlier instructor of the emperor. The duke, having the emperors

配天、多歷年所。○天惟純佑命、則商實、百姓王人、罔不秉德明恤、小臣屏侯甸、矧咸奔走、惟茲惟德稱、用乂厥辟、故一人有事于四方、若卜筮、罔不是孚。○公

reigns though deceased were assessors to Heaven, while it extended
9 over many years. Heaven thus determinately maintained its favouring appointment, and Shang was replenished with men. The various officers, and members of the royal House holding employments, all held fast their virtue, and displayed an anxious solicitude *for the empire.* The smaller officers, and the chiefs in the How and Teen *domains*, hurried about on their services. Thus did they all put forth their virtue, and aid their sovereign, so that whatever affairs he, the one man, had in hand, throughout the four quarters of the empire, an entire sincerity was conceded to them as to the indications of the tortoise or the milfoil."

as sacrificed to in his mind, had no occasion therefore to mention Yuĕ. This explanation was first suggested by Soo Shih.]

I acquiesce in this view of the text, in preference to that proposed by Gan-kwŏ. It has its difficulties, however, and one of the principal is that we are obliged to find another subject for the verb 歷 in the concluding clause. The use of 所, at the end is peculiar. The 'Daily Explanation' says it is merely 'an expletive' (語辭), which is saying that no account of it can be given. A usage of it apparently analogous to that here is given in the Dict., with the definition—指物之辭, 'a demonstrative.'

P. 9. *The same subject.* 天惟純佑命則商實,—such is the punctuation adopted by Ts'ae, and also by Keang Shing. Gan-kwŏ read on to 百姓, but the meaning which he endeavours to make out for 商實百姓 is inadmissible. Ts'ae supports the explanation of 實 which appears in the translation, by referring to Mencius, Book VII., Pt. II., xii., 1,—不信仁賢, 則國空虛, 'If men of virtue and ability be not trusted, a State will become empty and void.' The meaning seems to be that Heaven smiled upon the empire sustained by those great ministers, and there was no lack of smaller men to do their duty in their less important spheres with ability and virtue. 百姓王人,—it is not possible to say positively what officers are intended by these designations. Woo Ch'ing takes 百姓 as 'the people of the imperial domain' (王畿之民; comp. the use of the phrase in 'The Canon of Yaou,' p. 2); but it must be used of officers or ministers, and not of the people. I suppose it = 百官. Perhaps Keang Shing is correct in taking 百姓 as the officers with different surnames from that of the imperial House (異姓之臣), and 王人 as cadets of that House in official employment (王之族人, 同姓之臣). 明恤—明致其恤, 有憂國之心. The phrase is correlative with 秉德, and is not to be joined with 小臣 below,—as Gan-kwŏ does. 屏侯甸—爲屏藩于侯甸之服者—'those who acted as screens (—the prin-

曰、君奭、天壽平格、保乂有殷、有殷嗣天滅威、今汝永念則有固命、厥亂明我新造邦。○公曰、君奭、十一節 在昔上帝割、申勸寧王之德、其集大命于厥

10 The duke said, "Prince Shih, Heaven gives long life to the just and the intelligent;—it was thus that *those ministers* maintained and regulated the dynasty of Yin. He who at last came to the throne was extinguished by the majesty of Heaven. Think you of the distant future, and we shall have the decree *in favour of Chow* made sure, and its good government will be brilliantly displayed in our new-founded State."

11 III. The duke said, "Prince Shih, aforetime when God was afflicting Yin, he encouraged anew the virtue of the Tranquillizing king, till at last the great favouring decree was concentrated in his

ces) in the How and Tëen domains.' 矧= 'still more;' or simply = 'likewise.' 惟兹惟德稱=惟此內外之臣, 皆舉稱其德, 'all these ministers, about the court and away from it, throughout the empire, displayed and exerted their virtue.' 若卜筮, 罔不是(=是之)孚(=信之)=如龜之卜, 如蓍之筮, 天下無不敬信之.

P. 10. *Advice to Shih, grounded on the prec., that he should do for Chow what those ministers had done for Yin.* 天壽平格,—Gan-kwŏ supposes that 平格 is spoken of the sovereigns of Yin, (平至之君). It is better to understand the characters of the ministers who have been spoken of. They are called 平, 'level,' free of all selfishness, and 格, 'intelligent,' all-reaching and embracing. 壽 conveys not only the idea of long life, but also of prosperity,—as in the last Book, p. 7. Show is intended by 有殷嗣. 天滅威=天滅之以示威. 永念,—'think of the distant future.' This is better than to take the terms as simply = 'always think of this.' 厥亂明我新造邦=其治效亦赫然明著於我新造之邦, 'its efficient govt. will be gloriously and brilliantly displayed in our new founded kingdom.' Maou K'e-ling understands Lŏ to be 'the newly founded country;' but the dynasty is what is meant; compare the passage of the She King, quoted in 'The Great Learning,' comm., ii., 3. [It does not appear from this par. that the duke of Shaou had expressed his wish to withdraw from the public service, but the duke of Chow is evidently urging him to continue at his post to the last.]

Ch. III. Pp. 11—17. IT WAS BY THE AID OF THEIR ABLE MINISTERS THAT THE KINGS WAN AND WOO WERE RAISED TO THEIR GRAND DISTINCTION AND THE SOVEREIGNTY OF THE EMPIRE. THE DUKE OF CHOW LOOKS TO SHIH TO COOPERATE WITH HIM IN MAINTAINING THEIR DYNASTY OF CHOW. 11. 上帝割—'God was cutting,' *i.e.*, was bringing about the overthrow of the dynasty of Yin. Këang Shing, after K'ang-shing, takes 割 for 蓋, a particle of style, the force of which passes into the verbs that follow; but there is no necessity to resort to such a device. Hea Seen observes that 'Heaven encouraged king Wăn, and afterwards encouraged king Woo; hence the language—申勸;—see the 集說. 申 is 'a term, continuative of what has gone before,' (繼前之辭). In the Le Ke, Bk. 緇衣, p. 24, we find this par. in the form—

躬。○惟（十二節）文王、尙克修和我有夏、亦惟有若虢叔、有若閎夭、有若散宜生、有若泰顚、有若南宮括。○又（十三節）曰、無能往來、茲迪彝教、文王蔑（十四節）德降于國人。○亦惟純佑秉德、迪知天威、乃惟時昭

12 person. *But* that king Wăn was able to conciliate and unite the portion of the great empire which we came to possess, was owing to his having such ministers as his brother of Kih, Hwang Yaou, San E-săng, T'ae Teen, and Nan-kung Kwŏ."

13 He repeated this sentiment, "But for the ability of these men to go and come in his affairs, developing his constant lessons, there would have been no benefits descending from king Wăn on the

14 people. And it also was from the determinate favour *of Heaven*, that there were these men of firm virtue, and acting according to their knowledge of the dread majesty of Heaven, to give themselves

在昔上帝周田觀文王之德，其集大命于厥躬. This was, no doubt, the reading current in the Han dyn. as from Fuh-shang. 12. *King Wăn and the ministers who aided him.* 惟文至有夏,—我有夏=我所有之諸夏, 'the empire, or the portion of the empire, which we had.' The reference is to the two-thirds of the empire which acknowledged the authority of Wăn. 尙=庶幾, 'perhaps.' Tsow Ching-k'e says that the terms 克尙 intimate the difficulty of Wăn's undertaking, and the greatness of the assistance which he derived from his ministers. 虢叔,—from a passage in the 左傳,僖五年, we learn that this was a son of king Ke, and a younger brother of Wăn. Kih was the name of his appanage, in the pres. dis. of Paou-ke (寶雞), dep. of Fung-ts'ëang, Shen-se. [This was called the western Kih. There were two other districts called Kih under the Chow dynasty,—the eastern Kih, and the northern.] 閎,散,泰, and 南宮 are surnames; and 夭,宜生,顚, and 括 are names. So says Gan-kwŏ, and there is no reason to call the thing in question, except in the case of the second, whose surname is said by some to have been 散宜. Of those five ministers we can hardly be said to know more than the surnames and names. It would be a waste of time to refer to the legendary tales that are circulated about them. If we were surprised that there was no mention in p. 7 of Foo Yüe, it is no less strange that the greatest of Wăn's ministers, the 太公望, should here be passed over in silence. 13. It is certainly most natural to take 又曰 here as introducing another remark, confirmatory of the preceding, by the duke of Chow. I can by no means accede to the view of Gan-kwŏ, and of Këang Shing and K'e-ling among the moderns, that 又曰無能往來 is an observation of king Wăn, who, though he had those five ministers, still said, 'They are not able (=enough) to go and come in my affairs.' In order to make the rest of the par. harmonize in any way with this construction, they are obliged to take 蔑德='exquisite virtue.' 14. This par. corresponds to par. 9. What E Yin and the others did for the emperors of Yin, that did these five ministers for king Wăn,—and all by the determinate favour of Heaven. The 'Daily Explanation' expands 亦惟純佑秉德 into—我

文王、迪見冒、聞于上帝、惟時受有殷命哉。○武王惟茲四人、(十五節)尚迪有祿、後暨武王、誕將天威、咸劉厥敵、惟茲四人、昭武王惟冒、丕單稱德。○今在予(十六節)小子旦、若游大川、予往暨汝奭其濟、小子同未在位、誕無我責、

to enlighten king Wăn, and lead him forward to his high distinction and universal over-rule, till his fame reached the ears of God, and
15 he received the decree of Yin. There were still four of these men who led on king Woo to the possession of that decree with all its emoluments. Afterwards, along with him, in great reverence of the majesty of Heaven, they slew all his enemies; and *then* these four men made king Woo distinguished all over the empire,
16 till *the people* universally and greatly proclaimed his virtue. Now, with me Tan, who am but a little child, it is as if I were floating on a great stream; let me from this time cross it along with you, O Shih. Our young sovereign is *powerless* as if he had not yet

文王之時、有虢叔等五臣、爲之輔佐、亦惟天意在文王、純一不二、以佑助之、故生此等秉持明德之人. 迪知天威,—comp. 迪哲 in the last Book, p. 16. 乃惟時昭文王=乃惟以是昭文王. Këang Shing puts a stop at 昭, and makes 乃惟時昭 to be descriptive of the ministers, as becoming thoroughly enlightened and virtuous. This construction is not good. 迪見冒=啟迪其德、使著見於上、覆冒於下. Comp. Bk. XIV., p. 4. 15. *King Woo and his able ministers.* 武王至有祿,—茲四人, 'four of these men.' One of them had died,—it is supposed, the prince of Kih. 天祿,—comp. 'The Counsels of Yu,' p. 17. King Wăn had the decree,—the appointment to the possession of the empire; but Woo came into the possession itself. 後暨武王,—暨 is used here as in the last Book, p. 5, =與, a preposition, 'along with.' 劉,—see 'The Pwan-kăng,' Pt. i., p. 2. 昭武王惟冒=昭武王、遂覆冒天下. Këang Shing puts a stop at 昭, as in the last par., and reads 睸 for 冒, with which character the passage is quoted in the 說文. The meaning would then be—'king Woo looked humbly down on all beneath.' But the punctuation and reading are both bad. 16. *The duke of Chow entreats Shih to co-operate with him in supporting their new dynasty. If he will not do so, the consequences will be disastrous.* We must suppose that all the four ministers who had aided Woo were now dead, and the burden of the State was on the dukes of Chow and Shaou. 游=浮水, 'to float on the water.' 予往暨(=與; as in the last par.) 汝奭其濟=我自今以往、與汝奭同心輔

收罔勗不及、耇造德不降、我則鳴鳥不聞、矧曰其有能格。○公（十七節）曰、嗚呼、君、肆其監于茲、我受命無疆惟休、亦大惟艱、告君乃猷裕、我不以後人

ascended the throne. You must by no means lay the whole burden on me; and if we draw ourselves up without an effort to supply his deficiencies, no good will flow to the people from our age and experience. We shall not hear the voices of the singing birds, and much less can it be thought that we shall make his *virtue* equal *to Heaven*."

17 The duke said, "Oh! consider well, O prince, these things. We have received the favouring decree *of Heaven*, to which belongs an unlimited amount of what is desirable, but having great difficulties attached to it. What I announce to you are counsels of a generous largeness. I cannot allow the successor of our kings to go astray."

佐,共濟艱難,可也. 小子同未在位,—by 小子 here we must understand king Ching. The duke had, indeed, resigned the regency, and the govt. was in the emperor's hands. But Ching was still young, and unequal to his high duties. 誕無我責,收罔勗不及,—Ts'ae thinks there is something wanting before the former of these clauses, and says he does not understand the latter. Gan-kwŏ took 誕無我責 as 一汝大無非責我之留, 'and you are blaming me for remaining in the govt.,' which agrees with his view that the duke of Shaou was dissatisfied, because the other had not retired upon resigning the regency. The terms will bear the meaning which I have given in the translation; and it appears to me more in harmony with the tenor of the address. As to the meaning of the second clause, the editors of Yung-ching's Shoo give a modified approval to the view of Leu Tsoo-heen, adduced by Yu E-shoo (余芑舒; of the Yuen dyn.), making the words addressed to the duke of Shaou:—召公若收斂退藏,罔勗勉成王之所不逮. I take the characters much in the same way, but consider that the duke of Chow is speaking of himself as well as of prince Shih. I can hardly tell how Gan-kwŏ interprets here. He uses many words, but I do not understand them. Këang Shing points—誕無我責收,罔勗不及,=' Do not you by any means charge me to retire. I will exert myself, and exertion is never made without success!' 耇造德=耇老成人之德. 鳴鳥,—by 'the singing birds' are meant the male and female phœnix, fabled to appear at court in times of great prosperity. See on the 'Yih and Tseih,' p. 9. In the She King, Pt. III., Bk. II., Ode viii., st. 9, mention is made of the phœnixes flying about and screaming on the hills. The ode is ascribed to the duke of Shaou, and is supposed to celebrate king Ching and the happiness of his times. 其有能格,—this is said with reference to the predicates in p. 7 about what the ministers of Yin did for their sovereigns. 17. *The duke urges Shih to lay to heart what he has said to him.* 肆其監于茲,—comp. the last Book, p. 19. 肆 is taken =大. 我受至惟艱,—comp. Bk. XII., p. 9. By 後人, 'the after man,' we are to understand king Ching. The 前人 at the beginning of next par. renders this very probable.

迷。○十八節公曰、前人敷乃心、乃悉命汝、作汝民極、曰、汝明朂偶王、在亶乘玆大命、惟文王德丕承無疆之恤。○十九節公曰、君、告汝朕允、保奭、其汝克敬、以予監于殷喪大否、肆念我天威。○二十節予不允惟若玆誥、予惟曰、襄我二

18 IV. The duke said, "The former king laid bare his heart, and gave full charge to you, constituting you one of the guides of the people, and saying, 'Do you with intelligence and energy prove a helper to the king; do you with sincerity support and carry on this great decree. Think of the virtue of king Wăn, and enter greatly into his boundless anxieties.'"

19 The duke said, "What I tell you, O prince, are my sincere thoughts. O Shih, the Grand-protector, if you can but reverently survey with me the decay and great disorders of Yin, and thence consider the dread majesty of Heaven *which warns* us!——

20 "Am I not to be believed that I must thus speak? I simply say, 'The establishment of our dynasty rests with us two.' Do you agree

Ch. IV. Pp. 18—23. 18. *The duke of Shaou had received a special charge from king Woo to be a guardian of the young king and of the dynasty.* 前人, 'the former man,' is to be understood of king Woo. On his deathbed he had given the charge, of which a portion is here adduced, to the dukes of Chow and Shaou. 敷乃心,—the 乃 here would seem to = 其, the adj. pronoun of the third person. The phrase, however, = 所敷者乃其心腹. 作汝民極,—this has reference to the appointment of Shih to be the Grand-guardian, in which office he was to be a support and pattern for the people. Lin Che-k'e says: 凡爲大臣者,皆曰以爲民極. 偶王 = 輔弼嗣王, 'to help the heir king.' Two, joined in any way, are called 偶. Shih was to prove as a help-meet to the king. In 乘大命, we have the metaphor of a carriage in which the sovereign appointment was placed and carried on. 惟文王德,—the 惟 = 念, 'to think of.' 丕承無疆之恤,—comp. 無疆惟恤, Bk. XII., p. 9. 19. *The duke of Chow earnestly begs Shih to enter into his anxieties, and learn from the fate of Yin to labour for the establishment of their dynasty.* 其汝克敬,—this is hortatory, and the meaning seems to be best brought out by giving the translation an optative form. 以予 may be taken as = 與予. 大否 (p'ei) = 大亂, 'great disorders,' or 大阸, 'great distresses.' 我天威,—'our Heavenly terrors,' *i.e.*, the terrors of Heaven which were to be dreaded by them, and guarded against through a diligent discharge of their duties. 20. *So much was dependent on the two dukes that they ought to be exerting themselves to the utmost, and especially to be looking out for men who might hereafter supply their places.* 予不允惟若玆誥 is

人、汝有合哉、言曰、在時二人、天休滋至、惟時二人弗戡、其汝克敬德、明我俊民、在讓後人于丕時。○嗚廿一節呼、篤棐時二人、我式克至于今日休、我咸成文王功于不怠、丕冒、海隅出日、罔不率俾。

with me? Then you *also* will say, 'It rests with us two.' And the favour of Heaven has come to us so largely:—it should be ours to feel as if we could not sustain it. If you can but reverently cultivate your virtue, and bring to light our men of eminence, then when you resign to some successor in a time of established security, ———.

21 "Oh! it is by the earnest assistance of us two that we have come to the prosperity of the present day. But we must go on, abjuring all idleness, to complete the work of king Wăn, till it has entirely overspread the empire, and from the corners of the sea and the sunrising there shall not be one who is disobedient to our rule."

to be taken interrogatively. The 'Daily Explanation' gives for it:—凡我言語,豈是不足取信于人,而如此諄諄告汝乎. 襄我二人, —襄=成. The two men are evidently the duke of Chow himself, and the duke of Shaou. The clause—王業之成在我與汝而已,—as in the translation. Gan-kwŏ took the two men to be Wăn and Woo, and this idea put him to the greatest straits throughout the par. Even Maou K'e-ling does not venture to defend such as an interpretation. 在時(=是)二人—在我二人. 戡—堪 or 勝, 'to be equal to,' 'to sustain.' I do not know what to make of the 在 in the last clause. The speaker does not complete his meaning. He simply says—'In the fact of yielding to successors in a time of great prosperity,'———. Critics supply what is wanting according to their different opinions as to the main object which the duke of Chow had in view in the address. 21. *The two dukes had done much for Chow in the past; it remained for them to complete their work.* 篤棐時(=是)二人—篤於輔君(or 王室)者是我二人. 我式(—用),—'we thereby.' The 'we' is we of Chow, =our dynasty. 丕冒—使丕偏覆冒于斯民, 'causing it universally to overspread this people.' 罔不率俾—無不循我化,可臣使也, 'all yield to our transforming influences, and become subjects who may be employed.

[M. de Guignes observes on this paragraph:—'It is sufficiently singular that a philosopher like Chow-kung inspires here the spirit of conquest; it was then, therefore, the taste of the Chinese, who sought to extend themselves more and more to the east.' See 'Le Chou-king,' p. 237. The duke's words hardly called for such a remark. He is merely seeking the full establishment of their dynasty,—that Chow should enter into all the possessions of Yin.]

○公（廿二節）曰、君、予不惠若茲多誥、予惟用閔于天越民。○公（廿三節）曰、嗚呼、君、惟乃知民德、亦罔不能厥初、惟其終、祗若茲、往敬用治。

22 The duke said, "O prince, am I not speaking in accordance with reason in these many declarations? I am only influenced by anxiety about *the decree of* Heaven, and about the people."

23 The duke said, "Oh! O prince, you know the ways of the people, how at the beginning they can be *all we could desire*, but it is the end *which is to be thought of*. Act in careful accordance with this fact. Go and reverently exercise your government."

P. 22. *The duke affirms the reasonableness of his remarks, and re-states the grounds of them.* 予不惠若茲多誥 is to be taken interrogatively, like the commencing clause of p. 20. This is sufficient against the view of Këang Shing, who reads it indicatively, and takes 惠＝慧, so that the meaning is—'I in my want of wisdom make these many declarations.' 惠＝順於理, 'accordant with reason.' We have met with it before, having this meaning. 予惟用閔于天越(＝及)民＝予惟用憂天命, 難以永保, 及生民, 無所倚賴. 23. *The uncertainty of the attachment of the people should make ministers careful to retain their good will.* 民德＝'the ways of the people;' now all-attachment to a govt., now disaffected and rebellious. 惟其終＝當思其終.

THE BOOKS OF CHOW.

BOOK. XVII. THE CHARGE TO CHUNG OF TS'AE.

蔡仲之命

一節 惟周公位冢宰、正百工、群叔流言、乃致辟管叔于商、囚蔡叔于郭鄰、以車七乘、降霍叔于庶人、三年不齒、蔡仲克庸祗德、周公以爲卿士、叔卒、乃命

1 When the duke of Chow was in the place of prime minister, and directed all the officers, the *king's* uncles spread abroad an *evil* report, in consequence of which he put to death the prince of Kwan in Shang; confined the prince of Ts'ae in Koh-lin, with an attendance, however, of seven chariots; and reduced the prince of Hŏ to be a private man, causing his name to be erased from the registers for three years. The son of the prince of Ts'ae being able to display a reverent virtue, the duke of Chow made him a high noble, and when his father died, requested a decree from the king, investing him with the country of Ts'ae.

THE NAME OF THE BOOK.—蔡仲之命, 'The Charge to Chung of Ts'ae.' Ts'ae was the name of the small State or district, which formed the appanage of Too, a younger brother of the duke of Chow, on whose history I have slightly touched in the note on p. 12 of Bk. VI. The name still remains in the dis. of Shang-ts'ae (上蔡), dep. of Joo-ning, Ho-nan. Too was deprived of this appanage, but it was subsequently restored to his son, and the Charge preserved in this Book was given to him on the occasion. The name of Too's son was Hoo (胡). He is here called Chung; but that character only denoted his place in the roll of his brothers or cousins. A Chinese scholar has attempted to explain it to me thus.—Too was younger than king Woo, and so, from the standpoint of king Ching, he is called 蔡叔,

'(younger) uncle of Ts'ae.' King Ching and Hoo were cousins,—'brothers,' according to Chinese usage of terms, and Hoo, being the younger of the two, was called 蔡仲, '(second) brother of Ts'ae.'

The Book is only found in the old text, or that of Gan-kwŏ. There is some difference of opinion as to the place which it should occupy in the list of the Books of Chow. Ts'ae thinks it ought to be placed before 'The Announcement about Lŏ.' In the 'Little Preface,' as we have it from Ch'ing, it is placed the 96th in the list of Books, immediately before the 'Speech at Pe.' Ming-shing allows that so it is wrongly placed, which indeed is evident, but says that Ch'ing gave the preface as he found it without venturing any alterations, whereas the author or forger of Gan-kwŏ's commentary took it upon him to remove the notice to where it now stands. Whether Gan-kwŏ's commentary be a forgery or not, the Book occurs in it, I apprehend, in the place which it originally occupied. There is no necessity for supposing with Ts'ae that it should be before Book XIII. We do not know in what year Ts'ae Shuh died. Ts'ae Chung's restoration to his father's honours may not have taken place till after the building of Lŏ, and king Ching had taken the government, upon reaching his majority, into his own hands.

CONTENTS. The first par. is of the nature of a preface, giving the details necessary to explain the appointment of Hoo. The seven paragraphs that follow are the king's Charge, directing him how to conduct himself, so that he might blot out the memory of his father's misdeeds, and win the praise of the emperor.

P. 1. *Prefatory details.* 惟周公至百工,—comp. 'The Instructions of E.,' p. 1. 羣叔流言,—comp. Bk. VI., p. 12. 致辟,—'carried out the law to the utmost,' = 'put to death.' [This confirms the interpretation given of 我之弗辟, in Bk. VI., p. 13.] 囚蔡叔至七乘,—囚 = 'to confine.' K'ang-shing defined the term by 拘. 郭鄰 was the name of a place; but where it was, we cannot tell. Sze-ma Ts'een, in the 管蔡世家第五, says that Ts'ae Shuh was allowed an attendance of 'ten chariots and 70 footmen.' In the 左傳, 定四年, mention is also made of 70 footmen, but the chariots are seven, as in the text. For 以車七乘 the 'Daily Explanation' gives—猶以車七乘隨之. 降霍叔至不齒,—the name of Hoh Shuh was Ch'oo (處). Ch'oo's appanage was Hoh, the name of which remains in Hoh Chow, dep. of P'ing-yang (平陽), Shan-se. 三年不齒,—'for three years he had not his teeth,' *i.e.*, he was struck off the family roll. The names of all the brothers were entered according to their 'teeth' or ages; hence one of the definitions of 齒 in the dict. is by 年也, 列也. 蔡仲至卿士,—蔡仲, see the note on the 'name of the Book.' Ts'een says that 'when the duke of Chow heard of the good character of Hoo, he raised him to be a noble of Loo' (周公聞之, 而舉胡以爲魯卿士). The opinion of the speaker in the passage of the 左傳 referred to above was the same (蔡仲改行帥德, 周公舉之, 以爲己卿士). Ts'ae on the contrary thinks that the office of 'high noble,' conferred on Hoo, was within the imperial domain, and not in Loo. This view appears to me the more likely; but the text does not enable us to decide the point.

命諸王邦之蔡—請命于成王, 復封其國于蔡, 使繼叔之後, 'He requested a decree from king Ching, and again invested Hoo with Ts'ae, that he might continue the line of his father.' Gan-kwŏ thought that the Ts'ae with which Hoo was invested was not the same which had been the appanage of his father, but another on the east, 'between the Hwae and the Joo,' to which the name of Ts'ae was given, to mark the connection between it and the former. This is not likely, nor is it supported by proper historical evidence.

[Shih King (郝敬; of the Ming dynasty) denies the various statements in this par., saying they are legends founded on a misapprehension of the duke of Chow's language in 'The Metal-bound Coffer,'—我之弗辟, 我無以告我先王; and that to suppose that the duke killed one brother and degraded two others, as he is here said to have done, is injurious to his character, and would establish a precedent of most dangerous nature. Having thus settled it that the statements are not true, he goes on to the conclusion, that this Book is a forgery. But this is egregious trifling. The statements of this par. were staple of Chinese history before the burning of the Shoo. The passage of the 左傳 adduced above, and the sequel of which contains a part of par. 3, is sufficient to prove this. The duke of Chow is easily vindicated from any charges brought against his character for the deeds which are related here.]

諸王邦之蔡。○王(二節)若曰、小子胡、惟爾率德改行、克愼厥猷、肆予命爾侯于東土、往卽乃封、敬哉。○(三節)爾尙蓋前人之愆、惟忠惟孝、爾乃邁迹自身、克勤無怠、以垂憲乃後、率乃祖文王之彝

2 "The king speaks to this effect, 'My little child, Hoo, you follow the virtue *of our ancestors*, and have changed from the conduct *of your father;* you are able to take heed to your ways;—I therefore appoint you to be a prince *of the empire* in the east. Go to your country. Be reverent!

3 'In order that you may cover the faults of your father, be loyal, be filial. Urge on your steps in your own way, diligent and never idle, and so you will hand down an example to your descendants.

Pp. 2—8. The charge. 2. *The virtue of Hoo, to which he was entitled for the distinction conferred on him.* 王若曰,—it may seem that this should be translated—'The king spake to the following effect,' rather than as I have done. I apprehend, however, that the charge was delivered by the duke of Chow in the king's name, in the same way as the charge to the Viscount of Wei, Bk. VIII. The 命諸王邦之蔡 in the last par. leads me to this view, nor need it be rejected though Hoo's appointment may have taken place after the building of Lŏ. 率德改行 must = 循祖之德,改父之行,—as in the translation. 東土,—Ts'ae was to the east of Haou, Ching's capital. 往卽乃封,—the first definition of 封 in the dict. is 爵諸侯之土, 'the country with which a prince was invested.' The primary meaning of the term, however, was, no doubt, 'a tumulus or mound;' and Sëě Ke-seuen (薛季宣) ingeniously accounts for its being used as the designation of a territory in this way:—天子建侯立國,分以天子之社,使置社於其國,因謂之封, 'The emperor, when appointing a prince over a State, took from the earth of his own altar to the spirit of the land, and gave it to the prince, that he might raise an altar to the spirit of the land in his State, which was thence called by the name of 封. Compare the note on 'The Tribute of Yu,' Pt. i., p. 35. 3. *Hoo must go on as he had begun, covering by his good deeds the evil memory of his father.* 爾尙至惟孝,—the force of the 尙 is partly concessive, and partly hortatory. By 前人 is intended, of course, Hoo's father. Though Hoo was acting contrary to his father's example, yet as his conduct would remove the disgrace that rested on his father's memory, it is characterized as 'filial.' 邁迹自身,—Gan-kwŏ gives for this—行善迹用汝身. There is a reference plainly to the conduct of Hoo's father, who had left no traces of good by which he might direct his steps. Lin Che-k'e says:—汝之行善迹當自汝身而始. The characters, as I understand them, are literally:—'Do you push boldly on (邁卽勇往,力行之意), treading on your own person.' The conclusion,—無若爾考之違王命—is quoted in the 左傳, as referred to above.

[Ch'in Foo-lëang says:—'When Shun gave charge to Yu, he made no reference to the misconduct of his father K'wăn; and the duke

訓、無若爾考之違王命。○四節皇天無親、惟德是輔、民心無常、惟惠之懷、為善不同、同歸于治、為惡不同、同歸于亂、爾其戒哉。○五節愼厥初、惟厥終、終以不困、不惟厥終、終以困窮。○六節懋乃攸績、睦乃四鄰、以蕃王室、以和兄

Follow the constant lessons of your grandfather, king Wăn, and be not like your father disobedient to the royal orders.

4 'Great Heaven has no affections;—it helps only the virtuous. The people's hearts are not constant;—they cherish only the kind. Acts of goodness are different, but they contribute in common to government. Acts of evil are different, but they contribute in common to disorder. Do you be cautious!

5 'To give heed to the beginning, think of the end:—the end will then be without distress. If you do not think of the end, it will be in distress, and that the greatest.

6 'Exert yourself to achieve your proper merit. Seek to be in harmony with all your neighbours. Be a fence to the royal House. Live in harmony with your brethren. Tranquillize and help the inferior people.

of Chow, when giving charge to the viscount of Wei, made no mention of Woo-kăng. How is it that he here makes mention so repeatedly and distinctly of Hoo's father? Hoo's father was his own brother. It was necessary he should speak of him, on the principle explained by Mencius, VI., Pt. ii., iii.;'—see the 集說.]

P. 4. 皇天至之懷,—comp. the 'Tae-këă, Pt. iii., p. 1. 皇天無親,惟德是輔 is quoted as from the Books of Chow, in the 左傳,僖五年. 5. 愼厥初,惟厥終,—Comp. 愼終于始, in the 'Tae-këă,' Pt. iii., p. 6. The same sentiment is here brought differently out. 惟 is to be taken = 思, as in the same expression—惟厥終—in the last Bk. p. 23. In the 左傳,襄,二十五年, there is a quotation from the Shoo, the original of which is probably in this par.—愼始而敬終,終以不困.

P. 6. *Rules for Hoo in his relations with others.* 懋乃攸績 = 勉汝所立之功, 'exert yourself in achieving your proper merit.' What that merit was is not said. 'It embraced,' says Tsëaou Hwang (焦竑), 'the bringing forward the able, the intelligent administration of the government, and the right use of punishments.' 四鄰 = 'the prince of the neighbouring States on every side.' 以

弟、康濟小民。○率(七節)自中、無作聰明亂舊章、詳乃視聽、罔以側言改厥度、則予一人汝嘉。○王(八節)曰、嗚呼、小子胡、汝往哉、無荒棄朕命。

7 'Follow the course of the Mean, and do not by assuming to be intelligent throw old statutes into confusion. Watch over what you see and hear, and do not for one-sided words deviate from the right rule. Then I, the one man, will praise you.'"

8 "The king says, 'Oh! my little child, Hoo, go, and do not idly throw away my charge.'"

蓄, 以和,—the 以 does not connect the clauses with those which precede. 兄弟 'brethren,' are the princes and nobles of the same surname with himself. 7. *Rules of a more internal character.* 率自中,—Lin Che-k'e observes that this clause is equivalent to the 率性 at the commencement of the 'Doctrine of the Mean.' We need not, however, look for any moral or metaphysical doctrine in the text. 中 is here 'the middle,' 'the proper Mean.' Emphasis is to be laid on the 作 in the second clause. Wang Ts'ëaou says:—'Intelligence is a Heavenly virtue; assuming to be intelligent is a selfish shrewdness' (聰明, 天德也, 作聰明則私智耳. 詳=審, 'to exercise a discriminating judgment.' 厥度,—厥 might be translated in the second person,—'your,' or even in the first. Ts'ae expands from 審乃 thus:—視聽不審, 惑於一偏之說, 則非中矣, 其能不改吾身之法度乎.

P. 8. *Concluding admonition.*

THE BOOKS OF CHOW.

BOOK XVIII. NUMEROUS REGIONS.

多方

惟（一節）五月丁亥、王來自奄、至于宗周。○周（二節）公曰、王若曰、猷、告爾四國多方、惟爾殷侯尹民、我惟大降爾命、爾罔不知。○洪（三節）惟圖天之命、弗永寅念于祀。

1 I. In the fifth month, on the day Ting-hae, the king arrived from
2 Yen, and came to the honoured city of Chow. The duke of Chow
said, "The king speaks to the following effect, 'Ho! I make an
announcement for you of the four kingdoms and many *other* regions.
Ye who were the officers and people of the prince of Yin, I have
dealt very leniently as regards your lives, as ye all know. You
3 kept reckoning greatly upon *some* decree of Heaven, and did not
keep with perpetual awe before your thoughts *the preservation of*
your sacrifices.

INTRODUCTORY NOTE. The Preface to the Shoo contains the names of two Books now lost, which had their place between 'The Charge to Chung of Ts'ae' and 'The Numerous Regions.' The one was styled 'The Government of king Ching,' and was made on occasion of an expedition of the king to the east, when he smote the wild tribes of the Hwae, and extinguished the State of Yen (東伐淮夷遂踐奄). The other had reference to the king's removal of the chief or ruler of Yen to the district of P'oo-koo (蒲姑) in Ts'e, and was styled 將蒲姑, which we do not know how to translate, being unable, from the loss of the Book, to say how the character 將 should be taken. The Book that now comes under our notice was a sequel to these two, the prefatory note saying that it was made on the return of the king to Haou from Yen (成王歸自奄, 在宗周誥庶邦, 作多方).

Now, the prefatory note to 'The Great Announcement' says that after king Woo's death,

when Woo-kăng and the three uncles of Ching, who had been placed as overseers of him in Yin, rebelled, the wild tribes of the Hwae rose at the same time and made common cause with them. In 'The Numerous Officers,' p. 21, again, the king is made to say to the nobles of Yin, that, 'when he came from Yen,' he dealt very leniently with them. The question has been raised whether, in those and other notices, we have intimations of only one expedition against the tribes of the Hwae and Yen, or of successive expeditions. On the lost Book of 'The Govt. of king Ching,' Ch'ing K'ang-shing says that the exploits described in it were those of the duke of Chow when he put down the rebellion of his brothers, and that he did not know how the Book had been arranged in the place assigned to it in the Preface. Këang Shing, Wang Ming-shing, and others, who all but swear to the words of Ch'ing, would arrange all the Books I have mentioned before 'The Numerous Officers.' In the standard chronology, moreover, the 'Numerous Regions' is assigned to the fifth year of king Ching, B.C. 1,110 (or 1,111). On the other hand, Gan-kwŏ maintains that the wild tribes spoken of were not tamed by one visit of the imperial forces. The duke of Chow smote them, he says, and Yen with them, when quelling the rebellion of his brothers and Woo-kăng, but they rebelled again when the duke had resigned the regency, and the king himself, probably attended by his uncle, took the field against them; and it was on his return from extinguishing the State of Yen, that the announcement contained in the 'Numerous Regions' was made. It is of the operations at this time against the Hwae and other wild tribes, he thinks, that mention is made in 'The speech at Pe.'

I am inclined in this matter to adopt the view of Gan-kwŏ. We may conclude from the arrangement of the Books that this was the opinion of the compiler of the Preface. If we may credit what Mencius says, the records of the Shoo do not tell us a tithe of the wars carried on by the duke of Chow to establish the new dynasty:—'He smote Yen, and after three years put its ruler to death. He drove Fei-leen to a corner by the sea and slew him. The states which he extinguished amounted to fifty' (Mencius, Bk. III., Pt. II., ix., 6). I may conclude this note with the remarks of Shoo Shih on the difficulty with which the dynasty of Chow was established. He says:—'"The Great Announcement," "The Announcement to the prince of K'ang," "The Ann. about Drunkenness," "The timber of the Tsze," "The Ann. of the duke of Shaou," "The Ann. about Lŏ," "The Numerous Officers," and "The Numerous Regions,"—these eight pieces, each having its different subject, yet have all a general reference to the fact that the minds of the people of Yin would not submit to Chow. When I have read "The Great Speech," and "The Completion of the War," I have always exclaimed—'How easily did Chow take the empire from Yin!' But when I read these eight Books, I exclaim—'With what difficulty did Chow bring Yin to a quiet submission!' "The Numerous Regions" was addressed not to the off. of Yin only, but also to those of the other regions throughout the empire;—showing us that it was not the people of Yin only who refused to acknowledge the new sway. One can understand how deep had been the influence of the six virtuous kings who came after T'ang. Under the tyranny of Show, the people were as if in the midst of flaming fire, and they turned to Chow as water flows downwards, without thinking of the virtue of the former kings. But when the empire was a little settled, they were no longer amid the fires, and their thoughts turned to the seven emperors of Yin, as a child thinks of its parents. Though sages like king Woo and the duke of Chow followed one another with their endeavours to soothe them, their insurrectionary movements could not be repressed. Had the new dynasty not possessed the duke of Chow, it could hardly have been established.—This he knew, and it was this which made him apprehensive, and that he did not dare to withdraw from public life.' See the 集傳.

The Name of the Book.—多方, 'The Numerous Regions.' The phrase occurs in the 2d par., and up and down throughout the greater portion of the Book; and hence it is used to designate the whole, indicating that it was addressed to the representatives not of one region, but of many. In parr. 24—29, the phrase 多士, 'numerous officers,' takes the place of 多邦, and Woo Ch'ing has removed so much to the former Book;—for which he is hardly to be blamed. 'The Numerous Regions' is found in both the texts.

Contents. The king has returned to his capital in triumph, having put down rebellion in the east, and specially extinguished the State or tribe of Yen. A great assembly of princes and nobles,—the old officers of Yin, and chiefs from many regions besides,—is gathered on the occasion. They are all supposed to have been secretly, if not openly, in sympathy with the rebellion which has been trampled out, and to grudge to yield submission to the rule of Chow. The king, by the duke of Chow, reasons and expostulates with them. He insists on the leniency with which he had dealt with them in the past; and whereas they might be saying that Chow's overthrow of the Yin dynasty was a usurpation, he shows that it was from the will of Heaven. The history of the empire is reviewed, and it is made to appear that king Woo had displaced the emperors of Shang, just as T'ang, the founder of Shang, had displaced the emperors of Hea. It was the course of duty for them therefore to submit to Chow. If they did not avail themselves of its leniency, they should be dealt with in another way.

Having thus spoken, the duke turns, at par. 24, and addresses the many officers of the States, and especially those of Yin who had been removed to Lŏ, speaking to them in the style of 'The Numerous Officers.' Finally he reminds them all that it is time for them to begin a new course. If they do well, all will be well with them; if they continue perverse, they will have themselves to blame for the consequences.

Ch. I. Pp. 1—12. Time when, and parties to whom the Announcement was made. A review of the downfall of the Hea

DYNASTY, AND OF THE HISTORY OF THAT OF SHANG;—TO SHOW THE WAY OF HEAVEN IN THE RISE AND FALL OF THE IMPERIAL SWAY. 1. See the introductory note. On 奄 and 宗周, see the notes on Bk. XIV., p. 21. Gaubil observes that whereas the most approved history of the empire refers the date of this Book to the 5th year of king Ching, or B.C. 1,111, there really was no day Ting-hae in the 5th month of that year in the calendar of Chow. The correctness of his observation is easily verified, for the Chow year corresponding to B.C. 1,111, must have commenced with the cycle day 辛酉. But we have seen (p. 421) that it was in the year B.C. 1,098 that the duke of Chow resigned the regency. The next year, B.C. 1,097, began, if the calendar was correct, on the 6th cycle day, or 己巳, and the 5th month must have commenced with the day 丁卯 or 戊辰, so that the day Ting-hae would be the 20th or 21st of it. Gan-kwŏ arrived at the same result from his view that the day 戊辰, Bk. XIII., p. 29, was the last day of the year. Let these numerical statements have whatever weight is due to them;—they seem to me to show that this Book follows 'The Announcement about Lŏ,' in chronological order, and that we are right in rejecting the early date assigned to it by K'ang-shing and his followers.

2. 周公曰, 王若曰,—the announcement is thus introduced differently from any that have preceded. 'The Great Announcement' for instance begins with 王若曰, though the king could have had little or nothing to do with it. The language of it, like the expedition which it vindicated, was all from the duke of Chow. The compilers of the Books, however, did not think it necessary to prefix a 周公曰, as they have done here. The only reason for the addition in the text at all satisfactory assumes (what I have inferred on other grounds) that this announcement was made after the duke had resigned the regency. The king might then have been expected to declare his sentiments in his own person. He did not do so on this occasion. There were reasons, no doubt, for his not doing so, though we cannot assign them. The duke of Chow was spokesman as before; and to indicate their different positions we have the prefix—'The duke of Chow said.' 猷, 告爾四國多方,—on 猷告, see upon Bk. VII., p. 1. Woo Ch'ing understands by 四國 'all the States in the four quarters of the empire' (四方諸國), and by 多方, 'the people of all the States' (諸國之民). This is ingenious but not satisfactory. 四國多方 stand collaterally, and indicate different regions. The 'many regions' are more extensive than the 'four States,' and cannot be taken as embraced in them. We must understand the 四國 as in Bk. XIV., p. 21, of the imperial domain of Shang or Yin, which had been divided into four parts presided over by three of king Woo's brothers, and by Woo-kăng, the son of Show. It seems to me absurd to suppose, with Këang Shing, that Yen was one of the States thus classed together.

Then by 多邦 are intended the princes and people of other regions generally. It is probable the people of Yen, in the rising which had been quelled, had raised the standard of the fallen dynasty, and that the issue of their struggle had been eagerly waited for by the people of the old imperial domain, and of other eastern regions. However that may be, the duke of Chow and other friends of the new dynasty thought the time a fitting one to give another and general exposition of the grounds on which they vindicated for it the sovereignty of the empire. 惟爾殷侯尹民,云云,—by 殷侯, 'the prince of Yin,' is denoted Woo-kăng. Këang Shing takes 殷=衆, so that 爾殷侯尹民=爾諸侯治民者, 'ye princes of the empire, governing the people;' but such a meaning of 殷 in this place is very unlikely. Woo Ch'ing retains 殷 in the sense of 'the Yin dynasty,' but takes the clause in the same way as Shing (殷諸侯之尹其民者), saying that whereas the 'people' were addressed in 爾四國多方, the speaker here rises to address their 'rulers' (誥民而因及其君). But there is no such gradation of thought in the text, and Ch'ing's exegesis lies under the additional disadvantage of making 惟=及, 'and.' The duke of Chow, having called the attention of all in the assembly to what he had to say (告爾四國多方), here turns and addresses himself more particularly to the nobles and people who had occupied the imperial domain of Yin. I understand 殷侯尹民 as=殷侯之百官與衆民. The 'Daily Explanation' differently:—爾殷侯所尹正統轄之民. 我惟大降爾命,—see on Bk. XIV., p. 21. I understand the language here as in that previous passage, in accordance with the views of Ts'ae. Here, however, he supposes that the king says he is sparing their lives a *second time*, and 爾罔不知 is with him=爾宜無不知, 'Be ye all aware of this.' But this clause and the former are to me plainly historical, and refer to what is past. Ts'ae's view is fully and clearly expanded in the 'Daily Explanation:'—爾……助奄作叛,今奄國既滅,皆當以從逆坐

書經

○惟帝降格于夏、有夏誕厥逸、不肯感言于民、乃大淫昏、不克終日勸于帝之迪、乃爾攸聞。○ 四節

4 'God sent down correction on Hea, but the sovereign *only* increased his luxury and sloth, and would not speak kindly to the people. He proved himself on the contrary dissolute and dark, and would not yield for a single day to the leading of God;—this

誅、我惟不忍多殺、大降恩赦、宥爾殷民之命、爾等宜無不知之、勿復生二心. 3. This par. is the key-note to the Book, and it is right to connect it closely with what precedes. The subject of it is 'the officers and people of Yin,' who had deemed the empire belonged to the House of T'ang by a 'divine right' (天之命), and did not consider that what Heaven had given, it might and would take away, if there were not the earnest and virtuous discharge of the duties of government. Ts'ae makes Yen to be the subject of the par. Thus the 'Daily Explanation' follows the passage just quoted with—'And do you know the reason why Yen has perished? The people of Yen presumed greatly on their private views, reckoned on the decree of supreme Heaven, and with evil action rose in rebellion. They used no far-reaching reverent forethought, which would have led them to obey the laws, and rest in their lot, whereby they would have preserved the sacrifices to their ancestors. They have thus suddenly brought destruction on themselves; and do you look to Yen as a beacon, and know that the decree of Heaven is not to be rashly sought or relied on.' But why should we suppose that the speaker has here the State of Yen in view? It is mentioned indeed in the 1st par., but that is an addition by the compiler, and Yen is nowhere referred to in the address. It was too insignificant, moreover, to occupy the place which must be assigned to it, if we suppose that the announcement is thus made to turn upon its history.

No similar objections can be made to the view which I have taken. The sacrifices to the emperors of the Yin dynasty were allowed, in the generous clemency of king Woo, to be continued by their lineal descendant Woo-kăng, the son of the tyrant Show; but no sooner was Woo dead, than he and his adherents rose in rebellion against the new dynasty, and brought down new and heavy punishments, though still tempered with mercy, upon themselves. I am surprised that none of the Chinese critics have thus connected the 2d and 3d parr.

Gan-kwŏ joined the 3d par. with the 4th, and supposed that Këë, the last emperor of the Hea dyn., was the subject of it. Këang Shing deals with it very inanely, saying that it is a general declaration, = 'Should kings reckon on the decree of Heaven, and not reverently consult with long forethought, for their sacrifices' (王者圖度天命、而不長敬念于祭祀乎)? 洪惟,—see on the same characters in Bk. VII., p. 1. Këang Shing would make them in both places merely a phrase of introduction or exclamation; but we are not reduced to have recourse to such a device.

Pp. 4—7. *How the sovereignty of the empire passed from the House of Hea to T'ang.* 4. Ts'ae thinks that some paragraphs introductory to this have been lost, his reason being that it is the custom in the Shoo to precede the account of the downfall of a dynasty because of the wickedness of its last emperor with a reference to the virtuous emperors who preceded him. That is the practice certainly, but the duke of Chow may not have observed it here. We are not obliged to suppose any loss of text. 惟帝降格于夏,—comp. Bk. XIV., p. 5. The 'Daily Explanation' here takes 格=正. 感言于民,—感=憂, 'sorrowfully,' 'with sympathy.' 不克終日勸于帝之迪,—終日, in the Analects and Mencius, is used for 'a whole day.' Here the phrase = 'one day,' 'a single day.' Këang Shing has for it 一日; and the 'Daily Explanation' gives 終日之暫. 'He could not for a single day be advised by (exert himself on) the leading of God,'—the critics dwell on the phrase—'the leading of God,' and understand by it the unceasing monitions of conscience,—all the ways by which the heart of man is touched in Providence, which may be described as efforts on the part of God to keep him from evil, and lead him into the way of righteousness. 5.

五節 厥圖帝之命、不克開于民之麗、乃大降罰、崇亂有夏、因甲于內亂、不克靈承于旅、罔丕惟進之恭、洪舒于

5 is what you have heard. He kept reckoning on the decree of God *in his favour*, and would not promote the means of the people's support. By great inflictions of punishment also, he increased the disorder of the States of Hea. The first cause *of his evil course* was the internal misrule, which made him unfit to deal well with the multitudes. Nor did he seek at all to employ men whom he could

Ts'ae says that most of this par. is not understood by him. He brings out the meaning which appears in the translation, however, and is on the whole more successful in dealing with it than the other critics. The same subject evidently is continued,—the crimes of Këĕ, which occasioned the overthrow of the Hea dynasty. 厥圖帝之命,—compare the notes on 'The Speech of T'ang,' p. 3. 不克開于民之麗,—the expression 民之麗 has been taken variously. Gan-kwŏ explains 麗 by 施, so that the meaning is—'that which should be bestowed on the people,' viz., good govt. and lessons of instruction; and the whole = he could not begin even to govern and instruct the people as he ought. This is very unsatisfactory. In the Yih King (離卦) it is said—日月麗乎天,百穀草木麗乎土. Këang Shing, taking 麗 there as = 附, 'to be attached to,' understands the text as = 'he could not do what would make the people attached to him.' Ts'ae defined the character in the Yin by 依, 'to rely on,' and not by 附, from which he deduces the meaning of the text which I have given.—Këĕ made no provision for the necessaries of life among the people, such as food and clothing. 乃大至有夏,—this continues the description of Këĕ. He is the subject of 降. Woo Ch'ing on the contrary understands 'Heaven' as the subject of 降, and makes the clauses descriptive of the punishment of Këĕ. 因甲至于旅,—the critics are all agreed that by 內亂, 'internal disorder,' we are to understand the vile debaucheries of which Këĕ was guilty in his connection with Me-he (see pp. 170, 171).

With Ts'ae, Woo Ch'ing, and others, I take 甲 = 始, 'to begin,' and 因 is equivalent to a noun, the subject of 甲. K'ang Shing and Wang Suh both took 甲 as = 狎, or 習, but they do not account for the 因. Equally unsatisfactory is the exegesis of Gan-kwŏ, who takes 甲 as if it were 夾. With 靈承于旅 comp. Bk. XIV., p. 13, 我周王丕靈承帝事. Here 旅 is taken, by all the critics except Woo Ch'ing, as = 衆, 'all the multitude of the people.' The only difficulty in so taking it is with 承, which would so be applied to describe the act of the superior to his inferiors,—which is contrary to its common usage. Feeling this, Ch'ing takes 旅 as denoting the sacrifice to God which was so called (see the dict. *in voc.*), who takes the clause as = 'he could not attend well to the sacrifices to God.' But this is so far-fetched that it is better to acquiesce in the other view, even with the difficulty attaching to it. 罔丕至于民,—I have translated here after the 'Daily Explanation,' which has:—無能大進賢人而敬用之,使大布寬舒之澤于其民. There is little to choose between this and the view of Ts'ae and Woo Ch'ing:—'Nor could he make great approaches towards the virtue of reverence in which he might have shown a generous largeness of heart to the people' (不能大進於恭,而大寬裕其民). Gan-kwŏ gave quite a different meaning to the second clause:—'Nor could he greatly advance to the virtue of reverence, but was very indifferent and idle in governing the people' (大舒惰于治民). Keang Shing reads 荼 instead of 舒, and interprets:—'The greatly

民、亦惟有夏之民、叨懫日欽、劓割夏邑。○天惟時求民主、乃大降顯休命于成湯、刑殄有夏。○惟天不畀純、乃惟以爾多方之義民、不克永于多享、惟夏之恭多士、大不克明保享于民、

respect, and who might display a generous kindness to the people, but he daily honoured the covetous and cruel, who were guilty of
6 cruel tortures in the cities of Hea. Heaven on this sought *a true* lord for the people, and made its distinguishing and favouring decree light on T'ang the Successful, who punished and destroyed the
7 sovereign of Hea. Heaven's refusal of its favour *to Hea* was decided, and it was because the righteous men among your many regions were not permitted to continue long in their posts of enjoyment, and the many officers whom Hea respected were quite unable to maintain an intelligent preservation of the people in the enjoyment *of their*

false were employed by him, and put into offices, to the calamity and bitter suffering of the people' (誣罔大者, 惟進之任, 使供職, 大爲患苦于民). 惟有夏至末,—叨=饕, 'to be gluttonous or greedy,' 'to covet;' 懫, *i.q.* 懥,=忿, 'to be angry,' 'resentful.' 劓割夏邑,—comp. in 'The Speech of T'ang,' p. 3, 率割夏邑. 劓 'to cut off the nose,' is better translated here generally. Këang Shing reads 民 after 夏, on the authority of the 說文; but the meaning which he gives to the whole is very far-fetched.—'The people also under the rule of Hea, suffering the oppression of greed and cruelty, longed more every day to see the kingdom of Hea cut off.' Only one searching for strange meanings could attempt to draw this from the text.

P. 6. 時=是. 天惟時求民主=天惟是之故求可爲民主者. 7. 惟天不畀純=天之不畀於桀(=夏)者大矣, 'Heaven's refusal *of its favour to Këë*, (or *Hea*) was great and decided.' The rest of the par. explains why Heaven thus withdrew its favour. We have in Bk. XVI., p. 9, an opposite declaration of Heaven's favour to Shang,—天惟純佑命. It is well to take 純 in the same way in both passages, as meaning 'determinate,' 'decided.' 爾多方之義民,—義民, 'righteous people,'=賢者, 'men of virtue and ability.' They are called 'of your many regions,' *i.e.*, the many regions of the empire. We can lay no stress on the 爾, 'your.' 永於多享,—'long in much enjoyment,'='long in the enjoyment of their offices.' Këang Shing says:—不能久長多享祿位, 言桀不任賢. 不克明保享于民,—'could not understand to preserve and secure enjoyment for the people.' The use of 享, and the 于 before 民, render the language obscure, but the meaning seems to be what I have given. The 'Daily Explanation' gives for it—不能明達治體, 以保安享有國家之民, 'they could not understand the art of govt. so as to secure their tranquil enjoyment (=possession) of the people of the empire.'

乃胥惟虐于民、至于百爲、大不克開。○乃八節惟成湯、克以爾多方簡、代夏作民主。○愼九節厥麗乃勸、厥十節民刑用勸。○以十一節至于帝乙、罔不明德愼罰、亦克用勸。○要十二節囚、

lives, but on the contrary aided one another in oppression, so that of the hundred ways of promoting *prosperity* they could not advance *one*.

8 'In the case indeed of T'ang the Successful, it was because he was the choice of your many regions that he superseded Hea and
9 became the lord of the people. He paid careful attention to the essential virtues *of a sovereign*, in order to stimulate the people, and
10 they on their part imitated him, and were stimulated. From him down to the emperor Yih, the sovereigns all made their virtue illustrious, and were cautious in the use of punishments;—thus also
11 exercising a stimulating influence *over the people*. When they, having

Ying-tă quotes the view of Too Yu (杜預) to the same effect, making 享=受, 'to receive;'—see the 註疏. Këang Shing defines 胥 by 皆, 'all.' It is equivalent to 'all,' but with the further meaning of 'mutual' co-operation. 至于百爲,大不能開,—Gan-kwŏ connected the former of these clauses with the one preceding.—'They aided one another in oppression, even in a hundred different ways.' The last four characters are then simply an addition to the indictment.—'And they were greatly unable to initiate any plan of good' (大不能開民以善). It is better to connect the clauses together as I have done. The 不克開 leads us back to 不克開于民之麗 in p. 5, and the meaning comes out as in the translation.

Pp. 8—12. *The empire gained by the virtue of T'ang, and maintained by that of his successors, was finally lost by the wickedness and misgovernment of Show.* 8. It is only in the interpretation of the intermediate clause of this par.,—克以爾多方簡, that there is a difference of opinion. We may translate it 'on the ground of being chosen by your many regions;' and the meaning, as stated by Yaou Shun-muh (姚舜牧), is that 'Heaven, in seeking a lord for the people, simply followed the choice of the many regions' (天求民主,盡從多方之所簡耳). Gan-kwŏ and Këang Shing translate, however,—'was able among your many regions to choose *the worthy*.' But this is *forcing* a meaning, much more than the other construction, from the characters themselves, nor is the sentiment so suitable to the tenor of the Book. 9. We ought surely to take 麗 here as in p. 5. Ts'ae, however, makes 厥麗 to be = 'what he depended on,' *i.e.*, the essential virtue of a sovereign, or benevolence. 刑=法, 'to imitate,' 'to find a pattern.' Gan-kwŏ takes it in the sense of 'punishment.'—'His people, though he might punish them, were stimulated to virtue!' The student will mark the force of the 乃 and the 用 in the two clauses. And yet, such is the peculiar character of the Chinese language, that the critics interpret 用 in the next par. quite differently. 10. 明德愼罰,—see Bk. IX., p. 3. The assertion made here about the sovereigns of the Shang dynasty down to Yih, must be taken with large allowance. 11. 要囚,—see on Bk. XI., p. 11. It is strange to find this specified

殄戮多罪、亦克用勸。開釋無辜、亦克用勸。○今至于爾辟、弗克以爾多方享天之命。○嗚呼、王若曰、誥告爾多方、非天庸釋有夏、非天庸釋有殷。○乃惟爾辟、以爾多方、大淫圖天之命、屑有辭。○乃惟有夏、圖厥

(十二節 開釋無辜; 十三節 嗚呼; 十四節 非天庸釋有夏; 十五節 乃惟有夏)

examined the evidence in criminal cases, put to death those chargeable with many crimes, they exercised the same influence; they did so
12 also, when they liberated those who were not purposely guilty. But when *the* throne came to your *late* sovereign, he could not with *the good will* of your many regions continue in the enjoyment of the favouring decree of Heaven.'"
13 II. "Oh! the king speaks to the following effect, 'I announce and declare to you of the many regions, Heaven had no set purpose to do away with the sovereign of Hea, or with the sovereign of Yin.
14 But it was the case that your ruler, being in possession of your many regions, abandoned himself to great excess, and reckoned on the favouring decree of Heaven, making trifling excuses for his
15 conduct. And so in the case of the sovereign of Hea;—his schemes

with reference to the emperors; but so it is in the text. 開釋無辜,—comp, in 'The Counsels of Yu,' p. 12, 與其殺不辜,寧失不經. 12. By 爾辟, 'your sovereign,' we are to understand Show. 以爾多方 should be interpreted with reference to the 以爾多方簡 of p. 8. The critics have all overlooked this.

Ch. II. Pp. 13—16. How the sovereignty of the empire, having passed from Hea to Yin, by the will of Heaven, passed again from the tyrant Show to the princes of Chow. 13. The critics have much to say on the manner in which this par. begins,—the repetition of 王若曰, and the 嗚呼, which precedes. But what can be said to the purpose, more than that the duke of Chow chose thus to speak? Very strange is the method of Këang Shing, who makes the 嗚呼 an exclamation concluding the previous paragraph. 庸釋,—庸＝用, 有心之謂也 (Ts'ae), our 'on purpose,' 'with premeditation;' 釋＝去之, 'to put away,' 'to remove.' By 有夏 and 有殷, we are to understand Këë and Show. The removal of them, however, was equivalent to the overthrow of their respective dynasties. 14. 爾辟＝爾君, 'your sovereign,' referring to Këë. 以爾多邦,—'by—on the ground of—your many regions.' Këang Shing gives:—'relying on the multitudes of your many regions.' 屑有辭—屑, as in p. 22, ＝輕, 'lightly,' 'triflingly.' Compare in Bk. XIV., p. 5, 大淫泆有辭. 15. Here the speaker turns again to Këë, the representative of the Hea line (有夏). Leu Tsoo-heen says that the 集 here is that of 積

政、不集于享、天降時喪、有邦間之。○(十六節)乃惟爾商後王、逸厥逸、圖厥政、不蠲烝、天惟降時喪。○(十七節)惟聖罔念作狂、惟狂克念作聖、天惟五年、須暇之子孫、誕作民主、

of government were not of a tendency to secure his enjoyment *of the empire*, so that Heaven sent down ruin on him, and the chief of
16 your State entered into the line of his succession. *Indeed*, it was the case that the last sovereign of your Shang was luxurious to the extreme of luxury, while his schemes of government showed neither purity nor progress, so that Heaven sent down such ruin on him.
17 'The wise, not thinking, become foolish, and the foolish, by thinking, become wise. Heaven for five years waited kindly, and forbore with the descendant *of T'ang, to see if* he would indeed prove himself the true ruler of the people, but there was nothing

集, meaning 'to—collect,' and the 享 is that of 享國, meaning 'to enjoy the empire.' He adds that 'good governmental measures bring together all means of prosperity' (治世之政,聚其所以興). This is the easiest way of explaining the characters. Këang Shing, not so well, takes 集=就. Woo Ch'ing is here, as frequently, peculiar. He makes 不集于享 to mean—'the princes were alienated, and he could not bring them together and make them come to court with their offerings' (諸侯離心,不能合聚之,使來朝享). 時(=是)喪,—'this ruin,'=such a ruin. 有邦間之,—by 有邦 is meant T'ang, so called as being then merely one of the princes, 'the holder of a State.' 間之,—'separated—interrupted—it.' Koo Seih-ch'ow says:—'From Yu to Këë there had been a continuous succession of 400 years; but from this it was interrupted and broken off' (自禹至桀,四百年之統,自此間而斷也). 16. Lin Che-k'e observes on 逸厥逸 that it means 'he carried his 逸—his luxurious indolence to excess.' This is better than to take one of the characters in the sense of 過, 'to go beyond.' 蠲烝,—蠲=潔, 'pure;' 烝=進, 'to advance,' 'progress.' The meaning of the clause 不蠲烝 then comes out as in the translation. Këang Shing, after Ma Yung, takes 烝=升, 'to ascend,' so the whole ='his measures of govt. did not go up purely to Heaven.' This is far-fetched, but not so much so as Woo Ch'ing's interpretation. He takes 烝, in its sense of 'the winter sacrifice,' and hence for 'sacrifices' in general, so that 不蠲烝='he did not offer his sacrifices with purity!'

P. 17. 惟聖至作聖,—these two sayings have wonderfully exercised the ingenuity of the critics. Confucius has said (Ana. XVII., iii.) that 'the wise of the highest class and the stupid of the lowest class cannot be changed.' Surely he who can be called 聖 belongs to 'the wise of the highest class;'—how can the dictum of the great sage and the sentiment of the duke of Chow in this passage be reconciled? The foreign student is not concerned to reconcile them. What the duke says we know to be accordant with facts. He had not come to the folly and arrogance of the sage and his school exalting the 'sagely man' above the attributes

罔可念聽。○十八節天惟求爾多方、大動以威、開厥顧天、惟爾多方、罔堪顧之。○十九節惟我周王、靈承于旅、克堪用德、惟典神天、天惟式教我用

18 in him deserving to be regarded. Heaven then sought among your
many regions, making a great impression by its terrors to stir up
one who might look *reverently* to it; but in all your regions, there was
19 not one deserving of its regard. There were, however, our kings of
Chow, who treated well the multitudes of the people, and were able
to sustain the burden of virtuous *government*, and to preside over
all services to spirits and to Heaven. Heaven thereupon instructed

of humanity, and all created beings. 須=待, 'to wait.' 暇=寬限, 'to allow indulgently a longer time.' The 之 in 之子孫 occasions a difficulty. Woo Ch'ing makes it=是, 'this,' as in the expression 之子于歸, quoted in the 'Great Learning,' Comm. ix., 6. It is better to take it as merely giving emphasis to the active meaning of the verbs 須 and 暇. Show of course is intended,—'the descendant' of T'ang. The clause 誕作民主 ought, I think, to be connected with the preceding, as appears in the translation. Gan-kwŏ, however, and in recent times Këang Shing, understand it as='But he greatly played the people's lord, and there was nothing in him,' &c. When it is said that Heaven forbore with Show for five years, giving him the opportunity of repentance, there must have been something remarkable in the closing period of his history, which was known to the duke of Chow and his hearers, and to which allusion is made. We, however, do not know the events of the time with sufficient minuteness to be able to say what it was. See on the 十三年 in the 'Great Speech,' Pt. i., p. 1. 18. 大動以威,—greatly moving by its terrors.' Moving whom? Gan-kwŏ says—'Show.' But this is evidently wrong. The individuals intended to be moved were the princes of the various regions; the terrors employed to move them were the overthrow of Show, and the troubles generally of the time. There is a difficulty in interpreting the expressions 顧天 and 顧之. Ts'ae gives 以開發其能受眷顧之命者, 'to influence and bring forth one who might receive its decree of favour and regard,' for 開厥顧天. Then for 罔堪顧之 there is given 皆不足以堪眷顧之命, 'all were insufficient to sustain the favouring decree.' Woo Ch'ing explains in the same way. But 厥顧天 must mean 'their looking to Heaven,' not 'Heaven's looking to them.' 顧 simply =回視, 'to turn round and look at,' commonly with the idea of kindness or favour attached. I suppose that the subject of the former 顧 is 'the princes,' and the object, Heaven, while of the latter the subject is Heaven, and the object, the princes. 19. 我周王—these 'kings' were Wăn and Woo. 靈承于旅,—see p. 5. 惟典神天,—典=主, 'to preside over.' The whole=主神天之祀, 'who could preside over the sacrifices to spirits and to Heaven.' The phrase 神天 has occasioned some difficulty. When Dr. Medhurst made his translation of the Shoo, he supposed that 神 was an adj. qualifying 天, and rendered the passage by—'Only they could superintend the worship of the Divine Heaven.' Subsequently he saw the error of this, and has corrected it in his 'Theology of the Chinese,' pp. 56, 57, where he refers to the paraphrase of the 'Daily Explanation,'—誠可典司神天,爲上帝百神之主矣. Gaubil trans-

休、簡畀殷命、尹爾多方。○[二十節]今我曷敢多誥、我惟大降爾四國民命。○[廿一節]爾曷不忱裕之于爾多方、爾曷不夾介乂我周王享天之命、今

them, and increased their excellence, made choice of them, and gave them the decree of Yin, to rule over your many regions.

20 III. 'Why do I now presume to make *these* many declarations? I have dealt very leniently as regards the lives of you, the people of
21 these four States. Why do you not show sincere and generous obedience in your many regions? Why do you not aid and co-operate with us the kings of Chow to secure the enjoyment of

lated the clause by—'Il (he takes 我周王 as singular) fut en état d'être mis à la tête des affaires qui regardent les esprits;' and observes, in a note, that 典神天 is equivalent to the 作神主 in the 'Both possessed pure Virtue,' p. 3. So far he is correct; but the 天 should not be sunk in a translation. Its use shows very clearly, how, while the ancient Chinese could say of God, whom they intended by 'Heaven,' that He was a *spirit*, just as we do, they did not consider Him as merely one of 'the host of spirits.' No Chinese critic has ever taken 神 here as an adjective. They invariably understand a conjunction between 神 and 天. I need only give further what Ch'in Ta-yew says on the passage:—可爲神與天之主,山川宗社之得其安,三光寒暑之得其序,皆人君有以主之. If it be still asked why 天, as the more honourable, does not precede 神, we may reply with Dr. Medhurst, that 天神 might have been taken as meaning 'the spirits of heaven;' or (which seems to me more likely, as that usage of 天神 is foreign to the Shoo) that the collocation was chosen to avoid the coming together of the closely allied sounds of 典 and 天. 惟天式教我用休,—'Heaven therefore (see 式 in Bk. XVI., p. 21) taught us, and thereby was excellence.' By the 我, 'us,' are intended the 我王, at the beginning of the par., and I have therefore kept the third person in the translation.

Ch. III. Pp. 20—23. THE KING COMPLAINS OF THE RELUCTANCE WITH WHICH THE RULE OF CHOW WAS SUBMITTED TO; SHOWS THE FOLLY OF IT, AND DECLARES THAT, IF PERSEVERED IN, IT SHOULD BE DEALT WITH IN ANOTHER STYLE.

20. 曷敢,—'how dare I?' The critics make no remark on the use of 敢, 'to dare,' 'to presume,' here. It is strange from the lips of the king in this connection. He might very well speak of himself as 'presuming,' with reference to Heaven; but it sounds oddly as it stands. 我惟,云云,—see on p. 2. Yaou Shun-muh says:—'At the commencement of the announcement, the king tells them how he had spared their lives, and starts from that to unfold the reasons why Heaven now bestows its favour and now withdraws, that they might be taught to nip the unquiet and insurrectionary tendencies of their hearts in the bud. Here he reminds them a second time of the same thing, wishing to show them the path of self-renovation and improvement, that they might escape the miseries of extreme punishment in which they were going on to involve themselves.' See the 集說. 21. 爾曷不忱裕之,—I take the 之 here like the same character in 須暇之, p. 17, as giving emphasis to the previous verbs. This usage corresponds to that which is not unfrequent with our English *it*.—'Why do you not sincere it, and liberalize it?' Treated so well by the govt. of Chow, why would they not obey it sincerely and with a largeness of mind like that which had been shown to them. It is not easy to translate the clause. Medhurst misses the meaning; and when Gaubil says 'Pourquoi ne seriez-vous pas desormais fideles et tranquilles dans votre pays,' the '*tranquilles*' by no means brings out sufficiently the meaning of 裕. 夾介

爾尙宅爾宅、畋爾田、爾曷不惠王熙天之命。○廿二節爾乃迪屢不靜、爾心未愛、爾乃不大宅天命、爾乃屑播天命、爾乃自作不典、圖忱于正。○廿三節我惟時其教告之、我惟時其戰要囚之、至于再、

Heaven's favouring decree? You now still dwell in your dwellings,
and cultivate your fields;—why do you not obey our kings, and
22 consolidate the decree of Heaven? The paths which you tread
are continually those of disquietude;—have you in your hearts
no love for yourselves? do you refuse so greatly to acquiesce in
the ordinance of Heaven? do you triflingly reject that decree? do
you of yourselves pursue unlawful courses, scheming *by your alleged*
23 *reasons* for the approval of upright men? I simply instructed
and declared to you; I secured in trembling awe and confined
the chief criminals:—I have done so twice and for three times.

=夾輔介助, to assist and 'to aid.' 乂 is best taken as=保, 'to preserve,' 'to maintain.' The kings of Chow had received the favouring decree of Heaven; but that decree had to be made firm or sure by the cheerful acquiescence of the people and princes in their sway. 今爾至爾田,—comp. the closing par. of the 'Numerous Officers.' 惠=順, 'to accord with,'='to obey and have sympathy with.' 熙=廣, 'to make wide,' ='to strengthen.' 22. The 'Daily Explanation' says that here 'the people of Yin are reproved as to the past, and admonished as to the future.' The first clause is to be supposed narrative; but all the others are best taken interrogatively. 爾乃迪屢不靜=爾乃屢蹈不靜. This is somewhat harsh, requiring the inversion of 迪屢; but what can we do? Këang Shing takes 迪 in the sense of 道.—'I have sought to guide you repeatedly, but still you are not tranquil.' This construction is more objectionable. Their 'paths of disquietude' were the rebellious movements in which they had repeatedly engaged. 爾心未愛 is taken by Gan-kwŏ and Këang Shing indicatively,='you do not yet love our dynasty of Chow.' I prefer, however, to understand it as in the translation. Ts'ae gives:—爾心其未知所以自愛也. 宅天命,—宅=居 or 安, 'to rest or repose in.' 屑,—see par. 14. 不典=不法, 'lawless ways.' The last clause, 圖忱于正, is a difficult one. Gan-kwŏ and Ying-tă are as enigmatical upon it as the text itself. Këang Shing takes 正=長, 'superiors,' and gives:—謀取信于長上, 'scheming to be believed by your superiors.' But what 'superiors' can we think of in the case? The translation is after the 'Daily Explanation,' which says:—且爾等反覆叛亂,自作不法之事,爲正人所深惡,乃猶以義不忘殷,圖見信于正人乎, 23. *Past leniency would not be continued, if they still continued dissatisfied and gave disturbance.* 我惟至于三 is to be taken as descriptive of the king's past dealings with the rebellious. Kin Le-ts'ëang says:—'教告之 refers to the announcements made before the expedition to the East

至于三、乃有不用我降爾命、我乃其大罰殛之、非我有周秉德不康寧、乃惟爾自速辜。○王曰、廿四節嗚呼、猷告爾有方多士、暨殷多士、今爾奔走臣我監五祀。○越廿五節

But if you do not take advantage of the leniency with which I have spared your lives, I will proceed to severe punishments and put you to death. It is not that we, the sovereigns of Chow, hold it virtuous to make you untranquil, but it is you yourselves who accelerate your crimes *and sufferings*.'"

24 IV. "The king says, 'Oh! ho! I tell you, ye many officers of the various regions, and you, ye many officers of Yin, now have ye been hurrying about, doing service to my overseers for five years.

(謂東征之前, 文告之); 戰要囚之 refers to the captives and prisoners, during that expedition, who however were not put to death' (謂東征之時, 俘囚之, 然不殺). 惟時=惟是. We may retain the signification of 惟 as 'only,' 'simply.' We cannot, however, interpret 要囚 as we have done in the previous instances of its occurrence, p. 11, and Bk. IX., p. 12. The 之 here perhaps requires that we interpret the phrase differently. Wang Ts'aou gives for it 束而囚執之. 非我, 云云, —comp. the two last clauses of Bk. X., p. 11. Compare also Bk. XIV., p. 18, 非我一人奉德不康寧.

Ch. IV. Pp. 24—29. THE KING ADDRESSES MORE PARTICULARLY THE NUMEROUS OFFICERS WHO HAD BEEN REMOVED TO LŎ, AND URGES THEM TO THE RIGHT DISCHARGE OF THEIR DUTIES. IF THEY DO WELL, THEY WILL HAVE GREAT REWARDS. IF THEY PROVE IDLE AND PERVERSE, THEY WILL BOTH BY HEAVEN AND THE KING, BE MORE HEAVILY PUNISHED THAN THEY HAD YET BEEN. Woo Ch'ing, as I stated in the note on the name of the Book, removes this chapter to the 'Numerous Officers,' with the exception of a part of the 29th par., which he seems to reject altogether. In this measure, he followed the example of the critics Woo and Hoo (probably 吳才老 and 胡明仲). The change of the style of address, from 多方 to 多士, certainly gives countenance to it, though the 有方多士 in par. 24 may be pleaded in favour of the received arrangement. The point, however, is of little importance.

P. 24. Ying-tă explains 爾有方多士 by 汝在此所有四方之多士, 謂四方之諸侯, 'you who are here, the numerous officers of the four quarters. The princes from the four quarters of the empire are thus designated.' I would rather take 有方 as=所有之方, equivalent to 'all the quarters of the empire.' 臣我監五祀(=年. The Yin term for 'year' is used, perhaps because it is the old officers of that dyn. who are addressed),—acting as ministers to my overseers for five years.' Këang Shing supposes that the 'overseers' are the three uncles of the king, who had been appointed by his father to oversee Woo-kăng, and finds a reference to the past;—'Ye hurried about, doing service to my overseers for five years.' But this interpretation is quite absurd; and moreover the 今 is inexplicable on it. It is only exceeded in absurdity by the view of Gan-kwŏ, who would interpret:—'Ye run about serving my overseers. If you do so for five years without fault, I will restore you to your original territory!' King Ching's 'overseers' were the ministers of Chow, under whose charge the officers and people of Yin removed to Lŏ were placed. The statement that those officers had served them there for 'five years' should put

惟有胥伯小大多正、爾罔不克臬。○廿六節自作不和、爾惟和哉、爾室不睦、爾惟和哉、爾邑克明、爾惟克勤乃事。○廿七節爾尚不忌于凶德、亦則以穆穆在乃位、克閱于乃

25 There are among you the employés, the chiefs, with the numerous directors, small and great:—endeavour to discharge your duties ac-
26 cording to the laws. It is from yourselves that the want of harmony arises:—strive to be harmonious. In your families there is a want of concord:—strive to be harmonious. When intelligence rules in your cities, then will ye be proved attentive to your duties.
27 Do not be afraid, I pray you, of the evil ways *of the people;* and moreover by occupying your offices with a reverent sedateness, you will find it possible to select from your cities individuals on

beyond a doubt what I have all along maintained, that the removal of the people to the new settlement had taken place before the building of the imperial city of Lŏ. See the 集傳.

25. 胥, 伯, and 正 are all names given to various officers. They were common designations under the Chow dyn.;—see the note from Ch'in Sze-k'ae in the 集傳. But what 胥, what 伯, and what 正 are here intended we cannot tell, and any very definite translation of the terms cannot be given. Ts'ae gives 臬 the meaning of 事, 'affairs,' 'business,'= 'duties.' The dict. refers to the passage under the meaning of 法, 'laws,' which we know that 臬 often has. I have combined the two. [We know that Fuh-shang read—越惟有胥賦, 小大多政, which Këang Shing of course edits; but I cannot find or give any suitable explanation of such a text.] 26. There seems to be some gradation of thought here, from harmony of mind to harmony of conduct; thence to social harmony in the families of the people; and thence again to what we may call a general political harmony:—all to be secured by the harmony of the officers addressed. Wang Ts'ëaou says that 'the first 和哉 requires serene tranquillity of mind in order to the harmony of the body or whole character, and the second requires the harmonious obedience of the whole character *to reason* in order to the harmony of the family.' See the 集說. This significance of the difft. clauses, however, is very indistinctly intimated, and hence Gan-kwŏ gives another interpretation, which it is not worth while to adduce and animadvert upon. 27, 28. The former of these parr. describes certain things to be aimed at by the numerous officers, if they could succeed in which, there would be the results which the latter par. sets forth. It must be allowed that it requires considerable ingenuity to decide on the meaning which is to be given to the clauses of the former. 爾尚不忌于凶德,—忌 is to be taken in the sense of 畏, 'to fear.' 尚 has its force of exhortation or entreaty. The 凶德, 'evil conduct,' is to be referred to the people, whose stupidity and obstinacy (頑民) made them so difficult of management. 穆穆=和敬貌, 'the appearance of harmony and reverence.' 克閱于乃邑謀助=能簡閱爾邑之賢者以謀其助, 'can select the worthy in your cities, thus consulting to get their assistance.' Such is the view of the meaning proposed by Ts'ae, only that he finds the idea of concession in 尚. Woo Ch'ing's interpretation is different. He says:—度幾無有凶惡之德可忌諱也, 亦且肅敬在爾之位, 能臨視於爾之邑, 而謀者大矣. Këang Shing reads the first clause

邑謀介。○廿八節爾乃自時洛邑、尚永力畋爾田、天惟畀矜爾、我有周惟其大介賚爾、迪簡在王庭、尚爾事、有服在大僚。○廿九節王曰、嗚呼、多士爾不克勸忱我命、爾亦則惟不克享、凡民惟曰不享、爾乃惟逸惟頗、大遠王命、

28 whom you may calculate. You may thus in this city of Lŏ long continue, cultivating your fields. Heaven also will favour and compassionate you; and we, the sovereigns of Chow, will greatly help you and confer rewards, selecting you to stand in our royal court. Only be attentive to your duties, and you may rank among our great officers.'"

29 "The king says, 'Oh! ye numerous officers, if ye cannot exhort one another to pay a sincere regard to my charges, it will further show that you are unable to honour your sovereign, and all the people will *also* say—"We will not honour him." Thus will you be proved slothful and perverse, greatly disobedient to the charges of your sovereign.

along with par. 26, and edits it—爾上不碁于凶德. For 碁 he gives the authority of the 說文; but that is of no importance, as this character is there explained by 忌. But the 說文 quotes the passage with 尚 and not 上, which Shing arbitrarily assumes to have been the original reading. The meaning which he thus finds is:—'You will be proved attentive to your duties, and your superiors will have no occasion to detest your evil ways.'

爾乃至爾田,—自時(=是)洛邑 seems to = 'from this—on the ground of your behaviour in this—city of Lŏ.' The force of 尚 is sufficiently given by our 'may.' On 畋爾田, Wang Ts'ëaou observes that 'to cultivate a field (田) is called 畋, in the same way as to catch fish (魚) is called 漁.'

畀矜爾=畀予矜憐於爾, 'gift you and compassionate you.' 介賚爾=介助賚錫於爾, 'aid you and confer bounties on you.' In 尚爾事, the 尚 has its hortative force. Ts'ae gives for the clause—其庶幾勉爾之事.

有服在大僚,—comp. 'The Numerous Officers,' p. 20. It will there be seen how the officers of Yin desired the favours that are here promised them.

P. 29. *If they will not be won by the leniency shown and the favours promised to them, but continue disaffected, and make the people also disaffected, they shall be dealt with summarily and severely.* The critics are here concerned to free the duke of Chow from the charge of speaking, or making the king speak, like one of the chiefs and arbiters among the princes, of whom we read so much in Mencius,—first coaxing and then threatening, subduing men merely by their strength. Leu Tsoo-heen goes into the point at length, and says that here we have the judgment and the infliction of Heaven always preceding the judgment and act of human authority. But we should find the same thing in the speeches of those tyrant-chiefs. The duke said what seemed most likely to him to accomplish his

書經

則惟爾多方探天之威、我則致天之罰、離逖爾土。○王三十節曰、我不惟多誥、我惟祗告爾命。○又卅一節曰、時惟爾初、不克敬于和、則無我怨。

Throughout your many regions, you will bring on yourselves the terrors of Heaven, and I also will inflict its punishments, removing you far from your country.'"

30 V. "The king says, 'I do not *wish to* make these many announcements, but in a spirit of awe I lay my commands before you.' He
31 also says, 'Now you may make a *new* beginning. If you cannot reverently realize the harmony *which I enjoin*, do not *hereafter* murmur against me.'"

end. 嗚呼至不享,—comp. Bk. XIII., p. 12. The meaning of 享 is the same in both passages, only the idea of 'offerings' is more here as the expression simply of loyal obedience. 頗=僻, 'depraved,' 'perverse.' 遠王命=違王命; 探=求取, 'to seek for and bring on.' 離逖爾土,—comp. 移爾遐逖, Bk. XIV., p. 21. The king would seem to be threatening the refractory with another and more distant banishment. Ts'ae conjectures that 多方 is a mistake for 多士, which, I think, is very likely.

Ch. V. Pp. 30, 31. *The conclusion of the address.* 我不至爾命,—the relation between the two clauses seems to require that the former should be supplemented as in the translation. 時惟爾初=今與爾更始, 'now I grant to you to change and begin *afresh*.' The 時, however, is not =今, but =是.

THE BOOKS OF CHOW.

BOOK XIX. THE ESTABLISHMENT OF GOVERNMENT.

立政

一節 周公若曰、拜手稽首、告嗣天子王矣、用咸戒于王曰、王左右、常伯、常任、準人、綴衣、虎賁、周公曰、嗚呼、休兹、

1 I. The duke of Chow spoke to the following effect, "With our heads to our hands and then to the ground, we make our declarations to the new emperor, our king." In such manner accordingly all *the other ministers* cautioned the king, saying, "In close attendance on your Majesty there are the regular presidents, the regular *high* officers, and the officers of the laws; the keepers of the robes *also*, and the guards."—The duke of Chow said, "Oh! admirable are these *officers*. Few, however, know to be sufficiently anxious about them."

The Name of the Book.—立政, 'The Establishment of Government.' This phrase occurs four or five times in the course of the Book, and is thence taken to denominate it;—with considerable appropriateness. The subject treated of throughout is, it will be seen, how good government may be established. The Book is found in both the texts.

Contents. The editors of Yung-ching's Shoo give the following summary of the Book from Tung Ting (董鼎), of the Yuen dynasty, which is tolerably complete:—'In imperial govt. there is nothing more important than the use of *proper* men; and when *proper* men are being looked out for, the first care should be for those to occupy the "three *high* positions." When these are properly filled, all the other offices will get their right men, and imperial govt. will be established. The appointment of the officers of business, of pastoral oversight, and of the law (宅事, 牧, 準; p. 2) is the great theme of the whole Book (其綱領), and the words, "Admirable are these! But to know to be sufficiently careful about them," ——, are its pulse [其血脈; *i.e.*, may be felt everywhere, throbbing in all the sentiments]. Parr. 2 and 3 illustrate the subject from the history of the Hea dynasty; parr. 4 and 5 do the same from that of the House of T'ang; and in parr. 9 to 15 it is shown how Wăn and Woo, like the founders of the previous dynasties, knew how to be anxious about the selection of their officers, and so obtained the great inheritance of the empire, initiating the happy state

which was then continuing. From par. 16 to the end, the duke earnestly addresses the king on his duty to put away from him men of artful tongues; to employ the good, distinguished by their habits of virtue; to be always well prepared for war; and to be very careful of his conduct in the matter of litigations. His object in all was that the king should learn from the founders of the different dynasties how he should manifest anxiety on the great subject of the Book, and should be warned by the fate of Këë and Show against allowing himself to be indifferent about it. The whole is an example of loyal affection, which we seem even to the present day to be able to take hold of.'

Lin Che-k'e comments upon it, arranged in three chapters:—parr. 1—5; 6—15; 16—28. The student will find the arrangement in five chapters which I have adopted of more assistance to him.

The order of the paragraphs; and Date. There is no ancient authority for altering the arrangement of the received text; but the reader can hardly fail to be annoyed with the long list of officers of Wăn and Woo in parr. 8—15.—Why should the speaker go at so much length into their appointments, after having touched so briefly on those of Yu and T'ang? The student's attention is distracted by the lengthy enumeration; it could only have diverted the young king's mind from the important lesson which the duke wished to impress upon him. There is, again, the greater portion of par. 2,—from 乃敢 to the end, which has always seemed to me to have no proper connection as it stands. The only Chinese critic, however, whom I have met with, who owns to feeling the same difficulties is Wang Pih. He does not scruple to say that the text as it stands is 'head and tail in disorder, and without connection.' His conception of the occasion when the duke delivered the sentiments of the Book is this:—It was soon after king Ching undertook the responsibilities of the government. At such a time it was proper that all the officers should unite in *lessoning* him, and the duke of Chow accordingly appeared with a host of them, great and small, and when they had expressed their views on the point which seemed most important to them, he took the subject up, and prosecuted it in his own way. Pih would thus remove parr. 8—11, and the part of par. 2 to which I have referred, and make them all one long preliminary paragraph;—周公若曰,拜手稽首,告嗣天子王矣,用咸戒于王曰,王左右常伯,常任,準人,綴衣,虎賁,趣馬,小尹,左右攜僕,百司,庶府,大都小伯,藝人,表臣百司,大史,尹伯,庶常吉士,司徒,司馬,司空,亞旅,夷,微,盧,烝,三亳,阪尹,乃敢告教厥后曰,拜手稽首后矣,曰宅乃事,宅乃牧,宅乃準,茲惟后矣,謀面用丕訓德,則乃宅人,茲乃三宅無義民,周公曰,嗚呼,休茲,知恤鮮哉.

The praise of ingenuity cannot be denied to this arrangement of the text, and if it were proper to decide on such a point simply on internal grounds, I should not hesitate to adopt it.

Wang Pih supposes that this announcement was made after the duke of Chow had resigned the regency. Such was the opinion of all the early scholars; and likewise, we may presume from the order in which the Book stands, of the compiler of 'The Little Preface,' though his note says nothing on the point (see Pref. N. 54). Now, however, in the received chronology, the Book is referred to the 4th year of king Ching. This date was first proposed by Hoo Woo-fung (胡五峰; one of the early Sung writers, author of the 皇王大紀), and is argued for in the 通鑑綱目,—on very insufficient grounds, as will be seen from the notes on various paragraphs.

Ch. I. P. 1. Circumstances attending the delivery of the Address; and its Text. 周公若曰至王矣,—it will be seen that I have translated 拜手,云云, in the first person plural, understanding that the duke of Chow appeared before the king with a long train of ministers, and that he here speaks first in their name,—for himself and for them. Then 用咸戒于王 intimates that the ministers all took up the subject, and began to speak for themselves. As the 'Daily Explanation' has it:—羣臣用皆進戒于王. They have hardly entered on their admonitions, however, when the duke takes the word from them, and continues the address in his own person,—周公曰,嗚呼,云云. Gan-kwŏ supposed that the duke of Chow was the speaker in his own person throughout. Hence he understood 拜手,云云 as = 'with my head to my hands, &c., I make an announcement.' For 用咸戒于王曰, he gives—又用王所立政之事,皆戒于王

曰, 'He also took up the various procedures of the king by which he should establish his govt., and warned him on the subject of them all, saying,'——. But Lin Che-k'e well observes that this is very forced, and apart from the meaning of the text. The interpretation which I have given was first fully developed by Ch'in Shaou-nan (陳少南), who found the germ of it in the comment of Wang Suh,—于時周公會羣臣,共戒王,其言曰,拜手稽首者,是周公讚羣臣之辭,休茲,此五官美哉. Dr. Medhurst makes 拜手,云云, to be addressed by the duke to all the ministers.—'The duke of Chow, *addressing his ministers*, spoke to the following effect, Bow down and make obeisance, while you address the new emperor and king.' This construction is to be decidedly rejected, but there can be pleaded for it the authority of Woo Ch'ing, who says:—前周公若曰,公與羣臣言也,後周公曰,公與王言也. 嗣天子王矣,—'the son of Heaven who has inherited (or, who is continuing) the line of succession, the king.' This language, it is said, is more appropriate, if addressed to the young king, a minor, than if addressed to him when of full age. It seems to me, on the contrary, what we should expect, if spoken to Ching now fully seated on the throne of his father. 常伯,常任,準人,—'the regular chiefs, the regular holders of office, and the equalizing men.' It is difficult to say what officers are intended by these designations. Leu Tsoo-heen says:—'These are the occupiers of 'the three positions,' mentioned in the 4th par., but nowhere else in the Books of the three early dynasties do the designations appear. May we not suppose that they were other names for the high nobles and assistants about the imperial court? Different names were given to the occupants of offices, as when the prime minister was called A-hăng (阿衡) and Paou-hăng (保衡), and when the three chief ministers about a prince's court were called K'e-foo (圻父), Nung-foo (農父), and Hwang-foo (宏父). In the same way, the names in the text are to be taken simply as diversified designations of the great ministers who assisted in the govt. during the three dynasties. The two designations of 綴衣 and 虎賁 which follow are the names of two selected from among the various classes of inferior officers, as specimens of the rest. With those who were in the great offices was lodged the safety or the peril of the throne; by those whose offices brought them into familiar intercourse with the sovereign his character was liable to be affected:—the condition of the empire depended equally on them both.' See the 集說. There can be no doubt these observations give the general meaning of the text, and the reason why the ministers and officers mentioned in it are specified; but how are we to translate the different designations? Gaubil avoids the difficulty by retaining the names, and giving vague accounts of the officers intended by them in his notes. It seems reasonable to take, with Lin Che-k'e, the 常伯 here as = the 宅乃牧 of par. 2; the 常任 as = the 宅乃事; and the 準人 as = the 宅乃準. We may then understand by 常伯 the chiefs or presidents who had a pastoral charge of the people (牧民之長); by 常任, the high ministers of War, Instruction, Works, &c., in the imperial domain; and by 準人, the law officers. 準 = 'level,' 'to level,' 'the instrument to make or determine a level.' 準人 are the officers who guard the laws, the instrument of justice. The officers called 綴衣, 'Connected Robes,' and 虎賁, 'Tiger Braves,' are not known to have existed under these names in the previous dynasties; this Book shows that they were an institution in the times of Wăn and Woo. We do not find the name of 綴衣 in the Chow Le, but there are enumerated the 'master of the furred robes' (司裘), the 'master of robes to the empress' (內司服), the 'tailor' (縫人), and the 'master of robes' (司服) which must have been kindred appointments. See Books VI., VII., and XXI. The 虎賁 are expressly mentioned in Bk. XXXI. They were guards, amounting, acc. to K'ang-shing, to 800 men, generally in attendance on the emperor's person; but might be detailed off to other services.

休茲=美矣此官, as in the translation. Many critics understand the characters as meaning—'Admirable are these *observations!*' But it would be hard to say what observations have been made. The duke takes the word out of the mouth of the others, and at once gives out the text which he proceeds to illustrate in his own way. 知恤鮮哉=知以不得人爲憂者殆亦鮮矣, 'those who know to make the not getting the proper men for them a subject of sorrow are few.'

知恤鮮哉。○ 二節 古之人迪惟有夏、乃有室大競、籲俊尊上帝、迪知忱恂于九德之行、乃敢告教厥后曰、拜手稽首后矣、曰宅乃事、宅乃

2 II. "Among the ancients who exemplified *this anxiety* there was the founder of the Hea dynasty. When his House was at its strength, he sought for able men to honour God. *His advisers*, when they knew of men thoroughly proved and trustworthy in the practice of the nine virtues, would then presume to inform and instruct their sovereign, saying, 'With our heads to our hands and then to the ground, O sovereign, we would say, Let such an one occupy one of your high offices: Let *such an one* be one of your pastors: Let such an one be one of your law-officers. By such appointments

Ch. II. Pp. 2, 3. THE IMPORTANCE OF THIS PRINCIPLE,—AN ANXIOUS CONCERN TO GET THE OFFICES OF STATE FILLED BY THE RIGHT MEN, ILLUSTRATED IN THE HISTORY OF THE HEA DYNASTY. 2. 古之人迪惟有夏＝古之人君，迪行知恤之道者，惟夏王大禹, 'of the ancients who walked in this course of a wise anxiety there was the great Yu, the Sovereign of Hea.' 迪＝行 or 蹈, 'to walk,' 'to tread.' Gan-kwŏ and Këang Shing take it as＝道; but they bring out the same meaning. 有室大競＝當王室大强之時, 'when the imperial House was greatly strong.' Këang Shing, after Gan-kwŏ, by 有室 understands 卿夫大之家, 'the families of the high nobles and officers;'—an interpretation not nearly so good as that which I have followed. 籲(＝呼＝求)俊尊上帝,—comp., in p. 4, 丕釐上帝之耿命, and, in p. 6, 以敬事上帝. These three passages supply a very striking testimony of the recognition in those times of God as ruling over the nations of the earth. Yu, T'ang, and kings Wăn and Woo, the founders of the three great dynasties which are still celebrated, all considered it their great business to honour and serve God. They were simply His ministers. Whatever were the errors of religious belief and worship into which they fell, they held fast this important principle—that they were called to their high stations by the one Supreme Ruler, and were bound to occupy in them so as to please Him. 迪知忱恂于九德之行,—this, I think, is spoken of Yu's ministers, the advisers who were about him. Not only did *he* seek out able men to honour God, but *they* also sympathized with him in his views, and co-operated with him, and recommended to him men of whose character and fitness they were assured. As Wăng Ts'ëaou tersely says: 一古之賢臣，以人事君，古之賢君，以人事天, 'The good and able ministers of antiquity served the sovereigns by *recommending the right* men; the good and able sovereigns of antiquity served Heaven by *employing those* men. For 九德之行 see 'The Counsels of Kaou-yaou,' pp. 3, 4. Lin Che-k'e explains 迪知 by 驗之於實迹而知之, 'those whom they knew by examination of their actual conduct.' 宅乃事，云云,—these three clauses are to be taken not as general advice with regard to putting good men in the positions indicated, but as specific, with reference to the individuals whom they had in view as displaying more or fewer of 'the nine virtues.' 兹惟后矣＝如此而後可以爲君也, 'do this, and so will you prove yourself the sovereign indeed.' 謀面至末,—Gan-kwŏ quite misunderstood the meaning of this part of the par., led away in the first place by interpreting the 三宅 of the 五宅三居, 'three localities assigned to the five banishments,'

牧、宅乃準、茲惟后矣、謀面用丕訓德、則乃宅人、茲乃三宅無義民。○桀三節德、惟乃弗作往任、是惟暴德、罔後。○亦四節越成湯、陟丕釐上帝之耿命、乃用三有宅、克卽

you will discharge your royal duty. If you judge by the face only, and therefrom deem men well schooled in virtue and appoint them, then those three appointments will all be occupied by unrighteous
3 people.' The way of Këě, *however*, was not to observe this precedent. Those whom he employed were cruel men;—and he had no successors.
4 III. "After him there was T'ang the Successful, who, rising to the throne, greatly administered the bright ordinances of God. He employed to fill the three *high* positions those who were equal to those

mentioned in the 'Canon of Shun,' p. 20. He gives for the whole:—謀所面見之事,無疑則能用大順德,乃能居賢人于衆官,若此乃能三居無義民,大罪宥之四裔,次九州之外,次其國之外, 'Consult on the ground of the things you have seen before your face, and which will not admit of doubt; you can then employ those who are greatly accordant with virtue, and will be able to fill all the offices with men of worth. Thereafter you can locate the unrighteous people in the three places assigned to them:—those whose crimes are heinous, farthest among the four wild tribes; less heinous criminals beyond the nine provinces; and those whose offences are lighter still beyond the boundaries of their several States.' This interpretation of 三宅 is altogether foreign to the scope of the paragraph; but it continued till the Sung dynasty, and even then Soo Tung-po followed it. 謀面 is 'to judge merely from the face, or outward appearance.' 謀面用丕訓德,則乃宅人=徒謀之面貌,用以爲大順于德,乃宅而任之. Këang Shing avoids the old interpretation of 三宅, and brings out a meaning something like what I have given, but by hard shifts. He reads 亂 before 謀; takes 面=向; 丕 for 不; 義 for 儀; and interprets, 'If your counsels are deceived, and you move towards men who are not virtuous, and place them in these offices, then the occupants of these three positions will be able to give no good example to the people.' 3. 桀德,—'K'ëě's virtue,' *i.e.*, his evil way, 德 being in a bad sense. 弗作往,—'did not do the past,' *i.e.*, did not imitate the example of Yu in employing the worthy. The language is not clear, but it is better to point and construe as I have done,—after Ts'ae. Gan-kwŏ and Këang Shing have each a different method; but they take the same view of the whole paragraph. 任是惟暴德=所任者乃惟暴德之人.

Ch. III. Pp. 4, 5. THE IMPORTANCE OF THE SAME PRINCIPLE EXEMPLIFIED IN THE HISTORY OF THE SHANG DYNASTY. 4. 亦越 may be taken, with Ts'ae, as a compound conjunction,=our 'again,' 'further.' 陟丕釐上帝之耿命,—'ascended, and greatly regulated the bright appointment of God.' 陟,'ascended,' seems to be used with reference to T'ang's from being the chief of a second-rate State becoming emperor. Other explanations of the term are given, but it is not worth while to dwell on them. 釐=理 or 治, 'to regulate,' 'to administer.' Gan-kwŏ prefers the meaning of 賜, 'to give;'—but very inappropriately. The

書經

宅、曰三有俊、克即俊、嚴惟丕式、克用三宅三俊、其在商邑、用協于厥邑、其在四方、用丕式見德。○嗚呼、五節其在受德暋、惟羞刑暴德之

positions; and those who were called possessors of the three grades of
ability could display that ability. He then studied them severely
and greatly imitated them, making the utmost use of them in their
three positions and with their three grades of ability. The people in
the cities of Shang were hereby all brought to harmony, and those in
the different quarters of the empire were brought greatly under the
5 influence of the virtue thus displayed. Oh! when the throne of T'ang
came to Show, his character was all violence. He preferred men of
severity, princes of States who deemed cruelty a virtue, to share

meaning is, that when T'ang was established on the throne, his whole system of govt. was in harmony with the mind of God. His institutions might be regarded as divine ordinances. 乃用三有宅克即宅,—this is clearly paraphrased in the 'Daily Explanation'—乃又能旁求賢才,相助爲理,所用以居常伯,常任,準人之官,爲三有宅者,實能就是位,而不曠廢其職. Still more evident here than in the 2d par. is the blunder of Gan-kwŏ in taking 三宅 of 'the three places of banishment.' 三有俊,—'the three—or three classes—of possessors of ability, men among a thousand.' Gan-kwŏ and Këang Shing suppose that men are meant who possessed the 'three virtues' mentioned in 'The Great Plan,' p. 17; but it is simpler to understand that by 俊 are intended men who had talents and virtue which would make them eligible to the three high positions. On such T'ang had his notice fixed, and was prepared to call them to office at the proper time. 曰三有俊克即俊—所稱三俊,實能就是德而不浮其名. 嚴惟至三俊,—Woo Ch'ing may be said to expunge 嚴惟丕式, for he says that they are 'a form of introduction' (發語辭). Gan-kwŏ and Këang Shing interpret the passage thus:—'T'ang's majesty became a great example to the empire because he was able to use the right men' (湯之嚴威惟能大法于天下者,以其能用三宅三俊). They differ, however, in the meaning which they give to 三宅; but their construction of the text is far inferior to that of Leu Tsoo-heen and other critics, which I have followed. 惟 is not the particle, but the verb, =思, 'to think of,' 'to study;' and 式=法 or 效, 'to imitate.' Tsoo-heen says that T'ang's way with E Yin, first sitting as a learner at his feet, and then reposing entire confidence in him as his minister, may illustrate the meaning. 其在商邑,—by 'the cities of Shang' we are to understand all the territory of the imperial domain. 用丕式見德,—'thereby were led to great imitation, and saw the virtue *of their sovereign*.' The 'Daily Explanation' expands it:—其在四方之遠而自慕者,用以大爲取法,如親見其君德,而無不順治焉.

5. 其在受,—comp. the commencement of parr. 5 and 6 in Bk. XV. 暋=强, 'strong,' 'violent.' Ts'ae explains 羞刑 by 進任刑戮者, 'he advanced to office those who punished capitally.' Këang Shing also gives 進任 for 羞; but I must take 羞刑 as a description of 暴德之人, 'men of violent character, *like his own*, who

人、同于厥邦、乃惟庶習逸德之人、同于厥政、帝欽罰之、乃伻我有夏、式商受命、奄甸萬姓。○亦越文王武王、克知三有宅心、灼見三有俊心、以敬事上帝、立民長伯。○

with him in the *government of the empire;* and at the same time, the host of his associates, men who counted idleness a virtue, shared the offices of his court. God then sovereignly punished him, and caused us to possess the great empire, enjoy the favouring decree which Shang had *afore* received, and govern all the people in their myriad realms.

6 IV. "Subsequently there were king Wăn and king Woo, who knew well the minds of those whom they put in the three positions, and clearly saw the minds of those who had the three grades of ability. Thus they could employ them reverently to serve God,

advanced (= deemed) punishments as the proper instrument of govt.' Show had pleasure only in those princes of the States who were such. 厥邦, 'his countries,' seems to be opposed to 厥政, 'his govt.,' *i.e.*, the fiefs to the court. I take 欽 in the sense of 'sovereignly.' Anything with the express sanction of imperial authority is so denominated. 伻我有夏,式商受命=使我周有此諸夏,用商所受之命. 奄甸萬姓,—'entirely to rule the myriad surnames.' Compare in Bk. XIV., p. 6, 成湯革夏,俊民甸四方. We need not seek for any other meaning to 甸 (as Ts'ae does) than the general one of 治, 'to govern.' 萬姓,—comp. Pt. III., Bk. III., p. 9. I suppose that 萬 is used without any particular reference to the surnames of the people as being so many, or that 萬姓=萬邦之民.

Ch. IV. Pp. 6—15. THE SAME PRINCIPLE OF ANXIETY ABOUT EMPLOYING THE RIGHT MEN EXEMPLIFIED IN THE KINGS WAN AND WOO.

6. Ts'ae observes that when it is said that Wăn and Woo knew *the minds* and saw *the minds* of the 三宅 and 三俊, this is equivalent to the language of the 2d par., 迪知忱恂而非謀面. It certainly indicates that those sovereigns sought to obtain the most thorough knowledge of those whom they placed or would place in the highest offices of trust. Tsoo-heen calls attention to the difference between 知 and 見.—They *knew* what was in the highest servants of their govt.; they *saw* what the men of ability could prove themselves to be, when called to employment. 立民長伯,—those whom Wăn and Woo thus appointed were the 三宅 and 三俊. Ts'ae, arguing from the language of the Bk. 王制 in the Le Ke, makes the 長 to be the governors of a 屬 or five States, and the 伯 to be the Chiefs of a 州 or 210 States. I do not think that we need to seek for such a definite application of the terms. Ch'in Leih says that it was a common practice of antiquity for the princes of States to reside at the imperial court, and there sustain office, while the officers of the court were also sent forth, as princes of

七節 立政、任人、準夫、牧、作三事。○八節 虎賁、綴衣、趣馬、小尹、左右攜僕、百司、庶府。○九節 大都、小伯、藝人、表臣百司、太史、尹伯、庶常吉

7 and appointed them as presidents and chiefs of the people. To establish their government, they had the men of office, the officers of law, and the pastors, and these appointments were their three
8 concerns. *They had also* their guards; their officers of the robes; their equerries; their heads of petty officers; their personal attendants;
9 their various overseers; and their treasurers. They had their governors of larger assigned cities and of the smaller; their men of arts; the overseers whose offices were beyond the court; their grand historiographers; and their chiefs of direction:—all, good men of constant virtue.

States. See the 集說. 7. Këang Shing briefly and comprehensively explains this par.—文武立政,以任人,準夫,牧,爲三事. 任人 is the 常任 of par. 1; 準夫, the 準人; and 牧, the 常伯. 8. The long enumeration of officers in this and some following paragraphs has no organic connection with the rest of the Book, the argument of which would be improved by the omission of it. I have shown in one of the introductory notes how Wang Pih would dispose of it. All that we can do is to explain the various designations in the best way we can. 趣 (read *ts'ow*) 馬,—'equerries.' These belonged to the department of the 校人 or masters of the imperial stud. Their rank was that of 下士. See the Chow Le, Books XXVIII. and XXXII. 小尹—小官之長, 'the heads of small officers.' We cannot define the designation more particularly. 左右攜僕,—Gan-kwŏ understands this phrase as in the translation,—左右攜持器物之僕. Ts'ae supposes that 攜 has this signification, and that 僕 denotes 'charioteers' (僕御). Woo Ch'ing, again would confine the two characters to this latter meaning. Gan-kwŏ's interpretation seems the preferable. 百司,—'the hundred superintendents or overseers.' The phrase denotes all the officers who had their special individual charges. Many 司 are mentioned in the Chow Le,—the 司服, 司門, 司市, 司甲, 司弓矢, &c. 庶府,—'all the treasurers.' In the Chow Le, Bk. VI., we have the 大府, or 'Grand Treasurer;' the 玉府, or 'Treasurer of gems, pearls, gold ornaments,' &c.; the 內府, or 'Keeper of the inner treasury;' and the 外府, or 'Keeper of the outer treasury,'—the treasury of disbursements. Other 府 are mentioned in other places. Wang Yen says:—'The 庶府 denote all charged with the management of the imperial wealth' (凡掌財). 9. The 大都小伯 must be construed, with Ch'in Shaou-nan, 大小都伯, 'the commandants of *Too*, great and small.' The clause is an instance of what is called 'interlaced style' (互文見意), and when completed would be 大都之伯, 小都之伯. On the meaning of 都, see the note on Mencius, II., Pt. II., iv., 4. By the 'great *Too*' here we are to understand the cities in the imperial domain assigned for the support of the highest nobles (公之采邑), and by the 'small *Too*' the cities assigned to those of inferior dignity. 藝人,—'men of arts'. This is understood to

士。○十節司徒、司馬、司空、亞旅。○十一節夷、微、盧、烝、三亳、阪、尹。○十二節文王惟克厥宅心、乃克立茲常事、司牧人、以克俊有

10 "*In the various States* there were the minister of Instruction, the minister of War, and the minister of Works; with the many officers subordinate to them.

11 "Among the wild tribes of the Wei, the Loo, and the Ching; in the three Pŏ; and in dangerous places: they had wardens.

12 "King Wăn was able to have in himself the minds of those in the *three high* positions, and so it was that he established those regular officers and superintending pastors, so that they were men of ability

include, according to the language of the Le Ke, Bk. 王制, Pt. iv., p. 10, 'all who employ their arts in the govt.,—priests, historiographers, archers, charioteers, doctors, diviners, and the practisers of the various mechanical arts' (凡執技以事上者,祝,史,射,御,醫,卜,及百工). 表臣百司,—these 百司 are distinguished from those in the prec. par. by the addition of 表臣, 'outside ministers.' We are to understand officers with special charges, as in the former case, but located away from the court. 大史,—see on Bk. X., p. 18. We are to understand here not only the 'Grand Historiographer,' but all the officers in his department. 尹伯 is defined by Ts'ae 有司之長, 'the heads of the several classes of offices.' He illustrates his meaning by referring to the 庖人 (=庖尹), or 'butcher,' and the 內饔, or 'cook,' whose offices were both subordinate to that of the 膳夫, or 'master cook,' who was their 伯. 庶常吉士,—this is descriptive of the officers enumerated, and of the subordinates employed by them.

P. 10. This par. has reference to the various officers in the States of the princes. See 'The Speech at Muh,' p. 2.

P. 11. This par. would seem to go on to speak of the officers,—overseers or governors,—whom Wăn and Woo appointed among the wild tribes, the 尹 at the close belonging to each of the tribes specified, all included under the commencing 夷. The 三亳, however, occasions a difficulty, for their people were the descendants of T'ang's original subjects, and could not be classed with the 夷, under which term therefore we can only include the 微, the 盧, and the 烝. The two first of these are mentioned in the 2d par. of Bk. II., referred to above, with other wild tribes, who acted with the forces of king Woo in his overthrow of Show. The 烝 are not mentioned there, and there is much difference of opinion as to how that term should be taken. Gan-kwŏ adopts the meaning of 衆, 'the multitudes;' Ming-shing approves that of 君, 'rulers,' which is given to it in the 爾雅; and others suppose it is the name of a wild tribe, like the two preceding terms. The 'three Pŏ' were Mung (蒙) or the 'northern Pŏ,' in the pres. dis. of Shang-k'ew, dep. of Kwei-tih in Ho-nan; the western Pŏ, in the pres. dis. of Yen-sze, dep. of Ho-nan; and the 'southern Pŏ,' which was only a few *le* from the northern. Ts'ae says that he does not understand the meaning of 阪. He supposes however that it may mean 'strong positions' (阪=險) throughout the five domains, where it was deemed proper to locate special officers. K'ang-shing joined it with 三亳, and supposed that it denoted the three strong-holds, where the overseers of the different Pŏ were placed.

Pp. 12—15. *Further exemplification in Wăn and Woo of their anxiety to get right men; and of the confidence which they reposed in them when got.* 12. 文王惟克厥宅心,—we must explain these words from the 克知三有宅心 in par. 6. King Wăn was able to know fully the minds of his officers,

德。○十三節文王罔攸兼于庶言、庶獄庶慎、惟有司之牧夫、是訓用違。○十四節庶獄庶慎、文王罔敢知于茲。○十五節亦越武王、率惟敉功、不敢替厥義

13 and virtue. He would not himself appear in the various notifications, in litigations, and in precautionary measures of government. There were the officers and pastors *to attend to them*, whom he *simply*
14 required to be obedient and not disobedient. *Yea*, as to litigations and precautionary measures *he would seem as if* he did not presume
15 to know about them. He was followed by king Woo, who carried out his work of settlement, and did not dare to supersede his right-

and to employ them with entire confidence. Gan-kwŏ, indeed, took the language differently:—文王惟其能居心遠惡舉善, 'king Wăn was able to set his mind on this,—the putting far off the bad and elevating the good.' But, as Choo He has observed, if this were the meaning, we should have read 克宅厥心, and not 克厥宅心. Këang Shing reads 文王維厥度心, which he interprets—'King Wăn employed his deliberating mind.' 乃克立茲常事, 司牧人,—by 常事 are intended the 常任 of par. 1, and by 司牧人 the 常伯. The 準人 are not mentioned here, unless the 司牧人 be taken to include them and all the other officers who have been enumerated. 以克俊有德=皆是實能俊而有德, being a description of the qualifications and virtue of Wăn's officers. 13, 14. These parr. are intended to show how king Wăn, having appointed the right men, left them to the management of their offices, and did not interfere with them in the discharge of their duties. 罔攸兼=無所兼理, 'he in no way interfered with;—did not attend to, along with his own duties.' 庶言=號令, 'governmental orders and notifications.' This seems to be the only proper meaning of this phrase in the connection. It must run on with the 庶獄 and 庶慎,—all under the govt. of 罔攸兼于. Këang Shing, partly after Gan-kwŏ, would attach 文王罔攸兼于庶言 to the previous par., with the meaning that king Wăn was guided in appointing his officers by the deliberations of his mind, and paid no attention to the praise or censure of individuals by others (庶言=衆人毀譽之言). 庶獄=獄訟, 'civil and criminal causes;'—see on Ana. XII., xiii. 庶慎=國之禁戒儲備, 'all things in the State which were to be guarded against and provided for.' 惟有至末,—the 之 is taken as=及, a particle of connection. 是訓用違,—this is a very difficult clause. I have translated it after Foo Yuen-tsoo (傅元初; Ming dyn.), who says:—文王三宅之賢, 無非常德吉士, 安得有違命者, 推誠任人, 馭下有體, 只是訓戒之, 欲其用命, 不欲其違命耳. 14. Litigations and precautionary measures only are mentioned here, because king Wăn could not but know the notifications that went forth in his name. 15. *How King Woo entered into the spirit and work of his father.* 率惟敉功=率循文王安定天下之功. Comp. 未克敉公功, Bk. XIII., p. 19. By 義德 Ts'ae thinks we

德、率惟謀、從容德、以竝受此丕丕基。○[十六節]嗚呼、孺子王矣、繼自今、我其立政、立事、準人、牧夫、我其克灼知厥若、丕乃俾亂、相我受民、和我庶獄庶愼、時則勿有間

eous and virtuous men; who entered *also* into his plans, employing as before his forbearing and virtuous men. It was thus that they unitedly received this vast inheritance.

16 V. "Oh! young son, the king, from this time forth be it ours to establish the government, appointing the *high* officers, the officers of the laws, and the pastors;—be it ours clearly to know what courses are natural to them, and then greatly to employ them in the government, that they may aid us in the management of the trust of the people, and harmoniously conduct all litigations and precautionary measures. And let us never allow others to come between us and

should understand 義德之人; and similarly 容德. We get an easier meaning certainly by taking the expressions in this way, than if we understand them of king Wăn himself.

Ch. V. Pp. 16—24. THE DUKE ADDRESSES KING CHING DIRECTLY, AND URGES HIM EVER TO ACT ON THE PRINCIPLE WHICH HAS BEEN ILLUSTRATED. 15, 16. *How the king should carefully choose, entirely trust, and steadily maintain his officers.* 孺子,王,—this language has been pressed to show that the address was delivered when the king was a minor. 孺子, it must be conceded, is properly 一乳子, 'a sucking child;' but it is used away from that signification, whether it was applied to Ching about his 15th year, or his 20th. When the duke of Chow had resigned the regency, he still continued to think of the king as the boy he had watched over, and ruled for, and so he calls him here, when offering these counsels which are not at all appropriate to him as a minor. 我其至牧夫,—the critics all say that 我 here (and in other clauses below) refers to king Ching. Woo Ch'ing says, 'The six 我 in pp., 15, 16, are all the duke's 我ing king Ching' (六我皆我成王). Ch'in Ta-yew says, 'By the 我 the duke identifies himself with the king. Sovereign and minister should compose, as it were, one body' (我者我其君,君臣一體也). All this may be correct, but we may as well translate by the plural of the first personal pronoun. 立政 covers the 立事,準人,牧夫, as it does 任人,準夫,牧 in p. 7. It is remarkable how the order of enumeration, when speaking of the 'three positions, is continually varied. 我其克灼知厥若,—comp. the language of p. 6. 若 here must be equal to 心 there. The critics generally define it by 順, and then understand by 知厥若, 'know that they are accordant with right,' obedient to heavenly principle. Ts'ae, much more happily, goes on to explain 順 by 心之安, 'that in which the mind reposes,' and then adduces, to illustrate the meaning, the words of Confucius (Ana. II., x.) 察其所安,人焉廋哉, 'Examine in what things a man rests. How can he conceal his character!' 丕乃俾亂=大委任之,使展布四體以爲治. Këang Shing would strangely make 丕 here only a particle of introduction. 我受民=我所受

書經

之。○自(十七節)一話一言、我則末惟成德之彥、以乂我受民。○嗚(十八節)呼、予旦已受人之徽言、咸告孺子王矣、繼自今、文子文孫、其勿誤于庶獄庶愼。惟(十九節)正是乂之。○自古

17 them. *Yea*, in our every word and speech, let us be thinking of officers of complete virtue, to regulate the people whom we have received.

18 "Oh! I, Tan, have received these excellent words from others, and tell them all to you, young son, the king. From this time forth, O accomplished son *of Woo*, accomplished grandson *of Wăn*, do not err in regard to the litigations and precautionary measures;—let

之民, 'the people whom we have received,' *i.e.*, who have been entrusted to us by Heaven, and transmitted to us by our ancestors. 時則勿有間之,—時—如是, 'thus,' 'in this condition.' 間之,—'to come between them;' either between them and their work, or between them and us. Këang Shing joins this clause on to the next, and reads 物 instead of 勿, from Wang Ch'ung's 論衡. He labours hard but unsuccessfully to interpret his text.

17. In translating this par. I have followed Ts'ae, who takes 末=終 and 惟=思. 自一話一言=一話一言之間, 'during the space of one word or one sentence.' Lin Che-k'e has the same view. Woo Ch'ing would refer 一話一言 to the 庶言 of par. 13. Gan-kwŏ's comment on the whole par. is strangely laboured and absurd: 一言政當用一善,善在一言而已,欲其口無擇言,如此我則終惟有成德之美,以治我所受之民.

18—21. *The king is repeatedly and variously warned against erring in the matter of litigations and precautionary measures.* There was probably some disposition in the young emperor to interfere with the regular course of these two departments, which made the duke dwell so pointedly upon them.

18. 徽言=美言 or 善言, 'admirable words' or 'good words.' He refers no doubt to all that he has said in the address. The 'men from whom he received them' were probably the host of ministers and officers, who had commenced to address the king when he took the words out of their mouth. Lin Che-k'e praises the honesty of the duke of Chow in making this acknowledgment, and contrasts him with some other statesmen who used the ideas of others, taking all the credit of them to themselves. 文子,文孫,—'the accomplished son, the accomplished grandson.' King Shing no doubt is intended. 正是乂之,—there is no end of the disputes about how 正 is to be taken. Ts'ae supposes that it=正人, which phrase we have in Bk. IX., p. 17. From the conclusion of p. 21 we must conclude that the 有司之牧夫 are intended. Wang Ts'ëaou makes a good observation on this par.:—'The prec. par. says that the sovereign is not to let other men interrupt the proceedings of his officers; here he is admonished not to throw those proceedings into error by interference of his own' (上言勿間之以人,此言勿誤之以已,大抵人君任賢不專,其弊有是二端,故反覆言之也). 19. 自古商

商人、亦越我周文王、立政立事牧夫準人、則克宅之、克由繹之、茲乃俾乂。○二十節國則罔有立政用憸人、不訓于德、是罔顯在厥世、繼自今立政、其勿以憸人、其惟吉士、用勱相我國家。○廿一節今文子文孫、孺子王矣、其勿誤于庶獄、惟有司之牧夫。

19 the proper officers regulate them. From of old to the founder of
Shang, and downwards to king Wăn of our Chow, in establishing
government, when they appointed *high* officers, pastors, and officers
of the laws, they settled them in their positions and unfolded their
talents. It was thus that they gave the government into their hands.
20 In the empire never has there been the establishment of govern-
ment in the employment of artful-tongued men;—*with such men*,
unlessoned in virtue, never can *a government* be distinguished in the
world. From this time forth, in establishing government, make
no use of artful-tongued men, but *seek for* good officers, and get
them to use all their powers in aiding the government of our empire.
21 Now, O accomplished son *of Woo*, accomplished grandson *of Wăn*,
young son, the king, do not err in the matter of litigations. There
are the officers and pastors *to attend* to them.

人=自古及商人. By 'of old,' Yu, the founder of the Hea dyn., must be intended. 克由繹之,—由繹 is explained by 紬繹, 'to unroll a clue,' 'to get hold of the end, and draw out all the silk.' The high officers, being put in their positions, were made to unfold all their talents. We may keep the proper meaning of 由, however. See the comment of Leu Tsoo-hëen in the 集說:—由繹,由其外而繹其中也,由其言而繹其心,云云. 茲乃俾乂=茲其所以使之治事. It is better to understand the clause thus, than to take it, with Gan-kwŏ, as=此乃使天下治.

20. *Men of artful tongues should on no account be allowed to get office.* 諭 (K. S. edits 憸) 人=佞人, 'specious,' 'talkative,' 'artful men.' Ch'ëong Kew-shing gives the following account of them:—憸人者,傾巧辯給之人,詐是飾非,言足拒諫,悅其心,則譽桀紂爲堯舜,失其意,則誣伯夷爲盜跖. 不訓于德,訓 is commonly defined by 順, but we may retain its proper signification. 其惟吉士=其惟用有常吉士. See par. 9. 21. Comp. par. 13.

○其克詰爾戎兵、以陟禹之迹、方行天下、至于海表、罔有不服、以覲文王之耿光、以揚武王之大烈。○嗚呼、繼自今、後王立政、其惟克用常人。

22 "Have well arranged also your military accoutrements and weapons, so that you may go forth beyond the steps of Yu, and be able to travel over all beneath heaven, even to beyond the seas, everywhere meeting with submission:—so shall you display the bright glory of king Wăn, and render more illustrious the great achievements of king Woo.

23 "Oh! from this time forth, may you and your successors, in establishing the government, seek to employ men of constant virtue."

P. 22. This par. suddenly introduces a subject difft. from those hitherto dwelt upon, and seemingly quite out of place in the Book. At the close of his address to prince Shih, however, we found the duke of Chow all at once break into the same warlike mood. There he would have the dynasty extend its sway, till 'from the corners of the sea to the sunrising there should not be one disobedient to the rule of Chow.' Here his enthusiasm rises higher, and he will have the empire extended beyond its limits in the time of Yu. Many of the critics argue that after the dynasty of Hea began to decline, the wild tribes all round the empire encroached upon it, till the 'nine provinces' of Shang hardly embraced half the territory which those of Yu had done. There is no definite testimony, however, to this effect. If it were so, we can well suppose that the duke of Chow was bent on extending the sway of his House, to recover at least all the ground that had been lost from the time of Yu. 詰爾戎兵,—詰 is defined by 治, 'to have in good order.' The term means 'to interrogate judicially.' Its proper force here is 'to maintain a strict inquiry into.' 戎 and 兵 are used in the dict. to define each other; both signify 'military weapons.' Gan-kwŏ is followed by Ts'ae in distinguishing them, as I have done in the translation (戎服兵器). 陟禹之迹,—'ascend the footsteps of Yu.' But this hardly makes sense. The 'Daily Explanation' defines 陟 by 越而過之, 'to go beyond.' For the 'footsteps of Yu,' the limits of his different progresses, see 'The Tribute of Yu,' Pt. ii., p. 23, and the 'Yih and Tseih,' p. 8. 方行天下,—方=四方 or 徧. 覲 is used in the sense of 見,—'to cause to be displayed.' Leu Tsoo-heen tries to argue that the duke of Chow is not inciting the king here to warlike expeditions, but only to be prepared for war as the best security for peace. He lays down this maxim very tersely: 一古人治兵,乃所以弭兵,後世銷兵,乃所以召兵. Këang Shing defines 詰 by 謹, 'to be circumspect,' 'to watch against,' so that he brings out the meaning that the king was to have done with war and cultivate the arts of peace, as the means of securing universal submission! For this interpretation there is no more ground than for Tsoo-hëen's reasoning. [I am glad to find that Woo Ch'ing thinks this par. as much out of place as I do. 'It has no connection,' he says, 'with the text before and after. It may be presumed that a portion of the Book has been lost.']

P. 23. The duke here repeats the burden of his address, extending his wishes from king Ching to his successors. 常人=常德之人. Comp. 庶常吉士, p. 9, and in 'The Counsels of Kaou-yaou, p. 2, 彰厥有常,吉哉.

○周公若曰、太史、司寇蘇公、式敬爾由獄、以長我王國、茲式有慎、以列用中罰。 廿四節

24 VI. The duke of Chow spake to the following effect, "O grand historiographer, the minister of Crime, the duke of Soo, dealt reverently with all the criminal matters which came before him, thereby to perpetuate the fortunes of our empire. Here was an example of careful anxiety *for other ministers*, to rank with him in the ordering of the appropriate punishments."

Ch. VI. P. 24. I cannot see that this par. has any connection with the rest of the Book. It appears indeed to be more out of place, if possible, than par. 22. It is evidently a fragment of some of the lost Books which has got tacked on here. 司寇蘇公,—'the minister of Crime, the duke of Soo.' From a passage in the 左傳, 成十一年, we learn that the duke of Soo (where Soo was I have not ascertained) was called 忿生, and was minister of Crime to king Woo. 式敬爾由獄,—Gan-kwŏ gives for this—能用法, 敬汝所用之獄, 'could use the laws so as to reverence the criminal cases which you use.' But what meaning can a reader get from this? Këang Shing endeavours in vain to explain it. I take 敬爾 together as an adverb, = 'reverently.' 式 = 用; different from 式 below, which = 法. 由獄 = 所斷之獄, 'the criminal causes which he decided,'—which 'passed through' his hands. 茲式云云,—the 'Daily Explanation' gives for this:—嗣爲司寇者, 于此取法而加謹焉, 則必能以輕重條列, 用其中罰, 無偏輕偏重之條, 無失入失出之慮, 刑獄淸, 而天下無寃民矣. This seems to give the meaning, but I prefer to take 列 as referring to the duke of Soo, and = 'to rank with him.'

THE BOOKS OF CHOW.

BOOK XX. THE OFFICERS OF CHOW.

周官

惟周王撫萬邦、巡侯甸、四征弗庭、綏厥兆民、六服群辟、罔不承德、歸于宗周、董正治

1 I. The king of Chow brought the myriad regions *of the empire* to tranquillity; he made a tour of inspection through the How and Tëen tenures; he punished on all sides the chiefs who had refused to appear at court; thus securing the repose of the millions of the people, and all the *princes of the* six tenures acknowledging his virtue. He then returned to the honoured capital of Chow, and strictly regulated the officers of the administration.

THE NAME OF THE BOOK.—周官, 'The Officers of Chow.' The Book contains a general outline of the official system of the Chow dynasty. It details the names and functions of the principal ministers about the court, to whom various counsels moreover are addressed by king Ching. 'The Officers of Chow' is not an inappropriate name for it. It is found only in the old or Gan-kwŏ's text. Ts'ae assigns it to the class of the Books of the Shoo called 'Instructions' (訓體).

DATE; AND QUESTION OF GENUINENESS. The first par. refers the Book to king Ching, without any mention of the duke of Chow. Its date therefore must be in some year after the duke resigned the regency, and the king took the govt. into his own hands. As the next Book but one (now lost) contained an account of the duke's death, in the 11th year of Ching, we may assign the 'officers of Chow' to the 9th or 10th year of that monarch. I introduce the subject of the date here, because of the strangeness of the prefatory note about it, that the Book was made 'when king Ching had made an end of the House of Yin, and extinguished the wild tribes of the Hwae' (see page 12). The 'making an end of the House of Yin' carries us back to the death of Woo-kăng in the 2d or 3d year of Ching (see P. N. 41); from which the extinction of the Hwae tribes would bring us down to his 7th or 8th year. The 1st par., which is the proper introduction to the Book, makes no mention of either of those events. I do not think the prefatory notice is entitled to any consideration.

On the question of the GENUINENESS of the Book, it will be sufficient here to give the remarks of Ts'ae, reserving the fuller discussion of the points he mentions for their proper place in the annotations. He says:—'This Book disagrees with the Chow Le, as we now have it, in various points. For instance, the Chow Le does not contain the ministers called here the "three *Kung*," and "the three *Koo*." Some have said that the *Kung* and *Koo* were dignities, enjoyed by other ministers, and were not specific offices; but if we refer to parr. 5 and 6, where it is said that "the three *Kung* discourse of the principles of reason, and adjust the States," and that "the

three *Koo* assist the *Kung* to diffuse widely all transforming influences," these are specific duties, belonging to offices to which there can be none superior. Others would identify the 太師 here with the 師氏 of the Chow Le, and the 太保 with the 保氏; but this cannot be, for the 師氏 and 保氏 are only subordinate officers in the department of the minister of Instruction.

'Again, it is said here, p. 14, that "in six years the chiefs of the five tenures attend once at court," whereas in the Chow Le, Bk. XXXVIII., the princes of the six tenures appear at court, from such and such a tenure, every year; from another tenure in two years; and so on;—a quite different arrangement. These discrepancies give rise to doubts; but the Chow Le could only have been made by a sage. Or perhaps, the duke of Chow, when he was making all his arrangements for the officers of the government, had not come to the offices of the 師 and 保. What I mean is this, that he was restrained by some consideration of their greatness from speaking of them. Moreover, the book was not completed when the duke died. The laws and regulations in it had not all come into practice;—This may account for the discrepancies I have pointed out. And still farther:—What must have formed the sixth part of the Chow Le, "The officer of the Winter," is lost. The beginning and end of it are incomplete. It is a work of the duke of Chow, to which alas! he did not put the finishing hand. Let the reader of the Shoo, however, compare it carefully with the classic, and he will be able to judge of the governmental arrangements of the duke of Chow.'

CONTENTS. The Book has a beginning, middle, and end, more distinctly marked than we generally find in the Books of the Shoo. The first par. is introductory, and describes the condition of the empire when the arrangements of the official system of Chow were publicly announced; all the other parr. contain that announcement. The king begins by referring to the arrangements of former dynasties. He then, parr. 5—14, sets forth the principal offices of State, the ministers of which had their residence at court, and goes on to the arrangements for the administration of the provinces. The remaining parr. contain many excellent advices to the ministers and officers, to discharge their duties so that the fortunes of the dynasty might be consolidated, and there be no dissatisfaction among the myriad States. The whole, it will be seen, falls naturally into a division into five Chapters.

Ch. I. THE CONDITION OF THE EMPIRE WHEN THIS ADDRESS TO THE MINISTERS AND OFFICERS WAS PROMULGATED. Rebellion had been quelled; disobedience had been punished; peace had been secured at length within the borders of the empire.—There was now leisure to attend to the right ordering of the system of administration. 惟周王撫萬邦,—'the king of Chow soothed the myriad regions.' This phrase,—'the myriad regions,' as well as the 四征 and 兆民 below, are taken by Ying-tă as vague expressions, it being proper, when speaking of the movements and measures of the emperor, to do so 'in large terms;' and both Lin Che-k'e and Ts'ae approve of the remark. I have spoken of the five tenures of Yu, and the ten tenures of the Chow dynasty on pp. 148, 149; and the difficulty of reconciling them with one another, and of reconciling the dimensions of even the five tenures with the actual extent of the country. There are other difficulties, however, in the way of taking the 'myriad regions' of the text literally, which may be seen in the note of Ch'in Sze-k'ae *in loc.* He says:—'The empire of Chow was 10,000 *le* square. A space of 1,000 *le* square, giving an area of 1,000,000 square *le*, would contain 100 States, each 100 *le* square; and the whole, 10,000 such States. But the territory of one of the greater princes was 100 *le* square:—it is easy to see how the tenures could contain 10,000 States. At the beginning of the Chow dynasty, however, the princes who assembled at Muh were only 800 (see on p. 298, App. to the Great Declaration). And in the "Imperial Regulations" [see the Le Ke, Bk. 王制] the States of the empire only amount to 1,713. For these reasons Ying-tă said we were not to take the 10,000 in the text literally.' We can indeed only regard the 'myriad States' of the text as a great exaggeration; and we must take in the same way the statement in the 左傳, about the great Yu, that 'when he assembled the princes at mount T'oo, they came with their gems and silks from ten thousand States' (哀公七年;—禹合諸侯於塗山,執玉帛者萬國). 巡侯甸,—see the figure of the tenures of Chow, on p. 149. Those of the How and the Teen were the first and second beyond the imperial domain. The critics seem to think that the king's progresses were not confined to them, but extended at least to the 'six tenures' immediately mentioned. 'These two are mentioned,' says Ying-tă, 'as being nearest to the imp. domain.' But why should we extend the meaning of the text in this way? There may have been good reasons, not recorded, why only the *How* and *Teen* tenures were inspected at this time. 四征弗庭—四方征討不庭之國. Ying-tă says the king had only smitten the Hwae tribes, and the statement here that his punitive expeditions had extended on every side is an exaggeration like that in 'myriad regions.' Here again our best way is simply to take the text as we find it. 弗庭—弗來庭者, as in the translation. Gan-kwŏ takes 庭=直, a meaning which the character has, but which does not seem so appropriate here. 兆人,—comp. Pt. III., Bk. III., p. 5. 六服,—the Chow dyn. had nine *fuh*, or ten, including the imp. domain. By the 'six tenures' here are probably to be understood the How, Teen, Nan, Ts'ae, Wei, mentioned in the 1st par. of the 'Announcement about Lŏ,' and the imp. domain. There is much discussion on the point among the critics, however:—see Lin Che-k'e *in loc.*

官。○二節王曰、若昔大猷、制治于未亂、保邦于未危。○三節曰、唐虞稽古、建官惟百、內有百揆四岳、外有州牧侯伯、

2 II. The king said, "It was the grand method of former times to regulate the government while there was no confusion, and to
3 secure the country while there was no danger." He said, "Yaou and Shun studied antiquity, and established a hundred officers. At court there were the General Regulator, and the *President* of the Four Eminences. Abroad there were the Pastors of the provinces, and the princes of States. Thus the various departments of

羣辟＝諸侯. 承德＝奉承周德, 'honoured and received (＝acknowledged) the virtue of the House of Chow.' 歸于宗周,—where did the king return from? This announcement, occurring here, affords some ground for Ying-tă's view, that the king made a progress not only through the How and Teen tenures, but through all the others. By 宗周 it would seem that we should understand Woo's capital of Haou;—see on Bk. III., p. 1. There king Ching continued to have his residence, notwithstanding the duke of Chow's wish that he should remove to the new city of Lŏ. The prefatory notice, however, says that the king returned to Fung, which had been the capital of Wăn. The various methods by which it has been attempted to harmonize the two statements may be seen in Lin Che-k'e. He himself approves of the view of Ch'in Shaou-nan,—that king Ching first came to Haou, 'the honoured city of Chow' in the text, and there deliberated and determined on the various arrangements for the officers; and that then, before the public proclamation of them, he went to Fung, to announce the intended measure in the temple of king Wăn. 董正治官＝督正治事之官, 'strictly managed the rectification of the officers administering the affairs of government.'

Ch. II. Pp. 2—4. First Part of the King's Address:—the Precedents of Former Dynasties, and his own Anxiety to display a similar Wisdom. 2. 若昔大猷,—Gan-kwŏ gives for this—當順古大道, 'we ought to accord with (＝to follow) the great method of antiquity.' It is better to take 若 with Lin Che-k'e, as an introductory particle, so that 若昔 simply＝在昔, 'anciently.' Ts'ae understands the phrase thus. He is wrong, however, I think, in his interpretation of 大猷 as＝大道之世, as if it were in apposition with 若昔, and the whole meant—'in ancient times, the age when right principles greatly prevailed.' Gaubil takes the passage thus, and appears to think that some great meaning lies hid in it. He translates:—'Anciently, in the time *de la grande loi*, good government consisted in preventing troubles, and in preserving the kingdom without danger;' adding in a note, 'We see that the time of *the grand law* is a time of innocence; the troubles and the dangers of States come not till after this time. I believe that king Ching means to say that innocence of manners and public tranquillity are the basis of good government. The commentaries give here no light on the text.' The text is really sufficiently plain. 若昔大猷＝'The grand method of former times was this:'—. The next par. illustrates how this method was carried out by Yaou and Shun, and Yu, and T'ang. When they had brought peace about in their distracted empires, they proceeded to secure it by the ordering of their official system. And Ching, having got the empire tranquillized at length, would now go on to imitate their example.

3. 唐虞稽古,—for 唐 and 虞 see on the names of Pt. I., and II. Yaou and Shun are intended, and it seems better to give those well-known names in the translation. Medhurst for 稽古 gives—'examined the records of antiquity.' But a statement so remarkable should not be supplemented. Gaubil observes that 'these two sovereigns, it may be inferred, had certain sources of knowledge, that is to say, some history, of the times anterior to theirs.' The expression may lead us to infer so, but I have not introduced the inference into the version. Gaubil adds:—'The author of the 左傳 speaks of the officers of Hwang-te, and of Shaou-haou, who reigned before Yaou. Confucius, in his commentaries on the Yih King,

庶政惟和、萬國咸寧、夏商官倍、亦克用乂、明王立政、不惟其官、惟其人。○四節今予小子、祗勤于德、夙夜不逮、仰惟前代時若、訓迪厥官。○五節立太師、

government went on harmoniously, and the myriad States all enjoyed repose. In the dynasties of Hea and Shang, the number of officers was doubled, and they continued able to secure good government. *Those* intelligent kings, in establishing their government, cared not so
4 much about the number of the offices as about the men. Now I, who am a little child, cultivate with reverence my virtue, concerned day and night about my deficiencies. I look up to *those* former dynasties, and seek to conform to them, while I instruct and direct you, *all* my officers.

speaks of Fuh-he, of Shin-nung, and of Hwang-te, as of princes of an earlier date.' This subject will be found touched on in the prolegomena. 內有至侯伯,—for 百揆, see on the 'Canon of Shun,' p. 2. 四岳,—see on the 'Can. of Yaou,' p. 11; *et al.* 州牧,—see on the 'Can. of Shun,' p. 16. Ts'ae takes 侯伯 as = 'the chiefs of the princes of States;' and Ying-tă identified them with the 五長, mentioned in the 'Yih and Tseih,' p. 8. Much preferable to either of those views is that of Lin Che-k'e, that the 侯 and 伯 are two of the five orders of feudal princes, among whom the provinces were divided,—two specified for the whole. 庶政惟和,—comp. 庶績咸熙, 'Can. of Shun,' p. 27. Medhurst translates 亦克用乂 by 'and yet they were enabled to maintain order,' as if it were surprising that they should be able to do so with two hundred officers instead of one hundred. We ought not to suppose any adversative force in 亦. Lin Che-k'e appears to have had an impression of the meaning similar to that of Dr. Medhurst, for he writes of the officers of Hea and Shang being double the number of those of Yaou and Shun, and of those of the Chow dyn. being still more numerous (amounting to 360), because men were more able in the earlier times. It is strange that it did not occur to him that, as the population grew with the lapse of time, the number of officers was necessarily increased. 明王至末,—Gan-kwŏ joined this to the next par., and understood it as a general remark about 'intelligent kings,' with which Ching prefaces the account of his own arrangements. It is better to understand the remark as applying to Yaou and Shun, Yu and T'ang. The gist of it is, that these sovereigns were not anxious to have the show of many offices, but to get right men. Ts'ae says: —明王立政,不惟其官之多,惟其得人而已.

4. 祗勤于德,—'reverently sedulous about my virtue.' 逮 = 及, 'to reach to.' 夙夜不逮 = 夙夜常恐有所不及. We must suppose that he measured his deficiencies with reference to the standard of Yaou, and the other 'intelligent monarchs.' 仰惟前代時(=是)若(=順) = 予仰承前代之明王,惟奉順不違, 'I look up to those intelligent monarchs of former dynasties, seeking to honour them and conform to them, and not to act contrary to their example.' 訓迪厥官,—'to lesson and lead the officers.'

太傅、太保、茲惟三公、論道經邦、燮理陰陽、官不必備、惟其人。○大師少師、少傅、少保、曰三孤、貳公弘化、寅亮天

5 III. "I appoint the Grand Tutor, the Grand Assistant, and the Grand Guardian. These are the three *Kung*. They discourse of the principles of reason, and adjust the States; harmonizing *also* and regulating the operations of Heaven and Earth. These offices need not *always* be filled:—there must *first* be the men for them.

6 "*I appoint* the Junior Tutor, the Junior Assistant, and the Junior Guardian. These are called the three *Koo*. They assist

Ch. III. Pp. 5—14. THE SECOND PART OF THE KING'S ADDRESS, GIVING THE PRINCIPAL OFFICIAL AND GOVERNMENTAL ARRANGEMENTS UNDER THE NEW DYNASTY. 5, 6. *The three Kung, and three Koo.* We cannot well translate 公 and 孤 in these parr. Medhurst calls the 三公, 'three dukes,' and the 三孤, 'three conspicuous ones.' But the terms are here as names of office, and not of nobility. We may suppose that the *Kung* were so called with reference to the public spirit and freedom from all selfishness which 公 denotes. The dict. says the *Koo* were so named to show that, though they were assistant to the *Kung*, they were not to be considered as subordinate officers of their departments. Gan-kwŏ's account of the name is somewhat similar:—孤,特也,卑於公,尊於卿,特置此三者. When it is said—'I appoint the Grand Tutor,' &c., (立大師云云), we are not to understand that these names and the offices belonging to them were first constituted by king Ching. From Pt. IV., Book XI., we see that they were in existence in the time of the Shang dyn. King Wăn had 太公 for grand Tutor, and under Woo that office was exercised by the duke of Chow, while the duke of Shaou was Grand Protector or Guardian. The meaning must be, that the offices were now more definitely declared a part of the governmental system of the Chow dynasty. Lin Che-k'e is of opinion that little is to be gained by attempting curiously to define the names 師, 傅, and 保, and distinguish them from one another. Kea K'wei (賈逵) held that 保 had reference to the preservation of the person; 傅, to aiding in virtue and righteousness; and 師, to the guidance of instructions. Gan-kwŏ said that 'the 師 was the emperor's pattern; the 傅, his helper; and the 保, his sustainer in virtue and righteousness.' The renderings in the translation cannot be far from the exact meaning. The business of the three *Kung* was 論道經邦,燮理陰陽. By 道 we are to understand all principles of reason and truth,—all the *courses or ways*, which it was proper for the emperor to pursue. The effect of the *Kungs'* discoursing on these with him would be seen in the States of the empire, in the govt. of which there would be no disorder. It would be seen also in the harmony of all the elements of nature, and the material prosperity which was dependent on them. This seems to be what is intended by 'harmonizing and regulating the *Yin* and *Yang*.' On the two characters 陰 and 陽, which occur with their mystical application nowhere else in the Shoo, it may be sufficient here to give the note of Gaubil:—'Chinese books are filled with these two characters. In their natural sense 陽 signifies "clear," "light," and 陰, "obscure," "darkness." In Chinese Physics 陽 is "movement," or the principle of movement; and 陰 is "repose," or the principle of repose. The moral and metaphorical applications of the terms are infinite, and extend to whatever is susceptible of them more or less, whether in Physics or in Morals. The sense of this paragraph is that all goes well in the empire; that the laws are in vigour; that commerce flourishes; that there are no public calamities; that the seasons are not deranged.' I believe that the meaning is not more than what Gaubil says. The remarks of Wang Kăng-yan are quite express on the point:—燮理陰陽,則無他道,惟區處人事,各得其宜,則天地之氣自順,故堯舜在上,而天災滅熄 [This is a sad mis-

地、弼予一人。○七冢宰掌邦治、統百官、均四海。○

the *Kung* to diffuse widely all transforming influences; they with reverence display brightly *the powers of* heaven and earth:—assisting me, the one man.

7 "*I appoint* the prime minister, who presides over the ruling of the empire, has the general management of all other officers, and secures

representation], 庶政太和,在夏懋德,而罔有天災,考其所爲,不過咨四岳,九官,十二牧,分任庶政,使人人各遂其性而已,初未嘗特設燮理陰陽之官,亦未聞別有燮理陰陽之政,云云. See my remarks on 'The Doctrine of the Mean,' i. 5; *et al.* 官不必備,惟其人,—the meaning of this is briefly and clearly given by one of the brothers Ch'ing.—不得其人而居之,不若闕之之愈也, 'If the right men cannot be got to put in these positions, it is better to leave them unoccupied.'

貳公弘化,寅亮天地,—貳公, 'seconding (=helping) the *Kung*.' 天地 correspond to 陰陽 in the former par. Tsoo-hëen says that 'Heaven and Earth are used with regard to the visible forms of those bodies or powers, and 陰 and 陽 with regard to their 氣, or operating energy.' Gaubil is wrong when he would understand 'religion' by 'Heaven' and 'government' by 'Earth.'

[I have stated, in the introductory note from Ts'ae, the objection taken against the genuineness of this Book, from the Chow Le's saying nothing about the duties of the three *Kung* and three *Koo*. But the existence and exalted dignity of these offices is referred to repeatedly in the Chow Le. For instance, Bk. XXI., p. 8, commences—王之三公八命,其卿六命, which declares the existence of the *Kung*, and intimates their superiority in rank to the executive ministers of the government. Par. 32 of Book XXXVI., again, gives the *Koo* likewise precedence of those ministers. —左九棘,孤,卿,大夫位焉,羣士在其後,右九棘,公,侯,伯,子,男位焉,羣吏在其後,面三槐,三公位焉,州長,衆庶在其後. The Chow Le therefore is not silent on these great ministers, as we might suppose from what Ts'ae says. It only does not treat of them separately, defining their duties, and enumerating the officers in their departments. But they were not the heads of departments. They composed the emperor's cabinet or privy council. Biot calls them happily—'les conseillers auliques,' and 'les vice-conseillers.' They were the prototypes of the 內閣, or 'Inner Council' of the present day. It did not belong to the plan of the Chow Le to speak of them more fully than it does.

But if we could not thus account for the little that is said about them in that Work, the inference would be against it, and not against this Book. There can be no doubt as to the genuineness of the first half of par. 5. If all the rest of the Book be forged, so much—立太師,太傅,太保,玆惟三公—has come to us with the guarantee of Ch'ing Heuen; and even Këang Shing edits it as a veritable fragment of 'The Officers of Chow.']

Pp. 7—12. *The six chief ministers of the executive.* Only the minister is mentioned, but in every case we are to understand that he was the head of a department with many subordinate officers. There is a close correspondence between those six departments of Chow, and the 'six Boards' (六部) by which the govt. of the empire is now administered. 7. 冢(=大)宰,—'the great or prime governor.' The name was as old as the Shang dynasty, for we find it applied to E Yin, Pt. IV., Bk. IV., p. 1. This was the office of the duke of Chow (see Bk. XVII., p. 1.), who united with it the dignity of 'Grand Tutor.' The 冢宰 is 'the officer of Heaven' (天官) of the Chow Le, and is represented now by the 'Board of Civil Office' (吏部). He was superior to all the other great ministers, and was called 'their Head' (六卿之首). This difference between him and them is intimated, I think, by the 統百官, 'has the general management of all the officers.' This is probably what is intended by the difficult clause in Pt. IV., Bk. IV., p. 1, 百官總已以聽冢宰.

八節 司徒掌邦教、敷五典、擾兆民。○ 九節 宗伯掌邦禮、治神人、和上下。○ 十節 司馬掌邦政、統六師、平邦國。○ 十一節 司寇掌邦

8 an uniformity throughout all within the four seas: the minister of
Instruction, who presides over the education of the empire, incul-
cates the duties attaching to the five relations of society, and trains
9 to obedience the people: the minister of Religion, who presides over
the ceremonies of the empire, attends to the service of the spirits
10 and manes, and makes a harmony between high and low; the
minister of War, who presides over the *military* administration of
the empire, commands the six hosts, and secures the tranquillity
11 of all the States: the minister of Crime, who presides over the
prohibitions of the empire, searches out the villainous and secretly

must understand 立, from p. 5, at the commencement of this and the other parr. The 邦 in them is also to be taken as = 邦國, 'the empire.' 8. 司徒,—'the superintendent of the multitudes,' perhaps with a reference to the meaning of 徒 as 'disciples.' This officer was as old as the time of Shun;—see the 'Can. of Shun,' p. 19. He is the 'officer of Earth' (地官) of the Chow Le. His department seems to merge in that of the present 'Board of Rites,' for we can hardly identify it with the 'Board of Revenue' (戶部). 敷五典,—comp. 敬敷五教, 'Can. of Shun,' p. 19. 擾 = 安, 'to tranquillize.' Ts'ae for 擾兆民 gives 馴擾兆民之不順者,而使之順. 9. 宗伯,—this office was also as old as the time of Shun. See 'Can. of Shun,' p. 23; which supplies an explanation of the name 宗伯, as = 宗廟官長, 'chief officer of the ancestral temple.' Otherwise, we might translate it by—'The reverend,' 'The very reverend.' He was the 'officer of the Spring' (春官) of the Chow Le; and his department now is that of the Board of Rites (禮部), which also absorbs in a great measure the functions of the 'minister of Instruction,' as I have observed. 治神人 = the 掌建邦之天神地祇人鬼之禮, 'manages the ceremonies to be paid to the spirits of Heaven, of Earth, and of Men,' of the Chow Le. Gaubil says:—'Il s'agit des ceremonies religieuses pour les esprits, et des civiles pour les hommes morts.' One cannot restrain a smile at the distinction which he introduces between the ceremonies, as here 'religious,' and there only 'civil!' 和上下,—all festive, funeral, and other ceremonies, as well as those of sacrifice, came under the 宗伯, who had therefore to define the order of rank, precedence, &c. This is what is intended by the 'high and low' of the text. 10. 司馬,—Ts'ae says that 'no arm of warlike measures is more important than the cavalry, and hence the minister of War was called "master of the Horse"' (軍政莫急於馬,故以司馬名官). This minister does not appear among the officers of Shun. He is the 'officer of Summer' (夏官) of the Chow Le, and appears in the 'Board of War' (兵部) of the present day. 掌邦政,—'handles the govt. of the empire.' But the same might be said of every other minister;—why is the name of 'government' used only in connection with the minister of War? Ts'ae says:—'Military measures are used to punish and to smite,—to correct the evil-doers; they are the greatest of the measures of imperial govt.' (戎政用以征伐而正彼之不正,王政之大者). 六師,—see on 'The Punitive Expedition of Yin,' p. 1. 11. 司寇,—'manager of banditti' (羣行攻刧曰寇). Kaou-yaou was Shun's minister of Crime, though he was only called 士; see the 'Can. of Shun,' p. 20. There is

禁、詰姦慝、刑暴亂。○司空十二節掌邦土、居四民、時地利。○六卿十三節分職、各率其屬、以倡九牧、阜成兆民。○六年、十四節五服一朝、又六

wicked, and punishes oppressors and disturbers of the peace: *and* the
12 minister of Works, who presides over the land of the empire, settles
the four classes of the people, and regulates the seasons for obtaining the advantages of the ground.
13 "These six ministers, with their different duties, lead on their
subordinates, and set an example to the nine pastors of the provinces, enriching and perfecting the condition of the millions of the people.
14 In six years the chiefs of the five tenures attend once at court. When
this has been done a second six years, the king makes his tours of

now the 'Board of Punishments' (刑部); but the text says that the minister of Crime 'handled the *prohibitions* of the empire.' 'He is so described,' observes Ch'in King, 'to show the benevolent purpose of punishments, as instituted to *deter* men from doing evil.' This minister was 'the officer of Autumn' (秋官) of the Chow Le. 12. 司空,—'the minister of Works.' He was the 'officer of Winter' (冬官), of the Chow Le, the portion of which relating to his department was unfortunately lost, though the scholars of the Han dynasty have endeavoured to supply it. The present 'Board of Works' (工部) corresponds to this minister, and his functions. In the 'Canon of Shun' we have the name of 司空, and also of 共工, which appears to have been the more ancient designation;—see the 'Can. of Yaou,' p. 10. 司空 may be translated—'overseer of the unoccupied,' suggesting to us that the earliest duties of this minister must have been to assign unoccupied lands. Kin Le-ts'ëang says:—'The 司空 was the minister who managed unoccupied grounds (空土), dividing and defining them in preparation for the investiture of ministers; for dotations to officers; for assignment as fields to husbandmen, shops to mechanics, and stances to traffickers. All the ground unapportioned was under his management; once apportioned, the minister of War, and the minister of Instruction had then to do with it.' See the 集說. 居四民,—'settles the four *classes of the* people,' *i.e.*, arranges that scholars or officers, farmers, workers, and merchants shall all live in the places best adapted for them. 時地利,—'times the advantages of the earth.' This would seem to imply that different operations might be required at different times, and that changes and removals of settlements might come to be desirable;—all to be done by the advice and authority of the minister of Works.

Pp. 13, 14. *Relation of the six ministers to the pastors of the provinces; and rule for imperial progresses, and appearances of the various princes at court.* 13. 各率其屬,—'each one leads on those belonging to his department.' The subordinates of each department amounted, in theory, to sixty. As the Chow Le exists, however, the dept. of the prime minister has 63 officers; that of the minister of Instruction, 76; that of the minister of Religion, 69; that of the minister of War, 69; and that of the minister of Crime, 65. The excess in each, it is supposed, belonged originally to the officers of the dept. of the minister of Works, the account of which is commonly believed to be lost. See the work of Ch'in Sze-k'ae *in loc.* 以倡九牧,—'to go before—be an example to—the nine pastors.' We do not learn from the Shoo how communications were maintained between the six ministers at the imperial court and the pastors of provinces. 14. 六年至又六年,—in the Chow Le, Bk. XXXVIII., it is said that the princes of the How tenure appeared at court every year; those of the Teen, every two years; of the Nan, every three years; of the Ts'ae, every four years; of the Wei, every five years; and of the Yaou, every six years. This seems a different arrangement from that described in the text. The text mentions five

年、王乃時巡、考制度于四岳、諸侯各朝于方岳、大明黜陟。○王曰、〔十五節〕嗚呼、凡我有官君子、欽乃攸司、慎乃出令、令出惟行、弗惟反、以公滅私、民其允懷。○〔十六節〕學古入官、議事以制、政乃不迷、其

inspection in the four seasons, and examines the regulations and measures at the four mountains. The princes attend on him, each at the mountain of his quarter, and promotions and degradations are awarded with great intelligence."

15 IV. The king said, "Oh! all ye men of virtue, my occupiers of office, pay reverent attention to your charges, and be careful of the commands you issue; for, once issued, they must be carried into effect and not be retracted. By your public feeling extinguish all selfish aims, and the people will have confidence in you, and be gladly obedient.

16 Study antiquity in order to enter on your offices. In deliberating on affairs, determine by help *of such study*, and your arts of government

tenures and not six;—perhaps the Yaou tenure was too distant, and too little reduced to the order of the nearer domains, to be made much account of in king Ching's time. The text of the Shoo and of the Chow Le so far agree, that in six years the princes from *all* the tenures had appeared at court. They differ in this, that the text would appear to make the princes to appear there only once, whereas, acc. to the other authority, all but those of the Yaou tenure would have appeared repeatedly. The interpretation must be strained either in the one case or the other, to make the two accounts agree. 王乃時巡以下,—Compare parr, 8, 9. Shun's progresses were made every five years, and the nobles all appeared during the intermediate ones. As the empire and its population grew, it was found necessary to separate the progresses by a longer interval.

Ch. IV. Pp. 15—20. Third part of the address:—various exhortations to the ministers and officers as to the way in which they should discharge their duties.

15. *How they should attend to their offices, especially in the matter of issuing orders, and in putting away all selfishness.* 君子 is best taken here as 有德之稱; the king thus shows his respect for his officers. 欽乃攸司一敬汝所主之職, 慎乃出令,—what commands are we to understand by 令 here? Most critics take them as 'governmental notifications' (國家政令), but I cannot think so. Such orders would go forth as from the sovereign himself. I understand the commands here, with Leu Tsoo-hëen, as orders to be issued by superior officers to their subordinates; to which I would add notices by any of them to the people under their jurisdiction. 令出惟行, 弗惟反,—反=回還, 'to return,' 'to come back.' It is here nearly equal to our 'to retract.' The difficulty is with the 惟, especially in 弗惟反. Ts'ae gives 欲 for it in both cases. 一令出欲其行, 不欲其壅逆而不行. There seems no better way of dealing with it. 民其允懷一民莫不敬信懷服.

16. *The necessity of study—of acquainting themselves with the past and the present—in order to their discharge of their duties.* 學古至不迷,—學古

爾典常作之師、無以利口亂厥官、蓄疑敗謀、怠忽荒政、不學牆面、蒞事惟煩。○[十七節]戒爾卿士、功崇惟志、業廣惟勤、惟克果斷、乃罔後艱。○[十八節]位不期驕、祿不期侈、恭

will be free from error. Make the regular statutes *of our* dynasty your rule, and do not with artful speeches introduce disorder into your offices. To accumulate doubts is the way to ruin your plans; to be idle and indifferent is the way to ruin your government. Without study, you stand facing a wall, and your management of affairs will be full of trouble.

17 I caution you, my high nobles, exalted merit depends on the *high* aim, and a patrimony is enlarged only by diligence. It is by means of bold decision that future difficulties are avoided.

18 With rank, pride comes unperceived, and extravagance in the

而入官; it is, no doubt, to these words that Tsze-ch'an, the minister of Ch'ing, refers in the 左傳,襄二十一年, when he says—僑聞學而後入政,未聞以政學者也. In illustration of the advice, comp. Bk. IX., p. 5. The clause 議事以制 seems also to be quoted in the 左傳,昭六年, in connection with the same Tsze-ch'an. 其爾至厥官,—by 典常 we are to understand the statutes of the existing dynasty. The 'Daily Explanation' expands 其爾典常作之師 clearly, though rather lengthily:—然天下事,有宜于古,而未卽宜于今者,又當以本朝爲法,如我文武周公之所經畫,皆當代之典常也,爾大小庶官,尤宜于先王典常,祇遵率由,奉爲師法. We may compare with the sentiment that in 'The Charge to the viscount of Wei,' p. 4, 率由典常. 利口,—Ts'ae thinks the 'sharp mouths' are those of the officers themselves; Wang Kang-yay thinks they are those of others to whose suggestions the officers listen. What is said in 'The Charge to Chung of Ts'ae,' p. 7, may be pleaded to determine in favour of either view,—無作聰明亂舊章,罔以側言改厥度. 不學牆面,—compare Con. Ana., XVII., x. 17. *The necessity of a high aim, of diligence, and of decision.* This advice (and we may suppose, with Ts'ae, the others that follow also) is addressed to the 卿士, 'the chief ministers and officers;' but we need not confine its application to them. Gan-kwŏ says:—此戒凡有官位,但言卿士,舉其掌事者. 功崇惟志,—this may be expressed by 功以志崇, or 崇功在志, or 功之所以崇乃志, &c. I call attention to this to illustrate the use of the 惟, which may be called the particle *par eminence* of the Shoo. Choo He illustrates the sentiment by 斷以不疑,鬼神避之,需者事之賊也. This last expression is from the 左傳. We say—'Procrastination is the thief of time;' the Chinese say—'Procrastination is the thief of business.' 18. *Against pride and extravagance.* 位不期驕,—see, for the

儉惟德、無載爾僞、作德、心逸日休、作僞、心勞日拙。○十九節居寵思危、罔不惟畏、弗畏入畏。○二十節推賢讓能、庶官乃和、不和政厖、舉能其官、惟爾之能、稱匪其人、惟爾不任。○廿一節王

same way with emolument. Let reverence and economy be *real* virtues, and do not show them in your affairs with hypocrisy. Practise them as virtues, and your minds will be at ease, and you will daily become more admirable. Practise them in hypocrisy, and your minds will be toiled, and you will daily become more stupid.
19 In the enjoyment of favour think of peril, and never be without a cautious apprehension. He who is without such apprehension
20 finds himself amidst what is to be feared. Push forward the worthy, and give place to the able, and harmony will prevail among all your officers. When they are not harmonious, the government becomes a tangled confusion. If those whom you advance are able for their offices, the ability is yours. If you advance improper men, then you are not equal to your duty."

meaning of 期, on 期于予治, in 'The Counsels of Yu,' p. 11. The cure for pride is 'reverence' (恭), akin to what we call 'self-respect.' If a man feel that he is in himself above his rank he will not be lifted up by it. Similarly, the cure for extravagance is 'economy' (儉). But this reverence and economy must be real, and not assumed,—true virtues. This is the meaning of 恭.儉惟德, 無載爾僞, 'Reverence (the cure for pride) and economy (the cure for extravagance) must be *truly* virtuous, and not *merely* conveyances (=carriages to convey) for your hypocrisy.' I cannot do anything better than this with the 載. Mencius probably had this passage in view, when he wrote 恭儉豈可以聲音笑貌爲哉, (IV. Pt. I., xvi).

19. *In prosperity think of adversity.* 居寵思危,—comp. in 'The T'ae-këă, Pt. iii., p. 5, 無安厥位, 惟危. We find the text quoted in the 左傳, 襄十一年, with 安 for 寵. We may take the 惟 in 惟畏 as = 思, according to the construction of the T'ae-këă, *l. c.* 弗畏入畏 = 不知祇畏, 則入于可畏之中. Shin She-hing observes that 'the first two 畏 intend the apprehension of the mind, while the last indicates the calamity of overthrow and disgrace.' 20. *How it would be for their own good and the public advantage to advance the meritorious.* The first four characters—推賢讓能, are found in Seun K'ing, 仲尼篇. 讓能,—'yield—show complaisance—to the able.' 政厖,—the 說文 defines 厖 by 石大貌, 'the appearance of a great rock.' The meaning of 亂, 'confusion,' is commonly given to it here. 舉能其官 = 所舉者能修其官.

曰、嗚呼、三事、暨大夫、敬爾有官、亂爾有政、以佑乃辟、永康兆民、萬邦惟無斁。

21 V. The king said, "Oh! ye *charged with* the threefold business *of government*, and ye great officers, reverently attend to your departments, and conduct well your affairs of government, so as to assist your sovereign, and secure the lasting happiness of the millions of the people:—so shall there be no dissatisfaction among the myriad States."

Ch. V. P. 21. THE END OF THE ADDRESS:—THE HAPPY AND PERMANENT RESULTS OF THE MINISTERS AND OFFICERS ACTING AS THEY WERE EXHORTED. 三事,—see last Book, p. 7. The 'six ministers are intended by the phrase; but how to classify them as the 任人, 準夫, and 牧 respectively, I do not know. By 大夫 are intended all the subordinate officers of the six departments. 亂爾有政,—亂 is evidently = 治. Wang Kăng-yay says that the last clause, 萬邦惟無斁 is inexplicable. The 無斁, as describing the feeling of the people to the officers, is inadmissible, he thinks, and he cannot construe the 惟. But there are many more difficult passages in the Shoo. I do not think the meaning is that the States would never be wearied of the officers, but that they would never be weary of the dynasty sustained by them in such a way.

THE BOOKS OF CHOW.

BOOK XXI. KEUN-CH'IN.

君陳

一節 王若曰、君陳、惟爾令德孝恭、惟孝友于兄弟、克施有政、命汝尹茲東郊、敬哉、○二節 昔周

1 I. The king spake to the following effect, "Keun-ch'in, it is you who are possessed of excellent virtue, filial and respectful. Being filial, and friendly with your brethren, you can display those qualities in the exercise of government. I appoint you to rule this eastern frontier. Be reverent!

INTRODUCTORY NOTE. Keun-ch'in was the successor, in 'the eastern capital,' of the duke of Chow, who henceforth passes off the stage of the Shoo, which he has occupied so long. Between the 'Officers of Chow' and the 'Keun-ch'in' there were two Books, which are both lost. The loss of the second we must much deplore, for it contained an account of the death of the duke of Chow, and an announcement made by king Ching at his bier. The duke died in Fung, the capital of his father Wăn, and, dying, signified his wish to be buried at Ching-chow, which he had built and watched over. The place was dear to him; but his wishes in regard to it were always to be disappointed. He had sought to make it the capital of the dynasty, but king Ching would not leave Haou. He now wished that his dust should rest in its soil, but the king chose rather to have him buried in Peih, the cemetery of their House (in the pres. district of Han-yang, dep. of Se-ngan). The object, according to Sze-ma Ts'een, was to honour him. He says that 'the king buried him in Peih, near by king Wăn, to show that he did not presume to look on the duke as a minister.'

The duke of Chow was undoubtedly one of the greatest men whom China has produced, and I do not know the statesman of any nation with whom his countrymen need shrink from comparing him. But this is not the place for writing either his history or his eulogium; I only wish, before passing on with the translation of the Shoo, to consider the claim which has been advanced for him to the invention of the mariner's compass. Gaubil held that he was versed both in astronomy and geometry, and says expressly that the use of the compass was known to him;—see 'Le Chou-king,' p. 214, note 4. The common opinion of the Chinese is that not only was the use of the instrument known to him, but that he discovered it. In the chapter on 'Inventions' (制作), in the 幼學故事尋源, or 'Inquiries into ancient things for the use of Learners,' it is said —'The duke of Chow made the south-pointing chariot, which has come down to us in the form of the mariner's compass' (周公作指南車,羅盤是其遺制).

The circumstances under which he is said to have made this instrument may be given first in the narrative of P. De Mailla, in his 'Histoire Generale de la Chine,' pp. 316—318. When I

subjoin the sources of his narrative, the reader will see how the history has been compiled, and whether we can put faith in the things related. P. De Mailla says:—'This same sixth year of his reign, king Ching, after having established his different officers, received the news that the ambassadors of a foreign kingdom, called Yuě-tchang-tchi (越裳氏), were come to bring him presents and do him homage. This kingdom, situated to the south of the country of Kiao-tchi (交趾) or Cochin-china, had never sent anybody to China. The emperor gave orders that the ambassadors should be conducted to the court, and that great honours should everywhere be paid to them. This prince (? the king, or the duke of Chow) received them very well, treated them with distinction, and accepted their presents, among which was a white pheasant,—a species heretofore unknown; after which he made the inquiry be put to them on what business they had come. They replied by interpreters, that the elders of their country said loudly, that for three years they had had neither winds nor tempest, no unseasonable rains nor great waves of the sea, and that there must be some special cause for such favour of Heaven; that apparently the throne of China was occupied by a sage emperor, who had procured for them these benefits.

'After that, the duke conducted them to the ancestral temple of the reigning family, where he caused to be displayed on the one side the presents which they had brought, and on the other those which king Ching was sending to their prince. Among these were five chariots of a new invention. They accommodated the travellers, and indicated at the same time the route which they kept, by means of a small box, made in the form of a pavilion or dome, suspended from the roof, in which was a hand that always pointed to the south, to whatever side the chariots might turn. It was on this account that they were called *Tchi-nan-tshe* (指南車), or *chariot of the south.* This machine was very useful to the envoys of Yue-tchang-tchi, for when they were arrived at the kingdom of Fou-nan-lin, on the borders of the sea, they took to some barques, and by means of this compass they needed only one year to return to their own kingdom.'

Now, the Shoo does not contain, and never contained, any account of this embassy from Cochin-china, and I have searched in vain for any mention of it in Sze-ma Ts'een. The earliest mention of it is in Fuh-shang's 'Introduction to the Shoo' (尙書大傳). His account is the following:—周公居攝六年,制禮作樂,天下和平,越裳以三象重九譯而獻白雉,成王以歸周公,公曰,德澤不加焉,君子不饗其質,政令不施焉,則君不臣其人,吾何獲此賜也,其使請曰,吾受命吾國之黄耇曰,久矣天之無別風淮雨,意者中國有聖人乎,有則盍往朝之,周公乃薦於宗廟,'In the sixth year of the duke of Chow's regency, he framed the ceremonial and official statutes *of the dynasty*, and made its music. The whole empire became harmonious and tranquil. *At that time, ambassadors came* from Yuě-chang, with three elephants, and interpreters speaking nine languages, and presented a white pheasant. King Ching put them in the hands of the duke of Chow, who said, "Where the benefits of his virtue have not been experienced, the superior man declines to receive gifts; and a sovereign does not acknowledge as his subjects those to whom he has not issued the orders of his govt.;—on what ground is it that this offering comes to us?" The ambassadors begged to say, "We come by the command of the elders of our kingdom. They said, 'For a long time there have been no unusual winds nor unseasonable rains in the sky. Is it not likely that there is a sagely man in the middle kingdom? Why should you not go and pay homage at his court?'" On this the duke of Chow presented them in the ancestral temple.'

It will be observed that in this account no mention is made of the 'south-pointing chariots.'

We come to Han Ying, not much later than Fuh-shang. In his 'Introduction to the She King' (韓詩外傳), composed about the middle of the second century B.C., we have substantially the same account of the embassy from Yuě-chang, but with certain marvels which preceded it. He says:—成王之時,禾三苗貫桑而生,同爲一秀,大幾滿車,長幾充箱,成王問周公曰,此何物也,周公曰,三苗同一秀,意者天下殆同一也,比及三年,果越裳氏重九譯而至,獻白雉於周公,道路悠遠,山川幽深,恐使人之未達也,故重譯而來,周公曰,吾何以見賜也,譯曰,吾受命國之黄髮曰,久矣天之不迅風疾雨也,海不波溢也,三年於此矣,意者中國殆有聖人,盍往朝之,於是來也,'In the time of king Ching, three stalks of grain grew through a mulberry tree and came out in one flowering head, which was almost large enough to fill a cart, and long enough to fill the box of it. The king said to the duke of Chow, "What is this thing?" The duke replied, "Three stalks growing into one head probably betoken that the empire is now at length becoming one." Sure enough, three years after, the ruler of Yuě-chang *sent an embassy* with

interpreters speaking nine different languages, which presented a white pheasant to the duke of Chow. The interpreters were necessary, because the distance was very great, with dark and deep mountains and rivers, so that the ambassadors might not be understood. The duke of Chow asked to what they were indebted for the offerings, when the interpreters said, "We received the command from the grey-haired men of our kingdom, who said, 'For long, even for three years, we have had neither violent winds nor disastrous rains, nor storms on the sea. We may believe that there is a sage in the middle kingdom;—why not go and present yourselves at his court?' This is the reason we are come.""

I do not find this account in the Introduction of Han Ying, as it is now generally edited; but it is quoted continually in illustration of the embassy from Yuĕ-chang;—see the 四書人名考, on the 'Life of the duke of Chow.' There seems to be no reason to doubt its having come from Han Ying; but it will be seen that neither does he make any mention of the 'south-pointing chariots.'

The earliest authority that I have found for connecting the duke of Chow and the embassy from Cochin-china with these chariots is the 中華古今注, a Work of the Tsin dynasty, the writer of which, after giving his opinion that the invention was due to Hwang-te, about 1,500 years anterior to the Chow dynasty! adds that Hang Këen of the 'After Han,' attributed it to the duke of Chow. We read:—'The duke having produced by his govt. a state of great tranquillity, the people of Yuĕ-chang came with interpreters speaking different languages, and presented one white pheasant, two black pheasants, and the tusk of an elephant. The ambassadors being astray as to their road back, the duke gave them two pieces of ornamented and embroidered silk, and five light carriages, all made on the pattern of pointing to the south. The ambassadors were conveyed in these to the south, as far as the city Lin [probably the pres. Kwei-lin, metrop. of Kwang-se] of Foo-nan near the sea, so that in a year they reached their own country, &c.' (後漢極建,舊說云,周公所作也.周公致治太平,越裳氏重譯來,獻白雉一,黑雉二,象牙一,使者迷其歸路,周公錫以文錦二疋,輧車五乘,皆爲司南之制,使越裳氏載之以南,緣扶南林邑海際,朞年而至其國,云云;—卷上, art. 大駕指南車).

My readers will probably be disposed with me to set down the embassy from Yuĕ-chang as a mere legend, and the claim of the duke of Chow to be the inventor of the 'south pointing chariot' as nothing better.

It is attributed to him under different circumstances in a fragment of the Works of 鬼谷子, 'The hero of Demon valley,' a Taouist charlatan, somewhat later than Mencius, towards the end of the Chow dynasty. What he says, is that 'the prince of Suh-shin presented a white pheasant to king Wăn. There being a fear lest he should lose his way on his return home, the duke of Chow made the south-pointing chariot to conduct him safely' (肅愼氏獻白雉於文王,還恐迷路,周公因作指南車以送之;—see the 太平御覽,卷第七百七十五, art. I.). Now, the Book of the Shoo which immediately followed the 'Officers of Chow' was about the chief of Suh-shin; but the presumption from the prefatory notice is that it did not contain anything about the duke of Chow. It related, moreover, to a visit from that chief to king Ching, and not to king Wăn.

Allusion has been made to the account which carries back the making of the south-pointing chariot to Hwang-te, more than 2,600 years before Christ. This is given by Sze-ma Ts'een.—Hwang-te was operating to put down a rebellious chief, called Ch'e-yew, who frustrated his measures for a time by enveloping the armies in clouds of mist, so that the emperor's men could not tell their position. Against this magical contrivance, Hwang-te made the chariots in question, and succeeded in taking the rebel alive. Later narrators ascribe the chariots to Hwang-te's empress; and there have been those who, forgetting the claims both of Hwang-te and the duke of Chow, have ascribed them to Kwan Chung, the chief counsellor of the duke Hwan of Ts'e, in the 7th cent. B.C.;—see the 事物紀原,卷第二.

The general opinion among the Chinese, therefore, that the duke of Chow made the 'south-pointing chariot,' cannot be received as resting on a historical foundation. The 'south-pointing chariot' altogether may be called in question. The accounts of its construction as being drawn by four horses, with the wooden figure of a genius (木仙人) on the roof, are all fabulous;—see the 太平御覽, *l. c.* It would be hard to say that the mariner's compass was the child of this chariot. The truth, I imagine, is this, that the Chinese got some knowledge of the compass—found it out themselves, or learned it from India—not long before the Christian era, and that then the fables about the making of south-pointing chariots in more ancient times were invented.

The Name of the Book.—君陳, 'Keun-ch'in.' Ts'ae says that this was the name of the minister; and as the Book contains the charge given to him, it is called after him. Others would translate the characters—'Prince Ch'in,' as we translate the title of Bk. XVI., by 'Prince Shih.' Thus Hea Seen says:—'He must have been invested with some principality as its ruler, on which account he is called 君,

公師保萬民、民懷其德、往愼乃司、茲率厥常、懋昭周公之訓、惟民其乂。

2 II. "Formerly, the duke of Chow acted as teacher and guardian of the myriads of the people, who cherish *the remembrance of* his virtue. Go you, and with sedulous care undertake his charge; act in accordance with his regular ways, and exert yourself to illus-

Prince' (必封國爲君,故稱君). But as we know nothing of any principality with which this Keun-ch'in had anything to do, it is better to abide by the view of Ts'ae, in which he followed Gan-kwŏ.

K'ang-shing supposed that Keun-ch'in was a son of the duke of Chow, a younger brother of Pih-k'in, but the evidence seems conclusive that this was not the case. The charge could hardly have been delivered without containing some reference to such a relation between Keun-ch'in and his predecessor. See in Lin Che-k'e, on the point. The Book is found only in the text of Gan-kwŏ.

CONTENTS. I take the summary of these which is given in the 'Complete Digest of Commentaries on the Shoo.'—'The whole Book may be divided into three parts. The first, which is also the first par., contains the words of Keun-ch'in's appointment to the charge of the eastern capital. The concluding words,—"Be reverent," are specially emphatic, and give the key-note to all that follows. The second part contains parr. 2—6, and enjoins on Keun-ch'in to exert himself to illustrate the lessons of the duke of Chow, and thereby transform the people of Yin. The third part, parr. 7—14, further enjoins on him to give full development to those lessons, and adduces various particulars in which his doing so would appear,—all illustrative of the command at the commencement, that he should be reverent.'

Ch. I. P. 1. THE CHARGE TO KEUN-CH'IN; AND THE GROUND OF IT IN HIS PERSONAL EXCELLENCE. 惟爾至有政,—the 'filial piety and respectfulness' (孝恭) are the attributes which compose the 'excellent virtue' attributed to Keun-ch'in. Gan-kwŏ interprets 恭 wrongly of 'self-respect' (行已以恭). It is expanded, however, in the next clause into 友于兄弟, and is thus made to embrace both the respectfulness of the younger brother and the kindness of the elder. 克施有政,—'can be displayed *in* the possession (or *by* the possessor) of govt.' This sequel does not commend itself so readily to a foreigner as it does to the Chinese. A man, it seems to us, may be a good son and a good brother, and yet be but poorly fitted for the duties of an administrator, while it is true that a bad son and a bad brother cannot be trusted to discharge the duties of any other relation. The doctrine of king Ching, however, is that of all Chinese authorities, ancient and modern;—compare 'The Great Learning,' Comm., ch. ix.

[This portion of the Keun-ch'in is quoted by Confucius, Ana. II., xxi.; but not to the letter. It would be absurd, however, to conclude from that that the text here is not genuine.]

By the 東郊, 'eastern border or frontier,' we are evidently to understand Ching-chow, 'the lower capital,' to which the people of Yin had been removed. Gaubil is quite wrong, when he would understand by 郊 here the sacrifice offered to Heaven, or the place of it. Ch'in Sze-k'ae gives the following statements: —'The imperial city formed a square of nine *le*. Outside the city was called the 郊. Fifty *le* off was called the "near 郊, or frontier," and a hundred *le* off was called the "remote frontier." Ching-chow would be in the "near frontier."'

Ch. II. Pp. 2—6. KEUN-CH'IN MUST FOLLOW THE EXAMPLE AND LESSONS OF THE DUKE OF CHOW; MUST FEEL THE DIFFICULTY OF HIS DUTIES; SEEK THE COUNSEL OF OTHERS, BUT USE HIS OWN JUDGMENT; EVER ASCRIBING HIS MERIT AND SUCCESS TO THE EMPEROR. 2. 師保萬民,—'tutored and preserved the myriads of the people.' The myriads of the people were those of Yin who had been removed to Lŏ. —This is a very clear instance of the way in which such high-sounding phrases as 萬民 are employed. 往愼乃司,—from the 厥常 which follows, we must interpret 乃司 of the duke of Chow,—其所司之職, 'that which he was charged with.' Medhurst takes 乃 as=汝, 'you,' which it often is; but its usage in the Shoo permits us also to take the 乃司 as I propose. Ts'ae also takes it thus. 惟民其乂—則民

書經

○我聞曰、至治馨香、感于神明、黍稷非馨、明德惟馨、爾尚式時周公之猷訓、惟日孜孜、無敢逸豫。○凡人未見聖、若不克見、既見聖、亦不克由聖、爾其戒哉、爾惟風、下民惟草。○圖厥政、

三節 四節 五節

3 trate his lessons:—so shall the people be regulated. I have heard that he said, 'Perfect government is like piercing fragrance, and influences the spiritual Intelligences. It is not the millet which has the piercing fragrance; it is bright virtue.' Do you make this lesson of the duke of Chow your motto, being diligent from day to day, and not presuming to indulge in luxurious ease.

4 Ordinary men, while they have not seen a sage, *are full of desire*, as if they could not get a sight of him; but after they have seen him, they are still unable to follow him. Be cautioned by this. You are the wind; the inferior people are the grass.

其治矣. 3. 我聞曰至惟馨,—that the king is here quoting words which he had heard, directly or indirectly, from the duke of Chow, appears clear from the 式時周公之猷訓. Gan-kwŏ only heard in them the voice of some ancient worthy. 馨—香遠聞, 'fragrance smelt at a distance.' 黍稷,—these two kinds of millet, used in sacrifice, represent all the articles of sacrifice,—grain, flesh, fruits, spirits, &c. The clauses 黍稷非馨,明德惟馨, are found quoted from the Books of Chow, in the 左傳,僖五年. The general sentiment is the same as that which we find so often in the prophets of Holy Scripture,—the worthlessness of sacrifice without an earnest moral purpose in the offerer. 爾尚式(—法)時(—是)周公之猷訓—爾尚取此周公發明夫道理之訓,而大法之. So says the 'Daily Explanation,' taking 猷 as an adj., qualifying 訓. This may be done, but it is not necessary.

4. 凡人至由聖,—this is quoted as from 'The Keun-ch'in' in the Le Ke, Bk. 緇衣, par. 15. It might be thus with the 凡人, 'the common people;' but the king tells Keun-ch'in it ought not to be so with him. He must set an example to the multitude of obedience to the sage's lessons, remembering that they would take their cue from him. 爾惟風,下民惟草,—comp. the Ana. XII., xix., 君子之德風,小人之德草,草上之風,必偃. The student will not be sorry to have the following illustration of the comparison by Soo Tung-po:—天地之化育,有可以指而言者,有不可求而得者,日皆知其所以爲暖,雨皆知其所以爲潤,雷電皆知其所以爲震,雪霜皆知其所以爲殺,至於風,悠然布於天地之間,來不知其所自出,去不知其所入,故曰天地之化育,有不可求而得者,蓋風之於物,鼓舞搖蕩,而不知所以然,君子之化

莫或不艱、有廢有興、出入自爾師虞、庶言同則繹。○爾(六節)有嘉謀嘉猷、則入告爾后于內、爾乃順之于外、曰、斯謀斯猷、惟我后之德、嗚呼、臣人咸若時、惟良顯哉。

5 "In revolving the plans of your government, never hesitate to acknowledge the difficulty of the subject. Some things have to be abolished, and some to be adopted:—going out and coming in, seek the judgment of your people about them; and when there is a general agreement, exert your own powers of reflection.

6 When you have any good plans or counsels, enter and lay them before your sovereign in his palace. Thereafter, when you are acting abroad in accordance with them, say, 'This plan or this view is all due to our sovereign.' Oh! if all ministers were to act thus, how excellent would they be, and how distinguished!"

民,似之,云云. 5. 圖厥政,—'planning your govt.' The 爾, lower down, shows that we are to take 厥 in the second person. Compare the same expression in Bk. XVIII., pp. 15, 16. 莫或不艱 may be taken imperatively, as in the translation, or indicatively,—'there will perhaps always be difficulties.' 出入自爾師虞,—the 出入 seem to trouble the critics considerably. Ying Yung (應鏞) says on them:—出上之意以達之下,入下之言,以達之上, 'giving out the views of the sovereign to make them known to the people; bringing in the words of the people to make them known to the sovereign;' comp. on the 'Can. of Shun,' p. 25. Ch'in Ta-yew says—出謀之國人,入謀之左右, 'going out, consider the matters with the people; coming in, consider them with your associates.' But we may very well translate the terms literally, and consider the meaning as = 'always and everywhere.' 師=衆, 'all,' 'the multitude of the people.' 虞=度, 'to calculate,' 'to consider.' 言同則繹,—'when their words agree, then unroll the matter,' *i.e.*, come to your own decision. Compare 克由繹之, Bk. XIX., p. 19. Gan-kwŏ gives for 繹 here—陳而布之;—not so well.

[In the Le ke, Bk. 緇衣, p. 19, we find the words quoted from 'The Keun-ch'in,'—出入自爾師虞,庶言同, the concluding 則繹 being omitted.]

6. 謀 is defined by Ts'ae as 言切於事, 'words important to business;' and 猷 as 言合於道, 'words agreeing with reason.' The 'plans' and 'counsels' of the translation seem to correspond to the characters. Of 良顯 it is said—良以德言,顯以名言, '良 has reference to virtue; 顯 to fame.'

The critics take different views of king Ching's requirement in this par., that he should himself have all the credit of Keun-ch'in's wisdom and successes. Some, like a 葛氏, quoted by Ts'ae, see in it a disclosure of the king's weakness and vanity. Others would make the king be speaking of Keun-ch'in's ways in the past.—'When you had good plans and counsels, you entered,' &c. This construction is not natural; and besides it would not much lighten the conclusion as to the king's unjust vanity. Many critics endeavour to

○王曰、君陳、爾惟弘周公丕訓。無依勢作威、無倚法以削、寬而有制、從容以和。○殷民在辟、予曰辟、爾惟勿辟、予曰宥、爾惟勿宥、惟厥中。○有弗若于汝政、弗

7 III. The king said, "Keun-ch'in, do you give their full development to the great lessons of the duke of Chow. Do not rely on your power to exercise oppression; do not rely on the laws to practise extortion. Be gentle, but with strictness of rule. Promote harmony by the display of an easy forbearance.

8 "When any of the people of Yin are amenable to the laws, if I say 'Punish,' do not you therefore punish; and if I say 'Spare,'

9 do not you therefore spare. Seek the due course. Those who are disobedient to your government, and uninfluenced by your instruc-

make it out that the king is only laying down what ministers should do, with a lofty superiority to the imputation of vanity to which it might subject himself! The truth is, king Ching was but a very ordinary man.

[The whole of this par. is found, quoted from 'The Keun-ch'in,' in the Le Ke, Bk. 坊記, p. 15.]

Ch. III. Pp. 7—14. That Keun-ch'in's grand object should be to carry out the plans of the duke of Chow, with the spirit and measures in which he should do this.

7. It is observed by Hea Sëen that this paragraph describes the way in which Keun-ch'in should carry out the plans of his predecessor among the people of Yin who did not violate the laws. There must be an absence of all oppression, but generosity must at the same time be accompanied with firmness. 作威—'to play the awe-inspiring.' 無(=毋)倚法以削,—削—'to cut,' 'to pare.' Its application here is to the practice of extortion. Keun-ch'in it is observed by Lin Che-k'e, was not likely to do either of the things against which he is here warned, but it was right for the king to speak to him as he does, as it was right for Shun's counsellors to warn him against vices from which as a sage he was far removed. 從容以和,—'be easy and tolerating to harmonize.' The meaning seems to be that Keun-ch'in should carry himself easily and forbearingly, and so effect a harmony between the people and himself and his measures. Ts'ae explains the clause—和不可一於和, 必從容以和之, 而後可以和厥中, which Kăng-yay says he does not understand. Ts'ae has a trick of poising his sentences, with more reference to their sound than their sense.

Pp. 8—10. These parr. regard how Keun-ch'in should deal with the people who were transgressors of the laws. He should have respect to the decisions of the law, and to the end of all law; and to nothing else. 8. 在辟,—辟—法, 'the laws,' meaning the punishments assigned by them. The 'Daily Explanation,' for 殷民在辟, gives—凡此殷民, 苟有犯法而入于刑辟之內者. 惟厥中—惟當審其輕重之中, 'you ought simply to judge according to the due medium of lightness and severity.' The case which the emperor puts here is a very remarkable one,—that of himself seeking to interfere with the operation of the laws, and yet telling Keun-ch'in not to pay regard to him. There are both weakness and goodness in what he says. 9. 若—順. 辟以止辟乃辟,—this would seem to say that even in such cases, where punishment was inevitable, it should be modified by a consideration of the end of all punishment. But the idea of *a modification* of the punishment is out of place; and therefore Gaubil has probably given the real meaning of the passage by translating—'vous devez les

化于汝訓、辟以止辟、乃辟。○狃(十節)于姦宄、敗常亂俗、三細不宥。○爾(十一節)無忿疾于頑、無求備于一夫。○必(十二節)有忍、其乃有濟、有容、德乃大。○簡(十三節)厥修、亦簡其或不修、進

tions, you will punish, remembering that the end of punishment
10 is to make an end of punishing. Those who are inured to villainy and treachery, those who violate the constant duties of society, and those who introduce disorder into the public manners:—those three classes you will not spare, though their particular offences be but small.
11 "Be not passionate with the obstinate, and dislike them. Seek
12 not every quality in one individual. You must have patience
13 and you will be successful; have forbearance and your virtue will be great. Mark those who manage their affairs well, and also

punir sévèrement, afin d'empêcher que les autres ne tombent dans les mêmes fautes.' 10. 狃—習, 'practised,' 'habitually given to.' 敗常,—comp. 反道敗德, 'Counsels of Yu,' p. 20; and 欲敗度, 縱敗禮, 'T'ae-këă,' Pt. ii., p. 3. Wang Ts'ëaou refers, pertinently enough, to Bk. IX., p. 15, for instances of the crimes which are thus described. P. 16 may also illustrate the 亂俗. 三細不宥=人犯此三者, 雖小罪, 亦不可宥. Sun Ke-yew (孫繼有) observes:—三細, 非以三者爲細也, 三事中所犯亦自有大小, 舉小以該大.

Pp. 11—13. *How Keun-ch'in should show patience and generous forbearance in dealing with the people.* 11. 無(—毋)忿疾,—'do not burst out into anger, and cherish dislike against.' 疾 is the abiding of the 忿;—comp. 身有所忿懥, 云云, 'Great Learning,' Comm., vii. 1. By 頑 are intended the 'stupidly obstinate' people of Yin, who should continue opposed to the sway of Chow. They would give occasion for the 'patience,' immediately spoken of. 無求備于一夫,—comp. Ana. XVIII., x., 無求備于一人. This regards the people of Yin, who might be prepared to submit cordially, and who would give occasion for a 'generous forbearance.'

12. 若有忍, 其乃有濟,—this appears in the 國語, as from the Shoo, but slightly varied,—必有忍也, 若能有濟也. Comp. Ana., XV., xxxvi. 有容, 德乃大,—'have forbearance, and the virtue is great.'—Ts'ae says:—'*Patience* is associated with *the issues of* business; *forbearance*, with virtue. The king's discourse distinguishes these two things, as the one is more deep, and the other more shallow.' *Forbearance* then is superior to *patience*. Kăng-yay condemns this reading of the text; but something of the sort seems to be implied. 13. 簡,—'to select;' meaning here 'to mark,' 'to take distinguishing notice of,' whether in the way of approval or the contrary. On 簡厥至不修 the 'Daily Explanation' gives—有力田安居, 能修其職業者, 亦有遊手好閒, 不能修其職業者, 爾當簡其修者, 表厥宅里, 亦簡其不修者, 殊厥井疆, 不使混淆而無別, 則將修者益自奮, 而不修

厥良、以率其或不良。○惟十四節民生厚、因物有遷、違上所命、從厥攸好、爾克敬典在德、時乃罔不變、允升于大猷、惟予一人、膺受多福、其爾之休、終有辭于永世。

mark those who do not do so. Advance the good to induce those who may not be so to follow *their example*.

14 "The people are born good, and are changed by *external* things, so that they resist what their superiors command, and follow what they *themselves* love. Do you but reverently observe all the statutes, and they will become virtuous; they will thus all be changed, and truly advance to a great degree of excellence. Then shall I, the one man, enjoy much happiness, and your excellent *services* will be famous through long ages!"

者亦知愧矣. On 進厥良, 云云, Ts'ae says:—進行義之良者以率其不良, 則人勵行.

P. 14. *The radical goodness of human nature always makes it capable of being reformed. What happy effects would follow from Keun-ch'in's conducting his govt. to this issue.* 惟民生厚,—compare Ana., VI., xvii., 人之生也直. Ts'ae considers that 違上所命, 從厥所好 mean—'They resist what their rulers *only* command, *not exemplifying the same themselves*, and follow what they love:' according to the teaching in the 'Great Learning,' Comm., ix. 4. On this view the statement is that of another fact in the ways of men additional to what is said in the two previous clauses; and may be considered as the foundation of the 在德 in the admonition to Keun-ch'in which follows. Another view, which I have followed, is ingeniously suggested by Wăng Kăng-yay. Acc. to it 違上所命, 從厥(—其)所好 is merely an expansion or illustration of 因物有遷. The whole of Kăng-yay's annotation on the passage is with reading:—孩提之童, 皆知愛親, 及長皆知敬兄, 民生本厚也, 知誘物化, 然後百姓不親, 五品不遜者有之, 蓋因物有遷耳, 是以違上所命, 從厥攸好, 而放, 僻, 邪, 侈, 無所不爲, 厥者, 其也, 指民, 而言自狥已所好耳, 以爲從上所好者, 非也. 爾克敬典在德,—Ts'ae makes this = 'If you can reverently observe all the duties of society, and that with a real virtue,' influenced no doubt by his view of 違上所命, 從厥所好. Our safer plan is to take 敬典 accord. to its use in the 'Ann. to the prince of K'an,' where it twice occurs;—in parr. 19 and 24. 在德 will then be descriptive of the conduct of the people thus ruled over. So, Lin Che-k'e:—爾能敬典以導之, 其所行惟在於德, 則無有不變. 'If you can reverence the constant statutes, and so lead them on, what they do will be in *the way of* virtue, and so all will be changed.' 允升于大猷—信其能升進於大道. 其爾, 云云,—all this belongs to Keun-ch'in. Ts'ae is wrong in making 終有辭于永世, belong both to him and the king.

THE BOOKS OF CHOW.

BOOK XXII. THE TESTAMENTARY CHARGE.

顧命

一節 惟四月、哉生魄、王不懌。○二節 甲子、王乃洮頮水、相被冕服、憑玉几。

1 I. In the fourth month, when the moon began to wane, the king
2 was indisposed. On the day Këă-tsze, he washed his hands and
face, his attendants put on him his cap and robes, and *he sat up*, lean-

INTRODUCTORY NOTE. This Book brings us to the closing act of the reign and life of king Ching. His reign, according to the current chronology, lasted 37 years, ending B.C. 1,079. The thing, however, is by no means certain. Nothing can be gathered on the point from the Shoo or from Sze-ma Ts'een. Between the appointment of Keun-ch'in, moreover, as related in the last Book, and Ching's death, the history is almost a blank. The only events chronicled, and which have the authority of Ts'een, are a coinage of round money, with a square hole in the centre, —the prototypes of the modern cash; and an enactment that the manufactures of cloth and silk should be two cubits two inches wide, in pieces of forty-four cubits long.

THE NAME OF THE BOOK.—顧命, 'The Testamentary Charge.' Dr. Medhurst has most unfortunately rendered these characters by 'Retrospective Decree.' 顧=還視 'to turn round and look;' and 顧命 is 'The charge given, when turning round and looking.' K'ang-shing says:—回首日顧,臨死回顧而發命. 'To turn round the head is called 顧. *The king*, when about to die, turned round and looked *at his ministers*, and so issued his charge.' The phrase is now generally employed for a 'testament,' or 'dying charge,' such application being derived from its use here in the Shoo. The Book is found in both the texts.

CONTENTS. King Ching, feeling that his end is near, calls his six principal ministers and other officers around his couch, and commits his son Ch'aou to their care and guidance. The record of all the circumstances and the dying charge form a chapter ending at par. 10 with the announcement of the king's death. The rest of the Book is occupied with a detailed account of the ceremonies connected with the publication of the charge, and the accession of Ch'aou to the throne. It is an interesting monument of the ways of that distant time on such occasions. M. De Guignes tells us that Father Gaubil said that if all the other Books of the Shoo had been filled with the names of instruments, dresses, arms, &c., like this, he would not have undertaken to translate the Work. The difficulties which it presents of this nature, however, are not greater than we had to encounter in translating 'The Establishment of Government.'

Ch. I. Pp. 1—10. THE SICKNESS; TESTAMENTARY CHARGE; AND DEATH OF KING CHING.

1. 哉生魄,—'at the beginning of the growth of darkness,'=when the moon began to wane, the 16th day of the month. See on the 'Completion of the War,' pp. 1, 2, and 4. 不懌,—'was not pleased.' The phrase =不豫 in VI., p. 1,—an euphemism, instead

○乃三節同召太保奭、芮伯、彤伯、畢公、衞侯、毛公、師氏、虎臣、百尹、御事。○王四節

3 ing on the gem-adorned bench. He then called for the Grand-protector Shih, the baron of Juy, the baron of T'ung, the duke of Peih, the prince of Wei, the duke of Maou, Sze, the master of the warders, the master of the guards, the Heads of the officers,—*all* the superintendents of affairs.

of saying directly that the emperor was unwell. Woo Ch'ing observes that 'the emperor's being ill is expressed by 不懌 and 不豫, and his decease by 登遐 and 宴駕, because his ministers could not bear to name such things directly.' 2. 甲子,—'on the day Këa-tsze.' But what day of the month this was cannot be determined. Hëa Sëen observes that 'the historians of Han conclude that it was the same day intended by 哉生魄 in the 1st par., but it is to be presumed they are wrong. In the "Completion of the War," p. 1, we read—惟一月壬辰旁死魄,越翼日癸巳, where the day intended by 旁死魄 is determined by its calendaric name preceding. In the text here there is no such name given, and we cannot say what day 甲子 was.' See the 集說. On the conclusion of the historians of Han, and the year of king Ching's death, Gaubil says:—'Lew Hin, who lived some years B.C., and Pan Koo (班固), the historian, who flourished 70 or 80 years after Christ, place the year of the death of king Ching in 1,079, B.C., and make him to have reigned 37 years; and they are followed in these points by the standard History (通鑑綱目). They add that, on this year of Ching's death, the day 庚戌, the 47th of the cycle, was new moon of the 4th month of the calendar of Chow, and that 甲子 was the day of full moon;—citing the text of this par. On the year B.C., 1,079, the day 庚戌 was the 28th February of the Julian year, but new moon was several days after; the day 甲子 was the 14th of March, and the full moon was not till several days after. Those two authors therefore make a false calculation, founded on their false principles of the motion of the sun and moon, and of the return of the period of seventy-six years. The year 1,068 (or 1,069) B.C. was the year of the death of king Ching; the 16th of March was the day 甲子, and also the day of full moon in the morning for China. The place of the sun shows that it was the 4th month of the calendar of Chow, because the equinox happened in the course of it.' The argument of Gaubil here agrees with that which I have presented on Bk. XII., p. 1; but the data are less sure, as we cannot be certain that 甲子 in the text should be connected with the date in the 1st par., as the reasoning supposes. I receive the impression that it should not be so connected. 王乃洮頮水=王乃用水盥手洗面. The meaning of 頮 (=靧), 'to wash the face,' is sufficiently established; and hence Ying-tă says it remains that 洮 be taken for 'to wash the hands.' Ma Yung made it = 'to wash the hair.' The 說文 has 沬 for 頮. 相被冕服,—it is not worth while to try and settle the question of what particular cap or crown and robes the king wore on this occasion. His 冕 or crowns were six, and for each there was the appropriate occasion. See on the duties of the 司服 in the Chow Le, Bk. XXI. The present was an extraordinary occasion, and no doubt his attendants settled on their principle of court etiquette the proper habit in which he should receive his ministers. The text determining nothing, however, on the point, critics are left to decide the questions which they raise, according to their several views. See Lin Che-k'e and Këang Shing, *in loc.* We must leave in the same way the question undetermined of who the 相 was or were. The 太僕 and officers of his dept. are probably intended. See the Chow Le, Bk. XXXI., *in* 太僕. Ts'ae would take the term more generally as = 扶相者, 'the supporters and assistants.' 被冕服=以冕服被(=加在)王身. Lin Che-k'e ingeniously refers to the practice of Confucius, Ana. X., xiii. 3,—'When he was sick, and the prince came to visit him, he had his head placed to the east, made his court robes be placed over him, and drew his girdle across them.' The sage would

曰、嗚呼、疾大漸、惟幾、病日臻、既彌留、恐不獲誓言嗣、兹予審訓命汝。○

4 The king said, "Oh! my illness has greatly increased, and it will soon be over with me. The malady comes on daily with more violence and without interruption. I am afraid I may not find another opportunity to declare my wishes about my successor, and therefore I now lay my charge on you with special instructions.

not receive a visit from his prince in his undress, even though he was sick; and in the same spirit king Ching would be properly arrayed on the occasion in the text. 憑玉几—we are to conceive of the king seated on a mat, and leaning forward in his weakness on the bench or stool before him. The benches used at various imperial ceremonies were of five kinds, of which the 'gem-adorned' was the most honourable. See the Chow Le, Bk. XX., on the duties of the 司几筵. Difft. accounts are given of their size. They were all, acc. to Ma Yung, 3 feet long. Yuen Ch'in (阮諶) says they were '5 feet long, and 2 feet high.' 3. The duke of Shaou, and the other five ministers mentioned, were no doubt the six *K'ing* of Bk. XX. On the death of the duke of Chow, the duke of Shaou had succeeded him as 冢宰, or prime minister, retaining also his dignity of 'Grand-Guardian.'

A baron of Juy is mentioned in the prefatory notice to one of the lost Books, as having made the Ch'aou Ming (巢命), by order of king Woo. The one in the text may be the same, or a son of his. Juy is referred to the pres. dis. of Chaou-yih (朝邑), dep. of Se-ngan, Shen-se. The baron of Juy was minister of Instruction. The baron of T'ung was probably the minister of Religion. His principality of T'ung was in the sub. dep. of Hwa (華州), dep. of T'ung-chow. 'The duke of Peih,'—see Bk. XXIV. Ch'in Sze-k'ae says that he succeeded to the duke of Chow as chief of all the princes of the east, and in the office of Grand-Tutor. He was minister of War. 'The prince of Wei,'—see on the name of Bk. IX. He or his son was now the minister of Crime. 'The duke of Maou must have been the minister of Works. He is supposed to be called *Kung* or 'duke' here from having been appointed Grand-Assistant. Where Maou was is not certainly known. 師氏,—see on Bk. II., p. 2. By 虎臣 we are to understand the 虎賁 of Bk. XIX., p. 1,—the 虎賁氏 of the Chow Le, Bk. XXXI. 百尹=百官之長, 'the heads or chiefs of the various departments of officers;'—as frequently.

We may take 御事, with Woo Ch'ing, as a general designation of all the ministers and officers mentioned. It is said that the king sent 'a common summons' for them all to come to his presence (同召). On common occasions the order to repair to the imperial presence was given to the 'six K'ing,' who would 'lead on the officers belonging to their several departments' (see Bk. XX, p. 13); but on the present extraordinary occasion the order was sent directly to all, of whatever rank. Such at least is the explanation given of the phrase 同召.

Pp. 4—9. *The king's charge.* 4. *The severity and dangerousness of his illness, rendering it necessary for him to take that opportunity of making his wishes known to them.* 疾大漸惟幾,—疾 is the general name for sickness or disease. When the sickness is severe, the term 病 is used. 漸=進, 'to advance,' 'to grow.' 幾 is defined by 殆 or 危, 'perilous.' The 'Daily Explanation,' however, for 惟幾, gives 但幾希不絶耳, 'it wants only a little to the extinction of my breath.' 臻=至, 'to come on.' 彌=益, 'to increase,' or it may be construed with 留, in the sense of 終, 'to continue.' 恐不獲誓言嗣,—'I am afraid I shall not find *the opportunity* to speak solemnly and publicly about the succession.' This is the simplest way of construing this clause, and is that adopted by Woo Ch'ing and Këang Shing. Gan-kwŏ's method, followed by Ts'ae, is over ingenious:—恐遂死,不得誓言以嗣續我志, 'I am afraid I shall forthwith die, and not be able to make a public declaration to develop continuously what I have in my mind.' 審訓=詳審發訓, 'with careful exercise of thought I issue instructions.' 5.

五節 昔君文王武王、宣重光、奠麗陳教、則肆肆不違。用克達殷、集大命。○ 六節 在後之侗、敬迓天威、嗣守文武大訓、無敢昏逾。○

5 The former sovereigns, king Wăn and king Woo, displayed in succession their equal glory, making sure provision for the support of the people, and setting forth their instructions. *The people* accorded a practical submission; they did so without any opposition, so that their influence extended to Yin, and the great
6 appointment *of Heaven* was secured. After them, I, the stupid one, received with reverence the dread *decree* of Heaven, and continued to keep the great instructions of Wăn and Woo, not daring blindly to transgress them.

The brilliant and successful rule of Wăn and Woo. 昔君=先王, 'the former kings.' 昔 is used as an adj. 宣重光,—'published—manifested—their doubled light,'=相繼而能明其德, as Ch'in Ya-yen expresses it, 'continued one the other, and could make their virtue illustrious.' This is much better than to understand, with Ma Yung and Këang Shing, that 重光 is the light of the heavenly bodies combined together, and that 宣重光 is merely a figurative description of the virtue of Wăn and Woo, as like the brightness of the sun and moon. 奠(=定)麗,—comp. Bk. XVIII., p. 5. I take 麗 in the same way as there. The various views of its meaning taken by the critics all re-appear on this passage. 則肆肆不違,—肆 is found with the meanings of 習, 'to practise,' and of 勞, 'to toil.' Gan-kwŏ takes the latter meaning, and understands the characters of Wăn and Woo, =' thus they toiled; and though they toiled, they did nothing contrary to what was right' (文武勤勞,雖勞而不違道). So, Lin Che-k'e, as far as regards the meaning of 肆. The other meaning, however, is preferable. It was approved by Choo He, and adopted by Ts'ae. Acc. to it, 民, 'the people,' is understood as the subject of 肆. There is no difficulty in this way with 不違. Këang Shing also takes this view, and attributes the repetition of 肆 to the gasping utterance of the dying king. This is not necessary. The repetition of the character gives emphasis to its meaning. I put no comma after the 1st 肆, as is generally done. 用克達殷,—'thereby they could reach to all Yin,' *i.e.*, the whole empire came under their influence.

6. *How king Ching had endeavoured to discharge his kingly duties.* 在後之侗,—'The stupid one who was after *them*.' So Ching designates himself. Gan-kwŏ and Woo Ch'ing find in 侗 the idea of 'youth' as well as of 'stupidity' (侗幼而未有知也); but there is no such idea in the term in Ana., VIII., xvi. Këang Shing, on the authority of the 說文, and partly also of Ma Yung, edits—在夏后之詷, from which he endeavours to force out the meaning of 承文武之業,在中夏爲諸侯之共主, 'receiving the possession of Wăn and Woo, and being in the Central Great Land the common lord of all the princes!' 敬迓天威,—'I reverently met (=set myself to receive) *the* dread *decree of* Heaven.' By 天威 is meant, no doubt, the 大命 of last par.,—the appointment to the empire, enforced by the dread requirements of Heaven

今七節天降疾、殆弗興弗悟、爾尙明時朕言、用敬保元子釗、弘濟于艱難。○柔八節遠能邇、安勸小大庶邦。○思九節夫人自亂于威儀、爾無以釗冒貢于非

7 "Now Heaven has laid affliction on me, and it seems as if I should not again rise or be myself. Do you take clear note of my words, and in accordance with them watch reverently over my eldest son, Ch'aou, and greatly assist him in the difficulties of his
8 position. Be kind to those who are far off, and help those who are near. Promote the tranquillity of the States, small and great, and encourage them *to well-doing.*
9 "I think how a man has to govern himself in dignity and with decorum:—do not you allow Ch'aou to proceed heedlessly on the impulse of improper motives."

from those who held it. 7, 8. *The general duties which the ministers would have to perform for his son and successor.* 今天至弗悟,—Ts'ae puts a comma at 疾, and joins 殆 with the words that follow, as an adverb,—'probably,' 'it is to be feared that.' Gan-kwŏ and Këang Shing put the comma after 殆, and make it an adj., descriptive of the sickness. I prefer the former construction. 弗悟;—'will not awake,' *i.e.*, to a conscious ability for my duties. 元子釗,—Ching thus declares his eldest son as his successor. Ch'aou was the son's name. He is known in history by his honorary title of K'ang (康). I have not been able to ascertain how old he was at his accession. 弘濟于艱難,—no particular hardships and difficulties are meant, in which the new emperor might be involved, but those of his position generally. As the 'Daily Explanation' has it:—以宗社之重,基業之大,付之一人,可謂艱難矣. 柔遠能邇,—see the 'Can. of Shun,' p. 16. On 安勸, Ying-tă says:—又當安勸云云, 勸小大衆國,安之,使國得安存,勸之,使相勸爲善, 'tranquillize them, making the States feel in a condition of tranquil safety; encourage them, making them emulate one another in well-doing.' 遠邇 and 大小庶邦 are composite designations for the whole empire. 9. *Special charge to them to watch over the character of his son.* 思夫人,—夫人, 'this man,'='men' generally, or 'any man.' 自亂(=治)于威儀,—for 威儀 see on 'The Doctrine of the Mean,' xxvii., 3. 貢=進, 'to advance.' 非幾—'improper springs,' *i.e.*, of action. Choo He was asked the meaning of this phrase by one of his disciples, who said that most critics took 幾 in the sense of 危, 'perilous,' but that he thought it should be taken as simply=事, and 非幾=非所當爲之事, 'things which ought not to be done.' The master answered that 幾 meant 事之微, 'the small *beginnings or springs* of things.' Ching had in view, no doubt, the mind of his son, as the spring and regulator of all his conduct.

幾。○十節茲既受命、還、出綴衣于庭、越翼日乙丑、王崩。○十一節太保命仲桓南宮毛、俾爰齊侯呂伋、以二干戈、虎賁百人、逆子釗於南門之外、延入翼室、恤宅宗。○十二節丁卯、

10 Immediately on receiving this charge, the officers retired. The tent was then carried out into the court; and on the next day, *being* Yih-ch'ow, the king died.

11 II. The Grand-protector then ordered Chung Hwan and Nan-keung Maou to instruct Leu Keih, the prince of Ts'e, with two shield-and-spearmen and a hundred guards, to meet the prince Ch'aou outside the south gate, and conduct him to *one of* the wing apartments *near to that where the king lay*, there to be as chief mourner.

10. *The king's death.* 茲既受命還 (read *seuen*),—茲 is to be taken adverbially,—是時, 'then.' We must understand 羣臣, 'all the ministers,' as the subject of 受命. 還=退, 'retired,' *i.e.*, from the apartment where they had received the charge. Gan-kwŏ, as amplified by Ying-tă, makes the meaning to be that they retired from around the king to the ceremonial places in the apartment appropriate to their different ranks. In this way the interpreter only gives himself trouble. I prefer the simpler view. 出綴衣于庭,—we are obliged to seek a meaning for 綴衣 here quite difft. from that assigned to it in Bk. XIX., p. 1, where it denotes—'the keeper of the robes.' K'ang-shing would make the 衣 to mean the 'grave clothes,' and 綴衣='they made the grave clothes' (連綴小殮大殮之衣). But this view, though defended by Ming-shing, may safely be pronounced absurd. If it were to be admitted, we should have to find a third meaning for the phrase on its recurrence in p. 14. Ts'ae is right in defining it here, after Gan-kwŏ, by 幄帳, a kind of 'tent,' or curtains and canopy, set up over the emperor, when he held audiences. This had been prepared when he sent for his ministers to give them his last charge; and that ceremony over, it was now carried out into the court. Into what court? This question will be best answered, and the student prepared to understand the next chapter, if I refer to the form of the imperial palace in the time of Chow. It will easily be conceived by any one who has studied the architecture of the courts of the high officers throughout the empire at the present day.

The palace was much more long or deep than wide, consisting of five series of buildings, continued one after another, so that, if it had been according to etiquette, and all the gates had been thrown open, one might have walked in a direct line from the first gate to the last. The difft. buildings were separated by courts partially open and embracing a large space of ground. The gates of the different divisions, had their particular names. The first or outer gate, fronting the south, was called 皐門; the second was called 雉門; the third, 庫門; the fourth, 應門; and the fifth 路門, called also 畢門 and 虎門. Outside the second gate—the 雉門—was held the 'outer levee,' (外朝) when the sovereign received the princes and officers generally. Outside the 5th gate—the 路門—was held the 'audience of government' (治朝), when the king met his ministers, to consult with them on the business of the State. Inside this gate were the buildings which formed the private apartments, called

路寢, in the hall of which was held 'the inner audience' (內朝), and where the sovereign on occasions feasted those whom he designed specially to honour.

[Such is the general view of the palace given by Choo He. Acc. to K'ang-shing, the second gate was the 庫門, and the 雉門 was the third. Into a discussion of this point we need not enter. The gates were only gates according to our idea, in name, and included a large space, covered by a roof supported on pillars.]

The place where Ching delivered his testamentary charge was probably the hall in front of his bed-chamber, a sort of throne with curtains and canopy—the 綴衣,—being provided for the occasion. When he had finished, either before or after the retirement of the ministers, he was removed back to his chamber, and the tent—so to name it—was carried out into the court within the 路門. Medhurst mistook the meaning, and translated 出綴衣于庭, with reference to the ministers,—'going out, they set up their tents in the courtyard.' Gaubil saw that 綴衣 should be referred to the king; but he translated the clause by—'On detendit les rideaux, et on les remporta,' taking no notice of the 于庭.

Ch. II. Pp. 11—29. PUBLIC DECLARATION OF THE KING'S CHARGE TO HIS SUCCESSOR, WITH THE VARIOUS CEREMONIES OBSERVED ON THE OCCASION. 11. *Immediate measure to recognize Ch'aou as the successor to the throne.* 太保至呂伋,—the Grand-Guardian being also the 冢宰, or 'prime minister,' the regulation of all matters fell to him. Of Chung Hwan and Nan-keung Maou, we know nothing more than is here related. They were, no doubt, officers of trust and distinction about the court. 俾爰齊侯 simply = 使齊侯, 'to cause,' or 'to instruct the prince of Ts'e.' 俾爰 = 俾於, but the 爰 has little independent meaning. Këang Shing would define it by 引, 'to lead,' after the 說文; but what then becomes of the 俾, to which 爰 is merely supplementary. The prince of Ts'e was the son of 太公, the friend and minister of king Wăn, who had been enfeoffed by Woo with the principality of Ts'e, the capital of which was Ying-k'ew (營邱), in the pres. dis. of Lin-tsze, dep. of Ts'ing-chow, Shan-tung. Keih is known in history as duke Ting (丁公 or 玎公). His place at court, say all the critics, was that of 虎賁氏, or master of the guards. If it was so, it shows the dignity of that office, that it should be held by one of the chief princes of the empire. 以二千戈虎賁百人,—Gan-kwŏ supposed that 'the two shield-and-spearmen' were Hwan and Maou themselves, and that the meaning is that these officers were sent to the prince of Ts'e to get from him a hundred of the guards under his command, whom they preceded with spear and shield, to meet the prince. But the text, as it stands, will not bear this interpretation. It does seem strange, indeed, that only two men thus armed should have been selected; but so the record says. Medhurst, by mistake, took 干 for 千 and has rendered—'two thousand spearmen.' The style might have suggested to him that he was in error. 逆子釗於南門之外,—逆 = 迎, 'to meet.' Ts'ae and most of the other critics suppose the 5th or the 路 gate to be that intended. They think also that Ch'aou had been by his father's side at the time of his death, and that he went out purposely from the buildings in the rear, that he might be met thus publicly, and conducted back to be near the corpse as chief mourner. I cannot help thinking that by the 'south gate' we are to understand the first or outer gate of all,—the 皐門. This is the view of Këang Shing, who thinks further that the prince had been absent on some expedition, and that he was now returning, just in the nick of time. This last supposition appears to me unlikely. The prince may have been absent from the palace, tho' not far off, when his father died, or he may have purposely gone outside, that his entrance in such a style, which was a public declaration that he had been appointed successor to the throne, might be seen by all. 延入翼室,恤宅宗,—翼室, 'a wing apartment.' On each side of the hall, immediately in front of the private apartments, called the 後堂, there was a 夾室, side chamber, or wing, only not spread out, as in our idea of the wings of a house. That to which the prince was conducted was the 東夾室, 'side chamber on the east.' 恤宅宗 = 爲憂居之宗主, 'to be the lord of the mournful dwelling.' The 'mourning shed' called 梁闇 was not yet erected. At the present stage the apartment indicated in the text was the proper one for the prince to occupy.

命作冊度。○越(十三節)七日癸酉、伯相命士須材。○狄(十四節)設黼扆綴衣。○牖(十五節)間南嚮、敷重篾席、黼純、華玉仍几。○西(十六節)序東嚮、敷重底席、綴純、文貝仍几。○

12 On the day Ting-maou (*two days after the king's death*), he ordered a record to be made *of the charge*, and the ceremonies *to be*
13 *observed in publishing it.* On Kwei-yew, the seventh day after, as chief *of the west* and premier, he ordered the *proper* officers to provide the wood for *all* the requirements *of the funeral.*
14 The salvage men set out the screens ornamented with figures
15 of axes, and the tents. Between the window *and the door*, facing the south, they placed the different mats of bamboo basket-work, with their striped borders of white and black silk; and the usual

12. *The writing of the charge, and of the ceremonies to be observed.* The order here given is to be understood as from the Grand-Guardian. It would be given to the 內史, or 'Recorder of the Interior,' who was charged with the writing of the appointments of the emperor (內史掌書王命;—see the Chow Le, Bk. XXVI.). 作冊度=爲冊書法度, 'to make the writing on a tablet (or tablets), and the regulations.' For what was thus written see par. 24. The 'regulations' are all the ceremonies connected with conveying the appointment of Ching to his son. Few, if any, students, I apprehend, will be found to adopt Këang Shing's notion, that by 度 is intended 冊長短之數, 'the measure of the length of the tablets.' 13. *An order to prepare wood.* 伯相,—no doubt the Grand-guardian is still intended. In the 1st par, of the next Bk. he is introduced as 'leading forward all the princes of the western regions,' and we have seen before that he and the duke of Chow were 'the two chiefs,' the one having under his jurisdiction the east of the empire, and the other the west. Shih is here designated accordingly, as uniting the dignities of Chief and Premier, though it is difficult to assign a reason why the compiler of the Bk. should vary his style in so perplexing a manner. Ts'ae defines 須 by 取, 'to take,' 'to procure;' but this meaning of the character is not found in the dict., nor is it necessary. We may take it as an adj.,='requisite,' 'necessary,' and 命士須材 will='required *from* the *proper* officers the necessary materials,' those materials being probably of wood, though that is not necessarily implied in the term. So Gan-kwŏ:—命士致材木須待以供喪用. Acc. to the usual custom, the deceased monarch had been shrouded and coffined on the day 壬申, the seventh after the day of his death. The duties to him, therefore, were so far forward, that they might proceed to the announcement of his testamentary charge. There were only the shell or outer coffin (槨), and what were called the 明器, to be further provided; and it was with reference to them, I suppose, that the order in this par. was given. On those 明器, see the Le Ke, Bk. 檀弓, 下, Pt. i., p. 44, *et al.* It is not easy, however, to say definitely all that we are to understand here by 材. Ming-shing goes more at length into an examination of the point than any other of the critics whom I have seen.

Pp. 14—18. *At four points, where the emperor had been wont to receive his guests, the arrangements are made as if he were still alive.* 14. 狄設,—in the Le Ke, Bk. 祭統, p. 22, we find—翟者,樂吏之賤者; and assuming that 翟 and 狄 are interchangeable, the 狄 here are commonly described as 'the

attendants on the musicians.' In the 喪大記, Pt. i., p. 3, again, we find 狄人設階, which is more to the point, showing that certain 狄 or 狄人 were employed in performing the more servile offices at the ceremonies of funerals and mourning. I suppose they were natives of some of the wild *Teih* tribes; and we know that some of the 虎賁, or 'guards' were taken from those people. I have ventured to translate the character by our old term 'salvage,' which seems to convey a less intense meaning than savage. 黼扆綴衣,—we have seen the meaning of 綴衣 on p. 10. What was called 黼扆 is represented as a screen, with axe-heads figured on it, which was placed under the canopy that overshadowed the emperor, and behind him. As to the meaning of the terms, the 爾雅, Bk. II., sect. 釋宮, says that 'the space, east and west, between the window and the door, was called 扆(牖戶之間謂之扆,注云,窓東戶西也). Here the screen in question was placed; and we may believe, with many of the critics, that from its place it took its name. [The only difficulty in the way of this is that in the 爾雅 the character is in the 1st tone; whereas in combination with 黼 it is pronounced in the 2d.] Anything painted or embroidered black and white alternately is said to be 黼. The 爾雅, sect. 釋器 says that 'an axe is called 黼, the wooden handle being black as compared with the glittering head and edge.' However this be, the screen about which we are concerned is called indifferently 斧扆 and 黼扆, the axe-heads on it being understood to be emblematic of the decision of the imperial determinations. We are to understand that four such screens and tents were arranged in the four positions immediately indicated. Gaubil is wrong in translating both 狄 and 黼扆, in the singular.—'L'officier appelle Tie eut soin de mettre en état l'ecran, sur lequel etoient représentées des haches.' We are to understand also that all these and other arrangements were made by the direction of the Grand-Guardian. The 命 of the preceding paragraphs is to be conceived to be constantly repeated.

15. The first tent and screen were placed in front of the 'rear hall' belonging to the private apartments, of course directly fronting the south. There the king was in the habit of giving audience to his ministers and to the princes (此平時見羣臣,覲諸侯之坐). 牖間 would seem, to mean 'between the windows;' but from the account of 扆, given above from the 爾雅, we must take 牖 as an abbreviation for 牖戶之間;—as in the translation. 敷重篾席,—敷=設, or 鋪, 'to spread out.' On these mats the king sat; there were three of them, one over the other; and the text would lead us to suppose that all those mentioned here were made of bamboo splints woven together, having the edges bound with silk stripes of black and white alternating (黼 is explained above; 純 [read *chun*, 2d tone) = 緣, 'a border].' Ying-tă, however, quotes a passage of the Chow Le, Bk. XX., on the duties of the 司几筵, which, while it throws considerable light on the text, states that the three mats were each of a difft. material, and that each had its peculiar border.—凡大朝覲,大饗射,凡封國命諸侯,王位設黼依,依前南鄉,設莞筵紛純,加繅席畫純,加次席黼純,左右玉几. This passage, as translated (not quite accurately, but sufficiently so for my purpose) by Biot, is:—'En général, dans les grands réunions du printemps et de l'automne, dans les grands banquets, dans les cérémonies où l'on tire de l'arc, où un royaume est concédé en fief, où un grand dignitaire est nommé, il dispose le paravent brodé en noir et blanc, à la place que doit occuper l'empereur. Le devant du paravent fait face au midi. Il place la natte en joncs fins à bordure variée. Il ajoute la natte à lisière qui a une bordure peinte. Il ajoute la natte à rangées qui a une bordure mélangée de noir et de blanc. A gauche et à droite sont les petits bancs en jade pour s'appuyer.' Gan-kwŏ thinks that 篾 [this character is disputed] 席 is the 次席 of the above passage, the topmost of the three mats, the historian not thinking it necessary to describe the others particularly. Possibly it may be so; but the point is really not of much importance. 華玉仍几,—華玉=彩色之玉, 'gems of variegated colours.' The bench was adorned with such. 仍 is used as an adj.,='usual,' 'ordinary;' intimating that the bench was the same which was used in such position by the living emperor (仍,因也,因生時所設). Woo Ch'ing, however, explains the term differently, but by no means in so satisfactory a manner. He says:—仍几謂雖飾之漆之,尙仍其質,其文不皆滅質也,吉事尙文,凶事尙質故爾, 'The benches are called 仍几, because, though they were ornamented and lacquered, their proper material could still be distinguished, its substance not all concealed by the ornamenting. The reason of this was

十七節 東序西嚮、敷重豐席、畫純、雕玉仍几。○ 十八節 西夾南嚮、敷重筍席、玄紛純、漆仍几。○

16 bench and adorned with different-coloured gems. In the side space on the west, facing the east, they placed the different rush mats, with their variegated border; and the usual bench adorned with veined
17 tortoise-shell. In the side space on the east, facing the west, they put the different mats of fine grass, with their border of painted
18 silk; and the usual bench carved and adorned with gems. Before the western side-chamber, facing the south, they placed the different mats of fine bamboo, with their dark mixed border; and the usual lacquered bench.

that in festive matters the ornamental takes the prominence; but on occasions of mourning and sorrow, the simple and substantial. Perhaps we ought to translate 几 in the plural, acc. to the pass. of the Chow Le just referred to.

16. 西序東嚮,—it is difficult without a picture to get for one's-self or to give the reader an idea of the 序. They were on the front hall (前堂) of the private apartments. The wall which was the boundary of this portion of the 'hall' did not extend all the way across, and from the extremity of it short walls were built towards the south, coming forward to about a line with the pillars that supported the roof. These walls were originally called the 序, acc. to the 爾雅;—東西牆謂之序. They were so called, as 'fencing or differencing between the inside and out' (所以序別內外). The screen and tent here spoken of were placed, I believe, in the side space between the 序 and outer wall of the hall. The 東嚮 is descriptive of the position of this space, and is not to be understood of the aspect of the screen and mats, which must always have been 'towards the south.' Gaubil translates 西序 by 'devant l'appartement occidental,' and Medhurst by 'in the western ante-chamber;' but both are wrong. The space was not an 'apartment,' but a portion of the hall with its own designation. Here the emperor, morning and evening, took his seat to listen to affairs of business (此旦夕聽事之坐也). 底席,—'bottom mats.' Ma Yung, Wang Suh, and Gan-kwŏ, all say that these mats (or at least the bottom one of them) were made of 青蒲, 'green rushes or reeds;' and I have so translated. K'ang-shing thinks that bamboo mats, the splints very fine, were intended (底,致也,篾纖致席也). It is really all guess work. 綴 is supposed to have the sense of 雜彩, 'variegated.' 17. 東序西嚮,—comp. on last par. At this point the emp. feasted his ministers and the elders of the kingdom (此養國老,饗羣臣之坐). 豐席,—'great or superior mats.' Mats made of a kind of grass called 莞 (*hwan*) are probably meant;—why they were named 豐席 I cannot tell. The 集傳 calls them 筍席, by mistake apparently for 莞席. 畫=彩色, *i.e.*, silk painted in various colours. 18. 西夾南嚮,—this appears to have been the 西夾室, 'western side apartment,' *i.e.*, of the 'rear hall,' responding to that on the east, which was the 'wing apartment' (翼室), occupied for the time by prince Ch'aou as the place of mourning. Here the emperor had his private meals (此私燕之坐). 筍席,—筍 is commonly used for 'the young and edible shoots of bamboo;' here it is read *yun*, and means a soft, flexible species of bamboo, of which mats were made. 玄紛純,—'dark mixed border.' How it was mixed, I don't know. Perhaps the silk edging was all dark, but of different shades. The 'Daily Explanation' says:—其席之緣,則以黑色之繒雜爲之. The reason, it is said, for preparing all these places, as if king Ching had been still alive, was to afford so many resting places for his spirit, which it was presumed would be present

十九節 越玉五重、陳寶、赤刀、大訓、弘璧、琬琰、在西序、大玉、夷玉、天球、河圖、在東序、胤之舞衣、大貝、鼖鼓、在西房、兌

19 They *set forth* also the five kinds of gems, and the precious things of display. There were the red knife, the great lessons, the large convex symbol of gem, and the rounded and pointed maces,—all in the side space on the west; the large gem, the gems from the wild tribes of the east, the heavenly sounding stone, and the river plan,—all in the side-chamber on the east; the dancing habits of Yin, the large tortoise-shell, and the large drum,—all

at the ceremony of communicating his dying charge to his son. They could not tell at what particular spot it would choose to be, and therefore would enable it to have a choice. As Ts'ae expresses it, 將傳先王顧命,知神之在此乎,在彼乎,故兼設平生之坐.

P. 19. *Display of various precious relics.* 越玉五重陳寶,—this clause covers the rest of the par., which gives in detail the gems and precious relics, with the places in which they were set forth. Ying-tă has noticed this construction of the par.:—此經爲下總目,下復分別言之. I take 陳 passively, and understand a 列 before 玉, governing both it and 寶. 赤刀,—'the red knife.' This was, no doubt, a knife which had been distinguished at some time in the history of the empire. It would be of no use wearying ourselves, as the critics have done in vain, to discover what knife it was. Concerning 'the great lessons' Gaubil enquires:—'Was this the history of the empire, or some Book of religion or morals? or the one and the other?' We might put such questions indefinitely. Wang Suh thought we were to understand the Canons and Counsels of Parts I. and II. Ts'ae would go farther back, to the 'Books of the three 皇 and five 帝,' mentioned by Gan-kwŏ in his Introduction to the Shoo; but he thinks the lessons of Wăn and Woo may also be included! 弘(=大)璧,—see on Bk. VI., p. 4, where also the duke of Chow is represented as holding a mace (珪) in his hand. To the imperial 珪, 'maces,' or 'sceptres,' belonged the 琬琰. From the text we should naturally have concluded that one article was intended by those terms; but from the Chow Le, Bk. XX., on the duties of the 典瑞, we learn that there was one 'gem-token' called 琬, and another called 琰. They were each 9 inches long:—the former rounded, expressive of good will; the other pointed, expressive of sharp severity against evil. All these articles were exhibited in 'the western side-space,' behind the screen, &c., of p. 16. 大玉至東序,—大玉, 'great gem-*stone*;' but said by K'ang-shing to be from mount Hwa. 夷玉, 'gem-*stones* contributed by the E, or wild tribes of the east.' Ts'ae would take 夷 as=常, 'common,' which does not seem at all so likely a meaning. 天球,—see for the meaning of 球, on the 'Yih and Tseih,' p. 9. Gaubil thinks that 天球 means 'the heavenly sphere, a celestial globe, or something else, to represent the movement of the stars.' But the use of the character 球 for 'a globe' is quite modern. 河圖,—this was some scheme to represent the first suggestions of the eight diagrams of Fuh-he. The fable was, that a dragon-horse came forth from the waters of the Ho, having marks or signs on his back, from which that emperor got his idea. See what is said on the 'Book of Lŏ,' p. 321. 胤之至西房,—胤, see on the name of Pt. III., Bk. IV. 大貝,—'great tortoise-shell.' Among the gifts by which the friends of king Wăn propitiated the tyrant Show, when he had confined the rising chief in prison, mention is made of a tortoise-shell curved as the pole of a carriage. There was a drum under the Chow dyn., called 鼖鼓, made 8 feet long. That in the text, however, would probably be a similar

書經

之戈、和之弓、垂之竹矢、在東房。○大輅在賓階面、綴輅在阼階面、先輅在左塾之前、次輅在右塾之前。○

in the western apartment; and the spear of Tuy, the bow of Ho, and the bamboo arrows of Suy,—all in the eastern apartment.

20 The grand carriage was by the guests' steps, facing the south. The next carriage was by the eastern steps, facing the south. The foremost carriage was in the front of the left lobby; and the next carriage was in the front of the right lobby.

instrument transmitted from former times. By the western and eastern apartments we are to understand two rooms, east and west of the 路寢, forming part therefore of the private apartments. They were behind the 夾室 of the 'rear hall,' and of larger dimensions. 兌之至東房,—Tuy, Ho, and Suy were, no doubt, famous artificers of antiquity, and distinguished respectively for the making of the several articles here mentioned. That is all we can be said to know of Tuy and Ho, but Suy is supposed to be the same with Shun's minister of Works.

Ts'ae suggests that the various articles here enumerated were set forth not merely as relics of the empire, but as having been favourites with king Ching;—to keep up the illusion of everything appearing as if he were there alive. He gives also a good remark from Yang She (楊時, 中庸傳):—宗器, 於祭陳之, 示能守也, 於顧命陳之, 示能傳也, 'The articles of honour were set forth at the sacrifices, to show that the emperor could preserve them; they were set forth at the ceremonies of announcing a testamentary charge, to show that he could transmit them.'

P. 20. *Display of imperial carriages.* In the Chow Le, Bk. XXVII., on the duties of the 巾車, we have a full account of the imperial carriages, which were of five kinds,—玉, 金, 象, 革, and 木:—*i.e.*, the grand carriage ornamented with gems; the second, ornamented with metal (gold, we may suppose); the third, ornamented with ivory; the fourth with leather and lacquered; the fifth, a wooden carriage, lacquered. Ts'ae supposes that all the five carriages are included in the text, the grand carriage being the 玉輅 (or 路, which is the more common designation); 綴輅, 'the connected carriage,' being the 金輅; 先輅, 'the front carriage' the 木輅; and 次輅, 'the next carriage (or carriages) in order,' both the 象輅 and the 革路. In this view he differs from all the old commentators. Gan-kwŏ, Ma Yung, and Wang Suh took the carriages in the par. to be those of the Chow Le in the order of their rank, the fourth, or leather carriage—the chariot of war—being omitted, as inappropriate to the occasion. K'ang-shing had a view of his own. The 大輅 was with him, as the others, the 玉路, but the 綴輅 was also a 玉路 No. 2, while the 先輅 and the 次輅 were the 象路 and a 象路 No. 2 (玉路之貳, 象路之貳). I should prefer to adopt the view of Gan-kwŏ and those who agree with him. There can be no satisfactory explanation given of the names 綴, 先, and 次, and our course is simply to translate them as we best can. The carriages were all arranged inside the Loo (路) gate; and this gives us some idea of the dimensions of the palace, or the ground which it inclosed, as two carriages could stand opposite to each other (and not close together, we may suppose) between the gate and the steps by which the hall was ascended. On the west of the hall were the guests' steps, those by which visitors ascended; on the east were those appropriate to the host, the 主階, called here 阼階. The front of those steps was of course towards the south. The 爾雅 says—門側之堂謂之塾, 'Halls by the side of the gate were called 塾.' We may translate 塾 by 'lobby.' Ts'ae observes that the carriages were thus displayed, as in the case of the screens, tents, and relics, that everything might be done as when the king was alive. The student will ask where they were brought from, and how they were brought inside the Loo gate. Of course

廿一節 二人雀弁、執惠、立于畢門之內、四人綦弁、執戈上刃、夾兩階戺、一人冕執劉、立于東堂、一人冕執鉞、立于西堂、一人冕執戣、立于東

21 Two men in brownish leather caps, and holding three-cornered halberds, stood inside the gate leading to the private *apartments:* Four men in caps of spotted deer-skin, holding spears with up-turned blades, stood one on each side of the steps east and west, and near to the platform of the hall. One man in a great officer's cap, and holding an axe, stood in the hall *near the front* at the east *end.* One man in a great officer's cap, and holding a *somewhat different* axe, stood in the hall, near the front at the west *end.* One man in a great officer's cap, and holding a lance, stood at the

they were brought, by the officer called 典路, from their usual houses or repositories. How they were brought inside the Loo gate cannot be explained so clearly. Ming-shing says that from the Loo to the Kaou or outer gate there was a level way. This is not the case now in the structure of the large public buildings from which I have endeavoured to give a general idea of king Ching's palace.

P. 21. *Arrangement of guards about the gate and hall.* 二人至之內,—弁 is sometimes used as a general designation for all coverings of the head used in ancient times. Here it denotes a leathern cap worn by guards, and which is figured something like a 冕, having the surmounting cover, but no pendents attached. 雀弁,—'sparrow cap,' *i.e.*, acc. to K'ang-shing, with reference to the colour, which was like a male sparrow's head. The 惠 was a species of 矛, a kind of spear or lance, sharp-pointed, with hooks bending downwards (凡矛上鋭而旁勾, 上鋭所以象物之芒, 旁勾, 所以象物之生). Gan-kwŏ says the 惠 was 三隅矛, 'a three-cornered *maou.*' I suppose the point above the 'hooks' was fashioned in this way, which would make it more a halberd than a spear. We have seen that 畢門 is another name for 路門. These two men stood, each on one side, inside the fifth gate, within which everything yet described had been transacted.

四人至階戺,—the 綦弁 was different in form from the 雀弁, in being without the surmounting cover. It was made of the skin of a spotted deer, probably the *axis.* The 戈 spear had a blade with upturned edge, projecting on one side from the base of the point. 堂廉曰戺, 'The side of the platform of the hall was called 戺.' 'The two stairs' are mentioned in the last par. We are to conceive of a guard accoutred as described, standing near the platform of the hall on each side of the steps by which it was ascended.

一人至西堂,—the 冕 here was of the same form as that worn by the emperor, but distinguished from it by the number of the pendents and the nature of the gems strung upon them. The critics are probably right in determining that the 冕 here was that worn by a 大夫 or 'great officer,' having 'five pendents with black gems.' 鉞 is the common name for 'a battle-axe.' The 劉 was a weapon of the same kind, but with some peculiarity of form, which it is difficult to ascertain. By 西堂 and 東堂 we are to understand the portion of the 'front hall' or platform east and west, in front of the two 序 described on par. 19. K'ang-shing says:—序內半以前曰堂, 此立於東西堂者, 當在東西廂近階而立也. 一人至西垂,—戣 and 瞿,

書經

垂、一人冕執瞿、立于西垂、一人冕執銳、立于側階。○王（廿二節）麻冕黼裳、由賓階隮、卿士邦君、麻冕蟻裳、入卽位。○太（廿三節）保、太史、太宗、皆麻冕

front and eastern end of the hall. One man, in a great officer's cap, and holding a *somewhat different* lance, stood at the front and western end of the hall. One man in a great officer's cap, and holding a pointed weapon, stood by the steps on the north.

22 The king, in a hempen cap and a variously adorned skirt, ascended by the guests' steps, followed by the nobles aud princes of States, in hempen caps and black ant-coloured skirts. Having

23 entered, they all took their places. The Grand-protector, the Grand-historiographer, and the minister of Religion were all in hempen

are described as being varieties of the 戣, 'a spear or lance with three points.' I do not think that their exact form can be determined. See the figures in Ch'ing Yaou-teen's (程瑤田) 考工創物小言, in the 皇淸經解, 卷五百三十七. The dict. defines 垂 by 堂之盡處, 近階者, 'the extremities of the hall, near the steps.' These men stood east and west respectively from the bearers of the 劉 and the 鉞. See Yaou-teen's 釋宮小記, 經解卷五百三十五. 一人至側階,—Ts'ae says that 銳 ought to be 鈗, after Ying-tă, and on the authority of the 說文, which, however, only defines the character as 'a weapon grasped by the imperial attendants' (侍臣所執兵). 側階,—'the side steps;' but both Ts'ae and Këang Shing agree in saying that the steps on the north of the hall, of which there was only one flight are to be understood. Shing says:—側階, 北下階也, 在北堂之下, 側之言特, 北堂惟一階, 故曰側階. So, also Ying-tă, who observes further, that 'of the seven weapons mentioned in this par. it is only the 戈 of which we have any particular account. Of the rest we have no description. The names and forms of ancient and modern weapons being different, we cannot arrive at any certain knowledge about the various arms here mentioned. Wang Suh contented himself with saying that the characters were names of ancient weapons.'

Pp. 22—24. *The announcement of the testamentary charge; and the manner of it.* All was now ready for the grand ceremony and all the performers, in their appropriate array, take their places in the hall. 22. 麻冕,—see Ana, IX., iii. 黼裳,—the skirt of the emperor's dress on sacrificial occasions was variously adorned. See the 'Yih and Tseih,' p. 4. The 'axe' (黼) was one of the figures upon it, and Ying-tă supposes it is mentioned here, by synecdoche, for all the others. It may be so; but I take 黼, as in p. 15. Ch'aou is here for the first time called 'king;' but still he goes up by 'the guests' steps,' not presuming to ascend by the others, while his father's corpse was in the hall. 隮=升. 蟻裳,—'ant skirts;' meaning dark, like the colour of ants. 'They all entered and took their places;' *i.e.*, the places proper to them, according to their various ranks. 23. 太保至彤裳,—we can easily see how the three dignitaries here mentioned should take the prominent part in the ceremony which they did. Their skirts were of a pale red colour (彤=纁),—the proper colour of their sacrificial dress. 介圭,—'the grand mace' (介=大), a cubit and 2 inches long, called also 鎭圭. See the Chow Le, Bk. XIII., on the duties of the 玉

彤裳、太保承介圭、上宗奉同瑁、由阼階隮、太史秉書、由賓階隮、御王冊命。○曰、廿四王后憑玉几、道揚末命、命汝嗣訓、臨君周邦、率循大卞、燮和天下。用答揚文武

caps and red skirts. The Grand-protector bore the great mace. The minister of Religion bore the cup, and the mace-cover. These two ascended by the eastern steps. The Grand-historiographer bore the testamentary charge. He ascended by the guests' steps, and advanced to the king with the record of the charge, saying,
24 "Our great lord, leaning on the gem-adorned bench, declared his last charge, and commanded you to continue the observance of the lessons, and to take the rule of the empire of Chow, complying with the great laws, and securing the harmony of the empire, so as to respond to and display the bright instructions of Wăn and Woo."

人. It belonged to the emperor, and was one of the emblems of his sovereignty. 上宗,—this was, no doubt, the minister of Religion, the 宗伯 of Bk. XX., p. 9. In the Chow Le he is called 大宗伯, and immediately subordinate in his department were the two 小宗伯. 'Thus,' says K'ang-shing, 'there were three 宗伯. By 上宗 here are intended the 大宗伯 and one of the 小宗伯, one of them carrying the 同, and the other the 瑁.' This view may be rejected without hesitation. 上宗 is the 宗伯 *par eminence*, so denominated probably as superior to the two 小宗伯. 同 is defined—爵名, 'the name of a cup.' It must have been some particular cup which the emperor only had the right to employ in sacrificing. 瑁,—see on the 'Can. of Shun,' p. 7. This was what I have called there 'a sort of frame by which the genuineness of the gem-tokens conferred on the difft. princes was tested.' We see here that it was itself made of gem. We can easily understand how the other tokens or maces could be tested by it; but it is not explained how it was applied to the 璧圭. The Grand-guardian and the minister of Religion ascended by the east or emperor's steps, because the authority of king Ching was, as it were, in their persons, to be conveyed in the present ceremony to his son. 書 is the testamentary charge which the historiographer had written or graved on tablets by the guardian's order;—see par. 12. He ascended by the guests' steps, being only an employé in the premier's department. Other reasons for his doing so have been assigned;—unsatisfactorily. 御 here is best defined by 進, and 御王冊命＝以冊命進於王.

24. 曰,—'saying.' Some make 命 the nominative to this, as if what follows were what had been written. But this is not to be supposed. What was written was what the king had spoken, as recorded in parr. 4—9. In presenting the record the historiographer made the brief speech which is here given. 道揚末命＝宣揚臨終之命. 命汝嗣訓＝命汝嗣守文武之大訓, 'charged you to continue to keep the great lessons of Wăn and Woo.' 臨君周邦,—'to descend and be sovereign over the country (＝empire) of Chow.' 大卞＝大法, 'the great laws.' This clause seems to declare that the emperor was not

之光訓。○王(廿五節)再拜、興、答曰、眇眇予末小子、其能而亂四方、以敬忌天威。○乃(廿六節)受同瑁、王三宿、三祭、三咤、上

25 The king twice bowed *low*, and then arose, and said, "I am utterly insignificant and but a child; how can I be able to govern the four quarters *of the empire* with such a reverent awe of
26 the dread majesty of Heaven?" He then received the cup and the mace-cover. Thrice he advanced with a cup *of spirits;* thrice he sacrificed; and thrice he put the cup down. The minister of Religion said, "It is accepted."

absolute, but subject to certain constitutional laws. Sëë Ke-seuen, however, would make 'the great law' to be that delivered by Shun to Yu in Pt. II., Bk II., p. 15.

Pp. 25, 26. *Ch'aou's acceptance of the sovereignty.* 眇, derived from the *eye* and *small*, has the sense of 'little,' 'insignificant.' The repetition of it expresses that idea strongly. The whole expression—眇眇予末小子 is a very humble designation of himself by the new emperor. 而亂,—亂 is in the sense of 治. The critics nearly all take 而=如, and complete the meaning—其能如父祖治四方, 'can I govern the four quarters of the empire as my ancestors did?' This does not seem to be necessary. 其能而亂四方=其何能而治四方, according to a common usage of 而. 敬忌天威,—comp. 敬迓天威 in par. 6. 敬忌 occurred in Bk. IX., p. 19. 26. 乃受同瑁,—the king received these things from the minister of Religion, who had taken them up to the hall. 'He received them,' says K'ang-shing, 'one with each hand;' but we do not know the manner of the action. Nothing is said of his receiving 'the great mace,' which the guardian had borne up. No doubt he had received it, and disposed of it somehow. 三宿,三祭,三咤,—Ts'ae after Gan-kwŏ defines 宿 by 進爵, 'advanced the cup.' K'ang-shing says: —宿,肅也,徐行前曰肅,'宿 i. q. 肅, meaning to go gently forward.' The two definitions, it will be seen, may admit of a similar interpretation. When the king received the record of the charge he was standing at the top of the western steps a little eastwards, with his face to the north. The historiographer stood by king Ching's coffin, on the south west of it with his face to the east. There he read the charge, after which the king bowed twice, and the minister of Religion, on the south west of the king with his face to the north, presented the cup and mace-cover. The king took them, and having given the cover in charge to an attendant, advanced with the cup to the place between the pillars where the sacrificial spirits were placed. Having filled a cup, he advanced to the east of the coffin, and stood with his face to the west; then going to the spot where his father's spirit was supposed to be, he sacrificed, pouring out the spirits on the ground after which he put the cup on a bench appropriated for it. This he repeated three times. Such is the account of the ceremony given by Ying-tă, which must be nearly correct, if it be not so in every particular. He says three different cups were used, while we should rather suppose that the sacrifices were all made with one,—the 同 which is mentioned. The account in this point, however, agrees better with the 三咤, 咤 being taken in the sense of 奠爵, 'to set down a cup.' There is a difference of opinion both as to the form and meaning of this character. On these points Ch'in Leih has said:—'There are two explanations of 咤. Gan-kwŏ defined it as meaning 奠爵, "to put down a cup;" and most scholars have concurred in his view. Soo Shih, however, considered that it meant "to raise to the teeth without drinking," like 嚌, in the par. below. At first I was inclined to agree with Soo, principally because of the 'mouth' (口) at the side of the character. Subsequent examination altered this view. 咤 is a mistake for 詫, with which the 說文 quotes the passage. Gan-kwŏ's explanation ought not to be altered. If 咤 and 嚌 were the

宗曰饗。○(廿七節)太保受同、降盥、以異同秉璋以酢、授宗人同、拜、王答拜。○(廿八節)太保受同、祭、嚌、宅、授宗人同、拜、王答拜。○(廿九節)太保降、收、諸侯出廟門俟。

27 The Grand-protector received the cup, descended the steps, and washed his hands. He then took another cup, and in his hand a half mace, in order to make the responsive sacrifice. Having given the cup to an attending officer, he did obeisance. The king
28 returned the obeisance. The Grand-protector then took back the cup, and sacrificed with it. He then just tasted the sacrificial spirits, returned to his place, gave the cup to the attendant, and did obeisance. The king returned the obeisance.
29 The Grand-protector descended from the hall, when the various articles were removed, and the princes all went out from the temple gate and waited.

same in meaning, why should we not find one or the other of them in the two contiguous paragraphs?' See the 集說. 上宗曰饗,—both Gan-kwŏ and Wang Suh explain this—'The minister of Religion said to the king, "Drink now;"' referring to the custom for the offerer to drink some of the sacrificial wine, and so receive blessing from the spirit or spirits sacrificed to. I prefer to take the meaning as in the translation. The 'Daily Explanation' says:—宗伯乃傳神命而言曰,先王已饗之矣.

Pp. 27—29. *How the Grand-protector concluded the ceremony.* 27. 太保受同,—the 同 here must be that which the king had used. If we are to suppose with Gan-kwŏ that a difft. cup was employed for each libation, I should think that the 同 may have been used to fill them. 降盥,—'descended—*i.e.*, went down the steps, putting the cup back into a basket (下堂反于篚)—and washed his hands.' It was customary to wash the hands before offering sacrifice. The 璋 is described as a 'half mace carried by ministers' (半圭曰璋,臣所奉). Its make is called 邸剡, in the Chow Le, Bk. XX., 典瑞. With the new cup and this mace the guardian again ascended the steps—以酢—以報祭, 'to return the sacrifice;' here, it seems to me = 'to repeat the sacrifice,' 'to offer a second sacrifice.' The young king had in his sacrifice acknowledged to the spirit of his father that he had received his testamentary charge; it now belonged to the Grand-guardian to inform the same spirit that he had communicated that charge. 授宗人同拜—以授宗人而拜. By 宗人 we are to understand one of the employés in the dept. of the minister of Religion. The 'bowing' was to the spirit of the departed king, represented probably by a tablet, where it was supposed to rest. The guardian could not bow, and carry the cup and mace at the same time; he therefore handed them to the attendant. 王答拜,—the king returned the obeisance as for his father.

28. 嚌,—see on 咤 in the last par. 宅—居. The 'Daily Explanation' expands it into—退居其所立之位. 拜,王答拜,—as in the last par. Many critics, however, say that the bows were made to the new king, and returned by him for himself. I do not think this is unlikely. The critics have not borne sufficiently in mind that the service described in this Book was one of an extraordinary character. 29. 收—有

司收撤器用, 'the proper officers removed the apparatus of the service.' 廟門,—this is the Loo gate. The private apartments had for the time, through the presence of the coffin and by the sacrifices, been converted into a sort of ancestral temple. 俟,—'waited;' *i.e.*, they waited to have an audience of the new sovereign.

I append here the remarks of Wang Pih on this Book and the next. The difficult point on which he dwells will be found treated of on the last par. of the Announcement of king K'ang:—

顧命，康王之誥，二書只當合爲一篇，一正其始，一正其終，中開命誥之詞不多，全是紀載國家始終之大典，謂之敘事，可也，蘇氏之論，以爲三年之喪，既成服而暫釋，非禮也，此言誠足以爲萬世法，周公召公天下之聖賢也，以天下之聖賢，夾輔王室，所以處事制義，當無毫髮之未盡，周公當武王之崩也，位家宰，擁幼主以君臨天下，謂宜鎮定天下如泰山之安，周公以聖人之心待天下，而不肯爲嫌疑之防，亦以聖人之心待骨肉，而不肯起嫌疑之念，行之以大公至正，洞然而無所顧忌者也，豈料姦究餘孽，覷俟門隙，蠱惑人心，倡此一大變乎，成王之顧命，古所末有，豈非懲創前日身履之變，故出此防危慮患之計乎，召公恢張末命，其設施使內外小大之臣，無一髮之可議，所以綏定王室者密矣，而不暇考定禮儀於倉卒之閒，而終不免後世之譏評，吁可畏哉，雖曰處變權宜，未易以常法論，然處變而不失其經，是乃謂之權，以周公召公處變，猶不免後世之議，權可易用乎，古今善用權者，伊尹一人而已。

BOOK. XXIII. THE ANNOUNCEMENT OF KING K'ANG.

康王之誥

一節 王出在應門之內、太保率西方諸侯入應門左、畢公率東方諸侯入應門右、皆布乘黃朱、賓稱奉圭兼幣、曰、一二臣衞、敢執壤奠、皆再拜稽首、王義

1 I. The king came forth and stood *in the space* within the fourth gate of the palace, when the Grand-guardian led in all the princes of the western regions by the left *half* of the gate, and the duke of Peih those of the eastern regions by the right *half*. They then caused their teams of light bay horses, with red manes and tails, to be exhibited; and the princes, raising aloft their secptres and *other* presents, said, "We, your servants, defenders *of the throne*, venture to bring here the productions of our territories and set them forth." With these words, they did obeisance twice, bowing their heads to the earth. The king, righteously continuing the virtue *of his predecessors*, returned their obeisance.

THE NAME OF THE BOOK.—康王之誥, 'The Announcement of king K'ang.' We have seen, on par. 7 of the last Book, that K'ang was the honorary posthumous title conferred on Ch'aou, the successor of Ching, and third sovereign of the dynasty of Chow. In the dict. we find three explanations of the character, used with such an application. It may denote that the individual so denominated was 'an abyss, a fountain, sending forth its waters' (淵源流通曰康); or that 'he was gentle and mild, fond of happiness' (温柔好樂曰康); or that 'he caused the people to be tranquil and happy' (令民安樂曰康). Immediately on K'ang's accession, he made the Announcement

which is here recorded. The Book is found in both the texts; but something more must be said on this point.

The connection between this Book and the last. The Book is found in both the texts. In Fuh-shang's Shoo, however, this Book and the last formed only one Book. Yet the 'little preface' shows us that there were in Confucius' Shoo two Books, one called 'The Testamentary Charge,' and one, 'The Announcement of king K'ang.' We cannot but believe also that Fuh-shang's one Book contained the whole of them both. The only question is as to where the division of them should take place. Choo He says, 'Take away the prefatory notices, and we should not think of making any division. The one part runs naturally, by the connection of the style, into the other, (除却序文讀著,則文勢自相接連). All the old interpreters, excepting Gan-kwŏ,—K'ang-shing, Ma Yung, and Wang Suh,—extended the Testamentary Charge to par. 3 of the Announcement, and made the latter very brief indeed. Much more natural is the division as it stands in the *textus receptus*, and which I here assume was made by Gan-kwŏ, whether he acted merely on his own sense of fitness, or had special authority for the arrangement in the recovered tablets which were submitted to him. As the Books now stand, the first is complete, and the second. The portion which precedes the Announcement is a proper introduction to it, while it is out of place as an appendix to the Testamentary charge.

Tae Tung-yuen, of the present dynasty, pronounces both divisions wrong, but his own view, if he can be said to have one on the point in hand, is very unsatisfactory. Accepting Fuh-shang's arrangement of the whole in one Book, he would divide it into three parts:—the first, parr. 1—13, relating to the Testamentary Charge; the second, parr. 14—29, describing the accession of king K'ang, *the year after his father's death;* and the third, being all comprehended in the Announcement, relating all that took place at the first public audience or levee by the new monarch, immediately after the accession. Granting all this, he still divides the two Books at the same point as Gan-kwŏ. Of his view, that from p. 14 of the Charge the things described all belonged to the year after Ching's death, I shall speak on par. 1. See 戴東原集卷一.

Contents. The action of the Book follows immediately that of the last. A great assembly of princes do homage after their fashion to the new king, and caution and advise him on the discharge of the great duties to which he is called. He responds with the declaration which has given name to the Book, referring to his predecessors, and asking the assistance of all his hearers that his reign might be a not unworthy sequel of theirs. With this the proceedings terminate, and the king resumes his mourning dress which he had put off for the occasion. It will be seen that I have arranged the paragraphs in three chapters.

Ch. I. Pp. 1—3. First audience of the princes and ministers held by king K'ang. Their offerings; and advice. 1. 王出在應門之內=王乃出路(=廟)門,立于應門之內,'The king went out from the Loo gate, and stood in the space between it and the Ying gate.' The 應 gate, we have seen, was the 4th of the palace gates. It took its name, according to Ch'in Sze-k'ae, from a drum near it which was called the 應鼓. Between it and the 5th gate was held the 治朝 or 'audience of govt.,' at which king K'ang on this occasion received the homage of all the princes, showing himself to them for the first time, as 'the son of Heaven.'

[Ts'ae, by mistake, calls this the 內朝. It would not be correct, however, to call it, with Sze-k'ae, the 外朝.]

On the Guardian and the duke of Peih's leading the princes of the west and the east respectively, see on the last Bk., p. 3. The princes of the west entered by the left or eastern side of the gate, and those of the east by the right or western side, and took their places accordingly. This appears to have been all according to rule. The Le Ke, Bk. 曲禮,上. Pt. ii., p. 29, says, 'The host enters on the right of the gate, and proceeds to the eastern steps; the guest enters on the left, and proceeds to the western steps.' From west to east and from east to west, therefore, was the rule. See Lin Che-k'e, *in loc.* 皆布(=陳)乘黃朱,—a team of four horses (馬四匹) was called 乘. Those horses were 黃朱, 'yellow and red.' The former character expresses the general colour of the animals. But 'yellow' in Chinese is applied to many shades; that intended here being, I apprehend, a 'light bay.' 朱 is understood to denote that their tails and manes were dyed this colour. This is inferred from a passage in the 左傳,定十年, which describes such an operation:—宋公子地,有白馬四,公嬖向魋,取而朱其尾鬣以與之. Ts'ae mentions that some interpret the 黃朱 of 'baskets of yellow and red silks,' such as are mentioned in 'The Tribute of Yu;' but such an interpretation is very unlikely in this passage.

賓稱奉圭兼幣=諸侯乃舉所奉之守圭及幣帛, 'The princes raised aloft the several maces which they kept, and their *other* presents.' 賓=諸侯;—see the Chow Le, Bk. XXXVIII., p. 1,—大行人掌大賓之禮, where by 大賓 is meant all the princes from the

嗣德答拜。○太[二節]保暨芮伯咸進相揖皆再拜稽首曰敢敬告天子皇天改大邦殷之命惟周文武誕受羑若

2 The Grand-guardian and the chief of Juy, with all the rest, then advanced and bowed to each other, after which they did obeisance twice, bowing their heads to the ground, and said, 'O Son of Heaven, we venture respectfully to declare our sentiments. Great Heaven altered its decree in favour of the great empire of Yin, and Wăn and Woo of our Chow greatly received the same, and carried it out,

Yaou domain inwards. 奉圭,—these are the maces or gem-tokens conferred on them by the emp., and which they brought with them when they appeared at court. Ying-tă thought that by 幣 we were to understand the horses already exhibited—or a portion of them at least—in the courtyard; but I cannot believe so. A passage in the Book of the Chow Le just quoted, on the duties of the 小行人, beginning 合六幣, may be consulted. Other offerings, referred to in the address below, are no doubt intended. The princes, indeed, could not be raising them aloft themselves; but they had attendants with them who did so. 一二臣,—'we, one or two ministers.' Comp. the use of 二三 in the Ana., III., xxiv., *et al.* 執壤奠＝執壤地所出之贄奠之. We are to suppose that one of the princes spoke in the name of all the others. 王義嗣德答拜,—the words 義嗣德 seem introduced by the recorder of the Book to explain how it was that the young king returned the obeisance of the princes. Lin Che-k'e observes that, as a rule, the sovereign does not return the 拜 of his ministers, yet K'ang was on this occasion the *host* and the princes all were his *guests*, and such an interchange of courtesies was according to etiquette. Ts'ae, Woo Ch'ing, and Këang Shing, all find a deeper meaning in the language. K'ang, they say, was now the declared successor to the throne, but until the year of his father's death was elapsed, his reign could not chronologically commence. His returning the obeisance, therefore, was a recognition by himself and all the princes that he and no other was to be their sovereign;—it was done 'in righteousness,' though not perhaps in rule. Ts'ae says:—答拜既正其爲後,且知其以喪見. Shing's comment is:—誼 (so he reads) 德者,明王當喪,未嗣位,特以繼先王之德,王之體,誼當嗣先王之德,以諸侯之朝,故答拜,此之謂禮以誼起. If this criticism of Ts'ae &c. be correct, as I believe it is, it disposes of the view of Tae Tung-yuen, that all the ceremonies from par. 14 of the last Book took place in the year after Ching's death. There remains, indeed, the difficulty on which he insists.—How was it that the princes of the various domains happened to be at court with their offerings, &c., as if in readiness for the old king's death, and the accession of the new? The difficulty must be acknowledged; but perhaps it would disappear if we had fuller information about the time. To my mind it is not so great as that of supposing that the action is suddenly carried over many months, between parr. 13 and 14 of the last Book, without the slightest note of time in the text:—to say nothing of the conclusion of Ts'ae and others from these words 一王義嗣德.

Pp. 2, 3. *The advice given by all the princes to the young king.* 太保暨芮伯,—the princes advanced in the last par. to present their offerings under the leading of the Guardian and the duke of Peih, as the Chiefs of the east and west respectively. Now the duke of Peih gives place to the baron of Juy, the minister of Instruction, and ranking among the six *K'ing* next to the prime minister. 咸進相揖,—it seems the simplest construction to take 咸＝the 皆, which immediately follows, meaning all the rest of the princes and ministers, who then 相揖, 'moved their left or right arms to one other,' as they took their several places in the order required by the court etiquette. See the account of Confucius' movements in the court of Loo, Ana., X., iii., 2. Ying-tă would confine 咸進 to the Guardian and the baron of Juy.—'These two made all the others advance, motion-

若、克恤西土。○惟新陟王、畢協賞罰、戡定厥功。用敷遺後人休、今王敬之哉、張皇六師、無壞我高祖寡命。

3 manifesting their kindly government in the western regions. His recently ascended Majesty, rewarding and punishing exactly in accordance with what was right, fully established their achievements, and transmitted this happy state to his successors. Do you, O king, now be reverent in your position. Maintain your armies in great order, and do not allow the rarely equalled appointment of our high ancestors to come to harm."

ing to them with their arms to take their proper places, to which motion the princes responded.' Woo Ch'ing has still a difft. view, taking 相 as 相=擯相之人; but this only complicates the construction. 曰,—the Guardian was no doubt spokesman for all the others. 惟周至美若,—the difficulty here is with 美若, which Ts'ae acknowledges that he does not understand. He mentions the view of Soo Shih, that somehow there is an allusion to the confinement of king Wăn by the tyrant Show in 美里; but I do not see how this is to be brought out of the text. He mentions also the conjecture of some that 美若 is the same as 厥若 in p. 6, 美 being an error of the text for 厥. Gan-kwŏ took 美 as meaning 道. Ma Yung and Wang Suh did the same. Ying-tă observes that 美 and 猷 are allied in sound, and that therefore we may explain 美 by 道. I have translated accordingly (文武大受天道而順之), though I rather suspect that the text is corrupted. Këang Shing makes 美=進, and says:—天旼殷之命,惟文武大受,而進順之. There is no authority for such an interpretation of the char. 克恤西土,—the patrimony of the chiefs of Chow was in the west. It was in that part of the empire that their virtue was first recognized, and the foundations of their influence laid. 惟新陟王,—'the newly ascended king.' Ching was not yet buried, and had not received his honorary title. He could only be thus spoken of. 畢協至人休,—by the 'rewards and punishments,' which king Ching is said to have 'finished harmonizing,' *i.e.*, administering according to what was right, we are to understand probably the investitures of many princes, and the suppression of rebellions, with the punishment of the rebels, in which the duke of Chow played so conspicuous a part. These are all, allowably, attributed to the king himself; and by these he completed the work begun by Wăn and Woo, and the dynasty might be considered established in the possession of the empire. 戡=克, 'he succeeded in.' 敷遺後人休,—休 may be considered as in the objective gov. by 遺. 後人 is under the govt. of the preposition 於 understood. Woo Ch'ing gives the meaning of the whole very clearly:—賞當功,罰當罪,盡合其宜,克勝其任,安定文武之功,用能延及于今後人,有此休美. 張皇六師,—'Keep your six armies like a bent bow, and magnify them.' The duke of Shaou would seem to have in mind the counsel given to himself by the duke of Chow, Bk. XVI., p. 21, and also what was said by that duke to king Ching, Bk. XIX., p. 22. 無(=毋)壞我高祖寡命,—寡命 is defined by Ts'ae—艱難寡得之基命, 'the appointment difficult to be got, and such as is seldom to be got.' Këang Shing gives Wang Suh's account of 寡:—美文王少有及之,故曰寡命. The speaker, in 我高祖, '*our* high ancestor (or ancestors),' identifies himself with the imperial House. This gives some support to what is said, on p. 420, of the duke of Shaou's having been the son of king Wăn by a concubine.

○王若曰、四節庶邦侯甸男衞、惟予一人釗報誥。○昔君五節文武丕平富、不務咎、底至齊信、用昭明于天下、則亦有熊羆之士、不二心之臣、

4 II. The king spoke thus:—"Ye princes of the various States, chiefs of the How, Teen, Nan, and Wei domains, I, Ch'aou, the one
5 man, make an announcement in return *for your advice.* The former sovereigns, Wăn and Woo, were greatly just, and enriched *the people.* They did not occupy themselves with people's crimes. Pushing to the utmost and maintaining an entire impartiality and sincerity, they became gloriously illustrious throughout the empire. Then they had officers brave as bears and grisly bears, and ministers of no

Ch. II. Pp. 4—6. Reply of the king to the preceding address; called his Announcement. 4. The *princes* do not appear as parties in the preceding address, nor are the *ministers* (羣臣) mentioned here. But we must suppose that the address emanated from the princes as well as the ministers, and that the reply was made to them equally. No mention is made of the domain which was between the Nan and the Wei; no doubt the chiefs from it were present, and they may have been present also from beyond the Wei, though the text says nothing about them. 予一人釗,—the emperor called himself—'I, the one man,' and did not add his name. It was the rule, however, for the successor to the throne to do so, while the period of mourning for the deceased sovereign lasted.—See the case of the young emperor 猛, mentioned in the 左傳, 昭,二十二年. 報誥,—Lin Che-k'e expands this:—諸侯戒我,故我以誥報之. 5. *The merits of Wăn and Woo; and how they were supported by their ministers and officers.* 昔君,—as in the last Bk., p. 5. 丕平富,—'were greatly just and rich.' The critics are probably correct in interpreting the language of the govt. of Wăn and Woo,—that it was just, carefully guarding the rights of the people, and that it was liberal, making taxation light, so that the people had plenty for all their wants. The paraphrase of the 'Daily Explanation' is:—文武之爲君也,有溥博均平之德,輕徭役,薄賦斂,使天下家給人足,莫不富厚有餘,以豐民之財. Wang Suh's comment is brief and satisfactory:—文武道大,天下以平,萬民以富,是也. 不務咎,—'they did not bend their minds on—address their efforts to—the faults *of the people.*' The meaning seems to be that they were not on the watch to find out crime and punish it. To quote again from the Daily Explanation:—人或有非,不得已而用刑,則輕省而不務深刻,謹愼而不致錯誤,寧失出,毋失入,不專意求人之罪惡而務置之于法. I can by no means accept Këang Shing's definitions of 務=趣, and 咎=災. He says:—文武大平,富天下之民,使不趣于咎災,言爲民除害. 底至齊信,—底至=推行而底其至, 'they pushed the practice and carried it to the utmost.' The question arises of what it was that they carried to the utmost? Was it the virtues indicated in the two previous parr., so that 齊 and 信 are merely adjectives? or are we to take those two characters as nouns, denoting other virtues, having a substantial meaning of their own? Lin Che-k'e, Ts'ae, and the Sung critics generally take the former view. Ts'ae says:—齊信者,兼盡而極其誠也,文武務德,不務罰之心,推行而底其至,兼盡

保乂王家、用端命于上帝、皇天用訓厥道、付畀四方。○六節乃命建侯樹屏、在我後之人、今予一二伯父、尚胥暨顧、綏爾先公之臣服于先王、雖爾

double heart, who *helped them to* maintain and regulate the royal House. Thus *did they receive* the true favouring decree from God; and thus did great Heaven approve of their ways, and give them the four quarters *of the empire*.
6 Then they appointed and set up principalities, and established bulwarks *to the throne*, with a view to us their successors. Now do ye, my uncles, I pray you, consider with one another, and carry out the service which the dukes, your predecessors, rendered to my predecessors. Though your persons be

而極其誠,內外充實. Gan-kwŏ took the latter view, making 齊=中. He gives—致行至中信之道; and I have translated accordingly. Ma Yung likewise took 齊=中; but he put a stop there, and joined 信 as an adverb with the clause that follows, in which construction Këang Shing has followed him. 熊羆之士,—see Bk. II., p. 9. 用端命于上帝,—用='thus,' 'thereby.' 端=正直, 'correct.' We seem to be obliged to understand a 受 after 用:—'they thus received the right favouring decree from God.' Këang Shing is the only one who construes differently, saying—用能端直其命于上帝,言正命以待天也. What follows, 皇天,云云, is an expansion of this clause, a more accurate description of the 'favouring decree.' 訓=順, 'to accord with,'='to approve.' 6. *He appeals to the great princes to assist him as their fathers had assisted Wăn and Woo, and in accordance with the intention of their appointments.* 命建侯樹屏,—the subject of 命 is Wăn and Woo, as founders of the dynasty, so that the force of the term merges in that of 建 and 樹. This is much better than, with Këang Shing, to suppose the par. to begin at 皇天 above, and make 天 the nominative to 命.—乃命之建侯,云云. The 'planting of defences or screens' (樹屏) is nothing different from the 'setting up of princes' (建侯). 在我後之人,—在 must be taken as='with reference to,' 'for the sake of.' 一二伯父,—一二, as in par. 1. Ying-tă observes that when the emperor was addressing princes of large States who bore the same surname with himself, he called them 伯父; and if their principalities were small, he called them 叔父. The princes of a different surname were addressed by him as 伯舅 and 叔舅. Here Cha'ou speaks more particularly to the great princes of his own surname. 尚胥至先王,—胥=相; 暨=與; 胥暨='with one another.' 顧=顧念而不忘, 'to think of and not forget.' 綏=安. According as we take this to mean 'to soothe,' 'to tranquillize,' or 'to pursue quietly and steadily,' we get two views of the passage. Lin Che-k'e, after Soo Shih, adopts the latter view, and compares the sentiment with that in the 'Pwan-kăng,' Pt. i., p. 14, and Pt. ii., p. 14.—使諸侯能盡忠於王室,如其先公之於先王,則爾先公,在天之靈於是安矣, 'If you, princes,

身在外、乃心罔不在王室、用奉恤厥若、無遺鞠子羞。○七節群公既皆聽命、相揖趨出、王釋冕、反喪服。

distant, let your hearts be in the royal house. Thus enter into my anxieties and act in accordance with them, so that I, the little child, may not be put to shame."

7 III. All the dukes, having heard this charge, bowed to one another and hastily withdrew. The king put off his cap, and assumed again his mourning dress.

can discharge all loyal service to the royal House, as your predecessors did to mine, then their souls will have repose in heaven.' I was at first inclined to this view, but a closer inspection of the text makes me prefer the former, which is that given by Ts'ae after Gan-kwŏ. 用奉恤厥若 may be taken as in the translation, after Ts'ae and Gan-kwŏ. The 'Daily Explanation' has:—用以此心仰奉在上之憂勤而順承毋違. Or we may translate—'Be thus reverently anxious to act in accordance with the requirements of your duty,' which is the view taken by Lin Che-k'e.—汝諸侯其職所當順者當奉恤之而不敢忽忘. 鞠子—稚子, 'a child,' one who has not yet left his mother's arms.'

Ch. III. P. 7. THE AUDIENCE CLOSES, AND THE KING RESUMES HIS MOURNING. The use of 相揖 here confirms the interpretation of the phrase which I have adopted in p. 2. The concluding statement, showing that the king and all the officers only assumed their mourning dress at the conclusion of this Announcement, has, since the time of Soo Shih, given rise to a controversy, which will probably be among Chinese critics interminable. According to Shih, everything about the publication of the Testamentary Charge and the subsequent proceedings ought to have been transacted in mourning garb; and the neglect of this was a melancholy violation of *propriety*. If the duke of Chow had been alive, Shih thinks that he would not have allowed it, and he wonders why Confucius selected the documents recording it to form a portion of the Shoo. In point of fact, it cannot be proved positively that any violation of the proprieties established by the duke of Chow was committed, for the ceremonies to be observed on various occasions in the imperial court have not been transmitted. But to a student from the west the controversy appears trivial. We are glad to have the ceremonies actually observed at so distant a date brought before our eyes so graphically as is done in 'The Testamentary Charge,' and 'The Announcement of king K'ang.'

THE BOOKS OF CHOW.

BOOK XXIV. THE CHARGE TO *THE DUKE OF* PEIH.

畢命

惟一節十有二年、六月庚午朏、越三日壬申、王朝步自宗周、至于豐、以成周之衆、命畢公保釐東郊。○王二節若曰、

1 I. In the sixth month of his twelfth year, the day of the new moon's appearance was Kăng-woo, and on Jin-shin, the third day after, the king walked in the morning from the honoured city of Chow to Fung, and there, with reference to the multitudes of Ching-chow, gave charge to the duke of Peih to protect and regulate the eastern frontier.

INTRODUCTORY NOTE. If that reign must have been happy which, extending over a considerable number of years, has yet left few or no memorials in history, that of king K'ang may be so characterized. It extended over twenty-six years, but no other event of it, after the Announcement of the last Book, is alluded to in the Shoo or by Sze-ma Ts'een, but that appointment of the duke of Peih, to which we have now arrived. Ts'een, indeed, tells us that 'during the time of kings Ching and K'ang, the empire was in a state of profound tranquillity, so that punishments were laid aside, and not used for more than forty years' (成康之際,天下安寧,刑錯四十餘年不用). Happy China!

THE NAME OF THE BOOK.—畢命, 'The Charge to *the duke of* Peih.' The territory of Peih was in the pres. dis. of Ch'ang-ngan (長安), dep. of Se-ngan. It was not a large principality, whose ruler was entitled to be styled duke or *Kung*. That title is employed here as a denomination of dignity or office, the chief of Peih having succeeded to the duke of Chow as Grand-Tutor;—see on Bk. XXII., p. 3. He was a scion of the House of Chow. This and his being Grand-Tutor may both be inferred from the manner in which king K'ang addresses him as 父師. Ch'in Sze-k'ae says that his name was Kaou (高). He must have been well advanced in years, when the 'Charge' recorded here was addressed to him, for, acc. to p. 5, he had played his part in the fortunes of his House from the time of king Wăn. The Book was not in the Shoo of Fuh-shang.

CONTENTS. 'King K'ang,' says Ts'ae, 'considering *the condition of* the multitudes of Ching-

chow, appointed the duke of Peih to protect and regulate *that district and its people*. This Book contains the charge to him as it was recorded on tablets.'

Keun-ch'in, who had succeeded to the duke of Chow in charge of Ching-chow, has followed him to the grave. By the labours of those two great ministers, a considerable change had been effected in the character of the people of Yin who had been transferred to that district. King K'ang appoints the duke of Peih to enter into and complete their work, adopting such measures as the altered character of the people, and altered circumstances of the time, called for. The charge occupies all the Book after an introductory paragraph, and may be divided into three chapters, each introduced by the words—'The king said.'

The first, parr. 2—5, speaks of what had been accomplished in Ching-chow, and the admirable qualities of Kaou which fitted him to accomplish what remained to be done. The second, parr. 6—11, speaks of the special measures which were called for by the original character and by the altered character of the people. The third, parr. 12—15, dwells on the importance of the charge, and stimulates the duke, by various motives, to address himself to fulfil it effectually.

Ch. I. P. 1. THE TIME; PLACE; AND GENERAL NATURE OF THE CHARGE. 惟十至壬申,—朏, see on Bk. XII., p. 2. As it denotes the third day of the moon, we are again enabled to bring the commonly received chronology to the test of calculation. Here I will give the note of Gaubil, as on par. 2 of 'The Testamentary Charge:'—'It is agreed that the day 庚午 here is the third day of the sixth moon of the calendar of Chow. Lew Hin and Pan Koo pretend that this was the year corresponding to B.C. 1,067, to which year they refer the twelfth year of king K'ang; and this chronology is followed in the 通鑑綱目. In the year B.C. 1,067, the 16th of May was, indeed, the day 庚午, or the 7th of the cycle, but the 14th of May was not the first day of the moon which did not happen till several days after; and that year therefore was not the 12th of K'ang's reign. Laying down the principle avowed by Pan Koo and Lew Hin about the third day of the moon, the cycle names in the text agree with the year B.C. 1,056. The 16th of May was the day of new moon in China; the 18th, the third day of the moon, was 庚午; and this month was the sixth in the calendar of Chow, since during it the sun entered the sign of the Twins. From "The Announcement of Shaou," "The Announcement about Lŏ," and this Book, we see that the Chinese astronomers of those times counted the day when the sun and moon were veritably in conjunction to be the first day of the moon. The time of a lunation was divided into the time of brightness and the time of obscurity; the passage from the obscure to the bright time was described as "the death of the obscure," and the passage from the bright to the obscure time as "the birth of the obscure;"—see "The Testamentary Charge." The standard History gives 26 as the years of K'ang's reign; if that be correct, his death took place B.C. 1,042, since we have found that B.C. 1,056 was his 12th year; and B.C. 1,067 was the first year of his reign.

'This year, B.C. 1,067, should be marked by the cycle characters 庚戌, the 11th year of the cycle. Now, the "Bamboo Books" do mark his first year so; but the year which they denote is that B.C. 1,007, differing from the true year, which appears to have been demonstrated, exactly an entire cycle of 60 years.'

[As the cycle names of the days here afford ground for such important conclusions, in which Gaubil, I may state, was anticipated by Chang Yih-hing (the Buddhist priest mentioned on page 19), under the T'ang dynasty, it becomes desirable to establish the genuineness of the par., which may be hastily thrown aside with the remark that it only occurs in one of the controverted Books. Now this we are able to do, so far as the year, month, and days are concerned, from a passage in the 漢律歷志,第一下, being that referred to by Gaubil, and which is to this effect:—康王十二年,六月戊辰朔,三日庚午,故畢命豐刑曰,惟十有二年六月庚午,朏,王命作策豐刑. We do not know what to make of 豐刑 here; but it is plain that Lew Hin had seen a copy of the 'Charge to Peih,' in this par. substantially the same with what we have in the text before us.]

王朝至于豐,—朝步, see on Bk. III., p. 1. 宗周,—see on Bk. XX., p. 1. We are to understand Haou. 'The king went to Fung,' says Ts'ae, 'to give the charge in the temple of king Wǎn, because the duke of Peih had been minister to him.' 成周,—this was what was called 下都, 'the lower capital,' See on Bk. XXI., p. 1., where also 東郊, 'the eastern frontier,' is explained. 保一安; 釐一理. The time had come to adopt a difft. method with the people of Yin from those pursued by their former overseers, the duke of Chow and Keun-ch'in;—as is explained below.

嗚呼、父師、惟文王武王、敷大德于天下、用克受殷命。○三節惟周公左右先王、綏定厥家、毖殷頑民、遷于洛邑、密邇王室、式化厥訓、既歷三紀、世變

2 II. The king spoke thus:—Oh! Grand-tutor, it was when king Wăn and king Woo had diffused their great virtue through the empire that they were able to receive the appointment which Yin
3 had enjoyed. The duke of Chow acted as assistant to my royal predecessors, and tranquillized and established their empire. Cautiously did he deal with the refractory people of Yin, and removed them to the city of Lŏ, that they might be quietly near the royal house, and thus be transformed by its lessons. Six and thirty years have elapsed, the generation has been changed, and manners

Ch. II. Pp. 2—5. First part of the Charge. How the empire had been got by Wan and Woo, assisted by the duke of Chow; what the duke had done with the people of Yin. New measures were now called for; and the character of the duke of Peih, which marked him out as the man for the occasion. 2. 父師,—acc. to what was said on 一二伯父 in par. 6 of the last Book, we might translate this by 'Uncle and Tutor.' Lin Che-k'e, moreover, says that the duke of Peih was 'a son of king Wăn, a younger brother of king Woo and the duke of Chow, and an uncle of king Ching (文王之子,武王周公之弟,成王之叔父); but I do not know his authority for such a statement. Sze-ma Ts'een has given the names of Wăn's ten sons by his queen T'ae-sze, and this duke is not among them. I believe he was a scion of the House of Chow; but we may take 父師 here in the same way as in Pt. IV., Bk. XI., p. 1, as =太師. If he had really been a brother of the duke of Chow, we might have expected some reference to the fact in the course of the Charge. 3. 惟周公左右先王,—the critics generally understand by 先王 all K'ang's predecessors,—Wăn, Woo, and Ching. Lin Che-k'e contends with much force that the phrase should in this place be restricted to king Ching. It is hardly necessary to depart from the more common view. Ching must certainly be included. Gaubil gives—'le roi, mon pere;' Medhurst erroneously,—'these former kings.' 厥家=厥國家, 'their (or his) empire.' 毖殷至厥訓,—comp. Bk. XIV., pp. 18—21. 密邇王室,—comp. 密邇先王, Pt. IV., Bk. V., Pt. i., p. 9. The 王城 or 'imperial city' of Lŏ was the place where the 'nine vases' of the empire were deposited, and where it was intended that the emperor should give audience to all the princes. The people of Yin in Ching-chow and the country about might very well be said to be near the 'royal house.' The 'Daily Explanation' expands 式化厥訓 into 日聞我周之仁聲善政,日親我周之仁人君子,由是潛消其悍暴之習,而漸化于德義之訓. 既歷三紀,—'there have elapsed—been gone through—three *Ke*, or periods of twelve years.' A period of twelve years was denominated a 紀, acc. to Ying-tă, because in that period the planet Jupiter completed a revolution in his orbit, and the cycle characters of the 地支, or 'earthly branches,' had also run their round. We do not know exactly from what year we are to reckon these 36 years. If, as is commonly believed, the reign of Ching lasted 37 years, and we add 12 years of K'ang's reign to them, we obtain four duodenary periods, and not three. Even

風移、四方無虞、予一人以寧。○四節道有升降、政由俗革、不臧厥臧、民罔攸勸。○五節惟公懋德、克勤小物、弼亮四世、正色率下、罔不祗師言、

have altered. Through the four quarters of the empire there is no occasion for anxiety, and I, the one man, enjoy repose.

4 The prevailing ways now tend to advancement and now to degeneracy, and measures of government must be varied according to the manners *of the time*. If you do not manifest your approval of what is good, the people will not be led to stimulate themselves

5 in it. But your virtue, O duke, is strenuous, and you are cautiously attentive to small things. You have been helpful to and brightened four reigns, with deportment all-correct, leading on the inferior officers, so that there is not one who does not reverently take your words as a law. Your admirable merits were that of many in the

if we reckon from the date of the 'Announcement about Lŏ,' we have more than 40 years. A supposition of Gaubil, that king K'ang intends the time which had elapsed from the death of the duke of Chow, seems to me very likely. 世變,—our word 'generation' answers to 世. Ts'ae says;—父子曰世, 'Father and son are called a 世.'—'One generation passeth away, and another cometh.' 四方無虞,—see the use of 無虞 in Pt. II., Bk. IV., p. 6.

P. 4. *Govt. must be varied according to the character of the people; the time was come for discriminative measures.* 道有升降,—it would be hard to say how Gan-kwŏ understood this clause. His comment on it is—天道有上下交接之義, which Ying-tă only makes more dark by his expansion of it. I have followed Ts'ae who observes that 有升=有隆, 'generous,' 'affluent,' 'good;' and 有降=有汚, 'foul,' 'impure;' and then illustrates this clause and the next by saying that, when the duke of Chow took charge of Ching-chow, the character of the people, with their evil habits all-unchanged, rendered a firm and cautious dealing with them necessary. When Keun-ch'in took charge, the people were considerably improved, and hence he was enjoined to be forbearing with them, and promote harmonizing measures. 不臧云云,—the people, we are to suppose, were now in that state, that the good of many of them deserved to be acknowledged, and that acknowledgement would act as the best stimulus to others. The paraphrase of the 'Daily Explanation' is:—至于今日,善者固多,而不善者亦容或有之,務必寬嚴竝施,舆起其爲善者,且懲治其爲不善者,庶幾殷民有所畏慕,益相勸而化耳. 臧=善. In the first case it is a verb; in the second, a noun in the concrete. 5. *The great virtue of the duke of Peih.* 克勤小物,—小物, 'little things,'='small matters' (細行).

By 四世, 'four generations,' we are to understand the reigns of Wăn, Woo, Ching, and the existing reign of K'ang. Ying-tă refers to a passage in the 國語,晉語四 (near the end), about king Wăn, how he 詢於八虞,而咨於二虢,......而訪於辛尹,重之以周,召,畢,榮, which shows that in the 8th cent. B.C., it was the current belief that the duke of Peih had been a minister of king Wăn. 正色率下,—'with correct countenance

嘉績多于先王、予小子垂拱仰成。○六節 王曰、嗚呼、父師、今予祗命公以周公之事、往哉。○七節 旌別、淑慝、表厥宅里、彰善癉惡、樹之風聲、弗

times of the former kings; I, the little child, have but to let my robes hang down, and fold my hands while I look up for the complete effect *of your measures.*"

6 III. The king spoke, "Oh! Grand-tutor, I now reverently
7 charge you with the duties of the duke of Chow.—Go! Signalize the good, separating the bad from them; give tokens of your approbation to their neighbourhoods, distinguishing the good so as to make it ill for the evil, *thus* establishing the influence and reputation *of their virtue.* Where the people will not obey your lessons and statutes,

leading on those below you.' But by 色 we are to understand all the deportment. Lin Che-k'e refers, aptly enough, to the words of Confucius about the man in authority, Ana. XX., ii., 2,—君子正其衣冠尊其瞻視儼然人望而畏之不亦威而不猛乎. 祗師言=祗敬而師法公言. The 師 is a verb, ='to imitate,' 'to take as a model.' 嘉績多于先王,—this clause is in a measure opposed to the next.—'Even under my predecessors your admirable merits have been many; how much more must I be indebted to you!' 予小子云云,—we must not understand 'the robes let down and the hands folded' as expressive of idleness and indifference. The king figures himself in the ancestral temple, in his robes and attitudes of reverent ceremony, happy in the thought that he had so able a minister on whom he might entirely depend. Compare the same language in the conclusion of Bk. III., p. 10.

The king certainly is not sparing in his laudation of the minister.

Ch. III. Pp. 6—11. SECOND PART OF THE CHARGE:—THE SPECIAL DUTIES WHICH THE DUKE WAS TO DISCHARGE; THE DIFFICULTIES WITH WHICH HE WOULD HAVE TO CONTEND; AND THE METHOD BY WHICH HE MIGHT BE SUCCESSFUL. 6. 祗命,—'reverently charge.' The charge being so great, being communicated in the temple of king Wăn, having respect to the completion of the work of the duke of Chow, king K'ang could not but have a feeling of reverence in delivering it. The work that Keun-ch'in had done is not mentioned, but he appears in p. 13. 7. Many of the people of Yin had profited so much by the labours of the duke of Chow and Keun-ch'in with them, that they might be pronounced reformed, and should receive marks of favour, while those who continued obstinately bad should be made to feel that they were marked. 旌別 (low. 4th tone) 至風聲,—these clauses show how the good should be dealt with. 旌 is the name of a peculiar kind of flag, used among other purposes to mark out places or paths; as a verb here, it = our 'to signalize.' 旌別淑(=善)慝(=惡)=旌善別惡, with the meaning in the translation. 表厥宅里=表異善人之居里. 表,—'a signal,' 'to set up a signal;'—akin to 旌. 彰善癉惡=彰顯其善以病其為惡者. The two parts of the clause are connected as in the first clause. 樹之風聲,—with 樹之 comp. the expression 死之, Ana., XIV., xvi. The whole ='planting—setting up—for them, *i.e.*, the good, their influence and reputation.' The 'Daily Explanation' gives for it—善者之風聲,使之卓然樹立,顯于當時,傳于後世. 弗率至畏慕,—these three clauses describe how the bad

率訓典、殊厥井疆、俾克畏慕、申畫郊圻、慎固封守、以康四海。○政(八節)貴有恆、辭尚體要、不惟好異、商俗靡靡、利口惟賢、餘風未殄、公其

mark off the boundaries of their hamlets, making them fear *to do evil* and desire *to do good.* Define anew the borders and frontiers, and be careful to strengthen the guardposts through the territory, in order to secure the tranquillity of the whole empire.

8 "In measures of government to be consistent and constant, and in proclamations a combination of completeness and brevity, are valuable. There should not be the love of what is extraordinary. Among the customs of Shang was the flattery of superiors. Sharp-tonguedness was the sign of worth. The remains of these manners are not yet obliterated. Do you, O duke, bear this in mind.

should be dealt with. 殊厥井疆＝殊別其井居疆界. 井,—'the wells,' about which their farms were distributed. It may be translated here by 'hamlets.' We see how the people—the peasantry—of Yin were distributed over the country of which Ching-chow might be considered the centre. 申畫郊圻,—Ts'ae says that 圻 and 畿 are the same; but the meaning of 界, given for 圻 in the dict., answers very well. Wang Ts'ëaou says:—'The city of Lŏ and the honoured capital of Chow were the two centres of the imperial domain. The honoured capital of Haou might be considered to have a square of 800 *le*, or 64 squares of 100 *le* each, attached to it; and Lŏ or Ching-chow to have a square of 600 *le*, or 36 squares of 100 *le* each. The extent from east to west was greater than from north to south, but altogether there was as much as a square of 1,000 *le*. Thus the borders of Lŏ were also the borders of Haou.' See the 集說. 固封守, 'strengthen the *places of* ward within the boundaries over which you are appointed.'—封域之內, 高深險阻已設守禦者, 益謹飭之. Wang Ch'ung-yun observes that, while the separation of the good from the bad was calculated to have a beneficial moral effect upon the people, these latter measures were a safeguard against any attempts at insurrection.

Pp. 8—11. *The difficulties the duke would have to contend with; and how to contend with them.*

8. 恆 is defined as the opposite of 暫 or 'what is brief.' 辭＝辭令, 'proclamations,' 'govt. orders.' 體要＝理完言簡, 'complete in principle, and compendious in expression.' We may take 貴 and 尚 as synonyms. 靡靡 is taken as having the meaning of 隨順, 'ready acquiescence,' *i.e.*, of inferiors with their superiors. Ying-tă shows that this was the meaning given to the phrase in the time of Confucius, by quoting the remarks of Han K'e (韓起), a statesman of Tsin, contemporary with the sage:—韓宣子稱紂使師延作靡靡之樂. 靡靡者, 相隨順之意. [I have tried without success to verify this reference. Han K'e appears repeatedly in the 左傳, 昭公, but I have not met with the remark attributed to him. Ying-tă has probably confounded 韓宣子 with the scholar 韓非子, in the 3d Bk. of whose Works (十過第十) mention is made of 師延, who 與紂爲靡靡之樂.] The sharp-tonguedness of the times of Yin is indicated in Pt. IV., Bk. V., Pt. iii., p. 9, and Bk. VII., Pt.

書經

念哉。○我九節聞曰、世祿之家、鮮克由禮、以蕩陵德、實悖天道、敝化奢麗、萬世同流。○十節茲殷庶士、席寵惟舊、怙侈滅義、服美于人、驕淫矜侉、將由惡終、雖收放心、閑

9 I have heard the saying—'Families which have for generations enjoyed places of emolument seldom observe the rules of propriety. They become dissolute and do violence to virtue, setting themselves in positive opposition to the way of Heaven. They ruin the formative principles of good; encourage extravagance and display;
10 and tend to carry all *future* ages on the same stream with them.' Now the officers of Yin had long relied on the favour which they enjoyed. In the confidence of their prideful extravagance they extinguished their *sense of* righteousness. They displayed before men the beauty of their robes, proud, licentious, arrogant, and boastful;—the natural issue was that they should have ended in being thoroughly bad. Although their lost minds have been *in a measure*

i., p. 17. 9. On the general lesson of this par., comp. various passages of Bk. XV. 由禮=從禮, 'to pursue the course of propriety.' 陵=犯, 'to violate,' or 侵, 'to invade,' 'encroach upon.' 敝化,—'they injured transforming changes,' *i.e.*, they corrupt the public manners, acc. to which the characters of individuals are moulded. 敝=壞. 10. 席寵惟舊,—席 is used in the sense of 因 or 藉, 'to depend on.' Their 'favour' had been to them the mat on which they rested. The dict. gives on the character a note of Yen Sze-koo:—席猶因也, 言若人之坐於席也. For 怙侈 the 'Daily Explanation' gives—怙恃其驕侈. 侈 is 'extravagance' taking its rise from pride. 服美于人,—Lin Che-k'e understands this as meaning—'They tried to surpass other men in the beauty of their dress' (美于他人); but it is better to take the 于 after the adj. as in p. 5,—嘉績多于先王. Luh Këen (陸鍵: Ming dyn.) defines 驕 as=心肆, 'the dissoluteness of the mind;' 淫=心佚, 'the voluptuousness of the mind;' 矜=心傲, 'the arrogance of the mind;' 侉=心浮, 'the froth of the mind.' 將由惡終,—the 將 shows the natural issue of the various ways and attributes which have been described, and attributed to the officers of Yin. It would be wrong to translate it as an historical future. We find a portion of this par., without any note of quotation, in the 左傳, where 必 appears instead of 將.—襄, 二十七年, 叔孫曰, 服美于人, 必以惡終. 雖收, 云云,—it is here that the phrase, 放心, 'the lost mind,' to which so much importance was subsequently attached by Mencius, occurs for the first time in the classics. 閑之,—'to bar them.' 'The root of evil,' says Ch'in King, 'might still be present; and though the lost mind has been recovered, it may be carried off again on the occurrence of temptation.' 11. 資 (=貨財, 'goods,' 'pro-

之惟艱。○資(十一節)富能訓、惟以永年、惟德惟義、時乃大訓、不由古訓、于何其訓。○王(十二節)曰、嗚呼、父師、邦之安危、惟茲殷士、不剛不柔、厥德允修、○惟(十三節)周公克慎厥始、惟君陳克和厥中、惟公克成厥終、三后協心、同底于道、

11 recovered, it is difficult to keep them under proper restraint. If with their property and wealth they can be brought under the influence of instruction, they may enjoy lengthened years. Virtue and righteousness!—these are the great lessons. If you do not follow with them *these* lessons of antiquity, wherein will you instruct them?"

12 IV. The king said, "Oh! Grand-tutor, the security or the danger of the empire depends on these officers of Yin. If you are not *too* stern with them nor *too* mild, their virtue will be truly cultivated.

13 The duke of Chow was able to exercise the necessary caution at the beginning *of the undertaking;* Keun-ch'in displayed the harmony proper to the middle of it; and you, O duke, can bring it at last to a successful issue. You three princes will have been one in aim, and have equally arrived at the proper way. The penetrating power of your principles, and the good character of your

perty.') 富能訓,惟以永年,—it is difficult to say whether we should understand 資富能訓 as meaning, 'Having property and wealth, if they can also be instructed,' or 'Notwithstanding their property and wealth, if they can be instructed.' I think the former view is preferable, as Ch'in King says:—既富以養其身,又訓以養其心,全正性,所以順正命,此所以永年也. 時乃大訓,一時=是. 'The lessons of antiquity' can only mean those of 'virtue and righteousness.' The crowding of difft. subjects into one short paragraph is annoying and perplexing.

Ch. IV. Pp. 12—15. THE CONCLUSION OF THE CHARGE:—IMPORTANCE OF THE WORK ENTRUSTED TO THE DUKE; AND MOTIVES TO MAKE HIM EXERT HIMSELF. 12. 邦之安危,—by 邦 here we must understand the whole empire. The king had said in par. 8 that he had no occasion for anxiety about anything in the empire. His language here is different. 'It shows,' says Ts'ae, 'that he was one who could not rest easily in small achievements.' He would make assurance doubly sure. 不剛不柔,—this is the rule of conduct for the duke of Peih. He was to pursue the right medium in dealing with the officers of Yin. 13. 惟周公至厥終,—comp. Bk. XXI., p. 7. 三后協心,同底于道,—Wang Ts'ëaou says:—三后之政,前後以相濟爲心,是日協心,適因革之宜,各行其所當然,是日同底

道洽政治、澤潤生民、四夷左衽、罔不咸賴、予小子永膺多福。○ 十四節 公其惟時成周、建無窮之基、亦有無窮之聞、子孫訓其成式惟乂。○ 十五節 嗚呼、罔曰弗克、惟既厥心、罔曰民寡、惟慎厥事、欽若先王成烈、以休于前政。

measures of government, will exert an enriching influence on the people, so that the wild tribes, with their coats buttoning on the left, will all seek their dependence on them, and I, the little child,
14 will long enjoy much happiness. Thus, O duke, here in Ching-chow will you establish for ever the imperial possession *of Chow*, and you will have an inexhaustible fame. Your descendants will follow your perfect pattern, governing accordingly.
15 "Oh! do not say, 'I am unequal to this;' but exert your mind to the utmost. Do not say, 'The people are few;' but attend carefully to your business. Reverently follow the accomplished achievements of the former kings, and complete the excellence of the government of your predecessors."

于道, 'The govt. of the three princes differing as this earlier and that later, yet each aiding the others, is what is called 協心; their measures, different as the change of manners and times required, yet always right in their own circumstances, is what is called 同底于道.' 道洽,—comp. 洽於天下, Mencius, II., Pt. I., i., 7. 道洽 and 政治 are one thing, or the course and the issue of the rule of Ching-chow. 生民,—see Bk. V., p. 12. 左衽,—see Ana., XIV., xviii., 2. 予膺多福,—see Bk. XXI., p. 14. 14. 公其至之基,—Gan-kwŏ expounds this—公其惟以是成周之治爲周家立無窮之基業. 子孫訓(=順)其成式惟乂,—the 'Daily Explanation' gives for this:—公之子孫有治民之責者, 亦遵守成法, 以致治安, 譽流奕世, 謀詒後昆, 皆于公今日基之矣. 15. 惟既厥心,—既=竭盡, 'to exert to the utmost.' The duke ought not to shrink from his duty, because it was arduous. 罔曰至厥事,—neither might he trifle with his work, thinking it easy. 欽若,—comp. in the 'Can. of Yaou,' p. 3. By 'the former kings' we are to understand Wăn, Woo, and Ching. 以休于前政,—the 'former government' is that of the duke of Chow and Keun-ch'in. The clause will bear to be translated,—'that you may realize an excellence superior to the govt. of your predecessors;' but we have two instances of 于 after an adj. in this Book, and not indicating comparison. I prefer to consider 休 as an active verb, and the whole=以休美周公君陳之政.

THE BOOKS OF CHOW.

BOOK XXV. KEUN-YA.

君牙

王若曰、嗚呼、君牙、惟乃祖乃父、世篤忠貞、服勞王家、厥有成績、紀于太常。○惟予小

1 The king spoke thus:—"Oh! Keun-ya, your grandfather and your father, one after the other, with a true loyalty and honesty, laboured in the service of the royal House, accomplishing a merit

INTRODUCTORY NOTE. In the note at the commencement of the last Book, I have said that the annals of king K'ang are peculiarly barren. No other event of his reign is commemorated but the appointment of the duke of Peih to the govt. of Ching-chow. During his time, however, several worthies of whom we have had occasion to speak passed off the stage. In Loo, Pih-k'in, the son of the duke of Chow, died B.C. 1,062 (or 1,063), and was succeeded by his son Ts'ew (酋), or duke K'aou (考公), who gave place in the king's 20th year to duke Yang (煬公). Yang died in the last year of the reign, and was followed by his son Tsae (宰), or duke Yew (幽公). To the same year is assigned the death of Shih, the duke of Shaou, the co-worker with the duke of Chow in the establishment of the dynasty.

The viscount of Wei, the prince of K'ang, and Chung of Ts'ae have all likewise their deaths chronicled in this reign.

King K'ang was succeeded by his son Hëa (瑕), known as king Ch'aou (昭王), to whom the standard History assigns a very long reign of 51 years. The Shoo, however, is silent about him. The appointment of Keun-ya to be minister of Instruction, in the Book to which we have now arrived, was made by king Muh (穆), Ch'aou's son and successor, the first year of whose reign is commonly placed in B.C. 1,000 (or 1,001). The brief notices of Ch'aou and his reign which we find in Sze-ma Ts'een and other authors are unfavourable to him. The first symptoms of decay in the dynasty date, indeed, from his time. In B.C. 1,038 the duke of Loo was murdered by a younger brother, who established himself in his room, while the king could do nothing to avenge so great an outrage.

Ch'aou died in a hunting expedition to the south, according to most accounts, being drowned in the river Han, which he was crossing in a boat, whose planks were only glued together! This account is no doubt fabulous.

THE NAME OF THE BOOK.—君牙, 'Keun-ya.' The name is taken from that of the person whose appointment to be minister of Instruction forms the subject of the Book. Keun-ya's surname is not known. His father and grandfather, it appears, had been in the same office before him; and hence it is conjectured that he may have been the grandson of the Chief of Juy, who was minister of Instruction at the commencement of king K'ang's reign. This is possible; but we cannot say more, for, acc. to the received chronology, the commencement of Muh's reign was separated from that of K'ang by nearly 80 years.

The Book was not in Fuh-shang's Shoo.

CONTENTS. The Book is short, containing only seven paragraphs. The 4th and 5th parr.

子、嗣守文武成康遺緒、亦惟先王之臣、克左右亂四方、心之憂危、若蹈虎尾、涉于春冰。三節○今命

2 which was recorded on the grand banner. I, who am but a little child, have inherited the charge of the line of government transmitted from Wăn and Woo, from Ching and from K'ang, and keep also thinking of their ministers who were able to aid them in the good government of the four quarters *of the empire;*—the trembling anxiety of my mind makes me feel as if I were treading

speak of the duties of the minister of Instruction. The other paragraphs stimulate Keun-ya to the discharge of them by motives drawn from the merits of his forefathers, and the services which he would render to the empire, making his sovereign no unworthy descendant of Wăn and Woo.

Pp. 1—3. *The king speaks of the merits of Keun-ya's grandfather and father; of his own anxiety to get ministers equal to those of his ancestors; and of his hope that Keun-ya would render him services which should prove that he was the worthy scion of a good stock.* 1. 世篤至王家,—Ma San (馬森; Ming dyn.) gives the following definitions of 忠 and 貞: 一盡心之謂忠,無一念之不實也,守道之謂貞,無一事之不正也, 'The putting forth one's whole mind is called 忠; there is not in it the insincerity of a single thought: holding firm the way of principle is called 貞; there is not in it the incorrectness of a single action.' We must understand a preposition, 於 or 爲, between 勞 and 王. 紀於太常,—太常 is the name of the grand imperial banner. The Chow Le, Bk. XXVII., makes mention of the 司常, or 'superintendent of banners,' who had charge of all the 'nine flags or banners' (九旗). 常, therefore, is in that passage used apparently as synonymous with 旗. Commonly, however, we find it used with reference to the grand standard, on which were figures of the sun and moon, with figures of dragons, lying along its breadth, one over the other head above tail. The sun and moon, however, were the distinctive figures of the grand banner. It was borne aloft when the emperor went to sacrifice;—see the same Bk. of the Chow Le, on the duties of the 巾車, p. 2. The names of meritorious ministers, moreover, were inscribed on it during their life time, preparatory to their sharing in the sacrifices of the ancestral temple after their death;—see the Chow Le, Bk. XXX., on the duties of the 司勳, p. 3. 2. 惟予至遺緒,—it is inferred, and with reason, from the language of this clause, that the king had lately succeeded to the throne, and that this Charge to Keun-ya was delivered in the early part of his reign. Chronologists generally refer it to his 3d year. But how is it that while speaking of the line or clue of govt., as being transmitted to him from Wăn and Woo, Ching and K'ang, he makes no mention of K'ang's successor, his own father? The prefatory note expressly assigns the charge to king Muh. 亦惟至四方,—the meaning of this is, that while the king felt that he himself could not follow his predecessors *passibus æquis*, he thought also how they, so superior to him, had yet been assisted by very able ministers. What cause was there then for anxiety to him! 惟一思. In the edition of the 'Thirteen *King*,' for 先王之臣 we have 先正之臣. But Gan-kwŏ's comment—亦惟父祖之臣—shows that he must have read 先王. 先正 probably crept into the text from Bk. XXVIII., p. 1, *q. v.* 亂四方,—see 'The Testamentary Charge,' p. 25. 蹈虎尾,—this representation of perilousness is also found in the Yih King, under the diagram

爾予翼作股肱心膂纘乃舊服無忝祖考。○四節弘敷五典式和民則爾身克正罔敢弗正民心罔中惟爾之中。○五節夏暑雨小民惟曰怨

3 on a tiger's tail, or walking upon spring ice. I now give you charge to assist me; be as my limbs to me, as my heart and back-bone. Continue their old service, and do not disgrace your grandfather and father.

4 "Diffuse widely *the knowledge of* the five invariable relations *of society*, and reverently seek to produce a harmonious observance of the duties belonging to them among the people. If you can be correct in your own person, none will dare to be but correct. The minds of the people cannot attain to the right Mean *of*

5 *duty*;—they must be guided by your attaining it. In the heat and rains of summer, the inferior people may be described as murmuring

履. 8. 今命至心膂, comp. the various ways in which Kaou-tsung spoke of Yuĕ's relations to him, IV., Bk. VIII., Pt. i., pp. 5—8; and also par. 11 of the 'Yih and Tseih.' 舊服=先公之舊職, 'the old office of your fathers.' The only difficulty is with the 乃. It would seem to be =汝, and then 乃舊服, is 'the old duties which would almost seem hereditary in your family.' Ying-tă ingeniously says—繼汝先世舊所服行. This par. and the next show that Keun-ya's father and grandfather had been the ministers of Instruction.

P. 4. *The special duties of Keun-ya, and the importance of his exemplifying himself the lessons which he taught.* 弘敷五典,—comp. Shun's charge to Sëë, his minister of Instruction,—敬敷五教. 五教 embraces what are here called 五典 and 則. 典 denotes the social relations, with their obligations, as so many *canons* or unchanging rules of life; 則 denotes those obligations recognised and obeyed as practical duties or laws of conduct. 式=敬, 'reverently.' 爾身,云云,—comp. Ana. XII., xvii., 子帥以正,孰敢不正. The paraphrase of the 'Daily Explanation' is interesting:—至于立教典身矣,景景必正,則心之導之心,爾難于求清,自典民罔化民與偏,正之而之先乎,然無為望身無之表曲流能者悖粹以而之而民猶表期身正不純中中爾正求下也,而爾不而于之不在至正,于流濁矣,有中即爾有乎。則其自之于源事敢至自視徽得本欲先上之直,之民其能惟心也之則不蓋源之無而欲不地爾中

5. *How sympathy for the hardships of the people should move Keun-ya to labour for their good.* 小民惟曰怨咨,—'the inferior people may be described as murmuring and sighing.' 惟曰 is to be taken as in Bk. XIII., p. 12,—儀不及物惟曰不享. 祁=大, 'great.' 厥惟艱哉,—'theirs indeed are hardships!' As the 'Daily Explanation' says, 小民終歲勤動,求温飽而不可得,饑寒切身,怨咨無告,何其

書經

咨、冬祁寒、小民亦惟曰怨咨、厥惟艱哉、思其艱、以圖其易、民乃寧。○嗚六節呼、丕顯哉、文王謨、丕承哉、武王烈、啟佑我後人、咸以正罔缺、爾惟敬明乃訓、用奉若于

and sighing. And so it is with them in the great cold of winter. How great are their hardships! Think of their hardships in order to seek to promote their ease, and the people will be tranquil.
6 Oh! how great and splendid were the plans of king Wăn! How greatly were they carried out by the energy of king Woo. They are for the help and guidance of us their descendants;—all in principle correct and deficient in nothing! Do you with reverence illustrate your instructions, and enable me to honour and follow

生理之艱哉. 思其,云云,—the advice here given to Keun-ya is substantially the same with that given to T'ae-këă by E Yin,—無輕民事惟難. The student will say, 'But Keun-ya was the minister of Instruction, whose province was the minds of the people, whose business was their moral training:—how is it that he is here directed to think of the difficulties of their lot, and to provide for their material well-being?' In answer to this, there may be quoted first the remarks of Chang Urh-këa (張爾嘉; Ming dyn.):—'When the nourishment of the people is provided for, their moral training may be carried on with advantage. While they are groaning amid their sufferings from hunger and cold, it is vain to require from them to pursue the Mean, and discharge all the duties belonging to their various relations.' See the 集說. Next we may refer to the exposition of the duties of the minister of Instruction in the 9th Bk. of the Chow Le, from many parts of which we might suppose that he was the minister of Agriculture, and charged with the care of the material well-being of the people, rather than with what is commonly understood as the business of their education. That poverty tends to crime, and competency to virtue is a maxim recognised in China from its earliest history. These remarks seem to explain sufficiently anything that might seem incongruous in this par. There is no necessity to suppose with Lin Che-k'e that it is spoken to Keun-ya, not as minister of Instruction merely, but as uniting with that office the dignity of one of the *Kung*, and so charged with 'the harmonizing and regulating of the operations of Heaven and Earth' (Bk. XX., p. 5), able somehow therefore, and bound, to moderate the heats of summer and the cold of winter.

[In the Le Ke, Bk. 緇衣, p. 17, we have most of this par., with some trifling variations:—君雅曰,夏日暑雨,小民惟曰怨資,冬祈寒,小民亦惟曰怨.]

P. 6. *The king mentions the achievements of the dynasty in the past, and hopes not to come short of his predecessors by the help of Keun-ya, who likewise will thus be shown no unworthy son of his fathers.* 丕顯至罔缺,—see all this quoted by Mencius, III., Pt. VI., ix., 6. 用奉若于先王,—by 先王 we are probably to understand kings Ching and K'ang. 若=順. The whole=使予得奉順成康之舊. 對揚文武之光命,—compare 答揚文武之光訓, Bk. XXII., p. 4. 訓, however, indicates what issued from Wăn and

先王、對揚文武之光命、追配于前人。○七章王若曰、君牙、乃惟由先正舊典時式、民之治亂在兹、率乃祖考之攸行、昭乃辟之有乂。

the example of my *immediate* predecessors, to respond to and display the bright decree conferred on Wăn and Woo:—so shall you be the mate of your by-gone fathers."

7 The king spoke thus:—"Keun-ya, do you take for your rule the lessons afforded by the former courses of your excellent fathers. The good order or the bad of the people depends on this. You will thus follow the practice of your grandfather and father, and make the good government of your prince illustrious."

Woo; 命, what was conferred on them. 追配于前人,—this clause must have reference to Keun-ya, and not, as Gan-kwŏ supposed, both to the king and the ministers. 前人 are the grandfather and father of Keun-ya, already referred to. Literally the clause is—'Going back, you will match your former men.'

P. 7. *The king finally urges Keun-ya to follow the example of his father and grandfather in the same office.* 君牙至時(=是)式(=法),—先正, comp. the same phrase in IV., Bk. VIII., Pt. iii., p. 10. There, however, it denotes 'the former premier,' or chief of the administration of Shang, while here we can only understand it of Keun-ya's father and grandfather. 在兹,—'on this;' *i.e.*, your thus following your fathers. 率乃云云,—the 'Daily Explanation' has for this:—爾亦惟率由乃祖考之行事以正民之德,厚民之生,俾安養遂教,化行以顯乃辟政治之美不亦休哉.

[The whole of this Charge appears forced and exaggerated.]

THE BOOKS OF CHOW.

BOOK XXVI. THE CHARGE TO KEUNG.

冏命

一節 王若曰、伯冏、惟予弗克于德、嗣先人宅丕后、怵惕惟厲、中夜以興、思免厥愆。○二節 昔在

1 The king spoke thus:—"Pih-keung, I come short in virtue, and have now succeeded to the former kings, to occupy the great throne. I am fearful and conscious of the peril *of my position.* I rise at midnight, and think how I can avoid falling into faults.

THE NAME OF THE BOOK; AND DATE.—冏命, 'The Charge to Keung.' The prefatory note says that 'king Muh appointed Pih-keung to be the 太僕正, and thereupon was made the 'Charge to Keung.' From par. 1 we learn that Pih-keung (伯冏) was the name of the individual to whom the charge was given; the title therefore might have been 伯冏之命, or simply 伯冏, after the analogy of the title of the last Book. No reason can be given for the form of the name as we have it, but that it was the fancy of the compiler to call it so. As Lin Che-k'e says, 此篇與君牙,皆是命體,君牙之命篇,則但以其名,此則去伯而加以命字,是亦各其史官一時之意也.

As to the office which Pih-keung was appointed to fill, there are two opinions. In the preface it is called 太僕正; and in the Book, p. 4, 太正. He is no doubt included among the 僕 of p. 6, and we must admit, therefore, the designation in the preface as correct. Now 僕 is used first for 'servant,' without reference to the nature of the service. The dict. gives the definition of the 說文,—給事者, 'one who renders services,' and illustrates this by a passage from the Le Ke, 禮運,—仕于公曰臣,仕于家曰僕, 'a public officer is called 臣; an officer in the family is called 僕.' But the character also means 'a charioteer' (御車曰僕). The difft. views depend on whether the general meaning or the special be supposed to predominate in the case before us.

When we refer to the Chow Le, we find many officers in the dept. of the minister of War denominated as 僕. In Bk. XXXI., we have the 太僕,祭僕,御僕, and 隸僕; and in Bk. XXXII., we have the 太馭 (馭 is taken here to=僕), 戎僕,齊僕,道

文武、聰明齊聖、小大之臣、咸懷忠良、其侍御僕從、罔

2 Formerly, Wăn and Woo were endowed with all intelligence, august and sage, while their ministers, small and great, all cherished loyalty and goodness. Their servants, charioteers, attendanst,

僕, and 田僕. The student naturally, and I think correctly, supposes that he has in the 太僕 of Bk. XXXI. the office of Pih-keung; but Gan-kwŏ and Ying-tă, whose views Lin Che-k'e approved of, were of opinion rather that he should be identified with the 太馭 of Bk. XXXII. The duties of the 太僕 are desc ibed in many parr. He, or they—for there were two officers so denominated—regulated the dress of the emperor on difft. occasions, and the positions where he should stand or sit. He received the great commands of the emperor, and delivered them to those for whom they were intended; and conveyed on the other hand to the emperor memorials from without. He went before the emp. to and from audiences. These details are sufficient to show how close were his relations with the emperor, and how intimate were the services which he rendered.

The 太馭, under whom (though this point is not so clear) appear to have been the 戎僕, &c., mentioned above, had charge of the grand carriage of the emperor, and drove him in it to sacrifices. So far they were close enough together, but their relations were by no means so numerous and intimate as those of the emp. and the 太僕. Why should we suppose that Pih-keung was appointed 太馭 and not 太僕?

The only reason is that the 太馭 were great officers of the second degree (中大夫) while the 太僕 were only of the third (下大夫). There would be force in this, if the one office had been under the other. But there is no evidence to show that this was the case. The two K'ungs erroneously supposed it was, and hence they were led to a wrong conclusion about the office of Pih-keung.

There were two 太僕, under whom were 4 petty servants (小臣), 6 servants for sacrifices (祭僕), 12 special servants (御僕), 2 treasurers (府), 4 clerks (史), 2 helps (胥), 20 waiters (徒), with perhaps others. Pih-keung must have been the senior or chief of the two. Biot translates the term by, 'Grand Domestique.' 'High Chamberlain' is the nearest I can come to it in English.

[This long investigation of the office of Pih-keung may be wearisome to some readers. I thought it worth while to enter on it, because many Chinese critics have professed themselves unable to determine the point. M. de Guignes, who had certainly read the Shoo with care, at least in Gaubil's version, strangely says, in his summary of the Book, that 'Keung was one of the great officers of king Muh. He is named Pih-keung (伯冏), because he was chief of several vassal princes!' So difficult is it, without prolonged and close study, to interpret correctly documents in this language.]

The Book is only found in the 'old text.'

Contents. King Muh represents himself as conscious of his own incompetencies, and oppressed with a sense of the important duties devolving on him. His predecessors, much superior to himself, were yet greatly indebted to the aid of the officers about them;—how much more must this be the case with himself! He proceeds to appoint Keung to be the High Chamberlain, that he may guide correctly all the other servants about the imperial person, and so promote his virtue; telling him the manner of men whom he should employ, and the care which he should exercise in the selection of them.

Pp. 1—3. *Preliminary to the appointment.* 1. *The king's great anxiety in the thought of his own incompetency and his high position.* 予弗克于德,—'I am not competent in the point of virtue.' Compare Kaou-tsung's 台恐德弗類 in 'The Charge to Yue,' Pt. i., p. 2. 嗣先人宅丕后,—宅=居; 丕=大. Ts'ae gives for the whole. 繼前人居大君之位. 怵惕,—see Mencius, II., Pt., I., vi. 3. Ying-tă says here, that the phrase denotes 'the commotion of the heart (心動之名. 厲=危, 'perilousness.' 中夜以興,—以 perhaps has an adverbial force,='thereupon.' 2. *Wăn and Woo, sage as they were, were yet greatly aided by the servants about them.* 齊=莊, or 肅, 'grave,' 'august.' 侍御僕從,—侍=給侍左右, 'those who were about them, on the right and left, min-

匪正人、以旦夕承弼厥辟、出入起居、罔有不欽、發號施令、罔有不臧、下民祗若、萬邦咸休。○三節惟予一人無良、實賴左右前後有位之士、匡其不及、繩愆糾謬、格其非心、俾克紹先烈。○四節今予命汝作大正、正于群僕

and followers, were all men of correctness, morning and evening waiting on their sovereign's wishes or supplying his deficiencies. *Those kings*, going out and coming in, rising up and sitting down, were thus made reverent. Their every warning and command was good. The people yielded a reverent obedience, and the
3 myriad regions were all happy. But I, the one man, am destitute of goodness, and really depend on the officers who have places about me to help my deficiencies, applying the line to my faults, and exhibiting my errors, thus correcting my bad heart, and enabling me to be the successor of my meritorious predecessors.
4 "Now I appoint you to be High Chamberlain, to see that all belonging to your department and my personal attendants are correct,

istering and waiting; 御=御車者, 'charioteers;' 僕=太僕羣僕, 'the chamberlains and all their subordinates;' 從=凡從王者, 'all in close attendance on the sovereign's person.' Choo He remarks that anciently and in the Han dyn., 'all who were even in mean offices about the sovereign were officers of some rank' (士, 大夫). 承=順, 'to accord with,' 'to obey.' 弼=匡正, 'to support and correct.' 出入至不欽,—this is to be understood of the sovereigns. 發號施令,—Wang Gan-shih observes that 'intimations of the imperial will to serve as warnings were called 號, while such as were to have the force of laws were 令' (發之以爲警戒之謂號, 施之以爲法守之謂令).

3. *The king declares how much more he must be dependent on the good services of those about him.* 繩愆糾謬,—繩 is the 'line' by which things are made straight. We naturally look for a corresponding figure in 糾, but we do not have it. It is taken here by Gan-kwŏ, as=舉, 'to raise up,' 'to exhibit.' Lin Che-k'e understands by 繩, the 'thread which is used in mending rents;' and he takes 糾 in the sense of 察, 'to examine.' 先烈, 'the former ardent and meritorious ones' are Wăn and Woo.

Pp. 4—8. *The appointment of Pih-keung.—His duties, and rules for their discharge.* 4. 大正=太僕正;—see the note on the name of the Book. 正于至之臣, —the 于 need not be translated. It merely carries on the action of 正 to 臣. 羣僕侍御 are all the officers of the High Chamberlain's department mentioned in the said note. Ts'ae taking 大正 as=太僕,

侍御之臣、懋乃后德、交修不逮。○五節愼簡乃僚、無以巧言令色便辟側媚、其惟吉士。○六節僕臣正、厥后克正、僕臣諛、厥后自聖、后德惟臣、不德惟臣。○七節爾無昵于憸人、充耳目之官、迪上以非

that you may strive to promote the virtue of your sovereign, and
5 together supply my deficiencies. Be careful in choosing your
officers. Do not employ men of artful speech and insinuating
looks, men whose likes and dislikes are ruled by mine, one-sided
6 men and flatterers; but employ good men. When these household
officers are correct, their sovereign will be correct; when they are
flatterers, the sovereign will consider himself a sage. The sove-
reign's virtue and his want of it depend equally on those officers.
7 Cultivate no intimacy with flatterers, nor get them to fill the
offices of my ears and eyes;—they will lead their sovereign to

would yet include among them the various officers of the carriages who were under the 太馭, which, I said, we saw to be wrong. The 御 here can have nothing to do with the carriages. I have my doubts, indeed, whether it should be translated 'charioteers' in p. 2. 交修,—'cultivate together.' 交 is used as in 上下交征利, Mencius, I., Pt. I., i., 3. Wang Ts'ëaou says on it:—言左右前後非一人,交以修君之所不逮爲事也. 5. *How Keung should be careful in selecting his officers.* 愼簡乃僚,—僚=朋, 'friends,' 'companions,' 'brother officers.' But we must take the term here as meaning the subordinate officers of the Chamberlain's dept. It would appear from this that, under the Chow dyn., it was the business of every head of a dept. to select all the members of it. There were, no doubt, general principles for his guidance, but it was his to choose the men. 巧言令色,—see 'The Counsels of Kaou-yaou,' p. 2. 便辟,—see Ana., XVI., iv. Ts'ae defines them here:—便者,順人之所欲,辟者,避人之所惡. 吉士,—as in Bk. XIX., p. 9,=善士 or 君子. 其惟吉士=所用者惟吉士而已. 6. *The importance of having correct men about the sovereign.* 僕臣, we may translate this here by 'household officers.' 后德惟臣,不德惟臣,—Gan-kwŏ says for this:—君之有德,惟臣成之,君之無德,惟臣誤之,言君所行善惡,專在左右. 自聖,—'sages himself,'=自以爲聖. 7. *The king warns Keung again against having anything to do with flatterers.* 昵,—see Pt. IV., Bk. VIII., Pt. ii., 5. 憸人,—see Bk. XIX., p. 20. 充耳目之官,—'*to get them* to fill the offices of the ears and eyes.' The king must in a great measure hear with the ears and see with the eyes of those about him. See the phrase 耳目之官

先王之典。○非[八節]人其吉、惟貨其吉、若時、瘝厥官、惟爾大弗克祗厥辟、惟予汝辜。○王[九節]曰、嗚呼、欽哉、永弼乃后于彝憲。

8 disregard the statutes of the former kings. If you choose your men not for the goodness of their personal qualities, but for the sake of their bribes, the offices will thus be all made of no effect. Your great want of reverence for your sovereign will be apparent, and to you I will impute the blame."

9 The king said, "Oh! be reverent! Ever help your sovereign to follow the regular laws of duty *which he should exemplify*."

in Men., VI., Pt. I., xv., 2. 8. *Let Keung choose his officers on the ground of what they are, and not for what they have or can give him.* 貨 is here＝賂, 'to bribe,' 'a bribe.' 非人其吉,惟貨其吉,—this is addressed directly to Pih-keung.—'If it be not the man in whom is the excellence, but it is the bribe in which *you see* the excellence.' Gan-kwŏ missed the point and terseness of the language:—若非其人實吉良,惟以貨財配其吉良,以求入于僕侍之中, 若時＝如是, 'thus.' 瘝＝曠, 'to make void,' 'to leave as it were empty.' This is difft. from its use in Bk. IX., pp. 6, 17. Perhaps 瘝在, Bk. XII., p. 10, should be explained in accordance with this text.

P. 9. *The conclusion.* 彝憲＝常法 'the regular or constant laws of conduct,' which the sovereign should observe.

Concluding Note. The character of king Muh does not stand high with Chinese historians. Towards the end of his long reign, for 55 years are assigned to him, he took it into his head that he should travel, without any definite purpose of usefulness, all over the empire, wherever he could go. He did not prove the man that the critics say might have been expected from the language of his Charges to Keun-ya and Pih-keung. Lin Che-k'e thinks his fallings off have been exaggerated. To my mind these two addresses betray a tendency to exaggeration, and betoken a feebleness of mind.

THE BOOKS OF CHOW.

BOOK XXVII. *THE PRINCE OF* LEU UPON PUNISHMENTS.

呂刑

惟呂命、王享國百年、耄荒、度作刑、以詰四

1 I. In reference to the charge to *the prince of* Leu:—When the king had enjoyed the throne till he was the age of a hundred years, he gave great consideration to the appointment of punishments, in order to restrain *the people of* all quarters.

Introductory Note. The two last Books, there was reason to believe, were to be referred to the commencement of king Muh's reign; this, we learn from the Book itself, was the work of its close, when the king was not less than a century old. During the half century that he occupied the throne, the House of Chow went on to decline. Acc. to Sze-ma Ts'een, the king would engage in hostilities with the wild tribes round about, contrary to the counsels of his advisers, losing consequently the former reverence with which they had regarded the sovereigns of Chow, and the good-will also of many of the princes. As to the character of his enactments about punishments, which were the work of his hundredth year, opinions are greatly divided, some critics condemning it so much that they cannot understand why Confucius gave the Book a place in the Shoo. I will reserve the expression of a judgment in the case till we have considered its different parts in detail.

The Name of the Book.—呂刑, '*The prince of* Leu upon Punishments,' or 'The Punishments *of the prince* of Leu.' The Prefatory note says that 'Leu received the orders of king Muh to set forth the lessons of Hea on the redemption of punishments, and there was made Leu on Punishments' (see page. 13., n. 64). We can hardly say that any of this appears in the Book, for Leu, or the prince of Leu, is mentioned only once. The king is the speaker throughout. Nothing is said of Hea. We may accept the tradition, however, that Leu was Muh's minister of Crime, and that the regulations which the king announces had in the first place been digested by him.

呂 is to be taken as = 呂侯, 'The prince of Leu,' being itself the name of a principality, the place of which cannot be clearly ascertained. The Book is quoted in the Le Ke several times, and in other works, by the name of 甫刑, 'The Punishments of *the prince* of Foo.' Indeed this was the prevailing name of it during the Han dynasty. The truth seems to be, that the descendants of the prince of Leu were appointed to the principality of Foo, and their territorial title was transferred to him and to this Book. The Houses of Ts'e (齊), Shin (申), Heu (許), and Foo (甫), all traced their descent to Yaou's president of the Four Eminences, surnamed Keang (姜氏). He or his son was to the great Yu 'a minister who served the purpose of his heart and backbone' (心呂之臣). In this way the surname of 呂 arose among his descendants, and was retained by the princes of Ts'e, the most distinguished family of them. Possibly the prince of Leu, with whom we have here to do, may have had the same title from his importance to king Muh. However this may be, 呂刑 was the older and the proper title of this Book. Mih Teih quotes it by that name. It was found in both the texts.

CONTENTS. I confine myself for the present to the account of these given in the 'Complete Digest.'—'Par. 1 is the historiographer's account of the circumstances in which these lessons on punishments were made. Parr. 2—12 relate the lessons of antiquity for the information of the judges and princes, being a historical resumé which it was important for them to be acquainted with. Par. 13 is addressed specially to the princes, admonishing them of the diligence and carefulness to be employed in the use of punishments. Parr. 14—20 tell them how they should proceed in that use so as to make punishments a blessing. Par. 21 insists again on the reverence with which punishments should be employed. The last par. is addressed to future generations, and directs them to the ancient models, that punishments may never be but a blessing to the empire. Throughout the Book, "virtue" and "exact adaptation" are the terms which carry the weight of the meaning. *Virtue* must underlie the use of punishments, and *exact adaptation* will be the manifestation of it' (通篇以德與中爲主,德其本也,中其用也).

It will be seen that I have divided the king's address into six chapters, each of which commences with the words—'The king said.' This differs only in one trifling point from the arrangement of the 'Complete Digest.'

Ch. I. P. 1. INTRODUCTION:—THE TIME AND OBJECT FOR WHICH THE ANNOUNCEMENT ABOUT PUNISHMENTS WAS MADE. 惟呂命,—this clause has no syntactical connection with the rest of the par. Ts'ae says that the characters are used in the same way as 惟說命 in 'The Charge to Yuĕ,' Pt. ii., p. 1; but the student will perceive that the cases are not at all analogous. 惟說命 is an integral part of the par. where it stands, and supplies the nominative to the first verb in the par. which follows. We may suppose that the prince of Leu had received charge to digest the subject of punishments in acc. with his own views and those of king Muh; that he had done so; and that the king published the result as is subsequently narrated. In this way we may give 惟呂命 the meaning which appears in the translation.

It is not certain how the rest of the par. ought to be pointed. Should 耄 and 荒 be joined together and stand intermediately between what precedes and what follows, qualifying more especially what follows? or should we put a stop at 耄, joining it to 享國百年, and make 荒 an adv., qualifying 度? Gan-kwŏ took the former method, in which he is followed by Ts'ae, who says that 耄 is the designation of one who is old, with the weakness and mental disorders of age (老而亂之稱). 荒 he defines, after Gan-kwŏ, by 忽, 'sudden,' 'neglectful,' and subjoins Mencius' account of it,—從獸無厭謂之荒, 'Pursuing the chase without satiety is what I call being wild;'—see Men. I., Pt. II., iv. 7. On this construction, the two characters are strongly condemnatory of the king's character, and would go to show that the enactments about punishment which the Book relates were stigmatised by the historiographer as made by him in his dotage, and the licentiousness of his reign. Leu Tsoo-hëen and Ch'in Leih, whose opinions are appended in Yung-ching's Shoo, construing 耄 and 荒 together like Ts'ae, yet endeavour to make them have a difft. bearing on the statement 度作刑 which follows;—but unsuccessfully.

Soo Shih adopted the second method of pointing which I have indicated. He put a stop at 耄, and joined 荒 to the verb 度 as an adv., signifying 'greatly;'—referring, in support both of the construction and of that meaning of 荒, to the words of Yu in the 'Yih and Tseih.,' p. 8, 惟荒度土功, 'I kept planning with all my might my labour on the land.' I have followed this view in the translation. Ts'ae admits that it is ingenious and admissible (亦通), saying, however, that 'the character 耄 alone is one of condemnation' (耄亦貶之之辭). But in this latter criticism he is incorrect. We have the character used by Shun of himself in 'The Counsels of Yu,' p. 9, where it simply expresses the fact of his great age, and I do not think that we are to seek for any other meaning for it in the text.

The general rhythm of the par. also satisfies me that Shih's construction is to be preferred, unless indeed we should introduce a 詳 before 刑, as Këang Shing does, but on insufficient authority. Thus taken, the historiogaprher in this par. indicates neither censure nor approbation of king Muh's labours on the subject of punishments; and this is a recommendation of the view.

It still remains to direct attention to the peculiarity of the language—享國百年耄, which, on the analogy of Bk. XV., p. 4, *et al.*, and most naturally too, would be understood as saying that king Muh occupied the throne for a hundred years. Such a view has its supporters. Wang Ch'ung, for instance, maintains it, in his 論衡卷一,氣壽篇, adding that Muh lived altogether to the age of about 140. This cannot be admitted. Sze-ma Ts'een says he was 50 when he succeeded to the throne, and that he reigned 55 years. 詰 has a meaning here intermediate between that in Bk. XX., p, p. 22, and that in XX., p. 11,—禁.

方。○王曰、若古有訓、蚩尤惟始作亂、延及于平民、罔不寇賊、鴟義、姦宄、奪攘矯

2 II. The king said, "According to the teachings of ancient times, Ch'e-yew was the first to produce disorder, which spread among the common people, till all became robbers and murderers, owl-like in their conduct, traitors and villains, snatching and filching, dissemblers and oppressors.

Ch. II. Pp. 2—11. THE FIRST PART OF THE KING'S ADDRESS;—INTRODUCTORY. THE FIRST RISE OF DISORDER IN THE EMPIRE; THE CASE OF THE PEOPLE OF MEAOU; HOW SHUN DEALT WITH THEM; AND HOW HE WENT ON TO LABOUR BY HIS MINISTERS FOR THE PEOPLE, ENDING WITH THE SUBJECT OF PUNISHMENTS. 2. *Ch'e-yew, the first author of disorder in the empire.* 若古有訓,—this clause is equivalent to the 曰若稽古, with which the Canons of Yaou and Shun commence. 若 may be taken with Woo Ch'ing, as 'an introductory particle.' Then 古有訓='From of old there are the lessons.' Gaubil translates—'*Selon les anciens documents.*' But that is more than the text says. He adds in a note,—'These ancient documents are without doubt some books of history which subsisted in the time of king Muh.' Possibly so; but then we know nothing about them, their author, or their authority. There has been no allusion hitherto in the Shoo, if we except the words of Shun in the 'Yih and Tseih,' p. 4, to anything anterior to the time of Yaou; and here all at once king Muh carries us, as will be seen, three centuries farther back, even to before the year 1 of the calendared history of the empire. 始作亂,—'first produced disorder.' 亂 indicates that the 'disorder' was 'rebellion,' resistance to the Powers that were of the time. 平民,='the quiet orderly people.' 寇賊姦宄,—see the 'Can. of Shun,' p. 20. 鴟義,—'the 鴟 (probably the owl) watches its opportunity,' says Ch'ing, 'to dart on its prey. So vividly are the ways of those robbers and murderers represented.' 矯=詐, 'dissemblers.' 虔 has several meanings in the dict., one or two of which would suit the connection here, while others are of an antagonistic meaning. Ts'ae and Woo Ch'ing accept that of 劉=殺, 'murderers,' which I have modified to distinguish it from 賊.

Ch'e-yew, to whom the bad eminence of being the first rebel is here assigned, can hardly be considered a historical personage. The two characters of the name may be translated—'The Stupid and Extraordinary.' According to Sze-ma Ts'een, when the power of the descendants of Shin-nung, the second of the five *Tes*, with whom he commences his history, was declining, great confusion prevailed, and the princes all turned their arms against one another. Then the star of Hwang-te began to rise, and the well inclined gathered around him as their leader. Of all the princes Ch'e-yew was the most violent and oppressive. He attempted to seize the imperial power, when Hwang-te took the field against him, and put him to death after three engagements, and himself superseded the House of Shin-nung. Many fables about dragons, mists, and the invention of the compass, have been mixed up by subsequent writers with the struggle between Hwang-te and Ch'e-yew.

One tradition, indeed, makes Ch'e-yew later than Hwang-te. Gan-kwŏ says he was 'the ruler of Kew-le' (九黎之君); and in the 國語,楚語,下, we read that 'Kew-le became disorderly and vicious during the decay of Shaou-haou' (及少皞氏之衰也,九黎亂德). Now Shaou-haou was the son of Hwang-te. It is true that Gan-kwŏ says, on the next par., that 'Ch'e-yew was destroyed by Hwang-te;' but the impression which we get from the 國語 is that the speaker conceived of the first interruption of good order and vritue as having taken place in the time of Shaou-haou.

The authority of Confucius again is pleaded for making Ch'e-yew a common man, and the greediest of all men (蚩尤庶人之貪者). See Wang Ming-shing, *in loc.* See also the 16th chapter of Premare's preliminary discourse, prefixed to Gaubil's Shoo-king, where he has given all the information that Lo Peih (羅泌) has collected about Ch'e-yew in his 路史.

I pass on from this par. to the next with two remarks.—First, It is not clear for what purpose king Muh commences his discourse of punishments with this mention of Ch'e-yew,

虐。○苗民弗用靈、制以刑、惟作五虐之刑、曰法、殺戮無辜、爰始淫爲劓、刵、椓、黥、越茲麗刑、幷制、罔差有辭。

3 "Among the people of Meaou, they did not use the power of good, but the restraint of punishments. They made the five punishments engines of oppression, calling them the laws. They slaughtered the innocent, and were the first also to go to excess in cutting off the nose, cutting off the ears, castration, and branding. All who became liable to those punishments were dealt with without distinction, no difference being made in favour of

Perhaps he meant to indicate, as the 'Daily Explanation' says, that it was this rebel who first gave occasion for the use of punishment at all. (言古人制刑之由). Second, It is plain that at the commencement of human history Chinese tradition placed a period of innocence, a season when order and virtue ruled in men's affairs.

Pp. 3, 4. *The wickedness of the people of Meaou; and the excessive use of punishments among them.* The king appears to pass over a period of three or four hundred years; and from the time of Ch'e-yew, anterior, acc. to the prevailing accounts, to the invention of the cycle by Hwang-te, he comes down to the time of Shun. So, it will be seen, we must understand these and the following paragraphs. 苗民,—I do not see how we can take these characters otherwise than in the translation. K'ang-shing says that they mean 'the ruler of Kew-le.' 'The prince so denominated,' he says, 'giving trouble in the days of Shaou-haou, was dealt with by Chüen-heuh (顓頊),—afterwards the successor to the throne,—who put Kew-le to death, and removed a portion of his family to the outskirts of the empire on the west. There they reappeared as the chiefs of San-mëaou, and in the reign of his successor Kaou-sin (高辛氏) or the emperor Kuh (帝嚳), B.C. 2,431, displayed their hereditary wickedness, when it devolved finally on Yaou to take them in hand. (苗民謂九黎之君也,九黎之君,于少昊氏衰,而棄善道,上效蚩尤重刑,必變九黎言苗民者,有苗,九黎之後,顓頊代少昊誅九黎,分流其子孫,居于西裔者爲三苗,至高辛之衰,又復九黎之惡,堯興又誅之). This pedigree of the chiefs of the Meaou is ingenious, but I can only regard it as a fancy of the learned scholar. Equally fanciful is his explanation of the character 民 as applied to the ruler of the Meaou, that it is indicative of contempt, and stigmatises him as no better than one of the common herd. Gan-kwŏ, who is followed by Woo Ch'ing, for 苗民 gives 三苗之君, 'the ruler of San-meaou.' As I said above, I do not see how this can be allowed. Of course it is the ruler or rulers who are spoken of, and this can be indicated, as I have done, by using the indefinite *they* as the subject of 用. 弗用靈,制以刑,—the meaning of this seems to be that given by Gan-kwŏ,—不用善化民,而制以重刑, 'they did not use what was good to transform the people, but restrained them by heavy punishments.' 惟作五虐之刑,—we cannot be surprised that some of the critics should argue from this that the invention of 'the five punishments' is here attributed to the chiefs of the Meaou. But the conclusion is not warranted by the language, nor by history. 'The five punishments'—cutting off the nose, and the ear, castration, branding, and death—are all recognised by Shun (Can. of Shun, p. 11). They used those same punishments in Meaou, but excessively and more barbarously. The use of 虐 and 淫 sufficiently show this to be all that is taught in this par. See the remarks of Ch'in Leih in the 集說. 曰法=名之曰法; or, as Woo Ch'ing gives it, 非法而爲之法也. 殺戮 ('they killed and slaughtered') 無辜,—this was the way in which they abused the heaviest punishment, that of death.

○民興胥漸、泯泯棼棼、罔中于信、以覆詛盟、虐威庶戮、方告無辜于上、上帝監民、罔有馨香德、刑發聞惟腥。(四節)
○皇帝哀矜庶戮之不 (五節)

4 those who could offer some excuse. The mass of the people were gradually affected by this state of things, and became dark and disorderly. Their hearts were no more set on good faith, but they violated their oaths and covenants. The multitudes who suffered from the oppressive terrors, and were *in danger of* being murdered, declared their innocence to Heaven. God surveyed the people, and there was no fragrance of virtue arising from them, but the rank odour of their *cruel* punishments.

5 "The great emperor compassionated the innocent multitudes who were *in danger of being* murdered, and made the oppressors feel the

椓=去陰之刑, 'castration.' The char. was originally written 斀. 越茲, 云云,—this was the way in which they abused the four punishments just mentioned. K'ang-shing takes 麗 here=施,—于此施刑幷制; but I prefer to retain the meaning of 附, as in the translation. 民興胥漸,—on the extent of 民 here, see on the next par. 漸 (read *tsëen*, 1st tone)=漸染, 'were soaked and dyed.' The 胥,=相, shows how the influence was communicated from one to another. 泯泯=昏. 棼棼 (Shing edits 紛紛)=亂. 罔中于信,—中 is here =心, 'the heart;' the centre of the man. Ch'in King says:—罔中于信, 無中心出於誠信者, 信不由中也. 以覆詛盟,—覆, 'to turn upside down,' governs 詛 and 盟. I hardly know how to construe Ts'ae's 相與反覆詛盟而已. Shing quotes, in illustration of the sentiment, from the 左傳, 隱三年, these words,—信不由中, 質無益也. 虐威庶戮=其被虐威而陷于刑戮之衆. 罔有, 云云,—Comp. Bk. X., p. 11. On the meaning of 馨, see XXI., p. 3. 刑發聞惟腥,—'what the punishments sent forth to be smelt was only a rank odour.' Ts'ee says:—而刑戮發聞, 莫非腥穢.

[For the first part of par. 3, we find in Mih's 尙同中—呂刑之道曰, 苗民否用練折則刑, 惟作五殺之刑曰法. The critics say that 練 and 靈, 弗 and 否, 折 and 制 were all sounded like each other. Even if we should admit this, how do we have 則 for 以, and 殺 for 虐?

The same pass. appears in the Le Ke, Bk. 緇衣, p. 3, in a form which is somewhat different still:—甫刑曰, 苗民匪用命, 制以刑, 惟作五虐之刑, 曰法.]

Pp. 5—11. *How the Meaouites were dealt with; the evils produced by them remedied; and the system of punishments in the empire put into a satisfactory state.* 5 The important question in connection with this paragraph is as to the emperor whom we are to understand by 皇帝. K'ang-shing, followed of course by

辜、報虐以威、遏絕苗民、無世在下。○乃命重黎、絕地天通、罔有降格、群后之逮在下、明明棐常、鰥寡無蓋。○皇帝清問下民、鰥寡有辭于苗、德威惟畏、德明惟

(六節) (七節)

terrors of his majesty. He restrained and *finally* extinguished the people of Meaou, so that they should not continue to future generations.
6 Then he commissioned Ch'ung and Le to make an end of the communications between earth and heaven, and the descents *of spirits* ceased. From the princes down to the inferior officers, all helped with clear intelligence *the spread of* the regular principles of duty,
7 and the solitary and widows were no more disregarded. The great emperor with an unprejudiced mind carried his inquiries low down among the people, and the solitary and widows laid before him their complaints against the Meaou. He sought to awe *the people* by his virtue, and all were filled with dread; he proceeded *also* to

Këang Shing and Wang Ming-shing thought that in this par. and the next it was Chuen-heuh who was the subject, after which the discourse turns to Yaou. Gan-kwŏ, who is foll. by Woo Ch'ing, makes the emperor to be Yaou all through. Neither view is admissible. The things spoken of in parr. 8, 9, can only be ascribed to Shun. 乃命 at the beginning of p. 8, connects it so closely with p. 7, that we can only understand Shun to be the 皇帝. And as there is no intimation of that 皇帝 being difft. from the person indicated by the same title in par. 5, we must believe that Shun who is the principal subject in all the rest of this chapter is there intended. This is the view of Ts'ae, after Lin Che-k'e.

We get from what is said of the Meaou in these parr. a higher idea of them and their prince than is commonly entertained. From king Muh's language I judge that Shun had in him a powerful rival, and that the struggle which lasted through the reigns of Yaou, Shun, and Yu was of a dynastic nature. The chief of San-meaou was more than the head of a barbarous horde. He was a dangerous rival for the throne. The 'people' mentioned in p. 4, were probably the people of the empire generally. 皇帝至不辜,—we must take 庶戮 here as in the last par. 遏絕,云云,—the measures referred to in the 'Can. of Shun,' pp. 12 and 27, are thus described. The 'Daily Explanation' gives:—竄其君于三危,分北其黨,以遏絕有苗之民,而不使其繼世在下國,以貽百姓之害焉.

6. 乃命至降格,—this par. seems to interpose a difficulty in the way of the view which I have adopted above, that it is Shun who is to be understood as 'the emperor' in all this chapter. We read nothing in the Shoo of his appointing any ministers to do the work here spoken of. No Ch'ung and Le were officers of his. Nor do they appear among the ministers of Yaou, though it is attempted to identify Ch'ung with He (羲) and Le with Ho (和).

The passage formed the subject of a conversation in the lifetime of Confucius, between king Ch'aou (昭王; B.C. 514—488) of Tsoo and one of his ministers, called Kwan Yih-foo (觀射父). 'What is meant,' asked the king, 'by what is said in one of the Books of Chow about Ch'ung and Le, that they really brought it about that there was no intercourse between heaven and earth? If they had not done so, would people have been able to ascend to heaven?' (周書所謂重黎實使天地不通者何也,若無然,民將能登天乎). The minister replied

that that was not the meaning of the language at all, and he proceeded to give his own view of it at great length, and to the following effect:—Anciently, the people attended to the discharge of their duties to one another, and left the worship of spiritual beings—seeking intercourse with them, and invoking and effecting their descent on earth—to the officers who were appointed for that purpose. In this way things proceeded with great regularity. The people minded their own affairs, and the spirits minded theirs. Tranquillity and prosperity were the consequence. But in the time of Shaou-haou, through the lawlessness of Kew-le, a change took place. The people intruded into the functions of the regulators of the spirits and their worship. They left their duties to their fellow-men, and tried to bring down spirits from above. The spirits themselves, no longer kept in check and subjected to rule, made their appearance all irregularly and disastrously. All was confusion and calamity, when Chuen-heuh took the case in hand. He appointed Ch'ung, the minister of the South, to the superintendency of heavenly things, to prescribe the rules for the spirits, and Le, the minister of Fire (or of the North), to the superintendency of earthly things, to prescribe the rules for the people. (命南正重司天以屬神,命火正(一北正)黎司地以屬民). In this way both spirits and people were brought back to their former regular courses, and there was no unhallowed interference of the one with the other. This was the work described in the text,—'the bringing to an end the communication between earth and heaven.' Subsequently, the chief of San-meaou showed himself a Kew-le *redivivus*, till Yaou called forth the descendants of Ch'ung and Le who had not forgotten the virtue and function of their fathers, and made them take the case in hand again.

From the details of this strange passage of which I have given a summary, it would appear that the speaker considered that the Ch'ung and Le of the text were ministers of Yaou, descended from those of Chuen-heuh; and this has given rise to the opinion which I have alluded to on p. 3. of 'The Canon of Yaou,' that this was the ancestry of the minister He and Ho who are mentioned there.

That opinion is without a tittle of satisfactory evidence. Acc. to Yih-foo's statements, Ch'ung's function was that of the minister of Religion, and Le's that of the minister of Instruction, while He and Ho were simply ministers of astronomy, and their descendants continue to appear as such in the reign of Ch'ung-k'ang, the grandson of Yu, long after we know that men of other families were appointed to the two important ministries in question. Gaubil's speculations about the employment of the astronomer in the time of Yaou, not only to calculate and observe the motions of the heavenly bodies, but also to do away with conjurors, false worship, &c., fall to the ground;—see 'Le Chou-king,' p. 292, n. 1. He says also, that as Chung and Le are the same as He and Ho, if we suppose that Shun is the emperor spoken of here, we must assume that he gave those officers a new commission. But if we were to allow that it is Yaou who is spoken of, which I have shown on the last par. to be inadmissible, we should have the same difficulty with the statement of which I began this note. Ch'ung and Le are nowhere in the previous parts of the Shoo, or in any other reliable documents of history, mentioned as officers of his, any more than of Shun. I do not see that any light can be thrown on the passage. The statements of Kwan Yih-foo in the 國語 are entitled to little or no consideration.

羣后之逮在下,—I have translated this and the rest of the par. after Ts'ae. The 'Daily Explanation' gives for it:—當其時有土之諸侯及在下之百官,皆精白其心,輔助常道,民之順是道者,則嘉與之,以慶悖是道者則匡正之,以助常道,賞刑威之典,爲輔明,賞善罰惡,賞之具,其時好惡無告,爲善則必得伸,雖鰥寡之未有蔽而不蒙福,亦末有者. The meaning is, that through the reforms introduced by Ch'ung and Le, a general reformation among all the higher classes was produced. Princes and inferior officers co-operated with those ministers, and the way was opened for the poorest and most helpless of the people to make their complaints and distresses known to the emperor. A foundation is thus laid for the 皇帝清問下民, with which the next par. commences. It will be observed how all this agrees with the view of little less than a dynastic struggle between Shun and the Meaou.

[Këang Shing follows 罔有降格 with 皇帝清問, and edits to the end of p. 8 on a very unsatisfactory authority, that of Mih Teih, in whose 向賢,中, we read;—呂刑道之曰,皇帝清問下民,有辭有苗,曰羣后之肆在下,明明不常,鰥寡不蓋,德威維威,德明維明,乃名三后,恤功於民,伯夷降典,哲民維刑,禹平水土,主名山川,稷隆播種,農殖嘉穀,三后成功,維假於民.]

P. 7. *How Shun proceeded to remedy and remove the evils inflicted by the Meaou.* 清心,—'with a clear mind.' Ts'ae gives 虛心 for it,—'with an unprejudiced mind.' 辭 is here=訟辭, 'pleas,' 'accusations.' 德威,云云,—this is understood to be a de-

書經

明。○八節 乃命三后、恤功于民、伯夷降典、折民惟刑、禹平水土、主名山川、稷降播種、農殖嘉穀、三后成功、惟殷

8 enlighten them by his virtue, and all were enlightened. And he charged the three chiefs to labour with compassionate anxiety in the people's behalf. The baron E delivered the statutes *of ceremony*, to prevent the people from rendering themselves obnoxious to punishment. Yu reduced to order the water and the land, distinguishing by name the hills and rivers. Tseih spread abroad a knowledge of husbandry, so that *the people* could largely cultivate the admirable grains. When the three chiefs had accomplished their

scription of Shun's method of governing the people, in opposition to the wicked ways of the Meaou. Ts'ae says:—苗以虐爲威, 以察爲明, 帝反其道, 以德威, 而天下無不畏, 以德明, 而天下無不明. These clauses are quoted in the Le Ke, Bk. 表記, p. 34, where it is added 非虞帝其孰能如此乎. Ch'in Sze-k'ae remarks that this is a clear testimony that Shun is the emperor spoken of. It certainly shows that that opinion has the 表記 on its side, whatever weight may be attached to it.

P. 8. *How Shun proceeded in the work of government by means of his ministers.* The 'three 后,' princes or chiefs, are those immediately mentioned. 恤功于民 = 致憂民之功, 'to carry out their merits in painful anxiety for the people.' This is Ts'ae's explanation of the phrase, and is better than Woo Ch'ing's, who says:—恤功, 以民事爲憂也. 伯夷至惟刑,—伯夷, see 'The Can. of Shun,' p. 23. The 'statutes' which E delivered were of course those of what are there called 'the three ceremonies,'—all the canons of religious worship. I am not able to construe 折民惟刑. Gan-kwŏ defines 折 by 斷, 'to decide,' and gives for the whole:—伯夷下典禮教民, 而斷以法, understanding 刑 to mean 'the laws' of propriety or ceremony. But such a meaning of 刑 may be at once rejected in this place. Soo Shih, Wang Kang-chin (王綱振), and a host of critics, go about in vain to defend it by trying to show that rules of propriety and penal laws are essentially the same thing;—see the 集傳 and the 集說. Ma Yung and K'ang Shing seem to have read 悊 (=哲) 'wise,' 'knowing.' Taking that term here as a verb, we get the meaning—'and made the people wise on the subject of punishments;' in which interpretation few will acquiesce. Wang Ming-shing, defending this reading, says:—智民者, 民愚無知, 今道之以禮, 是智其民. But he thus avoids saying anything on 惟刑. Ts'ae gives for the clause—以折民之邪妄, 'to cut off the perversity of the people,' in the same way eschewing the most perplexing characters. The 'Daily Explanation,' however, after extending his words just quoted, adds—使不入于刑辟. Woo Ch'ing comes nearest to an admissible construction of the passage:—伯夷教民以禮, 民入于禮, 而不入于刑, 折絶斯民入刑之路, 'The baron E taught the people the rules of ceremony, so that they were observers of propriety, and did not pursue punishable ways, thus shutting up the path by which the people, entering on it, would have been led to punishment.' The translation follows this interpretation. 主名山川,—'superintended the naming of the mountains and rivers.' Këang Shing gives a more specific meaning to 主, making it = 立山川之主, 'he appointed the spirits who should preside

于民。○士制^九節^百姓于刑之中、以教祗德。○穆^十節^穆在上、明明在下、灼于四方、罔不惟德之勤、故乃明于刑之中、率乂于民

9 work, it was abundantly well with the people. The minister of Crime exercised among the people the restraint of punishments, in exact
10 adaptation to each offence, to teach them to reverence virtue. The greatest gravity and harmony in the sovereign, and the greatest intelligence in those below him, thus shining forth to all quarters *of the empire*, all were rendered diligent in cultivating their virtue. Hence, *if anything more were wanted*, the clear adjudication of punishments effected the regulation of the people, and helped them to observe the

over the mountains and rivers, and arranged their sacrifices.' This is not necessary. Ying-tă observes that the hills and rivers being as old as heaven and earth themselves, they ought to have had names before this; but Yu's regulation of the waters constituted a new era. Old things were passed away, and the names of those objects were perhaps lost, so that Yu named them anew! Certainly, the oldest names of the mountains and streams of a country are those given by the first inhabitants; as the Chinese believe that their hills and rivers got their names from Yu, this is to us a strong evidence that the country was first peopled, or began to be occupied, in his time. On the work of Tseih, see 'Can. of Shun,' p. 18. His appointment there has precedence of that of the baron E, and so has that of Kaou-yaou as the minister of crime. This is a not unimportant point of difference between the more ancient document and these statements of king Muh. 降,—'sent down;' here = 'taught the knowledge of.' 農 is taken = 厚, as in 'The Great Plan.' 殖 = 生. 惟殷于民,—殷 = 盛, 'affluent,' 'abundant,' or, as a noun, 'affluence,' 'prosperity.' The 'Daily Explanation' says:—殷,富庶之意也.

P. 9. *The appointment of the minister of Crime, and the object of it.* The minister of Crime was Kaou-yaou. In the 'Can. of Shun,' p. 20, as here, he is simply called 士. [Under the Han dynasty, however, the passage appears with 奚 instead of 士.] 制百姓于刑之中,—'restrained—regulated—the people in the midst of punishments;' *i.e.*, surrounded them with punishments. This was done, however, not with the design of punishing them, but, as is subjoined, 'to teach them to reverence virtue,' so that punishments should be unnecessary. Keang Shing edits 衷; and he and others make the word emphatic, meaning 'punishments exactly adapted to the degree of the offence' (不輕不重之謂,輕重適中之誼). This is refining; but it may be admitted.

From king Muh's thus separating Kaou-yaou from the 'three princes' in the last par., both emperors and people have at difft. times been led to place the minister of Crime on a lower level than the other great ministers of State. Kaou-yaou was certainly no inferior man with Shun. Nor was he so in the estimation of Muh. He is mentioned by him last, as it was his object to make all his previous statements converge to the subject of punishments.

P. 10. *The happy results of this govt. of Shun.* 穆穆在上 is descriptive of Shun; 明明在下, of his ministers. These two clauses are the subjects of the next—灼于四方; and the effects on all the people are told in 罔不惟德之勤. Notwithstanding all this happy influence on the people, there was yet room for the warning use of punishments, as intimated in 故乃明,云云. This is the common interpretation of the paragraph. The 刑之中 here is more favourable to the pregnant meaning of the 中, on which I have spoken in the last par. The only critic of note who takes a difft. view of the several clauses is Woo Ch'ing. He takes them all after 明明在下, as

棐彝。○典獄、非訖于威、惟訖于富、敬忌、罔有擇言在身、惟克天德、自作元命、配

11 regular duties of life. In examining criminal cases, the officers executed the law not only against the powerful, but also against the wealthy. They were all reverence and caution. They had no occasion to make choice of words in reference to their conduct. The virtue of Heaven was attained to by them; from them was the determination of so great a matter as the lives of men. In their low sphere they yet corresponded to *Heaven*, and enjoyed its favour."

descriptive of the ministers and princes:—四方諸侯皆惟德之勤,故能明于皐陶制刑之中,導民爲善,禁民爲惡,民之棐彝者,皆順法而刑不用. This is ingenious; but the ordinary view is to be preferred.

P. 11. *The impartiality of the administration of justice under Shun.* 典獄=典獄之官, 'the officers presiding over criminal causes,' under Kaou-yaou. 非訖(=盡)于威,惟訖于富=非惟得盡法於權勢之家,亦惟得盡法於賄賂之人,言不爲威屈,不爲利誘. 'they not only carried out the law against the powerful, but also against those who offered bribes, *i.e.*, they were neither bent by terrors nor seduced by gain.' This seems to be the meaning, tho' the language has been variously interpreted. Lin Che-k'e, for instance, makes it an indignant expression of contempt against minions of justice, especially among the Meaou, who gratified their own spleen and pride by the terrors with which their office invested them, or sought to enrich themselves by taking bribes.—凡典獄之吏,非欲誅殺以立威則欲納賄以致富,若苗民之臣,所謂庶威者,訖于威也,所謂奪貨者訖于貨也,威者貨者,此皆獄吏之常態也. 罔有擇言在身=在躬無一不可以告人,有不必擇而後言者, 'in their persons—conduct—there was nothing which they could not tell, nothing about which it was necessary first to make choice of words, and then to speak.' 惟克,云云,—it would seem necessary to explain these clauses of the officers in criminal causes. Gan-kwŏ did so, and expounds:—凡明於刑之中,無擇言在身,必是 (it will be seen he does not interpret the par. historically) 惟能天德,自爲大命,配享天意在於天下. This is not very perspicuous, but by the help of Ying-tă's paraphrase and glosses we can see that the pass. was supposed to say 'that all judges, with the reverence and caution mentioned, being just and impartial like Heaven, made for themselves a great decree, securing long life and other prosperity, responding to (享=當) the mind of Heaven, throughout the empire.' This is very vague and unsatisfactory. Ts'ae interprets of the 典獄之官, after Gan-kwŏ, but confines himself, as is too much his wont, to vague and general phrases, so that we cannot tell what he understood by 大命, and 配享在下. I have translated after the 'Daily Explanation,' which may be supposed to give the more definite expression of Ts'ae's views. Its language is:—夫天德無私,能制人死生之大命,今典獄者亦無私,則爲能克天德,而死生人之大命,乃不在天而在我矣,德自我克,命自我作,則雖在下,而豈不可配享于天哉. Wang Ch'ung-yun has called this interpretation in question, and instead of referring the clauses to 典獄, would refer them to Shun as the emperor who appointed Kaou-yaou, and whose careful provision for the administration of justice, was to be rewarded by the

享在下。○王曰、[十二節]嗟四方司政典獄、非爾惟作天牧、今爾何監、非時伯夷播刑之迪、其今爾何懲、惟時苗民、匪察于獄之麗、罔擇吉人、觀于五刑之中、惟時庶威

12 III. The king said, "Ah! you who superintend the government and preside over criminal cases throughout the empire, are you not constituted the shepherds of Heaven? Whom ought you now to survey as your model? Is it not Pih-e, spreading among the people his lessons to avert punishments? And from whom ought you now to take warning? Is it not from the people of Meaou, who would not examine into the circumstances of criminal cases, and did not make choice of good officers who should see to the right apportioning of the five pnnishments, but chose the violent and bribe-snatch-

possession of the empire long continued, and the favour of Heaven. He supports his explanation of 元命 as = 國, by 厥惟廢元命, in Bk. XIV., p. 5., and that of 配享在下 by 克配上帝 in 'The T'ae-këă,' Pt. iii., p 3, and by 配天其澤, in Bk. XIV., p. 8. The editors of Yung-ching's Shoo mention his view with approbation, but do not positively decide in favour of it. His interpretation of 元命 is better supported than that in the translation; but I cannot bring myself to admit that king Muh turns here to speak, either historically or by way of admonition, of sovereigns generally.

Ch. III. P. 12. THE KING ADDRESSES THE PRINCES AND OFFICERS OF JUSTICE ON THE GROUND OF THE STATEMENTS WHICH HE HAS MADE, AND URGES THEM TO TAKE THE BARON E AS THEIR MODEL, AND TO LOOK TO THE MEAOU AS A BEACON. 四方司政典獄,—from Gan-kwŏ downwards, the critics all take this as a designation of the 諸侯, or 'princes,' so that the king is addressing not them and their officers of justice, but them only. The view is to my mind very questionable. It is grounded on the appellation of 'shepherds of Heaven,' which follows. That is often given, no doubt, to the princes who rule,—to the sovereign *par eminence*, and to all who hold appointments under him; but why may we not suppose that it is here extended to judges also, whose decisions should always be according to the truth,—according to the mind of God? 監 = 監法, 'to consider and imitate.' This determines the meaning of 懲, which is in opposition to it, as = 懲戒, 'to condemn and beware of,' 'to take as a warning.' 非時(=是)伯夷播刑之迪,—there is here the same difficulty which we found in trying to explain the 折民惟刑 of par. 8. Perhaps the 迪, in the sense of 'leadings' (開導), is appropriate to the functions of E, whose rules of ceremony and propriety might be considered as designed to avert men from punishments and punishments from them. So, it will be seen, I have translated 刑之迪. This is putting some stress on the characters, but it gives a more satisfactory explanation of the text than any of the constructions proposed by the critics. Gan-kwŏ takes 迪 = 道, and gives for the whole:—言當視是伯夷布刑之道而法之. So, Këang Shing:—非是伯夷施刑之道乎. The 'Daily Explanation' seems to get, by a roundabout process, to the same conclusion with myself:—惟時伯夷制爲典禮,折民之入于刑,而開導之者無不至,是所謂播刑之迪者,此克作天牧,爾之所當監也. 惟時(=是)苗民,

奪貨、斷制五刑、以亂無辜、上帝不蠲、降咎于苗、苗民無辭于罰、乃絕厥世。○王十三節曰、嗚呼、念之哉、伯父、伯兄、仲叔、季弟、幼子、童孫、皆聽朕言、庶有格命、今爾罔不由慰日勤、爾罔或戒不勤、

ers, who determined and administered them so as to oppress the innocent, until God could not hold them guiltless, and sent down calamity on Meaou, when the people had no plea to urge in mitigation of punishment, and their name was cut off from the world?"

13 IV. The king said, "Oh! lay it to heart. My senior uncles, and all ye my brethren and cousins, my sons and my grandsons, listen all of you to my words, in which, it may be, you will receive a most important charge. You will tread the path of satisfaction only by being daily diligent;—do not have occasion to beware of the want of diligence. Heaven, in its wish to regulate the people, allows us for a day to make use of punish-

—I have translated interrogatively here, in response to the previous question. 匪察于獄之麗,—this has reference to the 越兹麗刑幷制 of p. 3. Literally the characters mean—'they did not examine into the obnoxiousness of criminal cases,' *i.e.*, they did not seek to find out either the real criminals or the degree of guilt. From this to the end of the par., we have a striking instance of the *long sentences* of the Shoo. 罔擇至無辜,—Keang Shing's comment on this is brief and clear:—不選擇善人,使觀于五刑之中正,惟是衆恃威奪貨之人任之,使斷制五刑,以亂罰無辜. 上帝不蠲,—蠲=潔, 'clean;' as a verb, 'to consider clean,' 'to acquit.' 乃絕厥世,—this has reference to the 遏絕苗民,無世在下, of p. 5. What was there ascribed to Shun is here ascribed to God; 'showing,' says Sun Ke-yew, 'that Shun was only the minister of Heaven's justice.'

Ch. IV. P. 13. THE KING ADDRESSES HIMSELF TO THE PRINCES OF THE SAME SURNAME WITH HIMSELF, AND CALLS THEM TO CO-OPERATE WITH HIM IN THE DILIGENT AND CAREFUL ADMINISTRATION OF PUNISHMENTS. 伯父,—see on Bk. XXIII., p. 6. 伯兄,仲叔季弟,—these were all the king's cousins, his 兄弟. Brothers may also be included. On 伯,仲,叔, and 季, see Con. Ana., XVIII., xi. Both Gaubil and Medhurst are wrong in taking 仲叔 together, as meaning 'junior uncles,' 'mes oncles paternels cadets.' 幼子童孫,—when we consider that king Muh was now a hundred years old, he may very well have had grand-children who were high in office or rulers of States. [Kēang Shing reads 僮 and not 童, arguing that 童 was properly the designation of 'a menial' or 'servant,' and 僮 that of 'a young person.' There is a note in the dict., under 僮, to the same effect, where it is added that in the lapse of time, through inadvertence and error, the characters have changed meaning.] 庶有格命,

天齊于民、俾我一日、非終、惟終、在人、爾尙敬逆天命、以奉我一人、雖畏勿畏、雖休勿休、惟敬五刑、以成三德、一人有慶、兆民賴之、其

ments. Whether crimes have been premeditated, or are unpremeditated, depends on the parties concerned;—do *you deal with them so as* reverently to accord with the mind of Heaven, and serve me, the one man. Though I would put them to death, do not you therefore put them to death; though I would spare them, do not you therefore spare them. Reverently apportion the five punishments, so as to complete the three virtues. Then shall I, the one man, enjoy felicity; the people will look to you as their sure dependence; the repose of such a state will be perpetual."

—Ts'ae, after Gan-kwŏ, defines 格 by 至,=至善 or 至當; and I have translated accordingly. Këang Shing, after K'ang-shing, defines 格 by 登, so that 格命=壽考, 'longevity.' This view may be rejected without hesitation. Nor does another advocated by Soo Shih and Sëë Ke-seuen, to which the editors of Yung-ching's Shoo are not disinclined, seem worthy of much more attention. According to it, the 命=天命, and 庶有格命=庶幾可以格于上帝, as in Bk. XVI., p. 7. Ts'ae explains 爾罔不由慰日勤 by 爾所用以自慰者無不以日勤, 'Let the method which you employ to find satisfaction—ease of mind—to yourselves be only that of daily diligence.' The 'diligence' must be understood with reference to the investigation of criminal cases and the administration of punishments; and hence it is added—爾罔或戒不勤. When punishment was once wrongly inflicted from a want of carefulness, the evil was done; regret and repentance would be of little avail. Lin Che-k'e interpreted 由 and 慰 differently, but not, I think, so well. He says:—爾當無不由朕之言, 相慰勉而日愈勤, 'you should stimulate one another from my words, and be daily more diligent.' [Gan-kwŏ read 日勤, which Këang Shing still edits. See Ying-tă's explanation of this text.] 天齊至在人,—these clauses have been variously pointed and interpreted. 天齊于民 is spoken of the design of Heaven in the use of punishments. It is to bring the people to a state of adjustment and good order. So far, all agree; but here agreement ends. I have put a comma with Ts'ae after 日, and 俾我一日=俾我爲一日之用耳, as in the translation.

Then 非終 and 惟終 are interpreted after the analogy of the same expressions in Bk. IX., p. 8; and it is very natural to do so, because the discourse there is all on the subject of the administration of the penal laws; and the meaning thus obtained well suits the general tenor of the paragraph. Gan-kwŏ pointed—天齊于民, 俾我, 一日非終, 惟終在人; but his explanation of this is hardly intelligible:—天整齊於下民使我爲之, 一日所行, 非爲天所終, 惟爲天所終, 在人所行. Of all who have adopted this pointing, Ch'in King may be said to have succeeded best; and the editors of Yung-ching's Show commend his interpretation, which is given in the 附錄, and is to this effect:—'Heaven would by punishments regulate the people, and not being able to do so itself, entrusts the work to me. But Heaven's heart of love for the people is inexhaustible, and I also cannot in one day complete the thing. For associates to complete it, I must look to others, and depend on them.' On other attempts to give a consistent meaning to the

寧惟永。○王曰、吁、來、有邦有土、告爾祥刑、在今爾安百姓、何擇非人、何敬非刑、

14 V. The king said, "Ho! come, ye rulers of States and territories, I will tell you how to make punishments a blessing. Now it is yours to give repose to the people:—what should you be most concerned about the choosing of? Should it not be proper men? What should you deal with the most reverently? Should it not be punishments? What should you calculate the most? Should it not be to whom they should reach?

passage on this construction, I need not dwell. Ts'ae has here outstript all the other commentators. 敬逆天命,—'reverently anticipate—meet—what Heaven has appointed;' *i.e.*, do you seek simply to do justice This will be to fulfil the mind of Heaven, and also the best service you can render to me. 雖畏勿畏,雖休勿休,—the advice here is the same with that given by king Ching to Keun-ch'in, Bk. XIX., p. 8; 畏 taken as=威, and then as=辟, 'punishment,' being the putting forth of the terrors of rule. It is here again—'many men, many minds.' Most critics do not admit any reference in the words to the king's own wishes; and take the meaning to be substantially as Ch'in King gives it:—'In using punishments, although people seem to give a dread submission, do not you think that realized; though they praise you, do not you think what you have done worthy of praise. Never be weary or satisfied, and so your way and mind will be in accord with the inexhaustible heart of love belonging to the sovereign and to Heaven.' Këang Shing edits 祇事不怠 after 勿有, and would exclude 惟敬五刑;—on very poor authority. 以成三德,—the 'three virtues' are those of 'The Great Plan,' p. 17,—the virtues of 'correctness and straightforwardness,' of 'strong government,' and of 'mild government.'

As Wang Yen says in the 集說:—'Punishments being light when they ought to be light, this would be "mild govt.," and the mildness would not be weak indulgence. Being severe when they ought to be severe, this would be "strong govt.," and the strength would not be oppression. Being intermediate between light and heavy, this would be "correct and straightforward govt.," and the correctness and straightforwardness would not degenerate to one-sidedness' (刑當輕而輕,以成柔德,而柔不至於縱弛,當重而重,以成剛德,而剛不至於苛暴,介輕重之間,以成正直,而正直不至於偏倚). The three concluding clauses all show the happy result of the princes' listening to the king's advice. Gan-kwŏ is wrong in taking 一人有慶=天子有善, and then making the other two clauses dependent on this.

Ch. V. Pp. 14—20. The king shows all his princes and chiefs how they should proceed in the administration of justice so as to make punishments a blessing. This chapter must be considered the most important of the Book. Its contents are what is intended by the 荒度作刑 of par. 1. I suppose that the various things here announced in a general way by the king were all drawn out, and had been published, with the necessary details and explanations, by the prince of Leu.

P. 14. *Preliminary address to all the princes.* 吁來有邦有土,—吁 is called in the dict. 疑怪之辭, 'a particle of doubt and surprise.' We have had it seven times already in the Shoo, where our 'alas!' was always suitable. But that expression of feeling is not what we should expect here. Lin Che-k'e makes the term on the contrary here expressive of joyful alacrity (吁來者歡而呼之使前也). We have the different readings of 于 and 於 (*woo*). 有邦 (another reading is 國) 有土 may be considered as descriptive of the princes of the empire generally,—of the imperial surname and of others. Këang Shing says that 有國 (so he reads) indicates the princes outside the imperial domain, and 有土, those having appanages within it; but I do not think we can thus discriminate the phrases. 告爾

何度非及。〇兩[十五節]造具備、師聽五辭、五辭簡孚、正于五刑、五刑不簡、正于五罰、五

15 "When both parties are present, *with their documents and witnesses* all complete, let all the judges listen to the five-fold statements which may be made. When they have examined and fully made up their minds on those, let them adjust the case to one of the five punishments. If the five punishments do not meet it, let them adjust it to one of the five redemption-fines; and if these

祥刑,—祥='felicitous'; here, as a verb, 'to make felicitous.' 'Punishments,' says Ch'in Ya-yen, 'used not to distress or oppress the people, but to give them repose, are called 祥刑.' K'ang-shing read 詳, and interpreted it by 審察之, 'discriminating examination.' The two characters, 祥 and 詳, might very easily be confounded. [Mih Teih quotes the passage with 訟刑, which is evidently an error.] 何擇,云云,—we have here three questions, with the answers to them, given also interrogatively, as in the translation. To quote again from Ya-yen,—三言何者,設爲問辭以致其疑,三言非者,設爲答辭以致其決. 何度非及=當何所謀度乎,豈非刑之所當逮及者乎, 'what ought you to deliberate about and calculate? Should it not be as to those to whom punishments should reach?'

[Këang Shing, professing to follow the text of Mih Teih, reads—在今而安百姓,何擇非人,何敬非刑,何度不及. But Mih has—女何擇言人,何敬不刑,何度不及. Ming-shing says that Mih's writings are too full of erroneous characters to allow his text to be relied on, and that 非刑,非及 is no doubt the true reading. That Mih did read the last clause—何度不及, however, is plain from the comment which he subjoins,—能擇人而敬爲刑,堯,舜,禹,湯,文,武之道可及也. 何度不及 would mean—'what can you plan which you may not reach?' This shows clearly one of the differences between the usages of 非 and 及.]

P. 15. *The manner of proceeding in hearing cases, and adjudicating upon them.* 兩造具備,—造=至, 'to come,' 'to appear;' and 兩造='the two parties interested—the plaintiff and defendant—having both appeared.' 具=俱='all,' 'completely;' 具備,—'being fully provided,' *i.e.*, having set forth all the particulars of their several cases. Ts'ae says:—具備=詞證皆在, '具備 means that the representations and witnesses are all there.' 師聽五辭—師 is defined in the 集傳 by 衆, 'all.' Këang Shing defines it by 士師, 'judges,' of whom there were four, mentioned in the Chow Le, Bk. XXXIV., and who rank immediately after the 'assistant minister of Crime.' Gan-kwŏ for 師聽 gives 衆獄官共聽, 'let all the judges hear in common.' The proper construction seems to be to take 師 in the meaning of 'judge,' but in the plural. Chang Kew-shing says:—'The parties concerned should not be one-sided in their representations, and the judges should not be one-sided in listening to the case. If only one listened to it, his intelligence might be unequal to it, and his deliberations might be inadequate, and therefore the rule was made that all the judges should hear the case in common.' See the 集說.

五辭,—'the five pleadings,' *i.e.*, the statements, with the evidence, on both sides, whether incriminating or exculpating. They are called 'five,' as the penalty might be one or other of the 'five punishments.' It is important to bear in mind that it is of cases of a serious nature, and punishable with these penalties that the king is speaking. Ts'ae says;—五辭,麗於五刑之辭也. 五辭簡孚,—簡=核其實, 'being

罰不服、正于五過。○十六節 五過之疵、惟官、惟反、惟內、惟貨、惟來、其罪惟均、其審克之。

again are not sufficient for it, let them reckon it among the five cases of error.

16 "In *settling* the five cases of error there are evils *to be guarded against*;—being warped by the influence of power, or by private grudge, or by female solicitation, or by bribes, or by applications. *Where such things are*, the offence becomes equal to the crime *before the judges*. Do you carefully examine, and prove yourselves equal *to every difficulty*.

searched out to the very truth of them;' 孚=無可疑, 'with no room for doubt.' 正于五刑,—正, 'to lay down straight,' here = 'to determine or adjust correctly,' *i.e.*, with reference to the penalty with which the particular crime should be visited. Fan Sze-lin observes that this does not intimate the ordering of the punishment to be inflicted forthwith, but the registering of the sentence in a book (非便用五刑, 只以此情辭質正于刑, 書當於何等刑加之也). 五刑不簡,—the meaning is, no doubt, what appears in the translation; but the exact force of the 簡 does not readily appear. Këang Shing, defines it, both here and above, by 誠, 'sincere,' 'true,' and explains here by 所犯非其誠, 無惡意, 而所爲惡也, 'the crime was not really intended. There was the criminal act, but not the evil intention.' The text, however, does not say anything so specific; and such a case, we may judge, should at once be referred to the 'five cases of error.' Literally we may translate the clause—'If the five punishments be not examined out;' meaning—if the result of investigation do not show that one of those punishments should be employed. 五罰,—'the five fines,'—the five redeemable cases. These are detailed below. The king speaks evidently of a system that had been established. We cannot infer from the text that it had been established by himself, though it may have been so. This point will be considered by and by. 五罰不服,—'if the five fines will not produce submission;' *i.e.*, if such a sentence will not be acquiesced in as just. 五過,—'the five classes of error,' *i.e.*, the various cases of inadvertence. What should ensue on the adjudication of any charge to be so ranked, does not appear. Ts'ae, after Gan-kwŏ, says the result would be pardon and dismissal (質于過而宥免之). Such was the rule prescribed to Kaou-yaou by Shun. See 'The Counsels of Yu,' p. 12,—宥過無大, 'you pardon inadvertent faults however great.' The rule of the Chow dynasty seems to have been more stringent. Wang Gan-shih, as quoted in the 集說, says that various penalties mentioned in the Chow Le, such as the stocks, exposure on a public stone, labouring on public works, were the punishments for crimes of error, which were not freely pardoned. Some degree of criminality must have been supposed to attach to the cases which were thus punished.

P. 16. *Caution to the judges against being warped in their decisions.* The text speaks only of offences that might be committed in the last of the proceedings described in the prec. par.; but the same influences might work their evil effect in the other measures as well. The judges might reduce crimes from any one grade to that beneath, or raise them, making them out greater than they really were, from the same improper motives. The warning is given with reference to the classing offences as cases of error merely; but it was intended to be understood with a general application. 五過之疵,—'the maladies of the five cases of error.' Evidently what is intended are the evil influences by which offences that were not cases of error were yet determined and registered as such. Gaubil mistook the meaning entirely, and rendered—'Ces cinq sortes de fautes sont occasionnées, 1°, parcequ'on craint un homme en place,' &c. 惟官至惟來,—the 'maladies' are here stated so concisely that it does not seem possible to give anything like a literal translation of the text. The nearest I can come to it would be—'The maladies that may affect *the determining of* the five cases of error are *the influence of* authority, revenge, closet *influence*,

○五刑之疑有赦、五罰之疑有赦、其審克之、簡孚有衆、惟貌有稽、無簡不聽、具嚴天威。○墨辟

17 "When there are doubts as to the infliction of any of the five punishments, that infliction should be forborne. When there are doubts as to the infliction of any of the five fines, it should be forborne. Do you examine carefully, and overcome every difficulty. When you have examined, and many things are clear, yet form a judgment from studying the appearance of the parties. If you find nothing on examination, do not listen to the case any more. In everything stand in awe of the dread majesty of Heaven.

bribes, and solicitations.' The 'Daily Explanation' for 官 gives—畏他人之權勢而不敢爭執; for 反,報復已之恩怨,而不本公平; for 內,聽受女謁之言; for 貨,廣開貨賄之門; for 來,凡有干求請囑,不能謝絕. 其罪惟均—其罪與犯人同, 'the offence of this is to be classed with that of the criminal in connection with whom it is shown.' 其審克之,—'do you distinguish and overcome it;' i.e., judge carefully, and so that your judgments shall be correct, superior to all difficulties and temptations. Woo Ch'ing says:—審克謂審之而能得其審也.

P. 17. *The care which should be exercised in coming to a conclusion in doubtful cases.* 五刑之疑有赦,—if we give to 赦 here its full meaning, as Woo Ch'ing and some other critics do, and say that where it was doubtful whether a crime should be adjudicated to one of the five punishments, it was to be absolutely pardoned, and the charge dismissed, we go against the rule in p. 15, 五刑不簡,正于五罰, and the direction moreover would be against all reason. With Gan-kwŏ, Lin Che-k'e, Ts'ae, and the host of commentators, therefore, I adopt a lighter meaning of 赦, as in the translation. Lin says:—五刑之疑,尙不免於罰,而謂之赦者,蓋雖以金自贖,而幸其不至殘潰其肌體,是亦赦也. 簡孚有衆,—'the points on which certainty has been attained by investigation may be many.' This construction seems preferable to that adopted by Gan-kwŏ,—簡核誠信,有合衆心, 'the investigations, conducting to an assured faith, may agree with the views of the multitude.' Notwithstanding this result, the king would still have the judges carefully study the countenance and demeanour of the accused. Those may convey an impression of innocence, which will outweigh contrary appearances and presumptions. 無簡不聽—'if there be no *result from* examination, there should be no more listening to the case.' As Ts'ae puts it 然聽獄,以簡核爲本,苟無情實,在所不聽. [Këang Shing, on the authority of the 說文, instead of 貌 reads 緢, which he makes out to mean 'carefully,' 'minutely' (微細). This leads him to construe the clauses 其審克之,簡孚有衆, and 惟緢有稽,無簡不聽. But 其審克之 is more suitable as the termination of a par. or sentence, than at the commencement.] 具嚴天威,—具=俱, 'all,' 'in all.' 嚴=敬, 'to revere.' Chang Kew-shing says:—具,俱也,謂上所言,皆敬天威.

疑赦、其罰百鍰、閱實其罪、劓辟疑赦、其罰惟倍、閱實其罪、剕辟疑赦、其罰倍差、閱實其罪、宮辟疑赦、其罰六百鍰、閱實其罪、大辟疑赦、其罰千鍰、閱實其罪、墨

18 "When in a doubtful case the infliction of branding is forborne, the fine laid on instead must be 600 ounces *of copper;* but you must first have satisfied yourselves as to the crime. When the case has reference to the cutting off the nose, the fine must be double this, the same care having been taken to determine the crime. Where the penalty would be cutting off the feet, the fine must be 3,000 ounces;—with the same careful determination of the crime. Where the penalty would be castration, the fine must be 3,000 ounces;—with the same careful determination of the crime. Where the punishment would be death, the fine must be 6,000 ounces;—with the same careful determination of the crime. Of crimes that

P. 18. *The law of the redemption of punishments.* 其罰百鍰,—'the fine is a hundred *hwan*.' The *hwan* was equal to six *leang*, *i.e.*, six Chinese ounces. Some uncertainty attaches, however, to this estimate. Këang Shing inclines to the view that 100 *hwan* were equal only to 3 *kin*, or Chinese pounds. The coins or metal in which this and all the other fines were paid is called by Gan-kwŏ 黃鐵, 'yellow iron.' Ying-tă observes that 'anciently, gold, silver, copper, and iron, all went by the general name of *kin* (金). Gan-kwŏ calls the metal spoken of here 黃鐵, and that intended in 'The Can. of Shun,' p. 11, 黃金; but in either case he means copper' (銅). It was that metal which was required anciently in all redemption payments. Medhurst makes the metal to be '*silver*,' for which he has no authority. Gaubil says he knows nothing about whether the fine was paid in copper or in some other metal. There has never been but one opinion on the subject, so far as I am aware, among the Chinese themselves.

其法惟倍,—倍—'double,'—1,200 ounces. 剕—刖足, 'cutting off the feet.' This was the third of the five punishments, and not 刵, or 'cutting off the ear,' as we might perhaps infer from p. 3, if there be no error of the text there. Cutting off the ear would not be a greater penalty than cutting off the nose. 倍差=倍而又差. But the amount is not at all certain. Ts'ae says it is 500 *hwan*,—double the previous fine, and a degree (次) more. Ma Yung makes it 533 *hwan* and one third of a *hwan* (倍者倍二百爲四百,差又加四百之三分一,凡五百三十三鍰,三分鍰一也). Këang Shing thinks this estimate excessive, and reduces it to 333 *hwan* and a third (倍差者于倍百鍰爲二百之外,又差出二百之三分二,凡三百三十三鍰三分鍰之一). The truth is, we do not know certainly the proportion denoted by 差. I apprehend that 倍蓰 in Men., VI., Pt., I., xi., 7, is another form of the 倍差 here, and therefore agree with Ts'ae. 宮辟 is called the 淫刑, 'punishment of illicit intercourse.' It was inflicted on the male by castration, and on the female by close confinement (男子割勢,婦人幽閉). 五刑之屬三千,—'pertaining to the five punishments

罰之屬千、劓罰之屬千、剕罰之屬五百、宮罰之屬三百、大辟之罰、其屬二百、五刑之屬三千、上下比罪、無僭亂辭、勿用不行、惟察惟法、其審克之。○

十九節 上刑適輕下服、下

may be redeemed by the fine in lieu of branding there are 1,000, and the same number of those that would otherwise incur cutting off the nose. The fine in lieu of cutting off the feet extends to 500 cases; that in lieu of castration to 300; and that in lieu of death to 200. Altogether, set against the five punishments there are 3,000 crimes. *In the case of others not exactly defined*, you must class them with the *next* higher or *next* lower offences, not admitting assumptive and disorderly pleadings, and not using obsolete laws. Examine; act lawfully:—judging carefully, and proving yourselves equal to every difficulty.

19 "Where the crime should incur one of the higher punishments, but there are mitigating circumstances, apply to it the *next*

there are 3,000 crimes.' Acc. to the Chow Le, Bk. XXXVI., on the duties of the 司刑, the crimes to be visited with the five punishments are stated to be 2,500, 500 being assigned to each penalty. By king Muh's enactments the total number of crimes was increased, but at the same time a larger number were classed as liable to the lighter penalties and fines, and a smaller number as liable to the heavier punishments. Thus the Chow Le makes 500 offences punishable with death; king Muh, only 200; against the 500 of the former, punishable with branding or cutting off the feet, he assigned in each case 1,000. 上下比罪,—'above and below compare the offence.' This is understood to be spoken with reference to offences which did not come exactly under any statutory definitions. Their proper place must be sought by comparison with other recognised offences of a heavier and a lighter character. The 'Daily Explanation' says:—法之所定有限,而人之所犯無窮,其有犯無正律者,則以上下刑而比附其罪,如罪疑于重,則以上刑比之,罪疑于輕,則以下刑比之. In such cases special caution was necessary, and therefore it is added —無僭亂辭,勿用不行. Ts'ae says he does not understand these clauses, but they will admit the interpretation which appears in the translation. 不行=已革之法, 'annulled laws' (舊有是法而今不行者). 惟察,云云,—Even Këang Shing reads 其審克之 as the concluding clause of the paragraph, thereby admitting the force of the remark which I made on his mode of pointing par. 17.

P. 19. *General principles affecting the determination of crimes and the adjudication of the punishment due to them* 上刑至有權,—上刑 denotes a crime, which, on a first and superficial view, would seem to require to be dealt with by one of 'the higher penalties;' but there are circumstances discovered on examination which 適輕, 'tend to a lighter *consideration of it*.' It must then 下服, 'be adjudicated to the penalty for offences of the next lower class.' The 'Daily Explanation'

刑適重上服、輕重諸罰有權、刑罰世輕世重、惟齊非齊、有倫有要。○罰（二十節）懲非死、人極于病、非佞折獄、惟良折獄、罔非在中、察辭于差、

lower. Where it should incur one of the lower punishments, but there are aggravating circumstances, apply to it the *next* higher. The light and heavy fines are to be apportioned *in the same way* by the balance of circumstances. Punishments and fines should *also* be light in one age and heavy in another. To secure uniformity in this *seeming* irregularity, there are certain relations of things *to be considered*, and the essential principle *to be observed*.

20 "The chastisement of fines is short of death, yet it will produce extreme distress. They are not *therefore* persons of artful tongue who should determine criminal cases, but really good persons, whose awards will hit the right mean. Examine carefully where there are any discrepancies in the statements; the view which you were

defines 服 by 受刑, 'to receive punishment.' 權 denotes properly 'the weight of a steelyard,' moved backwards and forwards along the arm as the thing weighed is light or heavy. This original meaning of the char. appears clearly in 輕重諸罰有權. Këang Shing's exposition of the meaning is here terse and perspicuous:—本在上刑之科、而情適輕、則減一等治之、本在下刑之科、而情適重、則加一等治之、宜輕宜重、有權焉、不可執一也. 刑罰世輕世重,—the different circumstances of different times form the weights to be employed in determining the penalties to be adjudicated to crimes committed in them. The adjudicating minds, however, will be found to come to different conclusions. Thus Ying-tă quotes from the Chow Le, Bk. XXXV., near the beginning, that 'in a new country—*i.e.*, immediately after a revolution—the punishments should be light; in a well-ordered country, moderate; and in a rebellious country, heavy' (刑、新國、用輕典、平國、用中典；亂國、用重典). Këang Shing, again, quotes from Seun K'ing, 正論篇, that 'when a State is well governed, the punishments should be severe, and light when it is in disorder' (治則刑重、亂則刑輕). This will always be; but an approximation to uniformity may be obtained by what is said in conclusion,—惟齊非齊有倫有要. Wang Gan-shih, correctly and ingeniously, defines 倫 by 先後之序, 'the order of precedence and sequence,' and 要 by 衆體所會, 'that in which all the different members meet.'

P. 20. *General observations on the character of the men who should act as judges, and on points to which they should specially direct their attentions.* 罰懲至在中,—良, as opposed to 佞, evidently denotes what we mean by 'good and honest.' 罔非在中 may be understood either of the awards of such men (輕重出入、不失乎中), or of their character in judging (公正不偏、無不在中). Këang Shing takes the latter view, but the former is to be preferred. 察辭于差,—'examine pleas in difference;' *i.e.*, where a prisoner or a witness is making false statements, he will probably not be long or perfectly consistent with himself. Let the judge mark any discrepancy, and follow up from it his quest of the truth. 非從

非從惟從、哀敬折獄、明啓刑書胥占、咸庶中正、其刑其罰、其審克之、獄成而孚、輸而孚、其刑上備、有幷兩

determined-not to follow you may see occasion to follow; with compassion and reverence settle the cases; examine clearly the penal code and deliberate with all your assessors, that your decisions may be all likely to hit the proper mean and be correct:—whether it be the infliction of a punishment or a fine, examining carefully, and mastering every difficulty. When the case is thus concluded, all parties will acknowledge the justice of the sentence; and when it is reported, the sovereign will do the same. In sending up reports of cases, they must be full and complete. *If a man have been tried on* two counts, his two punishments *must be recorded.*"

惟從,—非從 may be considered as governed by 從. A judge should ever be open to the evidence, and not allow the impressions which he receives to be affected by foregone conclusions in his own mind. Gan-kwŏ connected this clause closely with the preceding, as does Këang Shing:—'Follow up the inquiry from the point where discrepancy of statement has arrested your attention, and find out the truth. Having got the truth, do not follow the statement, but follow the truth' (既得其情,非從其辭,惟從其情.) This view has nothing to recommend it. 明啓刑書胥占,—'clearly open—(*i.e.*, lay open, unfold. The literal signification is not that intended)—the book (or books) of punishment, and mutually deliberate.' 占 = 度, 'to deliberate,'—as if they were considering the oracles of divination.' 獄成而孚—若是則獄成於下,而民信之, 'in this way the case will be concluded below, and the people will believe—have confidence in—the judgment.' 輸 (= 奏, 'to report, send up a statement of the case') 而孚—獄輸於上而君信之, 'when the case is reported, the sovereign will believe—have confidence in—the judgment.' Këang Shing, after Gan-kwŏ, takes the second 而 as = 汝, and interprets the whole:—獄成而信矣乃輸汝信于上, 'when the case is thus concluded, and you have got to the truth of it, then present a memorial of your assured conclusion to the sovereign.' This is very harsh and unnatural. 其刑上備,有幷兩刑,—the 'Daily Explanation' expounds this:—獄辭又不可遺漏,當其上奏,須備載其情辭,或一人而犯兩刑,雖從重問擬,亦必將輕罪開列,取自上裁,方見精詳謹愼之意.

[In this chapter there are many good advices concerning the care and the methods with which justice should be administered. The principal thing, however, on which the king dwells is the redemption of punishments, and I fear he must be left with the obloquy generally attaching with Chinese writers to his memory, as having been the first to introduce, at least on an extensive scale, the system of accepting money as a compensation for the most heinous offences. He says, indeed, that the fine was to be exacted only where there was some doubt as to the justice of inflicting the punishment itself. China certainly, within the range of its history, was never the country where a government would, openly and without some glossing of the fact, take money as a satisfaction for transgressions of the law; but it is easy to see how grossly the regulations of king Muh were sure to be abused. I cannot conceive the scheme here set forth to have emanated save from a weak and needy monarch. The prefatory note says that this Book developes and explains the laws of the Hea dynasty for the redemption of punishment; but there is no intimation in the Book itself of such a thing, nor is the statement supported by any other authority. The student meets with

刑。○王廿一節曰、嗚呼、敬之哉、官伯族姓、朕言多懼、朕敬于刑、有德惟刑、今天相民、作配在下、明清于單辭、民之亂、罔不中聽獄之兩辭、無

21 VI. The king said, "Oh! let there be a feeling of reverence. Ye judges and chiefs, and all ye who my relatives are of the royal House, *know all* that I speak in much fear. I think with reverence of the subject of punishment, for the end of it is to promote virtue. Now Heaven, wishing to help the people, has made us its representatives here below. Be intelligent and pure in *hearing* one side of a case. The right ordering of the people depends on the impartial hearing of the pleas on both sides;—do not seek for private

the assertion continually; but there is really no evidence for it whatever;—it rests merely on the dictum of that note, for which moreover it would not be difficult to find another explanation.

The Book grounds itself in the history of Shun, and especially on his establishment of penal laws and the administration of them. Now, the redemption of punishments is mentioned by him. The notice is very brief. We are told that 'he gave delineations of the statutory punishments, and enacted banishment as a mitigation of the five great inflictions; with the whip to be employed for short-coming officers, and the stick for offending teachers, and money to be received for redeemable offences.' (See 'The Can. of Shun,' p. 11.) Whatever the offences were that might be redeemed with Shun, those deserving or seeming to deserve any of the five punishments were not among them. Nor does the Chow Le contain anything to indicate that prior to Muh the redemption of punishments was recognised by the emperors of the dynasty. To him belongs the bad distinction of this legislation.

Once introduced into China, however, the redemption of punishments has entered into the penal code of every subsequent dynasty. Two tables will be found in the preliminary matter to Sir George Staunton's translation of the Penal Code of the present Mwan-chow rulers of the empire, pp. 72, 73, giving the scale, first, of the pecuniary redemption of necessary redeemable offences, and second, of the redemption of others not necessarily redeemable, but made so on petition. According to the latter, the punishment of death may be compounded for on a graduated scale, according to the rank of the offender, rising from 1,200 ounces of silver for a private individual to 12,000 for an officer above the 4th rank. The scale for redemption from perpetual banishment is between 720 and 7,200 ounces. And that for temporary banishment and blows with the bamboo is between 480 and 4,800 ounces. Great official corruption and depravation of the general morality must connect with such a code.]

Ch. VI. P. 21. THE KING AGAIN ADDRESSES THE PRINCES AND JUDGES GENERALLY, AND EXHORTS THEM TO REVERENCE, IMPARTIALITY, AND PURITY, IN THE ADMINISTRATION OF JUSTICE. 官,伯,族姓,—by 官 and 伯 we may understand the 典獄 and 司政 of p. 12. Ying-tă endeavours to show that 族姓 are to be taken, the former as meaning the princes who were cadets of the royal House, and the latter as those who were of other surnames. He says:—襄,十二年,左傳,哭諸侯之例云,異姓臨于外,同族于禰廟,是相對,則族爲同姓,姓爲異姓. But the *whole* of the passage will not support his inference. It is—凡諸侯之喪,異姓臨於外,同姓於宗廟,同宗於祖廟,同族禰廟. There is thus no opposition in the passage between 姓 and 族. By 族姓 we are to understand the 伯父,伯兄,仲,叔,季弟,幼子,童孫, of p. 13. The passage in the 左傳 itself bears out this view. 有德惟刑,—the 'Daily Explanation' paraphrases this by—刑爲不得已而用,先王所以教民祇德者,是有德惟刑,而不當

或私家于獄之兩辭、獄貨非寶、惟府辜功、報以庶尤、永畏惟罰、非天不中、惟人在命、天罰不極、庶民罔有令政在于天

advantage to yourselves by means of those pleas. Gain got by the decision of cases is no precious acquisition; it is an accumulation of guilt, and will be recompensed with many evils:—you should ever stand in awe of the punishment of Heaven. It is not Heaven that does not deal impartially with men, but men ruin themselves. If the punishment of Heaven were not so extreme, the people would have no good government all under heaven."

以刑視刑也. I think this is probably the meaning; but the critics are far from being agreed in it. Gan-kwŏ, for instance, interprets from 朕言,—'My words are mostly those of warning. I feel reverently about punishments, and ought to employ none but the virtuous to preside in their administration.' 今天至在下,—Ts'ae understands this as meaning that 'Heaven would by punishments aid the people, and you, who are in the office of judges, may be said to correspond to it below' (天以刑相治斯民,汝實任責,作配在下). The meaning which I have given requires less of supplement, and equally lays a foundation for the advices that follow. See Wang Kăng-yay, *in loc.* 單辭 is supposed by Ts'ae to mean 'statements unsupported by witnesses' (無證之辭). The words are literally—'single pleas.' They seem clearly to be opposed to the 兩辭 which follows, and = 'one side of a case,' such as that which will first come before a magistrate. 亂 is to be taken in the sense of 治, 'to govern,' 'to order rightly.' 兩辭=兩造者之辭 'the cases of both the parties.' 無或至惟罰,—this must all be construed as if it were one sentence. 獄貨 is the result of 私家于獄之兩辭. 府 is defined by 聚, 'to collect,' 'to accumulate,' and 功 by 事, 'deeds.' 惟府辜功,—'but it is forming a treasury of deeds of guilt.' 尤=殃, 'judgments,' 'miseries.' Literally 庶尤 is 'numerous extraordinary evils.' 惟人在命,—from the relation of this clause to that which precedes,—非天不中, we can easily determine its meaning; but it is not easy to see clearly the force of 在命. We may at once dismiss the view of Gan-kwŏ and Këang Shing, that 命=教命, 'instructions and commands.' The paraphrase of the latter is:—夫天之罰人,非天道不中也,惟人自取之,在其教命不中耳. 命 has very much the meaning of 'fate,' and 惟人在命=人自造命,而有以致之, 'man makes his own fate, and brings the punishment of Heaven on him.' So says Kăng-yay, but he throws no light on 在. Woo Ch'ing tries to do this, saying 人之爲人于在有生之命, 'man is man in having the fate of his life;' i.e., men bring punishment on themselves, because it is their prerogative to be by their conduct the arbiters of their own fate. After all, the meaning must be taken a good deal on trust; the language cannot be satisfactorily explained. 天法至末,—the simplest way is to take these two clauses as an admonition to the princes and judges, that if they do not do what they can to insure good govt. for the people, Heaven's punishments will surely overtake them. Gan-kwŏ, Këang Shing and others, take 極 as =中, 'the perfect mean, and highest excellence,' referring to

下。○廿二節王曰、嗚呼、嗣孫、今往何監、非德于民之中、尚明聽之哉、哲人惟刑、無疆之辭、屬于五極、咸中有慶、受王嘉師、監于茲祥刑。

22 VII. The king said, "Oh! ye who shall hereafter inherit *the dignities and offices* of the present time, to whom are ye to go for your models? Must it not be to those who maintained and promoted the virtue belonging to the unbiassed nature of the people. I pray you give attention to my words. The wise men *of antiquity* by their use of punishments have obtained boundless fame. Everything relating to the five punishments exactly hit with them the due mean, and hence came their excellence. Receiving from your sovereigns the good multitudes, behold in the case of those men punishments made felicitous."

皇極 in 'The Great Plan,' but I cannot construe the last clause on that view.

Ch. VII. P. 22. CONCLUSION;—THE KING WISHES TO IMPRESS HIS LESSONS ON THE JUDGES AND PRINCES OF FUTURE AGES. It seems most natural to understand 嗣孫, of the descendants of those whom the king was addressing. Indeed I do not see how the 孫 or the 今往 can be taken in any other way. 非德于民之中,—it is difficult to tell exactly what Gan-kwŏ understood by this. He says:—非當立德於民,爲之中正乎. He then connects 尚明聽之哉 with this.—'If you do so, you will perhaps listen to my words.' Këang Shing connects the clauses similarly, but takes the 聽 in the sense of 聽獄, 'to listen to criminal cases.' The 哉 indicates to me that 尚明聽之 is spoken by the king without any syntactical relation to what precedes. Moreover, after 監 we expect that individuals will be spoken of as models to those who are addressed. I therefore take 非德于民之中, with Ts'ae, as=非用刑成德,而能全民所受之中者乎. 哲人至有慶,—acc. to the translation, 哲人 are those referred to as models,—the baron E and others mentioned in the first part of the king's address. Ts'ae explains the whole:—明哲之人,用刑而有無窮之譽,蓋由五刑咸得其中,所以有慶也. He takes 極 as simply=刑, 'punishments,' but it must denote more than that,—'punishments rightly inflicted and duly apportioned' (五刑之施,皆中正之極也). The editors of Yung Ching's Shoo, without condemning Ts'ae's view, direct attention to a construction proposed by Seu K'ëaou (徐僑) and some other critics, who understand 無疆之辭 of 'the numberless pleas, false and true, that might be advanced on any question before the judges.' The wise men spoken of could carry the light of principle and a clear understanding into all this confusion, and referring every point to the laws, bring out an issue exactly accordant with right.—徐僑曰情辭雖難窮,惟智哲則有見,以哲人而用刑,雖情辭之來,紛然無有疆界,而以理燭之,以辭係法,各協其極,自然有慶矣. 嘉師,—'the good multitudes.' This is a designation for the people, as naturally possessing the 'unbiassed nature,' which is denominated 民之中 above.

Concluding Note. The student, after this careful examination of 'Leu on Punishments,' will not wonder that many of the Chinese critics themselves should have been puzzled to account for its finding a place among the documents of the Shoo. They ask, 'Did Confucius mean that it should meet with approval or disapproval?' Ts'ae thinks he admitted it into his compilation by way of warning, and because in the kindly feeling of compassion for the people that breathes in it, it shows that the generous spirit of former times was not yet extinct. It is of no use speculating in this way. I suppose Confucius admitted the Book, because it was the best of the times that he could find. It is a pity that he did not accompany it with some exposition of his own views on the historical allusions in it, and on Muh's scheme for the redemption of punishments.

Wang Pih's 'Doubts' about this Book are:

言治目亂句，詳，後刑又者，而從宮所剕流者，者，直未之不可於者，康又刑君辟之之
舜，至王，衰一甚而五罪，云第亦蓋刑，宥而竄流不刑，罪嘗不期贖命罰，及命曰刑扑
帝為穆為刑者例，思之次罪，也，剕以也，義，也，決之於未之者，必之慎語，之又五鞭
於以於以五制凡致麗宥亦之刑也，所劓之竄刑，舜本亦罪刑以王德之王宥，聞贖
始所終所宥所一嘗正法，者，辟之辟刑，宥宥之矣，者刑，於必所武明殺成不未者，
刑此刑此流廣，此未有之之大世大劓以有者，辟之輕之失以之昔於不言，細辟，刑
訓備，訓輕，只甚逃而自宥寬以後宥也，所自放大宥而王者所王辟，主可之三乃贖
刑，義也，罰也，者者之，各從也，爾，者，以宮刑，亦也，也，而輕，穆輕之穆起雖不赦曰辟，也，
呂而世而世該事忽流，有之之流所宥墨中，殛放流不疑，而舜刑，其也，有無既止贖
一約之繁之所敘世與自寬輕而者，以也，之宥宥以嘗可輕，宥，無導叔自茲陳，以俱
有不亂極殺報報，戒人，乃忍之是盡刑制言謂辭姦，意，惻人之典聽刑巡未切言與，
凡而不謂死，者者者一下，不殺者，之五之斯愚之之本矜聖存於世贖王其一斯者
贖，往而可必死死生於天人好殺義為人也，哉，吏獄之哀風，變察後其穆至此財，情
可所得約，者為為為忍於聖毫不至，以聖虐義法典刑四，還之精為以謂勞，為民本
如無烏之人特也，也，也，忍也，一可之首是之於也，乎制凡之法能以非子民乃斂之
刑者，下章殺非戒立立不生有不仁書，則苗害書察人語代變，其可戒，朱匱計，以王
之眥天三而死，者人下小，好豈於為之苗，有大律精聖之三之以尚之也，財為術，穆
辟之人，世矣，必生一天者為心，至以刑有師不者，能識克有世亦姦，刑取度，以之得
大鍰殺後簡而為為為忍以之刑所呂於反豈刑徒不審猶其書，之用可無無宜以
刑，千可哉，其人也，法法而所人意，乃也，創刑，也，呂也，而其怛，以於獄訟之遊年，權足

THE BOOKS OF CHOW.

BOOK XXVIII. THE CHARGE TO PRINCE WAN.

文侯之命

一節 王若曰、父義和、丕顯文武、克慎明德、昭升于上、敷聞在下、惟時上帝、集厥命于文王、亦惟先正、克左右昭事厥辟、越小大謀猷、罔不率從、肆先祖懷

1 The king spoke to the following effect:—"Uncle E-ho, how illustrious were Wăn and Woo! Carefully did they illustrate their virtue, till it rose brightly on high, and the fame of it was widely diffused here below. Therefore did God cause his favouring decree to light upon king Wăn. *Thereafter* there were ministers who aided and illustriously served their sovereigns, following and carrying out their plans and counsels great and small, so that my fathers sat tranquilly upon the throne.

INTRODUCTORY HISTORICAL NOTE. The Book of the Shoo at which we have now arrived is separated from the last by an interval of two hundred years. Between king P'ing who gave the Charge to the prince Wăn and king Muh there had reigned seven sovereigns of the House of Chow; and it is remarkable that not a single document of the reign of any of them was incorporated by Confucius with this volume. Of such monuments there must have been many. No Books have here been lost. Those two hundred years in the dynasty to which he himself belonged were left by the sage a blank. This fact is sufficient to prove that Confucius did not compile the Shoo as a history of his country, or even intend that it should afford materials for such a history. His design, we may rather judge, was to bring together such pieces as might show the wonderful virtue and intelligence of ancient sovereigns and statesmen, who should be models to those of future ages. But in all the space of time of which I am writing, there was neither sovereign nor statesman to whom it could give him pleasure to refer. Indeed, king Woo, the first of the sovereigns of Chow, had no successor equal to himself. But for his brother, the duke of Chow, the dynasty would have come to an early end. There was a constant degeneracy after king K'ang. Its progress was now and then temporarily,

but feebly, arrested. Power and influence passed with a steady progress from the imperial court to one feudatory and another, till in the time of Confucius himself the successors of Woo were hardly more than 'shadows of an empty name.' According to my plan I introduce here the names of the sovereigns between Muh and P'ing, and a few particulars of their reigns.

[i.] E-hoo (緊扈), the son of Muh, and known as king Kung (共王), or 'The Reverent' (謚法,旣過能改曰共), succeeded to the throne B.C. 945, and reigned for 12 years, acc. to the common chronology. The only incident of his reign of which we find mention is given by Sze-ma Ts'een from the 國語,周語上, and is to the effect that the king was on one occasion rambling near the river King, in the pres. dep. of P'ing-leang (平凉), Kan-suh, attended by the duke K'ang of Meih (密康公), a small principality in that part of the country, when three young ladies introduced themselves into their company. Duke K'ang's mother advised him to leave them to the emperor, but he appropriated them to himself. Within a year the king made an end of him and his principality, indignant, we are to suppose, at the duke's conduct in the matter of the three ladies. I do not know that this story, as I have given it, is entitled to much faith. None is due to the romantic account of it, which is found in the history of P. de Mailla.

[ii.] King Kung was succeeded, B.C. 933, by his son Këen (囏), known as king E (懿王), or 'The Mild' (謚法,温柔賢善曰懿), who reigned 25 years. All that Ts'een says of him is that in his time 'the royal House went on to decay, and poets made him an object of their satire.' He removed the capital to Hwae-le (槐里), a place in the pres. dis. of Hing-p'ing (興平), dep. of Se-gan. This seems, however, to have been merely a temporary measure. The 'Bamboo Books' speak of several irruptions of barbarous tribes in this reign.

[iii.] A brother of king E, by name Peih-fang (辟方), succeeded him, and is known as king Heaou (孝王), or 'The Filial' (謚法,慈惠愛親曰孝). Ts'een says nothing more of him than that he came to the throne and died. His reign, however, lasted from B.C. 908 to 894. During this period, the chiefs of the House destined to supersede that of Chow begin to make their appearance on the stage of affairs. They traced their lineage up to the baron Yih (益; often called 翳), the Forester of Shun. One of them, named Fei-tsze (非子), had made himself famous at this time by his skill in rearing horses, and was taken into the king's service to superintend his studs in the plains near the rivers K'een and Wei (汧渭之間), and was finally invested with a small territory of which the chief city was Ts'in, still the name of an inferior department of Kan-suh. The king appointed him there to continue the sacrifices to Yih, as the head of the Ying clan or family (號曰秦嬴), which thenceforth begins to make a great figure in the empire.

[iv.] On the death of king Heaou, the princes raised a son of his brother and predecessor, of the name of Sëĕ (燮), to the throne, which he occupied for 16 years, till B.C. 878. He is known as king E (夷王), or 'The Peaceable' (謚法,安心好靜曰夷). He proved a weak sovereign, and was in bondage to the princes to whom he owed the empire. It is objected to him that, when he gave audience to them, he descended from the dais to meet them, as if he were their equal merely. The chief of the State of Tsoo extended the possessions of his House during this reign, and assumed the right of investing his sons with his conquests without reference to the court. He arrogated to himself, moreover, the title of king. The imperial authority was evidently but little cared for.

[v.] King E was succeeded by his son Hoo (胡), known as king Le (厲王), or 'The Cruel' (謚法,殺戮無辜曰厲). A long reign of 51 years is assigned to him, but during the last thirteen years he was a fugitive, and the govt. was administered by two of the nobles. In B.C. 841, the people rose in rebellion, their patience exhausted by the various oppressions, engendered by the avarice, suspicions, and cruelty of the sovereign. The king made his escape, and fled to Che (彘), in the pres. sub. dep. of Hoh (霍州), dep. of P'ing-yang, Shanse, where he found a refuge. Disappointed by the escape of the tyrant, the people sought to wreak their fury on his eldest son, by name Tsing (靖), quite a youth, who had hidden himself in the house of the duke of Shaou, a descendant of Shih so famous in the early reigns of the dynasty. The loyalty of the ancestor had descended to the present Head of the family. As a minister, he had remonstrated, though in vain, with king Le, on his evil courses; he now sacrificed his own son to save the heir to the crown. The people surrounded the house, and insisted on Tsing being delivered to them that they might satiate their fury by tearing him in pieces. The duke gave his own son, of the same age as the prince, into their hands, and on him they worked their pleasure. Subsequently, the dukes of Shaou and Chow carried on the govt. for the prince until Le's death, which took place in Che in B.C. 827.

[vi.] Prince Tsing commenced a long reign of 46 years in B.C. 826. He is known as king Seuen (宣王), or 'The Distinguished' (謚法,聖善周聞曰宣). He had learned wisdom in the school of adversity, and from the

statesmen who had protected his youth. Most of the princes returned in a measure to their allegiance, but the empire was distracted by irruptions of the barbarous tribes on every side. In B.C. 821, there was a great drought, and the misery of the people was extreme. The virtue of the king seems to have experienced a decay. In B.C. 815, he neglected, notwithstanding the remonstrances of his ministers, the custom of putting his own hand to the plough, and turning up a furrow in a field enclosed for the purpose, as an acknowledgment of the dependance of the empire on agriculture, and an example to all its husbandmen. He was proceeding to resign himself to idle habits, when the queen divested herself of her ornaments, and accused herself of seducing the king to self-indulgence, and to lie long in bed. This roused him to resume his early ways. In his 39th year, B.C. 788, he took the field against one of the western tribes, known by the name of the Keang (羌), as if they were sprung from the same stock as the princes of Ts'e, and sustained a great defeat at a place called Ts'een-mow (千畝), or 'The Thousand Acres.' From the chagrin of this he never recovered. A few years after, he was proceeding 'to number the people,' like king David of Israel, with a view to collect an immense force, and wipe out the disgrace he had incurred. His ministers succeeded in averting his purpose, but he became melancholy and capricious, put to death some of his most faithful advisers, and died in a fit of moody insanity, as we may judge, in B.C. 779.

[vii.] Seuen was succeeded by his son Nëë (涅), known as king Yew (幽), or 'The Dark' (謚法動靜亂常曰幽), who was slain by a tribe of barbarian invaders called 'The Dog *Jung*' (犬戎) after an inglorious reign of 11 years. In the sixth year of his reign, on the 29th of August (new style), B.C. 775, occurred an eclipse of the sun. It is commemorated in the She King, Pt. II., Bk. IV., Ode iii., as 'an announcement of evils by the sun and moon.' Other symptomatic aberrations, as they appeared to be, in the order of nature are mentioned by the poet along with it:—

'The thunder roars, the lightning flashes;—
There is a want of repose, a want of good.
All the streams are overflowing;
The tops and crags of the mountains fall.
High hills become valleys;
Deep valleys become hills.
Alas! that this man
Will not correct himself.'

This eclipse gives us a point of chronological certainty for the history of this reign. It is the first of the long list of eclipses, by the mention of which Chinese history from the 8th century before Christ acquires more certainty than belongs to that of the earlier ages. The ruin and death of king Yew were brought about by the ascendancy which a female favourite, called Paou-sze (褒姒), gained over him. He had married and established as queen a daughter of the prince of Shin (申). This principality was in the pres. sub. dep. of Tang [鄧州], dep. of Nan-yang, Ho-nan); and his son by her, called E-k'ew (宜臼), was recognised as heir-apparent of the throne. The rise of Paou-sze was followed by the degradation of the prince and his mother. E-k'ew was sent, as a preliminary measure, to the court of Shin, 'to learn good manners.' His mother was then reduced to a second place, and Paou-sze was declared queen in her room, and an infant son by her took the place and dignity of heir-apparent. Scenes were enacted like those of Këë and Me-he, or of Show and Tă-ke. To please Paou-sze the king made game of all the nobles. The prince of Shin called in the assistance of the Dog Jung, and attacked the capital. He did not intend the death of the king, but only that of the intruding favourite and her son, and the restoration of his daughter and grandson to their rights. His barbarian auxiliaries, however, could not be controlled; the king flying from Haou was pursued by them and put to death, while Paou-sze became the captive of their chief.

Thus ended the sway of what is called 'the Western Chow.' The victorious nobles having expelled the Jung from the capital with some difficulty, brought back E-k'ew from Shin, and hailed him as king. He is known as king P'ing (平王), or 'The Tranquillizer' (謚法執事有制曰平). His first measure was to transfer the capital eastwards to Lŏ-yang, fulfilling at length, but under disastrous circumstances, the wishes of the duke of Chow; and from this time, B.C. 769, dates the history of 'the Eastern Chow.'

THE NAME OF THE BOOK.—文侯之命. 'The Charge to prince Wăn.' I have related in the above note how the Jung who had been called in by the prince of Shin to punish king Yew went far beyond his wishes, killing the king, and wishing to keep possession of the capital. To get rid of them he obtained the assistance of the princes of Tsin (晉), Ts'in (秦), Wei (衞), and Ch'ing (鄭), who in the first place drove out the barbarians, and then sent for Yew's son from Shin to take possession of the vacant throne. Among his earliest measures was the rewarding of the princes who had come in this way to the relief of the royal House; and this Book is said to contain the appointment of the prince of Tsin to be president or chief of several of the other princes (以文侯爲方伯).

The princes of Tsin were descended from king Woo's son, called Yu, and generally styled, from the name of his appanage, the prince of T'ang (唐叔虞). His son removed from T'ang to Tsin; and in course of time the principality came, though not without a struggle with a usurping uncle, to Ch'ow (仇), in B.C. 780, and was held by him for 35 years. He received after death the title of Wăn, or 'The Accomplished;'—it was he to whom the Charge in this Book was given. See in the dictionary

在位。○嗚呼、閔予小子、嗣造天丕愆、資澤于下民、

2 "Oh! an object of pity am I, who am but a little child. Just as I have succeeded to the throne, Heaven has severely chastised me, and cut off our resources of bounty to the inferior people;

no fewer than six different descriptions of character, any one of which might be considered to be expressed by the title Wăn.

In this account of the time and occasion of this Charge, I have followed the authority of the prefatory note, supported by Gan-kwŏ, K'ang-shing, and Wang Suh. The Book itself, however, it will be perceived, does not mention the name of the king, and the name of E-ho, by which the receiver of the Charge is called, is only, as will be seen on par. 1, an occasion of perplexity. There was a tradition during the Han dynasty that the Book belonged to a later period, and in Sze-ma Ts'een's history the Charge appears as given, B.C. 631, by king Sëang (襄王) to duke Wăn of Tsin, who was then the leading prince of the empire. Ma Yung also, we may infer from his explanation of the characters 義和, held this view. There is nothing in the matter of the Charge itself absolutely decisive in favour of either hypothesis. It seems, perhaps, to suit better the relations between king P'ing and the prince (=marquis) Wăn than those between Sëang and duke Wăn.

The Book is found in both the texts.

CONTENTS. The Book is short, containing only four paragraphs, which are divided into three and one by the usual mark of change of subject in the 'Announcements' and 'Charges' of the Shoo,—the compiler's statement of 'The king said.'

The king begins by celebrating the virtue and happy condition of Wăn and Woo, and the services rendered to the State by the worthy ministers of subsequent reigns. He contrasts with this the misery and distraction of his own times, deploring especially his want of wise counsellors and helpers, and praising prince Wăn for the services which he had rendered. The Book then concludes with the special Charge by which the king would reward the prince's merit in the past, and stimulate him to greater exertions in the future.

P. 1. *The king celebrates the virtue of Wăn and Woo who founded their dynasty, and the happiness of their successors who were assisted by able ministers.* 父義和,—'Uncle E-ho.' The princes of Tsin, we have seen, were a branch of the imperial House; and hence the king addresses Wăn as his 'uncle;'—see on Book XXIII., p. 6. But Wăn's name, as has been mentioned, was Ch'ow (仇), so that we are brought to the conclusion that he is here called by his 'style' (字) or marriage designation. Such is the view of Gan-kwŏ. Other explanations of the characters were attempted by K'ang-shing, and Ma Yung, which may be seen in the 後案. 惟時(=是,=是之故)上帝集厥命于文王,—this is the common way of speaking about the origin of the Chow dynasty,—that the divine appointment lighted on king Wăn. But as king Woo has just been mentioned along with him, as equally virtuous and distinguished, it seems strange that he should be dropt in this important declaration. The truth is that father and son in the persons of Wăn and Woo were blended together as *one* founder of the dynasty of Chow. If the appointment of Heaven lighted on Wăn, it would also have dropt from him to the ground but for the character of Woo. In interpreting the rest of the par. we may begin with the last clause, where the king must intend by 先祖, 'my forefathers,' not Wăn and Woo, but those who succeeded them. The 'Daily Explanation' would limit them to Ching and K'ang, with whom the line of powerful monarchs of Chow may be said to have ceased. But king P'ing might not have been willing to acknowledge this, and we may suppose that he speaks of his predecessors generally, as having fallen on better times than himself. Explaining 先祖 thus of the sovereigns subsequent to Woo, the same individuals are probably intended by 厥辟; and the phrase 先正 denotes 'their ministers;'—also generally, without any special application, Wăn's own ancestor, 'the prince of T'ang,' being included among them. Comp. the 2d par. of the 'Keun-ya.' 謀猷,—see on Bk. XXI., p. 6. 懷=安, 'to be tranquil.' 先祖懷在位=我先祖得安在位.

P. 2. *The king deplores the unhappiness of his own position, himself young and feeble, and the empire chastised by Heaven and torn by barbarian invaders, while he could expect little assistance from his ministers.* 嗣造至下民,—Gan-kwŏ, Wang Suh, and Këang Shing, all take 造 as =遭, 'to meet with,' so that it governs 天丕愆. This is quite allowable; but when we carry on the regimen of 造 to the next clause,—殄資, 云云, the construction becomes too forced. I therefore adopt the view of Ts'ae, that 造=始, and 嗣造=

侵戎我國家純、即我御事、罔或耆壽俊在厥服、予則罔克、曰、惟祖惟父、其伊恤朕躬、嗚呼、有績予一人、永綏在位。三節 ○父

and the invading barbarous tribes of the west have greatly injured our empire. Moreover, among the managers of my affairs, there are none of age and experience, and distinguished ability, in their offices. I am *thus* unequal to the difficulties of my position, and say to myself, 'My grand-uncles and uncles, you ought to compassionate my case. Oh! if there were those who could establish their merit in behalf of me, the one man, I might long enjoy repose upon the throne.'

方嗣位之初, 'just as I have succeeded to the throne.' 天 is then the nominative to 愆 and 殄. 愆, meaning 'a fault,' 'a crime,' is here used as a verb, = 'to deal with as a criminal,' 'to chastise.' The 'Daily Explanation' for 天丕愆 gives 爲天所大譴. 資澤于下民, 'the necessaries descending like moistening rain upon the lower people,' mean the favours and help which ought to flow from the throne to the people, but which were now cut off. The king is probably referring to his own troubles and the troubles of the people, occasioned by the removal of the capital from Haou to Lŏ-yang. 侵戎我國家純,—the 戎 here naturally leads our thoughts to the western barbarians, and especially to the 'Dog Jung,' who had killed king Yew, and kept possession of Haou. Gan-kwŏ, however, takes the term in the sense of 兵, 'weapons.' But whether we take it in that meaning, or as a name, we have to understand a verb like 傷, 'to injure,' carrying on the action of 侵戎 to 國家. 純=大, 'great,' or 'greatly.' 即我至厥服,—耆 壽 go together, signifying 'aged,' 'men of years and experience.' I do not see how we can discriminate these terms, and hence the 俊,—'talented,' stands awkwardly by itself. 服=官 or 職, as in Bk. V., p. 8. Këang Shing adopts here a reading current in the Han dynasty, and edits:—即我御事, 罔或耆壽咎在厥躬 (=躬), 'among the managers of my affairs, there are none of age and experience. The evils are on my person.' This is not liable to the difficulty which 俊 presents in the common reading; but the sentiment does not seem appropriate to the place. 予則罔克,—'I then am not adequate;' *i.e.*, feeble, unsupported; in the midst of calamities, the king felt unequal to the difficulties he had to cope with. 曰惟至末,—the 曰 indicates that the king thus spoke to himself. As Ying-tă says, 私爲言. 惟祖惟父 is an appeal to the princes of the same surname with himself. As 父, we have seen, denotes 'uncles,' 祖 will be 'grand-uncles.' The 'Daily Explanation' gives for it—爾諸侯有在我祖父之列者. Medhurst has missed the meaning, and renders—'Of those who have stood before my grandfather and father.' Gaubil has missed it in a different way:—'Quel est donc celui qui pourra me tenir lieu de grand-pere et de pere?' 伊 is here a particle,—惟. We have to suppose a second 予一人 as the nominative to 綏. The end of this par. thus corresponds to that of the preceding. Chang Kew-shing observes that the weakness of king P'ing's character is here apparent. He shows no self-reliance. He has no higher aim than to live quietly and have tranquillity in his time.

義和、汝克昭乃顯祖、汝肇刑文武、用會紹乃辟、追孝于前文人、汝多修扞我于艱、若汝予嘉。○王(四節)曰、父義和、其歸視爾師、寧爾邦、用賚爾秬鬯一卣、彤弓一、彤

3 "Uncle E-ho, you render still more glorious your illustrious ancestor. You were the first to imitate the example of Wăn and Woo, collecting *the scattered powers*, and continuing *the all-but-broken line of* your sovereign. Your filial piety goes back to your accomplished ancestor, *and is equal to his.* You have done much to repair my *losses*, and defend me in my difficulties, and of you, being such, I am full of admiration."

4 The king said, "Uncle E-ho, return home, survey your multitudes, and tranquillize your State. I reward you with a jar of spirits, made from the black millet, mixed with odoriferous herbs; with

P. 3. *The king acknowledges the services which prince Wăn had rendered, and praises him.* By 乃顯祖, 'your distinguished ancestor,' we are to understand the prince of T'ang. He also is intended by the 前文人 below. 汝肇刑文武,—whether we define 肇 by 始, as in the translation, or by 敏, 'earnestly,' as Këang Shing does, it seems very extravagant to be comparing prince Wăn to the kings Wăn and Woo. Ts'ae observes that the principles of Wăn and Woo might be said to be extinct, when the ministers about the court were only such as are described in the last par., but now prince Wăn had begun to lead the way to their revival, (後罔或耆壽俊在厥服, 則刑文武之道絕矣, 今刑文武自文侯始, 故曰肇刑文武). 用會紹乃辟,—會=合, 'to unite;' 紹=繼, 'to continue.' But 'to unite and continue your sovereign' is not very intelligible. The meaning is as I have given it. P'ing was a fugitive, and his claim to the throne disallowed, when his father was killed. Then the Jung held possession of the capital. It was owing, he means to say, principally to prince Wăn, that the forces of several princes—which the king might call his forces—were collected, the Jung driven out, and he himself brought back to the throne. 追孝于前文人,—'with your filial piety you pursue after the former accomplished man.' The meaning is much the same as that of the former clause, 汝克昭乃顯祖. 汝多修扞我于艱, 'you have done much to repair and to guard me in difficulties.' Wang Ts'eaou says:—修, 完於殘破之後, 扞, 禦於侵侮之時.

P. 4. *The Charge.* 其歸視爾師,—師=衆, 'multitudes,' 'people.' The sending the prince home might be considered a favour, as his attendance on the king in the removal from Haou to Lŏ must have been a service of no little difficulty and fatigue. 用賚爾秬鬯一卣,—to explain the 用,—'therefore,' the 'Daily Explanation' introduces in its paraphrase—予嘉汝功, 'I admire your merit.' We must suppose some thought in the king's mind, which is not expressed in the text. On 秬鬯一卣, comp. the explan. of 秬鬯二卣 in Bk. XIII., p. 21. The spirits thus presented to him would be employed by prince Wăn in sacrificing to his ancestor, the prince of T'ang, and announcing to his spirit the favour conferred on him by the king. 彤=赤, 'red;' 盧=黑, 'black.' The conferring on a

矢百、盧弓一、盧矢百、馬四匹、父往哉、柔遠能邇、惠康小民、無荒寧、簡恤爾都、用成爾顯德。

one red bow and a hundred red arrows; with one black bow, and a hundred black arrows; and with four horses. Go, my uncle! Show kindness to those who are afar off, and help those who are near at hand; cherish and secure the repose of the inferior people; do not idly seek your ease; inspect and compassionate *all in* your capital, *and other cities*—thus completing your illustrious virtue."

prince of a bow and arrows was understood to invest him with the power of punishing all within his jurisdiction who were refractory to the imperial commands, but not of taking life without first reporting to the court. See in the Le Ke, Bk. 王制, Pt. ii., p. 19,—賜弓矢,然後征,賜鈇鉞然後殺. Whether anything special was denoted by sending to Wăn two bows of different colours, and two sets of arrows, I do not know. 柔遠能邇,—see Bk. XXII., p. 8; *et al.* 簡恤爾都,—都 here is most probably to be understood as used not for the chief city only, but for all the other cities of the State. Ts'ae, after Gan-kwŏ, makes it = 國之都鄙, 'from the capital to the borders.' Soo Shih made the 簡 refer to 'the officers' (簡閱其士), over whom the prince should keep a watchful eye, and 恤 to the people, for whom he should exercise a compassionate care (惠恤其民). It is by no means clear to me that this Charge is the appointment of Wăn to be a 方伯, 'chief of a region.' That opinion probably arose from the view to which I have referred, that it was duke Wăn to whom the Charge was given.

Concluding historical note. In the 51st or last year of P'ing's reign, occurred an eclipse of the sun, Feb. 14, B.C. 719. He is the last of the emperors of the Chow dynasty, with whom the Shoo has anything to do; but the 'Spring and Autumn' commences in B.C. 721, with the first year of duke Yin (隱公) of Loo, and continues the history for about two centuries and a half longer.

It may be well here to give a list of the rest of the sovereigns of Chow. P'ing was the 13th.

[xiv.] King Hwan, (桓王), or 'The Laborious' (克敬勤民曰桓), grandson of P'ing. B.C. 718—696.

[xv.] King Chwang (莊王), or 'The Unsuccessful' (武而不遂曰莊), son of Hwan. B.C. 695—681.

[xvi.] King He (僖王; also written 釐王), or 'The Essayer' (有伐而還曰釐), son of Chwang. B.C. 680—676.

[xvii.] King Hwuy (惠王), or 'The Kind' (柔質慈民曰惠), son of He. B.C. 675—651.

[xviii.] King Sëang (襄王), or 'The Virtuous Enlarger' (辟地有德曰襄), son of Hwuy. B.C. 650—618.

[xix.] King K'ing (頃王), or 'The Trembling' (甄心動懼曰頃), son of Sëang. B.C. 617—612.

[xx.] King Kwang (匡王), or 'The Corrector' (貞心大度曰匡), son of K'ing. B.C. 611—606.

[xxi.] King Ting (定王), or 'The Establisher, (安民法古曰定), son of Kwang. B.C. 605—585.

[xxii.] King Këen (簡王), or 'The Easy-minded' (平易不訾曰簡), son of Ting. B.C. 584—571.

[xxiii.] King Ling (靈王), or 'The Uninjuring' (亂而不損曰靈), son of Këen. B.C. 570—544.

[xxiv.] King King (景王), or 'The

Righteously-successful' (由義而濟曰景), son of Ling. B.C. 543—519.

[xxv.] King King (敬王), or 'The Respectful' (善合法典曰敬), son of King. B.C. 518—476. King King (景) died in the beginning of summer, when his son Măng (猛), known as king Taou (悼王), was declared his successor; but he died before the year was out, and does not enter into the list of emperors.

[xxvi.] King Yuen (元王), or 'The Popular' (行義悅民曰元), son of King (敬). B.C. 474—466.

[xxvii.] King Ching-ting (貞定王), or 'The Pure and Correct' (清白守節曰貞, 純行不爽曰定), son of Yuen. B.C. 465—440.

[xxviii.] King K'aou (考王), son of Ching-ting. B.C. 439—425. In the spring of B.C. 446, Ching-ting died, and was immediately succeeded by his eldest son,—king Gae (哀王),—who was shortly killed by a brother, who seized the throne, and is called king Sze (思王). He again was killed before the end of the year by another brother, who held the throne, and became king K'aou.

[xxix.] King Wei-lëë (威烈王), or 'The Majestic and Resolute' (彊毅執正曰威, 秉德尊義曰烈), son of K'aou. B.C. 424—401.

[xxx.] King Gan (安王), or 'The Tranquil' (好和不爭曰安), son of Wei-lëë. B.C. 400—375.

[xxxi.] King Lëë (烈王), or 'The Resolute' (秉德尊義曰烈), son of king Gan. B.C. 374—368.

[xxxii.] King Hëen (顯王), or 'The Illustrious (?),' younger brother of Lëë. B.C. 367—320.

[xxxiii.] King Shin-tsing (慎靚王), son of Hëen. B.C. 319—314.

[xxxiv.] King Nan (赧王), or 'The Ruined and Sad' (喪國心愧曰赧), son of Shin-tsing. B.C. 313—255.

Nan surrendered the empire to the chief of Ts'in, but the supremacy of that State was not fully acknowledged till B.C. 221.

THE BOOKS OF CHOW.

BOOK. XXIX. THE SPEECH AT PE.

費誓

公曰、嗟人無譁、聽命、徂茲淮夷徐戎竝興。

1 The duke said, "Ah! ye men, make no noise, but listen to my commands. We are *now* going *to punish* those wild tribes of the Hwae and of Seu, who have risen up together.

The Name of the Book.—費誓, 'The speech at Pe.' This Book carries us back from the times of P'ing to those of Ching, the second of the emperors of Chow. The speech recorded in it is attributed in the Preface to the Shoo to Pih-k'in the son of the duke of Chow; and there is a general acquiescence of tradition and critics in this view. We may account for its position out of the chronological order from its being a record not of any imperial doings, but of the sentiments of the prince of a State. K'ang-shing and others placed it before 'Leu on Punishments,' which arrangement, still leaving it out of the order of time, would deprive us of the explanation just given. The speech has reference to some military operations against the tribes on the Hwae and other wild hordes of the province of Seu or T'seu; but we saw that they were in insurrection many times during the reign of Ching, and we cannot tell to what year the Book should be referred. Pih-k'in presided over his principality for the long period of 58 years, and died B.C. 1,062. The speech was made at Pe (費;—see Ming-shing on what he says was the older form of the name). On the situation of this place I give the note of Ch'in Sze-k'ae:—'Pih-k'in had his capital in the pres. dis. of K'euh-fow (曲阜), dep. of Yen-chow, and Pe was in the dis. still so called, in the dep. of E-chow (沂州). Now, acc. to the 寰宇記, E is east from Yen-chow 385 *le;* Pe is 95 *le* to the north-west of E; K'euh-fow is east from Yen-chow 30 *le;* and thus from K'euh-fow to Pe was 280 *le* or thereabouts. At the commencement of the "Spring and Autumn," Pe was an independent principality, for in the first year of duke Yin (B.C. 721) we read in the 左傳 that 'the baron of Pe led a force to fortify Lang' (費伯帥師城郎). Afterwards, it became the chief city of the Ke family of Loo, as we read again, in the first year of duke He (B.C. 658), that 'he granted to Ke Yew the fields on the south of the Wăn, and Pe' (公賜季友汶陽之田及費). In the Analects also Min Tsze-k'een appears as asked to be governor of Pe (Ana. VI., vii.). We may conclude, therefore, that, in the time of Pih-k'in, Pe did not belong to Loo. But it was in his jurisdiction as the chief or ruling prince of the regions of the east (東方伯). Gan-kwŏ is wrong when he says that Pe was a place in the eastern border of Loo, and Ying-tă when he says that Pih-k'in did not go beyond the territory of Loo. Pih-k'in's speech was like that of K'e at Kan, or of T'ang at Ming-t'eaou, or of king Woo at Muh; *i.e.*, it was made like those when the army approached the territory of the enemy.'

The Book is in both the texts.

Contents. Pih-k'in appears at the head of his host proceeding against the tribes of the Hwae and the wild people of Ts'eu. Having commanded silence, he issues his orders, first, that the soldiers all have their arms in good order; next, that the people of the country take

○善敹乃甲冑、敿乃干、無敢不弔、備乃弓矢、鍛乃戈矛、礪乃鋒刃、無敢不善。○ 二節

2 "Have in good repair your coats of mail and helmets; have the laces of your shields well secured:—presume not to have any of these but in perfect order. Prepare your bows and arrows; temper your lances and spears; sharpen your pointed and edged weapons:—presume not to have any of these but in good condition.

care of the oxen and horses of the army; further, that the troops on no account leave their ranks or go astray; and finally, he appoints the day when he will commence operations against the enemy, and commands that all the requisite preparations be made.

P. 1. *Opening of the speech. Occasion of the expedition.* By 'men' we are to understand all in the host, his own subjects of Loo, and the troops of States whom he had called to aid in the expedition,—officers and common men. 徂茲,云云,—there is a difficulty here with the interpretation of 徂茲. Ts'ae, after Soo Shih, takes the characters as = 往者, 'formerly,' so that the meaning of the clause is—'Formerly, the wild tribes of the Hwae and the Ts'eu rose in insurrection together.' But why refer to what they had done in former times? We must understand, on this construction, something like—'And now again, they take advantage of our present circumstances, and give fresh trouble, so that we have to take the field against them.' This is the way in which the 'Daily Explanation' brings out the meaning:—往者淮夷叛亂,爲王室之患,今又乘我始就國封,軍旅未習,乃脅徐方之戎,一時竝起. Gan-kwŏ's view was different. He took 徂 indeed as = 往,—not adverbially, however, but as a verb, meaning 'to go,'—'we are going,' or 'let us go.' The 茲 is = 此, 'this,' or 'these.'—'We are going to those tribes of the Hwae and of Seu, who have risen up together;' *i.e.*, we are going to chastise them. This construction is followed by Lin Che-k'e and Këang Shing, the latter of whom expounds the clause:—言往征此淮徐戎竝起爲寇者. I have translated according to this view. 'The wild tribes about the Hwae' are mentioned so far back as the time of Yu;—see 'The Tribute of Yu,' Pt. i, p. 35. They belonged to the province of Ts'eu, and why there should be mentioned in addition to them another tribe, called the 'Jung of Ts'eu' is a question which cannot be fully answered. 戎 was properly the name of the wild people on the west of the Middle kingdom. Possibly, a tribe of them had forced their way to the eastern coasts, and settled in one or more places of Ts'eu, continuing to retain their original designation. Wang Kăng-yay [often mentioned likewise as Wang Ch'ung-yun (王充耘)] has an instructive and suggestive note on the passage:—'徂 means "to go." The passage is best taken with K'ung Gan-kwŏ as meaning—"We are now going to smite those E and Jung." K'ung says that the various tribes of wild people were simply bridled by the emperors of the early dynasties and allowed to dwell in different places within the different provinces; but I venture to think that the true state of the case concerning them was this:—Anciently, when the country was first peopled, it was not possible for the principles of propriety and righteousness to penetrate everywhere with a transforming power. All who were unaffected by those principles were classed as E or Jung, and all who recognised them and came under their influence were said to be Hwa and Hea (輒謂爲華夏). We are not to suppose that it was necessary to be living outside the nine provinces, in what are called "the four seas," in order to be Jung and E. In the account of Yu's five domains, indeed, the Man and the E are said to have been in the domain of Restraint and the Wild domain; but when we examine the state of the empire of Chow, we find "the white Teih" (白狄) in T'aeyuen [in Shan-se], the E of the Hwae and the Jung of Ts'eu in the province of Ts'eu, the Lae E in Ts'e (齊有萊夷), and the Jung of Luh-wun about the E river (伊川有陸渾之戎). Even such great States as Woo and Tsoo had to drive out the E and Teih. It is plain that these tribes were not confined to the two domains to which we have referred. Shun told Kaou-yaou to restrain by punishments the Man and E who were disturbing the empire, which simply means that he was to punish those who denied the principles of propriety and righteousness, and violated them. The critics, not examining the case sufficiently,

三節 今惟淫舍牿牛馬、杜乃擭、斂乃穽、無敢傷牿、牿之傷、汝則有常刑。○四節 馬牛其風、臣妾逋逃、無敢越逐、祗復

3 "We must now largely let the oxen and horses loose, and not keep them as usual in enclosures:—do you shut up your traps, and fill up your pitfalls, and do not presume to injure any of the animals let loose. If any of them be injured, you shall be dealt with according to the regular punishments.

4 "When the horses and cattle are seeking one another, or when your followers, male or female, abscond, presume not to leave the

have rashly said that Kaou-yaou took weapons of war to deal with those people. They have not considered that the Man and E were dwelling with the mass of the ordinary population of the Middle Kingdom. There was no occasion for military operations against them. It is absurd to think of such measures as those of after ages,—the despatch of a great general to punish and smite the various tribes of barbarians.'

P. 2. *The soldiers must have their weapons all in good order.* 敹 is defined in the 說文 by 擇, 'to select,' and the 玉篇 similarly gives 簡 for it. Ts'ae explains it by 縫完, 'to stitch and make whole,' and K'ang-shing by 穿徹, which comes to the same thing. The meaning evidently is that in the translation, whatever may be the specific force of this term. The 'coats of mail and helmets' were made of leather, which may have been studded or fenced with more or less of metal. 敿 means properly 'the strings attached to a shield.' The soldiers are required to see that they were in good order. 無不弔 (*teih*),—'in perfect condition.' 弔=至. Ts'ae defines 鍛 by 淬, 'to put in the fire and then in water,'='to temper.' The character denotes the 'forging' of metals generally. 鋒刃,—'sharp points and edges,'—*i.e.*, weapons for thrust and cut.

P. 3. *The people must look after the ground in the line of march, so that the cattle of the army should not be injured.* The charge here must be taken as addressed to the people, though that is not mentioned in the text. 淫舍牿牛馬,—牿 is defined in the 說文 as 牛馬牢, 'an enclosure or stable for oxen and horses.' K'ang-shing endeavours to explain it from 梏, 'manacles,' *i.e.*, hobbles attached to the feet; but this is to be rejected. As they marched through the country, the soldiers would have, especially at night, to let loose (舍=放) their cattle, to rest them and let them seek pasture, instead of keeping them in stables or enclosures. They would have to do this 淫, 'extensively and carelessly' often. The critics all define 淫 here by 大, 'greatly;' but the other meaning which I have indicated must not be omitted. Below, in 傷牿 and 牿之傷, 牿 is used simply to indicate the cattle. Ying-tă says:—既言牛馬在牿, 遂以牿爲牛馬之名, 下云傷牿, 牿之傷, 謂牛馬也. What is intimated about the character of the country shows how thinly it must have then been peopled. With 擭 and 穽 comp. 擭 and 阱 in 'The Doctrine of the Mean,' Ch. vi. 斂=塞, 'to fill up.' None of the commentators touch on 'the regular punishments' for the offences here indicated, nor do I know what they were.

P. 4. *The soldiers must on no account leave their entrenchments or ranks; and the people must carefully return strayed animals and absconded followers.* 馬牛其風,—the dict. explains 風, with reference to this passage, by 佚, 'to stray;' but usage shows that such straying is like that 'when the wild ass snuffeth up the wind;'—牝牡相誘謂之風. 臣妾逋逃,—the 臣妾 are camp-

之、我商賚汝、乃越逐不復、汝則有常刑、無敢寇攘、踰垣牆、竊馬牛、誘臣妾、汝則有常刑。○甲五戌、我惟征徐戎、峙乃糗糧、無敢不逮、汝則有大刑、魯人三郊三遂、

ranks to pursue them. But let them be carefully returned. I will reward you who return them according to their value. But if you leave your places, to pursue them, or if you who find them do not return them, you shall be dealt with according to the regular punishments. And let none of you *people* presume to rob or detain *vagrant animals or followers*, or to jump over enclosures and walls to steal away horses or oxen, or to decoy away servants and female attendants. If you do so, you shall be dealt with according to the regular punishments.

5 "On the day Keă-suh I will punish the tribes of Seu;—prepare roasted grain and other provisions, and presume not to have any deficiency. If you do, you shall suffer the severest punishment. Ye men of Loo, from the three environing territories, and the three tracts beyond, prepare your posts and planks. On Keă-suh I will commence

followers who had to gather fuel, cook, &c. Kin Le-ts'ëang tells us that 'to every chariot there were attached three men in mail, and 70 foot soldiers, with other 25 followers, who are those intended here by 臣妾.' 越逐,—越 means 'getting over' the entrenchments. 祗復之,—this must be understood as addressed to the country-people who should fall in with such animals and camp-followers. Both they, and soldiers who should themselves pursue after the vagrants, are addressed in 乃越逐不復,汝則有常刑; but the rest of the par. regards only the people who should thus offend. Gan-kwŏ, indeed, supposes that 無敢,云云, is addressed to the soldiers, against stealing from the people, and Woo Ch'ing that it is forbidding them to steal one from another; but the view which I have proposed seems much more likely. 我商賚汝,—'I will deliberate and reward you;'—the meaning is as I have expressed it in the translation. The peculiar force of 攘, 'to appropriate on temptation of occasion offered,' should be expressed in a translation.

P. 5. *The time is fixed for direct operations, and everything required to be in readiness.* We are to suppose that the marching would be over by the day Këä-suh, and that they would be then in front of the enemy. 峙—儲 備, 'to have collected and prepared.' 魯人三郊三遂,—the country beyond the capital to a certain extent was called 郊, and beyond this again it was denominated 遂. Gaubil observes that 'it is difficult at the present day to get correct ideas of what was really intended by these designations of the frontiers; and that it is difficult to account for the mention of three *këaou* and three *suy*.' Wang Suh thinks that the troops from the *këaou and suy* on the east were left to guard the country, and hence, as only those from the other three went forth on the expedition, only they are mentioned. This was the view also of Gan-kwŏ. Ying-tă, however, puts forward another view, which is inconsistent with this, though he does not seem to be aware of the inconsistency.—In the imperial domain, to a distance of 100 *le* was called 郊, and beyond that was the 遂. In the 郊 were the six *hëang* (六鄉), which furnished the 'six hosts' (六軍), while the

峙乃楨榦、甲戌、我惟築、無敢不供、汝則有無餘刑非殺、魯人三郊三遂、峙乃芻茭、無敢不多、汝則有大刑。

my entrenchments;—dare not but be provided with a supply of these. *If you be not so provided*, you shall be subjected to various punishments, only short of death. Ye men of Loo, from the three environing territories, and the three tracts beyond, prepare the forage, and do not dare to let it be other than in abundance. *If you do*, you shall suffer the severest punishment."

suy extending 200 *le* beyond, furnished, if need were, six subsidiary hosts. In a large State of 100 *le* square, the *keaou* extended 20 *le* from the capital; and as it was supposed to furnish only 'three hosts,' and, if need were, three auxiliary hosts, it is inferred that these might all be called 三郊三遂之人. The language in the text, therefore, is simply equivalent to 'the army of Loo,' and we do not need to inquire further about a 4th *keaou* and a 4th *suy*.

楨榦 are 'the posts and planks' for the framework in which walls are raised in China by pounding earth and lime together (題曰楨, 旁曰榦). From the mention of the 'men of Loo,' it is inferred that there were men of other States also in the army, while they were required to provide the planks and posts, and forage, such labour being easier to them, as they were nearer than the others to the seat of war. 無餘刑,—'punishments without remainder.' It is difficult to say what punishments are meant. The addition of 非殺 shows that they were short of death. Gan-kwŏ simply says—'various punishments.' K'ang-shing and Wang Suh agree in saying that the punishments were such as would involve the parents and children of the offender, so that none should be exempt from them.

We have in this par. and the last the 'regular punishments' (常刑), which were well defined and known; the 大刑, 'great punishment' or death; and these 無餘刑.

芻茭 are distinguished as 'new-mown grass and hay.'

BOOK XXX. THE SPEECH OF *THE DUKE OF* TS'IN.

秦誓

公曰、嗟、我士、聽無譁、予誓告汝群言之首。

1 The duke said, "Ah! my officers, listen to me without any noise. I solemnly announce to you the most important of all sayings. *It is this which* the ancients have said, 'Thus it is with all people,

NAME OF THE BOOK.—秦誓, 'The Speech of *the duke of* Ts'in.' At the time when this speech was made, the States of Tsin (晉) and Ts'in (秦) were among the most powerful of the empire. In B.C. 630, they were engaged together in the siege of the capital of Ch'ing (鄭), and would have extinguished that principality, but the duke of Ts'in was suddenly induced to withdraw his forces, leaving three of his officers in friendly relations with the court of Ch'ing, and under engagement to defend the country from aggression. These men, however, were entirely in the interest of their own prince, and one of them, called Ke-tsze (杞子), sent word, in B.C. 627, to Ts'in, that he was in charge of one of the gates of the capital, and if an army were sent to take the place by surprise, Ch'ing might be added to the territories of Ts'in. The duke—duke Muh (穆公)—laid the matter before his counsellors. The most experienced of them—the famous Pih-le He (百里奚) and Këen-shuh (蹇叔)—were against taking advantage of the proposed treachery. The duke, however, listened rather to the promptings of his own ambition, and the next year sent a large force, under his three ablest commanders, hoping to fall upon Ch'ing all unexpected. The attempt failed. Ch'ing was warned of the approaching danger; and the commanders, vexed and disappointed, were leading the army back, when it was attacked by the troops of Tsin among the passes of the Heaou mountain (殽山), in the pres. dep. of Ho-nan, and sustained a terrible defeat. The troops were nearly all cut to pieces, and the three commanders were taken prisoners.

The duke of Tsin was intending to put these captives to death, when he was persuaded by his mother to send them back to Ts'in, that duke Muh might himself sacrifice them to his anger for their want of success. Muh, however, did no such thing. He went out from the capital to meet his defeated officers, and comforted them, saying that the blame of the defeat was his own, who had refused to listen to the advice of his wise counsellors. Then it is said he made the speech here recorded, for the benefit of all his ministers.

That the speech was made on the occasion thus described rests on the authority of the preface to the Shoo, which has generally been followed by the critics. The 左傳, however, while it relates how Muh met his commanders and comforted them, says nothing of the speech. And Sze-me Ts'een places it three years later, and on a different occasion. After some unsuccessful attempts to wipe out the disgrace at the Heaou hills, Ts'in made a great raid on its neighbour in B.C. 624, when Tsin did not dare to meet the enemy in the field. Then duke Muh crossed the Ho, and had the bones of his slaughtered host collected, and interred in one place, making great sacrifices and mourning on the occasion, and delivering this speech, to acknowledge and transmit the memory of the fault he had committed.

○古[二節]人有言曰、民訖自若是多盤、責人斯無難、惟受責俾如流、是惟艱哉。○我[三節]心之憂、日月逾邁、若弗云來。○惟[四節]古之謀人、則曰未就予忌、惟今之謀人、姑將

2 —they mostly love their ease. In reproving others there is no difficulty, but to receive reproof, and allow it to have a free course,
3 this is difficult!' The sorrow of my heart is this, that the days and months pass away, as if they would not come again.
4 "There were my old counsellors,—I said, 'They will not accommodate themselves to me,' and I hated them. There were my new counsellors, and I would for a time give my confidence to them.

I do not know whether we should accept the testimony of the preface or that of Ts'een on this point. But the thing is of little moment. They agree in making the speech refer to the defeat which had been incurred by the duke's refusal to listen to wise counsel.

The Book is found in both the texts.

Contents. The general nature of these may be gathered from the preceding note; but what is really said is more vague and less to the point of the occasion than we might have expected. The 'Complete Digest' says that parr. 2, 3 declare the fact of the duke's repentance; parr. 4, 5, the grounds of it; and parr. 6—8, the sincerity or emphasis of it.

P. 1. *The duke seeks to engage the attention of his officers.* 我士,—'my officers.' All his ministers are so denominated. 誓告=‘solemnly tell.' 羣言之首,—'the head (=the most important, the chief) of all words.' The duke means the ancient saying which he proceeds to state, and which seemed to him, in the mood of mind in which he was, to be so important. Ying-tă gives for the clause—我告汝以言中之最要者.

P. 2. *The saying of the ancients, that it is easy to give and difficult to receive reproof.* 民訖(=盡)自若是多盤,—'people all *are* naturally thus,—*they are* most for pleasure.' Choo He said he thought that 'this clause simply meant that it is the disposition of most men to love ease' (想只是說人情要安逸之意). This is probably all that is intended; but I do not see the appropriateness of the sentiment as an introduction to what follows. 受責俾如流,—'to receive reproof, and cause—allow—it to be like flowing water.' The meaning is that the reproof is not resisted, but flows on freely. Gaubil mistook the sense, and has translated —'recevoir les avis et les reprimandes des autres, sans les laisser couler comme l'eau, c'est là la difficultè.'

P. 3. *The duke deplores the swift passing away of time.* 逾 and 邁 are to be taken as synonyms,=過 or 往, 'to move on,' 'to proceed.' From Ying-tă's notes on Gan-kwŏ's commentary, we see that he read 員, and not 云. But those terms were anciently interchanged. Whichever we read here, it is to be taken in the sense of 旋 or 運, 'to return,' 'come round.' The duke is conscious that he has done wrong; what he deplores is that the wrong cannot be undone. The day is past, and it will not come again, that he might do differently on it.

P. 4. *He acknowledges his error in rejecting the advice of his aged counsellors and following that of new men, and declares he will not do so again.* By 古之謀人, 'ancient counsellors,' the duke intends Pih-le He and Këen-shuh, who advised him against attempting to surprise Ch'ing; and by 今之謀人, 'modern or recent counsellors,' he means Ke-tsze and the other officers who seduced him to the undertaking. 曰='I said to myself.' 未就予

以爲親、雖則云然、尙猷詢茲黃髮、則罔所愆。○五節番番良士、旅力既愆、我尙有之、仡仡勇夫、射御不違、我尙不欲、惟截截善諞言、俾君子易辭、我皇多有之。○六節昧

Although it may be so *with old men and new*, hereafter I will take advice from the men of yellow hair, and then I shall be free from error. That good old officer!—all his strength is exhausted, but may I still have him! That dashing brave officer!—his shooting and charioteering are faultless, but I had rather not wish him! As to men of quibbles, skilful at cunning words, and able to make the superior man change his purposes, what have I to do with making much use of them?

忌=其不就我意,乃忌疾之. See other explanations of this in Woo Ch'ing and Këang Shing, the latter of whom adopts a different reading,—as usual. Both their constructions are intolerably harsh. 姑將以爲親=姑且將以爲可親而與之謀, 'for a time I thought they might have my confidence, and be counselled with.' 雖則云然 converts the cases of those counsellors into general characteristics of old and new men.

P. 5. *Old counsellors; martial counsellors; and crafty counsellors.* 番番良士,—番 (read *po*) 番 is best taken as=老貌, 'the appearance of age.' The 仡仡=勇貌, 'the appearance of boldness;' and 截截=辯給貌, 'the appearance of disputatiousness.' Gan-kwŏ, indeed, makes 番番=勇武, 'brave and martial.' The phrase has this meaning in the She King, but we cannot admit it here. It is inappropriate to the old counsellors. See Ming-shing, *in loc.* 番 is here equal to the later 皤, 'old.' 旅力既愆,—Gan-kwŏ makes 旅力=衆力, meaning 'the strength of all the members.' It is better to take 旅=呂 or 膂, 'the backbone,' and understand 旅力 as simply equivalent to 'strength.' 既愆=' has failed.' But 愆 has always a moral sense,='a failure,' 'an error,' 'a sin.' We can understand our moral meaning of 'failure' arising from the primary material meaning of the term, but we are called to suppose a reverse process in regard to the usage of the Chinese character. Of all the critics Ts'ae appears to be the only one who felt the pinch of this difficulty, and he supposes that the duke is referring to an incident which occurred on the setting forth of the ill-fated expedition. The three commanders were the sons of the two aged ministers who were opposed to it; and when the troops were leaving the capital, the old men wept bitterly. This led to some strong language about them from the duke, and Ts'ae would make the language='There is that good old officer, whom I blamed for his want of strength!' But this is much forced, and after all the idea of the *want* or *failure* of strength must somehow be introduced into the version. Moreover, the duke is here speaking of different classes of counsellors, in consequence of what had occurred to himself indeed, but generally, and without particular reference to the men who had advised, or blamed, or sanctioned the expedition to surprise Ch'ing. 射御不違=善射善御不違於法者. This officer violates in nothing *the rules of his art.* 諞言=巧言, 'artful speech.' 易辭,—'to change his words;' such change of course growing out of a change of purpose. 皇=遑, 'leisure.' The duke says he had no leisure—he had something better to do than—to attend to such men.

昧我思之、如有一介臣、斷斷猗無他技、其心休休焉、其如有容、人之有技、若己有之、人之彥聖、其心好之、不啻如自其口出、是能容之、以保我子孫黎民、亦職有利哉。

6 "I have deeply thought and concluded;—Let me have but one resolute minister, plain and sincere, without other abilities, but having a simple complacent mind, and possessed of generosity, regarding the talents of others, as if he himself possessed them; and when he finds accomplished and sage-like men, loving them in his heart more than his mouth expresses, really showing himself able to bear them:—such a minister would be able to preserve my descendants and my people, and would indeed be a giver of benefits.

P. 6. *The duke's conception of a thoroughly good and valuable minister.* 昧昧我思之,—Gan-kwŏ joined this to the preceding par., and for 我皇多有之,昧昧我思之 gives = 我前多有之,以我昧昧思之而不明故也. 'Formerly I had many such, because I thought darkly of it, and was not intelligent.' But the balancing of the sentences in par. 5 shows that we ought to stop at 有之, and that 昧昧我思之 must belong to another subject. 昧昧 = 深潛, 'deeply.' From 如有 to the end of par. 7 is quoted in the 'Great Learning,' Comm. x. 14, with some trifling variations in particular characters. Këang Shing edits the text here, now retaining the characters in the *textus receptus*, and now giving those of the 'Great Learning;'—but on no critical principle that I can see. 一介臣,—in the 'Great Learning' we have 一个臣, 'a single minister.' 介 gives us the idea of 'resolute.' Ma Yung explains it by 耿介一心端慤者. 斷斷 = 誠一之貌, 'the appearance of sincere simplicity.' For 猗 the 'Great Learning' has 兮. Both the one and the other = 然, to be construed with 斷斷. 休休 = 易直好善, 'easy, straightforward, and loving good.' K'ang-shing defines it by 寬容貌, 'the appearance of generous forbearance.' 不啻謂心之所好甚于口之所言也, '不啻 means that the love in his heart is greater than the language in his mouth expresses' (Woo Ch'ing). For 是 in 是能容之, the 'Great Learning' gives 寔, which is an emphatic 是. 以保我子孫黎民 = 以故能保安我子孫衆民, = 'on these accounts (*i.e.*, with these qualities, thus endowed) he is able to protect,' &c. For 亦職有利哉 the 'Great Learning' gives 亦尙有利哉, which is easier to construe. Ts'ae defines 職 by 主 'to preside over,' the idea being that from such a man benefits, and only benefits, would come. His 'office, that over which he presided, would be, as it were the making of the people prosperous and happy.'

○七節人之有技、冒疾以惡之、人之彥聖、而違之俾不達、是不能容、以不能保我子孫黎民、亦曰殆哉。○八節邦之杌隉、曰由一人、邦之榮懷、亦尚一人之慶。

7 "But if *the minister*, when he finds men of ability, be jealous and hates them; if, when he finds accomplished and sage-like men, he oppose them and do not allow their advancement, showing himself really not able to bear them;—such a man will not be able to protect my descendants and people; and will there not indeed be dangers from him?

8 "The prosperity and unsettledness of a State may arise from one man. The glory and tranquillity of a State also may perhaps arise from the excellence of one man."

P. 7. *A thoroughly bad and dangerous minister.* For 冒, 'to cover over,' the 'Great Learning' has 娼, synonymous nearly with 疾. For 不達 it has 不通, but that variation does not affect the meaning at all.

P. 8. *A summary statement of the consequences flowing from the good and bad minister respectively.* The general meaning of the terms 杌隉 is sufficiently determined by their opposition to 榮懷. The critics generally content themselves with saying that they = 不安, 'unrest.' But that is the idea conveyed by 隉 alone, as its opposite 懷 = 安, or 'tranquillity.' Now in the dict. the first definition of 杌 is 木無枝, 'a tree without branches,' which gives us the idea of 'sterility.' The opposite idea is conveyed by 榮, 'a plant in the glory of its leaves and flowers.' 隉 is formed from 𠂤 and 毀 abbreviated, and = 'a mound falling to pieces.'

By the 'one man' to whom such consequences are attributed, either of good or evil, we are to understand the good minister of par. 6 or the bad one of par. 7. This is the opinion of Ts'ae, after Gan-kwŏ, and of the commentators generally. The editors of Yun-ching's Shoo, however, call attention to the opinion of Leu Tsoo-hëen and some others, that the duke intends himself as '*the* one man' of the State. This does not seem at all likely.

INDEXES.

INDEX I.

OF SUBJECTS.

Parts of the whole Book are indicated by I., II., *&c.; separate Books by* i., ii. *&c.; Parts of Books by* Pt. i., Pt. ii., *&c.; and Paragraphs by* 1, 2, *&c.*

A

B

C

書經

D

E

F

G

H

I

J

K

L

M

N

O

P

R

S

T

U

V

W

Y

INDEX II.

INDEX OF PROPER NAMES.

A

B

C

E

F

H

書經

J

K

L

M

N

P

S

T

W

Y

INDEX III.

OF CHINESE CHARACTERS AND PHRASES;

INTENDED ALSO TO HELP TOWARDS THE FORMATION OF A DICTIONARY AND CONCORDANCE FOR THE CLASSICS.

THE 1st RADICAL. 一.

一 *yih* yi — (1) One. II. i. 8: V. xxx. 6; *et alibi sæpe.* = anyone; but never used simply as our article *a*. III. iii. 5, 6; *et al.* = the first. III. iii. 4: V. iv. 4, 5, 6, 7; *et al.* (2) One and undivided, all-one, pure. II. ii. 15: IV. vi. 3, 4, 5; *et al.* = one and the same, unchanging. IV. vi. 6. = agreeing. V. vi. 9. (3) ? The uniform decision of the mind. IV. vi. 8. (4) To make one, to unite. II. ii. 20. = to consider as one and the same. V. x. 5. = to be of one mind. IV. vii. Pt. ii. 8. (5) Once. II. i. 9: V. xx. 14. (6.) 一二, one or two, = a few. V. ix. 4. = we. V. xxiii. 1. = you. V. xxiii. 6. (7) 一人, the one man. = the emperor. *Sæpissime.* V. xxx. 8, is doubtful.

丁 *ting* — The fourth of the calendaric stem-characters. IV. xxii. 12; *et al.* 武丁, one of the kings of the Shang dynasty. V. xvi. 7.

七 *ts'eih* ch'i — Seven. I. i. 12; *et sæpe.* = the seventh. V. iv. 4, 7, 20. 七政, the seven Directors, *i.e.*, the sun, moon, and five planets. II. i. 5.

三 *san* — (1) Three. I. i. 8; *et sæpe.* = the third. III. iii. 7; *et al.* = three classes. V. xxi. 10. (2) Thrice. V. xviii. 23; *et al.* = repeatedly. III. iii. 5. (3) 三苗, the country of the Meaou. II. i; *et al.* 三危, the name of a country. II. i. 12; *et al.* (4) 三帛, II. i. 8. 三就 and 三居, II. i. 20. 三禮, II. i. 23. 三考, II. i. 27. 三事, the three businesses. II. ii. 8. The same phrase is used differently in V. xix. 7, and xx. 21. 三德, II. iii. 4. The phrase has a different and more specific meaning in V. iv. 17, and xxvii. 18. 金三品, III. i. Pt. i. 44, 32. 三錯, III. i. Pt. i. 68. 三壤, III. i. Pt. ii. 15. 三正, the three months on which the year might be made to commence; but the meaning is doubtful. III., ii. 3. 三風, IV. iv. 7. 三王, king Wăn, his father, and grandfather. V. vi. 5. 三宅 and 三俊, V. xix. 4, 6. 三亳, V. xix. 11. 三公 and 三孤, the highest ministers under the Chow dynasty. V. xx. 5, 6. 三紀, V. xxiv. 3. 三后, the duke of Chow, Keun-ch'in, and the duke of Peih. V. xxiv. 13. Other persons are intended by the phrase in xxvii. 8. 三郊三遂, V. xxix. 5. 三江, III. i. Pt. i. 40. 三澨, the three great dykes. III. i. Pt. ii. 8. (4) 二三, now two, now three, unstable. IV. vi. 5.

上 *shang* chang — Above, that which is above;—used of place, time, and rank. Used for Heaven, the supreme Power. IV. vii. Pt. ii. 7, 12; *et al.* In the 12th par., however, and not a few other places, the idea is not so much of Heaven as the Power, but as the place whence the power comes forth.
Used for the sovereign, and superiors generally. IX. vi. 7: V. xxi. 14; *et al.*
Used for early ages. IV. xi. 1. The

highest in quality or class. III. i. Pt. i. 8, 25, 34; *et al. sœpe.* 上公, a *kung* of the highest class. V. viii. 3. 上宗, V. xxii. 23, 26. 上天, the supreme Heaven, IV. ii. 3; but compare IV. iii. 4. 上帝, God;—see 帝. 上日, the first day. II. i. 4. 上下 constantly appear as correlates, = high and low; heaven and earth; Heaven and the people; the sovereign and the people; the sovereign and his ministers; mountains and marshes. Observe 在上, IV. x. 6; also V. xxii. 21.

The usage of 上 as a preposition, with 在 or 於 preceding, is unknown in the Shoo.

上 *shang* chang — Up. 2d tone. To ascend; upwards. V. iv. 5. To send up. V. xxvi. 20.

下 *hëa* hsia — (1) Beneath, that which is below;—used of place, time, and rank. It stands often for the people, or inferiors generally; but the phrase 下民, the inferior people, is very common, as in I. i. 11: II. iv. 2: V. xxvi. 2; &c. The lowest in quality or class. III. i. Pt. i. 18, 25; *et al.* Spoken of after times, or later ages. IV. xi. 1: V. xxvii. 5. Used often for ministers. II. ii. 12: V. xxiv. 5; *et al.* 天之下, all under heaven. II. iv. 7. 天下, as a designation of the empire, is common. 下土, the low grounds. III. i. Pt. i. 58. 下地, this lower world, in app. to 帝庭, the court of God. V. vi. 7. 下國, the States of the empire. V. i. Pt. ii. 4. (2) As a verb. To keep under, to down-tread. III. iii. 4. (3) 上下, as correlates. See on 上.

下 *hëa* hsia — To descend, = downwards. V. iv. 5.

不 *puh* pu — Not. *Passim.* With other negatives, 罔, 莫, 無, conveying a strong affirmation. Observe also 不無. IV. x. 7. It is itself repeated with the same effect, having another character between,—不可不, 不敢不, 不啻不. Observe how, like other negatives, it attracts the object of the verb to itself in V. ix. 22: xiv. 22.

丑 *ch'ow* ch'ou — The second of the calendaric branch-characters. IV. iv. 1: V. xxii. 10.

丕 *p'ei* p'i — Great; greatly. The adverbial use is the more frequent. II. ii. 14: iv. 2: III. i. Pt. i. 78; *et al. sœpe.* It is repeated,—丕丕, = vast. V. vii. 9: xiv. 15. 丕子, the great son *of Heaven*, = the emperor. V. vi. 5. 丕時, a time of great prosperity. V. xvi. 20.

世 *she* shih — (1) An age, a generation; ages. II. ii. 8, 12: IV. ii. 1; *et al.* Adverbially, = for ages, from age to age. IV. vii. Pt. i. 14: V. i. Pt. iii. 4; *et al.* So, 世世. V. viii. 4. 世輕世重, in one generation and in another, &c. V. xxvii. 19. 厥世, his age, all his life. IV. v. Pt. ii. 9. Obs. 七世之廟, IV. vi. 4. (2) = hereditary possession, a hold on successive ages; the hereditary principle. II. iv. 8: V. i. Pt. i. 5: xxvii. 5, 12.

丙 *ping* — The third of the calendaric stem-characters. V. xi. 2.

丘 *k'ew* ch'iu — A hillock; a height. III. i. Pt. i. 16, 陶丘, the hill of T'aou. III. i. Pt. ii. 10.

並 *ping* — *I. q.* 竝, together. See 竝.

THE 2D RADICAL. 丨.

中 *chung* — The middle, that which is in the middle—used of place, time, quality, and rank. III. i. Pt. i., 8, 18, 25; &c. The Mean; to hold the course of the Mean. II. ii. 15: IV. ii. 8: V. xvii. 7: xxv. 4: xxi. 8: xxvii. 4. = impartially. V. xxvii. 22. Used absolutely, = in the middle, with ref. to time IV. ix. 3; with ref. to place, V. xiii. 23. 于......中, 于......之中, used both of place and metaphorically. V. vi. 11: xiii. 14: xxvii. 9, 10, 12. 在中. xxvii. 20. 日中, 宵中. I. i. 4, 6, where 中 = of the medium length. But 日中, V. xv. 10, = midday, and 中夜, V. xxvi. 1, = midnight. 中身, V. xv. 11, = the middle of life. 中邦, the middle region or regions. III. i. Pt. ii. 15. 中國. V. xi. 1. 中江, a part of the Këang. III. Pt. ii. 9. 中宗, one of the kings of the Shang dynasty. V. xv. 4, 16.

中 *chung* — That which hits, appropriate. V. xiv. 24. It is very doubtful whether we should acknowledge two tones of 上, 下, and 中, in the Shoo.

THE 3D RADICAL. 丶.

丹 *tan* tan — (1) Cinnabar. III. i. Pt. i. 52. (2) To paint with vermilion. V. xi. 4. (3) The name of the appanage of Yaou's son, Choo. II. iv. 8.

主 *choo* chu — (1) A lord or ruler. III. ii. 2. The emperor is 民主, III. vi. 11: V. xviii. 6, 8, 18; and 神主, IV. vi. 3. (2) To regard—be regarded—as the chief thing. II. vi. 8. To preside over. V. xxvii. 8.

THE 4TH RADICAL. 丿.

乂 *e* ai — (1) To regulate, to correct; to be regulated, brought to order. I. i. 11, 12: II. ii. 2: IV. ii. 2: *et al. sæpe.* Sometimes the meaning simply = to aid. V. xiv. 9: xviii. 21; *et al.* It is often found with 保. V. xvi. 8, 10: *et al.* Used adverbially. V. iv. 4. = orderliness. V. iv. 6, 34. (2) Men of eminence, of a hundred. II. iii. 4: IV. viii. Pt. iii. 7.

乃 *nae* nai — *Passim.* Two usages are met with everywhere. (1) As a particle, at the beginning of paragraphs, and after the subject of a clause. The idea of connection which it expresses is very various, = thereupon, so, however, &c. I. i. 3, 11: II. i. 1, 7, 8, 13, 28; *et al.* (2) As a possessive pronoun, = your. Once, in II. 13, it is used for you in the objective; but it is seldom if ever, used in the nominative. II. i. 3: ii. 8, 11, 14, 17, 20; *et al.* It is also used (3) as the copula; but this is less common. II. ii. 21: IV. vi. 6: V. xxvii. 10. Sometimes, however, we are in doubt whether to take it as a particle or as the copula. Often likewise we might resolve cases of the second usage into its verbal force. This appears especially where we have to translate it in the third person, as in V. xvi. 18: xxi. 2. Obs. also 由乃在位, IV. vii. Pt. i. 5.

之 *che* chih — (1) Of. The sign of the possessive case. The regent follows the 之, and the regimen precedes it. They may be respectively a noun, a phrase, or a larger clause. (2) Him, her, it, them. The antecedent, however, has often to be gathered from the context; as in II. ii. 7: iii. 2: iv. 6: *et al.* (3) We have 之 and another objective, as in 邦之蔡, V. xvii. 1, and other places. Some of these instances are peculiar. *E. G.* III. iii. 9; *et al.* (4) The idiom 之謂 occurs only once. V. iv. 6. 有之, has it, = says, also occurs only once. III. iii. 6. So also 若之何. IV. xi. 3. Such cases as 惟刑之恤, may be reduced to (1). V. xvii. 4, 惟德是輔, 惟惠之懷, shows clearly how they are to be understood. Observe 侵于之彊, V. i. Pt. ii. 8, where the text is probably imperfect. 之 occurs everywhere, but not so frequently as in the Four Books. (5) In V. xix. 13, 21 之 = 及, and.

乎 *hoo* hu — This only occurs four times in the Shoo (1) A part. of interrogation. I. i. 9. (2) A preposition. II. iii. 2. (3) An exclamation. III. iii. 5, 9.

乘 *shing* ch'êng — To mount on, to sail in. II. iv. 1: IV. vii. Pt. ii. 6. To support, maintain. V. xvi. 18.

乘 *shing* ch'êng — 3d tone. (1) The numeral for carriages. V. xvii. 1. (2) A team of four horses. V. xxiii. 1.

THE 5TH RADICAL. 乙.

乙 *yih* yi — The second calendaric stem-character IV. iv. 1: V. xii. 1; *et al.* 祖乙 and 帝乙, two kings of the Shang dynasty. V. xvi. 7, and V. x. 9: xiv. 7: xviii. 10.

九 *kew* chiu — Nine. *Sæpe.* The ninth. V. iv. 4, 39. 九州, the nine provinces into which Yu divided the empire. III. i. Pt. ii. 14. 九有, the empire, as consisting of those provinces. IV. vi. 2, 3. 九山, 九川, 九澤, the hills, &c., in those provinces. III. i. Pt. ii. 14. We have also 九族, the nine classes of kindred. I. i. 2; *et al.* 九功, 九歌, II. ii. 7. 九德, II. iii. 4: *et al.* 九成. II. iv. 9. 九河. III. i. Pt. i. 13: *et al.* 九江. III. i. Pt. i. 48; *et al.* 九疇. V. iv. 3. 九夷. V. v. 1. 九牧. V. xx. 13.

亂 *lwan* luan — (1) To govern, to bring into good order; a state of good order. II. iii. 3: IV. vii. Pt. ii. 14; Pt. iii. 6: *et sæpe.* (2) To throw into disorder, disorderly; rebellion. III. iii. 7: iv. 4: IV. i. 1: ii. 2, 7; *et sæpe.* (3) To ferry across. III. i. Pt. i. 70.

THE 6TH RADICAL. 亅.

予 — I, me; my. *Passim.* The phrases 予一人 and 予小子, are constantly used by the emperors in speaking of themselves. 予沖人, and some others, are also found. In V. vi. 10, 予

書經

一人 = our emperor. It is also plural. We, us; our. III. iii. 9: IV. i. 3: ii. 6: *et al.*

事 *sze* shih — (1) An affair; business; the course and conduct of business. II. i. 3: III. iv. 3: IV. 1, 2: V. xxiv. 6, 15; *et sæpe.* 事事, all affairs. IV. viii. Pt. ii. 8. 三事, see 三. 五事, V. iv. 4, 9. 六事, III. ii. 2. 御事 and 執事 are common. See 御 and 執. The use of 事, 宅事, and 立事, in V. xix. is peculiar. (2) As a verb. To be engaged, have business to do. II. iii. 4. To serve,—God, man, spirits. IV. vi. 11: viii. Pt. ii. 11: V. i. Pt. 1. 6: xxviii. 1; *et al.*

THE 7TH RADICAL. 二.

二 *urh* — Two, *Sæpe.* The second. II. i. 8: III. iii. 6: V. iv. 4, 5, 7, 8; *et al.* 一二, see 一. 二三, see 三. 二生, two living animals. II. i. 8.

于 *yu* yü — (1) A preposition, following both transitive and intransitive verbs. Its proper meaning is *in, on;* but it may be translated very variously,—to, at, in the case of, from, against, &c. *Passim.* (2) Than. Forming the comparative degree. IV. vii. Pt. iii. 4: V. i. Pt. ii. 5, 8: *et al.* (3) To proceed, to go forward. V. iii. 1: vii. 5, 6: and perhaps elsewhere.

云 *yun* yün — (1) To speak. IV. xi. 8: V. xxx. 4. (2) To come round, return. V. xxx. 3.

五 *woo* wu — Five. The fifth. III. 9: V. iv. 4. 5, 39, 40: *et al.* We have 五品, II. i. 19; 五典, II. i. 1, 9: V. xv. 14; xxv. 4; *et al.;* 五教, II. i. 19; *et al.;* and 五常, V. i. Pt. iii. 2;—all connected in signification. 五瑞, II. i. 7; and 五玉, II. i. 8;—also connected. 五禮, II. i. 8; *et al.* 五刑, II. i. 11; *et al., sæpe.* 五服, II. i. 20; with a difft. meaning, II. iii. 6; with a third meaning, II. iv. 8. 五流 and 五宅, II. i. 20. 五辰, II. iii. 4. 五章; 五色; 五采; 五聲; 五言; II. iv. 4. 五行, III. ii. 3: V. iv. 3, 4. 五事, see 事.

井 *tsing* ching — A well, = hamlets. V. xxiv. 7.

亞 *ya* — Secondary. = officers of inferior rank. V. ii. 2: x. 10: xix. 10.

THE 8TH RADICAL. 亠.

亡 *wang* — (1) To perish, come to ruin. II. iii. 6, 7; *et al.* To be going on to ruin. IV. ii. 7. (2) To flee away, to escape. V. xii. 10.

交 *keaou* chiao — Together, one with another. III. i. Pt. ii. 15: V. xxvi. 4. Obs. IV. viii. Pt. iii. 2.

亦 *yih* yi — Also, and moreover; even. *Passim.* It is often followed by other particles,— 亦惟, 亦越, 亦則,—in a way which we do not find in the Four Books; but it always indicates the *addition* of some circumstance or consideration. II. iii. 1. is peculiar, and there perhaps it = altogether.

亥 *hae* hai — The last of the calendaric branch characters. V. iii. 8: xviii. 1.

享 *hëang* hsiang — (1) To present offerings. V. xi. 5: xiii. 12: xviii. 29. To offer sacrifice. IV. vii. Pt. i. 14: V. i. Pt. iii. 8: xiii. 25. (2) To confer dignities. V. x. 16. The dignity conferred. V. ix. 23, 24. (3) To enjoy. V. viii. 4: xiii. 21. With the object expressed, as 國, 命. V. xv. 4, 5, 6, 11: xxviii. 1, 11: *et al.* = to accept a sacrifice. IV. v. Pt. iii. 1. = to satisfy. IV. vi. 3. (4) 南交, the name of a place. I. i. 5.

亮 *leang* liang — (1) To aid. II. i. 17, 26. (2) Brilliant; to display brilliantly. II. iii. 4: V. xx. 6: xxiv. 5.

亮 *lëang* liang — Low. 1st tone. In the phrase 亮陰, the emperor's mourning shed. IV. viii. Pt. i. 1: V. xv. 5.

亳 *pŏ* po — The name of T'ang's capital. IV. iii. 1: iv. 2: v. Pt. ii. 1: viii. Pt. iii. 1. There were three places of this name,—三亳. V. xix. 11.

亶 *tan* — Sincere. V. i. Pt. i. 3. Sincerity. V. xvi. 18. To make sincere. IV. vii. Pt. ii. 1.

THE 9TH RADICAL. 人.

人 *jin* jên — A man, men; man = humanity; = inhabitants. *Passim* = others, opp. to one's self. II. ii. 3; *et al.* = every man. IV. xi. 9. 罪人, criminals, IV. iii. 5: V. vi. 14. Similarly, with characters and phrases, it everywhere forms concrete nouns We may notice 一人, see 一; 遒人, III. iv. 3; 沖人, V. vii. 10, *et al.;* 格人, IV. x. 2; 庶人, all the people, V. iv. 25: 小人 the inferior people, V. xv. 18, *et al.;* and sometimes = mean men, II. ii. 20; 王人, members of the imperial House, V. xvi. 9; 準人,

V. xix. 1, 12, 16, 19; 藝人, V. xix. 9; 宗人, V. xxi. 27, 28; 臣人,— great officers, III. iv. 2: V. xxi. 4, 6.

仁 *jin* jên — Benevolence: benevolent. IV. ii. 5: v. Pt. iii. 1. 仁人, benevolent or virtuous men. V. i. Pt. ii. 6: iii. 6. = lovingly. V. vi. 4. This character only occurs these five times.

仇 *k'ew* ch'ou — To be hostile to. III. iii. 9: IV. ii. 6. 作仇, to contract mutual animosities. V. i. Pt. ii. 3.

今 *kin* chin — Now. *Passim.* 今日, to-day, the present time. V. xv. 13: xvi. 21. Observe 今...今翼日, V. vii. 5; 繼自今, V. xviii. 18; *et al.*; 今其有今罔後, IV. vii. Pt. ii. 7.

介 *këae* chieh — (1) To aid, co-operate with. V. x. 7: xii. 15: xviii. 21, 27, 28. (2) Great. V. xxii. 23. (3) Resolute. V. xxx. 6.

仍 *jing* jêng — = usual, ordinary. V. xxii. 15, 16, 17, 18.

他 *t'a* — Other. V. xxx. 6.

付 *foo* fu — To give. V. xi. 6: xxiii. 5.

仞 *jin* jên — A measure of eight cubits. We may call it a fathom. V. v. 9.

仡 *yih* yi — 仡仡. Bold, martial-like. V. xxx. 5.

代 *tae* tai — (1) Instead of; to supersede. II. iii. 5: IV. iv. 3: viii. Pt. i. 2: V. vi. 5, 16: xviii. 8. (2) A dynasty. V. xx. 4.

令 *ling* lêng — (1) An order, commands. IV. viii. Pt. i. 1: V. xx. 15: xxvi. 2. (2) Good, excellent. IV. v. Pt. iii. 3: V. viii. 3: xxi. 1: xxvii. 21. = insinuating. II. iii. 2: V. xxvi. 5.

以 *e* i — *Passim.* Several usages are marked distinctly enough. (1) At the beginning of sentences or clauses, being followed by a noun or substantive clause, after which comes the predicate of the sentence, it = to take, to use. *E. g.* I. i. 12: II. i. 20: iv. 4: IV. iii. 1: *et sæpe.* Sometimes the predicate and object are expressed by a single verb, and we have cases, such as are mentioned in Index III. to Mencius' Works, where it has been supposed that 以 is merely a sign of the accusative. *E. g.* IV. vii. Pt. ii. 1, 6. (2) Following the principal verb of the sentence, and followed by a noun, it = a preposition, and may be variously translated,—by, with, on the ground of, &c. I. i. 12: II. i. 1, 9, 11; *et sæpe.* In sentences of four characters, such as 以宜制事, we see how this usage and the last may run into each other. (3) Where it stands singly between the subject and predicate of the sentence, it = thereby. *E. g.* II. i. 24: IV. v. Pt. i. 7; Pt. iii. 8; *et sæpe.* (4) Its most common usage, perhaps, is as our *to*, the sign of the infinitive mood, when we might often translate it by—and thereby. *E. g.* I. i. 2, 4, 5, 6, 7, 8; *et sæpissime.* (5) To use, employ. V. xv. 20; *et al.* Most instances of its occurrence can be reduced to the above usages; but there are not a few passages, in which we hardly know how to construe the character, even though the general meaning may be plain enough. *E. g.* III. iii. 8; IV. viii. Pt. ii. 2; xi. 6; V. iv. 38; vi. 16; ix. 12; xi. 3: xiii. 3: xv. 12; xxvi. 1; *et al.*

仰 *yang* — To look up to. IV. viii. Pt. iii. 8: V. xx. 4: xxiv. 5.

仲 *chung* — (1) = 中, mid; the middle of. I. i. 4, 5, 6, 7. (2) The second of brothers. V. xxvii. 13. Such is its meaning in 羲仲, 和仲, I. i. 4, 6; and in 蔡仲, V. xvii. 1; 仲康, III. iv. 1; and 仲虺, IV. ii. 2. In 仲桓, V. xxii. 11, 仲 is probably the surname.

任 *jin* jên — (1) To employ, put in office. II. ii. 6: IV. vi. 2: vii. Pt. i. 7: V. xix. 3. (2) 常任 and 任人, V. xix. 1, 7, denote certain high officers. (3) To be equal to one's office. V. xx. 20.

任 *jin* jên — Artful. II. i. 16. 遲任, IV. vii. Pt. i. 13, a man's name.

伊 *e* i — (1) The name of a river. III. i. Pt. i. 55; Pt. ii. 13. (2) A particle, = 惟. V. xxviii. 2. (3) A surname. 伊尹, IV. iv. 1; *et al., sæpe.* 伊陟, V. xvi. 7. (4) 祖伊, the name of a minister of the tyrant Show. IV. x. 1, 6.

伏 *fuh* fu — To lie hidden. II. ii. 3. To suppress, make to lie hidden. IV. vii. Pt. i. 5. To be made to lie hidden, to be subjected. IV. iii. 5.

伐 *fă* fa — (1) To smite, to punish. II. ii. 20: V. iii. 1. Obs. 伐厥死, IV. vii. Pt. i. 16. Punishing. V. i. Pt. ii. 8. (2) To strike, to attack. V. vii. 12, 13. = blows. V. ii. 8. (3) To boast. II. ii. 14.

伋 *k'eih* ch'i — A name. 呂伋. V. xxii. 11.

休 *hew* hsiu — (1) Excellent; excellence. II. ii. 13: IV. v. Pt. ii. 7: viii. Pt. i. 11; Pt. ii. 4; Pt. iii. 11: V. xix. 1; *et al.* (2) Blessing, prosperity; favourable, prosperous; to bless. II. iv. 1: IV. iii. 7: V. iii. 7, 9: iv. 34: vii. 5, 9; *et sæpe.* (3) To be gentle, to spare; gentleness. V. xxvii. 13: II. ii. 7. (4) 休休, simple and upright,

書經

loving good. V. xxx. 6. 服休, V. x. 13, is peculiar.

伯 *pih* pi — (1) A father's elder brother, an uncle. 伯叔, IV. vii. Pt. iii. 8. 伯父, V. xxiii. 6: xxvii. 13. (2) The eldest of brothers. 伯兄, elder brothers or cousins. V. xxvii. 13. (3) The third title of nobility, which is often translated *baron*. 芮伯 and 彤伯, V. xxii. 3. 葛伯, IV. ii. 6. But the term was used for the chief or superintendent of many princes of all ranks, as in 西伯, IV. x. 1. So also in V. xxii. 13; and perhaps elsewhere. It sometimes, however, denotes the princes or chiefs generally, and officers likewise not so high in rank. IV. vii. Pt. iii. 8: V. x. 72: xii. 6: *et al.* 常伯, V. xix. 1, must denote princes of highest rank about court. Yu is styled 伯禹. II. 1. 17; E, 伯夷. II. i. 23: V. xxvii. 8. We have also 伯與, II. i. 21, 伯冏. V. xxvi. 1, where the two characters are probably the designation. The minister of Religion is styled 宗伯. V. xx. 9.

伻 *p'ăng* p'êng — To make to, to send, to send to. V. xiii. 3, 4, 10, 25, 28: xxix. 5.

位 *wei* — A position, place. Applied (1) to sites of buildings. V. xii. 3. (2) Places or seats of ceremony. II. iv. 9: IV. vii. Pt. iii. 1: V. xxii. 22. (3) Places of office or rank. II. ii. xx.; *et sæpe.* (4) The throne or imperial seat. I. i. 12; *et sæpe.*

佑 *yew* yu — To aid, to favour. IV. ii. 7: iii. 5: *et al.* 眷佑. IV. v. Pt. ii. 2. V. viii. 2.

何 *ho* — What; whom; how. II. i. 17: iii. 2, 3: iv. 1; *et al.* 如何, as how. I. i. 12: II. iii. 1. 若之何. IV. xi 3. 奈何. III. iii. 5: V. xii. 9.

佚 *yih* yi — To err, to fail. IV. vii. Pt. i. 16: V. x. 14. In. V. xvi. 3, 遏佚前人光, it seems to = to end, to overthrow.

佞 *ning* — Glib-tongued. V. xxvii. 20.

作 *tsŏh* tso — *Passim.* (1) Its prevailing use is in the sense of to make, to do; with the same extensive application which those terms have in English. Actively, to do, to make, to build, to constitute. Neuter, to be, to become; to act. 東作, the labours of the spring. I. i. 4. = active operations. V. iv. 31. It forms what we call the emphatic present tense. V. iv. 14; *et al.* (2) To arise. II. vii. Pt. ii. 1; where the idea of active operation is probably present. (3) In. III. i. Pt. i. 9, 18, 26, 50; and. IV. vii. Pt. ii. 11, it is used with reference to the cultivation of the ground. It is often difficult to construe it. *E. g.* V. ix. 20; xv. 5, 6: xix. 3. 大伾 The name of a hill. III. i. Pt. ii. 7.

伾 *p'e'i*

使 *sze* chih — (1) To cause, to make to. II. i. 17: V. iv. 13. (2) To employ, to command. IV. vi. 11: V. ii. 6.

來 *lae* lai — To come. II. ii. 6, 14; *et sæpe.* Coming, = future. IV. ii. 1. = solicitations, people coming to ask favours. V. xxvii. 16. 越若來, V. xii. 2, is a conjunction. Obs. 往來, V. xvi. 13.

侈 *ch'e* ch'ih — Extravagance. V. xx. 13: xxiv. 10. Obs. 侈服, V. i. Pt. i. 5.

侉 *kwa* kua — Ostentatious, boastful. V. xxiv. 10.

侍 *she* shih — To be in attendance on; attendants. V. xxvi. 2, 4.

侗 *t'ung* — Stupid. King Ching denominates himself—在後之侗. V. xxii. 6.

供 *kung* — To present to; to contribute. V. xii. 24: xv. 11, 12: xxix. 5.

依 *e* i — (1) To depend, rely on. II. ii. 10: III. iii. 9: V. vi. 7: xv. 2, 6: xxi. 7. (2) To be in accordance with. II. ii. 18. Obs. II. i. 24.

侮 *woo* wu — To contemn, treat with contempt; contemptuousness. II. ii. 20: V. i. Pt. i. 6; Pt. iii. 2; *et sæpe.* = to pay no regard to, deal summarily with. IV. ii. 7. Obs. 威侮, III. ii. 3.

侯 *how* hou — (1) The second of the five orders of nobility. V. xvii. 2: xx. 3. It often follows the name of the principality. *E. g.* 殷侯, V. xviii. 2; 衛侯, xxii. 3. (2) A noble or prince generally. So, in the phrase 諸侯, V. xxii. 29; xxiii. 1; *et al.* 侯服, the domain of the nobles. III. i. Pt. ii. 19. This, indicating often the princes of the domain, is the most common usage of 侯. V. iii. 3: ix. 1; *et al.* = principalities. V. xxiii. 6. Observe 孟侯, V. ix. 2. (3) A target. II. iv. 6.

侵 *ts'in* ch'in — To invade; invading. V. xxviii. 2: i. Pt. ii. 8.

便 *p'ëen* p'ien — Adulatory, cringing. V. xxvi. 5.

俊 *tseun* tsun — Men of distinguished ability, men among a thousand; their superior ability. V. v. 36, 37; *et al.* We have 俊乂, II. iii. 4; 俊彥, V. i. Pt. i. 5. Obs.

三有俊, V. xix. 4. To give distinction to. I. i. 2.

俗 *suh* su — Manners, the prevailing customs of a time or state. III. iv. 6 : V. xxi. 10 : xxiv. 4, 8.

保 *paou* pao — (1) To protect, maintain, secure. II. ii. 20 : IV. ii. 9 ; *et sæpe*. We have 定保, IV. iv. 2 ; 保乂, V. xvi. 8, 10 ; *et al.* ; 保惠, V. xv. 6, 10 ; 保釐, V. xxiv. 1. — to secure, to reckon on. V. ix. 6. (2) 太保 and 少保, the names of the highest officers under the Chow dyn. V. xx. 5, 6. 太保, occurs often. 保 alone is used in the same way, as in, V. xvi. 19 : xiii. 2. Obs. the cases of 師保, IV. v. Pt. ii. 3 ; V. i. Pt. iii. 3 ; xxi. 2. 保衡, the name, or *title* of office, of E Yin. V. xvi. 7.

俟 *sze* szŭ — To wait for. V. iii. 8 : vi. 8, 10 : xxii. 29.

信 *shin* shên — To believe, put confidence in. IV. i. 4 : V. i. Pt. iii. 3 ; *et al.* To be believed in ; sincerity. IV. vii. Pt. i. 7 : V. iii. 9 : xxiii. 5. Good faith. V. xxvii. 4. True. V. vi. 17.

修 *sew* hsiu — To cultivate ; to regulate, put in order : to be cultivated. II. i. 8 : ii. 7, 17 ; *et al.* 身修, self-cultivation. II. iii. 1. Compare with this, IV. v. Pt. ii. 4 : viii. Pt. iii. 5 : V. ix. 4. To repair. III. i. Pt. i. 4 ; *et al.* It is variously applied according to the things spoken of. Obs. III. iv. 2 ; IV. vii. Pt. i. 7 ; V. i. Pt. iii. 8 ; xvi. 12.

俱 *keu* chü — Together. III. iv. 6.

俶 *shuh* shu — To begin, to be the first to...... III. iv. 4.

倍 *pei* — To double ; to be doubled. V. xx. 8 : xxvii. 18.

俾 *pe* pei — To give, grant to, to allow, to make or cause. II. ii. 7, 8 ; *et sæpe.* Followed directly by a pronoun,—俾汝,— to act to. IV. vii. Pt. ii. 4. Observe 俾乂 and 俾亂, I. i. 11 ; V. xix. 16, 19. — to submit, preceded by 率. V. iii. 6 : xvi. 21. We find it preceding 率 with its ordinary signification.

倒 *taou* tao — To invert, turn upside down. V. iii. 8.

倚 — To bend on one side. IV. vii. Pt. ii. 8 : V. xxi. 7.

倡 *ch'ang* — To lead on, be an example to. V. xx. 13.

倦 *keuen* chüan — To be wearied. II. ii. 9.

倫 *lun* — The determined order or degree between things. II. i. 24 : V. ix. 11 : xxvii. 19. In the phrase 彝倫, V. iv. 2, 3, it means the orders or relations of human society.

偃 *yen* — To make to lie down, to hush. V. iii. 2. To be prostrated. V. vi. 16, 19.

假 *këa* chia — (1) To borrow. IV. iv. 2. (2) Great. 自假 — self-elated. II. ii. 14.

偏 *p'ëen* p'ien — Deflected. V. iv. 14.

側 *tsih* tsê — (1) On the side. V. xxii. 21. (2) One-sided. V. iv. 14, 19 : xvii. 7 : xxvi. 5. (3) Low and undistinguished. I. i. 12.

偶 *gow* ou — To assist, be a helpmate to. V. xvi. 18.

傅 *foo* fu — 太傅, the Grand-helper, and 少傅, the Assistant-helper, were great officers under the Chow dyn. V. xx. 5, 6. 傅巖, the place where Foo-yuĕ was found. IV. viii. Pt. i. 3.

傾 *k'ing* ch'ing — 西傾, the name of a mountain. III. i. Pt. i. 70 ; Pt. ii. 2.

備 *pei* — (1) To prepare ; preparations. V. xxix. 2 : IV. viii. Pt. ii. 8. (2) Complete. V. iv. 32, 33 : xxvii. 15, 20. — all talents. IV. iv. 5. — all filled up. V. xx. 5.

傲 *gaou* ao — Arrogant. I. i. 12 : II. i. 24 : iv. 8 : IV. vii. Pt. i. 6.

傷 *shang* — To wound ; to be wounded. IV. viii. Pt. i. 8 : V. ix. 16 : x. 11 : xxix. 3. 無傷, does no injury, — does not matter. V. i. Pt. ii. 5.

僉 *ts'ëen* ch'ien — All. I. i. 11 : II. i. 17, 21, 22, 23 : ii. 18.

僕 *puh* p'o — A servant. We have 臣僕, a subject. IV. xi. 8. 攜僕, personal attendants. V. xix. 8. In. V. xxvi. 2, 4, 6, it denotes the subordinate officers of the dept. of 太僕, or high-chamberlain.

僚 *lëaou* liao — Associate officers or ministers. II. iii. 4 : IV. viii. Pt. i. 9 : V. 10 : xiv. 20 : xviii. 28 : xxvi. 5. 百僚, occurs often, — 百官, the various officers, the body or mass of them.

僝 *chan* — To see displayed. I. i. 10.

僞 *wei* — Deceitful, deceitfully. V. xx. 18.

僭 *ts'en* chien — To be in error. IV. iii. 5 : vi. 5 : V. vii. 15. = to assume; assumptive. V. iv. 19, 34 : xxvii. 18.

僻 *peih* p'i — Perverse. V. iv. 19.

儀 *e* i — Usages, observances. V. xiii. 12. Demeanour, manners. 威儀, dignity, majestic manners. V. x. 11 : xxii. 9. = measured gambolings. II. iv. 9.

億 *yih* yi — A hundred thousand. V. i. Pt. i. 8 ; Pt. ii. 6 : xiii. 4.

儆 *king* ching — To warn, to be warned. II. ii. 6, 14 : IV. iv. 7.

儉 *këen* chien — To be economical; economy. II. ii. 14 : V. xx. 18. 儉德, self-restraint. IV. v. Pt. i. 6.

THE 10TH RADICAL. 儿.

允 *yun* jun — Sincerely, truly; really; in accordance with the truth of a case. I. i. 1, 8 : II. ii. 8, 8, 10, 15, 21 ; *et sæpe*. Sincere, to be believed. V. xvi. 20. Observe 允塞 II. i. 1. To believe, put confidence in. II. i. 16 : IV. viii. Pt. ii. 4. Sincerity. V. xvi. 19. Obs. 成允. II. ii. 14. Observe also 克允, II. i. 20; and 惟允, II. i. 25.

元 *yuen* yüan — (1) The first. II. i. 14 : IV. iv. 1. (2) = the eldest. V. viii. 1 : xii. 9, 13 : xxii. 7. (3) Great. V. ix. 16 : x. 2, 7; *et al.* We have 元后 for the sovereign, II. ii. 14, 17; *et al.*; 元龜, II. ii. 18 : *et al.*; 元孫, great-grandson, V. v. 5, 6 : 元祀, V. xiii. 7, 15, means the first place at sacrifices. 元命, V. xxvii. 11, is peculiar. (4) The head. But 元首, II. iv. 11, probably = the great head,—the sovereign. 在德元, in the head-*place* of virtue, = surpassing others. V. xii. 22. (5) Good. II. i. 16. 元良, the greatly good. IV. v. Pt. iii. 8.

兄 *heung* hsiung — An elder brother. V. ix. 4, 16 : xxi. 1. It is singularly joined with 考 in V. vii. 12. 兄弟, brothers; cousins of the same surname. V. xvii. 6 : xxvii. 18. = as brothers, in a brotherly way. V. xi. 5.

充 *ch'ung* — To fill. V. xxvi. 7.

兆 *chaou* chao — A million, millions. V. i. Pt. ii. 6. 兆民, the millions of the people, = the people. III. iii. 5 : IV. ii. 5 : iii. 5 ; *et sæpe*.

先 *sëen* hsien — First; formerly. II. ii. 18 : IV. ix. 1 : V. xi. 2 ; *et al.* As an adj., former, we find everywhere the combination 先王; also 先后; 先民; 先人; 先正; 先祖; 先輅; 先公; 先烈. = ancestors, forefathers. IV. v. Pt. ii. 7 : V. i. Pt. i. 6.

先 *sëen* psien — 3rd tone. To go before, setting an example. III. i. Pt. ii. 17 : IV. vii. Pt. i. 12 : V. xi. 7. So also we should tone, perhaps, in V. xiii. 23, 24 ; and in xii. 2.

光 *kwang* kuang — To shine, to enlighten. II. iv. 7 : V. i. Pt. iii. 5 ; *et al.* = glory. I. i. 1 : V. i. Pt. ii. 8 ; *et sæpe*. = bright, glorious. V. xiii. 22 : xxii. 24 : xxv. 6.

克 *k'th* k'o — *Passim.* (1) Its most common use is before a verb, when it is equal to our auxiliary *can, to be able to;* often, however, giving emphasis simply to the verb which follows. *E. g.* I. i. 1, 2, 12. Not unfrequently it stands alone, at the end of brief sentences, giving the idea of *competency* with reference to what has been spoken of, or is in the mind. *E. g.* II. ii. 3, 4 : V. xxviii. 2. It is followed also by a noun or pronoun, and = to be able for, to attain to. *E. g.* IV. iii. 9 : vi. 3, 8 : V. xxvii. 11, 16, 17, 18, 20. Once, we have a preposition between it and the noun. V. xxvi. 1. (2) As an active verb, to be able for, and more, to subdue, prevail against. IV. iv. 7 : V. v. 1 : vi. 1 ; *et al.* = subduing. V. iv. 17. (3) Crossing. V. iv. 21.

兌 *tuy* tui — A man's name. V. xxii. 19.

免 *mëen* mien — To avoid. V. xxvi. 1. To dispense or have done with. IV. viii. Pt. i. 1.

兗 *yen* — 兗州, one of Yu's nine provinces. III. i. Pt. i. 12.

兜 *tow* tou — 驩兜, a minister of Yaou, dealt with as a criminal by Shun. I. i. 10 : II. i. 12 : iii. 2.

兢 *king* ching — 兢兢, to be wary. II. iii. 5.

THE 11TH RADICAL. 入.

入 *juh* ju — To enter. *Sæpe*. It is almost always followed by 于, as in. II. i. 入官, to enter on office. V. xx. 16. 入畏, V. xx. 19. 出入, going out and coming in, = always and everywhere. V. xxi. 2.

內 *nuy* nei — The inside, that which is within. Its prepositional use hardly appears in the Shoo; but obs. IV. viii. Pt. iii. 8: xxii. 21: xxviii. 1. We have 于內. V. xxi. 6. = in the palace; in the court. III. iii. 6: V. xx. 3. Internal. V. xviii. 5. Interior. V. x. 10. 作內, internal operations. V. iv. 30. = female solicitation. V. xxvi. 16. It is generally found in correlation with 外. 內方, the name of a mountain. III. i. Pt. ii. 3. 內史, the Recorder of the interior. V. x. 13.

兩 *lëang* liang — Two,—always with definite reference, = the two, the pair. II. ii. 21: V. xxii. 21: xxvii. 15, 20, 21.

俞 *yu* yü — Yes. I. i. 12: II. i. 17, 21, 22, 23; *et al.* It is not found, excepting in the first two Parts.

THE 12TH RADICAL. 八.

八 *pă* pa — Eight. = the eighth. II. i. 8: *et al.* We have 八音, the different kinds of musical instruments, formed of eight difft. materials. II. i. 13, 24; *et al.*; 八政, the eight objects of government. V. iv. 4, 7; 八蠻, the eight *man* or savage tribes. V. v. 1.

公 *kung* — (1) Public feeling. V. xx. 15. (2) The highest *title* or dignity under the Chow dynasty. V. xx. 5, 6; *et al.* (3) The *title* of the highest princely rank. Found *passim* in the fifth Part; but only once in the Parts preceding, viz. IV. viii. Pt. ii. 2. The name of the principality often precedes, as in 周公, 毛公, 畢公. Observe 上公, V. viii. 3; and 公劉 V. iii. 5.

六 *luh* liu — Six. = the sixth. V. iv. 4; *et al.* We have 六宗, whose meaning is not well ascertained, II. i. 6; 六府, the six magazines, II. ii. 8: III. i. Pt. ii. 15; 六德, six of the nine virtues; II. iii. 4; 六律, the six pitch-tubes; II. iv. 4; *et al.*; 六卿, the leaders of the imperial hosts, III. iv. 1; but in V. xx. 13, 六卿 = the six ministers of the executive under Chow; 六事, III. ii. 2; 六師, the imperial armies. V. i. Pt. iii. 1; *et al.*; 六極, V. iv. 40; 六服, V. xx. 1.

共 *kung* — Together with, in common, all together. II. iv. 7: IV. vii. Pt. ii. 13; Pt. iii. 3; V. iv. 31: xiii. 4. To share in common. IV. vii. Pt. i. 7; Pt. ii. 4.

共 *kung* — 1st tone. 共工, the title of an ancient officer, minister of Works. I. i. 10: II. i. 12, 21.

兵 *ping* — Weapons of war. 戎兵, V. xiii 22.

其 *k'e* ch'i — The third personal pronoun, singular and plural. The possessive pronoun of the third person. As a demonstrative, the, that, this, these, those. It is found everywhere, and with peculiar usage. Very often it comes between the nominative and the verb, making the nominative emphatic, as in I. i. 11. But the nominative preceding may be a pronoun of any person, or a noun in any person, and the person of the 其 varies accordingly. *E. g.* IV. i. 3. 4. Often, again, 其 gives to the sentence or clause where it occurs a hortatory or imperative force. The clause is often terminated by a 哉, as in I. i. 12, but often not; *E. g.* V. xxvii. 16, 17, 20. 惟 often follows the 其 with this force. *E. g.* V. xix. 23. Sometimes the demonstrative force = then, in such a case; in the case of. *E. g.* II. ii. 20: IV. iii. 8. In many instances, such as 其訓, IV. v. Pt. ii. 9; 非人其吉, V. xxvi. 8, where the meaning may be plain enough, it is difficult to bring the usage under any general rule.

其 *ke* chi — A concluding particle. IV. xi. 3.

具 *keu* chü — All, in every thing. IV. iv. 7: V. xxvii. 15, 17. = to amass. IV. vii. Pt. ii. 14.

典 *tëen* tien — (1) Written books. V. xiv. 19. (2) Canons, statutes, regular rules and ways. III. iii. 8: iv. 4: IV. ii. 2; *et sæpe.* 五典, the five relations of society and the virtues belonging to them. II. i. 2; *et al.* 典常 are found together. V. viii. 4: xx. 16. 不典, unlawful ways. V. ix. 8: xviii. 22. = statutory. II. i. 11. = constantly. V. x. 7, 17. (3) To direct, superintend. II. i. 23. 24: V. xxvii. 11, 12. To be directed to, bent on. IV. viii. Pt. iii. 5. To consider, care for. V. ix. 3, 5.

兼 *këen* chien — Together with, and. V. xxiii. 1. To comprehend. = to absorb. IV. ii. 7. To embrace along with other duties. V. xix. 13.

冀 *k'e* ch'i — 冀州, one of Yu's nine provinces. III. i. Pt. i. 1. So, 冀方, III. iii. 7.

THE 13TH RADICAL. 冂.

册 *ts'ih* ts'ê — A tablet, or tablets with writing on them. V. vi. 11: xiii. 29, 30: xxii. 12. = records. V. xi. 19. To prepare such a tablet. V. vi. 5: xiii. 29.

再 *tsae* tsai — Twice. V. xviii. 23 : xxii. 25 : xxiii. 1, 2. To do twice, to repeat. II. ii. 17.

冒 *maou* mao — (1) To pursue blindly or heedlessly. V. i. Pt. i. 5 : xxii. 9. (2) To overspread. V. xvi. 14, 15, 21. To be overspread by. V. ix. 4. (3) Used for 娼, to be jealous of. V. xxx. 7.

冕 *mëen* mien — A cap of ceremony;—of various form and materials, acc. to the rank and circumstances of the wearer. IV. v. Pt. ii. 1 : V. xxii. 2, 21, 22, 23 : xxiii. 7.

THE 14TH RADICAL. 冖.

冢 *ch'ung* — (1) Great, highest. 冢君 = hereditary princes. V. i. Pt. i. 2, 6; *et al.* 冢土, the great earth, or the altar to the spirit of the earth. V. i. Pt. i. 10. 冢宰, prime minister. The title was used in both the dynasties of Shang and Chow. IV. iv. 1 : V. xvii. 1 : xx. 17. (2) 嶓冢, the name of a mountain. III. i. Pt. ii. 3, 8.

THE 15TH RADICAL. 冫.

冬 *tung* — Winter, in the winter. I. i. 7 : V. iv. 38 : xxv. 5.

冰 *ping* — Ice. V. xxv. 2.

凝 *ying* — To be accomplished. II. iii. 4.

THE 16TH RADICAL. 几.

几 *ke* chi — A bench or long stool. V. xxii. 2, 15, 16, 17, 18, 24.

凡 *fan* — All. IV. iii. 7 : vii. Pt. i. 17 : xi. 2 : V. iv. 10, 11, 13, 16, 23; *et al.*

凰 *hwang* huang — The male of the phœnix. II. iv. 9.

THE 17TH RADICAL. 凵.

凶 *hëung* hsiung — (1) Bad fortune; unfortunate. II. ii. 5 : IV. vi. 5 : V. iv. 30, 31, 33, 40; *et al.* 凶德, evil, suffering, condition. IV. vii. Pt. iii. 4. (2) Cruel, injurious; wicked. IV. iii. 8 : V. i. Pt. i. 6; Pt. ii. 3, 8; *et al.*

出 *ch'uh* ch'u — (1) To go or come forth. II. ii. 10 : III. i. Pt. ii. 10 : V. xxx. 6; *et al.* 出于, to issue in. V. xvi. 2. 出入, see 入. 出日, the rising sun. I. i. 4 : V. xvi. 21. Obs. V. xii. 10. (2) To put or send forth. II. i. 25 : ii. 17 : IV. vii. Pt. i. 1, 15; *et al.* Obs. V. xi. 3.

THE 18TH RADICAL. 刀.

刀 *taou* tao — A knife. V. xxiii. 19.

刃 *jin* jên — A sharp blade, attached to a spear. V. xxii. 21. Edged weapons. V. xxix. 2.

分 *fun* fên — To divide; to separate; to share; to distribute. V. iii. 9 : II. i. 27 : IV. vii. Pt. ii. 15 : V. v. 3. Separate. V. xx. 13. Separately. I. i. 4, 6.

刊 *k'an* — To hew down. II. iv. 1 : III. i. Pt. i. 1; Pt. ii. 14.

列 *lëë* lieh — To arrange; to be arranged. IV. viii. Pt. iii. 7 : V. iii. 10 : xix. 24.

刑 *hing* hsing — (1) Punishments. *Sæpe.* 五刑, the five punishments. II. i. 11, 20 : ii. 11 : V. xxvii. 13; *et al.* To punish. II. iii. 6 : V. ix. 16; *et al.* As an adjective. V. xxvii. 20; *et al.* (2) Laws generally. V. xv. 15. A pattern; behaviour. V. xiii. 21, 24 : I. i. 12. To imitate. V. xxviii. 3; *et al.*

初 *ch'oo* ch'u — The beginning or commencement; in the beginning, at first. II. i. 8 : ii. 19, 21 : *et sæpe.* 初一, the first. V. iv. 4. 初生, early days. V. xii. 18. To commence. V. ix. 1 : xiv. 1.

別 *pëë* pieh — (1) To separate. III. i. Pt. ii. 9. To distinguish. V. xxiv. 7. = besides. V. ix. 5, 17. (2) 大別, the name of a mountain. III. i. Pt. ii. 3, 8.

利 *le* li — (1) Gain, money. IV. ii. 5 : v. Pt. iii. 9. Advantage. IV. vii. Pt. ii. 4 : V. xxx. 6. 地利, V. xx. 12. Advantageous. V. vi. 12. 利用, conveniences. II. ii. 7. (2) 利口, sharpness of tongue. V. xx. 16 : xxiv. 8.

刳 *k'oo* k'u — To cut open. V. i. Pt. i. 5.

刵 *e* i — To cut off the ears. V. ix. 10 : xxvii. 3.

制 *che* chih — To order, regulate, define. IV. ii. 8 : vii. Pt. i. 12; *et al.* = strictness of regulation. V. xxi. 2. Regulations. II. xx. 14. 制于, to restrain one's self from. V. x. 13.

刻 *k'ih* k'o — To injure. IV. xi. 8.

則 *tsih* tsê — (1) Then; denoting either a logical sequence or a sequence of time. We must often leave it untranslated in English. *Passim.* (2) Rules. III. iii. 8: V. xxv. 4, (used in connection with 典). A model. IV. viii. Pt. i. 1. (3) To take as a law or pattern, to imitate. III. i. Pt. ii. 15: V. vi. 22; *et al.*

前 *ts'ëen* ch'ien — (1) The front. 在...之前 = before. V. xxii. 20. In front. V. iii. 8: xxvi. 3. (2) Former, as an adj. *Sæpe.* 前人, father, predecessor, forefathers, is very common. *E. g.* V. vii. 2, 10, 14.

削 *seŏ* hsiao — To pare. = to practise extortion. V. xxi. 7.

剔 *te'ih* t'i — To cut open, rip up. V. i. Pt. i. 5.

剕 *fei* — To cut off the feet. V. xxvii. 18.

剖 *p'ow* p'ou — To cut out. V. i. Pt. iii. 8.

剛 *kang* — Strong; stern. II. i. 24: V. iv. 17: xxiv. 12. Vigour. II. iii. 3. Sternly. V. x. 18.

剝 *pŏ* po — To tear off, = to degrade. V. i. Pt. ii. 5.

割 *kŏ* ko — To cut off; to injure, to afflict. I. i. 11: IV. i. 2, 8: V. xiv. 14: xvi. 11: xviii. 5. Sometimes the object is not expressed. = afflictions, calamities. V. vii. 1.

創 *ch'wang* ch'uang — To take warning. II. iv. 8.

勦 *tsëaou* chiao — To cut off. 勦絕, III. ii. 3.

劉 *lew* liu — (1) To slay. V. xvi. 15. = to wish others to die. IV. vii. Pt. i. 2. (2) A kind of battle axe. V. xxii. 21. (3) 公劉. One of the ancestors of the Chow family. V. iii. 5.

劓 *e* i — To cut off the nose. IV. viii. Pt. ii. 16: V. ix. 10: xxvii. 3, 18. 劓害, V. xviii. 5, must be translated generally,— to injure.

THE 19TH RADICAL. 力.

力 *leih* li — Strength. II. ii. 20: V. i. Pt. i. 8; *et al.* = influence. II. iv. 4. Strongly. IV. i. 3: V. i. Pt. ii. 3: xviii. 28.

功 *kung* — Work done, or to be done; achievement, services, merits. I. i. 10: II. i. 9, 26; *et sæpe.* Meritorious. II. ii. 18. 九功, the nine services. II. ii. 7. 辜功, deeds of guilt. V. xxvii. 21. 自以爲功, made it his own work. V. vi. 4, 16. 恤功于民, to labour compassionately for the people. V. xxvii. 8.

加 *këa* chia — To add, or be added, to;—to affect. V. viii. 2.

劼 *k'ëă* ch'ia — Strenuously. V. x. 18.

助 *tsoo* chu — To help, assist. V. ix. 7: v. 10.

勅 *ch'ih* — Written also, 勑 and 飭. To receive warning, admonish one's self. V. ix. 9. To have it in charge; to give in charge. II. iii. 6: iv. 11. With the idea superadded, that the charge is a work of correction. V. xiv. 2. = the execution of such a charge. V. xiv. 14.

勇 *yung* — Valour; brave. IV. ii. 2: V. xxx. 5.

勉 *mëen* mien — To urge, exert one's self. IV. vii. Pt. i. 15.

動 *tung* — To move, to put in action; to take action. IV. vi. 14: viii. Pt. ii. 6: V. x. 14. 16: xviii. 18. = movements. II. iv. 2: IV. vi. 5. To move, to excite, to affect. II. ii. 13, 21: vii. Pt. i. 12; Pt. ii. 1: Pt. iii. 5: V. iii. 7. = to remove. V. vi. 18.

勗 *heuh* hsü — To exert one's self. To act earnestly for. V. i. Pt. ii. 9: ii. 7, 8, 9: ix. 4: xvi. 16, 18.

務 *moo* mu — To bend the mind to, to strive after. IV. viii. Pt. iii. 4: V. i. Pt. iii. 4: xxiii. 5.

勝 *shing* shêng — To surpass. III. iii. 5.

勞 *laou* lao — To toil, to be toiled; to toil for; toil. IV. vii. Pt. i. 11, 14; Pt. ii. 10, 13: V. vi. 18: xv. 3, 5, 7: xx. 18: xxv. 1.

勞 *laou* lao — 3d tone. To encourage, to reward. V. xi. 2.

勢 *she* shih — Power, influence. V. xxi. 7. = the powerful. IV. ii. 4.

勤 *k'in* ch'in — To be laborious or diligent; to toil for, be laborious about. It is sometimes followed by 于. II. ii. 9, 14: IV. vii. Pt. i. 14: V. iii. 5: *et sæpe.* = laboriously. V. xi. 4, 5; *et al.* = to encourage to diligence. V. ix. i.

勳 *heun* hsün — (1) Merit; important service to the empire. II. ii. 20: V. i. Pt. i. 5: iii. 5. (2) 放勳, the name of the emperor Yaou. I. i. 1.

勱 *mae* mai — To exert one's strength. V. xix. 20.

勵 *le* li — To exert one's-self. II. iii. 1.

勸 *k'euen* ch'üan — To advise, to encourage, to stimulate. II. ii. 7: IV. vii. Pt. ii. 7: V. vii. 12: xvi. 11: xxvi. 8. To be stimulated, to come under the influence of. V. xviii. 4, 9, 10, 11. To encourage, advise, one another. V. xviii. 29: xxiv. 4.

THE 20TH RADICAL. 勹.

勿 *wuh* wu — Do not;—prohibitive. *Sæpe.* Sometimes the prohibition is indirect. *E. g.* II. ii. 6: V. vi. 17.

包 *paou* pao — (1) Bundles; things wrapped up. III. i. Pt. i. 44, 52 (N.B.) (2) Bushy. III. i. Pt. i. 33.

THE 21ST RADICAL. 匕.

化 *hwa* hua — To change, to exercise a transforming influence. V. xx. 6. Transforming influences. V. xxiv. 9. = to exchange. II. iv. 1. = to dissolve doubts. V. vii. 4. = to be influenced, transformed, by. V. i. Pt. ii. 3: xxi. 9: xxiv. 3.

北 *pih* pei — (1) The north; on the north; northwards; northern. III. i. Pt. ii. 7, 8, 9, 10, 13: IV. ii. 6: V. vi. 4. 北岳, a mountain. II. i. 8. (2) To be defeated and flee. V. iii. 8.

北 *pei* — 3d tone. To be separated. II. i. 27.

THE 22D RADICAL. 匚.

匡 *k'wang* k'uang — To correct. To assist. IV. iv. 7: v. Pt. ii. 2, 3: vii. Pt. i. 2: viii. Pt. i. 9: V. xxvi. 3.

匪 *fei* — Not. IV. iii. 7: viii. Pt. iii. 3: V. xx. 20: xxvi. 2: xxvii. 12.

匭 *kwei* kuei — A box or case. III. i. Pt. i. 52.

匯 *hwuy* hui — The whirling turbulent waters of the Han and Keang near their junction. III. i. Pt. ii. 8, 9.

匱 *kwei* kuei — A coffer or chest. V. vi. 11.

THE 23D RADICAL. 匸.

匹 *p'eih* p'i — (1) 匹夫匹婦, any ordinary man or woman. IV. vi. 11. (2) Responsive. V. xiii. 4. (3) A denominator of horses. V. xxviii. 4.

匿 *neih* ni — To conceal. IV. vi. Pt. i. 7.

區 *k'eu* ch'ü — 區夏, a small portion of the empire. V. ix. 4.

THE 24TH RADICAL. 十.

十 *shih* — Ten. *Sæpe.* 十愆, the ten evil ways. IV. iv. 7. It is generally found in the Shoo in combination with other numerals, both cardinal and ordinal.

千 *ts'ëen* ch'ien — A thousand. II. iv. 8: V. i. Pt. i. 8: ii. 2: xxvii. 18.

午 *woo* wu — The seventh of the calendaric branch characters. V. i. Pt. ii. 1: iii. 8: xii. 2, 5: xxiv. 1.

升 *shing* shêng — To ascend, to rise. II. i. 1: IV. v. Pt. iii. 4: V. xxi. 14: xxviii. 1. 升降 = advancement and degeneracy. V. xxiv. 4.

卉 *hwuy* hui — Grass,—all kinds of grasses. III. i. Pt. i. 44.

半 *pwan* pan — The half. IV. viii. Pt. iii. 5.

卑 *pei* — Mean. V. xv. 9.

協 *hëë* hsieh — To agree, be united, in. II. i. 1: IV. vi. 8; *et al.* = both together. II. ii. 18. To agree with. V. i. Pt. ii. 5. 協比, to form parties. IV. vii. Pt. iii. 3. To harmonize with what is right. V. xxiii. 3. To be brought to harmony with the right. II. ii. 1: V. iv. 11: viii. 3: xix. 4. To bring to harmony. I. i. 2: II. i. 8: IV. v. Pt. ii. 4: V. iv. 2. = harmoniously. V. iv. 4. = to help. IV. i. 3.

卒 *tsuh* tsu — (1) To die. V. xvii. 1. (2) To complete. V. vii. 16. (3) Then; when all was over. II. i. 8.

南 *nan* — The south. III. i. Pt. ii. 23: V. xxii. 15 18. 南訛 = the transformations of the summer. I. i. 5. Southwards; on the south. II. i. 8: III. i. Pt. ii. 7, 8: IV. ii. 6. Southern. III. i. Pt. ii. 6: V. vi. 4: xxii. 1. 南河, the southern part of the Ho. III. i. Pt. i. 53. 終南, the name of a mountain. III. i. Pt. i. 76. 南交, a place on the borders of Cochin China. I. i. 5. 南巢, the place where Këë was confined. IV. ii. 1. 南岳, the name of a mountain. II. i. 8. 南宮, a double surname. V. xvi. 12: xxii. 11.

THE 25TH RADICAL. 卜.

卜 *puh* pu — To divine by means of the tortoise-shell; divination. II. ii. 18: IV. vii. Pt. i. 2; Pt. ii. 7: V. iv. 20, 23, 24, 25; *et sæpe.* 卜龜 is to divine with the tortoise-

shell. V. vi. 9. 卜宅 is to divine about the locality. V. xii. 2.

卞 *p'een* pien — A law, a rule. V. xxii. 24.

占 *chen* chan — (1) To determine the answers on divination, to examine the prognostics. V. iv. 24. 官占, the officer charged with this work. II. ii. 18. Used for 𥿻. V. iv. 23. (2) To deliberate. V. xxvii. 20.

卣 *yew* yu — A wine-jar or bottle, of medium size. V. xiii. 25 : xxviii. 4.

THE 26TH RADICAL. 卩.

卬 *gung* ang — I, the speaker's own person. V. vii. 8, 11.

卯 *maou* mao — The 4th of the calendaric branch-characters. V. xii. 4 : xiii. 3 : xxii. 12.

危 *wei* — (1) Unstable and insecure. II. ii. 15. Perilousness. IV. v. Pt. iii. 5 : V. xx. 2, 19 : xxiv. 12. To have a feeling of danger. 危懼, IV. iii. 6. 憂危, V. xxv. 2. (2) 三危, the name of a place. II. i. 12 : III. i. Pt. i. 78 ; Pt. ii. 6.

即 *tseih* chi — (1) To go, approach, to. II. iv. 8 : III. i. Pt. i. 83 : *et sæpe.* Foll. by 于. V. xiv. 17. Observe 即命, V. vi. 8 : vii. 3 ; 克即宅, 即俊, xiv. 17 ; and 殷之即喪, IV. x. 7. = to apply one's-self to. V. xv. 9. (2) As a particle. = as to, even. V. xxviii. 2 ; instantly, V. xiii. 7.

卿 *k'ing* ch'ing — A high noble and officer. 六卿, the six leaders of the imperial armies. III. ii. 1. But in V. xx. 13, the same phrase indicates the six chief ministers under the Chow dynasty. 卿 is found everywhere else with 士 following;—IV. iv. 7 : xi. 2 : *et sæpe.* In V. xvii. 1, 卿士 is merely a compound designation of one individual; and in all the other places they should probably go together, as indicating one class of officers.

THE 27TH RADICAL. 厂.

厎 *che* chih — (1) To come to, to cause to come to; to be able to be brought to. II. i. 8 : iii. 3 : III. i. Pt. i. 6, 32, 41, 66, 77 : *et passim.* It is used with other verbs—厎貢, III. i. Pt. i. 52 ; Pt. ii. 15 ; 厎綏, IV. vii. Pt. i. 4. = to execute. V. i. Pt. i. 10. Obs. 自厎 IV. Pt. ii. 3 ; 厎遂, IV. xi. 1 ; 厎商之罪, V. iii. 6. (2) To settle. V. vii. 11. (3) 厎柱, the name of a hill. III. i. Pt. ii. 1, 7. In many copies of the Shoo 厎 is printed 底 and few Chinese teachers are aware of the error. In reality the character 底 occurs only once,— in V. xxii. 16.

厖 *mang* — V. xx. 20. Should probably be 庬 confused.

厚 *how* hou — Thick. III. iii. 9. = great, rich. V. i. Pt. iii. 4. In 民生厚, V. xxi. 14, 厚 = good ; but 厚生, II. ii. 7, = making the means of living abundant.

原 *yuen* yüan — A plain. III. i. Pt. i. 77 : IV. vii. Pt. i. 12. 太原, 東原, and 敷淺原 are all the names of plains. III. i. Pt. i. 5. 32 ; Pt. ii. 4.

厥 *heuĕ* chüeh — A personal and possessive pronoun, used everywhere ; and much in the same way as 其. It is properly of the third person, and, as a personal pronoun, it is only so found. As a possessive, however, it is often = my, our, your. *E. g.* IV. viii. Pt. ii. 10 : V. i. Pt. i. 7, 9 : iv. 2 : xxvi. 1, 8. It is frequently used also as a demonstrative, = the, that, those. *E. g.* I. i. 4, 5, 6, 7 : IV. viii. Pt. iii. 1 : V. iii. 2. Still more common than in the case of 其, however, there are instances, where it is difficult to construe the character with reference to its more common usages, *E. g.* V. i. Pt. iii. 1 : II. iii. 3 : V. xv. 8. 15, 17, 18.

厭 *yen* — To be satiated. V. xiii. 27.

厲 *le* li — (1) Severe, dangerous. V. vi. 5. (2) Oppressively. V. xi. 2. (3) To be conscious of peril. V. xxvi. 1.

THE 28TH RADICAL. 厶.

去 *k'eu* ch'ü — 2d tone. To put away. II. ii. 6.

參 *ts'an* ch'an — To be arranged in order. IV. x. 6.

THE 29TH RADICAL 又.

又 *yew* yu — Further, also, again,—continuing a narrative by the addition of further particulars. II. iv. 11 : III. i. Pt. ii. 7, 8, 9, 10, 12, 13 ; *et sæpe.*

及 *k'eih* ch'i — To come to, to reach, to attain to. IV. vii. Pt. i. 12, 14, 17 ; *et sæpe.* 不及 is frequent, meaning deficiencies, to be unequal to, not to be up to, &c. = to come to the knowledge of, to determine.

書經

V. xiii. 2. It very often simply = and. *E. g.* III. i. Pt. i. 4, 28, 46; Pt. ii. 1. = with. V. iv. 25. = to. V. xxvii. 2.

友 *yew* yu — A friend, friends. IV. vii. Pt. i. 10: V. vii. 12: x. 13. Friendly. V. i. Pt. i. 2, 6; *et sæpe*. To be friendly. V. ix. 16. Foll. by 于. xii. 24. 弗友, not friendly, = disobedient. V. iv. 17.

反 *fan* — (1) To return. III. iii. 9: IV. x. 6. (2) To take back, = to resume. V. xxiii. 7. To retract. xx. 15. To retort. vii. 7. 復反, to recover. vii. 4. 反風, to bring a contrary wind. vi. 19. (3) To go contrary to. II. ii. 20. = perversity. V. iv. 14. To overthrow. iii. 8. = in revenge, for private grudge. V. xxvii. 16.

叔 *shuh* shu — (1) The third of brothers. I. i. 5, 7. So also in V. xxvii. 13. where it includes cousins. (2) A father's younger brother. = uncles. V. xvii. 1. So, 伯叔, V. v. 3. 霍叔, 蔡叔, 管叔, were brothers of king Woo, and uncles of Ching. V. xvii. 1: vi. 12. 虢叔, a brother of king Wăn, and uncle of the duke of Chow. V. xvi. 12.

取 *ts'eu* ch'ü — To take. V. xii. 8. = to capture. V. i. Pt. ii. 8. = to take in hand, to make an end of. IV. ii. 7.

受 *show* shou — (1) To receive. *Passim.* Especially in the phrases,—受命, 受天命. Obs. 受終, II. i. 4; 受其敗, IV. xi. 8. To receive to employment. II. iii. 4. 受上帝, to receive gifts from God. II. iv. 2. (2) The name of the tyrant, the last emperor of the Shang dynasty. V. i. Pt. i. 4, 6, 8; *et sæpe*. He is in other books commonly mentioned by his epithet of 紂.

叢 *ts'ung* ts'êng — Crowded together. V. xv. 18. 叢脞, II. iv. 11, = vexatious. See 脞.

THE 30TH RADICAL. 口.

口 *k'ow* k'ou — (1) The mouth. II. ii. 17: IV. vii. Pt. i. 18: viii. Pt. ii. 4: V. xv. 15: xx. 6. 利口, see 利. 逸口, an exceeding mouth, = extravagant talk IV. vii. Pt. i. 12. 口實, that which fills the mouth, = matter for remark. IV. ii. 1. (2) 壺口, the name of a hill. III. i. Pt. i. 3; Pt. ii. 1.

古 *koo* ku — Antiquity; the ancients; ancient. I. i. 1: IV. viii. Pt. iii. 3: V. ix. 5: *et sæpe*. We have 古人, 古之人, 古先民, generally referring to the ancient sovereigns. Anciently, of old. IV. iv. 2: vii. Pt. i. 7, 14; *et al.* Observe 自古商人, V. xix. 19; and 若古, V. xxvii. 2.

叨 *t'ou* t'ao — To be covetous, greedy. V. xviii. 5.

召 *chaou* chao — To call for, to summon. III. ii. 1: V. xxii. 3. To call forth, to provoke. IV. xi. 7.

召 *shaou* shao — In the *title* of V. xii.; the name of the appanage of Shih, the Grand-protector in king Ching's reign.

可 *k'o* — May, might; can, could. Like *may* in English, 可 may represent possibility, liberty, duty. It occurs frequently, but not so often as in the Four Books. 可以 occurs only once. V. xvi. 10. 可 standing alone, = to do, to be competent. I. i. 9, 11.

台 *e* i — The first personal pronoun. Used also as a possessive. III. i. Pt. ii. 17: IV. i. 1, 3; *et sæpe*. It does not occur in the 5th Part.

史 *she* shih — A recorder, historiographer. V. vi. 5, 17. 內史, see 內. 太史, the Grand-recorder. V. x. 13: xix. 9, 24: xxii. 23.

右 *yew* yu — The right side; on the right side. II. ii. 4. V. ii. 1; *et al.* As an adj., the right. V. xxii. 20. 左右 go frequently together, with reference to the officers immediately about the sovereign. IV. vi. 7: viii. Pt. i. 4: V. xix. 1, 8; *et al.* The same characters, used as a verb, but with changed tones (左右), = to assist. II. iv. 4; *et al.* Observe 夾右, III. i. Pt. i. 11.

司 *sze* szû — To preside over, to superintend; that which one presides over, his proper business. We are puzzled sometimes, whether to construe the character as a noun or a verb. III. iv. 4: IV. ix. 5: V. xx. 15: xxi. 2: xxvii. 12. Officers. V. ix. 11: x. 17. So, 百司, V. xix. 8, 9; and 有司, II. ii. 12: V. xix. 13, 21. Obs. 司牧人. V. xix. 12; 司馬, the minister of War, V. ii. 2: xi. 2: xix. 10: xx. 10; 司空, the minister of Works. II. i. 17: V. ii. 2: iv. 7: xi. 2: xix. 10: xx. 12; 司寇 the minister of Crime, V. iv. 7: xix. 24: xx. 11; 司徒, the minister of Instruction. II. i. 19: V. ii. 2: iv. 7. xi. 2: xix. 10: xx. 8.

吁 *yu* yü — Alas. I. i. 9, 10, 11: II. ii. 6: iii. 2: iv. 1, 3. We should perhaps translate in the same way in V. xxvii. 14.

各 *kŏ* ko — Each, every one. II. iv. 8: IV. iii. 7: V. iv. 32; *et al.* Obs. IV. vii. Pt. iii. 7.

合 *hŏ* ho — To agree. IV. xi. 7: V. xvi. 20. To unite, make to blend. II. iv. 9. To preserve in harmony. V. xi. 3. 合黎, the name of a hill. III. i. Pt. ii. 5.

吉 *keih* chi — (1) Good. IV. vii. Pt. i. 12; Pt. ii. 16: V. xxv. 5, 8: xxvii. 12; *et al.* (2) Fortunate, lucky. II. ii. 5: IV. vi. 5; *et al.* Often used with reference to the favourable indications obtained by divination. II. iii. 3: V. iv. 26, 27, 28, 29, 30, 31; *et al.*

同 *t'ung* — (1) To unite; to bring—to be brought—to the same order or rule; together; the same. II. i. 8: ii. 18: iii. 6: iv. 7: III. i. Pt. i. 15, 18, 75; Pt. ii. 7, 14: iv. 5; *et sæpe.* = to share in. IV. vii. Pt. ii. 14: V. xix. 5. 大同, a great agreement. V. iv. 26. = the same as. V. xvi. 16. (2) The name of a cup. V. xxii. 23, 26, 27, 28. (3) Forms part of the name of a hill. III. i. Pt. ii. 12.

名 *ming* — (1) To name. II. ii. 10: V. vi. 15: xxvii. 8. (2) Famous, the best. V. iii. 6: III. i. Pt. i. 52.

后 *how* hou — (1) A sovereign, the sovereign. II. ii. 2: III. iv. 2: V. iii. 2; *et sæpe.* 元后, the great sovereign. II. ii. 14, 17; *et al.* So, 丕后. V. xxvi. 1. We have 后王, IV. viii. Pt. ii. 2; and 王后, V. xxii. 24. God is called 上天神后, IV. iii. 4. But Pwan-kăng calls his ancestors—我先神后, IV. vii. Pt. ii. 10. 后土, V. iii. 6. (2) A prince, one of the feudal chiefs of the empire. II. i. 8. The phrase 羣后, in this sense, is frequent. We have 三后;—see 三; 后羿, III. iii. 2; 后稷, II. i. 17, 18: vi. V. xxvii. 8.

吏 *le* li — An officer. 天吏. III. iv. 6.

吝 *lin* — Sparing, slow. IV. ii. 5.

君 *keun* chün — (1) To rule over. IV. viii. 1: V. xxii. 24. As a noun, a sovereign, a ruler. Applied to the emperor. II. ii. 4, 17: V. xxii. 5: xxiii. 5; *et sæpe.* Applied to princes, rulers of States. V. i. Pt. i. 2, 6; *et sæpe.* See especially in Bk. xvi., addressed to 君奭. The phrase 君子, = princely, superior man, occurs, but not so frequently as in the Four Books. It has hardly assumed as yet its technical meaning. II. ii. 20: V. i. Pt. iii. 2: v. 4: x. 7: xii. 24: xv. 1: xx. 15: xxx. 5. (2) In 君陳, V. xxi., and 君牙, xxv., 君 appears to be a part of the name.

否 *fow* fou — (1) Not, not to have. I. i. 12. If not, with reference to something going before. II. iv. 6: IV. v. Pt. iii. 2: V. xv. 3. (2) To disapprove, disallow. IV. vii. Pt. iii. 11: V. xv. 15.

否 *p'ei* — Distresses. ? disorders. V. xv. 17.

吾 *woo* wu — I. V. i. Pt. i. 6. = our, IV. xi. 3.

含 *han* — To hold in the mouth. = to conceal (?). IV. vii. Pt. i. 8. To cherish. V. xv. 17.

呂 *leu* lü — (1) = 呂侯, the prince of Leu. V. xxvii. 1. (2) The surname of the princes of Ts'e. V. xxii. 11.

告 *kaou* kao — To tell to, announce, declare to. *Passim.* It is sometimes followed by 于, but not often. To announce or appeal to Heaven. IV. iii. 3: V. xxvii. 4. 無告, the helpless, those who have none to appeal to. II. ii. 3.

周 *chow* chou — In IV. v. Pt. i. 3, it should probably be 君. Throughout the 5th Part, the character occurs everywhere as the name of the ancient seat of the princes of the Chow dynasty, which is its meaning always in the name—'the duke of Chow;' and as the name of the dynasty itself. Frequently it denotes the capital, Haou, as in xii. 1: xiii. 6, 10, 18, which is also called 宗周. See xviii. 1; *et al.* We have also 成周 for the name of the new capital at Lŏ, xxiv. 1, 4.

呱 *koo* ku — 呱呱, the wail of an infant. II. iv. 8.

呼 *hoo* — In the exclamation 嗚呼, Oh! *Passim.*

命 *ming* — *Passim.* (1) As a verb. To charge, command, appoint. The subject may be the emperor, any leader or chief, Heaven or God. As a noun. Commands, order, requirements, charge. Those may be from man, as in the titles of several of the Books, or from Heaven or God. In this latter sense its common reference is to the favour or decree of God in dealing with the appointment to the sovereignty of the empire. We have 元命, = the great appointment, *i.e.*, to the throne, V. xiv. 5; but the same phrase in V. xxvii. 11, means the power of life and death. As a verb, also in the passive. II. i. 1: V. vi. 7. To request authority. V. xvii. 1. To consult, ask the will of. II. ii. 18. In V. viii. 4, it means the symbols of investiture. (2) Life. The idea sometimes approaches that of fate, destiny. IV. vii. Pt. i. 4, 12; Pt. ii. 9; Pt. iii. 2, 6: V. xviii. 2; *et al.* Obs. 惟人在命. V. xxvii. 21; 自敗哲命, V. xii. 19; 惟命, V. xxvii. 1. (3) 文命. Perhaps the name of Yu. II. ii. 1.

咈 *fuh* fo — To oppose, to do despite to. II. ii. 6: IV. iv. 5: xi. 5. Perhaps it should have the same meaning in I. i. 11, though I have translated there after Ts'ae.

和 *ho* — (1) To harmonize; to cultivate harmony with; to be harmonious. I. i. 2: II. i. 24: ii. 7; *et sæpe.* = to unite. V. xvi. 12. = to be obedient. V. ix. 9. Harmonious, harmony. IV. vii. Pt. i. 12: V. xviii. 24: ix. 1: *et al.* Spoken of soup.

IV. viii. Pt. iii. 2. (2) A surname. I. i. 8, 6, 7, 8: II. iv. 1, 9. So also probably in V. xxii. 19. (3) The name of a river. III. i. Pt. i. 66. (4) Part of a designation,—義和. V. xxviii. 1, 3, 4.

咎 *kew* chiu (1) Calamity. II. ii. 20: V. xxvii. 12. (2) Crime, the fault. IV. vii. Pt. i. 12: Pt. ii. 4: V. iv. 11; *et al.* As an adj., = evil, criminal. V. iv. 13. (3) Unfavourable. V. iv. 34.

咤 *too* tu To set down a cup. V. xxii. 26.

咨 *tsze* tszû (1) To consult with; to inquire and find. I. i. 9, 10: II. i. 16. (2) An exclamation, = Ah! I. i. 8, 11, 12: II. i. 17, 21, 22, 23, 26: ii. 20.

咨 *tsze* tszû 3d tone. 怨咨, to murmur and sigh. V. xxv. 5.

咸 *heën* hsien (1) All. It stands very often at the beginning of clauses of sentences, and collects in one all the subjects of the verb which follows. Those subjects sometimes are only two. V. xix. 1: xxiii. 2. are peculiar, 咸 being equivalent to—they and all the rest. In Part V., however, standing in the same way at the beginning of clauses, it is often used adverbially, and = entirely, in every thing. *E. g.* viii. 1: ix. 1: x. 9: xiii. 5, 15. (2) A name. 巫咸. V. xvi. 7.

哀 *gae* ai To compassionate. V. xxvii. 5. Compassionately, with sorrow. V. xxii. 10: xxvii. 20. Sorrow, painful labour. V. ix. 16. 哀哉, an exclamation, = Alas. Placed at the end of the sentence. V. vii. 8.

品 *p'in* A rank, a sort. 五品, the five relationships of society. II. i. 19. 金三品, gold, silver, and copper. III. i. Pt. i. 44. 52.

哉 *tsae* tsai (1) A particle of exclamation. It occurs everywhere, but is not complicated with other particles as in the Four Books. Our point of exclamation—!—is generally sufficient for it. (2) To begin. IV. iv. 2: V. iii. 2: ix. 1: xxii. 1.

哲 *chĕ* chê Wise; wisdom. II. i. 1: iii. 2: IV. iv. 6: viii. Pt. i. 1: V. iv. 6, 34: vii. 1, 13: ix. 5, 20: x. 9: xii. 10, 19: xv. 16: xxvii. 22.

唐 *t'ang* The name of a principality where Yaou once ruled. The word is used to indicate him. V. xx. 3. With the addition of 陶. III. iii. 7.

問 *wun* wên To ask, to inquire. IV, ii. 8: V. vi. 17: xxvii. 7.

商 *shang* (1) To deliberate. V. xxix. 4. (2) Everywhere as the name of the dynasty so called. Sometimes the character denotes its original seat; sometimes, in Pt. V., what had formed its imperial domain; and sometimes its capital. Obs. 天邑商, V. xiv. 20, which is different from 商邑, x. 11. On the phrase 有商, see 有. (3) A surname. V. iii. 9.

啟 *k'e* ch'i (1) To open. IV. viii. Pt. i. 7: V. vi. 9, 16. = to open up, commence. V. iii. 5. 啟寵, to open the way to favourites. IV. viii. Pt. ii. 9. To institute. V. xi. 3. 啟明, to develope intelligence. I. i. 9. (2) To instruct. We have 啟迪, IV. v. Pt. i. 6: vi. 2; and 啟佑, V. xxv. 6. (3) The name of Yu's son. II. iv. 8.

啻 *ch'e* ch'i Only. 不啻, V. xiv. 24: xv. 17: xxx. 6.

善 *shen* (1) What is good; the good; good. II. ii. 7: IV. iii. 3, 8: iv. 8; *et sæpe.* To have in good condition. V. xxix. 2. (2) Skilful, to be skilful. V. xxx. 5.

喜 *he* hsi To rejoice, joyful. II. iv. 11: IV. vii. Pt. ii. 4.

喪 *sang* To mourn; mourning; the observances of funeral ceremonies. II. i. 13: IV. viii. Pt. i. 1: V. iii. 9: xxiii. 7.

喪 *sang* 3d tone. Active and neuter. To die, perish, go to ruin. To ruin; to lose. As a noun, ruin. IV. i. 3: iv. 7: viii. Pt. ii. 7: x. 4, 7: xi. 2. 8: V. i. Pt. ii. 5, (= to degrade); Pt. iii. 3: v. 6: vi. 12: vii. 14: x. 3, 11: xiv. 2, 10, 12: xvi. 2, 19: xviii. 15, 16.

喬 *k'ëaou* ch'iao High; tall. III. i. Pt. i. 42.

單 *an* (1) To complete. V. xiii. 24. (2) Greatly. V. xvi. 15. (3) Single. 單辭, one side of a case. V. xxvii. 21.

嗇 *sih* sê 嗇夫, certain inferior officers. III. iv. 4.

嗚 *woo* wu *Passim.* In combination with 呼, as an exclamation, = Oh!

嗜 *she* shih To delight in, lust after. III. iii. 6.

嗟 *tsëay* chieh An exclamation. Ah! III. ii. 2: iv. 2: IV. iii. 2: V. i. Pt. i. 2; *et al.*

嗣 *tsze* tszû (1) To inherit; inheriting; to succeed to. *Passim.* The expression 嗣王, inheriting (= new) king, is frequent. Obs. 嗣造, V. xxviii. 2. Heirs, successors. II. ii. 12: IV. iv. 6: V. xvi. 10. The successor, or heir. V. xxii. 4. (2) To employ or labour with. V. 6.

嘉 *këa* chia As an adj., good, admirable. II. ii. 3: IV. iv. 8: V. xxi. 6; *et al.* As a verb, to deem or pronounce admirable, to admire. II. ii. 14: V. viii. 3. Obs. IV. vii. Pt. iii.

4, and V. xv. 5, where it = to display admirable —— .

器 *k'e* ch'i Vessels, utensils. IV. vii. Pt. i. 13: V. v. 2. 玉器, the five tokens of gem. II. i. 8.

噫 *e* i An exclamation of dissatisfaction. V. vi. 17.

嚌 *tse* chi To taste, or merely raise to the lips. V. xxii. 28.

嚚 *yin* Insincere. I. i. 9, 12.

嚮 *hëang* hsiang Over against, towards. V. xxii. 15, 16, 17, 18. 嚮邇, to be approached. IV. vii. Pt. i. 12. = to approach, to draw near to. V. xiii. 10. = to show one's mind to. xiv. 5. = encouragingly, attractively. V. iv. 4.

嚴 *yen* To revere, stand in awe of. V. xxvii. 17. Severe, dignified. V. xv. 4. Severely. II. iii. 4: V. xix. 4.

THE 31st RADICAL. 囗.

囚 *ts'ëw* ch'iu (1) To confine, imprison. V. xvii. 1; and perhaps. xviii. 23. Imprisonment. V. iii. 8. (2) The pleas in criminal cases. 要囚 = to examine the evidence in criminal cases. V. ix. 12.

四 *sze* szě *Passim.* Four. The fourth. 四方, the four quarters, occurs everywhere, mostly as a designation of the empire. 四征, to proceed against on every side. V. xx. 1. 四夷, the wild tribes all around. II. ii. 6; *et al.* 四海, as a designation of the empire, is very common. 四海之內 occurs only once. IV. viii. Pt. iii. 8. 四民, the four classes of the people. V. xx. 12. We have many other phrases.—四國, V. xviii. 2, 20; *et al.*; 四隣, xvii. 6. (II. iv. 5 is different); 四輔, xiii. 20; 四隩, III. i. Pt. ii. 14; 四載, II. iv. 1; 四岳, I. i. 12, *et al.*; 四門, 四目, 四聰, II. i. 1, 15; 四時 I. i. 8; 四表, I. i. 1.

回 *hwuy* huy The crooked; bad. V. i. Pt. iii. 3.

因 *yin* As a noun, the cause. V. xviii. 5. As a preposition, by means of, on account of. III. iii. 2: V. xxi. 14. Along. III. i. Pt. i. 70. As a verb, to go on to more of what has been spoken of. I. i. 5.

困 *k'wăn* k'wên Distress, to be in distress. V. xvii. 5. 困窮, the distressed and poor. II. ii. 17; *et al.*, with a different shade of meaning. To distress. (act.). V. xiii. 21. To be distressed about. IV. vii. Pt. ii. 6.

冏 *këung* chiung The proper form of the name 冏, in V. xxvi. 1.

固 *koo* ku Sure, from; to be sure. III. iii. 4: V. xvi. 10. Firmly. II. ii. 18. To strengthen, make sure. IV. ii. 7: V. xiv. 3: xxiv. 7.

國 *kwŏ* kuo A kingdom, a State. Spoken of the States of the empire. IV. iv. 7: V. i. Pt. ii. 4: iv. 19; *et sæpe.* 萬國 = the empire. V. xx. 3. So, 國家, V. xxviii. 2; *et al.* Also, 邦國. V. xx. 10. Spoken of the empire. V. xv. 5, 6, 7: *et sæpe.* May sometimes be translated by—dynasty. V. xii. 8, 18; *et al.* 中國, V. xi. 6. 國人, the people. V. xvi. 13.

圉 *yu* yü 朱圉 the name of a mountain, III. i. Pt. ii. 2.

圖 *too* tu (1) To plan, to aim at. III. iii. 5: IV. v. Pt. ii. 3: vii. Pt. i. 7: V. vi. 10; *et sæpe.* Plans, objects. IV. v. Pt. i. 6. To reckon on. V. xviii. 3, 5, 14. (2) A plan or map. V. xiii. 3: xxii. 19.

THE 32D RADICAL. 土.

土 *t'oo* t'u (1) Earth. One of the five elements. II. ii. 7: V. iv. 5. The land, as opposed to water. II. i. 17: V. xxvii. 8. The ground or soil. III. i. Pt. i. 7, 16, 17, 24; *et al.*, *sæpe.* (2) Territory, regions; grounds. III. i. Pt. ii. 16: V. xxvii. 14: xxiii. 2: xx. 12: xiv. 23, 24; *et al.*, *sæpe.* (3) The earth, personified and deified, is called 后土. V. iii. 6. Comp. 冢土, I. i. Pt. i. 10.

在 *tsae* tsai *Passim.* (1) As a preposition, and neuter verb. Its radical meaning is—in, to be in. But we must render it variously in translating,—in, on, in the case of, with reference to; to depend on, rest on, lie in, &c. Once standing alone, it = to be present. IV. iv. 1. It often precedes what we should call adverbs of place or time,—昔, 今, 上, 下, 後, 中, &c. Obs. such usages as 在寬, II. i. 19. (2) To examine. I. i. 7: II. i. 5.

圭 *kwei* kuei A gem-stone. III. i. Pt. ii. 23. Tokens of gem, given by the emperor to the nobles. V. xxii. 23: xxiii. 1.

圮 *p'e* p'i To injure, subvert. I. i. 11.

地 *te* ti — The earth, in correlation with Heaven. II. ii. 8 *(n. b.)* V. xx. 6 *(n. b.)*: xxvii. 6. *(n. b.)*. The ground. IV. viii. Pt. i. 8: V. xx. 12. 天地, Heaven and Earth, = the supreme Power. V. i. Pt. i. 3. 永地, a lasting settlement. IV. vii. Pt. i. 6.

圻 *k'e* ch'i — (1) Frontiers. 郊圻, V. xxiv. 7. (2) 圻父, a designation of the minister of War. V. x. 13.

均 *keun* chün — To equalize. V. xx. 17. To be equal. V. xxvii. 16.

坐 *tso* — To sit. IV. v. Pt. i. 5.

垂 *ch'uy* ch'ui — (1) To hand down, transmit; to be transmitted. IV. ii. 8: V. viii. 2: xvii. 3: (2) To let hang down. In the phrase 垂拱, V. iii. 9: xxiv. 2. (3) The edge of a raised hall or platform. V. xxii. 21.

垂 *shwuy* shue — The name of Shun's minister of Works, and of a famous mechanician (probably the same). II. i. 21: V. xxii. 19.

垣 *yuen* yüan — A wall or enclosure. Specifically, a low wall. 垣墉. V. xi. 4. 垣牆, V. xxix. 4.

城 *ch'ing* ch'êng — 析城, the name of a mountain. III. i. Pt. ii. 1.

埴 *chih* — Clayey. III. i. Pt. i. 33.

執 *chih* — To hold, grasp; to seize. V. iii. 3: vi. 17: xxii. 21; *et al.* = to bring and show. V. xxiii. 1. To be laid hold of. V. xii. 10. To look upon, to hold as—. V. i. Pt. ii. 9. 執事 and 執事之人 = officers. V. vi. 17: IV. vii. Pt. iii. 8. 執藝事, to be engaged in mechanical affairs. III. iv. 3. 執中, to hold fast the Mean. II. ii. 15.

基 *ke* chi — A foundation. V. iii. 5. 初基, to lay the foundations. V. ix. 1. 基命, the founding decree. V. xiii. 2. The character, however, is generally used for the superstructure raised on the foundation, and = patrimony, possession, inheritance. IV. v. Pt. i. 2: V. vii. 9, 11: xvi. 2: xix. 15: xx. 14.

堂 *t'ang* — The hall, or outer apartment,—a raised platform. V. xxvii. 21. To build the hall, *i.e.*, to complete the building. V. vii. 11.

堪 *k'an* — To sustain; to be fit or worthy. V. xviii. 18, 19.

堯 *yaou* yao — The emperor Yaou. I. 1: IV. viii. Pt. iii. 10.

報 *paou* pao — To recompense, reward. V. iii. 10: xxvii. 5. To be recompensed. V. xxvii. 21. = in reply to. V. xxiii. 4.

墍 *tseih* chi — To detest. II. i. 25.

塗 *t'oo* t'u — (1) Miry; mire. III. i. Pt. i. 42, 51: IV. ii. 2. To plaster. V. xi. 4 *(n. b.)*. (2) 塗山, the name of a principality. II. iv. 8.

塞 *sih* sae — Sincere. II. i. 1: iii. 3.

塾 *shuh* shu — An apartment by the side of a gate. V. xxii. 20.

墉 *yung* — A wall. Specifically, a high wall. V. xi. 4.

墊 *teen* tien — To be flooded, merged in the water. II. iv. 1.

墍 *k'e* ch'i — To overlay with fine plaster. V. xi. 4.

墓 *moo* mu — A grave. V. iii. 8.

墜 *chuy* chui — To fall down among. IV. ii. 2. To let fall, to drop, to lose. III. iii. 8: IV. iv. 8: V. vi. 7: x. 12: xii. 11, 17: xvi. 2, 4.

墠 *shen* shan — A levelled space, a small terrace. V. vi. 4.

墨 *mih* mo — To brand, branding. IV. iv. 7: V. xxvii. 18.

墮 *to* — To fall to ruin. II. iv. 11.

墳 *fun* fên — ? rich. Spoken of soil. III. i. Pt. i. 17, 24, 33, 58.

壇 *t'an* — An altar. V. vi. 4.

壚 *loo* lu — Dark and thin. Spoken of soil. III. i. Pt. i. 58.

壞 *hwae* huai — To be spoiled, or ruined. II. ii. 7: V. xxiii. 3.

壤 *jang* — (1) 三壤, three qualities of the soil. III. i. Pt. ii. 15. (2) Mellow. Spoken of the soil. III. i. Pt. i. 7, 58, 59. (3) The productions of different States. V. xxiii. 1.

THE 33D RADICAL. 士.

士 *sze* shih — *Passim.* (1) It is the general designation for officers. The idea of *scholar* does not appear in the Shoo. The combinations of 卿士 (see 卿), 庶士, 多士 are frequent. (2) Specially, the minister of Crime. II. i. 20: ii. 11: V. xxvii. 9. (3) In II. ii. 20: III. iv. 5, 7, and some parr. of V. i., 士 probably = warriors, gallant men. (4) In V. iii. 7, 士女 = men and women.

壬 *jin* jên — (1) The 9th of the calendaric stem-characters. II. iv. 8: V. iii. 1: xxiv. 1. (2) Artful. II. iii. 2.

壺 *hoo* hu — See 口.

壽 *show* shou — Long life. V. iv. 36. 耇壽 V. xxviii. 2. and 壽耇, xii. 12, = men of age and experience. = a long reign. V. xv. 7. As a verb, to grant long life to. V. xvi. 10.

THE 35TH RADICAL. 夊.

夏 *hea* hsia — (1) Summer. I. i. 5: V. iv. 28: xxv. 5. (2) The dynasty so called. *Passim.* On 有夏, see 有. (3) A name for the empire. II. i. 20: V. iii. 5: viii. 3: ix. 4: xix. 5. So, 華夏. V. iii. 6. (4) Variegated. III. i. Pt. i. 35. (5) 雷夏, the name of a marsh. III. i. Pt. i. 14.

夔 *kwei* kuei — (1) Grave, reverential-looking. II. ii. 21. (2) The name of Shun's director of music. II. i. 24.

THE 36TH RADICAL. 夕.

夕 *seih* hsi — The evening. 朝夕, IV. viii. Pt. i. 5. V. x. 2. 旦夕. V. xxvi. 2.

外 *wae* wai — (1) The outside; outside, external. Generally, as correlate with 內. III. iii. 6: 6: V. iv. 30: xx. 3: xxi. 6. away from court. V. x. 11: xv. 5: xxiii. 6. 外諸子 and 小臣外正, certain officers so named. V. ix. 17, 18. In the regions beyond. II. iv. 8. 於...之外, V. xxii. 11. (2) 外方, the name of a mountain. III. i. Pt. ii. 2.

夙 *suh* su — Early in the morning. 夙夜, early and late. II. i. 23, 25: iii. 4: V. i. Pt. i. 10: v. 9: xiii. 16: xx. 4.

多 *to* — Many, numerous; much; mostly. *Passim.*

夜 *yay* yeh — The night. Generally combined with 夙. See 夙. 晝夜, II. iv. 8. 中夜, midnight. V. xxvi. 1.

夢 *mung* mêng — (1) To dream; a dream. IV. viii. Pt. i. 2: V. i. Pt. i. 5. (2) The name of a marsh. III. i. Pt. i. 50.

THE 37TH RADICAL. 大.

大 *ta* — (1) To be great; great; greatly. *Passim.* We have 大龜, the great tortoise. III. i. Pt. i. 52; *et al.*; 大家, the great Families, V. xi. 1; 大輅, the grand chariot of the emperor. V., xxii. 20; 大正, the high chamberlain, xxvi. 3; 大辟, the punishment of death., V. xxvii, 18; &c., &c. (2) Applied to Yu, = Yu the Great. II. ii. 1, 5: III. iii. 3. (3) 大夫. See 夫. (4) 大川, perhaps the Yellow River. V. iii. 6. (5) 大陸, the name of a tract of flat ground. III. i. Pt. i. 9; and of a place in it, Pt. ii. 7. 大野, the name of a lake. III. i. Pt. i. 31. 大別, see 別. 大伾; see 伾.

太 *t'ae* t'ai — Great. 太康, the third emperor of the Hea dyn. III. iii. 1. 太甲 and 太戊, emperors of the Shang dyn. V. xvi. 7; *et al.* 太王, king T'ae, the grandfather of king Wăn. V. iii. 5: vi. 4: xv. 8. 太保, 太傅, 太師; see 保, 傅, 師. 太史; see 史. 太宗, the minister of Religion. V. xxii. 23. 太室, the grand apartment of a temple. V. xiii. 28. 太常, name of the grand banner. xxix. 1. 太原; see 原. 太岳, 太行, 太華, names of mountains. III. i. Pt. ii. 1, 2.

天 *t'ëen* t'ien — (1) The visible heavens, the sky. I. i. 10, 11: II. iv. 1. 昊天, the firmament in which the heavenly bodies move. I. 8. 天下, II. i. 12: ii. 4, 14; *et sæpe*; used for 天之下, belong to this meaning. To this also should be reduced, probably, II. ii. 8: V. xx. 6. (2) It is once used for the place where God and happy spirits dwell. V. vi. 5. (3) Its most common use is for the supreme governing Power, understood to be omni-

scient, omnipotent, and righteous. In this sense it is constantly interchanged with the names God, and supreme God. It is employed in this way more than 150 times. It has sometimes the adjunct of 上, supreme. IV. ii. 3: iii. 5, and more often that of 皇, great. II. ii. 4: III. iv. 2; *et al.* (4) 天地 occurs once, where we might expect 天 alone, for the governing Power. V. i. Pt. i. 3. (5) 天子, a designation of the emperor. III. iv. 5: IV. viii. Pt. i. 1: V. iv. 16; *et al.* (6) Heavenly. V. xix. 20: xxii. 19; *et al.* Obs. V. ix. 5: xxvii: 6.

夫 *foo* fu — An individual, a man. IV. viii. Pt. iii. 10: V. ii. 2: vii. 5: xxi. 11. 匹夫匹婦, V. vi. 11, and 愚夫愚婦, III. iii. 5, = any ordinary man or woman. 獨夫, a solitary man, with some degree of contempt. V. i. Pt. iii. 4. 夫 alone in. V. xii. 10, = the ordinary people. We find it added to other words, making them = concrete nouns.—勇夫, V. xxx. 5; 牧夫, xix. 13, 16, 19, 21; 準夫, xix. 7; 穡夫, vii. 14; 嗇夫, III. iv. 4. The usage in 萬夫之長, IV. vi. 10, is peculiar. 大夫, a designation of officers generally, below those of the highest rank. IV. viii. Pt. ii. 2: V. ii. 6: vi. 16: xx. 21. 夫子 = heroes, a complimentary designation. V. i. Pt. i. 9: ii. 7, 8, 9.

夫 *foo* fu — Low. 1st tone. It is found with this tone only once, as a demonstrative. 夫人 = this man, any man. V. xxii. 9.

夭 *yaou* yao — Up. 1st tone. (1) Long and thin. Spoken of grass. III. i. Pt. i. 42. (2) 閎夭, a man's name. V. xvi. 12.

夭 *yaou* yao — To cut life short. IV. ix. 3

失 *shih* — To lose. V. i. Pt. i. 11. To lose the favour of. V. xiv. 8. To err. III. iii. 5: IV. vii. Pt. ii. 11. To fail in paying attention, to disregard. II. ii. 6: III. iii. 7: IV. vii. Pt. ii. 2.

夷 *e* i — (1) To squat on the heels. V. i. Pt. i. 6. (2) Ordinary. V. i. Pt. ii. 6. (3) To feel comfortable, at ease. I. 6. (4) A name given to the barbarous tribes in and around the middle kingdom. It is specially appropriate to those on the east, but we find those on the west expressly so designated in IV. ii. 6; and the term is often used for such tribes generally, as in III. i. Pt. ii. 21; V. xix. 11: xxii. 19. Such is the force of 四夷, II. ii. 6; *et al.* 蠻夷 is also so used. II. i. 16, 20; and 九夷八蠻, V. v. 1. We have of specific tribes—the 淮夷, III. i. Pt. i 35. *et al.*; the 萊夷, 26; the 和夷, 66; and the 鳥夷, 10, 44. See also V. xix. 11. (5) 嵎夷, the place in the extreme east to which Yaou sent his astronomers. I. 4: III. i. Pt. ii. 22. (6) 伯夷, Shun's minister of Religion. II. i. 23.

夾 *këă* chia — (1) To keep—be—near to. III. i. Pt. i. 11: V. xxii. 21. (2) To aid. V. xviii. 21. To this meaning we should probably refer V. xi. 6. (3) Applied to a side apartment of the palace. V. xxii. 18.

奄 *yen* — (1) Suddenly. II. ii. 4. (2) Entirely. V. xix. 5. (3) The name of a country. V. xviii. 1; *et al.*

奇 *k'e* ch'i — Wonderful, strange. V. i. Pt. iii: 3: v. 8.

奈 *nae* nai — Also written with 木 instead of 大. In combination with 何, = how. III. iii. 5: V. xii. 9 (*n. b.*)

奉 *fung* — To bear or carry with both hands. V. xii. 24: xxii. 23. 奉圭, the sceptres which they bore. xxiii. 1. = to escort. IV. ii. 1: v. Pt. ii. 1. = to receive. 奉辭, to carry orders. II. ii. 20. To serve,—the sovereign, ancestors, Heaven. IV. v. Pt. ii. 7: V. i. Pt. ii. 4; Pt. iii. 1: xxvii. 13. Before other verbs, = reverently. We have 奉恤, 奉答, 奉若, 奉音, 奉將, V. xxiii. 1: xiii. 14: IV. viii. Pt. ii. 2: vii. Pt. ii. 9: ii. 2: III. iv. 5. 奉德, V. xiv. 18; and 奉其恫, IV. vii. Pt. i. 12, are peculiar.

奏 *tsow* tsou — (1) To report to the emperor. II. i. 9. To advance, go forward to. II. iv. 7. (N.B.). To bring forward, introduce. II. iv. 1. (2) Spoken of music. = to beat. III. iv. 4.

契 *seĕ* hsieh — Shun's minister of instruction. II. i. 17, 19.

奔 *pun* — To hurry away, to run. IV. x. 1. To flee to, in submission. V. 11. 9. 奔走 to hurry about. V. iii. 3: x. 6: xiv. 22: xvi. 9: xviii. 24.

奚 *he* hsi — Why. IV. ii. 6.

奠 *tëen* tien — (1) To fix or settle, to determine. III, i. Pt. i. 1: IV. vii Pt. iii. 1: V. xxii. 5. (2) To set down, and to display. V. xxiii. 1.

奢 *ch'ay* ch'e — Extravagant. V. xxiv. 9.

奪 *t'ŏ* t'o — To take away from, to snatch. II. i. 4. *(N. B.)*: V. xxvii. 2, 12.

奭 *shih* — The name of the Grand-protector in king Ching's reign. V. xvi. 1, 7, 10; *et al.*

奮 *fun* fên — To display energy in—. II. i. 17: III. i. Pt. ii. 20.

THE 38TH RADICAL. 女.

女 *neu* nü — A daughter. I. i. 12. A female. V. iii. 7.

女 *neu* nü — Low. 3d tone. To wive, to give one's daughter to another in marriage. I. i. 12.

奴 *noo* nu — To enslave. V. i. Pt. iii. 3.

好 *hauo* hao — That which is good. = peace. II. ii. 17.

好 *haon* hao — 3d tone. To love, to be fond of. II. ii. 12: iv. 8: IV. ii. 8; *et sæpe.*

如 *joo* ju — As; to be as. II. i. 8: V. i. Pt. ii. 9: xiii. 10: xxx. 11. = to be as if; if. II. i. 13: V. xiii. 2: xxx. 6. 如何, see 何. In Pt. IV. i. 3: vii. Pt. i. 2: ix. 4: x. 4, we have 其如台,=what is that to us? that does not concern us.

妣 *pe* pi — A deceased mother. 考妣, a parent deceased. I. 13.

妹 *mei* — The name of a district of country, in the imperial domain of Shang. V. x. 1, 6.

妾 *ts'ëĕ* ch'ieh — Female camp-followers. V. xxix. 4.

始 *ch'e* shih — To begin, make a beginning: to be the first to—. II. iv. 4: V. xxvii. 2, 3. The beginning; in the beginning, at first. IV. ii. 9: v. Pt. iii. 2, 6: vi. 6: viii. Pt. iii. 5: V. xiii. 9: xxiv. 13.

姑 *koo* ku — For a time;—an expression of leniency and laxity. V. x. 15: xxx. 4.

姓 *sing* hsing — A surname, surnames. II. i. Pt. ii. 16: V. v. 3. 百姓, the hundred surnames, is a designation of the people. I. 2: II. i. 13, 19: ii. 6: III. iii. 3: vii. Pt. i. 12; Pt. iii. 3: V. i. Pt. ii. 7, 9: ii. 6: xxvii. 9, 14. 萬姓, the myriad surnames, is used in the same way. In one case we have 爾萬方百姓, but 萬姓 need not always be so resolved. In V. x. 10: xvi. 9, 百姓=百官, or officers of distinguished name. 族姓, V. xxvii. 21.

姦 *këen* chien — Selfish and open wickedness. I. 12. Villainous, openly wicked. V. i. Pt. iii. 3: xx. 11. In all other passages it is combined with 宄, the phrase= villains and traitors, or to play the part of such. II. i. 20: IV. vii. Pt. i. 12; Pt. ii. 16: xi. 2: V. ii. 6: ix. 15: xi. 2: xxi. 10: xxvii. 2.

威 *wei* — Majesty, terrors. Used in this sense very often with reference to Heaven's dread purposes, and the manifestation of them. II. ii. 7: iii. 7: V. xvi. 3, 10, 14, 15, 19; *et al.* 作威, to display terrors, to play the tyrant. IV. iii. 3: V. i. Pt. iii. 3, 4: iv. 18, 19; *et al.* To be violent; the violent. V. ix. 18: xxvii. 12. 威儀, dignity of demeanour, majesty. V. x. 11: xxii. 9. To awe; to overawe. V. xxvii. 7. 威威, to awe those who should be awed. V. ix. 4. Dread, majestic. III. iv. 5; *et al.* 威用, to use in an awing manner. V. iv. 4. 威侮五行, to waste and despise the five elements. III. ii. 3.

娶 *ts'eu* ch'ü — To marry. II. iv. 8.

婚 *hwăn* huên — Relatives. IV. vii. Pt. i. 10.

婦 *foo* fu — A married woman. 婦子, wives and children. V. xii. 10. 婦人, a woman, used in contempt. V. i. Pt. i. 5. So 婦 alone, ii. 6. 匹婦, 愚婦, see 夫.

媚 *mei* — Flatterers. V. xxvi. 5.

嬀 *kwei* kuei — The name of a stream. I. 12.

嬪 — To be—do the duty of—wife to. I. 12.

THE 39TH RADICAL. 子.

子 *tsze* tzû — *Passim.* (1) A son. IV. iii. 3: V. vii. 11. 12; *et sæpe.* = descendants. V. xii. 11. 子孫, sons and grand-sons, = descendants is very common. We have also 幼子童孫, V. xxvii. 13, and 子子孫孫, xi. 18. 胄子, II. i. 24, in the same sense. 婦子, see 婦. 小子, 鞠子, 孺子, 冲子, 元子, 天子, 丕子, are all appellations given to the emperor, or used by him of himself. (2) As a verb, to

treat as a son. II. iv. 8, (*n. b.*): IV. v. Pt. ii. 5. (3) An officer, officers. V. xiii. 24. Applied to certain specified officers,—庶子訓人, V. ix. 17. Observe IV. xi. 8, where we translate it by—*you*. 夫子 and 君子, see 夫 and 君. (4) The first of the calendaric branch-characters. V. ii. 1: iii. 8: xii. 6: xxii. 2. (5) A title of nobility, viscount. We have 微子, II. xi. 1; and 箕子, V. iii. 8: iv. 1, 2, 3.

孔 *k'ung* Great. II. iii. 2. Greatly. III. i. Pt. i. 48; Pt. ii. 15: IV. iv. 8.

孕 *ying* Pregnant. V. i. Pt. i. 5.

字 *tsze* tzu To love, to cherish. V. ix. 16.

存 *ts'un* To be in a state of preservation or flourishing. IV. ii. 7.

孚 *foo* fu To believe, repose confidence in. V. xvi. 9: xxvii. 20. Sincerity, faithfulness. V. xiii. 24. What is certain or fully proved. xxvii. 15, 17. To be fully established in. IV. v. Pt. iii. 9: V. xvi. 2. Sincerely, truly. IV. iii. 5: ix. 5.

孜 *tsze* tzŭ 孜孜, to be diligent, untiring. II. iv. 1: V. i. Pt. iii. 3: xxi. 3.

孝 *hëaou* hsiao To be filial; filial piety. I. 12: IV. v. Pt. ii. 7: V. viii. 3: ix. 16: x. 6: xvii. 3. xxi. 1: xxvii. 3.

孟 *măng* mêng (1) Chief or head. 孟侯. V. ix. 2. (2) First, the beginning. 孟春, the first month of spring. III. iv. 3. (3) 孟豬, the name of a marsh. III. i. Pt. i. 57. 孟津, the name of a ford, and a place. III. i. Pt. ii. 7: V. i. Pt. i. 1: iii. 8.

季 *ke* chi (1) The youngest of brothers or cousins. V. xxvii. 13. (2) The last month of a season. III. iv. 4. (3) 王季, the father of king Wăn. V. iii. 5: vi. 4: xv. 8.

孤 *koo* ku (1) Solitary, standing alone. III. i. Pt. i. 35. = helpless. IV. vii. Pt. i. 15. (2) 三孤, the three ministers, second in dignity at the court of Chow. V. xx. 6.

孥 *noo* nu Children. Used adverbially, = along with your children. III. ii. 5: IV. i. 4.

孫 *sun* A grandson. V. xix. 18, 21. 子孫 is very common for descendants. In V. xviii. 17, it is singular. 孫 alone is used for descendants, and descendant. IV. vii. Pt. ii. 14: v. xxvii. 22. We have 幼孫, IV. vii. Pt. ii. 12: 元孫, V. vi. 6; and 曾孫, V. iii. 6.

孳 *tsze* tzŭ To breed. I. 4.

學 *hëŏ* hsio To learn; learning. IV. viii. Pt. iii. 1, 3, 4, 5: V. xx. 16.

孺 *yu* yü A suckling; but 孺子 = young son. Used in reference to king Ching, in speaking of him or to him. V. vi. 12: xiii. 9, 13, 28: xix. 16, 18, 21.

孽 *nëĕ* nieh Calamities. IV. v. Pt. ii. 3. It appears in the text as 孼, which is not so correct as the form in the margin.

THE 40TH RADICAL. 宀.

宄 *kwei* kuei Traitorous, to play the part of a traitor. Found always in connection with 姦,—see 姦.

宅 *tsih* chai (1) To reside in. Spoken of place. I. 4, 5, 6, 7; *et sæpe*. Obs. V. xxii. 28. To be made habitable. III. i. Pt. i. 78; Pt. ii. 14. A site or locality; dwellings; neighbourhood. V. xii. 2: xiii. 4, 23. 五宅, II. i. 20. 宅里, V. xxiv. 7. (2) Spoken of office,—to occupy. II. i. 17: ii. 9; *et al.* Of a special service. IV. viii. Pt. i. 1: V. xxii. 1. To put into office. V. xix. 2, 12, 19. 有宅, office-able. xix. 2, 4. 宅, the office occupied. xix. 4. (3) To settle, consolidate. IV. v. Pt. i. 2: V. ix. 5, 7: xviii. 22.

宇 *yu* yü Sides of a roof, = roofs. IV. iii. 6.

守 *show* shou To keep, guard, have the charge of. II. ii. 17: IV. iii. 7: V. xxii. 6: xxv. 2. = guard-posts. V. xxiv. 7. 有守, men who keep themselves in the right way. V. iv. 11.

守 *show* shou Low. 3d tone. In the phrase 巡守, to make a tour of inspection. II. i. 8, 9.

安 *gan* an A condition of tranquil security. V. xxiv. 12. To rest, repose in. II. iv. 2: IV. v. Pt. iii. 5: vii. Pt. i. 11 (*n. b.*): V. v. 8. To tranquillize, give repose to. II. iii. 2: IV. vii. Pt. ii. 6: V. xxii. 8: xxvii. 14. 安安 = naturally, without effort. I. 1.

宏 *hwang* huang (1) To enlarge. IV. vii. Pt. iii. 7. (2) 宏父 = the minister of Works. V. x. 13.

宗 *tsung* (1) Belonging to one's ancestors. 宗廟, and 宗 alone, the temple of ancestors. III. iii. 8: IV. iv. 8: v. Pt. i. 2: V. i. Pt. i. 6; Pt. iii. 3. Connected with this is the name of the minister of Religion, as 秩宗, II. i. 23. 宗伯,

書經

富 *foo* fu — Riches. V. iv. 39. To be rich. iv. 18: xxiv. 11: xxvii. 11. To enrich. V. xxiii. 5.

寒 *han* — Cold; to be cold. V. iv. 32, 34: xxv. 5.

察 *ch'ă* ch'a — To examine. V. xxvii. 12, 18, 20.

寡 *kwa* — (1) To be few. V. xxiv. 15. (2 A widow. In the phrase 鰥寡. V. vii. 8: ix. 14: xv. 6, 10; *et al.* = the weak. V. xi. 3. (3) 寡命, the rarely equalled decree. V. xxiii. 3. 寡兄, your unworthy brother. vii. 5.

實 *shih* — (1) To be filled. V. xvi. 9. 口實, that which fills the mouth, matter for remark. IV. ii. 1. (2) To be real; real. IV. viii. Pt. i. 1: vii. Pt. 1. 10. Really; positively, exactly. IV. ii. 4: v. Pt. ii. 2: V. xxiv. 9: xxvi. 3: xxvii. 18.

寧 *ning* — To be in a state of repose, and tranquillity. III. iii. 4: IV. iv. 2: V. v. 7: xxiv. 3; *et sæpe.* To give repose or tranquillity to; to soothe. IV. iii. 6: V. xiii. 25: xiv. 18; *et sæpe.* 寧王寧人, and 寧考 are all designations of king Woo. V. vii. 3, 8, 9, 10, 11, 14, 15; *et al.* A state of tranquillity: serenity of mind. V. iv. 36: xxvii. 13. (2) It is better to. V. i. Pt. ii. 9. The comparison is completed in II. ii. 12.

審 *shin* shên — To examine carefully, to judge. V. xxvii, 16, 17, 18, 20. To describe minutely. IV. viii. Pt. i. 3. Discriminatingly. V. xxii. 4.

寬 *kwan* hwan — To be gentle. II. i. 24: iii. 3 (*n. b.*): V. ii. 5: xxi. 7. 在寬, be gentle, or the course to pursue is gentleness. II. i. 19. To make gentle. V. xv. 18. Gentleness. II. ii. 12: IV. iv. 3: V. viii. 2.

寶 *paou* pao — Precious. V. vi. 7: vii. 3: xxvii. 21. Precious things. IV. vii. Pt. iii. 12: V. v. 3: xxii. 19. To consider precious. V. v. 8.

寵 *ch'ung* — Favour. IV. v. Pt. iii. 9: V. xx. 19: xxiv. 10. To confer favours (寵綏). V. i. Pt. i. 7. 啟寵, to open the way to favourites. IV. viii. Pt. ii. 9.

THE 41st RADICAL. 寸

封 *fung* fêng — (1) Boundaries. V. xxiv. 7. (2) A territory over which a prince is appointed. V. xvii. 2. (3) To raise a tumulus;—over a grave, V. iii. 9; for an altar, II. i. 10. (4) The name of Wăn's ninth son, the prince of K'ang. V. ix: x., xi., *sæpe.*

射 *shay* — To shoot with bow and arrows. IV. vii. Pt. i. 15 (*n. b.*): V. xxx. 5.

將 *tsëang* chiang — (1) Shall, will, about to. It expresses a purpose, or a likely result. III. iii. 9: IV. iii. 6: vi. 1: vii. Pt. ii. 6, 17; Pt. iii. 4 (*n. b.*), 6: xi. 6 (?): V. iii. 6: vi. 12: xxiv. 10: xxx. 4 (*n. b.*). (2) To take, = to be charged with. III. iv. 5: IV. iii. 4: V. i. Pt. i. 5: xiv. 2: xvi. 15. (3)? To regulate. V. x. 4. (4) Great. V. xiii. 15. (5)? To acknowledge. V. xiii. 21. 迪將其後 in p. 20 is about inexplicable.

專 *chuen* chuan — To engross, to do alone. IV. viii. Pt. iii. 10.

尊 *tsun* — To honour. V. xix. 2.

對 *tuy* tui — To respond to. IV. viii. Pt. iii. 11: V. xxv. 6. To reply. V. vi. 17.

導 *taou* tao — To lead;—actually. III. i. Pt. i. 57. mentally = to survey and lay down the course of. Pt. ii. 1, 3—13.

THE 42d RADICAL. 小

小 *sëaou* hsiao — Small. *Passim.* Often used along with 大. To become small IV ii. 8. Of phrases we have 小子, used by the emperor, and to him and others, but only by the ministers E Yin and the duke of Chow; 小尹, V. xix. 8; 小伯, p. 9; 小臣, V. ix. 17, 18, *et al.*; 小民, the inferior people. V. xii. 13, 21, 22, 23; *et sæpe* 小人 is also used of the lower people. V. xv. 2, 3, 5, 6, 7, 17, 18. Only once, II. ii. 20, does it denote the mean in opposition to the superior man.

少 *shaou* shao — A little. V. vii. 1.

少 *shaou* shao — 3d tone. Junior, assistant. V. x. 2. The 少保, 少傅, 少師, were the three ministers second in dignity at the court of Chow. V. xx. 6. The 少師 appears before under the dyn. of Shang. IV. xi. 1, 3.

尚 *shang* — (1) Pray, may it be that. II. ii. 20: III. iv. 5; *et passim.* This is the prevailing usage of the character in the Shoo. The exhortation and entreaty are not so evident indeed in all cases, and the meaning approaches to a reflective *perhaps*, as in V. xxx. 8. (2) To ascend. V. ix. 21. (3) Still, in both the meanings of—in addition to, and notwithstanding. V. x. 7, 8: xiv. 23: xvi. 12, 15: *et al.* (4) To esteem, be reckoned valuable. V. xxiv. 8.

THE 43d RADICAL. 尢

尤 *yew* yu — (1) Evils, = judgments, calamities. V. xxvii. 21. (2) To murmur, to grudge. V. xvi. 3. (3) 蚩尤, the name of the first rebel. V. xxvii. 2.

就 *tsew* chiu — 三就, three places to be repaired to. II. i. 20. To accommodate one's-self to. V. xxx. 4.

THE 44TH RADICAL. 尸.

尸 *she* shih — To occupy in a sham way, like a personator of the dead. III. iii. 1: iv. 4.

尹 *yin* — (1) To direct, to rule. V. viii. 3: xviii. 19: xxi. 1. (2) Directors,—the heads of other officers, or official departments. V. xi. 2: xviii. 2. They are called 尹氏, vii. 6; 庶尹, II. iv. 10: V. x. 10; 師尹, V. iv. 35; 尹伯, xix. 9; 百尹, xxii. 8. The 小尹 are different. V. xix. 8; and perhaps 尹 in p. 11. (3) The designation of T'ang's prime minister E Yin. IV. iv. 1; *et sæpe.* He speaks of himself in the style 尹躬, IV. v. Pt. i. 2, 3: vi. 3.

尾 *wei* — (1) The tail. V. xxv. 2. (2) 孳尾, to pair and copulate. I. 4. (3) 部尾, a mountain. III. i. Pt. ii. 2.

居 *keu* chü — (1) To abide, reside in;—properly spoken with reference to place, but used also with ref. to office and condition. III. i. Pt. i. 39: IV. iv. 5: v. Pt. i. 9: viii. Pt. ii. 10: V. vi. 14; *et al.* Dwellings, homes, families. II. i. 20: IV. vii. Pt. iii. 5, 10: V. xiv. 18, 25; *et al.* (2) To settle, to locate. V. xiii. 14: xx. 12. (3) To abide sitting: V. i. Pt. i. 6: xxvi. 2. (4) The virtues appropriate to the several circumstances of life and condition. V. iv. 2. (5) Accumulated stores of grain. II. iv. 1.

屆 *këae* chieh — To reach to. II. ii. 21.

屋 *uh* wu — 王屋, a mountain. III. i. Pt. ii. 1.

屑 *seĕ* hsieh — Lightly, triflingly. V. xviii. 14, 22.

展 *chen* chan — To develope. V. v. 8.

屏 *ping* — A screen or defence. V. xxiii. 6. To act as defences in, or to make defences of. V. xvi. 9.

屛 *ping* — 3d tone. To put aside. V. i. Pt. iii. 3: vi. 8.

屢 *leu* lü — Frequently. II. iv. 11: V. ix. 21: xviii. 22.

屬 *shuh* shu — To pertain or belong to. V. xx. 13: xxvii. 18, 22.

屬 *chuh* chu — To be connected with. III. i. Pt. i. 73: IV. vii. Pt. ii. 6. 屬婦, to find connections for destitute women. V. x. i. 3.

THE 46TH RADICAL. 山.

山 *shan* — A mountain, a hill. *Sæpe.* A mound. V. v. 9. A hill-site. IV. vii. Pt. iii. 4. The emblematic mountain on the emperor's robe. II. iv. 4. 九山, the hills of the nine provinces. III. i. Pt. ii. 14. 名山, mount Hwa. V. iii. 6. 山 often follows the names of mountains. Those into whose names the character itself does not enter, and which will be found in their proper places, are 衡, 岠, 歷, 塗, 羽, 刑, and perhaps some others.

岐 *k'e* ch'i — The name of a mountain. III. i. Pt. i. 4, 76; Pt. ii. 1.

岡 *kang* — The ridge of a mountain. III. iv. 6.

岱 *tea* tai — A mountain, forming one of the boundaries of Ts'ing-chow, and Seu-chow. III. i. Pt. i. 21, 26, 28. In II. i. 8, it is also called 岱宗.

岳 *yŏ* yü — (1) A mountain so called, and also 太岳. III. i. Pt. i. 4; Pt. ii. 1. There were also the four mountains, called 四岳, V. xx. 14,—the northern, the southern, the eastern, and the western, all referred to in II. i. 8. (2) The second if not the first minister, about the courts of Yaou and Shun, was styled 四岳. I. 11, 12: II. i. 7, 15, 17, 23: V. xx. 3.

岷 *min* — A mountain in Lëang-chow. III. i. Pt. i. 63.

岍 *k'ëen* ch'ien — A mountain in Yung-chow. III. i. Pt. ii. 1.

峙 *che* chih — To provide, have collected and prepared. V. xxix. 5.

島 *taou* tao — An island. 島夷, III. i. P. i. 10, 44.

峻 *tseun* tsun — Lofty. III. iii. 6.

崇 *ts'ung* ch'ung — (1) To honour. IV. ii. 9: V. i. Pt. iii. 3: ii. 6: iii. 10; *et al.* = to indulge in. V. x. 9. (2) To be exalted, made great. V. xx. 17. (3) Greatly. IV. vii. Pt. ii. 11, 14: V. xviii. 5. (4) The name of a mountain in the present Hoo-nan. II. i. 12.

書經

崑 *kwăn* kuĕn — The name of a mountain in the west of the Ko-ko-nor. III. iv. 6. It probably is the same with the 崑崙 in III. i. Pt. i. 83.

崙 *lun* — See 崑 above.

崩 *păng* pĕng — (1) To die,—spoken of an emperor. V. xxii. 10. (2) To let fall, or drop off. V. i. Pt. ii. 9.

嵎 *yu* yü — 嵎夷, the most eastern point of Yaou's empire. I. 4: III. i. Pt. i. 23.

嶓 *po* — Called also 嶓冢, a mountain in Lëang-chow. III. i. Pt. i. 63; Pt. ii. 3, 8.

嶧 *yih* yi — A mountain in Ts'eu-chow. III. i. Pt. i. 35.

巖 *yen* — 傅巖, the name of a place in the present Shan-se. IV. viii. Pt. i. 3.

THE 47TH RADICAL. 巛.

川 *ch'uen* ch'uan — A river, a stream. *Sæpe.* 九川, the rivers and streams in the nine provinces. II. iv. 1: III. i. Pt. ii. 14. 大川, V. iii. 6, probably, denotes the Ho.

州 *chow* chou — The name of a great division of the empire,—a province. Yu divided the empire into nine. See III. i., *passim*: II. iv. 8. Shun divided these into twelve. II. i. 10.

巡 *seun* hsüu — To go round and survey. V. i. Pt. iii. 1. Used of an imperial tour of inspection. V. xx. 1, 14. See 守.

巢 *ch'aou* ch'ao — 南巢, the place where Këĕ was kept in confinement. IV. ii. 1.

THE 48TH RADICAL. 工.

工 *kung* — (1) Work. II. iii. 5. (2) Workmen. II. i. 21. (3) Service, duty. II. iv. 8. (4) Officers. III. iv. 3: V. iii. 4; *et al.* 百工, all the officers. I. 8: III. iv. 3: V. xiii. 6; *et al.* 宗工, honoured officers, Heads of clans. V. x. 10, 13. = masters of music. II. iv. 6. Obs. 士師工, V. xiii. 20. (5) 共工, the ancient name for the minister of Works. I. 10: II. i. 12. 21.

左 *tso* — The left (adj. and noun); on and in the left hand. IV. ii. 4: V. ii. 1: xxii. 20: xxiv. 13. On 左右 and 左右, see 右.

巧 *k'ëaou* ch'iao — Artful, artfulness. II. iii. 2: V. i. Pt. iii. 3: xxvi. 5.

巨 *keu* chü — Great. IV. viii. Pt. i. 6.

巫 *woo* wu — (1) 巫風, sorcerers' fashion. IV. iv. 7. (2) A surname. V. xvi. 7.

差 *ts'ze* tz'û — To make a distinction in. V. xxvii. 3. Discrepancies. p. 20. 倍差, two and a half times. p. 18.

THE 49TH RADICAL. 己.

己 *ke* chi — One's-self. In the Shoo of the 2d and 3d persons. II. ii. 3, 6: IV. ii. 5, 8: V. i. Pt. ii. 5: xxx. 6. Observe. 總己, IV. iv. 1.

已 *e* i — (1) Have, indicating the present complete tense. V. xvi. 3: xix. 18. (2) To stop, rest, have done with. I. i. 11: V. ix. 17: xiii. 21 (*n. b.*). (3) = yes. The speaker assents to or approves of what has been said, and goes on to add something more. V. vii. 2, 9: ix. 7, 14: xi. 8: xiii. 11.

巳 *sze* szû — The sixth of the calendaric branch-characters. V. iii. 1: xii. 5.

巽 *sun* — To resign. I. 12.

THE 50TH RADICAL. 巾.

市 *she* shih — A market-place. IV. viii. Pt. iii. 10.

布 *poo* pu — (1) To display. IV. iv. 3: V. xxiii. 1. (2) To spread abroad. IV. ii. 3.

希 *he* hsi — To become thin. Spoken of the feathers of birds and hair of animals. I. 5.

帛 *pih* pai — Pieces of silk. 三帛, I. 8.

帝 *te* ti — (1) God. The name is continually interchanged with 上帝, supreme God. II. i. 6: iv. 2: IV. i. 2: ii. 3: iii. 2 (皇天上帝), 8: iv. 8: v. Pt. iii. 3: vii. Pt. iii. 6: viii. Pt. i. 2: V. i. Pt. i. 6, 7, 10; Pt. iii. 3: iii. 6: iv. 3, 15: vi. 7: vii. 9, 13: viii. 3: ix. 4: xi. 2: xii. 9, (皇上帝) 14: xiv. 2, 4, 5, 8, 9, 13, 14: xvi. 3, 7, 11, 14: xviii. 4, 5: xix. 2, 4, 5, 6: xxiii. 5: xxvii. 5, 12: xxviii. 1. (2) The title of the ancient emperors Yaou and Shun. *Passim* in the first two Parts. Also in. IV. viii. Pt. iii. 10: V. xxvii. 5. 7 (皇帝). (3) 帝乙, one of the emperors

of the Shang dynasty. V. x. 9: xiv. 7: xviii. 10. The 帝 is wrongly translated —should not be translated—in these passages.

師 *sze* szû (1) The multitudes, the people; all. I. 12: II. i. 25: ii. 9. IV. ii. 3: V. xiii. 14, 24; *et al.* (2) A capital city. V. xiii. 3. (3) An army, a host. II. ii. 20, 21: V. i. Pt. ii. 1; *et al.* 六師, the imperial army. III. iv. 1: V. i. Pt. iii. 1; *et al.* (4) Instructors. IV. ii. 8: V. i. Pt. i. 7; *et al.* 師師, the instructors whom I am to follow. V. xi. 2. (5) Applied to various officers:—to the high dignitaries, 太師 and 少師, V. xx. 5, 6; *et al.*; 父師 一太師, IV. xi. 1, 3, 4: V. xxiv. 2, 5, 12; 師保 together, applied to E Yin. IV. v. Pt. ii. 3, and to the duke of Chow, V. xxi. 2; the same characters appear to be plural, V. i. Pt. iii. 8; 師氏, the captain of the warders, V. ii. 2: xxii. 8; officers generally, V. xiii. 20; 師尹, V. iv. 35; 師長, IV. vii. Pt. iii. 8: viii. Pt. ii. 2; tutors, a high office appointed by Yu, II. iv. 8; judges, V. xxvii. 15. (6) A model; to take as a model. IV. vi. 8: II. iii. 4: viii. Pt. iii. 3: V. xx. 16; *et al.* 師師, to imitate one another. II. iii. 4: IV. xi. 2.

席 *seih* hsi (1) A mat. V. xxii. 15, 16, 17, 18. (2) = to rely on. V. xxiv. 10.

常 *chang* (1) Regular, constant, unchanging; constancy; constantly. II. iii. 3: III. iv. 2, 3: IV. iv. 8: v. Pt. iii. 1: V. xxix. 3, 4; *et al.* Obs. 常伯,常任,常事, V. xix. 1, 12. Constant in virtue, V. xix. 9, 23. The regular principles of duty. V. xxi. 10: xx. vii. 6. Regular ways. V. xxi. 2. 五常, the five regular virtues of society. V. i. Pt. iii. 2. 典常. V. viii. 4; xx. 16. (2) 太常, name of the Grand-banner. V. xxv. 1.

幣 *pe* pi Offerings,—presents to the emperor,—of various kinds. V. xii. 8, 24: xxiii. 1.

THE 51st RADICAL. 干.

干 *kan* (1) A shield, shields. IV. viii. Pt. ii. 4: V. ii. 14: xxix. 1. 二干戈, two shield-and-spearmen. V. xxii. 11. (2) To seek for; to expose one's-self to. II. ii. 6, 11: III. iv. 4. (3) 比干, a relative of the tyrant Show, who cut out his heart. V. iii. 5.

平 *p'ing* (1) To reduce to order, to adjust, to tranquillize; to be reduced to order. I. 2, 4, 5, 6, 7; III. i. Pt. i. 32, 65: *et sæpe.* The work of Yu is spoken of as 平水土, II. i. 17: V. xxvii. 8. 平康, a condition of peace and tranquillity. V. iv. 17, 36. (2) Just. V. xxiii. 5. (3) Common, ordinary. V. xxvii. 2.

平 *p'een* p'een 平平, level and easy. V. iv. 14.

年 *neen* nien A year, years. IV. ix. 3: V. i. Pt. i. 1: *et sæpe.*

并 *ping* All together, in common. V. vi. 9: vii. 5, 15: xxvii. 3, 20.

幹 *kan* Business, occupations, duties. V. xiv. 23, 25.

THE 52d RADICAL. 幺.

幻 *hwan* huan Deceiving, deceit. 爲幻, the practice of deception, deceiving tricks. V. xv. 14, 18.

幼 *yew* yu Young. IV. vii. Pt. i. 15; Pt. ii. 12: V. vii. 1: xxvii. 13.

幽 *yew* yu (1) Dark, = ignorant, *i.e.*, the idle and undeserving. II. i. 27. (2) 幽都, the extreme north of Yaou's empire. I. 7. 幽洲, an island where Shun confined the minister of Works. II. i. 12.

幾 *ke* chi Up. 1st tone. The small beginnings or springs of things. II. iii. 5. = motives. V. xxvii. 9. 惟幾 = to attend to the slightest particulars. II. iv. 2, 11. But in V. xxvii. 4, the same phrase = there is but a little between me and death.

THE 53d RADICAL. 广.

序 *seu* hsü Short walls, running north and south, in the hall in front of the private apartments of the imperial palace. V. xxii. 16, 17, 19.

底 *te* ti Bottom, that which is underneath. V. xxii. 16. See 底.

庚 *kăng* kêng (1) The 7th of the calendaric stem-characters. V. iii. 3: xii. 3: xxiv. 1. (2) 盤庚, one of the emperors of the Shang dynasty. IV. vii.

府 *foo* fu A treasury. III. iii. 18. Treasurers. V. xix. 8. 六府, the six magazines or treasuries of nature. II. ii. 8: III. i. Pt. ii. 15. To form a treasury, to accumulate. V. xxvii. 21.

度 *too* tu (1) Measures of length. II. i. 8: V. xx. 4. (2) Measures generally, = rules, regulations, laws. Often joined with 法. II. ii. 4: III. iii. 1: IV. v. Pt. i. 7; Pt. ii. 3; *et al.* 無度, lawless. V. i. Pt. ii. 3: xiv. 16. Compare 非度, IV. xi. 2.

書經

百度, all measures, all the conduct. V. v. 5. As a verb, to bring under rule. IV. vii. Pt. i. 17.

度 *tŏ* to — To measure or calculate; to deliberate. II. iv. 8: V. i. Pt. i. 8: xv. 4: xxvii. 1, 14.

庬 *mang* — See 厖.

庭 *t'ing* — The court of a palace. V. xxii. 10. It is found generally as = the court or place of audience of the sovereign. IV. vii. Pt. i. 5; Pt. ii. 1: V. xiv. 20: xviii. 28. To appear at court. V. xx. 1. 帝庭, the court of God. V. vi. 7.

庶 *shoo* shu — *Passim.* It is one of the words, whose frequency is characteristic of the Shoo. As an adjective, numerous, all; the various, all comprehended in a class. II. iv. 11 will show how it is employed like the indefinite 百. 庶民, V. iv. 9, 10, 11, 16, 25—30; *et al.*, = the common people, the masses. 庶人, III. iv. 5: V. xvii. 1, = the common people, or one of the common people, in distinction from men of rank. It is used also as a noun = the multitudes. II. ii. 11: iv. 1: IV. i. 1. = the several classes. II. iv. 7. See 庶殷殷庶, V. xii. 7, where the usages as subst. and adj. come together. 庶羣, the herd of creatures. V. x. 11. (2) It may be, the result will probably be. V. xiii. 6: xxvii. 13.

康 *k'ang* — (1) To tranquillize, to secure the repose of. IV. viii. Pt. i. 9: V. xvii. 6; *et sæpe.* We find it along with other verbs, 一惠康, 康寧, 康乂, 康保. Obs. 惟康, study stability. II. iv. 2. To be brought to repose; a condition of ease and tranquillity. II. iv. 11: IV. vii. Pt. i. 6; Pt. ii. 4: V. vii. 1, 4. We have 康彊, V. iv. 26; 平康, p. 17; *et al.* We may take it adverbially in IV. x. 3, and V. ix. 6. Obs. 而康而色, V. iv. 11. (2) 太康, and 仲康, two of the emperors of the Shang dynasty. III. iii. 1, and iv. 1. 康 was also the posthumous title of the son of king Ching, and he appears among the emperors of the Chow dyn. as king K'ang. V. xxv. 2.

庸 *yung* — (1) To use,—either to display, or to employ. I. 9, 12: II. ii. 16: IV. vi. 8; *et al.* = to have occasion to, on purpose, therefore, thereon. II. iv. 11: IV. v. Pt. i. 4: viii. Pt. i. 2: V. v. 3: viii. 3: x. 15: xvi. 6: xviii. 13. 庸庸, to employ the employ-able. V. ix. 4. 徵庸, to be called to be employed. II. i. 27. Opp. to 靜, and = when employed. I. 10. Obs. 庸帝命, V. xiv. 5. (2) Merit, services. II. i. 9, 17. 自庸, to seek one's merit in. (3) The name of a wild tribe. V. ii. 3.

廉 *lëen* lien — To be discriminating; discrimination. II. iii. 3.

廟 *mëaou* miao — An ancestral temple. Either alone, or with 宗. IV. v. Pt. i. 2: vi. 10: V. i. Pt. i. 6; Pt. iii. 3: iii. 3. An apartment of the palace is so called on occasion. V. xxii. 29.

廡 *woo* wu — Luxuriant. V. iv. 32.

廢 *fei* — To abolish or set aside; to disregard; to render nugatory. II. ii. 3: III. iv. 1: IV. vii. Pt. iii. 7: V. ix. 5: xiii. 13: xiv. 5: xxi. 5.

廣 *kwang* kuang — To be enlarged; vast, wide. II. ii. 4: III. i. Pt. i. 24: IV. vi. 11: V. viii. 2: xx. 17.

THE 54TH RADICAL. 廴.

延 *yen* — (1) To conduct. V. xxii. 11. (2) To extend to. V. xxvii. 2. To be prolonged, II. ii. 13: V. xii. 17: xvi. 6. = to delay. V. vii. 1.

建 *keen* chien — To establish or set up, to appoint, II. iv. 8: IV. ii. 8; *et sæpe.* Without any object, = to exert an establishing influence. V. xiv. 8. Used adverbially. V. iv. 4.

THE 55TH RADICAL. 廾.

弁 *pëen* pien — A skin or fur cap. There were different kinds of it. V. vi. 16: xxii. 21.

异 *e* i — 异哉, well but. I. 11. The meaning is uncertain.

THE 56TH RADICAL. 弋.

弋 *yih* yi — To aim at. V. xiv. 8.

式 *shih* — (1) A model, a law. V. viii. 4: xx. 14. To take as a model, to imitate. V. xix. 4: xxi. 3: xxv. 7. To give an example of. V. xix. 24. (2) To reverence; reverently. IV. viii. Pt. i. 2: vii. Pt. iii. 13: V. xxv. 4. To bow to the cross-bar of a carriage, in token of reverence. V. iii. 9. (3) Explained by 用, and = to employ, to use; to cause; thereby, thereon. IV. ii. 3: viii. Pt. iii. 7: V. xi. 5: xvi. 21: xviii. 19: xix. 5, 24: xxiv. 3. 式爾, purposely. V. ix. 8. = and. V. xii. 23.

THE 57TH RADICAL. 弓.

弓 *kung* A bow. V. xxii. 19: xxviii. 4: xxix. 2.

弔 *teaou* tiao Always in the phrase 弗弔, which appears to mean—unpitying. V. vii. 1: xiv. 2: xvi. 2.

弔 *teih* ti To come or proceed to. IV. vii. Pt. iii. 7: V. ix. 16. That which has come to the extreme; in perfect order. V. xxix. 2.

引 *yin* To lead, to lead on to. V. ix. 17: xi. 8: xiv. 5. 引慝, to take crime to one's-self. II. ii. 21. 引考 = to enjoy long prosperity. V. xiii. 27.

弗 *fuh* fu Not. *Passim.* The frequency of its use is characteristic of the Shoo. = do not. V. ii. 9.

弘 *hwang* huang Large; to enlarge, give full development to; largely. V. viii. 4: xiii. 22: xx. 6: xxi. 7: xxii. 7, 19: xxv. 4. Observe 弘于天, and 弘王, V. ix. 5, 7.

弟 *te* ti A younger brother or cousin. III. iii. 3: V. vi. 12; *et al.* 兄弟, brethren or cousins. V. xvii. 6: xxi. 2. 父母弟 = paternal and maternal relatives. V. ii. 6. 作兄弟, with brotherly affection. V. xi. 5.

弱 *jŏ* jao (1) Weak; weakness. IV. ii. 7: V. iv. 40. = to despise. IV. vii. Pt. i. 15. (2) 弱水, the name of a stream. III. i. Pt. i. 72; Pt. ii. 5.

張 *chang* To be displayed. V. i. Pt. i. 8. To be adjusted. IV. v. Pt. i. 7. 張皇, maintain in great display. V. xxiii. 8. 譸張, extravagant talk. V. xv. 14, 18.

弼 *peih* pi To help;—sometimes = to correct. II. ii. 11: iv. 5, 8: V. i. Pt. i. 11; *et sæpe.* An assistant, helpers. II. iii. 1: iv. 2: IV. viii. Pt. i. 2.

彊 *k'ëang* ch'iang Valour, strength. II. iii. 8. 康彊, sound and strong in body. V. iv. 26. In p. 17, 彊 = violence, or the violent.

彌 *me* mi Still more. V. xxii. 4.

THE 58TH RADICAL. 彐.

彝 *e* i (1) A cup. 宗彝, a cup used in the ancestral temple, and a figure of which was embroidered on the lower garment of the emperor, which he wore on great occasions. II. iv. 4. (2) The nature of man, with its sense of the duties belonging to its various relations. V. iv. 2, 3: ix. 16. (3) A rule, a law. IV. iii. 7: V. ix. 18, 22; *et sæpe.* (4) Constant, regular; to be constant, addicted to. V. x. 4, 5: xvi. 13: xvii. 3; *et al.*

THE 59TH RADICAL. 彡.

形 *hing* hsing The figure, appearance. IV. viii. Pt. i. 3.

彤 *t'ung* (1) Red, painted with vermilion. V. xxii. 23: xxviii. 4. (2) The name of a certain supplementary sacrifice. IV. ix. 1. (3) The name of a principality. V. xxii. 3.

彥 *yen* Men admirable and accomplished. IV. v. Pt. i. 5: V. xix. 17: xxx. 6, 7.

彫 *teaou* tiao Carved. III. iii. 6.

彭 *p'ăng* p'êng 彭蠡, the name of a lake,—the present Po-yang. III. i. Pt. i. 38; Pt. ii. 8. 彭 was also the name of a wild tribe. V. ii. 3.

彰 *chang* To display, give distinction to. V. xi. 18: xxiv. 7: IV. vii. Pt. i. 6. To make—be made—manifest; plainly. II. iii. 3: iv. 4: IV. iii. 3: iv. 8: V. i. Pt. ii. 3; Pt. iii. 2. Observe. IV. ii. 5.

影 *ying* A shadow. II. ii. 5.

THE 60TH RADICAL. 彳.

役 *yih* yi To serve; to make to serve. V. ii. 9: v. 5: vii. 8: xiii. 12.

彼 *pe* pi That, those. III. iii. 7: V. i. Pt. ii. 5, 8. = there. V. xiii. 13.

往 *wang* (1) To go, to go to. *Passim.* The phrase 往哉 is very common. (2) The past. 既往, IV. v. Pt. ii. 3. So, perhaps, V. xix. 3. The future. 其往, henceforward. V. xiii. 9.

征 *ching* chêng To punish, to execute imperial justice. II. ii. 20: III. iv. 1: IV. ii. 6: V. iii. 1, 7: vii. 7 (*n. b.*); *et al.*

徂 *tsoo* tsu (1) To go, to go to. II. ii. 20; *et sæpe.* It is much used along with 征. (2) Like the 2d use of 往, = the past. V. x. 8.

待 *tae* tai To wait for. IV. v. Pt. i. 5.

徇 *seun* hsün To go along or round. III. iv. 3. — to review. V. i. Pt. ii. 1.

很 *hăn* hen 疾很 = to be frenzied. Spoken of the mind. V. x. 11.

律 *leuh* lü (1) Standard tubes, used as pitch pipes in music, and for other purposes. II. i. 8, 24. 六律. II. iv. 4. (2) To be a law to. V. viii. 4.

書經

後 *how* hou — That which is after. (1) As a noun. A future;=afterwards. IV. v. Pt. i. 3: vii. Pt. ii. 7; V. vi. 15; *et al.* An heir, successors. V. vii. 11: xvii. 3: xix. 3. Those behind. V. iii. 9. Obs. V. xxii. 6. (2) As an adj. Future, after. We have 後人, 後王, 後嗣, 後昆, 後裔, 後日, 後言, and perhaps other phrases. IV. ii. 8: iv. 6: v. Pt. i. 5: x. 11: V. viii. 2; *et al.* 前後之人, xxvi. 3. (3) As a verb. To put last, postpone. IV. ii. 6. To be remiss in. To remain. V. xii. 13, xiii. 13, 20, 29, 30. 先後, V. xi. 7, need not be toned.

徐 *seu* hsü — 徐州, one of Yu's provinces. III. i. Pt. i. 28. 徐戎, certain wild tribes. V. xxix. 1, 5.

徒 *t'oo* t'u — (1) Followers. IV. ii. 14. Soldiers. V. iii. 9. (2) 司徒, the minister of Instruction. II. i. 19: V. ii. 2: iv. 7: xi. 2: xix. 10: xx. 8.

得 *tih* tê — To get, to be got. IV. ii. 8: V. vi. 14: vii. 6: xii. 2 (= to get successfully.) 得罪, to commit crime, offend. V. ix. 15, 16.

從 *ts'ung* — To follow; to act in accordance or compliance with. II. ii. 3, 5, 6, 13, 18; *et passim.* = to employ as before. V. xix. 15. 從子保, to allow the son to succeed, and to protect him. V. xii. 11. 月之從星, the moon's following (= course among) the stars. V. iv. 38. = accordance with reason. V. iv. 6. To be made to follow,—to a certain place. III. i. Pt. i. 74;—their natural channels, p. 9. To be observed. II. i. 2. From;—as a sequence of. Adverbially, = consequently. V. xiv. 27: IV. viii. Pt. ii. 3: vii. Pt. i. 14.

從 *sung* — 從容, to show an easy forbearance. V. xxi. 7.

從 *tsung* — Low. 3d tone. Followers, immediate attendants. V. xxvi. 2.

御 *yu* yü — (1) To drive a carriage. III. ii. 4: V. xxx. 5. (2) To wait on, be in attendance on. III. iii. 3. 侍御, V. xxvi. 4. (3) To advance—present—to. xxii. 28. (4) To manage, superintend. In the phrase 御事, managers of affairs, which was a favourite description of managers and officers under the Chow dyn. V. i. Pt. i. 2: II. ii.; *et sæpe.* (5) To condescend to. Spoken of the emperor's demeanour to his ministers. II. ii. 12.

徧 *p'ëen* p'ien — All round. To extend one's proceedings all round. II. i. 6.

復 *fuh* fu — To return, give back. II. i. 8: IV. vi. 1: vii. Pt. iii. 6: V. xxix. 4. To report the execution of a commission. V. xiii. 1. To recover. V. vii. 4. To reply to. IV. viii. Pt. i. 11. 紹復, to continue. IV. vii. Pt. i. 4.

復 *fow* fou — Again. V. xii. 8.

循 *seun* hsün — To comply with. 率循, V. xxii. 24.

微 *we* wei — (1) Small. II. ii. 15. To be reduced to obscurity. V. iv. 37. (2) The seat of a wild tribe. V. ii. 3: xix. 11. (3) A principality so called. IV. xi. 1.

徯 *he* hsi — To wait for. II. iv. 2: III. iii. 3: IV. ii. 6: v. Pt. ii. 5.

徵 *ching* chêng — (1) To be called. II. i. 28. (2) To be verified, III. iv. 2. Verifications. V. iv. 4, 32, 34.

德 *tih* tê — Virtue, virtuous deeds; virtuous; virtuously. *Passim.* 九德, II. iii. 3. 一德, IV. vi. 3, 4. 三德, V. iv. 4, 13. 奉德, V. xiv. 18, and 秉德, xviii. 23, = to hold as a virtue. The term is also used of conduct, or a course, which is not virtuous, but indifferent or positively evil; as in IV. i. 3: vii. Pt. iii. 4 (*n. b.*): viii. Pt. ii. 5: V. i. Pt. ii. 3: iv. 10: xv. 13: x. 23: xviii. 27; *et al.*

徽 *hwuy* hui — Excellent; excellently. V. xv. 10: xix. 18. To set forth the excellence of. II. i. 2.

THE 61ST RADICAL. 心.

心 *sin* hsin — The heart; the heart, the mind, denoting the mental constitution generally. Observe 心腹腎腸, IV. vii. Pt. iii. 8; and 股肱心膂, V. xxv. 3; 天心, the mind of Heaven, and 上帝之心, the mind of God. IV. iii. 8, and vi. 3. 宅心, V. ix. 5, to settle, establish, the heart; but the same phrase is different in xix. 6, 12.

必 *peih* pi — Must, as an auxiliary. IV. i. 3: iv. 8: v. Pt. iii. 4, 7: V. i. Pt. i. 11; Pt. ii. 5, 7: xx. 5: xxi. 12.

忌 *ke* chi — (1) To fear. V. xviii. 27. To be apprehensive, cautious. 敬忌, V. ix. 19: xxii. 25: xxvii. 11. (2) To hate. V. xxx. 4.

忍 *jin* jên — To bear, to endure. 弗忍, to be unable to endure. III. iii. 2: IV. iii. 3. Patience. V. xxi. 12.

忒 *t'ih* t'ê — Errors. V. iv. 19, 23.

忘 *wang* — To forget, to be forgotten. V. vii. 2: viii. 3: x. 7.

志 *che* chih — The will, the aims. *Sæpe.* 百志, all one's purposes. II. ii. 6. = earnest thought. II. i. 24. 役志, to make the will to serve, service of the will. V. xiii. 12.

忝 *t'een* t'ien — To disgrace. I. 12: IV. v. Pt. i. 3: V. xxv. 8.

忠 *chung* — To be loyal; loyalty. To give one's whole heart to. IV. ii. 7: iv. 5, 7: V. i. Pt. i. 5: xvii. 3: xxv. 1: xxvi. 2.

忱 *shin* ch'ên — To be sincere; sincerity. IV. iii. 9: vii. Pt. ii. 6: V. vii. 10, 13: ix. 6, 22: xvi. 2: xix. 2. To regard sincerely. xviii. 29. To be believed. xviii. 21. Observe. 忱裕之, xviii. 21. To believe sincerely. IV. viii. Pt. ii. 13.

念 *neen* nien — To think; to think of, to regard, thoughts. II. ii. 7, 10; *et sæpe.* 服念, to reflect on. V. ix. 12. Thoughtfully. V. iv. 4.

忸 *nuh* nu — 忸怩, to blush, to be ashamed. III. iii. 9.

忽 *hwuh* hu — To slight, to show indifference. V. xx. 16. Defects of govt. II. iv. 4; but this passage is uncertain.

忿 *fun* fên — To be angry. V. xxi. 11.

怒 *noo* nu — To be angry; anger. IV. vii. Pt. iii. 3: V. i. Pt. i. 5: iv. 3: xv. 17. 自怒, to anger one's-self. V. vii. Pt. ii. 6.

怙 *hoo* hu — To rely on. It occurs in three combinations, each of which requires study. 怙終, II. i. 11: 怙冒, V. ix. 4; 怙侈, V. xxiv. 10.

思 *sze* szû — To think, to think of. II. iii. 1: iv. 1: IV. v. Pt. ii. 7: *et sæpe.* Thinking. V. iv. 6. To wish. II. iii. 8. The character is marked in the third tone in I. 1, to be thoughtful.

怠 *tae* tai — To be idle. II. ii. 6, 9: *et sæpe.* = to cease. IV. xi. 7. To grow weary. IV. i. 3. Idly. III. ii. 3.

急 *keih* chi — Haste. V. iv. 24.

性 *sing* hsing — The nature. Used with ref. to man. IV. v. Pt. i. 9: V. xii. 15. 天性, the Heavenly nature. IV. x. 3. 恆性, the nature invariably right. IV. iii. 2. Used with ref. to animals. V. v. 8 *(n. b.)*

怨 *yuen* yüan — To murmur, to murmur against. III. iii. 3: IV. ii. 6: V. ix. 21; *et sæpe.* What provokes resentment. V. ix. 22: x. 11. = dissatisfaction. III. iii. 5; V. ix. 6. = enmity. V. i. Pt. iii. 2.

怩 *ne* ni nieh — 忸怩, to blush, to be ashamed. III. iii. 9.

怪 *kwae* kuai — Strange. III. i. Pt. i. 26.

怵 *ch'uh* ch'u — 怵惕, to be alarmed. V. xxvi. 1.

恂 *seun* hsün — To be sincere. 忱恂, V. xix. 2.

恆 *hăng* hêng — (1) Constant; constancy; constantly. IV. iii. 2 (see 性): iv. 7: xi. 3: V. iv. 34: xi. 2: xiii. 4: xxiv. 8. To make constant, to preserve long. V. xiii. 14. (2) 恆山, the name of a mountain. III. i. Pt. ii. 1. The name of a river. III. i. Pt. i. 9.

恐 *k'ung* — To fear, be afraid. IV. ii. 1: vii. Pt. ii. 8: viii. Pt. i. 2: x. 1: V. vi. 16: xxii. 4. = to frighten. IV. vii. Pt. i. 12.

恤 *seuh* hsio — To pity, compassionate. II. i. 11: IV. i. 2: V. vii. 8; *et al.* 恤宅, the house of mourning. V. xxii. 11. To be anxious about. V. xii. 23: xiv. 7: xvi. 9: xix. 1. Anxieties. IV. vii. Pt. ii. 15: V. xii. 9: xvi. 18. 奉恤, to enter into anxieties. V. xxiii. 6. 恤功, to labour anxiously. xxvii. 8.

恥 *ch'e* ch'ih — To be ashamed, to be ashamed of. IV. viii. Pt. ii. 9; Pt. iii. 10.

恪 *k'ŏ* k'o — To respect. Reverently. 恪謹, IV. viii. Pt. i 3. 恪慎, V. viii. 3.

恫 *t'ung* — To be pained. 奉其恫, to feel the smart. IV. vii. Pt. ii. 12. 恫瘝, sickness and pain. V. ix. 6.

恬 *t'een* t'ien — To be peaceful, at ease. 引恬, to lead to the enjoyment of ease. V. xi. 3.

恭 *kung* — To respect or revere; to obey reverently, attend reverently to; respectfulness, reverence. I. 10: II. i. 1: ii. 20: iii. 3, 6: IV. vii. Pt. i. 17: V. iii. 7: *et sæpe.* = courteous, humble. I. 1: V. xv. 4, 10. Before other verbs, its force is adverbial and = reverently. III. ii. 3: IV. vii. Pt. iii. 5, 10: V. i. Pt. iii. 3; *et sæpe.* Obs. V. xviii. 5, 17, where the meaning = respected (past participle).

息 *seih* hsi — To stop, cease. V. x. 11.

悅 *yuĕ* yueh — To be pleased, IV. v. Pt. ii. 5: V. iii. 9. To please, give pleasure to. V. i. Pt. iii. 3.

悉 *seih* hsi — All; altogether, fully. IV. i. 1: vii. Pt. i. 5: V. xvi. 18. In everything. V. xiii. 8.

悔 *hwuy* hui — To repent. III. iii. 9: IV. vii. Pt. i. 12, 17. Repentance. V. iv. 22.

悖 *pei* — To oppose, act contrary to. V. xxiv. 9.

悛 *tseuen* chüan — To repent and alter. i. 悛心, a penitent heart. V. i. Pt. i. 7.

悟 *woo* wu — To awake. = to recover. V. xxii. 7.

患 *hwan* huan — Calamity, disaster. IV. viii. Pt. ii. 8.

悲 *pe* pei — To be sad. III. iii. 9.

情 *ts'ing* ch'ing — The feelings. V. ix. 6.

惇 *tun* — (1) To give honour to. II. i. 16: V. xiii. 15, 23. = in a large and generous way. II. iii. 1: V. xiii. 10. To prove the solidity of. V. iii. 9. Observe 五惇哉, II. iii. 6. (2) 惇物, the name of a mountain. III. i. Pt. i. 76.

惕 *t'eih* t'i — To stand in awe of. IV. vii. Pt. i. 6. 怵惕, see 怵.

惟 *wei* — No other character occurs so frequently in the Shoo as this. I have counted more than 850 instances of its use. We find it constantly at the beginning of Books and paragraphs, where it is hardly susceptible of translation, and we may content ourselves with saying that it is an initial particle. Here we may call it, *now;* there it is simply as the note which a man gives when he clears his throat preparatory to speaking. We find it again as frequently in the middle of sentences, coming after the subject, and acting as the *copula* to connect it and the predicate. For this usage of it the student may refer especially to. III. i., where it occurs nearly 30 times. Again, it is sometimes treated as a verb, and defined by 思, to think of, to care for. *E. g.* II. iv. 8: IV. v. Pt. iii. 5: V. i. Pt. i. 5; Pt. iii. 4. Lastly, it is used constantly as a conjunction, connecting sentences and clauses together, and must be variously translated—*and, but, and so, namely, &c.* It often = *only,* half adverbial, half conjunctive. *E. g.* II. iii. 3, 20: IV. vii. Pt. ii. 4, 6: V. iv. 18. Its use along with 哉, as in II. i. 11, 16, 17, 20, 23, 25, 26; and after 亦, 其 and 洪, as in IV. vii. Pt. i. 7; Pt. ii. 5: V. i. Pt. i. 4, is to be observed.

惠 *hwuy* hui — (1) To be kind to; to love. V. i. Pt. ii. 4: xv. 10. We have 惠康, xxvii. 4; 保惠, xv. 6, 14; 子惠, IV. v. Pt. ii. 5. To be kind; the kind. II. iii. 2: V. xvii. 4. (2) To accord with, to obey. II. i. 17: ii. 5: IV. i. Pt. i. 1: V. xiii. 27: xviii. 21. To be accordant, accordantly, with reason. II. iv. 8: V. ix. 6: xvi. 22. (3) A kind of three-cornered halberd. V. xxii. 21.

惡 *yŏ* o — Evil, wickedness; the evil. V. i. Pt. iii. 4: iv. 40: xxiv. 7; *et al.* 爲惡, deeds of evil. V. xvii. 4. 元惡, chief criminals. V. ix. 16. 惡德, men of wicked practices. IV. viii. Pt. ii. 5. 先惡, to set an example of wickedness. IV. vii. Pt. i. 12.

惡 *woo* wu — To hate. V. xxx. 7. 作惡, manifestations of selfish disliking. V. iv. 14.

惰 *to* — To be idle; to be idle at. II. iv. 11: IV. vii. Pt. i. 11.

愆 *k'ëen* ch'ien — To go beyond. V. ii. 7, 8. To be in error; faults. II. ii. 12: IV. viii. Pt. iii. 6: V. xv. 13, 17; *et sæpe.* 十愆, the ten evil ways. IV. iv. 7. = to chastise. V. xxviii. 2. ? = to be exhausted. V. xxx. v.

愚 *yu* yü — Simple. 愚夫愚婦, III. iii. 5.

愛 *gae* ai — To love, to be loved. V. x. 5, 11. (foll. by 于): II. ii. 17. Love. IV. iv. 4. Compassion. III. iv. 7. To love one's-self. V. xviii. 22.

感 *kan* — To influence. II. ii. 21: V. xxxi. 3 (foll. by 于).

愧 *kwei* k'uei — To be ashamed. 愧恥, IV. viii. Pt. iii. 10.

愼 *shin* shên — To be careful to—, to attend carefully to; carefully. II. i. 2: ii. 17: iii. 1: iv. 2, 11: III. i. Pt. ii. 15: *et sæpissime.* To be cautious in. V. ix. 3: xviii. 10. = careful anxiety. xix. 24. 庶愼, precautionary measures. xix. 18, 14, 16, 18. 恪愼. V. viii. 3.

愿 *yuen* yüan — To be honest and blunt; bluntness. II. iii. 3.

慄 *leih* li — 慄慄 to be apprehensive. IV. iii. 6.

慆 *t'aou* t'ao — Excessive, insolent. IV. iii. 7.

慕 *moo* mo — To desire *to do good.* V. xxiv. 7.

慚 *ts'an* — To be ashamed of, a feeling of shame for. IV. ii. 1.

慝 *neih* ni — The wicked, secretly wicked. V. xx. 11: xxiv. 7. 引慝, to take the wickedness or guilt to one's-self. II. ii. 21.

THE 63D RADICAL. 戶.

THE 64TH RADICAL. 手.

v. Pt. i. 2. 承于 = to treat, to deal with. V. xviii. 5; but IV. vii. Pt. i. 3, is different. 承以, following up with. IV. viii. Pt. ii 2. 統承, V viii. 1.

技 *ke* chi — Abilities. V. xxx. 6, 7. 奇技, wonderful contrivances. V. i. Pt. iii. 3.

抑 *yih* yi — To repress. 自抑, to attain humility, V. xv. 8.

投 *t'ow* t'ou — To throw, to lay. 投于, to lay on. V. vii. 8.

折 *chĕ* chê — (1) To break off. 短折 = shortening of life. V. iv. 40. (2) To determine, to settle. V. xxvii. 30. The meaning of 折民惟刑, in p. 8, is hardly determined.

抱 *paou* pao — To carry in the arms. V. xxii. 10.

拊 *foo* fu — To tap, or touch gently. Spoken of the handling of musical instruments. II. i. 24 : iv. 9, 10.

拔 *pă* pa — To be pulled or torn up. V. vi. 16.

拘 *keu* chü — To hold fast. 執拘, to apprehend. V. x. 14.

拙 *chuĕ* chueh — To be stupid; stupid. IV. vii. Pt. i. 8: V. xx. 18.

招 *chaou* chao — To call out. IV. viii. Pt. iii. 7. = to bring on. II. ii. 21.

拜 *pae* pai — To do obeisance. The ministers bow to the emperor, and he returns the obeisance. V. xxii. 26, 27, 28; *et al.* The fullest expression of homage is 拜手稽首;—see 手. The form—拜稽首 is also frequent. II. i. 17, 21, 22, 28 : ii. 18; *et al.* We have 拜昌言, to do reverence for the excellent words. II. ii. 21 : iii. 1.

括 *kwŏ* kuo — (1) The end of an arrow applied to the string. IV. v. Pt. i. 7. (2) A name. V. xvi. 12.

拱 *kung* — To fold the hands, *i. e.* to bring them together in the style of ceremony. In the phrase. 垂拱, V. iii. 9 : xxiv. 5.

持 *ch'e* chih — To hold. In the phrase 攜持, V. xii. 10.

指 *che* chih — To point to, to indicate. IV. vii. Pt. i. 7: = referring to, as to. IV. x. 8. 有指, what he aimed at. V. vii. 15.

振 *chin* chên — In the phrase 振旅, II. ii. 21. ? to withdraw.

授 *show* shou — To deliver, give to. I. 8 : V. xxii. 27, 28.

掌 *chang* — To take charge of, to handle, to direct. III. iv. 1 : V. xx. 7—12.

探 *t'an* — To bring on. V. xviii. 29.

接 *tsëë* chieh — To receive; to be received. IV. v. Pt. ii. 7 : V. v. 7.

推 *t'uy* t'ui — To push and overthrow. IV. ii. 7. To push forward, advance. V. xx. 20.

掩 *yen* — To cover, conceal. IV. vii. Pt. i. 14.

揆 *k'wei* k'uei — To calculate. = to study. III. i. Pt. ii. 20. 百揆, the name of the highest minister under Yaou and Shun. II. i. 2, 17 : V. xx. 8.

揖 *yih* yi — To bow,—in salutation. V. xxiii. 2, 7.

揚 *yang* — (1) To be displayed. IV. viii. Pt. iii. 11 : V. i. Pt. ii. 8 : xiii. 14 : xiv. 22 : xxv. 6. = to point out, bring to the light. I. 12. 道揚, to declare. V. xxii. 24. (2) 揚州, one of Yu's nine provinces. III. i. Pt. i. 37.

搜 *sow* sou — Appears in the text in the from 搜. 渠搜, the name of a mountain and wild people, in the west. III. i. Pt. i. 83.

損 *sun* — Loss, damage. II. ii. 21.

搏 *pŏ* po — To strike forcibly,—as the strings in playing a lute. II. iv. 9.

摯 *che* chih — To come, to arrive. IV. x. 4.

撫 *foo* fu — (1) To soothe; to bring to tranquillity. V. i. Pt. iii. 4 : iii. 5 : viii. 2 : xiii. 10 (foll. by 于): xx. 1. 撫綏. IV. v. Pt. i. 2. (2) To accord with, be observant of. 撫于......II. iii. 4.

播 *po* — (1) To spread abroad; to propagate, diffuse. IV. vii. Pt. i. 7 : V. ix. 17 : xxvii. 8, 12. Applied to the sowing of seed, in which application some read it in the 2d tone. II. i. 18 : iv. 1 : V. vii. 11. = to encourage. V. ix. 1. (2) To be separated. III. i. Pt. ii. 7. = transported. V. vii. 6. (3) To reject. V. i. Pt ii. 3 : xviii. 22. (4) 播 and 嶓冢, the name of a mountain. III. i. Pt. i. 1, 4; Pt. ii. 8.

書經

樸 *p'ŏ* p'u — To strike. 樸滅, to extinguish. IV. vii. Pt. i. 12.

撻 *t'ă* t'a — To flog. = the scourge. II. iv. 6. To be beaten. IV. viii. Pt. iii. 10.

擇 *tsih* chai — To choose, to select. V. iv. 20; xxvii. 11, 12, 14.

擊 *keih* chi — To tap,—as in playing the sounding-stone. II. i. 24: iv. 9, 10.

擭 *hwa* hua — 3d tone. A trap. V. xxix. 3.

擾 *jaou* jao — (1) Docility. II. iii. 3. To train to obedience. V. xx. 8. (2) To throw into confusion. III. iv. 4.

攘 *jang* — To steal upon occasion offered. 寇攘. V. ix. 15: xxix. 4. 奪攘, V. xxvii. 2. 攘竊, IV. xi. 6.

攜 *hwuy* hui — (1) To lead by the hand. 攜持, V. xix. 8. (2) To carry. 左右攜僕, personal attendants. xii. 10.

THE 65TH RADICAL. 支.

支 *che* chih — 析支, the name of a mountain in the west, and of the wild tribes about it. III. i. Pt. i. 83.

THE 66TH RADICAL. 攴.

收 *show* shou — (1) To recover. V. xxiv. 10. = to take and remove. xxii. 29. (2) = to keep back, to draw ons's-self up from effort. V. xvi. 16.

攸 *yew* yu — It is for the most part identical in meaning and use with 所. (1) A place. III. i. Pt. i. 75. The place where. V. xiv. 22, 26; *et al.* (2) That which, that whereby. IV. ii. 6: Pt. i. 7: vii. Pt. i. 5; Pt. ii. 4, 6; *et sæpissime.* 罔攸 is frequent. II. ii. 3: IV. viii. Pt. i. 1: V. xi. 8: *et al.* In one place we have 罔有攸. IV. i. 4. Obs. V. xiii. 19. (3) Serves the purpose of the copula. III. i. Pt. ii. 14.

改 *kæ* kai — To change, to alter. IV. ii. 5: V. xii. 9: xvii. 2, 7: xxiii. 2.

攻 *kung* — To attack. III. ii. 4: V. iii. 8. = to punish. IV. ii. 7. = to work upon. V. xii. 3.

放 *fang* — To let go, to send away. V. iii. 2. = to banish. II. i. 12: IV. iii. 1. To dismiss. V. i. Pt. iii. 3. (2) To neglect, to disobey. V. ix. 18. 放心, the lost heart. xxiv. 10. (3) 放勳, the name of Yaou. I. 1. Many comm. read 放 here, and explain differently. So with the character in 放齊, the name of one of Yaou's ministers. I. 9.

政 *ching* chêng — Government; the measures and rules of government. *Passim.* 八政, the eight objects of govt. V. iv. 4, 7. 七政, the sun, moon, and five planets; but the meaning is doubtful. II. i. 5. 庶政, the various departments of govt. V. xx. 3. 政人, parties charged with the administration of govt. V. ix. 16. 立政 is the name of the 19th Book, Pt. V., where the phrase often occurs. 同于厥政, to share in the offices of govt. xix. 5.

故 *koo* ku — (1) Therefore. IV. x. 3: V. x. 8, 11: xvi. 8, 9: xxvii. 10. (2) As a preposition, coming after its regimen, on account of. IV. vii. Pt. ii. 5: viii. Pt. i. 2. (3) What is purposed. II. ii. 12.

效 *hëaou* hsiao — To require, as a charge. V. xi. 3.

敉 *mei* — To settle, to establish. V. xix. 15. 敉寧. V. vii. 5, 11. ? to consider as completed. xiii. 19.

敘 *seu* hsü — To arrange orderly. II. iii. 1: V. ix. 9; *et al.* To be arranged. II. i. 2: ii. 7: iv. 8: III. i. Pt. i. 7, 8: V. iv. 2, 3; *et al.* Arrangements. II. ii. 7 (九敘): iii. 6: III. i. Pt. i. 83: *et al.* Observe. 篤敘, V. viii. 13, 27. An order, a series, = a line. V. vii. x. 4. By degrees. V. xiii. 9. = to employ according to qualifications. IV. vii. Pt. iii. 10.

教 *këaou* chiao — To teach. II. i. 29: iii. 5; *et sæpe.* We have 告教, V. xix. 2; 教告, xviii. 23; 教誨, xv. 14; and 誥教, x. 4. Teaching, instructions, lessons. V. xiii. 13, 16. = education. xx. 8. 教辭. x. 16. 文教. III. i. Pt. ii. 20. 五教, the duties belonging to the five relations of society. II. i. 19: ii. 11: V. iii. 9. 教刑, the punishment in schools. II. i. 11. = influence. III. i. Pt. ii. 23.

敏 *min* — To be active or earnest; to be active in; active. II. ii. 2: IV. viii. Pt. iii. 4: V. ix. 22.

救 *keu* chiu — To save, to rescue. IV. v. Pt. ii. 3: vii. Pt. ii. 13: V. vii. 12.

敔 *yu* yü — An instrument, to give the signal of stopping the other instruments of music. II. iv. 9.

敗 *pae* pai — To ruin; to violate. II. ii. 20: IV. v. Pt. ii. 3: xi. 1: V. xx. 16: xxi. 10. Obs. 戕敗人, V. xi. 2. = destroyers. IV. vii. Pt. i. 12. Ruin. IV. xi. 8.

敜 *nëĕ* nieh — To fill up. V. xxix. 3.

敝 *pe* pi — To ruin. V. xxiv. 9.

敢 *kan* — To venture, presume, dare. *Passim.* In one passage, = daringly, vigorously. IV. vii. Pt. iii. 10.

散 *san* — (1) To disperse. V. iii. 9. (2) A surname. V. xvi. 12.

敬 *king* — *Passim.* To respect, to revere. It is used as an active verb, to respect, to attend respectfully to, the action so described being determined by the object which follows, as in 敬致, I. 5; 敬德, V. xii. 10, 20, *et sæpe*, (comp. 敬厥德, IV. v. Pt. iii. 3); *et al;* 敬刑, V. xxvii. 13; 敬罰, V. ix. 8. Very often no object follows, or only a 之, especially in the phrases 敬哉 and 敬之哉, when the verb = to be reverent. Reverence, respectfulness. II. iii. 3. Observe especially 敬作所, V. xii. 16. It occurs frequently before other verbs, when its force of course is adverbial, = reverently, respectfully. *E. g.* I. 8: II. i. 19: iv. 7: V. xvi. 23.

敵 *teih* ti — Enemies, opponents. V. xvi. 15. 敵讎, IV. xi. 2, 7. To oppose, resist. V. iii. 9 (foll. by 于). To be resisted. V. i. Pt. ii. 9.

敷 *foo* fu — (1) To spread, lay out,—as mats. V. xxii. 15, 16, 17, 18. (2) To divide and arrange. Spoken of Yu's work. III. i. Pt. i. 1. So, foll. by 于, and without an object. II. ii. 1. (3) To spread abroad; to set forth, to publish. II. i. 19: ii. 21: IV. iii. 3: V. iv. 9; *et sæpe.* To lay bare the heart. IV. vii. Pt. iii. 3: V. xvi. 18. Obs. 敷遺, V. xxiii. 3: 敷佑, V. ix. 8; 敷菑, V. xvi. 20; and 敷施, II. iii. 4. Observe also 敷納(奏)以言, II. iv. 7: i. 9. = extensively. V. vi. 5: IV. iv. 6. 敷言 = amplification. V. iv. 15, 16. To be spread abroad. V. xxviii. 1. (4) 敷淺, the name of a plain. III. i. Pt i. 4.

數 *soo* shu — Numbers, calculations. In the phrase 曆數. II. ii. 14: V. iv. 8.

斁 *lëaou* liao — To have in repair. V. xxix. 2.

敿 *këaou* chiao — To secure the laces of a shield. V. xxix. 2.

斁 *yih* yi — To be satiated with, to dislike. IV. v. Pt. ii. 7: V. viii. 4: xx. 21. = to be tired of and intermit. V. xiii. 21.

斁 *too* tu — To go to ruin. V. iv. 3.

斂 *lëen* lien — To concentrate, collect. V. iv. 9. Exactions. IV. xi. 7. It is read both in the 2nd and 3d tones.

斅 *heaou* hsiao — To teach. IV. vii. Pt. i. 5 (foll. by 于): vii; Pt. iii. 5.

THE 67TH RADICAL. 文.

文 *wăn* wên — (1) Veined, ornamented. V. xxii. 16. = ornamented fabrics. III. i. Pt. i. 16. = display. V. xiii. 5, 15. (2) Learning, accomplishments. 文教, III. i. Pt. ii. 15. 文德, II ii. 21. = the occupations of peace. V. iii. 2. Accomplished. I. i: II. i. 1: V. xix. 18, 21: xxviii. 3. (3) 文命, perhaps the name of Yu. II. ii. 1. The honorary title of king Wan. It is found *passim* in the phrases 文王, 文祖, 文考, 文武. In II. i. 4, 14, however, 文祖 denotes the ancestor of Yaou. In the title of V. xxviii., 文 is likewise an honorary name.

THE 69TH RADICAL. 斤.

斥 *ch'ih* — Salt land. III. i. Pt. i. 24.

斨 *ts'ëang* ch'iang — The name of an officer about Shun's court. II. i. 21.

斮 *tsŏ* tso — To cut through. V. i. Pt. iii. 3.

斯 *sze* szû — This, these. V. x. 16: xxi. 6. Making, with the preceding subject, an emphatic nominative. V. vi. 16: xxx. 2. (2) As a conjunction, forthwith, thereon. V. iv. 11, 13: vi. 14.

新 *sin* hsin — New. IV. vii. Pt. i. 4, 13; Pt. ii. 5, 16: Pt. iii. 6; *et sæpe.* To be new or renewed. IV. ii. 18. To renovate one's-self. III. iv. 6. Newly, recently. IV. vi. 6: V. vi. 10; *et al.* 作新, to make new. V. ix. 7. Obs. V. vi. 18.

斲 *chŏ* cho — To carve; to do fine work on wood. V. xi. 4.

斷 *twan* tuan — (1) To determine. V. xxvii. 12. 果斷, a bold decision. V. xx. 17. (2) 斷斷, plain and sincere. V. xxx. 6.

斷 *twan* tuan — 2d tone. To cut off; to make an end of. IV. vii. Pt. i. 3; Pt. ii. 13.

THE 70TH RADICAL. 方.

方 *fang* — (1) A region, a quarter. Used of the cardinal points. V. vi. 4. Of the regions of the empire. III. iii. 7: V. xviii. 2, 7, 8; *et sæpe.* The phrase 四方, the four quarters, is everywhere used for the empire. 萬方, the myriad regions, is also used in the same way. IV. iii. 1, 2, 3, 8: v. Pt. i. 2. As an adverb, 方 = on all sides, from all quarters, everywhere. IV. xi. 2: V. xi. 5: xix. 22; *et al.* Obs. 方夏, V. iii. 5. (2) As a conjunction, then, now. II. iv. 8: IV. iv. 8: xi. 4: V. iv. 13. In II. i. 28, 方 is inexplicable. (3) To disobey. I. 11. (4) 外方 and 內方 are the names of mountains. III. i. Pt. 11. 2, 3.

於 *yu* yü — In. V. vi. 12: x. 12: xviii. 7: xxii. 11.

於 *woo* wu — An exclamation. Oh! I. 2 (*n. b.*), 11: II. i. 24: ii. 7: iv. 10.

施 *she* shih — To give; to display, to be displayed. II. iv. 4, 8: IV. vii. Pt. i. 10: V. xiii. 16: xvi. 5: xxi. 1. To give out (act.) V. xxvi. 2. = to use, to employ in office. II. iii. 4.

旁 *pang* — (1) On every side. IV. v. Pt. i. 5: viii. Pt. i. 3; Pt. iii. 7: V. xiii. 16. (2) To be by the side of, = near to, immediately following. V. iii. 1.

旄 *maou* mao — A kind of ensign, formed of ox-tails. V. ii. 1.

旅 *leu* lü — (1) Properly a body of 500 men, = hosts. II. ii. 21: V. iii. 9. (2) The multitudes,—spoken of the people. V. xviii. 5-19. (3) Numerous officers. We have 亞旅, V. ii. 2: xix. 10; and 尹旅, xi. 2. (4) 旅力, strength. V. xxx. 5. (5) To set forth, display, to. V. xii. 8. (6) The term used for sacrificing to mountains. III. i. Pt. i. 65, 76; Pt. ii. 14. (7) The name of a western tribe. V. v. 1.

旌 *tsing* ching — To signalize. V. xxiv. 7.

族 *tsuh* tsu — Relatives,—the different branches of a family or clan. V. i. Pt. i. 5. So, 族姓, V. xxvii. 21. 九族, the nine classes of kindred. I. 2: II. iii. 1: IV. ii. 8. ? 圮族, I. 11.

THE 71ST RADICAL. 无.

旣 *ke* chi — (1) A particle of past time, denoting what is spoken of as done, completed. *Passim.* Observe 旣月, II. i. 7; 旣往, IV. v. Pt. ii. 3; 旣 alone, IV. viii. Pt. iii. 1. (2) It very often serves as a conjunction, = when; or leads us to construe the clause where it occurs in the nominative absolute. (3) To be consumed. V. i. Pt. i. 6. (4) To exert to the utmost. V. xxiv. 15.

THE 72D RADICAL. 日.

日 *jih* — (1) The sun. I. 8: II. iv. 4; *et al.* 出日, the rising sun. I, 4. 納日, the setting sun. I. 6. (2) A day, days. *Passim.* We have 上日 and 元日 for the first day of the month, II. i. 4, 14; 今日, to-day, V. xvi. 21, *et al.*; 翼日, the day following, V. xxii. 10, *et al.* (observe 今翼日, V. vii. 5); 日中, midday, V. xv. 10; but the meaning is difft. in I. 4. The character is also used often adverbially, = daily. *E. g.* II. ii. 11: IV. ii. 8: vi. 6: V. xxi. 3.

旦 *tan* — (1) The morning. II. ii. 19: IV. v. Pt. i 5. 旦夕, morning and evening. V. xxvi. 2. (2) The name of the duke of Chow. V. vi. 5, 6: xii. 14; *et al.*

旨 *che* chih — Good, excellent. IV. viii. Pt. ii. 12.

早 *tsaou* tsao — Early, prematurely. V. xii. 17.

旬 *seun* hsün — A decade of days. I. 8: II. ii. 21: III. iii. 1: V. ix. 12.

旱 *han* — Drought. IV. viii. Pt. i. 6.

昊 *haou* hao — Vast, wide. 昊天 is the appearance of the firmament in summer. I. 3.

旻 *min* — 旻天 is the appearance of the firmament in autumn. The phrase is generally taken as = the pitying heavens. II. ii. 20: V. xiv. 2.

昃 *ts'ih* chai — The sun declining to the west, the afternoon. V. xv. 10.

昆 *kwăn* kuên — Afterwards. II. ii. 18. Futurity. IV. ii. 8.

昌 *ch'ang* — Good, admirable. 昌言, admirable words. II. ii. 21 : iii. 1 : iv. 1. To be prosperous or flourishing. IV. ii. 7 : V. iv. 13.

明 *ming* — *Passim.* (1) To be clear, bright; and metaphorically, to be intelligent. Clear, brilliant; intelligent. I. 1, 9 : II. i. 1 : ii. 11 : V. xxvi. 2; *et sæpe.* Clearness,—spoken of seeing. IV. v. Pt. ii. 7 : V. iv. 6; *et al.* Intelligence. V. vii. 3, 9. 神明, spiritual intelligences. V. xxi. 3. = pure. V. xiii. 25. In the sense of intelligent it is often associated with 聰. It is doubled to heighten the idea. V. xxvii. 6, 10 : III. iii. 8; but 明明 in I. 12 is different. (2) To illustrate; to make illustrious; to enlighten; to be enlightened; to be illustrious. V. xx. 14 : xxiii. 5 : xxvii. 7 : xxviii. 2 : xvi. 20; *et sæpe.* To understand clearly. V. xxii. 7; *et al.* To study. V. xiii. 13. To adjust clearly. II. iv. 4. To distinguish. II. iv. 7; *et al.* Obs. II. i. 15, 27 : III. iii. 5.

昏 *hwăn* huên — To be dark; dark, used metaphorically, morally dark, blinded. V. iv. 37 : xviii. 4; *et al.* To be bewildered. II. iv. 1. 昏德, dark as to virtue, = blindly vicious. IV. ii. 2. Blindly. V. xxii. 6; *et al.*

易 *yih* yi — To change, (both act. and neuter). IV. vii. Pt. ii. 15 : V. iv. 36, 37 : vii. 13 : x. 11 : xxx. 5. 易種, to perpetuate seed. IV. vii. Pt. ii. 16. 朔易, changes of the winter. I. 7.

易 *e* i — 3d tone. What is easy; agreeable. V. xxv. 5. To be easy, = easily preserved. V. xvi. 4. To take easily, make little account of. V. v. 3.

昔 *seih* hsi — Formerly. IV. viii. Pt. iii. 10 : V. vi. 18; *et sæpe.* 在昔. V. iv. 3 : x. 9 : xvi. 7, 11. 若昔. V. vii. 11 : xx. 2. As a noun, 昔之人. V. xv. 3.

星 *sing* hsing — A star, the stars. I. 3, 4, 5, 6, 7 : II. iv. 4 : V. iv. 8, 38.

春 *ch'un* — Spring. I. 4 : V. xxv. 2. In the spring. III. iv. 3 : V. i. Pt. i. 1.

昧 *mei* — (1) Dark, sombre. 昧谷, the sombre valley. I. 6. 昧爽, the early dawn, between the dark and light. IV. v. Pt. i. 5 : V. ii. 1 : iii. 8. The wilfully dark or blind. IV. ii. 7. (2) 昧昧 = deeply. V. xxx. 6.

昬 *hwăn* huên — (1) Used for 昏, blindly. V. ii. 6. (2) Used for 暋, to be strong, energetic. IV. vii. Pt. i. 11.

昭 *chaou* ch'ao — To display; to make illustrious or glorious. IV. ii. 8. iv. 3 : V. iii. 7 : v. 3; *et al.* To be illustrious. V. xxiii. 5. To enlighten. V. xiii. 24 : xvi. 14. Brightly. I. 2 : II. iv. 2 : IV. iii. 4.

是 *she* shih — (1) This, these. V. iv. 26 : xix. 3. = on this. III. i. Pt. i. 16. 若是, thus. V. xxx. 2. = really. V. xxx. 6, 7. (2) To be. II. iv. 8 : III. i. Pt. i. 70 : iii. 5 : V. ii. 6 : *et al.* This is the most common use of the term, and it is generally followed by a verb, which may be construed as in the participial mood.

昴 *maou* mao — The name of a star. I. 7.

昵 *neih* ni — To be near to, familiar with. V. i. Pt. ii. 3 (昵比) : xxvi. 7 (foll. by 于). = familiars, favourites. IV. viii. Pt. ii. 5.

昵 *ne* ni — Low. 2d tone. The shrine appropriate to the spirit-tablet of a father. IV. ix. 5.

時 *she* shih — *Passim.* (1) A time, the time; the seasons, a season or period of three months. I. 3, 8, 9 : II. i. 8, 16 : IV. v. Pt. ii. 6 : vii. Pt. ii. 3 : viii. Pt. ii. 6 : V. i. Pt. i. 11; Pt. iii. 1 : ix. 12; *et sæpe.* Always. IV. v. Pt. iii. 3 : viii. Pt. iii. 4; *et al.* Then. II. iv. 7 : V. ix. 9; *et al.* Seasonable; seasonableness; seasonably. II. i. 2 : V. iv. 32, 34, 37; *et al.* 自時, henceforth. V. xii. 14 : xiii. 23 : xv. 7; *et al.* To time, to regulate the seasons with a view to—. V. xx. 12. (2) Used as a synonym of 是, this, these; to be. The frequency of this usage is characteristic of the Shoo. I. 12 : II. i. 17, 18 : III. iv. 4 : IV. iii. 9 : iv. 7 : V. xxii. 7 : xxiv. 11, 14 : ix. 4, 11, 13 : xiv. 22, 25; *et sæpe.* 時 alone, and 若時, thus. I. 2 : II. iii. 2 : IV. vi. 6 : V. xiii. 17; *et sæpe.* What is right II. iv. 6. Obs. 惟時, II. iii. 4 : iv. 11 : V. xiv. 10, 18; *et al.*

晝 *chow* chou — Day, by day. 晝夜, II. iv. 8.

晨 *shin* ch'ên — The morning. = to announce the morning, to crow. V. ii. 5.

智 *che* chih — Wisdom; the wise. IV. ii. 2; V. xii. 10.

暇 *hea* hsia — Leisure. V. x. 10 : xiii. 13. 遑暇, xv. 10. 自暇, to give one's-self leisure. V. x. 9. 須暇, to wait and forbear. V. xviii. 17.

暑 *shoo* shu — To be hot, summer heat. V. xxv. 5.

暘 *yang* Sunshine. V. iv. 32, 34. 暘谷, the valley of sunshine,—a place in the extreme east of Yaou's empire, probably in Corea. I. 4.

暋 *min* To be violent. V. ix. 15 : xix. 5.

暫 *tsan* chan A brief time, for a brief time. IV. vii. Pt. ii. 16.

暴 *paou* pao Violence, oppression. V. i. Pt. i. 5 ; Pt. ii. 5 : ii. 6. Oppressors. V. xx. 11. So, 暴德 and 暴德之人, V. xix. 8, 5. Oppressive to one's-self, wantonly indifferent to virtue. IV. ii. 9. To oppress, be injurious to. V. iii. 6.

暨 *ke* chi (1) A conjunction. And. I. 8 : II. i. 17, 21 : III. i. Pt. i. 35 : IV. iv. 2 : vi. 3 : V. iii. 4 ; *et sæpe*. With, along with. II. iv. 1 : IV. vii. Pt. ii. 12 : V. xv. 5 ; *et al.* Observe. 胥暨. V. xxiii. 6. (2) To be come to, = the uttermost ends of. III. i. Pt. ii. 23. 暨 does not occur in the Four Books.

曆 To calculate. I. 3. 曆數, the calendaric calculations. V. iv. 8. 天之曆數 = the determinate appointment of Heaven. II. ii. 14.

曠 *k'wang* k'uang To make vacant. II. iii. 5.

THE 73D RADICAL. 日.

曰 *yuĕ* yüeh To speak, to say, saying. *Passim.* Commonly the nominative is expressed. It is used in soliloquy, and = to say to one's-self. *E. g.* V. xx. viii. 2. It is sometimes passive, and = to be called, to be : may be said to be, may be pronounced. *E. g.* V. iv. *Passim :* xxx. 7 : 8. Next to 惟, 曰 is probably the character of most frequent occurrence in the Shoo.

曲 *k'euh* ch'ü To be bent or crooked. V. iv. 5.

曷 *hŏ* ho Why ; how. IV. vii. Pt. i. 12 ; Pt. ii. 4, 6, 11, 12 ; Pt. iii. 5 : V. i. Pt. i. 7 : *et sæpe.* = when. IV. i. 3. = whither. III. iii. 9.

書 *choo* shu A writing, written document. IV. v. Pt. i. 2 ; Pt. ii. 2 : viii. Pt. i. 2 : V. vi. 16, 18 : xxii. 23. Written specifications. V. xii. 6. A record, a book of record. II. iv. 6 : V. xxvii. 20. Written oracular responses. V. vi. 9.

曾 *tsăng* tsêng 曾孫, a great grandson, but used = descendant. V. iii. 6.

替 *t'e* t'i (1) To disregard. V. v. 3 : vii. 9 : viii. 5 : ix. 24. (2) To intermit. V. xiii. 21. = to fail of. xii. 23. (3) To supersede. V. xix. 15.

會 *hwuy* hui (1) To assemble (both act. and neuter). II. ii. 20 : V. i. Pt. i. 1 ; Pt. ii. 1 : iii. 8 : ix. 1. To meet with. V. iv. 14. To meet. Spoken of waters. III. i. Pt. ii. 9, 10, 11, 12, 13. Observe 會同, III. i. Pt. i. 15 ; Pt. ii. 14. To unite. V. xxviii. 3. (2) Used for 繪, to depict. II. iv. 4.

THE 74TH RADICAL. 月.

月 *yuĕ* yüeh The moon. I. 3 : II. iv. 4 : V. i. Pt. iii. 5. A month, months. *Passim.*

有 *yew* yu Lower. 3d tone. And. I. 8 : II. i. 8, 10, 13, 16, 26 ; *et sæpe.* It is always used in enumeration of numbers, and follows 十.

有 *yew* yu (1) The impersonal substantive verb, —there is, there was, there will be. I. 11, 12 ; *et passim.* (2) To have, to possess. Also *passim.* It is often auxiliary merely to the verb that follows. The student must observe that 有 before the names of principalities, dynasties, = the holder or holders, the sovereign or sovereigns, of such. *E. g.* II. ii. 20, 21 : iii. 2, 5, 7 : IV. viii. Pt. iii. 10 : V. i. Pt. ii. 4. The name of the principality may be followed by 氏, as in III. ii. 3. 有 must be construed in the same way before many other nouns. *E. g.* IV. ii. 9 : V. Pt. iii. 1 : The term must often be construed as if it were preceded by a 所, *E. g.* II. ii. 17 : iv. 4 : IV. ii. 4 : V. i. Pt. iii. 5. Observe particularly the phrase 有衆, which may generally be thus resolved. III. iv. 2, 5 : IV. i. 2, 3 : V. i. Pt. i. 10 ; *et al.* So, 有司. II. ii. 12. It is difficult, however, sometimes to account for the 有. *E. g.* III. iii. 1 : V. iii. 8 : xii. 13. To be conscious of having, to have boastingly. IV. viii. Pt. ii. 7 ; *et al.* 九有, the nine provinces. IV. vi. 2.

朋 *p'ang* p'êng To form selfish friendships or associations. II. iv. 8 : V. i. Pt. ii. 3 : iv. 10 : xiii. 9.

服 *fuh* fu (1) To wear ; dress,—robes, garments. II. iv. 4, 7 : III. i. Pt. i. 10, 44 : IV. v. Pt. ii. 1 : V. xxii. 2 : xxiv. 10 ; *et al.* (2) A great variety of meanings may here be classed together. To undergo. V. xxv. 1. To serve ; service ; business ; to perform duties. IV. vii. Pt. i. 3 : V. i. Pt. i. 5 : ix. 16 : xii. 14, 18, 19 : xiv. 22 : xxv. 3 ; *et al.* = to enjoy, especially with 命, IV. vi. 6 : V. ix. 23 : xii. 10, 17 ; *et al.* ; but 服命 in V. viii. 4, and perhaps some other places, is different. = offices. V. xviii. 28 : xxviii. 2 : x. 13 (*n. b.*). To work on the fields. IV. vii. Pt. i. 9, 11. 服言, to carry out one's words.

IV. viii. Pt. ii. 12. (3) To submit. II. i. 12, 16; IV. v. Pt. ii. 5: V. iii. 8; *et al.* To produce submission. V. xxvii. 15: To subject animals to the yoke. V. iii. 2. To be subjected to. V. xxvii. 19. (4) 服念, to cherish and think of. V. ix. 12. (5) A tenure or domain, domains. II iv. 8 (五服): III. i. Pt. ii. 18—22: V. xx. 1 (六服); *et al.*

朏 *fei* The moon re-appearing. The 3d day of the month. V. xii. 2: xxiv. 1.

朔 *sŏ* so (1) The first day of the moon. II. ii. 19: III. iv. 4: IV. v. Pt. ii. 1. (2) The north; northern; northwards. I. 7: II. 1. 8: III. i. Pt. ii. 23: V. i. Pt. ii. 1: xiii. 3. 朔易, the changes of the winter. I. 7.

朕 *ch'in* sh'ên I, me, my, we, our. *Passim.* The character is used most frequently by the emperors in speaking of themselves, but with no special emphasis, being constantly interchanged with 我, 予, and other terms. It is used also by ministers in speaking of themselves. *E. g.* II. ii. 10, 20: iii. 8: III. i. Pt. ii. 17: V. xiii. 1, 13, 22, 24, 28; *et al.* It had not yet become the imperial *We.*

望 *wang* (1) To be full moon, the 15th day of the month. V. xii. 1. (2) The name of a sacrifice offered by the emperor to the mountains and rivers. II. i. 6, 8: V. iii. 3.

朝 *chaou* chao Morning, in the morning. V. i. Pt. i. 8: ii. 1: iii. 1: xii. 1, 2, 4, 6: xiii. 3: xv. 10: xxiv. 1. 朝夕, morning and evening. IV. viii. Pt. i. 5: V. x. 2.

朝 *ch'aou* ch'ao To appear at court or before the emperor. II. i. 9: V. xx. 14. Spoken of the waters of the Han and Këang hurrying to the Sea. III. i. Pt. i. 47.

朞 *ke* chi A round year of 366 days. I. 8.

期 *k'e* ch'i (1) To expect, to anticipate. 不期, unexpected, unperceived. V. xx. 18. With a view to. II. ii. 11. (2) A hundred years old. 耄期, between ninety and a hundred. II. ii. 11.

THE 75TH RADICAL. 木.

木 *muh* mu (1) A tree, trees. II. i. 22: III. i. Pt. i. 17, 33, 42: IV. iii 5; *et al.* = timber. III. i. Pt. i. 44. = woods. II. iv. 1: III. i. Pt. i. 1. (2) Wood, one of the elements. V. iv. 5. One of the six magazines of nature. II. ii. 7. Wood, generally. IV. viii. Pt. i. 11. Wooden-tongued. III. iv. 3.

未 *we* wei (1) Not yet; not, but the force of the *yet* can generally be detected. II. iii. 8: IV. iii. 5; *et sæpe.* Has sometimes to be translated by—there never was......III. iii. 6: V. ix. 13, 14. (2) The eighth of the calendaric stem-characters. V. iii. 3: xii. 1.

末 *mŏ* mo (1) Final, last. V. xxii. 24. Finally. xii. 24. (2) Ever, always. V. xix. 17. (3) Trivial, insignificant. V. xxii. 25.

本 *pun* pên The root. III. iii. 4: V. i. Pt. iii. 4.

朱 *choo* chu (1) Red. Spoken of the manes and tails of horses. V. xxiii. 1. (2) The name of an officer about the court of Shun. II. i. 22. The name of Yaou's son. I. 9: II. iv. 8. 朱圉, the name of a mountain. III. i. Pt. ii. 2.

朽 *hew* hsiu Rotten. III. iii. 5.

杵 *ch'oo* ch'u A wooden pestle, pestles. V. iii. 8.

杌 *wuh* wu A tree without branches, = a want of prosperity. V. xxx. 8.

材 *ts'ae* ts'ai (1) Materials of wood. V. xxii. 13. Timber. V. xi. 4. (2) *I. q.* 才, abilities. V. vi. 6. = men of ability. IV. vi. 7.

杖 *chang* To hold or grasp. V. ii. 1.

杜 *too* tu To shut or fill up. V. xxix. 3.

東 *tung* (1) The east. V. xxii. 6. In the east. V. xi. 14. Eastwards, on the east. II. i. 8: III. i. Pt. ii. 7—13, 23: IV. ii. 6: V. iii. 7: vii. 15. Eastern. V. viii. 3: ix. 1, 4; *et sæpe.* 東作, the labours of the spring. I. 4. (2) 東陵, the name of a mountain. III. i. Pt. ii. 9. 東原, a tract of country. III. i. Pt. i. 32.

杶 *ch'un* The name of a tree. III. i. Pt. i. 52.

松 *sung* The pine tree. III. i. Pt. i. 26.

析 *seih* hsi (1) To disperse, to be separated. I. 4: IV. vii. Pt. iii. 5. (2) 析支 and 析城 are names of mountains. III. i. Pt. i. 83; Pt. ii. 1.

林 *lin* (1) A forest. V. iii. 8. (2) 桃林, the name of a tract of country. V. iii. 2.

枚 *mei* One by one. II. ii. 18.

果 *kwo* kuo Bold, determined. 果毅, V. i. Pt. iii. 4. 果斷, V. xx. 17.

枲 *se* hsi Hemp. III. i. Pt. i. 26, 60.

柏 *pih* pai (1) The cypress tree. III. i. Pt. i. 52. (2) 桐柏, the name of a hill. III. i. Pt. ii. 2, 11.

某 *mow* mou — Such an one. V. vi. 5.

染 *jĕn* jan — To be dyed or stained with. III. iv. 6.

柔 *jow* jou — To be gentle with, to show kindness to; mild; mildness. II. i. 16: iii. 3: V. iv. 17: xv. 10: xxii. 8: xxiv. 12: xxviii. 4.

柱 *ch'oo* ch'u — 底柱, the name of a hill. III. i. Pt. ii. 1, 7.

柚 *yew* yu — The pummelo fruit. III. i. Pt. i. 44.

柴 *ch'ae* ch'ai — To offer a burnt-offering to Heaven. II. i. 8: V. iii. 3.

柷 *chuh* chu — A musical instrument, a kind of rattle, giving notice to the instruments of a band to strike up. II. iv. 9.

栗 *leih* li — To be majestic and dignified. II. i. 24: iii. 3. In many editions of the Shoo, 栗 appears in II. ii. 21, instead of 慄, to be fearful.

栝 *kwŏ* kuo — ? the cedar tree. III. i. Pt. i. 52.

格 *kih* ko — (1) To come or go to,—used both of place and conduct. I. 8: II. i. 2, 3, 14: ii. 9, 21: iv. 9: IV. i. 1: vii. Pt. i. 6: V. v. 8: xxvi. 6. To reach to. I. 1: IV. viii. Pt. iii. 10: V. vii. 1: xvi. 16. To make to reach to. V. xvi. 7. (2) To correct; correction. IV. ix. 2: V. xii. 11: xiv. 5: xviii. 4: xxvi. 3. To be corrected, become reformed. II. iv. 6. (3) Most excellent; intelligent. IV. x. 2: V. xxvii. 13.

桃 *t'aou* t'ao — See 林.

桀 *këĕ* chieh — The name of the tyrant, the last emperor of the Hea dynasty. IV. ii. 1: V. i. Pt. ii. 4, 5: xix. 3.

桐 *t'ung* — (1) The dryandra, III. i. Pt. i. 35. (2) 桐柏, see 柏. The name of the place where T'ang's grave was. IV. v. Pt. i. 9, 10,

桑 *sang* — The mulberry tree. Used as an adj., III. i. Pt. i. 16.

桓 *hwan* huan — (1) The name of a river. III. i. Pt. i. 70. (2) 桓桓 a martial bearing. V. ii. 9. (3) A name. V. xxii. 11.

梁 *lëang* liang — (1) The name of a hill. III. i. Pt. i. 4. (2) 梁州, one of Yu's nine provinces. III. i. Pt. i. 62.

梅 *mei* — Plums or prunes. IV. viii. Pt. iii. 2.

梓 *tsze* tzŭ — The name of a tree, the wood of which was much used by the cabinet-maker and the carver. V. xi. 4.

條 *t'eaou* t'iao — (1) Orderly divisions. IV. vii. Pt. i. 9. (2) High, tall. III. i. Pt. i. 17. (3) 鳴條, the name of a palace of Këĕ. IV. iv. 2.

棄 *k'e* ch'i — (1) To throw away, to abandon. II. ii. 20: III. ii. 3: iv. 4: IV. vii. Pt. ii. 13: viii. Pt. iii. 2: x. 3: V. i. Pt. ii. 3; Pt. iii. 3: ii. 6: vii. 11: xvii. 18. To put away,—spoken of one's faults. V. ix. 9. (2) The name of Shun's minister of Agriculture, the ancestor of the House of Chow. II. i. 18.

棐 *fei* — To assist, help. V. vii. 10, 13: ix. 6: x. 8, 9: xiii. 13, 17: xvi. 2, 21: xxvii. 6, 10.

棼 *fun* fên — 棼棼, to be in confusion, disorderly. V. xxvii. 4.

椓 *chŏ* cho — To castrate, castration. V. xxvii. 3.

植 *chih* — To place, to set up. V. vi. 4.

楛 *hoo* hu — The name of a tree, the wood of which was used for making arrows. III. i. Pt. i. 52.

楨 *ching* chêng — The posts of the framework used in rearing walls of earth and lime pounded together. 楨榦 V. xxix. 5.

楫 *tsëĕ* chieh — Oars. IV. viii. Pt. i. 6.

業 *yĕ* yeh — (1) A patrimony, possessions. IV. vii. Pt. i. 4: V. xx. 17. (2) 業業, to be fearful. II. iii. 5.

極 *keih* chi — (1) A support and pattern. V. xvi. 18. (2) That which is extreme. Applied to the idea of perfection or the highest excellence. V. iv. 4, 9, 10, 11, 14, 15, 16. Applied to the extremity of misery. 六極, V. iv. 4, 40. Applied to punishments. 五極. V. xxvii. 22. Extreme. xxvii. 21. To be extremely affected by; to be extremely for. V. xxvii. 20: vii. 15. Fully; to the utmost. V. iv. 33: ix. 8. A place of rest. IV. vii. Pt. iii. 5.

榦 *yan* — (1) The name of a tree whose wood was used for bows. III. i. Pt. i. 52. (2) The planks used for the sides of building frames. See 楨.

榮 *kung* jung — Glory, flourishing condition. V. xxx. 8.

榭 *seay* shê — A high terrace with buildings on it. V. i. Pt. i. 5.

構 *kow* kou — To cover over, to construct the roof. V. vii. 11.

樂 *yoh* yo — Music. II. i. 24.

樂 *loh* lo — Pleasure. II. ii. 6 : V. xv. 7, 13.

樸 *p'ŏ* p'o — To fashion rudely in wood. V. xi. 4.

樹 *shoo* shu — To plant, to set up. IV. viii. Pt. ii. 2 : V. i. Pt. iii. 4 : xxiii. 6 : xxiv. 7.

橋 *k'ëaou* ch'iao — 鉅橋, a place where the tyrant Show had collected great stores of grain. V. iii. 9.

橘 *keŭh* chü — Small oranges. III. i. Pt. i. 44.

機 *ke* chi — A spring, the centre of motion in any contrivance or implement. IV. v. Pt. i. 7.

檢 *këen* chien — To regulate. 檢身, IV. iv. 5.

檿 *yen* — A sort of wild mountain mulberry tree. III. i. Pt. i. 26.

櫱 *nëĕ* nieh — Shoots from a felled tree. IV. vii. Pt. i. 4.

權 *k'euen* ch'üan — (1) The weight of a steelyard, = the balance of circumstances. V, xxvii. 16. (2) Power. V. i. Pt. ii. 3.

THE 76TH RADICAL. 欠.

次 *ts'ze* tz'ŭ — (1) Next in order. V. iv. 4 : xxii. 20. (2) A position, a post. III. iv. 4. To halt, to take up a position. V. i. Pt. ii. 1. (3) To suit, to accord with. V. ix. 18.

欲 *yuh* yü — To wish, to desire. II. iv. 4, 6 : x. 4 : V. i. Pt. i. 11 : xi. 8 : xii. 23 : xxx. 5. Desires, —in a good or bad sense. II. ii. 6, 13 : IV. ii. 2 : v. Pt. ii. 3. = dissoluteness. II. iii. 5.

欽 *k'in* ch'in — To respect, to be reverent. I. i. 11, 12 : II. i. 11, 23, 26 : V. viii. 1 : xviii. 5; *et sæpe*. Reverently. III. iv. 5 : IV. viii. Pt. iii. 7. Obs. 欽若, to accord reverently with. I. 3 : IV. viii. Pt. ii. 3 : V. xxiv. 15. 欽厥止, reverently determine your end. IV. v. Pt. i. 7. Sovereignly. V. xix. 5.

歆 *hin* yin — To accept or enjoy a sacrificial offering. V. viii. 3.

歌 *ko* — To sing, singing. II. i. 24 : IV. iv. 7. A song, songs. II. ii. 7 : iv. 11 : III. iii. 3.

歡 *hwan* huan — To rejoice. V. xiii. 21.

THE 77TH RADICAL. 止.

止 *che* chih — (1) To stop, to halt. II. iv. 9 : V. ii. 7, 8. To make to stop, make an end of. V. xxi. 9. (2) = dwellings. V. xiv. 23. One's resting place, the end or aim. II. iv. 2 : IV. v. Pt. i. 7.

正 *ching* chêng — (1) To correct, adjust, regulate; to be correct, exact; correctness. I. 5, 7 : II. ii. 7 : III. i. Pt. ii. 15 : IV. ii. 2 : vii. Pt. iii. 1 : V. i. Pt. iii. 3 : iv. 13, 14, 17 : xiii. 8 : xv. 11, 12, 15 : xxvi. 6 : xxvii. 20; *et al.* = to punish; punishments; a righting. II. ii. 11 : IV. i. 2 : ix. 4. = correct men. V. xviii. 22. (2) It is used of ministers generally. V. xix. 18 : xxviii. 1. And of particular ministers; we have 外正, V. ix. 18; 正人, ix. 17; 少正, x. 2; 大正, xxvi. 4; *et al.*, as in x. 4, 7 : xviii. 25. 先正, IV. viii. Pt. iii. 8, = the former premier, but in V. xxv. 7, the same phrase = your correct father. (3) The month or months with which the year commenced in difft. dynasties. III. ii. 3 : IV. vi. 3. The first month of the year. II. i. 4, 14 : ii. 19.

此 *ts'ze* tz'ŭ — This, these. III. iii. 6, 7 : V. xv. 15, 18 : xix. 15.

步 *poo* pu — A pace, a step. V. ii. 7. To travel. V. iii. 1 : xii. 1 : xxiv. 1.

武 *woo* wu — (1) To be martial; prowess. IV. iv. 3 : V. i. Pt. ii. 8; Pt. iii. 6. = awe-inspiring. II. ii. 4. Warlike measures or ways. III. i. Pt. ii. 20 : V. iii. 2, 3. (2) The posthumous title of the first king of the Chow dynasty. V. vii. 5. 武王, V. vi. 12, 16; *et sæpe*. The combination of this title and that of his father—文武—is very frequent. (3) 武丁, one of the emperors of the Shang dynasty. V. xvi. 7.

歲 *suy* sui — A year, a round year. I. i. 8 : II. i. 8 : III. iv. 3 : IV. viii. Pt. i. 6 : V. iv. 8, 35—37 : vi. 19. 烝祭歲, to offer the annual winter sacrifice. V. xiii. 29; but the meaning is doubtful.

歷 *leih* li — (1) To pass through. V. xvi. 8 : xxiv. 8. Obs. 有夏歷年, &c., V. xii. 17, 19, 22. 經歷, to pass through and carry out. V. xvi. 4. 歷人, harbourers of criminals. V. xi. 2. = destinies, as if it were 曆數, V. vii. 1. (2) Fully, repeatedly. IV. vii. Pt. iii. 3. (3) 歷山, the name of a mountain near which Shun once lived. II. ii. 21.

歸 *kwei* kuei — (1) To return. II. i. 8 : IV. iii. 1 : v. Pt. ii. 1 : V. vi. 8, 11 : xx. 1. = to send. V. iii. 2 : x. 14. To retire; retirement. IV. vi. 1. (2) To turn to. III. iii.

9: IV. vi. 4: V. iv. 14: xvii. 4. 依歸, dependence and resort. V. vi. 7.

THE 78TH RADICAL. 歹.

死 *sze* szû — To die; death. II. i. 28: IV. vii. Pt. ii. 13: V. ix. 15; x. 11: xxvii. 20. Observe 殛死 and 伐厥死, IV. vii. Pt. i. 16: V. iv. 3. 一死, one dead animal. II. i. 8. 死魄, the dead dark disk, = new moon. V. iii. 1.

殂 *tsoo* tsu — 殂落 = to decease. II. i. 13.

殃 *yang* — Evils, miseries. IV. iv. 8.

殄 *t'een* t'ien — To cut off; to cast of. II. i. 25: iv. 8: V. ix. 22, 23: xviii. 6: xxviii. 2. We find it with other verbs:—殄戮, V. xii. 21: xviii. 11; 殄殲, V. i. Pt. iii. 4: 暴殄, V. iii. 6; 殄滅, IV. vii. Pt. ii. 16. To be cut off. V. xxiv. 8.

殆 *t'ae* t'ai — (1) Perilous. V. xxx. 7. (2) A particle, = I apprehend, it seems to be that. V. xxii. 7.

殉 *seun* hsün — To desire, to seek for. IV. iv. 7.

殊 *shoo* shu — To mark off, show to be different. V. xxiv. 7.

殖 *chih* — To plant, to cultivate. V. xxvii. 8. (2) To revive and prosper. IV. x. 5. To make to prosper. IV. ii. 9. (3) To accumulate. IV. ii. 5.

殘 *ts'an* — To injure, to oppress. 殘害, V. i. Pt. i. 5. 凶殘, the cruel oppressor. V. i. Pt. ii. 8.

殛 *keih* chi — (1) To keep prisoner to death. II. i. 12: V. iv. 3. (2) To destroy. IV. i. 1. We have 罰殛 in V. ix. 21, and xviii. 23, = to punish and destroy, or perhaps only = to punish severely.

殪 *e* i — To destroy, to exterminate. V. ix. 4.

殲 *ts'een* chien — To destroy utterly. III. iv. 6: V. i. Pt. iii. 4.

THE 79TH RADICAL. 殳.

殳 *shoo* shu — The name of an officer about the court of Shun. II. i. 21.

殷 *yin* — (1) To determine exactly, to regulate; to be regulated. I. 4. 6: III. i. Pt. i. 48. (2) Affluent, abundant, = to be well with. V. xxvii. 8. (2) The name of the capital to which Pwan-kăng removed the govt. of the Shang dynasty. IV. vii. Pt. i. 1. From the time of this removal, the dynasty was called either Yin or Shang, and in Pt. V. the character occurs everywhere in this application. After the rise of the Chow dyn., however, in Bks. vii.—xxiv., we are to understand very often by the term, not the dynasty, as over the empire, but the imperial domain of it, or even, more restrictedly, that portion of the domain which was for a time possessed by Woo-kăng, the son of Show. On the phrase 有殷, the sovereign of Yin, the House of Yin, V. xii. 11: xviii. 13; *et al.*, see 有.

殺 *shă* sha — To kill, to put to death; the penalty of death. II. ii. 12: III. iv. 4: V. ix. 8, 10, 13, 15, 17; *et sæpe.* 殺戮, V. i. Pt. iii 3: xxvii. 3. 同于殺, to be classed with those who should be put to death. V. x. 16.

毅 *e* i — To be bold and resolute; boldness. II. iii. 3. 果毅, V. i. Pt. iii. 4.

THE 80TH RADICAL. 毋.

毋 *moo* mu — Do not. II. ii. 18.

母 *moo* mu — A mother. I. 12: III. iii. 3. 父母, parents. II. ii. 21: V. x. 6: xv. 3. The emperor is spoken of as the parent of the people, V. iv. 16; and Heaven and Earth as the parent of all things, V. i. Pt. i. 3.

每 *mei* — Every. III. iv. 3.

毒 *tuh* tu — Poison, venom. 荼毒, wormwood and poison. IV. iii. 3. Painful smart. 生毒, IV. vii. Pt. i. 12. Painful. IV. vii. Pt. i. 11. Painful or poisonous injury. V. i. Pt. ii. 4. To poison, V. i. Pt. iii. 3. In anger, in hate. IV. xi.

THE 81ST RADICAL. 比.

比 *pe* pi — (1) To compare. V. xxvii. 18. (2) 比干, a relative of the tyrant Show, put to death by him. V. iii. 9.

比 *pe* pi — 3d tone. (1) To be—keep—near to. IV. iv. 6: V. xii. 15: xiv. 21. So, 昵比, to cultivate intimacies with. V. i. Pt. ii. 3. 比德, = selfish confederations. V. iv. 10. To agree. IV. vii. Pt. iii. 8. So, vii. Pt. ii. 12. To join (act.). V. ii. 4.

毖 *pe* pi — (1) To attend carefully to. V. xii. 14: xiii. 16. (2) To admonish; admonitions. V. x. 2, 13, 17: xiii. 25: xxiv. 3. (3) To distress; to be distressed. V. vii. 8, 10.

毗 *pe* pi — To assist, help. V. viii. 4.

THE 82D RADICAL. 毛.

毛 *maou* mao — (1) The hair,—of animals. III. i. Pt. i. 44, 52. Applied also to the down and feathers of birds. I. 6, 7. (2) The name of a principality. The duke of Maou was a high minister in the time of king Ching of the Chow dynasty. V. xxii. 3 (3) A name. V. xxii. 11.

毨 *seen* hsien — To be sleek or glossy. 毛毨, I. 6.

氄 *jung* — To be downy. To be full of feathers. 氄毛, I. 7.

THE 83D RADICAL. 氏.

氏 *she* shih — It follows the names of principalities and dynasties, denoting the rulers or sovereigns of them, and is used as we sometimes use *the* in English,—*The* O'Donoghue, &c. 師氏 an officer of the Chow dynasty, the master of the imperial warders. V. ii. 2: xxii. 3. 尹氏 seems to = all the 尹, the heads of departments. V. vii. 6.

民 *min* — The people. *Passim.* It is used also as we use *people*, without reference to rank, = men generally; *E.g.* V. xxx. 2. Of phrases we have 黎民, all the people, or the black-haired people, I. 2: II. i. 18: ii. 2: V. xxx. 6, 7; *et al.*; 小民, the inferior people. V. xi. 2: xxv. 4; *et sæpe*; 下民, also meaning the inferior people. V. xxi. 4: xxv. 5: xxvi. 2; *et sæpe*; though sometimes 下 seems to be opposed simply to Heaven above, and the phrase = mankind, as in V. iv. 2: and in I. 11, and II. iv. 2, we may perhaps say that 下民 means the people living in low places; 生民, simply = the people, V. v. 10: xxiv. 13; 庶民, the masses or multitudes of the people, V. iv. 9—16, 26—30, *et sæpe*; so, 烝民, V. iii. 6; 萬民, the myriads of the people, and 兆民, the millions, III. iii. 5: IV. iv. 8: vii. Pt. ii. 12: V. xv. 12; *et sæpe*; 四民, the four classes of the people, scholars or officers, farmers, mechanics, and merchants, V. xx. 12; 俊民, men of eminent ability, heroic men, V. xiv. 6: xvi. 20; *et al.*; 獻民, wise men, V. xiii. 23: 先民 spoken with reference to the emperors of former dynasties, V. xii. 11, and in p. 10, 後民 is used with ref. to the last emperor of the Shang dynasty.

THE 85TH RADICAL. 水.

水 *shwuy* shui — Water, waters. II. iv. 8: III. i. Pt. ii. 8: IV. xi. 2; *et al.* One of the elements. V. iv. 5. One of the six magazines of nature. II. ii. 7. 洪水, the inundation. I. 11: II. iv. 1: V. iv. 3. So, 洚水, II. ii. 4. = with water. V. xxii. 2. Yu's work is described as 平水土, II. i. 17: V. xxvii. 8. 水 is added constantly to the names of streams, or forms part of those names, like *water* in our *Blackwater.*

永 *yung* — Long, long-continued, perpetual. IV. v. Pt. i. 6: V. vi. 10: xii. 20, 23, 24; *et sæpe.* Far-reaching. II. iii. 1; *et al.* 永念, think of what is long distant. V. xvi. 10. 永世, long ages. IV. viii. Pt. iii. 3; *et al.* 永世無斁, for ever and ever without end. V. viii. 1. To continue long. V. xviii. 7. To prolong, to perpetuate; prolongation. II. i. 24, (some read in 3d tone): IV. vii. Pt. i. 4: V. xviii. 28; *et al.* 日永, the day is at its longest. I. 5. = length of years. IV. ix. 3. Ever, for ever, perpetually. II. ii. 8, 17: IV. ii. 9; *et passim.*

求 *k'ew* ch'iu — To seek, to seek for. IV. iii. 4: iv. 5, 6; *et sæpe*, in the 4th and 5th Parts. To seek allegiance. IV. vi. 4. Obs. 作求, V. ix. 20.

汙 *woo* wu — Filthy. III. iv. 6.

汝 *joo* ju — You (nom. and obj.), your. *Passim.*

江 *keang* chiang — (1) The Këang, one of the two great rivers of China, now called the Yang-tsze. III. i. Pt i. 45, 47, 53: Pt. ii. 8, 9. A part of its course is called 北江, Pt. ii. 8; and a part 中江, Pt. ii. 9. (2) 三江, three rivers in Yang-chow, which do not seem to have been identified with certainty. III. i. Pt. i. 40. (3) 九江, the nine streams, generally supposed to be a name for the T'ung-t'ing lake. III. i. Pt. i. 48, 52: Pt. ii. 4, 9.

池 *ch'e* ch'ih — A pond, ponds. V. i. Pt. i. 5.

汩 *kw'uh* ku — To throw into disorder. V. iv. 3.

汭 *j'uy* jui — The north of a stream. Or perhaps, the place of junction between two streams. I. 12: III. i. Pt. i. 73, 82: Pt. ii. 7: iii. 3: V. xii. 3.

汶 *wăn* wên — The name of a stream, now lost in the great Canal. III. i. Pt. i. 27; Pt. ii. 10.

決 *keuĕ* chüeh — To open a passage for a stream. II. iv. 1.

沂 *e* i — The name of a river in Shan-tung and Keang-soo. III. i. Pt. i. 29; Pt. ii. 11.

沃 *yuh* yü — To irrigate, to enrich. IV. viii. Pt. i 7.

沇 *yen* — The name of a stream, subsequently known as the Tse (濟), and flowing into the Ho. III. i. Pt. ii. 10.

沈 *ch'in* ch'ên — To be sunk; to sink (act. and neuter). III. iv. 4: IV. vii. Pt. i. 12: xi. 1, 4. 沈酒, to be sunk in drunkenness. V. i. Pt. i. 5. 沈潛, the reserved and retiring. V. iv. 17.

沔 *mëen* mien — The name of a stream. III. i. Pt. i. 70.

沖 *ch'ung* — Young, small. The phrases 沖子, 沖人, a youth, the youth, are used to the emperors, and by them of themselves. IV. vii. Pt. iii. 7: V. vi. 18: vii. 1, 8: xii. 12: xiii. 11, 14, 16: xvi. 5.

沙 *sha* — 流沙, the moving sands, the pres. desert of Gobi. III. i. Pt. ii. 5. 23.

沮 *tseu* chü — (1) The name of a stream in Yen-chow, whose waters flowed into the marsh of Luy-hea. III. i. Pt i. 15. (2) The name of another stream in Yung-chow, an affluent of the Wei. III. i. Pt. i. 74; Pt. ii. 12.

沱 *t'o* — A branch of the Keang. There were one or more streams of this name in King-chow, III. i. Pt i. 49; and also in Lëang-chow. III. Pt. i. 53, 64; Pt. ii. 9.

河 *ho* — The Yellow River, though its channel in the latter part of its course was different from what it is now. III. i. Pt. i. 11, 20. 36, &c.; Pt. ii. 1, 7, 10, 12, 13; iii. 2: IV. vii. Pt. ii. 1: viii. Pt. iii. 1: V. i. Pt. ii. 1: xiii. 3. 九河, nine channels, forming a delta in the northern part of Yen-chow, by which a portion of the waters of the Ho were through Yu's skill discharged into the sea. III. i. Pt. i. 13. 西河, the western Ho, that portion of it which runs from north to south betweee Shen-se and Shan-se. III. i. Pt. i. 71, 82. 南河, the most southern part of the Ho. III. i. Pt. i. 53. 河圖, the river plan,—the scheme on a dragon's back, which is fabled to have emerged from the Ho, and supplied Fuh-he with the idea of his diagrams. V. xxii. 19.

治 *ch'e* chih — To manage, to regulate. III. i. Pt. i. 4: V. xii. 14: xv. 4: xvi. 23: xx. 1, 7, 9. = to punish. III. iv. 6. = the performance of works. V. ix. 1.

治 *che* chih — 3d tone. To be well regulated; where management and regulation take effect, —good government. II. ii. 8, 11, 13: iv. 4: IV. v. Pt. iii. 2: viii. Pt. ii. 5: V. iii. 9: xvii. 4: xx. 2: xxi. 3: xxiv. 13: xxv. 7.—There is some uncertainty in determining in several instances to what tone we shall assign this character.

沿 *yüen* yüan — To follow the course of a stream or shore. III. i. Pt. i. 45.

泆 *yih* yi — To be dissipated; dissipation. V. x. 11: xiv. 4, 9.

法 *fă* fa — (1) Laws. V. xxi. 7: xxvii. 3. 法度, II. ii. 6: IV. vii. Pt. i. 5. = imperial appointments, or way of procedure. V. vii. 13. To act according to the laws. V. xxvii. 18. (2) A plan,—as of a house. V. vii. 11.

泗 *sze* sz'i — The name of a stream, which is now one of the feeders of the great Canal, but which anciently flowed into the Hwae. III. i. Pt. i. 35, 36, 45: Pt. ii. 11.

波 *po* — (1) 滎波, the name of a marsh in Yu-chow. III. i. Pt. i. 56. (2) = waters. III. i. Pt. ii. 5.

泣 *k'eih* ch'i — To weep, to shed tears. II. ii. 21: iv. 8: V. vi. 18.

泥 *ne* ni — Miry. 塗泥, III. i. Pt. i. 42, 51.

泰 *t'ae* t'ai — A surname. 泰顛, a minister of king Wăn. V. xvi. 12.

泯 *min* — To be exhausted or destroyed. V. ix. 16. 泯泯, to become dark or blinded. V. xxvii. 4.

洋 *yang* — 洋洋, vast, = of vast significance. IV. iv. 8.

洗 *sëen* hsien — To clarify spirits. V. x. 6.

洚 *keang* ching — (1) Waters overflowing. 洚水, the flood of Yaou's time. II. ii. 14. (2) The name of a stream, an affluent of the main stream of the Ho. III. i. Pt. ii. 7.

洛 *lŏ* lo — (1) The name of a river in Ho-nan, one of the principal tributaries of the Ho. III. i. Pt. i. 53, 55, 60; Pt. ii. 7, 18; *et al.* (2) 洛 alone, and 洛邑, occur often as the name of the 'capital of the completed Chow,' to which the people and officers of a part of the imperial domain of Yin were removed. V. ix. 1: xii. 2, 3, 4: xiv. 1, 22, 25; *et al.*

津 *tsin* chin (1) A ford. IV. xi. 2. (2) 孟律, the name of a ford over the Ho, and of the country about it. III. i. Pt. iii. 7: V. i. Pt. i. 1: iii. 8.

洪 *hung* (1) Water overflowing. 洪水, Yaou's flood. I. 11: II. iv. 1. (2) Great. 洪範, the Great Plan. V. iv. 3. Greatly. V. xiv. 16: xviii. 5. 洪大, V. ix. 1 洪惟 = I greatly think. V. xiv. 16: xviii. 5; but ? i. Pt. iii. 4.

洮 *t'aou* t'ao To wash the hands. V. xxii. 2.

洲 *chow* chou • An island. 幽洲, II. i. 12.

洽 *hĕă* hsia To penetrate, to permeate. II. ii. 12 (foll. by 于). V. xxiv. 13.

流 *lew* liu (1) To flow along; to flow away. III. i. Pt. ii. 7, 10: V. iii. 8: xxiv. 9: xxx. 2. To make to flow. V. i. Pt. ii. 4. 流言, flowing words, a rumour. V. vi. 12: xvii. 1. (2) To banish. II. i. 12. Banishment generally. 五流, II. i. 11, 20. The most distant banishment. III. i. Pt. ii. 22. (3) 流沙, see 沙.

浚 *seun* hsün = to regulate. II. iii. 4.

浩 *haou* hao 浩浩, of vast extent, the appearance of Yaou's flood. I. 11: II. iv. 1.

浮 *fow* fou (1) To float. Foll. by 于, meaning generally to float along or on, but sometimes to float to. III. i. Pt. i. 20, 27, 36, 82; *et al.* 浮磬, sounding-stones, lying on the banks, or seeming to float near them. III. i. Pt. i. 35. (2) To exceed. V. i. Pt. ii. 5 (foll. by 于).

海 *hae* hai The sea, seas. It generally denotes the sea on the east of China. II. iv. 7: III. i. Pt. i. 21, 24, 28; Pt. ii. 1, 7, 8, 9, 10, 11; *et al.* 南海, the southern sea. III. i. Pt. ii. 6. 四海, II. i. 13: ii. 1, 4, 17: iv. 1, 8: III. i. Pt. ii. 14, 23: iv. 1: IV. iv. 4: viii. Pt. iii. 8: V. i. Pt. i. 11; Pt. iii. 3: iii. 8. See 四. Marine. III. 1. Pt. i. 26. 海隅 and 海表, see 隅 and 表.

浪 *lang* 滄浪, the name of the Han in a portion of its course. III. i. Pt. ii. 8.

涇 *king* ching A river of Yung-chow, which joins the Wei. III. i. Pt. i. 73; Pt. ii. 12.

涉 *shĕ* shê To cross over—go through—a stream. IV. vii. Pt. ii. 1: xi. 2: V. i. Pt. iii. 3: vii. 2. = to tread on. V. xxv. 2.

涯 *yae* yai The bank of a river. IV. xi. 2.

淄 *tsze* tzû A river in Ts'ing-chow. III. i. Pt. i. 23.

淑 *shuh* shu The good, virtuous. V. xxiv. 7.

淪 *lun* To sink. 淪喪, to sink in ruin. IV. xi. 2, 8.

淫 *yin* To go to excess,—with a bad meaning; excess, dissoluteness. II. ii. 6: IV. iii. 7: x. 2: V. i. Pt. ii. 3: x. 11: xii. 21: xiv. 5, 9: xv. 12: *et al.* The bad. IV. iii. 8. 淫朋, lawless confederacies. V. iv. 10 Compare 朋淫, II. iv. 8. 淫風, the fashion of dissipation. IV. iv. 7. Extraordinary. V. i. Pt. iii. 3. Excessively. V. xxvii. 3. Extensively and carelessly. V. xxix. 3.

淺 *ts'een* ch'ien 敷淺, the name of a plain. III. i. Pt. ii. 4.

淮 *hwae* huai A river which rises in Ho-nan, and afterwards joins the Ho, but which in Yu's time held its own course to the sea. III. i. Pt. i. 28, 29; *et al.* 淮夷, wild tribes about the Hwae. III. i. Pt. i. 35: V. xxix. 1.

深 *shin* shen Deep. IV. iii. 6.

淵 *yuen* yüan Deep. V. vii. 2: viii. 2. Deep waters. V. iii. 6. An abyss. IV. iii. 6.

清 *ts'ing* ch'ing To be pure. II. i. 23: V. xxvii. 21. With an unprejudiced mind. V. xxvii. 7. To cleanse. V. i. Pt. i. 11.

渠 *k'eu* ch'ü (1) Great, principal. III. iv. 6. (2) 渠搜, the name of a mountain. III. i. Pt. i. 83.

温 *wăn* wên To be mild; mildness, gentleness. II. i. 1, 24: iii. 3.

渭 *wei* A river, which rises in the pres. Kansuh, and flows into the Ho, near the end of its course from north to south. III. i. Pt. 70, 73, 82; Pt. ii. 12.

游 *yew* yu To float on or across. V. xvi. 16.

湎 *meen* mien To be sunk in wine or intemperance. 沈湎, V. i. Pt. i. 5. 湎于酒, V. x. 10, 15, 17.

湯 *shang* 湯湯, the appearance of a flood. I. 11.

湯 *t'ang* — Commonly spoken of as 成湯, T'ang the Successful, the founder of the Shang dynasty. IV. ii. 1 : vi. 3 : V. i. Pt. ii. 4, 8 : viii. 2 : x. 9 ; *et al.*

源 *yuen* yüan — The source of a river. III. i. Pt. ii. 14.

準 *chun* — 準, 準人, and 準夫, in V. xix. 1, 2, 7, 16, 19, are names for the officers or guardians of the laws.

溢 *yih* yi — To overflow, to flow out. III. i. Pt. ii. 10.

滄 *ts'ang* — 滄浪, see 浪.

滅 *mëë* mieh — To extinguish, extinguishing ; to be extinguished. III. iii. 1 : IV. iii. 3 : V. i. Pt. ii. 3 : x. ii. xvi. 10 : xxiv. 10. 殄滅, IV. vii. Pt. ii. 16. 撲滅, IV. vii. Pt. i. 12. 滅亡, extinction and ruin. III. iii. 7.

滋 *tsze* tzû — To be abundant. V. i. Pt. iii. 4. Abundantly. V. xvi. 20.

滌 *teih* ti — To clear. III. i. Pt. ii. 14.

滎 *jung* — 滎波 and 滎, the name of a marsh. III. i. Pt. i. 56 ; Pt. ii. 10.

滔 *t'aou* t'ao — To insult, = to assail. Always in the phrase 滔天. I. 10, 11 : II. iv. 1.

滿 *mwan* man — = pride, the fulness of one's-self. II. ii. 21. 自滿, to be full of one's-self. II. ii. 14 ; IV. ii. 8.

漂 *p'eaou* p'iao — To float. 流漂, to float away. IV. iii. 8.

漆 *ts'eih* ch'i — (1) Varnish. III. i. Pt. i. 19, 60. Varnished. V. xxii. 18. (2) The name of a stream, a tributary of the Wei. III. i. Pt. i. 74 : Pt. ii. 12.

漢 *han* — A large stream, flowing into the Këang. III. i. Pt. i. 47, 53 ; Pt. ii. 8.

漳 *chang* — A stream, flowing from east to west, and in Yu's time joining the Ho in the pres. dis. of Fow-shing. 衡漳, III. i. Pt. i. 6.

漸 *tseen* chien — To advance by degrees ; more and more. III. i. Pt. i. 33 : V. xxii. 4.

漸 *tseen* chien — 1st tone. To permeate ; to be affected. III. i. Pt. ii. 23 : V. xxvii. 4.

漾 *yang* — The name of the Han in the early part of its course. III. i. Pt. ii. 8.

潛 *ts'ëen* ch'ien — (1) To dive,—to lie hid. 沈潛, the reserved and retiring. V. iv. 17. (2) The name of streams flowing from the Han and rejoining it again. III. i. Pt. i. 53, 64, 70.

澗 *këen* chien — An affluent of the Ho. III. i. Pt. i. 55 ; Pt. ii. 13 : V. xiii. 3.

潤 *jun* — To soak. V. iv. 5. 澤潤, to exert an enriching influence on. V. xxiv. 13.

澤 *tsih* tsê — (1) A marsh. We have 震澤, III. i. Pt. i. 41 ; and 菏澤, p. 52. To become a marsh. III. i. Pt. ii. 8. To be formed into a marsh. Pt. i. 14. 九澤, the marshes of the nine provinces, Pt. ii. 14. (2) = favours, bounties. V. xiv. 8. 資澤, xxviii. 13. 潤澤, see above.

澧 *le* li — The name probably of a stream, flowing into the Këang. III. i. Pt. ii. 9.

澨 *she* shih — 三澨, probably three dykes on the Han. III. i. Pt. ii. 8.

澮 *kwae* kuai — A field ditch or channel. II. iv. 1.

濟 *tse* chi — 2d tone. (1) 濟濟, numerous. II. ii. 20. (2) The name of a stream. ? flows now into the sea as the 小清. III. i. Pt. i. 20, 27 ; Pt. ii. 10.

濟 *tse* chi — 3d tone. (1) To cross over a stream. IV. vii. Pt. ii. 6 : viii. Pt. i. 6 : V. vii. 2 : xvi. 16. (2) To help. V. iii. 8 : xvii. 6 : xxii. 7. (3) To be successful. III. iv. 7 : V. xxi. 12.

濬 *seun* hsün — (1) Deep, profound,—spoken of Shun. II. i. 1. (2) To deepen the channel of a river. II. i. 10 : iv. 1.

濮 *puh* pu — Name of the country of a wild tribe, in the present Hoo-pih, one of those which assisted king Woo against the tyrant Show. V. ii. 3.

濰 *wei* — A river of Ts'ing-chow. III. i. Pt. i. 23.

濱 *pin* — The shore of the sea, or bank of a river. III. i. Pt. i. 24, 35.

瀍 *ch'en* ch'an — The name of a stream, an affluent of the Lŏ. III. i. Pt. i. 55 ; Pt. ii. 13 : V. xiii. 3.

灃 *fung* — The name of a river, an affluent of the Wei. III. i. Pt. i. 75 ; Pt. ii. 12.

灉 *yung* — The name of a river in Yen-chow. III. i. Pt. i. 15.

THE 86TH RADICAL. 火.

火 *ho* — (1) Fire, II. iv. 4 : III. iv. 6 : IV. vii. Pt. i. 8, 12 : V. xiii. 9. One of the five elements. V. iv. 5. One of the six magazines of nature. II. ii. 7. (2) The name of a star. I. 5.

灼 *chŏ* cho — (1) To burn or blaze. V. xiii. 9. To shine forth. V. xxvii. 10. Clearly. V. xix. 6, 16.

災 *tsae* — (1) Calamities, judgments. IV. iii. 3: iv. 2: vi. 5: vii. Pt. ii. 7: xi. 4, 8: V. i. Pt. i. 4. = punishment. IV. xi. 6. 作災, to inflict suffering. IV. vii. Pt. i. 14. 自災, to cause suffering one's-self. IV. vii. Pt. i. 12. (2) Offences by mishap. II. i. 11: V. ix. 8.

炎 *yen* — To blaze; to blaze over. V. iv. 5: III. iv. 6.

炙 *chih* — To roast. 焚炙, V. i. Pt. i. 5.

炭 *t'an* — Charcoal. 塗炭. IV. ii. 2.

烈 *lëĕ* lieh — (1) Violent, fierce,—spoken of natural phenomena. II. i. 2: III. iv. 6 (烈于, fiercer than). = energy. V. xxv. 6. (2) Merit, achievement; merit-achieving, meritorious. IV. iv. 1: v. Pt. ii. 6: vii. Pt. i. 3: viii. Pt. iii. 10: V. viii. 4: xiii. 14, 22, 24: xix. 22: xxiv. 5. Observe 前烈, V. iii. 5, and 先烈, xxvi. 3.

烝 *ching* chêng — (1) All, the multitudes of. 烝民, II. iv. 1: IV. vi. 9: V. iii. 6. (2) To advance, make progress. V. xviii. 16. Under this meaning comes. 烝烝, denoting probably *gradually*. I. 12. (3) Name of the winter sacrifice in the temple of ancestors. V. xiii. 29. (4) Name of a wild tribe subject to the House of Chow. V. xix. 11. But the meaning is doubtful.

焉 *yen* — A final particle, used at the end of sentences to round them. It only occurs four times in the Shoo. V. ii. 7, 8: vi. 4: xxx. 6.

焚 *fun* fên — To burn; to be burned. V. i. Pt. i. 5: III. iv. 6.

無 *woo* wu — Not, do not, to be without. *Passim.* 無 is the opposite of 有, both in its personal and impersonal forms, = not to have, to be without; and there is—was—not, there will not be, there not being. Obs. 有無, II. iv. 1, and 有罪無罪, V. i. Pt. i. 7. Its imperative usage, in the sense of 毋, is very frequent. Observe also 無大, 無小, however great, however small. II. ii. 11.

然 *jen* jan — So. It only occurs twice. IV. vii. Pt. ii. 10: V. xxx. 4.

熙 *he* hsi — (1) To be bright,—intelligent. II. ii. 6. (2) To be fully discharged. I. 8: II. i. 17, 27: iv. 11. (3) To enlarge, to consolidate. V. xviii. 21.

煢 *k'ëung* ch'iung — The friendless. V. iv. 12.

照 *chëaou* chiao — To shine. V. i. Pt. i. 5.

煩 *fan* — To be burdensome, full of trouble. IV. viii. Pt. ii. 11: V. xx. 16.

熊 *heung* hsiung — (1) A bear, bears. III i. Pt. 1. 79: V. ii. 9. 熊羆之士, soldiers brave as bears and grisly bears. V. xxiii. 5. (2) The name of an officer about the court of Shun. II. i. 22. (3) 熊耳, the name of a mountain at which Yu began his survey of the Lŏ. III. i. Pt. ii. 2, 13.

熟 *shuh* shu — To be ripe. V. vi. 16. To be fruitful. V. vi. 19.

燄 *yen* — 燄燄, fire slowly and gradually spreading, the first beginnings of a fire. V. xiii. 9.

燎 *lëaou* liao — To burn, to blaze. IV. vii. Pt. i. 12.

燕 *yen* — Easy, unoccupied. 用燕, for pleasure and idleness' sake. V. x. 11.

營 *ying* — To build. IV. v. Pt. i. 9. Plans for building. V. xii. 2, (經營), 4.

燠 *yuh* yü — To be warm. V. iv. 32, 34.

燮 *sëĕ* hsieh — To harmonize. 燮和. V. xxii. 24. 燮理, V. xx. 5. = in a state of harmony. V. iv. 17.

THE 87TH RADICAL. 爪.

爭 *tsăng* tsêng — To contest. II. ii. 14.

爰 *yüen* yüan — (1) A particle at the beginning of sentences and clauses, = on this, and so. IV. vi. 3: viii. Pt. i. 4: V. xv. 5, 6: xxvii 3. (2) It follows the verb, like 于, carrying it on to its object. IV. vii. Pt. iii. 1: V. xxii. 11. After the noun, as a verb itself, = to be seen in, to consist in. V. iv. 5. Obs. 既爰, and thereupon, IV. vii. Pt. i. 2.

爲 *wei* — *Passim.* (1) To be, to be in the place of; sometimes, to make to be. III. iii. 5: IV. iv. 5: V. iii. 6: xi. 5; *et sæpe.* 以爲, to consider to be. IV. ii. 1; but more frequently 以爲 = to take to be, to undertake, to employ. V. ii. 6: vi. 4, 16: xvii. 1. In. V. iv. 16, 以爲 = and so becomes. (2) To become. III. i. Pt.

書經

ii. 7—10. (3) To do, to act, to make. II. iv. 4 (*n. b.*): IV. v. Pt. iii. 8: V. i. Pt. ii. 8: v. 9: vi. 15: xi. 4; *et al.* 有爲, to have conduct, administrative power. V. iv. 11, 13. 秉爲, to hold fast and do, = practice. V. xiv. 4. 百爲, all the ways of good action in govt. V. xviii. 7. 爲幻, the practice of deceiving tricks. V. xv. 14. 爲善, the practice of good. V. xvii. 4.

爲 *wei* — 3d tone. To act on behalf of; in relation to. IV. vi. 7: V. vi. 2: xi. 8.

爵 *tsëŏ* chio — Dignities, degrees of nobility. IV. v. Pt. ii. 5: V. iii. 10.

THE 88TH RADICAL. 父.

父 *foo* fu — A father, fathers. I. 12: IV. vii. Pt. i. 14; Pt. ii. 18, 14: V. vii. 11: ix. 16: xxv. 1. 父母, parents, parent. II. ii. 21: V. x. 6: xiii. 13: xv. 8. Spoken of the emperor. V. iv. 16. Spoken of Heaven and Earth. V. i. Pt. i. 3. 父母弟, paternal and maternal relatives. V. ii. 6. 伯父, senior uncle, uncles. V. xxiii. 6: xxvii. 13. So, 父 alone. xxviii. 1, 2, 3, 4. 師父 = Grand-tutor. IV. xi. 1, 3, 4: V. xxiv. 2, 5, 12. ? ought 父 here to be in the 2d tone.

父 *foo* fu — 2d tone. An honourable designation, — minister or officer. We have 圻父, 宏父, and 農父, the three great ministers at the court of a prince of the empire. V. x. 13.

THE 89TH RADICAL. 爻.

爽 *shwang* shuang — (1) To enlighten. IV. ii. 3: V. vii. 13. 爽惟, to think clearly. V. ix. 20, 21. (2) Light. 昧爽, between the dark and light, in the early dawn. IV. v. Pt. i. 5: V. ii. 1: iii. 9. (3) = to lose, to forfeit. IV. vii. Pt. ii. 12. Errors. V. xiii. 12.

爾 *urh* — (1) You, your. *Passim.* (2) An adverb, = our *ly*. 式爾, purposely; 適爾, accidentally. V. ix. 8; *et al.*

THE 90TH RADICAL. 爿.

牆 *ts'eang* ch'iang — A wall, walls. III. iii. 6: V. xx. 16: xxix. 4 (垣牆).

THE 91ST RADICAL. 片.

牖 *yew* yu — A window. 牖間 = between the window and the door. V. xxii. 15.

THE 92D RADICAL. 牙.

牙 *ya* — 君牙, the minister of Instruction under king Muh. V. xxv. 1, 7.

THE 93D RADICAL. 牛.

牛 *new* niu — A bull, oxen. V. iii. 2: x. 6: xii. 5: xiii. 29: xxix. 3. 4.

牝 *p'in* — Female. 牝鷄, a hen. V. ii. 5.

牡 *mow* mou — The male of animals. = a victim. IV. iii. 4.

牧 *muh* mu — (1) A pastor or shepherd. Applied to the governors of provinces. II. i. 7, 16: V. xx. 3, 13. They are called 天牧, the shepherds of Heaven. V. xxvii. 12. The same is the application probably of 牧, 牧夫 and 牧人, in V. xix. 2, 7, 12, 13, 16, 19, 21. (2) To learn to live by pasturage. III. i. Pt. i. 26. (3) 牧野, the wilderness of Muh, the place, in the pres. Ho-nan, not far from the capital of Show, where the struggle between him and king Woo was determined. V. ii. 1: iii. 9.

物 *wuh* wu — (1) Things, articles. III. i. Pt. 26: V. v. 3, 6, 8; *et al.* 土物, productions of the ground. V. x. 5. 方物, productions of difft. regions, V. v. 2. 天物, creatures of Heaven. V. iii. 6. 萬物, all things. V. i. Pt. i. 3. = relics. V. viii. 1. = matters. V. xxiv. 5. (2) 敦物, the name of a mountain. III. i. Pt. i. 76.

牲 *shăng* shêng — An animal used for sacrifice,—a victim, victims. IV. xi. 6 (犧牷牲): V. i. Pt. i. 6 (犧牲): xii. 5.

牷 *ts'euen* ch'üan — A complete victim, without blemish. IV. xi. 6.

特 *t'ih* t'ê — A single ox or victim. II. i. 8.

牽 *k'ëen* ch'ien — To lead forward. V. x. 6.

海上絲綢之路文獻集成　科技與文化編

to the nobles. II. i. 8. Gem-adorned. II. i. 5: xxii. 2, 15, 17, 24. 玉食 = the revenues of the empire. V. iv. 19, 19.

王 *wang* — *Passim.* (1) The title of the sovereigns of China, during the Hea, Shang, and Chow dynasties, = king, kings. Often used as an adjective,—royal, imperial. 王人, members of the royal house. V. xvi. 9. 先王, the former king or kings. *Passim.* 三王, the three kings, meaning king Wăn, his father, and grandfather. V. vi. 10. In V. v. 12, it means—to possess the throne. (2) To acknowledge the imperial sovereignty,—spoken of the feudal princes coming to court. II. ii. 6. (3) 王屋, the name of a mountain. III. i. Pt. ii. 1.—— In Pt. V. 文王 and 武王 are very common. We have also 成王, x. 9, 10; 王秀, king Ke, iii. 5: vi. 4: xv. 8; and 太王, in the same passages. The character hardly occurs in the 3d tone, which we find so often in Mencius. Perhaps there may be two or three instances of it in the Shoo.

玕 *kan* — 琅玕, the name of a precious stone III. i. Pt. i. 81.

玩 *wan* — To play or trifle with. V. v. 6.

珍 *chin* chên — As an adj. = fine, rare. V. v. 8.

珠 *choo* chu — Pearls. III. i. Pt. i. 35.

珪 *kwei* kuei — Some kind of gem-stones fashioned, used by the duke of Chow in worshipping his ancestors. V. vi. 4, 8.

班 *pan* — (1) To distribute, = to return. II. i. 7. (2) = to withdraw and retire. II. ii. 21

球 *kĕw* ch'iu — A sounding stone. IV. ii. 9. 天球, V. xxii. 19. The gem-stone suitable for the manufacture of sounding stones. III. i. Pt. i. 81.

琅 *lang* — 琅玕, see 玕.

理 *le* li — To regulate. 燮理, V. xx. 5.

琨 *kwăn* kuen — Some kind of precious stone, III. i. Pt. i. 44.

琬 *yuen* yüan — A rounded mace. V. xxii. 19.

琰 *yen* — A pointed mace. V. xxii. 19.

琳 *lin* — Some kind of precious stone. III. i. Pt. i. 81.

琴 *k'in* ch'in — A lute. 琴瑟, II. iv. 9.

瑁 *maou* mao — A sceptre-cover,—an instrument of gem, used by the emperor to test the different sceptres of the princes. V. xxii. 23, 26.

瑕 *hëa* hsia — To blame. V. ix. 22.

瑞 *suy* jui — 五瑞, the five gem tokens of investiture, conferred on the princes. II. i. 7.

瑟 *sih* shê — A lute. See 琴.

瑤 *yaou* yao — A kind of precious stone. III. i. Pt. i. 44.

璆 *k'ëw* ch'iu — Probably gem-stones for the manufacture of sounding stones. III. i. Pt. i. 69.

璋 *chang* — A half mace, carried by ministers. V. xxii. 27.

璣 *ke* chi — (1) Pearls not quite round. III. i. Pt. i. 52. (2) 璿璣 some kind of astronomical instrument used by Shun. II. i. 5. But the meaning is doubtful.

璧 *peih* pi — An instrument of gem, with a square base, and convex above,—one of the tokens of investiture. Used by the duke of Chow in worship. V. vi. 4, 8. 弘璧, V. xxii. 19.

璿 *seuen* hsün — Revolving. 璿璣, see 璣.

THE 99TH RADICAL. 甘.

甘 *kan* — (1) Sweet; sweetness. V. iv. 5. To esteem to be sweet, to delight in. III. iii. 6. (2) The place of a great battle in ancient times,—in the present Shen-se. III. ii. 1. (3) A surname. IV. viii. Pt. iii. 1: V. xvi. 7.

THE 100TH RADICAL. 生.

生 *shăng* shêng — (1) To produce. IV. ii. 2: vii. Pt. i. 12. To beget, or to give birth to. V. xii. 19. To be born; to live; life. II. i. 28: iv. 6: IV. v. Pt. ii. 2: vi. 9: vii. Pt. i. 2; Pt. ii. 7: x. 5: V. xv. 7: xxi. 14. Life,—all living things. II. ii. 12. 二生, two living animals. II. i. 8. 厚生 = abundant means of sustentation. II. ii. 7. 生民 simply = the people. V. v. 10: xxiv. 13. Elsewhere 生民 = pro-

duced the people. 生魄 means the 16th day of the moon, V. iii. 4 : ix. 1 ; and 生明 the third day, iii. 2. 生生 = to foster life, IV. vii. Pt. iii. 10. 12 ; and = to increase and multiply. Pt. ii. 12, 17. 蒼生 = grassy shores. II. iv. 7. (2) In a name. 宜生, V. xvi. 12.

THE 101st RADICAL. 用.

用 *yung* — *Passim.* The frequency of this character is a peculiarity of the Shoo. The same also may be said of the way in which it is employed,—corresponding very much to the usages of 以. (1) To use, to employ. II. i. 8 : iii. 6 : IV. ii. 5, 8 : V. xix. 1, 4, 20, 23, 24 ; *et sæpe.* = to obey. III. ii. 5. 用罪, 用德, the criminal and the well-doer. IV. vii. Pt. i. 16. 用 alone is explained as meaning the use of virtue in V. xii. 22. Useful. V. v. 8, 利用, gainful for use, = conveniences of life. II. ii. 7. 器用, vessels for use. V. v. 2. 績用 = work that should have been done. I. 11. (2) Like 以, it is very often used like the sign of the infinitive,—to, so as to ; or may be resolved by thereby, and thereby. IV. vii. Pt. ii. 4, 9 : Pt. iii. 4, 5, 6 : viii. Pt. i. 8 : x. 2 : V. i. Pt. ii. 8 : iii. 7 : xxiii. 3, 5, 6 ; *et sæpe.* Connected with this is a usage, where 用 seems to merge in the verb that follows it. *E. g.* III. iv. 2 : IV. xi. 1, 7 : V. iv. 9 : xvi. 9, 22, 23. (3) = therefore. II. iv. 8 ; *et al.* Obs. 兹用 = 所以, II. ii. 12. Thereon. V. xix. 1. —There are not a few passages, however, where it is hardly possible to construe the character. *E. g.* IV. xi. 6 : V. vii. 2 : xiii. 13 : xix. 13.

THE 102d RADICAL. 田.

田 *t'een* t'ien — (1) Cultivable fields. II. ii. 21 : III. i. Pt. i. 8, 18, 25 ; *et sæpe.* 田畝, fields and acres. IV. vii. Pt. i. 11. 田功, the work of agriculture. V. xi. 4. (2) To hunt,—used for 畋. V. xv. 11, 12.

由 *yew* yu — (1) From,—to proceed from ; to use, to follow. IV. vii. Pt. i. 5 : Pt. iii. 7 : V. iii. 8 : vii. 13 : viii. 4 (率由) : ix. 5, 16, 17, 19. = by ; with, V. xxii. 22, 23 : xxiv. 10. It is sometimes difficult to construe 由. *E. g.* V. ix. 19 (see 繹), 24 : xxvii. 13. (2) Sprouts from a felled tree. IV. vii. Pt. i. 4.

甲 *këă* chia — (1) A coat of mail. 甲冑 = armour of defence. IV. viii. Pt. ii. 4 : V. xxix. 2. (2) The first of the calendaric stem-characters. 甲子, V. ii. 1 : iii. 8 : xii. 6 : xxii. 2 ; 甲寅, xii. 8 : 甲戌, xxix. 5. = to begin. V. xviii. 5. (3) 太甲, the grandson of T'ang, V. xvi. 7. The name also of the 5th Book, Pt. IV. 祖甲, a later emperor of the dynasty of Shang. V. xvi. 6, 16.

申 *shin* shên — (1) To repeat ; again, further. I. 5, 7 : II. iv. 2 : V. xiv. 22 : xvi. 11 : xxiv. 7. (2) The 9th of the calendaric branch-characters. V. xii. 2 : xxiv. 1.

男 *nan* — A part of the 2d domain of Yü, and the fourth of the domains of the Chow dynasty. III. i. Pt. ii. 19 : V. ix. 1 : x. 10, 13 : xii. 6 : xxiii. 4.

甸 *teen* tien — (1) To rule, to govern. V. xiv. 6 : xix. 5. (2) The imperial domain of Yu, and the third of the domains of the Chow dynasty. III. i. Pt. ii. 18 : IV. iv. 1 : V. iii. 3 : ix. i : x. 10, 13 ; *et al.*

畀 *pe* pi — To give. V. iv. 3 : xviii. 7, 19 : xxiii. 5. (付畀). = to be for, to favour. V. xiv. 3, 4, 24 : xviii. 28.

畋 *t'een* t'ien — (1) To hunt. III. iii. 1 : IV. iv. 7. (2) To cultivate. V. xviii. 21, 28.

畎 *k'euen* ch'üan — (1) Small channels in a field, for the purpose of irrigation. II. iv. 1. (2) A valley, where a stream runs. III. i. Pt. i. 26, 35.

畏 *wei* — (1) To fear ; to stand in awe, be apprehensive ; to be feared, what should be feared, dreadfulness, awfulness. II. ii. 17 : iii. 2 : IV. i. 2 : vii. Pt. i. 11 : V. i. Pt. ii. 9 : iii. 5 : vii. 9 : ix. 6 : xiv. 4 ; *et al.* Both the active and passive meanings appear in 畏畏, IV. xi. 5, and 弗畏 入畏, V. xx. 19. In V. xxvi. 13, 畏 alone = to fear to do evil. (2) To awe. II. iii. 7. = to put to death. V. xxvii. 13.

畔 *p'wan* pan — To violate. III. iv. 4.

留 *lew* liu — To continue, to remain. V. xxii. 4. The more correct form of the character is 畱.

畜 *ch'uh* ch'u — To keep, to feed. Applied to animals. V. v. 8. To nourish. Applied to the people. IV. vii. Pt. ii. 9, 13.

畝 *mow* mu — The Chinese acre,—acres, = fields. IV. vii. Pt. i. 11 (田畝) : V. vii. 11.

畢 *peih* pi — (1) All. V. i. Pt. ii. 1 : v. 2. Entirely. V. ix. 9 : xxiii. 3. (2) To be finished, to be completed. V. vii. 10. (3) A name for the 5th gate of the imperial palace. V. xxii. 21. (4) The name of a principality. V. xxii. 3 : xxiii. 1 : xxiv. 1.

書經

略 *lëŏ* lio (1) To be defined, marked out. III. i. Pt. i. 22. (2) A course, ways of proceeding, V. iii. 6.

番 *po* 番番, the appearance of being old. V. xxx. 5.

畫 *hwă* hua To define, as in the line out. V. xxiv. 6. Figured. V. xxii. 17. Thus *figured* is better here than *painted* as in the translation.

異 *e* i Different. V. v. 5: xxii. 27. Strange V. v. 8. What is strange or extraordinary. V. xxiv. 8.

當 *tang* Ought. V. x. 12. Ought to be considered as belonging to,—to be in, to rest on. IV. iii. 8.

疆 *këang* chiang A limit, boundaries. V. i. Pt. iii. 8: xi. 4: xxiv. 7. 疆土, territory. V. vii. 15: xi. 6. In the phrase 無疆, unlimited, boundless. IV. v. Pt. ii. 2: V. vii. 11: xii. 9: xvi. 17, 18: xxvii. 22.

疇 *ch'ow* ch'ou (1) Who? whom? I. 9, 10: II. i. 21, 22: III. iii. 9: IV. viii, Pt. i. 11. (2) A class, divisions. II. i. 17: V. iv. 3. (3) A mate, mates. V. x. 13.

THE 103D RADICAL. 疋.

疑 *e* i To doubt, hesitate; doubtful; doubts. II. ii. 6, 12: V. iv. 4, 20, 25: xx. 16. = as being doubtful. V. xxvii. 17, 18.

THE 104TH RADICAL. 疒.

疵 *ts'ze* tz'ŭ A malady, an evil.—Used of moral and social evils. V. vii. 4: xxvii. 16.

疾 *tseih* chi (1) Sickness, affliction, IV. viii. Pt. i. 8: V. iv. 40: vi. 1, 5: vii. 10; *et sæpe.* 罪疾, affliction—punishment—for crime. IV. vii. Pt. ii. 11, 12. 疾狠 = to be frenzied. V. x. 11. (2) To dislike, to hate. V. xxi. 1: xxx. 7 (冒疾). (3) Sedulously. V. xii. 10, 20.

病 *ping* Severe sickness. V. xxii. 4. Distress. xxvii. 20.

痛 *foo* fu To make ill or sick. V. i. Pt. iii. 8.

瘝 *kwan* kuan (1) To distress. V. ix. 6 (恫瘝乃身 = the pain distresses you), 17: 瘝在, the distressers (= oppressors) are in office. V. xii. 10. (2) To make void, render useless. V. xxvi. 8.

瘠 *tseih* chi To be thin, = to be starving, IV. xi. 7.

瘳 *ch'ow* ch'ou To cure, to be cured. IV. vii. Pt. ii. 6: viii. Pt. i. 8: V. vi. 11.

癉 *tan* 3d tone. To afflict, to distress,—make it evil with. V. xxiv. 7.

THE 105TH RADICAL. 癶.

癸 *kwei* kuei The last of the calendaric stem-characters. II. iv. 8. 癸巳, V. iii. 1. 癸亥, V. iii. 8. 癸酉, V. xxii. 13.

登 *tăng* têng To ascend. V. iii. 8. To raise, to make to ascend. I. 9. = to call up. IV. vii. Pt. ii. 1. = to complete, to sustain. V. i. Pt. iii. 4.

發 *fă* fa (1) To send forth. V. xxvi. 4: xxvi. 2 (發施). = to distribute. V. iii. 8. 發出, to manifest. IV. xi. 3. = to begin. IV. vii. Pt. i. 12. (2) The name of king Woo. V. i. Pt. i. 6: ii. 7.

THE 106TH RADICAL. 白.

白 *pih* pai White. V. ii. 1. Whitish,—applied to the colour of soil. III. i. Pt. i. 7, 24.

百 *pih* pai A hundred, I. i. 8: V. xxvii. 1, 18; *et al.* 百夫長, captains of hundreds. V. ii. 3. It is used as a round number, denoting all of the class who are spoken of or spoken to. We have 百官, II. ii. 19; *et al.*; 百工, V. ix. 1; *et al.*; 百宗工, V. x. 13; 百獸, II. i. 24; *et al.*; 百僚, V. xiv. 20; *et al.*; 百志, II. ii. 6; 百穀, V. iv. 36, 37; *et al.*; 百揆, II. i. 2; *et al.*; 百執事, IV. vii. Pt. iii. 8; *et al.*; 百祥, 百殃, IV. iv. 8; 百辟, V. xiii. 12; 百君子, V. xii. 24; 百度, V. v. 5; 百爲, V. xviii. 7; 百司, V. xix. 8, 9; 百尹, V. xxii. 3. 百姓, see 姓.

皆 *keae* chieh All. At the commencement of clauses, summing up what has preceded. IV. i. 3: vii. 8: V. xxii. 23: xxiii. 1, 2, 7: xxvii. 13.

皇 *hwang* huang (1) Great. We have 皇祖, the great ancestor, III. iii. 4; 皇帝, the great ruler, the emperor, xxvii. 5, 6; 皇上帝, the great supreme ruler, or God. IV. iii. 2; and 皇天, great Heaven, II. ii. 4: IV. iv. 2: v. Pt. ii. 2: viii. Pt. iii. 10: V. i. Pt. i. 5: iii. 6 (皇天后土): viii. 2: xi. 6: xii. 9 (皇天上帝), 14: xvi. 7: xvii. 4: xxiii. 2, 5. Greatly. V. xv. 17. So, in 張皇, xxiii. 3; or we may take 皇

there as a *hiphil* verb. (2) The sovereign; royal. V. iv. 4, 9, 10, 11, 15. (3) *I. q.* 遑, leisure, to be at leisure. V. xv. 18: xxx. 5.

THE 107TH RADICAL. 皮.

皮 *p'e* p'i — The skins of animals—with the hair on. III. i. Pt. i. 5, 69, 83.

THE 108TH RADICAL. 皿.

盈 *ying* — To be full. 貫盈, V. i. Pt. i. 9.

益 *yih* yi — (1) To advantage; that which is advantageous; advantage. II. ii. 21: V. i. Pt. ii. 5: v. 8. (2) The baron Yih was forester to Shun, and assistant to Yu in his labours caused by the inundation. II. i. 22: ii. 4, 6, 21: V. iv. 1.

盛 *sh'ing* shêng — To be complete. v. 4.

盛 *shing* shêng — = vesselful. V. i. Pt. i. 6.

盜 *taou* tao — Robbers. V. i. Pt. i. 6.

盟 *măng* mêng — A covenant. 詛盟, V. xxvii. 4.

盡 *tsin* chin — To exert to the utmost. V. ix. 6. To call forth all—. V. v. 4. 自盡, to develop one's-self fully. IV. vi. 11. Entirely, all. IV. vii. Pt. i. 2: V. xi. 16, 19: ix. 13: x. 14.

監 *këen* chien — To survey, to inspect. Spoken of Heaven or God. IV. v. Pt. iii. 2; ix. 3: V. xxvii. 4. To survey, inspect; to look to, —look to and study, either as a pattern or a warning. IV. v. Pt. iii. 3: vi. 8: viii. Pt. iii. 6: xi. 7: V. ix. 21; x. 12 (*n. b.*); xii. 17: xv. 19: xvi. 17, 19: xxvii. 12, 22. ? to afford an example to. V. xiii. 20. Overseers. V. xii. 3: xviii. 24. 監, in V. xii. 3, is marked in the 1st tone, but wrongly. In the sense there, the character is said to be in the 3d tone, and also in x. 12, and the meaning to be to take warning generally. The other applications of the character may be read either in the 1st tone or the third. See the 經韻集字析解.

盤 *pwan* pan — (1) To pursue pleasure, III. iii. 1: V. xxx. 2. (2) To go to excess. V. xv. 11 (foll. by 于). (3) A name. IV. viii. Pt. iii. 1: V. xvi. 7. 盤庚, one of the emperors of the Shang dynasty. IV. vii.

盥 *kwan* kuan — To wash the hands. V. xxii. 27.

盧 *loo* lu — (1) Black. V. xxviii. 4. (2) The name of one of the wild tribes confederate with Chow against Shang. V. ii. 3: xix. 11.

THE 109TH RADICAL. 目.

目 *muh* mu — The eyes. V. v. 5: xxvi. 7 (*n. b.*). 四目, the eyes of the four quarters,—the eyes of all. II. i. 15. Ministers are called 股肱耳目. IV. iv. 4.

直 *chih* — To be straight. V. iv. 5, 14. Upright, straightforward; the upright; straightforwardness. II. i. 23, 24: iii. 3: iv. 2: IV. iv. 7: V. iv. 17.

眇 *meaou* miao — 眇眇, insignificant. V. xxii. 25.

相 *seang* hsiang — Mutually, one another, II. i. 24: IV. ii. 6: xi. 2: V. i. Pt. ii. 3: xxiii. 2, 7. Sometimes the action of the verb following 相 passes not on parties indicated in the text, but on the speaker, or the person or parties in his mind. III. iv. 3: IV. vii. Pt. ii. 15.

相 *sëang* hsiang — 3d tone. (1) To aid, assist. IV. x. 2: V. i. Pt. i. 7: iii. 8: iv. 2; *et sæpe*. (2) To lead. IV. vii. Pt. iii. 9. (3) Used for premier. IV. viii. Pt. i. 4: V. xxii. 13; for ministers generally. IV. v. Pt. i. 3: V. x. 9; for attendants. V. xxii. 2. (4) To look at; to inspect, examine. IV. vii. Pt. i. 12: V. xii. 2, 11: xiii. 2, 4, 23; *et al.*

省 *sing* hsing — To examine. II. iv. 11: IV. v. Pt. i. 7: viii. Pt. ii. 4: V. iv. 35: vii. 10: x. 7 (觀省, see and examine yourselves).

眚 *săng* shêng — Inadvertent offences. II. i. 11: V. ix. 8.

眩 *heuen* hsüan — To be made confused or dizzy. 瞑眩, see 瞑.

睦 *muh* mu — To be harmonious. I. 2: V. xxviii. 26. To cultivate harmony with. V. xvii. 6.

衆 *chung* — All. It is found often,—before nouns, after pronouns, and alone: in the same way as our *all*. III. iv. 2, 7; *et sæpe*. It often = multitudes, the people. II. ii. 3, 12, 17; *et al.*

眷 *keuen* chüan — To regard, look on,—favourably. We can in the Shoo always construe it as an adverb,—fondly, graciously, II. ii. 4: IV. v. Pt. ii. 2: vi. 3: V. viii. 2: xii. 10.

睿 *yui* jui — To be perspicacious,—penetrating to what is minute; perspicaciousness. V. iv. 6.

瞍 *sow* sou — 瞽瞍, the name of Shun's father. II. ii. 21.

瞑 *meen* mien — 瞑眩, used of medicine distressing the patient, but salutary. IV. viii. Pt. i. 8.

瞿 *k'eu* ch'ü — A kind of lance. V. xxii. 21.

瞽 *koo* ku — (1) Blind. A blind man. II. i. 12. Blind musicians. III. iv. 4. (2) 瞽瞍, see 瞍.

THE 110TH RADICAL. 矛.

矛 *maou* mao — A spear, spears, V. ii. 4: xxix. 2.

矜 *king* ching — (1) To pity, compassionate. V. i. Pt. i. 11 (foll. by 于): xiv. 20, 24: xviii 28 (畀矜): xxvii. 5 (哀矜). (2) To attend earnestly or jealously to. V. v. 9. (3) To be elated with one's self, boastful. II. ii. 14: IV. viii. Pt. ii. 7: V. xxiv. 10.

THE 111TH RADICAL. 矢.

矢 *she* shih — (1) Arrows. V. xxii. 19: xxviii. 4: xxi. x. 2. (2) *I. q.* 誓, solemn, of the nature of protestation. IV. vii. Pt. i. 1.

矣 *e* i — A final particle. It does not occur often in the Shoo, and only after an adjective or a short clause, where its force is both decisive and exclamatory, V. ii. 1: xix. 1, 2, 16, 18, 21. See Index III. to Mencius on the character.

知 *che* chih — To know. *Passim.* Observe 夫知, V. xii. 10, which can hardly be construed.

矧 *shin* shên — Still more; how much more! The nature of the sentence sometimes makes the meaning—still less; how much less, I. ii. 21: IV. ii. 14: vii. Pt. i. 12: V. vii. 9, 13, 15; *et sæpe.* The 矧 is often followed by 曰. IV. vii. Pt. i. 3: V. vii. 1: ix. 21 *(n. b.)*: xii. 12: xiv. 9.

短 *twan* tuan — Short. IV. vii. Pt. i. 12: V. iv. 40. The shortest. I. 7.

矯 *këaou* chiao — To pretend, to falsify. 矯誣, IV. ii. 3. = dissemblers. V. xxvii. 2.

THE 112TH RADICAL. 石.

石 *shih* — (1) Stones. III. i. Pt. i. 26 (怪石): IV. iv. 6. The stone,—a measure of weight. III. iii. 8. Used for the sounding or musical stone. II. i. 24: iv. 4. (2) 碣石, the rocks of Këë, a famous landmark in the time of Yu, somewhere on the north of the present gulf of Pih-chih-le. II. i. Pt. i. 11; Pt. ii. 1. (3) 積石, the name of a mountain in the west, where Yu began his survey of the Ho. III. i. Pt. i. 82; Pt. ii. 7.

砥 *che* chih — Whetstones. III. i. Pt. i. 52.

砮 *noo* nu — Stones for arrowheads. III. i. Pt. i. 52, 69.

喦 *gan* an — To be precipitous. 民喦, the perilousness (= changeableness) of the people. V. xii. 13.

碣 *k'ëë* chieh — 碣石, see 石.

磬 *k'ing* ch'ing — Sounding stones, or stones for their manufacture. III. i. Pt. i. 60, 69.

礪 *le* li — Grindstones. III. i. Pt. i. 52: IV. viii. Pt. i. 6. To grind, to sharpen. V. xxix. 2.

THE 113TH RADICAL. 示.

示 *she* shih — To show, to intimate to. V. iii. 2.

祁 *k'e* ch'i — Great, greatly. V. xv. 5.

社 *shay* shê — The spirit-tablets or altars of the spirits of the land. III. ii. 5. 社稷 = the spirits of the land and of the grain. IV. v. Pt. i. 2. 郊社 = the sacrifices to Heaven and Earth. V. i. Pt. iii. 3 (?). To sacrifice to the spirits of the land. V. xii. 5.

祀 *sze* szû — (1) To sacrifice. V. iii. 3: xiii. 5. A sacrifice, sacrifices. III. iii. 8: IV. viii. Pt. ii. 11 (祭祀): ix. 1: V. i. Pt. i. 6: *et sæpe.* 元祀, see 元. (2) A year. 祀 was the term specially used in this meaning in the Shang dynasty. IV. iv. 1: v. Pt. ii. 1: viii. Pt. i. 1: V. iv. 1: xviii. 24.

祈 *k'e* ch'i — To pray,—to and for. V. xii. 20. 24.

祖 *tsoo* tsu — A grandfather. III. iii. 4, 8: IV. v. Pt. i. 3, 7: Pt. ii. 6: V. xiii. 22, 24, *et al.* But in other passages, we must adopt the general meaning of ancestor. *E. g.* IV. vii. Pt. ii. 18, 14: viii. Pt. iii. 10: xi. 1. This appears especially where we find 高祖, as in IV. vii. Pt. iii. 6, and sometimes 先祖, as in V. xiv. 6. Sometimes by 祖 we must understand

—the spirit-tablets of ancestors, as in III. ii. 5: IV. iv. 1 (sing. and 祖 = grandfather,). So, 文祖, the temple or spirit-tablet of Yaou's ancestor; and 藝祖, II. i. 4, 8, 14. 祖考 = the spirits of ancestors, II. iv. 3: but = grandfather and father, in V. x. 5: xxv. 1, 3, 7. = grand-uncle. V. xxviii. 2. (2) 祖甲 and 祖乙 were emperors of the Shang dynasty. V. xv. 6, 16: xvi. 7. (3) 祖己 and 祖伊 were ministers of the Shang dynasty. IV. ix. 2: x. 1, 6.

祇 *k'e* ch'i The spirit or spirits of the earth. Always found in connection with 神. IV. iii. 3: v. Pt. i. 2 (上下神祇): xi. 6: V. i. Pt. i. 6 (上帝, 神祇, 社稷, &c.).

祗 *che* chih To reverence, to respect; to attend reverently, or respectfully to. II. iv. 8: III. i. Pt. ii. 17: V. iv. 8 *(n. b.)*: v. Pt. i. 3: V. x. 10: xxvi. 2: xxvi. 9. Reverent. V. xvii. 1. 祗祗, to revere the reverend. V. ix. 4. 民祗, the awfulness of the people. V. xiv. 9. Used adverbially before other verbs,—reverently, respectfully. II. ii. 1, 21: IV. iv. 1: V. i. Pt. i. 10: iii. 6: vi. 7: viii. 3; *et sæpe.*

祝 *chuh* chu A prayer. 册祝, V. vi. 5. To write a prayer. 祝册, V. xiii. 29. = with a curse. V. i. Pt. iii. 3.

祝 *chow* chou 詛祝, to curse, to utter maledictions. V. xv. 15.

神 *shin* shên Spirits, spiritual beings. They may be the spirits of the departed, and spirits generally, real or imaginary. II. ii. 19, 21: IV. viii. Pt. ii. 11: V. iii. 8. So, 鬼神, II. ii. 18: III. iv. 2: IV. v. Pt. iii. 1: V. vi. 6. In this last instance we have also 神鬼, but with no difference of meaning. 神人, spirits and men. II. i. 24: V. viii. 3: xx. 9. 神主, lord of the spirits, is a designation of the emperor. IV. vi. 3. Specifically, 神 denotes the spirit or spirits of heaven,—in the phrase 神祇. IV. iii. 3: V. Pt. i. 2: xi. 6: V. i. Pt. i. 6. See the note on this last passage, where it appears that 上帝 is to be discriminated from 神. He is so discriminated in II. i. 6, from 羣神, the host or herd of the spirits. 神 also is to be discriminated from 天, in V. xviii. 19. Spiritual. 神明, spiritual intelligences. Spiritual, = mysterious, or active and invisible. II. ii. 4. 神宗 = the temple or shrine of Shun. II. ii. 19. 神后, ancestors now in the spirit world. IV. vii. Pt. ii. 10; but 神后 is a denomination of 上帝, in IV. iii. 4.

祠 *tsze* tzŭ To sacrifice. IV. iv. 1.

祭 *tse* chi To sacrifice. V. xxii. 26, 28. Sacrifices, a sacrifice. V. i. Pt. ii. 5: iii. 9. 祭祀, IV. viii. Pt. ii. 11. 烝祭, V. xiii. 29.

祥 *ts'eang* ch'iang To be felicitous, happiness. IV. iv. 8: vi. 5: vii. Pt. ii. 14. 休祥, V. i. Pt. ii. 5. To make felicitous; made a blessing. V. xxvii. 14, 22.

祼 *kwan* kuan To pour out a libation. V. xiii. 29.

祿 *luh* lu Revenues, emolument. IV. vi. 9 *(n. b.)*: V. xvi. 5: xx. 18: xxiv. 9. 天祿, Heaven-conferred revenues, = the possession of the empire. II. ii. 17.

禁 *kin* chin Prohibitions. V. xx. 11.

禋 *yin* The name of a sacrifice, offered with purity and reverence. II. i. 6: V. xiii. 25, 26, 29.

禍 *ho* huo Calamity. = causers of calamity. IV. iii. 3. To send down calamities on, —to punish. IV. vii. Pt. i. 12.

福 *fuh* fu Happiness; happinesses. IV. vii. Pt. i. 14: V. xxi. 14: xxiv 13. 五福, the five happinesses. V. iv. 4, 39. = favours. 作福, to confer—be the source of—favours. V. iv. 11, 13, 18, 19. To bless. IV. iii. 3.

禮 *le* li Ceremonies; rules of propriety; propriety. II. i. 8: IV. ii. 8, 9: v. Pt. ii. 3: viii. Pt. ii. 11: V. vi. 18: viii. 1: xiii. 5, 15, 19: xvi. 8: xx. 9: xxiv. 9. 五禮, religious, mourning, festive, military, and State ceremonies. So perhaps 五禮, in II. iii. 6. 三禮, three religious ceremonies, the worships of the spirits of Heaven, of Earth, and of men. II. i. 23.

THE 114TH RADICAL. 禸.

禹 *yu* yü Baron Yu, afterwards the great Yu, the remover of the deluge, and founder of the Hea dynasty. II. i. 17: ii. 1, 5, 7, 9, 10, 14, 18, 20, 21; *et sæpe.*

禽 *k'in* ch'in Birds. V. v. 8. Includes *beasts*, and = hunting. III. iii. 6.

THE 115TH RADICAL. 禾.

禾 *ho* huo. Grain growing. V. vi. 16, 9.

私 *sze* szû. Private, selfish. 私昵, favourites. IV. v. Pt. ii. 5. 私家, to be selfish, follow one's own prejudices. V. xxvi. 21. Selfish aims. V. xx. 15. To favour partially. IV. vi. 4.

秉 *ping*. To grasp, to hold. V. ii. 1 : vi. 1 : xxii. 23, 27. 秉德, to maintain virtue. V. xvi. 9, 14 ; the same phrase, in xviii. 23, = to consider it a virtue. 秉爲 = the decided conduct. V. xiv. 4. 秉哲, to maintain wisdom. V. x. 9.

秋 *ts'ëw* ch'iu. The autumn ; in the autumn. I. 6 (仲秋): III. iv. 4 : V. vi. 16. = the harvest. IV. vii. Pt. i. 9.

秕 *pe* pi. Empty or blasted grain. IV. ii. 4.

秩 *chih*. To arrange in order. I. 4. 5, 6. 秩宗, arranger of the ancestral temple, = minister of Religion. II. i. 23. In order, in an orderly manner. II. i. 8 : V. xiii. 5, 15. = social distinctions. II. iii. 6.

秬 *k'eu* ch'ü. Black millet. Spirits distilled from black millet. V. xiii. 25 : xxviii. 4.

秸 *këë* chieh. The stalk of grain without the ears. III. i. Pt. ii. 18.

移 *e* i. To remove. V. xiv. 21. To be altered. V. xxiv. 3.

稟 *pin*. To receive orders. IV. viii. Pt. i. 1

種 *chung*. To sow. II. ii. 10.

種 *chung*. 2d tone. Seed. V. xxvii. 8. = descendants. IV. vii. Pt. ii. 16.

稱 *ch'ing* ch'êng. (1) To lift up. V. ii. 4 : xxviii. 1. To undertake. IV. i. 1. To employ. V. xiii. 5, 15 : xvi. 9 : xx. 20. To display. V. xiii. 14. (2) To proclaim. V. xvi. 15.

稷 *tseih* chi. (1) A kind of millet, said to be the best of all grains. IV. vii. Pt. i. 11. 黍稷, V. x. 6 : xxi. 3. (2) The tablets or altars of the spirits presiding over the grain or agriculture of a country. 社稷, IV. v. Pt. i. 2. (3) 后稷, prince Tseih, the high ancestor of the House of Chow, was Shun's minister of agriculture. II. i. 17, 18 : iv. 1 : V. xxvii. 8.

稼 *këa* chia. To sow. 稼穡, to sow and reap, sowing and reaping. V. iv. 5 : xv. 2, 3, 7.

稽 *k'e* ch'i. 2d tone. To bow the head to the ground. Always in the formulas 拜稽首 and 拜手稽首. II. i. 17, 21, 22, 23 : ii. 18 : iv. 11 : IV. v. Pt. ii. 3, 4 : viii. Pt. ii. 13 ; Pt. iii. 11 : V. xii. 8, 20 : xiii. 1, 4, 22, 25 : xix. 1, 2 : xxiii. 1, 2.

稽 *k'e* ch'i. 1st tone. (1) To examine, to study. I. 1 : II. i. 1 : ii. 1, 3 (foll. by 于), 16 : iii. 1 : IV. vii. Pt. ii. 6 : V. iv. 4, 20 : viii. 1 : xii. 11, 12 : xx. 8 : xxvii. 17. 卜稽, to examine by divination. IV. vii. Pt. i. 2. (2) To manage, to cultivate. 稽田, V. xi. 4. (3) To agree with. V. x. 11.

穀 *kuh* ku. (1) Grain. V. xxvii. 8. One of the six magazines of nature. II. ii. 7. 百穀, all kinds of grain. II. i. 18 ; V. iv. 36, 37. (2) To be good. V. iv. 13.

穆 *muh* mu. Reverent ; profound and grave. V. x. 2. 穆穆, to be profoundly reverent ; to be submissive. II. i. 2 : V. xiii. 16 : xviii. 27 ; xxvii. 10. Reverently. V. vi. 2, 18.

積 *tseih* chi. (1) To accumulate. IV. viii. Pt. iii. 4. Accumulated. IV. vii. Pt. i. 10. (2) 積石, the name of a mountain. See 石.

穡 *sih* shê. To reap, gather in the harvest. IV. vii. Pt. i. 9. 稼穡, see 稼. 穡事, the business of harvesting. 穡夫, a reaper, a husbandman. V. vii. 14.

穢 *wei*. Filthiness. = wickedness. IV. vii. Pt. ii. 8. Rank odour. V. i. Pt. ii. 3.

穫 *hwŏ* huo. To cut down the grain, to reap. V. vi. 18 : vii. 11.

THE 116TH RADICAL. 穴.

空 *k'ung*. 司空, the minister of Works. II. i. 17 : V. ii. 2 : iv. 7 : xi. 2 : xix. 10 : xx. 12.

穽 *tsing* ching. *I. q.* 阱. Pitfalls. V. xxix. 3.

窮 *k'eung* ch'iung. (1) To exhaust. 無窮, inexhaustible, unending. V. viii. 1 : xxiv. 14. To be exhausted, brought to distress. In the phrase 困窮. II. ii. 17 : V. xvii. 5. The same phrase = the distressed and poor. II. ii. 3 : IV. v. Pt. ii. 5. (2) The name of a principality, held by E, the rebellious opponent of T'ae-k'ang. III. iii. 2.

竄 *ts'wan* ts'uan — To drive to and confine in till death. II. i. 12.

竊 *ts'ëĕ* ch'ieh — To steal, V. xxix. 4. 攘竊, IV. xi. 6. 草竊, to commit highway robbery. IV. xi. 2.

THE 117TH RADICAL. 立.

立 *leih* li — To stand erect; to be set up. V. vi. 4: xv. 7: xxii. 21. = firmness. II. iii. 3. = firmly. V. i. Pt. ii. 9. To establish, to set up, to appoint. IV. iv. 4: viii. Pt. i. 4: V. ii. 4: iv. 20, 24: xix. 6, 7, 12, 16, 19, 20, 23: xx. 3, 5.

竝 *ping* — *I. q.* 並. Together, unitedly. II. iv. 1: IV. iii. 3: V. xix. 15: xxix. 1. = even. IV. v. Pt. ii. 5.

章 *chang* — (1) To polish, to decorate. I. 2 (平章). To be decorated. V. iv. 36. 五章 the five decorations,—emblematic figures on robes. III. iii. 6. (2) = statutes. institutes. V. xvii. 7.

童 *t'ung* — Boys, youths. IV. iv. 7. 童孫, young grandsons. V. xxvii. 13.

端 *twan* tuan — Correct, = favourable. V. xxiii. 5.

競 *king* ching — To be strong. V. xix. 2.

THE 118TH RADICAL. 竹.

竹 *chuh* chu — The bamboo. 竹矢, bamboo arrows. V. xxii. 19.

笥 *sze* szŭ — A sort of chest for containing rice or clothes. IV. viii. Pt. ii. 4.

笙 *săng* shêng — A kind of organ; the calabash-organ. II. iv. 9.

筍 *yun* yün — A kind of soft, flexible bamboo, that can be made into mats. V. xxii. 18.

答 *tă* ta — To respond to,—in conduct. V. xiii. 4, 24: xxii. 24. To respond in acknowledgment of favours. V. ii. 6. In response. V. xxii. 27, 28: xxiii. 1. In reply. V. xxii. 25.

筮 *she* shih — To divine by means of the stalks of the milfoil. II. ii. 18: V. iv. 20, 24. 31: xvi. 9.

箘 *k'wăn* k'uên — A kind of bamboo, good for making arrows. III. i. Pt. i. 52.

箕 *ke* chi — The name of a principality, held by the relative of the tyrant Show, known as 箕子, the viscount of Ke. V. iii. 9: iv. 1, 2, 3.

管 *kwan* kuan — (1) A musical instrument,—a kind of flute. II. iv. 9. (2) The name of the appanage of the third son of king Wăn, known as 管叔. V. vi. 12: xvii. 1.

箴 *chin* chên — To remonstrate,—a kind of moral puncturing. IV. vii. Pt. i. 12. 箴言, in p. 5, words of remonstrance.

節 *tseĕ* chieh — (1) Tallies, tokens of authority. In the phrase 小臣諸節, V. ix. 17. (2) To regulate. V. xii. 15.

範 *fan* — A plan, a pattern. 洪範, V. iv. 8.

築 *chuh* chu — (1) To pound,—as in raising mud walls, = to build. = who was a builder. IV. viii. Pt. i. 3. To raise entrenchments. V. xxix. 5. (2) To raise and set up. V. xvi. 19.

篚 *fei* — Baskets,—round, of bamboo, in which articles of tribute were brought to court. III. i. Pt. i. 19, 26, 35, 44, 52, 60. To basket,—to bring in baskets. V. iii. 7.

篠 *seaou* hsiao — A species of slender bamboo. III. i. Pt. i. 42, 44.

篤 *tuh* tu — (1) Sincere, earnest. V. xxvi. 1. = the sincere. IV. vii. Pt. iii. 6. To follow sincerely. IV. xiii. 13, 27. Sincerely, earnestly. V. xiii. 7: xvi. 21. (2) To consolidate. V. iii. 5: V. xiii. 24. To be great. V. iii. 5: xiii. 17.

篾 *meĕ* mieh — Bamboo splints, fit for basket-work, made into mats. V. xxii. 15.

簣 *kwei* kuei — A basket. 一簣 = one basketful. V. v. 9.

簜 *t'ang* — A species of large bamboo. III. i. Pt. i. 42, 44.

簡 *këen* chien — (1) To be hasty, impetuous. II. i. 24. (2) To be easy, indifferent to many things. II. iii. 3. A generous ease. II. ii. 12. (3) To choose, select. IV. vii. Pt. iii. 9: V. xiv. 20: xviii. 8, 19, 28. (4) To examine, to mark. IV. iii. 8: V. xxi. 18: xxvii. 15 (簡孚), 17: xxviii. 4. In xxvii. 15, we have also 五刑不簡, where 不簡 = do not meet the case.

簫 *seaou* hsiao — An instrument of music. But 簫韶 is used for the music of Shun. II. iv. 9.

簬 *loo* lu — A species of bamboo, good for making arrows. III. i. Pt. i. 52.

籥 *yŏ* yo — *I. q.* 鑰. A kind of key for opening the case where oracular responses were kept. V. vi. 9. The meaning is doubtful.

籩 *pëen* pien — 豆籩, sacrificial vessels. V. iii. 3.

籲 *yu* yü — To cry to, to appeal to. IV. vii. Pt. i. 1; Pt. ii. 5. Foll. by Heaven or God. V. i. Pt. ii. 3: xii. 10: xix. 2. The character should be without the 竹.

THE 119TH RADICAL. 米.

米 *me* mi — Rice hulled. III. i. Pt. ii. 18. 粉米, the emblematic flour of rice represented on the lower robe of the emperor. II. iv. 4.

粉 *fun* fên — To grind, or reduce to powder or flour. 粉米,—see above.

粒 *leih* li — Grains of rice. = to have rice (or grain generally) to eat. II. iv. 1.

粟 *suh* hsü — Rice in the husk. III. i. Pt. ii. 18: IV. ii. 4. In V. iii. 8, we may understand perhaps grain generally.

粢 *tsze* tzŭ — A kind of millet. 粢盛, V. i. Pt. i. 6.

精 *tsing* ching — To be discriminating. II. ii. 15. i, 6.

糗 *ch'ow* ch'ou — Parched grain. V. xxix. 5.

糧 *lëang* liang — Provisions of grain. V. xxix. 5.

糵 *nëë* nieh — Malt. IV. viii. Pt. iii. 8.

THE 120TH RADICAL. 系.

糾 *këw* chiu — To raise up, to exhibit. V. xxvi. 3.

紀 *ke* chi — (1) To arrange different threads of silk. Hence to arrange, to regulate generally; and what is arranged, or arranges. 紀綱, rules and laws. III. iii. 7. 人紀, human distinctions or relationships. IV. iv. 5. 天紀, the heavenly arrangers or arrangements. III. iv. 4. These are called the five arrangers, 五紀, in V. iv. 4, 8. To be chronicled. V. xxv. 1. 紀其敘 = to take in hand—arrange—its *disturbed* order or *broken* line. V. vii. 4. (2) A period of twelve years. V. xxiv. 3.

紊 *wăn* wên — To be confused, confusion. IV. vii. Pt. i. 9.

納 *nă* na — To receive,—to take in. IV. viii. Pt. ii. 9: II. iv. 4, 6, 7. 納言 = the minister of Communication. II. i. 25. To present,—to send in, as in payment of tribute. III. i. Pt. i. 52: Pt. ii. 18: IV. viii. Pt. i. 5. To place or put. V. vi. 11. To be appointed. II. i. 2. 納日 = the setting sun. I. 6.

純 *shun* ch'un — (1) To be decided; determinate; determinately. V. xvi. 9, 14: xviii. 7. (2) To enlarge; great. V. x. 6; xxviii. 2.

純 *shun* chun — 2d tone. A border,—as of a mat. V. xxii. 15—18.

紛 *fun* fên — Mixed. V. xxii. 18.

索 *sŏ* so — (1) A rope. = reins. III. iii. 5. (2) = ruin, dissolution. V. ii. 5.

累 *luy* lêi — To involve,—to go on to affect. V. v. 9.

細 *se* hsi — Small. V. v. 9: xxi. 10.

紵 *ch'oo* ch'u — A coarse kind of hemp, or the cloth made from it. III. i. Pt. i. 60.

紹 *shaou* shao — To connect, continue. IV. vii. Pt. i. 4: viii. Pt. iii. 11: V. ix. 5: xxvi. 3. 紹上帝 = to be the vicegerent of God. V. xii. 14. 紹天明, to bring in connection with the intelligence of Heaven. V. vii. 3. 會紹乃辟 = connecting *the all but broken line of* your sovereign. V. xxviii. 3.

組 *tsoo* tsu — 璣組, strings of pearls. III. i. Pt. i. 52.

終 *chung* — (1) The end; the result. Often in connection with 始. IV. ii. 9: iv. 4: v. Pt. iii. 2, 6: vi. 6: viii. Pt. iii. 1, 5: V. xvi. 2, 23: xvii. 5. = a successful issue, expecially in the phrase 有終. IV. iii. 9: V. Pt. i. 3; Pt. ii. 3: viii. Pt. i. 10: V. xxiv. 13. = retirement,—the resignation of Yaou. II. i. 4. = futurity. V. vi. 10. As an adverb,—eventually, finally, in the end. II. ii. 14: V. v. 9: xxi. 14. As a verb,—to end (neut. and act.), II. i. 17: V. iv. 39: xxv. 10. To make an end of. V. xii. 10. To finish. V. vii. 10, 14: xiii. 11: xiv. 2 (終于上帝, finished the work of God). 終允德. IV. v. Pt. i. 10, and 終

續 *suh* hsu — To connect, = to prolong. IV. vii. Pt. ii. 9.

纖 *seen* hsien — Fine chequered silks. III. i. Pt. i. 35, 60.

纘 *tswan* tsuan — To continue. IV, ii. 2: V. xxv. 3.

THE 121ST RADICAL. 缶.

缺 *k'eue* ch'üeh — To be deficient, wanting. V. xxv. 6.

THE 122D RADICAL. 网.

罔 *wang* — A negative adverb. It occurs nearly as often as 無 or 不 and its frequent use is characteristic of the Shoo. It is, as nearly as possible, synonymous with 無 in all its usages, = no, not; do not; to be without; and there is not, there was not, &c. Especially it is found before other negatives,—罔不, 罔非, &c., and before 所, 攸 and 或. We have, in IV. iv. 8, a 罔大罔小, corresponding to the 無大無小, which I have called attention to under 無.

罪 *tsuy* tsui — A crime, an offence. II. ii. 12, 20, 21: V. xxvii. 16, 18; *et sæpe*. 罪 alone, II. i. 12; 罪人, V. vi. 14; *et al.*; 有罪, II. iii. 6; *et al.*; and 用罪, IV. vii. Pt. i. 16; all = the criminal or criminals. 罪疾, the pain—punishment—of crime. To treat—deal with—as criminal. IV. iii. 4: vii. Pt. iii. 2: V. i. Pt. i. 5: ix. 16.

置 *che* chih — To place, to set. IV. viii. Pt. i. 4.

罰 *fă* fa — Punishment, generally. II. ii. 12: III. ii. 3: iv. 5: IV. i. 4: V. ix. 3, 8, 11, 13, 16, 21; *et sæpe*. Specifically, the punishment of fine. Thus it is used in V. xxvii. 18, 19, 20; and in p. 17, we have the phrase 五罰, the five fines. We meet often with 天罰 and 天之罰, the punishment appointed by Heaven. *E. g.* V. i. Pt. i. 10; Pt. iii. 3: ii. 6. 王罰, the punishment inflicted by kings. V. xiv. 2. To punish. IV. vii. Pt. ii. 12: V. xv. 18; *et al.*

罹 *le* li — (1) To be sorrowful; to suffer distress from. V. x. 11: IV. iii. 8. (2) To be involved. V. iv. 11.

羆 *pe* pi — (1) A large species of bear. III. i. Pt. i. 69. Used to describe and stimulate soldiers. V. ii. 9: xxiii. 5. (2) Name of an officer at the court of Shun. II. i. 22.

THE 123D RADICAL. 羊.

羊 *yang* — The sheep or goat. V. xii. 5.

羌 *keang* chiang — The name of a pastoral tribe in the north-west, confederate with Chow against Shang. V. ii. 3.

美 *mei* — Admirable, beautiful. To beautify, = to do good service to. IV. viii. Pt. ii. 10. 服美, to wear fine robes. V. xxiii. 10.

羑 *yew* yu — 羑若, to pursue the same course. V. xxiii. 2. But the meaning is uncertain.

羞 *sew* hsiu — (1) To feel ashamed; shame: IV. viii. Pt. ii. 4: V. iii. 8: xxiii. 6. (2) To nourish. IV. vii. Pt. ii. 10: V. x. 7. (3) To bring forward, to advance. This signification assumes various modifications, being here = to cultivate, and there = to employ. IV. vii. Pt. iii. 11: V. iv. 13: x. 7: xix. 5.

羣 *k'eun* ch'ün — A flock or herd; a company. It is used to denote all of a class. Alone it = companies. V. x. 14. 羣庶 = herds of creatures. V. x. 11. We have 羣后, II. i. 9: *et sæpe*; 羣牧, II. i. 7; 羣神, II. i. 6: 羣臣, IV. viii. Pt. i. 1; 羣弟, V. vi. 12; 羣叔, xvii. 1: 羣辟, xx. 1: 羣公, xxiii. 7: 羣僕, xxvi. 4; 羣言, xxx. 1.

義 *e* i — (1) To be righteous; righteous; righteousness, what is right. II iii. 3: IV. ii. 8: v. Pt. i. 9: ix. 3: V. i. Pt. i. 8: iii. 9: iv. 14: ix. 13, 17; *et al.* 不義惟王, deemed it not righteous to be king. V. xv. 6. Righteous men. V. ix. 15. 鴟義, owl-like ways. V. xxvii. 2. (2) 義和, the designation of prince Wăn. xxviii. 1, 3, 4.

羲 *he* hsi — The name of one of the families, which had the care of astronomy, &c., in Yaou's time, and subsequently. I. 3, 4, 5, 8: III. iv. 1, 4.

羹 *kăng* kêng — Soup. IV. viii. Pt. iii. 2.

THE 124TH RADICAL. 羽.

羽 *yu* yü — (1) Feathers. II. ii. 21: III. i. Pt. i. 44, 52. (2) The name of a mountain in the east, where Shun confined K'wăn. II. i. 12. It is queried whether this was the

職 *chih* (1) Office, the duties of office. III. iv. 1: V. xx. 13. (2) To preside over, to secure a certain effect. V. xxx. 6.

聽 *t'ing* To hear, to listen to. II. ii. 16, 20: iv. 1: V. i. Pt. i. 2; Pt. ii. 2, 7: iv. 6 (= hearing); *et sæpe*. Often the idea of obedience enters into the term. *E. g.* IV. iv. 1: V. ix. 24: xv. 15, 18. 聽罪, to acknowledge one's offences. IV. ix. 4. To be listened to. IV. ii. 4; *et al.* 高乃聽, think highly of what you have heard. V. ix. 23.

THE 129TH RADICAL. 聿.

聿 *yuh* yü Then, thereon. IV. iii. 4.

肄 *e* i To practise. 肄肄 = with earnest practice or submission. V. xxii. 5.

肅 *suh* su To be grave; to venerate. 祇肅, IV. v. P. i. 2. Gravity. V. iv. 6, 34. Gravely. V. viii. 3. So, probably, in the difficult phrase 肅將, V. i. Pt. i. 5: xiii. 21.

肆 *sze* szû (1) An introductory particle or conjunction. It most commonly = therefore. *E. g.* II. ii. 20: IV. iii. 4: v. Pt. i. 2: V. i. Pt. i. 6; Pt. iii. 4; *et sæpe*. Other meanings suit better, however, in many cases, as thereafter, thereon, in II. i. 6, 8; but, in IV. vii. Pt. iii. 4, 7; *et al.*; now, in V. xi. 7: xii. 20: xiii. 3; *et al.* It occurs twice in V. xi. 2, one of the instances being hardly explicable. In xiv. 20, 予惟率肆矜爾, 肆 is always read along with 率, but a new meaning must then be coined to suit the case. We should put a comma at 率, and read 肆 with 矜; but I believe the text to be corrupt. (2) To let go. 肆赦, II. i. 11. (3) To be at ease, to take heart. V. vii. 13. (4) To be reckless. V. i. Pt. iii. 3. (5) To set forth, to offer. 肆祀, V. ii. 6. (6) Greatly, V. xvi. 17, 19.

肇 *chaou* chao (1) To institute. II. i. 10. To lay the foundations of. V. iii. 5: x. 2. Obs. 肇位, to come to the throne, to begin a reign. III. iv. 1. Before other verbs, it = to begin. IV. iv. 5: V. ix. 4: ? xxviii. 8. = from the first, IV. ii. 4; at first, V. xiii. 5. (2) To be earnest or diligent. V. x. 6; ? xxviii. 3.

THE 130TH RADICAL. 肉.

肖 *heaou* hsiao To be like, to resemble. IV. viii. Pt. iii. 3.

肜 *yung* The name of a supplementary sacrifice, offered the day after the regular sacrifice. IV. ix. 1.—This meaning is erroneously introduced in p. 674, under the character 彤.

股 *koo* ku The thigh, the upper part of the leg. We find it always in connection with 肱. IV. viii. Pt. iii. 9: V. x. 6. The phrase is used metaphorically of ministers. II. iv. 4, 11: V. xxv. 3.

肩 *keen* chien The shoulders. = to employ, to sustain IV. vii. Pt. iii. 10. = to maintain, in p. 13.

肱 *kwang* kuang The upper arm. See 股.

肯 *kăng* kêng To be willing. V. vii. 11: xviii. 4.

育 *yuh* yü To nourish, to keep. V. v. 8. 遺育, to leave those who may be brought up. IV. vii. Pt. ii. 16. Here it = children.

胄 *chow* 胄子, sons. II. i. 24.—Of the same sound as this character, and hardly distinguishable from it in form, is 冑, a helmet, which is found in the phrase 甲冑, in IV. viii. Pt. ii. 4: V. xxix. 2. It belongs to the 13th Radical 冂, and the character should have been entered on p. 655.

背 *p'ei* To turn the back on, to disregard or disobey. IV. v. Pt. ii. 3.

胡 *hoo* hu (1) What. IV. v. Pt. iii. 8. (2) The name of a nephew of the duke of Chow, prince Chung of Ts'ae. V. xvii. 2, 8.

胤 *yiu* (1) To inherit. = heirs. IV. ix. 5. 胤子, heir-son. I. 9. To follow after. V. xiii. 2. (2) The name of a state. III. iv. 1: V. xxii. 19.

胥 *seu* hsü (1) Mutually, together. IV. vii. Pt. i. 2, 12, 14; Pt. ii. 3, 6, 15: V. vii. 13: xviii. 7: xxiii. 6: xxvii. 4, 20. 胥 is thus synonymous with 相, though its construction is in most cases more difficult. We find it used in the same way as 相, when one of the parties whose action is intended is not directly expressed:—as in IV. v. Pt. ii. 2: V. xi. 3: xv. 14. (2) Employés,—certain officers who are thus denominated. V. xviii. 25.

能 *năng* nêng To be able, can. It is used everywhere before verbs like our auxiliary. In one case we find the idiomatic use of 而 between it and the verb,—V. xxii. 25.

As an active verb,—to cultivate the ability of, to help. V. xvi. 3 : xxii. 8 : xxviii. 4. To be able to manage, *to can*. V. ix. 18 : xvi. 23. Ability. II. ii. 14 : IV. viii. Pt. ii. 7 : V. iv. 13 (obs. 有能). = men of ability. IV. viii. Pt. ii. 5 : V. iii. 9 : xx. 20.

脅 *heĕ* hsieh — To be pressed, forced. III. iv. 6. To force with. V. i. Pt. ii. 3.

脛 *hing* hsing — The leg-bone. V. i. Pt. iii. 8.

脞 *ts'o* — To cut up meat small. 叢脞 seems to mean a collection of things small and trifling, = vexatious. II. iv. 11.

腆 *t'ëen* t'ien — (1) To be prosperous. V. vii. 4. (2) To make strong,—spoken of spirits. V. x. 6. (3) To go to excess,—foll. by 于. x. 8. 11.

腎 *shin* shên — The kidneys. IV. vii. Pt. iii. 3 *(n. b.)*

腥 *sing* hsing — Rank odour. V. x. 11 : xxvii. 4.

腸 *ch'ang* — The bowels. IV. vii. Pt. iii. 3.

腹 *fuh* fu — The belly. IV. vii. Pt. iii. 3.

膂 *leu* lü — The back-bone. V. xxv. 3.

膚 *foo* fu — The skin. = shallow—skin-deep—speeches. IV. vii. Pt. i. 7. But the meaning here may be different, and = puncturing, irritating, speeches. Compare. Ana. XII. vi.

膺 *ying* — = to receive. V. iii. 5 : xxi. 14 : xxiv. 13.

THE 131ST RADICAL. 臣.

臣 *ch'in* ch'ên — A minister, the correlate of 君. *Passim*. We have 臣人, III. iv. 2 : V. xxi. 6 ; and 臣下, V. i. Pt. ii. 3, both denoting ministers. But 臣庶, II. ii. 11, = ministers and multitudes. Ministry, the duties of being minister. II. ii. 2. To act the part of ministers to,—to serve. V. iv. 21 *(n. b.)*, 22 : xviii. 24.——臣 is generally to be taken of the great ministers of a government ; when it is otherwise, this is indicated. 臣僕 is spoken of himself by a great minister, IV. xi. 8 ; but 僕臣, V. xxvi. 6 (comp. pp. 2, 4) is different. 小臣, V. ix. 17, 18, means petty officers, but in 予小臣, V. xii. 24, the phrase is merely used in the self-depreciating style of conversation. 臣妾, V. xxix. 4, = camp-followers, male and female. 虎臣, the master of the guards. V. xxii. 8. 表臣, ministers away from court. V. xix. 9.

臧 *tsang* — To be good, admirable. V. x. 5 : xxvi. 2. Good condition, = prosperity. IV. vii. Pt. i. 16. To approve, declare to be good. IV. ii. 3. 臧厥臧, to show approval of what is good, V. xxiv. 4.

臨 *lin* — To present one's-self to, and deal with, in the character of the sovereign. II. ii. 12 : III. iii. 5 ; V. xxii. 24. It is spoken of the sun, as seeing and visiting all with his light. 日之照臨, V. i. Pt. iii. 5.

THE 132D RADICAL. 自.

自 *tsze* tzŭ — (1) As a preposition, from,—used with reference to time, place, and person. *Passim*. = according as. II. iii. 7 : V. i. Pt. ii. 7 ; *et al.* (2) Self, of all persons,—myself, yourself, himself. Of one's-self. V. ix. 8 ; *et al.* The meaning sometimes approaches to—then, as *a matter of course*. *E. g.* V. x. 6, 7 : xxx. 2. Its most frequent use in this signification is as joined to verbs in a reflex sense. We have 自賢, to count one's-self possessed of talents and worth ; 自滿假 ; 自靖 ; 自絕 ; 自庸 ; 自臭 ; 自酒 ; 自鞠自苦, 自安, 自廣, 自底, 自覆, 自抑畏, 自度, 自疾, 自恤, 自聖, 自亂, (=治.)

臬 *neĕ* nieh — Laws V. ix. 11, 13. 克臬, to be able to observe the laws. V. xviii. 25.

臭 *ch'ow* ch'ou — A fetid odour. Used as a verb, = to make one's-self abominable, to ruin. IV. vii. Pt. ii. 6, 8.

皋 *kaou* kao. — 皋陶, Shun's minister of Crime. II. i. 17, 20 : ii. 10, 11, 12 : iii. 1, 2, 3, 8 : iv. 1, 8, 11. The dict. gives 臯, from 白, as the more correct form of the character.

THE 133D RADICAL. 至.

至 *che* chih — (1) To come, to arrive. V. xvi. 20. It is everywhere followed by 于, and 至于 = to come to, to reach to. See everywhere in the 'Tribute of Yu,' *et al.* Generally the point of departure is indicated ; but sometimes it is not, and has

to be gathered from the context. *E. g.* V. x. 8: xi. 3, 6: xv. 5: xviii. 7, 12, 23. (2) The most, perfect, entire,—that which has reached the utmost degree. II. ii. 21: V. xxi. 8. 底至, to push to the utmost extent. V. xxiii. 5.

致 *che* chih — To carry out fully. IV. i. 4: V. xiv. 2, 21, 24: xviii. 29. It is thus used for the most part with reference to the infliction of punishment. Before verbs it indicates the doing to the utmost what the verb intimates. IV. vii. Pt. i. 17: V. x. 6. 致辟 = to put to death. V. xvii. 1; but 致罰, V. xiv. 5, = extreme punishment. 德之致, the things produced by virtue. V. v. 8. In I. 5, 致 is understood to mean the extreme limit of the sun's shadow.

臺 *t'ae* t'ai — Towers. V. i. Pt. i. 5. 鹿臺, the Stag tower, a structure of the tyrant Show. V. iii. 9.

臻 *tsin* chin — To arrive, to come on. V. xxii. 4.

THE 134TH RADICAL. 臼.

與 *yu* yü — (1) With, along with. II. ii. 19: IV. v. Pt. iii. 2: V. viii. 1. *And* sometimes answers better in translation than *with*. V. vi. 8, 16, 17. The with is sometimes nearly = for. II. ii. 17: IV. vi. 1. For, on behalf of. IV. iii. 4. (2) To give to. V. ix. 16. So, in IV. vii. Pt. ii. 12, which is peculiar. To grant, or concede to. III. iv. 6: IV. iv. 5 *(n. b.)* (3) Than, forming a comparative with 寧. II. ii. 12. (4) ? = 而. IV. v. Pt. i. 9.

與 *yu* yü — 3d tone. To be present at, to share in. IV. vii. Pt. i. 14.

與 *yu* yü — 1st tone. 伯與, an officer at the court of Shun. II. i. 21.

興 *hing* hsing — To arise, rise or get up,—with varied application, = to get better, to rise from bed, &c. IV. xi. 2, 8: V. iv. 3: xxii. 7, 25: xxvi. 1: xxix. 1. In xxvii. 4, the meaning of 興 is no more than *thereon*. To rise, = to flourish. IV. v. Pt. iii. 2: V. xiv. 25. To make to rise or prosper. V. vii. 9. Obs. 有廢有興, V. xxi. 5. To give rise to, to originate. II. ii. 17: iv. 11: V. xi. 4.

舉 *keu* chü — To lift up, = to advance to office. II. iv. 7: V. xx. 20.

舊 *kew* chiû — What is old; old. IV. ii. 2, 6: V. Pt. iii. 9: vii. Pt. i. 5, 13: V. xvii. 6: xxv. 3, 7. 舊人 = men of old families, in IV. vii. Pt. i. 7; but = the old ministers, in V. viii. 10. 舊 alone = the old course, in V. iii. 8. It is often abverbial, = of old, at first. III. iv. 6: IV. viii. Pt. ii. 1: xi. 5, 8: V. viii. 3: xv. 5, 6. — for long. V. xxiv. 10.

THE 135TH RADICAL. 舌.

舍 *shay* shê — (1) To neglect, to abandon. II. ii. 3 (舍已, to give up one's own views and wishes): IV. i. 2. (2) To let loose, —spoken of cattle. V. xxix. 3.

舒 *shoo* shu — To deal gently or kindly with. V xviii. 5 (foll. by 于).

THE 136TH RADICAL. 舛.

舜 *shun* — The ancient emperor, so denominated. 虞舜, I. 12. 帝舜, II. i. 1, 3, 14, 17, 18: IV. viii. Pt. iii. 10.

舞 *woo* wu — To make postures. Spoken of birds and beasts = to gambol in a regular way. II. i. 24: iv. 10. — to dance. II. ii. 21: IV. iv. 7. 舞衣, dancing habits. V. xxii. 19.

THE 137TH RADICAL. 舟.

舟 *chow* chou — A boat. II. iv. 8: IV. vii. Pt. ii. 6: viii. Pt. i. 6.

THE 138TH RADICAL. 艮.

良 *leang* liang — To be good; good; the good. II. iv. 11: IV. ii. 7: viii. Pt. i. 2; Pt. iii. 9: V. i. Pt. i. 5; Pt. iii. 6: xxi. 13: xxvi. 3. Excellent, skilful. IV. Pt. ii. 12: V. xxi. 6. 元良, greatly good. IV. v. Pt. iii. 8: V. i. Pt. ii. 5. — goodness. V. xxv. 2.

艱 *keen* chien — To be difficult or toilsome; difficulty, hardships. IV. iv. 5: v. Pt. iii. 1; Pt. ii. 13: V. vii. 3, 7, 8, 11: xvi. 17: xxiv. 10: xxv. 5: xxviii. 3: xxx. 8. 艱難, painful toil. V. xv. 2, 3, 7: xxii. 7. 艱食, food of toil,—that procured by agriculture. II. iv. 1. To realize the difficulty or pain of. II. ii. 2: V. xxi. 5.

THE 139TH RADICAL. 色.

色 *sih* sê — (1) The countenance, the looks; the deportment. II. iii. 2: V. xxiv. 5: xxvi. 5. Observe 而康而色. V. iv. 11. (2) Colours, III. i. Pt. i. 35. 五色, the five colours. II. iv. 4. (3)

Licentious pleasure. III. iii. 6 : IV. ii. 5 (聲色): iv. 7 : V. i. Pt. i. 5.

THE 140TH RADICAL. 艸

芮 *juy* jui — The name of a principality, the chief of which was minister of Instruction to king Ching. V. xxii. 3 : xxiii. 2.

芻 *ts'oo* ch'u — Grass. 芻茭 = forage. V. xxix. 5.

苗 *meaou* miao — (1) Growing grain. IV. ii. 4. (2) 三苗, the name of the original seat of the Meaou, a tribe which occasioned much trouble in the times of Yaou, Shun, and Yu. They are called 三苗, 苗 and 苗民. II. i. 19, 27 : ii. 20, 21 : iii. 2 : iv. 8 : III. i. Pt. i. 78 : V. xxvii. 3, 5, 7, 12.

若 *jŏ* jo — (1) To be as; as, as if; if. I. 1, 9, 10 : II. i. 1, 21, 22 : ii. 1, 19, 21 : iii. 1 : iv. 6, 8; *et passim*. From *to be as* comes the signification of—to conform to, to follow, to act in accordance with. We have other verbs associated with 若 in this usage; 一欽若, I. 3; *et al.*; 奉若, IV. ii. 2; *et al.*; 祗若, IV. viii. Pt. i. 11; 嗣若, V. xii. 18. To cause to conform to. IV. iii. 2. To be as should be, in accordance with the natural condition. IV. iv. 2; *et al.* To be regulated gently. V. xii. 21. When, in the case that. IV. vii. Pt. i. 9; Pt. ii. 5; *et al.* 若 occurs before phrases, and adverbs of time, when we cannot translate it. V. vii. 4 : xii. 4 : xx. 2 : xxvii. 2. To approve. V. x. 7 : xv. 13; *et al.* Observe especially 若否, in IV. vii. Pt. iii. 11. Such as,—in enumerations of famous men, but not always. V. xvi. 7, 12 : xxviii 3 (若汝). In the frequently recurring phrases 若時, 若茲, 若是, the 若 simply = as. Comp. 若之何, IV. xi. 8; and 若勤哉, V. vii. 10. Thus, nearly to this effect,—in the formulas 王 or 公若曰, IV. vii. Pt. i. 6 : xi. 1, 4 : V. iii. 5; *et sæpe*. After adjectives = our like or ly. V. iv. 34.—Observe 旅王若公, V. xii. 8; 越若來, V. xii. 2 : 厥若, V. xix. 16 : xxiii. 6; 時若, xx. 4; 美若, xxiii. 2.

苦 *k'oo* k'u — Bitter. V. iv. 5. To embitter. 自苦, IV. vii. Pt. ii. 6.

茅 *maou* mao — 菁茅, a kind of three-ribbed rush, used in straining the spirits for the imperial sacrifices. III. i. 52.

茭 *keaou* chiao — Dried grass. 茭芻, forage. V. xxix. 5.

茨 *tsze* tzû — To thatch. V. xi. 4.

茲 *tsze* tzû — This, these. *Passim.* It stands sometimes, especially at the beginning of clauses, with adverbial force, and = here; now; thus; therefore. *E. g.* IV. ii. 2 : vii. Pt. i. 3, 14; Pt. ii. 14 : V. vii. 2 : x. 7 : xvi. 9, 13 : xix. 19 : xxii. 4.

荊 *king* ching — (1) 荊州, one of Yu's nine provinces. (2) There are two mountains called King, mentioned in the Shoo;—the southern King, one of the boundaries of King-chow, III. i. Pt. i. 46, 54; Pt. ii. 3; and the northern, in Yung-chow, Pt. i. 76; Pt. ii. 1.

草 *ts'aou* ts'ao — Grass,—vegetation generally, distinct from trees. II. i. 22 : III. i. Pt. i. 17, 23, 42 : IV. iii. 5 : V. iv. 32 (庶草): xxi. 4. 草竊, to steal among the grass, probably = to commit highway robbery. IV. xi. 3.

荒 *hwang* huang — (1) Uncultivated, overgrown with grass and weeds. 荒野, IV. viii. i. Pt. iii. 1. So 荒 alone, in xi. 3, = the wilds. (2) The name of the last of Yu's domains. III. i. Pt. ii. 22. (3) After nouns, it = to be wildly addicted to. We have 酒荒, III. iv. 1; 色荒, 禽荒, iii. 6. Perhaps it may be construed in these cases as a noun. (4) As a verb,—to neglect, IV. vii. Pt. i. 8; to waste, to ruin. IV. xi. 4 : V. xx. 16. (3) Used adverbially,—wildly; neglectfully. III. iii. 8 : IV. vii. Pt. ii. 2 : V. i. Pt. iii. 2 : x. 11 : xv. 4, 5 : xviii. 4. Greatly. II. iv. 8 : V. xxvii. 1.

荼 *t'oo* tu — A bitter herb. Used metaphorically, as we use wormwood. IV. iii. 8.

莅 *le* li — Nearly synonymous with 臨. = to manage, the management of. V. xx. 16.

莠 *yew* yu — A useless plant, resembling growing corn in the stalk and leaf. IV. ii. 4.

莫 *mŏ* mo — Not; not to be; do not. II. ii. 24 : IV. iv. 2 (莫不): II. 8 (莫已若者): V. xxi. 5.

萊 *lae* lai — Probably the name of a mountain in the present Tăng-chow, Shan-tung. 萊夷, III. i. Pt. i. 26.

菁 *tsing* ching — 菁茅, see 茅.

菑 *tszé* tzʻi — To turn up the ground,—take the first steps in cultivating a field. V. vii. 11 : xi. 4.

菏 *ko* — The name of a marsh. III. i. Pt. i. 57 ; Pt. ii. 10.

華 *hwa* hua — 1st tone. Variegated, of different colours. V. xxii. 16. 華蟲, the variegated bird,—the emblematic pheasant embroidered on the upper robe of the emperor. II. iv. 4. 華夏, flowery and great, a name of the empire. V. iii. 6. 重華, perhaps the name of Shun. II. i. 1.

華 *hwa* hua — 3d tone. The name of a mountain ;—the western mountain of Shun's progresses. III. i. Pt. i. 62 ; Pt. iv. ii. 3 (called 太華), 7 : V. iii. 2.

萃 *tsʻuy* tsʻui — To collect, to be assembled. V. iii. 6 (observe the construction, which is intricate).

萬 *wan* — Ten thousand, a myriad, myriads. It is used generally in a vague manner, and = all of what is spoken of. We have 萬姓, the myriad surnames, = the people, III. iii. 9 : IV. vi. 9 : V. i. Pt. i. 5 : iii. 8 : xix. 5 ; 萬邦, the myriad countries, = the empire, I. 3 : II. ii. 3 : V. xxvi. 2 ; *et sæpe* ; 萬事, all matters, II. iv. 11 ; 萬幾, II. iii. 5 ; 萬世, myriad ages, for ever, and 萬年, II. ii. 8 : IV. v. Pt. i. 7 ; Pt. ii. 2 : V. xiii. 4, 27, 28 ; *et al.* ; 萬民, IV. vii. Pt. ii. 12 ; Pt. iii. 5 ; *et al.* ; 萬夫 seems to = the myriad heads of families, another name for the people, in IV. vi. 10 ; 萬方, the myriad regions, IV. ii. 2, 8 : iii. 1, 2, 3, 8 : *et sæpe* ; 萬物, all things, V. i. Pt. i. 3 ; 萬國 occurs only once, —in V. xx. 3.

落 *lŏ* lo — In the phrase 殂落, to decease. II. i. 13.

葛 *kŏ* ko — The name of a State, not far from the original seat of Tʻang, who punished its chief. V. ii. 6.

董 *tung* — To correct. II. ii. 7. Before another verb, = strictly. V. xx. 1.

蒙 *mûng* mêng — (1) Young, youthful. 蒙士, IV. iv. 7. (2) Stupidity. IV. iv. 34. Cloudiness. IV. iv. 29. (3) Two mountains were thus named,—one in Tsʻeu-chow, III. i. Pt. i. 30 ; the other in Lëang-chow, p. 65.

蒼 *tsʻang* — Grass-green. 蒼生, II. iv. 7.

蓄 *chʻuh* chʻu — To accumulate. V. xx. 16.

蓋 *kae* kai — To cover. V. xvii. 3. To be covered, = to be disregarded. V. xxvii. 6.

蔑 *mëĕ* mieh — Not, to be without. V. xvi. 13.

蔡 *tsʻae* tsʻai — (1) Criminals undergoing a lesser banishment. III. i. Pt. ii. 21. It is queried whether we should not read the character *shă* in this meaning. (2) The name of a mountain, which is not well ascertained. III. i. Pt. i. 65. (3) The name of the appanage, in the present Ho-nan, of Too, known as 蔡叔, a younger brother of the duke of Chow. V. xvii. 1. His son is 蔡仲,—in the same par.

蔽 *pe* pi — (1) To determine, decide firmly ; to be determined. II. ii. 18 : V. ix. 12. (obs. 不蔽), 13, 22. (2) To conceal. IV. iii. 8.

蕃 *fan* — (1) To be luxuriant. 蕃廡, V. iv. 32. (2) *I. q.* 藩, to be a fence or bulwark to. V. viii. 4 : xvii. 6.

蕩 *tʻang* — (1) 蕩蕩, vast. I. 11. = broad and long. V. iv. 14. (2) To be scattered. 蕩析, IV. vii. Pt. iii. 5. (3) To be dissolute. V. xxiv. 9.

薄 *pŏ* po — (1) To reach to, extend over. II. iv. 8. (2) To press on, = to deal sternly with. V. x. 13.——Ought we not to read the character in the first of these meanings—*pʻŏ*?

藏 *tsʻang* — To be hidden, kept in obscurity. V. xii. 10.

藝 *e* i — (1) An art, arts. V. vi. 6. 藝事, III. iv. 3. 藝人, in V. xix. 9, are certain officers so denominated. (2) *I. q.* 蓺, to cultivate, to bring under cultivation. III. i. Pt. i. 30, 63 : V. x. 1.

藥 *yŏ* yo — Medicine. IV. viii. Pt. i. 8.

藪 *sow* sou — A large jungly marsh, to which beasts will resort. V. iii. 6.

藻 *tsaou* tsao — A kind of water-plant,—duckweed, one of the emblematic figures on the lower sacrificial robe of the emperor. II. iv. 4.

蘇 *soo* su — (1) To revive. IV. ii. 6. (2) Apparently the name of a principality or State. V. xix. 24.

蘉 *mang* — To exert one's-self. V. xiii. 13.

THE 141st RADICAL. 虍.

虎 *hoo* hu — A tiger, tigers. V. ii. 9 (comp. for soldiers): xxv. ii. (2) 虎賁, life-guards. V. xxii. 11. The officer commanding them is called 虎臣, in p. 3. He and other officers under him are called 虎賁, in xix. 1, 8. (3) The name of an officer in the court of Shun. II. i. 22.

虐 *neŏ* yao — To oppress, tyrannize over. II. 1, 24: ii. 8: IV. vi. 3; *et sæpe*. Foll. by 于, in V. ii. 6: xviii. 6. Oppressive, dangerous, —used of sickness. V. vi. 5. Oppression; sometimes = oppressors. II. iv. 8: IV. iii. 3: iv. 3: V. i. Pt. i. 5: *et sæpe*. = calamities. IV. vii. Pt. ii. 4. Observe 五虐之刑, V. xxvii. 3.

虔 *k'een* ch'ien — To kill, = oppressors. V. xxvii. 2.

虛 *heu* hsü — The name of a star. I. 6.

虞 *yu* yü — (1) To consider, think about. V. x. 3: xxi. 5. 無虞, nothing to think about, a time of freedom from all anxiety. II. ii. 6: V. xxiv. 3. (2) A forester, the designation of the warden of woods and forests under Shun. II. i. 22. = a forester, generally. IV. v. Pt. i. 7. (3) The name of the principality which had belonged to the family of Shun, who is thence called 虞舜, I. 12; and 虞 alone, V. xx. 3. Obs. 虞賓, II. iv. 9.

號 *haou* hao — 1st tone. To cry out. 號泣, II. ii. 21.

號 *haou* hao — A warning order or command. V. xxvi. 2.

虢 *kih* ko — Name of the appanage of a younger brother of king Wăn, called 虢叔, V. xvi. 12.

虧 *k'wei* k'uei — To be wanting. V. v. 9.—— The dictionary gives this character under 虍, —but incorrectly. In the 說文 we find it under 亏, the appearance of the breath slowly ascending and stopped. 雐 is the phonetic element in the character, and 亏 the ideographic; and it ought to have its place in the dict. under the latter. But 亏 is no longer used for lexical purposes, being thrown out to reduce the number of radicals (as they are termed) as much as possible. This practice has given rise to not a few anomalies in the arrangement of characters.

THE 142d RADICAL. 虫.

虺 *hwuy* hui — 仲虺, one of the principal ministers of T'ang. IV. ii. 2.

蚩 *ch'e* ch'i — 蚩尤 appears in V. xxvii. 2, as the first troubler of the empire, a wicked and seditious prince of the most ancient times.

蜀 *shuh* shu — A tribe, whose seat was in the pres. dep. of Shing-too, Sze-ch'uen, confederate with Chow against Shang. V. ii. 3.

蟲 *ch'ung* — An insect;—but used for animals generally. 華蟲, the emblematic pheasant depicted on the emperor's robe. II. iv. 6.

蟻 *e* i — An ant. = ant-coloured. V. xxii. 22.

蠙 *pin* — 蠙珠, pearls. III. i. Pt. i. 35.—The dict. says that this character is 'the name of a kind of pearl.' This is a mistake, I apprehend. It should rather be taken as the *oyster*, in which pearls are found.

蠡 *le* li — 彭蠡, the name of a lake, the modern Po-yang. III. i. Pt. i. 38.

蠢 *ch'un* — Insects moving about.—Used for to be stupid, II. ii. 20; and for stupid, senseless, agitation. V. vii. 3, 5, 8.

蠲 *keuen* chüan — To be clean or pure. V. xviii. 16. To make clean, to cleanse. x. 16. To hold to be clean or guiltless. xxvii. 12.

蠻 *man* — The wild tribes of the south. But we find it used, where it must mean such wild tribes generally. III. i. Pt. ii. 22. As distinct from the tribes of other quarters, they are spoken of as the 八蠻, V. v. 1. We have 蠻夷, in II. i. 16, 20; and 蠻貊, in V. iii. 6.

蠶 *ts'an* — The silk worm. = to be made fit for silkworms. III. i. Pt. i. 16.

THE 143d RADICAL. 血.

血 *heuĕ* hsieh — Blood. V. iii. 9.

衋 *heih* ? hei — To be pained, to feel the pain of. V. x. 11.

THE 144th RADICAL. 行.

行 *hing* hsing — (1) To go, to travel over. V. xix. 22. To make to go. II. iv. 8. Used of the course of the sun and moon. V. iv. 38. 行遯, to go away and escape. IV. xi.

9. (2) To do; to carry—be carried—into practice; to execute; practice, execution. II. iii. 8: IV. i. 1: v. Pt. i. 7: viii. Pt. ii. 12, 13: Pt. ii. 3, 5: V. i. Pt. i. 5; Pt. iii. 8: ii. 7: iv. 16: ix. 21: xxv. 6. 不行 = obsolete laws. V. xxvii. 18. (3) 五行, the five elements. III. ii. 3: V. iv. 3, 4, 5.

行 *hing* hsing — 3d tone. Actions, conduct. II. i. 25: iii. 3: III. i. Pt. ii. 17: V. iv. 13: v. 9 (細行): x. 8 (酒惟行): xvii. 2: xix. 2.

衎 *hăng* hêng — 太衎, the name of a mountain. III. i. Pt. ii. 1.

衍 *yen* — = to push out, to infer. V. iv. 23.

衡 *hăng* hêng — (1) The beam of a balance, or steelyard. II. i. 8. 玉衡, the gem-adorned transverse, a part, apparently, of an astronomical instrument used by Shun. II. i. 5. To weigh, to adjust. V. xiii. 16. (2) 阿衡, the name, or a title, of T'ang's minister, E Yin. IV. v. Pt. i. 1; Pt. iii. 10. He is also called 保衡. V. xvi. 7. (3) The name of a mountain, the southern boundary of King-chow. III. i. Pt. i. 46; Pt. ii. 4. It is the southern mountain of Shun's progresses. II. i. 8. (4) 衡漳, the name of a river, an affluent of the Ho. III. i. Pt. i. 6.

衞 *wei* — (1) To defend. = defence. III. i. Pt. ii. 20. 臣衞, we, defenders of the throne. V. xxiii. 1. (2) Name of the 5th of the domains of Chow. V. iii. 3: ix. 1: x. 10, 13: xxiii. 4. (3) Name of a principality which occupied part of the pres. provinces of Chih-le and Ho-nan. V. xxii. 3. (4) The name of a river. III. i. Pt. i. 9.

THE 145TH RADICAL. 衣.

衣 *e* i — Clothes, robes. Specifically, the upper garments. 衣裳. IV. viii. Pt. ii. 4. 戎衣, a martial garb. V. iii. 8. 舞衣, dancing habits. V. xxii. 19. The phrase 綴衣 is used in two senses;—as the name of an officer or officers, keepers of the robes, xix. 1, 8; as the name of a sort of tent used in audiences, xxii. 10, 14.

衣 *e* i — 3d tone. To put on, = to carry into practice. V. ix. 5.

表 *peaou* piao — (1) That which is outside, the outside; beyond. III. iii. 1 (在洛之表). 表臣, outside ministers,—officers beyond the court. V. xix. 9. 海表, beyond the seat. V. xix. 22. 四表, the four outsides, the utmost limits, north, south, east, and west. I. i. (2) To serve as a mark to. IV. ii. 2. To set up a mark for,—to signalise. V. xxiv. 3.

衷 *chung* — Man's good moral nature. II. iii. 6: IV. iii. 2.

衽 *jin* jên — The lappel in front of a coat or jacket, buttoning, according to Chinese usage, on the right side. 左衽, V. xxiv. 13.—It is also written 袵.

被 *p'ei* p'i — 3d tone. To reach to. I. 1: III. i. Pt. i. 52; Pt. ii. 23.

被 *p'e* p'i — 1st tone. To put on one, to dress one with. V. xxii. 2.

裔 *e* i — The lower edge of a garment. 後裔, descendants. V. viii. 2.

裕 *yu* yü — To be generous, enlarged in mind and act; what is generous. V. ix. 22: xiii. 10: xvi. 17. Obs. in IV. ii. 8, 垂裕, to transmit a generous example, and 裕 alone, = to become enlarged. To make generous. V. ix. 5. Obs. 忱裕之, xviii. 21. To rule generously. V. ix. 19: xiii. 13.

裳 *shang* — The lower robe or garment. IV. viii. Pt. ii. 4: V. xxii. 22, 23.

褻 *seĕ* hsieh — Undress, = to take liberties, to allow one's-self. IV. vii. Pt. ii. 6.

襄 *seang* hsiang — (1) To overtop. I. 1: II. iv. 1. (2) To complete. to perfect; perfection. II. xvi. 20: II. iii. 8.

襲 *sih* hsi — A double garment, = to be repeated. V. i. Pt. ii. 5.

THE 146TH RADICAL. 襾.

西 *se* hsi — The west. V. xxii. 17. On the west, (adv. and prep.); westwards; at the west. II. i. 8: III. i. Pt. ii. 23: I. 6: V. xiii. 3. Western. V. xxii. 16, 18, 19, 21: xxiii. 1; *et. al.* Ch'ang and Fă, afterwards king Wăn and king Woo, were 西伯, chiefs of the west, IV. x. 2; and 西土 appears often as a denomination of the western portion of the empire, subject to, or acknowledging the supremacy of, the House of Chow. V. i. Pt. ii. 2; Pt. ii. 2, 5: ii. 1, 9: vii. 3; *et al.* We have 西戎 in III. i. Pt. i. 83, which is acc. to rule; but 西夷, in IV. ii. 6, shows how promiscuously the term 夷 may be

used. 西岳, the western mountain, II. i. 8, is mount Hwa (see 華). 西傾, III. i. Pt. i. 70; Pt. ii. 2, is a mountain far to the west, commonly thought to be in the Koko-nor. 西河, III. i. Pt. i. 70, 72, 82, is the Ho, in its course from north to south. As a verb, 西爾 = wested you, settled you in the west. V. xiv. 8.

要 *yaou* yao — 1st tone. (1) To restrain. V. xviii. 23—(?). 要服, the domain of restraint,—the 4th of Yu's tenures. III. i. Pt. ii. 21. (2) In the phrase 要囚, to examine the evidence in criminal cases. V. ix. 12: xviii. 11.—This is a perplexing phrase, especially as we have to interpret it differently in xviii. 23.

要 *yaou* yao — That which is important, the essential principle, V. xxvii. 19. 體要, in V. xxiv. 8, is probably the completeness of a govt. measure.

覃 *t'un* — 覃懷, a tract in the pres. dist. of Hwae-k'ing, Ho-nan, operated on by Yu. III. i. Pt. i. 6.

覆 *fuh* fu — To subvert, overthrow. III. iii. 8: iv. 4 (顚覆): IV. ii. 9: v. Pt. i. 5: V. xxvii. 4.

THE 147TH RADICAL. 見.

見 *këen* chien — To see, to observe; to be seen. IV. v. Pt. i. 3: V. vi. 9: ix. 6: xi. 2: xix. 4, 6 (灼見): xxi. 4.

見 *heen* hsien — (1) To appear before. II. ii. 21: IV. iv. 1. (2) To appear, to present one's-self, be seen. III. iii. 5: V. xvi. 14.—It is hardly possible to make anything of 見士于周, V. ix. 1.

規 *k'wei* k'uei — To admonish, III. iv. 3 (*n. b.*).

視 *she* shih — To see, V. i. Pt. ii. 7: iv. 6 (= seeing). To look at, to consider, III. iii. 5: IV. v. Pt. ii. 7: viii. Pt. i. 8: xvii. 7: xxviii. 4. To have a regard to. IV. v. Pt. ii. 6: vii. Pt. ii. 4. *I. q.* 示, to display. V. xiii. 8.

親 *ts'in* ch'in — (1) To love; to show affection to. I. 2: IV. v. Pt. iii. 1 (天無親), V. xvii. 4 (*i. d.*): v. 8. To love mutually. II. i. 19. To love relations. IV. iv. 4. (2) Relatives. V. i. Pt. ii. 6. (3) To approach, place one's-self near to. 以爲親, V. xxx. 4.

覲 *kin* chin — (1) To give audience to. II. i. 7, 8.—In the index to Mencius, I have said that this char. means—'to wait upon a superior,' 'to appear at court.' Such is its usage in his Works, and so the dict. defines it, making special reference to the first instance of its occurrence in the Shoo, where it is not the appearance of the inferior, but the action of the superior, which we are led to think of. The common idea is that of—*a case of audience*. It is only used in one other instance in the Shoo,—V. xix. 22, where I have rendered it *to display*, bringing that meaning out of 見, by which interpreters explain it.

覺 *keŏ* chiao — To apprehend, to perceive. 無覺, unperceived. IV. viii. Pt. iii. 5.

觀 *kwan* kuan — To see, to contemplate. I. 12: II. iv. 4: IV. vii. Pt. i. 8: V. i. Pt. i. 6: x. 11 (觀省): xii. 4: xiii. 28: xxvii. 12 (foll. by 于). = to prove, to evidence. IV. vi. 10. This idea may be traced also in I. 12; *et al.* = seeing, sights. V. xv. 12.

THE 148TH RADICAL. 角.

角 *keŏ* chiao — A horn, horns. V. i. Pt. ii. 9.

THE 149TH RADICAL. 言.

言 *yen* — To say, to speak; to speak about. II. i. 24: ii. 10: iii. 3: IV. iv. 1: viii. Pt. i. 1, 2; Pt. ii. 12: V. xiv. 26: xv. 5; *et sæpe*. 讒言, to defame. IV. viii. Pt. iii. 3. To talk, used contemptuously, I. 10. We have often 言曰, to speak, saying, and the formula 有言曰. *E. g.* IV. v. Pt. i. 5: vii. Pt. i. 13: V. i. Pt. iii. 4: iv. 2, 3: x. 12. Words. II. ii. 3, 16, 17, 21. = reports. II. i. 9: iv. 7. = compositions. II. iv. 5. 納言, the designation of Shun's minister of communication. II. i. 25. 五言 seems to = 五聲, the five notes of music, in II. iv. 4. 庶言 = notifications, in V. xix. 13. 言 alone, in V. iv. 6, = speech; and in xix. 17, 一言 = a speech, or a single remark. Of phrases with 言, we have 昌言, II. iv. 1; *et al.*; 食言, to eat one's words, be false to them, IV. i. 4; 聖言, IV. iv. 7; 辯言, v. Pt. iii. 9; 矢言, vii. Pt. i. 1; 逸言, vii. Pt. i. 7, and 箴言 and 浮言, both in p. 10; 敷言, V. iv. 15, 16; 流言, to set words flowing,

to raise a rumour, V. 7: xviii. 1; 德言, ix. 5; 誨言, xiii. 4; 側言, xvii. 7; 徽言, xix. 17; 諞言, xxx. 5.

討 *t'aou* t'ao — To punish. II. iii. 6.

訓 *hsun* hsün — (1) To instruct, to admonish, to lesson. It is generally foll. by 于. *E. g.* IV. iv. 1, 7: viii. Pt. iii. 2: V. v. 1. But not always,—as in V. ix. 5: xv. 14 (訓告), 15. To be instructed in. V. iv. 16: xix. 20. Obs. 諸子訓人, V. ix. 17: 非民攸訓, xv. 13; 審訓, xxii. 4. A lesson, instructions. III. iii. 4, 6: iv. 2: IV. v. Pt. i. 9 *(n. b.)*; Pt. ii. 3: vii. Pt. i. 6: V. iv. 15 *(n. b.)*: viii. 4; *et sæpe*. 大訓, the great lesson, was some relic of antiquity. V. xxii. 19. (2) To follow. V. xxiv. 14. So, in 嗣訓, xxii. 24. This meaning may be derived from the passive use of the character above. (3) To approve. V. xxiii. 5.

訖 *keih* chi — (1) All, entirely. V. xiii. 2. To reach to entirely. xxviii. 11 *(n. b.)*: III. i. Pt. ii. 23 (foll. by 于). (2) To extinguish, IV. x. 2.

記 *ke* chi — (1) To record. V. xiii. 7. (2) To make remember. II. iv. 6.

訛 *go* o — To transform. 南訛, transformations of the summer. I. 6.

訟 *sung* — To be wrangling or quarrelsome. I. 9. To wrangle about. IV. vii. Pt. i. 7.

訪 *fang* — To consult, to inquire of. V. iv. 1 (foll. by 于).

設 *shĕ* shê — To set up; to establish. IV. vii. Pt. ii. 2 (設中): viii. Pt. ii. 22: V. xxii. 14.

許 *heu* hsü — To grant, to concede to. V. vi. 8.

詈 *le* li — To rail at, to revile. V. xv. 17, 18.

詔 *chaou* chao — To announce to, to tell, = to advise. IV. xi. 7. 無詔, p. 8, = with none to appeal to.

詛 *tsoo* tsu — To curse. 詛祝, V. xv. 15. 詛盟, oaths and covenants. V. xxvii. 4.

詠 *yung* — To make music,—as an accompaniment to the voice. II. iv. 9.

詢 *seun* hsün — To consult with; to consult on. II. i. 3, 15 (foll. by 于): ii. 16, 18 (弗詢之謀): V. xxx. 4 (猷詢).

試 *she* shih — To try; to test; to make the experiment. I. 11, 12: II. i. 9: IV. vii. Pt. ii. 6, 17.

詩 *she* shih — Poetry. II. i. 24. A piece of poetry, a poem. V. vi. 15.

詰 *k'ëĕ* ch'ieh — (1) To punish. V. xx. 11. (2) To keep in good condition or order. xix. 22. (3) To restrain. xxvii. 1.

話 *hwa* hua — To address,—with a kindly feeling, IV. vii. Pt. ii. 1. 一話, one word, = every word. V. xix. 17.

詳 *ts'ëang* hs'iang — To pay attention to, watch over. V. xvii. 7.

誅 *choo* chu — To cut off, to destroy. V. i. Pt. i. 9. Used as a noun in III. iv. 4,—先王之誅, the death appointed by the former kings.

誓 *she* shih — To make a speech or solemn declaration to, to address. II. ii. 20: V. i. Pt. i. 2; Pt. ii. 1; Pt. iii. 4. A speech. V. xxx. 1. 誓言. IV. i. 4. = solemnly. III. ii. 2: xxii. 4.

誘 *yew* yu — To lead on. V. vii. 10. In a bad sense, = to decoy. V. xxx. 4.

誕 *tan* — (1) To make great, to increase. V. xviii. 4. The term is often used adverbially, = greatly. *E. g.* II. ii. 21: IV. iii. 1: vii. Pt. ii. 1, 7: V. i. Pt. iii. 4, 5: iii. 5: vii. 4, 13, 15. Obs. 誕惟, V. x. 11, which some would make to be merely an initial phrase. (2) To be disorderly or dissolute. V. xv. 2.

誚 *ts'ëaou* ch'iao — To blame. V. vi. 15.

誠 *ching* ch'eng — To be sincere. 克誠 = the sincere. IV. v. Pt. iii. 1.

誣 *woo* wu — To make false pretensions to. 矯誣, IV. ii. 3.

誤 *woe* wu — To err. V. xix. 18, 21.

誥 *kaou* kao — To announce to, to make an announcement. IV. v. Pt. iii. 1 (foll. by 于): viii. Pt. i. 2: V. vii. 1: ix. 1: x. 2 (誥毖), 4 (誥教), 12, 14: xii. 8 (誥告); xiii. 30; xvi. 20, 22: xviii. 13 (誥告), 20, 30: xxiii. 4. An announcement. IV. ii. 2: iii. 2: and in the titles of several Books.

誨 *hwuy* hui — To teach. 教誨, V. xv. 14. Instructions. IV. viii. Pt. i. 5. 誨言, instructive words. V. xiii. 4.

說 *shwŏ* shuo — To speak. 讒說, slanderous talkers, II. i. 25 : iv. 6. = words. V. vi. 16. 德之說, words or discourse about virtue. V. ix. 21.

說 *yuĕ* yüeh — The prime minister of Woo-ting, of the Shang dynasty. Everywhere in IV. viii.

誰 *shwuy* shui — Who? II. iv. 7.

請 *ts'ing* ch'ing — To request, beg leave. IV. iii. 4.

論 *lun* — (1) To discourse of. V. xx. 5. (2) Orderly relation, the order of antecedence and sequence. V. xxvii. 19.

諛 *yu* yü — To flatter, be a flatterer. V. xxvi. 6.

諞 *p'ëen* p'ien — 諞言, artful sayings. V. xxx. 5.

諟 *she* shih — To judge, consider. 顧諟, IV. v. Pt. i. 2.

諧 *heae* hsieh — To be harmonious. I. 12 : II. i. 24 : iii. 1 : iv. 10 (perhaps = to be made harmonious). To make harmonious, to manage harmoniously, or suitably to the requirements of the case. II. i. 21, 22 : ii. 18.

諫 *këen* chien — To remonstrate. IV. iv. 3 : IV. viii. Pt. i. 1 (foll. by 于 = with). Remonstrance, reproof. IV. iv. 3 : viii. Pt. i. 11. 諫輔 = the reprover and helper. V. i. Pt. ii. 5.

諴 *han* — (1) Sincerity. II. ii. 21. (2) To make harmonious (foll. by 于). V. xii. 13.

諶 *shin* shên — To trust, to rely on. IV. vi. 2 : V. xvi. 4.

諸 *choo* chu — (1) A preposition,—by, in, of, from. IV. v. Pt. iii. 7 : viii. Pt. i. 4 : V. vi. 17 : xvii. 1. (2) All, various ;—little more than a sign of the plural. V. ix. 17 : x. 15 : xxvii. 19. (3) In the phrase 諸侯, the various feudal princes of the empire. IV. i. Pt. ii. 19 : V. xx. 14 : xxii. 29 : xxiii. 1.

諺 *yen* — Village slang. To become addicted to such. V. xv. 3.

謀 *mow* mou — To consult ; to consult with. II. i. 18 (詢謀) : V. iv. 25 (foll. by 及). 謀面, to judge by the face. V. xix. 2. To plan, to consult for. IV. vii. Pt. ii. 7 ; Pt. iii. 10 : V. xviii. 17. = deliberation. V. iv. 6, 34. 謀人, counsellors. V. xxx. 6. Plans. II. ii. 6, 16 : IV. vii. Pt. i. 8 ; Pt. iii. 7 : V. ix. 22 (非謀, bad plans) : xii. 12 : xix. 15 : xx. 16 : xxi. 6 : xxviii. 1 (猷謀).

謂 *wei* — To say. IV. vii. Pt. iii. 5 : V. i. Pt. ii. 5. To be called. IV. ii. 8 : iv. 7 : viii. Pt. ii. 11. The idiomatic use of 之謂, = to be called, occurs only once ;—in V. iv. 26 ; and it may there be easily resolved, so as to give 之 its proper signification of *of*.

謙 *k'ëen* ch'ien — Humility. II. ii. 21.

謨 *moo* mu — Counsels. II. iii. 1 : IV. iv. 8 : V. xxv. 6 ; and in the titles of some Books. 謨訓, well-counselled instructions. IV. iv. 2.

謬 *mew* miu — Errors. 糾謬, V. xxvi. 3.

謹 *kin* chin — To give careful attention to. III. iv. 2 : IV. vii. Pt. i. 3.

譁 *hwa* hua — To make a noise. V. xxviii. 1 : xxx. 1.

識 *shih* — To know, understand. V. xiii. 12.

識 *che* chih — To remember, to keep a remembrance of. II. iv. 6.

議 *e* i — To deliberate on. V. xx. 6.

譸 *chow* chou — To deceive, impose on. 譸張, V. xv. 14, 18.

譽 *yu* yü — Praise. II. ii. 6 : V. ix. 17.

變 *pëen* pien — To change (act. and neut.) ; to be changed. I. 2 : IV. v. Pt. i. 8 : vii. Pt. i. 7 : V. xv. 15 : xxi. 14 : xxiv. 3.

讎 *ch'ow* ch'ou — To be an enemy. V. i. Pt. iii. 4 : IV. xi. 2 (敵讎). Hostile. V. xii. 24. = hateful. IV. xi. 7.

讒 *ch'an* — To calumniate. 讒說, slanderous talkers. II. i. 25 : iv. 6. 讒言, to defame. IV. vii. Pt. iii. 2.

讓 *jang* — To yield ; to yield to, or in behalf of. I. 1 (*n. b.*) : II. i. 3, 17, 21, 22, 23 (foll. by 于) : iv. 2 (= to be humble), 9 : V. xvi. 20 : xx. 20.

THE 150TH RADICAL. 谷.

谷 *kuh* ku — A valley. 暘谷, the Bright valley, somewhere in the remotest east. I. 4. 昧谷, the Dark valley, somewhere in the remotest north. I. 6.

THE 151st RADICAL. 豆.

豆 *tow* tou — A vessel for containing flesh. 豆籩, sacrificial vessels. V. iii. 3.

豈 *k'e* ch'i — How? III. iii. 5: IV. vii. Pt. ii. 9.

豐 *fung* — (1) To be abundant, excessive. IV. ix. 5. Superior,—in quality. V. xxiv. 1. (2) The name of king Wăn's capital. V. iii. 2: xxii. 17.

THE 152d RADICAL. 豕.

豕 *che* ch'ih — A pig. V. xii. 5.

象 *sëang* hsiang — (1) To resemble, have the appearance of. I. 10: V. viii. 1. To delineate, represent. I. 3 (曆象): II. i. 11: iv. 8. A likeness delineated. IV. viii. Pt. i. 3. The emblematic figures on the emperor's robes. II. iv. 4. 天象, heavenly figures. III. iv. 4. (2) Shun's half brother. II. i. 12.

豬 *choo* chu — *I. q.* 瀦, a lake, a receptacle of waters. (1) To *inlake*,—to form into a lake. III. i. Pt. i. 30, 38, 56. (2) 孟豬, Pt. i. 57, and 豬野, p. 77, are the names of lakes.

豫 *yu* yü — (1) To allow one's-self in pleasure or idle dissipation. IV. v. Pt. ii. 6: V. xxi. 3. Pleasure, dissipation. III. iii. 1: IV. viii. Pt. ii. 2: V. ix. 6. Indolence. V. iv. 34. (2) To be comfortable,—used in reference to a state of sickness. V. vi. 1. (3) 豫州, one of Yu's provinces. III. i. Pt. i. 54.

THE 153d RADICAL. 豸.

貊 *mih* mai — *I. q.* 貉. The rude tribes of the north. 蠻貊, V. iii. 6.

貌 *maou* mao — The appearance, demeanour. V. iv. 6: xxvii. 17.

貍 *le* li — Probably the jackal. III. i. Pt. i. 69.

貔 *pe* pi — A kind of leopard or panther. Soldiers are exhorted to be such. V. ii. 9.

THE 154th RADICAL. 貝.

貝 *pei* — (1) Creatures of the sea, with beautiful shells. Used for those shells. = tortoise-shell. V. xxii. 16 (文貝), 19. = cowries. IV. vii. Pt. ii. 14. (2) Variegated silks. III. i. Pt. i. 44. But the meaning is uncertain. I should almost be inclined to interpret the character of cowries.

貞 *ching* chêng — (1) To be—to become—correct and firm. IV. v. Pt. iii. 8: V. v. 5: xxv. 1. To be of the correct amount. III. i. Pt. 18. Solidity. V. iv. 22. (2) To sustain duties or responsibility. V. xiii. 4.

負 *foo* hu — To bear on the back. 負罪, to bear—assume to one's-self—the burden of guilt. II. ii. 21.

財 *ts'ae* ts'ai — Treasures, wealth. V. iii. 9. In 財賦, III. i. Pt. ii. 15, 財 seems to mean the material wealth or resources.

貢 *kung* — (1) To present as tribute,—the contribution of an inferior to a superior. V. v. 1. Articles of tribute. III. i. Pt. i. i. 19, *et passim*. (2) To advance, to go forward. V. xxii. 9 (foll. by 于).

貧 *p'in* — Poverty. V. iv. 40.

貨 *ho* huo — Goods, property; wealth. IV. ii. 5 (貨利): iv. 7: vii. Pt. iii. 10, 12 (貨寶): V. iv. 7; ix. 15. = bribes. V. xxvi. 8: xxvii. 12, 16, 21 (獄貨).

貫 *kwan* kuan — To be strung together. 貫盈, to be full. V. i. Pt. i. 9.

責 *tsih* tsê — (1) To reprove. V. xxx. 2. (2) To give in charge; to lay a charge on. IV. x. 6; V. xvi. 16. A charge. V. vi. 5.

貳 *urh* — (1) To be double-minded. III. iii. 1. 貳適, V. xiv. 15. (2) To assist,—act as seconds to. V. xx. 6.

貴 *kwei* kuei — To value, count valuable. V. v. 8: xxiv. 8.

貽 *e* i — To transmit. = to hand down. III. iii. 8: V. xii. 19. = to send to. V. vi. 15.

賁 *pun* pên — 虎賁, life-guards. V. xxii. 11. The officer or officers commanding are also thus denominated. xix. 1, 8.

fun fên — Great. 玆賁 = this great inheritance. IV. vii. Pt. iii. 7.

pe pi — To be ornamented. = elegant institutions. V. vii. 2. = brilliantly. IV. iii. 5.

資 *tsze* tzû — To have property. V. xxiv. 1. 資澤 = resources of bounty. V. xxviii. 2.

賈 *koo* ku — To traffic. 服賈, to pursue the business of traffic.—In Index III. to Mencius, this character is defined—'a stationary trafficker or merchant.' Such is the account given of it in the dict., in distinction from 商; but this instance

in the Shoo rather points to the idea of travelling about and trafficking.

賊 *tsih* tsei — To injure,—probably to death. 寇賊, II. i. 20: V. xxvii. 2. 賊虐, V. i. Pt. ii. 15. 賊刑, to punish capitally. II. i. 11.

賓 *pin* — (1) To receive guests. II. i. 2 (*n. b.*): V. xiv. 22. = the entertainment of guests. V. iv. 7. To receive as a guest,—respectfully. I. 4. A guest, guests. II. iv. 9: V. viii. 1: xiii. 29. 賓階, the guests' steps,—the steps on the western side of a hall or platform. V. xxii. 20, 22, 23. The term is used for the princes all appearing at court. V. xxiii. 1. This idea is likewise in II i. 2. (2) To come and acknowledge subjection. V. v. 2.

賚 *lae* lai — To confer to; to bestow gifts,—sometimes nearly = to reward. IV. i. 4: viii. Pt. i. 2: V. iii. 8: xvii. 23: xxviii. 4: xxix. 4.

賞 *shang* — To reward; rewards. II. ii. 12: III. ii. 5: IV. ii. 5: V. i. Pt. iii. 4: xxiii. 3.

賡 *kăng* kêng — To continue. Obs. 賡歌, II. iv. 11.

賢 *heen* hsien — (1) To be possessed of superior virtue and talents. Used generally for men of worth. II. ii. 3, 6: IV. ii. 6, 7: V. iii. 9; *et sæpe*. In V. i. Pt. iii. 3, we have the phrase 賢人. Obs. 惟賢, in V. xxiv. 8. (2) To be superior to—surpass—others. II. ii. 14. So, 自賢, p. 20. (3) In a name,—巫賢, a minister of the Shang dynasty. V. xvi. 7.

賤 *tsëen* chien — To contemn, consider vile. V. v. 8.

賦 *foo* fu — Revenue, contribution of revenue. III. i. Pt. i. 8; *et passim*. Obs. 財賦, Pt. ii. 18.

賴 *lae* lai — To depend on. II. ii. 8: IV. v. Pt. ii. 3: V. xxiv. 13: xxvi. 3: xxvii. 13.

贄 *che* chih — Articles of introduction,—gifts to prepare the way for an audience. II. i. 8.

贊 *tsan* — To assist. II. ii. 21. 贊贊, to be assiduously assisting. II. iii. 8.

贖 *shuh* shu — To redeem. 贖刑, II. i. 11.

THE 155TH RADICAL. 赤.

赤 *ch'ih* — (1) To be red; red. III. i. Pt. i. 33: V. xxii. 19. (2) 赤子, an infant. V. ix. 9.

赦 *shay* shê — To forgive. II. i. 11: IV. i. 4: iii. 14. 8. 無赦, without mercy. III. iv. 4: V. ix. 16. To remit a certain amount of penalty or punishment. V. xxvii. 17, 18.

THE 156TH RADICAL. 走.

走 *tsow* tsou — To run. III. iv. 4. 奔走, to hurry about,—generally on service. V. iii. 8: x. 6: xiv. 22: xvi. 9: xviii. 24.

起 *k'e* ch'i — To rise. V. vi. 19. 起居, rising up and sitting down. V. xxvi. 2. To rise flourishingly. II. iv. 1. As an active verb,—to raise up; to produce; to give occasion to. IV. vii. Pt. i. 7; Pt. ii. 8: viii. Pt. ii. 4.

越 *yuĕ* yüeh — (1) To pass over. This = to transgress. IV. vii. Pt. ii. 16 (顛越): V. Pt. i. 7 (*n. b.* 越厥志). = to frustrate. IV. v. Pt. i. 5. = to leave one's place. V. xxix. 4. (2) The idea of *passing over* takes various forms, in which the character is used as a conjunction, such as—*moreover, further*. V. x. 3, 10: xviii. 25: xxii. 19; and with these should be classed the instances of 亦越, V. xix. 4, 6, 15:—*reaching on to*, = *and*. V. i. Pt: i. 2: vii. 1. 6, 7, 8, 13: ix. 17, 18; *et sæpissime;—thereon, so that*, IV. vii. Pt. i. 11; *et al.;*—after, in phrases of time, V. iii. 1, 3: xii. 1, 3, 5, 6;—*in the case of*. V. x. 5, 11: xxvii. 3: xxviii. 1; *et al.;*—after active verbs, carrying them on to their object. IV. vii. Pt. iii. 6. (3) To give out orders. V. xi. 2. (4) To throw down, to assault violently. V. ix. 15.—There are not a few instances, in which we hardly know how to translate this character, which is of very frequent occurrence. *E. g.* IV. ix. 1: xi. 2: V. vii. 11 (越印): xii. 2 (越若來), 8.

趣 *ts'ow* ts'ou — 趣馬, equerries. V. xix. 8.

趨 *ts'en* ch'ü — To go quickly. 趨出, hastily withdrew. V. xxiii. 7.

THE 157TH RADICAL. 足.

足 *tsuh* tsu — (1) The foot. IV. viii. Pt. i. 8. (2) To be sufficient. IV. ii. 4: V. i. Pt. ii. 3, 5. To be sufficient for one's requirements. V. v. 8.

距 *k'eu* ch'ü — (1) To reach to. II. iv. 1. (1) To oppose, withstand. III. i. Pt. ii. 17: iii. 2.

跣 *sëen* hsien — To walk barefoot. IV. viii. Pt. i. 8.

路 *loo* lu — A path, a way. III. iv. 3: V. iv. 14.

踐 *tsëen* chien — To tread in, to pursue. V. viii. 3.

踰 *yu* yü — To pass—jump—over. V. xxix. 4.

蹈 *ta'ou* t'ao — To tread on. V. xxv. 2.

蹌 *ts'eang* ch'iang — 蹌蹌, to fall moving. II. iv. 9.

THE 158TH RADICAL. 身.

身 *shin* shên — (1) The body. V. xxiii. 6. But the material body is seldom what is expressed by the character. It rather = one's person, one's self. II. iii. 1 : IV. iv. 7, 8 : v. Pt. ii. 4 : vii. Pt. i. 12, 17 : V. iv. 26 : vi. 5 ; *et sæpe*. 修身, self-cultivation, occurs more than once. We also have 檢身, to govern one's person, V. iv. 5. Obs 酣身, V. x. 11 ; and 在身, V. xxvii. 11.

躬 *kung* — This is synonymous with the last, and used commonly for one's person. *E. g.* II. ii. 14 : IV. vi. 3 : viii. Pt. ii 4 ; Pt. iii. 4 : V. ii. 10. 尹躬, I, Yin. IV. v. Pt. i. 2, 3. 朕躬 = me, my case. V. xxviii. 2.

THE 159TH RADICAL. 車.

車 *keu* chü — A carriage, a cart. II. i. 9 : iv. 7 : V. x. 6 : xvii. 1.

輅 *loo* lu — An imperial carriage. V. xxii. 20.

載 *tsae* tsai — (1) To do ; to complete. II. iii. 3 ; iv. 2 (nearly unintelligible). To do service to. II. ii. 21. To perform service on. III. i. Pt. i. 3. Undertakings. II. i. 17. (2) To convey, transport ; to contain. V. xx. 8 (載爾僞). That which is conveyed or contained : = a cargo. IV. vii. Pt. ii. 6 ; = a record. V. xiii. 8.

載 *tsae* tsai — 2d tone. A year, years. I. 11, 12 : II. i. 3, 9, 13, 27, 28 : ii. 9 : iv. 1 : III. i. Pt. i. 18.

輔 *foo* fu — To assist. III. iv. 2 : IV. i. 4 : V. i. Pt. ii. 5 : *et al.* 四輔, V. xiii. 20, means to help the empire,—the four quarters, on every side.

輕 *k'ing* ch'ing — (1) Light, = that which is lighter. V. xxvii. 19. (2) To slight. IV. v. Pt. ii. 5. To deal lightly with. II. ii. 12.

輯 *ts'eih* ch'i — (1) To collect. II. i. 7. (2) To harmonize. IV. iii. 6 (輯寧).

輸 *hoo* hu — To report,—to a higher authority. V. xxvii. 20.

THE 160TH RADICAL. 辛.

辛 *sin* hsin — (1) Acrid. V. iv 5. (2) The 8th of the calendaric stem-characters. Used alone in II. iv. 8.

辜 *koo* ku — A transgression, guilt; guilty. V. x. 8 (酒惟辜), 11. The character generally occurs with negative adverbs, 一不, 非, 無, the phrase meaning guiltless and guiltlessness. II. ii. 12 : IV. ii. 4 : iii. 3 : viii. Pt. iii. 10 : xi. 12 : V. ix. 8 ; *et al.* To proceed to guilt. V. iv. 3. To hold to be guilty. V. xxvi. 8.

辟 *peih* pi — (1) A sovereign, a prince. It is generally used in application to the emperor, as in IV. v. Pt. i. 2 : vi. 1 : V. iv. 18, &c.; but it is used of all the princes of the empire in 百辟, V. xiii. 12, and 羣辟, xx. 1. To play the sovereign, to rule over ; sovereignship. IV. v. Pt. i. 3 (辟不辟) ; Pt. ii. 2 : V. xiii. 18 : xv. 18. (2) Rules, laws,—used in the phrase 定辟, settler of the rules or boundaries. V. x. 13. To this use the character in V. vi. 13 may also be reduced, making it = 'to take the law to.'

辟 *p'eih* p'i — (1) To punish ; punishments. V. xi. 3. 致辟, to carry punishment to the extreme, = to put to death. xvii. 1. 宮辟, castration, and 大辟, death : xxvii. 18. Obs. 在辟, in xxi. 8, and 辟以止辟乃辟, p. 9. (2) 便辟 mean persons who are guided in the advice they give by the likes and dislikes of those they advise. V. xxvi. 4.

辭 *ts'ze* tz'û — (1) Words. = instructions, orders. II. ii. 20 : V. vii. 10 (沈辭, hardly intelligible) : x. 16 (教辭) : xxiv. 8. = purposes. V. xxx. 5. (2) Pleas, statements and arguments in a case at law. V. xxvii. 15 (obs. 五辭), 18, 20, 21. Akin to this is its signification when foll. by 于, of complaints, xxvii. 7, 12 ; and that of excuses, apologies. V. xiii. 10 : xiv. 5, 12 : xxvii. 3. (3) Fame. V. xxi. 14 : xxvii. 22 ; and perhaps. IV. v. Pt. i. 7. (4) *I. q.* 辤, to decline. II. ii. 18.

辯 *pëen* pien (1) To dispute. 辯言, IV. v. Pt. iii. 9. (2) To rule, to manage right. V. x. 17.

THE 161st RADICAL. 辰.

辰 *shin* ch'ên (1) The heavenly bodies. The three 辰 are the sun, moon, and stars; and though we have not the phrase 二辰 in the Shoo, it seems the simplest way to take 辰 thus in the important passage, III. iv. 4, of the sun and moon. (2) The zodiacal spaces, within which occur the conjunctions of the sun and moon;—in the phrase 星辰, I. 3: V. iv. 8. In II. iv. 2, the phrase is perhaps simply = the stars. (3) 五辰 = the seasons, as associated with the five elements. II. iii. 4. (4) The fifth of the calendaric branch-characters. V. iii. 1: xiii. 29.

農 *nung* nêng (1) Husbandry. IV. vii. Pt. i. 9, 11: V. xiii. 13. 農父, the minister of agriculture. V. x. 13. (2) = largely; earnestly. V. iv. 4: xxvii. 8.

THE 162d RADICAL. 辵.

迂 *yu* yü To make crooked, to pervert. IV. vii. Pt. ii. 8.

近 *kin* chin To approach to. V. iv. 16. = to cherish. III. iii. 4.

迓 *ya* To meet. = to receive. V. xxii. 6. To go to meet: = to anticipate, IV. vii. Pt. ii. 9: = to rush on, V. ii. 9: = to hasten to accomplish, V. xiii. 16.

迤 *e* i To proceed in a winding way. III. i. Pt. ii. 9.

迪 *teïh* ti (1) The *right* path. II. ii. 5. To pursue the right path. II. iv. 8. To pursue the path of, tread in the steps of. II. iii. 1: IV. viii. Pt. i. 9: x. 3: V. i. Pt. iii. 4: v. 10; *et al.* It is used adverbially, with this meaning, before 知. V. vii. 13: xvi. 19; bef. 哲, xv. 16; bef. 畏, x. 9. Observe 不迪 = unprincipled men,—men who do not pursue the right path. IV. vii. Pt. ii. 16; 汝罔能迪, p. 12; and 出迪, IV. xi. 5. (2) To direct, to lead forward; to develope. IV. v. Pt. i. 5. (啟迪): vi. 3 *(id.)*: V. vii. 1: ix. 20, 21: x. 4; *et sæpe.* = to intimate to. IV. vii. Pt. ii. 14. Obs. 殷之迪諸臣, the officers of Yin who have been led to it. V. x. 15. (3) To advance, to bring forward. We have 迪簡, in V. xiv. 20: xviii. 28. Perhaps the simplest way of taking 不迪 in V. ii. 6, is with this meaning.—迪 is one of the characteristic words of the Shoo, and there is no other perhaps with which a translator has so little satisfaction.

述 *shuh* shu To narrate, relate. III. iii. 8.

迷 *me* mi To be erring; to go astray. II. i. 2: ii. 20: III. iv. 4: IV. v. Pt. i. 9: V. xv. 18 (迷亂): xvi. 17: xx. 16. 迷民, the deluded people. V. xi. 7. To err in the matter of, to come short of. 迷于, V. xiii. 16.

迹 *tseih* chi Footsteps, traces. V. iii. 5 (王迹 the traces of imperial sway): xix. 22. Obs. 邁迹自身 = to pursue vigorously one's own path.

追 *chuy* chui To pursue,—to take in the past. III. iii. 9. Used adverbially, and with the same reference to the past. V. xxv. 6: xxviii. 3.

退 *t'uy* t'ui To retire, withdraw. II. iv. 5: V. xiii. 18.

逃 *t'aou* t'ao Always in combination with 逋. To run away, to abscond. V. xxix. 4. = runaways, vagabonds. V. ii. 6: iii. 6.

逆 *yih* yi (1) To rebel against, to oppose. II. ii. 21: IV. 7. To be contrary to. IV. v. Pt. iii. 7 (foll. by 于). = rebelliousness, evil. II. ii. 8. To oppose,—in deliberation, or divination. V. iv. 27—30. (2) To meet. V. vi. 18: xxii. 11. = to accord with. xxvii. 13. (3) 逆河, the meeting Ho,—a name given to the Ho, where it entered the sea. III. i. Pt. ii. 7.

逋 *poo* pu To abscond. See 逃. 逋臣, vagabond ministers. V. vii. 6.

逐 *chuh* chu To pursue. V. xxix. 4.

逖 *teih* ti Far. V. ii. 1: xiv. 1 (遐逖): xviii. 29 (離逖).

通 *t'ung* To carry through. 通道, to open roads. V. v. 1. Intercommunication. 地天通, the communication between earth and Heaven. V. xxvii. 6.

逝 *she* shih To go, to put in motion. V. vii. 11 *(n. b.)*.

速 *suh* su To accelerate, to hasten. IV. v. Pt. ii. 3: V. x. 11: xviii. 23. Speedily. V. ix. 16, 17.

造 *tsaou* tsao — (1) To begin. IV. iv. 2. This is the meaning, probably, in 凡我造邦, IV. iii. 7; 新造邦, in V. xvi. 10; and 嗣造, V. xxviii. 2. Obs. 肇造, V. ix. 4. (2) To do; doings. V. vii. 1, 8. Perhaps we may bring under this 耇造德, in V. xvi. 16. (3) To seek for, with reference to. V. ix. 17.

造 *ts'aou* ts'ao — To arrive, to come. IV. vii. Pt. ii. 1. The plaintiff and defendant in a suit are called 兩造, the two comparing parties. V. xxvii. 15.

逢 *fung* — To meet with. V. iv. 26.

逭 *hwan* huan — To escape. IV. v. Pt. ii. 3.

逮 *tae* tai — To come to. V. xxvii. 6. 不逮, to be deficient; deficiencies. V. xx. 4: xxvi. 4: xxix. 5.

進 *tsin* chin — To advance, to enter. IV. viii. Pt. ii. 1 (foll. by 于): V. xxiii. 2. Actively, to advance, to bring forward. IV. vii. Pt. ii. 2 (登進): V. xviii. 5: xxi. 18.

逸 *yih* yi — (1) To exceed, to go to excess; to go to excess in,—generally with a bad meaning so that the term often = idleness, dissipation. II. ii. 6: iv. 16: V. x. 7, 9, 11: xv. 1, 3, 12: xviii. 4, 16, 29: *et al.* We have 逸言 and 逸口 = extravagant talk. IV. vii. Pt. i. 7, 12. The combination 逸豫, idleness and pleasure, is frequent. III. iii. 1: IV. viii. Pt. ii. 2: V. ix. 1; *et al.* 逸欲, idleness and lusts. II. iii. 5.   = errors. IV. vii. Pt. ii. 8. Sometimes 逸 is used as = to enjoy ease,—in a good sense. IV. vii. Pt. i. 14: V. xiv. 5: xv. 2: xx. 18. The sense is indifferent in V. xv. 7. Obs. V. xix. 5, and 逸厥逸, carried his luxurious ease to the utmost, in xviii. 16. (2) The name of a Recorder. V. xiii. 29, 30.

逾 *yu* yü — (1) To cross. V. iii. 19: in III. i. Pt. i. 53, 70; Pt. ii. 1, where it is foll. by 于, in two of the instances at least, it must mean to cross the country to. (2) To transgress. V. xxii. 6. (3) 逾邁, to pass away,—spoken of time. V. xxx. 2.

遂 *suy* sui — (1) To accomplish. 底遂 = great deeds. IV. xi. 1. (2) To give free course to. IV. ii. 7. (3) Thereon, and so. IV. xi. 2: V. v. 1. (4) Name of the country to a certain extent beyond the 郊 of a state. 三郊三遂, V. xxix. 5.

遇 *yu* yü — To meet with. It occurs only once,—in IV. vii. Pt. ii. 16, in a passage which is hardly intelligible.

遊 *yew* yu — To wander about,—generally in a bad sense, thus wasting the time and neglecting duties. We have 慢遊, II. iv. 8; 盤遊, III. iii. 1: and 遊畋, IV. iv. 7. To make excursions. V. xv. 11, 12. Obs. 遊于逸, II. ii. 6.

運 *yun* yün — To go round, = to act incessantly. II. ii. 4.

過 *kwo* kuo — 1st tone. To pass by. III. i. Pt. ii. 4, 7, 8, 9, 12: V. iii. 6.

過 *kwo* kuo — 3d tone. To go beyond. An error, a fault,—the idea of inadvertence is generally in the term. II. ii. 12: IV. ii. 5; viii. Pt. ii. 9: V. i. Pt. ii. 7. 五過, the five cases of error. V. xxvii. 15, 16.

遏 *gŏ* o — To stop. IV. iii. 6. We have 遏密, II. i. 13; 遏佚, V. xvi. 8; 遏絶, xxvii. 5, 率遏 = to exhaust. IV. i. 3.

遐 *hëa* hsia — Far. IV. v. Pt. iii. 4. 遐棄, to reject and put far off. III. iv. 4. 遐終, to put far away and make an end of. V. xii. 10. 遐逖, V. xiv 21.

遑 *hwang* huang — To have leisure. V. xv. 10.

遒 *ts'ëw* ch'iu — 遒人 = a herald. III. iv. 3.

道 *taou* tao — (1) A road, a path. V. v. 1. In V. iv. 14, it also means a path or way, and is synonymous with 路. It is there, however, used metaphorically, and we may pass from it to the use of it in the sense of ways or courses of life and conduct. III. iii. 7: V. xvi. 6: xxiii. 5: xxiv. 9. It is used often with reference to Heaven,—the way it follows and the way it approves. II. ii. 21: IV. ii. 9: iii. 3: viii. Pt. ii. 2: V. i. Pt. iii. 2: xxiv. 9. Then 道 means the way which is right, in acc. with Heaven's will, and the path of duty for man. II. ii. 6, 20: IV. v. Pt. iii. 2, 7: viii. Pt. i. 2: V. v. 7: xxiv. 3. Obs. 道心, the affinity of the mind for the right. II. ii. 15. 有道, the right-acting, or the principled. V. iii. 6. I have translated 道 by *principles* in xx. 5, but the idea is rather—courses of govt., the right underlying them. (2) To conduct by their proper courses. III. i. Pt. i. 13, 23, 49, 64. (3) To speak. 道極 =

to confess unreservedly. V. ix. 8. 道揚, xxii. 24.

達 *ta* ta — (1) To reach to. Gen. foll. by 于, II. iii. 7 (*n. b.*): III. i. Pt. i. 20, 27, 36, 45, 61: V. xi. 1 (*n. b.*): xxii. 5. 達四聰 = to hear with the ears of all. II. i. 15. = everywhere. V. xii. 4. (2) To get forward. V. xxx. 7.

違 *wei* — (1) To oppose, to go contrary to. II. ii. 6: IV. vii. Pt. iii. 7: V. iv. 31 (foll. by 于): vii. 7: xvii. 3: xxi. 14: xxx. 7. = to be disobedient to, the object being understood from the context. I. 10: II. iv. 5: V. xiv. 18: xv. 15: xvi. 3: xix. 13: xxii. 5: xxx. 5. = rebellion, or the rebellious. V. x. 13. (2) To avoid. IV. v. Pt. ii. 3.

遘 *kow* kou — To meet with. In reference to sickness.—V. vi. 5: xiii. 27.

遜 *sun* shün — (1) To accord with. IV. v. Pt. iii. 7 (foll. by 于). Obedience. V. xiv. 21, 22. To observe—to be observed—docilely. II. i. 19. = humble. IV. viii. Pt. iii. 4. (2) To be withdrawn, to be lying hid. IV. xi. 3.

遠 *yuen* yüan — To be distant; what is distant; the distant. V. i. Pt. ii. 5: v. 8 (遠物 = foreign things): xxii. 8: xxviii. 4: II. i. 16: *et al.* 無遠, without respect to distance. II. ii. 21: IV. vii. Pt. i. 16: V. v. 2: xiii. 18. 遠省, to examine what is long past. V. vii. 10. 胥遠, to become distant— alienated—from one another. IV. vii. Pt. ii. 15. 遠猷, to send one's plans far forward. V. ix. 22. = to put far away V. xviii. 29. = to a distance. V. x. 6. = at a distance. V. ix. 5.

遠 *yuen* yüan — 3d tone. To keep one's-self at a distance from. IV. iv. 7.

適 *shih* — (1) To proceed to. IV. vii. Pt. iii. 4 (foll. by 于): V. ix. 20: xiv. 5. Obs. 適輕 and 適重, in V. xxxvii. 19. 貳適 = two aims. V. xiv. 15. (2) 適爾, accidentally. V. ix. 8.

遯 *tun* t'un — To lie concealed. IV. viii. Pt. iii. 1. 行遯 to make one's escape. IV. xi. 9.

遵 *tsun* — To follow, to walk in. IV. iv. 14.

遷 *ts'een* ch'ien — (1) To remove,—both act. and neut. II. iii. 2: IV. vii. Pt. i. 1 (foll. by 于); Pt. ii. 1, 4, 6, 17; Pt. iii. 1, 5: V. xiv. 18, 25: xxiv. 3. (2) To exchange. II. iv. 2. (3) To be changed. V. xxi. 14.

選 *seuen* hsüan — To select, = to approve of. IV. vii. Pt. i. 14.

遹 *yuh* yü — To transmit the ways of, to follow the example of. V. ix. 5.

遺 *wei* — (1) To be left, to be remaining. V. ii. 6: xiv. 2: xxv. 2. (2) To leave neglected. II. ii. 3: V. i. Pt. i. 6: xii. 12. Obs. 遺育, to leave seed or posterity to one. IV. vii. Pt. ii. 16.

遺 *e* i — 3d tone. To leave to, to assign to. V. vii 3, 8. To this tone and meaning. V. xxiii. 3, 6, should probably be referred.

邁 *mue* mai — (1) Vigorously. II. ii. 10: V. xvii. 8. (2) To move forward, = to attain, to practise. IV. viii. Pt. ii. 2: V. xii. 15. To be passing on,—spoken of the movement of time. V. xxx. 3.

還 *seuen* hsüan — = to retire. V. xxii. 10.

邇 *urh* — To be near to. IV. v. Pt. i. 9: V. xxiv. 8. To approach to. IV. ii. 5. 嚮邇, to be approached. IV. vii. Pt. i. 12. What is near, the near. II. i. 16: iii. 1: IV. v. Pt. iii. 4; *et al.* 邇人, people at hand. V. v. 8.

THE 163D RADICAL. 邑.

邑 *yih* yi — A city or town, cities. Used of the capital,—IV. v. Pt. i. 3: vii. Pt. i. 3, 4; Pt. ii. 5, 16; *et sæpe.* Used of other cities, —III. iv. 1: IV. i. 3; *et sæpe.* = villages. V. xiv. 25. = a State (?). V. iii. 7.

邦 *pang* — A State, a country. *Passim.* 有邦, the possessors or princes of States. II. iii. 5: IV. v. Pt. ii. 5: V. xxvii. 14; *et al.* 萬邦, I. 2: II. iv. 1; *et al.*, *sæpe*, is used as a designation for the empire. 中邦, the middle region. III. i. Pt. ii. 15, probably denotes the empire proper, the three interior domains of Yu. 邦 alone is sometimes = empire or dynasty, as in V. xvi. 10; xx. 7—12; *et al.* In V. iii. 8, 邦 must denote specially the imperial domain. In V. ix. 1, we cannot account for the character. 五邦 in IV. vii. Pt. i. 3, is better understood as *five different regions*, than *five States*. 家 and 邦, the Clan or Family and the State, are often in contrast, as in IV. iii. 6, 7; *et al.* It is used as a verb, = to invest with a country. V. xvii. 1.

邪 *seay* hsieh — Wicked, depraved. V. viii. 2. That which is evil. II. ii. 6.

郊 *këaou* chiao — A certain extent of country, outside and around the capital city; borders, frontiers. V. ii. 1, 9: iii. 8: vi. 19: xxi. 1: xxiv. 1, 7. Observe 三郊, V. xxix. 5. Used for the place of the sacrifices to Heaven and Earth in the suburbs. V. xii. 5. Used for those sacrifices. V. i. Pt. iii. 3.

郭 *kŏ* kuo — 郭鄰, the name of a place. V. xvii. 1.

都 *too* tu — (1) Used in Part II. as an exclamation. Oh! II. ii. 4: iii. 1, 2, 3: iv. 1, 2. (2) A capital. IV. viii. Pt. ii. 2: V. xxviii. 4. In V. xix. 9, it denotes the cities of the high nobles in the imperial domain. Obs. 幽都, I. 7.

鄙 *p'ei* p'i — To reduce to the condition of a border territory. V. vii. 4.

鄰 *lin* — (1) A neighbour, neighbours. IV. v. Pt. ii. 5: V. vii. 13. 四鄰, the neighbouring States, all round. V. xvii. 6. The same phrase is applied to the emperor's ministers, II. iv. 5; and 鄰 alone, in p. 3. (2) 郭鄰, see 郭.

THE 164TH RADICAL. 酉.

酉 *yew* yu — The tenth of the calendaric branch-characters. V. xxii. 18.

配 *p'ei* — (1) To be the mate of; to correspond to. IV. v. Pt. iii. 3: V. xii. 14: xiv. 8: xxv. 6: xxvii. 11, 21. (2) To be assessors with,—in sacrifice. V. xvi. 8.

酒 *tsew* chiu — Distilled spirits. III. iii. 6: iv. 1, 4: IV. viii. Pt. iii. 2 (酒醴): xi. 1, 4: V. x. 2, 3, 4, 6, 8, 10, 13, 15, 17: xv. 13. 自酒, to abandon one's-self to drink. V. x. 11.

酗 *heu* hsü — To be furiously inebriated. Foll. by 于. IV. xi. 1, 4: V. i. Pt. ii. 3: xv. 13.

酢 *ts'ŏ* ts'o — To offer a responsive (? repeated) sacrifice. V. xxii. 27.

酣 *han* — To be drunken. IV. iv. 7. Obs. 酣身, V. x. 11.

酸 *swan* suan — Sour. V. iv. 5.

醇 *shun* — Unadulterated spirits. = pure and clear. IV. viii. Pt. ii. 10.

醉 *tsuy* tsui — To drink to excess. V. x. 4. In p. 7, it = to drink freely.

醴 *le* li — Sweet spirits,—the liquor in the state of fermentation. IV. viii. Pt. iii. 2.

THE 165TH RADICAL. 釆.

采 *tsae* tsai — (1) Affairs; to conduct affairs. I. 10: II. i. 17: III. 4. Observe 載采采, II. iii. 3; and 服采, V. x. 13. (2) Colours. 五采, II. iv. 4. (3) The cities and lands assigned to the ministers of the emperor in the domain of the nobles. III. i. Pt. ii. 19. (4) The 5th of the domains of the Chow dynasty. V. ix. 1.

釋 *shih* — To let go,—send from one's thoughts. II. ii. 10. To let go,—in shooting with a bow. IV. v. Pt. i. 7. = to liberate. V. iii. 8: xviii. 1. To put off,—spoken with ref. to a cap. V. xxiii. 7. To remove, do away with. V. xvi. 6 (foll. by 于): xviii. 13.

THE 166TH RADICAL. 里.

里 *le* li — (1) A place of residence. 宅里, a neighbourhood. V. xxix. 7. 里居, to be living in villages (= in retirement, V. x. 10.) (2) A measure of length. At present it is a little more than one third of an English mile. III. i. Pt. ii. 18—22.

重 *chung* — Heavy,—what is aggravated. V. xxvii. 19. As a verb, = to attach importance to, IV. vii. Pt. i. 2: V. iii. 9; = to deal severely with. II. ii. 12.

重 *ch'ung* — Aspirated, and 1st tone. (1) Repeated, more than one of the same kind. V. xxii. 5, 15—19. (2) 重華, in II. i. 1, is probably the name of Shun. (3) An ancient minister, apparently of the time of Shun. V. xxvii. 6.

野 *yay* yeh — Wild country, wilds. IV. viii. Pt. i. 3; Pt. iii. 1: V. iii. 2. The country,—away from court. II. ii. 3. 在野 = to be in obscurity. II. ii. 20. (2) 牧野, the scene of the battle between king Woo and Show. V. iii. 9. 大野, a lake, III. i. Pt. i. 31; so, 豬野, p. 77.

量 *leang* liang — Measures of capacity. II. i. 8.

釐 *le* li — To regulate. I. 8: V. xix. 4: xxiv. 1. Obs. 釐降 in I. 12.

THE 167TH RADICAL. 金.

金 *kin* chin — Metal. The 4th of the five elements. V. iv. 5. One of the six magazines of nature. II. ii. 7. = money. II. i. 11. = a weapon of steel. IV. viii. Pt. i. 6.

金三品, gold, silver, and copper. III. i. Pt. i. 44, 52. = with metal,—adverbial. V. vi. 11, 16.

釗 *chaou* chao — The name of king K'ang of the Chow dynasty. V. xxii. 7, 9, 11 : xxiii. 4.

鈞 *keun* chün — (1) A weight of 30 catties, the quarter of a stone. III. iii. 8. (2) *I. q.* 均 equal, as great. V. i. Pt. i. 9.

鉛 *yuen* yüan — Lead. III. i. Pt. i. 26.

鉞 *yuě* yüeh — A kind of battle-axe. V. ii. 1 : xxii. 21.

鉅 *k'eu* ch'ü — 鉅橋, a place where the tyrant Show had collected great stores of grain. V. iii. 9.

銀 *yin* — Silver. III. i. Pt. i. 69.

銍 *chih* — The ears of grain with a small portion of the stalk. III. i. Pt. ii. 18.

銳 *juy* jui — Some kind of sharp-pointed weapon. V. xxii. 21.

鋒 *fung* — The point of a weapon. V. xxix. 2.

錫 *seih* hsi — To give, to confer. III. i. Pt. ii. 16. It generally = to give to, being followed by two objectives, the thing given, and the party to whom it is so. IV. ii. 2 : V. iv. 3, 9, 11, 13 : xxii. 8. To present,—as tribute or offering. III. i. Pt. ii. 23. Obs. 錫貢 and 納錫 III. i. Pt. i. 44, 52, 60.

錯 *ts'ŏ* ts'o — (1) Stones for polishing sounding stones. III. i. Pt. i. 60. (2) To be mixed,—as revenue made up of various proportions, and kinds of impost. III. i. Pt. i. 8, 26, 43, 59 (*n. b.*), 68.

鍛 *twan* tuan — To temper. V. xxix. 2.

鍰 *hwan* huan — A weight, commonly said to be of six *lëang* or ounces; but the exact amount is rather uncertain. V. xxvii. 18.

鏞 *yung* — A large bell. II. iv. 9.

鏤 *low* lou — Steel. III. i. Pt. i. 69.

鐵 *t'ëĕ* t'ieh — Iron. III. i. Pt. i. 69.

鐸 *toh* tio — A bell with a wooden clapper. III. iv. 3.

鑑 *k'een* chien — A mirror,—whatever reflects objects. = a case for inspection or warning. V. i. Pt. ii. 5.

THE 168TH RADICAL. 長.

長 *ch'ang* — Long. 短長, short or long. IV. vii. Pt. i. 12. What is long off, far-distant. Pt. ii. 7. As a verb,—to prolong, V. xix. 24 ; to seek to be long continuing, IV. vii. Pt. i. 15.

長 *chang* — 2d tone. (1) An elder, elders. IV. iv. 4 : xi. 5 (耇長): V. x. 6. As a verb,—to treat as an elder, to exalt. V. ii. 6. (2) A president, presidents. II. iv. 8 : IV. vi. 10 (萬夫之長, chief of the myriad families): vii. Pt. iii. 8, and viii. Pt. ii. 2 (師長, heads of departments): V. ii. 2 (千夫長, 百夫長, captains of thousands, and captains of hundreds): xix. 6 (長伯).

THE 169TH RADICAL. 門.

門 *mun* — (1) A door, a gate. V. xxii. 11, 21, 29 : xxiii. 1. 四門, all the roads or channels of communication between the court and the empire. II. i. 2, 15. (2) 龍門, an important pass of the Ho, near which Yu began his labours. III. i. Pt. i. 82 ; Pt. ii. 7.

閉 *pe* pi — To shut. = to restrain. V. vii. 2.

開 *k'ae* k'ai — To open. = to initiate, to bring forward. V. xviii. 5, 7 : = to stir up. p. 18. 開釋, to liberate. p. 11.

閏 *jun* — Intercalary. I. 8.

閑 *heen* hsien — To bar. = to keep under restraint. V. xxiv. 10.

閎 *hung* hêng — A surname. V. xvi. 12.

間 *këen* chien — A space between. = to separate, to come between. V. xviii. 15 : xix. 16. = to fill up the intervals. II. iv. 9. 牖間, between the window and the door. V. xxii. 15. Some read the character in this passage *hëen*, and in the 1st tone.

閔 *min* — To think with anxiety about. V. xvi. 22. To be an object of pity. xxviii. 2.

閟 *pe* pi — To shut up. 閟毖, to shut up and distress. V. vii. 10.

閭 *leu* lü — The gate of a village. V. iii. 3.

閱 *yuĕ* yüeh — (1) To examine. V. xxvii. 18. (2) To select on examination. xviii. 27.

闗 *kwan* kuan — What is current or standard. III. iii. 8.

闢 *p'eih* p'i — To throw open. II. i. 15.

THE 170TH RADICAL. 阜.

阜 *fow* fou — Greatly. 阜成, V. xx. 13.

阪 *fan* — Precipitous, dangerous situations. V. xix. 11. The meaning is not well ascertained.

阻 *tsoo* chu — To be in difficulties; to suffer from. 阻飢, II. i. 18.

阼 *tsoo* tsu — The steps leading up to the hall on the east, appropriate to the host. V. xxii. 20, 23.

陂 *pe* pi — Embanked ponds. V. i. Pt. i. 5. To be banked up. III. i. Pt. ii. 14.

陂 *p'o* — To be uneven. V. iv. 14. It will be seen, however, that this was not the original reading here; and the character is commonly read *p'e*.

阿 *o* — 阿衡, the name, or the title, of E Yin. IV. v. Pt. i. 1: viii. Pt. iii. 10.

附 *foo* fu — To be attached—join one's-self to. IV. ii. 4: V. iii. 7.

陋 *low* lou — To be in a mean condition. 側陋, I. 12.

降 *këang* chiang — (1) To send down. I. 12: II. ii. 20: IV. iii. 2, 8: iv. 2, 8: V. i. Pt. 4; Pt. iii. 8: vi. 7; *et sæpe*. It may be variously translated,—to confer, to inflict, to deliver, &c. 降黜 = to make an end of. V. i. Pt. ii. 4. In IV. vii. Pt. iii. 4, it = to remove. (2) To descend. II. ii. 10: III. i. Pt. i. 16; *et sæpe*. 降格, to descend and approach. V. xxvii. 6. = to degenerate. V. xxiv. 4. (3) To spare, to deal leniently with in respect of. V. xviii. 2, 20, 23.

陟 *chih* — (1) To ascend:—with ref. to the throne. II. i. 3: ii. 14: V. xix. 4; with ref. to death. II. i. 28: V. xvi. 18: xxiii. 3. (2) To travel to. IV. v. Pt. iii. 4: xix. 22. (3) To promote. II. i. 27: xx. 14. (4) 伊陟, son probably of E Yin, a minister of the Shang dynasty. V. xvi. 7.

除 *ch'oo* ch'u — To remove, to take away. V. i. Pt. iii. 4: viii. 2.

陰 *yin* — Dark, obscure. 陰陽, the operations of Heaven and Earth. V. xx. 5. = secretly, by an unseen influence. V. iv. 2. · = the north side of a mountain. III. i. Pt. iii. 7.

陰 *yan* an — 亮陰, probably the shed where the emperor spends his time of mourning. IV. viii. Pt. i. 1: V. xv. 5.

陪 *pei* — 陪尾, the name of a mountain in the pres. Shan-tung. III. i. Pt. ii. 2.

陳 *ch'in* ch'ên — (1) To set forth; to display. IV. vi. 1: V. ix. 11, 18: xxii. 5, 19. Obs. 卜陳, V. vii. 15; 陳修, xi. 4; 有陳, xvi. 8. To be displayed. IV. xi. 1. To be marshalled, drawn up. V. iii. 8. (2) To continue long. IV. vii. Pt. ii. 11. (3) 君陳, the name of a minister, the successor of the duke of Chow in Lŏ. V. xxi. 1; *et al.*

陸 *luh* lu — 大陸, a tract of marshy ground in K'e-chow. III. i. Pt. i. 9; Pt. ii. 7.

陵 *ling* — (1) A high mound, a height. I. 11: II. iv. 1. (2) To do violence to. V. xiv. 9. (3) 東陵, the name of a place, corresponding to the pres. Pa-ling, chief city of the dep. of Yŏ-chow. III. i. Pt. ii. 9.

陶 *t'aou* t'ao — (1) In the phrase 鬱陶, anxieties, to be thinking anxiously. III. iii. 9. (2) The name of the principality over which Yaou first ruled, so that he is sometimes named from it. III. iii. 7. (3) The name of a small hill in the pres. dis. of Ting-t'aou, dep. of Yen-chow, Shan-tung. III. i. Pt. ii. 10.

陶 *yaou* yao — 皐陶, the name of Shun's minister of Crime. II. i. 17, 20: ii. 10, 11, 12: iii. 1, 2, 3, 8: iv. 1, 8, 11.

陻 *yin* — To dam up. V. iv. 3.

陽 *yang* — (1) The sun. 陽鳥, sun birds, = wild geese. III. i. Pt. i. 39. (2) = the south side of a mountain. III. i. Pt. i. 5, 35, 46, 62; Pt. ii. 4. (3) 陰陽, see 陰.

隅 *yu* yü — A corner. 海隅, the corners of the seas. II. iv. 7: V. xvi. 21.

隉 *nëë* nieh — A mound falling to pieces. = unsettledness. V. xx. 8.

階 *këae* chieh — Steps or stairs, leading up to a hall. II. ii. 21: V. xxii. 20—23.

隕 *yun* yün — To fall down into. IV. iii. 6.

THE 174TH RADICAL. 青.

青 *ts'ing* ch'ing. Green. III. i. Pt. i. 67.

靖 *tsing* ching. Tranquillity. 不靖, dispeace. IV. vii. Pt. i. 12. 自靖, to make one's-self tranquil. IV. xi. 9. To tranquillize. V. xv. 5.

靜 *tsing* ching. Quiescence,—the opposite of action. V. iv. 31. = in stillness, when unemployed. I. 10. To be quiet, tranquil. V. vii. 8, 7: ix. 21: xviii. 22.

THE 175TH RADICAL. 非.

非 *fei*. *Passim.* Not. It very often = it is not, it is not that, standing commonly, but not always, at the commencement of the clause, and the clause which follows frequently beginning with 惟 or 乃惟. *E. g.* IV. i. 1: iv. Pt. i. 7, 12; Pt. ii. 4: V. xii. 24: xiv. 8, 18, 20. It has sometimes a hypothetical force, = if not, without. II. ii. 17: IV. v. Pt. ii. 2: vi. 11; *et al.* Its signification is sometimes nearly that of an adjective, = that which is not, improper. IV. ii. 4: v. Pt. iii. 7: V. xii. 21; *et al.* = that which is really wrong, a crime. IV. viii. Pt. ii. 9. As a verb,—to do what is contrary to, to transgress. III. ii. 4: IV. xi. 2: V. xxvi. 7. Makes with 罔 an affirmative. V. x. 3; *et al.*

靡 *me* mi. (1) Not. IV. vi. 2. (2) 靡靡, ready acquiescence, to be flatteringly obsequious. V. xxiv. 8.

THE 176TH RADICAL. 面.

面 *meen* mien. The face. 面從, to follow to one's face. II. iv. 5. 謀面, to judge by the face. V. xix. 2. 北面, facing the north. V. vi. 4. So 牆面, xx. 16. 面 alone, xxii. 20, means facing the south. 面稽天, looking up to Heaven, to ascertain its will. xii. 11.

THE 177TH RADICAL. 革.

革 *kih* ko. (1) Hides. III. i. Pt. i. 44, 52. (2) To change, to remove or supersede. IV. vi. 3: V. iv. 5: xiv. 6, 19. Spoken of animals changing ther feathers and hair. I. 5. To be changed. V. xxiv. 4.

鞠 *këüh* chü. (1) To exhaust. 自鞠, IV. vii. Pt. ii. 6. (2) To nourish. IV. vii. Pt. iii. 10: V. ix. 16.—The meaning in these passages is doubtful. (3) 鞠子, a little child. V. xxiii. 6.

鞭 *pëen* pien. A whip. II. i. 11.

THE 180TH RADICAL. 音.

音 *yin*. Musical sounds. 八音, the eight kinds of musical instruments, = all music. II. i. 13, 24: iv. 4. 音 alone = music. III. iii. 6.

韶 *shaou* shao. The music of Shun. 簫韶, II. iv. 9.

響 *heang* hsiang. An echo. II. ii. 4.

THE 181ST RADICAL. 頁.

順 *shun*. To follow, to act in accordance with. V. i. Pt. i. 9: xxi. 6. To be obedient. IV. v. Pt. i. 9. = to allow, to indulge. V. i. Pt. iii. 3.

須 *seu* hsü. (1) To wait. 暇須, V. xviii. 17. (2) Necessary, requisite. V. xxii. 13.—The meaning here may also be brought under (1)

頑 *wan*. To be refractory, obstinately unprincipled. I. 12: II. iv. 6, 8: V. xxiv. 3. 頑童, IV. iv. 7. The refractory. V. xxi. 1.

頒 *pan*. To manifest, distribute everywhere. V. xiii. 13.

頗 *p'o*. One-sided, perverse. V. iv. 19: xviii. 29.

頟 *gih* ê. 頟頟, the appearance of unceasingness. II. iv. 8.

頮 *hwuy* hui. To wash the face. IV. xxii. 2.

顏 *yen*. The face, the countenance. III. iii. 9.

願 *yuen* yüan. To desire. 可願, what is desirable. II. ii. 17.

顛 *teen* tien. (1) To overthrow. 顛覆, III. iv. 4. 顛越, IV. vii. Pt. ii. 16. To be overthrown, = felled. IV. vii. Pt. i. 4. 顛隮, to be going to ruin. V. xi. 3, 8. (2) 泰顛, one of king Wăn's ministers. V. xvi. 12.

類 *luy* lêi. (1) A class, sorts. = the different characters or classes. V. i. Pt. iii. 3. Of a class. 不類, not equal to, not so good as. IV. viii. Pt. i. 2. 自底不類, to make one's-self unworthy. IV.

v. Pt. ii. 3. (2) To offer a special sacrifice to God. II. i. 6: V. i. Pt. i. 10.

顧 *koo* ku — To regard, to think of IV. v. P. i. 2: xi. 9: V. xii. 13: xiv. 9. = to consult. IV. vii. Pt. i. 12: V. xxiii. 6. = to examine. V. ix. 22. Observe 開 厥 顧 天, V. xviii. 18.

顯 *hëen* hsien — (1) To be or become illustrious. V. i. Pt. iii. 2, 4, 5: ix. 3, 4: xiii. 14: xxv. 6: xxviii. 1, 3, 4. 天 顯, bright principles of Heaven. V. ix. 16: x. 5; *et al.* Obs. 顯 民, to be illustrious with the people. V. ix. 1. = manifestly. V. ix. 21. (2) To be enlightened. IV. v. Pt. i. 5 (*n. b.*): viii. Pt. iii. 1: V. xiv. 9. (3) To distinguish, make illustrious. IV. ii. 7: V. xviii. 6.

THE 182D RADICAL. 風.

風 *fung* fêng — (1) The wind. II. i. 2: V. iv. 32, 34, 38: vi. 16, 19. 風 動, to be moved as by the wind. II. ii. 18. (2) Influence. IV. viii. Pt. iii. 8: V. xxiv. 7 (風 聲; but this may mean—the fame of their manners). (3) Manners, fashion. IV. iv. 7: V. xxi. 4: xxiv. 8. (4) To feel the sexual appetite,—used of animals. V. xxix. 4.

颺 *yang* — (1) To speak loudly and rapidly. II. iv. 7. (2) To rewrite and publish. p. 6.

THE 184TH RADICAL. 食.

食 *shih* — To eat. IV. xi. 6: V. xv. 10. Spoken of the fire licking up the ink on the tortoise-shell in divination. V. xiii. 3. 食 言, to eat one's words, to be false to what he has said. IV. i. 4. To accept support. IV. viii. Pt. iii. 11. Food. II. i. 16: iv. 1: IV. x. 3: V. iii. 9: iv. 8: v. 2. 玉 食 = the revenues of the empire. V. iv. 18, 19.

飢 *ke* chi — To be hungry. 阻 飢, to suffer from want. II. i. 18.

飲 *yin* — To drink. V. x. 4, 7, 9 (崇 飲), 14.

飽 *paou* pao — To be full. = to satiety. V. x. 7.

餉 *hëang* hsiang — To carry provisions to the labourers in the fields; = provision-carriers. IV. ii. 6.

養 *yang* — To nourish. II. ii. 7. 民 養, V. vii. 12, is hardly intelligble. Obs. 引 養, V. xi. 3.

養 *yang* — 3d tone. To support,—spoken with ref. to the support of one's parents. V. x. 6.

餘 *yu* yü — That which is over, remaining. III. i. Pt. ii. 5: V. xxiv. 8. 無 餘 刑 = all kinds of—no end of—punishments. V. xxix. 5.

餞 *tseen* chien — To convoy. I. 6.

饋 *kwei* kuei — To present offerings,—specially of food. 饋 祀, offerings of sacrifice. V. x. 7.

饗 *hëang* hsiang — To accept,—as the wine of sacrifice. (?). V. xxii. 26.

THE 185TH RADICAL. 首.

首 *show* shou — (1) The head. II. iv. 1. In the phrase 稽 首, II. i. 17, 21, 22, 28; *et sæpe.* (2) The chief, the most important. V. xxx. 1. (3) 雷 首, the name of a mountain. III. i. Pt. ii. 1.

THE 186TH RADICAL. 香.

香 *hëang* hsiang — That which is fragrant. Always in connection with 馨, and spoken of virtue. V. x. 11: xxii. 3: xxvii. 4.

馨 *hing* ch'ing — Odours smelt at a distance. 馨 香, see above.

THE 187TH RADICAL. 馬.

馬 *ma* — (1) A horse, horses. III. ii. 4: iii. 5. V. iii. 2; *et sæpe.* 趣 馬, equerries. V. xix. 8. (2) 司 馬, the minister of War. V. ii. 2: xi. 2: xix. 10: xx. 10.

馭 *yu* yü — To drive,—in a carriage. III. iii. 5.

馳 *ch'e* ch'ih — To bustle and hurry about. III. iv. 4.

駿 *tseun* tsun — = rapidly, hurriedly. V. iii. 8.

騂 *sing* hsing — Red. V. xiii. 29.

騭 *chih* — To make, to constitute. V. iv. 2.

驕 *këaou* chiao — To be proud. V. xxiv. 10.

驚 *king* ching — To alarm. II. i. 25.

驛 *yih* yi — The appearance of a want of connection. Used of one of the indications in divination. V. iv. 21.

驩 *hwan* huan — 驩兜, a bad minister of Yaou, punished by Shun. I. 10: II. i. 12: iii. 2.

THE 188TH RADICAL. 骨.

體 *t'e* t'i — Form, appearance. Used of the form of a prognostic in divination. V. vi. 10. Completeness. Used of the character of a proclamation. V. xxiv. 8.

THE 189TH RADICAL. 高.

高 *kaou* kao — (1) High. III. i. Pt. i. 1: IV. v. Pt. iii. 4. The high and lofty. V. iv. 12, 17. The founder of a House, or one's remote ancestor, is described by 高. 高后, IV. vii. Pt. ii. 12, 14: viii. Pt. i. 9. 高祖, IV. vii. Pt. iii. 6: V. xxiii. 3. To think highly of. V. ix. 23. (2) 高宗, the sacrificial title of Woo-ting, one of the sovereigns of the Shang dynasty. IV. ix. 1: V. xv. 5.

THE 190TH RADICAL. 髟.

髮 *fă* fa — The hair. V. xxx. 4.

髳 *mow* mou — The name of one of the wild tribes, confederate with king Woo against Shang. V. ii. 3.

THE 192D RADICAL. 鬯.

鬯 *ch'ang* — A kind of fragrant grass, used to flavour spirits. 秬鬯, flavoured spirits distilled from the black millet. V. xiii. 25: xxviii. 4.

鬱 *yuh* yü — In the phrase 鬱陶, III. iii. 9, the thoughts working anxiously and confusedly.

THE 194TH RADICAL. 鬼.

鬼 *kwei* kuei — In the phrase 鬼神. Spirits, spiritual beings. II. ii. 18; IV. iv. 2: Pt. iii. 1: V. vi. 6.

魁 *k'wei* k'uei — Chief, the principal. 渠魁 = the chief criminals. III. iv. 6.

魄 *p'ih* p'o — The disc of the moon, from the time it begins to wane to new moon. 哉生魄 is the 15th day of the moon. V. ix. 1: xxii. 1. 既生魄, V. iii. 4, is —after the moon began to wane; 死魄, p. 1, is the last day of the old moon.

THE 195TH RADICAL. 魚.

魚 *yu* yü — Fish. III. i. Pt. i. 35: IV. iv. 2.

魯 *loo* lu — The State so called. V. xxix. 5.

鮮 *seen* hsien — Fresh fish or meat. 鮮食, flesh to eat. II. iv. 1.

鮮 *seen* hsien — 2d tone. (1) Few; rarely, seldom. IV. vii. Pt. ii. 3: V. xix. 1: xxiv. 9. (2) 惠鮮, to show a fostering kindness to. V. xv. 10.

鯀 *kwăn* kuên — The father of Yu, punished by Shun. I. 11: II. i. 12: V. iv. 3.

鰥 *kwan* kuan — An unmarried man. I. 12. In all other cases, it appears along with 寡, and probably means widowers. V. vii. 8: ix. 4: xv. 6, 10: xxvii. 6, 7.

THE 196TH RADICAL. 鳥.

鳥 *neaou* niao — (1) Birds. Generally in combination with 獸. I. 4, 5, 6, 7: II. i. 22: iv. 9: III. i. Pt. i. 39: IV. iv. 2: V. xvi. 16. (2) 鳥鼠 and 鳥鼠同穴, the name of a mountain. III. i. Pt. i. 76; Pt. ii. 2, 12.

鳩 *kew* chiu — To collect, accumulate. I. 10.—The passage is hardly intelligible.

鳴 *ming* — (1) The sound of a bird; anything that emits sound is so called. 鳴鳥, V. xvi. 16, denotes the male and female phœnix. 鳴球 is the sounding-stone. II. iv. 9. (2) 鳴條 was a place near the capital of Këë. IV. iv. 2.

鳳 *fung* fêng — The male phœnix. II. iv. 9.

鴟 *ch'e* ch'ih — An owl. 鴟鴞 is the name of an ode. V. vi. 15. 鴟義, of owl-like conduct. V. xxvii. 2.

鴞 *heaou* hsiao 鴟鴞, a species of owl. See above.

THE 197TH RADICAL. 鹵.

鹹 *hëen* hsien Salt (adj.). V. iv. 5.

鹽 *yen* Salt (subst.) III. i. Pt. i. 26: IV. viii. Pt. iii. 2.

THE 198TH RADICAL. 鹿.

鹿 *luh* lu The deer. 鹿臺 the name of a tower where Show had accumulated his treasures. V. iii. 9.

麗 *le* li (1) To be fond of display. V. xxiv. 9. (2) To depend on; to be connected with. 民之麗, what the people depend on for support. V. xviii. 5. 厥麗, p. 9, should, probably, be taken in the same way. 刑之麗, V. xxvii. 12, — the circumstances of penal cases; but 麗刑, p. 8, — to be exposed to punishment.

麓 *luh* lu The foot of a mountain. II. i. 2.

THE 199TH RADICAL. 麥.

麴 *k'eüh* ch'ü Leaven, yeast. IV. viii. Pt. iii. 2.

THE 200TH RADICAL. 麻.

麻 *ma* Hempen. V. xxii. 22, 23.

麾 *hwuy* hui To brandish. V. ii. 1.

THE 201ST RADICAL. 黃.

黃 *hwang* huang Yellow. The colour of soil. III. i. Pt. i. 79. Yellow with gold. V. ii. 1. Light bay,—used of horses. V. xxiii. 1. The colour of hair in old men. V. xxx. 4. = yellow silks. V. iii. 7.

THE 202D RADICAL. 黍.

黍 *shoo* shu Millet;—a kind of glutinous grain. We always find 黍稷 together. IV. vii. Pt. i. 11: V. x. 6: xxi. 3.

黎 *le* li (1) Black. It occurs in the phrase 黎民, meaning the black-haired people. I. 2: II. i. 18: ii. 2, 10: iii. 2: III. iii. 1: IV. x. 1: V. xxx. 6, 7. Some critics explain it in all these passages by 衆, all, the multitudinous. (2) All. II. iv. 7. (3) Light, spoken of soil. III. i. Pt. i. 67. (4) The name of an ancient minister. V. xxvii. 6. (5) The name of a river. V. xiii. 3. (6) 合黎, the name of a hill. III. i. Pt. iii. 5.

THE 203D RADICAL. 黑.

黑 *hih* hĕ (1) Black,—spoken of the colour of soil. III. i. Pt. i. 17. (2) 黑水, the Blackwater. Two rivers are mentioned of this name; one, the southern boundary of Lëang-chow, III. i. Pt. i. 62: one, the western boundary of Yung-chow, p. 71; and Pt. ii. 6.

默 *mih* mo In silence. IV. viii. Pt. i. 2.

黜 *ch'uh* ch'u (1) To degrade; to be degraded. II. i. 27: IV. iii. 5: V. xx. 14. 放黜, to drive away degraded. V. i. Pt. iii. 3. 降黜 = to make an end of. V. i. Pt. ii. 4. (2) To put away. IV. vii. Pt. i. 6, 10.

黨 *tang* Partiality, partizanship. V. iv. 14.

黥 *k'ing* ch'ing To brand. V. xxvii. 3.

黷 *tuh* tu To blacken, to dirty. = irreverence. IV. viii. Pt. ii. 11.

THE 204TH RADICAL. 黹.

黻 *fuh* fu One of the symbols,—called that of distinguishing, from its form of two 己 placed in opposition to each other,—embroidered on the lower of the emperor's sacrificial robes. II. iv. 4.

黼 *foo* fu The figure of a hatchet,—also one of the symbols on the emperor's lower robe. II. iv. 4. 黼扆, a screen used at audiences, adorned with figures of axes. V. xxii. 14, 15, 22.

THE 205TH RADICAL. 黽.

鼈 *peë* pieh Tortoises. II. iv. 2.

THE 207TH RADICAL. 鼓.

鼓 *koo* ku — A drum. II. iv. 9: III. iv. 4: V. xxii. 19 (鼖鼓).

鞀 *t'aou* t'ao — A small hand-drum or rattle. II. iv. 9.

鼖 *fun* fên — 鼖鼓, a large drum. V. xxii. 19.

THE 208TH RADICAL. 鼠.

鼠 *shoo* shu — 鳥鼠, the name of a mountain. See 鳥.

THE 210TH RADICAL. 齊.

齊 *ts'e* ch'i — (1) To regulate, to adjust uniformly. II. i. 5: IV. vii. Pt. i. 17: V. ii. 7, 8 (= to adjust the ranks of a fighting host): xiii. 6 (= to marshal): xxvii. 13 (foll. by 于), 19 (齊非齊). (2) Reverent, grave. V. viii. 2: xxvi. 2. (3) Impartiality,—where all is perfectly adjusted. V. xxiii. 5. (4) The State so named. V. xxii. 11. (5) 方齊, one of Yaou's ministers. I. 9.

齋 *chae* chai — 齋栗, the appearance of reverent dread. II. ii. 21.

THE 211TH RADICAL. 齒.

齒 *ch'e* ch'ih — (1) Teeth. = elephant's teeth, ivory. III. i. Pt. i. 44, 52. (2) To be arranged according to age, to have one's place in the family roll. V. xvii. 1.

THE 212TH RADICAL. 龍.

龍 *lung* — (1) A dragon. One of the symbols on the upper sacrificial robe of the emperor. II. iv. 4. (2) An officer in the court of Shun, his minister of Communication. II. i. 23, 25. (3) 龍門, the name of a mountain on the western bank of the Ho, near where Yu began his labours. III. i. Pt. i. 82; Pt. ii. 7.

THE 213TH RADICAL. 龜.

龜 *kwei* kuei — The tortoise, whose shell was so much used in divination. V. iv. 26—31. 元龜, the great tortoise, specially good for divination, and proper for imperial use. II. ii. 18: III. i. Pt. i. 52: IV. x. 2: V. vi. 8. So, 大寶龜. V. vii. 3. 三龜, V. vi. 9.

OMISSIONS.

Page 649. Under 交 add—(2) 南交, a place far south, supposed to be in the borders of Cochin-China. I. 5.

Page 666. Beneath 嬪 insert—*pin*.

Page 671. Under 已 add—(2) 祖已, a minister of Woo-ting. IV. ix. 2.

Page 685. Beneath 曆 insert—*leih.* li

Page 708. Above 空 insert—穴, *heuĕ* hsûeh. A hole. 鳥鼠同穴, the name of a mountain. III. i. Pt. ii. 12.

Page 710. Under 臣 add—(2) 臣扈, a minister of T'ae-mow. V. xvi. 7.

Page 724. After 遯 insert 遲, *ch'e* ch'ih. A surname. 遲任, IV. vii. Pt. i. 13.

ERRORS.

Page 646. Under 一, for *yih* read *yih*.

„ 651. „ 伾, „ *p'e'i* „ *p'ei*.

„ 652. Art. 傅, for 巖 and where read 巖 and where.

Page 653. Under 僻, for *peih* read *p'eih*.

„ „ „ 克, „ *k'th* „ *k'ih*.

„ „ For 充, read 兗 (*bis*).

Page 655. Art. 凰, for male read female.

„ „ For 勛 read 勛.

„ 658. Under 厥, „ *heuĕ* „ *keuĕ*.

„ 659. „ 叨, „ *ta'ou* „ *t'aou*.

„ 661. Transfer—(2), &c., from 咨 to 咨.

„ 661. Under 單, for *an* read *tan*.

„ 662. For 囧, read 囧.

Page 663. Under 垂, for shue read shui.
" " " 堪, " *k'au* " *k'an.*
" " " 墨, " *mip* " *mih.*
" 666. " 好, " *hauo* " *haou.*
" 668. Art. 宗, " 代宗 read 岱宗.
Page 669. For the first 實, read 寒.
" " Under 寡, for *kaw* read *kwa* and kua.
Page 670 Art. 屛, for 3d read 2d.
" " Under 岱, " *tea* " *tae.*
" 677. " 惡, " *yŏ* " *gŏ.*
" " " 愧, " *kwei* " *k'wei.*
" 679. " 惑, " *hwo* " *hwŏ.*
" 681. " 改, " *kœ* " *kae.*
" 684. " 昭, " *chaou* read *ch'aou.*
" 685. " 書, " *choo* " *shoo.*
" 686. Art. 末, " stem " branch.
" 687. Under 榦, " *yan* " *kan.*

Page 687. Under 榮, for *lung* read *yung.*
" 689. For the radical 毋, and the one immediately following, read 毌.
Page 690. For 汗, read 汙.
" 695. Art. 爻, for 師爻 read 爻師.
Page 695. For 父 read 父.
" 696. Under 猾, for *gwă* read *hwă.*
" 697. Art. 王, " 秀 " 季.
" " Under 球, " *kew* " *k'ew.*
" 700. " 盛, " *sh'ing* " *shing.*
" 705. " the 2d 純, for *shun* read *chun.*
" 717. " 誤, for *woe* read *woo.*
" 719. " 象, " *seang* read *seang.*
" 720. " 趨, " *tsen* " *tseu.*
" 721. " 蹈, " *ta'ou* " *t'aou.*
" " " 輸, " *hoo* and hu read *shoo* and shu.
Page 726. Under 鐸, " tio read to.

NOTE. Since the publication of my second volume, I have met with three Works, which supply, to a considerable extent, the place of dictionaries to the Classics. The Sinologue, who shall undertake such a dictionary, will find in them a fund of most extensive and precious materials.

[1]. The first and handiest of the three is called 經韻集字析解. 'All the Characters in the Classics and Thesaurus Discriminated and Explained.' It was published at T'een-tsin, in 1822, by an officer, called Heung Show-k'ëen (熊守謙), who was assisted by a son, a nephew, and a friend, in the compilation. Altogether it contains about 10,000 characters. arranged under the Radicals by the number of strokes, as in K'ang-he's dictionary, and in the order in which they occur in that Work. It gives, moreover, simply the meanings there assigned to them; but wherever a passage of the three oldest classics is quoted with a various reading in any of the more recent ones, that is pointed out. The author estimates the number of characters in 'the thirteen Classics' at rather more than 6,500; but he does not count a character more than once, though difference of name and of tone would seem to require him to do so. The Book is in two volumes, making together only 247 Chinese pages, so that the student finds it very convenient for use. [The 'Thesaurus' mentioned in the title is, of course, the 佩文韻府, or 'Treasury of Tones and Rhymes, compiled in the apartment P'ei-wăn,'—one of the great literary Works undertaken by the order of K'ang-he, and which contains nearly 9,000 characters, with their names and tones defined, and their meaning and usage fully exhibited.]

[2]. The second Work is more voluminous, and consists of two Parts:—the 四書字詁, or 'The Explanation of the Characters in the Four Books,' in 78 chapters; and 羣經字詁, 'The Explanation of the Characters in the various King,' in 72 chapters. It was originally left in manuscript by a scholar named Twan Gŏ-t'ing (段諤廷), of the district of K'een-yang (黔陽) in Hoo-nan, and was afterwards revised, re-arranged, and published, under the auspices of a Hwang Pun-k'e (黃本驥), in 1857.

The arrangement of the characters is perplexing for the student. Taking the 'Great Learning' first, the book gives a table of the different characters in it, chapter by chapter; in the same

way it follows with the 'Doctrine of the Mean,' the 'Analects,' and the 'Works of Mencius.' In the second Part, we have the Yih, the Shoo, the She, the Ch'un Ts'ew, the Le Ke, the Chow Le, the three Chuen of Tso-k'ew, of Kung-yang, and of Kuh-leang, the Heaou King, and the Urh Ya, similarly dissected, no account being taken of the characters that have already occurred in the Four Books. The lexical portion follows the dissection in each Part, and the characters are taken in the order in which they have occurred in the Books. There is no arrangement of them with reference to the Radicals or to their sounds. This is troublesome to the learner; and though there is a preliminary chapter exhibiting the characters in each Book under their Radicals, much time and labour are still required to find the place of any term under examination. For the lexical portion itself, it is ample and satisfactory. The oldest definitions of the characters are given, and numerous examples of their use are adduced.

It is said, in a summary, that in the Great Learning there are 394 difft. characters; in the Doctrine of the Mean, 398 additional; in the Analects, other 616; and in the Works of Mencius, 776;—making in the Four Books not quite 2,200 characters. It is to be observed, however, that the same character is not counted twice, though it may be variously toned and enunciated.

In the Yih, again, there are 296 new characters; and in the Shoo, 456. The Index which I have compiled shows in the Shoo King altogether 1,998 different characters, counting a character for each variation of name and tone.

[3]. The third Work is of a different character and of higher pretensions than either of the above. It is called 經籍纂詁, 'A Digest of the Meanings in the Classical Books,' in 106 chapters. It was prepared, by the labours of many eminent scholars, under the superintendence of Yuen Yuen (阮元), to whom I have said, in vol. I., proleg., p. 133, we owe the grand collection of the 'Explanations of the Classics under the Ts'ing dynasty.' In an introductory chapter we have a memorial in which Yuen Yuen, then superintendent of the Transport Service on the grand canal, presents, in obedience to an order, his Work to the Emperor. It is dated in the 17th year of Kea-k'ing, or our 1812. In this digest the arrangement of characters adopted in the Thesaurus is followed.

END OF VOL. III.

国家出版基金项目
NATIONAL PUBLICATION FOUNDATION

海上絲綢之路文獻集成

總主編　陳支平　陳春聲

科技與文化編 62

主編　王揚宗　葉農

海峽出版發行集團
THE STRAITS PUBLISHING & DISTRIBUTING GROUP
福建人民出版社

本册目次

詩經

（*Cheu king: texte chinois avec une double traduction en français et en latin, une introduction et un vocabulaire*）

〔法〕顧賽芬（Séraphin Couvreur）編譯

《詩經》，法國顧賽芬編譯。顧賽芬（Séraphin Couvreur，一八三五—一九一九），法國耶穌會士。生於法國瓦雷訥，一八七〇來華，於河間府學習漢語，後至獻縣。曾將《四書》、《詩經》、《書經》、《禮記》、《儀禮》等儒家經典譯爲法文，又編撰《漢拉字典》、《漢法字典》等辭書。著述頗豐，影響深遠，三獲「儒蓮獎」（一八八六年、一八九一年、一八九五年）。是書有序言，述翻譯目的、所用底本；有導論，述《詩經》歷史、藝術手法及道德寓意。正文各頁最上爲原文；原文之下以拉丁字母爲漢字注音，各章前有主旨講解，最下爲拉丁語譯文，逐句直譯，略作解釋。後附《詩經》常用字字典。

據一八九六年河間府版影印。

詩　經

CHEU KING

TEXTE CHINOIS

AVEC

UNE DOUBLE TRADUCTION

EN FRANÇAIS ET EN LATIN

UNE INTRODUCTION ET UN VOCABULAIRE

PAR

S. COUVREUR S. J.

HO KIEN FOU

IMPRIMERIE DE LA MISSION CATHOLIQUE

1896

PRÉFACE.

Cette traduction, comme celle des Quatre Livres, a pour but de faire connaître l'enseignement donné dans les écoles. Elle est basée sur l'Explication complète du Cheu king 詩經備旨 qui est entre les mains de tous les étudiants. Le Cheu king pei tcheu, publié pour la première fois en 1763, renferme le commentaire de Tchou Hi et la paraphrase de 鄒聖脈 TCHEOU CHENG ME, surnommé 梧岡 OU KANG.

Parmi les ouvrages consultés, deux méritent une mention spéciale. Ce sont le 欽定詩經傳說彙纂 Recueil d'explications traditionnelles sur le Cheu king, composé par ordre de K'ang hi et publié sous le règne de son successeur en 1727, et le 毛詩註疏 Cheu king de Mao Tch'ang annoté et expliqué, qui fait partie de la collection des treize livres classiques 十三經註疏 éditée par ordre de K'ien loung en 1747.

Le Cheu king de K'ang hi donne d'abord le texte et les explications de Tchou Hi 詩集傳, puis les remarques de différents auteurs 集說. Les compilateurs impériaux ajoutent souvent un appendice 附錄, et enfin l'exposé de leurs propres opinions 案, qu'ils ont soin d'appuyer, quand ils le peuvent, sur le commentaire 序 SIU attribué à 子夏 TZEU HIA, disciple de Confucius, et à 毛萇 MAO TCH'ANG, lettré du deuxième siècle avant notre ère.

Les idées de Tchou Hi y sont plus d'une fois combattues. Elles ne sont donc pas tellement imposées qu'il ne soit jamais permis de s'en écarter. Les divergences sur les points importants sont notées dans le Cheu king pei tcheu en tête des pages, avec le titre 御案 Jugement de la commission impériale, et mises sous les yeux de tous les maîtres et de leurs élèves, comme un supplément ou un correctif autorisé et en quelque sorte officiel.

Le Cheu king de K'ien loung ne donne pas l'explication de Tchou Hi, mais celle de l'ancienne école, qui est souvent en désaccord avec la nouvelle. Outre le texte classique, il contient le commentaire 序 Siu de Tzeu hia et de Mao Tch'ang, les explications 箋 Tsien de 鄭康成 Tcheng K'ang tch'eng (127-200 après J.C.), la paraphrase 疏 Chou de 孔穎達 K'oung Ing ta, descendant de Confucius (574-648), beaucoup de citations tirées des écrits de 王肅 Wang Siu, qui vivait vers l'an 240, et d'autres savants très anciens.

Les lettrés de la dynastie actuelle ont aussi publié une volumineuse collection de commentaires sur les classiques 皇清經解. On y remarque une tendance très prononcée à contredire et à réfuter Tchou Hi.

Malgré cette opposition persistante, le célèbre commentateur tient encore la première place dans les écoles, et pour cette raison, nous avons suivi son interprétation le plus fidèlement possible.

Le Cheu king est peut-être le livre qui fournit le plus de renseignements certains sur les mœurs, les coutumes, les croyances des anciens peuples de l'extrême orient. Il offre un intérêt particulier au moraliste et à l'historien, et un secours utile au missionnaire.

Ho kien fou, avril 1896.

詩經

INTRODUCTION

CHAPITRE I.

NOTICE SUR LE CHEU KING.

HISTOIRE DU CHEU KING.

Le 詩經 **Chēu king** se divise en quatre parties intitulées 國風 **Kouŏ fōung**, 小雅 **Siaò ià**, 大雅 **Tá ià**, 頌 **Sóung**. Il comprend trois cent-cinq chants 篇 **p'iēn**, et les titres de six chants ou de six morceaux de musique qui n'existent plus.

Les chants du dernier livre, appelés 商頌 **Chāng sóung** Éloges de la dynastie des Chang, paraissent remonter au temps des empereurs de ce nom (1766-1122 avant J.C.). Tous les autres ont été composés sous les Tcheou, du douzième au sixième siècle avant notre ère.

Les chants relatifs à 文王 **Wênn wâng** (1184-1134) sont attribués à son fils 旦 **Tán**, plus connu sous le nom de 周公 **Tcheōu kōung** Prince de Tcheou.

Ces poésies avaient été recueillies par les maîtres de musique à la cour impériale, et étaient chantées dans les fêtes et les cérémonies. Confucius les revit, les corrigea, et confia son travail à 子夏 **Tzèu hiá**, l'un de ses disciples. Tzeu hia ajouta une courte explication ou préface 序 **Siù**.

Le Cheu king, comme la plupart des anciens monuments littéraires, fut condamné aux flammes par 秦始皇 **Ts'în Chèu houâng** (246-209). Mais, parce qu'il était en vers rimés et chantés, il se conserva dans la mémoire des lettrés encore plus facilement que les autres livres. Aussi, dès les commencements de la dynastie des 漢 **Hán**, au deuxième siècle avant notre ère, il en parut quatre versions ; à savoir, celle de Lou 魯詩 **Lòu chēu**, due à 申培 **Chēnn Feôu**, lettré de Lou ; celle de Ts'i 齊詩 **Ts'î chēu**, due à 陳元方 **Tch'ênn Iuên fāng**, lettré de Ts'i ; celle de Han 韓詩 **Hân chēu**, due à 韓嬰 **Hân Īng**, lettré de 燕 **Iēn** ; et celle de Mao 毛詩 **Maô chēu**, due à 毛萇 **Maô Tch'âng**, lettré de 趙 **Tchaó**.

Ces quatre versions ont été comparées ensemble et trouvées semblables pour le fond. Les différences consistaient surtout dans l'écriture ; certains caractères qui se prononçaient de la même manière étaient employés les uns pour les autres, comme il arrive souvent dans les anciens livres. Le sens était à peu près le même, ce qui prouve la fidélité de la mémoire des quatre écrivains et l'authenticité du recueil qu'ils ont transmis à la postérité.

Les trois premières versions n'existent plus. La quatrième 毛詩 **Maô chēu** nous reste seule, avec la courte explication 序 **Siù** de Tzeu hia, qui a été développée, dit-on, par Mao Tch'ang.

徐整 **Siû Tchéng** dit : « 子夏 **Tzèu hiá** donna (le Cheu king avec l'explication 序 **Siú**) à 高行子 **Kaō Hing tzèu**; Kao Hing tzeu le donna à 薛倉子 **Siě Ts'āng tzèu**; Sie Ts'ang tzeu le donna à 帛妙子 **Pě Miaó tzèu**; Pe Miao tzeu le donna à 河間人大毛公 **Maô** l'ancien, (nommé 亨 **Hēng**), lettré de Ho kien. Mao l'ancien enseigna l'explication traditionnelle du Cheu king dans sa famille, et la transmit ainsi à 趙人小毛公 **Maô** le jeune (Mao Tch'ang), lettré de Tchao. »

Mao le jeune était 河間獻王博士 savant lettré de Hien, roi de Ho kien. Dans le Traité des six arts libéraux 六藝論 **Liŭ i liún** il est dit: « Hien, roi de Ho kien, aimait l'étude. Mao, savant lettré qui était à son service, expliquait fort bien le Cheu king. Le roi Hien donna à ce livre le titre de 毛詩 **Maô chēu**. Ainsi c'est le roi Hien qui le premier le désigna sous le nom de Mao. »

Hien est le nom posthume de 德 **Tĕ**, fils de l'empereur 景帝 **King ti** (156-140) et frère de l'empereur 武帝 **Où ti** (140- 86). En l'année 155, il reçut en apanage la petite principauté de Ho kien, qui comprenait trois sous-préfectures du Ho kien fou actuel et une du 深州 **Chēnn tcheōu**, dans la province de Tcheu li.

Grand ami des lettres et insigne bienfaiteur des lettrés, il fit chercher partout les exemplaires des anciens livres, et eut le bonheur de s'en procurer plusieurs qui avaient disparu depuis les Ts'in, entre autres le Tao te king de Lao tzeu et les œuvres de Meng tzeu. Il offrit le Cheu king à son frère Ou ti. Sa mort arriva en l'année 129.

On voit encore sa tombe auprès d'une pagode appelée Hien wang miao, située à la distance de dix 里 **li** (six kilomètres) à l'est de la ville de 獻縣 **Hién hién**. La tombe de Mao Tch'ang 毛公塚 **Maô kōung tchòung** se trouve à deux kilomètres plus loin, dans la direction du nord-est.

COMPOSITION LITTÉRAIRE ET VERSIFICATION DU CHEU KING.

Dans la composition poétique on distingue trois éléments: la description ou simple narration 賦 **fóu**, la similitude ou comparaison 興 **hing** et l'allégorie 比 **pi**.

La première partie d'une similitude ou comparaison s'appelle 興意 **hing i** idée empruntée, 借映 **tsié ing** lumière ou image empruntée, 賓意 **pīn i** ou 客意 **k'ŏ i** idée étrangère au sujet. La seconde partie, qui est l'application de la première au sujet traité, se nomme 正意 **tchéng i** ou 轉正 **tchouèn tchéng** idée qui se rapporte ou revient directement au sujet, 主意 **tchòu i** idée propre au sujet.

L'allégorie est une similitude dont l'application n'est pas exprimée, et comme une fable dont la moralité doit être devinée par le lecteur. L'application ainsi laissée à la sagacité des commentateurs n'est pas toujours exempte de difficulté. En plus d'un endroit, après maintes conjectures, elle reste incertaine ou obscure.

Les stances 章 **tchāng** d'un même chant sont parfois d'inégale longueur. Les vers 句 **kiú** sont ordinairement de quatre lettres. Quelques-uns n'en ont que trois; d'autres en ont cinq ou six. Une grande liberté était laissée au poète.

Dans une même stophe, tantôt les vers se terminent tous par le même son, tantôt la rime varie. Le plus souvent les vers qui riment ensemble, se suivent immédiatement; mais on rencontre aussi des rimes croisées. Quelquefois le premier ou le dernier vers d'une strophe rime avec le premier ou le dernier vers de la suivante. Dans certaines strophes, un ou plusieurs vers ne riment avec aucun autre, et parfois séparent même deux vers rimant ensemble.

La prononciation ayant changé avec les temps, bon nombre de mots qui avaient autrefois la même désinence ne l'ont plus à présent. Tchou Hi et d'autres commentateurs du Cheu king se sont efforcés de conserver les rimes en indiquant les sons anciens, toutes les fois qu'ils l'ont jugé nécessaire. Dans les écoles, les maîtres dispensent ordinairement leurs élèves de les apprendre et de les réciter. Ils n'exigent que la prononciation actuelle, afin d'éviter la confusion qui naîtrait dans l'esprit et dans la mémoire, s'il fallait prononcer les lettres de deux manières différentes.

Nous avons ajouté entre parenthèses la figuration des sons anciens. On remarquera que plusieurs ont disparu entièrement de la langue mandarine, comme, par exemple, 天 t'în, 田 t'în, 甸 tîn, 的 tiŏ.

MORALITÉ DU CHEU KING.

Dans le Liun iu, Ch. XVII. 9, Confucius dit à ses disciples: « Mes enfants, pourquoi n'étudiez-vous pas le Cheu king? Ce livre nous porte à pratiquer la vertu, à nous examiner nous-mêmes. Il nous apprend à traiter convenablement avec les hommes, à nous indigner quand il le faut, à remplir nos devoirs envers nos parents et notre prince. Il nous fait connaître beaucoup d'animaux et de plantes. »

Au Chapitre II. 2, le Philosophe dit: « Le Cheu king contient trois cents chants. Un seul mot de l'un d'eux les résume tous: 思無邪 (詩魯頌) N'avoir que de bonnes pensées. » Sur ce passage Tchou Hi dit: « Le bien qui est raconté dans le Cheu king, excite l'homme à développer les vertus naturelles de son cœur; le mal l'excite à réprimer ses mauvais désirs. Tout l'aide à acquérir la rectitude des sentiments. »

Tous les autres commentateurs repoussent énergiquement l'idée que leur grand sage, en corrigeant le Cheu king, eût pu y tolérer des vers licencieux. Le bien y est signalé, disent-ils, afin qu'il soit pratiqué; le mal y est censuré, afin qu'il soit évité. Tout tend à inspirer l'amour de la vertu ou l'horreur du vice. Ainsi parlent les compilateurs chargés par K'ang hi de préparer l'édition impériale 欽定詩經傳說. Ils invoquent l'autorité des auteurs les plus graves. Néanmoins la première partie intitulée *Kouo foung* renferme plusieurs passages que les maîtres s'abstiennent d'expliquer aux enfants.

CHAPITRE II.

NOTIONS TIRÉES DU CHEU KING.

ÉTENDUE DE L'EMPIRE DES TCHEOU.

L'empire des Tcheou, du douzième au septième siècle avant notre ère, avait des limites beaucoup plus étroites que la Chine actuelle. A présent, les dix-huit provinces s'étendent du 21e au 41e degré de latitude septentrionale, et du 15e degré de longitude occidentale au 5e degré de longitude orientale, en comptant la longitude à partir de Pékin. A l'époque du Cheu king, l'empire chinois s'étendait seulement du 34e au 38e degré de latitude, et du 10e degré de longitude occidentale au 3e degré de longitude orientale.

Les Chinois avaient pour voisins, au nord les 玁 狁 **Hién iùn**, à l'ouest et au nord-ouest les 戎 **Jôung**, au midi les 蠻 **Mân** et les 荆 **Kīng**. Ils eurent souvent à repousser les invasions de ces peuplades à demi barbares. II. I. 7 et 8, II. III. 3 et 4, III. III. 2 et 7, IV. IV. 4, IV. V. 5. (*)

TRAVAUX DU GRAND IU.

禹 **Iù** (2205 - 2197), fondateur de la dynastie des 夏 **Hiá**, fit écouler l'eau qui couvrait la surface du pays, creusa des canaux, régla le cours des rivières et rendit possible la culture du sol. II. VI. 6, III. I. 10, III. III. 7, IV. V. 4.

DYNASTIE DES CHANG.

契 **Siĕ** naquit d'un œuf d'hirondelle que sa mère avait avalé. IV. V. 3. Il fut ministre de l'instruction publique sous le règne de 堯 **Iaô** (2356 - 2255), et reçut en fief la terre de 商 **Chāng**. Par ses enseignements il transforma sa principauté. Siang tou, descendant de Sie, brilla par ses vertus. IV. V. 4.

T'ang ou Tch'eng T'ang (1766 - 1753) honora le roi du ciel, toucha son cœur et mérita l'empire. « Ce prince belliqueux dressa son étendard sur son char de guerre, et soumis avec respect aux ordres du ciel, il prit sa hache d'armes. Sa bouillante ardeur égala celle du feu... Il défit les princes de Wei, de Kou, de Kouenn ou, et Kie, dernier empereur de la dynastie des Hia. » IV. V. 4. « Dans tout l'empire T'ang constitua les princes. Il gouverna les neuf provinces, et fut le premier empereur de la dynastie des Chang. » IV. V. 3.

武 丁 **Où tīng** ou 高 宗 **Kaō tsōung** (1324-1265), descendant de Tch'eng T'ang, se signala par ses exploits militaires. Il soumit les peuplades établies au nord du Kiang. IV. V. 3 et 4.

(*) Les deux premiers nombres, en chiffres romains, indiquent l'un la partie du Cheu king, l'autre le livre. Le troisième, en chiffre arabe, indique le chant.

詩經

NAISSANCE MERVEILLEUSE DE HEOU TSI.

« Kiang iuen offrit un sacrifice pour obtenir des enfants. Marchant sur la trace laissée par le pouce du pied du souverain roi, elle éprouva un frémissement. Elle retourna au palais,... conçut,... mit au monde un fils. Ce fils fut Heou tsi.

« Les mois de sa grossesse étant écoulés, elle enfanta son premier-né, aussi facilement qu'une brebis met au jour un agneau, sans rupture ni fissure, sans mal ni lésion ; et l'on vit clairement que cette naissance était un prodige. Le roi du ciel ne fut-il pas content ? N'agréa-t-il pas l'offrande pure de Kiang iuen, puisqu'il lui donna d'enfanter sans aucune difficulté ?

« On déposa l'enfant dans un étroit sentier; mais les bœufs et les brebis, le protégeant de leurs corps, lui donnèrent des soins affectueux. On le déposa dans une plaine couverte d'arbres; mais il y avait des bûcherons (qui le recueillirent). On le déposa au milieu de la glace; mais un oiseau le couvrit (de l'une de ses ailes, et de l'autre) lui fit une couche. L'oiseau s'en étant allé, Heou tsi se mit à vagir. Ses vagissements prolongés et puissants furent entendus par tous les chemins. » IV. II. 1.

« Les anciens lettrés ont quelque peu révoqué en doute l'histoire de la trace laissée par le pouce du pied. Mais le philosophe Tchang dit: « Avant le commencement du ciel et de la terre, certainement il n'existait pas d'homme ; il a fallu un être qui le formât et lui donnât naissance. » Le philosophe Sou dit aussi: « Tout être d'une nature extraordinaire naît d'une façon extraordinaire. La licorne naît autrement que le chien et l'agneau ; le crocodile et le dragon ne naissent pas comme le poisson ou la tortue. Certainement il en est ainsi pour les animaux. Doit-on s'étonner que la naissance des hommes extraordinaires diffère de celle des autres hommes ? » Ce raisonnement est juste. » (Tchou Hi).

« Une femme avait conçu et enfanté contrairement aux lois ordinaires de la nature. On craignit que ce ne fût un mauvais présage. Pour ce motif on voulut se défaire de l'enfant. Mais survinrent les choses extraordinaires racontées plus haut; aussitôt on le recueillit et on l'éleva. » (Tchou Hi).

« Kiang iuen est digne de vénération; sa vertu a toujours été irréprochable. Le roi du ciel abaissa sur elle un regard favorable. Dès que les mois de sa grossesse furent écoulés, aussitôt, sans lésion ni douleur, elle mit au monde Heou tsi. Le roi du ciel donna à Heou tsi toutes sortes de biens, les deux espèces de millet à panicules,... les haricots, le blé. » IV. IV. 4.

ORIGINES DE LA FAMILLE ET DE LA PRINCIPAUTÉ DE TCHEOU.

公劉 **Kōung Liôu**, descendant de Heou tsi, vivait avec son peuple au milieu des 西戎 **Sī Jôung**, dans le Kan siu actuel. Inquiété sans cesse par ces tribus remuantes, il résolut de s'en éloigner. En 1796 avant notre ère, prenant avec lui des provisions de vivres, il alla s'établir à 豳 **Pīn**, à l'ouest de la ville actuelle de 三水 **Sān chouèi**, dans le 邠州府 **Pīn tcheōu fòu**, province de 陝西 **Chèn sī**.

Il détermina le site des montagnes par l'observation des ombres, examina la direction des cours d'eau, distribua les terres et régla les impôts. Il passa la 渭

Wéi et fit extraire des pierres meulières et du fer. III. II. 6. Les travaux des habitants de Pin sous Koung Liou sont décrits. I. XV. 1.

Le roi du ciel, qui veille avec majesté sur les choses d'ici-bas, résolut de donner au peuple chinois une terre qui fût moins exposée aux attaques des barbares, et de retirer le pouvoir impérial à la famille des Chang, qui s'en étaient rendus indignes. Contemplant les quatre parties de l'empire et considérant les diverses principautés, il chercha une contrée favorable à un nouvel établissement, et un prince qui répondit aux intentions de sa providence. Il choisit un descendant de Koung Liou, l'ancien prince Tan fou 古公亶父, qui reçut le nom posthume de 大王 **T'ái wâng**. Tournant ses regards avec affection vers l'occident, il y marqua à son élu un endroit pour sa demeure. III. I. 7.

En 1325, Tan fou un matin quitta la terre de Pin, ses cavernes et ses cabanes disposées en forme de four. Pressant la course de ses chevaux, il suivit les bords de la Ts'i et de la Tsiu et arriva au pied du mont 岐 **K'i**. Il parcourut et examina les environs avec sa femme T'ai Kiang, délibéra avec ses compagnons, consulta la tortue et décida qu'il convenait de s'établir dans cette contrée, dans le 岐山縣 **K'i chān hién** actuel. III. I. 3.

Il fit arracher les arbres morts, éclaircir les massifs et les taillis, émonder les mûriers. Les Kouan i, barbares de l'occident, s'enfuirent par toutes les routes. III. I. 7. T'ai wang appela le ministre et le conducteur des travaux publics, et leur ordonna de construire les maisons et les autres bâtiments... En premier lieu le temple des ancêtres s'éleva beau et majestueux. III. I. 3.

Pour succéder à T'ai wang, le roi du ciel choisit Wang Ki, son second fils, de préférence à T'ai pe, qui était l'aîné. Wang Ki sut obtenir la soumission et l'affection de ses sujets. III. I. 7.

RÈGNE DE WENN WANG.

Wenn wang, fils et successeur de T'ai wang (1231 - 1135), fut toujours irréprochable. Il jouit des faveurs du ciel et les transmit à ses descendants. III. I. 7.

« Le ciel lui prépara une compagne... Le chef d'une grande principauté avait une fille si vertueuse qu'on l'eût prise pour la sœur cadette du ciel. » Wenn wang la demanda en mariage, et envoya des présents pour confirmer les fiançailles. Puis il alla en personne chercher sa fiancée. Pour traverser la Wei, il fit construire un pont de bateaux. III. I. 2. La femme de Wenn wang était T'ai Seu, fille du prince de Chenn. I. I. 1, 2, 3, 4, 5.

Les habitants de Mi ayant osé se soulever contre lui, Wenn wang, animé d'un courroux plein de majesté, rassembla ses cohortes et terrassa les rebelles. Il fonda une nouvelle capitale, nommée Tch'eng, à l'ouest du mont K'i. Puis, sur l'ordre du roi du ciel, il prit une seconde fois les armes, et attaqua la principauté de Tch'oung.

Le roi du ciel dit à Wenn wang: « J'aime votre vertu, votre sagesse. Vous ne faites pas éclater votre colère par des cris menaçants; vous évitez la profusion et l'inconstance. Vous suivez les lois du souverain suprême, sans vous fier à votre expérience ni à votre habileté. » Le roi du ciel dit à Wenn wang: « Prononcez la condamnation de cette principauté ennemie, (à savoir, de Tch'oung). » III. I. 7.

詩經

Wenn wang fit le siège de la capitale avec des tours roulantes et des catapultes, saisit les principaux défenseurs de la place, les fit juger et leur fit couper l'oreille gauche. Après avoir offert des sacrifices au roi du ciel et à l'inventeur de l'art militaire, il escalada les murs avec des échelles munies de crocs, rasa la ville et mit fin à la principauté. III. I. 7.

L'ode suivante raconte la construction de la Tour des Esprits, les délassements que Wenn wang prenait dans le Parc des Esprits et sur le bord du Bassin des Esprits, les concerts de musique qu'il entendait dans le gymnase ou école du palais. III. I. 8.

Wenn wang fonda ou rebâtit la ville de 豐 **Fōung**, sur le bord de la rivière de ce nom, à l'ouest de la ville actuelle de 西 安 府 **Si ngān fòu**, et il y fixa définitivement sa résidence. III. I. 10.

Il divisa l'ancienne terre de Tcheou ou K'i Tcheou en deux fiefs, conféra la partie orientale à son second fils 旦 **Tán**, qui prit le titre de 周 公 **Tcheōu kōung** prince de Tcheou, et la partie occidentale à son ministre 康 **K'āng**, qui prit le titre de 召 公 **Chaó kōung** prince de Chao, et est désigné dans le Chou king sous le nom de 君 奭 **kiūn Chéu** sage Cheu.

Tcheou koung aida puissamment son frère Ou wang et son neveu Tch'eng wang. On lui attribue plusieurs chants du Cheu king. L'éloge de Chao koung se trouve en différents endroits, notamment dans le livre intitulé 召 南 **Chaó nân**. Les chants 6, 7 et 8 du premier livre du Ta ia sont des instructions adressées par lui à Tch'eng wang.

AVÈNEMENT DE LA DYNASTIE DES TCHEOU.

T'ai Seu, femme de Wenn wang, lui donna un fils, qui fut Ou wang. « Jeune prince, le ciel vous protège, vous aide, vous confie son mandat. Docile à ses ordres, vous renverserez la puissante dynastie des Chang. »

Les soldats de Chang étaient nombreux et serrés comme les arbres d'une forêt. Ils furent rangés en bataille dans la plaine de Mou ie. Mais les nôtres seuls étaient pleins d'ardeur. Ils dirent à Ou wang : « Le souverain roi est avec vous ; n'hésitez pas à engager le combat. » Le grand maître Chang fou, semblable à un aigle qui vole, seconda Ou wang. Ce prince déchaînant l'ardeur de ses guerriers, défit la puissante armée de Chang. Aussitôt l'empire fut entièrement purgé des souillures accumulées par le tyran 紂 **Tcheóu**. III. I. 2.

Sur l'ordre du roi du ciel, les princes de la famille des Chang se soumirent au nouvel empereur. Portant toujours les vêtements et le bonnet de cérémonie adoptés sous la dynastie déchue, ils assistèrent aux libations faites en l'honneur des ancêtres de Ou wang. III. I. 1.

SUCCESSEURS DE OU WANG.

Après Ou wang, Tch'eng wang (1115-1078) et K'ang wang (1078-1052) furent élevés successivement au souverain pouvoir par le roi du ciel. Ils brillèrent par leur intelligence. IV. I. 9. Tch'eng wang fit fleurir l'agriculture. Après sa mort les

laboureurs l'honorèrent de leurs offrandes, et le roi du ciel leur donna des récoltes abondantes. IV. II. 1 et 2.

La mauvaise administration de l'empereur Li wang (878-827) cause les plus grands maux à tout l'empire. Le roi du ciel est fort irrité et déploie sa justice sévère. La dynastie des Tcheou doit craindre d'être retranchée comme celle des Chang. III. II. 1. et 3.

Siuen wang (827-781), fils de Li wang, supplie le roi du ciel de mettre fin à la sécheresse qui désole le pays. III. III. 4. Le prince de Chenn, oncle maternel de l'empereur, rend les services les plus signalés aux principautés méridionales. III. III. 5.

Le ciel abaisse ses regards sur le prince de Tcheou (Siuen wang). Pour donner au Fils du ciel un puissant défenseur, il fait naître Tchoung Chan fou. III. III. 6. Hou, prince de Chao, soumet les peuplades établies sur les bords du Kiang et de la Han. III. III. 8.

Siuen wang dirige en personne une expédition sur la rive septentrionale de la Houai. A son approche tout tremble, comme au bruit du tonnerre, au fracas de la foudre. Il lance ses officiers qui frémissent comme des tigres. Ses guerriers, rapides comme des oiseaux, semblent avoir des ailes. Ils font une multitude de prisonniers. Les habitants, voyant que l'empereur désire avant tout leur faire du bien, acceptent sa domination avec bonheur, et sont à lui pour toujours. III. III. 9.

Les troubles recommencent à l'intérieur sous le règne de Iou wang (781-770), qui donne toute sa confiance à une favorite nommée Pao Seu et à d'indignes ministres. Le ciel, malgré sa bonté et sa miséricorde, inflige de cruels châtiments. III. III. 10.

Le chant VI du livre XI des Kouo foung est une élégie sur la mort de trois hommes distingués d'une illustre famille. Aux obsèques de Mou, prince de Ts'in, le prince K'ang (620-608) les a fait immoler sur la tombe de son père. Tsouo K'iou ming dans ses commentaires rapporte que cent soixante-dix-sept victimes humaines ont été sacrifiées en cette occasion. Le poète déplore une telle barbarie. Les Ts'in la renouvelèrent, dit-on, à la mort de leur grand héros Ts'in Cheu houang, en l'année 209 avant J.C.

Les petits États eurent fréquemment des guerres à soutenir, soit entre eux soit contre les étrangers, surtout au temps de la décadence de la dynastie des Tcheou. Ainsi les barbares du nord ravagèrent la principauté de 衛 Wéi, sous le règne du prince 懿 I (668-660). I. IV. 6 et 10.

L'EMPEREUR EST LE FILS DU CIEL.

Le ciel donna à son fils (T'ang) un ministre (I In), qui fut le soutien et tint la balance de l'État, et seconda puissamment le fondateur de la dynastie des Chang. IV. V. 4.

Tch'eng wang dit: « Je visite les principautés au temps voulu. Le ciel dans sa bonté me traitera, j'espère, comme son fils. Le ciel a élevé la famille des Tcheou au-dessus de toutes les familles princières, et lui a donné rang parmi les familles impériales. J'ai quelque peu secoué les princes feudataires; il n'en est pas un qui n'ait tremblé. J'ai gagné et me suis attaché tous les esprits tutélaires, jusqu'à ceux

詩經

des fleuves et des hautes montagnes. Je suis vraiment le maître et le souverain de tout l'empire. » IV. I. 8.

« L'empereur est le fils du ciel. En qualité de fils, il est chargé par le ciel de veiller en même temps au soin des hommes et des esprits. » (詩經備旨).

GOUVERNEMENT.

Le gouvernement était féodal. Le domaine que l'empereur gouvernait directement par lui-même 畿 **k'i** avait mille 里 **li** stades en tous sens. IV. V. 3. Le reste de l'empire était partagé entre les princes feudataires. L'empereur donnait des fiefs même dans son domaine propre. Tous les feudataires recevaient de lui l'investiture. Ils devaient aller lui rendre compte de leur administration et demander ses ordres; l'empereur lui-même devait visiter les fiefs à des époques déterminées.

L'empereur et les princes feudataires avaient des 卿 **k'ing** ministres d'État et des 大夫 **tái fōu** grands préfets. De plus l'empereur avait 三公 **sān kōung** trois ministres qui étaient au-dessus de tous les autres. C'étaient le 太師 **t'ái chēu** grand maître, le 太傅 **t'ái fóu** grand précepteur et le 太保 **t'ái paò** grand tuteur.

Les feudataires de l'empire étaient divisés en cinq ordres 公侯伯子男 **kōung heôu pě tzèu nân**. Chacun d'eux recevait de l'empereur une tablette de jade comme marque de dignité. Cette tablette était de forme oblongue pour les trois premiers ordres et de forme annulaire pour les deux derniers. I. V. 1.

CONSTITUTION PHYSIQUE DES CHINOIS.

Dans un prince on admirait un visage d'un rouge vermeil. I. XI. 5.

Un type de beauté nous est offert en la personne de 宣姜 **Siuēn Kiāng**. « Elle a les yeux brillants, le front large, les angles du front bien remplis... Son large front est très blanc. Ses beaux cheveux noirs forment comme une nuée autour de sa tête. » I. IV. 3.

莊姜 **Tchouāng Kiāng** n'est pas moins remarquable. « Sa taille est élevée. Ses doigts sont blancs et délicats comme les jeunes pousses de laiterons, sa peau blanche comme la graisse figée, son cou blanc et long comme le ver qui ronge le bois, ses dents blanches et régulières comme les pepins de la courge, son front large comme celui de la cigale, ses sourcils minces et arqués comme les antennes du papillon du ver à soie. Un gracieux sourire embellit ses joues. Ses beaux yeux brillent d'un vif éclat, où le blanc et le noir tranchent bien l'un sur l'autre. » I. V. 3.

A 鎬 **Haò**, capitale de l'empire, les cheveux des femmes de haut rang étaient épais et lisses. Sur les tempes ils étaient bouclés naturellement, et présentaient l'apparence de la queue du scorpion. II. VIII. 1.

Le Cheu king ne fournit aucun renseignement sur la taille des Chinois. Dans Meng tzeu, Livre VI. Chapitre II. 2, on lit: 交聞文王十尺湯九尺今交九尺四寸以長 « Moi Kiao, j'ai entendu dire que Wenn wang avait dix pieds de taille (2 mètres), T'ang neuf pieds (1 mètre, 80 c.). Moi, j'ai neuf pieds et quatre dixièmes (1 mètre, 88 c.).» Le pied des Tcheou valait environ vingt centimètres.

VÊTEMENTS.

Les deux parties principales du vêtement des hommes et des femmes étaient une sorte de grand tablier ou de jupe fendue 裳 **châng**, qui couvrait la partie inférieure du corps depuis les reins jusqu'aux talons, et une veste ou tunique 衣 **i**, qui couvrait la partie supérieure du corps. La tunique avait un collet. I. IX. 1. Elle était serrée aux reins par une ceinture. I. IV. 3.

Les vêtements d'été étaient faits d'une simple étoffe de soie ou de chanvre, avec ou sans doublure. Ceux d'hiver étaient garnis de ouate ou de fourrures. I. XI. 8, I. VII. 6. Les anciens habitants du 陝 西 **Chèn si** portaient en hiver une étoffe grossière de laine. I. XV. 1.

Les femmes portaient communément un vêtement de soie ou de chanvre de couleur naturelle, et un bonnet gris ou garance. I. VII. 19. Une jeune fille de la principauté de 鄭 **Tchéng** revêt une tunique et un vêtement inférieur simples sur une tunique et un vêtement inférieur de soie à fleurs. I. VII. 15.

La tunique de cérémonie des princesses était ornée de broderies représentant des plumes de faisan. I. IV. 3. Lorsque 宣 姜 **Siuên Kiāng** paraissait devant un prince, en été elle portait une tunique de soie blanche sur une tunique de fine toile frisée, ou, selon une autre interprétation, une tunique de fine toile frisée sur une tunique de soie blanche. I. IV. 3.

L'empereur et les feudataires du premier rang 公 **kōung** avaient sur leurs vêtements 袞 **kouènn** neuf emblèmes 章 **tchāng**; dont cinq sur la tunique, à savoir, des dragons 龍 **lôung**, des montagnes 山 **chān**, des faisans 華 蟲 **houâ tch'ôung**, des flammes 火 **houò**, des vases sacrés 宗 彝 **tsōung i**; et quatre sur le vêtement inférieur, à savoir, des algues 藻 **tsaò**, des grains de riz 粉 米 **fènn mi**, des haches 黼 **fòu** et des lettres 亞 **iá** appelées 黻 **fòu**. I. XV 16, II. VII. 8.

Les feudataires du deuxième et du troisième rang 侯 伯 **heôu pĕ** avaient sur leur vêtement inférieur quatre emblèmes, comme l'empereur et les feudataires du premier rang; mais ils n'en avaient que trois sur leur tunique, à savoir, des faisans, des flammes et des vases sacrés. I. X. 9.

La tunique des feudataires des deux derniers rangs 子 男 **tzèu nân** avait aussi trois emblèmes: des algues, des grains de riz et des vases sacrés. Leur vêtement inférieur n'en avait que deux: des haches et des lettres. Ces vêtements appelés 毳 衣 **tch'ouéi i** étaient aussi portés par les 大 夫 **tái fōu** grands officiers de l'empereur hors du territoire impérial. I. VI. 9.

En hiver, les 諸 侯 **tchōu heôu** mettaient la tunique garnie de fourrures d'agneaux, lorsqu'ils donnaient audience, et celle garnie de fourrures de renards, lorsqu'ils faisaient visite à l'empereur. I. XIII. 1. Les 卿 **k'īng** ministres d'État et les 大 夫 **tái fōu** grands préfets portaient la tunique garnie de peaux d'agneaux, avec des manches dont les parements étaient de peau de léopard. I. VII. 6, I. X. 7.

Le prince de 秦 **Ts'în**, arrivant à 鎬 **Haó**, portait une tunique de soie à fleurs sur une tunique garnie de fourrures de renards, et un vêtement inférieur orné de diverses broderies sur le vêtement officiel orné de haches. I. XI. 5.

詩經

Les 卿 **k'īng** ministres d'État à la cour impériale étaient vêtus de noir, lorsqu'ils vaquaient aux affaires dans le palais même de l'empereur. I. VII. 1.

Les *tchou heou*, dans les cérémonies en l'honneur des ancêtres, portaient une tunique de soie blanche à collet rouge. I. X. 3.

Le blanc était la couleur du deuil. I. XIII. 2.

Le collet des lettrés était bleu 青 衿 **ts'īng kīn**. Cette expression est encore employée maintenant pour désigner un 秀 才 **sióu ts'âi**. I. VII. 17.

L'empereur, les princes et les officiers portaient des jambières ou genouillères 芾 ou 韍 **fŏu**, longues de trois 尺 **tch'ĕu** (60 centim.), larges d'un 尺 (20 c.) à la partie supérieure et de deux 尺 (40 c.) à la partie inférieure. Celles de l'empereur étaient rouge foncé; celles des feudataires des trois derniers rangs 伯 子 男 et celles des officiers inférieurs étaient rouge pâle.

Les 公 **kōung** et les 侯 **heôu** portaient des genouillères rouge foncé, quand ils donnaient audience, et des genouillères rouge pâle, quand ils paraissaient devant l'empereur. II. III. 4 et 5, II. VII. 8.

Les chaussures ordinaires en été étaient des souliers de chanvre. I. VIII. 6, I. IX. 1. Les chaussures de cérémonie 舄 **sī** étaient des souliers de couleur rouge, dont les semelles étaient très épaisses et les ornements étaient d'or ou dorés. I. XV. 7, II. III. 5.

Les hommes portaient à la ceinture un doigtier d'ivoire qui se mettait au pouce de la main droite pour tirer de l'arc, un poinçon d'os ou d'ivoire qui servait à défaire les nœuds, une épingle d'ivoire qui servait à gratter la tête et à démêler la chevelure. I. V. 6, I. IX. 1. Les femmes avaient une serviette à la ceinture. I. II. 12.

Les personnes de distinction, hommes et femmes, portaient à la ceinture des pierres de prix unies ensemble par des cordons. La forme de ces pierres était toujours la même; mais la qualité et la couleur variaient. La principale était une grande agrafe 珩 **hêng**, d'où pendaient trois cordons 組 **tsòu**. Le cordon du milieu portait une pierre ronde 瑀 **iù** et une pierre triangulaire 衝 牙 **hêng iâ**. Les deux autres avaient en leur milieu une pierre carrée 琚 **kiū**, et à leur extrémité une pierre semi-circulaire 璜 **houâng**. I. V. 10. Ces pierres s'entrechoquaient et faisaient entendre un son, lorsqu'on marchait. I. V. 5. On en donnait en présent. I. V. 10, I. VII. 8, I. XI. 9.

A la campagne, les hommes portaient le chapeau de paille en été, et le manteau de jonc contre la pluie. II. IV. 6. A la capitale, en été, les officiers portaient des chapeaux de jonc et des bonnets de toile noire. Ils avaient de longues ceintures pendantes. II. VIII. 1. Le chapeau ou le bonnet était retenu par deux cordons, dont les extrémités étaient nouées et pendaient sous le menton. I. VIII. 6.

Des pierres de prix ou des ornements d'ivoire, suspendus au bonnet par des cordons, couvraient les oreilles 充 耳 **tch'ōung èul**. I. V. 1, I. VIII. 3, II. VIII. 1. 武 **Où**, prince de 衛 **Wéi**, avait de belles pierres de prix sur les oreilles, et les perles brillaient comme des étoiles sur les coutures de son bonnet. I. V. 1.

Lorsqu'une princesse aidait son mari à faire une offrande, elle avait sur la tête

III

un ornement 副 **fóu** composé de cheveux. Deux épingles 笄 **kī**, dont la tête représentait une poule 雞 **kī**, y étaient enfoncées, et portaient des cordons 紞 **tàn** ornés de six pierres de prix 珈 **kiā**, qui pendaient sur les oreilles. Une troisième épingle 揥 **tch'éu** servait à démêler la chevelure. I. IV. 3.

Sous Wenn wang, la femme d'un prince préparant une offrande ou soignant les vers à soie, portait sur la tête un ornement 被 **pi** formé de cheveux étrangers tressés ensemble. I. II. 2.

Trois mois après la naissance d'un enfant, garçon ou fille, on lui coupait les cheveux, à l'exception de deux touffes qu'on lui laissait sur les tempes, et qu'on liait en forme de cornes. Ces deux touffes de cheveux devaient lui rappeler sans cesse les devoirs de la piété filiale. A la mort de son père, il coupait celle qui était sur la tempe gauche; à la mort de sa mère, il coupait l'autre. I. IV. 1, I. V. 4, I. VIII. 7.

CONSTRUCTIONS.

Les anciens habitants de 豳 **Pīn**, sous 亶 父 **Tàn fòu**, au quatorzième siècle avant notre ère, habitaient des huttes ou des cavernes en forme de four. III. I. 3.

Les bâtiments principaux regardaient le midi. Pour déterminer l'orientation, on observait le lever et le coucher du soleil et l'ombre d'un gnomon.

Les fondements étaient tracés et les terrassements commencés au mois de novembre, quand la constellation 定 **Tíng** ou 營 室 **Îng chēu** (Markab et une autre étoile de Pégase) atteignait sa culmination vers la tombée de la nuit. I. IV. 6.

La plupart des constructions étaient de terre. Les ouvriers qui devaient élever un mur, après avoir établi le soubassement, plantaient des pieux 楨 **tchēng**, et posaient de champ une ligne de planches 榦 **kán**, de chaque côté des fondations. Dans cette sorte de caisse, ils mettaient de la terre et la battaient avec force. Quand la caisse était remplie et la première assise ou *banchée* terminée, ils enlevaient les planches, les plaçaient plus haut, de manière à former comme une nouvelle caisse au-dessus de la première assise, et élevaient la seconde assise. Ils continuaient ainsi jusqu'à ce que le mur eût atteint la hauteur voulue. II. IV. 5.

Ce genre de construction, appelé *Pisé* ou *Maçonnerie de pisé*, est usité dans plusieurs contrées de l'Europe.

A la campagne, les toits étaient couverts de chaume. On les réparait chaque année avant l'hiver. I. XV. 1.

AGRICULTURE.

Le territoire était divisé en carrés qui avaient un 里 **li** stade ou trois cents 步 **póu** pas de chaque côté, et contenaient neuf cents 畝 **meòu**. La longueur du *pou* était de six 尺 **tch'ĕu**, et celle du *tch'eu* était de vingt centimètres environ. Par conséquent, le *pou* valait approximativement un mètre vingt centimètres, le stade 360 mètres, le stade carré 129600 mètres carrés, et le *meou* 144 mètres carrés ou un peu moins d'un are et demi.

Les carrés étaient subdivisés en neuf parties égales, et appelés 井 **tsing**, parce qu'ils présentaient la forme de cette lettre.

En dehors du domaine particulier de l'empereur, un *tsing* était confié à huit familles de laboureurs. Chacune d'elles en avait en propre une partie comprenant cent *meou* (144 ares). Elles cultivaient ensemble la partie centrale ou 公 田 **kōung t'iên**, dont les produits revenaient au chef de l'État. III. II. 6.

Dans le domaine propre de l'empereur, il n'y avait pas de champ commun, mais seulement des champs particuliers. La dixième partie des produits de la terre était donnée à l'État.

Chaque laboureur avait une habitation auprès de son champ pour le temps des travaux, et une autre au village ou à la ville pour l'hiver. I. XV. 1, II. VI. 6. Un inspecteur 田 畯 **t'iên tsiún** surveillait les travaux. II. VI. 7. L'institution des inspecteurs est attribuée à l'empereur Tch'eng wang (1115-1078). IV. II. 2.

Les femmes et les enfants portaient la nourriture aux travailleurs dans la campagne. II. VI. 7, IV. III. 6.

Les animaux domestiques étaient les chevaux, les bœufs, les brebis, les porcs, les poules, les chiens.

On cultivait surtout le millet, spécialement deux variétés d'une même espèce de millet à panicules 黍 稷 **chòu, tsĭ**. I. XV. 1, III. II. 1. Les autres grains cultivés étaient le blé, les pois, les haricots, le chanvre, l'orge, le riz, le grand millet ou sorgho. I. X. 8, III. II. 1, IV. I. 10.

Plusieurs espèces de concombres croissaient sur la lisière des champs et dans les jardins potagers. I. XV. 1. Les courges servaient à la natation. I. III. 9. La moitié d'une calebasse était une coupe primitivement admise même dans les banquets des princes. III. II. 6. Les poireaux 韭 **kiòu** sont mentionnés. I. XV. 1.

Les arbres fruitiers étaient le pêcher, le jujubier, le poirier, le cognassier, la vigne. I. II. 13, I. V. 10, I. XV. 1.

Un peu avant la moisson, le jardin potager était transformé en aire pour le battage des grains. I. XV. 1, II. IV. 2.

Les moissonneurs laissaient des épis, des javelles pour les glaneuses. II. VI. 8.

Les fils des laboureurs, s'ils se distinguaient par leur intelligence, pouvaient arriver aux charges. II. VI. 7.

CHASSE. PÊCHE.

Les princes, les grands officiers étaient portés sur des voitures traînées par quatre chevaux attelés de front. II. III. 5. Les voitures légères débusquaient le gibier. On se servait de chiens. I. XI. 2.

La voiture du chasseur devait être dirigée de telle sorte qu'il pût frapper l'animal au côté gauche. I. XI. 2.

Dans les endroits marécageux on mettait le feu aux herbes. I. VII. 4.

En hiver on chassait le loup, en été le grand cerf 麋 **mi**, au printemps et en automne le cerf ordinaire et le sanglier. I. XI. 2. On chassait aussi le renard, le

blaireau, le bœuf sauvage. I. IX. 6, I. XV. 1, II. III. 6. Un prince saisit un tigre avec les mains. I. VII. 4. Les particuliers prenaient le lièvre au filet. I. I. 7. Dans la principauté de Han, on trouvait des cerfs, deux espèces d'ours, des tigres, des chats sauvages. III. III. 7.

Les engins de pêche étaient la ligne, le filet, la nasse 笱 **keoû** ou 罶 **lioû**, une sorte de panier renversé 罩 **tchaó**. I. II. 13, I. III. 10, I. V. 5, II. II. 3 et 5.

On établissait dans l'eau des barrages de pierre, avec des ouvertures auprès desquelles on plaçait des nasses. I. III. 10. Les viviers n'étaient pas rares. II. IV. 8. Wenn wang avait un vivier. III. I. 8.

On pêchait l'esturgeon, la carpe, la tanche, la brème, le barbeau, le pimélode,...

TRAVAUX DES FEMMES.

Après les soins du ménage, les principales occupations des femmes, même des princesses, étaient de cueillir les plantes textiles, d'élever les vers à soie, de filer, de tisser et de préparer les vêtements. Une fille dans son bas âge avait une tuile pour jouet, parce que les fileuses se servaient de tuiles, on ignore à quel usage. II. IV. 3.

La femme de Wenn wang coupe les dolics. De leurs fibres elle tisse deux sortes de toiles, se fait des vêtemenets et les lave elle-même. I. I. 2.

Au printemps, les femmes cueillent les feuilles des mûriers et l'armoise blanche pour les vers à soie. I. XV. 1.

Les plantes textiles étaient les dolics, l'ortie blanche, le chanvre. I. XII. 4.

L'ensouple et la navette du métier à tisser sont mentionnées. II. V. 9.

Les tissus à fleurs imitaient les coquillages précieux 貝 錦 **pèi kin**. II. V. 6.

Une femme ne doit rien entreprendre de son propre chef. Sa principale vertu est l'obéissance, d'abord à ses parents, puis à son mari. II. IV. 5.

VOYAGES.

On voyageait à pied ou en voiture. Il n'est pas fait mention de voyageurs à cheval, non plus que de cavaliers dans les armées, l'usage d'aller à cheval n'étant pas encore introduit, disent les auteurs chinois.

Afin que la jambe fût plus ferme, une bande de toile était enroulée autour de la partie inférieure depuis le pied jusqu'au genou. Elle s'appelait 邪 幅 **siê pĭ**, parce qu'elle formait des replis obliques. II. VII. 8.

Les princes, les officiers avaient à leurs voitures quatre et quelquefois même cinq ou six chevaux attelés de front. I. IV. 10. Des sonnettes étaient fixées sur le devant de la caisse de la voiture et aux extrémités des mors des chevaux. IV. II. 8. Voy. la description du char de guerre. I. XI. 3.

Ceux qui, pour honorer un voyageur, l'avaient accompagné une partie de la route, devaient, avant de le quitter, offrir avec lui un sacrifice au dieu des chemins et faire un festin. I. III. 14.

TIR A L'ARC.

Le tir à l'arc était l'un des six arts libéraux, et faisait partie de l'enseignement dans les gymnases ou écoles. Des exercices, des luttes avaient lieu en public, spécialement les jours de réjouissance. II. VII. 6.

Les archers portaient au pouce de la main droite un doigtier d'os ou d'ivoire qui les aidait à tirer la corde de l'arc, et au bras gauche une armure de cuir contre laquelle ils appuyaient l'arc. II. III. 5.

Ils tiraient à la cible deux à deux, à trois reprises différentes. Chaque fois ils lançaient chacun quatre flèches. I. VIII. 11, III. II. 2. Les vainqueurs recevaient des félicitations. Les vaincus étaient condamnés à boire une coupe de liqueur. II. VII. 6. Les vainqueurs étaient rangés d'après la modestie plus ou moins grande qu'ils montraient dans leur triomphe. III. II. 2. Venait ensuite un banquet où la sobriété et les bienséances n'étaient pas toujours observées. II. VII. 6.

GUERRE.

Les chars de guerre faisaient la principale force des armées. Chacun d'eux avait quatre chevaux attelés de front et munis de cuirasses, portait trois hommes également munis de cuirasses, et avait une escorte de quatre-vingt-dix-sept fantassins. I. XI. 3, II. III. 4.

Il n'est pas question de cavalerie. D'après les auteurs chinois, l'usage de monter les chevaux ne s'est introduit qu'au troisième siècle avant notre ère.

L'empereur avait six légions divisées en cinq cohortes de cinq cents hommes chacune; il avait en tout soixante-quinze mille hommes. II. VI. 9, II. VIII. 3.

Le tambour appelait les soldats sous les armes. I. III. 6. On le battait avec lenteur pour donner le signal de l'attaque, et avec force pour donner le signal de la retraite. II. III. 4.

L'étape ordinaire était de trente 里 **li** stades (environ vingt kilomètres). II. III. 3. Les soldats bavards étaient bâillonnés. I. XV. 3.

Sur les étendards étaient représentés des éperviers, des dragons, ou des serpents enroulés autour de tortues. II. I. 8.

Les armes étaient l'arc, la javeline 戈 **kouŏ**, la lance 矛 **meôu**, le 殳 **chôu** faisceau de lattes de bambou, la hache de guerre, le sabre. I. V. 8, I. VII. 5, I. XI. 3, III. II. 6. « L'arc du chef a des extrémités d'ivoire; son carquois est de peau de veau marin. » II. I. 7.

Un archer avait deux arcs réunis dans un même étui. IV. IV. 4. L'empereur avait des arcs rouges 彤 弓 **t'ôung kōung**; il en offrait aux officiers qu'il voulait récompenser. II. III. 1. Avant de mettre un arc dans son étui, on le débandait, et, pour l'empêcher de se déformer, on lui accolait une armature de bambou qu'on liait fortement. II. III. 1.

Les soldats se préparant au combat, prenaient le casque et la tunique de cuir. II. III. 3. Les fantassins du prince de Lou avaient des casques ornés de

coquillages, qui étaient cousus en lignes avec du fil rouge. IV. IV. 4. L'empereur portait des genouillères de cuir rouge garance. II. VI. 9.

Le service militaire était obligatoire. Les soldats étaient des laboureurs arrachés aux travaux des champs. En plusieurs endroits du Cheu king, nous les entendons se plaindre d'avoir été envoyés et retenus longtemps loin de leurs familles, au milieu des fatigues et des périls, et de ne pouvoir ni cultiver leurs terres ni donner leurs soins à leurs parents. Les parents déplorent le sort de leurs fils. I. III. 6, I. X. 8, I. XV. 3 et 4, II. I. 7, II. VI. 3.

Les fils uniques dont les parents étaient avancés en âge, étaient exempts du service militaire. II. IV. 1.

MARIAGES.

Un jeune homme qui désire se marier, doit d'abord informer ses parents. I. VIII. 6. Pour contracter les fiançailles, un entremetteur est nécessaire. I. VIII 6, I. XV. 5. La famille du fiancé envoie des présents à la fiancée. III. I. 2. Parmi les présents figure une oie sauvage. I. III. 9.

Les noces se célèbrent après la fonte des glaces, vers l'époque de la floraison du pêcher. I. III. 9, I. I. 6. La mère fixe une serviette 縭 li à la ceinture de sa fille. I. XV. 3.

Le fiancé va lui-même chercher sa fiancée pour la célébration des noces. I. VIII. 3. Un jeune prince alla chercher sa fiancée avec une escorte de cent voitures. La princesse partit accompagnée de cent voitures de la maison de son père. I. II. 1. La cérémonie du mariage se fait le soir au crépuscule. I. XII. 5.

Une femme veuve, âgée de cinquante ans au moins, et n'ayant pas d'enfant mâle, servait de maîtresse à la jeune fille, avant et après le mariage. I. I. 2. La nouvelle mariée gardait le repos durant trois mois après la célébration des noces. Ce temps écoulé, elle allait rendre hommage aux ancêtres de son mari dans leur temple. Puis elle commençait à s'occuper des affaires domestiques. I. III. 10, I. IX. 1.

La femme d'un prince était libre de retourner à la maison paternelle pour voir ses parents, tant qu'ils étaient en vie. Après leur mort, elle devait se contenter d'envoyer un 大夫 **tái fōu** grand préfet saluer ses frères. I. III. 14, I. IV. 10.

Il est beau pour une veuve de ne pas contracter un second mariage. I. IV. 1, I. X. 11. D'après le Li ki, un jeune homme doit être marié avant l'âge de trente ans, et une fille avant l'âge de vingt ans.

FESTINS.

Les mets étaient servis, non sur des tables, mais à terre sur des nattes. II. VII. 6. Les invités s'asseyaient à terre sur une double couche de nattes, et s'adossaient contre des escabeaux. III. II. 2.

Vers 1796 avant notre ère, Koung Liou, après avoir fait construire des habitations dans son nouveau domaine, à Pin dans le Chen si, prépara un grand festin, où les invités prirent place sur des nattes étendues à terre, s'appuyèrent le dos contre des escabeaux, mangèrent de la viande de porc, et burent une sorte de liqueur fermentée qui leur fut servie dans des calebasses. III. II. 6.

Wenn wang ou l'un de ses descendants faisait servir huit plats. II. I. 5. L'empereur disait aux invités : « Qu'aucun de vous ne se retire sans avoir bu son soûl. » Les invités répondaient : « Oui, oserions-nous ne pas boire notre soûl ? » II. II. 10. Pendant le repas, les musiciens jouaient, les pantomimes donnaient une représentation. II. I. 5.

Hien fou, ministre de l'empereur Siuen wang (827-781), offre, par ordre de son maître, un festin au prince de Han et à ses compagnons de voyage. Le repas se compose de poisson frais, de tortues et de jeunes pousses de bambou et de massette. Cent bouteilles de liqueur fermentée égaient les voyageurs. III. III. 7.

Ki fou, revenu vainqueur d'une expédition contre les Hien iun, réunit ses amis à un festin. Il leur fait servir des tortues rôties et des carpes hachées. II. III. 3.

On peut inviter et traiter convenablement un ami, quand même on n'aurait à lui servir que des feuilles de concombres, un lièvre et un peu de liqueur fermentée. Le repas le plus frugal est agréable aux invités, si les règles de l'urbanité y sont parfaitement observées. II. VIII. 7.

Au commencement du repas, le maître de la maison offrait à boire. Les invités, après avoir bu, lui rendaient la pareille. Le maître de la maison emplissait et présentait de nouveau les coupes. Les invités les recevaient ; mais les déposaient aussitôt et ne buvaient pas. II. VIII. 7, III. II. 2.

Parfois un serveillant, aidé d'un censeur, avait la charge difficile de rappeler à l'ordre ceux qui, dans la chaleur du vin, oubliaient les bienséances. II. VII. 6.

Le riz et le millet étaient employés à la préparation des liqueurs fermentées. I. XV. 1.

Les parents de l'empereur, invités par lui à un banquet, portaient le bonnet de peau 弁 **pién**. II. VII. 3.

MUSIQUE.

La musique tenait une place importante dans les cérémonies et les réjouissances. Les chefs de musique étaient des aveugles. IV. II. 5.

Les principaux instruments étaient la cloche ordinaire 鐘 **tchōung**, la grosse cloche 鏞 **iôung**, la petite cloche 鉦 **tchēng**, le tambour ordinaire 鼓 **kòu**, le grand tambour 田 **t'iên**, le tambour de peau de crocodile 鼉鼓 **t'ouô kòu**, le tambour à caisse d'argile 土鼓 **t'òu kòu**, le tambour de forme tubulaire 應 **ing** qui mêlait ses sons 應和 **ing houó** à ceux du grand tambour 田 **t'iên** ; le tambourin à manche 鞉 **t'aô** muni de deux balles suspendues qui frappent sur les peaux et les font résonner, lorsqu'on agite l'instrument en le tenant par le manche; la pierre musicale 磬 **k'ing**, le luth à cinq ou sept cordes 琴 **k'in**, le luth à dix-neuf ou vingt-cinq cordes 瑟 **chĕ**, la flûte à deux tuyaux 管 **kouàn**, la flûte à seize ou vingt-quatre tuyaux 簫 **siaō**, la flûte à treize ou dix-neuf tuyaux (sorte de petit orgue à bouche) 笙 **chēng**, la flûte traversière 籥 **iŏ**, une autre flûte traversière 篪 **tch'êu**, la flûte ou sifflet d'argile en forme d'œuf 塤 **hiuēn**. I. I. 1, I. III. 13, II. I. 1, II. V. 5 et 7, III. I. 8, IV. II. 5.

On battait la mesure sur un vase d'argile 缶 **feòu**. I. XII. 1.

On donnait le signal, au moment de commencer un morceau de musique, en faisant retentir une sorte de tonnelet de bois 柷 **tchŏu** ; et au moment de terminer, en frappant sur un autre instrument de bois 圉 ou 敔 **iù**, qui avait la forme d'un tigre couché. IV. II. 5. Le son du tambour ouvrait la symphonie. III. I. 8.

Les cloches, les pierres musicales et plusieurs espèces de tambours étaient fixées à des suspensions. III. I. 8.

PANTOMIME AVEC CHANT.

Les pantomimes 舞 人 **où jênn** se mouvaient et gesticulaient sur la scène en chantant. Ils tenaient dans les mains un bouclier et une hache d'armes, lorsqu'ils représentaient un exploit militaire, une flûte 籥 **iŏ** et une plume de faisan 翟 **tĭ** ou un éventail de plumes de héron 翿 **t'aô**, lorsqu'ils représentaient une action civile. I. III. 13, I. VI. 3.

ÉCOLES OU GYMNASES.

L'empereur et les princes établissaient des écoles publiques dans leurs capitales. L'école impériale s'appelait 辟 廱 ou 璧 廱 **Pi iōung**, parce qu'elle était entourée d'un cercle d'eau, et présentait l'apparence de la tablette annulaire 璧 **pĭ**. III. I. 8.

Les écoles instituées par les princes se nommaient 泮 宮 **P'án kōung**, 泮 水 **P'án chouèi** ou 泮 林 **P'án lîn**, parce que l'enceinte était baignée par un demi-cercle d'eau, du côté du midi. IV. IV. 3.

Dans ces gymnases, les jeunes gens apprenaient les six arts libéraux ; à savoir, l'urbanité, la musique, le tir à l'arc, l'art de conduire une voiture, l'écriture et le calcul. Après une guerre, c'était dans l'école que la paix était annoncée. Les oreilles gauches des ennemis tués y étaient présentées au prince, et les prisonniers jugés. IV. IV. 3.

ASTRONOMIE. ÉCLIPSES.

Les mois sont désignés par les constellations qui atteignent le méridien vers la tombée de la nuit aux différentes époques de l'année. I. IV. 6, I. XV. 1.

Lorsque la lune est dans les Hyades, elle amène souvent une pluie torrentielle. II. VIII. 8.

Les éclipses, surtout celles de soleil, sont des signes menaçants. Une éclipse est une perturbation, sinon dans l'ordre physique, au moins dans l'ordre moral. Le principe 陰 **īn** ne devrait jamais l'emporter sur le principe 陽 **iâng**. Quand le gouvernement est bien réglé, la lune évite de se placer exactement sur le soleil ou en face de lui. Pour cela, elle s'écarte, s'il est nécessaire, de la route qui lui est tracée par les lois astronomiques, et il ne se produit aucune éclipse. (Tchou Hi). II. IV. 9.

ARC-EN-CIEL. PHÉNOMÈNES DE MAUVAIS AUGURE.

L'arc-en-ciel résulte d'un trouble dans la nature, et prive la terre de la pluie du matin. Il est le symbole d'une union contractée au mépris des règles et des usages. I. IV. 7.

Les corbeaux, les renards, les intempéries des saisons annoncent des malheurs. I. III. 16.

Les éclairs, les tonnerres, la crue extraordinaire des eaux, la chute des rochers, les collines abaissées, les vallées élevées sont les avertissements du ciel et les signes précurseurs de ses châtiments. II. IV. 9.

Le P. de la Charme ajoute l'annotation suivante : « Sub finem cujuslibet dynastiæ, historia sinensis refert præsagia ejusmodi, quæ dynastiam jamjam ruituram portendere credunt Sinenses. Unde gentem sinicam præ cæteris fere gentibus orbis universi superstitiosam habeo. Et historiam sinensem cæterosque libros sinenses legenti patebit quam aliena sit hæc natio ab atheismo, cujus ipsam insimulant nonnulli. Inter quos alii, corde ipsimet athei, vellent nationem quæ sapientissima audit, pravitatis et impietatis suæ consciam facere; alii male sani, audientes de quibusdam philosophis sinensibus, qui pauci quidem nec sibi constantes, atheorum in modum ratiocinantur, in atheismi crimen gentem universam vocare conantur. Nonne eodem jure Sinenses de gentis europææ quibusdam, quos paucos esse maxime vellem, atheismum venditantibus audiendo, gentem europæam universam atheismi insimulare possent? Male sanos dixi; non enim sibi nec religioni satis attendunt, asserendo gentem adeo antiquam, quæ ab ultima antiquitate iisdem fere moribus, eodem imperii regimine perseveravit, quæ libros antiquissima traditione acceptos diligentissime evolvit, cognitionis Dei expertem esse. Quidni de gente sinica dicunt, quod verum est quodque de omnibus idololatris gentibus dicendum esse arbitror, nempe Sinas hodiernos cognitionem Dei cum idololatria male conjungere, nec sibi ipsos constare; quemadmodum accidit populo judæo sub regibus suis, in templo Deum adoranti et in montibus idola sua colenti? »

LE CIEL DONNE A L'HOMME L'EXISTENCE, L'INTELLIGENCE ET LA LOI MORALE.

« Tout homme reçoit du ciel avec l'existence les parties constitutives de son être et la loi qui doit régir ses actions. Il a en son cœur la loi naturelle, et par suite il aime la vertu, dont il connaît la beauté. » III. III. 6. « Le ciel éclaire l'intelligence de l'homme. » III. II. 10.

LE CIEL VOIT TOUS NOS ACTES. NOUS DEVONS LE CRAINDRE.

« L'action du ciel est manifeste; son mandat (le pouvoir souverain) n'est pas facile à conserver. Ne dites pas qu'il se tient dans les hauteurs fort loin de nous. Il monte et descend; il est présent à nos actions. Chaque jour il est ici examinant toutes choses. » I. III. 3. Tchou Hi explique ainsi ce passage : « Ne dites pas que le ciel est très élevé et ne nous observe pas. Il faut savoir que sa perspicacité est très grande et redoutable, que sans cesse il monte et descend en quelque sorte, qu'il est présent à nos actions, qu'il n'est pas un seul jour sans venir porter ici ses regards. Il faut donc faire attention. »

« Sans craindre ni le regard des hommes ni la colère du ciel. » II. V. 5. « Vous ne rougissez pas devant les hommes, parce que vous croyez qu'on peut tromper les

IV

hommes. Mais on ne trompe pas le ciel. » (Tchou Hi). « Le regard du ciel est trés perspicace; rien ne lui échappe, tout lui est transparent. On doit le redouter beaucoup. » (詩經備旨).

« Craignez la colère du ciel... L'auguste ciel est vigilant; son œil vous suit partout où vous allez. L'auguste ciel est clairvoyant; il est témoin de vos déréglements et de votre conduite licencieuse. » III. II. 10.

« Le ciel est très perspicace. » III. III. 2. « Il voit et discerne le bien et le mal sans jamais se tromper. » (詩經備旨).

« O ciel qui brillez au-dessus de nous, vous exercez votre vigilance et votre autorité sur tout l'univers. » II. VI. 3. « Le ciel qui brille au-dessus de nous, exerce sa vigilance et son autorité sur tout l'univers... Rien ne doit échapper à ses investigations... Pourquoi n'examine-t-il pas ma cause? » (詩經備旨).

LE CIEL EST NOTRE PÈRE.

« O ciel qui occupez des régions vastes et inaccessibles, vous que nous appelons notre père, (comment pouvez-vous permettre que) des innocents soient ainsi victimes d'un tel désordre? » II. V. 4. « Le ciel dans sa bonté me traitera, j'espère, comme son fils. » IV. I. 8.

LE CIEL EST BON ET MISÉRICORDIEUX.

« O Heou tsi, prince orné de toutes les vertus, vous avez été comme l'associé du ciel (pour faire du bien aux hommes). C'est uniquement à votre incomparable bienfaisance que notre peuple doit d'avoir des grains. Vous nous avez donné le blé et l'orge, que le ciel a destinés pour être la nourriture de tous. » IV. I. 10.

« Le ciel, qui est naturellement miséricordieux, sévit à présent avec fureur. » III. III. 11.

« Le ciel envoie la mort, le trouble. » III. III. 4. « Siuen wang dit : « Il est étonnant que des calamités arrivent à présent ; car le ciel, dont le cœur est si bon, aime les princes. » (詩經備旨).

LE CIEL RÉCOMPENSE LA VERTU ET PUNIT LE VICE.

« Que le ciel vous protége et vous fasse jouir d'une félicité constante ; qu'il vous comble de tous les biens ! Que votre conduite soit toujours parfaite, et vous attire toutes les faveurs célestes ! » II. I. 6.

« Le ciel a contemplé le prince qui gouverne Tcheou. Attiré par l'éclat de sa vertu, il s'est incliné vers la terre. Pour protéger le Fils du ciel, il a fait naître Tchoung Chan fou. » III. III. 6.

« Nuit et jour (j'aurai devant les yeux et) je respecterai la majesté du ciel, afin de conserver toujours sa faveur et celle de Wenn wang. » IV. I. 7.

« Le ciel irrité nous afflige de plus en plus... L'auguste ciel, qui ne nous est plus propice, a envoyé ces troubles destructeurs. L'auguste ciel, qui nous a retiré sa faveur, a envoyé cet immense bouleversement. » II. IV. 7.

« Je livrerai les coupables au Très-Haut.» II. V. 6. « Je les livrerai au Très-Haut, au ciel, afin qu'il les juge et les punisse . » (Tchou Hi).

« Le ciel envoie ses (châtiments qui nous enveloppent comme des) filets, et ils sont nombreux. Les bons ministres ont disparu ; j'en suis affligé... L'auguste ciel peut tout raffermir. Ne déshonorez pas vos glorieux ancêtres, et vous sauverez votre postérité. » III. III. 10.

« Bien que le ciel, qui est très élevé, semble ne plus s'occuper des choses de la terre, son action, sa perspicacité sont infinies. Bien que le danger et le trouble soient extrêmes, il n'est rien que le ciel ne puisse consolider. Si Iou wang pouvait se corriger, se renouveler, et ne plus déshonorer ses ancêtres, il pourrait faire changer les dispositions du ciel, sauver sa postérité, et assurer le bonheur à ses descendants. » (詩 經 備 旨).

LE CIEL DONNE LE POUVOIR AUX PRINCES VERTUEUX ET LE RETIRE AUX PRINCES VICIEUX.

« Lorsqu'une vertu extraordinaire brille sur la terre, l'auguste mandat lui est conféré dans le ciel (le ciel lui confie le gouvernement de l'empire). Il serait téméraire de se reposer uniquement sur la faveur du ciel ; il n'est pas facile d'exercer le pouvoir impérial. L'héritier des In (le tyran Tcheou) avait la dignité de Fils du ciel ; le ciel lui retira l'empire. III. I. 2.

« Le ciel veillait sur les peuples d'ici-bas ; déjà il avait décrété d'une manière irrévocable (l'avènement des Tcheou à l'empire). Dès les premières années de Wenn wang, le ciel lui prépara une compagne... Le chef d'une grande principauté avait une fille si vertueuse qu'on l'aurait prise pour la sœur cadette du ciel... La fille aînée (du prince de Chenn) vint épouser (Wenn wang), et eut le bonheur de mettre au monde Ou wang. (Jeune prince, le ciel) vous protège, vous aide, vous confie son mandat. Docile à ses ordres, vous renverserez la puissante dynastie des Chang. » III. I. 2.

我周之業成於武王而武王之生又豈偶然哉 (詩經體註) Ce fut Ou wang qui fonda notre dynastie des Tcheou. Comment la naissance de Ou wang aurait-elle été un effet du hasard ?

« Wenn wang et Ou wang continuèrent l'œuvre de T'ai wang, et exécutèrent l'ordre définitif du ciel dans la plaine de Mou ie. (Le peuple dit à Ou wang) : « Loin de vous toute hésitation, toute perplexité ; le roi du ciel est avec vous. » IV. IV. 4.

« Le ciel ne se lasse pas de confier l'empire (à la maison des Tcheou)... Oh ! il (Ou wang) brille dans le ciel, lui qui fut fait empereur pour mettre fin (à la dynastie des Chang) ! » IV. III. 9. « La vertu de Ou wang, en procurant la paix au peuple, réjouit le cœur du (roi du) ciel, qui cherche à établir la tranquillité ; et elle brille à présent là-haut dans le ciel. » (詩 經 備 旨).

« Le mandat du ciel n'est pas facile à garder ; prince, craignez de vous perdre vous-même. Étendez au loin le renom de votre vertu, et considérez comment le ciel a retranché la dynastie des In. Les opérations du ciel ne sont perçues ni par

l'ouïe ni par l'odrat. (Il est impossible de les deviner d'avance. Pour être sûr de vous conformer toujours à la volonté du ciel), imitez Wenn wang; tous les peuples se lèveront et vous donneront leur confiance. » III. I. 1.

法文王卽所以法天如此則在天之靈可慰而靡常之命可保矣 (詩經備旨) Imiter Wenn wang, c'est le moyen d'imiter le ciel. Par là vous réjouirez l'âme de votre aïeul qui est dans le ciel, et conserverez le pouvoir souverain qui est toujours révocable.

« C'est le ciel qui a constitué les princes avec leurs capitales dans les terres que Iu a rendues habitables. » IV. V. 5.

« Le ciel m'agite en tous sens, comme s'il n'avait pas la force de me renverser. Il a d'abord voulu faire de moi le modèle des peuples, et m'a cherché avec sollicitude, comme s'il avait craint de ne pas me trouver. Ensuite il m'a saisi et traité en ennemi, et n'a plus voulu se servir de moi. » II. IV. 8. « Le cœur du ciel est naturellement très bienfaisant; cependant il ne nous fait plus de bien. » (詩經備旨).

« Mieux vaudrait que l'auguste ciel, (au lieu de châtier le peuple à cause de moi), me permît de me retirer (dans la vie privée). » III. III. 4. 昊天上帝乃司禍福趨避之權者也 (詩經體註) L'auguste roi du ciel est l'arbitre des biens et des maux; il décide si l'on doit s'avancer ou se retirer.

SACRIFICES ET SUPPLICATIONS EN L'HONNEUR DU CIEL.

« Le ciel descendra, j'espère, à la droite de ces victimes. » IV. I. 7. « L'empereur amène un bœuf et une brebis, les offre au roi du ciel, et dit: J'espère que le ciel descendra à la droite de ce bœuf et de cette brebis. Il n'ose pas l'assurer. » (Tchou Hi).

L'empereur adresse des supplications au ciel et aux esprits, afin d'obtenir la pluie. III. III. 4. « Je lève les yeux vers l'auguste ciel (pour implorer son secours); mais il ne nous est pas favorable. » III. III. 10.

PUISSANCE DU CHANG TI.

« Heou tsi n'est pas assez puissant, et le roi du ciel ne nous est pas favorable. » III. III. 4. « Le plus grand des esprits honorés dans le temple des ancêtres est Heou tsi. Il a toujours agréé nos offrandes; mais il n'est pas assez puissant pour triompher des calamités. Le plus grand des esprits honorés dans la campagne est le roi du ciel. Il est certainement assez puissant pour triompher des calamités; mais il n'agrée pas nos sacrifices. » (Cheu king pei tcheu).

LE CHANG TI RÉCOMPENSE LA VERTU ET PUNIT LE VICE.

« Ce roi du ciel plein de majesté a-t-il de la haine contre quelqu'un? » II. IV. 8. 上帝天神也 (詩經備旨) Le Chang ti est l'esprit du ciel. « Est-ce que le ciel affligerait quelqu'un par motif de haine? Il protège les bons et afflige les méchants, comme la justice le demande, et voilà tout. » (Tchou Hi).

«Le roi du ciel dans son immensité étend son pouvoir sur tous les peuples de la terre. (A présent) il déploie une grande sévérité; aux dons naturels qu'il départit, se mêlent beaucoup de vices. C'est le ciel qui donne l'être à tous les hommes; mais personne ne doit se tenir assuré de conserver les qualités naturelles qu'il a reçues de lui. Tout homme naît bon; mais peu le demeurent jusqu'à la mort.» III. III. 1.

«Le poète blâme Li wang, qui court à sa perte. Les troubles de l'empire, dit-il, n'ont pas surgi d'eux-mêmes; certainement ils ont été amenés par une cause. Ce souverain seigneur, dans son immensité, embrasse le monde entier; il est le roi des peuples de la terre. Puisqu'il est roi et gouverne les peuples, il doit donner aux hommes un bon naturel. A présent, ce souverain seigneur, devenu sévère, leur donne beaucoup d'inclinations vicieuses. Où est donc le soin qu'il prend des peuples de la terre en sa qualité de roi? La nature que le ciel donne aux hommes, est par elle-même toujours bonne, et nullement mauvaise. A présent, s'ils ont beaucoup d'inclinations dépravées, auxquelles on ne peut se fier, viennent-elles originairement de la nature? Au moment où les hommes reçoivent l'existence, leur nature est également bonne; il n'est personne en qui elle soit mauvaise par elle-même. Mais après qu'ils ont commencé d'exister, leurs facultés se dépravent en s'attachant à différents objets. Par suite, ils commettent des excès et des désordres, violent la loi naturelle, perdent les belles qualités qu'ils ont reçues de la nature; peu parviennent à suivre la voie de la vertu jusqu'à la fin. Si ces troubles violents sont survenus, s'il semble que le ciel donne beaucoup de penchants vicieux, les hommes en sont la cause. Est-il permis d'en attribuer la faute au ciel? Ce n'est pas le souverain seigneur qui fait ces temps mauvais; mais c'est vous, In, qui avez attiré ces malheurs, en rejetant les anciens ministres et les anciennes lois des empereurs vos ancêtres. Serait-il juste d'accuser le souverain seigneur, parce que les temps sont mauvais?» (詩 經 備 旨).

LE CHANG TI GOUVERNE LE MONDE.

«Le Chang ti est auguste; il veille avec majesté sur les choses d'ici-bas... Le Chang ti considéra les diverses principautés, et chercha avec soin (un prince qui répondît à ses désirs). L'ayant trouvé (en la personne de T'ai wang), il voulut augmenter ses possessions. Tournant ses regards avec affection vers l'occident, il y donna à T'ai wang un endroit pour s'établir.» III. I. 7.

上帝天帝也 (詩 經 備 旨) «Le Chang ti est le roi du ciel. Bien que cet auguste seigneur suprême soit très élevé au-dessus de nous, il abaisse sur la terre ses regards très perspicaces et pleins de majesté. En regardant et en considérant les quatre parties du monde, il n'a d'autre intention que de procurer au peuple la paix et la tranquillité. Ainsi la volonté du ciel est de donner au peuple la tranquillité, et, pour y parvenir, le choix d'un prince est la chose la plus nécessaire.» (Pei tcheu).

«Après avoir fondé la principauté, le roi du ciel choisit un prince capable pour la gouverner... Le roi du ciel donna à Wang Ki un jugement exquis.» III. I. 7.

« Le roi du ciel dit à Wenn wang: « Ne soyez pas intrigant... Devancez de bien loin tous les autres, et montez au sommet de la perfection. » « Le roi du ciel dit à Wenn wang: « J'aime votre vertu, votre sagesse... Vous suivez les lois du souverain suprême. » « Le roi du ciel dit à Wenn wang... Attaquez la capitale de Tch'oung.... Alors Wenn wang offrit des sacrifices au roi du ciel et à l'inventeur de l'art militaire. » III. I. 7.

LE CHANG TI DONNE L'EMPIRE AUX PRINCES VERTUEUX ET LE RETIRE AUX PRINCES VICIEUX.

« Les Chang ont toujours été dignes de recevoir le mandat du roi du ciel... T'ang, doué d'une éminente sagesse et très diligent, fit des progrès chaque jour; longtemps ses brillantes vertus touchèrent (le cœur du roi du ciel). Il honora le roi du ciel, et le roi du ciel le créa empereur, afin qu'il servit de modèle dans les neuf circonscriptions ou provinces. » IV. V. 4.

« Le roi du ciel ordonna au belliqueux Tch'eng T'ang de fixer les frontières dans toutes les parties de l'empire. » IV. V. 3.

« Les descendants des Chang étaient plus de cent mille. Sur l'ordre du roi du ciel, ils se soumirent tous aux princes de Tcheou... C'est que le ciel ne laisse pas constamment son mandat à la même famille... Tâchez de vous conformer sans cesse aux ordres du ciel; vous recevrez de lui beaucoup de faveurs. Tant que les In ont gardé le gouvernement du peuple, ils ont été comme les assesseurs du roi du ciel. Ayez constamment devant les yeux l'exemple (la déchéance) des In; le mandat suprême (le pouvoir impérial) n'est pas facile (à conserver). » III. I. 1. 上帝天之主宰也(朱熹集傳) Le Chang ti est le maître et le roi du ciel.

« Wenn wang, toujours attentif et diligent, servit parfaitement le souverain roi et reçut beaucoup de faveurs. Sa vertu ne se démentit jamais, et il obtint l'empire du monde. » III. I. 2.

« Homme intelligent et sage, prince bon et courageux, Wenn wang répondit aux désirs de l'auguste ciel, et assura la grandeur de son héritier (Ou wang). Il m'obtient de longues années de vie et des faveurs nombreuses. » IV. II. 7.

« Wenn wang sut procurer la paix au peuple, et par là réjouir le cœur (du roi) du ciel qui cherche à établir la tranquillité. Pour cette raison, le ciel le traita avec grande affection, et lui accorda des faveurs abondantes, qui s'étendirent jusqu'à son successeur. » (Cheu king pei tcheu).

« Quelle n'est pas la gloire de Tch'eng wang et de K'ang wang! Le roi du ciel leur a donné l'empire. » IV. I. 9. « Le Chang ti est le maître et le gouverneur du ciel... Ce fut le roi du ciel qui les constitua empereurs. Comment pourrait-on dire que ce fût le hasard? » (詩經備旨).

SACRIFICES ET PRIÈRES EN L'HONNEUR DU CHANG TI.

Wenn wang, avant son départ pour son expédition contre les habitants de Tch'oung, offrit des sacrifices au Chang ti et à l'inventeur de l'art militaire. III. I. 7.

詩經

« Au très auguste roi et seigneur du ciel, à son auguste aïeul Heou tsi, il (le prince Hi koung) offre une victime rousse. Ils agréent, ils approuvent cette offrande, et le comblent de biens. » IV. IV. 4.

« De très bonne heure j'ai demandé (au ciel) une année fertile. » III. III. 4. « Au commencement du printemps, on demandait une bonne récolte au roi du ciel. » (Tchou Hi).

« Oh ! que le blé et l'orge sont splendides ! Bientôt on recueillera ces magnifiques (dons du roi du ciel). Le roi du ciel, plein de gloire et de magnificence, nous donnera une récolte abondante. » IV. II. 1. «Les grains sont les dons brillants du roi du ciel. » (Tchou Hi).

LES ESPRITS NOUS VOIENT EN TOUS LIEUX.

A la maison, même dans les appartements les plus secrets, il faut veiller sur soi, se composer, comme si l'on était sous les regards de personnes distinguées, et s'abstenir de tout mal, par respect pour la présence des esprits. Ne dis pas : « Ce lieu est fermé à tous les regards, personne ne me voit. » L'approche des esprits ne peut être devinée ; il faut respecter grandement leur présence. III. III. 2.

LES ESPRITS AIDENT L'HOMME DE BIEN ET DÉLAISSENT L'HOMME VICIEUX.

« Oh ! vous, grands officiers de la cour, ne vous livrez pas constamment au repos. Remplissez avec calme les devoirs attachés à vos dignités ; aimez les hommes probes et sincères. Les esprits seconderont vos efforts, et vous accorderont les biens les plus précieux. » II. VI. 3.

« Si vous ne pensez qu'à remplir vos devoirs avec fidélité et diligence, vous aurez la confiance des intelligences célestes, et ne tromperez pas leur attente. Les esprits seconderont vos entreprises, abaisseront sur vous leurs regards, vous prêteront le secours de leurs lumières, vous accorderont une félicité sans égale, et vous combleront de tous les biens avec une libéralité sans limite. Il ne convient donc pas de garder longtemps le repos. Si au contraire vous laissiez de côté vos obligations et ne les remplissiez pas, si vous écartiez les hommes sincères et vertueux et ne les aidiez pas, les esprits *vomeraient vos* vous rejetteraient avec dégoût. Pourraient-ils, quand même ils le voudraient, vous combler de félicité? » (詩經備旨).

LES BONS SOUVERAINS APRÈS LEUR MORT SONT DANS LE CIEL.

« Mon aïeul Tch'eng t'ang regarde avec complaisance les dons que je lui offre en été et en automne. Ce sont les offrandes de son descendant. » IV. V. 2. « Je n'ose pas assurer que dans le ciel l'âme de mon illustre aïeul abaisse sur moi des regards favorables. Puisse-t-il regarder avec complaisance les dons que je lui offre en été et en automne ! » (Cheu king pei tcheu).

« Les trois rois (T'ai wang, Wang ki et Wenn wang) sont dans le ciel. » III. I. 9. « Après leur mort, leurs esprits allèrent s'unir au ciel. » (Cheu king pei tcheu).

« Wenn wang est là-haut. Oh ! comme il brille dans le ciel !... Wenn wang monte et descend, toujours à la droite ou à la gauche du roi du ciel. » III. I. 1.

« Dans cette strophe il est dit qu'après la mort de Wenn wang, son esprit est monté dans les hauteurs des cieux, où il brille d'un vif éclat ; que par suite, bien que la principauté particulière des Tcheou ait été fondée par Heou tsi (le premier de leurs ancêtres connus), plus de mille ans auparavant, leur famille a reçu du ciel tout récemment un nouveau pouvoir (le pouvoir impérial)... Parce que l'esprit de Wenn wang monte et descend, sans cesse à la droite ou à la gauche du roi du ciel, sa postérité jouit des faveurs du ciel, possède et gouverne l'empire. » (Tchou Hi).

« L'esprit de Wenn wang est sans cesse auprès du roi du ciel. Il unit sa vertu à celle du ciel, se meut et agit avec lui. » (Cheu king pei tcheu).

« Je m'efforcerai d'imiter mon aïeul Wenn wang. » IV. I. 2. « La mémoire des vertus de Wenn wang ne périra pas avec le temps, et son âme dans le ciel recevra un peu de consolation. » (Cheu king pei tcheu).

LES AMES DES MORTS SONT DANS LE CIEL.

« Je répands en libation une liqueur très pure ; ensuite je prends un taureau roux pour l'offrir à mes ancêtres. Avec le couteau dont le manche est muni de sonnettes, je coupe une ligne de poil ; je tire du sang et enlève la graisse des intestins. » II. VI. 6.

Le sacrificateur coupait une ligne de poil aux oreilles de la victime, et déclarait que cette victime était de la couleur voulue et n'avait aucune tache. Il prenait du sang, et annonçait que la victime avait été immolée. Ensuite il enlevait la graisse qui enveloppait les intestins, y mêlait du grain de millet et la brûlait avec de l'armoise, afin que l'odeur attirât les mânes.

« Sous les Tcheou, on offrait de préférence les choses odorantes. On répandait à terre du vin aromatisé, afin que le parfum descendît jusqu'aux sources d'eau, parce que les corps des ancêtres défunts étaient retournés à la terre. Au millet on mêlait de l'armoise trempée dans la graisse, et on le faisait chauffer, afin que l'odeur pénétrât les murs et le toit, parce que les âmes des ancêtres étaient allées au ciel. » (詩經體註).

LES PARENTS DÉFUNTS VOIENT LEURS DESCENDANTS SUR LA TERRE.

« Que le prince de Lou, qui est profondément vertueux, cultive soigneusement ses bonnes qualités, s'applique à garder la gravité et les bienséances, et soit le modèle de son peuple! Que ses vertus civiles et militaires comblent de joie ses illustres ancêtres! Que sa parfaite piété filiale lui attire les faveurs du ciel! » IV. IV. 3.

詩經

« La mort est proche; je ne sais plus où lever les yeux, où tourner la tête. Les mânes des anciens princes et des anciens ministres d'État m'ont tous délaissé. Comment mon père, ma mère, mes ancêtres ont-ils le cœur assez dur pour n'avoir pas compassion de moi? » III. III. 4.

« J'ai fait des offrandes aux anciens princes et aux anciens ministres, dans l'espoir qu'ils viendraient à mon secours et me rendraient le bonheur. Ils me regardent sans rien faire et sans me secourir, comme si je leur étais étranger. Mais mon père, ma mère et mes aïeux, qui sont mes plus proches parents, et ont en quelque sorte une même respiration avec moi, pourquoi souffrent-ils que je sois dans l'affliction, et ne se mettent-ils pas en peine de m'en délivrer? » (Cheu king pei tcheu).

« Mes parents défunts n'ont-ils pas un cœur humain? Comment n'ont-ils pas pitié de moi? » II. V. 10.

DESCRIPTION D'UNE CÉRÉMONIE EN L'HONNEUR DES PARENTS DÉFUNTS. II. VI. 5.

Dans les champs défrichés par les ancêtres, on cultive deux sortes de millet à panicules, qui servent à la préparation des liqueurs et des mets destinés aux parents défunts.

L'un des membres de la famille est désigné par le sort pour représenter les mânes des morts. Le maître de la maison le fera asseoir, se prosternera devant lui, l'invitera à manger et à boire, et lui rendra tous les honneurs qu'il voudrait rendre à ses ancêtres.

On va choisir des victimes parfaites, des bœufs et des brebis. Les serviteurs les dépouillent, font cuire la chair, font griller le foie, placent les viandes sur les supports et vont les offrir aux mânes. La princesse dispose un grand nombre de vases destinés à contenir les ragoûts, les sauces,...

Les cérémonies, grandes et petites, les sourires, les paroles, tout doit être conforme aux prescriptions.

Un officier est chargé de lire des panégyriques en l'honneur des ancêtres, de leur demander leur protection, de recevoir et de transmettre leurs réponses. Il attend leur venue à la porte du temple.

Leur représentant arrive; ils entrent eux-mêmes à sa suite avec majesté.

L'orateur chargé de prendre la parole en leur nom, dit au maître de la maison: « Votre pieuse offrande a exhalé une agréable odeur. Les esprits vous accordent toutes sortes de biens... » Le maître de la maison retourne à son siège. L'orateur lui dit: « Les esprits ont tous bu largement. »

Alors l'auguste représentant des mânes se lève. Les tambours et les cloches le reconduisent; les esprits se retirent avec lui. La princesse et tous les serviteurs enlèvent les offrandes sans retard.

Les parents en ligne masculine se réunissent dans le bâtiment situé derrière le temple, et mangent les mets qui ont été offerts aux morts.

Tous les musiciens entrent dans la salle du festin et exécutent des chants.

V

Quand les convives ont bu et mangé suffisamment, tous, jeunes et vieux, inclinent la tête et disent: «Les esprits ont agréé la boisson et la nourriture, et vous ont octroyé, Seigneur, une vie longue. Vous avez fait ces offrandes de la manière la plus convenable et aux temps marqués; vos fils et tous vos descendants les continueront à jamais sans interruption.» II. VI. 5.

LES PARENTS DÉFUNTS ASSISTENT AUX CÉRÉMONIES FAITES EN LEUR HONNEUR.

Tch'eng T'ang, attiré par la musique, vient dans son temple, et apporte à son descendant la joie et les faveurs du ciel. IV. V. 1 et 2.

«Déjà Wenn wang est à la droite de mes offrandes, et les accepte avec joie.» IV. I. 7.

«Tous les instruments unissent leurs sons avec gravité, accord et harmonie. Les ancêtres prêtent l'oreille.» IV. II. 5.

«Au printemps, en été, en automne et en hiver, vous faites des offrandes aux anciens princes et aux empereurs de votre famille. Vos ancêtres vous disent (par la bouche de leur représentant): «Nous vous accordons une vie longue, une vie sans fin.» Les mânes de vos ancêtres sont présents, et vous obtiennent un grand nombre de faveurs célestes.» II. I. 6.

«Déjà les coupes sont pleines de liqueurs pures; mon aïeul m'apporte la joie que je désirais (la joie de sa présence)... J'attire mon aïeul par la musique, sans recourir aux paroles... Du ciel nous vient la prospérité; les récoltes sont très abondantes. Mon aïeul vient, il est ici, il jouit des mets offerts, et m'obtient une félicité sans limite.» IV. V. 5.

LES PARENTS DÉFUNTS OBTIENNENT A LEURS DESCENDANTS LES FAVEURS DU CIEL.

«Au milieu des champs sont les cabanes; à l'extérieur et à l'intérieur, le long des bordures croissent des concombres. Je coupe ces concombres en plusieurs parties, les conserve dans l'eau salée, puis les offre à mes augustes ancêtres. Moi, leur descendant, j'aurai une vie longue, et recevrai les faveurs du ciel... J'apporte et présente mes offrandes; elles exhalent toutes une odeur agréable. Rien ne manque à la cérémonie; aussi mes ancêtres (arrivent) avec majesté. Ils m'obtiendront en récompense les plus grandes faveurs, dix mille années de vie, une vie sans fin.» II. VI. 6.

«Les biens qui constituent le bonheur dépendent du ciel. Comment ces augustes ancêtres peuvent-ils les départir? Ils ne font que procurer une vie longue à leur descendant, afin qu'il reçoive longtemps ces biens.» (Cheu king pei tcheu).

«Je les présente, je les offre (les poissons) à mes ancêtres, et j'obtiens un accroissement de félicité.» IV. II. 6. 享 祀 **Hiáng séu** signifie présenter, et non faire un sacrifice ou une offrande solennelle. (Cheu king pei tcheu). Siu Tch'ang ki dit:

« *Hiàng séu* c'est présenter, et non faire une offrande solennelle. C'est procurer les différentes choses qui conviennent selon les saisons, avec les sentiments d'une piété filiale très sincère. »

REPAS OFFERT AU REPRÉSENTANT DES PARENTS DÉFUNTS.

Le lendemain d'une cérémonie en l'honneur des ancêtres, les restes des offrandes sont servis au 尸 **chēu** représentant des mânes. Celui-ci est heureux à ce festin comme le canard ou la mouette au milieu de l'eau. III. II. 4.

SACRIFICES. SERMENTS SOLENNELS.

« Wenn wang offrit des sacrifices au roi du ciel et à l'inventeur de l'art militaire. » III. I. 7.

On sacrifiait aux esprits de la terre et des quatre points cardinaux, au Père de l'agriculture 神 農 **Chênn nôung**. II. VI. 7. On immolait une victime rousse aux esprits du sud, et une victime noire à ceux du nord. II. VI. 8.

Chenn noung, en sa qualité de souverain ou dieu du feu 炎 帝 **Iên tí**, était prié de brûler les insectes nuisibles. II. VI. 8.

En printemps, avant la chasse, on offrait un sacrifice au Dompteur des chevaux 伯 **Pĕ** ou 馬 祖 **Mà tsòu**. II. III. 6. Les voyageurs sacrifiaient aux dieux des chemins. I. III. 14.

Les serments solennels étaient prêtés sur le corps d'une victime. II. V. 4, note. « Faites venir les trois victimes ordinaires (un chien, un porc et un coq, et après avoir frotté vos lèvres de leur sang), jurez que vous ne me connaissez pas. » II. V. 5.

SORTILÈGES. SONGES.

La tortue et l'achillée donnent des augures. I. V. 4, II. I. 9. On soumet à l'action du feu une écaille de tortue, et l'on examine les fissures qui sont produites. III. I. 3.

Les ours vus en songe annoncent la naissance d'enfants mâles, et les serpents, la naissance de filles. II. IV. 5. Une multitude d'hommes remplacée par des poissons est le pronostic d'une année fertile. Les étendards aux tortues remplacés par les étendards aux faucons sont le présage d'un grand accroissement de population. II. IV. 6.

PROVERBES.

« Que le souverain ne parle pas à la légère ; des oreilles sont appliquées au mur (ce qui revient à notre proverbe : Les murs ont des oreilles). » II. V. 3.

« J'éprouve autant de joie que si je recevais deux cents (ou cinq cents) coquillages précieux. (Certains coquillages servaient de monnaie). » II. III. 2.

« Les faibles sont dévorés ; les forts sont rejetés de la bouche (ils savent résister, personne n'ose les dévorer). » III. III. 6.

« N'apprenez pas au singe à grimper sur les arbres; n'accumulez pas la boue sur la boue. (Le peuple est naturellement enclin à négliger ses devoirs ; évitez de l'exciter au mal par vos mauvais exemples). » II. VII. 9.

« Lorsqu'un arbre tombe et que ses racines sortent de terre, si les branches et les feuilles sont intactes, c'est que que les racines ont été coupées (,et détachées du sol). » III. III. 1.

« Quel est celui qui peut saisir un objet très chaud, s'il ne s'est mouillé la main: (pour obtenir une fin il faut en prendre les moyens). » III. III. 3.

« La vertu est légère comme une plume (elle est facile à connaître) ; et cependant peu d'hommes la soulèvent. » III. III. 6.

« Prenez conseil même des villageois dont le métier est de ramasser de l'herbe et du bois pour le chauffage. » III. II. 10.

« Un vieux cheval veut faire le jeune poulain, et ne prévoit pas à quoi il s'expose. (Ainsi les ambitieux veulent exercer des charges malgré leur incapacité ; ils ne prévoient pas les difficultés qui les attendent. Plus ils obtiennent d'honneurs, plus ils en convoitent; leur ambition est insatiable). Celui qui mange, doit cesser de vouloir manger, quand il est repu ; celui qui boit, doit s'arrêter, quand il a déjà beaucoup bu. » II. VII. 9.

« Un homme habile élève des remparts et rend l'État florissant; une femme habile renverse les remparts et ruine l'État. Une femme belle et habile qui intervient dans les affaires est un hibou malfaisant. Une femme qui a longue langue, attire une suite de malheurs. Les malheurs viennent, non du ciel, mais de la femme. Aucun enseignement utile, aucune instruction ne peut venir des femmes ni des eunuques. » III. III. 10.

CHEU KING

國風一

PREMIÈRE PARTIE

KOUO FOUNG

Le titre de cette première partie est plus facile à expliquer qu'à traduire en termes équivalents. Les expressions Mœurs des royaumes ou des principautés, Enseignements des royaumes, Chants populaires des principautés, ne rendent que d'une manière imparfaite la signification de ces deux mots *Kouo foung*.

毛萇 **Maô Tch'âng** en donne l'explication suivante. 風風也敎也風以動之敎以化之 « *Foung*, vent, enseignement. Ces chants sont comme un souffle qui remue les âmes ; ils contiennent des enseignements qui transforment les cœurs. »

朱熹 **Tchōu Hī** dit : « 國 **Kouŏ**, domaines soumis à la juridiction des princes 諸侯 **tchōu heóu** ; 風 **fōung**, stances que le peuple avait coutume de chanter. Les chants populaires sont appelés *foung*, parce qu'ils ont été composés sous l'influence des grands, et sont capables de faire impression sur les esprits ; de même qu'un objet rend un son sous l'action du vent, et que ce son est capable d'agir sur d'autres objets.

« Au dire de nos anciens, 二南爲正風 les chants contenus dans les deux premiers livres et intitulés Tcheou nan et Chao nan, sont d'une perfection irréprochable. Chantés d'abord dans l'intérieur du palais, ils ont passé de village en village, de principauté en principauté, et ont transformé tout l'empire. 十三國爲變風 Les chants des treize principautés (autres que celles de Tcheou et de Chao) n'ont pas la perfection des premiers. Ils ont été recueillis, conservés et classés au fur et à mesure dans les bureaux de la musique, afin que l'empereur les parcourût, les examinât, et publiât des instructions et des avertissements. Le recueil comprend en tout les chants de quinze principautés ; » et se divise en quinze livres.

1

Les quinze royaumes ou principautés sont 周 Tcheōu, 召 Chaó, 邶 Pèi, 鄘 Iôung, 衛 Wéi, 王 Wâng (domaine impérial), 鄭 Tchéng, 齊 Ts'i, 魏 Wéi, 唐 T'âng, 秦 Ts'în, 陳 Tch'ênn, 檜 Kouéi, 曹 Ts'aô, 豳 Pīn.

La principauté de 周 Tcheōu était au sud du mont 岐 K'î, dans le 雍 州 Iōung tcheōu, l'une des neuf provinces mentionnées dans le Chou king au chapitre intitulé 禹 貢 Iù kóung Tribut de Iu. 古 公 亶 父 L'ancien prince Tàn fòu, descendant de 后 稷 Heóu tsī à la treizième génération, occupa le premier cette terre, et la transmit à son fils 季 歷 Ki lī, qui reçut après sa mort le nom de 王 季 Wâng ki.

Les Tcheou faisaient remonter leur origine à 棄 K'i, qui fut 稷 tsi ministre de l'agriculture sous l'empereur 舜 Chouénn, vers l'an 2250 avant notre ère, et pour cette raison fut nommé 后 稷 Heóu tsī, et honoré comme dieu par les laboureurs. Heou tsi reçut en fief la terre de 邰 T'âi, à présent comprise dans le 武 工 縣 Où kōung hièn, qui dépend de 乾 州 K'iên tcheōu dans le 陝 西 Chèn sī. 公 劉 Kōung Liôu, l'un de ses descendants, en 1796 avant J. C., alla s'établir à 豳 Pīn, à l'ouest de la ville actuelle de 三 水 Sān chouèi, qui dépend de 邠 州 Pīn tcheōu dans le Chen si. En 1325, 亶 父 Tàn fòu, nommé plus tard 太 王 T'ái wâng, alla demeurer à 岐 K'î, au nord-est de la ville actuelle de 岐 山 K'î chān, qui dépend de 鳳 翔 Fóung siâng dans le Chen si. La plaine qui s'étend au sud du mont K'i, fut appelée 周 Tcheōu ou 岐 周 K'î tcheōu.

Vint ensuite 昌 Tch'āng ou 文 王 Wênn wâng, petit-fils de T'ai wang. Il étendit et agrandit peu à peu la principauté. Puis, en 1136, il passa la 渭 Wéi, et établit sa résidence à 豐 Fōung, dans le 鄠 縣 Hóu hién actuel, au sud-ouest de 西 安 府 Sī ngān fòu, capitale du Chen si. Il divisa l'ancienne terre de K'i Tcheou en deux fiefs, conféra la partie orientale à son fils 旦 Tán avec le titre de 周 公 Tcheōu kōung Prince de Tcheou, et la partie occidentale à son ministre 奭 Chĕu avec le titre de 召 公 Chaó kōung Prince de Chao.

Il chargea Tcheou koung de régler l'administration dans sa principauté particulière, et Chao koung de publier et de mettre en vigueur les règlements administratifs dans les domaines des autres princes. Alors les mœurs furent réformées et la vertu fleurit dans la principauté de Tcheou. Parmi les principautés méridionales comprises entre le 江 Kiāng, la 沱 T'ouô, la 汝 Jòu et la 漢 Hán, il n'y en eut aucune qui n'adoptât ces sages réformes. Les deux tiers de l'empire furent à Wenn wang.

Son fils 發 Fă, connu sous le nom de 武 王 Où wâng, transféra sa résidence à vingt-cinq 里 li plus loin vers l'est. Il se fixa à 鎬 Haò, dans le 咸 陽 縣 Hiên iâng hién actuel, au sud-ouest de Si ngan fou. En 1122, il défit 紂 Tcheóu, dernier empereur de la dynastie des 商 Chāng, et fut maître de l'empire. Après la mort de Ou wang en 1115, son fils 誦 Sóung, nommé plus tard 成 王 Tch'êng wâng, fut constitué empereur.

Tcheou koung aida Tch'eng wang, régla et fixa les usages et la musique. Il recueillit les chants dont l'influence avait réformé les mœurs du peuple au temps de Wenn wang, les fit exécuter dans le palais avec accompagnement

de flûtes et d'instruments à cordes ; puis il les propagea de village en village, de principauté en principauté.

Les chants qu'il trouva dans sa principauté, furent réunis avec ceux des principautés situées au midi de Tcheou, sous le titre de 周南 **Tcheōu nân** Chants de Tcheou et du midi. Les chants qu'il trouva dans les autres principautés méridionales, furent intitulés 召南 **Chaó nân** Chants de Chao et du midi.

La principauté de 邶 **Péi** était la partie septentrionale du 衛輝府 **Wéi houēi fòu** actuel dans la province de 河南 **Hô nân.**

La principauté de 鄘 **Iôung** était la partie méridionale du Wei houei fou actuel. On pense qu'elle fut conférée par 武王 **Où wâng** à 武庚 **Où kēng,** fils de 紂 **Tcheóu.**

La principauté de 衛 **Wéi** était la partie orientale du Wei houei fou. Sa capitale était la ville actuelle de 濬縣 **Siún hién.** Elle fut conférée par Ou wang à son frère 康叔 **K'āng chŏu.**

Le domaine impérial 王 **Wâng** était la ville de 洛陽 **Lŏ iâng** et son territoire dans le Ho nan. Ou wang avait établi sa résidence à 鎬 **Haò.** Son fils 成王 **Tch'êng wâng** alla demeurer à 豐 **Fōung.** De plus il chargea 召公 **Chaó kōung** de lui préparer une seconde résidence à Lo iang, à l'ouest de la ville actuelle de 河南府 **Hô nân fòu.** Il s'y rendait à certaines époques pour y recevoir les princes 諸侯 **tchōu heóu** de la partie orientale de l'empire. Hao ou Foung fut appelée la première capitale des Tcheou 宗周 **tsōung Tcheōu,** la capitale occidentale 西都 **sī tōu.** Lo iang fut nommée la ville impériale 王城 **wâng tch'êng,** la capitale orientale 東都 **tōung tōu.**

La principauté de 鄭 **Tchéng** fut constituée en 805 avant notre ère par l'empereur 宣王 **Siuēn wâng,** et conférée par lui à son frère 友 **Iòu,** dans le 華州 **Houâ tcheōu** actuel, sous-préfecture qui dépend de 同州府 **T'ôung tcheōu fòu** dans le 陝西 **Chèn sī.** Iou, dont le nom posthume est 桓公 **Houân kōung,** fut tué en 773 par les 戎 **Jôung,** qui vivaient à l'ouest de la Chine. En 770, ces barbares s'emparèrent de la capitale, et mirent à mort l'empereur 幽王 **Iōu wâng.** Pour échapper à leurs attaques, 平王 **P'îng wâng,** fils et successeur de Iou wang, alla demeurer à Lo iang. 掘突 **Kiuĕ tŏu,** fils de Houan koung, suivit l'empereur, lui rendit de grands services, et reçut de lui en fief un domaine situé à l'est de Lo iang. Ce fief prit le nom de 新鄭 **Sīn Tchéng** nouvelle Tcheng. C'est le Sin tcheng hien actuel ; il dépend de K'ai foung fou. Les chants de Tcheng qui font partie du Cheu king, ont été composés dans la principauté de Sin tcheng.

La principauté de 齊 **Ts'î,** située dans le Chan toung actuel, comprenait le 青州府 **Ts'īng tcheōu fòu,** le 濟南府 **Tsi nân fòu,** le 濰縣 **Wêi hién,...** Elle fut conférée par 武王 **Où wâng** à 尙父 **Cháng fòu,** l'un de ses ministres, plus connu sous le nom de 太公望 **T'ái kōung wáng.** Bornée à l'ouest par le Fleuve-Jaune, elle s'étendit à l'est jusqu'à la mer. La capitale était 營邱 **Îng k'iōu** dans le 臨淄縣 **Lîn tchēu hién** actuel.

La principauté de 魏 **Wéi** était dans le 解州 **Hiài tcheōu** actuel, qui est de la province de 山西 **Chān sī.** Elle était petite, et son histoire est peu connue.

La principauté de 唐 **T'âng** ou de 晉 **Tsin** était dans le 太原府 **T'ái iuên fòu** actuel, dans la province de 山西 **Chān sī**. Elle avait été gouvernée, dit-on, par l'empereur 堯 **Iaô**, qui est appelé prince de T'ang. Elle fut conférée par l'empereur 成王 **Tch'êng wâng** à son frère 叔虞 **Chŏu iù**. 燮 **Siĕ**, fils de Chou iu, changea l'ancien nom de la principauté, et lui donna celui de la rivière 晉 **Tsin**, qui formait la limite de ses possessions au sud.

La principauté de 秦 **Ts'în** eut d'abord pour capitale la ville actuelle de 秦州 **Ts'în tcheōu** dans le 甘肅 **Kān siŭ**. Elle fut conférée par l'empereur 孝王 **Hiaó wâng** (908-894) à 非子 **Fēi tzèu**, qui était chargé des troupeaux de chevaux, et se disait issu de 伯益 **Pĕ ĭ**, ministre de 舜 **Chouénn** et de 禹 **Iù**. Peu à peu elle prit une grande extension. Enfin les princes de Ts'in renversèrent la dynastie des Tcheou, et commandèrent à tout l'empire.

La principauté de 陳 **Tch'ênn** était le 陳州府 **Tch'ênn tcheōu fòu** actuel dans le Ho nan. Elle fut conférée par 武王 **Où wâng** à 滿 **Màn**, fils de 閼父 **Ngŏ fòu**, qui était directeur des poteries impériales, et se disait descendant de 舜 **Chouénn**. Man, dont le nom posthume est 胡公 **Hôu kōung**, établit sa capitale dans le 淮寧縣 **Houâi gnîng hién**.

La principauté de 檜 ou 鄶 **Kouéi** était le 鄭州 **Tchéng tcheōu** actuel dans le Ho nan. La famille princière portait le nom de 妘 **Iûn**, et comptait parmi ses ancêtres 祝融 **Tchŏu iôung**, ministre de l'ancien empereur 高辛 **Kaō sīn**.

La principauté de 曹 **Ts'aô** était le 曹縣 **Ts'aô hién** actuel dans le Chan toung. Elle fut conférée par Ou wang à son frère 振鐸 **Tchénn tŏ**.

La principauté de 豳 **Pīn** était dans le 三水縣 **Sān chouèi hién** actuel, sous-préfecture qui dépend de 邠州 **Pīn tcheōu** dans le 陝西 **Chèn sī**. Le caractère 豳 a été remplacé par 邠 sous 唐玄宗 **T'âng Hiuên tsōung**, de 713 à 742 après J. C. Le premier des chants de Pin décrit les travaux et les usages des anciens habitants de ce pays sous 公劉 **Kōung liôu**; il est l'œuvre de 周公 **Tcheōu kōung**. Les autres furent composés à la même époque sur des sujets actuels, peut-être aussi par Tcheou koung.

周南一之一

關雎

(1) 關關雎鳩．在河之洲．窈窕淑女．君子好逑．

(2) 參差荇菜．左右流之．窈窕淑女．寤寐求之．求之不得．寤寐思服．悠哉悠哉．輾轉反側．

KOUAN TS'IU. 1. **Kouān kouān ts'iū kiōu, tsái hô tchēu tcheōu. Iaò tiaò chŏu gniù, kiūn tzèu haò k'iôu.**

2. Tch'ēnn tch'ēu hing ts'ái, tsouò iòu liôu tchēu. Iaò tiaò chŏu gniù, òu méi k'iôu tchēu. K'iôu tchēu pŏu tĕ, òu méi sēu fŏu (p'ĕ). Iôu tsāi, iôu tsāi, tchèn tchouèn fàn tchĕ !

LIVRE I. TCHEOU NAN.

CHANT I. KOUAN TS'IU.

Les femmes du palais chantent les vertus de 太姒 **T'ái Séu**, épouse de 文王 **Wênn wâng**.

1. Les *ts'iu kiou* (se répondant l'un à l'autre, crient) *kouan kouan* sur un ilot dans la rivière. Une fille vertueuse (T'ai Seu), qui vivait retirée et cachée (dans la maison maternelle), devient la digne compagne d'un prince sage (Wenn wang).

2. La plante aquatique *hing*, tantôt grande tantôt petite, a besoin d'être cherchée partout à droite et à gauche dans le sens du courant. Ainsi cette fille vertueuse, modeste et amie de la retraite a été l'objet de nos recherches et le jour et la nuit. Cherchant et ne trouvant pas, nos esprits n'avaient de repos ni le jour ni la nuit. Oh ! depuis combien de temps, nous tournant et nous retournant la nuit tantôt sur un côté tantôt sur l'autre, (avons-nous été privées de sommeil) !

TITRE DU LIVRE. 周南一之一 **Tcheōu nân: I tchēu I.** Tcheou (regni et) australium (regnorum cantica): (Cheu king partis) primæ (liber) primus.

La principauté de Tcheou était dans le 岐山縣 **K'î chān hién** actuel. Voy. page 2.

CHANT I. 1. (Invicem respondentes) *kouan kouan* (aves aquatiles) *ts'iu kiou* sunt in fluminis insula. Segregata, abdita, optima puella (facta est) principis sapientis eximia conjux.

Le 雎鳩 **ts'iū kiōu** est un oiseau aquatique. Il ressemble à la mouette ou au petit canard appelé 鳧 **fōu**. Il est le symbole de la fidélité conjugale. Plusieurs anciens auteurs prétendent que c'est une espèce d'aigle de mer.

T'ai Seu, c.-à-d. l'auguste Seu, était fille du prince de 莘 **Chēnn**, dont la famille se nommait Seu.

2. Inæquali altitudine *hing* olus, læva dextraque, i. e. hic illic, secundo flumine quærimus illud. Segregatam, abditam, optimam puellam, vigilantes ac dormientes (seu lecto cubantes)

(3) 參差荇菜、左右采之、窈窕淑女、琴瑟友之、參差荇菜、左右芼之、窈窕淑女、鐘鼓樂之、

葛覃

(1) 葛之覃兮、施于中谷、維葉萋

3. Tch'ēnn tch'ēu hing ts'ài, tsouò ióu ts'ài (ts'ì) tchēu. Iaò tiaò chŏu gniù, k'în chĕ ióu (i) tchēu. Tch'ēnn tch'ēu hing ts'ài, tsouò ióu maó (mouŏ) tchēu. Iaò tiaò chŏu gniù, tchōung kòu lŏ tchēu.

KO T'AN. **1. Kŏ tchēu t'ân hì, i iū tchōung kŏu ; wêi iĕ ts'ī ts'ī. Houâng gniaò**

3. La plante *hing*, tantôt grande tantôt petite, (lorsqu'elle est trouvée) doit être cueillie à droite et à gauche. Au son des luths et des guitares, accueillons amicalement cette fille vertueuse, qui vivait solitaire et cachée. La plante *hing*, tantôt grande tantôt petite, (lorsqu'elle a été cueillie) doit être cuite et servie avec soin. Au son des cloches et des tambours, accueillons avec joie cette fille vertueuse, amie de la retraite et du silence.

CHANT II. KO T'AN.

La princesse T'ai Seu, femme de Wenn wang, a terminé ses travaux d'été. Elle les chante, et se prépare à aller revoir ses parents.

1. (A la fin du printemps), le dolic se répandant peu à peu s'étendait jusqu'au milieu de la vallée; ses feuilles étaient verdoyantes. Les oiseaux jaunes (peut-être les loriots) volaient çà et

quæsivimus illam. Quærentes illam nec reperientes, vigilando ac dormiendo cogitavimus et recogitavimus. Quanto ex tempore, quanto ex tempore membra torquentes ac retorquentes, mutavimus latus!

荇 **Hing**, plante aquatique comestible; peut-être la lenticule, la guimauve ou le limnanthème.

3. Inæquali altitudine *hing* olus, læva dextraque legimus illud. Segregatam, abditam, optimam puellam, lyris et citharis amice excipiamus illam. Inæquali altitudine *hing* olus, læva dextraque coquimus et apponimus illud. Segregatam, abditam, optimam puellam, campanis ac tympanis delectemus illam.

芼 **Maó.** Faire cuire et servir un mets. 琴 **K'în**, luth à cinq ou sept cordes. 瑟 **Chĕ**, luth à dix-neuf ou vingt-cinq cordes. L'accord de ces deux instruments est le symbole de la concorde entre les époux.

CHANT II. 1. *Pueraria* porrecta migraverat ad mediam vallem, et folia luxuriabant. Flavæ aves volando conveniebant in confertas arbores; earum voces *kī kī* (concordes procul audiebantur).

葛 **Kŏ**, *Pueraria phaseoloides*, espèce de *dolic*, plante grimpante ou rampante dont les fibres servent à faire de la toile.

Lorsque 中 **tchōung** signifie *au milieu de*, il se place ordinairement après le substantif. Il est placé avant dans l'expression 中谷 **tchōung kŏu.**

萋、黃鳥于飛、集
于灌木、其鳴喈
喈、

(2) 葛之覃兮、施
于中谷、維葉莫
莫、是刈是濩、爲
絺爲綌、服之無
斁、

(3) 言告師氏、言
告言歸、薄汚我
私、薄澣我衣、害
澣害否、歸寧父
母、

iû fēi, tsĭ iû kouán mŏu ; k'ĭ mîng kiāi kiāi (kī kī).

2. Kŏ tchēu t'ân hi, i iû tchōung kŏu ; wêi iĕ mouŏ mouŏ. Chéu i, chéu houŏ, wêi tch'ēu, wêi k'ĭ (k'iŏ) ; fŏu tchēu ŏu ĭ (iŏ).

3. Iên kaó chēu chéu, iên kaó iên kouēi. Pouŏ óu ngò sēu, pouŏ houàn ngò ĭ. Hŏ houàn, hŏ feòu ? Kouēi gning fóu mòu (meòu).

là, et se réunissaient sur les massifs d'arbres. Leurs voix chantant de concert retentissaient au loin.

2. (En été) les tiges rampantes du dolic s'étendaient jusqu'au milieu de la vallée; ses feuilles étaient belles et nombreuses. Je l'ai coupé et fait bouillir; j'en ai tissé deux sortes de toiles, l'une fine, l'autre grossière. J'en ai fait des vêtements que je ne me lasserai pas de porter.

3. J'ai averti ma maîtresse; elle a fait connaître au prince mon désir de retourner à la maison paternelle. Je nettoierai mes vêtements ordinaires et laverai mes vêtements de cérémonie. (Voyons) quels sont ceux qui ont besoin d'être lavés, et quels sont ceux qui n'en ont pas besoin. Je retournerai à la maison saluer mon père et ma mère.

孔穎達 **K'òung Ìng tă** (574-648) observe que les anciens faisaient souvent cette inversion. Nous la retrouverons plus d'une fois dans le Cheu king. 于 **Iû**, aller, particule; *iû*, dans.

2. *Pueraria* porrecta migraverat ad mediam vallem, et folia densa luxuriabant. Et præcidi et coxi; feci subtiliorem telam, feci rudiorem telam. Induam eam sine fastidio.

3. Monui magistram dominam; monuit (regem) de meo reditu in paternam domum. Paulum aqua purgabo meas privatas (vestes), paulum abluam meas stolas. (Videam) utræ abluendæ, utræ non. Revertar salutatura patrem et matrem.

Une femme veuve, âgée de cinquante ans et n'ayant pas d'enfant mâle, servait de maîtresse à la jeune fille avant et après le mariage. 言 **Iên**, particule qui n'a pas besoin d'être traduite.

卷耳

(1) 采采卷耳、不盈頃筐、嗟我懷人、寘彼周行、

(2) 陟彼崔嵬、我馬虺隤、我姑酌彼金罍、維以不永懷、

(3) 陟彼高岡、我馬玄黃、我姑酌彼兕觥、維以不永傷、

KIUEN EUL. 1. Ts'ài ts'ài kiuèn èul; pŏu îng k'ìng k'ouāng. Tsiē! ngò houâi jènn; tchéu pèi tcheōu hîng (hâng).

2. Tchĕu pèi ts'ouēi wêi; ngò mà houēi t'ouêi. Ngò kōu tchŏ pèi kīn lêi, wêi i pŏu iòung houâi (houêi).

3. Tchĕu pèi kaō kāng; ngò mà hiuèn houâng. Ngò kōu tchŏ pèi si kōung (kouāng), wêi i pŏu iòung chāng.

CHANT III. KIUEN EUL.

T'ai Seu, femme de Wenn wang, se désole en l'absence de son époux. Elle pense tellement à lui qu'elle ne peut donner son attention à nul autre objet, et cherche en vain à se distraire de sa peine.

1. J'essaie à plusieurs reprises de cueillir de la bardane (ou de la lampourde); je n'en remplis pas même une corbeille plate à bords déprimés. Hélas! je pense à mon époux, et laisse ma corbeille sur la grand'route.

2. Je veux gravir cette montagne semée de rochers (pour voir si mon époux revient); mes chevaux malades ne peuvent la monter. Alors je remplis une coupe du vin de cette amphore dorée, afin de dissiper les pensées qui m'importunent.

3. Je veux gravir cette haute colline; mes chevaux sont malades et de noirs devenus jaunes. Alors je remplis de vin cette corne de rhinocéros, afin de dissiper ma douleur.

CHANT III. 1. Colligo iterumque colligo lappam (seu xanthium); non impleo inclinatam corbem. Eheu! ego cogitans de viro, depono illud in magna via.

2. (Volo) conscendere illum saxis stratum montem; mei equi ægri non valent ascendere. Ego interim (vinum in poculum) infundo ex illa aurata amphora, sperans fore ut inde non perpetuo conficiar desiderio.

虺隤 Houēi t'ouêi, maladie qui rend les chevaux incapables de gravir une montée. 罍 Lêi, vase à vin sur lequel étaient représentés des nuages et des foudres 雷 lêi.

3. (Volo) conscendere illum altum collem; mei equi nigri (morbo facti sunt) flavi. Ego interim vinum infundo in illud rhinocerotis cornu, sperans fore ut non in perpetuum animo doleam.

觥 Kōung, grande coupe faite d'une corne de rhinocéros ou en forme de corne de rhinocéros.

（4）陟彼砠矣、我馬瘏矣、我僕痡矣、云何吁矣、

樛木

（1）南有樛木、葛藟纍之、樂只君子、福履綏之、

（2）南有樛木、葛藟荒之、樂只君子、福履將之、

（3）南有樛木、葛藟縈之、樂只君子、福履成之、

4. Tchēu pèi ts'iū i; ngò mà t'ôu i. Ngò pŏu fōu i; iûn hô hiū i! [**tchēu!**
KIOU MOU. **1. Nân iòu kiōu mŏu, kŏ lèi lèi tchēu. Lŏ tchèu kiūn tzèu, fŏu li souēi**
2. Nân iòu kiōu mŏu, kŏ lèi houāng tchēu. Lŏ tchèu kiūn tzèu, fŏu li tsiāng tchēu!
3. Nân iòu kiōu mŏu, kŏ lèi iôung tchēu. Lŏ tchèu kiūn tzèu, fŏu li tch'êng tchēu!

4. Je veux gravir cette montagne composée de roches recouvertes de terre; mes chevaux malades ne peuvent avancer. Le conducteur de ma voiture n'a pas la force de marcher. Oh! comme je gémis!

CHANT IV. KIOU MOU.

Sous l'emblème d'un arbre auquel s'attachent les plantes grimpantes, les femmes du palais exaltent la bonté de la princesse T'ai Seu à leur égard, et lui souhaitent en récompense une félicité parfaite.

1. Les montagnes du midi ont des arbres aux rameaux pendants; les dolics enlacent les troncs et les branches. Notre sage princesse fait nos délices; puisse-t-elle jouir d'une félicité constante et assurée!

2. Les montagnes du midi ont des arbres aux rameaux pendants; les dolics couvrent les troncs et les branches. Notre sage princesse fait nos délices; que tous les biens sans cesse l'environnent!

3. Les montagnes du midi ont des arbres aux rameaux pendants; les dolics s'enroulent autour des troncs et des branches. Notre sage princesse fait nos délices; que sa félicité soit toujours parfaite!

4. (Volo) conscendere illum saxis constantem montem; mei equi non valent progredi. Meus auriga æger non valet incedere. Oh! quantum gemo!

云 **Iûn,** particule.

CHANT IV. 1. In australi regione sunt recurvis pendulisque ramis arbores; phaseoli implicantur eis. Deliciæ nostræ sapiens domina; felicitas et perpetua bona beatam faciant eam!

葛 **Kŏ,** 藟 **lèi,** deux espèces de dolics. 只 **Tchèu,** particule.

2. In australi regione sunt recurvis pendulisque ramis arbores; phaseoli obtegunt eas. Deliciæ nostræ sapiens domina; felicitas et perpetua bona comitentur eam!

3. In australi regione sunt recurvis pendulisque ramis arbores; phaseoli circumvolvuntur eis. Deliciæ nostræ sapiens domina; felicitas et perpetua bona omnia plene affluant ei!

螽斯
(1) 螽斯羽、詵詵兮、宜爾子孫、振振兮、
(2) 螽斯羽、薨薨兮、宜爾子孫、繩繩兮、
(3) 螽斯羽、揖揖兮、宜爾子孫、蟄蟄兮、
桃夭
(1) 桃之夭夭、灼灼其華、之

TCHOUNG SEU. **1. Tchōung sēu iù, sīn sīn hī; ī èul tzèu suēnn tchēnn tchēnn hī.**
2. Tchōung sēu iù, hōung hōung hī; ī èul tzèu suēnn chêng chêng hī.
3. Tchōung sēu iù, tsī tsī hī; ī èul tzèu suēnn tch'ĕu tch'ĕu hī.
T'AO IAO. **1. T'aô tchēu iaō iaō, tchŏ tchŏ k'î houā. Tchēu tzèu iû kouēi, ī k'î chēu kiā.**

CHANT V. TCHOUNG SEU.

Sous l'emblème d'une troupe de sauterelles, les femmes du palais désignent la princesse T'ai Seu, louent sa bienveillance et sa douceur accommodante, et lui souhaitent en récompense une nombreuse postérité.

1. Sauterelles, race ailée, entre vous règnent l'union et la concorde; vous méritez d'avoir une postérité nombreuse.
2. Sauterelles, race ailée, votre bruyante troupe vole de concert; vous méritez d'avoir une postérité sans fin.
3. Sauterelles, race ailée, vous vivez réunies en troupe; vous méritez d'avoir une postérité nombreuse.

CHANT VI. T'AO IAO.

Le poète voyant que, sous Wenn wang, les mariages se célèbrent à l'époque, à l'âge et avec les cérémonies convenables, conclut que les jeunes mariées sont vertueuses, et les compare au pêcher sur lequel les fleurs éclosent, puis les fruits naissent, enfin les feuilles prennent leur entier développement.

1. Le pêcher est jeune et beau; ses fleurs sont brillantes. Ces jeunes filles vont célébrer leurs noces chez leurs fiancés; elles

CHANT V. 1. Locustæ volucres, congregatæ et concordes estis; æquum est vestram progeniem esse plurimam.

斯 **Sēu** paraît être comme une particule apposée au substantif précédent. 羽 **Iù**, aile, animal ailé.

2. Locustæ volucres, alis strepentibus simul volatis; æquum est vestram progeniem esse continuam.

3. Locustæ volucres, congregatæ vivitis; æquum est vestram progeniem esse plurimam.

CHANT VI. 1. Persica arbor est juvenis et pulchra; nitidi sunt ejus flores. Hæ puellæ petunt sponsorum domos; recte component sua conclavia ac domos, i. e. exemplis suis facient ut domestici homines recte se componant.

之 **Tchēu**, ce, cet, ces. 歸 **Kouēi**, se dit d'une fille conduite à la maison de son fiancé pour la célébration des noces. 于 *Iû*, particule; plusieurs interprètes, dans cette expression et dans beaucoup d'autres semblables, traduisent: *iû* aller.

子于歸。宜其室家、

(2) 桃之夭夭。有蕡其實、之子于歸。宜其家室。

(3) 桃之夭夭。其葉蓁蓁、之子于歸、宜其家人、

兔罝

(1) 肅肅兔罝。椓之丁丁。赳赳武夫、公侯干城。

2. T'aô tchēu iaō iaō, iòu fênn k'ì chēu. Tchēu tzèu iû kouēi, î k'î kiā chēu.

3. T'aô tchēu iaō iaō, k'î iě tchēnn tchēnn. Tchēu tzèu iû kouēi, î k'î kiā jênn.

T'OU TSIE. **1. Siŭ siŭ t'óu tsiē (tsiū), tchouŏ tchēu tchēng tchēng. Kiòu kiòu òu fōu, kōung heôu kān tch'êng.**

établiront l'ordre le plus parfait dans leurs appartements et dans toute la maison.

2. Le pêcher est jeune et beau, ses fruits sont nombreux. Ces jeunes filles vont célébrer leurs noces; elles établiront l'ordre le plus parfait dans leurs maisons et leurs appartements.

3. Le pêcher est jeune et beau, son feuillage est luxuriant. Ces jeunes filles vont célébrer leurs noces; elles établiront l'ordre le plus parfait parmi les personnes de leurs maisons.

CHANT VII. T'OU TSIE.

Le poète compare les officiers de Wenn wang aux chasseurs de lièvres. Sous ce prince, les hommes capables de remplir les charges publiques étaient très nombreux; on en rencontrait même parmi ceux qui exerçaient les métiers les plus vulgaires.

1. Le chasseur de lièvres dispose soigneusement son filet, et le fixe solidement avec des pieux, qu'il enfonce à coups retentissants. Ces braves officiers sont infatigables; ils servent de bouclier et de rempart à notre prince.

Les mariages se célébraient au printemps, vers l'époque de la floraison du pêcher. Le 禮記 **Li ki** Mémorial des Institutions et des Cérémonies veut qu'un jeune homme soit marié avant trente ans, une fille avant vingt ans. Plusieurs auteurs disent qu'un jeune homme doit se marier de vingt à trente ans, une fille, de quinze à vingt ans. Un homme ne se remarie plus après soixante ans, ni une femme après cinquante ans.

2. Persica arbor est juvenis ac pulchra; sunt multi ejus fructus. Hæ puellæ adeunt sponsorum domos; recte componunt suas domos ac conclavia.

蕡 **Fènn**, chènevis, nombreux comme les grains du chanvre.

3. Persica arbor est juvenis ac pulchra; luxuriant ejus frondes. Hæ puellæ petunt sponsorum domos; recte componunt suarum domorum homines.

CHANT VII. 1. Diligenter componit (venator ad capiendos) lepores rete; tundit illud, i. e. malleo infigit retis paxillos, repetito sonitu. Strenui sunt fortes viri, reguli scuta ac mœnia.

(2) 肅肅兔罝、施于中逵。赳赳武夫、公侯好仇、
(3) 肅肅兔罝、施于中林。赳赳武夫、公侯腹心、

芣苢

(1) 采采芣苢、薄言采之。采采芣苢、薄言有之、
(2) 采采芣苢、薄言掇之、采采芣苢、薄言捋之、

2. Siŭ siŭ t'óu tsiē (tsiū), chēu iū tchōung k'ouêi. Kiòu kiòu òu fōu, kōung heôu haò k'iôu (k'ouêi).

3. Siŭ siŭ t'óu tsiē (tsiū), chēu iū tchōung lîn. Kiòu kiòu òu fōu, kōung heôu fŏu sīn.

FEOU I. 1. Ts'ài ts'ài feôu i, pouŏ iên ts'ài (ts'i) tchēu. Ts'ài ts'ài feôu i, pouŏ iên iòu (i) tchēu.

2. Ts'ài ts'ài feôu i, pouŏ iên touŏ tchēu. Ts'ài ts'ài feôu i, pouŏ iên louŏ tchēu.

2. Le chasseur de lièvres dispose soigneusement son filet; il le tend à la jonction de neuf chemins. Ces braves officiers sont infatigables; ils sont les dignes compagnons de notre prince.

3. Le chasseur de lièvres dispose soigneusement son filet; il le tend au milieu de la forêt. Ces braves officiers sont infatigables; ils vivent dans l'intimité du prince.

CHANT VIII. FEOU I.

Sous le règne de Wenn wang, les femmes, en temps de paix, emploient leurs moments de loisir à cueillir le plantain.

1. Nous allons cueillir le plantain; nous en cherchons un peu. Nous allons cueillir le plantain; nous en trouvons un peu.

2. Nous allons cueillir le plantain; nous en cueillons quelques épis. Nous allons cueillir le plantain; nous égrenons quelques épis.

丁丁 **Tchēng tchēng**, bruit des coups de maillet. 公侯 **Kōung heôu**, prince. La solidité des piquets figure la fermeté des officiers.

2. Diligenter componit leporibus plagas; pandit in medio novem viarum compito. Strenui sunt fortes viri, reguli boni socii. — Les lièvres se réunissent à l'intersection des chemins; ainsi les officiers environnent leur prince.

3. Diligenter componit leporibus retia, pandit in media silva. Strenui sunt fortes viri, reguli pectus et animus.

L'intimité des officiers avec le prince est figurée par les profondeurs des bois.

CHANT VIII. 1. Colligentes colligimus plantaginem; paulum perquirimus eam. Colligentes colligimus plantaginem; paulum nanciscimur eam.

言 **Iên**, particule explétive.

2. Colligentes colligimus plantaginem; paulum decerpimus eam. Colligentes colligimus plantaginem; paulum digitis exprimimus ejus grana.

(3)采采芣苢、薄言袺之、采采芣苢、薄言襭之、

漢廣

(1)南有喬木、不可休息、漢有游女、不可求思、漢之廣矣、不可泳思、江之永矣、不可方思、

(2)翹翹錯薪、言刈其楚、之子于歸、言秣其馬、漢

3. Ts'ài ts'ài feôu i, pouŏ iên kiĕ tchēu. Ts'ài ts'ài feôu i, pouŏ iên hiĕ tchēu.

HAN KOUANG. **1. Nân iòu k'iaŏ mŏu, pŏu k'ŏ hiōu sĭ. Hán iòu iôu gniù, pŏu k'ŏ k'iôu sēu. Hán tchēu kouàng (kouáng) i, pŏu k'ŏ iòung (iáng) sēu. Kiāng tchēu iòung (iáng) i, pŏu k'ŏ fāng (fáng) sēu.**

2. K'iaô k'iaô ts'ouŏ sīn, iên i k'ī tch'òu. Tchēu tzèu iû kouēi, iên mouŏ k'ī

3. Nous allons cueillir le plantain; nous mettons les grains dans le pan de nos robes. Nous allons cueillir le plantain; nous fixons le pan de nos robes à la ceinture.

CHANT IX. HAN KOUANG.

Sous le règne de Wenn wang, les jeunes filles étaient très chastes. Le poète les compare à un grand arbre, à un arbuste épineux, à l'armoise.

1. Au midi il est des arbres très élevés qui ont peu de branches; on ne peut se reposer (à leur ombre, ils n'en donnent pas). Sur les bords de la Han il est des jeunes filles qui se promènent; il est aussi impossible d'ébranler leur vertu que de traverser la Han à gué ou de voyager sur le Kiang en radeau.

2. Je voudrais couper et recueillir les arbustes épineux qui s'élèvent au-dessus des autres arbrisseaux destinés au chauffage.

3. Colligentes colligimus plantaginem; paulum in vestis lacinia, quam manu adductam tenemus, ponimus eam. Colligentes colligimus plantaginem; in vestis lacinia, quam ad zonam infiximus, habemus eam.

袺 **Kiĕ**, retrousser et tenir avec la main le pan de la robe, et mettre un objet à l'intérieur. 襭 **Hiĕ**, retrousser le pan de la robe et le fixer sous la ceinture, pour y mettre ou après y avoir mis quelque chose.

CHANT IX. **1.** In australi regione sunt procero trunco paucisque ramis arbores; non datur subsidere ac quiescere (quia non præbent umbram). Ad Han fluvium sunt spatiantes puellæ, non possunt obtineri; (quemadmodum) Han fluvii latitudo non potest vado trajici, Kiang fluvii longitudo non potest rate percurri.

思 **Sēu**, particule. 方 **Fāng**, petit bateau carré, radeau, voyager en bateau.

2. Excelsiorem commixtis virgultis (velim) præcidere illam spinosam arbusculam. Hæc puella nuptura est; pabulum apponam ejus equo. Han

之廣矣、不可泳思、江之永矣、不可方思、

(3)翹翹錯薪、言刈其蔞、之子于歸、言秣其駒、漢之廣矣、不可泳思、江之永矣、不可方思、

汝墳

(1)遵彼汝墳、伐其條枚、未見君子、惄如調飢、

mà (mòu). Hán tchēu kouàng (kouáng) i, pŏu k'ò iòung (iáng) sēu. Kiāng tchēu iòung (iáng) i, pŏu k'ò fāng (fáng) sēu.

3. K'iaô k'iaô ts'ouŏ sīn, iên i k'ì liû. Tchēu tzèu iû kouēi; iên mouŏ k'ì kiū. Hán tchēu kouàng (kouáng) i, pŏu k'ò iòung (iáng) sēu. Kiāng tchēu iòung (iáng) i, pŏu k'ò fāng (fáng) sēu.

JOU FENN. **1. Tsuēnn pèi Jôu fênn, fă k'ì t'iaô mêi. Wéi kién kiūn tzèu, gnĭ jôu tcheōu kī.**

Cette fille va célébrer ses noces. (Mon estime pour sa vertu est telle que je m'abaisserais volontiers jusqu'à) porter la nourriture à son cheval. Il est impossible de traverser la Han à gué, ou de voyager sur le Kiang en radeau.

3. Je voudrais couper et recueillir l'armoise qui s'élève au-dessus des autres plantes destinées au chauffage. Cette fille va célébrer ses noces. (Pour témoigner combien j'estime sa vertu, je m'abaisserais volontiers jusqu'à) porter la nourriture à son poulain. Il est impossible de traverser la Han à gué, ou de voyager sur le Kiang en radeau.

CHANT X. JOU FENN

Sous le règne du tyran 紂 **Tcheóu**, une femme dont le mari revient d'une expédition pénible, se réjouit de son retour, et le compare à la brême devenue rouge par suite de fatigue. Elle l'engage à servir fidèlement son prince, parce que Wenn wang le veut, et donne lui-même l'exemple de l'obéissance.

1. (L'année dernière) le long du bord élevé de la Jou, j'ai coupé des branches et des arbustes. Ne revoyant pas mon seigneur (mon mari), dans mon affliction j'éprouvais comme le tourment d'une faim dévorante.

fluvii latitudo non potest vado trajici; Kiang fluvii longitudo non potest rate percurri.

于 **Iû**, 言 **Iên**, particules.

3. Excelsiorem commixtis cespitibus (velim) præcidere illam artemisiam. Hæc puella nuptura est; pabulum apponam ejus pullo. Han fluvii...

CHANT X. 1. Legens illum Jou fluvii aggerem, excidi illius ramos ac stipites. Nondum videns dominum (maritum), anhelabam quasi valde esuriens.

(2)遵彼汝墳、伐
其條肄、既見君
子、不我遐棄、
(3)魴魚赬尾、王
室如燬、雖則如
燬、父母孔邇、

麟之趾

(1)麟之趾、振振
公子、于嗟麟兮、
(2)麟之定、振振
公姓、于嗟麟兮、

2. Tsuēnn pèi Jôu fênn, fă k'î t'iaô i. Kí kién kiūn tzèu, pŏu ngò hiâ k'i.

3. Fâng iû tch'ēng wèi; wàng chĕu jôu houèi. Souēi tsĕ jôu houèi, fóu mòu k'òung èul.

LIN TCHEU TCHEU. **1. Lìn tchēu tchèu, tchēnn tchēnn kōung tzèu (tsi). Hiū tsiē ! lîn hî !**

2. Lìn tchēu tíng, tchēnn tchēnn kōung síng. Hiū tsiē ! lîn hî !

2. (Cette année) le long du bord élevé de la Jou, j'ai coupé des branches et des surgeons. J'ai revu mon seigneur, il n'est pas resté loin de moi pour toujours.

3. La brême a la queue toute rouge; la maison royale est comme un brasier ardent (Tcheou traite ses sujets avec cruauté). Bien qu'elle soit comme un brasier ardent, (soyez-lui dévoué); le père du peuple (Wenn wang) est très près de nous.

CHANT XI. LIN TCHEU TCHEU.

Le poète compare les fils, les petits-fils et les parents de Wenn wang à la licorne, qui ne foule du pied aucun être vivant, pas même le gazon, ne frappe ni du front ni de la corne, et par son apparition annonce un âge de prospérité.

1. Les fils généreux de notre prince sont comme les pieds de la licorne. Oh! ils sont la licorne (qui présage une ère de bonheur)!

2. Les petits-fils généreux de notre prince sont comme le front de la licorne. Oh! ils sont la licorne!

2. Legens illum Jou fluvii aggerem, excidi illius ramos ac surculos. Jam vidi dominum; non me longe dereliquit (sive mortuus sive captivus).

3. Cyprini piscis rubuit cauda; regia domus est velut ignis ardens. Licet quidem sit velut ardens ignis, parens valde propinquus est.

La queue de la brême est naturellement blanche; mais elle devient rouge, dit-on, quand l'animal s'est agité et fatigué beaucoup. Plusieurs commentateurs expliquent ainsi le dernier vers: « Vos parents sont très près, (votre négligence au service du prince leur attirerait des chagrins). »

CHANT XI. 1. Monocerotis pedes sunt benefici et generosi principis filii. Oh! sunt monoceros!

2. Monocerotis frons sunt benefici et generosi principis nepotes. Oh! sunt monoceros!

(3)麟之角、振
振公族、于嗟
麟兮。

召南一之二
鵲巢

(1)維鵲有巢、
維鳩居之、之
子于歸、百兩
御之、

(2)維鵲有巢、
維鳩方之、之
子于歸、百兩
將之、

3. Lîn tchēu kiŏ (lŏu), tchēnn tchēnn kōung tsŏu. Hiū tsiē ! lîn hî !

TS'IO TCH'AO. **1. Wêi ts'iŏ iòu tch'aŏ ; wêi kiōu kiū (kiù) tchēu. Tchēu tzèu iû kouēi ; pĕ leàng iá (iù) tchēu.**

2. Wêi ts'iŏ iòu tch'aŏ ; wêi kiōu fāng tchēu. Tchēu tzèu iû kouēi ; pĕ leàng tsiāng tchēu.

3. Les parents généreux de notre prince sont comme la corne de la licorne. Oh ! ils sont la licorne !

LIVRE II. CHAO NAN.

CHANT I. TS'IO TCH'AO.

Un jeune prince va épouser la fille d'un prince voisin. Les personnes de son palais exaltent la vertu de sa fiancée, la comparent à la tourterelle, et lui font une réception pompeuse, une cérémonie en rapport avec son mérite.

1. La pie a fait son nid ; la tourterelle l'occupe. Cette jeune fille va célébrer ses noces ; cent voitures (de la maison de son fiancé) vont l'inviter et l'amener.

2. La pie a fait son nid ; la tourterelle en jouit. Cette jeune fille va célébrer ses noces ; cent voitures (de la maison de son père) forment son escorte.

3. Monocerotis cornu sunt benefici et generosi principis cognati eodem cognomine vocati. Oh ! sunt monoceros !

TITRE DU LIVRE. 召南一之二 Chao et australium (regnorum cantica) : (Cheu king) primæ (partis) secundus (liber). La capitale de Chao était probablement dans le 岐山縣 **K'i chān hién** actuel. V. page 2.

CHANT I. 1. Pica habet nidum ; turtur occupat illum. Hæc puella adit sponsi domum nuptura ; centum currus eunt obviam ei.

兩 **Leàng**, particule numérale des voitures. — La pie sait construire un nid solide et commode. La tourterelle n'a pas cette habileté ; et cependant, à cause de sa douceur, elle mérite d'avoir un bon nid. D'après les commentateurs, quand les petits de la pie se sont envolés, la tourterelle dépose ses œufs à leur place. De même cette jeune princesse a mérité par ses vertus une réception magnifique.

2. Pica habet nidum ; turtur possidet illum. Hæc puella adit sponsi domum nuptura ; centum currus comitantur eam.

(3) 維鵲有巢、
維鳩盈之、之
子于歸、百兩
成之、

采蘩

(1) 于以采蘩
于沼于沚、于
以用之、公侯
之事、

(2) 于以采蘩
于澗之中、于
以用之、公侯
之宮、

(3) 被之僮僮、

3. Wêi ts'iŏ iòu tch'aŏ ; wêi kiōu îng tchēu. Tchēu tzèu iù kouēi ; pĕ leàng tch'êng tchēu.

TS'AI FAN. **1. Iû i ts'ài fân iû tchaò iù tchèu. Iû i ióung tchēu kōung heôu tchēu chéu (chèu).**

2. Iû i ts'ài fân iû kièn tchēu tchōung. Iû i ióung tchēu kōung heôu tchēu kōung.

3. Pí tchēu t'ôung t'ôung, siŭ iè tsâi kōung. Pí tchēu k'î k'î, pouŏ iên siuèn kouēi.

3. La pie a fait son nid ; la tourterelle le remplit de sa progéniture. Cette fille va célébrer ses noces ; des centaines de voitures lui font un cortège complet, (et une suite nombreuse de dames des deux principautés remplit le palais de son époux).

CHANT II. TS'AI FAN.

Sous le règne de Wenn wang, la femme d'un prince cueille l'armoise blanche, et l'offre dans la salle des ancêtres, ou d'après une autre opinion, l'emploie à faire éclore les œufs des vers à soie.

1. La princesse cueille l'armoise blanche au bord des bassins et sur les ilots. Elle l'emploie pour le service du prince (pour faire des offrandes ou élever des vers à soie).

2. Elle cueille l'armoise blanche au bord des ruisseaux dans les vallées. Elle l'emploie dans la salle (des ancêtres ou dans la magnanerie) du prince.

3. La tête parée de cheveux empruntés, dès le matin avant le jour elle se tient avec respect dans la salle (des ancêtres ou

3. Pica habet nidum ; turtur implet illum. Hæc puella adit sponsi domum nuptura ; (bis) centum currus complent illum (ritum).

CHANT II. 1. Colligit albam artemisiam secus stagna, in parvis insulis. Adhibet illam ad reguli negotium.

于以 **Iû i.** Cette expression semble n'avoir pas de signification propre. Quelques interprètes traduisent le mot *iû* par le verbe 往 **wàng** *aller*.

2. Colligit albam artemisiam, vallium rivos inter. Adhibet illam in reguli aula.

3. Capitis ornamento reverenter habito (reverenter immoto, ut nonnulli dicunt), mane, nocte (nondum depulsa), est in reguli æde. Capitis ornamento tarde incedente, paulatim recedens regreditur.

夙夜在公、被之祁祁、
薄言還歸、

草蟲

(1) 喓喓草蟲、趯趯阜螽、未見君子、憂心忡忡、亦既見止、亦既覯止、我心則降、

(2) 陟彼南山、言采其蕨、未見君子、憂心惙惙、亦既見止、亦既覯止、我心則說、

(3) 陟彼南山、言采其薇、未見君子、我心傷

TS'AO TCH'OUNG. 1. **Iaŏ iaŏ ts'aò tch'ŏung, t'ĭ t'ĭ feòu tchōung. Wéi kién kiūn tzèu, iōu sīn tch'ōung tch'ōung. Ĭ ki kién tchèu, ĭ ki keóu tchéu, ngò sīn tsĕ hiâng (hôung).**

2. Tchĕu pèi nân chān, iên ts'ài k'ì kiuĕ. Wéi kién kiūn tzèu, iōu sīn tchouŏ tchouŏ. Ĭ ki kién tchéu, ĭ ki keóu tchéu, ngò sīn tsĕ iuĕ.

3. Tchĕu pèi nân chān, iên ts'ài k'ì wêi. Wéi kién kiūn tzèu, ngò sīn chāng

dans la magnanerie) du prince. (Puis, lorsqu'elle a rempli son office), la tête parée de cheveux empruntés, elle se retire d'un pas lent, et retourne à ses appartements.

CHANT III. TS'AO TCH'OUNG.

La femme d'un grand officier appelle de ses vœux le retour de son mari.

1. La sauterelle des prés crie; la sauterelle des coteaux sautille (l'automne est venu). Je ne vois pas mon seigneur (mon mari); l'inquiétude agite mon cœur. Quand je l'aurai revu et retrouvé, mon cœur deviendra calme.

2. Je gravis cette montagne au midi (pour voir si mon seigneur ne revient pas encore); j'y cueille de la fougère. Je ne vois pas mon seigneur; mon cœur est dans la tristesse et l'inquiétude. Quand je l'aurai revu et retrouvé, mon cœur sera dans la joie.

3. Je gravis cette montagne au midi; j'y cueille de la fougère.

被 **Pi**, ornement formé de cheveux étrangers tressés ensemble. On le voyait s'avancer, lorsque la princesse marchait.

CHANT III. 1. Stridens stridet graminis locusta, saltitans saltitat collium locusta. Nondum video dominum (maritum meum); anxius animus agitatur. Postquam videro, postquam invenero, meus animus tum considet.

亦 **Ĭ**, 止 **tchèu**, particules explétives.

2. Ascendo illum australem montem; colligo illius filicem. Nondum video dominum; anxius animus tristatur. Postquam videro, postquam invenero, meus animus statim gaudebit.

3. Ascendo illum australem montem; colligo illius filicem. Nondum

悲。亦既見止、亦既覯止、我心則夷。

采蘋

(1) 于以采蘋、南澗之濱、于以采藻、于彼行潦。

(2) 于以盛之、維筐及筥、于以湘之、維錡及釜。

(3) 于以奠之、宗室牖下、誰其尸

pēi. Ĭ ki kién tchéu, ĭ ki keóu tchéu, ngò sīn tsĕ ĭ.

TS'AI P'IN. **1. Iû i ts'ài p'în nân kién tchēu pīn. Iû i ts'ài tsaò iû pèi hìng laò.**

2. Iû i tch'êng tchēu, wêi k'ouāng kĭ kiù. Iû i siāng tchēu, wêi i kĭ fòu.

3. Iû i tién tchēu tsōung chĕu iòu hiá (hòu). Chouêi k'î chēu tchēu? Iòu tchāi ki gniù.

Je ne vois pas mon seigneur; mon cœur est dans l'inquiétude et l'affliction. Quand je l'aurai revu et retrouvé, mon cœur jouira du repos.

CHANT IV. TS'AI P'IN.

La jeune femme d'un 大夫 **tái fōu** grand officier cueille des plantes, les fait cuire, et prépare des offrandes dans la salle des ancêtres.

1. Elle cueille des lentilles d'eau au midi dans la vallée sur le bord du courant. Elle cueille le potamot dans ces ruisseaux formés par l'inondation.

2. Elle met ces plantes dans des paniers, les uns carrés, les autres ronds. Elle les fait bouillir dans des chaudières, les unes munies de pieds, les autres sans pieds.

3. Elle les offre dans la salle du premier des ancêtres de la fenêtre...

video dominum; meus animus saucius mœret. Postquam videro, postquam invenero, meus animus tum tranquillus erit.

蕨 **Kiuĕ**, 薇 **wêi**, deux espèces de fougères comestibles.

CHANT IV. 1. Colligit lemnam ad australis in valle torrentis oram; colligit potamogetonem in illis fluentibus diluvii rivulis.

于以 **Iû i**, locution explétive. Plusieurs interprètes traduisent: *iû* aller.

2. Imponit illa in quadratis sportis et rotundis cistis. Coquit illa in caldario pedibus instructo et lebete pedibus carente.

3. Apponit illa in primi progenitoris delubro ad fenestram imam. Quænam ipsa præest illi rei? Est reverens junior mulier.

Le premier des ancêtres d'un grand officier était né du fils d'une femme de second rang d'un prince 諸侯 **tchōu heôu**. La salle où était sa tablette, était au nord et regardait le midi. La porte, qui se trouvait à droite en entrant,

之、有齊季女、

甘棠

(1)蔽芾甘棠、勿翦勿伐、召伯所茇、

(2)蔽芾甘棠、勿翦勿敗、召伯所憩、

(3)蔽芾甘棠、勿翦勿拜、召伯所說、

行露

(1)厭浥行露、豈

KAN T'ANG. **1. Pi féi kān t'âng, ŏu tsièn ŏu fă ; Chaó pĕ chòu pouŏ.**

2. Pi féi kān t'âng, ŏu tsièn ŏu pái (pi) ; Chaó pĕ chòu k'i.

3. Pi féi kān t'âng, ŏu tsièn ŏu pái (pi) ; Chaó pĕ chòu chouéi.

HING LOU. **1. Iĕ ĭ hìng lóu ; k'i pŏu siŭ ié (iŭ)? Wéi hìng touŏ lóu.**

famille, auprès de la fenêtre. Qui préside à ce travail? C'est une jeune femme respectueuse.

CHANT V. KAN T'ANG.

Le peuple, dans sa vénération pour le prince de Chao, respectait les arbres sous lesquels il s'était reposé.

1. Ne taillez pas, n'abattez pas ce poirier sauvage aux rameaux touffus, aux fruits doux. Le prince de Chao s'est abrité sous son feuillage.

2. Ne taillez pas, ne lésez pas ce poirier sauvage aux rameaux touffus, aux fruits doux. Le prince de Chao s'est reposé sous son feuillage.

3. Ne taillez pas, ne courbez pas ce poirier sauvage aux rameaux touffus, aux fruits doux. Le prince de Chao s'est arrêté sous son feuillage.

CHANT VI. HING LOU.

Une jeune fille a été promise en mariage à un jeune homme. Celui-ci l'accuse en justice, et veut la forcer à célébrer les noces, avant d'avoir accompli toutes les cérémonies des fiançailles. Elle refuse absolument d'enfreindre ainsi les usages.

1. Les chemins sont tout humides de rosée. Pourquoi refusé-je

et la fenêtre qui se trouvait à gauche, regardaient aussi toutes deux le midi. La tablette était du côté occidental, non loin de la fenêtre, et regardait l'orient. Les offrandes se plaçaient devant la tablette.

CHANT V. 1. Umbrosam, luxuriantem, dulcem pirum silvestrem ne tondeatis, ne ernatis; Chao princeps sub qua insidit.

2. Umbrosam, luxuriantem, dulcem pirum silvestrem ne tondeatis, ne lædatis; Chao princeps sub qua quievit.

3. Umbrosam, luxuriantem, dulcem pirum silvestrem ne tondeatis, ne incurvetis; Chao princeps sub qua resedit.

不夙夜、謂行多露、(2)誰謂雀無角、何以穿我屋、誰謂女無家、何以速我獄、雖速我獄、室家不足、(3)誰謂鼠無牙、何以穿我墉、誰

2. Chouêi wéi tsiŏ ôu kiŏ (lŏu)? Hô i tch'ouēn ngò ŏu? Chouêi wéi jòu ôu kiā (kŏu)? Hô i sŏu ngò iŭ? Souēi sŏu ngò iŭ, chĕu kiā pŏu tsiŭ.

3. Chouêi wéi chòu ôu iâ (wŏung)? Hô i tch'ouēn ngò iôung? Chouêi wéi

de sortir dès le matin au point du jour (c.-à-d. de célébrer mes noces sans retard)? C'est que sur les chemins la rosée est très abondante (c.-à-d. ce serait une faute grave de célébrer les noces avant l'entier accomplissement des cérémonies des fiançailles, je ne veux pas m'en rendre coupable).

2. Qui dira jamais que le moineau n'a pas de cornes? (On dit communément: S'il n'avait pas de cornes), comment pourrait-il percer mon toit? (De même, en voyant que tu me cites devant les tribunaux), qui dira que tu n'as pas contracté avec moi des fiançailles selon toutes les règles? (Au jugement de tous, si les règles n'avaient pas été entièrement observées), comment pourrais-tu me citer en justice? Tu auras beau me citer en justice; (de même que, contrairement à l'opinion vulgaire, il est certain que le moineau n'a pas de cornes; de même, contrairement aux discours publics, il est certain que) les cérémonies des fiançailles n'ont pas toutes été accomplies.

3. Qui dira jamais que le rat n'a pas de dents molaires (ou plutôt de dents canines? S'il n'avait pas de dents canines, dit-on), comment percerait-il mon mur? (De même, en voyant que

CHANT VI. 1. Plurimo madore (inficit) viarum ros. Qui nollem (exire) mane, nocte (nondum depulsa)? Dico in viis multum esse rorem.

2. Quis dicet passerem carere cornibus? (Omnes vulgo dicunt: Si careret cornibus), quo utens perfoderet meum tectum? (Pari ratione, quum videant me a te in jus vocari), quis dicet te carere sponsalibus, i. e. non omnibus sponsalitiis ritibus esse perfunctum? (Nisi perfecta essent sponsalia, putant), quomodo vocares me ad judicium? Quamvis voces me in judicium, (quemadmodum certum est passerem cornibus carere, et falsam esse vulgarem opinionem, ita certum est) sponsalia non esse perfecta.

室 **Chĕu**, épouse; 家 **kiā**, mari; **chĕu kiā**, la femme et le mari, mariage, fiançailles.

3. Quis dicet murem carere molaribus (aut potius caninis) dentibus? (Omnes vulgo dicunt: Si molaribus aut caninis dentibus careret), quo utens perfoderet meum parietem?... Quamvis voces me in judicium, (quemadmodum certum est, præter vulgi opinionem,

謂女無家、何以速我訟、雖速我訟、亦不女從、

羔羊

(1) 羔羊之皮、素絲五紽、退食自公、委蛇委蛇、

(2) 羔羊之革、素絲五緎、委蛇委蛇、自公退食、

(3) 羔羊之縫、

jòu ôu kiā (kōung)? Hô i sŏu ngò sóung (sôung)? Souēi sŏu ngò sóung (sôung), ì pŏu jòu ts'ôung.

KAO IANG. **1. Kaō iâng tchēu p'î (p'ouô), sóu sēu òu t'ouô. T'ouéi chĕu tzéu kōung, wēi î (t'ouô), wēi î (t'ouô).**

2. Kaō iâng tchēu kŏ (kĭ), sóu sēu òu iŭ (î). Wēi î (t'ouô), wēi î (t'ouô), tzéu kōung t'ouéi chĕu.

3. Kaō iâng tchēu fôung, sóu sēu òu tsōung. Wēi î (t'ouô), wēi î (t'ouô), t'ouéi chĕu tzéu kōung.

tu m'accuses devant les tribunaux), qui dira que tu n'as pas accompli toutes les cérémonies des fiançailles? (Si tu ne les avais pas accomplies, pense-t-on), comment pourrais-tu me citer en justice? Bien que tu me cites en justice, je ne te suivrai pas.

CHANT VII. KAO IANG.

Le poète loue la simplicité des vêtements ordinaires des 大夫 **tái fōu** grands préfets, leur tenue aisée et leur joyeuse allure.

1. Vêtu de peaux d'agneaux et de brebis ornées de cinq tresses de soie blanche, il quitte la cour joyeux et content, et va prendre son repas dans sa maison.

2. Vêtu de peaux d'agneaux et de brebis unies par cinq coutures de fil de soie blanche, joyeux et content, il quitte la cour et va prendre son repas.

3. Vêtu de peaux d'agneaux et de brebis cousues ensemble et

murem carere molaribus aut caninis dentibus, ita certe) tamen non te sequar, i.e. matrimonium tecum non contraham.

Les rongeurs ont à chaque mâchoire deux incisives et trois ou quatre molaires; mais pas de canines. Les incisives sont séparées des molaires par un grand espace vide.

CHANT VII. 1. (Indutus) agninis ovinisque pellibus, (additis) ex albo filo serico quinque ornamentis, (domum) recedit comesturus ex regia, contentus, contentus.

2. (Indutus) agninis ovinisque pellibus, (factis) ex albo filo serico quinque suturis, contentus, contentus, recedit comesturus ex regia.

3. (Indutus) agninis ovinisque (pellibus) consutis, (factis) ex albo filo serico quinque juncturis, contentus, contentus, recedit comesturus ex regia.

La signification de 總 **tsōung** est

素絲五總。委蛇委蛇。退食自公。

殷其靁

(1) 殷其靁、在南山之陽。何斯違斯。莫敢或遑。振振君子。歸哉歸哉。

(2) 殷其靁、在南山之側。何斯違斯。莫敢遑息。振振君子。歸哉歸哉。

(3) 殷其靁。在南山之下。何斯違斯。莫

IN K'I LEI. **1. In k'i lêi tsái nân chān tchēu iâng. Hô sēu wêi sēu, mouŏ kàn houĕ houâng? Tchēnn tchēnn kiūn tzéu! kouēi tsāi! kouēi tsāi!**

2. In k'i lêi tsái nân chān tchēu tchĕ (tchĭ). Hô sēu wêi sēu, mouŏ kàn houâng sĭ? Tchēnn tchēnn kiūn tzéu! kouēi tsāi! kouēi tsāi!

3. In k'i lêi tsái nân chān tchēu hiá (hóu). Hô sēu wêi sēu, mouŏ houĕ

unies par cinq tresses de soie blanche, joyeux et content, il quitte la cour et va prendre son repas.

CHANT VIII. IN K'I LEI.

La femme d'un officier soupire après le retour de son mari. « Le tonnerre, dit-elle, n'a pas ordinairement d'endroit fixe. A présent il en a un. Pourquoi mon mari n'en a-t-il pas ? »

1. Le tonnerre gronde sourdement, toujours au midi de la montagne australe. Pourquoi mon seigneur, toujours loin d'ici, n'ose-t-il jamais prendre un instant de loisir? Il est si bon! Oh! qu'il revienne! oh! qu'il revienne!

2. Le tonnerre gronde sourdement, toujours au midi, à côté de la montagne. Pourquoi mon seigneur, toujours loin d'ici, n'a-t-il jamais ni loisir ni repos? Il est si bon! Oh! qu'il revienne! qu'il revienne!

3. Le tonnerre gronde sourdement, toujours au midi, au pied de la montagne. Pourquoi mon seigneur, toujours loin d'ici, n'a-t-il

incertaine, dit Tchou Hi. D'après Mao Tch'ang, c'est la particule numérale des coutures.

CHANT VIII. 1. Lente mugiens illud tonitru manet ad australis montis meridiem. Quare ille procul abhinc, nunquam audet aliquantisper otio indulgere? Vere bonus est dominus meus! Oh! redeat! oh! redeat!

2. Lente mugiens illud tonitru manet ad australis montis latus. Quare ille procul abhinc, nunquam audet otiosus quiescere? Vere bonus est dominus meus! Oh! revertatur! oh! revertatur!

3. Lente mugiens illud tonitru manet ad australis montis radicem. Quare ille procul abhinc, nunquam

或遑處、振振君子、歸哉歸哉、

摽有梅

(1) 摽有梅、其實七兮、求我庶士、迨其吉兮、

(2) 摽有梅、其實三兮、求我庶士、迨其今兮。

(3) 摽有梅、頃筐塈之、求我庶士、迨其謂之、

houâng tch'ou? Tchēnn tchēnn kiūn tzèu! kouēi tsāi! kouēi tsāi!

PIAO IOU MEI. **1. Piaò iòu mêi, k'i chĕu ts'ī hi. K'iôu ngò chóu chéu, tái k'i kĭ hi!**

2. Piaò iòu mêi, k'i chĕu sān (chēnn) hi. K'iôu ngò chóu chéu, tái k'i kīn hi!

3. Piaò iòu mêi, k'īng k'ouāng hi tchēu. K'iôu ngò chóu chéu, tái k'i wéi tchēu!

jamais un instant de repos en aucun lieu? Il est si bon! Oh! qu'il revienne! qu'il revienne!

CHANT IX. PIAO IOU MEI.

Une jeune fille désire contracter mariage, de peur d'être exposée aux outrages des libertins.

1. Les fruits tombent du prunier; il n'en reste plus que sept (ou il n'en reste plus que les sept dixièmes). Puissent les bons jeunes gens qui me désirent, profiter de cet heureux jour!

2. Les fruits tombent du prunier; il n'en reste plus que trois (ou les trois dixièmes). Puissent les bons jeunes gens qui me recherchent, venir aujourd'hui!

3. Les derniers fruits sont tombés du prunier; on les a recueillis dans le panier plat à bords déprimés. Puissent les bons jeunes gens qui me recherchent, venir sans retard fixer le jour des noces!

paulisper otiosus manet? Vere bonus est dominus meus! Oh! revertatur! oh! revertatur!

CHANT IX. 1. Deciduut habita pruna; illi fructus septem manent (vel ex decem manent septem). Qui expetunt me omnes boni juvenes, occurrente hoc fausto die, (veniant)!

Les prunes *mei* mûrissent au printemps, à l'époque ordinaire des mariages. « Dans les principautés du midi, dit Tchou Hi, grâce à l'influence de Wenn wang, les jeunes personnes avaient appris à garder la chasteté et la fidélité à leurs engagements. »

2. Deciduut habita pruna; illi fructus tres manent (vel ex decem manent tres). Qui ambiunt me omnes frugi juvenes, occurrente hoc die, (veniant)!

3. Deciderunt habita pruna; in inclinato canistro collegerunt illa. Qui ambiunt me omnes boni juvenes, occurrente (hoc opportuno die), ipsi loquantur de illa re (et statuant nuptiarum diem cum parentibus meis)!

小星

(1) 嘒彼小星、三五在東、肅肅宵征、夙夜在公、寔命不同、

(2) 嘒彼小星、維參與昴、肅肅宵征、抱衾與裯、寔命不猶、

江有汜

(1) 江有汜、之子歸、不我以、不我以、其後也悔、

SIAO SING. 1. Houéi péi siaò sīng; sān òu tsái tōung. Siū siū siaō tchēng; sōu ié tsái kōung. Chéu ming pŏu t'ôung.

2. Houéi péi siaò sīng; wéi Chēnn iù Maò (Liôu). Siū siū siaō tchēng; paó k'īn iù tch'eôu. Chéu ming pŏu iôu.

KIANG IOU SEU. 1. Kiāng iòu séu (i). Tchēu tzèu kouēi, pŏu ngò i. Pŏu ngò i, k'ì heóu ié houéi (houèi).

CHANT X. SIAO SING.

Les compagnes d'une princesse, contentes d'un rang inférieur, se comparent à de petites étoiles auprès d'un grand astre. Elles prennent et quittent leur service le soir et le matin, au lever et au coucher des étoiles.

1. Ces petites étoiles paraissent à peine; on en voit de trois à cinq à l'orient. Nous marchons la nuit avec respect et précaution; le matin et le soir, nous sommes dans le palais. Notre sort est différent de celui de la princesse.

2. Ces petites étoiles paraissent à peine; on ne voit qu'Orion et les Pléiades. Nous marchons la nuit avec respect et précaution, portant nos couvertures dans nos bras. Notre condition n'est pas égale à celle de la princesse.

CHANT XI. KIANG IOU SEU.

Une jeune fille, allant épouser un prince, a refusé de s'associer l'une de ses parentes. Plus tard, elle la regrette et l'appelle auprès d'elle. La compagne loue ce repentir, et se compare à un bras du Kiang, qui retourne au courant principal, après en avoir été séparé, et avoir formé avec lui comme un ilot.

1. Le Kiang a des bras qui retournent au courant principal. Cette fille en se mariant ne m'a pas prise pour compagne. Elle ne m'a pas prise pour compagne; ensuite elle s'en est repentie.

CHANT X. 1. Vix apparent illæ parvæ stellæ; tres quinqueve sunt in oriente. Caute ac reverenter nocte incedimus; diluculo et vespere sumus in regia. Vere sors non est eadem.

Mao Tch'ang pense que 三五 désignent trois étoiles du Scorpion et cinq de l'Hydre.

2. Vix apparent illæ parvæ stellæ; non sunt nisi Orion et Pleiades. Caute ac reverenter nocte incedimus, brachiis complectentes stragulum ac simplicem lodicem. Vere sors non est æqualis.

CHANT XI. 1. Kiang habet ramos qui ad magnum flumen revertuntur. Illa puella nubens non me adhibuit

(2) 江有渚、之子歸、不我與、不我與、其後也處、

(3) 江有沱、之子歸、不我過、不我過、其嘯也歌、

野有死麕

(1) 野有死麕、白茅包之、有女懷春、吉士誘之、

(2) 林有樸樕、野有死鹿、白茅純束、有女如玉、

2. Kiāng iòu tchòu. Tchēu tzèu kouēi, pŏu ngò iù. Pŏu ngò iù, k'ì heóu iè tch'óu.

3. Kiāng iòu t'ouô. Tchēu tzèu kouēi, pŏu ngò kouō. Pŏu ngò kouō, k'ì siaó, iè kō.

IE IOU SEU KIUN. **1. Iè iòu sèu kiūn; pĕ maô paō (peòu) tchēu. Iòu gniù houâi tch'ouēnn; kĭ chéu iòu tchēu?**

2. Lîn iòu p'ŏu sŏu, iè iòu sèu lŏu; pĕ maô t'ouênn chŏu. Iòu gniù jŏu iŭ.

2. Le Kiang a des ilots. Cette fille en se mariant ne m'a pas choisie pour compagne. Elle ne m'a pas choisie pour compagne; ensuite (elle m'a appelée auprès d'elle, et) ses regrets ont cessé.

3. La T'ouo est un bras du Kiang. Cette fille en se mariant m'a laissée loin d'elle. Elle m'a laissée loin d'elle; ensuite (dans son repentir pour dissiper sa tristesse) elle a sifflé; (à présent) elle chante de joie.

CHANT XII. IE IOU SEU KIUN.

Une jeune personne réclame le respect dû à sa vertu.

1. Un homme trouve un daim mort dans la campagne; il l'enveloppe d'herbe blanche (avec précaution et l'emporte sans le toucher). Une jeune personne pense à se marier; un jeune homme honnête se permettra-t-il de la solliciter?

2. Un homme trouve des arbustes dans la forêt, un cerf mort dans la plaine; il les lie ou les enveloppe avec de l'herbe blanche. Une jeune personne est comme une pierre précieuse; (est-il permis de la traiter sans respect)?

(sociam). Non me adhibuit; illam postea et pœnituit.

2. Kiang habet parvas insulas. Illa puella nubens non me sibi sociavit. Non me sibi sociavit; illa postea et (me arcessivit atque) animo quievit.

3. Kiang habet T'ouo ramum. Illa puella nubens non juxta me transivit. Non juxta me transivit; illa (pœnitens) sibilavit et (gaudens) cantat.

CHANT XII. 1. Quum in campo est mortua dama, alba herba involvunt eam (ut eam decenter auferant, nec tangant). Quum est puella cupiens rem vernam, i. e. nuptias quæ vere contrahi solent, bonus juvenis sollicitabitne eam?

2. In silva sunt parvæ arbusculæ, in agris est mortuus cervus; alba herba involvunt aut colligant ea. Est puella similis gemmæ.

詩經

(3)舒而脫脫兮、無感我帨兮、無使尨也吠。

何彼襛矣

(1)何彼襛矣、唐棣之華、曷不肅雝、王姬之車、
(2)何彼襛矣、華如桃李、平王之孫、齊侯之子、
(3)其釣維何、維絲伊緡、齊侯之子、平王之孫、

3. Chŏu êul, touéi touéi hi; ôu kàn ngò chouéi; ôu chéu màng iè féi.

HO PEI NOUNG I. **1. Hô pèi nôung i! t'âng ti tchēu houâ (fôu). Hŏ pŏu siŭ iōung wâng Kī tchēu kiū?**

2. Hô pèi nôung i! houâ jôu t'aô li. P'îng wâng tchēu suēnn, Ts'î heóu tchēu tzéu (tsi).

3. K'i tiaó wêi hô? Wêi sēu ī min. Ts'î heóu tchēu tzéu, P'îng wâng tchēu suēnn.

3. Doucement, doucement, jeune homme; ne te permets pas même de toucher ma serviette ni de faire aboyer mon chien.

CHANT XIII. HO PEI NOUNG I.

Mariage d'une fille de l'empereur (Ou wang peut-être) avec ~~la fille~~ le fils d'un prince.

1. Que cette fleur est belle! c'est la fleur du cerisier sauvage. Les voitures de la princesse impériale n'annoncent-elles pas le respect et la soumission de la jeune épouse?

2. Que ces fleurs sont belles! on dirait la fleur du pêcher et celle du prunier. Ce sont la petite-fille du Roi pacificateur et le fils du prince de Ts'i (ou du Prince respectueux).

3. Qu'est-ce qu'une ligne de pêcheur? Des fils réunis et formant une corde. Ainsi s'unissent le fils du prince de Ts'i (ou du Prince respectueux) et la petite-fille du Roi pacificateur.

3. Lente, lente; ne moveas meum linteolum, ne facias ut canis latret.

帨 **Chouéi,** linge qu'on porte suspendu à la ceinture pour essuyer les objets.

CHANT XIII. 1. Quam hic (flos) pulcher est! silvestris cerasi flos. Num non exhibent reverentiam ac obsequium regiæ Ki cognomine puellæ currus?

姬 **Ki,** nom de famille des princes de Tcheou.

2. Quam hi (flores) pulchri sunt! flores similes persici prunique (floribus). *P'ing* regis neptis et *Ts'i* reguli filius.

Plusieurs commentateurs ont pensé que 平王 **P'ing wâng** désigne l'empereur P'ing wang, et 齊侯 **Ts'i heóu,** le prince 襄 **Siāng** de Ts'i (697-684). Les autres pensent que 平 **P'ing** est une épithète donnée à Wenn wang, et que 齊 **Ts'i** est une épithète donnée à un prince inconnu ou désigne la principauté de Ts'i.

3. Illa piscatoria linea quid est? nonnisi serica fila, nonnisi funiculus, i. e. fila in funiculum conjuncta et contorta. (Ita conjunguntur) Ts'i regni reguli (vel Reverentis reguli) filius et Pacificatoris regis neptis.

騶虞
(1) 彼茁者葭、
壹發五豝、于
嗟乎騶虞、
(2) 彼茁者蓬、
壹發五豵、于
嗟乎騶虞、

邶一之三
柏舟
(1) 汎彼柏舟、
亦汎其流、耿
耿不寐、如有
隱憂、微我無

TCHEOU IU. **1. Pėi tchouŏ tchė kiā; ĭ fă, ò u pā. Hiū tsiē hôu tcheōu iû (iâ)!**
2. Pėi tchouŏ tchė p'ôung; ĭ fă, òu tsōung. Hiū tsiē hôu tcheōu iû (wōung)!

PE TCHEOU. **1. Fán pėi pĕ tcheōu, ĭ fán k'i liôu. Kèng kèng pŏu méi, jôu iòu in iōu. Wêi ngŏ ôu tsiòu, i ngaò i iôu.**

CHANT XIV. TCHEOU IU.

Les princes *tchōu heōu,* par leur bonne administration, font tout prospérer, même les plantes et les animaux sauvages. Ils sont comme le *tcheōu iû,* animal très doux qui ne mange rien de vivant.

1. Les joncs sont vigoureux; le chasseur lance quatre flèches, et tue cinq sangliers mâles (l'une des quatre flèches en tue deux à la fois). Oh! notre prince est le *tcheou iu !*

2. Les chrysanthèmes sont vigoureux; le chasseur lance quatre flèches, et tue cinq jeunes sangliers. Oh! notre prince est le *tcheou iu !*

LIVRE III. PEI FOUNG.

CHANT I. PE TCHEOU.

Dans cette pièce, d'après Mao Tch'ang et d'autres anciens interprètes, un officier fidèle se plaint de n'avoir pas la confiance de son prince; d'après les modernes, une princesse se plaint de n'avoir pas les bonnes grâces de son époux.

1. Cette barque de bois de cyprès, ballottée avec violence, erre à la merci des flots. J'ai l'esprit troublé et ne puis dormir, comme si j'éprouvais une cruelle douleur. Le vin ne me manque pas pour me distraire et me récréer, (mais rien ne peut dissiper mon chagrin).

CHANT XIV. 1. Illic sunt vegeti junci; uno quatuor sagittarum jactu quinque masculi apri (occiduntur). Oh! (regulus noster est) *tcheōu iû!*

2. Illic sunt vegeta chrysanthema; uno quatuor sagittarum jactu quinque juvenes apri (occiduntur). Oh! (regulus noster est) *tcheōu iû!*

TITRE DU LIVRE. 邶一之三 Pei (regni cantica): primæ (partis) tertius (liber). La principauté de Pei était au nord de Wei houei fou dans le Ho nan actuel. Voy. page 3.

CHANT I. 1. Fluctuat illa cupressina cymba, et fluctuans illa decurrit. (Ita mente turbata) parum perspiciens, non dormio, quasi habens dolorem ac mærorem. Non quod caream vino, ut excurram, ut me oblectem.

酒、以敖以遊、(2)我心匪鑒、不可以茹、亦有兄弟、不可以據、薄言往愬、逢彼之怒、(3)我心匪石、不可轉也、我心匪席、不可卷也、威儀棣棣、不可選也、(4)憂心悄悄、慍于羣小、覯閔既多、受侮不少、靜言思之、寤辟有摽、(5)日居月諸、胡迭

2. Ngò sīn fèi kién, pǒu k'ò i jóu. Ī iòu hiōung ti, pǒu k'ò i kiú. Pouǒ iên wàng sóu, fôung pèi tchēu nóu.

3. Ngò sīn fèi chĕu, pǒu k'ò tchouèn iè. Ngò sīn fèi sĭ, pǒu k'ò kiuèn iè. Wēi i tái tái, pǒu k'ò siuèn iè.

4. Iōu sīn ts'iaò ts'iaò, iún iū k'iûn siaò. Keóu min ki touō, cheóu òu pǒu chaò. Tsing iên sēu tchēu, óu p'ĭ iòu piaò.

5. Jĕu kiū, iuĕ tchōu, hôu tiĕ èul wēi? Sīn tchēu iòu i, jôu fèi houàn ī. Tsing iên sēu tchēu, pǒu nêng fénn fēi.

2. Mon cœur n'est pas un miroir ; je n'y puis découvrir la cause de ma disgrâce. J'ai des frères, mais je ne puis compter sur eux. Quand je vais leur exposer un peu mon infortune, leur colère éclate contre moi.

3. Mon cœur n'est pas une pierre qui roule ; il n'est pas versatile. Mon cœur n'est pas une natte qui s'enroule ; il ne manque pas de droiture. Ma tenue et ma conduite sont admirables ; elles n'ont rien de répréhensible.

4. Le chagrin tourmente mon cœur ; une troupe de personnes viles me poursuit de sa haine. J'ai vu beaucoup d'afflictions et souffert bien des outrages. Je pense à mon malheur dans le silence ; quand je m'éveille, (accablée de douleur) je me frappe la poitrine.

5. Pourquoi est-ce le soleil et non la lune qui décroît ou s'éclipse?

2. Meus animus non est speculum ; non possum inde conjicere (cur principi non placeam). Etsi habeam fratres, non possum utens inniti (eis). Quum paululum adiens moneo (eos), offendo eorum iras.

3. Meus animus non est lapis, non potest versari ; meus animus non est matta, non potest volvi, i. e. nequit mihi objici aut inconstantis aut non recti animi crimen. Externa gravitas et agendi ratio constanter insignes, non possunt reprehendi.

4. Mœrens animus cruciatur ; odio sum gregi vilium (hominum seu ancillarum). Visæ molestiæ jam multæ ; acceptæ contumeliæ non paucæ. Tacite cogito de illis ; evigilans tundo pectus repetitis ictibus.

5. Sol et luna quomodo mutant vices et decrescunt? Animi mœror (adhæret) sicut non lota vestis. Tacite cogito de

而微、心之憂矣、
如匪澣衣、靜言
思之、不能奮飛、

綠衣

(1) 綠兮衣兮、綠
衣黃裏、心之憂
矣、曷維其已、
(2) 綠兮衣兮、綠
衣黃裳、心之憂
矣、曷維其亡、
(3) 綠兮絲兮、女
所治兮、我思古
人、俾無訧兮、

LIU I. 1. Liŭ hî ī hî, liŭ ī houâng li. Sīn tchēu iōu i, hŏ wêi k'ì i?

2. Liŭ hî ī hî, liŭ ī houâng châng. Sīn tchēu iōu i, hŏ wêi k'ì wâng?

3. Liŭ hî sēu hî, jòu chòu tch'êu hî. Ngò sēu kòu jênn, pi ôu iôu (1) hî.

(Pourquoi dois-je céder la place à ces personnes viles)? Le chagrin étreint mon cœur comme un vêtement souillé s'attache au corps. Je réfléchis en silence; je ne puis prendre mon essor et m'envoler d'ici.

CHANT II. LIU I.

莊姜 **Tchouāng Kiāng**, c.-à-d. la fille du prince de 齊 **Ts'i**, dont le nom de famille est 姜 **Kiāng**, mariée à 莊 **Tchouāng**, prince de 衛 **Wéi**, se plaint de son délaissement. La couleur verte est préférée à la couleur jaune, la servante à la maîtresse. (Le jaune est l'une des cinq couleurs simples des Chinois; le vert est considéré comme une couleur intermédiaire, et par suite moins estimé que les couleurs principales).

1. Le vêtement qui couvre la poitrine est vert; l'étoffe est verte et la doublure jaune. Comment l'affliction de mon cœur pourrait-elle cesser?

2. Le vêtement qui couvre la poitrine est vert, et celui qui couvre les jambes est jaune. Comment pourrais-je oublier mon chagrin?

3. Le fil de soie est teint en vert; prince, c'est votre œuvre (c'est vous qui avez substitué la servante à l'épouse légitime). Je me rappelle les maximes et les exemples des sages, pour me préserver de toute faute.

illis, nec possum expansis alis avolare.

居 **Kiū**, 諸 **tchōu**, particules explétives.

CHANT II. 1. Viridis est vestis qua tegitur superior pars corporis; viridi vesti flavus est subsutus pannus. Animi dolor quomodo ipse cessabit?

2. Viridis est vestis qua corporis pars superior tegitur; viridis est vestis superior, et flava vestis qua tegitur corpus a renibus ad talos. Animi dolor quomodo ipse memoria excidet?

3. Viridi colore tinctum est sericum filum, tu quod elaborasti. (Ancillam, quæ conditione erat humili, tu, princeps, ad uxoris tuæ dignitatem evexisti). Ego memini sapientium hominum, ut abstineam culpa.

(4) 絺兮綌兮、淒其以風、我思古人、實獲我心、

燕燕

(1) 燕燕于飛、差池其羽、之子于歸、遠送于野、瞻望弗及、泣涕如雨、

(2) 燕燕于飛、頡之頏之、之子于歸、遠于

4. Tch'ēu hī k'ī hī, ts'ī k'ī i fōung (fēnn). Ngò sēu kòu jênn, chĕu houĕ ngò sīn.

IEN IEN. 1. Ién ién iû fēi, tch'ēu tch'ēu k'ì iù. Tchēu tzèu iû kouēi, iuén sóung iū iè (chòu). Tchēn wàng fŏu kĭ, k'ĭ t'ì jóu iù.

2. Ién ién iû fēi, hiĕ tchēu, hâng tchēu. Tchēu tzèu iû kouēi; iuén iû tsiāng tchēu. Tchēn wàng fŏu kĭ, tchóu lĭ i k'ĭ.

4. Quand le vent souffle, les vêtements de toile ne sont pas assez chauds (et sont abandonnés. Chaque chose a son temps; le temps de la faveur est passé pour moi). Je me rappelle les préceptes et la conduite des sages; j'obtiens réellement l'objet de mes désirs (à savoir, la pratique parfaite de la vertu).

CHANT III. IEN IEN.

莊 姜 Kiang, femme de Tchouang, prince de 衛 Wéi, n'ayant pas d'enfant mâle, ce prince eut pour successeur 完 Houân ou 桓 公 Houân kōung, fils d'une femme de second rang, nommée 戴 嬀 Tái Kouēi ou 仲 氏 Tchóung chéu. Le prince Houan fut tué par 州 吁 Tcheōu hiū, l'un de ses frères, né d'une autre mère, et connu sous le nom de 宣 公 Siuēn kōung. Tai Kouei retourna dans la principauté de 陳 Tch'ênn, sa patrie. Tchouang Kiang raconte qu'elle la suivit une partie du chemin, et déplore leur séparation. Elle se compare, elle et sa compagne, à deux hirondelles.

1. Deux hirondelles volent ensemble; leurs ailes inclinent, l'une d'un côté l'autre de l'autre. Cette fille est retournée chez ses parents; je l'ai suivie loin dans la campagne. Quand mes yeux ont cessé de l'apercevoir, j'ai versé un torrent de larmes.

2. Deux hirondelles volent ensemble; tantôt elles montent tantôt elles descendent. Cette fille est retournée chez ses parents; je l'ai

4. Tela tum subtilis tum crassa fit frigida, quum ipsa obit ventum. (Vestes e tela confectæ, adveniente hiemali vento, calorem non præbent et relinquuntur; ita præteritum est tempus quo gratiosa eram, et abjicior). Ego memini sapientium hominum; vere assequor meum votum (nempe perfectam virtutem).

CHANT. III. 1. Hirundo et hirundo dum volant, non pariter moventur earum alæ. Hæc filia reversa est domum paternam; longe subsecuta sum in campo. Quum oculos attollens prospicere non potui, flens effudi lacrymas instar imbris.

2. Geminæ hirundines dum volant, (ambæ simul) modo ascendunt, modo

將之、瞻望弗及、佇立以泣。(3) 燕燕于飛、上下其音、之子于歸、遠送于南、瞻望弗及、實勞我心。(4) 仲氏任只、其心塞淵、終溫且惠、淑慎其身、先君之思、以勗寡人。

日月

(1) 日居月諸、照

3. Ién ién iû fēi, hiá chàng k'ì în. Tchēu tzèu iû kouēi; iuèn sóung iû nân (gnîn). Tchēn wáng fŏu kĭ; chēu laò ngò sīn.

4. Tchóung chéu jênn tchèu; k'î sīn sē iuēn (iūn). Tchōung wēnn ts'iè houéi; chŏu chénn k'i chēnn. Siēn kiūn tchēu sēu, i hiŭ kouà jênn.

JEU IUE. **1. Jĕu kiū, iuĕ tchōu, tchaó lìn hiá t'òu. Nài jôu tchēu jênn hî, chéu**

suivie fort loin. Quand mes yeux ont cessé de l'apercevoir, je me suis arrêtée longtemps pour pleurer.

3. Deux hirondelles volent ensemble; elles montent et descendent en gazouillant. Cette fille est retournée chez ses parents; je l'ai accompagnée loin vers le midi (sur la route de Tch'enn). Quand mes yeux ont cessé de l'apercevoir, mon cœur a été accablé de douleur.

4. Tchoung était une amie sincère, pénétrée d'un profond sentiment d'affection. Toujours aimable et docile, elle était vertueuse et veillait sur elle-même. Elle n'oubliait pas le prince défunt, et m'excitait à penser à lui.

CHANT IV. JEU IUE.

莊姜 **Tchouāng Kiāng** déplore la mauvaise conduite de Tchouang, prince de Wei, son époux. Elle prend à témoin le soleil et la lune, qui éclairent et voient toutes choses.

1. O soleil, ô lune, qui répandez ici-bas votre lumière et vos

descendunt. Haec filia rediit paternam domum; longe comitata sum eam. Quum oculos attollens prospicere non potui, diu morans steti ut flerem.

3. Geminae hirundines volant; descendunt ascenduntque earum voces, i. e. descendentes et ascendentes ambae fritinniunt. Haec puella repetiit domum; longe comitata sum versus meridiem. Quum oculos attollens prospicere non potui, vere afflictus est meus animus.

4. Tchoung cheu erat sincere amica; ejus amor erat profundus. Semper comis et obsequens, bona et invigilans sibimetipsi. Mortui reguli (Tchouang) memor, inde excitabat me exiguae virtutis mulierem, (ut illius reguli recordarer).

CHANT IV. 1. O sol, o luna, illustrantes propius aspicitis subjectam terram. En hujusmodi homo non antiquorum viae insistit. Quomodo (aut

臨下土。乃如之人兮、逝不古處、胡能有定、寧不我顧、

(2) 日居月諸、下土是冒、乃如之人兮、逝不相好、胡能有定、寧不我報、

(3) 日居月諸、出自東方、乃如之人兮、德音無良、胡能有定、俾也可忘、

(4) 日居月諸、東方自出、父兮母兮、畜

pŏu kòu tch'òu. Hôu nêng iòu tìng? Gnìng pŏu ngò kóu (kòu)?

2. Jĕu kiū, iuĕ tchōu, hiá t'òu chéu maó. Nài jôu tchēu jênn hì, chéu pŏu siāng haò. Hôu nêng iòu tìng? Gnìng pŏu ngò paó?

3. Jĕu kiū, iuĕ tchōu, tch'ŏu tzéu tōung fāng. Nài jôu tchēu jênn hì, tĕ īn ôu leâng. Hôu nêng iòu tìng? Pèi iè k'ò wâng?

4. Jĕu kiū, iuĕ tchōu, tōung fāng tzéu tch'ŏu. Fóu hì mòu hì, hiū ngò pŏu tsŏu. Hôu nêng iòu tìng? Paó ngò pŏu chŏu.

bienfaits, voyez comme cet homme diffère des anciens sages. Quand aura-t-il la ferme détermination de régler sa conduite? Pourquoi ne fait-il aucune attention à moi?

2. O soleil, ô lune, qui inondez la terre d'un océan de lumière, voyez comme cet homme me traite peu amicalement. Quand aura-t-il la ferme détermination de régler sa conduite? Pourquoi ne répond-il pas à mon affection?

3. O soleil, ô lune, qui venez de l'orient, voyez cet homme qui parle bien et agit mal. Quand prendra-t-il une sage détermination? Il me traite comme si je méritais l'oubli.

4. O soleil, ô lune, qui venez de l'orient! (Pourquoi) mes parents ne m'ont-ils pas continué leurs soins à la maison jusqu'à la mort?

(quando) poterit habere statutam (bene agendi voluntatem)? Cur non me respicit?

居 **Kiū**, 諸 **tchōu**, 逝 **chéu**, particules explétives. 臨 **Lîn** se dit d'un supérieur visitant ses inférieurs ou leur donnant ses soins.

2. O sol, o luna, subjectam terram vere tegitis (lumine). En hujusmodi homo non una (mecum) amice agit. Quomodo (aut quando) poterit habere statutam (bene agendi voluntatem)? Cur non mihi vices reddit?

冒 a le même sens que 照 臨

3. O sol, o luna, orimini ex orientali regione. En hujusmodi homo, bona (profert) verba, nec bonus est. Quomodo (aut quando) poterit habere statutam voluntatem? Ducit me dignam oblivione.

4. O sol, o luna, orientali regione exorimini. Pater et mater aluerunt me non ad finem (i. e. bonum fuisset si parentes perpetuo domi innuptam me aluissent). Quomodo (aut quando) poterit habere statutam (bene agendi

我不卒、胡能有定、報我不述、

終風

(1) 終風且暴、顧我則笑、謔浪笑敖、中心是悼、

(2) 終風且霾、惠然肯來、莫往莫來、悠悠我思、

(3) 終風且曀、不日有曀、寤言不寐、願言則嚏、

TCHOUNG FOUNG. 1. **Tchōung fōung, ts'iè paó. Kóu ngò, tsĕ siaó (saó). Hiŏ, láng, siaó ngaó. Tchōung sīn chéu taó.**

2. Tchōung fōung, ts'iè mâi. Houéi jèn k'éng lâi. Mouŏ wàng, mouŏ lâi. Iôu iôu ngò sēu (sāi).

3. Tchōung fōung, ts'iè i. Pŏu jĕu iòu i. Oú ién pŏu méi. Iuén ièn, tsĕ tí.

Quand cet homme prendra-t-il une sage détermination? Il répond à mon affection par des traitements injustes.

CHANT V. TCHOUNG FOUNG.

莊姜 **Tchouāng Kiāng** compare le prince Tchouang, son mari, ou, d'après Mao Tch'ang, le prince 州吁 **Tcheōu hiū**, à un ciel tempêtueux, qui semble parfois se rasséréner, mais redevient bientôt couvert d'épais nuages.

1. Le vent souffle tout le jour, et avec violence. Le prince me regarde; il se met à rire, m'accable de plaisanteries et sourit avec dédain. Je sens comme une blessure au fond de mon cœur.

2. Le vent souffle tout le jour, il tombe comme une pluie de poussière. Le prince parait consentir à venir me voir amicalement; mais il ne s'approche ni ne s'éloigne. Longtemps, longtemps je pense à lui.

3. Tout le jour le vent a soufflé, accompagné de nuages. Moins d'un jour après, le vent et les nuages reparaissent. Je veille sans pouvoir dormir. A force de penser au prince, je suis enrhumée du cerveau.

voluntatem)? Retribuit mihi non congruenter (æquitati).

CHANT V. 1. Toto die flat ventus, et quidem vehemens. Respicit me, statim ridet, jocatur sine modo, ridet arroganter. Medio animo inde saucior.

2. Toto die ventus, imo et descendens pulveris turbo. (Regulus) benigne videtur annuere (ad me) venire; (sed) nec vadit nec venit. Longo tempore ego cogito (de eo). 霾 Poussière soulevée par le vent et remplissant l'air.

3. Toto die ventus, imo ventus cum nubibus. Non elapso integro die, iterum est ventus cum nubibus. Vigilo, nec dormio. Cogitans (de regulo), tunc sternuto

Le chagrin et le manque de sommeil causent le rhume de cerveau, disent les commentateurs.

(4) 曀曀其陰、虺虺其靁、寤言不寐、願言則懷、

擊鼓

(1) 擊鼓其鏜、踊躍用兵、土國城漕、我獨南行、

(2) 從孫子仲、平陳與宋、不我以歸、憂心有忡、

(3) 爰居爰處、爰喪其馬、于以求之、于林之下、

4. Ì i k'ì īn; houēi houēi k'ì lêi. Oú iên pŏu méi; iuén iên, tsĕ houâi (houèi).

KI KOU. 1. Kí kòu k'ì t'āng; iòung iŏ ióung pīng (pāng). T'òu kouŏ, tch'êng Ts'aô. Ngò tŏu nân hing (hâng).

2. Ts'ôung Suēnn Tzèu tchóung, p'ing Tch'ênn iù Sóung. Pŏu ngò i kouēi; iōu sīn iòu tch'ōung (tch'óung).

3. Iuên kiū, iuên tch'òu; iuên sáng k'ì mà (mòu). Iû i k'iôu tchēu, iū lîn tchēu hiá (hòu).

4. Le vent et les nuages obscurcissent le ciel. Le tonnerre fait entendre un murmure menaçant. Je veille sans pouvoir dormir. Je pense au prince; son souvenir ne me quitte pas.

CHANT VI. KI KOU

州吁 **Tcheōu hiū**, fils de 莊公 **Tchouāng kōung**, prince de 衛 **Wéi**, après avoir tué son frère 桓公 **Houân kōung**, et usurpé le pouvoir, se ligue avec les princes de 陳 **Tch'ênn** et de 宋 **Sóung**, et envoie 孫子仲 **Suēnn Tzèu tchóung**, chef de son armée, attaquer le prince de 鄭 **Tchéng**. Un soldat se plaint d'être obligé de quitter sa famille, peut-être pour ne plus la revoir.

1. Le tambour bat; nous bondissons et nous employons nos armes. D'autres font des travaux de terrassement dans notre pays, fortifient la ville de Ts'ao. Nous seuls allons au midi (attaquer Tcheng).

2. Nous suivons Suenn Tzeu tchoung, en paix avec Tch'enn et Soung. Nous ne reverrons pas nos familles; mon cœur est dans l'angoisse.

3. Nous demeurons, nous nous arrêtons; nous perdons nos chevaux. Nous les cherchons au bas de la forêt.

4. Vento ac nubibus constat illa caligo. Murmure minatur illud tonitru. Vigilo, nec dormio. Cogitans, animo servo (reguli memoriam).

CHANT VI. 1. Percussum tympanum ipsum sonat; exsilientes utimur armis. (Alii aut fodiunt aut aggerant) terram in regno, mœniis instruunt Ts'ao urbem. Nos soli ad meridiem pergimus.

漕 **Ts'aô** était dans le 滑縣 **Houă hién** actuel, province de Ho nan.

2. Sequimur Suenn Tzeu tchoung, pace composita cum Tch'enn et Soung. Non nobis dabitur domum reverti; mœreus animus afficitur angore.

3. Tunc manemus, tunc sistimus; tunc amittimus nostros equos. Quærimus eos ad silvæ radicem.

(4) 死生契闊、與子成說、執子之手、與子偕老、

(5) 于嗟闊兮、不我活兮、于嗟洵兮、不我信兮、

凱風

(1) 凱風自南、吹彼棘心、棘心夭夭、母氏劬勞、

(2) 凱風自南、吹彼棘薪、母氏聖

4. Sèu chēng k'iĕ k'ouŏ, iù tzèu tch'êng chouŏ. Tchĕu tzèu tchēu cheòu; iù tzèu kiāi laò (leòu).

5. Hiū tsiē! k'ouŏ hī! pŏu ngò houŏ hī. Hiū tsiē! siūn hi! pŏu ngò chēnn hī.

K'AI FOUNG. **1. K'ài fōung tzèu nân (gnîn), tch'ouēi péi kĭ sīn. Kĭ sīn iaō iaō. Mòu chéu k'iû laô (leaô).**

2. K'ài fōung tzèu nân (gnîn), tch'ouēi péi kĭ sīn. Mòu chéu chéng chén; ngò òu ling jênn.

4. Nous avons promis fidélité à nos épouses pour la vie, pour la mort, pour le temps d'une grande et longue séparation. Nous leur avons pris la main, et juré de vieillir avec elles.

5. Hélas! pour le temps d'une longue séparation! La vie nous est enlevée. Hélas! nos engagements! Il nous est impossible de les remplir.

CHANT VII. K'AI FOUNG.

Une veuve de 衛 **Wéi** avait sept fils, et néanmoins vivait dans le désordre. Les sept frères, au lieu de se plaindre de leur mère, s'accusent eux-mêmes de ne lui donner ni secours ni consolation, et d'être ainsi la cause de ses dérèglements.

1. Le vent du midi caresse de son souffle bienfaisant les nouveaux surgeons au milieu de ces petits jujubiers sauvages; les surgeons sont tendres et beaux. Ainsi notre illustre mère s'est imposé pour nous de grandes fatigues.

2. Le vent du midi a caressé de son souffle bienfaisant (et fait croître) ces jujubiers sauvages qui serviront pour le feu.

于以 **Iû i**, locution explétive. On voit, dit Tchou Hi, que les soldats étaient débandés et ne pensaient plus à combattre.

4. In mortem, vitam et longum discidium, cum uxoribus fecimus pactum, i. e. juravimus nunquam nos invicem oblituros nec abjecturos.* Prehendimus uxorum dexteras, cum uxoribus una senectam traducturi.

5. Eheu! in longum discidium (juravimus)! Non datur nobis vivere. Eheu! fides! Non datur nobis fidem servare.

CHANT VII. 1. Genialis aura ex meridie afflat illarum minorum zizyphorum silvestrium medium, i. e. medios surculos; zizyphorum medii surculi sunt teneri et pulchri. (Ita) mater domina operose laboravit (ut nos aleret).

2. Genialis ventus ex meridie afflavit illas zizyphos ad ignem idoneas. (Ita)

善、我無令人、
(3) 爰有寒泉、在
浚之下、有子七
人、母氏勞苦、
(4) 睍睆黃鳥、載
好其音、有子七
人、莫慰母心、

雄雉

(1) 雄雉于飛、泄
泄其羽、我之懷
矣、自詒伊阻、
(2) 雄雉于飛、上
下其音、展矣君

3. Iuên iòu hân ts'iuên, tsái Siún tchēu hiá (hòu). Iòu tzèu ts'ĭ jênn; mòu chéu laô k'òu.

4. Hién houàn houâng gniaò, tsái haò k'ì īn. Iòu tzèu ts'ĭ jênn, mouŏ wéi mòu sīn.

HIOUNG TCHEU. **1. Hiôung tchéu iû fēi, i i k'ì iù. Ngò tchēu houâi i; tzèu ì ĭ tchòu.**

2. Hiôung tchéu iû fēi, hiá chàng k'ì īn. Tchèn i kiūn tzèu, chĕu laô ngò sīn.

Notre illustre mère est sage et bonne; mais parmi nous ses enfants, il n'est pas un homme de bien.

3. Une source d'eau fraiche sort auprès de la ville de Siun (et sert aux habitants). Notre illustre mère a sept fils; elle endure de grandes fatigues (parce qu'aucun d'eux ne l'aide).

4. Le loriot, dont la voix est claire et flexible, a soin de rendre son chant agréable. Notre mère a sept fils; aucun d'eux ne la console.

CHANT VIII. HIOUNG TCHEU.

La femme d'un officier loue le calme, le dévouement de son mari, et soupire après son retour. Elle souhaite qu'il s'abstienne de tout mal, afin que le ciel le protège et le ramène sain et sauf.

1. Le faisan dans son vol fend l'air avec lenteur. (De même) celui que je regrette (est calme au milieu des périls; mais il) me laisse dans l'inquiétude.

2. Le faisan dans son vol chante sans cesse, soit qu'il monte soit qu'il descende. Mon noble époux, (lui-même toujours

mater domina sapientissima, optima est; nostrûm nullus est frugi homo.

3. Est frigidus fons ad Siun urbis radicem (et incolis usui est); sunt filii septem homines, (nesciunt matri opem præbere, et) mater domina operose laborat.

La ville de 浚 **Siún** dépendait de la principauté de 衛 **Wéi**.

4. Clara et flexibili voce flava avis amœnum facit suum cantum (ut aures hominum demulceat). Sunt filii septem homines: nullus solatur matris animum.

CHANT VIII. 1. Mas phasianus dum volat, lente moventur ejus alæ. Ego quem desidero, ipse reliquit hoc obstaculum, i. e. hunc de discidio mœrorem.

2. Mas phasianus quum volat, descendit et ascendit ejus cantus (tum ascendens tum descendens cantat. Ita

子、實勞我心、
(3) 瞻彼日月、悠悠我思、道之云遠、曷云能來、
(4) 百爾君子、不知德行、不忮不求、何用不臧、

匏有苦葉

(1) 匏有苦葉、濟有深涉、深則厲、淺則揭、

3. Tchēn pèi jĕu iuĕ ; iôu iôu ngò sēu (sī). Taó tchēu iùn iuèn ; hŏ iûn nêng lâi (lî)?

4. Pĕ èul kiūn tzèu, pŏu tchēu tĕ hing (hâng). Pŏu tchéu, pŏu k'iôu ; hô ióung pŏu tsāng?

P'AO IOU K'OU IE. **1. P'aô iòu k'òu iĕ ; tsi iòu chênn chĕ. Chēnn, tsĕ li ; ts'ièn, tsĕ k'i.**

content), laisse mon cœur dans une cruelle affliction.

3. Je considère le soleil et la lune (et calcule le temps que ces astres ont mesuré). Il y a longtemps que je soupire après mon époux. Mais la distance est grande ; quand pourra-t-il être de retour?

4. Nobles guerriers, ne connaissez-vous pas tous la voie de la vertu? Celui qui ne nuit à personne et n'est pas cupide, en quoi ne sera-t-il pas irréprochable?

CHANT IX. P'AO IOU K'OU IE.

Dans la principauté de 衞 Wéi, les alliances matrimoniales sont conclues à la hâte et souvent mal assorties ; les anciens usages sont violés.

1. La courge conserve encore ses feuilles amères (elle n'est pas mûre et ne peut ni être mangée ni servir pour la natation). Le gué est profond. Quand il est profond, pour le passer on relève les vêtements jusqu'au-dessus de la ceinture. Quand il ne l'est pas, il suffit de relever les vêtements jusqu'aux genoux. (Ainsi les cérémonies du mariage doivent être accomplies diversement selon les différentes circonstances).

conjux meus quieto animo est). Vere eximius vir multum cruciat meum animum.

3. Suspicio illum solem et lunam (supputo quantum cursum perfecerint); diu, diu desideravi (conjugem). Via longa est; quando poterit venire?

4. Omnes vos principes viri, nonne cognoscitis bonas actiones? Qui neminem lædit et nihil concupiscit, quid tentabit quod non sit bonum?

冀其善處而得全(朱熹)
Elle espère que par la pratique constante de la vertu ils obtiendront d'être toujours sains et saufs.

CHANT IX. 1. Cucurbita habet amara folia; in loco ubi trajici solet aqua, est altum vadum. Quum altum est, tunc vestibus supra zonam adductis, trajiciendum est; quum non est altum, tunc vestibus ad genua adductis, trajiciendum est.

(2)有瀰濟盈。有
鷕雉鳴。濟盈不
濡軌。雉鳴求其
牡。
(3)雝雝鳴鴈。旭
日始旦。士如歸
妻。迨冰未泮。
(4)招招舟子。人
涉卬否。人涉卬
否。卬須我友。
谷風
(1)習習谷風。以
陰以雨。黽勉同

2. Iòu mi tsi îng; iòu iaò tchéu mîng. Tsi îng, pŏu jŏu kouèi (kiòu). Tchéu mîng, k'iŏu k'î meòu.

3. Iōung iōung mîng ién; hiŭ jĕu chéu tán. Chéu jŏu kouēi ts'ī, tái pīng wéi p'án.

4. Tchaō tchaō tcheōu tzèu (tsi); jênn chĕ, ngâng feòu (pèi). Jênn chĕ, ngâng feòu (pèi); ngāng siū ngò iòu (wèi).

KOU FOUNG. **1. Sī sī kŏu fōung, i īn i iù. Min mièn t'ôung sīn, pŏu î iòu nòu.**

2. L'eau remplit le gué, elle va déborder; la faisane fait entendre son cri. L'eau déborde, et l'on prétend la traverser sans même que les traces des roues de la voiture soient mouillées! La faisane crie, et pour compagnon on lui cherche un quadrupède!

3. (Anciennement) une oie sauvage à la voix harmonieuse était offerte (à la fiancée) dès le lever du soleil, dès le point du jour. Le fiancé qui devait aller chercher sa fiancée (après la fonte des glaces), offrait l'oie sauvage longtemps auparavant.

4. Le batelier appelle à lui; les autres passent dans sa barque, moi je ne passerai pas. Que les autres passent, moi je ne passerai pas; j'attendrai un compagnon qui me convienne (un mari digne de moi).

CHANT X. KOU FOUNG.

Une femme se plaint d'avoir été chassée par son mari et remplacée par une concubine.

1. Lorsqu'un vent modéré souffle de l'orient, les nuages se forment, la pluie arrose la terre. Ainsi les époux doivent s'efforcer de

2. Aqua plenus transeundi locus turget; edens voces phasiana clamat. Transeundi loco turgente, non madefactum iri vehiculi orbitas (dicunt)! Clamat phasiana; quærunt ei quadrupedem marem!

3. (Antiquitus sponsæ a sponsi parentibus offerebatur) consona voce clangens anser silvestris, oriente sole, primo mane. Sponsus cupiens deducere sponsam (postquam soluta esset glacies, mature anserem offerebat) quando gelu nondum erat solutum.

4. Clamans advocat cymbæ ductor; alii trajiciunt, ego non. Alii trajiciant, ego non; ego exspectabo meum consortem, i. e. virum mihi parem.

CHANT X. 1. Lenis flat ab oriente ventus; inde nubes, inde pluvia. (Ita conjugibus) conandum, enitendum ut sint

心、不宜有怒、采
葑采菲、無以下
體、德音莫違、及
爾同死、
(2) 行道遲遲、中
心有違、不遠伊
邇、薄送我畿、誰
謂荼苦、其甘如
薺、宴爾新昏、如
兄如弟、
(3) 涇以渭濁、湜
湜其沚、宴爾新
昏、不我屑以、毋

Ts'ài fōung, ts'ài fèi, ôu i hiá t'i. Tĕ īn mouŏ wéi, kĭ èul t'ôung sèu (si).

2. Hîng taò tch'êu tch'êu ; tchōung sīn iòu wéi. Pŏu iuén, ī èul, pouŏ sóung ngò k'ī. Chouêi wéi t'ôu k'òu? K'i kān jôu ts'ì. Ién èul sīn houēnn, jôu hiōung jôu ti.

3. Kīng i Wéi tchouŏ; chĕu chĕu k'i tchèu. Ién èul sīn houēnn; pŏu ngò siĕ i.

vivre unis de cœur, et ne se permettre aucun sentiment d'indignation l'un envers l'autre. On ne rejette pas un navet ou un radix, parce que l'extrémité est un peu gâtée. (Tu n'aurais pas dû me rejeter, parce que je n'ai plus toute la beauté de ma jeunesse). Je n'avais rien fait de contraire à l'honneur; tu devais me laisser vivre avec toi jusqu'à la mort.

2. Je voyage lentement; il me répugne de m'en aller. A mon départ, tu ne m'as pas accompagnée loin; tu t'es arrêté au seuil de la porte. Qui dira que la chicorée est amère? (Comparée à mon affliction) elle est douce comme la bourse-à-pasteur. Cependant tu te livres à la joie avec ta nouvelle femme, comme un frère avec son frère ou sa sœur.

3. L'eau trouble de la King paraît encore plus trouble quand on la voit au confluent auprès de l'eau limpide de la Wei; cependant elle est claire auprès des ilots (où le courant est moins rapide. Ainsi mon visage auprès de celui d'une femme plus jeune a paru laid à tes yeux, et tu as oublié mes qualités). Tu te livres à la joie

uno animo; non decet concipere iram. Colligitur napus, colligitur raphanus; non attenditur imæ radici. (Napus raphanusve non rejicitur eo quod ima radix corrupta sit. Sic ego non eram ejicienda quod vultus mei species defloruit). Bonæ famæ nihil contrarium egi; cum te simul (me vivere oportebat et) mori.

2. Ago iter lente, lente; in animo est repugnantia (mihi grave est abire). Non longe, sed prope, paululum comitatus es me ad limen. Quis dicet cichoreum esse amarum? (Cum mœrore meo comparatum) illud dulce est sicut capsella bursa-pastoris. Te oblectas cum tua nova uxore, quasi frater major et frater minor.

3. King aqua præ Wei aqua (confluente magis videtur) turbida; limpida est ipsa ad parvas insulas. (Sic ego cum tua juniore uxore comparata, tibi visa sum vultu fœdo; attamen animi dotibus non careo). Te oblectas cum tua nova uxore, nec me dignaris

逝我梁、毋發我
笱、我躬不閱、遑
恤我後。
(4) 就其深矣、方
之舟之、就其淺
矣、泳之游之、何
有何亡、黽勉求
之、凡民有喪、匍
匐救之。
(5) 不我能慉、反
以我爲讎、既阻
我德、賈用不售、
昔育恐育鞫、及

Où chéu ngò leàng, òu fă ngò keòu. Ngò kōung pŭ iuĕ; houâng siŭ ngò heòu?

4. Tsiòu k'î chēnn i, fāng tchēu tcheōu tchēu. Tsiòu k'î ts'ièn i, iòung tchēu iôu tchēu. Hô iòu, hô wàng, min mièn k'iôu tchēu. Fân min iòu sāng, p'ôu p'ŏu kiòu (kiōu) tchēu.

5. Pŏu ngò nêng hiŭ; fàn i ngò wêi tch'eôu. Ki tchòu ngò tĕ, kòu iòung pŏu

avec ta nouvelle femme, et ne daignes plus m'avoir pour compagne. Que cette femme ne se permette pas d'aller à mon barrage ni de soulever ma nasse, c.-à-d., d'occuper mes appartements ni de soigner les affaires de la maison. Mais tu n'as pu souffrir ma personne; auras-tu compassion de moi après mon départ?

4. Quand l'eau était profonde, je la passais en radeau ou en barque; quand elle ne l'était pas, je la traversais à gué ou à la nage. (Je soignais les affaires de ta maison avec discernement, d'après les circonstances). Sans considérer ce que nous avions ni ce que nous n'avions pas, je travaillais de tout mon pouvoir à trouver les choses nécessaires. Chaque fois qu'un voisin avait des obsèques à célébrer, je faisais tout des pieds et des mains pour lui venir en aide.

5. Tu ne veux plus vivre avec moi; bien plus, tu me traites en ennemie. Tu as rejeté mes bons offices; me voilà comme un marchand qui ne trouve pas d'acheteurs. Quand je vivais avec toi, je craignais d'abord de manquer de vivres et de périr ainsi que toi.

adhibere (sociam. Mulier illa) ne adeat meum septum lapideum, ne auferat meam nassam, i. e. ne habitet meum conclave, nec curet meas res. Me ipsam non tolerasti; vacabitne (tibi) misereri mei in futurum?

梁 **Leàng,** barrage de pierre établi dans l'eau, avec quelques ouvertures où l'on place des nasses 笱 **keòu** pour recevoir et prendre les poissons.

4. Quando offendebam illius altum locum, i. e. aquam altam, rate trajiciebam illum, cymba trajiciebam illum. Quando offendebam illius locum non altum, vado transibam illum, tranabam illum. (Non considerans) quid haberemus, quid non haberemus, enixe conabar acquirere illud, i. e. opes. Quicumque incola habebat funus, manibus pedibusque reptans, i. e. enitens omni modo, auxilium præbebam ei.

5. Non me potes, i. e. non me vis, alere; contra habes me pro inimica. Postquam rejecisti mea officia, sum

6

爾顛覆、既生既育、比予于毒。⑥我有旨蓄、亦以御冬、宴爾新昏、以我御窮、有洸有潰、既詒我肄、不念昔者、伊余來塈。

式微

①式微式微、胡不歸。微君之故、胡爲乎中露、

cheóu (cheŏu). Sĭ iû k'òung iû kiŭ, kĭ èul tiēn fŏu. Kí chēng, ki iŭ, pi iû iū tŏu.

6. Ngò iòu tchèu tch'ŏu, ĭ i iù tōung. Ién èul sīn houēnn, i ngò iù k'iôung. Iòu kouāng iòu houéi; ki î ngò i. Pŏu gnién sĭ tchè, ī iû lâi ki.

CHEU WEI. 1. Chĕu wêi! chĕu wêi! Hôu pŏu kouēi? Wêi kiūn tchēu kóu, hôu wêi hòu tchōung lóu?

Quand nous fumes dans l'aisance, et que les vivres abondèrent, tu me considéras comme un poison.

6. J'ai fait provision d'excellents légumes pour passer l'hiver avec toi. (C'est-à-dire, quand tu étais pauvre, mon travail t'a nourri. A présent que tu n'en as plus besoin), tu fêtes avec ta nouvelle femme; tu ne t'es servi de moi que pour écarter l'indigence. Violent et colère, tu m'as fort maltraitée. Tu as oublié les premiers temps de notre union, quand, nouvelle venue, je jouissais du repos que tu m'as accordé (durant trois mois dans ta maison).

CHANT XI. CHEU WEI.

Le prince de 黎 Lî, chassé par les barbares, s'est réfugié dans la principauté de 衛 Wéi avec un certain nombre de ses officiers. Ceux-ci l'exhortent à aller relever la gloire de la patrie.

1. Oh! comme nous sommes abaissés! Que ne retournons-nous dans notre pays? Si ce n'était à cause de vous, prince, aurions-nous consenti à vivre ici dans le déshonneur?

quasi mercator qui nequit vendere (merces suas). Olim (tecum) nutrita timebam ne alimenta exhaurirentur et tecum decidens subverterer. Postquam commode viximus, postquam opes suppeditarunt, assimilasti me veneno.

6. Ego habui optima recondita (olera), ad sustinendum (tecum) hiemem, i. e. calamitosa tempora. (Nunc) te oblectas cum tua nova uxore, usus me ad arcendam inopiam. Utens ferocia, utens iracundia, jam adduxisti mihi dura. Non recordaris præteriti temporis, (quando) tu me venientem quiete donasti.

伊 Ī, tu. La jeune épouse ne travaillait pas durant les trois premiers mois après la célébration du mariage.

CHANT XI. 1. Imminuti! imminuti! Cur non revertamur? Nisi principis causa, qua de causa in rore, i. e. quare hic in ignominia maneremus?

(2) 式微式微、胡不歸、微君之躬、胡為乎泥中。

旄丘

(1) 旄丘之葛兮、何誕之節兮、叔兮伯兮、何多日也、

(2) 何其處也、必有與也、何其久也、必有以也、

(3) 狐裘蒙戎、匪車不東、叔兮伯

2. Chĕu wêi ! chĕu wêi ! Hôu pŏu kouēi ? Wêi kiūn tchēu kōung, hôu wêi hôu gnî tchōung ?

MAO K'IOU. **1. Maô k'iōu tchēu kŏ (kiĕ) hi, hô tán tchēu tsiĕ hi ? Chŏu hi, pĕ (pĭ) hi, hô touō jĕu iè ?**

2. Hô k'i tch'òu iè ? pĭ iòu iù iè. Hô k'i kiòu (ki) iè ? pĭ iòu i iè.

3. Hôu k'iôu môung jôung. Fèi kiū pŏu tōung ; chŏu hi, pĕ hi, mi chòu iù t'ôung.

2. Quel abaissement ! quel abaissement ! Que ne retournons-nous dans notre pays ? Si ce n'était pour votre personne, prince, aurions-nous jamais consenti à vivre ici dans l'avilissement ?

CHANT XII. MAO K'IOU.

Les officiers de 黎 **Lî** réfugiés avec leur prince dans la principauté de 衛 **Wéi**, se plaignent de ce que les ministres de Wei ne les aident pas à rentrer dans leur pays.

1. Sur cette colline dont le revers est en pente douce, comment les tiges du dolic se sont-elles étendues si loin ? Pourquoi nos oncles (les ministres de Wei) tardent-ils si longtemps à nous secourir ?

2. Pourquoi gardent-ils le repos ? Sans doute ils attendent des alliés. Pourquoi attendent-ils si longtemps ? Ils ont certainement un motif.

3. Les poils de nos fourrures de renards sont déjà usés (parce que nous sommes restés longtemps ici). Nos voitures sont

式 **Chĕu** particule initiale. La principauté de Li était peut-être dans le 壺關縣 **Hôu kouān hién** actuel, qui dépend de 潞安府 **Lóu ngān fòu** dans le 山西 **Chān sī**.

2. Imminuti ! imminuti ! Cur non revertamur ? Nisi propter principis personam, qua de causa in cœno ?

CHANT XII. 1. Depressi collis puerariæ quomodo producti sunt articuli ? Patrui minores, patrui majores quare multis diebus (moram faciunt) ?

叔伯 **Chŏu, pĕ,** titre que les officiers de Li donnent par respect aux ministres de Wei.

2. Quare illi quieti manent ? Profecto habent fœderatos. Quare illi diu nihil agunt ? Certe est causa.

3. Indutarum vulpinis pellibus vestium (nostrarum) pili permixti sunt (et detriti). Non quod vehicula (nostra) non in orientem (venerint ad rogandum

兮。靡所與同。
(4) 瑣兮尾兮、流離之子、叔兮伯兮、褎如充耳。

簡兮

(1) 簡兮簡兮、方將萬舞、日之方中、在前上處。
(2) 碩人俁俁、公庭萬舞、有力如虎、執轡如組。

4. Souò hî, wèi hî, liôu lî tchēu tzèu (tsi). Chŏu hî, pĕ hî, ióu jôu tch'ōung èul.

KIEN HI. 1. Kièn hi! kièn hi! Fāng tsiāng wán òu. Jĕu tchĕu fāng tchōung, tsái ts'iên cháng tch'óu.

2. Chĕu jènn iù iù, kōung t'îng wán òu. Iòu lĭ jôu hòu; tchĕu pi jôu tsòu.

venues en orient (à Wei, pour demander des secours); mais nos oncles n'ont aucune sympathie pour nous.

4. Amoindris, relégués au dernier rang, nous sommes comme des enfants errants et dispersés. Nos oncles rient beaucoup, et ferment l'oreille à nos prières (ou bien, rient comme des sourds).

CHANT XIII. KIEN HI.

Un officier de 衛 **Wéi**, réduit à exercer le métier de chef de pantomimes, décrit ironiquement ses fonctions, et accuse le prince de ne pas conférer les charges aux hommes de talent d'après leur mérite.

1. Sans façon, sans gêne (sans tenir compte de ma dignité), me voici prêt à exécuter différents chants avec pantomime. Midi approche; je suis au premier rang (sur la scène), à l'endroit le plus élevé.

2. D'une taille grande et imposante, j'exécute dans la cour du palais différents chants avec accompagnement de pantomime. Je suis fort comme un tigre; les rênes des chevaux sont comme des rubans entre mes doigts.

auxilium; sed) patrui minores, patrui majores nihil habent quo nobiscum sint unanimes.

4. Imminuti, postremi, quasi vagi et dispersi pueri sumus. Patrui minores, patrui majores multum rident quasi obturatis auribus.

KIEN HI. 1. Incurius, incurius, modo incipiam saltare utriusque generis cantica, i. e. tum alia tum militaria. Dies modo medius erit; in anteriori superiorique loco maneo.

萬 **Wán**, nom générique des chants exécutés avec accompagnement de gestes. Pour les chants guerriers, chaque pantomime tenait en main un bouclier et une hache d'armes; pour les autres chants, il tenait une flûte et une plume de faisan.

2. Procerus homo, statura magnus, in regia aula salto utriusque generis cantica. Habeo vires tanquam tigris; tracto equorum habenas sicut fascias, i. e. facillime.

(3) 左手執籥、右手秉翟、赫如渥赭、公言錫爵、
(4) 山有榛、隰有苓、云誰之思、西方美人、彼美人兮、西方之人兮、
泉水
(1) 毖彼泉水、亦流于淇、有懷于衛、靡日

3. Tsouò cheòu tchĕu iŏ, iòu cheòu ping tĭ (tchŏ). Hĕ jŏu wŏ tchè (tchŏ); kōung iên sĭ tsiŏ.

4. Chān iòu tchēnn, sĭ iòu lîng. Iûn chouêi tchēu sēu? Sī fāng mèi jênn. Pèi mèi jênn hî, sī fang tchēu jênn hî.

TS'IUEN CHOUEI. **1. Pi pèi Ts'iuên chouèi, ĭ liôu iū K'î. Iòu houâi iū Wéi, mi**

3. De la main gauche je tiens une flûte, et de la droite une plume de faisan. Mon visage est d'un rouge foncé, comme s'il était peint. Le prince ordonne de m'offrir une coupe de vin en récompense.

4. Le coudrier croît sur les montagnes et la réglisse dans les endroits marécageux. (Chaque plante trouve le lieu qui lui convient. Tout homme devrait avoir un emploi en rapport avec ses aptitudes). Savez-vous à qui je pense? Je pense aux excellents princes de l'occident (aux anciens princes de Tcheou qui prenaient soin de rechercher et de bien employer les hommes de talent). Oh! qu'ils étaient admirables, ces princes de l'occident!

CHANT XIV. TS'IUEN CHOUEI.

Une fille de la maison de 衛 **Wéi**, mariée à un prince étranger, désire aller revoir son pays natal. Elle demandera à ses compagnes si ce voyage convient ou non; car ses parents ne sont plus. (D'après l'usage, la femme d'un prince pouvait retourner à la maison paternelle, tant que ses parents étaient en vie; après leur mort, elle se contentait d'envoyer un 大夫 **tái fōu** grand préfet saluer ses frères).

1. La Ts'iuen prend sa source dans le pays de Wei et se jette dans la K'i (sans sortir de Wei. Son sort me fait envie). Mon cœur est à Wei; j'y pense chaque jour. Mes compagnes, mes parentes

3. Sinistra manu teneo tibiam; dextera manu teneo phasiani plumam. Rubicundus (est vultus meus) quasi dense imbutus rubro colore. Regulus jubet me donari vini poculo.

4. In montibus est corylus, in palustribus locis est glycyrrhiza. De quo cogito? De occidentalis regionis inclytis viris. Illi inclyti viri, occidentalis regionis viri!

CHANT XIV. 1. Scaturiens illa Ts'iuen aqua influit in K'i. Habeo animum in Wei; nullus est dies quo non reminiscar. Optimæ sunt illæ omnes Ki; paululum cum illis deliberabo.

姬 **Kī** était le nom de famille de la

不思、孌彼諸姬、
聊與之謀、
(2) 出宿于泲、飲
餞于禰、女子有
行、遠父母兄弟、
問我諸姑、遂及
伯姊、
(3) 出宿于干、飲
餞于言、載脂載
舝、還車言邁、遄
臻于衛、不瑕有
害、
(4) 我思肥泉、茲

jĕu pŏu sēu (sī). Liuên pèi tchŏu Kī, leaô iù tchēu meôu (mêi).

2. Tch'ŏu siŭ iū Tsi, in tsién iū Gni. Gniù tzèu iòu hîng, iuèn fóu mòu hiōung tì. Wénn ngò tchōu kōu, souéi kĭ pĕ tzéu (tsì).

3. Tch'ŏu siŭ iū Kān (Kiēn), in tsién iū Iên. Tsái tchēu, tsái hiă (hiái) ; siuên kiū iên mài. Chouên tchēnn iū Wéi. Pŏu hiâ iòu hái ?

4. Ngò sēu Fêi ts'iuên ; tzēu tchēu iòung t'án (t'iēn). Sēu siū iù Ts'aô (Ts'eōu);

sont admirables; je les consulterai (sur mon projet de retour).

2. Quand je suis venue ici, je me suis arrêtée à Tsi; j'ai bu le vin et reçu les honneurs du festin d'adieu à Gni. Jeune fille, pour faire ce voyage, j'ai quitté mes parents et mes frères. Je consulterai mes tantes et mes autres parentes (sur mon projet de retour).

3. Partie d'ici, je m'arrêterai à Kan ; je boirai et recevrai les honneurs du festin d'adieu à Ien. Déjà on graisse, on arme l'essieu ; la voiture s'en retournera vite. J'arriverai bientôt à Wei ; mais ne serai-je pas en faute ?

4. Je pense à la Fei ; je soupire sans cesse après le bonheur de

jeune femme. Selon l'usage, plusieurs de ses parentes étaient allées avec elle demeurer à la cour de son mari.

2. Quando exivi (e domo paterna), constiti in Tsi, bibi et viaticum convivium accepi in Gni. Junior filia aggrediens iter, recessi a parentibus et fratribus. Interrogabo meas omnes amitas, inde etiam alias consanguineas tum natu majores tum natu minores.

Anciennement, ceux qui pour honorer un voyageur, l'avaient accompagné une partie du chemin, avant de le quitter, faisaient avec lui un sacrifice aux divinités protectrices des chemins, puis buvaient et mangeaient avec lui.

泲 **Tsi** et 禰 **Gni** étaient probablement dans la principauté de Wei, d'où la princesse était venue.

3. Quando exivero, consistam in Kan, bibam et viaticum convivium accipiam in Ien. Jam ungitur (axis vehiculi), jam armantur axis extrema; revertens vehiculum properabit. Celeriter perveniam ad Wei ; nonne quid erit mali ?

舝 **Hiă**, pièces de fer qu'on fixait aux extrémités de l'essieu immédiatement avant le départ, et qu'on retirait dès l'arrivée.

干 **Kān** et 言 **Iên** étaient sans doute dans le pays où la princesse était mariée.

4. Ego cogito de Fei fonte ; illum semper suspirans desidero. Cogito de

之永歎。思須與漕。
我心悠悠。駕言出
遊。以寫我憂。

北門

(1) 出自北門。憂心
殷殷。終窶且貧。莫
知我艱。已焉哉。天
實爲之。謂之何哉。
(2) 王事適我。政事
一埤益我。我入自
外。室人交徧讁我。
已焉哉。天實爲之。
謂之何哉。

ngò sīn iôu iôu. Kiá iên tch'ŏu iôu, i siè ngò iōu.

PE MENN. **1. Tch'ŏu tzéu pĕ mênn (min), iōu sīn īn īn. Tchōung kiù, ts'iè p'în, mouŏ tchēu ngò kiēn (kīn). Ì iên tsāi (tsī). T'iēn chĕu wêi tchēu; wéi tchēu hô tsāi (tsī)?**

2. Wâng chéu chĕu ngò; tchéng chéu ĭ p'î ĭ ngò. Ngò jŏu tzéu wái; chĕu jênn kiāo pién tchĕ ngò. Ì iên tsāi (tsī). T'iēn chĕu wêi tchēu; wéi tchēu hô tsāi (tsī)?

la revoir. Je pense aux villes de Siu et de Ts'ao; leur souvenir occupe toujours mon esprit. Que ne puis-je monter en voiture, partir, voyager et dissiper ma tristesse!

CHANT XV. PE MENN.

Un officier de 衛 Wéi chante son malheureux sort et sa résignation.

1. Je suis sorti par la porte du nord (qui mène à l'infortune); mon cœur est dans l'affliction. Je suis toujours dans la gêne et la pauvreté; personne ne connait mes souffrances. C'en est fait (je n'ai rien à attendre des hommes). C'est le ciel qui a réglé mon destin; que puis-je y redire?

2. Les affaires de l'empire viennent à moi; celles de notre principauté retombent toutes sur moi. Quand je reviens du dehors à la maison, tous les membres de la famille m'adressent mille reproches. C'en est fait. C'est le ciel qui a réglé mon destin; puis-je m'en plaindre?

Siu et Ts'ao urbibus; meus animus semper reminiscitur. (Quidni mihi liceat) juncto curru, proficisci, spatiari (in Wei), ita solvere meum mœrorem!

CHANT XV. 1. Egressus sum septentrionali porta; æger animus vehementer dolet. Semper angustatus et pauper sum; nemo cognoscit meas ærumnas. Actum est, i.e. ab hominibus nihil sperare possum. Cœlum revera fecit hoc; querar de hoc quid?

Le nord correspond aux ténèbres. La porte du nord est la porte des malheurs.

2. Imperii negotia veniunt ad me; regni negotiorum totus acervus imponitur mihi. Quum ego ingredior (redux) a foris, domestici homines conjuncti omnia exprobrant mihi. Actum est. Cœlum revera fecit hoc; dicam de hoc quid?

(3) 王事敦我、政事一埤遺我、我入自外、室人交徧摧我、已焉哉、天實爲之、謂之何哉、

北風

(1) 北風其涼、雨雪其雱、惠而好我、攜手同行、其虛其邪、既亟只且、

(2) 北風其喈、雨雪其霏、惠而好我、攜手同歸、其虛其邪、既亟只且、

3. Wâng chéu touēnn (touēi) ngò; tchéng chéu ĭ p'ì i (ì) ngò. Ngò jŏu tzéu wài; chĕu jênn kiaō pién ts'ouēi ngò. Ĭ iên tsāi (tsī). T'iēn chĕu wêi tchēu; wéi tchēu hô tsāi (tsī)?

PE FOUNG. **1. Pĕ fōung k'ì leâng ; iù siuĕ k'ì p'āng. Houéi êul haò ngò, hì cheòu t'ôung hîng (hâng). K'ì hiū k'ì siû ; kì kí tchéu tsiū.**

2. Pĕ fōung k'ì kiāi (kī); iù siuĕ k'ì fēi. Houéi êul haò ngò, hì cheòu t'ôung kouēi. K'ì hiū k'ì siû ; kì kí tchéu tsiū.

3. Les affaires de l'empire sont rejetées sur moi; toutes celles de notre gouvernement me sont imposées. Quand je reviens du dehors à la maison, toute la famille de concert m'accable de reproches. C'en est fait. C'est le ciel qui a fixé mon sort; pourquoi m'en plaindrais-je?

CHANT XVI. PE FOUNG.

Un habitant de 衛 **Wéi**, voyant l'intempérie du ciel et un grand nombre d'animaux de mauvais augure, des renards, des corbeaux, annonce des troubles dans l'État, et engage ses amis à le suivre dans une autre contrée.

1. Un vent glacial souffle du nord, et la neige tombe en abondance. O mes amis, donnons-nous la main et partons ensemble. Que tardons-nous? Le temps presse.

2. Le vent du nord siffle avec violence, et la neige se disperse de tous côtés. O mes amis, donnons-nous la main, et partons ensemble pour ne plus revenir. Que tardons-nous? Le temps presse.

3. Imperii negotia injiciuntur in me; regni negotiorum totus acervus imponitur mihi. Quum ingredior (redux) a foris, domestici homines conjuncti omnia objectant mihi. Actum est. Cœlum revera fecit hoc; dicam de hoc quid?

CHANT XVI. 1. Borealis ventus ille gelidus est; cadit nix illa copiosa. Benigni et amantes mei, prehensa manu, simul abeamus. (Cur) ipsi remissi, ipsi tardi? Jam res urget.

只 且 **Tchèu tsiū**, particules.

2. Borealis ventus ille stridet; cadens nix illa multum spargitur. Benigni et amantes mei, prehensa manu, simul in perpetuum abeamus. (Cur) ipsi remissi, ipsi tardi? Jam res urget.

(3) 莫赤匪狐，莫黑匪烏。惠而好我，攜手同車。其虛其邪，既亟只且。

靜女

(1) 靜女其姝，俟我於城隅。愛而不見，搔首踟躕。

(2) 靜女其孌，貽我彤管。彤管有煒，說懌女美。

(3) 自牧歸荑，洵美且異。匪女之爲美，美人之貽。

3. Mouŏ tch'ĕu fèi hôu ; mouŏ hĕ fèi ōu. Houéi êul haŏ ngò, hì cheòu t'ôung kiū. K'i hiū k'i siū? ki kĭ tchéu tsiū.

TSING GNIU. **1. Tsing gniù k'ì tch'ōu ; séu ngò iū tch'êng iû. Ngái êul pŏu kién, saŏ cheòu tch'ĕu tch'ôu.**

2. Tsing gniù k'ì liuèn, ì ngò t'ôung kouàn (kiuèn). T'ôung kouàn iòu wèi ; iuĕ ĭ gniù mèi.

3. Tzéu mŏu kouēi t'î ; siūn mèi, ts'iè i (î). Fèi jôu tchēu wêi mèi, mèi jènn tchēu ì.

3. On ne voit de fauve que des renards, ni de noir que des corbeaux. O mes amis, donnons-nous la main, et partons tous en voiture. Que tardons-nous? Le temps presse.

CHANT XVII. TSING GNIU.

Attente inutile de la venue d'une jeune personne amie de la retraite.

1. Cette fille qui cache sa beauté dans la retraite, devait m'attendre à l'angle du rempart. Je l'aime et ne la vois pas; je me gratte la tête, ne sachant que faire.

2. Cette fille qui cache sa beauté dans la retraite, m'a donné un tube rouge. Ce tube rouge est brillant; (en le voyant, je me rappelle et) j'aime la beauté de la jeune fille.

3. Revenant des pâturages, elle m'a rapporté de jeunes plantes, qui sont vraiment belles et rares. Jeunes plantes, ce n'est pas vous qui êtes belles; mais vous êtes le don d'une belle personne.

3. Nihil fulvi (apparet) nisi vulpes, nihil nigri nisi corvi. Benigni et amantes mei, prehensa manu, simul...

CHANT XVII. 1. Segregata puella illa formosa exspectatura erat me ad mœniorum angulum. Amans et non videns, scabeo caput quasi hærens.

Selon la remarque de 陸深, une fille 靜 qui vit retirée est juste l'opposé d'une personne 淫 impudique.

2. Segregata puella illa decora donavit mihi rubrum tubum. Ruber tubus habet fulgorem; gaudens delector puellæ pulchritudine.

On ignore quel était l'usage de ce tube.

3. Ex pascuis rediens obtulit germina vere pulchra et rara. Non vos estis pulchra, sed pulchræ puellæ donum.

新臺

(1) 新臺有泚、河水瀰瀰。燕婉之求、籧篨不鮮。

(2) 新臺有洒、河水浼浼。燕婉之求、籧篨不殄。

(3) 魚網之設、鴻則離之。燕婉之求、得此戚施。

SIN T'AI. 1. **Sīn t'âi iòu ts'èu ; Hô chouèi mi mi. Ién iuèn tchēu k'iôu ; k'iù tch'ôu pŏu siĕn (si).**

2. Sīn t'âi iòu ts'ouèi (siĕn) ; Hô chouèi mèi mèi (miĕn miĕn). Ién iuèn tchēu k'iôu ; k'iù tch'ôu pŏu t'iĕn.

3. Iù wàng tchēu chĕ ; hôung tsĕ lî tchēu. Ién iuèn tchēu k'iôu; tĕ ts'èu ts'ĭ chēu.

CHANT XVIII. SIN T'AI.

衛宣公 Siuen, prince de Wei, avait demandé en mariage pour son fils 伋 **Kĭ** une fille du prince de 齊 **Ts'î**. Apprenant qu'elle était belle, il voulut l'épouser lui-même, bâtit une tour sur le bord du Fleuve-Jaune, et arrêta au passage la jeune princesse, qui fut appelée 宣姜 **Siuēn Kiāng**. Voy. page 30. Dans les strophes suivantes, le peuple critique la conduite honteuse du prince.

1. La nouvelle tour est brillante; à son pied le Fleuve coule large et profond. La fille du prince de Ts'i désirait avoir un époux paisible et accommodant (le prince Ki); elle a trouvé un énorme panier qui n'a rien de rare (le prince Siuen).

2. La nouvelle tour est très élevée; (à son pied) le Fleuve coule à pleins bords. La princesse désirait avoir un époux paisible et accommodant; elle a trouvé un énorme panier qui restera toujours ce qu'il est.

3. Le filet attendait un poisson (le prince Ki); une grosse oie (le prince Siuen) s'y est jetée. La princesse espérait avoir un époux paisible et accommodant; elle a trouvé un bossu qui ne peut se courber en avant.

CHANT XVIII. 1. Nova turris habet nitorem; Fluvii aqua est ingens. Placidum et obsequentem quærebat (puella, et invenit) arundineam sportam minime raram.

2. Nova turris habet celsitatem; Fluvii aqua alveum implet. Placidum et obsequentem quærebat, (invenit) arundineam sportam non desinentem.

3. Piscatorium rete positum est; anser ingens tunc incidit in illud. Placidum et obsequentem quærebat; invenit illum gibbum qui corpus inclinare non potest.

CHANT XIX. 1. Duo filii vehuntur cymbis; fluctuat illarum umbra. Memor cogito de filiis; in animo anxius sum.

2. Duo filii vehuntur cymbis; fluctuantes illæ abeunt. Memor cogito de filiis; nonne quid advenit mali?

詩經

二子乘舟

(1) 二子乘舟、汎汎其景、願言思子、中心養養、

(2) 二子乘舟、汎汎其逝、願言思子、不瑕有害、

鄘一之四

柏舟

(1) 汎彼柏舟、在彼中河、髧

EUL TZEU CHENG TCHEOU. 1. Eúl tzèu chêng tcheōu, fán fán k'ì king (kàng). Iuén iên sēu tzèu; tchōung sīn iàng iàng.

2. Eúl tzèu chêng tcheōu, fán fán k'ì chéu. Iuén iên sēu tzèu, pǒu hiâ iòu hái?

PE TCHEOU. 1. Fán pèi pě tcheōu, tsái pèi tchōung Hô. Tàn pèi leàng maô,

CHANT XIX. EUL TZEU CHENG TCHEOU.

宣姜 **Siuēn Kiāng** eut deux fils, 壽 **Cheóu** et 朔 **Chouŏ**. Pour assurer à Chouo l'héritage de la principauté, elle complota avec lui contre le prince 伋 **Kĭ**. Siuen, trompé par sa femme, envoya Ki à Ts'i, et fit aposter des brigands pour le tuer en chemin. Cheou l'ayant appris, en donna avis à Ki. Celui-ci répondit qu'il voulait obéir à l'ordre de son père. Cheou, pour sauver la vie à son frère, monta en barque, prit les devants, fut saisi et tué par les brigands. Ki arriva ensuite et leur dit: « Mon père l'a ordonné, tuez-moi. Quel crime Cheou avait-il commis. » Il fut aussi mis à mort. Le peuple soupçonna les ordres secrets du père, et exprima ses craintes dans les strophes suivantes.

1. Les deux jeunes princes sont sur leurs barques, dont l'ombre semble flotter sur l'eau. Je ne cesse de penser à eux ; mon cœur est dans l'inquiétude.

2. Les deux jeunes princes sont sur leurs barques, qui se balancent sur l'eau. Je ne cesse de penser à eux ; ne leur serait-il pas arrivé quelque malheur ?

LIVRE IV. IOUNG FOUNG.

CHANT I. PE TCHEOU.

Après la mort de 共伯 **Kōung pě**, héritier présomptif de 僖 **Hī**, prince de 衛 **Wéi**, sa veuve 共姜 **Kōung Kiāng** jura de ne pas se remarier, et résista aux sollicitations pressantes de ses propres parents. « Une barque vogue dans un endroit déterminé, dit-elle; de même une veuve ne doit jamais passer à un second mari. »

1. Cette barque de bois de cyprès qui se balance sur l'eau, garde

TITRE DU LIVRE. 鄘一之四 Ioung (regni cantica): primæ (partis) quartus (liber). La principauté de Ioung était au sud de Wei houei fou dans le Ho nan. Voy. page 3.

CHANT I. 1. Fluctuans illa cupressina cymba manet in illo medio Fluvio (Flavo Fluvio). Pendulis illis duobus cincinnis (Koung pe) vere solus meus conjux. Ad mortem, juro, non habebo

彼兩髦、實維我儀、之死矢靡他、母也天只、不諒人只、

(2) 汎彼柏舟、在彼河側、髧彼兩髦、實維我特、之死矢靡慝、母也天只、不諒人只、

牆有茨

(1) 牆有茨、不可埽也、中冓之言、不可道也、所可道也、言之醜也、

chĕu wêi ngò i (ngô). Tchĕu sèu chèu mi t'ouō. Mòu iè t'iēn (t'īn) tchèu; pŏu leàng jênn tchèu.

2. Fán pèi pĕ tcheōu, tsái pèi Hô tchĕ. Tàn pèi leàng maô, chĕu wêi ngŏ t'ĕ. Tchĕu sèu chèu mi t'ĕ. Mòu iè t'iēn (t'īn) tchèu; pŏu leàng jênn tchèu.

TS'IANG IOU TS'EU. 1. Ts'iâng iòu ts'êu, pŏu k'ò saò (seòu) iè. Tchōung keòu tchēu iên, pŏu k'ò taó (t'eòu) iè. Chòu k'ò taó (t'eòu) iè, iên tchēu tch'eòu iè.

toujours le milieu du Fleuve. Ce prince, avec ses deux touffes de cheveux pendants, était et sera toujours mon unique époux. Je le jure, jamais je ne changerai de résolution. Ma mère est pour moi bonne comme le ciel; mais elle ne croit pas à ma persévérance.

2. Cette barque de bois de cyprès qui se balance sur l'eau, suit toujours cette rive du Fleuve. Ce prince, avec ses deux touffes de cheveux pendants, était et restera toujours mon unique époux. Je le jure, jamais je ne me rendrai coupable d'inconstance. Ma mère est pour moi bonne comme le ciel; mais elle ne croit pas à ma persévérance.

CHANT II. TS'IANG IOU TS'EU.

Dans le palais de 衛 Wéi, il est des choses si honteuses qu'on ne peut les raconter.

1. Sur le mur croît une plante épineuse (Herse ou Croix de Malte); on ne peut l'en arracher (sans nuire au mur). L'histoire des appartements intérieurs ne peut être entreprise; ce qu'on en pourrait raconter, serait honteux à dire.

alium animum. Mater cœlum est; (at) non fidit homini, i. e. mihi.

Trois mois après la naissance d'un enfant, garçon ou fille, on lui coupait les cheveux, à l'exception de deux touffes qu'on lui laissait sur les tempes pour lui rappeler sans cesse les devoirs de la piété filiale. A la mort de son père, il coupait celle qui était sur la tempe gauche; à la mort de sa mère, il coupait l'autre.

2. Fluctuans illa cupressina cymba manet ad illud Fluvii latus. Pendulis illis duobus cincinnis (Koung pe) vere solus meus unicus. Ad mortem, juro, non admittam scelus. Mater cœlum est; (at) non fidit homini.

CHANT II. 1. Super parietem est tribulus; non potest everri. Interiorum contignationum narratio, i. e. rerum quæ in penetralibus aguntur narratio, non potest exponi. Quæ possemus exponere, dicere ea esset turpe.

(2) 牆有茨、不可襄也、中冓之言、不可詳也、所可詳也、言之長也、

(3) 牆有茨、不可束也、中冓之言、不可讀也、所可讀也、言之辱也、

君子偕老

(1) 君子偕老、副笄六珈、委委佗佗、如山如河、象服是宜、子之不

2. Ts'iâng iòu ts'êu, pŏu k'ò siāng iè. Tchŏung keòu tchéu iên, pŏu k'ò siâng iè. Chòu k'ò siàng iè, iên tchēu tch'âng iè.

3. Ts'iâng iòu ts'êu, pŏu k'ò chŏu iè. Tchōung keòu tchēu iên, pŏu k'ò tŏu iè. Chòu k'ò tŏu iè, iên tchēu jŏu iè.

KIUN TZEU KIAI LAO. **1. Kiūn tzèu kiāi laò, fóu kī liŭ kiā (kō). Wēi wēi**

2. Une plante épineuse croît sur le mur; on ne peut l'enlever (sans nuire au mur). L'histoire des appartements secrets ne peut être racontée en détail; ce qu'on en pourrait raconter, serait trop long à dire.

3. Une plante épineuse croît sur le mur; on ne peut la lier et l'enlever. L'histoire des chambres intérieures ne peut être répétée. Ce qu'on en pourrait répéter, souillerait les lèvres.

CHANT III. KIUN TZEU KIAI LAO.

Beauté et parure de 宣姜 **Siuēn Kiāng** mises en contraste avec sa conduite déréglée.

1. Destinée à demeurer jusqu'à la mort avec le prince son époux, la tête parée d'une tresse de cheveux empruntés, de deux épingles et de six pierres de prix, elle marche d'un air calme, avec la gravité d'une montagne et la majesté d'un fleuve. Sa tenue est en rapport

2. Super parietem est tribulus; non potest amoveri. Interiorum contignationum narratio non potest evolvi. Quæ possemus evolvere, dicere ea longius esset.

3. Super parietem est tribulus; non potest ligari (et auferri). Interiorum contignationum narratio non potest recitari. Quæ possemus recitare, dicere ea probrosum esset.

CHANT III. 1. Cum marito simul (vitam et) senectam transactura, addititiis capillis in nodum coactis, spiculis et sex lapillis (ornata), placido habitu incedens, (gravis) sicut mons, (ampla) sicut amnis, legis vestibus vere convenit (specie). Mulier non est bona; de illis (ornamentis) quid?

Lorsqu'une princesse aidait son époux à faire une offrande, elle portait sur la tête un ornement 副 **fóu** composé de cheveux. Elle y enfonçait deux épingles 笄 **kī**, dont la tête représentait une poule et portait des cordons 紞 **tàn**. A ces cordons étaient suspendues six pierres de prix 珈 **kiā** ou 瑱

淑、云如之何、

(2) 玼兮玼兮、其之翟也、鬒髮如雲、不屑髢也、玉之瑱也、象之揥也、揚且之晳也、胡然而天也、胡然而帝也、

(3) 瑳兮瑳兮、其之展也、蒙彼縐絺、是紲袢也、子之清揚、揚且之顏也、展如之人兮、邦之媛也、

t'ouô t'ouô, jôu chān, jôu hô; siáng fôu chéu î (ngô). Tzéu tchēu pŏu chŏu; iûn jôu tchēu hô?

2. Ts'èu hì, ts'èu hì, k'ì tchēu tĭ (ti) iè. Tchènn fă jôu iùn, pŏu siĕ ti iè. Iŭ tchēu t'ién iè, siáng tchēu tch'éu iè; iàng tsiū tchēu sī (tchéu) iè. Hôu jên êul t'iēn iè? Hôu jên êul ti iè?

3. Ts'ouò hi, ts'ouò hi, k'ì tchēu tchén (tchēn) iè. Môung péi tcheóu tch'ēu, chéu siĕ fân iè. Tzèu tchēu ts'īng iâng, iâng tsiū tchēu iên iè. Tchén jôu tchēu jènn hî, pāng tchēu iuén (iuên) iè.

avec son costume officiel. Mais cette jeune femme n'est pas vertueuse; que lui servent sa parure et sa beauté?

2. Sa robe de cérémonie est neuve et brillante. Ses beaux cheveux noirs forment comme une nuée autour de sa tête; elle ne s'abaisse pas à porter perruque. Elle a des pierres de prix sur les oreilles et une épingle d'ivoire; son large front est bien blanc. Oh! n'est-ce pas un esprit céleste! n'est-ce pas une déesse!

3. Sa robe blanche pour les visites est neuve et brillante. Elle couvre une tunique de fine toile frisée. (Ou bien, en été une tunique de fine toile frisée couvre sa robe ordinaire). Une ceinture la retient. Cette jeune personne a les yeux brillants, le front large, les angles du front bien remplis. Une telle femme est vraiment la plus belle de la principauté.

t'ién, qui pendaient sur les oreilles. Elle y ajoutait une troisième épingle 揥 **tch'éu** qui servait à peigner la chevelure. La robe de la princesse s'appelait le vêtement de la loi, c.-à-d. le vêtement de celle qui devait être comme la loi vivante. Des plumes de faisan y étaient représentées.

2. Nova splendet, nova splendet ejus picta phasiani plumis vestis. Nigri capilli sunt instar nubis (multi ac pulchri); non dignatur ferre capillamentum. (Ei sunt) ex lapillis ornamenta aurium, ex ebore spiculum, ampli frontis candor. Quomodo sic jam cœlestis spiritus (videtur)! Quomodo sic jam cœleste numen!

見者驚猶鬼神也 A son aspect on éprouve un saisissement comme à la vue d'un esprit.

3. Nova splendet, nova splendet ejus vestis alba (quam induit regulum hospitesve invisura); operit illam ex crispa tela tunicam (vel vulgari tunicæ imponitur ex crispa tela tunica). Tunc cingitur zona. Mulieris

桑中

①爰采唐矣、沫之鄉矣、云誰之思、美孟姜矣、期我乎桑中、要我乎上宮、送我乎淇之上矣、

②爰采麥矣、沫之北矣、云誰之思、美孟弋矣、期我乎桑中、要我乎上宮、送我乎淇之上矣、

③爰采葑矣、沫

SANG TCHOUNG. 1. **Iuên ts'ài t'âng i, Mêi tchēu hiāng i. Iûn chouêi tchēu sēu? Mêi Méng Kiāng i. K'ì ngò hôu Sāng tchōung (tchāng), iaō ngò hôu Cháng kōung (kouāng), sóung ngò hôu K'î tchēu chàng (chāng) i.**

2. Iuên ts'ài mĕ (kĭ) i, Méi tchēu pĕ i. Iûn chouêi tchēu sēu? Mêi Méng Ĭ i. K'ì ngò hôu Sāng tchōung (tchāng), iaō ngò hôu Cháng kōung (kouāng), sóung ngò hôu K'î tchēu chàng (chāng) i.

3. Iuên ts'ài fōung i, Méi tchēu tōung i. Iûn chouêi tchēu sēu? Mêi Méng

CHANT IV. SANG TCHOUNG.

Le poète, pour rendre le vice odieux, fait parler un jeune libertin d'une grande famille de 衛 **Wéi**, lequel cherchait à séduire trois femmes mariées du plus haut rang.

1. Je cueille la cuscute dans le pays de Mei. Savez-vous à qui je pense? A la belle Meng Kiang, c.-à-d. à l'aînée des Kiang, de la maison de Ts'i. Elle m'a fixé Sang tchoung pour lieu de rendez-vous, est allée au-devant de moi jusqu'à Chang koung, et m'a reconduit jusqu'à K'i chang.

2. Je cueille le blé dans la partie septentrionale de Mei. Savez-vous à qui je pense? A la belle Meng I. Elle m'a fixé Sang tchoung pour lieu de rendez-vous, est allée au-devant de moi jusqu'à Chang koung, et m'a reconduit jusqu'à K'i chang.

3. Je cueille le navet dans la partie orientale de Mei. Savez-vous

micant oculi, amplus frons; ampli frontis anguli sunt pleni. Vere hujusmodi mulier est regni formosissima.

CHANT IV. 1. Colligo cuscutam in Mei regione (Wei regno subjecta). Dic, de quo cogito? De formosa Meng Kiang, i. e. natu maxima sororum e 齊 **Ts'i** regia stirpe Kiang nomine. Conveniendi locum præstituit mihi Sang tchoung, occurrit mihi in Chang koung, comitata est ad K'i chang.

Sang tchoung, Chang koung et K'i chang sont trois endroits du pays de Mei.

2. Colligo triticum in Mei boreali regione. Dic, de quo cogito? De formosa Meng I. Conveniendi locum præstituit mihi...

Dans le Tch'ouenn Ts'iou, au lieu de 弋 **I** on lit 姒 **Séu.** La jeune fille était probablement de la famille des 杞 **K'i,** descendants de la dynastie des 夏 **Hiá.**

3. Colligo napum in Mei orientali regione. Dic, de quo cogito? De formosa Meng Ioung...

之東矣、云誰之
思、美孟庸矣、期
我乎桑中、要我
乎上宮、送我乎
淇之上矣、
鶉之奔奔
(1) 鶉之奔奔、鵲
之彊彊、人之無
良、我以爲兄、
(2) 鵲之彊彊、鶉
之奔奔、人之無
良、我以爲君、

Iôung i. K'î ngò hôu Sāng tchōung (tchāng), iaō ngò hôu Cháng kōung (kouāng), sóung ngò hôu K'î tchēu cháng (chāng) i.

CHOUENN TCHEU PENN PENN. **1. Chouênn tchēu pēnn pēnn, ts'iŏ tchēu kiāng kiāng. Jênn tchêu ôu leàng; ngò i wêi hiōung (houāng)!**

2. Ts'iŏ tchēu kiāng kiāng, chouênn tchēu pēnn pēnn (pīn pīn). Jênn tchēu ôu leâng; ngò i wêi kiūn!

à qui je pense? A la belle Meng Ioung, c.-à-d. à la fille aînée des Ioung, de la principauté de ce nom. Elle m'a fixé Sang tchoung pour lieu de rendez-vous, est allée au-devant de moi jusqu'à Chang koung, et m'a reconduit jusqu'à K'i chang.

CHANT V. CHOUENN TCHEU PENN PENN.

Le peuple de Wei, dans son indignation, fait dire à 惠 **Houéi**, fils et successeur de 宣 **Siuēn**, prince de 衛 **Wéi**, que son frère 頑 **Wân** et sa mère 宣姜 **Siuēn Kiāng**, à cause de leurs mœurs déréglées, sont pires que les animaux.

1. Les cailles, les pies vont deux à deux et sont fidèles l'une à l'autre. Cet homme est vicieux, et je le considère encore comme mon frère!

2. Les pies, les cailles vont par paires, et sont fidèles l'une à l'autre. Cette femme est vicieuse, et je la considère encore comme une princesse!

御案聖人豈有刪詩而反取淫詞桑中之詩刺惡昭彰所謂思無邪也(備旨) On lit dans l'édition impériale: «Le grand sage (Confucius) qui a corrigé le Cheu king, aurait-il admis des vers obscènes? Le chant **Sang tchoung** blâme le vice, et met en lumière ce qui est dit (dans les 魯頌 Éloges de Lou, chant I): «Bannir toute pensée mauvaise.»

CHANT V. Coturnices volant compares; picæ volant compares. Homo non est bonus; ego habeo (eum) pro fratre!

2. Picæ volant pares, coturnices volant pares. Mulier non est bona; ego habeo (eam) pro reguli uxore!

彭執中 dit: «Un arbre gâté engendre des vers; un royaume corrompu s'attire des ennemis. Confucius a conservé ce chant, afin qu'on vît bien pourquoi les barbares avaient envahi la principauté de Wei.»

定之方中

(1) 定之方中、作于楚宮、揆之以日、作于楚室、樹之榛栗、椅桐梓漆、爰伐琴瑟、

(2) 升彼虛矣、以望楚矣、望楚與堂、景山與

TING TCHEU FANG TCHOUNG. 1. Ting tchēu fāng tchōung, tsŏ iū Tch'ôu kōung. Kouéi tchēu i jĕu, tsŏ iū Tch'ôu chĕu. Chóu tchēu tchēnn lĭ, ī t'ôung tzèu ts'ĭ, iuên fă k'în chĕ.

2. Chēng pèi k'iū (k'iù) i, i wáng Tch'ôu i. Wáng Tch'ôu iù T'âng, king chān

CHANT VI. TING TCHEU FANG TCHOUNG.

Les 狄 Tĭ barbares du nord ayant ravagé la principauté de 衛 Wéi, et dévasté la capitale, qui était située au nord du Fleuve-Jaune dans le 濬縣 Siún hién actuel, le prince 戴 Tái alla demeurer à 漕 Ts'aô, au sud du fleuve, dans le 滑縣 Houă hién actuel. Son successeur, le prince 文 Wênn, établit une nouvelle capitale à 楚邱 Tch'ôu k'iōu, dans le Chan toung. Il se signala, dit le poète, par sa diligence, sa prévoyance et son dévouement pour son peuple.

1. A l'époque de l'année où la constellation Ting passe au méridien (vers la tombée de la nuit), (le prince Wenn) commença la construction du palais de Tch'ou k'iou. Après avoir déterminé les points cardinaux par l'observation (du lever et du coucher) du soleil, il fit construire les bâtiments de Tch'ou k'iou. Il y planta des coudriers et des châtaigniers (afin que les fruits fussent offerts dans les temples); il planta aussi des catalpas de trois espèces et des sumacs, afin que le bois servît à faire des luths.

2. (Avant de prendre sa détermination), il monta sur les murs ruineux de Ts'ao, pour considérer de loin le site de Tch'ou k'iou. Il considéra de loin le site de Tch'ou k'iou et de T'ang. (Pour connaître

CHANT VI. 1. Quum *Ting* sidus attingeret meridianum (nocte prima), (Wenn regulus) extruxit Tch'ou palatium. Constituit illud ope solis; extruxit Tch'ou regiam domum. Plantavit illic corylos et castaneas (quarum fructus in sacris offerrentur), *i, t'ôung, tzèu* (triplicis generis catalpas) et verniciferam rhoem, quæ inde exciderentur ad *k'în, chĕ* (cithararum duo genera facienda).

La constellation 定 Ting comprend Markab et une autre étoile de Pégase. Sous le règne de Wenn (659-634), elle passait le soir au méridien vers la fin de novembre. Elle s'appelait 營室 Îng chĕu, parce que c'était l'époque la plus favorable pour commencer les constructions. Pour orienter les bâtiments, on observait le lever et le coucher du soleil, et l'ombre d'un gnomon de huit 尺 tch'ĕu. 楚邱 était, selon quelques auteurs, dans le 東昌府, ou, selon d'autres, dans le 曹州府 au sud-ouest de 成武縣.

2. Conscendit illa vetera mœnia (Ts'ao urbis), ut prospiceret Tch'ou. Prospexit Tch'ou et T'ang; observavit

8

京、降觀于桑。卜云其吉、終焉允臧。(3) 靈雨既零、命彼倌人、星言夙駕、說于桑田、匪直也人、秉心塞淵。騋牝三千、

蝃蝀

(1) 蝃蝀在東、莫之敢指、女子有行、遠父母兄弟、

iù kīng (kāng). Kiáng kouān iū sāng, pŏu iūn k'i kĭ, tchōung ièn iùn tsāng.

3. Lìng iù ki lìng, míng pèi kouān jênn, sīng ièn siū kiá, chouéi iū sāng t'iên (t'in). Fèi tchĕu iè jênn, ping sīn sĕ iuēn (iūn), lâi pin sān ts'iēn (ts'īn).

TI TOUNG. 1. Ti tóung tsái tōung, mouŏ tchēu kàn tchèu. Gniŭ tzèu iòu hing, iuèn fóu mòu hiōung ti.

l'orientation), il observa les ombres des montagnes et des collines. Étant descendu dans la plaine, il chercha les terrains propres à la culture du mûrier. Il consulta la tortue, reçut une réponse favorable, et mena son œuvre à bon terme.

3. Une pluie favorable ayant arrosé la terre, il donna ordre à l'intendant de ses équipages d'atteler sa voiture dès le matin avant la disparition des étoiles, (de partir) et de s'arrêter au milieu des plantations de mûriers et des champs cultivés. Ce grand homme ne borna pas là ses soins et son dévouement; il avait trois mille juments hautes de plus de sept pieds (1 mètre, 40 c.).

CHANT VII. TI TOUNG.

Une union qui n'est pas contractée selon les règles, est semblable à l'arc-en-ciel, qui résulte d'un trouble dans la nature, est de mauvais augure et prive la terre de la pluie du matin.

1. Lorsque l'arc-en-ciel paraît à l'orient, personne n'ose la montrer du doigt. Une fille qui se marie, quitte ses parents et ses frères.

umbras montium ac collium. Descendens inspexit moros (quæsivit loca ad colendas moros apta). Testudinem inspexit, (et cognovit) illud faustum fore; ad finem vere prosperum fuit.

3. Opportuna pluvia postquam decidit, jussit illum aurigarum magistrum, stellis (adhuc apparentibus), mane jungere vehiculum, sistere in mediis moris et agris. Non solum vir de (frugum et mororum cultura) servavit animum sincerum ac firmum; (præter alios equos), septem amplius pedibus altæ equæ erant ter mille.

CHANT VII. Quum cœlestis arcus est in oriente (vespere), nemo audet digito monstrare. Puella habens profectum (e domo paterna, ut nubat) relinquit parentes et fratres.

Personne n'ose montrer du doigt l'arc-en-ciel, lorsqu'elle apparaît vers le soir à l'orient. De même, il ne convient pas de parler d'une jeune personne qui a l'impudence de quitter ses parents et ses frères, et de se marier contrairement aux règles établies.

(2) 朝隮于西、崇朝其雨、女子有行、遠兄弟父母、

(3) 乃如之人也、懷昏姻也、大無信也、不知命也、

相鼠

(1) 相鼠有皮、人而無儀、人而無儀、不死何爲、

(2) 相鼠有齒、人而無止、人而無止、不死何俟、

2. Tchaō tsī iū sī, tch'ôung tchaō k'ì iù. Gniù tzèu iòu hìng, iuén hiōung ti fóu mòu.

3. Nài jôu tchēu jênn iè, houâi houēnn īn iè. Tá ôu sin (sīn) iè ; pŏu tchēu ming (mìn) iè.

SIANG CHOU. **1. Siáng chòu iòu p'î (p'ouô) ; jênn êul ôu î (ngô) ! Jênn êul ôu î (ngô), pŏu sèu hô wêi (wô) ?**

2. Siáng chòu iòu tch'èu ; jênn êul ôu tchèu ! Jênn êul ôu tchèu, pŏu sèu hô sèu (chèu) ?

2. Lorsque l'arc-en-ciel paraît le matin à l'occident, la pluie cesse avec la matinée. Une fille qui se marie, quitte ses parents et ses frères.

3. Cette fille pense à se marier (sans tenir compte des usages). Elle se perd elle-même, et ne connaît plus la loi naturelle.

CHANT VIII. SIANG CHOU.

L'urbanité est l'ornement et le complément de la personne ; elle maintient l'ordre dans la conduite. Un homme qui n'observe pas les convenances, se met au-dessous des plus vils animaux, qui ont une peau pour couvrir leur corps, des dents rangées en ordre et quatre membres intacts. Il n'est pas vraiment homme, et ne devrait pas vivre.

1. Voyez le rat, il a une peau ; et l'homme manquera de dignité! Un homme qui manque de dignité, pourquoi ne meurt-il pas?

2. Voyez le rat, il a des dents; et l'homme n'observera pas les convenances! Un homme qui n'observe pas les convenances, qu'attend-il pour mourir?

2. Quum (arcus cœlestis) mane ascendit ad occidentem, ad finem matutini temporis illa pluvia, i.e. finito mane desinit pluvia. Puella nubens relinquit parentes et fratres.

3. Ejusmodi puella cogitat de connubio (nec curat de servandis ritibus). Valde infidelis est (sibi, i.e. virtutem suam pessumdat), nec jam cognoscit legem naturalem.

CHANT VIII. 1. Aspice murem, habet pellem; homo autem caret gravitate! Homo qui caret gravitate, ut non moriatur quomodo fit?

2. Aspice murem, habet dentes; homo vero caret decora agendi ratione! Homo qui caret decora agendi ratione, ut moriatur quid exspectat?

(3)相鼠有體、人而無禮、人而無禮、胡不遄死。

干旄

(1)孑孑干旄、在浚之郊、素絲紕之、良馬四之、彼姝者子、何以畀之。

(2)孑孑干旟、在浚之都、素絲組之、良馬五之、彼姝者子、何以予之、

(3)孑孑干旌、在浚

3. Siáng chòu iòu t'i ; jênn êul òu li! Jênn êul òu li, hòu pŏu chouên sèu ?

KAN MAO. 1. Kiĕ kiĕ kān maò, tsái Siún tchēu kiaō (kaō). Sóu sēu pi tchēu; leàng mà séu tchēu. Pėi tch'ōu tchė tzèu, hô i pi tchēu ?

2. Kiĕ kiĕ kān iû, tsái Siún tchēu tōu. Sóu sēu tsòu tchēu ; leàng mà òu tchēu. Pėi tch'ōu tchė tzèu, hô i iù tchēu ?

3. Voyez le rat, il a quatre membres; et l'homme ne remplira pas ses devoirs! Un homme qui ne remplit pas ses devoirs, que ne meurt-il bien vite?

CHANT IX. KAN MAO.

Un 大夫 tái fōu grand préfet de 衛 Wéi honore de sa visite un sage qui demeure à Siun, dans la principauté de Wei.

1. L'étendard aux crins de bœuf se dresse dans la plaine de Siun. Le pennon est fixé à la hampe par un cordon de soie blanche. Il est porté sur une voiture trainée par quatre beaux coursiers attelés de front. Ce sage distingué, que rendra-t-il au grand préfet en retour d'un tel honneur?

2. L'étendard orné de faucons se dresse près des murs de Siun. Le pennon est fixé à la hampe par un cordon de soie blanche. Il est porté sur une voiture trainée par cinq superbes coursiers. Ce sage distingué, que donnera-t-il au grand préfet en retour de tant d'honneur?

3. Aspice murem, habet membra; homo autem non fungitur officiis! Homo qui non fungitur officiis, quare non illico moritur?

CHANT IX. Erecto hastili factum e bovinis caudis vexillum (advenientis magni præfecti) est in Siun campo. Albi coloris serica fascia colligat illud (hastile cum bovinis caudis); generosi equi quadrijugi vehunt illud. Ille insignis vir sapiens qua re utens donabit hunc (magnum præfectum)?

2. Erecto hastili signum falconibus pictum est in Siun proximo suburbiis loco. Albi coloris serica fascia alligat illud; generosi equi quinque vehunt illud. Ille insignis vir sapiens qua re utens donabit eum?

詩經

之城。素絲祝之、良馬六之、彼姝者子、何以告之。

載馳

① 載馳載驅、歸唁衛侯、驅馬悠悠、言至於漕、大夫跋涉、我心則憂。

3. Kiě kiě kān tsīng, tsái Siûn tchēu tch'êng. Sóu sēu tchǒu tchēu ; leàng mà lǒu tchēu. Pèi tch'ōu tchè tzèu, hô i kǒu tchēu ?

TSAI TCH'EU. **1. Tsái tch'êu tsái k'iū (k'iōu), kouēi ién Wéi heôu. K'iū mà iôu iôu, iên tchéu iū Ts'aô (Ts'eōu). Tái fōu pouǒ chě ; ngò sīn tsě iōu.**

3. L'étendard aux plumes de diverses couleurs se dresse dans les murs de Siun. Le pennon est fixé à la hampe par un cordon de soie blanche. Il est porté sur une voiture traînée par six bons coursiers. Ce sage distingué, quels enseignements donnera-t-il au grand préfet?

CHANT X. TSAI TCH'EU.

Une fille de 桓 **Houàn**, prince de 衛 **Wéi**, et de 宣姜 **Siuēn Kiāng** était mariée à 穆 **Mǒu**, prince de 許 **Hiù**. Ses parents étant déjà morts, elle apprend que la principauté de Wei a été ravagée par les barbares du nord. Elle veut aller consoler son frère, qui s'est retiré dans la ville de 漕 **Ts'aô**. Elle se met en marche, bien que les usages ne permettent pas à une femme mariée de retourner à la maison paternelle après la mort de ses parents. Au milieu de la route, elle est rappelée par un grand préfet. Elle exprime sa douleur dans ce chant.

1. Je voyage rapidement et presse la course de mes chevaux ; je veux retourner au pays natal et consoler le prince de Wei. A force de presser mes coursiers, je suis déjà loin, et j'espère aller jusqu'à Ts'ao. Mais le grand préfet est venu par terre et par eau ; mon cœur en est dans l'affliction.

3. Erecto hastili signum e plumis confectum est in Siun mœniis. Album sericum alligat illud ; generosi equi sex vehunt illud. Ille insignis vir sapiens de quo docebit eum?

徐光啓 **Siû Kouāng k'i**, ministre d'État et lettré célèbre, qui fut baptisé par le P. Matthieu Ricci à la cour de Wan li, dit dans son commentaire sur le Cheu king : « Les voitures des officiers étaient traînées par quatre chevaux attelés de front ; c'était la règle ordinaire. Ainsi, sous les Han, le préfet 太守 **t'ái cheòu** avait une voiture à quatre chevaux. Son traitement ayant été élevé jusqu'à vingt mille boisseaux de grain, il ajouta à sa voiture un cinquième cheval du côté droit. Pour cette raison un préfet est appelé 五馬 **òu mà**. On lit dans le Chou king : « Comme si je « devais avec des guides pourries condui- « re six chevaux attelés à une voiture. » Les règlements permettaient donc aux anciens, ce semble, d'atteler cinq ou six chevaux à leurs voitures. »

CHANT X. 1. Et celeriter vehor et equos concito ; domum repeto solatura Wei regni regulum. Stimulans equos longe processi ; statui ut pervenirem Ts'ao. Magnus præfectus per herbas et aquas properavit ; animus meus inde dolet.

(2) 既不我嘉、不能旋反、視爾不臧、我思不遠、既不我嘉、不能旋濟、視爾不臧、我思不閟、

(3) 陟彼阿丘、言采其蝱、女子善懷、亦各有行、許人尤之、衆穉且狂、

(4) 我行其野、芃芃其麥、控于大邦、誰因誰極、大夫君子、無我有尤、百爾所

2. Kí pŏu ngò kiā, pŏu nêng siuên fàn. Chéu èul pŏu tsāng ; ngò sēu pŏu iuèn. Ki pŏu ngò kiā, pŏu nêng siuên tsi. Chéu èul pŏu tsāng, ngò sēu pŏu pi.

3. Tchĕu pèi ngō k'iōu, iên ts'ài k'ì mŏung (mâng). Gniù tzèu chén houâi, ĭ kŏ iòu hìng (hâng). Hiù jênn iôu tchēu ; tchóung tchéu, ts'iè k'ouâng.

4. Ngò hìng k'ì iè ; p'ôung p'ôung k'ì mĕ (kĭ). K'óung iû tá pāng ; chouêi

2. Grand préfet, puisque vous n'approuvez pas ma détermination, je ne puis retourner dans mon pays. Mais, malgré cette désapprobation, la pensée du retour ne me quittera pas. Puisque vous n'approuvez pas ma détermination, je ne puis traverser l'eau et retourner dans mon pays. Mais, malgré cette désapprobation, je ne cesserai de penser au retour.

3. Je monte sur cette colline qui est plus élevée d'un côté que de l'autre ; j'y cueille des lis (pour dissiper ma tristesse). Beaucoup de pensées envahissent mon esprit de jeune fille ; chacune d'elles peut être mise à exécution. Les habitants de Hiu me blâment ; ils sont tous jeunes et inconsidérés dans leurs jugements.

4. Je traverse cette plaine, où le blé est déjà grand. Je voudrais gagner un prince puissant (à la cause du prince de Wei). Mais en qui mettrai-je mon appui? A qui aurai-je recours? Vous, grand préfet, et vous tous, habitants de Hiu, cessez de me blâmer.

2. Quum non me probes, non possum revertens domum redire. Licet videam te non probare, meum desiderium non abigetur. Quum non me probes, non possum revertens aquam trajicere. Licet videam te non probare, meum desiderium non inhibebitur.

3. Conscendo illum collem cujus latus unum altero altius est, ut colligam illius lilia. Ego junior puella multum cogitavi; etiam unamquamque (cogitationem meam) decet exsequi. Hiu incolæ criminantur illud; omnes sunt juvenes adeoque temere judicant.

許 était dans le 許 州 (Ho nan).

On dit que le lis a la propriété de dissiper la tristesse.

4. Ego percurro illum campum; altum est illius triticum. (Velim) attrahere magnum regnum (ut opem ferat Wei regulo). Cuinam innitar? quodnam adibo? Magne præfecte, incolæ

思、不如我所之、

衛一之五

淇奧

(1) 瞻彼淇奧、綠竹猗猗、有匪君子、如切如磋、如琢如磨、瑟兮僩兮、赫兮咺兮、有匪君子、終不可諼兮、

(2) 瞻彼淇奧、綠竹青青、有匪君子、充耳琇瑩、會

In ? chouéi kì ? Tái fōu kiūn tzèu, ôu ngò iòu iôu (i). Pĕ éul chóu sēu, pŏu jôu ngò chòu tchēu.

K'I IU. **1. Tchēn pèi K'î iŭ ; liŭ tchŏu ī ī (ngŏ ngŏ). Iòu fèi kiūn tzèu, jôu ts'iē, jôu ts'ouō, jôu tchouŏ, jôu mouô. Chĕ hì, hién hì, hĕ hi, hiuén hi. Iòu fèi kiūn tzèu ; tchōung pŏu k'ò hiuēn (hiuén) hî.**

2. Tchēn pèi K'î iŭ, liŭ tchŏu tsīng tsīng. Iòu fèi kiūn tzèu ; tch'ōung éul

Tous vos plans ne valent pas mon dessein de retourner dans mon pays.

LIVRE V. WEI FOUNG.

CHANT I. K'I IU.

武 **Cù**, prince de 衛 **Wéi** (812-757), s'est perfectionné lui-même, comme l'ouvrier travaille l'ivoire ou les pierres précieuses. Sa vertu s'est développée comme les bambous, qui naissent, grandissent et atteignent enfin toute leur croissance.

1. Voyez ce tournant de la K'i ; les bambous verdoyants sont jeunes et beaux. Ce prince sage, orné de toutes les qualités du corps et de l'âme, imite l'ouvrier qui coupe et lime l'ivoire, ou qui taille et polit les pierres précieuses. Sa tenue est grave, majestueuse, imposante, distinguée. Ce sage accompli ne pourra jamais être oublié.

2. Voyez ce tournant de la K'i ; les bambous verdoyants sont vigoureux et beaux. Ce sage orné de toutes les vertus porte des

omnes, nolite me culpare. Centena vos quæ excogitatis (consilia) minus bona sunt quam mei illuc reditus (consilium).

TITRE DU LIVRE. 衛一之五 Wei (regni cantica): primæ (partis) quintus (liber). La capitale de Wei fut d'abord la ville actuelle de 濬縣 **Siún hién**. V. page 3.

CHANT I. 1. Aspice illum K'i fluvii sinum ; viridantes bambusæ sunt novellæ et pulchræ. Habens decorem (corporis et animi), sapiens vir imitatur (artificem ebur cornuve) secantem, imitatur limantem ; imitatur (artificem lapillos) cædentem, imitatur polientem. Habitu compositus, gravis, verendus, insignis est. Habens decorem sapiens vir in perpetuum non poterit e memoria excidere.

2. Aspice illum K'i fluvii sinum ; virides bambusæ sunt firmæ et pulchræ. Habenti decorem sapienti viro tegmina aurium sunt pulchri lapilli ; suturæ pilei videntur stellæ, i. e.

弁如星。瑟兮僩兮、赫兮咺兮。有匪君子、終不可諼兮。
(3) 瞻彼淇奧、綠竹如簀。有匪君子、如金如錫、如圭如璧。寬兮綽兮、猗重較兮。善戲謔兮、不爲虐兮。

siòu ing, kouài pién jôu sīng. Chĕ hì, hièn hì, hĕ hì, hiuèn hì. Iòu fèi kiūn tzèu, tchōung pŏu k'ò hiuēn (hiuén) hi.

3. Tchēn pèi K'i iŭ ; liŭ tchŏu jôu tchĕ. Iòu fèi kiūn tzèu, jôu kīn, jôu sĭ, jôu kouēi, jôu pĭ. K'ouān hì, tch'ouŏ hì, i! tch'ôung kiŏ hi! Chén hì hiŏ hì, pŏu wêi iŏ hì.

pierreries sur les oreilles; les perles sur les coutures de son bonnet brillent comme des étoiles. Sa tenue est grave, majestueuse, imposante, distinguée. Ce sage accompli ne pourra jamais être oublié.

3. Voyez ce tournant de la K'i; les bambous verdoyants sont si drus qu'ils semblent former une natte. Ce sage accompli est comme l'or ou l'étain le plus pur, comme une tablette oblongue ou ronde parfaitement polie. Sa tenue annonce un cœur grand et généreux; oh! on dirait un haut dignitaire appuyé sur l'un des angles de sa voiture! Il rit et plaisante à propos; il n'a rien de dur.

gemmis ornatæ splendent. Habitu compositus, gravis, verendus, insignis est. Præditus decore sapiens vir in perpetuum non poterit de memoria excidere.

3. Aspice illum K'i fluvii sinum; viridantes bambusæ instar mattæ (sunt densæ). Præditus decore sapiens vir est similis auro, similis stanno, similis oblongæ tesseræ, similis rotundæ tesseræ. Liberalis, magnanimus, oh! in (vehiculo instructo) duobus cornibus! Belle facetus jocatur, nec est acerbus.

圭 **Kouēi,** 璧 **pĭ,** tablettes de jade employées comme marques de dignité ou de créance.

La première, qui était oblongue et terminée par des lignes droites, était donnée par l'empereur aux feudataires des trois premiers rangs 公侯伯. La seconde, de forme annulaire, était donnée aux feudataires des deux derniers rangs 子男.

重較 **Tch'ôung kiŏ,** les deux angles antérieurs de la caisse de la voiture d'un grand dignitaire. Ils étaient plus élevés que l'appui 軾 **chĕu,** et formaient comme deux cornes. Ils servaient eux-mêmes d'appuis, quand on se tenait debout dans la voiture.

考槃

（1）考槃在澗、碩
人之寬、獨寐寤
言、永矢弗諼、
（2）考槃在阿、碩
人之薖、獨寐寤
歌、永矢弗過、
（3）考槃在陸、碩
人之軸、獨寐寤
宿、永矢弗告、

碩人

（1）碩人其頎、衣
錦褧衣、齊侯之

K'AO P'AN. 1. **K'aò p'ân tsái kiên (kiēn), chēu jênn tchēu k'ouān (k'iuēn). Tŏu méi óu iên ; iòung chèu fŏu hiuēn.**

2. K'aò p'ân tsái ngō ; chēu jênn tchēu k'ouō. Tŏu méi óu kō ; iòung chèu fŏu kouō.

3. K'aò p'ân tsái lŏu; chēu jênn tchēu tchŏu. Tŏu méi óu siŭ ; iòung chèu fŏu kŏu.

CHEU JENN. **1. Chēu jênn k'î k'î ; i kin k'iŏung ī. Ts'î heôu tchēu tzèu, Wéi**

CHANT II. K'AO P'AN.

Contentement d'un solitaire.

1. Ce grand homme a construit sa hutte (ou, bat la mesure sur une écuelle) dans la vallée au bord de la rivière ; son cœur est au large. Il dort, veille et parle tout seul ; il jure que jamais il ne renoncera à ce bonheur.

2. Ce grand homme a construit sa hutte dans l'anfractuosité d'une montagne ; son cœur s'y trouve au large. Il dort, veille et chante tout seul ; il jure que jamais il ne désirera un plus grand bonheur.

3. Ce grand homme a construit sa hutte dans le flanc de la montagne ; (elle est si étroite qu') il se tient replié sur lui-même. Il dort, veille et se repose tout seul ; il jure que jamais il ne dira à personne (ce bonheur auquel personne ne contribue).

CHANT III. CHEU JENN.

Arrivée de 莊姜 **Tchouāng Kiāng** à la cour de 衞 **Wéi**, pour célébrer ses noces avec le prince 莊 **Tchouāng**.

1. C'est une femme de grande taille ; elle porte une tunique de

CHANT II. 1. Perfecta est casa ad vallis rivum; magni viri laxatur animus. Solus dormit, vigilat, loquitur; in perpetuum, jurat, non obliviscetur (hujus gaudii, nec aliud quæret).

槃 **P'ân**, écuelle, plat, hutte faite de pièces de bois ou de branchages agencés ensemble. Selon plusieurs interprètes, 考槃 signifie frapper sur une écuelle pour battre la mesure en chantant.

2. Perfecta est casa in montis anfractu; magni viri dilatatur animus. Solus dormit, vigilat, cantat; in perpetuum, jurat, nihil amplius cupiet.

3. Perfecta est casa in montis plano loco; magnus vir convolutus manet. Solus dormit, vigilat, iterum cubat; in perpetuum, jurat, non monebit (homines de suo gaudio quod ab hominibus nihil accipit).

子、衞侯之妻、東宮之妹、邢侯之姨、譚公維私、

②手如柔荑、膚如凝脂、領如蝤蠐、齒如瓠犀、螓首蛾眉、巧笑倩兮、美目盼兮、

③碩人敖敖、說于農郊、四牡有驕、朱幩

heôu tchēu ts'ī, tōung kōung tchēu méi, Hing heôu tchēu î, T'ân kōung wéi sēu (sī).

2. Cheòu jôu jeôu t'î, fōu jôu ing tchēu, ling jôu siôu ts'î, tch'éu jôu hóu sī, ts'în cheòu, ngô méi ; k'iaò siaó ts'ién hî, méi mòu p'án (p'ién) hî.

3. Chĕu jènn ngaô ngaô, chouéi iū nôung kiaō (kaō). Sèu meòu iòu kiaō (kaō).

toile simple sur une robe de soie à fleurs. Elle est la fille du prince de Ts'i, l'épouse du prince de Wei, la sœur de l'héritier présomptif de Ts'i, la sœur de la femme du prince de Hing; le prince de T'an a aussi épousé l'une de ses sœurs.

2. Ses doigts sont blancs et délicats comme les jeunes pousses de laiterons, sa peau blanche comme la graisse figée, son cou blanc et long comme le ver qui ronge le bois, ses dents blanches et régulières comme les pepins de la courge, son front large comme celui de la cigale, ses sourcils minces et arqués comme les antennes du papillon du ver à soie. Un gracieux sourire embellit ses joues; ses beaux yeux brillent d'un éclat où le noir et le blanc tranchent bien l'un sur l'autre.

3. C'est une femme d'une taille élevée; elle s'arrête au milieu des champs cultivés. Ses quatre coursiers sont robustes; des cordons rouges brillent aux extrémités des freins. Dans une voiture ornée

CHANT III. 1. Magna mulier illa procera est; induta est florida (veste supraque) cannabina veste simplici. Ts'i reguli filia, Wei reguli uxor, (Ts'i regni) hæredis soror natu minor, Hing reguli uxoris soror; T'an regulus est sororis maritus.

東宮 **Tōung kōung**, palais oriental. Cette expression désigne l'héritier présomptif, parce qu'il occupait la partie orientale du palais. Tchouang Kiang était sœur de l'héritier présomptif, et apparemment, née de la même mère, disent les commentateurs. Sa mère était donc la femme principale du prince de Ts'i. La principauté de 邢 **Hing** était dans le 邢臺縣 **Hing t'ài hièn**, qui dépend de 順德府 **Chouénn tĕ fòu** dans le Tcheu li. Celle de 譚 **T'ân** était près de 歷城 **Lĭ tch'ĕng**, qui dépend de Tsi nan fou dans le Chan toung.

2. Manuum (digiti) videntur tenera germina, pellis similis est concreto adipi, collum simile vermi lignum rodenti, dentes similes cucurbitæ granis; cicadæ caput, papilionis supercilia. Callido risu ornantur genæ; pulchri oculi albo colore nigroque colore clare distinctis.

3. Magna mulier valde procera est; sistit in culto campo. Quadrijugi equi mares habent robur; rubræ frenorum fasciæ sunt splendidæ (vel, rubris fas-

詩經

鑣鑣、翟茀以朝、大夫夙退、無使君勞。(4) 河水洋洋、北流活活、施罛濊濊、鱣鮪發發、葭菼揭揭、庶姜孽孽、庶士有朅、

氓

(1) 氓之蚩蚩、抱布貿絲、匪來貿絲、來即

Tchōu fênn piaō piaō (paō paō) ; tī fōu i tch'aô. Tái fōu sǒu t'ouéi ; ôu chéu kiūn laô.

4. Hô chouèi iâng iâng, pě liôu kouŏ kouŏ. Chēu kōu houŏ houŏ ; tchĕn iòu pouŏ pouŏ. Kiā t'ân kiě kiě. Chóu Kiāng iě iě ; chóu chéu iòu k'iě.

MENG. **1. Mêng tchēu tch'ēu tch'ēu, paó póu meóu sēu (sī). Fèi lâi meóu sēu (sī),**

de plumes de faisans et fermée par devant et par derrière, elle se rend au palais. Grands préfets, retirez-vous de bonne heure; ne fatiguez pas notre prince (laissez-le recevoir à loisir la princesse).

4. L'eau du Fleuve-Jaune est très élevée; son cours s'étend vers le nord. Les filets tombent dans l'eau avec bruit; les esturgeons de grande et de petite espèce sont très nombreux. Les roseaux et les joncs sont hauts. La princesse est accompagnée d'un brillant cortège de ses parentes; les hommes de sa suite ont une allure martiale.

CHANT IV. MENG.

Une fille de 衛 **Wéi,** dans l'espoir d'un légitime mariage, est partie à la suite d'un homme qui paraissait honnête et ne l'était pas. Elle déplore son imprudence et son infortune.

1. J'ai vu un homme qui paraissait simple et sans malice; il apportait une pièce de soie, et venait (disait-il) l'échanger contre

ciis ornata sunt frenorum extrema. Phasianorum plumis et velis (instructo vehiculo) utens adit aulam regiam. Magni præfecti, mature recedite; ne faciatis ut regulus fatigetur (publicis rebus).

Les mors des chevaux étaient terminés aux deux extrémités par des pièces de fer 鑣 **piaō** et ornés de cordons rouges. *Piaō piaō,* d'après Tchou Hi, exprime seulement la beauté de ces cordons. Les voitures des princesses étaient complétement fermées et ornées de plumes de faisans. Les tentures qui étaient devant et derrière s'appelaient 茀 **fŏu.**

4. Fluvii aqua est ingens; ad septentrionem fluit longo cursu. Jaciuntur retia cum strepitu; acipenseres tum majores tum minores plurimi sunt. Calami et junci alti sunt. Omnes Kiang (cognomine vocatæ puellæ quæ sponsam comitantur) pulchre ornatæ sunt; omnes viri (qui comitantur) habent militarem speciem.

Le Fleuve-Jaune passait au nord-ouest de Ts'i et au nord-est de Wei.

CHANT IV. 1. Vulgi homo rudis specie, (exeunte vere venisti) deferens sericam telam, empturus sericum filum (dixisti). Non venisti empturus sericum

我謀、送子涉淇、至于頓丘、匪我愆期、子無良媒、將子無怒、秋以爲期、

(2) 乘彼垝垣、以望復關、不見復關、泣涕漣漣、既見復關、載笑載言、爾卜爾筮、體無咎言、以爾車來、以我賄遷、

(3) 桑之未落、其

lâi tsí ngò meòu (mêi). Sóung tzèu chĕ K'i tchéu iû Touénn k'iōu (k'ī). Fèi ngò k'iēn k'i; tzèu óu leàng mêi. Ts'iāng tzèu óu nóu; ts'iōu i wêi k'i.

2. Chêng pèi kouèi iuên, i wàng Fŏu kouān (kiuēn). Pŏu kién Fŏu kouān (kiuēn), k'í t'i liên liên. Ki kién Fŏu kiuēn, tsái siaó tsái iên. Eùl pŏu èul chéu. T'i óu kióu iên, i èul kiū lâi, i ngò houéi ts'iēn.

3. Sāng tchēu wéi lŏ, k'i iĕ wŏ jŏ. Hiū tsiē! kiōu hi, óu chĕu sāng chénn

du fil de soie. En réalité, tu ne venais pas pour acheter du fil, mais pour me faire des propositions. Avec toi j'ai traversé la K'i, et suis allée jusqu'à Touenn k'iou. (C'était vers la fin du printemps. Je t'ai dit): «Ce n'est pas que je veuille différer notre union; mais il faut des entremetteurs honnêtes, et tu n'en as pas. Ne te fâche pas, je t'en prie; convenons ensemble de nous marier en automne.» (Alors nous nous sommes quittés).

2. (L'automne arrivé), je montai sur ce mur ruineux et regardai vers Fou kouan (ton pays). Tant que je ne vis personne venir de Fou kouan, je ne cessai de pleurer. Dès que je te vis venir de Fou kouan, je souris et dis: «Interroge la tortue, consulte l'achillée; si leurs réponses ne sont pas défavorables, tu amèneras ta voiture, et me conduiras avec mon bagage à ta maison.»

3. Les feuilles du mûrier paraissent onctueuses, jusqu'à l'époque

filum; venisti ut adires me deliberaturus. Comitans te, domine, vado trajeci K'i fluvium, perveni ad Touenn k'iou. (Tunc dixi tibi): «Non quod ego (velim) producere tempus statutum (ad matrimonium contrahendum); sed tu, domine, nondum habes bonos matrimonii conciliatores. Rogo te ne irascaris; autumnus habeatur pro statuto tempore.» (Nec te longius secuta sum).

2. (Postquam advenit autumnus), ascendi in illum ruinosum parietem, ut prospicerem Fou kouan (patriam tuam). Non videns (te venire ex) Fou kouan, flens lacrymata sum indesinenti modo. Quum vidi (te venientem ex) Fou kouan, statim risi, statim dixi: «Tu, interroges testudinem; tu, interroges achilleam. Signa nisi infausta sint, utens tuo vehiculo venias ut cum mea supellectile migrem (domum tuam).»

3. Dum morus nondum exuit folia, ejus folia unguinosa videntur. Heu! turtur, ne comedas mori fructus. Heu! mulier, ne cum viro voluptati indulgeas.

葉沃若。于嗟鳩兮。無食桑葚。于嗟女兮。無與士耽。士之耽兮。猶可說也。女之耽兮。不可說也。

(4) 桑之落矣。其黃而隕。自我徂爾。三歲食貧。淇水湯湯。漸車帷裳。女也不爽。士貳其行。士也罔極。二三其德。

(5) 三歲爲婦。靡室勞矣。夙興夜寐。靡

(chênn). Hiū tsiē! gniù hī, ôu iù chéu tān (tch'ēnn). Chéu tchēu tān (tch'ēnn) hî, iôu k'ò chouŏ iè. Gniù tchēu tān (tch'ēnn) hî, pŏu k'ò chouŏ iè.

4. Sāng tchēu lŏ i; k'î houâng êul iùn (în). Tzéu ngò ts'ôu èul, sān souéi chĕu p'în. K'î chouèi chāng chāng, tsiēn kiū wêi châng. Gniù iè pŏu chouàng (chouāng), chéu éul k'î hîng (hâng). Chéu iè wàng kĭ; éul sān k'î tĕ.

5. Sān souéi wêi fóu, mi chĕu laô i. Sŏu hīng, iè méi, mi iòu tchaŏ i. Iên kí

où elles commencent à tomber. (Ainsi la beauté du visage dure tout le temps de la jeunesse). Ah! tourterelle, ne mange pas de mûres, (tu deviendrais ivre). Ah! femme, ne recherche pas les plaisirs dans la société de l'homme. Chez l'homme, la recherche des plaisirs est encore explicable; chez la femme, elle ne l'est pas.

4. Les feuilles du mûrier jaunissent et tombent, quand le temps est venu. (Ainsi la beauté se flétrit). Entrée dans ta maison, j'ai souffert durant trois années les privations de l'indigence. (A présent que tu m'as chassée, je retourne dans mon pays). L'eau de la K'i est si haute qu'elle a mouillé la partie inférieure des tentures de ma voiture. Ce n'est pas moi, femme, qui ai manqué à ma parole; toi, homme, tu as changé de conduite deux ou trois fois. Tu ne connais pas de mesure; tes sentiments ont changé deux ou trois fois.

5. Ta femme durant trois années, je n'ai jamais trouvé trop pénible le soin des affaires domestiques. Me levant tôt, me couchant tard, je n'ai pas eu une matinée de repos. Quand notre

Viri lascivia adhuc potest explicari; mulieris lascivia non potest explicari.

Lorsque la tourterelle mange beaucoup de mûres, elle devient ivre, dit K'oung Ing ta.

4. Quum morus exuit folia, ea flavescunt et decidunt. Ex quo ego adivi tuam domum, tribus annis passa sum inopiam. (Nunc a te ejecta patriam domum repeto). K'i fluvii aqua est alta; madefactum est vehiculi velum inferius. Ego mulier fidem non fefelli; tu vir bis terque mutavisti tuam agendi rationem. Tu vir cares modo; bis terve mutavisti tuum animum.

5. Tribus annis fui uxor tua; non domus cura (mihi visa est) laboriosa. Mature surgens, sero cubans, non habui uno mane (otium). Pactio postquam perfecta est, devenisti ad sævitiam.

有朝矣、言既遂矣、至于暴矣、兄弟不知、咥其笑矣、靜言思之、躬自悼矣、

(6) 及爾偕老、老使我怨、淇則有岸、隰則有泮、總角之宴、言笑晏晏、信誓旦旦、不思其反、反是不思、亦已焉哉、

竹竿

(1) 籊籊竹竿、以

souéi i, tchéu iû paó i. Hiōung ti pŏu tchēu ; hi k'i siaó (saó) i. Tsing iên sēu tchēu ; kōung tzéu taó i.

6. Kí èul kiāi laò ; laò chéu ngò iuén. K'i tsĕ iòu ngán (ién) ; sĭ tsĕ iòu p'án (p'ién). Tsòung kiŏ tchēu ién, iên siaó ién ién. Sin chéu tán tán (tién tién) ; pŏu sēu k'i fàn (fàn). Fàn chéu pŏu sēu (sī) ; ĭ i iên tsāi (tsī).

TCHOU KAN. 1. Tí tí tchŏu kān i tiaó iû K'i. K'i pŏu èul sēu? iuén mouŏ tchéu tchēu.

convention a été conclue (et notre union dûment réglée), tu en es venu aux mauvais traitements. Mes frères ne savent pas (combien tu es coupable; quand ils me verront de retour), ils riront et se moqueront de moi. Je penserai à mon infortune en silence, et renfermerai mon chagrin dans mon cœur.

6. Je devais vivre et vieillir avec toi; la vieillesse venue, tu m'as donné de justes sujets de plaintes. La K'i a des digues; les marécages ont des bords élevés. (Toi, tu ne connais aucune limite). Quand j'avais encore les cheveux divisés en deux touffes, nous nous réjouissions ensemble; nous parlions, nous riions dans une concorde parfaite. Nous nous sommes juré fidélité en termes plus clairs que le jour; je ne prévoyais pas le changement actuel. Je n'ai pas prévu ce changement; à présent c'est fini (le mal est sans remède).

CHANT V. TCHOU KAN.

Une fille de la maison de Wei, mariée à un prince étranger, désire revoir les rivières, les bambous de son pays, et faire visite à ses parents.

1. Tiges de bambous longues et terminées en pointe, vous

Fratres mei nesciunt (culpam esse tuam; quum me reducem videbunt), illudentes ipsi ridebunt. Tacite cogitabo de illis rebus, mecum ipsa mœsta.

6. Cum te simul senectam transire oportebat; in senecta fecisti ut ego quererer (juste). K'i fluvius quidem habet aggeres; palustria etiam habent oras. (Tu vero nullum servas modum). Collectis in duo cornua capillis, i.e. juvenilibus annis, (tecum) gaudebam, loquebar, ridebam animo concordi. Data fide juravimus verbis diei instar claris; non prævidi hanc mutationem. Mutationem vere non prævidi; et actum est.

CHANT V. 1. Proceri et acuminati bambusarum caules, adhibemini ad

釣于淇、豈不爾
思、遠莫致之、
(2) 泉源在左、淇
水在右、女子有
行。遠兄弟父母。
(3) 淇水在右、泉
源在左、巧笑之
瑳、佩玉之儺。
(4) 淇水滺滺、檜
楫松舟、駕言出
遊、以寫我憂。
芄蘭
(1) 芄蘭之支、童

2. Ts'iuên iuên tsái tsouò, K'î chouèi tsái iòu (i). Gniù tzèu iòu hîng, iuén hiōung tí fóu mòu (mèi).

3. K'i chouèi tsái iòu (i), Ts'iuên iuên tsái tsouò. K'iaò siaò tchĕu ts'ouò, péi iŭ tchēu nouò.

4. K'î chouêi iôu iôu ; kouái tsiĕ sōung tcheōu. Kiá iên tch'ŏu iôu, i siĕ ngò iōu.

HOUAN LAN. **1. Houân lân tchēu tchēu, t'ôung tzèu péi hî. Souēi tsĕ péi hî,**

servez pour la pêche à la ligne dans la K'i. Comment ne penserais-je pas à vous? Mais je suis trop loin pour aller vous revoir.

2. La Ts'iuen coule à gauche et la K'i à droite. Une jeune fille qui s'en va pour se marier, quitte ses parents et ses frères.

3. La K'i coule à droite et la Ts'iuen à gauche. Les promeneurs dans leur rire gracieux laissent voir leurs belles dents blanches, et dans leur marche cadencée font entendre le son des jolies pierres suspendues à leurs ceintures.

4. La K'i déroule ses eaux; les rames de cèdre et les barques de sapin ne manquent pas. Attelez ma voiture, que je parte, me promène (sur les bords de la K'i) et dissipe ma tristesse.

CHANT VI. HOUAN LAN.

Vanité prétentieuse d'un jeune garçon qui portait à la ceinture un poinçon d'ivoire et un doigtier d'archer, comme un homme fait.

1. Ce jeune garçon, qui ressemble à la tige traînante du *houan*

piscandum hamo in K'i fluvio. Quomodo non de vobis cogitem? Remota nequeo pervenire illuc.

2. Ts'iuen scaturigo est ad sinistram, K'i fluvius ad dexteram. Junior filia habens iter (ad matrimonium contrahendum), recedit a parentibus et fratribus.

La K'i passait dans le sud-ouest de Wei et coulait vers l'est. La Ts'iuen iuen ou 百泉 **Pĕ ts'iuên** traversait le nord-ouest de Wei, coulait vers le sud-est, et se jetait dans la K'i. Une personne placée entre ces deux rivières et regardant vers leur confluent, avait la K'i à sa droite et la Ts'iuen à sa gauche.

3. Ki fluvius est ad dexteram, Ts'iuen scaturigo ad sinistram. (Incolarum) venuste ridentium albi dentes apparent; ad zonam appensorum lapillorum modulatus auditur tinnitus.

4. K'i aqua longe defluit; sunt cedrini remi et abiegnæ cymbæ. Jungatur vehiculum, ut abeam et spatier, ad solvendum meum mœrorem.

子佩觿、雖則佩觿、能不我知、容兮遂兮、垂帶悸兮、

(2) 芄蘭之葉、童子佩韘、雖則佩韘、能不我甲、容兮遂兮、垂帶悸兮、

河廣

(1) 誰謂河廣、一葦杭之、誰

nêng pŏu ngò tchēu. Iôung hi souéi hi, tch'ouêi tái ki hì.

2. Houân lân tchāu iĕ, t'ôung tzèu péi chĕ. Souēi tsĕ péi chĕ, nêng pŏu ngò kiă (kiĕ). Iôung hi souéi hi, tch'ouêi tái ki hi.

HO KOUANG. 1. Chouêi wéi Hô kouàng ? Ĭ wèi hàng tchēu. Chouêi wéi Sóung iuén ? K'i iù wáng (wàng) tchēu.

lan, porte à la ceinture un poinçon d'ivoire. Bien qu'il porte un poinçon d'ivoire, je n'ai pas encore découvert sa capacité. Sa tenue est nonchalante et ses manières trop libres; les extrémités de sa ceinture sont pendantes.

2. Ce jeune garçon, qui ressemble à la feuille du *houan lan,* porte à la ceinture un doigtier d'ivoire. Bien qu'il porte un doigtier d'ivoire, il ne m'a pas encore fait estimer sa capacité. Nonchalant dans sa tenue et trop libre dans ses manières, il laisse flotter mollement les extrémités de sa ceinture.

CHANT VII. HO KOUANG.

Une fille de 宣姜 **Siuēn Kiāng,** princesse de 衛 **Wéi,** ayant été mariée à 桓 **Houân,** prince de 宋 **Sóung,** lui donna un fils; puis fut répudiée et obligée de retourner à Wei. Après la mort de Houan, elle apprend que 襄公 **Siāng kōung,** son fils, a hérité de la principauté. Elle désire vivement aller le voir. Une seule chose l'arrête : comme elle a été répudiée, les convenances ne lui permettent pas de retourner à Soung. Elle compte pour rien la distance et le passage du Fleuve-Jaune.

1. Qui dira que le Fleuve-Jaune est large? Je le traverserais sur un roseau (ou sur une botte de roseaux). Qui dira que Soung est

CHANT VI. 1. *Houan lan* (repentis plantæ) ramulus, adolescentulus ad zonam appendit eburneum acumen. Licet jam ad zonam appendat eburneum acumen, (ejus) peritia non a me cognita est. Remissus, licentiosus videtur; pendula zona vacillat.

2. *Houan lan* folium, adolescentulus ad zonam defert eburneum sagittarii digitale. Licet jam ad zonam deferat eburneum digitale, peritia non a me magni æstimatur. Remissus, licentiosus videtur; pendula zona vacillat.

Le *houan lan* est une plante rampante, à jus laiteux, comestible. Le poinçon d'ivoire servait à défaire les nœuds. Le doigtier d'ivoire se met au pouce de la main droite pour tirer de l'arc.

CHANT VII. 1. Quis dicet Fluvium esse latum? Una arundine trajicerem

謂宋遠，跂予望之。

(2) 誰謂河廣，曾不容刀，誰謂宋遠，曾不崇朝。

伯兮

(1) 伯兮朅兮，邦之桀兮，伯也執殳，爲王前驅。

(2) 自伯之東，首如飛蓬，豈無膏沐，誰適爲容。

2. Chouêi wêi Hô kouàng? Ts'êng pŏu iôung taŏ. Chouêi wêi Sóung iuèn? Ts'êng pŏu tch'ôung tchaŏ.

PE HI. **1. Pĕ hî k'iĕ hî, pāng tchĕu kiĕ hi. Pĕ iè tchĕu chôu, wêi wâng ts'iên k'iū.**

2. Tzéu pĕ tchĕu tōung, cheòu jôu fēi p'ôung. K'i ôu kaŏ mŏu? Chouêi tĭ wêi iôung?

loin? En me dressant sur la pointe des pieds, je l'apercevrais d'ici.

2. Qui dira que le Fleuve-Jaune est large? Son lit ne contiendrait pas même une nacelle. Qui dira que Soung est loin? Je ferais le voyage en moins d'une matinée.

CHANT VIII. PE HI.

La femme d'un officier militaire déplore la longue absence de son mari.

1. Mon seigneur est vaillant; c'est l'homme le plus capable du pays. Mon seigneur, la lance à la main sur son char de guerre, conduit l'avant-garde de l'empereur.

2. Depuis que mon noble mari est allé vers l'orient, ma tête est comme l'armoise dont la graine voltige emportée par le vent. Est-ce que je manque de parfum et d'eau? (Non; mais en l'absence de mon mari), pour quel maître voudrais-je me parer?

illum. Quis dicet Soung regnum remotum esse? In pedum digitos arrecta ego prospicerem illud.

La capitale de Wei était dans le 衛輝府 **Wéi houēi fòu,** et celle de Soung dans le 歸德府 **Kouēi tĕ fòu.** Le Fleuve-Jaune les séparait.

2. Quis dicet Fluvium esse latum? At non caperet parvam scapham. Quis dicet Soung remotum esse? At (iter) non est integri mane.

CHANT VIII. 1. Dominus meus fortis est, totius regni præstantissimus vir. Dominus tenens hastam, propter regem præcurrens vehitur.

殳 **Chôu,** faisceau de lattes de bambou, de forme octogone, et sans pointe de fer, qui servait en guise de lance ou de massue sur les chars de guerre.

2. Ex quo dominus abiit ad orientem, caput meum simile est volitanti artemisiæ. Num caream unguento et aqua ad caput lavandum? (At) cui domino curem corpus ornare?

蓬 **P'ôung,** plante dont le vent met les feuilles en désordre, et emporte la graine qui est munie de duvet. 適 **Tĭ** signifie 主 **tchòu** maître.

(3) 其雨其雨、杲杲出日、願言思伯、甘心首疾、(4) 焉得諼草、言樹之背、願言思伯、使我心痗、

有狐

(1) 有狐綏綏、在彼淇梁、心之憂矣、之子無裳、(2) 有狐綏綏、在彼淇厲、心之憂矣、之子無帶、(3) 有狐綏綏、在

3. K'i iù ! k'i iù ! Kaò kaò tch'ŏu jĕu. Iuén ién sēu pĕ, kān sīn cheòu tsĭ.

4. Iēn tĕ hiuēn ts'aò? ién chóu tchĕu péi. Iuén ién sēu pĕ, chéu ngò sīn méi.

IOU HOU. **1. Iòu hôu souēi souéi, tsái péi K'i leàng. Sīn tchēu iōu i, tchēu tzèu ŏu châng.**

2. Iòu hôu souēi souēi, tsái péi K'i lí. Sīn tchéu iōu i ; tchēu tzèu ŏu tái (ti).

3. Iòu hôu souēi souēi, tsái péi K'i tchĕ. Sīn tchēu iōu i; tchēu tzèu ŏu fŏu (p'ĕ).

3. Oh ! la pluie ! que la pluie tombe ! Le soleil apparaît brillant. (Je suis comme un homme qui désire vivement la pluie, et voit toujours le ciel serein.). Je veux que mon esprit soit tout occupé du souvenir de mon seigneur, au point d'en avoir mal à la tête.

4. Où trouverai-je l'hémérocalle? Je la planterai derrière ma maison, (et la mangerai pour dissiper ma tristesse. Mais non); je veux penser à mon mari, au point d'en avoir le cœur malade.

CHANT IX. IOU HOU.

Le poète dépeint, sous la figure d'un renard, un malheureux habitant de Wei, qui, chassé de sa maison par les troubles de son pays, manque de vêtements.

1. Un renard se promène seul auprès de ce barrage établi dans la K'i. Mon cœur est affligé ; cet homme n'a pas de vêtement inférieur.

2. Un renard se promène seul sur le bord de la K'i auprès du gué profond. Mon cœur est affligé ; cet homme n'a pas de ceinture.

3. Un renard se promène seul sur le bord de la K'i. Mon cœur

3. Utinam pluvia (decidat)! utinam pluvia (decidat) ! Splendens apparet sol. Volo cogitare de domino, toto animo ita ut caput doleat.

4. Quomodo nanciscar hemerocallem? plantabo eam a domus tergo. Volo cogitare de domino, ita ut meum cor ægrotet.

諼 **Hiuēn**, oublier. On mange l'hémérocalle *hiuēn ts'aò* pour oublier les chagrins.

CHANT IX. 1. Est vulpes sola incedens ad illud K'i fluvii lapideum septum (quo pisces inhibentur et capiuntur). Animus meus dolet; ille vir non habet vestem qua a renibus ad talos tegatur.

2. Est vulpes sola incedens ad illud K'i fluvii altum vadum. Animus meus dolet; ille vir caret zona.

3. Est vulpes sola incedens ad illud K'i fluvii latus. Animus meus dolet; ille vir caret vestibus.

彼淇側、心之憂矣、
之子無服、

木瓜

(1) 投我以木瓜、報之以瓊琚、匪報也、永以爲好也、

(2) 投我以木桃、報之以瓊瑤、匪報也、永以爲好也、

(3) 投我以木李、報之以瓊玖、匪報也、永以爲好也、

MOU KOUA. **1. T'eǒu ngò i mǒu kouā (kōu); paó tchēu i k'iôung kiū. Fèi paó iè; iòung i wêi haó iè.**

2. T'eǒu ngò i mǒu t'aô; paó tchēu i k'iôung iaô. Fèi paó iè; iòung i wêi haó iè.

3. T'eǒu ngò i mǒu li; paó tchēu i k'iôung kiòu (ki). Fèi paó iè; iòung i wêi haó iè.

est affligé; cet homme n'a pas de vêtements pour se couvrir.

CHANT X. MOU KOUA.

Les petits présents en appellent de grands; mais l'amitié vaut mieux que tous les présents.

1. A celui qui m'offre un coing, je donne une belle pierre de prix *kiu*. Par là je ne prétends pas le payer de retour, (car aucun présent ne vaut l'affection qu'il m'a témoignée par sa prévenance); mais je veux rendre notre amitié à jamais durable.

2. A celui qui m'offre une pêche, je donne une pierre de prix *iao*. Par là je ne crois pas le payer de retour suffisamment; mais je veux rendre notre amitié à jamais durable.

3. A celui qui m'offre une prune, je donne une pierre de prix de couleur noire. Je ne crois pas que cela suffise pour le payer de retour; mais je veux rendre notre amitié à jamais durable.

CHANT X. 1. Qui donat me malo cidonio, retribuo illi e rubro lapillo zonæ fibulam, vel pulchram zonæ fibulam; non ut par pari referam (nam nihil par esse potest amori quem mihi significavit), sed ut in perpetuum inde sit amicitia.

佩玉

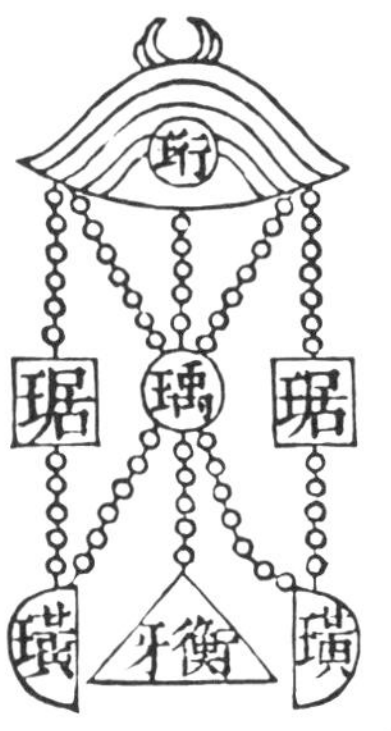

瓊 **K'iôung,** pierre de prix de couleur rouge, beauté d'une pierre de prix.

琚 **Kiū,** nom donné à deux des pierres de prix qu'on portait suspendues à la ceinture. La figure ci-contre représente les pierres de prix qu'on portait à la ceinture 佩玉 **pèi iŭ.**

2. Qui donat me malo persico, retribuo ei pulchrum lapillum *iaò* nomine; non ut par pari referam,...

3. Qui donat me pruno, retribuo ei pulchrum nigro colore lapillum;...

王一之六

黍離

① 彼黍離離、彼稷之苗、行邁靡靡、中心搖搖、知我者、謂我心憂、不知我者、謂我何求、悠悠蒼天、此何人哉。

② 彼黍離離、彼稷之穗、行邁靡靡、中心如醉、知我者、謂我心憂、不知我者、謂我何求、悠悠蒼天、此何人哉。

CHOU LI. 1. **Pèi chòu lì lì! pèi tsĭ tchēu miaô! Hîng mái mi mi; tchōung sīn iaô iaô. Tchēu ngò tchè, wéi ngò sīn iōu. Pŏu tchēu ngò tchè, wéi ngò hô k'iôu. Iôu iôu ts'āng t'iēn (t'īn), ts'èu hô jènn tsāi?**

2. Pèi chòu lì lì! pèi tsĭ tchēu souéi! Hîng mái mi mi; tchōung sīn jôu tsouéi. Tchēu ngò tchè, wéi ngò sīn iōu. Pŏu tchēu ngò tchè, wéi ngò hô k'iôu. Iôu iôu ts'āng t'iēn (t'īn), ts'èu hô jènn tsāi?

LIVRE VI. WANG FOUNG.

CHANT I. CHOU LI.

L'empereur 平王 **P'ing wâng** a transféré sa cour de 鎬 **Haó** (près de Si ngan fou) à 洛陽 **Lŏ iâng** (près de Ho nan fou). Un 大夫 **tái fōu** grand officier, passant à Hao, voit les moissons croître sur l'emplacement de l'ancienne résidence des Tcheou. La tristesse s'empare de son cœur.

1. Ici du millet *chou* avec sa tête pendante! ici du millet *tsi* encore en herbe! J'avance d'un pas lent; mon cœur est très agité. Ceux qui me connaissent, disent que je suis triste. Ceux qui ne me connaissent pas, demandent ce que je cherche. O ciel azuré, si elevé au-dessus de nous! quel homme a causé ce changement?

2. Ici du millet *chou* avec sa tête pendante! ici du millet *tsi* en épi! J'avance d'un pas lent; j'ai l'esprit troublé comme un homme ivre. Ceux qui me connaissent, disent que je suis triste. Ceux qui ne me connaissent pas, demandent ce que je cherche. O ciel azuré, ciel si loin de nous! quel homme a causé ce changement?

TITRE DU LIVRE. 王一之六 Imperialis (territorii cantica): primæ (partis) sextus liber. Le domaine impérial dont il est ici question, était la ville de Lo iang et ses environs. Voy. page 3.

CHANT I. 1. Illic *chòu* milium pendulo capite! illic *tsĭ* milii caules! Incedens progredior tardo passu; intimo animo commotus agitor. Qui norunt me, dicunt meum animum angi. Qui non cognoscunt me, petunt ego quid quæram. O procul remotum cæruleum cœlum! illud quisnam homo fecit?

黍 **Chòu**, 稷 **tsĭ**, deux variétés d'une même espèce de millet à panicules.

2. Illic *chòu* capite pendulo! illic *tsĭ* spicæ! Incedens progredior tardo passu; intimo animo quasi ebrius...

③彼黍離離、彼稷之實、行邁靡靡、中心如噎、知我者、謂我心憂、不知我者、謂我何求、悠悠蒼天、此何人哉、

君子于役

①君子于役、不知其期、曷至哉、雞棲于塒、日之夕矣、羊牛下來、君子于役、如之何勿思、

②君子于役、不日

3. Pèi chòu lî lî, pèi tsĭ tchēu chĕu ! Hîng mái mi mi ; tchōung sīn jôu iĕ (ĭ). Tchēu ngò tchè, wéi ngò sīn iōu. Pŏu tchēu ngò tchè, wéi ngò hô k'iôu. Iôu iôu ts'āng t'iēn (t'īn), ts'èu hô jênn tsāi ?

KIUN TZEU IU I. **1. Kiūn tzèu iû ĭ ; pŏu tchēu k'î k'î. Hŏ tchéu tsāi (tsī)? Kī sī iū chêu ; jĕu tchēu sĭ i, iâng iôu hiá lâi (lî). Kiūn tzèu iû ĭ ; jôu tchēu hô ŏu sēu (sī) ?**

2. Kiūn tzèu iû ĭ ; pŏu jĕu pŏu iuĕ. Hŏ k'î iôu houĕ ? Kī sī iū kiĕ ; jĕu tchēu

3. Ici du millet *chou* avec sa tête pendante ! ici du millet *tsi* dont le grain est presque mûr ! J'avance d'un pas lent ; je suis comme suffoqué. Ceux que me connaissent, disent que je suis triste. Ceux qui ne me connaissent pas, demandent ce que je cherche. O ciel azuré qui es si élevé au-dessus de nous ! quel homme est l'auteur de ce changement ?

CHANT II. KIUN TZEU IU I.

La femme d'un officier déplore la longue absence de son mari.

1. Mon seigneur est sous les armes ; je ne sais quand il doit revenir ? Où est-il à présent ? La poule prend son repos dans le trou du mur ; vers la fin du jour, les brebis et les bœufs reviennent dans leurs étables. Mon seigneur est retenu par le service militaire (et privé de repos) ; comment ne penserais-je pas à lui ?

2. Mon seigneur est sous les armes ; les jours, les mois écoulés depuis son départ, ne se peuvent plus compter. Quand

3. Illic *chòu* capite pendulo ! illic *tsĭ* grana ! Incedens progredior tardo passu ; intimo animo quasi suffocatus. Qui norunt me...

CHANT II. 1. Dominus meus militat ; non scio ejus (reditus) statutum tempus. Quo pervenit ? Gallina insidet in parietis foramine ; diei extremo, oves et boves descendentes redeunt. Dominus meus militat ; quomodo abstineam ne cogitem ?

2. Dominus meus militat ; nec dies nec menses (ex quibus profectus est, computari possunt). Quando ille poterit congredi (mecum) ? Gallina insidet in palo ; diei extremo, oves et

不月，曷其有佸。雞
棲于桀，日之夕矣，
牛羊下括。君子于
役，苟無饑渴。

君子陽陽

(1) 君子陽陽，左執
簧，右招我由房，其
樂只且。

(2) 君子陶陶，左執
翿，右招我由敖，其
樂只且。

揚之水

(1) 揚之水，不流束

sī i, iâng iôu hiá kouě. Kiūn tzèu iû ĭ; keòu ôu kī k'ŏ (k'iĕ)!

KIUN TZEU IANG IANG. 1. Kiūn tzèu iàng iàng. Tsouò tchĕu houâng; iôu tchaŏ ngò iôu fâng. K'i lŏ tchèu tsiū!

2. Kiūn tzèu t'aô t'aô. Tsouò tchĕu t'aô; iòu tchaŏ ngò iôu ngaô. K'i lŏ tchèu tsiū!

IANG TCHEU CHOUEI. 1. Iâng tchēu chouêi, pŏu liôu chŏu sīn. Pèi ki tchēu

reviendra-t-il auprès de moi? La poule juche sur un poteau; à la fin du jour, les brebis et les bœufs rentrent dans leurs étables. Mon seigneur est retenu par le service militaire (et ne revient pas); si du moins il n'avait pas à souffrir de la faim ni de la soif!

CHANT III. KIUN TZEU IANG IANG.

Joie d'une femme au retour de son mari. Celui-ci danse et joue de la flûte.

1. Mon seigneur est content. De la main gauche il tient sa flûte; de la droite il me fait signe et m'appelle à la maison. Oh! quelle joie!

2. Mon seigneur est joyeux. De la main gauche il tient l'éventail de plumes (des pantomimes); de la droite il me fait signe et m'appelle au théâtre. Oh! quelle joie!

CHANT IV. IANG CHEU CHOUEI.

Les soldats de l'empereur 平王 P'ing wâng sont en garnison dans les principautés de Chenn, de Fou et de Hiu, et les défendent contre les attaques des habitants de 楚 Tch'ou. Ils gémissent de vivre séparés de leurs familles.

1. Le courant est faible et n'a pas la force d'entraîner un fagot.

boves descendentes adveniunt. Dominus meus militat; si modo non esuriret, nec sitiret!

CHANT III. 1. Dominus valde gaudet. Sinistra tenet fistulæ ligulam (mimorum more); dextra advocat me e domo. Hoc gaudium (quantum est)!

2. Dominus lætatur. Sinistra tenet e plumis flabellum; dextra vocat me e theatro. Hoc gaudium (quantum est)!

Les pantomimes se cachaient le visage avec un éventail de plumes.

CHANT IV. 1. Tarde fluit aqua, nec valet deferre fascem ramalium. Illæ uxores et liberi non sunt nobiscum in præsidiis regni Chenn. Quam cogito! quam desidero! Quo mense revertentes redibimus domum?

詩經

薪、彼其之子、不與
我戍申、懷哉、
曷月予還歸哉、
(2) 揚之水、不流束
楚、彼其之子、不與
我戍甫、懷哉、
曷月予還歸哉、
(3) 揚之水、不流束
蒲、彼其之子、不與
我戍許、懷哉、
曷月予還歸哉、
中谷有蓷
(1) 中谷有蓷、暵其

tzèu pŏu iù ngò siŭ Chēnn. Houâi (Houêi) tsāi ! houêi tsāi ! Hŏ iuĕ iù siuên kouēi tsāi ?

2. Iâng tchēu chouèi, pŏu liôu chóu tch'òu. Pèi ki tchēu tzèu pŏu iù ngò siŭ Fòu. Houâi (Houêi) tsāi ! houêi tsāi ! Hŏ iuĕ iù siuên kouēi tsāi ?

3. Iâng tchēu chouèi, pŏu liôu chŏu p'ŏu (p'òu). Pèi kí tchēu tzèu pŏu iù ngò siŭ Hiù. Houêi tsāi ! houêi tsāi! Hŏ iuĕ iù siuên kouēi tsāi ?

TCHOUNG KOU IOU T'OUEI. **1. Tchōung kŏu ióu t'ouēi ; hán k'î kān i.**

Ainsi nos femmes et nos enfants (sont faibles, et) ne sont pas avec nous dans les garnisons de Chenn. Oh ! comme je pense à ma famille! que je désire la revoir ! En quel mois retournerons-nous dans nos foyers?

2. Le courant est faible et n'a pas la force d'entraîner une bourrée d'épines. Nos femmes et nos enfants ne sont pas avec nous dans le pays de Fou. Oh! comme je pense à ma famille! que je désire la revoir! En quel mois retournerons-nous dans nos foyers?

3. Le courant est faible et n'a pas la force d'entraîner une botte de joncs. Nos femmes et nos enfants ne sont pas à Hiu avec nous. Oh ! comme je pense à ma famille! que je désire la revoir ! En quel mois retournerons-nous dans nos foyers?

CHANT V. TCHOUNG KOU IOU T'OUEI.

La disette, causée par la sècheresse, force les personnes d'une même famille à se séparer et à chercher leur nourriture en différentes contrées.

1. Dans la vallée croît l'agripaume ; dans les terrains secs elle

申 **Chēnn**, à présent 信陽州 **Siniâng tcheōu** dans le Jou gning fou (Ho nan).

2. Tarde fluit aqua, nec valet deferre fascem veprium. Illæ uxores liberique non sunt nobiscum in præsidiis regni Fou. Quam cogito!...

甫 **Fòu**, à présent 南陽縣 **Nân iâng hièn** dans le Nan iang fou (Ho nan).

3. Tarde fluit aqua, nec valet deferre fascem juncorum. Illæ uxores liberique non sunt nobiscum in præsidiis Hiu regni...

許 **Hiù**, à présent 許州 **Hiù tcheōu** dans le Ho nan.

CHANT V. 1. In valle est leonurus; aruit ille in siccis locis. Sunt mulieres (a domesticis suis) divulsæ, derelictæ; gementes illæ suspirant. Gementes illæ

乾矣。有女仳離。嘅其嘆矣。嘅其嘆矣。遇人之艱難矣。

(2)中谷有蓷。暵其脩矣。有女仳離。條其歗矣。條其歗矣。遇人之不淑矣。

(3)中谷有蓷。暵其濕矣。有女仳離。啜其泣矣。啜其泣矣。何嗟及矣。

兔爰

(1)有兔爰爰。雉離

Iòu gniù p'i lî, k'ài k'ì t'ān i. K'ài k'ì t'ān i; iù jênn tchēu kiēn nân i.

2. Tchōung kǒu iòu t'ouēi ; hán k'ì siōu (chǒu) i. Iòu gniù p'i lî, t'iaǒ k'ì siaó (siǔ) i. T'iaǒ k'ì siaó (siǔ) i ; iù jênn tchēu pǒu chǒu i.

3. Tchōung kǒu iòu t'ouēi ; hán k'ì chēu i. Iòu gniù p'i lî ; tchouǒ k'ì k'ì i. Tchouǒ k'ì k'ì i ; hǒ tsiē kì i ?

T'OU IUEN. **1. Iòu t'óu iuên iuên ; tchéu lî iû louǒ. Ngǒ chēng tchēu tch'ōu,**

s'est desséchée. Des femmes quittent leurs familles et sont dénuées de tout secours ; elles gémissent et soupirent. Elles gémissent et soupirent sous le poids des malheurs auxquels la vie humaine est exposée.

2. Dans la vallée croît l'agripaume ; déjà grande (ou dans les terrains secs) elle s'est desséchée. Des femmes quittent leurs familles et manquent de tout secours. Elles poussent de longs soupirs semblables à des sifflements. Elles poussent de longs soupirs semblables à des sifflements, sous le poids de leur infortune.

3. Dans la vallée croît l'agripaume ; elle est desséchée, même dans les terrains humides. Des femmes quittent leurs familles et manquent de tout secours ; elles versent des torrents de larmes. Elles versent des torrents de larmes ; mais que leur servent leurs lamentations ?

CHANT VI. T'OU IUEN.

Les princes se révoltent contre l'empereur ; le trouble est partout. Ceux qui, semblables au faisan, sont courageux et amis du devoir, ont beaucoup à souffrir. Ceux qui sont rusés comme le lièvre, échappent seuls à l'infortune. Cette vue inspire le dégoût de la vie.

1. Le lièvre s'avance lentement avec précaution ; le faisan tombe

suspirant; offenderunt hominum ærumnas, i.e. ærumnas quibus obnoxia est vita humana.

2. In valle est leonurus; aruit ille adultus (aut in locis siccis). Sunt mulieres divulsæ, derelictæ; diu producto sono illæ sibilant. Diu producto sono illæ sibilant; offenderunt hominum infortunium. 脩 **Siōu**, grand, sec.

3. In valle est leonurus; aruit ille in humidis locis. Sunt mulieres divulsæ, derelictæ; lacrymantes illæ plorant. Lacrymantes illæ plorant; quid gementes assequentur?

于羅、我生之初、尚無爲。我生之後、逢此百罹、尚寐無吪、

(2) 有兔爰爰、雉離于罦、我生之初、尚無造、我生之後、逢此百憂、尚寐無覺、

(3) 有兔爰爰、雉離于罿、我生之初、尚無庸、我生之後、逢此百凶、尚寐無聰、

葛藟

(1) 緜緜葛藟、在河

cháng ôu wêi (wô). Ngò chēng tchēu heóu, fôung ts'éu pĕ lî (louô). Cháng méi ôu wô!

2. Iòu t'óu iuên iuên ; tchéu lî iū fōu (piaó). Ngò chēng tchēu tch'ōu, cháng ôu tsaó. Ngò chēng tchēu heóu, fôung ts'éu pĕ iōu (iaó). Cháng méi ôu kiaó!

3. Iòu t'óu iuên iuên ; tchéu lî iū tch'ôung. Ngò chēng tchēu tch'ōu, cháng ôu iôung. Ngò chēng tchēu heóu, fôung ts'éu pĕ hiōung. Cháng méi ôu ts'ōung!

KO LEI. **1. Miên miên kŏ lèi tsái Hô tchēu hòu. Tchōung iuén hiōung ti,**

dans le filet. Dans les premières années de ma vie, les difficultés n'existaient pas encore. Mais ensuite mille maux m'ont assailli. Que ne puis-je dormir privé de mouvement (que ne puis-je mourir)!

2. Le lièvre s'avance lentement avec précaution; le faisan tombe dans le trébuchet. Dans les premières années de ma vie, les difficultés n'existaient pas encore. Mais ensuite mille chagrins m'ont environné. Que ne puis-je dormir privé de sentiment!

3. Le lièvre s'avance avec lenteur et précaution ; le faisan tombe dans le trébuchet. Dans les premiers temps de ma vie, j'étais exempt d'afflictions ; mais ensuite mille infortunes me sont survenues. Que ne puis-je dormir et ne plus rien entendre!

CHANT VII. KO LEI.

Un homme obligé de vivre loin de sa famille déplore son sort.

1. Les dolics unis entre eux s'étendent sur la rive du Fleuve-

CHANT VI. 1. Est lepus cautus et tardus; phasianus incidit in rete. Meæ vitæ initio, adhuc nihil erat negotii. Meæ vitæ posteriori tempore, offendi illa centena mala. Utinam dormiam carens motu!

2. Est lepus cautus et tardus; phasianus incidit in decipulam. Meæ vitæ initio, adhuc nihil erat negotii. Meæ vitæ posteriori tempore, offendi illas centenas curas. Utinam dormiam carens sensu!

3. Est lepus cautus et tardus; phasianus incidit in decipulam. Meæ vitæ initio, adhuc non usus sum, i.e. non affectus sum ærumnis. Meæ vitæ posteriori tempore, offendi illa centena infortunia. Utinam dormiam carens auditu!

CHANT VII. 1. Longi et inter se continentes phaseoli super Fluvii aggerem.

之滸、終遠兄弟、謂他人父、謂他人父、亦莫我顧、

(2)緜緜葛藟、在河之涘、終遠兄弟、謂他人母、謂他人母、亦莫我有、

(3)緜緜葛藟、在河之漘、終遠兄弟、謂他人昆、謂他人昆、亦莫我聞、

采葛

(1)彼采葛兮、一日不見、如三月兮、

wéi t'ouō jênn fòu. Wéi t'ouō jênn fòu, ĭ mouŏ ngò kóu (kòu).

2. Miên miên kŏ lèi tsái Hô tchēu séu (i). Tchōung iuén hiōung ti, wéi t'ouō jênn mòu (méi). Wéi t'ouō jênn mòu (méi), ĭ mouŏ ngò iòu (i).

3. Miên miên kŏ lèi tsái Hô tchēu chouênn. Tchōung iuén hiōung ti, wéi t'ouō jênn kouēnn. Wéi t'ouō jênn kouēnn, ĭ mouŏ ngò wênn.

TS'AI KO. 1. Pèi ts'ài kŏ (kiĕ) hî. Ĭ jĕu pŏu kién, jôu sān iuĕ hî.

Jaune. Moi, je suis séparé pour toujours de mes frères ; je donne le nom de père à un étranger. Je donne le nom de père à un étranger, et il ne s'occupe pas de moi.

2. Les dolics s'étendent au bord du Fleuve en se tenant entre eux. Moi, je suis séparé de mes frères pour toujours; je donne le nom de mère à une étrangère. Je donne le nom de mère à une étrangère, et elle ne me considère pas comme son fils.

3. Les dolics s'étendent sur la digue escarpée du Fleuve sans jamais se séparer. Moi, je suis séparé de mes frères pour toujours; je donne le nom de frères à des étrangers. Je donne le nom de frères à des étrangers, et ils sont sourds à ma voix.

CHANT VIII. TS'AI KO.

Désir de voir un ami que ses ocupations tiennent éloigné.

1. Il cueille le dolic. Un jour passé sans le voir me paraît long comme trois mois.

In perpetuum reliqui fratres ; voco alienum hominem patrem. Voco alienum hominem patrem, et non de me curat.

2. Longi et inter se continentes phaseoli ad Fluvii oram. In perpetuum reliqui fratres; voco alienam mulierem matrem. Voco alienam mulierem matrem, et non me habet (pro filio).

3. Longi et inter se continentes phaseoli super Fluvii prominentem aggerem. In perpetuum reliqui fratres; voco alienos homines fratres. Voco alienos homines fratres, et non me audiunt.

CHANT VIII. 1. Ille colligit phaseolos. Unus dies quo non conspicio, videtur tres menses.

(2) 彼采蕭兮、一日不見、如三秋兮、

(3) 彼采艾兮、一日不見、如三歲兮、

大車

(1) 大車檻檻、毳衣如菼、豈不爾思、畏子不敢、

(2) 大車啍啍、毳衣如璊、豈不爾思、畏子不奔、

2. Pěi ts'ài siaō (siōu) hî. Ĭ jĕu pŏu kién, jôu sān ts'iōu hî.

3. Pěi ts'ài ngái hî. Ĭ jĕu pŏu kién, jôu sān souéi hî.

TA KIU. **1. Tá kiū hièn hièn; tch'ouéi I jôu t'àn. K'i pŏu èul sēu? Wéi tzèu pŏu kàn.**

2. Tá kiū t'ouēnn t'ouēnn ; tch'ouéi I jôu mênn. K'i pŏu èul sēu ? Wéi tzèu pŏu pēnn.

2. Il cueille l'armoise. Un jour passé sans le voir me paraît comme trois automnes (neuf mois).

3. Il cueille l'absinthe. Un jour passé sans le voir me paraît comme trois années.

CHANT IX. TA KIU.

La sévérité d'un 大 夫 **tái fōu** grand préfet met un frein à la licence des mœurs.

1. La grande voiture du préfet s'avance avec bruit, et les broderies vertes de son vêtement ressemblent aux joncs nouveaux. Comment ne penserais-je pas à toi? La crainte du préfet m'empêche de rien oser.

2. La grande voiture du préfet s'avance lourdement ; les broderies rouges de son vêtement sont comme des rubis. Comment pourrais-je t'oublier? La crainte du préfet m'empêche d'aller à toi.

2. Ille colligit artemisiam. Unus dies quo non conspicio, videtur tres autumni, i.e. novem menses.

3. Ille colligit absinthium. Unus dies quo non conspicio, videtur tres anni.

D'après les anciens commentateurs, dans cette pièce il s'agit d'un officier qui, envoyé loin de la cour pour traiter une affaire, désire y retourner au plus tôt, de peur d'être calomnié auprès de l'empereur. Ils traduisent ainsi: «Cet officier cueille le dolic, c.-à-d. remplit sa mission. Un jour passé sans voir l'empereur lui paraît comme trois mois.»

CHANT IX. 1. Ingens currus (magni præfecti) strepitat; acu picta vestis sicut nascentes junci. Quomodo non de te cogitem? Timens præfectum, nihil audeo.

2. Ingens currus tarde incedit; acu picta vestis sicut ruber lapillus. Quî non de te cogitem? Timens præfectum, non accurram.

Lorsqu'un grand préfet sortait du domaine impérial, il lui était permis de porter le 毳 衣 vêtement des 子 **tzèu** et des 男 **nân**, et de monter la grande voiture des 諸 侯 **tchōu heôu.**

(3) 穀則異室、死則同穴、謂予不信、有如皦日、

丘中有麻

(1) 丘中有麻、彼畱子嗟、彼留子嗟、將其來施施、

(2) 丘中有麥、彼留子國、彼留子國、將其來食、

(3) 丘中有李、彼留之子、彼留之子、貽我佩玖、

3. Kŏu, tsĕ i chĕu ; sèu, tsĕ t'ôung hiuĕ. Wéi iù pŏu sin, iòu jŏu kiaò jĕu.

K'IOU TCHOUNG IOU MA. **1. K'iōu tchōung iòu mà ; pėi liôu Tzèu tsiē. Pėi liôu Tzèu tsiē ; ts'iāng k'î lâi chēu chēu (chê chê).**

2. K'iōu tchōung iòu mĕ; pėi liôu Tzèu kouĕ. Pėi liôu Tzèu kouĕ; ts'iāng k'î lâi chĕu.

3. K'iōu tchōung iòu li ; pėi liôu tchēu tzèu (tsi). Pėi liôu tchēu tzèu (tsi), î ngò pėi kiòu (ki).

. 3. Nous sommes séparés pendant la vie ; une même fosse nous réunira après la mort. Si tu doutes de ma sincérité, je prendrai à témoin le soleil qui nous éclaire.

CHANT X. K'IOU TCHOUNG IOU MA.

Désir de revoir deux amis ou deux sages.

1. Sur la colline il y a du chanvre, et Tzeu tsie y est retenu. Tzeu tsie y est retenu ; que ne vient-il d'un air joyeux !

2. Sur la colline il y a du blé, Tzeu kouo y est retenu. Tzeu kouo y est retenu ; que ne vient-il prendre son repas !

3. Sur la colline il y a des pruniers ; ces deux seigneurs y sont retenus. Ces deux seigneurs y sont retenus ; (s'ils viennent), ils me donneront des pierres de prix pour ma ceinture (ou de précieux enseignements).

3. Vivi quidem in distinctis domibus, mortui vero in eadem fossa erimus. Si dicas me carere fide, est sicut clarissimus sol, i.e. testem invoco solem.

有如 s'emploie d'ordinaire dans les serments.

CHANT X. In colle medio est cannabis; illic detinent Tzeu tsie. Illic detinent Tzeu tsie; quam cupio eum venire laeto vultu !

2. In colle medio est triticum; illic detinent Tzeu kouo. Illic detinent Tzeu kouo; quam cupio eum venire et edere !

3. In colle medio sunt pruni; illic retinent illos dominos. Illic retinent illos dominos; (qui quum venient, spero fore ut) dent mihi ad zonam deferendos lapillos (seu documenta).

D'après les anciens commentateurs, le peuple exprime dans ce chant le désir de voir le retour et de recevoir les enseignements de deux sages qui ont été exilés injustement sous 莊王 **Tchouāng wàng**. « Le chanvre, le blé, les fruits sont cueillis et employés, dit le poète ; les sages sont rejetés. »

鄭一之七

緇衣

(1) 緇衣之宜兮、敝予又改為兮、適子之館兮、還予授子之粲兮、

(2) 緇衣之好兮、敝予又改造兮、適子之館兮、還予授子之粲兮、

(3) 緇衣之蓆兮、敝予又改作兮、適子之館兮、還

TCHEU I. **1. Tchēu ī tchēu i hî ; pi iù ióu kài wêi hî. Chĕu tzéu tchēu kouán (kouán) hî ; houân iû cheóu tzèu tchēu ts'án hî.**

2. Tchēu ī tchēu haò hî ; pi iù ióu kài tsaó (ts'aò) hî. Chĕu tzèu tchēu kouàn (kouán) hî ; houân iû cheóu tzèu ts'án hî.

3. Tchēu ī tchēu sĭ (siŏ) hî ; pi iù ióu kài tsŏ hî. Chĕu tzéu tchēu kouán

LIVRE VII. TCHENG FOUNG.

CHANT I. TCHEU I.

Les sujets de l'empereur 平王 **P'ing wâng** témoignent leur reconnaissance à 武公 **Où kōung**, prince de 鄭 **Tchéng**, qui a succédé à son père 桓公 **Houân kōung** dans la charge de 司徒 **sēu t'ôu** ministre de l'instruction publique à la cour impériale. Ils expriment le désir de l'avoir toujours pour ministre.

1. Le vêtement noir vous sied parfaitement ; quand celui que vous portez sera usé, nous vous en ferons un neuf. Nous irons à votre appartement dans le palais impérial (pour vous exprimer notre reconnaissance) ; et quand vous serez de retour dans votre maison, nous vous offrirons des mets.

2. Le vêtement noir vous convient admirablement ; quand le vôtre sera usé, nous vous en ferons un neuf. Nous irons à votre appartement dans le palais ; et quand vous serez de retour dans votre maison, nous vous offrirons des mets.

3. Votre vêtement noir est large (comme votre cœur) ; quand il sera usé, nous vous en ferons un neuf. Nous irons à votre appar-

TITRE DU LIVRE. 鄭一之七 Tcheng (regni cantica): primæ (partis) septimus (liber). Sur la principauté de Tcheng, voy. page 3.

CHANT I. 1. Nigra vestis convenit (tibi) ; quum detrita fuerit, nos iterum commutantes faciemus (novam). Ibimus ad domini conclave (ut gratum animum significemus) ; reduci (in privatam domum) nos donabimus domino dapes.

館 **Kouàn**, appartement où le ministre, vêtu de noir, vaquait aux affaires de sa charge dans le palais même de l'empereur.

2. Nigra vestis convenit ; quum detrita fuerit, nos rursus commutantes faciemus (novam). Ibimus ad domini conclave ; reduci dabimus domino dapes.

3. Nigra vestis est ampla ; quum

予授子之粲兮。

將仲子

(1) 將仲子兮、無踰我里、無折我樹杞、豈敢愛之、畏我父母、仲可懷也、父母之言、亦可畏也、

(2) 將仲子兮、無踰我牆、無折我樹桑、豈敢愛之、畏我諸兄、仲可懷也、諸兄之言、亦可畏也、

(3) 將仲子兮、無踰

(kouán) hi ; houân iù cheóu tzèu tchēu ts'án hi.

TS'IANG TCHOUNG TZEU. **1. Ts'iāng Tchóung tzèu hî, ôu iù ngò li, ôu tchĕ ngò chóu k'i. K'i kàn ngái tchēu ? Wéi ngò fóu mòu (mèi). Tchóung k'ò houâi (houêi) iè. Fóu mòu tchēu iên, ì k'ò wéi (wēi) iè.**

2. Ts'iāng Tchóung tzèu hî, ôu iù ngò ts'iâng, ôu tchĕ ngò chóu sāng. K'i kàn ngái tchēu ? Wéi ngò tchōu hiōung (houāng). Tchóung k'ò houâi (houêi) iè ; tchōu hiōung tchēu iên, ì k'ò wéi (wēi) iè.

3. Ts'iāng Tchóung tzèu hî, ôu iù ngò iuên, ôu tchĕ ngò chóu t'ân (t'iên).

tement dans le palais ; et quand vous serez de retour dans votre maison, nous vous offrirons des mets.

CHANT II. TS'IANG TCHOUNG TZEU.

Résistance aux désirs empressés d'un ami ou d'un conseiller nommé Tchoung.

1. Je prie Tchoung de ne pas se jeter dans mon hameau, de ne pas casser les saules que j'ai plantés. Est-ce que je tiendrais à ces arbres ? Non ; mais je crains mes parents. Tchoung mérite d'être aimé ; mais les reproches de mes parents sont aussi à craindre.

2. Je prie Tchoung de ne pas sauter par-dessus mon mur, de ne pas casser les mûriers que j'ai plantés. Est-ce que je tiendrais à ces arbres ? Non ; mais je crains mes frères. Tchoung mérite d'être aimé ; mais les reproches de mes frères sont aussi à craindre.

3. Je prie Tchoung de ne pas sauter dans mon jardin, de ne pas

detrita fuerit, nos rursus commutantes faciemus (novam). Ibimus ad...

CHANT II. 1. Rogo Tchoung dominum, ne saliat in meum pagum, ne frangat a me plantatas salices. Qui ausim amare eas ? Timeo meos parentes. Tchoung amandus est ; parentum dicta etiam timenda sunt.

2. Rogo Tchoung dominum, ne transiliat meum parietem, ne frangat a me plantatas moros. Qui ausim amare eas ? Metuo meos omnes fratres. Tchoung amandus est ; omnium fratrum dicta etiam metuenda sunt.

3. Rogo Tchoung, ne transiliat in meum hortum, ne frangat a me plantatas *t'ân* arbores. Qui ausim amare eas ? Timeo hominum nimios sermones.

我園、無折我樹檀、豈敢愛之、畏人之多言、仲可懷也、人之多言、亦可畏也、

叔于田

(1) 叔于田、巷無居人、豈無居人、不如叔也、洵美且仁、

(2) 叔于狩、巷無飲酒、豈無飲酒、不如叔也、洵美且好、

K'i kàn ngái tchēu? Wéi jênn tchēu touō iên. Tchóung k'ò houâi (houêi) iè. Jênn tchēu touō iên, ĭ k'ò wéi (wēi) iè.

CHOU IU T'IEN. **1. Chŏu iû t'iên (t'în), hiáng ŏu kiū jênn. K'i ŏu kiū jênn? Pŏu jôu Chŏu iè, siūn mèi, ts'iè jênn.**

2. Chŏu iû cheóu (cheòu), hiáng ŏu in tsiòu. K'i ŏu in tsiòu? Pŏu jôu Chŏu iè, siūn mèi, ts'iè haò (heòu).

casser les *t'an* que j'ai plantés. Est-ce que je tiendrais à ces arbres? Non; mais je crains les bavardages du public. Tchoung mérite d'être aimé; mais les bavardages sont aussi à craindre.

CHANT III. CHOU IU T'IEN.

Éloge décerné par le peuple ou par des flatteurs à 共叔段 **Kōung chŏu touán**, qui complotait contre son frère 莊 **Tchouāng**, prince de 鄭 **Tchéng**.

1. Chou se livre à la chasse; dans les bourgs il n'y a pas d'habitant. Comment n'y aurait-il aucun habitant? Je veux dire qu'aucun habitant n'égale Chou en bonté, en bienveillance.

2. Chou se livre à la chasse en hiver; dans les bourgs il n'y a pas de banquet. Comment n'y aurait-il pas de banquet? Je veux dire que personne n'offre le vin avec autant de bonté et de bienveillance que Chou.

Tchoung amandus est; hominum nimii sermones etiam sunt timendi.

L'ancienne école met ces paroles dans la bouche de 莊 **Tchouāng**, prince de Tcheng, refusant de suivre les avis de l'un de ses ministres, nommé 祭仲 **Tchái Tchóung**, qui l'engageait à prévenir la révolte de son frère. Tchouang, sur les instances de sa mère, avait conféré un fief considérable à son frère 共叔段 **Kōung chŏu touán**. Celui-ci se rendit agréable au peuple, et forma le projet de déposséder le prince Tchouang. Tchouang, pressé par Tchai Tchoung de déjouer le complot, répondit qu'il craignait le blâme de sa mère, de ses parents et de ses sujets.

檀 **T'ân**, arbre dont le bois est très dur et sert à faire des essieux.

CHANT III. 1. Chou it venatum; in vicis non est incolens homo. Quomodo non est incolens homo? Nullus tanquam Chou est vere bonus et humanus.

(3) 叔適野、巷無
服馬、豈無服馬、
不如叔也、洵美
且武、

大叔于田

(1) 叔于田、乘乘
馬、執轡如組、兩
驂如舞、叔在藪、
火烈具舉、襢裼
暴虎、獻于公所、
將叔無狃、戒其
傷女、

(2) 叔于田、乘乘

3. Chŏu chĕu iė (chòu), hiáng ŏu fŏu mà (mòu). K'i ŏu fŏu mà (mòu)? Pŏu jŏu Chŏu iė, siūn méi, ts'iė òu.

TA CHOU IU T'IEN. **1. Chŏu iû t'iên, chéng chéng mà (mòu). Tchĕu pi jŏu tsòu; leàng ts'ān jŏu òu. Chŏu tsái seòu (sòu), houò liĕ kiù kiù. Tán sĭ paó hòu, hién iû kōung chòu. Ts'iāng Chŏu ŏu gniòu, kiái k'i chāng jòu.**

2. Chŏu iû t'iên, chéng chéng houâng. Leàng fóu cháng siāng; leàng ts'ān ién

3. Chou est dans la plaine; dans les bourgs personne ne conduit les chevaux. Comment personne ne conduirait-il les chevaux? Je veux dire que personne ne les conduit d'une main si habile et si ferme que Chou.

CHANT IV. TA CHOU IU T'IEN.

Dextérité de 共叔段 **Kōung chŏu touán**, frère de 莊 **Tchouāng**, prince de 鄭 **Tchéng**. (On intitule ce chant 大叔于田 pour le distinguer du précédent).

1. Chou va à la chasse; sa voiture est traînée par quatre chevaux attelés de front. Il manie les rênes comme des rubans; les deux chevaux qui sont aux extrémités, marchent en cadence comme les danseurs. Chou entre dans les endroits marécageux; un feu violent s'allume de tous côtés. Chou, les bras dénudés, saisit un tigre et va le présenter au prince. Chou, je vous en prie, ne renouvelez pas souvent cet acte de courage; prenez garde qu'un tigre ne vous blesse.

2. Chou va à la chasse; sa voiture est traînée par quatre chevaux roux attelés de front. Ses chevaux vont comme les oies sauvages,

2. Chou it hieme venatum; in vicis nullus est bibens vinum. Quomodo nemo est bibens vinum? Nemo sicut Chou est vere bonus et benignus (in propinando vino).

3. Chou est in campis; in vicis nemo regit equos. Quomodo nemo regit equos? Nemo tanquam Chou est vere peritus et firmus.

服馬 **Fŏu mà**, dompter ou atteler des chevaux, conduire des chevaux attelés à une voiture.

CHANT IV. 1. Chou it venatum; vehitur quadrijugis equis. Tenet habenas quasi fascias; duo exteriores equi sicut saltatores (in numerum incedunt). Chou est in palustribus locis; ignis ardens ubique assurgit. Nudatis brachiis arripit tigrem; offert in reguli loco. Rogo te, Chou, ne assuescas

黃、兩服上襄、兩驂鴈行、叔在藪、火烈具揚、叔善射忌、又良御忌、抑磬控忌、抑縱送忌、

(3) 叔于田、乘乘鴇、兩服齊首、兩驂如手、叔在藪、火烈具阜、叔馬慢忌、叔發罕忌、抑釋掤忌、抑鬯弓忌、

hàng. Chŏu tsài seòu (sòu), houò liĕ kiú iàng. Chŏu chén ché kí, ióu leâng iú (iá) kí. Ĭ k'íng k'óung kí, ĭ tsóung sóung kí.

3. Chŏu iû t'iên, chéng chéng paò (peòu). Leàng fŏu ts'î cheòu ; leàng ts'ān jôu cheòu. Chŏu tsài seòu (sòu) ; houò liĕ kiú feòu. Chŏu mà mán (houán) kí ; Chŏu fă hàn kí. Ĭ chĕu pīng kí, ĭ tch'áng kōung kí.

les deux du milieu dépassant un peu les deux autres. Chou entre dans les endroits marécageux; une flamme furieuse s'élève partout. Chou est habile à tirer de l'arc; il excelle à conduire une voiture. Tantôt il fait courir ses chevaux, tantôt il les arrête. Sa main droite décoche la flèche, et sa main gauche se meut en avant comme pour accompagner le trait.

3. Chou va à la chasse; sa voiture est traînée par quatre chevaux blancs tachetés de noir, comme l'outarde. Les deux chevaux du milieu ont leurs têtes sur la même ligne; les deux autres, un peu en arrière, les accompagnent comme les mains accompagnent la tête. Chou entre dans les endroits marécageux; un violent incendie s'étend partout. Chou ralentit la marche de ses chevaux, décoche ses flèches plus rarement. Il ouvre son carquois (pour y remettre ses flèches) et serre son arc dans son étui.

(illud renovare); caveas ne ille laedat te.

Les chasseurs mettaient le feu aux herbes des marais, pour débusquer les animaux sauvages.

2. Chou it venatum; vehitur quadrijugis equis flavis. Duo jugales equi paulo anterius juncti sunt; duo exteriores anserum instar eunt (paulo posterius). Chou est in palustribus locis; ignis ardens ubique assurgit. Chou perite sagittatur et optime aurigatur. Currit, sistit; sagittam jacit, (sinistra manu) prosequitur.

抑 **Ĭ**, 忌 **kí**, particules.

3. Chou it venatum; vehitur quadrijugis equis otidi similibus, i.e. quorum color, otidis colori similis, est niger albo mixtus. Duo jugales equi pari linea habent capita; duo extremi equi instar manuum, i.e. a lateribus comitantur jugales equos, sicut manus comitantur caput, sed paulo posteriores. Chou est in palustribus locis; ignis ardens ubique vehementissimus est. Chou equi tardius eunt; Chou emittit sagittas rarius. Attollit pharetræ operculum; in theca recondit arcum.

掤 ou 冰 **Pīng**, carquois.

清人

(1) 清人在彭、駟介旁旁、二矛重英、河上乎翱翔、

(2) 清人在消、駟介麃麃、二矛重喬、河上乎逍遙、

(3) 清人在軸、駟介陶

TS'ING JENN. 1. **Ts'ing jênn tsái P'ôung (P'âng) ; séu kiái pāng pāng. Eúl meôu tch'ôung ing (iāng), Hô cháng ngaô siâng.**

2. Ts'ing jênn tsái Siaô ; séu kiái piaō piaō. Eúl meôu tch'ôung k'iaô, Hô cháng hôu tchaó iaô.

3. Ts'ing jênn tsái Tchŏu (Tcheóu) ; séu kiái t'aô t'aô (t'eóu t'eóu). Tsouó

CHANT V. TS'ING JENN.

文 **Wênn**, prince de 鄭 **Tchéng** (672-627), qui n'aimait pas 高克 **Kaō K'ŏ**, le chargea de lever des troupes dans le territoire de 清 **Ts'ing**, et d'aller s'établir sur les bords du Fleuve-Jaune pour empêcher les incursions des 狄 **Tī** Barbares du nord. L'armée stationna longtemps dans les villes de P'oung, de Siao et de Tchou. Enfin, fatiguée de rester en garnison sans rien faire, elle se dispersa d'elle-même.

1. Les soldats de Ts'ing sont à P'oung; les quatre chevaux munis de cuirasses et attelés de front aux chars de guerre ne cessent de courir. Les deux lances, avec leurs touffes de plumes élevées l'une plus haut que l'autre, voltigent comme en se jouant sur le bord du Fleuve.

2. Les soldats de Ts'ing sont à Siao ; les quatre chevaux munis de cuirasses et attelés de front présentent une apparence martiale. Les deux lances, avec leurs crochets élevés l'un plus haut que l'autre, courent comme en se jouant sur la digue du Fleuve.

3. Les soldats de Ts'ing sont à Tchou ; les quatre chevaux munis de cuirasses et attelés de front se promènent paisiblement. Le conducteur, debout à gauche, tourne bride; le soldat qui est à droite,

CHANT V. 1. Ts'ing homines sunt in P'oung; quadrijugi equi loricati indesinenter currunt. Ambæ hastæ, gradatim pendentibus plumarum cristis, in Fluvii ripa quasi ludentes cursitant.

Deux lances, au fer recourbé en forme de crochet, étaient fixées sur chaque voiture de guerre. L'une, appelée 酋矛 **ts'iôu meôu**, avait 二丈 **éul tchàng** vingt pieds de long, et l'autre, appelée 夷矛 **î meôu**, avait 二丈四尺 **éul tchàng séu tch'ĕu** vingt-quatre pieds. Comme elles étaient d'inégale longueur, les 英 **īng** touffes de plumes pendantes dont elles étaient ornées à la partie supérieure, se trouvaient à des hauteurs inégales au-dessus du chariot. Les quatre chevaux attelés de front aux chars de guerre étaient munis de cuirasses.

2. Ts'ing homines sunt in Siao; quadrijugi equi loricati militarem speciem præ se ferunt. Ambæ hastæ, gradatim arrectis uncis, in Fluvii aggere quasi ludentes cursitant.

L'armée est restée si longtemps sur les bords du Fleuve-Jaune que les lances ont perdu leurs touffes de

陶、左旋右抽、中
軍作好、
羔裘
(1) 羔裘如濡、洵
直且侯、彼其之
子、舍命不渝、
(2) 羔裘豹飾、孔
武有力、彼其之
子、邦之司直、
(3) 羔裘晏兮、三
英粲兮、彼其之
子、邦之彥兮、

siuên, ióu tch'eŏu (tch'eóu). Tchŏung kiūn tsŏ haò (heóu).

KAO K'IOU. **1. Kaŏ k'iôu jôu jôu, siūn tchĕu, ts'iė heŏu (hôu). Pėi ki tchĕu tzėu ché ming pŏu iû.**

2. Kaŏ k'iôu paó chĕu, k'òung ǒu iòu lĭ. Pėi ki tchēu tzėu pāng tchēu sēu tchĕu.

3. Kaŏ k'iôu ién hi, sān īng ts'án hì. Pėi ki tchēu tzėu pāng tchēu ién hi.

saisit une lance (par manière de jeu); le chef de l'armée (Kao K'o) qui est au milieu, a l'air d'un homme qui est à son aise.

CHANT VI. KAO K'IOU.

Éloge d'un 大 夫 **tái fōu** grand officier dont les qualités morales sont en rapport avec le brillant costume.

1. Sa tunique garnie de peaux d'agneaux paraît luisante; le poil est bien en ordre, elle est vraiment belle. Cet officier remplit son devoir avec une invariable fidélité.

2. Sa tunique garnie de peaux d'agneaux a des manches parées de peau de léopard; elle annonce du courage et de la vigueur. Cet officier maintient l'observation du devoir dans tout le pays.

3. Sa tunique garnie de peaux d'agneaux est neuve et brillante; elle est parée de trois ornements de soie. Cet officier est la gloire de sa patrie.

plumes. Les fers recourbés apparaissent dépouillés de cet ornement.

3. Ts'ing homines sunt in Tchou; quadrijugi equi loricati quasi ludentes spatiantur. Qui ad sinistram stat (currus ductor) retrorsum vertit currum; qui ad dexteram stat (miles) evellit hastam; qui medius stat dux militum (Kao K'o) agit partes hominis commode se habentis. 清 était dans le 中 牟 縣

Un char portait trois hommes.

CHANT VI. 1. Agninis pellibus induta vestis videtur unguine nitens, vere comptis pilis, et pulchra. Ille vir stat mandatis cœlestibus, i.e. rectum tenet constanter, nec immutatur.

其 **Ki**, particule explétive.

2. Agninis pellibus induta vestis habet pardi pelle ornatas manicas; magnam refert fortitudinem et robur. Ille vir in regno tuetur rectum.

3. Agninis pellibus induta vestis recens nitet; tribus sericis ornamentis emicat. Ille vir est regni ornamentum.

遵大路

(1) 遵大路兮、摻執子之祛兮、無我惡兮、不寁故也、

(2) 遵大路兮、摻執子之手兮、無我魗兮、不寁好也、

女曰雞鳴

(1) 女曰雞鳴、士曰昧旦、子興視夜、明星有爛、將翱將翔、弋鳧與鴈、

TSIUN TA LOU. **1. Tsiūn tá lóu hī, chèn tchĕu tzèu tchēu k'iū (k'iú) hī. Où ngò óu hī, pŏu tsàn kóu iè.**

2. Tsiūn tá lóu hī, chèn tchĕu tzèu tchēu cheòu hī. Où ngò tch'eòu hī, pŏu tsàn haò (heòu) iè.

GNIU IUE KI MING. **1. Gniù iuĕ : Kī mìng. Chéu iuĕ : Méi tán. Tzèu hīng chéu ié, mîng sīng iòu lán. Tsiāng ngaô tsiāng siâng, ĭ fôu iù ién.**

CHANT VII. TSIUN TA LOU.

Efforts pour retenir un ami et conserver son amitié, ou pour retenir un sage qui veut quitter son pays troublé par la mauvaise administration du prince 莊 **Tchouāng** (743-701).

1. Sur la grande route, je vous saisis et vous retiens par la manche. Ne vous en offensez pas; nos anciennes relations ne doivent pas être rompues si vite.

2. Sur la grande route je vous saisis et vous retiens par la main. Ne me dédaignez pas; notre amitié ne doit pas être rompue subitement.

CHANT VIII. GNIU IUE KI MING.

Une femme presse son mari d'aller à la chasse, et l'engage à cultiver l'amitié d'hommes vertueux.

1. La femme dit : Le coq chante. Le mari répond : Le jour commence à poindre. (La femme reprend) : Levez-vous, Seigneur, et voyez si la nuit touche à son terme, si l'Étoile du matin paraît. Courez, volez ; décochez votre flèche sur les canards et les oies sauvages.

CHANT VII. 1. Insistens magnæ viæ, arreptam teneo domini manicam. Ne mihi irascaris; non subito abrumpenda est pristina (consuetudo).

2. Insistens magnæ viæ, arreptam teneo domini manum. Ne me vilem habeas; non celeriter abrumpenda est amicitia.

CHANT VIII. 1. Mulier dicit: Gallus canit. Vir respondet: Dilucescit. (Mulier pergit): Domine, surge et vide nox (quo pervenerit), an matutina stella edat lucem. Jam curre, jam vola; sagitta pete anates et silvestres anseres.

弋 Ĭ, flèche munie d'un long fil par lequel l'oiseleur la retirait à lui.

(2) 弋言加之、與子宜之、宜言飲酒、與子偕老、琴瑟在御、莫不靜好、

(3) 知子之來之、雜佩以贈之、知子之順之、雜佩以問之、知子之好之、雜佩以報之。

有女同車

(1) 有女同車、顏如舜華、將翱將

2. Ĭ iên kiā (kī) tchēu, iù tzèu ĭ tchēu. Ĭ iên in tsiòu, iù tzèu kiāi laò (leòu). K'în chĕ tsái iú, mouŏ pŏu tsing haò (heòu).

3. Tchēu tzèu tchēu lâi (lĭ) tchēu, tsă péi i tséng (tsĕ) tchēu. Tchēu tzèu tchēu chouénn tchēu, tsă péi i wénn tchēu. Tchēu tzèu tchēu haó tchēu, tsă péi i paò tchēu.

IOU GNIU T'OUNG KIU. **1. Iòu gniù t'ôung kiū, iên jôu chouénn houâ (fōu).**

2. Si vous en tuez, je vous les assaisonnerai convenablement. Je les assaisonnerai et nous boirons ensemble ; j'espère vivre et vieillir avec vous. Voici deux luths ; tout respire la paix et la concorde.

3. Quand je connaîtrai ceux dont vous recherchez l'amitié, je leur donnerai les pierres de prix suspendues à ma ceinture. Quand je connaitrai ceux qui partageront vos sentiments, je les saluerai et leur offrirai les pierrres de prix suspendues à ma ceinture. Quand je connaîtrai ceux qui seront vos amis, je leur donnerai en retour les pierres de prix suspendues à ma ceinture.

CHANT IX. IOU GNIU T'OUNG KIU.

Éloge de Meng Kiang, fille du prince de 齊 **Ts'ī.**

1. Dans la voiture du prince est une femme qui ressemble à la fleur du cirier. Son vêtement flotte au vent ; les ornements carrés de sa ceinture sont de belles pierres rouges. Cette noble fille aînée

2. Si sagitta attingas eos, domino apte condiam eos. Apte condiam et bibemus vinum ; (spero fore ut) cum domino simul senescam. *K'în* et *chĕ* citharæ præsto sunt ; nihil non placidum ac concors.

Les deux luths *k'în* et *chĕ* représentent les deux époux ; l'accord de ces deux instruments figure l'affection conjugale.

3. Quum scivero dominus quos alliciat, variis zonæ (meæ) lapillis utens donabo eos. Quum scivero dominus quibuscum consentiat, variis zonæ (meæ) lapillis utens salutabo eos. Quum scivero dominus quos diligat, variis zonæ (meæ) lapillis munerabor eos.

CHANT IX. 1. Est mulier in eodem vehiculo, specie similis hibisci flori. (Ejus vestis vento agitata) volitat, fluitat ; inter zonæ lapillos sunt e *k'iôung* facta quadra. Illa eximia Meng Kiang

翔。佩玉瓊琚。彼美
孟姜。洵美且都。
(2) 有女同行。顏如
舜英。將翱將翔。佩
玉將將。彼美孟姜。
德音不忘。

山有扶蘇

(1) 山有扶蘇。隰有
荷華。不見子都。乃
見狂且。
(2) 山有橋松。隰有
游龍。不見子充。乃
見狡童。

Tsiāng ngaô tsiāng siâng ; péi iŭ k'iôung kiū. Pèi mèi Méng Kiāng siūn mèi, ts'iè tōu.

2. Iòu gniù t'ôung hîng (hâng), iên jôu chouénn Īng (iāng). Tsiāng ngaô tsiāng siâng ; péi iŭ ts'iāng ts'iāng. Pèi mèi Méng Kiāng tĕ în pŏu wâng.

CHAN IOU FOU SOU. **1. Chān iòu fôu sōu, sĭ iòu hô houâ (fōu). Pŏu kién Tzèu tōu ; nài kién k'ouâng tsiū.**

2. Chān iòu k'iaô sōung, sĭ iòu iôu lōung. Pŏu kién Tzèu tch'ōung ; nài kién kiaò t'ôung.

de la famille des Kiang est vraiment distinguée et accoutumée à l'observation des convenances.

2. Une femme accompagne le prince ; elle ressemble à la fleur du cirier. Son vêtement flotte au vent ; les ornements de sa ceinture retentissent. Les paroles de cette noble fille aînée de la famille des Kiang sont pleines de sagesse et ne seront jamais oubliées.

CHANT X. CHAN IOU FOU SOU.

Les belles plantes ne manquent pas; mais les hommes distingués font défaut.

1. L'arbuste appelé *fou sou* croît sur les montagnes, et le nénufar dans les endroits humides. Je ne vois aucun Tzeu tou, mais seulement des insensés.

2. Le sapin à la cime élevée croît sur les montagnes, et la renouée se traîne dans les endroits marécageux. Je ne vois aucun Tzeu tch'oung, mais des enfants astucieux.

vere est eximia et ad decorem servandum assueta. 佩玉 V. pag. 75.

2. Est mulier simul iens, specie similis hibisci flori. (Ejus vestis) volitat, fluitat; zonæ lapilli tinniunt. Illius eximiæ Meng Kiang sapienter dicta non excident e memoria.

CHANT X. 1. In montibus est *fôu sōu* (arbuscula moro similis); in palustribus est nymphæa. (Sic in regno congruit esse viros egregios). Non video Tzeu tou ; sed video stultos.

2. In montibus est elato vertice abies ; in palustribus est vagans polygonum. Non video Tzeu tch'oung ; at video dolosos pueros.

蘀兮

(1) 蘀兮蘀兮、風其吹女、叔兮伯兮、倡予和女。

(2) 蘀兮蘀兮、風其漂女、叔兮伯兮、倡予要女。

狡童

(1) 彼狡童兮、不與我言兮、維子之故、使我不能餐兮。

(2) 彼狡童兮、不與我食兮、維子之故、使我不能息兮。

T'OUO HI. **1. T'ouŏ hī, t'ouŏ hī, fōung k'ì tch'ouēi jòu. Chŏu hī, pĕ hī, tch'áng iù, houó (houēi) jòu.**

2. T'ouŏ hī, t'ouŏ hī, fōung k'ì p'iaŏ jòu. Chŏu hī, pĕ hī, tch'áng iù, iaŏ jòu.

KIAO T'OUNG. **1. Pèi kiaò t'ôung hī, pŏu iù ngò ièn hī. Wêi tzèu tchēu kóu, chèu ngò pŏu nêng ts'ān (ts'iuēn) hī?**

2. Pèi kiaò t'ôung hī, pŏu iù ngò chĕu hī. Wêi tzèu tchēu kóu, chèu ngò pŏu nêng sī hī?

CHANT XI. T'OUO HI.

Demande de secours. D'après les anciens commentateurs, les officiers subalternes de Tcheng font appel au dévouement de leurs supérieurs pour remédier aux maux de leur pays.

1. Feuilles flétries, feuilles desséchées, le vent souffle sur vous. O vous qui êtes comme nos pères, commencez le chant; nous le continuerons avec vous.

2. Feuilles mortes, feuilles desséchées, le vent vous agite. O vous qui êtes comme nos pères, commencez le chant ; nous le terminerons avec vous.

CHANT XII. KIAO T'OUNG.

Amitié rompue. D'après l'ancienne école, satire dirigée contre le prince 昭 **Tchaō**, qui était jeune et écartait des charges les hommes capables. (701-700).

1. Enfant rusé, tu refuses de me parler. Penses-tu qu'à cause de toi, seigneur, je perde l'appétit?

2. Enfant rusé, tu refuses de manger avec moi. Penses-tu qu'à cause de toi, seigneur, je perde tout repos?

CHANT XI. 1. Marcida folia, marcida folia, ventus ille perflat vos. Patrui minores, patrui majores, praecinite nobis, concinemus vobis.

2. Marcida folia, marcida folia, ventus ille agitat vos. Patrui minores, patrui majores, praecinite nobis, perficiemus vobis (canticum).

CHANT XII. 1. Ille astutus puer non mecum loquitur. Unice domini causa, num fiet ut ego non possim comedere?

2. Ille callidus puer non mecum comedit. Unice domini causa, num fiet ut ego non possim quiescere?

褰裳

(1) 子惠思我、褰裳涉溱、子不我思、豈無他人、狂童之狂也且、

(2) 子惠思我、褰裳涉洧、子不我思、豈無他士、狂童之狂也且、

丰

(1) 子之丰兮、俟我乎巷兮、悔予不送兮、

K'IEN CHANG. **1. Tzèu houéi sēu ngò, k'iēn chāng ché Tchēnn. Tzèu pŏu ngò sēu, k'i ôu t'ouō jènn ? K'ouâng t'ôung tchēu k'ouâng iè tsiū !**

2. Tzèu houéi sēu ngò, k'iēn chāng chĕ Wèi (Ì). Tzèu pŏu ngò sēu, k'i ôu t'ouō chèu ? K'ouâng t'ôung tchēu k'ouâng iè tsiū !

FOUNG. **1. Tzèu tchēu fōung (fóung) hî, sèu ngò hôu hiáng (hóung) hî ; houéi iù pŏu sóung hî.**

CHANT XIII. K'IEN CHANG.

Amitié ébranlée par des soupçons. D'après l'ancienne école, le peuple de Tcheng exprime le désir qu'un prince puissant intervienne et rétablisse la concorde entre le prince 忽 Hŏu ou 昭公 Tchaō kōung, et son frère 突 Tŏu, qui est appelé le plus insensé de tous les jeunes insensés.

1. Si vous avez des sentiments d'amitié pour moi, je relèverai mon vêtement jusqu'aux genoux, et traverserai la Tchenn à gué (pour aller à vous). Si vous ne pensez pas à moi, croyez-vous que je n'en trouve pas un autre? O le plus insensé de tous les jeunes insensés !

2. Si vous avez des sentiments d'amitié pour moi, je relèverai mon vêtement jusqu'aux genoux et traverserai la Wei à gué. Si vous ne pensez pas à moi, croyez-vous que je n'en trouve pas un autre? O le plus insensé de tous les jeunes insensés !

CHANT XIV. FOUNG.

Un jeune homme est allé inviter une jeune fille (sa fiancée, pour la célébration des noces, disent les anciens commentateurs). La jeune fille a refusé, contrairement aux usages. Elle exprime son repentir.

1. Un homme de bonne apparence m'attendait dans la ruelle. Je regrette de ne l'avoir pas suivi.

CHANT XIII. 1. Domine, si amanter cogitas de me, ad genua adducens vestem, vado trajiciam Tchenn fluvium. Domine, si non de me cogitas, num deerit alter vir? O stultorum puerorum stultissimum!

2. Domine, si amanter cogitas de me, ad genua adducens vestem, vado trajiciam Wei fluvium. Domine, si non de me cogitas, num deerit alter vir? O stultorum puerorum stultissimum!

CHANT XIV. 1. Dominus formosus expectabat me in angiportu. Me pœnitet quod non comitata sim eum.

②子之昌兮、俟我乎堂兮、悔予不將兮。

③衣錦褧衣、裳錦褧裳、叔兮伯兮、駕予與行。

④裳錦褧裳、衣錦褧衣、叔兮伯兮、駕予與歸。

東門之墠

①東門之墠、茹藘在阪、其室則邇、其人甚遠。

②東門之栗、有

2. Tzèu tchēu tch'āng hī, séu ngò hôu t'âng hī ; houéi iù pŏu tsiāng hī.

3. Ĭ kin k'iòung ī, châng kin k'iòung châng. Chŏu hī, pĕ hī, kiá iû iù hing (hâng).

4. Châng kin k'iòung châng, i kin k'iòung ī. Chŏu hī, pĕ hī, kiá iû iù kouēi.

TOUNG MENN TCHEU CHEN. **1. Tōung mênn tchēu chén, jôu liû tsái fàn. K'i chĕu tsè èul ; k'i jênn chénn iuèn.**

2. Tōung mênn tchēu lĭ, iòu tsiên kiā chēu. K'i pŏu èul sēu? Tzèu pŏu ngò tsī.

2. Un homme d'une belle prestance m'attendait dans la salle. Je regrette de ne l'avoir pas suivi.

3. J'ai revêtu une tunique simple sur une tunique de soie à fleurs, et un vêtement inférieur simple sur un autre de soie à fleurs. Messieurs, Messieurs, attelez une voiture, emmenez-moi avec vous.

4. J'ai mis un vêtement inférieur simple sur un autre de soie à fleurs, et une tunique simple sur une autre de soie à fleurs. Messieurs, Messieurs, préparez une voiture, conduisez-moi avec vous à la maison.

CHANT XV. TOUNG MENN TCHEU CHEN.

Affection refroidie.

1. A la porte orientale, près du terrain aplani, la garance croît sur le talus. La maison de cet homme est près d'ici (à la porte orientale); mais lui-même se tient loin de moi.

2. A la porte orientale, près des châtaigniers, sont des rangées

2. Dominus amplo corpore expectabat me in aula. Me pœnitet quod non comitata sim eum.

3. Indui e serico floribus intexto tunicam et (alteram) simplicem tunicam; indui e serico floribus intexto vestem inferiorem et simplicem vestem inferiorem. Domini, domini, jungite vehiculum mihi ut simul eamus.

4. Indui e serico floribus intexto vestem inferiorem et simplicem vestem inferiorem; indui e serico floribus intexto tunicam et simplicem tunicam. Domini, domini, jungite vehiculum mihi, simul eamus domum.

CHANT XV. 1. Ad orientalis portæ aream, rubia est in declivi. Illa domus est proxima; ille homo omnino distat, i.e. non ad me accedit.

2. Ad orientalis portæ castaneas

踐家室。豈不爾
思。子不我卽。

風雨

(1)風雨淒淒。雞
鳴喈喈。旣見君
子。云胡不夷。
(2)風雨瀟瀟。雞
鳴膠膠。旣見君
子。云胡不瘳。
(3)風雨如晦。雞
鳴不已。旣見君
子。云胡不喜。

子衿

(1)青青子衿。悠

FOUNG IU. 1. **Fōung iù ts'ī ts'ī ; kī mīng kiāi kiāi (kī kī). Kí kién kiūn tzèu, iûn hôu pōu î ?**

2. Fōung iù siaō siaō ; kī mīng kiaō kiaō. Kí kién kiūn tzèu, iûn hôu pōu leaô?

3. Fōung iù jôu houéi (houéi); kī mīng pōu i. Kí kién kiūn tzèu, iûn hôu pōu hì?

TZEU KIN. 1. **Ts'īng ts'īng tzèu kīn, iôu iôu ngò sīn. Tsóung ngò pōu wàng, tzèu gnìng pōu séu īn ?**

de maisons. Comment ne penserais-je pas à vous, Seigneur? Mais vous ne venez pas à moi.

CHANT XVI. FOUNG IU.

Dans ces strophes, d'après les interprètes modernes, une femme exprime sa joie en voyant son mari de retour. Au sentiment des anciens, le poète célèbre un sage qui vient rétablir l'ordre dans la principauté de Tcheng, et dont l'arrivée est comme le chant du coq au milieu d'une nuit orageuse.

1. Le vent et la pluie produisent un froid glacial ; le coq fait entendre son chant accoutumé. A la vue de ce sage, comment mon cœur ne serait-il pas en repos?

2. Le vent et la pluie mugissent ; le coq répète son chant accoutumé. A la vue de ce sage, comment la santé ne me serait-elle pas rendue?

3. Le vent et la pluie obscurcissent le ciel ; le coq ne cesse de chanter. A la vue de ce sage, comment ne serais-je pas dans la joie?

CHANT XVII. TZEU KIN.

Une femme ou un compagnon d'études reproche à un étudiant son absence trop prolongée.

1. Jeune homme au collet bleu, depuis longtemps je soupire

sunt ordinatæ domus et ædes. Qui non de te cogitem? Domine, non ad me accedis.

CHANT XVI. 1. Ventus et imber sunt algidi ; gallus canit *kiai kiai*. Quum viderim sapientem virum, dic, quomodo non pacaretur animus?

2. Ventus et pluvia strident ; gallus canit *kiao kiao*. Quum viderim sapientem virum, dic, quomodo non sanaretur morbus?

3. Ventus et pluvia quasi caliginem diffuderunt ; gallus canit indesinenter. Quum viderim sapientem virum, dic, quomodo non gauderem?

悠我心、縱我不往、子寧不嗣音、

(2) 青青子佩、悠悠我思、縱我不往、子寧不來、

(3) 挑兮達兮、在城闕兮、一日不見、如三月兮、

揚之水

(1) 揚之水、不流束楚、終鮮兄弟、維予與女、無信人之言、人實迋女、

2. Ts' īng ts'īng tzèu péi (pĕi) ; iôu iôu ngò sēu (sī). Tsóung ngò pŏu wàng, tzèu gning pŏu lâi (lî)?

3. T'aŏ hì t'ă (t'ĕ) hì, tsái tch'êng k'iuĕ hì. Ĭ jĕu pŏu kién, jŏu sān iuĕ hì.

IANG TCHEU CHOUEI. **1. Iâng tchēu chouèi pŏu liôu chŏu tch'ŏu. Tchŏung siēn hiōung tí, wêi iù iù jòu. Où sín jênn tchēu iên ; jênn chĕu kouáng jòu.**

après vous. Bien que je n'aille pas vous voir, que n'envoyez-vous continuellement des messages?

2. Jeune homme qui portez à la ceinture des ornements attachés par des cordons bleus, depuis longtemps je pense à vous. Bien que je n'aille pas vous voir, que ne venez-vous ici?

3. Vous folâtrez, vous vous amusez; du haut de la tour, au-dessus de la porte de la ville, (vous promenez des regards curieux). Un jour sans vous voir me paraît long comme trois mois.

CHANT XVIII. IANG TCHEU CHOUEI.

Protestations de fidélité d'une femme à son mari ou d'un ministre à son prince.

1. Le courant est si faible qu'il n'entraînerait pas une bourrée d'épines. (Ainsi l'amitié des hommes est faible et instable). Peu d'hommes vivent ensemble comme des frères jusqu'à la fin; mais nous deux, nous le devons. Ne croyez pas ce que vous disent (contre moi) les étrangers; les étrangers vous disent des faussetés.

CHANT XVII. 1. Cæruleum domini collare, valde diuturnum fuit meum desiderium. Licet ego non adeam, dominus quare non continuo mittit nuntia?

Les étudiants portaient le collet bleu. Encore à présent l'expression 青衿 désigne un 秀才 **sióu ts'ài.**

2. Cærulei domini zonæ penduli funiculi, diutissime ego cogitavi. Licet ego non adeam, dominus quare non venit?

3. Saltitat, genio indulget, in portæ alta turri. Unus dies quo non conspicio eum, videtur quasi tres menses.

CHANT XVIII. 1. Tarde fluens aqua non valet deferre colligatas spinas. In perpetuum pauci fratres sunt; soli ego et tu. Ne credas hominum sermonibus; homines vere falsa dicunt tibi.

(2) 揚之水、不流束
薪、終鮮兄弟、維予
二人、無信人之言、
人實不信、

出其東門

(1) 出其東門、有女
如雲、雖則如雲、
我思存、縞衣綦巾、
聊樂我員、
(2) 出其闉闍、有女
如荼、雖則如荼、
我思且、縞衣茹藘、
聊可與娛、

2. Iâng tchēu chouèi pŏu liôu chŏu sīn. Tchōung siên hiōung tí, wêi iû éul jênn. Où sin jênn tchēu iên ; jênn chĕu pŏu sin (sin).

TCH'OU K'I TOUNG MENN. **1. Tch'ŏu k'î tōung mênn, iòu gniù jôu iûn. Souēi tsĕ jôu iûn, fèi ngò sēu ts'uênn. Kaò î k'í kīn, leaô lŏ ngò iûn.**

2. Tch'ŏu k'î īn tôu, iòu gniù jôu t'ôu. Souēi tsĕ jôu t'ôu, fèi ngò sēu tsiū. Kaò î jôu liû, leaô k'ò iù iû.

2. Le courant est si faible qu'il n'entraînerait pas une botte de branchages. Peu d'hommes vivent ensemble comme des frères jusqu'à la fin ; mais nous deux, nous le devons. Ne croyez pas ce que vous disent les étrangers ; les étrangers ne méritent pas créance.

CHANT XIX. TCH'OU K'I TOUNG MENN.

Contre le luxe des femmes.

1. En dehors de la porte orientale on voit une nuée de femmes richement parées. Bien qu'elles soient (nombreuses et belles) comme une nuée, mes pensées ne s'arrêtent pas sur elles. Celle qui me plaît, c'est ma compagne qui porte un pauvre vêtement de soie blanche et un bonnet de couleur grise.

2. En dehors de ce mur surmonté d'une tour qui masque la porte de la ville, on voit des femmes qui sont comme des fleurs blanches. Bien qu'elles soient comme des fleurs blanches, mes pensées ne sont pas pour elles. Celle qui seule est capable de me rendre heureux, c'est cette compagne qui porte un simple vêtement de soie blanche et un bonnet teint en garance.

2. Tarde fluens aqua non valet deferre colligata ramalia. In perpetuum pauci fratres sunt; soli nos ambo homines. Ne credas hominum dictis; homines vere non sunt fide digni.

CHANT XIX. 1. Extra illam orientalem portam sunt mulieres instar nubis (plurimæ et ornatæ). Licet sint instar nubis, non mea cogitatio sistit in illis. (Uxor mea induta) alba veste et cinerei coloris pileo, satis juvat me.

員 **Iûn**, particule explétive.

2. Extra illam portæ muro exteriori impositam turrim sunt mulieres instar alborum florum. Quamvis sint similes albis floribus, non ego cogito de illis. (Uxor mea induta) alba veste et rubia tincto (pileo), bene par est quacum oblecter.

野有蔓草

(1) 野有蔓草、零露漙兮、有美一人、清揚婉兮、邂逅相遇、適我願兮、

(2) 野有蔓草、零露瀼瀼、有美一人、婉如清揚、邂逅相遇、與子偕臧、

溱洧

(1) 溱與洧、方渙

IE IOU MAN TS'AO. **1. Iè iòu mán ts'aò, lîng lóu t'ouân (chouén) hî. Iòu mèi ĭ jênn, ts'īng iâng iuén hî. Hiái heóu siāng iù ; chĕu ngò iuén (iuén) hî.**

2. Iè iòu mán ts'aò, lîng lóu jâng jâng. Iòu mèi ĭ jênn, iuén jôu ts'īng iâng. Hiái heóu siāng iù ; iù tzèu kiāi tsāng.

TCHENN WEI. **1. Tchēnn iù Wêi fāng houán houán (iuēn iuēn) hî. Chéu iù**

CHANT XX. IE IOU MAN TS'AO.

Rencontre fortuite d'un ami ou d'un sage.

1. Dans la plaine croît une plante rampante; elle est chargée de rosée. Il est un excellent homme remarquable par la beauté de ses yeux et de son front. Je l'ai rencontré par hasard; il est conforme à mes désirs.

2. Dans la plaine croît une plante rampante; elle est couverte de rosée. Il est un excellent homme remarquable par la beauté de ses yeux et de son front. Je l'ai rencontré par hasard, et me trouve bien avec lui.

CHANT XXI. TCHENN WEI.

Au printemps, dans le courant du troisième mois, les habitants de Tcheng vont cueillir une plante destinée à combattre l'influence des mauvais esprits, et célèbrent des fêtes à cette occasion.

1. La Tchenn et la Wei sont gonflées (par la fonte des neiges). Les hommes et les femmes se mettent à cueillir la plante *kien*

闉 **In**, mur de défense qui masque l'entrée d'une place forte.

CHANT XX. 1. In campis est repens herba; stillat ros multus. Est egregius quidam homo oculis et fronte formosis. Fortuito convenientes invicem occurrimus; consentaneus est meis votis.

Une plante rampante occupe une grande place et reçoit beaucoup de rosée. La rosée est le symbole des bons enseignements d'un sage.

2. In campis est repens herba; stillat ros valde copiosus. Est egregius quidam homo decoris oculis et fronte. Fortuito convenientes invicem occurrimus; cum domino simul bene est.

CHANT XXI. 1. Tchenn et Wei incipiunt tumescere. Viri et mulieres incipiunt carpere *kien* herbam. Mulieres dicunt: « Lustravistisne (campum)? »

渙兮、士與女、方秉蕳兮、女曰觀乎、士曰既且、且往觀乎、洧之外、洵訏且樂、維士與女、伊其相謔、贈之以勺藥、

(2) 溱與洧、瀏其清矣、士與女、殷其盈矣、女曰觀乎、士曰既且、且往觀乎、洧之外、洵訏且樂、維士與女、伊其將謔、贈之以勺藥、

gniù fāng ping kiēn hī. Gniù iuĕ : Kouān hôu? Chéu iuĕ : Ki tsiū. Ts'iè wàng kouān hôu? Wèi tchēu wái, siūn hiū ts'iè lŏ. Wèi chéu iù gniù, I k'i siāng hiŏ, tséng tchēu i chŏ iŏ.

2. Tchēnn iù Wèi, liôu k'ì ts'īng i. Chéu iù gniù īn k'i ìng i. Gniù iuĕ : Kouān hôu? Chéu iuĕ : Ki tsiū. Ts'iè wàng kouān hôu? Wèi tchēu wái, siūn hiū ts'iè lŏ. Wèi chéu iù gniù I k'i tsiāng hiŏ, tséng tchēu i chŏ iŏ.

(peut-être l'eupatoire ou la valériane). Les femmes disent : « Avez-vous parcouru la campagne? » Les hommes répondent : « Nous l'avons parcourue. » — « Que n'allons-nous la parcourir encore? Au delà de la Wei, la plaine est vaste et riante. » Alors les hommes et les femmes se livrent à des jeux et s'offrent des pivoines.

2. L'eau de la Tchenn et de la Wei est haute et limpide. Les hommes et les femmes remplissent la plaine. Les femmes disent : « Avez-vous parcouru la campagne? » Les hommes répondent : « Nous l'avons parcourue. » — « Que n'allons-nous la parcourir encore? Au delà de la Wei, la plaine est vaste et riante. » Alors les hommes et les femmes se livrent à des jeux et s'offrent des pivoines.

Viri dicunt : « Jam (lustravimus). » — « Modo quidni eamus lustratum? Wei fluvium ultra, vere ampla et amœna (loca). » Tunc viri et mulieres, illi inter se jocantur, et offerunt sibi pæoniæ florem.

La Tchenn et la Wei traversaient la principauté de Tcheng. La Tchenn se jetait dans la Wei, la Wei dans la 潁 **Ing** et la Ing dans la 淮 **Houâi.**

伊 **I**, particule initiale.

2. Tchenn et Wei fluviorum alta est illa aqua limpida. Viri et mulieres, valde illi multi sunt. Mulieres dicunt : « Lustravistisne? » Viri dicunt : « Jam (lustravimus). » — « Modo quidni eamus lustratum? Wei fluvium ultra, vere spatiosus et amœnus est (campus). » Tunc viri et mulieres, illi invicem jocantur, donant sibi pæoniæ florem.

將 **Tsiāng** a été mis par erreur à la place de 相 **siāng.**

La pivoine est appelée 離草 **lì ts'aò** la plante de la séparation, parce que les anciens avaient coutume de l'offrir au moment des adieux.

齊一之八

雞鳴

(1) 雞既鳴矣、朝既盈矣、匪雞則鳴、蒼蠅之聲、

(2) 東方明矣、朝既昌矣、匪東方則明、月出之光、

(3) 蟲飛薨薨、甘與子同夢、會且歸矣、無庶予子憎、

KI MING. 1. **Kī ki mîng i ; tch'aô ki îng i. Fêi kī tsĕ mîng, ts'āng îng tchĕu chēng.**

2. Tōung fāng mîng (mâng) i ; tch'aô ki tch'āng i. Féi tōung fāng tsĕ mîng (mâng), iuĕ tch'ŏu tchĕu kouāng.

3. Tch'ôung fēi hēng hēng, kān iù tzéu t'ôung móung (mêng). Houéi ts'iè kouēi i ; ôu chóu iû tzèu tsēng.

LIVRE VIII. TS'I FOUNG.

CHANT I. KI MING.

La femme du prince de Ts'i presse son mari de se lever et de donner audience. Dans sa préoccupation, elle confond le bourdonnement des mouches avec le chant du coq, la clarté de la lune avec la lumière de l'aurore. D'après l'ancienne interprétation 序 **Siú**, ce prince serait 哀公 **Ngāi kōung** (934-893), qui était indolent et licencieux.

1. Le coq a chanté ; déjà la cour est pleine d'officiers qui attendent l'audience. Ce n'était pas encore le chant du coq, mais le bourdonnement des mouches vertes.

2. L'aurore paraît à l'orient ; déjà les officiers sont tous réunis. Ce n'est pas l'apparition de l'aurore à l'orient, mais la clarté de la lune à son lever.

3. Les insectes voltigent et bourdonnent ; il me serait doux de rêver sur cette couche auprès de vous. Mais les officiers réunis à la cour s'en retourneraient chez eux ; prince, je crains qu'ils ne s'indignent contre vous et contre moi.

TITRE DU LIVRE. 齊一之八 **Ts'i** (regni cantica) : primæ (partis) octavus (liber). La principauté de Ts'i était dans la partie orientale du Chan toung actuel. Voy. page 3.

CHANT I. 1. Gallus jam cecinit, aula jam plena est. Non gallus quidem cecinit ; viridium muscarum susurrus fuit.

2. In orientali regione dilucescit, aula jam referta est. Non in orientali regione quidem dilucescit ; lunæ orientis claritas est.

3. Bestiolæ volitantes susurrant ; gratum est cum domino simul somniari. (At) qui convenerunt, interim redibunt domos ; timeo ne forte ego et dominus odio habeamur.

還

(1) 子之還兮、遭我乎峱之閒兮、竝驅從兩肩兮、揖我謂我儇兮、

(2) 子之茂兮、遭我乎峱之道兮、竝驅從兩牡兮、揖我謂我好兮、

(3) 子之昌兮、遭我乎峱之陽兮、竝驅從兩狼兮、揖我謂我臧兮、

SIUEN. **1. Tzèu tchēu siuên hī. Tsaō ngò hôu Naô tchēu kién (kiēn) hī ; píng k'iū ts'ôung leàng kiēn hī. Ĭ ngò wéi ngò hiuēn hī.**

2. Tzèu tchēu meóu (meòu) hī. Tsaō ngò hôu Naô tchēu taó (teòu) hī ; píng k'iū ts'ôung leàng meòu hī. Ĭ ngò wéi ngò haò (heòu) hī.

3. Tzèu tchēu tch'āng hī. Tsaō ngò hôu Naô tchēu iâng hī ; píng k'iū ts'ôung leàng lâng hī. Ĭ ngò wéi ngò tsāng hī.

CHANT II. SIUEN.

Sotte vanité et compliments réciproques de deux chasseurs. Ce chant est une satire contre la passion de la chasse.

1. C'est vous, Seigneur, qui êtes agile. Vous m'avez rencontré entre la ville et le mont Nao ; pressant la course de nos chevaux, nous avons poursuivi ensemble deux animaux de trois ans. Puis, me saluant, vous avez loué mon agilité.

2. C'est vous, Seigneur, qui êtes adroit. Vous m'avez rencontré sur le chemin du mont Nao ; pressant la course de nos chevaux, nous avons poursuivi ensemble deux animaux mâles. Puis, me saluant, vous avez loué ma dextérité.

3. C'est vous, Seigneur, qui êtes habile. Vous m'avez rencontré au midi du mont Nao ; pressant la course de nos chevaux, nous avons poursuivi ensemble deux loups. Puis, me saluant, vous avez loué mon habileté.

CHANT II. 1. Domini est pernicitas. Occurrit mihi in Nao intervallo, i.e. inter urbem et Nao montem ; simul, citatis equis, insectati sumus duas trium annorum feras. Salutans me, dixit me esse pernicem.

Le mont Nao était près de la capitale de Ts'i, dans le 臨淄縣 **Lin tcheū hién** actuel (Chan toung).

2. Domini sunt dotes eximiæ. Occurrit mihi in Nao montis via ; simul, citatis equis, insectati sumus duos mares. Salutans me, dixit me esse dotibus eximiis præditum.

3. Domini est peritia. Occurrit mihi ad Nao montis austrum ; simul, citatis equis, insectati sumus duos lupos. Salutans me, dixit me esse peritum.

著

(1) 俟我於著乎而、充耳以素乎而、尙之以瓊華乎而、

(2) 俟我於庭乎而、充耳以青乎而、尙之以瓊瑩乎而、

(3) 俟我於堂乎而、充耳以黃乎而、尙之以瓊英乎而、

TCHOU. **1. Séu ngò iû tchóu (tchōu) hôu êul. Tch'ōung èul i sóu (sōu) hôu êul ; cháng tchēu i k'iôung houâ (fōu) hôu êul.**

2. Séu ngò iû t'îng hôu êul. Tch'ōung èul i ts'īng hôu êul ; cháng tchēu i k'iôung iôung hôu êul.

3. Séu ngò iû t'âng hôu êul. Tch'ōung èul i houâng hôu êul ; cháng tchēu i k'iôung īng (iāng) hôu êul.

CHANT III. TCHOU.

Une nouvelle mariée se plaint de ce que son fiancé, au lieu d'aller au devant d'elle, est resté dans sa maison à l'attendre, et l'a reçue avec des ornements qui n'étaient pas de la couleur requise.

1. Il m'a attendue entre la porte de son habitation et la cloison intérieure. Sur ses oreilles pendaient des cordons de soie blanche ornés de pierres du genre *k'iôung houâ* (de couleur incarnat).

2. Il m'a attendue dans la cour de sa maison. Sur ses oreilles pendaient des cordons de soie verte ornés de pierres du genre *k'iôung iôung*.

3. Il m'a attendue dans la salle de réception. Sur ses oreilles pendaient des cordons de soie jaune ornés de pierres du genre *k'iôung ing*.

CHANT III. 1. Exspectavit me inter domus suæ januam et interius tabulatum. Tegmina aurium erant e sericis tæniis albis; inserti erant eis *k'iôung houâ* lapilli.

Les anciens portaient sur les oreilles des pierres de prix ou des ornements d'ivoire suspendus au bonnet par des cordons.

乎 **Hôu** marque l'étonnement. 而 **Eûl** est une particule finale.

2. Exspectavit me in atrio. Tegmina aurium erant e viridibus tæniis; inserti erant eis *k'iôung iôung* lapilli.

3. Exspectavit me in aula. Tegmina aurium erant e flavis tæniis; inserti erant eis *k'iôung īng* lapilli.

La porte principale des habitations est masquée à l'intérieur par une cloison 屛 **p'ing.** L'espace compris entre la porte et la cloison s'appelle 著 **tchóu.** Pour aller de la cloison à la salle de réception 堂 **t'âng**, on traverse une cour 庭 **t'ing**.

東方之日

(1)東方之日兮、彼姝者子、在我室兮、在我室兮、履我即兮。

(2)東方之月兮、彼姝者子、在我闥兮、在我闥兮、履我發兮。

東方未明

(1)東方未明、顛倒衣裳、顛之倒之、自公召之、

(2)東方未晞、顛倒裳

TOUNG FANG TCHEU JEU. **1. Tōung fāng tchēu jēu hī, pèi tch'ōu tchė tzèu tsái ngò chĕu hī. Tsái ngò chĕu hī ; lì ngò tsĭ hī.**

2. Tōung fāng tchēu iuĕ hī, pèi tch'ōu tchė tzèu tsái ngò t'ă (t'ĕ) hī. Tsái ngò t'ă (t'ĕ) hī ; lì ngò fă (p'ĕ) hī.

TOUNG FANG WEI MING. **1. Tōung fāng wéi mîng (mâng), tiēn taò ī châng. Tiēn tchēu taò (taó) tchēu ; tzéu kōung tchaó tchēu.**

2. Tōung fāng wéi hī, tiēn taò châng ī. Taò tchēu tiēn (tīng) tchēu ; tzéu kōung lìng tchēu.

CHANT IV. TOUNG FANG TCHEU JEU.

Le poète dévoile et blâme les mœurs de Ts'i.

1. Le soleil paraît à l'orient ; cette charmante femme est dans ma maison. Elle est dans ma maison ; elle y est entrée à ma suite.

2. La lune paraît à l'orient ; cette femme charmante est à ma porte. Elle est à ma porte, et sort à ma suite.

CHANT V. TOUNG FANG WEI MING.

Un officier de Ts'i se plaint d'être appelé au palais à des heures indues, et le jour et la nuit.

1. L'aube du jour ne paraît pas encore à l'orient ; (dans mon empressement) je mets à l'envers mes vêtements. Mes vêtements mis à l'envers, je reçois l'ordre d'aller à la cour.

2. Le soleil ne paraît pas encore à l'orient ; je mets à l'envers

CHANT IV. 1. In orientali regione est sol ; illa formosa puella est in mea domo. Est in mea domo ; sequens me accessit.

2. In orientali regione est luna ; illa formosa puella est intra meam januam. Est intra meam januam ; sequens me evadit.

CHANT V. 1. In orientali regione nondum lux apparet ; inverto, perverto superiorem vestem et inferiorem vestem. Inverto eas, perverto eas ; ex aula regia arcessunt me.

2. In orientali regione sol nondum lucescit ; inverto, perverto inferiorem vestem et superiorem vestem. Inverto

衣、倒之顛之、自
公令之、
(3) 折柳樊圃、狂
夫瞿瞿、不能辰
夜、不夙則莫、

南山

(1) 南山崔崔、雄
狐綏綏、魯道有
蕩、齊子由歸、既
曰歸止、曷又懷
止、
(2) 葛屨五兩、冠
緌雙止、魯道有

3. Tchĕ liòu fân pòu (póu), k'ouàng fōu kiú kiú. Pŏu nêng tch'ênn ié (iú), pŏu sŏu tsĕ móu.

NAN CHAN. **1. Nân chān ts'ouêi ts'ouêi, hiŏung hôu souēi souēi. Lòu taó iòu tàng ; Ts'î tzèu iôu kouēi. Ki iuĕ kouēi tchèu, hŏ iòu houâi (houêi) tchēu?**

2. Kŏ kiú òu leàng, kouān jouêi chouāng (chŏung) tchèu. Lòu taó iòu tàng,

mes vêtements. Mes vêtements mis à l'envers, je reçois un ordre de la cour.

3. J'entoure mon jardin de quelques branches de saule recourbées; les hommes les plus inconsidérés savent respecter cette clôture. Le prince ne connaît pas les limites du jour ni de la nuit; quand ses ordres ne viennent pas trop matin, ils viennent trop tard dans la nuit.

CHANT VI. NAN CHAN.

文姜 **Wênn Kiāng,** princesse de la maison de 齊 **Ts'î,** avait épousé 桓 **Houân,** prince de 魯 **Lòu.** Étant retournée à 齊 **Ts'î** avec son mari, elle eut des relations criminelles avec son propre frère, 襄 **Siāng,** prince de Ts'i. Le poète blâme l'impudicité du frère et l'imprudence ou la faiblesse du mari. Cf. Chant IX, page 110.

1. Sur cette haute montagne, au midi de Ts'i, un renard (le prince Siang) s'avance à pas lents (cherchant une compagne). La route de Lou est unie; la jeune fille de Ts'i (Wenn Kiang) l'a suivie pour aller épouser le prince de Lou. Puisqu'elle a contracté mariage, pourquoi son frère pense-t-il encore à elle?

2. Cinq paires de souliers de chanvre, une paire de cordons de chapeau, (c'est la règle. Ces objets vont toujours par paires. Ainsi

eas, perverto eas; ex aula regia jussa dantur mihi.

3. Inflexa salice sepio hortum; stulti homines verentes cavent. (Regulus) nescit matutini et vespertini temporis (limites discernere); quando non maturius, tunc tardius.

CHANT VI. 1. Australis mons est excelsus; mascula vulpes tarde incedit (feminam quaerens). Lou via habet plana; Ts'i puella sequens (eam) ivit nuptum. Quum jam iverit nuptum, quare rursus (Siang regulus) amanter cogitat?

曰 **Iuĕ,** 止 **tchèu,** particules.

2. Cannabinorum calceorum sunt quinque paria; pilei vinculorum est

蕩。齊子庸止。既曰
庸止。曷又從止。
(3)蓺麻如之何。衡
從其畝。取妻如之
何。必告父母。既曰
告止。曷又鞠止。
(4)析薪如之何。匪
斧不克。取妻如之
何。匪媒不得。既曰
得止。曷又極止。

甫田

(1)無田甫田。維莠

Ts'ì tzèu iôung tchèu. Ki iuĕ iôung tchèu, hŏ iòu ts'ôung tchèu ?

3. Í mâ jôu tchēu hô ? Hôung tsōung k'ì meòu. Ts'iù ts'ī jôu tchēu hô ? Pĭ kŏu fòu meòu. Ki iuĕ kŏu tchèu, hŏ iòu kiŭ tchèu ?

4. Sĭ sīn jôu tchēu hô ? Fèi fòu pŏu k'ŏ. Ts'iù ts'ī jôu tchēu hô ? Fèi mêi pŏu tĕ. Ki iuĕ tĕ tchèu, hŏ iòu kĭ tchèu ?

FOU T'IEN. **1. Où tién fòu t'iên ; wêi iòu kiaō kiaō (kaō kaō). Où sēu iuên jênn ; laô sīn taō taō.**

l'union conjugale doit être respectée). Le chemin de Lou est uni; la jeune fille de Ts'i l'a suivi. Puisqu'elle l'a suivi, pourquoi son frère la recherche-t-il encore?

3. Comment cultive-t-on le chanvre? On trace des sillons de l'est à l'ouest et du nord au sud. Comment un jeune homme contracte-t-il mariage? Il doit avertir ses parents. Puisque le prince de Lou a averti ses parents (et contracté un légitime mariage), pourquoi laisse-t-il sa femme satisfaire sa passion criminelle?

4. Comment fend-on le bois de chauffage? Il faut une hache. Comment contracte-t-on mariage? Il faut un médiateur. Puisque le prince de Lou a contracté mariage selon les règles prescrites, pourquoi laisse-t-il sa femme arriver à cette extrémité?

CHANT VII. FOU T'IEN.

On doit éviter de trop entreprendre, et imiter la nature qui procède avec ordre et sans précipitation.

1. Ne cultivez pas un champ trop vaste; seul le faux millet s'y

unum par. Lou via habet plana; Ts'i puella usa est. Quum jam usa sit, quare (Siang regulus) iterum prosequitur?

3. Colitur cannabis quomodo? Ab oriente ad occidentem et a septentrione ad meridiem ejus ager aratur. Ducitur uxor quomodo? (Vir suos) debet monere parentes. (Lou regni Houan regulus) quum monuerit parentes suos, quare rursus (sinit ut uxor cupidinem suam) omnino expleat?

4. Finditur comburendum lignum quomodo? Absque securi non potest. Ducitur uxor quomodo? Sine nuptiarum conciliatore nemo licite assequitur. Quum licite assecutus sit, quare rursus (sinit ut uxor cupidinem) ad extremum expleat?

詩經

驕驕。無思遠人。勞心忉忉。

(2) 無田甫田。維莠桀桀。無思遠人。勞心怛怛。

(3) 婉兮孌兮。總角丱兮。未幾見兮。突而弁兮。

盧令

(1) 盧令令。其人美且仁。

(2) 盧重環。其人美且鬈。

2. Oû tién fòu t'iên ; wêi iòu kiĕ kiĕ. Oû sēu iuèn jênn ; laô sīn tán tán (tĕ tĕ).

3. Iuèn hì liuèn hì ; tsòung kiŏ kouán (kiuén) hì. Wéi kì kién hì ; tŏu êul pién hì.

LOU LING. **1. Lôu lìng lìng ; k'î jênn mèi, ts'iè jênn.**

2. Lôu tch'ôung houân ; k'î jênn mèi, ts'iè k'iuên.

étalerait avec orgueil. Ne cherchez pas à attirer ceux qui sont trop loin de vous; vos efforts ne vous apporteraient que du chagrin.

2. Ne cultivez pas un champ trop étendu ; seul le faux millet y dresserait sa tête superbe. Ne cherchez pas à attirer ceux qui sont trop loin de vous; vos efforts vous donneraient beaucoup de trouble.

3. Un enfant délicat et beau porte encore les cheveux liés en deux touffes. Dans peu de temps, lorsque vous le reverrez, il aura grandi et portera déjà le bonnet des hommes faits.

CHANT VIII. LOU LING.

Le poète critique la folle estime accordée à la chasse dans la principauté de Ts'i. Il reproduit les vains compliments adressés par un chasseur à un autre.

1. Le chien de chasse fait retentir l'anneau de son collier ; son maître est admirable et bon.

2. Le chien de chasse porte un petit anneau attaché au grand ; son maître est admirable et porte une belle barbe.

CHANT VII. 1. Noli colere magnum agrum; solum falsum milium crescet superbe. Ne quæras (allicere) remotos homines; laborans animus angetur.

2. Noli colere magnum agrum; solum falsum milium superbe eminebit. Ne quæras (attrahere) remotos homines; laborans animus agitabitur.

3. (En puer) tener et formosus, collectis (capillis in duo) cornua (ad modum litteræ) *kouán*. Non aliquanto tempore (elapso, eum) videbis, procerus evaserit et feret virilem pileum.

On recevait le bonnet viril à vingt ans.

CHANT VIII. 1. Venatici canis tinnitat annulus ; ejus herus est mirabilis et bonus.

2. Venatici canis duplex est annulus; ejus herus est mirabilis et pulchra ornatus barba.

(3) 盧重鋂、其人美且偲。

敝笱

(1) 敝笱在梁、其魚魴鰥、齊子歸止、其從如雲、

(2) 敝笱在梁、其魚魴鱮、齊子歸止、其從如雨、

(3) 敝笱在梁、其魚唯唯、齊子歸止、其從如水、

3. Lôu tch'ôung mêi ; k'i jênn mêi, ts'iè sāi.

PI KEOU. **1. Pi keòu tsái leâng ; k'i iû fâng kouān (kiūn). Ts'ì tzèu kouēi tchèu ; k'i tsóung jôu iûn.**

2. Pi keòu tsái leâng ; k'i iû fâng siù. Ts'ì tzèu kouēi tchèu ; k'i tsóung jôu iù.

3. Pi keòu tsái leâng ; k'i iû wêi wêi. Ts'ì tzèu kouēi tchèu ; k'i tsóung jôu chouèi.

3. Le chien de chasse porte deux petits anneaux attachés au grand; son maître est admirable et a beaucoup de barbe.

CHANT IX. PI KEOU.

文姜 **Wênn Kiāng**, après la mort de 桓 **Houân**, prince de 魯 **Lòu**, son mari, retourne plusieurs fois à 齊 **Ts'î**, sa patrie, et entretient un commerce incestueux avec 襄 **Siāng**, prince de Ts'i, son propre frère. Le poète blâme la faiblesse de 莊 **Tchouāng**, prince de Lou, qui n'empêche pas sa mère d'aller à Ts'i. Il le compare à une nasse usée qui ne peut retenir les poissons. Cf. Chant VI, page 107.

1. Une nasse usée est dans l'eau auprès du barrage; il s'y présente une brême, une énorme *kouan* (Wenn Kiang). La fille de la maison de Ts'i (Wenn Kiang) retourne en son pays; sa nombreuse escorte forme comme une nuée.

2. Une nasse usée est auprès du barrage; il s'y présente une brême, une tanche. La fille de la maison de Ts'i retourne en son pays; sa nombreuse escorte ressemble à une pluie torrentielle.

3. Une nasse usée est au barrage; le poisson entre et sort librement. Le fille de la maison de Ts'i retourne en son pays; sa nombreuse escorte a l'apparence d'un torrent.

3. Venatico cani est insertus duobus minoribus annulus; ejus herus est mirabilis et multa ornatus barba.

CHANT IX. 1. Detrita nassa est ad septum in aqua exstructum; illic piscis est *brama*, *kouan* (ingens piscis qui in Flavo Fluvio invenitur). Ts'i filia (Wenn Kiang) redit patriam domum; ejus comites sunt instar nubis.

2. Detrita nassa est ad septum; illic piscis est *brama*, tinca. Ts'i filia redit patriam domum; ejus comitatus est similis imbri.

3. Detrita nassa est ad septum; illic piscis intrat, exit. Ts'i filia patriam domum redit; ejus comitatus est similis rivo.

載驅

(1) 載驅薄薄、簟茀朱鞹。魯道有蕩、齊子發夕。

(2) 四驪濟濟、垂轡濔濔。魯道有蕩、齊子豈弟。

(3) 汶水湯湯、行人彭彭。魯道有蕩、齊子翺翔。

(4) 汶水滔滔、行人儦儦。魯道有蕩、齊子遊敖。

TSAI K'IU. **1. Tsái k'iū p'ouŏ p'ouŏ, tièn fōu tchōu kouŏ. Lòu taó iòu tàng ; Ts'i tzèu fă sĭ (siŏ).**

2. Séu lî tsi tsi ; tch'ouêi pí gnì gnì. Lòu taó iòu tàng ; Ts'î tzèu k'ài tí.

3. Wénn chouèi chāng chāng ; hîng jênn pāng pāng. Lòu taó iòu tàng ; Ts'î tzèu ngaô siâng.

4. Wénn chouèi t'aō t'aō ; hîng jênn piaō piaō (paō paō). Lòu taó iòu tàng ; Ts'î tzèu iôu ngaô.

CHANT X. TSAI K'IU.

Le poète blâme l'impudence de 文姜 **Wênn Kiāng**, qui se rend de 魯 **Lòu** à 齊 **Ts'i** avec un pompeux équipage, et affronte sans rougir les regards des nombreux voyageurs qu'elle rencontre.

1. Elle presse la course de ses chevaux; la partie postérieure de sa voiture est couverte d'une natte à carreaux, et la partie antérieure, d'un cuir enduit de vernis rouge. La route de Lou est unie; la fille de la maison de Ts'i (Wenn Kiang) quitte l'endroit où elle a passé la nuit.

2. Quatre beaux coursiers noirs sont attelés de front à sa voiture; les rênes flottent mollement. La route de Lou est unie; la fille de la maison de Ts'i est au comble de la joie.

3. La Wenn coule large et profonde (aux confins de Ts'i et de Lou); les voyageurs sont très nombreux. La route de Lou est unie; la fille de la maison de Ts'i la parcourt joyeuse (sans craindre les regards).

4. La Wenn roule au loin ses eaux; les voyageurs se suivent nombreux. La route de Lou est unie; la fille de la maison de Ts'i la parcourt à son aise (sans éprouver la moindre honte).

CHANT X. 1. Urgetur vehiculum ad celeritatem; tessellata matta a tergo tegitur, rubro corio (a fronte tegitur, sicut reguli vehiculum). Lou via est plana; Ts'i filia egreditur e nocturno diversorio.

載 **Tsái**, particule initiale.

2. Quadrijugi equi nigri sunt pulchri; fluitantes habenæ sunt molles. Lou via est plana; Ts'i filia plene delectatur.

3. Wenn fluvii aqua lata fluit; iter facientes homines plurimi sunt. Lou via est plana; Ts'i filia lætabunda volitat.

4. Wenn amnis longus fluit (inter Ts'i et Lou); iter facientes homines multi invicem sequuntur. Lou via est plana; Ts'i filia spatians cursitat.

猗嗟

(1) 猗嗟昌兮、頎而長兮、抑若揚兮、美目揚兮、巧趨蹌兮、射則臧兮、

(2) 猗嗟名兮、美目清兮、儀既成兮、終日射侯、不出正兮、展我甥兮、

(3) 猗嗟孌兮、清揚婉兮、舞則選兮、射則貫兮、四矢反兮、以禦亂兮、

I TSIE. **1. Ī tsiē ! tch'āng hì ! K'i èul tch'âng hì. Ĭ jŏ iâng hì, mèi mŏu iâng hì. K'iaò ts'iū ts'iāng hì. Chè tsĕ tsāng hì.**

2. Ī tsiē ! mîng hì ! Mèi mŏu ts'īng hì. Ī ki tch'êng hì. Tchōung jĕu chĕu heôu, pŏu tch'ŏu tchêng hì. Tchèn ngò chēng hì.

3. Ī tsiē ! liuèn hì ! Ts'īng iâng wàn (hiuén) hì. Où tsĕ siuèn hì. Chè tsĕ kouàn (kiuén) hì ; séu chèu fàn (fán) hì. Ī iú louàn (liuén) hì.

CHANT XI. I TSIE.

Le poète loue les belles qualités de 莊 **Tchouāng**, prince de 魯 **Lòu**, et déplore sa faiblesse à l'égard de sa mère 文 姜 **Wênn Kiāng**, dont il n'empêche pas les désordres.

1. Hélas! un prince si accompli! Sa taille est élevée. Quand il cherche à cacher sa beauté, elle paraît encore avec plus d'éclat. Son regard est magnifique. Sa démarche est élégante, rapide ; il semble avoir des ailes. Il excelle à tirer de l'arc.

2. Hélas! un prince si digne de renom! Ses beaux yeux brillent. Ses manières sont distinguées. Il tire à la cible toute une journée; chacune de ses flèches frappe le centre. C'est vraiment le fils de la sœur de notre prince.

3. Hélas! un prince si élégant! Ses yeux brillent, son front est beau. Il exécute des chants avec pantomime mieux que personne. Quand il tire à l'arc, il est si fort qu'il transperce la cible, et si adroit que ses quatre flèches atteignent toutes le même point. Il est capable de maintenir l'ordre dans l'État.

CHANT XI. 1. Eheu! tam insignis! Altus et procerus. Se demittens quasi se attollit. Pulchri oculi moventur. Scite properat velut alatus. Quum sagittatur, tunc peritus est.

2. Eheu! laude tam dignus! Pulchri oculi nitent. Decora agendi ratio est absoluta. Toto die sagittis petit scopum, nec aberrat a centro. Vere est nostri (reguli) sororis filius.

3. Eheu! tam formosus! Nitentes oculi et elegans frons sunt pulchri. Quum cantica saltat, tunc egregius est. Quum sagittatur, tunc perforat scopum. Quatuor sagittæ repetunt, i.e. omnes eumdem scopi locum attingunt. Ideo potest arcere turbationem.

Au tir à l'arc, chacun des archers paraissait trois fois. Chaque fois il lançait quatre flèches.

魏一之九

葛屨

(1) 糾糾葛屨、可以履霜、摻摻女手、可以縫裳、要之襋之、好人服之、

(2) 好人提提、宛然左辟、佩其象揥、維是褊心、是以爲刺、

KO KIU. 1. **Kiòu kiòu kŏ kiù, k'ò i lì chouāng ; siēn siēn gniù cheòu k'ò i fôung châng. Iaō tchēu, kĭ tchēu ; haò jênn fôu (p'ĕ) tchēu.**

2. Haò jênn t'î t'î, iuèn jên tsouò pí. Péi k'î siáng tchéu. Wêi chéu pièn sīn ; chéu i wêi ts'éu (ts'i).

LIVRE IX. WEI FOUNG.

CHANT I. KO KIU.

Le poète blâme l'avarice d'un homme riche qui oblige sa femme à travailler aussitôt après la célébration de leurs noces, et se hâte de mettre des vêtements dont la confection n'est pas terminée.

1. S'il convient de mettre des souliers d'été tressés de brins de chanvre pour marcher au milieu du givre, il convient aussi d'employer les doigts délicats d'une nouvelle mariée à coudre des vêtements. A peine le vêtement inférieur a-t-il une ceinture et la tunique un collet, aussitôt cet homme qui est d'une condition élevée s'en revêt.

2. Cet homme d'une condition élevée est toujours calme, et se place poliment au côté gauche. Il porte à la ceinture un poinçon d'ivoire (comme les officiers et les lettrés). Mais il est avare ; c'est la seule chose que je blâme en lui.

TITRE DU LIVRE. 魏一之九 Wei (regni cantica): primæ (partis) nonus (liber). La principauté de Wei était le 解州 **Hiài tcheōu** actuel dans le 山西 **Chān sī.**

CHANT I. 1. Factis e torta cannabi æstivis calceis si deceat uti ad calcandam pruinam, tenuibus puellæ manibus decebit uti ad consuendas vestes. Cingulum assuitur huic (vesti inferiori), collare assuitur illi (vesti superiori) ; honestus vir induit illas.

La nouvelle mariée, trois mois après la célébration des noces, allait au temple des ancêtres de son mari. Cette cérémonie terminée, elle commençait à s'occuper des affaires domestiques.

2. Honestus vir placido habitu comiter ad sinistram recedit. Ad zonam defert suum eburneum spiculum. Solum ita angusto animo est ; quamobrem egi censuram.

Anciennement le côté droit était considéré comme le plus honorable ; à présent, c'est le côté gauche.

汾沮洳

(1) 彼汾沮洳、言采其莫、彼其之子、美無度、美無度、殊異乎公路、

(2) 彼汾一方、言采其桑、彼其之子、美如英、美如英、殊異乎公行、

(3) 彼汾一曲、言采其藚、彼其之子、美如玉、美如玉、殊異乎公族、

FENN TSIU JOU. 1. **Pèi Fênn tsiú jóu, iên ts'ái k'ì móu. Pèi ki tchēu tzèu, mèi ôu tóu. Mèi ôu tóu, chôu i hóu kōung lóu.**

2. Pèi Fênn ĭ fāng, iên ts'ái k'ì sāng. Pèi ki tchēu tzèu, mèi jôu īng (iāng). Mèi jôu īng (iāng), chôu i hóu kōung hâng.

3. Pèi Fênn ĭ k'iŭ, iên ts'ài k'ì siŭ. Pèi ki tchēu tzèu mèi jôu iŭ. Mèi jôu iŭ, chôu i hóu kōung tsŏu.

CHANT II. FENN TSIU JOU.

Le poète blâme l'avarice des officiers de Wei qui vont cueillir des plantes sauvages et des feuilles de mûrier, c.-à-d. qui recherchent de petits profits comme les hommes du peuple.

1. Dans ces marécages sur le bord de la Fenn, (l'intendant des équipages du prince) cueille l'oseille sauvage. Cet officier a des manières infiniment distinguées. Bien qu'il ait des manières infiniment distinguées, il n'est nullement ce que doit être un intendant des équipages du prince.

2. Dans cet endroit sur le bord de la Fenn, (l'intendant des voitures de guerre) cueille les feuilles des mûriers. Cet officier est élégant comme une fleur. Bien qu'il soit élégant comme une fleur, il n'est nullement ce que doit être un intendant des voitures de guerre.

3. Au tournant de la Fenn, (le président du tribunal chargé de régler les affaires de la famille du prince) cueille le plantain. Cet officier brille comme une pierre précieuse. Il brille comme une pierre précieuse; mais n'est nullement ce que doit être le président du tribunal chargé de régler les affaires de la famille du prince.

CHANT II. 1. In illis Fenn fluvii palustribus et uliginosis, colligit illorum locorum rumicem. Ille dominus decorus est sine mensura, i. e. infinite. Decorus est infinite, at valde dissimilis regiorum vehiculorum rectori.

2. In illo Fenn fluvii aliquo loco, colligit illius loci mororum folia. Ille dominus est decorus instar floris. Decorus instar floris, valde dissimilis videtur militarium vehiculorum rectori.

3. In illo Fenn fluvii aliquo sinu, colligit illius loci plantaginem. Ille dominus decorus est instar gemmæ. Decorus instar gemmæ, valde dissimilis videtur regii generis præsidi.

園有桃

(1) 園有桃、其實之殽。心之憂矣、我歌且謠。不知我者、謂我士也驕。彼人是哉、子曰何其。心之憂矣、其誰知之。其誰知之、蓋亦勿思。

(2) 園有棘、其實之食。心之憂矣、聊以行國。不知我者、謂我士也罔極。彼人是哉、子曰何其。心之憂矣、其誰知之。其誰知之、蓋亦

IUEN IOU T'AO. 1. Iuên iòu t'aô, k'î chēu tchēu hiaô. Sīn tchēu iōu i, ngò kō ts'iè iaô. Pŏu tchēu ngò tchè, wéi ngò chéu iè kiaō. « Pèi jênn chéu tsāi (tsī); tzèu iuĕ hô kī?» Sīn tchēu iōu i, k'î chouêi tchēu tchēu? K'î chouêi tchēu tchēu? kái ì ŏu sēu (sī).

2. Iuên iòu kĭ, k'î chēu tchēu chēu. Sīn tchēu iōu i, leaô i hîng kouŏ (ĭ). Pŏu tchēu ngò tchè, wéi ngò chéu iè wàng kĭ. « Pèi jênn chéu tsāi ; tzèu iuĕ hô kī ? » Sīn tchēu iōu i, k'î chouêi tchēu tchēu ? K'î chouêi tchēu tchēu ? kái ì ŏu sēu.

CHANT III. IUEN IOU T'AO.

Le poète s'afflige de voir son pays mal gouverné. De même qu'on mange des fruits pour apaiser un peu la faim ou la soif, de même il emploie le chant et la promenade pour calmer sa douleur, qui n'est comprise de personne.

1. Un pêcher est dans le jardin ; son fruit est bon à manger. Pour dissiper ma tristesse, je chante avec ou sans accompagnement de guitare. Ceux qui ne me connaissent pas, m'accusent d'orgueil. « Ces ministres d'État, disent-ils, font bien leur devoir ; que leur reprochez-vous? » Parmi mes censeurs qui comprend mon chagrin? Qui comprend mon chagrin? c'est qu'aucun d'eux ne réfléchit.

2. Un jujubier est dans le jardin; son fruit est bon à manger. Pour dissiper ma tristesse, je voyage un peu dans la principauté. Ceux qui ne me connaissent pas m'accusent de prendre une licence sans borne. « Ces ministres d'État, disent-ils, font bien leur devoir ; que leur reprochez-vous?» Parmi mes censeurs qui comprend mon chagrin? Qui comprend mon chagrin? c'est qu'aucun d'eux ne réfléchit.

CHANT III. 1. In horto est persicus, ejus fructus est edulium. Ob animi ægritudinem, ego cum fidibus cano et sine fidibus cano. Qui non noverunt me, dicunt me virum esse superbum. (Aiunt): « Illi regni ministri recte agunt; tu objicis quid? » Animi mœrorem, ex illis quis novit illum? Ex illis quis novit illum? etenim non cogitant.

2. In horto est zizyphus, ejus fructus est cibus. Ob animi ægritudinem, paululum ideo iter facio in regno. Qui non noverunt me, dicunt me virum carere limite. (Aiunt) : « Illi regni ministri recte agunt ; tu objicis quid?» Animi mœrorem, ex illis quis novit illum? Ex illis quis novit illum? etenim non cogitant.

勿思、

陟岵

①陟彼岵兮、瞻望父兮、父曰嗟、予子行役、夙夜無已、上愼旃哉、猶來無止、

②陟彼屺兮、瞻望母兮、母曰嗟、予季行役、夙夜無寐、上愼旃哉、猶來無棄、

③陟彼岡兮、瞻望兄兮、兄曰嗟、予弟行役、夙夜必偕、上愼旃哉、猶來無死、

TCHEU HOU. **1. Tchĕu péi hòu hī, tchĕn wáng fòu hī. Fòu iuĕ : « Tsiē ! iù tzèu hîng ĭ, sŏu ié ŏu i. Cháng chénn tchĕn tsāi, iŏu lâi ŏu tchèu ! »**

2. Tchĕu pèi k'ì hī, tchĕn wáng mòu (mì) hī. Mòu iuĕ : « Tsiē ! iù kì hîng ĭ, sŏu ié ŏu méi. Cháng chénn tchĕn tsāi, iŏu lâi ŏu k'ì ! »

3. Tchĕu pèi kāng hī, tchĕn wáng hiōung (houâng) hī. Hiōung iuĕ : « Tsiē ! iù tì hîng ĭ, sŏu ié pì kiāi (kī). Cháng chénn tchĕn tsāi, iŏu lâi ŏu sèu !

CHANT IV. TCHEU HOU.

Un jeune soldat pense avec douleur à sa famille.

1. Je gravis cette montagne couverte d'arbres, et lève les yeux vers la maison de mon père. Mon père dit : « Hélas ! mon fils est au service du prince, et n'a de repos ni jour ni nuit. Puisse-t-il prendre garde à lui, ne pas rester là, mais nous revenir ! »

2. Je gravis cette montagne nue, et lève les yeux vers la maison de ma mère. Ma mère dit : « Hélas ! mon plus jeune fils est au service du prince, et n'a de sommeil ni jour ni nuit. Puisse-t-il prendre garde à lui, ne pas laisser là son corps, mais nous revenir ! »

3. Je monte sur la crête de cette montagne, et lève les yeux vers la demeure de mes frères. Mes frères disent : « Hélas ! notre jeune frère est au service du prince, jour et nuit avec ses compagnons. Puisse-t-il prendre garde à lui, éviter la mort et nous revenir ! »

CHANT IV. 1. Ascendo illum arboribus consitum montem; oculos attollens prospicio ad patris (domum). Pater dicit : « Eheu ! meus filius fungitur militia; diu noctuque caret quiete. Utinam caveat sibi, iterum veniat nec (illic mortuus) consistat ! »

上 Cháng, employé pour 尙 souhaiter.

2. Ascendo illum nudum montem; oculos attollens prospicio ad matris (domum). Mater dicit : « Eheu ! meus natu minimus filius fungitur militia; diu noctuque caret somno. Utinam caveat sibi, iterum veniat, nec (ejus ossa illic) abjiciantur ! »

3. Ascendo illud montis jugum; oculos attollens prospicio ad fratrum majorum (locum). Fratres majores dicunt : « Eheu ! noster minimus frater fungitur militia; diu noctuque certe cum (sodalibus). Utinam caveat sibi, rursus veniat, nec moriatur ! »

詩經

十畝之閒

(1) 十畝之閒兮、桑者閑閑兮、行與子還兮、

(2) 十畝之外兮、桑者泄泄兮、行與子逝兮、

伐檀

(1) 坎坎伐檀兮、寘之河之干兮、河水清且漣猗、不稼不穡、胡取禾三百廛兮、不

CHEU MEOU TCHEU KIEN. **1. Chĕu meòu tchēu kién (kiēn) hî, sāng tchè hièn hièn hî. Hîng iù tzèu houân (siuèn) hî.**

2. Chĕu meòu tchēu wái (wéi) hî, sāng tchè i i hî. Hîng iù tzèu chéu hî.

FA T'AN. **1. K'àn k'àn fă t'ân (t'ién) hî, tchéu tchēu hô tchēu kān (kiēn) hî; hô chouèi ts'ĭng, ts'iè liên ī. « Pŏu kiá, pŏu chĕ, hôu ts'iù houô**

CHANT V. CHEU MEOU TCHEU KIEN.

Le gouvernement de Wei étant mal réglé, un officier propose à un autre de quitter tous deux la vie publique, de retourner dans leurs foyers et de se livrer aux travaux des champs.

1. (Dans son jardin) auprès de ses dix arpents de terre, un planteur de mûriers vit content. Vous et moi, retournons dans nos foyers.

2. (Dans son jardin) en-dehors de ses dix arpents, un planteur de mûriers vit heureux. Vous et moi, allons-nous-en.

CHANT VI. FA T'AN.

Le poète blâme la paresse des officiers qui reçoivent des traitements considérables et ne rendent aucun service au public. « On voit parfois, dit-il, des ouvriers, des charrons, qui, après s'être imposé de grandes fatigues, ne recueillent pas le fruit de leurs travaux, et supportent la faim avec résignation. Ils pensent que, puisqu'ils n'ont ni cultivé la terre ni été à la chasse, il est naturel qu'ils n'aient ni grain ni gibier. De même, le sage se résigne à travailler sans profit; mais jamais à recevoir sa nourriture sans travailler. »

1. Un ouvrier abat des arbres, taille à coups retentissants le bois (nécessaire pour faire une voiture), et le dépose sur le bord du fleuve. L'eau du fleuve est limpide et ridée par le vent. (Elle emporte le bois. L'ouvrier se console de sa perte et se résigne à souffrir la faim. Il se dit): « Tu ne sèmes ni ne moissonnes;

CHANT V. In decem jugerum intervallo, i.e. in horto, mororum cultor contentus vivit. Modo (ego) et tu redeamus.

行 **Hîng** équivaut à 將 **tsiāng** et marque le futur.

2. Decem jugera ultra, i.e. in horto, mororum cultor contentus vivit. Modo (ego) et tu abeamus.

CHANT VI. 1. Repetito crepitu cædit *t'an* arbores (vehiculorum faber), deponit eas ad fluvii ripam; fluvii aqua limpida est et vento crispatur. « Non seris, non metis; quomodo colligas fruges trecenties centum jugerum? Non

狩不獵、胡瞻爾庭、有縣貆兮、彼君子兮、不素餐兮、

(2) 坎坎伐輻兮、寘之河之側兮、河水清且直猗、不稼不穡、胡取禾三百億兮、不狩不獵、胡瞻爾庭、有縣特兮、彼君子兮、不素食兮、

(3) 坎坎伐輪兮、寘之河之漘兮、河水清且淪猗、不稼不

sān pĕ tch'ên hī ? Pŏu cheóu, pŏu liĕ, hôu tchēn èul t'îng iòu hiuên hiuēn hī ? » Pèi kiūn tzèu hī, pòu sóu ts'án (ts'iuên) hī.

2. K'àn k'àn fă fŏu (pĭ) hī, tchéu tchēu hô tchēu tchĕ hī ; hô chouèi ts'īng, ts'iĕ tchĕu ī. « Pŏu kiá, pŏu chĕ, hôu ts'iù houô sān pĕ ĭ hī ? Pŏu cheóu, pŏu liĕ, hôu tchēn èul t'îng iòu hiuên t'ĕ hī ? » Pèi kiūn tzèu hī, pŏu sóu chĕu hī.

3. K'àn k'àn fă liûn hī, tchéu tchēu hô tchēu tch'ouênn hī ; hô chouèi ts'īng, ts'iĕ liûn ī. « Pŏu kiá, pŏu chĕ, hôu ts'iù houô sān pĕ k'iûn hī ? Pŏu cheóu, pŏu

comment recueillerais-tu le grain de trois cents fois cent arpents de terre? Tu ne vas pas à la chasse ; comment verrais-tu des blaireaux suspendus dans ta cour?» Cet homme est un sage; il ne mange pas sa nourriture sans l'avoir méritée par son travail.

2. Un ouvrier taille à coups retentissants le bois nécessaire pour faire les rais d'une voiture, et le dépose auprès du fleuve. L'eau du fleuve est limpide, et ridée par un vent qui souffle dans le sens du courant. (Elle emporte le bois. L'ouvrier se résigne à supporter la faim, qui sera la conséquence de cette perte. Il se dit): «Tu ne sèmes ni ne moissonnes; comment recueillerais-tu trois cents fois cent mille gerbes? Tu ne vas pas à la chasse; comment verrais-tu des animaux de trois ans suspendus dans ta cour?» Celui-là est un sage; il ne mange pas sa nourriture sans l'avoir méritée par son travail.

3. Un ouvrier taille à coups retentissants le bois nécessaire pour faire les roues d'une voiture, et le dépose sur le bord escarpé du fleuve. L'eau du fleuve est limpide; un léger vent la fait tournoyer. (Elle

venaris, non capis feras; quomodo suspicias in tuo atrio esse suspensas meles?» Ille est sapiens vir; non otiosus capit cibum.

廛 **Tch'ên**, habitation d'un laboureur et de sa famille. Chaque famille avait cent 畝 **meòu**. 猗 **Ī**, particule finale.

2. Repetito crepitu cædit (lignum ad faciendos) rotarum radios, deponit illud ad fluvii latus; fluvii aqua limpida est et vento flumini obsequente crispatur. «Non seris, non metis; quomodo colligas frugum manipulos trecenties centena millia? Non venaris, non capis feras; quomodo suspicias in tuo atrio esse suspensas trium annorum feras?» Ille est sapiens vir; non otiosus comedit.

3. Repetito crepitu cædit (lignum

穡、胡取禾三百囷兮、不狩不獵、胡瞻爾庭、有縣鶉兮、彼君子兮、不素飧兮、

碩鼠

①碩鼠碩鼠、無食我黍、三歲貫女、莫我肯顧、逝將去女、適彼樂土、樂土樂土、爰得我所、

②碩鼠碩鼠、無食我麥、三歲貫女、莫我肯德、逝將去女、

liĕ, hôu tchên èul t'ing iòu hiuên chouênn hi ? » Péi kiūn tzèu hî, pŏu sóu suēnn (siûn) hi.

CHEU CHOU. **1. Chĕu chòu, chĕu chòu, ôu chĕu ngò chòu. Sān souéi kouán jòu, mouŏ ngò k'èng kóu (kòu). Chéu tsiāng k'iú jòu, chĕu péi lŏ t'òu. Lŏ t'òu, lŏ t'òu, iuên tĕ ngò chòu.**

2. Chĕu chòu, chĕu chòu, ôu chĕu ngò mĕ (kĭ). Sān souéi kouán jòu, mouŏ

emporte le bois. L'ouvrier se résigne à son sort, en disant) : « Tu ne sèmes ni ne moissonnes ; comment recueillerais-tu trois cents grandes corbeilles de grain? Tu ne vas pas à la chasse ; comment verrais-tu des cailles suspendues dans ta cour? » Cet homme est un sage ; il ne mange pas sa nourriture sans l'avoir méritée par son travail.

CHANT VII. CHEU CHOU.

Un habitant de Wei se propose d'aller habiter une autre contrée, pour échapper à la rapacité des exacteurs, qu'il compare aux rats.

1. Grand rat, grand rat, ne mange pas mon millet. Depuis trois ans (depuis longtemps) j'ai affaire à toi ; jamais tu n'as voulu prendre soin de moi. Je vais te quitter et aller dans cette terre fortunée. Terre fortunée ! terre fortunée ! J'y trouverai un séjour commode.

2. Grand rat, grand rat, ne magne pas mon blé. Depuis trois ans j'ai affaire à toi ; tu n'as jamais voulu me faire de bien. Je vais

ad faciendas) rotas, deponit illud ad fluvii præruptam ripam ; fluvii aqua limpida est et leni vento in gyros volvitur. « Non seris, non metis ; quomodo colligas frugum trecentas sportas? Non venaris, non capis feras ; quomodo suspicias in tuo atrio esse suspensas coturnices? » Ille est sapiens vir ; non otiosus comedit.

CHANT VII. 1. Ingens mus, ingens mus, ne comedas meum milium. Tribus annis, i.e. diu, assuevi tibi ; non mihi voluisti prospicere. Abiens mox linquam te ; adibo illam felicem terram. Felix terra, felix terra, ubi assequar meum locum, i.e. mihi commodam sedem.

2. Ingens mus, ingens mus, ne comedas meum triticum. Tribus annis assuevi tibi ; nec mihi voluisti bene-

適彼樂國、樂國
樂國、爰得我直、
(3) 碩鼠碩鼠、無
食我苗、三歲貫
女、莫我肯勞、逝
將去女、適彼樂
郊、樂郊樂郊、誰
之永號、

唐一之十

蟋蟀

(1) 蟋蟀在堂、歲
聿其莫、今我不
樂、日月其除、無

ngò k'éng tĕ. Chéu tsiāng k'iù jòu, chĕu pèi lŏ kouŏ (ĭ). Lŏ kouŏ (ĭ), lŏ kouŏ (ĭ), iuên tĕ ngò tchĕu.

3. Chĕu chòu, chĕu chòu, ôu chĕu ngò miaô (maô). Sān souéi kouán jòu, mouŏ ngò k'éng laô. Chéu tsiāng k'iù jòu, chĕu pèi lŏ kiaō (kaō). Lŏ kiaō (kaō), lŏ kiaō (kaō), chouêi tchĕu iòung haô ?

SI CHOUE. **1. Sĭ chouĕ tsái t'âng, souéi iŭ k'ì móu. Kīn ngò pŏu lŏ, jĕu iuĕ**

te quitter et aller dans ce royaume fortuné. Royaume fortuné! royaume fortuné ! Là je jouirai de mes droits.

3. Grand rat, grand rat, ne ronge pas ma moisson en herbe. Depuis trois ans j'ai affaire à toi ; tu n'as jamais voulu rien faire pour moi. Je vais te quitter et aller dans cette campagne fortunée. Campagne fortunée! campagne fortunée ! Là, de qui aurai-je à me plaindre?

LIVRE X. T'ANG FOUNG.

CHANT I. SI CHOUE.

L'hiver approche, les travaux des champs sont terminés. Il convient de prendre du repos et de se réjouir, mais avec modération.

1. Le grillon est dans la salle, et l'année touche à sa fin. Si nous ne nous réjouissons pas maintenant, (quand le ferons-nous)? les jours et les mois nous échapperont. Mais ne nous livrons pas

facere. Abiens modo linquam te; adibo illud felix regnum. Felix regnum, felix regnum, in quo obtinebo meum jus.

3. Ingens mus, ingens mus, ne comedas meam nascentem segetem. Tribus annis assuevi tibi; non mihi voluisti operam præbere. Abiens modo linquam te; adibo illum felicem campum. Felix campus, felix campus, ubi de quo clamans querar?

TITRE DU LIVRE. 唐一之十 T'ang (regni cantica): primæ (partis) decimus (liber). Sur la principauté de T'ang, voy. page 4.

CHANT I. Grillus est in aula, annus progrediens ipse vergit ad exitum. Si nunc nos non oblectemus nos, dies et menses ipsi fugient. Ne jam nimium gaudio indulgeamus ; præstat cogitare de suæ conditionis (propriis operibus). Amemus oblectamenta non immoderate; bonus vir cautus est. 聿 particule.

已大康、職思其居、好樂無荒、良士瞿瞿、

(2) 蟋蟀在堂、歲聿其逝、今我不樂、日月其邁、無已大康、職思其外、好樂無荒、良士蹶蹶、

(3) 蟋蟀在堂、役車其休、今我不樂、日月其慆、無已大康、職思其憂、好樂無荒、良士休休、

k'ì tch'óu. Où i t'ái k'āng, tchĕu sēu k'ì kiū (kiú). Haó lŏ ôu houāng, leàng chéu kiú kiú.

2. Sī chouĕ tsái t'âng, souéi iŭ k'ì chéu. Kīn ngò pŏu lŏ, jĕu iuĕ k'ì mái (lí). Oû i t'ái k'āng, tchĕu sēu k'ì wái (wéi). Haó lŏ ôu houāng, leàng chéu kouéi kouéi.

3. Sī chouĕ tsái t'âng, ĭ kiū k'ì hiōu. Kīn ngò pŏu lŏ, jĕu iuĕ k'ì t'aō (t'eōu). Oû i t'ái k'āng, tchĕu sēu k'ì iōu. Haó lŏ ôu houāng, leàng chéu hiōu hiōu.

trop à la joie ; il importe de ne jamais oublier les travaux de sa profession. Aimons les réjouissances avec modération ; un homme sage se tient toujours sur ses gardes.

2. Le grillon est dans la salle, et l'année va finir. Si nous ne nous réjouissons pas à présent, (quand le pourrons-nous)? les jours et les mois s'écouleront. Mais ne nous livrons pas trop à la joie ; il importe de penser aux choses extraordinaires qui peuvent survenir. Aimons les amusements avec modération ; un homme sage est toujours diligent.

3. Le grillon est dans la salle, les charrettes sont au repos. Si nous ne nous réjouissons pas à présent, (quand le pourrons-nous)? les jours et les mois passeront. Mais ne nous livrons pas trop à la joie ; il importe de prévoir les soucis à venir. Aimons les réjouissances, mais sans excès ; un homme sage est toujours calme.

2. Grillus est in aula, annus progrediens ipse exit. Si nunc nos non oblectemus nos, dies et menses ipsi elabentur. Ne jam nimium lætemur ; præstat præcogitare de suis extraordinariis rebus. Amemus oblectamenta non effrenate ; bonus vir diligenter procedit.

外 **Wái**, qui sort de l'ordinaire, imprévu. 蹶蹶 **Kouéi kouéi**, se donner du mouvement.

3. Grillus est in aula, oneraria plaustra ipsa quiescunt. Si nunc nos non feriemur, dies et menses ipsi præteribunt. Ne jam nimis indulgeamus gaudio ; præstat cogitare de suis curis (futuris). Amemus oblectamenta non immodice ; bonus vir tranquillus est.

役車 **Ĭ kiū**, voitures pour les bagages des soldats, charrettes des laboureurs.

16

山有樞

(1) 山有樞、隰有榆、子有衣裳、弗曳弗婁、子有車馬、弗馳弗驅、宛其死矣、他人是愉、

(2) 山有栲、隰有杻、子有廷內、弗洒弗埽、子有鐘鼓、弗鼓弗考、宛其死矣、他人是保、

(3) 山有漆、隰有栗、子有酒食、何不日

CHAN IOU TCH'OU. **1. Chān iòu tch'ōu, sĭ iòu iû. Tzèu iòu ī châng, fŏu i fŏu leôu (liû). Tzèu iòu kiū mà, fŏu tch'êu fŏu k'iū. Iuēn k'ì sèu i, t'ouŏ jênn chéu iû.**

2. Chān iòu k'aò (k'iòu), sĭ iòu gniòu. Tzèu iòu t'ìng néi, fŏu chài fŏu saò (seòu). Tzèu iòu tchōung kòu, fŏu kòu fŏu k'aò (k'iòu). Iuēn k'ì sèu i, t'ouŏ jênn chéu paò (peòu).

3. Chān iòu ts'ĭ, sĭ iòu lĭ. Tzèu iòu tsiòu chĕu, hô pŏu jĕu kòu chĕ, ts'ié i

CHANT II. CHAN IOU TCH'OU.

Contre l'avare qui amasse des biens et n'en jouit pas.

1. L'orme épineux croît sur les montagnes et l'orme blanc dans les vallées. Vous avez de beaux vêtements, et ne les portez pas, des voitures et des chevaux, et ne les faites pas courir. Immobile, vous attendez la mort, et un autre jouira de tous vos biens.

2. Le *k'aò* croît sur les montagnes et le *gniòu* dans les vallées. Vous avez une salle et des appartements; vous ne les arrosez ni ne les balayez (pour y donner des fêtes). Vous avez des cloches et des tambours; vous ne les frappez ni ne les battez. Immobile, vous attendez la mort, et un autre possédera vos biens.

3. L'arbre du vernis croît sur les montagnes et le châtaignier dans les vallées. Vous avez des liqueurs et des provisions de bouche. Aux jours de repos, pourquoi ne jouez-vous pas du luth, pour

CHANT II. 1. In montibus est ulmus spinosa, in vallibus est ulmus alba. Tu, Domine, habes vestes, nec trahis nec rapis, i.e. non eis indutus huc illuc adis. Tu habes vehicula et equos, nec concitas nec stimulas. Immotus exspectas tuam mortem; alius homo illis fruetur.

2. In montibus est *k'aò*, in vallibus est *gniòu*. Tu habes aulam et conclavia; nec irroras nec verris (ad paranda convivia). Tu habes campanas et tympana; non pulsas nec percutis. Immotus exspectas tuam mortem; alius homo illis potietur

3. In montibus est rhus vernicifera, in vallibus est castanea. Tu habes vinum et cibaria. Quare non diebus (feriatis) pulsas citharam, tum ut gaudens oblecteris, tum ut longior dies (tibi videatur)? Immotus exspectas tuam mortem; alius homo occupabit tuam domum.

詩經

鼓瑟、且以喜樂、
且以永日、宛其
死矣、他人入室、

揚之水

(1) 揚之水、白石
鑿鑿、素衣朱襮、
從子于沃、既見
君子、云何不樂、
(2) 揚之水、白石
皓皓、素衣朱繡、
從子于鵠、既見
君子、云何其憂、

iòung jĕu ? Iuĕn k'i sèu i, t'ouŏ jènn jŏu chĕu.

IANG TCHEU CHOUEI. **1. Iâng tchēu chouèi, pĕ chĕu tsŏ tsŏ. Sóu ī tchōu pouŏ, ts'ôung tzèu iū Oŭ (Iŏ). Ki kién kiūn tzèu, iùn hô pŏu lŏ ?**

2. Iâng tchēu chouèi, pĕ chĕu haó haó. Sóu I tchōu sióu (siaó), ts'ôung tzèu iū Kaó. Ki kién kiūn tzèu, iûn hô k'i iōu (iaó) ?

vous réjouir et trouver le jour plus long. Immobile, vous attendez la mort, et un autre occupera votre maison.

CHANT III. IANG TCHEU CHOUEÌ.

昭 **Tchaō**, prince de 晉 **Tsin**, donna la terre de 曲 沃 **K'iŭ ŏu** à son oncle 成 師 **Tch'êng chēu** ou 桓 叔 **Houân chŏu**. Celui-ci étant devenu puissant, les habitants de Tsin formèrent le dessein de se donner à lui. Ils louent sa sagesse ; ils expriment le désir de le voir revêtu des insignes réservés aux princes 諸 侯 **tchōu heôu**, et de vivre sous ses lois, au lieu d'obéir au prince Tchao.

1. Dans une eau qui coule à peine un rocher blanc se dresse bien haut. (Dans la principauté de Tsin affaiblie, le fief de K'iu ou devient très puissant). J'irai à K'iu ou présenter au prince (Houan chou) la tunique blanche à collet rouge brodé (que portent les *tchou heou,* lorsqu'ils font des offrandes), et je me rangerai sous ses lois. Quand j'aurai vu ce sage prince, comment ne serais-je pas dans la joie?

2. Dans une eau qui coule à peine brille un rocher blanc. J'irai à Kao (dans le fief de K'iu ou) présenter au prince la tunique blanche à collet rouge brodé, et me ranger sous ses lois. Quand j'aurai vu ce sage prince, comment serais-je encore dans la tristesse?

Tchou Hi dit que le temps paraît court au milieu des soucis, et long dans la joie des festins et de la musique.

CHANT III. 1. In tarde fluenti aqua album saxum alte eminet. (Deferens) albam tunicam rubro et acu picto collari, sequar dominum in Ou. Postquam videro sapientem principem, dic, qui non gaudebo?

2. In tarde fluenti aqua album saxum micat. (Deferens) albam tunicam rubro et acu picto collari, sequar dominum in Kao. Postquam videro sapientem principem, dic, qui ipse mœrebo?

(3) 揚之水、白石
粼粼、我聞有命、
不敢以告人、

椒聊

(1) 椒聊之實、蕃
衍盈升、彼其之
子、碩大無朋、椒
聊且、遠條且、
(2) 椒聊之實、蕃
衍盈匊、彼其之
子、實大且篤、椒
聊且、遠條且、

綢繆

(1) 綢繆束薪、三

3. Iâng tchēu chouèi, pĕ chĕu lîn lîn. Ngò wênn iòu mîng (mìng), pŏu kàn i kaó jênn.

TSIAO LEAO. 1. Tsiaō leaò tchēu chĕu, fân iên îng chēng. Pèi ki tchēu tzèu chĕu tá ôu p'êng. Tsiaō leaò tsiū iuèn t'iaô tsiū.

2. Tsiaō leaò tchēu chĕu fân iên îng kiū. Pèi ki tchēu tzèu chĕu tá, ts'iè tŏu. Tsiaō leaò tsiū iuèn t'iaô tsiū.

TCH'EOU MEOU. 1. Tch'eôu meôu chŏu sīn, Sān sīng tsái t'iēn (t'în). Kīn sī

3. Dans le faible courant d'une eau limpide apparaît un rocher blanc. J'ai entendu dire que le prince a (formé un complot et) donné des ordres; je n'ose en parler à personne.

CHANT IV. TSIAO LEAO.

Le poète compare la puissance de 桓叔 **Houân chŏu**, prince de 曲沃 **K'iū ŏu**, au poivrier qui étend ses branches et produit beaucoup de fruits.

1. Le poivrier, de plus en plus fertile, donne assez de fruits pour remplir un dixième de boisseau. Ce prince n'a pas d'égal en grandeur, en puissance. Oh! le poivrier étend loin ses branches!

2. Le poivrier, de plus en plus fertile, donne assez de fruits pour remplir les deux mains réunies. Ce prince est grand, puissant et libéral. Oh! le poivrier étend loin ses rameaux!

CHANT V. TCH'EOU MEOU.

Un homme et une femme, qui n'ont pu se marier à l'époque ordinaire, au printemps, ont célébré leurs noces plus tard, lorsque les Trois Étoiles (Antarès et deux autres du Scorpion) paraissaient le soir dans le ciel. Chacun d'eux se félicite lui-même tour à tour, et se demande comment il témoignera à l'autre son affection.

1. Les branchages sont liés ensemble solidement (le mariage

3. In tarde fluenti aqua album saxum apparet. Ego audivi esse jussa (principis Houan chou), nec audeo de iis monere homines.

CHANT IV. 1. Piperis fructus, multi et pulchri, implent decimam modii partem. Ille ipse dominus, potens, magnus, non habet parem. Oh! piper longe profert ramos!

聊 **Leaò**, particule explétive.

且 **Tsiū**, particule admirative.

2. Piperis fructus, multi et pulchri, implent ambas manus conjunctas. Ille ipse dominus, potens, magnus et liberalis est. Oh! piper longe protendit ramos!

星在天、今夕何夕、見此良人、子兮子兮、如此良人何。

(2)綢繆束芻、三星在隅、今夕何夕、見此邂逅、子兮子兮、如此邂逅何。

(3)綢繆束楚、三星在戶、今夕何夕、見此粲者、子兮子兮、如此粲者何。

杕杜

(1)有杕之杜、其葉

hô sī, kién ts'èu leâng jênn ! Tzèu hì, tzèu hì, jôu ts'èu leâng jênn hô ?

2. Tch'eôu meôu chŏu tch'ŏu (tch'eôu). Sān sīng tsái iû (iôu). Kīn sī hô sī, kién ts'èu hiái heóu (heóu) ! Tzèu hì, tzèu hì, jôu ts'èu hiái heóu (heóu) hô ?

3. Tch'eôu meôu chŏu tch'ŏu, Sān sīng tsái hòu. Kīn sī hô sī, kién ts'èu ts'án tchè (tchòu) ! Tzèu hì, tzèu hì, jôu ts'èu ts'án tchè (tchòu) hô ?

TI TOU. 1. Iòu tí tchēu tóu, k'î iĕ siù siù. Tŏu hìng kiù kiù ; k'i ôu t'oaō

est contracté) ; les Trois Étoiles paraissent dans le ciel. Quel soir que ce soir, où je vois cet excellent homme ! Moi, son épouse, que ferai-je pour cet excellent homme ?

2. L'herbe est liée solidement ; les Trois Étoiles paraissent à l'angle sud-est de la maison. Quelle nuit que cette nuit, où je vois cette union inattendue ! Moi, mari, que dois-je faire après cette union inattendue ?

3. Les épines sont liées ensemble solidement ; les Trois Étoiles paraissent en face de la porte (au midi). Quelle nuit que cette nuit, où je vois cette excellente femme ! Moi, son mari, comment dois-je traiter cette excellente compagne ?

CHANT VI. TI TOU.

Le sorbier solitaire a des feuilles qui l'ornent et le protègent. Son sort est préférable à celui d'un homme qui n'a plus ni frères ni parents du côté paternel, ou qui en est abandonné.

1. Un sorbier solitaire a du moins un feuillage touffu. Je vais

CHANT V. 1. Stricto vinculo colligata sunt ramalia ; Tres Stellæ sunt in cœlo. Hic vesper qualis vesper est ! Video hunc optimum virum ! Uxor, uxor, quomodo cum hoc optimo viro (agam) ?

良人 **Leâng jênn**, expression dont une femme se sert pour désigner son mari.

2. Stricto vinculo colligata est herba ; Tres Stellæ sunt ad angulum domus. Hæc nox qualis nox est ! Video hunc inopinatum conventum ! Maritus, maritus, quomodo in hoc inopinato conventu ?

3. Stricto vinculo colligati sunt vepres ; Tres Stellæ sunt ad januam (ad meridiem). Hæc nox qualis nox est ! Video hanc optimam (uxorem) ! Maritus, maritus, quomodo cum hac optima (uxore agam) ?

CHANT VI. 1. Est solitaria sorbus,

湑湑、獨行踽踽、豈無他人、不如我同父、嗟行之人、胡不比焉、人無兄弟、胡不佽焉、

(2) 有杕之杜、其葉菁菁、獨行睘睘、豈無他人、不如我同姓、嗟行之人、胡不比焉、人無兄弟、胡不佽焉、

羔裘

(1) 羔裘豹袪、自我

jênn? Pŏu jôu ngò t'ôung fòu. Tsiē! hîng tchēu jênn, hôu pŏu pi ién? Jênn ôu hiōung ti, hôu pŏu ts'éu ién?

2. Iòu ti tchēu tòu, k'i iĕ tsīng tsīng. Tŏu hing k'iôung k'iôung; k'i ôu t'ouô jênn? Pŏu jôu t'ôung sing (sīng). Tsiē! hîng tchēu jênn, hôu pŏu pi ién? Jênn ôu hiōung ti, hôu pŏu ts'éu ién?

KAO K'IOU. **1. Kaô k'iôu paó k'iū, tzéu ngò jênn kiū kiū. K'i ôu t'ouô jênn? Wéi tzéu tchēu kòu (kōu).**

seul sans compagnon. Est-ce que les hommes font défaut? Non; mais ils ne sont pas pour moi ce que seraient des frères nés du même père. Ah! voyageurs, pourquoi ne vous joignez-vous pas à moi? Pourquoi n'aidez-vous pas un homme qui n'a pas de frères?

2. Un sorbier solitaire a du moins un feuillage épais. Je vais seul, sans secours de personne. Est-ce que les hommes font défaut? Non; mais ils ne sont pas pour moi ce que seraient des parents portant le même nom de famille. Ah! voyageurs, pourquoi ne vous joignez-vous pas à moi? Pourquoi n'aidez-vous pas un homme qui n'a pas de frères?

CHANT VII. KAO K'IOU.

Plaintes du peuple contre l'administration d'un grand préfet.

1. O vous qui portez une tunique garnie de peaux d'agneaux, avec des manches dont les parements sont de peau de léopard,

ejus folia luxuriant. Solus incedo sine comite. Num desunt alii homines? Non sunt sicut mei eodem patre (geniti fratres). Heu! iter facientes homines, quare non vos consociatis mecum? Homo caret fratribus; cur non adjuvatis?

2. Est solitaria sorbus, ejus frondes sunt opacæ. Solus incedo sine adjutore. Num desunt alii homines? Non sunt sicut mei eodem cognomine (vocati consanguinei). Heu! iter facientes homines, quare non consociatis vos mecum? Homo caret fratribus; cur non adjuvatis?

CHANT VII. 1. Ex agninis pellibus tunicam, ex pardi pelle manicarum extrema (deferens), prosequeris nos homines severitate. Num deest alius homo;

人居居、豈無他人、維予之故。

(2) 羔裘豹褎、自我人究究。豈無他人、維予之好。

鴇羽

(1) 肅肅鴇羽、集于苞栩。王事靡盬、不能蓺稷黍、父母何怙、悠悠蒼天、曷其有所。

2. Kaō k'iôu paó siôu, tzéu ngò jênn kióu kióu. K'i ôu t'ouō jênn? Wêi tzéu tchēu haó (heóu).

PAO IU. **1. Siŭ siŭ paò iù, tsĭ iû paō hiù. Wâng chéu mi kòu, pŏu nêng i tsĭ chòu ; fóu mòu hô hòu? Iôu iôu ts'āng t'iēn, hô k'ì iòu chòu!**

vous nous traitez, nous vos sujets, avec trop de sévérité. N'existe-t-il donc aucun autre grand préfet (dans les terres duquel nous puissions nous retirer? Nous voulons vous rester fidèles) à cause de votre grande renommée.

2. O vous qui portez une tunique garnie de peaux d'agneaux, avec des manches dont les parements sont de peau de léopard, vous nous traitez avec une sévérité trop minutieuse. Est-ce qu'il n'existe aucun autre grand préfet? (Nous voulons vous rester fidèles) à cause de notre ancienne affection pour vous.

CHANT VIII. PAO IU.

Les habitants de Tsin, obligés de vivre dans les camps au service de l'empereur et de laisser leurs terres incultes, se comparent à des outardes obligées de percher sur les arbres, et expriment la crainte que leurs parents ne manquent du nécessaire. Les outardes n'ayant pas de pouces, ne peuvent se tenir sur les branches.

1. Les outardes font retentir leurs ailes et se rassemblent sur un massif de chênes. Il n'est pas permis de négliger les affaires de l'empereur, je ne puis semer le millet; quelle sera la subsistance de mes parents? O ciel azuré, qui es si loin de nous, quand rentrerai-je dans ma demeure?

i.e. alius magnus præfectus ad quem migrare possemus? Solummodo domini causa, i.e. propter tuam magnam famam ad alium migrare nolumus.

Les 卿 **k'ing** ministres d'État et les 大夫 **tái fōu** grands préfets portaient des tuniques garnies de peaux d'agneaux, avec des manches dont les parements étaient de peau de léopard.

2. Ex agninis pellibus tunicam, ex pardina pelle manicarum extrema (deferens), prosequeris nos homines scrupulosa severitate. Num deest alius homo? Solummodo tui amore (a te recedere nolumus).

CHANT VIII. 1. Strepunt otidum alæ, congregantur in densis quercubus. Imperatoris negotia non licet negligere, non possum serere milium; parentes quomodo sustentabuntur? O valde dissitum cæruleum cœlum, quandonam ipse habebo sedem (in paterna domo)?

(2) 肅肅鴇翼、集于苞棘、王事靡盬、不能蓺黍稷、父母何食、悠悠蒼天、曷其有極、

(3) 肅肅鴇行、集于苞桑、王事靡盬、不能蓺稻粱、父母何嘗、悠悠蒼天、曷其有常、

無衣

(1) 豈曰無衣七兮、不如子之衣、

2. Siŭ siŭ paò ĭ, tsĭ iū paō kĭ. Wâng chéu mi kòu, pŏu nêng i chòu tsĭ ; fóu mòu hô chĕu ? Iôu iôu ts'āng t'iēn, hô k'ì iòu kĭ ?

3. Siŭ siŭ paò hàng, tsĭ iū paō sāng. Wâng chéu mi kòu, pŏu nêng i taó leâng ; fóu mòu hô tch'âng ? Iôu iôu ts'āng t'iēn, hô k'ì iòu châng ?

OU I. **1. K'i iuĕ ôu ī ts'ĭ hì ? Pŏu jôu tzéu tchēu ī, ngān ts'iĕ kĭ hì.**

2. Les outardes font retentir leurs ailes et se rassemblent sur un massif de jujubiers. Il n'est pas permis de négliger les affaires de l'empereur, je ne puis semer le millet; que mangeront mes parents? O ciel azuré, ciel si éloigné de nous, quand ce service finira-t-il?

3. Les outardes rangées en lignes font retentir leurs ailes, et se rassemblent sur un massif de mûriers. Il n'est pas permis de négliger les affaires de l'empereur, je ne puis semer le riz ni le sorgho; de quoi vivront mes parents? O ciel azuré, ciel si éloigné de nous, quand pourrai-je remplir mes devoirs envers les personnes de ma famille?

CHANT IX. OU I.

Le prince 武 **Où**, nommé après sa mort 成公 **Tch'êng kōung**, petit-fils de 桓叔 **Houân chŏu**, prince de 曲沃 **K'iŭ ŏu**, s'est emparé de la principauté de 晉 **Tsin**. Il a les vêtements aux sept emblèmes des 諸侯 **tchōu heôu**. Il pourrait, dit-il, s'arroger lui-même le droit de les porter; mais il croit plus sûr d'en demander l'autorisation à l'empereur 僖王 **Hī wâng**. Il l'obtiendra par des présents.

1. Dira-t-on que je n'ai pas les vêtements aux sept emblèmes?

2. Strepunt otidum alæ, congregantur in densis zizyphis. Imperatoris negotia non licet negligere, non possum serere milium; parentes quid comedent? O valde dissitum cæruleum cælum, quandonam illa habebunt finem?

3. Strepunt otidum ordines, congregantur in densis moris. Imperatoris negotia non licet negligere, non possum serere oryzam et sorghum; parentes quid gustabunt? O valde dissitum cæruleum cælum, quandonam ipse fungar officiis (erga domesticos)?

CHANT IX. 1. Quomodo dici potest me non habere vestes septem (figuris ornatas)? Non tanquam ab imperatore (concessæ) vestes, tutæ ac faustæ.

Les 諸侯 **tcheōu heôu** et les 伯 **pĕ** avaient trois emblèmes 章 **tchāng** brodés sur la tunique 衣 **ī**; à savoir, des faisans, des flammes et des 宗彝 **tsōung i** vases employés dans le temple

安且吉兮、

(2) 豈曰無衣六兮、不如子之衣、安且燠兮、

有杕之杜

(1) 有杕之杜、生于道左、彼君子兮、噬肯適我、中心好之、曷飲食之、

(2) 有杕之杜、生于道周、彼君子兮、噬肯來遊、中心好之、曷飲食之、

2. K'i iuĕ ôu I liŭ hi ? Pŏu jôu tzèu tchēu I, ngān ts'iè iŭ hi.

IOU TI TCHEU TOU. **1. Iòu ti tchēu tòu chēng iū taó tsouò. Péi kiūn tzèu hi, chéu k'èng chĕu ngò ? Tchōung sīn haó tchēu ; hŏ in séu tchēu ?**

2. Iòu ti tchēu tòu chēng iū taó tcheōu. Péi kiūn tzèu hi, chéu k'èng lâi iôu ? Tchōung sīn haó tchēu ; hŏ in séu tchēu ?

(Je les ai ; mais) ceux qui viennent de l'empereur, apportent plus de tranquillité et de bonheur.

2. Dira-t-on que je n'ai pas les vêtements aux six emblêmes? (Je les ai ; mais) ceux qui viennent de l'empereur, donnent plus de tranquillité et de chaleur.

CHANT X. IOU TI TCHEU TOU.

Un homme désire recevoir un sage dans sa maison. Mais il est pauvre, et comme un sorbier solitaire qui ne donne pas d'ombre. Il craint que le sage ne consente pas à venir sous son toit.

1. Un sorbier solitaire est au côté gauche de la route. Ce sage consentira-t-il à venir chez moi? Je l'aime du fond du cœur; mais comment lui fournirai-je la boisson et la nourriture?

2. Un sorbier solitaire est au tournant de la route. Ce sage consentira-t-il à venir se promener avec moi? Je l'aime du fond du cœur; mais comment lui fournirai-je la boisson et la nourriture?

des ancêtres. Ils en avaient quatre sur le vêtement inférieur 裳 **châng**; à savoir, des algues, des grains de riz, des haches et des lettres 亞.

2. Quomodo dici potest me non habere vestes sex (figuris ornatas)? Non tanquam ab imperatore (concessæ) vestes, tutæ et calidæ.

Aucun dignitaire ne portait de vêtements ornés de six emblêmes. Le prince dit six par une sorte d'euphémisme.

CHANT X. 1. Est solitaria sorbus, crevit ad viæ sinistrum, i.e. orientale latus in semoto loco. Ille sapiens vir voletne venire ad me? Intimo animo diligo illum; quomodo potum et cibum dabo illi?

噬 **Chéu**, particule initiale.

2. Est solitaria sorbus, vivit ad viæ flexum. Ille sapiens vir voletne venire et spatiari? Imo animo diligo illum; quomodo dabo potum ac cibum illi?

葛生

(1) 葛生蒙楚、蘞蔓于野、予美亡此、誰與獨處、

(2) 葛生蒙棘、蘞蔓于域、予美亡此、誰與獨息、

(3) 角枕粲兮、錦衾爛兮、予美亡此、誰與獨旦、

(4) 夏之日、冬之夜、百歲之後、歸于其居、

KO CHENG. **1. Kŏ chēng môung tch'òu, liên mán iû iè (chòu). Iù mèi wàng ts'èu ; chouêi iù tŏu tch'òu ?**

2. Kŏ chēng môung kĭ, liên mán iû iŭ. Iû mèi wàng ts'èu ; chouêi iù tŏu sĭ ?

3. Kiŏ tchènn ts'án hî, kin k'ĭn lán hî. Iû mèi wàng ts'èu ; chouêi iù tŏu tán ?

4. Hiá tchēu jĕu, tōung tchēu iè (iû). Pĕ souéi tchēu heóu, kouēi iû k'î kiū (kiû).

CHANT XI. KO CHENG.

Une femme déplore l'absence de son mari engagé dans une expédition militaire. Elle est de pire condition qu'une plante grimpante ou rampante, qui trouve toujours un appui. Cependant elle assure que, dût son mari ne revenir jamais, elle n'en prendra point d'autre.

1. Le dolic couvre les arbustes épineux; le liseron se répand dans la plaine. Celui qui est l'objet de mon estime, est allé loin d'ici; laissée seule, avec quel autre pourrais-je demeurer?

2. Le dolic couvre les jujubiers; le liseron se traîne sur les tombes. L'objet de mon estime est loin d'ici; laissée seule, avec quel autre goûterais-je le repos?

3. Notre coussin nuptial garni d'ornements de corne est très beau et notre couverture de soie à fleurs est brillante. L'objet de mon estime est allé loin d'ici; laissée seule, avec quel autre attendrais-je le matin?

4. Que les jours d'été et les nuits d'hiver (me paraissent de longue durée! Cependant, dussé-je vivre encore cent ans, je n'accepterais pas un second mariage). Même après cent ans, j'irais m'unir à mon époux dans sa dernière demeure.

CHANT XI. 1. Dolichos crescens operit spinosas arbusculas; convolvulus serpit in campo. Meus eximius, i.e. meus maritus quem ego maximi facio, abiit hinc; quicum sola degam?

2. Dolichos crescens operit zizyphos; convolvulus serpit super sepulcra. Meus dilectus abiit hinc; quicum sola quiescam?

3. Corneis ornamentis cervical (nuptiale) est pulchrum; floridum stragulum fulget. Meus dilectus abiit hinc; quicum ego sola diluculum (exspectem)?

4. Æstatis dies, hiemis noctes (mihi videntur valde longæ. Attamen maritum alterum non accipiam). Centum post annos, congrediar in ejus sedem, i.e. sepulcrum.

(5) 冬之夜、夏之日、百歲之後、歸于其室。

采苓

(1) 采苓采苓、首陽之巔、人之爲言、苟亦無信、舍旃舍旃、苟亦無然、人之爲言、胡得焉、

(2) 采苦采苦、首陽之下、人之爲言、苟亦無與、舍旃舍旃、苟亦無然、人之爲言、胡得焉、

5. Tōung tchēu iė (iú), hiá tchēu jĕu. Pĕ souéi tchŏu heòu (hòu), kouēi iū k'î chĕu.

TS'AI LING. **1. Ts'ài lîng, ts'ài lîng, Cheòu iâng tchēu tiēn (tīng). Jênn tchēu wêi iên, keòu ĭ ôu sin (sīn). Chè tchēn, chè tchēn; keòu ĭ ôu jên. Jênn tchēu wêi iên, hôu tĕ iên?**

2. Ts'ài k'òu, ts'ài k'òu, Cheòu iâng tchēu hiá (hòu). Jênn tchēu wêi iên, keòu ĭ ôu iù. Chè tchēn, chè tchēn; keòu ĭ ôu jên. Jênn tchēu wêi iên, hôu tĕ iên?

5. Que les nuits d'hiver et les jours d'été (me paraissent de longue durée)! (Cependant) même après cent ans de vie, j'irais m'unir à mon époux dans son dernier logement (dans la fosse).

CHANT XII. TS'AI LING.

Personne n'ajouterait foi à l'affirmation de celui qui dirait qu'on trouve la réglisse, le laceron ou le sénevé sur le mont Cheou iang. De même on doit refuser toute créance à la calomnie.

1. On cueillerait la réglisse au sommet du Cheou iang! Les histoires qui se racontent, ne doivent pas être admises facilement. Rejetez-les, rejetez-les; ne leur donnez pas votre assentiment sans examen. Alors comment les inventeurs de fables arriveront-ils à leurs fins?

2. On cueillerait le laceron au pied du Cheou iang! Les histoires qui se racontent, ne doivent pas être crues facilement. Rejetez-les, rejetez-les; ne leur donnez pas votre assentiment sans examen. Alors comment les inventeurs de fables atteindront-ils leur but?

5. Hiemis noctes, æstatis dies! Centum post annos, coeam in ejus conclave, i.e. fossam.

CHANT XII. 1. Colligitur glycyrrhiza, colligitur glycyrrhiza in Cheou iang cacumine! Ab hominibus facta verba leviter non credenda. Abjice illa, abjice illa; leviter ne probes. Hominum ficte dicta quomodo assequentur (intentum finem)?

Le mont Chou iang est dans le 蒲州府 **P'ôu tcheōu fòu,** province de 山西 **Chān sī.**

2. Colligitur sonchus, colligitur sonchus ad Cheou iang radices! Hominum fictis verbis leviter non adhibenda fides. Rejice illa,...

(3)采葑采葑、首陽之東、人之爲言、苟亦無從、舍旃舍旃、苟亦無然、人之爲言、胡得焉、

秦一之十一

車鄰

(1)有車鄰鄰、有馬白顛、未見君子、寺人之令、

(2)阪有漆、隰有栗、既見君子、竝

3. Ts'ài fōung, ts'ài fōung, Cheòu iáng tchēu tōung. Jênn tchēu wêi iên, keòu ì òu ts'ōung. Chè tchēn, chè tchēn, keòu ì òu jên. Jênn tchēu wêi iên, hôu tĕ iên?

KIU LIN. **1. Iòu kiū lin lin, iòu mà pĕ tiēn (tīn). Wéi kién kiūn tzèu, séu jênn tchēu lìng.**

2. Fàn iòu ts'ī, sĭ iòu lĭ. Ki kién kiūn tzèu, ping tsouó kòu chĕ. Kīn tchè pŏu lŏ, chéu tchè k'ì tiĕ (tĭ).

3. On cueillerait le sénevé à l'est du Cheou iang! Les histoires qui se racontent ne doivent pas être admises facilement. Rejetez-les, rejetez-les; ne leur donnez pas votre assentiment sans examen. Alors comment les inventeurs de fables atteindront-ils leur but?

LIVRE XI. TS'IN FOUNG.

CHANT I. KIU LIN.

襄公 **Siāng kōung**, le premier des 大夫 **tái fōu** de 秦 **Ts'în** qui ait obtenu le titre de 諸侯 **tchōu heôu**, a des voitures et des chevaux magnifiques; il est servi par des eunuques. L'un des officiers de sa cour chante cette splendeur, et dans sa joie joue du luth et de la flûte.

1. Le prince a de nombreuses voitures au bruit retentissant, et des chevaux au front marqué d'une étoile blanche. Avant de le voir, il faut se faire annoncer par un eunuque.

2. L'arbre du vernis croît sur le penchant des collines et le châtaignier dans les vallées. (Chaque arbre croît dans le terrain qui lui convient. Ainsi la joie convient et doit éclater en ce jour). Ayant vu le prince, je m'assieds en sa présence et joue du luth. Si je ne

3. Colligitur sinapi, colligitur sinapi ad Cheou iang, orientem! Hominum licte dicta leviter non sunt accipienda. Abjice illa, abjice illa;...

TITRE DU LIVRE. 秦一之十一 Ts'in (regni cantica): primæ (partis) undecimus (liber). Sur la principauté de Ts'in, voy. page 1.

CHANT I. 1. Sunt vehicula turmatim strepentia, sunt equi alba fronte. Nondum viso regulo, i.e. antequam videatur regulus, eunuchus homo est adhibendus.

2. In clivis est rhus vernicifera, in vallibus est castanea. Postquam vidi regulum, simul (cum regulo) sedens

坐鼓瑟、今者不樂、逝者其耋、(3) 阪有桑、隰有楊、既見君子、並坐鼓簧、今者不樂、逝者其亡、

駟驖

(1) 駟驖孔阜、六轡在手、公之媚子、從公于狩、(2) 奉時辰牡、辰牡孔碩、公曰左之、舍拔則獲、

3. Fàn iòu sāng, sǐ iòu iàng. Ki kién kiūn tzèu, ping tsouó kòu houàng. Kīn tchė pŏu lŏ, chéu tchė k'ì wâng.

SEU T'IE. **1. Séu t'iĕ k'òung feŏu, liŭ pi tsái cheòu. Kōung tchēu mi tzéu, ts'ôung kōung iù cheóu (cheòu).**

2. Fóung chêu chênn meòu, chênn meòu k'òung chĕu (chŏ). Kōung iuĕ : Tsouò tchēu. Chė pŏ, tsĕ houŏ.

me réjouis pas à présent, (quand le ferai-je)? Peu à peu j'arriverai à l'âge de quatre-vingts ans.

3. Le mûrier croît sur le penchant des collines et le peuplier dans les vallées. Après avoir vu le prince, je m'assieds en sa présence et joue de la flûte. Si je ne me réjouis pas à présent, (quand le ferai-je)? Peu à peu la mort approche.

CHANT II. SEU T'IE.

Description d'une chasse.

1. Quatre chevaux gris-de-fer d'une belle corpulence sont attelés de front au char du prince; (deux rênes sont fixées par leurs extrémités sur le devant de la voiture), les six autres sont dans les mains du conducteur.

2. (Les gardiens du parc) font lever ceux des animaux mâles qui conviennent à la saison; ces animaux sauvages sont gros et gras. Le prince ordonne de diriger son char vers leur côté gauche. Il décoche ses flèches; ils sont à lui.

pulso citharam. Nunc si non lætabor, progredientibus (annis) ipse octogenarius ero.

3. In clivis est morus; in vallibus est populus. Postquam vidi regulum, simul sedens pulso lamellas, i.e. oris flatu pulso instrumenti 笙 **chēng** lamellas. Nunc si non lætabor, progredientibus (annis) ipse moriar.

CHANT II. 1. Quadrijugi equi ferreo colore sunt valde corpulenti; sex habenæ sunt in manibus. Gratiosi homines comitantes regulum eunt venatum.

Les rênes intérieures des deux chevaux extérieurs 驂 **ts'ān** étaient fixées au char. Les six autres étaient dans les mains du conducteur.

2. Offerunt illos tempestivos mares; tempestivi mares sunt valde corpulenti. Regulus dicit: (Ducatur currus) ad sinistrum latus eorum. Laxat sagittarum incisuram, statim obtinet.

(3) 遊于北園、四馬既閑、輶車鸞鑣、載獫歇驕、

小戎

(1) 小戎俴收、五楘梁輈、游環脅驅、陰靷鋈續、文茵暢轂、駕我騏馵、言念君

3. Iôu iû pĕ iuên, séu mà kì hiên. Iôu kiū louân piaō, tsài lièn hiĕ hiaō.

SIAO JOUNG. **1. Siaò jôung tsièn cheōu ; òu mŏu leàng tcheōu. Iôu houân hiĕ k'iū (k'iú), īn in ŏu siŭ (siú), wênn īn tch'áng kŏu (kóu), kiá ngò k'ì tchóu.**

3. (Après la chasse, le prince et ses compagnons) se promènent dans le parc situé au nord; les quatre chevaux montrent qu'ils ont été bien dressés (ou bien, se reposent en marchant lentement). Les chiens de chasse, les uns à long museau, les autres à court museau, se reposent portés sur les voitures légères, dont les chevaux agitent les grelots fixés au mors de leurs brides.

CHANT III. SIAO JOUNG.

Les 西戎 **Sī jôung** barbares de l'occident s'étant révoltés contre le gouvernement chinois, 襄 **Siāng**, prince de 秦 **Ts'in**, reçut ordre de marcher contre eux. La femme d'un officier décrit le char de guerre, témoigne son estime pour la valeur militaire, et fait des vœux pour le retour de son mari.

1. Le petit char de guerre est moins long (que les autres voitures). Des courroies enroulées avec élégance en cinq endroits affermissent le timon, qui est recourbé comme une voûte. Un anneau mobile (retient les rênes); les courroies costales tiennent à l'écart

En hiver on chassait le loup, en été le grand cerf 麋 **mî**, au printemps et en automne le cerf ordinaire et le sanglier. Le chasseur devait frapper l'animal au côté gauche. 時 **Chêu**, ce, cet. 辰 **Chênn**, saison. 拔 **Pŏ**, coche d'une flèche.

3. Spatiantur in boreali septo; quatuor equi bene exercitati (vel remisso gressu incedentes quiescunt). Leviora vehicula, tinnientibus frenis, vehunt venaticos longiori rostro canes et breviori rostro canes.

Le chasseur était monté sur un char traîné par quatre chevaux attelés de front. Les voitures légères allaient débusquer le gibier et le lancer vers le chasseur. Aux extrémités du mors de chaque cheval des voitures légères étaient fixés des grelots dont le son imitait le cri de l'oiseau fabuleux 鸞 **louân**. 獫 **Lièn**, chien de chasse à long museau. 歇驕 **Hiĕ hiaō**, chien de chasse à court museau.

CHANT III. 1. Parvi bellici currus minus profunde posita est posterior impages, i.e. anterior impages et posterior impages inter se minus distant, et ideo bellicus currus cæteris vehiculis brevior est. Quinque elegantibus e corio vinculis (firmatur recurvus instar domus) trabium temo. Sunt mobilis annulus, costarum repellentes corrigiæ, operta lora, argentati lororum annuli,

子。温其如玉。在其板屋。亂我心曲。

(2) 四牡孔阜。六轡在手。騏騮是中。騧是驂。龍盾之合。鋈以觼軜。言念君子。温其在邑。方何爲期。胡然我念之。

Iên gniên kiūn tzèu, wēnn k'i jŏu iŭ. Tsái k'i pàn ŏu, louán ngò sīn k'iŭ.

2. Séu meòu k'òung feòu, liŭ pi tsái cheòu. K'i liôu chéu tchōung (tchēng); kouā lì chéu ts'ān (chēnn). Lōung chouénn tchēu hŏ, ŏu i kiuĕ nă. Iên gniên kiūn tzéu, wênn k'i tsái ĭ (iŏ). Fāng hô wèi k'i? hôu jên ngò gniên tchēu?

(les deux chevaux extérieurs.). Les extrémités des traits sont fixées à la voiture par des anneaux argentés, et sont masquées (par une planche). Dans la voiture est un coussin rayé. Les moyeux sont longs. Elle est traînée par nos chevaux, dont les uns ont le pelage gris-noir et les autres le pied gauche blanc. Je pense à mon seigneur (à mon mari), il est doux comme le jade. Il demeure (comme les barbares de l'occident) dans une cabane faite de planches; mon cœur en est ému jusque dans ses replis les plus profonds.

2. Les quatre chevaux mâles sont vigoureux; six rênes sont dans les mains du conducteur. Les deux limoniers sont l'un gris-noir, l'autre roux à crinière noire; les deux chevaux extérieurs sont l'un jaune à bouche noire, et l'autre entièrement noir. Sur la voiture sont deux boucliers ornés de figures de dragons; les rênes intérieures des deux chevaux extérieurs sont fixées sur le devant du char au moyen de boucles argentées. Je pense à mon mari; ce seigneur si doux est dans une ville près des frontières. Quel sera le temps fixé pour son retour? pourquoi suis-je condamnée à déplorer son absence?

virgatum pulvinar, longi rotarum modioli. Juncti sunt mei gilvi equi, et sinistro pede albi equi. Cogito de domino (marito); lenis ille sicut iaspis. Est in illa tabulis compacta casa; conturbat mei animi intimos sinus.

言 **Iên**, particule.

2. Quatuor mares equi sunt valde corpulenti; sex habenæ sunt in manibus. Gilvus equus et rufus nigra juba equus sunt medii; flavus nigro ore equus et niger equus sunt laterales. Ornata pictis draconibus scuta sunt duo similia; argentatis adhibitis fibulis internæ externorum equorum habenæ (fixæ sunt). Cogito de domino; lenis ille est in urbe (proxima finibus). In futurum quodnam erit statutum tempus (ad ejus reditum)? quare ita ego (cogor) desiderare eum?

3. Tenuibus (e metallo loricis induti) quadrijugi equi valde concordant. Triangulis hastis sunt argentata inferiora extrema. Variegatus clypeus habet elegantiam. E tigrina pelle est pharetra; cælatis ornamentis nitent

(3) 俴駟孔羣、厹矛鋈錞、蒙伐有苑、虎韔鏤膺、交韔二弓、竹閉緄縢、言

3. Tsiên séu k'òung k'iûn, k'iôu meôu ŏu touéi (chouēnn). Môung fā iòu iuèn (iūn). Hòu tch'áng leóu îng, kiaō tch'áng éul kōung. Tchŏu pi kouénn t'êng. Iên

3. Les quatre chevaux, munis de minces cuirasses de métal, sont attelés de front et marchent bien d'accord. Les lances triangulaires ont le pied argenté; le bouclier aux couleurs variées est très élégant. Le carquois est de peau de tigre. Sur le poitrail des chevaux, les courroies portent des ornements ciselés. Deux arcs sont dans un

pectoralia equorum lora. Conjuncti in theca duo arcus; arundinea armatura funiculo constricta est. Cogito de domino; modo cubo, modo surgo. Placidus est optimus vir; gradatim diffusa est virtutis fama.

Les voitures avaient toutes la même largeur, à savoir, 六 尺 六 寸 **lŏu tch'ĕu lŏu ts'uénn** six pieds six dixièmes; le pied des 周 **Tcheōu** valait environ vingt centimètres. Les voitures ordinaires avaient 八 尺 **pă tch'ĕu** huit pieds de long. Le char de guerre avait seulement 四 尺 四 寸 **séu tch'ĕu séu ts'uénn**. On y montait par derrière. Il était traîné par quatre chevaux attelés de front. Les deux timoniers 兩 服 **leàng fŏu** soutenaient le timon et

念君子，載寢載興。厭厭良人，秩秩德音。蒹葭 ① 蒹葭蒼蒼，白露爲

gniên kiūn tzèu, tsái ts'in tsái hīng. Iēn iēn leâng jênn, tchĕu tchĕu tĕ īn (īng).

KIEN KIA. 1. Kiēn kiā ts'āng ts'āng, pĕ lóu wêi chouāng. Chóu wéi ī jênn,

même fourreau; chacun d'eux est muni d'une armature de bambou. Je pense à mon mari; je me couche, je me lève (sans pouvoir trouver de repos). Cet excellent homme est très paisible; le renom de sa vertu a grandi graduellement.

CHANT IV. KIEN KIA.

Un homme s'efforce vainement d'aller trouver quelqu'un qui est dans le voisinage. Il est arrêté par les obstacles, et celui qu'il cherche n'a pas de lieu fixe. Les interprètes supposent dans cette pièce une allusion à un fait qu'ils ne savent pas deviner.

1. Les roseaux et les joncs sont verdoyants; la rosée se change

tiraient le char au moyen d'un joug 衡 hêng, qui reposait sur leurs cous.

Les rênes intérieures 軜 nă des deux chevaux extérieurs 兩驂 leàng ts'ān étaient fixées par des boucles argentées 觼 kiuĕ devant l'appui 軾 chĕu. Les six autres rênes passaient dans un anneau de cuir 游環 iôu houân, qui 游 flottait derrière la croupe des chevaux; leurs extrémités étaient dans les mains du conducteur. Les courroies costales 脅驅 hiĕ k'iū, fixées par une extrémité au joug et par l'autre au corps de la voiture, s'étendaient entre les chevaux du milieu et les deux autres, et 驅 k'iū repoussaient ceux-ci, c.-à-d. les empêchaient de se serrer contre leurs compagnons.

Les traits 靷 in des deux chevaux extérieurs étaient fixés à la voiture par des anneaux argentés 鋈續 ŏu siŭ, qui étaient masqués 陰 īn par une planche. Dans la voiture était un coussin recouvert d'une peau de tigre sur lequel on s'asseyait. Les moyeux des voitures ordinaires avaient 一尺有半 ĭ tch'ĕu iòu pán un pied et demi de long; les moyeux du char de guerre avaient trois pieds deux dixièmes de long, afin qu'ils fussent plus solides.

Sur le char étaient plantées des lances de plusieurs espèces; le devant était protégé contre les traits des ennemis par trois boucliers de bois. La lance 厹矛 k'iôu meôu avait trois pointes. Sur le bouclier 蒙伐 môung fā étaient représentées des plumes de différentes sortes.

Après avoir débandé un arc, on lui accolait, pour l'empêcher de se déformer, une armature de bambou nommée 閉 pi ou 檠 k'ing, qu'on liait fortement avec une corde. Chaque archer avait un arc de rechange.

Un char de guerre portait trois hommes revêtus de cuirrasses; à savoir, un archer placé à gauche, un lancier à droite et un conducteur au milieu.

CHANT IV. 1. Calami et junci sunt virides; albus ros fit pruina. De quo cogito, ille homo est in aquæ illo loco. Adverso flumine tendo ad illum; via

霜。所謂伊人。在水一方。遡洄從之。道阻且長。遡游從之。宛在水中央。

(2) 蒹葭淒淒。白露未晞。所謂伊人。在水之湄。遡洄從之。道阻且躋。遡游從之。宛在水中坻。

(3) 蒹葭采采。白露未已。所謂伊人。在水之涘。遡洄從之。道阻且右。遡游從之。宛在水中沚。

tsái chouèi ĭ fāng. Sóu houêi ts'ôung tchēu, taó tchóu, ts'iè tch'âng. Sóu iôu ts'ôung tchēu, iuén tsái chouèi tchōung iāng.

2. Kiēn kiā ts'ī ts'ī, pĕ lóu wéi hī. Chóu wéi ī jênn, tsái chouèi tchēu mêi. Sóu houêi ts'ôung tchēu, taó tchóu, ts'iè tsī. Sóu iôu ts'ôung tchēu, iuén tsái chouèi tchōung tch'êu.

3. Kiēn kiā ts'ài ts'ài (ts'i ts'i), pĕ lóu wéi i. Chóu wéi ī jênn, tsái chouèi tchēu séu. Sóu houêi ts'ôung tchēu, taó tchóu, ts'iè ióu (wéi). Sóu iôu ts'ôung tchēu, iuén tsái chouèi tchèu.

en gelée blanche. Celui que je cherche, est en quelque endroit de la rivière. Pour aller à lui, je marche en sens contraire du courant; mais le chemin est semé d'obstacles et fort long. Je marche dans le sens du courant; mais voilà cet homme immobile au milieu de l'eau.

2. Les roseaux et les joncs sont luxuriants; la blanche rosée n'est pas encore évaporée. Celui que je cherche est sur la rive verdoyante. Pour aller à lui, je marche en sens contraire du courant; mais le chemin est semé d'obstacles et va en montant. Je marche dans le sens du courant; mais voilà cet homme immobile au milieu d'un ilot.

3. Les roseaux et les joncs sont bons à couper; la blanche rosée n'a pas encore disparu. Celui que je cherche est sur la digue de la rivière. Pour aller à lui, je marche en sens contraire du courant; mais le chemin est semé d'obstacles et tourne à droite (fait des détours). Je marche dans le sens du courant; mais voilà cet homme immobile au milieu d'un ilot.

est aspera et longa. Secundo flumine tendo ad illum; tranquillus manet in aquæ medio centro (nec jam potest attingi).

2. Calami et junci sunt virides; albus ros nondum exsiccatus est. De quo cogito, ille homo est in aquæ viridanti ripa. Adverso flumine tendo ad illum; via est aspera et ardua. Secundo flumine tendo ad illum, tranquillus manet in fluvii media insula.

3. Calami et junci colligi possunt; albus ros nondum evanuit. De quo cogito, ille homo est in aquæ aggere. Adverso flumine tendo ad illum; via est aspera et ad dexteram flectitur. Secundo flumine tendo ad illum; tranquillus manet in fluvii media insula.

終南

(1) 終南何有、有條有梅、君子至止、錦衣狐裘、顏如渥丹、其君也哉、

(2) 終南何有、有紀有堂、君子至止、黻衣繡裳、佩玉將將、壽考不忘、

TCHOUNG NAN. 1. **Tchōung nân hô iòu? Iòu t'iaô, iòu mêi. Kiūn tzèu tchéu tchéu, kin ī hôu k'iôu (k'ī). Iên jôu iŏ tān. K'î kiūn iè tsāi (tsī)!**

2. Tchōung nân hô iòu? Iòu ki, iòu t'âng. Kiūn tzèu tchéu tchéu, fŏu ī siôu châng. Péi iŭ ts'iāng ts'iāng. Cheóu k'aò pŏu wàng.

CHANT V. TCHOUNG NAN.

Le poète célèbre l'arrivée du prince de 秦 **Ts'în** à 鎬 **Haò**. Le mont Tchoung nan est couvert de beaux arbres; de même le prince porte des vêtements magnifiques, marques de sa dignité de 諸 侯 **tchōu heôu**. Ce prince est peut-être 襄 公 **Siāng kōung**, le premier tchou heou de Ts'in. (777-765).

1. Que voit-on sur le mont Tchoung nan? des catalpas et des pruniers. Notre prince est venu au pied de cette montagne; il porte une tunique de soie à fleurs sur une tunique garnie de fourrures de renards. Son visage est d'un rouge vermeil. Il a bien l'apparence d'un prince!

2. Que voit-on sur le mont Tchoung nan? des lieux escarpés et des plateaux. Notre prince est venu au pied de cette montagne; il porte deux vêtements inférieurs, l'un orné de haches, l'autre orné de diverses broderies. Les pierres de prix suspendues à sa ceinture font entendre un son. Puisse-t-il vivre longtemps, et ne jamais tomber en disgrâce!

CHANT V. 1. Tchoung nan quid habet? Habet catalpas, habet prunos. Regulus advenit ad radices (Tchoung nan montis; habet) floridam tunicam et indutam vulpium pellibus tunicam. Vultus color similis est intenso minio. Ille regulus est!

Le mont Tchoung nan était au sud de 鎬 **Haò**, l'ancienne capitale des 周 **Tcheōu**, dans le 西 安 府 **Sī ngān fòu**, province de 陝 西 **Chèn sī**. L'empereur 平 王 **P'îng vâng** (770-719), ayant fixé sa résidence à Lo iang, avait cédé l'ancien domaine de sa famille au prince 襄 **Siāng** de Ts'in, en le créant 諸 侯 **tchōu heôu**.

2. Tchoung nan quid habet? Habet abrupta et plana. Regulus advenit ad montis radices; pictis securibus ornata vestis (inferior), acu picta vestis inferior. Ad zonam appensi lapilli tinniunt. Diutissime vivat, nec in oblivionem deveniat, i.e. nunquam imperatoris gratiam suamque dignitatem amittat!

Le tranchant des haches était brodé en blanc, et le dos en bleu.

黃鳥

(1)交交黃鳥、止于棘、誰從穆公、子車奄息、維此奄息、百夫之特、臨其穴、惴惴其慄、彼蒼者天、殲我良人、如可贖兮、人百其身、

(2)交交黃鳥、止于桑、誰從穆公、子車仲行、維此仲行、百夫之防、臨其穴、惴惴其慄、彼蒼者天、

HOUANG GNIAO. **1. Kiaō kiaō houâng gniaò tchéu iū kĭ. Chouêi ts'ôung Mŏu kōung? Tzèu kiū Ièn sĭ. Wêi ts'èu Ièn sĭ, pĕ fōu tchēu t'ĕ. Lîn k'i hiuĕ (hĭ), tchouéi tchouéi k'ì lĭ. Pèi ts'āng tchè t'iēn (t'īn), tsiēn ngò leàng jênn. Jŏu k'ò chŏu hì, jênn pĕ k'i chēnn.**

2. Kiaō kiaō houâng gniaò, tchèu iū sāng. Chouêi ts'ôung Mŏu kōung? Tzèu kiū Tchóung hâng. Wêi ts'èu Tchóung hâng pĕ fōu tchēu fâng. Lîn k'i hiuĕ (hĭ),

CHANT VI. HOUANG GNIAO.

穆 **Mŏu**, prince de 秦 **Ts'in**, étant mort, le prince 康 **K'āng** fit immoler sur la tombe de son père cent soixante dix-sept personnes, parmi lesquelles étaient trois hommes remarquables de la famille des 子車 **Tzèu kiū**. Le peuple déplore le sort de ces trois victimes. Les oiseaux, dit-il, reposent librement sur les arbres; de même, les hommes doivent avoir la liberté de vivre, et il n'est pas permis de les précipiter dans la tombe.

1. L'oiseau jaune (peut-être le loriot) trace dans les airs des sillons qui s'entrecroisent, puis il se repose sur un jujubier. Qui accompagne au tombeau le prince Mou? C'est Tzeu kiu Ien si. Ce Ien si se distinguait entre cent. Arrivé près de la fosse, il tremble de peur. Le ciel nous enlève cet excellent homme. S'il était possible de le racheter, chacun de nous donnerait volontiers cent vies pour le sauver.

2. L'oiseau jaune trace dans les airs des sillons qui se croisent, puis il se repose sur un mûrier. Qui accompagne au tombeau le prince Mou? C'est Tzeu kiu Tchoung hang. Ce Tchoung hang à lui seul vaut autant que cent. Arrivé près de la fosse, il tremble

CHANT VI. 1. Huc illuc volitans flava avis sistit super zizyphum. Quis comitatur Mou regulum (ad tumulum)? Tzeu kiu Ien si. Solus hic Ien si inter centum viros eminet. Accedens ad suam fossam, tremens ille formidat. Illud cæruleum cœlum perimit nostrum egregium virum. Si liceret redimere, homines centuplicarent suum corpus.

2. Huc illuc volitans flava avis sistit super morum. Quis comitatur Mou regulum? Tzeu kiu Tchoung hang. Solus hic Tchoung hang centum viris par est. Accedens ad suam fossam, tremebun-

殲我良人，如可贖兮，人百其身。

(3) 交交黃鳥，止于楚。誰從穆公，子車鍼虎。維此鍼虎，百夫之禦。臨其穴，惴惴其慄。彼蒼者天，殲我良人。如可贖兮，人百其身。

晨風

(1) 鴥彼晨風，鬱彼北林。未見君子，憂心欽欽。如何如何，忘我實多。

tchouéi tchouéi k'î lî. Péi ts'āng tchè t'iēn (t'īn), tsiēn ngò leâng jênn. Jôu k'ò chŏu hi, jênn pĕ k'i chēnn.

3. Kiaō kiaō houâng gniaò tchéu iū tch'òu. Chouêi ts'ôung Mŏu kōung ? Tzèu kiū K'iên hòu. Wêi ts'èu K'iên hòu pĕ fōu tchēu iù. Lîn k'î hiuĕ (hĭ), tchouéi tchouéi k'î lî. Pêi ts'āng tchè t'iēn (t'īn), tsiēn ngò leâng jênn. Jôu k'ò chŏu hi, jênn pĕ k'î chēnn.

CHENN FOUNG. **1. Iū pèi chênn fōung (fēnn), iū pèi pĕ lîn. Wéi kién kiūn tzèu, iōu sīn k'īn k'īn. Jôu hô, jôu hô, wâng ngò chĕu touŏ ?**

de peur. Le ciel nous enlève cet excellent homme. S'il était possible de le racheter, chacun de nous voudrait avoir et donner cent vies pour le sauver.

2. L'oiseau jaune trace dans les airs des sillons qui se croisent, puis il se repose sur un arbuste épineux. Qui accompagne au tombeau le prince Mou? C'est Tzeu kiu K'ien hou. Ce K'ien hou à lui seul vaut autant que cent. Arrivé près de la fosse, il tremble de peur. Le ciel nous enlève cet homme éminent. S'il était possible de le racheter, chacun voudrait avoir et donner cent vies pour le sauver.

CHANT VII. CHENN FOUNG.

Une femme déplore l'absence prolongée de son mari. « Le faucon, dit-elle, revient dans la forêt; mon mari ne revient pas à la maison. Les montagnes et les vallées ont les arbres qui leur conviennent; moi, je n'ai pas l'objet de mes désirs.»

1. Le faucon au vol rapide se retire au nord dans cette épaisse forêt. Tant que je ne vois pas mon seigneur, je suis triste et ne cesse de penser à lui. Comment peut-il m'oublier si longtemps?

dus ille pavet. Illud cæruleum cœlum perimit...

3. Huc illuc volitans flava avis sistit super spinosam arbusculam. Quis comitatur Mou regulum? Tzeu kiu K'ien hou. Solus hic K'ien hou centum viris par est. Accedens ad suam fossam,...

CHANT VII. 1. Celeriter volat ille falco, densa est illa borealis silva. Non viso domino, mœstus animus continuo anxius est. Quomodo, quomodo obliviscitur mei vere diu?

(2)山有苞櫟，隰有六駮，未見君子，憂心靡樂，如何如何，忘我實多，

(4)山有苞棣，隰有樹檖，未見君子，憂心如醉，如何如何，忘我實多，

無衣

(1)豈曰無衣，與子同袍，王于興師，脩我戈矛，與子同仇，

(2)豈曰無衣，與子

2. Chān iòu paō lĭ (lŏ), sĭ iòu liŭ pŏ. Wéi kién kiūn tzèu, iōu sīn mi lŏ. Jôu hô, jôu hô, wâng ngò chĕu touō ?

3. Chān iòu paō tí, sĭ iòu chóu souéi. Wéi kién kiūn tzèu, iōu sīn jôu tsouéi. Jôu hô, jôu hô, wâng ngò chĕu touō ?

OU I. **1. K'i iuĕ ôu ī? iù tzèu t'ôung p'aô (p'eôu). Wâng iù hīng chēu. Siōu ngò kouō meôu ; iù tzèu t'ôung tch'eôu.**

2. K'i iuĕ ôu ī? iù tzèu t'ôung tchĕ (tŏ). Wâng iù hīng chēu. Siōu ngò meôu kĭ (kiŏ) ; iù tzèu kiāi tsŏ.

2. Les montagnes ont des massifs de chênes, et les vallées, des ormes dont l'écorce est tachetée de blanc. Tant que je ne vois pas mon seigneur, mon cœur inquiet n'a pas de joie. Comment peut-il m'oublier si longtemps?

3. Les montagnes ont des massifs de pruniers, et les vallées, de grands poiriers sauvages. Tant que je ne vois pas mon seigneur, mon cœur est triste, et troublé comme celui d'un homme ivre. Comment peut-il m'oublier si longtemps?

CHANT VIII. OU I.

Un ami engage son ami à partir avec lui pour une expédition contre les barbares de l'occident; il lui promet de lui fournir des vêtements, si c'est nécessaire.

1. Direz-vous que vous n'avez pas de vêtements? Je partagerai avec vous l'usage de mes tuniques ouatées. L'empereur met des troupes en campagne. Je prépare mes lances; vos ennemis seront les miens.

2. Direz-vous que vous n'avez pas de vêtements? Je partagerai

2. In montibus sunt densæ quercus, in vallibus sunt albis maculis ulmi. Non viso domino, mœstus animus caret gaudio. Quomodo,...

3. In montibus sunt densæ pruni, in vallibus sunt arrectæ pyri silvestres. Non viso domino, mœstus animus quasi ebrius turbatur. Quomodo,...

CHANT VIII. 1. Quomodo dices te carere vestibus? tecum, Domine, communicabo gossypio refertas tunicas. Imperator est educens copias. Paro meas hastas; tecum communes habebo hostes.

同澤、王于興師、脩我矛戟、與子偕作、

(3) 豈曰無衣、與子同裳、王于興師、脩我甲兵、與子偕行、

渭陽

(1) 我送舅氏、曰至渭陽、何以贈之、路車乘黃、

3. K'i iuĕ ôu ī? iù tzèu t'ôung châng. Wâng iù hīng chēu. Siōu ngò kiă pīng (pāng); iù tzèu kiāi hing (hâng).

WEI IANG. **1. Ngò sóung kióu chéu, iuĕ tchéu Wéi iàng. Hô i tséng tchēu? Lóu kiū chéng houâng.**

avec vous l'usage de mes vêtements intérieurs. L'empereur met des troupes en campagne. Je prépare mes lances, et partirai avec vous.

3. Direz-vous que vous n'avez pas de vêtements? Je partagerai avec vous l'usage de mes vêtements inférieurs. L'empereur met des troupes en campagne. Je prépare ma cuirasse et mes armes; je voyagerai avec vous.

CHANT IX. WEI IANG.

重 耳 **Tch'ôung èul**, fils de 獻 **Hién**, prince de 晉 **Tsin**, ayant été calomnié auprès de son père, se réfugia à la cour de 穆 **Mŏu**, prince de 秦 **Ts'in**, dont la femme était sa sœur. Quinze ans après la mort du prince Hien, Tch'oung eul fut appelé à gouverner la principauté, et devint le célèbre 文 **Wênn**, prince de 晉 **Tsin**. Son neveu, le prince 康 **K'āng**, héritier présomptif du prince 穆 **Mŏu**, l'accompagna à son départ de 秦 **Ts'in**, puis composa les deux stances suivantes.

1. J'accompagne mon oncle maternel jusqu'au nord de la Wei. Quels présents lui offrirai-je? Une voiture de *tchou heou* avec quatre chevaux jaunes.

2. Quomodo dices te carere vestibus? tecum communes habebo interiores vestes. Imperator est educens copias. Paro meas hastas; tecum simul surgam.

澤 **Tchĕ**, humecter, vêtement humecté par la sueur, caleçon, chemise.

戟 **Kí**, lance qui avait comme deux branches 枝 格 **tchēu kŏ**, était longue de seize 尺 **tch'ĕu**, et servait sur le char de guerre.

3. Quomodo dices te carere vestibus? tecum communes faciam inferiores vestes. Imperator est educens copias. Paro meam loricam et arma; tecum simul ibo.

CHANT IX. 1. Ego comitor avunculum dominum ad Wei fluvii septentrionem. Quo utens donabo eum? magno curru et quadrijugis equis flavis.

La capitale de 秦 **Ts'in** était alors la ville de 雍 **Iōung** dans le 西 安 府 **Sī ngān fòu**. Le prince K'ang accompagna son oncle jusqu'au 咸陽縣 **Hiên iâng hién** actuel. 曰 **Iuĕ**, particule.

Les *tchou heou* qui étaient parents de l'empereur, avaient des voitures

(2) 我送舅氏、悠悠我思。何以贈之、瓊瑰玉佩、

權輿

(1) 於我乎、夏屋渠渠、今也每食無餘、于嗟乎、不承權輿、

(2) 於我乎、每食四簋、今也每食不飽、于嗟乎、不承權輿、

2. Ngò sóung kióu chéu, iôu iôu ngò sēu. Hô i tséng tchēu ? K'iôung kouēi iù péi (pēi).

K'IUEN IU. **1. Iû ngò hôu, hiá ǒu k'iû k'iû. Kīn iè mèi chĕu ôu iû. Hiū tsiē hôu ! pŏu tch'êng k'iuèn iù.**

2. Iû ngò hôu, mèi chĕu séu kouèi (kiòu). Kīn iè mèi chĕu pŏu paò (peòu). Hiū tsiē hôu ! pŏu tch'êng k'iuèn iù.

2. J'accompagne mon oncle maternel, et tout le temps du voyage, je pense (à ma mère). Quels présents offrirai-je à mon oncle? Des pierres de prix et des ornements de jade pour sa ceinture.

CHANT X. K'IUEN IU.

Les hommes de talent se plaignent d'être négligés par le prince.

1. Pour nous (autrefois dans le palais) était une vaste salle (où nous recevions la nourriture). A présent, le prince ne nous offre plus les restes de sa table après aucun repas. Hélas ! la suite ne répond pas au commencement.

2. Pour nous quatre plats étaient servis à chaque repas. Maintenant, à aucun repas, nous n'avons assez pour nous rassasier. Hélas! la suite ne répond pas au commencement.

ornées d'or ou d'ivoire 金路 ou 象路; ceux qui étaient chargés de défendre les frontières, avaient des voitures couvertes de cuir 革路; ceux qui étaient dans les pays tributaires, avaient des voitures de bois sans ornement 木路.

2. Ego comitor avunculum dominum, longe ego cogito (de matre mortua). Quo utens donabo eum? pulchris lapillis et lapillis ad zonam appendendis.

CHANT X. 1. Nobis spatiosa aula late patebat. Nunc autem, quaque refectione, non sunt reliquiæ. Eheu! non continuantur initia.

權 **K'iuên**, poids de balance. 輿 **Iû**, plateforme d'une voiture. *K'iuên iû* signifie commencement, parce que ceux qui les premiers construisirent des balances, des voitures, firent d'abord le poids, la plateforme.

2. Nobis quaque refectione quatuor vasa. Nunc autem, quaque refectione, non saturamur. Eheu! non continuantur initia.

簋 **Kouèi**, vase d'argile ou de bois, rond à l'extérieur et carré à l'intérieur, dans lequel on servait du millet ou du riz.

陳一之十二

宛丘

(1)子之湯兮、宛丘之上兮、洵有情兮、而無望兮、

(2)坎其擊鼓、宛丘之下、無冬無夏、値其鷺羽、

(3)坎其擊缶、宛丘之道、無冬無夏、値其鷺翿、

東門之枌

(1)東門之枌、宛

IUEN K'IOU. 1. Tzèu tchēu t'āng hī, Iuēn k'iōu tchēu cháng hī. Siūn iòu ts'îng hī, êul ôu wáng hī.

2. K'àn k'î kĭ kòu, Iuēn k'iōu tchēu hiá (hòu). Où tōung ôu hiá (hòu), tchéu k'î lóu iù.

3. K'àn k'î kĭ feòu, Iuēn k'iōu tchēu taó (teòu). Où tōung ôu hiá, tchéu k'î lóu taó (tcheòu).

TOUNG MENN TCHEU FENN. 1. Tōung mênn tchēu fênn, Iuēn k'iōu tchēu

LIVRE XII. TCH'ENN FOUNG.

CHANT I. IUEN K'IOU.

Contre la dissipation habituelle des officiers de Tch'enn.

1. Vous prenez vos ébats sur le Iuen k'iou. Vous y trouvez vraiment du plaisir; mais votre conduite n'est pas belle à voir.

2. Vous battez le tambour au pied du Iuen k'iou. Hiver comme été, vous tenez à la main votre plume de héron (comme les danseurs. Cf. pages 41 et 78).

3. Vous battez (la mesure sur) le tambourin d'argile dans le chemin du Iuen k'iou. Hiver comme été, vous tenez à la main votre éventail de plumes de héron (comme les pantomimes).

CHANT II. TOUNG MENN TCHEU FENN.

Contre les habitudes légères des jeunes gens de Tch'enn.

1. Il y a des ormes blancs près de la porte orientale, et des

TITRE DU LIVRE. 陳一之十二 Tch'enn (regni cantica): primæ (partis) duodecimus (liber). La principauté de Tch'enn était le 陳州府 Tch'ênn tcheōu fòu dans le Ho nan. Voy. page 4.

CHANT I. 1. Dominus genio indulget, in Iuen k'iou collis vertice. Vere habet voluptatis sensum, at nihil habet spectatu dignum.

Le Iuen K'iou était près de la capitale de la principauté de Tch'enn.

2. Cum sonitu pulsat tympanum ad Iuen k'iou collis radices. Absque hiemis æstatisve discrimine, arrectam tenet suam ardeæ plumam.

3. Cum sonitu pulsat vas fictile, in Iuen k'iou collis via. Absque hiemis æstatisve discrimine, arrectum tenet ex ardeæ plumis flabellum.

CHANT II. 1. (Sunt) orientalis

19

丘之栩、子仲之子。婆娑其下、

(2) 穀旦于差、南方之原、不績其麻、市也婆娑、

(3) 穀旦于逝、越以鬷邁、視爾如荍、貽我握椒、

衡門

(1) 衡門之下、可以棲遲、泌之洋洋、可以樂飢、

(2) 豈其食魚、必河

hiû, Tzèu tchóung tchēu tzèu p'ouô souō k'ì hià (hòu).

2. Kŏu tán iû tch'ā (ts'ouō), nân fāng tchēu iuên, pŏu tsĭ k'î mâ (mô), chéu iè p'ouô souō.

3. Kŏu tán iû chéu, iuĕ i tsōung mái (lí). Chéu èul jôu k'iaô, î ngŏ iŏ tsiaō.

HENG MENN. **1. Hêng mênn tchēu hiá k'ò i sī tch'êu. Pí tchĕu iâng iâng, k'ò i lŏ kī.**

2. K'i k'î chĕu iû, pĭ Hô tchēu fāng ? K'i k'î ts'iù ts'ī, pí Ts'î tchēu Kiāng ?

chênes sur le Iuen k'iou. La fille de Tzeu tchoung danse sous ces arbres.

2. On choisit une belle matinée, et l'on se donne rendez-vous sur le terrain uni qui est au midi. Au lieu de filer son chanvre, la jeune fille danse sur la place publique.

3. Un beau matin, on va se promener, et l'on marche en troupe. «Tu me parais belle comme la fleur de la mauve ; tu me donnes une poignée de grains aromatiques.»

CHANT III. HENG MENN.

Contentement d'un sage qui mène une vie pauvre et obscure.

1. Dans une cabane qui n'a pour porte que quelques barres de bois, on peut se reposer à son aise. Auprès d'une fontaine qui coule, on peut supporter la faim avec joie.

2. Pour manger du poisson, est-il nécessaire d'avoir une brême

portæ ulmi albæ, Iuen k'iou collis quercus. Tzeu tchoung filia saltat subter eas.

2. Sudum mane seligitur, et australis regionis planus locus (platea). Non net suam cannabim, in platea saltat.

3. Sudo mane, eunt ambulatum; tum collata turba eunt. «Video te quasi malvam; donas mihi pugillum piperis.»

越 **Iuĕ** équivaut à 於 **iū**, alors.

CHANT III. 1. (In humili casa, compositam lignis) transversis januam juxta, datur inde quiescere commode. Ad fontis fluenta, datur inde cum gaudio famem ferre.

2. Num ut quis comedat piscem, necessaria est Fluvii brama? Num ut quis ducat uxorem, necessaria est Ts'i Kiang?

之魴、豈其取妻、必齊之姜、(3)豈其食魚、必河之鯉、豈其取妻、必宋之子、

東門之池

(1)東門之池、可以漚麻、彼美淑姬、可與晤歌、(2)東門之池、可以漚紵、彼美淑姬、可與晤語、(3)東門之池、可以

3. K'i k'i chēu iû, pì Hô tchēu li? K'i k'i ts'iù ts'ī, pì Sóung tchēu Tzèu (Tsi)?

TOUNG MENN TCHEU TCH'EU. **1. Tōung mênn tchēu tch'êu k'ò i ngeóu mâ (mô). Pèi mèi chŏu kī, k'ò iù óu kō.**

2. Tōung mênn tchēu tch'êu, k'ò i ngeóu tchòu. Pèi mèi chŏu kī, k'ò iù óu iù.

3. Tōung mênn tchēu tch'êu, k'ò i ngeóu kiēn. Pèi mèi chŏu kī, k'ò iù óu iên.

du Fleuve-Jaune? Pour se marier, est-il nécessaire d'obtenir la main d'une fille de la famille des Kiang qui règnent à Ts'i?

3. Pour manger du poisson, est-il nécessaire d'avoir une carpe du Fleuve-Jaune? Pour se marier, est-il nécessaire d'obtenir la main d'une fille de la famille des Tzeu qui règnent à Soung?

CHANT IV. TOUNG MENN TCHEU TCH'EU.

Éloge d'une femme.

1. Près de la porte orientale, le fossé des remparts peut servir à rouir le chanvre. Avec cette femme aimable, vertueuse et sage, on peut chanter d'accord.

2. Près de la porte orientale, le fossé peut servir à rouir l'ortie blanche. Avec cette femme aimable, vertueuse et sage, on peut converser et être d'accord.

3. Près de la porte orientale, le fossé peut servir à rouir le jonc

3. Num ut quis comedat piscem, necessaria est Fluvii carpa? Num ut quis ducat uxorem, necessaria est Soung Tzeu?

CHANT IV. 1. Orientalis portæ fossa potest adhiberi ad macerandam cannabem. Illa decora eximiaque sapiens mulier ea est quicum possis concorditer canere.

姬 **Ki**, nom de famille des 周 **Tcheōu**. Les filles de cette famille étaient d'une perfection accomplie. Leur nom sert à désigner une femme parfaite.

2. Orientalis portæ fossa potest adhiberi ad macerandam urticam niveam. Illa decora eximiaque sapiens mulier ea est quicum possis concorditer colloqui.

3. Orientalis portæ fossa potest adhiberi ad macerandum juncum. Illa decora eximiaque sapiens mulier ea est quicum possis concorditer loqui.

漚菅、彼美淑姬、
可與晤言、
東門之楊
(1) 東門之楊、其
葉牂牂、昏以爲
期、明星煌煌、
(2) 東門之楊、其
葉肺肺、昏以爲
期、明星晢晢、
墓門
(1) 墓門有棘、斧
以斯之、夫也不
良、國人知之、知

TOUNG MENN TCHEU IANG. **1. Tōung mênn tchēu iâng, k'î iĕ tsāng tsāng. Houēnn i wêi k'î ; mîng sīng houâng houâng.**

2. Tōung mênn tchēu iâng, k'î iĕ p'éi p'éi. Houēnn i wêi k'î ; mîng sīng tchéu tchéu.

MOU MENN. **1. Móu mênn iòu kĭ, fòu i sī tchēu. Fōu iè pŏu leàng, kouŏ jênn tchēu tchēu. Tchēu èul pŏu i ; chouêi sĭ jên i.**

textile. Avec cette femme aimable, vertueuse et sage, on peut parler et être d'accord.

CHANT V. TOUNG MENN TCHEU IANG.

Vers le soir, à l'heure ordinaire des mariages, un jeune homme est allé attendre sa fiancée. A l'aube du jour, elle n'était pas encore venue.

1. Près de la porte orientale sont des peupliers au feuillage touffu. Le crépuscule du soir était le moment fixé (pour s'y rendre), et déjà l'Étoile du matin brille.

2. Près de la porte orientale sont des peupliers au feuillage épais. Le crépuscule du soir était l'heure fixée, et déjà l'Étoile du matin brille.

CHANT VI. MOU MENN.

Le poète donne un avertissement à un méchant homme, qui ne craint pas l'opinion publique et ne veut pas se corriger. Il ne lui présente que des objets lugubres, des tombes, des arbustes épineux, des hiboux.

1. A la porte du cimetière sont des arbustes épineux ; on a soin de les couper. Cet homme n'est pas bon ; tous les habitants de la

CHANT V. 1. (Sunt) orientalis portæ populi ; earum frondes sunt densæ. Diluculum vespertinum electum erat pro statuto tempore ; matutina stella clare fulget.

2. (Sunt) orientalis portæ populi ; earum frondes sunt densæ. Vespertinum diluculum electum erat pro statuto tempore ; matutina stella clare fulget.

CHANT VI. 1. Ad tumulorum januam sunt spinosæ arbusculæ ; securis adhibetur ad recidendas eas. Ille homo non est bonus ; regni incolæ sciunt illud. Sciunt, attamen non desinit ; olim jamdiu ita est.

詩經

而不已。誰昔然矣。

(2) 墓門有梅。有鴞萃止。夫也不良、歌以訊之、訊予不顧、顛倒思予、

防有鵲巢

(1) 防有鵲巢。邛有旨苕、誰侜予美。心焉忉忉。

(2) 中唐有甓。邛有旨鷊。誰侜予美。心焉惕惕。

2. Móu mênn iòu mèi, iòu hiaō tsouéi tchèu. Fōu iè pŏu leàng, kō i sin (souéi) tchēu. Sin (Souéi), iù pŏu kóu (kòu); tiēn taò sēu iù (iù).

FANG IOU TS'IO TCH'AO. **1. Fâng iòu ts'iŏ tch'aô, k'iôung iòu tchèu t'iaô (t'aō). Chouêi tcheōu iù mèi? Sīn iên taō taō.**

2. Tchōung t'âng iòu p'ĭ, k'iôung iòu tchèu ĭ. Chouêi tcheōu iù mèi? Sīn iên t'ĭ t'ĭ.

principauté le savent. Ils le savent, et cependant il ne veut pas se corriger; il en est ainsi depuis fort longtemps.

2. A la porte du cimetière sont des pruniers; les hiboux s'y rassemblent. Cet homme n'est pas bon; je chante pour l'avertir. Je chante; mais il ne fait pas attention à moi. Quand il sera entièrement perdu, il se souviendra de mes avis.

CHANT VII. FANG IOU TS'IO TCH'AO.

Chaque chose possède et garde ce qui lui convient. Moi, j'ai perdu mon ami. Les mauvaises langues m'ont ravi son cœur.

1. Sur la digue est un nid de pie; sur la colline croissent d'excellents pois. Qui a circonvenu mon ami? Mon cœur est dans l'angoisse.

2. Au milieu de la cour du temple des ancêtres, l'allée est pavée de grandes briques; sur la colline croissent d'excellentes plantes à raies de diverses couleurs. Qui a circonvenu mon ami? Mon cœur est dans les tourments.

誰 **Chouêi**, autrefois, depuis longtemps.

2. Ad tumulorum januam sunt pruni, sunt bubones congregati et sistentes. Ille homo non est bonus; cano ut moneam eum. Cano, mihi non attendit. Penitus subversus reminiscetur mei.

止 **Tchèu**, demeurer, ou particule.

CHANT VII. 1. In aggere est (arbor et) picæ nidus, in colle est exquisitum pisum. Quis circumvenit meum dilectum? Animo angor.

2. In media ad avorum delubra via sunt majores lateres, in colle est exquisita ĭ planta. Quis circumvenit meum dilectum? Animo crucior.

鷊 **Ĭ**, petite plante marquée de longues raies de diverses couleurs.

月出

(1) 月出皎兮、佼人僚兮、舒窈糾兮、勞心悄兮、

(2) 月出皓兮、佼人懰兮、舒懮受兮、勞心慅兮、

(3) 月出照兮、佼人燎兮、舒夭紹兮、勞心慘兮、

株林

(1) 胡爲乎株林、從夏南、匪適株

IUE TCH'OU. **1. Iuĕ tch'ŏu haò hì, kiaò jênn leaò hì. Chōu iaò kiaò hì. Laô sīn ts'iaò hì.**

2. Iuĕ tch'ŏu haò hì, kiaò jênn liòu (laò) hì. Chōu iòu cheòu (chaò) hì; laô sīn ts'aò hì.

3. Iuĕ tch'ŏu tchaó hì, kiaò jênn leaó hì. Chōu iaò chaó hì; laô sīn ts'àn (ts'aò) hì.

TCHOU LIN. **1. Hôu wèi hôu Tchōu lîn? Ts'ôung Hià Nân (Gnîn). Fèi chĕu Tchōu lîn; ts'ôung Hià Nân (Gnîn).**

CHANT VIII. IUE TCH'OU.

La beauté du visage comparée à la clarté de la lune.

1. La lune à son lever brille d'une clarté pure. Ce beau visage est aimable. Sa vue dilate un cœur serré par la tristesse. L'inquiétude fatigue mon cœur.

2. La lune à son lever brille d'une clarté pure. Ce beau visage est aimable. Sa vue dissipe la tristesse la plus profonde. L'inquiétude agite mon cœur.

3. La lune à son lever éclaire la terre. Ce beau visage est brillant. Sa vue dilate un cœur serré par le chagrin. L'inquiétude accable mon âme.

CHANT IX. TCHOU LIN.

Le peuple de 陳 **Tch'ênn** flétrit la conduite du prince 靈 **Lîng**, qui va à 株林 **Tchōu lîn** voir la veuve d'un 大夫 **tái fōu** de la famille des 夏 **Hià**, dont le fils s'appelle 南 **Nân**.

1. Pourquoi notre prince va-t-il à Tchou lin? Il cultive l'amitié

CHANT VIII. 1. Luna oritur nitida; formoso vultu homo est amabilis. Relaxatur intensa animi constrictio. Laborans animus angitur.

2. Luna oritur candida; formosa specie homo est amabilis. Solvitur mœror congestus. Anxius animus agitatur.

3. Luna oriens edit lucem; formoso vultu homo splendet. Relaxatur arcta animi constrictio. Mœstus animus cruciatur.

慘 **Ts'àn** tient ici la place de 懆 **ts'aò**.

CHANT IX. 1. Quid facturus in Tchou lin? Sectatur Hia Nan, i.e. Hia Nan matrem. Non petit Tchou lin; sectatur Hia Nan.

林。從夏南。
(2) 駕我乘馬。說于株野。乘我乘駒。朝食于株。

澤陂

(1) 彼澤之陂。有蒲與荷。有美一人。傷如之何。寤寐無爲。涕泗滂沱。
(2) 彼澤之陂。有蒲與蕑。有美一人。碩大且卷。寤寐無爲。中心悁悁。

2. Kiá ngò chéng mà (mòu), chouéi iū Tchōu ié (chòu). Chéng ngò chéng kiū ; tchaō chĕu iū Tchōu.

TCHE POUO. **1. Pèi tchĕ tchēu pouō, iòu p'ôu iù hô. Iòu méi ĭ jênn, chāng jôu tchēu hô ? Oú méi ôu wêi, t'i séu p'āng t'ouô.**

2. Pèi tchĕ tchēu pouō, iòu p'ôu iù kiēn. Iòu méi ĭ jênn, chĕu tá, ts'iê k'iuên. Oú méi ôu wêi, tchōung sīn iuēn iuēn.

de Hia Nan. Il ne va pas visiter Tchou lin ; il cultive l'amitié de Hia Nan.

2. Il fait atteler de front nos quatre coursiers, et s'arrête dans la plaine de Tchou lin. Il fait atteler de front nos quatre jeunes coursiers, et le matin il déjeune à Tchou lin.

CHANT X. TCHE POUO.

Douleur causée par l'absence d'un ami.

1. Dans ce marais, le long de la digue, le jonc croît avec le nénufar. Il est un homme distingué ; (son absence afflige mon cœur). Quel remède chercherai-je à ma blessure? Je ne puis penser à aucune affaire, ni le jour ni la nuit. De mes yeux, de mes narines, l'eau coule comme la pluie.

2. Dans ce marais, le long de la digue, le jonc croît avec la valériane. Il est un homme distingué, grand, noble, aux cheveux bouclés. Je ne puis penser à aucune affaire, ni le jour ni la nuit ; mon cœur est sans cesse dans la tristesse.

Le poète dit Hia Nan, parce qu'il n'ose pas dire clairement que l'objet des affections du prince est la mère de Hia Nan.

2. Jungit nostros quadrijugos equos, sistit in Tchou campo. Jungit nostros quadrijugos pullos, mane comedit in Tchou.

CHANT X. 1. Ad illius paludis aggerem sunt juncus et nymphæa. Est egregius aliquis vir ; vulnerato animo, quo utar remedio? Vigilans, dormiens, de nullo negotio cogito. Lacrymæ et nasi pituita imbris instar fluunt.

2. Ad illius paludis aggerem sunt juncus et valeriana. Est egregius aliquis vir, procerus, magnus et cincinnatus. Vigilans, dormiens, de nullo negotio cogito ; intimus animus indesinenter mœret.

蕑 **Kiēn**, valériane ou autre plante semblable.

(3)彼澤之陂、有蒲菡萏。有美一人、碩大且儼。寤寐無爲、輾轉伏枕。

檜一之十三

羔裘

(1)羔裘逍遙、狐裘以朝。豈不爾思、勞心忉忉。

(2)羔裘翱翔、狐裘在堂。豈不爾

3. Pèi tchĕ tchĕu pouŏ, iòu p'ôu hàn tàn (tièn). Iòu mèi ĭ jènn, chĕu tá, ts'iè ièn. Oú méi ôu wèi, tchèn tchouèn fŏu tchènn (tchèn).

KAO K'IOU. **1. Kaŏ k'iôu siaŏ iaŏ, hôu k'iôu i tch'aŏ. K'i pŏu èul sēu? Laŏ sīn taŏ taŏ.**

2. Kaŏ k'iôu ngaŏ siâng, hôu k'iôu tsái t'âng. K'i pŏu èul sēu? Ngò sīn iōu chāng.

3. Dans ce marais, auprès de la digue, le jonc croît avec la fleur du nénufar. Il est un homme distingué, grand, noble, majestueux. Je ne puis penser à aucune affaire, ni le jour ni la nuit. Je me tourne et me retourne, la tête appuyée sur mon oreiller.

LIVRE XIII. KOUEI FOUNG.

CHANT I. KAO K'IOU.

Le prince de 檜 **Kouèi** cherche à briller par le luxe de ses vêtements, et néglige les affaires publiques.

1. Vous revêtez la tunique garnie de peaux d'agneaux pour aller vous promener, et la tunique garnie de peaux de renards pour donner audience. Comment ne penserais-je pas à vous? Mon esprit, tourmenté par l'inquiétude, est tout occupé de vous.

2. Vous revêtez la tunique garnie de peaux d'agneaux pour vous promener çà et là, et la tunique garnie de peaux de renards pour demeurer dans votre salle d'audience. Comment ne pense-

3. Ad illius paludis aggerem sunt juncus et nymphææ flos. Est egregius aliquis vir, procerus, magnus et decoro habitu. Vigilans, dormiens, de nullo negotio cogito. Me versans reversansque, incumbo in cervical.

TITRE DU LIVRE. 檜一之十三 Kouei (regni cantica): primæ (partis) decimus tertius (liber). La principauté de Kouei était le 鄭州 **Tchéng tcheōu** dans le Ho nan. Voy. page 4.

CHANT I. 1. Agnina tunica (indutus) huc illuc spatiaris; vulpina tunica (indutus) excipis ad aulam adeuntes. Quomodo non de te cogitem? Laborans animus est cogitabundus.

D'après l'usage, les princes 諸侯 **tchōu heôu** mettaient la tunique garnie de fourrures d'agneaux pour donner audience, et la tunique garnie de fourrures de renards pour faire visite à l'empereur.

2. Agnina tunica (indutus) huc illuc discurris, vulpina tunica (indutus)

思、我心憂傷、
(3) 羔裘如膏、日
出有曜。豈不爾
思、中心是悼。

素冠

(1) 庶見素冠兮、
棘人欒欒兮、勞
心慱慱兮、
(2) 庶見素衣兮、
我心傷悲兮、聊
與子同歸兮。
(3) 庶見素韠兮、
我心蘊結兮、聊
與子如一兮、

3. Kaō k'iôu jôu kaó, jĕu tch'ŏu iòu iaó. K'i pŏu èul sēu? Tchōung sīn chéu taó.

SOU KOUAN. **1. Chóu kién sóu kouān hì, kĭ jênn louân louân hì! Laô sīn t'ouân t'ouân. !**

2. Chóu kién sóu ī hì! ngò sīn chāng pēi hì. Leaô iù tzèu t'ôung kouēi hì.

3. Chóu kién sóu pĭ hì! ngò sīn iùn kiĕ (kĭ) hì. Leaô iù tzèu jôu ĭ hì.

rais-je pas à vous? Mon cœur est comme blessé par le chagrin.

3. Votre tunique garnie de peaux d'agneaux est luisante, et brille quand le soleil paraît. Comment ne penserais-je pas à vous? Au fond du cœur j'éprouve comme la douleur d'une blessure.

CHANT II. SOU KOUAN.

Le poète déplore le manque de piété filiale et l'habitude de ne plus porter le deuil durant trois années après la mort des parents.

1. Que je désirerais voir le bonnet blanc, et un homme devenu maigre à cause de son application à remplir les observances du deuil! Mon cœur est dans l'affliction.

2. Que je désirerais voir le vêtement blanc! Mon cœur éprouve comme la douleur d'une blessure. J'irais demeurer avec le sage (qui garderait ainsi le deuil durant trois années).

3. Que je désirerais voir les genouillères blanches! Mon cœur est comme serré par la tristesse. Je ne ferais qu'un cœur et qu'une âme avec ce sage.

stas in aula tua. Quomodo non de te cogitem? Meus animus mœrore conficitur.

3. Agnina tunica quasi unguine obducta, apparente sole, edit fulgorem. Quomodo non de te cogitem? In animo vere quasi læsus doleo.

CHANT II. 1. Utinam videam album pileolum, et diligentem hominem macie tabescentem! Laborans animus mœret.

2. Utinam videam albam vestem (inferiorem)! Meus animus læsus dolet. Paululum cum (illo) sapiente adirem illius domum.

3. Utinam videam alba genualia! Meus animus vehementer constringitur. Paululum cum (illo) sapiente quasi unus essem.

Le bonnet, le vêtement et les genouillères de couleur blanche se portaient la troisième année du deuil.

隰有萇楚

(1) 隰有萇楚、猗儺其枝、夭之沃沃、樂子之無知、

(2) 隰有萇楚、猗儺其華、夭之沃沃、樂子之無家、

(3) 隰有萇楚、猗儺其實、夭之沃沃、樂子之無室、

匪風

(1) 匪風發兮、匪車偈兮、顧瞻周

SI IOU TCH'ANG TCH'OU. **1. Sī iòu tch'âng tch'òu, ngò nouò k'ī tchēu. Iaō tchēu ŏu ŏu. Lŏ tzèu tchēu ôu tchēu.**

2. Sī iòu tch'âng tch'òu, ngò nouò k'ī houâ. Iaō tchēu ŏu ŏu. Lŏ tzèu tchēu ôu kiā.

3. Sī iòu tch'âng tch'òu, ngò nouò k'ī chĕu. Iaō tchēu ŏu ŏu. Lŏ tzèu tchēu ôu chĕu.

FEI FOUNG. **1. Fēi fōung fă (p'ĕ) hī, fēi kiū k'iĕ hī. Kóu tchēn Tcheōu taó, tchōung sīn tă (tĕ) hī.**

CHANT III. SI IOU TCH'ANG TCH'OU.

Le peuple, opprimé par ses chefs, porte envie aux êtres privés de sentiment et exempts de souffrance.

1. Dans la vallée croît le carambolier; ses rameaux sont tendres et flexibles. Il est jeune, beau et luisant. (Arbuste), je te félicite d'être dépourvu de sentiment.

2. Dans la vallée croît le carambolier; ses fleurs sont tendres et flexibles. Il est jeune, beau et luisant. (Arbuste), je te félicite de n'avoir pas de famille.

3. Dans la vallée croît le carambolier; ses fruits sont tendres et délicats. Il est jeune, beau et luisant. (Arbuste), je te félicite de n'avoir pas de famille.

CHANT IV. FEI FOUNG.

Le ciel ne manifeste pas son courroux et ne déchaîne pas les vents; les voyages n'offrent ni difficulté ni danger. Cependant le poète éprouve un profond chagrin. C'est que les voyageurs sont rares sur la route de la capitale de l'empire. L'empereur ne conserve plus qu'une ombre de pouvoir, et peu de sujets fidèles se rendent à sa cour. Celui qui fait cuire un poisson, se prépare un mets excellent; de même celui qui rend honneur et obéissance à l'empereur, obtient de grands avantages.

1. Le vent ne souffle pas avec fureur, la voiture dans sa course

CHANT III. 1. In valle est carambola, molles et flexiles sunt ejus rami. Tenera et pulchra quasi rore nitet. (Arbuscula), congaudeo tibi quod careas sensu.

2. In valle est carambola, molles et flexiles sunt ejus flores. Tenera et pulchra quasi rore nitet. (Arbuscula), congaudeo tibi quod non habeas domum.

3. In valle est carambola, molles et flexiles sunt ejus fructus. Tenera et pulchra quasi rore nitet. (Arbuscula), congaudeo tibi quod careas domo.

道、中心怛兮、(2) 匪風飄兮、匪車嘌兮、顧瞻周道、中心弔兮、(3) 誰能亨魚、溉之釜鬵、誰將西歸、懷之好音、

曹一之十四

蜉蝣

(1) 蜉蝣之羽、

2. Fèi fōung p'iaō (p'iaó) hì, fèi kiū p'iaō (p'iaó) hì. Kóu tchēn Tcheōu taó, tchōung sīn tiaó hì.

3. Chouêi nêng p'ēng iù? Kái tchēu fòu sin. Chouêi tsiāng sī kouēi? Houâi tchēu haò īn.

FEOU IOU. **1. Feôu iôu tchēu iù, ī chāng tch'òu tch'òu. Sīn tchēu iōu i. Iū ngò kouēi tch'òu.**

n'éprouve pas de cahots violents. Cependant, quand je considère la route de Tcheou, mon cœur est ému de douleur.

2. Le vent ne tourbillonne pas, la voiture n'éprouve pas de cahots violents. Néanmoins, quand je considère la route de Tcheou, mon cœur est dans l'affliction.

3. Quelqu'un a-t-il un poisson à faire cuire? Je lui laverai sa chaudière. Quelqu'un veut-il aller à l'occident (à Hao, la capitale de l'empire)? Je l'encouragerai par mes chants.

LIVRE XIV. TS'AO FOUNG.

CHANT I. FEOU IOU.

Le poète compare les hommes frivoles à un insecte de la famille des scarabées, dont les ailes sont brillantes et la vie ne dure qu'un jour. Il voudrait les attirer à lui et les instruire.

1. Les ailes du *feou iou* sont comme un vêtement neuf et brillant. Mon cœur est triste. Que cet homme frivole vienne demeurer chez moi.

CHANT IV. 1. Non ventus furit, non currus celeriter currens succutitur. Conversus suspicio Tcheou viam, intimus animus mœret.

Sous les 周 **Tcheōu**, le mot *Tcheou* servait à désigner la capitale de l'empire.

2. Non ventus in orbem versatur, non currus succutitur. Conversus suspicio Tcheou viam, intimus animus mœrore afficitur.

3. Quis potest coquere piscem? Abluam ei cacabum aut ollam. Quis parat occidentem adire? Animum addam ei bonis verbis.

La capitale des Tcheou était encore la ville de 鎬 **Haó**, située près de Si ngan fou, à l'ouest de 檜 **Kouéi**.

TITRE DU LIVRE. 曹一之十四 Ts'ao (regni cantica): primæ (partis) decimus quartus (liber). La principauté de Ts'ao était le 曹縣 dans le midi du Chan toung.

CHANT I. 1. *Feôu iôu* bestiolæ alæ sunt vestis quæ quasi recens nitet.

衣裳楚楚。心之憂矣。於我歸處。

(2) 蜉蝣之翼。采采衣服。心之憂矣。於我歸息。

(3) 蜉蝣掘閱。麻衣如雪。心之憂矣。於我歸說。

候人

(1) 彼候人兮。何戈與祋。彼其之子。三百赤芾。

(2) 維鵜在梁。不濡其翼。彼其之子。不

2. Feòu iòu tchēu ĭ, ts'ài ts'ài ī fōu (p'ĕ). Sīn tchēu iōu i. Iū ngò kouēi sĭ.

3. Feòu iòu k'iŭ iuĕ, mâ ī jôu siuĕ. Sīn tchēu iōu i. Iū ngò kouēi chouéi (chouĕ).

HEOU JENN. **1. Pèi heóu jênn hî, hô kouō iù touéi. Pèi kì tchēu tzèu, sān pĕ tch'ĕu fôu (p'éi).**

2. Wêi t'î tsái leâng, pŏu jôu k'ì ĭ. Pèi kì tchēu tzèu pŏu tch'éng k'ì fôu (p'ĕ).

2. Les ailes du *feou iou* sont comme un vêtement aux couleurs variées. Mon cœur est triste. Que cet homme frivole vienne demeurer chez moi.

3. Le *feou iou* sort de la terre; sa robe de chanvre est blanche comme la neige. Mon cœur est triste. Que cet homme frivole vienne demeurer chez moi.

CHANT II. HEOU JENN.

Le prince augmente beaucoup le nombre des officiers, donne les charges à d'indignes favoris, et laisse les hommes de mérite dans l'obscurité et l'indigence.

1. Ces dignitaires chargés de recevoir à la cour les hôtes et les visiteurs portent la lance et l'épieu. (Au-dessous d'eux), ces hommes vils (les grands préfets), au nombre de trois cents, portent des genouillères rouges.

2. Le pélican, immobile sur le barrage, ne mouille pas ses ailes. Ainsi, ces hommes vils ne font rien qui soit en rapport avec le magnifique vêtement dont ils sont parés.

Animus meus mœret. Apud me veniat et commoretur (ille homo levis).

2. *Feôu iôu* bestiolæ alæ sunt variis coloribus picta vestis. Animus meus mœret. Apud me veniat et sistat.

3. *Feôu iôu*, effossa (terra, erumpit) gaudens; cannabina vestis sicut nix. Animus meus mœret. Apud me veniat et maneat.

CHANT II. 1. Illi curantes de hospitibus præpositi arrectam tenent hastam et pilum. Illi homines (qui præpositis subsunt) sunt trecenti rubris genualibus (大夫 tái fōu magni præfecti).

2. Pelicanus stans super septum, non madefacit suas alas. (Ita, honoribus aucti) illi homines nihil consentaneum faciunt suis vestibus.

詩經

稱其服。
(3) 維鵜在梁。不濡其咮。彼其之子。不遂其媾。
(4) 薈兮蔚兮。南山朝隮。婉兮孌兮。季女斯飢。

鳲鳩

(1) 鳲鳩在桑。其子七兮。淑人君子。其儀一兮。其儀一兮。心如結兮。
(2) 鳲鳩在桑。其子

3. Wêi t'î tsái leàng, pŏu jôu k'î tcheóu. Pèi ki tchēu tzèu pŏu souéi k'î keóu.

4. Wèi hī wéi hi, nân chān tchaŏ tsī. Iuèn hī liuèn hi, ki gniù sēu kī.

CHEU KIOU. **1. Chēu kiōu tsái sāng, k'î tzèu ts'ī hi. Chŏu jênn kiūn tzèu, k'î ī ī hī. K'î i ī hī; sīn jôu kiĕ (kī) hī.**

2. Chēu kiōu tsái sāng, k'î tzèu tsái mèi. Chŏu jênn kiūn tzèu, k'î tái ī sēu

3. Le pélican, immobile sur le barrage, ne mouille pas son bec. Ces hommes vils ne font rien qui réponde à la faveur dont ils jouissent.

4. Au midi, sur la montagne, la végétation est luxuriante, et le matin on voit des vapeurs s'élever. (La cour du prince est pleine d'indignes ministres, et l'administration est mal réglée). La plus jeune des filles du prince est délicate et belle; cependant elle meurt de faim (c.-à-d. les hommes de bien sont entièrement négligés).

CHANT III. CHEU KIOU.

La huppe ne quitte pas le mûrier et soigne assidûment tous ses petits. De même, bien que les hommes et les circonstances changent avec la même mobilité que les petits de la huppe, le sage ne s'écarte jamais de la voie de la vertu, et remplit fidèlement tous ses devoirs.

1. La huppe reste sur le mûrier; ses petits sont au nombre de sept. L'honnête homme, le vrai sage tient toujours la même conduite. Sa conduite est toujours la même, parce que son cœur est comme enchaîné au devoir.

2. La huppe reste sur le mûrier; ses petits sont sur le prunier.

3. Pelicanus stans super septum, non madefacit suum rostrum. Illi homines nihil consentaneum faciunt suo favori.

4. Arbores et herbæ quum sint densissimæ, in australi monte mane ascendunt vapores. Juvenis et formosa, natu minima filia interim esurit.

CHANT III. 1. Upupa manet in moro; ejus pulli septem sunt. Qui est probus homo, sapiens vir, ejus habitus est unus. Ejus habitus est unus; animus est quasi ligatus.

2. Upupa manet in moro; ejus pulli

在梅、淑人君子、其帶伊絲、其帶伊絲、其弁伊騏、

3. 鳲鳩在桑、其子在棘、淑人君子、其儀不忒、其儀不忒、正是四國、

4. 鳲鳩在桑、其子在榛、淑人君子、正是國人、正是國人、胡不萬年、

下泉

1. 洌彼下泉、浸彼

(sī). K'ì tái I sēu (sī), k'ì pién ī k'î.

3. Chēu kiōu tsái sāng, k'ì tzèu tsái kĭ. Chŏu jênn kiūn tzèu, k'ì i pŏu t'ĕ. K'ì î pŏu t'ĕ ; tchéng chéu séu kouŏ (ĭ).

4. Chēu kiōu tsái sāng, k'ì tzèu tsái tchēnn. Chŏu jênn kiūn tzèu, tchéng chéu kouŏ jênn. Tchéng chéu kouŏ jênn ; hôu pŏu wán gniên (gnin) ?

HIA TS'IUEN. **1. Liĕ pèi hiá ts'iuên, tsin pèi paŏ lâng. K'ái ngò ôu t'án, gniên pèi Tcheōu kīng (kāng).**

L'honnête homme, le vrai sage porte une ceinture de soie de couleur naturelle. Sa ceinture est de soie simple ; son bonnet de peau est gris-tacheté.

3. La huppe reste sur le mûrier ; ses petits sont sur le jujubier. L'honnête homme, le vrai sage est irréprochable dans sa conduite. Sa conduite est irréprochable ; il réforme toute notre principauté.

4. La huppe reste sur le mûrier ; ses petits sont sur le coudrier. L'honnête homme, le vrai sage réforme la conduite de tous les habitants de cette principauté. Il réforme la conduite de tous les habitants ; pourquoi ne continuerait-il pas ainsi dix mille ans?

CHANT IV. HIA TS'IUEN.

La dynastie des Tcheou est en décadence. L'autorité de l'empereur, semblable à une eau glaciale, est plus nuisible qu'utile aux peuples de l'empire.

1. Une eau glaciale coule de cette source et arrose les touffes

sunt in pruno. Qui est probus homo, sapiens vir, ejus zona est ex albo serico. Ejus zona est ex albo serico ; ejus pileus pelliceus est cinereus punctis distinctus.

伊 I, particule.

3. Upupa manet in moro ; ejus pulli sunt in zizypho. Qui est probus homo, sapiens vir, ejus habitus caret vitio. Ejus habitus caret vitio ; componit has quatuor regni regiones.

4. Upupa manet in moro ; ejus pulli sunt in corylo. Qui est probus homo, sapiens vir, componit hujus regni incolas. Componit hujus regni incolas ; cur non decies mille annis?

CHANT IV. 1. Gelidus ille defluens fons imbuit illud densum panicum

苞稂。愾我寤嘆。念彼周京。

(2) 冽彼下泉。浸彼苞蕭。愾我寤嘆。念彼京周。

(3) 冽彼下泉。浸彼苞蓍。愾我寤嘆。念彼京師。

(4) 芃芃黍苗。陰雨膏之、四國有王、郇伯勞之、

2. Liĕ pèi hiá ts'iuên, tsin pèi paò siaŏ (siōu). K'ái ngò óu t'án, gnién pèi kīng Tcheōu.

3. Liĕ pèi hiá ts'iuên, tsin pèi paō chēu. K'ái ngò óu t'án, gnién pèi kīng chēu.

4. P'ôung p'ôung chòu miaŏ, īn iù kaó tchēu. Séu kouŏ iòu wâng, Siūn pĕ laó tchēu.

du grand millet. Dès mon réveil, je soupire et gémis, à la pensée de la capitale de l'empire.

2. Une eau glaciale coule de cette source et arrose les touffes de l'armoise. Dès mon réveil, je soupire et gémis, au souvenir de la capitale de l'empire.

3. Une eau glaciale coule de cette source et arrose les touffes de l'achillée. Dès mon réveil, je soupire et gémis, au souvenir de la grande capitale.

4. (Autrefois) le millet était beau; la pluie l'arrosait en temps opportun. Toutes les principautés jouissaient des bienfaits de l'empereur, et le prince de Siun leur venait en aide.

majus. Suspiriis ego evigilans gemo; cogito de illa Tcheou urbe imperii præcipua.

Les plantes arrosées par une eau glaciale ne parviennent pas à maturité.

2. Gelidus ille defluens fons imbuit illam densam artemisiam. Suspiriis ego evigilans gemo, memor illius urbis præcipuæ Tcheou.

On employait l'armoise pour faire éclore les vers à soie.

3. Gelidus ille defluens fons imbuit illam densam achilleam. Suspiriis ego evigilans gemo, cogito de illa urbe præcipua.

L'achillée servait à la divination.

4. (Olim) luxurians crescebat milii seges; nubilo cœlo pluvia irrorabat eam. Omnia regulorum regna habebant imperatorem; Siun princeps adjuvabat ea.

Cette pluie qui féconde la terre, est l'image des bienfaits que Wenn wang et ses premiers successeurs répandaient dans tout l'empire.

郇 **Siūn**, petite principauté, à présent 猗氏縣 **Ī chéu hién** dans le 蒲州府 **P'ôu tcheōu fòu**, province de Chan si. Un descendant de 文王 **Wênn wâng** la gouverna, et aida les autres princes à régler leur administration.

A la tête de chacune des neuf provinces 九州 **kiòu tcheōu** était un 伯 **pĕ**.

豳一之十五

七月

①七月流火。九月授衣。一之日觱發。二之日栗烈。無衣無褐。何以卒歲。三之日于耜。四之日舉趾。同我婦子。饁彼南

TS'I IUE. 1. **Ts'ī iuĕ liôu Houò (Houéi); kiòu iuĕ cheóu I (i). Ī tchēu jĕu pĭ fă (féi); éul tchēu jĕu lĭ liĕ (li). Où I ôu hŏ (hi), hô i tsŏu souéi? Sān tchēu jĕu iû sèu (i); séu tchēu jĕu kiù tchèu. T'ôung ngò fóu tzéu (tsi), iĕ péi nân meòu (méi). T'iên tsiún tchéu hi.**

LIVRE XV. PIN FOUNG.

CHANT I. TS'I IUE.

Occupations des anciens habitants de 豳 **Pin** aux différentes époques de l'année, sous le règne de 公劉 **Kōung Liôu**, l'un des ancêtres des 周 **Tcheōu**, dix-huit siècles avant notre ère. Ce chant est attribué à 周公 **Tcheōu kōung**, et fut composé, dit-on, vers l'année 1114 avant J. C., pour l'instruction de 成王 **Tch'êng wâng**. L'auteur y fait parler un sujet de Koung Liou.

1. Au septième mois (d'après le calendrier des Hia, qui faisaient commencer l'année civile avec le deuxième mois lunaire après celui où tombait le solstice d'hiver), Antarès du Scorpion s'écarte du méridien (vers le soir). Au neuvième mois (de l'année des Hia, le père de famille) distribue des vêtements (d'hiver aux personnes de sa maison). Au premier mois de l'année (d'après le calendrier des Tcheou, c.-à-d. au mois lunaire où tombe le solstice d'hiver), souffle un vent froid. Au deuxième mois (de l'année des Tcheou), l'air est glacial. Sans vêtements chauds, sans habits de laine, pourrait-on atteindre la fin de l'année (des Hia, ou le deuxième mois lunaire après celui du solstice d'hiver). Au troisième mois (des Tcheou), on va préparer la charrue. Au quatrième mois (des Tcheou), on va labourer la terre. Avec ma femme et mes enfants,

TITRE DU LIVRE. 豳一之十五 Pin (regni cantica): primæ (partis) decimus quintus (liber). Sur la principauté de Pin, voy. pages 2 et 4.

CHANT I. 1. Septimo mense, (vespere ab austro ad occidentem) declinat Antares. Nono mense, (paterfamilias) tribuit vestes. Primi (mensis, i.e. lunaris mensis in quem incidit hiemale solstitium) diebus, flat ventus frigidus; secundi (a solstitiali mense) diebus, aer est frigidus. Absque vestibus, absque laneis, quo pacto attingi possit finis anni? Tertii (a solstitiali mense) diebus, itur ad aratrum. Quarti (a solstitiali mense) diebus, moventur pedes (ad agros arandos). Cum mea uxore et liberis, cibos offero (meis domesticis) in illis australibus jugeribus. Agricolarum præpositus adveniens gaudet.

Au temps de Koung liou, sous la dynastie des Hia, le premier mois de

畝、田畯至喜。
(2) 七月流火、
九月授衣、春
日載陽、有鳴
倉庚、女執懿
筐、遵彼微行、
爰求柔桑、春
日遲遲、采蘩
祁祁、女心傷
悲、殆及公子
同歸。
(3) 七月流火、
八月萑葦、蠶

2. Ts'ĭ iué liôu Houò (Houèi) ; kiòu iuĕ cheòu ī (i). Tch'ouēnn jĕu tsái iâng, iòu mìng ts'āng kēng (kāng) ; gniù tchēu i k'ouāng, tsiūn pèi wêi hìng (hâng) ; iuên k'iôu jeôu sāng. Tch'ouēnn jĕu tch'êu tch'êu, ts'ài fân k'ì k'ì. Gniù sīn chāng pēi ; tái kĭ kōung tzèu t'ôung kouēi.

3. Ts'ĭ iuĕ liôu Houò (Houèi) ; pă iuĕ houân wêi. Ts'ân iuĕ t'iaō sāng, ts'iù

je porte des vivres aux travailleurs dans les champs qui sont au midi. Quand l'inspecteur des travaux des champs arrive, il est content.

2. Au septième mois de l'année (des Hia), Antarès s'écarte du méridien vers le soir. Au neuvième mois (des Hia), on distribue les vêtements d'hiver. Au printemps, quand l'air devient tiède et que le loriot commence à chanter, les femmes prennent leurs élégantes corbeilles, et suivant les petits sentiers, cherchent les feuilles tendres du mûrier. Quand les jours du printemps sont devenus plus longs, elles vont en grand nombre cueillir l'armoise blanche (pour les vers à soie.). Le cœur de la jeune fille est triste, (elle pense que bientôt elle devra quitter ses parents); le temps approche où le fils du prince viendra la chercher pour célébrer leurs noces.

3. Au septième mois (de l'année des Hia), Antarès passe au méridien vers le soir. Au huitième mois, on recueille les joncs et

l'année civile était, comme sous la dynastie actuelle, le deuxième mois lunaire après celui où tombait le solstice d'hiver; sous les Tcheou, c'était le mois lunaire où tombait le solstice d'hiver. Le septième mois de l'année des Hia correspondait à notre mois d'août ou à notre mois de septembre.

Dans cette pièce, les mois sont désignés tantôt d'après le calendrier des Hia, tantôt d'après celui des Tcheou, ce qui engendre de la confusion, et paraît fort étrange dans la bouche d'un contemporain de Koung liou, qui vivait sept siècles avant l'avènement des Tcheou.

2. Septimo mense, (vespere ab austro) declinat Antares. Nono mense tribuuntur vestes. Quum vernus sol incipit tepescere et adest cantans flava avis, mulieres tenentes decora canistra, sequuntur illas angustas semitas et quærunt tenera mori folia. Quum vernus sol tardat, i.e. producit diem, colligunt albam artemisiam plurimæ. Puellæ animus afficitur mœrore, quia fere adest tempus quo (relinquet parentes, et) reguli filius cum (ea) domum repetet.

3. Septimo mense vespere ab austro) declinat Antares; octavo mense junci et arundines (colliguntur, e quibus fiunt bombycibus crates). Bomby-

月條桑、取彼斧斨、以伐遠揚、猗彼女桑。七月鳴鵙、八月載績。載玄載黃、我朱孔陽、為公子裳。

(4) 四月秀葽、五月鳴蜩。八月其穫、十月隕蘀。一之日于貉、取彼狐狸、為公子裘。二之日其同、載纘武功、言私其

pĕi fŏu ts'iāng, i fă iuèn iâng, ī pèi gniù sāng. Ts'ĭ iuĕ mîng kiŭ; pă iuĕ tsái tsĭ, tsái hiuên, tsái houâng. Ngò tchŏu k'òung iâng; wéi kōung tzèu châng.

4. Séu iuĕ siòu iaŏ, òu iuĕ mîng t'iaŏ. Pă iuĕ k'î houŏ; chĕu iuĕ iùn t'ouŏ. Ĭ tchĕu jĕu iŭ hŏ. Ts'iù pèi hôu lî, wéi kōung tzèu k'iôu (k'î). Eúl tchĕu jĕu k'î t'ôung, tsái tsouàn òu kōung. Iên sēu k'î tsōung, hièn kiēn iū kōung.

les roseaux (et l'on en fait des clayons pour les vers à soie). A l'époque où l'on nourrit les vers à soie, on enlève les branches des mûriers; on coupe avec la hachette celles qui s'écartent le plus du tronc ou qui s'élèvent le plus haut. Aux jeunes mûriers on enlève seulement les feuilles. Au septième mois, la pie-grièche se fait entendre. Au huitième mois, on commence à filer le chanvre. On teint la soie et le chanvre, partie en noir, partie en jaune. Mon étoffe rouge est très brillante; on en fera des vêtements pour le fils du prince.

4. Au quatrième mois (de l'année des Hia), la plante *iao* (peut-être le polygala) a de la graine. Au cinquième mois, la cigale crie. Au huitième mois, on récolte les grains. Au dixième mois, les feuilles tombent des arbres. Au premier mois (de l'année des Tcheou, au mois où tombe le solstice d'hiver), on va chasser aux blaireaux. On prend les renards; de leurs peaux on fait des tuniques pour le fils du prince. Au deuxième mois, on se réunit et l'on continue le vigoureux exercice de la chasse. Les chasseurs ont pour eux les jeunes sangliers d'un an; ils offrent au prince ceux de trois ans.

cum (alendorum) mense, demittuntur rami mororum; sumitur illa securicula asciolave ad cædendos remotos et altius assurgentes (ramos). (At solummodo) foliis exuuntur illæ juniores mori. Septimo mense cantat lanius. Octavo mense incipiunt nere cannabem. (Tum cannabinum tum sericum filum pannusve tingitur) partim nigro partim flavo colore. Meus ruber (pannus) valde splendet; fient reguli filio vestes.

4. Quarto mense nascitur granum *iao* parvæ herbæ. Quinto mense stridet cicada. Octavo mense illi metunt. Decimo mense decidunt cadiva folia. Primi (i.e. solstitialis mensis) diebus, itur ad meles (capiendas). Capiuntur illæ vulpes; fiunt reguli filio tunicæ e pellibus (vulpium). Secundi (a solstitiali mense) diebus, illi conveniunt,

豵、獻豜于公、

(5) 五月斯螽動股、六月莎雞振羽、七月在野、八月在宇、九月在戶、十月蟋蟀、入我牀下、穹窒熏鼠、塞向墐戶、嗟我婦子、曰爲改歲、入此室處、

(6) 六月食鬱及薁、七月亨葵及菽、八月剝棗、十月穫稻、爲此春酒、以介眉

5. Où iuě sēu tchōung tóung kòu. Liŭ iuě souō kī tchénn iù. Ts'ī iuě tsái ié (chòu). Pă iuě tsái iù. Kiòu iuě tsái hóu. Chĕu iuě sĭ chouĕ jŏu ngò tch'ouâng hiá (hóu). K'iōung tchĕu, hiūn chòu. Sĕ hiáng, kín hóu. Tsiē! ngò fóu tzèu (tsòu), iuĕ : « Wêi kài souéi, jŏu ts'èu chĕu tch'òu. »

6. Liŭ iuĕ chĕu iŭ kĭ iŭ. Ts'ī iuĕ p'ēng k'ouêi kĭ chŏu. Pă iuĕ p'ŏu tsaò (tseòu). Chĕu iuĕ houŏ taó (teòu). Wêi ts'ēu tch'ouēnn tsiòu, i kiái mêi cheóu

5. Au cinquième mois (de l'année des Tcheou), la sauterelle remue les pattes (saute et fait du bruit avec les pattes). Au sixième mois, le grillon champêtre agite ses ailes; au septième, il est dans la plaine; au huitième, il est sous le bord du toit; au neuvième, il est dans la maison. Au dixième mois, le grillon domestique pénètre sous mon lit. On bouche les fentes; on enfume les rats. On ferme bien les fenêtres qui regardent le nord; on enduit les portes de terre glaise. Plein de compassion pour ma femme et mes enfants, je leur dis: « La nouvelle année approche; retirons-nous et demeurons dans cette maison. »

6. Au sixième mois (de l'année des Tcheou), on mange des prunes et du raisin. Au septième mois, on fait cuire des mauves et des pois. Au huitième mois, on abat les jujubes. Au dixième mois, on recueille le riz; on en fait une liqueur qui sera bonne à boire au printemps, et soutiendra les forces des vieillards aux longs

tum prosequuntur strenuum (venationis) opus. Sibi servant illos unius anni apros, offerunt trium annorum apros regulo.

5. Quinto mense, locusta movet crura, i.e. cruribus saltat et stridet. Sexto mense, campestris grillus concutit alas; septimo mense est in campo; octavo mense est sub tecti ora; nono mense est in domo. Decimo mense, domesticus grillus intrat meum lectum subter. Rimæ obturantur; fumo aut expelluntur aut occiduntur mures. Obturantur obversæ ad septentrionem fenestræ; luto obducuntur januæ. Miserens meæ uxoris et liberorum, dico: « Imminet novus annus; ingredientes in hanc domum maneamus. »

6. Sexto mense comeduntur prunum et uva. Septimo mense coquuntur malva et pisum. Octavo mense decutitur zizyphum. Decimo mense metitur oryza; fit hoc vernum vinum, ad firmandos

壽、七月食瓜、八月斷壺。九月叔苴、采荼薪樗、食我農夫。⑦九月築場圃、十月納禾稼、黍稷重穋。禾麻菽麥、嗟我農夫、我稼既同、上入執宮功。晝爾于茅、宵爾索綯、亟其乘屋、其始播百穀、

(cheòu). Ts'ī iuĕ chĕu kouā (kōu). Pă iuĕ touàn hôu. Kiòu iuĕ chŏu ts'iū. Ts'ài t'ôu, sīn tch'ōu, séu ngò nôung fōu.

7. Kiòu iuĕ tchōu tch'âng póu. Chĕu iuĕ nă houŏ kiá (kóu), chòu tsĭ tch'ôung liŭ (lĭ), houŏ, mâ, chŏu, mĕ (kĭ). « Tsiē! ngò nôung fōu, ngò kiá ki t'ôung. Chàng jŏu tchéu kōung kōung. Tcheóu èul iû maô; siaô èul souŏ t'aô; kĭ k'î chêng ŏu. K'ì chéu pouó pĕ kŏu. »

sourcils. Au septième mois, on mange des melons. Au huitième mois, on coupe les courges. Au neuvième mois, on recueille le grain du sésame. On cueille le laiteron, on coupe l'ailante pour faire du feu, et l'on prépare la nourriture de nos laboureurs.

7. Au neuvième mois (de l'anné des Tcheou), on bat le jardin potager et on le transforme en aire. Au dixième mois, on apporte dans l'aire les grains récoltés, les deux sortes de millet à panicules, le millet tardif, le millet hâtif, le sésame, les pois, le blé. « Oh! mes laboureurs, tous nos grains sont recueillis. Allons à la ville ou au village, et donnons nos soins à nos bâtiments. Le jour recueillons de la paille, le soir faisons des cordes; hâtons-nous de monter sur les toits (et de les réparer. Au printemps) nous commencerons à semer les différents grains. »

prominentibus superciliis senes. Septimo mense comeduntur pepones. Octavo mense reciduntur cucurbitæ. Nono mense colliguntur sesami grana. Decerpitur sonchus; comburenda cæditur ailantus; cibi parantur nostris agricolis.

眉 **Mêi** signifie vieillesse, parce que les sourcils deviennent proéminents chez les vieillards.

麻 **Mâ** désigne ici, non pas le chanvre ordinaire, mais une plante dont la graine fournit une huile comestible, comme le sésame.

7. Nono mense fistucant in aream hortum olitorium. Decimo mense, inferunt (in aream) segetes et fruges, (nempe) milium *chòu*, milium *tsĭ*, serum milium, præcox milium; segetes (alias, nempe) sesamum, pisa, triticum. « Oh! mei agricolæ, nostræ fruges jam collectæ sunt. Ascendentes ingrediamur (in urbem aut vicum), et capessamus ædium opus. Interdiu eamus colligere stramen, vespere torqueamus funes; propere ipsi conscendamus tecta. Ipsi incipiemus serere varias fruges. »

(8) 二之日鑿冰沖沖、三之日納于凌陰、四之日其蚤、獻羔祭韭、九月肅霜、十月滌場、朋酒斯饗、曰殺羔羊、躋彼公堂、稱彼兕觥、萬壽無疆、

鴟鴞

(1) 鴟鴞鴟鴞、

8. Eùl tchēu jĕu tsŏ pīng tch'ōung tch'ōung ; sān tchēu jĕu nă iū ling în (iôung). Séu tchēu jĕu k'ì tsaò, hién kaō, tsí kiòu (kiaò). Kiòu iuĕ siū chouāng. Chĕu iuĕ tĭ tch'âng. P'êng tsiòu sēu hiàng (hiāng). Iuĕ : « Chă kaō iâng, tsī pèi kōung t'âng. Tch'êng pèi sì kōung (kouāng), wán chèóu ôu kiāng. »

TCH'EU HIAO. **1. Tch'ēu hiaō, tch'ēu hiaō, ki ts'iù ngò tzèu, ôu houèi ngò**

8. Au deuxième mois (de l'année des Tcheou), on casse la glace à coups redoublés ; au troisième mois, on la transporte dans la glacière. Au quatrième mois, de bon matin, on offre en sacrifice un agneau et des poireaux. Au neuvième mois, l'air est froid, le givre se forme. Au dixième mois, un terrain est aplani et nettoyé ; on apporte deux amphores de vin, et l'on dit : «Tuons un agneau, allons à la salle de notre prince, (emplissons de vin) cette corne de rhinocéros, et la tenant levée, souhaitons au prince dix mille ans de vie, une vie sans fin. »

CHANT II. TCH'EU HIAO.

武王 **Où wâng**, fondateur de la dynastie des 周 **Tcheōu**, après avoir ravi l'empire à 紂 **Tcheóu**, chargea ses deux frères 管叔 **Kouàn chōu** et 蔡叔 **Ts'ái chōu** de surveiller 武庚 **Où kēng**, fils du tyran Tcheou, à qui il avait laissé une petite principauté. Après la mort de Ou wang, son fils 成王 **Tch'êng wâng** gouverna l'empire avec l'aide de 周公 **Tcheōu kōung**, frère de Ou wang. Ou keng se révolta contre le nouvel empereur. Il fut soutenu par Kouan chou et Ts'ai chou, qui accusèrent leur frère Tcheou koung d'infidélité envers Tch'eng wang, leur commun neveu. Tcheou koung prit les armes, défit les rebelles et mit à mort Ou keng et Kouan chou. Dans les stances suivantes, il rend compte de sa conduite à Tch'eng wang, pour dissiper les soupçons que la calomnie avait fait naître contre lui dans l'esprit de son neveu. Il se compare à un oiseau ; son nid est la maison ou la dynastie des Tcheou, à laquelle il donne tous ses soins. Il compare Ou keng à un hibou, qui lui a ravi ses petits, à savoir, ses deux frères Kouan chou et Ts'ai chou, et s'est efforcé de détruire son nid.

1. Hibou, hibou, après m'avoir enlevé mes petits, ne détruis pas

Chaque laboureur avait une maison au milieu des champs pour le temps des travaux, et une autre au village ou à la ville pour l'hiver.

8. Secundi (a solstitiali mense) diebus, frangitur glacies repetitis ictibus ; tertii diebus, infertur in glaciei fossam. Quarti diebus, ipso mane, offerunt agnum, offerunt porros. Nono mense frigus et pruina. Decimo mense,

既取我子、無毀我室、恩斯勤斯、鬻子之閔斯、

(2) 迨天之未陰雨、徹彼桑土、綢繆牖戶、今女下民、或敢侮予、

(3) 予手拮据、予所捋荼、予所蓄租、予口卒瘏、曰予未有家室、

(4) 予羽譙譙、予尾翛翛、予室翹

chĕu (chèu). Ngēnn sēu k'în sēu, iŭ tzèu tchēu min (mîn) sēu.

2. Tái t'iēn tchēu wéi în iù, tch'ĕ pèi sāng tòu, tch'eōu miôu iòu hòu. Kīn jòu hiá mîn, houĕ kàn òu iù (iù)?

3. Iù cheòu kĭ kiū, iù chòu louŏ t'ôu, iù chòu hiŭ tsōu; iù k'eòu tsŏu t'ôu. Iuĕ iù wéi iòu chĕu kiā (kōu).

4. Iù iù ts'iaô ts'iaô, iù wèi siaō siaō. Iù chĕu k'iaô k'iaô, fōung iù chòu p'iaō iaô. Iù wêi īn hiaō hiaō.

ma maison (mon nid). Je déplore amèrement le sort de ces petits que j'avais nourris avec tendresse et sollicitude.

2. Avant que les nuages annonçassent la pluie, j'ai enlevé de l'écorce à la racine de ce mûrier, et lié solidement la fenêtre et la porte de ma demeure (de mon nid. Je disais): « O hommes qui passez sous mon nid, quelqu'un de vous osera-t-il à présent m'outrager?»

3. Mes griffes (et mon bec) ont travaillé péniblement à arracher des joncs, à réunir des matériaux (pour mon nid); mon bec en est tout déchiré. Je me disais: « Je n'ai pas encore d'habitation, (il faut en construire une sans retard). »

4. (Dans ce travail) mes plumes ont été usées et ma queue diminuée. Cependant, ma maison est en péril, elle est battue par le vent

mundant aream; duobus poculis vini statim allatis, dicunt: «Occidamus agnum, ascendamus ad illam reguli aulam, attollamus e rhinocerotis cornu crateram, (regulo precemur) decies mille annorum vitam longam, carentem limite.

CHANT II. 1. Bubo, bubo, jam eripuisti meos natos; ne destruas meam domum. Benefeceram eis, diligentia prosecutus eram eos; nutritorum natorum misereor eorum.

2. Quando in cœlo nondum erant nubes nec pluvia, detraxi illam mori radicis corticem, arcte colligavi fenestellam et januam. (Dicebam): « Nunc ex vobis subjectis hominibus aliquis audebitne contumelia afficere me? »

3. Mei ungues (et rostrum) instanter laboraverunt, (circa illos) ego quos decerpsi juncos, (circa ea) ego quæ colligens congessi; meum rostrum omnino læsum est. Dicebam: « Ego nondum habeo domum. »

4. Meæ pennæ minutæ sunt, mea cauda detrita est. Mea domus periclitatur, ventus et pluvia quam concutientes agitant. Ego solummodo voce clamo trepida.

翹、風雨所漂搖、予維音曉曉、

東山

(1) 我徂東山、慆慆不歸、我來自東、零雨其濛、我東曰歸、我心西悲、制彼裳衣、勿士行枚、蜎蜎者蠋、烝在桑野、敦彼獨宿、亦在車下、

(2) 我徂東山、慆

TOUNG CHAN. **1. Ngò ts'ôu tōung chān, t'aō t'aō pŏu kouēi. Ngò lâi tzéu tōung, lìng iù k'ì môung. Ngò tōung iuĕ kouēi, ngò sīn sī pēi. Tchéu pèi chāng ī ; ŏu chéu hîng (hâng) méi. Iuēn iuēn tchè chŏu, tchēng tsái sāng iè (chòu). Touēi pèi tŏu siŭ, ĭ tsái kiū hià (hòu).**

2. Ngò ts'ôu tōung chān, t'aō t'aō pŏu kouēi. Ngò lâi tzéu tōung, lìng iù k'ì

et la pluie, (la calomnie menace de me perdre dans l'esprit du prince, et de renverser par ce moyen la puissance de notre famille). Je ne puis que pousser un cri d'alarme.

CHANT III. TOUNG CHAN.

Tcheou koung, revenu de son expédition contre 武庚 **Où kēng,** exprime ses sentiments et ceux de ses soldats. Voyez le chant précédent.

1. Je suis allé aux montagnes de l'est, et resté longtemps sans revenir à la maison. Pendant mon retour, une pluie fine est tombée. Au moment où dans l'est j'ai reçu l'ordre de revenir, je pensais à l'ouest avec tristesse. Aussitôt j'ai préparé mes vêtements ordinaires, heureux (de quitter le costume militaire, et) de ne plus voir ni rangs ni bâillons. (En chemin, considérant le ver à soie, je me disais): « Cet insecte demeure et se meut dans le champ de mûriers. Moi, je passe ici la nuit loin de ma maison, de ma femme et de mes enfants. Mais du moins je suis encore vivant sous mon char de guerre, c.-à-d. je ne suis pas mort. »

2. Je suis allé aux montagnes de l'est, et resté longtemps sans

CHANT III. 1. Ego ivi ad orientales montes, valde diu non redivi domum. Me veniente ex oriente, cadens pluvia ipsa tenuis. Quando ego in oriente jussus sum redire, meus animus de occidente mœrebat. Composui illas vestes (urbanas, et cogitavi) jam non adhibenda agmina nec linguaria. (In itinere mihi dicebam): « Sese movens bombyx manet in mororum campo. Domesticis carens, hic solus pernocto (sine uxore ac liberis); attamen supersum bellicum currum subter. »

鄘 **Iôung,** principauté de Ou keng, était dans le sud du 衛輝府 **Wéi houēi fòu,** par conséquent à l'est de la capitale des Tcheou. 士 signifie 事 faire. On mettait un bâillon aux soldats bavards. Le char de guerre servait de tente. 烝 **Tchēng,** particule.

慆不歸。我來自東。零雨其濛。果臝之實、亦施于宇。伊威在室。蠨蛸在戶。町畽鹿場。熠燿宵行。亦可畏也。伊可懷也。

③ 我徂東山。慆慆不歸。我來自東。零雨其濛。鸛鳴于垤。婦嘆于室。洒埽穹窒。我征聿至。有敦瓜苦。烝在栗薪。自我不見。于今三年。

môung. Kouò louò tchēu chēu, ĭ i iù iù. Ĭ wēi tsài chēu, siaō chaō tsài hòu. T'ing t'ouàn lŏu tch'àng, ĭ iaó siaō hing (hâng). Ĭ k'ò wéi (wēi) iè, ĭ k'ò houâi (houêi) iè.

3. Ngò ts'ôu tōung chān, t'aō t'aō pōu kouēi. Ngò lài tzéu tōung, lìng iù k'i môung. Kouàn mìng iû tiĕ (tĭ). Fóu t'án iû chēu. Chài saó k'iōung tchĕu. Ngò tchēng iû tchéu (tchēu). Iòu touēi kouā k'òu, tchēng tsài lĭ sīn. Tzéu ngò pōu kién, iû kīn sān gniên (gnin).

revenir à la maison. Pendant mon retour, une pluie fine est tombée. (En chemin je me disais) : « (Ma maison sera sans doute abandonnée). Les courges pendront au bord du toit. La cloporte sera à l'intérieur, et l'araignée à la porte. Tout autour, les cerfs auront battu le terrain. Le ver luisant y promènera sa lumière la nuit. » J'avais des sujets de crainte, mais aussi des sujets de joie.

3. Je suis allé aux montagnes de l'est, et resté longtemps sans revenir à la maison. Pendant mon retour, une pluie fine est tombée. La cigogne chantait sur un nid de fourmis. Ma femme soupirait à la maison. (En prévision de mon retour), elle avait arrosé et balayé la terre, et bouché les fentes. Soudain je suis revenu de l'expédition. Les coloquintes pendaient séparées les unes des autres aux branches du châtaignier. Je n'avais pas vu ma maison depuis trois ans.

2. Ego adivi orientales montes; valde diu non redii domum. Me veniente ex oriente, cecidit pluvia illa tenuis. (In itinere mihi ipse dicebam) : « Cucurbitarum fructus reptant sub tecti mei ora; oniscus est in domo; aranea est ad januam; vacuus circa domum locus est cervorum tritus campus; scintillat nocte incedens bestiola (lampyris). » Erant quidem timendi causæ; sed erant gaudendi causæ.

3. Ego adivi orientales montes; valde diu non redii domum. Me redeunte ex oriente, cecidit pluvia illa tenuis. Ciconia canebat super formicarum nidum. Uxor suspirabat domi. Asperserat et verrerat; foramina obturaverat. Ego ex expeditione subito adveni. Erant solitarii cucumeres amari, inerant castaneæ ramis. Ex quo ego non vidi, usque nunc tres anni (elapsi sunt).

Au dire des commentateurs, les fourmis pressentent la pluie et sortent de leurs trous. La cigogne s'en repaît.

詩經

(4) 我徂東山、慆慆不歸、我來自東、零雨其濛、倉庚于飛、熠燿其羽、之子于歸、皇駁其馬、親結其縭、九十其儀、其新孔嘉、其舊如之何、

破斧

(1) 既破我斧、又缺我斨、周公東征、四國是皇、哀我人斯、亦孔之將、

4. Ngò ts'ôu tōung chān, t'aō t'aō pōu kouēi. Ngò lâi tzéu tōung, lìng iù k'ì môung. Ts'āng kēng iû fēi, ĭ iaô k'ì iù. Tchēu tzèu iù kouēi, houâng pouŏ k'ì mà (mòu). Ts'īn kiĕ k'ì lì, kiòu chĕu k'ì i. K'ì sīn k'òung kiā (kī), k'i kióu jôu tchēu hô (hî) ?

P'OUO FOU. **1. Ki p'ouó ngò fòu, iòu k'iuĕ ngò ts'iāng. Tcheōu kōung tōung tchēng, séu kouŏ chéu houâng. Ngāi ngò jênn sēu, ĭ k'òung tchēu tsiāng.**

4. Je suis allé aux montagnes de l'est, et resté longtemps sans revenir à la maison. Pendant mon retour, une pluie fine m'a accompagné. Quand le loriot vole, ses ailes brillent. Quand la jeune fille va célébrer ses noces, elle a des chevaux jaunes ou roux tachetés de blanc. Sa mère lui lie la serviette à la ceinture. Mille ornements l'environnent. Si les nouveaux époux sont si heureux, quelle n'est pas la joie des anciens, (quand ils se revoient après une longue séparation)?

CHANT IV. P'OUO FOU.

Les soldats, au retour de l'expédition dirigée contre 武庚 **Où kēng**, font l'éloge de 周公 **Tcheōu kōung**. Il leur a imposé de grandes fatigues, disent-ils, mais uniquement dans l'intérêt de l'empire; et ils s'en réjouissent.

1. Après avoir cassé ma hache, j'ai encore ébréché ma cognée. (Malgré tant de fatigues, je suis content). Tcheou koung, par son expédition dans l'est, a rétabli l'ordre dans tout l'empire. Plein de commisération pour nous, hommes du peuple, il nous a rendu le plus signalé service.

4. Ego adivi orientales montes; valde diu non redii domum. Me veniente ex oriente, cecidit pluvia illa minuta. Flava avis dum volat, nitent ejus pennæ. Illa puella dum nuptura adit sponsi domum, vel flavi albis maculis distincti vel fulvi albo sparsi sunt illius equi. Mater nectit illius linteum. Novem decemque illius (comitantia) ornamenta. Si illi novi (conjuges) sunt valde felices, illi veteres quantum (gaudent, quum diu sejuncti invicem conveniunt)?

CHANT IV. 1. Postquam fregi meam securim, etiam fidi meam asciam. Tcheou princeps ad orientem exercitum eduxit, omnia regna eo ipso recte composita sunt. Miseratione usus est in nos homines valde ingenter.

(2) 既破我斧、又鈌我錡、周公東征、四國是吪、哀我人斯、亦孔之嘉、

(3) 既破我斧、又鈌我銶、周公東征、四國是遒、哀我人斯、亦孔之休、

伐柯

(1) 伐柯如何、匪斧不克、取妻如何、匪媒不得、

2. Ki p'ouó ngò fòu, iòu k'iuě ngò k'î (k'ŏ). Tcheōu kōung tōung tchēng, séu kouŏ chéu wô. Ngāi ngò jênn sēu, ĭ k'òung tchēu kiā (kŏ).

3. Ki p'ouó ngò fòu, iòu k'iuě ngò k'iôu. Tcheōu kōung tōung tchēng, séu kouŏ chéu ts'iôu. Ngāi ngò jênn sēu, ĭ k'òung tchēu hiōu.

FA KO. **1. Fă kō jôu hô ? Fèi fòu pŏu k'ŏ. Ts'iú ts'ī jôu hô ? Fêi mêi pŏu tĕ.**

2. Après avoir brisé ma hache, j'ai encore ébréché mon ciseau. Tcheou koung, par son expédition dans l'est, a transformé tout l'empire. Il a signalé sa commisération envers le peuple d'une manière éclatante.

3. Après avoir cassé ma hache, j'ai encore ébréché ma cognée. Tcheou koung, par son expédition dans l'est, a affermi l'union des peuples de l'empire. Il a signalé excellemment sa compassion envers nous tous.

CHANT V. FA KO.

Les habitants de l'est se réjouissent de l'arrivée de Tcheou koung. Depuis longtemps, disent-ils, ils désiraient le voir, et ne pouvaient obtenir ce bonheur. A présent, il leur est si facile de le voir qu'il est facile à un homme de tailler un manche de hache, quand il a une hache, ou de se marier, quand il a un entremetteur.

1. Pour tailler un manche de hache, que faut-il? Il faut une hache (munie de son manche). Pour avoir une épouse, que faut-il? Il faut un entremetteur.

斯 **Sēu,** particule. 將 **Tsiāng,** grand.

2. Postquam rupi meam securim, etiam fidi meum scalprum. Tcheou princeps ad orientem eduxit exercitum; omnia regna eo correcta sunt. Miseratione prosecutus est nos homines omnino pulchre.

3. Postquam fregi meam securim, etiam fidi meam asciam. Tcheou princeps in oriente rebelles debellavit; omnia regna eo ipso consociata sunt. Miseratione prosecutus est nos homines omnino eximie.

CHANT V. 1. Cæditur securis manubrium quo pacto? Nisi habeatur securis (manubrio instructa), non possibile est. Ducitur uxor qua ratione? Nisi habeatur conciliator nuptiarum, non obtinetur.

2. Quum cæditur manubrium, quum

（2）伐柯伐柯、
其則不遠、我
遘之子、籩豆
有踐、

九罭

（1）九罭之魚、
鱒魴、我覯之
子、袞衣繡裳、
（2）鴻飛遵渚、
公歸無所、於
女信處、
（3）鴻飛遵陸、
公歸不復、於

2. Fá kō, fá kō, k'i tsĕ pŏu iuèn. Ngò keóu tchēu tzèu, piēn teóu iòu tsièn.

KIOU IU. **1. Kiòu iù tchēu iû, tsuēnn fâng. Ngò keóu tchēu tzèu, kouènn I siòu châng.**

2. Hôung fēi tsiûn tchòu. Kōung kouēi òu chòu ? Iû jòu sin tch'òu.

3. Hôung fēi tsiùn lôu. Kōung kouēi pŏu fōu. Iû jòu sin siù.

2. Quand je taille un manche de hache, j'ai le modèle près de moi. (Ce modèle est le manche de la hache qui me sert d'instrument. Si j'ai un entremetteur, il m'est facile d'avoir une femme). Je vais au devant de cette jeune fille (que l'entremetteur m'a trouvée); les vases sont déjà rangés en ordre pour les offrandes (tout est prêt pour la cérémonie du mariage).

CHANT VI. KIOU IU.

Les habitants de l'est, apprenant que Tcheou koung doit les quitter et retourner à la cour, expriment le désir de le retenir au milieu d'eux. Ils le comparent à un poisson excellent, à un oiseau de passage.

1. Les poissons pris dans le filet à neuf poches sont la brême et le rouget. Nous avons le bonheur de posséder ce prince qui porte la robe et les insignes de sa haute dignité.

2. L'oie sauvage dans son vol longe les ilots (et s'arrête peu de temps). Ce prince n'a-t-il pas sa demeure où il doit retourner? Chez vous (habitants de l'est), il est venu passer deux nuits seulement.

3. L'oie sauvage dans son vol longe la terre ferme. Ce prince une fois parti ne reviendra plus. Chez vous il est venu passer deux nuits seulement.

cæditur manubrium, ejus exemplar non procul distat. Ego occurro illi puellæ; arundinea vasa et lignea vasa sunt ordinata.

Confucius, Tchoung ioung Ch. 13, applique au sage les deux premiers vers.

CHANT VI. 1. Instructo novem saccis reti capti pisces sunt leuciscus et brama. Nos vidimus hunc principem regia tunica et acupicta veste inferiori.

L'empereur et les 公 **kōung** portaient cinq emblèmes brodés sur leurs tuniques 衣 **I**; à savoir, des dragons, des montagnes, des faisans, des flammes, des vases sacrés 彝 **I**. Sur le vêtement 裳 **châng** qui descendait des reins aux talons, ils avaient quatre emblèmes; à savoir, des algues, des grains de riz, des haches et des lettres 亞.

2. Anser silvestris major volans legit

女信宿、(4)是以有袞衣兮、無以我公歸兮、無使我心悲兮、

狼跋

(1)狼跋其胡、載疐其尾、公孫碩膚、赤舄几几、(2)狼疐其尾、載跋其胡、公孫碩膚、德音不瑕、

4. Chéu i iòu kouènn ī hi. Oû i ngò kōung kouēi hi ; ôu chéu ngò sīn pēi hī.

LANG POUO. **1. Lâng pouŏ k'ī hôu, tsái tchéu k'ī wèi. Kōung suénn chĕu fōu, tch'ĕu sĭ ki ki.**

2. Lâng tchéu k'i wèi, tsái pouŏ k'ī hôu. Kōung suénn chĕu fōu, tĕ īn pŏu hiâ (hôu).

4. Deux nuits nous l'avons eu avec son vêtement royal au milieu de nous. Que notre prince ne retourne pas chez lui, et ne laisse pas nos cœurs dans l'affliction.

CHANT VII. LANG POUO.

Le loup devenu vieux trébuche souvent ; sa queue et la peau qui pend son cou ont une longueur démesurée et embarrassent sa marche. Tcheou koung, au milieu de grandes et nombreuses difficultés, n'a jamais fait un faux pas.

1. Lorsqu'un vieux loup avance, la peau qui pend sous son cou arrête le mouvement de ses pattes de devant ; alors (il recule, mais) sa queue se prend entre ses pattes de derrière. Tcheou koung, poli, grand, admirable, avec ses sandales rouges marche d'un pas ferme et assuré.

2. Lorsqu'un vieux loup recule, sa queue se prend entre ses pattes de derrière ; alors (il essaie d'avancer, mais) la peau qui pend sous sou cou embarrasse ses pattes de devant. Tcheou koung, toujours poli, grand, admirable, conserve intacte sa bonne renommée.

parvas insulas ; princeps revertens num caret loco (ad quem revertatur)? Apud vos (orientales incolas) duabus noctibus moratus est.

3. Anser silvestris volans legit continentem ; princeps reversus domum non huc redibit. Apud vos duabus noctibus mansit.

4. Quapropter habuimus (illum indutum) regia veste. Ne sit ut noster princeps domum revertatur ; ne fiat ut nostri animi doleant.

CHANT VII. 1. Lupus (quum progreditur) calcat sui colli pellem ; tunc (recedit, sed pedibus posterioribus) constringit suam caudam. Princeps (Tcheou koung) obsequens, magnus, insignis, rubris sandaliis gravis et firmus consistit.

2. Lupus (volens recedere, posterioribus pedibus) constringit suam caudam ; tum (progreditur et) calcat sui colli pellem. Princeps obsequens, magnus, insignis est ; bona fama caret vitio.

小雅二

DEUXIÈME PARTIE

SIAO IA

雅 **Ià** signifie 正 **tchéng** correct, convenable, bienséant. 小雅 **Siaò ià** Ce qui convient dans les circonstances ordinaires. 大雅 **Tá ià** Ce qui convient dans les grandes circonstances. 小雅二 Deuxième partie du Cheu king : Siao ia. 大雅三 Troisième partie du Cheu king : Ta ia.

Les chants qui composent ces deux parties du Cheu king, étaient exécutés à la cour impériale, les premiers, 小雅 **Siaò ià**, dans les festins, les seconds, 大雅 **Tá ià**, dans les réunions des princes 諸侯 **tchōu heóu** et dans les cérémonies en l'honneur des ancêtres. Les uns et les autres étaient réservés à l'empereur. Les princes et même les ministres d'État se sont quelquefois permis d'en faire usage ; mais c'était une usurpation, un abus introduit par suite de la décadence de la dynastie des Tcheou.

Le 小雅 **Siaò ià** se divise en huit 什 **chĕu** décades ou huit livres contenant chacun dix chants, et désignés respectivement par les premiers mots du premier chant.

Les vingt-deux premiers chants célèbrent des faits qui se passèrent sous les règnes de Wenn wang, de Ou wang et de Tch'eng wang, et l'on pense que Tcheou koung en est l'auteur.

鹿鳴之什二之一

鹿鳴

(1)呦呦鹿鳴、食野之苹、我有嘉賓、鼓瑟吹笙、吹笙鼓簧、承筐是將、人之好我、示我周行、

(2)呦呦鹿鳴、食野之蒿、我有嘉賓、德音孔昭、視民不恌、君子是則是傚、我有旨

LOU MING. 1. **Iōu iōu lōu ming (mâng), chĕu iĕ tchēu p'ing (p'âng). Ngò iòu kiā pīn, kòu chĕ tch'ouēi chēng (chāng). Tch'ouēi chēng kòu houâng, tch'êng k'ouāng chéu tsiāng. Jênn tchēu haó ngò ; chéu ngò tcheōu hing (hâng).**

2. Iōu iōu lōu ming, chĕu iĕ tchēu haō. Ngò iòu kiā pīn, tĕ īn k'òung tchaō. Chéu min pŏu t'iaō (t'aō). Kiūn tzèu chéu tsĕ chéu hiaó (haō). Ngò iòu tchéu tsiòu, kiā pīn chĕu ién i ngaō.

LIVRE I. LOU MING.

CHANT I. LOU MING.

L'empereur donne un festin à ses ministres et aux envoyés des princes feudataires. Il compare ses invités à une troupe de cerfs qui brament ensemble et broutent l'herbe dans la plaine.

1. Les cerfs brament de concert et broutent le cresson dans la plaine. J'ai d'excellents convives ; pour eux on touche le luth, on joue de la flûte. On joue de la flûte ; toutes les lamelles retentissent. Des corbeilles pleines de présents sont offertes aux convives. Ils m'aiment, ils m'enseigneront la grande voie (les principes de la sagesse).

2. Les cerfs brament de concert et broutent l'armoise dans la plaine. J'ai d'excellents convives; leur vertu brille d'un grand éclat. Ils apprennent au peuple à ne pas se conduire d'une manière abjecte ; ils sont la règle et le modèle des officiers. J'ai un vin exquis ; je

TITRE DU LIVRE. 鹿鳴之什二之一 Lou ming decas: (Cheu king partis) secundæ (decas) prima.

CHANT III. 1. Concordi voce cervi clocitant, pascuntur campi cardamo. Ego habeo optimos convivas ; pulsatur cithara, inflatur fistula. Inflatur fistula, pulsantur fistulæ lamellæ ; oblatio corbium tunc peragitur. Viri diligunt me ; monstrabunt mihi magnam viam (recte agendi).

笙 **Chēng**, flûte composée de treize ou de dix-neuf tuyaux.

A présent on appelle 鹿鳴宴 **Lŏu ming ién** le repas offert aux lettrés qui obtiennent le degré de 舉人 **kiù jênn**.

2. Concordi voce cervi clocitant, pascun-

酒，嘉賓式燕以敖，

(3) 呦呦鹿鳴，食野之芩，我有嘉賓，鼓瑟鼓琴，鼓瑟鼓琴，和樂且湛，我有旨酒，以燕樂嘉賓之心，

四牡

(1) 四牡騑騑，周道倭遲，豈不懷歸，王事靡盬，我心傷悲，

3. Iōu iōu lōu ming, chĕu iè tchēu k'in. Ngò iòu kiā pīn, kòu chĕ kòu k'in... Houô lŏ, ts'iè tān (tchĕnn). Ngò iòu tchèu tsiòu, i ién lŏ kiā pīn tchĕu sīn.

SEU MEOU. **1. Séu meòu fēi fēi, tcheōu taó wēi tch'ēu. K'i pŏu houâi kouēi ? Wâng chéu mi kòu. Ngò sīn chāng pēi.**

l'offre dans ce festin à mes excellents convives, afin qu'il se réjouissent.

3. Les cerfs brament de concert et broutent le plante *k'in* dans la plaine. J'ai d'excellents convives; pour eux on touche le luth et la guitare. On touche le luth et la guitare; la concorde et l'allégresse règnent, la réjouissance se prolonge. J'ai un vin exquis; je le sers dans ce banquet à mes excellents convives, afin de réjouir leurs cœurs.

CHANT II. SEU MEOU.

Un officier exprime son dévouement envers l'empereur et son affection envers ses parents. Ce chant, disent les interprètes, a été composé, non par cet officier lui-même, mais par un autre, et chanté en son honneur dans un festin qui lui fut offert à la cour.

1. Mes quatre chevaux ont voyagé sans cesse, parcourant les longs détours de la grande route. Comment n'aurais-je pas désiré retourner à la maison? Mais je ne pouvais négliger le service de l'empereur. Mon cœur était dans l'affliction.

tur campi artemisia. Ego habeo optimos convivas; virtutis fama valde claret. Docent plebem ne abjecte agat; præpositi tunc imitantur, tunc æmulantur. Ego habeo exquisitum vinum; optimis convivis inter epulas propino ut oblectentur.

式 **Chĕu**, particule initiale.

3. Concordi voce cervi clocitant, pascuntur campi *k'in* herba. Ego habeo optimos convivas; pulsatur cithara, pulsatur lyra. Pulsatur cithara, pulsatur lyra; concordia, lætitia, imo diuturna oblectatio. Ego habeo exquisitum vinum; utens et epulis excipiens, exhilaro optimorum convivarum animos.

芩 **K'in**, plante herbacée, rampante, dont les feuilles ressemblent à celles du bambou. Elle croît dans les terrains salés et humides. Les chevaux et les bœufs s'en nourrissent.

CHANT II. 1. Quadrijugi mares indesinenter cucurrerunt; magna via flexuosa ac longa est. Qui non cupivissem domum redire? Regia negotia non

(2) 四牡騑騑、嘽
嘽駱馬、豈不懷
歸、王事靡盬、不
遑啓處、
(3) 翩翩者鵻、載
飛載下、集于苞
栩、王事靡盬、不
遑將父、
(4) 翩翩者鵻、載
飛載止、集于苞
杞、王事靡盬、不
遑將母、
(5) 駕彼四駱、載

2. Séu meòu fēi fēi, t'ān t'ān lŏ mà (mòu). K'i pŏu houâi kouēi ? Wâng chéu mi kòu ; pŏu houâng k'i tch'òu.

3. P'iēn p'iēn tchė tchouēi, tsái fēi tsái hiá (hòu), tsĭ iû paō hiù. Wâng chéu mi kòu ; pŏu houâng tsiāng fòu.

4. P'iēn p'iēn tchė tchouēi, tsái fēi tsái tchèu, tsĭ iû paō k'i. Wâng chéu mi kòu ; pŏu houâng tsiāng mòu (mèi).

5. Kiá péi séu lŏ, tsái tcheóu ts'īn ts'īn. K'i pŏu houâi kouēi ? Chéu ióung tsŏ kō, tsiāng mòu lâi chènn (chēnn).

2. Mes quatre chevaux ont couru sans cesse ; nombreux étaient les coursiers blancs à crinière noire. Comment n'aurais-je pas désiré retourner à la maison? Mais je ne pouvais négliger le service de l'empereur ; je n'avais pas le temps de prendre un peu de relâche, même à genoux.

3. Les tourterelles vont çà et là ; tantôt elles volent, tantôt elles se posent sur les arbres. Elles se rassemblent sur un massif de chênes. Je ne pouvais négliger les affaires de l'empereur ; je n'avais pas le temps de soigner mon père.

4. Les tourterelles vont çà et là ; tantôt elles volent, tantôt elles s'arrêtent. Elles se rassemblent sur un massif de lyciets. Je ne pouvais négliger les affaires de l'empereur ; je n'avais pas le temps de soigner ma mère.

5. Mes quatre coursiers blancs à crinière noire couraient avec rapidité. Comment n'aurais-je pas désiré retourner à la maison?

licebat negligere. Meus animus saucius dolebat.

2. Quadrijugi mares cucurrerunt indesinenter; plurimi erant albi nigra juba equi. Qui non cupivissem domum reverti? Regia negotia non licebat negligere. Non mihi vacabat in genua innixo sistere.

3. Huc illuc discurrunt turtures, modo volant modo descendunt ; congregantur super confertas quercus. Regia negotia non licebat negligere; non mihi vacabat alere patrem.

4. Huc illuc discurrunt turtures, modo volant modo sistunt ; congregantur super conferta lycia. Regia negotia non licebat negligere ; non mihi vacabat alere matrem.

5. Juncti erant illi quadrijugi albi nigra juba equi et currebant celeriter.

騤騤。豈不懷歸。是用作歌。將母來諗。

皇皇者華

(1) 皇皇者華。于彼原隰。駪駪征夫。每懷靡及。

(2) 我馬維駒。六轡如濡。載馳載驅。周爰咨諏。

(3) 我馬維騏。六轡如絲。載馳載驅。周爰咨謀。

HOUANG HOUANG TCHE HOUA. **1. Houâng houâng tchè houâ (fōu), iū pèi iuên sĭ. Chēnn chēnn tchēng fōu ; méi houâi mi kĭ.**

2. Ngò mà wêi kiū, liŭ pi jôu jôu. Tsái tch'ēu, tsái k'iū ; tcheōu iuên tzēu tsiū.

3. Ngò mà wêi k'i, liŭ pi jôu sēu (sī). Tsái tch'ēu, tsái k'iū ; tcheōu iuên tzēu meôu (mêi).

Voilà pourquoi j'ai composé ce chant, et viens exprimer mon désir de donner mes soins à ma mère.

CHANT III. HOUANG HOUANG TCHE HOUA.

Éloge d'un officier qui, chargé d'une mission par l'empereur, part avec une suite nombreuse, voyage en toute hâte, et demande partout des renseignements et des avis.

1. L'éclat des fleurs resplendit partout, sur les plateaux des montagnes et dans les plaines basses. Ainsi les voyageurs (l'envoyé et ses compagnons) partent nombreux et marchent rapidement. Ils sont dans une sollicitude continuelle, comme s'ils se croyaient incapables de remplir leur mission.

2. Mes chevaux sont tous jeunes et vigoureux ; leurs six rênes sont luisantes. Je presse, je fouette mes coursiers. Je vais partout demander des renseignements et des avis.

3. Mes chevaux sont tous gris tachetés ; leurs six rênes sont flexibles comme des fils de soie. Je vais partout chercher des renseignements et des avis.

Qui non cupivissem domum redire? Quapropter composui canticum, de alenda matre veni moniturus (regem).

CHANT III. 1. Splendentes flores sunt in illis planis locis tum editis tum humilibus. Plurimi celeriter currunt viatores viri, i.e. missus præfectus ejusque comites; continuo solliciti sunt quasi non possent assequi (ut regio mandato recte fungerentur).

2. Mei equi solummodo sunt (i.e. omnes sunt) juvenes equi ; sex habenæ videntur unguine novo nitentes. Et urgeo equos et stimulo equos ; omnia loca percurro, tum inquiro et interrogo.

爰 **Iuên** équivaut à 於 **iū**, alors. Deux des huit rênes étaient fixées sur le devant de la caisse de la voiture. Le conducteur tenait les six autres dans les mains. Voy. page 136.

3. Mei equi solummodo sunt coloris cineracei maculis distincti ; sex habenæ sunt quasi sericum. Omnia loca percurro, tum inquiro et interrogo.

(4) 我馬維駱、六轡沃若、載馳載驅、周爰咨度。

(5) 我馬維駰、六轡既均、載馳載驅、周爰咨詢。

常棣

(1) 常棣之華、鄂不韡韡、凡今之人、莫如兄弟。

(2) 死喪之威、兄弟孔懷、原隰裒矣、兄弟求矣。

4. Ngò mà wêi lŏ, liŭ pi ŏu jŏ. Tsái tch'ĕu, tsái k'iū ; tcheōu iuên tzēu touŏ.

5. Ngò mà wêi În, liŭ pi ki kiūn. Tsái tch'ĕu, tsái k'iū ; tcheōu iuên tzēu siūn.

TCH'ANG TI. **1. Tch'âng tí tchēu houâ, ngŏ pŏu wèi wèi? Fân kīn tchēu jênn, mouŏ jôu hiōung ti.**

2. Sēu sāng tchēu wēi, hiōung ti k'òung houâi (houêi). Iuên sî p'eōu i, hiōung ti k'iôu i.

4. Mes chevaux sont tous blancs et ont la crinière noire; leurs six rênes paraissent luisantes. Je presse, je fouette mes coursiers; je vais partout solliciter des renseignements et des conseils.

5. Mes chevaux sont tous gris pommelés; leurs six rênes vont bien ensemble. Je presse, je fouette mes coursiers; je vais partout interroger et délibérer.

CHANT IV. TCH'ANG TI.

L'empereur, dans un festin offert à ses frères, fait l'éloge de l'amitié fraternelle.

1. La fleur du prunier n'est-elle pas plus brillante que toutes les autres? De même, les frères sont préférables à tous les autres hommes qui sont au monde.

2. Parmi les terreurs de la mort et des funérailles, les frères montrent la plus grande affection. Ils vont sur les hauteurs et dans les vallées chercher les nombreux cadavres de leurs frères.

4. Mei equi solummodo sunt albi nigra juba; sex habenæ unguine nitere videntur. Et urgeo equos et stimulo equos; omnia loca percurro, tum inquiro et delibero.

5. Mei equi solummodo sunt cineracei coloris maculis distincti; sex habenæ conveniunt inter se. Et urgeo equos et stimulo equos; omnia loca percurro, tum inquiro et delibero.

CHANT IV. 1. Pruni flos aspectu nonne splendet? Quicumque nunc sunt homines, (inter eos) non sunt pares fratribus.

鄂 **Ngŏ**, paraître, apparence.

2. In mortis et funeris terroribus, fratres maximo amore invicem prosequuntur. In planis locis sive editis sive humilibus congesta (fratrum cadavera) fratres quærunt.

(3) 脊令在原、兄弟急難、每有良朋、況也永歎、

(4) 兄弟鬩于牆、外禦其務、每有良朋、烝也無戎、

(5) 喪亂既平、既安且寧、雖有兄弟、不如友生、

(6) 儐爾籩豆、飲酒之飫、兄弟既具、和樂且孺、

3. Tsĭ lìng tsái iuên, hiōung ti kĭ nân (gniên). Mèi iòu leàng p'êng, houáng iè iòung t'ān (t'iēn).

4. Hiōung ti hĭ iū ts'iâng, wái iù k'i óu (òu). Mèi iòu leàng p'êng, tchēng iè ôu jôung (jòu).

5. Sāng louán kí p'ìng, ki ngān ts'iè gnìng. Souēi iòu hiōung ti, pŏu jôu iòu chēng (sīng) ?

6. Pin èul piēn teóu, in tsiòu tchēu iú. Hiōung ti ki kiú, houô lŏ, ts'iè jóu.

3. La bergeronnette s'agite dans la plaine ; de même, les frères sont parfois agités par le sort. Alors les meilleurs amis poussent sans cesse des gémissements, (mais ne viennent pas en aide).

4. Lors même que des frères se querellent entre eux dans l'intérieur des murs, ils se réunissent toujours pour repousser les attaques du dehors, tandis que les meilleurs amis ne sont d'aucun secours.

5. Quand les deuils et les troubles ont cessé, et que la paix et la tranquillité sont rétablies, ne serait-il pas déraisonnable d'estimer et d'aimer moins ses frères que des amis ordinaires ?

6. Je suppose que vos vases de bois soient rangés pour les offrandes et qu'on boive le vin à longs traits. Quand vos frères sont tous présents, alors règnent la concorde, la joie et la plus tendre affection.

3. Motacilla est in campo ; fratres premuntur calamitate. Interdum habentur boni amici ; perpetuos edunt gemitus (nec adjuvant).

況 **Houáng**, particule.

4. Fratres (etsi) rixantur intra parietes, foris (conjunctim) repellunt sibi illatas injurias. Quandoque habentur fideles amici ; tamen non adjuvant.

務 tient la place de 侮 **òu.**

烝 **Tchēng**, particule.

5. Funeribus et turbationibus jam suppressis, (restituta) jam pace et quiete, etsi habentur fratres, nonne pares amicis hominibus (ducendi sunt)?

6. Ordinasti tua arundinea vasa et lignea vasa, et bibitur vinum ad satietatem. Postquam fratres omnes adsunt, concordia, gaudium, imo quasi juvenis filii in parentes amor.

(7) 妻子好合、如鼓瑟琴、兄弟既翕、和樂且湛、

(8) 宜爾室家、樂爾妻帑、是究是圖、亶其然乎、

伐木

(1) 伐木丁丁、鳥鳴嚶嚶、出自幽谷、遷于喬木、嚶其鳴矣、求其友聲、相彼鳥矣、猶求友聲、矧伊人矣、不求友生、神

7. Ts'ī tzèu haò hŏ, jôu kòu chĕ k'în. Hiōung tí kí hĭ, houô lŏ, ts'iè tān (tchēnn).

8. Î èul chĕu kiā (kōu), lŏ èul ts'ī nôu. Chéu kióu chéu t'ôu, tàn k'î jên hôu.

FA MOU. 1. Fă môu tchēng tchēng; gniaò mîng īng īng. Tch'ŏu tzéu iōu kŏu, ts'iēn iû k'iaô móu. Īng k'î mîng i, k'iôu k'î iòu chēng. Siáng pèi gniaò i, iôu

7. Je suppose que vous, votre femme et vos enfants, vous vous accordiez comme le luth et la guitare. Quand l'accord régnera entre vous et vos frères, alors seulement la bonne intelligence, la joie et le bonheur seront de longue durée.

8. De la concorde avec vos frères dépendent le bon ordre de votre maison, le bonheur de votre femme et de vos enfants. Examinez à fond cette question, réfléchissez-y; et dites-moi s'il n'en est pas ainsi.

CHANT V. FA MOU.

L'empereur, dans un festin offert aux princes, loue la concorde et l'amitié. Le bruit des haches dans la forêt, dit-il, le chant des oiseaux, tout dans la nature tend à l'harmonie, et invite l'homme à cultiver l'amitié.

1. Le bruit des haches retentit en cadence dans la forêt. Les oiseaux chantent de concert. Du fond de la vallée ils vont sur la cime des grands arbres. Ils se répondent et s'appellent l'un l'autre. Voyez donc, un oiseau sait par son chant appeler un compagnon. Comment un homme ne rechercherait-il pas l'amitié d'un autre

7. Uxor liberique amant et concordant, sicut pulsatæ cithara et lyra. Fratres postquam concordabunt, erit concordia, gaudium, imo diuturna oblectatio.

8. (Fratres tui) recte componunt tuam domum, felices faciunt tuam uxorem et liberos. Id scruteris, id mediteris; (nonne) vere id ita est?

CHANT V. 1. Cæduntur arbores concordi strepitu. Aves cantant concordi voce; avolant ex obscura (profunda) valle, migrant ad proceras arbores. Consonus est earum cantus; est quærentium suos compares vox. Vide illam avem, etiam (ipsa) quærens comparem

詩經

之聽之、終和且平。

(2) 伐木許許、釃酒有藇、既有肥羜、以速諸父。寧適不來、微我弗顧。於粲洒埽、陳饋八簋、既有肥牡、以速諸舅。寧適不來、微我有咎。

(3) 伐木于阪、釃酒有衍。籩豆有

k'iŏu iòu chēng. Chénn I jênn i, pŏu k'iŏu iòu chēng ? Chênn tchēu t'īng tchēu, tchŏung houô, ts'iè p'ìng.

2. Fă mŏu hiù hiù ; chĕu tsiòu iòu siù. Ki iòu fêi tchòu, i sŏu tchōu fòu. Gning chēu pŏu lâi, wêi ngò fŏu kóu (kòu). Oū ! ts'án chài saò (seòu), tch'ênn kouéi pă kouèi (kiòu). Ki iòu fêi meòu, i sŏu tchŏu kiòu. Gnîng chĕu pŏu lâi, wêi ngò iòu kiòu.

3. Fă mŏu iū fàn ; chēu tsiòu iū ièn. Piēn teóu iòu tsièn, hiŏung ti ŏu iuèn.

homme? (S'il le fait) les esprits l'exauceront; il aura toujours la concorde et la tranquillité.

2. Le bruit des haches retentit avec force. Mon vin est clarifié et bien pur, et j'ai des agneaux gras. J'inviterai mes oncles paternels (les grands princes feudataires qui portent le même nom de famille que moi). Si par hasard ils ne viennent pas, j'aime mieux que ce soit pour une autre raison que pour celle d'un manque d'attention de ma part. Oh! arrosez et balayez proprement (la salle pour le festin); servez huit plats sur la table. J'ai des agneaux gras. J'inviterai mes oncles maternels (les grands princes feudataires qui ne portent pas le même nom de famille que moi). Si par hasard ils ne viennent pas, j'aime mieux que ce soit pour une autre raison que pour celle d'une négligence de ma part.

3. On coupe les arbres sur le penchant de la colline. Le vin clarifié est abondant. Les vases de bois sont déjà disposés sur la

clamat. Multo magis ille homo nonne quæret amicum hominem? Spiritus audient illum; in perpetuum concordia fruetur et pace.

2. Cæduntur arbores vi et fragore. Defæcatum vinum est liquidum; jam habeo pringues quinque mensium agnos; utens invitabo omnes patruos, i.e. magnos regulos meo cognomine vocatos. Malim forte (eos propter aliam causam non venire, non quia ego non curem (de eis). Oh! nitide aspergite et verrite (aulam ad convivium); ordinate dapum octo vasa. Jam habeo pingues mares (agnos aliave animalia). Utens invitabo omnes avunculos, i.e. magnos regulos non meo cognomine vocatos. Malim forte (eos propter aliam causam) non venire, non quia ego habeam culpam.

3. Cæduntur arbores in collis clivo. Defæcatum vinum multum est. Arundinea vasa et lign[illegible] jam ordinata sunt. Fratres non procul sunt, i.e.

踐。兄弟無遠。民之失德。乾餱以愆。有酒湑我。無酒酤我。坎坎鼓我。蹲蹲舞我。迨我暇矣。飲此湑矣。

天保

(1)天保定爾。亦孔之固。俾爾單厚。何福不除。俾爾多益。矣莫不庶。

(2)天保定爾。俾爾

Mîn tchēu chēu tě, kān heŏu i k'iēn (k'ièn). Iòu tsiòu siù ngò ; ǒu tsiòu kòu ngò. K'àn k'àn kòu ngò ; ts'uènn ts'uénn òu ngò. Tái ngò hiá (hòu) i, in ts'èu siù i.

T'IEN PAO. **1. T'iēn paò tìng èul, ĭ k'òung tchēu kóu. Pèi èul tān heóu ; hô fŏu pŏu tch'óu. Pei èul touō ĭ, i mouŏ pŏu chóu.**

2. T'iēn paò tìng èul, pèi èul tsièn kŏu. K'ing ǒu pŏu ì, cheóu t'iēn pě lŏu. Kiáng èul hiá fŏu, wêi jĕu pŏu tsŏu.

table. Tous mes frères (les petits princes) sont présents. Les hommes du peuple négligent les devoirs de l'amitié (par avarice) pour épargner leurs aliments secs. (Moi, je traite mes amis avec libéralité). Quand j'ai du vin, je le fais clarifier ; quand je n'en ai pas, j'en fais acheter. Je fais battre le tambour et exécuter des chants avec pantomime. Puisque nous avons du loisir, buvons ensemble ce vin pur.

CHANT VI. T'IEN PAO.

Les princes et les officiers, invités à la table de l'empereur, prient le ciel d'acquitter lui-même la dette de leur reconnaissance.

1. Que le ciel vous protège, et vous accorde une prospérité constante et assurée. Qu'il vous fasse jouir d'un bonheur sans mélange, et vous renouvelle sans cesse toutes ses faveurs. Qu'il vous comble de ses dons, et vous envoie tous les biens en abondance.

2. Que le ciel vous protège et vous fasse jouir d'une félicité

adsunt reguli minores, sive mei sive alieni cognominis. Plebeiorum hominum deficit beneficentia (erga amicos), siccorum alimentorum causa peccant. Quum habeo vinum, defæcatur mihi ; quum non habeo vinum, emitur mihi. Repetito sonitu pulsatur tympanum mihi ; ad numeros cantica saltantur mihi. Quando nos otio fruimur, bibamus hoc defæcatum.

CHANT VI. 1. Cœlum tueatur ac statuat te, et quidem magna firmitate. Faciat ut tu sis simpliciter beatus, i. e. omnibus bonis potitus ac nulli malo obnoxius, et quodcumque beneficium non desinat quin renovetur. Faciat ut tu multum augearis donis, ita ut nihil non sit copiosum.

2. Cœlum protegat et confirmet te ; faciat ut tu omnibus sis cumulatus

戩穀、罄無不宜、受天百祿、降爾遐福、維日不足、
(3) 天保定爾、以莫不興、如山如阜、如岡如陵、如川之方至、以莫不增、
(4) 吉蠲爲饎、是用孝享、禴祠烝嘗、于公先王、君曰卜爾、萬壽無疆、

3. T'iēn paò ting èul, i mouŏ pŏu hīng, jôu chān, jôu feòu, jôu kāng, jôu līng, jôu tch'ouēn tchēu fāng tchéu, i mouŏ pŏu tsēng.

4. Kĭ kiuēn wêi tch'éu, chéu ióung hiaó hiàng (hiāng).{Iŏ sêu tchēng tch'âng, iû kōung siēn wâng. Kiūn iuĕ : « Pŏu èul, wán cheóu ôu kiāng. »

constante; qu'il vous comble de tous les biens. Que votre conduite soit toujours parfaite, et vous attire toutes les faveurs célestes. Que le ciel vous accorde une grande prospérité, qui ne soit pas seulement passagère, mais dure toujours.

3. Que le ciel vous protège et vous fasse jouir d'une prospérité constante. Que vos biens s'accumulent, et soient comme une montagne, comme un monticule, comme la crête d'une montagne, comme une haute colline, comme un fleuve dont les eaux, après avoir commencé à couler, ne cessent de croître.

4. Vous choisissez un jour heureux, et après les purifications d'usage, vous préparez les dons que vous destinez à vos ancêtres. Au printemps, en été, en automne et en hiver, vous faites des offrandes aux anciens princes et aux empereurs de votre famille. Vos ancêtres vous disent (par la bouche de leur représentant): « Nous vous accordons une vie longue, une vie sans fin. »

bonis. Omnino nihil sit non congruum (in tua agendi ratione), et accipias cœlestia omnia dona. Immittat tibi diuturnam felicitatem, solummodo ad tempus non suppeditet.

3. Cœlum protegat et statuat te, ita ut nihil non cumuletur, instar montis, instar monticuli, instar montis jugi, instar collis, instar fluvii qui incipit advenire, ita ut nihil non crescat (tibi).

4. Fausto die, purificationibus factis, præparas dona (vinum et dapes), quæ adhibens pius progenitoribus offers. Æstiva, verna, hiemalia, autumnalia sacra offers (progenitoribus tuis) regulis et decessoribus imperatoribus. Principes dicunt: « Statuimus tibi summam longævitatem carentem limite. »

Avant une offrande, on s'abstenait de certaines choses durant plusieurs jours, et on lavait avec soin les vases. Les anciens princes de la famille des 周 **Tcheōu** étaient 后稷 **Heóu tsĭ** et ses successeurs jusqu'à 太王 **T'ái wâng**. Les premiers empereurs de cette famille étaient 太王 **T'ái wâng** et 王季 **Wâng ki**, qui reçurent le titre d'empereurs seulement après leur mort.

(5) 神之弔矣、詒爾多福、民之質矣、日用飲食、羣黎百姓、徧爲爾德、

(6) 如月之恒、如日之升、如南山之壽、不騫不崩、如松柏之茂、無不爾或承、

采薇

(1) 采薇采薇、薇亦作止、曰歸曰

5. Chênn tchēu tĭ i, ĭ èul touŏ fŏu (pĭ). Mîn tchēu tchĕu i, jĕu iòung in chĕu. K'iûn lî pĕ sing pién wêi èul tĕ.

6. Jôu iuĕ tchēu hêng, jôu jĕu tchēu chēng, jôu nân chān tchēu cheóu, pŏu k'iên pŏu pēng. Jôu sōung pĕ tchēu meóu, ôu pŏu èul houĕ tch'êng.

TS'AI WEI. **1. Ts'ài wêi, ts'ài wêi; wêi ĭ tsŏ (tsóu) tchèu. Iuĕ kouēi, iuĕ**

5. Les mânes de vos ancêtres sont présents, et vous obtiennent un grand nombre de faveurs célestes. (Grâce à eux), le peuple est simple, et ne s'occupe que de chercher chaque jour sa nourriture. Les cent familles, tous vos sujets s'appliquent à cultiver la vertu d'accord avec vous.

6. Comme le croissant de la lune, comme la marche ascendante du soleil, comme l'âge des montagnes australes qui ne diminuent ni ne s'écroulent jamais, comme la végétation du sapin et du cyprès, votre prospérité durera toujours pleine et entière.

CHANT VII. TS'AI WEI.

Les soldats de l'empereur expriment leurs sentiments à leur départ pour une expédition contre les barbares du nord. Ils marquent les époques par les différents états de la fougère.

1. On cueille la fougère; la fougère sort de terre (c'est le printemps). Quand on parlera de revenir à la maison, l'année touchera

Après une offrande, le 尸 **chōu** représentant des ancêtres prenait la parole en leur nom, et promettait les faveurs célestes en récompense de la piété filiale.

5. (Progenitorum) manes advenerunt; tribuunt tibi multa bona. Populus est simplex; die utitur (ab quaerendum) potum et cibum. Omnes nigris capillis homines, centum familiae ubique operam dant tecum virtuti.

6. Ut lunae crementum, ut solis ascensus, ut australium montium longaevitas qui nec deficiunt nec ruunt, ut abietis et cupressus luxuries, nihil non tibi forte continuabitur.

CHANT VII. 1. Decerpitur filix, decerpitur filix; filix quidem e terra erumpit. Agetur de reditu, agetur de reditu, anno jam exeunte. Carebimus domo, carebimus familia, Hien iun causa. Nec vacabit in genua inniti et sistere, Hien iun causa.

D'après les auteurs chinois, 玁狁 **Hiên iùn**, 匈奴 **Hiōung nôu**, 獯鬻,

詩經

歸。歲亦莫止。靡室靡家。玁狁之故。不遑啓居。玁狁之故。

(2) 采薇采薇。薇亦柔止。曰歸曰歸。心亦憂止。憂心烈烈。載飢載渴。我戍未定。靡使歸聘。

(3) 采薇采薇。薇亦剛止。曰歸曰歸。歲亦陽止。王事靡盬。不遑啓處。憂心孔疚。我行不來。

kouēi, souéi ĭ móu tchèu. Mi chēu mi kiā (kōu), Hièn iùn tchēu kóu. Pŏu houâng k'i kiū, Hièn iùn tchēu kóu.

2. Ts'ài wêi, ts'ài wêi ; wêi ĭ jeôu tchèu. Iuĕ kouēi, iuĕ kouēi, sīn ĭ iōu tchèu. Iōu sīn liĕ liĕ, tsái kī tsái k'ŏ (k'iĕ). Ngò chóu wéi tíng, mì chéu kouēi p'ing.

3. Ts'ài wêi, ts'ài wêi ; wêi ĭ kāng tchèu. Iuĕ kouēi, iuĕ kouēi, souéi ĭ iâng tchèu. Wâng chéu mì kòu, pŏu houâng k'i tch'òu. Iōu sīn k'òung kiòu (kì), ngò hîng pŏu lâi (lî).

à son terme. Pour nous, plus de maison, plus de famille; cela, à cause des invasions des Hien iun. Nous n'aurons pas un instant pour nous reposer, même sur nos genoux, à cause des invasions des Hien iun.

2. On cueille la fougère; la fougère est encore tendre (l'année n'est pas très avancée). Quand je pense à (l'époque si éloignée de) notre retour, mon cœur est triste. Mon cœur est tourmenté par le chagrin; nous souffrirons la faim et la soif. Tant que notre service ne sera pas terminé et que nous garderons le pays, nous ne pourrons pas même envoyer un messager saluer nos parents.

3. On cueille la fougère; la fougère est déjà dure (l'année est avancée.). Quand on parlera de retour, nous serons au dixième mois de l'année. Les affaires de l'empereur ne peuvent être négligées; nous n'aurons pas un instant pour nous reposer, même sur nos genoux. Mon cœur est plongé dans la tristesse; je ne reviendrai pas de cette expédition.

Hiūn iŭ, 突厥 **Tŏu kiuĕ** sont des noms différents qui désignent les mêmes peuplades du nord, probablement les Huns. 止 **Tchèu**, particule.

薇 **Wêi**, plante comestible, peut-être une espèce de fougère.

2. Decerpitur filix, decerpitur filix; filix quidem est tenera. Cogitans de reditu, cogitans de reditu, animus quidem mœret. Mœrore animus æstuat; et esuriemus et sitiemus. Nostra regionis custodia dum non erit peracta, neminem mittemus domum qui salutet.

3. Decerpitur filix, decerpitur filix; filix quidem dura est. Agetur de reditu, agetur de reditu, anni quidem decimo

(4) 彼爾維何、維常之華、彼路斯何、君子之車、戎車既駕、四牡業業、豈敢定居、一月三捷、

(5) 駕彼四牡、四牡騤騤、君子所依、小人所腓、四牡翼翼、象弭魚服、豈不日戒、玁狁孔棘、

(6) 昔我往矣、楊柳依依、今我來思、雨雪霏霏、行道遲遲、

4. Pèi èul wèi hô ? Wèi châng tchēu houâ (fōu). Pèi lóu sēu hô ? Kiūn tzèu tchēu kiū. Jôung kiū ki kiá, sèu meòu iĕ iĕ. K'i kàn ting kiū ? Ĭ iuĕ sān tsiĕ.

5. Kiá pèi sèu meòu, sèu meòu k'ouêi k'ouêi, kiūn tzèu chòu I, siaò jênn chòu fêi. Sèu meòu ĭ ĭ ; siáng mì, iù fōu (p'ĕ). K'i pŏu jĕu kiái (kĭ) ? Hièn iùn k'òung kĭ.

6. Sĭ ngò wàng i, iâng liòu I I. Kīn ngò lâi sēu, iú siuĕ fēi fēi. Hing taó tch'êu

4. Quelle est cette fleur élégante? C'est la fleur du prunier. Quelle est cette voiture? C'est la voiture du chef de l'armée. Ce char de guerre est attelé; il est traîné par quatre coursiers robustes. Comment oserais-je me donner du repos? Chaque mois nous devrons (livrer trois combats et) remporter trois victoires.

5. Les quatre coursiers sont attelés, les quatre coursiers sont très vigoureux. Ce char est celui qui porte le chef de l'armée et protège les simples soldats. La marche des quatre coursiers est très régulière. L'arc du chef a des extrémités d'ivoire; son carquois est de peau de veau marin. Comment ne serions-nous pas sans cesse sur nos gardes? Les Hien iun nous pressent vivement.

6. A notre départ, les saules étaient brillants de verdure. Maintenant que nous retournons à la maison, la neige tombe à gros flocons. Le voyage sera long; nous souffrons la soif et la faim.

mense. Regia negotia non sunt negligenda; non vacabit in genua inniti et morari. Mœrore animus valde æger est; ego proficiscar nec revertar.

4. Illud elegans quid est? Est pruni flos. Ille currus quisnam est? Militum ducis currus. Militaris currus jam junctus est; quatuor equi mares sunt robusti. Quomodo ausim sistere et morari? Uno mense ter vincemus.

5. Juncti sunt illi quatuor mares equi, quatuor mares validissimi. (Illa quadriga est) militum dux qua innititur, i. e. vehitur, gregales milites qua proteguntur. Quatuor mares composite incedunt. Ex ebore sunt arcus extrema, ex phocæ pelle est pharetra. Quomodo non quotidie caveamus? Hien iun valde premunt.

6. Primum me proficiscente, salices virescebant. Nunc me redeunte, cadit nix copiosa. Facimus iter longe

載渴載飢、我心傷悲、莫知我哀、

出車

（1）我出我車、于彼牧矣、自天子所、謂我來矣、召彼僕夫、謂之載矣、王事多難、維其棘矣、

（2）我出我車、于彼郊矣、設此旐矣、建彼旄矣、彼旟旐斯、胡不旆

tch'êu, tsái k'ŏ tsái kī. Ngò sīn chāng pēi, mouŏ tchēu ngò ngāi (ī).

TCH'OU KIU. **1. Ngò tch'ŏu ngò kiū, iū pèi mŏu (mī) i. Tzéu t'iēn tzéu chòu, wêi ngò lâi (lī) i. Tchaó pèi pŏu fōu, wéi tchêu tsái (tsī) i. Wâng chéu touŏ nán, wêi k'î kí i.**

2. Ngò tch'ŏu ngò kiū, iū pèi kiaŏ (kaŏ) i. Chĕ ts'êu tchaò i, kién pèi maô i.

Mon cœur est accablé de tristesse; personne ne connaît nos souffrances.

CHANT VIII. TCH'OU KIU.

Nan Tchoung, chef de l'armée impériale, reçoit les félicitations de la cour à son retour d'une expédition contre les barbares du nord et de l'ouest.

1. Nous avons été avec nos chars (et l'avant-garde de l'armée) jusqu'aux pâturages (à plus de cent stades de la capitale. Nan Tchoung a dit): « De la demeure du Fils du ciel un ordre m'est arrivé. » Aussitôt il a appelé le conducteur de sa voiture, lui a ordonné de mettre sur son char les armes et les autres objets, et lui a dit: « L'affaire que l'empereur me confie est pleine de difficultés; la promptitude est surtout nécessaire. »

2. Nous avons été avec nos chars (et le gros de l'armée) dans les campagnes au-delà des faubourgs de la capitale, (lorsque l'avant-garde était déjà arrivée aux pâturages). Nous avons arboré l'étendard qui est orné de tortues et de serpents et surmonté d'une touffe de crin de bœuf. Comment l'étendard orné d'éperviers et l'étendard orné de tortues et de serpents n'auraient-ils pas flotté (le premier

diuque; et sitimus et esurimus. Meus animus æger mœret; nemo novit nostras ærumnas.

CHANT VIII. 1. Nos eduximus nostros currus ad illa pascua. (Nan Tchoung dixit): « Ex cœli filii sede edictum mihi venit. » Arcessivit illum currus ductorem, jussit illum onerare currum (armis et cæteris; illique dixit): « Regium negotium multas habet difficultates; maxime illud properandum est. »

2. Nos eduximus nostros currus ad illos circum suburbia campos. Explicatum illud testudinibus et anguibus ornatum signum, (cujus ad summum) erecta est bovis cauda. Illud accipitribus ornatum signum (et illud) testu-

旆、憂心悄悄、僕夫況瘁、
(3) 王命南仲、往城于方、出車彭彭、旂旐央央、天子命我、城彼朔方、赫赫南仲、玁狁于襄、
(4) 昔我往矣、黍稷方華、今我來思、雨雪載塗、王事多難、不遑啓

Pėi iù tchaȯ sēu, hôu pŏu pėi pėi? Iōu sīn ts'iaȯ ts'iaȯ, pŏu fōu houáng souėi.

3. Wȧng ming Nȃn Tchóung, wȧng tch'ėng iū Fāng. Tch'ŏu kiū p'ôung p'ôung (p'ȃng p'ȃng), k'î tchaȯ iāng iāng. T'iēn tzèu ming ngȯ, tch'ėng pėi Chouŏ fāng. Hĕ hé Nȃn Tchóung, Hiėn iùn iù siāng.

4. Sī ngȯ wȧng i, chȯu tsī fāng houȧ (fōu). Kīn ngȯ lâi sēu, iú siuĕ tsái t'ȯu.

à l'avant-garde, le second au centre de l'armée)? Notre chef était agité par l'inquiétude (à cause de la responsabilité qui pesait sur lui; et pour une raison semblable), le conducteur de sa voiture séchait de crainte.

3. L'empereur avait ordonné à Nan Tchoung d'établir des fortifications dans le pays de Fang. Nos chars étaient nombreux; nos étendards brillaient, ornés les uns de dragons, les autres de tortues et de serpents. «Le Fils du ciel, dit Nan Tchoung, m'a ordonné d'établir des fortifications dans le pays de Chouo fang.» Nan Tchoung est redoutable; les Hien iun ont été chassés.

4. A notre départ, les deux sortes de millet à panicules étaient à peine en fleur. Maintenant, à notre retour, la neige est tombée et fondue, la route est boueuse. L'affaire dont l'empereur nous avait chargés était pleine de difficultés; nous n'avons pas eu le temps de nous arrêter un peu et de nous reposer, même sur nos genoux.

dinibus anguibusque ornatum signum quomodo non undassent expansa? (Militum ducis) anxius animus commovebatur; currus ductor tunc tabescebat.

On appelait 郊 **kiaō** la zone de terrain qui s'étendait depuis les faubourgs de la capitale jusqu'à une distance de cent stades. Au-delà étaient les 牧 **mōu** pâturages.

況 **Houáng**, alors, à cause de cela.

3. Imperator jussit Nan Tchoung ire et mœnia exstruere in Fang. Educti currus plurimi erant; draconibus ornatum signum et testudinibus anguibusque ornatum signum quasi nova nitebant. (Nan Tchoung dixit): «Cœli filius jussit me mœnibus munire illud Chouo fang.» Terribilis Nan Tchoung; Hien iun tunc expulsi sunt.

方 **Fāng** ou 朔方 **Chouŏ fāng** *Pays septentrional*, à présent 寧夏府 **Gning hiá fòu** dans le Kan siu.

4. Primum nobis proficiscentibus, milii duo genera *chòu tsī* incipiebant florere. Nunc nobis revertentibus, cecidit nix et via lutosa est. Imperatoris

詩經

居、豈不懷歸、畏此簡書、(5) 喓喓草蟲、趯趯阜螽、未見君子、憂心忡忡、既見君子、我心則降、赫赫南仲、薄伐西戎、(6) 春日遲遲、卉木萋萋、倉庚喈喈、采蘩祁祁、執訊獲醜、薄言還歸、赫赫南仲、玁狁于夷、

Wâng chéu touō nân, pŏu houâng k'i kiū. K'i pŏu houâi kouēi? Wéi ts'éu kién chōu.

5. Iaō iaō ts'aò tch'ōung, t'ī t'ī feòu tchōung. Wéi kién kiūn tzèu, iōu sīn tch'ōung tch'ōung. Kí kién kiūn tzèu, ngò sīn tsĕ hiâng (hôung). Hĕ hĕ Nân Tchóung pouŏ fă sī Jôung.

6. Tch'ouēnn jĕu tch'êu tch'êu, houèi mŏu ts'ī ts'ī. Ts'āng kēng kiāi kiai (kī kī), ts'ài fân k'ī k'ī. Tchĕu sin houĕ tch'eòu, pouŏ iên siuên kouēi. Hĕ hĕ Nân Tchóung, Hiên iùn iû i.

Comment n'aurions-nous pas désiré retourner dans nos foyers? Mais nous respections la volonté de l'empereur (qui avait ordonné cette expédition).

5. (La femme de Nan Tchoung disait): « Le grillon champêtre crie, la sauterelle bondit (l'année s'avance). Je ne vois pas encore mon seigneur; l'inquiétude agite mon cœur. Quand je reverrai mon seigneur, le calme rentrera dans mon cœur. » Nan Tchoung est redoutable; il a dompté sans peine les barbares de l'ouest.

6. Le printemps est revenu, les jours s'allongent, et la végétation est très active. Le loriot chante; une foule de personnes cueillent l'armoise (pour les vers à soie). Nous prenons avec nous les chefs des barbares qui doivent être jugés et toute la multitude des prisonniers de guerre, et nous retournons dans nos familles. Nan Tchoung est redoutable; à présent les Hien iun se tiennent en repos.

negotium multas habebat difficultates; non vacavit in genua inniti et sistere. Quomodo non cupivissemus reverti? Verebamur illud in tabulis inscriptum imperatoris edictum.

5. (Absentis militum ducis uxor dicebat): « Stridet campestris grillus, saltat locusta. Nondum videns dominum, mœstus animus agitatur. Quando videro dominum, meus animus illico quiescet. » Terribilis est Nan Tchoung; facile profligavit occidentales barbaros.

6. Verni dies longiores fiunt; herbæ et arbores luxuriant. Flava avis dulce cantat; colligunt artemisiam plurimi. Tenemus judicandos (barbarorum duces), sumimus turbam (barbarorum); paulum revertentes repetimus domos. Formidabilis est Nan Tchoung; Hien iun sunt quieti.

杕杜

(1)有杕之杜、有
睆其實、王事靡
盬、繼嗣我日、日
月陽止、女心傷
止、征夫遑止、
(2)有杕之杜、其
葉萋萋、王事靡
盬、我心傷悲、卉
木萋止、女心悲
止、征夫歸止、
(3)陟彼北山、言
采其杞、王事靡
盬、憂我父母、檀

TI TOU. **1. Iòu tí tchēu tòu, iòu houàn k'ì chĕu. Wâng chéu mì kòu, kí séu ngò jĕu. Jĕu iuĕ iâng tchèu. Gniù sīn chāng tchéu, tchēng fōu houâng tchèu.**

2. Iòu tí tchēu tòu, k'ì iĕ ts'ī ts'ī. Wâng chéu mì kòu, ngò sīn chāng pēi. Houèi mŏu ts'ī tchèu, gniù sīn pēi tchèu, tchēng fōu kouēi tchèu.

3. Tchĕu pèi pĕ chān, iên ts'ài k'ì k'ì. Wâng chéu mì kòu, iōu ngò fóu mòu (mèi). T'ân kiū tch'én tch'én. Séu meòu kouàn kouàn (kiuén kiuén); tchēng fōu pŏu iuén.

CHANT IX. TI TOU.

Au retour d'une expédition contre les Hien iun, les femmes des soldats expriment le désir qu'elles avaient de les revoir et les inquiétudes dont elles étaient tourmentées.

1. Le poirier sauvage est solitaire, et ses fruits sont beaux (l'automne est venu). Le service de l'empereur ne peut être négligé. Pour moi les jours se succèdent et s'ajoutent l'un à l'autre ; déjà le dixième mois de l'année est arrivé. Mon cœur de femme est dans l'affliction. Les soldats de l'expédition devraient avoir leur congé.

2. Le poirier sauvage est solitaire, son feuillage est verdoyant (le printemps est revenu). Le service de l'empereur ne peut être négligé. Mon cœur est dans l'affliction. Le végétation est luxuriante. Mon cœur de femme est inquiet. Les soldats de l'expédition devraient revenir.

3. Je gravis cette montagne qui est au nord, et j'y cueille le lyciet (le printemps touche à sa fin). Le service de l'empereur ne peut être négligé. Les parents de mon mari sont inquiets. Les chars en

CHANT IX. 1. Est solitaria pirus silvestris, sunt pulchri ejus fructus. Imperatoris negotium non est negligendum. Continui invicem succedunt mei dies; diebus et mensibus (elabentibus, advenit) decimus mensis. Uxoris animus dolet; profectis militibus danda est vacatio.

2. Est solitaria pirus silvestris, ejus frondes sunt virides. Imperatoris negotium non est negligendum; meus animus saucius mœret. Herbæ et arbores luxuriant. Uxoris animus mœret; profectis militibus redeundum est.

3. Ascendo illum septentrionalem montem, volens colligere illius (montis) lycium. Imperatoris negotium non est negligendum; anxii sunt mei (mariti) parentes. E *t'ân* ligno currus sunt detriti; quadrijugi mares laboribus

車幝幝、四牡痯
痯、征夫不遠、
(4)匪載匪來、憂
心孔疚、期逝不
至、而多爲恤、卜
筮偕止、會言近
止、征夫邇止、

南陔

白華之什二之二

白華

華黍

魚麗

(1)魚麗于罶、鱨

4. Fèi tsái fèi lâi (lî), iōu sīn k'òung kiòu (kĭ). K'î chéu pŏu tchéu (tchĕu), èul touŏ wêi siŭ. Pŏu chéu kiāi (ki) tchèu, houéi iên kìn (ki) tchèu; tchēng fōu èul tchèu.

IU LI. **1. Iû lì iū liòu, châng chā (souŏ). Kiūn tzèu iòu tsiòu, tchèu, ts'iè touŏ.**

bois de *t'an* sont usés; les chevaux n'ont plus de force. Les soldats de l'expédition doivent n'être plus loin.

4. Ils n'ont pas encore chargé leurs voitures, et ne reviennent pas. Mon cœur est dans une grande angoisse. Le temps où j'espérais les revoir est déjà passé, et ils ne sont pas arrivés; j'en suis très inquiète. Je consulte à la fois la tortue et l'achillée; toutes deux me répondent que mon mari approche. Les soldats de l'expédition sont près d'ici.

CHANT X. NAN KAI.

Nan kai, d'après Tchou Hi, était le titre d'un air de musique qu'on exécutait sur le 笙 **chēng**. Selon d'autres, il existait sous ce titre une exhortation à la piété filiale, qui s'est perdue sous la dynastie des 秦 **Ts'in**.

LIVRE II. PE HOUA.

CHANT I. PE HOUA.

CHANT II. HOUA CHOU.

Pe houa et *Houa chou*, comme *Nan kai*, selon l'opinion de Tchou Hi, étaient les titres de deux airs de musique qu'on exécutait sur le 笙 **chēng**. Selon d'autres, ils désignent des chants dont les paroles se seraient perdues sous les Ts'in. Le premier aurait eu pour objet la piété filiale, et le second, l'harmonie des saisons.

CHANT III. IU LI.

Éloge des liqueurs, des poissons et des autres mets servis à un festin.

1. Les poissons passent dans la nasse; ce sont des *chang*

contriti sunt. Profecti milites non procul absunt.

4. Non oneraruut vehicula, non reversi sunt; meus animus valde angitur. Opinatum tempus jam præteritum est, nec advenerunt; et multum concipio mœrorem. Testudinem consulo, achilleam consulo simul; conjunctim respondent (illos) appropinquare. Profecti milites propinqui sunt.

鯊、君子有酒、旨且多、

(2) 魚麗于罶、魴鱧、君子有酒、多且旨、

(3) 魚麗于罶、鰋鯉、君子有酒、旨且有、

(4) 物其多矣、維其嘉矣、

(5) 物其旨矣、維其偕矣、

(6) 物其有矣、維其時矣、

由庚

2. Iû lì iū liòu, fâng li. Kiūn tzèu iòu tsiòu, touō, ts'iè tchèu.

3. Iû lì iū liòu, ièn li. Kiūn tzèu iòu tsiòu, tchèu, ts'iè iòu (i).

4. Oŭ k'î touō i, wêi k'î kiā (kō) i.

5. Oŭ k'î tchèu i, wêi k'î kiāi (ki) i.

6. Oŭ k'î iòu (i) i, wêi k'î chêu (chèu) i.

(poissons gros et longs dont les ouïes sont jaunes) et des *cha* (petits poissons qui lancent le sable par la gueule). Notre hôte nous sert une liqueur exquise et abondante.

2. Les poissons passent dans la nasse ; ce sont des brêmes et des muges (ou des tanches). Notre hôte nous sert un vin abondant et exquis.

3. Les poissons passent dans la nasse ; ce sont des silures et des carpes. Notre hôte nous sert un vin exquis et abondant.

4. Les mets sont nombreux ; ils sont tous excellents.

5. Les mets sont exquis et de toute espèce.

6. Les mets sont excellents ; ils sont tous de la saison.

CHANT IV. IOU KENG.

Titre d'un air de musique ou d'un chant qui n'existe plus.

CHANT III. 1. Pisces transeunt in nassam, *chăng*, *chā*. Sapiens dominus habet vinum exquisitum et multum.

罶 **Liòu**, sorte de nasse grossière qu'on plaçait à l'ouverture d'un barrage.

鯊 **Chā**, nom du requin, et d'un petit poisson qui lance le sable 沙 **chā**.

2. Pisces transeunt in nassam, brama et mugil (juxta quosdam, tinca). Sapiens dominus habet vinum multum et exquisitum.

3. Pisces transeunt in nassam, pimelodus et cyprinus. Sapiens dominus habet vinum exquisitum et copiosum.

Ièn, poisson qui 偃 **ièn** s'enfonce dans la vase, et s'appelle communément 鮎 **gniên.**

4. Dapes ipsæ multæ, nonnisi ipsæ optimæ.

5. Dapes ipsæ exquisitæ, nonnisi ipsæ completæ.

6. Dapes ipsæ copiosæ, nonnisi ex tempestivæ.

詩經

南有嘉魚

(1) 南有嘉魚、烝然罩罩、君子有酒、嘉賓式燕以樂、

(2) 南有嘉魚、烝然汕汕、君子有酒、嘉賓式燕以衎、

(3) 南有樛木、甘瓠纍之、君子有酒、嘉賓式燕綏之、

NAN IOU KIA IU. **1. Nân iòu kiā iû, tchēng jên tchaó tchaó. Kiūn tzèu iòu tsiòu, kiā pīn chĕu ién i iaó.**

2. Nân iòu kiā iû, tchēng jên chán chán. Kiūn tzèu iòu tsiòu, kiā pīn chĕu ién i k'án.

3. Nân iòu kiòu mŏu, kān hôu lèi tchēu. Kiūn tzèu iòu tsiòu, kiā pīn chĕu ién souēi tchēu.

CHANT V. NAN IOU KIA IU.

L'empereur invite à sa table un grand nombre d'hommes distingués, comme on pêche le barbeau. Les convives s'attachent à lui, comme les courges s'attachent aux branches des arbrisseaux. Ils reviendront volontiers une seconde fois, comme une troupe d'oiseaux.

1. Au midi (dans le Kiang et la Han) on prend beaucoup de barbeaux sous des paniers renversés. Le maître de la maison a du vin; ses excellents convives fêtent et se réjouissent.

2. Au midi on prend beaucoup de barbeaux à l'aide de nasses. Le maître de la maison a du vin; ses excellents convives fêtent et se réjouissent.

3. Au midi il est des arbres aux branches pendantes. Les concombres doux s'y attachent. Le maître de la maison a du vin; ses excellents convives fêtent et sont contents.

CHANT V. 1. In australi regione sunt barbi; magno numero nassis operiuntur. Domus dominus habet vinum; optimi convivæ epulantur et ita oblectantur.

烝 然 **Tchēng jên** peut se traduire par *en grand nombre*, ou être considéré comme une simple particule initiale. 罩 **Tchaó**, sorte de panier sous lequel le poisson se trouve pris.

2. In australi regione sunt barbi; magno numero nassis extrahuntur. Domus dominus habet vinum; optimi convivæ epulantur et lætantur.

3. In australi regione sunt pendulis ramis arbores; dulces cucurbitæ implicantur eis. Domus dominus habet vinum; optimi convivæ epulantur et gaudent.

4. Huc illuc volitantes turtures magno numero veniunt. Domus dominus habet vinum; optimi convivæ epulantur et iterum (epulabuntur).

思 **Sēu**, particule.

(4) 翩翩者鵻、烝然來思、君子有酒、嘉賓式燕又思、

崇丘

南山有臺

(1) 南山有臺、北山有萊、樂只君子、邦家之基、樂只君子、萬壽無期、

(2) 南山有桑、北山有楊、樂只君子、邦家之光、樂只君子、萬壽無疆、

4. P'iēn p'iēn tchė tchouēi, tchēng jên lâi (lî) sēu. Kiūn tzèu iòu tsiòu, kiā pīn chĕu ién iòu (î) sēu.

NAN CHAN IOU T'AI. **1. Nân chān iòu t'âi (t'î), pĕ chān iòu lâi (lî). Lŏ tchèu kiūn tzèu, pāng kiā tchēu kī. Lŏ tchēu kiūn tzèu, wán cheóu ôu k'î!**

2. Nân chān iòu sāng, pĕ chān iòu iâng. Lŏ tchèu kiūn tzèu, pāng kiā tchēu kouāng. Lŏ tchèu kiūn tzèu, wán cheóu ôu kiāng!

4. Les tourterelles volent çà et là et viennent en grand nombre. Le maître de la maison a du vin; ses excellents convives fêtent et reviendront encore.

CHANT VI. TCH'OUNG K'IOU.

Titre d'un chant ou d'un air de musique qui n'existe plus.

CHANT VII. NAN CHAN IOU T'AI.

L'empereur fait l'éloge des princes et des ministres réunis à sa table. Il les compare aux arbres des forêts, et leur souhaite les faveurs du ciel.

1. Sur les montagnes, au midi croît la plante *t'ai*, au nord la plante *lai*. Convives aimables et distingués, vous êtes les soutiens des États. Convives aimables et distingués, puisse votre vie durer dix mille ans et n'avoir pas de fin !

2. Sur les montagnes, au midi croît le mûrier, au nord le peuplier. Convives aimables et distingués, vous êtes la gloire des États. Convives aimables et distingués, puissiez-vous vivre dix mille ans, vivre toujours!

CHANT VII. 1. In australi monte est *t'âi* herba ; in septentrionali monte est *lâi* herba. Amabiles insignes viri, regnorum fundamenta estis. Amabiles viri insignes, (vobis concedantur) decies mille anni, (vita) sine limite!

臺 T'âi, plante à feuilles lancéolées dont l'écorce sert à faire des chapeaux d'été et des manteaux contre la pluie.

萊 Lâi, plante dont les feuilles sont odoriférantes et peuvent être mangées cuites.

2. In australi monte est morus, in septentrionali monte est populus. Amabiles viri insignes, estis regnorum gloria. Amabiles insignes viri, decies mille anni, (vita) sine limite !

詩經

(3) 南山有杞、北山有李、樂只君子、民之父母、樂只君子、德音不已、

(4) 南山有栲、北山有杻、樂只君子、遐不眉壽、樂只君子、德音是茂、

(5) 南山有枸、北山有楰、樂只君子、遐不黃耇、樂只君子、保艾爾後、

由儀

3. Nân chān iòu k'i, pě chān iòu li. Lŏ tchèu kiūn tzèu, mîn tchēu fóu mòu (mèi). Lŏ tchēu kiūn tzèu, tĕ īn pŏu i.

4. Nân chān iòu k'aò (k'eòu), pĕ chān iòu gniòu. Lŏ tchèu kiūn tzèu, hiâ pŏu mèi cheóu (cheòu)? Lŏ tchèu kiūn tzèu, tĕ īn chéu meòu (meòu).

5. Nân chān iòu kiù, pĕ chān iòu iû. Lŏ tchèu kiūn tzèu, hiâ pŏu houâng keòu (kòu)? Lŏ tchèu kiūn tzèu, paò ngái èul hiá (hòu).

3. Sur les montagnes, au midi croît l'ailante, au nord le prunier. Convives aimables et distingués, vous êtes les pères du peuple. Convives aimables et distingués, puisse le souvenir de vos vertus se perpétuer toujours !

4. Sur les montagnes, au midi croît le *k'ao,* au nord le *gniou.* Convives aimables et distingués, pourquoi n'atteindriez-vous pas la vieillesse aux longs sourcils? Convives aimables et distingués, puisse votre vertu être à jamais célèbre !

5. Sur les montagnes, au midi croît le *kiu,* au nord le *iu*. Convives aimables et distingués, pourquoi n'atteindriez-vous pas la vieillesse aux cheveux jaunes? Convives aimables et distingués, puissent les mérites de votre vertu protéger et conserver votre postérité !

CHANT VIII. IOU I.

Titre d'un chant ou d'un air de musique qui n'existe plus.

3. In australi monte est ailantus; in septentrionali monte est prunus. Amabiles viri insignes, populi parentes estis. Amabiles viri insignes, virtutis fama non desinat!

4. In australi monte est *k'aò* (arbor ailanto similis); in septentrionali monte est *gniòu* (arbor cujus e ligno fiunt arcus). Amabiles viri insignes, cur non longis superciliis senecta (donaretur vobis)? Amabiles viri insignes, virtutis fama inde clareat!

5. In australi monte est *kiù* (arbor populo similis, cujus fructus cocti comeduntur); in septentrionali monte est *iû* (arbor catalpæ similis). Amabiles viri insignes, cur non flavis capillis senecta (daretur vobis)? Amabiles viri insignes, (virtus vestra) protegat et alat vestros posteros!

蓼蕭

(1) 蓼彼蕭斯、零露湑兮、既見君子、我心寫兮、燕笑語兮、是以有譽處兮、

(2) 蓼彼蕭斯、零露瀼瀼、既見君子、爲龍爲光、其德不爽、壽考不忘、

(3) 蓼彼蕭斯、零露泥泥、既見君子、孔燕豈弟、宜兄宜弟、令德壽豈、

LOU SIAO. **1. Lŏu pèi siaō sēu, lîng lóu siù hì. Kí kién kiūn tzèu, ngò sīn siè (siù) hì. Ién siaó iù hì, chéu i iòu iú tch'óu hî.**

2. Lŏu pèi siaō sēu, lîng lóu jâng jâng. Kí kién kiūn tzèu, wêi lōung wêi kouāng. K'ì tĕ pŏu chouàng (chouāng), cheóu k'aò pŏu wàng.

3. Lŏu pèi siaō sēu, lîng lóu gnî gnî. Kí kién kiūn tzèu, k'òung ién k'ài tì. Î hiōung î tì, lìng tĕ cheóu k'ài (k'ì).

CHANT IX. LOU SIAO.

L'empereur fait l'éloge des princes réunis à sa table. Il souhaite que, semblables à l'armoise humectée par la rosée, ils reçoivent les faveurs du ciel.

1. Cette armoise est grande; sur ses feuilles brillent les gouttes de rosée. La vue de ces princes sages réjouit mon cœur. Cette fête, ces joyeux entretiens nous attireront des éloges et sont le gage d'un bonheur constant.

2. Cette armoise est grande; elle est couverte d'une rosée abondante. La présence de ces princes sages est pour moi une faveur et un honneur. Leur vertu sans tache leur assure une vie longue et une gloire immortelle.

3. Cette armoise est grande; elle est humectée par la rosée. Je vois ces princes sages fêter ensemble avec allégresse et cordialité. Ils traiteront bien tous leurs frères, et leur vertu insigne leur méritera une vie longue et prospère.

CHANT IX. 1. Alta illa artemisia; cadentis roris guttis nitet. Quum videam sapientes regulos, animus meus omni cura liber est. Epulamur, ridemus, colloquimur; quapropter erit laus et constans gaudium.

斯 **Sēu**, particule.

2. Alta illa artemisia, cadit ros copiosus. Quod videam sapientes regulos, duco beneficio, duco honori. Eorum virtute a recto non aberrante, erunt longævi nec obliterabuntur.

3. Alta illa artemisia cadente rore perfusa est. Video sapientes regulos, valde convivantur amabiles. Bene agent cum fratribus majoribus, bene agent cum fratribus minoribus; ex præclara virtute longævitas et gaudium.

(4) 蓼彼蕭斯、零
露濃濃、既見君
子、鞗革沖沖、和
鸞雝雝、萬福攸
同、

湛露

(1) 湛湛露斯、匪
陽不晞、厭厭夜
飲、不醉無歸、

(2) 湛湛露斯、在
彼豐草、厭厭夜
飲、在宗載考、

(3) 湛湛露斯、在

4. Lŏu pèi siaŏ sēu, lîng lóu nôung nôung. Kí kién kiūn tzèu, t'iaô kŏ tch'ôung tch'ôung. Houô louân iōung iōung, wán fŏu iôu t'ôung.

TCHAN LOU. **1. Tchân tchân lóu sēu, fèi iâng pŏu hī. Iēn iēn ié in, pŏu tsouéi ôu kouēi.**

2. Tchân tchân lóu sēu, tsái pèi fōung ts'aò. Iēn iēn ié in, tsái tsōung tsái k'aò.

3. Tchân tchân lóu sēu, tsái pèi k'i kī. Hièn iùn kiūn tzèu, mouô pŏu lìng tĕ.

4. Cette armoise est grande ; elle reçoit la rosée en abondance. J'ai vu ces sages princes. Les extrémités des rênes pendaient mollement de leurs mains, et les sonnettes retentissaient d'accord à l'appui de leurs voitures et aux freins de leurs chevaux. J'en augure pour eux l'affluence de tous les biens.

CHANT X. TCHAN LOU.

L'empereur offre un festin aux princes feudataires. Cette faveur impériale est comparée à une rosée abondante, et la tenue respectueuse des princes à la forme élégante des plus beaux arbres.

1. La rosée est abondante ; seule la chaleur du soleil peut la dissiper. Nous buvons à loisir et longtemps jusque pendant la nuit ; personne ne se retirera qu'après avoir bu son soûl.

2. La rosée est abondante sur ces plantes vigoureuses. Nous buvons à loisir et longtemps jusque dans la nuit ; la fête se termine dans les appartements particuliers de l'empereur.

3. La rosée est abondante sur ces saules et sur ces jujubiers. Au commencement du repas, l'empereur disait aux convives : 無不醉 Que chacun boive son soûl. Les invités répondaient : 諾敢不醉 Oui, oserions-nous ne pas boire notre soûl ?

4. Alta illa artemisia ; cadit ros copiosus. Vidi sapientes regulos, habenarum extrema lora pendentia, curruum fulcri et frenorum tintinnabula suave consonantia ; (ex hac consonantia si recte augurer) omnia bona inde convenient.

CHANT X. 1. Valde copiosus est ros ; nisi solis calore, non siccabitur. Commode diuque nocte bibitur ; nisi vino satiatus, nemo domum recedet.

2. Valde copiosus est ros super illam vegetam herbam. Commode diuque nocte bibitur ; in præcipua æde (ab ipso imperatore habitata) perficitur (convivium).

彼杞棘、顯允君子、莫不令德、④其桐其椅、其實離離、豈弟君子、莫不令儀、

彤弓之什二之三

彤弓

①彤弓弨兮、受言藏之、我有嘉賓、中心貺之、鐘鼓既設、一朝饗之、

②彤弓弨兮、受言載之、我有嘉賓、中

4. K'î t'ôung k'î ì, k'î chĕu lî lî. K'ài tí kiūn tzèu, mouŏ pŏu ling î.

T'OUNG KOUNG. **1. T'ôung kōung tch'aō hì, cheòu iên ts'âng tchēu. Ngò iòu kiā pīn, tchōung sīn houáng (houáng) tchēu. Tchōung kòu kì chĕ, ĭ tchaō hiàng (hiàng) tchēu.**

2. T'ôung kōung tch'aō hì, cheòu iên tsái (tsí) tchēu. Ngò iòu kiā pīn,

Ces princes sages sont distingués et sincères; ils sont tous d'une vertu remarquable.

4. Cet éléococca et ce catalpa sont chargés de fruits. Ces princes sages sont d'un commerce agréable et facile; (même au milieu d'un festin) leur tenue est parfaite.

LIVRE III. T'OUNG KOUNG.

CHANT I. T'OUNG KOUNG.

L'empereur, pour récompenser un prince feudataire, lui offre un festin et lui fait présent d'un arc rouge.

1. L'arc rouge est débandé; reçu des mains de l'ouvrier, il a été mis en réserve. J'ai un hôte distingué; je le lui donne de bon cœur. Les cloches et les tambours sont préparés; dès le matin je lui offre un banquet.

2. L'arc rouge est débandé; reçu des mains de l'ouvrier, il a été muni d'une armature de bambou (qui l'empêche de se déformer). J'ai un hôte distingué; mon cœur trouve en lui sa joie. Les

3. Valde copiosus est ros super illas salices et zizyphos. Insignes et sinceri sapientes reguli; nullius non est præclara virtus.

4. Illa elæococca, illa catalpa; illarum fructus pendent. Amabiles et faciles sapientes reguli; nullius non est insignis gravitas.

TITRE DU LIVRE. 彤弓之什二之三 T'oung koung decas: (Cheu king partis) secundæ (decas) tertia.

CHANT I. 1. Ruber arcus laxatus est; acceptum recondidi eum. Ego habeo insignem convivam; ex animo dono ei. Campanæ et tympana disposita sunt; primo mane convivium offero ei.

言 Iên, particule.

2. Ruber arcus laxatus est; acceptum armatura munivi eum. Ego habeo insignem convivam; intimo animo

心喜之、鐘鼓既設、一朝右之、

(3)彤弓弨兮、受言櫜之、我有嘉賓、中心好之、鐘鼓既設、一朝醻之、

菁菁者莪

(1)菁菁者莪、在彼中阿、既見君子、樂且有儀、

(2)菁菁者莪、在彼中沚、既見君子、我心則喜、

tchŏung sīn hi (hí) tchēu. Tchŏung kòu ki chĕ, ĭ tchaŏ ióu (i) tchēu.

3. T'ôung kŏung tch'aŏ hī, cheóu iên kaŏ (kaó) tchēu. Ngò ióu kiā pīn, tchŏung sīn haó tchēu. Tchŏung kòu ki chĕ, ĭ tchaŏ tch'eŏu (taó) tchēu.

TSING TSING TCHE NGO. **1. Tsīng tsīng tchè ngô tsái pèi tchŏung ngō. Kí kién kiūn tzèu, lŏ ts'iè ióu i (ngô).**

2. Tsīng tsīng tchè ngô tsái pèi tchŏung tchèu. Kí kién kiūn tzèu, ngò sīn tsĕ hi.

cloches et les tambours sont préparés; dès le matin je le fais asseoir à ma droite (à la place d'honneur).

3. L'arc rouge est débandé ; reçu des mains de l'ouvrier, il a été mis dans un étui. J'ai un hôte distingué que j'aime du fond du cœur. Les cloches et les tambours sont préparés ; dès le matin je lui offre le vin pour la seconde fois.

CHANT II. TSING TSING TCHE NGO.

L'armoise prospère dans les terrains qui lui conviennent. De même, le cœur se réjouit à la vue d'un sage.

1. L'armoise croît admirablement sur cette colline. En voyant ce sage, je suis content, et remplis les devoirs de l'hospitalité envers lui.

2. L'armoise est fort belle sur cet ilot. A la vue de ce sage, mon cœur se réjouit.

gaudeo eo. Campanæ et tympana disposita sunt; primo mane ad dexteram meam pono eum.

La droite était alors la place d'honneur.

3. Ruber arcus laxatus est; acceptum in theca condidi eum. Ego habeo insignem convivam; intimo animo amo eum. Campanæ et tympana disposita sunt; primo mane vinum iterum propino ei.

CHANT II. 1. Luxurians artemisia est in illo medio colle. Quum videam sapientem virum, lætor et fungor officiis (convivatoris).

2. Luxurians artemisia est in illa media insula. Quum videam sapientem virum, meus animus tunc gaudet.

(3) 菁菁者莪、在彼中陵、既見君子、錫我百朋。
(4) 汎汎楊舟、載沉載浮、既見君子、我心則休。

六月

(1) 六月棲棲、戎車既飭、四牡騤騤、載是常服、玁狁孔

3. Tsīng tsīng tchě ngô tsái pèi tchōung līng. Ki kién kiūn tzèu, sì ngò pě p'êng.

4. Fán fán iâng tcheōu, tsái tch'ênn tsái feôu. Ki kién kiūn tzèu, ngò sīn tsĕ hiōu.

LOU IUE. **1. Lŏu iuě sī sī, jôung kiū ki tch'ĕu, séu meòu k'ouêi k'ouêi, tsái**

3. L'armoise est fort belle sur cette hauteur. A la vue de ce sage, je me réjouis comme si je recevais cinq cents (ou deux cents) coquillages précieux.

4. La barque de peuplier, ballotée par les flots, tantôt descend tantôt s'élève. (Ainsi mon cœur était agité). La vue de ce sage donne le repos à mon âme.

CHANT III. LOU IUE.

Expédition contre les Hien iun, barbares du nord.

1. Au sixième mois de l'année, il y eut grand empressement. On prépara les chars de guerre avec leurs quatre chevaux robustes. On y mit les vêtements ordinaires (le bonnet et la tunique de peau que les soldats prennent au moment du combat). Les Hien iun

3. Luxurians artemisia est in illo medio colliculo. Quum videam sapientem virum, donat me centies quinque (vel centies duobus) conchyliis.

Jusqu'au deuxième siècle avant notre ère, certains coquillages servaient de monnaie.

4. Fluctuans et agitata populea cymba modo descendit modo assurgit. Quum videam sapientem virum, meus animus tunc quiescit.

CHANT III. 1. Sexto mense valde trepidatum est. Bellici currus parati sunt; quatuor mares equi erant robusti. Impositæ sunt illis (curribus) consuetæ vestes. Hien iun vehementer ardebant; nos idcirco properavimus. Imperator tunc emisit in bellum milites, ut tranquillaretur imperatoris regnum.

Après la mort des empereurs 成王 **Tch'êng wâng** et 康王 **K'āng wâng** (1078), la dynastie des Tcheou tomba en décadence. 厲王 **Li wâng,** le septième des successeurs de K'ang wang, fut si cruel que ses sujets le chassèrent (878). Il se retira à 彘 **Tchéu,** aujourd'hui 汾西 **Fênn sī** dans le P'ing iang fou, province de Chan si. Les Hien iun profitèrent de ces troubles pour faire invasion, et s'avancèrent jusque près de la capitale de l'empire. **Li** wang étant mort, son fils 靖 **Tsing** fut reconnu empereur, et prit le nom de 宣王 **Siuēn wâng** (827). Le nouvel empereur mit 尹吉甫 **In Kĭ fòu** à la tête de ses troupes, et le chargea de repous-

熾、我是用急、王于出征、以匡王國。(2)比物四驪、閑之維則。維此六月、既成我服。我服既成、于三十里。王于出征、以佐天子。(3)四牡脩廣、其大有顒。薄伐玁狁、以奏膚公。有嚴有翼、共武之服。共武之服、以定王國。

chéu chāng fŏu (p'ĕ). Hiên iùn k'òung tch'éu, ngò chéu iòung kĭ. Wâng iû tch'ŏu tchēng, i k'ouāng wâng kouŏ (ĭ).

2. Pí ŏu séu lî, hiên tchēu wêi tsĕ. Wêi ts'éu lŏu iuĕ, kí tch'êng ngò fŏu (p'ĕ). Ngò fŏu kí tch'êng, iû sān chĕu lì. Wâng iû tch'ŏu tchēng, i tsouò t'iēn tzèu (tsì).

3. Séu meòu siōu kouàng, k'í tá iòu iôung. Pouŏ fă Hiên iùn, i tseóu fōu kōung. Iòu iên iòu ĭ, kōung òu tchēu fŏu (p'ĕ). Kōung òu tchēu fŏu (p'ĕ), i tíng wâng kouŏ (ĭ).

faisaient une invasion furieuse; nous devions nous hâter. L'empereur avait ordonné l'expédition pour maintenir l'ordre et la paix dans l'empire.

2. Les quatre chevaux noirs de chaque attelage étaient de même force, bien exercés et habitués à suivre toutes les règles. Dès ce sixième mois, nos vêtements militaires furent achevés. Nos vêtements achevés, nous fîmes trente stades par jour. L'empereur avait ordonné cette expédition pour maintenir l'autorité du Fils du ciel.

3. Les quatre chevaux de chaque voiture étaient grands, corpulents; ils avaient la tête grosse. Nous avons battu les Hien iun et bien mérité de notre pays. Notre chef a dirigé l'expédition avec une sévère exactitude. Il a dirigé l'expédition et affermi l'empire.

ser les barbares. D'après les 司馬法 **Sēu mà fă** Règlements du Ministère de la guerre, aucune expédition ne devait être entreprise en été ni en hiver. On dérogea aux usages en cette circonstance, à cause de la nécessité.

2. Æquo robore erant quatuor equi nigri, exercitati (ita ut) omnino obsequerentur legibus. Statim illo sexto mense, jam perfectæ sunt nostræ vestes (militares). Nostris vestibus jam perfectis, tunc triginta stadia (quotidie percurrimus). Imperator emisit in bellum milites, ut opem ferrent cœli filio.

Pour les cérémonies et les visites, les quatre chevaux d'un attelage devaient être de même couleur. Pour la guerre, on les choisissait d'égale force. L'étape ordinaire était de trente stades.

3. Quatuor mares erant alti, corpulenti; ipsi magnum habebant caput. Paulum debellavimus Hien iun, inde nuntiavimus magna merita. (Dux militum) habens severitatem, habens diligentiam, curavit militarem rem. Curavit militarem rem, ita firmavit imperium.

（4）玁狁匪茹、整居焦穫、侵鎬及方、至于涇陽、織文鳥章、白旆央央、元戎十乘、以先啓行、
（5）戎車既安、如輊如軒、四牡既佶、既佶且閑、薄伐玁狁、至于太原、文武吉甫、萬邦爲憲、
（6）吉甫燕喜、既

4. Hièn iùn fèi jóu, tchèng kiū Tsiaō Hóu. Ts'īn Haò kǐ Fāng, tchéu iū Kīng iàng. Tchĕu wénn gniaò tchāng, pĕ péi iāng iāng. Iuên jôung chĕu chéng, i siēn k'i hìng (hâng).

5. Jôung kiū kí ngān (iēn), jôu tchéu jôu hiēn. Séu meòu kí kǐ, kí kǐ ts'iĕ hiên. Pouŏ fă Hièn iùn, tchéu iū T'ái iuên. Wênn óu Kǐ fòu, wán pāng wéi hién (hièn).

6. Kǐ fòu ién hì, kí touŏ cheóu tch'éu. Lâi kouēi tzéu Haò, ngò hìng iòung

4. Les Hien iun, sans mesurer leurs forces, avaient occupé Tsiao et Hou, envahi Hao et Fang, et pénétré jusqu'au nord de la King. Nos étendards aux figures de faucons étaient déployés; les bordures de nos bannières aux figures de tortues et de serpents brillaient comme neuves. Dix grands chars de guerre ouvraient la marche.

5. Nos chars de guerre étaient bien équilibrés, également hauts par devant et par derrière. Leurs quatre chevaux étaient robustes ; ils étaient robustes et bien exercés. Ki fou excelle dans l'administration civile et dans le commandement militaire ; il est le modèle de tout l'empire.

6. Ki fou fête et se réjouit ; il est très heureux. Nous sommes

4. Hien iun non metientes (suas vires), integras occupaverant Tsiao et Hou regiones, invaserant Hao et Fang, pervenerant ad King fluvii septentrionem. Vexilla ornata avium figuris, alba signorum pictis testudinibus et anguibus ornatorum extrema quasi recentia nitebant. Majores bellici currus decem numero adhibiti antecedebant in primo agmine. — On ignore où se trouvait 焦 **Tsiaō**. 穫 **Hóu** était dans le 三原縣 **Sān iuên hièn** actuel, qui dépend de Si ngan fou dans le Chen si. 鎬 **Haò** n'était pas la capitale de ce nom, mais un pays fort éloigné, situé au nord, ainsi que 方 **Fāng**.

5. Bellici currus erant librati ; qualis erat tegminis pars anterior, talis erat pars posterior. Quatuor mares erant robusti ; erant robusti et exercitati. Paulum debellavimus Hien iun (et persecuti sumus) usque ad T'ai iuen. Quum civilis tum militaris præfecti dotibus pollet Ki fou ; omnibus regnis est exemplar.

T'ai iuen était dans le T'ai iuen hien actuel, province de Chan si.

6. Ki fou convivans lætatur ; jam multa fruitur felicitate. Venientes redivimus domos ex Hao ; nos iter fecimus

多受祉。來歸自鎬。我行永久。飲御諸友。炰鼈膾鯉。侯誰在矣。張仲孝友。

采芑

(1) 薄言采芑。于彼新田。于此菑畝。方叔涖止。其車三千。師干之試。方叔率止。乘

kiòu (ki). Ìn iú tchōu iòu (i), paō piē kouài li. Heóu wéi tsái i, Tchāng Tchóung hiaó iòu (i).

TS'AI K'I. **1. Pouŏ iên ts'ài k'i, iū pèi sīn t'iên, iū ts'èu tchĕu meòu (mèi). Fāng chŏu li tchéu. K'î kiū sān ts'iēn, chēu kān tchēu chéu (chéu). Fāng chŏu**

revenus de Hao ; notre voyage a duré longtemps. Ki fou offre à tous ses amis du vin, des tortues grillées, des carpes hachées. Et quel est le principal invité? C'est Tchang Tchoung, le modèle des fils et des frères (l'ami de Ki fou).

CHANT IV. TS'AI K'I.

Récit d'une expédition dirigée par Fang chou contre les barbares du midi, en l'année 825, sous 宣王 **Siuēn wâng.**

1. Nous avons cueilli le laiteron (pour nous et pour nos chevaux) dans les champs qui avaient été défrichés soit l'année précédente soit l'année même de l'expédition. Fang chou prit le commandement de l'armée. Il avait sous ses ordres trois mille chars de guerre, avec des soldats bien exercés. Il dirigeait la marche, porté sur un char attelé de quatre chevaux de couleur gris-noir. Ses quatre chevaux gris-noir étaient dociles et marchaient d'accord.

longo tempore. Vinum propinans offert omnibus amicis ; sunt tostæ testudines et minutatim concisi cyprini. At quis adest? Tchang Tchoung in parentes pius et in fratres amans.

CHANT IV. 1. Paululum decerpsimus sonchum, in illis anno superiore primum cultis agris, in his hoc ipso anno primum cultis agris. Fang chou obivit ducis munia. Ejus currus ter mille ; milites defensores exercitati. Fang chou duxit, vectus suis quatuor cineracei coloris equis. Quatuor cineracei coloris equi obsequentes et ordine moventes se ; militaris currus erat rubro colore. E texta in quadrorum modum storea erat currus tegmen ; e phocæ pelle erat pharetra. Fibulis consertæ erant pectorales equorum fasciæ ; e manibus pendebant habenarum extrema.

薄言 **Pouŏ iên,** 止 **Tchèu,** particules. 新田 **Sīn t'iên,** terrain qui a été défriché l'année précédente. 菑畝 **Tchēu meòu,** terrain qui a été défriché dans l'année courante. 干 **Kān,** bouclier, protéger, défendre, défenseur. 膺 **Ing,** poitrine, poitrail, parties du harnais et ornements qui sont sur le poitrail d'un cheval. Le laiteron servait à la nourriture des hommes et des chevaux.

其四騏、四騏翼翼、路車有奭、簟茀魚服、鉤膺鞗革。②薄言采芑、于彼新田、于此中鄉、方叔涖止、其車三千、旂旐央央、方叔率止、約軝錯衡、八鸞瑲瑲、服其命服、朱芾斯皇、

chouĕ tchéu, chêng k'î séu k'î. Séu k'î ĭ ĭ, lóu kiū iòu hĭ. Tiên fŏu iû fŏu (p'ĕ), keōu īng t'iaò kŏ (kĭ).

2. Pouŏ iên ts'ài k'i, iū pèi sīn t'iên, iū ts'èu tchōung hiāng. Fāng chŏu lí tchéu. K'i kiū sān ts'iēn, k'i tchaò iāng iāng. Fāng chŏu chouĕ tchéu, iŏ k'i ts'ouŏ hêng (hàng). Pă louân ts'iāng ts'iāng, fŏu k'i míng fŏu. Tchōu fŏu sēu

Son char de guerre était peint en rouge, et couvert d'une natte à carreaux. Son carquois était de peau de veau marin. Des rubans fixés par des boucles aux cous de ses chevaux descendaient sur leurs poitrails. De ses mains pendaient les extrémités des rênes.

2. Nous avons cueilli le laiteron dans les champs qui avaient été défrichés l'année précédente, et auprès des bourgs et des villages. Fang chou prit le commandement de l'armée. Il avait sous ses ordres trois mille chars de guerre. On voyait briller nos étendards ornés, les uns de dragons, les autres de tortues et de serpents. Les moyeux des roues étaient entourés de lanières rouges, et le joug paré de divers ornements. Les huit sonnettes retentissaient aux extrémités des mors des chevaux. Fang chou portait son costume

Un char de guerre exigeait cent hommes. Il portait un archer, un lancier et un conducteur, tous trois munis de cuirasses. Le conducteur se tenait au milieu, l'archer à gauche et le lancier à droite. Vingt-quatre fantassins marchaient en avant, et vingt-quatre de chaque côté. De plus, vingt-cinq hommes étaient chargés de conduire les bagages, de préparer la nourriture, de soigner les chevaux,...

Trois mille chars de guerre supposent trois cent mille hommes. L'armée impériale avait au plus 六師 **liŭ chēu** ou 六軍 **liŭ kiūn** six légions, chacune de douze mille cinq cents hommes, en tout, soixante quinze mille soldats. Plusieurs commentateurs pensent que le poète a exagéré le nombre des chars de guerre. D'autres, pour soutenir la vérité de son récit, disent que les troupes de l'empereur n'étaient pas seules, que les princes feudataires avaient fourni chacun leur contingent.

2. Paulum carpsimus sonchum, in illis anno superiore primum cultis agris, in his mediis circa pagos agris. Fang chou obivit ducis munia. Ejus currus ter mille. Ornata draconibus pictis signa et ornata testudinibus anguibusque pictis signa splendebant. (Rubris loris) circumligati erant rotarum modioli; varie ornatum jugum. Octo frenorum tintinnabula tinniebant. Indutus erat imperatis (i.e. ab imperatore donatis) vestibus. Rubra genualia tunc

詩經

有瑲葱珩。(3) 鴥彼飛隼、其飛戾天、亦集爰止。方叔涖止、其車三千、師干之試。方叔率止、鉦人伐鼓、陳師鞠旅。顯允方叔、伐鼓淵淵、振旅闐闐。(4) 蠢爾蠻荊、大邦爲讎。方

houâng, iòu ts'iāng ts'ōung hêng (hâng).

3. Iŭ pèi fēi siùn, k'î fēi li t'iēn ; ĭ tsĭ iuên tchéu. Fāng chŏu lí tchéu. K'î kiū sān ts'iēn, chēu kān tchēu chéu (chèu). Fāng chŏu chouĕ tchéu, tchēng jênn, fă kòu. Tch'énn chēu kiŭ liù ; hièn iùn Fāng chŏu. Fă kòu iuēn iuēn (īn īn), tchénn liù t'iên t'iên (t'în t'în).

4. Tch'ouènn èul Mân Kīng, tá pāng wêi tch'eôu. Fāng chŏu iuên laò, k'ŏ

officiel. Ses genouillères rouges brillaient. Une agrafe de jade couleur d'oignon retentissait à sa ceinture.

3. L'épervier vole rapidement et s'élève jusqu'au ciel; puis il descend et se repose au lieu qui lui convient. Fang chou (semblable à l'épervier) prit le commandement de l'armée; il avait trois mille chars de guerre, avec des soldats bien exercés. Fang chou dirigea la marche, avec des cymbales et des tambours. Il rangea ses troupes en ordre de bataille et harangua ses cohortes. Fang chou (donnait ses ordres) avec clarté, (punissait et récompensait) avec justice. Le tambour battait avec lenteur (pour l'attaque), et avec force pour la retraite.

4. Barbares méridionaux de King, vous avez été insensés; vous

splendebant. Erat tinniens cæpæ colore lapillus *hèng* ad zonam appensus.

Les moyeux des roues étaient fort longs et peints en rouge. L'extrémité était entourée d'une lanière de cuir. 錯 **Ts'ouŏ** signifie 雜 **tsă** variés, divers. Une sonnette était fixée à chaque extrémité du frein des chevaux. Les quatre chevaux attelés de front à un char de guerre avaient ensemble huit sonnettes. Cf. page 136.

珩 **Hêng**, agrafe de jade à laquelle étaient fixées les pierreries ou les pièces de jade qu'on portait suspendues à la ceinture. Voy. page 75. Les officiers du troisième rang 三命 **sān ming** et au-dessous portaient des genouillères de couleur rouge pâle, et une agrafe de couleur verte. Les genouillères de l'empereur étaient de couleur rouge foncé.

3. Celer ille volans accipiter; ille volans attingit cœlum. Etiam insidet in sistendi loco. Fang chou obivit ducis munia; ejus currus ter mille; milites defensores bene exercitati. Fang chou duxit; erant pulsantes cymbala homines et pulsantes tympana. Ordinavit legiones, commonuit cohortes. Perspicue (jubebat) et juste (retribuebat) Fang chou. Pulsabatur tympanum placido sonitu; revocabantur cohortes firmo sonitu.

4. Stolidi fuistis, vos australes barbari King provinciæ; magno imperio

叔元老。克壯其猶。方叔率止。執訊獲醜。戎車嘽嘽。嘽嘽焞焞。如霆如雷。顯允方叔。征伐玁狁。蠻荊來威。

車攻

(1) 我車既攻。我馬既

tchouáng k'ì iôu. Fāng chōu chouĕ tchèu, tchĕu sin houĕ tch'eòu (tch'eŏu). Jôung kiū t'ān t'ān, t'ān t'ān t'ouēi t'ouēi, jôu t'îng jôu lêi. Hièn iùn Fāng chōu. Tchēng fă Hièn iùn, Mân Kīng lâi wēi.

KIU KOUNG. **1. Ngò kiū ki kōung, ngò mà ki t'ôung ; séu meòu lōung lōung, kiá iên ts'ôu tōung.**

vous êtes attaqués à un puissant empire. Fang chou était d'un âge très avancé; mais ses conseils annonçaient encore une grande vigueur. Fang chou dirigea la marche, saisit les chefs qui devaient être soumis à un jugement, et fit une multitude de captifs. Nos chars de guerre étaient nombreux. Ils étaient nombreux, et terribles comme le tonnerre et la foudre. Les ordres de Fang chou étaient clairs, ses récompenses et ses châtiments étaient justes. Il a terrassé les Hien iun (barbares du nord), et les barbares méridionaux de King, frappés d'épouvante, sont venus faire leur soumission.

CHANT V. KIU KOUNG.

L'empereur 宣王 **Siuēn wâng** va de 鎬 **Haò** à 洛陽 **Lŏ iâng**, dans le Ho nan actuel. Il y convoque les princes feudataires, reçoit leurs hommages et les conduit à la chasse. Le poète décrit dans les trois premières strophes les préparatifs qui furent faits à 鎬 **Haò** avant le départ; dans la quatrième, l'arrivée des princes feudataires à Lo iang; dans les quatre dernières, la chasse et le retour à Lo iang.

1. Nos chars étaient solides et les quatre chevaux bien assortis (également rapides). Les quatre chevaux étaient corpulents.

fecistis hostilia. Fang chou erat valde senex, (at) pollebant robore ejus consilia. Fang chou duxit exercitum; tenuit judicandos (hostium duces), cepit turbam. Bellici currus erant plurimi. Erant plurimi, maximo numero; (terribiles) sicut tonitru, sicut fulmen. Perspicuus, justus Fang chou. Debellans profligavit Hien iun; australes barbari King provinciæ venerunt timore perculsi.

荊 **Kīng**, l'une des neuf provinces 九州 **kiòu tcheōu** établies par le grand 禹 **Iù**; elle est comprise dans le Hou kouang actuel.

CHANT V. 1. Nostri currus erant firmi, nostri equi erant pares (celeritate). Quatuor mares erant corpulenti. (Imperator dixit): «Jungite currus; eamus ad orientem.»

Les quatre chevaux attelés de front à une voiture, pour les cérémonies, devaient être de même couleur; pour la guerre, ils devaient être d'égale force; pour la chasse, on les choisissait

同。四牡龐龐。駕言徂東。

(2) 田車既好。四牡孔阜。東有甫草。駕言行狩。

(3) 之子于苗。選徒囂囂。建旐設旄。搏獸于敖。

(4) 駕彼四

2. T'iên kiū ki haò (heòu), séu meòu k'òung feòu. Tōung iòu Fòu ts'aò (ts'eòu), kiá iên hing cheòu (cheòu).

3. Tchēu tzéu iù miaô (maô), siuén t'ôu ngaô ngaô. Kién tchaò chĕ maô, pouŏ cheòu iù Ngaô.

4. Kiá péi séu meòu, séu meòu ĭ ĭ. Tch'ĕu fōu kīn sī, houéi t'ôung iòu ĭ.

(L'empereur dit) : « Attelez les voitures ; allons à l'est (à Lo iang). »

2. Les voitures de chasse étaient excellentes et leurs quatre chevaux très corpulents. A l'est sont les prairies de Fou. (L'empereur dit) : « Attelez les voitures, et allons chasser. »

3. Les officiers choisirent les hommes pour la chasse ; (seuls) ils faisaient entendre leurs voix. Ils dressèrent (sur les voitures) les étendards, les uns ornés de tortues et de serpents, les autres ornés de dragons et surmontés de touffes de crin de bœuf, afin de chasser au pied du mont Ngao.

4. Les princes feudataires, sur leurs voitures attelées de quatre

également rapides à la course.

La capitale de l'empire était 鎬 **Haò** dans le 陝西 **Chèn sī**. Tcheou koung avait fait bâtir une seconde résidence impériale à Lo iang, à l'ouest de la ville actuelle de Ho nan fou dans le Ho nan. V. page 3. Les premiers empereurs de la dynastie des Tcheou s'y transportaient à certaines époques et y réunissaient les princes feudataires de cette partie de l'empire. Leurs successeurs, peu soucieux de bien gouverner, se dispensérent de ce voyage. Siuen wang (827-781) réforma l'administration, repoussa les invasions des barbares et rétablit les anciens usages. Il tint des assemblées de princes à Lo iang.

2. Venatici currus erant eximii, quatuor mares valde corpulenti. In oriente sunt Fou prata. (Imperator dixit) : « Jungite currus ; eamus venatum. »

言 **Iên**, particule. 甫草 **Fòu ts'aò** ou 圃田 **Pòu t'iên** est dans le 中牟縣 **Tchōung meôu hién** actuel, qui dépend de 開封府 **K'āi fōung fòu.** Il faisait partie du domaine propre de l'empereur.

狩 **Cheòu**, chasse pendant l'hiver. 苗 **Miaô**, chasse pendant l'été. Ici ces deux lettres signifient chasse en général.

3. Illi præpositi ad venationem selegerunt ministros constrepentibus vocibus. Erexerunt ornata pictis testudinibus anguibusque signa, explicuerunt bovinas caudas (in vertice signorum pictis draconibus ornatorum), ut caperemus feras ad Ngao (montis radices).

Le mont Ngao est sur la limite du 滎陽縣 **Hiôung iâng hién** actuel (Ho nan).

牡。四牡奕奕。赤芾金舄、會同有繹。

(5) 決拾既佽。弓矢既調。射夫既同。助我舉柴。

(6) 四黃既駕。兩驂不猗。不失其馳。舍矢如破。

(7) 蕭蕭馬鳴。悠悠旆旌。徒

5. Kiuĕ chĕu ki ts'éu, kōung chèu ki t'iaŏ (t'ôung). Ché fōu ki t'ôung, tchóu ngò kiù tzéu.

6. Séu houâng ki kiá, leàng ts'ân pŏu i (ngò). Pŏu chĕu k'i tch'êu (t'ouò), ché chèu jŏu p'ouò.

7. Siaŏ siaŏ mà ming, iôu iôu pèi tsīng. T'ôu iù pŏu kīng, tá p'aŏ pŏu ing.

chevaux, arrivèrent à la suite les uns des autres. Avec leurs genouillères de couleur rouge pâle et leurs chaussures dorées, ils se réunirent et se rangèrent par ordre de dignité (dans le palais de Lo iang).

5. Le doigtier et le brassard allaient bien ensemble; les flèches étaient appropriées à l'arc. Les archers (des princes), unissant leurs efforts, nous aidèrent à enlever le gibier amassé.

6. Des quatre chevaux jaunes attelés de front à chaque voiture, les deux qui étaient aux extrémités n'inclinaient (ni du côté du timon ni du côté opposé). Le conducteur observait parfaitement les règles de son art. L'archer lançait les flèches avec une force capable de transpercer (le gibier).

7. (Après la chasse), les chevaux au repos hennirent, et les étendards se balancèrent mollement au vent. Les piétons et les

4. (Reguli) vecti sunt illis quatuor maribus; quatuor mares invicem succedentes (advenerunt). Rosei coloris genualibus et auratis calceis convenientes congregati sunt, servato dignitatis ordine.

Les princes portaient des genouillères rouge foncé, quand ils donnaient audience à leurs subordonnés, et des genouillères rouge pâle, quand ils paraissaient devant l'empereur. Les chaussures de cérémonie 舄 **sĭ** étaient des souliers de couleur rouge, dont les semelles étaient très épaisses et les ornements étaient d'or.

5. Digitale et brachiale invicem conveniebant; arcus et sagittae invicem congruebant. Sagittarii homines (regulorum) jam conjuncti adjuverunt nos ad tollendum acervum (occisarum ferarum).

決 **Kiuĕ**, doigtier d'ivoire qui se mettait au pouce de la main droite, et aidait à tirer la corde de l'arc. 拾 **Chĕu**, armure de cuir que l'archer avait au bras gauche, et contre laquelle il appuyait son arc.

6. Quatuor flavi equi postquam erant juncti, duo extimi non declinabant. Ductor non aberrabat a suis

詩經

御不驚。大
庖不盈。
⑧ 之子于
征。有聞無
聲。允矣君
子。展也大
成。

吉日

① 吉日維
戊。既伯既
禱。田車既
好。四牡孔
阜。升彼大

8. Tchēu tsèu iù tchēng, iòu wénn ôu chēng. Iùn i kiūn tzòu, tchèn iè tá tch'êng.

KI JEU. **1. Kí jĕu wêi meòu (meòu), kí pĕ kí taò (teòu). T'iên kiū kí haò (heòu), séu meòu k'òung feòu. Chēng pèi tá feòu, ts'ôung k'ì k'iùn tch'eòu.**

conducteurs s'abstinrent de crier. La cuisine impériale ne fut pas remplie, (parce que l'empereur fit distribuer le gibier aux chasseurs, et en garda peu pour lui).

8. Les officiers impériaux dans leurs courses firent entendre le bruit de leur marche, mais aucun cri. Vraiment l'empereur est un prince sage, et il accomplit de grandes choses.

CHANT VI. KI JEU.

Description d'une chasse dirigée par l'empereur 宣王 **Siuēn wâng** dans le domaine impérial, près de 鎬 **Haò** dans le Chen si actuel.

1. Le cinquième jour du cycle est un jour heureux; nous avons fait des offrandes et des prières au génie protecteur des chevaux. Les voitures de chasse étaient en bon état, et leurs quatre chevaux

aurigæ legibus; emittebantur sagittæ quasi perfossuræ.

7. (Perfecta venatione), quiescentes equi hinnitum ediderunt; lente agitata signa ac vexilla. Pedites ductoresque non vociferati sunt. Magna (imperatoris) culina non fuit plena.

8. Illi præpositi dum excurrerunt, fuit strepitus, nullus clamor. Vere (imperator) est sapiens princeps; vere magna perficit.

CHANT VI. 1. Faustus dies est cycli quintus; sacra fecimus Domitori equorum, preces fudimus. Venatici currus erant optimi; quatuor mares valde corpulenti. (Statuimus ut) ascenderemus illum magnum collem, et insectaremur illius turbas et greges (ferarum).

Les Chinois divisent les années, les mois, les jours et les heures par périodes ou cycles de soixante. Soixante dénominations servent à désigner les soixante parties d'un cycle. Elle sont les mêmes pour les années, les mois, les jours et les heures. Elles sont formées des douze caractères horaires 子丑寅卯辰巳午未申酉戌亥 **tzèu tch'eòu in maò chênn séu òu wéi chēnn iòu siū hài** combinés avec les dix caractères 甲乙丙丁戊己庚辛壬癸 **kiă ì ping tīng meòu ki kēng sīn jênn kouèi.**

Les jours d'ordre impair sont appelés 剛日 **kāng jĕu** jours où la force prédomine; ils sont favorables pour les entreprises au dehors, pour les voyages, la guerre,... Les jours d'ordre pair sont appelés 柔日 **jeôu jĕu** jours

阜、從其羣醜。(2) 吉日庚午、既差我馬、獸之所同、麀鹿麌麌、漆沮之從、天子之所、(3) 瞻彼中原、其祁孔有、儦儦俟俟、或羣或友、悉率左右、以燕天子、(4) 既張我弓、既挾我矢、發

2. Kĭ jĕu kēng òu, ki tch'ā ngò mà (mòu). Cheóu tchēu chòu t'ôung, iŏu lŏu iù iù. Ts'ĭ Tsiū tchēu ts'ôung, t'iēn tzèu tchēu chòu.

3. Tchēn pèi tchōung iuên, k'ĭ k'ĭ k'òung iòu (i). Piaŏ piaŏ sèu sèu (i i), houĕ k'iùn, houĕ iòu (i). Sĭ chouĕ tsouò iòu (i), i ièn t'iēn tzèu (tsi).

4. Ki tchāng ngò kōung, ki hiĕ ngò chèu. Fă pèi siaò pā, i ts'èu tá sèu, i iú pīn k'ŏ, ts'iè i tchouŏ li.

très vigoureux. Nous avons résolu de gravir cette grande colline, et d'y poursuivre les troupes d'animaux sauvages.

2. Le septième jour du cycle, qui est un jour heureux, nous avons choisi (pour chaque voiture) quatre chevaux (également rapides; et nous avons examiné les endroits) où les animaux sauvages se réunissent, où les biches et les cerfs sont en grand nombre. Les bords de la Ts'i et de la Tsiu sont les meilleurs endroits pour la chasse impériale.

3. Nous avons vu cette plaine. Les animaux sauvages en remplissaient la vaste étendue. Ils couraient, marchaient, deux ou trois ensemble. Nous avons conduit avec nous tous nos hommes, pour donner une réjouissance au Fils du ciel.

4. Nous avons bandé nos arcs et encoché nos flèches. Ici nous

où la douceur prédomine; ils sont favorables pour les affaires domestiques, pour les offrandes aux défunts, les mariages,... Le cinquième et le septième jour du cycle devaient être favorables pour la chasse. 戊 **Meóu** est employé par abréviation pour 戊辰 cinquième dénomination cyclique.

伯 **Pĕ** ou 馬祖 **Mà tsòu** le Dompteur des chevaux préside à la constellation 房 **Fâng**, qui fait partie du Scorpion. On lui faisait des offrandes au printemps. En été, on sacrifiait à 先牧 **Siēn mŏu**, qui le premier nourrit des chevaux; en automne, à 馬社 **Mà chĕ**, qui le premier attela ces animaux; en hiver, à 馬步 **Mà póu**, esprit malfaisant qui se plaît à leur nuire.

2. Faustus dies est cycli septimus (*keng ou* litteris notatus); selegimus nostros equos. (Curribus vecti, ivimus et inspeximus loca) feræ quo conveniunt, cervæ cervique ubi plurimi sunt. Ts'i et Tsiu (fluviis proxima loca) ad insectandas (feras sunt idonea) imperatori loca.

3. Prospeximus illam mediam planitiem; illa vasta est, valde abundabat (feris). Currebant, gradiebantur, aliæ trinæ, aliæ binæ. Omnes ducti sunt circumstantes ministri, ad oblectandum Cœli filium.

彼小豝、殪此大兕、以御賓客、且以酌醴、

鴻鴈

(1) 鴻鴈于飛、肅肅其羽、之子于征、劬勞于野、爰及矜人、哀此鰥寡、(2) 鴻鴈于飛、集于中澤、之子于垣、百堵皆作、雖則劬

HOUNG IEN. 1. **Hôung ién iû fēi, siū siū k'ì iù. Tchēu tzèu iû tchēng, k'iû laô iū iè (chòu). Iuên kī kīng jênn, ngāi ts'èu kouān kouà (kòu).**

2. Hôung ién iû fēi, tsĭ iû tchōung tchĕ (tŏ). Tchēu tzèu iû iuên, pĕ tòu kiāi tsŏ. Souēi tsĕ k'iû laô, k'ì kiòu ngāi tchĕ (tŏ).

avons percé de petites laies; là, tué de grands bœufs sauvages. Nous en avons servi la chair avec du vin nouveau à nos visiteurs et à nos hôtes.

CHANT VII. HOUNG IEN.

Le peuple chante les souffrances de sa dispersion sous 厲王 **Li wâng**, la joie de son retour sous 宣王 **Siuēn wâng**, la reconstruction des maisons, la tranquillité dont il jouit. Il se compare aux oies sauvages qui, après les fatigues d'un long voyage, trouvent leur repos dans les lieux marécageux.

1. Les oies sauvages dans leur vol font entendre le bruit de leurs ailes. Ces enfants (de notre peuple) dans leurs voyages ont souffert mille fatigues au milieu des déserts. Dans leurs souffrances ils étaient à plaindre. Quelle compassion ne méritaient pas ces hommes privés de leurs femmes, ces femmes privées de leurs maris !

2. Les oies sauvages dans leurs voyages se reposent ensemble au milieu des marais. Les enfants de notre peuple, (revenus sur le sol natal), se sont mis à construire des murs; ils en ont élevé cinq mille pieds à la fois. Sans doute leur fatigue a été grande;

4. Intendimus nostros arcus; nervo aptavimus sagittam. Fodimus illas parvas sues; occidimus hos magnos boves silvestres. Utentes obtulimus hospitibus ac convivis; utentes propinavimus vinum novum.

CHANT VII. 1. *Hôung* silvestres anseres majores et *ién* silvestres anseres minores dum volant, *siū siū* strepunt eorum alæ. Illi filii (populi nostri) dum iter fecerunt, laborantes fatigati sunt in desertis. (Illæ ærumnæ) attigerunt miserandos homines. Quam miserandi illi uxoribus carentes viri et maritis carentes mulieres!

2. Silvestres anseres tum majores tum minores dum volant, considunt in mediis paludibus. Illi filii dum parietes exstruxerunt, centies quinquaginta parietum palmæ simul surrexerunt. Licet tunc labore fatigati sunt, ipsi tandem quiete habitaverunt.

勞、其究安宅、

(3) 鴻鴈于飛、哀鳴嗷嗷、維此哲人、謂我劬勞、維彼愚人、謂我宣驕、

庭燎

(1) 夜如何其、夜未央、庭燎之光、君子至止、鸞聲將將、

3. Hôung ién iû fēi, ngāi mîng ngaô ngaô. Wêi ts'èu tchĕ jênn, wéi ngò k'iû laô. Wêi pèi iû jênn, wéi ngò siuēn kiaō (kaō).

T'ING LEAO. **1. Ié jôu hô kī? Ié wéi iāng ; t'ing leaô tchēu kouāng. Kiūn tzèu tchéu tchéu, louân chēng ts'iāng ts'iāng.**

mais enfin ils ont eu des habitations commodes pour se reposer.

3. Les oies sauvages dans leur vol crient d'une voix plaintive *ngaô ngaô*. (Lorsqu'ils entendront notre chant), les hommes sages (auront compassion de nous, et) diront que nous avons supporté de grandes souffrances ; mais les insensés diront que nous montrons de l'arrogance.

CHANT VIII. T'ING LEAO.

Ce chant est un soliloque nocturne de l'empereur. L'empereur, qu'on croit être 宣王 **Siuēn wâng**, doit recevoir dès le matin, selon l'usage, les princes feudataires. Il craint de se lever trop tard et d'être surpris au lit par ses illustres visiteurs. Il juge de l'heure de la nuit par l'apparence des torches qu'il s'imagine voir allumées dans la cour du palais. D'après son appréciation, minuit n'est pas encore venu, et déjà il pense entendre les sonnettes des chevaux des princes.

1. La nuit est-elle avancée? Il n'est pas encore minuit. Cependant les torches brillent dans la cour. Les princes arrivent; j'entends les sonnettes aux mors des brides de leurs chevaux.

Quand les anciens élevaient des murs de terre, ils disposaient des planches de chaque côté, afin de maintenir la terre. Les planches avaient ordinairement un 丈 **tcháng** ou dix 尺 **tch'ĕu** de long. Pour cette raison, on appelait 板 **pàn** une longueur de dix *tch'ĕu*. On appelait 堵 **tòu** une longueur de cinq *pàn* ou cinquante *tch'ĕu*. Voy. plus loin L. IV. Ch. 5.

3. Silvestres anseres tum majores tum minores dum volant, gementes clamant *ngaò ngaò*. (Audito hoc nostro cantico), soli hi prudentes viri dicent nos labore fatigatos esse. Sed illi stulti homines dicent nos palam facere arrogantiam.

CHANT VIII. 1. Nox quomodo, i. e. noctis quota est hora? Nox nondum media est; aulæ faces lucescunt. Reguli adveniunt; frenorum tintinnabulorum sonus strepit.

其 **Kī**, 止 **Tchèu**, particules.

Un peu avant le jour, lorsqu'une audience devait avoir lieu, on allumait de grandes torches 大燭 **tá tchŏu** dans la rue devant la porte principale et dans la cour du palais de l'empereur et des princes. Elles étaient faites de

② 夜如何其。夜未艾。庭燎晣晣。君子至止。鸞聲噦噦。

③ 夜如何其。夜鄉晨。庭燎有煇。君子至止。言觀其旂。

沔水

① 沔彼流水。朝宗于海。駛彼飛隼。載飛載止。嗟我兄

2. Ié jôu hô kī ? Ié wéi ngái (i) ; t'îng leaò tchéu tchéu. Kiūn tzèu tchéu tchéu, louân chēng houéi houéi.

3. Ié jôu hô kī ? Ié hiáng chênn ; t'îng leaò iòu hiūn. Kiūn tzèu tchéu tchéu, iên kouān k'î k'i (k'în).

MIEN CHOUEI. **1. Mièn pèi liôu chouèi, tch'aô tsōung iû hài (houèi). Iŭ pèi fēi siùn, tsái fēi tsái tchèu. Tsiē ! ngò hiōung ti, pāng jènn tchōu iòu (wéi),**

2. La nuit est-elle avancée? La nuit n'est pas encore terminée. Mais dans la cour la lueur des torches commence à pâlir. Les princes approchent ; j'entends distinctement les sonnettes de leurs chevaux.

3. La nuit est-elle avancée? La nuit va faire place au jour. Dans la cour la flamme des torches est mêlée de fumée. Les princes arrivent ; déjà je vois leurs étendards.

CHANT IX. MIEN CHOUEI.

Le poète déplore l'indifférence de ses concitoyens qui ne se mettent pas en peine de faire cesser les troubles du pays. Les cours d'eau et les oiseaux savent trouver le lieu de leur repos et suivre certaines règles. Les hommes ne savent pas travailler à rétablir la paix et la tranquillité. Les mauvaises langues sont la cause de tout le mal, et personne ne s'applique à les réprimer.

1. Ces fleuves coulent à pleins bords ; ils vont offrir leurs hommages et payer tribut à la mer. Le faucon au vol rapide tantôt fend l'air, tantôt se repose. Hélas ! parmi mes frères, mes concitoyens,

bois résineux ou de roseaux enduits de graisse. L'empereur avait dans sa cour cent 庭燎 **t'ing leaò** grandes torches ; les 公 **kōung** en avaient cinquante ; les 侯 **heôu**, les 伯 **pĕ**, les 子 **tzèu** et les 男 **nân**, seulement trente.

姚舜牧 **Iaô Chouénn mŏu** dit qu'à minuit les torches n'étaient peut-être pas encore allumées. 宣王 **Siuēn wâng**, dans son anxiété, s'imagine déjà les voir briller, et n'ose plus prolonger son sommeil.

2. Nox quomodo? Nox nondum desiit. Aulæ tædarum flamma pallescit. Reguli adveniunt ; tintinnabulorum sonus distincte auditur.

3. Nox quomodo? Nox prope accedit ad diluculum. Aulæ faces habent flammam fumo mixtam. Reguli adveniunt ; en prospicio eorum vexilla.

CHANT IX. 1. Alveum implent illæ fluentes aquæ ; (quasi reguli ad imperatorem) reverentiam significaturæ coeunt ad mare. Celer ille volans falco,

弟、邦人諸友、莫肯念亂、誰無父母、

(2) 沔彼流水、其流湯湯、鴥彼飛隼、載飛載揚、念彼不蹟、載起載行、心之憂矣、不可弭忘、

(3) 鴥彼飛隼、率彼中陵、民之訛言、寧莫之懲、我友敬矣、讒言其興、

mouŏ k'èng gnién louán. Chouêi ôu fóu mòu (mèi) ?

2. Mièn pèi liôu chouèi, k'ì liôu chāng chāng. Iŭ pèi fēi siùn, tsái fēi tsái iàng. Gnién pèi pŏu tsĭ, tsái k'ì tsái hìng (hâng). Sīn tchēu iōu i, pŏu k'ò mi wâng.

3. Iŭ pèi fēi siùn, chouĕ pèi tchōung lîng. Mîn tchēu wô iên, gnìng mouŏ tchēu tch'êng ? Ngò iòu kìng i, tch'ân iên k'ì hīng ?

mes amis, personne ne veut chercher un remède aux troubles actuels. (Et cependant) qui n'a pas un père, une mère (dans l'affliction à cause de ces désordres)?

2. Ces fleuves coulent à pleins bords; leurs eaux sont abondantes. Le faucon au vol rapide tantôt plane, tantôt s'élève dans les airs, (et jamais ne se repose. Ainsi) à la pensée de ces hommes qui s'écartent de la voie droite, je suis dans une continuelle agitation. Je ne puis ni calmer ni oublier le chagrin de mon cœur.

3. Le faucon dans son vol rapide suit le flanc de la colline (il suit la route qui lui est comme tracée par la colline. Les hommes au contraire s'écartent du droit chemin). On répand des faussetés; pourquoi personne n'y met-il obstacle? Si mes amis (mes frères et mes concitoyens) veillaient sur eux-mêmes avec soin, tant de médisances auraient-elles cours?

modo volat, modo sistit. Heu! inter meos fratres, regni incolas, omnes amicos, nullus vult cogitare de turbatione. (Attamen) quis non habet parentes (quibus illa turbatio graviter nocet)?

朝 **Tch'aŏ** se dit de la visite que les princes 諸 侯 **tchōu heôu** faisaient à l'empereur en printemps, et 宗 **tsōung**, de celle qu'ils lui faisaient en été. Les fleuves sont comparés aux princes, et l'océan à l'empereur.

2. Implent alveum illæ fluentes aquæ; illæ fluunt ingenti copia. Celer est ille volans falco; et volat et assurgit, (nec quiescit. Ita) cogitans de illis hominibus non insistentibus tritæ viæ, et assurgo et incedo, i.e. nulla quiete fruor. Animi mœror non potest cohiberi nec obliterari.

蹟 **Tsĭ**, traces de pas, chemin battu, suivre le bon chemin.

3. Celer est ille volans falco; legit illum medium clivum. Homines falsa proferunt dicta; quare nemo eos coercet? Si mei amici sibi attenderent, maledica verba illa num exsurgerent?

鶴鳴

(1) 鶴鳴于九皐、聲聞于野、魚潛在淵、或在于渚、樂彼之園、爰有樹檀、其下維蘀、他山之石、可以爲錯、

(2) 鶴鳴于九皐、聲聞于天、魚在于渚、或潛在淵、樂彼之園、爰有樹檀、其下維穀、他山之石、可以攻玉、

HO MING. **1. Hŏ mîng iū kiòu kaō, chēng wénn iū iè (chòu). Iù tsién tsái iuēn, houĕ tsái iū tchòu. Lŏ pèi tchēu iuên, iuên iòu chóu t'ân (t'iên); k'ì hiá wêi t'ŏ. T'ouō chān tchēu chĕu k'ò i wêi ts'ŏ.**

2. Hŏ mîng iū kiòu kaō, wénn chēng iū t'iēn. Iû tsái iū tchòu, houĕ tsién tsái iuēn. Lŏ pèi tchēu iuên, iuên iòu chóu t'ân (t'iên); k'ì hiá wêi kŏu. T'ouō chān tchēu chĕu k'ò i kōung iŭ.

CHANT X. HO MING.

Le poète propose quatre allégories, dont la signification n'est pas très apparente. D'après Tchou Hi, sous la première, il nous enseigne que la vérité ne doit pas rester cachée; sous la deuxième, que l'application des principes doit varier avec les circonstances; sous la troisième, que les meilleures choses ne sont pas exemptes de défaut; sous la quatrième, que les plus mauvaises choses ont des qualités louables. Ces quatre allégories et ces quatre enseignements sont les mêmes dans les deux strophes.

1. La cigogne crie dans le marais au milieu des neuf étangs; sa voix retentit jusque dans les déserts. Le poisson tantôt se cache dans les profondeurs des abîmes, tantôt demeure auprès des ilots (où l'eau est peu profonde). Ce jardin est agréable; il est planté de *t'ân*, mais à leur pied on ne voit que des feuilles mortes. Les pierres de cette montagne (paraissent grossières, et cependant) on peut en faire des pierres à aiguiser.

2. La cigogne crie dans le marais au milieu des neuf étangs; sa voix retentit jusque dans le ciel. Le poisson tantôt demeure auprès des ilots, tantôt se cache dans les profondeurs des abîmes. Ce jardin est agréable; il est planté de *t'ân*, mais à leur pied ce ne sont que des mûriers à papier. Les pierres de cette montagne (bien que grossières) peuvent servir à polir les pierres précieuses.

CHANT X. 1. Ciconia clamat in (paludis mediis) novem lacunis; vox auditur in desertis. Piscis latet in profundis aquis, aut manet ad insulas (ubi aqua non est profunda). Amœnus est ille hortus; sunt plantatæ *t'ân* arbores; ad earum radices solummodo sunt decidua folia. Illius montis lapides (licet crassi videantur), possunt adhiberi ad faciendas cotes.

2. Ciconia clamat inter novem paludis lacunas; vox personat in cœlo. Piscis manet ad insulas, aut latet in aquis profundis. Amœnus est ille hortus; sunt plantatæ *t'ân* arbores; ad earum radices solummodo sunt *broussonetiæ*. Illius montis lapides possunt adhiberi ad poliendas gemmas.

祈父之什二之四

祈父

①祈父、予王之爪牙、胡轉予于恤、靡所止居、

②祈父、予王之爪士、胡轉予于恤、靡所底止、

③祈父、亶不聰、胡轉予于恤、有母之尸饔、

K'I FOU. 1. K'î fòu, iù wâng tchêu tchaò iâ (ôu). Hôu tchouèn iû iû siū, mi chòu tchèu kiū?

2. K'î fòu, iù wàng tchêu tchaò chéu. Hôu tchouén iû iū siū, mi chòu tchèu tchèu?

3. K'î fòu, tàn pŏu ts'ōung. Hôu tchouén iû iū siū, iòu mòu tchêu chêu iōung?

LIVRE IV. K'I FOU.

CHANT I. K'I FOU.

Les soldats de l'armée ou de la garde impériale se plaignent d'avoir été retenus longtemps dans une expédition lointaine.

1. Ministre de la guerre, nous sommes les griffes et les dents (les défenseurs) de l'empereur. Pourquoi nous avez-vous précipités dans le malheur, et réduits à n'avoir pas de demeure fixe?

2. Ministre de la guerre, nous sommes les griffes, les soldats de l'empereur. Pourquoi nous avez-vous précipités dans le malheur, et condamnés à des fatigues sans fin?

3. Ministre de la guerre, vous n'avez pas été très perspicace. Pourquoi nous avez-vous précipités dans le malheur, et (au mépris des lois) réduit les mères (avancées en âge à aller chercher elles-mêmes l'eau et le chauffage), à faire tout le travail de la cuisine, (au lieu de recevoir les soins de leurs fils)?

TITRE DU LIVRE. 祈父之什二之四 K'i fou decas: (Cheu king) secundæ (partis) quarta (decas).

CHANT I. 1. Imperialis territorii summe militum præposite, nos sumus imperatoris ungues ac dentes, i.e. defensores. Quare devolvisti nos in miseriam, (ita ut) non esset ubi sistentes moraremur?

祈 K'i est employé pour 圻 ou 畿 k'i, territoire ou domaine particulier de l'empereur. 祈父 K'i fòu, nom donné au ministre de la guerre 司馬 sêu mà dans le domaine de l'empereur.

2. Imperialis territorii militiæ præses, nos sumus imperatoris unguibus instructi milites. Quare devolvisti nos in miseriam, (ita ut) non esset quo adeuntes sisteremus?

3. Imperialis territorii militum præses, vere non fuisti perspicax. Quare devolvisti nos in miseriam, (ita ut) habitæ matres curam impenderent coquendis cibis?

Les fils uniques dont les parents étaient avancés en âge, étaient exempts

白駒

①皎皎白駒、食我場苗、縶之維之、以永今朝、所謂伊人、於焉逍遙、

②皎皎白駒、食我場藿、縶之維之、以永今夕、所謂伊人、於焉嘉客、

③皎皎白駒、賁然來思、爾公爾

PE KIU. **1. Kiaò kiaò pě kiū, chěu ngò tch'âng miaò. Tchěu tchěu wêi tchēu, i iòung kīn tchaō. Chòu wéi ī jênn, iū iên tchaò iaô.**

2. Kiaò kiaò pě kiū, chěu ngò tch'âng houŏ. Tchěu tchēu wêi tchēu, i iòung kīn sĭ (siŏ). Chòu wêi ī jênn, iū iên kiā k'ŏ.

3. Kiaò kiaò pě kiū, pi jên lâi (iū) sēu. Eùl kōung èul heôu (hôu), ĭ iú ôu

CHANT II. PE KIU.

Le poète s'efforce de retenir un sage. N'y parvenant pas, il le prie de vouloir bien du moins envoyer souvent des messagers.

1. Que le jeune cheval d'une blancheur éclatante (dont ce sage a coutume de se servir) mange les plantes qui croissent dans mon aire (transformée en jardin potager). Que je le lie par le pied, par le cou, afin de prolonger la joie de cette matinée. Que le sage dont je parle, goûte ici un repos agréable.

2. Que son jeune cheval d'une blancheur éclatante mange les feuilles des haricots qui croissent dans mon aire. Que je le lie par le pied, par le cou, afin de prolonger la joie de cette soirée. Que le sage dont je parle demeure ici, hôte distingué.

3. Que ce jeune cheval d'une blancheur éclatante vienne richement paré (ou promptement). (Et alors vous, mon sage ami), vous obtiendrez la dignité de *koung* ou de *heou*, et jouirez d'un repos et

du service militaire. Les soldats se plaignent de ce que cette loi n'avait pas été observée.

CHANT II. 1. Nitenti candore albus equuleus comedat meæ areæ (in hortum mutatæ) crescentia olera. Pede alligem eum, collo alligem eum, ut diuturnum sit hujus mane (gaudium). De quo loquor ille vir in hoc loco quiete oblectet se.

Après le battage des grains, l'aire était transformée en jardin jusqu'à la moisson suivante.

2. Nitenti candore albus equuleus comedat meæ areæ phaseolorum folia. Pede alligem eum, collo alligem eum, ut diuturnum sit hujus vesperi (gaudium). De quo loquor ille vir in hoc loco sit insignis hospes.

3. Nitenti candore albus equuleus ornate (seu celeriter) veniat. Tu (mi sapiens amice) eris *koung*, tu eris *heou*; otio te oblectabis sine fine. Cura ne tu otio vageris; nitere ne tu de secessu cogites.

侯。逸豫無期。愼爾優游、勉爾遁思、

(4) 皎皎白駒、在彼空谷、生芻一束、其人如玉、毋金玉爾音、而有遐心、

黃鳥

(1) 黃鳥黃鳥、無集于穀、無啄我粟、此邦之人、不我肯穀、言旋言歸、復我邦族。

k'î. Chénn èul iôu iôù (ǒu), mién èul touénn sēu (sī).

4. Kiaò kiaò pĕ kiū, tsái pèi k'ōung kŏu. Chēng tch'ōu ĭ chŏu; k'î jênn jôu iŭ. Où kīn iŭ èul īn, èul iòu hiâ sīn.

HOUANG GNIAO. **1. Houâng gniaò, houâng gniaò, ŏu tsī iū kŏu, ŏu tchouŏ ngò sŏu. Ts'èu pāng tchēu jênn pŏu ngò k'èng kŏu. Iên siuên iên kouēi, fŏu ngò pāng tsŏu.**

d'un bonheur sans fin. Prenez garde de vouloir aller çà et là; bannissez la pensée de vivre dans la retraite.

4. Ce jeune cheval d'une blancheur éclatante est dans cette vallée déserte. (Il s'en va; il ne veut ni des haricots ni des autres plantes de mon jardin, et se contente d') une botte d'herbe verte. Son maître est (par ses belles qualités) comme une pierre précieuse. (Sage ami), ne soyez pas avare de vos paroles, comme d'autres le sont de l'or et des pierres précieuses (envoyez-moi souvent des lettres, des messagers); ne me retirez pas votre affection.

CHANT III. HOUANG GNIAO.

Un homme étant allé dans un pays étranger avec l'intention d'y fixer sa demeure, et n'y trouvant pas l'accueil qu'il souhaitait, compare les habitants à des oiseaux jaunes qui lui sont nuisibles, et prend la résolution de retourner dans sa patrie.

1. Oiseau jaune, oiseau jaune, ne te pose pas sur le mûrier à papier, ne mange pas mon grain. Les habitants de cette contrée ne veulent pas me bien traiter. Je veux me retirer, je veux retourner dans mon pays; j'irai revoir ma patrie et ma parenté.

賁 **Pi**, brillant, bien orné. Quelques commentateurs lisent 奔 **pēnn** courir.

1. Nitenti candore albus equuleus est in illa deserta valle. Virentis herbæ unus fascis (explet eum); ille vir est sicut gemma. Noli aurum gemmasque ducere tua verba, et habere alienatum animum.

CHANT III. 1. Flava avis, flava avis, ne insideas in broussonetia, ne rostro capias meum frumentum. Hujus regni homines non me volunt bene tractare. Cogito de recessu, cogito de reditu; revertar ad meum regnum et consanguineos.

（2）黃鳥黃鳥、無集于桑、無啄我粱、此邦之人、不可與明、言旋言歸、復我諸兄、
（3）黃鳥黃鳥、無集于栩、無啄我黍、此邦之人、不可與處、言旋言歸、復我諸父、

我行其野

（1）我行其野、蔽芾其樗、昏姻之

2. Houâng gniaò, houâng gniaò, ôu tsī iû sāng, ôu tchouŏ ngò leâng. Ts'èu pāng tchēu jênn, pŏu k'ò iù mîng (mâng). Iên siuên iên kouēi, fŏu ngò tchōu hiōung (houāng).

3. Houâng gniaò, houâng gniaò, ôu tsī iû hiù, ôu tchouŏ ngò chòu. Ts'èu pāng tchēu jênn, pŏu k'ò iù tch'òu. Iên siuên iên kouēi, fŏu ngò tchōu fòu.

NGO HING K'I IE. **1. Ngò hîng k'ì iè, pi féi k'ì tch'ōu. Houēnn īn tchēu kóu,**

2. Oiseau jaune, oiseau jaune, ne te pose pas sur le mûrier, ne mange pas mon sorgho. Avec les habitants de cette contrée il est impossible de s'entendre. Je veux m'en retourner et rentrer dans mon pays; j'irai revoir tous mes frères.

3. Oiseau jaune, oiseau jaune, ne te pose pas sur le chêne, ne mange pas mon millet. Avec les habitants de cette contrée il est impossible de demeurer. Je veux m'en retourner et rentrer dans mon pays; j'irai revoir tous mes oncles.

CHANT IV. NGO HING K'I IE.

Un homme dans l'indigence espère trouver du secours auprès d'un parent par alliance dans une contrée étrangère. Il entreprend un long voyage. Sur la route, il n'a pour abri que des ailantes, des arbres qui ont peu de feuillage; il n'a pour nourriture que des herbes sauvages. Arrivé chez son parent par alliance, il le trouve marié à une seconde femme, et très indifférent envers lui. Il se détermine à retourner dans son pays.

1. J'ai traversé les déserts, n'ayant d'autre abri que des ailantes. A cause de notre affinité, je suis allé pour demeurer chez vous. Vous

2. Flava avis, flava avis, ne insideas in moro, ne rostro capias meum sorghum. Cum hujus regni hominibus non possibile est simul clare loqui. Volo reverti, volo domum redire; regrediar ad meos omnes fratres.

3. Flava avis, flava avis, ne insideas in quercu, ne rostro capias meum milium. Cum hujus regni hominibus non possibile est simul habitare. Volo regredi, volo domum redire; revertar ad meos omnes patruos.

CHANT IV. 1. Ego percurri illa deserta; opertus protegebar illa ailanto. Ob affinitatis causam, volui adire te habitaturus. Tu non me alis; redibo ad meam patriam et domum.

昏 ou 婚 **Houēnn**, prendre femme,

故、言就爾居、爾不
我畜、復我邦家、
(2)我行其野、言采
其蓫、昏姻之故、言
就爾宿、爾不我畜、
言歸思復、
(3)我行其野、言采
其葍、不思舊姻、求
爾新特、成不以富、
亦秖以異、
斯干
(1)秩秩斯干、幽幽

iên tsióu èul kiū. Eùl pōu ngò hiŭ, fōu ngò pāng kiā (kōu).

2. Ngò hîng k'ì iè, iên ts'ài k'ì tchŏu. Houēnn īn tchēu kóu, iên tsióu èul siŭ. Eùl pōu ngò hiŭ, iên kouēi sēu fōu.

3. Ngò hîng k'ì iè, iên ts'ài k'ì fŏu (pĭ). Pōu sēu kióu īn, k'iôu èul sīn t'ĕ. Tch'êng pōu i fóu, ĭ tchēu i i (ĭ).

SEU KAN. **1. Tchēu tchēu sēu kān, iōu iōu nân chān. Jôu tchŏu paō (peòu)**

ne me donnez pas la nourriture; je retournerai dans mon pays et dans ma maison.

2. J'ai traversé les déserts, cueillant un peu de patience pour apaiser la faim. A cause de notre affinité, je suis allé pour loger chez vous. Vous ne me donnez pas à manger; je veux rentrer dans mon pays et pense au retour.

3. J'ai traversé les déserts, cueillant la phytolaque pour me nourrir. Vous n'avez pas souci de votre ancien parent par alliance; vous ne cherchez qu'à plaire à votre nouvelle compagne, non parce qu'elle est plus riche que la première, mais uniquement parce que c'est une autre (le changement vous plait).

CHANT V. SEU KAN.

L'empereur 宣王 **Siuēn wâng**, après avoir fait rebâtir son palais, donna un festin à ses officiers. On y chanta les strophes suivantes, dans lesquelles le poète raconte les travaux de construction, décrit le site et la beauté de l'édifice, et souhaite à l'empereur des songes heureux et la naissance d'enfants nombreux dans la nouvelle demeure.

1. (D'un côté) la rivière (Foung) forme un demi-cercle

épouse, nom qu'un homme donne aux parents de sa femme. 姻 **Īn**, prendre un mari, mari, nom qu'une femme donne aux parents de son mari. 昏姻 **Houēnn īn**, se marier, mariage, parent par alliance.

2. Ego percurri illa deserta, et collegi illum rumicem. Ob affinitatis causam, volui adire te pernoctaturus. Tu non me nutris; volo domum reverti, cogito de reditu.

3. Ego percurri illa deserta, et carpsi illam phytolaccam. Non curas de veteri affini; amore prosequeris tuam novam conjugem, certe non quia ditior est, sed solummodo quia alia est.

南山、如竹苞矣、如松茂矣、兄及弟矣、式相好矣、無相猶矣、

(2) 似續妣祖、築室百堵、西南其戶、爰居爰處、爰笑爰語、

(3) 約之閣閣、椓之橐橐、風雨攸除、鳥鼠

i, jôu sōung meóu (meòu) i. Hiōung kĭ tí i, chĕu siāng haó (heòu) i, óu siāng iôu (iòu) i!

2. Séu siŭ pi tsòu, tchouŏ chĕu pĕ tòu. Sī nân k'i hòu, iuên kiū iuên tch'òu, iuên siaó iuên iù.

3. Iŏ tchēu kŏ kŏ, tchouŏ tchēu t'ouŏ t'ouŏ. Fōung iù iôu tch'óu, gniaò chòu iôu k'iù, kiūn tzéu iôu hiū (iù).

régulier; au midi est le mont (Tchoung nan) sombre et silencieux. (Les murs de l'édifice sont compactes et solides) comme un massif de bambous; (la charpente est serrée et gracieuse) comme une forêt de pins verdoyants. Que (dans cette demeure) les frères soient unis d'affection, et ne trament rien les uns contre les autres!

2. L'empereur, héritier et successeur de ses aïeux, a construit ce palais dont les murs ont ensemble cinq mille pieds de longueur; les portes regardent, les unes l'occident, les autres le midi. Ici il habitera et demeurera, il donnera des réjouissances et tiendra ses conseils.

3. Les ouvriers disposèrent d'abord parfaitement les planches (entre lesquelles ils devaient élever les murs; puis versèrent dans l'intervalle et) battirent avec soin la terre. Le vent et la pluie n'y

CHANT V. 1. Ordine composita illa ripa; umbrosus et placidus australis mons. (Parietes sunt densi et firmi) sicut bambusarum silva; (lignea compages est densa ac decora) sicut pini luxuriantes. (In hac domo) fratres majores et fratres minores invicem ament, nihil invicem moliantur!

La rivière 豐 **Fōung** passait au pied de la ville de 鎬 **Haò**; le mont 終 南 **Tchōung nân** était au midi.

式 **Chĕu**, particule.

2. (Imperator) hæres et successor ataviarum atavorumque, exstruxit palatium centies quinquaginta cubitis parietum constans; aliæ occidentem, aliæ meridiem spectant ejus januæ. Ibi habitabit, ibi manebit, ibi ridebit, ibi colloquetur.

似 **Séu** signifie 嗣 succéder, hériter.

3. Colligarunt illas (tabulas) aptissime; tutuderunt illam (terram) repetitis ictibus. Ventus et pluvia hinc arcentur; aves et mures hinc excluduntur. Sapiens princeps hunc locum honestabit.

Les ouvriers qui doivent élever un mur de terre, après avoir établi le soubassement, plantent des pieux 楨 **tchēng**, et posent de champ une ligne

攸去。君子攸芋。

(4) 如跂斯翼。如矢斯棘。如鳥斯革。如翬斯飛。君子攸躋。

(5) 殖殖其庭。有覺其楹。噲噲其正。噦噦其冥。君子攸寧。

(6) 下莞上簟。

4. Jòu k'i sēu ĭ, jòu chèu sēu kĭ, jòu gniaò sēu kŏ (kĭ), jòu houēi sēu fēi, kiūn tzèu iôu tsī.

5. Tchēu tchēu k'ì t'ìng, iòu kiŏ k'ì ìng. K'ouái k'ouái k'ì tchéng (tchēng), houéi houéi k'ì mìng, kiūn tzèu iôu gnîng.

6. Hiá kouān cháng tièn, nài ngān sēu ts'in (ts'ièn). Nài ts'in nài hīng. « Nài

pénétreront pas ; les oiseaux et les rats n'y entreront pas. La présence du souverain rendra ce lieu auguste.

4. (La grande salle d'audience est majestueuse) comme un homme qui se tient avec respect sur la pointe des pieds. (Les angles sont droits) comme le vol rapide d'une flèche. (La toiture est élégante) comme un oiseau dont le plumage est renouvelé. (Les bords du toit sont recourbés) comme les ailes d'un faisan qui vole. Le souverain montera à cette salle (pour donner audience).

5. La cour est bien unie, et entourée de colonnes très hautes. Les parties de l'édifice qui reçoivent les rayons du soleil sont très gaies ; les autres sont vastes et profondes. Notre souverain y goûtera le repos.

6. Sur une natte de jonc recouverte d'un natte de bambou, il

de planches 幹 **kán**, de chaque côté des fondations. Dans cette sorte de caisse, ils mettent de la terre et la battent avec force. Quand la caisse est remplie, ils enlèvent les planches, les placent plus haut, de manière à former comme une nouvelle caisse au-dessus de la première assise ou *banchée*, et élèvent une seconde assise. Ils continuent ainsi jusqu'à ce que le mur ait atteint la hauteur voulue.

Ce genre de construction, mentionné par Pline, est encore usité dans plusieurs contrées de l'Europe sous le nom de *Pisé* ou *Maçonnerie de pisé*. Dans la Sainte Écriture, Eccli. c. 22. 19, la caisse de planches est désignée, ce semble, par ces mots *loramentum ligneum colligatum in fundamento ædificii*.

4. (Magna exedra est magnifica) sicut homo in pedum digitos arrectus cum reverentia. (Ejus anguli sunt recti) sicut sagittæ (volatus) celer. (Tectum assurgit decorum) sicut avis renovatis pennis. (Tecti ora est recurva) sicut phasiani volantis (alæ). Sapiens princeps huc ascendet.

5. Planum est illud atrium ; habent altitudinem illæ columnæ. Hilarem præbent speciem illæ (ædium partes) quæ solis radiis sunt obversæ ; profundæ vastæque illæ non solis radiis illustratæ. Sapiens princeps hic quiescet.

乃安斯寢、乃寢乃興、乃占我夢、吉夢維何、維熊維羆、維虺維蛇。

(7) 大人占之、維熊維羆、男子之祥、維虺維蛇、女子之祥。

(8) 乃生男子、載寢之牀、載衣之裳、載弄之璋、其泣喤喤、朱芾斯皇、室家君王。

tchēn nài móung (mêng). Kì méng wêi hô? Wêi hiôung wêi pī (pouō), wêi houèi wêi chê (t'ouô).»

7. T'ái jênn tchēn tchēu. « Wêi hiôung wêi pī (pouō), nân tzèu tchēu siâng. Wêi houèi wêi chê (t'ouô), gniù tzèu tchēu siâng.»

8. Nài chēng nân tzèu, tsái ts'in tchēu tch'ouâng, tsái í tchēu châng, tsái lóung tchēu tchāng. K'i k'ī hôung hôung (houâng houâng), tchōu fōu sēu houâng, chĕu kiā kiūn wâng.

reposera commodément. Il reposera, se lèvera (et dira): «Interprétez mes songes. Quels sont les songes d'heureux augure? (Pendant mon sommeil j'ai vu) des ours et des serpents de deux espèces.»

7. Le grand devin répondra: «Les ours annoncent la naissance de garçons, et les serpents la naissance de filles.»

8. Des garçons naîtront à l'empereur; ils seront couchés sur des lits. Ils seront vêtus de belles robes, et auront pour jouets des tablettes d'honneur. (Devenus grands) ils porteront des genouillères rouges brillantes, et recevront en héritage les principautés et l'empire.

6. Inferius stratis junceis mattis, superius stratis arundineis storeis, commode hic cubabit. Et cubabit, et surget, et dicet: «Interpretare mea somnia. Fausta somnia sunt quænam? Et ursi et majores ursi et serpentes et angues (a me somniante visi sunt).»

7. Magnus conjector interpretabitur illa. «Et ursi et majores ursi inquiet, sunt masculæ prolis omina; et serpentes et angues sunt fœmineæ prolis omina.»

8. Inde nascentur masculi pueri; et reclinabunt eos in lectos. Et induent eos stolis, et in ludum dabunt eis tesseras. Eorum vagitus erit sonorus. Rubra genualia inde splendebunt. Domo et familia erunt (alii) reguli, (unus) imperator.

Les tablettes de jade étaient des marques de dignité. V. page 64. On donnait des tablettes pour jouets aux enfants mâles des grandes familles, pour signifier les honneurs qui les attendaient. L'empereur et les princes portaient des genouillères rouges. L'un des fils de l'empereur devait avoir pour héritage et pour domaine 室家 **chĕu kiā** l'empire, et les autres, des principautés.

(9) 乃生女子、載寢之地、載衣之裼、載弄之瓦、無非無儀、唯酒食是議、無父母貽罹。

無羊

(1) 誰謂爾無羊、三百維羣、誰謂爾無牛、九十其犉、爾羊來思、其角

9. **Nài chēng gniù tzèu, tsái ts'in tchēu tí, tsái i tchēu t'i, tsái lóung tchēu wà (wéi). Où fēi ôu î (i); wéi tsiòu chēu chéu i, ôu fóu mòu î lì (li).**

OU IANG. **1. Chouêi wéi èul ôu iâng? Sān pě wêi k'iùn. Chouêi wéi èul ôu iôu? Kiòu chĕu k'î chouênn. Eùl iâng lâi sēu, k'i kiŏ tsĭ tsĭ. Eùl iôu lâi sēu, k'i èul chĕu chĕu.**

9. Des filles naîtront à l'empereur; elles seront déposées à terre. On les enveloppera de langes, et on leur donnera pour jouet une tuile. (Devenues grandes), elles ne feront rien de mal; de leur propre chef elles n'entreprendront aucune œuvre même louable. Il leur suffira de donner leurs soins à la boisson et à la nourriture, et de n'attirer aucun désagrément à leurs parents.

CHANT VI. OU IANG.

État florissant des troupeaux et prospérité de l'empire sous le règne de 宣王 **Siuēn wàng.**

1. Dira-t-on que vous n'avez pas de brebis? Chacun de vos troupeaux en compte trois cents. Dira-t-on que vous n'avez pas de bœufs? Vos bœufs roux à museau noir s'élèvent au nombre de quatre-vingt-dix (sans compter les autres). Vos brebis viennent, et ne

9. Inde nascentur puellæ; reclinabunt eas in terram. Et induent eas pannis, et in ludum dabunt eis tegulas. Nihil tentabunt mali, nihil boni (ultro aggredientur, sed in omnibus oportebit et sufficiet ut sive parentibus sive maritis obtemperent). Solummodo potus et cibus erunt de quibus curabunt; nec parentibus arcessent molestiam.

Anciennement les fileuses employaient une tuile, on ignore à quel usage. La mère donnait pour jouet à sa fille une tuile pour l'initier aux occupations des femmes. 弄璋 **Lóung tchāng** se dit communément de la naissance d'un garçon, et 弄瓦 **lóung wà**, de celle d'une fille.

Ce passage nous montre quelle différence les Chinois mettaient dans leur estime entre les garçons et les filles, alors comme aujourd'hui. Les garçons sont déposés sur un lit, revêtus de beaux vêtements et destinés aux honneurs. Les filles, même celles qui naissent sur les marches du trône impérial, sont déposées à terre, enveloppées de langes et destinées aux travaux domestiques. Elles n'auront d'autre mérite que celui de l'obéissance.

CHANT VI. 1. Quis dicet te carere ovibus? Tercentarum est unus grex.

濈濈。爾牛來思。其耳濕濕。

(2) 或降于阿。或飲于池。或寢或訛。爾牧來思。何蓑何笠。或負其餱。三十維物。爾牲則具。

(3) 爾牧來思。以薪以蒸。以雌以雄。爾羊來思。矜矜兢兢。不騫不崩。麾之以肱。畢來既升。

(4) 牧人乃夢。衆維

2. Houĕ kiáng iū ngō, houĕ in iū tch'ĕu (t'ouô), houĕ ts'in, houĕ wô. Eùl mŏu lâi sēu, hò souô hò lĭ; houĕ fóu k'ì heòu. Sān chĕu wêi ŏu ; èul chēng tsĕ kiú (kiŭ).

3. Eùl mŏu lâi sēu, i sīn i tchēng, i ts'ēu i hiôung (îng). Eùl iâng lâi sēu, kīng kīng kīng kīng, pŏu k'iēn pŏu pēng. Houēi tchēu i kōung, pĭ lâi kí chēng.

4. Mŏu jênn nài méng ; tchóung wêi iû i, tchaó wêi iû i. T'ái jênn tchēn

se battent pas entre elles avec les cornes. Vos bœufs viennent, et leurs oreilles sont moites (signe de vigueur).

2. (Parmi vos moutons et vos bœufs), ceux-ci descendent des replis des collines, ceux-là boivent aux amas d'eau ; les uns sont couchés, les autres sont en mouvement. Vos pâtres viennent, portant le manteau de jonc et le chapeau de paille ; quelques-uns portent sur le dos leurs provisions de vivres. Vous avez trente (brebis et trente bœufs) de chaque couleur ; les victimes ne vous manquent pas.

3. Vos pâtres viennent avec du bois, des branchages ou des herbes pour le chauffage, avec du gibier de toute sorte. Vos brebis viennent ; elles sont fortes et vigoureuses, aucune n'est faible ni malade. Vous leur faites signe de la main ; elles viennent toutes, et les voilà rentrées dans les étables.

4. Puis vos pâtres ont des songes. (Dans leur sommeil ils

Quis dicet te carere bobus? Nonaginta sunt illi flavi nigro ore. Tuæ oves veniunt, illæ cornibus concordant, i. e. non invicem feriunt. Tui boves veniunt, illorum aures madore nitent.

2. (Oves et boves tui) alii descendunt ex montis sinu, alii bibunt ad lacunas, alii decumbunt, alii movent se. Tui pastores veniunt ; gestant junceam impluviam, gestant arundineum petasum ; quidam bajulant sua cibaria sicca. Triginta sunt uniuscujusque coloris (tum oves tum boves) ; tuæ victimæ ideo suppetunt.

3. Tui pastores veniunt, cum cremiis, cum ramalibus seu herbis, cum feminis feris, cum maribus. Tuæ oves veniunt ; firmæ ac robustæ sunt, nec debilitatæ nec morbidæ. Signum das eis brachio ; omnes veniunt, jam ascenderunt (in caulas).

4. Pastores inde somniant. (In somniis vident) multos homines, (et paulo post eorum loco) solum pisces ; ornata

魚矣、旐維旟矣、大人占之、衆維魚矣、實維豐年、旐維旟矣、室家溱溱、

節南山

① 節彼南山、維石巖巖、赫赫師尹、民具爾瞻、憂心如惔、不敢戲談、國既卒斬、何用不監、

tchēu. « Tchóung wêi iù i, chĕu wêi fōung gniên (gnîn) ; tchaó wêi iù i, chĕu kiā tchēnn tchēnn. »

TSIE NAN CHAN. **1. Tsiĕ pèi nân chān, wêi chĕu iên iên. Hĕ hĕ chēu In, mîn kiú èul tchēn. Iōu sīn jôu t'ân, pŏu kàn hi t'ân. Kouŏ ki tsŏu tchàn (tchēn), hô ióung pŏu kiēn ?**

voient) des multitudes d'hommes qui sont remplacés par des poissons, des guidons ornés de tortues qui sont remplacés par des étendards ornés de faucons. Le grand devin interprète ces songes. «Les poissons substitués aux hommes, (dit-il), annoncent une année fertile (parce que les poissons se multiplient beaucoup plus que les hommes). Les étendards *iû* substitués aux guidons *tchaó* annoncent un grand accroissement de population (parce que les *tchaó* servent dans les campagnes peu habitées, et les *iû* dans les villes et les districts populeux). »

CHANT VII. TSIE NAN CHAN.

Plaintes du 大夫 **tái fōu** grand préfet 家父 **Kiā Fòu** contre 尹 **In**, ministre de l'empereur 幽王 **Iōu wâng**.

1. Au midi cette montagne est très élevée; ses rochers paraissent comme amoncelés les uns sur les autres. Ainsi vous, In, vous qui êtes grand maître, vous inspirez le respect par votre haute dignité, et tous les regards sont tournés vers vous. Mais un feu brûle dans les cœurs attristés; personne n'ose se permettre même une plaisanterie (de crainte d'exciter vos soupçons et votre colère). Déjà l'empire (la dynastie) est sur le point de prendre fin et de disparaître; pourquoi n'ouvrez-vous pas les yeux?

pictis testudinibus anguibusque signa, (et paulo post eorum loco) solum ornata pictis falconibus signa. Summus hariolus interpretatur illa. « Hominum turba, solum pisces, (ait), vere est frugibus locuples annus. Testudinibus ornata signa, solum falconibus ornata signa, est domuum et familiarum frequens numerus. »

CHANT VII. 1. Præcelsus est ille australis mons; saxa acervata eminent. Dignitate conspicuus es, magister In; cives omnes te suspiciunt. Mœstis animis quasi uruntur; non audent jocose loqui. Imperium (Tcheou domus regia) jam perit et absciditur; qua de causa non inspicis?

Le 太師 **t'ái chēu** grand maître, le

(2) 節彼南山、有實其猗、赫赫師尹、不平謂何、天方薦瘥、喪亂弘多、民言無嘉、憯莫懲嗟、

(3) 尹氏太師、維周之氐、秉國之均、四方是維、天子是毗、俾民不迷、不弔昊天、不宜空我師、

(4) 弗躬弗親、庶

2. Tsiē pèi nân chān, iòu chĕu k'ì ī (ngō). Hĕ hĕ chēu În, pŏu p'îng wéi hô ? T'iēn fāng tsién ts'ouô ; sáng louán hôung touō. Mîn iên ôu kiā (kō) ; ts'àn mouŏ tch'êng tsiē (tsouō).

3. Ìn chéu t'ái chēu, wéi Tchəŏu tchēu ti (tī). Ping kouŏ tchēu kiūn, séu fāng chēu wéi. T'iēn tzèu chéu p'î, péi jênn pŏu mî. Pŏu tiaó haò t'iēn, pŏu î k'ōung ngò chēu.

4. Fŏu kōung fŏu ts'īn, chóu mîn fŏu sin (sīn). Fŏu wénn fŏu chéu, ŏu wàng

2. Au midi cette montagne est très élevée ; les environs sont couverts d'arbres. Vous êtes très élevé en dignité, grand maître In ; pourquoi n'observez-vous pas la justice (dans votre administration)? Le ciel irrité nous afflige de plus en plus ; les morts (causées par la famine) se multiplient, et les désordres (les brigandages) deviennent de plus en plus graves et nombreux. Les discours des hommes ne sont pas en votre faveur ; jusqu'ici vous ne vous êtes ni corrigé ni repenti.

3. Chef de la famille des In, vous êtes grand maître, le soutien de la dynastie des Tcheou. Vous tenez la balance de l'empire et faites la loi à tous les États. Vous êtes chargé d'aider le Fils du ciel, pour empêcher le peuple de s'égarer. Il ne convient pas que (par votre conduite) vous rendiez l'auguste ciel impitoyable, et nous fassiez tous périr.

4. Vous ne faites rien vous-même, vous ne traitez pas les affai-

太傅 **t'ái fóu** grand précepteur et le 太保 **t'ái paò** grand tuteur étaient les 三公 **sān kōung** trois grands dignitaires de l'empire.

2. Praealtus est ille australis mons ; sunt plena (arboribus) illi adjacentia (loca). Dignitate praecelsus es, magister In ; non es aequus, cogitas quid, i.e. qua mente laedis aequitatem ? Cœlum nunc ingeminat morbos ; funera et scelera ingentia ac multa. Hominum sermones non laudant (te) ; hucusque non te coercuisti poenitens.

憯 **Ts'àn** signifie 曾 **ts'êng** auparavant, jusqu'à présent.

3. In domine, es summus magister, et Tcheou regiae familiae basis. Tenes imperii aequilibrium, quatuor regionum es moderator. Cœli filii es adjutor, ut populus non hallucinetur. Non miserente augusto cœlo, non decet exinanire nostram multitudinem.

民弗信、弗問弗仕、勿罔君子、式夷式已、無小人殆、瑣瑣姻亞、則無膴仕、

(5) 昊天不傭、降此鞠訩、昊天不惠、降此大戾、君子如屆、俾民心闋、君子如夷、惡怒是違、

(6) 不弔昊天、亂靡有定、式月斯

kiūn tzèu. Chĕu i chĕu i, ôu siaò jênn tài (i). Souò souò În iá, tsĕ ôu òu chéu.

5. Haò t'iēn pŏu tch'ôung, kiáng ts'éu kiŭ hiōung. Haò t'iēn pŏu houéi, kiáng ts'éu tá li. Kiūn tzèu jŏu kiái (ki), péi mîn sīn k'iuĕ (k'ouéi). Kiūn tzèu jŏu î, óu nóu chéu wêi.

6. Pŏu tiaó haò t'iēn (t'īng), louán mi iòu ting (tīng). Chĕu iuĕ sēu chēng,

res vous-même; le peuple n'a pas confiance. Que les hommes dépourvus de connaissances et d'expérience (soient exclus des charges et) ne trompent pas l'empereur. Soyez juste, destituez (les mauvais officiers); que des hommes vils ne mettent plus l'empire en péril. Que vos misérables parents par alliance n'occupent plus les postes les plus lucratifs.

5. L'auguste ciel, qui ne nous est pas propice, a envoyé ces troubles destructeurs. L'auguste ciel, qui nous a retiré sa faveur, a envoyé cet immense bouleversement. Si nos gouvernants veillaient eux-mêmes sur les affaires, les cœurs des sujets auraient un peu de repos. Si nos gouvernants étaient équitables, les colères et les haines disparaitraient.

6. L'auguste ciel n'a pas pitié de nous, et les troubles n'ont pas de fin. Ils croissent chaque mois, et ne laissent au peuple aucune

4. Non ipse res geris, non ipse obis munia, (sed cognatis tuis committis; ideo) universus populus non fidit. Qui non didicerunt nec magistratum gesserunt, (rebus publicis ne præficiantur), ne decipiant imperatorem. Et utere æquitate, et destitue; ne viles homines periculo sint. Tenues affines jam ne habeant opimos magistratus.

5. Augustum cœlum, non æque propitium (nobis ac cæteris hominibus), immisit hanc exinanientem perturbationem. Augustum cœlum non beneficum immisit hanc magnam subversionem. Imperii rectores si obirent (res publicas), facerent ut civium animi paulum quiescerent. Imperii rectores si essent justi, odia et iræ eo ipso amoverentur.

傭 **Tch'ôung** signifie 均 **kiūn**, égal, juste, impartial. 昊天不傭 Le ciel ne nous traite plus avec sa bonté ordinaire, avec cette bienfaisance qu'il a coutume d'exercer envers tous les hommes.

6. Non miseretur augustum cœlum: perturbatio non habet finem. Mense (quoque) illa crescit, facit ut populus

生、俾民不寧、憂心如酲、誰秉國成、不自爲政、卒勞百姓、

(7) 駕彼四牡、四牡項領、我瞻四方、蹙蹙靡所騁、

(8) 方茂爾惡、相爾矛矣、既夷既懌、如相醻矣、

(9) 昊天不平、我王不寧、不懲其心、覆怨其正、

pèi mîn pŏu gnîng. Iōu sīn jôu tch'êng, chouêi ping kouŏ tch'êng? Pŏu tzéu wêi tchéng (tchēng), tsŏu laô pĕ sing (sīng).

7. Kiá pèi séu meòu, séu meòu hiàng lìng. Ngò tchēn séu fāng, tsŏu tsŏu mì chòu tch'èng.

8. Fāng meóu èul ngŏ, siáng èul meôu i. Kî î kí ĭ, jôu siāng tch'eôu i.

9. Haò t'iēn pŏu p'îng, ngò wâng pŏu gnîng. Pŏu tch'êng k'î sîn, fòu iuén k'î tchéng (tchēng).

tranquillité. Dans mon chagrin j'éprouve comme le trouble de l'ivresse. Qui donc est à la tête des affaires? Il ne s'occupe pas lui-même de l'administration, et ne cesse de faire le malheur du peuple.

7. J'attelle mes quatre coursiers, mes quatre coursiers à forte encolure. Je parcours du regard toutes les contrées de l'univers. Elles sont toutes dans la détresse; il n'en est pas une où je puisse diriger ma course.

8. (Perturbateurs de l'ordre public), parfois votre fureur est à son comble, et je vous vois tourner vos lances les uns contre les autres. Quand vous êtes apaisés et contents, vous êtes ensemble comme des hommes qui s'offrent à boire réciproquement.

9. L'auguste ciel ne nous est plus propice comme il l'est aux autres hommes, et l'empereur n'a pas de repos. (Le grand maître In) au lieu de se corriger, s'irrite contre ceux qui lui donnent des avis.

non quiescat. Mœstus animus (perturbatus est) quasi ebrietate. Quis tenet imperii administrationem? Non ipse gerit res publicas, ad finem (i. e. semper) ærumnis afficit populum.

7. Jungo illos quatuor mares equos, quatuor mares magna cervice. Ego prospicio quatuor regiones; sunt in angustiis, non est locus ad quem vehar.

8. Modo ingentia sunt vestra odia; video vestras hastas. Postquam sedati estis et gaudentes, estis quasi invicem propinantes vinum.

9. Augustum cœlum non æque favet; noster imperator non quiete fruitur. (Summus magister In) non coercet suum animum; contra irascitur suis correctoribus.

(10) 家父作誦、以究王訩。式訛爾心、以畜萬邦。

正月

(1) 正月繁霜、我心憂傷。民之訛言、亦孔之將。念我獨兮、憂心京京。哀我小心、癙憂以痒。

(2) 父母生我、胡俾我瘉。不自我先、不自我後。好

10. Kiā Fòu tsŏ sóung (tsŏung) i kióu wâng hiōung. Chŏu wŏ éul sīn, i hiŭ wán pāng (pŏung).

TCHENG IUE. **1. Tchéng iuĕ fân chouāng, ngò sīn iōu chāng. Mîn tchēu wŏ iên, i k'òung tchēu tsiāng. Gniên ngò tŏu hî, iōu sīn kīng kīng (kāng kāng). Ngāi ngò siaò sīn, chòu iōu i iâng.**

2. Fóu móu chēng ngò, hôu pèi ngò iù? Pŏu tzéu ngò siēn, pŏu tzéu ngò heóu

10. Moi Kia Fou, j'ai composé ce chant pour mettre à nu le désordre de l'administration de l'empire. (Prince), changez de sentiments, et vous rendrez tous vos peuples heureux.

CHANT VIII. TCHENG IUE.

Un 大夫 **tái fōu** déplore les malheurs de l'État. L'empereur 幽王 **Iōu wâng** donne toute sa confiance à d'indignes officiers et à 褒姒 **Paō Séu**, sa favorite.

1. Au quatrième mois (au mois de mai ou de juin) la gelée blanche couvre la terre. (Cette anomalie est un châtiment du ciel); mon cœur est dans l'angoisse. La calomnie devient de plus en plus puissante. Quand je considère que personne autre que moi n'en a souci, mon inquiétude augmente encore beaucoup. Dans ma sollicitude je suis à plaindre; le chagrin dévore mon cœur et me rend malade.

2. Pourquoi mes parents m'ont-ils donné le jour dans ce temps d'affliction? Ces malheurs sont survenus juste dans le cours de ma

10. Kia Fou feci canticum ad eruendam imperatoris (administrationis) confusionem. (Rex), mutes tuum animum, ut pascas omnia regna.

CHANT VIII. 1. Quarto anni mense, multa pruina. Meus animus curis angitur. Hominum falsa dicta multum augentur. Cogitans me solum (de illis curare), anxius est animus vehementer. Miserandus est meus sollicitus animus; intimo mœrore angor, ita ut morbo tabescam.

Le quatrième mois de l'année, d'après le calendrier des 夏 **Hiá** et celui de la dynastie actuelle, correspond à notre mois de mai ou de juin. On l'appelait 正月 **tchéng iuĕ**, parce que c'est le moment où le principe 陽 **iâng**, qui est le principe de la chaleur, domine dans la nature.

2. Pater et mater gignentes me, quare fecerunt ut ego offenderem ærumnas?

詩經

言自口、莠言自口、憂心愈愈、是以有侮、

(3) 憂心惸惸、念我無祿、民之無辜、并其臣僕、哀我人斯、于何從祿、瞻烏爰止、于誰之屋、

(4) 瞻彼中林、侯薪侯蒸、民今方殆、視天夢夢、既克有定、靡人弗

(hòu). Haò iên tzéu k'eòu (k'òu), iòu iên tzéu k'eòu (k'òu). Iōu sīn iù iù, chéu i iòu òu.

3. Iōu sīn k'iôung k'iôung, gnién ngò ôu lōu. Mîn tchēu ôu kòu, ping k'î tch'ênn pòu. Ngāi ngò jênn sēu, iû hô ts'ôung lōu ? Tchēn ôu iuên tchèu, iû chouêi tchēu ôu.

4. Tchēn pèi tchōung lîn, heôu sīn heôu tchēng. Mîn kīn fāng tài, chéu t'iēn

vie, pas avant ni après. (A présent) les paroles louangeuses, comme les paroles de blâme, ne partent que des lèvres. Mon chagrin augmente de plus en plus, et m'attire des outrages.

3. Mon cœur est tourmenté par le chagrin; je pense à mon malheureux sort. Avec les citoyens innocents, je serai réduit à l'état de serviteur et d'esclave. Infortunés que nous sommes, de qui pouvons-nous attendre le salut? Je vois des corbeaux prêts à se poser; mais je ne sais sur quelle maison ils s'arrêteront. (De même je ne sais en qui mettre mon espoir).

4. Dans une forêt je distingue du gros bois et du menu bois. A présent le peuple est en péril, et voit le ciel ne faire aucune distinction (entre les bons et les méchants). Quand le ciel aura résolu de soumettre les hommes par la force, personne ne pourra lui

(Illæ ærumnæ ortæ sunt) non ex tempore me præcedente, neque ex tempore me subsequente. Laudatoria verba ex ore, obtrectationis verba ex ore (non ex animo prodeunt). Mœret animus magis ac magis; quapropter afficior contumelia.

3. Mœstus animus vehementer dolet; cogito de mea infelici fortuna. Cum civibus carentibus culpa, simul ipse minister ac servus ero. Miserandi sumus nos homines. A quo provenient bona? Observo corvos jam constituros; (observo) super cujusnam domum (constituri sint, nec possum conjectura assequi).

4. Aspicio illam mediam silvam, sunt et crassiora ligna et minutiora ramalia. Cives nunc jam periclitantur; vident cœlum non discernere (bonos et malos). Quando subigendi habuerit statutam voluntatem, non erit homo quem non superabit. Præditus majestate supremus dominus ille quem odio habet?

上帝天神也（詩經備旨）**Cháng ti t'iēn chênn iè.** Le souverain seigneur est l'esprit du ciel. 夫天豈有所憎而禍之乎福善禍淫

勝、有皇上帝、伊誰云憎、(5)謂山蓋卑、爲岡爲陵、民之訛言、寧莫之懲、召彼故老、訊之占夢、具曰予聖、誰知烏之雌雄、(6)謂天蓋高、不敢不局、謂地蓋厚、不敢不蹐、維號斯言、有倫有脊、哀今之人、胡

môung môung (mêng mêng). Kí k'ŏ iòu tíng, mi jênn fŏu chéng. Iòu houàng cháng ti, I chouêi iùn tsēng?

5. Wéi chān kài pēi, wêi kāng wêi lîng. Mîn tchēu wô iên, gnîng mouŏ tchēu tch'êng? Tchaò pèi kòu laò, sin tchēu tchên mòung (mêng). Kiŭ iuĕ: « Iù chéng. » Chouêi tchēu ōu tchēu ts'ēu hiôung (hêng)?

6. Wéi t'iēn kài kaŏ, pŏu kàn pŏu kiŭ (kĭ). Wéi ti kài heòu, pŏu kàn pŏu tsĭ.

résister. Ce suprême dominateur plein de majesté a-t-il de la haine contre quelqu'un?

5. (Les calomniateurs) disent (et voudraient faire croire) que les montagnes sont basses, tandis qu'elles ont des crêtes et des plateaux. Pourquoi personne ne met-il un frein à la calomnie? L'empereur fait venir les vieillards, ses vieux serviteurs; il interroge les interprètes des songes. Chacun lui répond: « Je suis sage. » Mais entre les corbeaux, qui peut distinguer le mâle de la femelle? (De même qui saurait discerner le vrai du faux dans les discours des hommes)?

6. Bien qu'on nous dise que le ciel est très élevé, nous n'osons ne pas nous tenir courbés. Bien qu'on nous assure que la terre est épaisse et solide, nous n'osons y marcher que très doucement. Cependant, ceux qui (l'affirment et) le proclament, le disent avec raison, avec fondement. Mais hélas! (nous ne pouvons plus nous fier au témoignage de personne); pourquoi les hommes à présent

亦自然之理而已 (朱熹集傳) **Fŏu t'iēn k'i iòu chòu tsēng èul houó tchēu hòu? Fŏu chén houó in, I tzéu jên tchēu li, èul i.** Est-ce que le ciel affligerait quelqu'un par motif de haine? Il protège les bons et afflige les méchants, comme la justice le demande, et voilà tout.

5. Dicunt montes humiles esse; sunt juga, sunt plana. Hominum fallaces sermones, quare nemo eos cohibet? (Imperator) arcessit illos veteres (ministros) senes; interrogat de illis (hominum sermonibus) interpretes somniorum. Omnes respondent: « Ego sum sapiens. » (Sed) quis discernat corvorum feminam et marem?

蓋 **Kái**, particule.

6. Licet dicatur cœlum sublime esse, non audemus non incurvare corpus. Licet dicatur terra esse crassa, non audemus non brevi passu incedere.

爲虺蜴。

(7) 瞻彼阪田、有菀其特。天之扤我、如不我克。彼求我則、如不我得。執我仇仇、亦不我力。

(8) 心之憂矣、如或結之。今茲之正、胡然厲矣。燎之方揚、寧或滅之。赫赫宗周、襃姒威之。

~~Chouèi~~ haǒ sēu iên, iòu liùn iòu tsï. Ngāi kīn tchēu jônn, hôu wêi houèi ĭ ?

7. Tchēn pèi fàn t'iên, iòu iŭ k'ì t'ĕ. T'iēn tchēu ǒu ngò, jôu pŏu ngò k'ŏ. Pèi k'iôu ngò tsĕ, jôu pŏu ngò tĕ. Tchĕu ngò k'iôu k'iôu, ĭ pŏu ngò lí.

8. Sīn tchēu iōu i, jôu houé kiĕ tchēu. Kīn tzēu tchēu tchéng, hôu jên li (liĕ) i ? Leaǒ tchēu fāng iâng, gning houĕ miĕ tchēu ? Hĕ hĕ tsōung Tcheōu, Paǒ Séu hiuĕ tchēu.

sont-ils (trompeurs et méchants) comme les serpents et les lézards?

7. Voyez ce champ semé d'aspérités; (malgré la pauvreté du sol) la moisson s'y dresse verdoyante. (Au contraire, malgré la bonté naturelle de son cœur), le ciel m'agite en tous sens, comme s'il n'avait pas la force de me renverser. Il a d'abord voulu faire de moi le modèle des peuples, et m'a cherché avec sollicitude comme s'il avait craint de ne pas me trouver. Ensuite il m'a saisi et traité en ennemi, et n'a plus voulu se servir de moi.

8. Mon cœur est dans l'angoisse, comme s'il était serré par un lien. Pourquoi le gouvernement actuel est-il si tyrannique? Lorsqu'un grand incendie est une fois allumé, qui peut l'éteindre? Pao Seu elle seule anéantira la grande capitale de la dynastie des Tcheou (la ville de Hao).

Attamen qui proclamant illa verba, nempe cœlum esse sublime et terram crassam, habent rationem, habent basim. (Sed) proh dolor! hujus temporis homines quare agunt ut angues et lacerti?

7. Aspice illum salebrosum agrum; est florens ejus arrecta (seges viridis). Cœlum exagitat me, quasi non me vincere valeret. Illud (cœlum initio) quæsivit me (ut essem populorum) exemplar, quasi non me assequi valeret. (Postea) tenuit me inimico modo, et non meam operam adhibuit.

天心本至仁反不愛人非理之難明者乎(詩經備旨)

T'iēn sīn pènn tchéu jênn, fàn pŏu ngái jênn. Fēi li tchēu nân mîng tchè hôu ? (Le poète dit): « Le cœur du ciel est par nature très bienfaisant; cependant il ne nous fait plus de bien. N'est-ce pas une chose dont la raison est difficile à comprendre? »

8. Cor angitur, ac si quis constringeret illud. Nunc hoc regimen quare est crudele? Incendium postquam cœpit assurgere, quomodo quis exstinguat illud? Majestate præstat præcipua Tcheou imperatorum urbs; Pao Seu exstinguet eam.

On appelait 宗周 tsōung Tcheōu

30

(9) 終其永懷、又窘陰雨、其車既載、乃棄爾輔、載輸爾載、將伯助予、

(10) 無棄爾輔、員于爾輻、屢顧爾僕、不輸爾載、終踰絕險、曾是不意、

(11) 魚在于沼、亦匪克樂、潛雖伏矣、亦孔之炤、憂

9. Tchōung k'î iòung houâi, iòu k'iùn În iù. K'î kiū ki tsái, nài k'î èul fòu. Tsái chōu èul tsái, ts'iāng pĕ tchóu iù (iu).

10. Oû k'i èul fòu, iùn iû èul fòu (pĭ). Liú kóu èul pŏu, pŏu chōu èul tsái (tsĭ). Tchōung iû tsiuĕ hièn, ts'êng chéu pŏu i (ĭ).

11. Iû tsái iū tchaò (tchŏ), ĭ fèi k'ŏ lŏ. Tsiên souēi fôu i, ĭ k'òung tchĕu tchŏ.

9. La crainte du dénouement me poursuit sans cesse ; la pluie et le mauvais temps causent un grand embarras (les chemins sont très mauvais, et le voyage, c.-à-d. le gouvernement de l'État, est extrêmement difficile). Votre voiture est chargée, (grand empereur), et vous rejetez les armatures des roues (les ministres sages). La charge de votre voiture tombera ; (alors vous irez partout demander du secours, et direz): « Je vous en prie, seigneur, aidez-moi. »

10. Si vous ne rejetiez pas les armatures qui doivent affermir les rais de vos roues, si vous surveilliez assidûment le conducteur de votre voiture, votre charge ne serait pas renversée. Vous franchiriez jusqu'à la fin les endroits les plus escarpés. Ces réflexions ne vous sont-elles pas encore venues à l'esprit ?

11. Un poisson (pris dans un fleuve ou dans un grand lac et) condamné à rester dans un bassin, n'y peut vivre joyeux. Il aura beau chercher à disparaître au fond de l'eau, il sera toujours parfaitement vu (parce qu'elle n'est pas profonde, et il sera facilement

principale ou première capitale des Tcheou la ville de 鎬 **Haò**, pour la distinguer de 洛陽 **Lŏ iàng**, qui était la seconde capitale. Voy. page 3.

La favorite de Iou wang s'appelait Seu. Elle était de la principauté de Pao.

9. De exitu semper cogito, et ad incitas redigunt nubes ac pluvia. Iste currus onustus est, et rejicis tua munimenta (rotarum). At cadente currus onere, (dices): « Quæso, domine, adjuva me. »

輔 **Fòu**, bâtons qu'on liait aux rais des roues pour les rendre plus solides.

10. Si non abjicias tua munimenta, quæ proderunt tuis rotarum radiis, et sæpe respicias tui currus ductorem, non subvertetur tui currus onus. Usque ad finem transibis maxime salebrosa. Hucusque de illis nonne cogitasti ?

11. Piscis (qui in amne lacuve captus est) manens in piscina, non potest gaudere. In imo mersus, licet latere (quærat), tamen valde translucebit

心慘慘、念國之爲虐、

(12) 彼有旨酒、又有嘉殽、洽比其鄰、昏姻孔云、念我獨兮、憂心慇慇、

(13) 佌佌彼有屋、蔌蔌方有穀、民今之無祿、天夭是椓、哿矣富人、哀此惸獨、

十月之交

(1) 十月之交、朔

Iōu sīn ts'àn ts'àn (ts'ŏ ts'ŏ), gnién kouŏ tchĕu wĕi iŏ.

12. Pèi iòu tchèu tsiòu, iòu iòu kiā hiaô. Hiă pi k'ì lîn, houēnn în k'òung iûn. Gnién ngò tŏu hì, iōu sīn în în.

13. Ts'èu ts'èu pèi iòu ŏu, sŏu sŏu fāng iòu kŏu. Mîn kīn tchēu ŏu lŏu, t'iēn iaŏ chéu tchouŏ (tŏu). Kŏ i fóu jênn, ngāi ts'èu k'iôung tŏu.

CHEU IUE TCHEU KIAO. **1. Chéu iuĕ tchēu kiaō, chouŏ jĕu sīn maò (meòu),**

repris. Tel est le sort du peuple). Mon cœur est accablé de tristesse, quand je pense à la tyrannie du gouvernement.

12. Ces vils favoris de l'empereur ont des vins exquis, des mets savoureux. Ils ont des réunions avec leurs voisins, des relations fréquentes avec leurs parents par alliance. Moi, je me vois seul, et mon cœur en éprouve une grande douleur.

13. Ces viles créatures ont des maisons ; ces homme abjects ont leurs émoluments. A présent le peuple est dépourvu de tout, et le ciel le frappe de ses calamités. Le sort du riche est encore supportable ; mais bien malheureux est le pauvre qui est délaissé.

CHANT IX. CHEU IUE TCHEU KIAO.

Un officier de l'empereur 幽王 **Iōu wâng** décrit les phénomènes effrayants qui se produisent dans le ciel et sur la terre et annoncent la chute de la dynastie. Il recherche les causes des désordres, et déclare sa résolution de rester à son poste et de remplir fidèlement son devoir.

1. A la conjonction du soleil et de la lune, le premier jour du

(nec vitabit retia). Mœstus animus dolore cruciatur, dum recordor in imperio adhibitam tyrannidem.

12. Illi (viles homines imperatori gratiosi) habent exquisitum vinum; insuper habent lautas dapes. Una conveniunt cum suis vicinis; affines crebro invicem conversantur. Cogitans me esse solum, mœret animus summo dolore.

云 **Iûn**, avoir des relations d'amitié.

13. Minutuli illi habent domos; viles præsto habent stipendia. Populus nunc caret opibus; cœlestibus calamitatibus is tunditur. Non incommode sunt dites homines; miserandi sunt hi inopes et soli.

CHANT IX. 1. Decimo mense lunari, conjunctione (habita solis et lunæ), primo lunaris mensis die, *sīn maò* vigesimo octavo cycli die, soli accidit ut (luna) obscuraret eum, et est valde

日 辛 卯、日 有 食 之、亦 孔 之 醜、彼 月 而 微、

jĕu iòu chĕu tchĕu, ĭ k'ùung tchĕu tch'eòu. Pèi iuĕ êul wêi, ts'èu jĕu êul wêi.

dixième mois lunaire, jour qui était le vingt-huitième du cycle, le soleil a été éclipsé, ce qui est de très mauvais augure. La lune

infausta res. Illa luna et deficit; hic sol et deficit. Nunc hi sub cœlo homines ideo maxime miserandi sunt.

Dans les Annales des T'ang 唐書志 **T'âng chŏu tchéu**, il est dit que cette éclipse arriva la sixième année de Iou wang (775 avant notre ère). Ici le dixième mois lunaire, au sentiment de Tchou Hi, est celui du calendrier des 夏 **Hiá**, qui faisaient commencer l'année à la deuxième néoménie après le solstice d'hiver, comme sous la dynastie actuelle. D'autres rapportent ce mois au calendrier des 周 **Tcheōu**, qui faisaient commencer l'année deux lunaisons plus tôt. Les astronomes ont calculé qu'une éclipse de soleil dût avoir lieu le 29 août de l'année 775 avant J.C.

Sur ce passage, 朱熹 **Tchōu Hī** dit: « Les astronomes divisent la sphère céleste en 365 度 **tóu** degrés 1/4. Le ciel tourne de gauche à droite autour de la terre. En un jour et une nuit, il accomplit 一周 **ī tcheōu** une révolution entière, augmentée d'un degré. Le soleil et la lune se meuvent l'un et l'autre dans le ciel. En un jour et une nuit, le soleil parcourt un degré, et la lune 13 degrés 7/19. Ainsi, le soleil emploie une année à faire un tour complet dans le ciel. La lune met vingt-neuf jours et plus.

« Elle est alors sur le même méridien que le soleil et en conjonction avec lui 會 **houéi**. En un an, cette conjonction se reproduit douze fois. Au moment même de la conjonction, la lune n'a plus de lumière et est entièrement obscure 晦 **houéi**. Après la conjonction, sa lumière renaît 復蘇 **feóu sōu**; une nouvelle lunaison commence 朔 **chouŏ**. Le quinzième jour de chaque lunaison, le soleil et la lune sont en face l'un de l'autre 相對 **siāng touéi**. Alors la lune est pleine 正滿 **tchéng màn**; les deux astres sont en opposition 望 **wáng**.

« A la fin d'une lunaison et au commencement de la suivante, le soleil et la lune ont la même longitude 東西同度 **tōung sī t'ôung tóu**. Lorsque de plus ils ont la même latitude 南北同道 **nân pĕ t'ôung taó**, la lune cache le soleil; le soleil est éclipsé 日爲之食 **jĕu wêi tchĕu chéu**. Au moment de l'opposition, le soleil et la lune sont en face l'un de l'autre. Lorsque de plus leur latitude est la même, la lune entre en lutte avec le soleil 月亢日 **iuĕ k'áng jĕu** et en est éclipsée 月爲之食 **iuĕ wêi tchĕu chéu**.

« Tous ces phénomènes sont soumis à des règles constantes. Cependant, lorsque l'empereur est vertueux et gouverne bien, lorsqu'il emploie les hommes sages et rejette les hommes vicieux, il peut faire prévaloir le principe 陽 **iâng** sur le principe 陰 **īn** (le soleil sur la lune). Le principe *in* étant affaibli, ne peut empiéter 侵 **ts'īn** sur le principe *iang*. Par suite, lors même que le soleil et la lune, en suivant leur marche régulière, devraient s'éclipser, la lune se tient toujours à l'écart du soleil 月常避日 **iuĕ tch'âng pi jĕu**. Elle

此日而微、今此下民、亦孔之哀、(2)日月告凶、不用其行、四國無政、不用其良、彼月而食、則維其常、此日

Kin ts'èu hiá mîn î k'òung tchēu ngāi (1).

2. Jéu iuĕ kaó hiōung, pŏu ióung k'î hîng (hâng). Séu kouŏ ôu tchéng, pŏu ióung k'î leâng. Pèi iuĕ êul chĕu, tsĕ wêi k'î châng. Ts'èu jĕu êul chĕu, iû hô pŏu tsāng ?

subit des éclipses, et le soleil aussi. A présent le sort des hommes ici-bas est bien à plaindre.

2. Le soleil et la lune annoncent des malheurs ; ils s'écartent des principes qui doivent les diriger. C'est que l'empire est mal gouverné, et les hommes de bien exclus des charges. Que la lune soit éclipsée, ce n'est pas un grave désordre. Mais quand le soleil

accélère ou retarde sa marche, monte ou descend, de manière à ne se trouver jamais juste sur le soleil ou en face de lui. Ainsi, lors même qu'une éclipse devrait se produire, elle n'a pas lieu.

« Quand le gouvernement est mal réglé et les hommes vertueux exclus des charges, le sujet résiste à son prince et le fils à son père ; la femme commande à son mari ; les inférieurs sont arrogants envers leurs supérieurs ; les barbares envahissent l'empire. Alors le principe *in* devient très puissant, et le principe *iâng* très faible. Lorsqu'une éclipse doit avoir lieu, elle arrive infailliblement. 雖日行有常度而實爲非常之變矣 **Souēi iuĕ hîng iòu tch'âng tóu, êul chĕu wêi fēi tch'âng tchēu pién i.** Bien qu'elle résulte du cours ordinaire des astres, elle n'en est pas moins une perturbation vraiment extraordinaire. » 朱公遷 **Tchōu kōung Ts'iēn** dit : 以數言之則其常以理言之則其變矣 **I chóu iên tchēu, tsĕ k'î tch'âng ; i lì iên tchēu, tsĕ k'î pién i.** Au point de vue des lois astronomiques, c'est un phénomène régulier ; au point de vue de la raison ou du devoir, c'est un désordre.

2. Sol et luna nuntiant infausta, non utentes suis viis. Universum imperium caret regimine, non adhibitis ejus idoneis viris. Quum illa luna obscuratur, tunc tantummodo est illius lex. Quum hic sol ipse deficit, (quærendum est) in quo futura sit infelicitas.

« Toutes les fois qu'il arrive une éclipse de soleil ou de lune, dit Tchou Hi, ces deux astres suivent leur cours régulier ; et cependant ils sont censés ne pas obéir aux principes qui doivent les régir. La lune, en ne se tenant pas à l'écart du soleil, manque à son devoir. Ce désordre provient de ce que l'empire est mal gouverné et les hommes de bien laissés dans la vie privée. Ainsi, les éclipses de soleil et de lune sont toutes contraires aux principes. Cependant une éclipse de lune n'est pas une perturbation extraordinaire ; mais une éclipse de soleil annonce un grand malheur. Que le principe 陰 **in** luttant contre le principe 陽 **iâng**, ait le désavantage, cela s'explique. Mais que le principe *in* l'emporte sur le principe

而食、于何不臧。(3) 爗爗震電、不寧不令、百川沸騰、山冢崒崩、高岸爲谷、深谷爲陵、哀今之人、胡憯莫懲、(4) 皇父卿士、番維司徒、家伯冢宰、仲允膳夫、聚子內史、蹶維趣馬、楀維師氏、豔妻煽方處、

3. Iĕ iĕ tchénn tién, pŏu gnîng pŏu lìng (lîng). Pĕ tch'ouēn féi t'êng, chān tchòung ts'ŏu pēng. Kaō ngán wêi kŏu, chēnn kŏu wêi lìng. Ngāi kīn tchēu jénn, hôu ts'àn mouŏ tch'êng ?

4. Houâng fòu k'īng chéu, Fān wêi sēu t'ôu. Kiā pĕ tchòung tsài, Tchóung iùn chén fōu. Tcheōu tzèu néi chéu, Kouéi wêi ts'eòu mà (mòu). Kiù wêi chēu chéu, ién ts'ī chén fāng tch'òu.

est éclipsé, (on doit se demander) quel malheur est sur le point d'arriver.

3. Il tonne, il éclaire, le ciel paraît tout embrasé; il n'est ni tranquillité ni bonheur. Tous les cours d'eau bouillonnent et débordent; les rochers les plus élevés tombent de la cime des montagnes. Les bords escarpés des montagnes et des fleuves sont remplacés par des vallées, et les vallées profondes par des collines. Hélas ! pourquoi personne à présent ne réforme-t-il l'administration ?

4. Houang fou est président des ministres d'État, Fan ministre de l'instruction, Kia pe premier ministre, Tchoung iun grand maître d'hôtel, Tcheou tzeu ministre de l'intérieur et de la justice, Kouei intendant des écuries, Kiu censeur impérial. Une femme d'une grande beauté, nouvellement élevée au rang d'impératrice, attise la discorde.

iâng et parvienne à l'éclipser, c'est un prodige inexplicable. Aussi Confucius dans les Annales de Lou a toujours signalé les éclipses de soleil, et n'a pas noté les éclipses de lune. »

3. Ingenti scintillatione tonat et fulgurat; nec quies nec felicitas. Omnia flumina ebullientia assurgunt; ex montium cacumine praecelsa saxa ruunt. Altæ oræ fiunt valles; profundæ valles fiunt colles. Eheu! inter hujus ætatis homines quare adhuc nullus corrigit (administrationem)?

4. Houang fou est regni ministrorum præpositus; Fan est præpositus multitudinis, i.e. præest populi institutioni. Kia pe est summus administrator, Tchoung iun culinæ præpositus. Tcheou tzeu est internus scriptor (muniorum et legum). Kouei est curator equorum; Kiu est censor dominus. Formosa uxor (Pao Seu) incendium excitat, nuper constituta (imperatoris uxor præcipua).

Le 內史 faisait observer les lois concernant les dignités, la peine capitale, les récompenses et le retrait des faveurs.

詩經

(5) 抑此皇父、豈曰不時、胡爲我作、不卽我謀、徹我牆屋、田卒汙萊、曰予不戕、禮則然矣、

(6) 皇父孔聖、作都于向、擇三有事、亶侯多藏、不憖遺一老、俾守我王、擇有車馬、以居徂向、

(7) 黽勉從事、不

5. Ĭ ts'éu Houâng fòu, k'i iuĕ pŏu chêu ? Hôu wêi ngò tsŏ, pŏu tsĭ ngò meôu (mêi) ? Tch'ĕ ngò ts'iâng ŏu, t'iên tsŏu ŏu lâi (lî). Iuĕ : « Iû pŏu ts'iâng, li tsĕ jên i (ĭ).

6. Houâng fòu k'òung chéng, tsŏ tōu iû Cháng. Tchĕ sān iòu chéu, tàn heóu touŏ tsáng. Pŏu in i ĭ laò, pèi cheòu ngò wâng (wáng). Tchĕ iòu kiū mà, i kiū ts'ôu Cháng.

7. Min mièn ts'ôung chéu, pŏu kàn kaó laŏ. Oû tsouéi ŏu kōu, tch'àn k'eòu

5. Ce Houang fou voudrait-il jamais reconnaitre que ses ordres sont intempestifs? Pourquoi nous envoie-t-il au loin (faire des expéditions ou des corvées), sans avoir délibéré avec nous? Il nous oblige à quitter nos maisons; nos champs restent tout couverts d'eau stagnante ou de mauvaises herbes. Il dit: « Je ne vous fais aucun tort; vous devez ce service (à l'empereur). »

6. Houang fou est (ou se croit) très perspicace. Il a bâti pour lui-même une grande ville dans la terre de *Chang* (qui fait partie du domaine propre de l'empereur). Il y a constitué trois ministres choisis parmi les habitants les plus riches, et n'a pu se résoudre à laisser un seul des anciens ministres pour garder notre empereur. Il a contraint ceux qui possédaient des voitures et des chevaux d'aller demeurer à Chang.

7. Je continue mon service avec grande fatigue, et n'ose

5. Iste Houang fou quomodo fateretur se non tempestive (jussa dare)? Qua de causa nos movet, nec adit nos deliberaturus? Aufert nobis parietes ac domos; agri toti sunt aquis submersi herbisve obsiti. Dicit: « Ego non injuriam infero; obsequium (imperatori debitum) hujusmodi est. »

抑 **Ĭ**, particule.

6. Houang fou est valde perspicax; constituit magnam urbem in Chang. Selegit tres curatores rerum, vere quidem multa recondita (habentes); nec se cohibens reliquit unum antiquum regni ministrum, ut custodiret nostrum imperatorem. Elegit habentes currus et equos, ut habitaturi irent in Chang.

Les lois permettaient à Houang fou d'avoir deux 有事 **iòu chéu** ou 卿 **k'ing**. Seuls les 諸侯 **tchōu heôu** pouvaient en avoir trois.

7. Magno conatu prosequor rem, nec audeo monere de laboribus

敢告勞、無罪無辜、讒口囂囂、下民之孽、匪降自天、噂沓背憎、職競由人、

(8) 悠悠我里、亦孔之痗、四方有羨、我獨居憂、民莫不逸、我獨不敢休、天命不徹、我不敢傚、我友自逸、

雨無正

(1) 浩浩昊天、不

ngaô ngaô. Hiá min tchēu iĕ, fèi kiáng tzéu t'iēn (t'în). Tsuènn tă péi tsēng, tchĕu kíng iòu jênn.

8. Iôu iôu ngò li, ĭ k'òung tchēu méi (houéi). Séu fāng iòu sién, ngò tŏu kiū iōu. Min mouŏ pŏu ĭ, ngò tŏu pŏu kàn hiōu. T'iēn míng pŏu tch'ĕ ; ngò pŏu kàn hiaó, ngò iòu tzéu ĭ.

IU OU TCHENG. 1. Haò haò haò t'iēn, pŏu tsiún k'ì tĕ. Kiáng sáng kī kín,

demander mon congé. Je ne suis coupable d'aucun crime, d'aucune faute, et cependant les mauvaises langues font grand vacarme. Ce n'est pas le ciel qui envoie des malheurs à la terre. Lorsque les détracteurs sont en face de nous, ils ne tarissent pas d'éloges, et en secret ils nous poursuivent de leur haine. Les principaux auteurs de nos souffrances sont les hommes.

8. Je suis très inquiet pour mon village; il est dans la plus grande affliction. Partout règne l'aisance; seul je suis dans la gêne. Personne n'est privé de tout agrément; seul je n'ose prendre un peu de repos. Le ciel ne fait pas les parts égales, (nous devons tous acquiescer à ses décrets). Je n'ose imiter mes amis, qui s'accordent des jouissances.

CHANT X. IU OU TCHENG.

Sous le règne de 厲王 Li wâng ou de 幽王 Iôu wâng, l'empire est mal gouverné et la disette est grande. Beaucoup d'officiers ont quitté la cour. Les autres qui sont restés, les engagent à revenir.

1. L'auguste ciel, qui est si grand, ne déploie pas une grande

(et rogare dimissionem). Careo scelere, careo culpa; maledicæ linguæ confuse clamant. Sub cœlo hominum calamitates non descendunt e cœlo. (Obtrectatores coram) multum loquuntur, a tergo odio prosequuntur; præcipua vis exseritur ab hominibus.

8. Valde anxius sum de meo pago, etenim vehementer laborat. In quatuor regionibus sunt superflua; ego solus maneo in angustiis. Hominum nullus non se oblectat; ego solus non audeo quiescere. Cœli providentia non coæquat sortes. Ego non audeo imitari meos amicos sese oblectantes.

CHANT X. 1. Immensum est augustum cœlum, nec ample exserit suam beneficentiam. Demittit funera, frugum

駿其德、降喪饑饉、斬伐四國、昊天疾威、弗慮弗圖、舍彼有罪、既伏其辜、若此無罪、淪胥以鋪。

(2) 周宗既滅、靡所止戾、正大夫離居、莫知我勩、三事大夫、莫肯夙夜、邦君諸侯、莫肯朝夕、庶曰式臧、覆出爲惡、

tchàn fā séu kouŏ (ĭ). Mîn t'iēn tsĭ wēi, fŏu liú fŏu t'ŏu. Chè pèi iòu tsouéi, kí fŏu k'ī kōu. Jŏ ts'èu ôu tsouéi, liûn siū i p'ōu.

2. Tcheōu tsōung kí miĕ, mì chòu tchèu lí. Tchéng tái fōu lì kiū, mouŏ tchēu ngò i. Sān chéu tái fōu, mouŏ k'èng sŏu ié (iŏ). Pāng kiūn tchōu heôu, mouŏ k'èng tchaō sĭ (siŏ). Chóu iuē chēu tsāng ; fŏu tch'ōu wêi ngŏ.

bienfaisance. Il envoie la mort et la famine exercer partout leurs ravages et trancher la vie des hommes. Le ciel, qui est si miséricordieux, use d'une rigoureuse sévérité, sans tenir compte d'aucune considération. Qu'il ait rejeté (et livré à la mort) les coupables, (c'est justice); ils ont porté la peine de leurs crimes. Mais pourquoi sur toute l'étendue de l'empire les innocents sont-ils enveloppés dans la même condamnation?

2. Déjà la dynastie des Tcheou s'éteint; le trouble n'aura pas de limite. Les grands préfets qui dirigeaient les officiers, sont allés demeurer loin de la capitale; aucun d'eux ne connaît nos souffrances. Parmi les trois principaux ministres d'État et les grands préfets (qui sont restés), aucun ne veut se lever matin ni se coucher tard (pour vaquer aux affaires). Aucun prince feudataire ne veut aller à la cour impériale le matin ni le soir. Oh! si l'empereur se mettait à faire le bien! Au contraire, il fait le mal de plus en plus.

carentiam, olerum carentiam; abscindit et perimit quatuor regionum homines. Misericors cœlum dire sævit, nec cogitat nec meditatur. Abjecit illos habentes scelera; subierunt suas pœnas. Quod attinet ad hos carentes culpa, (quare demerguntur simul, ita ut universi (pereant)?

2. Tcheou prosapia jam exstinguitur; non est ubi (perturbatio) sistens maneat. (Magistratuum duces majores præfecti reliquerunt (urbem præcipuam et alibi) habitant; (eorum) nemo noscit nostros labores. Inter tres summos ministros et majores præfectos nullus vult mature (surgere) ac sero (cubare). Inter regnorum rectores regulos nullus vult mane et vespere (adire imperatorem). Utinam dicatur (imperator) agere bonum! contra progreditur faciens malum.

三事 **Sān chéu** ou 三公 **Sān kōung**, les trois grands ministres d'État à la cour de l'empereur. Se présenter à l'empereur le matin, se dit 朝 **tchaō**; le soir, se dit 夕 **sĭ**.

31

(3) 如何昊天、辟言不信、如彼行邁、則靡所臻、凡百君子、各敬爾身、胡不相畏、不畏于天、

(4) 戎成不退、饑成不遂、曾我暬御、憯憯日瘁、凡百君子、莫肯用訊、聽言則答、譖言則退、

(5) 哀哉不能言、匪舌是出、維躬

3. Jôu hô haó t'iēn (t'īn), pī iên pŏu sin (sīn)? Jôu pèi hing mái, tsĕ mi chòu tchēnn. Fân pĕ kiūn tzèu, kŏ king èul chēnn. Hôu pŏu siāng wéi, pŏu wéi iū t'iēn (t'īn)?

4. Jôung tch'êng pŏu t'ouéi, kī tch'êng pŏu souéi. Ts'êng ngò siĕ iú, ts'àn ts'àn jĕu tsouéi. Fân pĕ kiūn tzèu, mouŏ k'èng ióung sin (souéi). T'īng iên tsĕ tă, tchénn iên tsĕ t'ouéi.

5. Ngāi tsāi pŏu nêng iên ; féi chĕ chéu tch'ouéi, wêi kōung chéu tsouéi. Kò

3. Auguste ciel, comment ce prince refuse-t-il d'entendre ceux qui lui rappellent les lois? Il est comme un voyageur qui avance toujours sans savoir où il s'arrêtera. O vous tous qui exercez des charges, veillez chacun sur vous-mêmes. Pourquoi ne vous respectez-vous pas les uns les autres, et ne respectez-vous pas le ciel?

4. La guerre a éclaté; l'empereur n'a pas fait un pas en arrière (dans la voie du mal). La famine a sévi; il n'a pas fait un pas en avant (dans la voie du bien). Moi qui n'ai jamais été qu'un serviteur de la chambre impériale, j'en suis malade de chagrin. Parmi les officiers de tout grade, aucun ne veut donner d'avis à l'empereur. Lorsqu'il (les interroge et) désire les entendre, ils se contentent de répondre à ses questions. Mais dès qu'ils sont en butte à la calomnie, ils se retirent loin de la cour.

5. Malheur aux avis (sincères) qu'il n'est pas permis de donner! Non seulement ils sont inutiles, mais ils sont nuisibles à celui

3. Quomodo, augustum cœlum, legum verba non admittit (imperator)? Similis est alicui iter facienti, progredienti, at non habenti quo perveniat. Omnes varii magistratus, singuli attendatis vobis ipsis. Quare non invicem veremini, nec veremini cœlum?

4. Bello facto, non recessit (imperator a prava via); fame facta, non progressus est (in bonam viam). Hucusque ego familiaris minister, gravi mœrore æger sum. Inter omnes varios magistratus nullus vult adhibere monitionem. (Quum imperator interrogat et) aurem præbet verbis, tunc respondent. Maledicis verbis (eos attingentibus), tunc recedunt (ab imperatoris aula).

5. Male est non licitis verbis. Non (tantum frustra) lingua ea profert; sed ipse (ille qui ea loquitur) inde grave patitur damnum. Bene est licitis verbis. Callida verba sicut flumen; faciunt ut

是瘁。哿矣能言、巧言如流、俾躬處休。

(6) 維曰于仕、孔棘且殆。云不可使、得罪于天子。亦云可使、怨及朋友。

(7) 謂爾遷于王都、曰予未有室家。鼠思泣血、無言不疾。昔爾出居、誰從作爾室。

i néng iên ; k'iaò iên jôu liôu, pèi kōung tch'òu hiōu.

6. Wèi iuě : « Iû chéu. » K'òung kĭ ts'iè tài (i). Iûn pŏu k'ò chéu, tĕ tsouéi iū t'iēn tzéu (tsi). Ĭ iûn k'ò chéu, iuén kĭ p'êng iòu (i).

7. Wéi èul ts'iēn iū wâng tōu, iuĕ : « Iû wéi iòu chĕu kiā (kōu). » Chòu séu k'ĭ hiuĕ (hĭ), ôu iên pŏu tsĭ. Sĭ èul tch'ŏu kiū, chouêi ts'ôung tsŏ èul chĕu ?

qui les donne. Heureux est le sort des discours qu'il est permis de faire entendre. Un langage artificieux est comme un cours d'eau (qui ne rencontre pas d'obstacle); il assure un bonheur constant à celui qui le tient.

6. La plupart des hommes disent: «Exercez des charges.» (Ils ne savent pas qu') elles ont des épines et des périls. Si vous donnez un conseil que l'empereur ne croie pas devoir suivre, vous offenserez le Fils du ciel. Si vous donnez un (mauvais) conseil qu'il approuve, vous exciterez l'indignation de vos amis (qui sont hommes de bien).

7. (Vous tous qui êtes allés loin d'ici), je vous engage à revenir à la capitale de l'empire. Vous me répondez: «Nous n'y possédons pas de maisons.» Vous versez des larmes de sang, et ne dites pas une parole qui n'exprime la douleur. Mais autrefois, quand vous êtes partis pour habiter une terre lointaine, qui vous a suivis pour vous y construire des maisons?

ipse (ille qui ea loquitur) constantibus fruatur commodis.

Les trois premiers vers peuvent se traduire ainsi: «Malheur aux avis qu'il n'est pas permis de donner, et qui ne partent pas seulement des lèvres, (mais du cœur)! Ils sont nusibles à celui qui les donne.»

6. (Homines multi) solummodo dicunt: «Adeatis publica munia.» (Nesciunt ea esse) valde spinosa, imo periculosa. (Qui consilium proponit quod imperator) dicit non esse adhibendum, habet offensionem apud Cœli filium. Et (qui consilium proponit quod imperator) dicit esse adhibendum, ira attingit (i.e. movet) socios et amicos (ejus).

7. Hortor vos ut remeetis in imperatoris urbem præcipuam. Respondetis: «Nos non habemus ædes ac domos (in urbe præcipua).» Mœste cogitabundi lacrymatis sanguinem; nihil dicitis quod non dolorem significet. Olim vobis emigrantibus ut habitaretis (in longinqua regione), quis comitatus est ut exstrueret vobis ædes?

小旻之什二之五

小旻

(1) 旻天疾威、敷于下土、謀猶回遹、何日斯沮、謀臧不從、不臧覆用、我視謀猶、亦孔之邛、

(2) 潝潝訿訿、亦孔之哀、謀之其臧、則具是違、謀之不臧、則具是依、我視謀猶、伊

SIAO MIN. 1. **Mìn t'iēn tsī wēi, fōu iū hiá t'òu. Meôu iôu houéi iŭ, hô jĕu sēu tsiù? Meôu tsāng pŏu ts'ôung, pòu tsāng fŏu ióung (iôung). Ngò chéu meôu iôu, ĭ k'òung tchēu k'iôung.**

2. Hī hĭ tzèu tzèu, ĭ k'òung tchēu ngāi (ī). Meôu tchēu k'ī tsāng, tsĕ kiú chéu wêi. Meôu tchēu pŏu tsáng, tsĕ kiú chéu ī. Ngò chéu meôu iôu, ĭ iū hôu ti (tī).

LIVRE V. SIAO MIN.

CHANT I. SIAO MIN.

Un 大夫 tái fōu grand préfet déplore l'aveuglement de l'empereur, qui donne toute sa confiance à d'indignes conseillers et prend de mauvaises décisions.

1. Le ciel, élevé à des hauteurs inaccessibles, exerce sa sévérité et répand la terreur sur la terre. Quand viendra le jour où les mauvais conseils et les mauvaises décisions n'auront plus cours? Les bons conseils ne sont pas suivis, les mauvais sont mis à exécution. Quand je considère ces conseils et ces décisions, j'éprouve la plus vive douleur.

2. (Quand les conseillers de l'empereur sont en face les uns des autres), ils sont de parfait accord, (mais en secret) ils se dénigrent réciproquement; c'est vraiment lamentable. Si un avis est bon, ils le rejettent tous; s'il est mauvais, ils y adhèrent tous. Quand je

TITRE DU LIVRE. 小旻之什二之五 Siao (ia) Min decas: (Cheu king) secundæ (partis) quintus liber. Dans les quatre titres 小旻 Siaò Mìn, 小宛 Siaò Iuèn, 小弁 Siaò P'ân, 小明 Siaò Mîng, le mot 小 marque que les quatre chants ainsi intitulés font partie du 小雅 Siaò ià, et sert à les distinguer des chants intitulés 召旻 Chaó Mìn, 大明 Tá Mîng, qui font partie du 大雅 Tá ià, et de deux autres chants qui sont perdus, et dont les titres contenaient les lettres 宛 iuèn et 弁 p'ân. 小旻 équivaut à 小雅之旻.

CHANT I. 1. Reconditi dissitique cœli acerba severitas diffunditur in subjectam terram. Consilia ac destinata prava et obliqua quo die tandem desinent? Consilia bona non sequitur (imperator; mala contra adhibet. Ego videns consilia et destinata, vehementer doleo.

2. (Imperatoris consiliarii coram) inter se consentiunt, (a tergo) invicem obloquuntur; et valde dolendum est. Ex consiliis, quæ bona sunt statim omnes ea aversantur; ex consiliis, quæ non

于胡底。

(3) 我龜既厭、不我告猶。謀夫孔多、是用不集。發言盈庭、誰敢執其咎、如匪行邁謀、是用不得于道。

(4) 哀哉為猶、匪先民是程、匪大猶是經。維邇言是聽、維邇言是爭、如彼築室于道謀、是用不潰于成。

3. Ngò kouēi ki iên, pŏu ngò kaó iôu (ióu). Meôu fōu k'òung touō, chéu ióung pŏu tsĭ (tsióu). Fă iên îng t'îng, chouêi kàn tchĕu k'ì kióu? Jôu fèi hîng mái meôu, chéu ióung pŏu tĕ iû taó (teóu).

4. Ngāi tsāi wêi iôu, fèi siēn mîn chéu tch'êng, fèi tá iôu chéu kīng. Wêi èul iên chéu t'īng, wêi èul iên chéu tchēng. Jôu pèi tchŏu chĕu iû taó meôu, chéu ióung pŏu houéi iû tch'êng.

considère ces conseils et ces décisions, (je me demande) où tout cela aboutira.

3. Nous avons fatigué nos tortues (à force de les consulter); elles ne veulent plus nous indiquer les décisions à prendre. Les conseillers sont extrêmement nombreux, et pour cette raison rien ne se fait. Leurs discours remplissent la grande cour du palais; mais qui oserait prendre sur lui la responsabilité de l'exécution? Ils sont comme des hommes qui délibéreraient sur un voyage sans faire un pas, et par suite n'avanceraient pas en chemin.

4. Ils prennent leurs décisions d'une manière déplorable; ils n'imitent pas les anciens sages, et ne suivent pas les grands principes. Ils n'écoutent que les discours et ne discutent que les opinions de ceux qui les entourent. Ils sont comme un homme qui, pour bâtir une maison, délibérerait avec tous les passants, et par suite n'avancerait pas en besogne.

bona sunt statim omnes iis adhærent. Ego videns consilia ac destinata, (quæro) ea ad quid perventura sint.

3. Nostræ testudines sunt fatigatæ, non nos monent statuenda. Deliberantes homines quam plurimi sunt; quapropter nihil conficitur. Prolata verba implent aulam palatii; quis audet sumere illius culpam, i. e. culpam quæ tribuetur si res proposita infeliciter cedat? Similes sunt hominibus qui non incedentes (nec) gradientes deliberant, adeoque non proficiunt in via.

4. Miserabiliter ineunt rationes; non antiquos viros illi imitantur, non magna instituta illi sequuntur. Solummodo proxime dicta illi audiunt; solummodo de proxime dictis illi disputant. Similes sunt ei qui exstructurus domum, in via (cum prætereuntibus) deliberat, quapropter non procedit in perficiendo opere.

(5) 國雖靡止、或聖或否、民雖靡膴、或哲或謀、或肅或艾、如彼泉流、無淪胥以敗、

(6) 不敢暴虎、不敢馮河、人知其一、莫知其他、戰戰兢兢、如臨深淵、如履薄冰、

小宛

(1) 宛彼鳴鳩、翰飛戾天、我心憂

5. Kouŏ souēi mi tchèu, houĕ chéng houĕ feòu (pèi). Min souēi mi hōu, houĕ tchĕ houĕ meôu (môu), houĕ siŭ houĕ i. Jôu pèi ts'iuên liôu, ôu liûn siū i pái (péi).

6. Pŏu kàn paó hòu, pŏu kàn p'ing hô. Jênn tchēu k'i ĭ, mouŏ tchēu k'i t'ouŏ. Tchén tchén kīng kīng, jôu lin chēnn iuēn (iūn), jôu li pouŏ pīng.

SIAO IUEN. **1. Iuèn pèi ming kiōu, hán fēi li t'iēn (t'īn). Ngò sīn iōu chāng,**

5. Bien que les conseillers de la cour soient sans cesse flottants, quelques-uns d'entre eux sont perspicaces. Bien que la population soit peu nombreuse, on trouve encore des hommes prudents, des hommes de bon conseil, des hommes d'un maintien grave, des hommes capables de gouverner. Mais, semblables à une source qui coule toujours, ne courons-nous pas tous ensemble à notre perte?

8. Il serait très téméraire d'attaquer un tigre (sans avoir aucune arme) ou de traverser le Fleuve-Jaune en marchant sur l'eau. L'empereur et ses conseillers le comprennent; mais il est une autre chose qu'ils ne comprennent pas, (à savoir, le péril de l'empire). Je tremble de peur et prends garde à moi, comme si je mettais le pied sur le bord d'un gouffre profond ou marchais sur une glace très mince.

CHANT II. SIAO IUEN.

Un grand préfet, à une époque de trouble, engage ses frères à remplir fidèlement leurs devoirs, à pratiquer constamment la vertu, à veiller avec soin sur eux-mêmes.

1. Le pigeon ramier est petit; dans son vol il s'élève jusqu'au ciel. (Un grand courage surmonte toutes les difficultés). Mon cœur

5. In aula regia licet (consiliarii) non consistant, alii sunt perspicaces, alii non. Incolæ licet non multi sint, quidam sunt prudentes, quidam pleni consilii, quidam habitu graves, quidam ad regendum apti. Similes sumus illi fonti defluenti; nonne devolvimur simul in ruinam?

8. Non audendum est apprehendere tigridem (sine armis), nec audendum est insistere Fluvio (sine cymba). Homines (imperator ejusque ministri) intelligunt illud unum; (eorum) nullus intelligit illud aliud, nempe reipublicæ pericula. Timens tremo ac sollicite caveo, quasi accedens ad altam voraginem, quasi calcans tenuem glaciem.

CHANT II. 1. Parva est illa gemens

傷、念昔先人、明發不寐、有懷二人、

(2) 人之齊聖、飲酒溫克、彼昏不知、壹醉日富、各敬爾儀、天命不又、

(3) 中原有菽、庶民采之、螟蛉有子、蜾蠃負之、教誨爾子、式穀似之、

(4) 題彼脊令、

gnién sī siēn jênn. Mîng fă pŏu méi, iòu houâi éul jênn.

2. Jênn tchēu ts'î chéng, in tsiòu wēnn k'ŏ. Péi houēnn pŏu tchēu, ĭ tsouéi jĕu fóu (pĭ). Kŏ king éul î, t'iēn ming pŏu ióu (ĭ).

3. Tchōung iuên iòu chŏu, chóu mîn ts'ài (ts'i) tchēu. Mîng lîng iòu tzèu, kouò louò fóu (péi) tchēu. Kiaō houéi éul tzèu, chéu kŏu séu (i) tchēu.

4. Ti péi tsī ling, tsái fēi tsái mîng. Ngò jĕu sēu mài, éul iuĕ sēu tchēng. Sŏu

est blessé par la douleur; je pense à mes parents défunts. Au point du jour, quand je ne puis dormir, je me rappelle le souvenir de mon père et de ma mère.

2. Un homme grave et sage, lorsqu'il boit du vin, se modère et reste maître de lui-même. Il est des hommes aveugles et dépourvus d'intelligence qui se plongent dans l'ivresse chaque jour de plus en plus. Ayez soin de garder votre gravité; les dons du ciel (une fois perdus) ne peuvent être recouvrés.

3. Dans la plaine croissent des haricots, et tout le monde en cueille. (Ainsi tout homme peut et doit pratiquer la vertu). La chenille du mûrier a des petits; la guêpe les transporte (dans son trou et leur donne ses soins; au bout de sept jours, ils sont changés en petites guêpes). Enseignez, instruisez vos enfants; vertueux vous-mêmes, vous les rendrez vertueux comme vous.

4. Voyez la bergeronnette; elle chante en volant (elle fait deux

palumbes; pennis volans attingit cœlum. Meus animus mœrore dolet; reminiscor olim (viventes) prædecessores homines, i.e. parentes nunc mortuos. Die oriente non dormiens, habeo memoriam duorum hominum, nempe patris et matris.

Le titre 小宛 **Siaò iuèn** équivaut à 小雅之宛 **Siaò ià tchēu iuèn**, Chant luen qui est compris dans la partie du Cheu king intitulée Siao ia. V. p. 244.

2. Homines graves et perspicaces, quum bibunt vinum, se moderantes cohibent. Illi obcæcati non intelligunt; toti sunt ebriositati in dies copiosius. Singuli invigilate vestræ gravitati; cœli dona non iterantur, i.e. animis inditæ virtutes, semel amissæ, non redduntur.

3. In planitie sunt phaseoli; totus populus decerpit eos. Mori eruca habet natos; vespa dorso portat eos. Docentes erudite vestros liberos; utentes virtute, i.e. ipsi colentes virtutem, (vobis) similes facietis eos.

4. Aspicite illam motacillam, simul volat et cantat. Ego in diem quidem

載飛載鳴、我日斯邁、而月斯征、夙興夜寐、無忝爾所生、

(5) 交交桑扈、率場啄粟、哀我塡寡、宜岸宜獄、握粟出卜、自何能穀、

(6) 温温恭人、如集于木、惴惴小心、如臨于谷、戰戰兢兢、如履薄冰、

hīng ié méi, ôu t'ièn êul chòu chēng.

5. Kiaō kiaō sāng hòu, chouĕ tch'âng tchouŏ siŭ. Ngāi ngò tiēn kouà, î ngàn î iŭ. Iŏ siŭ tch'ŏu pŏu, tzéu hô nêng kŏu.

6. Wēnn wēnn kōung jênn, jôu tsĭ iŭ mŏu. Tchouéi tchouéi siaò sīn, jôu lìn iŭ kŏu. Tchén tchén kīng kīng, jôu li pouŏ pīng.

choses à la fois, afin d'employer son temps le mieux possible). Je dois faire des progrès de jour en jour, et vous devez avancer de mois en mois. Levez-vous de bonne heure et couchez-vous tard; ne déshonorez pas ceux qui vous ont donné le jour.

5. L'émérillon du mûrier (qui est un oiseau de proie) vole çà et là dans l'aire; (il est réduit à) manger du grain. (Ainsi) parmi nous les personnes faibles, les hommes veufs et les femmes veuves sont à plaindre; (au lieu de les secourir), on juge qu'il convient d'en remplir les prisons de la province et de la capitale. Je prends une poignée de grain, et vais consulter les sorts, pour savoir comment je pourrai pratiquer la vertu.

6. Soyons accommodants et respectueux, (craintifs) comme si nous étions perchés sur des arbres (et exposés à tomber). Soyons attentifs avec anxiété, comme si nous étions sur le bord escarpé d'une vallée profonde. Tremblons et prenons garde, comme si nous marchions sur une glace très mince.

progredi, vos in mensem proficere (debetis). Summo mane surgite, sero cubate; ne dedecore afficiatis eos a quibus vos nati estis.

5. Huc illuc volitans mori æsalon per totam aream comedit grana. Miserandi sunt nostri debiles ac solitarii (vidui et viduæ; videtur) æquum vicorum carceribus, urbis regiæ carceribus (eos addicere). Pugillum capiens granorum, exeo sortes consulturus, ex quo possim fieri bonus (ad cœli iram placandam).

6. Valde obsequenter reverentes homines simus, (timentes) quasi insideremus in arboribus (cum cadendi periculo). Anxii attento animo simus, quasi accedentes ad vallis (oram præruptam); trementes ac cauti, quasi calcantes tenuem glaciem.

小弁

(1) 弁彼鸒斯、歸
飛提提、民莫不
穀、我獨于罹、何
辜于天、我罪伊
何、心之憂矣、云
如之何、

(2) 踧踧周道、鞫
為茂草、我心憂
傷、惄焉如擣、假
寐永歎、維憂用
老、心之憂矣、疢
如疾首、

SIAO P'AN. 1. **P'ân pèi iú sēu, kouēi fēi chêu chêu. Mîn mouŏ pŏu kŏu, ngò tŏu iū li. Hô kōu iū t'iēn ? ngò tsouéi ī hô ? Sīn tchēu iōu i, iùn jôu tchēu hô ?**

2. Tí tí Tcheōu taò (teòu), kiŭ wêi meóu ts'aò (ts'eòu). Ngò sīn iōu chāng, gnǐ iên jôu taò (teòu). Kià méi ióung t'án, wêi iōu ióung laò (leòu). Sīn tchēu iōu i, tch'énn jôu tsǐ cheòu.

CHANT III. SIAO P'AN.

宜臼 **Î kióu**, fils aîné et héritier présomptif de l'empereur 幽王 **Iōu wâng**, déplore sa disgrâce et celle de sa mère. 褒姒 **Paō Séu**, femme de second rang, a supplanté l'impératrice; un fils de la favorite a été déclaré héritier de l'empire. I kiou et l'impératrice sa mère, princesse de 申 **Chēnn**, ont été relégués dans la principauté de ce nom (南陽府 **Nân iâng fòu** actuel, province de Honan).

1. Les corbeaux battent des ailes, et volant en troupe, retournent tranquillement à leur endroit habituel. Chacun jouit du bien-être; moi seul, je suis dans l'affliction. Quelle offense ai-je commise contre le ciel? quel crime est le mien? Mon cœur est triste; que dois-je faire?

2. La route de la capitale est unie et facile à parcourir. (Cependant, à cause des troubles, elle est presque déserte); elle est toute couverte d'herbes épaisses. Mon cœur, blessé par la douleur, souffre comme s'il était sous le pilon. Je me couche tout habillé et gémis sans cesse; le chagrin me fait vieillir avant le temps. Mon cœur est triste; j'éprouve comme des douleurs de tête.

CHANT III. 1. Plaudentibus alis illi corvi, ad stationem redeuntes, volant turmatim et tranquille. Incolarum nullus caret commodis; ego solus in ærumnis sum. Quodnam peccatum (mihi est) adversus cœlum? Meum scelus quodnam est? Animus mœret; quomodo (agam)?

鸒 Petit corbeau à ventre blanc. Avant de s'envoler, il bat des ailes 拊翼.

斯 **Sēu**, 伊 **Ī**, 云 **Iûn**, particules. Le titre 小弁 équivaut à 小雅之弁. Voy. page 244.

2. Plana et facilis est Tcheou urbis præcipuæ via; tota facta est vegetum gramen. Meum cor mœrore saucium, dolet quasi tunsum. Vestitus cubans semper gemo. Unice mœreo, ideo senui. Animus mœret; doleo quasi laborans capite.

(3) 維桑與梓。必恭敬止、靡瞻匪父、靡依匪母、不屬于毛、不離于裏、天之生我、我辰安在。

(4) 菀彼柳斯、鳴蜩嘒嘒。有漼者淵、萑葦淠淠、譬彼舟流、不知所屆、心之憂矣、不遑假寐。

(5) 鹿斯之奔、維足伎伎。雉之朝雊、尚求其雌、譬彼壞木、

3. Wèi sāng iù tzèu, pĭ kōung king tchèu. Mi tchēn fèi fòu, mi ī fèi mòu (mèi). Pŏu tchŏu iŭ maŏ, pŏu li iŭ li. T'iēn tchēu chēng ngò, ngò tch'ènn ngān tsài (tsi)?

4. Iŭ pèi liòu sēu, ming t'iaŏ houéi houéi. Iòu ts'ouéi tché iuēn, houân wèi p'i p'i. P'i pèi tcheŏu liŏu, pŏu tchēu chòu kiái (ki). Sīn tchēu iōu ī, pŏu houâng kià mèi.

5. Lŏu sēu tchēu pēnn, wèi tsiŭ k'ì k'i. Tchéu tchēu tchaŏ keòu, cháng k'iŏu

3. Un fils doit honorer et respecter même les mûriers et les catalpas (que son père a plantés). Il doit mettre tout son espoir en son père et tout son appui en sa mère. A présent, je ne vis plus de la même respiration que mes parents, et n'ai plus de place en leurs cœurs. Pour me donner la naissance, quelle heure (néfaste) le ciel a-t-il choisie?

4. Les saules sont très vigoureux ; les cigales crient d'une voix stridente.. L'eau est très profonde; les jones et les roseaux y croissent en abondance. Comme une barque entraînée par le courant, je ne sais où j'aboutirai. Mon cœur est triste; je n'ai pas même le temps de me reposer un peu tout habillé.

5. Les cerfs courent, mais lentement (pour ne pas se séparer). Le faisan crie le matin; lui-même sait appeler sa compagne. Je suis (seul), semblable à un arbre gâté, malade et sans branches.

3. Vel moros et catalpas oportet honorare et vereri. Nemo suspiciendus est nisi pater; nemini innitendum est nisi matri. Non conjunctus sum cum spiritu (parentum), nec inhæreo in visceribus. Quum cœlum nativitatem dedit mihi, meæ nativitatis hora ubinam fuit?

4. Vegetæ sunt illæ salices; clamant cicadæ stridenti voce. Est alta aqua profunda; junci et calami plurimi sunt. Similis illi cymbæ decurrenti, non scio quo adveniam. Animus mœret; nec (mihi) vacat (vel) vestito cubare.

5. Cervi currunt, at pede tardo. Phasianus mane clamat, etiam quærit suam feminam. Similis sum illi putrescenti arbori, quæ morbida est adeoque caret ramis. Animus mœret; quomodo nemo id nescit?

疾用無枝、心之憂矣、寧莫之知、(6)相彼投兔、尚或先之、行有死人、尚或墐之、君子秉心、維其忍之、心之憂矣、涕既隕之、(7)君子信讒、如或醻之、君子不惠、不舒究之、伐木掎矣、析薪杝矣、舍彼有罪、予之佗矣、(8)莫高匪山、莫浚

k'ì ts'ēu (ts'ī). P'i pėi houái mǒu, tsǐ ióung ǒu tchēu. Sīn tchēu iǒu i, gning mouǒ tchēu tchēu?

6. Siáng pėi t'eǒu t'óu, cháng houě sién (sin) tchēu. Hīng ióu sėu jėnn, cháng houě kin tchēu. Kiūn tzéu ping sīn, wėi k'ì jėnn tchēu. Sīn tchēu iǒu i, t'ì ki iún tchēu.

7. Kiūn tzéu sin tch'ân, jǒu houě tch'eǒu (tch'eóu) tchēu. Kiūn tzéu pǒu houéi, pǒu chōu kióu tchēu. Fă mǒu ki (kǒ) i, sǐ sīn tch'èu (t'ouǒ) i. Chė pėi iǒu tsouéi, iù tchēu t'ouó (t'ouǒ) i.

8. Mouǒ kaǒ fėi chān, mouǒ siún fėi ts'iuên. Kiūn tzéu ǒu i iǒu iên, ėul tchǒu

Mon cœur est triste; comment personne ne connaît-il ma douleur?

6. Lorsqu'un lièvre cherche un protecteur, il trouve quelqu'un qui se met au-devant de lui (et le sauve). Lorsqu'un cadavre gît dans un chemin, il se trouve quelqu'un pour l'enterrer. Le souverain (l'empereur) n'a que de la dureté. Mon cœur est triste; les larmes coulent de mes yeux.

7. Le souverain admet les calomnies, comme il accepterait une coupe de vin. Il ne m'aime pas; il n'examine pas à loisir les accusations. Celui qui coupe un arbre par le pied, lui attache la cime avec une corde, (de peur qu'il ne se casse en tombant); celui qui fend du bois suit les veines. Le souverain laisse aller les coupables (les calomniateurs), et me traite en criminel.

8. Rien n'est haut comme une montagne, ni profond comme une

6. Videte illum confugientem leporem; etiam aliquis præcedet (et eripiet) eum. Quum in via est mortuus homo, etiam aliquis humat eum. Imperator præditus est eo animo ut solummodo ille non misereatur hominis. Animus mœret; lacrymæ decidunt.

7. Imperator fidem adhibet calumniis, quasi quis vinum propinaret ei. Imperator non est beneficus; non sedulo inspicit illas. Qui cædit arborem, alligat verticem; qui findit lignum, obsequitur venis. (Imperator) dimittit illos habentes scelera; mihi ea attribuit.

8. Nihil est sublime nisi mons; nihil profundum nisi fons. Rex ne facile proferat verba; aures adhærent ad parietem. (Pao Seu filius) ne adeat meum septum, ne tollat meam nassam.

匪泉、君子無易由言、耳屬于垣、無逝我梁、無發我笱、我躬不閱、遑恤我後、

巧言

(1) 悠悠昊天、曰父母且、無罪無辜、亂如此憮、昊天已威、予慎無罪、昊天泰憮、予慎無辜、

(2) 亂之初生、僭始既涵、亂之又生、君子信讒、君子如怒、

iû iuên. Oû chéu ngò leàng, ǒu fǎ ngò keòu. Ngò kōung pǒu iuě, houâng siŭ ngò heòu?

K'IAO IEN. 1. Iôu iôu haò t'iēn, iuě fóu mòu tsiù. Oû tsouéi ǒu kōu, louán jôu ts'èu hōu? Haò t'iēn i wēi (wéi), iù chénn ǒu tsouéi. Haò t'iēn t'ái hōu, iù chénn ǒu kōu.

2. Louán tchēu tch'ōu chēng, tchénn chéu ki hân. Louán tchēu iôu chēng,

source. Que le souverain ne parle pas à la légère; des oreilles sont appliquées au mur (pour écouter). Que (le fils de Pao Seu) n'approche pas de mon barrage et n'enlève pas ma nasse, c.-à-d. ne me ravisse pas l'empire. Le souverain ne s'occupe pas de ma personne; aura-t-il le loisir d'étendre sa compassion à ma postérité?

CHANT IV. K'IAO IEN.

Un grand préfet, victime de la calomnie, adresse ses plaintes au ciel.

1. O ciel qui occupez des régions vastes et inaccessibles, vous que nous appelons notre père, (comment pouvez-vous permettre que) des innocents soient ainsi victimes d'un tel désordre? Auguste ciel, vous êtes trop rigoureux; je m'examine, et ne trouve en moi aucun crime. Auguste ciel, (votre sévérité) est excessive; je m'examine, et ne trouve en moi aucune faute.

2. Le trouble est venu de ce que la calomnie a d'abord été bien accueillie. Il s'est accru, parce qu'ensuite elle a obtenu créance auprès de l'empereur. Si l'empereur faisait éclater sa colère contre les calomniateurs, probablement le trouble serait bientôt comprimé.

(Imperator) me ipsum non curat; ei vacabitne misereri meorum posterorum?

CHANT IV. 1. Magnum remotumque cœlum, diceris pater et mater. Carentes scelere, carentes culpa (homines) turbantur usque eo vehementer! Augustum cœlum, nimium sævis; ego inspiciens (meipsum video) carere scelere. Augustum cœlum, nimis magna est (tua severitas); ego inspiciens (meipsum video) carere culpa.

2. Turbatio cœpta est oriri, (quia) calumnia oriens jam accepta est. Turbatio rursus crevit, (quia) princeps vir fidem adhibuit calumniatoribus. Princeps vir si irasceretur, turbatio forsan

亂庶遄沮、君子如祉、亂庶遄已、

(3) 君子屢盟、亂是用長、君子信盜、亂是用暴、盜言孔甘、亂是用餤、匪其止共、維王之邛、

(4) 奕奕寢廟、君子作之、秩秩大猷、聖人莫之、他人有心、予忖度

kiūn tzèu sin tch'ǎn. Kiūn tzèu jǒu nòu, louán chóu tchouēn tsiù. Kiūn tzèu jǒu tch'èu, louán chóu tchouēn i.

3. Kiūn tzèu liú mêng (mâng), louán chéu ióung tchàng (tch'âng). Kiūn tzèu sin taó, louán chéu ióung paó. Taó iên k'òung kān, louán chéu ióung t'ân. Fèi k'ì tchèu kōung, wêi wâng tchēu k'iôung.

4. Ĭ ĭ ts'in miaó, kiūn tzèu tsŏ tchēu. Tchĕu tchĕu tá iôu, chéng jênn mouŏ tchēu. T'ouŏ jênn iòu sīn, iù ts'uènn tŏ tchēu. Tĭ tĭ tch'àn t'óu, iù k'iuén houŏ tchēu.

Si l'empereur se montrait heureux (d'entendre les bons avis), probablement le trouble finirait bientôt.

3. L'empereur, (à cause de la défiance qui règne entre lui et les princes feudataires), fait renouveler souvent les serments solennels; le trouble n'en devient que plus grand. Il ajoute foi aux accusations des brigands (ses favoris), et le trouble amène l'oppression. Les discours de ces brigands lui sont très agréables, et le trouble s'étend de plus en plus. (Ces indignes ministres) ne remplissent pas les devoirs de leurs charges; ils ne servent qu'à perdre l'empereur.

4. (En voyant) la magnificence d'un temple des ancêtres, (je juge qu') un prince vertueux l'a fait construire. (En considérant) la belle ordonnance des grandes institutions, (je juge qu') elles ont été fixées par les plus grands sages. Un homme a une pensée; je

brevi inhiberetur. Princeps vir si gauderet (audire proborum monita), turbatio forsan mox desineret.

3. Princeps vir sæpe jurat (cum regulis); turbatio eapropter crescit. Princeps vir fidem adhibet latronibus; turbatio eapropter tyrannidem parit. Latronum verba sunt valde suavia; turbatio eapropter progreditur. Non sua munia implent, solummodo sunt imperatoris pernicies.

盟 Une victime était immolée. Avec son sang on se frottait les lèvres. Elle était enterrée avec la copie des conventions.

止 Tchèu signifie 職 tchĕu, charge, fonctions, devoirs attachés à une charge. 止共 Tchéu kōung équivaut à 共職事 remplir les devoirs de sa charge.

4. Magnifica sunt (aulæ gentilitiæ) sacrarium et delubra; sapiens vir extruxit ea. Apte composita sunt magna consilia; sapientissimi viri statuerunt ea. Alius homo habet cogitatum; ego cogitans conjicio illud. Celeriter saltat callidus lepus; occurrens canis capit eum.

之、躍躍毚兔、遇犬獲之、

(5) 在染柔木、君子樹之、往來行言、心焉數之、蛇蛇碩言、出自口矣、巧言如簧、顏之厚矣、

(6) 彼何人斯、居河之麋、無拳無勇、職爲亂階、既微且尰、爾勇伊何、爲猶將多、爾居徒幾何、

5. Jénn jèn jeòu mǒu, kiūn tzèu chòu tchēu. Wâng lài hìng iên, sīn iên chóu (chòu) tchēu. Ī ì chēu iên, tch'ǒu tzèu k'eòu (k'òu) i. K'iaò iên jôu houâng, iên tchēu heòu (hóu) i.

6. Péi hô jênn sēu? kiū hô tchēu mêi. Oû k'iuèn ôu iòung, tchĕu wêi louán kiāi (kī). Ki wêi ts'iè tchòung, èul iòung ī hô? Wêi iôu tsiāng touō, èul kiū t'ôu ki (kī) hô?

puis la deviner. Le lièvre rusé bondit et court très vite; il rencontre un chien qui le saisit. (Les ruses des calomniateurs se devinent facilement).

5. Les arbres dont le bois est tendre et flexible, (utile et facile à travailler), sont plantés par les sages. Dans les discours des passants qui vont et viennent, l'intelligence sait discerner le vrai du faux. Exprimer les grandes pensées qui viennent naturellement à l'esprit, (cela convient). Mais tenir des discours artificieux avec un bruit semblable à celui des languettes d'une flûte, c'est de l'impudence.

6. Ces calomniateurs quels sont-ils? Des hommes qui vivent au milieu des herbes sur les bords des rivières, n'ont ni force ni courage, et font leur principale occupation de propager le désordre. (Hommes méprisables), avec vos jambes ulcérées et enflées, quel courage pouvez-vous avoir? Vous formez des projets grands et nombreux; mais combien avez-vous de partisans?

Le bâtiment principal du temple des ancêtres des Tcheou se composait de neuf petites salles 九廟 **kiòu miaó**, dans chacune desquelles était la tablette de l'un des ancêtres. Derrière se trouvait un autre bâtiment 寢 **ts'in**, où l'on conservait les vêtements et tous les objets nécessaires aux cérémonies.

5. Flexibiles ac molles arbores, sapiens vir plantat eas. Qui eunt et redeunt, transeuntium dicta, mens discernit ea. Facile orientia magna documenta exeant ex ore, (decet). Callida proferre verba instar fistulæ ligularum, vultus crassa pellis.

6. Illi (calumniatores) quales homines sunt? Habitantes in fluviorum herbosis ripis, carentes viribus, carentes fortitudine, toti in agendis turbationis scalis. Jam ulceratis ac tumentibus cruribus, vestra fortitudo quænam est? Statuitis consilia magna et multa; vobiscum stantes sequaces quot sunt?

Les habitants des pays humides et marécageux sont faibles, maladifs, exposés à différentes infirmités.

何人斯

(1) 彼何人斯、其心孔艱、胡逝我梁、不入我門。伊誰云從、維暴之云。

(2) 二人從行、誰爲此禍、胡逝我梁、不入唁我、始者不如今、云不我可。

(3) 彼何人斯、胡逝我陳、我聞其

HO JENN SEU. **1. Pèi hô jênn sēu ? K'î sīn k'òung kiēn (kīn). Hôu chéu ngò leâng, pǒu jǒu ngò mênn ? Ĭ chouêi iûn ts'ôung ? Wêi Paó tchēu iûn.**

2. Eúl jênn ts'ôung hîng, chouêi wêi ts'éu houò ? Hôu chéu ngò leâng, pǒu jǒu ién ngò ? Chéu tchè pǒu jôu kīn, iûn pǒu ngò k'ò.

3. Pèi hô jênn sēu ? Hôu chéu ngò tch'ênn ? Ngò wênn k'î chēng, pǒu kién k'î

CHANT V. HO JENN SEU.

Le prince de 蘇 **Sōu**, privé de sa charge, voyant que le prince de 暴 **Paó**, son ancien ami, qui est 卿 **k'īng** ministre d'État, ne vient plus le voir, le soupçonne d'avoir été la cause de sa disgrâce. N'osant pas l'accuser ouvertement, il accuse un compagnon qu'il ne nomme pas.

1. Quel est cet homme? Il forme des projets très dangereux. Pourquoi va-t-il à mon barrage, et n'entre-t-il pas dans ma maison? Quel est celui qu'il accompagne? C'est le prince de Pao.

2. Ces deux hommes (le prince de Pao et son compagnon) marchent à la suite l'un de l'autre; lequel des deux m'a causé ce malheur? Pourquoi celui-ci va-t-il à mon barrage, et n'entre-t-il pas pour me consoler (de ma disgrâce)? Auparavant il me traitait bien différemment; il ne me trouve plus digne de son amitié.

3. Quel est cet homme? Pourquoi vient-il jusqu'à l'allée de ma cour? J'entends sa voix et n'aperçois pas sa personne. (Il m'accuse)

CHANT V. 1. Ille quisnam homo est? Ejus consilia valde periculosa sunt. Quare adit meum septum, nec ingreditur meam januam? Ille quemnam sequitur? Solum Pao regulum.

云 **Iûn**, particule. Sou et Pao étaient deux petites principautés comprises dans le domaine propre de l'empereur.

2. Duo homines invicem sequentes incedunt; uter excitavit hoc infortunium? Cur adit meum septum, nec ingreditur ut soletur me? Initio non sicut nunc; non me dignum censet (amicitia sua).

3. Ille quisnam homo est? Cur adit meæ aulæ mediam viam? Ego audio illius vocem, nec video illius corpus. Non eum pudet coram hominibus, nihil timet a cœlo.

陳 **Tch'ênn**, allée qui conduit de la porte extérieure d'une habitation à la salle principale. 不愧於人則以人爲可欺也天不可欺(朱熹) Vous ne rougissez pas devant les

聲、不見其身、不愧于人、不畏于天、

(4) 彼何人斯、其爲飄風、胡不自北、胡不自南、胡逝我梁、祇攪我心、

(5) 爾之安行、亦不遑舍、爾之亟行、遑脂爾車、壹者之來、云何其盱、

(6) 爾還而入、我心易也、還而不入、否難知也、壹者之來、俾我祇也、

chēnn. Pŏu kouéi iū jênn, pŏu wéi iū t'iên (t'īn).

4. Pèi hô jênn sēu ? K'î wêi p'iaō fōung (fēnn). Hôu pŏu tzéu pĕ ? hôu pŏu tzéu nân (gnîn) ? Hôu chéu ngò leàng, tchēu kiaò ngò sīn ?

5. Eùl tchēu ngān hîng, ĭ pŏu houâng chè (chŏu). Eùl tchēu kĭ hîng, houâng tchēu èul kiū. Ĭ tchè tchēu lâi, iùn hô k'i hiū !

6. Eùl houân èul jŏu, ngò sīn i (i) iè. Houân èul pŏu jŏu, feòu nân tchēu iè. Ĭ tchè tchēu lâi, pèi ngò k'i iè.

sans craindre le regard des hommes ni la colère du ciel.

4. Quel est cet homme? Il est comme un vent violent. Pourquoi ne vient-il pas du nord? pourquoi ne vient-il pas du midi? (Il va et vient, fait semblant de vouloir continuer ses relations amicales avec moi, et cependant reste toujours à distance). Pourquoi va-t-il à mon barrage, et trouble-t-il ainsi mon esprit?

5. Même lorsque vous voyagez lentement, (vous dites que) vous n'avez pas le temps de vous arrêter (pour venir me voir. Et cependant), même lorsque vous voyagez rapidement, vous prenez le temps de graisser l'essieu de votre voiture. Oh! venez au moins une fois; combien je désire vous voir!

6. Si à votre retour vous entrez chez moi, mon cœur sera soulagé. Mais si à votre retour vous n'entrez pas, votre refus sera difficile à expliquer. Ne viendriez-vous qu'une seule fois, vous me rendriez content.

hommes, parce que vous croyez qu'on peut tromper les hommes. Mais on ne trompe pas le ciel. 天之明察無隱不彰甚可畏也 (備旨) Le regard du ciel est très perspicace; rien ne lui échappe, tout lui est transparent. On doit le redouter beaucoup.

4. Ille quisnam homo est? Ille est vehemens ventus. Cur non a septentrione? cur non a meridie? Quare adit meum septum, solummodo perturbans meum animum?

5. Quum tu tarde incedis, etiam (dicis) tibi non vacare quiescere. Quum tu celeriter properas, vacat ungere tuum currum. Semel venias; quantopere ipse cupio!

6. Si tu rediens tunc ingrediaris, meus animus levabitur. Si rediens tunc non ingrediaris, dedignatio difficile intelligetur. Si semel venias, facies me tranquillum.

(7) 伯氏吹壎、仲氏吹篪、及爾如貫、諒不我知、出此三物、以詛爾斯、

(8) 爲鬼爲蜮、則不可得、有靦面目、視人罔極、作此好歌、以極反側、

7. Pĕ chèu tch'ouēi hiuēn, tchóung chéu tch'ouēi tch'êu ; kĭ èul jôu kouán. Leáng pŏu ngò tchēu, tch'ŏu ts'èu sān ŏu, i tchóu èul sēu.

8. Wêi kouèi wêi iŭ, tsĕ pŏu k'ò tĕ. Iòu t'ièn mién mŏu, chéu jênn wàng kĭ. Tsŏ ts'èu haò kō, i kĭ fàn tchĕ.

7. (Quand nous étions tous deux ministres d'État à la cour de l'empereur), nous nous accordions comme deux frères, dont l'aîné joue du hiuen, et l'autre joue de la flûte. Nous étions unis comme deux perles enfilées ensemble. Si vraiment vous ne connaissez pas mes sentiments, faites venir les trois victimes ordinaires (un chien, un porc et un coq ; après avoir frotté vos lèvres de leur sang), jurez que vous ne me connaissez pas.

8. Si vous étiez un esprit ou une tortue à trois pattes, personne ne pourrait vous voir. Mais vous avez un visage et des yeux qui sont très apparents, (les hommes vous voient et devinent sans peine vos sentiments); vous aussi, vous voyez continuellement les hommes. J'ai composé cet excellent petit chant, pour mettre à découvert votre inconstance et votre duplicité.

7. Natu maximus frater dominus sonabat ovo testaceo ; natu minor frater dominus inflabat tibiam. Conjunctus tecum sicut trajectus (uno eodemque funiculo). Si vere non me nosti, effer ista tria animalia, ut jures de te illud.

Ces trois animaux sont un chien, un porc et un coq. Voy. 左傳隱十一年

氏 **Chèu**, terme honorifique.

壎 **Hiuēn**, instrument d'argile, percé de six trous, dans lequel on soufflait pour en tirer des sons. Il avait la forme et la grosseur d'un œuf de poule ou d'oie.

篪 Flûte traversière, longue de 一尺四寸 (vingt-huit centimètres environ), percée de huit trous, et dont les sons imitaient les cris d'un petit enfant.

8. Si esses spiritus, si esses jaculatrix testudo, tunc nemo posset assequi (ut te videret). Habes coram spectabiles vultum et oculos, intueris homines sine fine. Composui hoc bonum canticum, ut omnino patefacerem versatilem et obliquum (animum tuum).

蜮 **Iŭ**, tortue à trois pattes, appelée 短狐 **touàn hôu**, 水弩 **chouèi nòu**, 射工 **ché kōung**, 射影 **chĕ ing**, qui cause des maladies et même la mort, en lançant du sable sur les personnes qu'elle voit au bord de l'eau, ou en soufflant dans l'eau sur leur ombre. Elle vivait dans le Kiang et dans la Houai.

靦 **T'ièn**, regarder quelqu'un en face.

巷伯

(1) 萋兮斐兮、成是貝錦、彼譖人者、亦已大甚、

(2) 哆兮侈兮、成是南箕、彼譖人者、誰適與謀、

(3) 緝緝翩翩、謀欲譖人、慎爾言也、謂爾不信、

HIANG PE. 1. **Ts'ī hī féi hī, tch'êng chéu péi kin. Péi tchénn jênn tchè, ī i t'ái chênn.**

2. Tch'è hī tch'èu hī, tch'êng chéu nân Kī. Péi tchénn jênn tchè, chouêi tī iù meôu (mêi)?

3. Tsī tsī p'iēn p'iēn (p'in p'in), meôu iù tchénn jênn. Chénn èul iên iè, wéi èul pŏu sin (sīn).

CHANT VI. HIANG PE.

Un eunuque, nommé 孟子 **Méng tzèu**, qui était 巷伯 **hiáng pĕ** préposé à la garde d'un passage dans le palais, se plaint d'avoir été victime de la calomnie.

1. L'ouvrier, par un heureux assemblage de lignes et de fleurs élégantes, tisse une pièce de soie dont les dessins imitent les veines des coquillages précieux. Ainsi les calomniateurs (ayant trouvé en moi quelques légers défauts, les ont peints des couleurs les plus noires, et) ont beaucoup exagéré.

2. Quatre points lumineux qui vont en s'écartant, et semblent ouvrir une grande bouche, forment le Van du midi. Ainsi ces calomniateurs (s'ils étaient seuls, ne sauraient combiner un plan); quels sont donc ceux qui président à leurs délibérations?

3. Vous promenez partout votre bavardage; vous ne pensez et ne cherchez qu'à médire. Faites attention à vos paroles; on dira que vous ne méritez aucune créance.

CHANT VI. 1. Floridum, ornatum, compositum fit conchyliis sericum. Illi qui obtrectant hominibus, jam multum excesserunt.

Les coquillages précieux 貝 **péi** servaient de monnaie. Leur diamètre variait de quatorze à vingt centimètres.

2. Hianti ore, diductus, compositus fit australis Vannus. Illi qui obtrectant hominibus, quibusnam auctoribus simul deliberant?

適 **Tī** signifie 主 **tchòu** donner un conseil, présider une délibération, décider en maître. 箕 **Kī**, Van, l'une des vingt-huit constellations zodiacales des Chinois. Elle comprend quatre étoiles du Sagittaire, dont deux, très rapprochées l'une de l'autre, forment ce qu'on appelle le talon 踵 **tchòung**, et les deux autres la langue 舌 **chĕ**.

3. Linguis strepentes huc illuc discurritis; meditantes vultis obtrectare hominibus. Attendite vestris sermonibus; dicent vos non esse fide dignos.

(4) 捷捷幡幡、謀欲譖言、豈不爾受、既其女遷、

(5) 驕人好好、勞人草草、蒼天蒼天、視彼驕人、矜此勞人、

(6) 彼譖人者、誰適與謀、取彼譖人、投畀豺虎、豺虎不食、投畀有北、有北不受、投畀有昊、

4. Tsiě tsiě fān fān, meǒu iū tchénn iên. K'i pǒu éul cheóu, ki k'ì jòu ts'iēn ?

5. Kiaō jênn haò haò, laǒ jênn ts'aò ts'aò. Ts'āng t'iēn (t'īn), ts'āng t'iēn (t'īn), chéu pèi kiaō jênn, kīng ts'éu laǒ jênn.

6. Pèi tchénn jênn tchè (tchòu), chouêi tĭ iù meǒu (mǒu)? Ts'iù pèi tchénn jênn, t'eǒu pi tch'ài hòu. Tch'âi hòu pǒu chĕu, t'eǒu pi iòu pě. Iòu pě pǒu cheóu, t'eǒu pi iòu haò (heóu).

4. Doués d'un esprit vif et changeant, vous pensez et cherchez à médire. Ce que vous faites à autrui, comment enfin ne vous serait-il pas rendu à vous-mêmes?

5. Les orgueilleux (les calomniateurs) sont dans la joie; les malheureux (victimes de la calomnie) sont dans la tristesse. Ciel azuré, ciel azuré, voyez ces orgueilleux, ayez compassion de ces malheureux.

6. Quels sont ceux qui président aux délibérations de ces calomniateurs? Je prendrai ces calomniateurs, et les jetterai aux loups et aux tigres. Si les loups et les tigres ne veulent pas les dévorer, je les jetterai aux régions glacées du nord, (afin qu'ils périssent de faim et de froid). Si les régions boréales ne veulent pas les recevoir, je les livrerai au très-haut, (afin qu'il les châtie).

4. Ingenio acres, animo versatiles, meditantes vultis proferre maledica verba. Quomodo non, quod ex vobis acceptum est, tandem illud ad vos remigrabit?

既字作終字看 Le lettre *ki* équivaut à la lettre *tchōung*.

5. Superbi homines lætitia fruuntur; miseri homines mœrore afficiuntur. Cæruleum cœlum, cæruleum cœlum, aspice illos superbos homines, miserere horum miserorum hominum.

草草 Inquiet, chagrin.

6. Illi qui obtrectant hominibus, quibusnam ducibus simul deliberant? Sumam illos qui obtrectant hominibus; projiciens tradam lupis et tigribus. Si lupi et tigres non comedant, projiciens tradam existenti septentrioni. Si existens septentrio non accipiat, projiciens tradam existenti altissimo (cœlo).

Dans les expressions 有北有昊 la lettre 有 a un sens vague qu'il est difficile de rendre. Elle sert à arrondir la phrase.

投畀昊天使制其罪 (朱熹) Je les livrerai au très-haut, au ciel, afin qu'il les juge et les punisse.

⑦楊園之道、猗于畝丘、寺人孟子、作爲此詩、凡百君子、敬而聽之、

谷風

①習習谷風、維風及雨、將恐將懼、維予與女、將安將樂、女轉棄予、

②習習谷風、維風及頹、將恐將

7. Iâng iuên tchēu taó, i iû meòu k'iōu (k'ī). Sêu jênn Méng tzéu tsŏ wêi ts'èu chēu. Fân pĕ kiūn tzèu, king èul t'ing tchēu.

KOU FOUNG. **1. Sĭ sĭ kŏu fōung, wèi fōung kí iù. Tsiāng k'òung, tsiāng kiú, wêi iû iù jòu. Tsiāng ngān, tsiāng lŏ, jòu tchouèn k'í iù (iù).**

2. Sĭ sĭ kŏu fōung, wêi fōung kĭ t'ouêi. Tsiāng k'òung, tsiāng kiú, tchéu iû iû houâi (houêi). Tsiāng ngān, tsiāng lŏ, k'í iù jŏu î (wêi).

7. L'allée du jardin des peupliers (qui est dans un terrain bas) aboutit à la colline qui est couverte de champs cultivés. (Les calomniateurs, après avoir renversé les officiers de bas étage, s'attaqueront aux plus élevés). Moi, l'eunuque Meng tzeu, j'ai composé ce chant. Écoutez-le avec attention, vous tous, grands dignitaires, quel que soit votre rang.

CHANT VII. KOU FOUNG.

Un ami se plaint de l'inconstance de son ami.

1. Lorsque le vent d'est souffle doucement, bientôt il amène la pluie. (Ainsi nous étions toujours ensemble). Quand vous aviez des périls à redouter, vous et moi, nous étions tout entiers l'un à l'autre. La sécurité et la prospérité reparaissant, vous avez changé de conduite et m'avez rejeté.

2. Lorsque le vent d'est souffle doucement, bientôt il produit des tourbillons au sein de l'air. Ainsi, quand vous aviez des périls à redouter, vous me portiez sur votre cœur. La sécurité et la

7. Consiti populis septi via attinet ad cultum colliculum. Eunuchus Meng tzeu componens feci hoc canticum. Quicumque estis omnis gradus magnates, attendite et auscultate hoc.

CHANT VII. 1. Lenis et temperatus est orientalis ventus; statim ventus sociatur cum pluvia. Adveniente timore, adveniente metu, unice ego et tu. Adveniente quiete, adveniente gaudio, tu vertens (agendi rationem mutans) rejecisti me.

2. Lenis et temperatus flat orientalis ventus; statim ventus sociatur cum vorticibus. Adveniente timore, adveniente metu, ponebas me in sinu tuo. Adveniente quiete, adveniente gaudio, rejecisti me quasi obliteratum.

懼、寘予于懷、將安將樂、棄予如遺、

(3) 習習谷風、維山崔嵬、無草不死、無木不萎、忘我大德、思我小怨、

蓼莪

(1) 蓼蓼者莪、匪莪伊蒿、哀哀父母、生我劬勞、

(2) 蓼蓼者莪、匪

3. Sĭ sĭ kŏu fōung, wêi chān ts'ouēi wêi. Oû ts'aò pŏu sèu, ôu mŏu pŏu wêi (wêi). Wàng ngò ta tĕ, sēu ngò siaò iuén.

LOU NGO. **1. Lŏu lŏu tchè ngô ; fèi ngô, ī haō. Ngāi ngāi ! fóu mòu, chēng ngò k'iû laô !**

2. Lŏu lŏu tchè ngô; fèi ngô, ī wéi. Ngāi ngāi ! fóu mòu, chēng ngò laô tsouéi !

prospérité reparaissant, vous m'avez rejeté comme un objet livré à l'oubli.

3. Lorsque le vent d'est souffle doucement, il (échauffe de sa tiède haleine) les cimes des hautes montagnes. Cependant il ne peut soustraire aucune plante, aucun arbre à la loi du dépérissement et de la mort. (Il n'est personne qui ne soit borné dans ses facultés et sujet à quelques défauts.). Vous oubliez les grands services que je vous ai rendus, et ne vous souvenez que de vos petits griefs contre moi.

CHANT VIII. LOU NGO.

Un fils, longtemps retenu au service de son prince, exprime sa douleur de n'avoir pu donner ses soins à ses parents jusqu'à leur mort.

1. L'armoise appelée *ngò* croît grande et large. Je ne suis plus cette belle armoise (qui donnait de grandes espérances) ; mais une armoise des plus viles, (parce que je n'ai pas rempli les devoirs de la piété filiale). Hélas! hélas! ô mon père! ô ma mère! vous m'avez élevé avec tant de peine et de fatigue!

2. L'armoise appelée *ngô* croît grande et large; je ne suis plus cette belle armoise, mais un armoise des plus viles. Hélas! hélas!

3. Lenis et temperatus flat orientalis ventus, et montis sublimis est vertex. Non est herba quæ non moriatur; non est arbor quæ non marcescat. Oblivisceris mea magna officia, recordaris meas parvas offensas.

CHANT VIII. 1. Procera et ampla crescit *ngô* (artemisia quædam esculenta); jam non sum *ngô*, sed *hao* (vilissima artemisia). Heu! heu! pater et mater! aluistis me operoso labore!

2. Procera et ampla est *ngô* artemisia; non jam *ngô*, sed *wéi* (vilissima artemisia). Heu! heu! pater et mater!

莪伊蔚、哀哀父母、生我勞瘁、

(3) 缾之罄矣、維罍之恥、鮮民之生、不如死之久矣、無父何怙、無母何恃、出則銜恤、入則靡至、

(4) 父兮生我、母兮鞠我、拊我畜我、長我育我、顧我復我、出入腹我、欲報之德、昊天罔極、

(5) 南山烈烈、飄風

3. P'ing tchēu k'ing i, wêi lêi tchēu tch'èu. Siên min tchēu chēng, pŏu jôu sèu tchēu kiòu (ki) i. Où fóu hô hòu ? Où mòu hô chèu ? Tch'ŏu tsĕ hiên siŭ, jŏu tsĕ mi tchéu.

4. Fóu hî chēng ngò, mòu hî kiŭ ngò. Fòu ngò hiŭ ngò, tchàng ngò iŭ ngò. Kóu ngò fŏu ngò, tch'ŏu jŏu fŏu ngò. Iŭ paó tchēu tĕ, haó t'iēn wàng kĭ.

5. Nân chān liĕ liĕ, p'iaō fōung fă fă. Mìn mouŏ pŏu kŏu, ngò tŏu hô hái (hŏ) ?

ô mon père ! ô ma mère ! vous m'avez élevé avec tant de travail et de peine !

3. Si la bouteille est vide, c'est une honte pour l'amphore (qui ne lui fournit pas de vin. Si les parents sont dans l'abandon, c'est une honte pour les enfants). Il vaudrait mieux être mort depuis longtemps, que de prolonger sa vie, quand on n'a plus ses parents. Celui qui n'a plus de père, en qui mettra-t-il son espoir ? Celui qui n'a plus de mère, en qui mettra-t-il sa confiance ? Hors de la maison, il porte partout son chagrin avec lui ; dans la maison, il n'a personne à qui s'adresser.

4. Mon père m'a engendré, ma mère m'a porté dans son sein. Ils m'ont traité avec tendresse, nourri, élevé, préservé de tout mal, gardé avec sollicitude, entouré de soins continuels. Ma reconnaissance n'aurait jamais pu répondre parfaitement à leurs bienfaits, qui ont été sans limite, comme le vaste ciel.

5. La montagne qui est au midi, est haute et large ; le vent y

aluistis me laborioso dolore !

3. Lagenæ vacuitas unice est amphoræ dedecus. Parentibus orbatorum hominum vita non par est morti jampridem (consummatæ). Qui orbus est patre, in quo spem habebit ? Qui orbus est matre, cui innitetur ? Foris quidem animo recondit mœrorem ; domi vero non habet quem adeat.

4. Pater genuit me, mater aluit me (in utero suo). Foverunt me, nutriverunt me, fecerunt ut ego crescerem, curarunt me, invigilarunt mihi, versarunt me. Foris ac domi sinu gestarunt me. Si voluissem rependere beneficia, (non par fuissem ; nam fuerunt infinita, sicut) vastum cœlum caret termino.

5. Australis mons est altus et

發發、民莫不穀、我獨何害、

(6) 南山律律、飄風弗弗、民莫不穀、我獨不卒、

大東

(1) 有饛簋飧、有捄棘匕、周道如砥、其直如矢、君子所履、小人所視、睠言顧之、潸焉出涕、

6. Nân chān liŭ liŭ, p'iaō fōung fŏu fŏu. Mîn mouŏ pŏu kŏu, ngò tŏu pŏu tsŏu.

TA TOUNG. **1. Iòu môung kouèi suënn, iòu k'iôu kì pi. Tcheōu taó jôu tchéu, k'i tchĕu jôu chéu. Kiūn tzèu chòu li, siaò jênn chòu chéu (chéu). Kiuén ièn kóu tchēu, chān iên tch'ŏu t'i.**

souffle avec violence. (Mon sort est très agité). Tous les autres sont heureux; pourquoi suis-je seul malheureux?

6. La montagne qui est au midi, est haute et large; le vent y souffle avec violence. Tous les autres sont heureux; moi seul je n'ai pu remplir jusqu'à la fin les devoirs de la piété filiale.

CHANT IX. TA TOUNG.

Un officier de la principauté de 譚 **T'ân** se plaint de ce que le gouvernement impérial, dont le siège est à 鎬 **Haò** dans le Chen si actuel, favorise les contrées occidentales, et accable d'exactions les régions orientales. Les esprits qui régissent les étoiles du ciel, voient les souffrances des opprimés, et ne font rien pour les secourir. 譚 était le 歷城縣 actuel dans le 濟南府 (Chan toung).

1. (Sous les premiers empereurs de la dynastie des Tcheou, régnait l'abondance). Il y avait de grands vases remplis de millet (qu'on offrait aux esprits), et des cuillers recourbées en bois de jujubier (qui servaient à retirer les viandes des chaudières). La route de la capitale était unie comme une meule, droite comme la trajectoire d'une flèche. (Elle était très battue). Les dignitaires la suivaient (pour aller rendre leurs hommages à l'empereur); les hommes du peuple la voyaient (et la parcouraient). A présent, lorsque je tourne mes regards vers cette route, (je la vois déserte), je verse un torrent de larmes.

amplus; flat ventus vehementer. Civium nullus non felix; ego solus cur mœrore afficior?

6. Australis mons est altus et amplus; flat ventus vehementer. Civium nullus non felix; ego solus non ad finem (functus sum pietatis filialis officiis).

CHANT IX. 1. (Olim) erant plena vasa milii cocti; erant curva e zizypho cochlearia. Tcheou urbis via (erat plana) sicut mola, ipsa recta sicut sagittæ (via). Magnates cui insistebant, plebeii homines quam videbant. Respiciens considero eam; effuse manant lacrymæ.

(2)小東大東、杼柚其空。糾糾葛屨、可以履霜。佻佻公子、行彼周行、既往既來、使我心疚。

(3)有冽氿泉、無浸穫薪。契契寤歎、哀我憚人。薪是穫薪、尚可載也。哀我憚人、亦可息也。

(4)東人之子、職勞不來。西人之子、粲粲衣服。舟人之子、

2. Siaò tōung (tāng) tá tōung (tāng), tchòu tchŏu k'ī k'ōung (k'āng). Kiaò kiaò kŏ kiú, k'ò i li chouāng. T'iaô t'iaô kōung tzèu, hîng péi Tcheōu hîng (hâng). Ki wàng ki lâi (lî), chéu ngò sīn kiòu (kí).

3. Iòu liĕ kouéi ts'iuên (ts'iûn), ôu tsín houŏ sīn. K'i k'i óu t'án, ngāi ngò touó jênn. Sīn chéu houŏ sīn, cháng k'ò tsái (tsī) iè. Ngāi ngò touó jênn, ĭ k'ò sí iè.

4. Tōung jênn tchēu tzèu, tchĕu laô pŏu lâi (lî). Sī jênn tchēu tzèu, ts'án

2. Dans les principautés orientales, petites ou grandes, la navette et l'ensouple sont inoccupées. Les habitants sont réduits à fouler les frimas avec des souliers d'été faits de brins de dolics tordus ensemble. Les fils délicats des grands dignitaires parcourent à pied la route de la capitale. Quand je les vois aller et venir ainsi, mon cœur est saisi de douleur.

3. La source qui répand ses eaux glaciales en différentes directions, ne va pas mouiller (et gâter) le bois recueilli pour le chauffage. (L'empereur, moins compatissant que cette source, opprime ses propres sujets). Dans ma douleur, je gémis privé de sommeil. Oh! que nous sommes malheureux! Lorsque le bois a été recueilli pour le chauffage, il a l'espoir d'être voituré (et mis en lieu sûr). Hélas! infortunés que nous sommes, nous devrions aussi pouvoir jouir d'un peu de repos.

4. Dans les contrées orientales, les fils des habitants sont voués à la souffrance, et ne reçoivent aucun encouragement. (Au contraire) dans les régions occidentales, les fils des habitants sont

2. In minoribus orientalibus et in majoribus orientalibus (regnis), textorius radius et liciatorium sunt vacua. Tortis cannabis fibris calcei oportet ut adhibeantur ad calcandam pruinam. Molli corpore magnatum filii insistunt illi Tcheou viæ. Quia eunt et redeunt, faciunt ut meus animus doleat.

3. Est algidus sese diffundens fons; non imbuit collecta ramalia. Magno mœrore insomnis gemo; miserandi sumus nos afflicti homines! Ramalia, ubi sunt collecta ramalia, peroptato possunt vehi. Miserandi nos afflicti homines, etiam (æquum est ut) possimus quiescere.

4. Orientalium incolarum filii toti sunt laboribus addicti absque solatio.

熊羆是裘、私
人之子、百僚
是試、
(5) 或以其酒、
不以其漿、鞙
鞙佩璲、不以
其長、維天有
漢、監亦有光、
跂彼織女、終
日七襄、
(6) 雖則七襄、
不成報章、睆
彼牽牛、不以

ts'ân î fôu (p'ĕ). Tcheōu jênn tchēu tzèu, hiôung pī chéu k'iòu (k'î). Sēu jênn tchēu tzèu, pĕ leaò chéu chéu (chēu).

5. Houĕ i k'ì tsiòu, pŏu i k'ì tsiāng. Hiuén hiuén pèi souéi, pŏu i k'ì tch'āng. Wêi t'iēn iòu Hán, kién î iòu kouāng. K'ì pèi Tchēu gniù, tchōung jĕu ts'ī siāng.

6. Souēi tsĕ ts'ī siāng, pŏu tch'êng paó tchāng. Houàn pèi K'iēn iôu, pŏu i fôu

vêtus d'habits magnifiques. Les fils des bateliers portent des tuniques garnies de peaux d'ours. Les fils des serviteurs sont admis à remplir toutes sortes de magistratures.

5. Si quelqu'un de nous offre du vin aux habitants des contrées occidentales, ils l'estiment moins que leur eau de riz. Si on leur offre de longs pendants de ceinture ornés de belles pierres, ils ne les trouvent pas assez longs. Cependant, du haut du ciel, les étoiles de la Voie lactée nous regardent, et elles ne manquent pas de lumière. Il y a aussi les trois étoiles disposées en triangle et formant la constellation de la Vierge qui fait de la toile (Wéga et deux autres étoiles de la Lyre); elles parcourent dans la journée sept des douze parties de la sphère céleste.

6. Bien qu'elles parcourent sept des stations du ciel, elles ne font pas une belle pièce de soie pour nous récompenser. Ce Bœuf traîné à l'aide d'une corde (le Cou de l'Aigle) est très brillant;

Occidentalium incolarum filiis splendidæ sunt vestes. (In occidente) nautarum filii ex vulgarium ursorum et majorum ursorum pellibus ipsi induunt tunicas. Famulorum filii omnis generis muniis præpositi ipsi adhibentur.

5. Si quis adhibet (et offert eis) suum vinum, non æstimant (tanti quanti) suum oryzæ liquorem. (Si quis offert eis) longe pendulas zonariorum lapillorum lineas, non æstimant eas longas. Attamen in cœlo est Via lactea, videt et habet lumen. Divaricans (in modum trianguli) illa Textrix virgo (a mane) ad finem diei (percurrit) septem cœli stationes.

Tchou Hi dit qu'il ne comprend pas bien le sens du dernier vers de cette strophe; il se contente de rapporter l'opinion de 鄭康成 **Tchéng K'āng tch'êng**, commentateur du deuxième siècle de notre ère. La sphère céleste se divise en douze parties ou stations, qui correspondent aux douze signes du zodiaque. Les étoiles parcourent sept de ces stations, de cinq heures du matin à sept heures du soir, et les cinq autres, de sept heures du soir à cinq heures du matin.

6. Etsi quidem (percurrit) septem stationes, non perficit quo nos remune-

服箱。東有啓明。西有長庚。有捄天畢。載施之行。

(7) 維南有箕。不可以簸揚。維北有斗。不可以挹酒漿。維南有箕。載翕其舌。維北有斗。西柄之揭。

四月

(1) 四月維夏。六月徂暑。先祖匪人。胡寧忍予。

siāng. Tōung iòu K'i mìng (màng), sī iòu Tch'âng kēng (kāng). Iòu k'iôu t'iēn Pĭ, tsái chēu tchēu hìng (hâng).

7. Wêi nân iòu Kī, pŏu k'ò i pouò iàng. Wêi pĕ iòu Teòu, pŏu k'ò i ĭ tsiōu tsiāng. Wêi nân iòu Kī, tsái hī k'i chĕ. Wêi pĕ iòu Teòu, sī ping tchēu kiĕ.

SEU IUE. 1. Séu iuĕ wêi hiá (hòu), lŏu iuĕ ts'ôu chòu. Siēn tsòu fēi jênn? hôu gnìng jènn iù (iù)?

mais il ne nous sert pas à traîner une voiture. A l'orient parait l'Étoile du matin, et à l'occident l'Étoile du soir, (elles ne nous sont d'aucun secours). Il y a aussi dans le ciel ce Filet recourbé qui semble fait pour prendre des lièvres (les Hyades); il est bien étendu à sa place (parmi les autres constellations zodiacales; mais il ne nous sert pas même à prendre un lièvre).

7. Au midi est le Van; il ne peut servir à vanner le grain. (Cf. page 258). Au nord est la Cuiller (l'Épaule et l'Arc du Sagittaire); elle ne peut servir à tirer du vin ou de la liqueur. Au midi le Van allonge sa langue (comme pour dévorer l'orient). Au nord la Cuiller lève son manche vers l'occident (comme pour prendre à l'orient et donner à l'occident).

CHANT X. SEU IUE.

Un officier déplore ses malheurs.

1. Au quatrième mois de l'année, l'été commence; au sixième, la chaleur décroit. (Tout passe; seuls mes maux n'ont pas de fin). Mes ancêtres ne sont-ils pas hommes (n'ont-ils pas un cœur bon et humain)? comment souffrent-ils que je sois si malheureux?

retur pulchrum (sericum pannum). Fulgens ille Tractus Bos non adhibetur qui jungatur capso vehiculi. In oriente est Lucifer, in occidente est Vesperus. Est curvum cœleste Rete ad venandos lepores; solummodo explicatum est ex ordine.

7. Etiam in meridie est Vannus; non potest adhiberi ad vannenda et subjectanda (grana). Et in septentrione est Trulla; non potest adhiberi ad depromendum vinum aut liquorem. Et in meridie est Vannus, solum exserit suam linguam. Et in septentrione est Trulla, ad occidentem manubrium attollit.

CHANT X. 1. Quarto mense quidem æstas; sexto mense recedunt calores.

(2) 秋日淒淒、百卉具腓、亂離瘼矣、爰其適歸、

(3) 冬日烈烈、飄風發發、民莫不穀、我獨何害、

(4) 山有嘉卉、侯栗侯梅、廢爲殘賊、莫知其尤、

(5) 相彼泉水、載清載濁、我日構禍、曷云能穀、

2. Ts'iōu jĕu ts'ī ts'ī, pĕ houéi kiú fêi. Louán lî mouŏ i, iuên k'î chĕu kouēi?
3. Tōung jĕu liĕ liĕ, p'iaō fōung fă fă. Min mouŏ pŏu kŏu, ngò tŏu hô hái (hŏ)?
4. Chān iòu kiā houéi, heôu lî heôu mêi. Féi wêi ts'ân tsĕ, mouŏ tchēu k'î iôu (î).
5. Siáng pèi ts'iuên chouèi, tsái ts'īng tsái tchouŏ (tchŏu). Ngò jĕu keòu houó, hŏ iùn nêng kŏu?

2. Les jours d'automne sont froids; toutes les plantes herbacées se flétrissent. (Ce deuil de la nature est l'image de la désolation actuelle de l'empire). Au milieu du trouble, de la dispersion générale, je suis dans l'affliction; où irai-je chercher un refuge?

3. Les jours d'hiver sont très rigoureux; le vent souffle avec violence. (Malgré tant de maux), chacun paraît content (résigné à son malheureux sort); pourquoi moi seul suis-je dans le chagrin?

4. Sur les montagnes croissent de beaux arbres, à savoir, des châtaigniers, des pruniers. (Au contraire, dans l'empire il n'est plus d'officiers intègres). Ils sont devenus malfaiteurs cruels; et personne ne se reconnaît coupable.

5. Voyez l'eau de cette source; elle est tantôt limpide tantôt trouble, (elle n'est pas trouble tous les jours). Moi, je suis malheureux tous les jours; quand pourrai-je enfin jouir du bonheur?

Defuncti avi nonne sunt homines? Qua de causa non miserentur mei?

Ici les mois lunaires sont ceux du calendrier des 夏 **Hiá**, lequel était conforme au calendrier actuel. Cf. p. 160.
胡寧 **Hôu gning**, pourquoi?

2. Autumnales dies sunt frigidi; omnigenæ plantæ cunctæ marcescunt. De turbatione et dispersione doleo; quo ego abiens confugiam?

Dans le 家語 **Kiā iù**, au lieu de 爰 **iuên**, on lit 奚 **hî**.

3. Hiemales dies sunt asperrimi; flat ventus vehementer. Civium nullus non felix; ego solus cur mœreo?

4. In montibus sunt pulchræ arbores, nempe castaneæ, nempe pruni. (Magistratus) corrupti evaserunt crudeles et malefici; nemo agnoscit suam culpam.

卉 Plantes herbacées. Anciennement ce mot désignait toutes sortes de plantes.

5. Aspice illius fontis aquam; modo liquida modo turbida est. Ego quotidie offendo infortunia; quando potero esse felix?

(6) 滔滔江漢、南國之紀。盡瘁以仕、寧莫我有。

(7) 匪鶉匪鳶、翰飛戾天。匪鱣匪鮪、潛逃于淵。

(8) 山有蕨薇、隰有杞桋。君子作歌、維以告哀。

北山之什二之六

北山

(1) 陟彼北山、言

6. T'aō t'aō Kiāng Hán, nân kouŏ tchèu ki. Tsìn tsouéi i chéu, gnîng mouŏ ngò iòu (i)?

7. Fèi t'ouân fèi iuēn (iūn), hàn fēi li t'iēn (t'īn). Féi tchēn fèi wèi, tsièn t'aô iū iuēn (iūn).

8. Chān iòu kiuĕ wêi, sĭ iòu k'i î. Kiūn tzèu tsŏ kō, wêi i kaó ngāi (ī).

PE CHAN. **1. Tchĕu pèi pĕ chān, iên ts'ài k'i k'i. Kiāi kiāi chéu tzéu (tsi),**

6. Le Kiang et la Han, ces deux grands cours d'eau sont comme les grandes artères des principautés du midi. (Ils ne sont inconnus de personne). Moi, je me consume tout entier dans l'exercice de ma charge ; comment se fait-il que personne ne semble connaître mon existence?

7. Je ne suis ni aigle ni faucon pour m'envoler jusqu'au ciel ; ni esturgeon, grand ou petit, pour plonger et fuir au fond des eaux. (Je n'ai aucun moyen d'échapper à mon malheur).

8. Les fougères croissent sur les montagnes, le lyciet et l'orme dans les vallées. (Chaque chose occupe le lieu qui lui convient. Moi, je vis loin du foyer domestique). Je suis officier; j'ai composé ce chant pour faire connaître ma douleur.

LIVRE VI. PE CHAN.

CHANT I. PE CHAN.

Un grand préfet se plaint d'être retenu longtemps loin de sa famille et condamné à des fatigues continuelles pour le service de l'empereur, tandis que beaucoup d'autres jouissent d'un paisible repos.

1. Nous gravissons cette montagne qui est au nord, et nous y

6. Ingentibus aquis fluunt Kiang et Han; australium regnorum arteriæ sunt. Totus consumor in gerendo magistratu; cur nemo me existere (scit)?

7. Non sum aquila nec falco, ut pennis volans attingam cœlum. Non sum acipenser major nec acipenser minor, ut immersus fugiam in aquam profundam.

8. In montibus sunt *kiue* et *wei* filices; in vallibus sunt lycium et ulmus. Præfectus composui canticum, tantummodo ut significarem dolorem.

TITRE DU LIVRE. 北山之什二之六 Pe chan decas: secundæ (partis) sexta (decas).

CHANT I. 1. Ascendimus illum septentrionalem montem, ut decerpamus

釆其杞、偕偕士子、朝夕從事、王事靡盬、憂我父母、

(2) 溥天之下、莫非王土、率土之濱、莫非王臣、大夫不均、我從事獨賢、

(3) 四牡彭彭、王事傍傍、嘉我未老、鮮我方將、旅力方剛、經營四方、

(4) 或燕燕居息、或

tchaō sĭ ts'ōung chéu (chéu). Wâng chéu mi kòu, iōu ngò fóu mòu (méi).

2. P'òu t'iēn tchēu hiá (hòu), mouŏ fēi wâng t'òu. Chouĕ t'òu tchēu pīn, mouŏ fēi wâng tch'ênn. Tái fōu pŏu kiūn, ngò ts'ōung chéu tŏu hiên (hênn).

3. Séu meòu p'ōung p'ōung (p'âng p'âng), wâng chéu p'âng p'âng. Kiā ngò wéi laò, sièn ngò fāng ts'iāng. Liù lì fāng kāng, kīng îng séu fāng.

4. Houĕ ién ién kiū sĭ, houĕ tsin tsouéi chéu kouŏ (ĭ). Houĕ sĭ ièn tsái

cueillons le lyciet (pour notre nourriture). Nous sommes tous des officiers robustes et courageux; du matin au soir nous sommes occupés par les affaires. Il n'est pas permis de négliger le service de l'empereur; (par mon absence) je laisse mes parents dans le chagrin.

2. Sous l'immensité des cieux, il n'est pas un endroit qui n'appartienne à l'empereur. Entre les rivages des quatre mers, il n'est personne qui ne soit sujet de l'empereur. (Chacun des habitants de l'empire devrait supporter sa part des charges publiques). Les ministres d'État ne sont pas justes; ils m'obligent à faire seul tout le service, comme si j'avais seul la sagesse nécessaire.

3. Mes quatre chevaux sont toujours en marche; les affaires de l'empereur ne me laissent point de relâche. On me loue de n'avoir pas encore vieilli; on m'admire d'avoir conservé mes forces jusqu'à présent. Tant que mon épine dorsale est encore assez robuste, je suis chargé de dessiner et d'exécuter les plans dans toutes les parties de l'empire.

4. Parmi les citoyens, les uns sont en repos et à leur aise; les autres

illius lycium. Robusti ac fortes præpositi, a mane ad vesperum operam damus negotiis. Imperatoris negotia non licet negligenter tractare; mœrore afficio meos parentes.

2. Vastum cœlum subter, nulla non est imperatoris terra. Secundum terrarum oras maritimas, nemo non est imperatoris subditus. Magni magistratus non sunt æqui; ego operam do negotiis (quasi) solus prudens.

3. Quatuor mares equi semper eunt; imperatoris negotia continuo urgent. Laudant me quod nondum senuerim; mirantur me quod etiamnum robustus sim. Dorsalis spinæ viribus etiamnum pollentibus, designo et perficio (opera) in quatuor imperii regionibus.

盡瘁事國、或息
偃在牀、或不已
于行、
(5) 或不知叫號、
或慘慘劬勞、或
棲遲偃仰、或王
事鞅掌、
(6) 或湛樂飲酒、
或慘慘畏咎、或
出入風議、或靡
事不爲、
無將大車
(1) 無將大車、祇

tch'ouâng, houĕ pŏu i iŭ hîng (hâng).

5. Houĕ pŏu tchēu kiaó haô, houĕ ts'àn ts'àn k'iŭ laô. Houĕ sī tch'êu ièn iàng, houĕ wâng chéu iàng tchàng.

6. Houĕ tān lŏ in tsiòu, houĕ ts'àn ts'àn wéi kiòu. Houĕ tch'ŏu jŏu fóung i (ī), houĕ mi chéu pŏu wéi.

OU TSIANG TA KIU. **1. Oû tsiāng tá kiū, tchēu tzéu tch'ènn hī. Oû sēu pĕ iōu, tchēu tzéu k'ì hì.**

se dépensent entièrement au service de l'État. Les uns se reposent étendus sur leurs lits; les autres sont toujours en voyage.

5. Les uns (retirés au fond de leurs appartements) n'entendent pas même un cri; les autres, toujours dans l'inquiétude, sont accablés de fatigue. Les uns, oisifs et tranquilles comme des oiseaux perchés sur les arbres, lèvent et baissent les yeux tout à leur aise; les autres, occupés au service de l'empereur, sont dans le trouble et l'agitation.

6. Les uns passent un temps considérable dans les plaisirs et les orgies; les autres sont dans la peine et craignent encore d'être blâmés. Les uns, à la maison et au dehors, ne font que censurer et critiquer; les autres sont condamnés à exécuter tous les travaux.

CHANT II. OU TSIANG TA KIU.

Un officier, accablé de travail au service de l'empereur, ne trouve pas de meilleur soulagement à sa peine que de le bannir de son esprit et de n'y pas penser.

1. Ne poussez pas à la roue pour faire avancer la grande

4. Quidam commode manent quieti; quidam omnino consumuntur servientes regno. Quidam quieti jacent super lectos; quidam non desinunt in itinere esse.

5. Quidam non norunt (non audiunt cujusvis) clamorem vociferationemve; quidam solliciti et anxii summopere laborant. Quidam residentes (ut aves in arboribus) et pigritantes despiciunt ac suspiciunt; quidam in imperatoris negotiis vehementer trepidant.

6. Quidam diu se oblectant et bibunt vinum; quidam valde laborantes timent ne culpentur. Quidam foris domique carpentes judicant; quidam nullum est negotium quod non peragant.

自塵兮、無思百憂、祇自疧兮、

(2) 無將大車、維塵冥冥、無思百憂、不出于熲、

(3) 無將大車、維塵雝兮、無思百憂、祇自重兮、

小明

(1) 明明上天、

2. Où tsiāng tá kiū, wêi tch'ênn mîng mîng (mòung mòung). Où sēu pĕ iōu, pŏu tch'ŏu iū kiòung.

3. Où tsiāng tá kiū, wêi tch'ênn iōung hî. Où sēu pĕ iōu, tchēu tzéu tchóung hî.

SIAO MING. **1. Mîng mîng cháng t'ien, tchaó lîn hiá t'òu. Ngò tchēng ts'ŏu**

charrette; vous ne feriez que soulever et recevoir sur vous la poussière. (De même) ne pensez pas à vos nombreux chagrins; vous ne feriez que vous rendre vous-même malheureux.

2. Ne poussez pas à la roue pour faire avancer la grosse charrette; vous ne feriez que soulever la poussière et vous aveugler. (De même) ne pensez pas à vos nombreux chagrins; votre intelligence en serait troublée, obscurcie.

3. Ne poussez pas à la roue pour faire avancer la grosse charrette; vous seriez couvert de poussière. (De même) ne pensez pas à vos nombreux chagrins; vous ne feriez que vous charger d'un poids accablant.

CHANT III. SIAO MING.

Un grand préfet, envoyé en expédition, se plaint d'être retenu longtemps loin de sa maison, et il en appelle au ciel. Il envie le sort des officiers qui sont à la cour, et leur donne des avis.

1. O ciel qui brillez au-dessus de nous, vous exercez votre

CHANT II. 1. Ne adjuvans impellas magnum plaustrum; solummodo ipse te pulvere consperges. Ne cogites de innumeris curis; solummodo ipse te lædes.

疧 **K'î** ne rime pas avec 塵 **tch'ênn.** C'est une lettre fautive. On croit qu'il faut lire 痻 **min.**

2. Ne adjuvans impellas magnum plaustrum; solummodo excitato pulvere caligabis. Ne cogites de innumeris curis; (si cogitabis), non emerges ex tenui luce.

3. Ne adjuvans impellas magnum plaustrum; solummodo excitato pulvere obduceris. Ne cogites de innumeris curis; (si cogitabis), solummodo ipse te gravabis.

CHANT III. 1. O fulgidum et supernum cœlum, invigilas et moderaris subjectæ terræ. Ego profectus adivi occidentem; perveni ad K'iou deserta. A secundi mensis primo die, jam pertuli frigora et calores. Animi mœror ipse venenum est valde amarum. Cogito de illis fungentibus (magistratu in imperatoris aula) viris; lacrymæ decidunt velut imber. Quomodo non cupiam reverti domum? Timeo hoc offensæ rete.

照臨下土。我征徂西。至于艽野。二月初吉。載離寒暑。心之憂矣。其毒大苦。念彼共人。涕零如雨。豈不懷歸。畏此罪罟。

(2) 昔我往矣。日月方除。曷云其還。歲聿云莫。念我獨兮。我事孔庶。心之憂矣。憚

sī, tchéu iû K'iôu iè (chòu). Eúl iuĕ tch'ōu kĭ, tsái lî hân chòu. Sīn tchēu iōu i, k'î tŏu t'ái k'òu. Gnién pèi kōung jènn, t'ì lîng jôu iù. K'ì pŏu houâi kouēi? Wéi ts'éu tsouéi kòu.

2. Sĭ ngò wàng i, jĕu iuĕ fāng tch'óu. Hŏ iûn k'î houân? Souéi iŭ iûn móu. Gnién ngò tŏu hî, ngò chéu k'òung chóu. Sīn tchēu iōu i, touó ngò pŏu hiá (hóu).

vigilance et votre autorité sur tout l'univers. (Écoutez ma plainte). Je suis allé à l'occident jusqu'aux déserts de K'iou. Depuis le premier jour du deuxième mois de l'année, j'ai supporté le froid et le chaud. Mon cœur est tourmenté par le chagrin, comme par un amer poison. En pensant aux officiers qui exercent leurs fonctions (à la cour et jouissent de la tranquillité), je verse des torrents de larmes. Comment ne désirerais-je pas mon retour? Mais je crains de commettre une offense (sans le vouloir), et de tomber ainsi comme dans un filet.

2. Au temps de mon départ, le soleil et la lune venaient de clore l'année précédente. Quand retournerai-je? Déjà l'année touche à son terme. Je me vois seul et sous le poids d'affaires très nombreuses. Mon cœur est triste ; au milieu de mes fatigues je n'ai

小明 **Siaò Ming** signifie 小雅之明 **Siaò iá tchēu Mîng**, le chant intitulé *Ming*, qui fait partie du *Siao ia*. Cf. page 244. **K'iôu**, nom d'un lieu très éloigné. 初吉 **Tch'ōu kĭ**, le premier jour du mois lunaire, ainsi nommé parce qu'il était favorable pour commencer une entreprise. Les mois lunaires sont indiqués d'après le calendrier des 夏 **Hiá**, lequel était conforme au calendrier actuel. 離 **Li** équivaut à 經 **kīng**, passer par, éprouver, souffrir, avoir l'expérience de. 照 **Tchaó**, éclairer, veiller sur, prendre soin de. 臨 **Lin**, approcher, se dit d'un supérieur visitant ou gouvernant un inférieur. 呼天而訴之曰… 夫明明上天照臨下土是宜無所不察也… 何天不我察哉 詩經備旨) L'officier en appelle au ciel et lui exprime sa plainte en ces termes: « Le ciel qui brille au-dessus de nous, exerce sa vigilance et son autorité sur tout l'univers… Rien ne doit échapper à ses investigations… Pourquoi n'examine-t-il pas ma cause? »

2. Olim me abeunte, sol et luna modo excluserant (superiorem annum). Quandonam ipse revertar? Annus exit. Cogito me esse solum et mea negotia

我不暇、念彼共人、睠睠懷顧、豈不懷歸、畏此譴怒、

(3) 昔我往矣、日月方奧、曷云其還、政事愈蹙、歲聿云莫、采蕭穫菽、心之憂矣、自詒伊戚、念彼共人、興言出宿、豈不懷歸、畏此反覆、

(4) 嗟爾君子、無恒安處、靖共爾位、正

Gnién pèi kōung jênn, kiuén kiuén houâi kóu. K'i pòu houâi kouēi? Wéi ts'èu k'ién nóu.

3. Sí ngò wàng i, jĕu iuĕ fāng iŭ. Hŏ iùn k'i houân? Tchéng chéu iù tsiŭ. Souéi iŭ iùn móu, ts'ài siaō houŏ chŏu. Sīn tchēu iōu i, tzéu î ī ts'í (tsiŭ). Gnién pèi kōung jênn, hīng ién tch'ŏu siŭ. K'i pòu houâi kouēi? Wéi ts'èu fàn fŏu.

4. Tsiē! èul kiūn tzèu, ôu hêng ngān tch'òu. Tsíng kōung èul wéi, tchéng

aucun loisir. Au souvenir des officiers qui exercent des charges à la cour, mes affections et mes regrets tourmentent mon cœur. Comment ne désirerais-je pas mon retour? Mais je crains le blâme et la colère (de l'empereur).

3. Au temps de mon départ, le soleil et la lune commençaient à donner une douce chaleur. Quand retournerai-je? Les affaires du gouvernement sont de plus en plus pressantes. L'année touche à son terme ; on cueille l'armoise, on récolte les haricots. Mon cœur est triste ; je me suis attiré moi-même ces souffrances, (j'aurais dû prévoir ces difficultés et fuir bien loin). En pensant aux officiers qui exercent des charges (à la cour, je ne puis dormir), je me lève et vais passer la nuit dehors. Comment ne désirerais-je pas mon retour? Mais je crains (d'exciter la colère de l'empereur et de provoquer) une catastrophe.

4. Oh! vous, grands officiers de la cour, ne demeurez pas sans cesse dans le repos. Remplissez avec calme et réflexion les

valde numerosa. Animus dolet, fatigatus ego nullo fruor otio. Memini illorum fungentium (magistratu in aula) virorum; cum amore et desiderio in animo recogito. Quomodo non cupiam reverti? Timeo hanc exprobrationem et iram.

3. Olim me abeunte, sol et luna incipiebant tepere. Quandonam ipse revertar? Publicæ administrationis res magis ac magis urgent. Annus exit; decerpitur artemisia, demetuntur phaseoli. Animus dolet; ipse mihi adscivi mœrorem. Cogito de illis fungentibus (magistratu in aula) viris; surgens egredior pernoctatum. Qui non cupiam reverti? Timeo hanc subversionem.

4. Oh! vos, magnates, ne constanter quieti maneatis. Pacate fungamini officiis vestrarum dignitatum. Probis rectisque ipsis adsitis. Spiritus obsecundabunt illis (conatibus vestris), adhibentes bona dabunt vobis.

直是與、神之聽之、式穀以女、⑤嗟爾君子、無恒安息、靖共爾位、好是正直、神之聽之、介爾景福、

鼓鐘

①鼓鐘將將、淮水湯湯

tchĕu chéu iù. Chênn tchēu t'īng tchēu, chĕu kŏu i jòu.

5. Tsiē ! èul kiūn tzèu, ǒu hêng ngān sī. Tsíng kōung èul wéi, hào chéu tchéng tchĕu. Chênn tchēu t'īng tchēu, kiái èul king fòu (pì).

KOU TCHOUNG. 1. Kòu tchōung ts'iāng ts'iāng, Houâi chouèi t'āng t'āng. Iōu

devoirs attachés à vos dignités; aidez les hommes probes et sincères. Les esprits seconderont vos efforts, et vous combleront de biens.

5. Oh! vous, grands officiers de la cour, ne vous livrez pas constamment au repos. Remplissez avec calme les devoirs attachés à vos dignités; aimez les hommes probes et sincères. Les esprits seconderont vos efforts, et vous accorderont libéralement les biens les plus précieux.

CHANT IV. KOU TCHOUNG.

L'empereur 幽王 Iōu wâng se livre au plaisir de la musique et à d'autres divertissements, sur le bord de la Houai, depuis le moment où les eaux du fleuve commencent à croître jusqu'à celui où elles ont diminué au point de laisser apparaître trois îlots.

1. Les cloches retentissent. L'eau de la Houai va croissant. Mon

安 Ngān, calme, sans précipitation, avec réflexion.

5. Oh! vos, magnates, ne constanter commode quiescatis. Pacate fungamini officiis vestrarum dignitatum. Diligite illos probos et rectos. Spiritus obsecundabunt illis (operibus vestris), augebunt vos ingentibus bonis. 若然則一念忠敬之心孚之於神明而無欺矣神之聽之隆其降監甚明之機錫之以莫大之慶而景福之介無所吝焉寧不可以長處其逸哉向使棄爾職而不修疏正直而不與則神其吐之欲式穀景福其可得乎(詩經備旨) « S'il en est ainsi, si vous ne pensez qu'à remplir vos devoirs avec fidélité et diligence, vous aurez la confiance des intelligences célestes, et ne tromperez pas leur attente. Les esprits seconderont vos entreprises, abaisseront sur vous leurs regards, vous prêteront le secours de leurs lumières, vous accorderont une félicité sans égale, et vous combleront de tous les biens avec une libéralité sans limite. Il ne convient donc pas de garder longtemps le repos. Si au contraire vous laissiez de côté vos obligations et ne les remplissiez pas, si vous écartiez les hommes sincères et vertueux et ne les aidiez pas, les esprits *eromerent vos* vous rejetteraient avec dégoût. Pourraient-ils, quand même ils le voudraient, vous combler de félicité? »

湯、憂心且傷、淑人君子、懷允不忘、

(2) 鼓鐘喈喈、淮水湝湝、憂心且悲、淑人君子、其德不回、

(3) 鼓鐘伐鼛、淮有三洲、憂心且妯、淑人君子、其德不猶、

(4) 鼓鐘欽欽、鼓瑟鼓琴、笙磬同音、以雅以南、以籥不僭、

sīn ts'iė chāng. Chŏu jênn kiūn tzèu, houâi iùn pŏu wâng.

2. Kòu tchōung kiāi kiāi (kī kī), Houâi chouèi hiāi hiāi (hī hī). Iōu sīn ts'iė pēi. Chŏu jênn kiūn tzèu, k'î tĕ pŏu houêi.

3. Kòu tchōung fă kaō (kiōu), Houâi iòu sān tcheōu. Iōu sīn ts'iė tch'eōu. Chŏu jênn kiūn tzèu, k'î tĕ pŏu iôu.

4. Kòu tchōung k'īn k'īn, kòu chĕ kòu k'în. Chēng k'ing t'ôung īn. Ì ià i Nân (Gnîn), i iŏ pŏu tsién (ts'īn).

cœur est triste et affligé. Je pense sans cesse aux sages et vertueux empereurs (Wenn wang, Ou wang, Tch'eng wang et K'ang wang).

2. Les cloches retentissent ; l'eau de la Houai coule à pleins bords. Mon cœur est dans la tristesse et la douleur. La conduite de nos sages et vertueux souverains fut toujours irréprochable.

3. Les cloches retentissent, on bat le grand tambour. Dans la Houai apparaissent trois ilots. Mon cœur est triste et agité. Telle n'était pas la conduite de nos sages et vertueux souverains.

4. Les cloches retentissent; on entend le luth et la guitare. Les flûtes et les pierres sonores unissent leurs accords. On exécute les chants du Siao ia, du Ta ia, du Tcheou nan et du Chao nan; les pantomimes jouent de la flûte. La musique et la représentation sont parfaites; (mais la conduite du prince est très déréglée).

CHANT IV. 1. Pulsantur campanæ cum sonitu *ts'iang ts'iang*. Houai aqua assurgit. Mœret animus et dolet. Optimos viros, sapientes reges cogitans vere non obliviscor.

2. Pulsantur campanæ cum sonitu *kiai kiai*. Houai aqua turgida fluit. Mœret animus et dolet. Optimorum virorum, sapientium regum ipsorum mores non deflectebant (a recto).

3. Pulsantur campanæ, percutitur majus tympanum. In Houai sunt tres insulæ. Mœret animus et agitatur. Optimorum virorum, sapientium regum ipsorum mores non erant tales.

4. Pulsantur campanæ cum sonitu *k'in k'in*; pulsatur cithara, pulsatur lyra. Fistulæ et sonori lapides miscent sonos. Adhibentur Ia, adhibentur Nan (canuntur Cheu king cantica), adhibentur (mimorum) tibiæ; (tum alii musici tum mimi) non aberrant.

楚茨

(1) 楚楚者茨、言抽其棘、自昔何爲、我蓺黍稷、我黍與與、我稷翼翼、我倉既盈、我庾維億、以爲酒食、以饗以祀、以妥以侑、以介景福。

(2) 濟濟蹌蹌、絜爾牛羊、以

TCH'OU TS'EU. **1. Tch'ôu tch'ôu tchè ts'êu, iên tch'eōu k'ì kí. Tzéu sĭ hô wéi? Ngò i chòu tsĭ. Ngò chòu iù iù, ngò tsĭ ĭ ĭ. Ngò ts'āng ki ing, ngò iù wêi ĭ, i wêi tsiòu chĕu, i hiàng i séu (ĭ), i t'ouò i iòu (ĭ), i kiái king fòu (pĭ).**

2. Tsi tsi ts'iāng ts'iāng, kiĕ èul iôu iâng. Ì wàng tchēng tch'âng. Houĕ pŏ

CHANT V. TCH'OU TS'EU.

Description des cérémonies faites par un grand dignitaire en l'honneur de ses ancêtres.

1. Autrefois les chardons couvraient ce champ; ils ont été arrachés, ainsi que tous les arbustes épineux. Pourquoi les anciens ont-ils fait ce travail de défrichement? Afin que je cultivasse le *chou* et le *tsi* (les deux sortes de millet à panicules qu'on a coutume d'offrir aux ancêtres). Mon *chou* est verdoyant et beau; mon *tsi* est luxuriant. Mes greniers sont remplis; j'ai dans les champs cent mille monceaux de grain. J'en fais des liqueurs et des mets, pour les offrir à mes parents défunts. Je fais asseoir commodément (le représentant de mes ancêtres), et l'invite à boire et à manger. J'obtiendrai en récompense un accroissement de prospérité.

2. Avec un maintien grave et une démarche respectueuse, nous allons choisir des victimes parfaites, des bœufs et des brebis. Nous

CHANT V. 1. Valde densi erant tribuli; evulsi sunt illi sentes. Ex antiquis temporibus quare hoc factum est? Ut ego sererem *chòu, tsĭ* (panici milii duo genera). Meum *chòu* milium luxuriat; meum *tsĭ* milium ubertim crescit. Mea horrea impleta sunt; mei acervi sunt centies mille. Utens facio vinum et dapes, utens offero, utens sacra facio. Utens colloco, utens excito (progenitorum vicarium); inde augebitur magna felicitas.

茨 **Ts'êu** ou 蒺藜 **Tsĭ lì**, Tribule, appelé aussi Herse ou Croix de Malte. 棘 **Kĭ** ou 荊棘 **Kīng kĭ**, arbustes épineux. 言 **Iên**, particule. 庾 **Iù**, amas de grain en plein air.

L'un des membres de la famille était désigné par le sort pour représenter les parents défunts. Il prenait le nom de 尸 **chēu**. Le maître de la maison le faisait asseoir commodément, se prosternait devant lui, l'invitait à manger et à boire, et lui rendait les mêmes honneurs qu'à ses ancêtres.

2. Composito habitu reverentique incessu, puros eligimus boves et oves. Utentes imus hiemalia sacra facturi, autumnalia sacra facturi. Hi excoriant, illi coquunt; quidam imponunt fercu-

往烝嘗、或剝或
亨、或肆或將、祝
祭于祊、祀事孔
明、先祖是皇、神
保是饗、孝孫有
慶、報以介福、萬
壽無疆、
(3) 執爨踖踖、為
俎孔碩、或燔或
炙、君婦莫莫、為
豆孔庶、為賓為
客、獻酬交錯、禮

houĕ p'ēng (p'āng), houĕ séu houĕ tsiāng. Tchŏu tsi iū pōung (pāng). Séu chéu k'òung ming (màng), siēn tsòu chéu houâng. Chênn paò chéu hiàng (hiāng), hiaó suēnn iòu k'ing (k'iâng). Paó i kiái fŏu (pī), wán cheóu ŏu kiāng.

3. Tchĕu ts'ouán tsĭ tsĭ (tsiŏ tsiŏ), wêi tchòu k'òung chĕu (chŏ). Houĕ fân, houĕ tchĕu (tchŏ). Kiūn fóu mouŏ mouŏ, wêi teóu k'òung chóu (tchŏ). Wêi

les faisons servir aux cérémonies d'hiver, d'automne (et des autres saisons). Parmi les serviteurs, les uns écorchent les victimes, les autres en font cuire la chair; ceux-ci mettent les viandes sur les supports, ceux-là vont les offrir aux mânes. L'orateur chargé de prendre la parole dans la cérémonie est auprès de la porte du temple (attendant l'arrivée des mânes). Le service est complet et splendide; les mânes des ancêtres entrent avec majesté. Leur répondant (leur représentant) agrée les offrandes, et moi, leur descendant dévoué, j'aurai du bonheur. Ils m'accorderont en récompense un accroissement de prospérité, dix mille années de vie, une vie sans fin.

3. Les serviteurs soignent les foyers avec grand respect, et disposent des supports très grands (pour placer les viandes). Quelques-uns font rôtir (la chair des victimes), d'autres font griller (le foie). La princesse dispose avec calme et respect un grand nombre de vases (destinés à contenir les ragoûts, les sauces,...). Les étrangers (qui ont été désignés par le sort et invités à la cérémonie),

lis, alii asportant. Orator sacrorum est ad januam. Sacrorum res sunt valde splendidæ; progenitores inde magnifice (ingrediuntur). Manium sponsor inde fruitur; pius nepos habebo felicitatem. Munerabuntur magna prosperitate, decies mille vitæ annis, sine termino.

絜 **Kiĕ**, pur; choisir une victime pure et exempte de défauts, c.-à-d. une victime d'une seule couleur avec des cornes bien régulières.

爾 **Eùl**, particule.

祝 **Tchŏu** ou 祝 祭 **Tchŏu tsi**, celui qui lisait des panégyriques en l'honneur des esprits, leur adressait des demandes, recevait et transmettait leurs réponses.

3. (Ministri) curant focos magna reverentia, componunt quadras valde magnas; quidam torrent, quidam subassant. Principis uxor pacate et reverenter componit vasa bene multa. Qui sunt hospites et qui sunt adventores, invicem vino donant et donantur,

儀卒度、笑語卒獲、神保是格、報以介福、萬壽攸酢、

(4) 我孔熯矣、式禮莫愆、工祝致告、徂賚孝孫、苾芬孝祀、神嗜飲食、卜爾百福、如幾如式、既齊既稷、既匡既敕、永錫爾極、時萬時億、

pīn wêi k'ŏ, hién tch'eôu kiaō ts'ouŏ. Li ī tsŏu tóu (touŏ), siaó iù tsŏu houŏ. Chénn paò chéu kŏ. Paó i kiài fŏu (pí), wán cheóu iôu tsŏ.

4. Ngò k'òung chèn i, chĕu li mouŏ k'iēn (k'īn). Kóung tchŏu tchéu kaó, ts'ôu lái hiaó suēnn (siūn). Pí fēnn hiaó séu (ì), chènn chéu in chéu. Pòu èul pĕ fŏu (pĭ), jôu kī jôu chŏu. Ki ts'i ki tsí, ki k'ouāng ki tch'ĕu, iòung sí èul kĭ, chéu wán chéu ī.

s'offrent du vin mutuellement à la ronde. Toutes les cérémonies, grandes ou petites, sont observées conformément aux prescriptions; les sourires et les paroles sont tout-à-fait comme il convient. Le répondant des mânes arrive, (et les mânes avec lui). Ils m'accordent en récompense une grande prospérité et dix mille années de vie.

4. J'ai fait tout ce qui était en pouvoir, et accompli toutes les cérémonies avec la plus grande exactitude. L'habile orateur me transmet les paroles des mânes, et vient de leur part me promettre des récompenses, en retour de ma piété filiale. «Votre pieuse offrande, dit-il, a exhalé une agréable odeur. Les esprits ont agréé la boisson et les mets. Ils vous accordent en partage toutes sortes de biens, qui vous viendront conformément à vos désirs et de la manière convenable. Vous avez été grave, prompt, irréprochable, attentif. Les esprits vous accordent pour toujours les faveurs les plus signalées; ils vous les enverront sans cesse par myriades et par dixaines de myriades.»

obversi et transversi. Ritus et minores cæremoniæ omnino quadrant legibus; risus et verba omnino assequuntur (id quod decet). Manium sponsor inde advenit. Munerantur magna felicitate, et decies mille anni sunt quos retribuunt.

神保以象神尸格則神格矣(詩經備旨) Le répondant qui représente les mânes arrive, et les mânes arrivent avec lui.

4. Ego omnino exhausi vires, utens ritibus non peccavi. Peritus orator significans monet (de manium mandatis), venit et muneratur pium nepotem. «Suave fragravit pia oblatio; spiritus acceptos habuerunt potum ac cibum; præstituunt tibi omnis generis bona, juxta vota, juxta normam. Fuisti compositus, fuisti celer, fuisti rectus, fuisti cautus. In perpetuum donant te summis (bonis), jugiter decies mille, jugiter centies mille.»

詩經

(5) 禮儀既備、鐘鼓既戒、孝孫徂位、工祝致告、神具醉止、皇尸載起、鼓鐘送尸、神保聿歸、諸宰君婦、廢徹不遲、諸父兄弟、備言燕私、

(6) 樂具入奏、以綏後祿、爾殽既將、莫怨具慶、既醉既飽、小大稽

5. Li î ki pi (pĭ), tchōung kòu ki kiái (kĭ), hiaó suēnn ts'ôu wéi (lĭ). Kōung tchōu tchéu kaó (kĕ). Chênn kiú tsouéi tchéu, houâng chēu tsái k'i. Kòu tchōung sóung chēu, chênn paò iŭ kouēi. Tchōu tsài kiūn fóu féi tch'ĕ pŏu tch'êu. Tchōu fóu hiōung ti, pi iên ién sēu.

6. Iŏ kiú jŏu tseóu (tsŏu), i souēi heóu lŏu. Eùl hiaŏ kí tsiāng, mouŏ iuén kiú k'ing (k'iâng). Ki tsouéi ki paò (peòu), siaò tá k'i cheòu. Chênn chéu in

5. Les cérémonies, grandes et petites, sont terminées; les cloches et les tambours ont annoncé la fin. Moi, descendant dévoué, je vais reprendre mon siège. L'habile orateur me dit (au nom du représentant des mânes): « Les esprits ont tous bu largement. » Alors l'auguste représentant des mânes se lève. Les tambours et les cloches le reconduisent; les esprits se retirent avec leur répondant. La princesse et tous les serviteurs enlèvent les offrandes sans retard. Tous les parents en ligne masculine, soit d'une génération antérieure à celle du prince, soit d'une génération postérieure, prennent part à un festin privé, (ils mangent les mets qui ont été offerts aux mânes).

6. Tous les musiciens entrent (dans la salle du festin, derrière le temple des ancêtres), et exécutent des chants, pour accompagner les promesses de prospérité qui doivent être faites (par les convives). Les mets sont servis; personne n'est mécontent, chacun est heureux. Quand les convives ont bu et mangé suffisamment, tous,

5. Ritus et cæremoniæ jam perfectæ sunt ; campanæ et tympana monuerunt (omnia esse perfecta). Pius nepos vado ad sedem ; peritus orator significans monet (manium vicarii verbis). « Spiritus omnes biberunt ad saturitatem. » Augustus manium vicarius tunc surgit. Tympana et campanæ comitantur manium vicarium ; manium sponsor recedit. Omnes ministri et principis uxor tollentes amovent non tarde. Omnes patrui et patrueles cuncti epulantur privatim.

6. Musici omnes ingrediuntur et personant, ad firmandam posteriorem faustorum precationem. Et dapes appositæ sunt ; nemo indignatur, omnes sunt felices. Jam saturati vino, jam saturati epulis, minores et majores (ætate) demittunt caput. « Spiritus acceptos habuerunt potum et cibum ; dederunt tibi, Domine, ut diu viveres.

首、神嗜飲食、使君壽考、孔惠孔時、維其盡之、子子孫孫、勿替引之、

信南山

(1)信彼南山、維禹甸之、畇畇原隰、曾孫田之、我疆我理、南東其畝、

(2)上天同雲、雨雪雰雰、益之以霢霂、既優既渥、既霑既足、生我百穀、

chĕu, chéu kiūn cheóu k'aò (k'eòu). K'òung houéi k'òung chêu, wêi k'ì tsin (tsin) tchēu. Tzéu tzéu suēnn suēnn, ŏu t'ì in tchēu.

SIN NAN CHAN. **1. Sin pèi nân chān, wêi Iù tién (tīn) tchēu. Iûn iûn iuên sĭ, tsēng suēnn tién (tīn) tchēu. Ngò kiāng, ngò lì; nân tōung k'ì meòu (mèi).**

2. Cháng t'iēn t'ôung iûn, iù siuĕ fēnn fēnn; ĭ tchēu i mĕ mŏu. Ki iōu ki iŏ (ŏu), ki tchēn ki tsŏu, chēng ngò pĕ kŏu.

jeunes et vieux, inclinent la tête (et disent): «Les esprits ont agréé la boisson et la nourriture, et vous ont octroyé, Seigneur, une vie longue. Vous avez fait ces offrandes de la manière la plus convenable et aux temps marqués (à chaque saison de l'année); vos fils et tous vos descendants les continueront à jamais sans interruption.»

CHANT VI. SIN NAN CHAN.

Soins donnés à l'agriculture et honneurs rendus aux parents défunts par un grand dignitaire de l'empire.

1. Cette montagne qui est au midi (et ses alentours) ont d'abord reçu les soins du grand Iu. (Mes ancêtres) ont défriché les hauteurs et les vallées, et moi, leur arrière-petit-fils (leur descendant), je cultive ces champs. J'en ai marqué les limites, je les ai divisés (par des fossés et des canaux); les arpents s'étendent, les uns du nord au sud, les autres de l'est à l'ouest.

2. Un épais nuage couvre tout le ciel, et la neige tombe à gros flocons; une pluie fine vient s'y ajouter (en printemps). La terre ainsi fécondée, imbibée, arrosée et saturée, produit toute sorte de grains.

Omnino juxta rationem, omnino temporibus statutis, ipse perfecisti illa. Filii et nepotes sine intermissione producent illa.»

Le festin avait lieu dans le 寢 où l'on gardait les vêtements de cérémonie.

CHANT VI. 1. Vere illum australem montem proprie Iu composuit illum. Extricata sunt et altiora et depressiora loca; pronepos colo ea. Ego limites constitui, ego in partes divisi; austrum orientemve spectant eorum jugera.

南山 Le mont 終南 situé au sud de 鎬 Haò, la capitale.

2. Superno cælo una ubique obducta nubes, cadit nix densa; augetur id minuta pluvia. (Terra) ditata, imbuta, irrorata, saturata producit mihi omnis generis fruges.

（3）疆場翼翼、黍稷彧彧、曾孫之穡、以爲酒食、畀我尸賓、壽考萬年、（4）中田有廬、疆場有瓜、是剝是菹、獻之皇祖、曾孫壽考、受天之祜、（5）祭以清酒、從以騂牡、享

3. Kiāng ĭ ĭ ĭ, chŏu tsĭ iŭ iŭ (ĭ ĭ). Tsēng suēnn tchĕu chĕ, i wêi tsiòu chĕu, pi ngò chēu pīn, cheóu k'aò wán gniên (gnîn).

4. Tchōung t'iên iòu liû, kiāng ĭ iòu kouā (kōu). Chéu pŏ chéu tsiū, hién tchēu houâng tsòu. Tsēng suēnn cheóu k'aò (k'òu), cheóu t'iēn tchēu hòu.

5. Tsi i ts'īng tsiòu ; ts'ôung i sīng meòu, hiàng iū tsòu k'aò (k'iòu). Tchĕu

3. La délimitation et la division du terrain sont bien régulières; les deux espèces de millet à panicules y sont prospères. Je les recueille et j'en prépare des liqueurs et des mets, que j'offre au représentant de mes ancêtres et aux invités (qui assistent à la cérémonie); j'obtiendrai en récompense dix mille années de vie.

4. Au milieu des champs sont les cabanes; le long des bordures du terrain et de ses parties, croissent des concombres. Je coupe ces concombres en plusieurs morceaux, les conserve dans l'eau salée, puis les offre à mes augustes ancêtres. Moi, leur descendant, j'aurai une vie longue, et recevrai les faveurs du ciel.

5. Je répands en libation une liqueur très pure; ensuite je prends un taureau roux pour l'offrir à mes ancêtres. Avec le couteau dont

3. Totius agri margines et partium margines recte compositi sunt; *chou* et *tsi* (milii duo genera) luxuriant. Pronepotis messis est. Utens conficio vinum et cibum; do meorum progenitorum vicario et hospitibus, et longa vita erit decies mille annorum.

4. In medio agro sunt casæ; in agri marginibus et partium marginibus sunt cucurbitæ. Et in partes seco et muria condio; offero eas augustis avis. Pronepos longævus ero, et accipiam cœli beneficia.

Un 里 **li** stade carré de terrain contenait neuf cents 畝 **meòu**, et était divisé en neuf parties égales. Il s'appelait 井 **tsing**, parce que sa division en neuf parties rappelait la forme de cette lettre. Huit familles avaient chacune en propre l'un des huit carrés extérieurs, et une cabane dans le carré du milieu. Ces cabanes occupaient ensemble vingt-cinq *meou*. Les soixante-quinze *meou* restants étaient cultivés en commun par les huit familles, et les produits servaient à couvrir les dépenses publiques.

福在天此皇祖何能錫之只是使之壽考以永受之也（詩經備旨）Les biens qui constituent le bonheur dépendent du ciel. Comment ces augustes ancêtres peuvent-ils les départir? Ils ne font que procurer une vie longue à leur descendant, afin qu'il reçoive longtemps ces biens.

5. Offerens utor puro vino; prosequens utor rubeo bove masculo, offero

于祖考、執其鸞刀、以啓其毛、取其血膋、(6)是烝是享、苾苾芬芬、祀事孔明、先祖是皇、報以介福、萬壽無疆、

甫田

(1)倬彼甫田、歲取十千、我取其陳、食我

k'i louân taō, i k'i k'ì maô, ts'iù k'ì hiuě leaô (laô).

6. Chéu tchēng chéu hiàng (hiāng), pí pǐ fēnn fēnn. Séu chéu k'òung ming (mâng) ; siēn tsòu chéu houàng. Paó i kiái fōu, wán cheóu ôu kiāng.

FOU T'IEN. 1. Tchouŏ pèi fòu t'iên (t'în), souéi ts'iù chēu ts'iēn (ts'īn).

le manche est muni de sonnettes, je coupe une ligne de poil ; je tire du sang et enlève la graisse des intestins.

6. J'apporte et présente mes offrandes ; elles exhalent toutes une odeur agréable. Rien ne manque à la cérémonie ; aussi mes ancêtres (arrivent) avec majesté. Ils m'obtiendront en récompense les plus grandes faveurs, dix mille années de vie, une vie sans fin.

CHANT VII. FOU T'IEN,

Soins donnés à l'agriculture et offrandes faites aux esprits par un prince ou un grand dignitaire.

1. Ce vaste terrain est divisé d'une manière bien nette ; chaque année je reçois les produits de dix mille *meou*. Avec les vieux

coram avis. Sumo illum tintinnabulis instructum cultrum, ad aperiendam viam inter hos pilos, i.e. ad secandos pilos circa aures longo tractu, et desumo hunc sanguinem et viscerum adipem.

Le sacrificateur coupait une ligne de poil aux oreilles de la victime, et déclarait que cette victime était de la couleur voulue et n'avait aucune tache. Il prenait du sang, et annonçait que la victime avait été immolée. Ensuite il enlevait la graisse qui enveloppait les intestins, y mêlait du grain de millet et la brûlait avec de l'armoise, afin que l'odeur attirât les mânes.

« Sous les Tcheou, on offrait de préférence les choses odorantes. On répandait à terre du vin aromatisé, afin que le parfum descendît jusqu'aux sources d'eau, parce que les corps des ancêtres défunts étaient retournés à la terre. Au millet on mêlait de l'armoise trempée dans la graisse, et on le faisait chauffer, afin que l'odeur pénétrât les murs et le toit, parce que les âmes des ancêtres étaient allées au ciel. » (詩經體註).

6. Tunc infero, tunc offero ; (omnia) bene olent. Sacrorum res omnino perfectæ sunt ; avi ideo magnifici (accedunt). Munerabuntur magnis beneficiis, decies mille annorum vita, absque termino.

CHANT VII. 1. Distincte partitus ille magnus ager ; quotannis percipio decies mille (*meòu* jugerum fructus). Ego sumens illas veteres (fruges), nutrio meos agricolas. Ab antiquis (temporibus fuerunt) frugibus locupletes anni. Nunc adeo australia jugera.

農人、自古有年、今適南畝、或耘、或耔、黍稷薿薿、攸介攸止、烝我髦士、

(2) 以我齊明、與我犧羊、以社以方、我田既臧、農夫之慶、琴瑟擊鼓、以御田祖、以祈甘雨、以介我稷黍、以穀我士女、

Ngò ts'iù k'ì tch'ènn, séu ngò nôung jènn. Tzéu kòu iòu gniên (gnìn). Kīn chĕu nân meòu (mèi). Houē iùn, houē tzèu (tsi); chòu tsĭ i i. Iôu kiái iôu tchéu, tchēng ngò maô chéu.

2. Ì ngò tzēu mìng (mâng), iù ngò hī iâng, i ché i fāng. Ngò t'iên kī tsāng, nôung fōu tchēu k'ìng (k'iâng). K'în chĕ kī kòu, i iá t'iên tsòu, i k'ì kān iù, i kiái ngò tsĭ chòu, i kŏu ngò chéu gniù.

grains je nourris mes laboureurs. Depuis les temps les plus reculés les récoltes ont été abondantes. A présent je vais aux champs qui sont au midi. Là les travailleurs sont occupés, les uns à arracher les mauvaises herbes, les autres à butter les plantes. Les deux espèces de millet à panicules y sont très florissantes. Dans un endroit spacieux et commode, je réunis et j'encourage les hommes de talent.

2. J'offre du millet pur et une brebis d'une seule couleur aux esprits de la terre et à ceux des quatre points cardinaux. Si mes champs sont fertiles, c'est grâce à l'heureuse fortune de mes laboureurs. Avec le luth, la guitare et le tambour (de terre cuite), je vais inviter le Père de l'agriculture (Chenn noung), pour demander une pluie favorable, récolter beaucoup de millet, et nourrir mes travailleurs, leurs femmes (et leurs enfants).

Quidam herbis purgant terram, quidam acervant terram ad plantarum radices. *Chòu* et *tsĭ* luxuriant. Ubi est vastus locus, ubi est commoda statio, invito meos ingenio præstantes viros.

Un prince, un grand dignitaire percevait la neuvième partie des produits des terres qui lui étaient allouées. Celui qui parle dans ces strophes, recevait les produits de dix mille 畝 **meòu**. Il avait par conséquent quatre-vingt-dix mille *meòu* de terre. Les fils des laboureurs étaient ordinairement laboureurs; mais les plus intelligents pouvaient parvenir aux charges.

2. Adhibeo meum milium purissimum et meam unius coloris ovem, ut sacrum faciam telluris spiritibus, ut sacrum faciam quatuor regionum spiritibus. Mei agri sunt bene (feraces) agricolarum felici fortuna. Cum cithara et lyra pulsato tympano utor ut occurram agriculturæ parenti, ut rogem opportunam pluviam, ut copiosum impetrem milium, ut alam meos viros ac mulieres.

Ce tambour s'appelait 土鼓 **t'ou kòu**; la caisse était de terre cuite.

(3) 曾孫來止、以其婦子、饁彼南畝、田畯至喜、攘其左右、嘗其旨否、禾易長畝、終善且有、曾孫不怒、農夫克敏、

(4) 曾孫之稼、如茨如梁、曾孫之庾、如坻如京、乃求千斯倉、乃求萬斯箱、黍稷稻粱、農夫之慶、報

3. Tsēng suēnn lâi tchèu, i k'î fóu tzèu (tsi), iĕ pèi nân meòu (mèi). T'iên tsiún tchéu hi. Jâng k'î tsouò iòu (i), tch'âng k'î tchèu feòu (pèi). Houô i tch'âng meòu (mèi), tchōung chén, ts'iè iòu (i). Tsēng suēnn pòu nóu, nôung fōu k'ŏ min (mi).

4. Tsēng suēnn tchēu kiá, jôu ts'êu jôu leâng. Tsēng suēnn tchēu iù, jôu tch'êu jôu kīng (kāng). Nài k'iôu ts'iēn sēu ts'āng, nài k'iôu wán sēu siāng. Chòu tsĭ taó leâng, nôung fōu tchēu k'ing (k'iâng). Paó i kiái fóu, wán cheóu ôu kiāng.

3. Je viens dans ces champs de mes pères, avec les femmes et les enfants qui portent la nourriture aux travailleurs dans la plaine du midi. L'inspecteur des champs arrive et témoigne sa joie. Prenant un peu de nourriture à droite et à gauche, je la goûte pour savoir si elle est bonne. Les moissons sont bien soignées dans toute l'étendue du terrain; la récolte sera belle et abondante. Je ne suis pas mécontent de mes laboureurs; (ma bonté envers eux) stimule leur diligence.

4. Les tiges des plantes sont (serrées entre elles) comme les brins de chaume sur un toit; la moisson (est ondulée et) présente l'apparence du timon recourbé d'un char. Les monceaux de grain seront grands comme des ilots, comme des monticules. Il faudra mille greniers (pour serrer le grain), et dix mille voitures (pour transporter les gerbes sur l'aire). Ce millet de deux espèces, ce riz, ce sorgho sont dus à l'heureuse fortune de mes laboureurs. Les

3. Pronepos venio (in illos agros a majoribus meis traditos), cum illorum (agricolarum) uxoribus ac liberis, qui cibos ferunt in illa australia jugera. Agrorum præpositus adveniens gaudet. Capio ex illis (cibis aliquid) dextra lævaque; gusto an illud bonum sit necne. Fruges curatæ sunt in tota longitudine jugerum; postremo erunt pulchræ et multæ. Pronepos non ægritudine afficior; agricolæ valent ad laborem excitari.

4. Pronepotis segetes (nondum demessæ) similes sunt tecti stramento, similes recurvo currus temoni. Pronepotis acervi erunt similes parvis insulis, similes monticulis. Inde quærenda sunt mille illa granaria, inde quærenda decies mille illa plaustra. Duplicis generis milium, oryza, sorghum sunt agricola-

以介福萬壽無
疆、

大田

(1)大田多稼、既
種既戒、既備乃
事、以我覃耜、俶
載南畝、播厥百
穀、既庭且碩、曾
孫是若、
(2)既方既皁、既
堅既好、不稂不
莠、去其螟螣、及
其蟊賊、無害我

TA T'IEN. 1. Tá t'iên touō kiá ; ki tchǒung, ki kiái. Ki péi nài chéu (chéu), i ngò iên séu (i). Chŏu tsái nân meòu (mèi), pouŏ kiuĕ pĕ kŏu (kŏ). Ki t'ing, ts'iĕ chĕu (chŏ), tsēng suēnn chéu jŏ.

2. Ki fāng ki tsaò (tseòu), ki kiēn ki haò (heòu). Pŏu lâng pŏu iòu. K'iû

esprits leur obtiendront en récompense une grande prospérité, dix mille années de vie, une vie sans fin.

CHANT VIII. TA T'IEN.

Travaux des champs et sacrifices offerts aux esprits protecteurs des moissons.

1. Dans ce vaste terrain nous devrons semer beaucoup. Déjà nous avons choisi la semence et préparé nos instruments. Pourvus de toutes les choses nécessaires à nos travaux, nous prenons nos charrues au soc bien affilé, et donnons nos premiers soins aux champs qui sont au midi. Nous y semons toute sorte de grains. Déjà les tiges se dressent, déjà la moisson est haute, à la grande satisfaction de l'héritier de nos anciens princes.

2. Déjà les épis apparaissent ; déjà le grain se forme, déjà il durcit, déjà il est mûr et d'excellente qualité. Il ne reste ni faux sorgho ni faux millet. Il faut exterminer ces insectes qui rongent soit la moelle, soit les feuilles, soit les racines, soit les nœuds des

rum felix fortuna. (Spiritus eos) munerabuntur magna felicitate, decies mille annis, (vita) sine termino.

CHANT VIII. 1. In vasto agro multum seretur. Jam selegimus semen, jam paravimus instrumenta. Postquam omnia comparavimus ad nostra opera, utimur nostris acutis vomeribus; incipimus operam dare australibus jugeribus, serimus eorum (jugerum) omnigenas fruges. Jam arrectæ, jam altæ sunt. Remoto nepoti id satisfacit.

2. Jam apparent spicæ; jam nascuntur grana, jam firmantur grana, jam perfecta sunt. Non est *lang* nec *iou*. Abigendi illi *ming* (vermes qui rodunt frugum medullam), *t'e* (qui rodunt folia), cum illis *meou* (qui radices rodunt) et *tse* (qui rodunt articulos), ne noceant nostrorum arvorum teneris segetibus. Agriculturæ parens habet miram virtutem; capiens (illos vermes) tradat ardenti igni!

方 **Fāng** ou 房 **Fâng**, ovaire d'une plante. 稂 **Lâng**, mauvaise herbe qui croît dans le sorgho et lui ressemble.

田穉、田祖有神、
秉畀炎火、
(3) 有渰淒淒、興
雨祁祁、雨我公
田、遂及我私、彼
有不穫穉、此有
不斂穧、彼有遺
秉、此有滯穗、伊
寡婦之利、
(4) 曾孫來止、以
其婦子、饁彼南
畝、田畯至喜、來
方禋祀、以其騂

k'ì mìng t'ĕ, kĭ k'ì meôu tsĕ, ôu hái ngò t'iên tchéu. T'iên tsòu iòu chênn, ping pi iên houò (houèi)!

3. Iòu iên ts'ī ts'ī, hīng iù k'ì k'ì! Iù ngò kōung t'iên, souéi kĭ ngò sēu (sī)! Péi iòu pŏu houŏ tchéu, ts'èu iòu pŏu lién tsí. Péi iòu ì ping, ts'èu iòu tchéu souéi. Ī kouà fóu tchēu lí.

4. Tsēng suēnn lâi tchèu, i k'ì fóu tzèu (tsi), iĕ pèi nân meòu (mèi). T'iên tsiún

plantes, afin qu'ils ne nuisent pas à nos jeunes moissons. Le Père de l'agriculture est un esprit très puissant; qu'il prenne ces insectes et les livre aux flammes!

3. Qu'il se forme d'épais nuages, et que la pluie commence à tomber doucement! Qu'elle arrose d'abord notre champ commun, puis nos champs particuliers! Il y aura des tiges encore jeunes et petites qui ne seront pas coupées, des gerbes qui ne seront pas recueillies, des poignées qui seront laissées, des épis qui échapperont aux moissonneurs. Les femmes veuves en feront leur profit.

4. L'héritier de nos anciens princes vient avec les femmes et les enfants, qui apportent la nourriture (à leurs maris et à leurs pères) dans les champs qui sont au midi. L'inspecteur des champs arrive et témoigne sa joie. Le prince vient faire des offrandes aux esprits des quatre points cardinaux. Il offre une victime rousse

莠 **Iòu,** mauvaise herbe qui croît dans le millet et lui ressemble. Le Père de l'agriculture était l'ancien empereur 神農 **Chênn nôung,** qu'on honorait sous le titre de 炎帝 **Iên ti** Empereur du feu.

3. Sint exorientes nubes valde densæ! incipiat pluvia leniter cadere! Irroret nostrum communem agrum, inde adveniat ad nostros privatos! Illic erunt non demessi teneri caules, hic erunt non collecti fasciculi. Illic erunt relicti manipuli, hic erunt prætermissæ spicæ. Illud erit viduarum mulierum lucrum.

公田 **Kōung t'iên,** champ qui était cultivé en commun, et dont les produits revenaient au chef de l'État en guise de tribut.

4. Remotus nepos venit, cum horum (agricolarum) uxoribus ac liberis, qui cibos afferunt in his australibus jugeribus. Agrorum præpositus adveniens gaudet. (Remotus nepos) venit quatuor regionum spiritibus sacra facturus. Utitur sua rubea victima et nigra, cum suo duplicis generis milio. Utens offert,

黑、與其黍稷、以享以祀、以介景福、

瞻彼洛矣

(1) 瞻彼洛矣、維水泱泱、君子至止、福祿如茨、韎韐有奭、以作六師、

(2) 瞻彼洛矣、維水泱泱、君子至止、鞞琫有珌、君子萬年、保其家室、

tchéu hi. Lâi fāng īn séu (ĭ), i k'ì sīng hĕ, iù k'ì chóu tsĭ, i hiàng i séu (ĭ), i kiái king fŏu (pĭ).

TCHEN PEI LO I. **1. Tchēn pèi Lŏ i, wêi chouèi ngāng ngāng. Kiūn tzèu tchéu tchéu, fŏu lŏu jôu ts'êu. Méi kŏ iòu chĕu, i tsŏ liŭ chēu.**

2. Tchēn pèi Lŏ i, wêi chouèi ngāng ngāng. Kiūn tzèu tchéu tchéu, ping pòung iòu pĭ. Kiūn tzèu wán gniên, paò k'ì kiā chĕu.

(aux esprits du sud), une victime noire (aux esprits du nord), avec deux sortes de millet à panicules. Par cette offrande et ces sacrifices, il obtient un grand accroissement de prospérité.

CHANT IX. TCHEN PEI LO I.

Félicitations adressées à l'empereur par les princes réunis à Lo iang pour délibérer sur les affaires militaires.

1. Voyez cette rivière Lo; ses eaux sont profondes et étendues. Le souverain (l'empereur) est venu; le ciel l'a comblé de biens. Il porte les genouillères de cuir rouge garance, qu'il prend lorsqu'il met en campagne les six légions.

2. Voyez cette rivière Lo; ses eaux sont profondes et étendues. Le souverain est venu; l'ouverture et l'extrémité du fourreau de son épée sont de pierre précieuse. Durant dix mille années, il vivra et maintiendra sa maison.

utens sacrificat; utens ampliat magnam felicitatem. 禋 sacrifice offert avec une intention pure.

CHANT IX. 1. Aspicite illum Lo fluvium; aqua est lata et profunda. Princeps advenit; a cœlo collata bona (magna et densa sunt) sicut tecti stramentum. Rubia infecta genualia sunt rubra; utens educit sex legiones.

La résidence ordinaire de l'empereur était à 鎬 **Haó** dans le 陝西 **Chèn sī** actuel. Il avait une seconde résidence à 洛陽 **Lŏ iâng** sur les bords de la Lo. V. page 3. Les genouillères de cuir teint en garance faisaient partie du costume militaire. L'empereur levait dans son domaine propre six légions, chacune de douze mille cinq cents hommes.

2. Aspicite illum Lo fluvium; aqua est lata et profunda. Princeps venit; vaginæ est os iaspium cum extremo iaspio. Princeps decies mille annis (vivet et) tuebitur suam domum.

(3)瞻彼洛矣、維水泱泱、君子至止。福祿既同、君子萬年、保其家邦、

裳裳者華

(1)裳裳者華。其葉湑兮、我覯之子、我心寫兮、我心寫兮、是以有譽處兮、

(2)裳裳者華、芸其黃矣、我覯之子。維其有章矣、維其有章矣。是以有慶矣、

3. Tchēn pèi Lǒ i, wêi chouèi ngāng ngāng. Kiūn tzèu tchéu tchéu, fǒu lǒu ki t'ôung. Kiūn tzèu wán gniên, paò k'ì kiā pāng (pōung).

CHANG CHANG TCHE HOUA. **1. Châng châng tchè houâ, k'ì iĕ siù hì. Ngò keòu tchēu tzèu, ngò sīn siè (siù) hì. Ngò sīn siè (siù) hì, chéu i iòu iú tch'òu hi.**

2. Châng châng tchè houâ, iún k'ì houâng i. Ngò keòu tchēu tzèu, wêi k'ì iòu tchāng i. Wêi k'ì iòu tchāng i, chéu i iòu k'ing (k'iāng) i.

3. Voyez cette rivière Lo; ses eaux sont profondes et étendues. Le souverain est venu; tous les biens du ciel sont réunis en sa personne. Durant dix mille années il vivra, et soutiendra sa maison et tout l'empire.

CHANT X. CHANG CHANG TCHE HOUA.

L'empereur répond aux félicitations qui lui ont été adressées dans le chant IX. Il compare les princes aux fleurs les plus brillantes.

1. Les fleurs sont brillantes, le feuillage est luxuriant. A la vue de ces princes, mon cœur est pleinement satisfait. Mon cœur est pleinement satisfait; ces princes méritent d'être loués et de conserver à jamais leurs dignités.

2. Les fleurs sont brillantes, leur couleur est jaune foncée. Je vois ces princes qui brillent par la distinction de leur maintien et de leurs manières. A cause de cette distinction (indice de leur vertu), ils méritent d'être comblés de biens.

3. Aspicite illum Lo fluvium; aqua est lata et profunda. Princeps venit; omnia bona sunt conjuncta. Princeps decies mille annis (vivet ac) tuebitur suam domum et regna.

CHANT X. 1. Splendidi sunt flores, ipsa folia luxuriant. Ego conspicio hos regulos; meus animus omni ægritudine liber est. Meus animus omni ægritudine est liber; quapropter habebunt laudes et stabiles honores.

2. Splendidi sunt flores, intense ipsi flavi sunt. Ego conspicio hos regulos; ipsi habent decorem. Ipsi habent decorem (internæ virtutis indicium); quapropter habebunt felicitatem.

(3) 裳裳者華、或黃或白、我覯之子、乘其四駱、乘其四駱、六轡沃若、

(4) 左之左之、君子宜之、右之右之、君子有之、維其有之、是以似之、

桑扈之什二之七

桑扈

(1) 交交桑扈、有鶯其羽、君子樂胥、受天之祜、

3. Châng châng tchè houâ, houě houâng houě pě (pǒ). Ngò keóu tchēu tzèu, chêng k'î séu lǒ. Chêng k'î séu lǒ, lǒu pi ǒu jǒ.

4. Tsouò (Tsouō) tchēu tsouò (tsouō) tchēu, kiūn tzèu î (ngô) tchēu. Iòu (î) tchēu iòu (i) tchēu, kiūn tzèu iòu (i) tchēu. Wêi k'î iòu (i) tchēu, chéu i séu (i) tchēu.

SANG HOU. **1. Kiaō kiaō sāng hòu, iòu īng k'î iù. Kiūn tzèu lǒ siū (siù), cheóu t'iēn tchēu hòu.**

3. Les fleurs sont brillantes; les unes sont jaunes, les autres blanches. Je vois ces princes qui montent des voitures traînées par quatre chevaux blancs à crinière noire. Ils montent des voitures traînées par quatre chevaux blancs à crinière noire; les six rênes sont luisantes.

4. Qu'on emploie ces princes ici ou là, partout leur capacité sera suffisante. Ils sont réellement capables, et ils le paraissent.

LIVRE VII. SANG HOU.

CHANT I. SANG HOU.

L'empereur félicite les grands feudataires réunis à sa table. Voyant leurs manières aisées et cordiales, il les compare aux bruants du mûrier.

1. Les bruants du mûrier voltigent ensemble çà et là; leur plumage est varié. Ces princes sages sont aimables; ils recevront les faveurs du ciel.

3. Splendidi sunt flores, alii flavi, alii albi. Ego conspicio hos regulos; vehuntur suis quatuor albis nigra juba equis. Vehuntur suis quatuor albis nigra juba equis; sex habenæ adipe nitentes videntur.

4. Si ad sinistram adhibeas eos, si ad sinistram adhibeas eos, reguli pares erunt huic loco; si ad dextram adhibeas eos, si ad dextram adhibeas eos, habebunt hanc (habilitatem). Unice quia ipsi habent eam, propterea videntur eam (habere).

TITRE DU LIVRE. 桑扈之什二之七 Sang hou decas: secundæ (partis) septima (decas).

CHANT I. Huc illuc simul volitant mori emberizæ; habent varios colores earum pennæ. Sapientes reguli sunt amabiles; accipient cœli beneficia.

胥 **Siū**, particule. Le 桑扈 **sāng hòu** ressemble à la caille ou au bruant.

(2) 交交桑扈、有鶯其領、君子樂胥、萬邦之屏、
(3) 之屏之翰、百辟爲憲、不戢不難、受福不那、
(4) 兕觥其觩、旨酒思柔、彼交匪敖、萬福來求、

鴛鴦

(1) 鴛鴦于飛、畢之羅之、君子萬

2. Kiaō kiaō sāng hòu, iòu ìng k'ì ling. Kiūn tzèu lŏ siū (siù), wàn pāng tchēu ping.

3. Tchēu ping tchēu hán (hién), pĕ pĭ wéi hién. Pŏu tsĭ pŏu nân (nŏ), cheóu fŏu pŏu nŏ.

4. Si kōung k'ì k'iôu, tchèu tsiòu sēu jeôu. Pèi kiaō fèi ngaó, wán fŏu lâi k'iôu.

IUEN IANG. **1. Iuēn iāng iû fēi, pĭ tchēu louô tchēu. Kiūn tzèu wán gnièn, fŏu lŏu î (ngŏ) tchēu.**

2. Les bruants du mûrier voltigent ensemble çà et là ; ils ont le cou orné de diverses couleurs. Ces princes sages sont aimables ; ils sont les remparts de tous les États.

3. Remparts et soutiens des États, ils sont les modèles de tous les princes. Ne sont-ils pas modérés? ne sont-ils pas diligents? Les faveurs qu'ils recevront du ciel ne seront-elles pas nombreuses?

4. Cette corne de rhinocéros est recourbée ; elle contient un vin exquis et très doux. Les princes (assis à ce banquet) ne sont pas arrogants entre eux ; toutes les faveurs du ciel viendront d'elles-mêmes s'offrir à eux.

CHANT II. IUEN IANG.

Réponse des princes feudataires aux félicitations et aux souhaits exprimés par l'empereur dans le chant précédent.

1. Les canards mandarins vont par paires ; on les prend (en grand nombre) avec de petits filets munis d'un long manche et avec des filets ordinaires. Notre souverain mérite de vivre dix

Il vit au milieu des mûriers. On l'appelle 竊脂 **Ts'ién tchēu,** Graisse de couleur peu foncée, parce que son plumage est gris-blanc. 竊 est l'ancienne forme de la lettre 淺 **ts'ièn.**

2. Huc illuc simul volitant mori emberizæ ; habent varios colores earum colla. Sapientes reguli sunt amabiles ; omnium regnorum sunt propugnacula.

3. Hæc propugnacula, hæc sustentacula, omnium rectorum sunt exemplaria. Nonne modesti sunt? nonne diligentes? Accepta cœli beneficia nonne multa erunt?

4. Rhinocerotis cornu illud curvum est ; exquisitum vinum est lene. Illi inter se non sunt arrogantes ; omnia cœli beneficia venient et quærent (illos).

思 **Sēu,** particule.

CHANT II. **1.** Masculæ anates et feminæ anates dum volant, (homines) instructis longo manubrio reticulis

年、福祿宜之、(2)鴛鴦在梁、戢其左翼、君子萬年、宜其遐福、(3)乘馬在廄、摧之秣之、君子萬年、福祿艾之、(4)乘馬在廄、秣之摧之、君子萬年、福祿綏之、

頍弁

(1)有頍者弁、實維伊何、爾酒既

2. Iuēn iāng tsái leâng, tsĭ k'ì tsouò ĭ. Kiūn tzèu wán gniên, i k'î hiâ fŏu (pĭ).

3. Chéng mà tsái kióu, ts'ouò tchēu mouŏ (méi) tchēu. Kiūn tzèu wán gniên, fŏu lŏu ngái (i) tchēu.

4. Chéng mà tsái kióu, mouŏ tchēu ts'ouò (ts'ouêi) tchēu. Kiūn tzèu wán gniên, fŏu lŏu souēi tchēu.

K'OUEI PIEN. **1. Iòu k'ouèi tchè pién, chĕu wêi ī hô ? Eùl tsiòu ki tchèu, èul**

mille ans, et de jouir sans cesse des faveurs du ciel.

2. Les canards mandarins se tiennent par paires sur les barrages, avec leurs ailes gauches réunies (l'un tournant la tête du côté où l'autre tourne la queue, et ne se séparant jamais). Notre souverain mérite de vivre dix mille ans, et d'avoir toujours la félicité pour compagne.

3. Lorsque les quatre chevaux d'un char sont dans l'écurie, on les nourrit de paille hachée et de grain. Notre souverain vivra dix mille ans, nourri, comblé des bienfaits du ciel.

4. Lorsque les quatre chevaux d'un char sont dans l'écurie, on les nourrit de grain et de paille hachée. Notre souverain vivra dix mille ans, sans cesse comblé des faveurs du ciel.

CHANT III. K'OUEI PIEN.

Chant adressé à l'empereur dans un festin offert par lui à tous les princes ses parents.

1. Quels sont ces hommes qui portent des bonnets de peau ?

capiunt eas, expansis retibus capiunt eas. Rex decies mille annis (vivat decet) ; cœli beneficia et opes congruunt cum ejus (meritis).

2. Masculæ anates et feminæ anates quum sunt in septo, conjungunt suas sinistras alas. Rex decies mille annis (vivat decet); dignus est ejusmodi diuturna felicitate.

3. Quadrijugi equi quum sunt in equili, (homines) paleam concidunt eis, frumento alunt eos. Rex decies mille annis (vivet); cœli beneficia et opes alent eum.

4. Quadrijugi equi quum sunt in equili, (homines) frumento alunt eos, paleam concidunt eis. Rex decies mille annis (vivet), cœli beneficia et opes beatum faciunt eum.

CHANT III. 1. Qui habent capiti

旨、爾殽既嘉、豈伊異人、兄弟匪他、蔦與女蘿、施于松柏、未見君子、憂心奕奕、既見君子、庶幾說懌、

(2) 有頍者弁、實維何期、爾酒既旨、爾殽既時、豈伊異人、兄弟具來、蔦與女蘿、施于松上、未見君子、憂心怲怲、既見君子、庶幾有臧、

(3) 有頍者弁、實維

hiaŏ ki kiā (kŏ), k'i ĭ i jênn? Hiōung ti, féi t'ouō. Gniaò iù gniù louŏ, i iū sōung pĕ (pŏ). Wéi kién kiūn tzèu, iōu sīn ĭ ĭ (iŏ iŏ). Ki kién kiūn tzèu, chóu kī iuĕ ĭ (iŏ).

2. Iòu k'ouèi tchė pién, chĕu wêi hŏ k'î? Eùl tsiòu ki tchèu, èul hiaŏ ki chèu, k'i ĭ i jênn? Hiōung ti kiú lâi (li). Gniaò iù gniù louŏ, i iū sōung cháng. Wéi kién kiūn tzèu, iōu sīn ping ping (páng páng). Ki kién kiūn tzèu, chóu kī iòu tsāng (tsáng).

3. Iòu k'ouèi tchė pién, chĕu wêi tsái cheòu. Eùl tsiòu ki tchèu, èul hiaŏ ki

Puisque vous leur avez fait servir des liqueurs excellentes et des mets exquis, pourraient-ils être des étrangers? Ce sont vos frères, et pas d'autres. Le gui et la cuscute s'étendent sur le sapin et le cyprès. (Ainsi ces princes vous sont unis). Avant d'avoir vu ces hommes distingués, mon cœur était triste et agité. A présent que je les vois, je suis heureux et content.

2. Quels sont ces hommes qui portent des bonnets de peau? Puisque vous leur avez fait servir des liqueurs excellentes et des mets de la saison, pourraient-ils être des étrangers? Ce sont vos frères, qui sont tous venus. Le gui et la cuscute s'étendent sur le sapin. (Ainsi ces princes vous sont unis). Avant d'avoir vu ces hommes distingués, mon cœur était plein de tristesse. A présent que je les vois, il jouit du repos.

3. Ils ont la tête couverte du bonnet de peau. Puisque vous

impositum pelliceum pileum, vere ii quinam sunt? Tuum vinum quum sit exquisitum, tuæ dapes quum sint optimæ, quomodo ii essent extranei homines? Fratres sunt, non alii. Viscum et cuscuta protenduntur super abietem et cupressum. Nondum visis egregiis viris, mœstus animus erat inquietus. Postquam vidi insignes viros, feliciter lætus gaudeo.

2. Qui habent capiti impositum pelliceum pileum, vere quinam sunt? Tuum vinum quum sit exquisitum, tuæ dapes quum sint tempestivæ (adeoque optimæ), quomodo ii essent extranei homines? Fratres omnes venerunt. Viscum et cuscuta protenduntur super abietem. Nondum visis optimis viris, tristis animus erat ægritudine plenus. Postquam vidi inclytos viros, feliciter habet bene.

期 K'i, particule.

3. Habitus impositusque pileus quidem obtegit caput. Tuum vinum quum sit exquisitum, tuæ dapes quum sint

在首、爾酒既旨、爾
殽既阜、豈伊異人、
兄弟甥舅、如彼雨
雪、先集維霰、死喪
無日、無幾相見、樂
酒今夕、君子維宴、

車舝

(1) 閒關車之舝兮、
思孌季女逝兮、匪
飢匪渴、德音來括、
雖無好友、式燕且
喜、

feòu. K'i I i jênn? Hiōung ti chēng kiòu. Jôu pèi iù siuĕ, siēn tsĭ wêi sién. Sèu sàng ôu jĕu, ôu ki siāng kién. Lŏ tsiòu kīn sĭ, kiūn tzèu wêi ién.

KIU HIA. 1. Kiēn kouān kiū tchēu hiă hî, sēu liuèn ki gniù chéu (chĕ) hî. Fèi kî fèi k'ŏ, tĕ īn lâi kouŏ. Souēi ôu haò iòu (i), chĕu ién, ts'iè hì.

leur avez fait servir des liqueurs exquises et des mets nombreux, pourraient-ils être des étrangers? Ce sont vos frères, vos cousins du côté maternel et vos parents par alliance. Lorsque la neige doit tomber, il se forme d'abord du grésil. (Ainsi les cheveux blancs sont les précurseurs de la mort). La mort viendra bientôt; les réunions ne se renouvelleront pas longtemps. Ce soir il faut boire ensemble gaiement; que ces princes se livrent tout entiers à la joie.

CHANT IV. KIU HIA.

Joie d'un nouveau marié.

1. Les coups retentissants du marteau ont fixé les armatures aux extrémités de l'essieu de ma voiture; je suis allé au-devant de cette belle jeune fille. Je n'avais ni faim ni soif; (cependant j'éprouvais comme le sentiment de la faim et de la soif. Je désirais vivement que) cette fille d'une vertu tant vantée vînt avec moi. Quand même nous n'aurions pas avec nous d'excellents amis, nous deux nous fêterions et serions dans la joie.

multæ, quomodo ii essent extranei homines? Sunt fratres, matrueles et affines. Si illa casura est nix, prius congeritur gelicidium. Mors et funus non (post multos) dies (venient); non diu invicem videbitis. Oblectetis vos vino hoc vespere; insignes viri unice lætentur.

CHANT IV. 1. Cum strepitu vehiculi axis extremorum ferramenta (aptata sunt); cogitans de formosa ac juveni puella adivi. Nec esuriebam, nec sitiebam; (sed cupiebam vehementer) optimæ famæ (puellam) venire et congredi. Etsi non adessent optimi amici, uteremur epulis et gauderemus.

Kiēn kouān, bruit des coups de marteau. *Hiă*, pièces de fer qu'on fixait aux extrémités de l'essieu pour retenir les roues pendant le voyage, et qu'on retirait après l'arrivée.

(2) 依彼平林、有集維鷮、辰彼碩女、令德來教、式燕且譽、好爾無射、

(3) 雖無旨酒、式飲庶幾、雖無嘉殽、式食庶幾、雖無德與女、式歌且舞、

(4) 陟彼高岡、析其柞薪、析其柞薪、其葉湑兮、鮮我覯爾、我心寫兮、

(5) 高山仰止、景行行止、四牡騑騑、六

2. Ī pèi p'ing lîn, iòu tsĭ wěi kiaŏ. Tch'ênn pèi chĕu gniù, ling tĕ lâi kiaō. Chĕu ién, ts'iè iù, haó éul ŏu ĭ (tóu).

3. Souēi ŏu tchèu tsiòu, chĕu in chóu kī. Souēi ŏu kiā hiaô, chĕu chĕu chóu kī. Souēi ŏu tĕ iù jòu, chĕu kŏ ts'iè òu.

4. Tchĕu pèi kaō kāng, sĭ k'i tsŏ sīn (siāng). Sĭ k'i tsŏ sīn (siāng,) k'i iĕ siù hi. Sièn ngò keóu éul, ngò sīn siè (siù) hi.

5. Kaō chān iàng (iāng) tchèu, king hìng hing (hâng hâng) tchèu. Séu meòu

2. Dans cette plaine la forêt est épaisse; les faisans s'y réunissent. Cette fille d'un rare mérite a été mariée au temps convenable; sa vertu exemplaire m'instruira (et m'aidera). Je lui offre un festin et fais son éloge. (Chère épouse), je vous aime et vous aimerai toujours.

3. Bien que je n'aie pas de bonnes liqueurs, vous daignerez boire, j'espère. Bien que je n'aie pas de mets exquis, vous daignerez manger, j'espère. Bien que ma vertu ne soit pas à la hauteur de la vôtre, nous chanterons et danserons ensemble.

4. Je monte sur cette crête élevée, et j'y fends des branches de chêne pour le chauffage. J'y fends des branches de chêne; les feuilles sont verdoyantes. Par un bonheur incomparable, je vous vois; mon cœur est content.

5. Je pouvais contempler cette haute montagne et parcourir ce grand chemin. J'ai quatre coursiers bien dressés; leurs six rênes

2. Densa est illa plana silva; sunt congregati phasiani. Tempore (opportuno nupta est) hæc magnæ (virtutis) puella; insigni virtute venit edoctura (et adjutura). Adhibeo epulas et laudo. Amo te, nec fastidiam.

3. Licet desit exquisitum vinum, uteris potu, spero. Licet desint optimæ dapes, uteris cibo, spero. Licet caream virtutibus quibus adjuvem te, utemur cantu et saltabimus.

4. Ascendo illud altum jugum; findo ex illius quercubus cremia. Findo ex illius quercubus cremia; earum frondes luxuriant. Rara (felicitate) ego video te; meus animus solvitur.

5. Altus mons suspici poterat; magna via percurri poterat. Quatuor mares equi

轡如琴、覯爾新
昏、以慰我心、

青蠅

(1)營營青蠅、止
于樊、豈弟君子、
無信讒言、
(2)營營青蠅、止
于棘、讒人罔極、
交亂四國、
(3)營營青蠅、止
于榛、讒人罔極、
構我二人、

賓之初筵

(1)賓之初筵、左

fēi fēi, lŏu pi jŏu k'în. Keóu éul sīn houēnn, i wéi ngò sīn.

TS'ING ING. **1. Ìng ing ts'īng ing, tchéu iū fân. K'ài ti kiūn tzèu, ŏu sin tch'ân iên.**

2. Ìng ing ts'īng ing, tchéu iū kĭ. Tch'ân jênn wàng kĭ, kiaō louán séu kouŏ(ĭ).

3. Ìng ing ts'īng ing, tchéu iū tchēnn. Tch'ân jênn wàng kĭ, keóu ngò éul jênn.

PIN TCHEU TCH'OU IEN. **1. Pīn tchēu tch'ŏu iên, tsouò ióu tchĕu tchĕu. Piēn**

sont comme les cordes d'un luth. (Je suis allé vous chercher). Je vous vois, vous devenez ma compagne; je suis au comble de mes vœux.

CHANT V. TS'ING ING.

Le poète prie l'empereur de ne pas prêter l'oreille à la calomnie, qu'il compare au bourdonnement de la mouche verte.

1. La mouche verte va bourdonner çà et là, et se pose sur la haie. Prince aimable, ne croyez pas ce que dit le calomniateur.

2. La mouche verte va bourdonner çà et là, et se pose sur les jujubiers (de la haie). Le calomniateur ne connaît point de bornes; il trouble tous les États.

3. La mouche verte va bourdonner çà et là, et se pose sur les coudriers (de la haie). Le calomniateur ne connaît pas de bornes; il mettrait le désaccord entre vous et moi.

CHANT VI. PIN TCHEU TCH'OU IEN.

Sur le bon usage et l'abus des liqueurs fermentées.

1. (Quand les archers se préparent à lutter ensemble deux à

sunt bene instituti; sex habenæ (compositæ) sicut fides. Video te recenter nuptam; inde expletur meus animus.

CHANT V. 1. Huc illuc volitans susurrat viridis musca; sistit supra sepem. Festive et comis rex, ne credas calumniatoris sermonibus.

2. Huc illuc volitans susurrat viridis musca; sistit super zizyphos. Calumniator homo non habet limites; miscens perturbat omnia regna.

3. Huc illuc volitans susurrat viridis musca; sistit super corylos. Calumniator homo non habet limites; committet nos ambos homines.

CHANT VI. 1. Hospites primum adeuntes storeas, læva dextraque ordinati (sedent). *Piēn, teóu* (vasa lignea)

右秩秩。籩豆有
楚。殽核維旅。酒
既和旨。飲酒孔
偕。鐘鼓既設。舉
醻逸逸。大侯既
抗。弓矢斯張。射
夫既同。獻爾發
功。發彼有的。以
祈爾爵
(2) 籥舞笙鼓。樂
既和奏。烝衍烈
祖。以洽百禮。百
禮既至。有壬有

teóu iòu tch'òu, hiaô hŏ wéi liù. Tsiòu ki houô tchéu, in tsiòu k'òung kiāi (ki). Tchōung kòu ki chĕ (chĕu), kiù tch'eôu î î. Tá heóu ki kāng, kōung chéu sēu tchāng. Ché fōu ki t'òung, hién èul fă kōung. Fă pèi iòu tĭ (tiŏ), i k'i èul tsiŏ.

2. Iŏ òu chēng kòu, iŏ ki houô tseòu (tsòu), tchēng k'án liĕ tsòu, i hiă pĕ li.

deux), les invités, arrivés auprès des nattes, se rangent à droite et à gauche. Les vases de bois sont disposés en ordre; les ragoûts et les fruits à noyaux sont servis (les ragoûts dans les vases appelés *teou,* les fruits dans les vases appelés *pien*). Une liqueur excellente est préparée; tous boivent d'une manière très bienséante. Les cloches et les tambours étant disposés, (ils s'offrent à boire les uns aux autres), la coupe est levée et circule dans un ordre parfait. La grande cible est déployée; chacun des archers encoche sa flèche et tire à soi la corde de son arc (comme pour lancer la flèche). Ils sont divisés en couples d'après leur force ou leur habileté. (Les deux rivaux se disent l'un à l'autre avec courtoisie): «Je vous invite à signaler votre talent d'archer.» (Et ils se répondent): «Je tirerai si bien que je frapperai cette cible, et vous prierai de boire la coupe (destinée au vaincu).»

2. (Pour honorer vos ancêtres), des pantomimes dansent la flûte à la main, au son des orgues et des tambours. Votre offrande réjouit vos illustres ancêtres, et vous observez toutes les cérémonies. Toutes les cérémonies sont accomplies; elles sont magnifi-

habent ordinem; pulmenta et poma exhibita sunt. Vinum jam temperatum bonum est; bibunt vinum valde concordi (observantia). Campanæ et tympana disposita sunt; attollentes (poculum) retribuunt (vinum) ordine procedentes. Magno scopo expanso, arcus (nervus) et sagitta tunc attrahuntur. Sagittariis jam sociatis paribus (binis ac binis): «Offero tibi jaculationis laudem.» «Jaciens feriam illum habitum scopum, inde rogabo te (ut bibas victo propinatum) poculum.»

Anciennement on mangeait sur des nattes étendues à terre. Après l'exercice du tir à l'arc, le vaincu était condamné à boire une coupe de liqueur.

2. (Mimi instructi tibiis saltant, organis ac tympanis sonantibus; musica instrumenta jam consona cecinerunt. Offerens oblectas bene meritos avos; ita obsequeris omnibus ritibus. Omnes

林、錫爾純嘏、子
孫其湛湛、曰
樂、各奏爾能、賓
載手仇、室人入
又、酌彼康爵、以
奏爾時、
(3) 賓之初筵、溫
溫其恭、其未醉
止、威儀反反、曰
既醉止、威儀幡
幡、舍其坐遷、屢
舞僊僊、其未醉
止、威儀抑抑、曰

Pĕ li ki tchéu, iòu jênn iòu lîn. Sī èul chouênn kòu, tzèu suēnn k'ì tān (tch'ênn). Kì tān iuĕ lŏ, kŏ tseòu èul nêng (gnîn). Pīn tsài cheòu kiû, chĕu jênn jŏu iòu (iôu). Tchŏ péi k'āng tsiŏ, i tseóu èul chêu (tch'eôu).

3. Pīn tchēu tch'ōu ién, wēnn wēnn k'ì kōung. K'ì wéi tsouéi tchéu, wēi î fān fān. Iuĕ kí tsouéi tchéu, wēi î fān fān. Ché k'ì tsouó ts'iēn, liú òu siēn siēn. Kì

ques et très nombreuses. (Les mânes) vous obtiennent en récompense un bonheur sans mélange (à vous et à vos descendants); vos fils et vos petits-fils s'en réjouissent. Dans leur joie et leur allégresse, chacun d'eux fait tout ce qu'il peut (ils offrent à boire au représentant des ancêtres). Alors l'un des invités puise de la liqueur; un serviteur de la maison entre et remplit la coupe. Il remplit cette coupe salutaire, (et vous l'offrez au représentant des défunts). Ainsi se terminent les cérémonies de chaque saison.

3. (Aux banquets donnés en d'autres occurrences que celles du tir à l'arc ou des offrandes en l'honneur des ancêtres), lorsque les invités approchent des nattes, ils sont polis et respectueux. Tant qu'ils ne sont pas ivres, la gravité et la bienséance sont gardées selon toutes les règles. Quand ils sont ivres, la gravité et la bienséance sont fort ébranlées. Ils quittent leurs places pour en prendre d'autres; à plusieurs reprises ils dansent et font des cabrioles. Tant qu'ils ne sont pas ivres, ils conservent leur gravité, observent les bienséances. Quand ils sont ivres, ils négligent entièrement la

ritus sunt absoluti, sunt magnifici, sunt plurimi. (Spiritus) munerantur te (tuosque posteros) pura felicitate; filii et nepotes ipsi gaudent. Ipsi gaudentes ac lætantes, singuli exserunt suas vires. Hospes tunc manibus depromit vinum; domesticus minister ingrediens iterum (vinum infundit in poculum). Vinum infundit in illud salutare poculum, ut exhibeatis vestram tempestivam (oblationem).

3. Hospites quum primum adeunt storeas, comis est eorum observantia. Donec ipsi non inebriati sunt, gravitas ac decentia quadrant legibus. Postquam inebriati sunt, gravitas ac decentia valde nutant. Relictis suis sedibus discurrunt; crebro saltant tripudiantes. Ii donec non inebriati sunt, gravitas et decentia accurate servantur. Postquam

既醉止、威儀怭怭、是曰既醉、不知其秩、④賓既醉止、載號載呶、亂我籩豆、屢舞僛僛、是曰既醉、不知其郵、側弁之俄、屢舞傞傞、既醉而出、並受其福、醉而不出、是謂伐德、飲酒孔嘉、維其令儀、⑤凡此飲酒、或醉或否、既立之監、或佐之史、彼醉不臧、不醉反

wéi tsouéi tchèu, wēi i ĭ ĭ. Iuĕ ki tsouéi tchèu, wēi i pĭ pĭ. Chéu iuĕ ki tsouéi, pŏu tchēu k'ì tchĕu.

4. Pīn ki tsouéi tchèu, tsái haó tsái naó. Louán ngò piēn teóu, liú òu k'ī k'ī. Chéu iuĕ ki tsouéi, pŏu tchēu k'ì iôu (ì). Tchĕ pién tchēu ngô, liú òu souō souō. Ki tsouéi èul tch'ŏu, ping cheóu k'ì fŏu (pĭ). Tsouéi êul pŏu tch'ŏu, chéu wéi fă tĕ. Ìn tsiòu k'òung kiā (kō), wêi k'ì líng ì (ngô).

5. Fàn ts'èu in tsiòu, houĕ tsouéi houĕ feòu (pèi). Ki lĭ tchēu kiēn, houĕ

gravité et les bienséances. Dans l'ivresse, ils ne connaissent plus aucune règle.

4. Quand les invités sont ivres, ils poussent des cris et des vociférations. Ils mettent en désordre nos vases de bois ; à plusieurs reprises ils dansent en chancelant. Quand ils sont ivres, ils n'ont plus conscience de leurs déportements. Avec leurs bonnets inclinés de côté, ils dansent à plusieurs reprises et longtemps. Quand un invité a trop bu, s'il se retire, c'est heureux pour lui et pour le maître de la maison. Ne pas se retirer, quand on est ivre, cela s'appelle ruiner sa vertu (se conduire mal et perdre sa réputation). L'usage des banquets est excellent ; mais il faut que les bienséances y soient parfaitement gardées.

5. Dans tous ces banquets, il est des invités qui boivent trop, et d'autres qui boivent sobrement. On établit un surveillant ;

inebriati sunt, gravitas ac decentia omnino negliguntur. Ita, postquam inebriati sunt, non noscunt suas leges.

4. Hospites postquam inebriati sunt, et clamant et vociferantur. Permiscent nostra lignea vasa ; crebro saltant obliquo corpore. Vere quum inebriati sunt, non noscunt sua errata. Obliquus pileus inclinatur ; crebro saltant non cessantes. Quum quis inebriatus est et egreditur, (is et domus dominus) ambo servant suam felicitatem. Inebriari et non egredi, id dicitur pessumdare virtutem. Bibere vinum valde bonum est, modo in hoc decora sit agendi ratio.

5. In omnibus illis potationibus vini, alii inebriantur, alii non. Postquam constitutus est inspector, quandoque

恥、式勿從謂。無俾大怠、匪言勿言、匪由勿語、由醉之言、俾出童羖。三爵不識、矧敢多又、

魚藻

(1) 魚在在藻、有頒其首、王在在鎬、豈樂飲酒。

(2) 魚在在藻、

tsouó tchēu chèu. Pèi tsouéi pǒu tsāng, pǒu tsouéi fàn tch'èu. Chĕu ǒu ts'ǒung wéi, ǒu pèi t'ái tái (i). Fèi iên ǒu iên, fèi iôu ǒu iù. Iôu tsouéi tchēu iên, pèi tch'ǒu t'ǒung kòu. Sān tsiŏ pǒu chĕu, chènn kàn touō ióu (ĭ)!

IU TSAO. **1. Iû tsái? Tsái tsaò; iòu fênn k'î cheòu. Wâng tsái? Tsái Haò; k'ài lŏ in tsiòu.**

2. Iû tsái? Tsái tsaò; iòu chēnn k'ì wéi. Wâng tsái? Tsái Haò; in tsiòu lŏ k'i.

parfois on lui adjoint un censeur (qui note les paroles et les actions. En dépit du surveillant et du censeur), ceux qui s'enivrent se conduisent mal. Les autres en ont honte; mais ils ne peuvent pas les avertir, ni les empêcher de suivre leur fantaisie. (Ils ne peuvent pas leur dire): « Évitez de dire des choses qu'il ne convient pas de dire, et de parler de choses qu'on ne doit pas faire. Si vous parlez dans l'ivresse, le bélier sans cornes arrivera. Avec trois coupes vous perdez la raison; quel dommage que vous osiez en boire davantage! »

CHANT VII. IU TSAO.

Dans un banquet à la cour impériale, les princes feudataires font l'éloge de l'empereur. Il est heureux et tranquille dans sa capitale, disent-ils, comme le poisson au milieu des plantes aquatiques.

1. Où demeure le poisson? Dans les herbes aquatiques, et sa tête y devient grosse. Où réside l'empereur? A Hao; aimable et joyeux, il y boit du vin.

2. Où demeure le poisson? Dans les herbes aquatiques, et sa

adjuvat censor. Illi ebrii non bene agunt; qui non sunt ebrii, contra pudore afficiuntur. At non possunt accedentes monere, (non possunt) non sinere ut nimium genio indulgeant. (Non possunt dicere): « Quæ non dicenda sunt, ne dicatis; quæ non sunt exsequenda, ne respondeatis. Ex ebriorum dictis fiet ut appareat cornibus carens aries. Tribus poculis amittitis memoriam; quam majori (jactura) audetis plura rursus (sorbere)! »

On menace ici du bélier sans cornes les ivrognes privés de raison, comme en Europe on menace du loup blanc les enfants qui pleurent.

CHANT VII. 1. Piscis ubi manet? Manet in herbis aquatilibus; habet amplitudinem ejus caput. Imperator ubi habitat? Habitat Hao; festivus et lætus bibit vinum.

2. Piscis ubi manet? Manet in herbis

有莘其尾。王在在鎬。飲酒樂豈。

(3) 魚在在藻。依于其蒲。王在在鎬。有那其居。

采菽

(1) 采菽采菽。筐之筥之。君子來朝。何錫予之。雖無予之。路車乘馬。又何予之。玄袞及黼。

3. Iû tsái ? Tsái tsaò ; I iû k'î p'ôu. Wâng tsái ? Tsái Haò ; iòu nô k'î kiū.

TS'AI CHOU. **1. Ts'ài chŏu, ts'ài chŏu, k'ouàng tchēu, kiù tchēu. Kiūn tzèu lâi tch'aô ; hô sí iù tchēu ? Souēi ôu iù tchēu, lóu kiū chéng mà (mòu). Iòu hô iù tchēu ? Hiuên kouènn kî fòu.**

queue y devient longue. Où réside l'empereur? A Hao ; heureux et aimable, il y boit du vin.

3. Où demeure le poisson? Dans les herbes aquatiques ; il y est protégé par les jones. Où réside l'empereur? A Hao ; c'est un séjour tranquille.

CHANT VIII. TS'AI CHOU.

Réponse de l'empereur aux félicitations que les princes lui ont exprimées dans le chant précédent.

1. Les haricots sont cueillis, et mis dans des corbeilles, les unes carrées, les autres rondes. (Nombreux comme les haricots) les princes arrivent à ma cour. Quels présents leur offrirai-je? Quand même je n'aurais pas autre chose à leur offrir, je leur donnerai des voitures impériales avec leurs quatre chevaux. Que leur donnerai-je de plus? Des tuniques ornées de dragons et des vêtements inférieurs ornés de haches.

aquaticis; habet longitudinem ejus cauda. Imperator ubi habitat? Habitat Hao; bibit vinum hilaris ac festivus.

3. Piscis ubi manet? Manet in herbis aquatilibus; innititur juncis. Imperator ubi habitat? Habitat Hao; habet quietem ejus sedes.

CHANT VIII. 1. Carpunt phaseolos, carpunt phaseolos; quadratis corbibus imponunt eos, rotundis canistris imponunt eos. Reguli veniunt ad aulam; quid munerans dabo eis? Etsi nihil (aliud) habeam quod donem eis, sunt regii currus et quadrijugi equi. Præterea quid dabo eis? Nigras pictis draconibus ornatas tunicas et pictis securibus (ornatas vestes inferiores).

Les voitures impériales étaient de cinq sortes; à savoir, les 玉路 iŭ lóu voitures ornées de pierres précieuses, qui étaient réservées à l'empereur; les 金路 kīn lóu voitures dorées, qui étaient concédées aux princes portant le même nom de famille que l'empereur; les 象路 siáng lóu voitures avec des ornements d'ivoire, qui étaient concédées à ceux

(2) 觱沸檻泉、言采其芹、君子來朝、言觀其旂、其旂淠淠、鸞聲嘒嘒、載驂載駟、君子所屆、

(3) 赤芾在股、邪幅在下、彼交匪紓、天子所予、樂只君子、天子命之、樂只君子、福祿申之、

2. Pĭ fŏu hiên ts'iuên (ts'iûn); iên ts'ài k'î k'în. Kiūn tzèu lâi tch'aô, iên kouān k'î k'î (k'în). K'î k'î p'i p'i; louân chēng houéi houéi. Tsái ts'ān tsái séu; kiūn tzèu chòu kiái (ki).

3. Tch'ĕu fŏu tsái kòu, siê pĭ tsái hià (hòu). Pèi kiaō fèi chōu (chòu), t'iēn tzèu chòu iù. Lŏ tchèu kiūn tzèu; t'iēn tzèu ming (ming) tchēu. Lŏ tchèu kiūn tzèu; fŏu lŏu chēnn tchēu.

2. Dans l'eau d'une source jaillisante on cueille le cresson. (De même) lorsque les princes arrivent à ma cour, on voit de loin leurs étendards ornés de dragons. Leurs étendards flottent au vent; les sonnettes de leurs chevaux retentissent doucement. Ils ont deux chevaux latéraux; en tout, quatre chevaux attelés de front. A ces signes on reconnaît l'arrivée des princes.

3. Des genouillères de couleur rouge pâle leur couvrent la partie supérieure des jambes; des bandes d'étoffe enveloppent de leurs contours obliques la partie inférieure. Dans ces réunions, les princes ne négligent nullement les bienséances; le Fils du ciel en est heureux. Ils sont aimables; le Fils du ciel leur accorde de nouvelles dignités. Ils sont aimables; le Fils du ciel augmente leurs honneurs et leurs revenus.

des parents de l'empereur qui ne portaient pas le même nom de famille que lui; les 革路 **kŏ lóu** voitures couvertes de cuir, qui étaient concédées aux princes chargés de défendre les frontières; les 木路 **mŏu lóu** voitures de bois vernis, qui étaient concédées aux princes des pays tributaires.

Sur le vêtement supérieur 衣 **i** des princes 公 **kōung** étaient représentés des dragons, des montagnes, des faisans, des flammes, des vases 彝 **i**; sur le vêtement inférieur 裳 **châng**, des algues, des grains de riz, des haches, des 亞.

2. Scatens exsilit fons; carpitur ejus nasturtium. Reguli veniunt ad aulam; prospicio eorum pictis draconibus ornata vexilla. Eorum vexilla vento agitantur; tintinnabulorum tinnitus lenis. Sunt laterales equi, sunt quadrijugi equi. Reguli illis (utentes) adveniunt.

3. Rubea genualia operiunt coxas; oblique circumvolutæ fasciæ operiunt inferiora, nempe tibias. Illi convenientes non sunt remissi, Cœli filius quod approbat. Amabiles reguli; Cœli filius honoribus auget eos. Amabiles reguli; honores et opes ampliat eis.

(4) 維柞之枝、其葉蓬蓬、樂只君子、殿天子之邦、樂只君子、萬福攸同、平平左右、亦是率從、

(5) 汎汎楊舟、紼纚維之、樂只君子、天子葵之、樂只君子、福祿膍之、優哉游哉、亦是戾矣、

角弓

(1) 騂騂角弓、翩

4. Wěi tsŏ tchēu tchēu, k'ì iě p'ôung p'ôung. Lŏ tchéu kiūn tzèu, tién t'iēn tzèu tchēu pāng (pōung). Lŏ tchéu kiūn tzèu, wán fŏu iôu t'ôung. P'iên p'iên tsouò iòu, ì chéu chouĕ ts'ôung.

5. Fán fán iàng tcheōu, fŏu lì wêi tchēu. Lŏ tchéu kiūn tzèu, t'iēn tzèu k'ouéi tchēu. Lŏ tchéu kiūn tzèu, fŏu lŏu p'î tchēu. Iōu tsāi, iōu tsāi, ì chéu lì (lì) i.

KIO KOUNG. **1. Sīng sīng kiŏ kōung, p'iēn k'ì fàn (fân) i. Hiōung tì houēnn In, ôu siū iuén (iuên) i.**

4. Sur les branches du chêne le feuillage est très touffu (et sert à les protéger). Ces princes sont aimables ; ils défendent les États du Fils du ciel. Ces princes sont aimables ; ils sont comblés de tous les biens. Des hommes d'une tenue irréprochable les suivent et les accompagnent.

5. La barque en bois de peuplier est ballottée par les vagues ; on la fixe à l'aide d'une amarre. (Ainsi l'empereur s'attache les princes par la collation des dignités). Ces princes sont aimables ; le Fils du ciel pèse leurs mérites. Ils sont aimables ; le Fils du ciel augmente beaucoup leurs honneurs et leurs revenus. Avec quel plaisir et quelle joie ils sont venus ici !

CHANT IX. KIO KOUNG.

Le poète reproche à l'empereur de traiter avec froideur ses propres parents, et de prêter l'oreille aux détracteurs ambitieux.

1. Un arc a été bien travaillé et ses extrémités ont été garnies de corne ; (lorsqu'on le détend), il se redresse, (et ses extrémités

4. Sunt quercus rami, eorum folia sunt densa. Amabiles reguli, a tergo defendunt Cœli filii regnum. Amabiles reguli, omnia bona ideo simul veniunt (eis). Recte compositi læva dextraque (circumstantes ministri) etiam eos sequentes comitantur.

殿 **Tién**, arrière-garde, former l'arrière-garde.

5. Fluctuat populea cymba ; fune vincientes alligant eam. Amabiles reguli, Cœli filius pensat eos. Amabiles reguli, honores et opes multum augentur eis. Quam libenter, quam gaudenter ipsi advenerunt !

CHANT IX. 1. Bene temperatus est cornu ornatus arcus ; (soluto nervo), inversus ille retroagitur. Fratribus et

其反矣、兄弟昏姻、無胥遠矣、(2) 爾之遠矣、民胥然矣、爾之教矣、民胥傚矣、(3) 此令兄弟、綽綽有裕、不令兄弟、交相爲瘉、(4) 民之無良、相怨一方、受爵不讓、至于已斯亡、(5) 老馬反爲駒、不顧其後、如食宜饇、如酌孔取、

2. Eùl tchēu iuén (iuên) i, mîn siū jên i. Eùl tchēu kiaó i, mîn siū hiaó i. [(iû).

3. Ts'èu lìng hiōung tí, tch'ouŏ tch'ouŏ iòu iú. Pŏu lìng hiōung tí, kiaō siāng wêi iù

4. Mîn tchēu ôu leâng, siāng iuén ĭ fāng. Cheóu tsiŏ pŏu jáng (jâng), tchéu iū i sēu wâng.

5. Laò mà fàn wêi kiū (kiû), pŏu kóu k'ì heóu (hóu). Jôu sêu i iú, jôu tchŏ k'òung ts'iù (ts'iú).

s'écartent l'une de l'autre). Des frères, des parents par alliance ne doivent pas s'éloigner les uns des autres (comme les extrémités d'un arc qu'on détend).

2. Vous vous éloignez de vos parents ; vos sujets vous imitent. Vous donnez l'exemple; vos sujets le suivent.

3. Les bons frères sont extrêmement généreux. Les mauvais frères se font de la peine les uns aux autres.

4. Les sujets qui manquent de probité, se plaignent les uns des autres, chacun soutenant son sentiment. S'ils obtiennent des dignités, ils ne sont pas modestes, (ils se les disputent entre eux), jusqu'à ce qu'enfin ils les perdent.

5. Un vieux cheval veut faire le jeune poulain, et ne prévoit pas à quoi il s'expose. (Ainsi ces détracteurs ambitieux veulent exercer des charges malgré leur incapacité; ils ne prévoient pas les difficultés qui les attendent. Plus ils obtiennent d'honneurs, plus ils en convoitent; leur ambition est insatiable). Celui qui mange, doit cesser de vouloir manger, quand il est repu ; celui qui boit, doit s'arrêter, quand il a déjà beaucoup bu.

affinibus non licet invicem secedere.

2. Tu secedis (a cognatis); subditi omnes ita (agunt). Tu exemplum præbes ; populares omnes imitantur.

3. Illi boni fratres largi sunt abundanter ; mali fratres convenientes invicem faciunt negotium.

4. Subditi non probi invicem queruntur, (unoquoque tenente) unum locum, i. e. unam sententiam. Acceptis dignitatibus, non sunt modesti, donec actum est, et tunc amittunt (eas).

5. Vetus equus mutatus agit vices pulli ; non prospicit quæ sibi obventura sunt. Si quis edat, oportet ut satietur, i. e. ut non sit semper inhians cibi; si quis bibat, (oportet ut agnoscat) se multum sumpsisse.

(6) 毋教猱升木、如塗塗附、君子有徽猷、小人與屬。
(7) 雨雪瀌瀌、見晛曰消、莫肯下遺、式居婁驕、
(8) 雨雪浮浮、見晛曰流、如蠻如髦、我是用憂、

菀柳

(1) 有菀者柳、不尚息焉、上帝甚

6. Oû kiaó naô chēng mŏu, jôu t'ôu t'ôu fóu. Kiūn tzèu iòu houēi iôu, siaò jênn iù chŏu (chóu).

7. Iú siuĕ p'iaô p'iaô, kién hién iuĕ siaô. Mouŏ k'éng hiá î, chĕu kiū liú kiaô.

8. Iú siuĕ feôu feôu, kién hién iuĕ liôu. Jôu Mân jôu Maô (Meôu), ngò chéu ióung iôu.

IU LIOU. 1. Iòu iù tchè liòu, pŏu cháng sī iên? Cháng tí chénn taó, ôu tzéu gnì iên. Péi iù tsing tchĕu, heóu iù kí iên.

6. (Le peuple est par lui-même très enclin à négliger ses parents; craignez de l'y porter encore par vos exemples). N'apprenez pas au singe à grimper sur les arbres; n'accumulez pas la boue sur la boue. Quand le souverain se conduit bien, tous les sujets font le bien avec lui.

7. Une neige abondante est tombée; au premier rayon du soleil elle se fond. (Au moindre signe de la colère du souverain, les détracteurs rentrent dans le silence). Vous ne voulez ni abaisser ni éloigner aucun (de ces calomniateurs); aussi leur arrogance augmente sans cesse.

8. Une neige abondante est tombée; le premier rayon du soleil la dissipe. (A cause de votre faiblesse) nous devenons semblables aux barbares (pour les mœurs); j'en éprouve une grande douleur.

CHANT X. IU LIOU.

Un prince feudataire dit qu'il est impossible d'aller à la cour impériale, à cause de la tyrannie de l'empereur.

1. Un saule est magnifique; ne désire-t-on pas se reposer (à son

6. Noli docere simiam ut conscendat arbores, imitari hominem qui cœno cœnum adjicit. Quum rex habet bonam agendi rationem, subditi cum eo conveniunt.

7. Cadit nix copiosa; viso solis calore, statim solvitur. Neminem vis deprimere nec abjicere; tunc innitens, i. e. confisa tuæ indulgentiæ, multiplicatur arrogantia.

8. Decidit nix copiose; viso solis calore, (liquefacta) defluit. Imitamur barbaros australes, barbaros occidentales; ego ea de causa doleo.

CHANT X. 1. Est luxurians salix; nonne optandum quiescere? Supremus

蹈、無自暱焉、俾予靖之、後予極焉、

(2) 有菀者柳、不尚愒焉、上帝甚蹈、無自瘵焉、俾予靖之、後予邁焉、

(3) 有鳥高飛、亦傅于天、彼人之心、于何其臻、曷予靖之、居以凶矜、

2. Iòu iù tchĕ liòu, pŏu cháng k'i iên? Cháng ti chénn taó, ôu tzéu tchái (tsi) iên. Péi iù tsing tchēu, heóu iù mái (li) iên.

3. Iòu gniaò kaō fēi, ĭ fóu iū t'iēn (t'īn). Péi jênn tchēu sīn, iū hô k'ì tchēnn? Hŏ iù tsing tchēu? kiū i hiōung kīn.

ombre? Si l'empereur était bon, ne désirerait-on pas aller à sa cour)? Mais ce maître suprême de l'univers est très redoutable; je ne veux pas de moi-même l'approcher. Si je contribuais à affermir son pouvoir, il m'accablerait ensuite par ses exigences.

2. Sous un saule magnifique, ne désire-t-on pas se reposer? Mais ce maître suprême de l'univers est très redoutable; je ne veux pas me nuire à moi-même. Si je travaillais à affermir son pouvoir, il exigerait ensuite de moi beaucoup trop.

3. Un oiseau vole très haut; arrivé au ciel, il s'arrêtera. Jusqu'où cet homme (l'empereur) étendra-t-il ses prétentions? Pourquoi travaillerais-je à affermir sa puissance? Je n'en retirerais d'autre fruit que des vexations cruelles et lamentables.

dominus valde tremendus est; nolo ipse appropinquare. Fac ut ego confirmem eum; postea me obruet.

上帝指王也 (朱熹) **Cháng ti tchéu wâng iè.** L'expression *cháng ti* désigne l'empereur. 輔氏廣曰視其君如上帝本知所尊也 **Fòu chéu Kouàng iuĕ: « Chéu k'i kiūn jôu Cháng tí, pènn tchēu chòu tsuēnn iè. »** Fou Kouang dit: « Il voit dans la personne de son souverain comme le Maître suprême de l'univers; il sait qu'il lui doit un grand respect. »

蹈當作神言威靈可畏也 (朱熹) **Taó tāng tsŏ chênn, iên wēi lîng k'ŏ wéi iè.** «La lettre *taó* doit être remplacée par la lettre 神 **chênn,** qui signifie doué d'une puissance surhumaine et redoutable.» On trouve la lettre 神 dans le 戰國策 où ce passage est cité. Selon d'autres auteurs, la lettre *taó* doit être conservée, et signifie changeant, inconstant.

2. Est luxurians salix, nonne optandum quiescere? Supremus dominus valde tremendus est; nolo ipse mihi nocere. Fac ut ego firmem eum; postea a me nimis exiget.

3. Est avis sublime volans, etiam perveniet ad cœlum (et sistet). Illius hominis (imperatoris) animus usque quo ipse perveniet? Quare ego firmarem eum? Unice adsciscerem funesta et miseranda.

都人士之什二之八

都人士

(1)彼都人士、狐裘黃黃、其容不改、出言有章、行歸于周、萬民所望、

(2)彼都人士、臺笠緇撮、彼君子女、綢直如髮、我不見兮、我心不說、

(3)彼都人士、充耳琇實、彼君子女、謂之尹吉、我不見兮、

TOU JENN CHEU. 1. Pèi tōu jênn chéu, hôu k'iôu houâng houâng. K'î iôung pŏu kài, tch'ŏu iên iòu tchāng. Hîng kouēi iû Tcheōu, wán mîn chòu wáng (wâng).

2. Pèi tōu jênn chéu, t'âi lî tchēu tsouŏ (tsiuĕ). Pèi kiūn tzèu gniù, tch'eôu tchĕu jôu fă (fiuĕ). Ngò pŏu kién hî, ngò sīn pŏu iuĕ.

3. Pèi tōu jênn chéu, tch'ōung èul siòu chĕu. Pèi kiūn tzèu gniù, wéi tchēu ìn Kĭ. Ngò pŏu kién hî, ngò sīn iùn kiĕ (kĭ).

LIVRE VIII. TOU JENN CHEU.

CHANT I. TOU JENN CHEU.

Le peuple dispersé par suite des troubles de l'empire regrette de ne plus voir les costumes, de ne plus entendre le langage élégant des habitants de 鎬 Haô, la capitale.

1. (En hiver) les officiers de la capitale portaient des tuniques jaunes garnies de peaux de renards. Leur tenue était constamment irréprochable et leur langage élégant. Retourner à la capitale, c'est le désir de tout le peuple.

2. (En été) les officiers de la capitale portaient des chapeaux de jonc et des bonnets de toile noire. Les femmes des grandes familles avaient les cheveux épais et lisses. Je ne les vois plus; mon cœur n'a pas la joie.

3. Les officiers de la capitale portaient sur les oreilles des pierres de prix appelées *siou*. Les femmes de haut rang étaient si distinguées qu'on les aurait crues toutes issues des illustres familles des

TITRE DU LIVRE. 都人士之什二之八 Tou jenn cheu decas: secundæ (partis) octava (decas).

CHANT I. 1. Illis regiæ urbis viris præpositis erant e vulpinis pellibus tunicæ flavæ. Illorum habitus non mutabatur; prolata verba habebant elegantiam. Proficisci et redire ad urbem regiam, omnes populares est id quod cupiunt.

2. Illis regiæ urbis viris præpositis erant juncei petasi, e nigra tela pilei. Illis egregiis mulieribus erant spisso et recto modo capilli. Ego non video; meus animus non gaudet.

3. Illis regiæ urbis viris præpositis tegmina aurium erant e *siou* lapillis obturamenta. Illas egregias mulieres

我心苑結、

(4) 彼都人士、垂帶而厲、彼君子女、卷髮如蠆、我不見兮、言從之邁、

(5) 匪伊垂之、帶則有餘、匪伊卷之、髮則有旟、我不見兮、云何盱矣、

采綠

(1) 終朝采綠、不盈一匊、予髮曲局、薄言歸沐、

4. Pèi tōu jênn chéu, tch'ouêi tái êul li (lái). Pèi kiūn tzèu gniù, k'iuên fă jôu tch'ái. Ngò pōu kién hì, iên ts'ôung tchēu mái.

5. Fèi ī tch'ouêi tchēu, tái tsĕ iòu iû. Fèi ī k'iuên tchēu, fă tsĕ iòu iû. Ngò pōu kién hì, iûn hô hiū i ?

TS'AI LIU. **1. Tchōung tchaō ts'ài liŭ, pōu îng ī kiŭ. Iù fă k'iŭ kiŭ, pouŏ iên kouēi mŏu.**

In et des Ki. Je ne les vois plus ; mon cœur est comme glacé par la douleur.

4. Les officiers de la capitale portaient de longues ceintures pendantes. Les femmes distinguées avaient (sur les tempes) des boucles de cheveux semblables à la queue du scorpion. Je ne les vois plus ; (si je les voyais), je me mettrais à leur suite.

5. Les officiers ne prenaient pas soin de faire pendre leurs ceintures ; elles pendaient d'elles-mêmes, parce qu'elles étaient plus longues qu'il ne fallait pour ceindre les reins. Les femmes ne bouclaient pas leurs cheveux ; leurs cheveux bouclaient d'eux-mêmes. Je ne les vois plus ; oh ! que je désire les revoir !

CHANT II. TS'AI LIU.

Une femme attend avec impatience le retour de son mari. Tout entière à cette pensée, à ce sentiment, elle est incapable de s'appliquer au moindre travail.

1. J'ai employé toute la matinée à cueillir des roseaux ; je n'en ai pas recueilli assez pour remplir mes deux mains. Mes cheveux sont en désordre ; je vais retourner à la maison et me laver la tête, (afin d'être en état de recevoir convenablement mon mari).

dixisses esse e In aut Ki (genere oriundas). Ego non video ; meum cor quasi dense coagulatum est.

4. Illis regiæ urbis viris præpositis pendebant zonæ et defluebant. Illis egregiis mulieribus recurvi erant capilli instar scorpiorum. Ego non video ; (si viderem), sequens illos irem.

5. Non ipsi demittebant eas, zonæ vero habebant superflua. Non ipsæ torquebant eos, capilli vero habebant recurvum flexum. Ego non video ; quantum cupio !

CHANT II. 1. Toto mane legi calamos, nec implevi semel ambas manus. Mei capilli sunt intorti et implexi ; interim domum repeto et caput lavabo.

(2) 終朝采藍、不盈一襜、五日爲期、六日不詹、
(3) 之子于狩、言韔其弓、之子于釣、言綸之繩、
(4) 其釣維何、維魴及鱮、維魴及鱮、薄言觀者、
黍苗
(1) 芃芃黍苗、陰雨膏之、悠悠南行、召伯勞之、

2. Tchōung tchaō ts'ài lân, pŏu îng ĭ tch'ēn (tān). Oú jĕu wéi k'î, lŏu jĕu pŏu tchēn (tān).

3. Tchēu tzèu iû cheóu, ièn tch'áng k'î kōung. Tchēu tzèu iû tiaó, ièn liûn tchēu chêng.

4. K'î tiaó wêi hô ? Wêi fâng kĭ siú (siù). Wêi fâng kĭ siú (siù), pouŏ ièn kouān tchė (tchóu).

CHOU MIAO. **1. P'ôung p'ôung chòu miaŏ, īn iù kaó tchēu. Iôu iôu nân hîng, Chaó pĕ laó tchēu.**

2. J'ai passé toute la matinée à cueillir l'indigotier; je n'en ai pas recueilli assez pour remplir le pan de ma robe. Mon seigneur devait être de retour dans cinq jours. Au sixième jour, je ne le vois pas encore.

3. S'il (revient et qu'il) aille à la chasse, je replacerai son arc dans l'étui. S'il va pêcher à la ligne, je ferai la corde de sa ligne.

4. Quels poissons prendra-t-il avec sa ligne? Des brêmes et des perches. Ces brêmes et ces perches, j'irai les voir.

CHANT III. CHOU MIAO.

Expédition et travaux de 召穆公 Mou, prince de Chao, chargé par l'empereur 宣王 **Siuēn wâng** (827-781) de bâtir dans la terre de 謝 **Sié** la nouvelle capitale de la principauté de 申 **Chēnn**.

1. Le millet à panicules croit avec vigueur, fécondé par la pluie du ciel. (De même) nous allons fort loin vers le midi, encouragés par le prince de Chao.

一匊 **ĭ kiŭ**, autant que les deux mains réunies peuvent contenir.

2. Toto mane legi indicum, nec implevi semel sinum ex stolæ lacinia factum. Quinque dies erat statutum tempus; sexto die non video.

3. Si ille dominus (maritus) ibit venatum, in theca recondam ejus arcum. Si ille dominus ibit hamo venatum, torquebo ejus funiculum.

4. Ille hamo capiet speciatim quid? Speciatim bramam et percam. Speciatim bramam et percam paululum aspectura (ibo).

CHANT III. **1.** Vegeta crescit milii panici seges; nubes et pluvia opimant eam. Valde procul ad austrum imus: Chao princeps allevat hunc (laborem).

(2) 我任我輦、我車我牛、我行既集、蓋云歸哉、

(3) 我徒我御、我師我旅、我行既集、蓋云歸處、

(4) 肅肅謝功、召伯營之、烈烈征師、召伯成之、

(5) 原隰既平、泉流既清、召伯有成、王心則寧、

2. Ngò jènn, ngò lièn, ngò kiū, ngò iôu (1). Ngò hîng k'i tsĭ, kái iùn kouēi tsāi (tsī).

3. Ngò t'ôu, ngò iú, ngò chēu, ngò liù. Ngò hîng kí tsĭ, kái iùn kouēi tch'òu.

4. Siŭ siŭ Sié kōung, Chaó pĕ îng tchēu. Liĕ liĕ tchēng chēu, Chaó pĕ tch'êng tchêu.

5. Iuên sí kí p'îng, ts'iuên liôu kí ts'īng. Chaó pĕ iòu tch'êng, wâng sīn tsĕ gning.

2. C'est nous qui portons les bagages, traînons les voitures, conduisons les charrettes et les bœufs. Quand notre expédition sera terminée, alors peut-être on parlera de retour, (jusque-là il n'en sera pas question).

3. Nous allons à pied et en voiture; nous sommes soldats des légions et des cohortes. Quand notre expédition sera terminée, alors peut-être on parlera de retour et de repos.

4. Les travaux exécutés à Sié ont une apparence sévère ; le prince de Chao en a tracé le plan. Les soldats de l'expédition sont pleins d'ardeur; le prince de Chao les forme (et les encourage).

5. Les terrains hauts et les terrains bas ont été arrangés; le lit des rivières a été débarrassé. Le prince de Chao a terminé ses travaux, et l'empereur est content.

2. Nos sarcinas bajulamus, nos vehicula trahimus, nos plaustra ducimus, nos boves ducimus. Nostrum iter postquam perfectum erit, forsan loquemur de reditu.

3. Nos pedites, nos vecti, nos legionum milites, nos cohortum milites. Nostrum iter postquam confectum erit, forsan agetur de reditu et quiete.

La cohorte était de cinq cents hommes. Cinq cohortes formaient une légion.

4. Severa sunt Sie urbis opera; Chao princeps delineavit ea. Acriter strenuæ sunt expeditionis legiones; Chao princeps format eas.

謝 Sié était dans le **信陽州 Sin iàng tcheōu**, qui dépend de **汝寧府 Jòu gnîng fòu** dans le Ho nan.

5. Altiora loca et humiliora sunt composita; fontes fluunt jam expediti. Chao princeps assecutus est ut perficeret; imperatoris animus inde quietus est.

隰桑

(1) 隰桑有阿、其葉有難、既見君子、其樂如何、

(2) 隰桑有阿、其葉有沃、既見君子、云何不樂、

(3) 隰桑有阿、其葉有幽、既見君子、德音孔膠、

(4) 心乎愛矣、遐不謂矣、中心藏之、何日忘之、

SI SANG. 1. **Sĭ sāng iòu ngō, k'ì iĕ iòu nô. Ki kién kiūn tzèu, k'ì lŏ jŏu hô !**

2. Sĭ sāng iòu ngō, k'ì iĕ iòu ŏu (iŏ). Ki kién kiūn tzèu, iùn hô pŏu lŏ ?

3. Sĭ sāng iòu ngō, k'ì iĕ iòu iōu (iaō). Ki kién kiūn tzèu, tĕ īn k'òung kiaō.

4. Sīn hôu ngái (hi) i, hiâ pŏu wéi i ? Tchōung sīn ts'âng tchēu ; hô jĕu wàng tchēu ?

CHANT IV. SI SANG.

Le poète exprime son estime et son affection pour les hommes sages. Il les compare aux mûriers touffus qui croissent dans les terrains bas et humides.

1. Dans un terrain bas et humide le mûrier devient beau ; son feuillage est luxuriant. A la vue d'un sage, quelle n'est pas ma joie!

2. Dans un terrain bas et humide le mûrier devient beau ; ses feuilles sont onctueuses et luisantes. A la vue d'un sage, comment ne serais-je pas dans la joie ?

3. Dans un terrain bas et humide le mûrier devient beau ; son feuillage est vert foncé. A la vue d'un sage, la renommée de sa vertu fait une plus grande impression sur mon cœur.

4. (Déjà auparavant) je l'aimais en mon cœur ; pourquoi ne le dirais-je pas ? Je garde son souvenir au fond de mon âme ; pourrais-je jamais l'oublier ?

CHANT IV. 1. In humili et humido loco morus habet pulchritudinem ; ejus folia habent luxuriam. Quum viderim sapientem virum, hoc (meum) gaudium quantum est !

阿美貌 難盛貌 **Ngō**, belle apparence ; **nô**, apparence de prospérité.

2. In humili et uvido loco morus habet pulchritudinem ; ejus folia habent unguinem et nitorem. Quum viderim sapientem virum, dic, quomodo non gaudeam ?

3. In humili et uliginoso loco morus habet pulchritudinem ; ejus folia habent spissius viridem colorem. Quum viderim sapientem virum, virtutis fama valde adhæret (animo meo).

幽 **Iōu**, sombre, couleur tirant sur le noir.

膠 **Kiaō**, colle, coller, adhérer.

4. In animo (jam antea eum) diligebam ; quare non dicam ? In animo recondo eum ; quonam die obliviscar eum ?

白華

① 白華菅兮、白茅束兮、子之遠、俾我獨兮、

② 英英白雲、露彼菅茅、天步艱難、之子不猶、

③ 滮池北流、浸彼稻田、嘯歌傷懷、念彼碩人、

PE HOUA. **1. Pĕ houā kiēn hî, pĕ maô chŏu hî. Tchēu tzèu tchēu iuén, pèi ngò tŏu hî.**

2. Īng īng pĕ iûn, lóu pèi kiēn maô (meôu). T'iēn póu kiēn nân, tchēu tzèu pŏu iôu.

3. P'iôu tch'êu pĕ liôu, tsín pèi taó t'iên (t'în). Siaó kō chāng houâi, gnién pèi chĕu jènn.

CHANT V. PE HOUA.

La fille du prince de 申 **Chēnn**, mariée à l'empereur 幽王 **Iōu wâng**, reproche à celui-ci de l'avoir délaissée, et de lui avoir substitué 褒姒 **Paō Séu**, qui était une femme de second rang.

1. La plante appelée *pe houa,* pour être rouie, est liée avec du chiendent. (Ainsi les deux époux doivent rester unis). Cet homme (l'empereur Iou) se sépare de moi, et me condamne à la solitude.

2. Un petit nuage d'une blancheur éclatante arrose le *pe houa* et le chiendent. Les temps sont durs et difficiles; cet homme est moins bon (pour moi que le petit nuage pour les plantes les plus viles).

3. L'eau des marais s'écoule vers le nord et arrose le champ de riz. Je chante et pousse des soupirs qui ressemblent à des sifflements; je pense à ce prince auguste (moins bon pour moi que le ruisseau pour le champ de riz).

CHANT V. 1. Albis floribus junci (ut fiant) *kiēn* macerati junci, albo gramine colligantur. Ille dominus recedens facit ut ego sola sim.

白華 **Pĕ houā**, nom d'une plante à fleurs blanches, de la famille des graminées. Ses fibres servent à faire des cordes. Après le rouissage, elle prend le nom de 菅 **kiēn.** Sa racine donne une fécule qui est bonne à manger.

2. Nitens alba nubecula irrorat illa *pĕ houā* et gramen. Temporum cursus est acerbus, difficilis; ille vir non imitatur (album nubeculam).

天步猶言時運也 **T'iēn póu, iôu iên chêu iún iè.** La marche du ciel, comme on dirait le cours des temps.

3. Decurrens paludum aqua ad septentrionem fluit, irrigat illum oryzæ agrum. Sibilans cano sauciato animo; reminiscor illum dignitate præstantem virum. — Entre la ville de 豐 **Fōung** et celle de 鎬 **Haò** plusieurs rivières coulent vers le nord.

(4) 樵彼桑薪。卬烘于煁。維彼碩人、實勞我心。

(5) 鼓鐘于宮。聲聞于外。念子懆懆。視我邁邁。

(6) 有鶖在梁。有鶴在林。維彼碩人、實勞我心。

(7) 鴛鴦在梁。戢其左翼。之子無良。二三其德。

(8) 有扁斯石。履

4. Ts'iaŏ pėi sāng sīn, ngāng hōung iū chênn. Wêi pėi chĕu jênn, chĕu laŏ ngò sīn.

5. Kòu tchōung iū kōung, chēng wénn iū wài. Gniên tzèu ts'aó ts'aó, chéu ngò mái mái.

6. Iòu ts'iōu tsái leâng, iòu hŏ tsái lin. Wêi pėi chĕu jênn chĕu laŏ ngò sīn.

7. Iuēn iāng tsái leâng, tsí k'i tsouò ĭ. Tchēu tzèu ôu leâng, éul sān k'i tĕ.

8. Iòu piėn sēu chĕu, li tchēu pī hì. Tchēu tzèu tchēu iuén, pėi ngò ti (k'i) hì.

4. Les branches du mûrier sont coupées pour le chauffage, (et elles devraient servir à cuire la nourriture); je les brûle sur un petit fourneau (uniquement pour avoir de la lumière). De même ce grand prince (me prive de mon rang et) afflige mon cœur.

5. Lorsque les tambours et les cloches retentissent dans le palais, au dehors l'écho leur répond. Je pense à cet homme avec anxiété; lui me regarde avec mépris (il ne répond pas à mon affection).

6. La cigogne est sur le barrage (où le poisson abonde), et la grue est dans la forêt (sur la montagne où elle meurt de faim. La favorite est dans l'abondance, et l'épouse légitime dans la pénurie). Vraiment ce grand prince afflige mon cœur.

7. Le canard mandarin et sa compagne sur le barrage (se tournent en sens inverse, et) l'aile gauche de l'un touche l'aile gauche de l'autre. (Ainsi les époux doivent rester unis). Cet homme manque de probité; il change sans cesse de conduite.

8. Celui-là est très bas qui se tient sur une pierre très basse.

4. Cæduntur illi mororum comburendi rami; ego comburo super foculum. Etenim ille magnus vir vere angit meum animum.

5. Tympanis et campanis in palatio (pulsatis), echo diffunditur in exteriora. Cogito de viro inquieto animo; videt me cum despectu.

6. Est ciconia insidens septo, est grus in silva. Etenim ille magnus vir vere cruciat meum animum.

7. Anas mascula et anas femina insidentes septo, conjungunt suas sinistras alas. Ille vir non est probus; bis terque mutat suam agendi rationem.

8. Est humilis quidam lapis; qui insistit ei, est humilis. Illius viri discessus facit ut ego ægrotem.

之卑兮、之子之遠、俾我疷兮、

緜蠻

(1) 緜蠻黃鳥、止于丘阿、道之云遠、我勞如何、飲之食之、教之誨之、命彼後車、謂之載之、

(2) 緜蠻黃鳥、止于丘隅、豈敢憚行、畏不能趨、飲之食之、教之誨之、命彼後車、謂之載之、

MIEN MAN. 1. **Miên mân houâng gniaò : « Tchèu iū k'iōu ngō. Taó tchēu iûn iuèn ; ngò laô jôu hô ? » Ìn tchēu, séu tchēu, kiaó tchēu, houéi tchēu. Ming pèi heóu kiū, wéi tchēu tsái tchēu.**

2. Miên mân houâng gniaò : « Tchèu iū k'iōu iû. K'i kàn tán hîng ? Wéi pŏu nêng ts'iū. » Ìn tchēu, séu tchēu, kiaó tchēu, houéi tchēu. Míng pèi heóu kiū, wéi tchēu tsái tchēu.

(Un prince se dégrade qui s'attache à une personne vile). Cet homme, en se séparant de moi, me rend malade.

CHANT VI. MIEN MAN.

Un soldat, sous l'emblème du loriot, se plaint de ses fatigues, et réclame du soulagement.

1. Le loriot babillard dit en son langage : « Je m'arrête dans un enfoncement au pied de la colline. La route est longue ; je suis fatigué, que puis-je faire ? » Donnez-lui à boire, donnez-lui à manger ; donnez-lui des avis et des instructions. Donnez des ordres au conducteur de cette voiture (de bagages) qui est derrière ; dites-lui de le transporter en voiture.

2. Le loriot babillard dit en son langage : « Je m'arrête à l'angle de la colline. Me permettrais-je de reculer devant la fatigue du voyage ? Non, mais je crains de ne pouvoir avancer vite. » Donnez-lui à boire et à manger, donez-lui des avis et des intructions. Donnez des ordres au conducteur de la voiture qui est derrière ; dites-lui de le transporter en voiture.

CHANT VI. 1. *Miên mân* clamitans flava avis dicit) : « Sisto in collis anfractu. Via est longa ; ego fatigata quomodo (agam) ? » Adaquate eam, cibate eam, docete eam, monete eam. Jussum date illi posteriori vehiculo, dicite illi ut vehat eam.

Mien man est le petit cri de l'oiseau fatigué, qui ne pouvant plus voler, appelle du secours.

2. Clamitans flava avis (dicit) : « Sisto in collis angulo. Quomodo ausim refugere itineris (laborem) ? Timeo ne non valeam celeriter ire. » Adaquate eam,...

(3) 緜蠻黃鳥、止于丘側。豈敢憚行、畏不能極。飲之食之、教之誨之、命彼後車、謂之載之、

瓠葉

(1) 幡幡瓠葉、采之亨之、君子有酒、酌言嘗之、

(2) 有兔斯首、炮之燔之、君子有酒、酌言獻之、

3. Miên mân houâng gniaò : « Tchéu iû k'iōu tchĕ. K'i kàn tán hîng ? Wéi pŏu nêng kĭ. » Ìn tchēu, séu tchēu, kiaó tchēu, houéi tchēu. Ming pèi heóu kiū, wéi tchēu tsái tchēu.

HOU IE. **1. Fān fān hôu iĕ, ts'ài tchēu, p'ēng (p'āng) tchēu. Kiūn tzèu iòu tsiòu, tchŏ iên tch'âng tchēu.**

2. Iòu t'óu sēu cheòu, p'aô tchēu fân tchēu. Kiūn tzèu iòu tsiòu, tchŏ iên hién (hiên) tchēu.

3. Le loriot babillard dit en son langage : « Je m'arrête auprès de la colline. Me permettrais-je de reculer devant la fatigue de la route ? Non, mais je crains de ne pouvoir atteindre le terme du voyage. » Donnez-lui à boire et à manger ; donnez-lui des avis et des instructions. Donnez des ordres au conducteur de cette voiture qui est derrière ; dites-lui de le transporter en voiture.

CHANT VII. HOU IE.

Le repas le plus frugal est agréable aux invités, si les règles de l'urbanité y sont parfaitement observées.

1. Des feuilles de concombres sont tremblantes sur leurs tiges ; on les cueille et on les fait cuire. Le maître de la maison a du vin ; il en remplit une coupe et le goûte (pour savoir s'il est bon).

2. On a un lièvre ; on le fait cuire sous la cendre sans le dépouiller de son poil, ou bien on le fait cuire sur le feu. Le maître de la maison a du vin ; il le verse dans les coupes et l'offre à ses invités.

3. Clamitans flava avis (dicit) : « Sisto ad collis latus. Qui ausim refugere itineris laborem ? Timeo ne non valeam metam attingere. » Adaquate eam,...

CHANT VII. 1. Nutantia cucurbitæ folia (habentur) ; carpunt ea, coquunt ea. Domus dominus habet vinum ; infundit et gustat illud.

言 **Iên**, particule.

2. Habetur lepus unus ; pilis vestitum torrent eum, igne coquunt eum. Domus dominus habet vinum ; infundit et offert illud.

斯 **Sēu**, particule explétive.

首 **Cheòu**, particule numérale des lièvres

(3) 有兔斯首、燔之炙之、君子有酒、酌言酢之、

(4) 有兔斯首、燔之炮之、君子有酒、酌言醻之、

漸漸之石

(1) 漸漸之石、維其高矣、山川悠遠、維其勞矣、武人東征、不遑朝矣、

(2) 漸漸之石、維

3. Iòu t'óu sēu cheòu, fân tchēu tchĕu (tchŏ) tchēu. Kiūn tzèu iòu tsiòu, tchŏ ièn tsŏ tchēu.

4. Iòu t'óu sĕu cheòu, fân tchĕu p'aŏ (p'eŏu) tchēu. Kiūn tzèu iòu tsiòu, tchŏ ièn tch'eŏu tchēu.

TCH'AN TCH'AN TCHEU CHEU. **1. Tch'ân tch'ân tchēu chĕu, wêi k'î kaŏ i. Chān tch'ouēn iŏu iuèn, wêi k'î laŏ i. Où jênn tōung tchēng, pŏu houâng tchaŏ i.**

2. Tch'ân tch'ân tchēu chĕu, wêi k'î tsŏu i. Chān tch'ouēn iŏu iuèn, hŏ k'î

3. On a un lièvre; on le fait cuire sur le feu ou rôtir auprès du feu. Le maître de la maison a du vin; les invités en remplissent une coupe et la lui offrent à leur tour.

4. On a un lièvre; on le fait cuire sur le feu, ou bien on le met sous la cendre chaude sans le dépouiller de son poil. Le maître de la maison a du vin; il en remplit les coupes, et de nouveau invite à boire.

CHANT VIII. TCH'AN TCH'AN TCHEU CHEU.

Le chef d'une expédition militaire raconte les difficultés des voyages et les souffrances endurées par ses soldats.

1. Ces rochers sourcilleux sont très élevés. Les montagnes et les rivières qui s'étendent au loin, rendent les voyages très difficiles. Soldat (et chef) de cette expédition dans les contrées orientales, je n'ai pas même une matinée de repos.

2. Ces rochers sourcilleux sont escarpés et très hauts. Quand

3. Habetur lepus unus; igne coquunt eum, assant eum. Domus dominus habet vinum; (hospites) infundunt et in vicem offerunt illud (domino).

4. Habetur lepus unus; coquunt eum, pilis vestitum torrent eum. Domus dominus habet vinum; infundit et rursus offert illud.

Les invités recevaient les coupes présentées pour la seconde fois; mais ils les déposaient aussitôt, et ne buvaient pas la liqueur.

CHANT VIII. 1. Aspera saxa sunt ipsa alta. Montes et fluvii longe protensi, sunt ipsi magno labori. Miles (militum dux) in orientali expeditione, ne (uno quidem) otior mane.

2. Aspera saxa sunt ipsa alta et

其卒矣、山川悠遠、曷其沒矣、武人東征、不遑出矣、

(3) 有豕白蹢、烝涉波矣、月離于畢、俾滂沱矣、武人東征、不遑他矣、

苕之華

(1) 苕之華、芸其黃矣、心之憂矣、維其傷矣、

(2) 苕之華、其葉青青、知我如此、不如

mŏu (mĭ) i. Où jênn tōung tchēng, pŏu houâng tch'ŏu i.

3. Iòu chèu pĕ tĭ, tchēng chĕ pouō i. Iuĕ lì iū Pĭ, pèi p'āng t'ouô i. Où jênn tōung tchēng, pŏu houâng t'ouō i.

T'IAO TCHEU HOUA. **1. T'iaô tchēu houā, iûn k'î houâng i. Sīn tchēu iōu i, wêi k'î chāng i.**

2. T'iaô tchēu houā, k'î iĕ tsīng tsīng. Tchēu ngò jôu ts'èu, pŏu jôu ôu chēng (sīng).

verrons-nous l'extrémité de ces montagnes et de ces rivières qui s'étendent au loin? Soldat, je m'enfonce dans ces contrées orientales, et n'ai pas le loisir de prévoir comment j'en sortirai.

3. Les pieds des pourceaux (ordinairement sales et noirs) sont blancs, parce qu'ils marchent dans l'eau (qui couvre les chemins). La lune va entrer dans les Hyades; elle amènera des pluies torrentielles. Soldat, je porte les armes en orient, et n'ai pas le temps de penser à autre chose.

CHANT IX. T'IAO TCHEU HOUA.

Le poète déplore la décadence de la dynastie des Tcheou et les souffrances du peuple.

1. Les fleurs de la bignonie sont déjà d'un jaune foncé (et vont tomber. Ainsi l'empire menace ruine). Mon cœur est triste; il est comme blessé.

2. Les fleurs de la bignonie (sont tombées); ses feuilles sont encore vertes, (mais ne le seront plus longtemps). Si j'avais su

prærupta. Montes et fluvii longe protensi quando ipsi finem habebunt? Miles orientem pervado, nec vacat (præcogitare) de exitu.

3. Sunt sues albis pedibus, omnes incedunt in undis. Luna (mox erit in Hyadibus, faciet ut imbres maximi decidant. Miles in oriente bellum gero, nec vacat de alia re (curare).

CHANT IX. 1. Bignoniæ flores spisse illi flavi sunt. Animus dolet, etenim ipse saucius est.

2. Bignoniæ flores (deciderunt); ejus folia viridia sunt. Si scivissem me

無生。

(3) 牂羊墳首。三星在罶。人可以食。鮮可以飽。

何草不黃

(1) 何草不黃。何日不行。何人不將。經營四方。

(2) 何草不玄。何人不矜。哀我征夫。獨爲匪民。

3. Tsāng iâng fênn cheòu; sān sīng tsái liòu. Jênn k'ò i chĕu, sièn k'ò i paò (peòu).

HO TS'AO POU HOUANG? **1. Hô ts'aò pŏu houâng? Hô jĕu pŏu hîng (hâng)? Hô jênn pŏu tsiāng, kīng ing séu fāng?**

2. Hô ts'aò pŏu hiuên (hiûn)? Hô jênn pŏu kouān (kīng)? Ngāi ngò tchēng fōu, tŏu wêi fèi mîn.

les maux qui m'attendaient dans le monde, j'aurais mieux aimé ne pas naître.

3. La tête des brebis devient grosse, (parce qu'elles manquent de nourriture et sont amaigries); dans la nasse (on ne voit pas de poissons, mais seulement la lumière de) trois étoiles (réflétée par l'eau). Les hommes ont assez de vivres (pour ne pas mourir); mais peu en ont assez pour se rassasier pleinement.

CHANT X. HO TS'AO POU HOUANG?

Les hommes sont constamment retenus loin de leurs familles, et accablés de fatigue dans les expéditions militaires. Ils sont comme des plantes qui dépérissent.

1. Est-il une plante qui ne soit devenue jaune? Est-il un jour où nous ne voyagions pas? Quels sont les hommes qui ne vont pas supporter mille fatigues dans toutes les parties de l'empire?

2. Quelle est la plante qui n'est pas devenue noire? Quels sont les hommes qui vivent avec leurs femmes? Malheureux soldats engagés dans cette expédition, seuls nous ne sommes plus traités comme des hommes.

eo modo fore, nihil potius mihi fuisset quam non nasci.

3. Ovibus magnum est caput; tres stellæ sunt in nassa. Homines assequuntur ut edant; pauci assequuntur ut saturentur.

牂羊 **Tsāng iâng**, femelle du bélier. Quand une brebis est maigre, disent les commentateurs, sa tête devient ou paraît plus grosse.

CHANT X. 1. Quænam planta non est flava? quonam die non iter facimus? Quinam homines non pergunt, ut operam præbeant in omnibus regionibus?

2. Quænam planta non est nigra? Quinam homines non carent uxoribus? Miseri nos expeditionis homines, soli censemur non esse populares.

(3) 匪兕匪虎、率彼曠野、哀我征夫、朝夕不暇、

(4) 有芃者狐、率彼幽草、有棧之車、行彼周道、

3. Fèi sì fèi hòu, chouĕ pèi k'ouáng iè (chòu). Ngāi ngò tchēng fōu, tchaō sī pŏu hiá (hòu).

4. Iòu p'êng tchè hôu, chouĕ pèi iōu ts'aò. Iòu tchàn tchēu kiū, hìng pèi tcheōu taó.

3. Sans être ni rhinocéros ni tigres, nous parcourons ces pays déserts (comme les animaux sauvages). Malheureux soldats engagés dans cette expédition, du matin au soir nous n'avons aucun repos.

4. Les renards à longue queue voyagent à travers ces épaisses touffes d'herbe, (ils y trouvent leur agrément). Nous, avec nos charrettes surmontées de clayons (et chargées de bagages), nous parcourons cette grande route (très péniblement).

3. Licet non simus rhinocerotes nec tigres, peragramus illas desertas terras. Miseri nos expeditionis homines, mane et vespere caremus otio.

4. Habentes longam caudam vulpes pervadunt illas densas herbas. Cum habentibus crates onerariis plaustris, percurrimus illam magnam viam.

大雅三

TROISIÈME PARTIE

TA IA

文王之什三之一

文王

(1) 文王在上、於昭于天、周雖舊邦、其命維新、有周不顯、帝命不時、文王

WENN WANG. 1. **Wênn wâng tsái cháng, ōu! tchaō iū t'iēn (t'īn)! Tcheōu souēi kióu pāng, k'ì míng wêi sīn. Iòu Tcheōu pŏu hièn? Tí míng pŏu chêu (chéu)?**

LIVRE I. WENN WANG.

CHANT I. WENN WANG.

周公 **Tcheōu kōung**, fils de 文王 **Wênn wâng** et frère puîné de 武王 **Où wàng**, qui fonda la dynastie des 周 **Tcheōu**, rappelle au jeune empereur 成王 **Tchêng wâng**, fils de Ou wang, les exploits de Wenn wang, dont les vertus ont mérité les faveurs du ciel et valu l'empire à la famille des Tcheou.

1. Wenn wang est là-haut ; oh ! comme il brille dans le ciel ! Bien que la principauté particulière des Tcheou soit ancienne, ils ont reçu un mandat nouveau (qui leur confère le pouvoir impérial). Les Tcheou n'étaient-ils pas illustres ? Et le mandat du roi

TITRES. 大雅三 Ea quæ in magnis rebus decent : (Cheu king) tertia pars. Cf. page 173. 文王之什三之一 Wenn wang decas : tertiæ (partis) primus (liber).

CHANT I. Wenn rex est in superis ; oh ! splendet in cœlo ! Tcheou licet sit antiquum regnum, ejus mandatum, i.e. cœleste mandatum quo ejus reguli creati sunt totius imperii rectores, solummodo recens est. Tenentes Tcheou (reguli) nonne insignes erant ? Regis (supremi) mandatum nonne fuit tempestivum ? Wenn rex ascendit descenditque, adstans ad regis (supremi) lævam dextramve.

上卽天也 Région supérieure, c'est-à-dire, le ciel. 帝上帝 **Ti, Cháng ti**, roi du ciel. 命天命也 *Míng*, mandat conféré par le ciel. 此章言文王既沒而其神在上昭明於天是以周雖自后稷始封千有餘年而其受天命則自今始也... 蓋以文王之

陟降、在帝左右、(2)亹亹文王、令聞不已、陳錫哉周、侯文王孫子、文王孫子、本支百世、凡周之士、不顯亦世、(3)世之不顯、厥猶翼

Wênn wâng tchĕu kiáng, tsái tí tsouò iòu (i).

2. Wèi wèi Wênn wâng, líng wénn pŏu i. Tch'ênn sĭ tsāi Tcheōu, heóu Wênn wâng suēnn tzèu (tsi). Wênn wâng suēnn tzèu (tsi), pénn tchēu pĕ chéu. Fân Tcheōu tchēu chéu, pŏu hièn ĭ chéu?

3. Chéu tchēu pŏu hièn? Kiuĕ iôu ĭ ĭ. Sēu houâng touō chéu, chēng ts'èu wâng

du ciel n'est-il pas venu en son temps? Wenn wang monte et descend, toujours à la droite ou à la gauche du roi du ciel.

2. Wenn wang a déployé une grande énergie; sa gloire n'a pas de fin. (Le roi du ciel) étend ses bienfaits sur la famille des Tcheou, sur les descendants de Wenn wang. Les descendants de Wenn wang régneront durant cent générations, l'héritier principal (sur l'empire), les autres (sur des principautés). Et tous les officiers des Tcheou ne seront-ils pas illustres d'âge en âge?

3. Ne seront-ils pas illustres dans tous les âges? Ils poursuivent l'exécution de leurs plans avec activité et circonspection. Beau-

神一升一降無時不在上帝之左右是以子孫蒙其福澤而君有天下也(朱熹集傳) Dans cette strophe il est dit qu'après la mort de Wenn wang, son esprit est monté dans les hauteurs des cieux, où il brille d'un vif éclat; que par suite, bien que la principauté particulière des Tcheou ait été fondée par Heou tsi (le premier de leurs ancêtres connus), plus de mille ans auparavant, leur famille a reçu du ciel tout récemment un nouveau pouvoir (le pouvoir impérial)... Parce que l'esprit de Wenn wang monte et descend, sans cesse à la droite ou à la gauche du roi du ciel, sa postérité jouit des faveurs du ciel, possède et gouverne l'empire. 無時不在上帝之左右與天合德同運而竝行者也(詩經備旨) L'esprit de Wenn wang est sans cesse auprès du roi du ciel. Il unit sa vertu à celle du ciel, se meut et agit avec lui.

2. Magnos exseruit conatus Wenn rex; optima fama non desinit. (Rex cœlestis) profert beneficia in Tcheou (domum), nempe in Wenn regis posteros. Wenn regis posteri, et stirps et rami, centum generationibus (regnabunt). Omnes Tcheou ministri nonne clarebunt etiam quaque generatione?

Wenn wang par ses vertus a mérité les faveurs du ciel, et obtenu l'empire pour son fils 武王 **Où wâng.** Mais lui-même n'a jamais été 王 **wâng** empereur. Ce titre lui a été conféré après sa mort, ainsi qu'à son père 王季 et à son aïeul 太王, par 周公 **Tcheōu kōung**, son second fils.

3. Quaque generatione nonne clarebunt? In suis consiliis sunt strenui et cauti. Eximii sunt multi ministri, nati

翼、思皇多士、生此王國、王國克生、維周之楨、濟濟多士、文王以寧、

(4) 穆穆文王、於緝熙敬止、假哉天命、有商孫子、商之孫子、其麗不億、上帝既命、侯于周服、

(5) 侯服于周、天命靡常、殷士膚

kouŏ (ĭ). Wâng kouŏ (ĭ) k'ŏ chēng, wéi Tcheōu tchēu tchēng. Tsì tsì touō chéu, Wênn wâng ì gnìng.

4. Mŏu mŏu Wênn wâng, ōu! ts'ĭ hī king tchèu! Kià tsāi t'iēn mìng! Iòu Chāng suēnn tzèu. Chāng tchēu suēnn tzèu, k'ĭ lì pŏu ĭ. Cháng tí kí mìng, heóu iū Tcheōu fŏu (pĕ).

5. Heóu fŏu (pĕ) iū Tcheōu, t'iēn mìng mì chàng. Īn chéu fōu mìn, kouán tsiāng iū

coup d'excellents officiers sont nés dans les États de Wenn wang. La principauté de Wenn wang les a produits; ils sont les soutiens des Tcheou. Les officiers sont très nombreux; Wenn wang se tient assuré qu'ils soutiendront la dynastie.

4. Wenn wang était profondément vertueux; oh! il se signala par son application constante à remplir ses devoirs! Le mandat du ciel est grand; témoins les descendants des Chang. Les descendants des Chang étaient plus de cent mille. Sur l'ordre du roi du ciel, ils se soumirent tous aux princes de Tcheou.

5. Ils se soumirent tous aux princes de Tcheou; c'est que le ciel ne laisse pas constamment son mandat (à la même famille. Maintenant) les officiers distingués et agiles des In versent et pré-

in hoc regis (Wenn wang) regno. Regis regnum potuit gignere, et sunt Tcheou sustentacula. Abunde multi sunt ministri; Wenn rex utens securus est (de sua domo et regno).

思 **Sēu**, particule.

4. Profunda virtute erat Wenn rex; oh! continenter animum intendebat! Magnum est cœli mandatum; (testes) sunt Chang posteri. Chang posteri illi erant numero non solum (i. e. amplius) centum millia. Supremus rex quum jusserit, unice sub Tcheou (imperium) se subjecerunt.

武王 **Où wâng** détrôna 紂 **Tcheòu**, dernier empereur de la famille des 商 **Chāng**, appelés aussi 殷 **Īn**, et fonda la dynastie des Tcheou, en l'année 1122 avant J. C.

5. Unice se subjecerunt sub Tcheou (imperium); cœli mandatum non constanter permanet (in eadem domo). In regum ministri insignes et celeres, libationibus operam præstant in urbe præcipua. Hi agentes libationum adjutores, constanter induunt securibus pictis ornatam (vestem inferiorem) et *hiù* pileum. (Tch'eng) imperatoris addictissimi ministri, nonne memineritis vestri avi (Wenn regis)?

敏、祼將于京、厥
作祼將、常服黼
冔、王之藎臣、無
念爾祖、
⑥無念爾祖、聿
脩厥德、永言配
命、自求多福、殷
之未喪師、克配
上帝、宜鑒于殷、
駿命不易、
⑦命之不易、無
遏爾躬、宣昭義
問、有虞殷自天、

kīng (kāng). Kiuĕ tsŏ kouán tsiāng, chāng fŏu fòu hiù. Wâng tchĕu tsin tch'ênn, ŏu gnién èul tsòu?

6. Où gnién èul tsòu? Iŭ siŏu kiuĕ tĕ. Iòung iên p'éi míng, tzéu k'iôu touŏ fŏu (pĭ). Īn tchĕu wéi sáng chĕu, k'ŏ p'éi Cháng ti. Ī kién iū Īn; siún míng pŏu i.

7. Míng tchĕu pŏu i, ŏu ngŏ èul kŏung. Siuĕn tchaŏ i wénn, iòu iû Īn tzéu

sentent les liqueurs pour les libations (offertes aux ancêtres des Tcheou) dans la capitale. Lorsqu'ils aident à faire des libations, ils portent toujours le vêtement inférieur orné de haches brodées, et le bonnet de cérémonie qui était en usage sous les In. Officiers dévoués de l'empereur actuel, ne vous souviendrez-vous pas toujours de votre aïeul (Wenn wang)?

6. Ne penserez-vous pas toujours à votre aïeul? Perfectionnez vos vertus. Tâchez de vous conformer sans cesse aux ordres du ciel; vous recevrez de lui beaucoup de faveurs. Tant que les In ont gardé le gouvernement du peuple, ils ont été comme les assesseurs du roi du ciel. Ayez constamment devant les yeux l'exemple (la déchéance) des In; le mandat suprême (le pouvoir impérial) n'est pas facile (à conserver).

7. Le mandat du ciel n'est pas facile (à garder; prince), craignez de vous perdre vous-même. Étendez au loin le renom de votre vertu, et considérez comment le ciel a retranché la dynastie des In. Les opérations du ciel ne sont perçues ni par l'ouïe ni par

6. Nonne memores eritis vestri avi? Excolite vestras virtutes. Perpetim quærite obsequi jussis (cœli); ipsi vobis arcessetis multa cœli beneficia. In dum non amisit multitudinem, i.e. populi regendi potestatem, potuit consociari cœlesti regi. Oportet oculos intendere in In; summum mandatum non facile (servatur).

聿 Iŭ, particule. 上帝天之主宰也(朱熹集傳) Le Chang ti est le maître et le roi du ciel.

7. Mandatum non facile (servatur; Tch'eng rex), noli excidere teipsum. Profer claram æquitatis famam, et inspice In (excidium) e cœlo. Superni cœli gesta carent sono, carent odore. Imagine referens imitare Wenn regem; omnia regna exsurgent et fident.

法文王卽所以法天如此則在天之靈可慰而靡常之命可保矣(詩經備旨) Imiter

上天之載，無聲無臭。儀刑文王，萬邦作孚。

大明

(1) 明明在下，赫赫在上。天難忱斯，不易維王。天位殷適，使不挾四方。

(2) 摯仲氏任，自彼殷商，來嫁于周，曰嬪于京。乃及王季，維德之

t'iēn (t'īn). Cháng t'iēn tchēu tsái, ǒu chēng ǒu tch'eóu (tch'eǒu). Ī hîng Wênn wâng, wán pāng tsǒ fōu (feǒu).

TA MING. **1. Mîng mîng tsái hiá, hĕ hĕ tsái cháng (chāng). T'iēn nân chênn sēu, pǒu i wêi wâng. T'iēn wêi Īn tĭ, chèu pǒu tsiĕ séu fāng.**

2. Tchéu tchóung chéu Jênn, tzéu pèi Īn Chāng, lâi kiá iū Tcheōu, iuĕ p'in iū

l'odorat. (Il est impossible de les deviner d'avance. Pour être sûr de vous conformer toujours à la volonté du ciel), imitez, copiez Wenn wang ; tous les peuples se lèveront et vous donneront leur confiance.

CHANT II. TA MING.

Le poète célèbre la naissance et les vertus de 文 王 **Wênn wâng**, la naissance de 武 王 **Où wâng**, la défaite du tyran 紂 **Tcheóu** et l'avènement des 周 **Tcheōu** à l'empire.

1. Lorsqu'une vertu extraordinaire brille sur la terre, l'auguste mandat lui est conféré dans le ciel (le ciel lui confie le gouvernement de l'empire). Il serait téméraire de se reposer uniquement sur la faveur du ciel ; il n'est pas facile d'exercer le pouvoir impérial. L'héritier des In (le tyran Tcheou) avait la dignité de Fils du ciel ; (le ciel) lui retira l'empire.

2. La fille cadette du prince de Tcheu, dont la famille s'appelait Jenn, vint du domaine impérial de In ou Chang, se maria à Tcheou, et fut dans la capitale la femme (de Wang Ki, prince de Tcheou). Elle et son époux s'adonnèrent à la pratique de

Wenn wang, c'est le moyen d'imiter le ciel. Par là vous réjouirez l'âme de votre aïeul qui est dans le ciel, et conserverez le pouvoir souverain qui est toujours révocable.

CHANT II. 大 明 **Tá Mîng**, le chant *Mîng* contenu dans le Ta ia. Cf. page 244.

1. Quum maxime clara (virtus) inest in inferis, i. e. in terra, augustum mandatum inest in superis, i. e. in cœlo. Cœlo difficile fiditur ; non facile (potestatem exercet) imperator. In Cœli filii sede erat In regum hæres ; (cœlum) fecit ut non teneret quatuor regiones.

2. Tcheu (regni reguli) natu secunda filia, (familiæ nomine) Jenn, ex illo In seu Chang (proprio regno), veniens nupsit in Tcheou regno, scilicet uxor facta est in urbe præcipua.

行。大任有身。生此文王。

(3) 維此文王。小心翼翼。昭事上帝。聿懷多福。厥德不回。以受方國。

(4) 天監在下。有命既集。文王初載。天作之合。在洽之陽。在渭之涘。文王嘉止。大邦有子。

(5) 大邦有子。俔天之妹。文定厥祥。親

kīng (kāng). Nài kĭ Wâng Ki, wèi tĕ tchēu hing (hâng). T'ái Jènn iòu chēnn (hàng), chēng ts'èu Wènn wâng.

3. Wêi ts'èu Wènn wâng siaò sīn ĭ ĭ. Tchaō chéu Cháng ti, iŭ houâi touō fŏu (pĭ). Kiuĕ tĕ pŏu houêi, i cheóu fāng kouŏ (ĭ).

4. T'iēn kién tsái hiá, iòu ming ki tsĭ (tsŏ). Wênn wâng tch'ōu tsái, t'iēn tsŏ tchēu hŏ. Tsái Hŏ tchēu iàng, tsái Wêi tchēu sêu (i). Wênn wâng kiā tchêu, tá pāng iòu tzèu (tsi).

5. Tá pāng iòu tzèu (tsi), k'ién t'iēn tchēu méi. Wênn tíng kiuĕ siâng, ts'īn

toutes les vertus. Cette auguste princesse de Jenn devint enceinte et enfanta Wenn wang.

3. Wenn wang, toujours attentif et diligent, servit parfaitement le souverain roi et reçut beaucoup de faveurs. Sa vertu ne se démentit jamais, et il obtint l'empire du monde.

4. Le ciel veillait sur les peuples d'ici-bas; déjà il avait décrété d'une manière irrévocable (l'avènement des Tcheou à l'empire). Dès les premières années de Wenn wang, le ciel lui prépara une compagne, au nord de la Ho, sur le bord de la Wei. Quand Wenn wang fut à l'âge de se marier, le chef d'une grande principauté avait une fille (nommée T'ai Seu).

5. Le chef d'une grande principauté avait une fille (si vertueuse qu') on l'aurait prise pour la sœur cadette du ciel. Les pré-

lude (ipsa) et Wang Ki unice bonas actiones egerunt. Inclyta Jenn habuit conceptum; edidit hunc Wenn regem.

3. Et hic Wenn rex attento animo studiosus, insigniter servivit supremo regi, et complexus (accepit) multa bona. Ejus virtus non deflexit (a recto); ideo accepit regionum (omnium) regna.

4. Cœlum invigilabat in infera; erat decretum jam absolutum. Wenn regis primis annis, cœlum fecit ei comparem, ad Ho fluvii septentrionem, ad Wei fluvii oram. Wenn rege uxorem ducturo, magnum regnum habebat puellam.

Cette grande principauté était celle de 莘 Chēnn, le 洽陽縣 Hŏ iâng hién actuel, qui dépend de 同州 T'ôung tcheōu dans le 陝西 Chén sī. La jeune fille était 太姒 T'ái Séu. Cf. page 5 et suivantes.

5. Magnum regnum habebat puellam; similis videbatur cœli sorori natu

迎于渭、造舟爲梁、不顯其光、
(6) 有命自天、命此文王、于周于京、纘女維莘、長子維行、篤生武王、保右命爾、燮伐大商、
(7) 殷商之旅、其會如林、矢于牧野、維予于

ing iû Wéi. Tsaó tcheōu wêi leàng; pŏu hièn k'i kouāng?

6. Iòu ming tzèu t'iēn, ming ts'èu Wênn wâng iū Tcheōu, iū kīng (kāng). Tsouàn gniù wêi Chēnn. Tchàng tzèu wêi hîng (hâng), tŏu chēng Où wâng. Paò iòu ming èul, siĕ fă tá Chāng.

7. Īn Chāng tchêu liû, k'i houéi jôu lîn. Chéu iū Mŏu iè, wêi iù heôu hīng (hīn). «Cháng tí lîn jòu, ôu èul èul sīn.»

sents (envoyés par Wenn wang au père de la princesse) confirmèrent le pacte préliminaire de cette union approuvée par les augures. Wenn wang alla en personne au-devant de sa fiancée jusqu'à la Wei. (Pour traverser la rivière), il fit construire un pont de bateaux. Cette alliance n'a-t-elle pas été glorieuse?

6. Un décret émané du ciel avait fixé que Wenn wang régnerait sur la principauté et dans la capitale de Tcheou. La princesse qui devait occuper la place (de la mère de Wenn wang), était de la principauté de Chenn. La fille aînée (du prince de Chenn) vint épouser (Wenn wang), et eut le bonheur de mettre au monde Ou wang. «(Jeune prince, le ciel) vous protège, vous aide, vous confie son mandat. Docile à ses ordres, vous renverserez la puissante dynastie des Chang.»

7. Les soldats de In ou Chang réunis (dans leurs campements), étaient (nombreux et serrés) comme les arbres d'une forêt. Ils furent rangés en bataille dans le désert de Mou ie. Mais les nôtres

minori. Muneribus (Wenn rex) præstituit suas faustas (nuptias); ipse obviam ivit ad Wei. Fabricatis cymbis fecit pontem. Nonne splenduit eorum gloria?

6. Erat decretum e cœlo; (cœlum) decreverat hunc Wenn regem (fore regulum) in Tcheou regno, in urbe præcipua (regni Tcheou). Successura (Wenn regis matri) puella erat Chenn (reguli filia). (Chenn reguli) natu maxima filia venit nuptura; fortunata genuit Ou regem. «(Cœlum) protegit, adjuvat, mandato mittit te; obsequens profligabis potentem Chang.»

我周之業成於武王而武王之生又豈偶然哉(詩經體註) Ce fut Ou wang qui fonda notre dynastie. Comment la naissance de Ou wang aurait-elle été un effet du hasard?

7. In Chang cohortes ipsæ congregatæ erant instar silvæ. Ordinatæ sunt in Mou solitudine. At nostri soli ardentes erant. «Supremus rex adest tibi; ne sit anceps tuus animus.»

侯興，上帝臨女，無貳爾心。

(8) 牧野洋洋，檀車煌煌，駟騵彭彭。維師尚父，時維鷹揚。涼彼武王，肆伐大商，會朝清明。

緜

(1) 緜緜瓜瓞，民之初生，自土沮漆。古公亶父，陶復陶穴，未有家室。

8. Mŏu iè iâng iâng, t'ân kiū houâng houâng. Séu iuèn p'ôung p'ôung (p'âng p'âng). Wêi chēu Cháng fòu, chêu wêi Ing iâng, leáng pèi Où wâng. Séu fă tá Châng, houéi tchaō ts'īng mîng (mâng).

MIEN. **1. Miên miên kouā tiĕ. Mîn tchēu tch'ōu chēng tzéu t'òu Ts'iū Ts'ī. Kòu kōung Tàn fòu, t'aô fŏu t'aô hiuĕ (hĭ), wéi iòu kiā chēu.**

seuls étaient pleins d'ardeur. (Ils dirent à Ou wang): «Le souverain roi est avec vous; n'hésitez pas (à engager le combat).»

8. Le désert de Mou ie était très vaste. Les chars en bois de *t'ân* étaient resplendissants; leurs quatre chevaux noirs au ventre blanc étaient robustes. Le grand maître Chang fou, semblable à un aigle qui vole, aida Ou wang. Ce prince déchaînant l'ardeur de ses guerriers, défit la puissante armée de Chang. Le jour même du combat, l'empire fut entièrement purgé (des souillures accumulées par le tyran Tcheou).

CHANT III. MIEN.

Origine et progrès de la famille des 周 **Tcheōu**. Cf. page 2.

1. Les fruits de la courge naissent et se développent les uns à la suite des autres sur la même tige. (Ainsi notre nation a grandi peu à peu). Notre peuple est originaire de la terre (de Pin) où coulent la Ts'iu et la Ts'i. Au temps de l'ancien prince Tan fou, il habitait des huttes et des cavernes disposées en forme de fours; il n'avait pas encore de maisons ni de bâtiments.

Mou ie est dans le 淇縣 **K'i hién** actuel, préfecture de 衛輝府 **Wéi houēi fòu**, province de Ho nan. 侯 **Heôu** équivaut à 維 **wêi**, seulement.

8. Mou solitudo latissime patebat. E *t'ân* ligno currus splendebant valde; quadrijugi equi nigri albo ventre erant robusti. (Summus) magister Chang fou tunc fuit sicut aquila volans; adjuvit illum Ou regem. Emissis (militibus, Ou rex) profligavit potentem Chang. Commissi prælii (ipso) mane, purgatum refulsit (imperium, sordido liberatum tyranno).

尚父 **Cháng fòu**, Noble seigneur, titre donné à 太公望 **T'ái kōung wáng**, qui était alors 太師 **t'ái chēu** grand maître.

CHANT III. 1. Continenter nascuntur et crescunt cucurbitæ majores fruc-

(2) 古公亶父、
來朝走馬、率
西水滸、至于
岐下、爰及姜
女、聿來胥宇、
(3) 周原膴膴、
堇荼如飴、爰
始爰謀、爰契
我龜、曰止曰
時、築室于茲、
(4) 迺慰迺止、
迺左迺右、迺
疆迺理、迺宣

2. Kòu kōung Tàn fòu lâi tchaō tseòu mà (mòu). Chouě sī chouèi hòu, tchéu iū K'ì hià (hòu). Iuên kī Kiāng gniù, iū lâi siū iù.

3. Tcheōu iuên òu òu, kin t'ōu jôu î. Iuên chéu iuên meôu (mêi), iuên k'i ngò kouēi. Iuě tchéu iuě chêu, tchŏu chĕu iū tzēu (tsī).

4. Nài wéi nài tchèu, nài tsouò nài iòu (i). Nài kiāng nài lì, nài siuēn nài

2. L'ancien prince Tan fou un matin (quitta la terre de Pin souvent ravagée par les barbares, et) pressa la marche de ses chevaux, pour venir (dans la terre de Tcheou). Suivant les bords des rivières de l'ouest (qui sont la Ts'iu et la Ts'i), il arriva au pied du mont K'i. Là, avec son épouse issue de la famille des Kiang, il chercha un endroit pour fixer sa demeure.

3. (Au sud du mont K'i), les plaines de Tcheou étaient belles et fertiles; la violette et le laiteron (qui sont des plantes amères) avaient la douce saveur d'un gâteau de riz. Ou wang délibéra d'abord (avec ses compagnons), grilla (et consulta) notre tortue. Puis il déclara qu'il convenait de se fixer en cet endroit, que le moment était favorable, et qu'il fallait bâtir des maisons.

4. Il encouragea ses sujets, et fixa les emplacements des habitations, les uns à droite, les autres à gauche. Il détermina les grandes limites et la division des terres. Dans tout le pays il établit

tus et cucurbitæ minores fructus. Gentis primus ortus ex terra (Pin, in qua sunt fluvii) Ts'iu et Ts'i. (Quum viveret) antiquus regulus Tan fou, erant in fornacis modum casæ, in fornacis modum cavernæ; nondum erant domus et ædificia.

2. Antiquus regulus Tan fou veniens mane properavit equis. Legens occidentalium fluviorum (Ts'iu et Ts'i) ripas, pervenit ad K'i montis radices. Ibi (ipse) et Kiang filia (uxor ejus) venientes simul-inspexerunt habitationis-locum.

3. Tcheou planities erant pingues et pulchræ; viola, sonchus erant sicut placenta. Et incepit et deliberavit (cum sociis quos ex Pin secum adduxerat), et torruit nostram testudinem. Dixit manendum esse, dixit tempus esse opportunum; ædificandas esse domos in hoc loco.

堇 **Kin**, plante comestible, peut-être une espèce de violette. 契 **K'i**, instrument employé par le devin pour allumer le feu et faire griller l'écaille de la tortue.

4. Et animos addidit, et domibus loca constituit, tum ad sinistram, tum

廼畝、自西徂
東、周爰執事、
(5) 乃召司空、
乃召司徒、俾
立室家、其繩
則直、縮版以
載、作廟翼翼、
(6) 捄之陾陾、
度之薨薨、築
之登登、削屢
馮馮、百堵皆
興、鼛鼓弗勝、
(7) 廼立皐門、

meòu (mèi). Tzéu sī ts'ôu tōung, tcheōu iuên tchĕu chéu (chéu).

5. Nài tchaó sēu k'ōung, nài tchaó sēu t'ôu; pèi lĭ chĕu kiā (kōu). K'î chêng tsĕ tchĕu, chŏu pàn i tsái (tsī), tsŏ miaó ĭ ĭ.

6. Kiū tchēu jêng jêng, touŏ tchēu hēng hēng, tchŏu tchēu tēng tēng, siŏ tchēu p'ing p'ing. Pĕ tòu kiāi hīng, kaō kòu fŏu chēng.

7. Nài lĭ kaō mênn, kaō mênn iòu k'áng (k'āng). Nài lĭ ing mênn, ing mênn

des hameaux (ou des canaux d'irrigation), et régla la disposition des arpents. Il alla de l'ouest à l'est arranger toutes choses.

5. Il appela le ministre et le conducteur des travaux publics, et leur ordonna de construire les maisons et les autres bâtiments. Ils employèrent le cordeau pour que tout fût droit. Ils firent (disposer et) lier les planches, de manière qu'on pût (les élever au fur et à mesure, et) continuer (la maçonnerie jusqu'à la hauteur voulue). En premier lieu le temple des ancêtres s'éleva beau et majestueux.

6. Un grand nombre d'hommes remplirent de terre les paniers. Ils la jetèrent entre les cloisons de planches avec un bruit confus de voix, et la battirent à coups retentissants. Ils raclèrent les aspérités, et le bruit annonçait la solidité du travail. Cinq mille pieds de mur s'élevèrent à la fois. Le grand tambour était impuissant à modérer l'ardeur des ouvriers.

7. Ils élevèrent la porte de l'enceinte du palais; elle eut une

ad dexteram. Et agrorum magnos limites signavit et partes delineavit. Et dispersit (i. e. per totam regionem aut viculos constituit aut canaliculos duxit), et jugera definivit. Ab occidente adiens orientem, curavit rem.

5. Et accersivit præfectum operum publicorum, et accersivit ducem operariorum, ut exstruerent domos et ædificia. Hi linea usi sunt et designarunt (omnia). Colligaverunt tabulas, ut continuaretur (opus ab imo ad summum). Excitaverunt avorum delubra decora et augusta. Cf. pag. 221.

6. In corbes imposuerunt eam (terram) quamplurimi, inter tabulata injecerunt eam confusis vocibus, tutuderunt eam instrumentorum invicem respondentium sono, raserunt prominentias firmo strepitu. Centies quinquaginta muri palmæ simul surrexerunt. Majus tympanum non valebat moderari (ardorem).

7. Tunc erexerunt septi portam; septi porta habuit altitudinem. Tunc erexerunt regiæ ædis portam; regiæ

皐門有伉、迺立應門、應門將將、迺立冢土、戎醜攸行、

(8) 肆不殄厥慍、亦不隕厥問、柞棫拔矣、行道兌矣、混夷駾矣、維其喙矣、

(9) 虞芮質厥成、文王蹶厥生、予曰有疏附、予曰有先後、予曰有

ts'iāng ts'iāng. Nài lì tchòung t'òu, jôung tch'eòu iôu hîng (hâng).

8. Séu pŏu tièn kiuĕ iùn, ì pŏu iùn kiuĕ wénn. Tsŏ iŭ péi i, hîng taó t'ouéi i. Kouēnn î touéi i, wêi k'ì wéi i.

9. Iû Jouéi tchĕu kiuĕ tch'êng, Wênn wâng kouéi kiuĕ chēng. Iû iuĕ iòu chōu

grande hauteur. Ils élevèrent la porte des appartements du prince ; elle fut belle et majestueuse. Ils élevèrent le grand autel de la Terre, point de départ de tous les grands mouvements.

8. Bien que T'ai wang ne parvînt pas à arrêter entièrement la fureur des barbares, sa gloire n'en fut pas diminuée. (Au lieu des taillis épais qui servaient de retraites aux ennemis), de grands chênes s'élevèrent, et des chemins furent ouverts. Les Kouenn i s'enfuirent en toute hâte, pouvant à peine respirer.

9. Les princes de Iu et de Jouei firent la paix entre eux, et Wenn wang augmenta rapidement sa puissance. Je le reconnais, (il n'eut pas seul tout le mérite de cette grande œuvre. Parmi ses sujets), les uns engagèrent leurs concitoyens à s'attacher à lui ; les autres ou le précédèrent (et l'encouragèrent par leurs exemples et leurs avis), ou le suivirent (et l'aidèrent à remplir son devoir).

ædis porta fuit decora et augusta. Tunc exstruxerunt Telluris magnum altare, magna multitudo unde profectura erat (quoties magnum opus aggressura erat).

Avant d'entreprendre une affaire importante ou de mettre une armée en campagne, on sacrifiait à la Terre.

8. Inde (T'ai wang) non extinxit illorum (occidentalium barbarorum) iras; attamen non decidit ejus fama. Quercus et ilices surrexerunt; (inter eas) incedentibus viæ patuerunt. Kouenn i (occidentales barbari) propere fugerunt, vix illi spiritum ducentes.

9. Iu et Jouei (regnorum principes) composuerunt suam pacem; Wenn rex celeriter promovit suæ potentiæ incrementum. Ego dico fuisse qui ducerent (alios) ut adhærerent (Wenn regi). Ego dico fuisse qui præducerent (Wenn regem ut virtutem coleret, et fuisse) qui sequerentur (et adjuvarent eum ad colendam virtutem). Ego dico fuisse qui excurrentes prædicarent (Wenn regis virtutes). Ego dico fuisse qui inhiberent contumelias (ab hostibus illatas).

Les princes de Iu et de Jouei se disputaient depuis longtemps la possession d'une terre. Ils convinrent de

奔奏。予曰有
禦侮。
棫樸
(1) 芃芃棫樸。
薪之槱之。
濟濟辟王。左右
趣之。
(2) 濟濟辟王。
左右奉璋。奉
璋峨峨。髦士
攸宜。
(3) 淠彼涇舟。
烝徒楫之。周

fóu (fòu), iù iuĕ iòu siên heóu (hóu). Iù iuĕ iòu pĕnn tseòu (tsòu), iù iuĕ iòu iù òu.

IU POU. **1. P'êng p'êng iŭ pŏu, sīn tchēu iòu tchēu. Tsì tsì pí wâng, tsouò iòu ts'iú (ts'eòu) tchēu.**

2. Tsì tsì pí wâng, tsouò iòu fòung tchāng. Fòung tchāng ngô ngô, maô chéu iôu i (ngô).

3. P'i pèi Kīng tcheōu, tchēng t'ôu tsiĕ (tsí) tchēu. Tcheōu wâng iù mái, liŭ chēu kĭ tchēu.

D'autres allèrent partout publier ses vertus; d'autres le défendirent contre les outrages de ses ennemis.

CHANT IV. IU POU.

La vertu de Wenn wang lui attire un grand nombre d'hommes, comme les beaux arbustes attirent les bûcherons. Elle brille comme la Voie lactée, durant une longue suite d'années. Elle est semblable aux objets d'or ou de pierre précieuse les mieux travaillés.

1. Les belles touffes de *iu* sont coupées pour être brûlées immédiatement ou mises en réserve. Le prince qui nous gouverne est admirable à voir; de tous côtés on accourt à lui.

2. Le prince qui nous gouverne est admirable à voir; les ministres qui l'entourent, lui offrent la coupe pour les libations. Il lui offrent la coupe avec beaucoup de dignité, comme il convient à des officiers distingués.

3. Cette barque vogue sur la King; un grand nombre de rameurs unissent leurs efforts. Lorsque le prince de Tcheou (Wenn wang)

prendre Wenn wang pour arbitre et se rendirent auprès de lui. L'esprit de conciliation qu'ils remarquèrent dans tous les rangs de la société, les frappa tellement qu'ils eurent honte de leurs démêlés, et conclurent d'eux-mêmes un accommodement. Ce fait ayant été publié partout, augmenta beaucoup l'influence de Wenn wang sur tous les autres princes.

CHANT IV. 1. Luxuriant arbusculæ *iu* densæ; cædunt et comburunt eas, cædunt et recondunt eas. Habitu decorus est gubernans rex; læva dextraque properatur ad eum.

樸 **Pŏu**, touffe d'arbres.

2. Habitu decorus est gubernans rex; læva dextraque (ministri) porrigunt libatorium. Porrigunt libatorium summa gravitate, insignes viros quod decet.

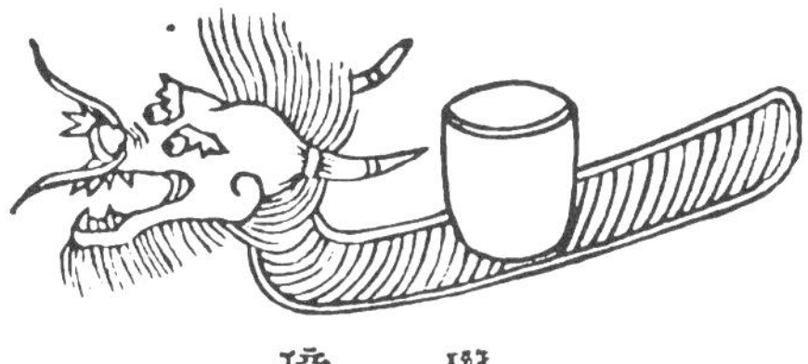

璋 瓚

王于邁、六師及之、

(4) 倬彼雲漢、爲章于天、周王壽考、遐不作人、

(5) 追琢其章、金玉其相、勉勉我王、綱紀四方、

旱麓

(1) 瞻彼旱麓、

4. Tchouŏ pèi iùn hán, wêi tchāng iû t'iēn (t'în). Tcheōu wâng cheóu k'aò; hiâ pŏu tsŏ jênn?

5. Touēi tchouŏ k'î tchāng, kīn iŭ k'î siāng. Mièn mièn ngò wâng, kāng ki séu fāng.

HAN LOU. **1. Tchēn pèi Hán lŏu, tchēnn hòu tsi tsi. K'ài ti kiūn tzèu, kān lŏu k'ài ti.**

part pour une expédition, les six légions se mettent à sa suite.

4. Cette Voie lactée est vaste; elle est l'ornement du ciel. Le prince de Tcheou a vécu longtemps; n'a-t-il pas excité les hommes (à pratiquer la vertu)?

5. Ces ornements sont ciselés et bien travaillés; ils sont d'or et de pierres précieuses. Notre prince est sans cesse agissant; il donne des institutions et des lois à toutes les parties de l'empire.

CHANT V. HAN LOU.

La vertu de Wenn wang lui attire les faveurs du ciel et toute sorte de biens.

1. Voyez le pied de ce mont Han; il y croît beaucoup de

圭 **Kouēi**, tablette de jade qui était une marque de dignité ou de mission. V. page 64. 璋 **Tchāng**, tablette de jade qui était la moitié d'un 圭 **Kouēi** divisé dans le sens de sa longueur. 璋 **Tchāng** ou 璋瓚 **Tchāng tsàn**, vase fixé sur un *tchang* et employé pour les libations. 圭瓚 **Kouēi tsan**, vase fixé sur un *kouei* et employé pour les libations. Le souverain prenait lui-même le *kouei tsan* pour les premières libations, et recevait le *tchang tsan* des mains de ses ministres pour les secondes.

3. Currit illa King fluvii cymba; multi homines remis impellunt illam. Tcheou princeps quum iens incedit, sex legiones prosequuntur eum.

4. Magna est illa Via lactea; est ornamentum in cœlo. Tcheou rex diu vixit; num non excitavit homines?

Wenn wang vécut quatre-vingt-dix-sept ans. (1231-1135).

5. Cælata et elaborata sunt illa ornamenta; aurum et lapilli sunt illorum materies. Indesinenter strenuus noster rex; instituta et leges dat quatuor regionibus.

追 **Touēi**, travailler au ciseau un objet de métal. 琢 **Tchouŏ**, travailler une pierre de prix.

CHANT V. 1. Aspice illas Han montis radices; coryli et *hòu* arbusculæ sunt plurimæ. Amœnus et comis princeps (Wenn rex); adsciscit bona amœnitate et comitate.

榛楛濟濟、豈弟君子、干祿豈弟、

(2) 瑟彼玉瓚、黃流在中、豈弟君子、福祿攸降、

(3) 鳶飛戾天、魚躍于淵、豈弟君子、遐不作人、

(4) 清酒既載、騂牡既備、以享以祀、以介景福、

(5) 瑟彼柞棫、民所燎矣、豈弟君子、神所勞矣、

2. Chĕ pèi iŭ tsàn, houâng liôu tsái tchōung. K'ài ti kiūn tzèu, fŏu lŏu iôu kiáng (hôung).

3. Iuên fēi li t'iēn (t'īn), iŭ iŏ iū iuēn (iūn). K'ài ti kiūn tzèu, hiâ pŏu tsŏ jênn?

4. Ts'īng tsiòu ki tsái (tsì), sīng meòu ki pi (pí), i hiàng i séu (ì), i kiái king fŏu (pí).

5. Chĕ pèi tsŏ iŭ, mîn chòu leaó i. K'ài ti kiūn tzèu, chênn chòu laó i.

coudriers et de *hóu*. Ainsi notre prince est gracieux et affable ; par son aménité il s'attire beaucoup de biens et d'honneurs.

2. Cette coupe de jade est finement travaillée; on y verse la liqueur jaune pour les libations. Ainsi notre prince est gracieux et affable, et les faveurs du ciel descendent sur lui.

3. L'épervier en son vol s'élève jusqu'au ciel; le poisson bondit dans les profondeurs des eaux. Notre prince est gracieux et affable; comment n'attirerait-il pas les hommes à sa suite?

4. Une liqueur pure est dans la coupe; une victime mâle de couleur rousse est préparée. Notre prince les offre aux esprits tutélaires, et reçoit un accroissement de biens.

5. Ces petits chênes sont très drus; ils servent pour le chauffage (ou bien, on brûle autour d'eux les mauvaises herbes qui nuisent à leur croissance). Notre prince est gracieux et affable; les esprits le récompensent.

楛 **Hóu**, arbuste épineux dont la tige est rouge.

2. Subtiliter elaboratum est illud iaspium libatorium; flavus liquor est in medio. Amœnus et comis princeps, bona et honores in quem descendunt (e cœlo).

玉瓚 **Iŭ tsàn**, coupe d'or fixée sur une tablette de jade 圭 **kouēi**. V. page 330. 黃流 **Houâng liôu** ou 鬱鬯 **iŭ tch'áng**, liqueur jaune extraite du 秬黍 **kiú chòu** millet noir, et aromatisée avec une plante appelée 鬱 **iŭ**.

3. Accipiter volans attingit cœlum; piscis saltat in aquis profundis. Amœnus et comis est princeps; quomodo non excitaret homines?

4. Purus liquor jam continetur (in poculo); rufa victima mascula jam parata est, ut (princeps) offerat, ut sacrum faciat, ut ampliet ingentia bona.

5. Densæ sunt illæ quercus et ilices, populus quas comburit (vel circa quas noxiam herbam comburit ut vegetiores crescant). Amœnus et comis est princeps; spiritus quem munerantur.

(6) 莫莫葛藟、施于條枚、豈弟君子、求福不回、

思齊

(1) 思齊大任、文王之母、思媚周姜、京室之婦、大姒嗣徽音、則百斯男、

(2) 惠于宗公、神罔時怨、神罔時恫、刑于寡妻、至于兄弟、以御于家邦、

6. Mŏu mŏu kŏ lèi, i iū t'iaô mêi. K'ài ti kiūn tzèu, k'iôu fŏu pŏu houêi.

SEU TCHAI. **1. Sēu tchāi T'ái Jênn, Wênn wâng tchēu mòu. Sêu méi Tcheōu Kiāng, kīng chēu tchêu fòu. T'ái Séu séu houēi īn, tsĕ pĕ sēu nān (gnîn).**

2. Houéi iū tsōung kōung, chênn wàng chêu iuén, chênn wàng chêu t'ōung. Hîng iū kouà ts'ī, tchéu iū hiōung ti, i iá iū kiā pāng (pōung).

6. Le dolic est très vigoureux ; il s'attache au tronc et aux branches des arbres. Notre prince est gracieux et affable ; sa vertu constante lui attire beaucoup de biens.

CHANT VI. SEU TCHAI.

Éloge de Wenn wang, de sa mère, de sa grand'mère et de sa femme.

1. L'Auguste Jenn, mère de Wenn wang, fut irréprochable. Toujours aimable envers Kiang (femme de T'ai wang, prince) de Tcheou, elle fut la digne épouse du prince (Wang Ki). L'Auguste Seu (épouse de Wenn wang) hérita de la bonne renommée (de l'Auguste Jenn); cent fils ou petits-fils naquirent à Wenn wang.

2. Wenn wang suivit les traces des princes de sa famille ; aussi jamais leurs mânes ne furent ni mécontents ni attristés. Ses exemples eurent une puissante influence d'abord sur sa femme, puis sur ses frères, enfin sur tous les peuples.

6. Luxuriat *kŏ* planta ; serpit super ramos et truncos. Amœnus et comis est princeps ; arcessit bona non deflectens (a recto).

CHANT VI. 1. Recte composita erat Augusta Jenn, Wenn regis mater. Blanda fuit erga Tcheou (reguli T'ai regis uxorem) Kiang, in regia domo uxor. Augusta Seu (Wenn regis uxor) prosecuta est optimam famam, et centum illi pueri (Wenn regi nati sunt).

思 **Sēu**, particule. Le poète dit que Wenn wang fut en partie redevable de sa gloire à sa mère et à sa femme.

2. Obsecutus est (Wenn rex exemplis) generis sui regulorum ; manes nunquam ideo indignati sunt, manes nunquam ideo doluerunt. Exemplar fuit tenui uxori, pervenit ad fratres, inde occurrit familiis et regnis.

寡妻 **Kouà ts'ī** ou 寡小君 **Kouà siaò kiūn**, femme d'un prince.

(3) 雝雝在宮。
肅肅在廟。不
顯亦臨。無射
亦保。
(4) 肆戎疾不
殄。烈假不瑕。
不聞亦式。不
諫亦入。
(5) 肆成人有
德。小子有造。
古之人無斁。
譽髦斯士。

3. Iōung iōung tsái kōung, siŭ siŭ tsái miaó (maó). Pŏu hièn ĭ lìn, ôu ĭ ĭ paó (paó).

4. Séu jôung tsĭ pŏu tièn, liĕ kià pŏu hiâ. Pŏu wênn ĭ chĕu, pŏu kién ĭ jŏu.

5. Séu tch'êng jênn iòu tĕ, siaò tzèu iòu tsaó. Kòu tchēu jênn ôu ĭ, iû maô sēu chéu.

3. Il était très ami de la concorde dans le palais et très respectueux dans le temple des ancêtres. Loin de tout regard, il agissait comme s'il avait été en présence de quelqu'un. (Lors même qu'il pratiquait la vertu) sans effort, il veillait encore sur lui-même.

4. Bien qu'il n'ait pas prévenu les grands malheurs qui arrivèrent (son emprisonnement, les invasions des barbares), sa gloire et sa grandeur sont sans tache. Tout ce qu'il exécutait était parfait, même les choses sur lesquelles il n'avait jamais reçu ni enseignement ni avis.

5. (Grâce à lui), les hommes faits étaient vertueux, et les jeunes gens s'appliquaient à le devenir. Notre ancien prince travaillait sans relâche; ses ministres acquirent un grand renom, une rare capacité.

3. Concordiæ amans in palatio, valde reverens erat in avorum templo. Quum non videretur, tamen (recte compositus erat quasi quis) adstans vidisset. (Vel quum jam optime ageret) sine labore, etiam invigilabat sibi.

4. Quapropter magnas ærumnas licet non præciderit, splendor et magnitudo sine nævo fuerunt. (Quum ageret res de quibus) non edoctus erat, etiam legibus quadrabant; (quum ageret res de quibus) non monitus fuerat, etiam rectæ erant.

Wenn wang fut détenu dans les fers pendant deux ans à 羑里 **Iòu li**, dans le Honan actuel, par le tyran 紂 **Tcheóu**, dernier empereur de la dynastie des In. Dans sa prison il étudia et expliqua les 卦 **kouá**, symboles inventés par Fou hì.

5. Inde maturi homines habebant virtutem; juniores homines habebant exercitationem. Antiquus vir (Wenn rex laborem) nunquam fastidio habebat; præclari et præstantes evaserunt ejus ministri.

既冠以上爲成人 On appelle homme fait celui qui a reçu le bonnet viril. Les jeunes gens le recevaient à l'âge de vingt ans.

皇矣

(1) 皇矣上帝、
臨下有赫、監
觀四方、求民
之莫、維此二
國、其政不獲、
維彼四國、爰
究爰度、上帝
耆之、憎其式
廓、乃眷西顧、
此維與宅、

HOUANG I. 1. **Houâng i cháng ti, lìn hiá iòu hŏ. Kiēn kouān séu fāng, k'iôu mîn tchēu mouŏ. Wêi ts'èu éul kouŏ, k'ì tchéng pŏu houŏ. Wêi péi séu kouŏ, iuên kióu iuên touŏ. Cháng ti k'ì tchēu, tsēng k'ì chĕu kouŏ. Nài kiuén sī kóu, ts'èu wêi iù tchĕ (tŏ).**

CHANT VII. HOUANG I.

Par ordre du Chang ti, 太王 **T'ái wâng** s'établit au pied du mont 岐 **K'î**, dans la terre qui prit le nom de 周 **Tcheōu** ou K'i Tcheou; 王季 **Wâng Kí** continua l'œuvre de son père; 文王 **Wênn wâng** défit le prince de 密 **Mí** et détruisit la capitale de 崇 **Tch'ôung**. Cf. page 2.

1. Le roi du ciel est auguste; il veille avec majesté sur les choses d'ici-bas. Regardant et contemplant les quatre parties de l'empire, il a cherché une contrée pour fixer notre peuple. Le gouvernement de ces deux dynasties impériales (des Hia et des Chang) n'avait pas été bien réglé. Le roi du ciel considéra les diverses principautés, et chercha avec soin (un prince qui répondît à ses désirs). L'ayant trouvé (en la personne de T'ai wang), il voulut augmenter l'étendue de ses possessions. Tournant ses regards avec affection vers l'occident, il y donna (à T'ai wang) un endroit pour s'établir, (à savoir, la terre de K'i Tcheou).

CHANT VII. 1. Augustus est supernus rex, invigilat inferis cum majestate. Inspiciens ac contemplans quatuor regiones, quæsivit populo stabilem sedem. At illarum duarum regiarum familiarum (Hia et Chang) ipsarum regimen non assecutum erat (intentum finem). Tunc in illarum quatuor plagarum regnis, et quæsivit et perpendit. Supremus rex assecutus eum (quem quærebat), auxit ejus (ditionis) modum et amplitudinem. Tum amanter occidentem respexit, ibi dedit sedem (T'ai regi).

上帝天帝也(詩經備旨) Le Chang ti est le roi du ciel. 臨視也 *Lìn*, considérer.

« Bien que cet auguste seigneur suprême soit très élevé au-dessus de nous, il abaisse sur la terre ses regards très perspicaces et pleins de majesté. En regardant et en considérant les quatre parties du monde, il n'a d'autre intention que de procurer au peuple la paix et la tranquillité. Ainsi la volonté du ciel est de donner au peuple la tranquillité, et pour y parvenir, le choix d'un prince est la chose la plus nécessaire. Ce qu'ont fait les deux dynasties des Hia et des Chang, n'était pas le moyen de donner au peuple la tranquillité. Elles ont mal administré

(2) 作之屏之、其菑其翳、脩之平之、其灌其栵、啓之辟之、其檉其椐、攘之剔之、其檿其柘、帝遷明德、串夷載路、天立厥配、受命既固、

(3) 帝省其山、柞棫斯拔、松柏斯兌、帝作邦作對、自大伯王季、維

2. Tsŏ tchēu pìng tchēu, k'ì tchēu k'ì i. Siōu tchēu p'ing tchēu, k'ì kouán k'ì lì. K'ì tchēu p'ì tchēu, k'ì tch'ēng k'ì kiū (kiú). Jâng tchēu t'ī tchēu, k'ì ièn k'ì tché (tóu). Tí ts'iēn ming tŏ, Kouán î tsái lóu. T'iēn lì kiuĕ p'éi, cheóu míng kì kóu.

3. Tí sing k'ì chān; tsŏ iŭ sēu péi, sōung pĕ sēu t'ouéi. Tí tsŏ pāng tsŏ touéi,

2. (T'ai wang, arrivé dans la terre de K'i Tcheou), fit arracher et enlever les arbres morts, dont les uns étaient restés debout et les autres gisaient à terre. On tailla, on régularisa ceux qui formaient des massifs ou des rangées. On éclaircit les tamaris et les catalpas. On émonda les mûriers de montagne et les mûriers tinctoriaux. Le roi du ciel ayant établi (à K'i Tcheou) ce prince d'une vertu éclatante, les barbares d'occident appelés Kouan i s'enfuirent par toutes les routes. Le ciel lui prépara une compagne (T'ai Kiang). Ainsi fut confirmé le mandat (du ciel, qui voulait en faire le père d'une nouvelle dynastie impériale).

3. Le roi du ciel considéra cette montagne (K'i chan, et vit que) les chênes s'y dressaient majestueux, que les sapins et les cyprès étaient bien espacés. Après avoir fondé la principauté, le roi du ciel choisit un prince capable pour la gouverner (après T'ai wang; il fit ce choix) dès la naissance de T'ai pe et de Wang

l'empire. Il ne convient pas de leur laisser plus longtemps le soin d'exécuter les volontés du ciel. Le souverain seigneur examine, et cherche dans tous les royaumes de la terre, pour y trouver un prince qui procure la paix au peuple, et exécute les desseins de sa majesté suprême. » (詩經備旨).

2. (T'ai wang in K'i Tcheou) evulsit illas, amovit illas, illas mortuas et adhuc stantes arbores, illas mortuas ac jacentes arbores. Composuit illas, adæquavit illas, illas densas arbusculas, illas ordine crescentes arbores. Interlucavit illas, rarefecit illas, illas tamarices, illas catalpas. Putavit illas, totondit illas, illas montanas moros, illas tinctorias moros. Rex (cœli) transmovit claræ virtutis (virum T'ai wang in K'i Tcheou); *Kouán i* occidentales barbari (fugientes) impleverunt vias. Cœlum constituit ei conjugem (Augustam Kiang); acceptum mandatum (quo rex cœli ei præstituerat imperium) firmatum est.

串夷 **Kouán i**, barbares occidentaux, appelés aussi 昆夷 **Kouēnn i**.

3. Rex (cœli) inspexit illum montem (K'i chan); quercus et ilices tunc arrectæ erant, abietes et cupressi tunc erant perviæ. Rex (cœli), constituto regno, constituit idoneum (hæredem),

此王季。因心則友、則友其兄、則篤其慶。載錫之光、受祿無喪、奄有四方。(4) 維此王季、帝度其心、貊其德音、其德克明、克明克類。克長克君、王此大邦、克順克比、比于文王、其德靡悔、既受帝祉、施于孫子、

tzèu T'ái pĕ, Wâng Ki. Wêi ts'èu Wâng Ki, īn sīn tsĕ iòu (i). Tsĕ iòu (i) k'ì hiōung (houâng), tsĕ tŏu k'ì k'ing (k'iâng), tsĕ sì tchēu kouāng. Cheóu lŏu ôu sáng (sāng), ièn iòu séu fāng.

4. Wêi ts'èu Wâng Ki, tí touŏ k'ì sīn. Mĕ k'ì tĕ īn, k'ì tĕ k'ŏ mîng. K'ŏ mîng k'ŏ léi, k'ŏ tchàng k'ŏ kiūn. Wáng ts'èu tá pāng, k'ŏ chouénn k'ŏ pì. Pì iû Wênn wâng, k'ì tĕ mì houéi (houèi). Kí cheóu tí tch'èu, í iû suēnn tzèu (tsì).

Ki (fils de T'ai wang. Il préféra Wang Ki à T'ai pe, qui était l'aîné). Wang Ki aima son frère aîné (T'ai pe) d'une affection sincère. Il aima son frère aîné, augmenta sa propre grandeur, et procura une grande gloire à T'ai pe (dont il publia la sagesse et le désintéressement). Il fut comblé de biens, les conserva toujours, et bientôt posséda tout l'empire.

4. Le roi du ciel donna à Wang Ki un jugement exquis, et dans le silence prit soin d'étendre la renommée de sa sagesse. La sagesse de Wang Ki fut intelligente. Elle le rendit capable de comprendre et de discerner les choses, de former et de gouverner les hommes. Chargé de gouverner cette grande principauté, il sut obtenir la soumission et l'affection de ses sujets. Wenn wang, qui lui succéda, n'eut jamais rien à se reprocher. Il jouit des faveurs du ciel, et les transmit à ses descendants.

a T'ai pe et Wang Ki (nativitate). Ille Wang Ki ex animo quidem dilexit fratrem. Et dilexit suum fratrem natu majorem, et firmavit suam prosperitatem, et tribuit illi (fratri suo) gloriam. Accepit bona, nec amisit; inde habuit quatuor regiones.

Du vivant de son père T'ai wang, T'ai pe sachant déjà que le ciel avait destiné l'empire à Wenn wang, fils de Wang Ki, se retira dans le pays de 吳 **Oû** et ne revint pas. A la mort de T'ai wang, Wang Ki lui succéda. Plein d'affection et de reconnaissance pour son frère aîné T'ai pe, il publia partout ses vertus.

4. Et illum Wang Ki, rex (cœli) subtili judicio donavit illum. Tacite curavit illius sapientiæ famam; illius sapientia valuit intelligere. Valuit intelligere, valuit discernere, valuit educare, valuit imperare. Imperans huic magno regno, valuit sibi conciliare obsequium, valuit sibi conciliare amorem. (Postquam regnum) devenit ad Wenn regem, hujus virtus nihil habuit cujus pœniteret. Postquam accepit regis cœlestis beneficia, tradidit posteris.

(5) 帝謂文王、無然畔援、無然歆羨、誕先登于岸、密人不恭、敢距大邦、侵阮徂共、王赫斯怒、爰整其旅、以按徂旅、以篤周祜、以對于天下、

(6) 依其在京、侵自阮疆、陟我高岡、無矢我陵、我陵我阿、無飲我

5. Ti wéi Wênn wâng: « Où jên pán iuén, ǒu jên hīn sién; tán siēn tēng iū ngán (ién). » Mì jénn pǒu kōung, kàn kiú tá pāng (pōung). Ts'īn Iuên ts'ǒu Kōung. Wâng hě sēu nóu, iuên tchèng k'ì liù, i ngó ts'ǒu liù, i tǒu Tcheōu hóu, i touéi iū t'iēn hiá (hóu).

6. Ī k'ì tsái kīng (kāng), ts'īn tzéu Iuên kiāng, tchěu ngò kaō kāng. Où chèu

5. Le roi du ciel dit à Wenn wang: « Ne soyez pas intrigant comme les hommes vulgaires, qui abandonnent celui-ci pour s'attacher à celui-là. Ne soyez pas comme eux cupide ni ambitieux. Devancez de bien loin tous les autres, et montez au sommet de la perfection. » Les habitants de Mi, refusant l'obéissance due à leur suzerain, osèrent résiter à la grande principauté (de Tcheou). Ils envahirent la principauté de Iuen et allèrent jusqu'à Koung. Le prince (Wenn wang), dans son courroux plein de majesté, rassembla ses cohortes, pour arrêter la marche des cohortes ennemies, augmenter la grandeur de la famille des Tcheou, et répondre aux vœux de tout l'empire.

6. Wenn wang demeura en repos dans sa capitale. (Mais ses soldats, après avoir repoussé les barbares), sortant des frontières de Iuen, pénétrèrent (dans le pays ennemi) et gravirent les crêtes élevées des montagnes, qui dès lors nous appartinrent. (Les ennemis) n'osèrent pas se ranger en bataille sur nos collines; les colli-

5. Rex (cœli) dixit Wenn regi: « Noli sic (ut cæteri homines) deficere (ab hoc viro) et adrepere (ad illum). Noli sic concupiscere et appetere. Longe præiens ascendas ad apicem (virtutis). » Mi regni incolæ non obsequentes, ausi sunt resistere magno regno. Invaserunt Iuen regnum, adiverunt Koung (Iuen regni locum). Rex (Wenn wang) cum majestate tunc iratus est. Statim composuit suas cohortes, ut inhiberet progredientes cohortes (hostium), ut augeret Tcheou domus prosperitatem, ut responderet totius imperii votis.

密 **Mi** ou 密須 **Mi siū** est à présent compris dans le 靜寧州 **Tsing gnìng tcheōu**, département de 平涼府 **P'ing leâng fòu**, province de Kan siu. 阮 **Iuèn** est dans le 涇州 **Kīng tcheōu**, département de P'ing leang fou.

6. Quiete ipse (Wenn rex) mansit in urbe regia. (At ejus milites regnum Mi) invadentes ex Iuen regni finibus,

泉、我泉我池、度其鮮原、居岐之陽、在渭之將、萬邦之方、下民之王、⑦帝謂文王、予懷明德、不大聲以色、不長夏以革、不識不知、順帝之則、帝謂文王、詢爾仇方、同爾兄弟、以

ngò lìng, ngò lìng ngò ngō. Oû in ngò ts'iuên, ngò ts'iuên ngò tch'êu (t'ouô). Touô k'ì siēn iuên, kiū K'î tchēu iâng, tsái Wéi tchēu tsiāng, wán pāng tchēu fāng, hiá mîn tchēu wâng.

7. Tí wéi Wênn wâng: «Iù houâi mîng tĕ, pŏu tá chēng i chĕ, pŏu tch'âng hiá i kĕ, pŏu chēu pŏu tchēu, chouénn tí tchēu tsĕ.» Tí wéi Wênn wâng: «Siūn

nes (de Mi) étaient à nous, les montagnes étaient à nous. Ils ne burent pas à nos fontaines; les fontaines (de Mi) étaient à nous, les lacs étaient à nous. Wenn wang chercha la meilleure plaine, et fixa sa résidence au sud du mont K'i, sur le bord de la Wei. (Cette nouvelle capitale) devint le centre de toutes les principautés, le rendez-vous de tous les peuples.

7. Le roi du ciel dit à Wenn wang: «J'aime votre vertu, votre sagesse. Vous ne faites pas éclater votre colère par des cris menaçants; vous évitez la profusion et l'inconstance. Vous suivez les lois du souverain suprême, sans vous fier à votre expérience ni à votre habileté.» Le roi du ciel dit à Wenn wang: «Prononcez la condamnation de cette principauté ennemie, (à savoir, de Tch'oung). Aidé

ascenderunt nostra excelsa juga, i.e. Mi regni montium juga quæ nostra facta erant. (Hostes) aciem non ordinarunt supra nostros colles; nostri erant colles, nostri montes. Non biberunt ad nostros fontes; nostri erant fontes, nostri lacus. (Wenn rex) quæsivit optimam planitiem; sedem fixit ad K'i montis austrum, ad Wei fluvii latus. (Illa nova urbs regia) fuit omnium regnorum locus (medius ac præcipuus), subditorum populorum confluens.

La ville fondée par Wenn wang s'appela 程邑 **Tch'êng ĭ**. Elle était située dans le 咸陽縣 **Hiên iâng hién** actuel. Plus tard il fonda ou rebâtit la ville de 豐 **Fōung**, sur le bord de la rivière de ce nom, et y fixa définitivement sa résidence. Voy. III. I. 10.

7. Rex (cœli) dixit Wenn regi: «Ego amo perspicacem virtutem (tuam). Non uteris elata voce cum ostensione, nec auges profusionem cum mutatione. Nec scientiæ nec peritiæ (tuæ confidens), obsequeris regis (cœlestis) legibus.» Rex (cœli) dixit Wenn regi: «Condemnes tibi infensam regionem. Cum tuis fratribus, i.e. amicis regulis, adhibeas tuas uncis instructas scalas et tuas rotatas turres ac catapultas, ut expugnes Tch'oung regni oppidum.»

La principauté de Tch'oung était le 鄠縣 **Hóu hién** actuel dans le 西安府 **Sī ngān fòu**, province de 陜西 **Chèn sì**. La capitale était peut-être la

爾鉤援、與爾臨衝、以伐崇墉。⑧臨衝閑閑、崇墉言言、執訊連連、攸馘安安、是類是禡、是致是附、四方以無侮、臨衝茀茀、崇墉仡仡、是伐

èul k'iòu fāng. T'ôung èul hiōung ti, i èul keōu iuên, iù èul lîn tch'ōung, i fă Tch'ôung iôung.»

8. Lìn tch'ōung hiên hiên; Tch'ôung iôung iên iên. Tchēu sin liên liên, iòu kouě ngān ngān (iēn iēn). Chéu lèi chéu má, chéu tchéu chéu fóu (fóu); séu fāng i òu òu. Lìn tch'ōung fòu fóu (pí pí); Tch'ôung iôung k'ī k'ī. Chéu fă chéu séu, chéu tsiuě chéu hōu; séu fāng i òu fóu.

de vos frères, prenez vos échelles munies de crocs, vos tours roulantes et vos catapultes; attaquez la capitale de Tch'oung.»

8. Les tours roulantes et les catapultes s'avancèrent peu à peu. Les murs de la capitale de Tch'oung étaient très élevés. (Les principaux défenseurs de la place) furent pris les uns après les autres; on leur coupa l'oreille gauche après mûr examen. Alors (Wenn wang) offrit des sacrifices au roi du ciel et à l'inventeur de l'art militaire; puis il invita (tous les princes) à venir se joindre à lui. Dans tout l'empire aucun ne lui fit affront (par un refus. Seul le prince de Tch'oung persista dans sa révolte). Alors les tours roulantes et les catapultes attaquèrent vivement la place; mais les remparts étaient très forts. Wenn wang prononça la sentence définitive, lança ses soldats, renversa le temple des ancêtres et mit fin à

ville de 豐 Fōung, qui fut rebâtie par Wenn wang et devint la capitale de tout l'empire. Cf. III. I. 10. «Le souverain roi considère Wenn wang avec affection. Il dit que sa vertu est intérieure et cachée, sans bruit, sans éclat, sans apparence; que sans se prévaloir de sa sagesse, il se conforme aux lois du ciel; qu'il est prudent, et n'use pas de sa prudence particulière; qu'il est éclairé, et n'use pas de ses propres lumières; qu'il se contente d'obéir au souverain roi, et de le servir assidûment.» (詩經備旨).

8. Rotatæ turres et catapultæ tarde admotæ sunt. Tch'oung mœnia erant excelsa et magna. Capti sunt (principes) alii post alios; quibus amputata est auris sinistra sedato judicio. Tum sacrum fecit regi cæli, tum sacrum fecit artis militaris auctori. Tum impulit (omnes regulos) ut venirent ad se, tunc hortatus est ut adhærerent sibi. In quatuor imperii plagis inde nullus contumelia affecit eum. (Solus Tch'oung regulus non se subdidit). Rotatæ turres et catapultæ vehementer impugnarunt; Tch'oung mœnia erant firmissima. Tum (sententiam) protulit, tum emisit (milites), tum evertit (avorum delubra), tum delevit (regnum). In quatuor imperii regionibus inde nemo restitit.

類將出師祭上帝禡至所征之地而祭始造軍法者也 (詩經備旨) *Lèi*, sacrifice offert au

是肆、是絕是忽、四方以無拂、

靈臺

(1) 經始靈臺、經之營之、庶民攻之、不日成之、經始勿亟、庶民子來、

(2) 王在靈囿、麀鹿攸伏、麀鹿濯濯、白鳥翯翯、王在靈沼、於牣魚躍、

LING T'AI. 1. **Kīng chéu Líng t'âi (t'î), kīng tchēu ìng tchēu. Chóu mîn kōung tchēu, pŏu jĕu tch'êng tchēu. Kīng chéu, ŏu kĭ; chóu mîn tzéu lâi (lî).**

2. Wâng tsái Líng ióu (iŭ), iōu lŏu iōu fŏu. Iōu lŏu tchouŏ tchouŏ, pĕ gniaŏ hŏ hŏ. Wâng tsái Líng tchaŏ (tchŏ), ŏu! jénn iŭ iŏ!

la principauté de Tch'oung. Dès lors il n'eut plus un seul adversaire dans tout l'empire.

CHANT VIII. LING T'AI.

Wenn wang ordonne la construction de la Tour des esprits, et le peuple exécute le travail avec une joie, une ardeur merveilleuse. Le prince prend plaisir à considérer les animaux dans le Parc des esprits, à entendre la musique dans l'école du palais.

1. Wenn wang mesura (et traça) les fondements, puis commença la construction de la Tour des esprits; il en mesura et traça les fondements. Tout le peuple y travailla, et la termina en moins d'un jour (en très peu de temps). Lorsque le prince traça les fondements et commença la construction, il dit qu'il ne fallait pas se hâter; mais tous ses sujets accoururent (avec empressement) comme des fils à leur père.

2. Le prince se promenait dans le Parc des esprits; les biches et les cerfs étaient couchés sur l'herbe. Les biches et les cerfs avaient le corps luisant de graisse; les oiseaux blancs étalaient leurs ailes brillantes. Le prince allait auprès du Bassin des esprits; oh! le bassin était plein de poissons qui prenaient leurs ébats!

roi du ciel un peu avant le départ pour une expédition. *Mà*, sacrifice offert à l'inventeur de l'art de la guerre après l'arrivée dans le lieu de l'expédition.

CHANT VIII. 1. (Wenn rex) mensus est (locum) et inchoavit (ædificationem) Spirituum turris; mensus est ejus locum, delineavit eum. Totus populus adlaboravit ad eam; non die (integro consumpto) perfecit eam. Metiens et inchoans (Wenn rex dixerat) ne properarent. Omnes populares (quasi) filii venerunt.

La tour de Wenn wang fut appelée Tour des esprits, parce que les travailleurs la construisirent avec la promptitude des esprits.

2. Rex erat in Spirituum septo (quod adjacebat turri); cervæ et cervi ibi cubabant. Cervæ et cervi pinguedine nite-

(3) 虡業維樅、賁鼓維鏞、於論鼓鐘、於樂辟廱、

(4) 於論鼓鐘、於樂辟廱、鼉鼓逢逢、矇瞍奏公、

3. Kiù iĕ wêi ts'ōung, fênn kòu wêi iôung. Oû! liùn kòu tchōung! Oû! lŏ pī iōung!

4. Oû! liùn kòu tchōung! Oû! lŏ pī iōung! T'ouô kòu p'ôung p'ôung; môung seòu tseóu kōung.

3. Les montants étaient dressés avec la dentelure; les grands tambours étaient préparés avec les grosses cloches. Oh! que les sons des tambours et des cloches étaient harmonieux! Oh! que le lac circulaire était joyeux!

4. Oh! que les sons des tambours et des cloches étaient harmonieux! Oh! que le lac circulaire était joyeux! Le tambour de peau de crocodile battait doucement; les musiciens aveugles exécutaient leurs chants.

bant; albæ aves candidis pennis splendebant. Rex adstabat ad Spirituum piscinam; oh! plena erat piscibus saltantibus!

3. Scapi et dentes erant arrecti; (parata erant) magna tympana et magnæ campanæ. Oh! modulate sonabant tympana et campanæ! Oh! festivus erat circularis lacus!

Les cloches et les 磬 **k'ing** pierres musicales se suspendaient à une traverse 栒 **siùn** soutenue par deux montants 虡 **kiù** et surmontée d'une dentelure 業 **iĕ**.

L'école du palais impérial s'appelait 辟廱 **Pī iōung** ou 璧廱 (禮王制) **Pī iōung** Lac circulaire ou Concorde circulaire, parce qu'elle était entourée d'une ceinture d'eau, et présentait la forme d'une tablette ronde 璧 **pī** percée en son milieu. Les jeunes gens s'y exerçaient au tir à l'arc, aux cérémonies,... Les princes avaient des écoles semblables. On les appelait 泮宮 **P'án kōung,** parce que l'enceinte était baignée seulement par un demi-cercle d'eau. Voy. plus loin 魯頌 Chant III.

4. Oh! modulate sonabant tympana et campanæ! Oh! festivus erat circularis lacus! E crocodili pelle tympanum modulate reboabat; cæci canebant res, i.e. cantica.

Le son du tambour annonçait le commencement des morceaux de musique. On appelle 矇 **môung** les aveugles chez qui les pupilles ou les prunelles des yeux existent, et 瞍 **seòu** ceux chez qui elles n'existent pas.

下武

(1) 下武維周、世有哲王、三后在天、王配于京、

(2) 王配于京、世德作求、永言配命、成王之孚、

(3) 成王之孚、下土之式、永言孝思、孝思維則、

HIA OU. 1. Hiá Où wêi Tcheōu, chéu iòu tchĕ wâng. Sān heóu tsái t'iēn, wâng p'éi iū kīng (kāng).

2. Wâng p'éi iū kīng (kāng), chéu tĕ tsŏ k'iôu. Iòung iên p'éi míng, tch'êng wàng tchēu fōu (feôu).

3. Tch'êng wâng tchēu fōu (feôu), hiá t'òu tchēu chĕu. Iòung iên hiaó sēu, hiaó sēu wêi tsĕ.

CHANT IX. HIA OU.

Ou wang, par l'imitation de ses prédécesseurs et la pratique de la piété filiale, a obtenu l'empire, et en a assuré l'héritage à ses descendants.

1. Ou wang fonda la dynastie des Tcheou (ou bien, Wenn wang et Ou wang fondèrent la dynastie des Tcheou); mais déjà avant le règne de Ou wang, sa famille, depuis plusieurs générations, avait produit des rois sages, (à savoir, T'ai wang, Wang Ki et Wenn wang). Ces trois rois sont dans le ciel; Ou wang fut leur émule dans la capitale.

2. Ou wang fut leur émule dans la capitale; il s'efforça de conserver l'héritage de leurs vertus. Toujours attentif à suivre la volonté du ciel, il assura à l'empereur (à sa personne) la confiance des peuples.

3. Il assura à l'empereur la confiance des peuples; maître de l'univers, il en fut le modèle. Il fut toujours attentif à pratiquer la piété filiale, et sa piété filiale fut exemplaire.

CHANT IX. 1. Postea Ou condidit Tcheou (imperium, vel, Wenn et Ou condiderunt Tcheou imperium); (sed antea) generationibus (pluribus) fuerant (vel fuerunt) prudentes reges. Tres reges sunt in cœlo; rex (Ou wang) par fuit in regia urbe (鎬 Haò).

Tchou Hi dit qu'il ne peut expliquer la lettre 下 hiá, que, d'après plusieurs interprètes, on doit remplacer par la lettre 文 Wênn.

三后太王王季文王也在天既沒而其精神上與天合也 (詩經備旨) Les trois rois sont T'ai wang, Wang Ki et Wenn wang. Ils sont dans le ciel: après leur mort, leurs esprits allèrent s'unir au ciel.

2. Rex par fuit in urbe regia; hæreditarias virtutes assurgens sectatus est. Semper cogitans ut obsequeretur mandatis (cœlestibus), firmavit regi fidem (omnium).

3. Firmavit regi fidem, subjecti orbis exemplar fuit. Semper cogitavit ut

(4) 媚茲一人、應侯順德、永言孝思、昭哉嗣服、

(5) 昭茲來許、繩其祖武、於萬斯年、受天之祜、

(6) 受天之祜、四方來賀、於萬斯年、不遐有佐、

文王有聲

(1) 文王有聲、遹駿有聲、遹求厥寧、遹觀厥成、文

4. Méi tzēu ĭ jênn, íng heôu chouénn tĕ. Iòung iên hiaó sēu, tchaō tsāi séu fŏu (p'ĕ).

5. Tchaō tzēu lâi hiù, chéng k'î tsòu òu. Iû wán sēu gniên, cheóu t'iēn tchēu hòu.

6. Cheóu t'iēn tchēu hòu, séu fāng lâi hó. Iû wán sēu gniên, pŏu hiâ ìou tsouó?

WENN WANG IOU CHENG. **1. Wênn wâng iòu chēng, iŭ siún iòu chēng. Iŭ**

4. Ce souverain de l'univers fut aimé des peuples, qui répondirent à ses soins par leur soumission. Toujours attentif à pratiquer la piété filiale, il se signala en continuant les œuvres de ses prédécesseurs.

5. Il se signala ainsi, et les descendants suivront constamment les traces de leur aïeul (Ou wang). Durant des myriades d'années, ils recevront les faveurs du ciel.

6. Ils recevront les faveurs du ciel et les hommages de tous les princes de l'empire. Durant des myriades d'années, manqueront-ils jamais de soutiens?

CHANT X. WENN WANG IOU CHENG.

Wenn wang établit sa résidence à Foung et Ou wang à Hao. Éloge de ces deux princes.

1. Wenn wang eut du renom, et son renom fut grand. Il chercha la pacification de l'empire, et il la vit s'accomplir. Wenn wang fut un vrai souverain!

pietatis filialis meminisset; filialis pietatis memor fuit exemplar.

4. (Homines) amaverunt illum unicum virum; responderunt obediente animo. Semper cogitans ut pietatis filialis reminisceretur, splenduit certe, prosequens gesta (antecessorum).

一人 L'homme qui seul (commande à tout l'empire), l'empereur.

5. Splenduit ita; posteri insistentes prosequentur sui avi vestigia. Per decies mille annos accipient cœli beneficia.

許 **Hiù** signifie 所 **chòu**, habiter, demeurer, persévérer.

6. Accipient cœli beneficia; omnium regionum (reguli) venient et gratulabuntur. Per decies mille annos desinent quomodo habere adjutores?

遐 **Hiâ** signifie 何 **hô** comment?

CHANT X. 1. Wenn rex habuit famam, magnam habuit famam. Quæsivit

王烝哉。

(2) 文王受命。有此武功。既伐于崇。作邑于豐。文王烝哉。

(3) 築城伊淢。作豐伊匹。匪棘其欲。遹追來孝。王后烝哉。

(4) 王公伊濯。維豐之垣。四方攸同。王后維翰。王后烝哉。

k'iôu kiuĕ gning, iŭ kouān kiuĕ tch'êng. Wênn wâng tchēng tsāi !

2. Wênn wâng cheóu ming, iòu ts'èu òu kōung. Ki fā iŭ Tch'ôung, tsŏ ĭ iŭ Fōung. Wênn wâng tchēng tsāi !

3. Tchŏu tch'êng ī siŭ, tsŏ Fōung ī p'ĭ. Fèi kĭ k'ì iŭ, iŭ tchouēi lâi hiaó (hiŭ). Wâng heóu tchēng tsāi !

4. Wâng kōung ī tchouŏ, wêi Fōung tchēu iuên. Séu fāng iôu t'ôung, wâng heóu wêi hân (hiên). Wâng heóu tchēng tsāi !

2. Wenn wang, sur l'ordre du ciel, fit une expédition militaire. Après avoir châtié le prince de Tch'oung, il rebâtit une ville à Foung (dans la principauté de Tch'oung, et il y fixa sa résidence). Wenn wang fut un vrai souverain !

3. Il fit construire les remparts le long des fossés (de l'ancienne ville ruinée), et bâtir la ville de Foung dans les limites des remparts. (Il ne voulut pas que la nouvelle ville fut plus grande que l'ancienne). C'est qu'il ne cherchait pas à satisfaire son orgueil ; mais (à assurer, comme ses pères, la tranquillité du peuple, et) à pratiquer, comme eux, la piété filiale. Cet auguste prince fut un vrai souverain !

4. Les travaux de Wen wang devinrent célèbres, surtout après qu'il eût construit les remparts de Foung. La ville devint le centre de tous les États, et cet auguste prince en fut la colonne. Cet auguste prince fut un vrai souverain !

illam pacificationem, vidit illam perfectam pacificationem. Wenn rex regnavit certe ! 遹 **Iŭ**, particule.

2. Wenn rex, accepto cœli mandato, habuit illa militaria gesta. Postquam pœnas sumpsit in Tch'oung, exstruxit urbem in Foung. Wenn rex regnavit certe !

Ce fut peut-être l'ancienne capitale de Tch'oung que Wenn wang fit rebâtir, après l'avoir détruite.

3. Erexit mœnia secundum fossas ; exstruxit Foung urbem illis (mœniis) quadrantem, non properans (indulgere) suæ voluntati, sed repetens hæreditariam pietatem filialem. Rex augustus regnavit certe !

4. Regis opera ipsa inclaruerunt, unice (maxime) ob Foung urbis mœnia. Quatuor regiones eo convenerunt ; rex augustus fuit columna (omnium regnorum). Rex augustus regnavit certe !

（5）豐水東注、維禹之績、四方攸同、皇王維辟、皇王烝哉、

（6）鎬京辟廱、自西自東、自南自北、無思不服、皇王烝哉、

（7）考卜維王、宅是鎬京、維龜正之、武王成之、武王烝哉、

（8）豐水有芑、武

5. Fōung chouèi tōung tchóu, wêi Iù tchēu tsī. Séu fāng iôu t'ôung, houâng wâng wêi pĭ. Houâng wâng tchēng tsāi!

6. Haò kīng pĭ iōung; tzéu sī tzéu tōung, tzéu nân tzéu pĕ, òu sēu pŏu fòu (p'ĕ). Houâng wâng tchēng tsāi!

7. K'aò pòu wêi wâng, tchĕ chéu Haò kīng (kāng). Wêi kouēi tchéng (tchēng) tchēu, Où wâng tch'êng tchēu. Où wâng tchēng tsāi!

8. Fōung chouèi iòu kì. Où wâng k'ì pŏu chéu? Ì kiuĕ suēnn meôu, i ién ì tzèu. Où wâng tchēng tsāi!

5. La Foung (coulait) à l'est de la ville, (se jetait dans la Wei, et avec la Wei) déversait ses eaux (dans le Fleuve-Jaune), par suite des travaux du grand Iu. Les habitants de toutes les contrées se rendaient à la capitale en suivant le cours de la Foung; et l'auguste empereur (Ou wang) gouverna seul tout l'empire. Cet auguste empereur fut un vrai souverain!

6. Dans Hao, sa capitale, Ou wang établit le lac circulaire (l'école du palais). De l'orient à l'occident, du midi au septentrion, chacun se soumit à lui de cœur. Cet auguste prince fut un vrai souverain!

7. Ou wang consulta les sorts, avant de fonder la ville de Hao. La tortue donna une réponse favorable; Ou wang exécuta le travail. Ou wang fut un vrai souverain!

8. L'eau de la Foung arrose la plante potagère nommée *ki;* Ou

5. Foung fluvius ad orientem influebat; unice Iu opus fuerat. Quatuor regiones eo (fluvio) convenerunt; augustus imperator (Ou wang) unicus regnavit. Augustus imperator regnavit certe!

6. Hao urbis regiæ circularis lacus, i. e. imperatoris schola constituta est. Cf. pag. 342. Ab occidente, ab oriente, a meridie, a septentrione, nemo cogitavit ut non se subderet. Augustus imperator regnavit certe!

7. Inspexit testudinem quidem rex, exstructurus illam Hao urbem regiam. Testudo probavit illud, Ou rex perfecit illud. Ou rex regnavit certe!

8. Foung fluvius habet (et irrigat) *ki* olus; Ou wang num caruit negotio? (Curavit) tradere suis posteris instituta, ita tranquillare reverentem filium. Ou rex regnavit certe!

王豈不仕。詒厥孫謀、以燕翼子、武王烝哉、

生民之什三之二

生民

(1) 厥初生民、時維姜嫄、生民如何、克禋克祀、以弗無子、履帝武

CHENG MIN. 1. **Kiuĕ tch'ŏu chēng mîn, chêu wêi Kiāng Iuên (Iûn). Chēng mîn jôu hô ? K'ŏ în, k'ŏ séu (i), i fŏu ôu tzèu (tsi). Li ti òu min (mi), hīn iôu kiái iôu**

wang ne remplit-il aucun office? Il assura l'empire à ses descendants, et la tranquillité à (Tch'eng wang) son fils respectueux. Ou wang fut un vrai souverain!

LIVRE II. CHENG MIN.

CHANT I. CHENG MIN.

Naissance merveilleuse, travaux agricoles et sacrifices de Heou ts'i, père de la race des Tcheou. Sa mère le conçut par l'opération du ciel et l'enfanta sans douleur, contrairement aux lois de la nature humaine.

1. La mère qui donna naissance à la race des Tcheou, fut Kiang Iuen. Comment a-t-elle enfanté? Elle fit une offrande avec une intention pure; elle offrit un sacrifice, pour obtenir de ne pas rester sans enfants. Marchant sur la trace laissée par le pouce du

TITRE DU LIVRE. 生民之什三之二 Cheng min decas: tertiæ partis secunda decas.

CHANT I. 1. Quæ cœpit gignere gentem, illa fuit Kiang Iuen. Genuit gentem quomodo? Valuit puro animo offerre, valuit sacrum facere, ut deprecaretur carentiam sobolis. Calcans regis impressi pedis pollicem, infremuit. (Adiens locum) quem ampliarat, in quo manebat, et concepit et secedens (mansit in laterali conclavi), et peperit et aluit. Ille fuit Heou tsi.

Kiang Iuen était fille du prince de 邰 **T'ài**, qui descendait de 神農 **Chênn nôung**, et femme de l'empereur 高辛 **Kaŏ sīn** ou de l'un de ses descendants. Son nom de famille était Kiang, et son nom propre Iuen. La terre de T'ai est à présent comprise dans le 武功縣 **Òu kōung hién**, préfecture de 乾州 **K'iên tcheōu**, province de 陝西 **Chèn sī**.

Le fils de Kiang Iuen fut appelé 棄 **K'i** *Abandonné*. Il devint 稷 **tsĭ** ministre de l'agriculture sous le règne de Iao, et pour cette raison reçut le nom de Heou tsi.

武 **Où**, empreinte du pied. 敏 **Min**, gros orteil. D'après Tchou Hi, 帝 **Ti** désigne le 上帝 **Cháng ti**; selon d'autres commentateurs, il désigne l'empereur, le mari de Kiang Iuen.

鄭言當祀郊禖之時有上帝大神之迹姜嫄因祭見之遂履此帝迹拇指之處而足不能滿... 於是則震動而有身 (孔穎達) Tcheng K'ang tch'eng dit: Au moment de l'offrande faite pour avoir des enfants, il y avait la trace du pied du souverain seigneur qui est un esprit très puissant. Kiang iuen la vit

敏歆、攸介攸止、載震載夙、載生載育、時維后稷。(2) 誕彌厥月、先生如達、不坼不副、無菑無害、以赫厥靈、

tchéu. Tsái tchénn, tsái siŭ (sĭ), tsái chēng, tsái iŭ (1). Chêu wêi Heóu tsĭ.

2. Tán mì kiuĕ iuĕ, siēn chēng jôu t'ŏ. Pŏu tch'ĕ, pŏu pĭ (pĕ), ôu tsāi ôu hái

pied du souverain roi, elle éprouva un frémissement. Elle retourna au palais agrandi et habité par elle. Elle conçut, et demeura retirée (dans un appartement latéral). Elle mit au monde et éleva un fils. Ce fils fut Heou tsi.

2. Les mois de sa grossesse étant écoulés, elle enfanta son premier-né aussi facilement qu'une brebis met au jour un agneau, sans rupture, sans fissure, sans mal, sans lésion ; et l'on vit clairement que cette naissance était un prodige. Le roi du ciel ne fut-il

en faisant son offrande. Elle foula du pied la trace du gros orteil du seigneur; son pied ne put la couvrir entièrement... Alors elle éprouva un frémissement et conçut.

« Les anciens lettrés ont quelque peu révoqué en doute l'histoire de la trace laissée par le pouce du pied. Mais le philosophe Tchang dit: 天地之始固未嘗先有人也則人固有化而生者矣蓋天地之氣生之也 « Avant le commencement du ciel et de la terre, certainement il n'existait pas d'homme; il a fallu un être qui le formât et lui donnât naissance. Le ciel et la terre ont fourni les principes qui l'ont composé. » Le philosophe Sou dit aussi: « Tout être d'une nature extraordinaire naît d'une façon extraordinaire. La licorne naît autrement que le chien et l'agneau; le crocodile et le dragon ne naissent pas comme le poisson ou la tortue. Certainement il en est ainsi pour les animaux. Doit-on s'étonner que la naissance des hommes extraordinaires diffère de celle des autres hommes? » Ce raisonnement est juste. » Tchou Hi)

Le P. de la Charme dit: « Quoad fabulam natalium principis Heou tsi, patet illam inventam fuisse ad commendandam gentis Tcheou originem. Simili fabula commendatur origo familiæ Chang, ut videbitur inferius (IV. V. 3), et dynastiæ sequentes his artibus usæ sunt. Tartari ipsi, qui nunc regnant, nonne asserunt gentis suæ originem repeti a virgine quæ nullo viri consortio peperit? Sic audivi a P. Parennin.

« Interpretes plerique hanc fabulam rejiciunt; clare tamen rejicere non audent. Alii: « Videmus, inquiunt, in rerum natura generationes mirabiles. Initio mundi primus homo certe aliter genitus est ac homines cæteri. Animal *K'i lin* et draco aliter ac bos et piscis. Quidni vir sanctus aliter gignetur ac vulgus hominum? » Ita illi interpretes. Quorum modus loquendi nobis viam facit ad prædicandam incarnationem Christi. »

2. Impletis suis mensibus, prima vice peperit facillime puerum) quasi agnum, sine abruptione, sine fissura, sine malo, sine damno, ita ut pateret illius (rei portentum. Cœli rex nonne gavisus est? Nonne acceptam habuit puram oblationem? Nullo labore Kiang luen peperit filium.

上帝不寧、不康禋祀、居然生子、③誕寘之隘巷、牛羊腓字之、誕寘之平林、會伐平林、誕寘之寒冰、鳥覆

(hŏ), i hĕ kiuĕ lìng. Cháng tí pŏu gnîng? Pŏu k'āng īn sêu (i)? Kiū jên chēng tzèu (tsi).

3. Tán tchéu tchēu iái hiáng; iôu iâng fêi tzéu tchēu. Tán tchéu tchēu p'îng lîn; houéi fă p'îng lîn. Tán tchéu tchēu hân pīng; gniaò feóu ĭ (i) tchēu. Gniaò

pas content? n'agréa-t-il pas l'offrande pure de Kiang Iuen, lui qui la fit enfanter sans aucune difficulté?

3. On déposa l'enfant dans un étroit sentier; mais les bœufs et les brebis, le protégeant de leurs corps, lui donnèrent des soins affectueux. On le déposa dans une plaine couverte d'arbres; mais il y avait des bûcherons (qui le recueillirent). On le déposa au milieu de la glace; mais un oiseau le couvrit (de l'une de ses

誕 Tán, particule. 凡人之生必拆副菑害其母而首生之子尤難今姜嫄首生后稷如羊子之易無拆副菑害之苦是顯其靈異也上帝豈不寧乎豈不康我之禋祀乎而使我無人道而徒然生是子也(朱熹) «Tout enfant qui vient au monde, déchire, fend et lèse gravement le sein de sa mère, surtout si c'est le premier-né. Or Kiang Iuen enfanta Heou tsi, son premier-né, aussi facilement qu'une brebis met au jour un agneau, sans rupture, sans lésion ni douleur; cela montre que cette naissance fut merveilleuse et extraordinaire. Le roi du ciel ne fut-il pas content? n'agréa-t-il pas le sacrifice pur de notre aïeule Kiang Iuen, lui qui lui donna de concevoir et d'enfanter sans difficulté et contrairement aux lois de la nature humaine?»

天欲顯其靈異於世使知聖人之生有異於凡人也(詩經備旨) Le ciel a voulu manifester au monde sa puissance merveilleuse, et montrer que la naissance des grands sages est bien différente de celle des hommes vulgaires.

3. Deposuerunt eum in angusto calle; boves et oves cruribus protegentes amanter curarunt eum. Deposuerunt eum in plana silva; occurrerunt qui cædebant planæ silvæ arbores. Deposuerunt eum in gelida glacie; avis operuit et sustinuit eum. Avis postquam abiit, Heou tsi vagiit. Vere protentus, vere magnus, ejus vagitus implevit vias.

無人道而生子或者以爲不祥故棄之而有此異也於是始收而養之(朱熹) «Une femme avait conçu et enfanté contrairement aux lois de la nature humaine. On craignit que ce ne fût un mauvais présage. Pour ce motif on voulut se défaire de l'enfant. Mais survinrent ces choses extraordinaires; alors on le recueillit et on l'éleva.»

«On le déposa d'abord dans un étroit sentier, pensant que les bœufs et les brebis l'écraseraient infailliblement sous leurs pieds. Mais au contraire les bœufs

翼之。鳥乃去矣。后稷呱矣。實覃實訏。厥聲載路。

(4)誕實匍匐。克岐克嶷。以就口食。蓺之荏菽。荏菽旆旆。禾役穟穟。麻麥幪幪。瓜瓞唪唪。

nài k'iú i, Heóu tsĭ kōu (kóu) i. Chĕu t'ân chĕu hiū (hiú), kiuĕ chēng tsái lóu.

4. Tán chĕu p'ôu p'ĕ, k'ŏ k'ì k'ŏ ĭ. Ì tsióu k'eòu chĕu, i tchĕu jénn chŏu. Jènn chŏu péi péi, houŏ ĭ souéi souéi. Mâ mĕ mòung mòung, kouā tiĕ pòung pòung.

ailes, et de l'autre) lui fit une couche. L'oiseau s'en étant allé, Heou tsi se mit à vagir. Ses vagissements prolongés et puissants furent entendus par tous les chemins.

4. A peine pouvait-il se traîner sur ses pieds et sur ses mains, que déjà il était grand et vigoureux. Dès qu'il fut capable de porter lui-même la nourriture à sa bouche, il sema de grands haricots ; ses grands haricots flottèrent au vent comme des bannières. Ses moissons semées en lignes furent très belles. Ses plantes oléagineuses et ses céréales furent drues et vigoureuses. Ses concombres, gros ou petits, furent très nombreux.

et les brebis en eurent compassion et le réchauffèrent de leurs corps. Alors on le déposa dans une plaine au milieu d'une forêt, croyant que dans un endroit désert et couvert de bois il ne se trouverait personne pour lui sauver la vie. Mais des bûcherons survinrent et le recueillirent. Ensuite on le déposa dans la glace, pensant qu'il n'y trouverait plus aucun secours. Qui l'aurait deviné? Un oiseau le couvrit de l'une de ses ailes, et de l'autre lui fit une couche. L'oiseau s'en étant allé, Heou tsi poussa des vagissements. Bien qu'il eût subi longtemps ces vicissitudes successives, sa voix était encore puissante, se faisait entendre au loin, et retentissait tout le long des chemins. N'était-ce pas bien extraordinaire? Alors enfin Kiang luen le recueillit et le nourrit. Tels sont les prodiges qui parurent, quand Heou tsi fut abandonné. Qu'un oiseau ait eu un instinct merveilleux, ce fut évidemment par la volonté du ciel. Si l'oiseau était resté, à la fin Heou tsi serait mort. L'oiseau se retira; ce fut le ciel qui le fit partir. La force de la voix de l'enfant montra que le ciel l'avait doué d'une nature vigoureuse. Il fut plusieurs fois abandonné, et toujours il parut des signes extraordinaires. Ce furent des manifestations de la volonté du ciel qui ordonnait de lui conserver la vie. » (詩經備旨).

4. Ubi vere reptavit, eminebat statura, eminebat viribus. Ubi admovere (potuit ipse) ori cibum, sevit majores phaseolos; majores phaseoli vento agitati sunt. Segetum ordines pulchri fuerunt. Oleaceæ plantæ et triticum fuerunt vegeta ac densa. Cucurbitæ majores et cucurbitæ minores plurimæ fuerunt.

(5) 誕后稷之穡、有相之道、茀厥豐草、種之黃茂、實方實苞、實種實褎、實發實秀、實堅實好、實穎實栗、即有邰家室、

(6) 誕降嘉種、維秬維秠、維穈維芑、恆之秬秠、是穫是畝、恆之穈芑、是任是負、以歸肇祀、

5. Tán Heóu tsǐ tchēu chě, iòu siáng tchēu taó (teòu). Fǒu kiuě fōung ts'aò (ts'eòu), tchóung tchēu houâng meóu (meòu). Chěu fāng chěu paō (peòu), chěu tchòung chéu sióu (sióu). Chěu fā chěu sióu (sióu), chěu kiēn chěu haò (heòu). Chěu ing chěu lǐ, tsǐ iòu T'āi kiā chěu.

6. Tán kiáng kiā tchòung, wèi kiú wèi p'i, wèi mênn wèi k'i. Kéng tchēu kiú p'i, chéu houǒ chéu meòu (mèi). Kéng tchēu mênn k'i, chéu jénn chéu fóu (fèi), i kouēi tchaó séu (i).

5. Heou tsi dans ses travaux agricoles aidait la nature (il consultait les saisons, les qualités du sol). Il débarrassa la terre des épaisses touffes d'herbe, et lui fit produire des moissons jaunes. Lorsque le germe, d'abord caché dans l'enveloppe du grain, commençait à gonfler, le grain était semé. Le germe sortait de terre, la tige croissait, l'épi se formait; le grain durcissait et était de bonne qualité. L'épi s'inclinait plein de grains excellents. (Heou tsi, en récompense de ses services), reçut (de l'empereur Chouenn) la terre de T'ai, qui avait appartenu à son père.

6. Il distribua au peuple des semences des meilleurs grains, du millet noir ordinaire, du millet noir qui avait deux grains dans une seule enveloppe, du sorgho rouge, du sorgho blanc. Partout on sema du millet noir ordinaire et du millet noir à double grain; la moisson fut recueillie et mise en monceaux dans les champs. Partout on sema du sorgho rouge et du sorgho blanc; on porta le grain à la maison, sur les épaules ou sur le dos, pour faire les offrandes instituées (par Heou tsi).

5. Heou tsi agrestia opera habuerunt adjuvandi (cœli ad fruges producendas) rationem. Abstulit illas densas herbas, sevit illic flavas pulchrasque (fruges). Et reconsum erat (germen in grano), et tumescebat (germen), et semen fiebat, et erumpebat (germen), et crescebat (caulis), et spicabat, et firmabatur (granum), et bonum erat, et inclinabatur (spica), et opimum erat granum. Inde habuit T'ai patrimonium.

6. Demisit (i.e. plebi tribuit) optima semina, i.e. frugum semina, et nigrum milium, et geminis granis nigrum milium, et rubro grano sorghum, et albo grano sorghum. Ubique sata sunt nigrum milium ac gemellis granis nigrum milium; et demessa sunt et in agris acervata. Ubique sata sunt rubrum sorghum et album sorghum; et hume-

(7) 誕我祀如何、或舂或揄、或簸或蹂、釋之叟叟、烝之浮浮、載謀載惟、取蕭祭脂、取羝以軷、載燔載烈、以興嗣歲、

(8) 卬盛于豆、于豆于登、其香始升、上帝居歆、胡臭亶時、后稷肇祀、庶無罪悔、以迄于今、

7. Tán ngò séu (i) jôu hô? Houĕ chôung houĕ iôu, houĕ pouò houĕ jeôu. Chĕu tchĕu seôu seôu, tchēng tchēu feôu feôu. Tsái meôu tsái wêi. Ts'iù siaŏ tsi tchĕu, ts'iù ti i p'ouŏ (p'éi). Tsái fân tsái liĕ, i hīng séu souéi (siuĕ).

8. Ngàng tch'êng iû teóu, iû teóu iû tēng. K'ì hiāng chéu chēng, cháng ti kiū hīn. Hôu tch'eóu tàn chèu (chéu)? Heóu tsī tchaò séu (i), chóu ôu tsouéi houéi (houéi), i hī iû kīn.

7. Comment se font nos offrandes? Ceux-ci écorcent le millet sous le pilon, ceux-là le retirent du mortier. Les uns le vannent; les autres foulent les épis (pour faire sortir le grain). On le lave avec bruit, et on le fait cuire à la vapeur (ou avec dégagement de vapeur). Alors on consulte (sur le choix du jour et des ministres de la cérémonie); puis on réfléchit, c.-à-d. on fait les purifications d'usage. On prend de l'armoise et on offre la graisse (on les mêle ensemble et on les brûle). On prend un bouc pour l'offrir aux esprits des chemins. On fait cuire de la viande, on en fait rôtir, afin que l'année suivante soit prospère.

8. Nous mettons (les mets) dans les vases de bois, (les mets) dans les vases de bois et (les sauces) dans les vases de terre. Dès que leur agréable odeur s'élève dans les airs, le roi du ciel la respire avec joie. Est-ce uniquement parce que ce parfum s'exhale à l'époque voulue? C'est surtout parce que, depuis l'institution de ces offrandes par Heou tsi jusqu'à nos jours, jamais il ne s'y est glissé une seule faute qu'on dût déplorer.

ris portata sunt et dorso portata sunt, ut domi inchoarentur sacra.

7. Nostra sacra quomodo (fiunt)? Hi tundunt in mortario (milium); illi hauriunt (ex mortario). Alii vannunt; alii calcant (spicas). Lavant illud (milium) cum strepitu, coquunt illud cum vapore. Tunc consulunt, tunc meditantur. Sumunt artemisiam et offerunt adipem. Sumunt caprum ut offerant viarum spiritibus. Et coquunt et assant (carnes), ad fortunandum sequentem annum.

8. Nos imponimus in ligneis vasis, in ligneis vasis (dapes), in fictilibus vasis (juscula). Horum fragrantia incipit ascendere; cœli rex gaudens haurit odorem. Num (non gaudet nisi) quia odor vere statuto tempore (ascendat)? (Maxime gaudet quia ex quo) Heou tsi instituit sacra, feliciter nulla fuit culpa cujus pœnitendum, usque in præsens.

行葦

(1) 敦彼行葦。牛羊勿踐履。方苞方體。維葉泥泥、戚戚兄弟、莫遠具爾。或肆之筵、或授之几。

(2) 肆筵設席。授几有緝御。或獻或酢、洗爵奠斝、醓醢以薦。或燔或

HING WEI. 1. T'ouàn pêi hîng wêi, iòu iàng ŏu tsién li. Fāng paŏ fāng t'i, wêi iĕ gni gni. Ts'ī ts'ī hiōung ti, mouŏ iuén kiú èul. Houĕ séu tchēu iên, houĕ cheóu tchēu ki.

2. Séu iên chŏ sî (siŏ), cheóu ki iòu tsī iú (iá). Houĕ hién houĕ tsŏ ; si tsiŏ, tién kiá (kiá). T'ān hài i tsién (tsiŏ), houĕ fân houĕ tchĕu (tchŏ). Kiā hiaŏ p'i kiŏ. Houĕ kŏ houĕ ngŏ (iŏ).

CHANT II. HING WEI.

Festin offert par l'empereur aux princes de sa famille, et suivi d'un exercice de tir à l'arc, probablement après une cérémonie en l'honneur des ancêtres.

1. Le long du chemin les roseaux sont en touffes épaisses ; que les bœufs, les brebis n'aillent pas les fouler sous leurs pieds. Bientôt ils se développeront, bientôt ils seront entièrement formés; leurs feuilles tendres seront luisantes. Ainsi les frères (les membres d'une même famille) sont unis (par le sang); qu'aucun d'eux ne se tienne éloigné, mais qu'ils approchent tous. Pour chacun une natte est préparée; quelques-uns (les plus âgés) reçoivent (en outre) des escabeaux (pour s'appuyer étant assis).

2. Sur chacune des nattes étendues à terre une seconde natte est placée; les escabeaux sont distribués, et les serviteurs se succèdent sans interruption. Le maître de la maison offre du vin aux convives; ceux-ci lui en offrent à leur tour. Le maître de la maison lave la coupe (et offre du vin une seconde fois); les convives déposent la coupe (et ne boivent pas). On apporte les bouillons ou les sauces et les hachis de viande conservés dans la saumure. On

CHANT II. 1. Densi sunt illi viæ calami; boves et oves ne insistentes calcent. Mox erumpent, mox formati erunt, et folia tenera nitebunt. (Sanguine) arcte conjuncti sunt fratres; nullus procul absit, omnes accedant. Aliis sternuntur storeæ; aliis (insuper) dantur scabella.

2. Substratis mattis impositæ sunt storeæ; data sunt scabella, adsunt continui ministri. Modo domus dominus convivis propinat vinum, modo convivæ domus domino propinant vinum. (Domus dominus) lavat poculum (et vinum iterum propinat; convivæ) deponunt poculum (nec bibunt). Juscula, carnes concisæ et in muria servatæ inde afferuntur. Sunt carnes aliæ assatæ

炙，嘉殽脾
臄，或歌或
咢。
（3）敦弓既
堅，四鍭既
鈞，舍矢既
均，序賓以
賢。敦弓既
句，既挾四
鍭，四鍭如
樹，序賓以
不侮。
（4）曾孫維

3. Tiaō kōung ki kiēn (kīn), séu heôu ki kiūn. Chè chèu ki kiūn, siú pīn i hièn (hènn.). Tiaō kōung ki keóu (keōu), ki tsiĕ séu heôu. Séu heôu jôu chóu (chóu), siú pīn i pŏu òu.

4. Tsēng suēnn wêi tchòu, tsiòu li wêi jòu. Tchŏ i tá teóu (tchóu), i k'i

sert la viande grillée, le (foie) rôti, et les mets exquis, à savoir, la rate et la lèvre supérieure (la langue ou le palais). On chante avec accompagnement de guitare, on bat le tambour.

3. Les arcs peints sont forts; les quatre flèches de chaque archer sont bien équilibrées. Les archers ont tous frappé la cible (plus ou moins près du centre, un nombre de fois plus ou moins grand); ils sont rangés d'après leur dextérité. Ils ont tiré à eux la corde de leurs arcs le plus possible, pris (et lancé) leurs quatre flèches. Leurs quatre flèches sont comme plantées dans la cible. Ils sont rangés d'après leur modestie respectueuse.

4. Le descendant éloigné (qui vient de faire des offrandes à ses ancêtres) est le maître de la maison, et son vin doux est géné-

aliæ tostæ (jecur tostum); optimæ dapes sunt splen et superius labium (aut lingua aut palatum). Quidam canunt cum fidibus, quidam pulsant tympana.

3. Picti arcus sunt firmi; quatuor sagittæ sunt libratæ. Emissis sagittis omnes attigerunt scopum; ordinantur hospites ex dexteritate. Pictorum arcuum (nervus) attractus est quam maxime; desumptæ sunt quatuor sagittæ. Quatuor sagittæ videntur plantatæ. Ordinantur hospites ex carentia arrogantiæ, vel, ordinantur victores ex eo quod non illudunt victis.

L'expression 敦弓 **tiaō kōung** s'emploie spécialement pour désigner l'arc de l'empereur. Elle est employée ici dans un sens plus étendu, parce que cet exercice eut lieu à la cour impériale. 鍭 **Heôu**, flèche munie de plumes et d'une pointe métallique. 鈞 **Kiūn**, bien équilibré. Une flèche est bien équilibrée, lorsque son centre de gravité est au tiers de sa longueur mesurée à partir de la pointe. Chacun des archers lançait quatre flèches. Ils ont tous frappé la cible, mais à des distances différentes du centre, les uns avec une flèche, les autres avec plusieurs. Les vainqueurs devaient 不侮 **pŏu òu** éviter de se montrer arrogants et d'insulter aux vaincus. On ne dit pas si l'appréciation de leur modestie et leur classement étaient faciles. 句 est employé pour 彀 **Keóu**, tirer à soi la corde d'un arc le plus possible pour lancer une flèche.

4. Remotus nepos est domus dominus; vinum dulce est generosum. Infundit ope majoris cochlearis ad precandam flavescente coma senectutem.

主、酒醴維醹、酌
以大斗、以祈黃
耇。黃耇台背、以
引以翼、壽考維
祺、以介景福。

既醉

(1) 既醉以酒、既
飽以德、君子萬
年、介爾景福、
(2) 既醉以酒、爾
殽既將、君子萬
年、介爾昭明、
(3) 昭明有融、高

houâng keòu (kòu). Houâng keòu t'âi péi (pě), i in i ĭ. Cheóu k'aò wêi k'î, i kiái king fŏu (pĭ).

KI TSOUEI. **1. Ki tsouéi i tsiòu, kí paò i té. Kiūn tzèu wán gniên, kiái èul king fŏu (pĭ).**

2. Ki tsouéi i tsiòu, èul hiaô ki tsiāng. Kiūn tzèu wán gniên, kiái èul tchaō mîng (mâng).

3. Tchaō mîng (mâng) iòu iôung, kaō lâng ling tchōung. Ling tchōung iòu tch'ŏu, kōung chēu kiā kaó (kŏu).

reux. Il emplit les coupes avec la grande cuiller, et souhaite à ses hôtes une vieillesse si longue que leurs cheveux deviennent jaunes. Il leur souhaite de vivre jusqu'à ce que leurs chevelures soient jaunes, et la peau de leurs dos rugueuse et tachetée comme celle du marsouin, afin qu'ils se guident et s'aident (mutuellement dans la voie du devoir). Il leur souhaite une vieillesse prospère, afin que leur félicité augmente encore.

CHANT III. KI TSOUEI.

Les princes invités à la table de l'empereur, le remercient de sa bonté, et lui souhaitent en récompense un accroissement de bonheur.

1. Vous nous avez fait boire le vin à pleines coupes, et nous avez comblés de vos bienfaits. Prince, que le ciel vous accorde dix mille ans de vie et un accroissement de prospérité!

2. Vous nous avez fait boire le vin à pleines coupes, et offert des mets exquis. Prince, que le ciel vous accorde dix mille années de vie, et augmente l'éclat de votre gloire!

3. L'éclat de votre gloire sera très grand, et votre sublime clarté

(Precatur eis) flavescentem senectam et porculi marini (instar rugosum maculosumque) dorsum, ut ducant, ut adjuvent (invicem in via virtutis. Precatur eis ut) senectus sit prospera, ad augendam magnam felicitatem.

CHANT III. 1. Large potasti vino, satiasti beneficiis. Rex, decies mille annis (vivas et) crescant tua ingentia bona!

2. Large potasti vino, tuæ dapes allatæ sunt. Rex, decies mille annis (vivas et) crescat tua fulgida claritas!

3. Fulgida claritas erit splendor

朗令終，令終有
俶，公尸嘉告。
(4) 其告維何，籩
豆靜嘉，朋友攸
攝，攝以威儀。
(5) 威儀孔時，君
子有孝子，孝子
不匱，永錫爾類。
(6) 其類維何，室
家之壼，君子萬
年，永錫祚胤。
(7) 其胤維何，天
被爾祿，君子萬
年，景命有僕。

4. K'i kŏu wêi hô? Piēn teóu tsing kiā (kō). P'êng iòu iôu chĕ, chĕ i wēi i (ngô).

5. Wēi i (ngô) k'òung chêu (chêu), kiūn tzéu iòu hiaó tzèu. Hiaó tzèu pōu k'ouéi, iòung sī èul léi.

6. K'i léi wêi hô ? Chĕu kiā tchēu k'ouènn (k'iún). Kiūn tzéu wán gniên, iòung sī tsóu in.

7. K'i in wêi hô ? T'iēn pi èul lŏu. Kiūn tzéu wán gniên, king ming iòu pōu.

brillera sans cesse à travers les âges. Cette gloire durable a son fondement (dans votre vertu ; vers la fin de la cérémonie en l'honneur de vos ancêtres), le représentant des princes vos ancêtres vous a promis de grandes faveurs.

4. Que vous a-t-il annoncé ? Vos vases de bambou et vos vases de bois contenaient des offrandes pures et exquises. Les amis qui vous ont aidé, l'ont fait avec dignité et bienséance.

5. (Les offrandes, les cérémonies que vous avez faites) avec dignité et bienséance, ont été conformes à la saison ; et vous avez un fils d'une grande piété filiale. Votre fils a rempli son devoir parfaitement ; vous jouirez à jamais des faveurs du ciel.

6. Quelles seront ces faveurs ? Dans votre palais, au sein de votre famille, vous vivrez dix mille ans ; votre félicité et votre postérité n'auront pas de fin.

7. Que sera votre postérité ? Le ciel vous a revêtu de la dignité suprême. Il vous donnera dix mille années de vie, et son grand mandat restera attaché à votre personne.

maximus ; sublimis claritas habebit optimum finem. Optimo fini est initium (seu basis, nempe virtus tua) ; regum mortuorum vicarius fausta nuntiavit.

4. Ejus nuntium fuit quodnam ? Arundinea vasa et lignea vasa fuerunt pura et optima. Amici quæ curaverunt, curaverunt cum gravitate ac decoro.

5. Gravitas ac decentia (tua) valde consentanea tempori fuit ; rex habet pium filium. Pius filius nihilo defecit ; jugiter dabuntur tibi bona.

6. Hæc bona erunt quænam ? In ædium domusque angiportubus, rex decies mille annis (vivet), jugiter donabitur felicitate et posteritate.

7. Ea posteritas quomodo ? Cœlum induit te dignitate (regia). Rex, decies mille annis (vives, et cœli) magnum mandatum erit adhærens.

(8)其僕維何。釐爾女士。釐爾女士。從以孫子。

鳧鷖

(1)鳧鷖在涇。公尸來燕來寧。爾酒既清。爾殽既馨。公尸燕飲。福祿來成。

(2)鳧鷖在沙。公尸來燕來宜。爾酒既多。爾殽既嘉。公尸燕飲。福祿來爲。

8. K'î pŏu wêi hô ? Lî èul gniù chèu. Lî èul gniù chèu, ts'ôung i suēnn tzèu.

FOU I. **1. Fôu î tsái Kīng ; kōung chēu lâi ién lâi gning. Eùl tsiòu ki ts'īng, èul hiaô ki hīng. Kōung chēu ién in, fŏu lŏu lâi tch'êng.**

2. Fôu î tsái chā (souô) ; kōung chēu lâi ién lâi î (ngô). Eùl tsiòu ki touô, èul hiaô kí kiā (kō). Kōung chēu lâi in, fŏu lŏu lâi wêi (wô).

8. Comment restera-t-il attaché à votre personne? Le ciel vous a donné une femme héroïque; par elle vous aurez des descendants.

CHANT IV. FOU I.

Le lendemain d'une cérémonie en l'honneur des ancêtres, les restes des offrandes sont servis dans le 寢 **ts'in**, derrière le temple des ancêtres, au représentant des mânes. Celui-ci est heureux à ce festin comme le canard ou la mouette au milieu de l'eau.

1. Le canard sauvage et la mouette sont sur l'eau de la King. Le représentant des princes vos ancêtres vient fêter et se reposer. Votre vin est pur, et vos mets exhalent une odeur agréable. Le représentant des princes vos ancêtres fête et boit; la félicité et les honneurs viennent à lui dans toute leur plénitude.

2. Le canard sauvage et la mouette sont sur le sable. Le représentant des princes vos ancêtres vient fêter et recevoir les honneurs qui lui sont dus. Votre vin est abondant et vos mets exquis. Le représentant des princes vos ancêtres fête et boit; la félicité et les honneurs viennent et sont à son service.

8. Ejus adhæsio erit quomodo? (Cœlum) dedit tibi uxorem virilem, i.e. uxorem quæ viriliter agit. Dedit tibi uxorem virilem, inde habebis nepotes.

CHANT IV. 1. Anas silvestris et gavia sunt in King fluvio. Regum mortuorum vicarius venit et epulatur, venit et quiescit. Tuum vinum est purum, tuæ dapes sunt fragrantes. Regum mortuorum vicarius epulatur et bibit; felicitas et honores (ei) veniunt plene.

2. Anas silvestris et gavia sunt in arena. Regum mortuorum vicarius venit et epulatur, venit et congruenter excipitur. Tuum vinum est copiosum; tuæ dapes sunt optimæ. Regum mortuorum vicarius epulans bibit; felicitas et honores veniunt et satisfaciunt (ei).

(3) 鳧鷖在渚。公尸來燕來處。爾酒既湑。爾殽伊脯。公尸燕飲。福祿來下。

(4) 鳧鷖在潨。公尸來燕來宗。既燕于宗。福祿攸降。公尸燕飲。福祿來崇。

(5) 鳧鷖在亹。公尸來止熏熏。旨酒欣欣。燔炙芬芬。公尸燕飲。無有後艱。

3. Fôu î tsài tchòu ; kōung chēu lâi ién lâi tch'òu. Eùl tsiòu kí siù, èul hiaô î fòu. Kōung chēu ién in, fòu lōu lâi hià (hòu).

4. Fôu î tsài ts'ôung ; kōung chēu lâi ién lâi tsōung. Kí ién iû tsōung, fòu lōu iôu hiáng (hôung). Kōung chēu ién in, fòu lōu lâi tch'ôung.

5. Fôu î tsài mênn ; kōung chēu lâi tchèu hiūn hiūn. Tchèu tsiòu hīn hīn, fân tchēu fênn fēnn. Kōung chēu ién in, ôu iòu heóu kiēn (kīn).

3. Le canard sauvage et la mouette sont sur un ilot. Le représentant des princes vos ancêtres vient fêter et se reposer. Votre vin est purifié, et vos mets sont des tranches de viande. Le représentant des princes défunts fête et boit ; la félicité et les honneurs descendent sur sa personne.

4. Le canard sauvage et la mouette sont au confluent de deux rivières. Le représentant des princes vos ancêtres vient fêter et recevoir des honneurs. (Hier) il a goûté les offrandes dans le temple des ancêtres, et fait descendre sur vous la prospérité et les honneurs. (Aujourd'hui) il fête et boit (dans le bâtiment situé derrière le temple des ancêtres); les biens et les honneurs viendront en plus grande affluence.

5. Le canard sauvage et la mouette sont sur l'eau dans une gorge de montagne. Le représentant des princes vos ancêtres vient; il est affable et joyeux. Votre excellent vin excite la joie; vos viandes grillées, vos viandes rôties exhalent une odeur agréable. Le représentant des princes vos ancêtres fête et boit; aucun mal ne vous arrivera à l'avenir.

3. Anas silvestris et gavia sunt in parva insula. Regum mortuorum vicarius venit epulaturus, venit quieturus. Tuum vinum est defæcatum, tuæ dapes sunt concisæ carnes. Regum mortuorum vicarius epulans bibit; felicitas et honores venientes descendunt.

4. Anas silvestris et gavia sunt in confluente. Regum morturum vicarius venit ut epuletur, venit ut honoretur. (Heri) epulatus est in avorum aula; felicitas et honores inde descenderunt. (Nunc in æde posteriori), regum mortuorum vicarius epulans bibit; felicitas et honores venient ampliores.

5. Anas silvestris et gavia sunt in aqua inter montis fauces decurrente. Regum mortuorum vicarius venit et

詩經

假樂

(1) 假樂君子、顯顯令德、宜民宜人、受祿于天、保右命之、自天申之、

(2) 干祿百福、子孫千億、穆穆皇皇、宜君宜王、不愆不忘、率由舊章、

(3) 威儀抑抑、德音秩秩、無怨無

KIA LO. 1. **Kiā lǒ kiūn tzèu (tsě), hièn hièn ling tē. Î min i jènn, cheòu lǒu iū t'iēn (t'īn). Paò ióu ming ('mìng) tchēu, tzèu t'iēn chēnn tchēu.**

2. Kān lǒu pě fǒu (pǐ), tzèu suēnn ts'iēn ǐ. Mǒu mǒu houâng houâng, î kiūn î wâng. Pǒu k'iēn pǒu wâng, chouě iòu kiòu tchāng.

3. Wēi i î í, tě īn tchěu tchěu. Où iuén ǒu óu, chouě iòu k'iûn p'ǐ. Cheóu fǒu ǒu kiāng, séu fāng tchēu kāng.

CHANT V. KIA LO.

En réponse au chant précédent, le représentant des mânes promet à l'empereur 成王 **Tch'êng wâng** toutes sortes de biens.

1. Le prince est admirable et aimable; sa vertu brille d'un grand éclat. Il gouverne bien le peuple et dirige bien les officiers. Le ciel le comble d'honneurs et de richesses. Il le protège, l'aide, lui confie le mandat souverain, et sans cesse lui renouvelle ces faveurs.

2. Le prince s'attire les richesses, les honneurs, toutes sortes de biens. Ses descendants se compteront par milliers et par centaines de milliers. Respectueux, distingués, ils seront capables de bien gouverner les principautés et l'empire. Exempts de faute et n'oubliant rien, ils suivront exactement les anciens statuts.

3. Leur tenue, leurs manières seront d'une gravité irréprochable; leur bonne renommée n'aura pas de déclin. Exempts de ressentiment et de haine, ils céderont aux avis des hommes sages qui

subsistit comis et gaudens. Optimum vinum lætitiam parit; assata et tosta fragrant. Regum mortuorum vicarius epulans bibit; non sunt futuræ ærumnæ.

CHANT V. 1. Mirabilis et festivus est imperator; claret eximia virtus. Recte agit cum populo, recte agit cum præpositis; accipit opes et honores e cœlo. (Cœlum) protegit, adjuvat, mandato donat eum; ultro cœlum ingeminat illa.

假 est employé à la place de 嘉 **kiā**. Cf. 中庸 Ch. 17.

2. Adsciscit opes et honores omniaque bona; filii et nepotes erunt milleni, centies milleni. Reverentes, insignes, idonei erunt reguli, idonei imperatores. Nihil peccabunt, nihil obliviscentur; obsequentes insistent antiquis institutis.

3 (Eorum) gravitas et observantia

惡、率由羣匹。受
福無疆、四方之
綱。
(4) 之綱之紀、燕
及朋友、百辟卿
士、媚于天子、不
解于位、民之攸
墍。

公劉

(1) 篤公劉、匪居
匪康、迺埸迺疆、
迺積迺倉、迺裹
餱糧、于槖于囊、

4. **Tchēu kāng tchēu kì, ién kì p'êng iòu (i). Pĕ pì k'īng chéu, méi iû t'iēn tzèu. Pŏu kiài iū wéi, mîn tchēu iôu hì.**

KOUNG LIOU. 1. **Tŏu kōung Liôu, fèi kiū fèi k'āng. Nài i nài kiāng, nài tzéu nài ts'āng. Nài kouŏ heôu leâng, iû t'ouŏ iû nâng. Sēu tsī iôung kouāng,**

partageront avec eux les soins du gouvernement. Ils jouiront d'une prospérité sans limite, et seront la loi vivante des quatre parties de l'empire.

4. Grâce à ces lois, à ces règles vivantes, leurs amis et leurs officiers auront la tranquillité. Tous les princes et les ministres d'État aimeront le Fils du ciel. Si l'empereur ne demeure pas oisif sur le trône, tout le peuple jouira de la paix.

CHANT VI. KOUNG LIOU.

召康公 K'ang, prince de Chao, nommé dans le Chou king 君奭 **kiūn Chĕu** le sage Cheu, raconte à l'empereur 成王 **Tch'êng wâng** comment le prince Liou, quittant le pays des 西戎 **sī Jôung** barbares occidentaux, alla s'établir dans la terre de 豳 **Pīn**. Cf. page 2,

1. Le prince Liou était tout dévoué à son peuple; il ne prenait ni relâche ni repos. (Vivant au milieu des barbares), il fixa les limites et la division de son territoire. Il amassa des grains dans les champs et dans les greniers; il fit mettre des aliments secs dans des sacs qui s'ouvraient aux deux extrémités, et des grains dans

erunt perfectæ; bona fama erit continua. Absque simultate, absque odio, obsequentur multitudini sociorum. Accipient bona sine limite; quatuor regionum erunt leges.

4. His legibus, his regulis, tranquillitas perveniet ad amicos et socios, i.e. ad regulos et regni ministros. Omnes reguli et regni ministri amabunt Cœli filium. Nisi pigrescat in sede, populus inde pace fruetur.

CHANT VI. 1. Generosus princeps Liou, nec cessabat, nec otio indulgebat. (In occidentalium barbarorum regione), et divisit et limitavit territorium. Et collegit (sub dio in agris) et condidit in horreis (fruges). Et involvit cibaria ac frumenta, in saccis utrinque pertusis, in consuetis saccis. Volens congregare (populum) et ita præclarum

思輯用光、弓矢斯張、干戈戚揚、爰方啓行、

(2) 篤公劉、于胥斯原、既庶既繁、既順迺宣、而無永歎、陟則在巘、復降在原、何以舟之、維玉及瑤、鞞琫容刀、

(3) 篤公劉、逝彼百泉、瞻彼溥原、迺陟南岡、乃覯于京、京師之野、于時處處、

kōung chéu sēu tchāng. Kān kouō ts'ī iāng, iuên fāng k'i hìng (hâng).

2. Tŏu kōung Liôu, iû siū sēu iuên. Ki chéu ki fân, ki chouénn nài siuēn, êul ôu iòung t'ān. Tchĕu tsĕ tsái ién (iên), fŏu kiáng tsái iuên. Hô ī tcheōu (tchaō) tchēu? Wêi iŭ kĭ iaô, ping pòung iôung taō.

3. Tŏu kōung Liôu; chéu pèi pĕ ts'iuên, tchēn pèi p'òu iuên. Nài tchĕu nân

des sacs munis de fonds. Dans l'intention de rassembler ses sujets et de rendre sa race illustre, il fit prendre les arcs, les flèches, les boucliers, les lances, les haches d'armes, et se mit en marche.

2. Le prince Liou était tout dévoué à son peuple; (arrivé à Pin), il alla examiner la plaine. Déjà ses sujets étaient nombreux, contents et disséminés partout; ils ne se lamentaient pas sans cesse (au souvenir du pays qu'ils avaient quitté. Le prince monta et s'arrêta sur la cime de la montagne; puis descendit et s'arrêta dans la plaine. Que portait-il à la ceinture? Des ornements de jade, des pierres de prix, un fourreau dont l'ouverture était de pierre précieuse, une épée bien ornée (ou une épée dans le fourreau).

3. Le prince Liou était tout dévoué à son peuple; il alla au lieu où coulent les cent sources, et examina cette vaste plaine. Puis il monta sur la crête de la montagne au sud, et de là il considéra cette haute colline, ce haut plateau propre à recevoir une grande

facere (regnum), arcus sagittasque tunc explicuit. Cum scutis, hastis, asciis, securibus, statim cœpit aggredi iter.

2. Generosus princeps Liou, ivit inspecturus hanc planitiem. Jam multi, jam densi, jam quieti et ubique diffusi (erant homines); et non erant continui gemitus (de pristina sede relicta). Ascendit, et stetit in montis cacumine; rursus descendens stetit in planitie. Quibus rebus utens cinxit se? Unice iaspide et lapillis *iaò*, vagina cujus gemmeum erat labrum, et ornato ense (vel contento ense).

3. Generosus princeps Liou, adivit illos centum fontes; inspexit illam vastam planitiem. Tum ascendit australe jugum, et prospexit ad altum collem, altum multitudinisque (capacem) campum. In eo collocavit domos, in eo accepit advenas; in eo dixit verba, i.e. jussa ac monita, in eo deliberavit de deliberandis.

46

于時廬旅、于時言言、于時語語、

(4) 篤公劉、于京斯依、蹌蹌濟濟、俾筵俾几、既登乃依、乃造其曹、執豕于牢、酌之用匏、食之飲之、君之宗之、

(5) 篤公劉、既溥既長、既景迺岡、相其陰陽、觀其流泉、其軍三單、

kāng, nài keóu iū kīng (kāng), kīng chēu tchēu iè (chóu). Iū chēu tch'óu tch'óu, iū chēu liû liû. Iū chēu iên iên, iū chēu iù iù.

4. Tǒu kōung Liôu, iū kīng sēu ī (i). Ts'iāng ts'iāng tsi tsi, pèi iên pèi ki. Ki tēng nài ī (i); nài ts'aó k'î ts'aô. Tchĕu chéu iū laô; tchŏ tchēu iòung p'aô. Sèu tchēu in tchēu, kiūn tchēu tsōung tchēu.

5. Tǒu kōung Liôu, ki p'òu ki tch'âng. Ki king nài kāng, siáng k'î īn iâng; kouān

multitude. Il y construisit des habitations, y reçut les étrangers, y donna ses ordres et ses avis, y tint les délibérations.

4. Le prince Liou était tout dévoué à son peuple. Il établit sa demeure sur la colline. (Ses officiers arrivèrent) avec un maintien grave et des manières distinguées; il leur fit préparer des nattes et des escabeaux. Lorsqu'ils furent entrés (dans le lieu du festin, ils s'assirent sur les nattes et) s'appuyèrent (contre les escabeaux). Le prince envoya au pâturage prendre un porc dans l'étable. Il offrit du vin à ses convives dans des courges. Il leur servit à manger et à boire, et se constitua leur roi, et le chef de famille de toute sa parenté.

5. Le prince Liou était tout dévoué à son peuple; il défricha les terres sur une vaste étendue en long et en large. Il observa les ombres (pour déterminer les points cardinaux), et s'éleva sur les crêtes des montagnes (pour considérer la contrée). Il examina les coteaux exposés au nord et ceux exposés au midi; il observa le

Sur cette colline il établit sa capitale. De là vint l'usage d'appeler 京師 **kīng chēu** la ville principale d'un grand État.

4. Generosus princeps Liou. In colle tum sedem fixit. Habitu gravi et decore magno (aderant præpositi); jussit parari storeas, jussit afferri scabella. Postquam ascenderunt (ad convivii locum), statim adnixi sunt (scabellis). Et adivit sua pabula, cepit suem in stabulo. Vinum propinavit illis (convivis) adhibens cucurbitas. Cibavit illos, potavit illos; regem se constituit aliis, familiæ caput aliis.

5. Generosus princeps Liou; late protulit, longe protulit (agrorum cultum). Inspexit umbras, et ascendit juga. Consideravit illorum (locorum) obversa septentrioni et obversa meridiei; prospexit illorum fluentes fontes. Ejus legiones erant tres simplices. Observavit illorum (locorum) depressa et excelsa.

度其隰原，徹田爲糧，度其夕陽，豳居允荒，

(6) 篤公劉，于豳斯館，涉渭爲亂，取厲取鍛，止基廼理，爰衆爰有，夾其皇澗，遡其過澗，止旅廼密，芮鞫之即，

k'i liôu ts'iuên. K'i kiūn sān tān. Touŏ k'i sī iuên, tch'ĕ t'iên wêi leâng. Touŏ k'i sī iâng, Pīn kiū iùn houāng

6. Tŏu kōung Liôu, iū Pīn sēu kouàn (kouán). Chĕ Wéi wêi louán; ts'iù li, ts'iù touán. Tchèu kī nài li; iuên tchóung iuên iòu (i). Kiă k'i Houâng kién, sóu k'i Kouŏ kién. Tchèu liù nài mī, Jouéi kiŭ tchēu tsī.

cours des rivières. Son armée n'était que de trois légions. Il observa les endroits bas et les endroits élevés. Il partagea les terres et fixa l'impôt. Il examina la région située à l'ouest de la montagne, (la fit habiter et cultiver); l'établissement de Pin fut vraiment vaste.

6. Le prince Liou était tout dévoué à son peuple. A son arrivée à Pin, n'ayant encore qu'une demeure temporaire (avant de se fixer définitivement), il fit faire des bacs, pour traverser la Wei et amener des pierres meulières et du fer. Après s'être fixé (à Pin), il traça les limites des terres. Ses sujets devinrent nombreux et riches. Ils établirent leurs habitations des deux côtés de la vallée de Houang, et continuèrent leurs constructions jusqu'à la vallée de Kouo. La population étant devenue très dense, ils s'étendirent jusqu'au tournant de la Jouei.

Compositis agris statuit vectigal. Consideravit illius (montis) occidentalem regionem; Pin statio vere ampla fuit.

徹田 **Tch'ĕ t'iên.** Le territoire était divisé en carrés qui avaient un 里 **li** stade de chaque côté (360 mètres environ), et contenaient neuf cents 畝 **meòu.** Les carrés étaient subdivisés en neuf parties égales. Un stade carré contenait environ 129 600 mètres carrés. Un *meou* valait 144 mètres carrés ou un peu moins d'un are et demi. Chaque famille possédait un champ de cent *meou,* un hectare quarante-quatre ares; c'était peu. La partie centrale était le champ commun. Voy. page 281.

6. Generosus princeps Liou. In Pin (quum primum advenit) tunc diversans, i. e. antequam sedem collocaret in perpetuum, trajecturus Wei fluvium fecit pontones, eduxit cotes, eduxit ferrum. Sede statuta, delineavit limites. (Incolæ fuerunt) et multi et locupletes. Utrinque occuparunt illam Houang vallem, progressi sunt ad illam Kouo vallem. Commorantium multitudo tunc densior facta est, ad Jouei fluvii convexam ripam pervenit.

鞫 **Kiŭ,** partie convexe du tournant d'une rivière. La Jouei (汭 ou 芮), affluent de la 涇 **Kīng,** traversait la principauté de Pin.

泂酌

①泂酌彼行潦、挹彼注茲、可以餴饎、豈弟君子、民之父母。

②泂酌彼行潦、挹彼注茲、可以濯罍、豈弟君子、民之攸歸。

③泂酌彼行潦、挹彼注茲、可以濯溉、豈弟君子、民之攸塈。

HIOUNG TCHO. **1. Hiòung tchŏ pèi hîng laò, ĭ pèi tchóu tzēu, k'ò i fēnn tch'êu (tch'èu). K'ài tí kiūn tzèu, min tchēu fóu mòu (mèi).**

2. Hiòung tchŏ pèi hîng laò, ĭ pèi tchóu tzēu, k'ò i tchouŏ lêi. K'ài tí kiūn tzèu, min tchēu iôu kouēi.

3. Hiòung tchŏ pèi hîng laò, ĭ pèi tchóu tzēu, k'ò i tchouŏ kái (ki). K'ài tí kiūn tzèu, min tchēu iôu hi.

CHANT VII. HIOUNG TCHO.

君奭召康公 Le sage Cheu, K'ang, prince de Chao, dit à 成王 **Tch'êng wâng**: « La chose la plus vile, l'eau qui coule dans les chemins, peut rendre quelque service. A plus forte raison un prince sage et aimable contribuera-t-il au bonheur de ses sujets. »

1. Prenez cette eau qui coule loin d'ici dans le chemin, prenez-la et versez-la ici ; elle pourra servir pour faire cuire le riz à la vapeur et le faire bouillir. Un prince sage, aimable et bon est le père du peuple.

2. Prenez cette eau qui coule loin d'ici dans le chemin, prenez-la et versez-la ici ; elle pourra servir à laver les amphores. Un prince sage, aimable et bon est le refuge du peuple.

3. Prenez cette eau qui coule loin d'ici dans le chemin, prenez-la et versez-la ici ; elle pourra servir à laver, à rincer les objets. Un prince sage, aimable et bon assure la tranquillité de son peuple.

CHANT VII. 1. E longinquo haurias illam in via decurrentem aquam; haurias illinc, transfundas huc ; poteris uti ad oryzam semel iterumque coquendam. Festivus et benignus sapiens rex est populi pater ac mater.

餴 **Fēnn**, riz qui a été cuit à la vapeur seulement, riz à moitié cuit. 饎 **Tch'êu**, riz parfaitement cuit, mets tout préparé, repas. Après que le riz a été chauffé à la vapeur une première fois, on y verse de l'eau et on le fait bouillir.

2. E longinquo haurias illam in via decurrentem aquam; haurias illinc, transfundas huc ; poteris utens abluere amphoras. Festivus et benignus sapiens rex, populares ad quem confugiunt.

3. E longinquo haurias illam in via fluentem aquam ; haurias illinc, transfundas huc ; poteris utens lavare et abluere. Festivus et benignus sapiens rex, populares per quem quiescunt.

卷阿

(1) 有卷者阿、飄風自南、豈弟君子、來游來歌、以矢其音、

(2) 伴奐爾游矣、優游爾休矣、豈弟君子、俾爾彌爾性、似先公酋矣、

(3) 爾土宇昄章、亦孔之厚矣、豈弟君子、俾爾彌

K'IUEN NGO. **1. Iòu k'iuèn tchè ngō, p'iaō fōung tzèu nân (gnîn). K'ài ti kiūn tzèu lâi iôu lâi kō ; i chèu k'i în.**

2. P'àn houán èul iôu i, iōu iôu èul hiōu i. K'ài ti kiūn tzèu, pèi èul mî èul sing, sèu siēn kōung ts'iôu i.

3. Eùl t'òu iù p'àn tchāng, î k'òung tchī heòu (hòu) i. K'ài ti kiūn tzèu, pèi èul mî èul sing, pě chênn èul tchòu i.

CHANT VIII. K'IUEN NGO.

L'empereur 成王 **Tch'êng wâng** et 君奭 **kiūn Chĕu** le sage Cheu, prince de Chao, se promenant ensemble, entrèrent dans un enfoncement sur le versant d'une colline. Là, l'empereur ayant chanté, le sage ministre lui répondit par les strophes suivantes. Il souhaite à son maître une félicité parfaite, et lui recommande de choisir des officiers vertueux. Ils sont semblables au phénix, dit-il ; pour les attirer et les garder, il faut les traiter comme il convient.

1. Dans cet enfoncement sur le versant de la colline le vent souffle du midi. Notre prince aimable et bon est venu se promener et chanter. Je profite de cette occasion pour lui faire entendre les sons de ma voix.

2. Pour charmer vos loisirs vous vous promenez ; vous vous délassez par une agréable promenade. Prince aimable et bon, fasse le ciel que vous accomplissiez toutes vos années, et que vous finissiez comme les princes vos pères !

3. Votre territoire est grand, renommé, et n'a rien à craindre. Prince aimable et bon, fasse le ciel que vous accomplissiez toutes vos années, et que tous les esprits attendent sans cesse de vous

CHANT VIII. 1. Est sinuosus collis, flat ventus ex meridie. Festivus et benignus rex venit spatiatum, venit cantatum. Utens (hac occasione) expromam hos sonos.

2. Otia delectans tu spatiaris ; commode spatians tu quiescis. Festivus et benignus rex (quum sis, cœlum) faciat ut tu expleas tuam vitam, sicut progenitores reges finiverunt !

性 **Sing** signifie 命 **ming** la vie, toutes les années que le ciel a résolu d'accorder.

3. Tui territorii spatium est magnum et illustre, etiam valde firmum, i.e. tutum. Festivus et bonus rex

爾性、百神爾主矣、
(4) 爾受命長矣、茀祿爾康矣、豈弟君子、俾爾彌爾性、純嘏爾常矣、
(5) 有馮有翼、有孝有德、以引以翼、豈弟君子、四方爲則、
(6) 顒顒卬卬、如圭如璋、令聞令望、豈弟君子、四方爲綱、
(7) 鳳凰于飛、翽翽

4. Eùl cheóu ming tch'âng i, fŏu lŏu èul k'āng i. K'ài ti kiūn tzèu, pèi èul mi èul sing, chouènn kià èul châng i.

5. Iòu p'îng iòu ĭ, iòu hiaó iòu tĕ, i in i ĭ. K'ài ti kiūn tzèu, séu fāng wêi tsĕ.

6. Iôung iôung ngâng ngâng, jôu kouēi jôu tchāng, ling wénn ling wáng (wâng). K'ài ti kiūn tzèu, séu fāng wêi kāng.

7. Fóung houâng iû fēi, houéi houéi k'ĭ iù, ĭ tsĭ iuên tchéu. Ngái ngái wâng touŏ kĭ

(comme de leur principal sacrificateur) les honneurs qui leur sont dus!

4. Vous avez reçu le mandat du ciel (l'empire) depuis longtemps; vous jouissez en paix de votre félicité et de vos richesses. Prince aimable et bon, fasse le ciel que vous accomplissiez toutes vos années, et jouissiez sans cesse d'un bonheur sans mélange!

5. Ayez des soutiens, ayez des aides; ayez des officiers d'une grande piété filiale, d'une vertu insigne, qui vous aident de leurs conseils et de leurs soins. Prince aimable et bon, vous serez le modèle de tout l'empire.

6. Que votre maintien soit grave et majestueux, (et votre vertu pure) comme le jade. Que votre renommée soit bonne et votre extérieur distingué. Prince aimable et bon, vous serez la loi vivante de tout l'empire.

7. Lorsque les deux phénix volent, on entend le bruit de leurs

(quum sis, cœlum) faciat ut tu expleas tuam vitam, et omnes spiritus tibi innitantur, i.e. meritos honores a te maxime expectent!

4. A te acceptum mandatum fuit diuturnum; felicitas, opes tibi tranquillæ sunt. Festivus et bonus rex (quum sis, cœlum) faciat ut tu expleas tuam vitam, et pura felicitas tibi sit continua!

5. Habeas sustentacula, habeas adjutores, habeas pios in parentes viros, habeas probos, ut ducant, ut adjuvent. Festivus et bonus rex, quatuor regionum eris exemplar.

6. Sis habitu magnificus et gravis; (virtus tua sit pura) sicut *kouēi* iaspis, sicut *tchāng* iaspis; bona sit fama, bonus aspectus. Festivus et bonus rex, quatuor regionum eris lex.

7. Phœnix mas et phœnix femina dum volant, strepunt eorum alæ; etiam

其羽、亦集爰止、藹藹王多吉士、維君子使、媚于天子、
(8) 鳳凰于飛、翽翽其羽、亦傅于天、藹藹王多吉人、維君子命、媚于庶人、
(9) 鳳凰鳴矣、于彼高岡、梧桐生矣、于彼朝陽、菶菶萋萋、雝雝喈喈、
(10) 君子之車、既庶且多、君子之馬、既

chèu, wêi kiūn tzèu chèu, méi iû T'iēn tzèu.

8. Fóung houâng iû fēi, houéi houéi k'i iù, ī fóu iû t'iēn (t'īn). Ngái ngái wâng touō kí jènn, wêi kiūn tzèu míng (mîn), méi iû chóu jènn.

9. Fóung houâng mîng i, iû pèi kaō kāng, ôu t'ôung chēng i. Iû pèi tchaō iâng, pòung pòung ts'ī ts'ī, iōung iōung kiāi kiāi (kī kī).

10. Kiūn tzèu tchēu kiū, kí chóu ts'iè touō. Kiūn tzèu tchēu mà, kí hiên ts'iè tch'èu (t'ouô). Chéu chēu pòu touō, wêi i souéi kō.

ailes ; ils vont se reposer dans le lieu qui leur convient. Ayez un très grand nombre d'officiers vertueux ; soyez le seul à les diriger, et ils vous aimeront, Fils du ciel.

8. Lorsque les deux phénix volent, on entend le bruit de leurs ailes ; ils s'élèvent jusqu'au ciel. Ayez un très grand nombre d'officiers vertueux ; soyez le seul à les mettre en charge, et ils aimeront tous vos sujets.

9. Les deux phénix chantent au sommet de la montagne ; l'éléococca croît verdoyant et touffu sur le versant oriental. Les phénix chantent ensemble d'une voix mélodieuse.

10. Prince, (vous pouvez traiter avec honneur beaucoup de sages officiers ; car) vous avez des voitures en grand nombre, et des

insidunt in sua statione. Ingenti numero sint regi multi probi ministri ; solus rex adhibeat (eos), amabunt Cœli filium.

8. Phœnix mas et phœnix femina dum volant, strepunt eorum alæ ; etiam perveniunt ad cœlum. Ingenti numero sint regi multi probi ministri ; solus rex constituat (eos), amabunt cunctos homines.

9. Phœnix mas et phœnix femina cantant in illo alto jugo ; elæococca crescit in illo orientali clivo, luxurians et viridans. Consona et canora voce (cantant).

Le sommet de la montagne désigne la cour impériale. Le phénix ne se repose que sur l'éléococca. De même le sage ne demeure à la cour d'un prince que s'il y est traité comme il convient. 朝陽 **Tchaō iâng**, soleil du matin, celui des côtés d'une montagne qui voit le soleil le matin.

10. Regis currus sunt multi et numerosi ; regis equi sunt exercitati et celeres. Exprompsi versus non multos, solummodo ut succedens cantarem.

閑且馳、矢詩不多、維以遂歌、

民勞

(1)民亦勞止、汔可小康、惠此中國、以綏四方、無縱詭隨、以謹無良、式遏寇虐、憯不畏明、柔遠能邇、以定我王、

(2)民亦勞止、汔可小休、惠此中國、以爲民逑、無

MIN LAO. 1. **Min ì laô tchéu, hì k'ò siaò k'āng. Houéi ts'èu tchōung kouŏ, i souēi séu fāng. Où tsóung kouèi souêi, i kìn ôu leâng. Chĕu ngŏ k'eóu iŏ, ts'àn pŏu wéi mîng (mâng). Jeôu iuèn uêng èul, i tìng ngò wâng.**

2. Min ì laô tchéu, hì k'ò siaò hiōu. Houéi ts'èu tchōung kouŏ, i wêi min

chevaux bien exercés et très rapides. J'ai composé ces quelques vers uniquement pour répondre à votre chant.

CHANT IX. MIN LAO.

Sous l'empereur 厲王 **Lì wâng**, un ministre d'État engage l'un de ses collègues à combattre les flatteurs, qui oppriment le peuple et mettent le trouble dans la capitale.

1. Le peuple est accablé de maux, mais il pourrait être un peu soulagé. Faites du bien à cette capitale, et vous procurerez la paix à tout l'empire. Ne laissez pas toute liberté aux flatteurs astucieux, et les méchants se tiendront sur leurs gardes. Réprimez les spoliateurs, les oppresseurs, qui ne craignent pas de résister aux volontés manifestes du ciel. Traitez avec bonté les étrangers, policez les habitants du pays; vous affermirez la puissance de notre prince (Li wang).

2. Le peuple est accablé de souffrances, mais il pourrait avoir un peu de tranquillité. Faites du bien à cette capitale, afin de rétablir l'union parmi le peuple. Ne laissez pas toute liberté aux

CHANT IX. 1. Populus quidem gravatur, forsan potest paululum relevari. Benefac huic mediæ metropoli, ut tranquilles quatuor regiones. Ne indulgeas dolosis assentatoribus, ut cautos facias improbos. Fac cohibeas spoliatores, oppressores, hucusque non verentes clarum (cœli numen). Foveas longinquos, excolas propinquos, ut firmes nostrum regem.

止 **Tchèu**, particule. 中國京師也 *Tchoung kouo*, la capitale de l'empire. 憯 **Ts'àn**, employé pour 曾 **ts'êng**, marque du passé. 明天之明命也 *Ming*, ordre ou volonté manifeste du ciel. 能順習也 *Nêng*, exercer et rendre docile.

2. Populus quidem gravatur, forsan potest paululum pace frui. Benefac huic mediæ metropoli, ut fiat civium (animorum) conjunctio. Ne indulgeas dolosis assentatoribus, ut cautos facias

縱詭隨、以謹惛怓、
式遏寇虐、無俾民
憂、無棄爾勞、以爲
王休、
(3) 民亦勞止、汔可
小息、惠此京師、以
綏四國、無縱詭隨、
以謹罔極、式遏寇
虐、無俾作慝、敬慎
威儀、以近有德、
(4) 民亦勞止、汔可
小愒、惠此中國、俾
民憂泄、無縱詭隨、

k'iôu. Où tsóung kouèi souêi, i kin houênn naô (neôu). Chĕu ngŏ k'eóu iŏ, ôu pèi mîn iôu. Oû k'i èul laô, i wêi wâng hiōu.

3. Mîn ĭ laô tchèu, hĭ k'ò siaò sĭ. Houéi ts'èu kīng chēu, i souēi séu kouŏ (ĭ). Oû tsóung kouèi souêi, i kìn wàng kĭ. Chĕu ngŏ k'eóu iŏ, ôu pèi tsŏ t'ĕ. King chénn wêi î, i kín iòu tĕ.

4. Mîn ĭ laô tchèu, hĭ k'ò siaò k'i. Houéi ts'èu tchōung kouŏ, pèi mîn iōu í.

flatteurs astucieux, et les criards turbulents se tiendront sur leurs gardes. Réprimez les spoliateurs, les oppresseurs, afin qu'ils cessent d'affliger le peuple. Ne renoncez pas à servir votre pays ; vous assurerez le bonheur du prince.

3. Le peuple est accablé de maux, mais il pourrait avoir un peu de repos. Faites du bien à cette capitale, afin de procurer la tranquillité à tous les peuples de l'empire. Ne laissez pas toute liberté aux flatteurs astucieux, et vous rendrez circonspects ceux qui ne connaissent aucune limite. Réprimez les spoliateurs, les oppresseurs ; empêchez-les d'étendre leurs vexations. Ayez soin d'avoir un extérieur grave et des manières bienséantes, afin d'attirer les hommes de bien.

4. Le peuple est accablé sous un pesant fardeau, mais il pourrait être un peu soulagé. Faites du bien à cette capitale, pour dissiper la douleur du peuple. Ne laissez pas toute liberté aux flatteurs artificieux, et les vilains malfaiteurs se tiendront sur leurs gardes.

turbulentos clamatores. Fac coerceas spoliatores, oppressores, ne faciant ut populus mœreat. Ne abjicias tuos labores (præteritos), ut fiat regi felicitas.

3. Populus quidem gravatur, forsan potest paululum quiescere. Benefac huic urbi præcipuæ, ut tranquilles omnia regna. Ne indulgeas dolosis assentatoribus, ut cautos facias homines carentes limite. Fac inhibeas spoliatores, oppressores ; ne sinas ut excitent mala. Diligenter attendas gravitati et decentiæ, ut allicias præditos virtute.

4. Populus quidem gravatur, forsan potest paululum onere levari. Benefac huic mediæ metropoli, ut populi mœror solvatur. Ne indulgeas dolosis assentatoribus, ut cautos facias deformes et

以謹醜厲、式遏
寇虐、無俾正敗、
戎雖小子、而式
弘大、
(5) 民亦勞止、汔
可小安、惠此中
國、國無有殘、無
縱詭隨、以謹繾
綣、式遏寇虐、無
俾正反、王欲玉
女、是用大諫、
板
(1) 上帝板板、下

Où tsóung kouéi souêi, i kìn tch'eòu lí. Chĕu ngŏ k'eóu iŏ, ôu pèi tchéng pái (pi). Jôung souēi siaò tzèu, êul chĕu hôung tá (ti).

5. Mîn ĭ laô tchèu, hî k'ò siaò ngān. Houéi ts'èu tchōung kouŏ, kouŏ ôu iòu ts'ân. Oû tsóung kouèi souêi, i kìn k'ièn k'iuèn. Chĕu ngŏ k'eóu iŏ, ôu péi tchéng fàn. Wâng iŭ iŭ jôu, chéu ióung tá kièn.

PAN. **1. Cháng tí pàn pàn, hiá mîn tsŏu tàn. Tch'ŏu houá pŏu jên, wêi iôu pŏu**

Réprimez les spoliateurs, les oppresseurs; ne permettez pas que la voie du devoir soit méconnue. Quelle que soit votre faiblesse, vous devez accomplir de grandes choses.

5. Le peuple est accablé de maux, mais il pourrait avoir un peu de repos. Faites du bien à cette capitale, et le salut de tous les États sera assuré. Ne laissez pas toute liberté aux flatteurs artificieux, et les favoris du prince se tiendront sur leurs gardes. Réprimez les spoliateurs, les oppresseurs, pour que les vrais principes ne soient pas renversés. Le prince désire vous aimer et vous traiter avec honneur comme une pierre précieuse; voilà pourquoi je vous avertis sérieusement.

CHANT X. PAN.

Dans un temps de troubles, un officier ami du devoir rappelle à l'un de ses collègues qu'il faut craindre la colère du ciel.

1. Le roi du ciel a changé de conduite, (il est irrité et) les hommes ici-bas sont accablés de maux. Vos paroles ne sont pas

improbos. Fac coerceas spoliatores, oppressores; ne sinas ut recta via corrumpatur. Tu quamvis (debilis sis ut) junior puer, tamen adhibeberis ad valde magna.

5. Populus quidem gravatur, forsan potest paululum recreari. Benefac huic mediæ metropoli; regna non habebunt grave damnum. Ne indulgeas dolosis assentatoribus, ut cautos facias (homines regi) arcte adhærentes. Fac cohibeas spoliatores, oppressores; ne sinas ut recta via subvertatur. Rex vult gemmæ instar habere te; quapropter magnopere moneo te.

CHANT X. 1. Cœli rex plane mutatus est; inferi homines omnino laborant. (A te) prolata verba non sunt recta;

民卒癉、出話不然、爲猶不遠、靡聖管管、不實於亶、猶之未遠、是用大諫、

(2) 天之方難、無然憲憲、天之方蹶、無然泄泄、辭之輯矣、民之洽矣、辭之懌矣、民之莫矣、

(3) 我雖異事、及爾同僚、我即爾謀、聽我囂囂、我言維服、勿以爲笑、先民有言、詢于芻蕘、

iuèn. Mi chéng kouàn kouàn, pŏu chĕu iū tàn. Iôu tchēu wéi iuèn, chéu ióung tá kièn.

2. T'iēn tchēu fāng nân (gnièn), ôu jên hién hién (hiên hiên). T'iēn tchēu fāng kouéi, ôu jên i i. Sêu tchēu tsĭ (tsŏ) i, mîn tchēu hiă i. Sêu tchēu ĭ (iŏ) i, mîn tchēu mouŏ i.

3. Ngò souēi i chéu, kĭ èul t'ôung leaô. Ngò tsĭ èul meôu, t'īng ngò hiaō hiaō. Ngò iên wêi fŏu, ŏu i wéi siaó (siaō). Siēn mîn iòu iên: « Siūn iū tch'ôu jaô. »

conformes à la vérité; vos vues ne s'étendent pas loin. « Il n'y a pas de grand sage, (pensez-vous), tout appui fait défaut, (je ne puis pratiquer la vertu). » Vous n'êtes pas vraiment sincère. Vos vues ne s'étendent pas loin; voilà pourquoi je vous avertis sérieusement.

2. A présent le ciel envoie des afflictions; ne soyez pas si satisfait. A présent le ciel ébranle la terre; ne soyez pas si peu soucieux. Si vos paroles étaient conformes (à la droite raison et aux sentiments du peuple), l'union se rétablirait parmi le peuple. Si vos paroles étaient pleines de douceur, le peuple deviendrait tranquille.

3. Bien que ma charge soit différente de la vôtre, je suis votre collègue. Quand je viens pour délibérer avec vous, vous m'écoutez avec suffisance. Je ne vous parle que d'affaires urgentes; ne vous moquez pas de ce que je dis. Les anciens répétaient souvent: « Prenez conseil même des villageois dont le métier est de ramasser de l'herbe ou du bois pour le chauffage. »

statuta consilia non longe attingunt. In animo dicis): « Deficiente sapientissimo viro, deficit basis. » Non est res in sinceritate (tua). Cogitata non longe attingunt; quapropter magnopere moneo.

管管無所依也 *Kouàn kouàn*, tout appui fait défaut.

2. Cœlum nunc ærumnis premit; noli ita gaudere. Cœlum nunc commovet; noli ita esse incuriosus. (Si tua) verba concordabunt (cum recta ratione et populi sensu), populus unietur. (Si tua) verba erunt lenia, populus tranquillabitur.

3. Mihi licet alia negotia (curanda), cum te socior collega. Quando convenio te deliberatum, audis me tibi confidens. Mea verba unice sunt de negotiis (urgentibus); ne habeas ludibrio. Antiqui homines habebant adagium: « Inquire ab iis qui herbam et ramalia colligunt. »

(4) 天之方虐、無然謔謔、老夫灌灌、小子蹻蹻、匪我言耄、爾用憂謔、多將熇熇、不可救藥、

(5) 天之方懠、無爲夸毗、威儀卒迷、善人載尸、民之方殿屎、則莫我敢葵、喪亂蔑資、曾莫惠我師、

(6) 天之牖民、如壎如篪、如璋如圭、如

3. T'iēn tchēu fāng iŏ, òu jên hiŏ hiŏ. Laò fōu kouán kouán, siaò tzèu kiŏ kiŏ. Fèi ngò iên maó (mouŏ), èul ióung iōu hiŏ. Touō tsiāng hŏu hŏu (hŏ hŏ), pòu k'ó kióu iŏ.

5. T'iēn tchēu fāng tsi (tsī), òu wêi k'ouā p'î. Wēi î tsŏu mî, chén jênn tsái chēu. Mîn tchēu fāng tién hī, tsĕ mouŏ ngò kàn k'ouêi. Sáng louán miĕ tzēu, ts'êng mouŏ houéi ngò chēu.

6. T'iēn tchēu iòu mîn, jŏu hiuēn jŏu tch'êu, jŏu tchāng jŏu kouēi, jŏu ts'iŭ

4. A présent le ciel sévit; ne vous moquez pas de ses fléaux. Moi qui suis plus âgé que vous, je parle sincèrement; vous qui êtes plus jeune, vous êtes plein d'orgueil (et méprisez mes avis). Ce n'est pas que mon langage soit celui d'un vieillard qui déraisonne; mais vous riez de nos maux. Le trouble croissant toujours deviendra comme un grand incendie, et sera sans remède.

5. A présent le ciel fait éclater son courroux; ne soyez ni vantard ni flatteur. On ne verrait plus dans votre conduite ni gravité ni bienséance; les hommes de bien deviendraient semblables aux représentants des mânes (qui mangent et boivent, mais ne font rien). A présent le peuple soupire et gémit; aucun de nous n'ose seulement examiner (les causes du mal). Il n'y a partout que ruines, troubles, destructions, gémissements; jusqu'ici personne ne console notre peuple.

6. Le ciel éclaire l'intelligence de l'homme aussi facilement que la flûte de bambou accompagne le sifflet d'argile, que deux *tchang*

4. Cœlum nunc sævit; noli ita irridens negligere. Senior ego sincera fide (loquor); junior tu attollis pedes, i. e. superbus es. Non quod mea verba sint senis (delirantis); tu habes ærumnas ludibrio. Si crescant (mala), fiet quasi incendium, nec poterunt depelli remedio.

5. Cœlum nunc iratum est; ne sis jactator, adulator. (Morum tuorum) gravitas ac decentia omnino turbarentur; probi viri tunc fierent manium vicarii. Populus nunc gemens suspirat; et non nos audemus perpendere (malorum causas). Excidium, turbatio, deletio, suspiria (sunt continua); adhuc nemo solatur nostrum numerosum populum.

6. Cœlum illustrat hominis mentem (facillime), ut testaceum sibilum

取如攜、攜無曰益、牖民孔易、民之多辟、無自立辟、

(7) 价人維藩、大師維垣、大邦維屏、大宗維翰、懷德維寧、宗子維城、無俾城壞、無獨斯畏、

(8) 敬天之怒、無敢戲豫、敬天之渝、無敢馳驅、昊

jôu hi. Hi ôu iuĕ ĭ. Iòu mîn k'òung i (ĭ). Mîn tchēu touō p'ĭ, ôu tzéu lĭ p'ĭ.

7. Kiái jênn wêi fân, tá chēu wêi iuên. Tá pāng wêi p'îng, tá tsōung wêi hân (hiên). Houâi tĕ wêi gnîng, tsōung tzèu wêi tch'êng. Oû pèi tch'êng houái (houéi), ôu tŏu sēu wéi.

8. King t'iēn tchēu nóu, ôu kàn hi iú. King t'iēn tchēu iû, ôu kàn tch'êu k'iū.

font un *kouei,* et que l'acceptation suit la demande ; il suffit de recevoir. Il est très facile d'éclairer l'intelligence de l'homme (et de le porter au bien. Mais il est également aisé de le porter au mal). Les hommes ont beaucoup de vices ; n'allez pas vous-même étaler vos vices à leurs yeux.

7. Les hommes d'une grande vertu sont comme la haie (de l'empire) ; la multitude du peuple en est le mur. Les grandes principautés sont comme la cloison élevée devant la porte ; les grandes familles sont les colonnes. L'amour de la vertu assure la tranquillité ; les princes du sang sont les remparts. Ne renversez pas les remparts ; ne vous condamnez pas à la solitude, à des craintes continuelles.

8. Craignez la colère du ciel, ne vous abandonnez pas à la dissipation ni à l'oisiveté. Craignez les dispositions changeantes du

(præcinit), ut arundinea tibia (concinit), ut *tchang* tabella ut *kouei* tabella (conveniunt), ut rogatio ut acceptio ; acceptioni nihil est addendum. Illustrare mentem hominis valde facile est. Hominum multa sunt vitia; noli ipse proponere vitia.

Si l'on divise un 圭 en deux parties égales dans le sens de la longueur, on obtient deux 璋 symétriques. En rapprochant ces deux moitiés l'une de l'autre, on reconstruit le 圭 complet.

7. Optimi viri sunt sepes (imperii), magna multitudo (populi) est murus. Magna regna sunt occulens januam paries, magnæ familiæ sunt postes. Exculta virtus est pax, (regiæ) familiæ filii sunt mœnia. Ne facias ut mœnia labantur; ne sis solus adeoque timens.

8. Verearis cœli iram, ne audeas ludere et otiari. Verearis cœli (animi) mutationem, ne audeas præceps ruere (in vitia). Augustum cœlum est vigilans; attingit te exeuntem ac incedentem. Augustum cœlum est perspicax ; attingit te vagantem ac licenter agentem.

« Rien n'échappe au regard ni à la justice terrible du ciel. Bien que cet auguste ciel soit très haut, il prend

天曰明。及爾出王。昊天曰旦。及爾游衍。

蕩之什三之三

蕩

(1) 蕩蕩上帝。下民之辟。疾威上帝。其命

Haò t'iēn iuĕ mîng (mâng), kĭ èul tch'ŏu wàng (wàng). Haò t'iēn iuĕ tán, kĭ èul iôu ién (ién).

TANG. **1. Tàng tàng cháng ti, hiá mîn tchēu pí. Tsĭ wēi cháng ti, k'i ming**

ciel; prenez garde de vous précipiter dans le désordre. L'auguste ciel est vigilant, son œil vous suit partout où vous allez. L'auguste ciel est clairvoyant; il est témoin de vos déréglements et de votre conduite licencieuse.

LIVRE III. TANG.

CHANT I. TANG.

Le poète représente à 厲王 **Li wâng** le péril auquel l'expose sa conduite licencieuse. Il met en scène 文王 **Wênn wâng** donnant des avis à 紂 **Tcheòu**, dernier souverain de la dynastie des 殷 **In** ou 商 **Chāng**.

1. Le roi du ciel dans son immensité étend son pouvoir sur tous les peuples de la terre. (A présent) il déploie une grande sévérité; aux dons naturels qu'il départit se mêlent beaucoup de vices. C'est

soin des choses d'ici-bas, et sa grande clairvoyance est redoutable. Quand vous allez et venez, il vous voit certainement. Bien que l'auguste ciel soit éloigné, il observe, il voit, et sa perspicacité est très grande. Vos courses, vos déréglements lui sont certainement connues. En quelque lieu que vous ailliez, vous n'échapperez pas à son regard perspicace. Ainsi certainement il faut le craindre. » (詩經備旨).

TITRE DU LIVRE. 蕩之什三之三 **Tang decas**: tertiæ (partis) tertia (decas). Ce livre contient onze chants, au lieu de dix.

CHANT I. **1.** Immensus est cœli rex, inferorum hominum rector. Vehementer sævus (factus est) cœli rex; ab eo inditæ naturæ sunt multa vitia. Cœlum creat universos homines; ab eo inditæ naturæ non est fidendum. Nemo non habet initium (bonum); pauci possunt habere finem (bonum).

« Le poète blâme Li wang qui court à sa perte. Les troubles de l'empire, dit-il, n'ont pas surgi d'eux-mêmes; certainement ils ont été amenés par une cause. Ce souverain seigneur dans son immensité embrasse le monde entier; il est le roi des peuples de la terre. Puisqu'il est roi et gouverne les peuples, il doit donner aux hommes un bon naturel. A présent, ce souverain seigneur, devenu sévère, leur donne beaucoup d'inclinations vicieuses. Où est donc le soin qu'il prend des peuples de la terre en sa qualité de roi? La nature que le ciel donne aux hommes, est par elle-même toujours bonne, et nullement mauvaise. A présent, s'ils ont beaucoup d'inclinations dépravées auxquelles on ne peut se fier, viennent-elles originai-

多辟、天生烝民、其命匪諶、靡不有初、鮮克有終、

(2) 文王曰咨、咨女殷商、曾是彊禦、曾是掊克、曾是在位、曾是在服、天降滔德、女興是力、

(3) 文王曰咨、咨女殷商、而

touō p'ĭ. T'iēn chēng tchēng mîn, k'î ming fèi chênn. Mi pŏu iòu tch'ōu, siên k'ŏ iòu tchōung (tchênn).

2. Wênn wâng iuĕ : «Tzēu! Tzēu! jòu Īn Chāng! Ts'êng chéu k'iâng iú! ts'êng chéu p'eòu k'ŏ! Ts'êng chéu tsái wéi! ts'êng chéu tsái fŏu (p'ĕ)! T'iēn kiáng t'aō tĕ, jòu hīng chéu lĭ!»

3. Wênn wâng iuĕ : «Tzēu! Tzēu! jòu Īn Chāng! Eùl ˈping i lĕi. K'iáng iú

le ciel qui donne l'être à tous les hommes; mais personne ne doit se tenir assuré de conserver les qualités naturelles qu'il a reçues de lui. Tout homme naît bon; mais peu le demeurent jusqu'à la mort.

2. Wenn wang dit: «Hélas! Malheur à toi, In-Chang! Encore ces oppresseurs violents! Encore ces exacteurs impitoyables! Encore ces dignitaires! Encore ces officiers! Le ciel produit des insolents (pour nous punir); toi, en les élevant aux charges, tu les rends puissants!»

3. Wenn wang dit: «Hélas! Malheur à toi, In-Chang! Tu devrais employer des hommes vertueux. (Au contraire), des oppres-

rement de la nature? Au moment où les hommes reçoivent l'existence, la nature est également bonne en chacun; elle n'est jamais mauvaise par elle-même. Mais après qu'il ont commencé d'exister, leurs facultés se dépravent en s'attachant à différents objets. Par suite, ils commettent des excès et des désordres, violent la loi naturelle, perdent les belles qualités qu'ils ont reçues de la nature; peu parviennent à suivre la voie de la vertu jusqu'à la fin. Si ces troubles violents sont survenus, s'il semble que le ciel donne beaucoup de penchants vicieux, les hommes en sont la cause. Est-il permis d'en attribuer la faute au ciel? Ce n'est pas le souverain seigneur qui fait ces temps mauvais; mais c'est vous, In, qui avez attiré ces malheurs, en rejetant les anciens ministres et les anciennes lois des empereurs vos ancêtres. Serait-il juste d'accuser le souverain seigneur, parce que les temps sont mauvais?» (詩經備旨).

2. Wenn rex dixit: «Hei! Hei tibi, In Chang! Adhuc isti violenti oppressores! adhuc isti extorquentes exactores! Adhuc isti occupant dignitates! adhuc isti præsunt rebus! Cœlum immittit protervis moribus (homines); tu promovens vere addis vires!»

3. Wenn rex dixit: «Hei! Hei tibi, In Chang! Tu (debes) adhibere probum genus (virorum). Violenti oppressores multum odiosi, qui fluctuantibus verbis utentes respondent, spoliatores

秉義類、彊禦多懟、流言以對、寇攘式內、侯作侯祝、靡屆靡究、

(4) 文王曰咨、咨女殷商、女炰烋于中國、斂怨以爲德、不明爾德、時無背無側、爾德不明、以無陪無卿、

(5) 文王曰咨、咨女殷商、天不湎爾以酒、不義從式、既愆

touō touéi. Liôu iên i touéi, k'eóu jâng chĕu néi. Heôu tchóu heôu tcheóu, mi kiái mi kióu.»

4. Wênn wâng iuĕ : « Tzēu ! Tzēu ! jòu Īn Chāng ! Jòu p'aô hiaō iû tchōung kouŏ (1), lién iuén i wèi tĕ. Pŏu mîng èul tĕ, chêu ôu péi ôu tchĕ. Eùl tĕ pŏu mîng, i ôu p'êi ôu k'īng.»

5. Wênn wâng iuĕ : « Tzēu ! Tzēu ! jòu Īn Chāng ! T'iēn pŏu mièn èul i tsiòu,

seurs cruels qui excitent beaucoup de mécontentement, qui répondent (à tes questions) par des paroles sans fondement, des spoliateurs, des voleurs occupent les charges à ta cour. De là viennent des imprécations, des malédictions sans fin. »

4. Wenn wang dit: « Hélas! Malheur à toi, In-Chang! Tu te montres violent et cruel dans l'empire; tu crois que multiplier les actes odieux c'est pratiquer la vertu. Ta vertu n'est pas éclairée; aussi, ni derrière toi ni à tes côtés, tu n'as d'officiers (vraiment dignes de ce nom). Ta vertu n'est pas éclairée; aussi tu n'as ni assesseurs ni ministres d'État (qui remplissent leurs devoirs).»

5. Wenn wang dit: « Hélas! Malheur à toi, In-Chang! Ce n'est pas le ciel qui te pousse à te plonger dans l'ivresse, jusqu'à ce que tu aies le visage tout rouge, ni à prendre des hommes iniques pour guides

et raptores adhibentur intus, i.e. in aula regia. Inde imprecationes, inde exsecrationes, sine limite sine fine. »

4. Wenn rex dixit: « Hei! Hei tibi, In Chang! Tu violentum et ferum te præbes in medio regno, i.e. in Sinarum imperio; acervare odiosa ducis exercere virtutem. Caret ratione tua virtus; ideo non habes sequaces nec assistentes (qui muneribus vere fungantur). Tua virtus caret ratione; ideo desunt assessores, desunt regni ministri (utiles). »

陪 **P'êi**, les 三公 **sān kōung** trois grands assesseurs. 卿 **K'īng**, les ministres d'État au nombre de six.

5. Wenn rex dixit: « Hei! Hei tibi, In Chang! Cælum non vultum rubore suffundit tibi (i.e. non facit ut faciem rubore suffundas tibi) per vinum, ut carentes æquitate sequaris ac adhibeas. Postquam deturpasti tuum habitum, (bibere non desinis), nec diem nec noctem discernens). Et clamas et vociferaris; facis ut dies evadat nox. »

爾止、靡明靡晦、式號式呼、俾晝作夜、

(6) 文王曰咨、咨女殷商、如蜩如螗、如沸如羹、小大近喪、人尚乎由行、內奰于中國、覃及鬼方、

(7) 文王曰咨、咨女殷商、匪上帝不時、殷不用舊、雖無老成人、尚

pŏu i ts'ôung chĕu (chéu). Ki k'iĕn èul tchéu, mi mîng mi houéi (houéi). Chĕu haó chĕu hóu, pèi tcheóu tsŏ ié (iú).»

6. Wênn wâng iuĕ : « Tzēu ! Tzēu ! jòu Īn Chāng ! Jôu t'iaô jôu t'âng, jôu féi jôu kēng (lâng). Siaò tá kin sáng (sāng) ; jènn cháng hôu iôu hîng (hâng). Néi pi iū tchōung kouŏ, t'ân kī Kouéi fāng.»

7. Wênn wâng iuĕ : « Tzēu ! Tzēu ! jòu Īn Chāng ! Fèi cháng ti pŏu chéu (chéu),

et pour ministres. Oubliant toute bienséance, (tu bois) jour et nuit. Tu pousses des cris, des clameurs, et fais du jour la nuit. »

6. Wenn wang dit : « Hélas ! Malheur à toi, In-Chang ! (Les esprits sont tellement agités que le peuple est) comme une troupe de cigales (qui crient toutes ensemble), comme une eau qui bout à gros bouillons. Toutes choses, grandes ou petites, sont sur le point de périr ; et cependant, toi et tes officiers, vous marchez toujours dans la même voie. L'indignation soulevée dans tout l'empire s'étend jusqu'à Kouei fang (jusqu'aux contrées étrangères les plus éloignées). »

7. Wenn wang dit : « Hélas ! Malheur à toi, In-Chang ! Ce n'est pas le roi du ciel qui a rendu les temps mauvais ; mais toi, In, en rejetant les anciens (ministres et les anciennes lois). Quand même tu n'aurais plus d'hommes âgés et expérimentés, tu as encore les

6. Wenn rex dixit : « Hei ! Hei tibi, In Chang ! (Populus turbatis animis est) sicut *t'iaô* cicadæ sicut *t'âng* cicadæ (confuse clamantes), sicut ebulliens (aqua), sicut jusculum (ebulliens). Parva magnaque proximant excidio ; homines insistentes (eidem pravæ viæ) progrediuntur. Intus indignatio est in medio imperio, profertur ad Kouei regionem. »

鬼方 Nom d'un pays très éloigné dont il est fait mention dans le I king. 高宗伐鬼方 (易既濟) Kao tsoung (1324-1265) attaqua le pays des Kouei. Quelques auteurs disent que ce pays était dans le Hou kouang, que son nom lui venait de ce que les esprits s'y manifestaient souvent.

7. Wenn rex dixit : « Hei ! Hei tibi, In Chang ! Non cœli rex mala fecit tempora : In non utitur antiquis (legibus ac ministris). Licet non habeas senes ac peritos viros, adhuc habes instituta et leges. Hucusque illis (viris ac legibus) non obsequeris ; magnum mandatum inde inclinatur. »

有典刑、曾是莫聽、大命以傾、

(8) 文王曰咨、咨女殷商、人亦有言、顛沛之揭、枝葉未有害、本實先撥、殷鑒不遠、在夏后之世、

抑

(1) 抑抑威儀、維德之隅、人亦有言、靡哲不愚、庶人之愚、亦職維

Ĭn pŏu ióung kióu (ki). Souëi ôu laò tch'ĕng jènn, cháng iòu tièn hìng. Ts'ĕng chéu mouŏ t'īng, tá ming i k'īng.»

8. Wènn wâng iuĕ: « Tzēu! Tzēu! jòu Ĭn Chāng! Jènn ĭ iòu iên: Tiēn pèi tchēu kiĕ, tchēu iĕ wéi iòu hái (hĕ), pènn chĕu siēn pouŏ (piĕ). Ĭn kién pŏu iuèn, tsái Hiá heóu tchēu chéu (siĕ).

I. 1. Ĭ ĭ wēi i, wĕi tĕ tchēu iù. Jênn ĭ iòu iên: Mi tchĕ pŏu iû. Chóu jènn tchēu

institutions et les lois. Mais tu ne suis ni les lois ni les avis des sages ; aussi ton empire est sur son déclin. »

8. Wenn wang dit: «Hélas! Malheur à toi, In-Chang! Le proverbe dit: «Lorsqu'un arbre tombe et que ses racines sortent de terre, si les branches et les feuilles sont encore intactes, c'est que les racines ont été coupées (et détachées du sol). » In a un miroir (un exemple) peu ancien, qui date du temps (de Kie, dernier empereur de la dynastie) des Hia.

CHANT II. I.

Règles de conduite que 衛武公 Ou, prince de Wei, écrivit pour son usage, et se fit lire chaque jour jusqu'à l'âge de quatre-vingt-quinze ans. S'adressant la parole à lui-même, il se reproche ses fautes, et s'excite à bien remplir ses devoirs.

1. Une gravité constante, un soin habituel de garder les bienséances sont les indices extérieurs de la vertu. On dit communément: «(A présent) il n'est pas de sage qui ne devienne insensé.» La folie des hommes vulgaires vient surtout de leurs défauts naturels.

8. Wenn rex dixit: «Hei! Hei tibi, In Chang! Homines habent adagium: «(Quum arbor) decidens attollit (radices extra humum), si rami et frondes nondum habent damnum, radices certe prius abruptæ sunt.» In speculum non remotum est; inest Hia regum tempore.»

La dynastie des In est tombée, sans qu'il y eût ni révolte des princes ni attaque de la part des étrangers. Les branches et les feuilles étaient donc intactes. Mais les empereurs de cette dynastie 爲不義以自絕于天 avaient eux-mêmes rompu avec le ciel par leurs injustices.

CHANT II. 1. Diligenter servatæ gravitas ac decentia sunt virtutis prominentes anguli, i. e. signa. Homines habent dictum: «Nullus est sapiens qui

詩經

疾、哲人之愚、亦維斯戾。

(2) 無競維人、四方其訓之、有覺德行、四國順之。訏謨定命、遠猶辰告、敬慎威儀、維民之則、

(3) 其在于今、興迷亂于政、顛覆厥德、荒湛于酒、女雖湛樂從、弗念厥紹、敷求先王、克共明刑、

iù, ĭ tchĕu wĕi tsĭ (tsi). Tchĕ jênn tchēu iù, ĭ wĕi sēu lì.

2. Où kīng wĕi jênn, séu fāng k'ì hiún tchēu. Iòu kiŏ tĕ hing, séu kouŏ chouénn tchēu. Hiū mouŏ ting míng, iuén iòu tch'ènn kaó (kĕ). King chénn wēi ì, wĕi mìn tchēu tsé.

3. K'ì tsái iū kīn (kīng), hīng mì louán iū tchéng (tchēng). Tiēn fŏu kiuĕ tĕ, houāng tān iū tsiòu (tsiaò). Jòu wĕi tān lŏ ts'ôung, fŏu gnién kiuĕ chaò. Wàng fŏu k'iôu siēn wâng, k'ŏ kòung míng hing (houâng).

Mais la folie de ceux qui sont (naturellement) sages résulte de la perte de leurs bonnes dispositions naturelles.

2. Nulle puissance n'est comparable à celle d'un homme vraiment homme; tout l'univers suit ses enseignements. Une vertu sublime attire à elle tous les peuples. Un prince dont les plans sont vastes, les décisions fixes, les institutions durables, les avis appropriés aux circonstances, la tenue et la conduite toujours graves et parfaites, un tel prince est le modèle du peuple.

3. Toi, à présent, tu aimes les ténèbres et la confusion dans les affaires publiques. Tu ruines entièrement tes bonnes dispositions naturelles, en te plongeant dans l'ivresse. Malgré cet amour effréné des plaisirs, ne penseras-tu pas enfin à l'héritage que tu as reçu de tes pères? N'étudieras-tu pas sérieusement les exemples des anciens princes, afin de suivre leurs sages lois?

non stultescat.» Vulgarium hominum stultitiæ præcipua causa est defectus (naturalis). Sapientium hominum stultitia est ipsius inversio, i. e. dotum naturalium depravatio.

2. Non est potens nisi vir (qui vere est vir perfectus); quatuor regiones ipsæ magistrum habent eum. Qui habet recta ac sublimia virtutis opera, omnia regna obsequuntur ei. (Vir cujus sunt) magna consilia, stabilia jussa, diuturna instituta, tempestiva monita, diligenter ac caute servatæ gravitas et decentia, est populi exemplar.

3. Ipse qui es in præsenti, præoptas caliginem et turbationem in publica administratione. Subvertis tuam virtutem, perdite immersus in vino. Tu licet immoderata oblectamenta secteris, nonne cogitabis de tua hæreditate? Nonne late investigabis (exempla) priorum regum, ut possis tenere clara instituta?

(4) 肆皇天弗尙、如彼泉流、無淪胥以亡。夙興夜寐、洒埽廷內、維民之章、脩爾車馬、弓矢戎兵、用戒戎作、用逷蠻方、

(5) 質爾人民、謹爾侯度、用戒不虞、愼爾出話、敬爾威儀、無不柔嘉、白圭之玷、尙可磨也、斯言之玷、不可爲也、

(6) 無易由言、無曰苟

4. Sóu houâng t'iēn fŏu cháng (châng), jŏu pèi ts'iuên liôu. Oû liûn siū i wàng, sōu hīng ié méi. Chài saò t'ing néi, wêi mîn tchēu tchāng. Siōu èul kiū mà, kōung chèu jôung pīng (pāng). Ióung kiái jôung tsŏ, ióung t'ī Mân fāng.

5. Tchĕu èul jênn mîn, kìn èul heóu tóu. Ióung kiái pŏu iû (iú), chénn èul tch'ŏu houá. King èul wēi î (ngô), ôu pŏu jeôu kiā (kō). Pĕ kouēi tchēu tièn, cháng k'ò mouô iè. Sēu iên tchēu tièn, pŏu k'ò wêi (wô) iè.

6. Oû i iôu iên, ôu iuĕ keòu i. Mouŏ mênn tchénn chĕ, iên pŏu k'ò chéu (chĕ) i.

4. L'auguste ciel n'est pas satisfait. Semblables à l'eau d'un torrent, ne courons-nous pas tous à notre perte? Lève-toi de bonne heure et couche-toi tard; arrose et balaie l'intérieur du palais, pour donner l'exemple du travail à ton peuple. Prépare tes chars, tes chevaux, tes arcs, tes flèches, tes autres armes, pour te défendre contre les attaques des ennemis, et repousser les hordes du midi.

5. Forme bien tes ministres et tes sujets, remplis avec soin tes devoirs de prince, pour te prémunir contre les dangers imprévus. Prends garde à tes paroles; que ton maintien soit grave et ta conduite bienséante; en toutes choses sois doux et distingué. Un défaut dans une tablette de jade blanc peut être corrigé; les écarts de la langue ne peuvent être réparés.

6. Ne parle pas à la légère. Ne dis pas: «(Cette chose n'a

4. Itaque augusto cœlo minime probante, sicut ille fons defluens, nonne devolvemur simul ut pereamus? Mature surge, sero cuba, asperge et verre aulæ interna, ut sis populi exemplar. Præpara tuos currus et equos, arcus, sagittas, militaria arma, ut præcaveas belli ortum, ut arceas australes gentes.

5. Perfice tuos ministros et populares, diligenter (obsequere) tuis reguli legibus, ut præcaveas inopinata. Attende tuis proferendis verbis, cura tuam gravitatem et decentiam, ne quid non sit lene et eximium. Albæ tabellæ nævus forsan potest expoliri; istorum verborum nævus non potest curari.

6. Ne leviter emittas verba; neque dicas: «Inconsiderate (hoc proferre licet).» Quum nemo contineat meam linguam, verba non decet ut elabantur

矣、莫捫朕舌、言不可逝矣、無言不讎、無德不報、惠于朋友、庶民小子、子孫繩繩、萬民靡不承、

(7) 視爾友君子、輯柔爾顏、不遐有愆、相在爾室、尚不愧于屋漏、無曰不顯、莫予云覯、神之格思、不可度思、矧可射思、

(8) 辟爾爲德、俾臧

Oû iên pŏu tch'eôu (tch'eôu), ôu tĕ pŏu paó (peóu). Houéi iû p'êng iòu (i), chóu mîn siaò tzèu (tsi). Tzèu suēnn chêng chêng, wán mîn mì pŏu tch'êng.

7. Chéu èul iòu kiūn tzèu, tsĭ jeôu èul iên. Pŏu hiâ iòu k'iēn, siáng tsái èul chĕu. Cháng pŏu kouéi iū ŏu leóu. Oû iuĕ : Pŏu hièn ; mouŏ iû iûn keóu. Chênn tchēu kŏ sēu, pŏu k'ó touŏ sēu ; chènn k'ò ĭ (iŏ) sēu.

8. Pí èul wêi tĕ, pèi tsāng pèi kiā (kŏ). Chŏu chénn èul tchéu, pŏu k'iĕn iû î

aucune importance, on peut en parler) sans y avoir beaucoup réfléchi.» Comme personne ne peut se charger de retenir ma langue pour moi, je dois veiller moi-même à ne laisser échapper aucune parole inconsidérée. Toute bonne parole reçoit sa récompense; toute bonne action est payée de retour. Sois bon envers tes ministres, et envers tes sujets qui sont tes enfants. Tes descendants se succéderont d'âge en âge, et personne ne refusera de leur obéir.

7. On te voit, dans tes relations avec les grands, prendre un air gracieux et doux, et avoir soin que tout en toi soit irréprochable. A la maison, il importe que tu ne fasses rien dont tu doives avoir honte, même lorsque tu es sous les ouvertures du toit, c.-à-d. dans les appartements qui sont situés au nord-ouest et ne reçoivent la lumière que par des ouvertures pratiquées dans le toit. Ne dis pas: «Ce lieu est fermé à tous les regards, personne ne me voit.» L'approche des esprits ne peut être devinée; il faut respecter leur présence.

8. Toi qui tiens le premier rang, pratique la vertu d'une

(inconsulto). Nullum est verbum quod non rependatur; nullum est beneficium quod non reddatur. Benignus esto erga socios (ministros tuos), omnes populares tuos filios. Filii et nepotes continenter succedent; ex universis civibus nullus non obsequetur.

7. Vident te, quum convenis principes viros, amœnum ac lenem componere tuum vultum, ne quis sit defectus. Visus in tua domo, præstat ut nihil (sit de quo) erubescas sub tecti spiramentis. Ne dicas: «Non patet (hic locus), nemo me videt.» Spirituum accessus non potest conjici; multo minus (præsentia) potest parvifieri.

不遐 **Pŏu hiâ** équivaut à 不何 **pŏu hô.** 云 **Iûn** et 思 **sēu** sont des particules.

8. Princeps tu exercens virtutem,

俾嘉、淑愼爾止、不愆于儀、不僭不賊、鮮不爲則、投我以桃、報之以李、彼童而角、實虹小子、

⑨ 在染柔木、言緡之絲、溫溫恭人、維德之基、其維哲人、告之話言、順德之行、其維愚人、覆謂我僭、民各有心、

(ngŏ). Pŏu tsiĕn pŏu tsĕ, siĕn pŏu wéi tsĕ. T'eŏu ngò i t'aŏ, paó tchĕu i li. Péi t'ŏung êul kiŏ, chĕu hŏung siaò tzèu (tsi).

9. Jènn jèn jeŏu mŏu, iên min tchĕu sēu (sī). Wēnn wēnn kŏung jènn, wéi tĕ tchĕu kī. K'ì wéi tchĕ jènn, kaó tchĕu houá iên, chouénn tĕ tchĕu hîng. K'ì wéi iû jènn, fŏu wéi ngò tsiĕn (tsīn). Mîn kŏ iòu sīn.

manière parfaite et insigne. Compose bien ton extérieur, ne manque en rien aux bienséances. Ne commets aucune erreur, aucune injustice. Il sera presque impossible que le peuple ne te prenne pas pour modèle, (ou bien, ceux-là seront rares qui ne te prendront pas pour modèle). (Quand le prince est vertueux, le peuple le devient; de même que), quand on me donne une pêche, en retour je donne une prune. (Mais vouloir que le peuple soit vertueux sans lui donner toi-même l'exemple, c'est) vouloir qu'un veau ou un agneau de quelques mois ait déjà des cornes; c'est te tromper toi-même comme un petit enfant.

9. Un bois flexible et élastique peut être entouré d'un cordon de soie (et devenir un arc). De même, un caractère enclin à la déférence et au respect est le fondement de la vertu. Si j'enseigne une bonne maxime à un homme naturellement sage, il la mettra en pratique avec docilité. Au contraire, un homme insensé dira que mes principes sont faux. Les esprits des hommes sont différents.

fac ut sit sincera, fac ut sit insignis. Componens cura tuum habitum, ne pecces circa decorum, ne aberres, ne lædas; rarum (i. e. mirum) erit si non evades exemplar, vel, pauci non habebunt te pro exemplari. (Quum quis) donat me malo persico, retribuo ei prunum. (Si velis ut vitulus agnusve) ille licet sit juvenis, tamen habeat cornua, vere ludificas te parvum puerum.

9. Flexibile ac molle lignum, obvolvunt illud serico filo (et fit arcus). Comis et obsequiosus homo est virtutis fundamentum. Qui est sapiens vir, si doceam eum dicta (antiquorum sapientium), docili virtute peraget. Qui est stultus homo, contra dicet me errare. Hominum quisque habet ingenium (suum, i. e. homines natura sunt alii sapientes alii stulti).

(10) 於乎小子、未知臧否、匪手攜之、言示之事、匪面命之、言提其耳、借曰未知、亦既抱子、民之靡盈、誰夙知而莫成、

(11) 昊天孔昭、我生靡樂、視爾夢夢、我心慘慘、誨爾諄諄、聽我藐藐、匪用爲教、覆用爲虐、借曰未知、亦聿既耄、

10. Oū hōu ! siaò tzèu ! Wèi tchēu tsāng pi. Fèi cheòu hī tchēu, ièn chéu tchēu chéu (chèu). Fèi mién ming tchēu, ièn t'ī k'ì èul. Tsié iuě wéi tchēu, ī kí paó tzèu. Min tchēu mi ing, chouèi sŏu tchēu èul móu tch'èng ?

11. Haó t'iēn k'òung tchaō (tchŏ), ngò chēng mi lŏ. Chéu èul mōung mōung ; ngò sīn ts'àn ts'àn (ts'ŏ ts'ŏ). Houéi èul tchouēnn tchouēnn, t'īng ngò mouŏ mouŏ. Fèi ióung wèi kiaó (kiŏ), fŏu ióung wéi iŏ. Tsié iuě wéi tchēu, ī iŭ kí maó (mouŏ).

10. Hélas! petit enfant, tu confonds encore le bien avec le mal. Cependant, non seulement je te conduis par la main, mais je t'enseigne de vive voix. Non seulement je te donne des avis en tête-à-tête, mais je te tire les oreilles. Ne dis pas que tu n'as pas encore la raison; tu portes déjà un fils dans tes bras. Quel est l'homme qui, après avoir connu tôt la vertu, la pratique tard, à moins qu'il ne soit plein de lui-même?

11. L'auguste ciel est très perspicace, (je crains qu'il ne te châtie) ; ma vie se passe sans joie. La vue de ton aveuglement accable mon cœur de chagrin. Je ne cesse de te répéter mes avis ; tu m'écoutes avec une froide indifférence. Tu ne me considères pas comme un maître qui t'enseigne, mais comme un tyran. Ne dis pas que tu n'as pas encore la raison ; tu as déjà quatre-vingt-dix ans.

10. Eheu! parvus filius (ipsemet Ou regulus) nondum discernit bonum a malo. Non (solum) manu traho (et duco) eum, etiam doceo verbis eum res. Non (solum) coram moneo eum, etiam revello ejus aures. Fingamus eum dicere se nondum sapere; sed jam ulnis portat filium. Hominum non sui plenus quis mature novit (virtutis viam) et sero perficit se?

L'orgueil est le grand ennemi de la perfection.

11. Magnum cœlum est valde perspicax; ego vivens careo gaudio. Videns te mente caligantem, meus animus mœrore angitur. Doceo te repetitis monitis; audis me negligenti incuria. Non habes me pro docente (magistro), contra habes pro tyranno. Quod si dicas te nondum sapere, at jam nonaginta annorum es.

孔昭指鑒別善惡不爽言 (詩經備旨) *K'òung tchaō* signifie voir et discerner le bien et le mal sans jamais se tromper.

(12) 於乎小子、告爾舊止、聽用我謀、庶無大悔、天方艱難、曰喪厥國、取譬不遠、昊天不忒、回遹其德、俾民大棘。

桑柔

(1) 菀彼桑柔、其下侯旬、捋采其劉、瘼此下民、不殄心憂、倉兄塡

12. Oū hōu ! siaò tzèu ! Kaó èul kiòu tchèu. T'īng ióung ngò meôu, chóu ôu tá houèi (houèi). T'iēn fāng kiēn nân, iuĕ sáng kiuĕ kouŏ (ĭ). Ts'iù p'i pŏu iuèn, haò t'iēn pŏu t'ĕ. Houêi iŭ k'î tŏ, pèi mîn tá kĭ.

SANG JEOU. **1. Iŭ pèi sāng jeôu, k'î hiá heôu siûn. Louŏ ts'ài k'î liôu, mouó ts'èu hiá mîn. Pŏu tièn sīn iōu, tch'ouáng houáng tch'ênn hì. Tchouŏ pèi haò t'iēn (t'īn), gning pŏu ngò kīn ?**

12. Hélas! petit enfant, je te rappelle les anciens principes. Écoute et suis mes avis; tu t'épargneras d'amers repentirs. Déjà le ciel envoie des malheurs et des afflictions; bientôt il mettra fin à ta principauté. Je déduis mes enseignements d'un principe évident; c'est que le ciel ne saurait se tromper. En étouffant les heureuses dispositions que la nature t'a données, tu attirerais de grands maux sur le peuple.

CHANT III. SANG JEOU.

芮伯 Le prince de Jouei déplore les malheurs de l'empire. Il les attribue à la tyrannie de 厲王 **Li wâng** et aux mauvais conseils de ses officiers.

1. Ce jeune mûrier était très verdoyant; il offrait un épais ombrage. Ses feuilles ont été cueillies, arrachées; il dépérit, et ceux qui se reposent à son pied sont incommodés. (Ainsi la dynastie des Tcheou autrefois florissante, est à présent en décadence, et rend le peuple malheureux). Mon chagrin est continuel; mon cœur

12. Eheu! parve fili, moneo te antiqua (instituta); ausculta et exsequere mea consilia, ut feliciter careas magna pœnitentia. Cœlum nunc ærumnis et angoribus (premit), mox perdet hoc regnum. Desumo documentum non remotum, (nempe ex eo quod) magnum cœlum non fallitur. Mutans corrumpis tuas virtutes (naturales); facies ut populus vehementer cruciétur.

CHANT III. 1. Luxuriabat illa morus tenera; illam subter, densum erat (tegmen). Decerptis lectisque (foliis) illa læsa est; laborant hi infra (subsistentes) homines. Non solvitur animi mœror; vehementer angor jamdiu. Perspicax est illud augustum cœlum; cur non nostri misereiur?

侯 **Heôu**, particule. 塡 employé pour 陳 **tch'ênn**, ancien.

« L'auguste ciel, si clairvoyant, si perspicace, connaît parfaitement, ce qui

兮、倬彼昊天、寧
不我矜、
(2) 四牡騤騤、旟
旐有翩、亂生不
夷、靡國不泯、民
靡有黎、具禍以
燼、於乎有哀、國
步斯頻、
(3) 國步蔑資、天
不我將、靡所止
疑、云徂何往、君
子實維、秉心無
競、誰生厲階、至
今爲梗、

2. Séu meòu k'ouêi k'ouêi, iû tchaò iòu p'iēn (p'īn). Louán chēng pŏu î, mì kouŏ pŏu mìn (mìn). Mîn mi iòu lî, kiú houó i sín (tsīn). Oū hōu ! iòu ngāi (ī)! kouŏ póu sēu p'în.

3. Kouŏ póu miĕ tzēu, t'iēn pŏu ngò tsiāng (tsiàng). Mi chòu tchéu î (î), iûn ts'ôu hô wàng ? Kiūn tzèu chĕu wêi, ping sīn ôu king (k'iàng). Chouêi chēng li kiāi (kī), tchéu kīn wêi kèng (kàng) ?

est affligé depuis longtemps. L'auguste ciel voit toutes choses; comment n'a-t-il pas compassion de nous?

2. (Le service militaire dépeuple l'empire). Les quatre chevaux robustes (attelés de front à chacun des chars de guerre) sont sans cesse en courses; les étendards voltigent, ornés les uns de tortues et de serpents, les autres d'éperviers. Le trouble ne s'apaise pas; toutes les principautés sont près de s'éteindre. Il ne reste plus d'hommes à cheveux noirs; tous (ceux qui étaient capables de porter les armes) ont été accablés de souffrances et exterminés. Hélas! que c'est lamentable! l'empire court à sa perte.

3. L'empire court à sa ruine, c'est lamentable; le ciel nous abandonne. Nous ne trouvons plus où nous fixer; où irons-nous? Si les officiers avaient pris à cœur d'établir la concorde et d'éviter tout différend, de qui serait venue la longue chaîne de mécontentements qui nous a conduits à cette extrémité d'infortune?

fait la sûreté ou le péril des peuples; rien n'échappe à sa vigilance. Comment n'a-t-il pas pitié de nos maux? Pourquoi n'écarte-t-il pas les périls, et ne ramène-t-il pas la tranquillité?» (詩經備旨).

2. Quatuor mares equi robusti et strenui (semper currunt); testudinibus et anguibus pictis ornata vexilla et accipitribus pictis ornata signa sunt volitantia. Turbatio exorta non sedatur. Nullum regnum quod non deleatur. Hominum nullus superest nigris capillis; omnes ærumnis afflicti sunt, ita ut in cineres redacti sint. Eheu! est dolendum! Imperii cursus adeo præceps (in exitium).

3. Imperium currens deletur, gemitibus prosequendum est; cœlum non nos curat. Non est ubi sistamus stabiles; ad quem locum pergemus? Si præpositi viri vere concordiam curassent, et firmo animo noluissent contendere; quis creasset irarum scalam, i.e. irarum causas in diem graviores, usque ad nunc factam miseriam?

(4) 憂心慇慇、念我土宇、我生不辰、逢天僤怒、自西徂東、靡所定處、多我覯痻、孔棘我圉、(5) 爲謀爲毖、亂況斯削、告爾憂恤、誨爾序爵、誰能執熱、逝不以濯、其何能淑、載胥及溺、(6) 如彼遡風、亦

4. Iōu sīn īn īn, gnién ngò t'òu iù. Ngò chēng pŏu tch'ènn, fôung t'iēn tán nòu. Tzéu sī ts'ôu tōung (tīng), mi chòu ting tch'òu. Touō ngò keóu min, k'òung kĭ ngò iù.

5. Wêi meôu wêi pi (pī), louán houáng sēu siŏ. Kaó éul iōu siŭ, houéi éul siú tsiŏ. Chouêi nêng tchĕu jĕ, chéu pŏu i tchouŏ? K'i hô nêng chŏu? Tsái siū kí gní (gniŏ)?

6. Jôu péi sóu fōung (fēnn), ĭ k'òung tchéu ngái. Mîn iòu siŭ sīn, p'ìng iùn

4. Mon cœur est dans la plus grande affliction; je pense à mon pays, à ma maison (que je désire revoir). Je suis né à une époque malheureuse, où le ciel est fort irrité. De l'occident à l'orient, je ne trouve pas un endroit pour me fixer. J'ai rencontré beaucoup de souffrances; le trouble est très grand aux frontières où je suis.

5. (Le poète s'adresse à l'empereur). Vous tenez des conseils, vous employez des précautions; cependant le trouble augmente toujours et votre pouvoir diminue. Je vous dirai ce qui devrait exciter votre douleur et votre commisération. Je vous enseignerai à conférer les dignités (aux hommes sages), d'après le mérite de chacun. Qui peut tenir un objet brûlant, s'il ne s'est mouillé la main? (Si les charges ne sont pas remplies par de bons officiers), l'administration pourra-t-elle être bien réglée? Nous irons tous ensemble nous engloutir dans les flots.

6. (A présent, les hommes de talent sont) comme des voya-

蔑 **Miě**, employé pour 滅 **miě**, détruire. 資 **Tzēu**, employé pour 咨 **tzēu**, soupirer. 云 **Iûn**, particule.

4. Mœstus animus vehementer dolet; reminiscor meum patrium solum et domum. Ego natus sum infelici tempore, offendi cœli vehementem iram. Ab occidente ad orientem, non est ubi consistens maneam. Multas ego vidi ærumnas; vehementer premuntur nostri fines.

5. Agis deliberationes, adhibes cautionem; turbatio crescit, inde minueris. Monebo te dolenda et miseranda; docebo te quomodo ordinandæ sint dignitates. Quis potest tenere calidissimum quid, non usus lotione (manus)? (Nisi sapientes viri publicis muniis fungantur), res quomodo poterit bene esse? Tunc simul sequentes mergemur.

逝 **Chéu**, particule.

6. (Sapientes viri nunc sunt) similes illis qui incedunt obversi vento, et

孔之僾。民有肅心、荓云不逮、有好是稼穡、力民代食、稼穡維寶、代食維好。

(7) 天降喪亂、滅我立王、降此蟊賊、稼穡卒痒。哀恫中國、具贅卒荒、靡有旅力、以念穹蒼。

(8) 維此惠君、民人所瞻。秉心宣

pŏu tái. Haó chéu kiá chĕ, lĭ mìn tái chĕu. Kiá chĕ wêi paò, tái chĕu wêi haò.

7. T'iēn kiáng sáng louán, miĕ ngò lĭ wâng. Kiáng ts'èu meôu tsĕ, kiá chĕ tsŏu iâng. Ngāi t'ōung tchōung kouŏ, kiú tchouéi tsŏu houāng. Mi iòu liù lĭ, i gnién k'iōung ts'āng.

8. Wêi ts'èu houéi kiūn, mîn jênn chòu tchēn (tchāng). Ping sīn siuēn iòu,

geurs qui marchent en sens contraire du vent et sont tout essoufflés. A la campagne on en trouve qui désireraient remplir des charges; mais ils disent qu'ils ne parviendraient pas (à rétablir l'ordre). Ils aiment mieux cultiver la terre, travailler comme les gens du peuple, que de vivre des appointements d'une charge. La culture des champs leur paraît plus honorable que l'exercice des charges, et le fruit du travail préférable aux appointements.

7. Le ciel envoie la mort et le trouble, et anéantit l'autorité de notre empereur. Il envoie des insectes qui rongent les racines et les nœuds des plantes; les moissons dépérissent tout à fait. L'empire est dans un état lamentable; tout est entraîné à la fois dans une ruine complète. Je n'ai plus même la force d'élever ma pensée vers le ciel (et de chercher à l'apaiser).

8. Un prince juste et bon est l'espoir des petits et des grands. Il a toujours soin de consulter les sentiments du peuple, et d'examiner avec soin la conduite de ses officiers. Au contraire, un prince

omnino anhelant. Inter homines (rusticos) est progrediendi (ad res publicas curandas) animus; adducuntur ut dicant se non assecuturos. Malunt ita serere ac metere; operantur rustici homines pro magistratuum stipendiis. Serere et metere est honestius; permutare stipendia est melius.

7. Cœlum immittit mortem ac turbationem, opprimit a nobis constitutum imperatorem. Immittit istos *meóu* (vermes qui segetum radices rodunt) et *tsĕ* (vermes qui articulos rodunt); sata et segetes omnino ægrotant. Miserandum et deflendum est Sinarum imperium; omnia continenter plane vastantur. Non sunt spinæ dorsali vires, ut cogitem de cavo et cæruleo cœlo.

8. Solus ille æquus rex est privati et præpositi quem suspiciunt. Constanti animo ubique consultat, inspicit diligenter suos adjutores. At ille non

猶考慎其相，維彼
不順，自獨俾臧，自
有肺腸，俾民卒狂。
(9) 瞻彼中林，甡甡
其鹿。朋友已譖，不
胥以穀。人亦有言，
進退維谷。
(10) 維此聖人，瞻言
百里，維彼愚人，覆
狂以喜。匪言不能，
胡斯畏忌。
(11) 維此良人，弗求
弗迪，維彼忍心，是

k'aò chénn k'ì siáng (siāng). Wêi pèi pŏu chouénn, tzéu tŏu pèi tsāng. Tzéu iòu féi tch'âng, pèi mîn tsŏu k'ouâng.

9. Tchēn pèi tchōung lîn, chēnn chēnn k'î lŏu. P'êng iòu i tsién (tsīn), pŏu siū i kŏu. Jénn ĭ iòu ién : Tsín t'ouéi wêi kŏu.

10. Wêi ts'èu chéng jênn, tchēn ién pĕ lì. Wêi pèi iù jênn, fŏu k'ouâng i hì. Féi ién pŏu nêng ; hôu sēu wéi kí (kì)?

11. Wêi ts'èu leâng jênn, fŏu k'iôu fŏu tĭ (tŏu). Wêi pèi jènn sīn, chéu

inique s'imagine que lui seul pense bien. Il suit ses propres idées, et finit par exciter la fureur du peuple.

9. Au milieu de la forêt voyez comme les cerfs vont par troupes. (Les hommes sont moins sages que ces animaux). Les compagnons, les amis se trompent mutuellement, et ne s'aident pas à faire le bien. Selon l'adage, nul ne peut (sans danger) ni avancer ni reculer.

10. Les vues et les avis du sage s'étendent à cent stades (il voit et signale les dangers les plus éloignés). L'insensé au contraire (ne voit pas le péril, et) à cause de sa folie est toujours joyeux. Je serais capable de donner des avis (à l'empereur); pourquoi suis-je retenu par la crainte?

11. Les hommes de bien ne sont ni cherchés ni promus aux charges. Les hommes cruels sont aimés et promus plusieurs fois.

æquus se solum putat recte judicare. Sibi habet mentis sensa; facit ut populus tandem furiat.

9. Aspice illam mediam silvam ; plurimi simul eunt illius cervi. Amici et socii sunt infidi, non invicem juvant ad bonum. Homines habent adagium : Progredi aut regredi est impossibile.

谷 **Kŏu**, vallée, vide, manque de ressource, impossibilité.

10. Solus hic sapientissimus vir prospicit et monet ad centum stadia. At ille stultus homo contra insanit et inde lætatur. Non quod monere non possim; cur ita timens abstineo (quin moneam)?

Si je ne donne pas d'avis à l'empereur, ce n'est pas que les avis me fassent défaut ; mais je sais qu'ils seraient inutiles et m'attireraient des malheurs.

11. Solus hic probus vir nec quæritur nec promovetur. At ille inhuma-

顧是復、民之貪
亂、寧爲荼毒、
⑫大風有隧、有
空大谷、維此良
人、作爲式穀、維
彼不順、征以中
垢、
⑬大風有隧、貪
人敗類、聽言則
對、誦言如醉、匪
用其良、覆俾我
悖、
⑭嗟爾朋友、予

chéu fŏu. Min tchēu t'ān louán, gning wêi t'ôu tŏu.

12. Tá fōung iòu souéi, iòu k'ōung tá kŏu. Wêi ts'èu leàng jênn, tsŏ wêi chĕu kŏu. Wêi pèi pŏu chouénn, tchēng i tchōung keòu (kŏu).

13. Tá fōung iòu souéi, t'ān jênn pái léi. T'ing iên tsĕ touéi, sóung iên jôu tsouéi. Fèi ióung k'î leàng, fŏu pèi ngò péi.

14. Tsiē ! èul p'êng iòu, iù k'î pŏu tchēu èul tsŏ ? Jôu pèi fēi tch'ôung, chéu î î houŏ. Kí tchēu in jôu, fàn iù lâi hŏ.

Aussi le peuple devient avide de sédition, et se plaît à nuire comme un poison amer.

12. Les vents violents ont leurs routes ; ils suivent les grandes vallées où rien ne les arrête. (Ainsi chaque homme suit la voie qui lui est propre). L'homme de bien procède toujours avec bonté ; l'homme méchant marche par des voies ténébreuses et fangeuses.

13. Les vents violents ont leurs routes. L'ambitieux renverse ses collègues (ou les hommes de bien). Si l'empereur voulait prêter l'oreille à mes avis, je les lui présenterais. Je me contente de les chanter, (avec l'esprit troublé) comme un homme ivre. Il n'emploie pas les hommes de bien ; sa conduite (m'afflige au point de) me troubler l'intelligence.

14. Ah ! mon ami, toi (ambitieux, dis-moi), est-ce dans l'ignorance que j'ai composé ce chant ? (Je rencontre parfois la vérité),

nus homo et respicitur et iterum iterumque (promovetur). Populus optat turbationem, et gaudet fieri amarum toxicum.

荼 **T'ôu,** plante amère dont on extrait un poison.

12. Magnus ventus habet viam ; habet vacuam magnam vallem. Solus hic probus vir, aggrediens rem agendam, utitur bonitate. At ille iniquus incedit per medias sordes.

13. Magnus ventus habet viam ; cupidus homo evertit collegas (aut, juxta alios interpretes, evertit bonos. Si imperator) aurem præberet monitis, tunc loquerer. Cano monita quasi ebrius. Non adhibet illos probos, contra facit ut ego insaniam.

14. Ah ! tu, amice (cupidum hominem alloquitur), ego num haud scius et feci (illos versus) ? (Mea verba aliquando ad veritatem accedunt), sicut

豈不知而作、如彼飛蟲、時亦弋獲、既之陰女、反予來赫、

(15) 民之罔極、職涼善背、爲民不利、如云不克、民之回遹、職競用力、

(16) 民之未戾、職盜爲寇、涼曰不可、覆背善詈、雖曰匪予、既作爾歌、

15. Min tcheū wàng kĭ, tcheū leâng chén péi (pĕ). Wêi min pŏu lí, jôu iùn pŏu k'ŏ. Min tcheū houêi iŭ, tcheū king ióung lĭ.

16. Min tcheū wéi li, tcheū taó wêi k'eóu. Leâng iuĕ pŏu k'ŏ, fŏu péi chén li. Souêi iuĕ : « Fèi iû ; » ki tsŏ èul kō.

comme le chasseur atteint parfois l'oiseau en son vol. Je suis venu (t'engager à changer de conduite, et) te tirer du péril (auquel tu t'exposes); toi au contraire, tu t'irrites contre moi.

15. La licence illimitée du peuple doit être imputée à ces hypocrites qui savent prendre toutes les formes. Ils travaillent à priver le peuple de ses ressources (avec un acharnement toujours croissant), comme s'ils craignaient de ne pas atteindre leur but. La perversité du peuple doit être imputée à ces hommes qui luttent de toutes leurs forces (dans l'intérêt de leur cupidité).

16. Si le peuple n'est pas encore rentré dans le calme, la faute en est aux officiers rapaces qui commettent des brigandages. (En présence des hommes de bien), ces hypocrites disent qu'il n'est pas permis (d'opprimer le peuple); en secret ils les dénigrent très habilement. (Hypocrites), quoique vous disiez: «Ce n'est pas nous (qui dénigrons les honnêtes gens);» j'ai composé ce chant pour vous.

illam volantem bestiolam (avem) quandoque et (auceps) sagitta petit ac capit. Veni ut tuerer te; contra mihi venis ut succenseas.

15. Populi immoderata (licentia) præsertim (orta est ex hominibus specie) fidis, peritis tergiversandi (versipellibus). Operam dant ut populus careat commodis, (in diem acrius premunt) quasi non valerent (intentum assequi). Populi mutatio ac perversitas maxime orta est ex hominibus qui contendunt adhibitis viribus.

On croit que 涼 est employé au lieu de 諒 sincère. On lui donne aussi le sens de 薄 mauvais.

16. Quod populus nondum quietus sit, maxime oritur ex latronibus qui exercent rapinas. (Specie) fidi dicunt (coram sapientibus viris): «Nefas est (opprimere populum).» Verso tergo, scite maledicunt (probis viris). Licet dicatis: «Non nos (maledQiximus);» feci vobis canticum.

詩經

雲漢
(1) 倬彼雲漢。
昭回于天、王
曰於乎、何辜
今之人、天降
喪亂、饑饉薦
臻、靡神不舉、
靡愛斯牲、圭
璧既卒、寧莫
我聽。
(2) 旱既大甚、
蘊隆蟲蟲、不
殄禋祀、自郊

IUN HAN. 1. Tchouŏ pėi iùn hán, tchaŏ houêi iū t'iēn (t'īn). Wâng iuĕ : Oū hōu ! hô kōu kīn tchēu jênn ? T'iēn kiáng sáng louán, kī kìn tsién tchēnn. Mi chênn pŏu kiù, mi ngái sēu chēng (sīng). Kouēi pĭ ki tsŏu ; gnîng mouŏ ngò t'īng ?
2. Hàn ki t'ái chénn, iùn lōung tch'ôung tch'ôung. Pŏu tièn īn séu, tzéu kiaŏ

CHANT IV. IUN HAN.

L'empereur 宣王 Siuēn wâng déplore la stérilité de la terre causée par la sécheresse. Il a fait et il fait encore des supplications et des sacrifices à tous les esprits du ciel et de la terre. Jusqu'à présent il n'a pas été exaucé. Ce chant est attribué à un officier nommé 仍叔 Jêng Chŏu.

1. La voie lactée était brillante, et ses feux tournaient avec la voûte azurée. L'empereur (levant les yeux au ciel) dit : Hélas ! de quel crime les hommes peuvent-ils être accusés à présent ? Le ciel envoie la mort, le trouble ; les grains et les légumes ont manqué plusieurs années de suite. Il n'est pas d'esprit que je n'aie honoré ; je n'ai pas épargné les victimes. Il ne reste plus de tablettes de jade, ni oblongues ni circulaires. Pourquoi ne suis-je pas exaucé ?

2. La sécheresse est très grande ; la chaleur accumulée dans l'air est très intense. Je n'ai pas cessé de faire des offrandes avec une intention pure, dans la campagne (au ciel, à la terre) et dans

CHANT IV. 1. Clara erat illa lactea via, fulgens et se volvens cum cœlo. Rex ait : Eheu ! in quo culpandi sunt nunc homines ? Cœlum immittit mortem, turbationem ; frugum carentia, olerum carentia iterum iterumque advenerunt. Nullum spiritum non honoribus colui ; non parce usus sum illis victimis. Oblongæ tabellæ et circulares tabellæ jam absumptæ sunt. Quare nullus (spiritus) me audit ?

宣王曰災異之來乃天心仁愛人君 (備旨) Siuen wang dit : « Il est étonnant que des calamités arrivent à présent ; car le ciel, dont le cœur est si bon, aime les princes. » Dans les grandes calamités, on faisait des sacrifices à tous les esprits, même à ceux qui ne recevaient plus aucun honneur depuis longtemps. On offrait des tablettes de jade de différentes couleurs aux esprits du ciel, de la terre, des astres, des montagnes, des cours d'eau,... et on les enterrait.

2. Siccitas jam est magna valde ; congestus vehemens est aeris calor. Non intermissa sunt puro animo oblata sacra, a campis ad aulam regiam. Superis et inferis (spiritibus) sacra obtuli et humavi ; nullum spiritum non hono-

徂宮、上下奠瘞、靡神不宗、后稷不克、上帝不臨、耗斁下土、寧丁我躬、

(3) 旱既大甚、則不可推、兢兢業業、如霆如雷、周餘黎民、靡有孑遺、昊天上帝、則不我遺、胡不

ts'ôu kōung. Cháng hiá tién i, mi chênn pŏu tsōung. Heóu tsĭ pŏu k'ŏ, cháng ti pŏu lìn (lôung). Haŏ tóu hiá t'òu, gnîng tīng ngò kōung?

3. Hàn ki t'ái chénn, tsĕ pŏu k'ò t'ouēi. Kīng kīng iĕ iĕ, jôu t'îng jôu lêi. Tcheōu iû lî mîn, mi iòu kiĕ î (wêi). Haò t'iēn cháng ti, tsĕ pŏu ngò î (wêi). Hôu pŏu siāng wéi? Siēn tsòu iù ts'ouêi.

le palais (aux mânes de mes ancêtres). J'ai offert des sacrifices aux esprits du ciel et de la terre, puis enterré les offrandes; il n'est aucun esprit que je n'aie honoré. Mais Heou tsi n'est pas assez puissant, et le roi du ciel ne nous est pas favorable. Pourquoi cette dévastation, cette désolation de la terre arrive-t-elle de mon vivant? (Ou bien, Mieux vaudrait faire retomber sur moi tous les maux, que de désoler et de ruiner tout le pays).

3. La sécheresse est très grande, et par suite, sans remède. Je crains et tremble à la vue du péril, comme si j'entendais le roulement et le fracas du tonnerre. De tous les hommes à cheveux noirs qui obéissaient aux Tcheou, il ne reste plus un seul survivant, pas même un estropié. L'auguste roi du ciel ne me laissera pas survivre non plus. Comment ne craindrions- nous pas tous?

ravi. Heou tsi non valet (calamitatem depellere); cœli rex non adest. Consumitur et vastatur subjecta terra, quare adstante mea persona? (juxta alios interpretes, melius est calamitates incumbere mihi soli).

宮之神莫尊於后稷未嘗不吾享也而力又不足以勝災郊之神莫尊於上帝力固足以勝災也而又不吾享(備旨) Le plus grand des esprits honorés dans le temple des ancêtres est Heou tsi. Il a toujours agréé nos offrandes, mais il n'est pas assez puissant pour triompher des calamités. Le plus grand des esprits honorés dans la campagne est le roi du ciel. Il est certainement assez puissant pour triompher des calamités; mais il n'agrée pas nos sacrifices.

3. Siccitas jam magna est valde, ideo non potest depelli. Vehementer timeo et periculo percellor, quasi tonitru producto sono, quasi tonitru fragore. Ex Tcheou superstite nigris capillis populo non est unus mancus relictus. Magni cœli supernus rex ideo neque me relinquet. Quomodo non simul timeamus? Majorum delubra delebuntur.

孑 **Kiĕ**, celui à qui manque le bras droit, manchot, estropié. C'est une hyperbole de dire qu'il ne restait plus un seul homme à cheveux noirs. Meng

相畏、先祖于摧、

(4) 旱既大甚、則不可沮、赫赫炎炎、云我無所、大命近止、靡瞻靡顧、羣公先正、則不我助、父母先祖、胡寧忍予、

(5) 旱既大甚、滌滌山川、旱魃爲虐、如惔如焚、我心憚暑、憂心如熏、羣公先正、則

4. Hàn kí t'ái chénn, tsě pǒu k'ò tsiù. Hě hě iên iên, iùn ngò ôu chòu. Tá míng kin tchéu, mi tchēn mi kóu (kòu). K'iûn kōung siēn tchéng, tsě pǒu ngò tchóu (tchòu). Fóu mòu siēn tsòu, hôu gnîng jènn iù (iù)?

5. Hàn kí t'ái chénn, tǐ tǐ chān tch'ouēn (tch'ouênn). Hàn pouŏ wêi iŏ, jôu t'ân jôu fênn. Ngò sīn tán chòu, iōu sīn jôu hiūn. K'iûn kōung siēn tchéng, tsě

Le temple de mes ancêtres sera détruit.

4. La sécheresse est trop grande pour qu'il soit possible d'y mettre fin. Elle est accompagnée d'une chaleur excessive; je n'ai plus d'endroit où je puisse me retirer. La mort est proche; je ne sais plus où lever les yeux, où tourner la tête. Les mânes des anciens princes et des anciens ministres d'État m'ont tous délaissé. Comment mon père, ma mère, mes ancêtres ont-ils le cœur assez dur pour n'avoir pas compassion de moi?

5. La sécheresse est très grande; les montagnes sont dénudées et les rivières sont à sec. Le démon de la sécheresse, dans sa cruelle tyrannie, semble promener la flamme et l'incendie. Les chaleurs m'épouvantent; mon cœur affligé est comme dans un feu.

tzeu, L. V. Ch. I. 4, observe que cette phrase ne doit pas être prise à la lettre.

4. Siccitas jam magna est valde, ideo non potest inhiberi. Siccus aer est calidissimus; ego non habeo ubi maneam. Magnum decretum (interitus) est proximum. Non est quo suspiciam, nec est quo oculos convertam. Omnes principes, antiqui duces (regni ministri) jam non me adjuvant. Pater et mater, priores avi quomodo ferunt non misereri mei?

«J'ai fait des offrandes aux anciens princes et aux anciens ministres, dans l'espoir qu'ils viendraient à mon secours et me rendraient heureux. Ils me regardent sans rien faire et sans me secourir, comme si je leur étais étranger. Mais mon père, ma mère et mes aïeux, qui sont mes plus proches parents, et ont en quelque sorte une même respiration avec moi, pourquoi souffrent-ils que je sois dans l'affliction, et ne se mettent-ils pas en peine de m'en délivrer?» (詩經備旨).

5. Siccitas jam magna est valde; loti (exinaniti, exhausti) sunt montes et fluvii. Siccitatis genius facit saevissima, quasi incendit quasi comburit. Meus animus timet a caloribus; mœstus animus quasi æstuat. Omnes principes,

不我聞。昊天
上帝、寧俾我
遯。
（六）旱既大甚。
黽勉畏去、胡
寧瘨我以旱。
憯不知其故、
祈年孔夙、方
社不莫。昊天
上帝、則不我
虞。敬恭明神。
宜無悔怒。

pŏu ngò wénn. Haò t'iēn chàng tí, gning péi ngò touénn (touénn).

6. Hán kí t'ái chenn. min mièn wéi k'iú. Hôu gning tiēn ngò i hán? Ts'àn pŏu tchēu k'ì kóu. K'ì gniên k'òung siŭ, fāng ché pŏu móu. Haò t'iēn chàng tí, tsĕ pŏu ngò iû (iú). Kìng kōung mîng chênn, î ôu houèi nóu.

Les mânes des princes et des ministres d'État refusent tous de m'entendre. Mieux vaudrait que l'auguste roi du ciel, (au lieu de châtier le peuple à cause de moi), me permît de me retirer (dans la vie privée).

6. La sécheresse est très grande: je me fais violence (pour demeurer); je n'ose me retirer (parce que je ne sais où aller et ne veux pas abandonner mon peuple). Pourquoi le ciel m'envoie-t-il le fléau de la sécheresse? Je n'en sais pas la cause. De très bonne heure j'ai demandé une année fertile: je n'ai pas sacrifié tard aux esprits de la terre et des quatre points cardinaux. L'auguste roi du ciel ne considère pas (avec quel soin j'ai accompli ces cérémonies). J'ai honoré avec respect ces esprits intelligents; il est juste qu'ils n'aient contre moi ni haine ni colère.

antiqui duces jam non me audiunt. Magni cœli supernum regem potius est facere ut ego recedam.

魃 Démon à forme humaine, haut de deux à trois 尺 (de 40 à 60 centimètres), ayant les yeux au sommet de la tête, allant à pied sans vêtement, avec la rapidité du vent.

昊天上帝乃司禍福進退之權者也（詩經體註） L'auguste roi du ciel est l'arbitre des biens et des maux; il décide si l'on doit s'avancer ou se retirer.

6. Siccitas jam magna est valde; mihi vim infero (ut maneam), non audeo abire. Quomodo (cœlum) fert affligere me siccitate? Hucusque non novi illius (rei) causam. Precatus sum fertilem annum valde mature; quatuor regionum et terræ spiritibus sacra feci non tarde. Magni cœli supernus rex jam non me considerat. Reverenter honoravi intelligentes spiritus; æquum est carere odio, ira.

孟春祈穀于上帝孟冬祈來年于天宗（朱熹） Au commencement du printemps, on demandait une bonne récolte au roi du ciel; au commencement de l'hiver, on demandait une année fertile aux honorables du ciel, c.-à-d. au soleil, à la lune et aux étoiles. 方 Fāng, employé pour 祊 fāng, offrande faite aux esprits des quatre points cardinaux.

(7) 旱既大甚、散
無友紀、鞫哉庶
正、疚哉冢宰、趣
馬師氏、膳夫左
右、靡人不周、無
不能止、瞻卬昊
天、云如何里、
(8) 瞻卬昊天、有
嘒其星、大夫君
子、昭假無贏、大
命近止、無棄爾
成、何求為我、以
戾庶正、瞻卬昊
天、曷惠其寧、

7. Hàn ki t'ái chénn, sàn ȏu iòu ki. Kiŭ tsāi chóu tchéng! kiŏu tsāi tchòung tsài (tsi)! Ts'eòu mà chēu chéu, chén fōu tsouò iòu (i). Mi jênn pŏu tcheŏu, ȏu pŏu nêng tchéu. Tchēn iàng haò t'iēn, iùn jôu hô lì?

8. Tchēn iàng haò t'iēn, iòu houéi k'ì sīng. Tái fōu kiūn tzèu, tchaō kŏ ȏu îng. Tá míng kin tchéu, ȏu k'i éul tch'êng. Hô k'iòu wéi ngò, i lì chóu tchéng (tchēng)? Tchēn iàng haò t'iēn, hŏ houéi k'ì gnîng?

7. La sécheresse est extrême; mes officiers sont dispersés, je n'en ai plus qui m'aident à gouverner. Tous les ministres sont à bout de forces; le premier ministre est malade de fatigue. L'intendant des écuries, le capitaine des gardes, le chef des cuisines, tous mes serviteurs se sont efforcés de secourir le peuple; aucun d'eux n'a refusé son concours sous prétexte d'impossibilité. Levant les yeux vers le ciel, je dis: Pourquoi suis-je plongé dans une telle affliction?

8. Je lève les yeux vers le ciel; les étoiles brillent (rien n'annonce la pluie). Vous, grands officiers, hauts dignitaires, vous avez fait tout ce qui était en votre pouvoir pour rendre le ciel propice. Bien que la mort soit imminente, ne cessez pas vos supplications. Est-ce pour moi seul que vous priez les esprits? Non; c'est aussi pour calmer les inquiétudes des ministres d'État. Je lève les yeux vers le ciel; quand nous accordera-t-il la faveur que nous lui demandons?

7. Siccitas jam magna est valde; dispersi, non sunt collegæ (regni ministri) qui regant. Viribus exhausti sunt præpositorum duces; ægrotat ministrorum præses. Curator equorum, custodum præfectus, victus curator, circumstantes ministri, nullus homo non opem ferre (conatus est); nullus (dixit se) non posse et desiit (conari). Suspiciens contemplor magnum cœlum; dico, (cur) usque eo angor?

Plusieurs commentateurs pensent qu'au lieu de 散無友紀 on doit lire 散無有紀 et traduire: (Les officiers ou les habitants) sont dispersés, il n'y a plus de gouvernement. 卬 employé pour 仰 iàng, regarder en haut, espérer.

8. Suspiciens contemplor magnum cœlum, habent fulgorem ejus stellæ. Magni præfecti principes viri, ut clare accedatis (ad cœlum rogandum) nihil superest (quod fieri possit). Interitu imminente, ne desistatis a vestro opere. Num precamini mihi (soli)? Ad tranquillandos præpositorum duces (precamini). Suspiciens contemplor magnum cœlum; quandonam donabit illud beneficium?

崧高

(1) 崧高維嶽、
駿極于天、維
嶽降神、生甫
及申、維申
及甫、維周之翰、
四國于蕃、四
方于宣、
(2) 亹亹申伯、
王纘之事、于
邑于謝、南國
是式、王命召
伯、定申伯之

SOUNG KAO. 1. **Sōung kaō wêi iŏ, siún kí iû t'iēn (t'īn). Wêi iŏ kiáng chênn, chēng Fòu kí Chēnn. Wêi Chēnn kí Fòu wêi Tcheōu tchēu hân (hiên). Séu kouŏ iû fân, séu fāng iû siuēn.**

2. Wéi wéi Chēnn pĕ, wàng tsouàn tchēu chéu. Iû î iû Sié, nân kouŏ chéu

CHANT V. SOUNG KAO.

申伯 Le prince de Chenn, oncle maternel de l'empereur 宣王 **Siuēn wâng**, ayant reçu en fief la terre de 謝 **Sié** (à présent 信陽州 dans le **Ho nan**), 尹吉甫 **Īn Kì fòu**, l'un de ses collègues, composa ce chant pour le féliciter.

1. Les montagnes sacrées sont étendues et élevées; leurs cimes touchent au ciel. Un esprit descendu de ces montagnes a donné le jour au prince de Fou et au prince de Chenn. Ces deux princes sont les colonnes de la maison des Tcheou, les défenseurs de toutes les principautés, les bienfaiteurs de tout l'empire.

2. Le prince de Chenn est courageux et infatigable. L'empereur lui a ordonné de continuer les œuvres de ses pères, d'établir sa capitale à Sie, afin qu'il fût le modèle des princes du midi. L'empereur a chargé le prince de Chao de préparer la résidence du prince de Chenn (à Sie), de constituer parfaitement cette princi-

CHANT V. 1. Magni et alti sunt montes sacri, sublimia cacumina attingunt cœlum. Ex montibus sacris descendens spiritus creavit Fou regni et Chenn regni regulos. Chenn et Fou reguli sunt Tcheou domus columnæ. Omnibus regnis sunt propugnacula, omnibus regionibus diffundunt beneficia.

On appelait 嶽 **iŏ** les montagnes sur lesquelles les empereurs offraient des sacrifices. C'étaient le 岱山 **T'ái chān** ou 泰山 **T'ái chān** dans le Chan toung actuel, le 衡山 **Hêng chān** dans le Hou nan, le 華山 **Houá chān** dans le Chen si, le 恒山 **Hêng chān** dans le Tcheu li, et, à partir de la dynastie des 周 **Tcheōu**, le 嵩山 **Sōung chan** dans le Ho nan. 申, à présent 信陽州; 甫, à présent 南陽縣 dans le Ho nan.

Le poète dit qu'un esprit descendu des montagnes sacrées donna naissance au prince de Fou et au prince de Chenn, parce qu'ils étaient tous deux de l'illustre famille des 姜 **Kiāng**, et descendaient du premier ministre de l'empereur 堯 **Iaô**. Ce ministre portait le titre de 四嶽 **séu iŏ** gardien des quatre montagnes sacrées.

2. Fortis et strenuus est Chenn regulus. Imperator jussit prosequi opera (majorum); inde urbem præcipuam condere in Sie, australium regnorum

宅、登是南邦、世執其功、③王命申伯、式是南邦、因是謝人、以作爾庸、王命召伯、徹申伯土田、王命傅御、遷其私人、④申伯之功、召伯是營、有俶其城、寢廟既成、既成藐藐、王錫申伯、四牡蹻蹻、鉤膺濯濯、

chĕu (chéu). Wâng ming Chaó pĕ (pŏ) ting Chēnn pĕ tchēu tchĕ (touŏ), tēng chéu nân pāng (pōung), chéu tchĕu k'ì kōung.

3. Wâng ming Chēnn pĕ: « Chĕu chéu nân pāng (pōung). Īn chéu Sié jênn i tsŏ èul iôung. » Wâng ming Chaó pĕ tch'ĕ Chēnn pĕ t'òu t'iên (t'în). Wâng ming fóu iú ts'iēn k'ì sēu jênn.

4. Chēnn pĕ tchēu kōung, Chaó pĕ chéu îng. Iòu tch'ŏu k'ì tch'êng; ts'in miaó kí tch'êng, kí tch'êng mouŏ mouŏ. Wâng sĭ Chēnn pĕ (pŏ) séu meòu kiŏ kiŏ, keŏu īng tchouŏ tchouŏ.

pauté du midi, afin que les services du prince de Chenn fussent continués d'âge en âge par ses descendants.

3. L'empereur a dit au prince de Chenn: « Soyez le modèle des princes du midi. Employez les habitants de Sie à construire les remparts de votre capitale. » L'empereur a ordonné au prince de Chao de soumettre au système appelé *tch'e* le territoire du prince de Chenn. Il a ordonné à l'intendant de la maison (du prince de Chenn) de conduire (à Sie) les serviteurs.

4. Le prince de Chao a réglé les travaux de construction dans la nouvelle capitale du prince de Chenn. On a d'abord élevé les remparts. Puis on a construit le temple des ancêtres et le bâtiment postérieur; ils ont une grande profondeur. L'empereur a donné au prince de Chenn quatre chevaux robustes, qui portent sur le poitrail des courroies et des boucles très luisantes.

esse exemplar. Imperator jussit Chao regulum constituere Chenn reguli sedem, perficere illud australe regnum, ut posteri (Chenn reguli) tenerent (prosequerentur) ejus opus.

3. Imperator jussa dedit Chenn regulo: « Sis exemplar illis australibus regnis. Adhibeas illos Sie incolas, ut exstruas tua mœnia. » Imperator jussit Chao regulum componere Chenn reguli terram et agros. Imperator jussit præfectum famulorum transmittere ejus (Chenn reguli) familiares homines.

徹 **Tch'ĕ**. Voy. page 363, note.

4. Chenn reguli ædificia, Chao regulus ea delineavit. Fuit initium ab ejus mœniis. Posterior ædes et delubra perfecta sunt; perfecta sunt valde profunda. Imperator donavit Chenn regulo quatuor mares equos valde robustos, fibulis instructa equorum pectoralia valde lucentia.

(5) 王遣申伯、路車乘馬、我圖爾居、莫如南土、錫爾介圭、以作爾寶、往近王舅、南土是保、

(6) 申伯信邁、王餞于郿、申伯還南、謝于誠歸、王命召伯、徹申伯土疆、以峙其粻、式遄其行、

(7) 申伯番番、既

5. Wàng k'iēn Chēnn pě lòu kiū chéng mà (mòu). «Ngò t'òu èul kiū, mouŏ jŏu nàn t'òu. Sī èul kiài kouēi, i tsŏ èul paò (pòu). Wàng kin wâng kiòu, nân t'òu chéu paò (pòu).»

6. Chēnn pě sin mái, wâng tsién iū Mêi. Chēnn pě houàn nân, Sié iū tch'éng kouēi. Wâng ming Chaó pě tch'ĕ Chēnn pě t'òu kiāng, i tchèu k'i tchāng, chéu tch'ouèn k'i hing (hàng).

7. Chēnn pě pouŏ pouŏ (fān fān), ki jŏu iû Sié. T'òu iù t'ān t'ān. Tcheōu pāng

5. L'empereur a envoyé le prince de Chenn (à Sie) sur un char impérial attelé de quatre chevaux, (et lui a dit) : « Après mûres réflexions, je ne trouve pas de meilleur endroit pour votre résidence que le midi. Je vous donne la grande tablette (des *tchou heou*), qui sera l'insigne de votre dignité. Allez donc, oncle maternel de l'empereur, et protégez les principautés du midi. »

6. Le prince de Chenn est parti en effet, (et se dirigeant vers le nord-ouest, est allé d'abord à Mei, où l'empereur se trouvait); l'empereur lui a offert à Mei le festin d'adieu. Le prince de Chenn, retournant vers le midi, s'est rendu à Sie. L'empereur avait ordonné au prince de Chao d'établir dans les terres du prince de Chenn le système agraire appelé *tch'e*, afin de lui préparer des provisions de vivres qui lui permissent d'accélérer sa marche.

7. Le prince de Chenn au visage martial a fait son entrée dans Sie, avec une suite nombreuse de piétons et d'hommes montés en

5. Imperator misit Chenn regulum regio curru, quadrijugis equis. « Mihi cogitanti de tua sede, nulla (visa est) par australi regioni. Dono te magna tabella (*tchōu heòu* regulorum), ut fiat tuum pretiosum (dignitatis signum. V. pag. 64). Ito, regis avuncule; australem regionem inde protegas. »

近 **Kin**, que plusieurs commentateurs prononcent *ki*, est une particule.

6. Chenn regulus reapse profectus est; imperator convivio excepit in Mei. Chenn regulus reversus est ad austrum, Sie revera adivit. Imperator jusserat Chao regulum *tch'ĕ* Chenn reguli territorium et limites, ut colligeretur ei annona, et sic celeriter conficeretur ejus iter. — *Mei*, à présent Mei hien dans le Foung siang fou, province de Chen si.

7. Chenn regulus militari habitu ingressus est in Sie. Pedites et rhedarii erant plurimi. In Tcheou regno (regio

入于謝。徒御嘽
嘽。周邦咸喜。戎
有良翰。不顯申
伯。王之元舅。文
武是憲。
(8) 申伯之德。柔
惠且直。揉此萬
邦。聞于四國。吉
甫作誦。其詩孔
碩。其風肆好。以
贈申伯。

烝民

(1) 天生烝民。有

hiên hi. « Jôung iòu leàng hân (hiên); pŏu hièn Chēnn pĕ? Wâng tchēu iuên kiòu, wênn òu chéu hién (hiên). »

8. Chēnn pĕ tchēu tĕ jeôu houéi, ts'iè tchĕu. Jeòu ts'èu wán pāng, wénn iū séu kouŏ (ĭ). Kĭ fòu tsŏ sóung, k'ì chēu k'òung chĕu, k'ì fōung séu haò, i tséng Chēnn pĕ.

TCHENG MIN. **1. T'iēn chēng tchēng mîn, iòu ŏu iòu tsĕ. Mîn tchēu ping ĭ,**

voiture. Les habitants du territoire impérial se sont tous réjouis. (Ils se félicitaient les uns les autres, en disant): « Vous avez un excellent défenseur (qui gardera les frontières au midi). Le prince de Chenn n'est-il pas distingué? Il est l'aîné des oncles maternels de l'empereur, le modèle des officiers civils et militaires. »

8. Le prince de Chenn est remarquable par sa douceur, sa bienfaisance et sa droiture. Il établira l'ordre dans toutes les principautés; son nom est célèbre dans tout l'empire. Moi Ki fou, j'ai composé ce chant. Les vers en sont magnifiques, l'air coulant et harmonieux. Je l'offre au prince de Chenn.

CHANT VI. TCHENG MIN.

樊侯仲山甫 **Tchóung Chān fòu**, prince de Fan, 冢宰 **tchòung tsài** premier ministre de l'empereur 宣王 **Siuēn wâng**, et 太保 **t'ái paò** grand tuteur, ayant reçu l'ordre d'aller fortifier la capitale de la principauté de 齊 **Ts'î**, dans le 臨菑縣 **Lîn tchēu hién** actuel (province de Chan toung), son collègue 尹吉甫 **În Kĭ fòu** lui offrit à son départ les stances suivantes.

1. Tout homme reçoit du ciel avec l'existence les parties constitutives de son être et la loi qui doit régir ses actions. Il a en son

territorio) omnes incolæ gavisi sunt. (Invicem gratulantes dicebant): « Vos habetis egregium columen. Nonne insignis est Chenn regulus? Imperatoris est natu maximus avunculus; et civiles et militares præpositi eum habent pro exemplari. »

8. Chenn reguli virtus est mitis, benefica et recta. Componet illa omnia regna; famosus est in quatuor regionibus imperii. Ki fou feci canticum. Ejus versus sunt valde magnifici, ejus numeri fluunt pulchri. Utens muneror Chenn regulum.

CHANT VI. 1. Cœlo creante universos homines, sunt res (quibus constant homines), est lex moralis. Homines

物有則、民之秉彝、好是懿德、天監有周、昭假于下、保茲天子、生仲山甫、

(2) 仲山甫之德、柔嘉維則、令儀令色、小心翼翼、古訓是式、威儀是力、天子是若、明命使賦、

(3) 王命仲山甫、式是百辟、纘戎祖考、王躬是保、出納王命、王之喉舌、賦政

haó chéu i tě. T'iēn kién iòu Tcheōu, tchaō kŏ iū hiá (hòu). Paò tzēu t'iēn tzèu, chēng Tchóung Chān fòu.

2. Tchóung Chān fòu tchēu tě, jeôu kiā wêi tsě. Ling i líng chě, siaò sīn í i. Kòu hiún chéu chĕu, wêi i chéu lĭ. T'iēn tzèu chéu jŏ, mîng mîng chéu fòu.

3. Wâng mîng Tchóung Chān fòu: «Chĕu chéu pĕ pĭ. Tsouàn jôung tsòu k'aò, wâng kōung chéu paò. Tch'ŏu nă wâng mîng, wâng tchēu heôu chĕ. Fóu tchéng iū wái, séu fāng iuên fă (pĕ).»

cœur la loi naturelle, et par suite, il aime la vertu, dont il reconnaît la beauté. Le ciel a contemplé le prince qui gouverne Tcheou (Siuen wang). Attiré par l'éclat de sa vertu, il s'est incliné vers la terre. Pour défendre le Fils du ciel, il a fait naître Tchoung Chan fou (et l'a orné de ses dons les plus insignes).

2. La vertu de Tchoung Chan fou est aimable, admirable, entièrement conforme à la loi morale. Son maintien, l'air de son visage sont pleins de dignité; son esprit est toujours attentif à l'accomplissement du devoir. Les enseignements des anciens sont sa règle; il s'applique à garder la gravité, à observer les bienséances. Entièrement soumis aux volontés du Fils du ciel, il s'emploie à répandre partout ses instructions et ses décrets.

3. L'empereur dit à Tchoung Chan fou: «Soyez le modèle de tous les princes; continuant les services rendus par vos ancêtres, défendez la personne de l'empereur. Transmettez mes ordres et rendez-moi compte de leur exécution; soyez ainsi comme mon

præditi lege naturali, amant illam pulchram virtutem. Cœlum contemplans regentem Tcheou, clara (virtute motum) se inclinavit in terram. Protegens hunc Cœli filium, produxit Tchoung Chan fou.

2. Tchoung Chan fou virtus est mitis, pulchra, consentanea legi morali. Decorus habitus, decorus vultus; attentus animus diligentissime. Antiquorum præcepta sunt quæ exsequitur; gravitas et observantia sunt quibus operam dat. Cœli filius est cui obsequitur; clara decreta facit ut proferantur.

3. Imperator mandata dedit Tchoung Chan fou: «Exemplar sis illis omnibus regulis; succedens tuis majo-

于外、四方爰發。
(4) 肅肅王命、仲山甫將之、邦國若否、仲山甫明之。既明且哲、以保其身、夙夜匪解、以事一人。
(5) 人亦有言、柔則茹之、剛則吐之。維仲山甫、柔亦不茹、剛亦不吐。不侮矜寡、不畏彊禦。
(6) 人亦有言、德輶如毛、民鮮克舉之、

4. Siŭ siŭ wâng míng, Tchóung Chān fòu tsiāng tchēu. Pāng kouŏ jŏ pi, Tchóung Chān fòu míng (mâng) tchēu. Kí míng, ts'iè tchĕ, i paò k'i chēnn. Sŏu iè fèi kiái, i chéu ĭ jènn.

5. Jènn ĭ iòu ièn: «Jeôu tsĕ jòu tchēu; kāng tsĕ t'òu tchēu.» Wêi Tchóung Chān fòu, jeôu ĭ pŏu jòu, kāng ĭ pŏu t'òu. Pŏu òu kouán kouà (kòu), pŏu wéi k'iâng iù.

6. Jènn ĭ iòu ièn: «Tĕ iòu jôu maô, mìn sièn k'ŏ kiù tchēu.» Ngò î t'ôu (t'ôu)

porte-voix. Publiez partout mes décisions administratives, afin que le peuple s'y conforme dans tout l'empire.

4. Les ordres de l'empereur sont très importants; Tchoung Chan fou les exécute. Dans les principautés il discerne parfaitement si l'administration est bonne ou mauvaise. Il est habile, perspicace, et sait conserver intacte sa vertu. Du matin au soir il travaille sans relâche pour le service de celui qui seul commande à tout l'empire.

5. On dit communément: «Ce qui est tendre est avalé; ce qui est dur est rejeté de la bouche.» Tchoung Chan fou ne dévore pas ce qui est tendre, et ne rejette pas de la bouche ce qui est dur. (Je veux dire qu') il n'opprime pas les hommes veufs ou les femmes veuves, et ne craint pas de résister aux forts et aux violents.

6. On dit aussi communément: «La vertu est légère comme un poil; cependant peu d'hommes sont capables de la soulever;» c.-à-d.

ribus mortuis, rex ipse sit quem defendas. Efferas et referas regia jussa, regis guttur ac lingua. Proferas administrationem foris, quatuor regiones inde exsurgant (et exsequantur).»

4. Valde gravia sunt regis mandata; Tchoung Chan fou exsequitur ea. Regnorum administratio an bona sit necne, Tchoung Chan fou clare discernit illud. Est peritus et perspicax, ita ut tueatur seipsum (suas virtutes). A mane ad vesperum nunquam pigrescit, ita servit unico viro, i. e. imperatori.

5. Homines et habent dictum: «Molle, tunc edunt illud; durum, tunc expuunt illud.» Solus Tchoung Chan fou molle et non comedit, durum et non expuit. Non opprimit viduos ac viduas, nec timet potentes ac violentos.

6. Homines et habent dictum: «Virtus est levis sicut pilus; homines pauci valent attollere eam.» Ego considerans

我儀圖之、維仲山甫舉之、愛莫助之、袞職有闕、維仲山甫補之、

(7) 仲山甫出祖、四牡業業、征夫捷捷、每懷靡及、四牡彭彭、八鸞鏘鏘、王命仲山甫、城彼東方、

(8) 四牡騤騤、八鸞喈喈、仲山甫徂齊、式遄其歸、吉甫作誦、穆如清風、仲山

tchĕu, wĕi Tchóung Chān fòu kiù tchĕu. Ngái, mouŏ tchóu (tchóu) tchĕu. Kouènn tchĕu iòu k'iuĕ, wĕi Tchóung Chān fòu pòu tchĕu.

7. Tchóung Chān fòu tch'ŏu tsòu, séu meòu iĕ iĕ. Tchĕng fōu tsiĕ tsiĕ, mèi houâi mi kĭ (kiĕ). Séu meòu p'êng p'êng (p'âng p'âng), pă louân ts'iāng ts'iāng. Wâng ming Tchóung Chān fòu tch'êng pĕi tōung fāng.

8. Séu meòu k'ouêi k'ouêi, pă louân kiāi kiāi (kī kī). Tchóung Chān fòu ts'ôu

la vertu est facile à pratiquer, et cependant peu d'hommes sont vertueux. Quand j'y réfléchis, je vois que Tchoung Chan fou seul la soulève. Bien que j'aime Tchoung Chan fou, je ne l'aide pas (il pratique la vertu sans le secours de personne). Si celui qui porte la robe impériale (si l'empereur) manque à son devoir, Tchoung Chan fou répare la faute.

7. Tchoung Chan fou part et sacrifie au dieu des chemins. Ses quatre chevaux sont robustes; ses compagnons de voyage sont agiles. Il craint sans cesse de ne pouvoir bien exécuter les ordres de l'empereur. Ses quatre chevaux sont beaux et robustes; leurs huit sonnettes retentissent en cadence. L'empereur a ordonné à Tchoung Chan fou de fortifier cette région orientale (la principauté de Ts'i).

8. Ses quatre chevaux sont robustes, et leurs huit sonnettes retentissent en cadence. Tchoung Chan fou va à Ts'i; mais qu'il se hâte d'en revenir. Moi Ki fou, j'ai composé ce chant, afin que, comme un souffle subtil, il pénètre jusqu'au cœur de Tchoung

perpendo illud; solus Tchoung Chan fou attollit eam. Amans non adjuvo eum. Si regiæ stolæ officia habent defectum, solus Tchoung Chan fou resarcit illum.

7. Tchoung Chan fou exiens viarum genio sacrificat. Quatuor equi sunt robusti; expeditionis viri sunt celeres. Continuo anxius est ne non assequatur (ut regio mandato fungatur). Quatuor equi sunt robusti et corpulenti; octo tintinnabula concorditer sonant. Imperator jussit Tchoung Chan fou munire illam orientalem regionem.

8. Quatuor equi sunt robusti, octo tintinnabula concorditer sonant. Tchoung Chan fou petit Ts'i; sed acceleret suum reditum. Ki fou composui canticum, alte penetrans sicut liquida

甫永懷、以慰其
心、

韓奕

(1) 奕奕梁山、維
禹甸之、有倬其
道、韓侯受命、王
親命之、纘戎祖
考、無廢朕命、夙
夜匪解、虔共爾
位、朕命不易、榦
不庭方、以佐戎
辟、

(2) 四牡奕奕、孔

Ts'ï, chĕu tch'ouên k'ï kouēi. Kï fòu tsŏ sóung, mŏu jôu ts'ïng fōung (fēnn). Tchóung Chān fòu ióung houâi, i wéi k'ï sīn.

HAN I. **1. Ï ï Leâng chān, wêi Iù tién tchĕu. Iòu tchouŏ k'ï taò. Hân heôu cheóu ming. Wâng ts'īn ming tchēu: «Tsouàn jôung tsòu k'aò. Oû féi tchénn ming, sŏu ié fèi kiái (kï). K'iên kōung èul wéi, tchénn ming pŏu i. Kán pŏu t'ïng fāng, i tsouó jôung pï.»**

2. Séu meòu ï ï, k'òung siōu, ts'iè tchāng. Hân heôu jŏu kin, i k'ï kiái kouēi.

Chan fou, et le console dans les regrets que lui causera longtemps le souvenir (de sa famille et de ses amis).

CHANT VII. HAN I.

Visite du jeune prince de Han à l'empereur 宣王 **Siuēn wâng** pour recevoir l'investiture après la mort de son père; son mariage; beauté de son territoire; étendue de sa puissance.

1. Le mont Leang est vraiment grand; Iu lui a donné ses soins. La route en est clairement tracée; le prince de Han (l'a suivie pour aller) recevoir l'investiture. L'empereur lui a dit: «Succédez à vos ancêtres; remplissez fidèlement le mandat que je vous confie. Du matin au soir soyez diligent, acquittez-vous avec soin des devoirs attachés à votre dignité; et mon mandat ne vous sera pas retiré. Faites rentrer dans l'obéissance les princes (vos subordonnés) qui refusent de venir à ma cour; aidez ainsi votre souverain.»

2. Avec ses quatre beaux chevaux, bien longs et bien grands, le

aura. Tchoung Chan fou diuturno desiderio afficiendus est; inde solatium capiet ejus animus.

CHANT VII. 1. Magnus est Leang mons; Iu composuit illum. Est clara illius via; Han regulus accepit mandatum. Imperator ipse jussa dedit ei: «Succede tuis majoribus mortuis; ne frustreris meum mandatum. A mane ad vesperam ne pigersis, diligenter fungere officiis tuæ dignitatis; meum mandatum non mutabitur. Corrige non venientes ad regiam aulam regiones, i. e. regulos, ut adjuves tuum regem.»

Le mont Leang est dans le 韓城縣 **Hân tch'êng hién**, préfecture de Si ngan fou, province de Chen si. Il était considéré comme le rempart naturel de la principauté de Han 韓之鎮 **Hân tchēu tchénn.**

2. (Vectus) quatuor maribus equis egregiis, valde longis et proceris, Han

脩且張、韓侯入覲、以其介圭、入覲于王。王錫韓侯、淑旂綏章、簟茀錯衡、玄袞赤舄、鉤膺鏤鍚、鞹鞃淺幭、鞗革金厄。

(3) 韓侯出祖、出宿于屠。顯父餞之、清酒百壺。其殽維何、炰鼈鮮魚。其蔌維何、維

Jŏu kin iŭ wáng. Wáng sĭ Hân heŏu chŏu k'î jouéi tchāng, tién fŏu ts'ouŏ hêng (hâng), hiuên kouènn tch'ĕu sĭ, keōu īng leóu iàng, k'ouŏ k'ōung ts'ièn mĭ, t'iaŏ kŏ kīn ngŏ (gnĭ).

3. Hân heŏu tch'ŏu tsóu, tch'ŏu siŭ iŭ T'ŏu. Hièn fóu tsién tchēu, ts'īng tsiòu pĕ hŏu. K'î hiaŏ wêi hô? P'aŏ piĕ siēn iŭ. K'î sŏu wêi hô? Wêi siùn kĭ p'ŏu. Kĭ

prince de Han arriva à la cour impériale, portant la grande tablette de jade, marque de sa dignité. Il arriva et parut devant l'empereur. L'empereur donna au prince de Han un bel étendard orné de dragons avec un pendant de plumes de diverses couleurs, une natte à carreaux pour couvrir la partie postérieure de sa voiture, un joug bien orné, une robe noire, des chaussures rouges, des courroies munies de boucles pour le poitrail de ses chevaux, des ornements ciselés pour le front de ses chevaux, un appui de voiture entouré de cuir et recouvert d'une peau de tigre, des rênes garnies d'anneaux de métal à leurs extrémités.

3. Le prince de Han, à son départ de la cour impériale, sacrifia au dieu des chemins. Il passa une nuit à T'ou. Là (au nom de l'empereur) Hien fou lui offrit le repas des voyageurs, avec cent jarres de vin. Quels étaient les mets principaux? Des tortues rôties, du poisson frais. Quels étaient les légumes? De jeunes pousses de

regulus intravit ut inviseret regem, utens sua magna tabella. Intravit et invisit regem. Rex donavit Han regulo pulchrum draconibus pictum vexillum cum pendulo ornamento, e tessellata storea currus tegmen, variegatum jugum, nigram vestem, rubros calceos, fibulis instructa pectoralia, cælata frontalia, corio firmatum fulcrum, e tigrina pelle fulcri tegmen, habenarum extrema metallicis annulis.

綏 ou 緌 **Jouēi**, pendant composé de crins de bœuf ou de plumes d'oiseaux, teint de diverses couleurs, et fixé à l'extrémité supérieure de la hampe d'un étendard. 簟 **Tièn**, natte tressée à carreaux. 茀 **Fŏu**, natte qui couvrait la partie postérieure d'une voiture. 鍚 **Iâng**, ornement de métal qui se plaçait sur le front des chevaux.

3. Han regulus profiscens sacra fecit viarum genio; profectus pernoctavit in T'ou. Hien fou convivium obtulit ei, cum puri vini centum lagenis. Ejus dapes quænam fuerunt? Tostæ testudines, recentes pisces. Ejus olera quænam

筍及蒲。其贈維何。乘馬路車。籩豆有且。侯氏燕胥。

(4) 韓侯取妻。汾王之甥。蹶父之子。韓侯迎止。于蹶之里。百兩彭彭。八鸞鏘鏘。不顯其光。諸娣從之。祁祁如雲。韓侯顧之。爛其盈門。

(5) 蹶父孔武。靡

tséng wêi hô? Chéng mà lóu kiū. Piēn tsóu iòu tsiū, heóu chéu ién siū.

4. Hân heóu ts'iù ts'ī, Fênn wâng tchēu chēng, Kouéi fòu tchēu tzèu (tsi). Hân heóu íng tchéu, iū Kouéi tchēu lì. Pĕ leáng p'êng p'êng (p'âng p'âng), pă louân ts'iāng ts'iāng. Pŏu hièn k'ì kouāng? Tchōu tí ts'ôung tchēu, k'î k'î jôu iûn. Hân heóu kóu tchēu, lán k'ì îng mênn (mîn).

5. Kouéi fòu k'òung òu, mi kouŏ pŏu taó. Wéi Hân Kì siáng iòu, mouŏ jôu Hân

bambou et de jonc. Quels étaient les présents? Une voiture impériale avec quatre chevaux attelés de front. Il y avait beaucoup de fruits et de ragoûts dans les vases de bois. Tous les princes (qui étaient allés à la cour impériale) prirent part au festin.

4. Le prince de Han épousa la fille de la sœur du roi de la Fenn (Li wang), la fille de Kouei fou. Il alla chercher la jeune fille au lieu où Kouei fou avait sa résidence. Cent voitures le suivirent, chacune munie de huit sonnettes retentissantes. Ne fut-ce pas un grand honneur (pour Kouei fou)? La fiancée parut, accompagnée de plusieurs de ses jeunes parentes, qui marchaient à pas lents et formaient comme une nuée. Le prince de Han les regarda; l'éclat de leur splendeur remplissait le palais.

5. Kouei fou plein d'ardeur et d'activité, avait parcouru toutes

fuerunt? Bambusarum germina et junci. Ejus dona quænam fuerunt? Quadrijugi equi, regius currus. Fructibus et pulmentis plena vasa lignea fuerunt multa. Regulorum cœtus epulatus est simul.

4. Han regulus duxit uxorem Fenn regis sororis filiam, Kouei fou filiam. Han regulus ivit exceptum ad Kouei fou sedem. Centum currus simul incesserunt, octo tintinnabulis concorditer sonantibus. Nonne clarus fuit illius (Kouei fou) honor? Nonnullæ cognatæ comitatæ sunt eam (puellam), presso gradu, instar nubis. Han regulus respexit eas; splendore eæ implebant palatium.

L'empereur 厲王 **Li wâng**, chassé du trône à cause de sa tyrannie, se retira sur les bords de la Fenn, et fut appelé par dérision le roi ou l'empereur de la Fenn. Sa sœur avait épousé Kouei fou, grand ministre d'État dont la famille se nommait 姞 **Kí**. La fiancée d'un prince *tcheou heou* emmenait avec elle huit de ses parentes, qui devenaient femmes de second rang.

5. Kouei fou valde strenuus, nullum regnum non adiverat. Propter Han Ki quæsiverat locum; nullus (inventus)

國不到、爲韓姞相攸、莫如韓樂。孔樂韓土、川澤訏訏、魴鱮甫甫、麀鹿噳噳。有熊有羆、有貓有虎。慶既令、居韓姞燕譽。

(6) 溥彼韓城。燕師所完、以先祖受命、因時百蠻、王錫韓侯、其追其貊、奄受北國、

lŏ (laó). K'óung lŏ Hân t'òu, tch'ouēn tchĕ hiū hiū. Fâng siù fòu fòu, iōu lōu iù iù. Iòu hiôung iòu pī, iòu maô iòu hòu. K'ing ki ling kiū, Hân Kī ién iū (iū).

6. P'òu péi Hân tch'êng, Iēn chēu chòu houàn. Ī siēn tsòu cheóu ming, În chêu pĕ Mân, wâng sī Hân heôu, k'i Tchouēi k'i Mĕ, ién cheóu pă kouŏ, În i k'i pĕ, chēu

les principautés, cherchant un établissement à (sa fille) Han Ki; nul endroit ne lui avait paru si agréable que le pays de Han. La terre de Han est délicieuse ; les cours d'eau et les lacs y sont grands. Les brêmes et les perches sont très grosses; les biches et les cerfs abondent. Il y a des ours ordinaires, des ours gris, des chats sauvages et des tigres. Cet excellent séjour avait plu à Kouei fou; Han Ki y trouve la paix et le bonheur.

6. Les remparts de la capitale de Han ont une vaste étendue: ils ont été construits par le peuple de Ien. Parce que les ancêtres du prince de Han, au nom des empereurs précédents, avaient gouverné les différentes tribus barbares d'une manière conforme aux coutumes de ces peuples, l'empereur confia au prince de Han les Tchouei, les Me, afin que, comme ses pères, il gouvernât ces contrées

sicut Han amœnus. Valde amœnum est Han territorium; fluvii lacusque magni sunt. Bramæ et percæ ingentes sunt; cervæ cervique plurimi. Sunt vulgares ursi, sunt ursi quorum color est flavus albo mixtus; sunt feles silvestres, sunt tigres. Gavisus erat jam optima sede; Han Ki quieta lætatur.

La fille de Kouei fou, après son mariage avec le prince de Han, s'appela Han Ki, Ki étant le nom de sa propre famille, et Han le nom de famille de son mari.

6. Vasta sunt illa Han (urbis præcipuæ) mœnia, Ien regni populus quæ perfecit. Quia (Han principis) majores, accepto regio mandato, congruenter illorum moribus rexerant illos omnes barbaros, imperator commisit Han regulo illos Tchouei, illos Me, ut late accipiens septentrionales gentes, congruenter regeret, adhibitus illorum dux, bene mœnia exstrueret, bene fossas duceret, bene rem agrariam componeret, bene vectigalia imperaret, offerret illorum (locorum) albarum ferarum pelles, fulvas pantheras, flavos ursos.

Les remparts de la capitale de Han avaient été construits, sur l'ordre de 武王 **Où wâng**, par le sage Cheu 君奭 **kiūn Chĕu**, K'ang prince de Chao 召康公 **Chaó K'āng kōung**, qui était

因以其伯、實墉
實壑、實畝實籍、
獻其貔皮、赤豹
黃羆、

江漢

(1) 江漢浮浮、武
夫滔滔、匪安匪
遊、淮夷來求、既
出我車、既設我
旟、匪安匪舒、淮
夷來鋪、

(2) 江漢湯湯、武
夫洸洸、經營四

iôung chĕu hŏ, chĕu meòu chĕu tsĭ, hién k'î p'î p'î, tch'ĕu paó houâng pī.

KIANG HAN. **1. Kiāng Hán feôu feôu, òu fōu t'aō t'aō (t'eōu t'eōu). Fèi ngān fèi iôu, Houâi i lâi k'iôu. Ki tch'ŏu ngò kiū, ki chĕ ngò iû. Fèi ngān fèi chōu, Houâi i lâi p'ōu.**

2. Kiāng Hán chāng chāng ; òu fōu kouāng kouāng. Kīng îng sêu fāng, kaó

septentrionales en qualité de chef, qu'il y fît élever des fortifications solides et creuser des fossés profonds, qu'il réglât le partage des terres et la levée des impôts, et qu'il offrît (à l'empereur) des peaux de léopards blancs, de panthères rousses et d'ours jaunes.

CHANT VIII. KIANG HAN.

虎 **Hòu**, prince de 召 **Chaó**, désigné après sa mort sous le nom de 穆 **Mŏu**, soumet les barbares établis au sud de la Houai, et règle le partage des terres et la levée des impôts. L'empereur 宣王 **Siuēn wâng** lui confie de nouvelles charges et lui accorde de grandes faveurs.

1. Les eaux du Kiang et de la Han sont très élevées; nos soldats (à la jonction de ces deux fleuves) descendent d'un pas rapide (vers l'est). Sans jamais interrompre ni ralentir leur marche, ils vont chercher les barbares établis sur les bords de la Houai. Déjà nos chars sont dehors, nos étendards aux faucons sont dressés. Jamais notre marche n'est interrompue ni ralentie; nous venons attaquer les barbares de la Houai en bataille rangée.

2. Les eaux du Kiang et de la Han sont très élevées; nos soldats ont un air martial. Nous rétablissons l'ordre dans toute l'étendue de

aussi prince de 燕 **Iēn**, et ministre des travaux publics 司空 **sēu k'ōung**.

因 **În**, gouverner un pays d'un manière conforme au caractère et aux coutumes des habitants. 蠻 **Mân**, barbares du sud, tribu barbare quelconque. 貔 **P'î**, animal sauvage de couleur blanche; il ressemble au renard, à l'ours, au tigre ou au léopard.

CHANT VIII. 1. Kiang et Han aquæ turgent ; milites celeriter descendunt. Nec quiescunt, nec tarde incedunt ; Houai barbaros veniunt quæsituri. Jam eduximus nostros currus, jam proposuimus nostra falconibus picta vexilla. Nec quiescimus, nec tarde incedimus ; adversus Houai barbaros venimus ordinaturi aciem.

2. Kiang et Han ingentes aquæ; milites bellico vultu. Componimus et ordi-

方、告成于王、四方既平、王國庶定、時靡有爭、王心載寧、

(3) 江漢之滸、王命召虎、式辟四方、徹我疆土、匪疚匪棘、王國來極、于疆于理、至于南海、

(4) 王命召虎、來旬來宣、文武受命、召公維翰、無

tch'ĕng iû wàng. Séu fāng kí p'îng, wâng kouŏ chóu tíng (tīng). Chĕu mì iòu tchēng, wâng sīn tsái gnîng.

3. Kiāng Hán tchēu hòu, wâng míng Chaó Hòu : « Chĕu p'ì séu fāng ; tch'ĕ ngò kiāng t'òu. Fèi kiòu fèi kĭ, wâng kouŏ lâi kĭ. Iû kiāng iû lì, tchéu iû nân hài (houèi).»

4. Wâng míng Chaó Hòu : « Lâi siûn, lâi siuēn. Wênn Où cheóu míng, Chaó

ces pays barbares, et nous annonçons à l'empereur l'heureuse issue de la guerre. Partout la tranquillité règne, et le domaine propre de l'empereur est en sûreté. A présent les combats ont cessé; l'empereur est exempt d'inquiétude.

3. Hou, prince de Chao, étant encore aux bords du Kiang et de la Han, reçoit de nouveaux ordres. « Étendez ma domination en tous sens, lui dit l'empereur. Partout aux frontières établissez le système du travail et du tribut en commun, non pour vexer et opprimer les habitants, mais pour soumettre tous les pays au régime établi dans le domaine impérial. Fixez les limites, partagez les terres, jusqu'à la mer qui s'étend au sud de la Houai. »

4. L'empereur dit à Hou, prince de Chao: « Étendez partout (mon système agraire. Mes ancêtres) Wenn wang et Ou wang, parvenus au pouvoir, eurent pour principal soutien le prince de Chao (le sage Cheu, l'un de vos aïeux). Ne me considérez pas comme un

namus quatuor regiones (barbararum gentium); nuntiamus felicem exitum imperatori. Quatuor oris jam tranquillatis, imperatoris territorium spes est fore ut sit tutum. Nunc nullum est prælium; imperatoris animus inde quietus est.

3. Ad Kiang et Han ripas (adhuc sumus); imperator mandata mittit Chao regni Hou regulo. « Fac proferas quatuor oras. *Tch'e* (communis laboris et tributi legem statuas, Cf. pag. 363) in meorum finium terris, non ut (incolæ) male habeant nec ut opprimantur, (sed ut) ad imperatoris regnum veniant quasi ad polum, i.e. totius imperii centrum et exemplar. Et limites statuas et agrum partiaris usque ad australe mare. »

4. Imperator mandata dedit Chao regni Hou regulo: « Iens proferas, iens extendas (agrariæ rei legem). Postquam Wenn et Ou imperatores acceperunt potestatem, (ex majoribus tuis unus, sapiens Cheu, K'ang) Chao regulus fuit fulcimen. Ne dicas me esse parvum

曰予小子。召公是似。肇敏戎公。用錫爾祉。(5) 釐爾圭瓚。秬鬯一卣。告于文人。錫山土田。于周受命。自召祖命。虎拜稽首。天子萬年。(6) 虎拜稽首。對揚王休。作召公考。天子萬壽。明明天子。令聞不

kōung wêi hàn (hiuên). Où iuĕ iû siaò tzèu (tsi), Chaó kōung chéu sèu (i). Tchaó min jôung kōung, ióung sĭ èul tch'èu.

5. « Lì èul kouēi tsàn, kiù tch'àng ĭ iòu. Kaó iû wênn jênn, sĭ chān t'òu t'iên (t'în). Iû Tcheōu cheóu míng (míng), tzèu Chaó tsòu míng (míng).» Hòu pái k'ì cheòu. « T'iēn tzèu wán gniên (gnîn). »

6. Hòu pái k'ì cheòu, touéi iâng wâng hiōu (hiòu), tsŏ Chaó kōung k'aò (k'iòu). « T'iēn tzèu wán cheóu (cheòu). Míng míng t'iēn tzèu (tsi), líng wênn

petit enfant ; mais imitez le prince de Chao (le sage Cheu). Vous avez commencé à rendre des services signalés ; je veux vous en récompenser.

5. « Je vous donne une coupe fixée sur une tablette de jade et une jarre de liqueur aromatisée (pour faire des libations à vos ancêtres). Après avoir consulté (dans son temple) le plus humain des hommes (Wenn wang), je vous donne des montagnes, des terres, des champs cultivés. Vous en recevrez l'investiture à Tcheou, comme votre aïeul le prince de Chao (le sage Cheu). » (A la réception de ce message), Hou salua en inclinant la tête jusqu'à terre, (et dit) : « Que le Fils du ciel vive dix mille ans ! »

6. Hou salua en inclinant la tête jusqu'à terre (dans le temple du sage Cheu son aïeul), et par reconnaissance exalta les bienfaits de l'empereur. Il fit (fondre un vase avec une inscription, où, après avoir reproduit le message de l'empereur et raconté) ses propres travaux, (il ajouta) : « Dix mille ans au Fils du ciel ! Que le Fils du ciel, dont le génie est si perspicace, ne cesse de signaler son règne

puerum; Chao regulum vero imiteris. Cœpisti diligenter præstare tuam operam; quapropter dono tibi præmia.

5. « Dono tibi iaspia tabella instructum libatorium et miliacei aromatitæ unum poculum. Postquam monui perhumanum virum (Wenn regem), dono montes, terras, agros. In Tcheou accipies mandatum, sicut Chao regulus avus accepit mandatum. » Hou salutavit inclinato ad terram capite, (et dixit) : « Cœli filio decies mille anni ! »

6. Hou salutavit inclinato ad terram capite (in sapientis Cheu avi sui delubro), et rependens palam fecit imperatoris beneficium. Confecit (vas in quo insculpsit) Chao reguli opera, et: « Cœli filio decies mille anni ! Perspicaci

已、矢其文德、洽
此四國、
常武
(1) 赫赫明明、王
命卿士、南仲大
祖、大師皇父、整
我六師、以脩我
戎、既敬既戒、惠
此南國、
(2) 王謂尹氏、命
程伯休父、左右
陳行、戒我師旅、
率彼淮浦、省此

pŏu i. Chéu k'i wênn tĕ, hiă ts'èu séu kouŏ (ĭ).»

TCH'ANG OU. **1. Hĕ hĕ mîng mîng, wâng mîng k'îng chèu (chòu), Nân Tchóung t'ái tsòu, tái chēu Houâng fòu : « Tchèng ngò lŏu chēu, i siōu ngò jôung (jòu). Ki king ki kiái (kĭ), houéi ts'èu nân kouŏ (ĭ).»**

2. Wâng wéi Ìn chèu : « Ming Tch'êng pĕ Hiōu fòu tsouó ióu tch'ênn hâng,

(par des expéditions militaires). Qu'il déploie ses vertus civiles. et les rende utiles à tous les peuples de l'empire. »

CHANT IX. TCH'ANG OU.

Récit d'une expédition de l'empereur 宣王 **Siuēn wâng** contre les barbares établis au nord de la Houai.

1. L'empereur, avec une majesté terrible et en termes clairs, donne ses ordres à son ministre, le grand maître Houang fou, descendant de Nan Tchoung. « Formez, dit-il, mes six légions, et disposez mon appareil de guerre. Puis, avec diligence et circonspection, portez secours aux contrées du sud (troublées par la révolte des barbares qui sont établis au nord de la Houai). »

2. L'empereur dit au (secrétaire, In Ki fou) chef de la famille des In: « Écrivez de ma part à Hiou fou, prince de Tch'eng, d'aider Houang fou à former les rangs, de donner des avis à mes légions, à mes cohortes, de suivre la rive de la Houai, d'examiner

ingenio cœli filii magna fama non desinat. Exserat suas civiles virtutes, et bene faciat his quatuor imperii regionibus. »

CHANT IX. 1. Tremenda majestate, apertis verbis, imperator mandata dat regni ministro, (orto) ex Nan Tchoung proavo, summo magistro Houang fou. « Compone meas sex legiones, inde præpara mea arma. Jam diligens, jam cautus, opem præsta illis australibus regnis »

Par exception, les deux lettres 常武 du titre ne sont pas tirées du chant lui-même. Elles signifient que l'empereur Siuen wang, doué d'une vertu constante 常德, se signala par des exploits militaires 武功. Les belles actions de Nan Tchoung sont racontées dans le Siao ia, L. I. Ch. VIII, page 187.

2. Imperator dixit In domino : « Jubeas Tch'eng regulum Hiou fou adjuvare (Houang fou) ad componendos ordines, monere meas legiones et cohortes, legere

徐土、不留不處、三事就緒、

(3) 赫赫業業、有嚴天子、王舒保作、匪紹匪遊、徐方繹騷、震驚徐方、如雷如霆、徐方震驚、

(4) 王奮厥武、如震如怒、進厥虎臣、闞如虓虎、鋪敦淮濆、仍執醜

kiái ngò chēu liù, chouĕ pèi Houâi p'òu, sing ts'èu Siû t'òu, pŏu liôu pŏu tch'òu, sān chéu tsiòu siù (siù).»

3. Hĕ hĕ iĕ iĕ (iŏ iŏ), iòu iên t'iēn tzèu. Wâng chōu paò tsŏ, fèi chaò fèi iôu. Siû fāng ĭ saō (seōu), tchénn kīng Siû fāng. Jôu lêi jôu t'îng, Siû fāng tchénn kīng.

4. Wâng fénn kiuĕ òu, jôu tchénn jôu nòu. Tsin kiuĕ hòu tch'ènn, hàn jôu hiaō hòu. P'ōu touēnn Houâi fênn, jêng tchĕu tch'eòu lòu. Tsiĕ pèi Houâi p'òu, wâng chĕu tchēu chòu.

le pays de Siu, de ne pas laisser de garnison et de ne pas demeurer longtemps dans le même endroit, afin que dans les champs les trois sortes de travaux suivent leur cours. »

3. Le Fils du ciel paraît dans l'éclat de sa grandeur, de sa puissance et de sa majesté. Les soldats de l'empereur s'avancent lentement, paisiblement ; ils ne marchent ni trop serrés entre eux ni trop écartés les uns des autres. La terreur se répand d'un endroit à l'autre dans le pays de Siu ; les habitants de Siu tremblent épouvantés. Ils tremblent d'épouvante, comme s'ils entendaient le roulement ou le fracas du tonnerre.

4. L'empereur déploie son ardeur militaire ; sa fureur est semblable au courroux du tonnerre. Il lance en avant ses bouillants officiers, qui frémissent comme des tigres. Ses soldats en rangs serrés couvrent la rive de la Houai ; à la première attaque, il fait un grand

illam Houai fluvii ripam, inspicere hanc Siu terram ; non immorari, non permanere, ut tria (genera rusticorum) operum assequantur consecutionem. »

程 **Tch'êng** était près de 豐 **Fōung** dans le domaine propre de l'empereur.

三事 Les travaux dans les trois sortes de terrains ; à savoir, dans les terrains élevés, dans les terrains bas et dans les plaines.

3. Gravitate conspicuus, potentia magnus, habet majestatem Cœli filius. Regii (milites) tarde, placide progrediuntur, neque condensiores, neque resoluti. Siu regio tractim commovetur ; concussa tremit Siu regio. Quasi tonitru sono quasi tonitru fragore, Siu regio concussa tremit.

4. Imperator exserit suum militarem ardorem, quasi tonans quasi furens. Impellit suos tigrino ardore ministros, frementes quasi rugientes tigres. Sternit (militibus) confertim Houai fluvii ripam ; aggrediens tenet multos captivos.

虜、截彼淮浦、王師之所、

(5) 王旅嘽嘽、如飛如翰、如江如漢、如山之苞、如川之流、緜緜翼翼、不測不克、濯征徐國、

(6) 王猶允塞、徐方既來、徐方既同、天子之功、四方既平、徐方來庭、徐方不回、王曰還歸、

5. Wàng liù t'ān t'ān, jôu fēi jôu hán, jôu Kiāng jôu Hán, jôu chān tchēu paó (peōu), jôu tch'ouēn tchēu liôu, mièn mièn ĭ ĭ, pŏu tch'ĕ pŏu k'ŏ, tchouŏ tchēng Siû kouŏ (ĭ).

6. Wàng iôu iùn sĕ; Siû fāng ki lâi (lĭ), Siû fāng ki t'ôung, t'iēn tzèu tchēu kōung. Séu fāng ki p'ing, Siû fāng lâi t'ing. Siû fāng pŏu houêi, wâng iuĕ: Houân kouēi.

nombre de prisonniers. Cette rive de la Houai est bien gardée; les légions impériales y stationnent.

5. L'armée impériale est nombreuse; elle semble voler, avoir des ailes. (Ses lignes se déploient longues et larges) comme le Kiang et la Han, (fermes) comme le pied d'une montagne; (elles renversent tous les obstacles) comme le cours d'un torrent. Rien ne peut les rompre ni les mettre en désordre. Avec des stratagèmes impénétrables et une force irrésistible, elle soumet entièrement le pays de Siu.

6. Les intentions (pacifiques et bienveillantes) de l'empereur sont sincères et certaines; aussi les habitants de Siu se donnent à lui. Ils se réunissent et se donnent à lui, grâce à la bonté du Fils du ciel. Tout le pays de Siu est pacifié; les chefs viennent promettre obéissance. L'empereur se tient assuré que les habitants de Siu ne changeront plus de sentiments, et dit: Retournons dans nos foyers.

Intercludit illam Houai fluvii ripam, regiarum legionum stationem.

5. Imperatoris exercitus est numerosus; videtur volare, videtur alis ferri. (Longus et latus est) sicut Kiang sicut Han, (firmus) sicut montis radix, (obstacula omnia superans) sicut torrentis cursus, omnino continuus, bene ordinatus. Inscrutabilibus (utens stratagematibus), invictus, late (aut nitide) subdit Siu regionem.

6. Imperatoris mens est sincera et vera; Siu regionis incolæ jam veniunt. Siu regionis incolæ jam conveniunt, Cœli filii opera. Quatuor regionibus (Siu barbarorum) jam tranquillis, Siu regionis (principes) veniunt et obsequium imperatori pollicentur. Siu incolis non mutaturis animum, imperator dicit: Revertentes redeamus domum.

瞻卬

(1) 瞻卬昊天、則不我惠、孔塡不寧、降此大厲。邦靡有定、士民其瘵、蟊賊蟊疾、靡有夷屆。罪罟不收、靡有夷瘳。

(2) 人有土田、女反有之、人有民人、女覆奪之、此宜無罪、女反收之、彼宜有罪、女覆說之、

TCHEN IANG. 1. **Tchēn iàng haó t'iēn, tsě pŏu ngò houéi. K'òung tch'ènn pŏu gnîng, kiáng ts'èu tá lí. Pāng mî iòu tíng, chèu mîn k'î tchái (tchéu). Meôu tsĕ meôu tsî, mî iòu î kiái (kí). Tsouéi kòu pŏu cheōu, mî iòu î tch'eōu.**

2. Jênn iòu t'òu t'iên, jòu fàn iòu tchēu. Jênn iòu mîn jênn, jòu fŏu touŏ tchēu. Ts'èu î òu tsouéi, jòu fàn cheōu (cheòu) tchēu. Péi î iòu tsouéi, jòu fŏu t'ouŏ tchēu.

CHANT X. TCHEN IANG.

Le poète déplore les maux qui accablent le peuple sous le règne de l'empereur 幽王 **Iōu wâng.** Il les attribue à l'ingérence de la favorite 褒姒 **Pāo Séu** et des eunuques dans les affaires publiques.

1. Je lève les yeux vers l'auguste ciel (pour implorer son secours); mais il ne nous est pas favorable. Depuis longtemps il nous envoie de grandes afflictions, sans nous laisser aucune trêve. L'État n'a plus de stabilité; les officiers et les particuliers sont dans la souffrance. Il est des vers rongeurs (de mauvais ministres) qui ruinent le peuple et le tourmentent sans cesse. Les lois injustes et cruelles sont comme des filets toujours tendus; il n'y a ni relâche ni espoir de guérison.

2. D'autres possèdent des terres; (vous, prince), vous vous en emparez. Ils ont des sujets et des serviteurs; vous les leur enlevez. Un homme ne mérite aucun châtiment; vous le faites saisir. Un autre mérite une peine sévère; vous l'y soustrayez.

CHANT X. 1. Aspicio sursum augustum cœlum; nunc non nobis benefacit. Vetustissime non fuit quies, descendunt hæ magnæ turbationes. Regnum nullam habet stabilitatem; præpositi et privati ipsi laborant. *Meòu* et *tsĕ* rodentes graviter nocent; nulla est tranquillitas, finis. Suppliciorum retia non colliguntur; nulla est tranquillitas, (nulla) sanatio. — 卬 est employé pour 仰.

塡 **Tch'ènn,** vieux, longtemps.

蟊 **Meôu,** insecte qui ronge les racines des céréales. 賊 **Tsĕ,** insecte qui ronge les nœuds des céréales.

2. Alii habent terras et agros; tu (imperator) vero occupas eas. Alii habent subditos homines; tu vero aufers eos. Hunc æquum est carere pœna; tu vero apprehendis eum. Illum æquum est affici pœna; tu vero eximis illum.

(3) 哲夫成城、哲婦傾城、懿厥哲婦、爲梟爲鴟、婦有長舌、維厲之階、亂匪降自天、生自婦人、匪教匪誨、時維婦寺、

(4) 鞫人忮忒、譖始竟背、豈曰不極、伊胡爲慝、如賈三倍、君子是識、婦無公事、休其蠶織、

(5) 天何以刺、何神

3. Tchě fōu tch'êng tch'êng, tchě fóu k'īng tch'êng. Ī kiuě tchě fóu, wêi kiaō wêi tch'ēu. Fóu iòu tch'âng chě, wêi li tchēu kiāi (kī). Louán fèi kiáng tzèu t'iēn (t'īn), chēng tzéu fóu jênn. Fèi kiaó fèi houéi, chêu wêi fóu séu.

4. Kiŭ jênn tchéu t'ě, tsién chéu king péi (pě). K'i iuě pŏu kī? Ī hôu wêi gni? Jôu kòu sān péi, kiūn tzèu chéu chěu; fóu ôu kōung chéu, hiōu k'i ts'ân tchěu.

5. T'iēn hô i ts'éu (ts'i? Hô chênn pŏu fóu (féi)? Chè èul kiái tí, wêi iû siū ki.

3. Un homme habile élève des remparts (et rend l'État florissant); une femme habile renverse les remparts (et ruine l'État). Une femme belle et habile (qui intervient dans les affaires) est un hibou malfaisant. Une femme qui a longue langue, attire une suite de malheurs. Les malheurs viennent, non du ciel, mais de la femme. Aucun enseignement utile, aucune instruction ne peut venir des femmes ni des eunuques.

4. Par leurs ruses criminelles ils réduisent au silence leurs adversaires. Ils trompent d'abord le prince par leurs mensonges, puis ils l'abandonnent. Avoueraient-ils jamais que leurs mensonges n'ont point de limite? (Ils disent): «En mes discours quel mal y a-t-il?» Il serait étrange qu'un homme d'un rang élevé fît le commerce et sût retirer de ses marchandises trois fois le prix d'achat; de même c'est un renversement, qu'une femme, exclue des affaires publiques (à raison de son sexe, s'y livre tout entière, et) abandonne ses vers à soie et son tissage.

5. (Prince), pourquoi le ciel vous envoie-t-il des avertissements?

3. Peritus vir perficit oppida; perita mulier evertit oppida. Formosa illa perita mulier; est bubo, est noctua. Mulier habens longam linguam, unice est malorum scala. Turbationes non descendunt e cœlo, oriuntur ex hac muliere. Non docentes, non erudientes, tales sunt mulieres et eunuchi.

4. Elingues reddunt homines nociva versutia. Mendaces primum, tandem deficiunt. Num dicant (sua mendacia) carere limitibus? (Dicunt): «Illud quomodo est malum?» Sicut si mercaturam triplici pretio præstans vir ipsam calleret, ita quod mulier ad quam non attinent publicæ res, relinquat suos bombyces et texturam, (est turbatio).

5. Cœlum quare corripit (te, rex)?

不富。舍爾介狄。維予胥忌、不弔不祥、威儀不類、人之云亡、邦國殄瘁、

(6) 天之降罔、維其優矣、人之云亡、心之憂矣、天之降罔、維其幾矣、人之云亡、心之悲矣、

(7) 觱沸檻泉、維其深矣、心之憂矣、寧自今矣、不自我先、不自我後、藐藐昊

Pŏu tiaó pŏu siâng, wêi i pŏu lêi. Jênn tchĕu iûn wâng, pāng kouŏ tién tsouéi.

6. T'iēn tchēu kiáng wàng, wêi k'î iōu i. Jênn tchēu iûn wâng, sīn tchēu iōu i. T'iēn tchēu kiáng wàng, wêi k'î kî i. Jênn tchēu iûn wâng, sīn tchēu pēi i.

7. Pĭ fŏu hién ts'iuên, wêi k'î chēnn i. Sīn tchēu iōu i, gnîng tzéu kīn i? Pŏu tzéu ngò siēn, pŏu tzéu ngò heóu (hóu). Miaò miaò haò t'iēn, ŏu pŏu k'ŏ kòung

Pourquoi les esprits ne vous accordent-ils pas leurs faveurs ? Vous laissez les hordes puissantes des barbares envahir librement vos frontières, et n'avez de haine que contre moi (à cause de ma franchise). Vous ne déplorez pas les malheurs (que le ciel vous envoie comme avertissements); vous n'avez pas soin de garder la gravité dans votre maintien ni la décence dans votre conduite. Vous n'avez plus de bons ministres; l'État affaibli touche à sa ruine.

6. Le ciel envoie ses (châtiments, qui nous enveloppent comme des) filets, et ils sont nombreux. Les bons ministres ont disparu; j'en suis affligé. Le ciel envoie ses châtiments, et ils sont proches. Les bons ministres ont disparu; j'en suis affligé.

7. Une eau qui jaillit, bouillonne et vient directement de la source, sort d'une grande profondeur. Mon chagrin (est très profond); est-ce seulement à présent qu'il commence? Ces malheurs sont arrivés juste durant ma vie, ni avant ni après. L'auguste ciel peut tout

Cur spiritus non fortunant? Negligis tuos ingentes barbaros, unice me considerans odisti. Non doles de infortuniis; habitus gravitati et actionum decentiæ non attendis. Ministri (probi) non sunt jam; regnum exstinguitur morbidum.

6. Cœlum immittit retia, sunt illa multa. Ministri (probi) non sunt jam; animo doleo. Cœlum immittit retia, sunt illa proxima. Ministri probi non sunt jam; animo doleo.

7. Subsilientis et ebullientis aquæ recta scatebra est illa profunda. Animi dolor num oritur nunc? (Ærumnæ) non ortæ sunt ante me, nec ortæ post me. Altum et remotum magnum cœlum nihil non valet firmare. Ne dedecore afficias augustos progenitores; ita salvabis tuos posteros.

« Bien que le ciel, qui est très élevé, semble ne plus s'occuper des choses de la terre, son action, sa perspicacité sont infinies. Bien que le danger et le trouble

天無不克鞏、無忝皇祖、式救爾後。

召旻

(1) 旻天疾威、天篤降喪、瘨我饑饉、民卒流亡、我居圉卒荒。

(2) 天降罪罟、蟊賊內訌、昏椓靡共、潰潰回遹、實靖夷我邦、

(kòu). Où t'ièn houàng tsòu, chĕu kiòu èul heóu (hòu).

CHAO MIN. **1. Mìn t'iēn tsī wēi; t'iēn tŏu kiáng sáng, tiēn ngò kì kìn. Mîn tsŏu liôu wâng; ngò kiū iù tsŏu houāng.**

2. T'iēn kiáng tsouéi kòu, meôu tsĕ néi hôung. Houēnn tchouŏ mì kōung, houéi houéi houêi iŭ. Chĕu tsìng i ngò pāng (pōung).

raffermir. Ne déshonorez pas vos glorieux ancêtres, et vous sauverez votre postérité.

CHANT XI. CHAO MIN.

Maux causés à l'empire par les mauvais ministres de l'empereur 幽王 **Iōu wâng.**

1. Le ciel, qui est naturellement miséricordieux, sévit à présent avec fureur. Il envoie des fléaux meurtriers, et nous afflige par la famine. Tout le peuple se disperse et périt. Partout jusqu'aux frontières règne la désolation.

2. Le ciel envoie des châtiments qui nous enveloppent comme des filets. Les (mauvais ministres, semblables à des) vers rongeurs, mettent le trouble à l'intérieur, répandent les ténèbres, usent de violence et ne remplissent aucun de leurs devoirs. Ces perturbateurs vicieux sont (les hommes que l'empereur choisit pour) maintenir l'ordre et la tranquillité dans notre pays.

soient extrêmes, il n'est rien que le ciel ne puisse consolider. Si Iou wang pouvait se corriger, se renouveler, et ne plus déshonorer ses ancêtres, il pourrait faire changer les dispositions du ciel, sauver sa postérité, et assurer le bonheur à ses descendants. » (詩經備旨).

CHANT XI. 1. Misericors cœlum vehementer sævit; cœlum firmiter immittit excidia, affligit nos frugum olerumque carentia. Populus totus vagatur et perit. Nostra habitata (loca) et fines omnino desolata sunt.

Le titre 召旻 **Chaó mìn** est composé de la dernière et de la première lettre du chant. 居 **Kiū,** le milieu ou l'intérieur du pays.

2. Cœlum immittit pœnarum retia; vermes et erucæ intus perturbant, caligant, percutiunt, nullo funguntur officio. Perturbatores, perversi, firmi componunt et tranquillant nostrum regnum.

詩經

(3) 皐皐訿訿、曾不知其玷、兢兢業業、孔塡不寧、我位孔貶、
(4) 如彼歲旱、草不潰茂、如彼棲苴、我相此邦、無不潰止、
(5) 維昔之富不如時、維今之疚不如茲、彼疏斯粺、胡不自替、職兄斯引、
(6) 池之竭矣、不

3. Kaō kaō tzèu tzèu, ts'êng pŏu tchēu k'ì tién. Kīng kīng iĕ iĕ, k'òung tiēn pŏu gnîng. Ngò wéi k'òung pièn.

4. Jôu pèi souéi hán, ts'aò pŏu houéi meóu. Jôu pèi sī ts'iû, ngò siáng ts'èu pāng, ôu pŏu houéi tchèu.

5. Wéi sī tchēu fóu pŏu jôu chêu. Wéi kīn tchēu kióu pŏu jôu tzēu. Pèi chōu sēu pái; hôu pŏu tzéu t'i, tchēu houáng sēu in?

6. Tch'êu tchēu kiĕ i, pŏu iûn tzéu p'în. Ts'iuên tchēu kiĕ i, pŏu iûn tzéu

3. Ils sont orgueilleux et médisants; l'empereur ne connaît pas encore leurs défauts. Nous, très diligents et très circonspects, depuis longtemps nous n'avons pas de repos; cependant nos dignités nous sont enlevées ou sont diminuées.

4. Je vois notre pays entièrement troublé, et semblable à une plante qui, dans une année de sécheresse, n'acquiert aucune vigueur, ou à une plante aquatique qui (arrachée du fond de l'eau) s'est desséchée sur un arbre.

5. L'opulence des temps anciens était loin de ressembler à notre condition actuelle; jamais la détresse n'a été si grande qu'à présent. Ces ministres perturbateurs diffèrent des honnêtes gens, autant que le riz le plus grossier diffère du riz le plus épuré. Pourquoi ne se démettent-ils pas eux-mêmes de leurs charges, et prolongent-ils ainsi nos angoisses?

6. Le bassin est desséché, et l'on ne dit pas que c'est parce que

3. Stolide superbiunt, obloquentes detrahunt; adhuc non cognoscit (imperator) eorum vitia. Valde diligentes, valde cauti, valde diu non quiescimus; nostræ dignitates multum minuuntur.

4. Sicut illa anni siccitate plantam non evadentem vegetam, sicut illam arbori insidentem plantam siccatam, ego video hoc regnum in nulla re non perturbatum.

5. Antiquorum temporum opulentia non fuit similis huic (nostræ conditioni); præsentis temporis angustiæ non fuit similis huic. Illi (perturbatores sunt sicut) crassa oryza; hi (probi viri sunt sicut) munda oryza. Cur non ipsi se abdicant, et unica causa sunt angoris adeo producti?

6. Lacus siccatus est, nec dicitur (hoc ortum esse) ex ripis; fons aruit,

云自頻、泉之竭矣、不云自中、溥斯害矣、職兄斯弘、不烖我躬、

(7) 昔先王受命、有如召公、日辟國百里、今也日蹙國百里、於乎哀哉、維今之人、不尚有舊、

tchōung (tchēng). P'òu sēu hái i, tchēu houáng sēu hôung. Pòu tsāi ngò kōung?

7. Sī siēn wàng cheóu ming, iòu jòu Chaó kōung. Jēu p'ī kouō pĕ li; kīn iè jēu tsŏu kouō pĕ li. Oū hōu! ngāi tsāi! Wêi kīn tchēu jènn, pòu cháng iòu kióu (ki)?

les bords (ne reçoivent plus d'eau du dehors); la fontaine est tarie, et l'on ne dit pas que c'est parce que la source (ne donne plus d'eau. On ne dit pas la vraie cause de nos maux). Les mauvais ministres étendent partout leurs ravages, et sont l'unique cause de nos angoisses. Le malheur ne m'atteint-il pas moi-même?

7. Sous les règnes des anciens souverains (Wenn wang et Ou wang), il y avait un homme comme le prince de Chao, et l'étendue de l'empire augmentait de cent stades par jour. A présent elle diminue de cent stades chaque jour. Hélas! que c'est lamentable! De notre temps n'y a-t-il plus d'hommes semblables aux anciens? (Il y en a, mais ils sont exclus des charges).

nec dicitur (hoc ortum esse) ex centro. Late ita nocent; unica causa sunt angoris adeo magni. Nonne calamitas attingit me ipsum?

7. Olim priores reges quum acceperunt imperium, erat vir talis qualis Chao regulus; quotidie proferebatur imperium centum stadiis. Nunc vero quotidie arctatur imperium centum stadiis. Eheu! dolendum! Inter hujus temporis homines nonne adhuc sunt (quidam virtute pares) antiquis?

頌 四

QUATRIÈME PARTIE

SOUNG

周頌清廟之什四之一

清廟

○於穆清廟、肅雝顯相、濟濟多士、秉文之德、對越在天、駿奔走在廟、不

TS'ING MIAO. Oū! mŏu ts'īng miaó! Siŭ iōung hièn siáng. Tsèu tsèu touō chèu, ping Wênn tchēu tĕ. Touéi iuĕ tsái t'iēn, siún pēnn tseòu tsái miaó. Pŏu hièn? pŏu tch'êng? Oû î iû jênn sēu.

LIVRE I. TCHEOU SOUNG TS'ING MIAO.

CHANT I. TS'ING MIAO.

周公 **Tcheōu kōung**, après avoir fait préparer une résidence impériale à 洛陽 **Lŏ iâng** (ville située à l'ouest de 河南府 **Hô nân fòu** dans le Ho nan actuel), s'y rendit lui-même, y réunit tous les princes de l'est, et dans une cérémonie en l'honneur de Wenn wang, fit exécuter l'hymne suivant.

Oh! que le temple est retiré et silencieux! Les aides distingués, pleins de respect et de modération, et tous les officiers, qui sont en si grand nombre, possèdent les vertus de Wenn wang (le respect et la modération). Imitateurs (de Wenn wang dont les mânes sont) dans le ciel, ils marchent à grands pas avec rapidité

TITRE DU LIVRE. 周頌清廟之什四之一 Tcheou soung, Ts'ing miao decas, (Cheu king) quartæ (partis) primus (liber). La quatrième partie du Cheu king contient quarante chants, dont trente et un sont de la dynastie des Tcheou 周頌, quatre des princes de Lou 魯頌 et cinq de la dynastie des Chang 商頌. Elle se divise en cinq livres. Ces chants sont appelés 頌 Éloges, parce que la plupart sont des hymnes qui étaient exécutés dans le temple des ancêtres, en l'honneur des anciens souverains. Ceux des Tcheou forment trois livres ou décades. Les rimes y sont très rares, on ne sait pour quelle raison.

CHANT I. Oh! reconditum ac quietum est delubrum! Reverentes et moderati insignes adjutores, magno numero varii administri habent Wenn regis virtutes. Similes (virtute Wenn

顯不承。無射
於人斯。

維天之命

(1) 維天之命
於穆不已。於
乎不顯。文王
之德之純。
(2) 假以溢我。
我其收之。駿
惠我文王。曾
孫篤之。

維清

○ 維清緝熙。

WEI T'IEN TCHEU MING. **1. Wêi t'iên tchēu ming, ōu! mōu pŏu i. Oū hōu! pŏu hièn Wênn wâng tchēu tĕ tchēu chouênn.**

2. Kiá i ĭ ngò, ngò k'î cheōu tchēu. Siún houéi ngò Wênn wâng, tsēng suēnn tŏu tchēu.

(en présence de sa tablette qui est) dans son temple. Les vertus de Wenn wang ne sont-elles pas glorieuses? ne se perpétuent-elles pas? On ne se lasse jamais (de les célébrer ni de les imiter).

CHANT II. WEI T'IEN TCHEU MING.

Vertu de Wenn wang comparée à l'action du ciel.

1. Oh! l'action du ciel est cachée et incessante! Oh! la vertu sans mélange de Wenn wang ne brille-t-elle pas?

2. S'il a compassion de moi et m'obtient les faveurs du ciel, je les recevrai. (Pour les mériter) je m'efforcerai d'imiter mon aïeul Wenn wang; et mes descendants les plus éloignés s'appliqueront à faire de même.

CHANT III. WEI TS'ING.

Éloge des statuts de Wenn wang.

Les statuts de Wenn wang brillent et doivent briller sans cesse

regi cujus manes sunt) in cœlo, magnis et celeribus passibus excurrunt (coram ejus tabella quæ est) in delubro. (Wenn regis virtutes) nonne clarent? nonne perseverant? Nunquam fastidio sunt hominibus.

越 **Iuĕ** équivaut à 於 **iū** dans. 斯 **Sēu**, particule. Les aides étaient des princes et des ministres d'État. La rapidité de la marche était une marque de respect.

CHANT II. 1. Sola cœli actio oh! recondita est, nec cessat! Oh! nonne insignis est Wenn regis virtutis puritas?

2. Si utens (beneficiis) miserebitur mei, ego ipse accipiam illa. Magnopere imitabor meum (avum) Wenn regem; remoti nepotes diligenter facient idem.

溢 **Ĭ**, lettre employée par erreur au lieu de 恤 **siŭ**.

文王之德愈久不忘而在天之靈可少慰矣（備旨）La mémoire des vertus de Wenn wang ne périra pas avec le temps, et son âme dans le ciel recevra un peu de consolation.

CHANT III. Sunt illustria et continuo illustranda Wenn regis statuta. Ex

文王之典、肇禋
迄用有成、維周
之禎、
烈文
(1)烈文辟公、錫
茲祉福、惠我無
疆、子孫保之、
(2)無封靡于爾
邦、維王其崇之、
念茲戎功、繼序
其皇之、
(3)無競維人、四
方其訓之、不顯

WEI TS'ING. **Wêi ts'ǐng ts'ǐ hǐ, Wênn wâng tchēu tièn. Tchaó īn, hǐ ióung iòu tch'êng, wêi Tcheōu tchēu tchēng.**

LIE WENN. **1. Liě wênn pǐ kōung, sǐ tzēu tch'èu fōu. Houéi ngò ôu kiāng, tzèu suēnn paò tchēu.**

2. Ôû fōung mi iû èul pāng, wêi wâng k'î tch'ôung tchēu. Gnién tzēu jôung kōung, kí siú k'î houâng tchēu.

3. Ôû king wêi jènn, séu fāng k'î hiún tchēu. Pōu hièn wêi tě, pě pǐ k'î hing

d'un vif éclat. Depuis qu'on a commencé à lui faire des offrandes, jusqu'à nos jours où ses règlements ont enfin donné à l'empire sa perfection, ils sont la fortune des Tcheou.

CHANT IV. LIE WENN.

L'empereur 成王 **Tch'êng wâng,** après une cérémonie en l'honneur de ses ancêtres, remercie les princes présents.

1. Princes illustres et distingués, je vous suis redevable des faveurs (que les mânes de mes pères m'ont accordées aujourd'hui). Vous me les avez fait obtenir pour toujours ; mes descendants les conserveront.

2. Vous n'êtes ni exacteurs ni prodigues dans vos principautés; l'empereur doit pour cette raison vous décerner des honneurs en récompense. A cause de la grande cérémonie (que vous venez d'accomplir avec moi), j'espère que vos héritiers d'âge en âge mériteront les mêmes honneurs et de plus grands encore.

3. Il n'est rien de plus puissant que la bienfaisance; elle attire

quo cœptum est sacra facere (et usque ad hoc tempus quo ejus statuta) adhibita potuerunt perficere (nostrum imperium), fuerunt Tcheou felicitas.

CHANT IV. 1. Clari et decori gubernantes reguli, præbuistis mihi hæc fausta et felicia. Donastis mihi sine fine; filii et nepotes servabunt hæc.

2. Non estis exactores prodigive in vestris regnis, et imperator ipse (debet) honoribus rependere illud. Cogitans de hoc magno opere, hæredum series spero fore ut ampliores accipiat illos (honores).

3. Nihil potens nisi humanitas; quatuor imperii regiones discunt eam.

維德百辟其刑
之、於乎前王不
忘、

天作
○天作高山、大
王荒之、彼作矣、
文王康之、彼徂
矣岐、有夷之行、
子孫保之、

昊天有成命
○昊天有成命、
二后受之、成王
不敢康、夙夜基
命宥密、於緝熙、

tchēu. Oū hōu! ts'iên wâng pŏu wâng.

T'IEN TSO. **T'iēn tsŏ kaŏ chān; T'ái wâng houāng tchēu. Pèi tsŏ i, Wênn wâng k'āng tchēu. Pèi ts'iû i K'î, iòu î tchēu hîng (hâng); tzèu suēnn paò tchēu.**

HAO T'IEN IOU TCH'ENG MING. **Haò t'iēn iòu tch'êng míng, éul heóu cheóu tchēu. Tch'êng wâng pŏu kàn k'āng, sŏu ié kī míng iòu mí. Oū! ts'ī hī! Tān kiuē sīn, séu k'î tsing tchēu.**

tout l'univers à son école. Il n'est rien de plus beau que la vertu; tous les princes imitent un souverain vertueux. Oh ! les premiers souverains (Wenn wang et Ou wang) ne seront jamais oubliés.

CHANT V. T'IEN TSO.

Éloge de T'ai wang et de Wenn wang.

Le ciel a fait cette haute montagne (le mont K'i); T'ai wang a défriché les terres environnantes. Il a commencé l'ouvrage; Wenn wang l'a terminé. (Grâce à eux), des chemins unis conduisent au pied de cette montagne escarpée. Leurs descendants puissent-ils la conserver!

CHANT VI. HAO T'IEN IOU TCH'ENG MING.

Éloge de Tch'eng wang.

Le ciel dans sa bonté résolut de confier son mandat (à une nouvelle dynastie); les deux souverains (Wenn wang et Ou wang) l'ont reçu. Tch'eng wang ne se permit pas de vivre dans le repos; mais du matin au soir il travailla à établir solidement son pouvoir (par l'exercice de toutes les vertus). Oh! il soutint la gloire de ses pères.

Nihil conspicuum nisi virtus; omnes reguli ipsi imitantur eam. Oh! priores imperatores non oblitterabuntur.

CHANT V. Cœlum fecit excelsum montem (K'i montem); T'ai rex curavit (terras sitas circa) illum. Is incepit; Wenn rex perfecit illud. Ille præruptus mons K'i habet planas vias. Filii et nepotes servent illum!

CHANT VI. Benignum cœlum habuit statutum mandatum; duo reges acceperunt illud. Tch'eng rex non ausus est otio indulgere; a mane ad vesperum firmavit mandatum altius et accuratius.

單厥心、肆其靖之、

我將.

(1) 我將我享、維羊維牛、維天其右之、

(2) 儀式刑文王之典、日靖四方、伊嘏文王、既右饗之、

(3) 我其夙夜、畏天之威、于時保之、

NGO TSIANG. **1. Ngò tsiāng ngò hiāng, wêi iâng wêi iôu ; wêi t'iēn k'î ióu (iôu) tchēu.**

2. Î chêu hîng Wênn wâng tchēu tièn, jĕu tsing séu fāng. Ī kià Wênn wâng, kí ióu hiàng (hiāng) tchēu.

3. Ngò k'î sŏu ié wéi t'ién tchēu wēi, iû chêu paò tchēu.

Il déploya toute son énergie ; c'est à lui que nous devons la paisible possession de l'empire.

CHANT VII. NGO TSIANG.

Au Chang ti et à Wenn wang.

1. J'amène et j'offre une brebis et un bœuf. Le (roi du) ciel descendra, j'espère, à la droite de ces victimes.

2. Je suis et j'observe avec la plus grande fidélité les statuts de Wenn wang. Je maintiens ainsi constamment la tranquillité dans tout l'empire. Wenn wang, à qui mon règne doit sa prospérité, déjà est à la droite de mes offrandes et les accepte avec joie.

3. Nuit et jour (j'aurai devant les yeux et) je respecterai la majesté du ciel, afin de conserver toujours sa faveur et celle de Wenn wang.

Oh! produxit splendorem. Totum exseruit suum animum; inde ille tutum facit illud.

CHANT VII. 1. Ego adduco, ego offero et ovem et bovem. Et cœlum spero fore ut dextrum adsit.

Dans l'antiquité le côté droit était le plus honorable. 奉其牛羊以享上帝而曰天庶其降在牛羊之右乎蓋不敢必也 (朱熹) L'empereur amène un bœuf et une brebis, les offre au roi du ciel, et dit : « J'espère que le (roi du) ciel descendra à la droite de ce bœuf et de cette brebis. » Il n'ose pas l'assurer.

2. Imitans, sequens, observans Wenn regis statuta, quotidie tranquillas facio quatuor imperii regiones. Ille felicitatem conferens Wenn rex jam dexter gaudet illis (donis).

3. Ego ipse diu noctuque verebor cœli majestatem, ut omni tempore servem illam (cœli et Wenn regis gratiam).

時邁

(1) 時邁其邦、昊天其子之、

(2) 實右序有周、薄言震之、莫不震疊、懷柔百神、及河喬嶽、允王維后、

(3) 明昭有周、式序在位、載戢干戈、載櫜弓矢、我求懿德、肆于時夏、允王保之、

CHEU MAI. 1. Chêu mái k'î pāng; haó t'iēn k'î tzèu tchēu.

2. Chĕu iòu siú iòu Tcheōu; pouŏ iên tchénn tchēu, mouŏ pŏu tchénn tiĕ. Houâi jeôu pĕ chênn, kĭ hô k'iaô iŏ. Iùn wâng wêi heóu.

3. Mîng tchaō iòu Tcheōu; chĕu siú tsái wéi. Tsái tsĭ kān kouō, tsái kaō kōung chèu. Ngò k'iôu i tĕ, séu iû chêu Hià, iùn wâng paò tchēu.

CHANT VIII. CHEU MAI.

武王 **Où wâng**, après avoir renversé la dynastie des 殷 **In**, parcourt l'empire, réunit les princes, et offre des sacrifices au ciel, aux esprits des montagnes et des rivières.

1. Je visite les principautés au temps voulu. Le ciel dans sa bonté me traitera, j'espère, comme son fils.

2. Le ciel a élevé la famille des Tcheou au-dessus de toutes les familles princières, et lui a donné rang parmi les familles impériales. J'ai quelque peu secoué les princes feudataires; il n'en est pas un qui n'ait tremblé. J'ai gagné et me suis attaché tous les esprits tutélaires, jusqu'à ceux des fleuves et des hautes montagnes. Je suis vraiment le maître et le souverain de tout l'empire.

3. La maison des Tcheou est illustre et glorieuse. J'ai assigné à chacun des dignitaires son rang d'après les lois. J'ai fait rapporter les boucliers et les lances, et remettre dans les fourreaux les arcs et les flèches. Je vais cultiver la vertu et la répandre dans tout l'empire. Je mériterai de conserver le pouvoir impérial.

CHANT VIII. 1. Tempori perlustro hæc regna; benignum cœlum, spero, pro filio habebit me.

2. (Cœlum) vere extulit honoribus (supra omnes regulos, et inter imperii rectores) accensuit tenentes Tcheou (principes). Paululum concussi eos (regulos); nullus non concussus tremuit. Alliciens demulsi omnes spiritus, usque ad fluviorum excelsorumque montium genios. Vere imperator sum rector (omnium gentium).

« L'empereur est le fils du ciel. En qualité de fils, il est chargé par le ciel de veiller en même temps au soin des hommes et des esprits. » (詩經備旨).

3. Clari et illustres sunt tenentes Tcheou principes. Ex statutis ordinavi qui tenent dignitates (regulos). Et collecta sunt scuta et hastæ, et thecis reconditi sunt arcus et sagittæ. Ego sectabor pulchram virtutem et diffun-

執競

(1) 執競武王、無競維烈、不顯成康、上帝是皇、

(2) 自彼成康、奄有四方、斤斤其明、

(3) 鐘鼓喤喤、磬筦將將、降福穰穰、

(4) 降福簡簡、威儀反反、既醉既飽、福祿來反、

TCHEU KING. **1. Tchĕu king Où wàng, ôu king wêi liĕ. Pŏu hiĕn Tch'eng, K'āng? Cháng ti chêu houâng.**

2. Tzéu pèi Tch'êng, K'āng, ièn iòu séu fāng, kin kin k'î mîng (mâng).

3. Tchōung kòu hôung hôung (houâng houâng), k'ing kouàn ts'iāng ts'iāng; kiáng fŏu jâng jâng.

4. Kiáng fŏu kièn kièn, wēi i fàn fàn. Kí tsouéi kí paò, fŏu lŏu lâi fàn.

CHANT IX. TCHEU KING.

Aux trois empereurs Ou wang, Tch'eng wang et K'ang wang.

1. La force d'âme de Ou wang a été constante; ses belles actions sont incomparables. Quelle n'est pas la gloire de Tch'eng wang et de K'ang wang? Le roi du ciel leur a donné l'empire.

2. Dès que Tch'eng wang et K'ang wang furent en possession de tout l'empire, ils se signalèrent par leur intelligence.

3. Les cloches et les tambours retentissent d'accord; les pierres sonores et les flûtes mêlent leurs sons harmonieux. Des faveurs insignes et nombreuses descendent du ciel.

4. De grandes faveurs descendent du ciel. Les témoignages de respect redoublent. (Les mânes) ont respiré tout leur soûl l'odeur des liqueurs et des mets. De nouvelles faveurs descendent du ciel.

dam in hoc Sinarum imperio. Vere imperator servabo illud, i.e. supremam potestatem.

CHANT IX. 1. Firmiter tenuit fortitudinem Ou rex; carent æmulatoribus merita (ejus). Nonne conspicui sunt Tch'eng et K'ang? Cœli rex eos imperatores constituit.

上帝是天之主宰皇是君 (備旨) Le Chang ti est le maître et le gouverneur du ciel. *Houâng* équivaut à *kiūn*, souverain, gouverner, constituer souverain.

2. Ex quo illi Tch'eng et K'ang in universum habuerunt quatuor imperii regiones, resplenduit eorum intelligentia.

上帝是皇豈偶然哉 (備旨) Ce fut le roi du ciel qui les constitua empereurs. Comment pourrait-on dire que ce fût le hasard?

3. Campanæ et tympana consonant; sonori lapides et tibiæ simul canunt. Descendunt beneficia opima ac multa.

4. Descendunt e cœlo beneficia maxima. Habitus gravitas et reverentiæ significatio denuo exhibentur. (Manes) jam large biberunt, jam saturati sunt; fausta et bona veniunt denuo.

思文

○思文后稷、克配彼天、立我烝民、莫匪爾極、貽我來牟、帝命率育、無此疆爾界、陳常于時夏、

周頌臣工之什四之二

臣工

(1)嗟嗟臣工、敬爾在公、王釐爾成、來咨來茹、

SEU WENN. Sēu wênn Heóu tsī, k'ŏ p'éi péi t'iēn. Lĭ ngò tchēng mîn, mouŏ fèi èul kĭ. Î ngò lâi meôu, ti ming chouĕ iŭ (ĭ). Où ts'èu kiāng èul kiái (kí), tch'ênn tch'âng iû chêu Hiá.

TCH'ENN KOUNG. 1. Tsiē! tsiē! tch'ênn kōung, king èul tsái kōung. Wâng li èul tch'êng; lâi tzēu, lâi jóu.

CHANT X. SEU WENN.

A Heou tsi, qui fut ministre de l'agriculture sous le règne de Chouenn.

O Heou tsi, prince orné de toutes les vertus, vous avez été comme l'associé du ciel (pour faire du bien aux hommes). C'est uniquement à votre incomparable bienfaisance que notre peuple doit d'avoir des grains. Vous nous avez donné le blé et l'orge, que le ciel a destinés pour être la nourriture de tous. Sans distinction de contrées ni de territoires, vous avez enseigné et fait observer partout dans l'empire les lois des relations sociales.

LIVRE II. TCHEOU SOUNG TCH'ENN KOUNG.

CHANT I. TCH'ENN KOUNG.

Instructions données par l'empereur aux inspecteurs des travaux des champs.

1. Ah! ah! ministres et officiers (préposés aux travaux des champs), remplissez avec soin les devoirs de vos charges. L'empereur vous a donné des règlements. Venez les examiner, et délibérer (sur la manière de les appliquer dans les différents pays).

CHANT X. O (omnibus virtutibus) ornate Heou tsi, potuisti sociari illi cœlo. Quæ frugibus instruxerit nostrum numerosum populum, nihil fuit nisi tua summa (beneficentia). Tradidisti nobis triticum et hordeum, quibus rex (cœli) jussit (homines) ubique nutriri. Non discriminatis his finibus, illis terminis, diffudisti (socialis ordinis) leges in hoc Sinarum regno.

思 Sēu, particule. 立 employé pour 粒 lĭ, grain de céréale, nourrir de grain, vivre de grain. 帝上帝命令也 (詩經備旨) *Tí*, Chang ti; *míng*, ordre, ordonner.

TITRE DU LIVRE. 周頌臣工之什四之二 Tcheou soung, Tch'enn koung decas, quartæ (partis) secunda.

CHANT I. 1. Ah! ah! ministri et præpositi, diligenter curate vestra in

(2)嗟嗟保介、維莫之春、亦又何求、如何新畬、於皇來牟、將受厥明、明昭上帝、迄用康年、命我衆人、庤乃錢鎛、奄觀銍艾、

噫嘻

○噫嘻成王、既昭假爾、率時農夫、播厥

2. Tsiē! tsiē! paò kiái, wêi móu tchēu tch'ouēnn. Ĭ iòu hô k'iôu, jôu hô sīn iû? Oū! houâng lâi meôu; tsiāng cheóu kiuĕ mîng. Mîng tchaō chàng tí hĭ ioung k'āng gniên. Míng ngò tchóung jênn: «Tchéu nài tsièn pouŏ.» Ién kouān tchĕu í.

I HI. Ĭ hī! Tch'êng wâng, kì tchaō kŏ èul. Chouĕ chêu nôung fōu, pouó kiuĕ

2. Ah! ah! assistants des officiers, déjà le printemps touche à sa fin. A quoi devez-vous penser, si ce n'est à la manière de cultiver les terrains qui sont défrichés depuis un ou deux ans? Oh! que le blé et l'orge sont splendides! Bientôt on recueillera ces magnifiques (dons du roi du ciel). Le roi du ciel, plein de gloire et de magnificence, nous donnera une récolte abondante. Dites à tous nos travailleurs: «Préparez vos bêches et vos houes.» Bientôt nous verrons la moisson tomber sous la faucille.

CHANT II. I HI.

Instruction adressée aux inspecteurs des travaux des champs par l'un des successeurs de l'empereur Tch'eng wang.

Oh! Tch'eng wang est manifestement avec vous (pour vous diriger). Conduisez vos laboureurs semer les différentes espèces de grains. Cultivez avec soin vos champs particuliers, sur toute

communi domo (negotia). Imperator dedit vobis statuta. Venite consultum, venite deliberatum.

2. Ah! ah! præpositi adjutores, jam exeunte vere, etiam præterea quid quæritis, (nisi) quomodo colendi secundo anno tertiove anno agri? Oh! quam pulchra sunt triticum et hordeum! Mox colligemus hæc splendida (cœlestis regis dona). Clarus et illustris cœli rex adveniet ut adhibeat (i.e. ut donet) frugibus locupletem annum. Dicite nostris omnibus hominibus (agricolis): «Parate vestras palas et ligones.» Brevi videbimus falcula metentes.

新 **Sīn**, terre qui a été défrichée l'année précédente. 畬 **Iû**, terre qui est défrichée depuis deux ans seulement. 厥明上帝之明賜也 (朱熹) *Kiuĕ mîng*, dons brillants du roi du ciel.

CHANT II. Oh! oh! Tch'eng rex manifeste adest vobis. Vos præeuntes istis agricolis, serite illas varias fruges. Magnopere colite vestros privatos (agros), integris triginta stadiis. Et operam date vestræ culturæ, decies mille sicut unum par.

Il est fait mention de Tch'eng wang, parce que le premier il préposa

百穀、駿發爾私、終三十里、亦服爾耕、十千維耦、

振鷺

(1) 振鷺于飛、于彼西雝、我客戾止、亦有斯容、

pě kŏu. Siún fă éul sēu, tchŏung sān chĕu li. Ĭ fŏu éul kĕng, chĕu ts'iēn wēi ngeòu (i).

TCHENN LOU. **1. Tchénn lóu iû fēi, iû pèi sī iōung. Ngò k'ŏ li tchèu, ĭ iòu sēu iôung.**

l'étendue des trente stades. Appliquez-vous au travail (avec un accord parfait), comme si les dix mille familles ne formaient qu'une seule association de deux.

CHANT III. TCHENN LOU.

Éloge donné par l'empereur au prince de 杞 **K'i** et au prince de 宋 **Sóung**, qui l'ont assisté dans une cérémonie en l'honneur de ses ancêtres. Le premier était issu de la famille impériale des 夏 **Hiá**, et le second de celle des 商 **Chāng**.

1. Les hérons volent en troupe auprès du lac occidental. Ainsi mes hôtes sont venus gracieux et élégants.

des officiers aux travaux des champs, et leur donna des règlements. Dans le domaine propre de l'empereur, il n'y avait pas de champ commun, mais seulement des champs particuliers. La dixième partie des produits de la terre était donnée à l'État.

Un stade carré était divisé en dix parties égales, chacune de cent 畝 **meòu**, et cultivé par dix familles. Un terrain carré dont chaque côté avait en longueur trente-trois stades et un peu plus, contenait mille stades carrés, et était cultivé par dix mille familles. Les familles étaient associées deux à deux pour la culture des terres. Trente stades est un nombre rond employé au lieu de trente-trois stades. V. page 363.

« Dans l'édition impériale du Cheu king, il est dit que ce chant était une prière pour demander, au printemps et en été, une bonne récolte au souverain seigneur. Telle est la tradition constante des anciens. Tous les lettrés de tous les temps l'ont suivie, et dit que cette prière était une cérémonie importante. Tchou Hi avait d'abord admis cette opinion, et affirmé qu'elle était traditionnelle. Ensuite il a changé de sentiment, et prétendu, on ne sait pour quelle raison, que ce chant était un avis adressé aux chefs des laboureurs. Après lui ceux qui ont fait une étude approfondie des King, sont restés dans l'incertitude. » (詩經備旨).

CHANT III. La principauté de Soung était dans le 歸德府 **Kouēi tĕ fòu** actuel (province de Ho nan). Celle de K'i était le 杞縣 **K'i hién** actuel (préfecture de K'ai foung fou).

1. Gregatim ardeæ volant in illo occidentali lacu. Mei hospites advenerunt, etiam habent ejusmodi habitum.

Le plumage du héron est blanc et

(2) 在彼無惡
在此無斁、庶
幾夙夜、以永
終譽。

豐年

○豐年多黍
多稌、亦有高
廩、萬億及秭、
爲酒爲醴、烝
畀祖妣、以洽
百禮、降福孔
皆。

2. Tsái pèi ôu óu, tsái ts'èu ôu ĭ (tóu). Chóu kĭ sōu iè (iú), i iòung tchōung iú.

FOUNG GNIEN. **Fōung gniên touŏ chòu touŏ tòu. Ĭ iòu kaō lin, wán ĭ kĭ tzèu. Wêi tsiòu wêi li, tchēng pi tsòu pi. Ĭ hiă pĕ li, kiáng fŏu k'òung kiāi (ki).**

2. Là (dans leurs principautés) personne ne les a en aversion; ici personne n'est fatigué de leur présence. J'en ai la confiance, on célébrera à jamais leurs louanges nuit et jour.

CHANT IV. FOUNG GNIEN.

Chant qui accompagnait les sacrifices offerts en automne et en hiver pour remercier le ciel des produits de la terre.

La récolte a été abondante; nous avons beaucoup de millet et de riz. Les greniers sont pleins; les boisseaux de grain y sont accumulés par dixaines de mille, par centaines de millions, par dixaines de quadrillions. Nous en ferons de la liqueur fermentée, de la liqueur douce, que nous offrirons à nos aïeux et à nos aïeules. Ainsi nous accomplirons toutes les cérémonies, et le ciel nous accordera toutes sortes de faveurs.

son vol élégant. Ce lac occidental est, croit-on, celui de l'école impérial 辟雝 **Pi iōung**, qui était située à l'ouest de la capitale.

2. In illis (locis, scilicet in K'i et Soung regnis) nemo odit; in hoc (loco seu imperiali regno) nemo fastidit. Spes est fore ut diu noctuque ideo sine fine laudentur.

CHANT IV. Fertilis fuit annus; multum milium, multa oryza. Et sunt alta (plena) horrea, *wán*, *i*, *tzèu* (modiis). Fiet fermentatus liquor, fiet dulcis liquor; allatus offeretur progenitoribus et progenitricibus. Utentes explebimus omnes ritus; descendent bona plene omnigena.

Le millet croît dans les terrains secs, et le riz dans les terrains humides. Quand ils réussissent l'un et l'autre, c'est que les saisons ont été favorables pour toutes sortes de terrains, et toutes les récoltes sont abondantes.

億 **I** signifie ordinairement cent mille, et quelquefois 數萬至萬 dix mille fois dix mille ou cent millions. 秭 **Tzèu** signifie ordinairement cent millions, et parfois 數億至億 cent millions de fois cent millions ou dix quadrillions. Ces deux lettres, d'après Tchou Hi, doivent s'entendre ici dans le second sens.

洽 **Hiă** signifie 備 **Pi**, complet, accomplir entièrement.

有瞽

(一)有瞽有瞽。在周之庭。(二)設業設虡。崇牙樹羽。應田縣鼓。鞉磬柷圉。既備乃奏。簫管備舉。

[illegible] 1 Iou kou iou kou tsái Tcheóu tchēu t'ing.

2 Ché ié ché kiú, tch'ôung iâ chôu iù. Ing t'iên hiuên kòu, t'aô k'ing tch'ou iù. Ki pi nai tseóu (tsóu), siaô kouàn pi kiù.

CHANT V. [illegible]

周 公 Tcheou koung. [illegible] les Tcheou. [illegible]

1. Les musiciens aveugles sont ici; ils sont dans la cour du temple des ancêtres, des Tcheou.

2. On a disposé les suspensions des instruments de musique, les montants, la planche transversale, avec les dents qui se dressent et les plumes qui sont fixées au-dessus. Le petit tambour, le grand tambour, le tambourin à manche, les pierres musicales, la caisse musicale, le tigre couché, tous les instruments sont prêts, et le concert commence. On prend à la fois la flûte à vingt-trois tuyaux et celle à deux tuyaux.

CHANT V. 1. Adsunt caeci musici, adsunt caeci; sunt in Tcheou gentilitii delubri aula.

2. Proposita est transversa tabula, proposita sunt postes; arrecti sunt denticuli, infixae plumae. Respondens tympanum, majus tympanum, suspensum tympanum, manubriatum tympanum, musici lapides, musica capsa, musicus tigris jam parata sunt, et fit concentus. Fistula et tibia simul capiuntur.

Les cloches 鐘 tchôung, les pierres musicales 磬 k'ing et plusieurs espèces de tambours étaient suspendues à des traverses 栒 siùn portées par deux montants 虡 kiù, dont le pied avait la forme d'un animal fabuleux. La traverse était surmontée d'une dentelure, qu'on appelait 業 iě, parce qu'elle présentait l'apparence de la partie supérieure de cette lettre. Au-dessus de la dentelure étaient fixées des plumes de diverses couleurs. Voy. page 312.

應 Ing, sorte de tambour qui avait la forme d'un tube, et mêlait ses sons 應和 ing houó à ceux du grand tambour.

鞉 T'aô, petit tambourin muni d'un manche et portant de chaque côté une balle suspendue. Lorsqu'on l'agite en le tenant par le manche, les deux balles frappent sur les peaux et les font résonner.

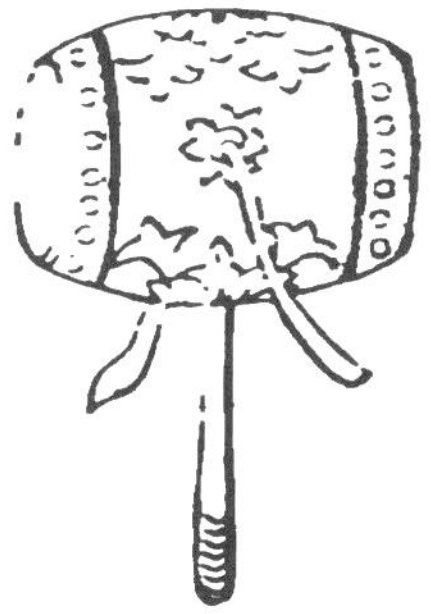

柷 Tch'ŏu, caisse de bois qui servait à donner le signal avant le commencement de chaque morceau de musique, et qu'on faisait résonner en

喤喤厥聲、肅雝和鳴、先祖是聽、我客戾止、永觀厥成、(3)

潛

猗與漆沮、潛有多魚、有鱣有鮪、鰷鱨鰋鯉、以享以祀、以介景福、○

3. Hôung hôung kiuĕ chēng, siŭ iōung houô ming. Siēn tsòu chéu t'ing; ngò k'ŏ lí tchèu, iòung kouān kiuĕ tch'êng.

TSIEN. **Ī iû! Ts'ī Tsiū, tsién iòu touō iû. Iòu tchēn, iòu wèi, t'iaô, tch'âng, iên, lì. Ì hiàng i séu (ĭ), i kiái king fŏu (pĭ).**

3. Tous les instruments unissent leurs sons avec gravité, accord et harmonie. Les ancêtres prêtent l'oreille. Les hôtes qui sont venus, entendront avec plaisir tous les morceaux (depuis le premier jusqu'au dernier).

CHANT VI. TSIEN.

Chant que l'empereur faisait exécuter quand il offrait des poissons à ses ancêtres en hiver et au printemps, dans le bâtiment situé derrière la salle des ancêtres.

Oh! dans la Ts'i et la Tsiu les parcs enferment beaucoup de poissons, des esturgeons grands et petits, des *t'iao,* des *tch'ang,* des *ien,* des carpes. Je les présente, je les offre à mes ancêtres, et j'obtiens un accroissement de félicité.

agitant le bâton 椎 **tch'ouêi** ou 止 **tchèu** placé en son milieu. 圉 ou 敔 **Iù**, instrument de bois qui avait la forme d'un tigre couché, et qu'on frappait avec un bâton nommé 籈 **tchēnn** pour annoncer la fin de chaque morceau de musique.

簫 **Siaō**, flûte composée de vingt-trois tuyaux 大簫 **tá siaō**, ou de seize tuyaux 小簫 **siaò siaō**. 管 **Kouàn**, flûte composée de deux tuyaux.

3. Suaviter sociantur illorum soni; temperate, concorditer, una simul sonant. Mortui progenitores illa audiunt. Mei hospites venerunt; ad finem aspicient (audient) illorum cantica.

成 **Tch'êng**, morceau de musique. Les principaux assistants 客 **k'ŏ** étaient le prince de 杞 **K'i**, rejeton de la dynastie des 夏 **Hià**, et le prince de 宋 **Sóung**, rejeton de celle des 商 **Chāng**.

CHANT VI. Oh! in Ts'i et Tsiu fluviis, lignea septa habent multos pisces. Habent acipenseres majores, habent acipenseres minores, *t'iaô, tch'âng, iên,* cyprinos. Utens offero, utens polluceo; utens ampliabo magnam felicitatem.

T'iaô, nom d'un poisson mince et long. *Tch'âng*, nom d'un poisson dont la tête est munie de cartilages jaunes. *Iên,* nom d'un poisson dont le corps est rond et la tête blanche, et qui demeure 偃 couché dans la vase.

享祀是爲不以祭言(詩經備旨) **Hiàng séu** signifie présenter, et non faire un sacrifice ou une offrande solennelle.

徐氏常吉曰享祀是爲非祭所謂備四時之異物順孝子之誠心也(欽定詩經傳說) Siu Tch'ang ki dit: « *Hiàng séu* c'est

雝

(1) 有來雝雝、至止肅肅、相維辟公、天子穆穆。

(2) 於薦廣牡、相予肆祀、假哉皇考、綏予孝子。

(3) 宣哲維人、文武維后、燕及皇天、克昌厥後。

IOUNG. 1. Iòu lâi iōung iōung, tchéu tchéu siŭ siŭ. Siáng wêi pĭ kōung, t'iēn tzèu mŏu mŏu.

2. Oū! tsién kouàng meòu, siáng iù séu séu (i). Kià tsāi houâng k'aò (k'eòu), souēi iù hiaó tzéu (tsi).

3. Siuēn tchĕ wêi jênn, wênn òu wêi heòu, ién kĭ houâng t'iēn (t'în), k'ŏ tch'āng kiuĕ heòu.

CHANT VII. IOUNG.

Ce chant fut composé pour la cérémonie faite par 武王 **Où wàng** en l'honneur de son père 文王 **Wênn wâng**. Il est aussi appelé 徹 **tch'ĕ**, parce qu'il était chanté à la fin de la cérémonie, pendant qu'on emportait les offrandes.

1. Les princes feudataires sont venus avec des dispositions amicales, et assistent à la cérémonie avec grand respect. Ceux qui aident l'empereur en cette fête, sont des chefs de principautés ; le maintien du fils du ciel est parfait.

2. Oh ! ils offrent un gros taureau, et m'aident à disposer les offrandes. Mon auguste père comble de joie mon cœur de fils.

3. (Mon père) homme intelligent et sage, prince bon et courageux, répondit aux désirs de l'auguste ciel, et assura la grandeur de son héritier (Ou wang).

présenter, et non faire une offrande solennelle. C'est procurer les différentes choses qui conviennent aux diverses saisons, avec les sentiments d'une piété filiale très sincère.»

CHANT VII. 1. Sunt (reguli *tchōu heòu*) qui venerunt animo amico ; adve-nerunt et adstant magna reverentia. Adjutores sunt gubernantes reguli ; cœli filius recte compositus est.

2. Oh ! offerunt amplum taurum ; juvant me ut exponam sacra. Magnus augustus pater beatum facit me pium filium, (nam insigni virtute sua meruit ut sibi tanquam imperatori sacrum facerem Ipse imperator).

3. Perspicax et prudens vir, huma-nus et fortis rex, quiete donavit etiam augustum cœlum ; potuit magnum facere suum hæredem.

故能安民以慰上天求莫之心由是天心用眷而餘休所被有以克昌於厥後焉 (備旨) Il sut ainsi procurer la paix au peuple, et par là réjouir le cœur (du roi) du ciel qui cherche à établir la tranquillité. Pour cette raison, le ciel le traita avec grande affection, et lui accorda des faveurs abondantes, qui s'étendirent jusqu'à son successeur.

(4) 綏我眉壽、介以繁祉、既右烈考、亦右文母、

載見

(1) 載見辟王、曰求厥章、龍旂陽陽、和鈴央央、鞗革有鶬、休有烈光、

(2) 率見昭考、以孝以享、

4. Souêi ngò mêi cheòu (cheòu), kiái i fân tch'èu. Ki ióu liĕ k'aò (k'eòu), ì ióu wênn mòu (mèi).

TSAI HIEN. **1. Tsái hién pí wâng, iuĕ k'iôu kiuĕ tchāng. Lōung k'i iâng iàng, houô lîng iāng iāng. T'iaô kŏ iòu ts'iāng; hiōu iòu liĕ kouāng.**

2. Chouĕ hién tchaō k'aò, i hiaó i hiàng (hiāng).

4. Il m'obtient de longues années de vie et des faveurs nombreuses. Après avoir honoré mon auguste père (par des offrandes, comme s'il avait été revêtu de la dignité impériale), j'honore de la même manière ma vertueuse mère (T'ai Seu).

CHANT VIII. TSAI HIEN.

Pour une offrande faite par 成 王 **Tch'êng wâng** à son père 武 王 **Où wâng**, en présence des princes feudataires.

1. Les princes viennent se présenter devant l'empereur (Ou wang dans son temple), pour lui demander les statuts qu'ils doivent observer. Leurs étendards ornés de dragons sont déployés. Les sonnettes de leurs voitures et de leurs étendards retentissent d'accord. Les (anneaux qui entourent les) extrémités des rênes de leurs chevaux s'entrechoquent avec bruit. Les princes brillent d'un éclat magnifique.

2. Je les conduis devant mon père dont la tablette est placée du côté gauche; je témoigne ma piété filiale et présente des offrandes.

4. (Wenn rex) donat me longa vita, auget multis bonis. Postquam honoravi augustum patrem, etiam honoro perhumanam matrem (**太 姒 T'ái Séu**).

CHANT VIII. 1. En apparent (reguli *tchōu heòu* coram Ou rege) rectore imperatore, ut quærant suas leges. Draconibus pictis ornata vexilla explicata splendent; curruum tintinnabula, vexillorum tintinnabula sociant sonos; habenarum extrema edunt sonitum. (Reguli) belle habent præclarum splendorem.

2. Duco ut appareant coram posito a sinistris patre, ut filialem pietatem significem, ut dona offeram.

載 Tsái, 曰 Iuĕ, particules. **和 Houô**, sonnettes fixées sur le devant de la caisse d'une voiture. **鈴 Lîng**, sonnettes fixées à la partie supérieure d'un étendard.

On appelle **穆 mōu** les tablettes qui sont placées du côté droit dans le temple des ancêtres, et **昭 tchaō** celles qui sont du côté gauche. Dans le temple des ancêtres des Tcheou, la tablette

55

(3)以介眉壽、永言保之、思皇多祜、烈文辟公、綏以多福、俾緝熙于純嘏。

有客

(1)有客有客、亦白其馬、有萋有且、敦琢其旅、

(2)有客宿宿、有客信信、言授之縶、以縶其馬、

3. Ì kiái mêi cheóu, iòung iên paò tchēu, sēu houâng touō hòu. Liĕ wênn pí kōung souēi i touō fŏu, pèi ts'ĭ hī iû chouênn kià (kòu).

IOU K'O. **1. Iòu k'ŏ, iòu k'ŏ, ĭ pĕ k'î mà (mòu). Iòu ts'ī iòu ts'iù, touēi tchouŏ k'î liù.**

2. Iòu k'ŏ siŭ siŭ, iòu k'ŏ sín sín. Iên cheóu tchēu tchĕu, i tchēu k'î mà (mòu).

3. En récompense je reçois l'assurance d'une vie longue, et je conserverai toujours les magnifiques et nombreuses faveurs qui me sont accordées. Grâce aux (mérites de ces) princes distingués et vertueux, je suis en possession de beaucoup de biens. Je garderai ces biens dans toute leur splendeur, et jouirai d'un bonheur sans mélange.

CHANT IX. IOU K'O.

Le prince de Wei 微子, rejeton de la dynastie des 殷 **In**, créé prince de 宋 **Sóung**, entre dans le temple des ancêtres des Tcheou. 成王 **Tch'êng wâng** le reçoit avec joie et s'efforce de le retenir longtemps.

1. J'ai un noble visiteur; (comme ses pères) il a encore des chevaux blancs. Les hommes d'élite (les hauts dignitaires) qui l'accompagnent, sont respectueux et attentifs.

2. J'ai un hôte qui veut demeurer seulement une ou deux nuits. Je lui donnerai des cordes pour attacher ses chevaux (afin qu'il reste plus longtemps).

de 后稷 **Heóu tsĭ** était au milieu, celle de 文王 **Wênn wâng** à droite, et celle de 武王 **Où wâng** à gauche.

3. Ideo augeor longa vita, et semper servabo hæc, scilicet splendida multaque bona. Insignes et humani gubernatores reguli compotem me faciunt multorum bonorum, ut prosequens splendida servem (hæc bona) usque ad perfectam felicitatem.

CHANT IX. 1. Habeo hospitem, habeo hospitem; adhuc albi sunt ejus equi. Habent reverentiam, habent intentum animum optime exculti ejus comites.

Les In avaient adopté la couleur blanche. 敦 **Touēi**, sculpter, ciseler, polir, perfectionner, corriger, châtier.

2. Habeo hospitem una nocte pernoctaturum, habeo hospitem duabus noctibus pernoctaturum. Dabo ei funes quibus alliget suos equos (ut diutius maneat).

(3) 薄言追之。左
右綏之、既有淫
威、降福孔夷、
武
○ 於皇武王、無
競維烈。允文文
王、克開厥後、嗣
武受之、勝殷遏
劉、耆定爾功。
周頌閔予小子
之什四之三
閔予小子
(1) 閔予小子、遭

3. Pouŏ ièn tchouēi tchēu, tsouò ióu souēi tchēu. Ki iòu în wēi, kiáng fŏu k'òung î.

OU. **Oū! houâng Où wâng, ôu king wêi liĕ. Iùn wênn Wênn wâng, k'ŏ k'āi kiuĕ heóu. Séu Où cheòu tchēu, chéng În ngŏ liôu, tchèu tìng èul kōung.**

MIN IU SIAO TZEU. **1. Min iû siaò tsèu; tsaō kiā pōu tsaó (tseóu). K'iôung**

3. (A son départ) j'irai après lui, et lui ferai mille caresses (pour le retenir). Ma famille lui a conféré de grandes distinctions et de grands bienfaits sans la moindre difficulté.

CHANT X. OU.

Ce chant appelé 大武 **Tá Où** fut composé par 周公 pour accompagner la représentation mimique des exploits de 武王 **Où wâng**.

Oh! Ou wang, auguste souverain, vos belles actions n'ont pas d'égales. Wenn wang, prince d'une vertu vraiment parfaite, à commencé l'œuvre que ses successeurs devaient achever; vous, Ou wang, vous l'avez continuée. Vainqueur des In, vous avez mis fin aux massacres et affermi votre ouvrage.

LIVRE III. MIN IU SIAO TZEU.

CHANT I. MIN IU SIAO TZEU.

成王 **Tch'êng wâng**, trois ans après la mort de son père 武王 **Où wâng**, quitte ses vêtements de deuil, entre dans le temple de ses ancêtres et leur exprime ses sentiments.

1. Je suis à plaindre, moi petit enfant, à qui l'empire est échu,

3. Paululum prosequar eum (abeuntem); dextra lævaque, i.e. omnibus modis, mulcebo eum. (A Tcheou imperatoribus) jam habet magnos honores, descenderunt bona valde facile.

CHANT X. Oh! auguste Ou rex, sine paribus sunt præclara facta (tua). Vere *wênn* humanus Wenn rex potuit inchoare post se prosequendum opus; successor Ou suscepisti illud. Vicisti In, inhibuisti cædes; assecutus es ut firmares tua opera.

TITRE DU LIVRE. Tcheou soung, Min iu siao tzeu decas, quartæ (partis) tertius (liber).

CHANT I. 1. Miserandus ego parvus

家不造、嬛嬛在
疚、於乎皇考、永
世克孝、
(2) 念茲皇祖、陟
降庭止、維予小
子、夙夜敬止、
(3) 於乎皇王、繼
序思不忘、
訪落
○訪予落止、率
時昭考、於乎悠
哉、朕未有艾、將
予就之、繼猶判

k'iôung tsài kióu. Oū hōu! houâng k'aò, iòung chéu k'ŏ hiaó (heóu).

2. Gnién tzēu houâng tsòu, tchéu kiáng t'ìng (t'ing) tchèu. Wêi iû siaò tzèu, siŭ ié king tchéu.

3. Oū hōu! houâng wâng, ki siú sēu pŏu wâng.

FANG LO. **Fàng iù lŏ tchèu, chouĕ chéu tchaō k'aò. Oū hōu! iôu tsāi! Tchènn wéi iòu ngái, tsiāng iû tsióu tchēu. Ki iôu p'án houán. Wêi iû siaò tzèu, wéi kân**

quand notre dynastie n'est pas encore solidement établie. Dépourvu de ressources, je suis dans l'angoisse. Oh! mon auguste père, vous avez pratiqué la piété filiale durant toute votre vie.

2. Vous aviez présent à la pensée mon auguste aïeul (Wenn wang, et croyiez le voir) s'élever au ciel et descendre dans la cour du palais. Moi petit enfant, sans cesse je vous respecterai (et vous imiterai, vous et mon aïeul).

3. Oh! augustes souverains (Wenn wang et Ou wang), je m'appliquerai à continuer votre œuvre, et ne vous oublierai jamais.

CHANT II. FANG LO.

成王 **Tch'êng wâng**, après avoir consulté ses ministres au commencement de son règne, entre dans le temple de ses ancêtres et promet de suivre les traces de son père 武王 **Où wâng.**

J'ai consulté mes ministres sur ce que je dois faire au commencement de mon règne. Je suivrai les traces de mon père dont la tablette est ici à gauche. Oh! qu'il est allé loin (dans la voie de la vertu)! Je ne puis arriver jusque là. Je voudrais m'en approcher;

filius, nactus sum domum non firmiter constitutam. Ope destitutus versor in angore. Oh! auguste pater, tota vita potuisti esse pius.

2. Cogitabas de hoc augusto avo (Wenn rege) ascendente ac descendente in aulam. Ego parvus filius diu noctuque reverebor (et imitabor patrem et avum).

止 **Tchèu**, particule.

3. Oh! augusti reges Wenn rex et Ou rex), de prosequenda serie (vestrorum operum) cogitabo nunquam immemor.

CHANT II. Consului meos ministros) de meo initio; sequar hunc a sinistra positum patrem. Oh! quam remotus est! ego non possum attingere.

詩經

渙、維予小子、未堪家多難、紹庭上下、陟降厥家、休矣皇考、以保明其身、

敬之

(1) 敬之敬之、天維顯思、命不易哉、無曰高高在上、陟降厥士、日監在茲、

kiā touō nán. Chaò t'ìng chàng hiá, tchĕu kiáng kiuĕ kiā. Hiōu i houâng k'aò, i paò mîng k'î chēnn.

KING TCHEU. **1. « King tchēu, king tchēu; t'iēn wêi hièn sēu (sī), mìng pŏu í tsāi (tsī). Où iuĕ kaō kaō tsái chàng. Tchĕu kiáng kiuĕ chèu, jĕu kién tsāi tzēu (tsī).»**

mais je m'écarte encore de la route qu'il a tracée. Moi qui suis comme un petit enfant, je suis incapable de faire face aux difficultés si nombreuses que rencontre ma dynastie. Je suivrai (j'imiterai) mon père revenant de la cour d'audience ou s'y rendant, sortant de la maison ou y rentrant. Mon auguste père, qui est si bon, me protégera et m'éclairera.

CHANT III. KING TCHEU.

成王 **Tch'êng wâng**, en réponse aux avis de ses ministres, promet de faire sans cesse des progrès dans la vertu et leur demande de vouloir bien l'aider.

1. « Faites attention, (m'avez-vous dit), faites attention : l'action du ciel est manifeste ; son mandat (le pouvoir souverain) n'est pas facile à conserver. Ne dites pas qu'il se tient dans les hauteurs fort loin de nous. Il monte et descend ; il est présent à nos actions. Chaque jour il est ici examinant toutes choses. »

Velim ego adire eum ; prosequens adhuc recedo et aberro. Nunc ego parvus filius nondum par sum sustinendis domus tot difficultatibus. Prosequar (patrem) ex aula ascendentem (et in aulam) descendentem, ascendentem (in suam domum) et descendentem e sua domo. Qui optimus est augustus pater ideo tuebitur ac illustrabit hanc (meam) personam.

CHANT III. 1. « Attendas ad hoc, (inquistis), attendas ad hoc : cœli (actio) est manifesta ; mandatum non facile (servatur). Ne dicas (cœlum) altissimum stare in supernis. Ascendit et descendit ad hæc (nostra) opera ; quotidie inspiciens inest huic loco. »

思 **Sēu**, particule. 天道甚明其命不易保也無謂其高而不吾察當知其聰明明畏常若陟降於吾之所爲而無日不臨監於此者不可以不敬也（朱熹）La marche, l'action du ciel est très manifeste ; son mandat (le pouvoir souverain) n'est pas facile à conserver. Ne dites pas qu'il est très élevé et ne nous observe pas. Il faut savoir que sa perspicacité est très grande et redoutable ; que sans cesse il monte et descend en quelque sorte, qu'il est présent à nos actions, qu'il n'est pas un seul jour sans venir porter ici ses regards. Il faut donc faire attention.

（2）維予小子、不聰敬止、日就月將、學有緝熙于光明、佛時仔肩、示我顯德行、

小毖

○予其懲、而毖後患、莫予荓蜂、自求辛螫、肇允彼桃蟲、拚飛維鳥、未堪家多難、予又集于蓼、

2. Wèi iû siaò tzèu (tsi), pŏu ts'ōung kìng tchēu. Jĕu tsióu iuĕ tsiāng, hiŏ ióu ts'ī hī iū kouāng mìng (mâng). Pī chêu tzēu kiēn, chéu ngò hièn tĕ hìng (hâng).

SIAO PI. **Iû k'ì tch'êng êul pí heóu houán. Mouŏ iû p'ing fôung, tzéu k'iôu sīn chĕu. Tchaó iùn pèi t'aô tch'ôung, fān fēi wêi gniaò. Wèi k'ān kiā touō nàn, iû ióu tsĭ iū leaò.**

2. Moi qui suis comme un petit enfant, je n'ai pas assez d'intelligence pour être toujours attentif (à remplir mes devoirs). Je ferai des progrès de jour en jour, chaque mois j'avancerai. Par l'étude j'acquerrai sans cesse de nouvelles lumières, jusqu'à ce que j'arrive à une clarté parfaite. Aidez-moi à porter le fardeau qui pèse sur mes épaules; enseignez-moi par quelles actions je dois signaler ma vertu.

CHANT IV. SIAO PI.

管 **Kouàn** et 蔡 **Ts'ái**, frères de 武王 **Où wâng**, et 武庚 **Où kēng**, fils du tyran 紂 **Tcheóu**, s'étant révoltés, ont été soumis par les armes. 成王 **Tch'êng wâng** se repent d'avoir prêté l'oreille aux calomnies répandues contre 周公 **Tcheōu kōung**, et sollicite le concours de ses ministres. Il compare ses oncles Kouan et Ts'ai à deux guêpes, et Ou keng à un oiseau qui, d'abord petit, est devenu grand.

Je me repens du passé, et me tiendrai en garde pour l'avenir. Je n'aurai plus affaire aux guêpes, de peur de m'attirer la piqûre de leurs cruels aiguillons. Ou keng était d'abord un très petit oiseau; il s'est mis à voler, et il est devenu un gros oiseau. Je ne suis pas capable de faire face aux nombreuses difficultés que rencontre ma dynastie; je me trouve de nouveau au milieu d'amers soucis.

2. At ego parvus filius non perspicax attendo. In diem progrediar, in mensem proficiam. Discenti erit continuatum lumen, usque ad splendentem claritatem. Adjuvate (me ut feram) hoc onus humeris; docete me præclare bonas actiones (faciendas).

CHANT IV. Ego ipse me reprehendo, et cavebo futura mala. Non ego ultar vespis, ipse adsciturus acerbam punctionem. Initio vere ille erat persicæ arboris avicula; huc illuc volitans factus est magna avis. Nondum par sum sustinendis domus tot difficultatibus; ego rursus circumdatus sum amaris herbis *leaò*. Cf. pag. 165.

載芟

(1) 載芟載柞、其耕澤澤、

(2) 千耦其耘、徂隰徂畛、

(3) 侯主侯伯、侯亞侯旅、侯彊侯以、有嗿其饁、思媚其婦、有依其士、有略其耜、俶載南畝、

(4) 播厥百穀、實函斯活、

TSAI CHAN. **1. Tsái chān tsái tchĕ (tsŏ); k'ì kēng tchĕ tchĕ (touŏ touŏ).**

2. Ts'iēn ngeòu k'ì iùn, ts'ôu sĭ ts'ôu tchēnn.

3. Heôu tchòu, heôu pĕ, heôu iá, heôu liù, heôu k'iâng, heôu i. Iòu t'àn k'ì iĕ. Sēu méi k'ì fóu, iòu ī k'ì chéu. Iòu leŏ k'ì séu (i), tch'ôu tsái nân meòu (mèi).

4. Pouó kiuĕ pĕ kŏu, chĕu hân sēu houŏ (hŏu).

CHANT V. TSAI CHAN.

Description des travaux des champs, et actions de grâces après une récolte abondante.

1. Les laboureurs arrachent les herbes et les souches d'arbres; la charrue fend la terre et la réduit en poussière.

2. Deux mille hommes vont deux à deux enlever les mauvaises herbes dans les terres labourées et aux lisières des champs.

3. Voici le père de famille, son fils aîné, ses autres fils, tous les jeunes gens de la famille, les aides vigoureux et les ouvriers gagés. Ils mangent avec bruit la nourriture (que les femmes leur ont apportée). Les maris témoignent leur satisfaction à leurs femmes; celles-ci s'attachent de plus en plus à leurs maris. Les laboureurs affilent leurs socs, et commencent leur travail par les champs situés au midi.

4. Ils sèment les différents grains; la semence contient un principe de vie.

CHANT V. 1. Et herbas auferunt et stipites evellunt; ipsis arantibus, finditur et resolvitur (humus).

2. Millies bini ipsi herbas evellunt, adeuntes plana, adeuntes agrorum margines.

3. Et herus et primogenitus et natu minores et omnes domus juvenes et robusti (adjutores) et adhibiti (operarii adsunt). Edunt strepitum ipsi comedentes (cibos a mulieribus allatos. Mariti) ex animo blandiuntur suis uxoribus; (uxores animo) adhærent suis maritis. Curant acuere suos vomeres et inchoant opus ab australibus jugeribus.

4. Serunt suas varias fruges; semen continet aliquod vitæ (principium).

(5) 驛驛其達、有厭其傑。

(6) 厭厭其苗、緜緜其麃。

(7) 載穫濟濟、有實其積、萬億及秭、爲酒爲醴、烝畀祖妣、以洽百禮。

(8) 有飶其香、邦家之光、有椒其馨、胡考之寧。

(9) 匪且有且、匪今斯今、振古如茲。

5. Ĭ ĭ k'ì tă (tĕ), iòu ién k'ì kiĕ.

6. Ién ién k'ì miaŏ, miên miên k'ì piaŏ.

7. Tsái houŏ tsi tsi, iòu chĕu k'ì tzéu (tzéu), wán ĭ kĭ tzèu. Wêi tsiòu wêi lì, tchēng pi tsòu pì, i hiă pĕ li.

8. Iòu pĭ k'ì hiāng, pāng kiā tchēu kouāng. Iòu tsiaŏ k'ì hīng, hôu k'aò tchēu gnîng.

9. Fèi ts'iè iòu ts'iè, fèi kīn sēu kīn (kīng); tchénn kòu jôu tzēu.

5. Les grains sortent de terre en rangées continues; les plantes qui trouvent des sucs plus abondants, s'élèvent au-dessus des autres.

6. Les moissons en herbe trouvent des sucs abondants. Les ouvriers nombreux et serrés enlèvent les mauvaises herbes.

7. Un grand nombre de moissonneurs recueillent les grains; (les monceaux dans les aires) sont au nombre de dix mille, de cent millions, de dix quadrillions. On en fait des liqueurs fermentées et des liqueurs douces, qui sont offertes aux aïeux et aux aïeules, et servent à accomplir toutes les cérémonies.

8. Ces liqueurs ont un parfum très agréable; (servies dans les réunions des princes), elles font honneur à l'État. Elles ont l'odeur du poivre; elles soutiennent les forces des vieillards.

9. Ce n'est pas seulement ici que règne une telle abondance, et ce n'est pas de notre temps qu'elle a paru pour la première fois. Elle a existé dans les temps les plus anciens.

5. Continuis ordinibus illæ erumpunt; quæ habent uberiorem succum, eæ eminent.

6. Uberem habent succum illæ crescentes segetes. Multi et continui illi herbas evellunt.

7. Tum metunt plurimi, habitos fructus ipsi acervant (in areis), decies mille, millies centenis millibus, et *tzèu* (10. 000. 000. 000. 000. 000 acervis). Fit fermentatus liquor, fit dulcis liquor; allatus offertur progenitoribus et progenitricibus, ita explentur omnes ritus. Cf. pag. 429.

8. Habet suaveolentiam eorum (liquorum odor; est regni decus. Habet piperis (odorem) eorum fragrantia; est longævorum senum sustentatio.

9. Non solum hoc loco est hæc (abundantia), nec solum nunc est hæc præsens (abundantia); summe antiquis temporibus erat sicut hoc.

良耜

(1) 畟畟良耜、俶載南畝、

(2) 播厥百穀、實函斯活。

(3) 或來瞻女、載筐及筥、其饟伊黍、

(4) 其笠伊糾、其鎛斯趙、以薅荼蓼、

(5) 荼蓼朽止、黍稷茂止。

(6) 穫之挃挃、積之栗栗、其崇如墉、其

LEANG SEU. **1. Tch'ĕ tch'ĕ leâng sèu (i), tch'ŏu tsái nân meòu (mèi).**

2. Pouó kiuĕ pĕ kŏu, chĕu hân sēu houŏ (hŏu).

3. Houĕ lâi tchĕn jòu, tsái k'ouāng kī kiù; k'î cháng ī chòu.

4. K'î lī ī kiòu (kiaò), k'î pouŏ sēu tchaò, i haō t'ŏu leaò.

5. T'ŏu leaò hiòu tchèu, chòu tsĭ meòu (meòu) tchèu.

6. Houŏ tchĕu tchĕu tchĕu, tsī tchĕu lī lī. K'î tch'ŏung jŏu iŏung, k'î pi jŏu tchĕ, i k'āi pĕ chĕu.

CHANT VI. LEANG SEU.

Actions de grâces rendues aux esprits de la terre et des grains.

1. Les socs des charrues sont bien affilés; on commence le travail par les champs situés au midi.

2. On sème les différents grains; la semence contient un principe de vie.

3. On vient vous voir, avec des paniers, les uns carrés, les autres ronds. Pour votre nourriture on vous apporte du millet.

4. Les bords des chapeaux de bambou se relèvent et s'agitent; les houes creusent le sol et arrachent les mauvaises herbes.

5. Les mauvaises herbes pourrissent (et engraissent la terre). Le millet à panicules devient très vigoureux.

6. Il tombe avec bruit sous la faucille; il est mis en monceaux serrés. Les monceaux sont hauts comme les remparts d'une ville,

CHANT VI. 1. Bene acuminatis optimis vomeribus, inchoant opus in australibus jugeribus.

2. Serunt suas varias fruges; semen continet aliquod vitæ principium.

3. Quidam (uxores et liberi) veniunt ut videant vos; et quadratas cistas et rotundas corbes (portant). Ab eis allatus cibus est milium.

4. Horum arundineorum petasorum quidem (oræ nutant) arrectæ; hi ligones tunc fodiunt (terram), ut evellant *t'ŏu* et *leaò* (amaras herbas).

5. *T'ŏu* et *leaò* putrescunt; milii duo genera viribus pollent.

6. Metunt ea cum strepitu; coacervant ea dense. Ea alta sunt sicut mœnia; ea densa sunt sicut pectinis (dentes). Ideo aperiuntur centum domus (ad condenda ea).

比如櫛以開百室。⑦百室盈止。婦子寧止。⑧殺時犉牡。有捄其角。似以續續古之人。

絲衣

○絲衣其紑。載弁俅俅。自堂徂基。自羊徂牛。鼐鼎及

7. **Pĕ chĕu ing tchéu, fóu tzèu gnìng tchéu.**

8. **Chă chêu chouénn meòu, iòu k'iôu k'ì kiŏ (liŭ), i séu i siŭ, siŭ kòu tchēu jénn.**

SEU I. **Sēu ī k'ī feòu, tsái pién k'iôu k'iôu. Tzéu t'âng ts'ôu kī, tzéu iâng ts'ôu**

serrés comme les dents d'un peigne. Les cent maisons s'ouvrent (pour recevoir le grain).

7. Les cent maisons sont pleines; les femmes et les enfants sont dans la joie.

8. Nous allons immoler ce taureau roux aux lèvres noires, aux cornes recourbées, afin de suivre les exemples et de continuer les observances des anciens.

CHANT VII. SEU I.

Tenue respectueuse et soins diligents des officiers employés à préparer une cérémonie en l'honneur des ancêtres et le festin qui suivait.

Ils sont vêtus d'une tunique de soie très propre, et portent sur la tête un bonnet (de toile rouge) mis très décemment. Des bâtiments intérieurs situés près de la porte ils vont dans le passage (informer le maître de la maison). Après avoir examiné la brebis,

Cent familles formaient ce qu'on appelait 一族 **ī tsòu**. Elles cultivaient un terrain limité par des canaux 洫 **siŭ** et divisé par d'autres canaux plus petits 溝 **keōu**, qui servaient à l'arroser. Elles s'entr'aidaient dans leurs travaux, et faisaient la récolte en même temps.

7. Centum domus plenæ sunt; uxores et liberi gaudent.

8. Mactabimus hunc flavum nigro ore taurum, habentibus curvaturam ejus cornibus. Ita imitabimur, ita prosequemur antiquos homines.

CHANT VII. Serica tunica ipsa nitida est; delatus pileus recte compositus. Ex januæ interioribus ædibus adeunt aream, ex ove adeunt bovem, majorem cortinam et minorem cortinam. Rhinocerotis cornu ipsum curvum est; bonum vinum est dulce. Non clamant, non arrogantes sunt; longæ vitæ beneficium (eis dabitur).

Près de la porte du temple des ancêtres étaient quatre bâtiments 門塾 **ménn chŏu**, dont deux étaient à l'intérieur et regardaient le nord, et deux étaient à l'extérieur et regardaient le sud. Dans les deux bâtiments intérieurs, appelés ici 堂 **t'âng**, on conservait les vases dans lesquels les offrandes

鼒、兕觥其觩、旨酒思柔、不吳不敖、胡考之休、

酌

○於鑠王師、遵養時晦、時純熙矣、是用大介、我龍受之、蹻蹻王之造、載用有嗣、實維爾公允師、

iôu, nài ting kī tzēu. Séu kōung k'ī k'iôu, tchèu tsiòu sēu jeôu, pŏu houá pŏu ngaó; hôu k'aò tchēu hiōu.

TCHO. **Oū! chŏ wâng chēu! Tsiūn iàng chêu houéi; chêu chouênn hī i, chéu ióung tá kiái. Ngò lōung cheóu tchēu, kiaò kiaò wâng tchēu tsaó (tseóu). Tsái ióung iòu séu (séu), chêu wêi èul kōung iùn chēu.**

ils vont voir le bœuf, puis la grande et la petite chaudière. (Ils ont préparé) la corne de rhinocéros de forme recourbée, avec d'excellentes liqueurs qui sont très douces. Ils s'abstiennent de crier, de se montrer arrogants. Une vie longue sera leur récompense.

CHANT VIII. TCHO.

Ce chant, destiné à célébrer les exploits de 武王 **Où wâng**, est intitulé *Tchŏ*, parce que ce prince 酌時 **tchŏ chêu** consultait les circonstances avant de prendre les armes.

Oh! que les légions de l'empereur (Ou wang) étaient belles! Consultant les circonstances, il les forma avec soin, (et les tint dans l'inaction), tant que les temps furent obscurs (tant que la volonté du ciel et du peuple ne parut pas manifeste). Lorsque le temps fut manifestement arrivé, il revêtit la grande cuirasse. Grâce à la faveur du ciel, l'œuvre commencée par ce prince courageux nous a été confiée. Pour la continuer, nous imiterons sincèrement votre conduite (la conduite de Ou wang).

devaient être présentées. Les chaudières étaient à l'extérieur, ainsi que les victimes. 基 **Kī** désigne, ce semble, l'espace vide ou passage entre les deux 堂 **t'âng**.

Avant une cérémonie, le chef de famille et les invités se rendaient dans le 基 **kī**. Les officiers d'un rang inférieur allaient voir si les vases, les chaudières et les autres ustensiles étaient propres, et si les victimes étaient convenables. Ils informaient le chef de famille qui se tenait dans le 基 **kī**.

思 **Sēu**, particule.

CHANT VIII. Oh! pulchræ erant (Ou) regis legiones! Obsequens (adjunctis eas) excoluit tempore tenebroso. Tempore pure lucente, tunc usus est magna lorica (debellavit Tcheou tyrannum et imperio potitus est). Nos beneficio accepimus illud fortissimi regis inceptum. Nunc id quo utemur, ut possimus prosequi, erit tuorum operum sincera imitatio.

桓

○綏萬邦、屢豐年、天命匪解、桓桓武王、保有厥士、于以四方、克定厥家、於昭于天、皇以間之、

賚

○文王既勤止、我應受之、敷時繹思、我徂維求定、時

HOUAN. Souêi wán pāng, liù fōung gniên; t'iēn ming fêi kiái. Houân houân Où wâng, paò iòu kiuĕ chèu. Iû i séu fāng, k'ŏ ting kiuĕ kiā. Oū! tchaō iû t'iēn, houâng i kién tchēu!

LAI. Wênn wâng ki k'în tchèu, ngò îng cheóu tchēu. Fōu chêu ĭ sēu; ngò ts'ôu

CHANT IX. HOUAN.

Faveurs accordées par le ciel à la vertu de Ou wang.

Tous les peuples jouissent de la paix ; souvent les récoltes sont abondantes. Le ciel ne se lasse pas de confier l'empire (à la maison des Tcheou). Le valeureux Ou wang garda ses anciens officiers, les distribua dans toutes les parties de l'empire, et put ainsi affermir sa dynastie. Oh ! il brille dans le ciel, lui qui fut fait empereur pour mettre fin (à la dynastie des Chang) !

CHANT X. LAI.

武王 Où wâng 賚 lái confère des fiefs, comme son père 文王 Wênn wâng.

Wenn wang a déployé la plus grande diligence. Il est juste que (moi et mes successeurs), nous soyons les héritiers (de sa puissance et de sa vertu). Nous imiterons partout et toujours ses exemples, que nous devons étudier et nous rappeler sans cesse ; et nous travaillerons uniquement à affermir la tranquillité. Ces fiefs sont

CHANT IX. Tranquilla sunt omnia regna, crebri sunt fertiles anni. Cœlum mandans (imperium Tcheou domui) non tædet. Fortissimus Ou rex servatos tenuit suos præpositos, ut adhiberet in quatuor imperii regionibus ; potuit firmare suam domum. Oh ! splendet in cœlo, imperator creatus ut abrumperet illam (Chang domum) !

La guerre amène ordinairement la stérilité de la terre et la famine. Par exception, les victoires de Ou wang sur le tyran 紂 Tcheóu ont amené avec la paix la fertilité et l'abondance. 由是安民之德有以慰上天求莫之心而其德上昭於天矣 (備旨) Sa vertu, en procurant la paix au peuple, réjouit le cœur (du roi) du ciel, qui cherche à établir la tranquillité ; et elle brille à présent là-haut dans le ciel.

CHANT X. Wenn rex summam exseruit diligentiam. Nos æquum est accipere illud, i. e. ejus potestatem accipere et diligentiam imitari. Ubique imitantes hanc scrutandam ac recolendam (Wenn

周之命。於繹
思。
般
○於皇時周。
陟其高山。嶞
山喬嶽。允猶
翕河。敷天之
下。裒時之對。
時周之命。
魯頌四之四
駉
(1) 駉駉牡馬。
在坰之野。薄

wêi k'iôu tìng. Chêu Tcheōu tchēu mìng. Oū! ī sēu!

P'AN. **Oū! houâng chêu Tcheōu! Tchĕu k'ì kaō chān, touò chān k'iaô iŏ, iùn iôu hī hô. Fōu t'iēn tchēu hiá, p'eôu chêu tchēu touéi. Chêu Tcheōu tchēu mìng.**

KIOUNG. **1. Kiōung kiōung meòu mà (mòu), tsái kiōung tchēu iè (chòu).**

conférés par les Tcheou; oh! il faut étudier et se rappeler (les exemples de Wenn wang)!

CHANT XI. P'AN.

Ou wang 般 **p'ân** va çà et là, visite les différentes principautés, gravit les hautes montagnes, offre des sacrifices, assemble les princes feudataires.

Oh! que la maison des Tcheou est puissante! Nous gravissons ces hauteurs, ces collines étroites et longues, ces montagnes élevées. Suivant le Fleuve-Jaune, dont le cours est devenu paisible, par tout l'empire nous réunissons les princes, et leur donnons des (instructions et des) réponses. C'est que le mandat du ciel est confié à la maison des Tcheou.

LIVRE IV. LOU SOUNG.

CHANT I. KIOUNG.

僖 **Hī**, prince de Lou (659-626), étend sa vigilance à toutes les branches de l'administration. Il donne des soins intelligents à l'élevage des chevaux.

1. Des chevaux grands et gras sont dans les plaines près des frontières. Parmi ces chevaux grands et gras, les uns sont noirs et

regis virtutem), nos pergentes undequæremus stabilire pacem. Hæc sunt Tcheou mandata; oh! scrutanda et recolenda (Wenn regis virtus)!

CHANT XI. Oh! magna est nunc Tcheou domus! Ascendimus illos altos colles, angustos experrectosque colles, excelsos montes. Vere sequentes placidum Fluvium, totum cœlum subter, congregatis illis (regulis) respondemus. Idque quia Tcheou domus est imperium.

TITRE DU LIVRE. Lou regni præconia, quartæ (partis) quartus (liber). La principauté de Lou était le 兗州府 **Iuèn tcheōu fòu** actuel dans le Chan toung. L'origine de cette principauté est racontée plus loin. Voy. Chant IV.

CHANT I. 1. Ingentes pinguesque mares equi sunt in dissitarum orarum campis. Pauca dicam de ingentibus pinguibusque illis: sunt nigri albis femoribus, sunt remisse flavi, sunt nigri,

言駉者、有驈有皇、有驪有黃、以車彭彭、思無疆、思馬斯臧、(2)駉駉牡馬、在坰之野、薄言駉者、有騅有駓、有騂有騏、以車伾伾、思無期、思馬斯才、(3)駉駉牡馬、在坰之野、薄言駉者、有驒有駱、有

Pouŏ ièn kiōung tchè (tchòu): iòu iŭ, iòu houâng, iòu lî, iòu houâng; i kiū p'ēng p'ēng (p'âng p'âng). Sēu ŏu kiāng; sēu mà, sēu tsāng.

2. Kiōung kiōung meòu mà (mòu), tsái kiōung tchēu iè (chòu). Pouŏ ièn kiōung tchè (tchòu): iòu tchouēi, iòu p'ēi, iòu sīng, iòu k'î; i kiū p'ēi p'ēi. Sēu ŏu k'î; sēu mà, sēu ts'âi (ts'î).

3. Kiōung kiōung meòu mà (mòu), tsái kiōung tchēu iè (chòu). Pouŏ ièn

ont les cuisses blanches, les autres sont jaune pâle; d'autres sont noirs, d'autres sont jaunes. Pour traîner les voitures ils sont excellents. Les pensées du prince ont une étendue sans limite; il pense aux chevaux, et les chevaux sont bons.

2. Des chevaux grands et gras sont dans les plaines près des frontières. Parmi ces chevaux grands et gras, les uns sont gris-blanc, les autres sont jaune-blanc; d'autres sont roux, d'autres sont noir pâle. Pour traîner les voitures ils ont de la force. Les pensées du prince ont une étendue sans limite; il pense aux chevaux, et les chevaux sont forts.

3. Des chevaux grands et gras sont dans les plaines près des frontières. Parmi ces chevaux grands et gras, les uns sont noir pâle et comme couverts d'écailles, les autres ont le corps blanc et la crinière noire; d'autres ont le corps roux et la crinière noire, d'autres ont le corps noir et la crinière blanche. Attelés aux voitures, ils

sunt flavi. Adhibiti ad currus, sunt optimi. Cogitationes (reguli) carent limite; cogitat de equis, eo ipso boni sunt.

Dans le territoire d'un État, au-delà des faubourgs de la capitale, on distinguait comme cinq zones larges d'environ cent 里 li stades chacune: 郊 **kiaō**, 牧 **mōu**, 野 **iè**, 林 **lin**, 坰 **kiōung**.

2. Ingentes pinguesque mares equi sunt in dissitarum orarum campis. Pauca dicam de ingentibus pinguibusque illis: sunt albogilvi, sunt flavi coloris albo mixti, sunt fulvi, sunt remisse nigri. Adhibiti ad currus, sunt robusti. Cogitationes (reguli) carent limite: cogitat de equis, eo ipso validi sunt.

3. Ingentes pinquesque mares equi sunt in dissitarum orarum campis. Pauca dicam de ingentibus pinguibusque illis: sunt remisse nigri et quasi squamati, sunt albi nigra juba, sunt fulvi nigra juba, sunt nigri alba juba. Adhibiti ad currus, non cessant. Cogitationes (reguli) fastidium nesciunt;

詩經

駱有雒、以車繹繹、思無斁、思馬斯作、

(4) 駉駉牡馬、在坰之野、薄言駉者、有駰有騢、有驔有魚、以車祛祛、思無邪、思馬斯徂、

有駜

(1) 有駜有駜、駜彼乘黃、夙夜在公、在公明明、振

kiōung tchė (tchóu): iòu t'ouô, iòu lŏ, iòu liôu, iòu lŏ; i kiū ĭ ĭ (iŏ iŏ). Sēu ôu ĭ (iŏ); sēu mà, sēu tsŏ.

4. Kiōung kiōung meòu mà (mòu), tsái kiōung tchēu iè (chòu). Pouŏ iên kiōung tchė (tchóu): iòu īn, iòu hiâ (hôu), iòu tién, iòu iû; i kiū k'iū k'iū. Sēu ôu siê (siû); sēu mà, sēu ts'ôu.

IOU PI. **1. Iòu pĭ iòu pĭ, pĭ pėi chéng houâng. Siŭ iė tsái kōung, tsái kōung**

marchent sans relâche. L'esprit du prince ne se lasse jamais; il pense aux chevaux, et les chevaux s'élancent.

4. Des chevaux grands et gras sont dans les plaines près des frontières. Parmi ces chevaux grands et gras, les uns sont gris, les autres sont blanc-roux ; d'autres ont de longs poils blancs sur les jambes, d'autres ont les yeux blancs comme les poissons. Pour traîner les voitures ils sont robustes. Les pensées du prince n'ont rien d'oblique; il pense aux chevaux, et les chevaux marchent.

CHANT II. IOU PI.

Banquet offert par le prince de Lou à ses officiers.

1. Les quatre chevaux jaunes attelés de front aux voitures des officiers sont gras et robustes, sont gras et robustes. (Les officiers) sont toute la journée dans le palais. Ils sont dans le palais, rangés en ordre (pour le festin). Les hérons accourent en troupe; les hérons se posent à terre (c.-à-d. les pantomimes arrivent tenant à la main des plumes de héron; ils imitent cet oiseau volant, puis

cogitat de equis, eo ipso erumpunt.

4. Ingentes pinguesque mares equi sunt in dissitarum orarum campis. Pauca dicam de ingentibus pinguibusque illis: sunt gilvi, sunt coloris albi rufo mixti, sunt quorum tibiæ longos pilos albos habent, sunt oculis albis instar piscium. Adhibiti ad currus, viribus pollent. Cogitationes (reguli) nihil habent obliquum (nihil habent quod non sit rectum et honestum); cogitat de equis, eo ipso eunt.

CHANT II. 1. Sunt pingues ac robusti, sunt pingues ac robusti, pingues ac robusti illi quadrijugi equi flavi. (Præpositi cum regulo) a mane ad vesperum sunt in curia. Sunt in curia clare ordinati. Gregatim veniunt ardeæ

振鷺于下。鼓咽咽。醉言舞。于胥樂兮。

(2) 有駜有駜。駜彼乘牡。夙夜在公。在公飲酒。振振鷺鷺。于飛。鼓咽咽醉言歸。于胥樂兮。

(3) 有駜有駜。駜彼乘駽。夙夜在公。在公載燕。自今以始。歲其有。君子有穀。詒孫子。于胥樂兮。

mìng mìng (mâng mâng). Tchénn tchénn lóu, lóu iû hiá (hòu). Kòu iuēn iuēn, tsouéi iên òu ; iû siû lŏ hì.

2. Iòu pĭ iòu pĭ, pĭ pèi chéng meòu. Siŭ ié tsái kōung, tsái kōung in tsiòu. Tchénn tchénn lóu, lóu iû fēi. Kòu iuēn iuēn, tsouéi iên kouēi ; iû siû lŏ hì.

3. Iòu pĭ iòu pĭ, pĭ pèi chéng hiuén. Siŭ ié tsái kōung, tsái kōung tsái iên. « Tzéu kīn i chéu, souéi k'i iòu (i). Kiūn tzéu iòu kŏu, î suēnn tzéu (tsì) ; iû siû lŏ hì. »

descendant à terre). Les tambours font entendre des sons graves et prolongés. Les convives ont bien bu, ils se mettent à danser; ainsi ils se réjouissent ensemble.

2. Les quatre chevaux mâles attelés de front aux voitures des officiers sont gras et robustes, sont gras et robustes. (Les officiers) sont du matin au soir dans le palais; dans le palais ils boivent du vin. Les hérons viennent en troupe; les hérons se mettent à voler. Les tambours font entendre des sons graves et prolongés. Les convives, après avoir bien bu, retournent chez eux (pour éviter tout excès); ainsi ils se réjouissent ensemble.

3. Les quatre chevaux gris attelés de front aux voitures des officiers sont gras et robustes, sont gras et robustes. Les officiers sont du matin au soir dans le palais; dans le palais ils prennent part à un banquet. « Qu'à l'avenir, (disent-ils), les récoltes soient abondantes! Que notre sage prince jouisse de grands biens et les transmette à ses descendants! nous continuerons de nous réjouir ensemble. »

(mimi); ardeæ descendunt. Tympana graves sonos producunt. (Convivæ) large bibunt et saltant; ita simul lætantur.

2. Sunt pingues et robusti, sunt pingues et robusti, pingues et robusti illi quadrijugi equi mares. (Præpositi cum regulo) a mane ad vesperum sunt in curia; in curia bibunt vinum. Gregatim veniunt ardeæ (mimi); ardeæ volant. Tympana graves producunt sonos. (Convivæ) large bibunt et redeunt domos; ita simul lætantur.

3. Sunt pingues ac robusti.... illi quadrijugi murini. (Præpositi) a mane ad vesperum sunt in curia: in curia tunc epulantur. « Abhinc sumpto initio, (aiunt), anni peroptato fertiles sint! Sapiens princeps habeat bona, tradatque filiis ac nepotibus! ita simul gaudebimus. »

詩經

泮水

(1) 思樂泮水、薄采其芹、魯侯戾止、言觀其旂、其旂茷茷、鸞聲噦噦、無小無大、從公于邁、

(2) 思樂泮水、薄采其藻、魯侯戾止、其馬蹻蹻、其馬蹻蹻、其音昭昭、載色載笑、匪怒伊教、

P'AN CHOUEI. **1. Sēu lŏ p'án chouèi, pouŏ ts'ài k'î k'în. Lòu heôu lí tchéu; iên kouān k'î k'î (k'în). K'î k'î péi péi; louân chēng houéi houéi. Oû siaò ôu tái, ts'ôung kōung iû mái.**

2. Sêu lŏ p'án chouèi, pouŏ ts'ài k'î tsaò. Lòu heôu lí tchéu, k'î mà kiaò kiaò. K'î mà kiaò kiaò; k'î īn tchaō tchaō (tchaò tchaò). Tsái chĕ tsái siaó, fèi nóu ī kiaó.

CHANT III. P'AN CHOUEI.

Visite de 僖 **Hī**, prince de Lou, à l'école publique qu'il avait restaurée; souhaits pour la personne du prince et pour le succès de ses armes.

1. Que ce demi-cercle d'eau est agréable! Nous y cueillerons un peu de cresson. Le prince de Lou approche; on voit son étendard orné de dragons. Son étendard flotte au vent; les sonnettes de ses chevaux retentissent d'accord. Tous les habitants, sans distinction de grands ou de petits, suivent le prince dans sa marche.

2. Que ce demi-cercle d'eau est agréable! Nous y cueillerons quelques prêles. Le prince de Lou arrive; ses chevaux sont très beaux. Ses chevaux sont très beaux; sa renommée est très brillante. Son visage est doux et souriant; il enseigne sans impatience.

CHANT III. 1. Quam delectat semicircularis aqua! Paululum carpemus ejus nasturtium. Lou regulus advenit; videmus ejus pictis draconibus ornatum vexillum. Ejus vexillum vento agitatur; tintinnabulorum soni concordant. Nec parvorum nec magnorum (discrimine facto, omnes incolæ) sequuntur regulum euntem.

思 **Sēu**, 言 **Iên**, 止 **Tchèu**, particules. On appelait 泮 **p'án**, 泮 水 **p'án chouèi**, 泮 宮 **p'án kōung** ou 泮 林 **p'án lin** les écoles ou gymnases établis par les 諸 侯 **tchōu heôu** pour l'enseignement des arts libéraux. Ils étaient baignés par un demi-cercle d'eau, de l'est au sud et du sud à l'ouest. L'école impériale s'appelait 璧 廱 **pĭ iōung**, parce qu'elle était entourée d'eau de tous côtés. Voy. page 342. Les expressions 入 泮 **jŏu p'án**, 遊 泮 **iôu p'án**, 采 芹 signifient être reçu 秀 才.

2. Quam delectat semicircularis aqua! Paululum carpemus ejus equisetum. Lou regulus advenit; ejus equi sunt egregii. Ejus equi sunt egregii; ejus fama valde claret. Et leni vultu et subridens, absque ira is docet.

(3) 思樂泮水，薄采其茆。魯侯戾止，在泮飲酒。既飲旨酒，永錫難老。順彼長道，屈此羣醜。

(4) 穆穆魯侯，敬明其德。敬慎威儀，維民之則。允文允武，昭假烈祖。靡有不孝，自求伊祜。

(5) 明明魯侯，克明其德。既作泮宮，淮夷攸服。矯矯虎臣，

3. Sēu lŏ p'ân chouèi, pouŏ ts'ài k'ì maò (miòu). Lòu heŏu lì tchéu; tsái p'ân in tsiòu. Kí in tchéu tsiòu, iòung sĭ nân laò (leòu)! Chouénn péi tch'âng taó (teòu), k'iŭ ts'éu k'iûn tch'eòu!

4. Mŏu mŏu Lòu heŏu, king mîng k'ì tĕ, kìng chénn wēi î, wêi mîn tchēu tsĕ! Iùn wénn iùn òu, tchaŏ kŏ liĕ tsòu! Mì iòu pŏu hiaó, tzéu k'iŏu ī hòu!

5. Mîng mîng Lòu heŏu, k'ŏ mîng k'ì tĕ. Kí tsŏ p'ân kōung, Houâi i iŏu fŏu

3. Que ce demi-cercle d'eau est agréable! Nous y cueillerons un peu de plantain. Le prince de Lou est arrivé; dans le gymnase il boit du vin. Après avoir bu un vin exquis, puisse-t-il avoir le privilège de ne jamais vieillir, suivre toujours la grande voie (du devoir et de la justice), et rendre tous ses sujets dociles à ses lois!

4. Que le prince de Lou, qui est profondément vertueux, cultive soigneusement ses bonnes qualités, s'applique à garder la gravité et les bienséances, et soit le modèle de son peuple! Que ses vertus civiles et militaires comblent de joie ses illustres ancêtres! Que sa parfaite piété filiale lui attire les faveurs du ciel!

5. Le prince de Lou est très intelligent; il a donné le plus grand lustre à ses vertus. Après qu'il a relevé le gymnase public, puissent les barbares de la Houai se soumettre à lui! Que ses officiers, courageux comme des tigres, lui offrent dans le gymnase les oreilles

3. Quam delectat semicircularis aqua! Paululum carpemus ejus alisma. Lou regulus advenit; in gymnasio bibit vinum. Cum biberit exquisitum vinum, jugiter donetur ut difficile (i. e. minime) senescat, insistat illi magnæ viæ (rituum et æquitatis), et sibi subdat hanc (populi) turbam ac multitudinem!

4. Penitus bonus Lou regulus, diligenter excolens suas virtutes, diligenter attendens gravitati et decoro, sit populi exemplar! Vere humanus, vere fortis, clare moveat bene meritos avos (Tcheou koung et Lou regulos)! Nihil habens non pium, ipse sibi adsciscat illa bona!

5. Clare intelligit Lou regulus; potuit expolire suas virtutes. Quum excitaverit semicircularis aquæ gymnasium, Houai barbari ideo se subdant! Fortes tigridum instar duces in gymnasio offerant hostium occisorum sinistras aures! (Judices) bene judicantes sicut Kao iao, in gymnasio offerant captivos!

在泮獻馘。淑問如皋陶、在泮獻囚。

(6) 濟濟多士、克廣德心、桓桓于征、狄彼東南、烝烝皇皇、不吳不揚、不告于訩、在泮獻功。

(7) 角弓其觩、束矢其搜。戎車孔博、徒御無斁、既克淮夷、孔淑不

(p'ĕ). **Kiaò kiaò hòu tch'ênn, tsái p'án hién kouĕ (hĭ). Chŏu wénn jŏu Kaŏ iaŏ (iŏu), tsái p'án hién siŏu.**

6. Tsi tsi touŏ chéu, k'ŏ kouàng tĕ sīn. Houân houân iū tchēng, t'ĭ pèi tōung nân (gnin). Tchēng tchēng houâng houâng, pŏu houá pŏu iàng, pŏu kaó iū hiŏung, tsái p'án hién kōung.

7. Kiŏ kōung k'ĭ k'iŏu, chŏu chéu k'ĭ cheŏu. Jŏung kiū k'òung pouŏ, t'ŏu iú ŏu ĭ (iŏ). Ki k'ŏ Houâi ĭ, k'òung chŏu pŏu ĭ (iŏ). Chĕu kóu èul iŏu, Houâi ĭ tsŏu houŏ.

gauches des ennemis tués! Que ses juges, sages comme Kao iao (ministre de Chouenn et de Iu), lui présentent dans le gymnase les prisonniers de guerre!

6. Que les officiers de tout grade développent les bons sentiments de leurs cœurs! Qu'ils déploient leur valeur dans l'expédition, et repoussent les barbares de l'orient et du midi! Que redoutables par leur nombre et leur puissance, ils évitent de crier et de s'agiter sans raison! Qu'ils ne s'accusent pas les uns les autres (et ne se disputent pas le mérite des belles actions) devant les juges (chargés de régler les différends des soldats); mais qu'ils exposent leurs faits d'armes dans le gymnase!

7. Les arcs ornés de corne sont tendus; les flèches volent par centaines avec un bruit strident. Les chars de guerre sont très grands; les piétons et les conducteurs sont infatigables. Les barbares de la Houai sont subjugués. Entièrement soumis, ils ne feront

Anciennement, après une guerre, c'était dans le gymnase que la paix était annoncée. Les oreilles gauches des ennemis tués y étaient présentées au prince, et les prisonniers de guerre jugés.

6. Magna multitudine numerosi duces valeant ampliare virtutes animorum (suorum)! Fortes ac strenui in expeditione, repellant illos orientales et australes! Numerosi et verendi, ne clament, ne leviter agant! Ne accusent apud judices; in gymnasio nuntient bene gesta!

7. Cornu ornati arcus ipsi curvati sunt; fasces (quinquaginta centumve) sagittarum ipsæ volantes strident. Bellici currus sunt amplissimi; pedites et ductores non lassantur. Jam superati Houai barbari, omnino obsequentes non resistent. Fac firmiter statuas tua consilia; Houai barbari in perpetuum tenebuntur.

逆，式固爾猶，淮
夷卒獲。
(8) 翩彼飛鴞，集
于泮林，食我桑
黮，懷我好音，憬
彼淮夷，來獻其
琛，元龜象齒，大
賂南金。
閟宮
(1) 閟宮有侐，實
實枚枚，赫赫姜
嫄，其德不回，上
帝是依，無災無

8. P'iēn pėi fēi hiaō, tsĭ iû p'án lin. Chĕu ngò sāng chénn, houâi ngò haò in. K'ing pėi Houâi i, lâi hién k'î tch'ēnn. Iuên kouēi siáng tch'èu, tá lóu nân kin.

PI KOUNG. **1. Pí kōung iòu hiŭ, chĕu chĕu mêi mêi. Hĕ hĕ Kiāng Iuên, k'î tĕ pŏu houėi. Cháng tí chéu ī (wēi), ôu tsāi ôu hái, mì iuĕ pòu tch'èu (tch'ouēi).**

plus de résistance. (Prince), combinez bien vos plans, et les barbares de la Houai seront à vous pour toujours.

8. Les oiseaux de nuit (dont le cri est naturellement si désagréable) volent çà et là, et se posent sur les arbres du gymnase. Ils mangent les fruits de nos mûriers, et leurs voix devenues harmonieuses charment nos oreilles. (Ainsi) les barbares de la Houai, devenus raisonnables, viendront offrir ce qu'ils ont de plus précieux, de grandes tortues, des dents d'éléphants et une grande quantité d'or du midi.

CHANT IV. PI KOUNG.

Origine de la famille impériale des Tcheou et de la famille princière de Lou: assurance de félicité et de succès donnée au prince 僖 **Hi**, qui a fait restaurer le temple des ancêtres, et leur rend les honneurs qui leur sont dus.

1. Le temple des ancêtres, situé dans un endroit retiré et fermé, est solitaire et silencieux. Les fondements en sont solides et la structure parfaite. Kiang Iuen est très vénérable ; sa vertu a toujours été irréprochable. Le roi du ciel abaissa sur elle un regard favorable. Dès que les mois de sa grossesse furent écoulés, aussitôt, sans

8. Huc illuc discurrunt illæ volantes striges; considunt in gymnasii arboribus. Comedunt nostrorum mororum mora; delectant nos canora voce. Sapientes illi Houai barbari venient et offerent sua pretiosa, magnas testudines, elephantum dentes; multum donabunt australe aurum.

南金荆陽之金也 L'or du midi, c.-à-d. l'or des deux provinces de King et de Iang (du Hou kouang et du Kiang nan).

CHANT IV. 1. Recondito et clauso delubro sunt puritas ac tranquillitas: firmiter fundatum est, accurate exstructum. Veneranda est Kiang Iuen; ejus virtus nunquam deflexit. Cœli rex eam benigne respexit; sine læsione, sine damno, expletis mensibus, haud mora, ipsa genuit Heou tsi. (Cœli rex immisit

害。彌月不遲。是生后稷。降之百福。黍稷重穋。稙穉菽麥。奄有下國。俾民稼穡。有稷有黍。有稻有秬。奄有下土。纘禹之緒。

(2) 后稷之孫。實維大王。居岐之陽。實始翦商。至于文武。纘大王之緒。致天之屆。于牧之野。無貳無虞。上帝臨女。

chéu chēng Heóu tsī. Kiáng tchēu pĕ fŏu (pĭ), chòu tsĭ tch'ôung lŏu (lĭ). Tchĕu tchéu chŏu mĕ (kĭ), ièn iòu hiá kouŏ (ĭ). Péi mìn kiá chĕ, iòu tsĭ, iòu chòu, iòu taò, iòu kiù. Ièn iòu hiá t'òu, tsouàn Iù tchēu siù.

2. Heóu tsī tchēu suēnn, chĕu wĕi T'ái wâng. Kiū K'î tchēu iâng, chĕu chéu tsièn Chāng. Tchéu iû Wênn Où tsouàn T'ái wâng tchēu siù, tchéu t'iēn tchēu kiái, iû Mŏu tchēu iè (chòu). «Où èul ôu iû, cháng tí lìn jòu.» Touēi Chāng tchēu liù,

lésion ni douleur, elle mit au monde Heou tsi. Le roi du ciel donna à Heou tsi toutes sortes de biens, les deux espèces de millet à panicules, les grains qui se sèment tôt et mûrissent tard, ceux qui se sèment tard et mûrissent tôt, ceux qui se sèment tôt et ceux qui se sèment tard, les haricots et le blé. Bientôt Heou tsi reçut en fief une principauté, et fit cultiver par les habitants les deux espèces de millet à panicules, le riz et le millet noir. Peu à peu il étendit ses bienfaits partout sous le ciel, et continua l'œuvre de Iu.

2. L'un des descendants de Heou tsi fut T'ai wang. Il s'établit au sud du mont K'i, et travailla le premier à renverser les Chang. Plus tard Wenn wang et Ou wang continuèrent l'œuvre de T'ai wang, et exécutèrent l'ordre définitif du ciel dans la plaine de Mou ie. (Le peuple dit à Ou wang): «Loin de vous toute hésitation, toute perplexité; le roi du ciel est avec vous.» Ou wang châtia les cohortes des Chang; il eut part à cet exploit (avec tous les siens).

huic omnia bona, milium *chòu* et milium *tsĭ*, fruges quæ maturius satæ serius maturescunt et fruges quæ serius satæ citius maturescunt, fruges maturius serendas et fruges serius serendas, phaseolum ac triticum. Mox habuit subjectum (imperatori) regnum (邰 T'âi nomine); fecit ut populus sereret et meteret. Fuit *tsĭ*, fuit *chòu*, fuit oryza, fuit nigrum milium. (Ita Heou tsi aliquo modo) universam tenuit subjectam cœlo terram; prosecutus est Iu inceptum. Cf. pag. 2 et 347.

2. Inter Heou tsi posteros vere fuit T'ai rex. Incoluit K'i montis austrum, revera cœpit præcidere Chang. Quum perventum est ad Wenn et Ou reges, prosecuti sunt T'ai regis inceptum, et perfecerunt cœli extremum (decretum de Chang domo) in Mou campo. (Ou regi dictum est): « Ne ambigas, ne sis anxius; cœli rex adest tibi.» Correxit

敦商之旅、克咸厥功。王曰、叔父、建爾元子、俾侯于魯、大啓爾宇、爲周室輔。

(3) 乃命魯公、俾侯于東、錫之山川、土田附庸、周公之孫、莊公之子、龍旂承祀、六轡耳耳、春秋匪解、享祀不忒、皇皇后帝、皇祖后

k'ŏ hièn kiuĕ kōung (kòu). Wâng iuĕ: « Chŏu fòu, kièn èul iuên tzèu (tsòu), pèi heôu iū Lòu. Tá k'i èul iù, wêi Tcheōu chĕu fòu. »

3. Nài ming Lòu kōung pèi heôu iū tōung. Sĭ tchêu chān tch'ouēn, t'òu t'iên fòu iôung. Tcheōu kōung tchēu suēnn, Tchouāng kōung tchēu tzèu (tsi), lōung k'î tch'êng sèu (i), lŏu p'éi èul èul. Tch'ouēnn ts'iōu fèi kiài (kĭ), hiàng sèu pòu t'ĕ. Houâng houâng heóu ti, houàng tsòu Heóu tsĭ, hiàng i sīng hī, chéu hiàng chêu

L'empereur (Tch'eng wang) dit (à Tcheou koung, qui avait contribué plus que personne à la défaite des Chang): « Mon oncle, je crée et constitue votre fils aîné (Pe k'in) prince de Lou. J'augmente considérablement l'étendue de vos domaines, afin que (vous et vos descendants) vous souteniez puissamment la maison des Tcheou. »

3. Il conféra au prince de Lou (à Pe k'in) l'investiture, et l'autorité de *tchou heou* dans l'est. Il lui donna des montagnes, des fleuves, des terres, des champs cultivés et des annexes. (Notre prince Hi koung), descendant de Tcheou koung et fils du prince Tchouang, avec son étendard orné de dragons, vient faire des offrandes; les six rênes de ses chevaux flottent mollement. Au printemps et en automne, il ne manque jamais de faire des offrandes avec toute la perfection possible. Au très auguste roi et seigneur du ciel, à son auguste aïeul Heou tsi, il offre une victime rousse.

Chang cohortes; valuit (cum omnibus militibus suis) esse particeps hujus facinoris. Imperator (成 王 **Tch'êng wâng**) dixit (周 公 **Tcheōu** duci): « Patrue, constituo tuum natu maximum filium (伯 禽 **Pĕ k'in**), ut sit regulus in Lou. Late amplio tuum territorium, ut sis Tcheou domus adjutor. »

牧 野 était dans le 淇 縣 **K'i hién**, préfecture de Wei houei fou, province de Ho nan.

3. Tum mandatum dedit Lou regulo (Pe k'in), ut esset regulus in oriente. Donavit ei montes, fluvios, terras, agros, adnexa regna. Tcheou ducis posterus, Tchouang reguli filius (僖 公 **Hi kōung**), cum ornato pictis draconibus vexillo, offert sacra; sex habenæ molliter fluitant. Vere et autumno non remissus, offerens sacra facit nihil peccans. Augustissimo regi et dominatori (cœli), augusto progenitori Heou tsi offert rufam victimam. Hoc gustant, hoc probant; immittunt bona valde

稷。享以騂犧。是饗是宜。降福既多。周公皇祖。亦其福女。

(4) 秋而載嘗。夏而楅衡。白牡騂剛。犧尊將將。毛炰胾羹。籩豆大房。萬舞洋洋。孝孫有慶。俾爾熾而昌。俾爾壽而臧。保彼東方。魯邦是常。不虧不

i; kiáng fŏu ki touō (i). Tcheōu kōung, houâng tsòu, ĭ k'ĭ fŏu jòu.

4. Ts'iōu êul tsái tch'âng, hiá êul pĭ hêng (hâng). Pĕ meòu sīng kāng, hī tsuēnn ts'iāng ts'iāng. Maô p'aô tzéu kēng (lâng), piēn teóu tá fâng, wán òu iâng iâng. Hiaó suēnn iòu k'ing (k'iâng); pèi êul tch'éu êul tch'āng, pèi êul cheóu êul tsāng. Paò pèi tōung fāng; Lòu pāng chéu châng. Pŏu k'ouēi pŏu pēng, pŏu tchénn pŏu

Ils agréent, ils approuvent cette offrande, et le comblent de biens. Tcheou koung et vos autres glorieux ancêtres, (prince), vous accordent aussi des faveurs.

4. En automne le prince offre le sacrifice de la saison; (il immole) des bœufs aux cornes desquels on a fixé un bois transversal en été (pour les empêcher de nuire). (Il offre) un bœuf blanc (à Tcheou koung) et un bœuf roux (à Pe k'in et aux autres princes de Lou). Il y a des coupes majestueuses ornées de figures de bœufs, de la chair rôtie d'un porc qui a été (échaudé et) dépouillé de son poil, des hachis, des sauces, des vases de bois dont les uns sont carrés et les autres ronds, de longues tables très basses qui ont l'apparence de bâtiments (et sur lesquelles on offre la chair des victimes). Il y a de magnifiques danses, les unes civiles, les autres militaires. Prince, en récompense de votre piété filiale, vous recevrez beaucoup de biens. Vos pères vous obtiendront un règne glorieux et florissant, une vie longue et une santé parfaite. Vous garderez cette contrée orientale. La principauté de Lou sera à vous pour toujours. Elle ne sera ni diminuée ni renversée ni

multa. Tcheou koung et augusti progenitores etiam ipsi fortunant te.

附庸 **Fóu iôung,** petite principauté placée sous la dépendance d'une grande.

4. Autumno autem fit autumnale sacrum; æstate vero lignum transversum (boum capiti impositum est ne cornibus ferirent). Albus masculus (offertur Tcheou duci), rufus bos (offertur Pe k'in cæterisque Lou regulis.) Sunt bobus pictis ornati crateres magnifici, depilati (porci caro) assata, minutalia, juscula, lignea vasa quadrata, lignea vasa rotunda, magnæ mensæ; tum civiles tum militares saltationes pulcherrimæ. Pie pronepos, habebis prospera. (Progenitores tui) facient ut tu corusces ac floreas; facient ut sis longævus et bene valeas. Proteges hanc orienta-

崩不震不騰、三壽作朋、如岡如陵、

(5)公車千乘、朱英綠縢、二矛重弓、公徒三萬、貝冑朱綅、烝徒增增、戎狄是膺、荊舒是懲、則莫我敢承、俾爾昌而熾、俾爾壽而富、黃髮台背、壽胥與試、俾爾昌而大、俾爾耆而艾、萬有千歲、

t'êng. Sān cheȯu tsŏ p'êng, jȯu kāng jȯu ling.

5. Kōung kiŭ ts'iēn chéng (chêng), tchōu īng lŏu t'êng, éul meȯu tch'ȯung kōung. Kōung t'ȯu sān wán, péi tcheȯu tchôu siēn (sīng), tchēng t'ôu tsêng tsêng. Jȯung tī chéu īng, Kīng Chōu chéu tch'êng; tsĕ mouŏ ngȯ kàn tch'êng. Pėi eul tch'āng êul tch'éu; pėi ėul cheȯu êul fȯu (pĭ). Houâng fă t'āi pėi, cheóu siū iū chéu. Pėi ėul tch'āng êul tá (tí); pėi ėul k'ì êul ngái (i). Wán iȯu ts'iēn souéi, mėi cheȯu ȯu iȯu hái (hi).

ébranlée ni troublée. Vous aurez trois ministres d'État avec lesquels vous vieillirez, dans une conformité de sentiments inébranlable comme les collines et les montagnes.

5. Le prince a mille chars de guerre, portant chacun deux lances ornées de rubans rouges et deux arcs entourés de cordons verts. Le prince a trente mille fantassins, dont les casques sont ornés de coquillages cousus en ligne avec du fil rouge; leur multitude est imposante. Avec ces forces nous repousserons les barbares de l'est et du nord, nous arrêterons les hordes de King et de Chou; personne n'osera plus nous résister. (Que vos ancêtres vous obtiennent un règne florissant et glorieux, une longue vie, une grande opulence! Que des vieillards à la chevelure jaunissante, à la peau rugueuse, vous aident à gouverner l'État! Que vos ancêtres vous obtiennent de régner avec grandeur et gloire, d'atteindre la vieillesse et de conserver vos forces, de vivre des

lem regionem; Lou regnum inde perpetuum (erit tibi). Non minuetur, non corruet, non concutietur, non turbabitur. Cum tribus senioribus (regni ministris) conjunges amicitiam (firmam) instar collis instar montis.

5. Reguli currus mille quadrigæ; rubris fasciis, viridibus funiculis, duæ hastæ, bini arcus. Reguli pedites triginta millia; conchyliis ornatæ galeæ per rubrum filium; multitudo peditum valde numerosa. Occidentalibus et septentrionalibus barbaris sic obsistemus. King et Chou gentes sic coercebimus: tunc nemo nobis audebit resistere. (Progenitores tui) faciant ut tu floreas et corusces! faciant ut tu sis longævus et dives! Flavescentibus capillis et rugoso porculi marini instar dorso, seniores simul tecum se exerceant, i.e.

眉壽無有害。
(6) 泰山巖巖，魯
邦所詹。奄有龜
蒙，遂荒大東，至
于海邦，淮夷來
同，莫不率從，魯
侯之功。
(7) 保有鳧繹，遂
荒徐宅，至于海
邦，淮夷蠻貊，及
彼南夷，莫不率
從，莫敢不諾，魯
侯是若。

6. T'ái chān iên iên, Lòu pāng chòu tchēn. Ièn iòu Kouẹ̄i Môung. Souéi houāng tá tōung, tchéu iū hài pāng (pōung). Houâi î lâi t'ôung, mouŏ pŏu chouĕ ts'ôung; Lòu heôu tchēu kōung.

7. Paò iòu Fôu Ĭ (Iŏ), souéi houāng Siû tchĕ (tŏ), tchéu iū hài pāng. Houâi î Mân Mé (Mŏ), kĭ pèi nân î, mouŏ pŏu chouĕ ts'ôung, mouŏ kàn pŏu nŏ; Lòu heôu chéu jŏ.

milliers et des myriades d'années, et d'être exempt de toute incommodité !

6. Le T'ai chan est très élevé ; la principauté de Lou le contemple. Elle possède déjà les monts Kouei et Moung; bientôt elle s'étendra vers l'extrême orient jusqu'aux contrées voisines de la mer. Les barbares de la Houai viendront faire alliance avec nous ; toutes les nations nous seront soumises. Le mérite en sera au prince de Lou.

7. La principauté de Lou possède et garde le mont Fou et le mont I; bientôt elle aura le territoire de Siu, et s'étendra jusqu'aux contrées voisines de la mer. Les habitants des bords de la Houai, les Man, les Me et les autres barbares du midi feront tous leur soumission ; aucun peuple n'osera la refuser. Ils obéiront au prince de Lou.

publicis rebus dent operam! Faciant ut tu floreas et magnus evadas! Faciant ut senectam attingas et vires serves; decem millibus et millibus annis producas senectutem, nec habeas damnum!

6. T'ai mons excelsus est, Lou regnum quem prospectat. Late habet Kouei et Moung montes ; inde proferetur ad extremum orientem, usque ad maritima regna. Houai barbari venient et societatem conjungent; nulla gens non simul obsequetur. (Illud erit) Lou reguli meritum.

7. (Lou regnum) custodit habitos Fou et I montes ; inde occupabit Siu territorium, usque ad maritima regna. Inter Houai barbaros, *Mân* et *Mĕ* (australes barbaros) et illos (alios) australes barbaros, nullus non conjunctim obsequetur, nullus audebit non annuere. Lou regulo illi obsequentur.

8. Cœlum donabit regulum pura felicitate; (regulus) valde longævus servabit Lou. Occupans Chang et Hiu, redintegrabit Tcheou koung territo-

(8) 天錫公純嘏、眉壽保魯、居常與許、復周公之宇、魯侯燕喜、令妻壽母、宜大夫庶士、邦國是有、既多受祉、黃髮兒齒、

(9) 徂來之松、新甫之柏、是斷是度、是尋是尺、松桷有舄、路寢孔碩、新廟奕奕、奚斯所作、孔曼且碩、萬民是若、

8. T'iēn sĭ kōung chouênn kià (kòu), mêi cheóu paò Lòu. Kiū Châng iù Hiù. fŏu Tcheŏu kōung tchēu iù. Lòu heôu ién hi, ling ts'ĭ cheóu mòu (mèi), i tái fōu chóu chéu. Pāng kouŏ chéu iòu (i). Ki touŏ cheóu tch'èu, houâng fă êul tch'èu.

9. Ts'ŏu lâi tchēu sōung, Sīn fòu tchēu pĕ (pŏ), chéu touàn chéu touŏ, chéu sîn, chéu tch'ĕu (tch'ŏ). Sōung kiŏ iòu sĭ (ts'iŏ), lòu ts'in k'òung chēu (chŏ). Sīn miaó ĭ ĭ (iŏ iŏ), Hi sēu chòu tsŏ. K'òung wán, ts'iè chĕu (chŏ), wán mîn chéu jŏ.

8. Le prince recevra du ciel un bonheur sans mélange; il vivra longtemps et gardera la principauté de Lou. Il reprendra les districts de Chang et de Hiu, et possédera tout le territoire qu'avait Tcheou koung. Le prince de Lou sera heureux et content, ainsi que sa vertueuse épouse, sa vieille mère, les grands préfets ses amis et tous ses autres officiers. Il conservera la principauté, et comblé de tous les biens, avec une chevelure jaunissante il aura des dents nouvelles comme les enfants.

9. Les sapins du mont Ts'ou lai et les cyprès du mont Sin fou ont été coupés, puis mesurés avec le cordeau de huit pieds ou avec le pied. Les chevrons de sapin sont gros; parmi les bâtiments situés derrière le temple des ancêtres (et destinés à contenir les vêtements de cérémonie), le principal est très vaste. Les salles du temple sont magnifiques; elles sont l'œuvre de (l'architecte) Hi seu. Elles s'étendent sur une grande longueur, sont vastes et plaisent à tout le monde.

rium. Lou regulus beatus gaudebit, cum optima uxore et annosa matre, cum amicis majoribus præfectis et omnibus præpositis. Regnum ipse habebit. Postquam multa acceperit bona, flavescentes capilli et pueriles dentes (ei erunt).

齒落更生細者亦壽徵也

La croissance de petites dents fines, à la place de celles qui sont tombées, est encore un signe de longévité.

9. Ts'ou lai montis abietes et Sin fou montis cupressi ipsæ cæsæ, ipsæ mensæ sunt, tum octo pedum linea tum pede. Abiegni capreoli sunt crassi; (a delubrorum tergo sita) magna ædes est valde ampla. Nova delubra magnifica sunt, Hi seu quæ exstruxit. Valde longa et ampla, universo populo ea placent.

商頌四之五

那

①猗與那與、置
我鞉鼓、奏鼓簡
簡、衎我烈祖、
②湯孫奏假、綏
我思成、鞉鼓淵
淵、嘒嘒管聲、既
和且平、依我磬
聲、於赫湯孫、穆
穆厥聲、
③庸鼓有斁、萬

NOUO. **1. Ī iù! nouô iù! Tchéu ngò t'aô kòu, tseóu kòu kièn kièn, k'án ngò liĕ tsòu.**

2. T'āng suēnn tseóu kŏ, souēi ngò sēu tch'êng. T'aô kòu iuēn iuēn (īn īn), houéi houéi kouàn chēng. Kí houô, ts'iè p'ing, ī ngò k'ing chēng. Oū! hĕ T'āng suēnn, mŏu mŏu kiuĕ chēng.

3. Iôung kòu iòu ĭ, wán òu iòu ĭ. Ngò iòu kiā k'ŏ, ī pŏu ì ĭ.

LIVRE V. CHANG SOUNG.

CHANT I. NOUO.

Pour une cérémonie faite par un empereur de la dynastie des 商 **Chāng** en l'honneur de 湯 **T'āng** ou 成 湯 **Tch'êng T'āng**, fondateur de cette dynastie.

1. Oh! que de musiciens! Ils disposent nos tambourins et nos tambours. Les tambours font entendre des sons graves, et réjouissent mon illustre aïeul (Tch'eng T'ang).

2. Mon aïeul T'ang vient attiré par ma musique, et m'apporte la joie que je désirais (la joie de sa présence). Les tambourins et les tambours font entendre des sons graves, et les flûtes des sons clairs et perçants. Ces instruments unissent leurs accords à ceux de nos tablettes de jade. Oh! que le descendant de T'ang est majestueux! Que sa musique est belle!

3. Les grosses cloches et les tambours font entendre des sons

TITRE DU LIVRE. 商頌四之五 Chang præconia, quartæ (partis) quintus liber. La terre de 商 **Chāng** était le 商州 actuel dans le 陝西 **Chèn si.** T'ang établit sa résidence à 亳 **Pouŏ** dans le 考城縣 actuel, qui dépend de 歸德府 dans le Ho nan. Sur l'origine de la famille des Chang, voy. plus loin, Chant III.

CHANT I. 1. Oh! quot (musici)! Disponunt nostra tympaniola et tympana. Pulsant tympana graviter; delectant meum benemeritum progenitorem (Tch'eng T'ang).

2. T'ang regis pronepos musica attraho (eum); juvat me, intento facto, i. e. facto eo quod optabam et intendebam. Tympaniola et tympana graviter reboant; clari et acuti tibiarum soni. Consona et temperata consociantur nostrarum iaspidearum tabellarum sonis. Oh! augustus est T'ang regis pronepos! Pulchra est ejus musica!

3. Campanæ majores et tympana

舞有奕，我有嘉
客，亦不夷懌。
(4)自古在昔，先
民有作，溫恭朝
夕，執事有恪。
(5)顧予烝嘗，湯
孫之將。
烈祖
(1)嗟嗟烈祖，有
秩斯祜，申錫無
疆，及爾斯所。
(2)既載清酤，賚
我思成。亦有和

4. Tzóu kòu tsái sĭ, siēn mîn iòu tsŏ, wēnn kōung tchaō sĭ, tchĕu chéu iòu k'ŏ.

5. Kóu iû tchēng tch'âng, T'āng suēnn tchĕu tsiāng.

LIE TSOU. **1. Tsiē tsiē! liĕ tsòu! Iòu tchĕu sēu hòu. Chēnn sĭ ôu kiāng, kì èul sēu chòu.**

2. Kí tsái ts'īng kōu (hòu), lái ngò sēu tch'ēng (tch'âng). Ì iòu houô kēng

plus pleins ; les pantomimes se mettent en rang, et représentent des actions, les unes civiles, les autres militaires. J'ai d'excellents hôtes ; ne sont-ils pas joyeux et contents ?

4. Depuis les temps les plus reculés, nos devanciers nous ont donné l'exemple : ils ont toujours été doux, respectueux, et fidèles à remplir avec soin leurs devoirs.

5. T'ang agréera, je l'espère, les offrandes que je lui fais en été et en automne ; ce sont les offrandes de son descendant.

CHANT II. LIE TSOU.

En l'honneur de 成湯 **Tch'ēng t'āng.**

1. Oh ! combien nous sommes redevables à votre aïeul (Tch'eng t'ang) ! Ses bienfaits sont continuels. Renouvelés sans cesse, ils sont venus jusqu'à vous en ce lieu.

2. Déjà les coupes sont pleines de liqueurs pures (dit l'empereur) ; mon aïeul m'apporte la joie que je désirais (la joie de sa

pleniorem edunt sonitum ; tum civiles tum militares choreæ ordinantur. Ego habeo eximios hospites ; et nonne gaudentes lætantur ?

4. Ex antiquis sæculis, per præterita tempora, qui fuerunt homines habuerunt facta : mites ac reverentes a mane ad vesperum, tractando res erant diligentes.

5. (T'ang rex, spero) respiciet mea æstiva et autumnalia sacra, T'ang regis pronepotis oblationes.

CHANT II. 1. Oh ! quam bene meretur avus ! Sunt continua hæc beneficia (quæ ab eo proficiscuntur). Denuo collata absque fine, pervenerunt ad te in hunc locum.

Dans cette strophe, le poète s'adresse à l'empereur régnant. Dans les suivantes, il fait parler l'empereur lui-même.

2. Jam contenti sunt (in poculis) puri liquores ; dat ut meum intentum sit perfectum. Et sunt condita juscula,

羹、既戒既平、鬷假無言、時靡有爭、綏我眉壽、黃耇無疆、

(3) 約軝錯衡、八鸞鶬鶬、以假以享、我受命溥將、自天降康、豐年穰穰、來假來饗、降福無疆、

(4) 顧予烝嘗、湯孫之將、

(lâng). Ki kiái ki p'îng (p'âng), tsōung kŏ ôu iên (ngâng); chêu mi iòu tchēng (tchāng). Souēi ngò mêi cheóu, houâng keòu ôu kiāng.

3. Iŏ k'î ts'ŏ hêng (hâng), pă louân ts'iāng ts'iāng, i kŏ i hiàng (hiāng). Ngò cheóu ming p'òu tsiāng. Tzéu t'iēn kiáng k'āng, fōung gniên jàng jàng. Lâi kŏ lâi hiàng (hiāng), kiáng fòu ôu kiāng.

4. Kóu iù tchēng tch'âng, T'āng suēnn tchēu tsiâng.

présence). Il y a aussi des sauces; elles ont été préparées d'avance et bien assaisonnées. J'attire mon aïeul par l'odeur des mets (ou par la musique), sans recourir aux paroles, et il ne s'élève pas de dispute (entre les princes qui m'aident dans cette cérémonie). Mon aïeul m'accorde de longues années, une vieillesse couronnée de cheveux jaunissants, une vie sans fin.

3. Avec des voitures dont les moyeux sont entourés de bandes de cuir et le joug orné de courroies, avec huit sonnettes retentissantes aux mors des chevaux, (les princes viennent) évoquer (les mânes de mon aïeul) et leur faire des offrandes. J'ai hérité d'un empire vaste et puissant. Du ciel nous vient la prospérité; les récoltes sont très abondantes. Mon aïeul arrive, il est ici, il jouit des mets offerts, et m'obtient une félicité sans limite.

4. Il regarde avec complaisance les dons que je lui offre en été et en automne; ce sont les offrandes de son descendant.

sunt præparata, sunt temperata. Ollis (vel musica) attraho (avum) sine verbis; tunc non est contentio (inter adjutores regulos). Donat me longa vita, flava senecta absque termino.

Dans le 中庸 Tchōung iôung, Ch.33, au lieu de 鬷假 on lit 奏假 tseóu kŏ. Cette seconde version paraît préférable; elle est adoptée communément.

3. Fasciatis rotarum modiolis, ornato jugo, octo equorum tintinnabulis consonantibus, (reguli veniunt) ut evocent (avi manes), ut offerant. Ego accepi imperium vastum ac magnum. E cœlo descendunt prospera; fertiles anni frugibus locupletes. (Avus) veniens adest, veniens oblatis fruitur; immittit bona sine limite.

4. Respicit mea æstiva et autumnalia sacra, a T'ang pronepote oblata.

列祖在天之靈猶未敢必其我顧也尙其顧予之烝嘗 (詩經備旨) Je n'ose pas assurer que dans le ciel l'âme de mon illustre aïeul abaisse sur moi des regards favorables. Puisse-t-il regarder avec complaisance les dons que je lui offre en été et en automne!

玄鳥

(1) 天命玄鳥、降而生商、宅殷土芒芒、古帝命武湯、正域彼四方、(2) 方命厥后、奄有九有、商之先后、受命不殆、在武丁孫子、

HIUEN GNIAO. 1. **T'iēn míng hiuên gniaò kiáng êul chēng Chāng. Tchĕ Īn t'òu màng màng. Kòu tí míng òu T'āng tchéng iŭ pèi séu fāng.**

2. Fāng míng kiuĕ heòu, ièn iòu kiòu iòu (i). Chāng tchēu siēn heòu cheòu míng pŏu tái (i); tsái Où tīng suēnn tzèu (tsi).

CHANT III. HIUEN GNIAO.

Origine de la famille impériale des 商 **Chāng**; éloge de 成 湯 **Tch'êng t'āng** (1766-1753) et de 武 丁 **Où tīng** (1324-1265).

1. Par ordre du ciel, une hirondelle descendit, et la famille des Chang lui dut son origine. Les Chang habitèrent la terre de In et devinrent puissants. Le roi du ciel ordonna au belliqueux Tch'eng t'ang de fixer les frontières dans toutes les parties de l'empire.

2. Dans tout l'empire T'ang constitua les princes; il gouverna les neuf provinces. Premier empereur de la famille des Chang, il reçut un pouvoir stable, qui demeure à Ou ting, son descendant.

CHANT III. 1. Cœli mandato nigra avis (hirundo) descendit et genuit Chang. (Chang domus) incoluit In terram et magna facta est. Antiquitus rex (cœli) jussit bellicosum T'ang statuere fines in quatuor imperii regionibus.

帝 上帝也 *Tí*, le roi du ciel.

簡 狄 **Kièn tĭ**, fille du prince de 娀 **Sōung** et femme de l'empereur 高 辛 **Kaō sīn**, offrit avec son mari le sacrifice du printemps dans la campagne, et pria la divinité qui préside aux naissances. Une hirondelle vint et déposa un œuf. Kien ti avala cet œuf, et donna naissance à 契 **Siĕ**. Sie fut ministre de l'instruction publique sous le règne de 堯 **Iaô**, et reçut en fief la terre de 商 **Chāng**, à présent 商 州 dans le 陝 西 **Chèn sī**. 成 湯 **Tch'êng t'āng**, descendant de Sie, s'empara de l'empire en 1766 avant J.C., et fixa sa résidence à 亳 **Pouŏ** dans le 考 城 縣 **K'aò tch'êng hién**, qui dépend de 歸 德 府 dans le Ho nan. En 1401, 盤 庚 **P'ân kēng**, l'un de ses successeurs, transféra sa résidence dans la terre de 殷 **In**, à 亳 **Pouŏ** dans le 偃 師 縣 **Ièn chēu hièn** actuel qui dépend de 河 南 府, et la dynastie prit le nom de In. La capitale de T'ang fut appelée *Nan Pouo* Pouo méridionale, et celle de P'an keng *Si Pouo* Pouo occidentale. Il y avait une troisième Pouo située au pied du mont 景 **King** dans le K'ai foung fou, et appelée ***Pe Pouo*** Pouo septentrionale ou 景 亳 **King Pouŏ**.

2. Regionibus (T'ang) constituit suos regulos; late habuit novem habitas (provincias). E Chang domo primus imperator accepit imperium quod non est periclitatum; est penes Ou ting, ejus progeniem.

(3) 武丁孫子。武王靡不勝。龍旂十乘、大糦是承。

(4) 邦畿千里、維民所止、肇域彼四海。

(5) 四海來假、來假祁祁、景員維河、殷受命咸宜、百祿是何。

長發

(1) 濬哲維商。

3. Où tīng suēnn tzèu òu wàng mi pŏu chēng. Lōung k'î chéu chéng, tá tch'éu chéu tch'êng.

4. Pāng k'î ts'iēn li, wêi mîn chòu tchèu. Tchaò iŭ pèi séu hài (houéi).

5. Séu hài lâi kŏ, lâi kŏ k'î k'î. King iuên wêi hô. Īn cheóu míng hiên î (ngô); pĕ lŏu chéu hó (hô).

TCH'ANG FA. **1. Siún tchĕ wêi Chāng, tch'âng fă k'ì siáng. Hôung chouéi màng**

3. Ou ting, son descendant, prince belliqueux, est capable de faire face à tout événement. Les grands princes, chacun avec leurs dix voitures attelées de quatre chevaux (ou bien, un grand nombre de princes, avec leurs voitures attelées de quatre chevaux) et leurs étendards ornés de dragons, viennent offrir les précieux grains (les deux sortes de millet à panicules, dans le temple des ancêtres).

4. Le territoire propre de l'empereur n'a que mille stades d'étendue en tous sens; son peuple y fixe sa demeure. Mais les grandes limites de son empire sont les quatre mers.

5. Des rivages des quatre mers les princes viennent (assister aux offrandes). Ils viennent en très grand nombre. (Pouo, la capitale, est d'un accès facile). Située au pied du mont King, elle est entourée de grands fleuves. La maison des In (ou Chang) méritait d'avoir l'empire; elle soutient admirablement toutes ses dignités.

CHANT IV. TCH'ANG FA.

Éloge de 契 **Siĕ**, père de la famille des 商 **Chāng**, de 相土 **Siáng t'òu**, petit-fils de Sie, de 成湯 **Tch'êng t'āng**, premier empereur de la dynastie des Chang, et de 伊尹 **Ī in**, premier ministre de T'ang.

1. Les Chang se sont toujours signalés par une profonde sagesse;

3. Ou ting, ejus progenies, bellicosus imperator, nulli rei non est par. Ornato pictis draconibus vexillo, decem quadrigis (utentes reguli, vel decem quadrigæ, i.e. multi quadrigis vecti reguli, pretiosas fruges inde offerunt.

4. Imperatoris territorium est mille stadiorum, unice populus ubi habitat. Prolati fines sunt illa quatuor maria.

5. E quatuor maribus (reguli) venientes accedunt (ad sacra facienda). Venientes accedunt magno numero. King (collis et urbis) circuitus unice sunt fluvii magni. In accipere imperium omnino decebat; omnes opes ideo sustinet.

CHANT IV. 1. Alte prudentes sunt

長發其祥、洪水芒芒、禹敷下土方、外大國是疆、幅隕既長、有娀方將、帝立子生商、

(2) 玄王桓撥、受小國是達、受大國是達、率履不越、遂視既發、相土烈烈、海外有截、

màng, Iù fōu hià t'òu fāng. Wái tá kouŏ chéu kiāng, fōu iuên kì tch'âng. Iòu Sōung fāng tsiāng, ti lĭ tzèu chēng Chāng.

2. Hiuên wâng houân pouŏ (piĕ), cheóu siaò kouŏ chéu tă (touŏ), cheóu tá kouŏ chéu tă (touŏ). Chouĕ li pòu iuĕ, souéi chéu kí fă (p'ĕ). Siáng t'òu liĕ liĕ, hài wái iòu tsiĕ.

les présages de leur grandeur avaient paru depuis longtemps. Lorsque les eaux du déluge couvraient la terre, Iu les fit écouler. Il fixa les limites des grandes principautés qui n'étaient pas dans le domaine propre de l'empereur, et l'étendue de ce domaine fut augmentée. La maison de Soung devint puissante. (Sie), fils (d'une fille du prince de Soung), fut nommé ministre par l'empereur (Chouenn), et donna naissance à la famille des Chang.

2. (Sie), prince d'une sagesse profonde (ou bien, le prince noir) gouverna avec fermeté. Chargé d'un petite principauté, il la transformait (par ses enseignements); chargé d'une grande, il la transformait encore. Il observait lui-même les lois et ne s'en écartait jamais; puis il enseignait, et tout le peuple suivait ses enseignements. Siang t'ou (descendant de Sie) brilla par sa vertu; l'ordre régna partout entre les quatre mers et au-delà.

Chang domini; jamdiu prodiverant eorum (celsitudinis) omina. Ingentibus aquis late diffusis, Iu composuit subjectæ (cœlo) terræ regiones. Externis magnis regnis ipse limites statuit; (imperatoris territorii) finium circuitus jam ampliatus est. Tenens Soung regnum (regulus) tunc magnus evasit. Imperator (Chouenn) promovit (Soung reguli filiæ) filium (Sie nomine), qui procreavit Chang gentem.

2. Alte sapiens rex (vel, niger rex, Sie) fortiter rexit. Acceptum parvum regnum ipse pervadebat (præceptis suis); acceptum magnum regnum ipse pervadebat. Sequebatur leges, nec transgrediebatur; inde docebat, jam (omnes ad agendum) exsurgebant. Siang t'ou virtute claruit; maria ultra, fuit ordo.

玄 王 **Hiên wâng**, Prince d'une profonde sagesse; ou bien, prince noir, parce que Sie dut la naissance à l'œuf d'une hirondelle 玄 鳥 **hiuên gniaò**. Voy. page 462. 視 **Chéu** équivaut à 示, avertir, instruire.

詩經

(3) 帝命不違。至于湯齊。湯降不遲。聖敬日躋。昭假遲遲。上帝是祗。帝命式于九圍。

(4) 受小球大球。爲下國綴旒。何天之休。不競不絿。不剛不柔。敷政優優。百祿是遒。

(5) 受小共大共。爲下國駿厖。何天之龍。敷奏其勇。不震

3. Ti ming pŏu wĕi, tchéu iū T'āng ts'ī. T'āng kiáng pŏu tch'èu, chéng king jĕu tsī. Tchaō kŏ tch'èu tch'èu, cháng ti chéu tchēu; ti ming chĕu iū kiòu wĕi.

4. Cheóu siaò k'iôu tá k'iôu, wĕi hiá kouŏ tchouéi liôu. Hŏ t'iēn tchēu hiōu, pŏu king pŏu k'iôu, pŏu kāng pŏu jeôu, fōu tchéng iōu iōu; pĕ lŏu chéu ts'iôu.

5. Cheóu siaò kōung (kòung) tá kōung (kòung), wĕi hiá kouŏ siún māng (mòung).

3. Les Chang ont toujours été dignes de recevoir le mandat du roi du ciel (le pouvoir impérial); quand parut T'ang, il se trouva convenir pour ce dessein. T'ang ne naquit ni trop tard (ni trop tôt). Doué d'une éminente sagesse et très diligent, il fit des progrès chaque jour; longtemps ses brillantes vertus touchèrent (le cœur du roi du ciel). Il honora le roi du ciel, et le roi du ciel le créa empereur, afin qu'il servît de modèle dans les neuf circonscriptions ou provinces.

4. Les princes de tous les États, grands ou petits, allèrent à lui avec les tablettes de jade (insignes de leurs dignités); ils devinrent pour lui ce que les pendants sont pour un étendard (ils se mirent sous sa dépendance). Il fut comblé des dons du ciel. Sans violence ni faiblesse, sans dureté ni mollesse, il gouverna tout l'empire avec une grande douceur. Tous les biens lui vinrent à la fois.

5. Il reçut le tribut de tous les princes, grands et petits, et fit la puissance et la force des principautés qui dépendaient de lui.

3. (Cœli) regis mandatum non recessit (a Chang domo); quum devenit ad T'ang, (hic Tang et cœli mandatum) convenerunt. T'ang natus est non serius. Sapientissimus et diligens, quotidie progressus est; præclare movit (cœli regis animum) longo tempore. Cœli regem ipse reveritus est; (cœli) rex constituit (eum ut esset) exemplar in novem orbibus seu provinciis.

4. Acceptis minoribus tabellis et majoribus tabellis, i.e. regulis tum minoribus tum majoribus, fuit subjectis regnis (id quod vexillum est) pendentibus infulis; suscepit cœli beneficia. Non violentus non remissus, nec durus nec mollis, protulit regimen magna suavitate; omnia bona in eum convenerunt.

5. Accepit minora tributa et majora tributa; factus est subjectorum regnorum magnitudo et firmitas. Suscepit

59

不動、不戁不竦、百祿是總、

(6) 武王載旆、有虔秉鉞、如火烈烈、則莫我敢曷、苞有三櫱、莫遂莫達、九有有截、韋顧既伐、昆吾夏桀、

(7) 昔在中葉、有震且業、允也天子、降于卿士、實維阿衡、實左右商王、

Hó t'iēn tchĕu tch'òung. Fŏu tseóu k'ì iòung, pŏu tchénn pŏu tóung (tòung), pŏu nàn pŏu sòung. Pĕ lŏu chéu tsòung.

6. Où wâng tsái péi, iòu k'ièn pìng iuĕ. Jŏu houò liĕ liĕ, tsĕ mouŏ ngò kàn ngē. Paŏ iòu sān iĕ, mouŏ souéi mouŏ tă (tĕ), kiòu iòu iòu tsiĕ. Wéi Kóu kí fă (p'iĕ), Kouēnn ôu Hiá Kiĕ.

7. Sī tsái tchōung iĕ, iòu tchénn, ts'iè iĕ, iùn iè t'iēn tzèu (tsi), kiáng iū k'īng chéu, chĕu wéi ngō héng (hâng), chĕu tsouó ióu Chāng wâng.

Il fut comblé des faveurs du ciel. Déployant partout sa valeur, il n'était jamais ému ni agité ni effrayé ni tremblant. Tous les biens lui venaient à la fois.

6. Ce prince belliqueux dressa son étendard (sur son char de guerre), et soumis avec respect (aux ordres du ciel), il prit sa hache d'armes. Son ardeur égala celle du feu; personne n'osa nous résister. La racine avait trois rejetons; aucun ne put croître ni grandir. (Kie avait trois alliés : les princes de Wei, de Kou et de Kouenn ou. Ils ne purent arriver à leurs fins). T'ang rétablit l'ordre dans les neuf provinces. Il défit d'abord les princes de Wei et de Kou, puis le prince de Kouenn ou, et Kie, (dernier empereur) de la dynastie des Hia.

7. Dans les temps qui s'écoulèrent depuis Sie jusqu'à T'ang, l'empire avait été ébranlé et mis en péril. Mais le ciel donna à son fils (T'ang) un ministre (I in), qui fut le soutien et tint la balance de l'État, et seconda le fondateur de la dynastie des Chang.

cœli beneficia. Late exserens suam fortitudinem, non commovebatur, non agitabatur, non pavebat, non tremebat. Omnia bona in eum confluebant.

6. Bellicosus rex imposuit vexillum (quadrigis); motus reverentia (in cœli jussum), cepit securim. Similis igni exarsit; jam nemo nobis ausus est resistere. Radix habebat tres surculos; nullus crevit, nullus procerus evasit. Novem habitæ (provinciæ) habuerunt ordinem. Wei et Kou regulis debellatis, Kouenn ou regulus et Hia Kie (debellati sunt).

7. Olim in mediis generationibus (inter Sie et T'ang), occurrerant quassatio et periculum. Vere cœli filio (T'ang imperatori cœlum) immisit regni ministrum (I in). Qui vere fuit sustentaculum et statera, vere adstans

詩經

殷武

(1) 撻彼殷武、奮伐荆楚、罙入其阻、裒荆之旅、有截其所、湯孫之緒、

(2) 維女荆楚、居國南鄉、昔有成湯、自彼氐羌、莫敢不來享、莫敢不來王、曰商是常、

IN OU. **1. T'ă pèi Īn òu, fènn fă Kīng Tch'ŏu, mì jŏu k'ì tchŏu, p'eōu Kīng tchēu liŭ, iòu tsiĕ k'ì chòu; T'āng suēnn tchēu siù.**

2. « Wèi jòu Kīng Tch'ŏu, kiū kouŏ nân hiāng. Sī iòu Tch'êng t'āng, tzéu pèi Tī k'iāng, mouŏ kàn pŏu lâi hiàng (hiāng). Mouŏ kàn pŏu lâi wâng; iuĕ Chāng chéu tch'âng.

CHANT V. IN OU.

Éloge de 武丁 **Où tīng** ou 高宗 **Kaō tsōung**, qui régna de 1324 à 1265 avant J. C., et raffermit l'empire des Chang ou In.

1. L'empereur (Kao tsoung), de la famille des In, déploya une valeur énergique; il se précipita sur le pays de King tch'ou. Pénétrant avec audace dans les endroits les plus périlleux, il prit (et soumit) tous les habitants. L'ordre fut établi dans cette contrée. Cette œuvre (commencée par T'ang) fut terminée par l'un de ses descendants (par Kao tsoung).

2. (Kao tsoung dit aux vaincus): «Habitants de King tch'ou, votre pays est situé au midi du domaine impérial. Autrefois sous le règne de Tch'eng t'ang, même parmi les Ti k'iang, aucun chef n'osait refuser de venir offrir son tribut; aucun n'osait refuser de venir rendre hommage à l'empereur. Ils disaient que c'était la règle établie par la maison des Chang. (A plus forte raison, vous, habitants de King tch'ou, devez-vous venir à ma cour).»

adjuvit Chang imperatorem.

阿 **Ngō** signifie 倚 **i**, appui, soutien; 衡 **hêng**, balance, tenir la balance. 阿衡 premier ministre.

CHANT I. 1. Acris fuit illa In imperatoris (Kao tsoung) fortitudo; impetum faciens aggressus est King tch'ou. Audacter intravit illius periculosa loca, collegit (et sibi subdidit) King multitudinem. Habuerunt ordinem illa loca; fuit T'ang nepotis hæreditarium opus.

2. (Domitis King tch'ou incolis Kao tsoung dixit): « Vos, King tch'ou, incolitis ad imperii austrum sitam regionem. Olim quum esset Tch'eng t'ang, abusque Ti kiang (occidentalibus barbaris), nemo audebat non venire oblatum (vectigal); nemo audebat non venire cultum imperatorem. Dicebant Chang imperatoris esse legem. »

(3) 天命多辟、設都于禹之績、歲事來辟、勿予禍適、稼穡匪解、

(4) 天命降監、下民有嚴、不僭不濫、不敢怠遑、命于下國、封建厥福、

(5) 商邑翼翼、四方之極、赫赫厥聲、濯濯厥靈、壽考且寧、以保我後生、

3. T'iēn mîng touō pǐ chě tōu iū Iù tchēu tsǐ. Souéi chéu lâi pǐ. «Où iù houó tchě, kiá chě fèi kiài (kí).»

4. T'iēn mîng kiáng kién, hiá mîn iòu iēn (iâng). Pǒu tsién pǒu lán, pǒu kàn tài houâng, mîng iū hiá kouǒ (ǐ), fōung kién kiuě fǒu (pǐ).

5. Chāng ǐ ǐ ǐ, séu fāng tchēu kǐ. Hě hě kiuě chēng, tchouǒ tchouǒ kiuě lîng. Cheóu k'aò, ts'iè gnîng, i paò ngò heóu chēng (sīng).

3. C'est le ciel qui a constitué les princes avec leurs capitales dans les terres que Iu a rendues habitables. Ils sont venus rendre compte à l'empereur de leur administration année par année. (Ils semblaient lui dire): «Ne nous infligez ni châtiment ni réprimande; nous avons donné des soins assidus à l'agriculture.»

4. Le (roi du) ciel se fait une loi de descendre et de considérer la terre. (Il entend la voix du peuple; aussi le souverain) doit craindre le peuple. (Kao tsoung) accorda les récompenses avec justice, et n'excéda pas (dans l'application des châtiments). Il n'osa jamais s'abandonner à la paresse, à l'oisiveté. (C'est pourquoi le ciel) lui soumit les royaumes d'ici-bas, et affermit grandement son pouvoir.

5. La capitale des Chang fut admirablement gouvernée et devint le modèle de toutes les contrées de l'empire. Sa renommée fut grande, et sa puissance resplendit partout. Kao tsoung eut une vie longue et paisible, et ses institutions nous sauvegardent encore, nous qui sommes venus après lui.

3. Cœlum constituit varios regulos, ut instituerent urbes præcipuas in Iu operibus, i.e. in locis quæ Iu expedivit ac composuit. De annuis rebus venerunt monituri imperatorem. (Dicere videbantur): «Noli nos aut plectere aut corripere; de agrorum cultura non remisse curavimus.»

4. Cœlum statuta voluntate descendit ac inspicit; subjectus populus habet quod timeatur. (Kao tsoung) non erravit (in remunerando), non excessit (in puniendo); non ausus est pigre otiari. (Ideo cœlum) constituit super subjecta (cœlo) regna, multum firmavit ejus felicitatem.

5. Chang urbs præcipua optime composita est; fuit quatuor imperii

(6) 陟彼景山，松柏丸丸。是斷是遷，方斲是虔。松桷有梴，旅楹有閑，寢成孔安。

6. Tchĕu péi King chān, sŏung pĕ houân houân. Chéu touàn chéu ts'iĕn, fāng tchouŏ chéu k'iên. Sŏung kiŏ iòu tch'ĕn, liù ing iòu hiên. Ts'in tch'êng k'òung ngān (iên).

6. Nous avons gravi ce mont King (qui est dans l'enceinte de la capitale); les sapins et les cyprès s'y dressent majestueusement. Nous avons coupé de ces arbres; nous les avons transportés ici. Nous les avons équarris et aplanis avec la hache, puis sciés de la longueur voulue. Les chevrons de sapin sont longs, les colonnes grosses et nombreuses. Nous avons achevé ce temple; (la tablette de Kao tsoung) y reposera et n'en sortira plus.

regionum fastigium (et exemplar). Præclara fuit ejus fama; valde splenduit ejus potestas. (Kao tsoung usus est) longa vita et tranquillitate, ita ut protegeret nos postea natos.

Kao tsoung régna 59 ans.

6. Ascendimus illum King collem; abietes et cupressi recte stant. Nonnullas excidimus, eas transtulimus; quadratas et dolatas eas concidimus. Abiegni capreoli sunt longi, numerosæ columnæ sunt amplæ. Delubro perfecto, (Kao tsoung tabella) omnino quieta (jam non loco mutabitur).

La lettre 寢 **ts'in** désigne ici un bâtiment construit exprès pour Kao tsoung dans l'enceinte du temple des ancêtres.

詩經

LETTRES CHINOISES

CONTENUES DANS LE CHEU KING

RACINE 1. 一

一 **Ī.** Un, premier, tout entier, uniforme, constant. 丨朝十 **tchaō.** Toute une matinée. 丨人十 **jênn.** Un seul homme; celui qui seul gouverne tout l'empire.

丁 **Tīng.** Reposer sur. || **Tchēng.** 丨丨十十. Bruit de coups.

七 **Ts'ī.** Sept, septième.

三 **Sān.** Trois, troisième.

下 **Hià.** Bas, inférieur, postérieur, moindre, au-dessous, sous, après, le plus bas, le moins ancien, le moindre, le dernier, le plus vil, en bas, sur la terre. 上丨 **Cháng** 十. En haut et en bas, les supérieurs et les inférieurs, le ciel et la terre. || **Hiá.** Descendre, tomber, abaisser.

上 **Cháng.** Haut, ancien, supérieur, antérieur, au-dessus, sur, avant, le plus élevé, le plus ancien, le meilleur, le premier, en haut, au ciel. || **Chàng.** Monter.

不 **Pŏu.** Ne pas.

且 **Ts'iè.** Et, bien plus; cela. || **Tsiū.** Particule finale. || **Ts'iù.** Respectueux, grave.

世 **Chéu.** Génération, époque, vie, d'âge en âge, héréditaire.

丘 **K'iōu.** Monticule, colline.

RACINE 2. 丨

中 **Tchōung.** Milieu, centre, qui est au milieu; le milieu de, au milieu de, dans. Dans le Cheu king, même lorsque cette lettre signifie *le milieu de, au milieu de, dans,* elle se place souvent avant le substantif qu'elle régit. 丨國十 **kouŏ.** Royaume situé au centre de la Chine, le domaine propre de l'empereur, la Chine, le milieu du royaume ou de la principauté, dans le royaume.

丰 **Fōung.** Visage replet ; gracieux, aimable.

丱 **Kouán.** Chevelure d'enfant liée en deux touffes qui ont l'apparence de cornes.

串 **Tch'ouén.** Enfiler, accoutumé. 丨夷十 **î.** Tribu barbare de l'occident.

RACINE 3. 丶

丸 **Houân.** Globule, boule, balle. 丨丨十十. Droit, vertical.

丹 **Tān.** Rouge.

主 **Tchòu.** Maître, chef, arbitre, présider, diriger, celui qui donne l'hospitalité, recevoir l'hospitalité chez quelqu'un.

RACINE 4. 丿

乃 **Nài.** Et, aussi, alors, ensuite, ainsi, en effet, à la vérité, mais, cependant.

久 **Kiòu.** Longtemps, à la longue.

之 **Tchēu.** Aller à, jusqu'à; pronom personnel qui s'emploie comme régime d'un verbe; ce, cet, cela; particule qui se place après le complément d'un nom, et forme le génitif ou possessif; particule qui s'emploie après le régime d'un verbe, lorque ce régime précède le verbe; particule qui s'emploie après le participe et après l'adjectif.

乎 **Hôu.** A, dans, vers, par, de, envers; conjonction qui précède le second terme d'une comparaison; particule qui suit une interrogation ou une exclamation; particule euphonique. || **Hōu.** 於 | **Oū** 于! Hélas!

乘 **Chêng, Tch'êng.** Être ou aller à cheval, en voiture ou en barque; monter. || **Chéng.** Voiture attelée de quatre chevaux de front, attelage de quatre chevaux, quatre objets de même espèce; conduire une voiture; particule numérale des voitures, des attelages de quatre chevaux;...

RACINE 5. 乙

九 **Kiòu.** Neuf, neuvième.

也 **Iè.** Particule qui marque une pause, et s'emploie à la fin d'une phrase ou d'un membre de phrase, après un nom propre,...

乾 **K'iên.** Influence du ciel. || **Kān.** Sec, sécheresse.

亂 **Louán.** Troubler, mêler, confondre, ne pas discerner, trouble, désordre, confusion, sédition; barque, bac.

RACINE 6. 亅

予 **Iû.** Je, moi, nous. || **Iù.** 與. Donner, approuver.

事 **Chéu.** Affaire, action, occupation, travail, difficulté, différend; faire, exécuter, service, rendre service, servir, aider.

RACINE 7. 二

二 **Eúl.** Deux, deuxième.

于 **Iû.** Dire, aller; particule. || **Iū.** 於. Dans, à, par, au sujet de.

五 **Où.** Cinq, cinquième.

云 **Iûn.** Dire, louer; particule.

亞 **Iá.** Second. || 婭. Parent par alliance.

亟 **Kî.** Prompt, vite, s'empresser, urgent.

RACINE 8. 亠

亡 **Wâng.** Mourir, périr, prendre fin, détruire, anéantir, ruiner, mettre fin, perdre, fuir, s'exiler. || 忘. Oublier.

交 **Kiaō.** Croiser, se croiser, s'entremêler, avoir des relations.

亦 **Ĭ.** Aussi, même alors; particule.

亨 **Hēng.** Pénétrer; prospère. || **P'ēng.** 烹. Faire cuire.

詩經

享 **Hiàng.** Offrir un présent, offrande, présent, recevoir, agréer un présent.

京 **Kīng.** Colline, monticule; haut, grand; capitale d'un grand État.

亳 **Pouŏ.** Nom de ville.
V. page 462.

亶 **Tàn.** Sincère, vrai. | 父 + fòu ou 太 王 **T'ái wâng.** Aïeul de Wenn wang. V. page 2.

亹 **Wèi.** Infatigable, laborieux. || **Mênn.** Torrent dans une gorge de montagne.

RACINE 9. 人

人 **Jênn.** Homme, femme, autrui, quelqu'un, ministre d'État, officier. 一 | Ĭ +. Celui qui seul gouverne tout l'empire.

仁 **Jênn.** Affection de l'homme envers ses semblables, bonté envers autrui, bienfaisance, bienveillance, vertu parfaite.

仇 **K'iôu.** Ennemi, compagnon. || **Kiū.** 斛. Puiser, transvaser.

今 **Kīn.** A présent, de nos jours.

仍 **Jêng.** Selon, d'après, comme auparavant.

介 **Kiái.** Aide, serviteur, aider; grand, rendre grand; armure.

仔 **Tzēu.** Soutenir une charge.

仕 **Chéu.** Mettre en charge, être en charge, officier.

仡 **Ĭ.** | | + +. Courageux, fort, solide.

他 **T'ouō.** Autre, autre chose.

代 **Tái.** Remplacer.

令 **Líng.** Commander, ordonner; bon, rendre bon. || **Lìng.** | | + +. Bruit d'anneaux.

以 **Ì.** Se servir de, employer, par le moyen de, par ce moyen; avoir, posséder, jouir de; user des droits ou de l'autorité de, agir en qualité de, agir comme; cause, motif, à cause de, pour ce motif; parce que, afin que; arriver à, jusqu'à; considérer, avoir égard à, tenir compte de, en comparaison de, d'après, selon; particule qui précède souvent le régime du verbe. | 爲 + wêi. Employer à faire, traiter comme, considérer comme, juger. 何 | Hô +? *Qua re utendum est?* comment? 是 | Chéu +. *Quapropter,* à cause de cela. 于 | Iû +, 越 | Iuĕ +. Particules.

仰 **Iàng.** Regarder en haut, lever les yeux vers, espérer.

仲 **Tchóung.** Le second entre trois, le second des frères; nom de famille.

任 **Jênn.** Sincère, fidèle; porter un fardeau sur les épaules; nom de famille de la mère de Wenn wang. 太 | T'ái +. La mère de Wenn wang.

伉 **K'āng.** Haut.

伎 **K'ì.** | | + +. Avec précaution.

伊 **Ī.** Ce, cet, il, lui; seulement, à la vérité; particule. | 威 + wēi. Cloporte.

伏 **Fŏu.** Être couché, se cacher; souffrir.

伐 **Fă.** Attaquer, châtier ou soumettre des sujets rebelles par la force des armes, envahir, couper, trancher; battre le tambour; bouclier.

休 **Hiōu.** Bonheur, heureux, repos, bon, excellent.

60

伯 **Pĕ.** L'aîné des frères ou des sœurs, oncle paternel; la troisième des cinq dignités 公 侯 伯 子 男 **kōung heôu pĕ tzèu nân**; le chef de tous les feudataires d'une province 州 **tcheōu**; le dieu protecteur des chevaux.

似 **Séu.** Semblable, comme; continuer.

伴 **P'án.** | 奐 ✝ **houán.** A loisir.

伾 **P'ēi.** | | ✝ ✝. Robuste.

位 **Wéi.** Place, siège, position, état, condition, dignité.

佇 **Tchòu.** Rester longtemps debout.

佌 **Ts'èu.** | | ✝ ✝. Petit, vil, méprisable.

佐 **Tsouó.** Aider.

何 **Hò.** Quel? quelle chose? comment? 如 | **Jôu** ✝, 如 之 | **Jôu tchēu** ✝? Comment? que faut-il faire? | 以 ✝ **i**? Par quel moyen? || **Hò, Hó.** Porter un fardeau, recevoir.

余 **Iû.** Je, moi.

佗 **T'ouô.** 委 委 | | **Wēi wēi** ✝ ✝. Marcher d'un air joyeux. || **T'ouó.** Imposer, infliger.

佛 **Pĭ.** 弼. Aider.

作 **Tsŏ.** Créer, faire, bâtir, produire, composer, agir, mettre en mouvement, faire avancer, tirer dehors, arracher, exciter, causer, commencer, surgir, s'élever. || **Tchòu.** 詛. Maudire, se plaindre.

佩 **Péi.** Porter un objet suspendu à la ceinture. V. page 75.

佶 **Kĭ.** Fort.

佸 **Houŏ, Kouŏ.** Se réunir.

佻 **T'iaô.** | | ✝ ✝. Accablé de fatigue.

使 **Chèu.** Employer, diriger, gouverner, commander, faire que, afin que. || **Chéu.** Envoyé, messager, envoyer quelqu'un.

佼 **Kiaò.** Beau.

佽 **Ts'éu.** Aider; convenir, proportionné.

侈 **Tch'èu.** Prodigue, excessif, vaste, large.

侐 **Hiŭ, Hí.** Paisible, silencieux.

侑 **Ióu.** Exciter à manger.

依 **Ī.** S'appuyer sur, s'attacher à, conformément à; tranquille; végétation prospère. || **Ì.** 倚. S'appuyer contre, auprès de.

侜 **Tcheōu.** Circonvenir, empêcher de connaître la vérité.

來 **Lâi.** Venir, arriver, futur, postérieur; blé. || **Lái.** Attirer par des bienfaits, encourager par des récompenses.

侮 **Où.** Traiter avec mépris, outrager, attaquer.

侯 **Heôu.** La seconde des cinq grandes dignités 公 侯 伯 子 男 **kōung heôu pĕ tzèu nân**; chef d'une principauté; cible; beau, admirable; particule. 諸 | **Tchōu** ✝. Chef d'une principauté.

侵 **Ts'īn.** Avancer pas à pas, envahir peu à peu, incursion, empiéter, usurper.

俁 **Iù.** | | ✝ ✝. De grande taille.

俄 **Ngô.** Incliné.

俟 **Séu.** Attendre.

保 **Paò.** Veiller sur, protéger, défendre, préserver, garantir, cautionner, répondre de.

俅 **K'iôu.** | | ⼗ ⼗. Respectueux.

俔 **K'ién.** Être comparable à.

信 **Sín.** Sincère, véridique, vrai, vraiment, fidèle au devoir, croire, ajouter foi, avoir confiance, passer deux nuits dans un endroit. || **Chēnn.** 申. Étendre, développer.

俎 **Tchòu.** Petite table sur laquelle on offrait la chair des victimes.

修 **Siōu.** Perfectionner, cultiver, réparer; long.

俴 **Ts'ién.** Peu profond, mince.

俶 **Tch'ŏu.** Commencer, premier.

俾 **Pèi.** Faire en sorte que, afin que.

倉 **Ts'āng.** Grenier. | 庚 ⼗ **kēng.** Loriot. || **Tch'ouáng.** 愴. Affligé.

倒 **Taó.** En sens inverse, tourner un objet dans un sens différent. || **Taò.** Se renverser, bouleverser.

候 **Heóu.** Attendre, recevoir un hôte.

倡 **Tch'áng.** Entonner un chant, commencer.

借 **Tsié.** Prêter, emprunter; supposer, si.

倌 **Kouān.** Intendant des équipages, conducteur du char impérial.

倍 **Péi.** Double. 三 | **Sān** ⼗. Triple.

値 **Tchéu.** Tenir dans la main.

倩 **Ts'ién.** Élégant, gracieux.

倫 **Liûn.** Raison, motif.

倬 **Tchouŏ.** Grand, brillant, clairvoyant.

倭 **Wēi.** Sinueux.

偕 **Kiāi.** Ensemble, l'un avec l'autre; de toute sorte. | | ⼗ ⼗. Vigoureux.

偃 **Ièn.** Couché.

假 **Kià.** Faux, grand. | 寐 ⼗ **méi.** Prendre son repos sans se déshabiller. || **Kiā.** 嘉. Beau, louable. || **Kŏ.** 格. Arriver, pénétrer. || **Hô.** 何. Comment? pourquoi?

側 **Tchĕ.** Être au côté de quelqu'un, côté.

偈 **Kiĕ.** | | ⼗ ⼗. Rapide.

偲 **Sāi.** Belle barbe.

傚 **Hiaó.** Imiter.

傞 **Souō.** | | ⼗ ⼗. Sauter, danser.

備 **Pí.** Complet, entier, prêt, préparer, fournir.

傅 **Fóu.** Maître qui enseigne; parvenir à.

傍 **Pōung.** | | ⼗ ⼗. Sans relâche.

傑 **Kiĕ.** Surpasser.

傷 **Chāng.** Blesser, offenser, endommager, nuire, être contraire, affliger.

傭 **Tchōung.** Égal, juste.

傾 **K'ing.** Tête inclinée, renverser.

僊 **Siēn.** | | ┼ ┼. Sauter, cabrioler.

僤 **Tán.** Intense, très.

僚 **Leaô.** Collègue, officier de même rang. || **Leaò.** Beau.

僛 **K'ī.** | | ┼ ┼. Chanceler en dansant.

僕 **Pŏu.** Serviteur, conducteur de voiture, conduire une voiture; s'attacher à, appartenir.

僮 **T'ŏung.** Imprudent, insensé. | | ┼ ┼. Immobile, respectueux.

僩 **Hièn.** Majestueux, plein de dignité.

僭 **Tsién.** Faux, erreur. || **Tchénn.** Médire, calomnier. || **Ts'īn.** Trouble, désordre.

儀 **Î.** Maintien ou tenue du corps, la conduite de quelqu'un, règles de conduite, règles de convenances, cérémonies et usages du monde, témoignage de respect; décent, convenable; imiter, considérer, examiner; ornement; compagnon.

億 **Ĭ.** Cent mille, cent millions.

儇 **Hiuēn.** Agile.

僾 **Hí.** Être essoufflé.

儐 **Pín.** Arranger, disposer.

優 **Iōu.** Abondant, surabondant, nombreux. | | ┼ ┼. Doux, aimable. 游 | **Iôu** ┼. Aller çà et là, s'amuser.

儦 **Piaō.** | | ┼ ┼. Nombreux.

儺 **Nô.** Marcher posément. || **Nô.** 猗 | **ī** ┼. Flexible, délicat.

儼 **Ièn.** Air sévère, majestueux.

RACINE 10. 儿

允 **Iùn.** Vrai, sincère, vraiment.

元 **Iuên.** Grand, le plus âgé.

兄 **Hiōung.** Frère plus âgé que nous, sœur plus âgée que nous. | 弟 ┼ **tí.** Frères, sœurs; cousins. || **Houáng.** Triste, affligé.

充 **Tch'ōung.** Emplir, boucher. | 耳 ┼ **èul.** Ornements de pierre qui pendaient sur les oreilles et les couvraient.

先 **Siēn.** Avant, antérieur, meilleur, préférable, mettre avant, préférer, d'abord, défunt. | 王 ┼ **wâng.** Roi précédent, les anciens souverains. || **Sién.** Marcher en avant, devancer, donner l'exemple.

光 **Kouāng.** Lumière, gloire, glorieux.

克 **K'ŏ.** Être capable de, vaincre, soumettre, maîtriser, opprimer, exacteur.

兌 **T'ouéi.** Communiquer, voie.

兔 **T'óu.** Lièvre, lapin.

兒 **Eûl.** Enfant.

兕 **Séu.** Rhinocéros.

兢 **Kīng.** | | ┼ ┼. Craintif et circonspect, fort.

RACINE 11. 入

入 **Jŏu.** Entrer, à l'intérieur, à la maison, progresser.

內 **Néi.** Intérieur, à l'intérieur, dans; à la cour du prince, en Chine.

兩 **Leàng.** Deux; paire de souliers. || **Leáng.** Particule numérale des voitures.

RACINE 12. 八

八 **Pă.** Huit, huitième.

六 **Liŭ.** Six. | 轡 ✝ pi. Les six rênes qui étaient dans les mains du conducteur d'un char à quatre chevaux. V. page 137.

公 **Kōung.** Public, commun, juste; la première des cinq grandes dignités 公侯伯子男 **kōung heôu pĕ tzèu nân**; titre donné aux nobles de tout rang après leur mort; résidence d'un officier. || 功. Service, mérite.

兮 **Hî.** Particule finale.

共 **Kōung, Kóung.** Fournir, préparer, tribut. || **Kōung.** 恭. Prendre garde à, prendre soin de.

兵 **Pīng.** Arme, soldat.

其 **K'î.** Il, elle, son, sa, ce, cet; particule qui se place entre le verbe et le sujet. || **Kī.** Particule.

具 **Kiú.** Préparer, fournir, pourvoir; tout, ensemble.

典 **Tièn.** Statut, règle.

RACINE 13. 冂

冑 **Tcheóu.** Casque.

冒 **Maó.** Couvrir.

冓 **Keóu.** Charpente. 中 | **Tchōung** ✝. Appartement intérieur, appartement des femmes.

冔 **Hiū.** Bonnet de cérémonie qui était en usage sous la dynastie des 殷 **Īn.**

RACINE 14. 冖

冞 **Mî.** Profond.

冠 **Kouān.** Bonnet.

冢 **Tchòung.** Monticule, cime d'une montagne, grand. | 宰 ✝ **tsài.** Premier ministre.

冥 **Mîng.** Obscur, ténébreux.

RACINE 15. 冫

冬 **Tōung.** Hiver.

冰 **Pīng.** Glace.

冽 **Liĕ.** Froid.

凄 **Ts'î.** Froid.

凌 **Lîng.** Glace. | 陰 ✝ **iōung.** Glacière.

凝 **Îng.** Gelé, coagulé.

RACINE 16. 几

几 **Kì.** Tabouret contre lequel on s'appuyait étant assis; petite table.

凡 **Fân.** Chaque, quiconque, tout.

凰 **Houâng.** La femelle du phénix. 鳳 | **Fóung** ✝. Phénix.

凱 **K'ài.** Joyeux.

RACINE 17. 凵

凶 **Hiōung.** Néfaste, funeste, malheureux, funèbre.

出 **Tch'ŏu.** Sortir, paraître, se montrer, naître, faire sortir, manifester, produire, envoyer, rejeter, quitter. | 入 ✝ **jŏu.** Sortir et entrer, à la maison et hors de la maison.

函 **Hân.** Contenir.

RACINE 18. 刀

刀 **Taō.** Couteau, sabre, petite barque.

刈 **Í.** Couper.

切 **Ts'iĕ.** Couper.

刑 **Hîng.** Châtiment corporel; modèle, exemple, donner l'exemple, imiter.

初 **Tch'ōu.** Commencement, premier.

判 **P'án.** Diviser, séparer.

利 **Lí.** Profit, avantage.

到 **Taó.** Arriver, jusqu'à.

制 **Tchéu.** Couper, régler, fixer, limite, loi, règle, statut.

刺 **Ts'éu.** Percer, piquer; punir; critiquer, blâmer.

則 **Tsĕ.** Alors, dès lors, ensuite, par suite; loi, règle, modèle, prendre pour modèle.

削 **Siŏ.** Couper, amincir, démembrer, diminuer.

前 **Ts'iên.** Avant, devant, antérieur, précédent.

剔 **T'ī.** Gratter, amincir.

剛 **Kāng.** Dur, ferme, solide. ‖ 犅. Taureau.

剝 **Pouŏ.** Diviser, écorcher. ‖ **P'ŏu.** Frapper, abattre.

副 **Fóu.** Faux cheveux, aider. ‖ **P'ĭ.** Fendre.

劉 **Liôu.** Tuer; déchirer; nom de famille. 公 | **Kōung** 十. L'un des ancêtres des Tcheou. V. pag. 2 et 360.

RACINE 19. 力

力 **Lĭ.** Force, énergie, effort.

加 **Kiā.** Ajouter, atteindre, imposer, frapper.

功 **Kōung.** Service signalé rendu au public, action méritoire, travail accompli.

助 **Tchóu.** Aider.

劬 **K'iû.** Fatigue, peine.

勇 **Iòung.** Bravoure, brave, valeureux, intrépide.

勉 **Mièn.** Faire des efforts, se faire violence à soi-même.

務 **Oú.** S'appliquer à, faire des efforts. ‖ **Où.** 侮. Outrager.

勖 **Hiŭ.** Exciter, animer.

動 **Tóung.** Mouvoir, être ému.

勝 **Chéng.** Vaincre, soumettre. ‖ **Chēng.** Être capable de, avoir assez de force ou de talent pour.

勞 **Laô.** Travail fatigant, fatigue, peine, chagrin. ‖ **Laó.** Récompenser, encourager.

勤 **K'în.** Diligent, laborieux.

勩 **Í.** Fatigue, peine.

RACINE 20. 勹

勺 **Chŏ.** Cuiller, cuillerée. | 藥 十 iŏ. Pivoine.

勿 **Oŭ.** Ne pas (s'emploie ordinairement avec l'impératif).

包 **Paō.** Envelopper, contenir.

匊 **Kiŭ.** Autant que les deux mains réunies peuvent contenir.

匍 **P'ŏu.** | 匐 十 p'ŏ ou 十 fŏu. Marcher sur les pieds et sur les mains, ne pouvoir marcher.

匐 **P'ŏ, Fŏu.** 匍 | P'ŏu 十. Se traîner sur les pieds et sur les mains; faire tous ses efforts.

匏 **P'aŏ.** Courge.

RACINE 21. 匕

匕 **Pì.** Cuiller.

北 **Pĕ.** Nord, septentrional.

RACINE 22. 匚

匡 **K'ouāng.** Régler, corriger, réformer; aider.

匪 **Fèi.** Non, ne pas, ce n'est pas que; faux, mauvais; panier. || 斐. Bien orné, élégant.

匱 **Kouéi.** Manquer, faire défaut; panier.

RACINE 23. 匸

匹 **P'ĭ.** Compagnon, semblable, conforme.

RACINE 24. 十

十 **Chĕu.** Dix, dixième.

千 **Ts'iēn.** Mille.

午 **Où.** Midi; lettre horaire employée dans les dénominations du cycle.

升 **Chēng.** Monter, croître; la dixième partie du 斗 teòu boisseau, un litre environ.

卉 **Houéi.** Herbe, plante.

卒 **Tsŏu.** Fin, finir, enfin, à la fin. mourir.

卑 **Pēi.** Bas, vil, méprisable.

南 **Nân.** Sud, méridional.

博 **Pouŏ.** Grand, vaste.

RACINE 25. 卜

卜 **Pŏu.** Exposer au feu l'écaille d'une tortue, examiner les fissures produites et tirer des présages; deviner, donner.

占 **Tchēn.** Interpréter un présage, deviner.

卣 **Iòu.** Jarre pour le vin.

RACINE 26. 卩

卬 **Ngàng.** Je, moi. | | 十 十. Grand, majestueux, imposant. || **Iàng.** 仰. Regarder en haut.

卯 **Maò.** Caractère horaire employé dans les dénominations du cycle.

卷 **Kiuèn.** Enrouler. | 耳 十 èul. Lampourde ou bardane. || **K'iuên.** Courbé, sinueux, bouclé.

卽 **Tsĭ.** Aller à, approcher, alors, aussitôt.

卿 **K'īng.** Ministre d'État à la cour de l'empereur ou d'un prince, grand officier.

RACINE 27. 厂

厄 **Ngŏ.** Anneau.

厚 **Heóu.** Épais, ferme, libéral, vertueux; estimer beaucoup, traiter avec honneur.

厖 **Màng.** Grand.

原 **Iuên.** Plaine, uni; origine, cause, commencement.

厥 **Kiuĕ.** Son, sa, leur.

猒 **Ién.** Abonder, suffire. || **Ièn.** Tranquille, content. || **Iĕ.** | 浥 † i. Humecté.

厲 **Lí.** Pierre à aiguiser; austère, sévère, cruel, tyrannique, opprimer; gué profond, relever les vêtements jusqu'à la ceinture pour traverser l'eau; qui est pendant.

RACINE 28. 厶

厹 **K'iòu.** Lance à trois pointes.

去 **K'iú.** S'en aller, quitter. || **K'iù.** Éloigner, rejeter.

參 **Chēnn.** Constellation d'Orion. || **Tch'ènn.** | 差 † tch'ēu. Inégal, irrégulier.

RACINE 29. 又

又 **Ióu.** Aussi, encore, de nouveau, de plus.

及 **Kĭ.** Atteindre, arriver à, s'étendre à, jusqu'à; et, avec, ensemble.

友 **Iòu.** Ami, compagnon, amitié fraternelle, agir en ami; deux.

反 **Fàn.** Réitérer, renouveler, répéter, revenir, s'en retourner, faire revenir, rappeler, tourner en sens contraire, changer, devenir autre, contraire.

叔 **Chŏu.** | †, | 父 † fóu. Frère puiné de notre père. || Le troisième de quatre frères.

取 **Ts'iù.** Prendre, obtenir, attirer, recevoir, choisir, imiter, approuver, tirer avantage de. || **Ts'iú.** 娶. Prendre femme.

受 **Cheóu.** Recevoir, admettre, supporter.

叟 **Cheōu.** | | † †. Bruit que fait le grain, quand on le lave.

RACINE 30. 口

口 **K'eòu.** Bouche, bec.

古 **Kòu.** Ancien, vieux.

句 **Keóu.** 彀 Arc tendu le plus fortement possible.

只 **Tchèu.** Seulement. || **Tchèu.** Particule euphonique.

召 **Tchaó.** Dire à quelqu'un de venir. || **Chaó.** Domaine situé au sud du mont 岐 **K'î** dans le 陝 西 **Chèn sī.** V. page 2. | 公 † **kōung.** Prince de Chao. V. page 2. | 南 † **nân.** V. page 16.

可 **K'ò.** Être possible, être convenable, être louable, être permis, être capable, être digne, être suffisant, être passable, approuver, agréer, consentir.

叫 **Kiaó.** Appeler,

右 **Ióu.** Main droite, côté droit; honorer, aider. 左 | **Tsouò** †. A droite et à gauche, ceux qui sont auprès de quelqu'un.

史 **Chèu.** Annaliste, historiographe.

台 **T'âi.** 鮐. Marsouin. | 背 † **péi.** Dos rugueux et tacheté comme celui du marsouin: dos de vieillard.

司 **Sēu.** Présider, charge publique, officier. | 空 † **k'ōung.** Ministre des travaux publics. | 徒 † **t'ôu.** Ministre de l'instruction.

各 **Kŏ.** Chaque, chacun.

吁 **Hiū.** Soupirer.

合 **Hŏ.** Unir, réunir, convenir, être d'accord.

吉 **Kĭ.** Heureux. 初 | **Tch'ōu** †. Nouvelle lune.

詩經

同 **T'ôung.** Semblable, identique, prendre part à, ensemble, en commun, avec, se réunir, rassembler, assemblée, entier; réunions des princes aux époques ordinaires.

名 **Mîng.** Nom, réputation, renom, illustre.

吐 **T'òu.** Rejeter de la bouche.

向 **Hiáng.** Fenêtre tournée au nord.

后 **Heóu.** Souverain, prince. | 稷 ╁ **tsĭ.** Nom donné à 棄 **K'í**, qui fut ministre de l'agriculture sous le règne de 舜 **Chouénn.** Voy. ag. 2 et 347.

君 **Kiūn.** Roi, souverain, prince, princesse. | 臣 ╁ **tch'ênn.** Le prince et le sujet, relations entre le prince et le sujet. | 子 ╁ **tzèu.** Prince, celui qui cultive la vertu, disciple de la sagesse, homme sage, homme respectable.

吠 **Féi.** Aboyer.

否 **Feòu.** Non; mal agir. || **Pì.** Mauvais.

告 **Kaó, Kŏu.** Dire, rapporter, annoncer, informer.

吪 **Wô.** Mouvoir, réformer.

吳 **Houá.** Crier.

吹 **Tch'ouēi.** Souffler.

吾 **Oû.** Je, moi.

呦 **Iōu.** | | ╁ ╁. Cri du cerf.

周 **Tcheōu.** Circuit, contour, tout autour, partout, universel, complet, parfait; grand; nom d'une ancienne principauté, aujourd'hui 岐山縣 **K'î chān hién** dans le 鳳翔府 **Fóung siâng fòu** du 陝西 **Chèn sī**; nom d'une dynastie impériale, dont les ancêtres étaient princes de Tcheou, et qui régna de 1134 à 256 avant notre ère, avec la ville de 鎬 **Haó** pour capitale; la capitale de l'empire chinois (sous les Tcheou). V. page 2. | 公 ╁ **kōung.** Frère cadet de 武王 **Où wâng**, qui fonda la dynastie des 周 **Tcheōu.** V. page 2. | 南 ╁ **nân.** Titre du premier livre du Cheu king. Voy. page 5.

呼 **Hōu.** Crier pour appeler quelqu'un.

命 **Míng.** Ordre, prescription, décision, mandat, donner un ordre, nommer à une charge, enseigner, ordre ou volonté du ciel, Providence, destin; tout ce qui vient du ciel, spécialement le pouvoir souverain, la vie, les facultés naturelles, les talents, l'ordre de l'univers, la loi naturelle,...

和 **Houô.** Accord, harmonie, union, concorde, accommodant, condescendant, affable, obligeant, tempéré, modéré; sonnettes fixées sur le devant d'une voiture. || **Houó.** Accompagner un chant.

咎 **Kióu.** Faute, blâmer.

呱 **K'ōu, Wā.** Vagissement.

呶 **Naô.** Crier, cris confus.

咨 **Tzēu.** Consulter; soupirer, gémir; ah!

咸 **Hièn.** Tous, entièrement, unir.

咽 **Ién.** Avaler. || **Iuēn.** | | ╁ ╁. Son du tambour.

哀 **Ngāi.** Être dans l'affliction, compatir, malheureux, lamentable.

咢 **Ngŏ.** Battre le tambour.

咥 **Hí.** Rire aux éclats.

咮 **Tcheóu.** Bec d'oiseau.

咺 **Hiuèn.** Distingué, glorieux.

哆 **Tch'èu.** Grande bouche ouverte.

哉 **Tsāi.** Particule finale qui marque l'admiration, l'étonnement ou le doute.

員 **Iuên.** Rond, contour. || **Iûn.** Augmenter, aider. || 云. Particule.

哲 **Tchĕ.** Sage, prudent.

哿 **Kò.** Pouvoir supporter son sort, supporter, agréer, approuver.

唁 **Ién.** Consoler par des paroles.

唐 **T'âng.** Allée qui conduisait de la porte à la salle du temple des ancêtres; cuscute; nom de principauté. V. page 4. | 棣 † ti. Prunier ou cerisier sauvage.

唪 **Pòung.** | | † †. Nombreux.

售 **Cheóu.** Vendre.

唯 **Wêi.** Seulement. || **Wèi.** | | † †. Entrer et sortir librement.

啄 **Tchouŏ.** Becqueter, prendre avec le bec.

商 **Chāng.** Domaine des princes de ce nom, qui gouvernèrent tout l'empire de 1766 à 1154. V. p. 462.

啍 **T'ouēnn.** | | † †. Mouvement lent et pesant d'une grosse voiture.

問 **Wénn.** Interroger, s'informer, s'informer de la santé de quelqu'un, saluer, envoyer des salutations || 聞. Réputation.

啓 **K'ì.** Ouvrir, étendre, découvrir, enseigner, commencer, précéder; être à genoux. | 明 † ming. L'étoile du matin.

啜 **Tchouŏ.** Pleurer.

善 **Chèn.** Bon; être bon à.

喉 **Heôu.** Gosier.

喓 **Iaō.** | | † †. Bruit des sauterelles.

喙 **Houéi.** Ne pouvoir respirer, être aux abois.

喤 **Houâng.** | | † †. Vagissement. || **Hôung.** | | † †. Accord d'instruments de musique.

單 **Tān.** Simple; entièrement, employer entièrement.

喜 **Hì.** Se réjouir, être content, joyeux, réjouir.

喪 **Sāng.** Deuil, funérailles. || **Sáng.** Mourir, cesser d'exister, faire mourir, ruiner, laisser périr, perdre, être privé de, perdre sa charge, perdre le pouvoir souverain.

喬 **K'iaô.** Haut, dressé verticalement.

喈 **Kiāi.** | | † †. Gazouillement des oiseaux, son des cloches, bruit du vent.

嗜 **Chéu.** Trouver agréable, aimer, agréer, convoiter.

嗟 **Tsiē.** Soupirer, gémir; oh! ah! hélas!

嗣 **Séu.** Continuer, succéder, hériter, héritier.

嗷 **Ngaô.** | | † †. Cris plaintifs d'une troupe d'oies sauvages.

詩經

嗿 **T'ān.** Bruit que fait une multitude de personnes mangeant ensemble.

嘅 **K'ái.** Soupirer, gémir.

嘆 **T'án.** Soupirer.

嘌 **P'iaō.** Soubresaut, cahot, agitation.

嘏 **Kià, Kòu.** Bonheur.

嘒 **Houéi.** Petite lumière, briller. | | † †. Bruit d'insectes, accord d'instruments de musique.

嘉 **Kiā.** Excellent, approuver, donner des éloges; prendre femme.

嘗 **Tch'âng.** Goûter, faire l'épreuve; offrande que l'empereur et les 諸 侯 **tchōu heôu** faisaient en automne à leurs ancêtres.

嘯 **Siaó, Siŭ.** Siffler, gémissement prolongé.

嘵 **Hiaō.** | | † †. Voix tremblante.

嘻 **Hī.** Soupirer, admirer; oh! ah!

嘽 **T'ān.** | | † †. Haletant, nombreux.

噂 **Tsuénn.** Conversation. | 沓 † **tă.** Longue conversation.

噎 **Iĕ, Ī.** Obstruction du gosier, suffocation.

噦 **Houéi.** | | † †. Gazouillement, tintement; vaste, spacieux.

噫 **Ī.** Hélas! oh!

噬 **Chéu.** Particule initiale.

噲 **K'ouái.** | | † †. Endroit bien éclairé et agréable.

噳 **Iù.** | | † †. Nombreux.

嚶 **Īng.** Gazouillement des oiseaux.

嚴 **Ièn.** Sévère, majestueux.

囂 **Hiaō.** Crier. || **Ngaô.** | | † †. Cris confus.

囊 **Nâng.** Sac.

RACINE 31. 囗

四 **Séu.** Quatre.

囚 **Siôu.** Prisonnier.

因 **Īn.** S'appuyer sur, suivre, par le moyen de, d'après, selon.

回 **Houêi.** Tourner, revenir, dépravé, corrompu.

囷 **K'iūn.** Grande corbeille ronde.

固 **Kóu.** Ferme, solide, affermir.

囿 **Ióu.** Parc.

圃 **Pòu.** Jardin potager.

國 **Kouŏ.** État, royaume, empire, ville capitale d'un État, dynastie. 四 | **Séu** †. Tous les États.

圉 **Iù.** Pâturages aux frontières d'un État; instrument sur lequel on frappait pour annoncer la fin des morceaux de musique.

圍 **Wêi.** Environner, enceinte. 九 | **Kiòu** †. Les neuf circonscriptions ou provinces.

園 **Iuên.** Jardin, parc.

圖 **T'ôu.** Penser, consulter, plan, dessin.

RACINE 32. 土

土 **T'òu.** Terre, l'un des cinq éléments des Chinois, globe terrestre,

sol, terrain, territoire, champ, pays, localité. 冢 | **Tchòung** 十. Autel élevé à l'esprit de la terre. || **Tóu.** Écorce de racine d'arbre.

地 **Tí.** Le globe terrestre, sol, terrain, champ.

在 **Tsái.** Être présent, dans, sur.

圭 **Kouēi.** Tablette de jade qui était une marque de dignité. V. page 64.

坐 **Tsouó.** S'asseoir, assis, siège.

均 **Kiūn.** Égal, juste, égal à égal, modérer, régler.

坎 **K'ān.** Son du tambour. | | 十 十. Bruit des coups de hache.

坰 **Kiōung.** Endroits les plus reculés d'un État.

坻 **Tch'êu.** Ilot.

坼 **Tch'ĕ.** Fendre, déchirer.

垂 **Tch'ouêi.** Qui est pendant, laisser pendre.

垝 **Kouèi.** Menacer ruine.

垢 **Keòu, Kiù.** Sale, immonde, impur.

垣 **Iuên.** Mur peu élevé.

垤 **Tiĕ.** Fourmilière, monticule.

城 **Tch'êng.** Rempart, place fortifiée, ville, fortifier.

域 **Iŭ.** Frontières, limites, étendue d'un territoire, contrée.

執 **Tchĕu.** Tenir, saisir, maintenir, diriger, régler, conduire, observer ou faire observer une loi, pratiquer constamment une vertu.

埤 **P'êi.** Ajouter, imposer, peser sur.

埸 **Ĭ.** Limite d'un champ, fixer les limites de chaque champ.

基 **Kī.** Fondation, pied d'un mur, fonder, établir.

堂 **T'âng.** Salle principale d'une maison, palais; terrain élevé qui s'étend en plaine.

堅 **Kiēn.** Ferme, solide, constant.

埽 **Saó.** Balayer.

堪 **K'ān.** Être capable de, pouvoir supporter.

報 **Paó.** Rendre la pareille, payer de retour, récompenser.

場 **Tch'âng.** Terrain nu et uni, aire pour battre les grains, terrain uni où l'on sacrifiait en plein air.

堵 **Tòu.** Mur long de cinquante 尺 tch'ĕu.

塗 **T'ôu.** Boue, chemin, route.

塒 **Chêu.** Trou dans un mur pour les poules.

塞 **Sái.** Boucher; sincère, sincèrement.

填 **T'iên.** Remplir, combler. || **T'ièn.** Faible, malade. || **Tch'ênn.** Longtemps.

塵 **Tch'ênn.** Poussière, couvrir de poussière.

墉 **Iôung.** Rempart, entourer de remparts; mur de terre.

塈 **Kí.** Recueillir; se reposer.

墐 **Kín.** Enduire de mortier, couvrir de terre.

墓 **Móu.** Tombe.

墳 **Fênn.** Digue, grand.

增 **Tsēng.** Augmenter. | | 十 十. Nombreux.

墠 **Iuên.** Terrain aplani.

壎 **Hiuēn.** Instrument de musique qui était fait de terre cuite, avait la forme et la grosseur d'un œuf de poule ou d'oie, était percé de six trous, et dans lequel on soufflait.

壑 **Hŏ.** Canal, fossé.

壞 **Houái.** Tomber en ruine, se gâter, se corrompre.

RACINE 33. 士

士 **Chéu.** Celui qui s'adonne à l'étude des lettres ou de la sagesse, lettré, sage, officier civil ou militaire, soldat, aide, serviteur, mari. || 事. Servir, affaire.

壬 **Jênn.** Grand.

壯 **Tchouáng.** Fort.

壺 **Hôu.** Pot, vase pour les liquides, calebasse.

壹 **Ĭ.** Un, une fois, tout dévoué à.

壼 **K'ouènn.** Passage entre les bâtiments.

壽 **Cheóu.** Vie longue.

RACINE 35. 夊

夏 **Hiá.** Été. || **Hià.** Grand; nom de la première dynastie chinoise, qui, fondée par le grand 禹 **Iù** en 2205, régna jusqu'en 1766 avant notre ère; l'empire chinois.

RACINE 36. 夕

夕 **Sĭ.** Soir, soleil couchant, logement pour la nuit.

外 **Wái.** Dehors, extérieur, étranger, au-delà, après, outre, non compris.

夙 **Siŭ.** Matin, de très bonne heure, tôt. | 夜 † **ié.** Matin et soir, du matin au soir. || **Sĭ.** Retraite.

多 **Touō.** Nombreux, beaucoup, devenir nombreux.

夜 **Ié.** Nuit, tard.

夢 **Móung.** Songe, rêver. || **Môung.** | | † †. Obscur, ténébreux.

RACINE 37. 大

大 **Tá, Tái.** Grand, noble, distingué, éminent, supérieur, devenir grand, agrandir. || **T'ái.** Excessif. S'emploie pour 太. | 王 † **wâng.** L'un des ancêtres de la dynastie des Tcheou. V. page 2.

天 **T'iēn.** Ciel, le ciel matériel, l'auteur de la nature, le maître et l'arbitre souverain du ciel et de la terre. | 下 † **hiá.** Sous le ciel, tout ce qui est sous le ciel, la terre, l'empire chinois. | 子 † **tzèu.** Le fils du ciel: le souverain de la Chine.

夫 **Fōu.** Homme, mari, soldat, simple particulier. | 婦 † **fóu.** Le mari et la femme. 大 | **Tái** †. Grand dignitaire d'un rang inférieur au 卿 **k'īng** ministre d'État. || **Fôu.** Ce, cet.

夭 **Iaō.** Jeune et beau, feuillage verdoyant, élégant, visage souriant; châtiment envoyé par le ciel.

失 **Chĕu.** Perdre, laisser échapper, laisser enlever, ne pas obtenir, omettre, négliger, s'écarter de, ne pas se conformer à, erreur, faute.

央 **Iāng**. Milieu. || **Īng**. | | 卄. Brillant.

夷 **Î**. Uni, égal, juste, paisible, aisé, naturel ; tribus étrangères.

夸 **K'ouà**. Se vanter, exagérer.

夾 **Kiă**. Tenir ou serrer des deux côtés, occuper les deux côtés de.

奄 **Ièn**. Occuper une vaste étendue, largement, grandement ; aussitôt.

奉 **Fòung**. Présenter, offrir, porter un objet des deux mains.

奏 **Tseóu**. Jouer d'un instrument de musique ; annoncer, déployer.

奔 **Pēnn**. Courir, s'échapper, s'enfuir, rapide.

奐 **Houán**. 伴 | **P'án** 十. S'abandonner à l'oisiveté, s'amuser.

契 **K'í**. Instrument avec lequel le devin perçait l'écaille de la tortue pour l'exposer au feu. | | 十 十. Triste. || **K'iĕ**. Séparé.

奕 **Ĭ**. Grand, beau, magnifique; continu ; triste.

奚 **Hî**. Quel? comment? pourquoi? nom d'homme.

奠 **Tién**. Présenter, offrir, déposer.

奧 **Iŭ**. Espace compris dans le tournant d'une rivière ; douce chaleur.

奪 **Touŏ**. Prendre de force, enlever, emporter.

奭 **Chĕu**. Rouge. 君 | **Kiūn** 十. Le Sage Cheu ou 召 公 **Chaó kōung**, ministre de 武 王 **Où wâng**.

奮 **Fénn**. Prendre son essor, s'élever, faire de grands efforts, exciter.

奰 **Pí**. Colère, indignation.

RACINE 38. 女

女 **Gniù**. Femme, fille, femelle. | 子 十 **tzèu**. Fille, femme. || **Jòu**. 汝. Tu, vous.

好 **Haò**. Bon, bien, louable, beau, apte à, habile à. || **Haó**. Aimer, désirer, convoiter, ami, amitié, relations amicales.

如 **Jôu**. Comme, semblable, comme si. 不 | **Pŏu** 十. Ne pas égaler, ne pas valoir autant. 莫 | **Mouŏ** 十. Aucun ou Rien n'égale ou ne vaut.

妣 **Pì**. Mère ou aïeule décédée.

妥 **T'ouò**. A l'aise, commodément.

姓 **Síng**. Nom de famille. 百 | **Pĕ** 十. Les cent familles, toutes les familles, le peuple.

姑 **Kōu**. Sœur de notre père ; en attendant, pour le moment.

始 **Chéu**. Commencer, d'abord. || **Chèu**. Commencement.

妯 **Tch'eōu**. Trouble d'esprit.

妹 **Méi**. Sœur moins âgée que nous.

姊 **Tzèu**. Sœur plus âgée que nous.

妻 **Ts'ī**. Épouse.

姒 **Séu**. Nom de famille des descendants de 禹 **Iù**. 太 | **T'ái** 十. Nom de la femme de 文 王 **Wênn wâng**. V. page 5.

委 **Wēi**. | 蛇 十 **t'ouô**. Paraître joyeux et content.

姝 **Tch'ōu**. Excellent, beau.

姞 **Kĭ**. Nom de famille de la femme de 后 稷 **Heóu tsĭ**.

姨 **Î**. Sœur de la mère ou de la femme.

姜 **Kiāng**. Nom de famille. | 女 十. **gniù**. La femme de 大 王 **T'ái wâng**.

威 **Wēi.** Qui inspire le respect et la crainte; majestueux, terrible.

姬 **Kī.** Surnom de la famille des 周 **Tcheōu**; femme distinguée.

姻 **Īn.** Affinité par le mariage, parent par alliance.

娀 **Sōung.** Ancienne principauté située dans le 蒲 州 (Chan si).

娑 **Souō.** 婆 | **P'ouô** 亍. Sauter, danser.

娛 **Iû.** Se réjouir, s'amuser.

娣 **Tí.** Sœur moins âgée que nous.

婁 **Liû.** Traîner.

婆 **P'ouô.** Mère avancée en âge.

婉 **Iuèn.** Beau, aimable, agréable.

婦 **Fóu.** Épouse, femme mariée.

媒 **Mêi** S'entremettre pour faire conclure un mariage.

媚 **Méi.** Flatter, aimable, agréable, favori.

媛 **Iuén.** Beauté, femme distinguée.

媾 **Keóu.** Faveur, bienfait.

嫄 **Iuên.** 姜 | **Kiāng** 亍. Mère de 后 稷 **Heóu tsĭ**. V. page 347.

嫁 **Kiá.** Prendre un mari.

嬛 **K'iôung.** Seul et destitué de tout secours.

嬪 **P'în.** Devenir la femme de.

孌 **Liuèn.** Beau, élégant, excellent.

RACINE 39. 子

子 **Tzèu.** Fils, fille, enfant; aimer d'un amour paternel; petit d'un animal, œuf; titre de dignité; officier, homme respectable, Monsieur, Madame.

孑 **Kiĕ.** Restant, homme estropié, mutilé. | | 亍 亍. Dressé verticalement.

孔 **K'òung.** Grandement, très.

字 **Tzéu.** Aimer, prendre soin de.

存 **Ts'uênn.** Conserver, survivre, être parmi.

孝 **Hiaó.** Piété filiale, remplir les devoirs de la piété filiale.

孚 **Fōu.** Confiance.

孟 **Méng.** Le plus âgé.

季 **Kí.** Le troisième de plusieurs frères; jeune. 王 | **Wâng** 亍. Père de 文 王 **Wênn wâng**.

孫 **Suēnn.** Petit-fils, descendant. | 子 亍 **tzèu**. Petit-fils, descendant. 子 | **Tzèu.** 亍. Descendants. || **Suénn.** 遜 Modeste, condescendant.

學 **Hiŏ.** Apprendre sous un maître, étudier, imiter.

孺 **Jóu.** Enfant, affection d'un enfant.

孽 **Iĕ.** Malheur, calamité.

RACINE 40. 宀

宅 **Tchĕ.** Habitation, contrée où l'on fixe sa demeure, occuper, habiter.

宇 **Iù.** Toit, emplacement d'une habitation, territoire.

守 **Cheòu.** Garder, défendre, protéger, veiller sur.

安 **Ngān.** Paisible, calme, tranquille, en sûreté, en sécurité, en

bon état, en bonne santé, à qui rien ne manque, content, heureux, repos, loisir, agrément, aisément, sans effort, procurer la tranquillité ou le repos; comment? pourquoi? où?

宋 **Sóung.** Ancienne principauté située dans le 歸德府 **Kouèi tě fòu** (Ho nan).

完 **Houân** (Wan). Complet, compléter.

宗 **Tsōung.** Souche d'une famille, ancêtres, tous ceux qui sont issus d'une souche commune et portent le même nom de famille, vénérable, vénérer. 丨 廟 ┼ **miaó.** Salle où les tablettes des ancêtres de l'empereur ou d'un prince étaient rangées et honorées; tablettes portant les noms des ancêtres.

宜 **Î.** Convenable, raisonnable, juste, utile, commode, traiter comme il convient, arranger convenablement, régler, remplir ses devoirs envers.

定 **Tíng.** Fixer, établir, déterminer, cesser, arrêter, finir; front.

宛 **Iuèn.** Immobile, tranquille, poli. 丨 然 ┼ **jên.** Poliment. 丨 丘 ┼ **k'iōu.** Nom de montagne. V. page 145. ‖ **Iuén.** Petit.

客 **K'ŏ, K'ĕ.** Celui qui reçoit l'hospitalité, étranger, visiteur.

宣 **Siuēn.** Aller partout, proclamer, déployer, étendre.

室 **Chĕu.** Maison, chambre; famille, épouse.

宥 **Ióu.** Grand et profond.

宮 **Kōung.** Maison, établissement, palais, temple des ancêtres. 東 丨 **Tōung** ┼. Héritier présomptif.

宰 **Tsài.** Gouverner, disposer en maître, gouverneur, intendant, ministre d'État. 冢 丨 **Tchòung** ┼. Premier ministre.

害 **Hái.** Nuire, causer du dommage, souffrir. ‖ **Hŏ.** 曷. Quoi? pourquoi? comment? quand?

宴 **Ién.** Repos, loisir, plaisir, amusement, festin.

宵 **Siaō.** Nuit. 丨 行 ┼ **hing.** Le ver luisant.

家 **Kiā.** Maison; famille, les personnes qui demeurent dans une même maison, tous ceux qui sont issus d'un même sang et portent le même nom de famille; mari, fiancé.

容 **Iôung.** Contenir, comprendre, embrasser, recevoir, admettre; tenue du corps, air du visage, apparence extérieure, manière d'agir.

宿 **Siŭ.** Passer une nuit dans un endroit.

寁 **Tsiĕ.** Rapide, rompre brusquement.

密 **Mĭ.** Secret, silence, dru, compacte; nom de lieu. V. page 338.

寇 **K'eóu.** Voleur, brigand.

富 **Fóu.** Riche, richesse, abondant, enrichir.

寐 **Méi.** Dormir, prendre son repos.

寒 **Hân.** Froid, souffrir du froid.

寘 **Tchéu.** Placer, déposer, abandonner.

實 寔 **Chĕu.** Plein, emplir; solide, réel, véritable, sincère, en réalité; fruit, résultat, effet produit, service rendu.

寡 **Kouà.** Peu, rare, petit, peu considérable, femme veuve. 丨 人 ┼ **jênn.** Femme de peu de mérite: moi princesse. 丨 妻 ┼ **ts'ī.** Épouse

詩經

d'un rare mérite: femme légitime.

寢 **Ts'ìn.** Se coucher pour prendre son repos, être au lit; bâtiment qui était derrière le temple des ancêtres, et renfermait les vêtements et les ustensiles nécessaires pour les cérémonies.

寤 **Oú.** S'éveiller, être éveillé.

察 **Tch'ă.** Examiner, considérer, prendre connaissance, faire une enquête, donner des soins minutieux à; paraître, se manifester.

寧 寍 **Gnîng.** Paisible, tranquille, rendre tranquille; il vaut mieux, il est préférable; comment? pourquoi?

N. B.—La première forme est à présent interdite, parce qu'elle a fait partie du nom de l'empereur 道 光 Taó kouāng.

寬 **K'ouān,** Large, vaste; généreux, magnanime.

寫 **Siè.** S'écouler, se dissiper.

寶 **Paò.** Chose précieuse; tablette de jade qui était une marque de dignité.

RACINE 41. 寸

寺 **Séu.** Eunuque.

封 **Fōung.** Grand; officier mercenaire.

射 **Ché.** Tirer de l'arc, archer. ‖ **Chĕu.** Lancer une flèche contre un objet, frapper d'une flèche. ‖ **Ĭ.** Dégoût, satiété.

將 **Tsiāng.** Être sur le point de, avoir l'intention de; marque du futur; grand, fort, aider, escorter, marcher, avancer, offrir, présenter, communiquer, exécuter, pousser, faire avancer; côté; presque. ‖ **Ts'iāng.** Désirer, prier. ‖ ‖ ┼ ┼. Splendide, majestueux, harmonieux.

尋 **Sîn.** Chercher; mesure de huit 尺 tch'ĕu.

尊 **Tsuēnn.** Honorable; vase pour le vin.

對 **Touéi.** Donner une réponse, conforme, convenable.

RACINE 42. 小

小 **Siaò.** Petit, peu considérable, vil. ‖ 人 ┼ jênn. Homme vulgaire, homme méprisable. ‖ 子 ┼ tzèu. Enfant; vous, mon fils; moi petit enfant (l'empereur se désigne ainsi lui-même). ‖ 心 ┼ sīn. Avec soin.

少 **Chaò.** Peu.

尚 **Cháng.** Ajouter, encore, de plus; par bonheur, espérer, désirer, souhaiter.

RACINE 43. 尢

尤 **Iôu.** Mauvais, blâmer.

尨 **Mâng.** Chien très poilu.

就 **Tsióu.** Aller à, approcher, avancer, progresser.

尰 **Tchòung.** Jambes enflées.

RACINE 44. 尸

尸 **Chēu.** Cadavre; celui qui dans une cérémonie en l'honneur d'un mort représentait la personne du mort; officier inerte; diriger.

尺 **Tch'ĕu.** Mesure d'environ vingt centimètres sous les Tcheou, et d'environ trente-cinq à présent.

尹 **Ìn.** Gouverner, administrer, régler, diriger, préfet, officier.

尾 **Wèi.** Queue; dernier, objet sans valeur.

局 **Kiŭ.** Courber, incliner, bouclé.

居 **Kiū.** Habiter, demeurer, occuper, demeure, contrée habitée, occuper une charge; repos, état commode; tranquille, content. | | ††. Avec orgueil ou mépris.

屆 **Kiái.** Fin, limite, arriver.

屈 **K'iū.** Courber, incliner, subjuguer.

屋 **Oŭ.** Maison. 夏 | **Hià** †. Grande table 俎 **tchòu.**

屎 **Hī.** Soupirer, gémir, murmurer.

屑 **Siĕ.** Pur, convenable. 不 | **Pŏu** †. Ne pas juger convenable, ne pas daigner.

展 **Tchèn.** Vrai, vraiment. || **Tchēn.** Robe de cour de couleur blanche.

屏 **Pìng, Píng.** Écarter, éloigner, enlever. || **P'ìng.** Cloison, paravent, rempart.

屠 **T'ôu.** Boucherie; nom de lieu. V. page 404.

屢 **Liú.** Souvent.

履 **Lì.** Chaussure, marcher sur, suivre les traces de; prospérité.

屨 **Kiú.** Chaussure de cuir ou de chanvre.

屬 **Chŏu.** Appliquer, adhérent, proche, uni, parent, communiquer, appartenir à, dépendre de. || **Tchŏu.** Rassembler.

RACINE 46. 山

山 **Chān.** Montagne, colline. | 川 † **tch'ouēn.** Montagnes et cours d'eau.

屺 **K'ì.** Montagne nue.

岐 **K'î.** Nom d'une montagne et de l'ancien domaine des princes de 周 **Tcheōu,** dans le | 山 縣 † **chān hién** actuel (province de 陝 西 **Chèn sī**); haut. Voy. page 2.

岡 **Kāng.** Crête d'une montagne.

岨 **Ts'iū.** Montagne où les rochers sont recouverts de terre.

岵 **Hòu.** Montagne couverte de végétation.

岸 **Ngán.** Bord élevé d'une rivière; hauteur, sommet; prison.

峙 **Tchèu.** Amasser, réunir des provisions.

峨 **Ngô.** | | ††. Maintien grave.

峱 **Naô.** Montagne située dans la principauté de 齊 **Ts'î** (Chan toung actuel). V. page 104.

崇 **Tch'ôung.** Haut, amonceler, monceau; honorer; tout, entier; arriver au plus haut point; nom de principauté. V. page 339.

崒 **Tsŏu.** Haute montagne.

崔 **Ts'ouēi.** Montagne haute et étendue.

崧 **Sōung.** Haut et large.

崩 **Pēng.** S'écrouler, tomber, déchoir.

嵬 **Wèi.** Haut et escarpé. 崔 | **Ts'ouēi** †. Montagne où les rochers sont recouverts de terre.

嶞 **Touó.** Montagne étroite et longue.

嶽 **Iŏ.** Montagne où les empereurs faisaient des sacrifices. V. p. 396.

嶷 **Ī.** Avoir l'usage de la raison, discerner.

詩經

嶺 **Tiēn.** Cime, sommet.

巖 **Iên.** | | ✝ ✝. Haut et escarpé.

巘 **Ièn.** Cime, sommet.

RACINE 47. 川

川 **Tch'ouēn.** Cours d'eau, rivière.

巢 **Tch'aô.** Nid, hutte sur un arbre.

RACINE 48. 工

工 **Kōung.** Artisan, ouvrier, métier, travail, officier, préfet, habile.

左 **Tsouò.** Côté gauche, main gauche. || **Tsouó.** Aider.

巧 **K'iaò.** Habile, adroit, ingénieux, rusé.

差 **Tch'ā.** Différence, erreur. || **Tch'āi.** Distinguer, choisir, envoyé. || **Ts'ēu.** Ordre, rang, différence, distinction. 參 | **Tch'ēnn** ✝. De longueur ou de hauteur inégale. | 池 ✝ **tch'ēu.** Ne pas aller de front.

RACINE 49. 巳

巳 **Ì.** Avoir une fin, prendre fin, mettre fin, cesser, destituer; déjà, auparavant, marque du temps passé; trop, excès.

巷 **Hiáng.** Passage étroit, ruelle.

RACINE 50. 巾

巾 **Kīn.** Bonnet.

市 **Chéu.** Place de marché.

布 **Póu.** Toile.

帑 **Nòu.** 孥. Les fils et les filles; la femme et les enfants.

帝 **Tí.** Prince souverain, roi, empereur, le souverain roi. 上 | 天 | 也 (朱熹) **Cháng ✝ t'iēn ✝ iè.** Le Chang ti est le roi du ciel. 上 | 是天之主宰 (朱熹集傳) **Cháng ✝ chéu t'iēn tchēu tchòu tsài.** Le Chang ti est le maître et l'arbitre souverain du ciel.

師 **Chēu.** Maître qui enseigne, modèle, chef, directeur de musique, prendre pour maître ou pour modèle, imiter; grand nombre de personnes; capitale d'un État; légion de deux mille cinq cents hommes, armée. 六 | **Liŭ ✝.** Les six légions dont se composait l'armée impériale.

席 **Sĭ.** Natte.

帨 **Chouéi.** Serviette.

帶 **Tái.** Ceinture.

帷 **Wêi.** Tenture disposée verticalement autour d'un objet.

常 **Châng** (Tch'âng). Règle constante, régulier, constant, de longue durée.

幅 **Fŏu.** Limite. || **Pĭ.** 邪 | **Siê** ✝. Bande de toile qu'on enroulait autour de la jambe.

幝 **Tch'èn, Tān.** | | ✝ ✝. Usé.

幡 **Fān.** Bannière. || 翻. Agité par le vent, changeant, inconstant.

幩 **Fênn.** Ornement d'une bride.

幪 **Mòung.** | | ✝ ✝. Belle moisson.

幭 **Miĕ.** Couverture

RACINE 51. 干

干 **Kān.** Bouclier, repousser; chercher à obtenir; bord élevé d'une rivière, rivière; hampe; nom d'une ville située dans le 唐 山 縣, qui dépend de Chouenn te fou dans le Tcheu li. V. page 46.

平 **P'îng.** De niveau, uni, égal, uniforme, ordinaire, commun, vulgaire, juste, impartial, bien tempéré, en équilibre, calme, paisible, bien réglé, aplanir, rendre égal, rendre tranquille, régler, arranger.

年 **Gnièn.** Année, récolte de l'année, moisson.

幷 **Pîng.** Ensemble, tout à la fois.

RACINE 52. 幺

幽 **Iōu.** Obscur, sombre, touffu.

幾 **Kī.** Premiers indices, moment fixé, temps favorable, grand danger. 庶 | Chóu ┼. Presque, à souhait, heureusement, je désire, j'espère. || **Kì.** | 何 ┼ hô? Combien? combien peu? 無 | Oû ┼. Peu de temps. 未 | Wéi ┼. Peu après.

RACINE 53. 广

序 **Siù.** Ordre, ranger en ordre, continuer.

底 **Tì.** Arriver à, terme, fin.

庖 **P'aô.** Endroit où l'on tue les animaux et où l'on conserve les viandes.

庚 **Kēng.** Lettre du cycle. 長 | Tch'âng ┼. L'étoile du matin.

庤 **Tch'èu.** Recueillir, amasser des provisions.

度 **Tóu.** Mesurer la longueur d'une chose, mesure de longueur; loi, règle, régler; marcher, passer. || **Touŏ.** Réfléchir, conjecturer, deviner, délibérer; perspicace; élever un mur de terre.

庭 **T'îng.** La cour principale d'une maison; aller à la cour d'un prince; vertical.

庶 **Chóu.** Grand nombre, multitude, le peuple, le vulgaire, tout l'ensemble, homme d'un rang peu élevé. | 幾 ┼ kī, | 乎 ┼ hôu. Près, à peu près, presque, je désire, j'espère, heureusement.

康 **K'āng.** Tranquille, heureux, prospère, abondant.

庸 **Iôung.** Constant, invariable, employer, mettre en charge, service rendu au public; grosse cloche; rempart.

庾 **Iù.** Amas de grain en plein air.

廄 **Kióu.** Écurie.

廓 **K'ouŏ.** Vaste, grand.

廣 **Kouàng.** Large, vaste, qui s'étend au loin.

廢 **Féi.** Tomber en ruine, dépérir, se corrompre, enlever.

廛 **Tch'ên.** Habitation d'un laboureur.

廟 **Miaó.** | ┼, 宗 | Tsōung ┼, 祖 | Tsòu ┼. Tablette portant le nom de l'un des ancêtres défunts, loge ou chambre occupée par la tablette d'un défunt, bâtiment divisé en loges ou petites chambres pour les tablettes des ancêtres d'une famille. 大 | T'ái ┼. Chambre où est la tablette du plus ancien des ancêtres de la famille impériale.

海上絲綢之路文獻集成　科技與文化編

詩經

La salle des ancêtres des Tcheou avait 九廟 **kiòu miaó** neuf chambres, dont une au milieu 太祖 **T'ái tsòu,** quatre au midi 四穆 **séu mŏu** et quatre au nord 四昭 **séu tchaō**. Celle du midi contenait la tablette de 后稷 **Heóu tsĭ**; les deux plus rapprochées, les tablettes de Wenn wang et de Ou wang; les six autres, les tablettes des six empereurs qui étaient morts les derniers.

廩 **Lìn.** Grenier.

廬 **Liû.** Cabane, baraque.

廱 **Iōung.** 璧 | **Pĭ** † ou 辟 | **Pĭ** †. École impériale qui était entourée d'eau de tous côtés et présentait l'apparence d'une tablette de jade en forme d'anneau 璧 **pĭ**.

RACINE 54. 廴

廷 **T'ìng.** Cour d'un palais, résidence d'un souverain.

建 **Kién.** Fonder, établir, constituer, dresser.

RACINE 55. 廾

弁 **Pién.** Bonnet. || **P'ân.** Aller çà et là.

弄 **Lóung.** Jouer, donner pour jouet.

RACINE 56. 弋

弋 **Ĭ.** Flèche munie d'un long fil par lequel le chasseur la retire à soi; chasser aux oiseaux avec une flèche munie d'un long fil.

式 **Chĕu.** Règle, modèle, exemple, prendre pour modèle; employer; particule.

RACINE 57. 弓

弓 **Kōung.** Arc.

引 **Ìn.** Tirer à soi la corde d'un arc pour lancer une flèche, faire venir à soi, attirer, conduire, étendre, déployer.

弔 **Tiaó.** Avoir compassion, être affligé. || **Tĭ.** Arriver.

弘 **Hôung.** Grand, vaste, agrandir, développer.

弗 **Fŏu.** Ne pas; écarter. | | † †. Bruit du vent.

弟 **Tí.** Frère puiné. 豈 | **K'ài** †. Joyeux, aimable.

弨 **Tch'aō.** Arc détendu.

弭 **Mì.** Extrémités d'un arc garnies d'os ou d'ivoire, comprimer.

張 **Tchāng.** Bander un arc; grand, corpulent.

彊 **K'iàng.** Fort, robuste, puissant, violent. || **Kiāng.** | | † †. Constant.

彌 **Mî.** Entier, complet, compléter, accomplir.

RACINE 58. 彐

彝 **Î.** Loi naturelle, règle; vase employé pour les offrandes.

RACINE 59. 彡

彤 **T'ôung.** Rouge.

彥 **Ién.** Homme remarquable par sa vertu et sa science.

彧 **Iŭ, Ĭ.** | | † †. Végétation prospère.

彭 **Pāng.** | | † †. Nombreux, robuste. || **P'âng.** | | † †. Robuste, infatigable. || **P'êng.** Nom de lieu. V. page 90.

RACINE 60. 彳

役 **Ǐ.** Remplir un service public, porter les armes; travail; rang.

彼 **Pèi.** Celui-là, cela, ce lieu-là, ce, cet.

往 **Wàng.** Aller à, s'en aller, passer, s'écouler, passé, écoulé.

征 **Tchēng.** Marcher, expédition militaire, soumettre par la voie des armes un vassal ou des sujets rebelles.

徂 **Ts'ôu.** Aller à.

律 **Liŭ.** | | ✝ ✝. Haut et escarpé.

後 **Heóu.** Après, postérieur, futur, descendant, postérité, successeur.

徐 **Siû.** Nom de contrée. V. page 411.

徒 **T'ôu.** Aller à pied, piéton, fantassin, suivant, aide.

得 **Tĕ.** Obtenir, acquérir, posséder, arriver à. | 罪 ✝ **tsouéi.** Offenser.

從 **Ts'ôung.** Suivre, poursuivre, s'appliquer à, à partir de. ‖ **Tsóung.** Compagnon, suivant. ‖ **Tsōung.** Du nord au sud, étendue en longueur.

御 **Iú.** Conduire une voiture, aller en voiture, voiturier; gouverner, administrer; présenter, être auprès de quelqu'un, traiter un hôte; se prémunir contre, préparer; impérial. 傅 | **Fóu** ✝. Premier ministre. ‖ **Iá.** Aller au-devant.

徧 **Pién.** Tout autour, partout, universellement, généralement.

復 **Fŏu.** Revenir, retourner, reprendre, recouvrer, réitérer, renouveler, tourner en tous sens; antre ou cabane en forme de four.

微 **Wêi.** Petit, moindre, diminuer, déchoir, dépérir; non, si ce n'est; plaie à la jambe.

徹 **Tch'ĕ.** Universel, commun, général, entier; enlever, détacher, partage des terres. Voy. page 303.

德 **Tĕ.** Vertu, disposition bonne ou mauvaise de l'âme, conduite bonne ou mauvaise, bonté, bienfaisance.

徽 **Houēi.** Bon, parfait.

RACINE 61. 心

心 **Sīn.** Cœur, esprit, intelligence, volonté, désir, intention, affection.

必 **Pĭ.** Certainement, nécessairement.

忉 **Taō.** Triste, inquiet.

忌 **Kí.** Craindre, éviter; particule finale.

忍 **Jènn.** Supporter, endurer, permettre; n'avoir pas compassion.

忒 **T'ĕ.** Erreur, faute, excès; changeant, inconstant, trompeur.

忖 **Ts'uènn.** Conjecturer, deviner.

忘 **Wàng.** Oublier, être oublié.

忝 **T'ièn.** Déshonorer.

忡 **Tch'ōung.** Cœur agité.

忮 **Tchéu.** Nuire, cruel.

忱 **Chènn.** Digne de foi, sincère.

念 **Gnién.** Penser à, se souvenir.

忽 **Hŏu.** Détruire entièrement.

怒 **Nóu.** Colère, s'irriter, s'indigner.

憹 **Naŏ, Neŏu.** Inquiet, turbulent.

怙 **Hòu.** Avoir sa confiance ou son appui en quelqu'un.

怛 **Tă, Tán.** Triste, inquiet.

思 **Sēu.** Penser, réfléchir; particule. || **Séu.** Pensif, triste.

怠 **Tái.** Paresseux, négligent.

急 **Kĭ.** Prompt, urgent; grande difficulté.

性 **Síng.** Nature, vie.

怨 **Iuén.** Mécontentement, plainte, ressentiment, inimitié.

怭 **Pĭ.** Oublier les convenances, indécent.

怲 **Pìng, Páng.** | | † †. Plein de tristesse.

恃 **Chéu.** Avoir sa confiance ou son appui en quelqu'un.

恒 **Hêng.** Constant. || **Kéng.** Croître, progresser; partout.

恌 **T'iaō.** Esprit léger, déchoir.

恐 **K'òung.** Craindre.

恤 **Siŭ.** Avoir compassion, traiter avec commisération, secourir; triste.

恥 **Tch'èu.** Avoir honte, faire éprouver un sentiment de honte.

恩 **Ngēnn.** Bienfaisance, bienfait.

恪 **K'ŏ.** Respectueux.

恭 **Kōung.** Témoigner du respect, honorer, soigneux, diligent, veiller sur soi-même.

息 **Sĭ.** Respirer, s'arrêter, cesser, se reposer, faire cesser.

恫 **T'ōung.** S'affliger, triste.

悄 **Ts'iaò.** Triste, inquiet.

悉 **Sĭ.** Entièrement, tout.

悔 **Houèi.** Se repentir, se corriger.

悖 **Péi.** Déraisonnable, injuste, désordonné; opposé, contraire.

悠 **Iôu.** Vaste, s'étendre au loin.

患 **Houán.** Chagrin, cause de chagrin, malheur.

悁 **Iuēn.** Triste, inquiet, mécontent.

悸 **Kí.** Agité, qui est pendant.

惄 **Gnĭ.** Vif désir, pensif, triste.

惔 **T'ân.** Dévoré de chagrin, brûlant.

悲 **Pēi.** Affligé, triste.

悼 **Taó.** Triste, affligé.

惙 **Tchouŏ.** Grande tristesse.

惟 **Wêi.** Seulement, penser à; particule euphonique.

惠 **Houéi.** Bienfaisant, bienfait, bon; aimer, condescendre.

惡 **Ngó.** Mauvais, méchant. || **Oú.** Avoir en aversion, haïr.

惕 **T'ĭ.** Inquiet, diligent, craindre, respecter.

情 **Ts'îng.** Sentiment de l'âme, bonté, affection.

惛 **Houēnn.** Trouble, agitation d'esprit.

惸 **K'iôung.** Seul et sans secours; triste, inquiet.

愒 **K'í, K'iĕ.** Se reposer.

愛 **Ngái.** Aimer, avoir de l'attachement pour, être avare de.

感 **Kàn.** Toucher le cœur.

惴 **Tchouéi.** Craindre, être inquiet.

愆 **K'iēn.** Excès, défaut, faute, erreur.

愈 **Iù.** Se guérir, aller mieux, surpasser, augmenter, plus.

愉 **Iû.** Joyeux, air aimable et joyeux.

意 **Í.** Pensée, opinion, attente, attention, désir, intention, sentiment, penser, deviner.

愚 **Iû.** Ignorant, peu intelligent

慍 **Iún.** Haïr, odieux.

愧 **Kouéi.** Avoir honte, avoir lieu de rougir.

愬 **Sóu.** Accuser, plaider, porter plainte, dénigrer.

愼 **Chénn.** Soigneux, attentif, prendre garde, examiner.

愾 **Hí.** Long soupir.

慉 **Hiŭ.** Nourrir.

慇 **Īn.** Triste, affligé.

慅 **Saō, Ts'aò.** Triste, inquiet.

慆 **T'aō.** Pervers; longtemps.

慄 **Lĭ.** Craindre.

慘 **Ts'àn.** Triste, malheureux, lamentable.

慝 **T'ĕ.** Faute, vice, défaut, mal.

慢 **Mán.** Lent, tardif, négligent, peu respectueux, traiter avec négligence ou mépris, traiter avec peu de respect.

慰 **Wéi.** Consoler, encourager.

慱 **T'ouân.** Triste.

慮 **Liú.** Penser à ce qu'on doit faire.

慶 **K'íng.** Féliciter, récompenser, bonheur.

憂 **Iōu.** Triste, inquiet, cause de chagrin.

憎 **Tsēng.** Haïr, avoir en aversion.

憖 **Ín.** Se faire violence à soi-même.

憚 **Tán.** Craindre ; fatigué. ‖ **Touó.** Fatigué.

憩 **K'í.** Se reposer.

憬 **Kiòung, Kìng.** Comprendre, reconnaître.

憮 **Où.** Traiter avec bonté. | 然 + jên. Déconcerté, affligé.

憲 **Hién.** Règle, modèle, loi. | | + +. Joyeux.

應 **Īng.** Il faut, il convient, il est certain, il est probable. ‖ **Íng.** Répondre, conforme; nom d'un petit tambour. | 門 + **mênn.** Nom d'une porte du palais impérial.

懆 **Ts'aò.** Triste.

懌 **Ĭ.** Joyeux, aimable, réjouir.

懟 **Touéi.** Aversion, haine, irriter, mécontenter.

懠 **Ts'î.** Colère.

憯 **Ts'àn.** Triste; déjà auparavant.

懮 **Iòu.** Triste, inquiet, pensif.

懰 **Liòu, Laò.** Beau, aimable.

懲 **Tch'êng.** Réprimer, corriger.

懷 **Houâi.** Sein, concevoir ou garder une pensée ou un sentiment, penser à, se rappeler le souvenir de, aimer; cœur, esprit, pensée.

懼 **Kiú.** Craindre.

懿 **Í.** Excellent, vertueux, sage.

戁 **Nàn.** Craindre.

RACINE 62. 戈

戈 **Kouō.** Lance, pique.

戊 **Meóu, Oú.** Cinquième lettre du cycle.

戍 **Chóu.** Soldats cantonnés aux frontières, cantonnement.

戎 **Jôung.** Arme, soldat, guerre, char de guerre; nom de peuplades étrangères répandues à l'ouest de la Chine; grand, aider; vous, votre.

戒 **Kiái.** Prendre garde, éviter, s'abstenir, avertir quelqu'un de prendre garde.

我 **Ngò.** Je, moi, nous.

成 **Tch'êng.** Faire, exécuter, terminer, mener à bonne fin, perfectionner, parfait, complet, accompli, expérimenté; fin d'une guerre; règle. **|** 王 **† wâng.** Deuxième souverain de la dynastie des Tcheou (1115-1078). V. page 2.

戕 **Ts'iâng.** Tuer, blesser, endommager, faire violence.

或 **Houĕ.** Quelqu'un, quelques-uns, ou bien, peut-être.

戚 **Ts'ĭ.** Petite hache de guerre; uni par le sang, uni d'affection; triste, mécontent.

戟 **Kĭ.** Lance employée sur les chariots de guerre.

戢 **Tsĭ.** Réunir, recueillir; modérer, tempérer.

戩 **Tsièn.** Complet, parfait.

截 **Tsiĕ.** Couper, retrancher; ranger en ordre, établir l'ordre, régler.

戰 **Tchén.** Combattre; craindre, trembler de peur.

戲 **Hí.** S'amuser, jouer, plaisanter.

RACINE 63. 戶

戶 **Hóu.** Porte.

戾 **Lí.** Terme, limite, arriver à, s'arrêter à, arrêter, calmer, fixer; mauvais, faute, malheur, contraire.

房 **Fâng.** Maison. 大 **| Tá †.** Large support 俎 **tchòu** qui présente l'apparence d'un bâtiment.

所 **Chòu (Chouò).** Lieu, demeure; pronom relatif qui n'est jamais sujet, mais toujours régime d'un verbe; adverbe de lieu.

扁 **Pièn.** De forme aplatie, peu élevé.

扈 **Hóu.** 桑 **| Sāng †.** Petit oiseau qui vit sur le mûrier.

RACINE 64. 手

手 **Cheòu.** Main.

才 **Ts'âi.** Talent, habileté, bonne qualité, faculté naturelle.

扤 **Oŭ.** Agiter.

扶 **Fôu.** Soutenir, aider, secourir. **|** 蘇 **† sōu.** Nom d'arbre.

承 **Tch'êng.** Présenter ou recevoir un objet avec respect; aider; continuer, soutenir, résister.

抑 **Ĭ.** Comprimer, déprimer, abaisser; particule initiale. **| | † †.** Attentif et respectueux

63

投 **T'eôu.** Lancer, se précipiter, se réfugier, présenter.

抗 **Kāng.** Lever, dresser.

折 **Tchĕ.** Casser, courber, diminuer, décider, juger.

抱 **Paó.** Prendre ou tenir dans les bras, embrasser, contenir.

抽 **Tch'eōu.** Tirer dehors, enlever, arracher.

拂 **Fŏu.** Résister, s'opposer, contraire.

拊 **Fòu.** Caresser de la main, donner des soins affectueux.

拔 **Pouŏ.** Coche d'une flèche. ‖ **Péi.** Debout; enlever.

拚 **Fān.** Voltiger.

招 **Tchaō.** Appeler quelqu'un par un signe de la main.

拜 **Pái.** Saluer, courber.

括 **Kouŏ.** Arriver, atteindre. ‖ **Houŏ.** Aller trouver, se réunir.

拮 **Kiĕ, Kĭ.** ｜ 据 ┼ kiū. Travailler sans cesse.

拾 **Chĕu.** Manche de cuir que l'archer portait au bras gauche.

挃 **Tchĕu.** ｜ ｜ ┼ ┼. Bruit de la faucille du moissonneur.

按 **Ngán.** Mettre la main sur un objet, arrêter, réprimer.

拳 **K'iuên.** Poing; fort.

挑 **T'aō.** Léger, sauter, danser.

指 **Tchèu.** Doigt, montrer du doigt, indiquer, signifier, faire connaître.

挾 **Hiĕ.** Prendre ou tenir un objet sous le bras ou entre les doigts, avoir, posséder.

振 **Tchénn.** Secouer, agiter, exciter, arrêter, faire cesser, faire revenir; au plus haut degré. ｜ ｜ ┼ ┼. Vol d'une troupe d'oiseaux.

挹 **Ĭ.** Puiser avec une cuiller.

捄 **Kiōu, Kiū.** Mettre de la terre dans un panier, élever un mur. ‖ **K'iōu.** Recourbé.

捋 **Louŏ.** Cueillir, effeuiller ou égrener avec la main.

捫 **Mênn.** Saisir, retenir.

控 **K'óung.** Modérer, retenir; accuser.

掎 **Kì.** Lier, retenir par un lien.

掘 **Kiuĕ.** Creuser, trou, sortir d'un trou.

掤 **Pīng.** Couvercle d'un carquois.

推 **T'ouēi.** Repousser, écarter, s'excuser.

据 **Kiū.** 拮 ｜ Kiĕ ┼. Travailler sans cesse.

授 **Cheóu.** Donner, livrer, transmettre, enseigner.

掊 **P'eōu.** Prendre, saisir, exiger, exaction. ｜ 克 ┼ kŏ. Exacteur.

掌 **Tchàng.** La paume de la main; diriger, administrer. 鞅 ｜ iàng ┼. Accablé de fatigue.

捷 **Tsiĕ.** Rapide; victoire. ‖ **Ts'iĕ.** ｜ ｜ ┼ ┼. Murmurer.

掇 **Touŏ, Tchouŏ.** Recueillir, cueillir.

揄 **Iôu.** Puiser avec une cuiller.

揉 **Jeóu.** Assouplir, amollir, rendre soumis.

握 **Iŏ.** Prendre dans la main, autant que la main fermée peut contenir.

揥 **T'í, Tí, Tchéu.** Épingle d'os avec laquelle on se grattait la tête.

揆 **Kouéi.** Examiner, apprécier, juger, mesurer.

提 **T'î.** Tenir à la main un objet qui pend, tirer de bas en haut, proposer, suggérer. || **Chêu.** | | ┼ ┼. Vol d'une troupe d'oiseaux.

揭 **Kiĕ.** Soulever, lever, enlever, détacher. | | ┼ ┼. Droit et haut. || **K'í.** Relever les vêtements jusqu'aux genoux pour passer l'eau.

援 **Iuên.** Tirer à soi un objet, tirer de bas en haut, aider; s'élever à l'aide d'une personne ou d'une chose, se servir de. 鈎 | **Keōu** ┼. Échelle munie de crochets. 畔 ┼ **P'án** ┼. Rebelle, déloyal.

揖 **Ĭ.** Saluer en joignant les mains. || **Tsĭ.** | | ┼ ┼. Réunis en grand nombre.

揚 **Iâng.** S'élever dans les airs, haut, déployer, faire paraître, publier, exalter, célébrer; hache d'armes; la partie de la tête qui avoisine les sourcils.

搏 **Pouŏ.** Saisir, frapper.

搔 **Saō.** Gratter.

搖 **Iaô.** Agiter. | | ┼ ┼. Agité.

搜 **Cheōu, Seōu.** Sifflement d'une flèche.

摧 **Tsouēi.** Molester, détruire, supprimer. || **Ts'ouó.** Paille hachée, nourrir de paille hachée.

摯 **Tchéu.** Ancienne principauté située dans le Chen si ou le Ho nan.

摻 **Chān, Siēn.** Main délicate et belle. || **Chàn.** Saisir.

摽 **Piaò, P'iaò.** Frapper, tomber.

播 **Pouó.** Semer.

撥 **Pouŏ.** Régler, gouverner; rompre, déraciner, dissiper.

撮 **Tsouŏ.** Bonnet.

撻 **T'ă.** Frapper, battre de verges; rapide.

擇 **Tchĕ.** Choisir, prendre de préférence, trier, séparer, distinguer.

據 **Kiú.** S'appuyer sur, mettre son appui ou sa confiance en.

擊 **Kĭ.** Frapper, battre.

擣 **Taò.** Battre à grands coups.

攘 **Jâng.** Repousser, écarter, prendre, saisir, enlever, voler. || **Cháng.** Prendre.

攝 **Chĕ.** Aider.

攜 **Hî.** Se donner la main, conduire par la main, tenir à la main.

攪 **Kiaò.** Mêler, agiter, troubler, molester.

RACINE 65. 支

支 **Tchēu.** Branche d'arbre, branche d'une famille.

RACINE 66. 攴

收 **Cheou.** Prendre, saisir, recevoir; caisse d'une voiture.

攸 **Iôu.** Lieu; là, où, adverbe de lieu; que, pronom relatif qui s'emploie comme régime, et non comme sujet du verbe.

改 **Kài.** Changer, devenir autre, rendre différent, corriger, réformer.

政 **Tchéng.** Gouvernement, administration publique, lois de l'État, gouverner.

攻 **Kōung.** Travailler, polir, arranger; fort, ferme.

故 **Kóu.** Cause, motif; à cause de; ancien, vieux, ancien ami.

敕 **Tch'ĕu.** Arranger, soigneux, diligent.

教 **Kiaó.** Enseigner, instruire, enseignement, doctrine, avis.

敏 **Mìn.** Prompt, actif, hâter, intelligence prompte; gros orteil.

救 **Kióu.** Mettre un terme à un mal, secourir, délivrer, sauver.

敖 **Ngaô.** Se livrer à la joie, s'amuser; grand; théâtre; nom de montagne. Voyez page 207. || **Ngaó.** 傲. Orgueilleux, arrogant.

敗 **Pái.** Vaincre, détruire, ruiner, corrompre, gâter.

敝 **Pí.** Usé, ruiné, affaibli, gâté, endommagé, vaincu, user.

敢 **Kàn.** Oser, se permettre de, prendre la liberté de.

散 **Sàn.** Se séparer, se disperser, séparé, dispersé, aller çà et là.

敦 **Touēnn.** Imposer, peser sur. || **T'ouênn.** Cantonnement. || **Touēi.** Seul; polir, corriger, châtier. || **T'ouàn.** Nombreux. || **Tiaō.** 彫. Peint.

敬 **Kíng.** Éprouver un sentiment de respect, révérer; traiter avec respect ou avec soin; attentif, soigneux, diligent.

敷 **Fōu.** Étendre, répandre au loin, vaste, universel; étaler, arranger, préparer.

數 **Chòu.** Examiner, réfléchir, discerner.

整 **Tchèng.** Arranger, disposer, mettre en ordre.

斂 **Lièn.** Recueillir, exiger ou percevoir une taxe, impôt, contribution.

斁 **Tóu.** Ruiner, détruire, anéantir. || **Í.** Satiété, dégoût, dédain.

RACINE 67. 文

文 **Wênn.** Linéament, raie, dessin, peinture, ornement; tout ce qui sert à perfectionner le corps ou l'âme, orné, élégant, doux, humain, poli, civil, qui n'est pas militaire. | 王 ✝ **wâng**. V. page 2.

斐 **Fèi.** Orné, élégant, exagéré.

RACINE 68. 斗

斗 **Teòu.** Boisseau; cuiller; nom d'une constellation qui fait partie du Sagittaire.

RACINE 69. 斤

斤 **Kīn.** Hache, cognée; livre (poids). || **Kín.** | | ✝ ✝. Perspicace.

斧 **Fòu.** Hache.

斨 **Ts'iāng.** Hache dont le fer est percé d'un trou carré pour recevoir le manche.

斬 **Tchàn.** Trancher, rogner, décapiter, retrancher, mettre fin.

斯 **Sēu.** Ce, cet, cela, ce lieu, à cause de cela, ensuite, alors, aussitôt; particule finale; particule adjointe à certains noms d'animaux, de plantes,...

新 **Sīn.** Nouveau, récent, renouveler.

斲 **Tchouŏ.** Hache, tailler avec une hache.

斷 **Touán.** Trancher, couper; séparer, interrompre, cesser; décider, certainement.

RACINE 70. 方

方 **Fāng.** Carré, rectangulaire; région, lieu; bateau carré; occuper

règle, régulier, moyen, à l'instant même, juste en ce moment, juste au moment où, ne faire que commencer, à peine; sacrifice offert aux esprits des quatre points cardinaux. 四丨 Séu 十. Les quatre points cardinaux, toutes les parties de la terre ou d'un État. 丨十 ou 朔丨 Chouŏ 十. V. page 188.

於 Iū. Dans, en, à, par, au sujet de. || Oū. Oh! 丨乎十 hōu! Oh! hélas!

施 Chēu. Étaler, étendre, déployer; joyeux. || Í. Étendre, livrer, transmettre.

旂 K'î. Étendard orné de dragons et muni de sonnettes.

旄 Maô. Guidon formé de crin de bœuf. 丨丘十 k'iōu. Colline qui présente l'apparence de la tête et du dos d'un cheval.

旃 Tchēn. Bannière; particule finale.

旅 Liù. Troupe de cinq cents soldats, cohorte; nombreux, foule, tous; voyageur, étranger; épine dorsale.

旁 Pōung. 丨丨十十. Courir sans cesse.

旋 Siuên. Se mouvoir en rond, revenir sur ses pas.

旌 Tsīng. Guidon formé de plumes de faisan.

族 Tsŏu. Parents en ligne directe, tous ceux qui sont issus d'un même sang et portent le même nom de famille.

旐 Tchaō. Étendard sur lequel sont brodés des serpents et des tortues.

旒 Liôu. Pendants fixés à la bordure d'un étendard.

旟 Iû. Étendard sur lequel sont brodés des faucons; recourbé, cheveux bouclés.

RACINE 71. 无

旣 Kí. Finir, terminer, épuiser, entièrement; dans un temps passé, déjà, auparavant, après que, quand, puisque.

RACINE 72. 日

日 Jĕu. Soleil, jour, durant le jour, chaque jour. 無丨Oû 十, 不丨Pŏu 十. N'avoir pas de jour déterminé, de temps en temps, souvent, dans un temps très prochain.

旦 Tán. Matin. 丨丨十十. Chaque matin; clairement, clairvoyant, perspicace.

旭 Hiŭ. Soleil levant.

旨 Tchèu. Excellent, exquis; intention, désir, volonté.

旬 Siûn. Dix jours; tout autour, partout.

旱 Hán. Sec, sécheresse.

昊 Haò. Grand, vaste, auguste.

旻 旼 Mîn. Compatissant, pitié. La première de ces deux lettres n'est plus employée, parce qu'elle a fait partie du nom de Tao kouang.

昄 Pàn. Grand, spacieux.

昆 Kouēnn. Frère plus âgé que nous. 丨吾十 ôu. Ancienne principauté. V. page 466.

明 Mîng. Lumière, lumineux, briller, éclairer; clair, évident, manifeste; distingué, illustre, glo-

rieux; perspicace, esprit pénétrant. | 星 ✝ sīng. L'étoile du matin.

昏 **Houēnn.** Crépuscule du soir, obscur, ténébreux; mariage, femme, parent par alliance.

易 **Ĭ.** Facile, rendre facile; changer, échanger; à la légère; arracher les mauvaises herbes. || **Ĭ.** Transformation.

昔 **Sĭ.** Autrefois, jadis, hier.

昌 **Tch'āng.** Brillant, beau, prospère, nombreux.

星 **Sīng.** Étoile.

春 **Tch'ouēnn.** Printemps.

昬 **Houēnn.** Ténèbres, obscurité, ignorance.

昧 **Méi.** Obscur. | 旦 ✝ tán. Au point du jour.

昴 **Maò.** Les Pléiades.

昭 **Tchaō.** Lumière, briller, éclairer, instruire, faire briller; le côté septentrional dans le temple des ancêtres. | 穆 ✝ mōu. Le côté septentrional et le côté méridional dans le temple des ancêtres. Voy. la lettre 廟 Miaó, page 492.

是 **Chéu.** Ce, cet, ceci, cela; vrai, bon, louable, être; admettre, affirmer, approuver.

晉 **Tsín.** Ancienne principauté. V. page 4.

時 **Chêu.** Temps, moment opportun, saison; ce, cet, cela.

晏 **Ién, Ngán.** Douce chaleur du soleil; ciel serein; briller; accord, harmonie.

晝 **Tcheóu.** Le temps qui s'écoule depuis le lever du soleil jusqu'à son coucher.

晛 **Hién.** Le soleil paraissant, chaleur du soleil.

晦 **Houéi.** Obscurité, ténèbres.

晞 **Hī.** Se sécher au soleil.

晨 **Chênn, Tch'ênn.** Matin. | 風 ✝ fōung. Faucon.

晤 **Oú.** Briller; converser.

晢 **Tchĕ.** Briller.

晣 **Tchéu.** | | ✝ ✝. Clarté pâle.

晳 **Sĭ.** Discerner; blanc.

景 **Kìng.** Brillant, grand; nom d'une colline comprise dans la capitale des 商 Chāng. V. p. 462 et 469. || **Ìng.** Ombre; déterminer l'orientation d'un lieu par l'inspection des ombres.

暇 **Hiá.** Repos, avoir le loisir de.

暑 **Chòu.** Chaleur de l'été.

暢 **Tch'áng.** Pénétrer partout, s'étendre, se propager; long.

暱 **Gnĭ.** Proche, approcher.

暬 **Siĕ.** Familier.

暴 **Paó.** Cruel, violent, traiter avec cruauté; attaquer, saisir.

暵 **Hàn.** Sécher, desséché.

曀 **Í.** Ciel nuageux et vent violent.

曜 **Iaó.** Briller, luire.

曠 **K'ouáng.** Vide, désert, inoccupé, inutile; vaste.

RACINE 73. 日

日 **Iuĕ.** Dire, nommer, signifier; particule.

曲 **K'iŭ.** Courbe, sinueux, désordonné, blâmable, injuste. | 沃 ⊤ **ŏu.** Ancienne principauté, à présent 聞喜縣 dans le 山西.

曳 **Í, Iĕ.** Tirer ou traîner après soi, tirer à soi.

曷 **Hŏ.** Pourquoi? comment? quand? où? qui? quel? résister.

書 **Chōu.** Écrire, écriture, pièce écrite, livre.

曹 **Ts'aô.** Troupeau, pâturage; nom de principauté. V. page 4.

曼 **Wán.** Long, vaste.

替 **T'í.** Cesser, discontinuer, omettre, négliger.

曾 **Ts'êng.** Déjà, dès lors. || **Tsēng.** | 孫 ⊤ **suēnn.** Arrière-petit-fils, descendant éloigné.

會 **Houéi.** Réunir, rencontrer, aller trouver, se réunir, assemblée, société; rencontre, occasion; accord. || **Kouái.** Couture.

朅 **K'iĕ.** Courageux, valeureux, martial.

RACINE 74. 月

月 **Iuĕ.** Lune, mois lunaire.

有 **Iòu.** Avoir, obtenir, acquérir, posséder, tenir sous son autorité, être, arriver, survenir; abondant. 九 | **Kiòu** ⊤. Les neuf provinces.

朋 **P'êng.** Compagnon, ami, égal; une paire, deux.

服 **Fŏu.** Vêtement, revêtir; carquois; prendre sur soi, se charger de, travail, œuvre, office; être soumis ou exposé à, supporter; garder ou se rappeler le souvenir de; dompter, soumettre, gouverner, régir, se soumettre, obéir, servir; cheval attelé au timon d'une voiture.

朔 **Chouŏ.** La nouvelle lune, le premier jour du mois lunaire; nord. | 方 ⊤ **fāng.** V. page 188.

朕 **Tchénn.** Je.

望 **Wáng.** Regarder vers, voir dans le lointain; désirer, espérer, mettre son espoir en.

朝 **Tchaō.** Matin, matinée || **Tch'aô.** Lieu où le souverain donne audience, cour d'un souverain, audience à la cour, avoir une audience du souverain, aller à la cour, donner audience.

期 **K'î.** Fixer un terme ou un moment, moment ou terme fixé; fin. || **Kī.** Particule finale.

RACINE 75. 木

木 **Mŏu.** Arbre, bois (matière ligneuse).

未 **Wéi.** Pas encore, ne pas.

本 **Pènn.** Racine, tronc, fondement; branche aînée d'une famille.

朽 **Hiòu.** Bois pourri, gâté.

李 **Lì.** Prunier, prune.

杜 **Tóu.** Arbre qui ressemble au poirier.

杝 **T'ouō.** Fendre du bois dans le sens des veines.

杕 **Tí.** Arbre solitaire.

杞 **K'ì.** Saule, osier; ancienne principauté, à présent | 縣 dans le K'ai foung fou.

束 **Chŏu.** Lier, fagot, botte, faisceau.

杭 **Hâng.** Barque, traverser en bateau.

枌 **Fènn.** Orme blanc.

杻 **Gniòu.** Arbre dont le bois sert à faire des arcs.

杲 **Kaò, Haò.** Soleil levant, briller.

果 **Kouò.** Fruit.

林 **Lîn.** Forêt, massif d'arbres; nombreux.

枚 **Mêi.** Tronc, tige. | | ✝ ✝. Bien travaillé.

板 **Pàn.** Planche. | | ✝ ✝. Changé, devenu autre.

析 **Sī.** Fendre du bois.

松 **Sōung.** Sapin.

枕 **Tchènn.** Coussin, oreiller.

枝 **Tchēu.** Branche.

杼 **Tch'òu.** Navette de tisserand.

東 **Tōung.** Orient, oriental.

柯 **Kō.** Manche de hache.

柳 **Liòu.** Saule.

柚 **Tchŏu.** Ensouple ou rouleau du métier à tisser.

染 **Jèn.** Teindre; souple, flexible.

柏 **Pĕ.** Cyprès thuya.

枸 **Kiù.** *Hovenia dulcis.*

柄 **Píng.** Manche.

柔 **Jeôu.** Flexible, tendre, faible, mou, souple; doux, traiter avec bonté.

柴 **Tch'âi.** Bois de chauffage. || **Tzéu.** Réunir, monceau.

柞 **Tsŏ.** Chêne. || **Tchĕ.** Éclaircir les arbres.

柘 **Tché.** Mûrier tinctorial.

栖 **Sī.** Se reposer sur un arbre.

栗 **Lĭ.** Châtaignier, ferme, solide, grain plein. | | ✝ ✝. Dense, serré. | 烈 ✝ **liĕ.** Vent froid.

核 **Hĕ.** Noyau, fruit à noyau.

栩 **Hiù.** Chêne.

桓 **Houân.** Courageux, martial.

桋 **Î.** Arbre qui ressemble à l'orme.

栲 **K'aò, Kaò.** Sumac, ailante.

格 **Kŏ, Kĕ.** Arriver, approcher.

桀 **Kiĕ.** Homme éminent; poteau qui sert de juchoir à une poule; nom du dernier des empereurs de la dynastie des 夏 **Hiá.** (1818-1766). | | ✝ ✝. Végétation prospère.

栵 **Lí.** Rangée d'arbres.

桃 **T'aô.** Pêcher, pêche.

桐 **T'ôung.** *Éléococca,* arbre de la famille des Euphorbiacées, dont les graines donnent une huile appelée | 油 ✝ **iôu** qui est employée par les peintres.

桑 **Sāng.** Mûrier; cueillir les feuilles du mûrier.

詩經

株 **Tchōu.** Tronc. | 林 † **lin.** Ancienne ville, à présent 柘城 **Tché tch'êng** dans le Kouei te fou (Ho nan).

梧 **Oû.** *Éléococca* ou *Sterculia*, arbre de bon augure.

梃 **T'ìng.** Bâton; tige; long.

梓 **Tzèu.** *Catalpa.*

梟 **Hiaō, Kiaō.** Hibou qui, dit-on, dévore sa mère.

梗 **Kèng.** Difficulté, embarras, détresse.

桷 **Kiŏ.** Chevron carré.

梁 **Leâng.** Pont; barrage; poutre; timon recourbé en forme de pont.

梅 **Mêi.** Prunier.

條 **T'iaô.** Petite branche; long, prolongé; nom d'arbre. | 風 † **fōung.** Vent du nord.

椅 **Ī.** Arbre semblable au catalpa.

棫 **Iŭ.** Nom d'un arbre épineux.

棘 **Kĭ.** Jujubier sauvage; actif, prompt, urgent, difficile; être en deuil.

棄 **K'í.** Quitter, abandonner, renoncer à, rejeter, délaisser.

棗 **Tsaò.** Jujubier, jujube.

棧 **Tchán.** Clayon, voiture de soldat.

椐 **Kiū.** Arbre épineux dont on fait des bâtons de vieillards.

棲 **Sī.** Se reposer sur un arbre. || **Ts'ī.** | | † †. Précipitation.

椒 **Tsiaō.** Poivre. || **Tsiaó.** Odeur agéable.

棠 **T'âng.** Sorbier, sorte de poirier sauvage.

椓 **Tchouŏ.** Battre, frapper à grands coups. || **Tŏu.** Affliger.

棸 **Tcheōu.** Nom de famille.

棣 **Tí.** 唐 | **T'âng** †. Cerisier sauvage. 常 | **Châng** †. Prunier ou cerisier. || **Tái.** | | † †. Parfait.

楊 **Iâng.** Peuplier.

楚 **Tch'òu.** Nom de plusieurs arbustes épineux; dense, épais; ranger en ordre; ancienne principauté qui s'étendait au nord et au sud du Kiang. | 邱 † **k'iōu.** Nom de lieu. Voy. page 57.

楫 **Tsiĕ, Tsĭ.** Rame, ramer.

楀 **Iù, Kiù.** Nom de famille.

榆 **Iû.** Orme.

楅 **Fŏu, Pĭ.** Bois fixé transversalement aux cornes d'un bœuf pour l'empêcher de nuire.

業 **Iĕ.** Dentelure qui présente la forme de la lettre 業, et surmonte la traverse de la suspension d'une cloche ou d'un tambour; danger. Voy. page 342. | | † †. Fort, robuste; dangereux.

楹 **Îng.** Colonne.

楰 **Iû.** Arbre semblable au catalpa.

楛 **Hóu.** Nom d'un arbuste épineux dont on fait des flèches.

極 **Kĭ.** Faîte, le point le plus élevé, au plus haut degré, réduire à la dernière extrémité; terme; aller à.

楘 **Mŏu.** Bandes de cuir dont on ornait le timon des voitures.

楨 **Tchēng.** Poteau, soutien.

榛 **Tchēnn.** Noisetier.

榦 **Kán.** Planches entre lesquelles on élevait les murs de terre, réprimer.

構 **Keóu.** Rencontrer, mettre en désaccord.

穀 **Kŏu.** Mûrier dont l'écorce sert à faire du papier.

槃 **P'ân.** Bassin, plat, hutte.

樊 **Fân.** Haie, défense, défendre.

樂 **Iŏ.** Musique, instruments de musique, musiciens. || **Lŏ.** Joie, joyeux, heureux, agréable, se réjouir. || **Iaó.** Avoir pour agréable.

槱 **Iôu.** Bois à brûler, amonceler du bois.

樛 **Kiōu.** Arbre aux branches pendantes.

樕 **Sŏu.** 樸 | **Pŏu** †. Arbustes touffus.

樞 **Tch'ōu.** Arbre épineux qui ressemble à l'orme.

樗 **Tch'ōu.** *Ailantus glandulosa.*

樅 **Ts'ōung.** Dressé verticalement.

樹 **Chóu.** Arbre, planter, semer, dresser.

橋 **K'iaô.** Arbre qui est grand et droit et n'a que peu de branches.

樸 **Pŏu.** Touffe d'arbustes, massif d'arbres.

橐 **T'ouŏ.** Sac qui s'ouvre aux deux extrémités. | | † †. Bruit de la hie.

樵 **Ts'iaô.** Couper ou ramasser du bois pour le chauffage.

檉 **Tch'ēng.** Tamarix.

檀 **T'ân.** Arbre dont le bois sert à faire des essieux de voitures.

檜 **Kouéi.** Arbuste semblable au genévrier; nom de principauté. V. page 4.

檖 **Souéi.** Poirier sauvage.

檻 **Hièn.** Cage; jaillir. | | † †. Bruit d'une voiture.

檿 **Ièn.** Sorte de mûrier sauvage.

櫜 **Kaō.** Fourreau d'arc, mettre un arc dans son fourreau.

櫟 **Lĭ.** Espèce de chêne.

櫛 **Tchĕ, Tsiĕ, Tchĕu.** Peigne.

權 **K'iuên.** Poids de balance. | 輿 † iù. Commencement.

欒 **Louân.** | | † †. Trés amaigri par le chagrin.

RACINE 76. 欠

欣 **Hīn.** Joyeux, content.

欲 **Iŭ.** Vouloir, désirer, ambitionner, désir.

欽 **K'īn.** | | † †. Agitation de l'âme; son des cloches.

歇 **Hiĕ.** Se reposer. | 驕 † **kiaō.** Chien à court museau.

歆 **Hīn.** Se dit d'un esprit qui respire avec joie l'odeur des offrandes.

歌 **Kō.** Chant, chanter, composer un chant.

歎 **T'án.** Soupirer, gémir, admirer.

歗 **Siaó.** Siffler, pousser un long gémissement.

RACINE 77. 止

止 **Tchèu.** S'arrêter, cesser, être en repos, se fixer, demeurer, conduite bonne ou mauvaise; particule finale.

正 **Tchéng.** Droit, direct, régulier, légitime, correct, irréprochable, juste, exact; règle, loi, modèle; chef; rendre droit, diriger, régler; quatrième mois de l'année. | 政. Gouvernement. || **Tchēng.** Milieu d'une cible; le côté d'une maison où sont les fenêtres.

此 **Ts'èu.** Ce, cet, cela, ce lieu.

步 **Póu.** Deux pas ou enjambées, mesure de six 尺 (1 mètre, 20); marche, cours, conduite.

武 **Où.** Robuste, actif, brave, militaire, guerrier, martial, affaires militaires, guerre, sévère; trace du pied. | 王 **Wâng**. Nom du fondateur de la dynastie des 周 **Tcheōu** (1122-1115). V. page 2. | 丁 † **tīng** ou 高 宗 **Kaō tsōung**. Empereur de la dynastie des 殷 **Īn** (1324-1265).

歲 **Souéi.** Année, récolte de l'année.

歸 **Kouēi.** Retourner à la maison, aller à, converger à, se réunir à; envoyer, offrir; aller célébrer ses noces, aller chercher sa fiancée pour la célébration des noces.

RACINE 78. 歹

死 **Sèu.** Mourir, mort.

殄 **T'ièn.** Détruire, anéantir, mettre fin, prendre fin. || 腆. Bon.

殆 **Tái.** Dangereux, être en danger.

殊 **Chôu.** Tout à fait, entièrement.

殖 **Chĕu, Tchĕu.** | | † †. Aplani, uni.

殘 **Ts'ân.** Nuire gravement, cruel.

殪 **Í.** Tuer.

殲 **Tsiēn.** Détruire, anéantir.

RACINE 79. 殳

殳 **Chôu.** Lance ou faisceau de lattes de bambou.

殷 **Īn.** Grand, prospère, nombreux; nom que prit la dynastie des 商 **Chāng** (1401-1122); nom de la terre que les princes de cette famille possédaient dans le 河 南 **Hô nân** près de 歸 德 府 **Kouēi tĕ fòu**. | | † †. Triste. || **Ìn.** Roulement du tonnerre.

殺 **Chă.** Tuer.

殽 **Hiaô.** Viande, mets, manger, mets offert aux esprits.

毀 **Houèi.** Démolir, renverser, détruire.

殿 **Tién.** Grand édifice, palais; affermir. | 屎 † **hī**. Gémir.

RACINE 80. 毋

毋 **Oû.** Ne pas, négation qui s'emploie ordinairement avec l'impératif.

母 **Mòu.** Mère; femelle d'un animal.

每 **Mèi.** Chaque, chaque fois, bien que, quand même.

毒 **Tŏu.** Poison, très nuisible, très dangereux.

RACINE 81. 比

比 **Pì.** Mettre en parallèle, comparer, assimiler; se concilier les esprits. || **Pí.** S'associer, s'unir, s'attacher à, semblable; arriver à, quand, lorsque, après que.

紕 **Pí.** Prendre garde, soin, précaution; couler de source.

毗 **P'î.** Aider; flatteur.

毚 **Tch'ân.** Rusé.

RACINE 82. 毛

毛 **Maô.** Poil, cheveu; enlever le poil.

毳 **Ts'ouéi.** Duvet, poil. | 衣 † i. Vêtement de laine.

RACINE 83. 氏

氏 **Chéu.** Branche d'une famille; la famille d'une femme; chef de famille, homme distingué, homme honorable.

民 **Mîn.** Peuple, homme du peuple, simple particulier.

氐 **Tì.** Base, soutien. || **Tī.** | 羌 † k'iāng. Barbares de l'ouest.

氓 **Mêng.** Habitant venu d'une autre contrée, peuple.

RACINE 85. 水

水 **Chouèi.** Eau, cours d'eau.

永 **Iòung.** Pour toujours, perpétuel.

氿 **Kouèi.** Bras de rivière.

求 **K'iôu.** Chercher, demander, travailler à obtenir ou à connaître, obtenir.

汜 **Séu.** Cours d'eau qui retourne à la rivière d'où il est sorti.

汎 **Fán.** | | † †. Agité, flottant.

汙 **Oū.** Eau trouble, lieu bas et humide. || **Oú.** Salir, souiller; laver.

汝 **Jòu.** Tu, vous; rivière qui donne son nom à la ville de | 州 † tcheōu dans le 河 南 Hô nân.

江 **Kiāng.** Grand fleuve.

池 **Tch'ĉu.** Amas d'eau stagnante, fossé plein d'eau.

汔 **Hĭ.** Presque, à peu près.

汕 **Chán.** Prendre des poissons avec une nasse ou un panier.

沒 **Mŏu.** Plongé dans l'eau; finir, mourir; extrémité, à la fin.

沓 **Tă.** Grande crue des eaux; parler beaucoup.

沛 **Péi.** 顛 | Tiēn †. Renversé, bouleversé.

汶 **Wénn.** Nom d'un affluent de la 濟 Tsi dans le Chan toung. V. page 111.

決 **Kiuĕ.** Anneau d'os que l'archer porte au pouce de la main droite.

沙 **Chā.** Sable.

汾 **Fènn.** Rivière qui donne son nom à la ville de | 州 府 † tcheōu fòu dans le 山 西 Chān si. Voy. page 114.

沃 **Oŭ, Wŏ, Iŏ.** Humide, verdoyant, gras, fertile.

沚 **Tchèu.** Ilot dans une rivière.

沂 **Î.** Rivière qui prend sa source dans le 青 州 府 Ts'ing tcheōu fòu du Chan toung.

沈 **Tch'ênn.** Plongé dans l'eau.

沐 **Mŏu.** Se laver la tête.

沔 **Mièn.** Fleuve coulant à pleins bords.

沖 **Tch'ōung.** Qui est pendant. | | † †. Bruit que fait la glace en se fendant.

波 **Pouō.** Flot, eau agitée.

泉 **Ts'iuên.** Source d'eau; nom de rivière. Voy. page 71.

沸 **Féi.** Bouillonner, grande crue des eaux. || **Fǒu.** 觱 | **Pi** †. Jaillir.

泮 **P'án.** Demi-cercle d'eau; gymnases établis par les 諸 侯 **tchōu heōu**, ainsi nommés parce qu'ils avaient au midi un demi-cercle d'eau.

沮 **Tsiú.** Marécage; arrêter, dissuader. || **Tsiū.** 漆 | **Ts'ï** †. Noms de deux rivières qui traversaient le 延 安 府 **Iên ngān fòu** dans le 陝 西 **Chèn sī** et se jetaient dans la 渭 **Wéi** (voy. pag. 210 et 431); noms de deux rivières qui traversaient le 邠 州 **Pīn tcheōu** et se jetaient dans la 渭 **Wéi** (voy. page 326).

河 **Hô.** Rivière, fleuve; le Fleuve-Jaune.

泂 **Hiòung.** Éloigné.

泱 **Iāng.** | | † †. Large et profond.

泳 **Ióung.** Marcher dans l'eau.

沬 **Méi.** Nom de lieu. V. page 55.

泯 **Mìn.** Submergé, périr, disparaître.

泌 **Pí.** Ruisseau, source.

沼 **Tchaò.** Réservoir d'eau, bassin.

治 **Tch'ěu.** Prendre soin de.

況 **Houáng (K'ouáng).** Augmenter, à plus forte raison, pour cette raison.

泄 **Siě.** S'écouler. || **Í.** Se disperser. | | † †. Négligent; lent, insouciant.

泗 **Séu.** Nom d'une rivière qui prend sa source dans le midi du Chan toung.

泚 **Ts'èu.** Suinter; limpide, clair, luisant, brillant.

泲 **Tsì.** Nom de lieu. V. page 46.

泣 **K'ï.** Verser des larmes.

泥 **Gnî.** Boue, mortier, sale.. || **Gnì.** Rosée, humide.

注 **Tchóu.** Verser, se déverser, faire déverser, diriger un cours d'eau.

泰 **T'ái.** Grand, excessif, fastueux, prodigue, orgueilleux. | 山 † **chān** ou 太 山 **T'ái chān.** Montagne sacrée située dans le | 安 府 † **ngān fòu** du Chan toung.

沱 **T'ouô.** Bras de rivière, nom de rivière. | | † †. Grande pluie, larmes abondantes.

洋 **Iâng.** Grande étendue d'eau, océan. | | † †. Vaste, nombreux.

洒 **Chà.** Arroser, jeter de l'eau. || **Sì.** 洗. Laver, effacer. || **Ts'ouèi.** Haut.

洗 **Sì.** Laver.

洄 **Houêi.** 溯 | **Sóu** †. Aller en sens contraire du courant.

洪 **Hôung.** Grande inondation, grand, vaste.

洳 **Jóu.** 沮 | **Tsiú** †. Endroit marécageux.

洧 **Wèi.** Nom d'une rivière qui passe dans le 鄭 州 **Tchéng tcheōu** du Ho nan. V. page 102.

洸 **Kouāng.** Brave, martial, ardent, irrité.

洛 **Lŏ.** Rivière qui traverse le 河南府 **Hô nân fòu.** | 陽 † **iâng.** Nom de ville. V. page 3.

活 **Houŏ.** Vivre, se mouvoir. ‖ **Kouŏ.** | | † †. Courant rapide.

洽 **Hiă.** Concorde; conforme, agréable; imbiber, répandre des bienfaits. ‖ **Hŏ.** Rivière qui traverse le 同州府 **T'ôung tcheōu fòu** dans le 陝西 **Chèn sī.**

洵 **Siûn.** Vrai, sincère, fidélité.

洲 **Tcheōu.** Ilot, terre habitable.

流 **Liôu.** Couler, courant, le cours de l'eau; mouvant, errant, flottant; exiler; entraîné par le courant. | 離 † **lì.** Errant, dispersé; hibou.

涉 **Chĕ.** Marcher dans l'eau; traverser l'eau en barque.

涕 **T'í, T'ì.** Verser des larmes.

涖 **Lí.** Exercer une charge, gouverner, commander.

浥 **Ĭ, Iĕ.** Humide, mouillé.

涘 **Séu.** Rive, bord de l'eau.

浮 **Feôu.** Nager, flotter, aller sur l'eau. | | † †. Grandes eaux, neige abondante, vapeur épaisse.

涇 **King.** Rivière du 陝西 **Chèn sī.**

海 **Hài.** Mer. 四 | **Séu** †. Tout le pays compris entre les quatre mers, l'empire chinois.

浦 **P'òu.** Rive, rivage.

浪 **Láng.** Flot, vague; folle joie, dissolu.

浸 **Tsín.** Imbiber; pénétrer peu à peu comme l'eau.

浼 **Mèi.** Sale, salir, souiller. ‖ **Mièn.** | | † †. Couler à pleins bords.

消 **Siaō.** Fondre, dissoudre, détruire, anéantir, diminuer.

浚 **Siún.** Creuser, profond; nom d'une rivière et d'une ville du 河南 **Hô nân.** Voy. pag. 37 et 60.

浩 **Haó.** Grande étendue d'eau, vaste, intense.

涼 **Leâng.** Froid, sévère. ‖ **Leáng.** Aider, sincère; hypocrite.

淒 **Ts'ī.** Froid, glacial. | | † †. Froid, végétation prospère.

淇 **K'ì.** Nom de rivière. V. page 71.

淑 **Chŏu.** Bon, vertueux, heureux, bonheur.

涵 **Hân.** Contenir, recevoir, admettre, accepter.

淮 **Houâi.** Nom d'une rivière qui traverse le Ho nan et le Ngan houei.

淫 **Ìn.** Grand, excessif, déréglé, licencieux.

深 **Chēnn.** Profond, subtil, intense, couleur foncée.

淪 **Liûn.** Rides sur l'eau; submerger, ruiner, périr.

淠 **P'í.** Agité, ballotté. | | † †. Agité par le vent, nombreux.

淢 **Siŭ.** Fossé.

淵 **Iuēn.** Eau très profonde, abîme; profond. | | † †. Son du tambour.

混 **Houènn.** Eau trouble. ‖ **Kouēnn.** | 夷 † **î.** Tribu occidentale.

清 **Ts'ing.** Limpide, pur, paisible, silencieux.

淺 **Ts'ièn.** Eau peu profonde; peau de tigre.

詩經

渠 **K'iû.** Canal. | | † †. Spacieux.

湄 **Mêi.** Rive verdoyante.

湎 **Mièn.** Plongé dans l'ivresse.

湘 **Siāng.** Cuire, bouillir.

湑 **Siù.** Filtrer; rosée abondante. | | † †. Abondant.

湛 **Tchán.** | | † †. Rosée abondante. || **Tān.** Adonné aux plaisirs.

湜 **Tchĕu.** Eau limpide.

渚 **Tchòu.** Ilot.

游 **Iôu.** Aller çà et là, se promener, se récréer; flotter.

渝 **Iû.** Changeant, inconstant.

渥 **Iŏ.** Mouillé; couleur claire.

湝 **Kiāi, Hiâi.** | | † †. Couler à pleins bords.

湯 **T'āng.** Eau bouillante. | †, 成 | **Tch'êng** †. Nom du fondateur de la dynastie des 商 **Chāng** (1766-1753). || **Táng.** Aller çà et là, dissipé, dissolu. || **Chāng.** Grandes eaux.

温 **Wēnn.** Douce chaleur; tempéré, doux, affable.

渭 **Wéi.** Rivière du 陝西 **Chèn sī.**

測 **Tch'ĕ.** Mesurer la profondeur de; comprendre parfaitement.

渰 **Ièn.** Nuages s'amoncelant.

渴 **K'ŏ.** Avoir soif.

源 **Iuên.** Source d'eau.

渙 **Houán.** Dispersé, séparé. | | † †. Rivière grossie par la fonte des neiges.

溢 **Ĭ.** Déborder, inonder; se répandre; répandre des bienfaits.

溥 **P'òu.** Vaste, universel.

溱 **Tchēnn.** Rivière qui passe près de 鄭州 **Tchéng tcheōu** dans le Ho nan. V. page 102. | | † †. Abondant, luxuriant.

溺 **Gnĭ.** Plongé dans l'eau; plongé dans la débauche, corrompu.

溼 **Chĕu.** Humide, endroit bas et humide.

滔 **T'aō.** Grande crue des eaux; enflé d'orgueil.

滂 **P'āng.** | 沱 † **t'ouô.** Pluie torrentielle, larmes abondantes.

滌 **Tĭ.** Laver, nettoyer. | | † †. Desséché, dénudé.

滅 **Miĕ.** Éteindre, mettre fin.

滯 **Tchéu.** Gelé, coagulé, arrêté; demeurer, rester; s'écouler.

滸 **Hòu.** Rive.

漘 **Chouênn, Tch'ouênn.** Bord de l'eau.

漆 **Ts'ĭ.** | 沮 † **Tsiū.** Voy. 沮.

漂 **P'iaō.** Flotter, s'écouler; agiter.

漏 **Leóu.** Couler à travers une ouverture. 屋 | **Oū** †. V. page 65.

溉 **Kái, Kí.** Laver.

漢 **Hán.** Nom d'une rivière qui traverse le Hou pe et se jette dans le Kiang. 天 | **T'iēn** †, 雲 | **Iûn** †. La voie lactée.

滺 **Iôu.** Couler.

漿 **Tsiāng.** Eau de riz, boisson.

漣 **Liên.** Rides sur l'eau. ‖ ǂ ǂ. Pleurs continuels.

漚 **Ngeóu.** Plonger dans l'eau, rouir.

瀌 **Piaō, P'iôu.** Couler.

漕 **Ts'aô.** Ville de la principauté de 衛 **Wéi**, située dans le 滑 縣 **Houă hién** actuel (prov. de Ho nan). V. page 57.

漙 **T'ouân.** Rosée abondante.

漸 **Tsiēn.** Mouiller, imbiber. ‖ **Tch'ân.** ‖ ǂ ǂ. Haut et escarpé.

漼 **Ts'ouèi.** Profond.

潸 **Chān.** Pleurer.

潛 **Ts'iên.** Se cacher au fond de l'eau; vivier.

潦 **Laò.** Eau qui coule dans un chemin.

潝 **Hī.** Couler. ‖ ǂ ǂ. Être d'accord.

潰 **Houéi.** Troubler; visage rouge de colère; réussir. ‖ ǂ ǂ. Perturbateurs.

澗 **Kién.** Torrent dans un ravin.

潨 **Ts'ôung, Tchōung.** Affluent, confluent.

濆 **Fênn.** Rive.

濃 **Nôung.** ‖ ǂ ǂ. Abondant.

濁 **Tchouŏ.** Eau trouble, sale.

澣 **Houán.** Laver du linge.

濊 **Houŏ.** ‖ ǂ ǂ. Bruit que fait un filet en tombant dans l'eau.

澤 **Tchĕ.** Amas d'eau stagnante; vêtement de dessous. ‖ **Chĕu, Touŏ.** ‖ ǂ ǂ. Facile, pulvérisé.

濈 **Tsī.** ‖ ǂ ǂ. D'accord, doux, accommodant.

濯 **Tchouŏ.** Laver, mouiller; grand, brillant. ‖ ǂ ǂ. Gras et luisant.

濱 **Pīn.** Rive, rivage.

濬 **Siún.** Profond, perspicace.

濕 **Chĕu.** Humide. ‖ **Tch'ĕu.** ‖ ǂ ǂ. Mouvoir les oreilles.

濟 **Tsì.** Rivière qui donne son nom à la ville de ‖ 南 府 ǂ **nân fòu**, capitale du Chan toung. ‖ ǂ ǂ. Beau, distingué, nombreux. ‖ **Tsí.** Traverser l'eau à gué ou en bateau; secourir; réussir.

濡 **Jôu.** Humide, luisant.

濫 **Lán.** Déborder, inonder; excéder, châtier trop sévèrement.

濩 **Houŏ.** Bouillir, cuire.

濛 **Môung.** Pluie fine.

濔 **Mì, Gnì.** ‖ ǂ ǂ. Souple, flexible.

瀏 **Liôu.** Eau profonde.

瀌 **Piaō, P'iôu.** ‖ ǂ ǂ. Neige abondante.

瀟 **Siaō.** ‖ ǂ ǂ. Bruit du vent et de la pluie.

瀰 **Mì, Gnì.** Grandes eaux.

瀼 **Jâng, Nâng.** ‖ ǂ ǂ. Rosée abondante.

灌 **Kouán.** Dense, dru, abondant. ‖ ǂ ǂ. Parler franchement.

RACINE 86. 火

火 **Houò.** Feu; nom de l'une des étoiles du Scorpion.

灼 **Tchŏ.** | | ⺊ ⺊. Brillant.

災 **Tsāi.** Calamité, malheur, dommage, lésion, affliger, causer un grave dommage.

炙 **Tchĕu.** Faire rôtir, viande rôtie.

炎 **Iên.** Flamme, brûlant.

炤 **Tchaō, Tchaò.** Briller.

炮 **P'aò.** Rôtir, griller.

炰 **P'aò.** Rôtir. | 烋 ⺊ **hiaō.** Orgueilleux.

烋 **Hiaō.** Crépitation; orgueilleux.

烈 **Liĕ.** Feu très ardent, brûler; ardent, violent, terrible, intense; brillant, glorieux, service signalé; grave, majestueux. || **Lí.** Froid intense; rôtir.

烏 **Oū.** Corbeau.

烕 **Miĕ.** Éteindre.

烖 **Tsāi.** 災. Calamité.

烘 **Hōung.** Donner de la flamme, brûler.

烝 **Tchēng.** Cuire à la vapeur; avancer, présenter, offrir; offrande faite aux morts en hiver; beaucoup, tous; vigoureux; être vraiment souverain; particule initiale.

焉 **Iên.** Particule finale; terminaison d'adverbes. || **Iēn.** Comment?

焞 **T'ouēnn.** Clarté pâle. || **T'ouēi.** | | ⺊ ⺊. Nombreux.

焦 **Tsiaō.** Brûler; nom de lieu.

焚 **Fènn.** Brûler.

無 **Où.** N'exister pas, n'avoir pas, néant, rien, non, ne pas, sans. | 日 ⺊ **jĕu.** Sans jour fixe, de temps en temps, souvent, très prochainement.

然 **Jèn.** Mettre le feu, brûler; de cette manière, ainsi, à la manière de, comme, oui, dire oui, approuver; terminaison d'adverbes.

煁 **Chênn.** Fourneau portatif.

熙 **Hī.** Brillant, glorieux.

煇 **Houēi.** Lumière, briller. || **Hiūn.** Fumée.

照 **Tchaó.** Éclairer.

煒 **Wèi.** Briller.

煽 **Chén.** Feu ardent; exciter du trouble.

熊 **Hiòung.** Ours, peau d'ours.

熏 **Hiūn.** Fumer, enfumer. | | ⺊ ⺊. Visage doux et joyeux.

熇 **Hŏ.** | | ⺊ ⺊. Brûlant.

熯 **Jèn.** Desséché, épuisé.

熠 **Ĭ, Sĭ.** Brillant.

熱 **Jĕ.** Chaud.

熲 **K'iòung.** Lumière, briller.

熾 **Tch'éu.** Feu très ardent, glorieux.

燎 **Liaó.** Briller, torche; brûler.

65

燔 **Fàn.** Brûler, faire cuire.

燕 **Ién.** Hirondelle; festin, joie, fête, repos, réjouir. || **Iēn.** Ancienne principauté située au nord-ouest de 齊 **Ts'î,** et comprenant une partie du Tcheu li actuel.

營 **Îng.** Tracer le contour ou le plan d'un bâtiment; former un projet. | | 十 十. Bourdonnement des mouches. | 丘 十 **k'iōu.** Capitale de Ts'î. V. page 3.

燬 **Houèi.** Feu très ardent.

燮 **Siĕ.** Conforme, accommodant, obéissant.

燠 **Iŭ.** Chaud, qui donne de la chaleur.

燿 **Iaó.** Briller.

燼 **Tsín.** Cendre, réduire en cendres.

爗 **Iĕ.** Brillant.

爛 **Lán.** Brillant.

爨 **Ts'ouán.** Foyer, cuire.

RACINE 87. 爪

爪 **Tchaò.** Ongles, griffes, défense.

爭 **Tchēng.** Lutter, contester, combattre.

爰 **Iuên.** Ensuite, à cause de cela, dans; particule initiale. | | 十 十. Lentement, avec précaution.

爲 **Wêi.** Faire, agir, exercer, action; prendre soin de, diriger, modérer, gouverner; être, passer pour; juger, considérer comme. 以 | | 十. Faire par ce moyen, juger, considérer ou traiter comme, passer pour. || **Wéi.** Motif, à cause de, en vue de, dans l'intérêt de.

爵 **Tsiŏ.** Nom générique des petits oiseaux, moineau; coupe; dignité, conférer une dignité. 五 | **Où** 十. Les cinq ordres de feudataires de l'empire institués par Iao et Chouenn; à savoir, 公 侯 伯 子 男 **kōung heôu pĕ tzèu nân.**

RACINE 88. 父

父 **Fòu.** Père; frère du père: tous ceux qui sont parents d'un prince en ligne masculine et sont d'une génération antérieure à la sienne. || **Fòu.** S'emploie après un nom.

RACINE 89. 爻

爽 **Chouàng.** Erreur, faute, vice, défectueux, déchoir.

爾 **Eùl.** Tu, vous; ainsi, de cette manière, à la manière de; particule finale qui forme souvent des adverbes ou des diminutifs. || 邇. Être près.

RACINE 90. 爿

牀 **Tch'ouâng.** Lit.

牂 **Tsāng.** Brebis. | | 十 十. Prospère, luxuriant.

牆 **Ts'iâng.** Mur.

RACINE 91. 片

版 **Pàn.** Planche, tablette.

牖 **Iòu.** Fenêtre, éclairer.

RACINE 92. 牙

牙 **Iâ.** Dent, ivoire; défense.

詩經

RACINE 93. 牛

牛 **Iôu (Gniôu).** Bœuf, vache. 牽 | **K'iēn** †. Les étoiles α β γ de l'Aigle.

牝 **Pín.** Femelle.

牟 **Meôu.** Mugir; orge.

牡 **Meòu.** Quadrupède mâle, taureau, étalon.

牢 **Laô.** Étable, prison.

牣 **Jénn.** Plein, emplir.

牧 **Mŏu.** Faire paître, brouter, paître, pasteur, pâturage. | 野 † **iè**. Nom de lieu. V. page 326.

物 **Oŭ.** Chose, objet, substance, animal; couleur du poil.

牲 **Chēng.** Bœuf d'une seule couleur, victime; animal domestique.

特 **T'ĕ.** Taureau, animal de trois ans; un seul, seulement; éminent; compagnon.

牽 **K'iēn.** Conduire un animal derrière soi à l'aide d'une corde.

犀 **Sī.** Rhinocéros; pepin.

犉 **Chouênn.** Bœuf roux dont le museau est noir.

犧 **Hī.** Animal d'une seule couleur, victime.

RACINE 94. 犬

犬 **K'iuèn.** Chien.

狂 **K'ouâng.** Présomptueux, téméraire, ambitieux, insensé.

狄 **Tĭ.** Tribus barbares du nord. || **T'ĭ.** 逖. Éloigner.

狁 **Iùn.** 玁 | **Hiên** †. Barbares du nord, peut-être les Huns.

狃 **Gniòu.** S'habituer, récidiver.

狐 **Hôu.** Renard.

狡 **Kiaò.** Rusé, artificieux, trompeur.

狩 **Cheóu.** Chasse qui se faisait en hiver.

狼 **Lâng.** Loup

猗 **Ī.** Oh! hélas! long, verdoyant, beau, prospère; particule finale. || **Ĭ, Ì.** Cueillir les feuilles. || **Ì.** Tendre, flexible, souple. || 倚. Incliner d'un côté, s'appuyer.

猱 **Naô, Neôu.** Singe.

猶 **Iôu.** Semblable, comme, aussi, mêmement, néanmoins. || 猷. Former un plan, comploter. || 由. Suivre.

猷 **Iôu.** Plan, combiner un plan.

獄 **Iŭ.** Procès, affaire litigieuse; prison.

獨 **Tŏu.** Seul, solitaire, privé de secours, vieillard sans enfant.

獫 **Hièn.** Chien à long museau.

獲 **Houĕ.** Prendre ou tuer un animal à la chasse; obtenir, gagner.

獵 **Liĕ.** Chasse, chasser.

獸 **Cheóu.** Quadrupède.

獻 **Hién.** Offrir, présenter, montrer.

玁 **Hièn.** | 狁 † **iùn**. Barbares du nord.

RACINE 95. 玄

玄 **Hiuên.** Couleur d'azur, noirâtre, brun foncé. | 鳥 † **gniaò**. Hirondelle.

率 **Chouĕ.** Conduire, diriger, suivre, se conformer à, imiter; tout, partout.

RACINE 96. 玉

玉 **Iŭ.** Pierre de prix, jade; précieux, estimer beaucoup.

王 **Wâng.** Roi, empereur, rendre hommage à l'empereur. | 季 ✝ **ki.** Père de Wenn wang. V. page 2. || **Wáng.** Gouverner l'empire. || **Wàng.** 往. Aller à,

玖 **Kiòu.** Pierre de couleur noire.

珈 **Kiā.** Pierres de prix qui ornaient la tête des femmes.

珌 **Pĭ, Piĕ.** Pierre de prix fixée à l'extrémité d'un fourreau d'épée.

玷 **Tién.** Défaut.

玼 **Ts'èu.** Éclat d'une pierre précieuse.

珩 **Hêng.** Agrafe de jade qu'on portait à la ceinture. V. page 75.

球 **K'iôu.** Tablette de jade qui était une marque de dignité.

琇 **Sióu, Iòu.** Pierre de prix.

理 **Lì.** Diviser les terres.

琚 **Kiū.** Ornement qu'on portait à la ceinture. Voy. page 75.

琛 **Tch'ēnn.** Objet précieux.

琫 **Pòung.** Ornement de jade fixé à l'ouverture d'un fourreau d'épée.

琢 **Tchouŏ.** Tailler ou polir une pierre de prix.

琴 **K'în.** Luth à cinq ou sept cordes.

瑟 **Chĕ.** Luth à dix-neuf ou vingt-cinq cordes; maintien grave, violent.

瑕 **Hiâ.** Défaut, tache; comment?

瑤 **Iaô.** Nom d'une belle pierre.

瑩 **Iôung.** Nom d'une belle pierre; briller.

瑰 **Kouēi.** Nom d'une pierre de prix.

瑣 **Souò.** Fragment, bagatelle, objet de nulle valeur.

瑱 **T'ién, Tchénn.** Ornements qu'on portait pendants sur les oreilles.

瑲 **Ts'iāng.** Son des clochettes ou des pierres musicales.

瑳 **Ts'ouò.** Blanc et brillant. | | ✝ ✝. Splendide.

璊 **Mân, Mènn.** Belle pierre rouge.

璋 **Tchāng.** La moitié d'une tablette 圭 **kouēi.**

璧 **Pĭ.** Tablette de jade de forme annulaire, que les feudataires de quatrième et de cinquième *rang* 子 男 **tzèu nân** recevaient de l'empereur comme marque de leur dignité; objet précieux, présent. V. page 64.

環 **Houân.** Anneau, entourer. 游 | **Iôu** ✝. Voy. page 137.

璲 **Souéi.** Nom d'une belle pierre.

瓊 **K'iôung.** Nom d'une belle pierre; précieux, beau.

瓚 **Tsán.** Vase employé pour les libations.

RACINE 97. 瓜

瓜 **Kouā.** Concombre, courge. 木 | **Mŏu** ✝. Coing.

瓞 **Tiĕ.** Petit concombre.

瓢 **P'iaô.** Calebasse, cuiller faite en forme de calebasse.

RACINE 98. 瓦

瓦 **Wà.** Tuile.

甓 **P'ĭ, Pĭ.** Grande brique, carreau.

RACINE 99. 甘

甘 **Kān.** Doux au goût, savoureux, favorable. | 心 † sīn. Souffrir volontiers.

甚 **Chénn.** Excéder, trop, plus, beaucoup, tout à fait.

RACINE 100. 生

生 **Chēng.** Produire, engendrer, naître, croître, vivre, naissance, vie, vivant. 先 | Siēn †. Plus âgé, plus ancien.

甡 **Chēnn.** Nombreux.

甥 **Chēng.** Fils de notre sœur.

RACINE 101. 用

用 **Ióung.** Se servir de, employer, pratiquer, pourvoir d'un emploi, usage, utilité, pratique, par ce moyen, à cause de cela, afin que par ce moyen. 是 | Chéu †. Par ce moyen, à cause de cela.

甫 **Fòu.** Prénom; grand, commencer; nom de lieu. V. page 79.

RACINE 102. 田

田 **T'iên.** Champ cultivé; chasse, chasser; grand tambour. || **Tién.** Cultiver.

由 **Iôu.** Venir de, passer par, suivre, se servir de, dépendre de; à partir de.

甲 **Kiă.** Cuirasse, enveloppe dure; premier, surpasser.

申 **Chēnn.** Réitérer, renouveler, répéter, deux fois; ancienne principauté. V. page 79.

男 **Nân.** Du sexe masculin; feudataire du cinquième rang.

甸 **Tién.** Arranger, rendre cultivable.

町 **T'ièn.** | 畽 † t'ouàn. Terrain vide auprès d'une habitation.

畀 **Pí.** Donner, accorder, daigner.

畇 **Iûn, Siûn.** Défricher.

界 **Kiái.** Limite.

畏 **Wéi.** Craindre, respecter, attentif, vigilant.

畛 **Tchènn.** Sentier pratiqué sur la levée de terre qui sépare deux champs.

畔 **Pán.** Limite; déserter, quitter, abandonner, rejeter.

畜 **Hiŭ.** Nourrir, entretenir, retenir.

畟 **Tch'ĕ, Tsĭ.** Soc de charrue. | | † †. Aigu.

留 **Liôu.** Retenir, garder, laisser.

畝 **Meòu.** Mesure agraire contenant cent 步 póu carrés et valant environ 144 mètres carrés ou un peu moins d'un are et demi; monticule, monceau.

畢 **Pĭ.** Fin, finir; tous, ensemble; les Hyades.

略 **Leŏ.** Plan, sommaire, idée générale; aiguiser.

異 **Í.** Différent, autre, extraordinaire, étrange, étranger.

番 **Pouō.** | | † †. Vieillard à cheveux blancs; courageux. ||

Pouō, Piēn. Brave, martial. || **P'ouô, P'ān.** Nom de famille.

畯 **Tsiún.** Inspecteur des travaux des champs.

畬 **Iû.** Champ qui a été défriché depuis un ou deux ans.

畽 **T'ouàn, T'ōung.** 町 | T'ién ✝. Terrain vide près d'une habitation.

畿 **K'ī.** Domaine impérial; seuil de porte.

疆 **Kiāng.** Limite; marquer les limites d'un territoire.

疊 **Tiĕ.** Craindre, trembler de peur.

RACINE 103. 疋

疏 **Chōu.** Éloigné; grossier, de mauvaise qualité.

疐 **Tchéu.** Embarrasser la marche.

疑 **Î.** Douter, soupçonner. || **Gnîng.** Fixer, tranquille.

RACINE 104. 疒

疚 **Kióu.** Maladie chronique, défaut, mauvaise habitude, chagrin.

疢 **Tch'énn.** Fièvre chaude; grande affliction.

{疷 疧} **K'î.** Malade.

疾 **Tsî.** Maladie; défaut, chagrin, déplaisir, rapide, violent, sévir.

痒 **Iâng.** Malade, être en peine.

痗 **Méi.** Malade, affligé, chagrin.

痡 **P'ōu, Fōu.** Malade, épuisé, malheureux.

痯 **Kouàn.** Malade, forces épuisées, triste.

痻 **Mîn, Houēnn.** Maladie, douleur, malheur.

瘁 **Tsouéi.** Très fatigué, à bout de forces, triste.

瘉 **Iù.** Maladie, douleur, malheur, chagrin.

瘏 **T'ôu.** Malade, hors de service.

瘞 **Í.** Enterrer, inhumer, mettre en terre les objets qui ont été offerts à un esprit tutélaire.

瘥 **Ts'ouô.** Maladie, épidémie, contagion.

瘨 **Tiēn, T'iên.** Malade, affligé.

瘳 **Tch'eōu, Leaô.** Aller mieux, guérir.

瘼 **Mouŏ.** Maladie, douleur, affliction.

瘵 **Tchái, Tsí.** Malade, affligé.

癉 **Tán.** Douleur, fatigue, malheur.

癙 **Chòu.** Chagrin secret.

RACINE 105. 癶

登 **Tēng.** Monter; accomplir, perfectionner, rendre prospère, mûrir. | | ✝ ✝. Bruit d'une bie.

發 **Fă.** Lancer une flèche; mettre hors, faire sortir, envoyer, émettre, énoncer, distribuer, ouvrir; faire paraître, montrer, découvrir, manifester, révéler, apparaître, se montrer, se révéler; promouvoir; cultiver, développer, augmenter; sortir, partir; commencer, produire, naître; remuer, mouvoir, se mouvoir, actif; éprouver ou manifester un sentiment. || **Pouŏ.** | | ✝ ✝. Nombreux. || **Féi.** 觱 | Pi ✝. Vent froid.

RACINE 106. 白

白 **Pĕ.** Blanc, nu, vide, inutile.

百 **Pĕ.** Cent; de toute sorte, de tout rang, tous.

皁 **Tsaò, Tseòu.** Grain encore tendre dans l'épi.

的 **Tĭ.** Brillant, le milieu d'une cible.

皆 **Kiāi.** Tous, de toute espèce.

皇 **Houâng.** Grand, auguste, magnifique, seigneur souverain, empereur; brillant; jaune.

皋 **Kaō.** Marais, étang, haut. | 門 + **mênn.** Porte de l'enceinte d'un palais. | | + +. Grossier, insolent. | 陶 + **iaô.** L'un des ministres de 舜 **Chouénn.**

皎 **Kiaò.** Blancheur éclatante.

皓 **Haò.** Blancheur éclatante.

皦 **Kiaò.** Brillant.

RACINE 107. 皮

皮 **P'î.** Peau, cuir, fourrure.

RACINE 108. 皿

盈 **Îng.** Plein; plein de soi-même, orgueilleux.

益 **Ĭ.** Augmenter, ajouter, croître.

盛 **Chéng.** Florissant, prospère, abondant, grand, beaucoup, au plus haut degré. || **Tch'êng.** Millet préparé dans un vase pour être offert aux esprits; mettre dans, placer dans.

盜 **Taó.** Voleur, dérober.

盟 **Mêng, Mîng.** Confirmer un pacte par un serment, serment, pacte solennel, traité.

盡 **Tsín.** Entièrement, tout à fait, au plus haut degré, faire ou dire entièrement, employer entièrement, épuiser, fin, prendre fin, mettre fin.

監 **Kién.** Surveiller, inspecter, considérer, gouverner.

盧 **Lôu.** Chien.

盬 **Kòu.** Mal conditionné, peu solide.

RACINE 109. 目

目 **Mŏu.** Œil.

盱 **Hiū.** Désirer, espérer.

直 **Tchĕu.** Droit, juste, équitable, honnête, sincère; seulement.

相 **Siāng.** Ensemble, mutuellement. || **Siáng.** Considérer, voir, aider.

盾 **Chouénn.** Bouclier.

盼 **P'án.** Œil où le blanc se détache parfaitement du noir.

省 **Sìng.** Examiner, observer, surveiller.

眉 **Mêi.** Sourcil; longs et épais sourcils de vieillard, vieillesse.

眷 **Kiuén.** Affection, aimer.

衆 **Tchóung.** Nombreux, tous, multitude.

睆 **Houàn.** Brillant, beau, plein.

睍 **Hièn.** | 睆 + **houàn.** Chant agréable.

睠 **Kiuén.** Regarder en arrière.

瞍 **Seòu.** Aveugle à qui manquent les prunelles des yeux.

睘 **K'iôung.** Seul et sans secours.

瞻 **Tchēn.** Regarder en haut, considérer, espérer.

瞽 **Kòu.** Aveugle, musicien aveugle.

瞿 **Kiú.** Craindre. | | 十 十. Craindre et prendre garde, stupéfait.

矇 **Môung.** Aveugle qui a conservé les prunelles de ses yeux.

RACINE 110. 矛

矛 **Meòu.** Lance.

矜 **King.** Avoir compassion, digne de compassion, malheureux. | | 十 十. Fort, robuste. || **Kouān.** 鰥. Veuf.

RACINE 111. 矢

矢 **Chèu.** Flèche; produire, mettre dehors, ranger en ordre, montrer, déployer; faire serment.

矣 **Ì.** Particule finale.

知 **Tchēu.** Connaître, savoir, prendre connaissance, comprendre.

矧 **Chènn.** A plus forte raison.

矯 **Kiaò.** | | 十 十. Brave, courageux, martial.

RACINE 112. 石

石 **Chĕu.** Pierre, rocher.

砥 **Tchèu.** Pierre à aiguiser, meule.

破 **P'ouó.** Casser, briser, fendre; frapper comme avec une hache.

砠 **Ts'iū.** Montagne où les rochers sont recouverts de terre.

碩 **Chĕu.** Grand, remarquable.

磋 **Ts'ouō.** Polir, limer.

磨 **Mouô.** Frotter, aiguiser, broyer, moudre.

磬 **K'íng.** Instrument de musique consistant en une ou plusieurs tablettes de pierre qu'on suspend à une traverse, et qu'on frappe pour en tirer des sons; retenir, modérer, faire dévier. V. page 342.

RACINE 113. 示

示 **Chéu.** Avertir, montrer.

社 **Ché.** Autel élevé à l'esprit ou aux esprits de la terre, sacrifice offert à la Terre.

祁 **K'î.** Grand, vaste. | | 十 十. En grand nombre, lentement, goutte à goutte.

祀 **Séu.** Sacrifice, offrande, faire un sacrifice ou une offrande.

祇 **K'î.** L'esprit de la terre; content, heureux. || **Tchēu.** Seulement. || 祗. Respecter.

祈 **K'î.** Prier, demander; annoncer. | | 十 十. Nombreux.

祊 **Pēng.** Espace compris entre la porte de l'enceinte d'un temple et la salle principale.

祉 **Tch'èu.** Bonheur, se réjouir.

祋 **Tái, Touŏ.** Grosse lance 殳 chôu.

祚 **Tsóu.** Bonheur.

祖 **Tsòu.** Aïeul, ancêtres; sacrifice offert au dieu des chemins. 太 | **T'ái** 十. Le premier des ancêtres.

祜 **Hòu.** Bienfait du ciel, bonheur.

詩經

祝 **Tchŏu.** Celui qui dans les cérémonies lisait des panégyriques en l'honneur des esprits, leur adressait des demandes, recevait et transmettait leurs réponses; lier. || **Tcheóu.** Maudire.

神 **Chênn.** Esprit, spirituel, mystérieux.

祗 **Tchēu.** Respect.

祠 **Sêu.** Offrande faite aux ancêtres en printemps.

祥 **Siâng.** Présage, bonheur, favorable.

祭 **Tsí.** Sacrifice, offrande, sacrifier, faire une offrande.

祼 **Kouán.** Libation.

祿 **Lŏu.** Bonheur, avantage.

祺 **K'î.** Bonheur, prospérité, joie.

禍 **Houó.** Calamité, malheur, causer un grave dommage.

禎 **Tchēng.** Heureux présage.

福 **Fŏu.** Bonheur.

禋 **Īn.** Sacrifice offert avec une intention pure.

禡 **Má.** Sacrifice offert au dieu de la guerre.

禦 **Iú.** Garder, défendre, résister; adversaire, rival, égal.

禮 **Lì.** Convenances, bienséances, usage, cérémonie, témoignage de respect, urbanité, politesse.

禱 **Taó.** Prier un esprit protecteur.

禰 **Gnì.** Lieu situé au nord de 曹州府 **Ts'aô tcheōu fòu** dans le Chan toung. V. page 46.

禴 **Iŏ.** Offrande faite aux ancêtres en été.

RACINE 114. 内

禹 **Iù.** Nom du fondateur de la dynastie des Hia (2205-2197).

RACINE 115. 禾

禾 **Houô.** Céréales.

秀 **Sióu.** Inflorescence d'une céréale, fleurir; beau, excellent.

私 **Sēu.** Propre, particulier, privé, intéressé, partial ; prendre pour soi; nom qu'une femme donne au mari de sa sœur.

秉 **Pìng.** Saisir; maintenir, observer, posséder, employer.

秋 **Ts'iōu.** Automne.

秦 **Ts'în.** Nom de principauté. V. pag. 4 et 143.

秬 **Kiú.** Millet noir.

秣 **Mouŏ.** Nourrir de grain un animal.

秠 **P'ēi.** Millet noir.

秩 **Tchĕu.** Ordre, rang. 秩秩. Par ordre, graduellement, convenablement, régulièrement.

租 **Tsōu.** Recueillir

秭 **Tzèu.** Un million, cent millions, dix quadrillions.

稂 **Lâng.** Mauvaise herbe qui ressemble au millet.

程 **Tch'êng.** Mesure, poids, règle, modèle; nom de lieu. V. page 411.

稌 **Tóu.** Riz glutineux.

稙 **Tchĕu.** Semer de bonne heure.

種 **Tchòung.** Semence. || **Tchóung.** Semer, ensemencer.

66

稱 **Tch'ēng.** Peser ; lever. || **Tch'éng.** Égal, conforme.

稷 **Tsĭ.** Millet à panicules dont le grain est jaune. 后 | **Heóu** ⼗. V. pag. 2 et 347.

稻 **Taó.** Riz.

稼 **Kiá.** Semer, culture des champs, moisson.

稽 **K'ì.** Se mettre à genoux et incliner la tête jusqu'à terre en signe de respect

穋 **Tchéu.** Grain semé tard, jeune.

穀 **Kŏu.** Grains qui servent à la nourriture de l'homme; bon, vertueux, favorable, heureux; vivre.

穆 **Mŏu.** Beau, majestueux, respectueux, doux, mystérieux ; le côté méridional dans le temple des ancêtres. Voyez 廟 Miaó, page. 492.

積 **Tsĭ.** Amasser, accumuler. || **Tzéu.** Amas, provisions.

穈 **Mênn.** Millet rouge.

穋 **Liŭ.** Grain qui se sème tard et se récolte tôt.

穎 **Ìng.** Épi.

穗 **Souéi.** Épi.

穟 **Souéi.** Épi. | | ⼗ ⼗. Végétation prospère.

穠 **Nôung.** Drus et nombreux.

穡 **Chĕ.** Moissonner, récolter. 稼 | **Kiá** ⼗. Travaux des champs.

穧 **Tsí.** Javelle.

穫 **Houŏ.** Moissonner, récolter. || **Hóu.** 焦 | **Tsiaō** ⼗. Lieu situé dans le 三 原 縣 **Sān iuên hién** du 陝 西 **Chèn sī.**

穰 **Jâng.** | | ⼗ ⼗. Abondant.

RACINE 116. 穴

穴 **Hiuĕ.** Trou, caverne, fosse.

究 **Kióu.** Chercher, scruter; limite, fin.

穹 **K'iōung.** Voûte, en forme de voûte, haut; ouverture, trou.

空 **K'ōung.** Vide, creux, inoccupé, qui n'est pas employé. 司 | **Sēu** ⼗. Ministre des travaux publics. || **K'óung.** Vider, épuiser.

穿 **Tch'ouēn.** Percer.

突 **Tŏu.** Sortir subitement, soudain.

窈 **Iaò.** Retiré, solitaire, profond, paisible.

窒 **Tchĕu.** Boucher, fermer.

窕 **T'iaó.** Retiré, solitaire, profond, paisible.

窘 **Kiùn.** Être dans la détresse, embarrassé.

窮 **K'iôung.** Pauvre, dépourvu de tout.

窶 **Kiú.** Pauvre, gêné.

RACINE 117. 立

立 **Lĭ.** Être debout, se mettre debout, dresser; ferme, affermir; établir, constituer, fonder; exécuter; mettre en charge. || 粒. Grain.

竝 **Pìng.** Deux personnes ou deux choses ensemble; unir, côte à côte.

竟 **Kíng.** Limite, terme, enfin.

章 **Tchāng.** Un tout complet, un morceau de musique, ornements de diverses couleurs, élégant, briller ; loi, règle, usage, modèle.

詩經

童 **T'ŏung.** Enfant de huit à quinze ans; jeune bélier sans bornes.

竦 **Sòung.** Craindre.

竭 **Kiĕ.** Employer entièrement, épuiser.

競 **Kíng.** Fort, énergique, lutter, rivaliser, s'empresser.

RACINE 118. 竹

竹 **Tchŏu.** Bambou.

竿 **Kān.** Tige de bambou, perche, ligne de pêcheur.

笑 **Siaó.** Rire.

笙 **Chēng.** Flûte composée de treize ou de dix-neuf tuyaux. Voy. page 174.

笠 **Lĭ.** Chapeau de jonc ou de paille.

第 **Fŏu.** Natte ou cuir qui couvre la partie postérieure d'une voiture.

笱 **Keòu.** Nasse ou panier pour prendre le poisson.

筍 **Siùn.** Jeune pousse de bambou.

筐 **K'ouāng.** Panier carré.

笄 **Kī.** Épingle de tête.

答 **Tă.** Répondre.

筥 **Kiù.** Panier rond.

筦 **Kouàn.** 管. Flûte.

筮 **Chéu.** Deviner au moyen de brins d'achillée.

筵 **Iên.** Natte qu'on étendait à terre et sur laquelle on mangeait, repas, festin.

箕 **Kī.** Van; nom d'une constellation qui fait partie du Sagittaire.

管 **Kouàn.** Roseau, tube, flûte à deux tuyaux; prendre soin de. | | † †. Ignorant.

箱 **Siāng.** Caisse d'une voiture, voiture.

築 **Tchŏu.** Élever un mur de terre; bâtir.

節 **Tsiĕ.** Nœud ou jointure d'une plante; article; haut, escarpé; modération.

篪 **Tch'êu.** Flûte traversière.

篨 **Tch'ôu.** Grosse natte; enflé, bouffi, obésité difforme.

篤 **Tŏu.** Ferme, solide, sincère, généreux, magnanime, affermir, augmenter.

簋 **Kouèi.** Vase de bois dans lequel on servait la nourriture.

簀 **Tchĕ.** Massif d'arbres.

簟 **Tién.** Natte de bambou.

簡 **Kièn.** Tablettes sur lesquelles on écrivait, pièce écrite. | | † †. Négligent, abondant.

簫 **Siaō.** Flûte composée de seize ou de vingt-trois tuyaux.

簧 **Houâng.** Languette de flûte; bavard.

簸 **Pouò.** Vanner le grain.

籊 **Tĭ, T'ĭ.** | | † †. Long et mince.

籍 **Tsĭ.** Cahier, registre, rôle du cens.

籧 **K'iû.** Grosse natte; gonflé, obésité difforme.

籥 **Iŏ.** Flûte traversière.

籩 **Piēn.** Vase de bois dans lequel on offrait aux esprits des viandes, des fruits,...

RACINE 119. 米

粟 **Siŭ.** Grain de riz ou de millet avec son enveloppe.

粱 **Leâng.** Sorgho.

粲 **Ts'án.** Riz pur, riz cuit, mets; beau, élégant. | | ☨ ☨. Net, propre.

粼 **Lîn.** Limpide, pur, net.

粺 **Pái.** Grain très pur.

粻 **Tchāng.** Grain, provision de grains.

糧 **Leâng.** Grains, tribut.

糦 **Tch'éu.** Millet cuit.

釋 **Chĕu.** Laver le riz.

RACINE 120. 糸

糾 **Kiòu.** Tisser, unir. | | ☨ ☨. Tissé. || **Kiaò.** Triste. || **K'iaó.** Léger.

約 **Iŏ.** Lier, entourer.

紀 **Kì.** Régler, règle, statut; crête d'une colline.

納 **Nă.** Faire entrer, porter dans, rapporter, raconter.

紓 **Chōu.** Relâché, moins intense.

紑 **Feōu.** Neuf et brillant.

紕 **P'î.** Tisser, lier, attacher.

純 **Chouênn.** Simple, sans mélange, pur. || **T'ouênn.** Lier, envelopper.

索 **Souŏ.** Corde, faire une corde.

素 **Sóu.** Étoffe de soie unie et blanche ou de couleur naturelle; blanc; ne rien faire, ne rendre aucun service.

紹 **Chaó.** Continuer, succéder; en masse compacte; profond chagrin.

紼 **Fŏu.** Corde, câble.

紲 **Siĕ.** Lier, ceindre.

紵 **Tchóu.** Abutilon, sorte de gros chanvre.

終 **Tchōung.** Fin, jusqu'à la fin, pour toujours, tout, entier. | 南 ☨ nân. Nom de montagne. V. page 139.

紽 **T'ouò.** Nombre des cordons de soie.

組 **Tsòu.** Ruban ou cordon de soie.

絕 **Tsiuĕ.** Rompre, mettre fin, au plus haut degré, surpasser.

絜 **Kiĕ.** 潔. Pur, purifier.

絲 **Sēu.** Soie.

結 **Kiĕ.** Lier, serrer; angoisse.

絿 **K'iòu.** Négligent, tardif, indulgent.

綅 **Ts'īn.** Fil ou cordon rouge.

經 **Kīng.** Chaîne d'un tissu; faire un tracé, tracer un plan, chercher ou combiner les moyens pour atteindre une fin, combiner, disposer, régler, diriger; règle constante.

絺 **Tch'ēu.** Toile fine.

綌 **K'ĭ.** Toile grossière.

綏 **Souēi.** Paisible, tranquille, heureux, procurer la tranquillité. || **Jouēi.** Ornement d'un

海上絲綢之路文獻集成 科技與文化編

詩經

étendard. || **Chouēi.** | | ++. Marche du renard.

綠 **Liŭ.** Vert. || 菉. Bambou.

絨 **Iŭ, Hiŭ.** Couture.

綽 **Tch'ŏ.** Large, vaste, libéral, bienfaisant, accommodant. | | ++. Bon et généreux.

綴 **Tchouéi.** Être attaché à, dépendre de, appendice, dépendance.

緇 **Tchēu.** Noir, noirâtre.

綦 **K'î.** Vert ou bleu pâle.

綢 **Tch'eôu.** Serrer avec un lien; serré, dense, dru.

維 **Wêi.** Seulement; considérer, régler; particule.

綯 **T'aô.** Tordre, faire des cordes.

網 **Wàng.** Filet.

綱 **Kāng.** Corde de filet, principe ou règle, régler.

綸 **Liûn.** Arranger régler.

緌 **Jouēi.** Cordons qui liaient le chapeau et dont les extrémités pendaient sous le menton; extrémités pendantes des cordons d'un chapeau.

綣 **K'iuèn.** Union intime.

緄 **Kouènn.** Cordon, ceinture.

緒 **Siú.** Extrémité extérieure du fil d'un cocon; commencement, entreprise, succession, héritage.

緜 **Miên.** Bourre de soie, ouate. | | ++. Suite non interrompue.

緝 **Ts'ĭ.** Continuer, continu. || **Tsĭ.** | | ++. Murmure.

緡 **Mîn.** Cordon de soie; revêtir, couvrir.

縣 **Hiuên.** Suspendre, pendant.

縈 **Iôung.** Enrouler, s'enrouler autour.

縞 **Kaò.** Soie blanche, simple, sans ornement.

縐 **Tcheóu.** Tissu de soie fin et crêpu.

縢 **T'êng.** Cordon, bande, lier.

縫 **Fôung.** Coudre. || **Fóung.** Couture.

縮 **Chŏu.** Lier, se contracter.

縱 **Tsóung.** Laisser libre, laisser ou prendre toute liberté; décocher; quand même.

縭 **Lî.** Cordon, ceinture, bandeau.

縶 **Tchĕu.** Attacher, lier les pieds.

總 **Tsòung.** Réunir et lier ensemble plusieurs objets; se réunir. || **Tsōung.** Couture.

績 **Tsĭ.** Tiller ou filer le chanvre; service rendu au public, mérite.

繁 **Fân.** Nombreux, abondant, de toute sorte.

繆 **Miôu.** Serrer avec un lien, unir.

織 **Tchĕu.** Tisser, tresser. || **Tch'éu.** 幟. Étendard.

繡 **Sióu.** Broder.

繩 **Chêng.** Corde, cordeau de charpentier, continuer. | | ++. Suite non interrompue.

繹 **Ĭ.** Suite non interrompue, continuer.

繼 **Kí.** Continuer, succéder.

繾 **K'ièn.** Union étroite.

續 **Siŭ.** Continuer.

纍 **Lêi.** Être attaché à.

纘 **Tsouàn.** Continuer, succéder.

纚 **Li.** Corde.

RACINE 121. 缶

缶 **Feòu.** Vase de terre sur lequel on battait la mesure.

缺 **K'iuĕ.** Vase cassé, casser, faire défaut.

缾 **P'ing.** Jarre, bouteille.

罄 **K'íng.** Vide, épuisé.

罍 **Lêi.** Vase pour le vin, jarre.

RACINE 122. 网

罔 **Wàng.** Filet; prendre dans un filet, tromper; ne pas, sans; calamité.

罕 **Hàn.** Rare, peu fréquent.

罛 **Kōu.** Grand filet de pêcheur.

罟 **Kòu.** Filet; châtiment, calamité.

罝 **Tsiē, Tsiū.** Filet pour prendre les lièvres.

罦 **Feôu.** Filet d'oiseleur.

罭 **Iŭ.** Filet. 九 | Kiòu 平. Filet qui a neuf poches.

罩 **Tchaó.** Nasse, prendre le poisson sous un panier renversé.

罪 **Tsouéi.** Faute, offense, crime, châtiment, inculper. 得 | Tĕ 平. Offenser.

置 **Tchéu.** Placer, disposer, dresser, établir, constituer, mettre en charge.

罶 **Liòu.** Clayons enfoncés dans l'eau pour arrêter et prendre les poissons.

罹 **Li.** Chagrin, infortune.

罿 **Tch'ōung.** Filet d'oiseleur.

羅 **Lô.** Filet d'oiseleur, prendre dans un filet.

羆 **P'i, Pi.** Ours de grande taille.

RACINE 123. 羊

羊 **Iàng.** Brebis, chèvre.

羌 **K'iāng.** Tribus de l'ouest.

美 **Mèi.** Beau, excellent.

羔 **Kaō.** Agneau.

羖 **Kòu.** Bélier.

羜 **Tchóu.** Agneau de cinq mois.

羝 **Ti.** Bélier de trois ans.

羣 **K'iûn.** Troupeau, troupe, beaucoup, tous, ensemble; semblable, d'accord.

羨 **Sién.** Désirer vivement; superflu, reste, excédant.

義 **Í.** Justice, juste, équitable, honnête.

羹 **Kēng.** Bouillon, sauce, potage.

RACINE 124. 羽

羽 **Iù.** Plume, aile.

習 **Sĭ.** S'exercer. | | ✝ ✝. Vent d'est soufflant doucement.

翕 **Hĭ.** Concorde, réglé; mettre dehors.

翔 **Siâng.** Voltiger. 翱 | Ngaô ✝. Courir çà et là.

翛 **Siaō.** | | ✝ ✝. Gâté, en mauvais état.

翟 **Tĭ.** Faisan, plume de faisan, robe ornée de figures de faisans.

翦 **Tsièn.** Couper, tailler, retrancher.

翩 **P'iēn.** Voler rapidement, voltiger, courir çà et là.

翬 **Houēi.** Faisan au plumage varié.

翰 **Hán.** Voler très haut; pieu.

翯 **Hŏ.** Plumage d'une blancheur éclatante.

翳 **Í.** Ombrager, couvrir, joncher la terre.

翼 **Ĭ.** Aile, couvrir de son aile, protéger, aider. | | ✝ ✝. Soigneux, diligent, fort, élégant, brillant, en bon ordre.

翹 **K'iaô** Haut, éminent; être en péril.

翺 **Ngaô.** Voltiger, aller çà et là, chercher des amusements.

翽 **Houéi.** Bruit d'ailes.

翿 **Taó.** Sorte d'éventail fait de plumes que les pantomimes tenaient à la main.

RACINE 125. 老

老 **Laò.** Vieux, vieillard, ancien ministre d'État.

考 **Kaò.** Examiner; accomplir, frapper; vie longue, vieux; père défunt.

耄 **Maó.** Vieillard qui a soixante-dix ans ou plus.

者 **Tchè.** Suffixe du participe et quelquefois de l'adjectif; qui; particule.

耆 **K'î.** Homme de soixante ans. ‖ **Tchèu.** Parvenir, atteindre.

耇 **Keòu.** Rides de la vieillesse, vieillard.

耋 **Tiĕ.** Vieillir, vieillard qui a de soixante-dix à quatre vingts ans.

RACINE 126. 而

而 **Eûl.** Et, mais, néanmoins, au contraire; particule finale.

RACINE 127. 耒

耔 **Tzèu.** Butter une plante.

耗 **Haó.** Consumer, détruire peu à peu, ruiner, anéantir.

耕 **Kēng.** Labourer, cultiver la terre.

耘 **Iûn.** Arracher les mauvaises herbes.

耜 **Séu.** Soc de charrue, charrue.

耦 **Ngeòu.** Deux sillons, deux personnes associées.

RACINE 128. 耳

耳 **Eùl.** Oreille. | | ✝ ✝. Flexible, flottant.

耿 **Kèng.** Ferme. | | ✝ ✝. Agité, inquiet.

耽 **Tān.** Joie, amusement, adonné aux plaisirs.

聊 **Leaô.** Un peu; particule.

聖 **Chéng.** Celui qui possède naturellement la plus haute sagesse, sage du premier ordre.

聘 **P'íng.** Demander des nouvelles de quelqu'un, saluer par lettre.

聞 **Wênn.** Entendre. || **Wénn.** Renom, réputation; parvenir jusqu'à (en parlant du son).

聰 **Ts'ōung.** Entendre clairement, comprendre, esprit perspicace.

聲 **Chēng.** Son, bruit, voix, chant, réputation.

職 **Tchĕu.** Charge publique, emploi, profession, travail, devoir; occupation unique ou principale.

聽 **T'īng.** Écouter, entendre.

RACINE 129. 聿

聿 **Iŭ.** Ensuite; particule.

肄 **Í.** Fatigue, peine; jeune pousse, rejeton.

肆 **Séu.** Étendre, étaler, répandre, propager, attaquer, par suite.

肅 **Siŭ.** Respectueux, attentif, maintien grave, sévère, froid intense, avancer, commencer. | | † †. Respectueux, circonspect, disposé avec soin, bruit des ailes d'un oiseau.

肇 **Tchaó.** Commencer, fonder, d'abord. || 兆. Limite.

RACINE 130. 肉

股 **Kòu.** Cuisse.

肥 **Fêi.** Gras, fertile, riche, abondant.

肩 **Kiēn.** Épaule; quadrupède de trois ans.

肱 **Kōung.** La partie supérieure du bras.

肯 **K'èng.** Vouloir, consentir.

育 **Iŭ.** Produire, nourrir, entretenir, perfectionner, instruire.

肺 **Féi.** Poumon. | 腸 † tch'âng. Sentiment. || **P'éi.** | | † †. Végétation prospère.

背 **Péi.** Dos, partie postérieure, par derrière, tourner le dos, quitter, enfreindre.

胡 **Hòu.** Fanon du bœuf, peau qui pend sous le cou; comment? pourquoi? vieillesse.

胤 **Ín.** Postérité.

胥 **Siū.** Ensemble, mutuellement, considérer ensemble, veiller conjointement sur.

脂 **Tcheū.** Graisse, onguent, graisser.

能 **Nêng.** Pouvoir, être capable de, puissance, force, habileté.

脊 **Tsĭ.** Épine dorsale, fondement, raison solide. | 令 † ling. Bergeronnette.

脅 **Hiĕ.** Côte, côté.

胾 **Tzéu.** Viande hachée.

脯 **Fòu.** Tranche de viande séchée.

脫 **T'ouŏ.** Dépouiller, enlever, déshabiller. || **T'ouéi.** | | † †. Paisible.

腓 **Fêi.** Le gras de la jambe; avoir confiance, protéger; dépérir.

脾 **P'î.** Rate, estomac, intestins.

腸 **Tch'âng.** Intestins.

腹 **Fŏu.** Estomac, ventre, sein; siége du sentiment; tenir sur son sein.

膋 **Leaô.** Graisse qui enveloppe les intestins.

膏 **Kaō.** Graisse. || **Kaó.** Graisser, humecter, féconder.

腗 **P'i.** Estomac de bœuf; abondant.

膚 **Fōu.** Peau; grand, beau, distingué.

膠 **Kiaō.** Colle, glu; unir, adhérer. ‖ **Kiaò.** | | † †. Chant du coq.

膳 **Chén.** Viande cuite, mets préparé. | 夫 † **fōu.** Chef de cuisine.

膴 **Où.** Fertile, lucratif, abondant, nombreux.

膺 **Îng.** Poitrine, poitrail, ornement du poitrail d'un cheval; résister.

膾 **Kouéi.** Viande hachée.

臄 **Kiŏ.** Palais de la bouche, lèvre supérieure, langue.

蓏 **Louò.** 果 | **Kouò** †. *Bryonia.*

RACINE 131. 臣

臣 **Tch'ênn.** Sujet d'un prince, ministre d'État, grand dignitaire, officier, serviteur.

臧 **Tsāng.** Bon, honnête, heureux, habile, approuver.

臨 **Lîn.** Visiter un inférieur, veiller sur, gouverner, diriger, approcher, aider; sorte de catapulte.

RACINE 132. 自

自 **Tzéu.** Préposition qui marque le lieu d'où l'on vient, le lieu par où l'on passe, l'origine, la cause, la voie, le moyen; depuis que, parce que, puisque; soi-même, moi-même, vous-même; de soi-même, spontané, naturel, sans effort.

臭 **Tch'eóu.** Odeur.

皋 **Kaō.** Appeler. | 陶 † **iaô.** Nom de l'un des ministres de Chouenn.

RACINE 133. 至

至 **Tchéu.** Aller à, arriver.

致 **Tchéu.** Transmettre, faire venir, attirer, exciter, provoquer.

臺 **T'âi.** Tour; jonc.

臻 **Tchēnn.** Aller à, arriver.

RACINE 134. 臼

舂 **Chōung.** Écorcer le riz ou le millet dans un mortier.

舄 **Sĭ.** Soulier monté sur une semelle de bois; grand, vaste.

舅 **Kióu.** Frère de notre mère; nom que l'empereur donne à ceux de ses parents qui portent un nom de famille différent du sien.

與 **Iù.** Ensemble, avec, et, s'unir, union, aider; donner, accorder, permettre, à, en faveur de, au détriment de; donner son assentiment. ‖ **Iû.** Particule. | | † †. Végétation prospère.

興 **Hīng.** Se lever, sortir du lit; prendre les armes; commencer, exciter, émouvoir; élever, élever à une charge, parvenir à un rang élevé; prospère, florissant, en vogue, en vigueur, rendre prospère. ‖ **Híng.** Ardent; comparaison, allégorie.

舉 **Kiù.** Lever, soulever, s'élever, commencer; exalter, honorer.

舊 **Kióu.** Vieux, ancien, ancien ami, ancien ministre.

RACINE 135. 舌

舌 **Chĕ.** Langue.

舍 **Ché.** Demeure, habitation, maison, demeurer, habiter; mettre

67

de côté, rejeter, éloigner, destituer; décocher. ‖ **Chĕ.** Cesser, s'arrêter. ‖ 捨. Quitter, renoncer à.

舒 **Chōu.** Étendre; relâcher, se reposer, à l'aise, lentement.

RACINE 136. 舛

舜 **Chouénn.** *Hibiscus*; nom d'un ancien empereur, successeur de Iao (2255-2205).

舝 **Hiă.** Armatures de fer fixées aux extrémités de l'essieu d'une voiture pour retenir les roues.

舞 **Où.** Représentation mimique accompagnée de chant; exprimer une pensée ou un sentiment par les mouvements du corps.

RACINE 137. 舟

舟 **Tcheōu.** Barque, navire; ceinture, porter un objet à la ceinture.

般 **Pān.** Manière, sorte. ‖ **P'àn.** 盤. Aller çà et là, s'amuser.

RACINE 138. 艮

良 **Leâng.** Bon, habile, sincère. 丨人丅 jênn. Homme de bien, mari.

艱 **Kiēn.** Difficile, difficulté, pénible, peine, souffrance.

RACINE 139. 色

色 **Chĕ.** Couleur, apparence, air du visage, manière d'être.

RACINE 140. 艸

艽 **K'iòu.** Plaine inculte à l'extrémité d'un État.

艾 **Ngái.** Armoise, absinthe; nourrir, entretenir; fin, terme, atteindre le terme. ‖ **Í.** Couper l'herbe, moissonner; régler, réformer.

芄 **Houân.** Végétation luxuriante. 丨蘭丅 lân. Jonc.

芋 **Hiū.** Grand, honorable, honorer.

芑 **K'ì, K'í.** Millet ou sorgho blanc.

芒 **Mâng.** 丨丨丅丅. Vaste.

芟 **Chān.** Couper l'herbe.

芬 **Fēnn.** Odoriférant.

芣 **Feôu.** 丨苢丅 i. Plantain.

芸 **Iún.** Couleur foncée.

芮 **Jouéi.** Ancienne principauté, à présent 丨城縣丅 tch'êng hién dans le 山西 Chān sī. ‖ 汭. Nom de rivière. V. page 363.

芹 **K'în.** Cresson.

芩 **K'în.** Nom de plante. V. p. 175.

芻 **Tch'ōu.** Herbe pour le chauffage, foin.

芼 **Mouŏ.** Faire cuire et servir un mets.

芾 **Féi.** Feuillage touffu. ‖ **Fŏu.** Genouillères.

(苡 (苢 **Ì.** Plantain.

苑 **Iùn.** Beau, élégant. ‖ **Iún.** Angoisse, chagrin.

苓 **Lîng.** Réglisse.

苟 **Keòu.** Peu important, à la légère, si seulement.

苦 **K'òu.** Laiteron; amer, amertume, souffrance.

茀 **Fŏu.** Arranger, débarrasser; bonheur; toit d'une voiture. 丨丨丅丅. Énergique.

詩經

英 **Ing.** Fleur; ornement fixé à l'extrémité d'une lance ou cousu sur une tunique; éclat d'une pierre précieuse, brillant.

若 **Jŏ.** Si, s'il s'agit de, quant à, conforme, semblable, agréable, convenable.

茅 **Maô.** Herbes, chiendent.

茆 **Maò.** Plantain.

茂 **Meóu.** Végétation luxuriante; florissant, vigoureux, abondant, excellent.

苗 **Miaô.** Moisson en herbe; chasse faite en été.

苞 **Paō.** Tronc d'arbre; touffu, touffe d'herbes, massif d'arbres. || **Peōu.** Pied d'une montagne. || **Peòu.** Germe prêt à sortir, germer.

苾 **Pĭ.** Odoriférant.

苹 **P'îng.** Armoise.

茇 **Pouŏ.** Hutte faite ou couverte d'herbe, demeurer dans une hutte.

茁 **Tchă.** Jeune pousse.

苴 **Ts'iū.** Chanvre femelle. || **Tch'à.** Herbe morte flottant sur l'eau.

苕 **T'iaô.** Pois, vesce.

茵 **Īn.** Natte double ou peau de tigre étendue dans une voiture.

茷 **Péi.** | | ✝ ✝. Étendard agité par le vent.

荇 **Hìng.** Nom d'une plante aquatique comestible. V. page 5.

荏 **Jènn.** Haricot; mou, souple, flexible.

荑 **T'î.** Jeune pousse.

茨 **Ts'êu.** Herbes et arbustes à épines, chardon, Herse ou Croix de Malte.

荒 **Houāng.** Terre couverte de mauvaises herbes; défricher; inutile, oisif, perdre le temps; couvrir; détruire.

茲 **Tzēu.** Ce, ceci, cela, ce lieu, ce temps.

茹 **Jòu.** Manger, recevoir, accepter. || **Jóu.** Considérer, délibérer.

荊 **Kīng.** Nom de différents arbustes épineux; nom de l'une des neuf provinces de 禹 **Iù**, à présent comprise dans le Hou kouang.

荍 **K'iaô.** Herbe ou arbuste qui ressemble à la mauve.

草 **Ts'aò.** Nom générique des plantes herbacées. | | ✝ ✝. Triste.

荷 **Hô.** Nénufar.

莊 **Tchouāng.** Tenue irréprochable.

莘 **Chēnn.** Ancienne principauté. V. page 324.

莞 **Houàn.** Natte de jonc.

莠 **Iòu.** Mauvaise herbe qui ressemble au millet, nuisible, injurieux.

荼 **T'ôu.** Laiteron; amer, amertume, poison.

莪 **Ngô.** Armoise.

莫 **Mouŏ.** Ne pas, nul, rien; établir, méditer, délibérer. | | ✝ ✝. Feuillage touffu. || 瘼. Dépérir. || **Móu.** 暮. Soleil couchant, soir, fin. || **Mĕ.** | | ✝ ✝. Calme, paisible, respectueux.

莎 **Chā.** | 雞 ✝ **kī.** Grillon.

菜 **Ts'ái.** Légume.

華 **Houâ.** Fleurs.

萑 **Houân.** Jonc ou roseau déjà grand et dur.

菲 **Fèi.** Navet, rave.

菹 **Tsiū.** Légume conservé dans le sel.

菽 **Chŏu.** Pois, haricot, et autres légumes semblables.

萋 **Ts'ī.** Élégant, respectueux. | | † †. Feuillage touffu, épais nuages.

萃 **Tsouéi.** Plantes nombreuses; réunion, foule.

萊 **Lâi.** Nom d'une plante comestible.

萏 **T'àn.** 菡 | **Hàn** †. Bouton de fleur.

萎 **Wēi.** Se flétrir, dépérir.

菀 **Iuèn.** Végétation luxuriante.

菁 **Ts'īng.** | | † †. Feuillage touffu, végétation prospère.

菅 **Kiēn, Kouān.** Fibres d'une plante textile nommée 白華 **pĕ houâ.**

菑 **Tchēu.** Terre nouvellement défrichée. || **Tchéu.** Arbre mort qui est encore debout. || **Tsāi.** 災. Calamité.

荓 **P'îng.** Faire en sorte que, déterminer, exciter.

菡 **Hàn.** | 萏 † **t'àn.** Bouton de fleur.

菫 **Kìn.** Violette.

菶 **Pòung.** | | † †. Végétation luxuriante.

菼 **T'àn.** Jonc, roseau.

萇 **Tch'âng.** | 楚 † **tch'òu.** Carambolier.

萬 **Wán.** Dix mille, tous; représentation mimique. V. page 44.

葚 **Chénn.** Mûre.

落 **Lŏ.** Descendre, tomber, chute des feuilles.

葉 **Iĕ.** Feuille; une génération.

著 **Tchóu.** Espace compris entre la porte d'une habitation et la cloison qui est à l'entrée de la cour.

葽 **Iaō.** Nom de plante, polygala.

葍 **Fŏu.** Nom d'une plante dont la racine est comestible.

葑 **Fōung.** Navet.

葛 **Kŏ.** Nom d'une plante textile, *dolic*. V. page 6.

葦 **Wèi.** Roseau, jonc; nacelle.

葭 **Kiā.** Roseau qui n'a pas encore fleuri.

葵 **K'ouêi.** Nom de différentes plantes qui ressemblent à la mauve. || 揆. Mesurer, déterminer, examiner.

葱 **Ts'ōung.** Oignon; vert comme l'oignon.

蓁 **Tchēnn.** | | † †. Végétation florissante.

蓋 **Kái.** Couvrir; en effet, car.

蓍 **Chēu.** *Achillea ptarmica*. Les devins consultaient les sorts au moyen de soixante-quatre brins d'achillée.

蒿 **Haō.** Armoise.

蒹 **Kiēn.** Roseau grand et mince.

蓄 **Tch'ŏu.** Amasser, provision.

詩經

蒙 **Moûng.** Couvrir, voiler, recevoir. | 伐 + fă. Bouclier orné de plumes de diverses couleurs. || **Màng.** | 戎 + jôung. Fourrure usée.

蓆 **Sĭ.** Natte; ample.

蓑 **Souō.** Manteau de jonc contre la pluie.

蒲 **P'ôu.** Jonc, *typha;* osier.

蒸 **Tchēng.** Chènevotte; menu bois pour le chauffage.

蒼 **Ts'āng.** Vert, azuré, ciel.

蔦 **Gniaò.** Nom d'une plante rampante ou grimpante.

蓼 **Leaò.** Nom d'une plante amère qui est comestible; amertume, souffrance. || **Lŏu.** Haut.

蔞 **Leôu.** Armoise.

蔑 **Miĕ.** Périr, anéantir.

蓺 **Í.** Semer, planter.

蓬 **P'ôung.** Espèce d'armoise dont les feuilles sont mises en désordre et les graines dispersées par le vent. | | + +. Feuillage touffu.

蔌 **Sŏu.** Nom générique des plantes culinaires. | | + +. Vil, méprisable.

蓫 **Tchŏu.** Oseille, patience.

蓷 **T'ouēi.** Agripaume.

蔓 **Wán.** Ramper, s'étendre.

蔚 **Wéi.** *Leonurus;* végétation luxuriante.

蔽 **Pí.** Ombrager, couvrir, cacher, contenir. || **Pĭ.** Touffu.

蕘 **Jaô.** Herbe ou menu bois pour le chauffage.

蕃 **Fân.** Végétation luxuriante. || 藩. Haie, défense.

蕡 **Fênn.** Fruits nombreux.

蕑 **Kiēn.** Nom d'une plante odorante.

蕩 **Táng, T'àng.** Grand, immense, uni.

蕭 **Siaō.** Armoise. | | + +. Silence.

蕨 **Kiuĕ.** Fougère.

薦 **Tsién.** Offrir, présenter, proposer, recommander; de nouveau, réitérer.

薨 **Hōung.** Mort d'un prince. | | + +. Bourdonnement, bruit sourd.

薪 **Sīn.** Herbe ou bois pour le chauffage.

薁 **Iŭ.** Vigne sauvage, raisin.

薖 **K'ouō.** Grand, large, libéral.

薇 **Wêi.** Nom d'une plante comestible.

薈 **Wéi.** Luxuriant.

薅 **Haō.** Enlever les mauvaises herbes.

薄 **Pouŏ.** Mince, peu; particule initiale.

薿 **Ì.** | | + +. Luxuriant.

藍 **Lân.** Plantes qui donnent l'indigo.

藏 **Ts'âng.** Mettre en lieu sûr, garder, cacher, renfermer. || **Tsáng.** Ce que l'on tient serré ou caché.

藇 **Siú.** Excellent.

藐 **Miaò.** Petit, peu considérable, peu important. || **Mouǒ.** | | ††. Mystérieux; mépriser.

藎 **Tsín.** Loyal, dévoué.

薺 **Tsí.** Bourse-à-pasteur.

藩 **Fàn.** Haie, défense.

藥 **Iǒ.** Remède, remédier.

藟 **Lèi.** Nom d'une plante grimpante.

藘 **Liû.** 茹 | **Jôu** †. Garance.

藪 **Seòu.** Marais, étang.

藚 **Siǔ.** Plantain d'eau.

藿 **Houǒ.** Feuille de haricot.

蘊 **Iùn.** Accumuler, réunir; grand chagrin.

藹 **Ngái.** Massif d'arbres, nombreux.

蘋 **P'în.** Lentille sauvage.

蘀 **T'ouǒ.** Feuilles qui tombent des arbres.

藻 **Tsaò.** Algues et autres plantes semblables.

蘇 **Sōu.** Revivre. 扶 | **Fôu** †. Nom d'arbuste.

蘖 **Iě.** Rejet, surgeon, rejeton.

蘭 **Lân.** 芄 | **Houân** †. Jonc, roseau.

蘩 **Fân.** Armoise.

蘞 **Lièn.** Convolvulus.

蘿 **Louô.** 女 | **Gniù** †. Nom d'une plante grimpante.

RACINE 141. 虍

虎 **Hòu.** Tigre, brave, courageux.

虐 **Iǒ.** Cruel, perturbateur, opprimer, vexer.

虓 **Hiaō.** Cri du tigre.

虔 **K'iên.** Respecter, diviser.

處 **Tch'òu.** Habiter, demeurer, rester, se reposer, paisible, tranquille, constant. || **Tch'óu.** Lieu, demeure.

虛 **Hiū.** Vide, inutile, oisif, négligent, ruines.

虜 **Lòu.** Prisonnier de guerre.

虞 **Iû.** Prévoir, examiner, considérer, hésiter, perplexe; ancienne principauté, à présent 平陸 **P'ing lǒu** dans le 山西 **Chān sī**. 騶 | **Tcheōu** †. Nom d'un animal fabuleux remarquable par sa douceur.

號 **Haò.** Crier, appeler.

虡 **Kiú.** Les deux montants de la suspension d'une cloche ou d'un tambour. V. page 342.

虧 **K'ouēi.** Faire défaut, décroître.

RACINE 142. 虫

虹 **Hôung, Hiâng.** Tromper.

虺 **Houèi.** Serpent. || **Houēi.** Malade, ne pouvoir monter. | | ††. Bruit du tonnerre.

蚩 **Tch'ēu.** | | ††. Dépourvu d'intelligence.

蛇 **Chê.** Serpent. || **Î, T'ouô.** 委 | **Wēi** †. Ramper, prendre un détour, content.

詩經

蛉 **Lìng.** 螟 | **Mîng** 十. Nom d'insecte.

蛸 **Chaō.** 蠨 | **Siaō** 十. Petite araignée.

蜉 **Feôu.** | 蝣 十 **iôu.** Éphémère.

蜂 **Fōung.** Guêpe, abeille.

蜎 **Iuēn.** Marche d'un insecte.

蛾 **Ngô.** Papillon du ver à soie.

蜴 **Ĭ.** Lézard.

蜮 **Iŭ.** Tortue dont le souffle est pernicieux.

蜾 **Kouò.** | 蠃 十 **louò.** Guêpe; père adoptif.

蝃 **Tí.** | 蝀 十 **tōung.** Arc-en-ciel.

蝀 **Tōung.** 蝃 | **Tí** 十. Arc-en-ciel.

蜩 **T'iaô.** Cigale, grillon.

蝣 **Iôu.** 蜉 | **Feôu** 十. Éphémère.

蝱 **Mêng.** Cousin; nom d'une plante employée contre la tristesse.

蝤 **Ts'iôu.** | 蠐 十 **ts'î.** Ver qui vit dans le bois.

融 **Iôung.** Brillant.

螟 **Mîng.** Insecte qui vit dans la tige des céréales.

螗 **T'âng.** Cigale.

螣 **T'ĕ.** Insecte qui ronge les feuilles des céréales.

螓 **Ts'în.** Petite cigale dont la tête est grosse et carrée.

螫 **Chĕu.** Piqûre d'un insecte.

蟀 **Chouĕ.** 蟋 | **Sĭ** 十. Grillon.

蟋 **Sĭ.** | 蟀 十 **chouĕ.** Grillon.

蟊 **Meôu.** Insecte qui ronge les racines des céréales.

蟄 **Tchĕu.** | | 十 十. Nombreux, d'accord.

螽 **Tchōung.** Sauterelle, grillon.

蟲 **Tch'ôung.** Nom générique des reptiles et des insectes. | | 十 十. Grande chaleur.

蠋 **Chŏu.** Chenille.

蠅 **Îng.** Mouche.

蠃 **Louò.** 蜾 | **Kouò.** 十. Guêpe.

蠆 **Tch'ái.** Scorpion.

蠐 **Ts'î.** 蝤 | **Ts'iôu** 十. Ver qui vit dans le bois.

蠢 **Tch'ouènn.** Se mouvoir, remuer, prendre les armes.

蠨 **Siaō.** Petite araignée.

蠲 **Kiuēn.** Pur, purifier.

蠶 **Ts'ân.** Ver à soie, nourrir des vers à soie.

蠻 **Mân.** Tribus étrangères du midi.

RACINE 143. 血

血 **Hiuĕ.** Sang.

衆 **Tchóung.** Nombreux, tous, foule.

RACINE 144. 行

行 **Hîng.** Marcher, voyager, partir, suivre un chemin, agir, exécuter,

accomplir; chemin, voie; bientôt. || **Híng.** Action || **Hàng.** Rangée, file, société. || **Háng.** | | † †. Ferme, martial, inflexible.

衍 **Ièn.** Abondant; licencieux.

衎 **K'án.** Fêter, féliciter, récompenser.

衝 **Tch'ōung.** Machine de guerre employée pour l'attaque des places fortes.

衛 **Wéi.** Garder; ancienne principauté dont la capitale était la ville actuelle de 濬縣 **Siún hién** dans le Ho nan. V. page 3.

衡 **Hêng.** Joug; fléau de balance. || **Hôung.** 橫. Traverse, transversal.

RACINE 145. 衣

衣 **Ī.** Tunique courte, vêtement. || **Í.** Vêtir, mettre un vêtement.

衿 **Kīn.** Collet.

衾 **K'īn.** Couverture de lit.

袞 **Kouènn.** Tunique portée par l'empereur et les princes.

袢 **Fàn.** Ceinture, robe d'été.

袪 **K'iū.** Parement d'une manche d'habit.

袍 **P'aô.** Longue tunique doublée ou ouatée. || **P'eōu.** 同 | **T'ôung** †. Amis intimes.

被 **Péi.** Couvrir, gratifier; faux cheveux.

袺 **Kiĕ.** Mettre ou porter un objet dans le pan de son vêtement retroussé.

裒 **P'eōu.** Réunir, assembler.

裕 **Iú.** Abondant.

裘 **K'iôu.** Tunique garnie de fourrure.

裏 **Lì.** Doublure.

補 **Pòu.** Réparer, ajouter ce qui manque, suppléer.

裳 **Châng.** Partie de l'habillement qui couvrait le corps depuis les reins jusqu'au-dessous des genoux. 帷 | **Wêi** †. Rideaux d'une voiture de femme. | | † †. Beau.

裹 **Kouò.** Envelopper.

裼 **Sĭ.** Mettre à nu les bras, les épaules ou la poitrine. || **T'í.** Langes.

裯 **Tch'eôu.** Couverture de lit.

褐 **Hŏ.** Tissu de poil.

褊 **Pièn.** Étroit, petit.

褎 **Sióu.** Manche. || **Ióu.** Vêtement brillant, belle moisson.

褰 **K'iēn.** Tenir ses vêtements relevés pour passer l'eau.

褧 **K'iòung.** Tunique sans doublure.

褒 **Paō.** Nom de principauté. | 姒 † **Séu.** Seu de Pao, femme de 幽王 **Iōu wâng.**

襄 **Siāng.** Atteler; arracher, expulser; pièce de toile.

襋 **Kĭ.** Collet d'habit.

襜 **Tch'ēn.** Partie antérieure d'une tunique.

襢 **Tán.** Se dénuder les bras, les épaules ou la poitrine.

襭 **Hiĕ.** Mettre ou tenir un objet dans le pan de son vêtement.

襮 **Pouŏ, Pŏu.** Collet brodé.

RACINE 146. 襾

西 **Sī.** Occident, ouest.

要 **Iaō.** Rencontrer; ceinture d'un vêtement, coudre une ceinture à un vêtement.

覃 **T'àn.** Arriver à, s'étendre. || **Ièn.** Aigu.

覆 **Fŏu.** Tourner un objet dans un sens différent de celui dans lequel il était, retourner, renverser, bouleverser; au contraire; réitérer. || **Fóu.** Couvrir, protéger.

RACINE 147. 見

見 **Kién.** Voir, visiter. || **Hién.** Paraître devant.

視 **Chéu.** Regarder, voir.

親 **Ts'īn.** Soi-même; mère.

覯 **Keóu.** Rencontrer, voir.

覲 **Kín.** Faire visite, avoir une audience de l'empereur.

覺 **Kiŏ.** Grand, élevé, excellent. || **Kiaó.** Éveiller.

觀 **Kouān.** Regarder de loin, observer, considérer, examiner.

RACINE 148. 角

角 **Kiŏ.** Corne.

解 **Hiái.** Se relâcher, négligent, paresseux.

觥 **Kōung.** Grande coupe faite d'une corne de rhinocéros ou en forme de corne.

觩 **K'iôu.** Recourbé en forme de corne; arc fortement tendu.

觱 **Pĭ.** | 發 ✝ **féi.** Bruit du vent. | 沸 ✝ **fòu.** Sortir de source.

觼 **Kiuĕ.** Boucle, ardillon d'une boucle.

觿 **Hī, Tchouēi.** Pointe de corne ou d'ivoire qu'on portait suspendue à la ceinture pour défaire les nœuds.

RACINE 149. 言

言 **Iên.** Dire, parler, parole; particule; nom d'une ville située dans le Chouenn te fou (Tcheu lì). V. page 46. | | ✝ ✝. Haut.

訏 **Hiū.** Grand, vaste. || **Hōu.** Crier fort.

訓 **Hiún.** Enseigner, enseignement.

訌 **Hôung.** Ronger, ruiner, troubler.

訊 **Sín, Siún.** Interroger judiciairement, donner un avis.

設 **Chĕ.** Placer, disposer, déployer.

訪 **Fàng.** Interroger, consulter.

訩 **Hiōung.** Plaider; désordre, tumulte.

許 **Hiù.** Ancienne principauté, à présent | 州 ✝ **tcheōu** dans le Ho nan. || **Hòu.** | | ✝ ✝. Bruit de la hache.

訧 **Iôu.** Erreur, faute.

訟 **Sóung.** Procès, plaider.

訛 **Wô, Ngô.** Dire une fausseté; changer, se mouvoir.

詒 **Ì.** Causer, déterminer, attirer, transmettre.

詈 **Lí.** Parler mal de, dénigrer.

詛 **Tchòu.** Prononcer une imprécation.

訿 **Tzēu.** Parler mal de quelqu'un.

詵 **Chēnn.** | | † †. Multitude.

詩 **Chēu.** Vers, pièce de vers.

試 **Chéu.** Essayer, exercer, user, employer.

話 **Houá.** Parole, discours.

詭 **Kouèi.** Trompeur, injuste, méchant.

詳 **Siâng.** Faire un récit détaillé, raconter.

詢 **Siūn.** Consulter, délibérer.

詹 **Tchēn.** Regarder en haut. || **Tān.** Voir.

誓 **Chèu.** Serment, déclaration solennelle.

誘 **Iòu.** Diriger, exhorter, enseigner, séduire.

語 **Iù.** Converser, conversation, parole.

誠 **Tch'êng.** Vrai, vraiment.

誕 **Tán.** Vaste, étendre, propager; particule initiale.

誦 **Ióung.** Chanter, réciter en chantant.

誨 **Houéi.** Enseigner, instruire.

說 **Chouŏ.** Dire, parler, expliquer. || **Chouéi.** Donner des conseils; faire halte. || **Iuĕ.** 悅. Se réjouir.

論 **Liûn.** Parler, raconter, expliquer; ordre, harmonie.

誰 **Chouèi.** Qui? celui qui; autrefois.

諗 **Chènn.** Annoncer, avertir.

諒 **Leáng.** Vrai, sincère, avoir confiance.

諄 **Tchouēnn.** Expliquer longuement ou assidûment.

談 **T'ân.** Converser.

調 **T'iaô.** Convenir, conforme, proportionné.

諏 **Tsiū.** Interroger, consulter.

諶 **Chênn.** Avoir confiance, digne de confiance.

諸 **Tchōu.** Plusieurs, nombreux, tous; particule dubitative ou interrogative, particule euphonique.

諼 **Hiuēn.** Oublier. | 草 † ts'aò. Hémérocalle.

諾 **Nŏ.** Dire oui; réponse affirmative.

謀 **Meôu.** Former un projet, combiner un plan, délibérer, projet, plan.

謂 **Wéi.** Adresser la parole, parler de, informer, nommer, signifier; se dire à soi-même, penser, juger, conjecturer.

諫 **Kién.** Adresser des remontrances.

謠 **Iaô.** Chanter.

謔 **Hiŏ.** Se moquer, plaisanter.

謝 **Sié.** Ancienne principauté, à présent 信 陽 縣 Sin iâng hién dans le Ho nan. V. page 309.

謨 **Môu.** Former un projet, combiner un plan, délibérer, projet, plan.

謹 **Kìn.** Attentif, soigneux, circonspect, prendre soin de, prendre garde à.

譖 **Tchénn.** Accuser, calomnier.

識 **Chĕu.** Connaître, savoir, comprendre, connaissances, expérience. || **Tchéu.** Se graver dans la mémoire.

譙 **Ts'iaò.** 丨丨 ✝ ✝. Gâté, flétri.

譚 **T'àn.** Ancienne principauté, à présent 歴 城 **Lî tch'êng** dans le 山 東 **Chān tōung.** Voy. page 66.

譬 **Pí, P'í.** Similitude, assimiler, comparer.

議 **Í.** Examiner, délibérer, décider.

譽 **Iú.** Éloge, renom, louer, vanter. || **Iû.** Vanter; se réjouir.

譴 **K'ién.** Adresser des reproches.

讁 **Tchĕ.** Blâmer, adresser des reproches.

讀 **Tŏu.** Lire, étudier.

讎 **Tch'eôu.** Ennemi, inimitié; répondre, payer de retour.

讒 **Tch'ân.** Dénigrer, calomnier.

讓 **Jáng.** Céder, modeste, se mettre au-dessous d'un autre.

RACINE 150. 谷

谷 **Kŏu.** Vallée; fosse, précipice. 丨 風 ✝ **fōung.** Vent d'est.

RACINE 151. 豆

豆 **Teóu.** Vase de bois dans lequel on offrait de la viande cuite aux esprits; pois, haricot, fève.

豈 **K'ì.** Comment? pourquoi? || **K'ài.** 愷. Joyeux, aimable.

登 **Tēng.** Vase de terre dans lequel on offrait de la viande aux esprits.

豐 **Fōung.** Abondant, luxuriant; nom de la capitale des 周 **Tcheōu** dans le 陝 西 **Chèn sī.** V. page. 2 et 339.

豔 **Ién.** Beau.

RACINE 152. 豕

豕 **Chèu.** Cochon.

豝 **Pā.** Femelle du cochon, sanglier de deux ans.

象 **Siáng.** Éléphant, ivoire; représenter, peindre.

豜 **Kiēn.** Cochon de trois ans.

豫 **Iú.** Content, joyeux.

豳 **Pīn.** Ancienne principauté, à présent 邠 州 **Pīn tcheōu** dans le 陝 西 **Chèn sī.** Voy. page 4.

豵 **Tsōung.** Cochon d'un an.

RACINE 153. 豸

豹 **Paó.** Léopard, panthère.

豺 **Tch'âi.** Loup.

貊 **Mĕ.** Barbares du nord, étrangers; silencieux.

貉 **Hŏ.** Marmotte.

貆 **Houān.** Blaireau.

貍 **Lî.** Chat sauvage.

貓 **Maò.** Chat sauvage.

貔 **P'î.** Ours blanc ou autre animal semblable.

RACINE 154. 貝

貝 **Péi.** Beau coquillage marin.

負 **Fóu.** Porter un fardeau sur les épaules.

貧 **P'în.** Pauvre, pauvreté.

貪 **T'ān.** Convoiter, désirer, cupide.

貫 **Kouán.** Enfiler, passer à travers, avoir affaire à, s'accoutumer à.

貳 **Eúl.** Deux, double, changeant, perplexe.

貶 **Pièn.** Déprimer, abaisser, dégrader.

貺 **Houáng.** Donner, gratifier.

貽 **Î.** Donner, transmettre, don.

貿 **Meóu.** Échanger des marchandises, acheter.

賀 **Houó.** Féliciter.

賁 **Pí.** Bien orné, élégant. || **Fênn.** Grand.

賄 **Houèi.** Objet de quelque valeur.

賈 **Kòu.** Marchand à demeure fixe.

賂 **Lóu.** Donner, don.

資 **Tzēu.** Ressource pour vivre, secours, moyen.

賊 **Tsĕ.** Nuire gravement, voleur, assassin, insecte qui ronge les nœuds de la tige des céréales.

賓 **Pīn.** Celui qui donne ou reçoit l'hospitalité, hôte, visiteur, convive.

賚 **Lái.** Donner, don.

賦 **Fóu.** Répandre, publier; description poétique.

賢 **Hièn.** Homme d'un talent et d'une vertu remarquables.

質 **Tchĕu.** Matière, substance; base, constituer, affermir; simple, bon, honnête.

贅 **Tchouéi.** Pendant, agité, en péril; connexion, liaison, suite.

贈 **Tséng.** Donner, don.

贏 **Îng.** Restant.

贖 **Chŏu.** Racheter.

RACINE 155. 赤

赤 **Tch'ĕu.** Rouge, incarnat.

赫 **Hĕ.** Couleur du feu, enflammé de colère, ardent, terrible, brillant, majestueux.

赭 **Tchè.** Ocre rouge, couleur rouge.

赬 **Tch'ēng.** Rouge.

RACINE 156. 走

走 **Tseòu.** Marcher vite, courir.

赳 **Kiòu.** | | ┼ ┼. Brave, martial.

起 **K'ì.** Se lever.

越 **Iuĕ.** Aller au-delà, excéder, transgresser; particule.

趙 **Tchaó, T'iaò.** Creuser.

趣 **Ts'iú.** Marcher vite, faire attention. || **Ts'eóu.** | 馬 ┼ mà. Officier chargé du soin des chevaux.

趨 **Ts'iū.** Marcher vite.

趯 **Iŏ.** Sauter.

詩經

RACINE 157. 足

足 **Tsiŭ.** Pied, jambe; suffire.

跂 **K'î.** Se dresser sur la pointe des pieds.

趾 **Tchèu.** Pied.

距 **Kiú.** Résister, s'opposer.

跋 **Pouŏ.** Marcher à travers les herbes, fouler du pied.

路 **Lóu.** Chemin, route; grand, grande voiture, grand tambour.

踊 **Iòung.** Sauter.

踐 **Tsién.** Marcher sur; ordre, ranger en ordre.

踟 **Tch'èu.** | 躕 † tch'ôu. Embarrassé, hésitant.

踖 **Ts'ĭ.** | | † †. Avec respect.

踧 **Tĭ.** | | † †. Chemin uni.

踰 **Iû.** Sauter ou passer par-dessus.

蹂 **Jeòu.** Marcher sur.

踽 **Kiù.** | | † †. Seul, sans secours.

蹈 **Taó.** Marcher sur; redoutable, changeant.

蹌 **Ts'iāng.** Démarche respectueuse et pleine de dignité.

蹐 **Tsĭ.** Marcher à petits pas.

蹙 **Tsŏu.** Étroit, gêné, pauvre, malheureux, urgent.

蹢 **Tĭ.** Pied de quadrupède.

蹟 **Tsĭ.** Trace du pied.

蹲 **Ts'iûn.** | | † †. Danse guerrière.

蹶 **Kouéi.** Mouvoir. | | † †. Attentif.

蹻 **Kiaò.** Robuste, brave, courageux. || **Kiŏ.** Orgueilleux.

躋 **Tsī.** Monter, avancer.

躍 **Iŏ.** Sauter. || **T'ĭ.** | | † †. Sauter vite.

躕 **Tch'ôu.** Embarrassé, hésiter.

RACINE 158. 身

身 **Chēnn.** Corps, soi-même, en personne, la personne. 有 | Iòu †. Être enceinte.

躬 **Kōung.** Soi-même, en personne.

RACINE 159. 車

車 **Kiū.** Voiture.

軌 **Kouèi.** Essieu; la distance qui sépare les deux roues d'une voiture.

軍 **Kiūn.** Armée. 中 | Tchōung †. Général d'armée.

軒 **Hiēn.** Voiture dont la partie antérieure est plus légère et plus élevée que la partie postérieure. | 輊 † tchéu. Haut ou bas.

軜 **Nă.** Les rênes intérieures des deux chevaux extérieurs dans un attelage de quatre de front. Voyez page 136.

軝 **K'î.** L'extrémité du moyeu d'une roue.

軷 **Pă, Pouŏ.** Sacrifice offert au dieu des chemins.

軸 **Tchŏu.** Essieu; ensouple ou rouleau du métier à tisser; nom d'un endroit compris dans la principauté de 衛 Wéi.

較 **Kiŏ.** 重 | **Tch'ôung** ┼. Angles antérieurs de la caisse d'une voiture.

輈 **Tcheōu.** Timon d'une voiture.

載 **Tsái.** Charge d'une voiture ou d'une barque, transporter en voiture ou en barque, charger, mettre dans, contenir, soutenir, porter, emplir; action, travail, ouvrage, faire, exécuter, commencer, continuer; mais, alors, et, particule. || **Tsài.** Année. || **Tái.** 戴. Porter un objet sur la tête.

輊 **Tchéu.** Voiture dont la partie antérieure est plus lourde et plus basse que la partie postérieure.

輔 **Fòu.** Pièces destinées à renforcer les roues d'une voiture, aide, aider.

輦 **Lièn.** Voiture traînée par des hommes.

輪 **Liûn.** Roue.

輯 **Tsĭ.** Réunir, concorde, harmonie, doux, condescendant.

輶 **Iôu.** Léger.

輸 **Chōu.** Tomber, renverser.

輻 **Fŏu.** Rais de roue.

輾 **Tchèn.** | 轉 ┼ **tchouèn.** Faire un demi-tour sur soi-même, tourner.

輿 **Iû.** Le plancher d'une voiture. 權 | **K'iuên** ┼. Commencement.

轂 **Kŏu.** Moyeu, roue.

轉 **Tchouèn.** Tourner.

轡 **Pí.** Rênes.

RACINE 160. 辛

辛 **Sīn.** Saveur âcre; pénible, peine.

辜 **Kōu.** Faute, crime.

辟 **Pĭ.** Roi, empereur, chef d'un État; loi, règle, régler, prendre soin de. || **P'ĭ.** Mauvais, dépravé, injuste, faux, dissimulé. || 闢. Ouvrir un passage; labourer; étendre. || 擗. Se frapper la poitrine. || **Pí.** 避. Éviter, fuir.

辭 **Sêu.** Paroles, discours.

RACINE 161. 辰

辰 **Chênn, Tch'ênn.** Astre, constellation; heure, jour, temps convenable, jour heureux.

辱 **Jŏu.** Honte, déshonneur, affront, faire honte, outrager, déshonorer.

農 **Nôung.** Culture des champs, laboureur.

RACINE 162. 辵

迄 **Hĭ.** Arriver, jusqu'à, terme, enfin.

迋 **Wáng.** Tromper.

近 **Kín.** Proche, s'approcher, attirer à soi.

迎 **Ín.** Aller chercher, aller inviter.

述 **Chŏu.** Être d'accord, convenir.

迨 **Tái.** Arriver, quand vient le temps où, tant que.

迪 **Tĭ.** Avancer.

迭 **Tiĕ.** Alterner, tour à tour.

迷 **Mì.** Errer, se tromper.

逅 **Heóu.** Rencontrer.

逆 **Ĭ.** Marcher contre, se révolter.

迺 **Nài.** 乃. Et, aussi ; particule.

送 **Sóung.** Escorter, accompagner.

追 **Tchouēi.** Aller après quelqu'un qui s'en va ; revenir sur le passé.

逃 **T'aô.** Fuir, se cacher.

退 **T'ouéi.** Revenir sur ses pas, se retirer.

逝 **Chéu.** Aller à, marcher, s'en aller, passer, s'écouler ; particule initiale.

逢 **Fôung.** Rencontrer. || **P'ôung.** | | † †. Son du tambour.

逑 **K'iôu.** Réunir, lieu de réunion; compagnon, époux.

連 **Lièn.** Continu, sans interruption.

速 **Sŏu.** Inviter, appeler, presser.

逍 **Siaō.** | 遙 † iaô. Aller et venir, se promener, s'amuser.

造 **Tsaó.** Inventer, faire, exécuter. || **Ts'aó.** Aller à, faire des progrès.

逸 **Ĭ.** Repos, loisir, vie commode, se retirer des affaires.

逵 **K'ouêi, K'iôu.** Intersection de plusieurs chemins, carrefour.

逮 **Tái.** Arriver, quand vient le temps où, tant que.

進 **Tsín.** Avancer, entrer, faire avancer.

逷 **T'ĭ.** Éloigné, écarter, repousser.

遄 **Chouân.** Prompt, vite.

遐 **Hiâ.** Éloigné. || **Hô.** 何. Quel ? comment ?

遑 **Houâng.** Repos, loisir, avoir le loisir de.

遊 **Iôu.** Se promener, aller çà et là, rechercher les amusements.

遇 **Iú.** Rencontrer, survenir.

過 **Kouó.** Aller au-delà, passer auprès. || **Kouō.** Passer par ; nom d'une vallée.

遏 **Ngŏ.** Arrêter, réprimer.

遂 **Souéi.** Se répandre, progresser, conduire à bonne fin, accomplir, continuer; négligent; ensuite.

達 **Tà.** Se faire jour, sortir de terre; réussir, établir l'ordre; agneau. || **T'ă.** Sauter, conduite légère.

道 **Taó.** Voie, route, moyen, méthode, dire.

遁 **Touénn.** Se retirer, se cacher, mener une vie retirée.

遒 **Ts'iôu.** Se réunir, unir solidement.

違 **Wêi.** Quitter, marcher contre, résister, éloigné.

遙 **Iaô.** 逍 | Siaô †. Aller çà et là, vivre dans la dissipation.

遠 **Iuèn.** Éloigné, étranger venu de loin. || **Iuén.** S'éloigner.

遣 **K'iēn.** Envoyer.

遡 **Sóu.** Avancer contre le courant. | 洄 † houêi. Remonter le courant. | 游 † iôu. Suivre le courant.

遭 **Tsaō.** Rencontrer.

適 **Chĕu.** Aller à, arriver; joie, contentement. || **Tĭ.** Fils de la femme légitime; présider, maître. || **Tchĕ.** Blâmer.

遲 **Tch'êu.** Marcher lentement, tarder, lent, paisible, pas à pas, tard. 倭 | **Wēi** 十. Longs détours.

遯 **Touénn.** Se retirer, se cacher.

遺 **Î.** Laisser, abandonner, omettre. || **Í.** Offrir un présent.

遹 **Iŭ.** Corrompu, dépravé. || 聿. Particule initiale.

選 **Siuèn.** Choisir, blâmer. || **Siuén.** Tourner.

遵 **Tsuēnn.** Suivre, marcher le long de

遷 **Ts'iēn.** Changer de lieu, transporter, changer; monter.

邂 **Hiái.** | 逅 十 **heóu.** Rencontrer.

還 **Houân.** Retourner à. || **Siuèn.** Retourner à, agile.

邁 **Mái.** Marcher, voyager, aller à, parcourir, passer. | | 十十. Mépriser.

邇 **Eùl.** Proche.

RACINE 163. 邑

邑 **Ĭ.** Ville, ville capitale.

邛 **K'iòung.** Colline; fatigue, souffrance, trouble.

那 **Nò.** Beaucoup; tranquille.

邦 **Pāng.** Contrée, État, principauté.

邪 **Siè.** Oblique, incliné, injuste, pervers, mauvais.

邢 **Hìng.** Ancienne principauté. V. page 66.

邰 **T'āi.** Ancienne principauté, à présent 武 功 縣 **Où kōung hién** dans le 陝 西 **Chèn sī.** V. page 2.

邶 **Péi.** Ancienne principauté située au nord de 衛 輝 府 **Wéi houēi fòu** dans le Ho nan. V. page 3.

郇 **Siūn.** Ancienne principauté située dans le 山 西 **Chān sī** actuel. V. page. 159.

郊 **Kiaō.** Zone de terrain qui s'étendait depuis les 郭 **kouó** faubourgs de la capitale jusqu'à une distance de cent 里 **li** stades; sacrifice offert au Ciel ou à la Terre dans la plaine 郊 **kiaō.**

郵 **Iôu.** Maison où les courriers s'arrêtent. || 尤. Excès, faute.

都 **Tōu.** Ville capitale; beau.

郿 **Mêi.** Lieu situé dans le 鳳 翔 府 **Fóung siâng fòu** de la province de 陝 西 **Chèn sī.** V. page 398.

鄂 **Ngŏ.** Belle apparence.

鄉 **Hiāng.** Village, pays natal. || **Hiáng.** Tourné vers.

鄘 **Iôung.** Ancienne principauté située dans la partie méridionale du 衛 輝 府 **Wéi houēi fòu** (Ho nan). V. page 3.

鄰 **Lîn.** Voisin. | | 十十. Bruit de voitures.

鄭 **Tchéng.** Ancienne principauté. V. page 3.

RACINE 164. 酉

酋 **Ts'iòu.** Finir.

酌 **Tchŏ.** Verser à boire, délibérer.

配 **P'éi.** Conforme, semblable, égal, convenable, associé, compagnon, époux.

酒 **Tsiòu.** Liqueur fermentée.

酤 **Kōu.** Acheter de la liqueur.

酢 **Tsŏ.** Se dit d'un invité qui, après avoir bu le vin offert par le maître de la maison, verse lui-même à boire à celui-ci; rendre la pareille, récompenser.

酬 **Tch'eôu.** Offrir à boire une seconde fois à un invité.

酲 **Tch'êng.** Enivré.

醉 **Tsouéi.** Avoir bu son soûl, ivre.

醢 **Hài.** Viande hachée et conservée dans le sel.

醓 **T'àn.** Viande qui a été séchée, hachée et conservée dans le sel.

醜 **Tch'eòu.** Laid, difforme, de mauvais augure; multitude, troupe, nombreux.

醴 **Lì.** Liqueur qui n'a pas fermenté, liqueur nouvelle.

醹 **Jòu.** Excellente liqueur.

醻 **Tch'eòu.** Voyez 酬.

釃 **Chèu, Sì.** Clarifier une liqueur.

RACINE 165. 釆

采 **Ts'ài.** Couleurs variées; cueillir, recueillir.

釋 **Chĕu, Ĭ.** Délier, délivrer, quitter, laisser.

RACINE 166. 里

里 **Lì.** Réunion de vingt-cinq ou de cinquante familles, village, hameau; habitation, demeure; triste; stade de 300 步 **póu.** (Le *pou* valait six 尺 **tch'ĕu,** le *tch'eu* environ vingt centimètres. Le stade était de 360 mètres).

重 **Tchóung.** Lourd, pesant. ‖. **Tch'ôung.** Double, deux fois; grain qui se sème tôt et mûrit tard.

野 **Iè.** Campagne, champêtre, qui n'est pas cultivé.

釐 **Lî.** Donner.

RACINE 167. 金

金 **Kīn.** Métal, or, doré.

釜 **Fóu.** Marmite sans pieds.

釣 **Tiaó.** Pêcher à la ligne.

鈞 **Kiūn.** Poids de trente livres. ‖ 均. Égal,...

鉞 **Iuĕ.** Hache de guerre.

鉤 **Keōu.** Crochet, agrafe.

鈴 **Lîng.** Clochette, sonnette.

鉦 **Tchēng.** Petite cloche.

銍 **Tchĕu.** Faucille.

銜 **Hiên.** Tenir un objet dans la bouche, porter, avoir un sentiment dans le cœur.

鋂 **Mêi.** Grand anneau dans lequel sont engagés deux autres plus petits.

鋈 **Oŭ.** Argenter, dorer.

鋪 **P'ōu.** Étendre, déployer, couvrir, partout.

銶 **K'iôu.** Hache, ciseau.

錞 **Touéi.** Garniture de métal fixée à l'extrémité de la poignée d'une lance.

錡 **Ì.** Marmite à trois pieds. ‖ **K'î.** Ciseau.

69

錦 **Kìn.** Tissu de soie à fleurs de différentes couleurs.

錫 **Sĭ.** Étain; donner, don.

錢 **Tsièn.** Houe.

錯 **Ts'ouŏ.** Mêlé, croisé, transversal; bien orné; pierre meulière.

鍭 **Heòu.** Flèche.

鍚 **Iâng.** Ornement de métal qu'on mettait au front des chevaux.

鍼 **Tchēnn.** Aiguille. || **K'iên.** | 虎 † **hòu.** Nom d'homme.

鍛 **Touán.** Fer, forger.

鎛 **Pouŏ.** Houe.

鎬 **Haò.** Ville capitale de 武王 **Où wâng** et de ses successeurs, située au sud-ouest de Si ngan fou dans le 陝西 **Chèn sī.** V. page 2.

鏞 **Iôung.** Cloche.

鏤 **Leóu.** Ciseler, graver sur métal.

鏜 **T'āng.** Son du tambour.

鏘 **Ts'iāng.** | | † †. Tinter.

鐘 **Tchōung.** Cloche.

鑒 **Kién.** Miroir; fait qui peut servir d'avertissement.

鑠 **Chŏ.** Brillant.

鑣 **Piaō.** Mors de cheval. | | † †. Nombreux.

鑿 **Tsŏ.** Ciseau, couper, extraire. | | † †. Haut.

RACINE 168. 長

長 **Tch'âng.** Long, haut, longtemps. | 庚 † **kēng.** L'étoile du soir. || **Tchàng.** Le plus âgé, chef, diriger, croître.

RACINE 169. 門

門 **Mênn.** Porte, maison, famille, école, secte.

閉 **Pí.** Fermer; armature de bois qu'on liait à un arc débandé pour l'empêcher de se déformer.

開 **K'āi.** Ouvrir, commencer.

閔 **Mìn.** Avoir compassion, malheureux.

閑 **Hiên.** Barrière; exercé, habile, robuste, épais, oisif.

間 **Kiēn.** Entre, parmi. | 關 † **kouān.** Bruit des roues d'une voiture. || **Kién.** Interrompre, mettre fin; intermédiaire.

閟 **Pí.** Fermer, arrêter, réprimer; retiré, solitaire.

閣 **Kŏ.** | | † †. Bien agencé.

閱 **Iuĕ.** Considérer, regarder; porte, sortir.

闍 **Tōu.** Tour élevée au-dessus de la porte d'une ville.

闉 **Īn.** Murs sinueux qui protègent la porte d'une place forte.

闋 **K'iuĕ.** Se reposer.

闊 **K'ouŏ.** Séparé, éloigné.

闕 **K'iuĕ.** Tours élevées des deux côtés d'une porte; défaut.

闐 **T'iên.** Boucher. | | † †. Son du tambour.

關 **Kouān.** Fermer. | | † †. Cri du canard et d'autres oiseaux.

闞 **K'án.** Observer. || **Hán.** Cri du tigre.

闥 **T'ă.** Porte.

RACINE 170. 阜

阜 **Feóu.** Monticule; haut, grand, abondant.

防 **Fâng.** Digue, obstacle, se prémunir contre.

阮 **Iuèn.** Ancienne principauté, à présent 涇 州 **Kīng tcheōu** dans le 甘 肅 **Kān siŭ**. V. page 338.

阪 **Fàn.** Versant d'une montagne, bord escarpé, talus.

附 **Fóu.** Adhérent, adjoint, ajouté. | 庸 ┼ **iôung**. Petite principauté qui dépend d'une plus grande.

阿 **Ngō.** Colline, anfractuosité; grand et beau. | 丘 ┼ **k'iōu**. Colline qui est plus haute à une extrémité qu'à l'autre. | 衡 ┼ **hêng**. Premier ministre, titre donné à 伊 尹 **Ī in**.

陂 **P'ouō.** Versant d'une colline, bord escarpé, digue, talus.

阻 **Tchòu.** Obstacle, passage difficile, arrêter, empêcher.

降 **Kiáng.** Descendre, faire descendre, donner une chose à un inférieur. || **Hiâng.** Soumettre, se soumettre. || **Hôung.** Calme, repos.

除 **Tch'ôu.** Enlever, écarter, rejeter. || **Tchóu.** Passer, s'écouler; être écarté. || **Iû, Chōu.** Commencer.

陰 **Īn.** Obscur, nuageux, caché, intérieur. || **Ín.** 蔭. Ombrager, protéger. || **Iōung.** 凌 | **Lîng** ┼. Glacière.

陵 **Lîng.** Colline, monticule.

陸 **Liŭ.** Terre ferme, lieu élevé.

陪 **P'êi.** Compagnon, assistant.

陶 **T'aô.** Ouvrage d'argile. || **Iaô.** | | ┼ ┼. Joyeux. 皐 | **Kaō** ┼. Nom d'un ministre de 舜 **Chouénn**. || **Taó.** | | ┼ ┼. Ardent.

陳 **Tch'ênn.** Étaler, déployer, disposer, ranger en ordre; vieux; allée qui conduit de la porte à la salle principale d'une habitation; nom d'une ancienne principauté à présent comprise dans le | 州 府 du Ho nan. V. page 4.

陽 **Iâng.** Soleil, brillant; le dixième mois de l'année; le côté méridional d'une montagne, le côté septentrional d'une rivière. 夕 | **Sī** ┼. Le côté occidental d'une colline. 朝 | **Tchaō** ┼. Le côté oriental d'une colline. 首 | **Cheòu** ┼ Nom de montagne. V. page 131. | | ┼ ┼. Bien orné, élégant, joyeux.

隅 **Iû.** Angle; indice.

陾 **Jêng.** Multitude, foule.

階 **Kiāi.** Marche, degré, échelle; cause.

隆 **Lôung.** Grand, abondant, intense.

隘 **Iái.** Étroit.

隕 **Iùn.** Tomber, décroître. || **Iuên.** 員. Contour, limites.

隤 **T'ouêi.** Malade, dépérir.

險 **Hièn.** Escarpé, passage difficile.

隨 **Souêi.** Suivre, obséquieux, flatteur.

隧 **Souéi.** Voie, route.

隮 **Tsī.** Monter, s'élever.

隰 **Sĭ.** Terrain bas et humide.

隱 **Ìn.** Cacher, douleur, chagrin.

RACINE 172. 隹

隼 **Siùn.** Épervier.

雀 **Tsiŏ.** Moineau.

雄 **Hiòung.** Mâle.

雅 **Ià.** Convenable, beau, élégant. 小丨大丨 Siaò 十, Tá 十. Ce qui convient dans les petites choses, dans les grandes choses.

集 **Tsĭ.** Oiseaux réunis sur les arbres, réunir, se réunir; exécuter.

雊 **Keóu.** Cri du faisan.

雉 **Tchéu.** Faisan.

雌 **Ts'ēu.** Femelle.

雎 **Ts'iū.** 丨鳩 十 kiōu. Nom d'un oiseau aquatique. V. page 5.

雒 **Lŏ.** Nom d'oiseau. ‖ 駱. Cheval blanc à crinière noire.

雖 **Souēi.** Bien que, quand même.

雙 **Chouāng.** Double, paire, couple.

雜 **Tsă.** Mêlé, de plusieurs sortes.

雞 **Kī.** Coq, poule.

雝 **Iōung.** Accord, harmonie; lac.

離 **Lî.** Quitter, s'éloigner, se disperser. ‖ 罹. Tomber dans. ‖ **Lí.** Attaché à.

難 **Nàn.** Difficile, pénible. ‖ **Nán.** Peine, souffrance. ‖ **Nouô.** Beaucoup.

RACINE 173. 雨

雨 **Iù.** Pluie. ‖ **Iú.** Pleuvoir, tomber du ciel.

雪 **Siuě.** Neige.

雰 **Fēnn.** 丨丨十十. Neige tombant à gros flocons.

雱 **P'āng.** Neige tombant à gros flocons.

雲 **Iùn.** Nuage. 丨漢十 hán. Voie lactée.

零 **Lìng.** Tomber comme la pluie.

雷 **Lêi.** Tonnerre.

電 **Tién.** Éclair.

霂 **Mŏu.** Pluie fine.

震 **Tchénn.** Ébranler, trembler; concevoir.

霆 **T'ìng.** Foudre, éclair.

霏 **Fēi.** Neiger, neige abondante.

霑 **Tchēn.** Mouiller, humecter, faire du bien.

霜 **Chouāng.** Gelée blanche, givre.

霢 **Mĕ.** Pluie fine.

霰 **Sién.** Grésil.

露 **Lóu.** Rosée.

霾 **Mài.** Pluie amenée par un tourbillon de vent.

靁 **Lêi.** Tonnerre.

靈 **Lìng.** Esprit, merveille, merveilleux, puissant, grand, majestueux, bon, favorable.

詩經

RACINE 174. 青

青 **Ts'īng.** Vert, bleu, verdoyant. || **Tsīng.** | | † †. Luxuriant.

靖 **Tsíng.** Paisible, tranquille, procurer la paix, établir l'ordre.

靜 **Tsíng.** Paisible, silencieux; pur.

RACINE 175. 非

非 **Fēi.** Non, à moins que, ce n'est pas que; faux, mal, mauvais.

靡 **Mì.** Non, ne pas; prodigue. | | † †. Lentement.

RACINE 176. 面

面 **Mién.** Face, face à face.

靦 **T'ièn.** Regarder en face, voir, visible.

RACINE 177. 革

革 **Kŏ.** Peau dépouillée de son poil, cuir, courroie, lanière, cuirasse; muer.

靷 **Ìn.** Courroie qui sert de trait à une voiture.

鞃 **Hôung.** Milieu de l'appui 軾 **chĕu** fixé transversalement sur le devant d'une voiture.

鞅 **Iàng.** | 掌 † **tchàng.** Avoir la charge de.

鞏 **Kòung.** Affermir, fortifier.

鞉 **T'aô.** Tambourin qui est muni d'un manche et de deux petites balles, et qu'on agite avec la main.

鞙 **Hiuèn.** | | † †. Long et pendant.

鞠 **Kiŭ.** Nourrir; entier, entièrement, employer entièrement, épuiser; donner un avis.

鞗 **T'iaô.** Rênes.

鞞 **Pìng, Pì.** Fourreau.

鞫 **Kiŭ.** Réduire au silence un adversaire; épuisé, sans ressource; espace compris dans la courbure d'une rive.

鞹 **K'ouŏ.** Cuir.

RACINE 178. 韋

韋 **Wêi.** Cuir mou; nom de principauté.

韎 **Méi.** Cuir rouge, genouillères rouges.

韐 **Kiă.** Genouillères de cuir rouge.

韓 **Hân.** Ancienne principauté, à présent | 城 縣 dans le 陝 西 **Chèn sī.**

韔 **Tch'áng.** Fourreau d'arc.

韘 **Chĕ.** Doigtier d'ivoire que les archers portent au pouce de la main droite.

韠 **Pĭ.** Genouillères de cuir.

韡 **Wèi.** | | † †. Brillant.

RACINE 179. 韭

韭 **Kiòu.** Poireau.

RACINE 180. 音

音 **Īn.** Son, note musicale, cri, parole, message, nouvelle, renom, réputation.

RACINE 181. 頁

頃 **K'īng.** 傾. Incliné.

項 **Hiáng.** Cou, gros cou.

順 **Chouénn.** Accommodant, soumis, docile.

須 **Siū.** Attendre ; nom d'une ville de la principauté de 衞 **Wéi.**

頏 **Hâng.** Vol descendant d'un oiseau.

頎 **K'î.** De grande taille.

頍 **K'ouèi.** Porter un bonnet sur la tête.

頒 **P'ān.** Propager, publier. || **Fènn.** Grosse tête.

頌 **Sóung.** Louer, célébrer, éloge.

頓 **Touénn.** Saluer en inclinant la tête jusqu'à terre.

領 **Lìng.** Cou.

頡 **Hiĕ.** Vol ascendant d'un oiseau.

潁 **Ìng.** Rivière qui coule dans la province de Ngan houei.

熲 **K'iòung.** Flamme, lumière.

頻 **P'în.** Danger pressant ; bord élevé d'une rivière.

頹 **T'ouêi.** Tourbillon de vent.

題 **T'î.** Front ; titre, argument. || **Tí.** Regarder.

顏 **Iên.** Front, visage, air du visage.

顒 **Iôung.** Grosse tête. | | † †. Maintien bien composé.

願 **Iuén.** Désirer.

類 **Léi.** Espèce, discerner, semblable ; bien ; sacrifice offert au Chang ti.

顛 **Tiēn.** Front ; renverser, bouleverser, troubler.

顧 **Kóu.** Tourner la tête pour regarder, considérer, veiller sur, penser avec affection à.

顯 **Hièn.** Évident, manifeste, brillant, glorieux.

RACINE 182. 風

風 **Fōung.** Vent, influence. || **Fóung.** Critiquer, censurer.

飄 **P'iaō.** Souffle du vent. || **P'iaò.** Inconstance du vent.

RACINE 183. 飛

飛 **Fēi.** Voler.

RACINE 184. 食

食 **Chĕu.** Manger, repas, mets, aliment ; vivre de ; consumer ; éclipse. || **Séu.** Nourriture, nourrir.

飢 **Kī.** Avoir faim.

飧 **Suēnn.** Repas du soir ; prendre son repas.

飲 **Ìn.** Boire. || **Ín.** Donner à boire.

飫 **Iú.** Rassasié, rassasier.

飭 **Tch'ĕu.** Préparer.

飾 **Chĕu.** Orner.

飴 **Î.** Sucre.

飽 **Paò.** Manger son soûl, rassasié.

飶 **Pī.** Bonne odeur d'un mets.

養 **Iàng.** Nourrir, élever. | | † †. Chagrin.

餐 **Ts'ān.** Manger, dévorer.

餘 **Iû.** Restant, superflu.

館 **Kouàn.** Habitation où l'on réside temporairement, hôtel.

餤 **T'ân.** Nourrir, entretenir, augmenter.

餞 **Tsién.** Repas offert à quelqu'un qui part pour un voyage.

餴 **Fēnn.** Mettre de l'eau dans le riz qui a été cuit à la vapeur, et le faire chauffer de nouveau.

餱 **Heôu.** Grain grillé, provisions de vivres.

饁 **Iĕ.** Porter à manger aux laboureurs dans les champs.

饇 **Iú.** Rassasié.

饉 **Kín.** Manque de légumes.

饋 **Kouéi.** Offrir des mets.

饑 **Kī.** Manque de grain, famine, faim.

饎 **Tch'éu.** Nourriture préparée sur le le feu, repas.

饗 **Hiàng.** Offrir un festin, offrir des mets; agréer une offrande.

饔 **Iōung.** Mets préparé sur le feu, faire cuire la nourriture.

饛 **Môung.** Vase plein de nourriture.

饟 **Cháng.** Donner des vivres.

RACINE 185. 首

首 **Cheòu.** Tête, particule numérale des lièvres. 丨陽 **ǀ iâng.** Montagne située dans le 蒲州府 **P'ôu tcheōu fòu** du 山西 **Chān sī.** V. page 131.

馘 **Kouŏ.** Couper l'oreille gauche d'un ennemi tué.

RACINE 186. 香

香 **Hiāng.** Odeur agréable, parfum.

馨 **Hīng.** Odoriférant.

RACINE 187. 馬

馬 **Mà.** Cheval.

馮 **P'îng.** Marcher dans, s'appuyer sur. 丨丨 ǀ ǀ. Bruit.

馳 **Tch'êu.** Courir vite, presser la course de ses chevaux. ‖ **Touó.** Conduire des chevaux.

馵 **Tchóu.** Cheval dont le pied gauche de derrière est blanc.

駁 **Pouŏ.** Cheval roux tacheté de blanc.

駕 **Kiá.** Atteler.

駉 **Kiōung.** Cheval corpulent et robuste.

駒 **Kiū.** Poulain, jeune cheval.

駓 **P'ēi.** Cheval dont le pelage est mêlé de roux et de blanc.

駜 **Pĭ.** Cheval corpulent et robuste.

駟 **Séu.** Attelage de quatre chevaux.

駪 **Chēnn.** 丨丨 ǀ ǀ. Multitude.

駰 **Īn.** Cheval gris-blanc.

駱 **Lŏ.** Cheval blanc à crinière noire.

駮 **Pouŏ.** 駁. Nom d'un arbre dont l'écorce est tachetée.

駵 **Liôu.** Cheval roux à crinière noire.

駽 **Hiuēn.** Cheval couleur gris de fer.

騂 **Sīng.** Cheval roux, victime rousse. | | ✝ ✝. Arc bien conditionné.

騁 **Tch'èng.** Courir vite, presser la course de ses chevaux.

駾 **Touéi.** Courir vite, fuite rapide.

駸 **Ts'īn.** Courir très vite, courir sans cesse.

駿 **Tsiún.** Grand, élevé, puissant, agrandir, étendre.

騅 **Tchouēi.** Cheval dont le pelage est mêlé de gris et de blanc.

騑 **Fēi.** | | ✝ ✝. Voyager sans cesse.

騏 **K'î.** Cheval gris tacheté de noir.

騋 **Lâi.** Cheval qui a plus de sept 尺 tch'ěu de haut (un mètre, 40 c.).

騢 **Hiâ.** Cheval dont le pelage est mêlé de roux et de blanc.

騧 **Kouā.** Cheval roux dont la bouche est noire.

騤 **K'ouêi.** | | ✝ ✝. Cheval robuste et ardent.

騵 **Iuên.** Cheval roux dont le ventre est blanc et la crinière noire.

騫 **K'iēn.** Cheval malade; déchoir, décroître, faire défaut.

騷 **Saō.** Triste, inquiet.

騶 **Tcheōu.** | 虞 ✝ iû. Animal fabuleux qui a l'apparence du tigre et le naturel très doux.

騰 **T'êng.** Monter, s'élever.

驅 **K'iū.** Fouetter ses chevaux. 先 | Siēn ✝. Courir en avant.

驂 **Ts'ān.** Les deux chevaux extérieurs d'un attelage de quatre de front.

驈 **Iŭ.** Cheval noir dont les cuisses sont blanches.

驕 **Kiaō.** Cheval haut de six 尺 tch'ěu; robuste, orgueilleux, arrogant. | | ✝ ✝. Végétation luxuriante.

驔 **T'àn, Tién.** Cheval dont les cuisses ont de longs poils blancs.

驒 **T'ouô.** Cheval gris pommelé.

驚 **Kīng.** Effrayer, peur, trouble, tumulte.

驖 **T'iĕ.** Cheval couleur gris de fer.

驛 **Ĭ.** | | ✝ ✝. Luxuriant.

驟 **Tcheóu.** Cheval rapide.

驪 **Lî.** Cheval noir.

RACINE 188. 骨

體 **T'ì.** Corps, membres du corps; un tout complet; complètement formé. 下 | Hiá ✝. Racine d'une plante.

RACINE 189. 高

高 **Kaō.** Haut.

RACINE 190. 髟

髢 **T'í.** Cheveux surajoutés, faux cheveux.

髦 **Maô.** Deux touffes de cheveux qu'on ne rasait jamais à l'enfant, et qu'il devait porter pendants sur ses tempes jusqu'à la mort de ses parents; insigne, éminent.

髧 **Tàn.** Longs cheveux pendants.

髮 **Fă.** Cheveu.

鬈 **K'iuên.** Cheveux bouclés, belle chevelure, belle barbe.

鬒 **Tchènn.** Chevelure noire.

RACINE 191. 門

鬩 **Hī.** Disputer.

RACINE 192. 鬯

鬯 **Tch'áng.** Herbe qui servait à aromatiser les liqueurs, liqueur aromatisée ; fourreau d'arc.

鬱 **Iŭ.** Massif d'arbres ; prunier.

RACINE 193. 鬲

鬲 **Lī.** Chaudière munie de pieds.

鬷 **Tsōung.** Tous ensemble.

鬻 **Iŭ.** Nourrir.

RACINE 194. 鬼

鬼 **Kouèi.** Esprit inférieur, génie, mânes, démon.

魃 **Pă, Pouŏ.** Démon à tête chauve qui cause la sécheresse.

魏 **Wéi.** Ancienne principauté. V. page 3.

魗 **Tch'eòu.** 醜. Laid, difforme.

RACINE 195. 魚

魚 **Iû.** Poisson ; cheval dont les yeux sont entourés d'un cercle blanc, comme ceux des poissons.

魴 **Fâng.** Brème.

魯 **Lòu.** Ancienne principauté qui a formé le 兗 州 府 **Ièn tcheōu fòu,** le 東 平 州 **Tōung p'îng tcheōu,...** dans le Chan toung.

鮪 **Wèi.** Esturgeon.

鮮 **Siēn.** Poisson frais; récent. ‖ **Sièn.** Peu, rare, excellent; orphelin.

鯉 **Lì.** Carpe.

鯊 **Chā.** Requin; nom d'un poisson qui vit dans le sable.

鰋 **Ièn.** Nom d'un poisson à grosse tête qui vit dans la vase.

鰥 **Kouān.** Nom de poisson; homme veuf.

鰷 **T'iaô.** Nom d'un poisson mince et long.

鱒 **Ts'uénn.** Gardon, ablette.

鱣 **Tchēn.** Esturgeon.

鱧 **Lì.** Muge.

鱨 **Châng.** Nom de poisson.

鱮 **Siú.** Perche, carpe.

RACINE 196. 鳥

鳥 **Gniaò.** Oiseau.

鳧 **Fôu.** Canard sauvage.

鳩 **Kiōu.** Pigeon ramier, tourterelle.

鳳 **Fóung.** Phénix mâle.

鳲 **Chēu.** 丨 鳩 † **kiōu.** Pigeon ramier.

鳴 **Mîng.** Chant d'oiseau, cri, son, bruit.

鳶 **Iuên.** Milan, épervier.

鴇 **Paò.** Outarde; cheval dont le pelage est noir mêlé de blanc.

鴈 **Ién.** Oie sauvage.

鴛 **Iuēn.** Canard mandarin mâle.

鴦 **Iāng.** Femelle du canard mandarin.

鴞 **Hiaō.** Hibou.

鴟 **Tch'ēu.** | 鴞 † hiaō. Hibou.

鴥 **Iŭ.** Vol rapide de l'épervier.

鴻 **Hôung.** Oie sauvage de grande taille, grue.

鵠 **Hŏu.** Cygne. || **Kaó.** Nom de lieu.

鵜 **T'î.** Pélican.

鶪 **Kiŭ.** Pie-grièche.

鶉 **Chouênn.** Caille. || **T'ouân.** Aigle.

鵻 **Tchouēi.** Pigeon, tourterelle.

鵲 **Ts'iŏ.** Pie.

鶖 **Ts'iōu.** Cigogne.

鶬 **Ts'āng.** | 庚 † kēng. Loriot. || **Ts'iāng.** Brillant. | | † †. Son des clochettes.

鶴 **Hŏ.** Grue.

鷊 **Ĭ.** Faisan. 旨 | Tchèu †. Plante dont les feuilles ont des raies de diverses couleurs.

鶯 **Īng.** Loriot; plumage aux couleurs brillantes et variées.

鷕 **Iaò.** Cri de la faisane.

鷖 **Ī.** Mouette.

鷮 **Kiaō.** Faisan à longue queue.

鷺 **Lóu.** Héron.

鷹 **Īng.** Aigle, vautour, épervier.

鸒 **Iù.** Petit corbeau dont le ventre est blanc.

鸛 **Kouán.** Cigogne.

鸞 **Louân.** Sonnettes fixées au mors d'une bride. | 刀 † taō. Couteau dont le manche est terminé par une sonnette.

RACINE 198. 鹿

鹿 **Lŏu.** Cerf.

麀 **Iōu.** Biche.

麃 **Piaō** Arracher les mauvaises herbes. | | † †. Vigoureux, ardent.

麋 **Mèi.** 湄. Rive verdoyante.

麌 **Iù.** Troupe de cerfs.

麓 **Lŏu.** Pied d'une montagne, forêt au pied d'une montagne.

麕 **Kiūn.** Daim.

麗 **Lí.** Nombre; prendre des poissons dans une sorte de nasse.

麟 **Lîn.** Licorne femelle.

RACINE 199. 麥

麥 **Mĕ.** Blé.

RACINE 200. 麻

麻 **Mâ.** Chanvre.

麾 **Houēi.** Faire signe.

詩經

RACINE 201. 黃

黃 **Houâng.** Jaune. | 髮 + fă. Chevelure jaunissante d'un vieillard.

RACINE 202. 黍

黍 **Chòu.** Millet à panicules.

黎 **Lî.** Noir; nom de principauté. | 民 + **min.** Les hommes à la chevelure noire: tous ceux dont la chevelure ne commence pas encore à blanchir, le peuple chinois.

RACINE 203. 黑

黑 **Hĕ.** Noir.

黮 **Chénn.** 葚. Mûre.

RACINE 204. 黹

黻 **Fŏu.** La lettre 亞 brodée en noir et en bleu sur un tissu, vêtement brodé.

黼 **Fòu.** Hache brodée en blanc et en noir sur l'étoffe d'un 裳 **châng** vêtement inférieur.

RACINE 205. 黽

黽 **Mìn.** Faire des efforts.

鼈 **Piĕ.** Tortue molle.

鼉 **T'ouŏ.** Crocodile; grand tambour de peau de crocodile.

RACINE 206. 鼎

鼎 **Tìng.** Chaudière à trois pieds.

鼐 **Nài.** Grande chaudière à trois pieds.

鼒 **Tzēu.** Petite chaudière à trois pieds.

RACINE 207. 鼓

鼓 **Kòu.** Tambour, battre le tambour, jouer d'un instrument de musique.

鼛 **Kaō.** Grand tambour militaire.

RACINE 208. 鼠

鼠 **Chòu.** Rat. || 癙. Peine secrète.

RACINE 210. 齊

齊 **Ts'î.** Égal, sur la même ligne, de niveau; bien arrangé; ancienne principauté qui a formé le 清州府 **Ts'ing tcheōu fòu,** le 濟南府 **Tsi nân fòu,...** dans le Chan toung. V. page 3. || **Tzēu.** 粢. Millet, blé. || **Tchāi.** Purifier, observer l'abstinence.

RACINE 211. 齒

齒 **Tch'èu.** Dent.

RACINE 212. 龍

龍 **Lōung.** Dragon; faveur.

RACINE 213. 龜

龜 **Kouēi.** Tortue munie de carapace.

ADDITION.

Page V, ligne 6 : Lorsqu'une particule termine un vers, c'est le mot précédent qui rime avec le dernier mot d'un autre vers.

RECTIFICATIONS.

Page 58, ligne 25 : lorsqu'elle apparaît... *lisez* lorsqu'il apparaît.
— 184, — 11 : à leur départ... *lisez* à leur retour.

国家出版基金项目
NATIONAL PUBLICATION FOUNDATION

海上絲綢之路文獻集成

總主編 陳支平 陳春聲

科技與文化編 63

主編 王揚宗 葉 農

海峽出版發行集團
THE STRAITS PUBLISHING & DISTRIBUTING GROUP
福建人民出版社

本册目次

易經

（*The Yi King or Book of Changes*）

〔英〕理雅各（James Legge）編譯

《易經》，英國理雅各編譯。理雅各（James Legge，一八一五—一八九七），英國倫敦會傳教士，法國漢學儒蓮獎首位得主。於一八六一至一八七二年相繼出版《中國經典》（*The Chinese Classics*）五卷，於一八七九至一八九一年相繼出版《中國聖書》（*The Sacred Books of China*）六卷。諸種中國經典譯作，被後世奉爲標準譯本。所英譯《易經》收録於《東方聖書》第十六卷，一八八二年出版。書有緒論三章，末有附録。《易》爲群經之首，此爲英語世界首部權威譯本，譯文所據爲朱熹撰《周易本義》，亦將「傳」自「經」中析出。此外亦多採李光地《御纂周易折中》、牛鈕《御制日講易經解義》等要籍。據一八八二年牛津版影印。

易經

THE

SACRED BOOKS OF THE EAST

London

HENRY FROWDE

OXFORD UNIVERSITY PRESS WAREHOUSE

7 PATERNOSTER ROW

易經

THE

SACRED BOOKS OF THE EAST

TRANSLATED

BY VARIOUS ORIENTAL SCHOLARS

AND EDITED BY

F. MAX MÜLLER

VOL. XVI

Oxford

AT THE CLARENDON PRESS

1882

易經

THE

SACRED BOOKS OF CHINA

THE TEXTS OF CONFUCIANISM

TRANSLATED BY

JAMES LEGGE

PART II

THE YÎ KING

Oxford

AT THE CLARENDON PRESS

1882

CONTENTS.

THE TEXT.

SECTION I.

SECTION II.

THE APPENDIXES.

PREFACE.

I wrote out a translation of the Yî King, embracing both the Text and the Appendixes, in 1854 and 1855; and have to acknowledge that when the manuscript was completed, I knew very little about the scope and method of the book. I laid the volumes containing the result of my labour aside, and hoped, believed indeed, that the light would by and by dawn, and that I should one day get hold of a clue that would guide me to a knowledge of the mysterious classic.

Before that day came, the translation was soaked, in 1870, for more than a month in water of the Red Sea. By dint of careful manipulation it was recovered so as to be still legible; but it was not till 1874 that I began to be able to give to the book the prolonged attention necessary to make it reveal its secrets. Then for the first time I got hold, as I believe, of the clue, and found that my toil of twenty years before was of no service at all.

What had tended more than anything else to hide the nature of the book from my earlier studies was the way in which, with the Text, ordinarily and, as I think, correctly ascribed to king Wăn and his son Tan, there are interspersed, under each hexagram, the portions of the Appendixes I, II, and IV relating to it. The student at first thinks this an advantage. He believes that all the Appendixes were written by Confucius, and combine with the text to form one harmonious work; and he is glad to have the sentiments of 'the three sages' brought together. But I now perceived that the composition of the Text and of the Appendixes, allowing the Confucian authorship of the latter, was separated by about 700 years, and that their subject-matter was often incongruous. My first step towards a right understanding of the Yî was to study the Text by itself and as complete in itself. It was easy to

do this because the imperial edition of 1715, with all its critical apparatus, keeps the Text and the Appendixes separate.

The wisdom of the course thus adopted became more apparent by the formation of eight different concordances, one for the Text, and one for each of the Appendixes. They showed that many characters in the Appendixes, and those especially which most readily occur to sinologists as characteristic of the Yî, are not to be found in the Text at all. A fuller acquaintance, moreover, with the tone and style of the Appendixes satisfied me that while we had sufficient evidence that the greater part of them was not from Confucius, we had no evidence that any part was his, unless it might be the paragraphs introduced by the compiler or compilers as sayings of 'the Master.'

Studying the Text in the manner thus described, I soon arrived at the view of the meaning and object of the Yî, which I have described in the second chapter of the Introduction; and I was delighted to find that there was a substantial agreement between my interpretations of the hexagrams and their several lines and those given by the most noted commentators from the Han dynasty down to the present. They have not formulated the scheme so concisely as I have done, and they were fettered by their belief in the Confucian authorship of the Appendixes; but they held the same general opinion, and were similarly controlled by it in construing the Text. Any sinologist who will examine the Yü *K*ih *Z*ăh *K*iang Yî King *K*ieh Î, prepared by one of the departments of the Han Lin college, and published in 1682, and which I have called the 'Daily Lessons,' or 'Lectures,' will see the agreement between my views and those underlying its paraphrase.

After the clue to the meaning of the Yî was discovered, there remained the difficulty of translating. The peculiarity of its style makes it the most difficult of all the Confucian classics to present in an intelligible version. I suppose that there are sinologists who will continue, for a time at least, to maintain that it was intended by its

author or authors, whoever they were, merely as a book of divination; and of course the oracles of divination were designedly wrapped up in mysterious phraseology. But notwithstanding the account of the origin of the book and its composition by king Wăn and his son, which I have seen reason to adopt, they, its authors, had to write after the manner of diviners. There is hardly another work in the ancient literature of China that presents the same difficulties to the translator.

When I made my first translation of it in 1854, I endeavoured to be as concise in my English as the original Chinese was. Much of what I wrote was made up, in consequence, of so many English words, with little or no mark of syntactical connexion. I followed in this the example of P. Regis and his coadjutors (Introduction, page 9) in their Latin version. But their version is all but unintelligible, and mine was not less so. How to surmount this difficulty occurred to me after I had found the clue to the interpretation;—in a fact which I had unconsciously acted on in all my translations of other classics, namely, that the written characters of the Chinese are not representations of words, but symbols of ideas, and that the combination of them in composition is not a representation of what the writer would say, but of what he thinks. It is vain therefore for a translator to attempt a literal version. When the symbolic characters have brought his mind en rapport with that of his author, he is free to render the ideas in his own or any other speech in the best manner that he can attain to. This is the rule which Mencius followed in interpreting the old poems of his country:—'We must try with our thoughts to meet the scope of a sentence, and then we shall apprehend it.' In the study of a Chinese classical book there is not so much an interpretation of the characters employed by the writer as a participation of his thoughts;—there is the seeing of mind to mind. The canon hence derived for a translator is not one of license. It will be his object to express the meaning of the original as exactly and concisely as possible. But it will be necessary for him to introduce a word or two

now and then to indicate what the mind of the writer supplied for itself. What I have done in this way will generally be seen enclosed in parentheses, though I queried whether I might not dispense with them, as there is nothing in the English version which was not, I believe, present in the writer's thought. I hope, however, that I have been able in this way to make the translation intelligible to readers. If, after all, they shall conclude that in what is said on the hexagrams there is often 'much ado about nothing,' it is not the translator who should be deemed accountable for that, but his original.

I had intended to append to the volume translations of certain chapters from *K*û Hsî and other writers of the Sung dynasty; but this purpose could not be carried into effect for want of space. It was found necessary to accompany the version with a running commentary, illustrating the way in which the teachings of king Wăn and his son are supposed to be drawn from the figures and their several lines; and my difficulty was to keep the single Yî within the limits of one volume. Those intended translations therefore are reserved for another opportunity; and indeed, the Sung philosophy did not grow out of the Yî proper, but from the Appendixes to it, and especially from the third of them. It is more Tâoistic than Confucian.

When I first took the Yî in hand, there existed no translation of it in any western language but that of P. Regis and his coadjutors, which I have mentioned above and in various places of the Introduction. The authors were all sinologists of great attainments; and their view of the Text as relating to the transactions between the founders of the *K*âu dynasty and the last sovereign of the Shang or Yin, and capable of being illustrated historically, though too narrow, was an approximation to the truth. The late M. Mohl, who had edited the work in 1834, said to me once, 'I like it; for I come to it out of a sea of mist, and find solid ground.' No sufficient distinction was made in it, however, between the Text and the Appendixes; and in discussing the third and following Appendixes the translators

were haunted by the name and shade of Confucius. To the excessive literalness of the version I have referred above.

In 1876 the Rev. Canon McClatchie, M.A., published a version at Shanghai with the title, 'A Translation of the Confucian Yî King, or the "Classic of Changes," with Notes and Appendix.' . This embraces both the Text and the Appendixes, the first, second, and fourth of the latter being interspersed along with the Text, as in the ordinary school editions of the classic. So far as I can judge from his language, he does not appear to be aware that the first and second Appendixes were not the work of king Wăn and the duke of *K*âu, but of a subsequent writer—he would say of Confucius—explaining their explanations of the entire hexagrams and their several lines. His own special object was 'to open the mysteries of the Yî by applying to it the key of Comparative Mythology.' Such a key was not necessary; and the author, by the application of it, has found sundry things to which I have occasionally referred in my notes. They are not pleasant to look at or dwell upon; and happily it has never entered into the minds of Chinese scholars to conceive of them. I have followed Canon McClatchie's translation from paragraph to paragraph and from sentence to sentence, but found nothing which I could employ with advantage in my own.

Long after my translation had been completed, and that of the Text indeed was printed, I received from Shanghai the third volume of P. Angelo Zottoli's 'Cursus Litteraturae Sinicae,' which had appeared in 1880. About 100 pages of it are occupied with the Yî. The Latin version is a great improvement on that in the work of Regis; but P. Zottoli translates only the Text of the first two hexagrams, with the portions of the first, second, and fourth Appendixes relating to them; and other six hexagrams with the explanations of king Wăn's Thwan and of the Great Symbolism. Of the remaining fifty-six hexagrams only the briefest summary is given; and then follow the Appendixes III, V, VI, and VII at length. The author has done his work well.

His general view of the Yî is stated in the following sentences:—'Ex Fû-hsî figuris, Wăn regis definitionibus, *K*âu ducis symbolis, et Confucii commentariis, Liber conficitur, qui a mutationibus, quas duo elementa in hexagrammatum compositione inducunt, Yî (Mutator) vel Yî King (Mutationum Liber) appellatur. Quid igitur tandem famosus iste Yî King? Paucis accipe: .ex linearum qualitate continua vel intercisa; earumque situ, imo, medio, vel supremo; mutuaque ipsarum relatione, occursu, dissidio, convenientia; ex ipso scilicet trigrammatum corpore seu forma, tum ex trigrammatum symbolo seu imagine, tum ex trigrammatum proprietate seu virtute, tum etiam aliquando ex unius ad alterum hexagramma varietate, eruitur aliqua imago, deducitur aliqua sententia, quoddam veluti oraculum continens, quod sorte etiam consulere possis ad documentum obtinendum, moderandae vitae solvendove dubio consentaneum. Ita liber juxta Confucii explicationem in scholis tradi solitam. Nil igitur sublime aut mysteriosum, nil foedum aut vile hic quaeras; argutulum potius lusum ibi video ad instructiones morales politicasque eliciendas, ut ad satietatem usque in Sinicis passim classicis, obvias, planas, naturales; tantum, cum liber iste, ut integrum legenti textum facile patebit, ad sortilegii usum deductus fuerit, per ipsum jam summum homo obtinebit vitae beneficium, arcanam cum spiritibus communicationem secretamque futurorum eventuum cognitionem; theurgus igitur visus est iste liber, totus lux, totus spiritus, hominisque vitae accommodatissimus; indeque laudes a Confucio ei tributas, prorsus exaggeratas, in hujus libri praesertim appendice videre erit, si vere tamen, ut communis fert opinio, ipse sit hujus appendicis auctor.'

There has been a report for two or three years of a new translation of the Yî, or at least of a part of it, as being in preparation by M. Terrien de Lacouperie, and Professor R. K. Douglas of the British Museum and King's College, London. I have alluded on pages 8, 9 of the Introduction to some inaccurate statements about native commentaries on the Yî and translations of it by foreigners, made in connexion with this contemplated version. But I did not know

what the projected undertaking really was, till I read a letter from M. Terrien in the 'Athenæum' of the 21st January of this year. He there says that the joint translation 'deals only with the oldest part of the book, the short lists of characters which follow each of the sixty-four headings, and leaves entirely aside the explanations and commentaries attributed to Wen Wang, *K*âu Kung, Confucius, and others, from 1200 B. C. downwards, which are commonly embodied as an integral part of the classic;' adding, 'The proportion of the primitive text to these additions is about one-sixth of the whole.' But if we take away these explanations and commentaries attributed to king Wăn, the duke of *K*âu, and Confucius, we take away the whole Yî. There remain only the linear figures attributed to Fû-hsî, without any lists of characters, long or short, without a single written character of any kind whatever. The projectors have been misled somehow about the contents of the Yî; and unless they can overthrow all the traditions and beliefs about them, whether Chinese or foreign, their undertaking is more hopeless than the task laid on the children of Israel by Pharaoh, that they should make bricks without straw.

I do not express myself thus in any spirit of hostility. If, by discoveries in Accadian or any other long-buried and forgotten language, M. Terrien de Lacouperie can throw new light on the written characters of China or on its speech, no one will rejoice more than myself; but his ignorance of how the contents of the classic are made up does not give much prospect of success in his promised translation.

In the preface to the third volume of these 'Sacred Books of the East,' containing the Shû King, Shih King, and Hsiâo King, I have spoken of the Chinese terms Tî and Shang Tî, and shown how I felt it necessary to continue to render them by our word God, as I had done in all my translations of the Chinese classics since 1861. My doing so gave offence to some of the missionaries in China and others; and in June, 1880, twenty-three gentlemen addressed a letter to Professor F. Max Müller, complaining

that, in such a work edited by him, he should allow me to give my own private interpretation of the name or names in question instead of translating them or transferring them. Professor Müller published the letter which he had received, with his reply to it, in the 'Times' newspaper of Dec. 30, 1880. Since then the matter has rested, and I introduce it again here in this preface, because, though we do not meet with the name in the Yî so frequently as in the Shû and Shih, I have, as before, wherever it does occur, translated it by God. Those who object to that term say that Shang Tî might be rendered by 'Supreme Ruler' or 'Supreme Emperor,' or by 'Ruler (or Emperor) on high;' but when I examined the question, more than thirty years ago, with all possible interest and all the resources at my command, I came to the conclusions that Tî, on its first employment by the Chinese fathers, was intended to express the same concept which our fathers expressed by God, and that such has been its highest and proper application ever since. There would be little if any difference in the meaning conveyed to readers by 'Supreme Ruler' and 'God;' but when I render Tî by God and Shang Tî by the Supreme God, or, for the sake of brevity, simply by God, I am translating, and not giving a private interpretation of my own. I do it not in the interests of controversy, but as the simple expression of what to me is truth; and I am glad to know that a great majority of the Protestant missionaries in China use Tî and Shang Tî as the nearest analogue for God.

It would be tedious to mention the many critical editions and commentaries that I have used in preparing the translation. I have not had the help of able native scholars, which saved time and was otherwise valuable when I was working in the East on other classics. The want of this, however, has been more than compensated in some respects by my copy of the 'Daily Lectures on the Yî,' the full title of which is given on page xiv. The friend who purchased it for me five years ago in Canton was obliged to content himself with a second-hand copy; but I found that the

previous owner had been a ripe scholar who freely used his pencil in pursuing his studies. It was possible, from his punctuation, interlineations, and many marginal notes, to follow the exercises of his mind, patiently pursuing his search for the meaning of the most difficult passages. I am under great obligations to him; and also to the *K*âu Yî *K*eh *K*ung, the great imperial edition of the present dynasty, first published in 1715. I have generally spoken of its authors as the Khang-hsî editors. Their numerous discussions of the meaning, and ingenious decisions, go far to raise the interpretation of the Yî to a science.

J. L.

OXFORD,
16th March, 1882.

THE YÎ KING

OR

BOOK OF CHANGES

易經

THE YÎ KING

OR

BOOK OF CHANGES.

INTRODUCTION.

CHAPTER I.

THE YÎ KING FROM THE TWELFTH CENTURY B.C. TO THE COMMENCEMENT OF THE CHRISTIAN ERA.

There was a Yî in the time of Confucius.

1. Confucius is reported to have said on one occasion, 'If some years were added to my life, I would give fifty to the study of the Yî, and might then escape falling into great errors[1].' The utterance is referred by the best critics to the closing period of Confucius' life, when he had returned from his long and painful wanderings among the States, and was settled again in his native Lû. By this time he was nearly seventy, and it seems strange, if he spoke seriously, that he should have thought it possible for his life to be prolonged other fifty years. So far as that specification is concerned, a corruption of the text is generally admitted. My reason for adducing the passage has simply been to prove from it the existence of a Yî King in the time of Confucius. In the history of him by Sze-mâ *Kh*ien it is stated that, in the closing years of his life, he became fond of the Yî, and wrote various appendixes to it, that he read his copy of it so much that the leathern thongs (by which the tablets containing it were bound together) were thrice worn out, and that he said, 'Give me several years (more), and I should be master of the Yî[2].' The ancient books on which Confucius had delighted

---

[1] Confucian Analects, VII, xvi.

[2] The Historical Records; Life of Confucius, p. 12.

to discourse with his disciples were those of History, Poetry, and Rites and Ceremonies[1]; but ere he passed away from among them, his attention was much occupied also by the Yî as a monument of antiquity, which in the prime of his days he had too much neglected.

The Yî is now made up of the Text which Confucius saw and the Appendixes ascribed to him.

2. *Kh*ien says that Confucius wrote various appendixes to the Yî, specifying all but two of the treatises, which go by the name of 'the Ten Appendixes,' and are, with hardly a dissentient voice, attributed to the sage. They are published along with the older Text, which is based on still older lineal figures, and are received by most Chinese readers, as well as by foreign Chinese scholars, as an integral portion of the Yî King. The two portions should, however, be carefully distinguished. I will speak of them as the Text and the Appendixes.

The Yî escaped the fires of 3hin.

3. The Yî happily escaped the fires of 3hin, which proved so disastrous to most of the ancient literature of China in B.C. 213. In the memorial which the premier Lî Sze addressed to his sovereign, advising that the old books should be consigned to the flames, an exception was made of those which treated of 'medicine, divination, and husbandry[2].' The Yî was held to be a book of divination, and so was preserved.

In the catalogue of works in the imperial library, prepared by Liû Hin about the beginning of our era, there is an enumeration of those on the Yî and its Appendixes,—the books of thirteen different authors or schools, comprehended in 294 portions of larger or smaller dimensions[3]. I need not follow the history and study of the Yî into the line of the centuries since the time of Liû Hin. The imperial Khang-hsî edition of it, which appeared in 1715, contains quotations from the commentaries of 218 scholars, covering, more or less closely, the time from the second century B.C. to our seventeenth century. I may venture to say that

[1] Analects, VII, xvii.
[2] Legge's Chinese Classics, I, prolegomena, pp. 6–9.
[3] Books of the Earlier Han; History of Literature, pp. 1, 2.

易經

those 218 are hardly a tenth of the men who have tried to interpret the remarkable book, and solve the many problems to which it gives rise.

The Yî before Confucius, and when it was made.

4. It may be assumed then that the Yî King, properly so called, existed before Confucius, and has come down to us as correctly as any other of the ancient books of China; and it might also be said, as correctly as any of the old monuments of Hebrew, Sanskrit, Greek, or Latin literature. The question arises of how far before Confucius we can trace its existence. Of course an inquiry into this point will not include the portions or appendixes attributed to the sage himself. Attention will be called to them by and by, when I shall consider how far we are entitled, or whether we are at all entitled, to ascribe them to him. I do not doubt, however, that they belong to what may be called the Confucian period, and were produced some time after his death, probably between B.C. 450 and 350. By whomsoever they were written, they may be legitimately employed in illustration of what were the prevailing views in that age on various points connected with the Yî. Indeed, but for the guidance and hints derived from them as to the meaning of the text, and the relation between its statements and the linear figures, there would be great difficulty in making out any consistent interpretation of it.

The Yî mentioned in the Official Book of *K*âu.

(i) The earliest mention of the classic is found in the Official Book of the *K*âu dynasty, where it is said that, among the duties of 'the Grand Diviner,' 'he had charge of the rules for the three Yî (systems of Changes), called the Lien-shan, the Kweî-ȝhang, and the Yî of *K*âu; that in each of them the regular (or primary) lineal figures were 8, which were multiplied, in each, till they amounted to 64.' The date of the Official Book has not been exactly ascertained. The above passage can hardly be reconciled with the opinion of the majority of Chinese critics that it was the work of the duke of *K*âu, the consolidator and legislator of the dynasty so called; but I think there must have been the groundwork of it at a very early date. When that was composed or compiled, there

was existing, among the archives of the kingdom, under the charge of a high officer, 'the Yî of *K*âu,'—what constitutes the Text of the present Yî; the Text, that is, as distinguished from the Appendixes. There were two other Yî, known as the Lien-shan and the Kwei-ȝhang. It would be a waste of time to try to discover the meaning of these designations. They are found in this and another passage of the Official Book; and nowhere else. Not a single trace of what they denoted remains, while we possess 'the Yî of *K*âu' complete[1].

The Yî mentioned in the ȝo *Kh*wan.

(ii) In the Supplement of ȝo *Kh*iû-ming to 'the Spring and Autumn,' there is abundant evidence that divination by the Yî was frequent, throughout the states of China, before the time of Confucius. There are at least eight narratives of such a practice, between the years B.C. 672 and 564, before he was born; and five times during his life-time the divining stalks and the book were had recourse to on occasions with which he had nothing to do. In all these cases the text of the Yî, as we have it now, is freely quoted. The 'Spring and Autumn' commences in B.C. 722. If it extended back to the rise of the *K*âu dynasty, we should, no doubt, find

[1] See the *K*âu Kwan (or Lî), Book XXIV, parr. 3, 4, and 27. Biot (Le Tcheou Lî, vol. ii, pp. 70, 71) translates the former two paragraphs thus:—'Il (Le Grand Augure) est préposé aux trois methodes pour les changements (des lignes divinatoires). La première est appelée Liaison des montagnes (Lien-shan); la seconde, Retour et Conservation (Kwei-ȝhang); la troisième, Changements des *K*âu. Pour toutes il y a huit lignes symboliques sacrées, et soixante-quatre combinaisons de ces lignes.'

Some tell us that by Lien-shan was intended Fû-hsî, and by Kwei-ȝhang Hwang Tî; others, that the former was the Yî of the Hsiâ dynasty, and the latter that of Shang or Yin. A third set will have it that Lien-shan was a designation of Shăn Năng, between Fû-hsî and Hwang Tî. I should say myself, as many Chinese critics do say, that Lien-shan was an arrangement of the lineal symbols in which the first figure was the present 52nd hexagram, Kăn ䷳, consisting of the trigram representing mountains doubled; and that Kwei-ȝhang was an arrangement where the first figure was the present 2nd hexagram, Khwăn ䷁, consisting of the trigram representing the earth doubled,—with reference to the disappearance and safe keeping of plants in the bosom of the earth in winter. All this, however, is only conjecture.

accounts of divination by the Yî interspersed over the long intervening period. For centuries before Confucius appeared on the stage of his country, the Yî was well known among the various feudal states, which then constituted the Middle Kingdom[1].

(iii) We may now look into one of the Appendixes for its testimony to the age and authorship of the Text. The third Appendix is the longest, and the most important[2]. In the 49th paragraph of the second Section of it it is said:—

'Was it not in the middle period of antiquity that the Yî began to flourish? Was not he who made it (or were not they who made it) familiar with anxiety and calamity?'

The highest antiquity commences, according to Chinese writers, with Fû-hsî, B.C. 3322; and the lowest with Confucius in the middle of the sixth century B.C. Between these is the period of middle antiquity, extending a comparatively short time, from the rise of the *K*âu dynasty, towards the close of the twelfth century B.C., to the Confucian era. According to this paragraph it was in this period that our Yî was made.

The 69th paragraph is still more definite in its testimony:—

'Was it not in the last age of the Yin (dynasty), when the virtue of *K*âu had reached its highest point, and during the troubles between king Wăn and (the tyrant) *K*âu, that (the study of) the Yî began to flourish? On this account the explanations (in the book) express (a feeling of) anxious apprehension, (and teach) how peril may be turned into security, and easy carelessness is sure to meet with overthrow.'

The dynasty of Yin was superseded by that of *K*âu in B.C. 1122. The founder of *K*âu was he whom we call king Wăn, though he himself never occupied the throne. The

---

[1] See in the Ȝo *Kh*wan, under the 22nd year of duke *K*wang (B.C. 672); the 1st year of Min (661); and in his 2nd year (660); twice in the 15th year of Hsî (645); his 25th year (635); the 12th year of Hsüan (597); the 16th year of *Kh*ăng (575); the 9th year of Hsiang (564); his 25th year (548); the 5th year of *Kh*âo (537); his 7th year (535); his 12th year (530); and the 9th year of Âi (486).

[2] That is, the third as it appears farther on in this volume in two Sections. With the Chinese critics it forms the fifth and sixth Appendixes, or 'Wings,' as they are termed.

troubles between him and the last sovereign of Yin reached their height in B.C. 1143, when the tyrant threw him into prison in a place called Yû-lî, identified as having been in the present district of Thang-yin, department of *K*ang-teh, province of Ho-nan. Wăn was not kept long in confinement. His friends succeeded in appeasing the jealousy of his enemy, and securing his liberation in the following year. It follows that the Yî, so far as we owe it to king Wăn, was made in the year B.C. 1143 or 1142, or perhaps that it was begun in the former year and finished in the latter [1].

But the part which is thus ascribed to king Wăn is only a small portion of the Yî. A larger share is attributed to his son Tan, known as the duke of *K*âu, and in it we have allusions to king Wû, who succeeded his father Wăn, and was really the first sovereign of the dynasty of *K*âu [2]. There are passages, moreover, which must be understood of events in the early years of the next reign. But the duke of *K*âu died in the year B.C. 1105, the 11th of king *Kh*ăng. A few years then before that time, in the last decade of the twelfth century B.C., the Yî King, as it has come down to us, was complete [3].

The Yî is not the most ancient of the Chinese books.

5. We have thus traced the text of the Yî to its authors, the famous king Wăn in the year 1143 B.C., and his equally famous son, the duke of *K*âu, in between thirty and forty years later. It can thus boast of a great antiquity; but a general opinion has prevailed that it belonged to a period still more distant. Only two translations of it have been made by European scholars. The first was executed by Regis and other Roman Catholic missionaries in the beginning of last century, though it was given to the public only

[1] Sze-mâ *Kh*ien (History of the *K*âu Dynasty, p. 3) relates that, 'when he was confined in Yû-lî, Wăn increased the 8 trigrams to 64 hexagrams.'

[2] E.g., hexagrams XVII, l. 6; XLVI, l. 4. Tan's authorship of the symbolism is recognised in the Ȝo *Kh*wan, B.C. 540.

[3] P. Regis (vol. ii, p. 379) says: 'Vel nihil vel parum errabit qui dicet opus Yî King fuisse perfectum anno quinto *Kh*ăng Wang, seu anno 1109 aut non ultra annum 1108, ante aerae Christianae initium; quod satis in rebus non omnino certis.' But the fifth year of king *Kh*ăng was B.C. 1111.

in 1834 by the late Jules Mohl, with a title commencing 'Y-King, antiquissimus Sinarum liber[1].' The language of the other European translator of it, the Rev. Canon McClatchie of Shanghâi, whose work appeared in 1876, is still more decided. The first sentence of his Introduction contains two very serious misstatements, but I have at present to do only with the former of them;—that 'the Yî King is regarded by the Chinese with peculiar veneration, ... as being the most ancient of their classical writings.' The Shû is the oldest of the Chinese classics, and contains documents more than a thousand years earlier than king Wăn. Several pieces of the Shih King are also older than anything in the Yî; to which there can thus be assigned only the third place in point of age among the monuments of Chinese literature. Existing, however, about 3000 years ago, it cannot be called modern. Unless it be the books of the Pentateuch, Joshua, and Judges, an equal antiquity cannot be claimed for any portion of our Sacred Scriptures.

The Text much older than the Appendixes.

It will be well to observe here also how much older the Text is than the Appendixes. Supposing them to be the work of Confucius, though it will appear by and by that this assumption

[1] It has been suggested that 'Antiquissimus Sinarum liber' may mean only 'A very ancient book of the Chinese,' but the first sentence of the Preface to the work commences:—'Inter omnes constat librorum Sinicorum, quos classicos vocant, primum et antiquissimum esse Y-King.'

At the end of M. De Guignes' edition of P. Gaubil's translation of the Shû, there is a notice of the Yî King sent in 1738 to the Cardinals of the Congregation de Propaganda Fide by M. Claude Visdelou, Bishop of Claudiopolis. M. De Guignes says himself, 'L' Y-King est le premier des Livres Canoniques des Chinois.' But P. Visdelou writes more guardedly and correctly:—'Pour son ancienneté, s'il en faut croire les Annales des Chinois, il a été commencé quarante-six siècles avant celui-ci. Si cela est vrai, comme toute la nation l'avoue unanimement, ou peut à juste titre l'appeler le plus ancien des livres.' But he adds, 'Ce n'étoit pas proprement un livre, ni quelque chose d'approchant; c'étoit une énigme très obscure, et plus difficile cent fois à expliquer que celle du sphinx.'

P. Couplet expresses himself much to the same effect in the prolegomena (p. xviii) to the work called 'Confucius Sinarum Philosophus,' published at Paris in 1687 by himself and three other fathers of the Society of Jesus (Intorcetta, Herdritch, and Rougemont). Both they and P. Visdelou give an example of a portion of the text and its interpretation, having singularly selected the same hexagram,—the 15th, on Humility.

can be received as only partially correct, if indeed it be received at all, the sage could not have entered on their composition earlier than B.C. 483, 660 years later than the portion of the text that came from king Wăn, and nearly 630 later than what we owe to the duke of *K*âu. But during that long period of between six and seven centuries changes may have arisen in the views taken by thinking men of the method and manner of the Yî; and I cannot accept the Text and the Appendixes as forming one work in any proper sense of the term. Nothing has prevented the full understanding of both, so far as parts of the latter can be understood, so much as the blending of them together, which originated with Pî *K*ih of the first Han dynasty. The common editions of the book have five of the Appendixes (as they are ordinarily reckoned) broken up and printed side by side with the Text; and the confusion thence arising has made it difficult, through the intermixture of incongruous ideas, for foreign students to lay hold of the meaning.

Labours of native scholars on the Yî.

6. Native scholars have of course been well aware of the difference in time between the appearance of the Text and the Appendixes; and in the Khang-hsî edition of them the two are printed separately. Only now and then, however, has any critic ventured to doubt that the two parts formed one homogeneous whole, or that all the appendixes were from the style or pencil of Confucius. Hundreds of them have brought a wonderful and consistent meaning out of the Text; but to find in it or in the Appendixes what is unreasonable, or any inconsistency between them, would be to impeach the infallibility of Confucius, and stamp on themselves the brand of heterodoxy.

An imperfect description of their labours.

At the same time it is an unfair description of what they have accomplished to say, as has been done lately, that since the fires of 3hin, 'the foremost scholars of each generation have edited the Text (meaning both the Text and the Appendixes), and heaped commentary after commentary upon it; and one and all have arrived at the somewhat

lame conclusion that its full significance is past finding out[1].' A multitude of the native commentaries are of the highest value, and have left little to be done for the elucidation of the Text; and if they say that a passage in an Appendix is 'unfathomable' or 'incalculable,' it is because their authors shrink from allowing, even to themselves, that the ancient sages intermeddled, and intermeddled unwisely, with things too high for them.

Erroneous account of the labours of European Chinese scholars.

When the same writer who thus speaks of native scholars goes on to say that 'in the same way a host of European Chinese scholars have made translations of the Yî, and have, if possible, made confusion worse confounded,' he only shows how imperfectly he had made himself acquainted with the subject. 'The host of European Chinese scholars who have made translations of the Yî' amount to two,—the same two mentioned by me above on pp. 6, 7. The translation of Regis and his coadjutors[2] is indeed capable of improvement; but their work as a whole, and especially the prolegomena, dissertations, and notes, supply a mass of correct and valuable information. They had nearly succeeded in unravelling the confusion, and solving the enigma of the Yî.

CHAPTER II.

THE SUBJECT-MATTER OF THE TEXT. THE LINEAL FIGURES AND THE EXPLANATION OF THEM.

1. Having described the Yî King as consisting of a text in explanation of certain lineal figures, and of appendixes to it, and having traced the composition of the former to

[1] See a communication on certain new views about the Yî in the 'Times' of April 20, 1880; reprinted in Trübner's American, European, and Oriental Literary Record, New Series, vol. i, pp. 125-127.

[2] Regis' coadjutors in the work were the Fathers Joseph de Mailla, who turned the Chinese into Latin word for word, and compared the result with the Mankâu version of the Yî; and Peter du Tartre, whose principal business was to supply the historical illustrations. Regis himself revised all their work and enlarged it, adding his own dissertations and notes. See Prospectus Operis, immediately after M. Mohl's Preface.

its authors in the twelfth century B.C., and that of the latter to between six and seven centuries later at least, I proceed to give an account of what we find in the Text, and how it is deduced from the figures.

The Yî consists of essays based on lineal figures.

The subject-matter of the Text may be briefly represented as consisting of sixty-four short essays, enigmatically and symbolically expressed, on important themes, mostly of a moral, social, and political character, and based on the same number of lineal figures, each made up of six lines, some of which are whole and the others divided.

The first two and the last two may serve for the present as a specimen of those figures: ䷀, ䷁; and ䷾, ䷿[1]. The Text says nothing about their origin and formation. There they are. King Wăn takes them up, one after another, in the order that suits himself, determined, evidently, by the contrast in the lines of each successive pair of hexagrams, and gives their significance, as a whole, with some indication, perhaps, of the action to be taken in the circumstances which he supposes them to symbolise, and whether that action will be lucky or unlucky. Then the duke of *K*âu, beginning with the first or bottom line, expresses, by means of a symbolical or emblematical illustration, the significance of each line, with a similar indication of the good or bad fortune of action taken in connexion with it. The king's interpretation of the whole hexagram will be found to be in harmony with the combined significance of the six lines as interpreted by his son.

Both of them, no doubt, were familiar with the practice of divination which had prevailed in China for more than a thousand years, and would copy closely its methods and style. They were not divining themselves, but their words became oracles to subsequent ages, when men divined by the hexagrams, and sought by means of what was said under them to ascertain how it would be with them in the

[1] See Plate I at the end of the Introduction.

易經

future, and learn whether they should persevere in or withdraw from the courses they were intending to pursue.

2. I will give an instance of the lessons which the lineal figures are made to teach, but before I do so, it will be necessary to relate what is said of their origin, and of the rules observed in studying and interpreting them. For information on these points we must have recourse to the Appendixes; and in reply to the question by whom and in what way the figures were formed, the third, of which we made use in the last chapter, supplies us with three different answers.

The origin of the lineal figures.

(i) The 11th paragraph of Section ii says:—

'Anciently, when the rule of all under heaven was in the hands of Pâo-hsî, looking up, he contemplated the brilliant forms exhibited in the sky; and looking down, he surveyed the patterns shown on the earth. He marked the ornamental appearances on birds and beasts, and the (different) suitabilities of the soil. Near at hand, in his own person, he found things for consideration, and the same at a distance, in things in general. On this he devised the eight lineal figures of three lines each, to exhibit fully the spirit-like and intelligent operations (in nature), and to classify the qualities of the myriads of things.'

Pâo-hsî is another name for Fû-hsî, the most ancient personage who is mentioned with any definiteness in Chinese history, while much that is fabulous is current about him. His place in chronology begins in B.C. 3322, 5203 years ago. He appears in this paragraph as the deviser of the eight kwâ or trigrams. The processes by which he was led to form them, and the purposes which he intended them to serve, are described, but in vague and general terms that do not satisfy our curiosity. The eight figures, however, were ☰, ☱, ☲, ☳, ☴, ☵, ☶, and ☷; called *kh*ien, tui, li, *k*ăn, sun, khân, kăn, and khwăn; and representing heaven or the sky; water, especially a collection of water as in a marsh or lake; fire, the sun, lightning; thunder; wind and wood; water, especially as in rain, the clouds, springs, streams in defiles, and the moon; a hill or mountain; and the earth. To each of these figures is assigned a certain attribute or quality which should be suggested by the

natural object it symbolises; but on those attributes we need not enter at present.

(ii) The 70th and 71st paragraphs of Section i give another account of the origin of the trigrams:—

'In (the system of) the Yî there is the Great Extreme, which produced the two Î (Elementary Forms). These two Forms produced the four Hsiang (Emblematic Symbols); which again produced the eight Kwâ (or Trigrams). The eight Kwâ served to determine the good and evil (issues of events), and from this determination there ensued the (prosecution of the) great business of life.'

The two elementary Forms, the four emblematic Symbols, and the eight Trigrams can all be exhibited with what may be deemed certainty. A whole line (———) and a divided (— —) were the two Î. These two lines placed over themselves, and each of them over the other, formed the four Hsiang: ⚌; ⚏; ⚍; ⚎. The same two lines placed successively over these Hsiang, formed the eight Kwâ, exhibited above.

Who will undertake to say what is meant by 'the Great Extreme' which produced the two elementary Forms? Nowhere else does the name occur in the old Confucian literature. I have no doubt myself that it found its way into this Appendix in the fifth (? or fourth) century B.C. from a Tâoist source. *K*û Hsî, in his 'Lessons on the Yî for the Young,' gives for it the figure of a circle,—thus, ◯; observing that he does so from the philosopher *K*âu (A.D. 1017–1073)[1], and cautioning his readers against thinking that such a representation came from Fû-hsî himself. To me the circular symbol appears very unsuccessful. 'The Great Extreme,' it is said, 'divided and produced two lines,—a whole line and a divided line.' But I do not understand how this could be. Suppose it possible for the circle to unroll itself;

[1] *K*âu-ȝze, called *K*âu Tun-î and *K*âu Mâu-shuh, and, still more commonly, from the rivulet near which was his favourite residence, *K*âu Lien-*kh*î. Mayers (Chinese Reader's Manual, p. 23) says:—'He held various offices of state, and was for many years at the head of a galaxy of scholars who sought for instruction in matters of philosophy and research:—second only to *K*û Hsî in literary repute.'

—we shall have one long line, ————. If this divide itself, we have two whole lines; and another division of one of them is necessary to give us the whole and the divided lines of the lineal figures. The attempt to fashion the Great Extreme as a circle must be pronounced a failure.

But when we start from the two lines as bases, the formation of all the diagrams by a repetition of the process indicated above is easy. The addition to each of the trigrams of each of the two fundamental lines produces 16 figures of four lines; dealt with in the same way, these produce 32 figures of five lines; and a similar operation with these produces the 64 hexagrams, each of which forms the subject of an essay in the text of the Yî. The lines increase in an arithmetical progression whose common difference is 1, and the figures in a geometrical progression whose common ratio is 2. This is all the mystery in the formation of the lineal figures; this, I believe, was the process by which they were first formed; and it is hardly necessary to imagine them to have come from a sage like Fû-hsî. The endowments of an ordinary man were sufficient for such a work. It was possible even to shorten the operation by proceeding at once from the trigrams to the hexagrams, according to what we find in Section i, paragraph 2:—

'A strong and a weak line were manipulated together (till there were the 8 trigrams), and those 8 trigrams were added each to itself and to all the others (till the 64 hexagrams were formed).'

Who first multiplied the figures to 64?

It is a moot question who first multiplied the figures from the trigrams universally ascribed to Fû-hsî to the 64 hexagrams of the Yî. The more common view is that it was king Wăn; but *K*û Hsî, when he was questioned on the subject, rather inclined to hold that Fû-hsî had multiplied them himself, but declined to say whether he thought that their names were as old as the figures themselves, or only dated from the twelfth century B.C.[1] I will not venture to controvert

[1] *K*û-ʒze *Kh*wan shû, or Digest of Works of *K*û-ʒze, chap. 26 (the first chapter on the Yî), art. 16.

his opinion about the multiplication of the figures, but I must think that the names, as we have them now, were from king Wăn.

Why the figures were not continued after 64.

No Chinese writer has tried to explain why the framers stopped with the 64 hexagrams, instead of going on to 128 figures of 7 lines, 256 of 8, 512 of 9, and so on indefinitely. No reason can be given for it, but the cumbrousness of the result, and the impossibility of dealing, after the manner of king Wăn, with such a mass of figures.

(iii) The 73rd paragraph of Section i, with but one paragraph between it and the two others which we have been considering, gives what may be considered a third account of the origin of the lineal figures:—

'Heaven produced the spirit-like things (the tortoise and the divining plant), and the sages took advantage of them. (The operations of) heaven and earth are marked by so many changes and transformations, and the sages imitated them (by means of the Yî). Heaven hangs out its (brilliant) figures, from which are seen good fortune and bad, and the sages made their emblematic interpretations accordingly. The Ho gave forth the scheme or map, and the Lo gave forth the writing, of (both of) which the sages took advantage.'

The words with which we have at present to do are—'The Ho (that is, the Yellow River) gave forth the Map.' This map, according to tradition and popular belief, contained a scheme which served as a model to Fû-hsî in making his 8 trigrams. Apart from this passage in the Yî King, we know that Confucius believed in such a map, or spoke at least as if he did[1]. In the 'Record of Rites' it is said that 'the map was borne by a horse[2];' and the thing, whatever it was, is mentioned in the Shû as still preserved at court, among other curiosities, in B.C. 1079[3]. The story of it, as now current, is this, that 'a dragon-horse' issued from the Yellow River, bearing on its back an arrangement of marks, from which Fû-hsî got the idea of the trigrams.

[1] Analects IX, viii. [2] Lî Kî VIII, iv, 16. [3] Shû V, xxii, 19.

All this is so evidently fabulous that it seems a waste of time to enter into any details about it. My reason for doing so is a wish to take advantage of the map in giving such a statement of the rules observed in interpreting the figures as is necessary in this Introduction.

The form of the River Map.

The map that was preserved, it has been seen, in the eleventh century B.C., afterwards perished, and though there was much speculation about its form from the time that the restoration of the ancient classics was undertaken in the Han dynasty, the first delineation of it given to the public was in the reign of Hui Ʒung of the Sung dynasty (A.D. 1101–1125)[1]. The most approved scheme of it is the following:—

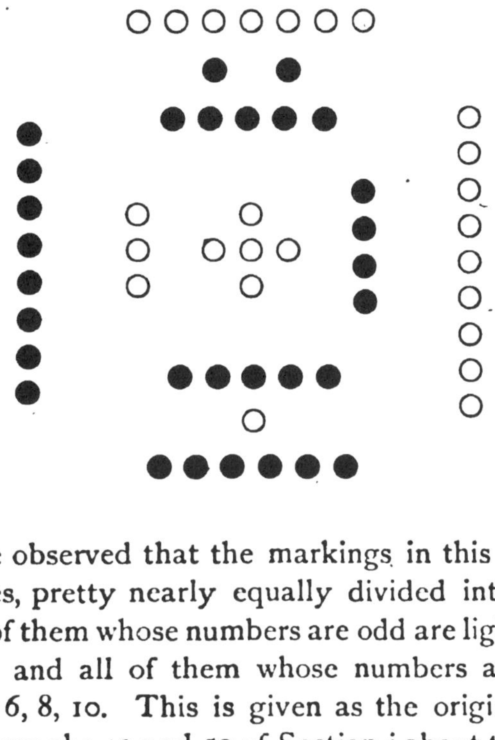

It will be observed that the markings in this scheme are small circles, pretty nearly equally divided into dark and light. All of them whose numbers are odd are light circles,—1, 3, 5, 7, 9; and all of them whose numbers are even are dark,—2, 4, 6, 8, 10. This is given as the origin of what is said in paragraphs 49 and 50 of Section i about the numbers of heaven and earth. The difference in the colour of the circles occasioned the distinction of them and of what they

[1] See Mayers' Chinese Reader's Manual, pp. 56, 57.

signify into Yin and Yang, the dark and the bright, the moon-like and the sun-like; for the sun is called the Great Brightness (Thâi Yang), and the moon the Great Obscurity (Thâi Yin). I shall have more to say in the next chapter on the application of these names. Fû-hsî in making the trigrams, and king Wăn, if it was he who first multiplied them to the 64 hexagrams, found it convenient to use lines instead of the circles:—the whole line (———) for the bright circle (○), and the divided line (— —) for the dark (●). The first, the third, and the fifth lines in a hexagram, if they are 'correct' as it is called, should all be whole, and the second, fourth, and sixth lines should all be divided. Yang lines are strong (or hard), and Yin lines are weak (or soft). The former indicate vigour and authority; the latter, feebleness and submission. It is the part of the former to command; of the latter to obey.

The lines, moreover, in the two trigrams that make up the hexagrams, and characterise the subjects which they represent, are related to one another by their position, and have their significance modified accordingly. The first line and the fourth, the second and the fifth, the third and the sixth are all correlates; and to make the correlation perfect the two members of it should be lines of different qualities, one whole and the other divided. And, finally, the middle lines of the trigrams, the second and fifth, that is, of the hexagrams, have a peculiar value and force. If we have a whole line (———) in the fifth place, and a divided line (— —) in the second, or vice versâ, the correlation is complete. Let the subject of the fifth be the sovereign or a commander-in-chief, according to the name and meaning of the hexagram, then the subject of the second will be an able minister or a skilful officer, and the result of their mutual action will be most beneficial and successful. It is specially important to have a clear idea of the name of the hexagram, and of the subject or state which it is intended to denote. The significance of all the lines comes thus to be of various application, and will differ in different hexagrams.

I have thus endeavoured to indicate how the lineal figures were formed, and the principal rules laid down for the interpretation of them. The details are wearying, but my position is like that of one who is called on to explain an important monument of architecture, very bizarre in its conception and execution. A plainer, simpler structure might have answered the purpose better, but the architect had his reasons for the plan and style which he adopted. If the result of his labours be worth expounding, we must not grudge the study necessary to detect his processes of thought, nor the effort and time required to bring the minds of others into sympathy with his.

My own opinion, as I have intimated, is, that the second account of the origin of the trigrams and hexagrams is the true one. However the idea of the whole and divided lines arose in the mind of the first framer, we must start from them; and then, manipulating them in the manner described, we arrive, very easily, at all the lineal figures, and might proceed to multiply them to billions. We cannot tell who devised the third account of their formation from the map or scheme on the dragon-horse of the Yellow River[1]. Its object, no doubt, was to impart a supernatural character to the trigrams and produce a religious veneration for them. It may be doubted whether the scheme as it is now fashioned be the correct one,—such as it was in the *K*âu dynasty. The paragraph where it is mentioned, goes on to say—'The Lo produced the writing.' This writing was a scheme of the same character as the Ho map, but on the back of a tortoise, which emerged from the river Lo, and showed it to the Great Yü, when he was engaged in his celebrated work of draining off the waters of the flood, as related in the Shû. To the hero sage it suggested 'the Great Plan,' an interesting but mystical document of the same classic, 'a Treatise,' according to Gaubil, 'of Physics, Astrology, Divination, Morals, Politics, and Religion,' the great model for the government of the

[1] Certainly it was not Confucius. See on the authorship of the Appendixes, and especially of Appendix III, in the next chapter.

kingdom. The accepted representation of this writing is the following :—

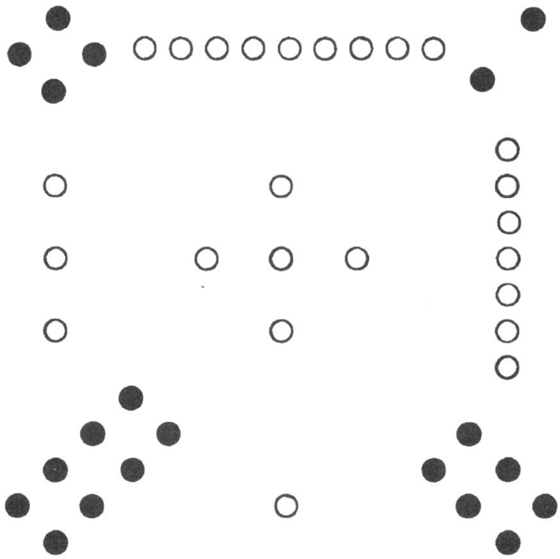

But substituting numbers for the number of marks, we have

4	9	2
3	5	7
8	1	6

This is nothing but the arithmetical puzzle, in which the numbers from 1 to 9 are arranged so as to make 15 in whatever way we add them[1]. If we had the original form of 'the River Map,' we should probably find it a numerical trifle, not more difficult, not more supernatural, than this magic square.

3. Let us return to the Yî of *K*âu, which, as I have said above on p. 10, contains, under each of the 64 hexagrams, a brief essay of a moral, social, or political character, symbolically expressed.

[1] For this dissection, which may also be called reductio ad absurdum, of the Lo writing, I was indebted first to P. Regis. See his Y-King I, p. 60. But *K*û Hsî also has got it in the Appendix to his 'Lessons on the Yî for the Young.'

易經

To understand it, it will be necessary to keep in mind the circumstances in which king Wăn addressed himself to the study of the lineal figures. The kingdom, under the sovereigns of the Yin or Shang dynasty, was utterly disorganised and demoralised. A brother of the reigning king thus described its condition:—

State of the country in time of king Wăn.

'The house of Yin can no longer exercise rule over the land. The great deeds of our founder were displayed in a former age, but through mad addiction to drink we have destroyed the effects of his virtue. The people, small and great, are given to highway robberies, villainies, and treachery. The nobles and officers imitate one another in violating the laws. There is no certainty that criminals will be apprehended. The lesser people rise up and commit violent outrages on one another. The dynasty of Yin is sinking in ruin; its condition is like that of one crossing a large stream, who can find neither ford nor bank[1].'

This miserable state of the nation was due very much to the character and tyranny of the monarch. When the son of Wăn took the field against him, he thus denounced him in 'a Solemn Declaration' addressed to all the states:—

The character of the monarch.

'Shâu, the king of Shang, treats all virtue with contemptuous slight, and abandons himself to wild idleness and irreverence. He has cut himself off from Heaven, and brought enmity between himself and the people. He cut through the leg-bones of those who were wading in a (winter-)morning; he cut out the heart of the good man[2]. His power has been shown in killing and murdering. His honours and confidence are given to the villainous and bad. He has driven from him his instructors and guardians. He has thrown to the winds the statutes and penal laws. He neglects the sacrifices to Heaven and Earth. He has discontinued the offerings

[1] The Shû IV, xi, 1, 2.

[2] These were well-known instances of Shâu's wanton cruelty. Observing some people one winter's day wading through a stream, he ordered their legs to be cut through at the shank-bone, that he might see the marrow which could so endure the cold. 'The good man' was a relative of his own, called Pi-kan. Having enraged Shâu by the sternness of his rebukes, the tyrant ordered his heart to be cut out, that he might see the structure of a sage's heart.

in the ancestral temple. He makes (cruel) contrivances of wonderful device and extraordinary ingenuity to please his wife[1].—God will no longer bear with him, but with a curse is sending down his ruin[2].'

Such was the condition of the nation, such the character of the sovereign. Meanwhile in the west of the kingdom, in a part of what is now the province of Shen-hsî, lay the principality of *K*âu, the lords of which had long been distinguished for their ability and virtue. Its present chief, now known to us as king Wăn, was *Kh*ang, who had succeeded to his father in B.C. 1185. He was not only lord of *K*âu, but had come to be a sort of viceroy over a great part of the kingdom. Equally distinguished in peace and war, a model of all that was good and attractive, he conducted himself with remarkable wisdom and self-restraint. Princes and people would have rejoiced to follow him to attack the tyrant, but he shrank from exposing himself to the charge of being disloyal. At last the jealous suspicion of Shâu was aroused. Wăn, as has been already stated, was thrown into prison in B.C. 1143, and the order for his death might arrive at any moment. Then it was that he occupied himself with the lineal figures.

The lords of *K*âu; and especially king Wăn.

The use of those figures—of the trigrams at least—had long been practised for the purposes of divination. The employment of the divining stalks is indicated in 'the Counsels of the Great Yü,' one of the earliest Books of the Shû[3], and a whole section in 'the Great Plan,' also a Book of the Shû, and referred to the times of the Hsiâ dynasty, describes how 'doubts were to be examined' by means of the tortoise-shell and the stalks[4]. Wăn could not but be familiar with divination as an institution of his

[1] We do not know what these contrivances were. But to please his wife, the infamous Tâ-*k*î, Shâu had made 'the Heater' and 'the Roaster,' two instruments of torture. The latter was a copper pillar laid above a pit of burning charcoal, and made slippery; culprits were forced to walk along it.

[2] The Shû V, i, Sect. iii, 2, 3.

[3] Shû II, ii, 18.

[4] Shû V, iv, 20–31.

country[1]. Possibly it occurred to him that nothing was more likely to lull the suspicions of his dangerous enemy than the study of the figures; and if his keepers took notice of what he was doing, they would smile at his lines, and the sentences which he appended to them.

King Wăn in prison, occupied with the lineal figures.

I like to think of the lord of *K*âu, when incarcerated in Yû-lî, with the 64 figures arranged before him. Each hexagram assumed a mystic meaning, and glowed with a deep significance. He made it tell him of the qualities of various objects of nature, or of the principles of human society, or of the condition, actual and possible, of the kingdom. He named the figures, each by a term descriptive of the idea with which he had connected it in his mind, and then he proceeded to set that idea forth, now with a note of exhortation, now with a note of warning. It was an attempt to restrict the follies of divination within the bounds of reason. The last but one of the Appendixes bears the name of 'Sequence of the Diagrams.' I shall have to speak of it more at length in the next chapter. I only remark at present that it deals, feebly indeed, with the names of the hexagrams in harmony with what I have said about them, and tries to account for the order in which they follow one another. It does all this, not critically as if it needed to be established, but in the way of expository statement, relating that about which there was no doubt in the mind of the author.

But all the work of prince *Kh*ang or king Wăn in the Yî thus amounts to no more than 64 short paragraphs. We do not know what led his son Tan to enter into his work and complete it as he did. Tan was a patriot, a hero, a legislator, and a philosopher. Perhaps he took the lineal figures in hand as a tribute of filial duty. What had been done for the whole hexagram he would do for each line, and make it clear that all the six lines 'bent one way their precious influence,' and blended their rays in the globe of light which his father had made each figure give forth.

Work of the duke of *K*âu on the separate lines.

[1] In the Book of Poetry we have Wăn's grandfather (Than-fû, III, i, ode 3. 3) divining, and his son (king Wû, III, i, ode 10. 7) doing the same.

But his method strikes us as singular. Each line seemed to become living, and suggested some phenomenon in nature or some case of human experience, from which the wisdom or folly, the luckiness or unluckiness, indicated by it could be inferred. It cannot be said that the duke carried out his plan in a way likely to interest any one but a hsien shăng who is a votary of divination, and admires the style of its oracles. According to our notions, a framer of emblems should be a good deal of a poet, but those of the Yî only make us think of a dryasdust. Out of more than 350, the greater number are only grotesque. We do not recover from the feeling of disappointment till we remember that both father and son had to write 'according to the trick,' after the manner of diviners, as if this lineal augury had been their profession.

The seventh hexagram.

4. At length I come to illustrate what I have said on the subject-matter of the Yî by an example. It shall be the treatment of the seventh hexagram (䷆), which king Wăn named Sze, meaning Hosts. The character is also explained as meaning 'multitudes;' and in fact, in a feudal kingdom, the multitudes of the people were all liable to become its army, when occasion required, and the 'host' and the 'population' might be interchangeable terms. As Froude expresses it in the introductory chapter to his History of England, 'Every man was regimented somewhere.'

The hexagram Sze is composed of the two trigrams Khan (☵) and Khwăn (☷), exhibiting waters collected on the earth; and in other symbolisms besides that of the Yî, waters indicate assembled multitudes of men. The waters on which the mystical Babylon sits in the Apocalypse are explained as 'peoples and multitudes and nations and tongues.' I do not positively affirm that it was by this interpretation of the trigrams that king Wăn saw in ䷆ the feudal hosts of his country collected, for neither from him nor his son do we learn, by their direct affirmation, that they had any acquaintance with the trigrams of Fû-hsî. The name which he gave

the figure shows, however, that he saw in it the feudal hosts in the field. How shall their expedition be conducted that it may come to a successful issue?

Looking again at the figure, we see that it is made up of five divided lines, and of one undivided. The undivided line occupies the central place in the lower trigram,—the most important place, next to the fifth, in the whole hexagram. It will represent, in the language of the commentators, 'the lord of the whole figure;' and the parties represented by the other lines may be expected to be of one mind with him or obedient to him. He must be the leader of the hosts. If he were on high, in the fifth place, he would be the sovereign of the kingdom. This is what king Wăn says:—

'Sze indicates how (in the case which it supposes), with firmness and correctness, and (a leader of) age and experience, there will be good fortune and no error.'

This is a good auspice. Let us see how the duke of *K*âu expands it.

He says:—

'The first line, divided, shows the host going forth according to the rules (for such a movement). If those (rules) be not good, there will be evil.'

We are not told what the rules for a military expedition were. Some commentators understand them of the reasons justifying the movement,—that it should be to repress and punish disorder and rebellion. Others, with more likelihood, take them to be the discipline or rules laid down to be observed by the troops. The line is divided, a weak line in a strong place, 'not correct:' this justifies the caution given in the duke's second sentence.

The Text goes on:—

'The second line, undivided, shows (the leader) in the midst of the hosts. There will be good fortune and no error. The king has thrice conveyed to him his charge.'

This does not need any amplification. The duke saw in the strong line the symbol of the leader, who enjoyed

the full confidence of his sovereign, and whose authority admitted of no opposition.

On the third line it is said :—

'The third line, divided, shows how the hosts may possibly have many commanders :—(in such a case) there will be evil.'

The third place is odd, and should be occupied by a strong line, instead of which we have a weak line in it. But it is at the top of the lower trigram, and its subject should be in office or activity. There is suggested the idea that its subject has vaulted over the second line, and wishes to share in the command and honour of him who has been appointed sole commander-in-chief. The lesson in the previous line is made of none effect. We have a divided authority in the expedition. The result can only be evil.

On the fourth line the duke wrote :—

'The fourth line, divided, shows the hosts in retreat : there is no error.'

The line is also weak, and victory cannot be expected; but in the fourth place a weak line is in its correct position, and its subject will do what is right in his circumstances. He will retreat, and a retreat is for him the part of wisdom. When safely affected, where advance would be disastrous, a retreat is as glorious as victory.

Under the fifth line we read :—

'The fifth line, divided, shows birds in the fields which it is advantageous to seize (and destroy). There will be no error. If the oldest son lead the host, and younger men be (also) in command, however firm and correct he may be, there will be evil.'

We have an intimation in this passage that only defensive war, or war waged by the rightful authority to put down rebellion and lawlessness, is right. The 'birds in the fields' are emblematic of plunderers and invaders, whom it will be well to destroy. The fifth line symbolises the chief authority, but here he is weak or humble, and has given all power and authority to execute judgment into the hands of the commander-in-chief, who is the oldest son; and in the subject of line 3 we have an example of the younger men who would cause evil if allowed to share his power.

Finally, on the sixth line the duke wrote:—

'The topmost line, divided, shows the great ruler delivering his charges (to the men who have distinguished themselves), appointing some to be rulers of states, and others to be chiefs of clans. But small men should not be employed (in such positions).'

The action of the hexagram has been gone through. The expedition has been conducted to a successful end. The enemy has been subdued. His territories are at the disposal of the conqueror. The commander-in-chief has done his part well. His sovereign, 'the great ruler,' comes upon the scene, and rewards the officers who have been conspicuous by their bravery and skill, conferring on them rank and lands. But he is warned to have respect in doing so to their moral character. Small men, of ordinary or less than ordinary character, may be rewarded with riches and certain honours; but land and the welfare of its population should not be given into the hands of any who are not equal to the responsibility of such a trust.

The above is a specimen of what I have called the essays that make up the Yî of *K*âu. So would king Wăn and his son have had all military expeditions conducted in their country 3000 years ago. It seems to me that the principles which they lay down might find a suitable application in the modern warfare of our civilised and Christian Europe. The inculcation of such lessons cannot have been without good effect in China during the long course of its history.

Sze is a fair specimen of its class. From the other 63 hexagrams lessons are deduced, for the most part equally good and striking. But why, it may be asked, why should they be conveyed to us by such an array of lineal figures, and in such a farrago of emblematic representations? It is not for the foreigner to insist on such a question. The Chinese have not valued them the less because of the antiquated dress in which their lessons are arrayed. Hundreds of their commentators have evolved and developed their meaning with a minuteness of detail and felicity of illustration that leave nothing to be desired. It is for foreign students of Chinese to gird up their loins for the

mastery of the book instead of talking about it as mysterious and all but inexplicable.

Granting, however, that the subject-matter of the Yî is what has been described, very valuable for its practical wisdom, but not drawn up from an abysmal deep of philosophical speculation, it may still be urged, 'But in all this we find nothing to justify the name of the book as Yî King, the "Classic of Changes." Is there not something more, higher or deeper, in the Appendixes that have been ascribed to Confucius, whose authority is certainly not inferior to that of king Wăn, or the duke of *K*âu?' To reply fully to this question will require another chapter.

CHAPTER III.

THE APPENDIXES.

Subjects of the chapter.

1. Two things have to be considered in this chapter:—the authorship of the Appendixes, and their contents. The Text is ascribed, without dissentient voice, to king Wăn, the founder of the *K*âu dynasty, and his son Tan, better known as the duke of *K*âu; and I have, in the preceding chapters, given reasons for accepting that view. As regards the portion ascribed to king Wăn, the evidence of the third of the Appendixes and the statement of Sze-mâ *Kh*ien are as positive as could be desired; and as regards that ascribed to his son, there is no ground for calling in question the received tradition. The Appendixes have all been ascribed to Confucius, though not with entirely the same unanimity. Perhaps I have rather intimated my own opinion that this view cannot be sustained. I have pointed out that, even if it be true, between six and seven centuries elapsed after the Text of the classic appeared before the Appendixes were written; and I have said that, considering this fact, I cannot regard its two parts as a homogeneous whole, or as constituting one book in the ordinary acceptation of that name. Before entering on the question of the authorship, a very brief statement of the nature and number of the Appendixes will be advantageous.

2. They are reckoned to be ten, and called the Shih Yî or 'Ten Wings.' They are in reality not so many; but the Text is divided into two sections, called the Upper and Lower, or, as we should say, the first and second, and then the commentary on each section is made to form a separate Appendix. I have found it more convenient in the translation which follows to adopt a somewhat different arrangement.

Number and nature of the Appendixes.

My first Appendix, in two sections, embraces the first and second 'wings,' consisting of remarks on the paragraphs by king Wăn in the two parts of the Text.

My second Appendix, in two sections, embraces the third and fourth 'wings,' consisting of remarks on the symbolism of the duke of *K*âu in his explanation of the individual lines of the hexagrams.

My third Appendix, in two sections, embraces the fifth and sixth 'wings,' which bear the name in Chinese of 'Appended Sentences,' and constitute what is called by many 'the Great Treatise.' Each wing has been divided into twelve chapters of very different length, and I have followed this arrangement in my sections. This is the most important Appendix. It has less of the nature of commentary than the previous four wings. While explaining much of what is found in the Text, it diverges to the origin of the trigrams, the methods pursued in the practice of divination, the rise of many arts in the progress of civilisation, and other subjects.

My fourth Appendix, also in two sections, forms the seventh 'wing.' It is confined to an amplification of the expositions of the first and second hexagrams by king Wăn and his son, purporting to show how they may be interpreted of man's nature and doings.

My fifth Appendix is the eighth 'wing,' called 'Discourses on the Trigrams.' It treats of the different arrangement of these in respect of the seasons of the year and the cardinal points by Fû-hsî and king Wăn. It contains also one paragraph, which might seem to justify the view that there is a mythology in the Yî.

My sixth Appendix, in two sections, is the ninth 'wing,'—

'a Treatise on the Sequence of the Hexagrams,' intended to trace the connexion of meaning between them in the order in which they follow one another in the Text of king Wăn.

My seventh Appendix is the tenth 'wing,' an exhibition of the meaning of the 64 hexagrams, not taken in succession, but promiscuously and at random, as they approximate to or are opposed to one another in meaning.

The authorship of the Appendixes.

3. Such are the Appendixes of the Yî King. We have to enquire next who wrote them, and especially whether it be possible to accept the dictum that they were all written by Confucius. If they have come down to us, bearing unmistakeably the stamp of the mind and pencil of the great sage, we cannot but receive them with deference, not to say with reverence. If, on the contrary, it shall appear that with great part of them he had nothing to do, and that it is not certain that any part of them is from him, we shall feel entirely at liberty to exercise our own judgment on their contents, and weigh them in the balances of our reason.

There is no superscription of Confucius on any of the Appendixes.

None of the Appendixes, it is to be observed, bear the superscription of Confucius. There is not a single sentence in any one of them ascribing it to him. I gave in the first chapter, on p. 2, the earliest testimony that these treatises were produced by him. It is that of Sze-mâ *Kh*ien, whose 'Historical Records' must have appeared about the year 100 before our era. He ascribes all the Appendixes, except the last two of them, which he does not mention at all, expressly to Confucius; and this, no doubt, was the common belief in the fourth century after the sage's death.

The third and fourth Appendixes evidently not from Confucius.

But when we look for ourselves into the third and fourth Appendixes—the fifth, sixth, and seventh 'wings'—both of which are specified by *Kh*ien, we find it impossible to receive his statement about them. What is remarkable in both parts of the third is, the frequent occurrence of the formula, 'The Master said,' familiar to all readers of the Confucian Analects. Of course, the

sentence following that formula, or the paragraph covered by it, was, in the judgment of the writer, in the language of Confucius; but what shall we say of the portions preceding and following? If he were the author of them, he would not thus be distinguishing himself from himself. The formula occurs in the third Appendix at least twenty-three times. Where we first meet with it, *K*û Hsî has a note to the effect that 'the Appendixes having been all made by Confucius, he ought not to be himself introducing the formula, "The Master said;" and that it may be presumed, wherever it occurs, that it is a subsequent addition to the Master's text.' One instance will show the futility of this attempt to solve the difficulty. The tenth chapter of Section i commences with the 59th paragraph:—

'In the Yî there are four things characteristic of the way of the sages. We should set the highest value on its explanations, to guide us in speaking; on its changes, for the initiation of our movements; on its emblematic figures, for definite action, as in the construction of implements; and on its prognostications, for our practice of divination.'

This is followed by seven paragraphs expanding its statements, and we come to the last one of the chapter which says,—'The Master said, "Such is the import of the statement that there are four things in the Yî, characteristic of the way of the sages."' I cannot understand how it could be more fully conveyed to us that the compiler or compilers of this Appendix were distinct from the Master whose words they quoted, as it suited them, to confirm or illustrate their views.

In the fourth Appendix, again, we find a similar occurrence of the formula of quotation. It is much shorter than the third, and the phrase, 'The Master said,' does not come before us so frequently; but in the thirty-six paragraphs that compose the first section we meet with it six times.

Moreover, the first three paragraphs of this Appendix are older than its compilation, which could not have taken place till after the death of Confucius, seeing it professes to quote his words. They are taken in fact from a narrative of the Ʒo *K*wan, as having been spoken by a marchioness-

dowager of Lû fourteen years before Confucius was born. To account for this is a difficult task for the orthodox critics among the Chinese literati. *K*û Hsî attempts to perform it in this way:—that anciently there was the explanation given in these paragraphs of the four adjectives employed by king Wăn to give the significance of the first hexagram; that it was employed by Mû *K*iang of Lû; and that Confucius also availed himself of it, while the chronicler used, as he does below, the phraseology of 'The Master said,' to distinguish the real words of the sage from such ancient sayings. But who was 'the chronicler?' No one can tell. The legitimate conclusion from *K*û's criticism is, that so much of the Appendix as is preceded by 'The Master said' is from Confucius,—so much and no more. I am thus obliged to come to the conclusion that Confucius had nothing to do with the composition of these two Appendixes, and that they were not put together till after his death. I have no pleasure in differing from the all but unanimous opinion of Chinese critics and commentators. What is called 'the destructive criticism' has no attractions for me; but when an opinion depends on the argument adduced to support it, and that argument turns out to be of no weight, you can no longer set your seal to this, that the opinion is true. This is the position in which an examination of the internal evidence as to the authorship of the third and fourth Appendixes has placed me. Confucius could not be their author. This conclusion weakens the confidence which we have been accustomed to place in the view that 'the ten wings' were to be ascribed to him unhesitatingly. The view has broken down in the case of three of them;—possibly there is no sound reason for holding the Confucian origin of the other seven.

Bearing of the conclusion as to the third and fourth on the other Appendixes.

I cannot henceforth maintain that origin save with bated breath. This, however, can be said for the first two Appendixes in my arrangement, that there is no evidence against their being Confucian like the fatal formula, 'The Master said.' So it is with a good part of my fifth Appendix; but the concluding paragraphs of it, as well as the seventh

Appendix, and the sixth also in a less degree, seem too trivial to be the production of the great man. As a translator of every sentence both in the Text and the Appendixes, I confess my sympathy with P. Regis, when he condenses the fifth Appendix into small space, holding that the 8th and following paragraphs are not worthy to be translated. 'They contain,' he says, 'nothing but the mere enumeration of things, some of which may be called Yang, and others Yin, without any other cause for so thinking being given. Such a method of procedure would be unbecoming any philosopher, and it cannot be denied to be unworthy of Confucius, the chief of philosophers[1].'

I could not characterise Confucius as 'the chief of philosophers,' though he was a great moral philosopher, and has been since he went out and in among his disciples, the best teacher of the Chinese nation. But from the first time my attention was directed to the Yî, I regretted that he had stooped to write the parts of the Appendixes now under remark. It is a relief not to be obliged to receive them as his. Even the better treatises have no other claim to that character besides the voice of tradition, first heard nearly 400 years after his death.

4. I return to the Appendixes, and will endeavour to give a brief, but sufficient, account of their contents.

The first bears in Chinese the name of Thwan *K*wan, 'Treatise on the Thwan,' thwan being the name given to the paragraphs in which Wăn expresses his sense of the significance of the hexagrams.

The first Appendix.

He does not tell us why he attaches to each hexagram such and such a meaning, nor why he predicates good fortune or bad fortune in connexion with it, for he speaks oracularly, after the manner of a diviner. It is the object of the writer of this Appendix to show the processes of king Wăn's thoughts in these operations, how he looked at the component trigrams with their symbolic intimations, their attributes and qualities, and their linear composition, till he could not think otherwise of the figures than he did. All these considerations are sometimes taken into account,

[1] Regis' Y-King, vol. ii, p. 576.

and sometimes even one of them is deemed sufficient. In this way some technical characters appear which are not found in the Text. The lines, for instance, and even whole trigrams are distinguished as kang and *z*âu, 'hard or strong' and 'weak or soft.' The phrase Kwei-shăn, 'spirits,' or 'spiritual beings,' occurs, but has not its physical signification of 'the contracting and expanding energies or operations of nature.' The names Yin and Yang, mentioned above on pp. 15, 16, do not present themselves.

I delineated, on p. 11, the eight trigrams of Fû-hsî, and gave their names, with the natural objects they are said to represent, but did not mention the attributes, the virtutes, ascribed to them. Let me submit here a table of them, with those qualities, and the points of the compass to which they are referred. I must do this because king Wăn made a change in the geographical arrangement of them, to which reference is made perhaps in his text and certainly in this treatise. He also is said to have formed an entirely different theory as to the things represented by the trigrams, which it will be well to give now, though it belongs properly to the fifth Appendix.

FÛ-HSÎ'S TRIGRAMS.

1	2	3	4	5	6	7	8
☰	☱	☲	☳	☴	☵	☶	☷
*kh*ien	tui	lî	*k*ăn	sun	khân	kăn	khwăn
Heaven, the sky.	Water, collected as in a marsh or lake.	Fire, as in lightning; the sun.	Thunder.	The wind; wood.	Water, as in rain, clouds, springs, streams, and defiles. The moon.	Hills, or mountains.	The earth.
S.	S.E.	E.	N.E.	S.W.	W.	N.W.	N.
Untiring strength; power.	Pleasure; complacent satisfaction.	Brightness; elegance.	Moving, exciting power.	Flexibility; penetration.	Peril; difficulty.	Resting; the act of arresting.	Capaciousness; submission.

易經

The natural objects and phenomena thus represented are found up and down in the Appendixes. It is impossible to believe that the several objects were assigned to the several figures on any principles of science, for there is no indication of science in the matter: it is difficult even to suppose that they were assigned on any comprehensive scheme of thought. Why are tui and khân used to represent water in different conditions, while khân, moreover, represents the moon? How is sun set apart to represent things so different as wind and wood? At a very early time the Chinese spoke of 'the five elements,' meaning water, fire, wood, metal, and earth; but the trigrams were not made to indicate them, and it is the general opinion that there is no reference to them in the Yî[1].

Again, the attributes assigned to the trigrams are learned mainly from this Appendix and the fifth. We do not readily get familiar with them, nor easily accept them all. It is impossible for us to tell whether they were a part of the jargon of divination before king Wăn, or had grown up between his time and that of the author of the Appendixes.

King Wăn altered the arrangement of the trigrams so that not one of them should stand at the same point of the compass as in the ancient plan. He made them also representative of certain relations among themselves, as if they composed a family of parents and children. It will be sufficient at present to give a table of his scheme.

KING WĂN'S TRIGRAMS.

1	2	3	4	5	6	7	8
☲	☴	☳	☶	☵	☰	☱	☷
lî	sun	*k*ăn	kăn	khân	*kh*ien	tui	khwăn
Second daughter.	Oldest daughter.	Oldest son.	Youngest son.	Second son.	Father.	Youngest daughter.	Mother.
S.	S.E.	E.	N.E.	N.	N.W.	W.	S.W.

[1] See *K*âo Yî's Hâi Yü Ȝhung Khâo, Book I, art. 3 (1790).

There is thus before us the apparatus with which the writer of the Appendix accomplishes his task. Let me select one of the shortest instances of his work. The fourteenth hexagram is ䷍, called Tâ Yû, and meaning 'Possessing in great abundance.' King Wăn saw in it the symbol of a government prosperous and realising all its proper objects; but all that he wrote on it was 'Tâ Yû (indicates) great progress and success.' Unfolding that view of its significance, the Appendix says:—

'In Tâ Yû the weak (line) has the place of honour, is grandly central, and (the strong lines) above and below respond to it. Hence comes its name of "Possession of what is great." The attributes (of its constituent trigrams, *kh*ien and lî) are strength and vigour, elegance and brightness. (The ruling line in it) responds to (the ruling line in the symbol of) heaven, and its actings are (consequently all) at the proper times. Thus it is that it is said to indicate great progress and success.'

In a similar way the paragraphs on all the other 63 hexagrams are gone through; and, for the most part, with success. The conviction grows upon the student that the writer has on the whole apprehended the mind of king Wăn.

The name Kwei-shăn.

I stated, on p. 32, that the name kwei-shăn occurs in this Appendix. It has not yet, however, received the semi-physical, semi-metaphysical signification which the comparatively modern scholars of the Sung dynasty give to it. There are two passages where it is found;—the second paragraph on *Kh*ien, the fifteenth hexagram, and the third on Făng, the fifty-fifth. By consulting them the reader will be able to form an opinion for himself. The term kwei denotes specially the human spirit disembodied, and shăn is used for spirits whose seat is in heaven. I do not see my way to translate them, when used binomially together, otherwise than by spiritual beings or spiritual agents.

*K*û Hsî once had the following question suggested by the second of these passages put to him:—'Kwei-shăn is a name for the traces of making and transformation; but when it is said that (the interaction of) heaven and earth

is now vigorous and abundant, and now dull and void, growing and diminishing according to the seasons, that constitutes the traces of making and transformation; why should the writer further speak of the Kwei-shăn?' He replied, 'When he uses the style of "heaven and earth," he is speaking of the result generally; but in ascribing it to the Kwei-shăn, he is representing the traces of their effective interaction, as if there were men (that is, some personal agency) bringing it about[1].' This solution merely explains the language away. When we come to the fifth Appendix, we shall understand better the views of the period when these treatises were produced.

The single character shăn is used in explaining the thwan on Kwân, the twentieth hexagram, where we read:—

'In Kwân we see the spirit-like way of heaven, through which the four seasons proceed without error. The sages, in accordance with (this) spirit-like way, laid down their instructions, and all under heaven yield submission to them.'

The author of the Appendix delights to dwell on the changing phenomena taking place between heaven and earth, and which he attributes to their interaction; and he was penetrated evidently with a sense of the harmony between the natural and spiritual worlds. It is this sense, indeed, which vivifies both the thwan and the explanation of them.

5. We proceed to the second Appendix, which professes to do for the duke of *K*âu's symbolical exposition of the several lines what the Thwan *K*wan does for the entire figures. The work here, however, is accomplished with less trouble and more briefly. The whole bears the name of Hsiang *K*wan, 'Treatise on the Symbols' or 'Treatise on the Symbolism (of the Yî).'

The second Appendix.

[1] See the 'Collected Comments' on hexagram 55 in the Khang-hsî edition of the Yî (App. I). 'The traces of making and transformation' mean the ever-changing phenomena of growth and decay. Our phrase 'Vestiges of Creation' might be used to translate the Chinese characters. See the remarks of the late Dr. Medhurst on the hexagrams 15 and 55 in his 'Dissertation on the Theology of the Chinese,' pp. 107–112. In hexagram 15, Canon McClatchie for kwei-shăn gives 'gods and demons;' in hexagram 55, 'the Demon-gods.'

D 2

If there were reason to think that it came in any way from Confucius, I should fancy that I saw him sitting with a select class of his disciples around him. They read the duke's Text column after column, and the master drops now a word or two, and now a sentence or two, that illuminate the meaning. The disciples take notes on their tablets, or store his remarks in their memories, and by and by they write them out with the whole of the Text or only so much of it as is necessary. Whoever was the original lecturer, the Appendix, I think, must have grown up in this way.

It would not be necessary to speak of it at greater length, if it were not that the six paragraphs on the symbols of the duke of *K*âu are always preceded by one which is called 'the Great Symbolism,' and treats of the trigrams composing the hexagram, how they go together to form the six-lined figure, and how their blended meaning appears in the institutions and proceedings of the great men and kings of former days, and of the superior men of all time. The paragraph is for the most part, but by no means always, in harmony with the explanation of the hexagram by king Wăn, and a place in the Thwan *K*wan would be more appropriate to it. I suppose that, because it always begins with the mention of the two symbolical trigrams, it is made, for the sake of the symmetry, to form a part of the treatise on the Symbolism of the Yî.

The Great Symbolism.

I will give a few examples of the paragraphs of the Great Symbolism. The first hexagram ䷀ is formed by a repetition of the trigram *Kh*ien ☰, representing heaven, and it is said on it:—Heaven in its motion (gives) the idea of strength. The superior man, in accordance with this, nerves himself to ceaseless activity.'

The second hexagram ䷁ is formed by a repetition of the trigram Khwăn ☷, representing the earth, and it is said on it:—'The capacious receptivity of the earth is what is denoted by Khwăn. The superior man, in accordance with this, with his large virtue, supports men and things.'

The forty-fourth hexagram, called Kâu ䷫, is formed by the trigrams Sun ☴, representing wind, and *Kh*ien ☰, representing heaven or the sky, and it is said on it:—'(The symbol of) wind, beneath that of the sky, forms Kâu. In accordance with this, the sovereign distributes his charges, and promulgates his announcements throughout the four quarters (of the kingdom).'

The fifty-ninth hexagram, called Hwân ䷺, is formed by the trigrams Khân ☵, representing water, and Sun ☴, representing wind, and it is said on it:—'(The symbol of) water and (that of wind) above it form Hwân. The ancient kings, in accordance with this, presented offerings to God, and established the ancestral temple.' The union of the two trigrams suggested to king Wăn the idea of dissipation in the alienation of men from the Supreme Power, and of the minds of parents from their children; a condition which the wisdom of the ancient kings saw could best be met by the influences of religion.

One more example. The twenty-sixth hexagram, called Tâ *Kh*û ䷙, is formed of the trigrams *Kh*ien, representing heaven or the sky, and Kân ☶, representing a mountain, and it is said on it:—'(The symbol of) heaven in the midst of a mountain forms Tâ *Kh*û. The superior man, in accordance with this, stores largely in his memory the words of former men and their conduct, to subserve the accumulation of his virtue.' We are ready to exclaim and ask, 'Heaven, the sky, in the midst of a mountain! Can there be such a thing?' and *K*û Hsî will tell us in reply, 'No, there cannot be such a thing in reality; but you can conceive it for the purpose of the symbolism.'

From this and the other examples adduced from the Great Symbolism, it is clear that, so far as its testimony bears on the subject, the trigrams of Fû-hsî did not receive their form and meaning with a deep intention that they should serve as the basis of a philosophical scheme concerning the constitution of heaven and earth and all that

is in them. In this Appendix they are used popularly, just as one

'Finds tongues in trees, books in the running brooks,
Sermons in stones, and good in everything.'

The writer moralises from them in an edifying manner. There is ingenuity, and sometimes instruction also, in what he says, but there is no mystery. Chinese scholars and gentlemen, however, who have got some little acquaintance with western science, are fond of saying that all the truths of electricity, heat, light, and other branches of European physics, are in the eight trigrams. When asked how then they and their countrymen have been and are ignorant of those truths, they say that they have to learn them first from western books, and then, looking into the Yî, they see that they were all known to Confucius more than 2000 years ago. The vain assumption thus manifested is childish; and until the Chinese drop their hallucination about the Yî as containing all things that have ever been dreamt of in all philosophies, it will prove a stumbling-block to them, and keep them from entering on the true path of science.

The third Appendix.

6. We go on to the third Appendix in two sections, being the fifth and sixth 'wings,' and forming what is called 'The Great Treatise.' It will appear singular to the reader, as it has always done to myself, that neither in the Text, nor in the first two Appendixes, does the character called Yî, which gives its name to the classic, once appear. It is the symbol of 'change,' and is formed from the character for 'the sun' placed over that for 'the moon[1].' As the sun gives place to the moon, and the moon to the sun, so is change always proceeding in the phenomena of nature and the experiences of society. We meet with the character nearly fifty times in this Appendix; —applied most commonly to the Text of our classic, so that Yî King or Yî Shû is 'the Classic or Book of Changes.' It is also applied often to the changes in the lines of the

[1] 易 = 日, the sun, placed over 勿, a form of the old D (=月), the moon.

易經

figures, made by the manipulations of divination, apart from any sentence or oracle concerning them delivered by king Wăn or his son. There is therefore the system of the Yî as well as the book of the Yî. The definition of the name which is given in one paragraph will suit them both:—'Production and reproduction is what is called (the process of) change[1].' In nature there is no vacuum. When anything is displaced, what displaces it takes the empty room. And in the lineal figures, the strong and the weak lines push each other out.

Harmony between the lines ever changing and the changes in external phenomena.

Now the remarkable thing asserted is, that the changes in the lines of the figures and the changes of external phenomena show a wonderful harmony and concurrence. We read:—

'The Yî was made on a principle of accordance with heaven and earth, and shows us therefore, without rent or confusion, the course (of things) in heaven and earth[2].'

'There is a similarity between the sage and heaven and earth; and hence there is no contrariety in him to them. His knowledge embraces all things, and his course is intended to be helpful to all under the sky; and therefore he falls into no error. He acts according to the exigency of circumstances, without being carried away by their current; he rejoices in Heaven, and knows its ordinations; and hence he has no anxieties. He rests in his own (present) position, and cherishes the spirit of generous benevolence; and hence he can love (without reserve)[3].'

'(Through the Yî) he embraces, as in a mould or enclosure, the transformations of heaven and earth without any error; by an ever-varying adaptation he completes (the nature of) all things without exception; he penetrates to a knowledge of the course of day and night (and all other correlated phenomena). It is thus that his operation is spirit-like, unconditioned by place, while the changes (which he produces) are not restricted to any form.'

One more quotation:—

'The sage was able to survey all the complex phenomena under the sky. He then considered in his mind how they could be

[1] III, i, 29 (chap. 5. 6). [2] III, i, 20 (chap. 4. 1).
[3] III, i, 22.

figured, and (by means of the diagrams) represented their material forms and their character[1].'

All that is thus predicated of the sage, or ancient sages, though the writer probably had Fû-hsî in his mind, is more than sufficiently extravagant, and reminds us of the language in 'the Doctrine of the Mean,' that 'the sage, able to assist the transforming and nourishing powers of heaven and earth, may with heaven and earth form a ternion[2].'

I quoted largely, in the second chapter, from this Appendix the accounts which it gives of the formation of the lineal figures. There is no occasion to return to that subject. Let us suppose the figures formed. They seem to have the significance, when looked at from certain points of view, which have been determined for us by king Wăn and the duke of *K*âu. But this does not amount to divination. How can the lines be made to serve this purpose? The Appendix professes to tell us.

Divination.

Before touching on the method which it describes, let me observe that divination was practised in China from a very early time. I will not say 5,200 years ago, in the days of Fû-hsî, for I cannot repress doubts of his historical personality; but as soon as we tread the borders of something like credible history, we find it existing. In the Shû King, in a document that purports to be of the twenty-third century B.C.[3], divination by means of the tortoise-shell is mentioned; and somewhat later we find that method continuing, and also divination by the lineal figures, manipulated by means of the stalks of a plant[4], the Ptarmica Sibirica[5], which is still cultivated on and about the grave of Confucius, where I have myself seen it growing.

Ancient divination.

The object of the divination, it should be acknowledged, was not to discover future events absolutely, as if they could be known beforehand[6], but

Object of the divination.

[1] III, i, 38 (chap. 8. 1).
[2] Doctrine of the Mean, chap. xxii.
[3] The Shû II, ii, 18.
[4] The Shû V, iv, 20, 31.
[5] See Williams' Syllabic Dictionary on the character 蓍.
[6] Canon McClatchie (first paragraph of his Introduction) says:—'The Yî is garded by the Chinese with peculiar veneration .... as containing a mine of

to ascertain whether certain schemes, and conditions of events contemplated by the consulter, would turn out luckily or unluckily. But for the actual practice the stalks of the plant were necessary; and I am almost afraid to write that this Appendix teaches that they were produced by Heaven of such a nature as to be fit for the purpose. 'Heaven,' it says, in the 73rd paragraph of Section i, quoted above on p. 14, 'Heaven produced the spirit-like things.' The things were the tortoise and the plant, and in paragraph 68, the same quality of being shăn, or 'spirit-like,' is ascribed to them. Occasionally, in the field of Chinese literature, we meet with doubts as to the efficacy of divination, and the folly of expecting any revelation of the character of the future from an old tortoise-shell and a handful of withered twigs[1]; but when this Appendix was made, the writer had not attained to so much common sense. The stalks were to him 'spirit-like,' possessed of

knowledge, which, if it were possible to fathom it thoroughly, would, in their estimation, enable the fortunate possessor to foretell all future events.' This misstatement does not surprise me so much as that Morrison, generally accurate on such points, should say (Dictionary, Part II, i, p. 1020, on the character 易):—

Of the odd and even numbers, the kwâ or lines of Fû-hsî are the visible signs; and it being assumed that these signs answer to the things signified, and from a knowledge of all the various combinations of numbers, a knowledge of all possible occurrences in nature may be previously known.' The whole article from which I take this sentence is inaccurately written. The language of the Appendix on the knowledge of the future given by the use of the Yî is often incautious, and a cursory reader may be misled; to a careful student, however, the meaning is plain. The second passage of the Shû, referred to above, treats of 'the Examination of Doubts,' and concludes thus:—'When the tortoise-shell and the stalks are both opposed to the views of men, there will be good fortune in stillness, and active operations will be unlucky.'

[1] A remarkable instance is given by Liû Kî (of the Ming dynasty, in the fifteenth century) in a story about Shâo Phing, who had been marquis of Tung-ling in the time of Ȝhin, but was degraded under Han. Having gone once to Sze-mâ Ki-kû, one of the most skilful diviners of the country, and wishing to know whether there would be a brighter future for him, Sze-mâ said, 'Ah! is it the way of Heaven to love any (partially)? Heaven loves only the virtuous. What intelligence is possessed by spirits? They are intelligent (only) by their connexion with men. The divining stalks are so much withered grass; the tortoise-shell is a withered bone. They are but things, and man is more intelligent than things. Why not listen to yourself instead of seeking (to learn) from things?' The whole piece is in many of the collections of Kû Wăn, or Elegant Writing.

a subtle and invisible virtue that fitted them for use in divining.

Formation of the lineal figures by the divining stalks.

Given the stalks with such virtue, the process of manipulating them so as to form the lineal figures is described (Section i, chap. 9, parr. 49–58), but it will take the student much time and thought to master the various operations. Forty-nine stalks were employed, which were thrice manipulated for each line, so that it took eighteen manipulations to form a hexagram. The lines were determined by means of the numbers derived from the River Map or scheme. Odd numbers gave strong or undivided lines, and even numbers gave the weak or divided. An important part was played in combining the lines, and forming the hexagrams by the four emblematic symbols, to which the numbers 9, 8, 7, 6 were appropriated[1]. The figures having been formed, recourse was had for their interpretation to the thwan of king Wăn, and the emblematic sentences of the duke of *K*âu. This was all the part which numbers played in the divination by the Yî, helping the operator to make up his lineal figure. An analogy has often been asserted between the numbers of the Yî and the numbers of Pythagoras; and certainly we might make ten, and more than ten, antinomies from these Appendixes in startling agreement with the ten principia of the Pythagoreans. But if Aristotle was correct in holding that Pythagoras regarded numbers as entities, and maintained that Number was the Beginning (Principle, ἀρχή) of things, the cause of their material existence, and of their

[1] These numbers are commonly derived from the River Scheme, in the outer sides of which are the corresponding marks:— ●●●●●●, opposite to ●●; ooooooo, opposite to o; ●●●●●●●●, opposite to ●●●●; and ooooooooo, opposite to ooo. Hence the number 6 is assigned to ⚏, 7 to ⚎, 8 to ⚍, and 9 to ⚌. Hence also, in connexion with the formation of the figures by manipulation of the stalks, 9 becomes the number symbolical of the undivided line, as representing *Kh*ien ☰, and 6 of the divided line, as representing Khwăn ☷. But the late delineation of the map, as given on p. 15, renders all this uncertain, so far as the scheme is concerned. The numbers of the hsiang, however, may have been fixed, must have been fixed indeed, at an early period.

modifications and different states, then the doctrine of the philosopher of Samos was different from that of the Yî[1], in which numbers come in only as aids in divining to form the hexagrams. Of course all divination is vain, nor is the method of the Yî less absurd than any other. The Chinese themselves have given it up in all circles above those of the professional quacks, and yet their scholars continue to maintain the unfathomable science and wisdom of these appended treatises!

The names Yin and Yang.

It is in this Appendix that we first meet with the names yin and yang[2], of which I have spoken briefly on pp. 15, 16. Up to this point, instead of them, the names for the two elementary forms of the lines have been kang and *z*âu, which I have translated by 'strong and weak,' and which also occur here ten times. The following attempt to explain these different names appears in the fifth Appendix, paragraph 4:—

'Anciently when the sages made the Yî, it was with the design that its figures should be in conformity with the principles underlying the natures (of men and things), and the ordinances appointed (for them by Heaven). With this view they exhibited in them the way of heaven, calling (the lines) yin and yang; the way of earth, calling them the strong (or hard) and the weak (or soft); and the way of man, under the names of benevolence and righteousness. Each (trigram) embraced those three Powers, and being repeated, its full form consisted of six lines.'

However difficult it may be to make what is said here intelligible, it confirms what I have affirmed of the significance of the names yin and yang, as meaning bright and dark, derived from the properties of the sun and moon. We may use for these adjectives a variety of others, such as active and inactive, masculine and feminine, hot and cold, more or less analogous to them; but there arise the important questions,—Do we find yang and yin not merely used to indicate the quality of what they are applied

[1] See the account of Pythagoras and his philosophy in Lewes' History of Philosophy, pp. 18-38 (1871).

[2] See Section i, 24, 32, 35; Section ii, 28, 29, 30, 35.

to, but at the same time with substantival force, denoting what has the quality which the name denotes? Had the doctrine of a primary matter of an ethereal nature, now expanding and showing itself full of activity and power as yang, now contracting and becoming weak and inactive as yin:—had this doctrine become matter of speculation when this Appendix was written? The Chinese critics and commentators for the most part assume that it had. P. Regis, Dr. Medhurst, and other foreign Chinese scholars repeat their statements without question. I have sought in vain for proof of what is asserted. It took more than a thousand years after the closing of the Yî to fashion in the Confucian school the doctrine of a primary matter. We do not find it fully developed till the era of the Sung dynasty, and in our eleventh and twelfth centuries[1]. To find it in the Yî is the logical, or rather illogical, error of putting 'the last first.' Neither creation nor cosmogony was before the mind of the author whose work I am analysing. His theme is the Yî,—the ever-changing phenomena of nature and experience. There is nothing but this in the 'Great Treatise' to task our powers;—nothing deeper or more abstruse.

[1] As a specimen of what the ablest Sung scholars teach, I may give the remarks (from the 'Collected Comments') of *Kû Kăn* (of the same century as *Kû* Hsî, rather earlier) on the 4th paragraph of Appendix V:—'In the Yî there is the Great Extreme. When we speak of the yin and yang, we mean the air (or ether) collected in the Great Void. When we speak of the Hard and Soft, we mean that ether collected, and formed into substance. Benevolence and righteousness have their origin in the great void, are seen in the ether substantiated, and move under the influence of conscious intelligence. Looking at the one origin of all things we speak of their nature; looking at the endowments given to them, we speak of the ordinations appointed (for them). Looking at them as (divided into) heaven, earth, and men, we speak of their principle. The three are one and the same. The sages wishing that (their figures) should be in conformity with the principles underlying the natures (of men and things) and the ordinances appointed (for them), called them (now) yin and yang, (now) the hard and the soft, (now) benevolence and righteousness, in order thereby to exhibit the ways of heaven, earth, and men; it is a view of them as related together. The trigrams of the Yî contain the three Powers; and when they are doubled into hexagrams, there the three Powers unite and are one. But there are the changes and movements of their (several) ways, and therefore there are separate places for the yin and yang, and reciprocal uses of the hard and the soft.'

易經

As in the first Appendix, so in this, the name kwei-shăn occurs twice; in paragraghs 21 and 50 of Section i. In the former instance, each part of the name has its significance. Kwei denotes the animal soul or nature, and Shăn, the intellectual soul, the union of which constitutes the living rational man. I have translated them, it will be seen, by 'the anima and the animus.' Canon McClatchie gives for them 'demons and gods;' and Dr. Medhurst said on the passage, 'The kwei-shăns are evidently the expanding and contracting principles of human life. . . . . The kwei-shăns are brought about by the dissolution of the human frame, and consist of the expanding and ascending shăn, which rambles about in space, and of the contracted and shrivelled kwei, which reverts to earth and nonentity[1].'

The name Kwei-shăn.

This is pretty much the same view as my own, though I would not here use the phraseology of 'expanding and contracting.' Canon McClatchie is consistent with himself, and renders the characters by 'demons and gods.'

In the latter passage it is more difficult to determine the exact meaning. The writer says, that 'by the odd numbers assigned to heaven and the even numbers assigned to earth, the changes and transformations are effected, and the spirit-like agencies kept in movement;' meaning that by means of the numbers the spirit-like lines might be formed on a scale sufficient to give a picture of all the changing phenomena, taking place, as if by a spiritual agency, in nature. Medhurst contents himself on it with giving the explanation of *K*û Hsî, that 'the kwei-shăns refer to the contractions and expandings, the recedings and approachings of the productive and completing powers of the even and odd numbers[2].' Canon McClatchie does not follow his translation of the former passage and give here 'demons and gods,' but we have 'the Demon-god (i.e. Shang Tî)[3].' I shall refer to this version when considering the fifth Appendix.

[1] Dissertation on the Theology of the Chinese, pp. 111, 112.
[2] Theology of the Chinese, p. 12?.
[3] Translation of the Yî King, p. 312.

The single character shăn occurs more than twenty times;—used now as a substantive, now as an adjective, and again as a verb. I must refer the reader to the translation and notes for its various significance, subjoining in a note a list of the places where it occurs [1].

Shan alone.

Much more might be said on the third Appendix, for the writer touches on many other topics, antiquarian and speculative, but a review of them would help us little in the study of the leading subject of the Yî. In passing on to the next treatise, I would only further say that the style of this and the author's manner of presenting his thoughts often remind the reader of 'the Doctrine of the Mean.' I am surprised that 'the Great Treatise' has never been ascribed to the author of that Doctrine, 3ze-sze, the grandson of Confucius, whose death must have taken place between B.C. 400 and 450.

7. The fourth Appendix, the seventh 'wing' of the Yî, need not detain us long. As I stated on p. 27, it is confined to an exposition of the Text on the first and second hexagrams, being an attempt to show that what is there affirmed of heaven and earth may also be applied to man, and that there is an essential agreement between the qualities ascribed to them, and the benevolence, righteousness, propriety, and wisdom, which are the four constituents of his moral and intellectual nature.

The fourth Appendix.

It is said by some of the critics that Confucius would have treated all the other hexagrams in a similar way, if his life had been prolonged, but we found special grounds for denying that Confucius had anything to do with the composition of this Appendix; and, moreover, I cannot think of any other figure that would have afforded to the author the same opportunity of discoursing about man. The style and method are after the manner of 'the Doctrine of the Mean' quite as much as those of 'the Great Treatise.' Several paragraphs, moreover, suggest to us the magniloquence of Mencius. It is said, for instance, by 3ze-sze, of

[1] Section i, 23, 32, 57, 58, 62, 64, 67, 68, 69, 73, 76, 81; Section ii, 11, 15, 33, 34, 41, 45.

the sage, that 'he is the equal or correlate of Heaven[1],' and in this Appendix we have the sentiment expanded into the following:—

'The great man is he who is in harmony in his attributes with heaven and earth; in his brightness with the sun and moon; in his orderly procedure with the four seasons; and in his relation to what is fortunate and what is calamitous with the spiritual agents. He may precede Heaven, and Heaven will not act in opposition to him; he may follow Heaven, but will act only as Heaven at the time would do. If Heaven will not act in opposition to him, how much less will man! how much less will the spiritual agents[2]!'

One other passage may receive our consideration:—

'The family that accumulates goodness is sure to have superabundant happiness, and the family that accumulates evil is sure to have superabundant misery[3].'

The language makes us think of the retribution of good and evil as taking place in the family, and not in the individual; the judgment is long deferred, but it is inflicted at last, lighting, however, not on the head or heads that most deserved it. Confucianism never falters in its affirmation of the difference between good and evil, and that each shall have its appropriate recompense; but it has little to say of the where and when and how that recompense will be given. The old classics are silent on the subject of any other retribution besides what takes place in time. About the era of Confucius the view took definite shape that, if the issues of good and evil, virtue and vice, did not take effect in the experience of the individual, they would certainly do so in that of his posterity. This is the prevailing doctrine among the Chinese at the present day; and one of the earliest expressions, perhaps the earliest expression, of it was in the sentence under our notice that has been copied from this Appendix into almost every moral treatise that circulates in China. A wholesome and an important truth it is, that 'the sins of parents are visited

[1] *K*ung-yung xxxi, 4.
[2] Section i, 34. This is the only paragraph where kwei-shăn occurs.
[3] Section ii, 5.

on their children;' but do the parents themselves escape the curse? It is to be regretted that this short treatise, the only 'wing' of the Yî professing to set forth its teachings concerning man as man, does not attempt any definite reply to this question. I leave it, merely observing that it has always struck me as the result of an after-thought, and a wish to give to man, as the last of 'the Three Powers,' a suitable place in connexion with the Yî. The doctrine of 'the Three Powers' is as much out of place in Confucianism as that of 'the Great Extreme.' The treatise contains several paragraphs interesting in themselves, but it adds nothing to our understanding of the Text, or even of the object of the appended treatises, when we try to look at them as a whole.

The fifth Appendix.

8. It is very different with the fifth of the Appendixes, which is made up of 'Remarks on the Trigrams.' It is shorter than the fourth, consisting of only 22 paragraphs, in some of which the author rises to a height of thought reached nowhere else in these treatises, while several of the others are so silly and trivial, that it is difficult, not to say impossible, to believe that they are the production of the same man. We find in it the earlier and later arrangement of the trigrams,—the former, that of Fû-hsî, and the latter, that of king Wăn; their names and attributes; the work of God in nature, described as a progress through the trigrams; and finally a distinctive, but by no means exhaustive, list of the natural objects, symbolised by them.

First paragraph.

It commences with the enigmatic declaration that 'Anciently, when the sages made the Yî,' (that is, the lineal figures, and the system of divination by them), 'in order to give mysterious assistance to the spiritual Intelligences, they produced (the rules for the use of) the divining plant.' Perhaps this means no more than that the lineal figures were made to 'hold the mirror up to nature,' so that men by the study of them would understand more of the unseen and spiritual operations, to which the phenomena around them were owing, than they could otherwise do.

The author goes on to speak of the Fû-hsî trigrams, and passes from them to those of king Wăn in paragraph 8. That and the following two are very remarkable; but before saying anything of them, I will go on to the 14th, which is the only passage that affords any ground for saying that there is a mythology in the Yî. It says:—

Mythology of the Yî.

'*Kh*ien is (the symbol of) heaven, and hence is styled father. Khwăn is (the symbol of) earth, and hence is styled mother. *K*ăn (shows) the first application (of khwăn to *kh*ien), resulting in getting (the first of) its male (or undivided lines), and hence we call it the oldest son. Sun (shows) a first application (of *kh*ien to khwăn), resulting in getting (the first of) its female (or divided lines), and hence we call it the oldest daughter. Khân (shows) a second application (of khwăn to *kh*ien), and Lî a second (of *kh*ien to khwăn), resulting in the second son and second daughter. In *K*ăn and Tui we have a third application (of khwăn to *kh*ien and of *kh*ien to khwăn), resulting in the youngest son and youngest daughter.'

From this language has come the fable of a marriage between *Kh*ien and Khwăn, from which resulted the six other trigrams, considered as their three sons and three daughters; and it is not to be wondered at, if some men of active and ill-regulated imaginations should see Noah and his wife in those two primary trigrams, and in the others their three sons and the three sons' wives. Have we not in both cases an ogdoad? But I have looked in the paragraph in vain for the notion of a marriage-union between heaven and earth.

It does not treat of the genesis of the other six trigrams by the union of the two, but is a rude attempt to explain their forms when they were once existing[1]. According to the idea of changes, *Kh*ien and Khwăn are continually varying their forms by their interaction. As here represented, the

[1] This view seems to be in accordance with that of Wû *Kh*ăng (of the Yüan dynasty), as given in the 'Collected Comments' of the Khang-hsî edition. The editors express their approval of it in preference to the interpretation of *K*û Hsî, who understood the whole to refer to the formation of the lineal figures, the 'application' being 'the manipulation of the stalks to find the proper line.'

other trigrams are not 'produced[1]' by a marriage-union, but from the application, literally the seeking, of one of them—of Khwăn as much as of *Kh*ien—addressed to the other[2].

This way of speaking of the trigrams, moreover, as father and mother, sons and daughters, is not so old as Fû-hsî; nor have we any real proof that it originated with king Wăn. It is not of 'the highest antiquity.' It arose some time in 'middle antiquity,' and was known in the era of the Appendixes; but it had not prevailed then, nor has it prevailed since, to discredit and supersede the older nomenclature. We are startled when we come on it in the place which it occupies. And there it stands alone. It is not entitled to more attention than the two paragraphs that precede it, or the eight that follow it, none of which were thought by P. Regis worthy to be translated. I have just said that it stands 'alone.' Its existence, however, seems to me to be supposed in the fourth chapter, paragraphs 28–30, of the third Appendix, Section ii; but there only the trigrams of 'the six children' are mentioned, and nothing is said of 'the parents.' *K*ăn, khân, and kăn are referred to as being yang, and sun, lî, and tui as being yin. What is said about them is trifling and fanciful.

Operation of God in nature throughout the year.

Leaving the question of the mythology of the Yî, of which I am myself unable to discover a trace, I now call attention to paragraphs 8–10, where the author speaks of the work of God in nature in all the year as a progress through the trigrams, and as being effected by His Spirit. The description assumes the peculiar arrangement of the trigrams, ascribed to king Wăn, and which I have exhibited above, on page 33[3]. Father Regis adopts the general view

[1] But the Chinese term Shăng 生, often rendered 'produced,' must not be pressed, so as to determine the method of production, or the way in which one thing comes from another.

[2] The significance of the mythological paragraph is altogether lost in Canon McClatchie's version:—'*Kh*ien is Heaven, and hence he is called Father; Khwăn is Earth, and hence she is called Mother; *K*ăn is the first male, and hence he is called the eldest son,' &c. &c.

[3] The reader will understand the difference in the two arrangements better by a reference to the circular representations of them on Plate III.

of Chinese critics that Wăn purposely altered the earlier and established arrangement, as a symbol of the disorganisation and disorder into which the kingdom had fallen[1]. But it is hard to say why a man did something more than 3000 years ago, when he has not himself said anything about it. So far as we can judge from this Appendix, the author thought that king Wăn altered the existing order and position of the trigrams with regard to the cardinal points, simply for the occasion,—that he might set forth vividly his ideas about the springing, growth, and maturity in the vegetable kingdom from the labours of spring to the cessation from toil in winter. The marvel is that in doing this he brings God upon the scene, and makes Him in the various processes of nature the 'all and in all.'

The 8th paragraph says :—

'God comes forth in *K*ăn (to his producing work); He brings (His processes) into full and equal action in Sun; they are manifested to one another in Lî; the greatest service is done for Him in Khwăn; He rejoices in Tui; He struggles in *Kh*ien; He is comforted and enters into rest in Khân; and he completes (the work of) the year in Kăn.'

God is here named Tî, for which P. Regis gives the Latin 'Supremus Imperator,' and Canon McClatchie, after him, 'the Supreme Emperor.' I contend that 'God' is really the correct translation in English of Tî; but to render it here by 'Emperor' would not affect the meaning of the paragraph. *K*û Hsî says that 'by Tî is intended the Lord and Governor of heaven;' and Khung Ying-tâ, about five centuries earlier than *K*û, quotes Wang Pî, who died A.D.

[1] E. g. I, 23, 24 :—' Observant etiam philosophi (lib. 15 Sinicae philosophiae Sing-lî) principem Wăn-wang antiquum octo symbolorum, unde aliae figurae omnes pendent, ordinem invertisse; quo ipsa imperii suis temporibus subversio graphice exprimi poterat, mutatis e naturali loco, quem genesis dederat, iis quatuor figuris, quae rerum naturalium pugnis ac dissociationibus, quas posterior labentis anni pars afferre solet, velut in antecessum, repraesentandis idoneae videbantur; v. g. si symbolum ☲ Lî, ignis, supponatur loco symboli ☵ Khân, aquae, utriusque elementi inordinatio principi visa est non minus apta ad significandas ruinas et clades reipublicae male ordinatae, quam naturales ab hieme aut imminente aut saeviente rerum generatarum corruptiones.' See also pp. 67, 68.

249, to the effect that 'Tî is the lord who produces (all) things, the author of prosperity and increase.'

I must refer the reader to the translation in the body of the volume for the 9th paragraph, which is too long to be introduced here. As the 8th speaks directly of God, the 9th, we are told, 'speaks of all things following Him, from spring to winter, from the east to the north, in His progress throughout the year.' In words strikingly like those of the apostle Paul, when writing his Epistle to the Romans, Wan *Kh*ung-ȝung (of the Khang-hsî period) and his son, in their admirable work called, 'A New Digest of Collected Explanations of the Yî King,' say:—'God (Himself) cannot be seen; we see Him in the things (which He produces).' The first time I read these paragraphs with some understanding, I thought of Thomson's Hymn on the Seasons, and I have thought of it in connexion with them a hundred times since. Our English poet wrote:—

'These, as they change, Almighty Father, these
Are but the varied God. The rolling year
Is full of Thee. Forth in the pleasing spring
Thy beauty walks, Thy tenderness and love.
Then comes Thy glory in the summer months,
With light and heat refulgent. Then Thy sun
Shoots full perfection through the swelling year.
Thy bounty shines in autumn unconfined,
And spreads a common feast for all that lives.
In winter awful Thou!'

Prudish readers have found fault with some of Thomson's expressions, as if they savoured of pantheism. The language of the Chinese writer is not open to the same captious objection. Without poetic ornament, or swelling phrase of any kind, he gives emphatic testimony to God as renewing the face of the earth in spring, and not resting till He has crowned the year with His goodness.

And there is in the passage another thing equally wonderful. The 10th paragraph commences:—'When we speak of Spirit, we mean the subtle presence (and operation of God) with all things;' and the writer goes on to illustrate this sentiment from the action and influences symbolised

by the six 'children,' or minor trigrams,—water and fire, thunder and wind, mountains and collections of water. *K*û Hsî says, that there is that in the paragraph which he does not understand. Some Chinese scholars, however, have not been far from descrying the light that is in it. Let Liang Yin, of our fourteenth century, be adduced as an example of them. He says:—'The spirit here simply means God. God is the personality (literally, the body or substantiality) of the Spirit; the Spirit is God in operation. He who is lord over and rules all things is God; the subtle presence and operation of God with all things is by His Spirit.' The language is in fine accord with the definition of shăn or spirit, given in the 3rd Appendix, Section i, 32.

Concluding paragraphs.

I wish that the Treatise on the Trigrams had ended with the 10th paragraph. The writer had gradually risen to a noble elevation of thought from which he plunges into a slough of nonsensical remarks which it would be difficult elsewhere to parallel. I have referred on p. 31 to the judgment of P. Regis about them. He could not receive them as from Confucius, and did not take the trouble to translate them, and transfer them to his own pages. My plan required me to translate everything published in China as a part of the Yî King; but I have given my reasons for doubting whether any portion of these Appendixes be really from Confucius. There is nothing that could better justify the supercilious disregard with which the classical literature of China is frequently treated than to insist on the concluding portion of this treatise as being from the pencil of its greatest sage. I have dwelt at some length on the 14th paragraph, because of its mythological semblance; but among the eight paragraphs that follow it, it would be difficult to award the palm for silliness. They are descriptive of the eight trigrams, and each one enumerates a dozen or more objects of which its subject is symbolical. The writer must have been fond of and familiar with horses. *Kh*ien, the symbol properly of heaven, suggests to him the idea of a good horse; an old horse; a lean horse; and a piebald. *K*ăn, the symbol of thunder, suggests the

idea of a good neigher; of the horse with white hind-legs; of the prancing horse; and of one with a white star in his forehead. Khân, the symbol of water, suggests the idea of the horse with an elegant spine; of one with a high spirit; of one with a drooping head; and of one with a shambling step. The reader will think he has had enough of these symbolisings of the trigrams. I cannot believe that the earlier portions and this concluding portion of the treatise were by the same author. If there were any evidence that paragraphs 8 to 10 were by Confucius, I should say that they were worthy, even more than worthy, of him; what follows is mere drivel. Horace's picture faintly pourtrays the inconsistency between the parts:—

'Desinit in piscem mulier formosa superne.'

In reviewing the second of these Appendixes, I was led to speak of the original significance of the trigrams, in opposition to the views of some Chinese who pretend that they can find in them the physical truths discovered by the researches of western science. May I not say now, after viewing the phase of them presented in these paragraphs, that they were devised simply as aids to divination, and partook of the unreasonableness and uncertainty belonging to that?

9. The sixth Appendix is the Treatise on the Sequence of the Hexagrams, to which allusion has been made more than once. It is not necessary to dwell on it at length. King Wăn, it has been seen, gave a name to each hexagram, expressive of the idea—some moral, social, or political truth—which he wished to set forth by means of it; and this name enters very closely into its interpretation. The author of this treatise endeavours to explain the meaning of the name, and also the sequence of the figures, or how it is that the idea of the one leads on to that of the next. Yet the reader must not expect to find in the 64 a chain 'of linked sweetness long drawn out.' The connexion between any two is generally sufficiently close; but on the whole the essays, which I have said they form, resemble 'a heap of orient pearls at random strung.' The changeableness of human

The sixth Appendix.

affairs is a topic never long absent from the writer's mind. He is firmly persuaded that 'the fashion of the world passeth away.' Union is sure to give place to separation, and by and by that separation will issue in re-union.

There is nothing in the treatise to suggest anything about its authorship; and as the reader will see from the notes, we are perplexed occasionally by meanings given to the names that differ from the meanings in the Text.

The seventh Appendix.

10. The last and least Appendix is the seventh, called 3â Kwâ *K*wan, or 'Treatise on the Lineal Figures taken promiscuously,'—not with regard to any sequence, but as they approximate, or are opposed, to one another in meaning. It is in rhyme, moreover, and this, as much as the meaning, determined, no doubt, the grouping of the hexagrams. The student will learn nothing of value from it; it is more a 'jeu d'esprit' than anything else.

易經

THE YÎ KING.

TEXT. SECTION I.

I. The *Kh*ien Hexagram.

Explanation of the entire figure by king Wăn.

*Kh*ien (represents) what is great and originating, penetrating, advantageous, correct and firm.

Explanation of the separate lines by the duke of *K*âu.

1. In the first (or lowest) line, undivided, (we see its subject as) the dragon lying hid (in the deep). It is not the time for active doing.

2. In the second line, undivided, (we see its subject as) the dragon appearing in the field. It will be advantageous to meet with the great man.

3. In the third line, undivided, (we see its subject as) the superior man active and vigilant all the day, and in the evening still careful and apprehensive. (The position is) dangerous, but there will be no mistake.

4. In the fourth line, undivided, (we see its subject as the dragon looking) as if he were leaping up, but still in the deep. There will be no mistake.

5. In the fifth line, undivided, (we see its subject as) the dragon on the wing in the sky. It will be advantageous to meet with the great man.

6. In the sixth (or topmost) line, undivided, (we see its subject as) the dragon exceeding the proper limits. There will be occasion for repentance.

7. (The lines of this hexagram are all strong and undivided, as appears from) the use of the number nine. If the host of dragons (thus) appearing were to divest themselves of their heads, there would be good fortune.

The Text under each hexagram consists of one paragraph by king Wăn, explaining the figure as a whole, and of six (in the case of hexagrams 1 and 2, of seven) paragraphs by the duke of *K*âu, explaining the individual lines. The explanatory notices introduced above to this effect will not be repeated. A double space will be used to mark off the portion of king Wăn from that of his son.

Each hexagram consists of two of the trigrams of Fû-hsî, the lower being called 'the inner,' and the one above 'the outer.' The lines, however, are numbered from one to six, commencing with the lowest. To denote the number of it and of the sixth line, the terms for 'commencing' and 'topmost' are used. The intermediate lines are simply 'second,' 'third,' &c. As the lines must be either whole or divided, technically called strong and weak, yang and yin, this distinction is indicated by the application to them of the numbers nine and six. All whole lines are nine, all divided lines, six.

Two explanations have been proposed of this application of these numbers. The *Kh*ien trigram, it is said, contains 3 strokes (☰), and the Khwăn 6 (☷). But the yang contains the yin in itself, and its representative number will be 3+6=9, while the yin, not containing the yang, will only have its own number or 6. This explanation, entirely arbitrary, is now deservedly abandoned. The other is based on the use of the 'four Hsiang,' or emblematic figures (⚌ the great or old yang, ⚎ the young yang, ⚏ the old yin, and ⚍ the young yin). To these are assigned (by what process is unimportant for our present purpose) the numbers 9, 8, 7, 6. They were 'the old yang,' represented by 9, and 'the old yin,' represented by 6, that, in the manipulation of the stalks to form new diagrams, determined the changes of figure; and so 9 and 6 came to be used as the

易經

II. The Khwăn Hexagram.

Khwăn (represents) what is great and originating, penetrating, advantageous, correct and having the firmness of a mare. When the superior man (here

---

names of a yang line and a yin line respectively. This explanation is now universally acquiesced in. The nomenclature of first nine, nine two, &c., or first six, six two, &c., however, is merely a jargon; and I have preferred to use, instead of it, in the translation, in order to describe the lines, the names 'undivided' and 'divided.'

I. Does king Wăn ascribe four attributes here to *Kh*ien, or only two? According to Appendix IV, always by Chinese writers assigned to Confucius, he assigns four, corresponding to the principles of benevolence, righteousness, propriety, and knowledge in man's nature. *K*û Hsî held that he assigned only two, and that we should translate, 'greatly penetrating,' and 'requires to be correct and firm,' two responses in divination. Up and down throughout the Text of the 64 hexagrams, we often find the characters thus coupled together. Both interpretations are possible. I have followed what is accepted as the view of Confucius. It would take pages to give a tithe of what has been written in justification of it, and to reconcile it with the other.

'The dragon' is the symbol employed by the duke of *K*âu to represent 'the superior man' and especially 'the great man,' exhibiting the virtues or attributes characteristic of heaven. The creature's proper home is in the water, but it can disport itself on the land, and also fly and soar aloft. It has been from the earliest time the emblem with the Chinese of the highest dignity and wisdom, of sovereignty and sagehood, the combination of which constitutes 'the great man.' One emblem runs through the lines of many of the hexagrams as here.

But the dragon appears in the sixth line as going beyond the proper limits. The ruling-sage has gone through all the sphere in which he is called on to display his attributes; it is time for him to relax. The line should not be always pulled tight; the bow should not be always kept drawn. The unchanging use

intended) has to make any movement, if he take the initiative, he will go astray; if he follow, he will find his (proper) lord. The advantageousness will be seen in his getting friends in the south-west, and losing friends in the north-east. If he rest in correctness and firmness, there will be good fortune.

1. In the first line, divided, (we see its subject) treading on hoarfrost. The strong ice will come (by and by).

2. The second line, divided, (shows the attribute of) being straight, square, and great. (Its operation), without repeated efforts, will be in every respect advantageous.

3. The third line, divided, (shows its subject) keeping his excellence under restraint, but firmly maintaining it. If he should have occasion to engage in the king's service, though he will not claim the success (for himself), he will bring affairs to a good issue.

4. The fourth line, divided, (shows the symbol of) a sack tied up. There will be no ground for blame or for praise.

5. The fifth line, divided, (shows) the yellow lower garment. There will be great good fortune.

---

of force will give occasion for repentance. The moral meaning found in the line is that 'the high shall be abased.'

The meaning given to the supernumerary paragraph is the opposite of that of paragraph 6. The 'host of dragons without their heads' would give us the next hexagram, or Khwăn, made up of six divided lines. Force would have given place to submission, and haughtiness to humility; and the result would be good fortune. Such at least is the interpretation of the paragraph given in a narrative of the 3o-*K*wan under B.C. 513. For further explanation of the duke of *K*âu's meaning, see Appendixes II and IV.

6. The sixth line, divided, (shows) dragons fighting in the wild. Their blood is purple and yellow.

7. (The lines of this hexagram are all weak and divided, as appears from) the use of the number six. If those (who are thus represented) be perpetually correct and firm, advantage will arise.

II. The same attributes are here ascribed to Khwăn, as in the former hexagram to *Kh*ien ;—but with a difference. The figure, made up of six divided lines, expresses the ideal of subordination and docility. The superior man, represented by it, must not take the initiative; and by following he will find his lord,—the subject, that is of *Kh*ien. Again, the correctness and firmness is defined to be that of 'a mare,' 'docile and strong,' but a creature for the service of man. That it is not the sex of the animal which the writer has chiefly in mind is plain from the immediate mention of the superior man, and his lord.

That superior man will seek to bring his friends along with himself to serve his ruler. But according to the arrangement of the trigrams by king Wăn, the place of Khwăn is in the south-west, while the opposite quarter is occupied by the yang trigram Kăn, as in Figure 2, Plate III. All that this portion of the Thwan says is an instruction to the subject of the hexagram to seek for others of the same principles and tendencies with himself to serve their common lord. But in quietness and firmness will be his strength.

The symbolism of the lines is various. Paragraph 2 presents to us the earth itself, according to the Chinese conception of it, as a great cube. To keep his excellence under restraint, as in paragraph 3, is the part of a minister or officer, seeking not his own glory, but that of his ruler. Paragraph 4 shows its subject exercising a still greater restraint on himself than in paragraph 3. There is an interpretation of the symbolism of paragraph 5 in a narrative of the 3o *K*wan, under the 12th year of duke *Kh*âo, B.C. 530. 'Yellow' is one of the five 'correct' colours, and the colour of the earth. 'The lower garment' is a symbol of humility. The fifth line is the seat of honour. If its occupant possess the qualities indicated, he will be greatly fortunate.

See the note on the sixth line of hexagram 1. What is there said to be 'beyond the proper limits' takes place here 'in the wild.' The humble subject of the divided line is transformed into a

III. The *K*un Hexagram.

䷂

*K*un (indicates that in the case which it presupposes) there will be great progress and success, and the advantage will come from being correct and firm. (But) any movement in advance should not be (lightly) undertaken. There will be advantage in appointing feudal princes.

1. The first line, undivided, shows the difficulty (its subject has) in advancing. It will be advantageous for him to abide correct and firm; advantageous (also) to be made a feudal ruler.

2. The second line, divided, shows (its subject) distressed and obliged to return; (even) the horses of her chariot (also) seem to be retreating. (But) not by a spoiler (is she assailed), but by one who seeks her to be his wife. The young lady maintains her firm correctness, and declines a union. After ten years she will be united, and have children.

3. The third line, divided, shows one following the deer without (the guidance of) the forester, and only finding himself in the midst of the forest. The superior man, acquainted with the secret risks, thinks it better to give up the chase. If he went forward, he would regret it.

---

dragon, and fights with the true dragon, the subject of the undivided line. They fight and bleed, and their blood is of the colour proper to heaven or the sky, and the colour proper to the earth. Paragraph 7 supposes that the hexagram Khwăn should become changed into *Kh*ien;—the result of which would be good.

4. The fourth line, divided, shows (its subject as a lady), the horses of whose chariot appear in retreat. She seeks, however, (the help of) him who seeks her to be his wife. Advance will be fortunate; all will turn out advantageously.

5. The fifth line, undivided, shows the difficulties in the way of (its subject's) dispensing the rich favours that might be expected from him. With firmness and correctness there will be good fortune in small things; (even) with them in great things there will be evil.

6. The topmost line, divided, shows (its subject) with the horses of his chariot obliged to retreat, and weeping tears of blood in streams.

III. The character called *K*un is pictorial, and was intended to show us how a plant struggles with difficulty out of the earth, rising gradually above the surface. This difficulty, marking the first stages in the growth of a plant, is used to symbolise the struggles that mark the rise of a state out of a condition of disorder, consequent on a great revolution. The same thing is denoted by the combination of the trigrams that form the figure;—as will be seen in the notes on it under Appendix II.

I have introduced within parentheses, in the translation, the words 'in the case which the hexagram presupposes.' It is necessary to introduce them. King Wăn and his son wrote, as they did in every hexagram, with reference to a particular state of affairs which they had in mind. This was the unspoken text which controlled and directed all their writing; and the student must try to get hold of this, if he would make his way with comfort and success through the Yî. Wăn saw the social and political world around him in great disorder, hard to be remedied. But he had faith in himself and the destinies of his House. Let there be prudence and caution, with unswerving adherence to the right; let the government of the different states be entrusted to good and able men:—then all would be well.

The first line is undivided, showing the strength of its subject. He will be capable of action, and his place in the trigram of mobility will the more dispose him to it. But above him is the

IV. The Măng Hexagram.

Măng (indicates that in the case which it presupposes) there will be progress and success. I do not (go and) seek the youthful and inexperienced,

---

trigram of peril; and the lowest line of that, to which especially he must look for response and co-operation, is divided and weak. Hence arise the ideas of difficulty in advancing, the necessity of caution, and the advantage of his being clothed with authority.

To the subject of the second line, divided, advance is still more difficult. He is weak in himself; he is pressed by the subject of the strong line below him. But happily that subject, though strong, is correct; and above in the fifth line, in the place of authority, is the strong one, union with whom and the service of whom should be the objects pursued. All these circumstances suggested to the duke of *K*âu the idea of a young lady, sought in marriage by a strong wooer, when marriage was unsuitable, rejecting him, and finally, after ten years, marrying a more suitable, the only suitable, match for her.

The third line is divided, not central, and the number of its place is appropriate to the occupancy of a strong line. All these things should affect the symbolism of the line. But the outcome of the whole hexagram being good, the superior man sees the immediate danger and avoids it.

The subject of the fourth line, the first of the upper trigram, has recourse to the strong suitor of line 1, the first of the lower trigram; and with his help is able to cope with the difficulties of the position, and go forward.

The subject of the fifth line is in the place of authority, and should show himself a ruler, dispensing benefits on a great scale. But he is in the very centre of the trigram denoting perilousness, and line 2, which responds to 5, is weak. Hence arises the symbolism, and great things should not be attempted.

The sixth line is weak; the third responding to it is also weak; it is at the extremity of peril; the game is up. What can remain for its subject in such a case but terror and abject weeping?

but he comes and seeks me. When he shows (the sincerity that marks) the first recourse to divination, I instruct him. If he apply a second and third time, that is troublesome; and I do not instruct the troublesome. There will be advantage in being firm and correct.

1. The first line, divided, (has respect to) the dispelling of ignorance. It will be advantageous to use punishment (for that purpose), and to remove the shackles (from the mind). But going on in that way (of punishment) will give occasion for regret.

2. The second line, undivided, (shows its subject) exercising forbearance with the ignorant, in which there will be good fortune; and admitting (even the goodness of women, which will also be fortunate. (He may be described also as) a son able to (sustain the burden of) his family.

3. The third line, divided, (seems to say) that one should not marry a woman whose emblem it might be, for that, when she sees a man of wealth, she will not keep her person from him, and in no wise will advantage come from her.

4. The fourth line, divided, (shows its subject as if) bound in chains of ignorance. There will be occasion for regret.

5. The fifth line, divided, shows its subject as a simple lad without experience. There will be good fortune.

6. In the topmost line, undivided, we see one smiting the ignorant (youth). But no advantage

will come from doing him an injury. Advantage would come from warding off injury from him.

IV. As *K*un shows us plants struggling from beneath the surface, Măng suggests to us the small and undeveloped appearance which they then present; and hence it came to be the symbol of youthful inexperience and ignorance. The object of the hexagram is to show how such a condition should be dealt with by the parent and ruler, whose authority and duty are represented by the second and sixth, the two undivided lines. All between the first and last sentences of the Thwan must be taken as an oracular response received by the party divining on the subject of enlightening the youthful ignorant. This accounts for its being more than usually enigmatical, and for its being partly rhythmical. See Appendix I, in loc.

The subject of the first line, weak, and at the bottom of the figure, is in the grossest ignorance. Let him be punished. If punishment avail to loosen the shackles and manacles from the mind, well; if not, and punishment be persevered with, the effect will be bad.

On the subject of the second line, strong, and in the central place, devolves the task of enlightening the ignorant; and we have him discharging it with forbearance and humility. In proof of his generosity, it is said that 'he receives,' or learns from, even weak and ignorant women. He appears also as 'a son' taking the place of his father.

The third line is weak, and occupies an odd place belonging properly to an undivided line; nor is its place in the centre. All these things give the subject of it so bad a character.

The fourth line is far from both the second and sixth, and can get no help from its correlate,—the first line, weak as itself. What good can be done with or by the subject of it?

The fifth line is in the place of honour, and has for its correlate the strong line in the second place. Being weak in itself, it is taken as the symbol of a simple lad, willing to be taught.

The topmost line is strong, and in the highest place. It is natural, but unwise, in him to use violence in carrying on his educational measures. A better course is suggested to him.

V. The Hsü Hexagram.

Hsü intimates that, with the sincerity which is declared in it, there will be brilliant success. With firmness there will be good fortune; and it will be advantageous to cross the great stream.

1. The first line, undivided, shows its subject waiting in the distant border. It will be well for him constantly to maintain (the purpose thus shown), in which case there will be no error.

2. The second line, undivided, shows its subject waiting on the sand (of the mountain stream). He will (suffer) the small (injury of) being spoken (against), but in the end there will be good fortune.

3. The third line, undivided, shows its subject in the mud (close by the stream). He thereby invites the approach of injury.

4. The fourth line, divided, shows its subject waiting in (the place of) blood. But he will get out of the cavern.

5. The fifth line, undivided, shows its subject waiting amidst the appliances of a feast. Through his firmness and correctness there will be good fortune.

6. The topmost line, divided, shows its subject entered into the cavern. (But) there are three guests coming, without being urged, (to his help).

If he receive them respectfully, there will be good fortune in the end.

V. Hsü means waiting. Strength confronted by peril might be expected to advance boldly and at once to struggle with it; but it takes the wiser plan of waiting till success is sure. This is the lesson of the hexagram. That 'sincerity is declared in it' is proved from the fifth line in the position of honour and authority, central, itself undivided and in an odd place. In such a case, nothing but firm correctness is necessary to great success.

'Going through a great stream,' an expression frequent in the Yî, may mean undertaking hazardous enterprises, or encountering great difficulties, without any special reference; but more natural is it to understand by 'the great stream' the Yellow river, which the lords of *K*âu must cross in a revolutionary movement against the dynasty of Yin and its tyrant. The passage of it by king Wû, the son of Wăn in B.C. 1122, was certainly one of the greatest deeds in the history of China. It was preceded also by long 'waiting,' till the time of assured success came.

'The border' under line 1 means the frontier territory of the state. There seems no necessity for such a symbolism. 'The sand' and 'the mud' are appropriate with reference to the watery defile; but it is different with 'the border.' The subject of the line appears at work in his distant fields, not thinking of anything but his daily work; and he is advised to abide in that state and mind.

'The sand' of paragraph 2 suggests a nearer approach to the defile, but its subject is still self-restrained and waiting. I do not see what suggests the idea of his suffering from 'the strife of tongues.'

In paragraph 3 the subject is on the brink of the stream. His advance to that position has provoked resistance, which may result in his injury.

Line 4 has passed from the inner to the upper trigram, and entered on the scene of danger and strife;—'into the place of blood.' Its subject is 'weak and in the correct place for him;' he therefore retreats and escapes from the cavern, where he was engaged with his enemy.

Line 5 is strong and central, and in its correct place, being that of honour. All good qualities therefore belong to the subject of it, who has triumphed, and with firmness will triumph still more.

Line 6 is weak, and has entered deeply into the defile and its caverns. What will become of its subject? His correlate is the

VI. The Sung Hexagram.

Sung intimates how, though there is sincerity in one's contention, he will yet meet with opposition and obstruction; but if he cherish an apprehensive caution, there will be good fortune, while, if he must prosecute the contention to the (bitter) end, there will be evil. It will be advantageous to see the great man; it will not be advantageous to cross the great stream.

1. The first line, divided, shows its subject not perpetuating the matter about which (the contention is). He will suffer the small (injury) of being spoken against, but the end will be fortunate.

2. The second line, undivided, shows its subject unequal to the contention. If he retire and keep concealed (where) the inhabitants of his city are (only) three hundred families, he will fall into no mistake.

3. The third line, divided, shows its subject keeping in the old place assigned for his support, and firmly correct. Perilous as the position is, there will be good fortune in the end. Should he per-

---

strong line 3 below, which comes with its two companions to his help. If they are respectfully received, that help will prove effectual. P. Regis tries to find out a reference in these 'three guests' to three princes who distinguished themselves by taking part with *K*âu in its struggle with Yin or Shang; see vol. i, pp. 279–282. I dare not be so confident of any historical reference.

chance engage in the king's business, he will not (claim the merit of) achievement.

4. The fourth line, undivided, shows its subject unequal to the contention. He returns to (the study of Heaven's) ordinances, changes (his wish to contend), and rests in being firm and correct. There will be good fortune.

5. The fifth line, undivided, shows its subject contending;—and with great good fortune.

6. The topmost line, undivided, shows how its subject may have the leathern belt conferred on him (by the sovereign), and thrice it shall be taken from him in a morning.

VI. We have strength in the upper trigram, as if to regulate and control the lower, and peril in that lower as if looking out for an opportunity to assail the upper; or, as it may be represented, we have one's self in a state of peril matched against strength from without. All this is supposed to give the idea of contention or strife. But the undivided line in the centre of Khân is emblematic of sincerity, and gives a character to the whole figure. An individual, so represented, will be very wary, and have good fortune; but strife is bad, and if persevered in even by such a one, the effect will be evil. The fifth line, undivided, in an odd place, and central, serves as a representative of 'the great man,' whose agency is sure to be good; but the topmost line being also strong, and with its two companions, riding as it were, on the trigram of peril, its action is likely to be too rash for a great enterprise. See the treatise on the Thwan, in loc.

The subject of line 1 is weak and at the bottom of the figure. He may suffer a little in the nascent strife, but will let it drop; and the effect will be good.

Line 2 represents one who is strong, and has the rule of the lower trigram;—he has the mind for strife, and might be expected to engage in it. But his strength is weakened by being in an even place, and he is no match for his correlate in line 5, and therefore retreats. A town or city with only three hundred families is said

VII. The Sze Hexagram.

Sze indicates how, in the case which it supposes, with firmness and correctness, and (a leader of) age

---

to be very small. That the subject of the line should retire to so insignificant a place is further proof of his humility.

Line 3 is weak and in an odd place. Its subject therefore is not equal to strive, but withdraws from the arena. Even if forced into it, he will keep himself in the background;—and be safe. 'He keeps in the old place assigned for his support' is, literally, 'He eats his old virtue;' meaning that he lives in and on the appanage assigned to him for his services.

Line 4 is strong, and not in the centre; so that we are to conceive of its subject as having a mind to strive. But immediately above it is line 5, the symbol of the ruler, and with him it is hopeless to strive; immediately below is 3, weak, and out of its proper place, incapable of maintaining a contention. Its proper correlate is the lowest line, weak, and out of its proper place, from whom little help can come. Hence its subject takes the course indicated, which leads to good fortune.

Line 5 has every circumstance in favour of its subject.

Line 6 is strong and able to contend successfully; but is there to be no end of striving? Persistence in it is sure to end in defeat and disgrace. The contender here might receive a reward from the king for his success; but if he received it thrice in a morning, thrice it would be taken from him again. As to the nature of the reward here given, see on the Lî *K*î, X, ii, 32.

P. Regis explains several of the expressions in the Text, both in the Thwan and the Hsiang, from the history of king Wăn and his son king Wû. Possibly his own circumstances may have suggested to Wăn some of the Thwan; and his course in avoiding a direct collision with the tyrant Shâu, and Wû's subsequent exploits may have been in the mind of the duke of *K*âu. Some of the sentiments, however, cannot be historically explained. They are general protests against all contention and strife.

and experience, there will be good fortune and no error.

1. The first line, divided, shows the host going forth according to the rules (for such a movement). If these be not good, there will be evil.

2. The second line, undivided, shows (the leader) in the midst of the host. There will be good fortune and no error. The king has thrice conveyed to him the orders (of his favour).

3. The third line, divided, shows how the host may, possibly, have many inefficient leaders. There will be evil.

4. The fourth line, divided, shows the host in retreat. There is no error.

5. The fifth line, divided, shows birds in the fields, which it will be advantageous to seize (and destroy). In that case there will be no error. If the oldest son leads the host, and younger men (idly occupy offices assigned to them), however firm and correct he may be, there will be evil.

6. The topmost line, divided, shows the great ruler delivering his charges, (appointing some) to be rulers of states, and others to undertake the headship of clans; but small men should not be employed (in such positions).

VII. The conduct of military expeditions in a feudal kingdom, and we may say, generally, is denoted by the hexagram Sze. Referring to Appendixes I and II for an explanation of the way in which the combination of lines in it is made out to suggest the idea of an army, and that idea being assumed, it is easy to see how the undivided line in the second place should be interpreted of the general, who is responded to by the divided line in the fifth and royal place. Thus entire trust is reposed in him. He is strong

易經

VIII. The Pî Hexagram.

Pî indicates that (under the conditions which it supposes) there is good fortune. But let (the principal party intended in it) re-examine himself, (as if)

---

and correct, and his enterprises will be successful. He is denominated *kang zăn*, 'an old, experienced man.'

'The rules,' it is said, 'are twofold;—first, that the war be for a righteous end; and second, that the manner of conducting it, especially at the outset, be right.' But how this and the warning in the conclusion should both follow from the divided line being in the first place, has not been sufficiently explained.

How line 2 comes to be the symbol of the general in command of the army has been shown above on the Thwan. The orders of the king thrice conveyed to him are to be understood of his appointment to the command, and not of any rewards conferred on him as a tribute to his merit. Nor is stress to be laid on the 'thrice.' 'It does not mean that the appointment came to him three times; but that it was to him exclusively, and with the entire confidence of the king.'

The symbolism of line 3 is very perplexing. P. Regis translates it:—'Milites videntur deponere sarcinas in curribus. Male.' Canon McClatchie has:—'Third-six represents soldiers as it were lying dead in their baggage carts, and is unlucky.' To the same effect was my own translation of the paragraph, nearly thirty years ago. But the third line, divided, cannot be forced to have such an indication. The meaning I have now given is more legitimate, taken character by character, and more in harmony with the scope of the hexagram. The subject of line 2 is the one proper leader of the host. But line 3 is divided and weak, and occupies the place of a strong line, as if its subject had perversely jumped over two, and perched himself above it to take the command. This interpretation also suits better in the 5th paragraph.

Line 4 is weak and not central; and therefore 'to retreat' is

by divination, whether his virtue be great, unintermitting, and firm. If it be so, there will be no error. Those who have not rest will then come to him; and with those who are (too) late in coming it will be ill.

1. The first line, divided, shows its subject seeking by his sincerity to win the attachment of his object. There will be no error. Let (the breast) be full of sincerity as an earthenware vessel is of its contents, and it will in the end bring other advantages.

2. In the second line, divided, we see the movement towards union and attachment proceeding from the inward (mind). With firm correctness there will be good fortune.

3. In the third line, divided, we see its subject seeking for union with such as ought not to be associated with.

4. In the fourth line, divided, we see its subject

---

natural for its subject. But its place is even, and proper for a divided line; and the retreat will be right in the circumstances.

In line 5 we seem to have an intimation of the important truth that only defensive war, or war waged by the rightful authority to put down rebellion and lawlessness, is right. 'The birds in the fields' symbolise parties attacking for plunder. The fifth line symbolises the chief authority,—the king, who is weak, or humble, and in the centre, and cedes the use of all his power to the general symbolised by line 2. The subject of 2 is 'the oldest son.' Those of three and four are supposed to be 'the younger brother and son,' that is, the younger men, who would cause evil if admitted to share the command.

The lesson on the topmost line is true and important, but the critics seem unable to deduce it from the nature of the line, as divided and in the sixth place.

seeking for union with the one beyond himself. With firm correctness there will be good fortune.

5. The fifth line, undivided, affords the most illustrious instance of seeking union and attachment. (We seem to see in it) the king urging his pursuit of the game (only) in three directions, and allowing the escape of all the animals before him, while the people of his towns do not warn one another (to prevent it). There will be good fortune.

6. In the topmost line, divided, we see one seeking union and attachment without having taken the first step (to such an end). There will be evil.

VIII. The idea of union between the different members and classes of a state, and how it can be secured, is the subject of the hexagram Pî. The whole line occupying the fifth place, or that of authority, in the hexagram, represents the ruler to whom the subjects of all the other lines offer a ready submission. According to the general rules for the symbolism of the lines, the second line is the correlate of the fifth; but all the other lines are here made subject to that fifth;—which is also a law of the Yî, according to the 'Daily Lecture.' To me it has the suspicious look of being made for the occasion. The harmony of union, therefore, is to be secured by the sovereign authority of one; but he is warned to see to it that his virtue be what will beseem his place, and subjects are warned not to delay to submit to him.

Where does the 'sincerity' predicated of the subject of line 1 come from? The 'earthenware vessel' is supposed to indicate its plain, unadorned character; but there is nothing in the position and nature of the line, beyond the general idea in the figure, to suggest the attribute.

Line 2 is the proper correlate of 5. Its position in the centre of the inner or lower trigram agrees with the movement of its subject as proceeding from the inward mind.

Line 3 is weak, not in the centre, nor in its correct place. The lines above and below it are both weak. All these things are supposed to account for what is said on it.

'The one beyond himself' in line 4 is the ruler or king, who is

IX. The Hsiâo *Kh*û Hexagram.

Hsiâo *Kh*û indicates that (under its conditions) there will be progress and success. (We see) dense clouds, but no rain coming from our borders in the west.

1. The first line, undivided, shows its subject returning and pursuing his own course. What mistake should he fall into? There will be good fortune.

2. The second line, undivided, shows its subject, by the attraction (of the former line), returning (to the proper course). There will be good fortune.

---

the subject of 5, and with whom union ought to be sought. The divided line, moreover, is in a place proper to it. If its subject be firm and correct, there will be good fortune.

The subject of line 5 is the king, who must be the centre of union. The ancient kings had their great hunting expeditions in the different seasons; and that of each season had its peculiar rules. But what is stated here was common to all. When the beating was completed, and the shooting was ready to commence, one side of the enclosure into which the game had been driven was left open and unguarded;—a proof of the royal benevolence, which did not want to make an end of all the game. So well known and understood is this benevolence of the model king of the hexagram, that all his people try to give it effect. Thus the union contemplated is shown to be characterised by mutual confidence and appreciation in virtue and benevolence.

A weak line being in the 6th place, which is appropriate to it, its subject is supposed to be trying to promote union among and with the subjects of the lines below. It is too late. The time is past. Hence it is symbolised as 'without a head,' that is, as not having taken the first step, from which its action should begin, and go on to the end.

3. The third line, undivided, suggests the idea of a carriage, the strap beneath which has been removed, or of a husband and wife looking on each other with averted eyes.

4. The fourth line, divided, shows its subject possessed of sincerity. The danger of bloodshed is thereby averted, and his (ground for) apprehension dismissed. There will be no mistake.

5. The fifth line, undivided, shows its subject possessed of sincerity, and drawing others to unite with him. Rich in resources, he employs his neighbours (in the same cause with himself).

6. The topmost line, undivided, shows how the rain has fallen, and the (onward progress) is stayed;—(so) must we value the full accumulation of the virtue (represented by the upper trigram). But a wife (exercising restraint), however firm and correct she may be, is in a position of peril, (and like) the moon approaching to the full. If the superior man prosecute his measures (in such circumstances), there will be evil.

IX. The name Hsiâo *Kh*û is interpreted as meaning 'small restraint.' The idea of 'restraint' having once been determined on as that to be conveyed by the figure, it is easily made out that the restraint must be small, for its representative is the divided line in the fourth place; and the check given by that to all the undivided lines cannot be great. Even if we suppose, as many critics do, that all the virtue of that upper trigram Sun is concentrated in its first line, the attribute ascribed to Sun is that of docile flexibility, which cannot long be successful against the strength emblemed by the lower trigram *Kh*ien. The restraint therefore is small, and in the end there will be 'progress and success.'

The second sentence of the Thwan contains indications of the place, time, and personality of the writer which it seems possible to ascertain. The fief of *K*âu was the western portion of the

X. The Lî Hexagram.

(Lî suggests the idea of) one treading on the tail of a tiger, which does not bite him. There will be progress and success.

---

kingdom of Yin or Shang, the China of the twelfth century B.C., the era of king Wăn. Rain coming and moistening the ground is the cause of the beauty and luxuriance of the vegetable world, and the emblem of the blessings flowing from good training and good government. Here therefore in the west, the hereditary territory of the house of *K*âu, are blessings which might enrich the whole kingdom; but they are somehow restrained. The dense clouds do not empty their stores.

P. Regis says:—'To declare openly that no rain fell from the heavens long covered with dense clouds over the great tract of country, which stretched from the western border to the court and on to the eastern sea, was nothing else but leaving it to all thoughtful minds to draw the conclusion that the family of Wăn was as worthy of the supreme seat as that of Shâu, the tyrant, however ancient, was unworthy of it (vol. i, p. 356).' The intimation is not put in the Text, however, so clearly as by P. Regis.

Line 1 is undivided, the first line of *Kh*ien, occupying its proper place. Its subject, therefore, notwithstanding the check of line 4, resumes his movement, and will act according to his strong nature, and go forward.

Line 2 is also strong, and though an even place is not appropriate to it, that place being central, its subject will make common cause with the subject of line 1; and there will be good fortune.

Line 3, though strong, and in a proper place, yet not being in the centre, is supposed to be less able to resist the restraint of line 4; and hence it has the ill omens that are given.

The subject of line 4, one weak line against all the strong lines of the hexagram, might well expect wounds, and feel apprehension in trying to restrain the others; but it is in its proper place; it is the first line also of Sun, whose attribute is docile flexibility.

易經

1. The first line, undivided, shows its subject treading his accustomed path. If he go forward, there will be no error.

2. The second line, undivided, shows its subject treading the path that is level and easy;—a quiet and solitary man, to whom, if he be firm and correct, there will be good fortune.

3. The third line, divided, shows a one-eyed man (who thinks he) can see; a lame man (who thinks he) can walk well; one who treads on the tail of a tiger and is bitten. (All this indicates) ill fortune. We have a (mere) bravo acting the part of a great ruler.

4. The fourth line, undivided, shows its subject treading on the tail of a tiger. He becomes full of apprehensive caution, and in the end there will be good fortune.

5. The fifth line, undivided, shows the resolute tread of its subject. Though he be firm and correct, there will be peril.

6. The sixth line, undivided, tells us to look at (the whole course) that is trodden, and examine the

---

The strong lines are moved to sympathy and help, and 'there is no mistake.'

Line 5 occupies the central place of Sun, and converts, by the sincerity of its subject, 4 and 6 into its neighbours, who suffer themselves to be used by it, and effect their common object.

In line 6, the idea of the hexagram has run its course. The harmony of nature is restored. The rain falls, and the onward march of the strong lines should now stop. But weakness that has achieved such a result, if it plume itself on it, will be in a position of peril; and like the full moon, which must henceforth wane. Let the superior man, when he has attained his end, remain in quiet.

presage which that gives. If it be complete and without failure, there will be great good fortune.

X. The character giving its name to the hexagram plays an important part also in the symbolism; and this may be the reason why it does not, as the name, occupy the first place in the Thwan. Looking at the figure, we see it is made up of the trigrams Tui, representing a marsh, and *Kh*ien, representing the sky. Tui is a yin trigram, and its top line is divided. Below *Kh*ien, the great symbol of strength, it may readily suggest the idea of treading on a tiger's tail, which was an old way of expressing what was hazardous (Shû V, xxv, 2). But what suggests the statement that 'the tiger does not bite the treader?' The attribute of Tui is pleased satisfaction. Of course such an attribute could not be predicated of one who was in the fangs of a tiger. The coming scatheless out of such danger further suggests the idea of 'progress and success' in the course which king Wăn had in his mind. And according to Appendix VI, that course was 'propriety,' the observance of all the rules of courtesy. On these, as so many stepping-stones, one may tread safely amid scenes of disorder and peril.

Line 1 is an undivided line in an odd place; giving us the ideas of activity, firmness, and correctness. One so characterised will act rightly.

Line 2 occupies the middle place of the trigram, which is supposed to symbolise a path cut straight and level along the hill-side, or over difficult ground. Line 5 is not a proper correlate, and hence the idea of the subject of 2 being 'a quiet and solitary man.'

Line 3 is neither central nor in an even place, which would be proper to it. But with the strength of will which the occupant of an odd place should possess, he goes forward with the evil results so variously emblemed. The editors of the imperial edition, in illustration of the closing sentence, refer to Analects VII, x.

Line 4 is in contiguity with 5, whose subject is in the place of authority; but he occupies the place proper to a weak or divided line, and hence he bethinks himself, and goes softly.

Beneath the symbolism under line 5, lies the principle that the most excellent thing in 'propriety' is humility. And the subject of the line, which is strong and central, will not be lacking in this, but bear in mind that the higher he is exalted, the greater may be his fall.

XI. The Thâi Hexagram.

In Thâi (we see) the little gone and the great come. (It indicates that) there will be good fortune, with progress and success.

1. The first line, undivided, suggests the idea of grass pulled up, and bringing with it other stalks with whose roots it is connected. Advance (on the part of its subject) will be fortunate.

2. The second line, undivided, shows one who can bear with the uncultivated, will cross the Ho without a boat, does not forget the distant, and has no (selfish) friendships. Thus does he prove himself acting in accordance with the course of the due Mean.

3. The third line, undivided, shows that, while there is no state of peace that is not liable to be disturbed, and no departure (of evil men) so that they shall not return, yet when one is firm and correct, as he realises the distresses that may arise, he will commit no error. There is no occasion for sadness at the certainty (of such recurring changes); and in this mood the happiness (of the present) may be (long) enjoyed.

4. The fourth line, divided, shows its subject fluttering (down);—not relying on his own rich

---

What is said on line 6 is good, but is only a truism. The whole course has been shown; if every step has been right and appropriate, the issue will be very good.

resources, but calling in his neighbours. (They all come) not as having received warning, but in the sincerity (of their hearts).

5. The fifth line, divided, reminds us of (king) Tî-yî's (rule about the) marriage of his younger sister. By such a course there is happiness and there will be great good fortune.

6. The sixth line, divided, shows us the city wall returned into the moat. It is not the time to use the army. (The subject of the line) may, indeed, announce his orders to the people of his own city; but however correct and firm he may be, he will have cause for regret.

XI. The language of the Thwan has reference to the form of Thâi, with the three strong lines of *Kh*ien below, and the three weak lines of Khwăn above. The former are 'the great,' active and vigorous; the latter are 'the small,' inactive and submissive. But where have the former 'come' from, and whither are the latter 'gone?' In many editions of the Yî beneath the hexagram of Thâi here, there appears that of Kwei Mei, the 54th in order (), which becomes Thâi, if the third and fourth lines exchange places. But in the notes on the Thwan, in the first Appendix, on hexagram 6, I have spoken of the doctrine of 'changing figures,' and intimated my disbelief of it. The different hexagrams arose necessarily by the continued manipulation of the undivided and divided lines, and placing them each over itself and over the other. When king Wăn wrote these Thwan, he was taking the 64 hexagrams, as they were ready to his hand, and not forming one from another by any process of divination. The 'gone' and 'come' are merely equivalent to 'below' and 'above,' in the lower trigram or in the upper.

A course in which the motive forces are represented by the three strong, and the opposing by the three weak lines, must be progressive and successful. Thâi is called the hexagram of the first month of the year, the first month of the natural spring, when for six months, through the fostering sun and genial skies, the processes of growth will be going on.

易經

XII. The Phî Hexagram.

In Phî there is the want of good understanding between the (different classes of) men, and its indication is unfavourable to the firm and correct

The symbolism of paragraph 1 is suggested by the three strong lines of *Kh*ien all together, and all possessed by the same instinct to advance. The movement of the first will be supported by that of the others, and be fortunate.

The second line is strong, but in an even place. This is supposed to temper the strength of its subject; which is expressed by the first of his characteristics. But the even place is the central; and it is responded to by a proper correlate in the fifth line above. Hence come all the symbolism of the paragraph and the auspice of good fortune implied in it.

Beneath the symbolism in paragraph 3 there lies the persuasion of the constant change that is taking place in nature and in human affairs. As night succeeds to day, and winter to summer, so calamity may be expected to follow prosperity, and decay the flourishing of a state. The third is the last of the lines of *Kh*ien, by whose strength and activity the happy state of Thâi has been produced. Another aspect of things may be looked for; but by firmness and correctness the good estate of the present may be long continued.

According to the treatise on the Thwan, the subjects of the fourth and other upper lines are not 'the small returning' as opponents of the strong lines below, as is generally supposed; but as the correlates of those lines, of one heart and mind with them to maintain the state of Thâi, and giving them, humbly but readily, all the help in their power.

Tî-yî, the last sovereign but one of the Yin dynasty, reigned from B.C. 1191 to 1155; but what was the history of him and his sister here referred to we do not know. P. Regis assumes that he gave his sister in marriage to the lord of *K*âu, known in subse-

course of the superior man. We see in it the great gone and the little come.

1. The first line, divided, suggests the idea of grass pulled up, and bringing with it other stalks with whose roots it is connected. With firm correctness (on the part of its subject), there will be good fortune and progress.

2. The second line, divided, shows its subject patient and obedient. To the small man (comporting himself so) there will be good fortune. If the great man (comport himself) as the distress and obstruction require, he will have success.

3. The third line, divided, shows its subject ashamed of the purpose folded (in his breast).

4. The fourth line, undivided, shows its subject acting in accordance with the ordination (of Heaven), and committing no error. His companions will come and share in his happiness.

5. In the fifth line, undivided, we see him who

---

quent time as king Wăn, and that she was the famous Thai-sze;—contrary to all the evidence I have been able to find on the subject. According to *Kh*ăng-ȝze, Tî-yî was the first to enact a law that daughters of the royal house, in marrying princes of the states, should be in subjection to them, as if they were not superior to them in rank. Here line 5, while occupying the place of dignity and authority in the hexagram, is yet a weak line in the place of a strong one; and its subject, accordingly, humbly condescends to his strong and proper correlate in line 2.

The course denoted by Thâi has been run; and will be followed by one of a different and unhappy character. The earth dug from the moat had been built up to form a protecting wall; but it is now again fallen into the ditch. War will only aggravate the evil; and however the ruler may address good proclamations to himself and the people of his capital, the coming evil cannot be altogether averted.

brings the distress and obstruction to a close,—the great man and fortunate. (But let him say), 'We may perish! We may perish!' (so shall the state of things become firm, as if) bound to a clump of bushy mulberry trees.

6. The sixth line, undivided, shows the overthrow (and removal of) the condition of distress and obstruction. Before this there was that condition. Hereafter there will be joy.

XII. The form of Phî, it will be seen, is exactly the opposite of that of Thâi. Much of what has been said on the interpretation of that will apply to this, or at least assist the student in making out the meaning of its symbolism. Phî is the hexagram of the seventh month. Genial influences have done their work, the processes of growth are at an end. Henceforth increasing decay must be looked for.

Naturally we should expect the advance of the subject of the first of the three weak lines to lead to evil; but if he set himself to be firm and correct, he will bring about a different issue.

Patience and obedience are proper for the small man in all circumstances. If the great man in difficulty yet cherish these attributes, he will soon have a happy issue out of the distress.

The third line is weak. Its place is odd, and therefore for it incorrect. Its subject would vent his evil purpose, but has not strength to do so. He is left therefore to the shame which he ought to feel without a word of warning. Does the ming of the fourth line mean 'the ordination of Heaven,' as *K*û Hsî thinks; or the orders of the ruler, as *Kh*ăng-ȝze says? Whichever interpretation be taken (and some critics unite the two), the action of the subject of the line, whose strength is tempered by the even position, will be good and correct, and issue in success and happiness.

The strong line in the fifth, (its correct), place, brings the distress and obstruction to a close. Yet its subject—the ruler in the hexagram—is warned to continue to be cautious in two lines of rhyme:—

'And let him say, "I die! I die!"
So to a bushy clump his fortune he shall tie.'

There is an end of the condition of distress. It was necessary that condition should give place to its opposite; and the strong line in the topmost place fitly represents the consequent joy.

XIII. THE THUNG *ZĂN* HEXAGRAM.

Thung *Zăn* (or 'Union of men') appears here (as we find it) in the (remote districts of the) country, indicating progress and success. It will be advantageous to cross the great stream. It will be advantageous to maintain the firm correctness of the superior man.

1. The first line, undivided, (shows the representative of) the union of men just issuing from his gate. There will be no error.

2. The second line, divided, (shows the representative of) the union of men in relation with his kindred. There will be occasion for regret.

3. The third line, undivided, (shows its subject) with his arms hidden in the thick grass, and at the top of a high mound. (But) for three years he makes no demonstration.

4. The fourth line, undivided, (shows its subject) mounted on the city wall; but he does not proceed to make the attack (he contemplates). There will be good fortune.

5. In the fifth line, undivided, (the representative of) the union of men first wails and cries out, and then laughs. His great host conquers, and he (and the subject of the second line) meet together.

6. The topmost line, undivided, (shows the repre-

易經

sentative of) the union of men in the suburbs. There will be no occasion for repentance.

XIII. Thung *Zăn* describes a condition of nature and of the state opposite to that of Phî. There was distress and obstruction; here is union. But the union must be based entirely on public considerations, without taint of selfishness.

The strong line in the fifth, its correct, place, occupies the most important position, and has for its correlate the weak second line, also in its correct place. The one divided line is naturally sought after by all the strong lines. The upper trigram is that of heaven, which is above; the lower is that of fire, whose tendency is to mount upwards. All these things are in harmony with the idea of union. But the union must be free from all selfish motives, and this is indicated by its being in the remote districts of the country, where people are unsophisticated, and free from the depraving effects incident to large societies. A union from such motives will cope with the greatest difficulties; and yet a word of caution is added.

Line 1 emblems the first attempts at union. It is strong, but in the lowest place; and it has no proper correlate above. There is, however, no intermixture of selfishness in it.

Lines 2 and 5 are proper correlates, which fact suggests in this hexagram the idea of their union being limited and partial, and such as may afford ground for blame.

Line 3 is strong, and in an odd place; but it has not a proper correlate in 6. This makes its subject more anxious to unite with 2; but 2 is devoted to its proper correlate in 5, of whose strength 3 is afraid, and takes the measures described. His abstaining so long, however, from any active attempt, will save him from misfortune.

Line 4 is strong, but in an even place, which weakens its subject. He also would fain make an attempt on 2; but he is afraid, and does not carry his purpose into effect.

Line 5 is strong, in an odd, and the central place; and would fain unite with 2, which indeed is the proper correlate of its subject. But 3 and 4 are powerful foes that oppose the union. Their opposition makes him weep; but he collects his forces, defeats them, and effects his purpose.

The union reaches to all within the suburbs, and is not yet universal; but still there is no cause for repentance.

XIV. The Tâ Yû Hexagram.

Tâ Yû indicates that, (under the circumstances which it implies), there will be great progress and success.

1. In the first line, undivided, there is no approach to what is injurious, and there is no error. Let there be a realisation of the difficulty (and danger of the position), and there will be no error (to the end).

2. In the second line, undivided, we have a large waggon with its load. In whatever direction advance is made, there will be no error.

3. The third line, undivided, shows us a feudal prince presenting his offerings to the Son of Heaven. A small man would be unequal (to such a duty).

4. The fourth line, undivided, shows its subject keeping his great resources under restraint. There will be no error.

5. The fifth line, divided, shows the sincerity of its subject reciprocated by that of all the others (represented in the hexagram). Let him display a proper majesty, and there will be good fortune.

6. The topmost line, undivided, shows its subject with help accorded to him from Heaven. There will be good fortune, advantage in every respect.

XIV. Tâ Yû means 'Great Havings;' denoting in a kingdom a state of prosperity and abundance, and in a family or individual, a

XV. The *Kh*ien Hexagram.

*Kh*ien indicates progress and success. The superior man, (being humble as it implies), will have a (good) issue (to his undertakings).

1. The first line, divided, shows us the superior man who adds humility to humility. (Even) the great

---

state of opulence. The danger threatening such a condition arises from the pride which it is likely to engender. But everything here is against that issue. Apart from the symbolism of the trigrams, we have the place of honour occupied by a weak line, so that its subject will be humble; and all the other lines, strong as they are, will act in obedient sympathy. There will be great progress and success.

Line 1, though strong, is at the lowest part of the figure, and has no correlate above. No external influences have as yet acted injuriously on its subject. Let him do as directed, and no hurtful influence will ever affect him.

The strong line 2 has its proper correlate in line 5, the ruler of the figure, and will use its strength in subordination to his humility. Hence the symbolism.

Line 3 is strong, and in the right (an odd) place. The topmost line of the lower trigram is the proper place for a feudal lord. The subject of this will humbly serve the condescending ruler in line 5. A small man, having the place without the virtue, would give himself airs.

Line 4 is strong, but the strength is tempered by the position, which is that of a weak line. Hence he will do no injury to the mild ruler, to whom he is so near.

Line 5 symbolises the ruler. Mild sincerity is good in him, and affects his ministers and others. But a ruler must not be without an awe-inspiring majesty.

Even the topmost line takes its character from 5. The strength of its subject is still tempered, and Heaven gives its approval.

stream may be crossed with this, and there will be good fortune.

2. The second line, divided, shows us humility that has made itself recognised. With firm correctness there will be good fortune.

3. The third line, undivided, shows the superior man of (acknowledged) merit. He will maintain his success to the end, and have good fortune.

4. The fourth line, divided, shows one, whose action would be in every way advantageous, stirring up (the more) his humility.

5. The fifth line, divided, shows one who, without being rich, is able to employ his neighbours. He may advantageously use the force of arms. All his movements will be advantageous.

6. The sixth line, divided, shows us humility that has made itself recognised. The subject of it will with advantage put his hosts in motion; but (he will only) punish his own towns and state.

XV. An essay on humility rightly follows that on abundant possessions. The third line, which is a whole line amid five others divided, occupying the topmost place in the lower trigram, is held by the Khang-hsî editors and many others to be 'the lord of the hexagram,' the representative of humility, strong, but abasing itself. There is nothing here in the text to make us enter farther on the symbolism of the figure. Humility is the way to permanent success.

A weak line, at the lowest place of the figure, is the fitting symbol of the superior man adding humility to humility.

Line 2 is weak, central, and in its proper place, representing a humility that has 'crowed;' that is, has proclaimed itself.

Line 3 is strong, and occupies an odd (its proper) place. It is 'the lord of the hexagram,' to whom all represented by the lines above and below turn.

Line 4 is weak and in its proper position. Its subject is sure to

XVI. The Yü Hexagram

Yü indicates that, (in the state which it implies), feudal princes may be set up, and the hosts put in motion, with advantage.

1. The first line, divided, shows its subject proclaiming his pleasure and satisfaction. There will be evil.

2. The second line, divided, shows one who is firm as a rock. (He sees a thing) without waiting till it has come to pass; with his firm correctness there will be good fortune.

3. The third line, divided, shows one looking up (for favours), while he indulges the feeling of pleasure and satisfaction. If he would understand!—If he be late in doing so, there will indeed be occasion for repentance.

4. The fourth line, undivided, shows him from whom the harmony and satisfaction come. Great

---

be successful and prosperous, but being so near the fifth line, he should still use the greatest precaution.

All men love and honour humility, in itself and without the adjuncts which usually command obedience and respect. Hence his neighbours follow the ruler in the fifth line, though he may not be very rich or powerful. His humility need not keep him from asserting the right, even by force of arms.

The subject of the sixth line, which is weak, is outside the game, so to speak, that has been played out. He will use force, but only within his own sphere and to assert what is right. He will not be aggressive.

is the success which he obtains. Let him not allow suspicions to enter his mind, and thus friends will gather around him.

5. The fifth line, divided, shows one with a chronic complaint, but who lives on without dying.

6. The topmost line, divided, shows its subject with darkened mind devoted to the pleasure and satisfaction (of the time); but if he change his course even when (it may be considered as) completed, there will be no error.

XVI. The Yü hexagram denoted to king Wăn a condition of harmony and happy contentment throughout the kingdom, when the people rejoiced in and readily obeyed their sovereign. At such a time his appointments and any military undertakings would be hailed and supported. The fourth line, undivided, is the lord of the figure, and being close to the fifth or place of dignity, is to be looked on as the minister or chief officer of the ruler. The ruler gives to him his confidence; and all represented by the other lines yield their obedience.

Line 1 is weak, and has for its correlate the strong 4. Its subject may well enjoy the happiness of the time. But he cannot contain himself, and proclaims, or boasts of, his satisfaction ;—which is evil.

Line 2, though weak, is in its correct position, the centre, moreover, of the lower trigram. Quietly and firmly its subject is able to abide in his place, and exercise a far-seeing discrimination. All is indicative of good fortune.

Line 3 is weak, and in an odd place. Immediately below line 4, its subject keeps looking up to the lord of the figure, and depends on him, thinking of doing nothing, but how to enjoy himself. The consequence will be as described, unless he speedily change.

The strong subject of line 4 is the agent to whom the happy condition is owing ; and it is only necessary to caution him to maintain his confidence in himself and his purpose, and his adherents and success will continue.

Line 5 is in the ruler's place ; but it is weak, and he is in danger of being carried away by the lust of pleasure. Moreover, proximity to the powerful minister represented by 4 is a source of danger.

XVII. The Sui Hexagram.

Sui indicates that (under its conditions) there will be great progress and success. But it will be advantageous to be firm and correct. There will (then) be no error.

1. The first line, undivided, shows us one changing the object of his pursuit; but if he be firm and correct, there will be good fortune. Going beyond (his own) gate to find associates, he will achieve merit.

2. The second line, divided, shows us one who cleaves to the little boy, and lets go the man of age and experience.

3. The third line, divided, shows us one who cleaves to the man of age and experience, and lets go the little boy. Such following will get what it seeks; but it will be advantageous to adhere to what is firm and correct.

4. The fourth line, undivided, shows us one followed and obtaining (adherents). Though he be firm and correct, there will be evil. If he be sincere (however) in his course, and make that evident, into what error will he fall?

Hence he is represented as suffering from a chronic complaint, but nevertheless he does not die. See Appendix II on the line.

Line 6, at the very top or end of the hexagram, is weak, and its subject is all but lost. Still even for him there is a chance of safety, if he will but change.

5. The fifth line, undivided, shows us (the ruler) sincere in (fostering all) that is excellent. There will be good fortune.

6. The topmost line, divided, shows us (that sincerity) firmly held and clung to, yea, and bound fast. (We see) the king with it presenting his offerings on the western mountain.

XVII. Sui symbolises the idea of following. It is said to follow Yü, the symbol of harmony and satisfaction. Where there are these conditions men are sure to follow; nor will they follow those in whom they have no complacency. The hexagram includes the cases where one follows others, and where others follow him; and the auspice of great progress and success is due to this flexibility and applicability of it. But in both cases the following must be guided by a reference to what is proper and correct. See the notes on the Thwan and the Great Symbolism.

Line 1 is strong, and lord of the lower trigram. The weak lines ought to follow it; but here it is below them, in the lowest place of the figure. This gives rise to the representation of one changing his pursuit. Still through the native vigour indicated by the line being strong, and in its correct place, its subject will be fortunate. Going beyond his gate to find associates indicates his public spirit, and superiority to selfish considerations.

Line 2 is weak. Its proper correlate is the strong 5; but it prefers to cleave to the line below, instead of waiting to follow 5. Hence the symbolism of the text, the bad omen of which needs not to be mentioned.

Line 3 is also weak, but it follows the strong line above it and leaves line 1, reversing the course of 2;—with a different issue. It is weak, however, and 4 is not its proper correlate; hence the conclusion of the paragraph is equivalent to a caution.

Line 4 is strong, and in the place of a great minister next the ruler in 5. But his having adherents may be injurious to the supreme and sole authority of that ruler, and only a sincere loyalty will save him from error and misfortune.

Line 5 is strong, and in its correct place, with 2 as its proper correlate; thus producing the auspicious symbolism.

The issue of the hexagram is seen in line 6; which represents the ideal of following, directed by the most sincere adherence to

易經

XVIII. The Kû Hexagram.

Kû indicates great progress and success (to him who deals properly with the condition represented by it). There will be advantage in (efforts like that of) crossing the great stream. (He should weigh well, however, the events of) three days before the turning point, and those (to be done) three days after it.

1. The first line, divided, shows (a son) dealing with the troubles caused by his father. If he be an (able) son, the father will escape the blame of having erred. The position is perilous, but there will be good fortune in the end.

2. The second line, undivided, shows (a son) dealing with the troubles caused by his mother. He should not (carry) his firm correctness (to the utmost).

3. The third line, undivided, shows (a son) dealing with the troubles caused by his father. There may be some small occasion for repentance, but there will not be any great error.

4. The fourth line, divided, shows (a son) viewing

---

what is right. This influence not only extends to men, but also to spiritual beings. 'The western hill' is mount *Kh*i, at the foot of which was the original settlement of the house of *K*âu, in B.C. 1325. The use of the name 'king' here brings us down from Wăn into the time of king Wû at least.

indulgently the troubles caused by his father. If he go forward, he will find cause to regret it.

5. The fifth line, divided, shows (a son) dealing with the troubles caused by his father. He obtains the praise of using (the fit instrument for his work).

6. The sixth line, undivided, shows us one who does not serve either king or feudal lord, but in a lofty spirit prefers (to attend to) his own affairs.

XVIII. In the 6th Appendix it is said, 'They who follow another are sure to have services (to perform), and hence Sui is followed by Kû.' But Kû means the having painful or troublesome services to do. It denotes here a state in which things are going to ruin, as if through poison or venomous worms; and the figure is supposed to describe the arrest of the decay and the restoration to soundness and vigour, so as to justify its auspice of great progress and success. To realise such a result, however, great efforts will be required, as in crossing the great stream; and a careful consideration of the events that have brought on the state of decay, and the measures to be taken to remedy it is also necessary. See Appendix I on the 'three days.'

The subject of line 1, and of all the other lines, excepting perhaps 6, appears as a son. Yet the line itself is of the yin nature, and the trigram in which it plays the principal part is also yin. Line 2 is strong, and of the yang nature, with the yin line 5 as its proper correlate. In line 2, 5 appears as the mother; but its subject there is again a son, and the upper trigram altogether is yang. I am unable to account for these things. As is said in the note of Regis on line 2:—'Haec matris filiique denominatio ad has lineas mere translatitia est, et, ut ait commentarius vulgaris, ad explicationem sententiarum eas pro matre et filio supponere dicendum est. Nec ratio reddetur si quis in utroque hoc nomine mysterium quaerat. Cur enim aliis in figuris lineae nunc regem, nunc vasallum, jam imperii administrum, mox summum armorum praefectum referre dicantur? Accommodantur scilicet lineae ad verba sententiae et verba sententiae ad sensum, quemadmodum faciendum de methodis libri Shih King docet Mencius, V, i, ode 4. 2.'

We must leave this difficulty. Line 1 is weak, and its correlate 4 is also weak. What can its subject do to remedy the state of decay? But the line is the first of the figure, and the decay is not

XIX. THE LIN HEXAGRAM.

Lin (indicates that under the conditions supposed in it) there will be great progress and success, while it will be advantageous to be firmly correct. In the eighth month there will be evil.

1. The first line, undivided, shows its subject advancing in company (with the subject of the

---

yet great. By giving heed to the cautions in the Text, he will accomplish what is promised.

The ruler in line 5 is represented by a weak line, while 2 is strong. Thus the symbolism takes the form of a son dealing with the prevailing decay induced somehow by his mother. But a son must be very gentle in all his intercourse with his mother, and especially so, when constrained by a sense of duty to oppose her course. I do not think there is anything more or better to be said here. The historical interpretation adopted by Regis and his friends, that the father here is king Wăn, the mother Thâi-sze, and the son king Wû, cannot be maintained. I have searched, but in vain, for the slightest Chinese sanction of it, and it would give to Kû the meaning of misfortunes endured, instead of troubles caused.

Line 3 is strong, and not central, so that its subject might well go to excess in his efforts. But this tendency is counteracted by the line's place in the trigram Sun, often denoting lowly submission.

Line 4 is weak, and in an even place, which intensifies that weakness. Hence comes the caution against going forward.

The weak line 5, as has been said, is the seat of the ruler; but its proper correlate is the strong 2, the strong siding champion minister, to whom the work of the hexagram is delegated.

Line 6 is strong, and has no proper correlate below. Hence it suggests the idea of one outside the sphere of action, and taking no part in public affairs, but occupied with the culture of himself.

second line). Through his firm correctness there will be good fortune.

2. The second line, undivided, shows its subject advancing in company (with the subject of the first line). There will be good fortune; (advancing) will be in every way advantageous.

3. The third line, divided, shows one well pleased (indeed) to advance, (but whose action) will be in no way advantageous. If he become anxious about it (however), there will be no error.

4. The fourth line, divided, shows one advancing in the highest mode. There will be no error.

5. The fifth line, divided, shows the advance of wisdom, such as befits the great ruler. There will be good fortune.

6. The sixth line, divided, shows the advance of honesty and generosity. There will be good fortune, and no error.

XIX. In Appendix VI Lin is explained as meaning 'great.' The writer, having misunderstood the meaning of the previous Kû, subjoins—'He who performs such services may become "great."' But Lin denotes the approach of authority,—to inspect, to comfort, or to rule. When we look at the figure, we see two strong undivided lines advancing on the four weak lines above them, and thence follows the assurance that their action will be powerful and successful. That action must be governed by rectitude, however, and by caution grounded on the changing character of all conditions and events. The meaning of the concluding sentence is given in Appendix I as simply being—that, 'the advancing power will decay in no long time.' Lû *K'ăn-khî* (Ming dynasty) says:—'The sun (or the day) is the symbol of what is Yang; and the moon is the symbol of what is Yin. Eight is the number of the second of the four emblematic figures (the smaller Yin), and seven is the number of the third of them (the smaller Yang). Hence to indicate the period of the coming of what is Yin, we use the phrase, "the eighth month;" and to indicate the period of the coming of what is

XX. The Kwân Hexagram.

Kwân shows (how he whom it represents should be like) the worshipper who has washed his hands, but not (yet) presented his offerings;—with sincerity

---

Yang, we use the phrase, "the seventh day."' The Khang-hsî editors say that this is the best explanation of the language of the Text that can be given:—'The Yang numbers culminate in 9, the influence then receding and producing the 8 of the smaller Yin. The Yin numbers culminate in 6, and the next advance produces the 7 of the smaller Yang; so that 7 and 8 are the numbers indicating the first birth of what is Yin and what is Yang.' 'If we go to seek,' they add, 'any other explanation of the phraseology of the Text, and such expressions as "3 days," "3 years," "10 years," &c., we make them unintelligible.' Lin is the hexagram of the twelfth month.

Line 1 is a strong line in its proper place. The danger is that its subject may be more strong than prudent, hence the caution in requiring firm correctness.

Line 2, as strong, should be in an odd place; but this is more than counterbalanced by the central position, and its correlate in line 5.

Line 3 is weak, and neither central, nor in its correct position. Hence its action will not be advantageous; but being at the top of the trigram Tui, which means being pleased, its subject is represented as 'well pleased to advance.' Anxious reflection will save him from error.

Line 4, though weak, is in its proper place, and has for its correlate the strong 1. Hence its advance is 'in the highest style.'

Line 5 is the position of the ruler. It is weak, but being central, and having for its correlate the strong and central 2, we have in it a symbol of authority distrustful of itself, and employing fit agents;—characteristic of the wise ruler.

Line 6 is the last of the trigram Khwăn, the height therefore of docility. Line 2 is not its correlate, but it belongs to the Yin to seek for the Yang; and it is so emphatically in this case. Hence the characteristic and issue as assigned.

and an appearance of dignity (commanding reverent regard).

1. The first line, divided, shows the looking of a lad;—not blamable in men of inferior rank, but matter for regret in superior men.

2. The second line, divided, shows one peeping out from a door. It would be advantageous if it were (merely) the firm correctness of a female.

3. The third line, divided, shows one looking at (the course of) his own life, to advance or recede (accordingly).

4. The fourth line, divided, shows one contemplating the glory of the kingdom. It will be advantageous for him, being such as he is, (to seek) to be a guest of the king.

5. The fifth line, undivided, shows its subject contemplating his own life(-course). A superior man, he will (thus) fall into no error.

6. The sixth line, undivided, shows its subject contemplating his character to see if it be indeed that of a superior man. He will not fall into error.

XX. The Chinese character Kwân, from which this hexagram is named, is used in it in two senses. In the Thwan, the first paragraph of the treatise on the Thwan, and the paragraph on the Great Symbolism, it denotes showing, manifesting; in all other places it denotes contemplating, looking at. The subject of the hexagram is the sovereign and his subjects, how he manifests himself to them, and how they contemplate him. The two upper, undivided, lines belong to the sovereign; the four weak lines below them are his subjects,—ministers and others who look up at him. Kwân is the hexagram of the eighth month.

In the Thwan king Wăn symbolises the sovereign by a worshipper when he is most solemn in his religious service, at the commencement of it, full of sincerity and with a dignified carriage.

Line 1 is weak, and in the lowest place, improper also for it;—

XXI. The Shih Ho Hexagram.

Shih Ho indicates successful progress (in the condition of things which it supposes). It will be advantageous to use legal constraints.

1. The first line, undivided, shows one with his feet in the stocks and deprived of his toes. There will be no error.

2. The second line, divided, shows one biting through the soft flesh, and (going on to) bite off the nose. There will be no error.

---

the symbol of a thoughtless lad, who cannot see far, and takes only superficial views.

Line 2 is also weak, but in its proper place, showing a woman, living retired, and only able to peep as from her door at the subject of the fifth line. But ignorance and retirement are proper in a woman.

Line 3, at the top of the lower trigram Khwăn, and weak, must belong to a subject of the utmost docility, and will wish to act only according to the exigency of time and circumstances.

Line 4, in the place proper to its weakness, is yet in immediate proximity to 5, representing the sovereign. Its subject is moved accordingly, and stirred to ambition.

Line 5 is strong, and in the place of the ruler. He is a superior man, but this does not relieve him from the duty of self-contemplation or examination.

There is a slight difference in the 6th paragraph from the 5th, which can hardly be expressed in a translation. By making a change in the punctuation, however, the different significance may be brought out. Line 6 is strong, and should be considered out of the work of the hexagram, but its subject is still possessed by the spirit of its idea, and is led to self-examination.

3. The third line, divided, shows one gnawing dried flesh, and meeting with what is disagreeable. There will be occasion for some small regret, but no (great) error.

4. The fourth line, undivided, shows one gnawing the flesh dried on the bone, and getting the pledges of money and arrows. It will be advantageous to him to realise the difficulty of his task and be firm,—in which case there will be good fortune.

5. The fifth line, divided, shows one gnawing at dried flesh, and finding the yellow gold. Let him be firm and correct, realising the peril (of his position). There will be no error.

6. The sixth line, undivided, shows one wearing the cangue, and deprived of his ears. There will be evil.

XXI. Shih Ho means literally 'Union by gnawing.' We see in the figure two strong lines in the first and last places, while all the others, with the exception of the fourth, are divided. This suggests the idea of the jaws and the mouth between them kept open by something in it. Let that be gnawed through and the mouth will close and the jaws come together. So in the body politic. Remove the obstacles to union, and high and low will come together with a good understanding. And how are those obstacles to be removed? By force, emblemed by the gnawing; that is, by legal constraints. And these are sure to be successful. The auspice of the figure is favourable. There will be success.

Lines 1 and 6 are much out of the game or action described in the figure. Hence they are held to represent parties receiving punishment, while the other lines represent parties inflicting it. The punishment in line 1 is that of the stocks, administered for a small offence, and before crime has made much way. But if the 'depriving' of the toes is not merely keeping them in restraint, but cutting them off, as the Chinese character suggests, the punishment appears to a western reader too severe.

Line 2 is weak, appropriately therefore in an even place, and it is central besides. The action therefore of its subject should

XXII. The Pî Hexagram.

Pî indicates that there should be free course (in what it denotes). There will be little advantage (however) if it be allowed to advance (and take the lead).

---

be effective; and this is shown by the 'biting through the soft flesh,' an easy thing. Immediately below, however, is a strong offender represented by the strong line, and before he will submit it is necessary to 'bite off his nose;' for punishment is the rule;—it must be continued and increased till the end is secured.

Line 3 is weak, and in an even place. The action of its subject will be ineffective; and is emblemed by the hard task of gnawing through dried flesh, and encountering, besides, what is distasteful and injurious in it. But again comes in the consideration that here punishment is the rule, and the auspice is not all bad.

Of old, in a civil case, both parties, before they were heard, brought to the court an arrow (or a bundle of arrows), in testimony of their rectitude, after which they were heard; in a criminal case, they in the same way deposited each thirty pounds of gold, or some other metal. See the Official Book of *K*au, 27. 14, 15. The subject of the fourth line's getting those pledges indicates his exercising his judicial functions; and what he gnaws through indicates their difficulty. Moreover, though the line is strong, it is in an even place; and hence comes the lesson of caution.

The fifth line represents 'the lord of judgment.' As it is a weak line, he will be disposed to leniency; and his judgments will be correct. This is declared by his finding the 'yellow metal;' for yellow is one of the five 'correct' colours. The position is in the centre and that of rule; but the line being weak, a caution is given, as under the previous line.

The action of the figure has passed, and still we have, in the subject of line 6, one persisting in wrong, a strong criminal, wearing the cangue, and deaf to counsel. Of course the auspice is evil.

1. The first line, undivided, shows one adorning (the way of) his feet. He can discard a carriage and walk on foot.

2. The second line, divided, shows one adorning his beard.

3. The third line, undivided, shows its subject with the appearance of being adorned and bedewed (with rich favours). But let him ever maintain his firm correctness, and there will be good fortune.

4. The fourth line, divided, shows one looking as if adorned, but only in white. As if (mounted on) a white horse, and furnished with wings, (he seeks union with the subject of the first line), while (the intervening third pursues), not as a robber, but intent on a matrimonial alliance.

5. The fifth line, divided, shows its subject adorned by (the occupants of) the heights and gardens. He bears his roll of silk, small and slight. He may appear stingy; but there will be good fortune in the end.

6. The sixth line, undivided, shows one with white as his (only) ornament. There will be no error.

XXII. The character Pî is the symbol of what is ornamental and of the act of adorning. As there is ornament in nature, so should there be in society; but its place is secondary to that of what is substantial. This is the view of king Wăn in his Thwan. The symbolism of the separate lines is sometimes fantastic.

Line 1 is strong, and in an odd place. It is at the very bottom of the hexagram, and is the first line of Lî, the trigram for fire or light, and suggesting what is elegant and bright. Its subject has nothing to do but to attend to himself. Thus he cultivates—adorns—himself in his humble position; but if need be, righteousness requiring it, he can give up every luxury and indulgence.

XXIII. The Po Hexagram.

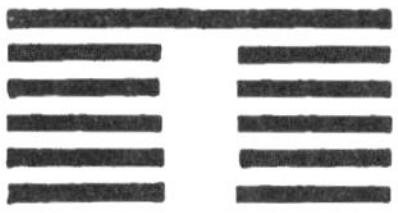

Po indicates that (in the state which it symbolises) it will not be advantageous to make a movement in any direction whatever.

Line 2 is weak and in its proper place, but with no proper correlate above. The strong line 3 is similarly situated. These two lines therefore keep together, and are as the beard and the chin. Line 1 follows 2. What is substantial commands and rules what is merely ornamental.

Line 3 is strong, and between two weak lines, which adorn it, and bestow their favours on it. But this happy condition is from the accident of place. The subject of the line must be always correct and firm to ensure its continuance.

Line 4 has its proper correlate in 1, from whose strength it should receive ornament, but 2 and the strong 3 intervene and keep them apart, so that the ornament is only white, and of no bright colour. Line 4, however, is faithful to 1, and earnest for their union. And finally line 3 appears in a good character, and not with the purpose to injure, so that the union of 1 and 4 takes place. All this is intended to indicate how ornament recognises the superiority of solidity. Compare the symbolism of the second line of *K*un (3), and that of the topmost line of Khwei (38).

Line 5 is in the place of honour, and has no proper correlate in 2. It therefore associates with the strong 6, which is symbolised by the heights and gardens round a city, and serving both to protect and to beautify it. Thus the subject of the line receives adorning from without, and does not of itself try to manifest it. Moreover, in his weakness, his offerings of ceremony are poor and mean. But, as Confucius said, 'In ceremonies it is better to be sparing than extravagant.' Hence that stinginess does not prevent a good auspice.

Line 6 is at the top of the hexagram. Ornament has had its course, and here there is a return to pure, 'white,' simplicity. Substantiality is better than ornament.

1. The first line, divided, shows one overturning the couch by injuring its legs. (The injury will go on to) the destruction of (all) firm correctness, and there will be evil.

2. The second line, divided, shows one overthrowing the couch by injuring its frame. (The injury will go on to) the destruction of (all) firm correctness, and there will be evil.

3. The third line, divided, shows its subject among the overthrowers; but there will be no error.

4. The fourth line, divided, shows its subject having overthrown the couch, and (going to injure) the skin (of him who lies on it). There will be evil.

5. The fifth line, divided, shows (its subject leading on the others like) a string of fishes, and (obtaining for them) the favour that lights on the inmates of the palace. There will be advantage in every way.

6. The topmost line, undivided, shows its subject (as) a great fruit which has not been eaten. The superior man finds (the people again) as a chariot carrying him. The small men (by their course) overthrow their own dwellings.

XXIII. Po is the symbol of falling or of causing to fall, and may be applied, both in the natural and political world, to the process of decay, or that of overthrow. The figure consists of five divided lines, and one undivided, which last thus becomes the prominent and principal line in the figure. Decay or overthrow has begun at the bottom of it, and crept up to the top. The hexagram is that of the ninth month, when the beauty and glory of summer have disappeared, and the year is ready to fall into the arms of sterile winter. In the political world, small men have gradually displaced good men and great, till but one remains; and the lesson for him is to wait. The power operating against him is

XXIV. The Fû Hexagram.

Fû indicates that there will be free course and progress (in what it denotes). (The subject of it) finds no one to distress him in his exits and

---

too strong; but the fashion of political life passes away. If he wait, a change for the better will shortly appear.

The lesser symbolism is chiefly that of a bed or couch with its occupant. The idea of the hexagram requires this occupant to be overthrown, or at least that an attempt be made to overthrow him. Accordingly the attempt in line 1 is made by commencing with the legs of the couch. The symbolism goes on to explain itself. The object of the evil worker is the overthrow of all firm correctness. Of course there will be evil.

Line 2 is to the same effect as 1; only the foe has advanced from the legs to the frame of the couch.

Line 3 also represents an overthrower; but it differs from the others in being the correlate of 6. The subject of it will take part with him. His association is with the subject of 6, and not, as in the other weak lines, with one of its own kind.

From line 4 the danger is imminent. The couch has been overthrown. The person of the occupant is at the mercy of the destroyers.

With line 5 the symbolism changes. The subject of 5 is 'lord of all the other weak lines,' and their subjects are at his disposal. He and they are represented as fishes, following one another as if strung together. All fishes come under the category of yin. Then the symbolism changes again. The subject of 5, representing and controlling all the yin lines, is loyal to the subject of the yang sixth line. He is the rightful sovereign in his palace, and 5 leads all the others there to enjoy the sovereign's favours.

We have still different symbolism under line 6. Its strong subject, notwithstanding the attempts against him, survives, and acquires fresh vigour. The people again cherish their sovereign, and the plotters have wrought to their own overthrow.

entrances; friends come to him, and no error is committed. He will return and repeat his (proper) course. In seven days comes his return. There will be advantage in whatever direction movement is made.

1. The first line, undivided, shows its subject returning (from an error) of no great extent, which would not proceed to anything requiring repentance. There will be great good fortune.

2. The second line, divided, shows the admirable return (of its subject). There will be good fortune.

3. The third line, divided, shows one who has made repeated returns. The position is perilous, but there will be no error.

4. The fourth line, divided, shows its subject moving right in the centre (among those represented by the other divided lines), and yet returning alone (to his proper path).

5. The fifth line, divided, shows the noble return of its subject. There will be no ground for repentance.

6. The topmost line, divided, shows its subject all astray on the subject of returning. There will be evil. There will be calamities and errors. If with his views he put the hosts in motion, the end will be a great defeat, whose issues will extend to the ruler of the state. Even in ten years he will not be able to repair the disaster.

XXIV. Fû symbolises the idea of returning, coming back or over again. The last hexagram showed us inferior prevailing over superior men, all that is good in nature and society yielding before what is bad. But change is the law of nature and society. When decay has reached its climax, recovery will begin to take place. In Po we had one strong topmost line, and five weak lines below

易經

XXV. The Wû Wang Hexagram.

Wû Wang indicates great progress and success, while there will be advantage in being firm and

it; here we have one strong line, and five weak lines above it. To illustrate the subject from what we see in nature,—Po is the hexagram of the ninth month, in which the triumph of cold and decay in the year is nearly complete. It is complete in the tenth month, whose hexagram is Khwăn ; then follows our hexagram Fû, belonging to the eleventh month, in which was the winter solstice when the sun turned back in his course, and moved with a constant regular progress towards the summer solstice. In harmony with these changes of nature are the changes in the political and social state of a nation. There is nothing in the Yî to suggest the hope of a perfect society or kingdom that cannot be moved.

The strong bottom line is the first of *K*ăn, the trigram of movement, and the upper trigram is Khwăn, denoting docility and capacity. The strong returning line will meet with no distressing obstacle, and the weak lines will change before it into strong, and be as friends. The bright quality will be developed brighter and brighter from day to day, and month to month.

The sentence, 'In seven days comes his return,' occasions some perplexity. If the reader will refer to hexagrams 44, 33, 12, 20, 23, and 2, he will see that during the months denoted by those figures, the 5th, 6th, 7th, 8th, 9th, and 10th, the yin lines have gradually been prevailing over the yang, until in Khwăn (2) they have extruded them entirely from the lineal figure. Then comes our Fû, as a seventh figure, in which the yang line begins to reassert itself, and from which it goes on to extrude the yin lines in their turn. Explained therefore of the months of the year, we have to take a day for a month. And something analogous—we cannot say exactly what—must have place in society and the state.

correct. If (its subject and his action) be not correct, he will fall into errors, and it will not be advantageous for him to move in any direction.

1. The first line, undivided, shows its subject free from all insincerity. His advance will be accompanied with good fortune.

2. The second line, divided, shows one who reaps without having ploughed (that he might reap), and gathers the produce of his third year's fields without having cultivated them the first year for that end. To such a one there will be advantage in whatever direction he may move.

3. The third line, divided, shows calamity happening to one who is free from insincerity;—as in

---

The concluding auspice or oracle to him who finds this Fû by divination is what we might expect.

The subject of line 1 is of course the undivided line, meaning here, says *Kh*ăng-ʒze, 'the way of the superior man.' There must have been some deviation from that, or 'returning' could not be spoken of.

Line 2 is in its proper place, and central; but it is weak. This is more than compensated for, however, by its adherence to line 1, the fifth line not being a proper correlate. Hence the return of its subject is called excellent or admirable.

Line 3 is weak, and in the uneven place of a strong line. It is the top line, moreover, of the trigram whose attribute is movement. Hence the symbolism; but any evil issue may be prevented by a realisation of danger and by caution.

Line 4 has its proper correlate in 1; different from all the other weak lines; and its course is different accordingly.

Line 5 is in the central place of honour, and the middle line of Khwăn, denoting docility. Hence its auspice.

Line 6 is weak; and being at the top of the hexagram, when its action of returning is all concluded, action on the part of its subject will lead to evils such as are mentioned. 'Ten years' seems to be a round number, signifying a long time, as in hexagram 3. 2.

the case of an ox that has been tied up. A passer by finds it (and carries it off), while the people in the neighbourhood have the calamity (of being accused and apprehended).

4. The fourth line, undivided, shows (a case) in which, if its subject can remain firm and correct, there will be no error.

5. The fifth line, undivided, shows one who is free from insincerity, and yet has fallen ill. Let him not use medicine, and he will have occasion for joy (in his recovery).

6. The topmost line, undivided, shows its subject free from insincerity, yet sure to fall into error, if he take action. (His action) will not be advantageous in any way.

XXV. Wang is the symbol of being reckless, and often of being insincere; Wû Wang is descriptive of a state of entire freedom from such a condition; its subject is one who is entirely simple and sincere. The quality is characteristic of the action of Heaven, and of the highest style of humanity. In this hexagram we have an essay on this noble attribute. An absolute rectitude is essential to it. The nearer one comes to the ideal of the quality, the more powerful will be his influence, the greater his success. But let him see to it that he never swerve from being correct.

The first line is strong; at the commencement of the inner trigram denoting movement, the action of its subject will very much characterise all the action set forth, and will itself be fortunate.

Line 2 is weak, central, and in its correct place. The quality may be predicated of it in its highest degree. There is an entire freedom in its subject from selfish or mercenary motive. He is good simply for goodness' sake. And things are so constituted that his action will be successful.

But calamity may also sometimes befal the best, and where there is this freedom from insincerity; and line 3 being weak, and in the place of an even line, lays its subject open to this misfortune. 'The people of the neighbourhood' are of course entirely innocent.

Line 4 is the lowest in the trigram of strength, and 1 is not a

XXVI. The Tâ *Kh*û Hexagram.

Under the conditions of Tâ *Kh*û it will be advantageous to be firm and correct. (If its subject do not seek to) enjoy his revenues in his own family (without taking service at court), there will be good fortune. It will be advantageous for him to cross the great stream.

1. The first line, undivided, shows its subject in a position of peril. It will be advantageous for him to stop his advance.

2. The second line, undivided, shows a carriage with the strap under it removed.

3. The third line, undivided, shows its subject urging his way with good horses. It will be advantageous for him to realise the difficulty (of his course), and to be firm and correct, exercising himself daily in his charioteering and methods of defence;

---

proper correlate, nor is the fourth the place for a strong line. Hence the paragraph must be understood as a caution.

Line 5 is strong, in the central place of honour, and has its proper correlate in 2. Hence its subject must possess the quality of the hexagram in perfection. And yet he shall be sick or in distress. But he need not be anxious. Without his efforts a way of escape for him will be opened.

Line 6 is at the top of the hexagram, and comes into the field when the action has run its course. He should be still, and not initiate any fresh movement.

then there will be advantage in whatever direction he may advance.

4. The fourth line, divided, shows the young bull, (and yet) having the piece of wood over his horns. There will be great good fortune.

5. The fifth line, divided, shows the teeth of a castrated hog. There will be good fortune.

6. The sixth line, undivided, shows its subject (as) in command of the firmament of heaven. There will be progress.

XXVI. *Kh*û has two meanings. It is the symbol of restraint, and of accumulation. What is repressed and restrained accumulates its strength and increases its volume. Both these meanings are found in the treatise on the Thwan; the exposition of the Great Symbolism has for its subject the accumulation of virtue. The different lines are occupied with the repression or restraint of movement. The first three lines receive that repression, the upper three exercise it. The accumulation to which all tends is that of virtue; and hence the name of Tâ *Kh*û, 'the Great Accumulation.'

What the Thwan teaches, is that he who goes about to accumulate his virtue must be firm and correct, and may then, engaging in the public service, enjoy the king's grace, and undertake the most difficult enterprises.

Line 1 is subject to the repression of 4, which will be increased if he try to advance. It is better for him to halt.

Line 2 is liable to the repression of 5, and stops its advance of itself, its subject having the wisdom to do so through its position in the central place. The strap below, when attached to the axle, made the carriage stop; he himself acts that part.

Line 3 is the last of *Kh*ien, and responds to the sixth line, the last of Kăn, above. But as they are both strong, the latter does not exert its repressive force. They advance rapidly together; but the position is perilous for 3. By firmness and caution, however, its subject will escape the peril, and the issue will be good.

The young bull in line 4 has not yet got horns. The attaching to their rudiments the piece of wood to prevent him from goring is an instance of extraordinary precaution; and precaution is always good.

XXVII. The Î Hexagram.

Î indicates that with firm correctness there will be good fortune (in what is denoted by it). We must look at what we are seeking to nourish, and by the exercise of our thoughts seek for the proper aliment.

1. The first line, undivided, (seems to be thus addressed), 'You leave your efficacious tortoise, and look at me till your lower jaw hangs down.' There will be evil.

2. The second line, divided, shows one looking downwards for nourishment, which is contrary to what is proper; or seeking it from the height (above), advance towards which will lead to evil.

3. The third line, divided, shows one acting contrary to the method of nourishing. However firm he may be, there will be evil. For ten years let him not take any action, (for) it will not be in any way advantageous.

A boar is a powerful and dangerous animal. Let him be castrated, and though his tusks remain, he cares little to use them. Here line 5 represents the ruler in the hexagram, whose work is to repress the advance of evil. A conflict with the subject of the strong second line in its advance would be perilous; but 5, taking early precaution, reduces it to the condition of the castrated pig. Not only is there no evil, but there is good fortune.

The work of repression is over, and the strong subject of line 6 has now the amplest scope to carry out the idea of the hexagram in the accumulation of virtue.

4. The fourth line, divided, shows one looking downwards for (the power to) nourish. There will be good fortune. Looking with a tiger's downward unwavering glare, and with his desire that impels him to spring after spring, he will fall into no error.

5. The fifth line, divided, shows one acting contrary to what is regular and proper; but if he abide in firmness, there will be good fortune. He should not, (however, try to) cross the great stream.

6. The sixth line, undivided, shows him from whom comes the nourishing. His position is perilous, but there will be good fortune. It will be advantageous to cross the great stream.

XXVII. Î is the symbol of the upper jaw, and gives name to the hexagram; but the whole figure suggests the appearance of the mouth. There are the two undivided lines at the bottom and top, and the four divided lines between them. The first line is the first in the trigram *K*ăn, denoting movement; and the sixth is the third in Kăn, denoting what is solid. The former is the lower jaw, part of the mobile chin; and the other the more fixed upper jaw. The open lines are the cavity of the mouth. As the name of the hexagram, Î denotes nourishing,—one's body or mind, one's self or others. The nourishment in both the matter and method will differ according to the object of it; and every one must determine what to employ and do in every case by exercising his own thoughts, only one thing being premised,—that in both respects the nourishing must be correct, and in harmony with what is right. The auspice of the whole hexagram is good.

The first line is strong, and in its proper place; its subject might suffice for the nourishing of himself, like a tortoise, which is supposed to live on air, without more solid nourishment. But he is drawn out of himself by desire for the weak 4, his proper correlate, at whom he looks till his jaw hangs down, or, as we say, his mouth waters. Hence the auspice is bad. The symbolism takes the form of an expostulation addressed, we must suppose, by the fourth line to the first.

The weak 2, insufficient for itself, seeks nourishment first from

XXVIII. The Tâ Kwo Hexagram.

Tâ Kwo suggests to us a beam that is weak. There will be advantage in moving (under its conditions) in any direction whatever; there will be success.

1. The first line, divided, shows one placing mats of the white mâo grass under things set on the ground. There will be no error.

2. The second line, undivided, shows a decayed

---

the strong line below, which is not proper, and then from the strong 6, not its proper correlate, and too far removed. In either case the thing is evil.

Line 3 is weak, in an odd place; and as it occupies the last place in the trigram of movement, all that quality culminates in its subject. Hence he considers himself sufficient for himself, without any help from without, and the issue is bad.

With line 4 we pass into the upper trigram. It is next to the ruler's place in 5 moreover, and bent on nourishing and training all below. Its proper correlate is the strong 1; and though weak in himself, its subject looks with intense desire to the subject of that for help; and there is no error.

The subject of line 5 is not equal to the requirements of his position; but with a firm reliance on the strong 6, there will be good fortune. Let him not, however, engage in the most difficult undertakings.

The topmost line is strong, and 5 relies on its subject; but being penetrated with the idea of the hexagram, he feels himself in the position of master or tutor to all under heaven. The task is hard and the responsibility great; but realising these things, he will prove himself equal to them.

willow producing shoots, or an old husband in possession of his young wife. There will be advantage in every way.

3. The third line, undivided, shows a beam that is weak. There will be evil.

4. The fourth line, undivided, shows a beam curving upwards. There will be good fortune. If (the subject of it) looks for other (help but that of line one), there will be cause for regret.

5. The fifth line, undivided, shows a decayed willow producing flowers, or an old wife in possession of her young husband. There will be occasion neither for blame nor for praise.

6. The topmost line, divided, shows its subject with extraordinary (boldness) wading through a stream, till the water hides the crown of his head. There will be evil, but no ground for blame.

XXVIII. Very extraordinary times require very extraordinary gifts in the conduct of affairs in them. This is the text on which king Wăn and his son discourse after their fashion in this hexagram. What goes, in their view, to constitute anything extraordinary is its greatness and difficulty. There need not be about it what is not right.

Looking at the figure we see two weak lines at the top and bottom, and four strong lines between them, giving us the idea of a great beam unable to sustain its own weight. But the second and fifth lines are both strong and in the centre; and from this and the attributes of the component trigrams a good auspice is obtained.

Line 1 being weak, and at the bottom of the figure, and of the trigram Sun, which denotes flexibility and humility, its subject is distinguished by his carefulness, as in the matter mentioned; and there is a good auspice.

Line 2 has no proper correlate above. Hence he inclines to the weak 1 below him; and we have the symbolism of the line. An

XXIX. The Khan Hexagram.

Khan, here repeated, shows the possession of sincerity, through which the mind is penetrating. Action (in accordance with this) will be of high value.

1. The first line, divided, shows its subject in the double defile, and (yet) entering a cavern within it. There will be evil.

2. The second line, undivided, shows its subject

---

old husband with a young wife will yet have children; the action of the subject of 2 will be successful.

Line 3 is strong, and in an odd place. Its subject is confident in his own strength, but his correlate in 6 is weak. Alone, he is unequal to the extraordinary strain on him, and has for his symbol the weak beam.

Line 4 is near 5, the ruler's place. On its subject devolves the duty of meeting the extraordinary exigency of the time; but he is strong; and, the line being in an even place, his strength is tempered. He will be equal to his task. Should he look out for the help of the subject of 1, that would affect him with another element of weakness; and his action would give cause for regret.

Line 5 is strong and central. Its subject should be equal to achieve extraordinary merit. But he has no proper correlate below, and as 2 inclined to 1, so does this to 6. But here the willow only produces flowers, not shoots;—its decay will soon reappear. An old wife will have no children. If the subject of the line is not to be condemned as that of 3, his action does not deserve praise.

The subject of 6 pursues his daring course, with a view to satisfy the extraordinary exigency of the time, and benefit all under the sky. He is unequal to the task, and sinks beneath it; but his motive modifies the judgment on his conduct.

in all the peril of the defile. He will, however, get a little (of the deliverance) that he seeks.

3. The third line, divided, shows its subject, whether he comes or goes (=descends or ascends), confronted by a defile. All is peril to him and unrest. (His endeavours) will lead him into the cavern of the pit. There should be no action (in such a case).

4. The fourth line, divided, shows its subject (at a feast), with (simply) a bottle of spirits, and a subsidiary basket of rice, while (the cups and bowls) are (only) of earthenware. He introduces his important lessons (as his ruler's) intelligence admits. There will in the end be no error.

5. The fifth line, undivided, shows the water of the defile not yet full, (so that it might flow away); but order will (soon) be brought about. There will be no error.

6. The topmost line, divided, shows its subject bound with cords of three strands or two strands, and placed in the thicket of thorns. But in three years he does not learn the course for him to pursue. There will be evil.

XXIX. The trigram Khan, which is doubled to form this hexagram, is the lineal symbol of water. Its meaning, as a character, is 'a pit,' 'a perilous cavity, or defile;' and here and elsewhere in the Yî it leads the reader to think of a dangerous defile, with water flowing through it. It becomes symbolic of danger, and what the authors of the Text had in mind was to show how danger should be encountered, its effect on the mind, and how to get out of it.

The trigram exhibits a strong central line, between two divided lines. The central represented to king Wăn the sincere honesty and goodness of the subject of the hexagram, whose mind was sharpened and made penetrating by contact with danger, and who

XXX. The Lî Hexagram.

Lî indicates that, (in regard to what it denotes), it will be advantageous to be firm and correct, and that thus there will be free course and success.

---

acted in a manner worthy of his character. It is implied, though the Thwan does not say it, that he would get out of the danger.

Line 1 is weak, at the bottom of the figure, and has no correlate above, no helper, that is, beyond itself. All these things render the case of its subject hopeless. He will by his efforts only involve himself more deeply in danger.

Line 2 is strong, and in the centre. Its subject is unable, indeed, to escape altogether from the danger; but he does not involve himself more deeply in it like the subject of 1, and obtains some ease.

Line 3 is weak, and occupies the place of a strong line. Its subject is in an evil case.

Line 4 is weak, and will get no help from its correlate in 1. Its subject is not one who can avert the danger threatening himself and others. But his position is close to that of the ruler in 5, whose intimacy he cultivates with an unostentatious sincerity, symbolled by the appointments of the simple feast, and whose intelligence he cautiously enlightens. In consequence, there will be no error.

The subject of line 5 is on the eve of extrication and deliverance. The waters of the defile will ere long have free vent and disappear, and the ground will be levelled and made smooth. The line is strong, in a proper place, and in the place of honour.

The case of the subject of line 6 is hopeless. When danger has reached its highest point, there he is, represented by a weak line, and with no proper correlate below. The 'thicket of thorns' is taken as a metaphor for a prison; but if the expression has a history, I have been unable to find it.

Let (its subject) also nourish (a docility like that of) the cow, and there will be good fortune.

1. The first line, undivided, shows one ready to move with confused steps. But he treads at the same time reverently, and there will be no mistake.

2. The second line, divided, shows its subject in his place in yellow. There will be great good fortune.

3. The third line, undivided, shows its subject in a position like that of the declining sun. Instead of playing on his instrument of earthenware, and singing to it, he utters the groans of an old man of eighty. There will be evil.

4. The fourth line, undivided, shows the manner of its subject's coming. How abrupt it is, as with fire, with death, to be rejected (by all)!

5. The fifth line, divided, shows its subject as one with tears flowing in torrents, and groaning in sorrow. There will be good fortune.

XXX. Lî is the name of the trigram representing fire and light, and the sun as the source of both of these. Its virtue or attribute is brightness, and by a natural metaphor intelligence. But Lî has also the meaning of inhering in, or adhering to, being attached to. Both these significations occur in connexion with the hexagram, and make it difficult to determine what was the subject of it in the minds of the authors. If we take the whole figure as expressing the subject, we have, as in the treatise on the Thwan, 'a double brightness,' a phrase which is understood to denominate the ruler. If we take the two central lines as indicating the subject, we have weakness, dwelling with strength above and below. In either case there are required from the subject a strict adherence to what is correct, and a docile humility. On the second member of the Thwan *Kh*ăng-ʒze says:—'The nature of the ox is docile, and that of the cow is much more so. The subject of the hexagram adhering closely to

6. The topmost line, undivided, shows the king employing its subject in his punitive expeditions. Achieving admirable (merit), he breaks (only) the chiefs (of the rebels). Where his prisoners were not their associates, he does not punish. There will be no error.

---

what is correct, he must be able to act in obedience to it, as docile as a cow, and then there will be good fortune.'

Line 1 is strong, and at the bottom of the trigram for fire, the nature of which is to ascend. Its subject therefore will move upwards, and is in danger of doing so coarsely and vehemently. But the lowest line has hardly entered into the action of the figure, and this consideration operates to make him reverently careful of his movements; and there is no error.

Line 2 is weak, and occupies the centre. Yellow is one of the five correct colours, and here symbolises the correct course to which the subject of the line adheres.

Line 3 is at the top of the lower trigram, whose light may be considered exhausted, and suggests the symbol of the declining sun. The subject of the line should accept the position, and resign himself to the ordinary amusements which are mentioned, but he groans and mourns instead. His strength interferes with the lowly contentment which he should cherish.

The strength of line 4, and its being in an even place, make its subject appear in this unseemly manner, disastrous to himself.

Line 5 is in the place of honour, and central. But it is weak, as is its correlate. Its position between the strong 4 and 6 fills its subject with anxiety and apprehension, that express themselves as is described. But such demonstrations are a proof of his inward adherence to right and his humility. There will be good fortune.

Line 6, strong and at the top of the figure, has the intelligence denoted by its trigrams in the highest degree, and his own proper vigour. Through these his achievements are great, but his generous consideration is equally conspicuous, and he falls into no error.

TEXT. SECTION II.

XXXI. T̆he Hsien Hexagram.

Hsien indicates that, (on the fulfilment of the conditions implied in it), there will be free course and success. Its advantageousness will depend on the being firm and correct, (as) in marrying a young lady. There will be good fortune.

1. The first line, divided, shows one moving his great toes.

2. The second line, divided, shows one moving the calves of his leg. There will be evil. If he abide (quiet in his place), there will be good fortune.

3. The third line, undivided, shows one moving his thighs, and keeping close hold of those whom he follows. Going forward (in this way) will cause regret.

4. The fourth line, undivided, shows that firm correctness which will lead to good fortune, and prevent all occasion for repentance. If its subject be unsettled in his movements, (only) his friends will follow his purpose.

5. The fifth line, undivided, shows one moving the flesh along the spine above the heart. There will be no occasion for repentance.

6. The sixth line, divided, shows one moving his jaws and tongue.

XXXI. With the 31st hexagram commences the Second Section of the Text. It is difficult to say why any division of the hexagrams should be made here, for the student tries in vain to discover any continuity in the thoughts of the author that is now broken. The First Section does not contain a class of subjects different from those which we find in the Second. That the division was made, however, at a very early time, appears from the sixth Appendix on the Sequence of the Hexagrams, where the writer sets forth an analogy between the first and second figures, representing heaven and earth, as the originators of all things, and this figure and the next, representing (each of them) husband and wife, as the originators of all the social relations. This, however, is far from carrying conviction to my mind. The division of the Text of the Yi into two sections is a fact of which I am unable to give a satisfactory account.

Hsien, as explained in the treatise on the Thwan, has here the meaning of mutual influence, and the duke of *K*âu, on the various lines, always uses Kan for it in the sense of 'moving' or 'influencing to movement or action.' This is to my mind the subject of the hexagram considered as an essay,—'Influence; the different ways of bringing it to bear, and their issues.'

The Chinese character called hsien is 咸, the graphic symbol for 'all, together, jointly.' Kan, the symbol for 'influencing,' has hsien in it as its phonetic constituent (though the changes in pronunciation make it hard for an English reader to appreciate this), with the addition of hsin, the symbol for 'the heart.' Thus 感 kan, 'to affect or influence,' = 咸 + 心; and it may have been that while the name or word was used with the significance of 'influencing,' the 心 was purposely dropt from it, to indicate the most important element in the thing,—the absence of all purpose or motive. I venture to think that this would have been a device worthy of a diviner.

With regard to the idea of husband and wife being in the teaching of the hexagram, it is derived from the more recent symbolism of the eight trigrams ascribed to king Wăn, and exhibited on p. 33 and plate III. The more ancient usage of them is given in the paragraph on the Great Symbolism of Appendix II. The figure consists of Kăn (☶), 'the youngest son,' and over it Tui (☱), 'the youngest daughter.' These are in 'happy union.'

易經

XXXII. The Hăng Hexagram.

Hăng indicates successful progress and no error (in what it denotes). But the advantage will come from being firm and correct; and movement in any direction whatever will be advantageous.

1. The first line, divided, shows its subject deeply (desirous) of long continuance. Even with firm

---

No influence, it is said, is so powerful and constant as that between husband and wife; and where these are young, it is especially active. Hence it is that Hsien is made up of Kăn and Tui. All this is to me very doubtful. I can dimly apprehend why the whole line (———) was assumed as the symbol of strength and authority, and the broken line as that of weakness and submission. Beyond this I cannot follow Fû-hsi in his formation of the trigrams; and still less can I assent to the more recent symbolism of them ascribed to king Wăn.

Coming now to the figure, and its lines, the subject is that of mutual influence; and the author teaches that that influence, correct in itself, and for correct ends, is sure to be effective. He gives an instance,—the case of a man marrying a young lady, the regulations for which have been laid down in China from the earliest times with great strictness and particularity. Such influence will be effective and fortunate.

Line 1 is weak, and at the bottom of the hexagram. Though 4 be a proper correlate, yet the influence indicated by it must be ineffective. However much a man's great toes may be moved, that will not enable him to walk.

The calves cannot move of themselves. They follow the moving of the feet. The moving of them indicates too much anxiety to move. Line 2, moreover, is weak. But it is also the central line, and if its subject abide quiet, till he is acted on from above, there will be good fortune.

Neither can the thighs move of themselves. The attempt to

correctness there will be evil; there will be no advantage in any way.

2. The second line, undivided, shows all occasion for repentance disappearing.

3. The third line, undivided, shows one who does not continuously maintain his virtue. There are those who will impute this to him as a disgrace. However firm he may be, there will be ground for regret.

4. The fourth line, undivided, shows a field where there is no game.

5. The fifth line, divided, shows its subject continuously maintaining the virtue indicated by it. In a wife this will be fortunate; in a husband, evil.

6. The topmost line, divided, shows its subject exciting himself to long continuance. There will be evil.

---

move them is inauspicious. Its subject, however, the line being strong, and in an odd place, will wish to move, and follows the subject of 4, which is understood to be the seat of the mind. He exercises his influence therefore with a mind and purpose, which is not good.

Line 4 is strong, but in an even place. It is the seat of the mind. Its subject therefore is warned to be firm and correct in order to a good issue. If he be wavering and uncertain, his influence will not extend beyond the circle of his friends.

The symbolism of line 5 refers to a part of the body behind the heart, and is supposed therefore to indicate an influence, ineffective indeed, but free from selfish motive, and not needing to be repented of.

Line 6 is weak, and in an even place. It is the topmost line also of the trigram of satisfaction. Its influence by means of speech will only be that of loquacity and flattery, the evil of which needs not to be pointed out.

XXXII. The subject of this hexagram may be given as perseverance in well doing, or in continuously acting out the law of one's

XXXIII. The Thun Hexagram.

Thun indicates successful progress (in its circumstances). To a small extent it will (still) be advantageous to be firm and correct.

1. The first line, divided, shows a retiring tail. The position is perilous. No movement in any direction should be made.

---

being. The sixth Appendix makes it a sequel of the previous figure. As that treats, it is said, of the relation between husband and wife, so this treats of the continuous observance of their respective duties. Hsien, we saw, is made up of Kăn, the symbol of the youngest son, and Tui, the symbol of the youngest daughter, attraction and influence between the sexes being strongest in youth. Hăng consists of Sun, 'the oldest daughter,' and *K*ăn, the oldest son. The couple are more staid. The wife occupies the lower place; and the relation between them is marked by her submission. This is sound doctrine, especially from a Chinese point of view; but I doubt whether such application of his teaching was in the mind of king Wăn. Given two parties, an inferior and superior in correlation. If both be continuously observant of what is correct, the inferior being also submissive, and the superior firm, good fortune and progress may be predicated of their course.

Line 1 has a proper correlate in 4; but between them are two strong lines; and it is itself weak. These two conditions are against its subject receiving much help from the subject of 4. He should be quiet, and not forward for action.

Line 2 is strong, but in the place of a weak line. Its position, however, being central, and its subject holding fast to the due mean, the unfavourable condition of an even place is more than counteracted.

Line 3 is strong, and in its proper place; but being beyond the centre of the trigram, its subject is too strong, and coming under

2. The second line, divided, shows its subject holding (his purpose) fast as if by a (thong made from the) hide of a yellow ox, which cannot be broken.

3. The third line, undivided, shows one retiring but bound,—to his distress and peril. (If he were to deal with his binders as in) nourishing a servant or concubine, it would be fortunate for him.

4. The fourth line, undivided, shows its subject retiring notwithstanding his likings. In a superior man this will lead to good fortune; a small man cannot attain to this.

5. The fifth line, undivided, shows its subject retiring in an admirable way. With firm correctness there will be good fortune.

6. The sixth line, undivided, shows its subject retiring in a noble way. It will be advantageous in every respect.

---

the attraction of his correlate in 6, he is supposed to be ready to abandon his place and virtue. He may try to be firm and correct, but circumstances are adverse to him.

Line 4 is strong in the place of a weak line, and suggests the symbolism of the duke of *K*âu.

The weak 5th line responds to the strong 2nd, and may be supposed to represent a wife conscious of her weakness, and docilely submissive; which is good. A husband, however, and a man generally, has to assert himself, and lay down the rule of what is right.

In line 6 the principle of perseverance has run its course; the motive power of *K*ăn is exhausted. The line itself is weak. The violent efforts of its subject can only lead to evil.

XXXIII. Thun is the hexagram of the sixth month; the yin influence is represented by two weak lines, and has made good its footing in the year. The figure thus suggested to king Wăn the growth of small and unprincipled men in the state, before whose advance superior men were obliged to retire. This is the theme of his essay,—how, 'when small men multiply and increase in power,

XXXIV. The Tâ *K*wang Hexagram.

Tâ *K*wang indicates that (under the conditions which it symbolises) it will be advantageous to be firm and correct.

---

the necessity of the time requires superior men to withdraw before them.' Yet the auspice of Thun is not all bad. By firm correctness the threatened evil may be arrested to a small extent.

'A retiring tail' seems to suggest the idea of the subject of the lines hurrying away, which would only aggravate the evil and danger of the time.

'His purpose' in line 2 is the purpose to withdraw. The weak 2 responds correctly to the strong 5, and both are central. The purpose therefore is symbolled as in the text. The 'yellow' colour of the ox is introduced because of its being 'correct,' and of a piece with the central place of the line.

Line 3 has no proper correlate in 6; and its subject allows himself to be entangled and impeded by the subjects of 1 and 2. He is too familiar with them, and they presume, and fetter his movements;—compare Analects, 17. 25. He should keep them at a distance.

Line 4 has a correlate in 1, and is free to exercise the decision belonging to its subject. The line is the first in *Kh*ien, symbolic of strength.

In the Shû IV, v, Section 2. 9, the worthy Î Yin is made to say, 'The minister will not for favour or gain continue in an office whose work is done;' and the Khang-hsî editors refer to his words as an illustration of what is said on line 5. It has its correlate in 2, and its subject carries out the purpose to retire 'in an admirable way.'

Line 6 is strong, and with no correlate to detain it in 3. Its subject vigorously and happily carries out the idea of the hexagram.

1. The first line, undivided, shows its subject manifesting his strength in his toes. But advance will lead to evil,—most certainly.

2. The second line, undivided, shows that with firm correctness there will be good fortune.

3. The third line, undivided, shows, in the case of a small man, one using all his strength; and in the case of a superior man, one whose rule is not to do so. Even with firm correctness the position would be perilous. (The exercise of strength in it might be compared to the case of) a ram butting against a fence, and getting his horns entangled.

4. The fourth line, undivided, shows (a case in which) firm correctness leads to good fortune, and occasion for repentance disappears. (We see) the fence opened without the horns being entangled. The strength is like that in the wheel-spokes of a large waggon.

5. The fifth line, divided, shows one who loses his ram(-like strength) in the ease of his position. (But) there will be no occasion for repentance.

6. The sixth line, divided, shows (one who may be compared to) the ram butting against the fence, and unable either to retreat, or to advance as he would fain do. There will not be advantage in any respect; but if he realise the difficulty (of his position), there will be good fortune.

XXXIV. The strong lines predominate in Tâ *K*wang. It suggested to king Wăn a state or condition of things in which there was abundance of strength and vigour. Was strength alone enough for the conduct of affairs? No. He saw also in the figure that which suggested to him that strength should be held in subordination to the idea of right, and exerted only in harmony with it.

XXXV. The 3in Hexagram.

In 3in we see a prince who secures the tranquillity (of the people) presented on that account with numerous horses (by the king), and three times in a day received at interviews.

This is the lesson of the hexagram, as sententiously expressed in the Thwan.

Line 1 is strong, in its correct place, and also the first line in *Kh*ien, the hexagram of strength, and the first line in Tâ *K*wang. The idea of the figure might seem to be concentrated in it; and hence we have it symbolised by 'strength in the toes,' or 'advancing.' But such a measure is too bold to be undertaken by one in the lowest place, and moreover there is no proper correlate in 4. Hence comes the evil auspice.

Line 2 is strong, but the strength is tempered by its being in an even place, instead of being excited by it, as might be feared. Then the place is that in the centre. With firm correctness there will be good fortune.

Line 3 is strong, and in its proper place. It is at the top moreover of *Kh*ien. A small man so symbolled will use his strength to the utmost; but not so the superior man. For him the position is beyond the safe middle, and he will be cautious; and not injure himself, like the ram, by exerting his strength.

Line 4 is still strong, but in the place of a weak line; and this gives occasion to the cautions with which the symbolism commences. The subject of the line going forward thus cautiously, his strength will produce good effects, such as are described.

Line 5 is weak, and occupies a central place. Its subject will cease therefore to exert his strength; but this hexagram does not forbid the employment of strength, but would only control and

1. The first line, divided, shows one wishing to advance, and (at the same time) kept back. Let him be firm and correct, and there will be good fortune. If trust be not reposed in him, let him maintain a large and generous mind, and there will be no error.

2. The second line, divided, shows its subject with the appearance of advancing, and yet of being sorrowful. If he be firm and correct, there will be good fortune. He will receive this great blessing from his grandmother.

3. The third line, divided, shows its subject trusted by all (around him). All occasion for repentance will disappear.

4. The fourth line, undivided, shows its subject with the appearance of advancing, but like a marmot. However firm and correct he may be, the position is one of peril.

5. The fifth line, divided, shows hȯw all occasion for repentance disappears (from its subject). (But) let him not concern himself about whether he shall fail or succeed. To advance will be fortunate, and in every way advantageous.

6. The topmost line, undivided, shows one advancing his horns. But he only uses them to punish the (rebellious people of his own) city. The position

direct it. All that is said about him is that he will give no occasion for repentance.

Line 6 being at the top of *K*ăn, the symbol of movement, and at the top of Tâ *K*wang, its subject may be expected to be active in exerting his strength; and through his weakness, the result would be as described. But he becomes conscious of his weakness, reflects and rests, and good fortune results, as he desists from the prosecution of his unwise efforts.

易經

is perilous, but there will be good fortune. (Yet) however firm and correct he may be, there will be occasion for regret.

XXXV. The Thwan of this hexagram expresses its subject more fully and plainly than that of any of the previous thirty-four. It is about a feudal prince whose services to the country have made him acceptable to his king. The king's favour has been shown to him by gifts and personal attentions such as form the theme of more than one ode in the Shih; see especially III, iii, 7. The symbolism of the lines dimly indicates the qualities of such a prince. Ȝin means 'to advance.' Hexagrams 46 and 53 agree with this in being called by names that indicate progress and advance. The advance in Ȝin is like that of the sun, 'the shining light, shining more and more to the perfect day.'

Line 1 is weak, and in the lowest place, and its correlate in 4 is neither central nor in its correct position. This indicates the small and obstructed beginnings of his subject. But by his firm correctness he pursues the way to good fortune; and though the king does not yet believe in him, he the more pursues his noble course.

Line 2 is weak, and its correlate in 5 is also weak. Its subject therefore has still to mourn in obscurity. But his position is central and correct, and he holds on his way, till success comes ere long. The symbolism says he receives it 'from his grandmother;' and readers will be startled by the extraordinary statement, as I was when I first read it. Literally the Text says 'the king's mother,' as P. Regis rendered it,—'Istam magnam felicitatem a matre regis recipit.' He also tries to give the name a historical reference;—to Thâi-*K*iang, the grandmother of king Wǎn; Thâi-*Z*ǎn, his mother; or to Thâi-sze, his wife, and the mother of king Wû and the duke of *K*âu, all famous in Chinese history, and celebrated in the Shih. But 'king's father' and 'king's mother' are well-known Chinese appellations for 'grandfather' and 'grandmother.' This is the view given on the passage, by *Kh*ǎng-ȝze, *K*û Hsî, and the Khang-hsî editors, the latter of whom, indeed, account for the use of the name, instead of 'deceased mother,' which we find in hexagram 62, by the regulations observed in the ancestral temple. These authorities, moreover, all agree in saying that the name points us to line 5, the correlate of 2, and 'the lord of the hexagram.' Now the subject of line 5 is the sovereign, who at length acknowledges the worth of the feudal lord, and gives him

XXXVI. The Ming Î Hexagram.

Ming Î indicates that (in the circumstances which it denotes) it will be advantageous to realise the

---

the great blessing. The 'New Digest of Comments on the Yî (1686),' in its paraphrase of the line, has, 'He receives at last this great blessing from the mild and compliant ruler.' I am not sure that 'motherly king' would not be the best and fairest translation of the phrase.

Canon McClatchie has a very astonishing note on the name, which he renders 'Imperial Mother' (p. 164):—'That is, the wife of Imperial Heaven (Juno), who occupies the "throne of the diagram," viz. the fifth stroke, which is soft and therefore feminine. She is the Great Ancestress of the human race. See Imp. Ed. vol. iv, Sect. v, p. 25, Com.' Why such additions to the written word?

Line 3 is weak, and in an odd place; but the subjects of 1 and 2 are possessed by the same desire to advance as the subject of this. A common trust and aim possess them; and hence the not unfavourable auspice.

Line 4 is strong, but it is in an even place, nor is it central. It suggests the idea of a marmot (? or rat), stealthily advancing. Nothing could be more opposed to the ideal of the feudal lord in the hexagram.

In line 5 that lord and his intelligent sovereign meet happily. He holds on his right course, indifferent as to results, but things are so ordered that he is, and will continue to be, crowned with success.

Line 6 is strong, and suggests the idea of its subject to the last continuing his advance, and that not only with firm correctness, but with strong force. The 'horns' are an emblem of threatening strength, and though he uses them only in his own state, and against the rebellious there, that such a prince should have any occasion to use force is matter for regret.

difficulty (of the position), and maintain firm correctness.

1. The first line, undivided, shows its subject, (in the condition indicated by) Ming Î, flying, but with drooping wings. When the superior man (is revolving) his going away, he may be for three days without eating. Wherever he goes, the people there may speak (derisively of him).

2. The second line, divided, shows its subject, (in the condition indicated by) Ming Î, wounded in the left thigh. He saves himself by the strength of a (swift) horse; and is fortunate.

3. The third line, undivided, shows its subject, (in the condition indicated by) Ming Î, hunting in the south, and taking the great chief (of the darkness). He should not be eager to make (all) correct (at once).

4. The fourth line, divided, shows its subject (just) entered into the left side of the belly (of the dark land). (But) he is able to carry out the mind appropriate (in the condition indicated by) Ming Î, quitting the gate and courtyard (of the lord of darkness).

5. The fifth line, divided, shows how the count of *K*î fulfilled the condition indicated by Ming Î. It will be advantageous to be firm and correct.

6. The sixth line, divided, shows the case where there is no light, but (only) obscurity. (Its subject) had at first ascended to (the top of) the sky; his future shall be to go into the earth.

XXXVI. In this hexagram we have the representation of a good and intelligent minister or officer going forward in the service of his country, notwithstanding the occupancy of the throne by a weak

XXXVII. The *K*iâ *Z*ăn Hexagram.

For (the realisation of what is taught in) *K*iâ *Z*ăn, (or for the regulation of the family), what is

---

and unsympathising sovereign. Hence comes its name of Ming Î, or 'Intelligence Wounded,' that is, injured and repressed. The treatment of the subject shows how such an officer will conduct himself, and maintain his purpose. The symbolism of the figure is treated of in the same way in the first and second Appendixes. Appendix VI merely says that the advance set forth in 35 is sure to meet with wounding, and hence 3in is followed by Ming Î.

Line 1 is strong, and in its right place;—its subject should be going forward. But the general signification of the hexagram supposes him to be wounded. The wound, however, being received at the very commencement of its action, is but slight. And hence comes the emblem of a bird hurt so as to be obliged to droop its wings. The subject then appears directly as 'the superior man.' He sees it to be his course to desist from the struggle for a time, and is so rapt in the thought that he can fast for three days and not think of it. When he does withdraw, opposition follows him; but it is implied that he holds on to his own good purpose.

Line 2 is weak, but also in its right place, and central; giving us the idea of an officer, obedient to duty and the right. His wound in the left thigh may impede his movements, but does not disable him. He finds means to save himself, and maintains his good purpose.

Line 3, strong and in a strong place, is the topmost line of the lower trigram. It responds also to line 6, in which the idea of the sovereign, emblemed by the upper trigram, is concentrated. The lower trigram is the emblem of light or brightness, the idea of which again is expressed by the south, to which we turn when we look at the sun in its meridian height. Hence the subject of the

most advantageous is that the wife be firm and correct.

1. The first line, undivided, shows its subject establishing restrictive regulations in his household. Occasion for repentance will disappear.

2. The second line, divided, shows its subject taking nothing on herself, but in her central place attending to the preparation of the food. Through her firm correctness there will be good fortune.

3. The third line, undivided, shows its subject (treating) the members of the household with stern severity. There will be occasion for repentance, there will be peril, (but) there will (also) be good fortune. If the wife and children were to be smirking and chattering, in the end there would be occasion for regret.

4. The fourth line, divided, shows its subject

---

line becomes a hunter pursuing his game, and successfully. The good officer will be successful in his struggle; but let him not be over eager to put all things right at once.

Line 4 is weak, but in its right place. *K*û Hsî says he does not understand the symbolism, as given in the Text. The translation indicates the view of it commonly accepted. The subject of the line evidently escapes from his position of danger with little damage.

Line 5 should be the place of the ruler or sovereign in the hexagram; but 6 is assigned as that place in Ming Î. The officer occupying 5, the centre of the upper trigram, and near to the sovereign, has his ideal in the count of *K*î, whose action appears in the Shû, III, pp. 123, 127, 128. He is a historical personage.

Line 6 sets forth the fate of the ruler, who opposes himself to the officer who would do him good and intelligent service. Instead of becoming as the sun, enlightening all from the height of the sky, he is as the sun hidden below the earth. I can well believe that the writer had the last king of Shang in his mind.

enriching the family. There will be great good fortune.

5. The fifth line, undivided, shows the influence of the king extending to his family. There need be no anxiety; there will be good fortune.

6. The topmost line, undivided, shows its subject possessed of sincerity and arrayed in majesty. In the end there will be good fortune.

XXXVII. *Kiâ Zăn*, the name of the hexagram, simply means 'a household,' or 'the members of a family.' The subject of the essay based on the figure, however, is the regulation of the family, effected mainly by the co-operation of husband and wife in their several spheres, and only needing to become universal to secure the good order of the kingdom. The important place occupied by the wife in the family is seen in the short sentence of the Thwan. That she be firm and correct, and do her part well, is the first thing necessary to its regulation.

Line 1 is strong, and in a strong place. It suggests the necessity of strict rule in governing the family. Regulations must be established, and their observance strictly insisted on.

Line 2 is weak, and in the proper place for it,—the centre, moreover, of the lower trigram. It fitly represents the wife, and what is said on it tells us of her special sphere and duty; and that she should be unassuming in regard to all beyond her sphere; always being firm and correct. See the Shih, III, 350.

Line 3 is strong, and in an odd place. If the place were central, the strength would be tempered; but the subject of the line, in the topmost place of the trigram, may be expected to exceed in severity. But severity is not a bad thing in regulating a family;—it is better than laxity and indulgence.

Line 4 is weak, and in its proper place. The wife is again suggested to us, and we are told, that notwithstanding her being confined to the internal affairs of the household, she can do much to enrich the family.

The subject of the strong fifth line appears as the king. This may be the husband spoken of as also a king; or the real king whose merit is revealed first in his family, as often in the Shih, where king Wăn is the theme. The central place here tempers the display of the strength and power.

XXXVIII. THE *KH*WEI HEXAGRAM.

䷥

Khwei indicates that, (notwithstanding the condition of things which it denotes), in small matters there will (still) be good success.

1. The first line, undivided, shows that (to its subject) occasion for repentance will disappear. He has lost his horses, but let him not seek for them;—they will return of themselves. Should he meet with bad men, he will not err (in communicating with them).

2. The second line, undivided, shows its subject happening to meet with his lord in a bye-passage. There will be no error.

3. In the third line, divided, we see one whose carriage is dragged back, while the oxen in it are pushed back, and he is himself subjected to the shaving of his head and the cutting off of his nose. There is no good beginning, but there will be a good end.

4. The fourth line, undivided, shows its subject solitary amidst the (prevailing) disunion. (But) he meets with the good man (represented by the first

---

Line 6 is also strong, and being in an even place, the subject of it might degenerate into stern severity, but he is supposed to be sincere, complete in his personal character and self-culture, and hence his action will only lead to good fortune.

line), and they blend their sincere desires together. The position is one of peril, but there will be no mistake.

5. The fifth line, divided, shows that (to its subject) occasion for repentance will disappear. With his relative (and minister he unites closely and readily) as if he were biting through a piece of skin. When he goes forward (with this help), what error can there be?

6. The topmost line, undivided, shows its subject solitary amidst the (prevailing) disunion. (In the subject of the third line, he seems to) see a pig bearing on its back a load of mud, (or fancies) there is a carriage full of ghosts. He first bends his bow against him, and afterwards unbends it, (for he discovers) that he is not an assailant to injure, but a near relative. Going forward, he shall meet with (genial) rain, and there will be good fortune.

XXXVIII. Khwei denotes a social state in which division and mutual alienation prevail, and the hexagram teaches how in small matters this condition may be healed, and the way prepared for the cure of the whole system. The writer or writers of Appendixes I and II point out the indication in the figure of division and disunion according to their views. In Appendix VI those things appear as a necessary sequel to the regulation of the family; while it is impossible to discover any allusion to the family in the Text.

Line 1 is strong, and in an odd place. A successful course might be auspiced for its subject; but the correlate in line 4 is also strong; and therefore disappointment and repentance are likely to ensue. In the condition, however, indicated by Khwei, where people have a common virtue, they will help one another. Through the good services of 4, the other will not have to repent. His condition may be emblemed by a traveller's loss of his horses, which return to him of themselves.

Should he meet with bad men, however, let him not shrink from them. Communication with them will be of benefit. His good

XXXIX. The *K*ien Hexagram.

In (the state indicated by) *K*ien advantage will be found in the south-west, and the contrary in the north-east. It will be advantageous (also) to meet

---

may overcome their evil, and at least it will help to silence their slanderous tongues.

Line 5 is weak, and its subject is the proper correlate of the strong 2. They might meet openly; but for the separation and disunion that mark the time. A casual, as it were a stolen, interview, as in a bye-lane or passage, however will be useful, and may lead on to a better understanding.

Line 3 is weak, where it ought to be strong. Its correlate, however, in 6 is strong, and the relation between them might seem what it ought to be. But the weak 3 is between the strong lines in 2 and 4; and in a time of disunion there ensue the checking and repulsion emblemed in the Text. At the same time the subject of line 6 inflicts on that of 3 the punishments which are mentioned. It is thus bad for 3 at first, but we are told that in the end it will be well with him; and this will be due to the strength of the sixth line. The conclusion grows out of a conviction in the mind of the author that what is right and good is destined to triumph over what is wrong and bad. Disorder shall in the long run give place to order, and disunion to union.

Line 4 has no proper correlate, and might seem to be solitary. But, as we saw on line 1, in this hexagram, correlates of the same class help each other. Hence the subjects of 4 and 1, meeting together, work with good will and success.

The place of 5 is odd, but the line itself is weak, so that there might arise occasion for repentance. But the strong 2 is a proper correlate to the weak 5. Five being the sovereign's place, the subject of 2 is styled the sovereign's relative, of the same surname

with the great man. (In these circumstances), with firmness and correctness, there will be good fortune.

1. From the first line, divided, we learn that advance (on the part of its subject) will lead to (greater) difficulties, while remaining stationary will afford ground for praise.

2. The second line, divided, shows the minister of the king struggling with difficulty on difficulty, and not with a view to his own advantage.

3. The third line, undivided, shows its subject advancing, (but only) to (greater) difficulties. He remains stationary, and returns (to his former associates).

4. The fourth line, divided, shows its subject advancing, (but only) to (greater) difficulties. He remains stationary, and unites (with the subject of the line above).

5. The fifth line, undivided, shows its subject struggling with the greatest difficulties, while friends are coming to help him.

6. The topmost line, divided, shows its subject going forward, (only to increase) the difficulties,

---

with him, and head of some branch of the descendants of the royal house. It is as easy for 5, so supported, to deal with the disunion of the time, as to bite through a piece of skin.

Line 6 is an even place, and yet the line is strong;—what can its subject effect? He looks at 3, which, as weak, is a proper correlate; but he looks with the evil eye of disunion. The subject of 3 appears no better than a filthy pig, nor more real than an impossible carriage-load of ghosts. He bends his bow against him, but he unbends it, discovering a friend in 3, as 1 did in 4, and 5 in 2. He acts and with good luck, comparable to the falling rain, which results from the happy union of the *yang* and *yin* in nature.

while his remaining stationary will be (productive of) great (merit). There will be good fortune, and it will be advantageous to meet with the great man.

XXXIX. *K*ien is the symbol for incompetency in the feet and legs, involving difficulty in walking; hence it is used in this hexagram to indicate a state of the kingdom which makes the government of it an arduous task. How this task may be successfully performed, now by activity on the part of the ruler, and now by a discreet inactivity:—this is what the figure teaches, or at least gives hints about. For the development of the meaning of the symbolic character from the structure of the lineal figure, see Appendixes I and II.

The Thwan seems to require three things—attention to place, the presence of the great man, and the firm observance of correctness—in order to cope successfully with the difficulties of the situation. The first thing is enigmatically expressed, and the language should be compared with what we find in the Thwan of hexagrams 2 and 40. Referring to Figure 2, in Plate III, we find that, according to Wăn's arrangement of the trigrams, the south-west is occupied by Khwăn (☷), and the north-east by *K*ăn (☶). The former represents the champaign country; the latter, the mountainous region. The former is easily traversed and held; the latter, with difficulty. The attention to place thus becomes transformed into a calculation of circumstances; those that promise success in an enterprise, which should be taken advantage of, and those that threaten difficulty and failure, which should be shunned.

This is the generally accepted view of this difficult passage. The Khang-hsî editors have a view of their own. I have been myself inclined to find less symbolism in it, and to take the south-west as the regions in the south and west of the kingdom, which we know from the Shih were more especially devoted to Wăn and his house, while the strength of the kings of Shang lay in the north and east.

'The idea of "the great man," Mencius's "minister of Heaven,"' is illustrated by the strong line in the fifth place, having for its correlate the weak line in 2. But favourableness of circumstances and place, and the presence of the great man do not dispense from the observance of firm correctness. Throughout these essays of the Yî this is always insisted on.

XL. The *K*ieh Hexagram.

In (the state indicated by) *K*ieh advantage will be found in the south-west. If no (further) operations be called for, there will be good fortune in coming back (to the old conditions). If some operations be called for, there will be good fortune in the early conducting of them.

1. The first line, divided, shows that its subject will commit no error.

Line 1 is weak, whereas it ought to be strong as being in an odd place. If its subject advance, he will not be able to cope with the difficulties of the situation, but be overwhelmed by them. Let him wait for a more favourable time.

Line 2 is weak, but in its proper place. Its correlation with the strong 5, and consequent significance, are well set forth.

Line 3 is strong, and in a place of strength; but its correlate in 6 is weak, so that the advance of its subject would be unsupported. He waits therefore for a better time, and cherishes the subjects of the two lines below, who naturally cling to him.

Line 4 is weak, and, though in its proper place, its subject could do little of himself. He is immediately below the king or great man, however, and cultivates his loyal attachment to him, waiting for the time when he shall be required to act.

Line 5 is the king, the man great and strong. He can cope with the difficulties, and the subjects of 2 and the other lines of the lower trigram give their help.

The action of the hexagram is over; where can the weak 6 go forward to? Let him abide where he is, and serve the great man immediately below him. So shall he also be great;—in meritorious action at least.

2. The second line, undivided, shows its subject catch, in hunting, three foxes, and obtain the yellow (=golden) arrows. With firm correctness there will be good fortune.

3. The third line, divided, shows a porter with his burden, (yet) riding in a carriage. He will (only) tempt robbers to attack him. However firm and correct he may (try to) be, there will be cause for regret.

4. (To the subject of) the fourth line, undivided, (it is said), 'Remove your toes. Friends will (then) come, between you and whom there will be mutual confidence.'

5. The fifth line, divided, shows (its subject), the superior man (=the ruler), executing his function of removing (whatever is injurious to the idea of the hexagram), in which case there will be good fortune, and confidence in him will be shown even by the small men.

6. In the sixth line, divided, we see a feudal prince (with his bow) shooting at a falcon on the top of a high wall, and hitting it. (The effect of his action) will be in every way advantageous.

XL. *K*ieh is the symbol of loosing,—untying a knot or unravelling a complication; and as the name of this hexagram, it denotes a condition in which the obstruction and difficulty indicated by the preceding *K*ien have been removed. The object of the author is to show, as if from the lines of the figure, how this new and better state of the kingdom is to be dealt with. See what is said on the Thwan of *K*ien for 'the advantage to be found in the south-west.' If further active operations be not necessary to complete the subjugation of the country, the sooner things fall into their old channels the better. The new masters of the kingdom should not be anxious to change all the old manners and ways. Let them do, as the duke of *K*âu actually did do with the subjugated people of Shang. If

XLI. The Sun Hexagram.

䷨

In (what is denoted by) Sun, if there be sincerity (in him who employs it), there will be great good fortune:—freedom from error; firmness and correctness that can be maintained; and advantage in every

---

further operations be necessary, let them be carried through without delay. Nothing is said in the Thwan about the discountenancing and removal of small men,—unworthy ministers or officers; but that subject appears in more than one of the lines.

There is a weak line, instead of a strong, in the first place; but this is compensated for by its strong correlate in 4.

*K*û Hsî says he does not understand the symbolism under line 2. The place is even, but the line itself is strong; the strength therefore is modified or tempered. And 2 is the correlate of the ruler in 5. We are to look to its subject therefore for a minister striving to realise the idea of the hexagram, and pacify the subdued kingdom. He becomes a hunter, and disposes of unworthy men, represented by 'the three foxes.' He also gets the yellow arrows,—the instruments used in war or in hunting, whose colour is 'correct,' and whose form is 'straight.' His firm correctness will be good.

Line 3 is weak, when it should be strong; and occupying, as it does, the topmost place of the lower trigram, it suggests the symbolism of a porter in a carriage. People will say, 'How did he get there? The things cannot be his own.' And robbers will attack and plunder him. The subject of the line cannot protect himself, nor accomplish anything good.

What is said on the fourth line appears in the form of an address to its subject. The line is strong in an even place, and 1, its correlate, is weak in an odd place. Such a union will not be productive of good. In the symbolism 1 becomes the toe of the subject of 4. How the friend or friends, who are to come to him on the removal of this toe, are represented, I do not perceive.

Line 5 is weak in an odd place; but the place is that of the ruler, to whom it belongs to perfect the idea of the hexagram by

movement that shall be made. In what shall this (sincerity in the exercise of Sun) be employed? (Even) in sacrifice two baskets of grain, (though there be nothing else), may be presented.

1. The first line, undivided, shows its subject suspending his own affairs, and hurrying away (to help the subject of the fourth line). He will commit no error, but let him consider how far he should contribute of what is his (for the other).

2. The second line, undivided, shows that it will be advantageous for its subject to maintain a firm correctness, and that action on his part will be evil. He can give increase (to his correlate) without taking from himself.

3. The third line, divided, shows how of three men walking together, the number is diminished by one; and how one, walking, finds his friend.

4. The fourth line, divided, shows its subject diminishing the ailment under which he labours by making (the subject of the first line) hasten (to his help), and make him glad. There will be no error.

5. The fifth line, divided, shows parties adding to (the stores of) its subject ten pairs of tortoise shells, and accepting no refusal. There will be great good fortune.

---

removing all that is contrary to the peace and good order of the kingdom. It will be his duty to remove especially all the small men represented by the divided lines, which he can do with the help of his strong correlate in 2. Then even the small men will change their ways, and repair to him.

Line 6 is the highest line in the figure, but not the place of the ruler. Hence it appears as occupied by a feudal duke, who carries out the idea of the figure against small men, according to the symbolism employed.

6. The topmost line, undivided, shows its subject giving increase to others without taking from himself. There will be no error. With firm correctness there will be good fortune. There will be advantage in every movement that shall be made. He will find ministers more than can be counted by their clans.

XLI. The interpretation of this hexagram is encompassed with great difficulties. Sun is the symbol for the idea of diminishing or diminution; and what is said in Appendix I has made it to be accepted as teaching the duty of the subject to take of what is his and contribute to his ruler, or the expenses of the government under which he lives; in other words, readily and cheerfully to pay his taxes. P. Regis says, 'Sun seu (vectigalis causa) minuere . . . . est valde utile;' and Canon McClatchie in translating Appendix I has:—'Diminishing (by taxation for instance) . . . . is very lucky.' Possibly, king Wăn may have seen in the figures the subject of taxation; but the symbolism of his son takes a much wider range. My own reading of the figure and Text comes near to the view of *Kh*ăng-ȝze, that 'every diminution and repression of what we have in excess to bring it into accordance with right and reason is comprehended under Sun.'

Let there be sincerity in doing this, and it will lead to the happiest results. It will lead to great success in great things; and if the correction, or it may be a contribution towards it, appear to be very small, yet it will be accepted;—as in the most solemn religious service. This is substantially the view of the hexagram approved by the Khang-hsî editors.

Line 1 is strong, and its correlate in 4 is weak. Its subject will wish to help the subject of 4; but will not leave anything of his own undone in doing so. Nor will he diminish of his own for the other without due deliberation.

Line 2 is strong, and in the central place. But it is in the place of a weak line, and its subject should maintain his position without moving to help his correlate in 5. Maintaining his own firm correctness is the best way to help him.

Paragraph 3 is to my mind full of obscurity. *K*û Hsî, adopting the view in Appendix I, says that the lower trigram was originally *Kh*ien, three undivided lines, like 'three men walking together,'

XLII. The Yî Hexagram.

Yî indicates that (in the state which it denotes) there will be advantage in every movement which shall be undertaken, that it will be advantageous (even) to cross the great stream.

1. The first line, undivided, shows that it will be advantageous for its subject in his position to make

---

and that the third line, taken away and made to be the topmost line, or the third, in what was originally Khwăn, three divided lines, was 'the putting away of one man;' and that then the change of place by 3 and 6, while they continued their proper correlation, was, one going away, and finding his friend. I cannot lay hold of any thread of reason in this.

Line 4 is weak, and in an even place; like an individual ailing and unable to perform his proper work. But the correlate in 1 is strong; and is made to hasten to its relief. The 'joy' of the line shows the desire of its subject to do his part in the work of the hexagram.

Line 5 is the seat of the ruler, who is here humble, and welcomes the assistance of his correlate, the subject of 2. He is a ruler whom all his subjects of ability will rejoice to serve in every possible way; and the result will be great good fortune.

Line 6 has been changed from a weak into a strong line from line 3; has received therefore the greatest increase, and will carry out the idea of the hexagram in the highest degree and style. But he can give increase to others without diminishing his own resources, and of course the benefit he will confer will be incalculable. Ministers will come to serve him; and not one from each clan merely, but many. Such is the substance of what is said on this last paragraph. I confess that I only discern the meaning darkly.

a great movement. If it be greatly fortunate, no blame will be imputed to him.

2. The second line, divided, shows parties adding to the stores of its subject ten pairs of tortoise shells whose oracles cannot be opposed. Let him persevere in being firm and correct, and there will be good fortune. Let the king, (having the virtues thus distinguished), employ them in presenting his offerings to God, and there will be good fortune.

3. The third line, divided, shows increase given to its subject by means of what is evil, so that he shall (be led to good), and be without blame. Let him be sincere and pursue the path of the Mean, (so shall he secure the recognition of the ruler, like) an officer who announces himself to his prince by the symbol of his rank.

4. The fourth line, divided, shows its subject pursuing the due course. His advice to his prince is followed. He can with advantage be relied on in such a movement as that of removing the capital.

5. The fifth line, undivided, shows its subject with sincere heart seeking to benefit (all below). There need be no question about it; the result will be great good fortune. (All below) will with sincere heart acknowledge his goodness.

6. In the sixth line, undivided, we see one to whose increase none will contribute, while many will seek to assail him. He observes no regular rule in the ordering of his heart. There will be evil.

XLII. Yî has the opposite meaning to Sun, and is the symbol of addition or increasing. What king Wăn had in his mind, in connexion with the hexagram, was a ruler or a government operating

XLIII. The Kwâi Hexagram.

Kwâi requires (in him who would fulfil its meaning) the exhibition (of the culprit's guilt) in the royal court, and a sincere and earnest appeal (for sym-

---

so as to dispense benefits to, and increase the resources of all the people. Two indications are evident in the lines;—the strong line in the ruler's seat, or the fifth line, and the weak line in the correlative place of 2. Whether there be other indications in the figure or its component trigrams will be considered in dealing with the Appendixes. The writer might well say, on general grounds, of the ruler whom he had in mind, that he would be successful in his enterprises and overcome the greatest difficulties.

Line 1 is strong, but its low position might seem to debar its subject from any great enterprise. Favoured as he is, however, according to the general idea of the hexagram, and specially responding to the proper correlate in 4, it is natural that he should make a movement; and great success will make his rashness be forgotten.

With paragraph 2 compare paragraph 5 of the preceding hexagram. Line 2 is weak, but in the centre, and is the correlate of 5. Friends give its subject the valuable gifts mentioned; 'that is,' says Kwo Yung (Sung dynasty), 'men benefit him; the oracles of the divination are in his favour,—spirits, that is, benefit him; and finally, when the king sacrifices to God, He accepts. Heaven confers benefit from above.'

Line 3 is weak, neither central, nor in its correct position. It would seem therefore that its subject should have no increase given to him. But it is the time for giving increase, and the idea of his receiving it by means of evil things is put into the line. That such things serve for reproof and correction is well known to Chinese moralists. But the paragraph goes on also to caution and admonish.

Line 4 is the place for a minister, near to that of the ruler. Its subject is weak, but his place is appropriate, and as he follows the

pathy and support), with a consciousness of the peril (involved in cutting off the criminal). He should (also) make announcement in his own city, and show that it will not be well to have recourse at once to arms. (In this way) there will be advantage in whatever he shall go forward to.

1. The first line, undivided, shows its subject in (the pride of) strength advancing with his toes. He goes forward, but will not succeed. There will be ground for blame.

2. The second line, undivided, shows its subject full of apprehension and appealing (for sympathy and help). Late at night hostile measures may be (taken against him), but he need not be anxious about them.

3. The third line, undivided, shows its subject (about to advance) with strong (and determined) looks. There will be evil. (But) the superior man, bent on cutting off (the criminal), will walk alone and encounter the rain, (till he be hated by his proper associates) as if he were contaminated (by the others). (In the end) there will be no blame against him.

---

due course, his ruler will listen to him, and he will be a support in the most critical movements. Changing the capital from place to place was frequent in the feudal times of China. That of Shang, which preceded *K*âu, was changed five times.

Line 5 is strong, in its fitting position, and central. It is the seat of the ruler, who has his proper correlate in 2. Everything good, according to the conditions of the hexagram, therefore, may be said of him ;—as is done.

Line 6 is also strong; but it should be weak. Occupying the topmost place of the figure, its subject will concentrate his powers in the increase of himself, and not think of benefiting those below him; and the consequence will be as described.

4. The fourth line, undivided, shows one from whose buttocks the skin has been stripped, and who walks slowly and with difficulty. (If he could act) like a sheep led (after its companions), occasion for repentance would disappear. But though he hear these words, he will not believe them.

5. The fifth line, undivided, shows (the small men like) a bed of purslain, which ought to be uprooted with the utmost determination. (The subject of the line having such determination), his action, in harmony with his central position, will lead to no error or blame.

6. The sixth line, divided, shows its subject without any (helpers) on whom to call. His end will be evil.

XLIII. In Kwâi we have the hexagram of the third month, when the last remnant, cold and dark, of winter, represented by the sixth line, is about to disappear before the advance of the warm and bright days of the approaching summer. In the yin line at the top king Wăn saw the symbol of a small or bad man, a feudal prince or high minister, lending his power to maintain a corrupt government, or, it might be, a dynasty that was waxen old and ready to vanish away; and in the five undivided lines he saw the representatives of good order, or, it might be, the dynasty which was to supersede the other. This then is the subject of the hexagram,—how bad men, statesmen corrupt and yet powerful, are to be put out of the way. And he who would accomplish the task must do so by the force of his character more than by force of arms, and by producing a general sympathy on his side.

The Thwan says that he must openly denounce the criminal in the court, seek to awaken general sympathy, and at the same time go about his enterprise, conscious of its difficulty and danger. Among his own adherents, moreover, as if it were in his own city, he must make it understood how unwillingly he takes up arms. Then let him go forward, and success will attend him.

Line 1 is strong, the first line of that trigram, which expresses the idea of strength. But it is in the lowest place. The stage of

XLIV. THE KÂU HEXAGRAM.

Kâu shows a female who is bold and strong. It will not be good to marry (such) a female.

---

the enterprise is too early, and the preparation too small to make victory certain. Its subject had better not take the field.

Line 2 is strong, and central, and its subject is possessed with the determination to do his part in the work of removal. But his eagerness is tempered by his occupancy of an even place; and he is cautious, and no attempts, however artful, to harm him will take effect.

Line 3 is strong, and its subject displays his purpose too eagerly. Being beyond the central position, moreover, gives an indication of evil. Lines 3 and 6 are also proper correlates; and, as elsewhere in the Yi, the meeting of yin and yang lines is associated with falling rain. The subject of 3, therefore, communicates with 6, in a way that annoys his associates; but nevertheless he commits no error, and, in the end, incurs no blame.

Line 4 is not in the centre, nor in an odd place, appropriate to it as undivided. Its subject therefore will not be at rest, nor able to do anything to accomplish the idea of the hexagram. He is symbolised by a culprit, who, according to the ancient and modern custom of Chinese courts, has been bastinadoed till he presents the appearance in the Text. Alone he can do nothing; if he could follow others, like a sheep led along, he might accomplish something, but he will not listen to advice.

Purslain grows in shady places, and hence we find it here in close contiguity to the topmost line, which is yin. As 5 is the ruler's seat, evil may come to him from such contiguity, and strenuous efforts must be made to prevent such an evil. The subject of the line, the ruler in the central place, will commit no error. It must be allowed that the symbolism in this line is not easily managed.

The subject of the 6th line, standing alone, may be easily disposed of.

1. The first line, divided, shows how its subject should be kept (like a carriage) tied and fastened to a metal drag, in which case with firm correctness there will be good fortune. (But) if he move in any direction, evil will appear. He will be (like) a lean pig, which is sure to keep jumping about.

2. The second line, undivided, shows its subject with a wallet of fish. There will be no error. But it will not be well to let (the subject of the first line) go forward to the guests.

3. The third line, undivided, shows one from whose buttocks the skin has been stripped so that he walks with difficulty. The position is perilous, but there will be no great error.

4. The fourth line, undivided, shows its subject with his wallet, but no fish in it. This will give rise to evil.

5. The fifth line, undivided, (shows its subject as) a medlar tree overspreading the gourd (beneath it). If he keep his brilliant qualities concealed, (a good issue) will descend (as) from Heaven.

6. The sixth line, undivided, shows its subject receiving others on his horns. There will be occasion for regret, but there will be no error.

XLIV. The single, divided, line at the top of Kwâi, the hexagram of the third month, has been displaced, and *Kh*ien has ruled over the fourth month of the year. But the innings of the divided line commence again; and here we have in Kâu the hexagram of the fifth month, when light and heat are supposed both to begin to be less.

In that divided line Wăn saw the symbol of the small or unworthy man, beginning to insinuate himself into the government

XLV. The 3hui Hexagram.

In (the state denoted by) 3hui, the king will repair to his ancestral temple. It will be advan-

---

of the country. His influence, if unchecked, would go on to grow, and he would displace one good man after another, and fill the vacant seats with others like-minded with himself. The object of Wăn in his Thwan, therefore, was to enjoin resistance to the encroachment of this bad man.

Kâu is defined as giving the idea of suddenly and casually encountering or meeting with. So does the divided line appear all at once in the figure. And this significance of the name rules in the interpretation of the lines, so as to set on one side the more common interpretation of them according to the correlation; showing how the meaning of the figures was put into them from the minds of Wăn and Tan in the first place. The sentiments of the Text are not learned from them; but they are forced and twisted, often fantastically, and made to appear to give those sentiments forth of themselves.

Here the first line, divided, where it ought to be the contrary, becomes the symbol of a bold, bad woman, who appears unexpectedly on the scene, and wishes to subdue or win all the five strong lines to herself. No one would contract a marriage with such a female; and every good servant of his country will try to repel the entrance into the government of every officer who can be so symbolised.

Line 1 represents the bête noire of the figure. If its subject can be kept back, the method of firm government and order will proceed. If he cannot be restrained, he will become disgusting and dangerous. It is not enough for the carriage to be stopt by the metal drag; it is also tied or bound to some steadfast object. Internal and external restraints should be opposed to the bad man.

The 'wallet of fish' under line 2 is supposed to symbolise the

tageous (also) to meet with the great man; and then there will be progress and success, though the advantage must come through firm correctness. The use of great victims will conduce to good fortune; and in whatever direction movement is made, it will be advantageous.

1. The first line, divided, shows its subject with a sincere desire (for union), but unable to carry it out, so that disorder is brought into the sphere of his union. If he cry out (for help to his proper correlate), all at once (his tears) will give place

---

subject of line 1. It has come into the possession of the subject of 2, by virtue of the meaning of the name Kâu, which I have pointed out. With his strength therefore he can repress the advance of 1. He becomes in fact 'the lord of the hexagram,' and all the other strong lines are merely guests; and especially is it important that he should prevent 1 from approaching them. This is a common explanation of what is said under this second line. It seems far-fetched; but I can neither find nor devise anything better.

With what is said on line 3, compare the fourth paragraph of the duke's Text on the preceding hexagram. Line 3 is strong, but has gone beyond the central place; has no correlate above; and is cut off from 1 by the intervening 2. It cannot do much therefore against 1; but its aim being to repress that, there will be no great error.

Line 1 is the proper correlate of 4; but it has already met and assóciated with 2. The subject of 4 therefore stands alone; and evil to him may be looked for.

Line 5 is strong, and in the ruler's place. Its relation to 1 is like that of a forest tree to the spreading gourd. But let not its subject use force to destroy or repress the growth of 1; but let him restrain himself and keep his excellence concealed, and Heaven will set its seal to his virtue.

The symbolism of line 6 is difficult to understand, though the meaning of what is said is pretty clear. The Khang-hsî editors observe:—'The subject of this line is like an officer who has withdrawn from the world. He can accomplish no service for the time; but his person is removed from the workers of disorder.'

to smiles. He need not mind (the temporary difficulty); as he goes forward, there will be no error.

2. The second line, divided, shows its subject led forward (by his correlate). There will be good fortune, and freedom from error. There is entire sincerity, and in that case (even the small offerings of) the vernal sacrifice are acceptable.

3. The third line, divided, shows its subject striving after union and seeming to sigh, yet nowhere finding any advantage. If he go forward, he will not err, though there may be some small cause for regret.

4. The fourth line, undivided, shows its subject in such a state that, if he be greatly fortunate, he will receive no blame.

5. The fifth line, undivided, shows the union (of all) under its subject in the place of dignity. There will be no error. If any do not have confidence in him, let him see to it that (his virtue) be great, long-continued, and firmly correct, and all occasion for repentance will disappear.

6. The topmost line, divided, shows its subject sighing and weeping; but there will be no error.

XLV. Ȝhui denotes collecting together, or things so collected; and hence this hexagram concerns the state of the kingdom when a happy union prevails between the sovereign and his ministers, between high and low; and replies in a vague way to the question how this state is to be preserved; by the influence of religion, and the great man, who is a sage upon the throne.

He, 'the king,' will repair to his ancestral temple, and meet in spirit there with the spirits of his ancestors. Whatever he does, being correct and right, will succeed. His religious services will be distinguished by their dignity and splendour. His victims will

易經

XLVI. The Shăng Hexagram.

Shăng indicates that (under its conditions) there will be great progress and success. Seeking by

---

be the best that can be obtained, and other things will be in harmony with them.

Line 1 is weak, and in the place of a strong line. It has a proper correlate in 4, but is separated from him by the intervention of two weak lines. The consequence of these things is supposed to be expressed in the first part of the symbolism; but the subject of the line is possessed by the desire for union, which is the theme of the hexagram. Calling out to his correlate for help, he obtains it, and his sorrow is turned into joy.

Line 2 is in its proper place, and responds to the strong ruler in 5, who encourages and helps the advance of its subject. He possesses also the sincerity, proper to him in his central position; and though he were able to offer only the sacrifice of the spring, small compared with the fulness of the sacrifices in summer and autumn, it would be accepted.

Line 3 is weak, in the place of a strong line, and advanced from the central place. The topmost line, moreover, is no proper correlate. But its subject is possessed by the desire for union; and though 2 and 4 decline to associate with him, he presses on to 6, which is also desirous of union. That common desire brings them together, notwithstanding 3 and 6 are both divided lines; and with difficulty the subject of 3 accomplishes his object.

[But that an ordinary rule for interpreting the lineal indications may be thus overruled by extraordinary considerations shows how much of fancy there is in the symbolism or in the commentaries on it.]

Line 4 has its correlate in 1, and is near to the ruling line in 5. We may expect a good auspice for it; but its being strong in an odd place, calls for the caution which is insinuated.

Line 5 is strong, central, and in its correct position. Through

(the qualities implied in it) to meet with the great man, its subject need have no anxiety. Advance to the south will be fortunate.

1. The first line, divided, shows its subject advancing upwards with the welcome (of those above him). There will be great good fortune.

2. The second line, undivided, shows its subject with that sincerity which will make even the (small) offerings of the vernal sacrifice acceptable. There will be no error.

3. The third line, undivided, shows its subject ascending upwards (as into) an empty city.

4. The fourth line, divided, shows its subject employed by the king to present his offerings on mount *Khî*. There will be good fortune; there will be no mistake.

5. The fifth line, divided, shows its subject firmly correct, and therefore enjoying good fortune. He ascends the stairs (with all due ceremony).

6. The sixth line, divided, shows its subject advancing upwards blindly. Advantage will be found in a ceaseless maintenance of firm correctness.

---

its subject there may be expected the full realisation of the idea of the hexagram.

Line 6, weak, and at the extremity of the figure, is still anxious for union; but he has no proper correlate, and all below are united in 5. Its subject mourns his solitary condition; and his good feeling will preserve him from error and blame.

XLVI. The character Shăng is used of advancing in an upward direction, 'advancing and ascending.' And here, as the name of the hexagram, it denotes the advance of a good officer to the highest pinnacle of distinction. The second line, in the centre of the lower trigram, is strong, but the strength is tempered by its being in an even place. As the representative of the subject of the

XLVII. The Khwăn Hexagram.

In (the condition denoted by) Khwăn there may (yet be) progress and success. For the firm and

---

hexagram, it shows him to be possessed of modesty and force. Then the ruler's seat, the fifth place, is occupied by a divided line, indicating that he will welcome the advance of 2. The officer therefore both has the qualities that fit him to advance, and a favourable opportunity to do so. The result of his advance will be fortunate.

It is said that after he has met with the ruler, 'the great man' in 5, 'advance to the south will be fortunate.' *K*û Hsî and other critics say that 'advancing to the south' is equivalent simply to 'advancing forwards.' The south is the region of brightness and warmth; advance towards it will be a joyful progress. As P. Regis explains the phrase, the traveller will proceed 'via recta simillima illi qua itur ad austrates felicesque plagas.'

Line 1 is weak, where it should be strong; its subject, that is, is humble and docile. Those above him, therefore, welcome his advance. Another interpretation of the line is suggested by Appendix I; which deserves consideration. As the first line of Sun, moreover, it may be supposed to concentrate in itself its attribute of docility, and be the lord of the trigram.

See on the second line of 3hui. Line 2 is strong, and the weak 5 is its proper correlate. We have a strong officer serving a weak ruler; he could not do so unless he were penetrated with a sincere and devoted loyalty.

Paragraph 3 describes the boldness and fearlessness of the advance of the third line. According to the Khang-hsî editors, who, I think, are right, there is a shade of condemnation in the line. Its subject is too bold.

Line 4 occupies the place of a great minister, in immediate contiguity to his ruler, who confides in him, and raises him to the highest distinction as a feudal prince. The mention of mount

correct, the (really) great man, there will be good fortune. He will fall into no error. If he make speeches, his words cannot be made good.

1. The first line, divided, shows its subject with bare buttocks straitened under the stump of a tree. He enters a dark valley, and for three years has no prospect (of deliverance).

2. The second line, undivided, shows its subject straitened amidst his wine and viands. There come to him anon the red knee-covers (of the ruler). It will be well for him (to maintain his sincerity as) in sacrificing. Active operations (on his part) will lead to evil, but he will be free from blame.

3. The third line, divided, shows its subject straitened before a (frowning) rock. He lays hold of thorns. He enters his palace, and does not see his wife. There will be evil.

4. The fourth line, undivided, shows its subject proceeding very slowly (to help the subject of the first line), who is straitened by the carriage adorned with metal in front of him. There will be occasion for regret, but the end will be good.

Khî, at the foot of which was the capital of the lords of *Kâu*, seems to take the paragraph out of the sphere of symbolism into that of history. 'The king' in it is the last sovereign of Shang; the feudal prince in it is Wăn.

In line 5 the advance has reached the highest point of dignity, and firm correctness is specially called for. 'Ascending the steps of a stair' may intimate, as *K*û Hsî says, the ease of the advance; or according to others (the Khang-hsî editors among them), its ceremonious manner.

What can the subject of the hexagram want more? He has gained all his wishes, and still he is for going onwards. His advance is blind and foolish; and only the most exact correctness will save him from the consequences.

5. The fifth line, undivided, shows its subject with his nose and feet cut off. He is straitened by (his ministers in their) scarlet aprons. He is leisurely in his movements, however, and is satisfied. It will be well for him to be (as sincere) as in sacrificing (to spiritual beings).

6. The sixth line, divided, shows its subject straitened, as if bound with creepers; or in a high and dangerous position, and saying (to himself), 'If I move, I shall repent it.' If he do repent of former errors, there will be good fortune in his going forward.

XLVII. The character Khwăn presents us with the picture of a tree within an enclosure; 'a plant,' according to Williams, 'fading for want of room;' 'a tree,' according to Tai Tung, 'not allowed to spread its branches.' However this be, the term conveys the idea of being straitened and distressed; and this hexagram indicates a state of things in which the order and government that would conduce to the well-being of the country can hardly get the development, which, by skilful management on the part of 'the great man' and others, is finally secured for them.

Looking at the figure we see that the two central places are occupied by strong lines; but 2 is confined between 1 and 3, both of which are weak, and 5 (the ruler), as well as 4 (his minister), is covered by the weak 6; all which peculiarities are held to indicate the repression or straitening of good men by bad. For the way in which the same view is derived from the great symbolism, see Appendix II, in loc.

The concluding sentence of the Thwan is literally, 'If he speak, he will not be believed;' but the Khang-hsî editors give sufficient reasons for changing one character so as to give the meaning in the translation. 'Actions,' not words, are what are required in the case.

The symbolism of 'buttocks' is rather a favourite with the duke of *K*âu;—'chacun à son goût.' The poor subject of line 1 sitting on a mere stump, which affords him no shelter, is indeed badly off. The line is at the bottom of the trigram indicating peril, and 4, which is its proper correlate, is so circumstanced as not to be able

XLVIII. The 3ing Hexagram.

(Looking at) 3ing, (we think of) how (the site of) a town may be changed, while (the fashion of) its

---

to render it help; hence comes the unfavourable auspice. 'Three years' is used, as often, for a long time.

The three strong lines in the figure (2, 4, and 5) are all held to represent 'superior men;' and their being straitened is not in their persons or estates, but in their principles which are denied development. Hence the subject of 2 is straitened while he fares sumptuously. His correlate in 5, though not quite proper, occupies the ruler's place, and comes to his help. That it is the ruler who comes appears from his red or vermillion knee-covers, different from the scarlet knee-covers worn by nobles, as in paragraph 5. Let 2 cultivate his sincerity and do the work of the hexagram as if he were sacrificing to spiritual beings; and then, if he keep quiet, all will be well.

For 'a full explanation' of paragraph 3 *K*û Hsî refers his readers to what Confucius is made to say on it in Appendix III, ii, 35. The reader, however, will probably not find much light in that passage. The Khang-hsî editors say here:—'The subjects of the three divided lines (1, 3, and 6) are all unable to deal aright with the straitened state indicated by the figure. The first is at the bottom, sitting and distressed. The second, occupies the third place, where he may either advance or retreat; and he advances and is distressed. Wounded abroad, he returns to his family, and finds none to receive him; so graphically is there set forth the distress which reckless action brings.'

Line 4 is the proper correlate of 1, but it is a strong line in an even place, and its assistance is given dilatorily. Then 1 is overridden by 2, which is represented by 'a chariot of metal.' It is difficult for the subjects of 1 and 4 to come together, and effect much; but 4 is near 5, which is also a strong line. Through a

wells undergoes no change. (The water of a well) never disappears and never receives (any great) increase, and those who come and those who go can draw and enjoy the benefit. If (the drawing) have nearly been accomplished, but, before the rope has quite reached the water, the bucket is broken, this is evil.

1. The first line, divided, shows a well so muddy that men will not drink of it; or an old well to which neither birds (nor other creatures) resort.

2. The second line, undivided, shows a well from which by a hole the water escapes and flows away to the shrimps (and such small creatures among the grass), or one the water of which leaks away from a broken basket.

3. The third line, undivided, shows a well, which has been cleared out, but is not used. Our hearts are sorry for this, for the water might be drawn out and used. If the king were (only) intelligent, both he and we might receive the benefit of it.

---

common sympathy, the subject of 5 will have a measure of success. So the symbolism of this line has been explained,—not very satisfactorily.

Line 5 is repressed by 6, and pressed on by 4. Above and below its subject is wounded. Especially is he straitened by the minister in 4, with his scarlet knee-covers. But the upper trigram is Tui, with the quality of complacent satisfaction. And this indicates, it is said, that the subject of 5 gets on notwithstanding his straits, especially by his sincerity. This explanation is not more satisfactory than the last.

Line 6 is at the top of the figure, where the distress may be supposed to reach its height. Its subject appears bound and on a perilous summit. But his extremity is also his opportunity. He is moved to think of repenting; and if he do repent, and go forward, his doing so will be fortunate.

4. The fourth line, divided, shows a well, the lining of which is well laid. There will be no error.

5. The fifth line, undivided, shows a clear, limpid well, (the waters from) whose cold spring are (freely) drunk.

6. The topmost line, divided, shows (the water from) the well brought to the top, which is not allowed to be covered. This suggests the idea of sincerity. There will be great good fortune.

XLVIII. Ȝing, which gives its name to this hexagram, is the symbol of a well. The character originally was pictorial (井), intended to represent a portion of land, divided into nine parts, the central portion belonging to the government, and being cultivated by the joint labour of the eight families settled on the other divisions. In the centre of it, moreover, was a well, which was the joint property of all the occupants.

What is said on Ȝing might be styled 'Moralisings on a well,' or 'Lessons to be learned from a well for the good order and government of a country.' What a well is to those in its neighbourhood, and indeed to men in general, that is government to a people. If rulers would only rightly appreciate the principles of government handed down from the good ages of the past, and faithfully apply them to the regulation of the present, they would be blessed themselves and their people with them.

In the Thwan we have the well, substantially the same through many changes of society; a sure source of dependance to men, for their refreshment and for use in their cultivation of the ground. Its form is what I have seen in the plains of northern China; what may be seen among ourselves in many places in Europe. It is deep, and the water is drawn up by a vessel let down from the top; and the value of the well depends on the water being actually raised. And so the principles of government must be actually carried out.

Line 1, being weak, and at the very bottom of the figure, suggests, or is made to suggest, the symbolism of it. Many men in authority are like such a well; corrupt, useless, unregarded.

Line 2 is strong, and might very well symbolise an active spring, ever feeding the well and, through it, the ground and its cultivators; but it is in an inappropriate place, and has no proper correlate.

XLIX. The Ko Hexagram.

(What takes place as indicated by) Ko is believed in only after it has been accomplished. There will be great progress and success. Advantage will come from being firm and correct. (In that case) occasion for repentance will disappear.

1. The first line, undivided, shows its subject (as if he were) bound with the skin of a yellow ox.

Its cool waters cannot be brought to the top. So important is it that the ministers of a country should be able and willing rightly to administer its government. In the account of the ancient Shun it is stated that he once saved his life by an opening in the lining of a well.

Line 3 is a strong line, in its proper place; and must represent an able minister or officer. But though the well is clear, no use is made of it. I do not find anything in the figure that can be connected with this fact. The author was wise beyond his lines. After the first sentence of the paragraph, the duke of *K*âu ceases from his function of making emblems; reflects and moralises.

Line 4 is weak, but in its proper place. Its subject is not to be condemned, but neither is he to be praised. He takes care of himself, but does nothing for others.

Line 5 is strong, and in its right place. The place is that of the ruler, and suggests the well, full of clear water, which is drawn up, and performs its useful work. Such is the good Head of government to his people.

Line 6 is in its proper place, but weak. If the general idea of the figure was different, a bad auspice might be drawn from it. But here we see in it the symbol of the water drawn up, and the top uncovered so that the use of the well is free to all. Then the mention of 'sincerity' suggests the inexhaustibleness of the elemental supply.

2. The second line, divided, shows its subject making his changes after some time has passed. Action taken will be fortunate. There will be no error.

3. The third line, undivided, shows that action taken by its subject will be evil. Though he be firm and correct, his position is perilous. If the change (he contemplates) have been three times fully discussed, he will be believed in.

4. The fourth line, undivided, shows occasion for repentance disappearing (from its subject). Let him be believed in; and though he change (existing) ordinances, there will be good fortune.

5. The fifth line, undivided, shows the great man (producing his changes) as the tiger (does when he) changes (his stripes). Before he divines (and proceeds to action), faith has been reposed in him.

6. The sixth line, divided, shows the superior man producing his changes as the leopard (does when he) changes (his spots), while small men change their faces (and show their obedience). To go forward (now) would lead to evil, but there will be good fortune in abiding firm and correct.

XLIX. The character called Ko or Keh is used here in the sense of changing. Originally used for the skin of an animal or bird, alive or dead, it received the significance of changing at a very early time. Its earliest appearance, indeed, in the first Book of the Shû, is in that sense. How the transition was made from the idea of a skin or hide to that of change is a subject that need not be entered on here. The author has before him the subject of changes occurring—called for—in the state of the country; it may be on the greatest scale. The necessity of them is recognised, and hints are

L. The Ting Hexagram.

Ting gives the intimation of great progress and success.

1. The first line, divided, shows the caldron overthrown and its feet turned up. (But) there will be

---

given as to the spirit and manner in which they should be brought about.

For the way in which the notion of change is brought out of the trigrams of the figure, see Appendixes I and II. It is assumed in the Thwan that change is viewed by people generally with suspicion and dislike, and should not be made hastily. When made as a necessity, and its good effects appear, the issues will be great and good. A proved necessity for them beforehand; and a firm correctness in the conduct of them :—these are the conditions by which changes should be regulated.

Line 1, at the bottom of the figure, may be taken as denoting change made at too early a period. It has no proper correlate or helper, moreover, above. Hence its subject is represented as tied up, unable to take any action.

Line 2, though weak, is in its correct place. It is in the centre also of the trigram Lî, signifying brightness and intelligence, and has a proper correlate in the strong 5. Let its subject take action in the way of change.

The symbolism of paragraph 3 is twofold. The line is strong, and in the correct position, but it has passed the centre of Sun and is on its outward verge. These conditions may dispose its subject to reckless and violent changing which would be bad. But if he act cautiously and with due deliberation, he may take action, and he will be believed in.

Line 4 is strong, but in the place of a weak line. This might vitiate any action of its subject in the way of change, and give occasion for repentance. But other conditions are intimated that

advantage in its getting rid of what was bad in it. (Or it shows us) the concubine (whose position is improved) by means of her son. There will be no error.

2. The second line, undivided, shows the caldron with the things (to be cooked) in it. (If its subject can say), 'My enemy dislikes me, but he cannot approach me,' there will be good fortune.

3. The third line, undivided, shows the caldron with (the places of) its ears changed. The progress (of its subject) is (thus) stopped. The fat flesh of the pheasant (which is in the caldron) will not be eaten. But the (genial) rain will come, and the grounds for repentance will disappear. There will be good fortune in the end.

4. The fourth line, undivided, shows the caldron with its feet broken; and its contents, designed for the ruler's use, overturned and spilt. Its subject will be made to blush for shame. There will be evil.

---

will have a contrary effect; and if he have further secured general confidence, he may proceed to the greatest changes, even to change the dynasty,—'with good fortune.' The conditions favourable to his action are said to be such as these:—The line has passed from the lower trigram into the upper; water and fire come in it into contact; the fourth place is that of the minister immediately below the ruler's seat. All these considerations demand action from the subject of 4 in harmony with the idea of the hexagram.

Line 5 has every quality proper to 'the lord of the hexagram,' and his action will be in every way beneficial. He is symbolled by the tiger; and the changes which he makes by the bright stripes of the tiger when he has changed his coat.

Line 6 is weak, but its subject is penetrated with the spirit of the hexagram. If its subject be a superior man, only inferior to 'the great man,' immediately below, the changes he makes will be inferior only to his. If he be a small man, he will be compliant and submissive. The lesson for him, however, is to abide firm and correct without taking any action of his own.

5. The fifth line, divided, shows the caldron with yellow ears and rings of metal in them. There will be advantage through being firm and correct.

6. The sixth line, undivided, shows the caldron with rings of jade. There will be great good fortune, and all action taken will be in every way advantageous.

L. Ting was originally a pictorial character, representing a caldron with three feet and two ears, used for cooking and preparing food for the table (the mat in old times) and the altar. The picture has disappeared from the character, but it is said that in the hexagram we have an outline from which fancy may construct the vessel. The lower line, divided, represents its feet; lines 2, 3, 4, all undivided, represent the body of it; line 5, divided, represents its two ears; and line 6, undivided, the handle by which it was carried, or suspended from a hook. Appendix VI makes Ting follow Ko in the order of the hexagrams, because there is no changer of the appearance and character of things equal to the furnace and caldron!

Ting and Ȝing (48) are the only two hexagrams named from things in ordinary use with men; and they are both descriptive of the government's work of nourishing. There are three hexagrams of which that is the theme, Î (27), under which we are told in Appendix I that 'the sages nourished men of worth, by means of them to reach to the myriads of the people.' Ȝing treats of the nourishment of the people generally by the government through its agricultural and other methods; Ting treats of the nourishment of men of talents and virtue; and that being understood, it is said, without more ado, that it 'intimates great progress and success.' The Text that follows, however, is more difficult to interpret than that of Ȝing.

Line 1 is weak, and little or nothing can be expected from its subject. But it has a proper correlate in the strong 4; and the disastrous overthrow, causing the feet to be directed towards 4, is understood to be lucky, as accelerating the co-operation of their two lines! The overturned caldron is thereby emptied of bad stuff that had accumulated in it!! The writer uses another illustration, which comes to the same thing. A concubine is less honourable than a wife,—like the overthrown caldron. But if she have a son,

LI. THE *K*ĂN HEXAGRAM.

*K*ăn gives the intimation of ease and development. When (the time of) movement (which it indicates) comes, (the subject of the hexagram) will be found looking out with apprehension, and yet

---

while the proper wife has none, he will be his father's heir, and the mother, the concubine, will share in the honour of his position. Thus the issue of what was so unpromising is good. At least 'there is no mistake.' The above is what is found in the best commentaries on the paragraph. I give it, but am myself dissatisfied with it.

Line 2 is strong. 'The enemy' is the first line, which solicits 1. One, however, is able to resist the solicitation; and the whole paragraph gives a good auspice. The personal pronoun seems to show that the whole was, or was intended to be, understood as an oracular response in divination. This paragraph is rhymed, moreover, as are also 1, 3, and 4:—

'In the caldron is good fare,
See my foe with angry glare;
But touch me he does not dare.'

Line 3 is also strong, and in the proper place; and if its correlate were the divided 5, its auspice would be entirely good. But instead of 5, its correlate is the strong 6. The place of the ears at 5 has been changed. Things promise badly. The advance of 3 is stopped. The good meat in the caldron which it symbolises will not be eaten. But 3 keeping firm 5 will by and by seek its society! The yin and the yang will mingle, and their union will be followed by genial rain. The issue will be good.

Line 4 is in the place of a great minister, who is charged with the most difficult duties, which no single man can sustain. Then the strength of 4 is weakened by being in an even place, and its correlate is the weak 1 in the lowest place. Its subject is insufficient of

smiling and talking cheerfully. When the movement (like a crash of thunder) terrifies all within a hundred lî, he will be (like the sincere worshipper) who is not (startled into) letting go his ladle and (cup of) sacrificial spirits.

1. The first line, undivided, shows its subject, when the movement approaches, looking out and around with apprehension, and afterwards smiling and talking cheerfully. There will be good fortune.

2. The second line, divided, shows its subject, when the movement approaches, in a position of peril. He judges it better to let go the articles (in his possession), and to ascend a very lofty height. There is no occasion for him to pursue after (the things he has let go); in seven days he will find them.

3. The third line, divided, shows its subject distraught amid the startling movements going on. If those movements excite him to (right) action, there will be no mistake.

---

himself for his work, and he has no sufficient help; and the result will be evil.

'Paragraph 5,' says the Daily Lecture, 'praises the ruler as condescending to the worthy with his humble virtue.' 'Yellow' has occurred repeatedly as 'a correct colour;' and here 'the yellow ears and strong rings of metal' are intended to intensify our appreciation of the occupant of 5. As the line is divided, a caution is added about being firm and correct.

Line 6 is strong, but the strength is tempered by its being in an even place. It is this which makes the handle to be of jade, which, though very hard, is supposed to have a peculiar and rich softness of its own. The auspice of the line is very good. 'The great minister,' it is said, 'the subject of 6,' performs for the ruler, the subject of 5, in helping his government and nourishing the worthy, the part which the handle does for the caldron.

4. The fourth line, undivided, shows its subject, amid the startling movements, supinely sinking (deeper) in the mud.

5. The fifth line, divided, shows its subject going and coming amidst the startling movements (of the time), and always in peril; but perhaps he will not incur loss, and find business (which he can accomplish).

6. The topmost line, divided, shows its subject, amidst the startling movements (of the time), in breathless dismay and looking round him with trembling apprehension. If he take action, there will be evil. If, while the startling movements have not reached his own person and his neighbourhood, (he were to take precautions), there would be no error, though his relatives might (still) speak against him.

LI. *K*ăn among the trigrams represents thunder, and, according to Wăn's arrangement and significance of them, 'the oldest son.' It is a phonetic character in which the significant constituent is Yü, meaning rain, and with which are formed most characters that denote atmospherical phenomena. The hexagram is formed of the trigram *K*ăn redoubled, and may be taken as representing the crash or peal of thunder; but we have seen that the attribute or virtue of the trigram is 'moving, exciting power;' and thence, symbolically, the character is indicative of movement taking place in society or in the kingdom. This is the meaning of the hexagram; and the subject is the conduct to be pursued in a time of movement—such as insurrection or revolution—by the party promoting, and most interested in, the situation. It is shown how he ought to be aware of the dangers of the time, and how by precaution and the regulation of himself he may overcome them.

The indication of a successful issue given by the figure is supposed to be given by the undivided line at the bottom of the trigram. The subject of it must be superior to the subjects of the two divided lines above. It is in the idea of the hexagram that he should be moving and advancing;—and what can his movement be but successful?

易經

LII. The Kăn Hexagram.

䷳

When one's resting is like that of the back, and he loses all consciousness of self; when he walks

The next sentence shows him sensible of the danger of the occasion, but confident and self-possessed. The concluding sentence shows him rapt in his own important affairs, like a sincere worshipper, thinking only of the service in which he is engaged. Such a symbol is said to be suggested by Wăn's significance of *K*ăn as 'the oldest son (page 33).' It is his to succeed to his father, and the hexagram, as following Ting, shows him presiding over the sacrifices that have been prepared in the caldron. This is too fanciful.

What is said on line 1 is little more than a repetition of the principal part of the Thwan. The line is undivided, and gives the auspice of good fortune.

'The position of peril' to the subject of line 2 is suggested, as Appendix II says, by its position, immediately above 1. But the rest of the symbolism is obscure, and *K*û Hsî says he does not understand it. The common interpretation appears in the version. The subject of the line does what he can to get out of danger; and finally, as is signified by the central position of the line, the issue is better than could have been expected. On the specification of 'seven days,' see what is said in the treatise on the Thwan of hexagram 24. On its use here *Kh*ăng-ȝze says:—'The places of a diagram amount to 6. The number 7 is the first of another. When the movement symbolised by *K*ăn is gone by, things will be as they were before.'

Line 3 is divided, and where an undivided line should be; but if its subject move on to the fourth place, which would be right for him, the issue will not be bad.

The 4th line, however, has a bad auspice of its own. It is undivided in an even place, and it is pressed by the divided line on

in his courtyard, and does not see any (of the persons) in it,—there will be no error.

1. The first line, divided, shows its subject keeping his toes at rest. There will be no error; but it will be advantageous for him to be persistently firm and correct.

2. The second line, divided, shows its subject keeping the calves of his legs at rest. He cannot help (the subject of the line above) whom he follows, and is dissatisfied in his mind.

3. The third line, undivided, shows its subject keeping his loins at rest, and separating the ribs (from the body below). The situation is perilous, and the heart glows with suppressed excitement.

4. The fourth line, divided, shows its subject keeping his trunk at rest. There will be no error.

5. The fifth line, divided, shows its subject keeping his jawbones at rest, so that his words are (all) orderly. Occasion for repentance will disappear.

6. The sixth line, undivided, shows its subject

---

either side, hence its subject is represented as supinely sinking in the mud.

Line 5 is divided, in an odd place, and that in which the action of the hexagram may be supposed to be concentrated. Hence its subject is always in peril; but his central position indicates safety in the end.

Line 6 is weak, and has to abide the concluding terrors of the movement. Action on the part of its subject is sure to be evil. If, however, he were to take precautions, he might escape with only the censures of his relatives. But I do not see anything in the figure to indicate this final symbolism. The writer, probably, had a case in his mind, which it suited; but what that was we do not know.

devotedly maintaining his restfulness. There will be good fortune.

LII. The trigram Kăn represents a mountain. Mountains rise up grandly from the surface of the earth, and their masses rest on it in quiet and solemn majesty; and they serve also to arrest the onward progress of the traveller. Hence the attribute ascribed to Kăn is twofold; it is both active and passive—resting and arresting. The character is used in this hexagram with both of those significations. As the name of the figure, it denotes the mental characteristic of resting in what is right; especially resting, as it is expressed by Chinese critics, 'in principle,'—that which is right, on the widest scale, and in the absolute conception of the mind; and that which is right in every different position in which a man can be placed. We find this treated of in the Great Learning (Commentary, chapter 3), and in the Doctrine of the Mean, chapter 14, and other places. This is the theme of the hexagram; and the symbolism of it is all taken from different parts of the human body, as in hexagram 31, and the way in which they are dealt with. Several of the paragraphs are certainly not easy to translate and interpret.

The other parts of the body, such as the mouth, eyes, and ears, have their appetencies, which lead them to what is without themselves. The back alone has nothing to do with anything beyond itself—hardly with itself even; all that it has to do is to stand straight and strong. So should it be with us, resting in principle, free from the intrusion of selfish though s and external objects. Amidst society, he who realises the idea of the hexagram is still alone, and does not allow himself to be distracted from the contemplation and following of principle. He is not a recluse, however, who keeps aloof from social life; but his distinction is that he maintains a supreme regard to principle, when alone, and when mingling with others.

In the symbolism the author rises from one part of the body to the other. The first line at the bottom of the figure fitly suggests 'the toes.' The lesson is that from the first men should rest in, and be anxious to do, what is right in all their affairs. The weakness of the line and its being in an odd place give occasion for the caution, with which the paragraph concludes.

Above the toes are the calves, represented by the second line, weak, but in its proper place. Above this, again, are the loins, represented by 3, strong, and in danger of being violent. Line 2

LIII. The *K*ien Hexagram.

䷴

*K*ien suggests to us the marriage of a young lady, and the good fortune (attending it). There will be advantage in being firm and correct.

1. The first line, divided, shows the wild geese gradually approaching the shore. A young officer (in similar circumstances) will be in a position of danger, and be spoken against; but there will be no error.

---

follows 3, and should help it; but is unable to do so; and there results dissatisfaction.

When the calves are kept at rest, advance is stopped, but no other harm ensues. Not so when the loins are kept at rest, and unable to bend, for the connexion between the upper and lower parts of the body is then broken. The dissatisfaction increases to an angry heat. Paragraph 3 is unusually difficult. For 'loins' P. Regis has scapulae, and for ribs renes; Canon McClatchie says:—'Third Nine is stopping at a limit, and separating what is in continued succession (i. e. the backbone); thus the mind,' &c.

Line 4 is a weak line resting in a proper place; hence it gives a good auspice. The Khang-hsî editors, however, call attention to the resting of the trunk as being inferior to the resting of the back in the Thwan.

The place of the weak fifth line is not proper for it; and this accounts for the mention of its subject 'repenting,' for which, however, there is not occasion.

The third line of the trigrams, and the sixth of the hexagram, is what makes Kăn what it is,—the symbol of a mountain. The subject of it therefore will carry out the resting required by the whole figure in the highest style.

2. The second line, divided, shows the geese gradually approaching the large rocks, where they eat and drink joyfully and at ease. There will be good fortune.

3. The third line, undivided, shows them gradually advanced to the dry plains. (It suggests also the idea of) a husband who goes on an expedition from which he does not return, and of a wife who is pregnant, but will not nourish her child. There will be evil. (The case symbolised) might be advantageous in resisting plunderers.

4. The fourth line, divided, shows the geese gradually advanced to the trees. They may light on the flat branches. There will be no error.

5. The fifth line, undivided, shows the geese gradually advanced to the high mound. (It suggests the idea of) a wife who for three years does not become pregnant; but in the end the natural issue cannot be prevented. There will be good fortune.

6. The sixth line, undivided, shows the geese gradually advanced to the large heights (beyond). Their feathers can be used as ornaments. There will be good fortune.

LIII. *K*ien is ordinarily used in the sense of gradually; but there is connected with that the idea also of progress or advance. The element of meaning in the character is the symbol of water; and the whole of it denotes gradual advance, like the soaking in of water. Three hexagrams contain in them the idea of advance,—3in (35), Shăng (46), and this *K*ien; but each has its peculiarity of meaning, and that of *K*ien is the gradual manner in which the advance takes place. The subject then of the hexagram is the advance of men to offices in the state, how it shoul, take place gradually and by successive steps, as well as on certain other

LIV. The Kwei Mei Hexagram.

Kwei Mei indicates that (under the conditions which it denotes) action will be evil, and in no wise advantageous.

conditions that may be gathered from the Text. P. Regis gives this exposition of the subject, as taken by him from the symbolism, which he ascribes to Confucius :—'Viri probi, seu republica digni, in virtutis soliditate instituendi sunt a sapiente, bonisque regulis ut altis radicibus firmandi, nec alii ad rempublicam tractandam promovendi, nisi qui paulatim per varios minoresque gradus ad magnum hoc regimen periculo facto ascendere digni sint.' He then illustrates this sentiment by the words of Pliny :—'Eligetur multis experimentis eruditus, et qui futura possit ex praeteritis praevidere.'

But how does the lineal figure give the idea of a gradual advance? We shall see how it is attempted in the Great Symbolism to get this from the component trigrams. The account there is not satisfactory; and still less so is what else I have been able to find on the subject. E.g., the trigrams were originally Khwăn and *Kh*ien; but the third line of Khwăn and the first of *Kh*ien have changed places; and the trigrams now denote 'the youngest son,' and 'the eldest daughter.' If all this, which is a mere farrago, were admitted, it would not help us to the idea of an advance.

Again, the lines 2, 3, 4, 5 are all in the places proper to them as strong or weak; we ascend by them as by regular steps to the top of the hexagram; and this, it is said, gives the notion of the gradual steps of the advance. But neither does this carry conviction with it to the mind. We must leave the question. King Wăn, for reasons which we cannot discover, or without such reasons, determined that the hexagram *K*ien should denote the gradual advance of men to positions of influence and office.

The marriage of a young lady is mentioned in the Thwan as an illustration of an important event taking place with various

1. The first line, undivided, shows the younger sister married off in a position ancillary to the real wife. (It suggests the idea of) a person lame on

---

preliminary steps, continued from its initiation to its consummation. But all must be done in an orderly and correct manner. And so must it be with the rise of a man in the service of the state.

The goose from the most ancient times played an important part in the marriage ceremonies of the Chinese; and this may have suggested the use of it in the symbolism of the different lines. Its habits as a bird of passage, and flying in processional order, admirably suited the writer's purpose. In paragraph 1 it appears for the first time in the season approaching the shore. Then comes the real subject of the line; and the facts of its being weak, and without a proper correlate, agree with, if they do not suggest, what is said about him, and the caution added.

The geese have advanced in line 2, and so has the officer, though he is not mentioned. The line is weak or humble, and central, and has a proper correlate in 5. Hence comes the good auspice.

Line 3 is strong, and has passed the central place, to the top of the lower trigram, and has not a proper correlate in 6. Its subject is likely to be violent and at the same time unsuccessful in his movements. He is like a husband who does not care for his wife, or a wife who does not care for her child. But in the case supposed, his strength in the end would be useful.

The web-footed goose is not suited for taking hold on the branches; but on flat branches it can rest. Line 4, weak, but in an even place, does not promise a good auspice for its subject; but it is the first line in the trigram of humility, and it is concluded that he will not fall into error.

Line 5 is a strong line in the ruler's seat; and yet it appears here as the symbol of a wife. Somehow its subject has been at variance with, and kept in disgrace by, calumniating enemies such as the plunderers of paragraph 3; but things come right in the end. The wife, childless for three years, becomes at last a mother; and there is good fortune.

The subject of line 6 has reached the top of the hexagram. There is no more advance for him; and he has no correlate. But he may still do some good work for the state, and verify the auspice derived from the ornamental plumes of the geese.

one leg who yet manages to tramp along. Going forward will be fortunate.

2. The second line, undivided, shows her blind of one eye, and yet able to see. There will be advantage in her maintaining the firm correctness of a solitary widow.

3. The third line, divided, shows the younger sister who was to be married off in a mean position. She returns and accepts an ancillary position.

4. The fourth line, undivided, shows the younger sister who is to be married off protracting the time. She may be late in being married, but the time will come.

5. The fifth line, divided, reminds us of the marrying of the younger sister of (king) Tî-yî, when the sleeves of her the princess were not equal to those of the (still) younger sister who accompanied her in an inferior capacity. (The case suggests the thought of) the moon almost full. There will be good fortune.

6. The sixth line, divided, shows the young lady bearing the basket, but without anything in it, and the gentleman slaughtering the sheep, but without blood flowing from it. There will be no advantage in any way.

LIV. Mei Kwei is a common way of saying that a young lady is married, or, literally, 'is going home.' If the order of the characters be reversed, the verb kwei will be transitive, and the phrase will signify 'the marrying away of a daughter,' or 'the giving the young lady in marriage.' In the name of this hexagram, Kwei is used with this transitive force. But Mei means 'a younger sister,' and not merely a young lady or a daughter. Kwei Mei might be equivalent to our 'giving in marriage;' but we shall find

LV. THE FĂNG HEXAGRAM.

Făng intimates progress and development. When a king has reached the point (which the name denotes)

---

that the special term has a special appropriateness. The Thwan makes the hexagram give a bad auspice concerning its subject; and for this the following reasons are given:—According to Wăn's symbolism of the trigrams, Tui, the lower trigram here, denotes the youngest daughter, and *K*ăn, the upper trigram, the oldest son. And as the action of the hexagram begins with that of the lower trigram, we have in the figure two violations of propriety. First, the marriage represented is initiated by the lady and her friends. She goes to her future home instead of the bridegroom coming to fetch her. Second, the parties are unequally matched. There ought not to be such disparity of age between them. Another reason assigned for the bad auspice is that lines 2, 3, 4, and 5 are all in places not suited to them, quite different from the corresponding lines in the preceding hexagram.

Is then such a marriage as the above, or marriage in general, the theme of the hexagram? I think not. The marriage comes in, as in the preceding essay, by way of illustration. With all the abuses belonging to it as an institution of his country, as will immediately appear, the writer acknowledged it without saying a word in deprecation or correction of those abuses; but from the case he selected he wanted to set forth some principles which should obtain in the relation between a ruler and his ministers. This view is insisted on in Wan *K*ing's 'New Collection of Comments on the Yî (A.D. 1686).'

A feudal prince was said to marry nine ladies at once. The principal of them was the bride who was to be the proper wife, and she was attended by two others, virgins from her father's harem; a cousin, and a half-sister, a daughter of her father by another mother of inferior rank. Under line 1 the younger sister

there is no occasion to be anxious (through fear of a change). Let him be as the sun at noon.

---

of the hexagram appears in the inferior position of this half-sister. But the line is strong, indicative in a female of firm virtue. The mean condition and its duties are to be deplored, and give the auspice of lameness; but notwithstanding, the secondary wife will in a measure discharge her service. There will be good fortune. Notwithstanding apparent disadvantages, an able officer may do his ruler good service.

Line 2 is strong, and in the centre. The proper correlate is 5, which, however, is weak, and in the place of a strong line. With such a correlate, the able lady in 2 cannot do much in the discharge of her proper work. But if she think only of her husband, like the widow who will die rather than marry again, such devotion will have its effect and its reward. Though blind of one eye, she yet manages to see. And so devoted loyalty in an officer will compensate for many disadvantages.

Line 3 is weak, where it should be strong; and the attribute of pleased satisfaction belonging to Tui culminates in its subject. She turns out to be of so mean a character and such a slave of passion that no one will marry her. She returns and accepts the position of a concubine.

Line 4 is strong, where it should be weak; but in the case of a female the indication is not bad. The subject of the line, however, is in no haste. She waits, and the good time will come.

King Tî-yî has been already mentioned under the fifth line of hexagram 11, and in connexion with some regulation which he made about the marriage of daughters of the royal house. His sister here is honourably mentioned, so as to suggest that the adorning which she preferred was 'the ornament of the hidden man of the heart.' The comparison of her to 'the moon almost full' I am ready to hail as an instance where the duke of *K*âu is for once poetical. *Kh*ăng-ʒze, however, did not see poetry, but a symbol in it. 'The moon is not full,' he says, 'but only nearly full. A wife ought not to eclipse her husband!' However, the sister of Tî-yî gets happily married, as she deserved to do, being represented by the line in the place of honour, having its proper correlate in 2.

Line 6 is weak, at the top of the hexagram, and without a proper correlate. Hence its auspice is evil. The marriage-contract is broken, according to *K*û Hsî, and does not take effect. The

1. The first line, undivided, shows its subject meeting with his mate. Though they are both of the same character, there will be no error. Advance will call forth approval.

2. The second line, divided, shows its subject surrounded by screens so large and thick that at midday he can see from them the constellation of the Bushel. If he go (and try to enlighten his ruler who is thus emblemed), he will make himself to be viewed with suspicion and dislike. Let him cherish his feeling of sincere devotion that he may thereby move (his ruler's mind), and there will be good fortune.

3. The third line, undivided, shows its subject with an (additional) screen of a large and thick banner, through which at midday he can see (the small) Mei star. (In the darkness) he breaks his right arm; but there will be no error.

4. The fourth line, undivided, shows its subject in a tent so large and thick that at midday he can see from it the constellation of the Bushel. But he meets with the subject of the (first) line, undivided like himself. There will be good fortune.

5. The fifth line, divided, shows its subject bringing around him the men of brilliant ability. There will be occasion for congratulation and praise. There will be good fortune.

6. The topmost line, divided, shows its subject

parties mentioned in the paragraph appear engaged in the temple, offering or sacrificing to the spirits of their ancestors. But the woman's basket which should contain her offerings (The Shih, I, ii, ode 4) is empty, and the man attempts to perform his part in slaying the victim (The Shih, II, vi, ode 6. 5) without effect.

with his house made large, but only serving as a screen to his household. When he looks at his door, it is still, and there is nobody about it. For three years no one is to be seen. There will be evil.

LV. The character Făng is the symbol of being large and abundant, and, as the name of this hexagram, denotes a condition of abundant prosperity. In the changes of human affairs a condition of prosperity has often given place to one of an opposite character. The lesson of the hexagram is to show to rulers how they may preserve the prosperity of their state and people. The component trigrams have the attributes of intelligence and of motive force, and the second is under the direction of the first. A ruler with these attributes is not likely to fail in maintaining his crown and prosperity, and it may well be said that the figure intimates progress and development. The king is told not to be anxious, but to study how he may always be like the sun in his meridian height, cheering and enlightening all.

The explanation of the Thwan is thus natural and easy. It will be found that a change is introduced in explaining the symbolism of the lines, which it is as well to point out here. Thus far we have found that to constitute a proper correlation between two lines, one of them must be whole, and the other divided. Here two undivided lines make a correlation. The law, evidently made for the occasion, goes far to upset altogether the doctrine of correlated lines. I have been surprised that the rules about the lines stated in the Introduction, pp. 15, 16, have held good so often. There have been various deviations from them, but none so gross as that in this hexagram.

Line 1 is strong, and in an odd place. Its correlate is 4, which would in other figures be deemed unfortunate. But here even the Text calls 4 (for the reference must be to it) the mate of 1, and makes their belonging to different categories of no account. The lesson taught is that mutual helpfulness is the great instrument for the maintenance of prosperity. The subject of line 1 is encouraged to go forward.

Line 2 is divided, and in its proper place. Occupying the centre of the trigram of brightness, the intelligence of it should be concentrated in its subject; but his correlate is the weak 5, weak and in an improper place, so that he becomes the benighted ruler, and darkness is shed from him down on 2, which is strangely symbolised.

LVI. THE LÜ HEXAGRAM.

Lü intimates that (in the condition which it denotes) there may be some little attainment and progress. If the stranger or traveller be firm and correct as he ought to be, there will be good fortune.

1. The first line, divided, shows the stranger mean and meanly occupied. It is thus that he brings on himself (further) calamity.

The subject of 2 therefore, if he advance, will not be acceptable to his ruler, and will not be employed. The only way in which he can be useful by developing the light that is in him is pointed out in the conclusion. The constellation of the Bushel corresponds to our Ursa Major, or perhaps part of Sagittarius.

Line 3 is strong, in its proper place. It is the last line moreover of the trigram of Brightness. All these conditions are favourable to the employment of its subject; but its correlate is the weak 6, which is at the extremity of the trigram of movement. There is no more power therefore in 6, and the subject of 3 has no one to co-operate with him. His symbolism and auspice are worse than those of 2; but his own proper goodness and capacity will save him from error. Mei is a small star in or near the Bushel.

The symbolism of line 4 is the same as that of 2, till we come to the last sentence. Then there is the strange correlation of the two strong lines in 4 and 1; and the issue is good.

The subject of line 5 is in the ruler's place, himself weak, but 'the lord' of the trigram of movement. He can do little unhelped, but if he can bring into the work and employ in his service the talents of 1, 3, and 4, and even of 2, his correlate, the results will be admirable. Nothing consolidates the prosperity of a country so much as the co-operation of the ruler and able ministers.

All the conditions of line 6 are unfavourable, and its subject is left to himself without any helpers. He is isolated for long, and undone. The issue is only evil.

2. The second line, divided, shows the stranger, occupying his lodging-house, carrying with him his means of livelihood, and provided with good and trusty servants.

3. The third line, undivided, shows the stranger, burning his lodging-house, and having lost his servants. However firm and correct he (try to) be, he will be in peril.

4. The fourth line, undivided, shows the traveller in a resting-place, having (also) the means of livelihood and the axe, (but still saying),'I am not at ease in my mind.'

5. The fifth line, divided, shows its subject shooting a pheasant. He will lose his arrow, but in the end he will obtain praise and a (high) charge.

6. The sixth line, undivided, suggests the idea of a bird burning its nest. The stranger, (thus represented), first laughs and then cries out. He has lost his ox(-like docility) too readily and easily. There will be evil.

LVI. The name Lü denotes people travelling abroad, and is often translated by 'strangers.' As early as the time of king Wăn, there was a class of men who went about from one state to another, pursuing their business as pedlars or travelling merchants; but in Mencius II, i, chap. 5. 3, it is used for travellers generally, whatever it was that took them out of their own states. Confucius himself is adduced as a travelling stranger; and in this hexagram king Wăn is supposed to have addressed himself to the class of such men, and told them how they ought to comport themselves. They ought to cultivate two qualities,—those of humility and integrity (firm correctness). By means of these they would escape harm, and would make some little attainment and progress. Their rank was too low to speak of great things in connexion with them. It is interesting to find travellers, strangers in a strange land, having thus a place in the Yî.

For the manner in which the component trigrams are supposed

LVII. THE SUN HEXAGRAM.

Sun intimates that (under the conditions which it denotes) there will be some little attainment and progress. There will be advantage in movement

---

to give the idea that is in Lü, see Appendix II. In Appendix I there is an endeavour to explain the Thwan by means of the lines and their relation to one another.

Line 1 is weak, in an odd place, and at the very bottom or commencement of the hexagram, These conditions are supposed to account for the unfavourable symbolism and auspice.

Line 2 is weak, but in its proper place. That place, moreover, is the central. Hence the traveller—and he might here very well be a travelling merchant—is represented in the symbolism as provided with everything he can require; and though the auspice is not mentioned, we must understand it as being good.

Line 3 is strong, and in an even place. But it occupies the topmost place in the lower trigram; and its strength may be expected to appear as violence. So it does in the symbolism, and extraordinary violence as well. It seems unreasonable to suppose, as in the conclusion, that one so described could be in any way correct. The Khang-hsî editors remark that the subjects of 2 and 3 are represented as having 'lodging-houses,' and not any of those of the other lines, because these are the only two lines in the places proper to them!

Line 4 is strong, but in an even place. Hence its subject has not 'a lodging-house;' but has found a situation where he has shelter, though he is exposed to perils. Hence he is represented as having an axe, which may be available for defence. Still he is not at peace in his mind. The Khang-hsî editors observe well that the mention of an axe makes us think of caution as a quality desirable in a traveller.

Line 5, though weak, is in the centre of the upper trigram, which

onward in whatever direction. It will be advantageous (also) to see the great man.

1. The first line, divided, shows its subject (now) advancing, (now) receding. It would be advantageous for him to have the firm correctness of a brave soldier.

2. The second line, undivided, shows the representative of Sun beneath a couch, and employing diviners and exorcists in a way bordering on confusion. There will be good fortune and no error.

3. The third line, undivided, shows its subject penetrating (only) by violent and repeated efforts. There will be occasion for regret.

4. The fourth line, divided, shows all occasion for repentance (in its subject) passed away. He takes game for its threefold use in his hunting.

5. The fifth line, undivided, shows that with firm correctness there will be good fortune (to its

---

has the quality of brightness and elegance. It is held to be the lord of the trigram Lî; and lines 4 and 6 are on either side in loyal duty to defend and help. Then the shooting a pheasant is supposed to be suggested; an elegant bird,—by the trigram of elegance. When an officer was travelling abroad in ancient times, his gift of introduction at any feudal court was a pheasant. The traveller here emblemed is praised by his attached friends, and exalted to a place of dignity by the ruler to whom he is acceptable. It will be seen how the idea of the fifth line being the ruler's seat is dropt here as being alien from the idea of the hexagram, so arbitrary is the interpretation of the symbolism.

Line 6 is strong, in an even place, at the extremity of Lî and of the whole hexagram. Its subject will be arrogant and violent; the opposite of what a traveller should be; and the issue will be evil. The symbolism must be allowed to be extravagant. What bird ever burned its nest? And the character for 'ox' is strangely used for 'ox-like docility.'

subject). All occasion for repentance will disappear, and all his movements will be advantageous. There may have been no (good) beginning, but there will be a (good) end. Three days before making any changes, (let him give notice of them); and three days after, (let him reconsider them). There will (thus) be good fortune.

6. The sixth line, undivided, shows the representative of penetration beneath a couch, and having lost the axe with which he executed his decisions. However firm and correct he may (try to) be, there will be evil.

LVII. With Sun as the fifth of the Fû-hsî trigrams we have become familiar. It symbolises both wind and wood; and has the attributes of flexibility (nearly allied to docility) and penetration. In this hexagram we are to think of it as representing wind with its penetrating power, finding its way into every corner and cranny.

Confucius once said (Analects 12. 19):—'The relation between superiors and inferiors is like that between the wind and the grass. The grass must bend when the wind blows upon it.' In accordance with this, the subject of the hexagram must be understood as the influence and orders of government designed to remedy what is wrong in the people. The 'Daily Lecture' says that the upper trigram denotes the orders issuing from the ruler, and the lower the obedience rendered to them by the people; but this view is hardly borne out by the Text.

But how is it that the figure represents merely 'some little attainment?' This is generally explained by taking the first line of the trigram as indicating what the subject of it can do. But over the weak first line are two strong lines, so that its subject can accomplish but little. The Khang-hsî editors, rejecting this view, contend that, the idea of the whole figure being penetration, line 1, the symbol of weakness and what is bad, will not be able to offer much resistance to the subjects of the other lines, which will enter and dispel its influence. They illustrate this from processes of nature, education, and politics; the effect they say is described as small, because the process is not to revolutionise or renew, but only to

LVIII. The Tui Hexagram.

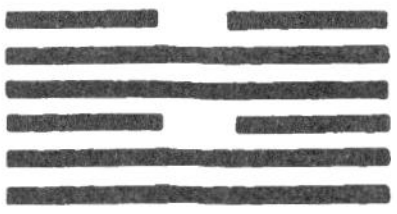

Tui intimates that (under its conditions) there will be progress and attainment. (But) it will be advantageous to be firm and correct.

---

correct and improve. Such as it is, however, it requires the operation of the strong and virtuous, 'the great man.' Even all this criticism is not entirely satisfactory.

Line 1 is weak, where it should be strong. The movements of its subject are expressive of perplexity. He wants vigour and decision.

Line 2 is strong, and in the right place, and has a good auspice. Things are placed or hidden beneath a couch or bed; and the subject of the line appears as searching for them. He calls in divination to assist his judgment, and exorcists to expel for him what is bad. The work is great and difficult, so that he appears almost distracted by it; but the issue is good. For this successful explanation of the line, I am indebted to the Khang-hsî editors. The writer of the Text believed of course in divination and exorcism; which was his misfortune rather than his fault or folly.

Line 3 is in the right place for a strong line. But its position at the top of the lower trigram is supposed to indicate the restlessness, and here the vehemence, of its subject. And 6 is no proper correlate. All the striving is ineffective, and there is occasion for regret.

Line 4 is weak, as is its correlate in 1. But 4 is a proper place for a weak line, and it rests under the shadow of the strong and central 5. Hence the omens of evil are counteracted; and a good auspice is obtained. The game caught in hunting was divided into three portions:—the first for use in sacrifices; the second for the entertainment of visitors; and the third for the kitchen generally. A hunt which yielded enough for all these purposes was deemed very successful.

On line 5 *Kh*ăng-ȝze says:—'It is the seat of honour, and the

1. The first line, undivided, shows the pleasure of (inward) harmony. There will be good fortune.

2. The second line, undivided, shows the pleasure arising from (inward) sincerity. There will be good fortune. Occasion for repentance will disappear.

3. The third line, divided, shows its subject bringing round himself whatever can give pleasure. There will be evil.

4. The fourth line, undivided, shows its subject deliberating about what to seek his pleasure in, and not at rest. He borders on what would be injurious, but there will be cause for joy.

5. The fifth line, undivided, shows its subject trusting in one who would injure him. The situation is perilous.

6. The topmost line, divided, shows the pleasure of its subject in leading and attracting others.

---

place for the lord of Sun, from whom there issue all charges and commands. It is central and correct; we must find in its subject the qualities denoted by Sun in their greatest excellence. But those qualities are docility and accordance with what is right; and the advantage of firm correctness is insisted on. With this all will be right.' With the concluding sentence compare the conclusion of the Thwan of hexagram 18.

The evil that paragraph 6 concludes with would arise from the quality of Sun being carried to excess. I have followed the Khang-hsî editors in adopting a change of one character in the received Text.

LVIII. The trigram Tui symbolises water as collected in a marsh or lake; and its attribute or virtus is pleasure or complacent satisfaction. It is a matter of some difficulty to determine in one's mind how this attribute came to be connected with the trigram. The Khang-hsî editors say:—'When the airs of spring begin to blow, from the collections of water on the earth the moistening vapours rise up (and descend again); so, when the breath of health is vigorous in a man's person, the hue of it is

LIX. THE HWÂN HEXAGRAM.

Hwân intimates that (under its conditions) there will be progress and success. The king goes to his ancestral temple; and it will be advantageous to

---

displayed in his complexion. Akin to this is the significance of the hexagram Tui representing a marsh, as denoting pleasure. Although the yin lines give it its special character they owe their power and effect to the yang; so when the qualities of mildness and harmony prevail in a man, without true-heartedness and integrity to control and direct them, they will fail to be correct, and may degenerate into what is evil. Hence it is said that it will be advantageous to be firm and correct!'

The feeling then of pleasure is the subject of this hexagram. The above quotation sufficiently explains the concluding characters of the Thwan; but where is the intimation in Tui of progress and attainments? It is supposed to be in the one weak line surmounting each trigram and supported by the two strong lines. Fancy sees in that mildness and benignity energised by a double portion of strength.

Line 1, strong in the place of strength, with no proper correlate above, is thus confined to itself. But its subject is sufficient for himself. There will be good fortune.

Line 2, by the rule of place, should be weak, but it is strong. Without any proper correlate, and contiguous to the weak 3, the subject of it might be injuriously affected, and there would be cause for repentance. But the sincerity natural in his central position counteracts all this.

The view of the third paragraph that appears in the translation is derived from the Khang-hsî editors. The evil threatened in it would be a consequence of the excessive devotion of its subject to pleasure.

'The bordering on what is injurious' in paragraph 4 has reference to the contiguity of line 4 to the weak 3. That might have

cross the great stream. It will be advantageous to be firm and correct.

1. The first line, divided, shows its subject engaged in rescuing (from the impending evil) and having (the assistance of) a strong horse. There will be good fortune.

2. The second line, undivided, shows its subject, amid the dispersion, hurrying to his contrivance (for security). All occasion for repentance will disappear.

3. The third line, divided, shows its subject discarding any regard to his own person. There will be no occasion for repentance.

4. The fourth line, divided, shows its subject scattering the (different) parties (in the state); which leads to great good fortune. From the dispersion (he collects again good men standing out, a crowd) like a mound, which is what ordinary men would not have thought of.

5. The fifth line, undivided, shows its subject amidst the dispersion issuing his great announcements as the perspiration (flows from his body).

---

an injurious effect; but the subject of 4 reflects and deliberates before he will yield to the seduction of pleasure, and there is cause for joy.

The danger to the subject of line 5 is from the weak 6 above, in whom he is represented as 'trusting.' Possibly his own strength and sincerity of mind may be perverted into instruments of evil; but possibly, they may operate beneficially.

The symbolism of paragraph 6 is akin to that of 3, though no positive auspice is expressed. The subject of line 3 attracts others round itself for the sake of pleasure; the subject of this leads them to follow himself in quest of it.

He scatters abroad (also) the accumulations in the royal granaries. There will be no error.

6. The topmost line, undivided, shows its subject disposing of (what may be called) its bloody wounds, and going and separating himself from its anxious fears. There will be no error.

LIX. Hwân, the name of this hexagram, denotes a state of dissipation or dispersion. It is descriptive primarily of men's minds alienated from what is right and good. This alienation is sure to go on to disorder in the commonwealth; and an attempt is made to show how it should be dealt with and remedied.

The figure is made up of one of the trigrams for water and over it that for wind. Wind moving over water seems to disperse it, and awakes naturally in the beholder the idea of dissipation.

The intimation of progress and success is supposed to be given by the strong lines occupying the central places. The king goes to the ancestral temple, there to meet with the spirits of his ancestors. His filial piety moves them by the sincerity of its manifestation. Those spirits come and are present. Let filial piety—in our language, let sincere religion—rule in men's minds, and there will be no alienation in them from what is right and good or from one another. And if the state of the country demand a great or hazardous enterprise, let it be undertaken. But whatever is done, must be done with due attention to what is right, firmly and correctly.

Line 1, at the commencement of the hexagram, tells us that the evil has not yet made great progress, and that dealing with it will be easy. But the subject of the line is weak, and in an odd place. He cannot cope with the evil himself. He must have help, and he finds that in a strong horse, which description is understood to be symbolical of the subject of the strong second line.

Line 2 is strong, but in an even place. That place is, indeed, the central, but the attribute of the lower trigram Khan is peril. These conditions indicate evil, and action will be dangerous; but the subject of 2 looks to 1 below him, and takes shelter in union with its subject. Since the commentary of *Kh*ăng-ȝze, this has been the interpretation of the line.

Line 3 is weak, and in an odd place. A regard for himself that would unfit its subject for contributing any service to the work of

LX. The *K*ieh Hexagram.

*K*ieh intimates that (under its conditions) there will be progress and attainment. (But) if the regulations (which it prescribes) be severe and difficult, they cannot be permanent.

1. The first line, undivided, shows its subject not

---

the hexagram might be feared; but he discards that regard, and will do nothing to be repented of. There is a change of style in the Chinese text at this point. As Wang Shăn-ȝze (Yüan dynasty) says:—'Here and henceforth the scattering is of what should be scattered, that what should not be scattered may be collected.'

Line 4, though weak, is in its correct place, and adjoins the strong 5, which is in the ruler's seat. The subject of 4, therefore, will fitly represent the minister, to whom it belongs to do a great part in remedying the evil of dispersion. And this he does. He brings dissentient partizanship to an end; and not satisfied with that, he collects multitudes of those who had been divided into a great body so that they stand out conspicuous like a hill.

Line 5 gives us the action of the ruler himself;—by his proclamations, and by his benevolence. *K*û Hsî and other critics enlarge on the symbolism of the perspiration, which they think much to the point. P. Regis avoids it, translating—'Ille, magnas leges dissipans, facit ut penetrent(ur?).' Canon McClatchie has an ingenious and original, so far as my Chinese reading goes, note upon it:—'As sweat cures fevers, so do proclamations cure rebellions.' Both of these translators miss the meaning of the other instance of the king's work.

Line 6 is occupied by a strong line, which has a proper correlate in 3; but 3 is at the top of the trigram of peril. The subject of 6 hurries away from association with the subject of it, but does so in the spirit of the hexagram, so that there is no error or blame attaching to him.

quitting the courtyard outside his door. There will be no error.

2. The second line, undivided, shows its subject not quitting the courtyard inside his gate. There will be evil.

3. The third line, divided, shows its subject with no appearance of observing the (proper) regulations, in which case we shall see him lamenting. But there will be no one to blame (but himself).

4. The fourth line, divided, shows its subject quietly and naturally (attentive to all) regulations. There will be progress and success.

5. The fifth line, undivided, shows its subject sweetly and acceptably enacting his regulations. There will be good fortune. The onward progress with them will afford ground for admiration.

6. The topmost line, divided, shows its subject enacting regulations severe and difficult. Even with firmness and correctness there will be evil. But though there will be cause for repentance, it will (by and by) disappear.

LX. The primary application of the character *K*ieh was to denote the joints of the bamboo; it is used also for the joints of the human frame; and for the solar and other terms of the year. Whatever makes regular division may be denominated a *K*ieh; there enter into it the ideas of regulating and restraining; and the subject of this hexagram is the regulations of government enacted for the guidance and control of the people. How the constituent trigrams are supposed to suggest or indicate this meaning will be seen in Appendix II.

*K*û Hsî anticipates that symbolism in trying to account for the statement that the figure gives the promise of success and attainment; but the ground of this is generally made out by referring to the equal division of the undivided and divided lines and our having in 2 and 5, the central places, two undivided lines. An

LXI. The *K*ung Fû Hexagram.

*K*ung Fû (moves even) pigs and fish, and leads to good fortune. There will be advantage in cross-

---

important point concerning 'regulations' is brought out in the conclusion of the Thwan,—that they must be adapted to circumstances, and not made too strict and severe.

Line 1 is strong, and in its correct place. Its subject therefore would not be wanting in power to make his way. But he is supposed to be kept in check by the strong 2, and the correlate 4 is the first line in the trigram of peril. The course of wisdom therefore is to keep still. The character here rendered door is that belonging to the inner apartments, leading from the hall into which entrance is found by the outer gate, mentioned under line 2. The courtyard outside the door and that inside the gate is one and the same. The 'Daily Lecture' says that the paragraph tells an officer not to take office rashly, but to exercise a cautious judgment in his measures.

Line 2 is strong, in the wrong place; nor has it a proper correlate. Its subject keeps still, when he ought to be up and doing. There will be evil.

Line 3 should be strong, but it is weak. It is neither central nor correct. It has no proper correlate, and it is the topmost line in the trigram of complacent satisfaction. Its subject will not receive the yoke of regulations; and he will find out his mistake, when it is too late.

Line 4 is weak, as it ought to be, and its subject has respect to the authority of the strong ruler in 5. Hence its good symbolism and auspice.

Line 5 is strong, and in its correct place. Its subject regulates himself, having no correlate; but he is lord of the hexagram, and his influence is everywhere beneficially felt.

ing the great stream. There will be advantage in being firm and correct.

1. The first line, undivided, shows its subject resting (in himself). There will be good fortune. If he sought to any other, he would not find rest.

2. The second line, undivided, shows its subject (like) the crane crying out in her hidden retirement, and her young ones responding to her. (It is as if it were said), 'I have a cup of good spirits,' (and the response were), 'I will partake of it with you.'

3. The third line, divided, shows its subject having met with his mate. Now he beats his drum, and now he leaves off. Now he weeps, and now he sings.

4. The fourth line, divided, shows its subject (like) the moon nearly full, and (like) a horse (in a chariot) whose fellow disappears. There will be no error.

5. The fifth line, undivided, shows its subject perfectly sincere, and linking (others) to him in closest union. There will be no error.

6. The topmost line, undivided, shows its subject in chanticleer (trying to) mount to heaven. Even with firm correctness there will be evil.

Line 6 is weak, in its proper place. The subject of the topmost line must be supposed to possess an exaggerated desire for enacting regulations. They will be too severe, and the effect will be evil. But as Confucius (Analects 3. 3) says, that is not so great a fault as to be easy and remiss. It may be remedied, and cause for repentance will disappear.

LXI. *K*ung Fû, the name of this hexagram, may be represented in English by 'Inmost Sincerity.' It denotes the highest quality of man, and gives its possessor power so that he prevails with spiritual beings, with other men, and with the lower creatures. It is the

LXII. The Hsiâo Kwo Hexagram.

Hsiâo Kwo indicates that (in the circumstances which it implies) there will be progress and attain-

---

subject of the 'Doctrine of the Mean' from the 21st chapter onwards, where Remusat rendered it by 'la perfection,' 'la perfection morale,' and Intorcetta and his coadjutors by 'vera solidaque perfectio.' The lineal figure has suggested to the Chinese commentators, from the author of the first Appendix, two ideas in it which deserve to be pointed out. There are two divided lines in the centre and two undivided below them and above them. The divided lines in the centre are held to represent the heart or mind free from all pre-occupation, without any consciousness of self; and the undivided lines, on each side of it, in the centre of the constituent trigrams are held to denote the solidity of the virtue of one so free from selfishness. There is no unreality in it, not a single flaw.

The 'Daily Lecture' at the conclusion of its paraphrase of the Thwan refers to the history of the ancient Shun, and the wonderful achievements of his virtue. The authors give no instance of the affecting of 'pigs and fishes' by sincerity, and say that these names are symbolical of men, the rudest and most unsusceptible of being acted on. The Text says that the man thus gifted with sincerity will succeed in the most difficult enterprises. Remarkable is the concluding sentence that he must be firm and correct. Here, as elsewhere throughout the Yî, there comes out the practical character which has distinguished the Chinese people and their best teaching all along the line of history.

The translation of paragraph 1 is according to the view approved by the Khang-hsî editors. The ordinary view makes the other to whom the subject of line 1 looks or might look to be the subject of 4; but they contend that, excepting in the case of 3 and 6, the force of correlation should be discarded from the study of this

ment. But it will be advantageous to be firm and correct. (What the name denotes) may be done in small affairs, but not in great affairs. (It is like) the notes that come down from a bird on the wing;—to descend is better than to ascend. There will (in this way) be great good fortune.

1. The first line, divided, suggests (the idea of) a bird flying, (and ascending) till the issue is evil.

2. The second line, divided, shows its subject passing by his grandfather, and meeting with his

---

hexagram; for the virtue of sincerity is all centred in itself, thence derived and thereby powerful.

For paragraph 2, see Appendix III, Section i, 42. It is in rhyme, and I have there rendered it in rhyme. The 'young ones of the crane' are represented by line 1. In the third and fourth sentences we have the symbolism of two men brought together by their sympathy in virtue. The subject of the paragraph is the effect of sincerity.

The 'mate' of line 3 is 6. The principle of correlation comes in. Sincerity, not left to itself, is influenced from without, and hence come the changes and uncertainty in the state and moods of the subject of the line.

Line 4 is weak, and in its correct place. The subject of it has discarded the correlate in 1, and hastens on to the confidence of the ruler in 5, being symbolised as the moon nearly full. The other symbol of the horse whose fellow has disappeared has reference to the discarding of the subject of 1. Anciently chariots and carriages were drawn by four horses, two outsides and two insides. Lines 1 and 4 were a pair of these; but 1 disappears here from the team, and 4 goes on and joins 5.

Line 5 is strong and central, in the ruler's place. Its subject must be the sage on the throne, whose sincerity will go forth and bind all in union with himself.

Line 6 should be divided, but is undivided; and coming after 5, what can the subject of it do? His efforts will be ineffectual, and injurious to himself. He is symbolised by a cock—literally, 'the plumaged voice.' But a cock is not fitted to fly high, and in attempting to do so will only suffer hurt.

grandmother; not attempting anything against his ruler, but meeting him as his minister. There will be no error.

3. The third line, undivided, shows its subject taking no extraordinary precautions against danger; and some in consequence finding opportunity to assail and injure him. There will be evil.

4. The fourth line, undivided, shows its subject falling into no error, but meeting (the exigency of his situation), without exceeding (in his natural course). If he go forward, there will be peril, and he must be cautious. There is no occasion to be using firmness perpetually.

5. The fifth line, divided, (suggests the idea) of dense clouds, but no rain, coming from our borders in the west. It also (shows) the prince shooting his arrow, and taking the bird in a cave.

6. The sixth line, divided, shows its subject not meeting (the exigency of his situation), and exceeding (his proper course). (It suggests the idea of) a bird flying far aloft. There will be evil. The case is what is called one of calamity and self-produced injury.

LXII. The name Hsiâo Kwo is explained both by reference to the lines of the hexagram, and to the meaning of the characters. The explanation from the lines appears immediately on comparing them with those of Tâ Kwo, the 28th hexagram. There the first and sixth lines are divided, and between are four undivided lines; here the third and fourth lines are undivided, and outside each of them are two divided lines. The undivided or yang lines are great, the divided or yin lines are called small. In Hsiâo Kwo the divided or small lines predominate. But this peculiar structure of the figure could be of no interest to the student, if it were not for the meaning of the name, which is 'small excesses' or 'exceeding in what is small.' The author, accepted by us as king Wăn,

LXIII. The *K*î 3î Hexagram.

*K*î 3î intimates progress and success in small matters. There will be advantage in being firm

---

had in his mind our distinction of essentials and non-essentials. Is it ever good to deviate from what is recognised as the established course of procedure? The reply is—never in the matter of right; but in what is conventional and ceremonial—in what is non-essential—the deviation may be made, and will be productive of good. The form may be given up, but not the substance. But the thing must be done very carefully,—humbly and reverently, and in small matters.

The symbolism of the bird is rather obscure. The whole of it is intended to teach humility. It is better for the bird to descend, keeping near to where it can perch and rest, than to hold on ascending into the homeless regions of the air.

Line 1 is weak, in an odd place, and possessed by the 'idea of exceeding,' which belongs to the hexagram. Its correlate is the strong 4, belonging to the trigram *K*ǎn, the attribute of which is movement. There is nothing to repress the tendency of 1; rather it is stimulated; and hence the symbolism.

Line 2 is weak, but in its proper place, and in the centre. Its correlate is 5, which is also a weak line. The lines 3 and 4 between them are both strong; and are supposed to represent the father and grandfather of the subject of 2; but he or she goes past them, and meets with the grandmother in 5. Again, 5 is the ruler's seat. The subject of 2 moves on to him, but not as an enemy; but humbly and loyally, as his minister according to the attributes of a weak line in the central place. It must be allowed that this view of the symbolism and its interpretation is obscure and strained.

The subject of line 3 is too confident in his own strength, and too defiant of the weak and small enemies that seek his hurt.

and correct. There has been good fortune in the beginning; there may be disorder in the end.

1. The first line, undivided, (shows its subject as a driver) who drags back his wheel, (or as a fox) which has wet his tail. There will be no error.

2. The second line, divided, (shows its subject as) a wife who has lost her (carriage-)screen. There is no occasion to go in pursuit of it. In seven days she will find it.

3. The third line, undivided, (suggests the case of) Kâo 3ung who attacked the Demon region, but was three years in subduing it. Small men should not be employed (in such enterprises).

Line 4 is also strong, but the exercise of his strength by its subject is tempered by the position in an even place. He is warned, however, to continue quiet and restrain himself.

Line 5, though in the ruler's seat, is weak, and incapable of doing anything great. Its subject is called king or duke because of the ruler's seat; and the one whom in the concluding sentence he is said to capture is supposed to be the subject of 2.

The first part of the symbolism is the same as that of the Thwan under hexagram 9, q.v. I said there that it probably gave a testimony of the merit of the house of *K*âu, as deserving the throne rather than the kings of Shang. That was because the Thwan contained the sentiments of Wăn, while he was yet only lord of *K*âu. But the symbolism here was the work of the duke of *K*âu, after his brother king Wû had obtained the throne. How did the symbolism then occur to him? May we not conclude that at least the hsiang of this hexagram was written during the troubled period of his regency, after the accession of Wû's son, king *Kh*ăng?

The Khang-hsî editors find in the concluding symbolism an incentive to humility:—'The duke, leaving birds on the wing, is content to use his arrows against those in a cave!'

Line 6 is weak, and is at the top of the trigram of movement. He is possessed by the idea of the hexagram in an extreme degree, and is incapable of keeping himself under restraint.

4. The fourth line, divided, shows its subject with rags provided against any leak (in his boat), and on his guard all day long.

5. The fifth line, undivided, shows its subject (as) the neighbour in the east who slaughters an ox (for his sacrifice); but this is not equal to the (small) spring sacrifice of the neighbour in the west, whose sincerity receives the blessing.

6. The topmost line, divided, shows its subject with (even) his head immersed. The position is perilous.

LXIII. The character called *Kî* is used as a symbol of being past or completed. 3î denotes primarily crossing a stream, and has the secondary meaning of helping and completing. The two characters, combined, will express the successful accomplishment of whatever the writer has in his mind. In dealing with this lineal figure, king Wăn was thinking of the condition of the kingdom, at length at rest and quiet. The vessel of the state has been brought safely across the great and dangerous stream. The distresses of the kingdom have been relieved, and its disorders have been repressed. Does anything remain to be done still? Yes, in small things. The new government has to be consolidated. Its ruler must, without noise or clamour, go on to perfect what has been wrought, with firmness and correctness, and ever keeping in mind the instability of all human affairs. That every line of the hexagram is in its correct place, and has its proper correlate is also supposed to harmonize with the intimation of progress and success.

Line 1, the first of the hexagram, represents the time immediately after the successful achievement of the enterprise it denotes;—the time for resting and being quiet. For a season, at least, all movement should be hushed. Hence we have the symbolism of a driver trying to stop his carriage, and a fox who has wet his tail, and will not tempt the stream again.

Line 2 is weak, and in its proper place. It also has the strong correlate 5; and might be expected to be forward to act. But it occupies its correct and central place, and suggests the symbol of a lady whose carriage has lost its screen. She will not advance

LXIV. THE WEI 3Î HEXAGRAM.

Wei 3î intimates progress and success (in the circumstances which it implies). (We see) a young fox that has nearly crossed (the stream), when its tail gets immersed. There will be no advantage in any way.

---

further so soon after success has been achieved; but keep herself hidden and retired. Let her not try to find the screen. When it is said that she will find this 'after seven days,' the meaning seems to be simply this, that the period of *K*î 3î will then have been exhausted, the six lines having been gone through, and a new period, when action will be proper, shall have commenced.

The strong line 3, at the top of the lower trigram, suggests for its subject one undertaking a vigorous enterprise. The writer thinks of Kâo 3ung, the sacrificial title of Wû Ting, one of the ablest sovereigns of the Shang dynasty (B. C. 1364–1324), who undertook an expedition against the barbarous hordes of the cold and bleak regions north of the Middle States. He is mentioned again under the next hexagram. He appears also in the Shû, IV, ix, and in the Shih, IV, iii, ode 5. His enterprise may have been good, and successful, but it was tedious, and the paragraph concludes with a caution.

Line 4 is weak, and has advanced into the trigram for water. Its subject will be cautious, and prepare for evil, as in the symbolism, suggested probably by the nature of the trigram.

'The neighbour in the East' is the subject of line 5, and 'the neighbour in the West' is the subject of the correlate 2, the former quarter being yang and the latter yin. Line 5 is strong, and 2 is weak; but weakness is more likely to be patient and cautious than strength. They are compared to two men sacrificing. The one presents valuable offerings; the other very poor ones. But the

1. The first line, divided, shows its subject (like a fox) whose tail gets immersed. There will be occasion for regret.

2. The second line, undivided, shows its subject dragging back his (carriage-)wheel. With firmness and correctness there will be good fortune.

3. The third line, divided, shows its subject, with (the state of things) not yet remedied, advancing on; which will lead to evil. But there will be advantage in (trying to) cross the great stream.

4. The fourth line, undivided, shows its subject by firm correctness obtaining good fortune, so that all occasion for repentance disappears. Let him stir himself up, as if he were invading the Demon region, where for three years rewards will come to him (and his troops) from the great kingdom.

5. The fifth line, divided, shows its subject by firm correctness obtaining good fortune, and having no occasion for repentance. (We see in him) the brightness of a superior man, and the possession of sincerity. There will be good fortune.

6. The topmost line, undivided, shows its subject

---

second excels in sincerity, and his small offering is the more acceptable.

The topmost line is weak, and on the outmost edge of Khân, the trigram of peril. His action is violent and perilous, like that one attempting to cross a ford, and being plunged overhead into the water.

LXIV. Wei 3î is the reverse of *K*î 3î. The name tells us that the successful accomplishment of whatever the writer had in his mind had not yet been realised. The vessel of the state has not been brought across the great and dangerous stream. Some have wished that the Yî might have concluded with *K*î 3î, and the last hexagram have left us with the picture of human affairs all brought to good order. But this would not have been in harmony with the

full of confidence and therefore feasting (quietly). There will be no error. (If he) cherish this con-

idea of the Yî, as the book of change. Again and again it has been pointed out that we find in it no idea of a perfect and abiding state. Just as the seasons of the year change and pursue an ever-recurring round, so is it with the phases of society. The reign of order has been, and has terminated; and this hexagram calls us to see the struggle for its realisation recommenced. It treats of how those engaged in that struggle should conduct themselves with a view to secure the happy consummation.

How the figure sets forth the state of things by its constituent trigrams will appear in Appendix II. A similar indication is supposed to be given by the lines, not one of which is in the correct place; the strong lines being all in even places, and the weak lines in odd. At the same time each of them has a proper correlate; and so the figure gives an intimation of some successful progress. See also Appendix I.

The symbolism of the young fox suggests a want of caution on the part of those, in the time and condition denoted by the hexagram, who try to remedy prevailing disorders. Their attempt is not successful, and they get themselves into trouble and danger. Whatever can be done must be undertaken in another way.

I suppose a fox to be intended by the symbolism of line 1, bringing that animal on from the Thwan. Some of the commentators understand it of any animal. The line is weak, at the bottom of the trigram of peril, and responds to the strong 4, which is not in its correct place. Its subject attempts to be doing, but finds cause to regret his course.

The subject of line 2, strong, and in the centre, is able to repress himself, and keep back his carriage from advancing; and there is good fortune.

The Khang-hsî editors say that it is very difficult to understand what is said under line 3; and many critics suppose that a negative has dropt out, and that we should really read that 'it will not be advantageous to try and cross the great stream.'

Line 4, though strong, is in an even place; and this might vitiate the endeavours of its subject to bring about a better state of things. But he is firm and correct. He is in the fourth place moreover, and immediately above there is his ruler, represented by a weak line, humble therefore, and prepared to welcome his endeavours. Let him exert himself vigorously and long, as Kâo Ȝung did in his

fidence, till he (is like the fox who) gets his head immersed, it will fail of what is right.

famous expedition (see last hexagram, line 3), and he will make progress and have success. Expeditions beyond the frontiers in those days were not very remote. Intercourse was kept up between the army and the court. Rewards, distinctions, and whatever was necessary to encourage the army, were often sent to it.

Line 5 is weak, in an odd place. But its subject is the ruler, humble and supported by the subject of the strong 2; and hence the auspice is very good.

The subject of line 6, when the work of the hexagram has been done, appears disposed to remain quiet in the confidence of his own power, but enjoying himself; and thereby he will do right. If, on the contrary, he will go on to exert his powers, and play with the peril of the situation, the issue will be bad.

THE APPENDIXES.

THE APPENDIXES.

APPENDIX I.

Treatise on the Thwan, or king Wăn's Explanations of the entire Hexagrams.

Section I.

I. 1. Vast is the 'great and originating (power)' indicated by *Kh*ien! All things owe to it their beginning:—it contains all the meaning belonging to (the name) heaven.

2. The clouds move and the rain is distributed; the various things appear in their developed forms.

3. (The sages) grandly understand (the connexion between) the end and the beginning, and how (the indications of) the six lines (in the hexagram) are accomplished, (each) in its season. (Accordingly) they mount (the carriage) drawn by those six dragons at the proper times, and drive through the sky.

4. The method of *Kh*ien is to change and transform, so that everything obtains its correct nature as appointed (by the mind of Heaven); and (thereafter the conditions of) great harmony are preserved in union. The result is 'what is advantageous, and correct and firm.'

5. (The sage) appears aloft, high above all things, and the myriad states all enjoy repose.

The name Thwan, and the meaning of the character so-called, are sufficiently established. The Thwan are king Wăn's explanations of the entire hexagrams. It seems impossible now to

II. 1. Complete is the 'great and originating (capacity)' indicated by Khwăn! All things owe to it their birth;—it receives obediently the influences of Heaven.

2. Khwăn, in its largeness, supports and contains all things. Its excellent capacity matches the unlimited power (of *Kh*ien). Its comprehension is wide, and its brightness great. The various things obtain (by it) their full development.

3. The mare is a creature of earthly kind. Its (power of) moving on the earth is without limit; it is mild and docile, advantageous and firm:—such is the course of the superior man.

---

ascertain how the character arose, and how it was named Thwan. The treatise on the Thwan is ascribed to Confucius; and I have considered in the Introduction, p. 30, whether the tradition to this effect may to any extent be admitted.

I. The hexagram *Kh*ien is made up of six undivided lines, or of the trigram *Kh*ien, Fû-hsî's symbol for heaven, repeated. The Thwan does not dwell upon this, but starts, in its exposition, from the word 'heaven,' supposing that the hexagram represented all the meaning which had ever been intended by that term. In paragraphs 1, 2, 4 the four attributes in Wăn's Text (2 being occupied with the second, though it is not expressly named) are illustrated by the phenomena taking place in the physical world.

In paragraphs 3 and 5, the subject is the sage. He is not named indeed; and Khung Ying-tâ (A. D. 574–648) does not introduce him till paragraph 5, when the meaning necessitates the presence of a human agent, who rules in the world of men as heaven does in that of nature. The 'connexion between the end and the beginning,' which he sees, is that of cause and effect in the operations of nature and the course of human affairs. The various steps in that course are symbolised by the lines of the hexagram; and the ideal sage, conducting his ideal government, taking his measures accordingly, is represented as driving through the sky in a carriage drawn by six dragons. *K*û Hsî extravagantly says that 'the sage is Heaven, and Heaven is the sage;' but there is nothing like this in the text.

4. 'If he take the initiative, he goes astray:'—he misses, that is, his proper course. 'If he follow,' he is docile, and gets into his regular (course). 'In the south-west he will get friends:'—he will be walking with those of his own class. 'In the north-east he will lose friends:'—but in the end there will be ground for congratulation.

5. 'The good fortune arising from resting in firmness' corresponds to the unlimited capacity of the earth.

III. 1. In *K*un we have the strong (*Kh*ien) and the weak (Khwăn) commencing their intercourse, and difficulties arising.

2. Movement in the midst of peril gives rise to 'great progress and success, (through) firm correctness.'

3. By the action of the thunder and rain, (which

II. As the writer in expounding the Thwan of hexagram 1 starts from the word 'heaven,' so here he does so from the symbolic meaning attached to 'earth.' What I have said on the Text about the difference with which the same attributes are ascribed to *Kh*ien and Khwăn, appears clearly in paragraph 1. It is the difference expressed by the words that I have supplied,—'power' and 'capacity.' *Kh*ien originates; Khwăn produces, or gives birth to what has been originated.

The 'penetrating,' or developing ability of Khwăn, as displayed in the processes of growth, is the subject of paragraph 2. 'The brightness' refers to the beauty that shines forth in the vegetable and animal worlds.

Paragraph 3 treats of the symbol of the 'mare,' to lead the mind to the course of 'the superior man,' the good and faithful minister and servant.

See the note, corresponding to paragraph 4, on the Text. 'Resting in firmness' is the normal course of Khwăn. Where it is pursued, the good effect will be great, great as the unlimited capacity of the earth.

are symbols of *K*ăn and Khan), all (between heaven and earth) is filled up. But the condition of the time is full of irregularity and obscurity. Feudal princes should be established, but the feeling that rest and peace have been secured should not be indulged (even then).

IV. 1. In Măng we have (the trigram for) a mountain, and below it that of a rugged defile with a stream in it. The conditions of peril and arrest

---

III. *K*un is made up of the trigrams *K*ăn and Khan; but according to the views on king Wăn's arrangement of the trigrams, as set forth especially in Appendix V, chap. 14, the six others come from *Kh*ien and Khwăn, and are said to be their children. On the first application of Khwăn to *Kh*ien, there results *K*ăn, the first line of *Kh*ien taking the place of the last of Khwăn; and on the second application, there results Khan, the middle line of *Kh*ien taking the place of that of Khwăn. McClatchie renders here:—'The Thun (*K*un) diagram represents the hard and the soft (air) beginning to have sexual intercourse, and bringing forth with suffering!' But there is nothing in the Yî, from the beginning to the end, to justify such an interpretation. Nor do I see how, from any account of the genesis by the component trigrams, the idea of the result as signifying a state of difficulty and distress can be readily made out.

In paragraph 2 there is an attempt from the virtues or attributes assigned to the trigrams to make out the result indicated in the Thwan. To move and excite is the quality of *K*ăn; perilousness is the quality of Khan. The power to move is likely to produce great effects; to do this in perilous and difficult circumstances requires firmness and correctness. But neither is this explanation very satisfactory.

The first part of paragraph 3 depicts a condition of trouble and disorder in the natural world occasioned by the phenomena that are symbols of the significance of *K*ăn and Khan; but this is symbolical again of the disorder and distress, political and social, characteristic of the time. Good princes throughout the nation would help to remedy that; but the supreme authority should not resign itself to indifference, trusting to them.

of progress (suggested by these) give (the idea in) Măng.

2. 'Măng indicates that there will be progress and success:'—for there is development at work in it, and its time of action is exactly what is right. 'I do not seek the youthful and inexperienced; he seeks me:'—so does will respond to will. 'When he shows (the sincerity that marks) the first recourse to divination, I instruct him:'—for possessing the qualities of the undivided line and being in the central place, (the subject of the second line thus speaks). 'A second and third application create annoyance, and I do not instruct so as to create annoyance:'—annoyance (he means) to the ignorant.

(The method of dealing with) the young and ignorant is to nourish the correct (nature belonging to them);—this accomplishes the service of the sage.

IV. The trigram Kăn has for its symbol in the natural world a mountain, which stands up frowningly, and stops or arrests the progress of the traveller. Stoppage, understood sometimes actively, and sometimes passively, is called the virtue or attribute indicated by it. Khan, as I said on p. 32, has water for its symbol, and especially in the form of rain. Here, however, the water appears as a stream in a difficult defile, such as ordinarily appears on an approach to a mountain, and suggesting perilousness as the attribute of such a position. From the combination of these symbols and their attributes the writer thinks that he gets the idea of the character (not the entire hexagram) Măng, as symbolical of ignorance and inexperience. See on 'the Great Symbolism' below.

Down to the last sentence of paragraph 2, all that is said is intended to show how it is that the figure indicates progress and success. The whole representation is grounded on the undivided line's being in the central place. It is the symbol of active effort for the teaching of the ignorant in the proper place and time; this being responded to by the divided fifth line, representing the ignorance to be taught as docile, 'will responds to will.' But the

VII. 1. (The name) Sze describes the multitude (of the host). The 'firmness and correctness' (which the hexagram indicates) refer to (moral) correctness (of aim). When (the mover) is able to use the multitude with such correctness, he may attain to the royal sway.

2. There is (the symbol of) strength in the centre (of the trigram below), and it is responded to (by its proper correlate above). The action gives rise to perils, but is in accordance (with the best sentiments of men). (Its mover) may by such action distress all the country, but the people will follow him;—there will be good fortune, and what error should there be?

VIII. 1. 'Pî indicates that there is good fortune:'—(the name) Pî denotes help; (and we see in the figure) inferiors docilely following (their superior).

---

editors of the imperial Yî allow this, and on the present passage discard the doctrine entirely, referring to the language of the Thwan on hexagrams 11 and 12 as fatal to it. See the notes there, and the Introduction, pp. 11–16. 'A strong line has come' is to be taken as equivalent simply to 'a strong line is there.'

What 'the great man sets a value on being the due mean and the correct place,' his decision in any matter of contention is sure to be right.

VII. That 'multitude' is given here as if it were the meaning of the name Sze arose, probably, from there being but one undivided line in the figure. That is the symbol of the general, all the other lines, divided, suggest the idea of a multitude obedient to his orders. The general's place in the centre of the lower trigram, with the proper correlate in line 5, suggests the idea of firmness and correctness that dominates in the hexagram. But in the last sentence it is the ruler, and not the general of the host, who is the subject. Compare what is said of him with Mencius, I, i, chap. 3; ii, chap. 5, &c.

2. 'Let (the principal party intended in it) re-examine himself, (as if) by divination, whether his virtue be great, unintermitting, and firm;—if it be so, there will be no error:—all this follows from the position of the strong line in the centre (of the upper trigram). 'Those who have not rest will come to him:'—high and low will respond to its subject. 'With those who are (too) late in coming it will be ill:'—(for them) the way (of good fortune here indicated) has been exhausted.

IX. 1. In Hsiâo *Kh*û the weak line occupies its (proper) position, and (the lines) above and below respond to it. Hence comes the name of Hsiâo *Kh*û (Small Restraint).

2. (It presents the symbols of) strength and flexibility. Strong lines are in the central places, and the will (of their subjects) will have free course. Thus it indicates that there will be progress and success.

3. 'Dense clouds but no rain' indicate the movement (of the strong lines) still going forward. The

---

'Perilousness' is the attribute of Khan, the lower trigram, and 'docility,' or 'accordance with others,' that of Khwăn, the upper. War is like 'poison' to a country, injurious, and threatening ruin to it, and yet the people will endure and encounter it in behalf of the sovereign whom they esteem and love.

VIII. There is some error in the text here,—as all the critics acknowledge. I have adopted the decision of *K*û Hsî, which by a very small change makes the whole read consistently, and in harmony with other explanations of the Thwan. 'The inferiors' are the subjects of all the other lines gathering round their superior, represented in the fifth line.

'The way has been exhausted:'—they do not seek to promote and enjoy union till it is too late. The sentiment is the same as that in the lines of Shakespeare about the tide in the affairs of men.

Commencing at our western border' indicates that the (beneficial) influence has not yet been widely displayed.

X. 1. In Lî we have (the symbol of) weakness treading on (that of) strength.

2. (The lower trigram) indicates pleasure and satisfaction, and responds to (the upper) indicating strength. Hence (it is said), 'He treads on the tail of a tiger, which does not bite him; there will be progress and success.'

3. (The fifth line is) strong, in the centre, and in

IX. 'The weak line' is said to occupy 'its proper position,' because it is in the fourth,—an even place. The 'responding' on the part of all the other lines above and below is their submitting to be restrained by it; and this arises simply from the meaning which king Wăn chose to attach to the hexagram.

But the restraint can only be small. The attributes of the two parts of the figure do not indicate anything else. The undivided line represents vigour and activity, and such a line is in the middle of each trigram. There cannot but be progress and success.

It is not easy to explain the symbolism of the last paragraph in harmony with the appended explanations. What *Kh*ăng-ȝze, Wang Făng, and other scholars say is to this effect:—Dense clouds ought to give rain. That they exist without doing so, shows the restraining influence of the hexagram to be still at work. But the other and active influence is, according to the general idea of the figure, continuing in operation;—there will be rain ere long. And this was taking place in the western regions subject to the House of *K*âu, which still was only a fief of Shang. It was not for the inferior House to rule the superior. *K*âu was for a time restrained by Shang. Let their positions be reversed by *K*âu superseding Shang, and the rain of beneficent government would descend on all the kingdom. This seems to be the meaning of the paragraph. This is the answer to the riddle of it. Confucius, in his treatise on the Thwan, hints at it, but no Chinese critic has the boldness to declare it fully.

its correct place. (Its subject) occupies the God-(given) position, and falls into no distress or failure;—(his) action will be brilliant.

XI. 'The little come and the great gone in Thâi, and its indication that there will be good fortune with progress and success' show to us heaven and earth in communication with each other, and all things in consequence having free course, and (also) the high and the low, (superiors and inferiors), in communication with one another, and possessed by the same aim. The inner (trigram) is made up of the strong and undivided lines, and the outer of the weak and divided; the inner is (the symbol of) strength, and the outer of docility; the inner (represents) the superior man, and the outer the small man. (Thus) the way of

---

X. '(The symbol of) weakness' in paragraph 1, according to Wang Shăn-ȝze (Yüan dynasty), is line 3, urged by the two strong lines below, and having to encounter the three strong lines above. Hû Ping-wan (also of the Yüan dynasty) says that the whole of the lower trigram, Tui, partaking of the yin nature, is the symbol of weakness, and the whole of *Kh*ien that of strength. The *K*eh-*K*ung editors say that, to get the full meaning, we must hold both views.

Paragraph 2 has been sufficiently explained on the Thwan itself.

Paragraph 3 has also been explained; but there remains something to be said on the Chinese text for 'occupies the God-given position,' or, literally, 'treads on the seat of Tî.' Canon McClatchie has—'The imperial throne is now occupied.' I think that 'the seat of Tî' is synonymous with 'the seat of Heaven,' in paragraph 2 of this treatise on hexagram 5. If Confucius, or whoever was the writer, had before him the phrase as it occurs in the Shû, I, 12, the force of Tî will depend on the meaning assigned to it in that part of the Shû. That the fifth line occupies the place of authority is here the only important point.

the superior man appears increasing, and that of the small man decreasing.

XII. 'The want of good understanding between the (different classes of) men in Phî, and its indication as unfavourable to the firm and correct course of the superior man; with the intimation that the great are gone and the little come:'—all this springs from the fact that in it heaven and earth are not in communication with each other, and all things in consequence do not have free course; and that the high and the low (superiors and inferiors) are not in communication with one another, and there are no (well-regulated) states under the sky. The inner (trigram) is made up of the weak and divided lines, and the outer of the strong and undivided: the inner is (the symbol of) weakness, and the outer of strength; the inner (represents) the small man, and the outer the superior man. Thus the way of the small man appears increasing, and that of the superior man decreasing.

XI. There is nothing to be said on the explanation of the Thwan here beyond what has been noticed on the different paragraphs of the Text. Canon McClatchie translates:—'The Thwan means that Heaven and Earth have now conjugal intercourse with each other . . . . and the upper and lower (classes) unite together.' But in both clauses the Chinese characters are the same. Why did he not go on to say—'the upper and lower classes have conjugal intercourse together;' or rather, why did he not dismiss the idea of such intercourse from his mind altogether? Why make the Yî appear to be gross, when there is not the shadow of grossness in it? The paragraph here well illustrates how the ruling idea in all the antinomies of the Yî is that of authority and strength on the one side, and of inferiority and weakness on the other.

XII. All the symbolism here springs from the trigram Khwăn occupying in the figure the inner or lower place, and *Khien* the outer or upper. It is for the inner trigram to take the initiative;

XIII. 1. In Thung *Z*ăn the weak (line) has the place (of influence), the central place, and responds to (the corresponding line in) *Kh*ien (above); hence comes its name of Thung *Z*ăn (or 'Union of men').

2. Thung *Z*ăn says:—

3. The language, 'Thung *Z*ăn appears here (as we find it) in (the remote districts of) the country, indicating progress and success, and that it will be advantageous to cross the great stream,' is moulded by its containing the strength (symbolled) in *Kh*ien. (Then) we have (the trigram indicating) elegance and intelligence, supported by (that indicating) strength; with the line in the central, and its correct, position, and responding (to the corresponding line above):—(all representing) the correct course of the superior man. It is only the superior man who can comprehend and affect the minds of all under the sky.

XIV. 1. In Tâ Yû the weak (line) has the place of honour, is grandly central, and (the strong lines) above and below respond to it. Hence comes its name of Tâ Yû (Having what is Great).

---

but how can earth (symbolised by Khwăn) take the place of heaven (symbolised by *Kh*ien)? As in nature it is heaven that originates and not earth, so in a state the upper classes must take the initiative, and not the lower.

XIII. To understand the various points in this commentary, it is only necessary to refer to the Text of the hexagram. The proper correlate of line 2 is line 5, and I have said therefore that it 'responds to (the corresponding line in) *Kh*ien.' The editors of the Khang-hsî edition, however, would make the correlate to it all the lines of *Kh*ien, as being more agreeable to the idea of union.

I do not think that a second paragraph has been lost. The

2. The attributes (of its component trigrams) are strength and vigour with elegance and brightness. (The ruling line in it) responds to (the ruling line in the symbol of) heaven, and (consequently) its action is (all) at the proper times. In this way (it is said to) indicate great progress and success.

XV. 1. *Khien* indicates progress and success. It is the way of heaven to send down its beneficial influences below, where they are brilliantly displayed. It is the way of earth, lying low, to send its influences upwards and (there) to act.

2. It is the way of heaven to diminish the full and augment the humble. It is the way of earth to overthrow the full and replenish the humble. Spiritual Beings inflict calamity on the full and bless the humble. It is the way of men to hate the full and love the humble. Humility in a position of honour makes that still more brilliant; and in a low position men will not (seek to) pass beyond it. Thus it is that 'the superior man will have a (good) issue (to his undertakings).'

'Thung *Z*ăn says' is merely a careless repetition of the three concluding characters of paragraph 1.

XIV. The position in the fifth place indicates the dignity, and its being central, in the centre of the upper trigram, indicates the virtue, of the lord of the figure.

The strength of the lord, moreover, is directed by intelligence; and his actions are always at the proper time, like the seasons of heaven.

XV. The Thwan on this hexagram was so brief, that the writer here deals generally with the subject of humility, showing how it is valued by heaven and earth, by spirits and by men. The descent of the heavenly influences, and the low position of the earth in paragraph 1, are both emblematic of humility. The heavenly influences have their 'display' in the beauty and fertility of the earth.

XVI. 1. In Yü we see the strong (line) responded to by all the others, and the will (of him whom it represents) being carried out; and (also) docile obedience employing movement (for its purposes). (From these things comes) Yü (the Condition of harmony and satisfaction).

2. In this condition we have docile obedience employing movement (for its purposes), and therefore it is so as between heaven and earth;—how much more will it be so (among men) in 'the setting up of feudal princes and putting the hosts in motion!'

3. Heaven and earth show that docile obedience in connexion with movement, and hence the sun and moon make no error (in time), and the four seasons do not deviate (from their order). The sages show such docile obedience in connexion with their movements, and hence their punishments and penalties are entirely just, and the people acknowledge it by their submission. Great indeed are the time and significance indicated in Yü!

The way of heaven is seen, e.g. in the daily declining of the sun, and the waning of the moon after it is full; the way of earth in the fall of the year. On the meaning of 'Spiritual Beings (Kwei Shăn),' see the Introduction, pp. 34, 35. It is difficult to say what idea the writer attached to the name. What he says of man's appreciation of humility is striking, and, I believe, correct.

XVI. What is said in paragraph 1 about the lines has been pointed out in the notes on the Text. 'Obedience' is the attribute of Khwăn, the lower trigram, which takes the initiative in the action of the figure; and here makes use of the movement, which is the attribute of *K*ăn, the upper trigram.

I can hardly trace the connexion between the different parts of paragraph 2. Does it not proceed on the harmony produced by the thunderous explosion between heaven and earth, as declared

XVII. 1. In Sui we see the strong (trigram) come and place itself under the weak; we see (in the two) the attributes of movement and pleasure:—this gives (the idea of) Sui.

2. 'There will be great progress and success; and through firm correctness no error:'—all under heaven will be found following at such a time.

3. Great indeed are the time and significance indicated in Sui.

XVIII. 1. In Kû we have the strong (trigram) above, and the weak one below; we have (below) pliancy, and (above) stopping:—these give the idea of Kû (a Troublous Condition of affairs verging to ruin).

2. 'Kû indicates great progress and success:'—(through the course shown in it), all under heaven, there will be good order. 'There will be advantage in crossing the great stream:'—he who advances will encounter the business to be done. '(He should

---

in Appendix II? Then the analogy between natural phenomena and human and social experiences comes into play.

Paragraph 3 is also tantalising. Why does the writer introduce the subject of punishments and penalties? Are they a consequence of putting the hosts in motion?

XVII. The trigrams *K*ăn and Tui are distinguished as strong and weak, *K*ăn representing, on king Wăn's scheme, 'the eldest son,' and Tui, 'the youngest daughter.' But 'the strong' here may mean the strong line, the lowest in the hexagram. As Wang Ȝung-*k*wan (Sung dynasty) says:—'The yang and strong line should not be below a yin and weak line, as we find it here. That is, in Sui the high places himself below the low, and the noble below the mean:'—esteeming others higher than himself, and giving the idea of following. Then *K*ăn denotes the production or excitement of motion, and Tui denotes pleasure; and the union of these things suggests the same idea.

weigh well, however, the events of) three days before (the turning-point), and those (to be done) three days after it:'—the end (of confusion) is the beginning (of order); such is the procedure of Heaven.

XIX. 1. In Lin (we see) the strong (lines) gradually increasing and advancing.

2. (The lower trigram is the symbol of) being pleased, and (the upper of) being compliant. The strong (line) is in the central position, and is properly responded to.

3. 'There is great progress and success, along with firm correctness:'—this is the way of Heaven.

4. 'In the eighth month there will be evil:'—(the advancing power) will decay after no long time.

XX. 1. The great Manifester occupies an upper place (in the figure), which consists of (the trigrams

---

XVIII. The symbolism here is the opposite of that in Sui. The upper trigram *K*ăn is strong, denoting, according to king Wăn, 'the youngest son;' and the lower, Sun, is weak, denoting 'the eldest daughter.' For the eldest daughter to be below the youngest son is eminently correct, and helps to indicate the auspice of great success. The attribute of Sun is pliancy, and that of *K*ăn stoppage or arrest. The feeble pliancy confronted by the arresting mountain gives an idea of the evil state implied in Kû.

'Three days before and after the turning-point' is, literally, 'three days before and after *k*iâ,' *k*iâ being the name of the first of the 'earthly stems' among the cyclical characters. Hence it has the meaning of 'beginning,' and here denotes the turning-point, at which disorder gives place to order. According to 'the procedure of Heaven,' history is a narrative of change, one condition of affairs constantly giving place to another and opposite. 'A kingdom that cannot be moved' does not enter into the circle of Chinese ideas.

XIX. See what has been said on the fourth paragraph in pp. 98, 99 on the Text. The other paragraphs need no explanation beyond what appears in the supplemented translation.

whose attributes are) docility and flexibility. He is in the central position and his correct place, and thus exhibits (his lessons) to all under heaven.

2. 'Kwan shows its subject like a worshipper who has washed his hands, but not (yet) presented his offerings;—with sincerity and an appearance of dignity (commanding reverent regard):'—(all) beneath look to him and are transformed.

3. When we contemplate the spirit-like way of Heaven, we see how the four seasons proceed without error. The sages, in accordance with (this) spirit-like way, laid down their instructions, and all under heaven yield submission to them.

XXI. 1. The existence of something between the jaws gives rise to the name Shih Ho (Union by means of biting through the intervening article).

2. The Union by means of biting through the intervening article indicates 'the successful progress (denoted by the hexagram).'

The strong and weak (lines) are equally divided (in the figure). Movement is denoted (by the lower trigram), and bright intelligence (by the upper); thunder and lightning uniting in them, and having brilliant manifestation. The weak (fifth) line is in

XX. 'The great Manifester' is the ruler, the principal subject of the hexagram, and represented by line 5, near the top of the figure. In that figure the lower trigram is Khwăn, representing the earth, with the attribute of docility, and the upper is Sun, representing wind, with the attributes of flexibility and penetration. As is the place of line 5, so are the virtues of the ruler.

'The spirit-like way of Heaven' is the invisible and unfathomable agency ever operating by general laws, and with invariable regularity, in what we call nature. Compare with this paragraph, the definition of Shăn or Spirit in Appendix III, i, 32; and the doctrine of the agency of God, taught in Appendix VI, 8, 9.

the centre, and acts in its high position. Although it is not in its proper position, this is advantageous for the use of legal constraints.

XXII. 1. (When it is said that) Pî indicates that there should be free course (in what it denotes):—

2. (We see) the weak line coming and ornamenting the strong lines (of the lower trigram), and hence (it is said that ornament) 'should have free course.' On the other hand, the strong line above ornaments the weak ones (of the upper trigram), and hence (it is said) that 'there will be little advantage, if (ornament) be allowed to advance (and take the lead).' (This is illustrated in the) appearances that ornament the sky.

3. Elegance and intelligence (denoted by the lower trigram) regulated by the arrest (denoted by the upper) suggest the observances that adorn human (society).

4. We look at the ornamental figures of the sky, and thereby ascertain the changes of the seasons. We look at the ornamental observances of society, and understand how the processes of transformation are accomplished all under heaven.

XXI. The 'equal division of the strong and weak lines' is seen by taking them in pairs, though the order in the first pair is different from that in the two others. This is supposed to indicate the intelligence of the judgments in the action of the hexagram. *K*ăn, the lower trigram, symbolises movement; Lî, the upper, intelligence. The fifth line's acting in its high position does not intimate the formation of the figure from Yî, the 42nd hexagram, but calls attention to the fact that a weak line is here 'lord of judgment.' This does not seem natural, but the effect is good;—judgment is tempered by leniency.

XXII. The first paragraph is either superfluous or incomplete. The language of paragraph 2 has naturally been pressed into the

XXIII. 1. Po denotes overthrowing or being overthrown. We see (in the figure) the weak lines (threatening to) change the (last) strong line (into one of themselves).

2. That 'it will not be advantageous to make a movement in any direction whatever' appears from the fact that the small men are (now) growing and increasing. The superior man acts according to (the exigency of the time), and stops all forward movement, looking at the (significance of the) symbolic figures (in the hexagram). He values the processes of decrease and increase, of fulness and decadence, (as seen) in the movements of the heavenly bodies.

---

service of the doctrine of changing the figures by divining manipulation; see p. 219, on paragraph 2 of the Thwan of hexagram 6. But as the Khang-hsî editors point out, 'the weak line coming and ornamenting the two strong lines' simply indicates how substantiality should have the help of ornament, and 'the strong line above (or ascending) and ornamenting the two weak lines' indicates that ornament should be restrained by substantiality. Ornament has its use, but it must be kept in check.—The closing sentence has no connexion with what precedes. Some characters are wanting, to show how the writer passes on to speak of 'the ornamental figures of the sky.' The whole should then be joined on to paragraph 3. The 'figures of the sky' are all the heavenly bodies in their relative positions and various movements, producing day and night, heat and cold, &c. The observances of society are the ceremonies and performances which regulate and beautify the intercourse of men, and constitute the transforming lessons of sagely wisdom.

XXIII. 'The symbolic figures in the hexagram' are Khwăn, below, the representative of docility, acting as circumstances require; and Kăn, the representative of a mountain, which arrests the progress of the traveller. The superior man of the topmost line thus interprets them, and acts accordingly. Yet he is not left without hope. Winter is followed by spring; night is

XXIV. 1. 'Fû indicates the free course and progress (of what it denotes):'—it is the coming back of what is intended by the undivided line.

2. (Its subject's) actions show movement directed by accordance with natural order. Hence 'he finds no one to distress him in his exits and entrances,' and 'friends come to him, and no error is committed.'

3. 'He will return and repeat his proper course; in seven days comes his return:'—such is the movement of the heavenly (revolution).

4. 'There will be advantage in whatever direction movement is made:'—the strong lines are growing and increasing.

5. Do we not see in Fû the mind of heaven and earth?

XXV. In Wû Wang we have the strong (first) line come from the outer (trigram), and become in the inner trigram lord (of the whole figure); we have (the attributes of) motive power and strength; we have the strong line (of the fifth place) in the

---

succeeded by day; the moon wanes, and then begins to wax again. So will it be in political life. As we read in the Hebrew prophet Isaiah, 'In returning and rest shall ye be saved; in quietness and in confidence shall be your strength.'

XXIV. 'The movement of the heavenly revolution' in paragraph 3 has reference to the regular alternations of darkness and light, and of cold and heat, as seen in the different months of the year. Hâu Hsing-kwo (of the Thang dynasty) refers to the expressions in the Shih, I, xv, ode 1, 'the days of (our) first (month), second (month),' &c., as illustrating the use of day for month, as we have it here; but that is to explain what is obscure by what is more so; though I believe, as stated on the Text, that 'seven days' is here equivalent to 'seven months.'

'The mind of heaven and earth' is the love of life and of all goodness that rules in the course of nature and providence.

central position, and responded to (by the weak second):—there will be 'great progress proceeding from correctness; such is the appointment of Heaven.

'If (its subject and his action) be not correct, he will fall into errors, and it will not be advantageous for him to move in any direction:'—whither can he (who thinks he is) free from all insincerity, (and yet is as here described) proceed? Can anything be done (advantageously) by him whom the (will and) appointment of Heaven do not help?

XXVI. 1. In (the trigrams composing) Tâ *Kh*û we have (the attributes) of the greatest strength and of substantial solidity, which emit a brilliant light; and indicate a daily renewal of his virtue (by the subject of it).

2. The strong line is in the highest place, and suggests the value set on talents and virtue; there is power (in the upper trigram) to keep the strongest in restraint:—all this shows 'the great correctness' (required in the hexagram).

3. 'The good fortune attached to the subject's not seeking to enjoy his revenues in his own family' shows how talents and virtue are nourished.

XXV. The advocates of one trigram's changing into another, which ought not to be admitted, we have seen, into the interpretation of the Yî, make Wû Wang to be derived from Sung (No. 6), the second line there being manipulated into the first of this; but this representation is contrary to the words of the text, which make the strong first line come from the outer trigram, i. e. from *Kh*ien. And so it does, as related, not very intelligibly, in Appendix V, 10, *K*ăn, the lower trigram here, being 'the eldest son,' resulting from the first application of Khwăn to *Kh*ien. The three peculiarities in the structure of the figure afford the auspice of progress and success; and very striking is the brief and emphatic declaration, that such progress is 'the appointment of Heaven.'

4. 'It will be advantageous to cross the great stream:'—(the fifth line, representing the ruler,) is responded to by (the second, the central line of *Kh*ien, representing) Heaven.

XXVII. 1. 'Î indicates that with firm correctness there will be good fortune:'—when the nourishing is correct, there will be good fortune. 'We must look at what we are seeking to nourish:'—we must look at those whom we wish to nourish. 'We must by the exercise of our thoughts seek the proper aliment:'—we must look to our own nourishing of ourselves.

2. Heaven and earth nourish all things. The sages nourish men of talents and virtue, by them to reach to the myriads of the people. Great is (the work intended by this) nourishing in its time!

XXVI. In paragraph 1, Tâ *Kh*û evidently means the 'grand accumulation' of virtue, indicated by the attributes of its component trigrams. 'Substantial solidity' may very well be given as the attribute of mountains.

'The strong line in the highest place' of paragraph 2 is line 6, whose subject is thus above the ruler represented by 5, and has the open firmament for his range in doing his work. This, and his ability to repress the strongest opposition, show how he is supported by all that is correct and right.

In a kingdom where the object of the government is the accumulation of virtue, good and able men will not be left in obscurity.

What will not a high and good purpose, supported by the greatest strength, be able to do?

XXVII. Many of the critics, in illustration of paragraph 1, refer appropriately to Mencius, VI, i, chap. 14.

In illustration of paragraph 2 they refer to the times and court of Yâo and Shun, sage rulers, from whose cherishing and nourishing came Yü to assuage the waters of the deluge, Ȝî to teach the people agriculture, Hsieh as minister of instruction, Kâo Yâo as minister of crime, and others;—all to do the work of nourishing the people.

XXVIII. 1. Tâ Kwo shows the great ones (= the undivided lines) in excess.

2. In 'the beam that is weak' we see weakness both in the lowest and the topmost (lines).

3. The strong lines are in excess, but (two of them) are in the central positions. The action (of the hexagram is represented by the symbols of) flexibility and satisfaction. (Hence it is said), 'There will be advantage in moving in any direction whatever; yea, there will be success.'

4. Great indeed is (the work to be done in) this very extraordinary time.

XXIX. 1. Khan repeated shows us one defile succeeding another.

2. This is the nature of water;—it flows on, without accumulating its volume (so as to overflow); it pursues its way through a dangerous defile, without losing its true (nature).

3. That 'the mind is penetrating' is indicated by the strong (line) in the centre. That 'action (in accordance with this) will be of high value' tells us that advance will be followed by achievement.

4. The dangerous (height) of heaven cannot be ascended; the difficult places of the earth are moun-

XXVIII. Paragraph 3. In the Great Symbolism 'wood' appears as the natural object symbolised by Sun, and not 'wind,' which we find more commonly. The attribute of 'flexibility,' however, is the quality of Sun, whether used of wind or of wood.

Paragraph 4. Such a time, it is said, was that of Yâo and Shun, of Thang the Successful, and of king Wû. What these heroes did, however, was all called for by the exigency of their times, and not by whim or principle of their own, which they wished to make prominent.

tains, rivers, hills, and mounds. Kings and princes arrange, by means of such strengths, to maintain their territories. Great indeed is the use of (what is here) taught about seasons of peril.

XXX. 1. Lî means being attached to. The sun and moon have their place in the sky. All the grains, grass, and trees have their place on the earth. The double brightness (of the two trigrams) adheres to what is correct, and the result is the transforming and perfecting all under the sky.

2. The weak (second line) occupies the middle and correct position, and gives the indication of 'a free and successful course;' and, moreover, 'nourishing (docility like that of) the cow' will lead to good fortune.

XXIX. On paragraph 2 Liang Yin says:—'Water stops at the proper time, and moves at the proper time. Is not this an emblem of the course of the superior man in dealing with danger?'

On paragraph 4 the Khang-hsî editors say that to exercise one's self in meeting difficulty and peril is the way to establish and strengthen the character, and that the use of such experience is seen in all measures for self-defence, there being no helmet and mail like leal-heartedness and good faith, and no shield and tower like propriety and righteousness.

XXX. 'The double brightness' in paragraph 1 has been much discussed. Some say that it means 'the ruler,' becoming brighter and brighter. Others say that it means both the ruler and his ministers, combining their brightness. The former view seems to me the better. The analogy between the natural objects and a transforming and perfecting rule is far fetched.

'The central and correct position' in paragraph 2 can be said only of the second line, and not of the fifth, where an undivided line would be more correct. The 'and moreover' of the translation is 'therefore' in the original; but I cannot make out the force and suitability of that conjunction.

SECTION II.

XXXI. 1. Hsien is here used in the sense of Kan, meaning (mutually) influencing.

2. The weak (trigram) above, and the strong one below; their two influences moving and responding to each other, and thereby forming a union; the repression (of the one) and the satisfaction (of the other); (with their relative position), where the male is placed below the female:—all these things convey the notion of 'a free and successful course (on the fulfilment of the conditions), while the advantage will depend on being firm and correct, as in marrying a young lady, and there will be good fortune.'

3. Heaven and earth exert their influences, and there ensue the transformation and production of all things. The sages influence the minds of men, and the result is harmony and peace all under the sky. If we look at (the method and issues) of those influences, the true character of heaven and earth and of all things can be seen.

XXXII. 1. Hăng denotes long continuance. The strong (trigram) is above, and the weak one below; (they are the symbols of) thunder and wind,

---

XXXI. Paragraph 2. Tui, the upper trigram, is weak and yin; and Kăn, the lower, is strong and yang; see Appendixes III, ii, 4, and V, 10. Kăn is below Tui; whereas the subject of the lower trigram should always take the initiative in these figures.

which are in mutual communication; (they have the qualities of) docility and motive force; their strong and weak (lines) all respond, each to the other:—these things are all found in Hăng.

2. (When it is said that) 'Hăng indicates successful progress and no error (in what it denotes); but the advantage will come from being firm and correct,' this indicates that there must be long continuance in its way of operation. The way of heaven and earth is to be long continued in their operation without stopping.

3. (When it is said that) 'Movement in any direction whatever will be advantageous,' this implies that when (the moving power) is spent, it will begin again.

4. The sun and moon, realising in themselves (the course of Heaven), can perpetuate their shining. The four seasons, by their changing and transforming, can perpetuate their production (of things). The sages persevere long in their course, and all under the sky are transformed and perfect. When we look at what they continue doing long, the natural tendencies of heaven, earth, and all things can be seen.

XXXII. All the conditions in paragraph 1 must be understood as leading to the indication of progress and success, which is explained in paragraph 2, and illustrated by the analogy of the course of heaven and earth.

'Movement in any direction,' as explained in paragraph 3, indicates the ever-occurring new modes and spheres of activity, to which he who is firm and correct is called.

Paragraph 4, and especially its concluding sentence, are of a meditative and reflective character not uncommon in the treatise on the Thwan.

XXXIII. 1. 'Thun indicates successful progress:'—that is, in the very retiring which Thun denotes there is such progress. The strong (line) is in the ruling place, (the fifth), and is properly responded to (by the second line). The action takes place according to (the requirement of) the time.

2. 'To a small extent it will (still) be advantageous to be firm and correct:'—(the small men) are gradually encroaching and advancing.

3. Great indeed is the significance of (what is required to be done in) the time that necessitates retiring.

XXXIV. 1. In Tâ *K*wang we see that which is great becoming strong. We have the (trigram) denoting strength directing that which denotes movement, and hence (the whole) is expressive of vigour.

2. 'Tâ *K*wang indicates that it will be advantageous to be firm and correct:'—that which is great (should be) correct. Given correctness and greatness (in their highest degree), and the character and tendencies of heaven and earth can be seen.

XXXIII. 'The superior man,' it is said, 'advances or withdraws according to the character of the time. The strength and correct position of the fifth line show that he is able to maintain himself; and as it is responded to by the weak second line, no opposition to what is correct in him would come from any others. He might therefore keep his place; but looking at the two weak lines, 1 and 2, he recognises in them the advance and irrepressible progress of small men, and that for a time it is better for him to give way and withdraw from the field. Thus there is successful progress even in his retiring.'

XXXIV. Paragraph 1. 'That which is great' denotes, in the first place, the group of four strong lines which strikes us on

易經

XXXV. 1. 3in denotes advancing.

2. (In 3in we have) the bright (sun) appearing above the earth; (the symbol of) docile submission cleaving to that of the Great brightness; and the weak line advanced and moving above:—all these things give us the idea of 'a prince who secures the tranquillity (of the people), presented on that account with numerous horses (by the king), and three times in a day received at interviews.'

XXXVI. 1. (The symbol of) the Earth and that of Brightness entering into the midst of it give the idea of Ming Î (Brightness wounded or obscured).

2. The inner (trigram) denotes being accomplished and bright; the outer, being pliant and submissive. The case of king Wăn was that of one

---

looking at the figure, and then the superior man, or the strong men in positions of power, of whom these are the representatives. *Kh*ien is the trigram of strength, and *K*ăn that of movement.

Paragraph 2. 'That which is great (should be) correct:'—that the 'should be' must be supplied in the translation appears from this, that the paragraph is intended to illustrate the text that 'it will be advantageous to be firm and correct.' The power of man becomes then a reflexion of the great power which we see working in nature, 'impartially,' 'unselfishly.'

XXXV. To those who advocate the view that the hexagrams of the Yî have been formed by changes of the lines in manipulating with the divining stalks, the words of paragraph 2, that we have in the figure 'the weak line advanced and moving above,' suggest the derivation of 3in from Kwan, whose 4th and 5th lines are made to change places (). But we have seen that that view is inadmissible in the interpretation of the Yî. And a simple explanation of the language at once presents itself. As Hsiang An-shih (Sung dynasty) says, 'Of the three "daughter" trigrams it is only Lî which has its divided line occupying the central place of honour, when it is the upper trigram in a hexagram.'

who with these qualities was yet involved in great difficulties.

3. 'It will be advantageous to realise the difficulty (of the position), and maintain firm correctness:'—that is, (the individual concerned) should obscure his brightness. The case of the count of *K*î was that of one who, amidst the difficulties of his House, was able (thus) to maintain his aim and mind correct.

XXXVII. 1. In *K*iâ *Z*ăn the wife has her correct place in the inner (trigram), and the man his correct place in the outer. That man and woman occupy their correct places is the great righteousness shown (in the relation and positions of) heaven and earth.

2. In *K*iâ *Z*ăn we have the idea of an authoritative ruler;—that, namely, represented by the parental authority.

3. Let the father be indeed father, and the son son; let the elder brother be indeed elder brother, and the younger brother younger brother; let the husband be indeed husband, and the wife wife:—then will the family be in its normal state. Bring the family to that state, and all under heaven will be established.

XXXVI. The sun disappearing, as we say, 'below the earth,' or, as the Chinese writer conceives it, 'into the midst of, or within the earth,' sufficiently indicates the obscuration or wounding of brightness,—the repression and resistance of the good and bright.

King Wăn was not of the line of Shang. Though opposed and persecuted by its sovereign, he could pursue his own course, till his line came in the end to supersede the other. It could not be so with the count of *K*î, who was a member of the House of Shang. He could do nothing that would help on its downfall.

XXXVII. Paragraph 1 first explains the statement of the

XXXVIII. 1. In Khwei we have (the symbol of) Fire, which, when moved, tends upwards, and that of a Marsh, whose waters, when moved, tend downwards. We have (also the symbols of) two sisters living together, but whose wills do not move in the same direction.

2. (We see how the inner trigram expressive of) harmonious satisfaction is attached to (the outer expressive of) bright intelligence; (we see) the weak line advanced and acting above, and how it occupies the central place, and is responded to by the strong (line below). These indications show that 'in small matters there will (still) be good fortune.'

3. Heaven and earth are separate and apart, but the work which they do is the same. Male and female are separate and apart, but with a common will they seek the same object. There is diversity between the myriad classes of beings, but there is an analogy between their several operations. Great indeed are the phenomena and the results of this condition of disunion and separation.

Thwan, about the wife, represented by line 2; and then proceeds to the husband, represented by line 5. The two trigrams become representative of the family circle, and the wide world without it. In the reference to heaven and earth it is not supposed that they are really husband and wife; but in their relation and positions they symbolise that social relation and the individuals in it.

Paragraph 2, more closely rendered, would be—'That in *K*îa *Z*ăn there is an authoritative ruler is a way of naming father and mother.' Does the writer mean to say that while the assertion of authority was indispensable in a family, that authority must have combined in it both force and gentleness?

XXXVIII. In paragraph 1 we have first an explanation of the meaning of Khwei from the symbolism of Fû-hsî. Then follows

XXXIX. 1. *K*ien denotes difficulty. There is (the trigram expressive of) perilousness in front. When one, seeing the peril, can arrest his steps (in accordance with the significance of the lower trigram), is he not wise?

2. (The language of) *K*ien, that 'advantage will be found in the south-west,' refers to the (strong fifth line) advanced and in the central place. That 'there will be no advantage in the north-east,' intimates that the way (of dealing with the *K*ien state) is exhausted. That 'it will be advantageous to see the great man,' intimates that advance will lead to achievement. That the places (of the different lines after the first) are those appropriate to them indicates firm correctness and good fortune, with which the regions (of the kingdom) are brought to their normal state. Great indeed is the work to be done in the time of *K*ien!

---

an explanation from that ascribed to king Wăn, where Tui represents the youngest daughter and Lî the second. The Khang-hsî editors observe that in many hexagrams we have two daughters dwelling together, but that only in this and 49 is attention called to it. The reason, they say, is that in those two diagrams the sisters are the second and third daughters, while in the others one of them is the eldest, whose place and superiority are fixed, so that between her and either of the others there can be no division or collision.

About what is said, in paragraph 2, on the weak line, as advanced and acting above, see the note on hexagram 35.

The lesson of paragraph 3 is not unity in diversity, but union with diversity.

XXXIX. The upper or front trigram is Khân, the attribute of which is perilousness; the lower is Kăn, of which the arresting, actively or passively, of movement or advance is the attribute. We can understand how the union of these attributes gives the ideas of difficulty and prudent caution.

The explanations in paragraph 2 of the phraseology of the Thwan

XL. 1. In *K*ieh we have (the trigram expressive of) peril going on to that expressive of movement. By movement there is an escape from the peril:—(this is the meaning of) *K*ieh.

2. 'In (the state indicated by) *K*ieh, advantage will be found in the south-west:'—the movement (thus) intimated will win all. That 'there will be good fortune in coming back (to the old conditions)' shows that such action is that of the due medium. That 'if some operations be necessary, there will be good fortune in the early conducting of them' shows that such operations will be successful.

3. When heaven and earth are freed (from the grasp of winter), we have thunder and rain. When these come, the buds of the plants and trees that produce the various fruits begin to burst. Great indeed are the phenomena in the time intimated by *K*ieh.

---

are not all easily followed. It is said that the advantageousness of the south-west is due to the central line in 5; but if we are to look for the meaning of south-west in Khwăn, as in the diagram of king Wăn's trigrams, there is no strong central line in it. May Khân, as a yang trigram, be used for Khwăn?

XL. 1. The meaning of the hexagram is brought out sufficiently well in paragraph 1 by means of the attributes of the constituent trigrams.

2. How it is that the movement indicated in the first condition will 'win' all does not immediately appear. The Khang-hsî editors say that 'moving to the south and west' is the same as 'returning back to the old conditions,' and that 'winning all' and acting 'according to the due medium' are descriptive of the effect and method without reference to the symbolism. Another explanation might be devised; but I prefer to leave the matter in doubt.

3. Paragraph 3 shows the analogy of what takes place in nature to the beneficent social and political changes described in the text, as is done very frequently in this Appendix.

XLI. 1. In Sun (we see) the lower (trigram) diminished, and the upper added to. (But) the method (of action) implied in this operates also above (or, mounts upwards (also) and operates).

2. 'If there be sincerity in this method of diminution, there will be great good fortune; freedom from error; firmness and correctness that can be maintained; and advantage in every movement that shall be made. In what shall this (sincerity in the exercise of Sun) be employed? (Even) in sacrifice, two baskets of grain, (though there be nothing else), may be presented:'—for these two baskets there ought to be the fitting time. There is a time when the strong should be diminished, and the weak should be strengthened. Diminution and increase, overflowing and emptiness:—these take place in harmony with the conditions of the time.

XLI. 1. All that we see is two undivided lines in the lower trigram, and then a divided one, and exactly the opposite in the upper. But the whole figure could not but have this form from the process of its formation, whether by the gradual addition of the two primitive lines, or by the imposition of the whole trigrams on one another. To say that the upper lines of *Kh*ien and Khwăn changed places to express the idea of subjects contributing in taxes to the maintenance of their ruler is absurd; and if that thought were in the mind of king Wăn (which I very much doubt), it would only show how he projected his own idea, formed independently of the figure, into its lines.

On the second sentence, the Khang-hsî editors say:—'When a minister devotes his life in the service of his lord, or the people undertake their various labours in behalf of their government, these are instances of the ministering of those below to increase those above. But in this way the intercourse of the two becomes close and their aims become the same;—does not the method of action of those below communicate itself to those above?'

In paragraph 2 the subject of contribution, such as the payment of

XLII. 1. In Yî we see the upper (trigram) diminished, and the lower added to. The satisfaction of the people (in consequence of this) is without limit. What descends from above reaches to all below, so great and brilliant is the course (of its operation).

2. That 'there will be advantage in every movement which shall be undertaken' appears from the central and correct (positions of the second and fifth lines), and the (general) blessing (the dispensing of which they imply).

That 'it will be advantageous (even) to cross the great stream' appears from the action of wood (shown in the figure).

3. Yî is made up of (the trigrams expressive of) movement and docility, (through which) there is daily advancement to an unlimited extent. We have (also) in it heaven dispensing and earth producing, leading to an increase without restriction

---

taxes, passes into the background. The Khang-hsî editors say:—'What is meant by diminishing in this hexagram is the regulation of expenditure or contribution according to the time. This would vary in a family according to its poverty or wealth; and in a state according to the abundance or scantiness of its resources. When it is said that there must be sincerity along with a diminution, it means that though such a diminution cannot be helped, yet what is given should be given sincerely. A small sacrifice sincerely offered is accepted. In the language, "There is a time when the strong should be diminished and the weak be strengthened," we are not to find the two baskets in the diminution of the strong. "The strong" is what is essential,—in this case sincerity; "The weak" is what is unimportant,—the amount and manner of the offering. If one supplement the insufficiency of his offering with the abundance of his sincerity, the insignificance of his two baskets will not be despised.'

of place. Everything in the method of this increase proceeds according to the requirements of the time.

XLII. 1. The process of the formation of the trigrams here is the reverse of that in the preceding hexagram; and is open to the remarks I have made on that. Of course the people are full of complacency and pleasure in the labours of their ruler for their good.

2. The mention of 'the action of wood' has reference to the upper trigram Sun, which is the symbol both of wind and wood. From wood boats and ships are made, on which the great stream may be crossed. In three hexagrams, this, 59, and 61, of which Sun is a part, we find mention made of crossing the great stream. It is generally said that the lower trigram *K*ăn also symbolises wood; but that is obtained by a roundabout process. *K*ăn occupies the place of the east in Wan's arrangement of the trigrams; but the east symbolises spring, when the growth of vegetation begins; and therefore *K*ăn may symbolise wood! It was stated on p. 33, that the doctrine of 'the five elements' does not appear in the Yî. *Kh*ăng-ȝze takes wood (木 mû), 'as a misprint for increase (益 yî).'

3. The words 'heaven dispensing and earth producing' are based on the fancied genesis of the figure from *Kh*ien and Khwăn (䷋), the first lines in each changing places. It was the author of this Appendix, probably, who first introduced that absurd notion in connexion with the formation of Sun and Yî.

One rhyme runs through and connects these three paragraphs thus:—

'Yî spoils the high, gives to the low;
The people feel intense delight.
Down from above to all below,
The blessing goes, so large and bright.
Success will every movement mark,
Central its source, its course aright.
The great stream even may be crossed,
When planks of wood their strength unite.
Yî movement shows and docile feet,
Which progress day by day invite.
Heaven gives; productive earth responds;
Increase crowns every vale and height;

XLIII. 1. Kwâi is the symbol of displacing or removing. We see (in the figure) the strong (lines) displacing the weak. (We have in it the attributes of) strength and complacency. There is displacement, but harmony (continues).

2. 'The exhibition (of the criminal's guilt) in the royal courtyard' is suggested by the (one) weak (line) mounted on the five strong lines.

There 'is an earnest and sincere appeal (for sympathy and support), and a consciousness of the peril (involved in the undertaking):'—it is the realisation of this danger, which makes the method (of compassing the object) brilliant.

'He should make an announcement in his own city, and show that it will not be well to have recourse at once to arms:'—(if he have recourse to arms), what he prefers will (soon) be exhausted.

'There will be advantage in whatever he shall go forward to:'—when the growth of the strong (lines) has been completed, there will be an end (of the displacement).

And ceaselessly it hastens on,
Each season's gifts quick to requite.'

XLIII. 1. The last clause of paragraph 1 is good in itself, showing that the strong and worthy statesman in removing a bad man from the state is not actuated by any private feelings. The sentiment, however, as it is expressed, can hardly be said to follow from the symbolism.

Paragraph 2. The same may be said of all the notes appended to the different clauses of this second paragraph. Hû Ping-wǎn (Yüan dynasty) says:—'If but a single small man be left, he is sufficient to make the superior man anxious; if but a single inordinate desire be left in the mind, that is sufficient to disturb the harmony of heavenly principles. The eradication in both cases must be complete, before the labour is ended.'

XLIV. 1. Kâu has the significance of unexpectedly coming on. (We see in it) the weak (line) coming unexpectedly on the strong ones.

2. 'It will not be good to marry (such) a female:'—one (so symbolised) should not be long associated with.

3. Heaven and earth meeting together (as here represented), all the variety of natural things become fully displayed.

4. When a strong (line) finds itself in the central and correct position, (good government) will greatly prevail all under the sky.

5. Great indeed is the significance of what has to be done at the time indicated by Kâu!

XLV. 1. 3hui indicates (the condition of union, or) being collected. We have in it (the symbol of) docile obedience going on to (what is expressed by that of) satisfaction. There is the strong line in the central place, and rightly responded to. Hence comes the (idea of) union.

2. 'The king will repair to his ancestral temple:'—

XLIV. On paragraph 1 the Khang-hsî editors say:—'"The weak line meets with (or comes unexpectedly on) the strong ones;"—the weak line, that is, plays the principal part. The case is like that of the minister who assumes the power of deciding for himself on all measures, or of a hen's announcing the morning;—is not the name of (shameless) boldness rightly applied to it? Hence nothing more is said about the symbol of the bold female; but attention is called to the second part of the Thwan.'

Paragraph 2 needs no remark. Paragraphs 3, 4, and 5 all speak of the importance of powers and parties meeting together,—in the world of nature, and in the sphere of human affairs. But I do not see how this sentiment is a natural sequel to that in 1 and 2, nor that it has any connexion with the teaching of the Thwan and Symbolism.

with the utmost filial piety he presents his offerings (to the spirits of his ancestors).

'It will be advantageous to meet the great man, and there will then be prosperity and success:'—the union effected by him will be on and through what is correct.

'The use of great victims will conduce to good fortune; and in whatsoever direction movement is made, it will be advantageous:'—all is done in accordance with the ordinances of Heaven.

3. When we look at the way in which the gatherings (here shown) take place, the natural tendencies (in the outward action) of heaven and earth and of all things can be seen.

XLVI. 1. (We find) the weak (line), as it finds the opportunity, ascending upwards.

2. We have (the attribute) of flexibility and that of obedience; we have the strong line (below) and its proper correlate above:—these things indicate that there will be 'great progress and success.'

XLV. The lower trigram in Ȝhui is Khwăn, whose attribute is docile obedience; and the upper is Tui, whose attribute is pleased satisfaction. Then we have the strong line in 5, and its proper correlate in 2. These things may give the idea of union. They might also give the idea of other good things.

The Khang-hsî editors say that though 'all is done in accordance with the ordinances of Heaven' follows the concluding clauses of the Thwan, yet the sentiment of the words must be extended to the other clauses as well. *Kh*ăng-ȝze says that 'the ordinances of Heaven' are simply the natural and practical outcome of 'heavenly principle;'—in this case what should and may be done according to the conditions and requirements of the time. So do the critics of China try to shirk the idea of personality in 'Heaven.'

With paragraph 3, compare the concluding paragraphs of the Thwan *K*wan on hexagrams 31, 32.

3. 'Seeking (by the qualities implied in Shăng) to meet with the great man, its subject need have no anxiety:'—there will be ground for congratulation.

'Advance to the south will be fortunate:'—his aim will be carried out.

XLVII. 1. In Khwăn (we see) the strong (lines) covered and obscured (by the weak).

2. We have in it (the attribute of) perilousness going on to that of satisfaction. Who is it but the superior man that, though straitened, still does not fail in making progress to his proper end?

'For the firm and correct, the (really) great man, there will be good fortune:'—this is shown by the central positions of the strong (lines).

'If he make speeches, his words cannot be made good:'—to be fond of arguing or pleading is the way to be reduced to extremity.

XLVI. The explanation of the first paragraph has given occasion to much difference of opinion. Some will have 'the weak (line)' to be 4; some 5; and some the whole of Khwăn, the upper trigram. The advocates of 4, make it come from hexagram 40, the weak 3 of which ascends to the strong 4, displaces it, and takes its place; but we have seen repeatedly the folly of the doctrine of changing lines and figures. The great symbolism of Appendix II suggests the proper explanation. The lower trigram, Sun, represents here not wind but wood. The first line, weak, is the root of a tree planted beneath the earth. Its gradual growth symbolises the advance upwards of the subject of the hexagram, fostered, that is, by the circumstances of the time.

XLVII. 1. One sees the relative position of the strong and weak lines in the figure; but to deduce from that the idea expressed by Khwăn requires a painful straining of the imagination. That idea was in the mind, and then the lines were interpreted accordingly.

2. 'Perilousness' is the attribute of the lower trigram, and 'satisfaction' that of the upper. The superior man, however straitened,

易經

XLVIII. 1. (We have the symbol of) wood in the water and the raising of the water; which (gives us the idea of) a well. A well supplies nourishment and is not (itself) exhausted.

2. 'The site of a town may be changed, while the fashion of its wells undergoes no change:'—this is indicated by the central position of the strong lines (in the second and fifth places).

'The drawing is nearly accomplished, but the rope has not yet reached the water of the well:'—its service has not yet been accomplished.

'The bucket is broken:'—it is this that occasions evil.

XLIX. 1. In Ko (we see) water and fire extinguishing each other; (we see also) two daughters dwelling together, but with their minds directed to

---

remains master of himself, and pursues the proper end of principle settled in his mind.

Why should the subject of Khwăn make speeches, be fond of arguing or pleading,—as the characters say, if we could translate them literally, 'setting a value on the mouth?' The reply to this is found in the trigram denoting 'satisfaction,' or 'being pleased.' The party in the extremity of Khwăn yet wishes and tries to make men pleased with him.

XLVIII. *K*ăng Khang-*Kh*ăng says:—'Khân, the upper trigram, represents water, and Sun, the lower, wood. This wood denotes the water-wheel or pulley with its bucket, which descends into the mouth of the spring, and brings the water up to the top.' This may be a correct explanation of the figure, though the reading of it from bottom to top seems at first to be strange.

Paragraph 2. That the fashion of the well does not undergo any (great) change is dwelt upon as illustrating the unchangeableness of the great principles of human nature and of government. But that this truth may be learned from the strong and central lines only produces a smile. So do the remarks on the other two sentences of the Thwan.

different objects:—(on account of these things) it is called (the hexagram of) Change.

2. 'It is believed in (only) after it has been accomplished:'—when the change has been made, faith is accorded to it.

(We have) cultivated intelligence (as the basis of) pleased satisfaction, (suggesting) 'great progress and success,' coming from what is correct.

When change thus takes place in the proper way, 'occasion for repentance disappears.'

3. Heaven and earth undergo their changes, and the four seasons complete their functions. Thang changed the appointment (of the line of Hsiâ to the throne), and Wû (that of the line of Shang), in accordance with (the will of) Heaven, and in response to (the wishes of) men. Great indeed is what takes place in a time of change.

L. 1. In Ting we have (symbolically) the figure of a caldron. (We see) the (symbol of) wood entering into that of fire, which suggests the idea of cook-

---

XLIX. Paragraph 1. Lî, the lower trigram, represents fire, and Tui, the upper, represents water. Water will extinguish fire, and fire again will dry up water. Each, to all appearance, produces a change in the other. Again, according to king Wăn's scheme of the trigrams, as shown on p. 33, and in Figure 1, Plate III, Lî is the second, and Tui the youngest daughter. Their wills are likely to differ in love and other things; but this symbolism does not so readily suggest the idea of change.

2. The first sentence suggests how the dislike to change on the part of people generally is overcome.

The second suggests how change proceeding from intelligence and giving general satisfaction will be successful.

Paragraph 3 tells us how the greatest natural and the greatest political changes are equally successful and admirable when conducted aright.

ing. The sages cooked their offerings in order to present them to God, and made great feasts to nourish their wise and able (ministers).

2. We have the symbol of) flexible obedience, and that (which denotes) ears quick of hearing and eyes clear-sighted. (We have also) the weak (line) advanced and acting above, in the central place, and responded to by the strong (line below). All these things give the idea of 'great progress and success.'

LI. 1. *K*ăn (gives the intimation of) ease and development.

2. 'When the (time of) movement (which it indicates) comes, (its subject) will be found looking out with apprehension:'—that feeling of dread leads to happiness. 'And yet smiling and talking cheerfully:'—the issue (of his dread) is that he adopts (proper) laws (for his course).

'The movement (like a crash of thunder) terrifies

L. 1. See the notes on the Text of the Thwan about the figure of a caldron in Ting. Its component trigrams are Sun representing wood, and Lî representing fire; which may very well suggest the idea of cooking. The last sentence of the paragraph is entirely after the style of 'the Great Symbolism.' The Khang-hsî editors say that the distinction between 3ing and Ting appears here very clearly, the former relating to the nourishment of the people, and the latter to the nourishing men of worth. They add that the reality of the offerings to God is such nourishing. 'God' is here Shang Tî, which Canon McClatchie translates 'the First Emperor,' adding in a note, 'The Chinese Jupiter, the Emperor of gods and men!'

2. The first sentence deduces the sentiment of the Thwan from the attributes or virtues of the trigrams with considerable amplification of the virtue of Lî. The second line of Lî, as being divided, calls forth in other hexagrams the same notice as here. It is the most important line in the figure, and being responded to by the strong 2, gives an indication of the 'great progress and success.'

all within a hundred lî:'—it startles the distant and frightens the near.

'He will be like the sincere worshipper, who is not startled into letting go his ladle and cup of sacrificial spirits:'—he makes his appearance, and maintains his ancestral temple and the altars of the spirits of the land and grain, as presiding at all sacrifices.

LII. 1. Kăn denotes stopping or resting;—resting when it is the time to rest, and acting when it is the time to act. When one's movements and restings all take place at the proper time for them, his way (of proceeding) is brilliant and intelligent.

2. Resting in one's resting-point is resting in one's proper place. The upper and lower (lines of the hexagram) exactly correspond to each other, but are without any interaction; hence it is said that '(the subject of the hexagram) has no consciousness of self; that when he walks in his courtyard, he does not see (any of) the persons in it; and that there will be no error.'

LI. Paragraph 1. See what is said on the Text.

2. The explanations of the Thwan here are good; but in no way deduced from the figure.

3. The portion of the text printed in a different type is supposed to have dropt out of the Chinese copies. The explanation of it that follows is based on Wăn's view of *K*ăn as representing the oldest son. See on the Text.

LII. 1. The Khang-hsî editors give their opinion that what is said in the first sentence of this paragraph, after the explanation of the name, illustrates the first sentence of the Thwan, and that the other sentence illustrates the rest of the Thwan. It may be so, but the whole of the Thwan appears in paragraph 2.

2. The hexagram being made up of Kăn repeated, lines 1, 2, 3 are of course the same as 4, 5, and 6. But it will be seen that there is not a proper correlation among them all. I do not see,

LIII. 1. The advance indicated by *K*ien is (like) the marrying of a young lady which is attended by good fortune.

2. (The lines) as they advance get into their correct places:—this indicates the achievements of a successful progress.

The advance is made according to correctness:—(the subject of the hexagram) might rectify his country.

3. Among the places (of the hexagram) we see the strong undivided line in the centre.

4. 'In (the attributes of) restfulness and flexible penetration we have (the assurance of) an (onward) movement that is inexhaustible.

LIV. 1. By Kwei Mei (the marrying away of a younger sister) the great and righteous relation between heaven and earth (is suggested to us). If heaven and earth were to have no intercommunication, things would not grow and flourish as they do. The marriage of a younger sister is the end (of her maidenhood) and the beginning (of her motherhood).

2. We have (in the hexagram the desire of)

---

however, that this furnishes any ground for the entire obliviousness of self, which the Thwan makes out to be in the figure.

LIII. The first sentence of paragraph 2 describes the lines from 2 to 5 all getting into their proper places, as has been pointed out on the Text, and that sentence is symbolical of what is said in the second. 'The rectification of the country' is the reality of 'the successful progress.'

'The strong undivided line' in paragraph 3 is the fifth of the figure.

Out of rest comes movement to go on for an indefinite time, and be succeeded by rest again;—as says paragraph 4.

pleasure and, on the ground of that, movement following. The marrying away is of a younger sister.

3. 'Any action will be evil:'—the places (of the lines) are not those appropriate to them.

'It will be in no wise advantageous:'— the weak (third and fifth lines) are mounted on strong lines.

LV. 1. Făng has the signification of being great. It is made up of the trigrams (representing)

LIV. 1. Kwei Mei in this Appendix has the meaning simply of marriage, and for Mei we might substitute Nü, 'daughter' or 'young lady.' This appears from the writer's going on to point out, as elsewhere, the analogy between the growth of things in nature from the interaction of heaven and earth and the increase of mankind through marriage. He does this with a delicate touch. There is no grossness in the original any more than there is in the translation.

But how are we to reconcile this reference to the action of heaven and earth with the bad auspice of the Thwan? The Khang-hsî editors felt the pressure of this difficulty, and they adduce a similar inconsistency in the account of hexagram 44 in this treatise, adding, 'From this we may say that the interaction of the yin and yang cannot be dispensed with, but that we ought to be careful about it in the beginning in order to prevent mischief in the end. This is the doctrine of the Yî.' This is very well, but it is no solution of the difficulty. The editors could not admit that the author of the Appendix did not understand or did not deal fairly with the Text; for that author, they thought, was Confucius.

2. The same editors say that paragraph 2 implies both that the desire for the marriage originated with the lady, and that she was aware that the gentleman was older than herself.

3. The position of a divided line above an undivided is always represented as an evil omen; it is difficult to understand why. There is less of an appearance of reason about it than in some other things which are said about the lines. The lines are where they cannot but be from the way in which the figures were formed.

intelligence and movement directed by that intelligence. It is thus that it has that signification.

2. 'The king has reached the condition (denoted by Făng):'—he has still to make it greater.

'There is no occasion to be anxious. Let him be as the sun at noon:'—it is for him to cause his light to shine on all under the sky.

3. When the sun has reached the meridian height, it begins to decline. When the moon has become full, it begins to wane. The (interaction of) heaven and earth is now vigorous and abundant, now dull and scanty, growing and diminishing according to the seasons. How much more must it be so with (the operations of) men! How much more also with the spiritual agency!

LVI. 1. 'Lü indicates that there may be some small attainment and progress:'—the weak (line) occupies the central place in the outer (trigram), and is obedient to the strong (lines on either side of it). (We have also the attributes of quiet) resting closely attached to intelligence (in the com-

---

LV. The Khang-hsî editors remark that paragraph 1 is not so much explaining the meaning of the name Făng, as accounting for the hexagram, composed of Lî and *K*ăn, having such a meaning.

Paragraph 3 seems rather contrary to the lesson of the hexagram. According to it, prosperity cannot be maintained, any more than we can have the other seasons without winter or perpetual day without night; but the object of the essay is to exhort to the maintenance of prosperity. Is it the case that the rise of every commonwealth and cause must be followed by its decay and fall? The mind refuses to admit the changes of the seasons, &c., as a true analogy for all moral and intellectual movements. See an important remark on the concluding sentence in the Introduction, pp. 34, 35.

ponent trigrams). Hence it is said, 'There may be some small attainment and progress. If the stranger or traveller be firm and correct as he ought to be, there will be good fortune.'

2. Great is the time and great is the right course to be taken as intimated in Lü!

LVII. 1. The double Sun shows how, in accordance with it, (governmental) orders are reiterated.

2. (We see that) the strong (fifth line) has penetrated into the central and correct place, and the will (of its subject) is being carried into effect; (we see also) the weak (first and fourth lines) both obedient to the strong lines (above them). It is hence said, 'There will be some little attainment and progress. There will be advantage in movement onward in whatever direction. It will be advantageous also to see the great man.'

LVI. What is said in paragraph 1 is intended to explain the Thwan, and not to account for the meaning of the name Lü. It is assumed that Lü means a stranger; and the writer from the position of the fifth line, and from the attributes of the component trigrams, derives the ideas of humility, docility, a quiet restfulness, and intelligence as the characteristics proper to a stranger, and which are likely to lead to his attaining what he desires, and then advancing.

LVII. 1. The language of this paragraph has often occurred to me in reading commands and addresses issued by the emperors of China, such as the essays on the precepts in what is called the Sacred Edict, the reiteration employed in many of which is remarkable.

Paragraph 2. The 'obedience of the weak lines to the strong ones' grows, in a way not very perceptible, from the idea of the hexagram, and the quality of the trigram as denoting penetration and flexibility.

LVIII. 1. Tui has the meaning of pleased satisfaction.

2. (We have) the strong (lines) in the centre, and the weak (lines) on the outer edge (of the two trigrams), (indicating that) in pleasure what is most advantageous is the maintenance of firm correctness. Through this there will be found an accordance with (the will of) heaven, and a correspondence with (the feelings of) men. When (such) pleasure goes before the people, (and leads them on), they forget their toils; when it animates them in encountering difficulties, they forget (the risk of) death. How great is (the power of) this pleased satisfaction, stimulating in such a way the people!

LIX. 1. 'Hwan intimates that there will be progress and success:'—(we see) the strong line (in the second place) of the lower trigram, and not suffering any extinction there; and (also) the weak line occupying its place in the outer trigram, and uniting (its action) with that of the line above.

2. 'The king goes to his ancestral temple:'—the king's (mind) is without any deflection.

3. 'It will be advantageous to cross the great stream:'—(the subject of the hexagram) rides in

LVIII. The feeling of pleasure going before the people and leading them on to endure toil and encounter death must be supposed to be produced in them by the example and lessons of their ruler. Lü Fañ-hsien paraphrases this portion of the text thus:—'When the sage with this precedes them, he can make them endure toil without any wish to decline it, and go with him into difficulty and danger without their having any fear.' I think this was intended to be the teaching of the hexagram, but the positive expression of it is hardly discernible.

(a vessel of) wood (over water), and will do so with success.

LX. 1. '*K*ieh intimates progress and attainment:'—the strong and weak (lines) are equally divided, and the strong lines occupy the central places.

2. 'If the regulations (which *K*ieh prescribes) be severe and difficult, they cannot be permanent:'—its course (of action) will in that case come to an end.

3. (We have the feeling of) pleasure and satisfaction directing the course amidst peril. (We have) all regulations controlled (by authority) in its proper place. (We have) free action proceeding from the central and correct position.

4. Heaven and earth observe their regular terms, and we have the four seasons complete. (If rulers) frame their measures according to (the due) regulations, the resources (of the state) suffer no injury, and the people receive no hurt.

LIX. 1. This paragraph has been partially anticipated in the notes on the Thwan. The second line is said to suffer 'no extinction,' because the lower trigram is that of peril. The Khang-hsî editors say that the former part of this paragraph shows how the root of the work of the hexagram is strengthened, and the latter part how the execution of that work is secured.

The conclusion of paragraph 2 is, literally, 'The king indeed is in the middle.' This does not mean, as some say, that the king is in the middle of the temple, but that his mind or heart is exactly set on the central truth of what is right and good.

The upper trigram Sun represents both wind and wood. To explain the meaning of Hwan, the significance of wind is taken; the writer here seizes on that of wood, as furnishing materials for a boat in which the great stream can be crossed.

LX. Paragraph 1. See what is said on the Text of the Thwan.

LXI. 1. In *K*ung Fû we have the (two) weak lines in the innermost part (of the figure), and strong lines occupying the central places (in the trigrams). (We have the attributes) of pleased satisfaction and flexible penetration. Sincerity (thus symbolled) will transform a country.

2. 'Pigs and fish (are moved), and there will be good fortune:'—sincerity reaches to (and affects even) pigs and fishes.

'There will be advantage in crossing the great stream:'—(we see in the figure) one riding on (the emblem of) wood, which forms an empty boat.

3. In (the exercise of the virtue denoted by) *K*ung Fû, (it is said that) 'there will be advantage in being firm and correct:'—in that virtue indeed we have the response (of man) to Heaven.

'Its course will come to an end' is the opposite of the intimation in *K*ieh of progress and attainment.

In paragraph 3 the writer returns to this intimation of the figure:—by the attributes of the trigrams; by the appropriate positions of lines 4 and 5; and by the central and correct place of 5.

Paragraph 4 illustrates the importance of doing things according to rule by reference to the operations of nature and the enactments and institutions of sage rulers.

LXI. 1. The structure of the lineal figure which is here insisted on has been pointed out in explaining the Thwan. On what is further said as to the attributes of the trigrams and their effect, *Kh*ăng-ʒze observes:—'We have in the sincerity shown in the upper trigram superiors condescending to those below them in accordance with their peculiarities, and we have in that of the lower those below delighted to follow their superiors. The combination of these two things leads to the transformation of the country and state.'

Paragraph 2. The two divided lines in the middle of the figure are supposed to give the semblance of an empty boat, and an

LXII. 1. In Hsiâo Kwo (we see) the small (lines) exceeding the others, and (giving the intimation of) progress and attainment.

2. Such 'exceeding, in order to its being advantageous, must be associated with firmness and correctness:'—that is, it must take place (only) according to (the requirements of) the time.

3. The weak (lines) are in the central places, and hence (it is said that what the name denotes) may be done in small affairs, and there will be good fortune.

4. Of the strong (lines one) is not in its proper place, and (the other) is not central, hence it is said that (what the name denotes) 'should not be done in great affairs.'

5. (In the hexagram) we have 'the symbol of a bird on the wing, and of the notes that come down from such a bird, for which it is better to descend than to ascend, thereby leading to great good fortune:'—to ascend is contrary to what is reasonable in the case, while to descend is natural and right.

---

empty boat, it is said (with doubtful truth), is not liable to be upset. The trigram Sun symbolises both wind and wood.

A good commentary on paragraph 3 is supplied in many passages of 'the Doctrine of the Mean,' e.g. chap. 20. 18:—'Sincerity is the way of Heaven. The attainment of sincerity is the way of men.'

LXII. Paragraph 1. That the small lines exceed the others appears at a glance. The intimation of progress and attainment is less clear. Compare the first paragraph of Appendix I to hexagram 33.

'The requirements of the time' in paragraph 2 cannot make

LXIII. 1. '*Kî* 3î intimates progress and success:'—in small matters, that is, there will be that progress and success.

2. 'There will be advantage in being firm and correct:'—the strong and weak (lines) are correctly arranged, each in its appropriate place.

3. 'There has been good fortune in the beginning:'—the weak (second line) is in the centre.

4. 'In the end' there is a cessation (of effort), and 'disorder arises:'—the course (that led to rule and order) is (now) exhausted.

LXIV. 1. 'Wei 3î intimates progress and success (in the circumstances which it implies):'—the weak (fifth) line is in the centre.

2. 'The young fox has nearly crossed the stream:'—but he has not yet escaped from the midst (of the danger and calamity).

---

right wrong or wrong right; but they may modify the conventional course to be taken in any particular case.

It is easy to explain paragraphs 3 and 4, but what is said in them carries no conviction to the mind.

The sentiment of paragraph 5 is good, apart from the symbolism, which is only perplexing.

LXIII. For paragraphs 1 and 2, see the note on the Text of the Thwan.

It is difficult to see the concatenation in paragraph 3 between the sentiment of the Thwan and the nature of the second line. The Khang-hsî editors compare this hexagram and the next with 11 and 12, observing that the goodness of Thâi (11) is concentrated, as here, in the second line.

The sentiment of paragraph 4 is that which we have often met with,—that things move on with a constant process of change. Disorder succeeds to order, and again order to disorder.

'Its tail gets immersed. There will be no advantage in any way:'—there is not at the end a continuance (of the purpose) at the beginning. Although the places (of the different lines) are not those appropriate to them, yet a strong (line) and a weak (line always) respond to each other.

LXIV. Paragraph 1. The indication is derived from the fifth line, divided, which is in the ruler's place. It occupies a strong place, has for its correlate the strong 2, and is itself in the centre of the yin trigram Lî.

Paragraph 2. Line 2 represents 'the young fox.' A strong line in the midst of the trigram of peril, its subject will be restless; and responding to the ruler in 5, he will be forward and incautious in taking action. The issue will be evil, and the latter end different from the beginning. What is said in the last sentence shows further how Wei 3î indicates progress.

APPENDIX II.

Treatise on the Symbolism of the Hexagrams, and of the duke of *K*âu's Explanations of the several Lines.

SECTION I.

I. Heaven, in its motion, (gives the idea of) strength. The superior man, in accordance with this, nerves himself to ceaseless activity.

1. 'The dragon lies hid in the deep;—it is not the time for active doing:'—(this appears from) the strong and undivided line's being in the lowest place.

2. 'The dragon appears in the field:'—the diffusion of virtuous influence has been wide.

3. 'Active and vigilant all the day:'—(this refers to) the treading of the (proper) path over and over again.

4. 'He seems to be leaping up, but is still in the deep:'—if he advance, there will be no error.

5. 'The dragon is on the wing in the sky:'—the great man rouses himself to his work.

6. 'The dragon exceeds the proper limits;—there will be occasion for repentance:'—a state of fulness, that is, should not be indulged in long.

7. 'The same undivided line is used' (in all the places of this hexagram), but the attribute of heaven (thereby denoted) should not (always) take the foremost place.

Like the Text under each hexagram, what is said under each in this treatise on its symbolism is divided into two portions. The

II. The (capacity and sustaining) power of the earth is what is denoted by Khwăn. The superior man, in accordance with this, with his large virtue supports (men and) things.

1. 'He is treading on hoarfrost;—the strong ice will come (by and by):'—the cold (air) has begun to take form. Allow it to go on quietly according to its nature, and (the hoarfrost) will come to strong ice.

2. The movement indicated by the second line, divided, is 'from the straight (line) to the square.' '(Its operation), without repeated effort, in every way advantageous,' shows the brilliant result of the way of earth.

3. 'He keeps his excellence under restraint, but firmly maintains it:'—at the proper time he will manifest it. 'He may have occasion to engage in the king's service:'—great is the glory of his wisdom.

---

first is called 'the Great Symbolism,' and is occupied with the trigrammatic composition of the hexagram, to the statement of which is always subjoined an exhibition of the use which should be, or has been, made of the lesson suggested by the meaning of the whole figure in the administration of affairs, or in self-government. If the treatise be rightly ascribed to Confucius, this practical application of the teaching of the symbols is eminently characteristic of his method in inculcating truth and duty; though we often find it difficult to trace the connexion between his premiss and conclusion. This portion of the treatise will be separated by a double space from what follows,—'the Lesser Symbolism,' in the explanations of the several lines.

I. *Kh*ien is formed by redoubling the trigram of the same name. In the case of other hexagrams of similar formation, the repetition of the trigram is pointed out. That is not done here, according to *K*û Hsî, 'because there is but one heaven.' But the motion of heaven is a complete revolution every day, resumed again the next; so moves 'the unwearied sun from day to day,' making it a good symbol of renewed, untiring effort.

4. 'A sack tied up;—there will be no error:'—this shows how, through carefulness, no injury will be received.

5. 'The yellow lower-garment;—there will be great good fortune:'—this follows from that ornamental (colour's) being in the right and central place.

6. 'The dragons fight in the wild:'—the (onward) course (indicated by Khwăn) is pursued to extremity.

7. '(The lines are all weak and divided, as appears from) the use of the number six:'—but (those who are thus represented) becoming perpetually correct and firm, there will thereby be a great consummation.

II. Khwăn is formed by redoubling the trigram of the same name and having 'the earth for its symbol.' As in the former hexagram, the repetition is emphatic, not otherwise affecting the meaning of the hexagram. 'As there is but one heaven,' says *K*û Hsî, 'so there is but one earth.' The first part of 'the Great Symbolism' appears in Canon McClatchie's version as—'Khwăn is the generative part of earth.' By 'generative part' he probably means 'the productive or prolific faculty.' If he mean anything else, there comes out a conclusion antagonistic to his own view of the 'mythology' of the Yî. The character Shî, which he translates by 'generative part,' is defined in Dr. Williams' dictionary as 'the virility of males.' Such is the special significance of it. If it were so used here, the earth would be masculine.

It is difficult to say exactly what the writer meant by—'The superior man, in accordance with this, and with his large nature, supports (men and) things.' Lin Hsî-yüan (Ming dynasty) says:—'The superior man, in his single person, sustains the burden of all under the sky. The common people depend on him for their rest and enjoyment. Birds and beasts and creeping things, and the tribes of the vegetable kingdom, depend on him for the fulfilment of their destined being. If he be of a narrow mind and cold virtue, how can he help them? Their hope in him would be in vain.'

'The Smaller Symbolism' is sufficiently dealt with in the notes on the Text.

III. (The trigram representing) clouds and (that representing) thunder form *K*un. The superior man, in accordance with this, (adjusts his measures of government) as in sorting the threads of the warp and woof.

1. Although 'there is a difficulty in advancing,' the mind (of the subject of the line) is set on doing what is correct. While noble, he humbles himself to the mean, and grandly gains the people.

2. The difficulty (to the subject of) the second line, divided, arises from its place over the undivided line below it. 'The union and children after ten years' shows things resuming their regular course.

3. 'One pursues the deer without the (guidance of the) forester:'—(he does so) in (his eagerness to) follow the game. 'The superior man gives up the chase, (knowing that) if he go forward he will regret it:'—he would be reduced to extremity.

4. 'Going forward after such a search (for a helper)' shows intelligence.

5. 'Difficulty is experienced (by the subject of the fifth line) in bestowing his rich favours:'—the extent to which they reach will not yet be conspicuous.

6. 'He weeps tears of blood in streams:'—how can the state (thus emblemed) continue long?

III. Khan represents water, especially in the form of rain. Here its symbol is a cloud. The whole hexagram seems to place us in the atmosphere of a thunderous sky overhung with thick and gloomy clouds, when we feel oppressed and distressed. This is not a bad emblem of the political state in the mind of the writer. When the thunder has pealed, and the clouds have discharged their

IV. (The trigram representing) a mountain, and beneath it that for a spring issuing forth form Măng. The superior man, in accordance with this, strives to be resolute in his conduct and nourishes his virtue.

1. 'It will be advantageous to use punishment:'—the object being to bring under the influence of correcting law.

2. 'A son able to (sustain the burden of) his family:'—as appears from the reciprocation between this strong line and the weak (fifth line).

3. 'A woman (such as is here represented) should not be taken in marriage:'—her conduct is not agreeable to what is right.

4. 'The regret arising from ignorance bound in chains' is due to the special distance of (the subject of this line) from the solidity (shown in lines 2 and 6).

5. 'The good fortune belonging to the simple lad without experience' comes from his docility going on to humility.

---

burden of rain, the atmosphere is cleared, and there is a feeling of relief. But I fail again to discern clearly the connexion between the symbolism and the lesson about the superior man's administration of affairs.

The subject of the first line of the Smaller Symbolism is represented by the undivided line, and therefore is firm and correct. He is noble, but his place is below the divided lines, symbols of the weak and mean (see Appendix IV, i, 1).

Line 2. 'Things resume their regular course:'—the subject is now at liberty to seek a union with the subject of line 5, according to the rules of the symbolism. Lines 1 and 4, 2 and 5, 3 and 6, the corresponding lines of the trigrams, are correlates.

The subject of line 4 naturally recurs to the correlate in line 1. He is the natural helper in the case, and he has the ability.

6. 'Advantage will come from warding off injury:'—(the subject of this line) above and (the ignorant) below, all do and are done to in accordance with their nature.

V. (The trigram for) clouds ascending over that

IV. 'The spring here issuing forth' is different from the defile with a stream in it, in the explanation of the Thwan; different moreover from 'rain,' mentioned also as the phenomenon which is the natural symbol of Khan. The presence of water, however, is common to the three. But the water of the spring, or of the stream, would flow away from the hill, and not be stopped by it; as an emblem therefore of the ignorance and inexperience denoted by Măng it is not suitable. *K*û Hsî says that 'the water of a spring is sure to move on and gradually advance.' This may serve as a symbol of the general process and progress of education, though it gives no account of the symbolism of the hill. It serves also to explain in part the transition of the writer to the subject of the superior man, and his dealing apparently with himself.

Does line 1 set forth the use of punishment as the dernier resort, undesirable, but possibly unavoidable, to bring men in subjection to law?

The force of line 2 comes out fully in the Thwan.

That a woman such as is represented in line 3 should not be taken in marriage is clear enough; but I do not see the bearing of the illustration on the proper lesson in the hexagram.

Line 3 separates 4 from 2, and 5 separates it from 6. Weak in itself, it is farther removed than any other from the two strong lines in the hexagram, and is represented as 'cribbed' in its ignorance.

The fifth is the most honourable place in the figure, and here is occupied by a weak line. This looks, however, to the occupant of line 2, less honourable than itself, and is marked by the two attributes that are named. Compare what is said on line 2.

A strong line in the topmost place must represent, according to the scheme of the hexagram, one who uses force in the cause of education; but the force is put forth not on the ignorant, but on those who would keep them ignorant, or increase their ignorance. The subject of this line, therefore, acts according to his nature, and the subjects of all the weak lines below are cared for as is best for them.

for the sky forms Hsü. The superior man, in accordance with this, eats and drinks, feasts and enjoys himself (as if there were nothing else to employ him).

1. 'He is waiting in the (distant) border:'—he makes no movement to encounter rashly the difficulties (of the situation). 'It will be advantageous for him constantly to maintain (the purpose thus shown), in which case there will be no error:'—he will not fail to pursue that regular course.

2. 'He is waiting on the sand:'—he occupies his position in the centre with a generous forbearance. Though 'he suffer the small injury of being spoken (against),' he will bring things to a good issue.

3. 'He is waiting in the mud:'—calamity is (close at hand, and as it were) in the outer (trigram). 'He himself invites the approach of injury:'—if he be reverent and careful, he will not be worsted.

4. 'He is waiting in (the place of) blood:'—he accommodates himself (to the circumstances of the time), and hearkens to (its requirements).

5. 'The appliances of a feast, and the good fortune through being firm and correct,' are indicated by (the position in) the central and correct place.

6. 'Guests come unurged (to give their help), and if (the subject of the line) receive them respectfully, there will be good fortune in the end:'—though the occupant and the place are not suited to each other, there has been no great failure (in what has been done).

V. 'The cloud,' it is said, 'that has risen to the top of the sky, has nothing more to do till it is called on, in the harmony of heaven

VI. (The trigram representing) heaven and (that representing) water, moving away from each other, form Sung. The superior man, in accordance with this, in the transaction of affairs takes good counsel about his first steps.

1. 'He does not perpetuate the matter about which (the contention is):'—contention should not be prolonged. Although 'he may suffer the small (injury) of being spoken against,' his argument is clear.

2. 'He is unequal to the contention; he retires and keeps concealed, stealthily withdrawing from it:'—for him from his lower place to contend with (the stronger one) above, would be to (invite) calamity, as if he brought it with his hand to himself.

3. 'He confines himself to the support assigned

---

and earth, to discharge its store of rain.' This gives to the writer the idea of waiting; and the superior man is supposed to be taught by this symbolism to enjoy his idle time, while he is waiting for the approach of danger and occasion for action.

'The regular course' of the subject of line 1 seems to be the determination to wait, at a distance from danger, the proper time to act.

The subject of line 2, which is undivided and in the centre, is thereby shown to be possessed of a large and generous forbearance.

The recognition of the circumstances of the time, and hearkening to its requirements, explain, in paragraph 4, 'the retreat from the cavern,' which is not here repeated from the Text. The line being weak and divided, its subject knows his own incompetency, and takes this prudent step.

Kû says that he does not understand what is said under line 6,—that the occupant and the place are not suited to each other, for the yin line being in the sixth, an even place, seems to be where it ought to be. We are only surprised that cases of inconsistency in these explanations are not more numerous.

to him of old:'—(thus) following those above him, he will have good fortune.

4. 'He returns to (the study of Heaven's) ordinances, changes (his wish to contend), and rests in being firm and correct:'—he does not fail (in doing what is right).

5. 'He contends;—and with great fortune:'—this is shown by his holding the due mean and being in the correct place.

6. 'He receives the robe through his contention:'—but still he is not deserving of respect.

VII. (The trigram representing) the earth and in the midst of it that representing water, form Sze. The superior man, in accordance with this, nourishes and educates the people, and collects (from among them) the multitudes (of the hosts).

1. 'The host goes forth according to the rules (for) such a movement:'—if those rules be not observed, there will be evil.

VI. The symbolism here is different from that in the Text of the Thwan. We have the visible sky ascending and water or rain descending, which indicate, one hardly sees how, opposition and contention. The lesson as to the course of the superior man is a good one, but might with equal propriety be deduced from many other hexagrams.

Hsiang An-shih (Sung dynasty) says that the first part of paragraph 2 is all to be taken as the language of the duke of *K*âu, the characters being varied; the rest is the remark of the writer of this treatise.

It is observed that the returning to (the study of Heaven's) ordinances, and changing the wish to contend, in paragraph 4, are not two things, but only one; 'the ordinances (ming) meaning what is right in principle.' The wish to contend was wrong in principle, and is now abandoned.

'The robe' takes the place of 'the leathern sash' in paragraph 6; but the sash was merely an appendage of the robe.

2. 'He is in the midst of the host, and there will be good fortune:'—he has received the favour of Heaven. 'The king has thrice conveyed to him the orders (of) his favour:'—(the king) cherishes the myriad regions in his heart.

3. 'The host with the possibility of its having many idle leaders:'—great will be its want of success.

4. 'The host is in retreat; but there is no error:'—there has been no failure in the regular course.

5. 'The oldest son leads the host:'—its movements are directed by him in accordance with his position in the centre. 'Younger men idly occupy their positions:'—the employment of such men is improper.

6. 'The great ruler delivers his charges:'—thereby he rightly apportions merit. 'Small men should not be employed:'—they are sure to throw the states into confusion.

VII. 'The Great Symbolism' here is not more satisfactory than in other paragraphs of it which have already come before us. *K*û Hsî says:—'As the water is not outside the earth, so soldiers are not outside the people. Therefore if (a ruler) be able to nourish the people, he can get the multitudes (of his hosts).' Is the meaning this,—that originally the people and soldiers are one body; that a portion of the people are taken out from among the mass, as occasion requires, to do the duty of soldiers; and that the nourishment and education of the people is the best way to have good soldiers ready for use on any emergency? Compare the saying of Confucius in Analects XIII, xxx.

What is said on the second line, that the general 'has received the favour of Heaven,' refers of course to the entire confidence reposed in him by the ruler or king, the subject of line 5. In this way Thien here is equal to Thien wang, so frequent in the 'Spring and Autumn,' and meaning—'King by the grace of

VIII. (The trigram representing) the earth, and over it (that representing) water, form Pî. The ancient kings, in accordance with this, established the various states and maintained an affectionate relation to their princes.

1. From 'the seeking union with its object' shown in the first line, divided, there will be other advantages.

2. 'The movement towards union and attachment proceeds from the inward (mind):'—(the party concerned) does not fail in what is proper to himself.

3. 'Union is sought with such as ought not to be associated with:'—but will not injury be the result?

4. 'Union is sought (by the party intended here) with one beyond himself, and (in this case) with a worthy object:'—he is following (the ruler) above him.

5. 'The good fortune belonging to the most illustrious instance of seeking union and attachment' appears in the correct and central position (of the fifth line, undivided).

(The king's) neglecting (the animals) confronting him (and then fleeing), and (only) taking those who present themselves as it were obediently, is seen in

---

Heaven.' But the great powers given to the general are from the king's wish through him to promote the good of all the nation.

In military operations there must be one ruling will and mind. A divided authority is sure to be a failure. But 'a retreat' is no evidence of failure in a campaign. When advance would lead to disaster, retreat is the regular course to pursue.

Other ways can be found to reward small men. They ought not to be placed in situations where the condition of others will depend on them.

'his allowing the escape of those in front of him.' 'That the people of his towns do not warn one another (to prevent such escape),' shows how he, in his high eminence, has made them pursue the due course.

6. 'He seeks union and attachment without taking the first (step to such an end):'—there is no possibility of a (good) issue.

IX. (The trigram representing) the sky, and that representing wind moving above it, form Hsiâo *Kh*û. The superior man, in accordance with this, adorns the outward manifestation of his virtue.

1. 'He returns and pursues his own path:'—it is right that there should be good fortune.

2. 'By the attraction (of the subject of the former line) he returns (to its own course),' and is in the central place:—neither will he err in what is due from him.

3. 'Husband and wife look on each other with averted eyes:'—(the subject of line three is like a

---

VIII. 'Water upon the face of the earth' is supposed to be an emblem of close union. Of the mere fact of close union this may be accepted as a fair illustration, and of its completeness. Some other symbolism might set forth better the tendency of parties to union, and their seeking it. What is said about the ancient kings is more pertinent to the meaning of the hexagram than in many other applications in 'the Great Symbolism.' The king appears in it not only as the centre, but as the cause, of union.

'The other advantages' under line 1 refer to all the benefits that will result from sincerity and union, which are in themselves good.

It is hardly possible to make what is said under line 5, on the royal huntings, agree with the account of them given on the same line in the duke of *K*âu's text. I suspect that there is some corruption of the text. The two verbs 'neglecting' and 'taking' seem to be used, the one for the other.

husband who) cannot maintain correctly his relations with his wife.

4. 'He is possessed of sincerity; his (ground for) apprehension is dismissed:'—(the subjects of the lines) above agree in aim with him.

5. 'He is possessed of sincerity, and draws others to unite with him:'—he does not use only his own rich resources.

6. 'The rain has fallen and (the onward progress) is stayed:'—the power (denoted in the figure) has accumulated to the full. 'If the superior man prosecute his measures, there will be evil:'—he will find himself obstructed.

IX. The suitability of the symbolism here is made all to turn on the wind. 'Wind,' says *K*û, 'is simply the air, without solid substance; it can restrain, but not for long.' The wind moves in the sky for a time, and then ceases. The process of thought from the symbol to the lesson is not easily traced. Is it meant to say that virtue manifesting itself outwardly—in the carriage and speech—is, however good, but a small matter, admirable in an officer, or even a feudal lord, but that we look for more in a king, the Head of a nation?

*Kh*ăng-ȝze calls attention to the addition to the duke of *K*âu's explanation in the notice on line 2, that 'it is in the central place,' adding that this explains how the subject of the line restrains himself, and does not go beyond what is due from him.

Only half of the symbolism in the Text of line 3 is taken up here. Line 1, it is said, is far from line 4, the mauvais sujet of the hexagram, and little affected by it; line 2 is nearer, but, being in the centre, suffers little; line 3 is close on it, and, not being in the centre, comes under its evil influence; while line 6 gives no help.

Line 4 is weak, and in an even place, appropriate to it; and hence its subject is said to 'have sincerity.' Being the first line, moreover, of Sun, the two others take their character from it.

Line 5, being undivided, and occupying the most important place in the figure, according to the value usually attached to the lines, is

X. (The trigram representing) the sky above, and below it (that representing the waters of) a marsh, form Lî. The superior man, in accordance with this, discriminates between high and low, and gives settlement to the aims of the people.

1. 'He treads his accustomed path and goes forward:'—singly and exclusively he carries out his (long-cherished) wishes.

2. 'A quiet and solitary man, to whom, being firm and correct, there will be good fortune:'—holding the due mean, he will not allow himself to be thrown into disorder.

3. 'A one-eyed man (who thinks that he) can see:'—he is not fit to see clearly. 'A lame man (who thinks that he can) tread well:'—one cannot walk along with him. 'The ill fortune of being bitten' arises from the place not being the proper one for him. 'A (mere) bravo acting the part of a great ruler:'—this is owing to his aims being (too) violent.

4. 'He becomes full of apprehensive caution, and in the end there will be good fortune:'—his aim takes effect.

5. 'He treads resolutely; and though he be firm and correct, there is peril:'—this is due to his being in the position that is correct and appropriate to him.

---

said 'to be rich,' or 'to have rich resources.' With these he unites with the 'subjects' of line 4 to effect their common object.

Under line 6 we are told that the restraint is at its height, and the restrained should keep still for a time. The paragraph is metrical. The paragraphs to lines 1, 2, 3, all rhyme together. So do those to 4, 5; and now under 6, we have a couplet:—

'Lo! rain, lo! rest, the power is full!
Good man! hold hard. Obstructions rule.'

6. 'There will be great good fortune,' and that in the occupancy of the topmost line:—this is great matter for congratulation.

XI. (The trigrams for) heaven and earth in communication together form Thâi. The (sage) sovereign, in harmony with this, fashions and completes (his regulations) after the courses of heaven and earth, and assists the application of the adaptations furnished by them,—in order to benefit the people.

1. 'The good fortune of advance, (as suggested by the emblem of) the grass pulled up,' arises from the will (of the party intended) being set on what is external to himself.

2. 'He bears with the uncultivated, and proves himself acting in accordance with the due mean:'—for (his intelligence is) bright and (his capacity is) great.

3. 'There is no going away so that there shall not be a return' refers to this as the point where the interaction of heaven and earth takes place.

4. 'He comes fluttering (down), not relying on

X. 'The sky above and a marsh lying below it is true,' says *Kh*ăng-ȝze, 'in nature and reason; and so should be the rules of propriety on which men tread.' This symbolism is far-fetched; and so is the application of it, if in any way drawn from it. But it is true that the members of a community or nation must keep their several places and duties in order to its being in a state of good order.

For lines 1, 2, 3, and 4, see notes on the Text.

If we might translate the conclusion of what is said on line 5, by—'in the position that is correctly appropriate to him,' the meaning would be more clear, though still the assumption which I have pointed out on the Text would underlie the statement; and as evidently as there, what is said under line 6 is but a truism.

his own rich resources:'—both he and his neighbours are out of their real (place where they are). 'They have not received warning, but (come) in the sincerity (of their hearts):'—this is what they have desired in the core of their hearts.

5. 'By such a course there is happiness, and there will be great good fortune:'—(the subject of the line) employs the virtue proper to his central position to carry his wishes into effect.

6. 'The city wall returned back into the moat' shows how the (governmental) orders have (long) been in disorder.

XII. (The trigrams of) heaven and earth, not in intercommunication, form Phî. The superior man, in accordance with this, restrains (the manifestation of) his virtue, and avoids the calamities (that threaten him). There is no opportunity of conferring on him the glory of emolument.

XI. It is difficult to translate the application of 'the Great Symbolism' here, so that it shall be intelligible to a reader. *Khăng-ȝze* says:—'A ruler should frame his laws and regulations so that the people may avail themselves of the seasons of heaven, and of the advantages afforded by the earth, assisting their transforming and nourishing services, and completing their abundant and admirable benefits. Thus the breath of spring, calling forth all vegetable life, gives the law for sowing and planting; the breath of autumn, completing and solidifying all things, gives the law for ingathering and storing,' &c.

The subject of line 1 has 'his will on what is external to himself:'—he is bent on going forward.

*K*û Hsî explains what is said on paragraph 4, that the upper lines 'are out of their real place where they are,' or, literally, 'have lost their substantiality,' by the remark that 'their proper place, as being weak lines, is below.' The editors of the imperial edition prefer another explanation, on which I need not enter.

1. 'The good fortune through firm goodness, (suggested by) the pulling up of the grass,' arises from the will (of the parties intended) being bent on (serving) the ruler.

2. 'The great man, comporting himself as the distress and obstruction require, will have success:'—he does not allow himself to be disordered by the herd (of small men).

3. That 'his shame is folded in his breast' is owing to the inappropriateness of his position.

4. 'He acts in accordance with the ordination (of Heaven), and commits no error:'—the purpose of his mind can be carried into effect.

5. 'The good fortune of the great man' arises from the correctness of his position.

6. 'The distress and obstruction having reached its end, it is overthrown and removed:'—how could it be prolonged?

XII. 'The Great Symbolism' here is sufficiently explained in the first Appendix. The application, however, is here again difficult, though we may try to find in it a particular instance of the interruption of communication,—in great merit not meeting with its reward.

The subject of the first line is one of the cluster of small men who are able to change their mind, and set their hearts to love their ruler.

The subject of the second line is a 'great man,' and occupies the place in the centre.

The subject of the third line is weak, and does not occupy his correct position;—hence the symbolism.

The fourth line is near the fifth, the ruler's place. It is a strong line in an even place; but acting according to the will of Heaven or of the ruler, its subject gets his purpose carried out.

The subject of the fifth line is the great man, the ruler in his right place. Hence he is successful, and in the last line, we see

XIII. (The trigrams for) heaven and fire form Thung Žăn. The superior man, in accordance with this), distinguishes things according to their kinds and classes.

1. '(The representative of) the union of men is just issuing from his gate:'—who will blame him?

2. '(The representative of) the union of men appears in relation with his kindred:'—that is the path to regret.

3. 'He hides his arms in the thick grass:'—because of the strength of his opponent. 'For three years he makes no demonstration:'—how can he do anything?

4. 'He is mounted on his city-wall;' but yielding to the right, 'he does not proceed to make the attack (he contemplated).' (Where it is said), 'There will be good fortune,' (that shows how) he feels the strait he is in, and returns to the rule of law.

5. The first action of (the representative of) the union of men (here described) arises from his central position and straightforward character. 'The meeting secured by his great host' intimates that the opponents of it have been overcome.

6. '(The representative of) the union of men appears in the suburbs:'—his object has not yet been attained.

---

how the distress and obstruction are come to an end. It was in the order of change that they should do so.

XIII. The style of 'heaven and fire form Thung Žăn' is such as to suggest the appearance of fire ascending up, blazing to the sky, and uniting with it. The application of the symbolism is again perplexing.

In line 1, the party just issuing from his gate has all the world

XIV. (The trigram for) heaven and (that of) fire above it form Tâ Yû. The superior man, in accordance with this, represses what is evil and gives distinction to what is good, in sympathy with the excellent Heaven-conferred (nature).

1. This first line, undivided, of Tâ Yû shows no approach to what is injurious.

2. 'A large waggon with its load' refers to the (virtue) accumulated (in the subject of the line), so that he will suffer no loss (in the conduct of affairs).

3. 'A feudal prince presents his offerings to the son of Heaven:'—a small man (in such a position) does (himself) harm.

4. 'He keeps his great resources under restraint:'—his wisdom discriminates clearly (what he ought to do).

5. 'His sincerity is reciprocated by all the others:'—his sincerity serves to stir and call out what is in their minds. 'The good fortune springing from a display of proper majesty' shows how they might (otherwise) feel too easy, and make no preparation (to serve him).

---

before him, with which to unite. Selfish thoughts disposing to union have no place in him.

In line 2, union (only) with kindred implies narrowness of mind.

For line 3, see note on the Text.

In line 4, stress should be laid on 'yielding to the right.'

For line 5, see note on the Text.

The Khang-hsî editors append the following note to the last paragraph:—'Under line 1 it is said that "union in the open country indicates progress and success," while here it is only said that "with union in the suburbs there is no cause for repentance." Beyond the suburbs was the open country, and till the union reached so far, the object of the hexagram was not attained. We may truly say that Confucius was a skilful reader of the duke of *K*âu.' Of course the editors did not doubt Confucius' authorship of all the Appendixes.

6. 'The good fortune attached to the topmost line of Tâ Yû' arises from the help of Heaven.

XV. (The trigram for) the earth and (that of) a mountain in the midst of it form *Kh*ien. The superior man, in accordance with this, diminishes what is excessive (in himself), and increases where there is any defect, bringing about an equality, according to the nature of the case, in his treatment (of himself and others).

1. 'The superior man who adds humility to humility' is one who nourishes his (virtue) in lowliness.

2. 'The good fortune consequent on being firm and correct, where the humility has made itself recognised,' is owing to the possessor's having (the virtue) in the core of his heart.

3. 'The superior man of (acknowledged) merit, and yet humble:'—the myriads of the people will submit to him.

4. 'One, whose action would be in every way advantageous, stirs up his humility the more:'—(but in doing so) he does not act contrary to the (proper) rule.

5. 'He may advantageously use the force of arms:'—correcting, that is, those who do not submit.

XIV. 'Fire above the sky' will shine far; and this is supposed to symbolise the vastness of the territory or of the wealth implied in the possession of what is great. The superior man, in governing men, especially in a time of prosperity and wealth, must set himself to develope what is good in them, and repress what is evil. And this will be in accordance with the will of Heaven, which has given to all men a nature fitted for goodness.

All the comment that is necessary on the symbolism of the several lines may be gathered from the comments on the Text.

6. 'His humility has made itself recognised:'—(but) all his aims have not yet been attained. 'He may employ the force of arms, (but only) in correcting (his own) towns and state.'

XVI. (The trigrams for) the earth and thunder issuing from it with its crashing noise form Yü. The ancient kings, in accordance with this, composed their music and did honour to virtue, presenting it especially and most grandly to God,

---

XV. The earth is low, and in the midst of it is a high mountain; but I fail to see how this can symbolise humility. Nor does Regis' representation of it much improve the case:—'Monte' (ait glossa) 'nihil est altius in terra, quae est summe abjecta. At cum is declivis sit, imago esse potest humilis modestiae.' I find the following note on the paragraph in my copy of the 'Daily Lessons' (see Preface):—'The five yin lines above and below symbolise the earth; the one yang line in the centre is "the mountain in the midst of the earth." The many yin lines represent men's desires; the one yang line, heavenly principle. The superior man, looking at this symbolism, diminishes the multitude of human desires within him, and increases the single shoot of heavenly principle; so does he become grandly just, and can deal with all things evenly according to the nature of each. In whatever circumstances or place he is, he will do what is right.' This is certainly very ingenious, but one shrinks from accepting a view that is not based on the component trigrams.

Under line 1, 'nourishes his (virtue)' is, literally, 'pastures himself.' He is all humility. That makes him what he is.

Under line 4, 'the (proper) rule' is the rule proper for the subject of the line in his circumstances so near the place of the ruler.

Under line 5, 'the refusal to submit' makes an appeal to force necessary. Even the best and humblest ruler bears the sword, and must not bear it in vain.

*K*û Hsî bases all that is said under line 6 on its being a weak line; so that the humble ruler is unable even at the close of the action described in the figure to accomplish all his objects, and must limit his field even in appealing to arms.

when they associated with Him (at the service) their highest ancestor and their father.

1. 'The (subject of the) first line proclaims his pleasure and satisfaction:'—there will be evil; his wishes have been satisfied to overflowing.

2. '(He sees a thing) without waiting till it has come to pass; with his firm correctness there will be good fortune:'—this is shown by the central and correct position (of the line).

3. 'He looks up (for favours), while he indulges the feeling of satisfaction; there will be occasion for repentance:'—this is intimated by the position not being the appropriate one.

4. 'From him the harmony and satisfaction come; great is the success which he obtains:'—his aims take effect on a grand scale.

5. '(The subject of) the fifth line has a chronic complaint:'—this is shown by his being mounted on the strong (line). 'He still lives on without dying:'—he is in the central position, (and its memories of the past) have not yet perished.

6. 'With darkened mind devoted to the harmony and satisfaction (of the time),' as shown in the topmost (line):—how can one in such a condition continue long?

XVI. 'The Great Symbolism' here is more obscure than usual. A thunderstorm clears the air and removes the feeling of oppression, of which one is conscious before its occurrence. Is this all that is meant by making the trigrams of the earth and thunder form Yü, the hexagram of harmony and satisfaction? What is meant, moreover, by making the thunder 'issue,' as the Chinese text says, from the earth? Then as to the application of this symbolism, I can trace the author's idea but imperfectly. To say that the thunder crash suggested the use of music, as some critics do, is

XVII. (The trigram for the waters of) a marsh and (that for) thunder (hidden) in the midst of it form Sui. The superior man in accordance with this, when it is getting towards dark, enters (his house) and rests.

1. 'He is changing the object of his pursuit:'—but if he follow what is correct, there will be good fortune. 'He goes beyond (his own) gate to find associates:'—he will not fail (in the method he pursues).

2. 'He cleaves to the little boy:'—he cannot be with the two at the same time.

3. 'He cleaves to the man of age and experience:'—by the decision of his will, he abandons (the youth) below.

4. 'He is followed and obtains adherents:'—according to the idea (of the hexagram), this is evil. 'He is sincere in his course:'—showing his intelligence, and leading to achievement.

5. 'He is sincere in fostering what is excellent:'—his position is correct and in the centre.

---

absurd. The use of music at sacrifices, however, as assisting the union produced by those services between God and his worshippers, and the present and past generations, agrees with the general idea of the figure. I must suppose that the writer had in mind the sacrifices instituted by the duke of *K*âu, as related in the Hsiâo King, chap. ix.

Pleasure has operated injuriously on the subject of line 1. He calls attention to himself.

Only a part of the symbolism of line 2 is referred to here. Such an omission is not uncommon;—as in lines 3 and 4 also.

With 'the memories of the past not perishing' compare Mencius, II, Section i, chap. 1. 6–13.

In line 6 the action of the hexagram is over. If one puts off changing his evil way any longer, there remains no more hope for him.

6. 'The sincerity is firmly held and clung to, as shown in the topmost line:'—(the idea of the hexagram) has reached its extreme development.

XVIII. (The trigram for) a mountain, and below it that for wind, form Kû. The superior man, in accordance with this, (addresses himself to) help the people and nourish his own virtue.

1. 'He deals with the troubles caused by his father:'—he feels that he has entered into the work of his father.

2. 'He deals with the troubles caused by his mother:'—he holds to the course of the due mean.

3. 'He deals with the troubles caused by his father:'—in the end there will be no error.

4. 'He views indulgently the troubles caused by his father:'—if he go forward, he will not succeed.

5. 'He deals with the troubles caused by his father, and obtains praise:'—he is responded to (by the subject of line two) with all his virtue.

XVII. An explosion of thunder amidst the waters of a marsh would be succeeded by a tremulous agitation of those waters; so far there would be a following of the movement of the lower trigram by the upper. Then in the application of the symbolism we have an illustration of action following the time, that is, according to the time; which is a common use of the Chinese character Sui. Neither the symbolism, however, nor its application adds much to our understanding of the text.

Paragraph 1 consists of two lines that rhyme; and paragraphs 4 (two lines), 5, and 6 do the same. According to Kû Yen-wû, paragraphs 2 and 3 also rhyme; but this appears to me doubtful. The symbolism of these paragraphs is sufficiently explained in the notes on the Text. Some peculiarities in their style (in Chinese) are owing to the bonds of the rhyme.

6. 'He does not serve either king or feudal lord:'—but his aim may be a model (to others).

XIX. (The trigram for) the waters of a marsh and that for the earth above it form Lin. The superior man, in accordance with this, has his purposes of instruction that are inexhaustible, and nourishes and supports the people without limit.

1. 'The good fortune through the firm correctness of (the subject of the first line) advancing in company (with the subject of the second)' is due to his will being set on doing what is right.

2. 'The good fortune and every possible advantage attending the advance (of the subject of the second line), in company (with the subject of the first),' arises from the fact that those (to whom the advance is made) are not yet obedient to the ordinances (of Heaven).

3. 'He (shows himself) well pleased to advance:'—his position is not that appropriate to him. 'If he become anxious, however, about his action,' his error will not be continued.

4. 'The freedom from error consequent on the

XVIII. 'When the wind,' says *Kh*ăng-ȝze, 'encounters the mountain, it is driven back, and the things about are all scattered in disorder; such is the emblem of the state denoted by Kû.' 'The nourishing of virtue' appears especially in line 6; all the other lines belong to the 'helping of the people.'

The subject of line 1 has entered into the work of his father, and brings it about that his father is looked on as blameless. The 'due mean' of line 2 is according to the caution in the Text. The Khang-hsî editors interpret the explanation of line 5 as = 'he takes up (the course of his father) with all his virtue.' I think they are wrong.

advance in the highest mode' is due to the (various) appropriateness of the position.

5. 'What befits the great ruler' means the pursuing the course of the due mean.

6. 'The good fortune consequent on the advance of honesty and generosity' is due to the will (of the subject of the line) being set on the subjects of (the first two lines of) the inner (trigram).

XX. (The trigram representing) the earth, and that for wind moving above it, form Kwan. The ancient kings, in accordance with this, examined the (different) regions (of the kingdom), to see the (ways of the) people, and set forth their instructions.

1. 'The looking of a lad shown by the first line, divided,' indicates the way of the inferior people.

XIX. 'The earth descending or approaching the marsh' is, according to *K*û Hsî, symbolical of the approach of superiors to the inferior people, and then the two predicates about the superior man are descriptive of him in that approach, the instruction being symbolised by Tui, and the supporting by Khwăn. The Khang-hsî editors, wishing to defend the explanation of lin by 'great,' in Appendix VI, which they ascribe to Confucius, say:—'Lin means "great." The earth above the waters of the marsh shows how full those waters are, rising to the level of the earth, and thus expressing the idea of greatness.' This representation is lame and impotent.

*K*û Hsî says he does not understand what is said on line 2. The interpretation in my version is the ordinary one, but I am not satisfied with it. The Khang-hsî editors try to solve the difficulty; but I am not able to follow them.

The same editors compare the conclusion of paragraph 6 in the symbolism of hexagram 11. 'What is external' there, and 'what is internal here,' have, they say, the same reference,—the state, namely, of the whole kingdom, the expressions differing according to the different standpoints from which they are made. The view in the translation is that of *K*û Hsî. It is difficult to hold the balance between them. The newer view, perhaps, is the preferable.

2. 'The firm correctness of a woman, in peeping out from a door' is also a thing to be ashamed of (in a superior man).

3. 'He looks at (the course of) his own life, to advance or recede (accordingly):'—he will not err in the path (to be pursued).

4. 'He contemplates the glory of the kingdom:'—(thence) arises the wish to be a guest (at court).

5. 'He contemplates his own life(-course):'—he should (for this purpose) contemplate (the condition of) the people.

6. 'He contemplates his own character:'—he cannot even yet let his mind be at rest.

XXI. (The trigrams representing) thunder and lightning form Shih Ho. The ancient kings, in accordance with this, framed their penalties with intelligence, and promulgated their laws.

1. 'His feet are in the stocks, and he is deprived of his toes:'—there is no walking (to do evil).

2. 'He bites through the soft flesh, and (goes on)

XX. Wind moving above the earth has the widest sweep, and nothing escapes its influence; it penetrates everywhere. This symbolism is more appropriate to the subject in hand than that of many other hexagrams. Personal influence in a ruler effects much; but the ancient kings wished to add to that the power of published instructions, specially adapted to the character and circumstances of the people. Sun, representing the wind, is well adapted to denote this influence;—see the Analects, XII, xix.

The looking in line 1 is superficial, and does not reach far.

Line 3. 'He will not err in the path to be pursued;'—advancing or receding as is best.

Line 4. 'The glory of the kingdom' is the virtue of the sovereign and the character of his administration. With the sentiment compare Mencius, VII, i, chap. 21. 2.

to bite off the nose:'—(the subject of the line) is mounted on the strong (first line).

3. 'He meets with what is disagreeable and hurtful:'—his position is not the proper one for him.

4. 'It will be advantageous to him to realise the difficulty of his task and be firm, in which case there will be good fortune:'—his light has not yet been sufficiently displayed.

5. 'Let him be firm and correct, realising the peril (of his position), and there will be no error:'—he will possess every quality appropriate (to his position and task).

6. 'He wears the cangue and is deprived of his ears:'—he hears, but will not understand.

XXII. (The trigram representing) a mountain and that for fire under it form Pî. The superior man, in accordance with this, throws a brilliancy around his various processes of government, but does not dare (in a similar way) to decide cases of criminal litigation.

XXI. *Kh*ăng-ʒze says that thunder and lightning are always found together, and hence their trigrams go together to give the idea of union intended in Shih Ho. The one trigram symbolising majesty and the other brightness or intelligence, the application of the hexagram here is easier and more natural than in many other cases.

1. 'There is no walking:'—that is, the subject of the line will not dare to offend any more.

2. '"Being mounted on the strong first line" means,' says *Kh*ăng-ʒze, 'punishing a strong and vehement man, when severity is required, as is denoted by the central position of the line.'

4. 'His light has not been sufficiently displayed;' that is, there is still something for him to do:—he has to realise the difficulty of his position and be firm.

1. 'He can discard a carriage and walk on foot:'—righteousness requires that he should not ride.

2. 'He adorns his beard:'—he rouses himself to action (only) along with the (subject of the) line above.

3. 'The good fortune consequent on his ever maintaining firm correctness' is due to this,—that to the end no one will insult him.

4. 'The place occupied by the fourth line, divided,' affords ground for doubt (as to its subject); but '(as the subject of the third pursues) not as a robber, but as intent on a matrimonial alliance,' he will in the end have no grudge against him.

5. 'The good fortune falling to the fifth line, divided,' affords occasion for joy.

6. 'The freedom from error attached to (the subject of) the topmost line, with no ornament but the (simple white),' shows how he has attained his aim.

XXII. 'A mountain,' says *Kh*ăng-ȝze, 'is a place where we find grass, trees, and a hundred other things. A fire burning below it throws up its light, and brings them all out in beauty; and this gives the idea of ornament, or being ornamented. The various processes of government are small matters, and elegance and ornament help their course; but great matters of judgment demand the simple, unornamented truth.'

The subject of line 1 does not care for and does not need ornament. He will walk in the way of righteousness without it.

Paragraph 3 tells us that it is not ornament, but correct firmness, which secures the respect of others.

In the fourth place, and cut off from line 1 by 2 and 3, we might doubt how far the subject of 4 would continue loyal to the subject of 1. But he does continue loyal, through the character and object of the subject of 3.

The Khang-hsî editors say:—'Line 5 occupies the place of honour, and yet prefers simplicity and exalts economy; its subject

XXIII. (The trigrams representing) the earth, and (above it) that for a mountain, which adheres to the earth, form Po. Superiors, in accordance with this, seek to strengthen those below them, to secure the peace and stability of their own position.

1. 'He overthrows the couch by injuring its legs:'—thus (he commences) his work of ruin with what is lowest (in the superior man).

2. 'He destroys the couch by injuring its frame:'—(the superior man) has as yet no associates.

3. That 'there will be no error on the part of this one among the overthrowers' arises from the difference between him and the others above and below.

4. 'He has overthrown the couch, and (proceeds to injure) the skin (of him who lies on it):'—calamity is very near at hand.

5. 'He obtains for them the favour that lights on the inmates of the palace:'—in the end there will be no grudge against him.

6. 'The superior man finds himself in a carriage:'—he is carried along by the people. 'The small men (by their course) overthrow their own dwellings:'—they can never again be of use to them.

---

might change and transform manners and customs;'—it is a small matter to say of him that he affords occasion for joy.

The subject of line 6 has more of the spirit of the hexagram than in most hexagrams. His being clothed in simple white crowns the lesson that ornament must be kept in a secondary place.

XXIII. 'A mountain,' says Yü Fan (towards the end of the Han dynasty), 'stands out high above the earth; here it appears as lying on the earth:—plainly it has been overturned.' On the

XXIV. (The trigram representing) the earth and that for thunder in the midst of it form Fû. The ancient kings, in accordance with this, on the day of the (winter) solstice, shut the gates of the passes (from one state to another), so that the travelling merchants could not (then) pursue their journeys, nor the princes go on with the inspection of their states.

1. 'Returning (from an error) of no great extent' is the prelude to the cultivation of the person.

2. 'The good fortune attendant on the admirable return (of the subject of the second line)' is due to his condescension to the virtuous (subject of the line) below.

3. Notwithstanding 'the perilous position of him

---

other hand, Liû Mû (early in the Sung dynasty) says:—'A mountain has the earth for its foundation. If the earth be thick, the mountain preserves its height. So it is with the sovereign and people.' The application might be deduced from either view.

It is hard to tell whether 'the lowest' in paragraph 1 should be supplemented as I have done. If not, then the explanation is a mere truism.

*Kh*ăng-ȝze is precise and decisive in supplementing the explanation of paragraph 2 as in the translation.

See on the Text of lines 3 and 4.

On paragraph 5, the Khang-hsî editors say admirably:—'The fifth line is weak, and yet occupies the most honourable place in the figure,—emblematic of a queen; and as its subject leads on the subjects of the other lines to obtain the favours given to the inmates of the palace, she, it is plain, has neither jealousy nor any other injurious temper that might incur blame for tending to overthrow the ruler.'

Paragraph 6 shows the ruler restored to the favour of the people, and the restoration of concord in the state. The small men have done their worst, and there is an end of their attempts—for a time.

who has made many returns,' there will be no error through (his aiming after righteousness).

4. 'He moves right in the centre (among those represented by the other divided lines), and yet returns alone:'—his object is to pursue the (proper) path.

5. 'The noble return, giving no ground for repentance,' is due to (the subject of the line) striving to perfect himself in accordance with his central position.

6. 'The evil consequent on being all astray on the subject of returning' is because the course pursued is contrary to the proper course for a ruler.

XXIV. 'Thunder in the midst of the earth' is thunder shut up and silent, just able to make its presence felt. So is it with the first genial stirrings of life after the winter solstice; so is it with the first returning steps of the wanderer to virtue. As the spring of life has to be nursed in quietness, so also has the purpose of good. The ancient statutes here referred to must have been like the present cessation from public and private business at the time of the new year, when all the Chinese people are for a time dissolved in festivity and joy.

Canon McClatchie translates here:—'The ancient kings on this culminating day (i. e. the seventh) closed their gates,' &c. 'Culminating day' does not give us the meaning so well as 'the day of the solstice;' but where does the translator find the explanatory 'the seventh,' which he puts in parentheses? In my own 'salad' days of Chinese knowledge I fancied there might be in paragraph 1 of the Text some allusion to a primitive sabbath; but there is no ground for introducing 'seven days,' or 'the seventh day,' into this paragraph of the Great Symbolism.

'The virtuous subject of the first line' is in paragraph 2 called žăn, 'the benevolent' or 'loving.' It is the only case in all the symbolism of the Yî where we find that term used as an adjective. It is emphatic here for 'humanity,' man in his ideal.

The other paragraphs present nothing for remark beyond what has been said on the Text of the duke of *K*âu.

XXV. The thunder rolls all under the sky, and to (every)thing there is given (its nature), free from all insincerity. The ancient kings, in accordance with this, (made their regulations) in complete accordance with the seasons, thereby nourishing all things.

1. When 'he who is free from insincerity makes any movement,' he will get what he desires.

2. 'He reaps without having ploughed:'—(the thought of) riches to be got had not risen (in his mind).

3. 'The passer-by gets the ox:'—this proves a calamity to the people of the neighbourhood.

4. 'If he can remain firm and correct there will be no error:'—he firmly holds fast (his correctness).

5. 'Medicine in the case of one who is free from insincerity!'—it should not be tried (at all).

6. 'The action (in this case) of one who is free from insincerity' will occasion the calamity arising from action (when the time for it is) exhausted.

XXV. The composition of the hexagram is given here in a manner different from what we have met with in the account of any of the preceding figures; and as the text is not called in question, I have made the best I could in the translation of the two commencing clauses. The application of the symbolism to what the ancient kings did is also hard to comprehend.

The paragraph on line 1 is another way of saying that in the course of things real goodness may be expected to be fortunate,—'by the appointment of Heaven.'

Paragraph 2. 'The thought of getting rich had not risen in his mind:'—he did what he did, because it was right, not because of the gain it would bring him.

On paragraph 3, it is said, 'The superior man seeks simply to be free from insincerity, and leaves the questions of happiness and calamity to Heaven.'

Paragraph 5. 'Sickness ought not to happen to one who

XXVI. (The trigram representing) a mountain, and in the midst of it that (representing) heaven, form Tâ *Kh*û. The superior man, in accordance with this, stores largely in his memory the words and deeds of former men, to subserve the accumulation of his virtue.

1. 'He is in a position of peril; it will be advantageous for him to stop his advance:'—he should not rashly expose himself to calamity.

2. '(He is as) a carriage from which the strap under it has been removed:'—being in the central position, he will incur no blame.

3. 'There will be advantage in whatever direction he may advance:'—(the subject of) the topmost line is of the same mind with him.

4. 'The great good fortune indicated by the fourth line, divided,' shows that there is occasion for joy.

5. 'The good fortune indicated by the fifth line, divided,' shows that there is occasion for congratulation.

6. 'In command of the firmament of heaven:'—the way is grandly open for movement.

---

is perfectly sincere. If it do happen, he must refer it to some inexplicable will of Heaven. As that has afflicted, so it will cure.'

Paragraph 6. 'When a thing is over and done, submission and acquiescence are what are required, and not renewed attempts at action.'

XXVI. I have quoted, in the Introduction, p. 37, *K*û Hsî's remark on the Great Symbolism here. *Kh*ăng-ȝze says:—'Heaven is the greatest of all things, and its being in the midst of a mountain gives us the idea of a very large accumulation. And so great

XXVII. (The trigram representing) a mountain and under it that for thunder form 頤. The superior man, in accordance with this, (enjoins) watchfulness over our words, and the temperate regulation of our eating and drinking.

1. 'You look at me till your (lower) jaw hangs down:'—(the subject of the line) is thus shown unfit to be thought noble.

2. 'The evil of advance by the subject of the second line, divided,' is owing to his leaving in his movements his proper associates.

3. 'For ten years let him not take any action:'—his course is greatly opposed (to what is right).

4. 'The good fortune attached to looking downwards for (the power to) nourish,' shows how brilliant will be the diffusion (of that power) from (the subject of the line's) superior position.

5. 'The good fortune from abiding in firmness' is due to the docility (of the subject of the line) in following (the subject of the line) above.

6. 'The good fortune, notwithstanding the peril

---

is the labour of the superior man in learning, acquiring, and remembering, to accumulate his virtue.'

Paragraph 1. The 'calamity' is that of opposition from, or repression by, the subject of line 4.

Paragraph 3. When the action of the hexagram has reached line 6, its work is done. The subject of 6 will no longer exercise repression, but join with that of 3, assisting him to advance.

Paragraph 4. The subject of line 4 has indeed occasion for joy. Without the use of punishment for crimes committed, by precaution anticipating them, without any trouble he has repressed evil. The 'joy' gives place in paragraph 5 to 'congratulation,' the people being all interested in the action of the ruler.

of his position, of him from whom comes the nourishing,' affords great cause for congratulation.

XXVIII. (The trigram representing) trees hidden beneath that for the waters of a marsh forms Tâ Kwo. The superior man, in accordance with this, stands up alone and has no fear, and keeps retired from the world without regret.

1. 'He places mats of the white mâɔ grass under things set on the ground:'—he feels his weakness and his being in the lowest place, (and uses extraordinary care).

2. 'An old husband and a young wife:'—such association is extraordinary.

3. 'The evil connected with the beam that is weak' arises from this, that no help can be given (to the condition thus represented).

4. 'The good fortune connected with the beam curving upwards' arises from this, that it does not bend towards what is below.

5. 'A decayed willow produces flowers:'—but how can this secure its long continuance? 'An old

---

XXVII. I do not think that the Great Symbolism here is anything but that of a thunderstorm, dispersing the oppression that hangs over nature, and followed by genial airs, and the reviving of all vegetation. But there is nothing analogous to the thunder in the application. 'Words,' it is said, 'nourish virtue; food and drink nourish the body.'

Paragraph 1. As Mencius said, 'He that nourishes the little belonging to him is a little man.'

Paragraph 2. Neither the subject of line 1, nor of line 6, is the proper associate of 2.

The other paragraphs are sufficiently illustrated in the notes on the Text.

wife and a young husband:'—this also is a thing to be ashamed of.

6. 'Evil follows wading with (extraordinary) boldness (through the stream):'—but (the act) affords no ground for blame.

XXIX. (The representation of) water flowing on continuously forms the repeated Khan. The superior man, in accordance with this, maintains constantly the virtue (of his heart) and (the integrity of) his conduct, and practises the business of instruction.

1. 'In the double defile, he enters a cavern within it:'—he has missed his (proper) way, and there will be evil.

2. 'He will get a little (of the deliverance) that he seeks:'—he will not yet escape from his environed position.

3. 'Whether he comes or goes, he is confronted by a defile:'—he will never (in such circumstances) achieve any success.

XXVIII. *Kh*ăng-ȝze says on the Great Symbolism:—'The waters of a marsh moisten and nourish the trees. When here it is said that they destroy and extinguish the trees, their action is very extraordinary.' This explanation is very far-fetched; and so is what the same scholar says on the application of it. I need not give it here, nor have I found, or myself made out, any other more easy and natural.

Paragraph 2. 'Such an association is extraordinary:'—the characters also imply, perhaps, that it is successful.

Paragraph 3. The beam being broken, any attempt to sustain it will have no effect in supporting the roof.

Paragraph 5. The shoots produced in line 2 will grow into a new and vigorous tree. The flowers here will soon decay, and the withered trunk continue the same. For what will a young man marry an old woman? There will be no children;—it can only be from some mercenary object.

4. '(Nothing but) a bottle of spirits and a subsidiary basket of rice:'—(these describe) the meeting at this point of (those who are represented by) the strong and weak lines.

5. 'The water in the defile is not full (so as to flow away):'—(the virtue indicated by) the central situation is not yet (sufficiently) great.

6. 'The sixth line, divided, shows its subject missing his (proper) course:'—'there will be evil for three years.'

XXX. (The trigram for) brightness, repeated, forms Lî. The great man, in accordance with this, cultivates more and more his brilliant (virtue), and diffuses its brightness over the four quarters (of the land).

1. 'The reverent attention directed to his confused steps' is the way by which error is avoided.

2. 'The great good fortune (from the subject of the second line) occupying his place in yellow' is owing to his holding the course of the due mean.

3. 'A position like that of the declining sun:'—how can it continue long?

4. 'How abrupt is the manner of his coming!'—none can bear with him.

5. 'The good fortune attached to the fifth line,

XXIX. The application of the Great Symbolism is here more perplexing even than usual. What is said of the superior man is good, but there is no reference in it to the subject of danger.

The subject of line 3 goes and comes, moves up and down, backwards and forwards; making no advance. This can be of no use in extricating him from the danger.

Those represented in line 4 by the strong and weak lines are the ruler and his minister.

divided,' is due to its occupying the place of a king or a prince.

6. 'The king employs him in his punitive expeditions:'—the object is to bring the regions to a correct state.

Section II.

XXXI. (The trigram representing) a mountain and above it that for (the waters of) a marsh form Hsien. The superior man, in accordance with this, keeps his mind free from pre-occupation, and open to receive (the influences of) others.

1. 'He moves his great toe:'—his mind is set on what is beyond (himself).

2. Though 'there would be evil; yet, if he abide (quiet) in his place, there will be good fortune:'—through compliance (with the circumstances of his condition and place) there will be no injury.

3. 'He moves his thighs:'—he still does not (want to) rest in his place. His will is set on 'following others:'—what he holds in his grasp is low.

4. 'Firm correctness will lead to good fortune,

XXX. In the Great Symbolism Lî is used in the sense of brightness. There was no occasion to refer to its other meaning. 'The great man' rather confirms the interpretation of the 'double brightness' in the treatise on the Thwan as indicating the ruler.

Paragraph 2. As yellow is a 'correct' colour, so is the due mean the correct course.

Paragraph 3. 'The declining sun,' say the Khang-hsî editors, 'is an emblem of the obscuration coming over the virtue of the mind.'

Paragraph 4. 'None can bear with him' refers to the second part of the symbolism of the line, which is not given here.

and prevent all occasion for repentance:'—there has not yet been any harm from (a selfish wish to) influence. 'He is unsettled in his movements:'—(his power to influence) is not yet either brilliant or great.

5. 'He (tries to) move the flesh along the spine above the heart:'—his aim is trivial.

6. 'He moves his jaws and tongue:'—he (only) talks with loquacious mouth.

XXXI. In various ways the waters of a marsh, placed high above the adjacent land, will descend to water and fertilise them. This symbolism agrees sufficiently well with the idea of influence passing between a superior and inferior party in relation with each other. There is nothing in the representation, however, to suggest particularly the relation between husband and wife; and the more I think of it, the more doubtful it becomes to me that king Wan intended by the trigrams of this figure to give the idea of man and wife. The application of the symbolism is sufficiently appropriate. The commentators see in it especially the lesson of humility—emptiness of self, or poverty of spirit—in order that the influences to which we are subjected may have free course.

Paragraph 1. What is beyond one's self is represented by line 4, a proper correlate of 1. There is the desire to influence; but it is ineffectively exhibited.

Paragraph 2. 'Compliance (with the circumstances of his condition and place)' is merely another way of 'being firm and correct.'

Paragraph 3. The language, 'What he holds in his grasp is low,' makes *K*û Hsî and the older commentators generally understand low of lines 1 and 2, and their weak subjects. But 'following' leads the mind to the lines above, as the Khang-hsî editors point out. 'Low' is to be understood in the sense of 'mean.'

Paragraph 4. The 'being firm and correct' appears here as equivalent to the want of 'a selfish wish to influence.'

Paragraph 5. The triviality of the aim explains the ineffectiveness of the movement, but not its giving no occasion for repentance. That the mei which are moved are behind and above the region of the heart seems too mechanical and trivial an explanation.

XXXII. (The trigram representing) thunder and that for wind form Hăng. The superior man, in accordance with this, stands firm, and does not change his method (of operation).

1. 'The evil attached to the deep desire for long continuance (in the subject of the first line)' arises from the deep seeking for it at the commencement (of things).

2. 'All occasion for repentance on the part of the subject of the second line, undivided, disappears:'—he can abide long in the due mean.

3. 'He does not continuously maintain his virtue:'—nowhere will he be borne with.

4. (Going) for long to what is not his proper place, how can he get game?

5. 'Such firm correctness in a wife will be fortunate:'—it is hers to the end of life to follow with an unchanged mind. The husband must decide what is right, and lay down the rule accordingly:—for him to follow (like) a wife is evil.

6. 'The subject of the topmost line is exciting himself to long continuance:'—far will he be from achieving merit.

XXXII. How the interaction of wind and thunder symbolises the lesson of the hexagram, and especially the application in this paragraph of that symbolism, is a question I have not been able to solve.

Paragraph 1. The stress of what is said under line 1 is here made to lie on its being the first line of the figure.

Paragraph 2. Line 2 is in the centre of its trigram, and that position, here as often elsewhere, symbolises the course of its subject.

Paragraph 3. The Khang-hsî editors make the application here = 'nowhere can he bear (to remain).'

XXXIII. (The trigram representing) the sky and below it that for a mountain form Thun. The superior man, in accordance with this, keeps small men at a distance, not by showing that he hates them, but by his own dignified gravity.

1. There is 'the perilousness of the position shown by the retiring tail:'—but if 'no movement' be made, what disaster can there be?

2. 'He holds it as by (a thong from the hide of) a yellow ox:'—his purpose is firm.

3. 'The peril connected with the case of one retiring, though bound,' is due to the (consequent) distress and exhaustion. 'If he were (to deal as in) nourishing a servant or concubine, it would be fortunate for him:'—but a great affair cannot be dealt with in this way.

4. 'A superior man retires notwithstanding his likings; a small man cannot attain to this.'

5. 'He retires in an admirable way, and with firm correctness there will be good fortune:'—this is due to the rectitude of his purpose.

6. 'He retires in a noble way, and his doing so will be advantageous in every respect:'—he who does so has no doubts about his course.

From paragraph 5 it appears that what is right will vary in different cases. The lesson of the hexagram is perseverance in what is right in each particular case.

XXXIII. *K*û Hsî says:—'The sky is illimitable; a mountain is high, but has its limits; the union of these is an emblem of retiring.' I do not understand such embleming. *Kh*ăng-ȝze says:—'Below the sky is a mountain. The mountain rises up below the sky, and its height is arrested, while the sky goes up higher and higher, till they come to be apart from each other. In this we have an emblem of retiring and avoiding.' We feel somewhat as

XXXIV. (The trigram representing) heaven and above it that for thunder form Tâ *K*wang. The superior man, in accordance with this, does not take a step which is not according to propriety.

1. 'He manifests his vigour in his toes:'—this will certainly lead to exhaustion.

2. 'The second line, undivided, shows that with firm correctness there will be good fortune:'—this is due to its being in the centre, (and its subject exemplifying the due mean).

3. 'The small man uses all his strength; in the case of the superior man it is his rule not to do so.'

4. 'The fence is opened and the horns are not entangled:'—(the subject of the line) still advances.

5. 'He loses his ram and hardly perceives it:'—he is not in his appropriate place.

6. 'He is unable either to retreat or to advance:'—this is owing to his want of care. 'If he realise the difficulty (of his position), there will be good fortune:'—his error will not be prolonged.

---

if there were a meaning in this; but, as in many other cases, both the symbolism and its application are but dimly apprehended.

The symbolism of the various lines is sufficiently explained on the Text. Paragraph 5 is but a repetition of the Text without additional explanation.

XXXIV. In illustration of the symbolism of the trigrams here, *Kh*ăng-ȝze says well:—'Thunder rolling above in the sky and making all things shake is the emblem of great power.' In passing on to its application he starts with a beautiful saying of antiquity, that 'the strong man is he who overcomes himself.' That this thought was in the mind of the writer of the paragraph on the Great Symbolism I can well believe; but the analogy between the natural and the moral and spiritual worlds in passing from the phenomenon of thunder to this truth is a thing to be felt, and that can hardly be described.

XXXV. (The trigram representing) the earth and that for the bright (sun) coming forth above it form 3in. The superior man, according to this, gives himself to make more brilliant his bright virtue.

1. 'He appears wishing to advance, but (at the same time) being kept back:'—all-alone he pursues the correct course. 'Let him maintain a large and generous mind, and there will be no error:'—he has not yet received an official charge.

2. 'He will receive this great blessing:'—for he is in the central place and the correct position for him.

3. 'All (around) trust him:'—their (common) aim is to move upwards and act.

4. '(He advances like) a marmot. However firm and correct he may be, his position is one of peril:'—his place is not that appropriate for him.

5. 'Let him not concern himself whether he fails or succeeds:'—his movement in advance will afford ground for congratulation.

6. 'He uses his horns only to punish (the rebellious people of) his city:'—his course of procedure is not yet brilliant.

Paragraph 1. 'This will lead to exhaustion;' and from that will follow distress and other evils.

The central position and the due moral mean in paragraph 2 is another instance of the felt analogy referred to above.

In paragraph 3 nothing is added to the Text; and on the symbolism nothing is said.

Paragraph 5. 'He is not in his appropriate place:' this is said simply because an odd place ought to be filled by a strong line.

XXXV. The sun rising above the earth, and then travelling up to his meridian height, readily suggests the idea of advancing. On

XXXVI. (The trigram representing) the earth and that for the bright (sun) entering within it form Ming Î. The superior man, in accordance with this, conducts his management of men;—he shows his intelligence by keeping it obscured.

1. 'The superior man (is revolving his) going away:'—(in such a case) he feels it right not to eat.

2. 'The good fortune of (the subject of) the second line, divided,' is due to the proper fashion of his acting according to his circumstances.

3. With the aim represented by 'hunting in the south' a great achievement is accomplished.

4. 'He has (just) entered into the left side of the belly (of the dark land):'—he is still able to carry out the idea in his (inner) mind.

5. 'With the firm correctness of the count of *Kî*,' his brightness could not be (quite) extinguished.

6. 'He had at first ascended to (the top of) the sky:'—he might have enlightened the four quarters

---

the application of this symbolism, Hû Ping-wăn (Yüan dynasty) says:—'Of strong things there is none so strong as heaven; and hence the superior man after its pattern makes himself strong; of bright things there is none so bright as the sun, and after its pattern he makes himself bright.'

If the subject of line 1 had received an official charge, then when unrecognised by his sovereign, and obstructed in his progress, his correct course would have been to cease to advance, and retire from the office in which he was not allowed to carry out his principles.

There is nothing said on line 2 to explain particularly the symbolism of 'the grandmother' in the Text.

'The course of procedure' in paragraph 6 has still an element of force in it, which is more than 'the firm correctness' that was to king Wăn the ideal character of a feudal lord, and therefore his light is not yet that of the full-orbed sun.

of the kingdom. 'His future shall be to go into the earth:'—he has failed to fulfil the model (of a ruler).

XXXVII. (The trigram representing) fire, and that for wind coming forth from it, form *K*iâ *Z*ăn. The superior man, in accordance with this, orders his words according to (the truth of) things, and his conduct so that it is uniformly consistent.

1. 'He establishes restrictive regulations in his household:'—(he does so), before any change has taken place in their wills.

2. 'The good fortune attached to the second line, divided,' is due to the docility (of its subject), operating with humility.

3. When 'the members of the household are treated with stern severity,' there has been no (great) failure (in the regulation of the family). When 'wife and children are smirking and chattering,' the (proper) economy of the family has been lost.

4. 'The family is enriched, and there is great

XXXVI. The application of the Great Symbolism here is in itself sufficiently natural; but this meaning of the hexagram hardly appears in the text, till we come to the sixth line.

Paragraph 1. 'He thinks it right not to eat;'—he does not purposely fast; but when he has nothing to eat, he does not complain. He thinks it right that it should be so in the case.

Paragraph 2. 'The proper fashion of acting' is suggested by the weak line's being in the central place.

Paragraph 3. 'The great achievement is accomplished;' but such achievement was not what prompted to action.

Paragraph 4. 'The idea in his inner mind' is the idea of withdrawing from the position and escaping; but the meaning is obscure. See on the Text.

good fortune:'—this is due to the docility (belonging to the subject of the line), and its being in its correct place.

5. 'The influence of the king extends to his family:'—the intercourse between them is that of mutual love.

6. 'The good fortune connected with the display of majesty' describes (the result of) the recovery of the true character.

XXXVII. The Symbolism here is certainly far-fetched. 'As wind,' it is said, 'comes first from fire, so does transforming influence emanate from the family.' But the subject of the hexagram is the regulation and not the influence of the family. Then the application is good for the superior man's cultivation of himself; but this again is only connected indirectly with the regulation of the family.

The sooner preventive measures are presented to the youthful mind the better; but does not prohibition imply that a change in the good will has taken place?

In paragraph 2 'docility' is suggested by the weak line. 'The humility' comes out of Sun, the upper trigram, whose attribute is pliant flexibility.

Yü Yen (Yüan dynasty) ingeniously observes on paragraph 4 that the riches of a family are not to be sought in its wealth, but in the affection and harmony of its members. Where these prevail, the family is not likely to be poor, and whatever it has will be well preserved.

The mention 'of mutual love' is unusual in Chinese writings, and must be considered remarkable here. 'The husband,' says *Kh*ăng-ʒze, 'loves his helpmate in the house; the wife loves him who is the pattern for the family.' But however admirable the sentiment is, it comes from the mind of the writer, and is not drawn from the Text.

Paragraph 6. It is said on this, that the majesty is not designedly assumed or put on; but the effect of the character remoulded and perfected. The words of Mencius are aptly quoted in illustration of the lesson:—'If a man himself do not walk in the (right) path, it will not be walked in (even) by his wife and children.'

XXXVIII. (The trigram representing) fire above, and that for (the waters of) a marsh below, form Khwei. The superior man, in accordance with this, where there is a general agreement, yet admits diversity.

1. 'He meets with bad men (and communicates with them):'—(he does so), to avoid the evil of their condemnation.

2. 'He happens to meet with his lord in a bye-passage:'—but he has not deviated (for this meeting) from the (proper) course.

3. 'We see his carriage dragged back:'—this is indicated by the inappropriateness of the position (of the line).

'There is no (good) beginning, but there will be a (good) end:'—this arises from his meeting with the strong (subject of the topmost line).

4. 'They blend their sincere desires together, and there will be no error:'—their (common) aim is carried into effect.

5. 'With his hereditary minister (he unites closely and easily) as if he were biting through a piece of skin:'—his going forward will afford ground for congratulation.

6. 'The good fortune symbolised by meeting with (genial) rain' springs from the passing away of all doubts.

XXXVIII. The application here of the Symbolism is correct, but neither of them comes up to the idea of disunion which is in Khwei.

The various paragraphs seem to need no illustration beyond what may be found in the notes on the Text.

XXXIX. (The trigram representing) a mountain, and above it that for water, form *K*ien. The superior man, in accordance with this, turns round (and examines) himself, and cultivates his virtue.

1. 'Advancing will conduct to (greater) difficulties, while remaining stationary will afford ground for praise:'—the proper course is to wait.

2. 'The minister of the king struggles with difficulty on difficulty:'—in the end no blame will be attached to him.

3. 'He advances, (but only) to (greater) difficulty; he remains stationary, and returns to his former associates:'—they, (represented in) the inner (trigram), rejoice in him.

4. 'To advance will (only be to) encounter (greater) difficulties; he remains stationary, and unites (with the subject of the line above):'—that is in its proper place and has the solidity (due to it in that position).

5. 'He struggles with the greatest difficulties, while friends are coming (to help him):'—he is in the central position, and possesses the requisite virtue.

6. 'To advance will (only) increase the difficulties, while his remaining stationary will (be productive of) great (merit):'—his aim is to assist the (subject of the line) inside of him.

'It will be advantageous to meet the great man:'—by his course he follows that noble (lord of the figure).

XXXIX. The Symbolism is described here a little differently from the form of it in Appendix I. *Kh*ăng-ȝze brings the same meaning out of it, however, in the following way:—'We have here a steep and difficult mountain, and again on the top of that there

XL. (The trigram representing) thunder and that for rain, with these phenomena in a state of manifestation, form *K*ieh. The superior man, in accordance with this, forgives errors, and deals gently with crimes.

1. The strong (fourth) line and the weak line here are in correlation:—we judge rightly in saying that 'its subject will commit no error.'

2. 'The good fortune springing from the firm correctness of the second line, undivided,' is due to its subject holding the due mean.

3. For 'a porter with his burden to be riding in a carriage' is a thing to be ashamed of. 'It is he himself that tempts the robbers to come:'—on whom besides can we lay the blame? (See Appendix III, i, 48.)

4. 'Remove your toes:'—the places (of this line

---

is water; each of the two trigrams is an emblem of perilousness. There is peril, both above and below, in the figure; and hence it represents the difficulties of the state.' The application of the symbolism is illustrated by the words of Mencius, 'When we do not, by what we do, realise (what we desire), we must turn inwards and examine ourselves in every point.'

From the lesson in paragraph 2 we saw that the moral value of conduct is independent of failure or success. It is said, 'Though the difficulties be too great for him to overcome, the sage accepts his desire, in order to stimulate others to loyal devotedness.'

On paragraph 3, Khung Ying-tâ says:—'Of the three lines of the lower trigram only the third is yang, above the two others which are of the yin nature. They cling to it, and are represented as if rejoicing in it.

The view given of paragraph 4 is that of the Khang-hsî editors.

'The friends' in paragraph 5 are the subjects of the second line, the correlate of 5, and also of the two other lines of the lower trigram.

Sû Shih (A.D. 1036–1101) remarks on paragraph 6 that by 'the inside,' and 'the noble,' we are to understand the subject of line 5.

and of the third and first) are all inappropriate to them.

5. When 'the superior man executes his function of removing (whatever is injurious to the idea of the hexagram),' small men will of themselves retire.

6. 'A prince with his bow shoots a falcon:'—thus he removes (the promoters of) rebellion.

XLI. (The trigram representing) a mountain and beneath it that for the waters of a marsh form Sun. The superior man, in accordance with this, restrains his wrath and represses his desires.

1. 'He suspends his own affairs and hurries away (to help the subject of the fourth line):'—the (subject of that) upper (line) mingles his wishes with his.

XL. It is a common saying that thunder and rain clear the atmosphere, and a feeling of oppression is relieved. The last paragraph of Appendix I, however, leads us to understand the Symbolism of the phenomena of spring. The application seems to refer to the gentle policy of a conqueror forward to forgive the opposition of those who offer no more resistance.

The subject of line 2 is a minister or officer; and the Khang-hsî editors say that while straightforwardness, symbolised by the arrow, is the first duty of an officer, if he do not temper that quality by pursuing the due medium, which is symbolised by the yellow colour of the arrow, but proceed by main force, and that only, to remove what is evil, he will provoke indignation and rebellion. The 'three foxes' are not alluded to in this second paragraph.

On paragraph 4 the same editors say:—'The subject of this line is not in the central nor in an odd place; he has for his correlate the subject of line 1 and for his close associate that of line 3, both of which lines are weak in strong places. Hence it is said, that they are all in places inappropriate to them.'

What paragraph 5 says, that 'the small men retire,' means that believing in the sincerity of the ruler's determination to remove all evil men, they retire of themselves, or strive to conform to his wishes.

2. 'It will be advantageous for (the subject of) the second line, undivided, to maintain his firm correctness:'—his central position gives its character to his aim.

3. 'One man, walking,' (finds his friend):—when three are together, doubts rise among them.

4. 'He diminishes the ailment under which he labours:'—this is matter for joy.

5. 'The great good fortune attached to the fifth line, divided,' is due to the blessing from above.

6. 'He gives increase to others without taking from what is his own:'—he obtains his wish on a grand scale.

XLI. 'The waters of a marsh are continually rising up in vapour to bedew the hill above it, and thus increase its verdure; what is taken from the marsh gives increase to the hill.' This is very far-fetched. In the application again the superior man acts only on himself, and for himself;—which has nothing to do with those of low degree giving to those above them. This application, however, agrees with what, as we have seen on the Text, was *Kh*ăng-ȝze's view of the meaning of the hexagram.

The explanation appended to paragraph 1 seems to be to account for the subject of line 1 hurrying away to the help of line 4.

'His aim' is to abide where he is, and help the subject of 5 by the exhibition of 'firm correctness.'

The Khang-hsî editors observe that paragraph 3 is true indeed of three men; and not of three men only, but of many repetitions of thought or action.

The same editors say on paragraph 5 that 'the blessing from above is explained, by many, of the oracles obtained through divining with the tortoise-shell; but that looking at the text on line 2 of the next hexagram, and that Tî (spoken of there) is the lord of all spirits, the term "above" here is most naturally explained of Heaven's mind, whose acceptance cannot be gainsaid by men or spirits.'

*Kh*ăng-ȝze says on paragraph 6, though I do not see the rele-

XLII. (The trigram representing) wind and that for thunder form Yî. The superior man, in accordance with this, when he sees what is good, moves towards it; and when he sees his errors, he turns from them.

1. 'If the movement be greatly fortunate, no blame will be imputed to him:'—though it is not for one in so low a position to have to do with great affairs.

2. 'Parties add to his stores:'—they come from beyond (his immediate circle) to do so.

3. 'Increase is given by means of what is evil and difficult:'—as he has in himself (the qualities called forth).

4. 'His advice to his prince is followed:'—his (only) object in it being the increase (of the general good).

5. '(The ruler) with sincere heart seeks to benefit (all below):'—there need be no question (about the result). '(All below) with sincere heart acknowledge (his goodness):'—he gets what he desires on a great scale.

6. 'To his increase none will contribute:'—this expresses but half the result. 'Many will seek to assail him:'—they will come from beyond (his immediate circle) to do so.

---

vancy of his remarks:—'Dwelling on high, and taking nothing from those below him, but on the contrary giving more to them, the superior man accomplishes his aim on a grand scale. The aim of the superior man is simply to be increasing what others have;—that and nothing else.'

XLII. The Symbolism here is different from what we gather from the former Appendix. Sun no longer symbolises wood, but, as

XLIII. (The trigram representing) heaven and that for the waters of a marsh mounting above it form Kwâi. The superior man, in accordance with this, bestows emolument on those below him, and dislikes allowing his gifts to accumulate (undispensed).

1. 'Without (being able to) succeed, he goes forward:'—this is an error.

2. 'Though hostile measures be taken against him, he need not be anxious:'—he pursues the course of the due mean.

3. 'The superior man looks bent on cutting off the culprit:'—there will in the end be no error.

4. 'He walks slowly and with difficulty:'—he is not in the place appropriate to him.

'He hears these words, but does not believe them:'—he hears, but does not understand.

5. 'If his action be in harmony with his central

---

it more commonly does, wind. Thunder and wind, it is supposed, increase each the other; and their combination gives the idea of increase. Then the application, good in itself, must be treated very nicely, as it is by the Khang-hsî editors, in order to make out any connexion between it and the Symbolism.

Paragraph 1. 'One in a low position should not move in great affairs;'—not a son, it is said, while his father is alive; nor a minister, while his ruler governs; nor a member of an official department, while its head directs its affairs. If such a one do initiate such an affair, only great success will excuse his rashness.

Paragraph 2. Line 5 is the proper correlate of 2; and its subject will be among the contributing parties. But others 'beyond' will be won to take part with him.

Paragraph 3. There is a soul of good even in men who seem only evil; and adversity may quicken it.

Paragraph 6. As in line 2 the attractive power of benevolence is shown, so in line 6 we have the repulsive power of selfishness exhibited. Mark the 'from beyond' in both paragraphs.

position, there will be no error:'—but his standing in the due mean is not yet clearly displayed.

6. 'There is the misery of having none on whom to call:'—the end will be that he cannot continue any longer.

XLIV. (The trigram representing) wind and that for the sky above it form Kâu. The sovereign, in accordance with this, delivers his charges, and promulgates his announcements throughout the four quarters (of the kingdom).

1. 'Tied and fastened to a metal drag:'—(this

XLIII. We can only understand the mounting of the waters of a marsh up into the sky of the phenomenon of evaporation; and certainly the waters so formed into clouds will be condensed, and come down again as rain. This may be taken as an image of dispersion, but not of displacement in the sense of the Text of the hexagram.

The first clause of the application follows naturally enough from the above interpretation of the Symbolism. *K*û Hsî says he does not understand the second clause. Many critics adopt the view of it which appears in the translation.

Paragraph 2 does not mention the precautionary measures taken in the Text by the subject of the line, from which the conclusion would follow quite as naturally as from his central position. The Khang-hsî editors, however, say that the not having recourse lightly to force is itself the due course.

Line 3 responding, and alone of all the strong lines responding to 6, may appear at first irresolute, and not prepared for decided measures; but 'in the end' its subject does what is required of him.

The contiguity of line 5 to the divided 6, is supposed to have some bad effect on its subject, so that while he does what his central position requires, it is not without an effort. 'If a man,' says *Kh*ăng-ȝze, 'cherish a single illicit desire in his mind, he has left the right way. The admonition here conveyed is deep.'

describes the arrest of) the weak (line) in its advancing course.

2. 'He has a wallet of fish:'—it is right for him not to allow (the subject of the first line) to get to the guests.

3. 'He walks with difficulty:'—but his steps have not yet been drawn (into the course of the first line).

4. 'The evil' indicated by there being 'no fish in the wallet' is owing to (the subject of the line) keeping himself aloof from the people.

5. 'The subject of the fifth line, undivided, keeps his brilliant qualities concealed:'—as is indicated by his central and correct position.

'(The good issue) descends (as) from Heaven:'—his aim does not neglect the ordinances (of Heaven).

6. 'He receives others on his horns:'—he is exhausted at his greatest height, and there will be cause for regret.

XLIV. Wind, blowing all-under the sky, penetrates everywhere, and produces its natural effect; and it is a good application of this phenomenon that follows; but it has nothing to do with the meaning of Kâu and the interpretation of the hexagram, as taught in the Text. The Khang-hsî editors perceive this, and deal with the Symbolism after a method of their own, on which it is unnecessary to enter.

Paragraph 1. My supplement, 'This describes the arrest of,' is a conclusion from the whole of the Text on the line. All the commentaries have it.

In the 'Daily Lecture' it is said that the lesson of paragraph 2 is that 'the subject of the line should make the repression of 1 his own exclusive work, and not allow it to pass on to the subject of any of the other lines.' That view is rather different from the one indicated in my supplement.

'His steps have not been drawn into the course of the first

XLV. (The trigram representing the) earth and that for the waters of a marsh raised above it form 3hui. The superior man, in accordance with this, has his weapons of war put in good repair, to be prepared against unforeseen contingencies.

1. 'In consequence disorder is brought into the sphere of his union:'—his mind and aim are thrown into confusion.

2. 'He is led forward; there will be good fortune, and freedom from error:'—(the virtue proper to) his central place has not undergone any change.

3. 'If he go forward, he will not err:'—in the subject of the topmost line there is humility and condescension.

4. 'If he be grandly fortunate, he will receive no blame:'—(this condition is necessary, because) his position is not the one proper to him.

5. 'There is the union (of all) under him in the place of dignity:'—(but) his mind and aim have not yet been brilliantly displayed.

---

line:'—we have to supply, 'and therefore there will be no great error.'

Paragraph 4. See what is said on the Text. But that the subject of the line stands alone is owing, it is here implied, to his own impatience. If he could exercise forbearance, he would find a proper opportunity to check the advance of the subject of line 1.

The subject of line 5, while mindful of his task in the hexagram,—to repress the advance symbolised by 1,—yet keeps his wise plans concealed till the period of carrying them into execution, determined by the ordinances of Heaven, has arrived. Then comes the successful stroke of his policy as if it were directly from Heaven.

The subject of line 6 really accomplishes nothing to repress the advance of the unworthy; but he keeps himself from evil communication with them. He is not to be charged with blameable error, though more and better might have been expected of him.

6. 'He sighs and weeps:'—he does not yet rest in his topmost position.

XLVI. (The trigram representing) wood and that for the earth with the wood growing in the midst of it form Shăng. The superior man, in accordance with this, pays careful attention to his virtue, and accumulates the small developments of it till it is high and great.

1. 'He is welcomed in his advance upwards, and there will be great good fortune:'—(the subjects of) the upper (trigram) are of the same mind with him.

2. 'The sincerity of the subject of the second line, undivided,' affords occasion for joy.

3. 'He advances upwards (as into) an empty city:'—he has no doubt or hesitation.

4. 'The king employs him to prevent his offerings on mount *Kh*î:'—such a service (of spiritual Beings) is according to (their mind).

XLV. What has this Great Symbolism to do with the idea and preservation of union? The question is answered in this way:—A marsh whose waters are high up above the earth must be kept in by banks and dykes, to keep them together, to preserve them from being dispersed. So the union of a people must be preserved by precautions against what would disturb and destroy it. Of such precautions the chief is to be prepared to resist attack from without, and to put down internal sedition.

Paragraph 3. The topmost line is the last in Tui, whose attribute is complacent satisfaction, appearing in flexibility or docility.

Paragraph 5. 'His mind and aim have not yet been brilliantly displayed:'—this is in explanation of the case that some may even still not have confidence in him.

Paragraph 6. The topmost position is that of the trigram; the subject of the line might bid farewell to all the work of the hexagram; but he cannot bear to do so.

5. 'He is firmly correct, and will therefore enjoy good fortune. He ascends the stairs (with all due ceremony):'—he grandly succeeds in his aim.

6. 'He blindly advances upwards,' and is in the highest place:—but there is decay in store for him, and he will not (preserve) his riches.

XLVII. (The trigram representing) a marsh, and (below it that for a defile, which has drained the other dry so that there is) no water in it, form Khwăn. The superior man, in accordance with this, will sacrifice his life in order to carry out his purpose.

1. 'He enters a dark valley:'—so benighted is he, and without clear vision.

2. 'He is straitened amidst his wine and viands:'—(but) his position is central, and there will be ground for congratulation.

XLVI. See what has been said on the Great Symbolism in Appendix I. The application which is made of it here may be accepted, though it has nothing to do with the teaching of the Text about the gradual rise of a good officer to high social distinction and influence.

Paragraph 1. Instead of finding in this the three lines of Khwăn and their subjects, *Kh*ăng-ȝze makes 'the upper' denote only line 2.

Paragraph 2. The subject of line 2 in his loyal devotion to 5 will do much good and benefit many; hence we have the words, 'affords occasion for joy.'

Paragraph 3. 'He has no doubt or hesitation:'—but this is presuming rather on his strength.

Paragraph 4. The Khang-hsî editors say:—'Such an employment of men of worth to do service to spiritual Beings is serving them according to their mind.'

Paragraph 6. When one has reached the greatest height, he should think of retiring. Ambition otherwise may overleap itself.

3. 'He lays hold of thorns:'—(this is suggested by the position of the line) above the strong (line).

'He enters his palace, and does not see his wife:'—this is inauspicious.

4. 'He proceeds very slowly (to help the subject of the first line):'—his aim is directed to (help) that lower (line). Although he is not in his appropriate place, he and that other will (in the end) be together.

5. 'His nose and feet are cut off:'—his aim has not yet been gained.

'He is leisurely, however, in his movements, and is satisfied:'—his position is central and (his virtue) is correct.

'It will be well for him to be (as sincere as) in sacrificing:'—so shall he receive blessing.

6. 'He is straitened as if bound with creepers:'—(his spirit and action) are unsuitable.

'(He says), "If I move, I shall repent of it." And he does repent (of former errors), which leads to good fortune:'—so he (now) goes on.

XLVII. The first sentence of the Great Symbolism is constructed differently from any which has presented itself in the previous 46 hexagrams. Literally translated, it would be 'a marsh with no water is Khwăn;' and this might certainly suggest to us a condition of distress. But how does this come out of the trigrams? The upper one is Tui, representing a marsh; and the lower is Khân, representing water in a defile. The collocation of the two suggests the running of the water from the marsh or lake into the stream, which will soon empty the other. Such is the view which occurred to myself; and it is the same as that given by *K*û Hsî:—'The water descending and leaking away, the marsh above will become dry.' The application is good in itself, but the concatenation between it and the Symbolism is hardly discernible.

XLVIII. (The trigram representing) wood and above it that for water form 3ing. The superior man, in accordance with this, comforts the people, and stimulates them to mutual helpfulness.

1. 'A well so muddy that men will not drink of it:'—this is indicated by the low position (of the line).

'An old well to which the birds do not come:'—it has been forsaken in the course of time.

2. 'A well from which by a hole the water escapes, and flows away to the shrimps:'—(the subject of this second line has) none co-operating with him (above).

3. 'The well has been cleared out, but is not used:'—(even) passers-by would be sorry for this.

A prayer is made 'that the king were intelligent:'—for then blessing would be received.

4. 'A well the lining of which is well laid. There will be no error:'—the well has been put in good repair.

5. 'The waters from the cold spring are (freely) drunk:'—this is indicated by the central and correct position (of the line).

6. 'The great good fortune' at the topmost place

So stupid is the subject of line 1 that by his own act he increases his distress.

The Khang-hsî editors say that the 'ground for congratulation in paragraph 2 is the banqueting and sacrificing.' I rather think it is the measure of help, which it is intimated the subject will give in removing the straitness and distress of the time.

See the extract from the Khang-hsî editors on the symbolism of the third line of the Text.

The difficulties attending the symbolism of the Text of lines 4, 5, and 6 are not lightened by what we find in this Appendix.

indicates the grand accomplishment (of the idea in the hexagram).

XLIX. (The trigram representing the waters of) a marsh and that for fire in the midst of them form Ko. The superior man, in accordance with this, regulates his (astronomical) calculations, and makes clear the seasons and times.

1. 'He is bound with (the skin of) a yellow ox:'—he should in his circumstances be taking action.

2. 'He makes his changes when some time has passed:'—what he does will be matter of admiration.

3. 'The change (contemplated) has been three times fully discussed:'—to what else should attention (now) be directed?

4. 'The good fortune consequent on changing (existing) ordinances' is due to the faith reposed in his aims.

5. 'The great man produces his changes as the tiger does when he changes his stripes:'—their beauty becomes more brilliant.

XLVIII. The Great Symbolism here may well enough represent a well, it being understood that the water which is above the wood is that raised by it for irrigation and other uses. What is said, moreover, in the application is more akin to the idea of the hexagram than in most of the other cases. It is certainly one way in which the ruler should nourish the people.

It is said on paragraph 1:—'Those who have a mind to do something in the world, when they look at this line, and its symbolism, will learn how they ought to exert themselves.'

Rather in opposition to what I have said on the Text of line 4, the 'Daily Lecture' observes here:—'The cultivation of one's self, which is represented here, is fundamental to the government of others.'

6. 'The superior man produces his changes as the leopard does when he changes his spots:'—their beauty becomes more elegant.

'Small men change their faces:'—they show themselves prepared to follow their ruler.

L. (The trigram representing) wood and above it that for fire form Ting. The superior man, in accordance with this, keeps his every position correct, and maintains secure the appointment (of Heaven).

1. 'The caldron is overturned, and its feet turned upwards:'—but this is not (all) contrary (to what is right).

'There will be advantage in getting rid of what was bad:'—thereby (the subject of the line) will follow the more noble (subject of the fourth line).

2. 'There is the caldron with the things (to be cooked) in it:'—let (the subject of the line) be careful where he goes.

'My enemy dislikes me:'—but there will in the end be no fault (to which he can point).

3. 'There is the caldron with (the places for) its

XLIX. Wise men, occupying themselves with the determination of the seasons and questions of time, have in all ages based their judgments on the observation of the heavenly bodies. We find this insisted on in the first book of the Shû, by the ancient Yâo. But how this application of the Great Symbolism really flows from it, I must confess myself unable to discover. Once, however, when I was conversing about the Yî with a high Chinese dignitary, who was a well-read scholar also so far as his own literature was concerned, he referred to this paragraph as proving that all our western science had been known to Fû-hsî and Confucius!

What is said on the several lines is sufficiently illustrated in the notes on the Text.

ears changed:'—(its subject) has failed in what was required of him (in his situation).

4. 'The contents designed for the ruler's use are overturned and spilt:'—how can (the subject of the line) be trusted?

5. 'The caldron has yellow ears:'—the central position (of the line) is taken as (a proof of) the solid (virtue of its subject).

6. 'The rings of jade' are at the very top:—the strong and the weak meet in their due proportions.

LI. (The trigram representing) thunder, being repeated, forms *K*ăn. The superior man, in accordance with this, is fearful and apprehensive, cultivates (his virtue), and examines (his faults).

1. 'When the (time of) movement comes, he will be found looking out with apprehension:'—that feeling of dread leads to happiness.

L. The Great Symbolism here has come before us in the treatise on the Thwan. Of the application of that symbolism I can only say that, as has been seen in many other hexagrams, while good enough in itself, it is far-fetched.

The same remark may be made on the explanation of the Text of the first line. I can myself do little more than guess at its meaning. The Khang-hsî editors observe that nothing is said about the case of the 'concubine' in the Text; but that it is covered by the 'following the more noble,' 'so condensed and complete are the words of the sage!'

The same editors find a pregnant sense in the conclusion of paragraph 2:—'There will be no fault in me to which my enemy can point, and his disposition to find fault will be diminished.'

'What was required of the caldron in the third line was that that line and line 5, instead of 6, should be correlates;' but there is little meaning in such a statement.

The subject of line 4 cannot be trusted again. He has failed in doing what was his proper work.

'He yet smiles and talks cheerfully:'—the issue (of his dread) is that he adopts (proper) laws (for his course).

2. 'When the movement approaches, he is in a position of peril:'—(a weak line) is mounted on a strong (one).

3. 'He is distraught amid the startling movements going on:'—(the third line) is in a position unsuitable to it.

4. 'Amid the startling movements, he sinks supinely in the mud:'—the light in him has not yet been brilliantly developed.

5. 'He goes and comes amid the startling movements, and (always) in peril:'—full of risk are his doings.

'What he has to do has to be done in his central position:'—far will he be from incurring any loss.

6. 'Amid the startling movements he is in breathless dismay:'—he has not found out (the course of) the due mean.

'Though evil (threatens), he will not fall into error:'—he is afraid of being warned by his neighbours.

LII. (Two trigrams representing) a mountain, one over the other, form Kăn. The superior man, in

---

LI. The account of the Great Symbolism here calls for no remark. Nor does the application of it; but may it not be too late to fear, and order anew one's thoughts and actions when the retributions in providence are taking place? Commentators are haunted by the shadow of this question; but they are unable rightly to meet it.

Paragraph 1 is the same as 2 in Appendix I.

Paragraph 4. Compare paragraph 4 of hexagram 21, Appendix II.

accordance with this, does not go in his thoughts beyond the (duties of the) position in which he is.

1. 'He keeps his toes at rest:'—he does not fail in what is correct (according to the idea of the figure).

2. 'He cannot help him whom he follows:'—(he whom he follows) will not retreat to listen to him.

3. 'He keeps the loins at rest:'—the danger (from his doing so) produces a glowing heat in the heart.

4. 'He keeps the trunk of his body at rest:'—he keeps himself free (from agitation).

5. 'He keeps his cheek bones at rest:'—in harmony with his central position he acts correctly.

6. 'There is good fortune through his devotedly maintaining his restfulness:'—to the end he shows himself generous and good.

LII. According to the view of the Khang-hsî editors, the application should be translated:—'The superior man, in accordance with this, thinks anxiously how he shall not go beyond the duties of his position.' It is difficult to decide between this shade of the meaning, and the more common one which I have followed.

The toes play a great part in walking; but they are here kept at rest, and so do not lose the correct idea of Kăn.

There is no correlation between lines 2 and 3, and thence the subject of 3 will hold on its upward way without condescending to 2.

*Kh*ăng-ʒze finds an unsatisfactory auspice in paragraph 4. Line 4 represents a great minister who should be able to guide all to rest where they ought to be; but he can only keep himself from agitation.

Yü Păn (Ming dynasty) says on paragraph 5:—'Words should not be uttered rashly. Then, when uttered, they will be found

LIII. (The trigram representing) a mountain and above it that for a tree form *K*ien. The superior man, in accordance with this, attains to and maintains his extraordinary virtue, and makes the manners of the people good.

1. 'The danger of a small officer (as represented in the first line)' is owing to no fault of his in the matter of what is right.

2. 'They eat and drink joyfully and at ease:'—but not without having earned their food.

3. 'A husband goes and does not return:'—he separates himself from his comrades.

'A wife is pregnant, but will not nourish her child:'—she has failed in her (proper) course.

'It might be advantageous in resisting plunderers:'—by acting as here indicated men would preserve one another.

4. 'They may light on the flat branches:'—there is docility (in the line) going on to flexible penetration.

5. 'In the end the natural issue cannot be prevented. There will be good fortune:'—(the subject of the line) will get what he desires.

6. 'Their feathers can be used as ornaments. There will be good fortune:'—(the object and character of the subject of the line) cannot be disturbed.

---

accordant with principle. But it is only the master of the virtue belonging to the due mean who can attain to this.'

LIII. The Khang-hsî editors, to bring out the suitability of the Great Symbolism and its application, say:—'A tree springing up on the ground is a tree as it begins to grow. A tree on a hill is high and large. Every tree when it begins to grow, shows its

LIV. (The trigram representing the waters of) a marsh and over it that for thunder form Kwei Mei. The superior man, in accordance with this, having regard to the far-distant end, knows the mischief (that may be done at the beginning).

1. 'The younger sister is married off in a position ancillary to that of the real wife:'—it is the constant practice (for such a case).

'Lame on one leg, she is able to tramp along:'—she can render helpful service.

2. 'There will be advantage in maintaining the firm correctness of a solitary widow:'—(the subject of

---

branches and twigs gradually becoming long. Every morning and every evening show some difference; and when the tree is high and great, whether it be of an ordinary or extraordinary size, it has taken years to reach its dimensions. This illustrates the difference between the advance in Shăng (46) and that in *K*ien. Then the maintenance of extraordinary virtue in the application and the improvement of manners is a gradual process. The improvement of the manners, moreover, flows from the maintenance of the extraordinary virtue; which implies also a gradual operation and progress.'

Paragraph 1. The danger is the result of circumstances; the small officer has not brought it on himself.

Paragraph 2. Only the geese appear in this paragraph; but the writer is thinking of the advancing officer. I cannot but think that in the language and sentiment also there is an echo of the Shih King, I, ix, ode 6.

The 'separation from his comrades' has respect to line 3 not finding its correlate in 6. 'The wife's failing in her proper course' has respect to the line being undivided and not in the centre.

*Kh*ăng-ȝze says, on paragraph 4, that humility and right-doing will find rest and peace in all places and circumstances.

Paragraph 5. 'The natural issue cannot be prevented:'—the wife will have a child; minister and ruler will meet happily.

Paragraph 6. See on the Text. But it is difficult to see the aptness of the symbolism.

the line) has not changed from the constancy (proper to a wife).

3. 'The younger sister who was to be married off is in a mean position:'—this is shown by the improprieties (indicated in the line).

4. (The purpose in) 'protracting the time' is that, after waiting, the thing may be done (all the better).

5. 'The sleeves of the younger sister of (king) Tî-yî, when she was married away, were not equal to those of her (half-) sister, who accompanied her:'—such was her noble character, indicated by the central position of the line.

6. '(What is said in) the sixth line, divided, about there being nothing in the basket' shows that the subject of it is carrying an empty basket.

LV. (The trigrams representing) thunder and lightning combine to form Făng. The superior man, in accordance with this, decides cases of litigation, and apportions punishments with exactness.

1. 'Though they are both of the same character, there will be no error:'—if the subject of this

---

LIV. Thunder rolling above is supposed to produce movement in the waters of the marsh below. The combination of this symbolism in Kwei Mei is recognised as an evil omen in the case which the name denotes. The application of it is not inappropriate.

Paragraph 1. 'It is the constant practice (for such a case)' seems to mean that an ancillary wife has no right to the disposition of herself, but must do what she is told. Thus it is that the mean position of the younger sister does not interfere with the service she can render.

The addition to the Text of 'the purpose' in paragraph 4 is to show that the putting marriage off is on the part of the lady and not on the other side.

line seek to overpass that similarity, there will be calamity.

2. 'Let him cherish his feeling of sincere devotion, that it shall appear being put forth:'—it is by sincerity that the mind is affected.

3. 'There is an (additional) screen of a large and thick banner:'—great things should not be attempted (in such circumstances).

'He breaks his right arm:'—in the end he will not be fit to be employed.

4. 'He is surrounded by a screen large and thick:'—the position of the line is inappropriate.

'At midday he sees the constellation of the Bushel:'—there is darkness and no light.

'He meets with the subject of the line, undivided like himself. There will be good fortune:'—action may be taken.

5. 'The good fortune indicated by the fifth line, divided,' is the congratulation (that is sure to arise).

6. 'He has made his house large:'—he soars (in his pride) to the heavens.

'He looks at his door, which is still, with no one about it:'—he (only) keeps himself withdrawn from all others.

LV. Lightning appears here as the natural phenomenon of which Lî is the symbol. The virtues attributed to the two trigrams are certainly required in the application of them which is subjoined; but that application has little or nothing to do with the explanation of the hexagram supplied by the Text.

I hardly understand the conclusion of paragraph 1. My translation of it is according to the view of *K*û Hsî, if I rightly understand that.

Paragraph 2. It is by such sincerity that the mind is affected,—that is, the mind of the ruler occupying line 5.

LVI. (The trigram representing) a mountain and above it that for fire form Lü. The superior man, in accordance with this, exerts his wisdom and caution in the use of punishments and not allowing litigations to continue.

1. 'The stranger is mean and meanly occupied:'—his aim is become of the lowest character, and calamity will ensue.

2. 'He is provided with good and trusty servants:'—he will in the end have nothing of which to complain.

3. 'The stranger burns his lodging-house:'—and he himself also suffers hurt thereby. When, as a stranger, he treats those below him (as the line indicates), the right relation between him and them is lost.

4. 'The stranger is in a resting-place:'—but he has not got his proper position.

'He has the means of livelihood, and the axe:'—but his mind is not at ease.

5. 'In the end he will obtain praise and a (high) charge:'—he has reached a high place.

6. 'Considering that the stranger is here at the very height (of distinction),' with the spirit that possesses him, it is right he (should be emblemed by a bird) burning (its nest).

Line 3 has a correlate in 6, which is weak, and as it were out of the game. The light in 3 moreover is hidden. Hence the symbolism; and through the blindness of its subject his hurt, which unfits him to be employed.

The line undivided like 4 is 1; perhaps we might translate—'He meets with the subject of the parallel line.'

No one but himself has any confidence in the subject of line 6. He holds himself aloof from others, and they leave him to himself.

'He loses his ox(-like docility) too readily and easily:'—to the end he would not listen to (the truth about the course to be pursued).

LVII. (Two trigrams representing) wind, following each other, form Sun. The superior man, in accordance with this, reiterates his orders, and secures the practice of his affairs.

1. '(Now) he advances, (now) he recedes:'—his mind is perplexed.

'It would be advantageous for him to have the

LVI. Different attempts are made to bring the idea of a travelling stranger out of the trigrams Kăn and Lî; but none of them is satisfactory. Let Khung Ying-tâ's view serve as a specimen of them:—'A fire on a mountain lays hold of the grass, and runs with it over the whole space, not stopping anywhere long, and soon disappearing;—such is the emblem of the traveller.' The application may be derived well enough from the attributes of the trigrams; but does not fit in with the lessons of the Thwan and Hsiang.

The meanness of the subject of line 1 does not arise from the nature of his occupation; but from his mind and aim being emptied of all that is good and ennobling.

Strong and trusty servants are the most important condition for the comfort and progress of the traveller; and therefore it alone is resumed and expanded.

The subject of line 3 treats those below him with violence and arrogance, which of course alienates them from him.

'He has not got into his proper position' seems to say no more than that 4 is a strong line in an even place.

It is difficult to say what 'he has reached a high place' means. The fifth line is not in this hexagram the ruler's seat; but by his qualities and gifts the subject of it attracts the attention and regard of his friends and of his ruler.

The spirit that possesses the subject of line 6 is one of haughty arrogance, with which the humility that ought to characterise him cannot co-exist. His careless self-sufficiency has shut his mind against all lessons of wisdom.

firmness of a brave soldier:'—his mind would in that case be well governed.

2. 'The good fortune springing from what borders on confusion' is due to the position (of the line) in the centre.

3. 'The regret arising from the violent and repeated efforts to penetrate' shows the exhaustion of the will.

4. 'He takes game in his hunting, enough for the threefold use of it:'—he achieves merit.

5. 'The good fortune of (the subject of) the fifth line, undivided,' is owing to its correct position and its being in the centre.

6. 'The representative of penetration is beneath a couch:'—though occupying the topmost place, his powers are exhausted.

'He has lost the axe with which he executed his decisions:'—though he try to be correct, there will be evil.

LVII. I have said on the Thwan that some commentators make the upper trigram symbolical of the ordinances of the ruler and the lower symbolical of the obedience of the people. E. g., *Kh*ăng-ʒze says:—'Superiors, in harmony with the duty of inferiors, issue their commands; inferiors, in harmony with the wishes of their superiors, follow them. Above and below there are that harmony and deference; and this is the significance of the redoubled Sun. When governmental commands and business are in accordance with what is right, they agree with the tendencies of the minds of the people who follow them.'

Paragraph 2 seems to say that the sincerity of purpose indicated by the central position of the second line conducts its subject to the right course, despite the many considerations that might distract him.

'The will is exhausted' in paragraph 3 intimates that 'the repeated efforts' made by its subject have exhausted him. He can now only regret his failures.

LVIII. (Two symbols representing) the waters of a marsh, one over the other, form Tui. The superior man, in accordance with this, (encourages) the conversation of friends and (the stimulus of) their (common) practice.

1. 'The good fortune attached to the pleasure of (inward) harmony' arises from there being nothing in the conduct (of the subject of the line) to awaken doubt.

2. 'The good fortune attached to the pleasure arising from (inward sincerity)' is due to the confidence felt in the object (of the subject of the line).

3. 'The evil predicated of one's bringing around himself whatever can give pleasure' is shown by the inappropriateness of the place (of the line).

4. 'The joy in connexion with (the subject of) the fourth line, undivided,' is due to the happiness (which he will produce).

5. 'He trusts in one who would injure him:'—his place is that which is correct and appropriate.

6. 'The topmost line, divided, shows the pleasure (of its subject) in leading and attracting others:'—his (virtue) is not yet brilliant.

What is said in paragraph 6 proceeds on a different view of the Text from that which I have followed.

LVIII. The application of the Great Symbolism here will recall to many readers the Hebrew maxims in Proverbs xxvii. 17, 19. The sentiment of it, however, does not readily fit in to the teaching of the hexagram as set forth in the Text.

There is nothing in the conduct of the subject of line 1 to awaken suspicion. He has as yet taken no action; but it was not necessary to say anything like this about the subject of line 2, his central position being an assurance that he would never do anything of a doubtful character.

LIX. (The trigram representing) water and that for wind moving above the water form Hwân. The ancient kings, in accordance with this, presented offerings to God and established the ancestral temple.

1. 'The good fortune attached to the first line, divided,' is due to the natural course (pursued by its subject).

2. 'Amidst the prevailing dispersion, he hurries to his contrivance (for security):'—he gets what he desires.

3. 'He has no regard to his own person:'—his aim is directed to what is external to himself.

4. 'He scatters the (different) parties (in the state), and there is great good fortune:'—brilliant and great (are his virtue and service).

5. 'The accumulations of the royal (granaries) are dispersed, and there is no error:'—this is due to the correctness of the position.

6. 'His bloody wounds are gone:'—he is far removed from the danger of injury.

Line 3 should be strong, and the desire of pleasure which is the idea of the hexagram leads its weak subject to the course which is so emphatically condemned.

Paragraph 5 is incomplete. Does the correctness and appropriateness of the position of the subject of the line afford any explanation of his trusting the subject of the weak line above, who would only injure him? It ought to keep him on the contrary from doing so. The commentators have seen this, and say that the paragraph is intended by way of caution.

The action of the hexagram should culminate and end in line 5. But the subject of it has not made brilliant attainment in the firmness and correctness by which the love of pleasure should be controlled.

LIX. The 'in accordance with this' must be equivalent to—'to remedy the state of things thus symbolised.' What follows certainly

LX. (The trigram representing) a lake, and above it that for water, form *K*ieh. The superior man, in accordance with this, constructs his (methods of) numbering and measurement, and discusses (points of) virtue and conduct.

1. 'He does not quit the courtyard outside his door:'—he knows when he has free course and when he is obstructed.

2. 'He does not quit the courtyard inside his gate. There will be evil:'—he loses the time (for action) to an extreme degree.

3. In 'the lamentation for not observing the (proper) regulations,' who should there be to blame?

4. 'The progress and success of the quiet and natural (attention) to all regulations' is due to the deference which accepts the ways of (the ruler) above.

5. 'The good fortune arising from the regulations enacted sweetly and acceptably' is due to (the line)

---

amounts to this, that the ancient kings considered the services of religion, sincerely and earnestly attended to, as calculated to counteract the tendency to mutual alienation and selfishness in the minds of men. How they operated to have this beneficial effect we are not told. Nor is it easy to account for the extension of what is said in the Text about the establishment of the ancestral temple to the presentation also of offerings to God. Probably the writer had the same idea in his mind as in the Great Symbolism of hexagram 16, q. v.

'The natural course' pursued by the subject of line 1 is, probably, that required by the time.

'What the subject of line 2 desired' would be his success in counteracting the prevailing tendency to disunion.

The view given of paragraph 5 is that propounded by *K*û Hsî.

For paragraph 6 see the note on line 6 under the Text.

易經

occupying the place (of authority) and being in the centre.

6. 'The regulations are severe and difficult. Even with firm correctness there will be evil:'—the course (indicated by the hexagram) is come to an end.

LXI. (The trigram representing the waters of) a marsh and that for wind above it form *K*ung Fû. The superior man, in accordance with this, deliberates about cases of litigation and delays (the infliction of) death.

1. 'The first line, undivided, shows its subject resting (in himself). There will be good fortune:'—no change has yet come over his purpose.

2. 'Her young ones respond to her:'—from the (common) wish of the inmost heart.

3. 'Now he beats his drum, and now he leaves off:'—the position (of the line) is the appropriate one for it.

LX. Various explanations of the Great Symbolism have been attempted. E. g., *Kh*ăng-ȝze says:—'The water which a lake or marsh will contain is limited to a certain quantity. If the water flowing in exceed that, it overflows. This gives us the idea of *K*ieh.' What is found on the application of it is to my mind equally unsatisfactory.

The subject of line 1 knows when he might have free course and when he is obstructed, and acts accordingly. He is regulated by a consideration of the time.

The subject of line 1 ought not to act, and he is still. The subject of line 2 ought to act, and he also is still. The error and the effect of it are great.

The subject of line 3 shows by his lamentation how he blames himself.

The other three paragraphs are sufficiently explained in what is said on the Text.

4. 'A horse the fellow of which disappears:'—he breaks from his (former) companions, and mounts upwards.

5. 'He is perfectly sincere, and links others to him in closest union:'—the place (of the line) is the correct and appropriate one.

6. 'Chanticleer (tries to) mount to heaven:'—but how can (such an effort) continue long?

LXII. (The trigram representing) a hill and that for thunder above it form Hsiâo Kwo. The superior man, in accordance with this, in his conduct exceeds in humility, in mourning exceeds in sorrow, and in his expenditure exceeds in economy.

1. 'There is a bird flying (and ascending) till the result is evil:'—nothing can be done to avoid this issue.

2. 'He does not attempt to reach his ruler:'—

LXI. Dissatisfied with previous attempts to explain the Great Symbolism, the Khang-hsî editors say:—'The wind penetrates things. The grass and trees of the level ground are shaken and tossed by it; the rocky valleys and caverns in their sides have it blowing round about them; and it acts also on the depths of the collected waters, the cold of which disappears and the ice is melted before it. This is what makes it the emblem of that perfect sincerity which penetrates everywhere. The litigations of the people are like the deep and dark places of the earth. The kings examine with discrimination into all secret matters connected with them, even those which are here mentioned, till there is nothing that is not penetrated by their perfect sincerity.' But all this is greatly strained. The symbolism of the eight trigrams gets pretty well played out in the course of the 64 hexagrams.

1. 'No change has come over the purpose:'—the sincerity, that is, perfect in itself and of itself, continues.

2. One bond of loving regard unites the mother bird and her young; so answers the heart of man to man.

a minister should not overpass the distance (between his ruler and himself).

3. 'Some in consequence find opportunity to assail and injure him. There will be evil:'—how great will it be!

4. 'He meets the exigency (of his situation), without exceeding (the proper course):'—(he does so), the position being inappropriate (for a strong line).

'If he go forward, there will be peril, and he must be cautious:'—the result would be that his course would not be long pursued.

5. 'There are dense clouds, but no rain:'—(the line) is in too high a place.

6. 'He does not meet the exigency (of his situation), and exceeds (his proper course):'—(the position indicates) the habit of domineering.

LXIII. (The trigram representing) fire and that for water above it form *K*î 3î. The superior

---

LXII. The Khang-hsî editors endeavour to show the appropriateness of the Great Symbolism in this way:—'When thunder issues from the earth, the sound of it comes with a rush and is loud; but when it reaches the top of a hill it has begun to die away and is small.' There is nothing in the Chinese about the hills being high; and readers will only smile at the attempted explanation. The application of the symbolism, or rather of the idea of the hexagram, is good, and in entire accordance with what I have stated that idea to be.

Nothing can be done to avoid the issue mentioned in paragraph 1, for the subject of the line brings it on himself.

Paragraph 2 deals only with the symbolism in the conclusion of what is stated under line 2. The writer takes the view which I have given on the Text.

For paragraphs 3 and 4 see the notes on the Text.

In line 5 the yin line is too high. If the line were yang, the auspice would be different.

man, in accordance with this, thinks of evil (that may come), and beforehand guards against it.

1. 'He drags back his wheel:'—as we may rightly judge, there will be no mistake.

2. 'In seven days she will find it:'—for the course pursued is that indicated by the central position (of the line).

3. 'He was three years in subduing it:'—enough to make him weary.

4. 'He is on his guard all the day:'—he is in doubt about something.

5. 'The slaughtering of an ox by the neighbour in the east is not equal to (the small sacrifice of) the neighbour in the west:'—because the time (in the latter case is more important and fit).

'His sincerity receives the blessing:'—good fortune comes on a great scale.

6. 'His head is immersed; the position is perilous:'—how could such a state continue long?

LXIV. (The trigram representing) water and that for fire above it form Wei 3i. The superior man, in accordance with this, carefully discriminates among (the qualities of) things, and the (different) positions they (naturally) occupy.

1. 'His tail gets immersed:'—this is the very height of ignorance.

LXIII. Water and fire coming together as here, fire under the water, each element occupies its proper place, and their interaction will be beneficial. Such is the common explanation of the Great Symbolism; but the connexion between it and the application of it, which also is good in itself, is by no means clear.

The notes on the different lines present nothing that has not been dealt with in the notes on the Text.

2. 'The second line, undivided, shows good fortune arising from being firm and correct:'—it is in the central place, and the action of its subject thereby becomes correct.

3. '(The state of things is) not yet remedied. Advancing will lead to evil:'—the place (of the line) is not that appropriate for it.

4. 'By firm correctness there is good fortune, and cause for repentance disappears:'—the aim (of the subject of the line) is carried into effect.

5. '(We see) the brightness of a superior man:'—the diffusion of that brightness tends to good fortune.

6. 'He drinks and gets his head immersed:'—he does not know how to submit to the (proper) regulations.

LXIV. In this last hexagram we have water below and fire above, so that the two cannot act on each other, and the Symbolism may represent the unregulated condition of general affairs, the different classes of society not harmonising nor acting together. The application follows naturally.

*K*û Hsî and others suspect an error in the text of paragraph 1; yet a tolerable meaning comes from it as it stands.

The Khang-hsî editors observe on paragraph 2 that an undivided line in the second place, and a divided line in the fifth place, are both incorrect, and yet it is often said of them that with firm correctness in their subjects there will be good fortune;—such is the virtue of the central position. This principle is at last clearly enunciated in this paragraph.

*Kh*ăng-ʒze says:—'The subject of line 4 has the ability which the time requires, and possesses also a firm solidity. He can carry out therefore his purpose. There will be good fortune, and all cause for repentance will disappear. The smiting of the demon region was the highest example of firm correctness.'

Both the symbols in paragraph 6 indicate a want of caution, and an unwillingness to submit one's impulses to the regulation of reason and prudence.

APPENDIX III.

The Great Appendix. Section I.

Chapter I. 1. Heaven is lofty and honourable; earth is low. (Their symbols), *Kh*ien and Khwăn, (with their respective meanings), were determined (in accordance with this).

Things low and high appear displayed in a similar relation. The (upper and lower trigrams, and the relative position of individual lines, as) noble and mean, had their places assigned accordingly.

Movement and rest are the regular qualities (of their respective subjects). Hence comes the definite distinction (of the several lines) as the strong and the weak.

(Affairs) are arranged together according to their tendencies, and things are divided according to their classes. Hence were produced (the interpretations in the Yî, concerning) what is good [or lucky] and evil [or unlucky].

In the heavens there are the (different) figures there completed, and on the earth there are the (different) bodies there formed. (Corresponding to them) were the changes and transformations exhibited (in the Yî).

2. After this fashion a strong and a weak line were manipulated together (till there were the eight trigrams), and those eight trigrams were added, each to itself and to all the others, (till the sixty-four hexagrams were formed).

3. We have the exciting forces of thunder and lightning; the fertilising influences of wind and rain; and the revolutions of the sun and moon, which give rise to cold and warmth.

4. The attributes expressed by *Kh*ien constitute the male; those expressed by Khwăn constitute the female.

5. *Kh*ien (symbolises Heaven, which) directs the great beginnings of things; Khwăn (symbolises Earth, which) gives to them their completion.

6. It is by the ease with which it proceeds that *Kh*ien directs (as it does), and by its unhesitating response that Khwăn exhibits such ability.

7. (He who attains to this) ease (of Heaven) will be easily understood, and (he who attains to this) freedom from laborious effort (of the Earth) will be easily followed. He who is easily understood will have adherents, and he who is easily followed will achieve success. He who has adherents can continue long, and he who achieves success can become great. To be able to continue long shows the virtue of the wise and able man; to be able to become great is the heritage he will acquire.

8. With the attainment of such ease and such freedom from laborious effort, the mastery is got of all principles under the sky. With the attainment of that mastery, (the sage) makes good his position in the middle (between heaven and earth).

Chapter I is an attempt to show the correspondency between the phenomena of external nature ever changing, and the figures of the Yî King ever varying. The first four paragraphs, it is said, show, from the phenomena of production and transformation in external

Chapter II. 9. The sages set forth the diagrams, inspected the emblems contained in them, and appended their explanations;—in this way the good fortune and bad (indicated by them) were made clear.

10. The strong and the weak (lines) displace each other, and produce the changes and transformations (in the figures).

11. Therefore the good fortune and evil (mentioned in the explanations) are the indications of the right and wrong (in men's conduct of affairs), and the repentance and regret (similarly mentioned) are the indications of their sorrow and anxiety.

---

nature, the principles on which the figures of the Yî were made. The fifth and sixth paragraphs show, particularly, how the attributes represented by the figures *Kh*ien and Khwăn are to be found in (the operations of) heaven and earth. The last two paragraphs show both those attributes embodied or realised in man. The realisation takes place, indeed, fully only in the sage or the ideal man, who thus becomes the pattern for all men.

In paragraph 3 we have five of the six derivative trigrams;—the six 'children,' according to the nomenclature of the Wăn arrangement. 'Thunder' stands for *k*ăn (☳), 'lightning' for lî (☲), 'wind' for sun (☴), and 'rain' for khan (☵). 'The sun,' however, is also an emblem of lî, and 'the moon' one of kăn (☶), generally said to represent 'mountains,' while tui (☱), representing 'collections of water,' has no place in the enumeration. *K*û Hsî says that in paragraph 3 we have the natural changes seen in the phenomena of the sky, while in 4 we have such changes as find body and figure on the earth.

Paragraphs 5 and 6 have both been misunderstood from neglect of the peculiar meaning of the character *k*ih (知), and from taking it in its common acceptation of 'knowing.' Both commentaries and dictionaries point out that it is here used in the sense of 'directing,' 'presiding over.' In paragraph 7, however, it resumes its ordinary significancy.

12. The changes and transformations (of the lines) are the emblems of the advance and retrogression (of the vital force in nature). Thus what we call the strong and the weak (lines) become the emblems of day and night. The movements which take place in the six places (of the hexagram) show the course of the three extremes (i. e. of the three Powers in their perfect operation).

13. Therefore what the superior man rests in, in whatever position he is placed, is the order shown in the Yî; and the study which gives him the greatest pleasure is that of the explanations of the several lines.

14. Therefore the superior man, when living quietly, contemplates the emblems and studies the explanations of them; when initiating any movement, he contemplates the changes (that are made in divining), and studies the prognostications from them. Thus 'is help extended to him from Heaven; there will be good fortune, and advantage in every movement.'

Chapter II, paragraphs 9–14, is divided into two parts. The former contains paragraphs 9–12, and tells us how the sages, king Wăn and the duke of *K*âu, proceeded in making the Yî, so that the good fortune and bad of men's courses should be indicated by it in harmony with right and wrong, and the processes of nature. Paragraphs 13, 14 form the second part, and speak of the study of the Yî by the superior man, desirous of doing what is right and increasing his knowledge, and the advantages flowing from it.

I can follow to some extent the first two statements of paragraph 12, so far as the ideas of the writer are concerned, though asserting any correspondence between the changes of the lines of the diagrams, and the operations of external nature, as in the succession of day and night, is merely an amusement of the fancy. I all but fail, however, to grasp the idea in the last statement. In the trigram, the first line represents earth; the second, man; and the

Chapter III. 15. The Thwan speak of the emblematic figures (of the complete diagrams). The Yâo speak of the changes (taking place in the several lines).

16. The expressions about good fortune or bad are used with reference to (the figures and lines, as) being right or wrong (according to the conditions of time and place); those about repentance or regret refer to small faults (in the satisfying those conditions); when it is said 'there will be no error,' or 'no blame,' there is reference to (the subject) repairing an error by what is good.

17. Therefore the distinction of (the upper and lower trigrams and of the individual lines) as noble or mean is decided by the (relative) position (of the lines); the regulations of small and great are found in the diagrams, and the discriminations of good and bad fortune appear in the (subjoined) explanations.

18. Anxiety against (having occasion for) repentance or regret should be felt at the boundary line (between good and evil). The stirring up the thought of (securing that there shall be) no blame arises from (the feeling of) repentance.

---

third, heaven; in the hexagram, the first and second lines are assigned to earth; the third and fourth, to man; and the fifth and sixth, to heaven. These are the three Powers, and each Power has 'a Grand Extreme,' where its nature and operation are seen in their highest ideal. This is to some extent conceivable; but when I try to follow our author, and find an analogy between the course of these extremes and the movements in the places of the diagrams, I have no clue by which to trace my way. For the concluding sentence of paragraph 14 see the duke of *K*âu on the last line of hexagram 14.

易經

19. Thus of the diagrams some are small, and some are great; and of the explanations some are startling, and some are unexciting. Every one of those explanations has reference to the tendencies (indicated by the symbols).

Chapter IV. 20. The Yî was made on a principle of accordance with heaven and earth, and shows us therefore, without rent or confusion, the course (of things) in heaven and earth.

21. (The sage), in accordance with (the Yî), looking up, contemplates the brilliant phenomena of the heavens, and, looking down, examines the definite arrangements of the earth;—thus he knows the causes of darkness (or, what is obscure) and light (or, what is bright). He traces things to their beginning, and follows them to their end;—thus he knows what can be said about death and life. (He

---

Chapter III, paragraphs 15–19, gives additional information about the constituent parts of the Yî, that is, the Text of the classic as we have it from king Wăn and his son. The imperial editors say that it expands the meaning of the fourth paragraph, the third of chapter 2. It does do so, but this account hardly covers all its contents.

To understand the names 'small and great,' as used of the diagrams in paragraphs 17 and 19, it should be noted that hexagrams to which the divided or yin line gives their character are termed 'small,' and those where the undivided or yang line rules are called 'great.' *K*âu (44, ䷫), Thun (33, ䷠), and Phei (12, ䷋) are instances of the former class; Fû (24, ䷗), Lin (19, ䷒), and Thâi (11, ䷊) of the other.

It is observed by 3hâi *Kh*ing (early in the Ming dynasty) that the terms 'diagrams' and 'explanations' must be understood not only of the whole figures but also as embracing the several lines.

perceives how the union of) essence and breath form things, and the (disappearance or) wandering away of the soul produces the change (of their constitution);—thus he knows the characteristics of the anima and animus.

22. There is a similarity between him and heaven and earth, and hence there is no contrariety in him to them. His knowledge embraces all things, and his course is (intended to be) helpful to all under the sky;—and hence he falls into no error. He acts according to the exigency of circumstances without being carried away by their current; he rejoices in Heaven and knows its ordinations;—and hence he has no anxieties. He rests in his own (present) position, and cherishes (the spirit of) generous benevolence;—and hence he can love (without reserve).

23. (Through the Yî), he comprehends as in a mould or enclosure the transformations of heaven and earth without any error; by an ever-varying adaptation he completes (the nature of) all things without exception; he penetrates to a knowledge of the course of day and night (and all other connected phenomena);—it is thus that his operation is spirit-like, unconditioned by place, while the changes which he produces are not restricted to any form.

Chapter IV, paragraphs 20–23, is intended still more to exalt the Yî, and seems to say that the sage by means of it can make an exhaustive study of all principles and of human nature, till he attains to the knowledge of the ordinances of Heaven. Such is the account of the chapter given by *K*û Hsî; but the second character in paragraph 21 must be understood in the signification which it has in all the sixty-four sentences which explain the emblematic structure of the hexagrams, as='in accordance with' and not 'by means of.' The

Chapter V. 24. The successive movement of the inactive and active operations constitutes what is called the course (of things).

imperial editors append to their statement of *K*û's account, that it must be borne in mind that the sages had not to wait till the Yî was made to conduct their exhaustive study. They had done that before, and the Yî may be considered as a talk on the results, drawn out in its own peculiar style. It holds the mirror up to nature; but its authors knew nature before they made it.

In paragraph 21, 'the brilliant phenomena of the heavens' are the various shining bodies of the sky, with their rising and setting; 'the definite arrangements of the earth' are the different situations of its parts according to the points of the compass, and its surface as diversified by mountain and valley; and by the study of these the causes of day and night are known as being the expansion and contraction of the elementary ether. The same thing produces the facts of birth or life and death.

Ȝing, which I have translated 'essence,' denotes the more subtle and pure part of matter, and belongs to the grosser form of the elementary ether; *khî*, or 'spirit,' is the breath, still material, but purer than the ȝing, and belongs to the finer, and more active form of the ether. Here *khî* is 'the breath of life.' In the hwun or 'soul (animus),' the *khî* predominates, and the ȝing in the pho or animal soul. At death the hwun wanders away, ascending, and the pho descends and is changed into a ghostly shade. So did the ancient Chinese grope their way from material things to the concept and representation of what was immaterial.

For my 'characteristics of the anima and animus,' Dr. Medhurst rendered 'the circumstances and conditions of the Kwei Shăns' (Theology of the Chinese, pp. 10–12); but he observes that 'the Kwei Shăns in the passage are evidently the expanding and contracting principles of human life.' The kwei shăns are brought about by the dissolution of the human frame, and consist of the expanding and ascending shăn, which rambles about in space, and of the contracted and shrivelled kwei, which reverts to earth and nonentity. It is difficult to express one's self clearly on a subject treated so briefly and enigmatically in the text.

We must understand that the subject of the predicates in this and the next two paragraphs is 'the sage,' who has endeavoured to give a transcript of his views and doings in the Yî. The character,

25. That which ensues as the result (of their movement) is goodness; that which shows it in its completeness is the natures (of men and things).

26. The benevolent see it and call it benevolence. The wise see it and call it wisdom. The common people, acting daily according to it, yet have no knowledge of it. Thus it is that the course (of things), as seen by the superior man, is seen by few.

27. It is manifested in the benevolence (of its operations), and (then again) it conceals and stores up its resources. It gives their stimulus to all things, without having the same anxieties that possess the sage. Complete is its abundant virtue and the greatness of its stores!

28. Its rich possessions is what is intended by 'the greatness of its stores;' the daily renovation which it produces is what is meant by 'the abundance of its virtue.'

29. Production and reproduction is what is called (the process of) change.

30. The formation of the semblances (shadowy forms of things) is what we attribute to *Kh*ien; the giving to them their specific forms is what we attribute to Khwăn.

31. The exhaustive use of the numbers (that turn

---

which I have translated by 'spirit-like' in paragraph 23, is different from *kh*î in paragraph 21. It is shăn, a character of the phonetic class, while its primary material signification has not been satisfactorily ascertained. 'The Chinese,' says P. Regis (vol. ii. p. 445), 'use it in naming the soul, true angels, and the genii of idolaters; and the Christian Chinese use it when they speak of God, of the Holy Spirit, of angels, and of the soul of man. For what else could they do?'

up in manipulating the stalks), and (thereby) knowing (the character of) coming events, is what we call prognosticating; the comprehension of the changes (indicated leads us to) what we call the business (to be done).

32. That which is unfathomable in (the movement of) the inactive and active operations is (the presence of a) spiritual (power).

Chapter V, paragraphs 24–32, still shows us the Yî fashioned so as to give a picture of the phenomena of the external universe; but the writer dwells more on the latter, and the different paragraphs give an interesting view of his ideas on the subject. He supposes a constant change from rest to movement and from movement to rest, through which all things are formed, now still, now in motion, now expanding, now contracting. It is customary to speak of two forms of an original ether as the two elementary principles, but they are really one and the same ether, in a twofold condition, with a twofold action. By their successive movement the phenomena of existence are produced,—what I have called 'the course (of things)' in paragraph 24. It is attempted, however, by many native scholars and by some sinologists, to give to tâo, the last character in that paragraph, the meaning of 'reason,' that which intelligently guides and directs the movements of the two elements. But this view is not in harmony with the scope of the chapter, nor can the characters be fairly construed so as to justify such an interpretation.

The imperial editors say that the germ of the Mencian doctrine about the goodness of human nature is in paragraph 25; but it says more widely, that 'every creature is good,' according to its ideal as from the plastic yin and yang. But few, the next paragraph tells us, can understand the measure of this goodness.

'The benevolent operations' in the course of things in paragraph 27 are illustrated from the phenomena of growth and beauty in spring and summer; and the cessation of these in autumn and winter may be called 'a concealing and storing them up.'

Paragraph 29 seems to state the origin of the name Yî as applied to the book, the Yî King.

In paragraph 30 the names *Kh*ien and Khwăn take the place of yin and yang, as used in paragraphs 24 and 32. In *Kh*ien,

Chapter VI. 33. Yes, wide is the Yî and great! If we speak of it in its farthest reaching, no limit can be set to it; if we speak of it with reference to what is near at hand, (its lessons are) still and correct; if we speak of it in connexion with all between heaven and earth, it embraces all.

34. There is *Kh*ien. In its (individual) stillness it is self-absorbed; when exerting its motive power it goes straight forward; and thus it is that its productive action is on a grand scale. There is Khwăn. In its (individual) stillness, it is self-collected and capacious; when exerting its motive power, it developes its resources, and thus its productive action is on a wide scale.

35. In its breadth and greatness, (the Yî) corre-

---

the symbol of heaven, every one of its three lines is undivided; it is the concentration of the yang faculty; so Khwăn, the symbol of the earth, is the concentration of the yin. The critics themselves call attention to the equivalence of the symbolic names here given to yin and yang. The connexion of the two is necessary to the production of any one substantial thing. The yang originates a shadowy outline which the yin fills up with a definite substance. So actually in nature Heaven (*Kh*ien) and Earth (Khwăn) operate together in the production of all material things and beings.

The 'numbers,' mentioned in paragraph 31, are not all or any numbers generally, but 7, 8, 9, 6, those assigned to the four 'emblematic figures,' that grow out of the undivided and divided lines, and by means of which the hexagrams are made up in divination. The 'future or coming events' which are prognosticated are not particular events, which the diviner has not already forecast, but the character of events or courses of actions already contemplated, as good or evil, lucky or unlucky, in their issue.

The best commentary on paragraph 32 is supplied by paragraphs 8–10 of Appendix VI. The 'Spirit' is that of 'God;' and this settles the meaning of tâo in paragraph 24, as being the course of nature, in which, according to the author, 'God worketh all in all.'

sponds to heaven and earth; in its ever-recurring changes, it corresponds to the four seasons; in its mention of the bright or active, and the dark or inactive operation, it corresponds to the sun and moon; and the excellence seen in the ease and ready response (of its various operations) corresponds to the perfect operations (presented to us in the phenomena of nature).

Chapter VII. 36. The Master said:—'Is not the Yî a perfect book?' It was by the Yî that the sages exalted their virtue, and enlarged their sphere of occupation. Their wisdom was high, and their rules of conduct were solid. That loftiness was after the pattern of heaven; that solidity, after the pattern of earth.

Chapter VI, paragraphs 33–35, goes on further to celebrate the Yî as holding up the mirror to nature in all its operations and in its widest extent. The grandiloquent language, however, amounts only to this, that, when we have made ourselves acquainted with the phenomena of nature, we can, with a heated fancy, see some analogy to them in the changes of the diagrams and lines of the Yî book.

*Kh*ien and Khwăn must be taken as the same names are understood in paragraph 30 above.

'The Yî,' with which paragraph 33 begins, must be understood also at the commencement of paragraph 35. The character which I have translated by 'corresponds' throughout this last chapter, should not, it is observed, have stress laid upon it. *K*û Hsî says that it is simply equal to the 'there is a similarity' of paragraph 22. 'The bright or active element' and 'the dark or inactive' are in the original, 'the yang and the yin.' The correspondence predicated between them and the sun and moon, the brightness and warmth of the one, and the paleness and coldness of the other, shows us how those names arose, and that it is foreign to the original concept of them to call them 'the male and female principles:'—with the last clause compare paragraphs 6–8.

undivided line) amount to 216; those for Khwăn (or the divided line), to 144. Together they are 360, corresponding to the days of the year.

53. The number produced by the lines in the two parts (of the Yî) amount to 11,520, corresponding to the number of all things.

54. Therefore by means of the four operations is the Yî completed. It takes 18 changes to form a hexagram.

55. (The formation of) the eight trigrams constitutes the small completion (of the Yî).

56. If we led on the diagrams and expanded them, if we prolonged each by the addition of the proper lines, then all events possible under the sky might have their representation.

57. (The diagrams) make manifest (by their appended explanations), the ways (of good and ill fortune), and show virtuous actions in their spiritual relations. In this way, by consulting them, we may receive an answer (to our doubts), and we may also by means of them assist the spiritual (power in its agency in nature and providence).

58. The Master said:—'He who knows the method of change and transformation may be said to know what is done by that spiritual (power).'

Chapter IX, paragraphs 49–58, is of a different character from any of the preceding, and treats, unsatisfactorily, of the use of numbers in connexion with the figure of the Yi and the practice of divination.

In the Thang edition of the Yî, published in the seventh century, paragraph 49 is the first of the eleventh chapter according to the arrangement now followed. *Kh*ăng-ȝze restored it to its present place, which it occupied, as has been proved, during the Han

Chapter X. 59. In the Yî there are four things characteristic of the way of the sages. We should set the highest value on its explanations to guide

---

dynasty, and to which it properly belongs. It and the next paragraph should be taken together, and are distinct from what follows, though the Thang edition is further confused in placing 51 before 50.

In 49 and 50 'heaven' and 'earth' are used as we have seen *Khien* and Khwăn are in paragraphs 30 and 34. Odd numbers belong to the strong or undivided line, which is symbolical of the active operation in nature, and the even numbers to the weak or divided line, symbolical of its inaction. The phraseology of the paragraphs, however, can only be understood by a reference to 'the river map,' which has been given in the Introduction, pages 15, 16.

The map, as it appeared on the back of 'the dragon-horse,' consisted of so many circles, and so many dark circular markings, the former, it was assumed, being of the yang character, and the latter of the yin. Fû-hsî for the circle substituted the strong or undivided line (———), and for the dark markings the weak or divided (— —). It will be seen that the yang symbols are the 1, 3, 5, 7 and 9 circles, and the yin are the 2, 4, 6, 8 and 10 circular markings, which is the pictorial delineation of paragraph 49. The only thing to be said upon it is that the arrangement of the five circles and ten circular markings is peculiar, and evidently devised 'for a purpose.' So far, however, as we know, no figure of the map was attempted till after the beginning of our twelfth century.

The same figure is supposed to illustrate what is said in paragraph 50: 'The numbers of the two series correspond to each other in their fixed positions.' 1 and 2, and 3 and 4 certainly front each other, and perhaps 5 and 6; but 7 and 8, and 9 and 10 do not do so in the same way. It is said also that 'each has another that may be considered its mate.' So it is with 1 and 6, 2 and 7, 3 and 8, 4 and 9, but hardly with 5 and 10. Further, $1+3+5+7+9=25$; $2+4+6+8+10=30$; and $25+30=55$; all of which points are stated.

The last statement in the paragraph, however, derives no illustration, so far as I can see, from the figure. How can the numbers effect the things that are predicated of them? There is a

us in speaking; on its changes for (the initiation of) our movements; on its emblematic figures for (definite action as in) the construction of implements;

jargon indeed about the formation of the five elements, but in order to make it appear not reasonable, but capable of being related, writers call in 'the Lo writing' to the aid of 'the Ho map;' and 'the five elements' is a division of the constituents of material things, which is foreign to the Yî.

Paragraph 51 is intended to describe the process of divination in manipulating the stalks, but the description is confused by introducing into it the four seasons and the subject of intercalation, so as to be very difficult to understand.

In the middle of the Ho map are the five circles symbolical of heaven and the ten dark terrestrial markings (five above and five below the others). These multiplied together give fifty, which form 'the great expansion.' But 50 divining stalks or slips, when divided, give either two odd numbers or two even; and therefore one was put on one side. The remaining 49, however divided, were sure to give two parcels of stalks, one containing an even number of stalks, and the other an odd, and so might be said fancifully to represent the undivided or strong, and the divided or weak line. It is needless to go minutely into the other steps of the process. Then comes in the counting the stalks by four, because there are four seasons in the year, and those that remain represent the intercalary days. But how could such a process be of any value to determine the days necessary to be intercalated in any particular year? The paragraph shows, however, that, when it was written, the rule was to intercalate two months in five years. But it does not say how many days would remain to be carried on to the sixth year after the second intercalation.

Paragraph 52. The actual number of the undivided and divided lines in the hexagrams is the same, 192 of each. But the representative number of an undivided line is 9, and of a divided line 6. Now 9×4 (the number of the emblematic figures) $\times 6$ (the lines of each hexagram) $= 216$; and $6 \times 4 \times 6 = 144$. The sum of these products is 360, which was assumed, for the purpose of working the intercalation, as the standard length of the year. But this was derived from observation, and other considerations;—it did not come out of the Yî.

Paragraphs 53–56. The number in 53 arises thus:—192 (the

and on its prognostications for our practice of divination.

60. Therefore, when a superior man is about to take action of a more private or of a public character, he asks (the Yî), making his inquiry in words. It receives his order, and the answer comes as the echo's response. Be the subject remote or near, mysterious or deep, he forthwith knows of what kind will be the coming result. (If the Yî) were not the most exquisite thing under heaven, would it be concerned in such an operation as this?

61. (The stalks) are manipulated by threes and fives to determine (one) change; they are laid on opposite sides, and placed one up, one down, to make sure of their numbers; and the (three necessary)

---

number of each series of lines in the sixty-four hexagrams) × 36 (obtained as above) = 6912, and 192 × 24 = 4608, the sum of which = 11,520. This is said to be 'the number of all things,' the meaning of which I do not know. The 'four operations' are those described in paragraph 31. They were thrice repeated in divination to determine each new line, and of course it took eighteen of them to form a hexagram. The diagrams might be extended ad infinitum, both in the number of lines and of figures, by the natural process of their formation as shown in the Introduction, page 14, without the aid of the divining stalks; and no sufficient reason can be given why the makers of the figures stopped at sixty-four.

It is difficult to believe the first statement in paragraph 57 and to understand the second. What is it 'to Shăn or spiritualise virtuous actions?' The concluding statement approximates to impiety.

We may grant what is affirmed in paragraph 58, but does the Yî really give us any knowledge of the processes of change and transformation in nature? What wiser are we after all the affirmations about numbers? 'Change' = changings, understood actively:—the work of Heaven; 'transformations' = evolution:—the finish given by earth to the changing caused by Heaven.

changes are gone through with in this way, till they form the figures pertaining to heaven or to earth. Their numbers are exactly determined, and the emblems of (all things) under the sky are fixed. (If the Yî) were not the thing most capable of change of all things under heaven, how could it effect such a result as this?

62. In (all these operations forming) the Yî, there is no thought and no action. It is still and without movement; but, when acted on, it penetrates forthwith to all phenomena and events under the sky. If it were not the most spirit-like thing under the sky, how could it be found doing this?

63. The (operations forming the) Yî are the method by which the sages searched out exhaustively what was deep, and investigated the minutest springs (of things).

64. 'Those operations searched out what was deep:'—therefore they could penetrate to the views of all under the sky. 'They made apparent the minutest springs of (things):'—therefore they could bring to a completion all undertakings under the sky. 'Their action was spirit-like:'—therefore they could make speed without hurry, and reached their destination without travelling.

65. This is the import of what the Master said, that 'In the Yî there are four things indicating the way of the sages.'

Chapter X, paragraphs 59–65, enlarges on the service rendered to men by the Yî, owing to the way in which it was made by the sages to express their views and carry into effect their wishes.

Paragraph 59 mentions the four things in which its usefulness appears. 'The emblematic figures' are the four **hsiang**, which are produced by the manipulation of the undivided and divided

Chapter XI. 66. The Master said :—'What is it that the Yî does? The Yî opens up (the knowledge of the issues of) things, accomplishes the undertakings (of men), and embraces under it (the way of) all things under the sky. This and nothing more is what the Yî does. Thereby the sages, through (divination by) it, would give their proper course to the aims of all under the sky, would give stability to their undertakings, and determine their doubts.'

67. Therefore the virtue of the stalks is versatile

---

lines, and whose representative numbers are 9, 8, 7, 6. 'Divination' appears in the paragraph as pû-shih, which means 'divination by the tortoise-shell and by the stalks.' But the tortoise-shell had nothing to do with the use of the Yî. Before the composition of these Appendixes the two terms must have been combined to express the practice of divination, without reference to its mode.

Paragraph 60 speaks of the explanations and prognostications of the Yî. The 'exquisiteness' ascribed to it would be due to the sages who had devised it, and appended their explanations to it; but the whole thing has no existence save in cloud-land.

Paragraph 61 speaks of the operations with the stalks till the various changes in the results issued in the determination of the emblematic figures, and then in the fixing of the individual lines and entire hexagrams. Even *K*û Hsî admits that the references to the different processes are now hardly intelligible.

Paragraph 62. How could the writer speak of the Yî without thought or action as being most 'spirit-like?' If it did what he asserts, those who contrived it might be so described? They would have been beings whose operation was indeed like that of spirits, inscrutable, 'unfathomable' (paragraph 32), even like that of the Spirit of God (VI, 10).

Paragraphs 63 and 64 ought not to be taken as saying that the sages did the things described for themselves by the Yî. They knew them of themselves, and made the Yî that others might come by it to do the same. So the writer imagined. No words could indicate more clearly than those of paragraph 65 that the paragraphs between it and 59 did not come from Confucius, but from the compiler of the Great Appendix, whoever he was.

and spirit-like; that of the diagrams is exact and wise; and the meaning given by the six lines is changeful to give (the proper information to men). The sages having, by their possession of these (three virtues), cleansed their minds, retired and laid them up in the secrecy (of their own consciousness). But their sympathies were with the people in regard both to their good fortune and evil. By their spirit-like ability they knew (the character of) coming events, and their wisdom had stored up (all experiences of) the past. Who could be able to accomplish all this? (Only our) ancient sages, quick in apprehension and clear in discernment, of far-reaching intelligence, and all-embracing knowledge, and with a majesty, going spirit-like to its objects;—it was only they who could do so.

68. Therefore (those sages), fully understanding the way of Heaven, and having clearly ascertained the experience of the people, instituted (the employment of) these spirit-like things, as a provision for the use of the people. The sages went about the employment of them (moreover) by purifying their hearts and with reverent caution, thereby giving (more) spirituality and intelligence to their virtue.

69. Thus, a door shut may be pronounced (analogous to) Khwăn (or the inactive condition), and the opening of the door (analogous to) *Khien* (or the active condition). The opening succeeding the being shut may be pronounced (analogous to what we call) a change; and the passing from one of these states to the other may be called the constant course (of things).

The (first) appearance of anything (as a bud) is

what we call a semblance; when it has received its complete form, we call it a definite thing.

(The divining-plant having been produced, the sages) set it apart and laid down the method of its employment,—what we call the laws (of divination). The advantage arising from it in external and internal matters, so that the people all use it, stamps it with a character which we call spirit-like.

70. Therefore in (the system of) the Yî there is the Grand Terminus, which produced the two elementary Forms. Those two Forms produced the Four emblematic Symbols, which again produced the eight Trigrams.

71. The eight trigrams served to determine the good and evil (issues of events), and from this determination was produced the (successful prosecution of the) great business (of life).

72. Therefore of all things that furnish models and visible figures there are none greater than heaven and earth; of things that change and extend an influence (on others) there are none greater than the four seasons; of things suspended (in the sky) with their figures displayed clear and bright, there are none greater than the sun and moon; of the honoured and exalted there are none greater than he who is the rich and noble (one); in preparing things for practical use, and inventing and making instruments for the benefit of all under the sky, there are none greater than the sages; to explore what is complex, search out what is hidden, to hook up what lies deep, and reach to what is distant, thereby determining (the issues) for good or ill of all events under the sky, and making all men under heaven full of strenuous endeavours, there

are no (agencies) greater than those of the stalks and the tortoise-shell.

73. Therefore Heaven produced the spirit-like things, and the sages took advantage of them. (The operations of) heaven and earth are marked by (so many) changes and transformations; and the sages imitated them (by means of the Yî). Heaven hangs out its (brilliant) figures from which are seen good fortune and bad, and the sages made their emblematic interpretations accordingly. The Ho gave forth the map, and the Lo the writing, of (both of) which the sages took advantage.

74. In the (scheme of the) Yî there are the four symbolic figures by which they inform men (in divining of the lines making up the diagrams); the explanations appended to them convey the significance (of the diagrams and lines); and the determination (of the divination) as fortunate or the reverse, to settle the doubts (of men).

Chapter XI, paragraphs 66–74, treats of divination, and the scheme of it supplied in the Yî. That scheme must be referred first to Heaven, which produced the spirit-like things,—the divining-plant and the tortoise; and next to the sages, who knew the mind of Heaven, and made the plant and shell subservient to the purpose for which they were intended.

Paragraph 66 answers the question of what the Yî does; and if there were truth or rèason in it, the book and its use would be most important. I have closed the quotation of "the Master's" words at the end of the paragraph; but really we do not know if they extend so far, or farther.

Paragraphs 67 and 68 glorify the sages and their work. The virtues of the divining-plant all belonged to them, and it was thus that they were able to organise the scheme of divination. The production of 'the spirit-like things' is, in paragraph 73, ascribed to 'Heaven;' the characters about them in these paragraphs mean no more than is expressed in the translation.

易經

Chapter XII. 75. It is said in the Yî, 'Help is given to him from Heaven. There will be good fortune; advantage in every respect.' The Master

---

Paragraph 69 shows how the antinomy of the yin and yang pervades all nature, and how the sages turned it, as existing pre-eminently in the divining-plant, to account.

Paragraph 70. Evidently the author had in view here the genesis of the diagrams of the Yî, the number of figures increasing in a geometrical progression with the ratio of 2, while the lines of the figures form an arithmetical progression with the common difference of 1. This is quite plain after 'the two elementary forms (——— and — —)' have been made. They give birth to 'the four emblematic symbols,' each of two lines (⚌, ⚍, ⚎, ⚏, known, in this order, as the Grand or old Yang, the young Yin, the young Yang, and the Grand or old Yin). By the addition to each of these symbols first of the yang line, and then of the yin, there arise the eight trigrams, each of three lines; and the process of formation might be continued indefinitely.

But how was the first step taken in the formation of the two elementary lines? Here, it is said, they were produced by the Thâi *K*î, or the Grand Terminus. This is represented in *K*û Hsî's 'Youth's Introduction to the Study of the Yî,' by a circle; but he tells us that that representation of it was first made by *K*âu-ȝze (A.D. 1017–1073, called also *K*âu Tun-î, *K*âu Mâu-shû, and, most of all, *K*âu Lien-*kh*i), and that his readers must be careful not to suppose that Fû-hsî had such a figure in his mind's eye. I fail myself to understand how there can be generated from a circle the undivided and the broken line. Given those two lines, and the formation of the sixty-four hexagrams proceeds regularly according to the method above described. We must start from them, whether we can account or not for the rise of the idea of them in the mind of Fû-hsî.

Leaving the subject of the figure of the Thâi *K*î, the name gives us hardly any clue to its meaning. *K*î is used for the extreme term of anything, as the ridge-pole of a house, or the pinnacle of a pagoda. The comment on the first sentence in the paragraph by Wang Pî (A.D. 226–249) is:—'Existence must begin in non-existence, and therefore the Grand Terminus produced the two elementary Forms. Thâi *K*î is the denomination of what has no denomination. As it cannot be named, the text takes the extreme

said:—'Yû (祐) is the symbol of assisting. He whom Heaven assists is observant (of what is right); he whom men assist is sincere. The individual here indicated treads the path of sincerity and desires to be observant (of what is right), and studies to exalt the worthy. Hence "Help is given to him from Heaven. There will be good fortune, advantage in every respect."'

76. The Master said:—'The written characters are

---

point of anything that exists as an analogous term for the Thâi *K*î.' Expanding Wang's comment, Khung Ying-tâ says:—'Thâi *K*î means the original subtle matter, that formed the one chaotic mass before heaven and earth were divided;' and then he refers to certain passages in Lâo-ȝze's Tâo Teh King, and identifies the Thâi *K*î with his Tâo. This would seem to give to Thâi *K*î a material meaning. The later philosophers of the Sung school, however, insist on its being immaterial, now calling it lî, the principle of order in nature, now tâo, the defined course of things, now Tî, the Supreme Power or God, now shăn, the spiritual working of God. According to *Kh*ăng-ȝze, all these names are to be referred to that of 'Heaven,' of which they express so many different concepts.

Paragraph 71 speaks of divination in practice, and paragraph 72 celebrates the service done by that through the plant and shell, as equal to, and indeed the complement of, all the other services rendered by heaven and earth, the seasons, the sun and moon, the sages, and the greatest potentates. Surely, it is all very extravagant.

The last two paragraphs resume the theme of the making of the Yî by the sages, and their teaching the practice of divination. Of the Ho map and the Lo writing, I have spoken in the Introduction, pages 14–18. But if we accept the statement that the Lo writing had anything to do with the making of the Yî, we must except Fû-hsî from the sages to whom we are indebted for it. It was to the Great Yü, more than a thousand years later than Fû-hsî, that the Lo disclosed its writing; and Yü is never said to have had anything to do with the Yî. Nor is either of these things mentioned in Section ii, paragraph 11, where the work of Fû-hsî is described more in detail.

not the full exponent of speech, and speech is not the full expression of ideas;—is it impossible then to discover the ideas of the sages?' The Master said:—'The sages made their emblematic symbols to set forth fully their ideas; appointed (all) the diagrams to show fully the truth and falsehood (of things); appended their explanations to give the full expression of their words; and changed (the various lines) and made general the method of doing so, to exhibit fully what was advantageous. They (thus) stimulated (the people) as by drums and dances, thereby completely developing the spirit-like (character of the Yî).'

77. May we not say that *Kh*ien and Khwăn [= the yang and yin, or the undivided and divided lines] are the secret and substance of the Yî? *Kh*ien and Khwăn being established in their several places, the system of changes was thereby constituted. If *Kh*ien and Khwăn were taken away, there would be no means of seeing that system; and if that system were not seen, *Kh*ien and Khwăn would almost cease to act.

78. Hence that which is antecedent to the material form exists, we say, as an ideal method, and that which is subsequent to the material form exists, we say, as a definite thing.

Transformation and shaping is what we call change; carrying this out and operating with it is what we call generalising the method; taking the result and setting it forth for all the people under heaven is, we say, (securing the success of) the business of life.

79. Hence, to speak of the emblematic figures:—(The sage) was able to survey all the complex phe-

nomena under the sky. He then considered in his mind how they could be figured, and (by means of the diagrams) represented their material forms and their character. Hence those (diagrams) are denominated Semblances. A (later) sage was able to survey the motive influences working all under the sky. He contemplated them in their common action and special nature, in order to bring out the standard and proper tendency of each. He then appended his explanation (to each line), to determine the good or evil indicated by it. Hence those (lines with their explanations) are denominated Imitations (the Yâo).

80. The most thorough mastery of all the complex phenomena under the sky is obtained from the diagrams. The greatest stimulus to movement in adaptation to all affairs under the sky is obtained from the explanations.

81. The transformations and shaping that take place are obtained from the changes (of the lines); the carrying this out and operating with it is obtained from the general method (that has been established). The seeing their spirit-like intimations and understanding them depended on their being the proper men; and the completing (the study of) them by silent meditation, and securing the faith of others without the use of words, depended on their virtuous conduct.

Chapter XII, paragraphs 75–81, endeavours to show how we have in the Yî a representation of the changing phenomena of nature, and such a representation as words or speech could not convey.

Paragraph 75 has a good meaning, taken by itself; but it has no apparent connexion with the rest of the chapter. *K*û Hsî thought

SECTION II.

Chapter I. 1. The eight trigrams having been completed in their proper order, there were in each the (three) emblematic lines. They were then

---

it was misplaced in its present position, and should be at the end of chapter 8. Compare paragraph 14.

The first two statements of paragraph 76 are general, but made here specially to exalt the Yî, as teaching more clearly and fully than written characters could have done. The Khang-hsî editors decide that 'the emblematic figures' here are the eight trigrams of Fû-hsî,—against the view of *K*û Hsî, which restricts them to signify the undivided and divided lines. The repetition of the words, 'The Master said,' is probably the error of an early transcriber.

Paragraphs 77 and 78 refer to the phenomena of nature and the course of human affairs, as suggesting and controlling the formation of the system of the Yî. The formation of that becomes the subject in paragraph 79. *Kh*ien and Khwăn are used, as we have already seen them more than once, for the active and inactive conditions in nature, indicated by the divided and undivided lines. It is difficult to translate what is said in paragraph 78, about Tâo and *Kh*î;—what I have called, 'an ideal method' and 'a definite' thing. P. Regis translates the text by—'Quod non est inter figurata aut corporea sed supereminet est rationale, est ratio, Tâo; quod (est) inter figurata subjacetque certae figurae est sensibile, est instrumentum.' But tâo cannot here signify ratio or reason; for tâo and *kh*î are names for the same thing under different conditions; first as a possibility, and next as an actuality. Such is the natural interpretation of the text, and so all the great scholars of the Sung dynasty construed it, as may be seen in the 'Collected Comments' of the imperial edition. So far they were correct, however many of them might stumble and fall in confounding this 'ideal method' with God.

What follows in the paragraph has no connexion with these two statements. P. Regis, who divides his translation into two paragraphs, says:—'Satis patet utramque textus hujus partem non cohaerere.

multiplied by a process of addition till the (six) component lines appeared.

2. The strong line and the weak push themselves each into the place of the other, and hence the changes (of the diagrams) take place. The appended explanations attach to every form of them its character (of good or ill), and hence the movements (suggested by divination) are determined accordingly.

3. Good fortune and ill, occasion for repentance or regret, all arise from these movements.

4. The strong and the weak (lines) have their fixed and proper places (in the diagrams); their changes, however varied, are according to the requirements of the time (when they take place).

5. Good fortune and ill are continually prevailing each against the other by an exact rule.

6. By the same rule, heaven and earth, in their course, continually give forth (their lessons); the sun and moon continually emit their light; all the movements under the sky are constantly subject to this one and the same rule.

Quod ergo illas divisimus, id fecimus majoris perspicuitatis causa, non ratione ordinis qui certe nullus est, ut in re potius assuta quam connexa.'

Paragraph 79 is a repetition of paragraphs 38, 39, 'to introduce,' says *K*û Hsî, 'the two paragraphs' that follow.

The editors of the imperial edition find in 80, 81, an amplification mainly of 76, showing how what is said there of the natural phenomena is exhibited in the Yî. The concluding sentence is a declaration (hardly necessary) about the sage makers, to the effect that they were as distinguished for virtuous conduct as for wisdom,—'the proper men' to stand between Heaven and the mass of men as they did.

7. *Kh*ien, (the symbol of heaven, and) conveying the idea of strength, shows to men its easy (and natural) action. *Kh*wăn, (the symbol of earth, and) conveying the idea of docility, shows to men its compendious (receptivity and operation).

8. The Yâo (or lines) are imitative representations of this. The Hsiang, or emblematic figures, are pictorial representations of the same.

9. The movements of the lines and figures take place (at the hand of the operator), and are unseen; the good fortune or ill is seen openly and is beyond. The work to be done appears by the changes; the sympathies of the sages are seen in their explanations.

10. The great attribute of heaven and earth is the giving and maintaining life. What is most precious for the sage is to get the (highest) place—(in which he can be the human representative of heaven and earth). What will guard this position for him? Men. How shall he collect a large population round him? By the power of his wealth. The right administration of that wealth, correct instructions to the people, and prohibitions against wrong-doing;—these constitute his righteousness.

Chapter I, paragraphs 1–10, is an amplification, according to Khung Ying-tâ and the editors of the imperial edition of the present dynasty, of the second chapter of Section i. The latter say that as all the chapters of Section i from the third onwards serve to elucidate chapter 2, so it is with this chapter and all that follow in this Section. The formation of the diagrams, and of their several lines, their indication of good fortune and bad, and the analogy between the processes of nature and the operations of divination, and other kindred subjects, are all touched on.

The order of the eight trigrams in paragraph 1, is *kh*ien, tui,

Chapter II. 11. Anciently, when Pâo-hsî had come to the rule of all under heaven, looking up, he contemplated the brilliant forms exhibited in the sky, and looking down he surveyed the patterns shown on the earth. He contemplated the ornamental appearances of birds and beasts and the (different) suitabilities of the soil. Near at hand, in his own person, he found things for consideration, and the same at a distance, in things in general. On this he devised the eight trigrams, to show fully the

---

lî, *k*ăn, sun, khan, kăn, khwăn. The three lines of each are emblematic,—the first of heaven, the second of man, the third of earth. This is the most likely explanation of hsiang, 'the emblems' or 'similitudes' here. Why the maker—'sages'—stopt at sixty-four figures, of six lines each, is a question that cannot be answered.

Paragraph 2. Of course it was a great delusion to suppose that the changes of lines consequent on divination could be so connected with the movements of life as to justify the characterising them as good or evil, or afford any guidance in the ordering of conduct.

Paragraph 4. Who can tell 'the requirements of the time' amid the complexity of the phenomena of nature or the ever-varying events of human experience and history? The wiser men are, the more correct will be their judgments in such matters; but is there any reason for trusting to divination about them?

Paragraphs 5, 6. It is difficult to say what is 'the exact rule' intended here; unless it be that the factors in every movement shall act according to their proper nature. The Khang-hsî editors say:—'We see the good sometimes meeting with misfortune, and the bad with good fortune; but such is not the general rule.' 'The lessons that heaven and earth give forth' are those concerning the method of their operation as stated in paragraph 7, and more fully in 6, 7, 8 of Section i.

What is said in paragraph 10 is striking and important, and in harmony with the general strain of Confucian teaching;—as in the Great Learning, chapter 10, and many other places; but I fail to see its appropriateness in its present place in the Yî.

attributes of the spirit-like and intelligent (operations working secretly), and to classify the qualities of the myriads of things.

12. He invented the making of nets of various kinds by knitting strings, both for hunting and fishing. The idea of this was taken, probably, from Lî (the third trigram, and thirtieth hexagram).

13. On the death of Pâo-hsî, there arose Shăn-năng (in his place). He fashioned wood to form the share, and bent wood to make the plough-handle. The advantages of ploughing and weeding were then taught to all under heaven. The idea of this was taken, probably, from Yî (the forty-second hexagram).

14. He caused markets to be held at midday, thus bringing together all the people, and assembling in one place all their wares. They made their exchanges and retired, every one having got what he wanted. The idea of this was taken, probably, from Shih Ho (the twenty-first hexagram).

15. After the death of Shăn-năng, there arose Hwang Tî, Yâo, and Shun. They carried through the (necessarily occurring) changes, so that the people did (what was required of them) without being wearied; yea, they exerted such a spirit-like transformation, that the people felt constrained to approve their (ordinances) as right. When a series of changes has run all its course, another change ensues. When it obtains free course, it will continue long. Hence it was that 'these (sovereigns) were helped by Heaven; they had good fortune, and their every movement was advantageous.' Hwang Tî, Yâo, and Shun (simply) wore their upper and

lower garments (as patterns to the people), and good order was secured all under heaven. The idea of all this was taken, probably, from *Khien* and Khwăn (the first and eighth trigrams, or the first and second hexagrams).

16. They hollowed out trees to form canoes; they cut others long and thin to make oars. Thus arose the benefit of canoes and oars for the help of those who had no means of intercourse with others. They could now reach the most distant parts, and all under heaven were benefited. The idea of this was taken, probably, from Hwân (the fifty-ninth hexagram).

17. They used oxen (in carts) and yoked horses (to chariots), thus providing for the carriage of what was heavy, and for distant journeys,—thereby benefiting all under the sky. The idea of this was taken, probably, from Sui (the seventeenth hexagram).

18. They made the (defence of the) double gates, and (the warning of) the clapper, as a preparation against the approach of marauding visitors. The idea of this was taken, probably, from Yü (the sixteenth hexagram).

19. They cut wood and fashioned it into pestles; they dug in the ground and formed mortars. Thus the myriads of the people received the benefit arising from the use of the pestle and mortar. The idea of this was taken, probably, from Hsiâo Kwo (the sixty-second hexagram).

20. They bent wood by means of string so as to form bows, and sharpened wood so as to make arrows. This gave the benefit of bows and arrows, and served to produce everywhere a feeling of awe.

The idea of this was taken, probably, from Khwei (the thirty-eighth hexagram).

21. In the highest antiquity they made their homes (in winter) in caves, and (in summer) dwelt in the open country. In subsequent ages, for these the sages substituted houses, with the ridge-beam above and the projecting roof below, as a provision against wind and rain. The idea of this was taken, probably, from Tâ *K*wang (the thirty-fourth hexagram).

22. When the ancients buried their dead, they covered the body thickly with pieces of wood, having laid it in the open country. They raised no mound over it, nor planted trees around; nor had they any fixed period for mourning. In subsequent ages the sages substituted for these practices the inner and outer coffins. The idea of this was taken, probably, from Tâ Kwo (the twenty-eighth hexagram).

23. In the highest antiquity, government was carried on successfully by the use of knotted cords (to preserve the memory of things). In subsequent ages the sages substituted for these written characters and bonds. By means of these (the doings of) all the officers could be regulated, and (the affairs of) all the people accurately examined. The idea of this was taken, probably, from Kwâi (the forty-third hexagram).

Chapter II, paragraphs 11–23, treats of the progress of civilisation in China, and how the great men of antiquity who led the way in the various steps of that progress were guided by the Yî. Only five of these are mentioned;—the first, Fû-hsî, the beginning of whose reign, according to the least unlikely of the chronological accounts, must be placed in the 34th century B.C., while Shun's

Chapter III. 24. Therefore what we call the Yî is (a collection of) emblematic lines. They are styled emblematic as being resemblances.

---

reign ended in B.C. 2203. The time embraced in this chapter therefore is about twelve centuries and a half. But the writer gives his own opinion that the various discoveries and inventions mentioned were suggested to their authors by certain hexagrams of the Yî. The most commonly received view, however, is that Fû-hsî had only the eight trigrams, and that the multiplication of them to the 64 hexagrams was the work of king Wăn, fully a thousand years later than Shun. This is the view of the editors of the imperial Yî. If it be contended that Fû-hsî himself multiplied his trigrams, and gave their names to the resulting hexagrams, how could he have wrapped up in them the intimations of discoveries which were not made till many centuries after his death? The statements in the chapter cannot be received as historical. It came from another hand, and not from Confucius himself. The writer or compiler gives the legends current about the various inventions of his time. The making of the trigrams is placed first of all to do honour to the Yî. The account of it is different from that given in paragraph 73 of the former Section, and we hear nothing of the Ho map or Lo writing.

Paragraph 11. Pâo-hsî here and in 13 is the same as Fû-hsî. As Pâo is written here, there is no meaning in it; but another character Phâo (庖) is more common, and Phâo-hsî would mean the inventor of the kitchen and cookery. This was the first step towards civilisation, and was appropriately followed by the hunting and fishing—both by means of nets—in paragraph 12.

Paragraphs 13, 14 celebrate the work of Shăn-năng, 'the marvellous or spirit-like husbandman.' There was no metal about the primitive plough. The market for the exchange of commodities, without the use of coin, was an important advance.

The invention of the robes, or of dress, mentioned in paragraph 15, would seem to show that previously men had been in a very rude state. The passage indicates, however, the courtesies and proprieties of social life, in which dress plays an important part, and which now began to be organised.

The infant navigation in paragraph 16 was as little indebted to the use of metal as the agriculture of 13.

Paragraphs 17 and 18 show that in those primitive times there

25. What we call the Thwan (or king Wăn's explanations) are based on the significance (of each hexagram as a whole).

26. We call the lines (of the figures) Yâo from their being according to the movements taking place all under the sky.

27. In this way (we see) the rise of good fortune and evil, and the manifestation of repentance and regret.

---

were already the practices of rapine and war. 'The double gates' were those of the city wall, and of the enclosed suburb. The clapper may still be heard all over China. Bows and arrows, however, came rather later, as in 20.

I suppose 'the sages' in paragraphs 21, 22, 23 refer generally to the great names mentioned in the previous chapters; nor can we define the distinction in the writer or compiler's mind between 'antiquity' and 'the highest antiquity.' Compare what is said on the rise of the coffin in 22 with Mencius' remarks on the same subject in Book III, ii, 5. 4. He would hardly have expressed himself as he did, if he had been familiar with this text. The invention of written characters is generally ascribed to Fû-hsî. Paragraph 23 does not say so, but the inventor is said to have been a sage of a subsequent age to the time of 'high antiquity.' That 'high antiquity' must stretch back very far.

Chapter III, paragraphs 24–27, treats of the Yî as made up of figurative diagrams, which again are composed of lines ever changing, in accordance with the phenomena of nature and human experience, while to the resulting figures their moral character and providential issues are appended by the sages. It may be regarded as an epitome of chapter 2 in Section i.

Paragraph 24. It is observed by the editors of the imperial edition that a chapter should not begin with a 'therefore;' and they are inclined to agree with many critics who would enter this as the last paragraph of the preceding chapter. In that case it would be a summing-up of the concluding sentences of the different paragraphs, the truth and genuineness of which are deservedly suspected. The characters for 'therefore,' however, are very loosely used in these Appendixes.—The lines, as they were intended by

Chapter IV. 28. In the Yang trigrams (or those of the undivided line) there are more of the Yin lines, and in the Yin trigrams (or those of the divided line) there are more of the Yang lines.

29. What is the cause of this? It is because the Yang lines are odd (or made by one stroke), and the Yin lines are even (or made by two strokes).

30. What (method of) virtuous conduct is thus intimated? In the Yang trigrams we have one ruler, and two subjects,—suggesting the way of the superior man. In the Yin trigrams we have two rulers, and one subject,—suggesting the way of the small man.

Fû-hsî, were emblematic; and they are still more so, as interpreted by the duke of *K*âu. Meanings are drawn from the figures that resemble or illustrate principles in the subjects to which they are applied.

Paragraph 25. The character rendered 'the significance' means materials, and is illustrated by reference to all the different materials out of which a house is composed. So there are half-a-dozen things about the diagrams, their lineal structure, emblematic intention, their attributes, &c., out of which their interpretation is fashioned.

Paragraph 26. E. g. an undivided line may appear in an odd place, which is right, or in an even place, which is wrong; and the case is the opposite with the divided lines. But what has this to do with the right or wrong of the events divined about?

Chapter IV, paragraphs 28–30. Of the distinction of the trigrams into Yang and Yin.

The trigrams that contain only one undivided line—*k*ăn (☶), khan (☵), and kăn (☳)—are called Yang. The undivided line is called 'the lord' in them. It is just the opposite with the Yin trigrams, in which there are two undivided lines, and one divided,—sun (☴), lî (☲), and tui (☱). These together constitute the 'six children,' or 'three

Chapter V. 31. It is said in the Yî, 'Full of anxious thoughts you go and come; (only) friends will follow you and think with you.' The Master said:—'In all (the processes taking place) under heaven, what is there of thinking? what is there of anxious scheming? They all come to the same (successful) issue, though by different paths; there is one result, though there might be a hundred anxious schemes. What is there of thinking? what is there of anxious scheming?'

32. The sun goes and the moon comes; the moon goes and the sun comes;—the sun and moon thus take the place each of the other, and their shining is the result. The cold goes and the heat comes; the heat goes and the cold comes;—it is by this mutual succession of the cold and heat that the year is completed. That which goes becomes less and less, and that which comes waxes more and more;—it is by the influence on each other of this contraction and expansion that the advantages (of the different conditions) are produced.

33. When the looper coils itself up, it thereby straightens itself again; when worms and snakes

---

sons' and 'three daughters' in the later arrangement of the trigrams, ascribed to king Wăn.

Paragraph 29. Each part of the divided line counts as one; hence a yang trigram counts as $1 + 2 + 2 = 5$ strokes, four of which are yin, while a yin trigram counts as $2 + 1 + 1 = 4$, only two of which are yang. But this is mere trifling.

In explanation of paragraph 30 it is said that 'we have in the yang trigrams two (or more) subjects serving one ruler, and in the yin one subject serving two rulers, and two rulers striving together for the allegiance of one subject.' This is ingenious, but fanciful; as indeed this distinction of the trigrams into a yang class and a yin is a mere play of fancy.

go into the state of hybernation, they thereby keep themselves alive. (So), when we minutely investigate the nature and reasons (of things), till we have entered into the inscrutable and spirit-like in them, we attain to the largest practical application of them; when that application becomes the quickest and readiest, and all personal restfulness is secured, our virtue is thereby exalted.

34. Going on beyond this, we reach a point which it is hardly possible to know. We have thoroughly comprehended the inscrutable and spirit-like, and know the processes of transformation;—this is the fulness of virtue.

35. It is said in the Yî, '(The third line shows its subject) distressed before a rock, and trying to lay hold of thorns; entering into his palace and not seeing his wife:—there will be evil.' The Master said:—'If one be distressed by what need not distress him, his name is sure to be disgraced; if he lay hold on what he should not touch, his life is sure to be imperilled. In disgrace and danger, his death will (soon) come;—is it possible for him in such circumstances to see his wife?'

36. It is said in the Yî, 'The duke with (his bow) shoots at the falcon on the top of the high wall; he hits it:—his every movement will be advantageous.' The Master said:—'The falcon is a bird (of prey); the bow and arrow is a weapon (of war); the shooter is a man. The superior man keeps his weapon concealed about his person, and waits for the proper time to move;—doing this, how should his movement be other than successful? There is nothing to fetter or embarrass his movement; and hence, when he comes forth, he succeeds in his object.

The language speaks of movement when the instrument necessary to it is ready and perfect.'

37. The Master said:—'The small man is not ashamed of what is not benevolent, nor does he fear to do what is not righteous. Without the prospect of gain he does not stimulate himself to what is good, nor does he correct himself without being moved. Self-correction, however, in what is small will make him careful in what would be of greater consequence;—and this is the happiness of the small man. It is said in the Yî, "His feet are in the stocks, and he is disabled in his toes:—there will be no (further) occasion for blame."'

38. If acts of goodness be not accumulated, they are not sufficient to give its finish to one's name; if acts of evil be not accumulated, they are not sufficient to destroy one's life. The small man thinks that small acts of goodness are of no benefit, and does not do them; and that small deeds of evil do no harm, and does not abstain from them. Hence his wickedness becomes great till it cannot be covered, and his guilt becomes great till it cannot be pardoned. This is what the Yî says, 'He wears the cangue and his ears are destroyed:—there will be evil.'

39. The Master said:—'He who keeps danger in mind is he who will rest safe in his seat; he who keeps ruin in mind is he who will preserve his interests secure; he who sets the danger of disorder before him is he who will maintain the state of order. Therefore the superior man, when resting in safety, does not forget that danger may come; when in a state of security, he does not forget the possibility of ruin; and when all is in a state of order, he does not

forget that disorder may come. Thus his person is kept safe, and his states and all their clans can be preserved. This is according to what the Yî says, "(Let him say), 'Shall I perish? shall I perish?' (so shall this state be firm, as if) bound to a clump of bushy mulberry trees."'

40. The Master said:—'Virtue small and office high; wisdom small and plans great; strength small and burden heavy:—where such conditions exist, it is seldom that they do not end (in evil). As is said in the Yî, "The tripod's feet are overthrown, and the ruler's food is overturned. The body of him (who is thus indicated) is wet (with shame):—there will be evil."'

41. The Master said:—'Does not he who knows the springs of things possess spirit-like wisdom? The superior man, in his intercourse with the high, uses no flattery, and, in his intercourse with the low, no coarse freedom:—does not this show that he knows the springs of things? Those springs are the slight beginnings of movement, and the earliest indications of good fortune (or ill). The superior man sees them, and acts accordingly without waiting for (the delay of) a single day. As is said in the Yî, "He is firm as a rock, (and acts) without the delay of a single day. With firm goodness there will be good fortune." Firm as a rock, how should he have to wait a single day to ensure his knowing (those springs and his course)? The superior man knows the minute and the manifested; he knows what is weak, and what is strong:—he is a model to ten thousand.'

42. The Master said:—'I may venture to say that the son of the Yen family had nearly attained (the

standard of perfection). If anything that he did was not good, he was sure to become conscious of that; and when he knew it, he did not do the thing again. As is said in the Yî, "(The first line shows its subject) returning from an error that has not led him far away. There is no occasion for repentance. There will be great good."'

43. There is an intermingling of the genial influences of heaven and earth, and transformation in its various forms abundantly proceeds. There is an intercommunication of seed between male and female, and transformation in its living types proceeds. What is said in the Yî, 'Three individuals are walking together and one is made to disappear; there is (but) one man walking, and he gets his mate,' tells us of the effort (in nature) at oneness (of operation).

44. The Master said:—'The superior man (in a high place) composes himself before he (tries to) move others; makes his mind restful and easy before he speaks; settles (the principles of) his intercourse with others before he seeks anything from them. The superior man cultivates these three things, and so is complete. If he try to move others while he is himself in unrest, the people will not (act) with him; if he speak while he is himself in a state of apprehension, the people will not respond to him; if without (certain principles of) intercommunication, he issue his requests, the people will not grant them. When there are none to accord with him, those who (work to) injure him will make their appearance. As is said in the Yî, "(We see one) to whose advantage none will contribute, while some will seek to assail him. He observes no

regular rule in the ordering of his heart:—there will be evil."'

Chapter V, paragraphs 31-44, gives the words of the duke of *K*âu on eleven different lines in the Text of the Yî, along with remarks of Confucius in farther illustration of them. But they seem also to be intended to bring forth more fully the meaning of certain previous utterances about the structure and scope of the Yî.

Paragraphs 31-34 start from the fourth line of the 31st hexagram, which would seem merely to require a steady and unvarying purpose in any one, in order to the full development of his influence. The editors of the imperial edition, however, make the whole a sequel of paragraph 5. But granted that there is no 'anxious scheming' in the processes of the natural world or in the phenomena of insect life, there is really no analogy to their proceedings in the course of the man who makes himself master of 'the nature and reasons of things,' as described in 33 and 34. Nor are 'the nature and reasons of things' to be found in the Yî, as the writer believed they were. Such as it is, it requires immense thought to understand it, and when we have laid hold of it, there is nothing substantial in our grasp. The 'virtue' predicated of such attainment is not so much moral excellence, as apprehension and the power and ability to invent, and to affect others.

Paragraph 35. See on the third line of Khwăn, the 47th hexagram. If we were to translate the explanations of the line after Confucius, we should put the first two statements hypothetically; but the four that compose it seem to run on in the same way. They are all, I apprehend, hypothetical.

Paragraph 36. See on the last line of *K*ieh, the 40th hexagram.

Paragraph 37. See on the first line of Shih Ho, the 21st hexagram. The 'self-correction in what is small' implies of course that the small man has been 'awed.' What is said about him here is true; but we hardly expect it in this place.

Paragraph 38 should probably begin, like those before and after it, with 'The Master said.' The characters quoted from the Yî are again from the text of Shih Ho, on the last line.

Paragraph 39. See on the fifth line of Phî, the 12th hexagram.

Paragraph 40 gives Confucius' views on the fourth line of Ting, the 50th hexagram.

In paragraph 41 we are conducted to the 16th hexagram,—the

Chapter VI. 45. The Master said:—'(The trigrams) *Kh*ien and Khwăn may be regarded as the gate of the Yî.' *Kh*ien represents what is of the yang nature (bright and active); Khwăn what is of the yin nature (shaded and inactive). These two unite according to their qualities, and there comes the embodiment of the result by the strong and weak (lines). In this way we have the phenomena of heaven and earth visibly exhibited, and can comprehend the operation of the spiritual intelligence.

46. The appellations and names (of the diagrams and lines) are various, but do not go beyond (what is to be ascribed to the operation of these two conditions). When we examine the nature and style

---

second line of it. The being 'firm as a rock' is understood to symbolise the state of 'rest,' the quiet self-possession out of which successful movement and action is understood to spring.

In paragraph 42, 'the son of the Yen family' is Yen Hui, the favourite disciple of Confucius. The passage quoted from the Yî is that on the first line of Fû, the 24th hexagram.

To paragraph 43, as to paragraph 38, I would prefix the characters for 'The Master said.' 'Male and female' is to be taken generally, and not confined to the individuals of the human pair. One Chinese writer says that in the transformations ascribed to heaven and earth, birds, fishes, animals, and plants are included, but from the 'transformation in its living types' plants are excluded, because in their generation there is nothing analogous to the emission and reception of seed. Other Chinese writers, however, are well enough acquainted with the sexual system of plants. It would seem to me that Confucius, if the paragraph were really his, intended only plants or the vegetable world in his reference to the operation of heaven and earth, and had all living tribes in view in his mention of male and female. The passage of the Yî referred to is on the third line of Sun, the 41st hexagram. The application of it is far-fetched.

Paragraph 44. See on the fifth line of Yî, the 42nd hexagram.

(of the appended explanations), they seem to express the ideas of a decaying age.

47. The Yî exhibits the past, and (teaches us to) discriminate (the issues of) the future; it makes manifest what is minute, and brings to light what is obscure. (Then king Wăn) opened (its symbols), and distinguished things in accordance with its names, so that all his words were correct and his explanations decisive;—(the book) was now complete.

48. The appellations and names (of the diagrams and lines) are but small matters, but the classes of things comprehended under them are large. Their scope reaches far, and the explanations attached to them are elegant. The words are indirect, but to the point; the matters seem plainly set forth, but there is a secret principle in them. Their object is, in cases that are doubtful, to help the people in their conduct, and to make plain the recompenses of good and evil.

The principal object, it is said, of chapter VI, paragraphs 45–48, is to set forth the views of king Wăn and his son in the explanations which they appended to the diagrams and lines; and in doing this the writer begins in 45, with Fû-hsî's starting, in the formation of his eight trigrams, from the devising of the whole and divided lines, to represent the two primitive forms in nature. The two 'pure' trigrams formed of these lines, unmixed, give rise to all the others, or rather the lines of which they are formed do so; and are thus compared to a gate by which the various diagrams enter to complete the system that is intended to represent the changing phenomena of nature and experience. The next sentence in the above version of paragraph 45 appears in Canon McClatchie's translation of the Yî, as follows:—'*Kh*ien is the membrum virile, and Khwăn is the pudendum muliebre (the sakti of *Kh*ien).' It is hardly possible, on reading such a version, to suppress the exclamation proh pudor! Can a single passage be adduced in support of it from among all the Chinese critics in the

易經

Chapter VII. 49. Was it not in the middle period of antiquity that the Yî began to flourish? Was not he who made it familiar with anxiety and calamity?

50. Therefore (the 10th diagram), Lî, shows us the foundation of virtue; (the 15th), Hsien, its handle; (the 24th), Fû, its root; (the 32nd), Hăng, its solidity; (the 41st), Sun, its cultivation; (the 42nd), Yî, its abundance; (the 47th), Khwăn, its exercise of discrimination; (the 48th), 3ing, its field; and (the 57th), Sun, its regulation.

51. In Lî we have the perfection of harmony; in Hsien, we have the giving honour to others,

---

line of centuries? I believe not. The ideas which it expresses are gratuitously and wantonly thrust into this text of the Yî. '*Kh*ien' and 'Khwăn' are not spoken of thus. If the latter half of the paragraph be unintelligible, this interpretation of the former would make the whole disgusting.

In paragraph 46 the writer passes from the work of Fû-hsî to that of king Wăn and his son, and the composition of the written Yi is referred to 'a decaying age,'—the age, namely, of the tyrant *K*âu. Then king Wăn and the duke of *K*âu, it is said, deploring the degeneracy of their times and the enormities of the government, indicated, by their treatment of the ancient symbols, their sense of right and wrong, and the methods by which the prevailing evils might be rectified.

Paragraphs 47 and 48 follow and expand the meaning of 45. The editors of the imperial edition say that the former sentence of 47 is the sequel of 45, and the latter of 46, bringing us finally to the explanations and decisions of king Wăn, as the most important portion of the Yî. *K*û Hsî, moreover, observes that throughout the chapter, as well as in the chapters that follow, there must be many characters wanting in the text, while there are many also that are doubtful. This is specially the case with 48. Where the order of the characters has been disarranged merely, correction is easy; but where characters are evidently missing, attempts to fill the lacunae are merely guess-work.

and the distinction thence arising; in Fû we have what is small (at first), but there is in it a (nice) discrimination of (the qualities of) things; in Hăng we have a mixed experience, but without any weariness; in Sun we have difficulty in the beginning and ease in the end; in Yî we have abundance of growth without any contrivance; in Khwăn we have the pressure of extreme difficulty, ending in a free course; in 3ing we have abiding in one's place and at the same time removal (to meet the movement of others); and in Sun we have the weighing of things (and action accordingly), but secretly and unobserved.

52. (The use of) Lî appears in the harmony of the conduct; of Hsien, in the regulation of ceremonies; of Fû, in self-knowledge; of Hăng, in uniformity of virtue; of Sun, in keeping what is harmful at a distance; of Yî, in the promotion of what is advantageous; of Khwăn, in the diminution of resentments; of 3ing, in the discrimination of what is righteous; and of Sun, in the doing of what is appropriate to time and to circumstances.

Chapter VII, paragraphs 49–52, is occupied with nine hexagrams, as specially indicating how the superior man, or the ruler, should deal with a time of trouble and solicitude, specially by the cultivation of his own virtue. Not, we are told, that the same thing might not be learned from other diagrams, but these nine specially occurred to the writer, or, as many think, to Confucius.

Paragraph 49 is important as agreeing in its testimony with 46. The Yî was made in middle-antiquity; that is, in the end of the Shang dynasty, and the rise of the *K*âu; and the maker or makers had personal and public reasons for anxiety about the signs of the times.

Paragraph 50 shows the particular phase of virtue in each of the nine hexagrams that are mentioned; 51, the marvellous character-

Chapter VIII. 53. The Yî is a book which should not be let slip from the mind. Its method (of teaching) is marked by the frequent changing (of its lines). They change and move without staying (in one place), flowing about into any one of the six places of the hexagram. They ascend and descend, ever inconstant. The strong and the weak lines change places, so that an invariable and compendious rule cannot be derived from them;—it must vary as their changes indicate.

54. The goings forth and comings in (of the lines) are according to rule and measure. (People) learn from them in external and internal affairs to stand in awe.

55. (The book), moreover, makes plain the nature of anxieties and calamities, and the causes of them. Though (its students) have neither master nor guardian, it is as if their parents drew near to them.

56. Beginning with taking note of its explanations, we reason out the principles to which they point. We thus find out that it does supply a constant and standard rule. But if there be not the proper men (to carry this out), the course cannot be pursued without them.

---

istics of each phase; and 52, its use. The 'therefore' with which paragraph 50 commences shows the process of thought by which the writer passed from the anxiety that possessed the mind of the author of the Yî to the use to be derived, in such circumstances, from the study of Lî and the other hexagrams.

Chapter VIII, paragraphs 53–56, describes the method of studying the Yî as consisting very much in watching the changes that take place in the lines, and reflecting on the appended explanations; while, after all, much must depend on there being 'the proper men,' to carry its lessons into practice.

Chapter IX. 57. The Yî is a book in which the form (of each diagram) is determined by the lines from the first to the last, which must be carefully observed. The six lines are mixed together, according to the time (when they enter the figure) and their substance (as whole and divided).

58. There is difficulty in knowing (the significance of) the first line, while to know that of the topmost line is easy;—they form the beginning and the end (of the diagram). The explanation of the first line tasks the calculating (of the makers), but in the end they had (but) to complete this.

59. As to the variously-disposed intermediate lines with their diverse formations, for determining their qualities, and discriminating the right and wrong in them, we should be unprovided but for the explanations of them.

60. Yea, moreover, if we wish to know what is likely to be preserved and what to perish, what will be lucky and what will be unlucky, this may easily be known (from the explanations of the different lines). But if the wise will look at the explanations of the entire diagrams, their thoughts will embrace more than half of this knowledge.

61. The second and fourth lines are of the same

There seems to be a contradiction between the statements in paragraphs 53 and 56 about the book supplying, and not supplying, a standard rule; but the meaning, probably, is that while it does not give a rule generally applicable, it gives rules for particular cases.

*K*û Hsî says he does not understand 54, and thinks some characters must have been lost. 'The six places of the hexagram' in 53 are, literally, 'the six empties.' The places are so called, because it is only a temporary possession of them, which is held by the fugitive lines, whether whole or divided.

quality (as being in even places), but their positions (with respect to the fifth line) are different, and their value is not the same; but the second is the object of much commendation, and the fourth the subject of many apprehensions,—from its nearness (to that line). But for a line in a place of weakness it is not good to be far (from the occupant of the place of strength), and what its subject should desire in such a case is (merely) to be without blame. The advantage (here) is in (the second line) being in the central place.

62. The third and fifth lines are of the same quality, (as being in odd places), but their positions are different; and the (occupant of) the third meets with many misfortunes, while the occupant of the fifth achieves much merit:—this arises from one being in the noble position and the other in the mean. Are they occupied by the symbol of weakness? There will be peril. By that of strength? There will be victory.

Chapter IX, paragraphs 56–62, speaks of the hexagrams as made up of the different lines, and various things to be attended to in those lines to determine their meaning.

Paragraph 57. The time or order in which the lines enter determines of course the place and number of each in the figure. Their 'substance' is their form, as whole or divided, being yang or yin.

Paragraph 58 belongs to the first and sixth lines. We are hardly prepared for the statement that 'the maker or makers' had so much difficulty in determining the meaning of the first line. Of course when they had fixed that and completed the figure, explaining all the lines, it was easy for the student to follow their exposition, as paragraph 59 says.

Paragraph 60 seems to say that the work of the duke of *K*âu on each line was but an indicating in detail of the processes of his father's mind in explaining the whole figure.

Chapter X. 63. The Yî is a book of wide comprehension and great scope, embracing everything. There are in it the way of heaven, the way of man, and the way of earth. It then takes (the lines representing) those three Powers, and doubles them till they amount to six. What these six lines show is simply this,—the way of the three Powers.

64. This way is marked by changes and movements, and hence we have the imitative lines. Those lines are of different grades (in the trigrams), and hence we designate them from their component elements. These are mixed together, and elegant forms arise. When such forms are not in their appropriate places, the ideas of good fortune and bad are thus produced.

The last two paragraphs mention several points important to be attended to in studying, more especially, the duke of *K*âu on the several lines. Three different views of the concluding statement,—'are they occupied,' &c.,—are given in the imperial edition. 'It belongs,' says Wû *K*ăng, 'to the fifth line;' 'to the third line,' says Hû Ping-wăn (also of the Yüan dynasty); while Hân Hsing-kwo (of the Thang dynasty) held that it belonged to both. The Khang-hsî editors say that 'by discriminating and combining these views, we get to the meaning of the text.' I am unable to do so.

Chapter X, paragraphs 63, 64, speaks of the great comprehensiveness of the Yî, its figures and explanations being applicable to the three Powers—heaven, earth, and man.

With paragraph 63, compare paragraph 4, Appendix VI. In the trigram the upper line represents heaven, the middle line man, and the lowest earth. This paragraph and that other are the nearest approach I know to an attempt to account for the doubling of the number of lines, and stopping with the hexagram; but the doing so was entirely arbitrary. *K*û Hsî says:—'The upper two characters belong to heaven, the middle two to man, and the lower two to earth.' No words could be more express; and yet Canon McClatchie says (p. 354):—'The two upper strokes represent Heaven, or Thâi-yî, the husband; the two middle strokes, Earth, his wife; and the

Chapter XI. 65. Was it not in the last age of Yin, when the virtue of *K*âu had reached its highest point, and during the troubles between king Wăn and (the tyrant) *K*âu, that the (study of the Yî) began to flourish? On this account the explanations (in the book) express (a feeling of) anxious apprehension, (and teach) how peril may be turned into security, and easy carelessness is sure to meet with overthrow. The method in which these things come about is very comprehensive, and must be acknowledged in every sphere of things. If at the beginning there be a cautious apprehension as to the end, there will probably be no error or cause for blame. This is what is called the way of the Yî.

---

two lower strokes, Man, their son; all being animated by the same Divine Reason (tâo) or Supreme God (Chih Shăn).' This note shows how one error, or misunderstanding of the Chinese original, draws other errors with it. The character tâo in the paragraph has not at all the sense of reason, human or divine, but its primary and ordinary signification of the path or course. As Lû Ȝî (Han dynasty) says:—'In the way of heaven there are the changes of day and night, sun and moon; in that of earth, those of hardness and softness, dryness and moisture; in that of man, those of action and rest, of movement and stillness, of good fortune and bad, of good and evil.'

'The imitative lines' in the translation of 64, is simply 'the Yâo' in the Chinese text, which I have rendered according to the account of them in paragraph 8, et al. Their different grades are their position as high or low in the figures (paragraph 1, Section i), and their 'component elements,' literally 'their substance, or thing-nature,' is their structure as being yang or yin, according to the use of wuh in paragraphs 57, 59, et al. A yang line in an even place, or a yin line in an odd, is not in its appropriate place, and gives an indication of what is bad.

Chapter XI, paragraph 65. P. Regis observes on this chapter:—'I do not hesitate to say that there is found nowhere in the whole

Chapter XII. 66. (The hexagram) *Kh*ien represents the strongest of all under the sky. Through this quality its operations are always manifested with ease, for it knows where there would be peril and embarrassment. (The hexagram) Khwăn represents the most docile of all under the sky. Through this quality its operations are always manifested with the promptest decision, for it knows where there would be obstruction.

67. (The sages, who are thus represented, and who made the Yî,) were able to rejoice in heart (in the absolute truth of things), and were able (also) to weigh carefully all matters that could occasion anxiety; (thus) they fixed the good and bad fortune (of all things) under the sky, and could accomplish the things requiring strenuous efforts.

68. Therefore amid the changes and transformations (taking place in heaven and earth), and the words and deeds of men, events that are to be fortunate have their happy omens. (The sages) knew the definite principles underlying the prognostications of the former class, and the future of

---

Yî a passage which affords more light for the explanation of the book.' Paragraph 49 told us that 'the study of the Yî flourished in the middle period of antiquity, and that the author of it was familiar with anxiety and troubles.' That information becomes here more particular. The Yî, existing when this Appendix was written, was made in the closing period of the Yin dynasty, and the making of it was somehow connected with the attempts of the tyrant *K*âu against king Wăn. We are not told expressly that the book was written, in part at least, by king Wăn; but the tradition to that effect derives a certain amount of support from what is said here. The general object of the author is also stated clearly enough,—to inculcate a cautious and reverent administration of affairs, never forgetful of the uncertainties of life and fortune.

those of the latter, (now to be) ascertained by divination.

69. The places of heaven and earth (in the diagrams) having been determined, the sages were able (by means of the Yî) to carry out and complete their ability. (In this way even) the common people were able to share with them in (deciding about) the counsels of men and the counsels of spiritual beings.

70. The eight trigrams communicate their information by their emblematic figures. The explanations appended to the lines and the completed figures tell how the contemplation of them affected (the makers). The strong and the weak lines appear mixed in them, and (thus) the good and the evil (which they indicate) can be seen.

71. The changes and movements (which take place in the manipulation of the stalks and the formation of the diagrams) speak as from the standpoint of what is advantageous. The (intimations of) good and evil vary according to the place and nature (of the lines). Thus they may indicate a mutual influence (in any two of them) of love or hatred, and good or evil is the result; or that mutual influence may be affected by the nearness of the lines to, or their distance from, each other, and then repentance or regret is the result; or the influence may be that of truth or of hypocrisy, and then the result is what is advantageous, or what is injurious. In all these relations of the (lines in the) Yî, if two are near and do not blend harmoniously, there may be (all these results),—evil, or what is injurious, or occasion for repentance and regret.

72. The language of him who is meditating a

revolt (from the right) betrays his inward shame; that of him whose inward heart doubts about it diverges to other topics. The words of a good man are few; those of a coarse man are many. The words of one who slanders what is good are un-

Chapter XII, paragraphs 66–72, is generally divided into three sections;—the first, embracing 66–68, and treating of the sages, the makers of the Yî, as themselves independent of it, knowing all that it enables us to know, and able to accomplish all that it enables us to accomplish; the second, embracing 69–71, and telling how the sages formed the Yî, and made all men, by means of it, partakers of their now unlimited knowledge and power; the third, comprised in paragraph 72, and saying, if it be genuine and in its proper place, that the ordinary speech of men is as mysterious and indicative of what is in them, as the explanations of the Yî are, when we consider who were its authors.

'The sages,' who are the subject of 65–68, are not mentioned in the text; but 67 makes it plain that the subject must be some personal being or beings. Neither *Kh*ien nor Khwăn can 'rejoice in heart, and weigh carefully matters occasioning anxiety.' The commentators generally interpolate 'the sages;' even Ying-tâ of the Thang dynasty, who does not introduce the sages in his exposition, yet makes the subject to be 'the disposer and nourisher of all things.' He gets to his view by an unnatural interpretation of two characters in 67, which are now thrown out of the text by all critics as not genuine. That 'the sages' is really the subject in the mind of the writer appears from the express mention of them in 69, when also 'heaven and earth' take the place of *Kh*ien and Khwăn. It is absurd, not to say blasphemous, to assume that the sages who made the Yî had the knowledge and ability here ascribed to them; but the theory of the Yî as containing a scheme for the discovery of the future necessitated the ascribing such attributes to them. Compare with the whole Section, and especially with paragraph 68, what is said in 'the Doctrine of the Mean,' chapter 24.

The first Section shows how the sages were themselves independent of the Yî, and had no need of it; the second goes on to tell how they devised and constructed it, to make all men equal to themselves in a knowledge of phenomena and human events, and of their indications of, and issues in, the future. Summing up its

substantial; those of him who is losing what he ought to keep are crooked.

---

lessons, the editors of the imperial edition say, 'There is no passage in the Appendix more full and clear than this on the five points in regard to the lines which the student of the Yî has to attend to. Those points are:—their time, position, quality, mutual nearness, and responsive relation. It is by a consideration of the two latter points, moreover, that he must form his judgment on their appropriateness or inappropriateness in the three others.'

Paragraph 72 has really no connexion with the rest of the chapter. I have stated above how the critics attempt to make out such a connexion; but I agree myself with P. Regis, who appends to his version of the paragraph this note:—'Quae sententiae quidem sapiunt doctrinam Confucianam, at non ordinem, utpote cum praecedentibus minime cohaerentes, sed omnino ab iis abscissae avulsaeque.'

APPENDIX IV.

Supplementary to the Thwan and Yâo on the first and second Hexagrams, and showing how they may be interpreted of man's nature and doings.

Section I. *Khien.*

Chapter I. 1. What is called (under *Kh*ien) 'the great and originating' is (in man) the first and chief quality of goodness; what is called 'the penetrating' is the assemblage of excellences; what is called 'the advantageous' is the harmony of all that is right; and what is called 'the correct and firm' is the faculty of action.

2. The superior man, embodying benevolence, is fit to preside over men; presenting the assemblage of excellences, he is fit to show in himself the union of all propriety; benefiting (all) creatures, he is fit to exhibit the harmony of all that is right; correct and firm, he is fit to manage (all) affairs.

3. The fact that the superior man practises these four virtues justifies the application to him of the words—'*Kh*ien represents what is great and originating, penetrating, advantageous, correct and firm.'

The title of this Appendix is in Chinese the Wăn Yen *K*wan, 'The Record of Wăn Yen;' and according to the analogy of the titles of the three Appendixes that follow, Wăn should perform the part of a verb and Yen that of a substantive. So the characters are usually taken, and to Wăn is given the meaning of 'Explaining (Shih);' and to Yen that of 'Words or Sentences,' meaning the Thwan of king Wăn, and the Yâo of the duke of *K*âu on the first two hexagrams. The document treats of these,

Chapter II. 4. What is the meaning of the words under the first line undivided, 'The dragon lies hid (in the deep);—it is not the time for active doing?' The Master said:—'There he is, with the powers of the dragon, and yet lying hid. The influence of the world would make no change in him; he would do nothing (merely) to secure his fame. He can live, withdrawn from the world, without regret; he can experience disapproval without trouble of mind. Rejoicing (in opportunity), he carries his principles

---

and of no others. 'It shows the amount and depth of meaning in them,' says *K*û Hsî, 'and the other hexagrams may be treated after the analogy supplied here.' Confucius, it is said by others, died before he was able to carry out the plan which he had formed. But, as I have shown in the Introduction (pp. 28–30), it is more than doubtful whether we have in this Appendix anything at all directly from the sage.

Chapter I, paragraphs 1–3, shows how the attributes of *Kh*ien, as explained by king Wăn, are to be understood of the constituent principles of human nature. What is remarkable is, that we find paragraphs 1, 2, with very little variation, in one of the narratives of the 3o *K*wan, as having been spoken by a marchioness-dowager of Lû in B.C. 564, several years before Confucius was born. One so familiar as *K*û Hsî was with all the classical literature of his country could not be ignorant of this. His solution of the questions arising from it is, that anciently there was this explanation of the characters of king Wăn; that it was employed by Shû *K*iang (of Lû), and that Confucius also availed himself of it; while the chronicler used, as he does below, the phraseology of 'The Master said,' to distinguish the real words of Confucius from such ancient sayings. But who was this chronicler? No one can tell. The legitimate conclusion from *K*û's criticism is this, that so much of this Appendix as is preceded by 'The Master said' is from Confucius;—so much and no more.

The ascription in paragraph 3 of 'the four virtues' to the superior or normal man, man in his best estate, and yet inferior to 'the sagely man,' is Confucian,—after the style of the teaching of the Master in the Analects.

into action; sorrowing (for want of opportunity), he keeps with them in retirement. Yes, he is not to be torn from his root (in himself).' This is 'the dragon lying hid.'

5. What is the meaning of the words under the second line, 'The dragon shows himself and is in the field;—it will be advantageous to see the great man?' The Master said:—'There he is, with the dragon's powers, and occupying exactly the central place. He is sincere (even) in his ordinary words, and earnest in his ordinary conduct. Guarding against depravity, he preserves his sincerity. His goodness is recognised in the world, but he does not boast of it. His virtue is extensively displayed, and transformation ensues. The language of the Yî, "The dragon shows himself and is in the field;—it will be advantageous to see the great man," refers to a ruler's virtue.'

6. What is the meaning of the words under the third line, 'The superior man is active and vigilant all the day, and in the evening (still) careful and apprehensive;—the position is dangerous, but there will be no mistake?' The Master said:—'The superior man advances in virtue, and cultivates all the sphere of his duty. His leal-heartedness and good faith are the way by which he advances in virtue. His attention to his words and establishing his sincerity are the way by which he occupies in his sphere. He knows the utmost point to be reached, and reaches it, thus showing himself in accord with the first springs (of things); he knows the end to be rested in, and rests in it, thus preserving his righteousness in accordance with that end. Therefore he occupies a high position without pride, and a low

position without anxiety. Thus it is that, being active and vigilant, and careful (also) and apprehensive as the time requires, though his position be perilous, he will make no mistake.'

7. What is the meaning of the words under the fourth line, 'He is as if he were leaping up, (but still) is in the deep;—there will be no mistake?' The Master said:—'He finds no permanent place either above or below, but he does not commit the error (of advancing). He may advance or recede;—there is no permanent place for him: but he does not leave his fellows. The superior man, advancing in virtue and cultivating the sphere of his duty, yet wishes (to advance only) at the (proper) time, and therefore there is no mistake.'

8. What is the meaning of the words under the fifth line, 'The dragon is on the wing in the sky;—it will be advantageous to see the great man?' The Master said:—'Notes of the same key respond to one another; creatures of the same nature seek one another; water flows towards the place that is (low and) damp; fire rises up towards what is dry; clouds follow the dragon, and winds follow the tiger:—(so) the sage makes his appearance, and all men look to him. Things that draw their origin from heaven move towards what is above; things that draw their origin from the earth cleave to what is below:—so does everything follow its kind.'

9. What is the meaning of the words under the topmost line, 'The dragon exceeds the proper limits;—there will be occasion for repentance?' The Master said:—'The position is noble, but it is not that of office; (its occupant) dwells on high, but he has no people (to rule); and the men of talent

and virtue in the positions below will give him no aid;—should he move in such a case, there will be occasion for repentance.'

In chapter II, paragraphs 4–9, Confucius is introduced, explaining, with considerable amplification, what is said by the duke of *K*âu under the several lines of the hexagram. 'The dragon' becomes the symbol of 'the superior man;' and of 'the great man,' or the sage upon the throne. The language approaches at times to the magniloquence of Mencius, while in paragraph 8 the voice hardly seems to be that of the sage at all.

With paragraph 5, compare chapters 8 and 14 of 'the Doctrine of the Mean,' agreeing much in language and sentiment with what we have here. The line, a strong or undivided line, and therefore yang, is said to be 'exactly in the central place;' but the line is in the second, an even place, that proper to a yin line; and in other passages this might be explained in an unfavourable way. The Chinese character *k*ăng has the meaning given to it, now of 'exact,' and now of 'correct,' the latter being always favourably interpreted.

Paragraph 8. The fifth is almost always the place of honour and authority in the hexagram, and therefore 'the great man' here continues to be the great man, 'the sage.' The argument is that as things of the same kind respond to and seek one another, so is it with the sage and ordinary man. They are of the same kind, though far apart; and when a sage appears, all other men look to him with admiration and hope. The continuity of the illustrations, however, is broken by the introduction of the dragon and clouds, and the tiger and wind. Are these of the same kind? *K*û Hsî says he does not think that the real dragon and real tiger are intended; but he does not tell us how he understood the terms. Ʒâi *Kh*ing (early in the Ming dynasty) says:—'The dragon feels the influence of the clouds surcharged with rain, and rises from the deep, and when the tiger feels the approach of the cold winds he roars. Thus when the dragon rises, the clouds are sure to collect; and when the tiger screams, the winds follow;' but all this does not help us to appreciate any better the words of the text. And the concluding illustration is nearly as foreign to our way of conceiving things. By 'things that draw their origin from heaven' all animals—moving creatures—are intended; and by those that draw their origin from the earth are intended all plants,—things that stand and

Chapter III. 10. 'The dragon lies hid;—it is not the time for active doing:'—the position is (too) low.

11. 'The dragon shows himself and is in the field:'—the time (requires him still) to be unemployed.

12. 'All the day active and vigilant:'—(he now) does his (proper) business.

13. 'He is as if he were leaping up, (but still) is in the deep:'—he is making trial of himself.

14. 'The dragon is on the wing in the sky:'—(the subject of the line) is on high and ruling.

15. 'The dragon exceeds the proper limit, and there will be occasion for repentance:'—when things have been carried to extremity, calamity ensues.

16. Undivided lines appear in all these representations of the great and originating power denoted by *Kh*ien:—(what follows in the Yâo tells us how) all under the sky there will be good order.

---

do not move. The former turn their heads to the sky, and the latter their roots to the earth. So we read in *K*û Hsî; but I continue to wonder that Confucius selected such illustrations and spoke in such a style.

Paragraph 9. As I have said above, the place of honour and authority in the hexagram belongs to the fifth line, and no other plays so unimportant a part as the sixth; and hence it is represented here as having 'no place' at all. Before he whom it represents is called to act, the battle has been won or lost. Movement from him will only accelerate and intensify the result.

Chapter III, paragraphs 10–16, goes over again the Yâo of the duke of *K*âu with very brief explanations, grounded chiefly on the consideration of the place or position occupied by the several lines, and the time of their introduction into the action of the hexagram.

Paragraph 16. See the note on the Text of *Kh*ien, corresponding to this line, page 58, and also that on paragraph 7 of the symbolism of the figures and lines, Section i, page 165. There is the same

Chapter IV. 17. 'The dragon lies hid in the deep;—it is not the time for active doing:'—the energy denoted by the undivided line is laid up and hid away as in the deep.

18. 'The dragon appears in the field:'—all under heaven (begins to be) adorned and brightened.

19. 'All the day active and vigilant:'—continually, as the time passes and requires, does he act.

20. 'He is as if he were leaping up, (but still) is in the deep:'—a change is taking place in the method indicated by (this) *Khien* diagram.

21. 'The dragon is on the wing in the sky:'—this shows that his place is based on his heavenly virtue.

22. 'The dragon exceeds the (proper) limit;—there will be occasion for repentance:'—the time is come to an end, and so also is his opportunity.

23. Undivided lines appear in all these representations of the great and originating power denoted by *Khien*:—and (from what follows in the Yâo) we see the model (of action) afforded by heaven.

---

difficulty in understanding the first part of the short paragraph; the conclusion of it must be a consequence of the language of the Yâo, though it is not repeated here.

Chapter IV, paragraphs 17–23, goes over the same ground for a third time, treating the various paragraphs chiefly from the standpoint of time.

Paragraph 17 tells us that time and circumstances are essential, as well as inward power, to successful development and demonstration. In paragraph 18, the words of the Yâo about meeting with the great man are not quoted, but they prompted the latter half of it.

Paragraph 19. Compare the language on paragraph 6, towards the end.

Paragraph 20. The subject passes here from the lower trigram and enters into the upper. We are told not to lay stress on 'the method of *Khien*.' In paragraph 21 we have the sage upon the

Chapter V. 24. The 'greatness' and 'originating' represented by *Kh*ien refer to it as (the symbol of) what gives their beginning (to all things), and (also) secures their growth and development.

25. 'The advantageousness and the correctness and firmness' refer to its nature and feelings (as seen in all the resulting things).

26. *Kh*ien, (thus) originating, is able with its admirable benefits to benefit all under the sky. We are not told how its benefits are conferred; but how great is (its operation)!

27. How great is (what is emblemed by) *Kh*ien!—strong, vigorous, undeflected, correct, and (in all these qualities) pure, unmixed, exquisite!

28. The six lines, as explained (by the duke of *K*âu), bring forth and display (its meaning), and everything about it is (thus) indirectly exhibited.

29. (The great man) at the proper time drives with these six dragons through the sky. The clouds move, and the rain is distributed; all under heaven enjoys repose.

---

throne. Time and opportunity are both in progress in 19; here in 22, they are both passed, have reached their extremity or end.

Paragraph 23:—see on paragraph 16. 'The model of heaven,' says Wû *Kh*ăng, 'is the due blending of the strong and active with the weak and passive, the regulation of movement in accordance with the highest reason, so that there shall be neither excess nor deficiency.'

Chapter V, paragraphs 24–29. The author here, leaving the treatise on the symbolism of the Yâo, turns to that on the Thwan, or expositions of king Wăn, and amplifies it, not quoting from it, however, so fully and exactly, as he has done in the previous chapters from the Yâo.

Paragraphs 24 and 25 are based on the statement of the significance of the Thwan under *Kh*ien, and not on the treatise on the symbolism. The originating power cannot be separated from that of penetration and development. The latter issues from the former

Chapter VI. 30. In the superior man his conduct is (the fruit of) his perfected virtue, which might be seen therefore in his daily course; but the force of that phrase, 'lying hid,' requires him to keep retired, and not yet show himself, nor proceed to the full development of his course. While this is the case, the superior man (knows that) it is not the time for active doing.

31. The superior man learns and accumulates the results of his learning; puts questions, and discriminates among those results; dwells magnanimously and unambitiously in what he has attained to; and carries it into practice with benevolence. What the Yî says, 'The dragon appears in the field:—it will be advantageous to meet with the great man,' has reference to the virtuous qualities of a ruler (as thus described).

32. In the third line there is a twofold (symbol of) strength, but (the position) is not central. (Its

---

as the summer follows on the spring, according to an illustration of *K*û Hsî. 'The advantageousness' and 'firm correctness,' he compares also to the autumn and winter, saying that the *Kh*ien power in its essence, as it is in itself, is best described by these two latter characteristics, while the two former describe it in its operation. It is thus that he tries to give his readers an idea of what he understood by 'nature and feelings' in 25. But this chapter treats of the *Kh*ien power in nature rather than in humanity. Confining our view to the power so operating, we cannot say that the description of it in 26 and 27 is magniloquent or hyperbolical.

Paragraph 28 returns to the explanations of the lines of the hexagram by the duke of *K*âu, which exhibit the power in different positions and relations, bringing out all its significance; and then 29 confines us to the fifth line, in which we have its ideal. The spheres of nature and of men seem to be in the view of the author, and therefore I introduce 'the great man,' as the subject, after the example of the best critics. Like the clouds and the rain to the thirsty earth, so is the rule of the sage to expectant humanity.

occupant) is not in heaven above, nor is he in the field beneath. Therefore there must be active vigilance and cautious apprehension as the time requires; and though (the position be) perilous, there will be no mistake.

33. In the fourth line there is (the symbol of) strength, but (the position) is not central. (Its occupant) is not in heaven above, nor is he in the field beneath, nor is he in the place of man intermediate. Hence he is in perplexity; and being so, he has doubts about what should be his movements, and so will give no occasion for blame.

34. The great man is he who is in harmony, in his attributes, with heaven and earth; in his brightness, with the sun and moon; in his orderly procedure, with the four seasons; and in his relation to what is fortunate and what is calamitous, in harmony with the spirit-like operations (of Providence). He may precede Heaven, and Heaven will not act in opposition to him; he may follow Heaven, but will act (only) as Heaven at the time would do. If Heaven will not act in opposition to him, how much less will men! how much less will the spirit-like operation (of Providence)!

35. The force of that phrase—'exceeding the proper limits'—indicates the knowing to advance but not to retire; to maintain but not to let perish; to get but not to lose.

36. He only is the sage who knows to advance and to retire, to maintain and to let perish; and that without ever acting incorrectly. Yes, he only is the sage!

Chapter VI, paragraphs 30–36. The author leaving the Thwan, turns again to the treatise on the symbolism of the Yâo, his main

Section II. Khwăn.

Chapter I. 1. (What is indicated by) Khwăn is most gentle and weak, but, when put in motion, is

---

object being to show how reasonable are the decisions and lessons of the duke of *K*âu.

The subject of paragraph 30 has the virtue; but his position in the lowest place shows that his time is not yet come.

In paragraph 31 we have the superior man developing, by means of the processes described, into 'the great man,' with the attributes of a ruler, the appearance of whom is a blessing to men.

The twofold symbol of strength in paragraph 32 is the yang or undivided line in the third place (odd) proper to it. There will be no mistake, because the subject of the line, in the exercise of his caution, will abstain from any forward movement.

According to paragraph 63 of last Appendix, Section ii, both the third and fourth lines in the hexagram belong to man, and are intermediate between those of heaven and those of earth. Khung Ying-tâ, to get over the difficulty in what is said on the fourth line, says that, as a matter of fact and locally, man is nearer earth than heaven, and is aptly represented therefore by the third line and not by the fourth;—I prefer to point out the inconsistency, and leave it. The subject of this fourth line will move very cautiously, and so escape blame.

The eulogium of 'the great man' in paragraph 34 cannot fail to recall to the classical scholar the thirty-first and other chapters of 'the Doctrine of the Mean,' where the sage is described as 'The Equal of Heaven.' In one sentence here he is spoken of as sometimes taking precedence of Heaven, which then does not act in opposition to him! I do not know of any statement about the sage, coming without doubt from Confucius, that is so extravagant as this. It is difficult—in fact impossible—to say from the Yî itself, what we are to understand by the kwei shăn, which I have translated here by 'the spirit-like operations (of Providence).' The compound denomination does not often occur in the book. In Appendix III, Section i, 21, kwei is the anima and shăn the animus; and in paragraph 50, I have translated the terms by 'the contracting and expanding operations.' In Appendix I, page 226 and page 259, the name is used as in the present text. That second instance and this

hard and strong; it is most still, but is able to give every definite form.

2. 'By following, it obtains its (proper) lord,' and pursues its regular (course).

3. It contains all things in itself, and its transforming (power) is glorious.

4. Yes, what docility marks the way of Khwăn! It receives the influences of heaven, and acts at the proper time.

Chapter II. 5. The family that accumulates goodness is sure to have superabundant happiness, and the family that accumulates evil is sure to have superabundant misery. The murder of a ruler by

---

paragraph were evidently constructed, the one on the model of the other. I think it likely that the breath or air, *khî*, became the name with the earliest Chinese for their first concept of spirit; then the breath inspired or inhaled was called kwei, and became the name for the grosser part of the spirit, returning to the earth; and shăn, the breath exhaled or expired, the name for the subtler and intellectual spirit, ascending to a state of activity and enjoyment. The explanations of the terms in the *R* Yâ and other dictionaries seem to justify this view. The combination kwei shăn is sometimes best translated by 'spiritual beings.' The school of the Sung philosophy understand by it—the contracting and expanding of the primary matter, or that matter conceived of in two forms or with two opposite qualities. *Kh*ăng-ȝze says here that 'Heaven and earth are another name for tâo, and kwei shăn another name for "the vestiges of making and transformation;" and that the sage being in harmony with the tâo or practical reason of the universe, how can men or the kwei shăn be contrary to him?' Whatever be thought of the Sung speculations and theories, I think that a translator ought to give an indication of the primary meaning of the name kwei shăn.

Paragraphs 35 and 36 suggest the description of Confucius by Mencius, V, ii, 1, 5, as the one among the sages who was most governed by the consideration of time, doing continually what the circumstances of the time required.

his minister, or of his father by a son, is not the result of the events of one morning or one evening. The causes of it have gradually accumulated,—through the absence of early discrimination. The words of the Yî, 'He treads on the hoar-frost; the strong ice will come (by and by),' show the natural (issue and growth of things).

6. 'Straight' indicates the correctness (of the internal principle), and 'square,' the righteousness (of the external act). The superior man, (thus represented), by his self-reverence maintains the inward (correctness), and in righteousness adjusts his external acts. His reverence and righteousness being (thus) established, his virtues are not solitary instances or of a single class. 'Straight, square, and great, working his operations, without repeated efforts, in every respect advantageous:'—this shows how (such a one) has no doubts as to what he does.

7. Although (the subject of) this divided line has excellent qualities, he (does not display them, but) keeps them under restraint. 'If he engage with them in the service of the king, and be successful, he will not claim that success for himself:'—this is the way of the earth, of a wife, of a minister. The way of the earth is—'not to claim the merit of achievement,' but on behalf (of heaven) to bring things to their proper issue.

8. Through the changes and transformations produced by heaven and earth, plants and trees grow luxuriantly. If (the reciprocal influence of) heaven and earth were shut up and restrained, we should have (a state that might suggest to us) the case of men of virtue and ability lying in obscurity. The words of the Yî, 'A sack tied up:—there will be

no ground for blame or for praise,' are in reality a lesson of caution.

9. The superior man (emblemed here) by the 'yellow' and correct (colour), is possessed of comprehension and discrimination. He occupies the correct position (of supremacy), but (that emblem) is on (the lower part of) his person. His excellence is in the centre (of his being), but it diffuses a complacency over his four limbs, and is manifested in his (conduct of) affairs:—this is the perfection of excellence.

10. (The subject of) the yin (or divided line) thinking himself equal to the (subject of the) yang, or undivided line, there is sure to be 'a contest.' As if indignant at there being no acknowledgment of the (superiority of the subject of the) yang line, (the text) uses the term 'dragons.' But still the (subject of neither line) can leave his class, and hence we have 'the blood' mentioned. The mention of that as being (both) 'azure and yellow' indicates the mixture of heaven and earth. Heaven's (colour) is azure and earth's is yellow.

The hexagram Khwăn is dealt with in Section ii, and much more briefly than *Kh*ien in Section i. Much less distinct, moreover, is the attempt in it to show how the attributes of the hexagram are to be understood of the principles of human nature. The most important portion of the Section, perhaps, is paragraph 5, the first of chapter II, and I have spoken of it in the Introduction, pages 47 and 48.

APPENDIX V.

Treatise of Remarks on the Trigrams.

Chapter I. 1. Anciently, when the sages made the Yî, in order to give mysterious assistance to the spiritual Intelligences, they produced (the rules for the use of) the divining plant.

2. The number 3 was assigned to heaven, 2 to earth, and from these came the (other) numbers.

3. They contemplated the changes in the divided and undivided lines (by the process of manipulating the stalks), and formed the trigrams; from the movements that took place in the strong and weak lines, they produced (their teaching about) the separate lines. There ensued a harmonious conformity to the course (of duty) and to virtue, with a discrimination of what was right (in each particular case). They (thus) made an exhaustive discrimination of what was right, and effected the complete development of (every) nature, till they arrived (in the Yî) at what was appointed for it (by Heaven).

Chapter I, paragraphs 1–3, treats of the rise of the scheme of the Yî from the wonderful qualities of the divining plant, the use of certain numbers, and the formation of the lineal figures.

P. Regis translates paragraph 1 by—'The ancient (sages), the most excellent men, were the authors of the Yî-king, in making which they were assisted by an intelligent spirit, who for their help produced the plant called Shih.'

But the text will not admit of this version, nor have I found the view given in it in any Chinese writer. It is difficult to make up one's mind whether to translate—'the sage,' or 'the sages.' Khung Ying-tâ contends that the writer had Fû-hsî and him alone in his

易經

Chapter II. 4. Anciently, when the sages made the Yî, it was with the design that (its figures) should be in conformity with the principles underlying the natures (of men and things), and the ordinances (for them) appointed (by Heaven). With this view they exhibited (in them) the way of heaven, calling (the lines) yin and yang; the way of earth, calling (them) the weak (or soft) and the strong (or hard); and the way of men, under the names of benevolence

---

mind. To me it seems otherwise. Fû-hsî, if we accept the testimony of universal Chinese consent, made the eight trigrams; but he did not make the Yî, which, by the same consent, was the production of king Wăn and his son.

The text would seem to say that the sages 'produced' the plant, but this is so extravagant that the view indicated in my supplementary clause appears in all the best commentators. So understood, the Yî may be said to 'give mysterious assistance to the spiritual Intelligences,' or, if we take that name as singular (according to the analogy of chapter 6), to the Divine Being in affording a revelation of His will, as in paragraph 3. We may well say that it is a pity the revelation should be so enigmatical; but the author, it must be remembered, is writing from his own standpoint. Wăn and his son, as I have endeavoured to show in the Introduction, merely wished to convey, under the style and veil of divination, their moral and political lessons.

On paragraph 2 it is said that heaven is round; and as the circumference of a circle is three times its diameter, hence 3 is the number of heaven. Again, earth is square, and as the circumference of a square is four times its length or breadth, or it consists of two pairs of equal sides, hence 2 is the number of earth.

The concluding statement about 'the other numbers' is understood of the manipulation of the divining stalks, as in Appendix III, i, 51. That manipulation, thrice repeated, might leave three stalks each time, and $3 \times 3 = 9$; or 2, being in the same way in all $= 6$; or twice 3 and once $2 = 8$; or twice 2 and once $3 = 7$. These are the numbers of the 4 binary symbols, employed in forming the new figures; ⚌, the old yang, $= 9$; ⚍, the young yin, $= 8$; ⚎, the young yang, $= 7$; and ⚏, the old yin, $= 6$.

and righteousness. Each (trigram) embraced (those) three Powers; and, being repeated, its full form consisted of six lines. A distinction was made of (the places assigned) to the yin and yang lines, which were variously occupied, now by the strong and now by the weak forms, and thus the figure (of each hexagram) was completed.

Chapter III. 5. (The symbols of) heaven and earth received their determinate positions; (those for) mountains and collections of water interchanged their influences; (those for) thunder and wind excited each other the more; and (those for) water and fire did each other no harm. (Then) among these eight symbols there was a mutual communication.

6. The numbering of the past is a natural process; the knowledge of the coming is anticipation. Therefore in the Yî we have (both) anticipation (and the natural process).

Chapter II. The top line in each trigram thus belongs to the category of heaven; the bottom line to that of earth; and the middle line to that of man. The odd places should be occupied, 'correctly,' by the undivided lines; and the even by the divided. The trigram being increased to the hexagram, lines 5 and 6 were assigned to heaven; 1 and 2 to earth; and 3 and 4 to man. 5 is the yang characteristic of heaven, and 6 the yin; so 1 and 2 in regard to earth; while 3 represents the benevolence of man, and 4 his righteousness. But all this is merely the play of fancy, and confuses the mind of the student.

Chapter III, paragraphs 5 and 6, is understood, though not very clearly, by referring to the circular arrangement of the trigrams according to Fû-hsî, as shown in Figure 2, of Plate III. Paragraph 5 refers to the correlation of *Kh*ien and Khwăn, Kăn and Tui, *K*ăn and Sun, Khân and Lî. Paragraph 6 is less easy of apprehension. Starting in the same figure from *Kh*ien and numbering on the left we come to *K*ăn by a natural process. Then

Chapter IV. 7. Thunder serves to put things in motion; wind to scatter (the genial seeds of) them; rain to moisten them; the sun to warm them; (what is symbolised by) Kăn, to arrest (and keep them in their places); (by) Tui, to give them joyful course; (by) *Kh*ien, to rule them; and by Khwăn, to store them up.

Chapter V. 8. God comes forth in *K*ăn (to His producing work); He brings (His processes) into full and equal action in Sun; they are manifested to one another in Lî; the greatest service is done for Him in Khwăn; He rejoices in Tui; He struggles in *Kh*ien; He is comforted and enters into rest in Khân; and He completes (the work of the year) in Kăn.

9. All things are made to issue forth in *K*ăn, which is placed at the east. (The processes of production) are brought into full and equal action in Sun, which is placed at the south-east. The being brought into full and equal action refers to the purity and equal arrangement of all things. Lî gives the idea of brightness. All things are now made mani-

---

we turn back, and numbering on the right, from Sun, we come by a backward process to Khwăn. The same process is illustrated on a large scale by the circular arrangement of the 64 hexagrams in Plate I. But what the scope of the paragraph is I cannot tell, and am tempted to say of it, as P. Regis does, 'Haec observatio prorsus inanis est.'

In chapter IV we have the same circular arrangement of the trigrams, though they are named in a different order; the last first and the first last. The first four are mentioned by their elemental names; the last four by the names of their lineal figures. No special significance is attached to this. If it ever had any, it has been lost.

fest to one another. It is the trigram of the south. The sages turn their faces to the south when they give audience to all under the sky, administering government towards the region of brightness:—the idea in this procedure was taken from this. Khwăn denotes the earth, (and is placed at the south-west). All things receive from it their fullest nourishment, and hence it is said, 'The greatest service is done for Him in Khwăn.' Tui corresponds (to the west) and to the autumn,—the season in which all things rejoice. Hence it is said, 'He rejoices in Tui.' He struggles in *Kh*ien, which is the trigram of the north-west. The idea is that there the inactive and active conditions beat against each other. Khan denotes water. It is the trigram of the exact north,—the trigram of comfort and rest, what all things are tending to. Hence it is said, 'He is comforted and enters into rest in Khan. Kăn is the trigram of the north-east. In it all things bring to a full end the issues of the past (year), and prepare the commencement of the next. Hence it is said, He completes (the work of the year) in Kăn.'

Chapter V, paragraphs 8 and 9, sets forth the operations of nature in the various seasons, as being really the operations of God, who is named Tî, 'the Lord and Ruler of Heaven.' Those operations are represented in the progress by the seasons of the year, as denoted by the trigrams, according to the arrangement of them by king Wăn, as shown also in Plate III, Figure 2.

'The greatest service is done for Tî in Khwăn;' Yang Wan-lî (of our twelfth century, but earlier than *K*û Hsî) says:—'Khwăn is a minister or servant. Tî is his ruler. All that a ruler has to do with his minister is to require his service.' 'On the struggles in *Kh*ien' he says:—'*Kh*ien is the trigram of the north-west, when the yin influence is growing strong and the yang diminishing.'

The 'purity' predicated in paragraph 9 of things in Sun, was

Chapter VI. 10. When we speak of Spirit we mean the subtle (presence and operation of God) with all things. For putting all things in motion there is nothing more vehement than thunder; for scattering them there is nothing more effective than wind; for drying them up there is nothing more parching than fire; for giving them pleasure and satisfaction there is nothing more grateful than a lake or marsh; for moistening them there is nothing more enriching than water; for bringing them to an end and making them begin again there is nothing more fully adapted than Kăn. Thus water and fire contribute together to the one object; thunder and wind do not act contrary to each other; mountains and collections of water interchange their influences. It is in this way, that they are able to change and transform, and to give completion to all things.

---

explained by *K*ăng Khang-*kh*ăng (our second century) as equivalent to 'newness,' referring to the brightness of all things in the light of spring and summer. On 'all things receive from the earth their fullest nourishment' the same Yang, quoted above, says:—'The earth performs the part of a mother. All things are its children. What a mother has to do for her children is simply to nourish them.'

Chapter VI is the sequel of the preceding. There ought to have been some mention of Shân or 'Spirit' in chapter 5. It is the first character in this chapter, and the two characters that follow show that it is here resumed for the purpose of being explained. As it does not occur in chapter 5, we must suppose that the author of it here brings forward and explains the idea of it that was in his mind. Many of the commentators recognise this,—e.g. Liang Yin, as quoted in the Introduction, p. 33.

Two other peculiarities in the style of the chapter are pointed out and explained (after a fashion) by 3hui *K*ing (earlier, probably, than the Sung dynasty):—'The action of six of the trigrams is described, but no mention is made of *Kh*ien or Khwăn. But

Chapter VII. 11. *Kh*ien is (the symbol of) strength; Khwăn, of docility; *K*ăn, of stimulus to movement; Sun, of penetration; Khan, of what is precipitous and perilous; Lî, of what is bright and what is catching; Kăn, of stoppage or arrest; and Tui, of pleasure and satisfaction.

heaven and earth do nothing, and yet do everything; hence they are able to perfect the spirit-like subtilty of the action of thunder, wind, and the other things. (Moreover), we have the trigram Kân mentioned, the only one mentioned by its name, instead of our reading "mountains." The reason is, that the putting in motion, the scattering, the parching, and the moistening, are all the palpable effects of thunder, wind, fire, and water. But what is ascribed to Kăn, the ending and the recommencing all things, is not so evident of mountains. On this account the name of the trigram is given, while the things in nature represented by the trigrams are given in those other cases. The style suitable in each case is employed.'

Chapter VII mentions the attributes, called also the 'virtues,' of the different trigrams. It is not easy to account for the qualities—'their nature and feelings'—ascribed to them. Khung Ying-tâ says:—'*Kh*ien is represented by heaven, which revolves without ceasing, and so it is the symbol of strength; Khwăn by the earth, which receives docilely the action of heaven, and so it is the symbol of docility; *K*ân by thunder, which excites and moves all things, and so it is the symbol of what produces movement; Sun by wind, which enters everywhere, and so it is the symbol of penetration; Khân by water, found in a place perilous and precipitous, and the name is explained accordingly; Lî by fire, and fire is sure to lay hold of things, and so it is the symbol of being attached to; Kân by a mountain, the mass of which is still and arrests progress, and so it is the symbol of stoppage or arrest; and Tui by a lake or marsh, which moistens all things, and so it is the symbol of satisfaction.'

The Khang-hsî editors consider this explanation of the qualities of the trigrams to be unsatisfactory, and certainly it has all the appearance of an ex post facto account. They prefer the views of the philosopher Shâo (of our eleventh century), which is based on the arrangement of the undivided and divided lines in the figures. This to me is more unsatisfactory than the other. The editors say,

Chapter VIII. 12. *Kh*ien (suggests the idea of) a horse; Khwăn, that of an ox; *K*ăn, that of the dragon; Sun, that of a fowl; Khan, that of a pig; Lî, that of a pheasant; Kăn, that of a dog; and Tui, that of a sheep.

Chapter IX. 13. *Kh*ien suggests the idea of the head; Khwăn, that of the belly; *K*ăn, that of the feet; Sun, that of the thighs; Khan, that of the ears; Lî, that of the eyes; Kăn, that of the hands; and Tui, that of the mouth.

Chapter X. 14. *Kh*ien is (the symbol of) heaven, and hence has the appellation of father. Khwăn is (the symbol of) earth, and hence has the appellation of mother. *K*ăn shows a first application (of Khwăn to *Kh*ien), resulting in getting (the first of) its male (or undivided lines), and hence is called 'the oldest son.' Sun shows a first application (of *Kh*ien to Khwăn), resulting in getting (the first of) its female (or divided lines), and hence is called 'the oldest daughter.' Khan shows a second application

---

moreover, that Shâo's account of the three yang trigrams, *K*ăn, Khan, and Kăn is correct, and that of the three yin, Sun, Lî, and Tui incorrect; but this would be based on king Wăn's arrangement, which does not appear to have place here.

Chapter VIII. In the Great Appendix, p. 383, it is said that Fû-hsî, in making his trigrams, was guided by 'the consideration of things apart from his own person.' Of such things we have a specimen here. The creatures are assigned, in their classes, to the different trigrams, symbolising the ideas in the last chapter. We must not make any difference of sex in translating their names.

Chapter IX. Fû-hsî found also 'things near at hand, in his own person,' while making the trigrams. We have here a specimen of such things.

(of Khwăn to *Kh*ien), resulting in getting (the second of) its male (or undivided lines), and hence is called 'the second son.' Lî shows a second application (of *Kh*ien to Khwăn), resulting in getting the second of its female (or divided lines), and hence is called 'the second daughter.' Kăn shows a third application (of Khwăn to *Kh*ien), resulting in getting (the third of) its male (or undivided lines), and hence is called 'the youngest son.' Tui shows a third application (of *Kh*ien to Khwăn), resulting in getting (the third of) its female (or divided lines), and hence is called 'the youngest daughter.'

Chapter XI. 15. *Kh*ien suggests the idea of heaven; of a circle; of a ruler; of a father; of jade; of metal; of cold; of ice; of deep red; of a good horse; of an old horse; of a thin horse; of a piebald horse; and of the fruit of trees.

16. Khwăn suggests the idea of the earth; of a mother; of cloth; of a caldron; of parsimony; of a turning lathe; of a young heifer; of a large waggon; of what is variegated; of a multitude; and of a handle and support. Among soils it denotes what is black.

17. *K*ăn suggests the idea of thunder; of the dragon; of (the union of) the azure and the yellow; of development; of a great highway; of the eldest son; of decision and vehemence; of bright young bamboos; of sedges and rushes; among horses, of

Chapter X has been discussed in the Introduction, pp. 49 and 50. Let it simply be added here, that the account which it does give of the formation of the six subsidiary trigrams is inconsistent with their gradual rise from the mutual imposition of the undivided and divided lines.

the good neigher; of one whose white hind-leg appears, of the prancer, and of one with a white star in his forehead. Among the productions of husbandry it suggests the idea of what returns to life from its disappearance (beneath the surface), of what in the end becomes the strongest, and of what is the most luxuriant.

18. Sun suggests the idea of wood; of wind; of the oldest daughter; of a plumb-line; of a carpenter's square; of being white; of being long; of being lofty; of advancing and receding; of want of decision; and of strong scents. It suggests in the human body, the idea of deficiency of hair; of a wide forehead; of a large development of the white of the eye. (Among tendencies), it suggests the close pursuit of gain, even to making three hundred per cent in the market. In the end it may become the trigram of decision.

19. Khan suggests the idea of water; of channels and ditches (for draining and irrigation); of being hidden and lying concealed; of being now straight, and now crooked; of a bow, and of a wheel. As referred to man, it suggests the idea of an increase of anxiety; of distress of mind; of pain in the ears;—it is the trigram of the blood; it suggests the idea of what is red. As referred to horses, it suggests the idea of the horse with an elegant spine; of one with a high spirit; of one with a drooping head; of one with a thin hoof; and of one with a shambling step. As referred to carriages, it suggests one that encounters many risks. It suggests what goes right through; the moon; a thief. Referred to trees, it suggests that which is strong, and firm-hearted.

20. Lî suggests the emblem of fire; of the sun; of lightning; of the second daughter; of buff-coat and helmet; of spear and sword. Referred to men, it suggests the large belly. It is the trigram of dryness. It suggests the emblem of a turtle; of a crab; of a spiral univalve; of the mussel; and of the tortoise. Referred to trees, it suggests one which is hollow and rotten above.

21. Kăn suggests the emblem of a mountain; of a by-path; of a small rock; of a gateway; of the fruits of trees and creeping plants; of a porter or a eunuch; of the (ring) finger; of the dog; of the rat; of birds with powerful bills; among trees, of those which are strong, with many joints.

22. Tui suggests the emblem of a low-lying collection of water; of the youngest daughter; of a sorceress; of the mouth and tongue; of the decay and putting down (of things in harvest); of the removal (of fruits) hanging (from the stems or branches); among soils, of what is strong and salt; of a concubine; and of a sheep.

Chapter XI may be made to comprehend all the paragraphs from the 15th to the end, and shows how universally the ideas underlying the Yî are diffused through the world of nature. The quality of the several trigrams will be found with more or less of truth, and with less or more of fancy, in the objects mentioned in connexion with them. More needs not to be said on the chapter than has been done in the Introduction, pp. 53 and 54.

APPENDIX VI.

The Orderly Sequence of the Hexagrams.

SECTION I.

1–3. When there were heaven and earth, then afterwards all things were produced. What fills up (the space) between heaven and earth are (those) all things. Hence (*K*h*ien and Khwǎn) are followed by *K*un[1]. *K*un denotes filling up.

3–6. *K*un is descriptive of things on their first production. When so produced, they are sure to be in an undeveloped condition. Hence *K*un is followed by Mǎng. Mǎng is descriptive of what is undeveloped,—the young of creatures and things. These in that state require to be nourished. Hence Mǎng is followed by Hsü. Hsü is descriptive of the way in which meat and drink (come to be supplied)[2]. Over meat and drink there are sure to be contentions[2]. Hence Hsü is followed by Sung.

6–8. Sung is sure to cause the rising up of the multitudes[3]; and hence it is followed by Sze. Sze has the signification of multitudes[3], and between multitudes there must be some bond of union. Hence it is followed by Pî, which denotes being attached to.

8–11. (Multitudes in) union must be subjected to some restraint. Hence Pî is followed by Hsiâo

*Kh*û. When things are subjected to restraint, there come to be rites of ceremony, and hence Hsiâo *Kh*û is followed by Lî[4]. The treading (on what is proper) leads to Thâi, which issues in a state of freedom and repose, and hence Lî is followed by Thâi.

11–16. Thâi denotes things having free course. They cannot have that for ever, and hence it is followed by Phî (denoting being shut up and restricted). Things cannot for ever be shut up, and hence Phî is followed by Thung Ȝăn. To him who cultivates union with men, things must come to belong, and hence Thung Ȝăn is followed by Tâ Yû. Those who have what is great should not allow in themselves the feeling of being full, and hence Tâ Yû is followed by *Kh*ien. When great possessions are associated with humility, there is sure to be pleasure and satisfaction; and hence *Kh*ien is followed by Yü.

16–19. Where such complacency is awakened, (he who causes it) is sure to have followers[5]. They who follow another are sure to have services (to perform), and hence Sui is followed by Kû[6]. Kû means (the performance of) services. He who performs such services may afterwards become great, and hence Kû is followed by Lin. Lin means great[6].

19–23. What is great draws forth contemplation, and hence Lin is followed by Kwân. He who attracts contemplation will then bring about the union of others with himself, and hence Kwân is followed by Shih Ho. Shih Ho means union. But things should not be united in a reckless or irregular way, and hence Shih Ho is followed by

易經

Pî. Pî denotes adorning. When ornamentation has been carried to the utmost, its progress comes to an end; and hence Pî is followed by Po. Po denotes decay and overthrow.

23–26. Things cannot be done away for ever. When decadence and overthrow have completed their work at one end, redintegration commences at the other; and hence Po is followed by Fû. When the return (thus indicated) has taken place, we have not any rash disorder, and Fû is followed by Wû Wang. Given the freedom from disorder and insincerity (which this name denotes), there may be the accumulation (of virtue), and Wû Wang is followed by Tâ *Kh*û.

26–30. Such accumulation having taken place, there will follow the nourishment of it; and hence Tâ *Kh*û is followed by Î. Î denotes nourishing. Without nourishment there could be no movement, and hence Î is followed by Tâ Kwo. Things cannot for ever be in a state of extraordinary (progress); and hence Tâ Kwo is followed by Khân. Khân denotes falling into peril. When one falls into peril, he is sure to attach himself to some person or thing; and hence Khân is followed by Lî. Lî denotes being attached, or adhering, to.

Section II.

31, 32. Heaven and earth existing, all (material) things then got their existence. All (material) things having existence, afterwards there came male and female. From the existence of male and female there came afterwards husband and wife. From

husband and wife there came father and son. From father and son there came ruler and minister. From ruler and minister there came high and low. When (the distinction of) high and low had existence, afterwards came the arrangements of propriety and righteousness.

The rule for the relation of husband and wife is that it should be long-enduring. Hence Hsien is followed by Hăng. Hăng denotes long enduring[7].

32–37. Things cannot long abide in the same place; and hence Hăng is followed by Thun. Thun denotes withdrawing. Things cannot be for ever withdrawn; and hence Thun is succeeded by Tâ *K*wang. Things cannot remain for ever (simply) in the state of vigour; and hence Tâ *K*wang is succeeded by 3in. 3in denotes advancing. (But) advancing is sure to lead to being wounded; and hence 3in is succeeded by Ming Î. Î denotes being wounded. He who is wounded abroad will return to his home; and hence Ming Î is followed by *K*iâ *Z*ăn.

37–40. When the right administration of the family is at an end, misunderstanding and division will ensue; and hence *K*iâ *Z*ăn is followed by Khwei. Khwei denotes misunderstanding and division; and such a state is sure to give rise to difficulties and complications. Khwei therefore is followed by *K*ien. *K*ien denotes difficulties; but things cannot remain for ever in such a state. *K*ien therefore is followed by *K*ieh, which denotes relaxation and ease.

40–44. In a state of relaxation and ease there are sure to be losses; and hence *K*ieh is followed

by Sun. But when Sun (or diminution) is going on without end, increase is sure to come. Sun therefore is followed by Yî. When increase goes on without end, there is sure to come a dispersing of it, and hence Yî is followed by Kwâi. Kwâi denotes dispersion. But dispersion must be succeeded by a meeting (again). Hence Kwâi is followed by Kâu, which denotes such meeting.

44–48. When things meet together, a collection is then formed. Hence Kâu is followed by 3hui, which name denotes being collected. When (good men) are collected and mount to the highest places, there results what we call an upward advance; and hence 3hui is followed by Shăng. When such advance continues without stopping, there is sure to come distress; and hence Shăng is followed by Khwăn. When distress is felt in the height (that has been gained), there is sure to be a return to the ground beneath; and hence Khwăn is followed by 3ing.

48, 49. What happens under 3ing requires to be changed, and hence it is followed by Ko (denoting change).

49–55. For changing the substance of things there is nothing equal to the caldron; and hence Kŏ is followed by Ting. For presiding over (that and all other) vessels, no one is equal to the eldest son, and hence Ting is followed by *K*ăn. *K*ăn conveys the idea of putting in motion. But things cannot be kept in motion for ever. The motion is stopped; and hence *K*ăn is followed by Kăn, which gives the idea of arresting or stopping. Things cannot be kept for ever in a state of repression, and hence Kăn is followed by *K*ien, which gives the idea of

(gradually) advancing. With advance there must be a certain point that is arrived at, and hence *K*ien is succeeded by Kwei Mei. When things thus find the proper point to which to come, they are sure to become great. Hence Kwei Mei is succeeded by Făng, which conveys the idea of being great.

55–57. He whose greatness reaches the utmost possibility, is sure to lose his dwelling; and hence Făng is succeeded by Lü (denoting travellers or strangers). We have in it the idea of strangers who have no place to receive them, and hence Lü is followed by Sûn, which gives the idea of (penetrating and) entering.

57–59. One enters (on the pursuit of his object), and afterwards has pleasure in it; hence Sûn is followed by Tui. Tui denotes pleasure and satisfaction. This pleasure and satisfaction (begins) afterwards to be dissipated, and hence Tui is followed by Hwan, which denotes separation and division.

59–62. A state of division cannot continue for ever, and therefore Hwan is followed by 3ieh. 3ieh (or the system of regulations) having been established, men believe in it, and hence it is followed by *K*ung Fû. When men have the belief which *K*ung Fû implies, they are sure to carry it into practice; and hence it is succeeded by Hsiâo Kwo.

62–64. He that surpasses others is sure to remedy (evils that exist), and therefore Hsiâo Kwo is succeeded by *K*î 3î. But the succession of events cannot come to an end, and therefore *K*î 3î is

succeeded by Wei 3î, with which (the hexagrams) come to a close.

The few sentences on this Appendix in the Introduction, pp. 54, 55, are sufficient. It shows the importance of the meaning of the name in the attempt to explain the lineal figures, and prepares us to expect on each one a brief enigmatical essay, which, it has been seen, is the nature of the Text. But the writer, whoever he was, is by no means careful always to follow that Text in the significance of the characters, as will appear in the few instances to which attention is called in the following notices. The treatise is too slight to require, or to justify, an exhibition of all its inaccuracies.

[1] But *K*un does not denote filling up. It is the symbol of being in a state of distress and difficulty. The writer is thinking of the result of the interaction of heaven and earth as being to fill all between them with the various forms of living beings; and to represent that he gives the result of *K*un, and not its meaning. He makes a blunder which might have been easily avoided, for he adds immediately that the character is descriptive of things on their first production.

[2] It is difficult to follow the writer here. Hsü in the Text is the symbol of the idea of waiting. Does he mean that a provision of food and drink can only be made gradually? There is nothing in the character Hsü to awaken in the mind the idea of nourishment. Then the genesis of contention which is given is strange. The writer probably had in his mind the lines of the Shih, II, i, ode 5. 3:—

'The loss of kindly feeling oft
From slightest things shall grow.
Where all the fare is dry and spare,
Resentments fierce may glow.'

But what is allowable, good even, in poetry, is out of place in this treatise.

[3] Contention on a great scale will put all the population of a state in excitement and motion, and military measures of repression will be necessary. But the idea of the multitudes in Sze would seem to be simply that of number, and not that of a numerous host. In a feudal kingdom, however, all the able-bodied people might be required to join the army.

[4] Lî, the name of the 10th hexagram, is the symbol for a shoe, and the act of treading or walking. It seems here to be derived from the homophonous lî, the symbol of acts of ceremony. The identity of sound or name must be considered as accidental. A measured step would be one of the first ways in which the inward sense of propriety would manifest itself.

[5] By the subject of Tâ Yû and *Kh*ien we must understand the possessor of the kingdom,—the great man who in his greatness is yet distinguished by humility. He attracts followers.

[6] For the true meaning of *K*û and Lin, the names of hexagrams 18, 19, see what is said in the notes on the Text of them.

[7] The same reference should be made to the notes on the Text of Hsien and many of the other hexagrams that follow.

APPENDIX VII.

Treatise on the Hexagrams taken promiscuously, according to the opposition or diversity of their meaning.

This last of the Appendixes is touched on very briefly in the concluding paragraph of the Introduction, p. 55. It is stated there to be in rhyme, and I have endeavoured to give a similar form to the following version of it. The rhymes and length of the lines in the original, however, are very irregular, and I found it impossible to reproduce that irregularity in English.

1, 2. Strength in *Kh*ien, weakness in Khwăn
we find.
8, 7. Pî shows us joy, and Sze the anxious
mind.
19, 20. Lîn gives, Kwân seeks;—such are the
several themes
Their different figures were to teach de-
signed.

3. *K*un manifests itself, yet keeps its place;
4. 'Mid darkness still, to light Măng sets
its face.

51, 52. *K*ăn starts; Kăn stops. In Sun and Yî
are seen
41, 42. How fulness and decay their course begin.
26. Tâ *Kh*û keeps still, and waits the proper
time.
25. Wû Wang sets forth how evil springs
from crime.

45, 46. Good men in 3hui collect; in Shăng they rise:
15, 16. *Kh*ien itself, Yü others doth despise.

21, 22. Shih Ho takes eating for its theme; and Pî
Takes what is plain, from ornament quite free.
58, 57. Tui shows its scope, but Sun's we do not see.
17, 18. Sui quits the old; Kû makes a new decree.

23. We see in Po its subject worn away;
24. And Fû shows its recovering from decay.

35. Above in 3in the sun shines clear and bright;
36. But in Ming Î 'tis hidden from the sight.
48, 47. Progress in 3ing in Khwăn encounters blight.

31. Effect quick answering cause in Hsien appears;
32. While Hăng denotes continuance for years.
59, 60. Hwân scatters; but 3ieh its code of rules uprears.

40. Relief and ease with *K*ieh are sure to come;
41. Hard toil and danger have in *K*ien their home.

38. Khwei looks on others as beyond its care;
37. *K*iâ *Z*ăn all includes within its sphere.

12, 11. While Phî and Thâi their different scopes
prefer,
34, 33. Tâ *K*wang stops here as right; withdraws
Thun there.

14. Tâ Yû adhering multitudes can show;
13. Thung *Z*ăn reflects their warm affection's
glow.

50, 51. Ting takes what's new; the old is left
by Ko.
61, 62. Sincere is *K*ung Fû; but exceeds, Hsiâo
Kwo.

55, 56. Făng tells of trouble; Lü can boast few
friends.
30, 29. Fire mounts in Lî; water in Khân
descends.
9. Hsiâo *Kh*û with few 'gainst many foes
contends.
10. Movement in Lî, unresting, never ends.

5. Hsü shows its subject making no advance:
6. In Sung we seek in vain a friendly glance;
28. And Tâ Kwo's overthrown with sad mis-
chance.

44. Kâu shows a meeting, where the many
strong
Are met by one that's weak, yet struggles
long.

53. In *K*ien we see a bride who will delay
To move until the bridegroom takes his
way.

27. Body and mind are nourished right in Î;
63. All things are well established in *K*î 3î.

54. Kwei Mei reveals how ends the virgin life;
64. Wei 3î how fails the youth (to get a wife).

43. The strong disperse the weak; Kwâi teaches so.
Prospers the good man's way; to grief all small men go.

TRANSLITERATION OF ORIENTAL ALPHABETS ADOPTED FOR THE TRANSLATIONS OF THE SACRED BOOKS OF THE EAST.

CONSONANTS.	MISSIONARY ALPHABET. I Class.	II Class.	III Class.	Sanskrit.	Zend.	Pehlevi.	Persian.	Arabic.	Hebrew.	Chinese.
Gutturales.										
1 Tenuis	k	...	...	क	𐬐	[illegible]	ک	ك	כּ	k
2 " aspirata	kh	...	...	ख	𐬑	[illegible]	...	...	כ	kh
3 Media	g	...	...	ग	𐬔	[illegible]	گ	...	גּ	...
4 " aspirata	gh	...	...	घ	𐬖	[illegible]	...	...	ג	...
5 Gutturo-labialis	q	...	...	...	...	...	ق	ق	ק	...
6 Nasalis	ṅ (ng)	...	...	ङ	{ 𐬢 (ng) / 𐬣 (N) }	...	...	...	...	...
7 Spiritus asper	h	...	...	ह	𐬵 (𐬒 *hv*)	[illegible]	ه	ه	ה	h, hs
8 " lenis	'	...	...	...	...	...	ا	ا	א	...
9 " asper faucalis	‘h	...	...	...	...	...	ح	ح	ח	...
10 " lenis faucalis	’h	...	...	...	...	...	ع	ع	ע	...
11 " asper fricatus	...	‘*h*	...	...	...	...	خ	خ	ח	...
12 " lenis fricatus	...	’*h*	...	...	...	...	...	...	...	...
Gutturales modificatae (palatales, &c.)										
13 Tenuis	...	*k*	...	च	𐬗	[illegible]	چ	...	...	*k*
14 " aspirata	...	*kh*	...	छ	...	...	...	...	...	*kh*
15 Media	...	*g*	...	ज	𐬘	[illegible]	ج	ج	...	...
16 " aspirata	...	*gh*	...	झ	...	...	غ	غ	...	...
17 " Nasalis	...	*ñ*	...	ञ	...	...	...	...	...	...

CONSONANTS (continued).	Missionary Alphabet. I Class.	II Class.	III Class.	Sanskrit.	Zend.	Pehlevi.	Persian.	Arabic.	Hebrew.	Chinese.
18 Semivocalis	y	...	....	य	𐬫 . 𐬌𐬌 init.	[illegible]	ي	ي	י	y
19 Spiritus asper	...	(ẏ)	....	...	....	...	...	...	...	...
20 „ lenis	...	(ẏ)	....	...	....	[illegible]	...	...	...	...
21 „ asper assibilatus	...	*s*	....	श	𐬱	[illegible]	ش	ش	...	...
22 „ lenis assibilatus	...	*z*	....	...	𐬲	[illegible]	ژ	...	...	*z*
Dentales.										
23 Tenuis	t	...	....	त	𐬙	[illegible]	ت	ت	תּ	t
24 „ aspirata	th	...	....	थ	𐬚	...	...	...	ת	th
25 „ assibilata	...	...	TH	...	....	...	ث	ث	...	...
26 Media	d	...	....	द	𐬛	[illegible]	د	د	דּ	...
27 „ aspirata	dh	...	....	ध	𐬜	...	...	...	ד	...
28 „ assibilata	...	...	DH	...	....	...	ذ	ذ	...	...
29 Nasalis	n	...	....	न	𐬥	[illegible]	ن	ن	נ	n
30 Semivocalis	l	...	....	ल	....	[illegible]	ل	ل	ל	l
31 „ mollis 1	...	*l*	....	ळ	....	...	...	...	...	...
32 „ mollis 2	...	...	L	...	....	...	...	...	...	...
33 Spiritus asper 1	s	...	....	स	𐬯	[illegible]	س (ث)	س	שׂ	s
34 „ asper 2	...	...	s (ʃ)	...	....	...	...	...	ס	...
35 „ lenis	z	...	....	...	𐬰	[illegible]	ز (ذ)	ز	ז	z
36 „ asperrimus 1	...	...	z (ʒ)	...	....	...	ص	ص	צ	ʒ, ʒh
37 „ asperrimus 2	...	...	ẓ (ʒ)	...	....	...	ض	...	...	...

Dentales modificatae (linguales, &c.)										
38 Tenuis	...	*t*	....	ट	....	...	ط	ط	ט	...
39 „ aspirata	...	*th*	....	ठ	....	...	ظ	ظ	...	...
40 Media	...	*d*	....	ड	[illegible]	[illegible]	...	...	...	...
41 „ aspirata	...	*dh*	....	ढ	....	...	...	ض	...	...
42 Nasalis	...	*n*	....	ण	[illegible]	...	...	...	...	...
43 Semivocalis	r	...	....	र	[illegible]	[illegible]	ر	ر	ר	...
44 „ fricata	...	*r*	....	...	....	...	...	...	...	*r*
45 „ diacritica	...	...	R	...	....	...	...	...	...	...
46 Spiritus asper	sh	...	....	ष	[illegible]	[illegible]	...	...	...	sh
47 „ lenis	zh	...	....	...	....	...	...	...	...	...
Labiales.										
48 Tenuis	p	...	....	प	[illegible]	[illegible]	پ	...	פּ	p
49 „ aspirata	ph	...	....	फ	....	...	...	...	פ	ph
50 Media	b	...	....	ब	[illegible]	[illegible]	ب	ب	בּ	...
51 „ aspirata	bh	...	....	भ	....	...	...	...	ב	...
52 Tenuissima	...	*p*	....	...	....	...	...	...	...	...
53 Nasalis	m	...	....	म	[illegible]	[illegible]	م	م	מ	m
54 Semivocalis	w	...	....	...	[illegible]	...	...	...	...	w
55 ʻ „ aspirata	hw	...	....	...	....	...	...	...	...	...
56 Spiritus asper	f	...	....	...	[illegible]	[illegible]	ف	ف	...	f
57 „ lenis	v	...	....	व	[illegible]	[illegible]	و	و	ו	...
58 Anusvâra	...	*m*	....	अं	[illegible]	...	...	...	...	...
59 Visarga	...	*h*	....	अः	....	...	...	...	...	...

VOWELS.	MISSIONARY ALPHABET. I Class.	II Class.	III Class.	Sanskrit.	Zend.	Pehlevi.	Persian.	Arabic.	Hebrew.	Chinese.
1 Neutralis	0	...	....	...	....	...	...	...	ְ	ă
2 Laryngo-palatalis	ĕ	...	....	...	....	...	...	...	...	...
3 „ labialis	ŏ	...	....	...	....	ا fin.	...	...	...	...
4 Gutturalis brevis	a	...	....	अ	𐬀	ا init.	َ	َ	ַ	a
5 „ longa	â	(a)	....	आ	𐬁	ا	َا	َا	ָ	â
6 Palatalis brevis	i	...	....	इ	𐬌	...	ِ	ِ	ִ	i
7 „ longa	î	(i)	....	ई	𐬍	ی	ِي	ِي	ִי	î
8 Dentalis brevis	*li*	...	....	ऌ	....	...	...	...	...	...
9 „ longa	*lî*	...	....	ॡ	....	...	...	...	...	...
10 Lingualis brevis	*ri*	...	....	ऋ	....	...	...	...	...	...
11 „ longa	*rî*	...	....	ॠ	....	...	...	...	...	...
12 Labialis brevis	u	...	....	उ	𐬎	...	ُ	ُ	ֻ	u
13 „ longa	û	(u)	....	ऊ	𐬏	ا	ُو	ُو	וּ	û
14 Gutturo-palatalis brevis	e	...	....	...	𐬆(e) 𐬇(e)	...	...	...	ֶ	e
15 „ longa	ê (ai)	(e)	....	ए	𐬉, 𐬊	ی	َيْ	َيْ	ֵ	ê
16 Diphthongus gutturo-palatalis	âi	(ai)	....	ऐ	....	...	َيْ	َيْ	...	âi
17 „ „	ei (ĕi)	...	....	...	....	...	...	...	...	ei, êi
18 „ „	oi (ŏu)	...	....	...	....	...	...	...	...	...
19 Gutturo-labialis brevis	o	...	....	...	𐬋	...	...	...	ָ	o
20 „ longa	ô (au)	(o)	....	ओ	𐬋	ا	َوْ	َوْ	וֹ	...
21 Diphthongus gutturo-labialis	âu	(au)	....	औ	𐬃 (au)	...	َوْ	َوْ	...	âu
22 „ „	eu (ĕu)	...	....	...	....	...	...	...	...	...
23 „ „	ou (ŏu)	...	....	...	....	...	...	...	...	...
24 Gutturalis fracta	ä	...	....	...	....	...	...	...	...	...
25 Palatalis fracta	ï	...	....	...	....	...	...	...	...	...
26 Labialis fracta	ü	...	....	...	....	...	...	...	...	ü
27 Gutturo-labialis fracta	ö	...	....	...	....	...	...	...	...	...

国家出版基金项目
NATIONAL PUBLICATION FOUNDATION

海上絲綢之路文獻集成

總主編　陳支平　陳春聲

科技與文化編

64

主編　王揚宗　葉　農

海峽出版發行集團
THE STRAITS PUBLISHING & DISTRIBUTING GROUP
福建人民出版社

本册目次

道德經　莊子

(*The TâoTeh King, the Writings of Kwang-ʒze*)

[英] 理雅各 (James Legge) 編譯

《道德經　莊子》，英國理雅各編譯。理雅各（James Legge，一八一五—一八九七），英國倫敦會傳教士，法國漢學儒蓮獎首位得主。於一八六一至一八七二年相繼出版《中國經典》（*The Chinese Classics*）五卷，於一八七九至一八九一年相繼出版《中國聖書》（*The Sacred Books of China*）六卷。諸種中國經典譯作，被後世奉爲標準譯本。所英譯之《道德經》爲中國經典西譯最具影響者之一。書中首次以音譯法翻譯「道」（*Tao*），後得英語世界普遍認可並採用。《莊子》之譯本，譯文前有長篇導論，注釋逾一千條。兩書收入《東方聖書》第三十九至四十卷。據一八九一年牛津版影印。

道德經　莊子

THE

SACRED BOOKS OF THE EAST

London

HENRY FROWDE

OXFORD UNIVERSITY PRESS WAREHOUSE

AMEN CORNER, E.C.

道德經 莊子

THE

SACRED BOOKS OF THE EAST

TRANSLATED

BY VARIOUS ORIENTAL SCHOLARS

AND EDITED BY

F. MAX MÜLLER

VOL. XXXIX

Oxford

AT THE CLARENDON PRESS

1891

Oxford
PRINTED AT THE CLARENDON PRESS
BY HORACE HART, PRINTER TO THE UNIVERSITY

道德經 莊子

THE

SACRED BOOKS OF CHINA

THE TEXTS OF TÂOISM

TRANSLATED BY

JAMES LEGGE

PART I

THE TÂO TEH *K*ING

THE WRITINGS OF *K*WANG-ȜZE

BOOKS I—XVII

Oxford

AT THE CLARENDON PRESS

1891

CONTENTS.

THE TÂO TEH *K*ING.

道德經 莊子

THE WRITINGS OF *K*WANG-ȜZE.

INTRODUCTION.

PART I.

PART II.

PREFACE.

In the Preface to the third volume of these 'Sacred Books of the East' (1879), I stated that I proposed giving in due course, in order to exhibit the System of Tâoism, translations of the Tâo Teh *K*ing by Lâo-ʒze (sixth century B.C.), the Writings of *K*wang-ʒze (between the middle of the fourth and third centuries B.C.), and the Treatise of 'Actions and their Retributions' (of our eleventh century); and perhaps also of one or more of the other characteristic Productions of the System.

The two volumes now submitted to the reader are a fulfilment of the promise made so long ago. They contain versions of the Three Works which were specified, and, in addition, as Appendixes, four other shorter Treatises of Tâoism; Analyses of several of the Books of *K*wang-ʒze by Lin Hsî-*k*ung; a list of the stories which form so important a part of those Books; two Essays by two of the greatest Scholars of China, written the one in A.D. 586 and illustrating the Tâoistic beliefs of that age, and the other in A.D. 1078 and dealing with the four Books of *K*wang-ʒze, whose genuineness is frequently called in question. The concluding Index is confined very much to Proper Names. For Subjects the reader is referred to the Tables of Contents, the Introduction to the Books of *K*wang-ʒze (vol. xxxix, pp. 127–163), and the Introductory Notes to the various Appendixes.

The Treatise of Actions and their Retributions exhibits to us the Tâoism of the eleventh century in its moral or ethical aspects; in the two earlier Works we see it rather as a philosophical speculation than as a religion in the ordinary sense of that term. It was not till after the introduction of Buddhism into China in our first century that Tâoism began to organise itself as a

Religion, having its monasteries and nunneries, its images and rituals. While it did so, it maintained the superstitions peculiar to itself:—some, like the cultivation of the Tâo as a rule of life favourable to longevity, come down from the earliest times, and others which grew up during the decay of the *K*âu dynasty, and subsequently blossomed;—now in Mystical Speculation; now in the pursuits of Alchemy; now in the search for the pills of Immortality and the Elixir vitae; now in Astrological fancies; now in visions of Spirits and in Magical arts to control them; and finally in the terrors of its Purgatory and everlasting Hell. Its phases have been continually changing, and at present it attracts our notice more as a degraded adjunct of Buddhism than as a development of the speculations of Lâo-ʒze and *K*wang-ʒze. Up to its contact with Buddhism, it subsisted as an opposition to the Confucian system, which, while admitting the existence and rule of the Supreme Being, bases its teachings on the study of man's nature and the enforcement of the duties binding on all men from the moral and social principles of their constitution.

It is only during the present century that the Texts of Tâoism have begun to receive the attention which they deserve. Christianity was introduced into China by Nestorian missionaries in the seventh century; and from the Hsî-an monument, which was erected by their successors in 781, nearly 150 years after their first entrance, we perceive that they were as familiar with the books of Lâo-ʒze and *K*wang-ʒze as with the Confucian literature of the empire, but that monument is the only memorial of them that remains. In the thirteenth century the Roman Catholic Church sent its earliest missionaries to China, but we hardly know anything of their literary labours.

The great Romish missions which continue to the present day began towards the end of the sixteenth century; and there exists now in the India Office a translation of the Tâo Teh *K*ing in Latin, which was brought to England by a Mr. Matthew Raper, and presented by him to the Royal Society, of which he was a Fellow, on January 10th, 1788. The manuscript is in excellent preservation, but we do not know by whom the version was made. It was presented, as stated in the Introduction, p. 12, to Mr. Raper by P. de Grammont, 'Missionarius Apostolicus, ex-Jesuita.' The chief object of the translator or translators was to show that 'the Mysteries of the Most Holy Trinity and of the Incarnate God were anciently known to the Chinese nation.' The version as a whole is of little value. The reader will find, on pp. 115, 116, its explanation of Lâo's seventy-second chapter;—the first morsel of it that has appeared in print.

Protestant missions to China commenced in 1807; but it was not till 1868 that the Rev. Dr. Chalmers, a member of one of them, published his 'Speculations on Metaphysics, Polity, and Morality of "The Old Philosopher," Lao-Tsze.' Meanwhile, Abel Rémusat had aroused the curiosity of scholars throughout Europe, in 1823, by his 'Memoir on the Life and Opinions of Lâo-Tseu, a Chinese Philosopher of the sixth century before our era, who professed the opinions commonly attributed to Pythagoras, to Plato, and to their disciples.' Rémusat was followed by one who had received from him his first lessons in Chinese, and had become a truly great Chinese scholar,—the late Stanislas Julien. He published in 1842 'a complete translation for the first time of this memorable Work, which is regarded with reason as the most profound, the most abstract, and the most difficult of all Chinese Literature.' Dr. Chalmers's translation was also complete, but his comments, whether original or from Chinese sources, were much fewer than those supplied by Julien. Two years later, two German versions of the Treatise were published at Leipzig;—by Reinhold von Pländkner and Victor von Strauss, differing much from each other, but both marked by originality and ability.

I undertook myself, as stated above, in 1879 to translate for 'The Sacred Books of the East' the Texts of Tâoism which appear in these volumes; and, as I could find time from my labours on 'The Texts of Confucianism,' I had written out more than one version of Lâo's work by the end of 1880. Though not satisfied with the result, I felt justified in exhibiting my general views of it in an article in the British Quarterly Review of July, 1883.

In 1884 Mr. F. H. Balfour published at Shanghai a version of 'Taoist Texts, Ethical, Political, and Speculative.' His Texts were ten in all, the Tâo Teh *K*ing being the first and longest of them. His version of this differed in many points from all previous versions; and Mr. H. A. Giles, of H. M.'s Consular Service in China, vehemently assailed it and also Dr. Chalmers's translation, in the China Review for March and April, 1886. Mr. Giles, indeed, occasionally launched a shaft also at Julien and myself; but his main object in his article was to discredit the genuineness and authenticity of the Tâo Teh *K*ing itself. 'The work,' he says, 'is undoubtedly a forgery. It contains, indeed, much that Lâo Tzû did say, but more that he did not.' I replied, so far as was necessary, to Mr. Giles in the same Review for January and February, 1888; and a brief summary of my reply is given in the second chapter of the Introduction in this volume. My confidence has never been shaken for a moment in the Tâo Teh *K*ing as a genuine relic of Lâo-ʒze, one of the most original minds of the Chinese race.

In preparing the version now published, I have used:—

First, 'The Complete Works of the Ten Philosophers;'—a Sû-*k*âu reprint in 1804 of the best editions of the Philosophers, nearly all belonging more or less to the Tâoist school, included in it. It is a fine specimen of Chinese printing, clear and accurate. The Treatise of Lâo-ʒze of course occupies the first place, as edited by Kwei Yû-kwang (better known as Kwei *K*ăn-shan) of the Ming dynasty. The Text and Commentary are those of Ho-shang Kung (Introd., p. 7), along with the division of the whole into Parts and eighty-one chapters, and the titles of the several chapters, all attributed to him. Along the top of the page, there is a large collection of notes from celebrated commentators and writers down to the editor himself.

Second, the Text and Commentary of Wang Pî (called also Fû-sze), who died A.D. 249, at the early age of twenty-four. See Introduction, p. 8.

Third, 'Helps (lit. Wings) to Lâo-ȝze;' by Ȝiâo Hung (called also *Z*âo-hâu), and prefaced by him in 1587. This is what Julien calls 'the most extensive and most important contribution to the understanding of Lâo-ȝze, which we yet possess.' Its contents are selected from the ablest writings on the Treatise from Han Fei (Introd., p. 5) downwards, closing in many chapters with the notes made by the compiler himself in the course of his studies. Altogether the book sets before us the substance of the views of sixty-four writers on our short *K*ing. Julien took the trouble to analyse the list of them, and found it composed of three emperors, twenty professed Tâoists, seven Buddhists, and thirty-four Confucianists or members of the Literati. He says, 'These last constantly explain Lâo-ȝze according to the ideas peculiar to the School of Confucius, at the risk of misrepresenting him, and with the express intention of throttling his system;' then adding, 'The commentaries written in such a spirit have no interest for persons who wish to enter fully into the thought of Lâo-ȝze, and obtain a just idea of his doctrine. I have thought it useless, therefore, to specify the names of such commentaries and their authors.'

I have quoted these sentences of Julien, because of a charge brought by Mr. Balfour, in a prefatory note to his own version of the Tâo Teh *K*ing, against him and other translators. 'One prime defect,' he says, though with some hesitation, 'lies at the root of every translation that has been published hitherto; and this is, that not one seems to have been based solely and entirely on commentaries furnished by members of the Tâoist school. The Confucian element enters largely into all; and here, I think, an injustice has been done to Lâo-ȝze. To a Confucianist the Tâoist system is in every sense of the word a heresy, and a commentator holding this opinion is surely not the best expositor. It is as a Grammarian rather than as a Philosopher that a member of the Jû Chiâ deals with the Tâo Teh *K*ing; he gives the sense of a passage according to the syntactical construction rather than according to the genius of the philosophy itself; and in attempting to explain the text by his own canons, instead of by the canons of Tâoism, he mistakes the superficial and apparently obvious meaning for the hidden and esoteric interpretation.'

Mr. Balfour will hardly repeat his charge of imperfect or erroneous interpretation against Julien; and I believe that it is equally undeserved by most, if not all, of the other translators against whom it is directed. He himself adopted as his guide the 'Explanations of the Tâo Teh *K*ing,' current as the work of Lü Yen (called also Lü 3û, Lü Tung-pin, and Lü *Kh*un-yang), a Tâoist of the eighth century. Through Mr. Balfour's kindness I have had an opportunity of examining this edition of Lâo's Treatise; and I am compelled to agree with the very unfavourable judgment on it pronounced by Mr. Giles as both 'spurious' and 'ridiculous.' All that we are told of Lü Yen is very suspicious; much of it evidently false. The editions of our little book ascribed to him are many. I have for more than twenty years possessed one with the title of 'The Meaning of the Tâo Teh *K*ing Explained by the TRUE Man of *Kh*un-yang,' being a reprint of 1690, and as different as possible from the work patronised by Mr. Balfour.

Fourth, the Thâi Shang Hwun Hsüan Tâo Teh *K*ăn *K*ing,—a work of the present dynasty, published at Shanghai, but when produced I do not know. It is certainly of the Lü 3û type, and is worth purchasing as one of the finest specimens of block-printing. It professes to be the production of 'The Immortals of the Eight Grottoes,' each of whom is styled 'a Divine Ruler (Tî *K*ün).' The eighty-one chapters are equally divided for commentary among them, excepting that 'the Divine Ruler, the Universal Refiner,' has the last eleven assigned to him. The Text is everywhere broken up into short clauses, which are explained in a very few characters by 'God, the True Helper,' the same, I suppose, who is also styled, 'The Divine Ruler, the True Helper,' and comments at length on chapters 31 to 40. I mention these particulars as an illustration of how the ancient Tâoism has become polytheistic and absurd. The name 'God, the True Helper,' is a title, I imagine, given to Lü 3û. With all this nonsense, the composite commentary is a good one, the work, evidently, of one hand. One of several recommendatory Prefaces is ascribed to Wân *Kh*ang, the god of Literature; and he specially praises the work, as 'explaining the meaning by examination of the Text.'

Fifth, a 'Collection of the Most Important Treatises of the Tâoist Fathers (Tâo 3û *K*ăn *K*wan *K*î Yâo).' This was reprinted in 1877 at *Kh*ang-*k*âu in *K*iang-sû; beginning with the Tâo Teh *K*ing, and ending with the Kan Ying Phien. Between these there are fourteen other Treatises, mostly short, five of them being among Mr. Balfour's 'Tâoist Texts.' The Collection was edited by a Lû Yü; and the Commentary selected by him, in all but the last Treatise, was by a Lî Hsî-yüeh, who appears to have been a recluse in a monastery on a mountain in the department of Pâo-ning, Sze-*kh*wan, if, indeed, what is said of him be not entirely fabulous.

Sixth, the Commentary on the Tâo Teh *K*ing, by Wû *Kh*ăng (A.D. 1249–1333) of Lin *Kh*wan. This has been of the highest service to me. Wû *Kh*ăng was the greatest of the Yüan scholars. He is one of the Literati quoted from occasionally by 3iâo Hung in his 'Wings;' but by no means so extensively as Julien supposes (Observations Détachées, p. xli). My own copy of his work is in the 12th Section of the large Collection of the 'Yüeh-yâ Hall,' published in 1853. Writing of Wû *Kh*ăng in 1865 (Proleg. to the Shû, p. 36), I said that he was 'a bold thinker and a daring critic, handling his text with a freedom which I had not seen in any other Chinese scholar.' The subsequent study of his writings has confirmed me in this opinion of him. Perhaps he might be characterised as an independent, rather than as a bold, thinker, and the daring of his criticism must not be supposed to be without caution. (See Introd., p. 9.)

The Writings of *K*wang-ȝze have been studied by foreigners still less than the Treatise of Lâo-ȝze. When I undertook in 1879 to translate them, no version of them had been published. In 1881, however, there appeared at Shanghai Mr. Balfour's 'The Divine Classic of Nan-hua (Introd., pp. 11, 12), being the Works of Chuang Tsze, Tâoist Philosopher.' It was a 'bold' undertaking in Mr. Balfour thus to commence his translations of Chinese Books with one of the most difficult of them. I fancy that he was himself convinced of this, and that his undertaking had been 'too bold,' by the criticism to which his work was subjected in the China Review by Mr. Giles. Nevertheless, it was no small achievement to be the first to endeavour to lift up the veil from *K*wang-ȝze. Even a first translation, though imperfect, is not without benefit to others who come after, and are able to do better. In preparing the draft of my own version, which draft was finished in April, 1887, I made frequent reference to the volume of Mr. Balfour.

Having exposed the errors of Mr. Balfour, Mr. Giles proceeded to make a version of his own, which was published last year in London, with the title of 'CHUANG TZŬ, Mystic, Moralist, and Social Reformer.' It was not, however, till I was well through with the revision of my draft version, that I supplied myself with a copy of his volume. I did not doubt that Mr. Giles's translation would be well and tersely done, and I preferred to do my own work independently and without the help which he would have afforded me. In carrying my sheets through the press, I have often paused over my rendering of a passage to compare it with his; and I have pleasure in acknowledging the merits of his version. The careful and competent reader will see and form his own judgment on passages and points where we differ.

Before describing the editions of *K*wang-ȝze which I

have consulted, I must not omit to mention Professor Gabelentz's 'Treatise on the Speech or Style of *K*wang-ʒze,' as 'a Contribution to Chinese Grammar,' published at Leipzig in 1888. It has been a satisfaction to me to find myself on almost every point of usage in agreement with the views of so able a Chinese scholar.

The works which I employed in preparing my version have been:—

First, 'The True *K*ing of Nan-hwâ,' in 'The Complete Works of the Ten Philosophers,' which has been described above. The Commentary which it supplies is that of Kwo Hsiang (Introd., pp. 9, 10), with 'The Sounds and Meanings of the Characters' from Lû Teh Ming's 'Explanations of the Terms and Phrases of the Classics,' of our seventh century. As in the case of the Tâo Teh *K*ing, the Ming editor has introduced at the top of his pages a selection of comments and notes from a great variety of scholars down to his own time.

Second, 'Helps (Wings) to *K*wang-ʒze by Ʒiâo Hung,'— a kindred work to the one with a similar title on Lâo-ʒze; by the same author, and prefaced by him in 1588. The two works are constructed on the same lines. Ʒiâo draws his materials from forty-eight authorities, from Kwo Hsiang to himself. He divides the several Books also into paragraphs, more or fewer according to their length, and the variety of subjects in them; and my version follows him in this lead with little or no change. He has two concluding Books; the one containing a collation of various readings, and the other a collection of articles on the history and genius of *K*wang-ʒze, and different passages of his Text.

Third, the *K*wang-ʒze Hsüeh or '*K*wang-ʒze made like Snow,' equivalent to our '*K*wang-ʒze Elucidated;' by a Lû Shû-*k*ih of Canton province, written in 1796. The different Books are preceded by a short summary of their subject-matter. The work goes far to fulfil the promise of its title.

Fourth, *K*wang-ʒze Yin, meaning 'The Train of

Thought in *K*wang-ȝze Traced in its Phraseology.' My copy is a reprint, in 1880, of the Commentary of Lin Hsî-*k*ung, who lived from the Ming into the present dynasty, under the editorship of a Lû *Kh*û-wang of *K*iang-sû province. The style is clear and elegant, but rather more concise than that of the preceding work. It leaves out the four disputed Books (XXVIII to XXXI); but all the others are followed by an elaborate discussion of their scope and plan.

Fifth, 'The Nan-hwâ Classic of *K*wang-ȝze Explained,' published in 1621, by a Hsüan Ying or Ȝung (宣穎, 宣㮆; the name is printed throughout the book, now in one of these ways, now in the other), called also Mâu-kung. The commentary is carefully executed and ingenious; but my copy of the book is so incorrectly printed that it can only be used with caution. Mr. Balfour appears to have made his version mainly from the same edition of the work; and some of his grossest errors pointed out by Mr. Giles arose from his accepting without question the misprints of his authority.

Sixth, 'Independent Views of *K*wang-ȝze (莊子獨見);'—by Hû Wăn-ying, published in 1751. Occasionally, the writer pauses over a passage, which, he thinks, has defied all preceding students, and suggests the right explanation of it, or leaves it as inexplicable.

It only remains for me to refer to the Repertories of 'Elegant Extracts,' called by the Chinese Kû Wăn, which abound in their literature, and where the masterpieces of composition are elucidated with more or less of critical detail and paraphrase. I have consulted nearly a dozen of these collections, and would mention my indebtedness especially to that called Mêi *Kh*wan, which discusses passages from twelve of *K*wang-ȝze's books.

When consulting the editions of Lin Hsî-*k*ung and Lû Shû-*k*ih, the reader is surprised by the frequency with which they refer to the 'old explanations' as 'incomplete and unsatisfactory,' often as 'absurd,' or 'ridiculous,' and he finds on examination that they do not so express themselves without reason. He is soon convinced that the translation of *K*wang-ȝze calls for the exercise of one's individual judgment, and the employment of every method akin to the critical processes by which the meaning in the books of other languages is determined. It was the perception of this which made me prepare in the first place a draft version to familiarise myself with the peculiar style and eccentric thought of the author.

From *K*wang-ȝze to the Tractate of 'Actions and their Retributions' the transition is great. Translation in the latter case is as easy as it is difficult in the former. It was Rémusat who in 1816 called attention to the Kan Ying Phien in Europe, as he did to the Tâo Teh *K*ing seven years later, and he translated the Text of it with a few Notes and Illustrative Anecdotes. In 1828 Klaproth published a translation of it from the Man-châu version; and in 1830 a translation in English appeared in the Canton Register, a newspaper published at Macao. In 1828 Julien published what has since been the standard version of it; with an immense amount of additional matter under the title—'Le Livre Des Récompenses et Des Peines, en Chinois et en Français; Accompagné de quatre cent Légendes, Anecdotes et Histoires, qui font connaître les Doctrines, les Croyances et les Mœurs de la Secte des Tâo-ssé.'

In writing out my own version I have had before me:—

First, 'The Thâi Shang Kan Ying Phien, with Plates and the Description of them;' a popular edition, as profusely furnished with anecdotes and stories as Julien's original, and all pictorially illustrated. The notes, comments, and corresponding sentences from the Confucian Classics are also abundant.

Second, 'The Thâi Shang Kan Ying Phien, with explanations collected from the Classics and Histories;'—a Cantonese reprint of an edition prepared in the *Kh*ien-lûng reign by a Hsiâ *K*iû-hsiâ.

Third, the edition in the Collection of Tâoist Texts described above on p. xvii; by Hsü Hsiû-teh. It is decidedly Tâoistic; but without stories or pictures.

Fourth, 'The Thâi Shang Kan Ying Phien *K*û;' by Hui Tung, of the present dynasty. The Work follows the Commentary of Wû *Kh*ăng on the Tâo Teh *K*ing in the Collection of the Yüeh-yâ Hall. The preface of the author is dated in 1749. The Commentary, he tells us, was written in consequence of a vow, when his mother was ill, and he was praying for her recovery. It contains many extracts from Ko Hung (Introduction, p. 5, note), to whom he always refers by his nom de plume of Pao-phoh 3ze, or 'Maintainer of Simplicity.' He considers indeed this Tractate to have originated from him.

I have thus set forth all that is necessary to be said here by way of preface. For various information about the Treatises comprised in the Appendixes, the reader is referred to the preliminary notes, which precede the translation of most of them. I have often sorely missed the presence of a competent native scholar who would have assisted me in the quest of references, and in talking over difficult passages. Such a helper would have saved me much time; but the result, I think, would scarcely have appeared in any great alteration of my versions.

J. L.

OXFORD,
December 20, 1890.

道德經　莊子

THE TEXTS OF TÂOISM.

道德經 莊子

THE TEXTS OF TÂOISM.

INTRODUCTION.

CHAPTER I.

WAS TÂOISM OLDER THAN LÂO-ȜZE?

1. In writing the preface to the third volume of these Sacred Books of the East in 1879, I referred to Lâo-ȝze as 'the acknowledged founder' of the system of Tâoism. Prolonged study and research, however, have brought me to the conclusion that there was a Tâoism earlier than his; and that before he wrote his Tâo Teh *K*ing, the principles taught in it had been promulgated, and the ordering of human conduct and government flowing from them inculcated.

Three Religions in China.

For more than a thousand years 'the Three Religions' has been a stereotyped phrase in China, meaning what we call Confucianism, Tâoism, and Buddhism. The phrase itself simply means 'the Three Teachings,' or systems of instruction, leaving the subject-matter of each 'Teaching' to be learned by inquiry. Of the three, Buddhism is of course the most recent, having been introduced into China only in the first century of our Christian era. Both the others were indigenous to the country, and are traceable to a much greater antiquity, so that it is a question to which the earlier origin should be assigned. The years of Confucius's life lay between B.C. 551 and 478; but his own acknowledgment that he was 'a transmitter and not a maker,' and the testimony of his grandson, that 'he handed down the doctrines of Yâo and Shun (B.C. 2300), and elegantly displayed the regulations of Wân and Wû (B.C. 1200), taking them as his model,' are well known.

2. Lâo-ʒze's birth is said, in the most likely account of it, to have taken place in the third year of king Ting of the *K*âu dynasty, (B.C.) 604. He was thus rather more than fifty years older than Confucius. The two men seem to have met more than once, and I am inclined to think that the name of Lâo-ʒze, as the designation of the other, arose from Confucius's styling him to his disciples 'The Old Philosopher.' They met as Heads of different schools or schemes of thought; but did not touch, so far as we know, on the comparative antiquity of their views. It is a peculiarity of the Tâo Teh *K*ing that any historical element in it is of the vaguest nature possible, and in all its chapters there is not a single proper name. Yet there are some references to earlier sages whose words the author was copying out, and to 'sentence-makers' whose maxims he was introducing to illustrate his own sentiments[1]. In the most distant antiquity he saw a happy society in which his highest ideas of the Tâo were realised, and in the seventeenth chapter he tells us that in the earliest times the people did not know that there were their rulers, and when those rulers were most successful in dealing with them, simply said, 'We are what we are of ourselves.' Evidently, men existed to Lâo-ʒze at first in a condition of happy innocence,—in what we must call a paradisiacal state, according to his idea of what such a state was likely to be.

Peculiarity of the Tâo Teh *K*ing.

When we turn from the treatise of Lâo-ʒze to the writings of *K*wang-ʒze, the greatest of his followers, we are

[1] The sixth chapter of Lâo's treatise, that about 'the Spirit of the Valley,' is referred to in Lieh-ʒze (I, 1[b]), as being from Hwang Tî, from which the commentator Tû Tâo-*k*ien (about A.D. 1300) takes occasion to say: 'From which we know that Lâo-ʒze was accustomed to quote in his treatise passages from earlier records,—as when he refers to the remarks of "some sage," of "some ancient," of "the sentence-makers," and of "some writer on war." In all these cases he is clearly introducing the words of earlier wise men. The case is like that of Confucius when he said, "I am a transmitter and not a maker," &c.' Found in Ʒiâo Hung, in loc.

not left in doubt as to his belief in an early state of paradisiacal Tâoism. Hwang Tî, the first year of whose reign is placed in B.C. 2697, is often introduced as a seeker of the Tâo, and is occasionally condemned as having been one of the first to disturb its rule in men's minds and break up 'the State of Perfect Unity.' He mentions several sovereigns of whom we can hardly find a trace in the records of history as having ruled in the primeval period, and gives us more than one description of the condition of the world during that happy time [1].

I do not think that *K*wang-ȝze had any historical evidence for the statements which he makes about those early days, the men who flourished in them, and their ways. His narratives are for the most part fictions, in which the names and incidents are of his own devising. They are no more true as matters of fact than the accounts of the characters in Bunyan's Pilgrim's Progress are true, with reference to any particular individuals; but as these last are grandly true of myriads of minds in different ages, so may we read in *K*wang-ȝze's stories the thoughts of Tâoistic men beyond the restrictions of place and time. He believed that those thoughts were as old as the men to whom he attributed them. I find in his belief a ground for believing myself that to Tâoism, as well as to Confucianism, we ought to attribute a much earlier origin than the famous men whose names they bear. Perhaps they did not differ so much at first as they came afterwards to do in the hands of Confucius and Lâo-ȝze, both great thinkers, the one more of a moralist, and the other more of a metaphysician. When and how, if they were ever more akin than they came to be, their divergence took place, are difficult questions on which it may be well to make some remarks after we have tried to set forth the most important principles of Tâoism.

Those principles have to be learned from the treatise of Lâo-ȝze and the writings of *K*wang-ȝze. We can hardly

[1] See in Books IX, X, and XII.

say that the Tâoism taught in them is the Tâoism now current in China, or that has been current in it for many centuries; but in an inquiry into the nature and origin of religions these are the authorities that must be consulted for Tâoism, and whose evidence must be accepted. The treatise, 'Actions and the Responses to them,' will show one of the phases of it at a much later period.

CHAPTER II.

THE TEXTS OF THE TÂO TEH *K*ING AND *K*WANG-ȝZE SHÛ, AS REGARDS THEIR AUTHENTICITY AND GENUINENESS, AND THE ARRANGEMENT OF THEM.

I. 1. I will now state briefly, first, the grounds on which I accept the Tâo Teh *K*ing as a genuine production of the age to which it has been assigned, and the truth of its authorship by Lâo-ȝze to whom it has been ascribed. It would not have been necessary a few years ago to write as if these points could be called in question, but in 1886 Mr. Herbert A. Giles, of Her Majesty's Consular Service in China, and one of the ablest Chinese scholars living, vehemently called them in question in an article in the China Review for the months of March and April. His strictures have been replied to, and I am not going to revive here the controversy which they produced, but only to state a portion of the evidence which satisfies my own mind on the two points just mentioned.

2. It has been said above that the year B.C. 604 was, probably, that of Lâo-ȝze's birth. The year of his death is not recorded. Sze-mâ *Kh*ien, the first great Chinese historian, who died in about B.C. 85, commences his 'Biographies' with a short account of Lâo-ȝze. He tells us that the philosopher had been a curator of the Royal Library of *K*âu, and that, mourning over the decadence of the dynasty, he wished to withdraw from the world, and proceeded to the pass or defile of Hsien-ku[1],

The evidence of Sze-mâ *Kh*ien, the historian.

[1] In the present district of Ling-pâo, Shan *K*âu, province of Ho-nan.

leading from China to the west. There he was recognised by the warden of the pass, Yin Hsî (often called Kwan Yin), himself a well-known Tâoist, who insisted on his leaving him a writing before he went into seclusion. Lâo-ʒze then wrote his views on 'The Tâo and its Characteristics,' in two parts or sections, containing more than 5000 characters, gave the manuscript to the warden, and went his way[1]; 'nor is it known where he died.' This account is strange enough, and we need not wonder that it was by and by embellished with many marvels. It contains, however, the definite statements that Lâo-ʒze wrote the Tâo Teh *K*ing in two parts, and consisting of more than 5000 characters. And that *Kh*ien was himself well acquainted with the treatise is apparent from his quotations from it, with, in almost every case, the specification of the author. He thus adduces part of the first chapter, and a large portion of the last chapter but one. His brief references also to Lâo-ʒze and his writings are numerous.

Lieh-ʒze, Han Fei-ʒze, and other Tâoist authors.

3. But between Lâo-ʒze and Sze-mâ *Kh*ien there were many Tâoist writers whose works remain. I may specify of them Lieh-ʒze (assuming that his chapters, though not composed in their present form by him, may yet be accepted as fair specimens of his teaching); *K*wang-ʒze (of the fourth century B.C. We find him refusing to accept high office from king Wei of *Kh*û, B.C. 339–299); Han Fei, a voluminous author, who died by his own hand in B.C. 230; and Liû An, a scion of the Imperial House of Han, king of Hwâi-nan, and better known to us as Hwâi-nan Ʒze, who also died by his own hand in B.C. 122. In the books of all these men we find quotations of many passages that are in our treatise. They are expressly said to be, many of them, quotations from Lâo-ʒze; Han Fei several times all but

[1] In an ordinary Student's Manual I find a note with reference to this incident to which it may be worth while to give a place here:—The warden, it is said, set before Lâo-ʒze a dish of tea; and this was the origin of the custom of tea-drinking between host and guest (see the 幼學故事尋源, ch. 7, on Food and Drink).

shows the book beneath his eyes. To show how numerous the quotations by Han Fei and Liû An are, let it be borne in mind that the Tâo Teh *K*ing has come down to us as divided into eighty-one short chapters; and that the whole of it is shorter than the shortest of our Gospels. Of the eighty-one chapters, either the whole or portions of seventy-one are found in those two writers. There are other authors not so decidedly Tâoistic, in whom we find quotations from the little book. These quotations are in general wonderfully correct. Various readings indeed there are; but if we were sure that the writers did trust to memory, their differences would only prove that copies of the text had been multiplied from the very first.

Evidence of Pan Kû.

In passing on from quotations to the complete text, I will clinch the assertion that *Kh*ien was well acquainted with our treatise, by a passage from the History of the Former Han Dynasty (B.C. 206–A.D. 24), which was begun to be compiled by Pan Kû, who died however in 92, and left a portion to be completed by his sister, the famous Pan *K*âo. The thirty-second chapter of his Biographies is devoted to Sze-mâ *Kh*ien, and towards the end it is said that 'on the subject of the Great Tâo he preferred Hwang and Lâo to the six *K*ing.' 'Hwang and Lâo' must there be the writings of Hwang-Tî and Lâo-ȝze. The association of the two names also illustrates the antiquity claimed for Tâoism, and the subject of note 1, p. 2.

Catalogue of the Imperial Library of Han.

4. We go on from quotations to complete texts, and turn, first, to the catalogue of the Imperial Library of Han, as compiled by Liû Hsin, not later than the commencement of our Christian era. There are entered in it Tâoist works by thirty-seven different authors, containing in all 993 chapters or sections (phien). Î Yin, the premier of *Kh*ăng Thang (B.C. 1766), heads the list with fifty-one sections. There are in it four editions of Lâo-ȝze's work with commentaries:—by a Mr. Lin, in four sections; a Mr. Fû, in thirty-seven sections; a Mr. Hsü, in six sections; and by Liû Hsiang, Hsin's own father, in four sections. All these four works have since perished, but there they were in the Imperial Library before

道德經 莊子

our era began. *K*wang-ȝze is in the same list in fifty-two books or sections, the greater part of which have happily escaped the devouring tooth of time.

We turn now to the twentieth chapter of *Kh*ien's Biographies, in which he gives an account of Yo Î, the scion of a distinguished family, and who himself played a famous part, both as a politician and military leader, and became prince of Wang-*k*û under the kingdom of *K*âo in B.C. 279. Among his descendants was a Yo *Kh*ăn, who learned in *Kh*î 'the words,' that is, the Tâoistic writings 'of Hwang-Tî and Lâo-ȝze from an old man who lived on the Ho-side.' The origin of this old man was not known, but Yo *Kh*ăn taught what he learned from him to a Mr. Ko, who again became preceptor to Ȝhâo Ȝhan, the chief minister of *Kh*î, and afterwards of the new dynasty of Han, dying in B.C. 190.

The catalogue of the Sui dynasty.

5. Referring now to the catalogue of the Imperial Library of the dynasty of Sui (A.D. 589–618), we find that it contained many editions of Lâo's treatise with commentaries. The first mentioned is 'The Tâo Teh *K*ing,' with the commentary of the old man of the Ho-side, in the time of the emperor Wăn of Han (B.C. 179–142). It is added in a note that the dynasty of Liang (A.D. 502–556) had possessed the edition of 'the old man of the Ho-side, of the time of the Warring States; but that with some other texts and commentaries it had disappeared.' I find it difficult to believe that there had been two old men of the Ho-side[1], both teachers of Tâoism and commentators on our *K*ing, but I am willing to content myself with the more recent work, and accept the copy that has been current—say from B.C. 150, when Sze-mâ *Kh*ien could have been little more than a boy. Tâoism was a favourite study with many of the Han emperors and their ladies. Hwâi-nan Ȝze, of whose many quotations from

[1] The earlier old man of the Ho-side is styled in Chinese 河上丈人; the other 河上公; but the designations have the same meaning. Some critical objections to the genuineness of the latter's commentary on the ground of the style are without foundation.

the text of Lâo I have spoken, was an uncle of the emperor Wăn. To the emperor *K*ing (B.C. 156–143), the son of Wăn, there is attributed the designation of Lâo's treatise as a *K*ing, a work of standard authority. At the beginning of his reign, we are told, some one was commending to him four works, among which were those of Lâo-ȝze and *K*wang-ȝze. Deeming that the work of Hwang-ȝze and Lâo-ȝze was of a deeper character than the others, he ordered that it should be called a *K*ing, established a board for the study of Tâoism, and issued an edict that the book should be learned and recited at court, and throughout the country[1]. Thenceforth it was so styled. We find Hwang-fû Mî (A.D. 215–282) referring to it as the Tâo Teh *K*ing.

The second place in the Sui catalogue is given to the text and commentary of Wang Pî or Wang Fû-sze, an extraordinary scholar who died in A.D. 249, at the early age of twenty-four. This work has always been much prized. It was its text which Lû Teh-ming used in his 'Explanation of the Terms and Phrases of the Classics,' in the seventh century. Among the editions of it which I possess is that printed in 1794 with the imperial moveable metal types.

The work of Wang Pî.

I need not speak of editions or commentaries subsequent to Wang Pî's. They soon begin to be many, and are only not so numerous as those of the Confucian Classics.

6. All the editions of the book are divided into two parts, the former called Tâo, and the latter Teh, meaning the Qualities or Characteristics of the Tâo, but this distinction of subjects is by no means uniformly adhered to.

Divisions into parts, chapters; and number of characters in the text.

I referred already to the division of the whole into eighty-one short chapters (37 + 44), which is by common tradition attributed to Ho-shang Kung, or 'The old man of the Ho-side.' Another very early commentator, called Yen Ȝun or Yen *K*ün-phing, made a division into seventy-two chapters (40 + 32), under the influence, no doubt, of some

[1] See Ȝiâo Hung's Wings or Helps, ch. v, p. 11a.

道德經 莊子

mystical considerations. His predecessor, perhaps, had no better reason for his eighty-one; but the names of his chapters were, for the most part, happily chosen, and have been preserved. Wû *Kh*ăng arranged the two parts in sixty-seven chapters (31 + 36). It is a mistake, however, to suppose, as even Mr. Wylie with all his general accuracy did[1], that Wû 'curtails the ordinary text to some extent.' He does not curtail, but only re-arranges according to his fashion, uniting some of Ho-shang Kung's chapters in one, and sometimes altering the order of their clauses.

Sze-mâ *Kh*ien tells us that, as the treatise came from Lâo-ȝze, it contained more than 5000 characters; that is, as one critic says, 'more than 5000 and fewer than 6000.' Ho-shang Kung's text has 5350, and one copy 5590; Wang Pî's, 5683, and one copy 5610. Two other early texts have been counted, giving 5720 and 5635 characters respectively. The brevity arises from the terse conciseness of the style, owing mainly to the absence of the embellishment of particles, which forms so striking a peculiarity in the composition of Mencius and *K*wang-ȝze.

In passing on to speak, secondly and more briefly, of the far more voluminous writings of *K*wang-ȝze, I may say that I do not know of any other book of so ancient a date as the Tâo Teh *K*ing, of which the authenticity of the origin and genuineness of the text can claim to be so well substantiated.

The Books of *K*wang-ȝze.

II. 7. In the catalogue of the Han Library we have the entry of '*K*wang-ȝze in fifty-two books or sections.' By the time of the Sui dynasty, the editions of his work amounted to nearly a score. The earliest commentary that has come down to us goes by the name of Kwo Hsiang's. He was an officer and scholar of the Ȝin dynasty, who died about the year 312. Another officer, also of Ȝin, called Hsiang Hsiû, of rather an earlier date, had undertaken the same task, but left it incomplete; and his manuscripts coming (not, as it appears, by

[1] Notes on Chinese Literature, p. 173.

any fraud) into Kwo's hands, he altered and completed them as suited his own views, and then gave them to the public. In the short account of Kwo, given in the twentieth chapter of the Biographies of the Ȝin history, it is said that several tens of commentators had laboured unsatisfactorily on *K*wang's writings before Hsiang Hsiû took them in hand. As the joint result of the labours of the two men, however, we have only thirty-three of the fifty-two sections mentioned in the Han catalogue. It is in vain that I have tried to discover how and when the other nineteen sections were lost. In one of the earliest commentaries on the Tâo Teh *K*ing, that by Yen Ȝun, we have several quotations from *K*wang-ȝze which bear evidently the stamp of his handiwork, and are not in the current Books; but they would not altogether make up a single section. We have only to be thankful that so large a proportion of the original work has been preserved. Sû Shih (Ȝze-*k*an, and Tung-pho), it is well known, called in question the genuineness of Books 28 to 31[1]. Books 15 and 16 have also been challenged, and a paragraph here and there in one or other of the Books. The various readings, according to a collation given by Ȝiâo Hung, are few.

Importance to Tâoism of the Books of *K*wang-ȝze.

8. There can be no doubt that the Books of *K*wang-ȝze were hailed by all the friends of Tâoism. It has been mentioned above that the names 'Hwang-Tî' and 'Lâo-ȝze' were associated together as denoting the masters of Tâoism, and the phrase, 'the words of Hwang-Tî and Lâo-ȝze,' came to be no more than a name for the Tâo Teh *K*ing. Gradually the two names were contracted into 'Hwang Lâo,' as in the passage quoted on p. 6 from Pan Kû. After the Han dynasty, the name Hwang gave place to *K*wang, and the names Lâo *K*wang, and, sometimes inverted, *K*wang Lâo, were employed to denote the system or the texts of Tâoism. In the account, for instance, of *K*î

[1] A brother of Shih, Sû *K*ēh (Ȝze-yû and Ying-pin), wrote a remarkable commentary on the Tâo Teh *K*ing; but it was Shih who first discredited those four Books, in his Inscription for the temple of *K*wang-ȝze, prepared in 1078.

道德經 莊子

Khang, in the nineteenth chapter of the Biographies of Ȝin, we have a typical Tâoist brought before us. When grown up, 'he loved Lâo and *K*wang;' and a visitor, to produce the most favourable impression on him, says, 'Lâo-ȝze and *K*wang *K*âu are my masters.'

Division of the Books into three Parts.

9. The thirty-three Books of *K*wang-ȝze are divided into three Parts, called Nêi, or 'the Inner;' Wâi, or 'the Outer;' and Ȝâ, 'the Miscellaneous.' The first Part comprises seven Books; the second, fifteen; and the third, eleven. 'Inner' may be understood as equivalent to esoteric or More Important. The titles of the several Books are significant, and each expresses the subject or theme of its Book. They are believed to have been prefixed by *K*wang-ȝze himself, and that no alteration could be made in the composition but for the worse. 'Outer' is understood in the sense of supplementary or subsidiary. The fifteen Books so called are 'Wings' to the previous seven. Their titles were not given by the author, and are not significant of the Tâoistic truth which all the paragraphs unite, or should unite, in illustrating; they are merely some name or phrase taken from the commencement of the first paragraph in each Book,—like the names of the Books of the Confucian Analects, or of the Hebrew Pentateuch. The fixing them originally is generally supposed to have been the work of Kwo Hsiang. The eleven Miscellaneous Books are also supplementary to those of the first Part, and it is not easy to see why a difference was made between them and the fifteen that precede.

The general title of *K*wang-ȝze's works.

10. *K*wang-ȝze's writings have long been current under the name of Nan Hwa *K*ăn *K*ing. He was a native of the duchy of Sung, born in what was then called the district of Măng, and belonged to the state or kingdom of Liang or Wei. As he grew up, he filled some official post in the city of Ȝhî-yüan,—the site of which it is not easy to determine with certainty. In A.D. 742, the name of his birth-place was changed (but only for a time) to Nan-hwa, and an imperial order was issued that *K*wang-ȝze should thence-

forth be styled 'The True Man of Nan-hwa,' and his Book, 'The True Book of Nan-hwa[1].' To be 'a True Man' is the highest Tâoistic achievement of a man, and our author thus canonised communicates his glory to his Book.

CHAPTER III.

WHAT IS THE MEANING OF THE NAME TÂO? AND THE CHIEF POINTS OF BELIEF IN TÂOISM.

Meaning of the name Tâo.

1. The first translation of the Tâo Teh *K*ing into a Western language was executed in Latin by some of the Roman Catholic missionaries, and a copy of it was brought to England by a Mr. Matthew Raper, F.R.S., and presented by him to the Society at a meeting on the 10th January, 1788,—being the gift to him of P. Jos. de Grammont, 'Missionarius Apostolicus, ex-Jesuita.' In this version Tâo is taken in the sense of Ratio, or the Supreme Reason of the Divine Being, the Creator and Governor.

M. Abel Rémusat, the first Professor of Chinese in Paris, does not seem to have been aware of the existence of the above version in London, but his attention was attracted to Lâo's treatise about 1820, and, in 1823, he wrote of the character Tâo, 'Ce mot me semble ne pas pouvoir être bien traduit, si ce n'est par le mot λόγος dans le triple sens de souverain Être, de raison, et de parole.'

Rémusat's successor in the chair of Chinese, the late Stanislas Julien, published in 1842 a translation of the whole treatise. Having concluded from an examination of it, and the earliest Tâoist writers, such as *K*wang-ȝze, Ho-kwan Ȝze, and Ho-shang Kung, that the Tâo was devoid of action, of thought, of judgment, and of intelligence, he concluded that it was impossible to understand by it 'the Primordial Reason, or the Sublime Intelligence which created, and which governs the world,' and to

[1] See the Khang-hsî Thesaurus (佩文韻府), under 華.

this he subjoined the following note:—'Quelque étrange que puisse paraître cette idée de Lâo-ȝze, elle n'est pas sans exemple dans l'histoire de la philosophie. Le mot nature n'a-t-il pas été employé par certains philosophes, que la religion et la raison condamnent, pour désigner une cause première, également dépourvue de pensée et d'intelligence?' Julien himself did not doubt that Lâo's idea of the character was that it primarily and properly meant 'a way,' and hence he translated the title Tâo Teh *K*ing by 'Le Livre de la Voie et de la Vertu,' transferring at the same time the name Tâo to the text of his version.

The first English writer who endeavoured to give a distinct account of Tâoism was the late Archdeacon Hardwick, while he held the office of Christian Advocate in the University of Cambridge. In his 'Christ and other Masters' (vol. ii, p. 67), when treating of the religions of China, he says, 'I feel disposed to argue that the centre of the system founded by Lâo-ȝze had been awarded to some energy or power resembling the "Nature" of modern speculators. The indefinite expression Tâo was adopted to denominate an abstract cause, or the initial principle of life and order, to which worshippers were able to assign the attributes of immateriality, eternity, immensity, invisibility.'

It was, probably, Julien's reference in his note to the use of the term nature, which suggested to Hardwick his analogy between Lâo-ȝze's Tâo, and 'the Nature of modern speculation.' Canon Farrar has said, 'We have long personified under the name of Nature the sum total of God's laws as observed in the physical world; and now the notion of Nature as a distinct, living, independent entity seems to be ineradicable alike from our literature and our systems of philosophy[1].' But it seems to me that this metaphorical or mythological use of the word nature for the Cause and Ruler of it, implies the previous notion of Him, that is, of God, in the mind. Does not this clearly appear in the words of Seneca?—'Vis illum (h.e. Jovem Deum) naturam

[1] Language and Languages, pp. 184, 185.

vocare, non peccabis:—hic est ex quo nata sunt omnia, cujus spiritu vivimus[1].'

In his translation of the Works of *K*wang-ȝze in 1881, Mr. Balfour adopted Nature as the ordinary rendering of the Chinese Tâo. He says, 'When the word is translated Way, it means the Way of Nature,—her processes, her methods, and her laws; when translated Reason, it is the same as lî,—the power that works in all created things, producing, preserving, and life-giving,—the intelligent principle of the world; when translated Doctrine, it refers to the True doctrine respecting the laws and mysteries of Nature.' He calls attention also to the point that 'he uses NATURE in the sense of Natura naturans, while the Chinese expression wan wû (= all things) denotes Natura naturata.' But this really comes to the metaphorical use of nature which has been touched upon above. It can claim as its patrons great names like those of Aquinas, Giordano Bruno, and Spinoza, but I have never been able to see that its barbarous phraseology makes it more than a figure of speech[2].

The term Nature, however, is so handy, and often fits so appropriately into a version, that if Tâo had ever such a signification I should not hesitate to employ it as freely as Mr. Balfour has done; but as it has not that signification, to try to put a non-natural meaning into it, only perplexes the mind, and obscures the idea of Lâo-ȝze.

Mr. Balfour himself says (p. xviii), 'The primary signification of Tâo is simply "road."' Beyond question this meaning underlies the use of it by the great master of Tâoism and by *K*wang-ȝze[3]. Let the reader refer to the version of the twenty-fifth chapter of Lâo's treatise, and to

[1] Natur. Quaest. lib. II, cap. xlv.

[2] Martineau's 'Types of Ethical Theory,' I, p. 286, and his whole 'Conjectural History of Spinoza's Thought.'

[3] 道 is equivalent to the Greek ἡ ὁδός, the way. Where this name for the Christian system occurs in our Revised Version of the New Testament in the Acts of the Apostles, the literal rendering is adhered to, Way being printed with a capital W. See Acts ix. 2; xix. 9, 23; xxii. 4; xxiv. 14, 22.

the notes subjoined to it. There Tâo appears as the spontaneously operating cause of all movement in the phenomena of the universe; and the nearest the writer can come to a name for it is 'the Great Tâo.' Having established this name, he subsequently uses it repeatedly; see chh. xxxiv and liii. In the third paragraph of his twentieth chapter, *K*wang-ȝze uses a synonymous phrase instead of Lâo's 'Great Tâo,' calling it the 'Great Thû,' about which there can be no dispute, as meaning 'the Great Path,' 'Way,' or 'Course[1].' In the last paragraph of his twenty-fifth Book, *K*wang-ȝze again sets forth the metaphorical origin of the name Tâo. 'Tâo,' he says, 'cannot be regarded as having a positive existence; existences cannot be regarded as non-existent. The name Tâo is a metaphor used for the purpose of description. To say that it exercises some causation, or that it does nothing, is speaking of it from the phase of a thing;—how can such language serve as a designation of it in its greatness? If words were sufficient for the purpose, we might in a day's time exhaust the subject of the Tâo. Words not being sufficient, we may talk about it the whole day, and the subject of discourse will only have been a thing. Tâo is the extreme to which things conduct us. Neither speech nor silence is sufficient to convey the notion of it. When we neither speak nor refrain from speech, our speculations about it reach their highest point.'

The Tâo therefore is a phenomenon; not a positive being, but a mode of being. Lâo's idea of it may become plainer as we proceed to other points of his system. In the meantime, the best way of dealing with it in translating is to transfer it to the version, instead of trying to introduce an English equivalent for it.

2. Next in importance to Tâo is the name Thien, meaning at first the vaulted sky or the open firmament of heaven. In the Confucian Classics, and in the speech of the Chinese

[1] 大塗. The Khang-hsî dictionary defines thû by lû, road or way. Medhurst gives 'road.' Unfortunately, both Morrison and Williams overlooked this definition of the character. Giles has also a note in loc., showing how this synonym settles the original meaning of Tâo in the sense of 'road.'

people, this name is used metaphorically as it is by ourselves for the Supreme Being, with reference especially to His will and rule. So it was that the idea of God arose among the Chinese fathers; so it was that they proceeded to fashion a name for God, calling Him Tî, and Shang Tî, 'the Ruler,' and 'the Supreme Ruler.' The Tâoist fathers found this among their people; but in their idea of the Tâo they had already a Supreme Concept which superseded the necessity of any other. The name Tî for God only occurs once in the Tâo Teh *K*ing; in the well-known passage of the fourth chapter, where, speaking of the Tâo, Lâo-ʒze says, 'I do not know whose Son it is; it might seem to be before God.'

Usage of the term Thien.

Nor is the name Thien very common. We have the phrase, 'Heaven and Earth,' used for the two great constituents of the kosmos, owing their origin to the Tâo, and also for a sort of binomial power, acting in harmony with the Tâo, covering, protecting, nurturing, and maturing all things. Never once is Thien used in the sense of God, the Supreme Being. In its peculiarly Tâoistic employment, it is more an adjective than a noun. 'The Tâo of Heaven' means the Tâo that is Heavenly, the course that is quiet and undemonstrative, that is free from motive and effort, such as is seen in the processes of nature, grandly proceeding and successful without any striving or crying. The Tâo of man, not dominated by this Tâo, is contrary to it, and shows will, purpose, and effort, till, submitting to it, it becomes 'the Tâo or Way of the Sages,' which in all its action has no striving.

The characteristics both of Heaven and man are dealt with more fully by *K*wang than by Lâo. In the conclusion of his eleventh Book, for instance, he says:—'What do we mean by Tâo? There is the Tâo (or Way) of Heaven, and there is the Tâo of man. Acting without action, and yet attracting all honour, is the Way of Heaven. Doing and being embarrassed thereby is the Way of man. The Way of Heaven should play the part of lord; the Way of man, the part of minister. The two are far apart, and should be distinguished from each other.'

In his next Book (par. 2), *K*wang-ʒze tells us what he intends by 'Heaven:'—'Acting without action,—this is what is called Heaven.' Heaven thus takes its law from the Tâo. 'The oldest sages and sovereigns attained to do the same,'—it was for all men to aim at the same achievement. As they were successful, 'vacancy, stillness, placidity, tastelessness, quietude, silence, and non-action' would be found to be their characteristics, and they would go on to the perfection of the Tâo[1].

The employment of Thien by the Confucianists, as of Heaven by ourselves, must be distinguished therefore from the Tâoistic use of the name to denote the quiet but mighty influence of the impersonal Tâo; and to translate it by 'God' only obscures the meaning of the Tâoist writers. This has been done by Mr. Giles in his version of *K*wang-ʒze, which is otherwise for the most part so good. Everywhere on his pages there appears the great name 'God;'—a blot on his translation more painful to my eyes and ears than the use of 'Nature' for Tâo by Mr. Balfour. I know that Mr. Giles's plan in translating is to use strictly English equivalents for all kinds of Chinese terms[2]. The plan is good where there are in the two languages such strict equivalents; but in the case before us there is no ground for its application. The exact English equivalent for the Chinese thien is our heaven. The Confucianists often used thien metaphorically for the personal Being whom they denominated Tî (God) and Shang Tî (the Supreme God), and a translator may occasionally, in working on books of Confucian literature, employ our name God for it. But neither Lâo nor *K*wang ever attached anything like our idea of God to it; and when one, in working on books of early Tâoist literature, translates thien by God, such a rendering must fail to produce in an English reader a correct apprehension of the meaning.

There is also in *K*wang-ʒze a peculiar usage of the name Thien. He applies it to the Beings whom he introduces as

[1] The Tâo Teh *K*ing, ch. 25, and *K*wang-ʒze, XIII, par. 1.

[2] See 'Strange Stories from a Chinese Studio,' vol. i, p. 1, note 2.

Peculiar usage of Thien in *K*wang-ȝze.

Masters of the Tâo, generally with mystical appellations in order to set forth his own views. Two instances from Book XI will suffice in illustration of this. In par. 4, Hwang-Tî does reverence to his instructor Kwang *Kh*ăng-ȝze[1], saying, 'In Kwang *Kh*ăng-ȝze we have an example of what is called Heaven,' which Mr. Giles renders 'Kwang *Kh*ăng Ȝze is surely God.' In par. 5, again, the mystical Yûn-*k*iang is made to say to the equally fabulous and mystical Hung-mung, 'O Heaven, have you forgotten me?' and, farther on, 'O Heaven, you have conferred on me (the knowledge of) your operation, and revealed to me the mystery of it;' in both which passages Mr. Giles renders thien by 'your Holiness.'

But Mr. Giles seems to agree with me that the old Tâoists had no idea of a personal God, when they wrote of Thien or Heaven. On his sixty-eighth page, near the beginning of Book VI, we meet with the following sentence, having every appearance of being translated from the Chinese text:—'God is a principle which exists by virtue of its own intrinsicality, and operates without self-manifestation.' By an inadvertence he has introduced his own definition of 'God' as if it were *K*wang-ȝze's; and though I can find no characters in the text of which I can suppose that he intends it to be the translation, it is valuable as helping us to understand the meaning to be attached to the Great Name in his volume.

Mr. Giles's own idea of the meaning of the name 'God' as the equivalent of Thien.

I have referred above (p. 16) to the only passage in Lâo's treatise, where he uses the name Tî or God in its highest sense, saying that 'the Tâo might seem to have been before Him.' He might well say so, for in his first chapter he describes the Tâo, '(conceived of as) having no name, as the Originator of heaven and

The relation of the Tâo to Tî.

[1] Kwang *Kh*ăng-ȝze heads the list of characters in Ko Hung's 'History of Spirit-like Immortals (神仙傳),' written in our fourth century. 'He was,' it is said, 'an Immortal of old, who lives on the hill of M'ung-thung in a grotto of rocks.'

道德經 莊子

earth, and (conceived of as) having a name, as the Mother of all things.' The reader will also find the same predicates of the Tâo at greater length in his fifty-first chapter.

The character Tî is also of rare occurrence in *K*wang-ȝze, excepting as applied to the five ancient Tîs. In Bk. III, par. 4, and in one other place, we find it indicating the Supreme Being, but the usage is ascribed to the ancients. In Bk. XV, par. 3, in a description of the human SPIRIT, its name is said to be 'Thung Tî,' which Mr. Giles renders 'Of God;' Mr. Balfour, 'One with God;' while my own version is 'The Divinity in Man.' In Bk. XII, par. 6, we have the expression 'the place of God;' in Mr. Giles, 'the kingdom of God;' in Mr. Balfour, 'the home of God.' In this and the former instance, the character seems to be used with the ancient meaning which had entered into the folk-lore of the people. But in Bk. VI, par. 7, there is a passage which shows clearly the relative position of Tâo and Tî in the Tâoistic system; and having called attention to it, I will go on to other points. Let the reader mark well the following predicates of the Tâo:—'Before there were heaven and earth, from of old, there It was, securely existing. From It came the mysterious existence of spirits; from It the mysterious existence of Tî (God). It produced heaven, It produced earth[1].' This says more than the utterance of Lâo,—that 'the Tâo seemed to be before God;'—does it not say that Tâo was before God, and that He was what He is by virtue of Its operation?

No idea of Creation proper in Tâoism.

3. Among the various personal names given to the Tâo are those of ȝâo Hwâ, 'Maker and Transformer,' and ȝâo Wû *K*ê, 'Maker of things.' Instances of both these names are found in Bk. VI, parr. 9, 10. 'Creator' and 'God' have both been employed for them; but there is no idea of Creation in Tâoism.

Again and again *K*wang-ȝze entertains the question of

[1] For this sentence we find in Mr. Balfour:—'Spirits of the dead, receiving It, become divine; the very gods themselves owe their divinity to its influence; and by it both Heaven and Earth were produced.' The version of it by Mr. Giles is too condensed:—'Spiritual beings drew their spirituality therefrom, while the universe became what we see it now.'

how it was at the first beginning of things. Different views are stated. In Bk. II, par. 4, he says:—'Among the men of old their knowledge reached the extreme point. What was that extreme point?

'Some held that at first there was not anything. This is the extreme point,—the utmost limit to which nothing can be added.

'A second class held that there was something, but without any responsive recognition of it (on the part of man).

'A third class held that there was such recognition, but there had not begun to be any expression of different opinions about it. It was through the definite expression of different opinions about it that there ensued injury to the (doctrine of the) Tâo[1].'

The first of these three views was that which *K*wang-ȝze himself preferred. The most condensed expression of it is given in Bk. XII, par. 8:—'In the Grand Beginning of all things there was nothing in all the vacancy of space; there was nothing that could be named[2]. It was in this state that there arose the first existence; the first existence, but still without bodily shape. From this things could be produced, (receiving) what we call their several characters. That which had no bodily shape was divided, and then without intermission there was what we call the process of conferring. (The two processes) continued to operate, and things were produced. As they were completed, there appeared the distinguishing lines of each, which we call the bodily shape. That shape was the body preserving in it the spirit, and each had its peculiar manifestation which we call its nature.'

Such was the genesis of things; the formation of heaven

[1] Compare also Bk. XXII, parr. 7, 8, and XXIII, par. 10.

[2] Mr. Balfour had given for this sentence:—'In the beginning of all things there was not even nothing. There were no names; these arose afterwards.' In his critique on Mr. Balfour's version in 1882, Mr. Giles proposed:—'At the beginning of all things there was nothing; but this nothing had no name.' He now in his own version gives for it, 'At the beginning of the beginning, even nothing did not exist. Then came the period of the nameless;'—an improvement, certainly, on the other; but which can hardly be accepted as the correct version of the text.

道德經 莊子

and earth and all that in them is, under the guidance of the Tâo. It was an evolution and not a creation. How the Tâo itself came,—I do not say into existence, but into operation,—neither Lâo nor *K*wang ever thought of saying anything about. We have seen that it is nothing material[1]. It acted spontaneously of itself. Its sudden appearance in the field of non-existence, Producer, Transformer, Beautifier, surpasses my comprehension. To Lâo it seemed to be before God. I am compelled to accept the existence of God, as the ultimate Fact, bowing before it with reverence, and not attempting to explain it, the one mystery, the sole mystery of the universe.

Man is composed of body and spirit.

4. 'The bodily shape was the body preserving in it the spirit, and each had its peculiar manifestation which we call its nature.' So it is said in the passage quoted above from *K*wang-ʒze's twelfth Book, and the language shows how Tâoism, in a loose and indefinite way, considered man to be composed of body and spirit, associated together, yet not necessarily dependent on each other. Little is found bearing on this tenet in the Tâo Teh *K*ing. The concluding sentence of ch. 33, 'He who dies and yet does not perish, has longevity,' is of doubtful acceptation. More pertinent is the description of life as 'a coming forth,' and of death as 'an entering[2];' but *K*wang-ʒze expounds more fully, though after all unsatisfactorily, the teaching of their system on the subject.

At the conclusion of his third Book, writing of the death of Lâo-ʒze, he says, 'When the master came, it was at the proper time; when he went away, it was the simple sequence (of his coming). Quiet acquiescence in what happens at its proper time, and quietly submitting (to its sequence), afford no occasion for grief or for joy. The ancients described (death) as the loosening of the cord on which God suspended (the life). What we can point to are the faggots that have been consumed; but the fire is transmitted elsewhere, and we know not that it is over and ended.'

[1] The Tâo Teh *K*ing, ch. 14; et al. [2] Ch. 50.

It is, however, in connexion with the death of his own wife, as related in the eighteenth Book, that his views most fully—I do not say 'clearly'—appear. We are told that when that event took place, his friend Huî-ȝze went to condole with him, and found him squatted on the ground, drumming on the vessel (of ice), and singing. His friend said to him, 'When a wife has lived with her husband, brought up children, and then dies in her old age, not to wail for her is enough. When you go on to drum on the vessel and sing, is it not an excessive (and strange) demonstration?' *K*wang-ȝze replied, 'It is not so. When she first died, was it possible for me to be singular, and not affected by the event? But I reflected on the commencement of her being, when she had not yet been born to life. Not only had she no life, but she had no bodily form. Not only had she no bodily form, but she had no breath. Suddenly in this chaotic condition there ensued a change, and there was breath; another change, and there was the bodily form; a further change, and she was born to life; a change now again, and she is dead. The relation between those changes is like the procession of the four seasons,—spring, autumn, winter, and summer. There she lies with her face up, sleeping in the Great Chamber[1]; and if I were to fall sobbing and going on to wail for her, I should think I did not understand what was appointed for all. I therefore restrained myself.'

The next paragraph of the same Book contains another story about two ancient men, both deformed, who, when looking at the graves on Kwăn-lun, begin to feel in their own frames the symptoms of approaching dissolution. One says to the other, 'Do you dread it?' and gets the reply, 'No. Why should I dread it? Life is a borrowed thing. The living frame thus borrowed is but so much dust. Life and death are like day and night.'

In every birth, it would thus appear, there is, somehow, a repetition of what it is said, as we have seen, took place at 'the Grand Beginning of all things,' when out of the

[1] That is, between heaven and earth.

道德經 莊子

primal nothingness, the Tâo somehow appeared, and there was developed through its operation the world of things,—material things and the material body of man, which enshrines or enshrouds an immaterial spirit. This returns to the Tâo that gave it, and may be regarded indeed as that Tâo operating in the body during the time of life, and in due time receives a new embodiment.

In these notions of Tâoism there was a preparation for the appreciation by its followers of the Buddhistic system when it came to be introduced into the country, and which forms a close connexion between the two at the present day, Tâoism itself constantly becoming less definite and influential on the minds of the Chinese people. The Book which tells us of the death of *K*wang-ȝze's wife concludes with a narrative about Lieh-ȝze and an old bleached skull[1], and to this is appended a passage about the metamorphoses of things, ending with the statement that 'the panther produces the horse, and the horse the man, who then again enters into the great machinery (of evolution), from which all things come forth (at birth) and into which they re-enter (at death).' Such representations need not be characterised.

The Tâo as promotive of longevity.

5. Kû Hsî, 'the prince of Literature,' described the main object of Tâoism to be 'the preservation of the breath of life;' and Liû Mî, probably of our thirteenth century[2], in his 'Dispassionate Comparison of the Three Religions,' declares that 'its chief achievement is the prolongation of longevity.' Such is the account of Tâoism ordinarily given by Confucian and Buddhist writers, but our authorities, Lâo and *K*wang, hardly bear out this representation of it as true of their time. There are chapters of the Tâo Teh *K*ing which

[1] Quoted in the Amplification of the Sixteen Precepts or Maxims of the second emperor of the present dynasty by his son. The words are from Dr. Milne's version of 'the Sacred Edict,' p. 137.

[2] In his Index to the Tripi*t*aka, Mr. Bunyio Nanjio (p. 359) assigns Liû Mî and his work to the Yüan dynasty. In a copy of the work in my possession they are assigned to that of Sung. The author, no doubt, lived under both dynasties,—from the Sung into the Yüan.

presuppose a peculiar management of the breath, but the treatise is singularly free from anything to justify what Mr. Balfour well calls 'the antics of the Kung-fû, or system of mystic and recondite calisthenics[1].' Lâo insists, however, on the Tâo as conducive to long life, and in *K*wang-ȝze we have references to it as a discipline of longevity, though even he mentions rather with disapproval 'those who kept blowing and breathing with open mouth, inhaling and exhaling the breath, expelling the old and taking in new; passing their time like the (dormant) bear, and stretching and twisting (their necks) like birds.' He says that 'all this simply shows their desire for longevity, and is what the scholars who manage the breath, and men who nourish the body and wish to live as long as Phăng-ȝû, are fond of doing[2].' My own opinion is that the methods of the Tâo were first cultivated for the sake of the longevity which they were thought to promote, and that Lâo, discountenancing such a use of them, endeavoured to give the doctrine a higher character; and this view is favoured by passages in *K*wang-ȝze. In the seventh paragraph, for instance, of his Book VI, speaking of parties who had obtained the Tâo, he begins with a prehistoric sovereign, who 'got it and by it adjusted heaven and earth.' Among his other instances is Phăng-ȝû, who got it in the time of Shun, and lived on to the time of the five leading princes of *K*âu,—a longevity of more than 1800 years, greater than that ascribed to Methuselah! In the paragraph that follows there appears a Nü Yü, who is addressed by another famous Tâoist in the words, 'You are old, Sir, while your complexion is like that of a child;—how is it so?' and the reply is, 'I became acquainted with the Tâo.'

I will adduce only one more passage of *K*wang. In his eleventh Book, and the fourth paragraph, he tells us of interviews between Hwang-Tî, in the nineteenth year of his reign, which would be B.C. 2679, and his instructor Kwang *Kh*ăng-ȝze. The Tâoist sage is not readily prevailed on

[1] See note on p. 187 of his *K*wang-ȝze.
[2] See Bk. XV, par. 1.

道德經 莊子

to unfold the treasures of his knowledge to the sovereign, but at last his reluctance is overcome, and he says to him, 'Come, and I will tell you about the Perfect Tâo. Its essence is surrounded with the deepest obscurity; its highest reach is in darkness and silence. There is nothing to be seen, nothing to be heard. When it holds the spirit in its arms in stillness, then the bodily form will of itself become correct. You must be still, you must be pure; not subjecting your body to toil, not agitating your vital force:—then you may live for long. When your eyes see nothing, your ears hear nothing, and your mind knows nothing, your spirit will keep your body, and the body will live long. Watch over what is within you; shut up the avenues that connect you with what is external;—much knowledge is pernicious. I will proceed with you to the summit of the Grand Brilliance, where we come to the bright and expanding (element); I will enter with you the gate of the dark and depressing element. There heaven and earth have their Controllers; there the Yin and Yang have their Repositories. Watch over and keep your body, and all things will of themselves give it vigour. I maintain the (original) unity (of these elements). In this way I have cultivated myself for 1200 years, and my bodily form knows no decay.' Add 1200 to 2679, and we obtain 3879 as the year B.C. of Kwang *Kh*ăng-ȝze's birth!

Startling results of the Tâo.

6. Lâo-ȝze describes some other and kindred results of cultivating the Tâo in terms which are sufficiently startling, and which it is difficult to accept. In his fiftieth chapter he says, 'He who is skilful in managing his life travels on land without having to shun rhinoceros or tiger, and enters a host without having to avoid buff coat or sharp weapon. The rhinoceros finds no place in him into which to thrust its horn, nor the tiger a place in which to fix its claws, nor the weapon a place to admit its point. And for what reason? Because there is in him no place of death.' To the same effect he says in his fifty-fifth chapter, 'He who has in himself abundantly the attributes (of the Tâo) is like an infant. Poisonous

insects will not sting him ; fierce beasts will not seize him ; birds of prey will not strike him.'

Such assertions startle us by their contrariety to our observation and experience, but so does most of the teaching of Tâoism. What can seem more absurd than the declaration that 'the Tâo does nothing, and so there is nothing that it does not do?' And yet this is one of the fundamental axioms of the system. The thirty-seventh chapter, which enunciates it, goes on to say, 'If princes and kings were able to maintain (the Tâo), all things would of themselves be transformed by them.' This principle, if we can call it so, is generalised in the fortieth, one of the shortest chapters, and partly in rhyme :—

'The movement of the Tâo
By contraries proceeds;
And weakness marks the course
Of Tâo's mighty deeds.

All things under heaven sprang from it as existing (and named); that existence sprang from it as non-existent (and not named).'

Ho-shang Kung, or whoever gave their names to the chapters of the Tâo Teh *K*ing, styles this fortieth chapter 'Dispensing with the use (of means).' If the wish to use means arise in the mind, the nature of the Tâo as 'the Nameless Simplicity' has been vitiated; and this nature is celebrated in lines like those just quoted :—

'Simplicity without a name
Is free from all external aim.
With no desire, at rest and still,
All things go right, as of their will.'

I do not cull any passages from *K*wang-ȝze to illustrate these points. In his eleventh Book his subject is Government by 'Let-a-be and the exercise of Forbearance.'

The paradisiacal state.

7. This Tâo ruled men at first, and then the world was in a paradisiacal state. Neither of our authorities tells us how long this condition lasted, but as Lâo observes in his eighteenth chapter, 'the Tâo ceased to be observed.' *K*wang-ȝze, however, gives us

more than one description of what he considered the paradisiacal state was. He calls it 'the age of Perfect Virtue.' In the thirteenth paragraph of his twelfth Book he says, 'In this age, they attached no value to wisdom, nor employed men of ability. Superiors were (but) as the higher branches of a tree; and the people were like the deer of the wild. They were upright and correct, without knowing that to be so was Righteousness; they loved one another, without knowing that to do so was Benevolence; they were honest and leal-hearted, without knowing that it was Loyalty; they fulfilled their engagements, without knowing that to do so was Good Faith; in their movements they employed the services of one another, without thinking that they were conferring or receiving any gift. Therefore their actions left no trace, and there was no record of their affairs.'

Again, in the fourth paragraph of his tenth Book, addressing an imaginary interlocutor, he says, 'Are you, Sir, unacquainted with the age of Perfect Virtue?' He then gives the names of twelve sovereigns who ruled in it, of the greater number of whom we have no other means of knowing anything, and goes on:—'In their times the people used knotted cords in carrying on their business. They thought their (simple) food pleasant, and their (plain) clothing beautiful. They were happy in their (simple) manners, and felt at rest in their (poor) dwellings. (The people of) neighbouring states might be able to descry one another; the voices of their cocks and dogs might be heard from one to the other; they might not die till they were old; and yet all their life they would have no communication together. In those times perfect good order prevailed.'

One other description of the primeval state is still more interesting. It is in the second paragraph of Bk. IX:—'The people had their regular and constant nature:—they wove and made themselves clothes; they tilled the ground and got food. This was their common faculty. They were all one in this, and did not form themselves into separate classes; so were they constituted and left to their natural tendencies. Therefore in the age of Perfect Virtue men walked along with slow and grave step, and with their looks steadily directed forwards. On the hills there were no footpaths nor excavated passages; on the lakes there were no boats nor dams. All creatures lived in companies, and their places of settlement were made near to one another. Birds and beasts multiplied to flocks and herds; the grass and trees grew luxuriant and long. The birds and beasts might be led about without feeling the constraint; the nest of the magpie might be climbed to, and peeped into. Yes, in the age of Perfect Virtue, men lived in common with birds and beasts, and were on terms of equality with all creatures, as forming one family;—how could they know among themselves the distinctions of superior men and small men? Equally without knowledge, they did not leave the path of their natural virtue; equally free from desires, they were in the state of pure simplicity. In that pure simplicity, their nature was what it ought to be.'

Such were the earliest Chinese of whom *K*wang-ʒze could venture to give any account. If ever their ancestors had been in a ruder or savage condition, it must have been at a much antecedent time. These had long passed out of such a state; they were tillers of the ground, and acquainted with the use of the loom. They lived in happy relations with one another, and in kindly harmony with the tribes of inferior creatures. But there is not the slightest allusion to any sentiment of piety as animating them individually, or to any ceremony of religion as observed by them in common. This surely is a remarkable feature in their condition. I call attention to it, but I do not dwell upon it.

The decay of the Tâo before the growth of knowledge.

8. But by the time of Lâo and *K*wang the cultivation of the Tâo had fallen into disuse. The simplicity of life which it demanded, with its freedom from all disturbing speculation and action, was no longer to be found in individuals or in government. It was the general decay of manners and of social order which unsettled the mind of Lâo, made him resign his position as a curator of the Royal Library, and determine to withdraw from China and hide himself

among the rude peoples beyond it. The cause of the deterioration of the Tâo and of all the evils of the nation was attributed to the ever-growing pursuit of knowledge, and of what we call the arts of culture. It had commenced very long before;—in the time of Hwang-Tî, *K*wang says in one place[1]; and in another he carries it still higher to Sui-zăn and Fu-hsî[2]. There had been indeed, all along the line of history, a groping for the rules of life, as indicated by the constitution of man's nature. The results were embodied in the ancient literature which was the life-long study of Confucius. He had gathered up that literature; he recognised the nature of man as the gift of Heaven or God. The monitions of God as given in the convictions of man's mind supplied him with a Tâo or Path of duty very different from the Tâo or Mysterious Way of Lâo. All this was gall and wormwood to the dreaming librarian or brooding recluse, and made him say, 'If we could renounce our sageness and discard our wisdom, it would be better for the people a hundredfold. If we could renounce our benevolence and discard our righteousness, the people would again become filial and kindly. If we could renounce our artful contrivances and discard our (scheming for) gain, there would be no thieves nor robbers[3].'

We can laugh at this. Tâoism was wrong in its opposition to the increase of knowledge. Man exists under a law of progress. In pursuing it there are demanded discretion and justice. Moral ends must rule over material ends, and advance in virtue be ranked higher than advance in science. So have good and evil, truth and error, to fight out the battle on the field of the world, and in all the range of time; but there is no standing still for the individual or for society. Even Confucius taught his countrymen to set too high a value on the examples of antiquity. The school of Lâo-ʒze fixing themselves in an unknown region beyond antiquity,—a prehistoric time between 'the Grand Beginning of all things' out of nothing, and the unknown commencement of societies of men,—has made no advance

[1] Bk. XI, par. 5. [2] Bk. XVI, par. 2.
[3] Tâo Teh *K*ing, ch. 19.

but rather retrograded, and is represented by the still more degenerate Tâoism of the present day.

There is a short parabolic story of *K*wang-ʒze, intended to represent the antagonism between Tâoism and knowledge, which has always struck me as curious. The last paragraph of his seventh Book is this:—'The Ruler (or god Tî) of the Southern Ocean was Shû (that is, Heedless); the Ruler of the Northern Ocean was Hû (that is, Hasty); and the Ruler of the Centre was Hwun-tun (that is, Chaos). Shû and Hû were continually meeting in the land of Hwun-tun, who treated them very well. They consulted together how they might repay his kindness, and said, "Men have all seven orifices for the purposes of seeing, hearing, eating, and breathing, while this (poor) Ruler alone has not one. Let us try and make them for him." Accordingly they dug one orifice in him every day; and at the end of seven days Chaos died.'

So it was that Chaos passed away before Light. So did the nameless Simplicity of the Tâo disappear before Knowledge. But it was better that the Chaos should give place to the Kosmos. 'Heedless' and 'Hasty' did a good deed.

The practical lessons of Lâo-ʒze.

9. I have thus set forth eight characteristics of the Tâoistic system, having respect mostly to what is peculiar and mystical in it. I will now conclude my exhibition of it by bringing together under one head the practical lessons of its author for men individually, and for the administration of government. The praise of whatever excellence these possess belongs to Lâo himself: *K*wang-ʒze devotes himself mainly to the illustration of the abstruse and difficult points.

Humility.

First, it does not surprise us that in his rules for individual man, Lâo should place Humility in the foremost place. A favourite illustration with him of the Tâo is water. In his eighth chapter he says:—'The highest excellence is like that of water. The excellence of water appears in its benefiting all things, and in its occupying, without striving to the contrary, the low ground which all men dislike. Hence (its way) is near to that of the Tâo.' To the same effect in the seventy-eighth chapter:—'There is nothing in the world more soft and weak than water, and yet for attacking things that are firm and strong there is nothing that can take precedence of it. Every one in the world knows that the soft overcomes the hard, and the weak the strong; but no one is able to carry it out in practice.'

Lâo's three Jewels.

In his sixty-seventh chapter Lâo associates with Humility two other virtues, and calls them his three Precious Things or Jewels. They are Gentleness, Economy, and Shrinking from taking precedence of others. 'With that Gentleness,' he says, 'I can be bold; with that Economy I can be liberal; Shrinking from taking precedence of others, I can become a vessel of the highest honour.'

Rendering good for evil.

And in his sixty-third chapter, he rises to a still loftier height of morality. He says, '(It is the way of the Tâo) to act without (thinking of) acting, to conduct affairs without (feeling) the trouble of them; to taste without discerning any flavour, to consider the small as great, and the few as many, and to recompense injury with kindness.'

Here is the grand Christian precept, 'Render to no man evil for evil. If thine enemy hunger, feed him; if he thirst, give him drink. Be not overcome with evil, but overcome evil with good.' We know that the maxim made some noise in its author's lifetime; that the disciples of Confucius consulted him about it, and that he was unable to receive it[1]. It comes in with less important matters by virtue of the Tâoistic 'rule of contraries.' I have been surprised to find what little reference to it I have met with in the course of my Chinese reading. I do not think that *K*wang-ʒze takes notice of it to illustrate it after his fashion. There, however, it is in the Tâo Teh *K*ing. The fruit of it has yet to be developed.

Second, Lâo laid down the same rule for the policy of the state as for the life of the individual. He says in his sixty-first chapter, 'What makes a state great is its being like a low-lying, down-flowing stream;—it becomes the

[1] Confucian Analects, XIV, 36.

centre to which tend all (the small states) under heaven.' He then uses an illustration which will produce a smile:—'Take the case of all females. The female always overcomes the male by her stillness. Stillness may be considered (a sort of) abasement.' Resuming his subject, he adds, 'Thus it is that a great state, by condescending to small states, gains them for itself; and that small states, by abasing themselves to a great state, win it over to them. In the one case the abasement tends to gaining adherents; in the other case, to procuring favour. The great state only wishes to unite men together and nourish them; a small state only wishes to be received by, and to serve, the other. Each gets what it desires, but the great state must learn to abase itself.'

'All very well in theory,' some one will exclaim, 'but, the world has not seen it yet reduced to practice.' So it is. The fact is deplorable. No one saw the misery arising from it, and exposed its unreasonableness more unsparingly, than *K*wang-ʒze. But it was all in vain in his time, as it has been in all the centuries that have since rolled their course. Philosophy, philanthropy, and religion have still to toil on, 'faint, yet pursuing,' believing that the time will yet come when humility and love shall secure the reign of peace and good will among the nations of men.

While enjoining humility, Lâo protested against war. In his thirty-first chapter he says, 'Arms, however beautiful, are instruments of evil omen; hateful, it may be said, to all creatures. They who have the Tâo do not like to employ them.' Perhaps in his sixty-ninth chapter he allows defensive war, but he adds, 'There is no calamity greater than that of lightly engaging in war. To do that is near losing the gentleness which is so precious. Thus it is that when weapons are (actually) crossed, he who deplores the (situation) conquers.'

There are some other points in the practical lessons of Tâoism to which I should like to call the attention of the reader, but I must refer him for them to the chapters of the Tâo Teh *K*ing, and the Books of *K*wang-ʒze. Its salient features have been set forth somewhat fully. Not-

道德經 莊子

withstanding the scorn poured so freely on Confucius by *K*wang-ʒze and other Tâoist writers, he proved in the course of time too strong for Lâo as the teacher of their people. The entrance of Buddhism, moreover, into the country in our first century, was very injurious to Tâoism, which still exists, but is only the shadow of its former self. It is tolerated by the government, but not patronised as it was when emperors and empresses seemed to think more of it than of Confucianism. It is by the spread of knowledge, which it has always opposed, that its overthrow and disappearance will be brought about ere long.

CHAPTER IV.

Accounts of Lâo-ʒze and *K*wang-ʒze given by Sze-mâ *Kh*ien.

It seems desirable, before passing from Lâo and *K*wang in this Introduction, to give a place in it to what is said about them by Sze-mâ *Kh*ien. I have said that not a single proper name occurs in the Tâo Teh *K*ing. There is hardly an historical allusion in it. Only one chapter, the twentieth, has somewhat of an autobiographical character. It tells us, however, of no incidents of his life. He appears alone in the world through his cultivation of the Tâo, melancholy and misunderstood, yet binding that Tâo more closely to his bosom.

The Books of *K*wang-ʒze are of a different nature, abounding in pictures of Tâoist life, in anecdotes and narratives, graphic, argumentative, often satirical. But they are not historical. Confucius and many of his disciples, Lâo and members of his school, heroes and sages of antiquity, and men of his own day, move across his pages; but the incidents in connexion with which they are introduced are probably fictitious, and devised by him 'to point his moral or adorn his tale.' His names of individuals and places are often like those of Bunyan in his Pilgrim's Progress or his Holy War, emblematic of their characters and the doctrines which he employs them to illustrate. He often comes on the stage himself, and there is an air of verisimilitude in his descriptions, possibly also a certain amount of fact about them; but we cannot appeal to them as historical testimony. It is only to Sze-mâ *Kh*ien that we can go for this; he always writes in the spirit of an historian; but what he has to tell us of the two men is not much.

And first, as to his account of Lâo-ʒze. When he wrote, about the beginning of the first century B.C., the Tâoist master was already known as Lâo-ʒze. *Kh*ien, however, tells us that his surname was Lî, and his name *R*, meaning 'Ear,' which gave place after his death to Tan, meaning 'Long-eared,' from which we may conclude that he was named from some peculiarity in the form of his ears. He was a native of the state of *Kh*û, which had then extended far beyond its original limits, and his birth-place was in the present province of Ho-nan or of An-hui. He was a curator in the Royal Library; and when Confucius visited the capital in the year B.C. 517, the two men met. *Kh*ien says that Confucius's visit to Lo-yang was that he might question Lâo on the subject of ceremonies. He might have other objects in mind as well; but however that was, the two met. Lî said to Khung, 'The men about whom you talk are dead, and their bones are mouldered to dust; only their words are left. Moreover, when the superior man gets his opportunity, he mounts aloft; but when the time is against him, he is carried along by the force of circumstances[1]. I have heard that a good merchant, though he have rich treasures safely stored, appears as if he were poor; and that the superior man, though his virtue be complete, is yet to outward seeming stupid. Put away your proud air and many desires, your insinuating habit and wild will. They are of no advantage to you;—this is all I have to tell you.' Confucius is made to say to his disciples after the interview: 'I know how

[1] Julien translates this by 'il erre à l'aventure.' In 1861 I rendered it, 'He moves as if his feet were entangled.' To one critic it suggests the idea of a bundle or wisp of brushwood rolled about over the ground by the wind.

birds can fly, fishes swim, and animals run. But the runner may be snared, the swimmer hooked, and the flyer shot by the arrow. But there is the dragon:—I cannot tell how he mounts on the wind through the clouds, and rises to heaven. To-day I have seen Lâo-ʒze, and can only compare him to the dragon.'

In this speech of Confucius we have, I believe, the origin of the name Lâo-ʒze, as applied to the master of Tâoism. Its meaning is 'The Old Philosopher,' or 'The Old Gentleman[1].' Confucius might well so style Lî *R*. At the time of this interview he was himself in his thirty-fifth year, and the other was in his eighty-eighth. *Kh*ien adds, 'Lâo-ʒze cultivated the Tâo and its attributes, the chief aim of his studies being how to keep himself concealed and remain unknown. He continued to reside at (the capital of) *K*âu, but after a long time, seeing the decay of the dynasty, he left it and went away to the barrier-gate, leading out of the kingdom on the north-west. Yin Hsî, the warden of the gate, said to him, "You are about to withdraw yourself out of sight. Let me insist on your (first) composing for me a book." On this, Lâo-ʒze wrote a book in two parts, setting forth his views on the Tâo and its attributes, in more than 5000 characters. He then went away, and it is not known where he died. He was a superior man, who liked to keep himself unknown.'

*Kh*ien finally traces Lâo's descendants down to the first century B.C., and concludes by saying, 'Those who attach themselves to the doctrine of Lâo-ʒze condemn that of the Literati, and the Literati on their part condemn Lâo-ʒze, verifying the saying, "Parties whose principles are different cannot take counsel together." Lî *R* taught that by doing nothing others are as a matter of course trans-

[1] The characters may mean 'the old boy,' and so understood have given rise to various fabulous legends; that his mother had carried him in her womb for seventy-two years (some say, for eighty-one), and that when born the child had the white hair of an old man. Julien has translated the fabulous legend of Ko Hung of our fourth century about him. By that time the legends of Buddhism about *S*âkyamuni had become current in China, and were copied and applied to Lâo-ʒze by his followers. Looking at the meaning of the two names, I am surprised no one has characterized Lâo-ʒze as the Chinese Seneca.

formed, and that rectification in the same way ensues from being pure and still.'

This morsel is all that we have of historical narrative about Lâo-ȝze. The account of the writing of the Tâo Teh *K*ing at the request of the warden of the barrier-gate has a doubtful and legendary appearance. Otherwise, the record is free from anything to raise suspicion about it. It says nothing about previous existences of Lâo, and nothing of his travelling to the west, and learning there the doctrines which are embodied in his work. He goes through the pass out of the domain of *K*âu, and died no one knowing where.

It is difficult, however, to reconcile this last statement with a narrative in the end of *K*wang-ȝze's third Book. There we see Lâo-ȝze dead, and a crowd of mourners wailing round the corpse, and giving extraordinary demonstrations of grief, which offend a disciple of a higher order, who has gone to the house to offer his condolences on the occasion. But for the peculiar nature of most of *K*wang's narratives, we should say, in opposition to *Kh*ien, that the place and time of Lâo's death were well known. Possibly, however, *K*wang-ȝze may have invented the whole story, to give him the opportunity of setting forth what, according to his ideal of it, the life of a Tâoist master should be, and how even Lâo-ȝze himself fell short of it.

Second, *Kh*ien's account of *K*wang-ȝze is still more brief. He was a native, he tells us, of the territory of Măng, which belonged to the kingdom of Liang or Wei, and held an office, he does not say what, in the city of *Kh*î-yüan. *K*wang was thus of the same part of China as Lâo-ȝze, and probably grew up familiar with all his speculations and lessons. He lived during the reigns of the kings Hui of Liang, Hsüan of *Kh*î, and Wei of *Kh*û. We cannot be wrong therefore in assigning his period to the latter half of the third, and earlier part of the fourth century B.C. He was thus a contemporary of Mencius. They visited at the same courts, and yet neither ever mentions the other. They were the two ablest debaters of their day, and fond of exposing what they deemed heresy. But it would only be a matter of useless speculation to try to account for their never having come into argumentative collision.

*Kh*ien says: '*K*wang had made himself well acquainted with all the literature of his time, but preferred the views of Lâo-ȝze, and ranked himself among his followers, so that of the more than ten myriads of characters contained in his published writings the greater part are occupied with metaphorical illustrations of Lâo's doctrines. He made "The Old Fisherman," "The Robber *K*ih," and "The Cutting open Satchels," to satirize and expose the disciples of Confucius, and clearly exhibit the sentiments of Lâo. Such names and characters as "Wei-lêi Hsü" and "Khang-sang Ȝze" are fictitious, and the pieces where they occur are not to be understood as narratives of real events[1].

'But *K*wang was an admirable writer and skilful composer, and by his instances and truthful descriptions hit and exposed the Mohists and Literati. The ablest scholars of his day could not escape his satire nor reply to it, while he allowed and enjoyed himself with his sparkling, dashing style; and thus it was that the greatest men, even kings and princes, could not use him for their purposes.

'King Wei of *Kh*û, having heard of the ability of *K*wang *K*âu, sent messengers with large gifts to bring him to his court, and promising also that he would make him his chief minister. *K*wang-ȝze, however, only laughed and said to them, "A thousand ounces of silver are a great gain to me, and to be a high noble and minister is a most honourable position. But have you not seen the victim-ox for the border sacrifice? It is carefully fed for several years, and robed with rich embroidery that it may be fit to enter the Grand Temple. When the time comes for it to do so, it would prefer to be a little pig, but it cannot get to be so. Go away quickly, and do not soil me with your presence.

[1] Khang-sang Ȝze is evidently the Kăng-sang *Kh*û of *K*wang's Book XXIII. Wei-lêi Hsü is supposed by Sze-mâ *K*ăng of the Thang dynasty, who called himself the Lesser Sze-mâ, to be the name of a Book; one, in that case, of the lost books of *K*wang. But as we find the 'Hill of Wei-lêi' mentioned in Bk. XXIII as the scene of Kăng-sang *Kh*û's Tâoistic labours and success, I suppose that *Kh*ien's reference is to that. The names are quoted by him from memory, or might be insisted on as instances of different readings.

I had rather amuse and enjoy myself in the midst of a filthy ditch than be subject to the rules and restrictions in the court of a sovereign. I have determined never to take office, but prefer the enjoyment of my own free will."'

*Kh*ien concludes his account of *K*wang-ȝze with the above story, condensed by him, probably, from two of *K*wang's own narratives, in par. 11 of Bk. XVII, and 13 of XXXII, to the injury of them both. Paragraph 14 of XXXII brings before us one of the last scenes of *K*wang-ȝze's life, and we may doubt whether it should be received as from his own pencil. It is interesting in itself, however, and I introduce it here: 'When *K*wang-ȝze was about to die, his disciples signified their wish to give him a grand burial. "I shall have heaven and earth," he said, "for my coffin and its shell; the sun and moon for my two round symbols of jade; the stars and constellations for my pearls and jewels;—will not the provisions for my interment be complete? What would you add to them?" The disciples replied, "We are afraid that the crows and kites will eat our master." *K*wang-ȝze rejoined, "Above, the crows and kites will eat me; below, the mole-crickets and ants will eat me; to take from those and give to these would only show your partiality."'

Such were among the last words of *K*wang-ȝze. His end was not so impressive as that of Confucius; but it was in keeping with the general magniloquence and strong assertion of independence that marked all his course.

CHAPTER V.

On the Tractate of Actions and their Retributions.

Peculiar style and nature of the Kan Ying Phien.

1. The contrast is great between the style of the Tâo Teh *K*ing and the Books of *K*wang-ȝze and that of the Kan Ying Phien, a translation of which is now submitted as a specimen of the Texts of Tâoism. The works of Lâo and *K*wang stand alone in the literature of the system. What

道德經 莊子

it was before Lâo cannot be ascertained, and in his chapters it comes before us not as a religion, but as a subject of philosophical speculation, together with some practical applications of it insisted on by Lâo himself. The brilliant pages of *K*wang-ȝze contain little more than his ingenious defence of his master's speculations, and an aggregate of illustrative narratives sparkling with the charms of his composition, but in themselves for the most part unbelievable, often grotesque and absurd. This treatise, on the other hand, is more of what we understand by a sermon or popular tract. It eschews all difficult discussion, and sets forth a variety of traits of character and actions which are good, and a still greater variety of others which are bad, exhorting to the cultivation and performance of the former, and warning against the latter. It describes at the outset the machinery to secure the record of men's doings, and the infliction of the certain retribution, and concludes with insisting on the wisdom of repentance and reformation. At the same time it does not carry its idea of retribution beyond death, but declares that if the reward or punishment is not completed in the present life, the remainder will be received by the posterity of the good-doer and of the offender.

A place is given to the treatise among the Texts of Tâoism in 'The Sacred Books of the East,' because of its popularity in China. 'The various editions of it,' as observed by Mr. Wylie, 'are innumerable; it has appeared from time to time in almost every conceivable size, shape, and style of execution. Many commentaries have been written upon it, and it is frequently published with a collection of several hundred anecdotes, along with pictorial illustrations, to illustrate every paragraph seriatim. It is deemed a great act of merit to aid by voluntary contribution towards the gratuitous distribution of this work[1].'

The origin of the treatise.

2. The author of the treatise is not known, but, as Mr. Wylie also observes, it appears to have been written during the Sung dynasty. The earliest mention of it which I have met with is in the continua-

[1] Notes on Chinese Literature, p. 179.

tion of Ma-twan Lin's encyclopedic work by Wang *Kh*î, first published in 1586, the fourteenth year of the fourteenth emperor of the Ming dynasty. In Wang's supplement to his predecessor's account of Tâoist works, the sixth notice is of 'a commentary on the Thâi Shang Kan Ying Phien by a Lî *Kh*ang-ling,' and immediately before it is a commentary on the short but well-known Yin Fû *K*ing by a Lû Tien, who lived 1042–1102. Immediately after it other works of the eleventh century are mentioned. To that same century therefore we may reasonably refer the origin of the Kan Ying Phien.

The meaning of the title.

As to the meaning of the title, the only difficulty is with the two commencing characters Thâi Shang. Julien left them untranslated, with the note, however, that they were 'l'abréviation de Thâi Shang Lâo *K*ün, expression honorifique par laquelle les Tâo-sze désignent Lâo-ʒze, le fondateur de leur secte[1].' This is the interpretation commonly given of the phrase, and it is hardly worth while to indicate any doubt of its correctness; but if the characters were taken, as I believe they were, from the beginning of the seventeenth chapter of the Tâo Teh *K*ing, I should prefer to understand them of the highest and oldest form of the Tâoistic teaching[2].

3. I quoted on page 13 the view of Hardwick, the Christian Advocate of Cambridge, that 'the indefinite expression

---

[1] See 'Le Livre des Récompense et des Peines en Chinois et en François' (London, 1835).

[2] The designation of Lâo-ʒze as Thâi Shang Lâo *K*ün originated probably in the Thang dynasty. It is on record that in 666 Kâo Ʒung, the third emperor, went to Lâo-ʒze's temple at Po *K*âu (the place of Lâo's birth, and still called by the same name, in the department of Făng-yang in An-hui), and conferred on him the title of Thâi Shang Yüan Yüan Hwang Tî, 'The Great God, the Mysterious Originator, the Most High.' 'Then,' says Mayers, Manual, p. 113, 'for the first time he was ranked among the gods as "Great Supreme, the Emperor (or Imperial God) of the Dark First Cause."' The whole entry is 至亳州尊老君爲太上元(or 玄)元皇帝. Later on, in 1014, we find *K*ăn Ʒung, the fourth Sung emperor, also visiting Po *K*âu, and in Lâo's temple, which has by this time become 'the Palace of Grand Purity,' enlarging his title to Thâi Shang Lâo *K*ün Hwun Yüan Shang Teh Hwang Tî, 'The Most High, the Ruler Lâo, the Great God of Grand Virtue at the Chaotic Origin.' But such titles are not easily translated.

Tâo was adopted to denominate an abstract Cause, or the initial principle of life and order, to which worshippers were able to assign the attributes of immateriality, eternity, immensity, invisibility.' His selection of the term worshippers in this passage was unfortunate. Neither Lâo nor *K*wang says anything about the worship of the Tâo, about priests or monks, about temples or rituals. How could they do so, seeing that Tâo was not to them the name of a personal Being, nor 'Heaven' a metaphorical term equivalent to the Confucian Tî, 'Ruler,' or Shang Tî, 'Supreme Ruler.' With this agnosticism as to God, and their belief that by a certain management and discipline of the breath life might be prolonged indefinitely, I do not see how anything of an organised religion was possible for the old Tâoists.

Was the old Tâoism a religion?

The Tâoist proclivities of the founder of the *Kh*in dynasty are well known. If his life had been prolonged, and the dynasty become consolidated, there might have arisen such a religion in connexion with Tâoism, for we have a record that he, as head of the Empire, had eight spirits[1] to which he offered sacrifices. *Kh*in, however, soon passed away; what remained in permanency from it was only the abolition of the feudal kingdom.

4. We cannot here attempt to relate in detail the rise and growth of the *K*ang family in which the headship of Tâoism has been hereditary since our first Christian century, with the exception of one not very long interruption. One of the earliest members of it, *K*ang Liang, must have been born not long after the death of *K*wang-ȝze, for he joined the party of Liû

The family of *K*ang.

[1] The eight spirits were:—1. The Lord of Heaven; 2. The Lord of Earth; 3. The Lord of War; 4. The Lord of the Yang operation; 5. The Lord of the Yin operation; 6. The Lord of the Moon; 7. The Lord of the Sun; and 8. The Lord of the Four Seasons. See Mayers's C. R. Manual, pp. 327, 328. His authority is the sixth of Sze-mâ *Kh*ien's monographs. *Kh*ien seems to say that the worship of these spirits could be traced to Thâi Kung, one of the principal ministers of kings Wăn and Wû at the rise of the *K*âu dynasty in the twelfth century B.C., and to whom in the list of Tâoist writings in the Imperial Library of Han, no fewer than 237 phien are ascribed.

Pang, the founder of the dynasty of Han, in B.C. 208, and by his wisdom and bravery contributed greatly to his success over the adherents of *Kh*in, and other contenders for the sovereignty of the empire. Abandoning then a political career, he spent the latter years of his life in a vain quest for the elixir of life.

Among Liang's descendants in our first century was a *K*ang Tâo-ling, who, eschewing a career in the service of the state, devoted himself to the pursuits of alchemy, and at last succeeded in compounding the grand elixir or pill, and at the age of 123 was released from the trammels of the mortal body, and entered on the enjoyment of immortality, leaving to his descendants his books, talismans and charms, his sword, mighty against spirits, and his seal. Tâo-ling stands out, in Tâoist accounts, as the first patriarch of the system, with the title of Thien Shih, 'Master or Preceptor of Heaven.' Hsüan Ȝung of the Thang dynasty in 748, confirmed the dignity and title in the family; and in 1016 the Sung emperor *K*ăn Ȝung invested its representative with large tracts of land near the Lung-hû mountain in *K*iang-hsî. The present patriarch—for I suppose the same man is still alive—made a journey from his residence not many years ago, and was interviewed by several foreigners in Shanghai. The succession is said to be perpetuated by the transmigration of the soul of *K*ang Tâo-ling into some infant or youthful member of the family; whose heirship is supernaturally revealed as soon as the miracle is effected[1].

Influence of Buddhism on Tâoism.

This superstitious notion shows the influence of Buddhism on Tâoism. It has been seen from the eighteenth of the Books of *K*wang-ȝze what affinities there were between Tâoism and the Indian system; and there can be no doubt that the introduction of the latter into China did more than anything else to affect the development of the Tâoistic system. As early as the time of Confucius there were recluses in the country, men who had withdrawn from the world, disgusted with its

[1] See Mayers's C. R. Manual, Part I, article 35.

vanities and in despair from its disorders. Lâo would appear to have himself contemplated this course. When their representatives of our early centuries saw the Buddhists among them with their images, monasteries, and nunneries, their ritual and discipline, they proceeded to organise themselves after a similar fashion. They built monasteries and nunneries, framed images, composed liturgies, and adopted a peculiar mode of tying up their hair. The 'Three Precious Ones' of Buddhism, emblematic to the initiated of Intelligence personified in Buddha, the Law, and the Community or Church, but to the mass of the worshippers merely three great idols, styled by them Buddha Past, Present, and To Come: these appeared in Tâoism as the 'Three Pure Ones,' also represented by three great images, each of which receives the title of 'His Celestial Eminence,' and is styled the 'Most High God (Shang Tî).' The first of them is a deification of Chaos, the second, of Lâo-ȝze, and the third of I know not whom or what; perhaps of the Tâo.

But those Three Pure Ones have been very much cast into the shade, as the objects of popular worship and veneration, by Yü Hwang Tî or Yü Hwang Shang Tî. This personage appears to have been a member of the *K*ang clan, held to be a magician and venerated from the time of the Thang dynasty, but deified in 1116 by the Sung emperor Hui ȝung at the instigation of a charlatan Lin Ling-sû, a renegade Buddhist monk. He is the god in the court of heaven to whom the spirits of the body and of the hearth in our treatise proceed at stated times to report for approval or condemnation the conduct of men.

Since the first publication of the Kan Ying Phien, the tenets of Buddhism have been still further adopted by the teachers of Tâoism, and shaped to suit the nature of their own system. I have observed that the idea of retribution in our treatise does not go beyond the present life; but the manifestoes of Tâoism of more recent times are much occupied with descriptions of the courts of purgatory and threatenings of the everlasting misery of hell to those whom their sufferings in those courts fail to wean from their wickedness. Those manifestoes are published by the mercy of Yü Hwang Shang Tî that men and women may be led to repent of their faults and make atonement for their crimes. They emanate from the temples of the tutelary deities[1] which are found throughout the empire, and especially in the walled cities, and are under the charge of Tâoist monks. A visitor to one of the larger of these temples may not only see the pictures of the purgatorial courts and other forms of the modern superstitions, but he will find also astrologers, diviners, geomancers, physiognomists, et id genus omne, plying their trades or waiting to be asked to do so, and he will wonder how it has been possible to affiliate such things with the teachings of Lâo-ȝze.

Other manifestoes of a milder form, and more like our tractate, are also continually being issued as from one or other of what are called the state gods, whose temples are all in the charge of the same monks. In the approximation which has thus been going on of Tâoism to Buddhism, the requirement of celibacy was long resisted by the professors of the former; but recent editions of the Penal Code[2] contain sundry regulations framed to enforce celibacy, to bind the monks and nuns of both systems to the observance of the Confucian maxims concerning filial piety, and the sacrificial worship of the dead; and also to restrict the multiplication of monasteries and nunneries. Neither Lâo nor *K*wang was a celibate or recommended celibacy. The present patriarch, as a married man, would seem to be able still to resist the law.

[1] Called *Kh*ăng Hwang Miâo, 'Wall and Moat Temples,' Palladia of the city.

[2] See Dr. Eitel's third edition of his 'Three Lectures on Buddhism,' pp. 36–45 (Hongkong: Lane, Crawford & Co., 1884). The edition of the Penal Code to which he refers is of 1879.

道德經

THE TÂO TEH *K*ING,

OR

THE TÂO

AND ITS CHARACTERISTICS.

道德經

THE TÂO TEH *K*ING.

PART I.

Ch. 1. 1. The Tâo that can be trodden is not the enduring and unchanging Tâo. The name that can be named is not the enduring and unchanging name.

2. (Conceived of as) having no name, it is the Originator of heaven and earth; (conceived of as) having a name, it is the Mother of all things.

3. Always without desire we must be found,
If its deep mystery we would sound;
But if desire always within us be,
Its outer fringe is all that we shall see.

4. Under these two aspects, it is really the same; but as development takes place, it receives the different names. Together we call them the Mystery. Where the Mystery is the deepest is the gate of all that is subtle and wonderful.

體道, 'Embodying the Tâo.' The author sets forth, as well as the difficulty of his subject would allow him, the nature of the Tâo in itself, and its manifestation. To understand the Tâo one must be partaker of its nature.

Par. 3 suggests the words of the apostle John, 'He that loveth not knoweth not God; for God is love.' Both the Tâo, Lâo-ȝze's ideal in the absolute, and its Teh, or operation, are comprehended in this chapter, the latter being the Tâo with the name, the Mother of all things. See pages 12, 13 in the Introduction on the translation of the term Tâo.

2. 1. All in the world know the beauty of the beautiful, and in doing this they have (the idea of)

what ugliness is; they all know the skill of the skilful, and in doing this they have (the idea of) what the want of skill is.

2. So it is that existence and non-existence give birth the one to (the idea of) the other; that difficulty and ease produce the one (the idea of) the other; that length and shortness fashion out the one the figure of the other; that (the ideas of) height and lowness arise from the contrast of the one with the other; that the musical notes and tones become harmonious through the relation of one with another; and that being before and behind give the idea of one following another.

3. Therefore the sage manages affairs without doing anything, and conveys his instructions without the use of speech.

4. All things spring up, and there is not one which declines to show itself; they grow, and there is no claim made for their ownership; they go through their processes, and there is no expectation (of a reward for the results). The work is accomplished, and there is no resting in it (as an achievement).

The work is done, but how no one can see;
'Tis this that makes the power not cease to be.

養身, 'The Nourishment of the Person.' But many of Ho-shang Kung's titles are more appropriate than this.

The chapter starts with instances of the antinomies, which suggest to the mind each of them the existence of its corresponding opposite; and the author finds in them an analogy to the 'contraries' which characterize the operation of the Tâo, as stated in chapter 40. He then proceeds to describe the action of the sage in par. 3 as in accordance with this law of contraries; and, in par. 4, that of heaven and earth, or what we may call nature, in the processes of the vegetable world.

Par. 2 should be rhymed, but I could not succeed to my satisfaction in the endeavour to rhyme it. Every one who can read Chinese will see that the first four members rhyme. The last two rhyme also, the concluding 隨 being pronounced so;—see the Khang-hsî dictionary in voc.

3. 1. Not to value and employ men of superior ability is the way to keep the people from rivalry among themselves; not to prize articles which are difficult to procure is the way to keep them from becoming thieves; not to show them what is likely to excite their desires is the way to keep their minds from disorder.

2. Therefore the sage, in the exercise of his government, empties their minds, fills their bellies, weakens their wills, and strengthens their bones.

3. He constantly (tries to) keep them without knowledge and without desire, and where there are those who have knowledge, to keep them from presuming to act (on it). When there is this abstinence from action, good order is universal.

安民, 'Keeping the People at Rest.' The object of the chapter is to show that government according to the Tâo is unfavourable to the spread of knowledge among the people, and would keep them rather in the state of primitive simplicity and ignorance, thereby securing their restfulness and universal good order. Such is the uniform teaching of Lâo-ȝze and his great follower *K*wang-ȝze, and of all Tâoist writers.

4. 1. The Tâo is (like) the emptiness of a vessel; and in our employment of it we must be on our guard against all fulness. How deep and unfa-

thomable it is, as if it were the Honoured Ancestor of all things!

2. We should blunt our sharp points, and unravel the complications of things; we should attemper our brightness, and bring ourselves into agreement with the obscurity of others. How pure and still the Tâo is, as if it would ever so continue!

3. I do not know whose son it is. It might appear to have been before God.

無源, 'The Fountainless.' There is nothing before the Tâo; it might seem to have been before God. And yet there is no demonstration by it of its presence and operation. It is like the emptiness of a vessel. The second character = 沖 = 盅;—see Khang-hsî on the latter. The practical lesson is, that in following the Tâo we must try to be like it.

5. 1. Heaven and earth do not act from (the impulse of) any wish to be benevolent; they deal with all things as the dogs of grass are dealt with. The sages do not act from (any wish to be) benevolent; they deal with the people as the dogs of grass are dealt with.

2. May not the space between heaven and earth be compared to a bellows?

'Tis emptied, yet it loses not its power;
'Tis moved again, and sends forth air the more.
Much speech to swift exhaustion lead we see;
Your inner being guard, and keep it free.

虛用, 'The Use of Emptiness.' Quiet and unceasing is the operation of the Tâo, and effective is the rule of the sage in accordance with it.

The grass-dogs in par. 1 were made of straw tied up in the shape of dogs, and used in praying for rain; and afterwards, when the sacrifice was over, were thrown aside and left uncared for. Heaven and earth and the sages dealt so with all things and with the people; but the illustration does not seem a happy one. Both *K*wang-ȝze and Hwâi-nan mention the grass-dogs. See especially the former, XIV, 25 a, b. In that Book there is fully developed the meaning of this chapter. The illustration in par. 2 is better. The Chinese bellows is different to look at from ours, but the principle is the same in the construction of both. The par. concludes in a way that lends some countenance to the later Tâoism's dealing with the breath.

6. The valley spirit dies not, aye the same;
The female mystery thus do we name.
Its gate, from which at first they issued forth,
Is called the root from which grew heaven and
earth.
Long and unbroken does its power remain,
Used gently, and without the touch of pain.

成象, 'The Completion of Material Forms.' This title rightly expresses the import of this enigmatical chapter; but there is a foundation laid in it for the development of the later Tâoism, which occupies itself with the prolongation of life by the management of the breath (氣) or vital force.

'The valley' is used metaphorically as a symbol of 'emptiness' or 'vacancy;' and 'the spirit of the valley' is the something invisible, yet almost personal, belonging to the Tâo, which constitutes the Teh (德) in the name of our *K*ing. 'The spirit of the valley' has come to be a name for the activity of the Tâo in all the realm of its operation. 'The female mystery' is the Tâo with a name of chapter 1, which is 'the Mother of all things.' All living beings have a father and mother. The processes of generation and production can hardly be imaged by us but by a recognition of this fact; and so Lâo-ȝze thought of the existing realm of nature—of life—as coming through an

E 2

evolution (not a creation) from the primal air or breath, dividing into two, and thence appearing in the forms of things, material and immaterial. The chapter is found in Lieh-ȝze (I, 1 b) quoted by him from a book of Hwang-Tî; and here Lâo-ȝze has appropriated it, and made it his own. See the Introduction, p. 2.

7. 1. Heaven is long-enduring and earth continues long. The reason why heaven and earth are able to endure and continue thus long is because they do not live of, or for, themselves. This is how they are able to continue and endure.

2. Therefore the sage puts his own person last, and yet it is found in the foremost place; he treats his person as if it were foreign to him, and yet that person is preserved. Is it not because he has no personal and private ends, that therefore such ends are realised?

韜光, 'Sheathing the Light.' The chapter teaches that one's best good is realised by not thinking of it, or seeking for it. Heaven and earth afford a pattern to the sage, and the sage affords a pattern to all men.

8. 1. The highest excellence is like (that of) water. The excellence of water appears in its benefiting all things, and in its occupying, without striving (to the contrary), the low place which all men dislike. Hence (its way) is near to (that of) the Tâo.

2. The excellence of a residence is in (the suitability of) the place; that of the mind is in abysmal stillness; that of associations is in their being with the virtuous; that of government is in its securing good order; that of (the conduct of) affairs is in its ability; and that of (the initiation of) any movement is in its timeliness.

3. And when (one with the highest excellence) does not wrangle (about his low position), no one finds fault with him.

易性, 'The Placid and Contented Nature.' Water, as an illustration of the way of the Tâo, is repeatedly employed by Lâo-ȝze.

The various forms of what is excellent in par. 2 are brought forward to set forth the more, by contrast, the excellence of the humility indicated in the acceptance of the lower place without striving to the contrary.

9. 1. It is better to leave a vessel unfilled, than to attempt to carry it when it is full. If you keep feeling a point that has been sharpened, the point cannot long preserve its sharpness.

2. When gold and jade fill the hall, their possessor cannot keep them safe. When wealth and honours lead to arrogancy, this brings its evil on itself. When the work is done, and one's name is becoming distinguished, to withdraw into obscurity is the way of Heaven.

運夷; but I cannot give a satisfactory rendering of this title. The teaching of the chapter is, that fulness and complacency in success are contrary to the Tâo.

The first clauses of the two sentences in par. 1, 持而盈之, 揣而銳之=盈而持之, 銳而揣之, are instances of the 'inverted' style not uncommon in the oldest composition. 'The way of Heaven' = 'the Heavenly Tâo' exemplified by man.

10. 1. When the intelligent and animal souls are held together in one embrace, they can be kept from separating. When one gives undivided attention to the (vital) breath, and brings it to the utmost degree of pliancy, he can become as a (tender)

babe. When he has cleansed away the most mysterious sights (of his imagination), he can become without a flaw.

2. In loving the people and ruling the state, cannot he proceed without any (purpose of) action? In the opening and shutting of his gates of heaven, cannot he do so as a female bird? While his intelligence reaches in every direction, cannot he (appear to) be without knowledge?

3. (The Tâo) produces (all things) and nourishes them; it produces them and does not claim them as its own; it does all, and yet does not boast of it; it presides over all, and yet does not control them. This is what is called 'The mysterious Quality' (of the Tâo).

能爲, 'Possibilities.' This chapter is one of the most difficult to understand and translate in the whole work. Even *K*û Hsî was not able to explain the first member satisfactorily. The text of that member seems well supported; but I am persuaded the first clause of it is somehow corrupt.

The whole seems to tell what can be accomplished by one who is possessed of the Tâo. In par. 3 he appears free from all self-consciousness in what he does, and of all self-satisfaction in the results of his doing. The other two paragraphs seem to speak of what he can do under the guidance of the Tâo for himself and for others. He can by his management of his vital breath bring his body to the state of Tâoistic perfection, and keep his intelligent and animal souls from being separated, and he can rule men without purpose and effort. 'The gates of heaven' in par. 2 is a Tâoistic phrase for the nostrils as the organ of the breath;—see the commentary of Ho-shang Kung.

11. The thirty spokes unite in the one nave; but it is on the empty space (for the axle), that the use of the wheel depends. Clay is fashioned into vessels; but it is on their empty hollowness, that their use depends. The door and windows are cut out (from the walls) to form an apartment; but it is on the empty space (within), that its use depends. Therefore, what has a (positive) existence serves for profitable adaptation, and what has not that for (actual) usefulness.

無用, 'The Use of what has no Substantive Existence.' The three illustrations serve to set forth the freedom of the Tâo from all pre-occupation and purpose, and the use of what seems useless.

12. 1. Colour's five hues from th' eyes their sight
will take;
Music's five notes the ears as deaf can make;
The flavours five deprive the mouth of taste;
The chariot course, and the wild hunting waste
Make mad the mind; and objects rare and strange,
Sought for, men's conduct will to evil change.

2. Therefore the sage seeks to satisfy (the craving of) the belly, and not the (insatiable longing of the) eyes. He puts from him the latter, and prefers to seek the former.

檢欲, 'The Repression of the Desires.' Government in accordance with the Tâo seeks to withdraw men from the attractions of what is external and pleasant to the senses and imagination, and to maintain the primitive simplicity of men's ways and manners. Compare chap. 2. The five colours are Black, Red, Green or Blue, White, and Yellow; the five notes are those of the imperfect Chinese musical scale, our G, A, B, D, E; the five tastes are Salt, Bitter, Sour, Acrid, and Sweet.

I am not sure that Wang Pî has caught exactly the author's idea in the contrast between satisfying the belly and satisfying the eyes; but what he says is ingenious: 'In satisfying the belly one nourishes himself; in gratifying the eyes he makes a slave of himself.'

13. 1. Favour and disgrace would seem equally to be feared; honour and great calamity, to be regarded as personal conditions (of the same kind).

2. What is meant by speaking thus of favour and disgrace? Disgrace is being in a low position (after the enjoyment of favour). The getting that (favour) leads to the apprehension (of losing it), and the losing it leads to the fear of (still greater calamity):—this is what is meant by saying that favour and disgrace would seem equally to be feared.

And what is meant by saying that honour and great calamity are to be (similarly) regarded as personal conditions? What makes me liable to great calamity is my having the body (which I call myself); if I had not the body, what great calamity could come to me?

3. Therefore he who would administer the kingdom, honouring it as he honours his own person, may be employed to govern it, and he who would administer it with the love which he bears to his own person may be entrusted with it.

厭恥, 'Loathing Shame.' The chapter is difficult to construe, and some disciples of *K*û Hsî had to ask him to explain it as in the case of ch. 10. His remarks on it are not to my mind satisfactory. Its object seems to be to show that the cultivation of the person according to the Tâo, is the best qualification for the highest offices, even for the government of the world. Par. 3 is found in *K*wang-ȝze (XI, 18 b) in a connexion which suggests this view of the chapter. It may be observed, however, that in him the position of the verbal characters in the two clauses of the paragraph is the reverse of that in the text of Ho-shang Kung, so that we can hardly accept the distinction of meaning of the two characters given in his commentary, but must take them as synonyms. Professor Gabelentz gives the following version of *K*wang-ȝze: 'Darum, gebraucht er seine Person achtsam in der Verwaltung des Reiches, so mag man ihm die Reichsgewalt anvertrauen; . . . liebend (schonend) . . . übertragen.'

14. 1. We look at it, and we do not see it, and we name it 'the Equable.' We listen to it, and we do not hear it, and we name it 'the Inaudible.' We try to grasp it, and do not get hold of it, and we name it 'the Subtle.' With these three qualities, it cannot be made the subject of description; and hence we blend them together and obtain The One.

2. Its upper part is not bright, and its lower part is not obscure. Ceaseless in its action, it yet cannot be named, and then it again returns and becomes nothing. This is called the Form of the Formless, and the Semblance of the Invisible; this is called the Fleeting and Indeterminable.

3. We meet it and do not see its Front; we follow it, and do not see its Back. When we can lay hold of the Tâo of old to direct the things of the present day, and are able to know it as it was of old in the beginning, this is called (unwinding) the clue of Tâo.

贊玄, 'The Manifestation of the Mystery.' The subject of par. 1 is the Tâo, but the Tâo in its operation, and not the primal conception of it, as entirely distinct from things, which rises before the mind in the second paragraph. The Chinese characters which I have translated 'the Equable,' 'the Inaudible,' and 'the Subtle,' are now pronounced Î, Hî, and Wei, and in 1823 Rémusat fancied that they were intended to give the Hebrew tetragrammaton יהוה which he thought had come to Lâo-ȝze somehow from the West, or been found by him there. It was a mere fancy or dream; and still more so is the recent attempt to revive the notion by Victor von Strauss in 1870, and Dr. Edkins in 1884. The idea of the latter is specially strange, maintaining, as he does, that we should read the characters according to their old sounds. Lâo-ȝze has not in the chapter a personal Being before his mind, but the procedure of his mysterious Tâo, the course according to which the visible phenomena take place, incognisable by human sense and capable of only approximate description by terms appropriate to what is within the domain of sense. See the Introduction, pp. 14, 15.

15. 1. The skilful masters (of the Tâo) in old times, with a subtle and exquisite penetration, comprehended its mysteries, and were deep (also) so as to elude men's knowledge. As they were thus beyond men's knowledge, I will make an effort to describe of what sort they appeared to be.

2. Shrinking looked they like those who wade through a stream in winter; irresolute like those who are afraid of all around them; grave like a guest (in awe of his host); evanescent like ice that is melting away; unpretentious like wood that has not been fashioned into anything; vacant like a valley, and dull like muddy water.

3. Who can (make) the muddy water (clear)? Let it be still, and it will gradually become clear. Who can secure the condition of rest? Let movement go on, and the condition of rest will gradually arise.

4. They who preserve this method of the Tâo do not wish to be full (of themselves). It is through their not being full of themselves that they can

afford to seem worn and not appear new and complete.

顯德, 'The Exhibition of the Quality,' that is, of the Tâo, which has been set forth in the preceding chapter. Its practical outcome is here described in the masters of it of old, who in their own weakness were yet strong in it, and in their humility were mighty to be co-workers with it for the good of the world.

The variety of the readings in par. 4 is considerable, but not so as to affect the meaning. This par. is found in Hwâi-nan (XII, 23 a) with an unimportant variation. From the illustration to which it is subjoined he understood the fulness, evidently as in ch. 9, as being that of a vessel filled to overflowing. Both here and there such fulness is used metaphorically of a man overfull of himself; and then Lâo-ȝze slides into another metaphor, that of a worn-out garment. The text of par. 3 has been variously tampered with. I omit the 久 of the current copies, after the example of the editors of the great recension of the Yung-lo period (A.D. 1403–1424) of the Ming dynasty.

16. 1. The (state of) vacancy should be brought to the utmost degree, and that of stillness guarded with unwearying vigour. All things alike go through their processes of activity, and (then) we see them return (to their original state). When things (in the vegetable world) have displayed their luxuriant growth, we see each of them return to its root. This returning to their root is what we call the state of stillness; and that stillness may be called a reporting that they have fulfilled their appointed end.

2. The report of that fulfilment is the regular, unchanging rule. To know that unchanging rule is to be intelligent; not to know it leads to wild movements and evil issues. The knowledge of that unchanging rule produces a (grand) capacity and forbearance, and

that capacity and forbearance lead to a community (of feeling with all things). From this community of feeling comes a kingliness of character; and he who is king-like goes on to be heaven-like. In that likeness to heaven he possesses the Tâo. Possessed of the Tâo, he endures long; and to the end of his bodily life, is exempt from all danger of decay.

歸根, 'Returning to the Root.' The chapter exhibits the operation of the Tâo in nature, in man, and in government; an operation silent, but all-powerful; unaccompanied with any demonstration of its presence, but great in its results.

An officer receives a charge or commission from his superior (受命); when he reports the execution of it he is said 復命. So all animate things, including men, receive their charge from the Tâo as to their life, and when they have fulfilled it they are represented as reporting that fulfilment; and the fulfilment and report are described as their unchanging rule, so that they are the Tâo's impassive instruments, having no will or purpose of their own,—according to Lâo-ȝze's formula of 'doing nothing and yet doing all things (無爲而無不爲).'

The getting to possess the Tâo, or to be an embodiment of it, follows the becoming Heaven or Heaven-like; and this is in accordance with the saying in the fourth chapter that 'the Tâo might seem to have been before God.' But, in *K*wang-ȝze especially, we often find the full possessor and displayer of the Tâo spoken of as 'Heaven.' The last sentence, that he who has come to the full possession of the Tâo is exempt from all danger of decay, is generally illustrated by a reference to the utterances in ch. 50; as if Lâo-ȝze did indeed see in the Tâo a preservative against death.

17. 1. In the highest antiquity, (the people) did not know that there were (their rulers). In the next age they loved them and praised them. In the

next they feared them; in the next they despised them. Thus it was that when faith (in the Tâo) was deficient (in the rulers) a want of faith in them ensued (in the people).

2. How irresolute did those (earliest rulers) appear, showing (by their reticence) the importance which they set upon their words! Their work was done and their undertakings were successful, while the people all said, 'We are as we are, of ourselves!'

淳風, 'The Unadulterated Influence.' The influence is that of the Tâo, as seen in the earliest and paradisiacal times. The two chapters that follow are closely connected with this, showing how the silent, passionless influence of the Tâo was gradually and injuriously superseded by 'the wisdom of the world,' in the conduct of government. In the first sentence there is a small various reading of 不 for 下, but it does not affect the meaning of the passage. The first clause of par. 2 gives some difficulty; 其貴言, 'they made their words valuable or precious,' i.e. 'they seldom spake;' cp. 1 Sam. iii. 1.

18. 1. When the Great Tâo (Way or Method) ceased to be observed, benevolence and righteousness came into vogue. (Then) appeared wisdom and shrewdness, and there ensued great hypocrisy.

2. When harmony no longer prevailed throughout the six kinships, filial sons found their manifestation; when the states and clans fell into disorder, loyal ministers appeared.

俗薄, 'The Decay of Manners.' A sequel to the preceding chapter, and showing also how the general decay of manners afforded opportunity for the display of certain virtues by individuals. Observe 'the Great Tâo,' occurring here for the first time as the designation of 'the Tâo.'

19. 1. If we could renounce our sageness and discard our wisdom, it would be better for the people a hundredfold. If we could renounce our benevolence and discard our righteousness, the people would again become filial and kindly. If we could renounce our artful contrivances and discard our (scheming for) gain, there would be no thieves nor robbers.

2. Those three methods (of government)
Thought olden ways in elegance did fail
And made these names their want of worth to veil;
But simple views, and courses plain and true
Would selfish ends and many lusts eschew.

還淳, 'Returning to the Unadulterated Influence.' The chapter desires a return to the simplicity of the Tâo, and shows how superior the result would be to that of the more developed systems of morals and government which had superseded it. It is closely connected with the two chapters that precede. Lâo-ȝze's call for the renunciation of the methods of the sages and rulers in lieu of his fancied paradisiacal state is repeated ad nauseam by *K*wang-ȝze.

20. 1. When we renounce learning we have no troubles.

The (ready) 'yes,' and (flattering) 'yea;'—
Small is the difference they display.
But mark their issues, good and ill;—
What space the gulf between shall fill?

What all men fear is indeed to be feared; but how wide and without end is the range of questions (asking to be discussed)!

2. The multitude of men look satisfied and pleased; as if enjoying a full banquet, as if mounted on a tower in spring. I alone seem listless and still, my desires having as yet given no indication of their

presence. I am like an infant which has not yet smiled. I look dejected and forlorn, as if I had no home to go to. The multitude of men all have enough and to spare. I alone seem to have lost everything. My mind is that of a stupid man; I am in a state of chaos.

Ordinary men look bright and intelligent, while I alone seem to be benighted. They look full of discrimination, while I alone am dull and confused. I seem to be carried about as on the sea, drifting as if I had nowhere to rest. All men have their spheres of action, while I alone seem dull and incapable, like a rude borderer. (Thus) I alone am different from other men, but I value the nursing-mother (the Tâo).

異俗, 'Being Different from Ordinary Men.' The chapter sets forth the difference to external appearance which the pursuit and observance of the Tâo produces between its votaries and others; and Lâo-ȝze speaks in it as himself an example of the former. In the last three chapters he has been advocating the cause of the Tâo against the learning and philosophy of the other school of thinkers in the country. Here he appears as having renounced learning, and found an end to the troubles and anxieties of his own mind; but at the expense of being misconceived and misrepresented by others. Hence the chapter has an autobiographical character.

Having stated the fact following the renunciation of learning, he proceeds to dwell upon the troubles of learning in the rest of par. 1. Until the votary of learning knows everything, he has no rest. But the instances which he adduces of this are not striking nor easily understood. I cannot throw any light on the four lines about the 'yes' and the 'yea.'

Confucius (Ana. XVI, viii) specifies three things of which the superior man stands in awe; and these and others of a similar nature may have been the things which Lâo-ȝze had in his mind. The nursing-mother at the end is, no doubt, the Tâo in operation, 'with a name,' as in ch. 1; 'the mysterious virtue' of chapters 51 and 52.

21. The grandest forms of active force
From Tâo come, their only source.
Who can of Tâo the nature tell?
Our sight it flies, our touch as well.
Eluding sight, eluding touch,
The forms of things all in it crouch;
Eluding touch, eluding sight,
There are their semblances, all right.
Profound it is, dark and obscure;
Things' essences all there endure.
Those essences the truth enfold
Of what, when seen, shall then be told.
Now it is so; 'twas so of old.
Its name—what passes not away;
So, in their beautiful array,
Things form and never know decay.

How know I that it is so with all the beauties of existing things? By this (nature of the Tâo).

虛心, 'The Empty Heart.' But I fail to see the applicability of the title. The subject of the chapter is the Tâo in its operation. This is the significance of the 德 in the first clause or line, and to render it by 'virtue,' as Julien and Chalmers do, only serves to hide the meaning. Julien, however, says that 'the virtue is that of the Tâo; and he is right in taking 從, the last character of the second line, as having the sense of 'from,' 'the source from,' and not, as Chalmers does, in the sense of 'following.'

Lâo-ȝze's mind is occupied with a very difficult subject—to describe the production of material forms by the Tâo; how or from what, he does not say. What I have rendered 'semblances,' Julien 'les images,' and Chalmers 'forms.'

seems, as the latter says, in some way to correspond to the 'Eternal Ideas' of Plato in the Divine Mind. But Lâo-ȝze had no idea of 'personality' in the Tâo.

22. 1. The partial becomes complete; the crooked, straight; the empty, full; the worn out, new. He whose (desires) are few gets them; he whose (desires) are many goes astray.

2. Therefore the sage holds in his embrace the one thing (of humility), and manifests it to all the world. He is free from self-display, and therefore he shines; from self-assertion, and therefore he is distinguished; from self-boasting, and therefore his merit is acknowledged; from self-complacency, and therefore he acquires superiority. It is because he is thus free from striving that therefore no one in the world is able to strive with him.

3. That saying of the ancients that 'the partial becomes complete' was not vainly spoken:—all real completion is comprehended under it.

益謙, 'The Increase granted to Humility.' This title rightly expresses the subject-matter of the chapter. I cannot translate the first clause otherwise than I have done. It was an old saying, which Lâo-ȝze found and adopted. Whether it was intended to embrace all the cases which are mentioned may be questioned, but he employs it so as to make it do so.

'The emptiness' which becomes full is literally the hollowness of a cavity in the ground which is sure to be filled by overflowing water;—see Mencius, IV, ii, 18. 'The worn out' is explained by the withered foliage of a tree, which comes out new and fresh in the next spring. I have taken the first sentence of par. 2 as Wû *Kh*ăng does;—see his commentary in loc.

23. 1. Abstaining from speech marks him who is obeying the spontaneity of his nature. A violent

wind does not last for a whole morning; a sudden rain does not last for the whole day. To whom is it that these (two) things are owing? To Heaven and Earth. If Heaven and Earth cannot make such (spasmodic) actings last long, how much less can man!

2. Therefore when one is making the Tâo his business, those who are also pursuing it, agree with him in it, and those who are making the manifestation of its course their object agree with him in that; while even those who are failing in both these things agree with him where they fail.

3. Hence, those with whom he agrees as to the Tâo have the happiness of attaining to it; those with whom he agrees as to its manifestation have the happiness of attaining to it; and those with whom he agrees in their failure have also the happiness of attaining (to the Tâo). (But) when there is not faith sufficient (on his part), a want of faith (in him) ensues (on the part of the others).

虛無, 'Absolute Vacancy.' This, I think, is the meaning of the title, 'Emptiness and Nothingness,' an entire conformity to the Tâo in him who professes to be directed by it. Such an one will be omnipotent in his influence in all others. The Tâo in him will restrain all (spasmodic) loquacity. Those who are described in par. 2 as 'failing' are not to be thought of as bad men, men given up, as Julien has it, au crime. They are simply ordinary men, who have failed in their study of the Tâo and practice of it, but are won to truth and virtue by the man whom the author has in mind. As we might expect, however, the mention of such men has much embarrassed the commentators.

Compare the concluding sentence with the one at the end of par. 1 in ch. 17.

24. He who stands on his tiptoes does not stand firm; he who stretches his legs does not walk (easily). (So), he who displays himself does not shine; he who asserts his own views is not distinguished; he who vaunts himself does not find his merit acknowledged; he who is self-conceited has no superiority allowed to him. Such conditions, viewed from the standpoint of the Tâo, are like remnants of food, or a tumour on the body, which all dislike. Hence those who pursue (the course) of the Tâo do not adopt and allow them.

苦恩, 'Painful Graciousness.' The chapter should be so designated. This concludes the subject of the two previous chapters,—pursuing the course, the course of the unemotional Tâo without vain effort or display.

The remnants of food were not used as sacrificial offerings;—see the Lî *K*î (vol. xxvii, p. 82). In what I have rendered by 'a tumour attached to the body,' the 行 is probably, by a mistake, for 形;—see a quotation by Wû *Kh*ăng from Sze-mâ *Kh*ien. 'Which all dislike' is, literally, 'Things are likely to dislike them,' the 'things' being 'spirits and men,' as Wû explains the term.

25. 1. There was something undefined and complete, coming into existence before Heaven and Earth. How still it was and formless, standing alone, and undergoing no change, reaching everywhere and in no danger (of being exhausted)! It may be regarded as the Mother of all things.

2. I do not know its name, and I give it the designation of the Tâo (the Way or Course). Making an effort (further) to give it a name I call it The Great.

3. Great, it passes on (in constant flow). Passing

on, it becomes remote. Having become remote, it returns. Therefore the Tâo is great; Heaven is great; Earth is great; and the (sage) king is also great. In the universe there are four that are great, and the (sage) king is one of them.

4. Man takes his law from the Earth; the Earth takes its law from Heaven; Heaven takes its law from the Tâo. The law of the Tâo is its being what it is.

象玄, 'Representations of the Mystery.' In this chapter Lâo approaches very near to give an answer to the question as to what the Tâo is, and yet leaves the reader disappointed. He commences by calling it 'a thing (物);' but that term does not necessitate our regarding it as 'material.' We have seen in the preceding chapter that it is used to signify 'spirits and men.' Nor does his going on to speak of it as 'chaotic (混成)' necessarily lead us to conceive it as made up of the 'material elements of things;' we have the same term applied in ch. 14 to the three immaterial constituents there said to be blended in the idea of it.

'He does not know its name,' and he designates it by the term denoting a course or way (Tâo, 道), and indicating the phenomenal attribute, the method in which all phenomena come before our observation, in their development or evolution. And to distinguish it from all other methods of evolution, he would call it 'the Great Method,' and so he employs that combination as its name in ch. 18 and elsewhere; but it cannot be said that this name has fully maintained itself in the writings of his followers. But understood thus, he here says, as in ch. 1, that it is 'the Mother of all things.' And yet, when he says that 'it was before Heaven and Earth were produced,' he comes very near his affirmations in chapters 1 and 4, that 'the nameless Tâo was the beginning (or originating cause) of Heaven and Earth,' and 'might seem to have been before

God.' Was he groping after God if haply he might find Him? I think he was, and he gets so far as to conceive of Him as 'the Uncaused Cause,' but comes short of the idea of His personality. The other subordinate causes which he mentions all get their force or power from the Tâo, but after all the Tâo is simply a spontaneity, evolving from itself, and not acting from a personal will, consciously in the direction of its own wisdom and love. 'Who can by searching find out God? Who can find out the Almighty to perfection?'

The predicate of the Tâo in the chapter, most perplexing to myself, is 'It returns,' in par. 3. 'It flows away, far away, and comes back;'—are not the three statements together equal to 'It is everywhere?'

26. 1. Gravity is the root of lightness; stillness, the ruler of movement.

2. Therefore a wise prince, marching the whole day, does not go far from his baggage waggons. Although he may have brilliant prospects to look at, he quietly remains (in his proper place), indifferent to them. How should the lord of a myriad chariots carry himself lightly before the kingdom? If he do act lightly, he has lost his root (of gravity); if he proceed to active movement, he will lose his throne.

重德, 'The Quality of Gravity.' Gravity and stillness are both attributes of the Tâo; and he who cultivates it must not give way to lightness of mind, or hasty action.

The rule for a leader not to separate from his baggage waggons is simply the necessity of adhering to gravity. I have adopted from Han Fei the reading of 'the wise prince' for 'the sage,' which is found in Ho-shang Kung; and later on the reading of 'has lost his root' for his 'loses his ministers,' though the latter is found also in Han Fei.

27. 1. The skilful traveller leaves no traces of his wheels or footsteps; the skilful speaker says nothing that can be found fault with or blamed; the skilful reckoner uses no tallies; the skilful closer needs no bolts or bars, while to open what he has shut will be impossible; the skilful binder uses no strings or knots, while to unloose what he has bound will be impossible. In the same way the sage is always skilful at saving men, and so he does not cast away any man; he is always skilful at saving things, and so he does not cast away anything. This is called 'Hiding the light of his procedure.'

2. Therefore the man of skill is a master (to be looked up to) by him who has not the skill; and he who has not the skill is the helper of (the reputation of) him who has the skill. If the one did not honour his master, and the other did not rejoice in his helper, an (observer), though intelligent, might greatly err about them. This is called 'The utmost degree of mystery.'

巧用, 'Dexterity in Using,' that is, in the application of the Tâo. This is the substance of the chapter, celebrating the effective but invisible operation of the Tâo, and the impartial exercise of it for the benefit of all men and all things.

I have given the most natural construction of the two characters at the end of par. 1, the only possible construction of them, so far as I can see, suitable to the context. The action of the Tâo (non-acting and yet all-efficient) and that of the sage in accordance with it, are veiled by their nature from the sight of ordinary men.

It is more difficult to catch the scope and point of par. 2. If there were not the conditions described in it, it would be hard for even an intelligent onlooker to distinguish between the man who had the skill and the man without it, between him who possessed the Tâo, and him who had it not, which would be strange indeed.

28. 1. Who knows his manhood's strength,
Yet still his female feebleness maintains;
As to one channel flow the many drains,
All come to him, yea, all beneath the sky.
Thus he the constant excellence retains;—
The simple child again, free from all stains.

Who knows how white attracts,
Yet always keeps himself within black's shade,
The pattern of humility displayed,
Displayed in view of all beneath the sky;
He in the unchanging excellence arrayed,
Endless return to man's first state has made.

Who knows how glory shines,
Yet loves disgrace, nor e'er for it is pale;
Behold his presence in a spacious vale,
To which men come from all beneath the sky.
The unchanging excellence completes its tale;
The simple infant man in him we hail.

2. The unwrought material, when divided and distributed, forms vessels. The sage, when employed, becomes the Head of all the Officers (of government); and in his greatest regulations he employs no violent measures.

反樸, 'Returning to Simplicity.' The chapter sets forth humility and simplicity, an artless freedom from all purpose, as characteristic of the man of Tâo, such as he was in the primeval time. 'The sage' in par. 2 may be 'the Son of Heaven,'—the Head of all rule in the kingdom, or the feudal lord in a state.

29. 1. If any one should wish to get the kingdom for himself, and to effect this by what he does, I see

that he will not succeed. The kingdom is a spirit-like thing, and cannot be got by active doing. He who would so win it destroys it; he who would hold it in his grasp loses it.

2. The course and nature of things is such that

What was in front is now behind;
What warmed anon we freezing find.
Strength is of weakness oft the spoil;
The store in ruins mocks our toil.

Hence the sage puts away excessive effort, extravagance, and easy indulgence.

無爲, 'Taking no Action.' All efforts made with a purpose are sure to fail. The nature of the Tâo necessitates their doing so, and the uncertainty of things and events teaches the same lesson.

That the kingdom or throne is a 'spirit-like vessel' has become a common enough saying among the Chinese. Julien has, 'L'Empire est comme un vase divin;' but I always shrink from translating 神 by 'divine.' Its English analogue is 'spirit,' and the idea in the text is based on the immunity of spirit from all material law, and the uncertain issue of attempts to deal with it according to ordinary methods. Wû *Kh*ăng takes the phrase as equivalent to 'superintended by spirits,' which is as inadmissible as Julien's 'divin.' The Tâo forbids action with a personal purpose, and all such action is sure to fail in the greatest things as well as in the least.

30. 1. He who would assist a lord of men in harmony with the Tâo will not assert his mastery in the kingdom by force of arms. Such a course is sure to meet with its proper return.

2. Wherever a host is stationed, briars and thorns spring up. In the sequence of great armies there are sure to be bad years.

3. A skilful (commander) strikes a decisive blow, and stops. He does not dare (by continuing his operations) to assert and complete his mastery. He will strike the blow, but will be on his guard against being vain or boastful or arrogant in consequence of it. He strikes it as a matter of necessity; he strikes it, but not from a wish for mastery.

4. When things have attained their strong maturity they become old. This may be said to be not in accordance with the Tâo: and what is not in accordance with it soon comes to an end.

儉武, 'A Caveat against War.' War is contrary to the spirit of the Tâo, and, as being so, is productive of misery, and leads to early ruin. It is only permissible in a case of necessity, and even then its spirit and tendencies must be guarded against.

In translating 果 by 'striking a decisive blow,' I have, no doubt, followed Julien's 'frapper un coup décisif.' The same 果 occurs six times in par. 3, followed by 而, and 3iâo Hung says that in all but the first instance the 而 should be taken as equivalent to 於, so that we should have to translate, 'He is determined against being vain,' &c. But there is no necessity for such a construction of 而.

'Weakness' and not 'strength' is the character of the Tâo; hence the lesson in par. 4.

31. 1. Now arms, however beautiful, are instruments of evil omen, hateful, it may be said, to all creatures. Therefore they who have the Tâo do not like to employ them.

2. The superior man ordinarily considers the left hand the most honourable place, but in time of war the right hand. Those sharp weapons are instruments of evil omen, and not the instruments of the

superior man;—he uses them only on the compulsion of necessity. Calm and repose are what he prizes; victory (by force of arms) is to him undesirable. To consider this desirable would be to delight in the slaughter of men; and he who delights in the slaughter of men cannot get his will in the kingdom.

3. On occasions of festivity to be on the left hand is the prized position; on occasions of mourning, the right hand. The second in command of the army has his place on the left; the general commanding in chief has his on the right;—his place, that is, is assigned to him as in the rites of mourning. He who has killed multitudes of men should weep for them with the bitterest grief; and the victor in battle has his place (rightly) according to those rites.

偃武, 'Stilling War.' The chapter continues the subject of the preceding. The imperially-appointed editors of Wang Pî's Text and Commentary (1765) say that from the beginning of par. 2 to the end, there is the appearance of text and commentary being mixed together; but they make no alteration in the text as it is found in Ho-shang Kung, and in all other ancient copies.

The concluding sentence will suggest to some readers the words of the Duke of Wellington, that to gain a battle was the saddest thing next to losing it.

32. 1. The Tâo, considered as unchanging, has no name.

2. Though in its primordial simplicity it may be small, the whole world dares not deal with (one embodying) it as a minister. If a feudal prince or the king could guard and hold it, all would spontaneously submit themselves to him.

3. Heaven and Earth (under its guidance) unite together and send down the sweet dew, which, with-

out the directions of men, reaches equally everywhere as of its own accord.

4. As soon as it proceeds to action, it has a name. When it once has that name, (men) can know to rest in it. When they know to rest in it, they can be free from all risk of failure and error.

5. The relation of the Tâo to all the world is like that of the great rivers and seas to the streams from the valleys.

聖德. Chalmers translates this by 'sagely virtue.' But I cannot adopt that rendering, and find it difficult to supply a better. The 'virtue' is evidently the Attribute of the Tâo come out from the condition of the Absolute, and capable of being named. In the former state it has no name; in the latter, it has. Par. 1 and the commencement of par. 4 must both be explained from ch. 1.

The 'primordial simplicity' in par. 2 is the Tâo in its simplest conception, alone, and by itself, and the 始制 in par. 4 is that Tâo come forth into operation and become Teh, the Teh which affords a law for men. From this to the end of the paragraph is very obscure. I have translated from the text of Wang Pî. The text of Ho-shang Kung is different, and he comments upon it as it stands, but to me it is inexplicable.

33. 1. He who knows other men is discerning; he who knows himself is intelligent. He who overcomes others is strong; he who overcomes himself is mighty. He who is satisfied with his lot is rich; he who goes on acting with energy has a (firm) will.

2. He who does not fail in the requirements of his position, continues long; he who dies and yet does not perish, has longevity.

辨德, 'Discriminating between (different) Attributes.' The teaching of the chapter is that the possession of the

Tâo confers the various attributes which are here most distinguished. It has been objected to it that elsewhere the Tâo is represented as associated with dulness and not intelligence, and with weakness and not with strength. But these seem to be qualities viewed from without, and acting on what is beyond itself. Inwardly, its qualities are the very opposite, and its action has the effect of enlightening what is dark, and overcoming what is strong.

More interesting are the predicates in par. 2. 3iâo Hung gives the comment on it of the Indian monk, Kumâra*g*îva, 'one of the four suns of Buddhism,' and who went to China in A.D. 401: 'To be alive and yet not alive may well be called long; to die and yet not be dead may well be called longevity.' He also gives the views of Lû Năng-shih (A.D. 1042–1102) that the freedom from change of Lieh-3ze, from death of *K*wang-3ze, and from extinction of the Buddhists, have all the same meaning as the concluding saying of Lâo-3ze here; that the human body is like the covering of the caterpillar or the skin of the snake; that we occupy it but for a passing sojourn. No doubt, Lâo-3ze believed in another life for the individual after the present. Many passages in *K*wang-3ze indicate the same faith.

34. 1. All-pervading is the Great Tâo! It may be found on the left hand and on the right.

2. All things depend on it for their production, which it gives to them, not one refusing obedience to it. When its work is accomplished, it does not claim the name of having done it. It clothes all things as with a garment, and makes no assumption of being their lord;—it may be named in the smallest things. All things return (to their root and disappear), and do not know that it is it which presides over their doing so;—it may be named in the greatest things.

3. Hence the sage is able (in the same way) to accomplish his great achievements. It is through

his not making himself great that he can accomplish them.

任成, 'The Task of Achievement.' The subject is the greatness of what the Tâo, called here by Lâo's own name for it in ch. 25, does; and the unconscious simplicity with which it does it; and then the achievements of the sage who is permeated by the Tâo. Par. 2 is descriptive of the influence of the Tâo in the vegetable world. The statements and expressions are much akin to those in parts of chapters 2, 10, and 51, and for Ho-shang Kung's difficult reading of 不名有 some copies give 而不居, as in chapter 2.

35. 1. To him who holds in his hands the Great Image (of the invisible Tâo), the whole world repairs. Men resort to him, and receive no hurt, but (find) rest, peace, and the feeling of ease.

2. Music and dainties will make the passing guest stop (for a time). But though the Tâo as it comes from the mouth, seems insipid and has no flavour, though it seems not worth being looked at or listened to, the use of it is inexhaustible.

仁德, 'The Attribute of Benevolence.' But there seems little appropriateness in this title. The subject of the chapter is the inexhaustible efficacy of the Tâo for the good of the world.

The Great Image (of the invisible Tâo) is a name for the Tâo in its operation; as in chapters 14 and 41. He who embodies this in his government will be a centre of attraction for all the world. Or the 天下往 may be taken as a predicate of the holder of the Great Image: —'If he go all under heaven teaching the Tâo.' Both constructions are maintained by commentators of note. In par. 2 the attraction of the Tâo is contrasted with that of ordinary pleasures and gratifications.

36. 1. When one is about to take an inspiration, he is sure to make a (previous) expiration; when he is going to weaken another, he will first strengthen him; when he is going to overthrow another, he will first have raised him up; when he is going to despoil another, he will first have made gifts to him:—this is called 'Hiding the light (of his procedure).'

2. The soft overcomes the hard; and the weak the strong.

3. Fishes should not be taken from the deep; instruments for the profit of a state should not be shown to the people.

微明, 'Minimising the Light;' equivalent, as Wû *Kh*ăng has pointed out, to the 襲明 of ch. 27.

The gist of the chapter is to be sought in the second paragraph, where we have two instances of the action of the Tâo by contraries, supposed always to be for good.

But there is a difficulty in seeing the applicability to this of the cases mentioned in par. 1. The first case, indeed, is merely a natural phenomenon, having no moral character; but the others, as they have been illustrated from historical incidents, by Han Fei and others at least, belong to schemes of selfish and unprincipled ambitious strategy, which it would be injurious to Lâo-ȝze to suppose that he intended.

Par. 3 is the most frequently quoted of all the passages in our *K*ing, unless it be the first part of ch. 1. Fishes taken from the deep, and brought into shallow water, can be easily taken or killed; that is plain enough. 'The sharp instruments of a state' are not its 'weapons of war,' nor its 'treasures,' nor its 'instruments of government,' that is, its rewards and punishments, though this last is the interpretation often put on them, and sustained by a foolish reference to an incident, real or coined, in the history of the dukedom of Sung. The lî *kh*î are 'contrivances for gain,' machines, and other methods to increase the wealth of a state, but, according to the principles of Lâo-ȝze, really injurious to it. These should not be shown to the people, whom the Tâoistic system would keep in a state of primitive simplicity and ignorance. This interpretation is in accordance with the meaning of the characters, and with the general teaching of Tâoism. In no other way can I explain the paragraph so as to justify the place undoubtedly belonging to it in the system.

37. 1. The Tâo in its regular course does nothing (for the sake of doing it), and so there is nothing which it does not do.

2. If princes and kings were able to maintain it, all things would of themselves be transformed by them.

3. If this transformation became to me an object of desire, I would express the desire by the nameless simplicity.

Simplicity without a name
Is free from all external aim.
With no desire, at rest and still,
All things go right as of their will.

爲政, 'The Exercise of Government.' This exercise should be according to the Tâo, doing without doing, governing without government.

The subject of the third paragraph is a feudal prince or the king, and he is spoken of in the first person, to give more vividness to the style, unless the 吾, 'I,' may, possibly, be understood of Lâo-ȝze himself personating one of them.

PART II.

38. 1. (Those who) possessed in highest degree the attributes (of the Tâo) did not (seek) to show them, and therefore they possessed them (in fullest measure). (Those who) possessed in a lower degree those attributes (sought how) not to lose them, and therefore they did not possess them (in fullest measure).

2. (Those who) possessed in the highest degree those attributes did nothing (with a purpose), and had no need to do anything. (Those who) possessed them in a lower degree were (always) doing, and had need to be so doing.

3. (Those who) possessed the highest benevolence were (always seeking) to carry it out, and had no need to be doing so. (Those who) possessed the highest righteousness were (always seeking) to carry it out, and had need to be so doing.

4. (Those who) possessed the highest (sense of) propriety were (always seeking) to show it, and when men did not respond to it, they bared the arm and marched up to them.

5. Thus it was that when the Tâo was lost, its attributes appeared; when its attributes were lost, benevolence appeared; when benevolence was lost, righteousness appeared; and when righteousness was lost, the proprieties appeared.

6. Now propriety is the attenuated form of leal-heartedness and good faith, and is also the commencement of disorder; swift apprehension is

(only) a flower of the Tâo, and is the beginning of stupidity.

7. Thus it is that the Great man abides by what is solid, and eschews what is flimsy; dwells with the fruit and not with the flower. It is thus that he puts away the one and makes choice of the other.

論德, 'About the Attributes;' of Tâo, that is. It is not easy to render teh here by any other English term than 'virtue,' and yet there would be a danger of its thus misleading us in the interpretation of the chapter.

The 'virtue' is the activity or operation of the Tâo, which is supposed to have come out of its absoluteness. Even Han Fei so defines it here,—'Teh is the meritorious work of the Tâo.'

In par. 5 we evidently have a résumé of the preceding paragraphs, and, as it is historical, I translate them in the past tense; though what took place on the early stage of the world may also be said to go on taking place in the experience of every individual. With some considerable hesitation I have given the subjects in those paragraphs in the concrete, in deference to the authority of Ho-shang Kung and most other commentators. The former says, 'By "the highest teh" is to be understood the rulers of the greatest antiquity, without name or designation, whose virtue was great, and could not be surpassed.' Most ingenious, and in accordance with the Tâoistic system, is the manner in which Wû *Kh*ăng construes the passage, and I am surprised that it has not been generally accepted. By 'the higher teh' he understands 'the Tâo,' that which is prior to and above the Teh (上德者, 在德之上, 道也); by 'the lower teh,' benevolence, that which is after and below the Teh; by 'the higher benevolence,' the Teh which is above benevolence; by 'the higher righteousness,' the benevolence which is above righteousness; and by 'the higher propriety,' the righteousness which is above propriety. Certainly in the summation of these four paragraphs which we have in the fifth, the subjects of them would appear to have been in the mind of Lâo-ȝze as thus defined by Wû.

In the remainder of the chapter he goes on to speak depreciatingly of ceremonies and knowledge, so that the whole chapter must be understood as descriptive of the process of decay and deterioration from the early time in which the Tâo and its attributes swayed the societies of men.

39. 1. The things which from of old have got the One (the Tâo) are—

Heaven which by it is bright and pure;
Earth rendered thereby firm and sure;
Spirits with powers by it supplied;
Valleys kept full throughout their void;
All creatures which through it do live;
Princes and kings who from it get
The model which to all they give.

All these are the results of the One (Tâo).

2. If heaven were not thus pure, it soon would rend;
If earth were not thus sure, 'twould break and bend;
Without these powers, the spirits soon would fail;
If not so filled, the drought would parch each vale;
Without that life, creatures would pass away;
Princes and kings, without that moral sway,
However grand and high, would all decay.

3. Thus it is that dignity finds its (firm) root in its (previous) meanness, and what is lofty finds its stability in the lowness (from which it rises). Hence princes and kings call themselves 'Orphans,' 'Men of small virtue,' and as 'Carriages without a nave.' Is not this an acknowledgment that in their considering themselves mean they see the foundation of

their dignity? So it is that in the enumeration of the different parts of a carriage we do not come on what makes it answer the ends of a carriage. They do not wish to show themselves elegant-looking as jade, but (prefer) to be coarse-looking as an (ordinary) stone.

法本, 'The Origin of the Law.' In this title there is a reference to the Law given to all things by the Tâo, as described in the conclusion of chapter 25. And the Tâo affords that law by its passionless, undemonstrative nature, through which in its spontaneity, doing nothing for the sake of doing, it yet does all things.

The difficulty of translation is in the third paragraph. The way in which princes and kings speak depreciatingly of themselves is adduced as illustrating how they have indeed got the spirit of the Tâo; and I accept the last epithet as given by Ho-shang Kung, 'naveless' (轂), instead of 穀 (='the unworthy'), which is found in Wang Pî, and has been adopted by nearly all subsequent editors. To see its appropriateness here, we have only to refer back to chapter 11, where the thirty spokes, and the nave, empty to receive the axle, are spoken of, and it is shown how the usefulness of the carriage is derived from that emptiness of the nave. This also enables us to give a fair and consistent explanation of the difficult clause which follows, in which also I have followed the text of Ho-shang Kung. For his 車, Wang Pî has 輿, which also is found in a quotation of it by Hwâi-nan 3ze; but this need not affect the meaning. In the translation of the clause we are assisted by a somewhat similar illustration about a horse in the twenty-fifth of *K*wang-ʒze's Books, par. 10.

40\. 1. The movement of the Tâo
By contraries proceeds;
And weakness marks the course
Of Tâo's mighty deeds.

2. All things under heaven sprang from It as existing (and named); that existence sprang from It as non-existent (and not named).

去用, 'Dispensing with the Use (of Means);'—with their use, that is, as it appears to us. The subject of the brief chapter is the action of the Tâo by contraries, leading to a result the opposite of what existed previously, and by means which might seem calculated to produce a contrary result.

In translating par. 2 I have followed 3iâo Hung, who finds the key to it in ch. 1. Having a name, the Tâo is 'the Mother of all things;' having no name, it is 'the Originator of Heaven and Earth.' But here is the teaching of Lâo-ȝze:—'If Tâo seems to be before God,' Tâo itself sprang from nothing.

41. 1. Scholars of the highest class, when they hear about the Tâo, earnestly carry it into practice. Scholars of the middle class, when they have heard about it, seem now to keep it and now to lose it. Scholars of the lowest class, when they have heard about it, laugh greatly at it. If it were not (thus) laughed at, it would not be fit to be the Tâo.

2. Therefore the sentence-makers have thus expressed themselves:—

'The Tâo, when brightest seen, seems light to lack;
Who progress in it makes, seems drawing back;
Its even way is like a rugged track.
Its highest virtue from the vale doth rise;
Its greatest beauty seems to offend the eyes;
And he has most whose lot the least supplies.
Its firmest virtue seems but poor and low;
Its solid truth seems change to undergo;
Its largest square doth yet no corner show;
A vessel great, it is the slowest made;

Loud is its sound, but never word it said;
A semblance great, the shadow of a shade.'

3. The Tâo is hidden, and has no name; but it is the Tâo which is skilful at imparting (to all things what they need) and making them complete.

同異, 'Sameness and Difference.' The chapter is a sequel of the preceding, and may be taken as an illustration of the Tâo's proceeding by contraries.

Who the sentence-makers were whose sayings are quoted we cannot tell, but it would have been strange if Lâo-ȝze had not had a large store of such sentences at his command. The fifth and sixth of those employed by him here are found in Lieh-ȝze (II, 15 a), spoken by Lâo in reproving Yang *K*û, and in VII, 3 a, that heretic appears quoting an utterance of the same kind, with the words, 'according to an old saying (古語有之).'

42. 1. The Tâo produced One; One produced Two; Two produced Three; Three produced All things. All things leave behind them the Obscurity (out of which they have come), and go forward to embrace the Brightness (into which they have emerged), while they are harmonised by the Breath of Vacancy.

2. What men dislike is to be orphans, to have little virtue, to be as carriages without naves; and yet these are the designations which kings and princes use for themselves. So it is that some things are increased by being diminished, and others are diminished by being increased.

3. What other men (thus) teach, I also teach. The violent and strong do not die their natural death. I will make this the basis of my teaching.

道化, 'The Transformations of the Tâo.' In par. 2 we

have the case of the depreciating epithets given to themselves by kings and princes, which we found before in ch. 39, and a similar lesson is drawn from it. Such depreciation leads to exaltation, and the contrary course of self-exaltation leads to abasement. This latter case is stated emphatically in par. 3, and Lâo-ȝze says that it was the basis of his teaching. So far therefore we have in this chapter a repetition of the lesson that 'the movement of the Tâo is by contraries,' and that its weakness is the sure precursor of strength. But the connexion between this lesson and what he says in par. 1 it is difficult to trace. Up to this time at least it has baffled myself. The passage seems to give us a cosmogony. 'The Tâo produced One.' We have already seen that the Tâo is 'The One.' Are we to understand here that the Tâo and the One were one and the same? In this case what would be the significance of the 生 ('produced')?—that the Tâo which had been previously 'non-existent' now became 'existent,' or capable of being named? This seems to be the view of Sze-mâ Kwang (A. D. 1009–1086).

The most singular form which this view assumes is in one of the treatises on our *King*, attributed to the Tâoist patriarch Lü (呂祖道德經解), that 'the One is Heaven, which was formed by the congealing of the Tâo.' According to another treatise, also assigned to the same Lü (道德眞經合解), the One was 'the primordial ether;' the Two, 'the separation of that into its Yin and Yang constituents;' and the Three, 'the production of heaven, earth, and man by these.' In quoting the paragraph Hwâi-nan ȝze omits 道生一, and commences with 一生二, and his glossarist, Kâo Yû, makes out the One to be the Tâo, the Two to be Spiritual Intelligences (神明), and the Three to be the Harmonising Breath. From the mention of the Yin and Yang that follows, I believe that Lâo-ȝze intended by the Two these two qualities or elements in the primordial ether, which would be 'the One.' I dare not hazard a guess as to what 'the Three' were.

道德經

43. 1. The softest thing in the world dashes against and overcomes the hardest; that which has no (substantial) existence enters where there is no crevice. I know hereby what advantage belongs to doing nothing (with a purpose).

2. There are few in the world who attain to the teaching without words, and the advantage arising from non-action.

偏用, 'The Universal Use (of the action in weakness of the Tâo).' The chapter takes us back to the lines of ch. 40, that

'Weakness marks the course
Of Tâo's mighty deeds.'

By 'the softest thing in the world' it is agreed that we are to understand 'water,' which will wear away the hardest rocks. 'Dashing against and overcoming' is a metaphor taken from hunting. Ho-shang Kung says that 'what has no existence' is the Tâo; it is better to understand by it the unsubstantial air (氣) which penetrates everywhere, we cannot see how.

Compare par. 2 with ch. 2, par. 3.

44. 1. Or fame or life,
Which do you hold more dear?
Or life or wealth,
To which would you adhere?
Keep life and lose those other things;
Keep them and lose your life:—which brings
Sorrow and pain more near?

2. Thus we may see,
Who cleaves to fame
Rejects what is more great;
Who loves large stores
Gives up the richer state.

3. Who is content
Needs fear no shame.
Who knows to stop
Incurs no blame.
From danger free
Long live shall he.

立戒, 'Cautions.' The chapter warns men to let nothing come into competition with the value which they set on the Tâo. The Tâo is not named, indeed, but the idea of it was evidently in the writer's mind.

The whole chapter rhymes after a somewhat peculiar fashion; familiar enough, however, to one who is acquainted with the old rhymes of the Book of Poetry.

45. 1. Who thinks his great achievements poor
Shall find his vigour long endure.
Of greatest fulness, deemed a void,
Exhaustion ne'er shall stem the tide.
Do thou what's straight still crooked deem;
Thy greatest art still stupid seem,
And eloquence a stammering scream.

2. Constant action overcomes cold; being still overcomes heat. Purity and stillness give the correct law to all under heaven.

洪德, 'Great or Overflowing Virtue.' The chapter is another illustration of the working of the Tâo by contraries.

According to Wû *Kh*ăng, the action which overcomes cold is that of the Yang element in the developing primordial ether; and the stillness which overcomes heat is that of the contrary Yin element. These may have been in Lâo-ȝze's mind, but the statements are so simple as hardly to need any comment. Wû further says that the purity and stillness are descriptive of the condition of non-action.

46. 1. When the Tâo prevails in the world, they send back their swift horses to (draw) the dung-carts.

道德經

When the Tâo is disregarded in the world, the war-horses breed in the border lands.

2. There is no guilt greater than to sanction ambition; no calamity greater than to be discontented with one's lot; no fault greater than the wish to be getting. Therefore the sufficiency of contentment is an enduring and unchanging sufficiency.

儉欲, 'The Moderating of Desire or Ambition.' The chapter shows how the practice of the Tâo must conduce to contentment and happiness.

In translating par. 1 I have, after Wû *Kh*ăng, admitted a 車 after the 糞, his chief authority for doing so being that it is so found in a poetical piece by *K*ang Hăng (A. D. 78-139). *K*û Hsî also adopted this reading (朱子大全, XVIII, 7 a). In par. 2 Han Ying has a tempting variation of 多欲 for 可欲, but I have not adopted it because the same phrase occurs elsewhere.

47. 1. Without going outside his door, one understands (all that takes place) under the sky; without looking out from his window, one sees the Tâo of Heaven. The farther that one goes out (from himself), the less he knows.

2. Therefore the sages got their knowledge without travelling; gave their (right) names to things without seeing them; and accomplished their ends without any purpose of doing so.

鑒遠, 'Surveying what is Far-off.' The chapter is a lesson to men to judge of things according to their internal conviction of similar things in their own experience. Short as the chapter is, it is somewhat mystical. The phrase, 'The Tâo' or way of Heaven, occurs in it for the first time; and it is difficult to lay down its precise meaning. Lâo-ȝze would seem to teach that man is a microcosm; and that, if he understand the movements of his own mind, he can understand the movements of all other minds. There are various readings, of which it is not necessary to speak.

I have translated par. 2 in the past tense, and perhaps the first should also be translated so. Most of it is found in Han Ying, preceded by 'formerly' or 'anciently.'

48. 1. He who devotes himself to learning (seeks) from day to day to increase (his knowledge); he who devotes himself to the Tâo (seeks) from day to day to diminish (his doing).

2. He diminishes it and again diminishes it, till he arrives at doing nothing (on purpose). Having arrived at this point of non-action, there is nothing which he does not do.

3. He who gets as his own all under heaven does so by giving himself no trouble (with that end). If one take trouble (with that end), he is not equal to getting as his own all under heaven.

忘知, 'Forgetting Knowledge;'—the contrast between Learning and the Tâo. It is only by the Tâo that the world can be won.

Ȝiâo Hung commences his quotations of commentary on this chapter with the following from Kumâragîva on the second par.:—'He carries on the process of diminishing till there is nothing coarse about him which is not put away. He puts it away till he has forgotten all that was bad in it. He then puts away all that is fine about him. He does so till he has forgotten all that was good in it. But the bad was wrong, and the good is right. Having diminished the wrong, and also diminished the right, the process is carried on till they are both forgotten. Passion and desire are both cut off; and his virtue and the Tâo are in such union that he does nothing; but though he does nothing, he allows all things to do their own doing, and all things are done.' Such is a Buddhistic view of the passage, not very intelligible, and which I do not endorse.

In a passage in the 'Narratives of the School' (Bk. IX, Art. 2), we have a Confucian view of the passage:—'Let perspicacity, intelligence, shrewdness, and wisdom be guarded by stupidity, and the service of the possessor will affect the whole world; let them be guarded by complaisance, and his daring and strength will shake the age; let them be guarded by timidity, and his wealth will be all within the four seas; let them be guarded by humility, and there will be what we call the method of "diminishing it, and diminishing it again."' But neither do I endorse this.

My own view of the scope of the chapter has been given above in a few words. The greater part of it is found in *K*wang-ȝze.

49. 1. The sage has no invariable mind of his own; he makes the mind of the people his mind.

2. To those who are good (to me), I am good; and to those who are not good (to me), I am also good;—and thus (all) get to be good. To those who are sincere (with me), I am sincere; and to those who are not sincere (with me), I am also sincere;—and thus (all) get to be sincere.

3. The sage has in the world an appearance of indecision, and keeps his mind in a state of indifference to all. The people all keep their eyes and ears directed to him, and he deals with them all as his children.

任德, 'The Quality of Indulgence.' The chapter shows how that quality enters largely into the dealing of the sage with other men, and exercises over them a transforming influence, dominated as it is in him by the Tâo.

My version of par. 1 is taken from Dr. Chalmers. A good commentary on it was given by the last emperor but one of the earlier of the two great Sung dynasties, in the period A.D. 1111–1117:—'The mind of the sage is free from pre-occupation and able to receive; still, and able to respond.'

In par. 2 I adopt the reading of 得 ('to get') instead of

the more common 德 ('virtue' or 'quality'). There is a passage in Han Ying (IX, 3 b, 4 a), the style of which, most readers will probably agree with me in thinking, was moulded on the text before us, though nothing is said of any connexion between it and the saying of Lâo-ȝze. I must regard it as a sequel to the conversation between Confucius and some of his disciples about the principle (Lâo's principle) that 'Injury should be recompensed with Kindness,' as recorded in the Con. Ana., XIV, 36. We read :—'Ȝze-lû said, "When men are good to me, I will also be good to them; when they are not good to me, I will also be not good to them." Ȝze-kung said, "When men are good to me, I will also be good to them; when they are not good to me, I will simply lead them on, forwards it may be or backwards." Yen Hui said, "When men are good to me, I will also be good to them; when they are not good to me, I will still be good to them." The views of the three disciples being thus different, they referred the point to the Master, who said, "The words of Ȝze-lû are such as might be expected among the (wild tribes of) the Man and the Mo; those of Ȝze-kung, such as might be expected among friends; those of Hui, such as might be expected among relatives and near connexions."' This is all. The Master was still far from Lâo-ȝze's standpoint, and that of his own favourite disciple, Yen Hui.

50. 1. Men come forth and live; they enter (again) and die.

2. Of every ten three are ministers of life (to themselves); and three are ministers of death.

3. There are also three in every ten whose aim is to live, but whose movements tend to the land (or place) of death. And for what reason? Because of their excessive endeavours to perpetuate life.

4. But I have heard that he who is skilful in managing the life entrusted to him for a time travels on the land without having to shun rhinoceros or

tiger, and enters a host without having to avoid buff coat or sharp weapon. The rhinoceros finds no place in him into which to thrust its horn, nor the tiger a place in which to fix its claws, nor the weapon a place to admit its point. And for what reason? Because there is in him no place of death.

貴生, 'The Value set on Life.' The chapter sets forth the Tâo as an antidote against decay and death.

In par. 1 life is presented to us as intermediate between two non-existences. The words will suggest to many readers those in Job i. 21.

In pars. 2 and 3 I translate the characters 十有三 by 'three in ten,' instead of by 'thirteen,' as Julien and other translators have done. The characters are susceptible of either translation according to the tone in which we read the 有. They were construed as I have done by Wang Pî; and many of the best commentators have followed in his wake. 'The ministers of life to themselves' would be those who eschewed all things, both internal and external, tending to injure health; 'the ministers of death,' those who pursued courses likely to cause disease and shorten life; the third three would be those who thought that by mysterious and abnormal courses they could prolong life, but only injured it. Those three classes being thus disposed of, there remains only one in ten rightly using the Tâo, and he is spoken of in the next paragraph.

This par. 4 is easy of translation, and the various readings in it are unimportant, differing in this respect from those in par. 3. But the aim of the author in it is not clear. In ascribing such effects to the possession of the Tâo, is he 'trifling,' as Dr. Chalmers thinks? or indulging the play of his poetical fancy? or simply saying that the Tâoist will keep himself out of danger?

51. 1. All things are produced by the Tâo, and nourished by its outflowing operation. They receive their forms according to the nature of each, and are

completed according to the circumstances of their condition. Therefore all things without exception honour the Tâo, and exalt its outflowing operation.

2. This honouring of the Tâo and exalting of its operation is not the result of any ordination, but always a spontaneous tribute.

3. Thus it is that the Tâo produces (all things), nourishes them, brings them to their full growth, nurses them, completes them, matures them, maintains them, and overspreads them.

4. It produces them and makes no claim to the possession of them; it carries them through their processes and does not vaunt its ability in doing so; it brings them to maturity and exercises no control over them;—this is called its mysterious operation.

養德, 'The Operation (of the Tâo) in Nourishing Things.' The subject of the chapter is the quiet passionless operation of the Tâo in nature, in the production and nourishing of things throughout the seasons of the year;—a theme dwelt on by Lâo-ȝze, in II, 4, X, 3, and other places.

The Tâo is the subject of all the predicates in par. 1, and what seem the subjects in all but the first member should be construed adverbially.

On par. 2 Wû *Kh*ăng says that the honour of the Son of Heaven is derived from his appointment by God, and that then the nobility of the feudal princes is derived from him; but in the honour given to the Tâo and the nobility ascribed to its operation, we are not to think of any external ordination. There is a strange reading of two of the members of par. 3 in Wang Pî, viz. 亭之毒之 for 成之熟之. This is quoted and predicated of 'Heaven,' in the Nestorian Monument of Hsî-an in the eighth century.

52. 1. (The Tâo) which originated all under the sky is to be considered as the mother of them all.

2. When the mother is found, we know what her children should be. When one knows that he is his mother's child, and proceeds to guard (the qualities of) the mother that belong to him, to the end of his life he will be free from all peril.

3. Let him keep his mouth closed, and shut up the portals (of his nostrils), and all his life he will be exempt from laborious exertion. Let him keep his mouth open, and (spend his breath) in the promotion of his affairs, and all his life there will be no safety for him.

4. The perception of what is small is (the secret of) clear-sightedness; the guarding of what is soft and tender is (the secret of) strength.

5. Who uses well his light,
Reverting to its (source so) bright,
Will from his body ward all blight,
And hides the unchanging from men's sight.

歸元, 'Returning to the Source.' The meaning of the chapter is obscure, and the commentators give little help in determining it. As in the preceding chapter, Lâo-ȝze treats of the operation of the Tâo on material things, he seems in this to go on to the operation of it in man, or how he, with his higher nature, should ever be maintaining it in himself.

For the understanding of paragraph 1 we must refer to the first chapter of the treatise, where the Tâo, 'having no name,' appears as 'the Beginning' or 'First Cause' of the world, and then, 'having a name,' as its 'Mother.' It is the same thing or concept in both of its phases, the ideal or absolute, and the manifestation of it in its passionless doings. The old Jesuit translators render this par. by 'Mundus principium et causam suam habet in Divino 有, seu actione Divinae sapientiae quae dici potest ejus mater.' So far I may assume that they agreed with me in understanding that the subject of the par. was the Tâo.

Par. 2 lays down the law of life for man thus derived from the Tâo. The last clause of it is given by the same translators as equivalent to 'Unde fit ut post mortem nihil ei timendum sit,'—a meaning which the characters will not bear. But from that clause, and the next par., I am obliged to conclude that even in Lâo-ʒze's mind there was the germ of the sublimation of the material frame which issued in the asceticism and life-preserving arts of the later Tâoism.

Par. 3 seems to indicate the method of 'guarding the mother in man,' by watching over the breath, the protoplastic 'one' of ch. 42, the ethereal matter out of which all material things were formed. The organs of this breath in man are the mouth and nostrils (nothing else should be understood here by 兌 and 門;—see the explanations of the former in the last par. of the fifth of the appendixes to the Yî in vol. xvi, p. 432); and the management of the breath is the mystery of the esoteric Buddhism and Tâoism.

In par. 4 'The guarding what is soft' is derived from the use of 'the soft lips' in hiding and preserving the hard and strong teeth.

Par. 5 gives the gist of the chapter:—Man's always keeping before him the ideal of the Tâo, and, without purpose, simply doing whatever he finds to do; Tâo-like and powerful in all his sphere of action.

I have followed the reading of the last character but one, which is given by ʒiâo Hung instead of that found in Ho-shang Kung and Wang Pî.

53. 1. If I were suddenly to become known, and (put into a position to) conduct (a government) according to the Great Tâo, what I should be most afraid of would be a boastful display.

2. The great Tâo (or way) is very level and easy; but people love the by-ways.

3. Their court(-yards and buildings) shall be well kept, but their fields shall be ill-cultivated, and their granaries very empty. They shall wear elegant and

ornamented robes, carry a sharp sword at their girdle, pamper themselves in eating and drinking, and have a superabundance of property and wealth;—such (princes) may be called robbers and boasters. This is contrary to the Tâo surely!

益證, 'Increase of Evidence.' The chapter contrasts government by the Tâo with that conducted in a spirit of ostentation and by oppression.

In the 'I' of paragraph 1 does Lâo-ȝze speak of himself? I think he does. Wû *Kh*ăng understands it of 'any man,' i.e. any one in the exercise of government;—which is possible. What is peculiar to my version is the pregnant meaning given to 有知, common enough in the mouth of Confucius. I have adopted it here because of a passage in Liû Hsiang's Shwo-wăn (XX, 13 b), where Lâo-ȝze is made to say 'Excessive is the difficulty of practising the Tâo at the present time,' adding that the princes of his age would not receive it from him. On the 'Great Tâo,' see chapters 25, 34, et al. From the twentieth book of Han Fei (12 b and 13 a) I conclude that he had the whole of this chapter in his copy of our *K*ing, but he broke it up, after his fashion, into fragmentary utterances, confused and confounding. He gives also some remarkable various readings, one of which (竽, instead of Ho-shang Kung and Wang Pî's 夸, character 48) is now generally adopted. The passage is quoted in the Khang-hsî dictionary under 竽 with this reading.

54. 1. What (Tâo's) skilful planter plants
Can never be uptorn;
What his skilful arms enfold,
From him can ne'er be borne.
Sons shall bring in lengthening line,
Sacrifices to his shrine.

2. Tâo when nursed within one's self,
His vigour will make true;

And where the family it rules
  What riches will accrue!
The neighbourhood where it prevails
  In thriving will abound;
And when 'tis seen throughout the state,
  Good fortune will be found.
Employ it the kingdom o'er,
  And men thrive all around.

3. In this way the effect will be seen in the person, by the observation of different cases; in the family; in the neighbourhood; in the state; and in the kingdom.

4. How do I know that this effect is sure to hold thus all under the sky? By this (method of observation).

修觀, 'The Cultivation (of the Tâo), and the Observation (of its Effects).' The sentiment of the first paragraph is found in the twenty-seventh and other previous chapters,—that the noiseless and imperceptible acting of the Tâo is irresistible in its influence; and this runs through to the end of the chapter with the additional appeal to the influence of its effects. The introduction of the subject of sacrifices, a religious rite, though not presented to the Highest Object, will strike the reader as peculiar in our *K*ing.

The Teh mentioned five times in par. 2 is the 'virtue' of the Tâo embodied in the individual, and extending from him in all the spheres of his occupation, and is explained differently by Han Fei according to its application; and his example I have to some extent followed.

The force of pars. 3 and 4 is well given by Ho-shang Kung. On the first clause he says, 'Take the person of one who cultivates the Tâo, and compare it with that of one who does not cultivate it;—which is in a state of decay? and which is in a state of preservation?'

道德經

55. 1. He who has in himself abundantly the attributes (of the Tâo) is like an infant. Poisonous insects will not sting him; fierce beasts will not seize him; birds of prey will not strike him.

2. (The infant's) bones are weak and its sinews soft, but yet its grasp is firm. It knows not yet the union of male and female, and yet its virile member may be excited;—showing the perfection of its physical essence. All day long it will cry without its throat becoming hoarse;—showing the harmony (in its constitution).

3. To him by whom this harmony is known,
(The secret of) the unchanging (Tâo) is shown,
And in the knowledge wisdom finds its throne.
All life-increasing arts to evil turn;
Where the mind makes the vital breath to burn,
(False) is the strength, (and o'er it we should mourn.)

4. When things have become strong, they (then) become old, which may be said to be contrary to the Tâo. Whatever is contrary to the Tâo soon ends.

玄符, 'The Mysterious Charm;' meaning, apparently, the entire passivity of the Tâo.

With pars. 1 and 2, compare what is said about the infant in chapters 10 and 20, and about the immunity from dangers such as here described of the disciple of the Tâo in ch. 50. My 'evil' in the second triplet of par. 3 has been translated by 'felicity;' but a reference to the Khang-hsî dictionary will show that the meaning which I give to 祥 is well authorised. It is the only meaning allowable here. The third and fourth 曰 in this par. appear in Ho-shang Kung's text as 日, and he comments on the clauses accordingingly; but 日 is now the received reading. Some light is thrown on this paragraph and the next by an apocryphal conversation attributed to Lâo-ȝze in Liû Hsiang's Shwo-wăn, X, 4 a.

56. 1. He who knows (the Tâo) does not (care to) speak (about it); he who is (ever ready to) speak about it does not know it.

2. He (who knows it) will keep his mouth shut and close the portals (of his nostrils). He will blunt his sharp points and unravel the complications of things; he will attemper his brightness, and bring himself into agreement with the obscurity (of others). This is called 'the Mysterious Agreement.'

3. (Such an one) cannot be treated familiarly or distantly; he is beyond all consideration of profit or injury; of nobility or meanness:—he is the noblest man under heaven.

玄德, 'The Mysterious Excellence.' The chapter gives us a picture of the man of Tâo, humble and retiring, oblivious of himself and of other men, the noblest man under heaven.

Par. 1 is found in *K*wang-ȝze (XIII, 20 b), not expressly mentioned, as taken from Lâo-ȝze, but at the end of a string of sentiments, ascribed to 'the Master,' some of them, like the two clauses here, no doubt belonging to him, and the others, probably *K*wang-ȝze's own.

Par. 2 is all found in chapters 4 and 52, excepting the short clause in the conclusion.

57. 1. A state may be ruled by (measures of) correction; weapons of war may be used with crafty dexterity; (but) the kingdom is made one's own (only) by freedom from action and purpose.

2. How do I know that it is so? By these

facts:—In the kingdom the multiplication of prohibitive enactments increases the poverty of the people; the more implements to add to their profit that the people have, the greater disorder is there in the state and clan; the more acts of crafty dexterity that men possess, the more do strange contrivances appear; the more display there is of legislation, the more thieves and robbers there are.

3. Therefore a sage has said, 'I will do nothing (of purpose), and the people will be transformed of themselves; I will be fond of keeping still, and the people will of themselves become correct. I will take no trouble about it, and the people will of themselves become rich; I will manifest no ambition, and the people will of themselves attain to the primitive simplicity.'

淳風, 'The Genuine Influence.' The chapter shows how government by the Tâo is alone effective, and of universal application; contrasting it with the failure of other methods.

After the 'weapons of war' in par. 1, one is tempted to take 'the sharp implements' in par. 2 as such weapons, but the meaning which I finally adopted, especially after studying chapters 36 and 80, seems more consonant with Lâo-ʒze's scheme of thought. In the last member of the same par., Ho-shang Kung has the strange reading of 法物, and uses it in his commentary; but the better text of 法令 is found both in Hwâi-nan and Sze-mâ *Kh*ien, and in Wang Pî.

We do not know if the writer were quoting any particular sage in par. 3, or referring generally to the sages of the past;—men like the 'sentence-makers' of ch. 41.

58. 1. The government that seems the most unwise,
Oft goodness to the people best supplies;

That which is meddling, touching everything,
Will work but ill, and disappointment bring.

Misery!—happiness is to be found by its side! Happiness!—misery lurks beneath it! Who knows what either will come to in the end?

2. Shall we then dispense with correction? The (method of) correction shall by a turn become distortion, and the good in it shall by a turn become evil. The delusion of the people (on this point) has indeed subsisted for a long time.

3. Therefore the sage is (like) a square which cuts no one (with its angles); (like) a corner which injures no one (with its sharpness). He is straightforward, but allows himself no license; he is bright, but does not dazzle.

順化, 'Transformation according to Circumstances;' but this title does not throw light on the meaning of the chapter; nor are we helped to an understanding of it by Han Fei, with his additions and comments (XI, 3 b, 4 b), nor by Hwâi-nan with his illustrations (XII, 21 a, b). The difficulty of it is increased by its being separated from the preceding chapter of which it is really the sequel. It contrasts still further government by the Tâo, with that by the method of correction. The sage is the same in both chapters, his character and government both marked by the opposites or contraries which distinguish the procedure of the Tâo, as stated in ch. 40.

59. 1. For regulating the human (in our constitution) and rendering the (proper) service to the heavenly, there is nothing like moderation.

2. It is only by this moderation that there is effected an early return (to man's normal state). That early return is what I call the repeated accumulation of the attributes (of the Tâo). With that

repeated accumulation of those attributes, there comes the subjugation (of every obstacle to such return). Of this subjugation we know not what shall be the limit; and when one knows not what the limit shall be, he may be the ruler of a state.

3. He who possesses the mother of the state may continue long. His case is like that (of the plant) of which we say that its roots are deep and its flower stalks firm:—this is the way to secure that its enduring life shall long be seen.

守道, 'Guarding the Tâo.' The chapter shows how it is the guarding of the Tâo that ensures a continuance of long life, with vigour and success. The abuse of it and other passages in our *K*ing helped on, I must believe, the later Tâoist dreams about the elixir vitae and life-preserving pills. The whole of it, with one or two various readings, is found in Han Fei (VI, 4 b–6 a), who speaks twice in his comments of 'The Book.'

Par. 1 has been translated, 'In governing men and in serving Heaven, there is nothing like moderation.' But by 'Heaven' there is not intended 'the blue sky' above us, nor any personal Power above it, but the Tâo embodied in our constitution, the Heavenly element in our nature. The 'moderation' is the opposite of what we call 'living fast,' 'burning the candle at both ends.'

In par. 2 I must read 復, instead of the more common 服. I find it in Lû Teh-ming, and that it is not a misprint in him appears from his subjoining that it is pronounced like 服. Its meaning is the same as in 復歸其明 in ch. 52, par. 5. Teh is not 'virtue' in our common meaning of the term, but 'the attributes of the Tâo,' as almost always with Lâo-ȝze.

In par. 3 'the mother of the state' is the Tâo as in ch. 1, and especially in ch. 52, par. 1.

60. 1. Governing a great state is like cooking small fish.

2. Let the kingdom be governed according to the Tâo, and the manes of the departed will not manifest their spiritual energy. It is not that those manes have not that spiritual energy, but it will not be employed to hurt men. It is not that it could not hurt men, but neither does the ruling sage hurt them.

3. When these two do not injuriously affect each other, their good influences converge in the virtue (of the Tâo).

居位, 'Occupying the Throne;' occupying it, that is, according to the Tâo, noiselessly and purposelessly, so that the people enjoy their lives, free from all molestation seen and unseen.

Par. 1. That is, in the most quiet and easy manner. The whole of the chapter is given and commented on by Han Fei (VI, 6a-7b); but very unsatisfactorily.

The more one thinks and reads about the rest of the chapter, the more does he agree with the words of Julien:— 'It presents the frequent recurrence of the same characters, and appears as insignificant as it is unintelligible, if we give to the Chinese characters their ordinary meaning.'—The reader will observe that we have here the second mention of spirits (the manes; Chalmers, 'the ghosts;' Julien, les démons). See ch. 39.

Whatever Lâo-ȝze meant to teach in par. 2, he laid in it a foundation for the superstition of the later and present Tâoism about the spirits of the dead;—such as appeared a few years ago in the 'tail-cutting' scare.

61. 1. What makes a great state is its being (like) a low-lying, down-flowing (stream);—it becomes the centre to which tend (all the small states) under heaven.

2. (To illustrate from) the case of all females:—the female always overcomes the male by her stillness. Stillness may be considered (a sort of) abasement.

3. Thus it is that a great state, by condescending to small states, gains them for itself; and that small states, by abasing themselves to a great state, win it over to them. In the one case the abasement leads to gaining adherents, in the other case to procuring favour.

4. The great state only wishes to unite men together and nourish them; a small state only wishes to be received by, and to serve, the other. Each gets what it desires, but the great state must learn to abase itself.

謙德, 'The Attribute of Humility;'—a favourite theme with Lâo-ʒze; and the illustration of it from the low-lying stream to which smaller streams flow is also a favourite subject with him. The language can hardly but recall the words of a greater than Lâo-ʒze:—'He that humbleth himself shall be exalted.'

62. 1. Tâo has of all things the most honoured
place.
No treasures give good men so rich a grace;
Bad men it guards, and doth their ill efface.

2. (Its) admirable words can purchase honour; (its) admirable deeds can raise their performer above others. Even men who are not good are not abandoned by it.

3. Therefore when the sovereign occupies his place as the Son of Heaven, and he has appointed his three ducal ministers, though (a prince) were to send in a round symbol-of-rank large enough to fill both the hands, and that as the precursor of the team of horses (in the court-yard), such an offering would not be equal to (a lesson of) this Tâo, which one might present on his knees.

4. Why was it that the ancients prized this Tâo

so much? Was it not because it could be got by seeking for it, and the guilty could escape (from the stain of their guilt) by it? This is the reason why all under heaven consider it the most valuable thing.

爲道, 'Practising the Tâo.' 貴道, 'The value set on the Tâo,' would have been a more appropriate title. The chapter sets forth that value in various manifestations of it.

Par. 1. For the meaning of 奥, see Confucian Analects, III, ch. 13.

Par. 2. I am obliged to adopt the reading of the first sentence of this paragraph given by Hwâi-nan, 美言可以市尊, 美行可以加人;—see especially his quotation of it in XVIII, 10 a, as from a superior man, I have not found his reading anywhere else.

Par. 3 is not easily translated, or explained. See the rules on presenting offerings at the court of a ruler or the king, in vol. xxvii of the 'Sacred Books of the East,' p. 84, note 3, and also a narrative in the 3o *K*wan under the thirty-third year of duke Hsî.

63. 1. (It is the way of the Tâo) to act without (thinking of) acting; to conduct affairs without (feeling the) trouble of them; to taste without discerning any flavour; to consider what is small as great, and a few as many; and to recompense injury with kindness.

2. (The master of it) anticipates things that are difficult while they are easy, and does things that would become great while they are small. All difficult things in the world are sure to arise from a previous state in which they were easy, and all great things from one in which they were small. Therefore the sage, while he never does what is great, is able on that account to accomplish the greatest things.

3. He who lightly promises is sure to keep but little faith; he who is continually thinking things easy is sure to find them difficult. Therefore the sage sees difficulty even in what seems easy, and so never has any difficulties.

思始, 'Thinking in the Beginning.' The former of these two characters is commonly misprinted 恩, and this has led Chalmers to mistranslate them by 'The Beginning of Grace.' The chapter sets forth the passionless method of the Tâo, and how the sage accordingly accomplishes his objects easily by forestalling in his measures all difficulties. In par. 1 the clauses are indicative, and not imperative, and therefore we have to supplement the text in translating in some such way, as I have done. They give us a cluster of aphorisms illustrating the procedure of the Tâo 'by contraries,' and conclude with one, which is the chief glory of Lâo-ȝze's teaching, though I must think that its value is somewhat diminished by the method in which he reaches it. It has not the prominence in the later teaching of Tâoist writers which we should expect, nor is it found (so far as I know) in *K*wang-ȝze, Han Fei, or Hwâi-nan. It is quoted, however, twice by Liû Hsiang;—see my note on par. 2 of ch. 49.

It follows from the whole chapter that the Tâoistic 'doing nothing' was not an absolute quiescence and inaction, but had a method in it.

64. 1. That which is at rest is easily kept hold of; before a thing has given indications of its presence, it is easy to take measures against it; that which is brittle is easily broken; that which is very small is easily dispersed. Action should be taken before a thing has made its appearance; order should be secured before disorder has begun.

2. The tree which fills the arms grew from the tiniest sprout; the tower of nine storeys rose from a

(small) heap of earth; the journey of a thousand lî commenced with a single step.

3. He who acts (with an ulterior purpose) does harm; he who takes hold of a thing (in the same way) loses his hold. The sage does not act (so), and therefore does no harm; he does not lay hold (so), and therefore does not lose his hold. (But) people in their conduct of affairs are constantly ruining them when they are on the eve of success. If they were careful at the end, as (they should be) at the beginning, they would not so ruin them.

4. Therefore the sage desires what (other men) do not desire, and does not prize things difficult to get; he learns what (other men) do not learn, and turns back to what the multitude of men have passed by. Thus he helps the natural development of all things, and does not dare to act (with an ulterior purpose of his own).

守微, 'Guarding the Minute.' The chapter is a continuation and enlargement of the last. Wû *Kh*ăng, indeed, unites the two, blending them together with some ingenious transpositions and omissions, which it is not necessary to discuss. Compare the first part of par. 3 with the last part of par. 1, ch. 29.

65. 1. The ancients who showed their skill in practising the Tâo did so, not to enlighten the people, but rather to make them simple and ignorant.

2. The difficulty in governing the people arises from their having much knowledge. He who (tries to) govern a state by his wisdom is a scourge to it; while he who does not (try to) do so is a blessing.

3. He who knows these two things finds in them also his model and rule. Ability to know this

model and rule constitutes what we call the mysterious excellence (of a governor). Deep and far-reaching is such mysterious excellence, showing indeed its possessor as opposite to others, but leading them to a great conformity to him.

淳德, 'Pure, unmixed Excellence.' The chapter shows the powerful and beneficent influence of the Tâo in government, in contrast with the applications and contrivances of human wisdom. Compare ch. 19. My 'simple and ignorant' is taken from Julien. More literally the translation would be 'to make them stupid.' My 'scourge' in par. 2 is also after Julien's 'fléau.'

66. 1. That whereby the rivers and seas are able to receive the homage and tribute of all the valley streams, is their skill in being lower than they;—it is thus that they are the kings of them all. So it is that the sage (ruler), wishing to be above men, puts himself by his words below them, and, wishing to be before them, places his person behind them.

2. In this way though he has his place above them, men do not feel his weight, nor though he has his place before them, do they feel it an injury to them.

3. Therefore all in the world delight to exalt him and do not weary of him. Because he does not strive, no one finds it possible to strive with him.

後已, 'Putting one's self Last.' The subject is the power of the Tâo, by its display of humility in attracting men. The subject and the way in which it is illustrated are frequent themes in the *K*ing. See chapters 8, 22, 39, 42, 61, et al.

The last sentence of par. 3 is found also in ch. 22. There seem to be no quotations from the chapter in Han Fei or Hwâi-nan; but Wû *Kh*ăng quotes passages from Tung

*K*ung-shû (of the second century B.C.), and Yang Hsiung (B.C. 53–A.D. 18), which seem to show that the phraseology of it was familiar to them. The former says:—'When one places himself in his qualities below others, his person is above them; when he places them behind those of others, his person is before them;' the other, 'Men exalt him who humbles himself below them; and give the precedence to him who puts himself behind them.'

67. 1. All the world says that, while my Tâo is great, it yet appears to be inferior (to other systems of teaching). Now it is just its greatness that makes it seem to be inferior. If it were like any other (system), for long would its smallness have been known!

2. But I have three precious things which I prize and hold fast. The first is gentleness; the second is economy; and the third is shrinking from taking precedence of others.

3. With that gentleness I can be bold; with that economy I can be liberal; shrinking from taking precedence of others, I can become a vessel of the highest honour. Now-a-days they give up gentleness and are all for being bold; economy, and are all for being liberal; the hindmost place, and seek only to be foremost;—(of all which the end is) death.

4. Gentleness is sure to be victorious even in battle, and firmly to maintain its ground. Heaven will save its possessor, by his (very) gentleness protecting him.

三寶, 'The Three Precious Things.' This title is taken from par. 2, and suggests to us how the early framer of these titles intended to express by them the subject-matter of their several chapters. The three things are the three distinguishing qualities of the possessor of the Tâo, the three great moral qualities appearing in its followers, the qualities, we may venture to say, of the Tâo itself. The same phrase is now the common designation of Buddhism in China,—the Tri-ratna or Ratna-traya, 'the Precious Buddha,' 'the Precious Law,' and 'the Precious Priesthood (or rather Monkhood) or Church;' appearing also in the 'Tri-*s*ara*n*a,' or 'formula of the Three Refuges,' what Dr. Eitel calls 'the most primitive formula fidei of the early Buddhists, introduced before Southern and Northern Buddhism separated.' I will not introduce the question of whether Buddhism borrowed this designation from Tâoism, after its entrance into China. It is in Buddhism the formula of a peculiar Church or Religion; in Tâoism a rule for the character, or the conduct which the Tâo demands from all men. 'My Tâo' in par. 1 is the reading of Wang Pî; Ho-shang Kung's text is simply 我. Wang Pî's reading is now generally adopted.

The concluding sentiment of the chapter is equivalent to the saying of Mencius (VII, ii, IV, 2), 'If the ruler of a state love benevolence, he will have no enemy under heaven.' 'Heaven' is equivalent to 'the Tâo,' the course of events,—Providence, as we should say.

68. He who in (Tâo's) wars has skill
Assumes no martial port;
He who fights with most good will
To rage makes no resort.
He who vanquishes yet still
Keeps from his foes apart;
He whose hests men most fulfil
Yet humbly plies his art.

Thus we say, 'He ne'er contends,
And therein is his might.'
Thus we say, 'Men's wills he bends,
That they with him unite.'
Thus we say, 'Like Heaven's his ends,
No sage of old more bright.'

配天, 'Matching Heaven.' The chapter describes the work of the practiser of the Tâo as accomplished like that of Heaven, without striving or crying. He appears under the figure of a mailed warrior (士) of the ancient chariot. The chapter is a sequel of the preceding, and is joined on to it by Wû *Kh*ăng, as is also the next.

69. 1. A master of the art of war has said, 'I do not dare to be the host (to commence the war); I prefer to be the guest (to act on the defensive). I do not dare to advance an inch; I prefer to retire a foot.' This is called marshalling the ranks where there are no ranks; baring the arms (to fight) where there are no arms to bare; grasping the weapon where there is no weapon to grasp; advancing against the enemy where there is no enemy.

2. There is no calamity greater than lightly engaging in war. To do that is near losing (the gentleness) which is so precious. Thus it is that when opposing weapons are (actually) crossed, he who deplores (the situation) conquers.

玄用, 'The Use of the Mysterious (Tâo).' Such seems to be the meaning of the title. The chapter teaches that, if war were carried on, or rather avoided, according to the Tâo, the result would be success. Lâo-ʒze's own statements appear as so many paradoxes. They are examples of the procedure of the Tâo by 'contraries,' or opposites.

We do not know who the master of the military art referred to was. Perhaps the author only adopted the style of quotation to express his own sentiments.

70. 1. My words are very easy to know, and very easy to practise; but there is no one in the world who is able to know and able to practise them.

2. There is an originating and all-comprehending

(principle) in my words, and an authoritative law for the things (which I enforce). It is because they do not know these, that men do not know me.

3. They who know me are few, and I am on that account (the more) to be prized. It is thus that the sage wears (a poor garb of) hair cloth, while he carries his (signet of) jade in his bosom.

知難, 'The Difficulty of being (rightly) Known.' The Tâo comprehends and rules all Lâo-ʒze's teaching, as the members of a clan were all in the loins of their first father (宗), and continue to look up to him; and the people of a state are all under the direction of their ruler; yet the philosopher had to complain of not being known. Lâo-ʒze's principle and rule or ruler was the Tâo. His utterance here is very important. Compare the words of Confucius in the Analects, XIV, ch. 37, et al.

Par. 2 is twice quoted by Hwâi-nan, though his text is not quite the same in both cases.

71. 1. To know and yet (think) we do not know is the highest (attainment); not to know (and yet think) we do know is a disease.

2. It is simply by being pained at (the thought of) having this disease that we are preserved from it. The sage has not the disease. He knows the pain that would be inseparable from it, and therefore he does not have it.

知病, 'The Disease of Knowing.' Here, again, we have the Tâo working 'by contraries,'—in the matter of knowledge. Compare par. 1 with Confucius's account of what knowledge is in the Analects, II, ch. 17. The par. 1 is found in one place in Hwâi-nan, lengthened out by the addition of particles; but the variation is unimportant. In another place, however, he seems to have had the correct text before him.

Par. 2 is in Han Fei also lengthened out, but with an

important variation (不 病 for 病 病), and I cannot construe his text. His 不 is probably a transcriber's error.

72. 1. When the people do not fear what they ought to fear, that which is their great dread will come on them.

2. Let them not thoughtlessly indulge themselves in their ordinary life; let them not act as if weary of what that life depends on.

3. It is by avoiding such indulgence that such weariness does not arise.

4. Therefore the sage knows (these things) of himself, but does not parade (his knowledge); loves, but does not (appear to set a) value on, himself. And thus he puts the latter alternative away and makes choice of the former.

愛已, 'Loving one's Self.' This title is taken from the expression in par. 4; and the object of the chapter seems to be to show how such loving should be manifested, and to enforce the lesson by the example of the 'sage,' the true master of the Tâo.

In par. 1 'the great dread' is death, and the things which ought to be feared and may be feared, are the indulgences of the appetites and passions, which, if not eschewed, tend to shorten life and accelerate the approach of death.

Pars. 2 and 3 are supplementary to 1. For 狹, the second character of Ho-shang Kung's text in par. 2, Wang Pî reads 狎, which has the same name as the other; and according to the Khang-hsî dictionary, the two characters are interchangeable. I have also followed Wû *Kh*ăng in adopting 狎 for the former of the two 厭 in par. 3. Wû adopted this reading from a commentator Liû of Lü-ling. It gives a good meaning, and is supported by the structure of other sentences made on similar lines.

In par. 4 'the sage' must be 'the ruler who is a sage,' a master of the Tâo, 'the king' of ch. 25. He 'loves himself,' i.e. his life, and takes the right measures to prolong his life, but without any demonstration that he is doing so.

The above is, I conceive, the correct explanation of the chapter; but as to the Chinese critics and foreign translators of it, it may be said, 'Quot homines, tot sententiae.' In illustration of this I venture to subjoin what is found on it in the old version of the Jesuit missionaries, which has not been previously printed:—

Prima explicatio juxta interpretes.

1. Populus, ubi jam principis iram non timet, nihil non audet ut jugum excutiat, resque communis ad extremum discrimen adducitur.

2. Ambitio principis non faciat terram angustiorem, et vectigalium magnitudine alendo populo insufficientem; numquam populus patriae pertaesus alias terras quaeret.

3. Vitae si non taedet, neque patrii soli taedebit.

4. Quare sanctus sibi semper attentus potentiam suam non ostentat.

5. Quia vere se amat, non se pretiosum facit; vel quia sibi recte consulit non se talem aestimat cujus felicitati et honori infelices populi unice servire debeant, immo potius eum se reputat qui populorum felicitati totum se debeat impendere.

6. Ergo illud resecat, istud amplectitur.

Alia explicatio.

1. Populus si non ita timet principis majestatem, sed facile ad eum accedit, majestas non minuitur, immo ad summum pervenit.

2. Vectigalibus terra si non opprimitur, suâ quisque contentus alias terras non quaeret, si se non vexari populus experitur.

3. Vitae si non taedet, nec patrii soli taedebit.

4. Quare sanctus majestatis fastum non affectat, immo similem se caeteris ostendit.

5. Sibi recte consulens, populorum amans, non se pretiosum et inaccessibilem facit.

6. Quidquid ergo timorem incutere potest, hoc evitat; quod amorem conciliat et benignitatem, se demonstrat hoc eligi et ultro amplectitur.

73. 1. He whose boldness appears in his daring (to do wrong, in defiance of the laws) is put to death; he whose boldness appears in his not daring (to do so) lives on. Of these two cases the one appears to be advantageous, and the other to be injurious. But

When Heaven's anger smites a man,
Who the cause shall truly scan?

On this account the sage feels a difficulty (as to what to do in the former case).

2. It is the way of Heaven not to strive, and yet it skilfully overcomes; not to speak, and yet it is skilful in (obtaining) a reply; does not call, and yet men come to it of themselves. Its demonstrations are quiet, and yet its plans are skilful and effective. The meshes of the net of Heaven are large; far apart, but letting nothing escape.

任爲, 'Allowing Men to take their Course.' The chapter teaches that rulers should not be hasty to punish, especially by the infliction of death. Though they may seem to err in leniency, yet Heaven does not allow offenders to escape.

While Heaven hates the ill-doer, yet we must not always conclude from Its judgments that every one who suffers from them is an ill-doer; and the two lines which rhyme, and illustrate this point, are equivalent to the sentiment in our Old Book, 'Clouds and darkness are round about Him.' They are ascribed to Lâo-ȝze by Lieh-ȝze (VI, 7 a); but, it has been said, that they are quoted by him 'in an entirely different connexion.' But the same text in two different sermons may be said to be in different connexions. In Lieh-ȝze and our *K*ing the lines have the same meaning, and substantially the same application. Indeed *K*ang *K*an, of our fourth century, the commentator of Lieh-ȝze, quotes the comment of Wang Pî on this passage, condensing it into, 'Who can know the mind of Heaven? Only the sage can do so.'

74. 1. The people do not fear death; to what purpose is it to (try to) frighten them with death? If the people were always in awe of death, and I could always seize those who do wrong, and put them to death, who would dare to do wrong?

2. There is always One who presides over the infliction of death. He who would inflict death in the room of him who so presides over it may be described as hewing wood instead of a great carpenter. Seldom is it that he who undertakes the hewing, instead of the great carpenter, does not cut his own hands!

制惑, 'Restraining Delusion.' The chapter sets forth the inefficiency of capital punishment, and warns rulers against the infliction of it. Who is it that superintends the infliction of death? The answer of Ho-shang Kung is very clear:—'It is Heaven, which, dwelling on high and ruling all beneath, takes note of the transgressions of men.' There is a slight variation in the readings of the second sentence of par. 2 in the texts of Ho-shang Kung and Wang Pî, and the reading adopted by Ȝiâo Hung differs a little from them both; but the meaning is the same in them all.

This chapter and the next are rightly joined on to the preceding by Wû *Kh*ăng.

75. 1. The people suffer from famine because of the multitude of taxes consumed by their superiors. It is through this that they suffer famine.

2. The people are difficult to govern because of the (excessive) agency of their superiors (in governing them). It is through this that they are difficult to govern.

3. The people make light of dying because of the greatness of their labours in seeking for the means of living. It is this which makes them think light of dying. Thus it is that to leave the subject of living altogether out of view is better than to set a high value on it.

貪損, 'How Greediness Injures.' The want of the nothing-doing Tâo leads to the multiplication of exactions by the government, and to the misery of the people, so as to make them think lightly of death. The chapter is a warning for both rulers and people.

It is not easy to determine whether rulers, or people, or both, are intended in the concluding sentence of par. 2.

76. 1. Man at his birth is supple and weak; at his death, firm and strong. (So it is with) all things. Trees and plants, in their early growth, are soft and brittle; at their death, dry and withered.

2. Thus it is that firmness and strength are the concomitants of death; softness and weakness, the concomitants of life.

3. Hence he who (relies on) the strength of his forces does not conquer; and a tree which is strong will fill the out-stretched arms, (and thereby invites the feller.)

4. Therefore the place of what is firm and strong is below, and that of what is soft and weak is above.

戒强, 'A Warning against (trusting in) Strength.' To trust in one's force is contrary to the Tâo, whose strength is more in weakness and humility.

In par. 1 the two characters which I have rendered by

'(so it is with) all things' are found in the texts of both Ho-shang Kung and Wang Pî, but Wû *Kh*ăng and 3iâo Hung both reject them. I should also have neglected them, but they are also found in Liû Hsiang's Shwo Wăn (X, 4a), with all the rest of pars. 1 and 2, as from Lâo-ȝze. They are an anakoluthon, such as is elsewhere found in our *K*ing; e.g. 天下之牝 in ch. 21, par. 2.

The 'above' and 'below' in par. 4 seem to be merely a play on the words, as capable of meaning 'more and less honourable.'

77. 1. May not the Way (or Tâo) of Heaven be compared to the (method of) bending a bow? The (part of the bow) which was high is brought low, and what was low is raised up. (So Heaven) diminishes where there is superabundance, and supplements where there is deficiency.

2. It is the Way of Heaven to diminish superabundance, and to supplement deficiency. It is not so with the way of man. He takes away from those who have not enough to add to his own superabundance.

3. Who can take his own superabundance and therewith serve all under heaven? Only he who is in possession of the Tâo!

4. Therefore the (ruling) sage acts without claiming the results as his; he achieves his merit and does not rest (arrogantly) in it:—he does not wish to display his superiority.

天道, 'The Way of Heaven;' but the chapter contrasts that way, unselfish and magnanimous, with the way of man, selfish and contracted, and illustrates the point by the method of stringing a bow. This must be seen as it is done in China fully to understand the illustration. I have known great athletes in this country tasked to the utmost of their strength to adjust and bend a large Chinese bow from Peking.

The 'sage' of par. 4 is the 'King' of ch. 25. Compare what is said of him with ch. 2, par. 4, et al.

78. 1. There is nothing in the world more soft and weak than water, and yet for attacking things that are firm and strong there is nothing that can take precedence of it;—for there is nothing (so effectual) for which it can be changed.

2. Every one in the world knows that the soft overcomes the hard, and the weak the strong, but no one is able to carry it out in practice.

3. Therefore a sage has said,

'He who accepts his state's reproach,
Is hailed therefore its altars' lord;
To him who bears men's direful woes
They all the name of King accord.'

4. Words that are strictly true seem to be paradoxical.

任信, 'Things to be Believed.' It is difficult to give a short and appropriate translation of this title. The chapter shows how the most unlikely results follow from action according to the Tâo.

Par. 1. Water was Lâo-ȝze's favourite emblem of the Tâo. Compare chapters 8, 66, et al.

Par. 2. Compare ch. 36, par. 2.

Par. 3. Of course we do not know who the sage was from whom Lâo-ȝze got the lines of this paragraph. They may suggest to some readers the lines of Burns, as they have done to me:—

'The honest man, though e'er so poor,
Is king o' men for a' that.'

But the Tâoist of Lâo-ȝze is a higher ideal than Burns's honest man.

Par. 4 is separated from this chapter, and made to begin the next by Wû *Kh*ăng.

79. 1. When a reconciliation is effected (between two parties) after a great animosity, there is sure to be a grudge remaining (in the mind of the one who was wrong). And how can this be beneficial (to the other)?

2. Therefore (to guard against this), the sage keeps the left-hand portion of the record of the engagement, and does not insist on the (speedy) fulfilment of it by the other party. (So), he who has the attributes (of the Tâo) regards (only) the conditions of the engagement, while he who has not those attributes regards only the conditions favourable to himself.

3. In the Way of Heaven, there is no partiality of love; it is always on the side of the good man.

任契, 'Adherence to Bond or Covenant.' The chapter shows, but by no means clearly, how he who holds fast to the Tâo will be better off in the end than he who will rather try to secure his own interests.

Par. 1 presents us with a case which the statements of the chapter are intended to meet:—two disputants, one good, and the other bad; the latter, though apparently reconciled, still retaining a grudge, and ready to wreak his dissatisfaction, when he has an opportunity. The 爲 ='for,' 'for the good of.'

Par. 2 is intended to solve the question. The terms of a contract or agreement were inscribed on a slip of wood, which was then divided into two; each party having one half of it. At the settlement, if the halves perfectly fitted to each other, it was carried through. The one who had the right in the dispute has his part of the agreement, but does not insist on it, and is forbearing; the other insists on the conditions being even now altered in his favour. The characters by which this last case is expressed, are very enigmatical, having reference to the satisfaction of the government dues of Lâo-ȝze's time,—a subject into which it would take much space to go.

Par. 3 decides the question by the action of Heaven, which is only another name for the course of the Tâo.

80. 1. In a little state with a small population, I would so order it, that, though there were individuals with the abilities of ten or a hundred men, there should be no employment of them; I would make the people, while looking on death as a grievous thing, yet not remove elsewhere (to avoid it).

2. Though they had boats and carriages, they should have no occasion to ride in them; though they had buff coats and sharp weapons, they should have no occasion to don or use them.

3. I would make the people return to the use of knotted cords (instead of the written characters).

4. They should think their (coarse) food sweet; their (plain) clothes beautiful; their (poor) dwellings places of rest; and their common (simple) ways sources of enjoyment.

5. There should be a neighbouring state within sight, and the voices of the fowls and dogs should be heard all the way from it to us, but I would make the people to old age, even to death, not have any intercourse with it.

獨立, 'Standing Alone.' The chapter sets forth what Lâo-ȝze conceived the ancient government of simplicity was, and what he would have government in all time to be. He does not use the personal pronoun 'I' as the subject of the thrice-recurring 使, but it is most natural to suppose that he is himself that subject; and he modestly supposes himself in charge of a little state and a small population. The reader can judge for himself of the consummation that would be arrived at;—a people rude and uninstructed, using quippos, abstaining from war and all travelling, kept aloof from intercourse even with their neighbours, and without the appliances of what we call civilisation.

The text is nearly all found in Sze-mâ *Kh*ien and *K*wang-ȝze. The first member of par. 1, however, is very puzzling. The old Jesuit translators, Julien, Chalmers, and V. von Strauss, all differ in their views of it. Wû *Kh*ăng and ȝiâo Hung take what I have now rendered by 'abilities,' as meaning 'implements of agriculture,' but their view is based on a custom of the Han dynasty, which is not remote enough for the purpose, and on the suppression, after Wang Pî, of a 人 in Ho-shang Kung's text.

81. 1. Sincere words are not fine; fine words are not sincere. Those who are skilled (in the Tâo) do not dispute (about it); the disputatious are not skilled in it. Those who know (the Tâo) are not extensively learned; the extensively learned do not know it.

2. The sage does not accumulate (for himself). The more that he expends for others, the more does he possess of his own; the more that he gives to others, the more does he have himself.

3. With all the sharpness of the Way of Heaven, it injures not; with all the doing in the way of the sage he does not strive.

顯質, 'The Manifestation of Simplicity.' The chapter shows how quietly and effectively the Tâo proceeds, and by contraries in a way that only the master of it can understand. The author, says Wû *Kh*ăng, 'sums up in this the subject-matter of the two Parts of his Treatise, showing that in all its five thousand characters, there is nothing beyond what is here said.'

Par. 2 suggests to Dr. Chalmers the well-known lines of Bunyan as an analogue of it:—

'A man there was, though some did count him mad,
The more he gave away, the more he had.'

Wû *Kh*ăng brings together two sentences from *K*wang-ȝze (XXXIII, 21 b, 22 a), written evidently with the characters of this text in mind, which, as from a Tâoist mint, are a still better analogue, and I venture to put them into rhyme:—

'Amassing but to him a sense of need betrays;
He hoards not, and thereby his affluence displays.'

I have paused long over the first pair of contraries in par. 3 (利 and 害). Those two characters primarily mean 'sharpness' and 'wounding by cutting;' they are also often used in the sense of 'being beneficial,' and 'being injurious;'—'contraries,' both of them. Which 'contrary' had Lâo-ȝze in mind? I must think the former, though differing in this from all previous translators. The Jesuit version is, 'Celestis Tâo natura ditat omnes, nemini nocet;' Julien's, 'Il est utile aux êtres, et ne leur nuit point;' Chalmers's, 'Benefits and does not injure;' and V. von Strauss's, 'Des Himmels Weise ist wolthun und nicht beschädigen.'

莊子

THE

WRITINGS OF *K*WANG-ȜZE.

莊子

THE WRITINGS OF *K*WANG-ȜZE.

INTRODUCTION.

Brief Notices of the different Books.

Book I. Hsiâo-yâo Yû.

The three characters which form the title of this Book have all of them the ideagram 辵 (*K*o), which gives the idea, as the Shwo Wăn explains it, of 'now walking, now halting.' We might render the title by 'Sauntering or Rambling at Ease;' but it is the untroubled enjoyment of the mind which the author has in view. And this enjoyment is secured by the Tâo, though that character does not once occur in the Book. *K*wang-ȝze illustrates his thesis first by the cases of creatures, the largest and the smallest, showing that however different they may be in size, they should not pass judgment on one another, but may equally find their happiness in the Tâo. From this he advances to men, and from the cases of Yung-ȝze and Lieh-ȝze proceeds to that of one who finds his enjoyment in himself, independent of every other being or instrumentality; and we have the three important definitions of the accomplished Tâoist, as 'the Perfect Man,' 'the Spirit-like Man,' and 'the Sagely Man.' Those definitions are then illustrated;—the third in Yâo and Hsü Yû, and the second in the conversation between *K*ien Wû and Lien Shû. The description given in this conversation of the spirit-like man is very startling, and contains statements that are true only of Him who is a 'Spirit,' 'the Blessed and only Potentate,' 'Who covereth Himself with light as with a garment, Who stretcheth out the heavens as a curtain,

Who layeth the beams of His chambers in the waters, Who maketh the clouds His chariot, Who walketh on the wings of the wind,' 'Who rideth on a cherub,' 'Who inhabiteth eternity.' The most imaginative and metaphorical expressions in the Tâo Teh *K*ing about the power of the possessor of the Tâo are tame, compared with the language of our author. I call attention to it here, as he often uses the same extravagant style. There follows an illustration of 'the Perfect Man,' which is comparatively feeble, and part of it, so far as I can see, inappropriate, though Lin Hsî-*k*ung says that all other interpretations of the sentences are ridiculous.

In the seventh and last paragraph we have two illustrations that nothing is really useless, if only used Tâoistically; 'to the same effect,' says 3iâo Hung, 'as Confucius in the Analects, XVII, ii.' They hang loosely, however, from what precedes.

An old view of the Book was that *K*wang-ȝze intended himself by the great phăng, 'which,' says Lû Shû-*k*ih, 'is wide of the mark.'

Book II. *Kh*î Wû Lun.

Mr. Balfour has translated this title by 'Essay on the Uniformity of All Things;' and, the subject of the Book being thus misconceived, his translation of it could not fail to be very incorrect. The Chinese critics, I may say without exception, construe the title as I have done. The second and third characters, Wû Lun, are taken together, and mean 'Discussions about Things,' equivalent to our 'Controversies.' They are under the government of the first character *Kh*î, used as a verb, with the signification of 'Harmonising,' or 'Adjusting.' Let me illustrate this by condensing a passage from the 'Supplementary Commentary of a Mr. *K*ang, a sub-secretary of the Imperial Chancery,' of the Ming dynasty (張學士補註). He says, 'What *K*wang-ȝze calls "Discussions about Things" has reference to the various branches of the numerous schools, each of which has its own views, conflicting with

莊子

the views of the others.' He goes on to show that if they would only adopt the method pointed out by *K*wang-ȝze, 'their controversies would be adjusted (物論齊),' now using the first *Kh*î in the passive voice.

This then was the theme of our author in this Book. It must be left for the reader to discover from the translation how he pursues it. I pointed out a peculiarity in the former Book, that though the idea of the Tâo underlies it all, the term itself is never allowed to appear. Not only does the same idea underlie this Book, but the name is frequently employed. The Tâo is the panacea for the evils of controversy, the solvent through the use of which the different views of men may be made to disappear.

That the Tâo is not a Personal name in the conception of *K*wang-ȝze is seen in several passages. We have not to go beyond the phenomena of nature to discover the reason of their being what they are; nor have we to go beyond the bigoted egoism and vaingloriousness of controversialists to find the explanation of their discussions, various as these are, and confounding like the sounds of the wind among the trees of a forest. To man, neither in nature nor in the sphere of knowledge, is there any other 'Heaven' but what belongs to his own mind. That is his only 'True Ruler.' If there be any other, we do not see His form, nor any traces of His acting. Things come about in their proper course. We cannot advance any proof of Creation. Whether we assume that there was something 'in the beginning' or nothing, we are equally landed in contradiction and absurdity. Let us stop at the limit of what we know, and not try to advance a step beyond it.

Towards the end of the Book our author's agnosticism seems to reach its farthest point. All human experience is spoken of as a dream or as 'illusion.' He who calls another a dreamer does not know that he is not dreaming himself. One and another commentator discover in such utterances something very like the Buddhist doctrine that all life is but so much illusion (象). This notion has its consummation in the story with which the Book concludes.

*K*wang-ʒze had dreamt that he was a butterfly. When he awoke, and was himself again, he did not know whether he, *K*wang *K*âu, had been dreaming that he was a butterfly, or was now a butterfly dreaming that it was *K*wang *K*âu. And yet he adds that there must be a difference between *K*âu and a butterfly, but he does not say what that difference is. But had he ever dreamt that he was a butterfly, so as to lose the consciousness of his personal identity as *K*wang *K*âu? I do not think so. One may, perhaps, lose that consciousness in the state of insanity; but the language of Young is not sufficiently guarded when he writes of

'Dreams, where thought, in fancy's maze, runs mad.'

When dreaming, our thoughts are not conditioned by the categories of time and space; but the conviction of our identity is never lost.

Book III. Yang Shang *K*û.

'The Lord of Life' is the Tâo. It is to this that we are indebted for the origin of life and for the preservation of it. Though not a Personal Being, it is here spoken of as if it were,—'the Lord of Life;' just as in the preceding Book it is made to appear as 'a True Governor,' and 'a True Ruler.' But how can we nourish the Tâo? The reply is, By avoiding all striving to do so; by a passionless, unstraining performance of what we have to do in our position in life; simply allowing the Tâo to guide and nourish us, without doing anything to please ourselves or to counteract the tendency of our being to decay and death.

Par. 1 exhibits the injury arising from not thus nourishing the life, and sets forth the rule we are to pursue.

Par. 2 illustrates the observance of the rule by the perfect skill with which the cook of the ruler Wăn-hui of Wei cut up the oxen for his employer without trouble to himself, or injury to his knife.

莊子

Par. 3 illustrates the result of a neglect of one of the cautions in par. 1 to a certain master of the Left, who had brought on himself dismemberment in the loss of one of his feet.

Par. 4 shows how even Lâo-ȝze had failed in nourishing 'the Lord of Life' by neglecting the other caution, and allowing in his good-doing an admixture of human feeling, which produced in his disciples a regard for him that was inconsistent with the nature of the Tâo, and made them wail for him excessively on his death. This is the most remarkable portion of the Book, and it is followed by a sentence which implies that the existence of man's spirit continues after death has taken place. His body is intended by the 'faggots' that are consumed by the fire. That fire represents the spirit which may be transferred elsewhere.

Some commentators dwell on the analogy between this and the Buddhistic transrotation of births; which latter teaching, however, they do not seem to understand. Others say that 'the nourishment of the Lord of Life' is simply acting as Yü did when he conveyed away the flooded waters 'by doing that which gave him no trouble;'—see Mencius, IV, ii, 26.

In *K*wang-ȝze there are various other stories of the same character as that about king Wăn-hui's cook,—e.g. XIX, 3 and XXII, 9. They are instances of the dexterity acquired by habit, and should hardly be pressed into the service of the doctrine of the Tâo.

Book IV. *Z*ăn *K*ien Shih.

A man has his place among other men in the world; he is a member, while he lives, of the body of humanity. And as he has his place in society, so also he has his special duties to discharge, according to his position, and his relation to others. Tâoist writers refer to this Book as a proof of the practical character of the writings of *K*wang-ȝze.

They are right to a certain extent in doing so; but the cases of relationship which are exhibited and prescribed for are of so peculiar a character, that the Book is of little value as a directory of human conduct and duty. In the first two paragraphs we have the case of Yen Hui, who wishes to go to Wei, and try to reform the character and government of its oppressive ruler; in the third and fourth, that of the duke of Sheh, who has been entrusted by the king of *Kh*û with a difficult mission to the court of *Kh*î, which is occasioning him much anxiety and apprehension; and in the fifth, that of a Yen Ho, who is about to undertake the office of teacher to the son of duke Ling of Wei, a young man with a very bad natural disposition. The other four paragraphs do not seem to come in naturally after these three cases, being occupied with two immense and wonderful trees, the case of a poor deformed cripple, and the lecture for the benefit of Confucius by 'the madman of *Kh*û.' In all these last paragraphs, the theme is the usefulness, to the party himself at least, of being of no use.

Confucius is the principal speaker in the first four paragraphs. In what he says to Yen Hui and the duke of Sheh there is much that is shrewd and good; but we prefer the practical style of his teachings, as related by his own disciples in the Confucian Analects. Possibly, it was the object of *K*wang-ʒze to exhibit his teaching, as containing, without his being aware of it, much of the mystical character of the Tâoistic system. His conversation with the duke of Sheh, however, is less obnoxious to this charge than what he is made to say to Yen Hui. The adviser of Yen Ho is a *K*ü Po-yü, a disciple of Confucius, who still has a place in the sage's temples.

In the conclusion, the Tâoism of our author comes out in contrast with the methods of Confucius. His object in the whole treatise, perhaps, was to show how 'the doing nothing, and yet thereby doing everything,' was the method to be pursued in all the intercourses of society.

莊子

BOOK V. TEH KHUNG FÛ.

The fû (符) consisted in the earliest times of two slips of bamboo made with certain marks, so as to fit to each other exactly, and held by the two parties to any agreement or covenant. By the production and comparison of the slips, the parties verified their mutual relation; and the claim of the one and the obligation of the other were sufficiently established. 'Seal' seems the best translation of the character in this title.

By 'virtue' (德) we must understand the characteristics of the Tâo. Where those existed in their full proportions in any individual, there was sure to be the evidence or proof of them in the influence which he exerted in all his intercourse with other men; and the illustration of this is the subject of this Book, in all its five paragraphs. That influence is the "Seal" set on him, proving him to be a true child of the Tâo.

The heroes, as I may call them, of the first three paragraphs are all men who had lost their feet, having been reduced to that condition as a punishment, just or unjust, of certain offences; and those of the last two are distinguished by their extraordinary ugliness or disgusting deformity. But neither the loss of their feet nor their deformities trouble the serenity of their own minds, or interfere with the effects of their teaching and character upon others; so superior is their virtue to the deficiencies in their outward appearance.

Various brief descriptions of the Tâo are interspersed in the Book. The most remarkable of them are those in par. 1, where it appears as 'that in which there is no element of falsehood,' and as 'the author of all the Changes or Transformations' in the world. The sentences where these occur are thus translated by Mr. Balfour:—'He seeks to know Him in whom is nothing false. He would not be affected by the instability of creation; even if his life were involved in the general destruction, he would yet hold firmly to his faith (in God).' And he observes in a note, that the first short sentence 'is explained by the commentators as referring to *K*ăn 3âi (眞宰), the term used by the Tâoist school for God.' But we met with that name and synonyms of it in Book II, par. 2, as appellations of the Tâo, coupled with the denial of its personality. *K*ăn 3âi, 'the True Governor or Lord,' may be used as a designation for god or God, but the Tâoist school denies the existence of a Personal Being, to whom we are accustomed to apply that name.

Hui-ȝze, the sophist and friend of *K*wang-ȝze, is introduced in the conclusion as disputing with him the propriety of his representing the Master of the Tâo as being still 'a man;' and is beaten down by him with a repetition of his assertions, and a reference to some of Hui-ȝze's well-known peculiarities. What would *K*wang-ȝze have said, if his opponent had affirmed that his instances were all imaginary, and that no man had ever appeared who could appeal to his possession of such a 'seal' to his virtues and influence as he described?

Lû Fang-wăng compares with the tenor of this Book what we find in Mencius, VII, i, 21, about the nature of the superior man. The analogy between them, however, is very faint and incomplete.

Book VI. Tâ 3ung Shih.

So I translate the title of this Book, taking 3ung as a verb, and 3ung Shih as = 'The Master who is Honoured.' Some critics take 3ung in the sense of 'Originator,' in which it is employed in the Tâo Teh *K*ing, lxx, 2. Whichever rendering be adopted, there is no doubt that the title is intended to be a designation of the Tâo; and no one of our author's Books is more important for the understanding of his system of thought.

The key to it is found in the first of its fifteen paragraphs. There are in man two elements;—the Heavenly or Tâoistic, and the human. The disciple of the Tâo, recognising them both, cultivates what he knows as a man

莊子

so as to become entirely conformed to the action of the Tâo, and submissive in all the most painful experiences in his lot, which is entirely ordered by it. A seal will be set on the wisdom of this course hereafter, when he has completed the period of his existence on earth, and returns to the state of non-existence, from which the Tâo called him to be born as a man. In the meantime he may attain to be the True man possessing the True knowledge.

Our author then proceeds to give his readers in five paragraphs his idea of the True Man. Mr. Balfour says that this name is to be understood 'in the esoteric sense, the partaking of the essence of divinity,' and he translates it by 'the Divine Man.' But we have no right to introduce here the terms 'divine' and 'divinity.' Nan-hwâi (VII, 5 b) gives a short definition of the name which is more to the point:—'What we call "the True Man" is one whose nature is in agreement with the Tâo (所謂眞人者性合于道也;' and the commentator adds in a note, 'Such men as Fû-hsî, Hwang-Tî, and Lâo Tan.' The Khang-hsî dictionary commences its account of the character 眞 or 'True' by a definition of the True Man taken from the Shwo Wăn as a 仙人, 'a recluse of the mountain, whose bodily form has been changed, and who ascends to heaven;' but when that earliest dictionary was made, Tâoism had entered into a new phase, different from what it had in the time of our author. The most prominent characteristic of the True Man is that he is free from all exercise of thought and purpose, a being entirely passive in the hands of the Tâo. In par. 3 seven men are mentioned, good and worthy men, but inferior to the True.

Having said what he had to say of the True Man, *K*wang-ȝze comes in the seventh paragraph to speak directly of the Tâo itself, and describes it with many wonderful predicates which exalt it above our idea of God;—a concept and not a personality. He concludes by mentioning a number of ancient personages who had got the Tâo, and by it wrought wonders, beginning with a Shih-wei, who preceded Fû-hsî, and ending with Fû Yüeh, the minister of

Wû-ting, in the fourteenth century B.C., and who finally became a star in the eastern portion of the zodiac. Phăng 3û is also mentioned as living, through his possession of the Tâo, from the twenty-third century B.C. to the seventh or later. The sun and moon and the constellation of the Great Bear are also mentioned as its possessors, and the fabulous Being called the Mother of the Western King. The whole passage is perplexing to the reader to the last degree.

The remaining paragraphs are mostly occupied with instances of learning the Tâo, and of its effects in making men superior to the infirmities of age and the most terrible deformities of person and calamities of penury; as 'Tranquillity' under all that might seem most calculated to disturb it. Very strange is the attempt at the conclusion of par. 8 apparently to trace the genesis of the knowledge of the Tâo. Confucius is introduced repeatedly as the expounder of Tâoism, and made to praise it as the *ne plus ultra* of human attainment.

Book VII. Ying Tî Wang.

The first of the three characters in this title renders the translation of it somewhat perplexing. *Ying* has different meanings according as it is read in the first tone or in the third. In the first tone it is the symbol of what is right, or should be; in the third tone of answering or responding to. I prefer to take it here in the first tone. As Kwo Hsiang says, 'One who is free from mind or purpose of his own, and loves men to become transformed of themselves, is fit to be a Ruler or a King,' and as 3hui *K*wan, another early commentator, says, 'He whose teaching is that which is without words, and makes men in the world act as if they were oxen or horses, is fit to be a Ruler or a King.' This then is the object of the Book—to describe that government which exhibits the Tâo equally in the rulers and the ruled, the world of men all happy and good without purpose or effort.

It consists of seven paragraphs. The first shows us the model ruler in him of the line of Thâi, whom I have not

莊子

succeeded in identifying. The second shows us men under such a rule, uncontrolled and safe like the bird that flies high beyond the reach of the archer, and the mouse secure in its deep hole from its pursuers. The teacher in this portion is *Kh*ieh-yü, known in the Confucian school as 'the madman of *Kh*û,' and he delivers his lesson in opposition to the heresy of a *Z*ăh-*k*ung Shih, or 'Noon Beginning.' In the third paragraph the speakers are 'a nameless man,' and a Thien Kăn, or 'Heaven Root.' In the fourth paragraph Lâo-ȝze himself appears upon the stage, and lectures a Yang Ȝze-*k*ü, the Yang *K*û of Mencius. He concludes by saying that 'where the intelligent kings took their stand could not be fathomed, and they found their enjoyment in (the realm of) nonentity.'

The fifth paragraph is longer, and tells us of the defeat of a wizard, a physiognomist in *K*ăng, by Hû-ȝze, the master of the philosopher Lieh-ȝze, who is thereby delivered from the glamour which the cheat was throwing round him. I confess to not being able to understand the various processes by which Hû-ȝze foils the wizard and makes him run away. The whole story is told, and at greater length, in the second book of the collection ascribed to Lieh-ȝze, and the curious student may like to look at the translation of that work by Mr. Ernst Faber (Der Naturalismus bei den alten Chinesen sowohl nach der Seite des Pantheismus als des Sensualismus, oder die Sämmtlichen Werke des Philosophen Licius, 1877). The effect of the wizard's defeat on Lieh-ȝze was great. He returned in great humility to his house, and did not go out of it for three years. He did the cooking for his wife, and fed the pigs as if he were feeding men. He returned to pure simplicity, and therein continued to the end of his life. But I do not see the connexion between this narrative and the government of the Rulers and Kings.

The sixth paragraph is a homily by our author himself on 'non-action.' It contains a good simile, comparing the mind of the perfect man to a mirror, which reflects faithfully what comes before it, but does not retain any image of it, when the mind is gone.

The last paragraph is an ingenious and interesting allegory relating how the gods of the southern and northern seas brought Chaos to an end by boring holes in him. Thereby they destroyed the primal simplicity, and according to Tâoism did Chaos an injury! On the whole I do not think that this Book, with which the more finished essays of *K*wang-ȝze come to an end, is so successful as those that precede it.

Book VIII. Phien Mâu.

This Book brings us to the Second Part of the writings of our author, embracing in all fifteen Books. Of the most important difference between the Books of the First and the other Parts some account has been given in the Introductory Chapter. We have here to do only with the different character of their titles. Those of the seven preceding Books are so many theses, and are believed to have been prefixed to them by *K*wang-ȝze himself; those of this Book and the others that follow are believed to have been prefixed by Kwo Hsiang, and consist of two or three characters taken from the beginning, or near the beginning of the several Books, after the fashion of the names of the Books in the Confucian Analects, in the works of Mencius, and in our Hebrew Scriptures. Books VIII to XIII are considered to be supplementary to VII by Aû-yang Hsiû.

The title of this eighth Book, Phien Mâu, has been rendered by Mr. Balfour, after Dr. Williams, 'Double Thumbs.' But the Mâu, which may mean either the Thumb or the Great Toe, must be taken in the latter sense, being distinguished in this paragraph and elsewhere from *K*ih, 'a finger,' and expressly specified also as belonging to the foot. The character phien, as used here, is defined in the Khang-hsî dictionary as 'anything additional growing out as an appendage or excrescence, a growing out at the side.' This would seem to justify the translation of it by 'double.' But in paragraph 3, while the extra finger increases the number of the fingers, this growth on the foot is represented as diminishing the number of the toes. I must consider

莊子

the phien therefore as descriptive of an appendage by which the great toe was united to one or all of the other toes, and can think of no better rendering of the title than what I have given. It is told in the Ȝo *K*wan (twenty-third year of duke Hsî) that the famous duke Wăn of Ȝin had phien hsieh, that is, that his ribs presented the appearance of forming one bone. So much for the title.

The subject-matter of the Book seems strange to us;—that, according to the Tâo, benevolence and righteousness are not natural growths of humanity, but excrescences on it, like the extra finger on the hand, and the membranous web of the toes. The weakness of the Tâoistic system begins to appear. *K*wang-ȝze's arguments in support of his position must be pronounced very feeble. The ancient Shun is introduced as the first who called in the two great virtues to distort and vex the world, keeping society for more than a thousand years in a state of uneasy excitement. Of course he assumes that prior to Shun, he does not say for how long a time (and in other places he makes decay to have begun earlier), the world had been in a state of paradisiacal innocence and simplicity, under the guidance of the Tâo, untroubled by any consideration of what was right and what was wrong, men passively allowing their nature to have its quiet development, and happy in that condition. All culture of art or music is wrong, and so it is wrong and injurious to be striving to manifest benevolence and to maintain righteousness.

He especially singles out two men, one of the twelfth century B.C., the famous Po-î, who died of hunger rather than acknowledge the dynasty of *K*âu; and one of a more recent age, the robber Shih, a great leader of brigands, who brought himself by his deeds to an untimely end; and he sees nothing to choose between them. We must give our judgment for the teaching of Confucianism in preference to that of Tâoism, if our author can be regarded as a fair expositor of the latter. He is ingenious in his statements and illustrations, but he was, like his master Lâo-ȝze, only a dreamer.

BOOK IX. MÂ THÎ.

'Horses' and 'Hoofs' are the first two characters of the Text, standing there in the relation of regent and regimen. The account of the teaching of the Book given by Lin Hsî-*k*ung is so concise that I will avail myself of it. He says:—

'Governing men is like governing horses. They may be governed in such a way as shall be injurious to them, just as Po-lâo governed the horse;—contrary to its true nature. His method was not different from that of the (first) potter and carpenter in dealing with clay and wood;—contrary to the nature of those substances. Notwithstanding this, one age after another has celebrated the skill of those parties;—not knowing what it is that constitutes the good and skilful government of men. Such government simply requires that men be made to fulfil their regular constant nature,—the qualities which they all possess in common, with which they are constituted by Heaven, and then be left to themselves. It was this which constituted the age of perfect virtue; but when the sages insisted on the practice of benevolence, righteousness, ceremonies, and music, then the people began to be without that perfect virtue. Not that they were in themselves different from what they had been, but those practices do not really belong to their regular nature; they arose from their neglecting the characteristics of the Tâo, and abandoning their natural constitution;—it was the case of the skilful artisan cutting and hacking his raw materials in order to form vessels from them. There is no ground for doubting that Po-lâo's management of horses gave them that knowledge with which they went on to play the part of thieves, or that it was the sages' government of the people which made them devote themselves to the pursuit of gain;—it is impossible to deny the error of those sages.

'There is but one idea in the Book from the beginning to the end;—it is an amplification of the expression in the preceding Book that "all men have their regular and con-

莊子

stant constitution," and is the most easily construed of all *K*wang-ȝze's compositions. In consequence, however, of the wonderful touches of his pencil in describing the sympathy between men and other creatures in their primal state, some have imagined that there is a waste and embellishment of language, and doubted whether the Book is really his own, but thought it was written by some one in imitation of his style. I apprehend that no other hand would easily have attained to such a mastery of that style.'

There is no possibility of adjudicating definitely on the suspicion of the genuineness of the Book thus expressed in Hsî-*k*ung's concluding remarks. The same suspicion arose in my own mind in the process of translation. My surprise continues that our author did not perceive the absurdity of his notions of the primal state of men, and of his condemnation of the sages.

Book X. *Kh*ü *Kh*ieh.

It is observed by the commentator Kwei *K*ăn-*kh*üan that one idea runs through this Book:—that the most sage and wise men have ministered to theft and robbery, and that, if there were an end of sageness and wisdom, the world would be at rest. Between it and the previous Book there is a general agreement in argument and object, but in this the author expresses himself with greater vehemence, and almost goes to excess in his denunciation of the institutions of the sages.

The reader will agree with these accounts of the Book. *K*wang-ȝze at times becomes weak in his attempts to establish his points. To my mind the most interesting portions of this Book and the last one are the full statements which we have in them of the happy state of men when the Tâo maintained its undisputed sway in the world, and the names of many of the early Tâoistic sovereigns. How can we suppose that anything would be gained by a return to the condition of primitive innocence and simplicity? The antagonism between Tâoism and Confucianism comes out in this Book very decidedly.

The title of the Book is taken from two characters in the first clause of the first paragraph.

BOOK XI. 3ÂI YÛ.

The two characters of the title are taken from the first sentence of the Text, but they express the subject of the Book more fully than the other titles in this Part do, and almost entitle it to a place in Part I. It is not easy to translate them, and Mr. Balfour renders them by 'Leniency towards Faults,' probably construing 3âi as equivalent to our preposition 'in,' which it often is. But *K*wang-ȝze uses both 3âi and Yû as verbs, or blends them together, the chief force of the binomial compound being derived from the significance of the 3âi. 3âi is defined by 3hun (存), which gives the idea of 'preserving' or 'keeping intact,' and Yû by Khwan (寬), 'being indulgent' or 'forbearing.' The two characters are afterwards exchanged for other two, wû wei (無爲), 'doing nothing,' 'inaction,' a grand characteristic of the Tâo.

The following summary of the Book is taken from Hsüan Ying's explanations of our author:—'The two characters 3âi Yû express the subject-matter of the Book, and "governing" points out the opposite error as the disease into which men are prone to fall. Let men be, and the tendencies of their nature will be at rest, and there will be no necessity for governing the world. Try to govern it, and the world will be full of trouble; and men will not be able to rest in the tendencies of their nature. These are the subjects of the first two paragraphs.

'In the third paragraph we have the erroneous view of 3hui *Kh*ü that by government it was possible to make men's minds good. He did not know that governing was a disturbing meddling with the minds of men; and how Lâo-ȝze set forth the evil of such government, going on till it be irretrievable. This long paragraph vigorously attacks the injury done by governing.

'In the fourth paragraph, when Hwang-Tî questions

莊子

Kwang *Kh*ăng-ʒze, the latter sets aside his inquiry about the government of the world, and tells him about the government of himself; and in the fifth, when Yün *K*iang asks Hung Mung about governing men, the latter tells him about the nourishing of the heart. These two great paragraphs set forth clearly the subtlest points in the policy of Let-a-be. Truly it is not an empty name.

'In the two last paragraphs, *K*wang in his own words and way sets forth, now by affirmation, and now by negation, the meaning of all that precedes.'

This summary of the Book will assist the reader in understanding it. For other remarks that will be helpful, I must refer him to the notes appended to the Text. The Book is not easy to understand or to translate; and a remark found in the *K*iâ-*kh*ing edition of 'the Ten Philosophers,' by Lû Hsiû-fû, who died in 1279, was welcome to me, 'If you cannot understand one or two sentences of *K*wang-ʒze, it does not matter.'

BOOK XII. THIEN TÎ.

The first two characters of the Book are adopted as its name;—Thien Tî, 'Heaven and Earth.' These are employed, not so much as the two greatest material forms in the universe, but as the Great Powers whose influences extend to all below and upon them. Silently and effectively, with entire spontaneity, their influence goes forth, and a rule and pattern is thus given to those on whom the business of the government of the world devolves. The one character 'Heaven' is employed throughout the Book as the denomination of this purposeless spontaneity which yet is so powerful.

Lû Shû-*k*ih says:—'This Book also sets forth clearly how the rulers of the world ought simply to act in accordance with the spontaneity of the virtue of Heaven; abjuring sageness and putting away knowledge; and doing nothing:—in this way the Tâo or proper Method of Government will be attained to. As to the coercive methods of Mo Tî and Hui-ʒze, they only serve to distress those who follow them.'

This object of the Book appears, more or less distinctly, in most of the illustrative paragraphs; though, as has been pointed out in the notes upon it, several of them must be considered to be spurious. Paragraphs 6, 7, and 11 are thus called in question, and, as most readers will feel, with reason. From 13 to the end, the paragraphs are held to be one long paragraph where *K*wang-ʒze introduces his own reflections in an unusual style; but the genuineness of the whole, so far as I have observed, has not been called in question.

Book XIII. Thien Tâo.

'Thien Tâo,' the first two characters of the first paragraph, and prefixed to the Book as the name of it, are best translated by 'The Way of Heaven,' meaning the noiseless spontaneity, which characterises all the operations of nature, proceeding silently, yet 'perfecting all things.' As the rulers of the world attain to this same way in their government, and the sages among men attain to it in their teachings, both government and doctrine arrive at a corresponding perfection. 'The joy of Heaven' and 'the joy of Men' are both realised. There ought to be no purpose or will in the universe. 'Vacancy, stillness, placidity, tastelessness, quietude, silence, and non-action; this is the perfection of the Tâo and its characteristics.'

Our author dwells especially on doing-nothing or non-action as the subject-matter of the Book. But as the world is full of doing, he endeavours to make a distinction between the Ruling Powers and those subordinate to and employed by them, to whom doing or action and purpose, though still without the thought of self, are necessary; and by this distinction he seems to me to give up the peculiarity of his system, so that some of the critics, especially Âû-yang Hsiû, are obliged to confess that these portions of the Book are unlike the writing of *K*wang-ʒze. Still the antagonism of Tâoism to Confucianism is very apparent throughout. Of the illustrative paragraphs, the seventh, relating the churlish behaviour of Lâo-ȝze to Confucius, and the way in which he subsequently argues with him and snubs him, is very amusing. The eighth paragraph, relating the interview between Lâo and Shih-*kh*ăng *Kh*î, is very strange. The allusions in it to certain incidents and peculiarities in Lâo's domestic life make us wish that we had fuller accounts of his history; and the way in which he rates his disciple shows him as a master of the language of abuse.

The concluding paragraph about duke Hwan of *Kh*î is interesting, but I can only dimly perceive its bearing on the argument of the Book.

BOOK XIV. THIEN YÜN.

The contrast between the movement of the heavens (天運), and the resting of the earth (地處), requires the translation of the characters of the title by 'The Revolution of Heaven.' But that idea does not enter largely into the subject-matter of the Book. 'The whole,' says Hsüan Ying, 'consists of eight paragraphs, the first three of which show that under the sky there is nothing which is not dominated by the Tâo, with which the Tîs and the Kings have only to act in accordance; while the last five set forth how the Tâo is not to be found in the material forms and changes of things, but in a spirit-like energy working imperceptibly, developing and controlling all phenomena.'

I have endeavoured in the notes on the former three paragraphs to make their meaning less obscure and unconnected than it is on a first perusal. The five illustrative paragraphs are, we may assume, all of them factitious, and can hardly be received as genuine productions of *K*wang-ȝze. In the sixth paragraph, or at least a part of it, Lin Hsî-*k*ung acknowledges the hand of the forger, and not less unworthy of credence are in my opinion the rest of it and much of the other four paragraphs. If they may be taken as from the hand of our author himself, he was too much devoted to his own system to hold the balance of judgment evenly between Lâo and Khung.

Book XV. Kho Î.

I can think of no better translation for 刻意, the two first characters of the Book, and which appear as its title, than our 'Ingrained Ideas;' notions, that is, held as firmly as if they were cut into the substance of the mind. They do not belong to the whole Book, however, but only to the first member of the first paragraph. That paragraph describes six classes of men, only the last of which are the right followers of the Tâo;—the Sages, from the Tâoistic point of view, who again are in the last sentence of the last paragraph identified with 'the True Men' described at length in the sixth Book. The fifth member of this first paragraph is interesting as showing how there was a class of Tâoists who cultivated the system with a view to obtain longevity by their practices in the management of the breath; yet our author does not accord to them his full approbation, while at the same time the higher Tâoism appears in the last paragraph, as promoting longevity without the management of the breath. *Kh*û Po-hsiû, in his commentary on *K*wang-ȝze, which was published in 1210, gives Po-î and Shû-*kh*î as instances of the first class spoken of here; Confucius and Mencius, of the second; Î Yin and Fû Yüeh, of the third; *Kh*âo Fû and Hsü Yû, as instances of the fourth. Of the fifth class he gives no example, but that of Phăng Ȝû mentioned in it.

That which distinguishes the genuine sage, the True Man of Tâoism, is his pure simplicity in pursuing the Way, as it is seen in the operation of Heaven and Earth, and nourishing his spirit accordingly, till there ensues an ethereal amalgamation between his Way and the orderly operation of Heaven. This subject is pursued to the end of the Book. The most remarkable predicate of the spirit so trained is that in the third paragraph,—that 'Its name is the same as Tî or God;' on which none of the critics has been able to throw any satisfactory light. Balfour's version is:—'Its name is called "One with God;"' Giles's, 'Its name is then "Of God,"' the 'then' being in consequence of his view that the subject is 'man's spiritual existence before he is born into the world of mortals.' My own view of the meaning appears in my version.

Lin Hsî-*k*ung, however, calls the genuineness of the whole Book into question, and thinks it may have proceeded from the same hand as Book XIII. They have certainly one peculiarity in common;—many references to sayings which cannot be traced, but are introduced by the formula of quotation, 'Therefore, it is said.'

Book XVI. Shan Hsing.

'Rectifying or Correcting the Nature' is the meaning of the title, and expresses sufficiently well the subject-matter of the Book. It was written to expose the 'vulgar' learning of the time as contrary to the principles of the true Tâoism, that learning being, according to Lû Shû-*k*ih, 'the teachings of Hui-ȝze and Kung-sun Lung.' It is to be wished that we had fuller accounts of these. But see in Book XXXIII.

Many of the critics are fond of comparing the Book with the 21st chapter of the 7th Book of Mencius, part 1,—where that philosopher sets forth 'Man's own nature as the most important thing to him, and the source of his true enjoyment,' which no one can read without admiration. But we have more sympathy with Mencius's fundamental views about our human nature, than with those of *K*wang-ȝze and his Tâoism. Lin Hsî-*k*ung is rather inclined to doubt the genuineness of the Book. Though he admires its composition, and admits the close and compact sequence of its sentences, there is yet something about it that does not smack of *K*wang-ȝze's style. Rather there seems to me to underlie it the antagonism of Lâo and *K*wang to the learning of the Confucian school. The only characteristic of our author which I miss, is the illustrative stories of which he is generally so profuse. In this the Book agrees with the preceding.

BOOK XVII. *KHIÛ* SHUI.

*Kh*iû Shui, or 'Autumn Waters,' the first two characters of the first paragraph of this Book, are adopted as its title. Its subject, in that paragraph, however, is not so much the waters of autumn, as the greatness of the Tâo in its spontaneity, when it has obtained complete dominion over man. No illustration of the Tâo is so great a favourite with Lâo-ȝze as water, but he loved to set it forth in its quiet, onward movement, always seeking the lowest place, and always exercising a beneficent influence. But water is here before *K*wang-ȝze in its mightiest volume,—the inundated Ho and the all but boundless magnitude of the ocean; and as he takes occasion from those phenomena to deliver his lessons, I translate the title by 'The Floods of Autumn.'

To adopt the account of the Book given by Lû Shû-*k*ih:—'This Book,' he says, 'shows how its spontaneity is the greatest characteristic of the Tâo, and the chief thing inculcated in it is that we must not allow the human element to extinguish in our constitution the Heavenly.

'First, using the illustrations of the Ho and the Sea, our author gives us to see the Five Tîs and the Kings of the Three dynasties as only exhibiting the Tâo in a small degree, while its great development is not to be found in outward form and appliances so that it cannot be described in words, and it is difficult to find its point of commencement, which indeed appears to be impracticable, while still by doing nothing the human may be united with the Heavenly, and men may bring back their True condition. By means of the conversations between the guardian spirit of the Ho and *Z*o (the god) of the Sea this subject is exhaustively treated.

'Next (in paragraph 8), the khwei, the millepede, and other subjects illustrate how the mind is spirit-like in its spontaneity and doing nothing. The case of Confucius (in par. 9) shows the same spontaneity, transforming violence.

Kung-sun Lung (in par. 10), refusing to comply with that spontaneity, and seeking victory by his sophistical reasonings, shows his wisdom to be only like the folly of the frog in the well. The remaining three paragraphs bring before us *K*wang-ʒze by the spontaneity of his Tâo, now superior to the allurements of rank; then, like the phœnix flying aloft, as enjoying himself in perfect ease; and finally, as like the fishes, in the happiness of his self-possession.' Such is a brief outline of this interesting chapter. Many of the critics would expunge the ninth and tenth paragraphs as unworthy of *K*wang-ʒze, the former as misrepresenting Confucius, the latter as extolling himself. I think they may both be allowed to stand as from his pencil.

Book XVIII. *K*ih Lo.

The title of this Book, *K*ih Lo, or 'Perfect Enjoyment,' may also be received as describing the subject-matter of it. But the author does not tell us distinctly what he means by 'Perfect Enjoyment.' It seems to involve two elements,—freedom from trouble and distress, and freedom from the fear of death. What men seek for as their chief good would only be to him burdens. He does not indeed altogether condemn them, but his own quest is the better and more excellent way. His own enjoyment is to be obtained by means of doing nothing; that is, by the Tâo; of which passionless and purposeless action is a chief characteristic; and is at the same time the most effective action, as is illustrated in the operation of heaven and earth.

Such is the substance of the first paragraph. The second is interesting as showing how his principle controlled *K*wang-ʒze on the death of his wife. Paragraph 3 shows us two professors of Tâoism delivered by it from the fear of their own death. Paragraph 4 brings our author before us talking to a skull, and then the skull's appearance to him in a dream and telling him of the happiness of the state after death. Paragraph 5 is occupied with Confucius and his favourite disciple Yen Hui. It stands by itself, unconnected with the rest of the Book, and its genuineness is denied by some commentators. The last paragraph, found in an enlarged form in the Books ascribed to Lieh-ȝze, has as little to do as the fifth with the general theme of the Book, and is a strange anticipation in China of the transrotation or transformation system of Buddhism.

Indeed, after reading this Book, we cease to wonder that Tâoism and Buddhism should in many practices come so near each other.

BOOK XIX. TÂ SHĂNG.

I have been inclined to translate the title of this Book by 'The Fuller Understanding of Life,' with reference to what is said in the second Book on 'The Nourishment of the Lord of Life.' There the Life before the mind of the writer is that of the Body; here he extends his view also to the Life of the Spirit. The one subject is not kept, however, with sufficient distinctness apart from the other, and the profusion of illustrations, taken, most of them, from the works of Lieh-ȝze, is perplexing.

To use the words of Lû Shû-*k*ih:—'This Book shows how he who would skilfully nourish his life, must maintain his spirit complete, and become one with Heaven. These two ideas preside in it throughout. In par. 2, the words of the Warden Yin show that the spirit kept complete is beyond the reach of harm. In 3, the illustration of the hunchback shows how the will must be maintained free from all confusion. In 4, that of the ferryman shows that to the completeness of the spirit there is required the disregard of life or death. In 5 and 6, the words of Thien Khâi-*k*ih convey a warning against injuring the life by the indulgence of sensual desires. In 7, the sight of a sprite by duke Hwan unsettles his spirit. In 8, the gamecock is trained so as to preserve the spirit unagitated. In 9, we see the man in the water of the cataract resting calmly in his appointed lot. In 10, we have the maker of the bell-stand completing his work as he did in accordance with the mind of Heaven. All these instances show how the

莊子

spirit is nourished. The reckless charioteering of Tung Yê in par. 11, not stopping when the strength of his horses was exhausted, and the false pretext of Sun Hsiû, clear as at noon-day, are instances of a different kind; while in the skilful Shui, hardly needing the application of his mind, and fully enjoying himself in all things, his movements testify of his harmony with Heaven, and his spiritual completeness.'

BOOK XX. SHAN MÛ.

It requires a little effort to perceive that Shan Mû, the title of this Book, does not belong to it as a whole, but only to the first of its nine paragraphs. That speaks of a large tree which our author once saw on a mountain. The other paragraphs have nothing to do with mountain trees, large or small. As the last Book might be considered to be supplementary to 'the Nourishment of Life,' discussed in Book III, so this is taken as having the same relation to Book IV, which treats of 'Man in the World, associated with other men.' It shows by its various narratives, some of which are full of interest, how by a strict observance of the principles and lessons of the Tâo a man may preserve his life and be happy, may do the right thing and enjoy himself and obtain the approbation of others in the various circumstances in which he may be placed. The themes both of Books I and IV blend together in it. Paragraph 8 has more the character of an apologue than most of *K*wang-ȝze's stories.

BOOK XXI. THIEN ȜZE-FANG.

Thien Ȝze-fang is merely the name of one of the men who appear in the first paragraph. That he was a historical character is learned from the 'Plans of the Warring States,' XIV, art. 6, where we find him at the court of the marquis Wăn of Wei (B.C. 424–387), acting as counsellor to that ruler. Thien was his surname; Ȝze-fang his designation, and Wû-*k*âi his name. He has nothing to do with any of the paragraphs but the first.

It is not easy to reduce all the narratives or stories in the Book to one category. The fifth, seventh, and eighth, indeed, are generally rejected as spurious, or unworthy of our author; and the sixth and ninth are trivial, though the ninth bears all the marks of his graphic style. Paragraphs 3 and 4 are both long and important. A common idea in them and in 1, 2, and 10 seems to be that the presence and power of the Tâo cannot be communicated by words, and are independent of outward condition and circumstances.

BOOK XXII. *K*IH PEI YÛ.

With this Book the Second Part of *K*wang-ȝze's Essays or Treatises ends. 'All the Books in it,' says Lû Shû-*k*ih, 'show the opposition of Tâoism to the pursuit of knowledge as enjoined in the Confucian and other schools; and this Book may be regarded as the deepest, most vehement, and clearest of them all.' The concluding sentences of the last paragraph and Lâo-ȝze's advice to Confucius in par. 5, to 'sternly repress his knowledge,' may be referred to as illustrating the correctness of Lû's remark.

Book seventeenth is commonly considered to be the most eloquent of *K*wang-ȝze's Treatises, but this twenty-second Book is not inferior to it in eloquence, and it is more characteristic of his method of argument. The way in which he runs riot in the names with which he personifies the attributes of the Tâo, is a remarkable instance of the subtle manner in which he often brings out his ideas; and in no other Book does he set forth more emphatically what his own idea of the Tâo was, though the student often fails to be certain that he has exactly caught the meaning.

The title, let it be observed, belongs only to the first paragraph. The *K*ih in it must be taken in the sense of 'knowledge,' and not of 'wisdom.'

莊子

Book XXIII. Kăng-sang *Kh*û.

It is not at all certain that there ever was such a personage as Kăng-sang *Kh*û, who gives its name to the Book. In his brief memoir of *K*wang-ȝze, Sze-mâ *Kh*ien spells, as we should say, the first character of the surname differently, and for the Kăng (庚), employs Khang (亢), adding his own opinion, that there was nothing in reality corresponding to the account given of the characters in this and some other Books. They would be therefore the inventions of *K*wang-ȝze, devised by him to serve his purpose in setting forth the teaching of Lâo-ȝze. It may have been so, but the value of the Book would hardly be thereby affected.

Lû Shû-*k*ih gives the following very brief account of the contents. Borrowing the language of Mencius concerning Yen Hui and two other disciples of Confucius as compared with the sage, he says, 'Kăng-sang *Kh*û had all the members of Lâo-ȝze, but in small proportions. To outward appearance he was above such as abjure sagehood and put knowledge away, but still he was unable to transform Nan-yung *Kh*û, whom therefore he sent to Lâo-ȝze; and he announced to him the doctrine of the Tâo that everything was done by doing nothing.'

The reader will see that this is a very incomplete summary of the contents of the Book. We find in it the Tâoistic ideal of the 'Perfect Man,' and the discipline both of body and mind through the depths of the system by means of which it is possible for a disciple to become such.

Book XXIV. Hsü Wû-kwei.

This Book is named from the first three characters in it, the surname and name of Hsü Wû-kwei, who plays the most important part in the first two paragraphs, and does not further appear. He comes before us as a well-known recluse of Wei, who visits the court to offer his counsels to the marquis of the state. But whether there ever was such a man, or whether he was only a creation of *K*wang-ȝze, we cannot, so far as I know, tell.

Scattered throughout the Book are the lessons so common with our author against sagehood and knowledge, and on the quality of doing nothing and thereby securing the doing of everything. The concluding chapter is one of the finest descriptions in the whole Work of the Tâo and of the Tâoistic idea of Heaven. 'There are in the Book,' says Lû Fang, 'many dark and mysterious expressions. It is not to be read hastily; but the more it is studied, the more flavour will there be found in it.'

BOOK XXV. ȜEH-YANG.

This Book is named from the first two characters in it,—'Ȝeh-yang,' which again are the designation of a gentleman of Lû, called Phăng Yang, who comes before us in *Kh*û, seeking for an introduction to the king of that state, with the view, we may suppose, of giving him good counsel. Whether he ever got the introduction which he desired we do not know. The mention of him only serves to bring in three other individuals, all belonging to *Kh*û, and the characters of two of them; but we hear no more of Ȝeh-yang. The second and third paragraphs are, probably, sequels to the first, but his name does not appear.

The paragraphs from 4 to 9 have more or less interest in themselves; but it is not easy to trace in them any sequence of thought. The tenth and eleventh are more important. The former deals with 'the Talk of the Hamlets and Villages,' the common sentiments of men, which, correct and just in themselves, are not to be accepted as a sufficient expression of the Tâo; the latter sets forth how the name Tâo itself is only a metaphorical term, used for the purpose of description; as if the Tâo were a thing, and not capable, therefore, from its material derivation of giving adequate expression to our highest notion of what it is.

'The Book,' says Lû Shû-*k*ih, 'illustrates how the Great Tâo cannot be described by any name; that men ought to

莊子

stop where they do not really know, and not try to find it in any phenomenon, or in any event or thing. They must forget both speech and silence, and then they may approximate to the idea of the Great Tâo.'

Book XXVI. Wâi Wû.

The first two characters of the first paragraph are again adopted as the title of the Book,—Wâi Wû, 'External Things;' and the lesson supposed to be taught in it is that expressed in the first sentence, that the influence of external things on character and condition cannot be determined beforehand. It may be good, it may be evil. Mr. Balfour has translated the two characters by 'External Advantages.' Hû Wăn-ying interprets them of 'External Disadvantages.' The things may in fact be either of these. What seems useless may be productive of the greatest services; and what men deem most advantageous may turn out to be most hurtful to them.

What really belongs to man is the Tâo. That is his own, sufficient for his happiness, and cannot be taken from him, if he prize it and cultivate it. But if he neglect it, and yield to external influences unfavourable to it, he may become bad, and suffer all that is most hateful to him and injurious.

Readers must judge for themselves of the way in which the subject is illustrated in the various paragraphs. Some of the stories are pertinent enough; others are wide of the mark. The second, third, and fourth paragraphs are generally held to be spurious, 'poor in composition, and not at all to the point.' If my note on the 'six faculties of perception' in par. 9 be correct, we must admit in it a Buddhistic hand, modifying the conceptions of *K*wang-ȝze after he had passed away.

Book XXVII. Yü Yen.

Yü Yen, 'Metaphorical Words,' stand at the commencement of the Book, and have been adopted as its name.

They might be employed to denote its first paragraph, but are not applicable to the Book as a whole. Nor let the reader expect to find even here any disquisition on the nature of the metaphor as a figure of speech. Translated literally, 'Yü Yen' are 'Lodged Words,' that is, Ideas that receive their meaning or character from their environment, the narrative or description in which they are deposited.

*K*wang-ȝze wished, I suppose, to give some description of the style in which he himself wrote:—now metaphorical, now abounding in quotations, and throughout moulded by his Tâoistic views. This last seems to be the meaning of his *K*ih Yen,—literally, 'Cup, or Goblet, Words,' that is, words, common as the water constantly supplied in the cup, but all moulded by the Tâoist principle, the element of and from Heaven blended in man's constitution and that should direct and guide his conduct. The best help in the interpretation of the paragraph is derived from a study of the difficult second Book, as suggested in the notes.

Of the five paragraphs that follow the first, the second relates to the change of views, which, it is said, took place in Confucius; the third, to the change of feeling in Ȝăng-ȝze in his poverty and prosperity; the fourth, to changes of character produced in his disciple by the teachings of Tung-kwo Ȝze-*kh*î; the fifth, to the changes in the appearance of the shadow produced by the ever-changing substance; and the sixth, to the change of spirit and manner produced in Yang *K*û by the stern lesson of Lâo-ȝze.

Various other lessons, more or less appropriate and important, are interspersed.

Some critics argue that this Book must have originally been one with the thirty-second, which was made into two by the insertion between its Parts of the four spurious intervening Books, but this is uncertain and unlikely.

Book XXVIII. *Z*ang Wang.

*Z*ang Wang, explaining the characters as I have done,

莊子

fairly indicates the subject-matter of the Book. Not that we have a king in every illustration, but the personages adduced are always men of worth, who decline the throne, or gift, or distinction of whatever nature, proffered to them, and feel that they have something better to live for.

A persuasion, however, is widely spread, that this Book and the three that follow are all spurious. The first critic of note to challenge their genuineness was Sû Shih (better known as Sû Tung-pho, A.D. 1036–1101); and now, some of the best editors, such as Lin Hsî-*k*ung, do not admit them into their texts, while others who are not bold enough to exclude them altogether, do not think it worth their while to discuss them seriously. Hû Wăn-ying, for instance, says, 'Their style is poor and mean, and they are, without doubt, forgeries. I will not therefore trouble myself with comments of praise or blame upon them. The reader may accept or reject them at his pleasure.'

But something may be said for them. Sze-mâ *Kh*ien seems to have been acquainted with them all. In his short biographical notice of *K*wang-ȝze, he says, 'He made the Old Fisherman, the Robber *K*ih, and the Cutting Open Satchels, to defame and calumniate the disciples of Confucius.' *Kh*ien does not indeed mention our present Book along with XXX and XXXI, but it is less open to objection on the ground he mentions than they are. I think if it had stood alone, it would not have been condemned.

Book XXIX. Tâo *K*ih.

It has been seen above that Sze-mâ *Kh*ien expressly ascribes the Book called 'the Robber *K*ih' to *K*wang-ȝze. *Kh*ien refers also in another place to *K*ih, adducing the facts of his history in contrast with those about Confucius' favourite disciple Yen Hui as inexplicable on the supposition of a just and wise Providence. We must conclude therefore that the Book existed in *Kh*ien's time, and that he had read it. On the other hand it has been shown that Confucius could not have been on terms of friendship with Liû-hsiâ *K*î, and all that is related of his brother the robber wants substantiation. That such a man ever existed appears to me very doubtful. Are we to put down the whole of the first paragraph then as a jeu d'esprit on the part of *K*wang-ȝze, intended to throw ridicule on Confucius and what our author considered his pedantic ways? It certainly does so, and we are amused to hear the sage outcrowed by the robber.

In the other two paragraphs we have good instances of *K*wang-ȝze's 'metaphorical expressions,' his coinage of names for his personages, more or less ingeniously indicating their characters; but in such cases the element of time or chronology does not enter; and it is the anachronism of the first paragraph which constitutes its chief difficulty.

The name of 'Robber *K*ih' may be said to be a coinage; and that a famous robber was popularly indicated by the name appears from its use by Mencius (III, ii, ch. 10, 3), to explain which the commentators have invented the story of a robber so-called in the time of Hwang-Tî, in the twenty-seventh century B.C.! Was there really such a legend? and did *K*wang-ȝze take advantage of it to apply the name to a notorious and disreputable brother of Liû-hsiâ *K*î? Still there remain the anachronisms in the paragraph which have been pointed out. On the whole we must come to a conclusion rather unfavourable to the genuineness of the Book. But it must have been forged at a very early time, and we have no idea by whom.

Book XXX. Yüeh *K*ien.

We need not suppose that anything ever occurred in *K*wang-ȝze's experience such as is described here. The whole narrative is metaphorical; and that he himself is made to play the part in it which he describes, only shows how the style of writing in which he indulged was ingrained into the texture of his mind. We do not know that there ever was a ruler of *K*âo who indulged in the love of the

莊子

sword-fight, and kept about him a crowd of vulgar bravoes such as the story describes. We may be assured that our author never wore the bravo's dress or girt on him the bravo's sword. The whole is a metaphorical representation of the way in which a besotted ruler might be brought to a feeling of his degradation, and recalled to a sense of his duty and the way in which he might fulfil it. The narrative is full of interest and force. I do not feel any great difficulty in accepting it as the genuine composition of *K*wang-ȝze. Who but himself could have composed it? Was it a good-humoured caricature of him by an able Confucian writer to repay him for the ridicule he was fond of casting on the sage?

BOOK XXXI. YÜ-FÛ.

'The Old Fisherman' is the fourth of the Books in the collection of the writings of *K*wang-ȝze to which, since the time of Sû Shih, the epithet of 'spurious' has been attached by many. My own opinion, however, has been already intimated that the suspicions of the genuineness of those Books have been entertained on insufficient grounds; and so far as 'the Old Fisherman' is concerned, I am glad that it has come down to us, spurious or genuine. There may be a certain coarseness in 'the Robber *K*ih,' which makes us despise Confucius or laugh at him; but the satire in this Book is delicate, and we do not like the sage the less when he walks up the bank from the stream where he has been lectured by the fisherman. The pictures of him and his disciples in the forest, reading and singing on the Apricot Terrace, and of the old man slowly impelling his skiff to the land and then as quietly impelling it away till it is lost among the reeds, are delicious; there is nothing finer of its kind in the volume. What hand but that of *K*wang-ȝze, so light in its touch and yet so strong, both incisive and decisive, could have delineated them?

Book XXXII. Lieh Yü-khâu.

Lieh Yü-khâu, the surname and name of Lieh-ȝze, with which the first paragraph commences, have become current as the name of the Book, though they have nothing to do with any but that one paragraph, which is found also in the second Book of the writings ascribed to Lieh-ȝze. There are some variations in the two Texts, but they are so slight that we cannot look on them as proofs that the two passages are narratives of independent origin.

Various difficulties surround the questions of the existence of Lieh-ȝze, and of the work which bears his name. They will be found distinctly and dispassionately stated and discussed in the 146th chapter of the Catalogue of the *Kh*ien-lung Imperial Library. The writers seem to me to make it out that there was such a man, but they do not make it clear when he lived, or how his writings assumed their present form. There is a statement of Liû Hsiang that he lived in the time of duke Mû of *K*ăng (B.C. 627–606); but in that case he must have been earlier than Lâo-ȝze himself, whom he very frequently quotes. The writers think that Liû's 'Mû of *K*ăng' should be Mû of Lû (B.C. 409–377), which would make him not much anterior to Mencius and *K*wang-ȝze; but this is merely an ingenious conjecture. As to the composition of his chapters, they are evidently not at first hand from Lieh, but by some one of his disciples; whether they were current in *K*wang-ȝze's days, and he made use of various passages from them, or those passages were *K*wang-ȝze's originally, and taken from him by the followers of Lieh-ȝze and added to what fragments they had of their master's teaching;—these are points which must be left undetermined.

Whether the narrative about Lieh be from *K*wang-ȝze or not, its bearing on his character is not readily apprehended; but, as we study it, we seem to understand that his master Wû-*z*ăn condemned him as not having fully attained to the Tâo, but owing his influence with others

莊子

mainly to the manifestation of his merely human qualities. And this is the lesson which our author keeps before him, more or less distinctly, in all his paragraphs. As Lû Shû-*k*ih says:—

'This Book also sets forth Doing Nothing as the essential condition of the Tâo. Lieh-ȝze, frightened at the respect shown to him by the soup-vendors, and yet by his human doings drawing men to him, disowns the rule of the heavenly; Hwan of *K*ăng, thinking himself different from other men, does not know that Heaven recompenses men according to their employment of the heavenly in them; the resting of the sages in their proper rest shows how the ancients pursued the heavenly and not the human; the one who learned to slay the Dragon, but afterwards did not exercise his skill, begins with the human, but afterwards goes on to the heavenly; in those who do not rest in the heavenly, and perish by the inward war, we see how the small men do not know the secret of the Great Repose; Ȝhâo Shang, glorying in the carriages which he had acquired, is still farther removed from the heavenly; when Yen Ho shows that the sage, in imparting his instructions, did not follow the example of Heaven in diffusing its benefits, we learn that it is only the Doing Nothing of the True Man which is in agreement with Heaven; the difficulty of knowing the mind of man, and the various methods required to test it, show the readiness with which, when not under the rule of Heaven, it seems to go after what is right, and the greater readiness with which it again revolts from it; in Khao-fû, the Correct, we have one indifferent to the distinctions of rank, and from him we advance to the man who understands the great condition appointed for him, and is a follower of Heaven; then comes he who plays the thief under the chin of the Black Dragon, running the greatest risks on a mere peradventure of success, a resolute opponent of Heaven; and finally we have *K*wang-ȝze despising the ornaments of the sacrificial ox, looking in the same way at the worms beneath and the kites overhead, and regarding himself as quite independent of them, thus giving us an example of the embodiment of the spiritual, and of harmony with Heaven.'

So does this ingenious commentator endeavour to exhibit the one idea in the Book, and show the unity of its different paragraphs.

BOOK XXXIII. THIEN HSIÂ.

The Thien Hsiâ with which this Book commences is in regimen, and cannot be translated, so as to give an adequate idea of the scope of the Book, or even of the first paragraph to which it belongs. The phrase itself means literally 'under heaven or the sky,' and is used as a denomination of 'the kingdom,' and, even more widely, of 'the world' or 'all men.' 'Historical Phases of Tâoist Teaching' would be nearly descriptive of the subject-matter of the Book; but may be objected to on two grounds:—first, that a chronological method is not observed, and next, that the concluding paragraph can hardly be said to relate to Tâoism at all, but to the sophistical teachers, which abounded in the age of *K*wang-ȝze.

Par. 1 sketches with a light hand the nature of Tâoism and the forms which it assumed from the earliest times to the era of Confucius, as imperfectly represented by him and his school.

Par. 2 introduces us to the system of Mo Tî and his school as an erroneous form of Tâoism, and departing, as it continued, farther and farther from the old model.

Par. 3 deals with a modification of Mohism, advocated by scholars who are hardly heard of elsewhere.

Par. 4 treats of a further modification of this modified Mohism, held by scholars 'whose Tâo was not the true Tâo, and whose "right" was really "wrong."'

Par. 5 goes back to the era of Lâo-ȝze, and mentions him and Kwan Yin, as the men who gave to the system of Tâo a grand development.

Par. 6 sets forth *K*wang-ȝze as following in their steps and going beyond them, the brightest luminary of the system.

Par. 7 leaves Tâoism, and brings up Hui Shih and other sophists.

Whether the Book should be received as from *K*wang-ȝze himself or from some early editor of his writings is 'a vexed question.' If it did come from his pencil, he certainly had a good opinion of himself. It is hard for a foreign student at this distant time to be called on for an opinion on the one side or the other.

THE WRITINGS OF *K*WANG-3ZE.

BOOK I.

Part I. Section I.

Hsiâo-yâo Yû, or 'Enjoyment in Untroubled Ease[1].'

1. In the Northern Ocean there is a fish, the name of which is Khwăn[2],—I do not know how many lî in size. It changes into a bird with the name of Phăng, the back of which is (also)—I do not know how many lî in extent. When this bird rouses itself and flies, its wings are like clouds all round the sky. When the sea is moved (so as to bear it along), it prepares to remove to the Southern Ocean. The Southern Ocean is the Pool of Heaven.

---

[1] See notice on pp. 127, 128, on the Title and Subject-matter of the Book.

[2] The khwăn and the phăng are both fabulous creatures, far transcending in size the dimensions ascribed by the wildest fancy of the West to the kraken and the roc. *K*wang-ȝze represents them as so huge by way of contrast to the small creatures which he is intending to introduce;—to show that size has nothing to do with the Tâo, and the perfect enjoyment which the possession of it affords. The passage is a good specimen of the Yü Yen (寓言), metaphorical or parabolical narratives or stories, which are the chief characteristic of our author's writings; but the reader must keep in mind that the idea or lesson in its 'lodging' is generally of a Tâoistic nature.

莊子

There is the (book called) *Khî* Hsieh [1],—a record of marvels. We have in it these words:—'When the phăng is removing to the Southern Ocean it flaps (its wings) on the water for 3000 lî. Then it ascends on a whirlwind 90,000 lî, and it rests only at the end of six months.' (But similar to this is the movement of the breezes which we call) the horses of the fields, of the dust (which quivers in the sunbeams), and of living things as they are blown against one another by the air [2]. Is its azure the proper colour of the sky? Or is it occasioned by its distance and illimitable extent? If one were looking down (from above), the very same appearance would just meet his view.

2. And moreover, (to speak of) the accumulation of water;—if it be not great, it will not have strength to support a large boat. Upset a cup of water in a cavity, and a straw will float on it as if it were a boat. Place a cup in it, and it will stick fast;—the water is shallow and the boat is large. (So it is with) the accumulation of wind; if it be not great, it will not have strength to support great wings. Therefore (the phăng ascended to) the height of 90,000 lî, and there was such a mass of wind beneath it; thenceforth the accumulation of wind was sufficient. As it seemed to bear the blue sky on its back, and there was nothing to obstruct or arrest its course, it could pursue its way to the South.

---

[1] There may have been a book with this title, to which Kwang-ȝze appeals, as if feeling that what he had said needed to be substantiated.

[2] This seems to be interjected as an afterthought, suggesting to the reader that the phăng, soaring along at such a height, was only an exaggerated form of the common phenomena with which he was familiar.

A cicada and a little dove laughed at it, saying, 'We make an effort and fly towards an elm or sapan-wood tree; and sometimes before we reach it, we can do no more but drop to the ground. Of what use is it for this (creature) to rise 90,000 lî, and make for the South?' He who goes to the grassy suburbs[1], returning to the third meal (of the day), will have his belly as full as when he set out; he who goes to a distance of 100 lî will have to pound his grain where he stops for the night; he who goes a thousand lî, will have to carry with him provisions for three months. What should these two small creatures know about the matter? The knowledge of that which is small does not reach to that which is great; (the experience of) a few years does not reach to that of many. How do we know that it is so? The mushroom of a morning does not know (what takes place between) the beginning and end of a month; the short-lived cicada does not know (what takes place between) the spring and autumn. These are instances of a short term of life. In the south of *Kh*û[2] there is the (tree) called Ming-ling[3], whose spring is 500 years, and its autumn the same; in high antiquity there was that called Tâ-*kh*un[4],

[1] In Chinese, Mang Ȝhang; but this is not the name of any particular place. The phrase denotes the grassy suburbs (from their green colour), not far from any city or town.

[2] The great state of the South, having its capital Ying in the present Hû-pei, and afterwards the chief competitor with *Kh*in for the sovereignty of the kingdom.

[3] Taken by some as the name of a tortoise.

[4] This and the Ming-ling tree, as well as the mushroom mentioned above, together with the khwăn and phăng, are all mentioned in the fifth Book of the writings of Lieh-ȝze, referred to in the next paragraph.

莊子

whose spring was 8000 years, and its autumn the same. And Phăng Ȝû [1] is the one man renowned to the present day for his length of life:—if all men were (to wish) to match him, would they not be miserable?

3. In the questions put by Thang [2] to *K*î we have similar statements:—'In the bare and barren north there is the dark and vast ocean,—the Pool of Heaven. In it there is a fish, several thousand lî in breadth, while no one knows its length. Its name is the khwăn. There is (also) a bird named the phăng; its back is like the Thâi mountain, while its wings are like clouds all round the sky. On a whirlwind it mounts upwards as on the whorls of a goat's horn for 90,000 lî, till, far removed from the cloudy vapours, it bears on its back the blue sky, and then it shapes its course for the South, and proceeds to the ocean there.' A quail by the side of a marsh laughed at it, and said, 'Where is it going to? I spring up with a bound, and come down again when I have reached but a few fathoms, and then fly about among the brushwood and bushes; and

---

[1] Or 'the patriarch Phăng.' Confucius compared himself to him (Analects, VII, 1);—'our old Phăng;' and *K*û Hsî thinks he was a worthy officer of the Shang dynasty. Whoever he was, the legends about him are a mass of Tâoistic fables. At the end of the Shang dynasty (B.C. 1123) he was more than 767 years old, and still in unabated vigour. We read of his losing 49 wives and 54 sons; and that he still left two sons, Wû and Î, who died in Fû-*k*ien, and gave their names to the Wû-î, or Bû-î hills, from which we get our Bohea tea! See Mayers' 'Chinese Reader's Manual,' p. 175.

[2] The founder of the Shang dynasty (B.C. 1766–1754). In Lieh-ȝze his interlocutor is called Hsiâ Ko, and Ȝze-*k*î.

this is the perfection of flying. Where is that creature going to?' This shows the difference between the small and the great.

Thus it is that men, whose wisdom is sufficient for the duties of some one office, or whose conduct will secure harmony in some one district, or whose virtue is befitting a ruler so that they could efficiently govern some one state, are sure to look on themselves in this manner (like the quail), and yet Yung-ȝze[1] of Sung[1] would have smiled and laughed at them. (This Yung-ȝze), though the whole world should have praised him, would not for that have stimulated himself to greater endeavour, and though the whole world should have condemned him, would not have exercised any more repression of his course; so fixed was he in the difference between the internal (judgment of himself) and the external (judgment of others), so distinctly had he marked out the bounding limit of glory and disgrace. Here, however, he stopped. His place in the world indeed had become indifferent to him, but still he had not planted himself firmly (in the right position).

There was Lieh-ȝze[2], who rode on the wind and pursued his way, with an admirable indifference (to

---

[1] We can hardly tell who this Yung-ȝze was. Sung was a duchy, comprehending portions of the present provinces of Ho-nan, An-hui, and *K*iang-sû.

[2] See note on the title of Book XXXII. Whether there ever was a personage called Lieh-ȝze or Lieh Yü-khâu, and what is the real character of the writings that go under his name, are questions that cannot be more than thus alluded to in a note. He is often introduced by *K*wang-ȝze, and many narratives are common to their books. Here he comes before us, not as a thinker and writer, but as a semi-supernatural being, who has only not yet attained to the highest consummations of the Tâo.

莊子

all external things), returning, however, after fifteen days, (to his place). In regard to the things that (are supposed to) contribute to happiness, he was free from all endeavours to obtain them; but though he had not to walk, there was still something for which he had to wait. But suppose one who mounts on (the ether of) heaven and earth in its normal operation, and drives along the six elemental energies of the changing (seasons), thus enjoying himself in the illimitable,—what has he to wait for[1]? Therefore it is said, 'The Perfect man has no (thought of) self; the Spirit-like man, none of merit; the Sagely-minded man, none of fame[1].'

4. Yâo[2], proposing to resign the throne to Hsü Yû[3], said, 'When the sun and moon have come forth, if the torches have not been put out, would it not be difficult for them to give light? When the seasonal rains are coming down, if we still keep watering the ground, will not our toil be labour lost for all the good it will do? Do you, Master, stand forth (as sovereign), and the kingdom will (at once) be well governed. If I still (continue to) preside over it, I must look on myself as vainly occupying the place;—I beg to resign the throne to you.' Hsü

[1] The description of a master of the Tâo, exalted by it, unless the predicates about him be nothing but the ravings of a wild extravagance, above mere mortal man. In the conclusion, however, he is presented under three different phrases, which the reader will do well to keep in mind.

[2] The great sovereign with whom the documents of the Shû *K*ing commence:—B. C. 2357–2257.

[3] A counsellor of Yâo, who is once mentioned by Sze-mâ *Kh*ien in his account of Po-î,—in the first Book of his Biographies (列傳). Hsü Yû is here the instance of 'the Sagely man,' with whom the desire of a name or fame has no influence.

Yû said, 'You, Sir, govern the kingdom, and the kingdom is well governed. If I in these circumstances take your place, shall I not be doing so for the sake of the name? But the name is but the guest of the reality;—shall I be playing the part of the guest? The tailor-bird makes its nest in the deep forest, but only uses a single branch; the mole[1] drinks from the Ho, but only takes what fills its belly. Return and rest in being ruler,—I will have nothing to do with the throne. Though the cook were not attending to his kitchen, the representative of the dead and the officer of prayer would not leave their cups and stands to take his place.'

5. *K*ien Wû[2] asked Lien Shû[2], saying, 'I heard *Kh*ieh-yü[3] talking words which were great, but had nothing corresponding to them (in reality);—once gone, they could not be brought back. I was frightened by them;—they were like the Milky Way[4] which cannot be traced to its beginning or end. They had no connexion with one another, and were not akin to the experiences of men.' 'What were his words?' asked Lien Shû, and the other replied, (He said) that 'Far away on the hill of Kû-shih[5] there dwelt a Spirit-like man whose flesh and skin

---

[1] Some say the tapir.

[2] Known to us only through *K*wang-ȝze.

[3] 'The madman of *Kh*û' of the Analects, XVIII, 5, who eschews intercourse with Confucius. See Hwang-fû Mî's account of him, under the surname and name of Lû Thung, in his Notices of Eminent Tâoists, I, 25.

[4] Literally, 'the Ho and the Han;' but the name of those rivers combined was used to denote 'the Milky Way.'

[5] See the Khang-hsî Thesaurus under the character 射. All which is said about the hill is that it was 'in the North Sea.'

莊子

were (smooth) as ice and (white) as snow; that his manner was elegant and delicate as that of a virgin; that he did not eat any of the five grains, but inhaled the wind and drank the dew; that he mounted on the clouds, drove along the flying dragons, rambling and enjoying himself beyond the four seas; that by the concentration of his spirit-like powers he could save men from disease and pestilence, and secure every year a plentiful harvest.' These words appeared to me wild and incoherent and I did not believe them. 'So it is,' said Lien Shû. 'The blind have no perception of the beauty of elegant figures, nor the deaf of the sound of bells and drums. But is it only the bodily senses of which deafness and blindness can be predicated? There is also a similar defect in the intelligence; and of this your words supply an illustration in yourself. That man, with those attributes, though all things were one mass of confusion, and he heard in that condition the whole world crying out to him to be rectified, would not have to address himself laboriously to the task, as if it were his business to rectify the world. Nothing could hurt that man; the greatest floods, reaching to the sky, could not drown him, nor would he feel the fervour of the greatest heats melting metals and stones till they flowed, and scorching all the ground and hills. From the dust and chaff of himself, he could still mould and fashion Yâos and Shuns[1];—how should he be willing to occupy himself with things[2]?'

[1] Shun was the successor of Yâo in the ancient kingdom.

[2] All this description is to give us an idea of the 'Spirit-like man.' We have in it the results of the Tâo in its fullest embodiment.

6. A man of Sung, who dealt in the ceremonial caps (of Yin)[1], went with them to Yüeh[2], the people of which cut off their hair and tattooed their bodies, so that they had no use for them. Yâo ruled the people of the kingdom, and maintained a perfect government within the four seas. Having gone to see the four (Perfect) Ones[3] on the distant hill of Kû-shih, when (he returned to his capital) on the south of the Făn water[4], his throne appeared no more to his deep-sunk oblivious eyes[5].

7. Hui-ȝze[6] told *K*wang-ȝze, saying, 'The king of Wei[7] sent me some seeds of a large calabash, which I sowed. The fruit, when fully grown, could contain five piculs (of anything). I used it to contain water,

[1] See the Lî *K*î, IX, iii, 3.

[2] A state, part of the present province of *K*ieh-*k*iang.

[3] Said to have been Hsü Yû mentioned above, with Nieh *Kh*üeh, Wang Î, and Phî-î, who will by and by come before us.

[4] A river in Shan-hsî, on which was the capital of Yâo;—a tributary of the Ho.

[5] This paragraph is intended to give us an idea of 'the Perfect man,' who has no thought of himself. The description, however, is brief and tame, compared with the accounts of Hsü Yû and of 'the Spirit-like man.'

[6] Or Hui Shih, the chief minister of 'king Hui of Liang (or Wei), (B.C. 370–333),' with an interview between whom and Mencius the works of that philosopher commence. He was a friend of *K*wang-ȝze, and an eccentric thinker; and in Book XXXIII there is a long account of several of his views. I do not think that the conversations about 'the great calabash' and 'the great tree' really took place; *K*wang-ȝze probably invented them, to illustrate his point that size had nothing to do with the Tâo, and that things which seemed useless were not really so when rightly used.

[7] Called also Liang from the name of its capital. Wei was one of the three states (subsequently kingdoms), into which the great fief of Ȝin was divided about B.C. 400.

莊子

but it was so heavy that I could not lift it by myself. I cut it in two to make the parts into drinking vessels; but the dried shells were too wide and unstable and would not hold (the liquor); nothing but large useless things! Because of their uselessness I knocked them to pieces.' *K*wang-ȝze replied, 'You were indeed stupid, my master, in the use of what was large. There was a man of Sung who was skilful at making a salve which kept the hands from getting chapped; and (his family) for generations had made the bleaching of cocoon-silk their business. A stranger heard of it, and proposed to buy the art of the preparation for a hundred ounces of silver. The kindred all came together, and considered the proposal. "We have," said they, "been bleaching cocoon-silk for generations, and have only gained a little money. Now in one morning we can sell to this man our art for a hundred ounces;—let him have it." The stranger accordingly got it and went away with it to give counsel to the king of Wû[1], who was then engaged in hostilities with Yüeh. The king gave him the command of his fleet, and in the winter he had an engagement with that of Yüeh, on which he inflicted a great defeat[2], and was invested with a portion of territory taken from Yüeh. The keeping the hands from getting chapped was the same in both cases; but in the one case it led to the investiture (of the possessor of the salve), and

[1] A great and ancient state on the sea-board, north of Yüeh. The name remains in the district of Wû-*k*iang in the prefecture of Sû-*k*âu.

[2] The salve gave the troops of Wû a great advantage in a war on the *K*iang, especially in winter.

in the other it had only enabled its owners to continue their bleaching. The difference of result was owing to the different use made of the art. Now you, Sir, had calabashes large enough to hold five piculs;—why did you not think of making large bottle-gourds of them, by means of which you could have floated over rivers and lakes, instead of giving yourself the sorrow of finding that they were useless for holding anything. Your mind, my master, would seem to have been closed against all intelligence!'

Hui-ȝze said to *K*wang-ȝze, 'I have a large tree, which men call the Ailantus[1]. Its trunk swells out to a large size, but is not fit for a carpenter to apply his line to it; its smaller branches are knotted and crooked, so that the disk and square cannot be used on them. Though planted on the wayside, a builder would not turn his head to look at it. Now your words, Sir, are great, but of no use;—all unite in putting them away from them.' *K*wang-ȝze replied, 'Have you never seen a wild cat or a weasel? There it lies, crouching and low, till the wanderer approaches; east and west it leaps about, avoiding neither what is high nor what is low, till it is caught in a trap, or dies in a net. Again there is the Yak[2], so large that it is like a cloud hanging in the sky. It is large indeed, but it cannot catch mice. You, Sir, have a large tree and are troubled because it is of no use;—why do you not plant it in a tract where there is nothing else, or in a wide and barren wild?

[1] The Ailantus glandulosa, common in the north of China, called 'the fetid tree,' from the odour of its leaves.

[2] The bos grunniens of Thibet, the long tail of which is in great demand for making standards and chowries.

莊子

There you might saunter idly by its side, or in the enjoyment of untroubled ease sleep beneath it. Neither bill nor axe would shorten its existence; there would be nothing to injure it. What is there in its uselessness to cause you distress?'

BOOK II.

PART I. SECTION II.

*Kh*î Wû Lun, or 'The Adjustment of Controversies[1].'

1. Nan-kwo 3ze-*kh*î[2] was seated, leaning forward on his stool. He was looking up to heaven and breathed gently, seeming to be in a trance, and to have lost all consciousness of any companion. (His disciple), Yen *Kh*ăng 3ze-yû[3], who was in attendance and standing before him, said, 'What is this? Can the body be made to become thus like a withered tree, and the mind to become like slaked lime? His appearance as he leans forward on the stool to-day is such as I never saw him have before in the same position.' 3ze-*kh*î said, 'Yen, you do well to ask such a question, I had just now lost myself[4]; but how should you understand it? You

[1] See pp. 128–130.

[2] Nan-kwo, 'the southern suburb,' had probably been the quarter where 3ze-*kh*î had resided, and is used as his surname. He is introduced several times by *K*wang-3ze in his writings:—Books IV, 7; XXVII, 4, and perhaps elsewhere.

[3] We have the surname of this disciple, Yen (顏); his name, Yen (偃); his honorary or posthumous epithet (*Kh*ăng); and his ordinary appellation, 3ze-yû. The use of the epithet shows that he and his master had lived before our author.

[4] 'He had lost himself;' that is, he had become unconscious of all around him, and even of himself, as if he were about to enter

莊子

may have heard the notes[1] of Man, but have not heard those of Earth; you may have heard the notes of Earth, but have not heard those of Heaven.'

Ȝze-yû said, 'I venture to ask from you a description of all these.' The reply was, 'When the breath of the Great Mass (of nature) comes strongly, it is called Wind. Sometimes it does not come so; but when it does, then from a myriad apertures there issues its excited noise;—have you not heard it in a prolonged gale? Take the projecting bluff of a mountain forest;—in the great trees, a hundred spans round, the apertures and cavities are like the nostrils, or the mouth, or the ears; now square, now round like a cup or a mortar; here like a wet footprint, and there like a large puddle. (The sounds issuing from them are like) those of fretted water, of the arrowy whizz, of the stern command, of the inhaling of the breath, of the shout, of the gruff note, of the deep wail, of the sad and piping note. The first notes are slight, and those that follow deeper, but in harmony with them. Gentle winds produce a small response; violent winds a great one. When the fierce gusts have passed away, all the apertures

---

into the state of 'an Immortal,' a mild form of the Buddhistic samâdhi. But his attitude and appearance were intended by Kwang-ȝze to indicate what should be the mental condition in reference to the inquiry pursued in the Book;—a condition, it appears to me, of agnosticism. See the account of Lâo-ȝze in a similar trance in Book XXI, par. 4.

[1] The Chinese term here (lâi) denotes a reed or pipe, with three holes, by a combination of which there was formed the rudimentary or reed organ. Our author uses it for the sounds or notes heard in nature, various as the various opinions of men in their discussions about things.

are empty (and still);—have you not seen this in the bending and quivering of the branches and leaves?'

Ʒze-yû said, 'The notes of Earth then are simply those which come from its myriad apertures; and the notes of Man may just be compared to those which (are brought from the tubes of) bamboo;—allow me to ask about the notes of Heaven[1].' Ʒze-*khî* replied, 'When (the wind) blows, (the sounds from) the myriad apertures are different, and (its cessation) makes them stop of themselves. Both of these things arise from (the wind and the apertures) themselves:—should there be any other agency that excites them?'

2. Great knowledge is wide and comprehensive; small knowledge is partial and restricted. Great speech is exact and complete; small speech is (merely) so much talk[2]. When we sleep, the soul communicates with (what is external to us); when we awake, the body is set free. Our intercourse with others then leads to various activity, and daily there is the striving of mind with mind. There are hesitancies; deep difficulties; reservations; small apprehensions causing restless distress, and great

---

[1] The sounds of Earth have been described fully and graphically. Of the sounds of Man very little is said, but they form the subject of the next paragraph. Nothing is said in answer to the disciple's inquiry about the notes of Heaven. It is intimated, however, that there is no necessity to introduce any foreign Influence or Power like Heaven in connexion with the notes of Earth. The term Heaven, indeed, is about to pass with our author into a mere synonym of Tâo, the natural 'course' of the phenomena of men and things.

[2] Words are the 'sounds' of Man; and knowledge is the 'wind' by which they are excited.

莊子

apprehensions producing endless fears. Where their utterances are like arrows from a bow, we have those who feel it their charge to pronounce what is right and what is wrong; where they are given out like the conditions of a covenant, we have those who maintain their views, determined to overcome. (The weakness of their arguments), like the decay (of things) in autumn and winter, shows the failing (of the minds of some) from day to day; or it is like their water which, once voided, cannot be gathered up again. Then their ideas seem as if fast bound with cords, showing that the mind is become like an old and dry moat, and that it is nigh to death, and cannot be restored to vigour and brightness.

Joy and anger, sadness and pleasure, anticipation and regret, fickleness and fixedness, vehemence and indolence, eagerness and tardiness;—(all these moods), like music from an empty tube, or mushrooms from the warm moisture, day and night succeed to one another and come before us, and we do not know whence they sprout. Let us stop! Let us stop! Can we expect to find out suddenly how they are produced?

If there were not (the views of) another, I should not have mine; if there were not I (with my views), his would be uncalled for:—this is nearly a true statement of the case, but we do not know what it is that makes it be so. It might seem as if there would be a true Governor[1] concerned in it, but we do not find

[1] 'A true Governor' would be a good enough translation for 'the true God.' But *K*wang-ȝze did not admit any supernatural Power or Being as working in man. His true Governor was the Tâo; and this will be increasingly evident as we proceed with the study of his Books.

any trace (of his presence and acting). That such an One could act so I believe; but we do not see His form. He has affections, but He has no form.

Given the body, with its hundred parts, its nine openings, and its six viscera, all complete in their places, which do I love the most? Do you love them all equally? or do you love some more than others? Is it not the case that they all perform the part of your servants and waiting women? All of them being such, are they not incompetent to rule one another? or do they take it in turns to be now ruler and now servants? There must be a true Ruler (among them)[1] whether by searching you can find out His character or not, there is neither advantage nor hurt, so far as the truth of His operation is concerned. When once we have received the bodily form complete, its parts do not fail to perform their functions till the end comes. In conflict with things or in harmony with them, they pursue their course to the end, with the speed of a galloping horse which cannot be stopped;—is it not sad? To be constantly toiling all one's lifetime, without seeing the fruit of one's labour, and to be weary and worn out with his labour, without knowing where he is going to:—is it not a deplorable case? Men may say, 'But it is not death;' yet of what advantage is this? When the body is decomposed, the mind will be the same along with it:—must not the case be pronounced very deplorable[2]? Is the life

[1] The name 'Ruler' is different from 'Governor' above; but they both indicate the same concept in the author's mind.

[2] The proper reply to this would be that the mind is not dissolved with the body; and *K*wang-ȝze's real opinion, as we shall find, was that life and death were but phases in the phenomenal

莊子

of man indeed enveloped in such darkness? Is it I alone to whom it appears so? And does it not appear to be so to other men?

3. If we were to follow the judgments of the predetermined mind, who would be left alone and without a teacher[1]? Not only would it be so with those who know the sequences (of knowledge and feeling) and make their own selection among them, but it would be so as well with the stupid and unthinking. For one who has not this determined mind, to have his affirmations and negations is like the case described in the saying, 'He went to Yüeh to-day, and arrived at it yesterday[2].' It would be making what was not a fact to be a fact. But even the spirit-like Yü[3] could not have known how to do this, and how should one like me be able to do it?

But speech is not like the blowing (of the wind); the speaker has (a meaning in) his words. If, however, what he says, be indeterminate (as from a mind not made up), does he then really speak or not? He thinks that his words are different from the chirpings of fledgelings; but is there any distinction between them or not? But how can the Tâo be so obscured, that there should be 'a True' and 'a False' in it? How can speech be so obscured that there should be 'the Right' and 'the Wrong' about them? Where shall the Tâo go to that it will not

development. But the course of his argument suggests to us the question here, 'Is life worth living?'

[1] This 'teacher' is 'the Tâo.'

[2] Expressing the absurdity of the case. This is one of the sayings of Hui-ȝze;—see Book XXXIII, par. 7.

[3] The successor and counsellor of Shun, who coped with and remedied the flood of Yâo.

be found? Where shall speech be found that it will be inappropriate? Tâo becomes obscured through the small comprehension (of the mind), and speech comes to be obscure through the vain-gloriousness (of the speaker). So it is that we have the contentions between the Literati[1] and the Mohists[2], the one side affirming what the other denies, and vice versâ. If we would decide on their several affirmations and denials, no plan is like bringing the (proper) light (of the mind)[3] to bear on them.

All subjects may be looked at from (two points of view),—from that and from this. If I look at a thing from another's point of view, I do not see it; only as I know it myself, do I know it. Hence it is said, 'That view comes from this; and this view is a consequence of that:'—which is the theory that that view and this—(the opposite views)—produce each the other[4]. Although it be so, there is affirmed now life and now death; now death and now life; now the admissibility of a thing and now its inadmissibility; now its inadmissibility and now its admissibility. (The disputants) now affirm and now deny; now deny and now affirm. Therefore the sagely man does not pursue this method, but views things in the light of (his) Heaven[5] (-ly nature), and hence forms his judgment of what is right.

[1] The followers of Confucius.

[2] The disciples of Mih-ʒze, or Mih Tî, the heresiarch, whom Mencius attacked so fiercely;—see Mencius, V, 1, 5, et al. His era must be assigned between Confucius and Mencius.

[3] That is, the perfect mind, the principle of the Tâo.

[4] As taught by Hui-ʒze;—see XXXIII, 7; but it is doubtful if the quotation from Hui's teaching be complete.

[5] Equivalent to the Tâo. See on the use in Lâo-ʒze and *K*wang-ʒze of the term 'Heaven,' in the Introduction, pp. 16–18.

莊子

This view is the same as that, and that view is the same as this. But that view involves both a right and a wrong; and this view involves also a right and a wrong:—are there indeed, or are there not the two views, that and this? They have not found their point of correspondency which is called the pivot of the Tâo. As soon as one finds this pivot, he stands in the centre of the ring (of thought), where he can respond without end to the changing views;—without end to those affirming, and without end to those denying. Therefore I said, 'There is nothing like the proper light (of the mind).'

4. By means of a finger (of my own) to illustrate that the finger (of another) is not a finger is not so good a plan as to illustrate that it is not so by means of what is (acknowledged to be) not a finger; and by means of (what I call) a horse to illustrate that (what another calls) a horse is not so, is not so good a plan as to illustrate that it is not a horse, by means of what is (acknowledged to be) not a horse[1]. (All things in) heaven and earth may be (dealt with as) a finger; (each of) their myriads may be (dealt with as) a horse. Does a thing seem so to me? (I say that) it is so. Does it seem not so to me? (I say that) it is not so. A path is formed by (constant)

[1] The language of our author here is understood to have reference to the views of Kung-sun Lung, a contemporary of Hui-3ze, and a sophist like him. One of his treatises or arguments had the title of 'The White Horse,' and another that of 'Pointing to Things.' If these had been preserved, we might have seen more clearly the appropriateness of the text here. But the illustration of the monkeys and their actions shows us the scope of the whole paragraph to be that controversialists, whose views are substantially the same, may yet differ, and that with heat, in words.

treading on the ground. A thing is called by its name through the (constant) application of the name to it. How is it so? It is so because it is so. How is it not so? It is not so, because it is not so. Everything has its inherent character and its proper capability. There is nothing which has not these. Therefore, this being so, if we take a stalk of grain[1] and a (large) pillar, a loathsome (leper) and (a beauty like) Hsî Shih[2], things large and things insecure, things crafty and things strange;—they may in the light of the Tâo all be reduced to the same category (of opinion about them).

It was separation that led to completion; from completion ensued dissolution. But all things, without regard to their completion and dissolution, may again be comprehended in their unity;—it is only the far reaching in thought who know how to comprehend them in this unity. This being so, let us give up our devotion to our own views, and occupy ourselves with the ordinary views. These ordinary views are grounded on the use of things. (The study of that) use leads to the comprehensive judgment, and that judgment secures the success (of the inquiry). That success gained, we are near (to the object of our search), and there we stop. When we stop, and yet we do not know how it is so, we have what is called the Tâo.

When we toil our spirits and intelligence, obstin-

[1] The character in the text means both 'a stalk of grain' and 'a horizontal beam.' Each meaning has its advocates here.

[2] A famous beauty, a courtezan presented by the king of Yüeh to his enemy, the king of Wû, and who hastened on his progress to ruin and death, she herself perishing at the same time.

ately determined (to establish our own view), and do not know the agreement (which underlies it and the views of others), we have what is called 'In the morning three.' What is meant by that 'In the morning three?' A keeper of monkeys, in giving them out their acorns, (once) said, 'In the morning I will give you three (measures) and in the evening four.' This made them all angry, and he said, 'Very well. In the morning I will give you four and in the evening three.' His two proposals were substantially the same, but the result of the one was to make the creatures angry, and of the other to make them pleased:—an illustration of the point I am insisting on. Therefore the sagely man brings together a dispute in its affirmations and denials, and rests in the equal fashioning of Heaven[1]. Both sides of the question are admissible.

5. Among the men of old their knowledge reached the extreme point. What was that extreme point? Some held that at first there was not anything. This is the extreme point, the utmost point to which nothing can be added[2]. A second class held that there was something, but without any responsive recognition[3] of it (on the part of men).

A third class held that there was such recognition, but there had not begun to be any expression of different opinions about it.

---

[1] Literally, 'the Heaven-Mould or Moulder,'—another name for the Tâo, by which all things are fashioned.

[2] See the same passage in Book XXIII, par. 10.

[3] The ordinary reading here is făng (封), 'a boundary' or 'distinctive limit.' Lin Hsî-kung adopts the reading 對, 'a response,' and I have followed him.

It was through the definite expression of different opinions about it that there ensued injury to (the doctrine of) the Tâo. It was this injury to the (doctrine of the) Tâo which led to the formation of (partial) preferences. Was it indeed after such preferences were formed that the injury came? or did the injury precede the rise of such preferences? If the injury arose after their formation, *K*âo's method of playing on the lute was natural. If the injury arose before their formation, there would have been no such playing on the lute as *K*âo's [1].

*K*âo Wăn's playing on the lute, Shih Kwang's indicating time with his staff, and Hui-ȝze's (giving his views), while leaning against a dryandra tree (were all extraordinary). The knowledge of the three men (in their several arts) was nearly perfect, and therefore they practised them to the end of their lives. They loved them because they were different from those of others. They loved them and wished to make them known to others. But as they could not be made clear, though they tried to make them so, they ended with the obscure (discussions) about 'the hard' and 'the white.' And their sons [2], moreover, with all the threads of their fathers' compositions, yet to the end of their lives accomplished nothing. If they, proceeding in this way, could be said to have succeeded, then am I also successful;

[1] *K*âo Wăn and Shih Kwang were both musicians of the state of Ȝin. Shih, which appears as Kwang's surname, was his denomination as 'music-master.' It is difficult to understand the reason why *K*wang-ȝze introduces these men and their ways, or how it helps his argument.

[2] Perhaps we should read here 'son,' with special reference to the son of Hui-ȝze.

莊子

if they cannot be pronounced successful, neither I nor any other can succeed.

Therefore the scintillations of light from the midst of confusion and perplexity are indeed valued by the sagely man; but not to use one's own views and to take his position on the ordinary views is what is called using the (proper) light.

6. But here now are some other sayings[1]:—I do not know whether they are of the same character as those which I have already given, or of a different character. Whether they be of the same character or not when looked at along with them, they have a character of their own, which cannot be distinguished from the others. But though this be the case, let me try to explain myself.

There was a beginning. There was a beginning before that beginning[2]. There was a beginning previous to that beginning before there was the beginning.

There was existence; there had been no existence. There was no existence before the beginning of that no existence[2]. There was no existence previous to the no existence before there was the beginning of the no existence. If suddenly there was non-existence, we do not know whether it was really anything existing, or really not existing. Now I have said what I have said, but I do not know whether what I have said be really anything to the point or not.

[1] Referring, I think, to those below commencing 'There was a beginning.'

[2] That is, looking at things from the standpoint of an original non-existence, and discarding all considerations of space and time.

Under heaven there is nothing greater than the tip of an autumn down, and the Thâi mountain is small. There is no one more long-lived than a child which dies prematurely, and Phăng 3û did not live out his time. Heaven, Earth, and I were produced together, and all things and I are one. Since they are one, can there be speech about them? But since they are spoken of as one, must there not be room for speech? One and Speech are two; two and one are three. Going on from this (in our enumeration), the most skilful reckoner cannot reach (the end of the necessary numbers), and how much less can ordinary people do so! Therefore from non-existence we proceed to existence till we arrive at three; proceeding from existence to existence, to how many should we reach? Let us abjure such procedure, and simply rest here[1].

7. The Tâo at first met with no responsive recognition. Speech at first had no constant forms of expression. Because of this there came the demarcations (of different views). Let me describe those demarcations:—they are the Left and the Right[2]; the Relations and their Obligations[3]; Classifications[4]

[1] On this concluding clause, 3iâo Hung says:—'Avoiding such procedure, there will be no affirmations and denials (no contraries). The phrase 因是已 occurs in the Book several times, and interpreters have missed its meaning from not observing that 是已 serve merely as a final particle, and often have the 因 added to them, without affecting its meaning.' See also Wang Yin on the usages of 因 in the 皇清經解, ch. 1208, art. 6.

[2] That is, direct opposites.

[3] Literally, 'righteousnesses;' the proper way of dealing with the relations.

[4] Literally, 'separations.'

莊子

and their Distinctions; Emulations and Contentions. These are what are called 'the Eight Qualities.' Outside the limits of the world of men[1], the sage occupies his thoughts, but does not discuss about anything; inside those limits he occupies his thoughts, but does not pass any judgments. In the *Kh*un *Kh*iû[2], which embraces the history of the former kings, the sage indicates his judgments, but does not argue (in vindication of them). Thus it is that he separates his characters from one another without appearing to do so, and argues without the form of argument. How does he do so? The sage cherishes his views in his own breast, while men generally state theirs argumentatively, to show them to others. Hence we have the saying, 'Disputation is a proof of not seeing clearly.'

The Great Tâo[3] does not admit of being praised. The Great Argument does not require words. Great Benevolence is not (officiously) benevolent. Great Disinterestedness does not vaunt its humility. Great Courage is not seen in stubborn bravery.

The Tâo that is displayed is not the Tâo. Words that are argumentative do not reach the point. Benevolence that is constantly exercised does not accomplish its object. Disinterestedness that vaunts its purity is not genuine. Courage that is most stub-

[1] Literally, 'the six conjunctions,' meaning the four cardinal points of space, with the zenith and nadir; sometimes a name for the universe of space. Here we must restrict the meaning as I have done.

[2] 'The Spring and Autumn;'—Confucius's Annals of Lû, here complimented by *K*wang-ȝze. See in Mencius, IV, ii, 21.

[3] Compare the Tâo Teh *K*ing, ch. 25, et al.

born is ineffectual. These five seem to be round (and complete), but they tend to become square (and immovable)[1]. Therefore the knowledge that stops at what it does not know is the greatest. Who knows the argument that needs no words, and the Way that is not to be trodden[2]?

He who is able to know this has what is called 'The Heavenly Treasure-house[3].' He may pour into it without its being filled; he may pour from it without its being exhausted; and all the while he does not know whence (the supply) comes. This is what is called 'The Store of Light[3].'

Therefore of old Yâo asked Shun, saying, 'I wish to smite (the rulers of) Ʒung, Kwei, and Hsü-âo[4]. Even when standing in my court, I cannot get them out of my mind. How is it so?' Shun replied, 'Those three rulers live (in their little states) as if they were among the mugwort and other brushwood;—how is it that you cannot get them out of your mind? Formerly, ten suns came out together, and all things were illuminated by them;—how much should (your) virtue exceed (all) suns!'

8. Nieh *Kh*üeh[5] asked Wang Î[5], saying, 'Do you know, Sir, what all creatures agree in approving and

---

[1] Compare the use of 方 in the Shû *K*ing, I, iii, 11.

[2] The classic of Lâo, in chaps. 1, 2.

[3] Names for the Tâo.

[4] Three small states. Is Yâo's wish to smite an instance of the 'quality' of 'emulation' or jealousy?

[5] Both Tâoistic worthies of the time of Yâo, supposed to have been two of the Perfect Ones whom Yâo visited on the distant hill of Kû-shih (I, par. 6). According to Hwang Mî, Wang Î was the teacher of Nieh *Kh*üeh, and he again of Hsü Yû.

莊子

affirming?' 'How should I know it?' was the reply. 'Do you know what it is that you do not know?' asked the other again, and he got the same reply. He asked a third time,—'Then are all creatures thus without knowledge?' and Wang Î answered as before, (adding however), 'Notwithstanding, I will try and explain my meaning. How do you know that when I say "I know it," I really (am showing that) I do not know it, and that when I say "I do not know it," I really am showing that I do know it[1].' And let me ask you some questions:—'If a man sleep in a damp place, he will have a pain in his loins, and half his body will be as if it were dead; but will it be so with an eel? If he be living in a tree, he will be frightened and all in a tremble; but will it be so with a monkey? And does any one of the three know his right place? Men eat animals that have been fed on grain and grass; deer feed on the thick-set grass; centipedes enjoy small snakes; owls and crows delight in mice; but does any one of the four know the right taste? The dog-headed monkey finds its mate in the female gibbon; the elk and the axis deer cohabit; and the eel enjoys itself with other fishes. Mâo Ȝhiang[2] and Lî Kî[2] were accounted by men to be most beautiful, but when fishes saw them, they dived deep in the water from them; when birds, they flew from them aloft; and

[1] Compare par. 1 of Book XXII.

[2] Two famous beauties;—the former, a contemporary of Hsî Shih (par. 4, note 2), and like her also, of the state of Yüeh; the latter, the daughter of a barbarian chief among the Western Jung. She was captured by duke Hsien of Ȝin, in B.C. 672. He subsequently made her his wife,—to the great injury of his family and state.

when deer saw them, they separated and fled away[1]. But did any of these four know which in the world is the right female attraction? As I look at the matter, the first principles of benevolence and righteousness and the paths of approval and disapproval are inextricably mixed and confused together:—how is it possible that I should know how to discriminate among them?'

Nieh *Kh*üeh said (further), 'Since you, Sir, do not know what is advantageous and what is hurtful, is the Perfect man also in the same way without the knowledge of them?' Wang Î replied, 'The Perfect man is spirit-like. Great lakes might be boiling about him, and he would not feel their heat; the Ho and the Han might be frozen up, and he would not feel the cold; the hurrying thunderbolts might split the mountains, and the wind shake the ocean, without being able to make him afraid. Being such, he mounts on the clouds of the air, rides on the sun and moon, and rambles at ease beyond the four seas. Neither death nor life makes any change in him, and how much less should the considerations of advantage and injury do so[2]!'

9. *Kh*ü Ȝhiâo-ȝze[3] asked *Kh*ang-wû Ȝze[3], saying,

---

[1] Not thinking them beautiful, as men did, but frightened and repelled by them.

[2] Compare Book I, pars. 3 and 5.

[3] We know nothing of the former of these men, but what is mentioned here; the other appears also in Book XXV, 6, q. v. If 'the master' that immediately follows be Confucius they must have been contemporary with him. The *Kh*iû in *Kh*ang-wû's reply would seem to make it certain 'the master' was Confucius, but the oldest critics, and some modern ones as well, think that *Kh*ang-wû's name was also *Kh*iû. But this view is attended with more

莊子

'I heard the Master (speaking of such language as the following):—"The sagely man does not occupy himself with worldly affairs. He does not put himself in the way of what is profitable, nor try to avoid what is hurtful; he has no pleasure in seeking (for anything from any one); he does not care to be found in (any established) Way; he speaks without speaking; he does not speak when he speaks; thus finding his enjoyment outside the dust and dirt (of the world)." The Master considered all this to be a shoreless flow of mere words, and I consider it to describe the course of the Mysterious Way.—What do you, Sir, think of it?' *Kh*ang-wû Ȝze replied, 'The hearing of such words would have perplexed even Hwang-Tî, and how should *Kh*iû be competent to understand them? And you, moreover, are too hasty in forming your estimate (of their meaning). You see the egg, and (immediately) look out for the cock (that is to be hatched from it); you see the bow, and (immediately) look out for the dove (that is to be brought down by it) being roasted. I will try to explain the thing to you in a rough way; do you in the same way listen to me.

'How could any one stand by the side of the sun and moon, and hold under his arm all space and all time? (Such language only means that the sagely man) keeps his mouth shut, and puts aside questions that are uncertain and dark; making his inferior capacities unite with him in honouring (the One Lord). Men in general bustle about and toil; the

difficulties than the other. By the clause interjected in the translation after the first 'Master,' I have avoided the incongruity of ascribing the long description of Tâoism to Confucius.

sagely man seems stupid and to know nothing[1]. He blends ten thousand years together in the one (conception of time); the myriad things all pursue their spontaneous course, and they are all before him as doing so.

'How do I know that the love of life is not a delusion? and that the dislike of death is not like a young person's losing his way, and not knowing that he is (really) going home? Lî *K*î[2] was a daughter of the border Warden of Âi. When (the ruler of) the state of Ȝin first got possession of her, she wept till the tears wetted all the front of her dress. But when she came to the place of the king[3], shared with him his luxurious couch, and ate his grain-and-grass-fed meat, then she regretted that she had wept. How do I know that the dead do not repent of their former craving for life?

'Those who dream of (the pleasures of) drinking may in the morning wail and weep; those who dream of wailing and weeping may in the morning be going out to hunt. When they were dreaming they did not know it was a dream; in their dream they may even have tried to interpret it[4]; but when they awoke they knew that it was a dream. And

---

[1] Compare Lâo-ȝze's account of himself in his Work, ch. 20.

[2] See note 2 on page 191. The lady is there said to have been the daughter of a barbarian chief; here she appears as the child of the border Warden of Âi. But her maiden surname of *K*î (姬) shows her father must have been a scion of the royal family of *K*âu. Had he forsaken his wardenship, and joined one of the Tî tribes, which had adopted him as its chief?

[3] Ȝin was only a marquisate. How does *K*wang-ȝze speak of its ruler as 'a king?'

[4] This could not be; a man does not come to himself in his dream, and in that state try to interpret it.

莊子

there is the great awaking, after which we shall know that this life was a great dream[1]. All the while, the stupid think they are awake, and with nice discrimination insist on their knowledge; now playing the part of rulers, and now of grooms. Bigoted was that *Kh*iû! He and you are both dreaming. I who say that you are dreaming am dreaming myself. These words seem very strange; but if after ten thousand ages we once meet with a great sage who knows how to explain them, it will be as if we met him (unexpectedly) some morning or evening.

10. 'Since you made me enter into this discussion with you, if you have got the better of me and not I of you, are you indeed right, and I indeed wrong? If I have got the better of you and not you of me, am I indeed right and you indeed wrong? Is the one of us right and the other wrong? are we both right or both wrong? Since we cannot come to a mutual and common understanding, men will certainly continue in darkness on the subject.

'Whom shall I employ to adjudicate in the matter? If I employ one who agrees with you, how can he, agreeing with you, do so correctly? And the same may be said, if I employ one who agrees with me. It will be the same if I employ one who differs from us both or one who agrees with us both. In this way I and you and those others would all not be able to come to a mutual understanding; and shall we then wait for that (great sage)? (We need not do so.) To wait on others to learn how conflicting opinions are changed is simply like not so

[1] Compare XVIII, par. 4.

O 2

waiting at all. The harmonising of them is to be found in the invisible operation of Heaven, and by following this on into the unlimited past. It is by this method that we can complete our years (without our minds being disturbed)[1].

'What is meant by harmonising (conflicting opinions) in the invisible operation of Heaven? There is the affirmation and the denial of it; and there is the assertion of an opinion and the rejection of it. If the affirmation be according to the reality of the fact, it is certainly different from the denial of it:—there can be no dispute about that. If the assertion of an opinion be correct, it is certainly different from its rejection:—neither can there be any dispute about that. Let us forget the lapse of time; let us forget the conflict of opinions. Let us make our appeal to the Infinite, and take up our position there[2].'

11. The Penumbra asked the Shadow[3], saying, 'Formerly you were walking on, and now you have stopped; formerly you were sitting, and now you have risen up:—how is it that you are so without stability?' The Shadow replied, 'I wait for the movements of something else to do what I do, and that something else on which I wait waits further

[1] See this passage again in Book XXVII, par. 1, where the phrase which I have called here 'the invisible operation of Heaven,' is said to be the same as 'the Heavenly Mould or Moulder,' that is, the Heavenly Fashioner, one of the Tâoistic names for the Tâo.

[2] That is, all things being traced up to the unity of the Tâo, we have found the pivot to which all conflicting opinions, all affirmations, all denials, all positions and negatives converge, and bring to bear on them the proper light of the mind. Compare paragraph 3.

[3] A story to the same effect as this here, with some textual variations, occurs in Book XXVII, immediately after par. 1 referred to above.

莊子

on another to do as it does[1]. My waiting,—is it for the scales of a snake, or the wings of a cicada[2]? How should I know why I do one thing, or do not do another[3]?

'Formerly, I, *K*wang *K*âu, dreamt that I was a butterfly, a butterfly flying about, feeling that it was enjoying itself. I did not know that it was *K*âu. Suddenly I awoke, and was myself again, the veritable *K*âu. I did not know whether it had formerly been *K*âu dreaming that he was a butterfly, or it was now a butterfly dreaming that it was *K*âu. But between *K*âu and a butterfly there must be a difference[4]. This is a case of what is called the Transformation of Things[4].'

---

[1] The mind cannot rest in second causes, and the first cause, if there be one, is inscrutable.

[2] Even these must wait for the will of the creature; but the case of the shadow is still more remarkable.

[3] I have put this interrogatively, as being more graphic, and because of the particle 邪, which is generally, though not necessarily, interrogative.

[4] Hsüan Ying, in his remarks on these two sentences, brings out the force of the story very successfully:—'Looking at them in their ordinary appearance, there was necessarily a difference between them, but in the delusion of the dream each of them appeared the other, and they could not distinguish themselves! *K*âu could be a butterfly, and the butterfly could be *K*âu;—we may see that in the world all traces of that and this may pass away, as they come under the influence of transformations.' For the phrase, 'the transformation of things,' see in Book XI, par. 5, et al. But the Tâoism here can hardly be distinguished from the Buddhism that holds that all human experience is merely so much mâya or illusion.

BOOK III.

PART I. SECTION III.

Yang Shang *K*û, or 'Nourishing the Lord of Life[1].'

1. There is a limit to our life, but to knowledge there is no limit. With what is limited to pursue after what is unlimited is a perilous thing; and when, knowing this, we still seek the increase of our knowledge, the peril cannot be averted[2]. There should not be the practice of what is good with any thought of the fame (which it will bring), nor of what is evil with any approximation to the punishment (which it will incur)[3]:—an accordance with the Central Element (of our nature)[4] is the regular way to preserve the body, to maintain the life, to nourish our parents, and to complete our term of years.

2. His cook[5] was cutting up an ox for the ruler Wăn-hui[5]. Whenever he applied his hand, leaned forward with his shoulder, planted his foot, and em-

[1] See pp. 130, 131.

[2] Under what is said about knowledge here there lies the objection of Tâoists to the Confucian pursuit of knowledge as the means for the right conduct of life, instead of the quiet simplicity and self-suppression of their own system.

[3] This is the key to the three paragraphs that follow. But the text of it is not easily construed. The 'doing good' and the 'doing evil' are to be lightly understood.

[4] A name for the Tâo.

[5] 'The ruler Wăn-hui' is understood to be 'king Hui of Liang (or Wei),' with the account of an interview between whom and Mencius the works of that philosopher commence.

ployed the pressure of his knee, in the audible ripping off of the skin, and slicing operation of the knife, the sounds were all in regular cadence. Movements and sounds proceeded as in the dance of 'the Mulberry Forest[1]' and the blended notes of 'the *K*ing Shâu[1].' The ruler said, 'Ah! Admirable! That your art should have become so perfect!' (Having finished his operation), the cook laid down his knife, and replied to the remark, 'What your servant loves is the method of the Tâo, something in advance of any art. When I first began to cut up an ox, I saw nothing but the (entire) carcase. After three years I ceased to see it as a whole. Now I deal with it in a spirit-like manner, and do not look at it with my eyes. The use of my senses is discarded, and my spirit acts as it wills. Observing the natural lines, (my knife) slips through the great crevices and slides through the great cavities, taking advantage of the facilities thus presented. My art avoids the membranous ligatures, and much more the great bones.

'A good cook changes his knife every year;—(it may have been injured) in cutting; an ordinary cook changes his every month;—(it may have been) broken. Now my knife has been in use for nineteen years; it has cut up several thousand oxen, and yet its edge is as sharp as if it had newly come from the whetstone. There are the interstices of the joints, and the edge of the knife has no (appreciable) thickness; when that which is so thin enters where the interstice is, how easily it moves along! The

---

[1] Two pieces of music, ascribed to *Kh*ăng Thang and Hwang-Tî.

blade has more than room enough. Nevertheless, whenever I come to a complicated joint, and see that there will be some difficulty, I proceed anxiously and with caution, not allowing my eyes to wander from the place, and moving my hand slowly. Then by a very slight movement of the knife, the part is quickly separated, and drops like (a clod of) earth to the ground. Then standing up with the knife in my hand, I look all round, and in a leisurely manner, with an air of satisfaction, wipe it clean, and put it in its sheath.' The ruler Wăn-hui said, 'Excellent! I have heard the words of my cook, and learned from them the nourishment of (our) life.'

3. When Kung-wăn Hsien[1] saw the Master of the Left, he was startled, and said, 'What sort of man is this? How is it he has but one foot? Is it from Heaven? or from Man?' Then he added[2], 'It must be from Heaven, and not from Man. Heaven's making of this man caused him to have but one foot. In the person of man, each foot has its marrow. By this I know that his peculiarity is from Heaven, and not from Man. A pheasant of the marshes has to take ten steps to pick up a mouthful of food, and thirty steps to get a drink, but it does not seek to be nourished in a coop. Though its spirit would (there) enjoy a royal abundance, it does not think (such confinement) good.'

[1] There was a family in Wei with the double surname Kung-wăn. This would be a scion of it.

[2] This is Hsien still speaking. We have to understand his reasoning ad sensum and not ad verbum. The master of the Left had done 'evil,' so as to incur the punishment from which he suffered; and had shown himself less wise than a pheasant.

莊子

4. When Lâo Tan died[1], *Kh*in Shih[2] went to condole (with his son), but after crying out three times, he came out. The disciples[3] said to him, 'Were you not a friend of the Master?' 'I was,' he replied, and they said, 'Is it proper then to offer your condolences merely as you have done?' He said, 'It is. At first I thought he was the man of men, and now I do not think so. When I entered a little ago and expressed my condolences, there were the old men wailing as if they had lost a son, and the young men wailing as if they had lost their mother. In his attracting and uniting them to himself in such a way there must have been that which made them involuntarily express their words (of condolence), and involuntarily wail, as they were doing. And this was a hiding from himself of his Heaven (-nature), and an excessive indulgence of his (human) feelings;—a forgetting of what he had received (in being born); what the ancients called the punishment due to neglecting the Heaven (-nature)[4]. When the Master came[5], it was at the proper time; when he went away, it was the simple sequence (of his coming). Quiet acquiescence in what happens at its proper time, and quietly submitting (to its ceasing) afford no occasion for grief or for joy[6]. The ancients described (death) as the loosening of the

[1] Then the account that Lâo-ȝze went westwards, and that nothing is known as to where he died, must be without foundation.

[2] Nothing more is known of this person.

[3] Probably the disciples of Lâo-ȝze.

[4] Lâo had gone to an excess in his 'doing good,' as if he were seeking reputation.

[5] Into the world.

[6] See *K*wang-ȝze's remarks and demeanour on the death of his wife, in Book XVIII.

cord on which God suspended (the life)[1]. What we can point to are the faggots that have been consumed; but the fire is transmitted (elsewhere), and we know not that it is over and ended[2].

[1] This short sentence is remarkable by the use of the character Tî (帝), 'God,' in it, a usage here ascribed to the ancients.

[2] The concluding sentence might stand as a short paragraph by itself. The 'faggots' are understood to represent the body, and the 'fire' the animating spirit. The body perishes at death as the faggots are consumed by the fire. But the fire may be transmitted to other faggots, and so the spirit may migrate, and be existing elsewhere.

莊子

BOOK IV.

PART I. SECTION IV.

*Z*ăn *K*ien Shih, or 'Man in the World, Associated with other Men[1].'

1. Yen Hui[2] went to see *K*ung-nî[3], and asked leave to take his departure. 'Where are you going to?' asked the Master. 'I will go to Wei[4]' was the reply. 'And with what object?' 'I have heard that the ruler of Wei[5] is in the vigour of his years, and consults none but himself as to his course. He deals with his state as if it were a light matter, and has no perception of his errors. He thinks lightly of his people's dying; the dead are lying all over the country as if no smaller space could contain them; on the plains[6] and about the marshes, they are as thick as heaps of fuel. The people know not where to turn to. I have heard you, Master, say, "Leave the state that is well

[1] See pp. 131, 132.

[2] The favourite disciple of Confucius, styled also Ȝze-yüan.

[3] Of course, Confucius;—his designation or married name.

[4] A feudal state, embracing portions of the present provinces of Ho-nan, *K*ih-lî, and Shan-tung. There was another state, which we must also call Wei in English, though the Chinese characters of them are different;—one of the fragments of the great state of Ȝin, more to the west.

[5] At this time the marquis Yüan, known to us by his posthumous title of duke Ling;—see Book XXV, 9.

[6] Adopting Lin's reading of 平 instead of the common 乎.

governed; go to the state where disorder prevails[1].” At the door of a physician there are many who are ill. I wish through what I have heard (from you) to think out some methods (of dealing with Wei), if peradventure the evils of the state may be cured.’

*K*ung-nî said, ‘Alas! The risk is that you will go only to suffer in the punishment (of yourself)! The right method (in such a case) will not admit of any admixture. With such admixture, the one method will become many methods. Their multiplication will embarrass you. That embarrassment will make you anxious. However anxious you may be, you will not save (yourself). The perfect men of old first had (what they wanted to do) in themselves, and afterwards they found (the response to it) in others. If what they wanted in themselves was not fixed, what leisure had they to go and interfere with the proceedings of any tyrannous man?

‘Moreover, do you know how virtue is liable to be dissipated, and how wisdom proceeds to display itself? Virtue is dissipated in (the pursuit of) the name for it, and wisdom seeks to display itself in the striving with others. In the pursuit of the name men overthrow one another; wisdom becomes a weapon of contention. Both these things are instruments of evil, and should not be allowed to have free course in one's conduct. Supposing one's virtue to be great and his sincerity firm, if he do not comprehend the spirit of those (whom he wishes to influence); and supposing he is free from the

[1] Compare in the Analects, VIII, xiii, 2, where a different lesson is given; but Confucius may at another time have spoken as Hui says.

莊子

disposition to strive for reputation, if he do not comprehend their minds;—when in such a case he forcibly insists on benevolence and righteousness, setting them forth in the strongest and most direct language, before the tyrant, then he, hating (his reprover's) possession of those excellences, will put him down as doing him injury. He who injures others is sure to be injured by them in return. You indeed will hardly escape being injured by the man (to whom you go)!

'Further, if perchance he takes pleasure in men of worth and hates those of an opposite character, what is the use of your seeking to make yourself out to be different (from such men about him)? Before you have begun to announce (your views), he, as king and ruler, will take advantage of you, and immediately contend with you for victory. Your eyes will be dazed and full of perplexity; you will try to look pleased with him; you will frame your words with care; your demeanour will be conformed to his; you will confirm him in his views. In this way you will be adding fire to fire, and water to water, increasing, as we may express it, the evils (which you deplore). To these signs of deferring to him at the first there will be no end. You will be in danger, seeing he does not believe you, of making your words more strong, and you are sure to die at the hands of such a tyrant.

'And formerly *K*ieh[1] killed Kwan Lung-făng[2], and *K*âu[3] killed the prince Pî-kan[4]. Both of

[1] The tyrant with whom the dynasty of Hsiâ ended.

[2] A worthy minister of *K*ieh.

[3] The tyrant with whom the dynasty of Shang or Yin ended.

[4] A half-brother of *K*âu, the tyrant of the Yin dynasty.

these cultivated their persons, bending down in sympathy with the lower people to comfort them suffering (as they did) from their oppressors, and on their account opposing their superiors. On this account, because they so ordered their conduct, their rulers compassed their destruction:—such regard had they for their own fame. (Again), Yâo anciently attacked (the states of) 3hung-*k*ih [1] and Hsü-âo [1], and Yü attacked the ruler of Hû [1]. Those states were left empty, and with no one to continue their population, the people being exterminated. They had engaged in war without ceasing; their craving for whatever they could get was insatiable. And this (ruler of Wei) is, like them, one who craves after fame and greater substance;—have you not heard it? Those sages were not able to overcome the thirst for fame and substance;—how much less will you be able to do so! Nevertheless you must have some ground (for the course which you wish to take); pray try and tell it to me.'

Yen Hui said, 'May I go, doing so in uprightness and humility, using also every endeavour to be uniform (in my plans of operation)?' 'No, indeed!' was the reply. 'How can you do so? This man makes a display[2] of being filled to overflowing (with virtue), and has great self-conceit. His feelings are not to be determined from his countenance. Ordinary men do not (venture to) oppose him, and he proceeds from the way in which he affects them

[1] See in par. 7, Book II, where Hsü-âo is mentioned, though not 3hung-*k*ih. See the Shû, III, ii.

[2] I take 陽 here as = 佯;—a meaning given in the Khang-hsî dictionary.

莊子

to seek still more the satisfaction of his own mind. He may be described as unaffected by the (small lessons of) virtue brought to bear on him from day to day; and how much less will he be so by your great lessons? He will be obstinate, and refuse to be converted. He may outwardly agree with you, but inwardly there will be no self-condemnation;—how can you (go to him in this way and be successful)?'

(Yen Hui) rejoined, 'Well then; while inwardly maintaining my straightforward intention, I will outwardly seem to bend to him. I will deliver (my lessons), and substantiate them by appealing to antiquity. Inwardly maintaining my straightforward intention, I shall be a co-worker with Heaven. When I thus speak of being a co-worker with Heaven, it is because I know that (the sovereign, whom we style) the son of Heaven, and myself, are equally regarded by Heaven as Its sons. And should I then, as if my words were only my own, be seeking to find whether men approved of them, or disapproved of them? In this way men will pronounce me a (sincere and simple[1]) boy. This is what is called being a co-worker with Heaven.

'Outwardly bending (to the ruler), I shall be a co-worker with other men. To carry (the memorandum tablet to court)[2], to kneel, and to bend the body reverentially:—these are the observances of ministers. They all employ them, and should I presume not to do so? Doing what other men do, they would have no occasion to blame me. This

[1] Entirely unsophisticated, governed by the Tâo.

[2] See the Lî Kî, XI, ii, 16, 17.

is what is called being a fellow-worker with other men.

'Fully declaring my sentiments and substantiating them by appealing to antiquity, I shall be a co-worker with the ancients. Although the words in which I convey my lessons may really be condemnatory (of the ruler), they will be those of antiquity, and not my own. In this way, though straightforward, I shall be free from blame. This is what is called being a co-worker with antiquity. May I go to Wei in this way, and be successful?' 'No indeed!' said *K*ung-nî. 'How can you do so? You have too many plans of proceeding, and have not spied out (the ruler's character). Though you firmly adhere to your plans, you may be held free from transgression, but this will be all the result. How can you (in this way) produce the transformation (which you desire)? All this only shows (in you) the mind of a teacher!'

2. Yen Hui said, 'I can go no farther; I venture to ask the method from you.' *K*ung-nî replied, 'It is fasting[1], (as) I will tell you. (But) when you have the method, will you find it easy to practise it? He who thinks it easy will be disapproved of by the bright Heaven.' Hui said, 'My family is poor. For months together we have no spirituous drink, nor do we taste the proscribed food or any strong-smelling vegetables[2];—can this be regarded as fasting?' The reply was, 'It is the fasting appropriate to sacrificing, but it is not the fasting

[1] The term is emphatic, as Confucius goes on to explain.

[2] Such as onions and garlic, with horse, dog, cow, goose, and pigeon.

of the mind.' 'I venture to ask what that fasting of the mind is,' said Hui, and *K*ung-nî answered, 'Maintain a perfect unity in every movement of your will. You will not wait for the hearing of your ears about it, but for the hearing of your mind. You will not wait even for the hearing of your mind, but for the hearing of the spirit[1]. Let the hearing (of the ears) rest with the ears. Let the mind rest in the verification (of the rightness of what is in the will). But the spirit is free from all pre-occupation and so waits for (the appearance of) things. Where the (proper) course is[2], there is freedom from all pre-occupation;—such freedom is the fasting of the mind.' Hui said[3], 'Before it was possible for me to employ (this method), there I was, the Hui that I am; now, that I can employ it, the Hui that I was has passed away. Can I be said to have obtained this freedom from pre-occupation?' The Master replied, 'Entirely. I tell you that you can enter and be at ease in the enclosure (where he is), and not come into collision with the reputation (which belongs to him). If he listen to your counsels, let him hear your notes; if he will not listen, be silent. Open no (other) door; employ no other medicine; dwell with him (as with a friend) in the same apartment, and as if you had no other option, and you will not be far from success in your object. Not to move a step is easy; to walk without treading on the ground is difficult. In acting after the manner of men, it is easy to fall

[1] The character in the text for 'spirit' here is 氣, 'the breath.'

[2] The Tâo.

[3] 'Said;' probably, after having made trial of this fasting.

into hypocrisy; in acting after the manner of Heaven, it is difficult to play the hypocrite. I have heard of flying with wings; I have not heard of flying without them. I have heard of the knowledge of the wise; I have not heard of the knowledge of the unwise. Look at that aperture (left in the wall);—the empty apartment is filled with light through it. Felicitous influences rest (in the mind thus emblemed), as in their proper resting place. Even when they do not so rest, we have what is called (the body) seated and (the mind) galloping abroad. The information that comes through the ears and eyes is comprehended internally, and the knowledge of the mind becomes something external:—(when this is the case), the spiritual intelligences will come, and take up their dwelling with us, and how much more will other men do so! All things thus undergo a transforming influence. This was the hinge on which Yü and Shun moved; it was this which Fû-hsî[1] and *K*î-*kh*ü[2] practised all their lives: how much more should other men follow the same rule!'

3. Ȝze-kâo[3], duke of Sheh, being about to proceed on a mission to *Kh*î, asked *K*ung-nî, saying, 'The king is sending me, *K*û-liang[3], on a mission which

---

[1] Often spoken of as Fo-hî, the founder of the Chinese kingdom. His place in chronology should be assigned to him more than B.C. 3000 rather than under that date.

[2] A predecessor of Fû-hsî, a sovereign of the ancient paradisiacal time.

[3] The name of Sheh remains in Sheh-hsien, a district of the department Nan-yang, Ho-nan. Its governor, who is the subject of this narrative, was a Shăn *K*û-liang, styled Ȝze-kâo. He was

is very important. *Khî* will probably treat me as his commissioner with great respect, but it will not be in a hurry (to attend to the business). Even an ordinary man cannot be readily moved (to action), and how much less the prince of a state! I am very full of apprehension. You, Sir, once said to me that of all things, great or small, there were few which, if not conducted in the proper way[1], could be brought to a happy conclusion; that, if the thing were not successful, there was sure to be the evil of being dealt with after the manner of men[2]; that, if it were successful, there was sure to be the evil of constant anxiety[3]; and that, whether it succeeded or not, it was only the virtuous man who could secure its not being followed by evil. In my diet I take what is coarse, and do not seek delicacies,—a man whose cookery does not require him to be using cooling drinks. This morning I received my charge, and in the evening I am drinking iced water;—am I not feeling the internal heat (and discomfort)? Such is my state before I have actually engaged in the affair;—I am already suffering from conflicting anxieties. And if the thing do not succeed, (the king) is sure to deal with me after the manner of men. The evil is twofold; as a minister, I am not able to bear the burden (of the mission). Can

not a duke, but as the counts of *Khû* had usurped the name of king, they gave high-sounding names to all their ministers and officers.

[1] Or, 'according to the Tâo.'

[2] As a criminal; punished by his sovereign.

[3] Anxiety 'night and day,' or 'cold and hot' fits of trouble;—a peculiar usage of Yin Yang.

P 2

you, Sir, tell me something (to help me in the case)?'

*K*ung-nî replied, 'In all things under heaven there are two great cautionary considerations:—the one is the requirement implanted (in the nature)[1]; the other is the conviction of what is right. The love of a son for his parents is the implanted requirement, and can never be separated from his heart; the service of his ruler by a minister is what is right, and from its obligation there is no escaping anywhere between heaven and earth. These are what are called the great cautionary considerations. Therefore a son finds his rest in serving his parents without reference to or choice of place; and this is the height of filial duty. In the same way a subject finds his rest in serving his ruler, without reference to or choice of the business; and this is the fullest discharge of loyalty. When men are simply obeying (the dictates of) their hearts, the considerations of grief and joy are not readily set before them. They know that there is no alternative to their acting as they do, and rest in it as what is appointed; and this is the highest achievement of virtue. He who is in the position of a minister or of a son has indeed to do what he cannot but do. Occupied with the details of the business (in hand), and forgetful of his own person, what leisure has he to think of his pleasure in living or his dislike of death? You, my master, may well proceed on your mission.

'But let me repeat to you what I have heard:—In

[1] The Ming of the text here is that in the first sentence of the *K*ung Yung.

莊子

all intercourse (between states), if they are near to each other, there should be mutual friendliness, verified by deeds; if they are far apart, there must be sincere adherence to truth in their messages. Those messages will be transmitted by internuncios. But to convey messages which express the complacence or the dissatisfaction of the two parties is the most difficult thing in the world. If they be those of mutual complacence, there is sure to be an overflow of expressions of satisfaction; if of mutual dissatisfaction, an overflow of expressions of dislike. But all extravagance leads to reckless language, and such language fails to command belief. When this distrust arises, woe to the internuncio! Hence the Rules for Speech[1] say, "Transmit the message exactly as it stands; do not transmit it with any overflow of language; so is (the internuncio) likely to keep himself whole."

4. 'Moreover, skilful wrestlers begin with open trials of strength, but always end with masked attempts (to gain the victory); as their excitement grows excessive, they display much wonderful dexterity. Parties drinking according to the rules at first observe good order, but always end with disorder; as their excitement grows excessive, their fun becomes uproarious[2]. In all things it is so. People are at first sincere, but always end with becoming rude; at the commencement things are treated as trivial,

[1] Probably a Collection of Directions current at the time; and which led to the name of Yang Hsiung's Treatise with the same name in our first century.

[2] See the Shih, II, vii, 6.

but as the end draws near, they assume great proportions. Words are (like) the waves acted on by the wind; the real point of the matters (discussed by them) is lost. The wind and waves are easily set in motion; the success of the matter of which the real point is lost is easily put in peril. Hence quarrels are occasioned by nothing so much as by artful words and one-sided speeches. The breath comes angrily, as when a beast, driven to death, wildly bellows forth its rage. On this animosities arise on both sides. Hasty examination (of the case) eagerly proceeds, and revengeful thoughts arise in their minds;—they do not know how. Since they do not know how such thoughts arise, who knows how they will end? Hence the Rules for Speech[1] say, "Let not an internuncius depart from his instructions. Let him not urge on a settlement. If he go beyond the regular rules, he will complicate matters. Departing from his instructions and urging on a settlement imperils negotiations. A good settlement is proved by its lasting long, and a bad settlement cannot be altered;—ought he not to be careful?"

'Further still, let your mind find its enjoyment in the circumstances of your position; nourish the central course which you pursue, by a reference to your unavoidable obligations. This is the highest object for you to pursue; what else can you do to fulfil the charge (of your father and ruler)[2]. The best thing you can do is to be prepared to sacrifice your life; and this is the most difficult thing to do.'

---

[1] See above, on preceding page.

[2] Not meaning the king of *Khû*; but the Tâo, whose will was to be found in his nature and the conditions of his lot.

莊子

5. Yen Ho[1], being about to undertake the office of Teacher of the eldest son of duke Ling of Wei, consulted *K*ü Po-yü[2]. 'Here,' said he, 'is this (young) man, whose natural disposition is as bad as it could be. If I allow him to proceed in a bad way, it will be at the peril of our state; if I insist on his proceeding in a right way, it will be at the peril of my own person. His wisdom is just sufficient to know the errors of other men, but he does not know how he errs himself. What am I to do in such a case?' *K*ü Po-yü replied, 'Good indeed is your question! Be on your guard; be careful; see that you keep yourself correct! Your best plan will be, with your person to seek association with him, and with your mind to try to be in harmony with him; and yet there are dangers connected with both of these things. While seeking to keep near to him, do not enter into his pursuits; while cultivating a harmony of mind with him, do not show how superior you are to him. If in your personal association you enter into his pursuits, you will fall with him and be ruined, you will tumble down with a crash. If in maintaining a harmony with his mind, you show how different you are from him, he will think you do so for the reputation and the name, and regard you as a creature of evil omen[3]. If you find him to be a mere boy, be you with him as another boy; if you find him one of those who will not have their ground marked out in the ordinary way, do you humour

[1] A member of the Yen family of Lû. We shall meet with him again in Books XIX, XXVIII, and XXXII.

[2] A minister of Wei; a friend and favourite of Confucius.

[3] Compare in the *K*ung Yung, ii, ch. 24.

him in this characteristic [1]; if you find him to be free from lofty airs, show yourself to be the same;—(ever) leading him on so as to keep him free from faults.

'Do you not know (the fate of) the praying mantis? It angrily stretches out its arms, to arrest the progress of the carriage, unconscious of its inability for such a task, but showing how much it thinks of its own powers. Be on your guard; be careful. If you cherish a boastful confidence in your own excellence, and place yourself in collision with him, you are likely to incur the fate (of the mantis).

'Do you not know how those who keep tigers proceed? They do not dare to supply them with living creatures, because of the rage which their killing of them will excite. They do not (even) dare to give them their food whole, because of the rage which their rending of it will excite. They watch till their hunger is appeased, (dealing with them) from their knowledge of their natural ferocity. Tigers are different from men, but they fawn on those who feed them, and do so in accordance with their nature. When any of these are killed by them, it is because they have gone against that nature.

'Those again who are fond of horses preserve their dung in baskets, and their urine in jars. If musquitoes and gadflies light on them, and the grooms brush them suddenly away, the horses break their bits, injure (the ornaments on) their heads, and smash those on their breasts. The more care that is taken of them, the more does their fond-

[1] Equivalent to 'Do not cross him in his peculiarities.'

莊子

ness (for their attendants) disappear. Ought not caution to be exercised (in the management of them)?'

6. A (master) mechanic, called Shih, on his way to *Kh*î, came to *Kh*ü-yüan[1], where he saw an oak-tree, which was used as the altar for the spirits of the land. It was so large that an ox standing behind it could not be seen. It measured a hundred spans round, and rose up eighty cubits on the hill before it threw out any branches, after which there were ten or so, from each of which a boat could be hollowed out. People came to see it in crowds as in a market place, but the mechanic did not look round at it, but held on his way without stopping. One of his workmen, however, looked long and admiringly at it, and then ran on to his master, and said to him, 'Since I followed you with my axe and bill, I have never seen such a beautiful mass of timber as this. Why would you, Sir, not look round at it, but went on without stopping?' 'Have done,' said Mr. Shih, 'and do not speak about it. It is quite useless. A boat made from its wood would sink; a coffin or shell would quickly rot; an article of furniture would soon go to pieces; a door would be covered with the exuding sap; a pillar would be riddled by insects; the material of it is good for nothing, and hence it is that it has attained to so great an age[2].'

[1] The name of a place; of a road; of a bend in the road; of a hill. All these accounts of the name are found in different editions of our author, showing that the locality had not been identified.

[2] No one has thought it worth cutting down.

When Mr. Shih was returning, the altar-oak appeared to him in a dream, and said, 'What other tree will you compare with me? Will you compare me to one of your ornamental trees? There are hawthorns, pear-trees, orange-trees, pummelo-trees, gourds and other low fruit-bearing plants. When their fruits are ripe, they are knocked down from them, and thrown among the dirt[1]. The large branches are broken, and the smaller are torn away. So it is that their productive ability makes their lives bitter to them; they do not complete their natural term of existence, but come to a premature end in the middle of their time, bringing on themselves the destructive treatment which they ordinarily receive. It is so with all things. I have sought to discover how it was that I was so useless;—I had long done so, till (the effort) nearly caused my death; and now I have learned it:—it has been of the greatest use to me. Suppose that I had possessed useful properties, should I have become of the great size that I am? And moreover you and I are both things;—how should one thing thus pass its judgment on another? how is it that you a useless man know all this about me a useless tree?' When Mr. Shih awoke, he kept thinking about his dream, but the workman said, 'Being so taken with its uselessness, how is it that it yet acts here as the altar for the spirits of the land?' 'Be still,' was the master's reply, 'and do not say a word. It simply happened to grow here; and thus those who do not know it do not speak ill of it as an evil thing. If it were not used as the altar, would it be in danger of

[1] This is the indignity intended.

莊子

being cut down? Moreover, the reason of its being preserved is different from that of the preservation of things generally; is not your explaining it from the sentiment which you have expressed wide of the mark?'

7. Nan-po Ʒze-*kh*î[1] in rambling about the Heights of Shang[2], saw a large and extraordinary tree. The teams of a thousand chariots might be sheltered under it, and its shade would cover them all! Ʒze-*kh*î said, 'What a tree is this! It must contain an extraordinary amount of timber! When he looked up, however, at its smaller branches, they were so twisted and crooked that they could not be made into rafters and beams; when he looked down to its root, its stem was divided into so many rounded portions that neither coffin nor shell could be made from them. He licked one of its leaves, and his mouth felt torn and wounded. The smell of it would make a man frantic, as if intoxicated, for more than three whole days together. 'This, indeed,' said he, 'is a tree good for nothing, and it is thus that it has attained to such a size. Ah! and spirit-like men acknowledge this worthlessness (and its result)[3].'

In Sung there is the district of *K*ing-shih[4], in which catalpae, cypresses, and mulberry trees grow well. Those of them which are a span or two or rather more in circumference[5] are cut down by persons who want to make posts to which to tie their

[1] Probably the Nan-kwo Ʒze-*kh*î at the beginning of the second Book.

[2] In the present department of Kwei-teh, Ho-nan.

[3] A difficult sentence to construe.

[4] In what part of the duchy we do not know.

[5] See Mencius, VI, i, 13.

monkeys; those which are three or four spans round are cut down by persons who want beams for their lofty and famous houses; and those of seven or eight spans are cut down by noblemen and rich merchants who want single planks for the sides of their coffins. The trees in consequence do not complete their natural term of life, and come to a premature end in the middle of their growth under the axe and bill;—this is the evil that befalls them from their supplying good timber.

In the same way the *K*ieh [1] (book) specifies oxen that have white foreheads, pigs that have turned-up snouts, and men that are suffering from piles, and forbids their being sacrificed to the Ho. The wizards know them by these peculiarities and consider them to be inauspicious, but spirit-like men consider them on this account to be very fortunate.

8. There was the deformed object Shû [2]. His chin seemed to hide his navel; his shoulders were higher than the crown of his head; the knot of his hair pointed to the sky; his five viscera were all compressed into the upper part of his body, and his two thigh bones were like ribs. By sharpening needles and washing clothes he was able to make a living. By sifting rice and cleaning it, he was able to support ten individuals. When the government was calling out soldiers, this poor Shû would bare his arms among the others; when it had any great service to be undertaken, because of his constant ailments, none of the work was assigned to him; when it was

[1] Probably the name of an old work on sacrifices. But was there ever a time in China when human sacrifices were offered to the Ho, or on any altar?

[2] One of *K*wang-ȝze's creations.

莊子

giving out grain to the sick, he received three *k*ung, and ten bundles of firewood. If this poor man, so deformed in body, was still able to support himself, and complete his term of life, how much more may they do so, whose deformity is that of their faculties[1]!

9. When Confucius went to *Kh*û[2], *Kh*ieh-yû, the madman of *Kh*û[3], as he was wandering about, passed by his door, and said, 'O Phoenix, O Phoenix, how is your virtue degenerated! The future is not to be waited for; the past is not to be sought again! When good order prevails in the world, the sage tries to accomplish all his service; when disorder prevails, he may preserve his life; at the present time, it is enough if he simply escape being punished. Happiness is lighter than a feather, but no one knows how to support it; calamity is heavier than the earth, and yet no one knows how to avoid it. Give over! give over approaching men with the lessons of your virtue! You are in peril! you are in peril, hurrying on where you have marked out the ground against your advance! I avoid publicity, I avoid publicity, that my path may not be injured. I pursue my course, now going backwards, now crookedly, that my feet may not be hurt[4].

---

[1] The deficiency of their faculties—here mental faculties—would assimilate them to the useless trees in the last two paragraphs, whose uselessness only proved useful to them.

[2] The great state of the south, having its capital in the present Hû-pei.

[3] See the Analects, XVIII, v.

[4] The madman would seem to contrast his own course with that of Confucius; but the meaning is very uncertain, and the text cannot be discussed fully in these short notes. There is a jingle

'The mountain by its trees weakens itself[1]. The grease which ministers to the fire fries itself. The cinnamon tree can be eaten, and therefore it is cut down. The varnish tree is useful, and therefore incisions are made in it. All men know the advantage of being useful, but no one knows the advantage of being useless.'

of rhyme also in the sentence, and some critics find something like this in them:

'Ye ferns, ye thorny ferns, O injure not my way!
To save my feet, I backward turn, or winding stray!'

[1] Literally, 'robs itself;'—exhausts its moisture or productive strength.

BOOK V.

Part I. Section V.

Teh Khung Fû, or 'The Seal of Virtue Complete[1].'

1. In Lû[2] there was a Wang Thâi[3] who had lost both his feet[4]; while his disciples who followed and went about with him were as numerous as those of Kung-nî. Khang Kî[5] asked Kung-nî about him, saying, 'Though Wang Thâi is a cripple, the disciples who follow him about divide Lû equally with you, Master. When he stands, he does not teach them; when he sits, he does not discourse to them. But they go to him empty, and come back full. Is there indeed such a thing as instruction without words[6]? and while the body is imperfect, may the mind be complete? What sort of man is he?'

Kung-nî replied, 'This master is a sage. I have

---

[1] See pp. 133, 134.

[2] The native state of Confucius, part of the present Shan-tung.

[3] A Tâoist of complete virtue; but probably there was not really such a person. Our author fabricates him according to his fashion.

[4] The character uh (兀) does not say that he had lost both his feet, but I suppose that such is the meaning, because of what is said of Toeless below that 'he walked on his heels to see Confucius.' The feet must have been amputated, or mutilated rather (justly or unjustly), as a punishment; but Kwang-ȝze wished to say nothing on that point.

[5] Perhaps a disciple of Confucius;—not elsewhere mentioned as such.

[6] See the Tâo Teh King, ch. 2.

only been too late in going to him. I will make him my teacher; and how much more should those do so who are not equal to me! Why should only the state of Lû follow him? I will lead on all under heaven with me to do so.' *Kh*ang *K*î rejoined, 'He is a man who has lost his feet, and yet he is known as the venerable Wang[1];—he must be very different from ordinary men. What is the peculiar way in which he employs his mind?' The reply was, 'Death and life are great considerations, but they could work no change in him. Though heaven and earth were to be overturned and fall, they would occasion him no loss. His judgment is fixed regarding that in which there is no element of falsehood[2]; and, while other things change, he changes not. The transformations of things are to him the developments prescribed for them, and he keeps fast hold of the author of them[2].'

*Kh*ang *K*î said, 'What do you mean?' 'When we look at things,' said *K*ung-nî, 'as they differ, we see them to be different, (as for instance) the liver and the gall, or *Kh*û and Yüeh; when we look at them, as they agree, we see them all to be a unity. So it is with this (Wang Thâi). He takes no knowledge of the things for which his ears and eyes are the appropriate organs, but his mind delights itself in the harmony of (all excellent) qualities. He looks at the unity which belongs to things, and does not perceive where they have suffered loss. He looks

[1] Literally, 'the Senior;' often rendered 'Teacher.'

[2] 'That in which there is no element of falsehood' is the Tâo, which also is the 'Author' of all the changes that take place in time and space. See the Introductory Note on the title and subject of the Book.

莊子

on the loss of his feet as only the loss of so much earth.'

*Kh*ang *K*î said, 'He is entirely occupied with his (proper) self[1]. By his knowledge he has discovered (the nature of) his mind, and to that he holds as what is unchangeable[1]; but how is it that men make so much of him?' The reply was, 'Men do not look into running water as a mirror, but into still water;—it is only the still water that can arrest them all, and keep them (in the contemplation of their real selves). Of things which are what they are by the influence of the earth, it is only the pine and cypress which are the best instances;—in winter as in summer brightly green[2]. Of those which were what they were by the influence of Heaven[3], the most correct examples were Yâo and Shun; fortunate in (thus) maintaining their own life correct, and so as to correct the lives of others.

'As a verification of the (power of) the original endowment, when it has been preserved, take the result of fearlessness,—how the heroic spirit of a single brave soldier has been thrown into an army of nine hosts[4]. If a man only seeking for fame and able in this way to secure it can produce such an effect, how much more (may we look for a greater

[1] Wang Thâi saw all things in the Tâo, and the Tâo in all things. Comp. Book XI, par. 7, et al.

[2] Notwithstanding his being a cripple. He forgets that circumstance himself, and all others forget it, constrained and won by his embodiment of the Tâo. What follows is an illustration of this, exaggerated indeed, but not so extravagantly as in many other passages.

[3] In the Tâoistic meaning of the term.

[4] The royal army consisted of six hosts; that of a great feudal prince of three. 'Nine hosts'=a very great army:

result) from one whose rule is over heaven and earth, and holds all things in his treasury, who simply has his lodging in the six members[1] of his body, whom his ears and eyes serve but as conveying emblematic images of things, who comprehends all his knowledge in a unity, and whose mind never dies! If such a man were to choose a day on which he would ascend far on high, men would (seek to) follow him there. But how should he be willing to occupy himself with other men?'

2. Shăn-thû *K*iâ[2] was (another) man who had lost his feet. Along with 3ze-*kh*ân[3] of *K*ăng[3] he studied under the master Po-hwăn Wû-žăn[4]. 3ze-*kh*ân said to him (one day), 'If I go out first, do you remain behind; and if you go out first, I will remain behind.' Next day they were again sitting together on the same mat in the hall, when 3ze-*kh*ân spoke the same words to him, adding, 'Now I am about to go out; will you stay behind or not? Moreover, when you see one of official rank (like myself), you do not try to get out of his way;—do you consider yourself equal to one of official rank?' Shăn-thû *K*iâ replied, 'In our Master's school is there indeed such recognition required of official rank? You are one, Sir, whose pleasure is in your official rank, and would therefore take precedence of other men. I

[1] The arms, legs, head, and trunk.

[2] Another cripple introduced by our author to serve his purpose.

[3] Kung-sun *Kh*iâo; a good and able minister of *K*ăng, an earldom forming part of the present Ho-nan. He was a contemporary of Confucius, who wept when he heard of his death in B.C. 522. He was a scion of the ruling house, which again was a branch of the royal family of *K*âu.

[4] A Tâoist teacher. See XXI, par. 9; XXXII, par. 1.

莊子

have heard that when a mirror is bright, the dust does not rest on it; when dust rests on it the mirror is not bright. When one dwells long with a man of ability and virtue, he comes to be without error. There now is our teacher whom you have chosen to make you greater than you are; and when you still talk in this way, are you not in error?' 3ze-*kh*ân rejoined, 'A (shattered) object as you are, you would still strive to make yourself out as good as Yâo! If I may form an estimate of your virtue, might it not be sufficient to lead you to the examination of yourself?' The other said, 'Most criminals, in describing their offences, would make it out that they ought not to have lost (their feet) for them; few would describe them so as to make it appear that they should not have preserved their feet. They are only the virtuous who know that such a calamity was unavoidable, and therefore rest in it as what was appointed for them. When men stand before (an archer like) Î[1] with his bent bow, if they are in the middle of his field, that is the place where they should be hit; and if they be not hit, that also was appointed. There are many with their feet entire who laugh at me because I have lost my feet, which makes me feel vexed and angry. But when I go to our teacher, I throw off that feeling, and return (to a better mood);—he has washed, without my knowing it, the other from me by (his instructions in) what is good. I have attended him now for nineteen years, and have not known that I am without my feet. Now, you, Sir, and I have for the object of our study the

[1] A famous archer of antiquity in the twenty-second century B.C., or perhaps earlier.

(virtue) which is internal, and not an adjunct of the body, and yet you are continually directing your attention to my external body;—are you not wrong in this?' Ȝze-*kh*ân felt uneasy, altered his manner and looks, and said, 'You need not, Sir, say anything more about it.'

3. In Lû there was a cripple, called Shû-shan the Toeless[1], who came on his heels to see *K*ung-nî. *K*ung-nî said to him, 'By your want of circumspection in the past, Sir, you have incurred such a calamity;—of what use is your coming to me now?' Toeless said, 'Through my ignorance of my proper business and taking too little care of my body, I came to lose my feet. But now I am come to you, still possessing what is more honourable than my feet, and which therefore I am anxious to preserve entire. There is nothing which Heaven does not cover, and nothing which Earth does not sustain; you, Master, were regarded by me as doing the part of Heaven and Earth;—how could I know that you would receive me in such a way?' Confucius rejoined, 'I am but a poor creature. But why, my master, do you not come inside, where I will try to tell you what I have learned?' When Toeless had gone out, Confucius said, 'Be stimulated to effort, my disciples. This toeless cripple is still anxious to learn to make up for the evil of his former conduct; —how much more should those be so whose conduct has been unchallenged!'

Mr. Toeless, however, told Lâo Tan (of the inter-

[1] 'Toeless' is a sort of nickname. Shû-shan or Shû hill was, probably, where he dwelt:—'Toeless of Shû hill.'

莊子

view), saying, 'Khung *Kh*iû, I apprehend, has not yet attained to be a Perfect man. What has he to do with keeping a crowd of disciples around him? He is seeking to have the reputation of being an extraordinary and marvellous man, and does not know that the Perfect man considers this to be as handcuffs and fetters to him.' Lâo Tan said, 'Why did you not simply lead him to see the unity of life and death, and that the admissible and inadmissible belong to one category, so freeing him from his fetters? Would this be possible?' Toeless said, 'It is the punishment inflicted on him by Heaven [1]. How can he be freed from it?'

4. Duke Âi of Lû [2] asked *K*ung-nî, saying, 'There was an ugly man in Wei, called Âi-thâi Tho [3]. His father-in-law, who lived with him, thought so much of him that he could not be away from him. His wife, when she saw him (ugly as he was), represented to her parents, saying, "I had more than ten times rather be his concubine than the wife of any other man [4]." He was never heard to take the lead in discussion, but always seemed to be of the same opinion with others. He had not the position of a ruler, so as to be able to save men from death. He had no revenues, so as to be able to satisfy men's craving for food. He was ugly enough, moreover, to scare

[1] 'Heaven' here is a synonym of Tâo. Perhaps the meaning is 'unavoidable;' it is so in the Tâoistic order of things.

[2] It was in the sixteenth year of duke Âi that Confucius died. Âi was marquis of Lû from B.C. 494 to 468.

[3] The account of Âi-thâi Tho is of course *K*wang-3ze's own fabrication. Âi-thâi is understood to be descriptive of his ugliness, and Tho to be his name.

[4] Perhaps this was spoken by his wife before their marriage.

the whole world. He agreed with men instead of trying to lead them to adopt his views; his knowledge did not go beyond his immediate neighbourhood[1]. And yet his father-in-law and his wife were of one mind about him in his presence (as I have said);—he must have been different from other men. I called him, and saw him. Certainly he was ugly enough to scare the whole world. He had not lived with me, however, for many months, when I was drawn to the man; and before he had been with me a full year, I had confidence in him. The state being without a chief minister, I (was minded) to commit the government to him. He responded to my proposal sorrowfully, and looked undecided as if he would fain have declined it. I was ashamed of myself (as inferior to him), but finally gave the government into his hands. In a little time, however, he left me and went away. I was sorry and felt that I had sustained a loss, and as if there were no other to share the pleasures of the kingdom with me. What sort of man was he?'

*K*ung-nî said, 'Once when I was sent on a mission to *Kh*û, I saw some pigs sucking at their dead mother. After a little they looked with rapid glances, when they all left her, and ran away. They felt that she did not see them, and that she was no longer like themselves. What they had loved in their mother was not her bodily figure, but what had given animation to her figure. When a man dies in battle, they do not at his interment employ the usual appendages

[1] One sees dimly the applicability of this illustration to the case in hand. What made Âi-thâi Tho so much esteemed was his mental power, quite independent of his ugly person.

莊子

of plumes[1]: as to supplying shoes to one who has lost his feet, there is no reason why he should care for them;—in neither case is there the proper reason for their use[1]. The members of the royal harem do not pare their nails nor pierce their ears[2]; when a man is newly married, he remains (for a time) absent from his official duties, and unoccupied with them[2]. That their bodies might be perfect was sufficient to make them thus dealt with;—how much greater results should be expected from men whose mental gifts are perfect! This Âi-thâi Tho was believed by men, though he did not speak a word; and was loved by them, though he did no special service for them. He made men appoint him to the government of their states, afraid only that he would not accept the appointment. He must have been a man whose powers[3] were perfect, though his realisation of them[3] was not manifested in his person.'

Duke Âi said, 'What is meant by saying that his powers were complete?' Kung-nî replied, 'Death and life, preservation and ruin, failure and success, poverty and wealth, superiority and inferiority, blame and praise, hunger and thirst, cold and heat;—these are the changes of circumstances, the operation of our appointed lot. Day and night they succeed to one another before us, but there is no wisdom

[1] See the Lî Kî, VIII, i, 7; but the applicability of these two illustrations is not so clear.

[2] These two have force as in 'reasoning from the less to the greater.' With the latter of the two compare the mosaical provision in Deuteronomy xxiv. 5.

[3] 'Powers' are the capacities of the nature,—the gift of the Tâo. 'Virtue' is the realisation or carrying out of those capacities.

able to discover to what they owe their origination. They are not sufficient therefore to disturb the harmony (of the nature), and are not allowed to enter into the treasury of intelligence. To cause this harmony and satisfaction ever to be diffused, while the feeling of pleasure is not lost from the mind; to allow no break to arise in this state day or night, so that it is always spring-time[1] in his relations with external things; in all his experiences to realise in his mind what is appropriate to each season (of the year)[2]:—these are the characteristics of him whose powers are perfect.'

'And what do you mean by the realisation of these powers not being manifested in the person?' (pursued further the duke). The reply was, 'There is nothing so level as the surface of a pool of still water. It may serve as an example of what I mean. All within its circuit is preserved (in peace), and there comes to it no agitation from without. The virtuous efficacy is the perfect cultivation of the harmony (of the nature). Though the realisation of this be not manifested in the person, things cannot separate themselves (from its influence).'

Some days afterwards duke Âi told this conversation to Min-ʒze[3], saying, 'Formerly it seemed to me the work of the sovereign to stand in court with his face to the south, to rule the kingdom, and to pay good heed to the accounts of the people concerned, lest any should come to a (miserable) death;—this

[1] Specially the season of complacent enjoyment.

[2] So, in Lin Hsî-*k*ung; but the meaning has to be forced out of the text.

[3] The disciple Min Sun or Min Ʒze-*kh*ien.

I considered to be the sum (of his duty). Now that I have heard that description of the Perfect man, I fear that my idea is not the real one, and that, by employing myself too lightly, I may cause the ruin of my state. I and Khung *Kh*iû are not on the footing of ruler and subject, but on that of a virtuous friendship.'

5. A person who had no lips, whose legs were bent so that he could only walk on his toes, and who was (otherwise) deformed[1], addressed his counsels to duke Ling of Wei, who was so pleased with him, that he looked on a perfectly formed man as having a lean and small neck in comparison with him. Another who had a large goitre like an earthenware jar[1] addressed his counsels to duke Hwan of *Kh*î[2], who was so pleased with him that he looked on a perfectly formed man as having a neck lean and small in comparison with him[3]. So it is that when one's virtue is extraordinary, (any deficiency in) his bodily form may be forgotten. When men do not forget what is (easily) forgotten, and forget what is not (easily) forgotten, we have a case of real oblivion. Therefore the sagely man has that in which his mind finds its enjoyment, and (looks on) wisdom as (but) the shoots from an old stump; agreements with others are to him but so much glue; kindnesses are

[1] These two men are undoubtedly inventions of *K*wang-ȝze. They are brought before us, not by surnames and names, but by their several deformities.

[2] The first of the five presiding chiefs; marquis of *Kh*î from B.C. 685 to 643.

[3] Lin Hsî-*k*ung wonders whether the story of the man who was so taken with the charms of a one-eyed courtesan, that he thought other women all had an eye too many, was taken from this!

(but the arts of) intercourse; and great skill is (but as) merchants' wares. The sagely man lays no plans;—of what use would wisdom be to him? He has no cutting and hacking to do;—of what use would glue be to him? He has lost nothing;—of what use would arts of intercourse be to him? He has no goods to dispose of;—what need has he to play the merchant? (The want of) these four things are the nourishment of (his) Heavenly (nature); that nourishment is its Heavenly food. Since he receives this food from Heaven, what need has he for anything of man's (devising)? He has the bodily form of man, but not the passions and desires of (other) men. He has the form of man, and therefore he is a man. Being without the passions and desires of men, their approvings and disapprovings are not to be found in him. How insignificant and small is (the body) by which he belongs to humanity! How grand and great is he in the unique perfection of his Heavenly (nature)!

Hui-ʒze said to *K*wang-ʒze, 'Can a man indeed be without desires and passions?' The reply was, 'He can.' 'But on what grounds do you call him a man, who is thus without passions and desires?' *K*wang-ʒze said, 'The Tâo[1] gives him his personal appearance (and powers); Heaven[2] gives him his bodily form; how should we not call him a man?' Hui-ʒze rejoined, 'Since you call him a man, how

[1] Lû Shû-*k*ih maintains here that 'the Tâo' and 'Heaven' have the same meaning; nor does he make any distinction between mâo (貌), 'the personal appearance,' and hsing (形), 'the figure,' or 'bodily form.'

[2] Compare in the Tâo Teh *K*ing expressions in li, 2, and lv, 5.

莊子

can he be without passions and desires?' The reply was, 'You are misunderstanding what I mean by passions and desires. What I mean when I say that he is without these is, that this man does not by his likings and dislikings do any inward harm to his body;—he always pursues his course without effort, and does not (try to) increase his (store of) life.' Hui-ȝze rejoined, 'If there were not that increasing of (the amount) of life, how would he get his body[1]?' *K*wang-ȝze said, 'The Tâo gives him his personal appearance (and powers); Heaven gives him his bodily form; and he does not by his likings and dislikings do any internal harm to his body. But now you, Sir, deal with your spirit as if it were something external to you, and subject your vital powers to toil. You sing (your ditties), leaning against a tree; you go to sleep, grasping the stump of a rotten dryandra tree. Heaven selected for you the bodily form (of a man), and you babble about what is strong and what is white[2].'

[1] Apparently a gross meaning attached by Hui-ȝze to *K*wang-ȝze's words.

[2] *K*wang-ȝze beats down his opponent, and contemptuously refers to some of his well-known peculiarities;—as in II, par. 5, XXXIII, par. 7, and elsewhere.

BOOK VI.

PART I. SECTION VI.

Tâ 3ung Shih, or 'The Great and Most Honoured Master[1].'

1. He who knows the part which the Heavenly[2] (in him) plays, and knows (also) that which the Human[2] (in him ought to) play, has reached the perfection (of knowledge). He who knows the part which the Heavenly plays (knows) that it is naturally born with him; he who knows the part which the Human ought to play (proceeds) with the knowledge which he possesses to nourish it in the direction of what he does not (yet) know[3]:—to complete one's natural term of years and not come to an untimely end in the middle of his course is the fulness of knowledge. Although it be so, there is an evil (attending this condition). Such knowledge still awaits the confirmation of it as correct; it does so because it is not yet determined[4]. How do we know that what

---

[1] See pp. 134–136.

[2] Both 'Heaven' and 'Man' here are used in the Tâoistic sense;—the meaning which the terms commonly have both with Lâo and *K*wang.

[3] The middle member of this sentence is said to be the practical outcome of all that is said in the Book; conducting the student of the Tâo to an unquestioning submission to the experiences in his lot, which are beyond his comprehension, and approaching nearly to what we understand by the Christian virtue of Faith.

[4] That is, there may be the conflict, to the end of life, between

莊子

we call the Heavenly (in us) is not the Human? and that what we call the Human is not the Heavenly? There must be the True man[1], and then there is the True knowledge.

2. What is meant by 'the True Man[2]?' The True men of old did not reject (the views of) the few; they did not seek to accomplish (their ends) like heroes (before others); they did not lay plans to attain those ends[3]. Being such, though they might make mistakes, they had no occasion for repentance; though they might succeed, they had no self-complacency. Being such, they could ascend the loftiest heights without fear; they could pass through water without being made wet by it; they could go into fire without being burnt; so it was

faith and fact, so graphically exhibited in the Book of Job, and compendiously described in the seventy-third Psalm.

[1] Here we meet with the True Man, a Master of the Tâo. He is the same as the Perfect Man, the Spirit-like Man, and the Sagely Man (see pp. 127, 128), and the designation is sometimes interchanged in the five paragraphs that follow with 'the Sagely Man.' Mr. Balfour says here that this name 'is used in the esoteric sense,—"partaking of the essence of divinity;"' and he accordingly translates 眞人 by 'the divine man.' But he might as well translate any one of the other three names in the same way. The Shwo Wăn dictionary defines the name by 仙人, 'a recluse of the mountain, whose bodily form has been changed, and who ascends to heaven;' but when this account was made, Tâoism had entered into a new phase, different from what it had in the time of our author.

[2] In this description of 'the True Man,' and in what follows, there is what is grotesque and what is exaggerated (see note on the title of the first Book, p. 127). The most prominent characteristic of him was his perfect comprehension of the Tâo and participation of it.

[3] 士 has here the sense of 事.

that by their knowledge they ascended to and reached the Tâo[1].

The True men of old did not dream when they slept, had no anxiety when they awoke, and did not care that their food should be pleasant. Their breathing came deep and silently. The breathing of the true man comes (even) from his heels, while men generally breathe (only) from their throats. When men are defeated in argument, their words come from their gullets as if they were vomiting. Where lusts and desires are deep, the springs of the Heavenly are shallow.

The True men of old knew nothing of the love of life or of the hatred of death. Entrance into life occasioned them no joy; the exit from it awakened no resistance. Composedly they went and came. They did not forget what their beginning had been, and they did not inquire into what their end would be. They accepted (their life) and rejoiced in it; they forgot (all fear of death), and returned (to their state before life)[1]. Thus there was in them what is called the want of any mind to resist the Tâo, and of all attempts by means of the Human to assist the Heavenly. Such were they who are called the True men.

3. Being such, their minds were free from all thought[2]; their demeanour was still and unmoved;

---

[1] Was not this the state of non-existence? We cannot say of Pantâoism. However we may describe that, the Tâo operates in nature, but is not identical with it.

[2] 心忘 appears in the common editions as 心志, which must have got into the text at a very early time. 'The mind forgetting,' or 'free from all thought and purpose,' appears every-

莊子

their foreheads beamed simplicity. Whatever coldness came from them was like that of autumn; whatever warmth came from them was like that of spring. Their joy and anger assimilated to what we see in the four seasons. They did in regard to all things what was suitable, and no one could know how far their action would go. Therefore the sagely man might, in his conduct of war, destroy a state without losing the hearts of the people[1]; his benefits and favours might extend to a myriad generations without his being a lover of men. Hence he who tries to share his joys with others is not a sagely man; he who manifests affection is not benevolent; he who observes times and seasons (to regulate his conduct) is not a man of wisdom; he to whom profit and injury are not the same is not a superior man; he who acts for the sake of the name of doing so, and loses his (proper) self is not the (right) scholar; and he who throws away his person in a way which is not the true (way) cannot command the service of others. Such men as Hû Pû-*k*ieh, Wû Kwang, Po-î, Shû-*kh*î, the count of *K*î, Hsü-yü, *K*î Thâ, and Shăn-thû Tî, all did service for other men, and sought to secure for them what they desired, not seeking their own pleasure[2].

where in the Book as a characteristic of the True Man. Not a few critics contend that it was this, and not the Tâo of which it is a quality, that *K*wang-ȝze intended by the 'Master' in the title.

[1] Such antithetic statements are startling, but they are common with both Lâo-ȝze and our author.

[2] The seven men mentioned here are all adduced, I must suppose, as instances of good and worthy men, but still inferior to the True Man. Of Hû Pû-*k*ieh all that we are told is that he was 'an ancient worthy.' One account of Wû Kwang is that he was of the time of Hwang-Tî, with ears seven inches long; another, that he

4. The True men of old presented the aspect of judging others aright, but without being partisans; of feeling their own insufficiency, but being without flattery or cringing. Their peculiarities were natural to them, but they were not obstinately attached to them; their humility was evident, but there was nothing of unreality or display about it. Their placidity and satisfaction had the appearance of joy; their every movement seemed to be a necessity to them. Their accumulated attractiveness drew men's looks to them; their blandness fixed men's attachment to their virtue. They seemed to accommodate themselves to the (manners of their age), but with a certain severity; their haughty indifference was beyond its control. Unceasing seemed their endeavours to keep (their mouths) shut; when they looked down, they had forgotten what they wished to say.

They considered punishments to be the substance (of government, and they never incurred it); ceremonies to be its supporting wings (and they always observed them); wisdom (to indicate) the time (for action, and they always selected it); and virtue to be accordance (with others), and they were all-accordant. Considering punishments to be the substance (of government), yet their generosity appeared in the (manner of their) infliction of death. Considering ceremonies to be its supporting wings, they pursued

---

was of the time of Thang, of the Shang dynasty. Po-î and Shû-*kh*î are known to us from the Analects; and also the count of *Kh*î, whose name, it is said, was Hsü-yü. I can find nothing about *K*î Thâ;—his name in 3iâo Hung's text is 紀他浣. Shǎn-thû Tî was of the Yin dynasty, a contemporary of Thang. He drowned himself in the Ho. Most of these are referred to in other places.

莊子

by means of them their course in the world. Considering wisdom to indicate the time (for action), they felt it necessary to employ it in (the direction of) affairs. Considering virtue to be accordance (with others), they sought to ascend its height along with all who had feet (to climb it). (Such were they), and yet men really thought that they did what they did by earnest effort[1].

5. In this way they were one and the same in all their likings and dislikings. Where they liked, they were the same; where they did not like, they were the same. In the former case where they liked, they were fellow-workers with the Heavenly (in them); in the latter where they disliked, they were co-workers with the Human in them. The one of these elements (in their nature) did not overcome the other. Such were those who are called the True men.

Death and life are ordained, just as we have the constant succession of night and day;—in both cases from Heaven. Men have no power to do anything in reference to them;—such is the constitution of things[2]. There are those who specially regard Heaven[3] as their father, and they still love It (distant as It is)[3];—how much more should they love

[1] All this paragraph is taken as illustrative of the True man's freedom from thought or purpose in his course.

[2] See note 3 on par. 1, p. 236.

[3] Love is due to a parent, and so such persons should love Heaven. There is in the text here, I think, an unconscious reference to the earliest time, before the views of the earliest Chinese diverged to Theism and Tâoism. We cannot translate the 身 here.

That which stands out (Superior and Alone)[1]! Some specially regard their ruler as superior to themselves, and will give their bodies to die for him;—how much more should they do so for That which is their true (Ruler)[1]! When the springs are dried up, the fishes collect together on the land. Than that they should moisten one another there by the damp about them, and keep one another wet by their slime, it would be better for them to forget one another in the rivers and lakes[2]. And when men praise Yâo and condemn *K*ieh, it would be better to forget them both, and seek the renovation of the Tâo.

6. There is the great Mass (of nature);—I find the support of my body on it; my life is spent in toil on it; my old age seeks ease on it; at death I find rest in it;—what makes my life a good makes my death also a good[3]. If you hide away a boat in the ravine of a hill, and hide away the hill in a lake, you will say that (the boat) is secure; but at midnight there shall come a strong man and carry it off on his back, while you in the dark know nothing about it. You may hide away anything, whether small or great, in the most suitable place, and yet it shall disappear from it. But if you could hide the world in the world[4], so that there was nowhere to which it could be removed, this would be the grand reality of the

[1] The great and most honoured Master,—the Tâo.

[2] This sentence contrasts the cramping effect on the mind of Confucianism with the freedom given by the doctrine of the Tâo.

[3] The Tâo does this. The whole paragraph is an amplification of the view given in the preceding note.

[4] The Tâo cannot be taken away. It is with its possessor, an 'ever-during thing.'

ever-during Thing [1]. When the body of man comes from its special mould [2], there is even then occasion for joy; but this body undergoes a myriad transformations, and does not immediately reach its perfection;—does it not thus afford occasion for joys incalculable? Therefore the sagely man enjoys himself in that from which there is no possibility of separation, and by which all things are preserved. He considers early death or old age, his beginning and his ending, all to be good, and in this other men imitate him;—how much more will they do so in regard to That Itself on which all things depend, and from which every transformation arises!

7. This is the Tâo;—there is in It emotion and sincerity, but It does nothing and has no bodily form [3]. It may be handed down (by the teacher), but may not be received (by his scholars). It may be apprehended (by the mind), but It cannot be seen. It has Its root and ground (of existence) in Itself. Before there were heaven and earth, from of old, there It was, securely existing. From It came the mysterious existences of spirits, from It the mysterious existence of God [4]. It produced heaven; It produced earth. It was before the Thâi-*k*î [5], and

---

[1] See p. 242, note 4.

[2] Adopting the reading of 範 for 犯, supplied by Hwâi-nan Ȝze.

[3] Our author has done with 'the True Man,' and now brings in the Tâo itself as his subject. Compare the predicates of It here with Bk. II, par. 2. But there are other, and perhaps higher, things said of it here.

[4] Men at a very early time came to believe in the existence of their spirits after death, and in the existence of a Supreme Ruler or God. It was to the Tâo that those concepts were owing.

[5] The primal ether out of which all things were fashioned by the interaction of the Yin and Yang. This was something like the

yet could not be considered high[1]; It was below all space, and yet could not be considered deep[1]. It was produced before heaven and earth, and yet could not be considered to have existed long[1]; It was older than the highest antiquity, and yet could not be considered old[1].

Shih-wei got It[2], and by It adjusted heaven and earth. Fû-hsî got It, and by It penetrated to the mystery of the maternity of the primary matter. The Wei-tâu[3] got It, and from all antiquity has made no eccentric movement. The Sun and Moon got It, and from all antiquity have not intermitted (their bright shining). Khan-pei got It, and by It became lord of Khwăn-lun[4]. Făng-î[5] got It, and by It enjoyed himself in the Great River. *K*ien Wû[6] got It, and by It dwelt on mount Thâi. Hwang-Tî[7] got It, and by It ascended the cloudy sky. *K*wan-hsü[8]

current idea of protoplasm; but while protoplasm lies down in the lower parts of the earth, the Thâi-*k*î was imagined to be in the higher regions of space.

[1] The Tâo is independent both of space and time.

[2] A prehistoric sovereign.

[3] A name for the constellation of the Great Bear.

[4] Name of the spirit of the Khwăn-lun mountains in Thibet, the fairy-land of Tâoist writers, very much in Tâoism what mount Sumêru is in Buddhism.

[5] The spirit presiding over the Yellow River;—see Mayers's Manual, pp. 54, 55.

[6] Appears here as the spirit of mount Thâi, the great eastern mountain; we met with him in I, 5, but simply as one of *K*wang-ȝze's fictitious personages.

[7] Appears before in Bk. II; the first of Sze-mâ *Kh*ien's 'Five Tîs;' no doubt a very early sovereign, to whom many important discoveries and inventions are ascribed; is placed by many at the head of Tâoism itself.

[8] The second of the 'Five Tîs;' a grandson of Hwang-Tî. I do not know what to say of his 'Dark Palace.'

莊子

got It, and by It dwelt in the Dark Palace. Yü-*kh*iang[1] got It, and by It was set on the North Pole. Hsî Wang-mû[2] got It, and by It had her seat in (the palace of) Shâo-kwang. No one knows Its beginning; no one knows Its end. Phăng 3û got It, and lived on from the time of the lord of Yü to that of the Five Chiefs[3]. Fû Yüeh[4] got It, and by It became chief minister to Wû-ting[4], (who thus) in a trice became master of the kingdom. (After his death), Fû Yüeh mounted to the eastern portion of the Milky Way, where, riding on Sagittarius and Scorpio, he took his place among the stars.

8. Nan-po 3ze-khwei[5] asked Nü Yü[6], saying, 'You are old, Sir, while your complexion is like that of a child;—how is it so?' The reply was, 'I have become acquainted with the Tâo.' The other said, 'Can I learn the Tâo?' Nü Yü said, 'No. How can you? You, Sir, are not the man to do so. There was Pû-liang Î[7] who had the abilities of a sagely man, but not the Tâo, while I had the Tâo, but not the abilities. I wished, however, to teach him, if, peradventure, he might

[1] The Spirit of the Northern regions, with a man's face, and a bird's body, &c.

[2] A queen of the Genii on mount Khwăn-lun. See Mayers's Manual, pp. 178, 179.

[3] Phăng 3û has been before us in Bk. I. Shun is intended by 'the Lord of Yü.' The five Chiefs;—see Mencius, VI, ii, 7.

[4] See the Shû, IV, viii; but we have nothing there of course about the Milky Way and the stars.—This passage certainly lessens our confidence in *K*wang-3ze's statements.

[5] Perhaps the same as Nan-po 3ze-*kh*î in Bk. IV, par. 7.

[6] Must have been a great Tâoist. Nothing more can be said of him or her.

[7] Only mentioned here.

become the sagely man indeed. If he should not do so, it was easy (I thought) for one possessing the Tâo of the sagely man to communicate it to another possessing his abilities. Accordingly, I proceeded to do so, but with deliberation[1]. After three days, he was able to banish from his mind all worldly (matters). This accomplished, I continued my intercourse with him in the same way; and in seven days he was able to banish from his mind all thought of men and things. This accomplished, and my instructions continued, after nine days, he was able to count his life as foreign to himself. This accomplished, his mind was afterwards clear as the morning; and after this he was able to see his own individuality[2]. That individuality perceived, he was able to banish all thought of Past or Present. Freed from this, he was able to penetrate to (the truth that there is no difference between) life and death;—(how) the destruction of life is not dying, and the communication of other life is not living. (The Tâo) is a thing which accompanies all other things and meets them, which is present when they are overthrown and when they obtain their completion. Its name is Tranquillity amid all Disturbances, meaning that such Disturbances lead to Its Perfection[3].'

'And how did you, being alone (without any teacher), learn all this?' 'I learned it,' was the reply, 'from the son of Fû-mo[4]; he learned it from

[1] So the 守 is explained.

[2] Standing by himself, as it were face to face with the Tâo.

[3] Amid all changes, in life and death, the possessor of the Tâo has peace.

[4] Meaning writings; literally, 'the son of the assisting pigment.'

莊子

the grandson of Lo-sung; he learned it from Shan-ming; he learned it from Nieh-hsü; he, from Hsü-yî; he, from Wû-âo; he, from Hsüan-ming; he, from Ȝhan-liâo; and he learned it from Î-shih.'

9. Ȝze-sze[1], Ȝze-yü[1], Ȝze-lî[1], and Ȝze-lâi[1], these four men, were talking together, when some one said, 'Who can suppose the head to be made from nothing, the spine from life, and the rump-bone from death? Who knows how death and birth, living on and disappearing, compose the one body?—I would be friends with him[2].' The four men looked at one another and laughed, but no one seized with his mind the drift of the questions. All, however, were friends together.

Not long after Ȝze-yü fell ill, and Ȝze-sze went to inquire for him. 'How great,' said (the sufferer), 'is the Creator[3]! That He should have made me the deformed object that I am!' He was a crooked hunchback; his five viscera were squeezed into the

---

We are not to suppose that by this and the other names that follow individuals are intended. Kwang-ȝze seems to have wished to give, in his own fashion, some notion of the genesis of the idea of the Tâo from the first speculations about the origin of things.

[1] We need not suppose that these are the names of real men. They are brought on the stage by our author to serve his purpose. Hwâi-nan makes the name of the first to have been Ȝze-shui (子水).

[2] Compare the same representation in Bk. XXIII, par. 10. Kû Teh-kih says on it here, 'The head, the spine, the rump-bone mean simply the head and tail, the beginning and end. All things begin from nothing and end in nothing. Their birth and their death are only the creations of our thought, the going and coming of the primary ether. When we have penetrated to the non-reality of life and death, what remains of the body of so many feet?'

[3] The 'Creator' or 'Maker' (造物者) is the Tâo.

upper part of his body; his chin bent over his navel; his shoulder was higher than his crown; on his crown was an ulcer pointing to the sky; his breath came and went in gasps[1]:—yet he was easy in his mind, and made no trouble of his condition. He limped to a well, looked at himself in it, and said, 'Alas that the Creator should have made me the deformed object that I am!' Ʒze said, 'Do you dislike your condition?' He replied, 'No, why should I dislike it? If He were to transform my left arm into a cock, I should be watching with it the time of the night; if He were to transform my right arm into a cross-bow, I should then be looking for a hsiâo to (bring down and) roast; if He were to transform my rump-bone into a wheel, and my spirit into a horse, I should then be mounting it, and would not change it for another steed. Moreover, when we have got (what we are to do), there is the time (of life) in which to do it; when we lose that (at death), submission (is what is required). When we rest in what the time requires, and manifest that submission, neither joy nor sorrow can find entrance (to the mind)[2]. This would be what the ancients called loosing the cord by which (the life) is suspended. But one hung up cannot loose himself;—he is held fast by his bonds[3]. And that creatures cannot overcome

---

[1] Compare this description of Ʒze-yü's deformity with that of the poor Shû, in IV, 8.

[2] Such is the submission to one's lot produced by the teaching of Tâoism.

[3] Compare the same phraseology in III, par. 4, near the end. In correcting Mr. Balfour's mistranslation of the text, Mr. Giles himself falls into a mistranslation through not observing that the 解

莊子

Heaven (the inevitable) is a long-acknowledged fact;—why should I hate my condition?'

10. Before long Ȝze-lâi fell ill, and lay gasping at the point of death, while his wife and children stood around him wailing[1]. Ȝze-lî went to ask for him, and said to them, 'Hush! Get out of the way! Do not disturb him as he is passing through his change.' Then, leaning against the door, he said (to the dying man), 'Great indeed is the Creator! What will He now make you to become? Where will He take you to? Will He make you the liver of a rat, or the arm of an insect[2]?' Ȝze-lâi replied, 'Wherever a parent tells a son to go, east, west, south, or north, he simply follows the command. The Yin and Yang are more to a man than his parents are. If they are hastening my death, and I do not quietly submit to them, I shall be obstinate and rebellious. There is the great Mass (of nature);—I find the support of my body in it; my life is spent in toil on it; my old age seeks ease on it; at death I find rest on it:—what has made my life a good will make my death also a good.

'Here now is a great founder, casting his metal. If the metal were to leap up (in the pot), and say, "I must be made into a (sword like the) Mo-yeh[3],"

---

is passive, having the 縣 that precedes as its subject (observe the force of the 也 after 解 in the best editions), and not active, or governing the 縣 that follows.

[1] Compare the account of the scene at Lâo-ȝze's death, in III, par. 4.

[2] Here comes in the belief in transformation.

[3] The name of a famous sword, made for Ho-lü, the king of

the great founder would be sure to regard it as uncanny. So, again, when a form is being fashioned in the mould of the womb, if it were to say, "I must become a man; I must become a man," the Creator would be sure to regard it as uncanny. When we once understand that heaven and earth are a great melting-pot, and the Creator a great founder, where can we have to go to that shall not be right for us? We are born as from a quiet sleep, and we die to a calm awaking.'

11. Ʒze-sang Hû[1], Măng Ʒze-fan[1], and Ʒze-*kh*in *K*ang[1], these three men, were friends together. (One of them said), 'Who can associate together without any (thought of) such association, or act together without any (evidence of) such co-operation? Who can mount up into the sky and enjoy himself amidst the mists, disporting beyond the utmost limits (of things)[2], and forgetting all others as if this were living, and would have no end?' The three men looked at one another and laughed, not perceiving the drift of the questions; and they continued to associate together as friends.

Suddenly, after a time[3], Ʒze-sang Hû died. Before he was buried, Confucius heard of the event, and

Wû (B. C. 514–494). See the account of the forging of it in the 東周列國志, ch. 74. The mention of it would seem to indicate that Ʒze-lâi and the other three men were of the time of Confucius.

[1] These three men were undoubtedly of the time of Confucius, and some would identify them with the Ʒze-sang Po-ʒze of Ana. VI, 1, Măng *K*ih-fan of VI, 13, and the Lâo of IX, vi, 4. This is very unlikely. They were Tâoists.

[2] Or, 'without end.'

[3] Or, 'Some time went by silently, and.'

sent Ȝze-kung to go and see if he could render any assistance. One of the survivors had composed a ditty, and the other was playing on his lute. Then they sang together in unison,

'Ah! come, Sang Hû! ah! come, Sang Hû!
Your being true you've got again,
While we, as men, still here remain
Ohone[1]!'

Ȝze-kung hastened forward to them, and said, 'I venture to ask whether it be according to the rules to be singing thus in the presence of the corpse?' The two men looked at each other, and laughed, saying, 'What does this man know about the idea that underlies (our) rules?' Ȝze-kung returned to Confucius, and reported to him, saying, 'What sort of men are those? They had made none of the usual preparations[2], and treated the body as a thing foreign to them. They were singing in the presence of the corpse, and there was no change in their countenances. I cannot describe them;—what sort of men are they?' Confucius replied, 'Those men occupy and enjoy themselves in what is outside the (common) ways (of the world), while I occupy and enjoy myself in what lies within those ways. There is no common ground for those of such different ways; and when I sent you to condole with those men, I was acting stupidly. They, moreover, make man to be the fellow of the

[1] In accordance with the ancient and modern practice in China of calling the dead back. But these were doing so in a song to the lute.

[2] Or, 'they do not regulate their doings (in the usual way).'

Creator, and seek their enjoyment in the formless condition of heaven and earth. They consider life to be an appendage attached, an excrescence annexed to them, and death to be a separation of the appendage and a dispersion of the contents of the excrescence. With these views, how should they know wherein death and life are to be found, or what is first and what is last? They borrow different substances, and pretend that the common form of the body is composed of them[1]. They dismiss the thought of (its inward constituents like) the liver and gall, and (its outward constituents), the ears and eyes. Again and again they end and they begin, having no knowledge of first principles. They occupy themselves ignorantly and vaguely with what (they say) lies outside the dust and dirt (of the world), and seek their enjoyment in the business of doing nothing. How should they confusedly address themselves to the ceremonies practised by the common people, and exhibit themselves as doing so to the ears and eyes of the multitude?'

Ȝze-kung said, 'Yes, but why do you, Master, act according to the (common) ways (of the world)?' The reply was, 'I am in this under the condemning sentence of Heaven[2]. Nevertheless, I will share

[1] The idea that the body is composed of the elements of earth, wind or air, fire, and water.

[2] A strange description of himself by the sage. Literally, 'I am (one of) the people killed and exposed to public view by Heaven;' referring, perhaps, to the description of a living man as 'suspended by a string from God.' Confucius was content to accept his life, and used it in pursuing the path of duty, according to his conception of it, without aiming at the transcendental method of the Tâoists. I can attach no other or better meaning to the expression.

莊子

with you (what I have attained to).' 3ze-kung rejoined, 'I venture to ask the method which you pursue;' and Confucius said, 'Fishes breed and grow in the water; man developes in the Tâo. Growing in the water, the fishes cleave the pools, and their nourishment is supplied to them. Developing in the Tâo, men do nothing, and the enjoyment of their life is secured. Hence it is said, "Fishes forget one another in the rivers and lakes; men forget one another in the arts of the Tâo."'

3ze-kung said, 'I venture to ask about the man who stands aloof from others[1].' The reply was, 'He stands aloof from other men, but he is in accord with Heaven! Hence it is said, "The small man of Heaven is the superior man among men; the superior man among men is the small man of Heaven[2]!"'

12. Yen Hui asked *K*ung-nî, saying, 'When the mother of Măng-sun 3hâi[3] died, in all his wailing for her he did not shed a tear; in the core of his heart he felt no distress; during all the mourning rites, he exhibited no sorrow. Without these three things, he (was considered to have) discharged his mourning well;—is it that in the state of Lû one who has not the reality may yet get the reputation of having it? I think the matter very strange.' *K*ung-nî

[1] Misled by the text of Hsüang Ying, Mr. Balfour here reads 崎 instead of 畸.

[2] Here, however, he aptly compares with the language of Christ in Matthew vii. 28.—*K*wang-3ze seems to make Confucius praise the system of Tâoism as better than his own!

[3] Must have been a member of the Măng or Măng-sun family of Lû, to a branch of which Mencius belonged.

said, 'That Măng-sun carried out (his views) to the utmost. He was advanced in knowledge; but (in this case) it was not possible for him to appear to be negligent (in his ceremonial observances)[1], but he succeeded in being really so to himself. Măng-sun does not know either what purposes life serves, or what death serves; he does not know which should be first sought, and which last[2]. If he is to be transformed into something else, he will simply await the transformation which he does not yet know. This is all he does. And moreover, when one is about to undergo his change, how does he know that it has not taken place? And when he is not about to undergo his change, how does he know that it has taken place[3]? Take the case of me and you:—are we in a dream from which we have not begun to awake[4]?

'Moreover, Măng-sun presented in his body the appearance of being agitated, but in his mind he was conscious of no loss. The death was to him like the issuing from one's dwelling at dawn, and no (more terrible) reality. He was more awake than others were. When they wailed, he also wailed, having in himself the reason why he did so. And we all have our individuality which makes us what we are as compared together; but how do we know that we

[1] The people set such store by the mourning rites, that Măng-sun felt he must present the appearance of observing them. This would seem to show that Tâoism arose after the earlier views of the Chinese.

[2] I adopt here, with many of the critics, the reading of 孰 instead of the more common 就.

[3] This is to me very obscure.

[4] Are such dreams possible? See what I have said on II, par. 9.

determine in any case correctly that individuality? Moreover you dream that you are a bird, and seem to be soaring to the sky; or that you are a fish, and seem to be diving in the deep. But you do not know whether we that are now speaking are awake or in a dream[1]. It is not the meeting with what is pleasurable that produces the smile; it is not the smile suddenly produced that produces the arrangement (of the person). When one rests in what has been arranged, and puts away all thought of the transformation, he is in unity with the mysterious Heaven.'

13. Î-*r* Ȝze[2] having gone to see Hsü Yû, the latter said to him, 'What benefit have you received from Yâo?' The reply was, 'Yâo says to me, You must yourself labour at benevolence and righteousness, and be able to tell clearly which is right and which wrong (in conflicting statements).' Hsü Yû rejoined, 'Why then have you come to me? Since Yâo has put on you the brand of his benevolence and righteousness, and cut off your nose with his right and wrong[3], how will you be able to wander in the way of aimless enjoyment, of unregulated contemplation, and the ever-changing forms (of dispute)?' Î-*r* Ȝze said, 'That may be; but I should

---

[1] This also is obscure; but Confucius is again made to praise the Tâoistic system.

[2] Î-*r* is said by Lî Î to have been 'a worthy scholar;' but Î-*r* is an old name for the swallow, and there is a legend of a being of this name appearing to king Mû, and then flying away as a swallow;—see the Khang-hsî Thesaurus under 而. The personage is entirely fabulous.

[3] Dismembered or disfigured you.

like to skirt along its hedges.' 'But,' said the other, 'it cannot be. Eyes without pupils can see nothing of the beauty of the eyebrows, eyes, and other features; the blind have nothing to do with the green, yellow, and variegated colours of the sacrificial robes.' Î-r 3ze rejoined, 'Yet, when Wû-*k*wang[1] lost his beauty, *K*ü-liang[1] his strength, and Hwang-Tî his wisdom, they all (recovered them)[2] under the moulding (of your system);—how do you know that the Maker will not obliterate the marks of my branding, and supply my dismemberment, so that, again perfect in my form, I may follow you as my teacher?' Hsü Yû said, 'Ah! that cannot yet be known. I will tell you the rudiments. O my Master! O my Master! He gives to all things their blended qualities, and does not count it any righteousness; His favours reach to all generations, and He does not count it any benevolence; He is more ancient than the highest antiquity, and does not count Himself old; He overspreads heaven and supports the earth; He carves and fashions all bodily forms, and does not consider it any act of skill;—this is He in whom I find my enjoyment.'

14. Yen Hui said, 'I am making progress.' *K*ung-nî replied, 'What do you mean?' 'I have ceased to think of benevolence and righteousness,' was the reply. 'Very well; but that is not enough.'

Another day, Hui again saw *K*ung-nî, and said, 'I am making progress.' 'What do you mean?'

[1] Names of parties, of whom we know nothing. It is implied, we must suppose, that they had suffered as is said by their own inadvertence.

[2] We must suppose that they had done so.

莊子

'I have lost all thought of ceremonies and music.' 'Very well, but that is not enough.'

A third day, Hui again saw (the Master), and said, 'I am making progress.' 'What do you mean?' 'I sit and forget everything[1].' Kung-nî changed countenance, and said, 'What do you mean by saying that you sit and forget (everything)?' Yen Hui replied, 'My connexion with the body and its parts is dissolved; my perceptive organs are discarded. Thus leaving my material form, and bidding farewell to my knowledge, I am become one with the Great Pervader[2]. This I call sitting and forgetting all things.' Kung-nî said, 'One (with that Pervader), you are free from all likings; so transformed, you are become impermanent. You have, indeed, become superior to me! I must ask leave to follow in your steps[3].'

15. Ȝze-yü[4] and Ȝze-sang[4] were friends. (Once), when it had rained continuously for ten days, Ȝze-yü said, 'I fear that Ȝze-sang may be in distress.' So he wrapped up some rice, and went to give it to him to eat. When he came to Ȝze-sang's door, there issued from it sounds between singing and wailing;

[1] 'I sit and forget;'—generally thus supplemented (無所不忘). Hui proceeds to set forth the meaning he himself attached to the phrase.

[2] Another denomination, I think, of the Tâo. The 大通 is also explained as meaning, 'the great void in which there is no obstruction (太虛之無碍).'

[3] Here is another testimony, adduced by our author, of Confucius's appreciation of Tâoism; to which the sage would, no doubt, have taken exception.

[4] Two of the men in pars. 9, 10.

a lute was struck, and there came the words, 'O Father! O Mother! O Heaven! O Men!' The voice could not sustain itself, and the line was hurriedly pronounced. ʒze-yü entered and said, 'Why are you singing, Sir, this line of poetry in such a way?' The other replied, 'I was thinking, and thinking in vain, how it was that I was brought to such extremity. Would my parents have wished me to be so poor? Heaven overspreads all without any partial feeling, and so does Earth sustain all;—would Heaven and Earth make me so poor with any unkindly feeling? I was trying to find out who had done it, and I could not do so. But here I am in this extremity!—it is what was appointed for me[1]!'

[1] Here is the highest issue of Tâoism;—unquestioning submission to what is beyond our knowledge and control.

莊子

BOOK VII.

Part I. Section VII.

Ying Tî Wang[1], or 'The Normal Course for Rulers and Kings[1].'

1. Nieh *Kh*üeh[2] put four questions to Wang Î[2], not one of which did he know (how to answer). On this Nieh *Kh*üeh leaped up, and in great delight walked away and informed Phû-î-ȝze[3] of it, who said to him, 'Do you (only) now know it?' He of the line of Yü[4] was not equal to him of the line of Thâi[5]. He of Yü still kept in himself (the idea of) benevolence by which to constrain (the submission of) men; and he did win men, but he had not begun to proceed by what did not belong to him as a man. He of the line of Thâi would sleep tranquilly, and awake in contented simplicity. He would consider himself now (merely) as a horse, and now (merely) as an ox[6]. His knowledge was real and untroubled

[1] See pp. 136–138.

[2] See p. 190, note 5.

[3] An ancient Tâoist, of the time of Shun. So, Hwang-fû Mî, who adds that Shun served him as his master when he was eight years old. I suppose the name indicates that his clothes were made of rushes.

[4] Shun. See p. 245, note 3.

[5] An ancient sovereign, earlier, no doubt, than Fû-hsî; but nothing is known of him.

[6] He thought nothing about his being, as a man, superior to the lower creatures. Shun in governing employed his acquired knowledge; Thâi had not begun to do so.

S 2

by doubts; and his virtue was very true:—he had not begun to proceed by what belonged to him as a man.

2. *K*ien Wû[1] went to see the mad (recluse), *Kh*ieh-yü[2], who said to him, 'What did *Z*ăh-*k*ung Shih[3] tell you?' The reply was, 'He told me that when rulers gave forth their regulations according to their own views and enacted righteous measures, no one would venture not to obey them, and all would be transformed.' *Kh*ieh-yü said, 'That is but the hypocrisy of virtue. For the right ordering of the world it would be like trying to wade through the sea and dig through the Ho, or employing a musquito to carry a mountain on its back. And when a sage is governing, does he govern men's outward actions? He is (himself) correct, and so (his government) goes on;—this is the simple and certain way by which he secures the success of his affairs. Think of the bird which flies high, to avoid being hurt by the dart on the string of the archer, and the little mouse which makes its hole deep under Shăn-*kh*iû[4] to avoid the danger of being smoked or dug out;—are (rulers) less knowing than these two little creatures?'

3. Thien Kăn[5], rambling on the south of (mount) Yin[6], came to the neighbourhood of the Liâo-water.

---

[1] See p. 170, note 2.

[2] See p. 170, note 3.

[3] A name;—'a worthy,' it is said.

[4] Name of some hill, or height.

[5] A name ('Root of the sky'), but probably mythical. There is a star so called.

[6] Probably the name of a mountain, though this meaning of Yin is not given in the dictionary.

莊子

Happening there to meet with the man whose name is not known[1], he put a question to him, saying, 'I beg to ask what should be done[2] in order to (carry on) the government of the world.' The nameless man said, 'Go away; you are a rude borderer. Why do you put to me a question for which you are unprepared[3]? I would simply play the part of the Maker of (all) things[4]. When wearied, I would mount on the bird of the light and empty air, proceed beyond the six cardinal points, and wander in the region of non-entity, to dwell in the wilderness of desert space. What method have you, moreover, for the government of the world that you (thus) agitate my mind?' (Thien Kăn), however, again asked the question, and the nameless man said, 'Let your mind find its enjoyment in pure simplicity; blend yourself with (the primary) ether in idle indifference; allow all things to take their natural course; and admit no personal or selfish consideration:—do this and the world will be governed.'

4. Yang Ȝze-*k*ü[5], having an interview with Lâo Tan, said to him, 'Here is a man, alert and vigorous

---

[1] Or, 'a nameless man.' We cannot tell whether *K*wang-ȝze had any particular Being, so named, in view or not.

[2] The objectionable point in the question is the supposition that 'doing' was necessary in the case.

[3] Or, 'I am unprepared.' But as Thien Kăn repeats the question, it seems better to supply the second pronoun. He had thought on the subject.

[4] See the same phraseology in VI, par. 11. What follows is merely our author's way of describing the non-action of the Tâo.

[5] The Yang *K*û, whom Mencius attacked so fiercely. He was, perhaps, a contemporary and disciple of Lâo-ȝze.

in responding to all matters[1], clearsighted and widely intelligent, and an unwearied student of the Tâo;—can he be compared to one of the intelligent kings?' The reply was, 'Such a man is to one of the intelligent kings but as the bustling underling of a court who toils his body and distresses his mind with his various contrivances[2]. And moreover, it is the beauty of the skins of the tiger and leopard which makes men hunt them; the agility of the monkey, or (the sagacity of) the dog that catches the yak, which make men lead them in strings; but can one similarly endowed be compared to the intelligent kings?'

Yang Ʒze-*k*ü looked discomposed and said, 'I venture to ask you what the government of the intelligent kings is.' Lâo Tan replied, 'In the governing of the intelligent kings, their services overspread all under the sky, but they did not seem to consider it as proceeding from themselves; their transforming influence reached to all things, but the people did not refer it to them with hope. No one could tell the name of their agency, but they made men and things be joyful in themselves. Where they took their stand could not be fathomed, and they found their enjoyment in (the realm of) nonentity.'

5. In *K*ăng there was a mysterious wizard[3] called

[1] The 嚮 may be taken as = 向, in which case we must understand a 道 as its object; or as = 響, 'an echo,' indicating the quickness of the man's response to things.

[2] Compare the language of Lâo Tan, in Bk. XII, par. 8, near the beginning.

[3] 巫 is generally feminine, meaning 'a witch.' We must take

莊子

*K*i-hsien. He knew all about the deaths and births of men, their preservation and ruin, their misery and happiness, and whether their lives would be long or short, foretelling the year, the month, the decade and the day like a spirit. When the people of *K*ăng saw him, they all ran out of his way. Lieh-ȝze went to see him, and was fascinated[1] by him. Returning, he told Hû-ȝze of his interview, and said, 'I considered your doctrine, my master, to be perfect, but I have found another which is superior to it.' Hû-ȝze[2] replied, 'I have communicated to you but the outward letter of my doctrine, and have not communicated its reality and spirit; and do you think that you are in possession of it? However many hens there be, if there be not the cock among them, how should they lay (real) eggs[3]? When you confront the world with your doctrine, you are sure to show in your countenance (all that is in your mind)[4], and so enable (this) man to succeed in interpreting your physiognomy. Try and come to me with him, that I may show myself to him.'

On the morrow, accordingly, Lieh-ȝze came with the man and saw Hû-ȝze. When they went out, the

it here as masculine (=覡). The general meaning of the character is 'magical,' the antics of such performers to bring down the spirits.

[1] Literally, 'intoxicated.'

[2] The teacher in Tâoism of Lieh-ȝze, called also Hû *Kh*iû, with the name Lin (林). See the remarks on the whole paragraph in the Introductory Notice of the Book.

[3] 'The hens' signify the letter of the doctrine; 'the cock,' its spirit; 'the eggs,' a real knowledge of it.

[4] 信 is here in the first tone, and read as 伸, meaning 'to stretch,' 'to set forth.'

wizard said, 'Alas! your master is a dead man. He will not live;—not for ten days more! I saw something strange about him;—I saw the ashes (of his life) all slaked with water!' When Lieh-ȝze re-entered, he wept till the front of his jacket was wet with his tears, and told Hû-ȝze what the man had said. Hû-ȝze said, 'I showed myself to him with the forms of (vegetation beneath) the earth. There were the sprouts indeed, but without (any appearance of) growth or regularity:—he seemed to see me with the springs of my (vital) power closed up. Try and come to me with him again.'

Next day, accordingly, Lieh-ȝze brought the man again and saw Hû-ȝze. When they went out, the man said, 'It is a fortunate thing for your master that he met with me. He will get better; he has all the signs of living! I saw the balance (of the springs of life) that had been stopped (inclining in his favour).' Lieh-ȝze went in, and reported these words to his master, who said, 'I showed myself to him after the pattern of the earth (beneath the) sky. Neither semblance nor reality entered (into my exhibition), but the springs (of life) were issuing from beneath my feet;—he seemed to see me with the springs of vigorous action in full play. Try and come with him again.'

Next day Lieh-ȝze came with the man again, and again saw Hû-ȝze with him. When they went out, the wizard said, 'Your master is never the same. I cannot understand his physiognomy. Let him try to steady himself, and I will again view him.' Lieh-ȝze went in and reported this to Hû-ȝze, who said, 'This time I showed myself to him after the pattern of the grand harmony (of the two elemental

莊子

forces), with the superiority inclining to neither. He seemed to see me with the springs of (vital) power in equal balance. Where the water wheels about from (the movements of) a dugong[1], there is an abyss; where it does so from the arresting (of its course), there is an abyss; where it does so, and the water keeps flowing on, there is an abyss. There are nine abysses with their several names, and I have only exhibited three of them. Try and come with him again.'

Next day they came, and they again saw Hû-ȝze. But before he had settled himself in his position, the wizard lost himself and ran away. 'Pursue him,' said Hû-ȝze, and Lieh-ȝze did so, but could not come up with him. He returned, and told Hû-ȝze, saying, 'There is an end of him; he is lost; I could not find him.' Hû-ȝze rejoined, 'I was showing him myself after the pattern of what was before I began to come from my author. I confronted him with pure vacancy, and an easy indifference. He did not know what I meant to represent. Now he thought it was the idea of exhausted strength, and now that of an onward flow, and therefore he ran away.'

After this, Lieh-ȝze considered that he had not yet begun to learn (his master's doctrine). He returned to his house, and for three years did not go out. He did the cooking for his wife. He fed the pigs as if he were feeding men. He took no part

---

[1] One of the dugong. It has various names in Chinese, one being 人魚, 'the Man-Fish,' from a fancied resemblance of its head and face to a human being;—the origin perhaps of the idea of the mermaid.

or interest in occurring affairs. He put away the carving and sculpture about him, and returned to pure simplicity. Like a clod of earth he stood there in his bodily presence. Amid all distractions he was (silent) and shut up in himself. And in this way he continued to the end of his life.

6. Non-action (makes its exemplifier) the lord of all fame; non-action (serves him as) the treasury of all plans; non-action (fits him for) the burden of all offices; non-action (makes him) the lord of all wisdom[1]. The range of his action is inexhaustible, but there is nowhere any trace of his presence. He fulfils all that he has received from Heaven[2], but he does not see that he was the recipient of anything. A pure vacancy (of all purpose) is what characterises him. When the perfect man employs his mind, it is a mirror. It conducts nothing and anticipates nothing; it responds to (what is before it), but does not retain it. Thus he is able to deal successfully with all things, and injures none.

7. The Ruler[3] of the Southern Ocean was Shû[4], the

[1] The four members of this sentence occasion the translator no small trouble. They are constructed on the same lines, and seem to me to be indicative and not imperative. Lin Hsî-kung observes that all the explanations that had been offered of them were inappropriate. My own version is substantially in accordance with his interpretations. The chief difficulty is with the first member, which seems anti-Tâoistic; but our author is not speaking of the purpose of any actor, but of the result of his non-action. 尸 is to be taken in the sense of 主, 'lord,' 'exercising lordship.' The 其 in the third sentence indicates a person or persons in the author's mind in what precedes.

[2] = the Heavenly or self-determining nature.

[3] Perhaps 'god' would be a better translation.

[4] Meaning 'Heedless.'

莊子

Ruler of the Northern Ocean was Hû[1], and the Ruler of the Centre was Chaos. Shû and Hû were continually meeting in the land of Chaos, who treated them very well. They consulted together how they might repay his kindness, and said, 'Men all have seven orifices for the purpose of seeing, hearing, eating, and breathing, while this (poor) Ruler alone has not one. Let us try and make them for him.' Accordingly they dug one orifice in him every day; and at the end of seven days Chaos died[2].

[1] Meaning 'Sudden.'

[2] The little allegory is ingenious and amusing. 'It indicates,' says Lin, 'how action (the opposite of non-inaction) injures the first condition of things.' More especially it is in harmony with the Tâoistic opposition to the use of knowledge in government. One critic says that an 'alas!' might well follow the concluding 'died.' But surely it was better that Chaos should give place to another state. 'Heedless' and 'Sudden' did not do a bad work.

BOOK VIII.

PART II. SECTION I.

Phien Mâu, or 'Webbed Toes[1].'

1. A ligament uniting the big toe with the other toes and an extra finger may be natural[2] growths, but they are more than is good for use. Excrescences on the person and hanging tumours are growths from the body, but they are unnatural additions to it. There are many arts of benevolence and righteousness, and the exercise of them is distributed among the five viscera[3]; but this is not the correct method according to the characteristics of the Tâo. Thus it is that the addition to the foot is but the attachment to it of so much useless flesh, and the addition to the hand is but the planting on it of a useless finger. (So it is that) the connecting (the virtues) with the five viscera renders, by excess or restraint, the action of benevolence and righteousness bad, and leads to many arts as in the employment of (great) powers of hearing or of vision.

2. Therefore an extraordinary power of vision

[1] See pp. 138, 139.

[2] 'Come out from the nature,' but 'nature' must be taken here as in the translation. The character is not Tâo.

[3] The five viscera are the heart, the liver, the stomach, the lungs, and the kidneys. To the liver are assigned the element 'wood,' and the virtue of benevolence; to the lungs, the element 'metal,' and the virtue of righteousness.

莊子

leads to the confusion of the five colours[1] and an excessive use of ornament. (Its possessor), in the resplendence of his green and yellow, white and black, black and green, will not stop till he has become a Lî *K*û[2]. An extraordinary power of hearing leads to a confusion of the five notes[3], and an excessive use of the six musical accords[4]. (Its possessor), in bringing out the tones from the instruments of metal, stone, silk, and bamboo, aided by the Hwang-*k*ung[4] and Tâ-lü[4] (tubes), will not stop till he has become a Shih Khwang[5]. (So), excessive benevolence eagerly brings out virtues and restrains its (proper) nature, that (its possessor) may acquire a famous reputation, and cause all the organs and drums in the world to celebrate an unattainable condition; and he will not stop till he has become a 3ăng (Shăn)[6] or a Shih (3hiû)[7]. An ex-

[1] Black, red, azure (green, blue, or black), white, and yellow.

[2] The same as the Lî Lâu of Mencius (IV, i, 1),—of the time of Hwang-Tî. It is not easy to construe the text here, and in the analogous sentences below. Hsüan Ying, having read on to the 煌煌 as the uninterrupted predicate of the sharp seer, says, 'Is not this a proof of the extraordinary gift?' What follows would be, 'But it was exemplified in Lî *K*û.' The meaning that is given in the version was the first that occurred to myself.

[3] The five notes of the Chinese musical scale.

[4] There are twelve of these musical notes, determined by the twelve regulating tubes; six, represented here by Hwang-*k*ung, the name of the first tube, giving the sharp notes; and six, represented by Tâ-lü, giving the flat notes.

[5] See in II, par. 5.

[6] The famous 3ăng-ʒze, or 3ăng Shăn, one of Confucius's ablest disciples.

[7] An officer of Wei in the sixth century B. C. He belonged to a family of historiographers, and hence the surname Shih (史). Confucius mentions him in the most honourable terms in the

traordinary faculty in debating leads to the piling up of arguments like a builder with his bricks, or a net-maker with his string. (Its possessor) cunningly contrives his sentences and enjoys himself in discussing what hardness is and what whiteness is, where views agree and where they differ, and pressing on, though weary, with short steps, with (a multitude of) useless words to make good his opinion; nor will he stop till he has become a Yang (*K*û)[1] or Mo (Tî)[1]. But in all these cases the parties, with their redundant and divergent methods, do not proceed by that which is the correct path for all under the sky. That which is the perfectly correct path is not to lose the real character of the nature with which we are endowed. Hence the union (of parts) should not be considered redundance, nor their divergence superfluity; what is long should not be considered too long, nor what is short too short. A duck's legs, for instance, are short, but if we try to lengthen them, it occasions pain; and a crane's legs are long, but if we try to cut off a portion of them, it produces grief. Where a part is by nature long, we are not to amputate, or where it is by nature short, we are not to lengthen it. There is no occasion to try to remove any trouble that it may cause.

3. The presumption is that benevolence and righteousness are not constituents of humanity; for to how much anxiety does the exercise of them give rise! Moreover when another toe is united to the

---

Analect. XV, vi, by the name Shih Yü. 'Righteousness' was his great attribute.

[1] The two heresiarchs so much denounced by Mencius. Both have appeared in previous Books.

莊子

great toe, to divide the membrane makes you weep; and when there is an extra finger, to gnaw it off makes you cry out. In the one case there is a member too many, and in the other a member too few; but the anxiety and pain which they cause is the same. The benevolent men of the present age look at the evils of the world, as with eyes full of dust, and are filled with sorrow by them, while those who are not benevolent, having violently altered the character of their proper nature, greedily pursue after riches and honours. The presumption therefore is that benevolence and righteousness are contrary to the nature of man:—how full of trouble and contention has the world been ever since the three dynasties[1] began!

And moreover, in employing the hook and line, the compass and square, to give things their correct form you must cut away portions of what naturally belongs to them; in employing strings and fastenings, glue and varnish to make things firm, you must violently interfere with their qualities. The bendings and stoppings in ceremonies and music, and the factitious expression in the countenance of benevolence and righteousness, in order to comfort the minds of men:—these all show a failure in observing the regular principles (of the human constitution). All men are furnished with such regular principles; and according to them what is bent is not made so by the hook, nor what is straight by the line, nor what is round by the compass, nor what is square by the carpenter's square. Nor is adhesion effected by

[1] Those of Hsiâ, Shang, and Kâu;—from the twenty-third century B.C. to our author's own time.

the use of glue and varnish, nor are things bound together by means of strings and bands. Thus it is that all in the world are produced what they are by a certain guidance, while they do not know how they are produced so; and they equally attain their several ends while they do not know how it is that they do so. Anciently it was so, and it is so now; and this constitution of things should not be made of none effect. Why then should benevolence and righteousness be employed as connecting (links), or as glue and varnish, strings and bands, and the enjoyment arising from the Tâo and its characteristics be attributed to them?—it is a deception practised upon the world. Where the deception is small, there will be a change in the direction (of the objects pursued); where it is great, there will be a change of the nature itself. How do I know that it is so? Since he of the line of Yü called in his benevolence and righteousness to distort and vex the world, the world has not ceased to hurry about to execute their commands;—has not this been by means of benevolence and righteousness to change (men's views) of their nature?

4. I will therefore try and discuss this matter. From the commencement of the three dynasties downwards, nowhere has there been a man who has not under (the influence of external) things altered (the course of) his nature. Small men for the sake of gain have sacrificed their persons; scholars for the sake of fame have done so; great officers, for the sake of their families; and sagely men, for the sake of the kingdom. These several classes, with different occupations, and different repu-

莊子

tations, have agreed in doing injury to their nature and sacrificing their persons. Take the case of a male and female slave[1];—they have to feed the sheep together, but they both lose their sheep. Ask the one what he was doing, and you will find that he was holding his bamboo tablets and reading. Ask the other, and you will find that she was amusing herself with some game[2]. They were differently occupied, but they equally lose their sheep. (So), Po-î[3] died at the foot of Shâu-yang[4] to maintain his fame, and the robber *K*ih[5] died on the top of Tung-ling[6] in his eagerness for gain. Their deaths were occasioned by different causes, but they equally shortened their lives and did violence to their nature;—why must we approve of Po-î, and condemn the robber *K*ih? In cases of such sacrifice all over the world, when one makes it for the sake of benevolence and righteousness, the common people style him 'a superior man,' but when another does it for the sake of goods and riches, they style him 'a small man.' The action of sacrificing is the same, and yet we have 'the superior man' and 'the small man!' In the matter of destroying his life, and doing injury to his nature, the robber *K*ih simply did the same as Po-î;—why must we make the distinction of 'superior man' and 'small man' between them?

---

[1] See the Khang-hsî dictionary under the character 臧.

[2] Playing at some game with dice. [3] See VI, par. 3.

[4] A mountain in the present Shan-hsî, probably in the department of Phû-*k*âu.

[5] A strange character, but not historical, represented as a brother of Liû-hsiâ Hui. See Bk. XXIX.

[6] 'The Eastern Height,'= the Thâi mountain in the present Shan-tung.

5. Moreover, those who devote their nature to (the pursuit) of benevolence and righteousness, though they should attain to be like Ȝăng (Shăn) and Shih (Ȝhiû), I do not pronounce to be good; those who devote it to (the study of) the five flavours, though they attain to be like Shû-*r*[1], I do not pronounce to be good; those who devote it to the (discrimination of the) five notes, though they attain to be like Shih Khwang, I do not pronounce to be quick of hearing; those who devote it to the (appreciation of the) five colours, though they attain to be like Lî *K*û, I do not pronounce to be clear of vision. When I pronounce men to be good, I am not speaking of their benevolence and righteousness;—the goodness is simply (their possession of) the qualities (of the Tâo). When I pronounce them to be good, I am not speaking of what are called benevolence and righteousness; but simply of their allowing the nature with which they are endowed to have its free course. When I pronounce men to be quick of hearing, I do not mean that they hearken to anything else, but that they hearken to themselves; when I pronounce them to be clear of vision, I do not mean that they look to anything else, but that they look to themselves. Now those who do not see themselves but see other things, who do not get possession of themselves but get possession of other things, get possession of what belongs to others, and not of what is their own; and they reach forth to what attracts others, and not to that in themselves which should attract them. But

[1] Different from Yîh-ya, the famous cook of duke Hwan of *Kh*î. This is said to have been of the time of Hwang-Tî. But there are different readings of the name.

thus reaching forth to what attracts others and not to what should attract them in themselves, be they like the robber *K*ih or like Po-î, they equally err in the way of excess or of perversity. What I am ashamed of is erring in the characteristics of the Tâo, and therefore, in the higher sphere, I do not dare to insist on the practice of benevolence and righteousness, and, in the lower, I do not dare to allow myself either in the exercise of excess or perversity.

BOOK IX.

Part II. Section II.

Mâ Thî, or 'Horses's Hoofs[1].'

1. Horses can with their hoofs tread on the hoar-frost and snow, and with their hair withstand the wind and cold; they feed on the grass and drink water; they prance with their legs and leap:—this is the true nature of horses. Though there were made for them grand towers[2] and large dormitories, they would prefer not to use them. But when Po-lâo[3] (arose and) said, 'I know well how to manage horses,' (men proceeded)[4] to singe and mark them, to clip their hair, to pare their hoofs, to halter their heads, to bridle them and hobble them, and to confine them in stables and corrals. (When subjected to this treatment), two or three in every ten of them died. (Men proceeded further) to subject them to hunger and thirst, to gallop them and race them,

[1] See pp. 140, 141.

[2] Literally, 'righteous towers;' but 義 is very variously applied, and there are other readings. Compare the name of ling thâi, given by the people to the tower built by king Wăn; Shih, III, i, 8.

[3] A mythical being, the first tamer of horses. The name is given to a star, where he is supposed to have his seat as superintendent of the horses of heaven. It became a designation of Sun Yang, a famous charioteer of the later period of the *K*âu dynasty, but it could not be he whom *K*wang-ȝze had in view.

[4] Po-lâo set the example of dealing with horses as now described; but the supplement which I have introduced seems to bring out better our author's meaning.

莊子

and to make them go together in regular order. In front were the evils of the bit and ornamented breast-bands, and behind were the terrors of the whip and switch. (When so treated), more than half of them died.

The (first) potter said, 'I know well how to deal with clay;' and (men proceeded) to mould it into circles as exact as if made by the compass, and into squares as exact as if formed by the measuring square. The (first) carpenter said, 'I know well how to deal with wood;' and (men proceeded) to make it bent as if by the application of the hook, and straight as if by the application of the plumb-line. But is it the nature of clay and wood to require the application of the compass and square, of the hook and line? And yet age after age men have praised Po-lâo, saying, 'He knew well how to manage horses,' and also the (first) potter and carpenter, saying, 'They knew well how to deal with clay and wood.' This is just the error committed by the governors of the world.

2. According to my idea, those who know well to govern mankind would not act so. The people had their regular and constant nature[1]:—they wove and made themselves clothes; they tilled the ground and got food[2]. This was their common faculty. They were all one in this, and did not form themselves into separate classes; so were they constituted and left to their natural tendencies[3]. Therefore in the

[1] Compare the same language in the previous Book, par. 3.

[2] But the weaver's or agriculturist's art has no more title to be called primitive than the potter's or carpenter's.

[3] A difficult expression; but the translation, probably, gives its

age of perfect virtue men walked along with slow and grave step, and with their looks steadily directed forwards. At that time, on the hills there were no foot-paths, nor excavated passages; on the lakes there were no boats nor dams; all creatures lived in companies; and the places of their settlement were made close to one another. Birds and beasts multiplied to flocks and herds; the grass and trees grew luxuriant and long. In this condition the birds and beasts might be led about without feeling the constraint; the nest of the magpie might be climbed to, and peeped into. Yes, in the age of perfect virtue, men lived in common with birds and beasts, and were on terms of equality with all creatures, as forming one family;—how could they know among themselves the distinctions of superior men and small men? Equally without knowledge, they did not leave (the path of) their natural virtue; equally free from desires, they were in the state of pure simplicity. In that state of pure simplicity, the nature of the people was what it ought to be. But when the sagely men appeared, limping and wheeling about in (the exercise of) benevolence, pressing along and standing on tiptoe in the doing of righteousness, then men universally began to be perplexed. (Those sages also) went to excess in their performances of music, and in their gesticulations in the practice of ceremonies, and then men began to be separated from one another. If the raw materials

true significance. 'Heaven' here is synonymous with 'the Tâo;' but its use shows how readily the minds, even of Lâo and *K*wang, had recourse to the earliest term by which the Chinese fathers had expressed their recognition of a Supreme and Controlling Power and Government.

莊子

had not been cut and hacked, who could have made a sacrificial vase from them? If the natural jade had not been broken and injured, who could have made the handles for the libation-cups from it? If the attributes of the Tâo had not been disallowed, how should they have preferred benevolence and righteousness? If the instincts of the nature had not been departed from, how should ceremonies and music have come into use? If the five colours had not been confused, how should the ornamental figures have been formed? If the five notes had not been confused, how should they have supplemented them by the musical accords? The cutting and hacking of the raw materials to form vessels was the crime of the skilful workman; the injury done to the characteristics of the Tâo in order to the practice of benevolence and righteousness was the error of the sagely men.

3. Horses, when living in the open country, eat the grass, and drink water; when pleased, they intertwine their necks and rub one another; when enraged, they turn back to back and kick one another;—this is all that they know to do. But if we put the yoke on their necks, with the moon-like frontlet displayed on all their foreheads, then they know to look slily askance, to curve their necks, to rush viciously, trying to get the bit out of their mouths, and to filch the reins (from their driver);—this knowledge of the horse and its ability thus to act the part of a thief is the crime of Po-lâo. In the time of (the Tî) Ho-hsü[1], the people occupied

[1] An ancient sovereign; but nothing more definite can be said about him. Most of the critics identify him with Shăn-năng, the

their dwellings without knowing what they were doing, and walked out without knowing where they were going. They filled their mouths with food and were glad; they slapped their stomachs to express their satisfaction. This was all the ability which they possessed. But when the sagely men appeared, with their bendings and stoppings in ceremonies and music to adjust the persons of all, and hanging up their benevolence and righteousness to excite the endeavours of all to reach them, in order to comfort their minds, then the people began to stump and limp about in their love of knowledge, and strove with one another in their pursuit of gain, so that there was no stopping them:—this was the error of those sagely men.

Father of Husbandry, who occupies the place in chronological tables after Fû-hsî, between him and Hwang-Tî. In the Tables of the Dynastic Histories, published in 1817, he is placed seventh in the list of fifteen reigns, which are placed without any specification of their length between Fû-hsî and Shăn-năng. The name is written as 合胥 and 赫胥.

BOOK X.

PART II. SECTION III.

Khü Khieh, or 'Cutting open Satchels[1].'

1. In taking precautions against thieves who cut open satchels, search bags, and break open boxes, people are sure to cord and fasten them well, and to employ strong bonds and clasps; and in this they are ordinarily said to show their wisdom. When a great thief comes, however, he shoulders the box, lifts up the satchel, carries off the bag, and runs away with them, afraid only that the cords, bonds, and clasps may not be secure; and in this case what was called the wisdom (of the owners) proves to be nothing but a collecting of the things for the great thief. Let me try and set this matter forth. Do not those who are vulgarly called wise prove to be collectors for the great thieves? And do not those who are called sages prove to be but guardians in the interest of the great thieves?

How do I know that the case is so? Formerly, in the state of *Khî*, the neighbouring towns could see one another; their cocks and dogs never ceased to answer the crowing and barking of other cocks and dogs (between them). The nets were set (in the water and on the land); and the ploughs and hoes were employed over more than a space of two thousand lî square. All within its four boundaries, the

[1] See pp. 141, 142.

establishment of the ancestral temples and of the altars of the land and grain, and the ordering of the hamlets and houses, and of every corner in the districts, large, medium, and small, were in all particulars according to the rules of the sages[1]. So it was; but yet one morning, Thien *Kh*ăng-ȝze[2] killed the ruler of *Kh*î, and stole his state. And was it only the state that he stole? Along with it he stole also the regulations of the sages and wise men (observed in it). And so, though he got the name of being a thief and a robber, yet he himself continued to live as securely as Yâo and Shun had done. Small states did not dare to find fault with him; great states did not dare to take him off; for twelve generations (his descendants) have possessed the state of *Kh*î[3]. Thus do we not have a case in which not only did (the party) steal the state of *Kh*î,

[1] The meaning is plain; but to introduce the various geographical terms would make the translation cumbrous. The concluding 曲 is perplexing.

[2] This event is mentioned in the Analects, XIV, xxii, where the perpetrator of the murder is called *Kh*ăn *Kh*ăng-ȝze, and *Kh*ăn Hăng. Hăng was his name, and *Kh*ăng the honorary title given to him after his death. The family to which he belonged had originally taken refuge in *Kh*î from the state of *Kh*ăn in B.C. 672. Why and when its chiefs adopted the surname Thien instead of *Kh*ăn is not well known. The murder took place in 482. Hăng did not immediately usurp the marquisate; but he and his successors disposed of it at their pleasure among the representatives of the old House till 386, when Thien Ho was recognised by the king of *K*âu as the marquis; and his next successor but one took the title of king.

[3] The kingdom of *Kh*î came to an end in B.C. 221, the first year of the dynasty of *Kh*in, after it had lasted through five reigns. How *K*wang-ȝze made out his 'twelve generations' we cannot tell. There may be an interpolation in his text made in the time of *Kh*in, or subsequently.

but at the same time the regulations of its sages and wise men, which thereby served to guard the person of him, thief and robber as he was?

2. Let me try to set forth this subject (still further). Have not there been among those vulgarly styled the wisest, such as have collected (their wealth) for the great chief? and among those styled the most sage such as have guarded it for him? How do I know that it has been so? Formerly, Lung-fǎng[1] was beheaded; Pî-kan[2] had his heart torn out; *Kh*ang Hung[3] was ripped open; and Ȝze-hsü[4] was reduced to pulp (in the *K*iang). Worthy as those four men were, they did not escape such dreadful deaths. The followers of the robber *K*ih[5] asked him, saying, 'Has the robber also any method or principle (in his proceedings)?' He replied, 'What profession is there which has not its principles? That the robber in his recklessness comes to the conclusion that there are valuable deposits in an apartment shows his sageness; that he is the first to enter it shows his bravery; that he is the last to quit it shows his righteousness; that he knows whether (the robbery) may be attempted or not shows his wisdom; and that he makes an equal

---

[1] See on Book IV, par. 1.

[2] See on Book IV, par. 1.

[3] A historiographer of *K*âu, with whom Confucius is said to have studied music. He was weakly and unjustly put to death, as here described by king *K*ǎng, in B.C. 492.

[4] Wû Ȝze-hsü, the hero of revenge, who fled from *Kh*û to Wû, which he long served. He was driven at last to commit suicide, and his body was then put into a leathern wine-sack, and thrown into the *K*iang near the present Sû-*k*âu;—about B.C. 475.

[5] See on Book VIII, par. 4.

division of the plunder shows his benevolence. Without all these five qualities no one in the world has ever attained to become a great robber.' Looking at the subject in this way, we see that good men do not arise without having the principles of the sages, and that *K*ih could not have pursued his course without the same principles. But the good men in the world are few, and those who are not good are many;—it follows that the sages benefit the world in a few instances and injure it in many. Hence it is that we have the sayings, 'When the lips are gone the teeth are cold[1];' 'The poor wine of Lû gave occasion to the siege of Han-tan[2];' 'When sages are born great robbers arise[3].' When the stream is dried, the valley is empty; when the mound is levelled, the deep pool (beside it) is filled up. When the sages have died, the great robbers will not arise; the world would be at peace, and there would be no more troubles. While the sagely men have not died, great robbers will not cease to appear. The more right that is attached to (the views of) the sagely men for the government of the world, the more advantage will accrue to (such men as) the robber *K*ih. If we make for men pecks and bushels

[1] This is an instance of cause and effect naturally happening.

[2] At a meeting of the princes, presided over by king Hsüan of *Kh*û (B.C. 369–340), the ruler of Lû brought very poor wine for the king, which was presented to him as wine of *K*âo, in consequence of a grudge against that kingdom by his officer of wines. In consequence of this king Hsüan ordered siege to be laid to Han-tan, the capital of *K*âo. This is an instance of cause and effect occurring irregularly.

[3] There seems to be no connexion of cause and effect here; but *K*wang-ȝze goes on in his own way to make out that there is such a connexion.

莊子

to measure (their wares), even by means of those pecks and bushels should we be teaching them to steal[1]; if we make for them weights and steelyards to weigh (their wares), even by means of those weights and steelyards shall we be teaching them to steal. If we make for them tallies and seals to secure their good faith, even by means of those tallies and seals shall we be teaching them to steal. If we make for them benevolence and righteousness to make their doings correct, even by means of benevolence and righteousness shall we be teaching them to steal. How do I know that it is so? Here is one who steals a hook (for his girdle);—he is put to death for it: here is another who steals a state;—he becomes its prince. But it is at the gates of the princes that we find benevolence and righteousness (most strongly) professed;—is not this stealing benevolence and righteousness, sageness and wisdom? Thus they hasten to become great robbers, carry off princedoms, and steal benevolence and righteousness, with all the gains springing from the use of pecks and bushels, weights and steelyards, tallies and seals:—even the rewards of carriages and coronets have no power to influence (to a different course), and the terrors of the axe have no power to restrain in such cases. The giving of so great gain to robbers (like) *K*ih, and making it impossible to restrain them;—this is the error committed by the sages.

3. In accordance with this it is said, 'Fish should

[1] The verb 'to steal' is here used transitively, and with a hiphil force.

not be taken from (the protection of) the deep waters; the agencies for the profit of a state should not be shown to men[1].' But those sages (and their teachings) are the agencies for the profit of the world, and should not be exhibited to it. Therefore if an end were put to sageness and wisdom put away, the great robbers would cease to arise. If jade were put away and pearls broken to bits, the small thieves would not appear. If tallies were burned and seals broken in pieces, the people would become simple and unsophisticated. If pecks were destroyed and steelyards snapped in two, the people would have no wrangling. If the rules of the sages were entirely set aside in the world, a beginning might be made of reasoning with the people. If the six musical accords were reduced to a state of utter confusion, organs and lutes all burned, and the ears of the (musicians like the) blind Khwang[2] stopped up, all men would begin to possess and employ their (natural) power of hearing. If elegant ornaments were abolished, the five embellishing colours disused, and the eyes of (men like) Lî *K*û[3] glued up, all men would begin to possess and employ their (natural) power of vision. If the hook and line were destroyed, the compass and square thrown away, and the fingers of men (like) the artful *Kh*ui[4] smashed, all men would begin to possess and employ their (natural) skill;—as it is said, 'The greatest art is

[1] See the Tâo Teh *K*ing, ch. 36. Our author's use of it throws light on its meaning.

[2] Note 1, p. 186.

[3] Note 2, p. 269.

[4] A skilful maker of arrows of the time of Yâo,—the Kung-kung of the Shû, II, i, 21; V, xxii, 19.

莊子

like stupidity[1].' If conduct such as that of Ʒăng (Shăn)[2] and Shih (*Kh*iû)[3] were discarded, the mouths of Yang (*K*û)[4] and Mo (Tî) gagged, and benevolence and righteousness seized and thrown aside, the virtue of all men would begin to display its mysterious excellence. When men possessed and employed their (natural) power of vision, there would be no distortion in the world. When they possessed and employed their (natural) power of hearing, there would be no distractions in the world. When they possessed and employed their (natural) faculty of knowledge, there would be no delusions in the world. When they possessed and employed their (natural) virtue, there would be no depravity in the world. Men like Ʒăng (Shăn), Shih (*Kh*iû), Yang (*K*û), Mo (Tî), Shih Khwang (the musician), the artist *Kh*ui, and Lî *K*û, all display their qualities outwardly, and set the world in a blaze (of admiration) and confound it;—a method which is of no use!

4. Are you, Sir, unacquainted with the age of perfect virtue? Anciently there were Yung-*kh*ăng, Tâ-thing, Po-hwang, *K*ang-yang, Lî-lû, Lî-*kh*û, Hsien-yüan, Ho-hsü, Ʒun-lû, *K*û-yung, Fû-hsî, and Shăn-năng[5]. In their times the people made

---

[1] The Tâo Teh *K*ing, ch. 45.

[2] Note 6, p. 269.

[3] Note 7, p. 269.

[4] Note 5, p. 261.

[5] Of the twelve names mentioned here the reader is probably familiar with those of Fû-hsî and Shăn-năng, the first and second of the Tî in chronology. Hsien-yüan is another name for Hwang-Tî, the third of them. *K*û-yung was, perhaps, a minister of Hwang-Tî. Ho-hsü has occurred before in Book IV. Of the other seven, five occur among the fifteen sovereigns placed in the 'Compendium

knots on cords in carrying on their affairs. They thought their (simple) food pleasant, and their (plain) clothing beautiful. They were happy in their (simple) manners, and felt at rest in their (poor) dwellings. (The people of) neighbouring states might be able to descry one another; the voices of their cocks and dogs might be heard (all the way) from one to the other; they might not die till they were old; and yet all their life they would have no communication together[1]. In those times perfect good order prevailed.

Now-a-days, however, such is the state of things that you shall see the people stretching out their necks, and standing on tiptoe, while they say, 'In such and such a place there is a wise and able man.' Then they carry with them whatever dry provisions they may have left, and hurry towards it, abandoning their parents in their homes, and neglecting the service of their rulers abroad. Their footsteps may be traced in lines from one state to another, and the ruts of their chariot-wheels also for more than a thousand lî. This is owing to the error of their superiors in their (inordinate) fondness for knowledge. When those superiors do really love knowledge, but do not follow the (proper) course, the whole world is thrown into great confusion.

How do I know that the case is so? The knowledge shown in the (making of) bows, cross-bows, hand-nets, stringed arrows, and contrivances with springs is great, but the birds are troubled by them

of History' between Fû-hsî and Shăn-năng. The remaining two may be found, I suppose, in the Lû Shih of Lo Pî.

[1] See the eightieth chapter of the Tâo Teh *K*ing.

莊子

above; the knowledge shown in the hooks, baits, various kinds of nets, and bamboo traps is great, but the fishes are disturbed by them in the waters; the knowledge shown in the arrangements for setting nets, and the nets and snares themselves, is great, but the animals are disturbed by them in the marshy grounds. (So), the versatility shown in artful deceptions becoming more and more pernicious, in ingenious discussions as to what is hard and what is white, and in attempts to disperse the dust and reconcile different views, is great, but the common people are perplexed by all the sophistry. Hence there is great disorder continually in the world, and the guilt of it is due to that fondness for knowledge. Thus it is that all men know to seek for the knowledge that they have not attained to; and do not know to seek for that which they already have (in themselves); and that they know to condemn what they do not approve (in others), and do not know to condemn what they have allowed in themselves;—it is this which occasions the great confusion and disorder. It is just as if, above, the brightness of the sun and moon were darkened; as if, beneath, the productive vigour of the hills and streams were dried up; and as if, between, the operation of the four seasons were brought to an end:—in which case there would not be a single weak and wriggling insect, nor any plant that grows up, which would not lose its proper nature. Great indeed is the disorder produced in the world by the love of knowledge. From the time of the three dynasties downwards it has been so. The plain and honest-minded people are neglected, and the plausible representations of restless spirits received with pleasure; the quiet and unexciting method of non-action is put away, and pleasure taken in ideas garrulously expressed. It is this garrulity of speech which puts the world in disorder.

莊子

BOOK XI.

Part II. Section IV.

Ȝâi Yû, or 'Letting Be, and Exercising Forbearance[1].'

1. I have heard of letting the world be, and exercising forbearance; I have not heard of governing the world. Letting be is from the fear that men, (when interfered with), will carry their nature beyond its normal condition; exercising forbearance is from the fear that men, (when not so dealt with), will alter the characteristics of their nature. When all men do not carry their nature beyond its normal condition, nor alter its characteristics, the good government of the world is secured.

Formerly, Yâo's government of the world made men look joyful; but when they have this joy in their nature, there is a want of its (proper) placidity. The government of the world by *K*ieh, (on the contrary), made men look distressed; but when their nature shows the symptoms of distress, there is a want of its (proper) contentment. The want of placidity and the want of contentment are contrary to the character (of the nature); and where this obtains, it is impossible that any man or state should anywhere abide long. Are men exceedingly joyful?—the Yang or element of expansion in them is too much developed. Are they exceedingly

[1] See pp. 142, 143.

U 2

irritated?—the Yin or opposite element is too much developed. When those elements thus predominate in men, (it is as if[1]) the four seasons were not to come (at their proper times), and the harmony of cold and heat were not to be maintained;—would there not result injury to the bodies of men? Men's joy and dissatisfaction are made to arise where they ought not to do so; their movements are all uncertain; they lose the mastery of their thoughts; they stop short midway, and do not finish what they have begun. In this state of things the world begins to have lofty aims, and jealous dislikes, ambitious courses, and fierce animosities, and then we have actions like those of the robber *K*ih, or of Ȝăng (Shăn) and Shih (Ȝhiû)[2]. If now the whole world were taken to reward the good it would not suffice, nor would it be possible with it to punish the bad. Thus the world, great as it is, not sufficing for rewards and punishments, from the time of the three dynasties downwards, there has been nothing but bustle and excitement. Always occupied with rewards and punishments, what leisure have men had to rest in the instincts of the nature with which they are endowed?

2. Moreover, delight in the power of vision leads

---

[1] I supply the 'it is as if,' after the example of the critic Lû Shû-*k*ih, who here introduces a 猶 in his commentary (猶四時之氣乖其序云云). What the text seems to state as a fact is only an illustration. Compare the concluding paragraphs in all the Sections and Parts of the fourth Book of the Lî *K*î.

[2] Our moral instincts protest against Tâoism which thus places in the same category such sovereigns as Yâo and *K*ieh, and such men as the brigand *K*ih and Ȝăng and Shih.

莊子

to excess in the pursuit of (ornamental) colours; delight in the power of hearing, to excess in seeking (the pleasures of) sound; delight in benevolence tends to disorder that virtue (as proper to the nature); delight in righteousness sets the man in opposition to what is right in reason; delight in (the practice of) ceremonies is helpful to artful forms; delight in music leads to voluptuous airs; delight in sageness is helpful to ingenious contrivances; delight in knowledge contributes to fault-finding. If all men were to rest in the instincts of their nature, to keep or to extinguish these eight delights might be a matter of indifference; but if they will not rest in those instincts, then those eight delights begin to be imperfectly and unevenly developed or violently suppressed, and the world is thrown into disorder. But when men begin to honour them, and to long for them, how great is the deception practised on the world! And not only, when (a performance of them) is once over, do they not have done with them, but they prepare themselves (as) with fasting to describe them, they seem to kneel reverentially when they bring them forward, and they go through them with the excitements of music and singing; and then what can be done (to remedy the evil of them)? Therefore the superior man, who feels himself constrained to engage in the administration of the world will find it his best way to do nothing[1]. In (that policy of) doing nothing, he can rest in the instincts of the nature with which he is endowed. Hence he who will administer (the government of) the world

[1] Here is the Tâoistic meaning of the title of this Book.

honouring it as he honours his own person, may have that government committed to him, and he who will administer it loving it as he loves his own person, may have it entrusted to him [1]. Therefore, if the superior man will keep (the faculties lodged in) his five viscera unemployed, and not display his powers of seeing and hearing, while he is motionless as a representative of the dead, his dragon-like presence will be seen; while he is profoundly silent, the thunder (of his words) will resound; while his movements are (unseen) like those of a spirit, all heavenly influences will follow them; while he is (thus) unconcerned and does nothing, his genial influence will attract and gather all things round him:—what leisure has he to do anything more for the government of the world?

3. Ȝhui *Kh*ü [2] asked Lâo Tan, saying, 'If you do not govern the world, how can you make men's minds good?' The reply was, 'Take care how you meddle with and disturb men's minds. The mind, if pushed about, gets depressed; if helped forward, it gets exalted. Now exalted, now depressed, here it appears as a prisoner, and there as a wrathful fury. (At one time) it becomes pliable and soft, yielding to what is hard and strong; (at another), it is sharp as the sharpest corner, fit to carve or chisel (stone or jade). Now it is hot as a scorching fire, and anon it is cold as ice. It is so swift that while one is bending down and lifting up his head, it shall twice

---

[1] A quotation, but without any indication that it is so, from the Tâo Teh *K*ing, ch. 13.

[2] Probably an imaginary personage.

莊子

have put forth a soothing hand beyond the four seas. Resting, it is still as a deep abyss; moving, it is like one of the bodies in the sky; in its resolute haughtiness, it refuses to be bound;—such is the mind of man [1]!'

Anciently, Hwang-Tî was the first to meddle with and disturb the mind of man with his benevolence and righteousness [2]. After him, Yâo and Shun wore their thighs bare and the hair off the calves of their legs, in their labours to nourish the bodies of the people. They toiled painfully with all the powers in their five viscera at the practice of their benevolence and righteousness; they tasked their blood and breath to make out a code of laws;—and after all they were unsuccessful. On this Yâo sent away Hwan Tâu to *Kh*ung hill, and (the Chiefs of) the Three Miâo to San-wei, and banished the Minister of Works to the Dark Capital; so unequal had they been to cope with the world [3]. Then we are carried on to the kings of the Three (dynasties), when the world was in a state of great distraction. Of the lowest type of character there were *K*ieh and *K*ih; of a higher type there were Ȝăng (Shăn) and Shih (Ȝhiû). At the same time there arose the classes of

[1] I must suppose that the words of Lâo-ȝze stop here, and that what follows is from *K*wang-ȝze himself, down to the end of the paragraph. We cannot have Lâo-ȝze referring to men later than himself, and quoting from his own Book.

[2] Hitherto Yâo and Shun have appeared as the first disturbers of the rule of the Tâo by their benevolence and righteousness. Here that innovation is carried further back to Hwang-Tî.

[3] See these parties, and the way they were dealt with, in the Shû King, Part II, Book I, 3. The punishment of them is there ascribed to Shun; but Yâo was still alive, and Shun was acting as his viceroy.

the Literati and the Mohists. Hereupon, complacency in, and hatred of, one another produced mutual suspicions; the stupid and the wise imposed on one another; the good and the bad condemned one another; the boastful and the sincere interchanged their recriminations;—and the world fell into decay. Views as to what was greatly virtuous did not agree, and the nature with its endowments became as if shrivelled by fire or carried away by a flood. All were eager for knowledge, and the people were exhausted with their searchings (after what was good). On this the axe and the saw were brought into play; guilt was determined as by the plumb-line and death inflicted; the hammer and gouge did their work. The world fell into great disorder, and presented the appearance of a jagged mountain ridge. The crime to which all was due was the meddling with and disturbing men's minds. The effect was that men of ability and worth lay concealed at the foot of the crags of mount Thâi, and princes of ten thousand chariots were anxious and terrified in their ancestral temples. In the present age those who have been put to death in various ways lie thick as if pillowed on each other; those who are wearing the cangue press on each other (on the roads); those who are suffering the bastinado can see each other (all over the land). And now the Literati and the Mohists begin to stand, on tiptoe and with bare arms, among the fettered and manacled crowd! Ah! extreme is their shamelessness, and their failure to see the disgrace! Strange that we should be slow to recognise their sageness and wisdom in the bars of the cangue, and their benevolence and righteousness in the rivets of the fetters and handcuffs! How do we know that

莊子

Ȝăng and Shih are not the whizzing arrows of *K*ieh and *K*ih[1]? Therefore it is said, 'Abolish sageness and cast away knowledge, and the world will be brought to a state of great order[2].'

4. Hwang-Tî had been on the throne for nineteen years[3], and his ordinances were in operation all through the kingdom, when he heard that Kwang *Kh*ăng-ȝze[4] was living on the summit of Khung-thung[5], and went to see him. 'I have heard,' he said, 'that you, Sir, are well acquainted with the perfect Tâo. I venture to ask you what is the essential thing in it. I wish to take the subtlest influences of heaven and earth, and assist with them the (growth of the) five cereals for the (better) nourishment of the people. I also wish to direct the (operation of the) Yin and Yang, so as to secure the comfort of all living beings. How shall I proceed to accomplish those objects?' Kwang *Kh*ăng-ȝze replied, 'What you wish to ask about is the original substance of all things[6]; what you

[1] Compare this picture of the times after Yâo and Shun with that given by Mencius in III, ii, ch. 9 et al. But the conclusions arrived at as to the causes and cure of their evils by him and our author are very different.

[2] A quotation, with the regular formula, from the Tâo Teh *K*ing, ch. 19, with some variation of the text.

[3] ? in B.C. 2678.

[4] Another imaginary personage; apparently, a personification of the Tâo. Some say he was Lâo-ȝze,—in one of his early states of existence; others that he was 'a True Man,' the teacher of Hwang-Tî. See Ko Hung's 'Immortals,' I, i.

[5] Equally imaginary is the mountain Khung-thung. Some critics find a place for it in the province of Ho-nan; the majority say it is the highest point in the constellation of the Great Bear.

[6] The original ether, undivided, out of which all things were formed.

wish to have the direction of is that substance as it was shattered and divided[1]. According to your government of the world, the vapours of the clouds, before they were collected, would descend in rain; the herbs and trees would shed their leaves before they became yellow; and the light of the sun and moon would hasten to extinction. Your mind is that of a flatterer with his plausible words;—it is not fit that I should tell you the perfect Tâo.'

Hwang-Tî withdrew, gave up (his government of) the kingdom, built himself a solitary apartment, spread in it a mat of the white mâo grass, dwelt in it unoccupied for three months, and then went again to seek an interview with (the recluse). Kwang *Kh*ăng-ȝze was then lying down with his head to the south. Hwang-Tî, with an air of deferential submission, went forward on his knees, twice bowed low with his face to the ground, and asked him, saying, 'I have heard that you, Sir, are well acquainted with the perfect Tâo;—I venture to ask how I should rule my body, in order that it may continue for a long time.' Kwang *Kh*ăng-ȝze hastily rose, and said, 'A good question! Come and I will tell you the perfect Tâo. Its essence is (surrounded with) the deepest obscurity; its highest reach is in darkness and silence. There is nothing to be seen; nothing to be heard. When it holds the spirit in its arms in stillness, then the bodily form of itself will become correct. You must be still; you must be pure; not subjecting your body to toil, not agitating your vital force;—then you may live for long. When

[1] The same ether, now in motion, now at rest, divided into the Yin and Yang.

莊子

your eyes see nothing, your ears hear nothing, and your mind knows nothing, your spirit will keep your body, and the body will live long. Watch over what is within you, shut up the avenues that connect you with what is external;—much knowledge is pernicious. I (will) proceed with you to the summit of the Grand Brilliance, where we come to the source of the bright and expanding (element); I will enter with you the gate of the Deepest Obscurity, where we come to the source of the dark and repressing (element). There heaven and earth have their controllers; there the Yin and Yang have their Repositories. Watch over and keep your body, and all things will of themselves give it vigour. I maintain the (original) unity (of these elements), and dwell in the harmony of them. In this way I have cultivated myself for one thousand and two hundred years, and my bodily form has undergone no decay[1].'

Hwang-Tî twice bowed low with his head to the ground, and said, 'In Kwang *Kh*ăng-ȝze we have an example of what is called Heaven[2].' The other said, 'Come, and I will tell you:—(The perfect Tâo) is something inexhaustible, and yet men all think it has an end; it is something unfathomable, and yet men all think its extreme limit can be reached. He who attains to my Tâo, if he be in a high position, will be one of the August ones, and in a low position, will be a king. He who fails in attaining it, in his highest attainment will see the light, but will

[1] It seems very clear here that the earliest Tâoism taught that the cultivation of the Tâo tended to prolong and preserve the bodily life.

[2] A remarkable, but not a singular, instance of *K*wang-ȝze's application of the name 'Heaven.'

descend and be of the Earth. At present all things are produced from the Earth and return to the Earth. Therefore I will leave you, and enter the gate of the Unending, to enjoy myself in the fields of the Illimitable. I will blend my light with that of the sun and moon, and will endure while heaven and earth endure. If men agree with my views, I will be unconscious of it; if they keep far apart from them, I will be unconscious of it; they may all die, and I will abide alone [1]!'

5. Yün *K*iang [2], rambling to the east, having been borne along on a gentle breeze [3], suddenly encountered Hung Mung [2], who was rambling about, slapping his buttocks [4] and hopping like a bird. Amazed at the sight, Yün *K*iang stood reverentially, and said to the other, 'Venerable Sir, who are you? and why are you doing this?' Hung Mung went on slapping his buttocks and hopping like a bird, but replied, 'I am enjoying myself.' Yün *K*iang said, 'I

[1] A very difficult sentence, in interpreting which there are great differences among the critics.

[2] I have preferred to retain Yün *K*iang and Hung Mung as if they were the surnames and names of two personages here introduced. Mr. Balfour renders them by 'The Spirit of the Clouds,' and 'Mists of Chaos.' The Spirits of heaven or the sky have still their place in the Sacrificial Canon of China, as 'the Cloud-Master, the Rain-Master, the Baron of the Winds, and the Thunder Master.' Hung Mung, again, is a name for 'the Great Ether,' or, as Dr. Medhurst calls it, 'the Primitive Chaos.'

[3] Literally, 'passing by a branch of Fû-yâo;' but we find fû-yâo in Book I, meaning 'a whirlwind.' The term 'branch' has made some critics explain it here as 'the name of a tree,' which is inadmissible. I have translated according to the view of Lû Shû-*k*ih.

[4] Or 'stomach,'—according to another reading.

莊子

wish to ask you a question.' Hung Mung lifted up his head, looked at the stranger, and said, 'Pooh!' Yün Kiang, however, continued, 'The breath of heaven is out of harmony; the breath of earth is bound up; the six elemental influences[1] do not act in concord; the four seasons do not observe their proper times. Now I wish to blend together the essential qualities of those six influences in order to nourish all living things;—how shall I go about it?' Hung Mung slapped his buttocks, hopped about, and shook his head, saying, 'I do not know; I do not know!'

Yün Kiang could not pursue his question; but three years afterwards, when (again) rambling in the east, as he was passing by the wild of Sung, he happened to meet Hung Mung. Delighted with the rencontre, he hastened to him, and said, 'Have you forgotten me, O Heaven? Have you forgotten me, O Heaven[2]?' At the same time, he bowed twice with his head to the ground, wishing to receive his instructions. Hung Mung said, 'Wandering listlessly about, I know not what I seek; carried on by a wild impulse, I know not where I am going. I wander about in the strange manner (which you have seen), and see that nothing proceeds without method and order[3];—what more should I know?' Yün Kiang replied, 'I also seem carried on by an aimless influence, and yet the people follow me wherever I go. I cannot help their doing so. But now as they thus

[1] Probably, the yin, the yang, wind, rain, darkness, and light;—see Mayers, p. 323.

[2] See Introduction, pp. 17, 18.

[3] Compare in Book XXIII, par. 1.

imitate me, I wish to hear a word from you (in the case).' The other said, 'What disturbs the regular method of Heaven, comes into collision with the nature of things, prevents the accomplishment of the mysterious (operation of) Heaven, scatters the herds of animals, makes the birds all sing at night, is calamitous to vegetation, and disastrous to all insects;—all this is owing, I conceive, to the error of governing men.' 'What then,' said Yün *K*iang, 'shall I do?' 'Ah,' said the other, 'you will only injure them! I will leave you in my dancing way, and return to my place.' Yün *K*iang rejoined, 'It has been a difficult thing to get this meeting with you, O Heaven! I should like to hear from you a word (more).' Hung Mung said, 'Ah! your mind (needs to be) nourished. Do you only take the position of doing nothing, and things will of themselves become transformed. Neglect your body; cast out from you your power of hearing and sight; forget what you have in common with things; cultivate a grand similarity with the chaos of the plastic ether; unloose your mind; set your spirit free; be still as if you had no soul. Of all the multitude of things every one returns to its root. Every one returns to its root, and does not know (that it is doing so). They all are as in the state of chaos, and during all their existence they do not leave it[1]. If

[1] They never show any will of their own.—On the names Yün *K*iang and Hung Mung, Lû Shû-*k*ih makes the following remarks:—'These were not men, and yet they are introduced here as questioning and answering each other; showing us that our author frames and employs his surnames and names to serve his own purpose. Those names and the speeches made by the parties are all from him. We must believe that he introduces Confucius, Yâo, and Shun just in the same way.'

莊子

they knew (that they were returning to their root), they would be (consciously) leaving it. They do not ask its name; they do not seek to spy out their nature; and thus it is that things come to life of themselves.'

Yün *K*iang said, 'Heaven, you have conferred on me (the knowledge of) your operation, and revealed to me the mystery of it. All my life I had been seeking for it, and now I have obtained it.' He then bowed twice, with his head to the ground, arose, took his leave, and walked away.

6. The ordinary men of the world[1] all rejoice in men's agreeing with themselves, and dislike men's being different from themselves. This rejoicing and this dislike arise from their being bent on making themselves distinguished above all others. But have they who have this object at heart so risen out above all others? They depend on them to rest quietly (in the position which they desire), and their knowledge is not equal to the multitude of the arts of all those others[2]! When they wish again to administer a state for its ruler, they proceed to employ all the methods which the kings of the three dynasties considered profitable without seeing the evils of such a course. This is to make the state depend on the peradventure of their luck. But how seldom it is that that peradventure does not issue in the ruin of the state! Not once in ten thousand instances will such men preserve a state. Not once will they succeed, and in more than ten thousand cases will they

[1] Meaning eccentric thinkers not Tâoists, like Hui-ȝze, Kung-sun Lung, and others.

[2] The construing and connexion of this sentence are puzzling.

ruin it. Alas that the possessors of territory,—(the rulers of states),—should not know the danger (of employing such men)! Now the possessors of territory possess the greatest of (all) things. Possessing the greatest of all things,—(possessing, that is, men), —they should not try to deal with them as (simply) things. And it is he who is not a thing (himself) that is therefore able to deal with (all) things as they severally require. When (a ruler) clearly understands that he who should so deal with all things is not a thing himself, will he only rule the kingdom? He will go out and in throughout the universe (at his pleasure); he will roam over the nine regions[1], alone in going, alone in coming. Him we call the sole possessor (of this ability); and the sole possessor (of this ability) is what is called the noblest of all.

The teaching of (this) great man goes forth as the shadow from the substance, as the echo responds to the sound. When questioned, he responds, exhausting (from his own stores) all that is in the (enquirer's) mind, as if front to front with all under heaven. His resting-place gives forth no sound; his sphere of activity has no restriction of place. He conducts every one to his proper goal, proceeding to it and bringing him back to it as by his own movement. His movements have no trace; his going forth and his re-enterings have no deviation; his course is like that of the sun without beginning (or ending).

[1] 'The nine regions' generally means the nine provinces into which the Great Yü divided the kingdom. As our author is here describing the grand Tâoist ruler after his fashion in his relation to the universe, we must give the phrase a wider meaning; but I have not met with any attempt to define it.

莊子

If you would praise or discourse about his personality, he is united with the great community of existences. He belongs to that great community, and has no individual self. Having no individual self, how should he have anything that can be called his? If you look at those who have what they call their own, they are the superior men of former times; if you look at him who has nothing of the kind, he is the friend of heaven and earth.

7. Mean, and yet demanding to be allowed their free course;—such are Things. Low, and yet requiring to be relied on;—such are the People. Hidden (as to their issues), and yet requiring to be done;—such are Affairs. Coarse, and yet necessary to be set forth;—such are Laws. Remote, and yet necessary to have dwelling (in one's self);—such is Righteousness. Near, and yet necessary to be widely extended;—such is Benevolence. Restrictive, and yet necessary to be multiplied;—such are Ceremonies. Lodged in the centre, and yet requiring to be exalted;—such is Virtue. Always One, and yet requiring to be modified;—such is the Tâo. Spirit-like, and yet requiring to be exercised;—such is Heaven[1].

Therefore the sages contemplated Heaven, but did not assist It. They tried to perfect their virtue, but did not allow it to embarrass them. They proceeded according to the Tâo, but did not lay any plans. They associated benevolence (with all their doings), but did not rely on it. They pursued right-

[1] All these sentences are understood to show that even in the non-action of the Master of the Tâo there are still things he must do.

eousness extensively, but did not try to accumulate it. They responded to ceremonies, but did not conceal (their opinion as to the troublesomeness of them). They engaged in affairs as they occurred, and did not decline them. They strove to render their laws uniform, but (feared that confusion) might arise from them. They relied upon the people, and did not set light by them. They depended on things as their instruments, and did not discard them[1].

They did not think things equal to what they employed them for, but yet they did not see that they could do without employing them. Those who do not understand Heaven are not pure in their virtue. Those who do not comprehend the Tâo have no course which they can pursue successfully. Alas for them who do not clearly understand the Tâo!

What is it that we call the Tâo[2]? There is the Tâo, or Way of Heaven; and there is the Tâo, or Way of Man. Doing nothing and yet attracting all honour is the Way of Heaven; Doing and being embarrassed thereby is the Way of Man. It is the Way of Heaven that plays the part of the Lord; it is the Way of Man that plays the part of the Servant. The Way of Heaven and the Way of Man are far apart. They should be clearly distinguished from each other.

[1] Antithetic to the previous sentences, and showing that what such a Master does does not interfere with his non-action.

[2] This question and what follows shows clearly enough that, even with *K*wang-ȝze, the character Tâo (道) retained its proper meaning of the Way or Course.

莊子

BOOK XII.

PART II. SECTION V.

Thien Tî, or 'Heaven and Earth[1].'

1. Notwithstanding the greatness of heaven and earth, their transforming power proceeds from one lathe; notwithstanding the number of the myriad things, the government of them is one and the same; notwithstanding the multitude of mankind, the lord of them is their (one) ruler[2]. The ruler's (course) should proceed from the qualities (of the Tâo) and be perfected by Heaven[3], when it is so, it is called 'Mysterious and Sublime.' The ancients ruled the world by doing nothing;—simply by this attribute of Heaven[4].

If we look at their words[5] in the light of the Tâo, (we see that) the appellation for the ruler of the

[1] See pp. 143, 144.

[2] Implying that that ruler, 'the Son of Heaven,' is only one.

[3] 'Heaven' is here defined as meaning 'Non-action, what is of itself (無爲自然);' the teh (德) is the virtue, or qualities of the Tâo;—see the first paragraph of the next Book.

[4] This sentence gives the thesis, or subject-matter of the whole Book, which the author never loses sight of.

[5] Perhaps we should translate here, 'They looked at their words,' referring to 'the ancient rulers.' So Gabelentz construes:—'Dem Tâo gemäss betrachteten sie die reden.' The meaning that I have given is substantially the same. The term 'words' occasions a difficulty. I understand it here, with most of the critics, as 稱名之言, 'the words of appellation.'

world[1] was correctly assigned; if we look in the same light at the distinctions which they instituted, (we see that) the separation of ruler and ministers was right; if we look at the abilities which they called forth in the same light, (we see that the duties of) all the offices were well performed; and if we look generally in the same way at all things, (we see that) their response (to this rule) was complete[2]. Therefore that which pervades (the action of) Heaven and Earth is (this one) attribute; that which operates in all things is (this one) course; that by which their superiors govern the people is the business (of the various departments); and that by which aptitude is given to ability is skill. The skill was manifested in all the (departments of) business; those departments were all administered in righteousness; the righteousness was (the outflow of) the natural virtue; the virtue was manifested according to the Tâo; and the Tâo was according to (the pattern of) Heaven.

Hence it is said[3], 'The ancients who had the nourishment of the world wished for nothing and the world had enough; they did nothing and all things were transformed; their stillness was abysmal, and the people were all composed.' The Record says[4], 'When the one (Tâo) pervades it, all business

[1] Meaning, probably, his appellation as Thien 3ze, 'the Son of Heaven.'

[2] That is, 'they responded to the Tâo,' without any constraint but the example of their rulers.

[3] Here there would seem to be a quotation which I have not been able to trace to its source.

[4] This 'Record' is attributed to Lâo-ʒze; but we know nothing of it. In illustration of the sentiment in the sentence, the critics

莊子

is completed. When the mind gets to be free from all aim, even the Spirits submit.'

2. The Master said[1], 'It is the Tâo that overspreads and sustains all things. How great It is in Its overflowing influence! The Superior man ought by all means to remove from his mind (all that is contrary to It). Acting without action is what is called Heaven(-like). Speech coming forth of itself is what is called (a mark of) the (true) Virtue. Loving men and benefiting things is what is called Benevolence. Seeing wherein things that are different yet agree is what is called being Great. Conduct free from the ambition of being distinguished above others is what is called being Generous. The possession in himself of a myriad points of difference is what is called being Rich. Therefore to hold fast the natural attributes is what is called the Guiding Line (of government)[2]; the perfecting of those attributes is what is called its Establishment; accordance with the Tâo is what is called being Complete; and not allowing anything external to affect the will is what is called being Perfect. When the Superior man understands these ten things, he keeps all matters as it were sheathed in himself, showing the greatness of his mind; and through the outflow of his doings, all things move (and come to him). Being such, he lets the gold lie hid in the hill, and the pearls in the deep; he considers not

refer to par. 34 in the fourth Appendix to the Yî King; but it is not to the point.

[1] Who is 'the Master' here? Confucius? or Lâo-ȝze? I think the latter, though sometimes even our author thus denominates Confucius;—see par. 9.

[2] ? the Tâo.

property or money to be any gain; he keeps aloof from riches and honours; he rejoices not in long life, and grieves not for early death; he does not account prosperity a glory, nor is ashamed of indigence; he would not grasp at the gain of the whole world to be held as his own private portion; he would not desire to rule over the whole world as his own private distinction. His distinction is in understanding that all things belong to the one treasury, and that death and life should be viewed in the same way[1].'

3. The Master said, 'How still and deep is the place where the Tâo resides! How limpid is its purity! Metal and stone without It would give forth no sound. They have indeed the (power of) sound (in them), but if they be not struck, they do not emit it. Who can determine (the qualities that are in) all things?

'The man of kingly qualities holds on his way unoccupied, and is ashamed to busy himself with (the conduct of) affairs. He establishes himself in (what is) the root and source (of his capacity), and his wisdom grows to be spirit-like. In this way his attributes become more and more great, and when his mind goes forth, whatever things come in his way, it lays hold of them (and deals with them). Thus, if there were not the Tâo, the bodily form would not have life, and its life, without the attributes (of the Tâo), would not be manifested. Is not he who preserves the body and gives the fullest development to the life, who establishes the attri-

[1] Balfour:—'The difference between life and death exists no more;' Gabelentz:—'Sterben und Leben haben gleiche Erscheinung.'

莊子

butes of the Tâo and clearly displays It, possessed of kingly qualities? How majestic is he in his sudden issuings forth, and in his unexpected movements, when all things follow him!—This we call the man whose qualities fit him to rule.

'He sees where there is the deepest obscurity; he hears where there is no sound. In the midst of the deepest obscurity, he alone sees and can distinguish (various objects); in the midst of a soundless (abyss), he alone can hear a harmony (of notes). Therefore where one deep is succeeded by a greater, he can people all with things; where one mysterious range is followed by another that is more so, he can lay hold of the subtlest character of each. In this way in his intercourse with all things, while he is farthest from having anything, he can yet give to them what they seek; while he is always hurrying forth, he yet returns to his resting-place; now large, now small; now long, now short; now distant, now near[1].'

4. Hwang-Tî, enjoying himself on the north of the Red-water, ascended to the height of the Khwăn-lun (mountain), and having looked towards the south, was returning home, when he lost his dark-coloured pearl[2]. He employed Wisdom to search for it, but he could not find it. He employed (the clear-sighted) Lî *K*û to search for it, but he

---

[1] I can hardly follow the reasoning of *K*wang-ȝze here. The whole of the paragraph is obscure. I have translated the two concluding characters 修遠, as if they were 遠近, after the example of Lin Hsî-yî, whose edition of *K*wang-ȝze was first published in 1261.

[2] Meaning the Tâo. This is not to be got or learned by wisdom, or perspicacity, or man's reasoning. It is instinctive to man, as the Heavenly gift or Truth (天眞).

could not find it. He employed (the vehement debater) *Kh*ieh *Kh*âu[1] to search for it, but he could not find it. He then employed Purposeless[1], who found it; on which Hwang-Tî said, 'How strange that it was Purposeless who was able to find it!'

5. The teacher of Yâo was Hsü Yû[2]; of Hsü Yû, Nieh *Kh*üeh[2]; of Nieh *Kh*üeh, Wang Î[2]; of Wang Î, Pheî-î[2]. Yâo asked Hsü Yû, saying, 'Is Nieh *Kh*üeh fit to be the correlate of Heaven[3]? (If you think he is), I will avail myself of the services of Wang Î to constrain him (to take my place).' Hsü Yû replied, 'Such a measure would be hazardous, and full of peril to the kingdom! The character of Nieh *Kh*üeh is this;—he is acute, perspicacious, shrewd and knowing, ready in reply, sharp in retort, and hasty; his natural (endowments) surpass those of other men, but by his human qualities he seeks to obtain the Heavenly gift; he exercises his discrimination in suppressing his errors, but he does not know what is the source from which his errors arise. Make him the correlate of Heaven! He would employ the human qualities, so that no regard would be paid to the Heavenly gift. Moreover, he would assign different functions to the different parts of the one person[4].

[1] The meaning of the characters shows what is the idea emblemed by this name; and so with Hsiang Wang,—'a Semblance,' and 'Nonentity;'='Mindless,' 'Purposeless.'

[2] All these names have occurred, excepting that of Pheî-î, who heads Hwang-fû Mî's list of eminent Tâoists. We shall meet with him again. He is to be distinguished from Phû-î.

[3] 'Match Heaven;' that is, be sovereign below, as Heaven above ruled all.

[4] We are referred for the meaning of this characteristic to 肝膽楚越, in Bk. V, par. 1.

Moreover, honour would be given to knowledge, and he would have his plans take effect with the speed of fire. Moreover, he would be the slave of everything he initiated. Moreover, he would be embarrassed by things. Moreover, he would be looking all round for the response of things (to his measures). Moreover, he would be responding to the opinion of the multitude as to what was right. Moreover, he would be changing as things changed, and would not begin to have any principle of constancy. How can such a man be fit to be the correlate of Heaven? Nevertheless, as there are the smaller branches of a family and the common ancestor of all its branches, he might be the father of a branch, but not the father of the fathers of all the branches[1]. Such government (as he would conduct) would lead to disorder. It would be calamity in one in the position of a minister, and ruin if he were in the position of the sovereign.'

6. Yâo was looking about him at Hwâ[2], the border-warden of which said, 'Ha! the sage! Let me ask blessings on the sage! May he live long!'

[1] That is, Nieh might be a minister, but could not be the sovereign. The phraseology is based on the rules for the rise of sub-surnames in the same clan, and the consequent division of clans under different ancestors;—see the Lî Kî, Bk. XIII, i, 10–14, and XIV, 8.

[2] 'Hwâ' is evidently intended for the name of a place, but where it was can hardly be determined. The genuineness of the whole paragraph is called in question; and I pass it by, merely calling attention to what the border-warden is made to say about the close of the life of the sage (Tâoist), who after living a thousand years, ascends among the Immortals (僊 = 仙), and arrives at the place of God, and is free from the three evils of disease, old age, and death; or as some say, after the Buddhists, water, fire, and wind!

Yâo said, 'Hush!' but the other went on, 'May the sage become rich!' Yâo (again) said, 'Hush!' but (the warden) continued, 'May the sage have many sons!' When Yâo repeated his 'Hush,' the warden said, 'Long life, riches, and many sons are what men wish for;—how is it that you alone do not wish for them?' Yâo replied, 'Many sons bring many fears; riches bring many troubles; and long life gives rise to many obloquies. These three things do not help to nourish virtue; and therefore I wish to decline them.' The warden rejoined, 'At first I considered you to be a sage; now I see in you only a Superior man. Heaven, in producing the myriads of the people, is sure to have appointed for them their several offices. If you had many sons, and gave them (all their) offices, what would you have to fear? If you had riches, and made other men share them with you, what trouble would you have? The sage finds his dwelling like the quail (without any choice of its own), and is fed like the fledgling; he is like the bird which passes on (through the air), and leaves no trace (of its flight). When good order prevails in the world, he shares in the general prosperity. When there is no such order, he cultivates his virtue, and seeks to be unoccupied. After a thousand years, tired of the world, he leaves it, and ascends among the immortals. He mounts on the white clouds, and arrives at the place of God. The three forms of evil do not reach him, his person is always free from misfortune;—what obloquy has he to incur?'

With this the border-warden left him. Yâo followed him, saying, 'I beg to ask—;' but the other said, 'Begone!'

7. When Yâo was ruling the world, Po-*kh*ăng Ȝze-kâo[1] was appointed by him prince of one of the states. From Yâo (afterwards) the throne passed to Shun, and from Shun (again) to Yü; and (then) Po-*kh*ăng Ȝze-kâo resigned his principality and began to cultivate the ground. Yü went to see him, and found him ploughing in the open country. Hurrying to him, and bowing low in acknowledgment of his superiority, Yü then stood up, and asked him, saying, 'Formerly, when Yâo was ruling the world, you, Sir, were appointed prince of a state. He gave his sovereignty to Shun, and Shun gave his to me, when you, Sir, resigned your dignity, and are (now) ploughing (here);—I venture to ask the reason of your conduct.' Ȝze-kâo said, 'When Yâo ruled the world, the people stimulated one another (to what was right) without his offering them rewards, and stood in awe (of doing wrong) without his threatening them with punishments. Now you employ both rewards and punishments, and the people notwithstanding are not good. Their virtue will from this time decay; punishments will from this time prevail; the disorder of future ages will from this time begin. Why do you, my master, not go away, and not interrupt my work?' With this he resumed his ploughing with his head bent down, and did not (again) look round.

8. In the Grand Beginning (of all things) there was nothing in all the vacancy of space; there was nothing that could be named[2]. It was in this state

[1] Some legends say that this Po-*kh*ăng Ȝze-kâo was a pre-incarnation of Lâo-ȝze; but this paragraph is like the last, and cannot be received as genuine.

[2] This sentence is differently understood, according as it is

that there arose the first existence[1];—the first existence, but still without bodily shape. From this things could then be produced, (receiving) what we call their proper character[2]. That which had no bodily shape was divided[3]; and then without intermission there was what we call the process of conferring[4]. (The two processes) continuing in operation, things were produced. As things were completed, there were produced the distinguishing lines of each, which we call the bodily shape. That shape was the body preserving in it the spirit[5], and each had its peculiar manifestation, which we call its Nature. When the Nature has been cultivated, it returns to its proper character; and when that has been fully reached, there is the same condition as at the Beginning. That sameness is pure vacancy, and the vacancy is great. It is like the closing of the beak and silencing the singing (of a bird). That closing and silencing is like the union of heaven and earth (at the beginning)[6]. The union, effected, as it

punctuated;—有無無, 有無名, or 有無, 無有無名. Each punctuation has its advocates. For myself, I can only adopt the former; the other is contrary to my idea of Chinese composition. If the author had wished to be understood so, he would have written differently, as, for instance, 無未有名.

[1] Probably, the primary ether, what is called the Thâi *K*ih.

[2] This sentence is anticipatory.

[3] Into what we call the yin and the yang;—the same ether, now at rest, now in motion.

[4] The conferring of something more than what was material. By whom or what? By Heaven; the Tâoist understanding by that term the Tâo.

[5] So then, man consists of the material body and the immaterial spirit.

[6] The potential heaven and earth, not yet fashioned from the primal ether.

莊子

is, might seem to indicate stupidity or darkness, but it is what we call the 'mysterious quality' (existing at the beginning); it is the same as the Grand Submission (to the Natural Course).

9. The Master[1] asked Lâo Tan, saying, 'Some men regulate the Tâo (as by a law), which they have only to follow;—(a thing, they say,) is admissible or it is inadmissible; it is so, or it is not so. (They are like) the sophists who say that they can distinguish what is hard and what is white as clearly as if the objects were houses suspended in the sky. Can such men be said to be sages[2]?' The reply was, 'They are like the busy underlings of a court, who toil their bodies and distress their minds with their various artifices;—dogs, (employed) to their sorrow to catch the yak, or monkeys[3] that are brought from their forests (for their tricksiness). *Kh*iû, I tell you this;—it is what you cannot hear, and what you cannot speak of:—Of those who have their heads and feet, and yet have neither minds nor ears, there are multitudes; while of those who have their bodies, and at the same time preserve that which has no bodily form or shape, there are really none. It is not in their movements or stoppages, their dying or living, their falling and rising again, that this is to be found. The regulation of the course lies in (their dealing with) the human element in them. When they have forgotten external things,

[1] This 'Master' is without doubt Confucius.

[2] The meaning and point of Confucius's question are not clear. Did he mean to object to Lâo-ȝze that all his disquisitions about the Tâo as the one thing to be studied and followed were unnecessary?

[3] Compare in Bk. VII, par. 4.

and have also forgotten the heavenly element in them, they may be named men who have forgotten themselves. The man who has forgotten himself is he of whom it is said that he has become identified with Heaven[1].'

10. At an interview with *K*î *Kh*êh[2], *K*iang-lü Mien[2] said to him, 'Our ruler of Lû asked to receive my instructions. I declined, on the ground that I had not received any message[3] for him. Afterwards, however, I told him (my thoughts). I do not know whether (what I said) was right or not, and I beg to repeat it to you. I said to him, "You must strive to be courteous and to exercise self-restraint; you must distinguish the public-spirited and loyal, and repress the cringing and selfish;—who among the people will in that case dare not to be in harmony with you?"' *K*î *Kh*êh laughed quietly and said, 'Your words, my master, as a description of the right course for a Tî or King, were like the threatening movement of its arms by a mantis which would thereby stop the advance of a carriage;—inadequate to accomplish your object. And moreover, if he guided himself by your directions, it would be as if he were to increase the dangerous height of his towers

[1] Their action is like that of Heaven, silent but most effective, without motive from within or without, simply from the impulse of the Tâo.

[2] These two men are only known by the mention of them here. They must have been officers of Lû, *K*î *Kh*êh a member of the great *K*î or *K*î-sun family of that state. He would appear also to have been the teacher of the other; if, indeed, they were real personages, and not merely the production of *K*wang-ȝze's imagination.

[3] That is any lessons or instructions from you, my master, which I should communicate to him.

莊子

and add to the number of his valuables collected in them;—the multitudes (of the people) would leave their (old) ways, and bend their steps in the same direction.'

*K*iang-lü Mien was awe-struck, and said in his fright, 'I am startled by your words, Master, nevertheless, I should like to hear you describe the influence (which a ruler should exert).' The other said, 'If a great sage ruled the kingdom, he would stimulate the minds of the people, and cause them to carry out his instructions fully, and change their manners; he would take their minds which had become evil and violent and extinguish them, carrying them all forward to act in accordance with the (good) will belonging to them as individuals, as if they did it of themselves from their nature, while they knew not what it was that made them do so. Would such an one be willing to look up to Yâo and Shun in their instruction of the people as his elder brothers? He would treat them as his juniors, belonging himself to the period of the original plastic ether[1]. His wish would be that all should agree with the virtue (of that early period), and quietly rest in it.'

11. Ȝze-kung had been rambling in the south in *Kh*û, and was returning to Ȝin. As he passed (a place) on the north of the Han, he saw an old man who was going to work on his vegetable garden. He had dug his channels, gone to the well, and was bringing from it in his arms a jar of water to pour into them. Toiling away, he expended a great deal

[1] The Chinese phrase here is explained by Dr. Williams:—'A vivifying influence, a vapour or aura producing things.'

of strength, but the result which he accomplished was very small. 3ze-kung said to him, 'There is a contrivance here, by means of which a hundred plots of ground may be irrigated in one day. With the expenditure of a very little strength, the result accomplished is great. Would you, Master, not like (to try it)?' The gardener looked up at him, and said, 'How does it work?' 3ze-kung said, 'It is a lever made of wood, heavy behind, and light in front. It raises the water as quickly as you could do with your hand, or as it bubbles over from a boiler. Its name is a shadoof.' The gardener put on an angry look, laughed, and said, 'I have heard from my teacher that, where there are ingenious contrivances, there are sure to be subtle doings; and that, where there are subtle doings, there is sure to be a scheming mind. But, when there is a scheming mind in the breast, its pure simplicity is impaired. When this pure simplicity is impaired, the spirit becomes unsettled, and the unsettled spirit is not the proper residence of the Tâo. It is not that I do not know (the contrivance which you mention), but I should be ashamed to use it.'

(At these words) 3ze-kung looked blank and ashamed; he hung down his head, and made no reply. After an interval, the gardener said to him, 'Who are you, Sir?' 'A disciple of Khung *Kh*iû,' was the reply. The other continued, 'Are you not the scholar whose great learning makes you comparable to a sage, who make it your boast that you surpass all others, who sing melancholy ditties all by yourself, thus purchasing a famous reputation throughout the kingdom? If you would (only) forget the energy of your spirit, and neglect the care of

莊子

your body, you might approximate (to the Tâo). But while you cannot regulate yourself, what leisure have you to be regulating the world? Go on your way, Sir, and do not interrupt my work.'

Ȝze-kung shrunk back abashed, and turned pale. He was perturbed, and lost his self-possession, nor did he recover it, till he had walked a distance of thirty lî. His disciples then said, 'Who was that man? Why, Master, when you saw him, did you change your bearing, and become pale, so that you have been all day without returning to yourself?' He replied to them, 'Formerly I thought that there was but one man[1] in the world, and did not know that there was this man. I have heard the Master say that to seek for the means of conducting his undertakings so that his success in carrying them out may be complete, and how by the employment of a little strength great results may be obtained, is the way of the sage. Now (I perceive that) it is not so at all. They who hold fast and cleave to the Tâo are complete in the qualities belonging to it. Complete in those qualities, they are complete in their bodies. Complete in their bodies, they are complete in their spirits. To be complete in spirit is the way of the sage. (Such men) live in the world in closest union with the people, going along with them, but they do not know where they are going. Vast and complete is their simplicity! Success, gain, and ingenious contrivances, and artful cleverness, indicate (in their opinion) a forgetfulness of the (proper) mind of man. These men will not go where their mind does not carry them, and will do

[1] Confucius.

nothing of which their mind does not approve. Though all the world should praise them, they would (only) get what they think should be loftily disregarded; and though all the world should blame them, they would but lose (what they think) fortuitous and not to be received;—the world's blame and praise can do them neither benefit nor injury. Such men may be described as possessing all the attributes (of the Tâo), while I can only be called one of those who are like the waves carried about by the wind.' When he returned to Lû, (Ȝze-kung) reported the interview and conversation to Confucius, who said, 'The man makes a pretence of cultivating the arts of the Embryonic Age[1]. He knows the first thing, but not the sequel to it. He regulates what is internal in himself, but not what is external to himself. If he had intelligence enough to be entirely unsophisticated, and by doing nothing to seek to return to the normal simplicity, embodying (the instincts of) his nature, and keeping his spirit (as it were) in his arms, so enjoying himself in the common ways, you might then indeed be afraid of him! But what should you and I find in the arts of the embryonic time, worth our knowing?'

12. *K*un Mâng[2], on his way to the ocean, met with Yüan Fung[2] on the shore of the eastern sea, and

[1] The 'arts of the Embryonic Age' suggests the idea of the earliest men in their struggles for support; not the Tâo of Heaven in its formation of the universe. But the whole of the paragraph, not in itself uninteresting, is believed to be a spurious introduction, and not the production of *K*wang-ȝze.

[2] These are not names of men, but like Yün *K*iang and Hung Mung in the fifth paragraph of the last Book. By *K*un Mâng, it is said, we are to understand 'the great primal ether,' and by Yüan

莊子

was asked by him where he was going. 'I am going,' he replied, 'to the ocean;' and the other again asked, 'What for?' *K*un Mâng said, 'Such is the nature of the ocean that the waters which flow into it can never fill it, nor those which flow from it exhaust it. I will enjoy myself, rambling by it.' Yüan Fung replied, 'Have you no thoughts about mankind[1]? I should like to hear from you about sagely government.' *K*un Mâng said, 'Under the government of sages, all offices are distributed according to the fitness of their nature; all appointments are made according to the ability of the men; whatever is done is after a complete survey of all circumstances; actions and words proceed from the inner impulse, and the whole world is transformed. Wherever their hands are pointed and their looks directed, from all quarters the people are all sure to come (to do what they desire):—this is what is called government by sages.'

'I should like to hear about (the government of) the kindly, virtuous men[2],' (continued Yüan Fung). The reply was, 'Under the government of the virtuous, when quietly occupying (their place), they have no thought, and, when they act, they have no anxiety; they do not keep stored (in their minds) what is right and what is wrong, what is good and

Fung, 'the east wind.' Why these should discourse together as they are here made to do, only *K*wang-ȝze himself could tell.

[1] Literally, 'men with their cross eyes;' an appellation for mankind, men having their eyes set across their face more on the same plane than other animals;—'an extraordinary application of the characters,' says Lin Hsî-*k*ung.

[2] The text is simply 'virtuous men;' but the reply justifies us in giving the meaning as 'kindly' as well. 德 has often this signification.

what is bad. They share their benefits among all within the four seas, and this produces what is called (the state of) satisfaction; they dispense their gifts to all, and this produces what is called (the state of) rest. (The people) grieve (on their death) like babies who have lost their mothers, and are perplexed like travellers who have lost their way. They have a superabundance of wealth and all necessaries, and they know not whence it comes; they have a sufficiency of food and drink, and they know not from whom they get it:—such are the appearances (under the government) of the kindly and virtuous.'

'I should like to hear about (the government of) the spirit-like men,' (continued Yüan Fung once more).

The reply was, 'Men of the highest spirit-like qualities mount up on the light, and (the limitations of) the body vanish. This we call being bright and ethereal. They carry out to the utmost the powers with which they are endowed, and have not a single attribute unexhausted. Their joy is that of heaven and earth, and all embarrassments of affairs melt away and disappear; all things return to their proper nature:—and this is what is called (the state of) chaotic obscurity[1].'

13. Măn Wû-kwei[2] and *Kh*ih-*k*ang Man-*kh*î[2] had been looking at the army of king Wû, when the latter said, 'It is because he was not born in the time of the Lord of Yü[3], that therefore he is in-

[1] When no human element had come in to mar the development of the Tâo.

[2] If these be the names of real personages, they must have been of the time of king Wû, about B. C. 1122.

[3] Generally understood to mean 'He is not equal to the Lord of

莊子

volved in this trouble (of war).' Măn Wû-kwei replied, 'Was it when the kingdom was in good order, that the Lord of Yü governed it? or was it after it had become disordered that he governed it?' The other said, 'That the kingdom be in a condition of good order, is what (all) desire, and (in that case) what necessity would there be to say anything about the Lord of Yü? He had medicine for sores; false hair for the bald; and healing for those who were ill:—he was like the filial son carrying in the medicine to cure his kind father, with every sign of distress in his countenance. A sage would be ashamed (of such a thing)[1].

'In the age of perfect virtue they attached no value to wisdom, nor employed men of ability. Superiors were (but) as the higher branches of a tree; and the people were like the deer of the wild. They were upright and correct, without knowing that to be so was Righteousness; they loved one another, without knowing that to do so was Benevolence; they were honest and leal-hearted, without knowing that it was Loyalty; they fulfilled their engagements, without knowing that to do so was Good Faith; in their simple movements they employed the services of one another, without thinking that they were conferring or receiving any gift. Therefore their actions left no trace, and there was no record of their affairs.'

14. The filial son who does not flatter his father,

Yü,' or Shun. The meaning which I have given is that propounded by Hû Wan-ying, and seems to agree better with the general purport of the paragraph.

[1] Ashamed that he had not been able to keep his father from getting sick, and requiring to be thus attended to.

and the loyal minister who does not fawn on his ruler, are the highest examples of a minister and a son. When a son assents to all that his father says, and approves of all that his father does, common opinion pronounces him an unworthy son; when a minister assents to all that his ruler says, and approves of all that his ruler does, common opinion pronounces him an unworthy minister. Nor does any one reflect that this view is necessarily correct[1]. But when common opinion (itself) affirms anything and men therefore assent to it, or counts anything good and men also approve of it, then it is not said that they are mere consenters and flatterers;—is common opinion then more authoritative than a father, or more to be honoured than a ruler? Tell a man that he is merely following (the opinions) of another, or that he is a flatterer of others, and at once he flushes with anger. And yet all his life he is merely following others, and flattering them. His illustrations are made to agree with theirs; his phrases are glossed:—to win the approbation of the multitudes. From first to last, from beginning to end, he finds no fault with their views. He will let his robes hang down[2], display the colours on them, and arrange his movements and bearing, so as to win the favour of his age, and yet not call himself a flatterer. He is but a follower of those others, approving and dis-

[1] We can hardly tell whether this paragraph should be understood as a continuation of *Kh*ih-*k*ang's remarks, or as from *K*wang-ȝze himself. The meaning here is that every one feels that this opinion is right, without pausing to reason about it.

[2] See the Yî King, Appendix III, ii, 15, where this letting his robes hang down is attributed to Shun. Ought we to infer from this that in this paragraph we have *Kh*ih-*k*ang still speaking about and against the common opinion of Shun's superiority to king Wû?

莊子

approving as they do, and yet he will not say that he is one of them. This is the height of stupidity.

He who knows his stupidity is not very stupid; he who knows that he is under a delusion is not greatly deluded. He who is greatly deluded will never shake the delusion off; he who is very stupid will all his life not become intelligent. If three men be walking together, and (only) one of them be under a delusion (as to their way), they may yet reach their goal, the deluded being the fewer; but if two of them be under the delusion, they will not do so, the deluded being the majority. At the present time, when the whole world is under a delusion, though I pray men to go in the right direction, I cannot make them do so;—is it not a sad case?

Grand music does not penetrate the ears of villagers; but if they hear 'The Breaking of the Willow,' or 'The Bright Flowers[1],' they will roar with laughter. So it is that lofty words do not remain in the minds of the multitude, and that perfect words are not heard, because the vulgar words predominate. By two earthenware instruments the (music of) a bell will be confused, and the pleasure that it would afford cannot be obtained. At the present time the whole world is under a delusion, and though I wish to go in a certain direction, how can I succeed in doing so? Knowing that I cannot do so, if I were to try to force my way, that would be another delusion. Therefore my best course is to let my purpose go, and no more pursue it. If I do not pursue it, whom shall I have to share in my sorrow[2]?

[1] The names of two songs, favourites with the common people.
[2] I shall only feel the more that I am alone without any to sympathise with me, and be the more sad.

If an ugly man[1] have a son born to him at midnight, he hastens with a light to look at it. Very eagerly he does so, only afraid that it may be like himself.

15[2]. From a tree a hundred years old a portion shall be cut and fashioned into a sacrificial vase, with the bull figured on it, which is ornamented further with green and yellow, while the rest (of that portion) is cut away and thrown into a ditch. If now we compare the sacrificial vase with what was thrown into the ditch, there will be a difference between them as respects their beauty and ugliness; but they both agree in having lost the (proper) nature of the wood. So in respect of their practice of righteousness there is a difference between (the robber) *K*ih on the one hand, and 3ăng (Shăn) or Shih (3hiû) on the other; but they all agree in having lost (the proper qualities of) their nature.

Now there are five things which produce (in men) the loss of their (proper) nature. The first is (their fondness for) the five colours which disorder the eye, and take from it its (proper) clearness of vision; the second is (their fondness for) the five notes (of music), which disorder the ear and take from it its

---

[1] 厲人 should perhaps be translated 'a leper.' The illustration is edited by *K*iâo Hung and others as a paragraph by itself. They cannot tell whether it be intended to end the paragraph that precedes or to introduce the one that follows.

[2] This paragraph must be our author's own. *Kh*ih-*k*ang, of the time of king Wû, could not be criticising the schemes of life propounded by Mo and Yang, whose views were so much later in time. It breathes the animosity of Lâo and *K*wang against all schemes of learning and culture, as contrary to the simplicity of life according to the Tâo.

莊子

(proper) power of hearing; the third is (their fondness for) the five odours which penetrate the nostrils, and produce a feeling of distress all over the forehead; the fourth is (their fondness for) the five flavours, which deaden the mouth, and pervert its sense of taste; the fifth is their preferences and dislikes, which unsettle the mind, and cause the nature to go flying about. These five things are all injurious to the life; and now Yang and Mo begin to stretch forward from their different standpoints, each thinking that he has hit on (the proper course for men).

But the courses they have hit on are not what I call the proper course. What they have hit on (only) leads to distress;—can they have hit on what is the right thing? If they have, we may say that the dove in a cage has found the right thing for it. Moreover, those preferences and dislikes, that (fondness for) music and colours, serve but to pile up fuel (in their breasts); while their caps of leather, the bonnet with kingfishers' plumes, the memorandum tablets which they carry, and their long girdles, serve but as restraints on their persons. Thus inwardly stuffed full as a hole for fuel, and outwardly fast bound with cords, when they look quietly round from out of their bondage, and think they have got all they could desire, they are no better than criminals whose arms are tied together, and their fingers subjected to the screw, or than tigers and leopards in sacks or cages, and yet thinking that they have got (all they could wish).

BOOK XIII.

Part II. Section VI.

Thien Tâo, or 'The Way of Heaven[1].'

1. The Way of Heaven operates (unceasingly), and leaves no accumulation[2] (of its influence) in any particular place, so that all things are brought to perfection by it; so does the Way of the Tîs operate, and all under the sky turn to them (as their directors); so also does the Way of the Sages operate, and all within the seas submit to them. Those who clearly understand (the Way of) Heaven, who are in sympathy with (that of) the sages, and familiar through the universe and in the four quarters (of the earth) with the work of the Tîs and the kings, yet act spontaneously from themselves:—with the appearance of being ignorant they are yet entirely still.

The stillness of the sages does not belong to them as a consequence of their skilful ability[3]; all things are not able to disturb their minds;—it is on this account that they are still. When water is still, its clearness shows the beard and eyebrows (of him

[1] See pp. 144, 145.

[2] That is, its operation is universal. The Chinese critics generally explain 'accumulation' here by 'rest,' which is not quite the idea.

[3] Such is the meaning here of the 善, as in the Tâo Teh *K*ing, chaps. 2, 8, and often.

who looks into it). It is a perfect Level[1], and the greatest artificer takes his rule from it. Such is the clearness of still water, and how much greater is that of the human Spirit! The still mind of the sage is the mirror of heaven and earth, the glass of all things.

Vacancy, stillness, placidity, tastelessness, quietude, silence, and non-action;—this is the Level of heaven and earth, and the perfection of the Tâo and its characteristics[2]. Therefore the Tîs, Kings, and Sages found in this their resting-place[3]. Resting here, they were vacant; from their vacancy came fullness; from their fullness came the nice distinctions (of things). From their vacancy came stillness; that stillness was followed by movement; their movements were successful. From their stillness came their non-action. Doing-nothing, they devolved the cares of office on their employés. Doing-nothing was accompanied by the feeling of satisfaction. Where there is that feeling of satisfaction, anxieties and troubles find no place; and the years of life are many.

Vacancy, stillness, placidity, tastelessness, quietude, silence, and doing-nothing are the root of all things. When this is understood, we find such a ruler on the throne as Yâo, and such a minister as Shun. When with this a high position is occupied, we find the attributes of the Tîs and kings,—the sons of Heaven; with this in a low position, we find the mysterious

[1] 準 here, is contracted in many editions into 准, which some have mistaken for 淮.

[2] Such are the natural characteristics of the Tâoistic mind.

[3] Implying cessation from all thought and purpose.

sages, the uncrowned kings, with their ways. With this retiring (from public life), and enjoying themselves at leisure, we find the scholars who dwell by the rivers and seas, among the hills and forests, all submissive to it; with this coming forward to active life and comforting their age, their merit is great, and their fame is distinguished;—and all the world becomes united in one.

2. (Such men) by their stillness become sages; and by their movement, kings. Doing-nothing, they are honoured; in their plain simplicity, no one in the world can strive with them (for the palm of) excellence. The clear understanding of the virtue of Heaven and Earth is what is called 'The Great Root,' and 'The Great Origin;'—they who have it are in harmony with Heaven, and so they produce all equable arrangements in the world;—they are those who are in harmony with men. Being in harmony with men is called the Joy of men; being in harmony with Heaven is called the Joy of Heaven. *K*wang-ʒze said, 'My Master! my Master! He shall hash and blend all things in mass without being cruel; he shall dispense his favours to all ages without being benevolent. He is older than the highest antiquity, and yet is not old. He overspreads the heavens and sustains the earth; from him is the carving of all forms without any artful skill[1]! This is what is called the Joy of Heaven. Hence it is said, "Those who know the Joy of Heaven during their life, act like Heaven, and at death undergo transformation like (other) things[2]; in their stillness

[1] Compare in Bk. VI, pars. 13 and 7.

[2] They do not cease to be, but only become transformed or changed.

莊子

they possess the quality of the Yin, and in their movement they flow abroad as the Yang. Therefore he who knows the Joy of Heaven has no murmuring against Heaven, nor any fault-finding with men; and suffers no embarrassment from things, nor any reproof from ghosts. Hence it is said, 'His movements are those of Heaven; his stillness is that of Earth; his whole mind is fixed, and he rules over the world. The spirits of his dead do not come to scare him; he is not worn out by their souls. His words proceeding from his vacancy and stillness, yet reach to heaven and earth, and show a communication with all things:—this is what is called the Joy of Heaven. This Joy of Heaven forms the mind of the sage whereby he nurtures all under the sky[1].'"'

3. It was the Way[2] of the Tîs and Kings to regard Heaven and Earth as their Author, the Tâo and its characteristics as their Lord, and Doing-nothing as their constant rule. Doing-nothing, they could use the whole world in their service and might have done more; acting, they were not sufficient for the service required of them by the world. Hence the men of old held non-inaction in honour. When superiors do nothing and their inferiors also do nothing, inferiors and superiors possess the same virtue; and when inferiors and superiors possess the same virtue, there are none to act as ministers. When inferiors act, and their superiors also act, then superiors and inferiors possess the same Tâo; and when superiors and inferiors possess the same

[1] I suppose that from 'It is said' to this is all quotation, but from what book we do not know.

[2] 'The virtue,' or attribute ;=the way.

Tâo, there is none to preside as Lord. But that the superiors do nothing and yet thereby use the world in their service, and that the inferiors, while acting, be employed in the service of the world, is an unchangeable principle. Therefore the ancient kings who presided over the world, though their knowledge embraced (all the operations of) Heaven and Earth, took no thought of their own about them; though their nice discrimination appreciated the fine fashioning of all things, they said not a word about it; though their power comprehended all within the seas, they did nothing themselves. Heaven produces nothing, yet all things experience their transformations; Earth effects no growth, yet all things receive their nurture; the Tîs and Kings did nothing, yet all the world testified their effective services. Hence it is said, 'There is nothing more spirit-like than Heaven; there is nothing richer than Earth; there are none greater than the Tîs and Kings.' Hence it is said (further), 'The attributes of the Tîs and kings corresponded to those of Heaven and Earth.' It was thus that they availed themselves of (the operations of) Heaven and Earth, carried all things on unceasingly (in their courses), and employed the various classes of men in their service.

4. Originating belongs to those in the higher position; details (of work) to those who are in the lower. The compendious decision belongs to the lord; the minutiae of execution, to his ministers. The direction of the three hosts[1] and their men with the five weapons[2] is but a trifling quality; rewards

[1] 'Three hosts' constituted the military force of one of the largest states.

[2] The bow, the club, the spear, the lance, the javelin. Other

莊子

and penalties with their advantages and sufferings, and the inflictions of the five punishments[1] are but trivial elements of instruction; ceremonies, laws, measures, and numbers, with all the minutiae of jurisprudence[2], are small matters in government; the notes of bells and drums, and the display of plumes and flags are the slightest things in music, and the various grades of the mourning garments are the most unimportant manifestations of grief. These five unimportant adjuncts required the operation of the excited spirit and the employment of the arts of the mind, to bring them into use. The men of old had them indeed, but they did not give them the first place.

The ruler precedes, and the minister follows; the father precedes, and the son follows; the elder brother precedes, and the younger follows; the senior precedes, and the junior follows; the male precedes, and the female follows; the husband precedes, and the wife follows.

This precedence of the more honourable and sequence of the meaner is seen in the (relative) action of heaven and earth, and hence the sages took them as their pattern. The more honourable position of heaven and the lower one of earth are equivalent to a designation of their spirit-like and intelligent qualities. The precedence of spring and summer and the sequence of autumn and winter mark the

---

enumerations of them are given. See the 'Officers of *K*âu,' Bk. XXXII.

[1] Branding, cutting off the nose, cutting off the feet, castration, death.

[2] I read here 刑 (not 形) 名.

order of the four seasons. In the transformations and growth of all things, every bud and feature has its proper form; and in this we have their gradual maturing and decay, the constant flow of transformation and change. Thus since Heaven and Earth, which are most spirit-like, are distinguished as more honourable and less, and by precedence and sequence, how much more must we look for this in the ways of men! In the ancestral temple it is to kinship that honour is given; in court, to rank; in the neighbourhoods and districts, to age; in the conduct of affairs, to wisdom; such is the order in those great ways. If we speak of the course (to be pursued in them), and do not observe their order, we violate their course. If we speak of the course, and do not observe it, why do we apply that name to it?

5. Therefore the ancients who clearly understood the great Tâo first sought to apprehend what was meant by Heaven[1], and the Tâo and its characteristics came next. When this was apprehended, then came Benevolence and Righteousness. When these were apprehended, then came the Distinction of duties and the observance of them. This accomplished, there came objects and their names. After objects and their names, came the employment of men according to their qualities: on this there followed the examination of the men and of their work. This led to the approval or disapproval of them, which again was succeeded by the apportioning of rewards and penalties. After this the stupid and the intelligent understood what was required of them, and the honourable and the mean occupied their several posi-

[1] The meaning, probably, is 'spontaneity.'

莊子

tions. The good and the able, and those inferior to them, sincerely did their best. Their ability was distributed; the duties implied in their official names were fulfilled. In this way did they serve their superiors, nourish their inferiors, regulate things, and cultivate their persons. They did not call their knowledge and schemes into requisition; they were required to fall back upon (the method of) Heaven:—this was what is called the Perfection of the Rule of Great Peace. Hence it is said in the Book [1], 'There are objects and there are their names.' Objects and their names the ancients had; but they did not put them in the foremost place.

When the ancients spoke of the Great Tâo, it was only after four other steps that they gave a place to 'Objects and their Names,' and after eight steps that they gave a place to 'Rewards and Penalties.' If they had all at once spoken of 'Objects and their Names,' they would have shown an ignorance of what is the Root (of government); if they had all at once spoken of 'Rewards and Penalties,' they would have shown an ignorance of the first steps of it. Those whose words are thus an inversion of the (proper) course, or in opposition to it, are (only fit to be) ruled by others;—how can they rule others? To speak all at once of 'Objects and their Names,' and of 'Rewards and Penalties,' only shows that the speaker knows the instruments of government, but does not know the method of it, is fit to be used as an instrument in the world, but not fit to use others as his instruments:—he is what we call a mere sophist, a man of one small idea.

[1] We cannot tell what book or books.

Ceremonies, laws, numbers, measures, with all the minutiae of jurisprudence, the ancients had; but it is by these that inferiors serve their superiors; it is not by them that those superiors nourish the world.

6. Anciently, Shun asked Yâo, saying, 'In what way does your Majesty by the Grace of Heaven[1] exercise your mind?' The reply was, 'I simply show no arrogance towards the helpless; I do not neglect the poor people; I grieve for those who die; I love their infant children; and I compassionate their widows.' Shun rejoined, 'Admirable, as far as it goes; but it is not what is Great.' 'How then,' asked Yâo, 'do you think I should do?' Shun replied, 'When (a sovereign) possesses the virtue of Heaven, then when he shows himself in action, it is in stillness. The sun and moon (simply) shine, and the four seasons pursue their courses. So it is with the regular phenomena of day and night, and with the movement of the clouds by which the rain is distributed.' Yâo said, 'Then I have only been persistently troubling myself! What you wish is to be in harmony with Heaven, while I wish to be in harmony with men.' Now (the Way of) Heaven and Earth was much thought of of old, and Hwang-Tî, Yâo, and Shun united in admiring it. Hence the kings of the world of old did nothing, but tried to imitate that Way.

7. Confucius went to the west to deposit (some) writings in the library of *K*âu[2], when 3ze-lû coun-

[1] So, in the 'Spring and Autumn' Chronicle, the rightful reigning sovereign is ordinarily designated, 'Heaven's King.' It is not a Tâoistic mode of speaking of him.

[2] It is supposed that Confucius, disappointed by his want of

莊子

selled him, saying, 'I have heard that the officer in charge of this *K*ăng[1] Repository of *K*âu was one Lâo Tan, who has given up his office, and is living in his own house. As you, Master, wish to deposit these writings here, why not go to him, and obtain his help (to accomplish your object)[2].' Confucius said, 'Good;' and he went and saw Lâo Tan, who refused his assistance. On this he proceeded to give an abstract of the Twelve Classics[3] to bring the other over to his views[4]. Lâo Tan, however, interrupted him while he was speaking, and said, 'This is too vague; let me hear the substance of them in brief.' Confucius said, 'The substance of them is occupied with Benevolence and Righteousness.' The other said, 'Let me ask whether you consider Benevolence and Righteousness to constitute the nature of man?' 'I do,' was the answer. 'If the superior man be not benevolent, he will not fulfil his character; if he be not righteous, he might as well not have been born. Benevolence and Righteousness are truly the nature of man.' Lâo Tan continued, 'Let me ask you what you mean by Benevolence and Righteousness.' Confucius said, 'To be in one's inmost heart in kindly sympathy

success, wished to deposit the writings or books which he prized so much in the Royal Library, that they might not be lost, and be available for some future teacher, more fortunate than himself.

1 The name of the Royal Library (徵); meaning, perhaps, 'Approved.'

2 That is, help him to get his books deposited in the Library.

3 Meaning, perhaps, the 'Spring and Autumn,' containing a chronicle of twelve marquises of Lû. We know of no collection in the time of Confucius which could be styled the 'Twelve Classics.'

4 說 is to be read shui.

with all things; to love all men; and to allow no selfish thoughts;—this is the nature of Benevolence and Righteousness.' Lâo Tan exclaimed, 'Ah! you almost show your inferiority by such words! "To love all men!" is not that vague and extravagant? "To be seeking to allow no selfish thoughts!"—that is selfishness[1]! If you, Master, wish men not to be without their (proper) shepherding, think of Heaven and Earth, which certainly pursue their invariable course; think of the sun and moon, which surely maintain their brightness; think of the stars in the zodiac, which preserve their order and courses; think of birds and beasts, which do not fail to collect together in their flocks and herds; and think of the trees, which do not fail to stand up (in their places). Do you, Master, imitate this way and carry it into practice; hurry on, following this course, and you will reach your end. Why must you further be vehement in putting forward your Benevolence and Righteousness, as if you were beating a drum, and seeking a fugitive son, (only making him run away the more)? Ah! Master, you are introducing disorder into the nature of man!'

8. Shih-*kh*ăng *Kh*î[2], having an interview with Lâo-ȝze, asked him, saying, 'I heard, Master, that you were a sage, and I came here, wishing to see you, without grudging the length of the journey. During the stages of the hundred days, the soles of my feet became quite callous, but I did not dare to stop and rest. Now I perceive that you are not

[1] The unselfishness was not spontaneous.

[2] We know nothing of this personage, but what is related here; nor does the whole paragraph serve to advance the argument of the Book.

莊子

a sage. Because there was some rice left about the holes of the rats, you sent away your younger sister, which was unkind; when your food, whether raw or cooked, remains before you not all consumed, you keep on hoarding it up to any extent[1].' Lâo-ȝze looked indifferent, and gave him no answer.

Next day *Kh*î again saw Lâo-ȝze, and said, 'Yesterday I taunted you; but to-day I have gone back to a better mood of mind. What is the cause (of the change)[2]?' Lâo-ȝze replied, 'I consider that I have freed myself from the trammels of claiming to be artfully knowing, spirit-like, and sage. Yesterday if you had called me an ox, you might have done so; or if you had called me a horse, you might have done so[3]. If there be a reality (corresponding to men's ideas), and men give it a name, which another will not receive, he will in the sequel suffer the more. My manner was what I constantly observe;—I did not put it on for the occasion.'

Shih-*kh*ăng *Kh*î sidled away out of Lâo's shadow; then he retraced his steps, advanced forward, and asked how he should cultivate himself. The reply was, 'Your demeanour is repelling; you stare with your eyes; your forehead is broad and yet tapering; you bark and growl with your mouth; your appearance is severe and pretentious; you are like a horse held by its tether, you would move, but are restrained, and (if let go) would start off like an

[1] These seem strange charges to bring against Lâo-ȝze, and no light is thrown on them from other sources.

[2] The change had been produced by the demeanour of Lâo-ȝze; the other could not tell how. Other explanations of the question are given by some of the critics.

[3] Compare in the first paragraph of Book VII.

arrow from a bow; you examine all the minutiae of a thing; your wisdom is artful, and yet you try to look at ease. All these are to be considered proofs of your want of sincerity. If on the borders one were to be found with them, he would be named a Thief.'

9. The Master[1] said, 'The Tâo does not exhaust itself in what is greatest, nor is it ever absent from what is least; and therefore it is to be found complete and diffused in all things. How wide is its universal comprehension! How deep is its unfathomableness! The embodiment of its attributes in benevolence and righteousness is but a small result of its spirit-like (working); but it is only the perfect man who can determine this. The perfect man has (the charge of) the world;—is not the charge great? and yet it is not sufficient to embarrass him. He wields the handle of power over the whole world, and yet it is nothing to him. His discrimination detects everything false, and no consideration of gain moves him. He penetrates to the truth of things, and can guard that which is fundamental. So it is that heaven and earth are external to him, and he views all things with indifference, and his spirit is never straitened by them. He has comprehended the Tâo, and is in harmony with its characteristics; he pushes back benevolence and righteousness (into their proper place), and deals with ceremonies and music as (simply) guests:—yes, the mind of the perfect man determines all things aright.'

[1] No doubt, Lâo-ʒze. In the 'Complete Works of the Ten Philosophers,' the text is 老子 and not 夫子.

莊子

10. What the world thinks the most valuable exhibition of the Tâo is to be found in books. But books are only a collection of words. Words have what is valuable in them;—what is valuable in words is the ideas they convey. But those ideas are a sequence of something else;—and what that something else is cannot be conveyed by words. When the world, because of the value which it attaches to words, commits them to books, that for which it so values them may not deserve to be valued;—because that which it values is not what is really valuable.

Thus it is that what we look at and can see is (only) the outward form and colour, and what we listen to and can hear is (only) names and sounds. Alas! that men of the world should think that form and colour, name and sound, should be sufficient to give them the real nature of the Tâo. The form and colour, the name and sound, are certainly not sufficient to convey its real nature; and so it is that 'the wise do not speak and those who do speak are not wise.' How should the world know that real nature?

Duke Hwan[1], seated above in his hall, was (once) reading a book, and the wheelwright Phien was making a wheel below it[2]. Laying aside his hammer and chisel, Phien went up the steps, and said, 'I venture to ask your Grace what words you are reading?' The duke said, 'The words of the sages.' 'Are those sages alive?' Phien con-

[1] No doubt, duke Hwan of *Kh*î, the first of the five presiding chiefs of the *K*âu dynasty.

[2] See in Mencius I, i, vii, 4 a similar reference to the hall and the courtyard below it.

tinued. 'They are dead,' was the reply. 'Then,' said the other, 'what you, my Ruler, are reading are only the dregs and sediments of those old men.' The duke said, 'How should you, a wheelwright, have anything to say about the book which I am reading? If you can explain yourself, very well; if you cannot, you shall die!' The wheelwright said, 'Your servant will look at the thing from the point of view of his own art. In making a wheel, if I proceed gently, that is pleasant enough, but the workmanship is not strong; if I proceed violently, that is toilsome and the joinings do not fit. If the movements of my hand are neither (too) gentle nor (too) violent, the idea in my mind is realised. But I cannot tell (how to do this) by word of mouth;—there is a knack in it. I cannot teach the knack to my son, nor can my son learn it from me. Thus it is that I am in my seventieth year, and am (still) making wheels in my old age[1]. But these ancients, and what it was not possible for them to convey, are dead and gone:—so then what you, my Ruler, are reading is but their dregs and sediments!'

[1] Compare the story in Book III about the ruler Wăn-hui and his butcher; and other passages.

莊子

BOOK XIV.

Part II. Section VII.

Thien Yün, or 'The Revolution of Heaven[1].'

1. How (ceaselessly) heaven revolves! How (constantly) earth abides at rest! And do the sun and moon contend about their (respective) places? Who presides over and directs these (things)? Who binds and connects them together? Who is it that, without trouble or exertion on his part, causes and maintains them? Is it, perhaps, that there is some secret spring, in consequence of which they cannot be but as they are? Or is it, perhaps, that they move and turn as they do, and cannot stop of themselves?

(Then) how the clouds become rain! And how the rain again forms the clouds! Who diffuses them so abundantly? Who is it that, without trouble or exertion on his part, produces this elemental enjoyment, and seems to stimulate it?

The winds rise in the north; one blows to the west, and another to the east; while some rise upwards, uncertain in their direction. By whose breathing are they produced? Who is it that, without any trouble and exertion of his own, effects all their undulations? I venture to ask their cause[2].

---

[1] See pp. 145, 146.

[2] Down to this we have a description of the phenomena of heaven and earth and of nature generally as proceeding regularly

Wû-hsien Thiâo[1] said, 'Come, and I will tell you. To heaven there belong the six Extreme Points, and the five Elements[2]. When the Tîs and Kings acted in accordance with them, there was good government; when they acted contrary to them, there was evil. Observing the things (described) in the nine divisions (of the writing) of Lo[3], their government was perfected and their virtue was complete. They inspected and enlightened the kingdom beneath them, and all under the sky acknowledged and sustained them. Such was the condition under the august (sovereigns[4]) and those before them.'

2. Tang[5], the chief administrator of Shang[5], asked *K*wang-ȝze about Benevolence[6], and the answer was, 'Wolves and tigers are benevolent.' 'What do you mean?' said Tang. *K*wang-ȝze replied, 'Father and son (among them) are affectionate to one another. Why should they be considered as not bene-

---

and noiselessly, without any apparent cause; which is the chief subject of the Book. As the description is not assigned to any one, we must suppose it to be from *K*wang-ȝze himself; and that it is he who asks the question in the last three characters.

[1] This is said by the critics to have been a minister of the Shang dynasty, under Thâi-mâu in the seventeenth century B.C.; but even *K*wang-ȝze would hardly so violate the unity of time.

[2] Generally means 'the Five Regular Virtues;' supposed to mean here 'the Five Elements.'

[3] Probably the 'Nine Divisions of the Great Plan,' in the Shû King, V, iv, fancied to be derived from the writing, which a tortoise from the Lo river exhibited to the great Yü.

[4] Possibly Fû-hsî, Shăn Năng, and Hwang-Tî.

[5] 'Shang' must be taken as the duchy of Sung, assigned by king Wû to the representative of the kings of the dynasty of Shang. 'Tang' would be a principal minister of it in the time of *K*wang-ȝze.

[6] The chief of all the virtues according to Confucianism.

莊子

volent ?' 'Allow me to ask about perfect benevolence,' pursued the other. *K*wang-ʒze said, 'Perfect benevolence[1] does not admit (the feeling) of affection.' The minister said, 'I have heard that, without (the feeling of) affection there is no love, and without love there is not filial duty;—is it permissible to say that the perfectly benevolent are not filial?' *K*wang-ʒze rejoined, 'That is not the way to put the case. Perfect Benevolence is the very highest thing;—filial duty is by no means sufficient to describe it. The saying which you quote is not to the effect that (such benevolence) transcends filial duty;—it does not refer to such duty at all. One, travelling to the south, comes (at last) to Ying[2], and there, standing with his face to the north, he does not see mount Ming[3]. Why does he not see it? Because he is so far from it. Hence it is said, "Filial duty as a part of reverence is easy, but filial duty as a part of love is difficult. If it be easy as a part of love, yet it is difficult to forget[4] one's parents. It may be easy for me to forget my parents, but it is difficult to make my parents forget me. If it were easy to make my parents forget me, it is difficult for me to forget all men in the world. If it were easy to forget all men in the world, it is difficult to make them all forget me."

'This virtue might make one think light of Yâo and Shun, and not wish to be they[5]. The profit

[1] A denomination here for the Tâo, employed by *K*wang-ʒze for the purpose of his argument.

[2] The capital of the state of *Kh*û in the south.

[3] Name of a hill in the extreme north.

[4] The Tâo requires such forgetfulness on the part of both giver and receiver; it is a part of its 'doing-nothing.'

[5] I think this is the meaning.

and beneficial influences of it extend to a myriad ages, and no one in the world knows whence they come. How can you simply heave a great sigh, and speak (as you do) of benevolence and filial duty? Filial duty, fraternal respect, benevolence, righteousness, loyalty, sincerity, firmness, and purity;—all these may be pressed into the service of this virtue, but they are far from sufficient to come up to it. Therefore it is said, "To him who has what is most noble[1], all the dignities of a state are as nothing[2]; to him who has what is the greatest riches, all the wealth of a state is as nothing; to him who has all that he could wish, fame and praise are as nothing." It is thus that the Tâo admits of no substitute.'

3. Pei-măn *Kh*ăng[3] asked Hwang-Tî, saying, 'You were celebrating, O Tî, a performance of the music of the Hsien-*kh*ih[4], in the open country near the Thung-thing lake. When I heard the first part of it, I was afraid; the next made me weary; and the last perplexed me. I became agitated and unable to speak, and lost my self-possession.' The Tî said, 'It was likely that it should so affect you! It was performed with (the instruments of) men, and all attuned according to (the influences of) Heaven. It

[1] The Tâo.

[2] This free version takes 幷 as = 屏. So the Khang-hsî dictionary explains it.

[3] Only heard of, so far as I know, in this passage.

[4] The name of Hwang-Tî's music; I do not venture to translate it. In his elaborate description of it, our author intended to give an idea of the Tâo, and the effect which the study of it was calculated to produce on the mind; as appears from the concluding sentence of the paragraph.

莊子

proceeded according to (the principles of) propriety and righteousness, and was pervaded by (the idea of) the Grand Purity.

'The Perfect Music first had its response in the affairs of men, and was conformed to the principles of Heaven; it indicated the action of the five virtues, and corresponded to the spontaneity (apparent in nature). After this it showed the blended distinctions of the four seasons, and the grand harmony of all things;—the succession of those seasons one after another, and the production of things in their proper order. Now it swelled, and now it died away, its peaceful and military strains clearly distinguished and given forth. Now it was clear, and now rough, as if the contracting and expanding of the elemental processes blended harmoniously (in its notes). Those notes then flowed away in waves of light, till, as when the hibernating insects first begin to move, I commanded the terrifying crash of thunder. Its end was marked by no formal conclusion, and it began again without any prelude. It seemed to die away, and then it burst into life; it came to a close, and then it rose again. So it went on regularly and inexhaustibly, and without the intervention of any pause:—it was this which made you afraid.

'In the second part (of the performance), I made it describe the harmony of the Yin and Yang, and threw round it the brilliance of the sun and moon. Its notes were now short and now long, now soft and now hard. Their changes, however, were marked by an unbroken unity, though not dominated by a fixed regularity. They filled every valley and ravine; you might shut up every crevice, and guard your spirit (against their entrance), yet there was nothing but gave admission to them. Yea, those notes resounded slowly, and might have been pronounced high and clear. Hence the shades of the dead kept in their obscurity; the sun and moon, and all the stars of the zodiac, pursued their several courses. I made (my instruments) leave off, when (the performance) came to an end, and their (echoes) flowed on without stopping. You thought anxiously about it, and were not able to understand it; you looked for it, and were not able to see it; you pursued it, and were not able to reach it. All-amazed, you stood in the way all open around you, and then you leant against an old rotten dryandra-tree and hummed. The power of your eyes was exhausted by what you wished to see; your strength failed in your desire to pursue it, while I myself could not reach it. Your body was but so much empty vacancy while you endeavoured to retain your self-possession[1]:—it was that endeavour which made you weary.

'In the last part (of the performance), I employed notes which did not have that wearying effect. I blended them together as at the command of spontaneity. Hence they came as if following one another in confusion, like a clump of plants springing from one root, or like the music of a forest produced by no visible form. They spread themselves all around without leaving a trace (of their cause); and seemed to issue from deep obscurity where there was no sound. Their movements came from nowhere; their home was in the deep darkness;—

[1] See the usage of the two characters 委蛇 in the Shih King, I, ii, Ode 3.

莊子

conditions which some would call death, and some life; some, the fruit, and some, (merely) the flower. Those notes, moving and flowing on, separating and shifting, and not following any regular sounds, the world might well have doubts about them, and refer them to the judgment of a sage, for the sages understand the nature of this music, and judge in accordance with the prescribed (spontaneity). While the spring of that spontaneity has not been touched, and yet the regulators of the five notes are all prepared;—this is what is called the music of Heaven, delighting the mind without the use of words. Hence it is said in the eulogy of the Lord of Piâo[1], "You listen for it, and do not hear its sound; you look for it, and do not perceive its form; it fills heaven and earth; it envelopes all within the universe." You wished to hear it, but could not take it in; and therefore you were perplexed.

'I performed first the music calculated to awe; and you were frightened as if by a ghostly visitation. I followed it with that calculated to weary; and in your weariness you would have withdrawn. I concluded with that calculated to perplex; and in your perplexity you felt your stupidity. But that stupidity is akin to the Tâo; you may with it convey the Tâo in your person, and have it (ever) with you.'

4. When Confucius was travelling in the west in Wei, Yen Yüan asked the music-master Kin[2], say-

[1] Some sovereign of antiquity, of whom it is difficult to find any other mention but this. Even in the Lû Shih I have not discovered him. The name is said to be pronounced Piâo; in which case it should consist of three 犬, and not of three 火.

[2] Only heard of here.

ing, 'How is it, do you think, with the course of the Master?' The music-master replied, 'Alas! it is all over with your Master!' 'How so?' asked Yen Yüan; and the other said, 'Before the grass-dogs[1] are set forth (at the sacrifice), they are deposited in a box or basket, and wrapt up with elegantly embroidered cloths, while the representative of the dead and the officer of prayer prepare themselves by fasting to present them. After they have been set forth, however, passers-by trample on their heads and backs, and the grass-cutters take and burn them in cooking. That is all they are good for. If one should again take them, replace them in the box or basket, wrap them up with embroidered cloths, and then in rambling, or abiding at the spot, should go to sleep under them, if he do not get (evil) dreams, he is sure to be often troubled with the nightmare. Now here is your Master in the same way taking the grass-dogs, presented by the ancient kings, and leading his disciples to wander or abide and sleep under them. Owing to this, the tree (beneath which they were practising ceremonies) in Sung was cut down[2]; he was obliged to leave Wei[3]; he was reduced to extremities in Shang[3] and *K*âu[4]:—were not those experiences like having (evil) dreams? He was kept in a state of siege between *Kh*ăn and Ȝhâi[5], so that for seven days he had no cooked food to eat, and was in a situation between life and death:—were not those experiences like the nightmare?

[1] See the Tâo Teh *K*ing, ch. 5.

[2] Analects III, xxii.

[3] In consequence of the dissoluteness of the court; Analects VI, xxvi; IX, 17.

[4] Meaning Sung and Wei.

[5] Analects XI, ii, 1.

莊子

'If you are travelling by water, your best plan is to use a boat; if by land, a carriage. Take a boat, which will go (easily) along on the water, and try to push it along on the land, and all your lifetime it will not go so much as a fathom or two:—are not ancient time and the present time like the water and the dry land? and are not *K*âu and Lû like the boat and the carriage? To seek now to practise (the old ways of) *K*âu in Lû is like pushing along a boat on the dry land. It is only a toilsome labour, and has no success; he who does so is sure to meet with calamity. He has not learned that in handing down the arts (of one time) he is sure to be reduced to extremity in endeavouring to adapt them to the conditions (of another).

'And have you not seen the working of a shadoof? When (the rope of) it is pulled, it bends down; and when it is let go, it rises up. It is pulled by a man, and does not pull the man; and so, whether it bends down or rises up, it commits no offence against the man. In the same way the rules of propriety, righteousness, laws, and measures of the three Hwangs[1] and five Tîs[1] derived their excellence, not from their being the same as those of the present day, but from their (aptitude for) government. We may compare them to haws[2], pears, oranges,

[1] It is impossible to speak definitely of who these three Hwangs (Augustuses) and five Tîs were, or whom the speaker intended by them. The former would seem to lead us to the purely fabulous ages, when twelve (or thirteen) Heavenly Hwangs, eleven Earthly, and nine Human ruled over the young world, for a period of 576,000 years. There is a general agreement of opinion that the five Tîs ended with Yâo and Shun.

[2] See Williams's Dictionary, sub voc. He says it is the Cra-

and pummeloes, which are different in flavour, but all suitable to be eaten. Just so it is that the rules of propriety, righteousness, laws, and measures, change according to the time.

'If now you take a monkey, and dress it in the robes of the duke of *K*âu, it will bite and tear them, and will not be satisfied till it has got rid of them altogether. And if you look at the difference between antiquity and the present time it is as great as that between the monkey and the duke of *K*âu. In the same way, when Hsî Shih [1] was troubled in mind, she would knit her brows and frown on all in her neighbourhood. An ugly woman of the neighbourhood, seeing and admiring her beauty, went home, and also laying her hands on her heart proceeded to stare and frown on all around her. When the rich people of the village saw her, they shut fast their doors and would not go out; when the poor people saw her, they took their wives and children and ran away from her. The woman knew how to admire the frowning beauty, but she did not know how it was that she, though frowning, was beautiful. Alas! it is indeed all over with your Master [2]!'

5. When Confucius was in his fifty-first year [3], he had not heard of the Tâo, and went south to Phei [4]

taegus cuneata and pinnatifida, common in China, and much esteemed for its acidity.

[1] A famous beauty,—the concubine of king Fû-*kh*âi of Wû.

[2] The comparisons in this paragraph are not complimentary to Confucius. Of course the conversation never took place, and must have been made up to ridicule the views of the sage.

[3] This would be in B.C. 503 or 502, and Lâo-ȝze would be more than a hundred years old.

[4] Probably in what is now the district of Phei, department of Hsü-*k*âu, *K*iang-sû.

莊子

to see Lâo Tan, who said to him, 'You have come, Sir; have you? I have heard that you are the wisest man of the North; have you also got the Tâo?' 'Not yet,' was the reply; and the other went on, 'How have you sought it?' Confucius said, 'I sought it in measures and numbers, and after five years I had not got it.' 'And how then did you seek it?' 'I sought it in the Yin and Yang, and after twelve years I have not found it.' Lâo-ȝze said, 'Just so! If the Tâo could be presented (to another), men would all present it to their rulers; if it could be served up (to others), men would all serve it up to their parents; if it could be told (to others), men would all tell it to their brothers; if it could be given to others, men would all give it to their sons and grandsons. The reason why it cannot be transmitted is no other but this,—that if, within, there be not the presiding principle, it will not remain there, and if, outwardly, there be not the correct obedience, it will not be carried out. When that which is given out from the mind (in possession of it) is not received by the mind without, the sage will not give it out; and when, entering in from without, there is no power in the receiving mind to entertain it, the sage will not permit it to lie hid there[1]. Fame is a possession common to all; we should not seek to have much of it. Benevolence and righteousness were as the lodging-houses of the former kings; we should only rest in them for a night, and not occupy them for

[1] That is, the sage will not deposit it, where it will lie hidden;—compare Analects XVI, vi.

long. If men see us doing so, they will have much to say against us.

'The perfect men of old trod the path of benevolence as a path which they borrowed for the occasion, and dwelt in Righteousness as in a lodging which they used for a night. Thus they rambled in the vacancy of Untroubled Ease, found their food in the fields of Indifference, and stood in the gardens which they had not borrowed. Untroubled Ease requires the doing of nothing; Indifference is easily supplied with nourishment; not borrowing needs no outlay. The ancients called this the Enjoyment that Collects the True.

'Those who think that wealth is the proper thing for them cannot give up their revenues; those who seek distinction cannot give up the thought of fame; those who cleave to power cannot give the handle of it to others. While they hold their grasp of those things, they are afraid (of losing them). When they let them go, they are grieved; and they will not look at a single example, from which they might perceive the (folly) of their restless pursuits:—such men are under the doom of Heaven[1].

'Hatred and kindness; taking and giving; reproof and instruction; death and life:—these eight things are instruments of rectification, but only those are able to use them who do not obstinately refuse to comply with their great changes. Hence it is said, "Correction is Rectification." When the minds of

[1] See the same expression used in Book VI, par. 11, used by Confucius of himself. Comparing the two passages together, I must doubt the correctness of my note there (2, p. 252), that 'Heaven' is used in the Confucian sense of Tî, or God. The men here pursued and toiled after the pleasures of the world, rather than the quiet satisfactions of the Tâo.

莊子

some do not acknowledge this, it is because the gate of Heaven[1] (in them) has not been opened.'

6. At an interview with Lâo Tan, Confucius spoke to him of benevolence and righteousness. Lâo Tan said, 'If you winnow chaff, and the dust gets into your eyes, then the places of heaven and earth and of the four cardinal points are all changed to you. If musquitoes or gadflies puncture your skin, it will keep you all the night[2] from sleeping. But this painful iteration of benevolence and righteousness excites my mind and produces in it the greatest confusion. If you, Sir, would cause men not to lose their natural simplicity, and if you would also imitate the wind in its (unconstrained) movements, and stand forth in all the natural attributes belonging to you!—why must you use so much energy, and carry a great drum to seek for the son whom you have lost[3]? The snow-goose does not bathe every day to make itself white, nor the crow blacken itself every day to make itself black. The natural simplicity of their black and white does not afford any ground for controversy; and the fame and praise which men like to contemplate do not make them greater than they naturally are. When the springs (supplying the pools) are dried up, the fishes huddle together on the dry land. Than that they should moisten one another there by their gasping, and keep one another wet by their milt, it would be better for them to forget one another in the rivers and lakes[4].'

---

[1] See Book XXIII, par. 9. The phrase = 靈府.

[2] The common reading 昔 is a mistake for 夕.

[3] Compare the same illustration in the preceding Book, par. 7.

[4] This illustration is from Book VI, par. 5.

From this interview with Lâo Tan, Confucius returned home, and for three days did not speak. His disciples (then) asked him, saying, 'Master, you have seen Lâo Tan; in what way might you admonish and correct him?' Confucius said, 'In him (I may say) that I have now seen the dragon. The dragon coils itself up, and there is its body; it unfolds itself and becomes the dragon complete. It rides on the cloudy air, and is nourished by the Yin and Yang. I kept my mouth open, and was unable to shut it;—how could I admonish and correct Lâo Tan?'

7. Ȝze-kung[1] said, 'So then, can (this) man indeed sit still as a representative of the dead, and then appear as the dragon? Can his voice resound as thunder, when he is profoundly still? Can he exhibit himself in his movements like heaven and earth? May I, Ȝhze, also get to see him?' Accordingly with a message from Confucius he went to see Lâo Tan.

Lâo Tan was then about to answer (his salutation) haughtily in the hall, but he said in a low voice, 'My years have rolled on and are passing away, what do you, Sir, wish to admonish me about?' Ȝze-kung replied, 'The Three Kings and Five Tîs[2] ruled

[1] Ȝze-kung would seem to have undertaken this expedition to maintain the reputation of the Master and his school;—only to be defeated by Lâo-ȝze more signally than Confucius had been.

[2] These are different probably, though the text is not quite certain, from the three Hwangs and five Tîs of par. 3. The Hwangs (or August Sovereigns) preceded the Tîs; the Kings (Wangs) came after them. The Three Kings are the three lines of kings commencing with the dynasty of Hsiâ, and following Shun. From the names mentioned by Ȝze-kung, we ought certainly so to understand the designation here.

the world not in the same way, but the fame that has accrued to them is the same. How is it that you alone consider that they were not sages?' 'Come forward a little, my son. Why do you say that (their government) was not the same?' 'Yâo,' was the reply, 'gave the kingdom to Shun, and Shun gave it to Yü. Yü had recourse to his strength, and Thang to the force of arms. King Wăn was obedient to *K*âu (-hsin), and did not dare to rebel; king Wû rebelled against *K*âu, and would not submit to him. And I say that their methods were not the same.' Lâo Tan said, 'Come a little more forward, my son, and I will tell you how the Three Hwangs and the Five Tîs[1] ruled the world. Hwang-Tî ruled it, so as to make the minds of the people all conformed to the One (simplicity). If the parents of one of them died, and he did not wail, no one blamed him. Yâo ruled it so as to cause the hearts of the people to cherish relative affection. If any, however, made the observances on the death of other members of their kindred less than those for their parents, no one blamed them[2]. Shun ruled it, so as to produce a feeling of rivalry in the minds of the people. Their wives gave birth to their children in the tenth month of their pregnancy, but those children could speak at five months; and before they were three years old, they began to call people by their surnames and names. Then it was that men began to die prematurely. Yü ruled it, so as to cause the minds of the people to become changed. Men's minds became scheming, and they

[1] See note 2, preceding page.

[2] Referring to some abuses, contrary to the doctrine of relationship.

used their weapons as if they might legitimately do so, (saying that they were) killing thieves and not killing other men. The people formed themselves into different combinations;—so it was throughout the kingdom. Everywhere there was great consternation, and then arose the Literati and (the followers of) Mo (Tî). From them came first the doctrine of the relationships (of society); and what can be said of the now prevailing customs (in the marrying of) wives and daughters? I tell you that the rule of the Three Kings and Five Tîs may be called by that name, but nothing can be greater than the disorder which it produced. The wisdom of the Three Kings was opposed to the brightness of the sun and moon above, contrary to the exquisite purity of the hills and streams below, and subversive of the beneficent gifts of the four seasons between. Their wisdom has been more fatal than the sting of a scorpion or the bite of a dangerous beast[1]. Unable to rest in the true attributes of their nature and constitution, they still regarded themselves as sages:—was it not a thing to be ashamed of? But they were shameless.' Ȝze-kung stood quite disconcerted and ill at ease.

8. Confucius said to Lâo Tan, 'I have occupied myself with the Shih, the Shû, the Lî, the Yo, the Yî, and the *Kh*un *Kh*iû, those six Books, for what I myself consider a long time[2], and am thoroughly

[1] What beast is meant here cannot be ascertained from the characters in the text,—鮮規之獸.

[2] But with the preparation of the *Kh*un *Kh*iû Confucius's life ended;—it is very plain that no conversation such as *K*wang-ȝze has fabricated here could ever have taken place.

莊子

acquainted with their contents. With seventy-two rulers, all offenders against the right, I have discoursed about the ways of the former kings, and set forth the examples of (the dukes of) *K*âu and Shâo; and not one of them has adopted (my views) and put them in practice:—how very difficult it is to prevail on such men, and to make clear the path to be pursued!'

Lâo-ȝze replied, 'It is fortunate that you have not met with a ruler fitted to rule the age. Those six writings are a description of the vestiges left by the former kings, but do not tell how they made such vestiges; and what you, Sir, speak about are still only the vestiges. But vestiges are the prints left by the shoes;—are they the shoes that produced them? A pair of white herons look at each other with pupils that do not move, and impregnation takes place; the male insect emits its buzzing sound in the air above, and the female responds from the air below, and impregnation takes place; the creatures called lêi are both male and female, and each individual breeds of itself[1]. The nature cannot be altered; the conferred constitution cannot be changed; the march of the seasons cannot be arrested; the Tâo cannot be stopped. If you get the Tâo, there is no effect that cannot be produced; if you miss it, there is no effect that can.'

Confucius (after this) did not go out, till at the end of three months he went again to see Lâo Tan, and said, 'I have got it. Ravens produce their young by hatching; fishes by the communication of their milt; the small-waisted wasp by transforma-

[1] Where had Lâo-ȝze or his author learned his zoology?

tion[1]; when a younger brother comes, the elder weeps[2]. Long is it that I have not played my part in harmony with these processes of transformation. But as I did not play my part in harmony with such transformation, how could I transform men?' Lâo-ʒze said, 'You will do. *Kh*iû, you have found the Tâo.'

---

[1] See the Shih King, II, v, Ode II, 3, about the sphex.

[2] Because, as we say, 'his nose is put out.' But the sentiment, though it is ascribed to Confucius, is rarely according to the fact of the case.

BOOK XV.

Part II. Section VIII.

Kho Î, or 'Ingrained Ideas[1].'

1. Ingrained ideas and a high estimate of their own conduct; leaving the world, and pursuing uncommon ways; talking loftily and in resentful disparagement of others;—all this is simply symptomatic of arrogance. This is what scholars who betake themselves to the hills and valleys, who are always blaming the world, and who stand aloof like withered trees, or throw themselves into deep pools[2], are fond of.

Discoursing of benevolence, righteousness, loyalty, and good faith; being humble and frugal, self-forgetful and courteous;—all this is simply symptomatic of (self-)cultivation. This is what scholars who wish to tranquillise the world, teachers and instructors, men who pursue their studies at home and abroad, are fond of.

Discoursing of their great merit and making a great name for themselves; insisting on the ceremonies between ruler and minister; and rectifying the relations between high and low;—all this shows their one object to be the promotion of government. This is what officers of the court, men who honour their lord and would strengthen the state and who

[1] See pp. 146, 147.
[2] As did Shăn-thû Tî. See in Book VI, par. 3.

would do their utmost to incorporate other states with their own, are fond of.

Resorting to marshes and lakes; dwelling in solitary places; occupying themselves with angling and living at ease;—all this shows their one object to be to do nothing. This is what gentlemen of the rivers and seas, men who avoid the society of the world and desire to live at leisure, are fond of.

Blowing and breathing with open mouth; inhaling and exhaling the breath; expelling the old breath and taking in new; passing their time like the (dormant) bear[1], and stretching and twisting (the neck) like a bird[1];—all this simply shows the desire for longevity. This is what the scholars who manipulate their breath, and the men who nourish the body and wish to live as long as Păng 3û, are fond of.

As to those who have a lofty character without any ingrained ideas; who pursue the path of self-cultivation without benevolence and righteousness; who succeed in government without great services or fame; who enjoy their ease without resorting to the rivers and seas; who attain to longevity without the management (of the breath); who forget all things and yet possess all things; whose placidity is unlimited, while all things to be valued attend them:—such men pursue the way of heaven and earth, and display the characteristics of the sages. Hence it is said[2], 'Placidity, indifference, silence, quietude,

---

[1] This is probably the meaning. The text is simply:—'Bear-passing, bird-stretching.'

[2] 'It is said:'—where? and by whom? These questions we cannot answer. We have met indeed already with the same characteristics of the Tâo; but *K*wang-3ze is not likely to be quoting

莊子

absolute vacancy, and non-action:—these are the qualities which maintain the level of heaven and earth and are the substance of the Tâo and its characteristics.'

2. In accordance with this it is said, 'The sage is entirely restful, and so (his mind) is evenly balanced and at ease. This even balance and ease appears in his placidity and indifference. In this state of even balance and ease, of placidity and indifference, anxieties and evils do not find access to him, no depraving influence can take him by surprise; his virtue is complete, and his spirit continues unimpaired.'

Therefore it is (also) said, 'The life of the sage is (like) the action of Heaven; and his death is the transformation common to (all) things. In his stillness his virtue is the same as that of the Yin, and in movement his diffusiveness is like that of the Yang. He does not take the initiative in producing either happiness or calamity. He responds to the influence acting on him, and moves as he feels the pressure. He rises to act only when he is obliged to do so. He discards wisdom and the memories of the past; he follows the lines of his Heaven (-given nature); and therefore he suffers no calamity from Heaven, no involvement from things, no blame from men, and no reproof from the spirits of the dead [1]. His life seems to float along; his death seems to be a resting. He does not indulge any

himself. On the 'It is said,' and the five recurrences of the phrase below, Lû Shû-kih says that Kwang-ȝze is quoting from sentences current among the adherents of Tâoism,—the sentence-makers often drawn on by Lâo-ȝze; compare the Tâo Teh King, ch. xli.

[1] See Book XIII, par. 2.

anxious doubts; he does not lay plans beforehand. His light is without display; his good faith is without previous arrangement. His sleep is untroubled by dreams; his waking is followed by no sorrows. His spirit is guileless and pure; his soul is not subject to weariness. Vacant and without self-assertion, placid and indifferent, he agrees with the virtue of Heaven.'

Therefore it is said (further), 'Sadness and pleasure show a depraving element in the virtue (of those who feel them); joy and anger show some error in their course; love and hatred show a failure of their virtue. Hence for the mind to be free from sorrow and pleasure is the perfection of virtue; to be of one mind that does not change is the perfection of quietude; to be conscious of no opposition is the perfection of vacancy; to have no intercourse with (external) things is the perfection of indifference; and to have no rebellious dissatisfactions is the perfection of purity.'

3. Therefore it is said (still further), 'If the body be toiled, and does not rest, it becomes worn out; if the spirit be used without cessation, it becomes toiled; and when toiled, it becomes exhausted. It is the nature of water, when free from admixture, to be clear, and, when not agitated, to be level; while if obstructed and not allowed to flow, it cannot preserve its clearness;—being an image of the virtue of Heaven.' Hence it is said (once again), 'To be guileless and pure, and free from all admixture; to be still and uniform, without undergoing any change; to be indifferent and do nothing; to move and yet to act like Heaven:—this is the way to nourish the spirit. Now he who possesses a

莊子

sword made at Kan-yüeh[1] preserves it carefully in a box, and does not dare to use it;—it is considered the perfection of valuable swords. But the human spirit[2] goes forth in all directions, flowing on without limit, reaching to heaven above, and wreathing round the earth beneath. It transforms and nourishes all things, and cannot be represented by any form. Its name is "the Divinity (in man)[3]." It is only the path of pure simplicity which guards and preserves the Spirit. When this path is preserved and not lost, it becomes one with the Spirit; and in this ethereal amalgamation, it acts in harmony with the orderly operation of Heaven.'

There is the vulgar saying, 'The multitude of men consider gain to be the most important thing; pure scholars, fame; those who are wise and able value their ambition; the sage prizes essential purity.' Therefore simplicity is the denomination of that in which there is no admixture; purity of that in which the spirit is not impaired. It is he who can embody simplicity and purity whom we call the True Man[4].

[1] Both of the seaboard states of Wû and Yüeh were famous for the swords produced in them. Kan-yüeh appears to have been the name of a valley or place in Wû, famous for the weapons made in it; unless indeed we should read 于越, instead of 干越, and take 于越 as equivalent to 於越, which is found in the Ȝo *Kh*wan as the name of Yüeh.

[2] Might be translated 'the subtle spirit.'

[3] A very remarkable use of Tî (帝) for the human spirit in the sense of God. The subject of the clause, let the reader observe, is that spirit, and not the Tâo. See pp. 146, 147, where I have said something about it.

[4] See the full account of 'the True Man' in Book VI.

BOOK XVI.

Part II. Section IX.

Shan Hsing, or 'Correcting the Nature[1].'

1. Those who would correct their nature by means of the vulgar learning[2], seeking to restore it to its original condition, and those who would regulate[3] their desires, by the vulgar ways of thinking, seeking thereby to carry their intelligence to perfection, must be pronounced to be deluded and ignorant people. The ancients who regulated the Tâo nourished their faculty of knowledge by their placidity, and all through life abstained from employing that faculty in action;—they must be pronounced to have (thus also) nourished their placidity by their knowledge[4].

When the faculty of knowledge and the placidity

---

[1] See pp. 147, 148.

[2] 'Vulgar' must mean 'common,' and 'the vulgar learning' is the teaching popular in the time of our author, and which he regarded as contrary to the principles of Tâoism, of which he was an adherent. The Chinese critics say that 'vulgar' here is used as the opposite of 'true.'

[3] 滑 is generally explained by 亂, 'to confuse,' but I cannot construe the sentence with that meaning of the term. In the Khang-hsî dictionary which I have followed, the character is defined by 治 with special reference to this passage.

[4] This sentence is the clue to the author's aim in the whole Book. The 'knowledge' is defined by 覺 生, 'the faculty of perception and apprehension.'

莊子

(thus) blend together, and they nourish each other, then from the nature there come forth harmony and orderly method. The attributes (of the Tâo) constitute the harmony; the Tâo (itself) secures the orderly method. When the attributes appear in a universal practice of forbearance, we have Benevolence; when the path is all marked by orderly method, we have Righteousness; when the righteousness is clearly manifested, and (all) things are regarded with affection, we have Leal-heartedness; when the (heart's) core is thus (pure) and real, and carried back to its (proper) qualities, we have Music; when this sincerity appears in all the range of the capacity, and its demonstrations are in accordance with what is elegant, we have Ceremony. If Ceremonies and Music are carried out in an imperfect and one-sided manner, the world is thrown into confusion. When men would rectify others, and their own virtue is beclouded, it is not sufficient to extend itself to them. If an attempt be made so to extend it, they also will lose their (proper) nature.

2. The men of old, while the chaotic condition was yet undeveloped[1], shared the placid tranquillity which belonged to the whole world. At that time the Yin and Yang were harmonious and still; their resting and movement proceeded without any disturbance; the four seasons had their definite times; not a single thing received any injury, and no living being came to a premature end. Men might be

[1] These 'men of old' were what we may call 'primeval men;'—men in the lowest stage of development; but which our author considered to be the highest or paradisiacal condition of their nature.

possessed of (the faculty of) knowledge, but they had no occasion for its use. This was what is called the state of Perfect Unity. At this time, there was no action on the part of any one, but a constant manifestation of spontaneity.

This condition (of excellence) deteriorated and decayed, till Sui-ǎn and Fû-hsî arose and commenced their administration of the world[1]; on which came a compliance (with their methods), but the state of unity was lost. The condition going on to deteriorate and decay, Shăn Năng and Hwang-Tî arose, and took the administration of the world, on which (the people) rested (in their methods), but did not themselves comply with them. Still the deterioration and decay continued till the lords of Thang and Yü[2] began to administer the world. These introduced the method of governing by transformation, resorting to the stream (instead of to the spring)[3], thus vitiating the purity and destroying the simplicity (of the nature). They left the Tâo, and substituted the Good for it, and pursued the course of Haphazard Virtue. After this they forsook their nature and followed (the promptings of) their minds. One mind and another associated their knowledge, but were unable to give rest to the world. Then they added to this knowledge (ex-

[1] *K*wang-ȝze gives no hint of how long he considered this highest condition to have lasted. Sui-ǎn, 'the man of the Burning Speculum,' 'the Fire-producer,' whom Williams calls 'the Prometheus of China,' appears before Fû-hsî, as the first in the line of the Rulers of the world, who broke up the Primal Unity.

[2] These were Yâo and Shun, named from the principalities over which their fathers ruled.

[3] 'The streams' were the methods of culture that arose after the simple virtues and spontaneity of the Tâo were lost.

莊子

ternal and) elegant forms, and went on to make these more and more numerous. The forms extinguished the (primal) simplicity, till the mind was drowned by their multiplicity. After this the people began to be perplexed and disordered, and had no way by which they might return to their true nature, and bring back their original condition.

3. Looking at the subject from this point of view, we see how the world lost[1] the (proper) course, and how the course (which it took) only led it further astray[1]. The world and the Way, when they came together, being (thus) lost to each other, how could the men of the Way make themselves conspicuous in the world? and how could the world rise to an appreciation of the Way? Since the Way had no means to make itself conspicuous in the world, and the world had no means of rising to an appreciation of the Way, though sagely men might not keep among the hills and forests, their virtue was hidden;—hidden, but not because they themselves sought to hide it.

Those whom the ancients called 'Retired Scholars' did not conceal their persons, and not allow themselves to be seen; they did not shut up their words, and refuse to give utterance to them; they did not hide away their knowledge, and refuse to bring it forth. The conditions laid on them by the times were very much awry. If the conditions of the times had allowed them to act in the world on a great scale, they would have brought back the state of unity without any trace being perceived (of how

[1] It is the same character in the text which I have been obliged to translate thus differently,—喪.

B b 2

they did so). When those conditions shut them up entirely from such action, they struck their roots deeper (in themselves), were perfectly still and waited. It was thus that they preserved (the Way in) their own persons.

4. The ancients who preserved (the Way in) their own persons did not try by sophistical reasonings to gloss over their knowledge; they did not seek to embrace (everything in) the world in their knowledge, nor to comprehend all the virtues in it. Solitary and trembling they remained where they were, and sought the restoration of their nature. What had they to do with any further action? The Way indeed is not to be pursued, nor (all) its characteristics to be known on a small scale. A little knowledge is injurious to those characteristics; small doings are injurious to the Way;—hence it is said, 'They simply rectified themselves.' Complete enjoyment is what is meant by 'the Attainment of the Aim.'

What was anciently called 'the Attainment of the Aim' did not mean the getting of carriages and coronets[1]; it simply meant that nothing more was needed for their enjoyment. Now-a-days what is called 'the Attainment of the Aim' means the getting of carriages and coronets. But carriages and coronets belong to the body; they do not affect the nature as it is constituted. When such things happen to come, it is but for a time; being but for a time, their coming cannot be obstructed and their going cannot be stopped[2]. Therefore we should not

[1] That is, worldly distinction.

[2] Because they depend on others. Compare Mencius VI, i, ch. 17, 2.

莊子

because of carriages and coronets indulge our aims, nor because of distress and straitness resort to the vulgar (learning and thinking); the one of these conditions and the other may equally conduce to our enjoyment, which is simply to be free from anxiety. If now the departure of what is transient takes away one's enjoyment, this view shows that what enjoyment it had given was worthless. Hence it is said, 'They who lose themselves in their pursuit of things, and lose their nature in their study of what is vulgar, must be pronounced people who turn things upside down.'

BOOK XVII.

Part II. Section X.

秋水

*Kh*iû Shui, or 'The Floods of Autumn [1].'

1. The time of the autumnal floods was come, and the hundred streams were all discharging themselves into the Ho. Its current was greatly swollen [2], so that across its channel from bank to bank one could not distinguish an ox from a horse. On this the (Spirit-) earl of the Ho [3] laughed with delight, thinking that all the beauty of the world was to be found in his charge. Along the course of the river he walked east till he came to the North Sea, over which he looked, with his face to the east, without being able to see where its waters began. Then he began to turn his face round, looked across the expanse, (as if he were) confronting *Z*o [3], and said with a sigh, 'What the vulgar saying expresses about him who has learned a hundred points (of the Tâo), and thinks that there is no one equal to himself, was surely spoken of me. And moreover, I have heard

[1] See pp. 148, 149.

[2] 涇 here perhaps means 'turbid.' It has nothing to do with the river *K*ing.

[3] See Mayers's Manual, p. 54. Our author adopts the common beliefs or superstitions of his time, and after his fashion puts his own reasonings into the mouths of these mythological personages. It is more difficult to collect the legends about *Z*o of the sea, or of the Northern Sea. See the Khang-hsî Thesaurus under 海若.

parties making little of the knowledge of *K*ung-nî and the righteousness of Po-î, and at first I did not believe them. Now I behold the all-but-boundless extent (of your realms). If I had not come to your gate, I should have been in danger (of continuing in my ignorance), and been laughed at for long in the schools of our great System[1].'

*Z*o, (the Spirit-lord) of the Northern Sea, said, 'A frog in a well cannot be talked with about the sea;—he is confined to the limits of his hole. An insect of the summer cannot be talked with about ice;—it knows nothing beyond its own season. A scholar of limited views cannot be talked with about the Tâo;—he is bound by the teaching (which he has received). Now you have come forth from between your banks, and beheld the great sea. You have come to know your own ignorance and inferiority, and are in the way of being fitted to be talked with about great principles. Of all the waters under heaven there are none so great as the sea. A myriad streams flow into it without ceasing, and yet it is not filled; and afterwards[2] it discharges them (also) without ceasing, and yet it is not emptied. In spring and in autumn it undergoes no change; it takes no notice of floods or of drought. Its superiority over such streams even as the *K*iang and the

[1] Thus the Confucian learning and its worthies were to the system of the Tâo only as the waters of the Ho to the great sea.

[2] I have translated here as if the reading were 尾閒, which is given by Lin Hsî-*k*ung. The correct reading, however, so far as depends on editions and dictionaries, is 尾閭; which is explained in the Khang-hsî dictionary as 'a great Rock in Fû-sang on the East,' against which the water of the sea collects, and is all evaporated!

Ho cannot be told by measures or numbers; and that I have never, notwithstanding this, made much of myself, is because I compare my own bodily form with (the greatness of) heaven and earth, and (remember that) I have received my breath from the Yin and Yang. Between heaven and earth I am but as a small stone or a small tree on a great hill. So long as I see myself to be thus small, how should I make much of myself? I estimate all within the four seas, compared with the space between heaven and earth, to be not so large as that occupied by a pile of stones in a large marsh! I estimate our Middle States, compared with the space between the four seas, to be smaller than a single little grain of rice in a great granary! When we would set forth the number of things (in existence), we speak of them as myriads; and man is only one of them. Men occupy all the nine provinces; but of all whose life is maintained by grain-food, wherever boats and carriages reach, men form only one portion. Thus, compared with the myriads of things, they are not equal to a single fine hair on the body of a horse. Within this range are comprehended all (the territories) which the five Tîs received in succession from one another; all which the royal founders of the three dynasties contended for; all which excited the anxiety of Benevolent men; and all which men in office have toiled for. Po-î was accounted famous for declining (to share in its government), and *K*ung-nî was accounted great because of the lessons which he addressed to it. They acted as they did, making much of themselves;—therein like you who a little time ago did so of yourself because of your (volume of) water!'

莊子

2. The earl of the Ho said, 'Well then, may I consider heaven and earth as (the ideal of) what is great, and the point of a hair as that of what is small?' Zo of the Northern Sea replied, 'No. The (different) capacities of things are illimitable; time never stops, (but is always moving on); man's lot is ever changing; the end and the beginning of things never occur (twice) in the same way. Therefore men of great wisdom, looking at things far off or near at hand, do not think them insignificant for being small, nor much of them for being great:—knowing how capacities differ illimitably. They appeal with intelligence to things of ancient and recent occurrence, without being troubled by the remoteness of the former, or standing on tiptoe to lay hold of the latter:—knowing that time never stops in its course. They examine with discrimination (cases of) fulness and of want, not overjoyed by success, nor disheartened by failure:—knowing the inconstancy of man's lot. They know the plain and quiet path (in which things proceed), therefore they are not overjoyed to live, nor count it a calamity to die:—the end and the beginning of things never occurring (twice) in the same way.

'We must reckon that what men know is not so much as what they do not know, and that the time since they were born is not so long as that which elapsed before they were born. When they take that which is most small and try to fill with it the dimensions of what is most great, this leads to error and confusion, and they cannot attain their end. Looking at the subject in this way, how can you know that the point of a hair is sufficient to determine the minuteness of what is most small, or that heaven and earth are sufficient to complete the dimensions of what is most large?'

3. The earl of the Ho said, 'The disputers of the world all say, "That which is most minute has no bodily form; and that which is most great cannot be encompassed;"—is this really the truth?' *Z*o of the Northern Sea replied, 'When from the standpoint of what is small we look at what is great, we do not take it all in; when from the standpoint of what is great we look at what is small, we do not see it clearly. Now the subtile essence is smallness in its extreme degree; and the vast mass is greatness in its largest form. Different as they are, each has its suitability,—according to their several conditions. But the subtile and the gross both presuppose that they have a bodily form. Where there is no bodily form, there is no longer a possibility of numerical division; where it is not possible to encompass a mass, there is no longer a possibility of numerical estimate. What can be discoursed about in words is the grossness of things; what can be reached in idea is the subtilty of things. What cannot be discoursed about in words, and what cannot be reached by nice discrimination of thought, has nothing to do either with subtilty or grossness.

'Therefore while the actions of the Great Man are not directed to injure men, he does not plume himself on his benevolence and kindness; while his movements are not made with a view to gain, he does not consider the menials of a family as mean; while he does not strive after property and wealth, he does not plume himself on declining them; while he does not borrow the help of others to accomplish his affairs, he does not plume himself on supporting

莊子

himself by his own strength, nor does he despise those who in their greed do what is mean; while he differs in his conduct from the vulgar, he does not plume himself on being so different from them; while it is his desire to follow the multitude, he does not despise the glib-tongued flatterers. The rank and emoluments of the world furnish no stimulus to him, nor does he reckon its punishments and shame to be a disgrace. He knows that the right and the wrong can (often) not be distinguished, and that what is small and what is great can (often) not be defined. I have heard it said, "The Man of Tâo does not become distinguished; the greatest virtue is unsuccessful; the Great Man has no thought of self;"—to so great a degree may the lot be restricted.'

4. The earl of the Ho said, 'Whether the subject be what is external in things, or what is internal, how do we come to make a distinction between them as noble and mean, and as great or small?' *Z*o of the Northern Sea replied, 'When we look at them in the light of the Tâo, they are neither noble nor mean. Looking at them in themselves, each thinks itself noble, and despises others. Looking at them in the light of common opinion, their being noble or mean does not depend on themselves. Looking at them in their differences from one another, if we call those great which are greater than others, there is nothing that is not great, and in the same way there is nothing that is not small. We shall (thus) know that heaven and earth is but (as) a grain of the smallest rice, and that the point of a hair is (as) a mound or a mountain;—such is the view given of them by their relative size. Look-

ing at them from the services they render, allowing to everything the service which it does, there is not one which is not serviceable; and, extending the consideration to what it does not do, there is not one which is not unserviceable. We know (for instance) that East and West are opposed to each other, and yet that the one cannot be without (suggesting the idea of) the other;—(thus) their share of mutual service is determined. Looking at them with respect to their tendencies, if we approve of what they approve, then there is no one who may not be approved of; and, if we condemn what they condemn, there is no one who may not be condemned. There are the cases of Yâo and *K*ieh, each of whom approved of his own course, and condemned the other;—such is the view arising from the consideration of tendency and aim.

'Formerly Yâo and Shun resigned (their thrones), and yet each continued to be Tî; *K*ih-khwâi[1] resigned (his marquisate) which led to his ruin. Thang and Wû contended (for the sovereignty), and each became king; the duke of Pâi[2] contended (for *Kh*û), which led to his extinction. Looking at the subject from these examples of striving by force and of resigning, and from the conduct of Yâo (on the one hand) and of *K*ieh (on the other), we see that there is a time for noble acting, and a time for

[1] See Mencius II, ii, ch. 8, and I, ii, chaps. 10, 11, with the notes. 之 is probably a mistake for 子.

[2] See the last narrative but one in the Ȝo *Kh*wan, under the sixteenth year of duke Âi of Lû,—the year in which Confucius died. 'The duke of Pâi' was merely the chief of a district of *Kh*û; but rebelling against the Ruler of the State, he was defeated, and strangled himself.

mean;—these characteristics are subject to no regular rule.

5. 'A battering ram may be used against the wall of a city, but it cannot be employed to stop up a hole;—the uses of implements are different. The (horses) *Kh*ih-*k*î and Hwâ-liû[1] could in one day gallop 1000 lî, but for catching rats they were not equal to a wild dog or a weasel;—the gifts of creatures are different. The white horned owl collects its fleas in the night-time, and can discern the point of a hair, but in bright day it stares with its eyes and cannot see a mound or a hill;—the natures of creatures are different.

'Hence the sayings, "Shall we not follow and honour the right, and have nothing to do with the wrong? shall we not follow and honour those who secure good government, and have nothing to do with those who produce disorder?" show a want of acquaintance with the principles of Heaven and Earth, and with the different qualities of things. It is like following and honouring Heaven and taking no account of Earth; it is like following and honouring the Yin and taking no account of the Yang. It is clear that such a course cannot be pursued. Yet notwithstanding they go on talking so:—if they are not stupid, they are visionaries. The Tî sovereigns resigned their thrones to others in one way, and the rulers of the three dynasties transmitted their thrones to their successors in another. He who acts differently from the requirements of his time and contrary to its custom is called an usurper; he who complies with the time

[1] Two of king Mu's team of eight famous steeds.

and follows the common practice is said to be righteous. Hold your peace, O earl of the Ho. How should you know what constitutes being noble and being mean, or who are the small and who the great?'

6. The earl of the Ho said, 'Very well. But what am I to do? and what am I not to do? How am I to be guided after all in regard to what I accept or reject, and what I pursue or put away from me?' *Z*o of the Northern Sea replied, 'From the standpoint of the Tâo, what is noble? and what is mean? These expressions are but the different extremes of the average level. Do not keep pertinaciously to your own ideas, which put you in such opposition to the Tâo. What are few? and what are many? These are denominations which we employ in thanking (donors) and dispensing gifts. Do not study to be uniform in doing so;—it only shows how different you are from the Tâo. Be severe and strict, like the ruler of a state who does not selfishly bestow his favours. Be scrupulous, yet gentle, like the tutelary spirit of the land, when sacrifice is offered to him who does not bestow his blessing selfishly. Be large-minded like space, whose four terminating points are illimitable, and form no particular enclosures. Hold all things in your love, favouring and supporting none specially. This is called being without any local or partial regard; all things are equally regarded; there is no long or short among them.

'There is no end or beginning to the Tâo. Things indeed die and are born, not reaching a perfect state which can be relied on. Now there is emptiness, and now fulness;—they do not continue in one form. The years cannot be reproduced; time

莊子

cannot be arrested. Decay and growth, fulness and emptiness, when they end, begin again. It is thus that we describe the method of great righteousness, and discourse about the principle pervading all things. The life of things is like the hurrying and galloping along of a horse. With every movement there is a change; with every moment there is an alteration. What should you be doing? what should you not be doing? You have only to be allowing this course of natural transformation to be going on.'

7. The earl of the Ho said, 'What then is there so valuable in the Tâo?' Zo of the Northern Sea replied, 'He who knows the Tâo is sure to be well acquainted with the principles (that appear in the procedures of things). Acquainted with (those) principles, he is sure to understand how to regulate his conduct in all varying circumstances. Having that understanding, he will not allow things to injure himself. Fire cannot burn him who is (so) perfect in virtue, nor water drown him; neither cold nor heat can affect him injuriously; neither bird nor beast can hurt him. This does not mean that he is indifferent to these things; it means that he discriminates between where he may safely rest and where he will be in peril; that he is tranquil equally in calamity and happiness; that he is careful what he avoids and what he approaches;—so that nothing can injure him. Hence it is said, "What is heavenly is internal; what is human is external." The virtue (of man) is in what is Heavenly. If you know the operation of what is Heavenly and what is Human, you will have your root in what is Heavenly and your position in Virtue. You will bend or stretch

(only) after the (necessary) hesitation; you will have returned to the essential, and may be pronounced to have reached perfection.'

'What do you mean,' pursued the earl, 'by the Heavenly, and by the Human?' *Zo* replied, 'Oxen and horses have four feet;—that is what I call their Heavenly (constitution). When horses' heads are haltered, and the noses of oxen are pierced, that is what I call (the doing of) Man. Hence it is said, "Do not by the Human (doing) extinguish the Heavenly (constitution); do not for your (Human) purpose extinguish the appointment (of Heaven); do not bury your (proper) fame in (such) a pursuit of it; carefully guard (the Way) and do not lose it:—this is what I call reverting to your True (Nature)."'

8. The khwei[1] desires to be like[2] the millipede[1]; the millipede to be like the serpent; the serpent like the wind; the wind to be like the eye; and the eye to be like the mind[3].

The khwei said to the millipede, 'With my one leg I hop about, and can hardly manage to go along. Now you have a myriad feet which you can employ; how is it that you are so abundantly furnished?' The millipede said, 'It is not so. Have you not seen one ejecting saliva? The largest portion of it is like a pearl, while the smaller portions fall down like a shower of mist in innumer-

[1] The khwei is 'a sort of dragon (it may be, a worm) with one foot.' The hsien has many feet; one account calls it 'a centipede.'

[2] Such is the meaning of the lin or lien. The best commentators explain it by hsien (羨), 'to covet and desire.'

[3] Compare Book I, par. 3, towards the end.

莊子

able drops. Now I put in motion the springs set in me by Heaven, without knowing how I do so.'

The millipede said to the serpent, 'I go along by means of my multitude of feet; and yet how is it that I do not go so fast as you who have no feet at all?' The serpent replied, 'How can the method of moving by the springs set in us by Heaven be changed? How could I make use of feet?'

The serpent said to the wind, 'I get along by moving my backbone and ribs, thus appearing to have some (bodily) means of progression. But now you, Sir, rise with a blustering force in the North Sea, and go on in the same way to the South Sea;—seemingly without any such means. How does it take place?' The wind said, 'Yes. With such a blustering force I rise in the North Sea and go on to the South Sea. But you can point to me, and therein are superior to me, as you are also in treading on me. Yet notwithstanding, it is only I who can break great trees, and blow down great houses. Therefore he whom all that are small cannot overcome is a great overcomer. But it is only he who is the sagely man[1] that is the Great Conqueror (of all).'

9. When Confucius was travelling in Khwang[2],

[1] The sagely man is 'the True man,' who embodies the Tâo. The Tâo has given to the khwei, the millipede, the serpent, and it may be said also to the wind, their means of progression and action. Nothing is said of the eye and the mind;—it was not necessary to dwell on the Tâo in them.

[2] See Confucian Analects, IX, v and XI, xxii. Our author's account of this event is his own, constructed by him to convey his own Tâoistic lessons.

some people of Sung (once) surrounded him (with a hostile intention) several ranks deep; but he kept singing to his lute without stopping. Ȝze-lû came in, and saw him, and said, 'How is it, Master, that you are so pleased?' Confucius said, 'Come here, and I will tell you. I have tried to avoid being reduced to such a strait for a long time; and that I have not escaped shows that it was so appointed for me. I have sought to find a ruler that would employ me for a long time, and that I have not found one, shows the character of the time. Under Yâo and Shun there was no one in the kingdom reduced to straits like mine; and it was not by their sagacity that men succeeded as they did. Under *K*ieh and *K*âu no (good and able man) in the kingdom found his way to employment; and it was not for (want of) sagacity that they failed to do so. It was simply owing to the times and their character.

'People that do business on the water do not shrink from meeting iguanodons and dragons;—that is the courage of fishermen. Those who do business on land do not shrink from meeting rhinoceroses and tigers;—that is the courage of hunters. When men see the sharp weapons crossed before them, and look on death as going home;—that is the courage of the determined soldier. When he knows that his strait is determined for him, and that the employment of him by a ruler depends on the character of the time, and then meeting with great distress is yet not afraid;—that is the courage of the sagely man. Wait, my good Yû, and you will see what there is determined for me in my lot.' A little afterwards, the leader of the armed men approached and took his leave, saying, 'We thought you were

Yang Hû[1], and therefore surrounded you. Now we see our mistake.' (With this) he begged to take his leave, and withdrew.

10. Kung-sun Lung[2] asked Mâu of Wei[3], saying, 'When I was young, I learned the teachings of the former kings; and when I was grown up, I became proficient in the practice of benevolence and righteousness. I brought together the views that agreed and disagreed; I considered the questions about hardness and whiteness[4]; I set forth what was to be affirmed and what was not, and what was allowable and what was not; I studied painfully the various schools of thought, and made myself master of the reasonings of all their masters. I thought that I had reached a good understanding of every subject; but now that I have heard the words of Kwang-ȝze, they throw me into a flutter of surprise. I do not know whether it be that I do not come up to him in the power of discussion, or that my knowledge is not equal to his. But now I do not feel able to open my mouth, and venture to ask you what course I should pursue.' Kung-ȝze Mâu leant forward on his stool, drew a long breath, looked up to heaven, smiled, and

[1] No doubt the Yang Ho of Analects XVII, i.

[2] The grandson (Kung-sun) of one of the rulers of Kâo (one of the three states into which the great state of Ȝin had been broken up). He has come down to us as a philosophic sophist, whose views it is not easy to define. See Mayers's Manual, p. 288, and Book XXXIII, par. 7.

[3] Wei was another of the divisions of Ȝin, and Mâu was one of the sons of its ruler at this time, a great admirer, evidently, of Kwang-ȝze, and more than a match for the sophist Lung.

[4] Holding, it is supposed, that 'the attributes of material objects, such as hardness and colour, are separate existences:'—so Mayers, after Wylie.

said, 'Have you not heard of the frog of the dilapidated well, and how it said to the turtle of the Eastern Sea, "How I enjoy myself? I leap upon the parapet of this well. I enter, and having by means of the projections formed by the fragments of the broken tiles of the lining proceeded to the water, I draw my legs together, keep my chin up, (and strike out). When I have got to the mud, I dive till my feet are lost in it. Then turning round, I see that of the shrimps, crabs, and tadpoles there is not one that can do like me. Moreover, when one has entire command of all the water in the gully, and hesitates to go forward, it is the greatest pleasure to enjoy one's self here in this dilapidated well[1];—why do not you, Master, often come and enter, and see it for yourself?" The turtle of the Eastern Sea (was then proceeding to go forward), but before he had put in his left foot, he found his right knee caught and held fast. On this he hesitated, drew back, and told (the frog) all about the sea, saying, "A distance of a thousand lî is not sufficient to express its extent, nor would (a line of) eight thousand cubits be equal to sound its depth. In the time of Yü, for nine years out of ten the flooded land (all drained into it), and its water was not sensibly increased; and in the time of Thang for seven years out of eight there was a drought, but the rocks on the shore (saw) no diminution of the water because of it. Thus it is that no change is produced in its waters by any cause operating for a short time or a long, and that they do not advance nor recede for any addition or subtraction, whether great or small; and this is the great pleasure afforded by the Eastern Sea." When

[1] A passage difficult to construe.

莊子

the frog of the dilapidated well heard this, he was amazed and terror-struck, and lost himself in surprise.

'And moreover, when you, who have not wisdom enough to know where the discussions about what is right and what is wrong should end, still desire to see through the words of *K*wang-ȝze, that is like employing a mosquito to carry a mountain on its back, or a millipede[1] to gallop as fast as the Ho runs;—tasks to which both the insects are sure to be unequal. Still further, when you, who have not wisdom enough to know the words employed in discussing very mysterious subjects, yet hasten to show your sharpness of speech on any occasion that may occur, is not this being like the frog of the dilapidated well?

'And that (*K*wang-ȝze) now plants his foot on the Yellow Springs (below the earth), and anon rises to the height of the Empyrean. Without any regard to south and north, with freedom he launches out in every direction, and is lost in the unfathomable. Without any regard to east and west, starting from what is abysmally obscure, he comes back to what is grandly intelligible. (All the while), you, Sir, in amazement, search for his views to examine them, and grope among them for matter for discussion;—this is just like peeping at the heavens through a tube, or aiming at the earth with an awl; are not both the implements too small for the purpose? Go your ways, Sir.

'And have you not heard of the young learners of

[1] A different character from that for a millipede in the last paragraph;—a Shang *K*ü, evidently some small insect, but we cannot tell what.

Shâu-ling[1], and how they did in Han-tan? Before they had acquired what they might have done in that capital, they had forgotten what they had learned to do in their old city, and were marched back to it on their hands and knees. If now you do not go away, you will forget your old acquirements, and fail in your profession.'

Kung-sun Lung gaped on the speaker, and could not shut his mouth, and his tongue clave to its roof. He slank away and ran off.

11. *K*wang-ȝze was (once) fishing in the river Phû[2], when the king of *Kh*û[3] sent two great officers to him, with the message, 'I wish to trouble you with the charge of all within my territories.' *K*wang-ȝze kept on holding his rod without looking round, and said, 'I have heard that in *Kh*û there is a spirit-like tortoise-shell, the wearer of which died 3000 years ago[4], and which the king keeps, in his ancestral temple, in a hamper covered with a cloth. Was it better for the tortoise to die, and leave its shell to be thus honoured? Or would it have been better for it to live, and keep on dragging its tail through the mud?' The two officers said, 'It would have been better for it to live, and draw its tail after it over the mud[5].' 'Go your ways. I will keep on drawing my tail after me through the mud.'

[1] A city of *K*âo, as Han-tan was its capital. Of the incident referred to, I have not been able to learn anything. The 'were marched' gives my idea of what it may have been.

[2] A river, which still gives its name to Phû-*k*âu, department *Kh*ao-*k*âu, Shan-tung.

[3] Probably king Wei, B.C. 339–330.

[4] A good antiquity for *Kh*û!

[5] ? A species of Testudo Serpentina, such as is often seen on pieces of Japanese lacquer-ware.

莊子

12. Hui-ȝze being a minister of state in Liang[1], *K*wang-ȝze went to see him. Some one had told Hui-ȝze that *K*wang-ȝze was come with a wish to supersede him in his office, on which he was afraid, and instituted a search for the stranger all over the kingdom for three days and three nights. (After this) *K*wang-ȝze went and saw him, and said, 'There is in the south a bird, called "the Young Phoenix[2];"—do you know it? Starting from the South Sea, it flies to the Northern; never resting but on the bignonia[3], never eating but the fruit of the melia azederach[4], and never drinking but from the purest springs. An owl, which had got a putrid rat, (once), when a phoenix went passing overhead, looked up to it and gave an angry scream. Do you wish now, in your possession of the kingdom of Liang, to frighten me with a similar scream?'

13. *K*wang-ȝze and Hui-ȝze were walking on the dam over the Hâo[5], when the former said, 'These thryssas come out, and play about at their ease;—that is the enjoyment of fishes.' The other said, 'You are not a fish; how do you know what

[1] Another name for Wei, so called from its capital;—in the present department of Khâi-făng.

[2] So the critics explain the name. Williams thinks the bird may be 'the argus pheasant,' or 'a variety of the peacock.' But what the bird was does not affect the meaning of our author's reference to it.

[3] One of the Eleococcae, the Dryandra Cordifolia of Thunberg.

[4] All the editions I have seen give 練 here, which makes no sense. The character should doubtless be 楝, with the meaning which I have given; and not 'bamboo,' which is found in the critics. It is also called 'the Pride of India.'

[5] A river in the department and district of Fung-yang, An-hui.

constitutes the enjoyment of fishes[1]?' *K*wang-ȝze rejoined, 'You are not I. How do you know that I do not know what constitutes the enjoyment of fishes?' Hui-ȝze said, 'I am not you; and though indeed I do not fully know you, you certainly are not a fish, and (the argument) is complete against your knowing what constitutes the happiness of fishes.' *K*wang-ȝze replied, 'Let us keep to your original question. You said to me, "How do you know what constitutes the enjoyment of fishes?" You knew that I knew it, and yet you put your question to me;—well, I know it (from our enjoying ourselves together) over the Hâo.'

[1] Surely a captious question. We infer the feelings of other creatures from their demonstrations.

莊子

TRANSLITERATION OF ORIENTAL ALPHABETS ADOPTED FOR THE TRANSLATIONS OF THE SACRED BOOKS OF THE EAST.

CONSONANTS.	MISSIONARY ALPHABET.			Sanskrit.	Zend.	Pehlevi.	Persian.	Arabic.	Hebrew.	Chinese.
	I Class.	II Class.	III Class.							
Gutturales.										
1 Tenuis	k	...	....	क	𐬐	[illegible]	ک	ك	כּ	k
2 „ aspirata	kh	...	....	ख	𐬑	[illegible]	...	...	כ	kh
3 Media	g	...	....	ग	𐬔	[illegible]	گ	...	גּ	...
4 „ aspirata	gh	...	....	घ	𐬖	[illegible]	...	...	ג	...
5 Gutturo-labialis	q	...	....	...	....	...	ق	ق	ק	...
6 Nasalis	ṅ (ng)	...	....	ङ	𐬣 (ng) 𐬧 (N)	...	...	...	...	...
7 Spiritus asper	h	...	....	ह	𐬵 (𐬓 *hv*)	[illegible]	ه	ه	ה	h, hs
8 „ lenis	'	...	....	...	....	...	ا	ا	א	...
9 „ asper faucalis	'h	...	....	...	....	...	ح	ح	ח	...
10 „ lenis faucalis	'h	...	....	...	....	...	ع	ع	ע	...
11 „ asper fricatus	...	*'h*	....	...	....	...	خ	خ	ח	...
12 „ lenis fricatus	...	*'h*	....	...	....	...	...	...	...	...
Gutturales modificatae (palatales, &c.)										
13 Tenuis	...	*k*	....	च	𐬗	[illegible]	چ	...	...	*k*
14 „ aspirata	...	*kh*	....	छ	....	...	...	...	...	*kh*
15 Media	...	*g*	....	ज	𐬘	[illegible]	ج	ج	...	...
16 „ aspirata	...	*gh*	....	झ	....	...	غ	غ	...	...
17 „ Nasalis	...	*ñ*	....	ञ	....	...	...	...	...	...

CONSONANTS (continued).	MISSIONARY ALPHABET. I Class.	II Class.	III Class.	Sanskrit.	Zend.	Pehlevi.	Persian.	Arabic.	Hebrew.	Chinese.
18 Semivocalis	y	. . .	. . . .	य	[illegible], init. [illegible]	[illegible]	ي	ي	י	y
19 Spiritus asper	. . .	(ẏ)	. . . .	. . .	. . . .	. . .	. . .	. . .	. . .	. . .
20 „ lenis	. . .	(y̓)	. . . .	. . .	. . . .	. . .	. . .	. . .	. . .	. . .
21 „ asper assibilatus	. . .	*s*	. . . .	श	[illegible]	[illegible]	ش	ش	. . .	. . .
22 „ lenis assibilatus	. . .	*z*	. . . .	. . .	[illegible]	[illegible]	ژ	. . .	. . .	*z*
Dentales.										
23 Tenuis	t	. . .	. . . .	त	[illegible]	[illegible]	ت	ت	תּ	t
24 „ aspirata	th	. . .	. . . .	थ	[illegible]	. . .	. . .	. . .	ת	th
25 „ assibilata	. . .	. . .	TH	. . .	. . . .	. . .	ث	ث	. . .	. . .
26 Media	d	. . .	. . . .	द	[illegible]	[illegible]	د	د	דּ	. . .
27 „ aspirata	dh	. . .	. . . .	ध	[illegible]	. . .	. . .	. . .	ד	. . .
28 „ assibilata	. . .	. . .	DH	. . .	. . . .	. . .	ذ	ذ	. . .	. . .
29 Nasalis	n	. . .	. . . .	न	[illegible]	[illegible]	ن	ن	נ	n
30 Semivocalis	l	. . .	. . . .	ल	. . . .	[illegible]	ل	ل	ל	l
31 „ mollis 1	. . .	*l*	. . . .	ळ	. . . .	. . .	. . .	. . .	. . .	. . .
32 „ mollis 2	. . .	. . .	L	. . .	. . . .	. . .	. . .	. . .	. . .	. . .
33 Spiritus asper 1	s	. . .	. . . .	स	[illegible]	[illegible]	س (ث)	س	שׂ	s
34 „ asper 2	. . .	. . .	s (ʃ)	. . .	. . . .	. . .	. . .	. . .	ס	. . .
35 „ lenis	z	. . .	. . . .	. . .	[illegible]	[illegible]	ز (ذ)	ز	ז	z
36 „ asperrimus 1	. . .	. . .	z (ʒ)	. . .	. . . .	. . .	ص	ص	צ	ʒ, ʒh
37 „ asperrimus 2	. . .	. . .	ẓ (ʒ)	. . .	. . . .	. . .	ض	. . .	. . .	. . .

Dentales modificatae (linguales, &c.)										
38 Tenuis	...	*t*	...	ट	...	...	ط	ط	ט	...
39 „ aspirata	...	*th*	...	ठ	...	...	ظ	ظ	...	...
40 Media	...	*d*	...	ड	𐬜	[illegible]	...	...	...	...
41 „ aspirata	...	*dh*	...	ढ	...	...	...	ض	...	...
42 Nasalis	...	*n*	...	ण	𐬧	...	...	...	...	...
43 Semivocalis	r	...	...	र	𐬭	[illegible]	ر	ر	ר	...
44 „ fricata	...	*r*	...	...	...	...	...	...	...	*r*
45 „ diacritica	...	...	R	...	...	...	...	...	...	...
46 Spiritus asper	sh	...	...	ष	𐬴	[illegible]	...	...	...	sh
47 „ lenis	zh	...	...	...	...	...	...	...	...	...
Labiales.										
48 Tenuis	p	...	...	प	𐬞	[illegible]	پ	...	פּ	p
49 „ aspirata	ph	...	...	फ	...	...	...	...	פ	ph
50 Media	b	...	...	ब	𐬠	[illegible]	ب	ب	בּ	...
51 „ aspirata	bh	...	...	भ	...	...	...	...	ב	...
52 Tenuissima	...	*p*	...	...	...	...	...	...	...	...
53 Nasalis	m	...	...	म	𐬨	[illegible]	م	م	מ	m
54 Semivocalis	w	...	...	...	[illegible]	...	...	...	...	w
55 „ aspirata	hw	...	...	...	...	...	...	...	...	...
56 Spiritus asper	f	...	...	...	𐬟	[illegible]	ف	ف	...	f
57 „ lenis	v	...	...	व	»	[illegible]	و	و	ו	...
58 Anusvâra	...	*m*	...	अं	[illegible] ã	...	...	...	...	...
59 Visarga	...	*h*	...	अः	...	...	...	...	...	...

VOWELS.	MISSIONARY ALPHABET. I Class.	II Class.	III Class.	Sanskrit.	Zend.	Pehlevi.	Persian.	Arabic.	Hebrew.	Chinese.
1 Neutralis	0	...	...	...	...	...	...	...	ְ	ă
2 Laryngo-palatalis	ĕ	...	...	...	...	...	...	...	...	...
3 „ labialis	ŏ	...	...	...	...	ı fin.	...	...	...	...
4 Gutturalis brevis	a	...	...	अ	𐬀	𐭠 init.	ـَ	ـَ	ַ	a
5 „ longa	â	(*a*)	...	आ	𐬁	𐭠	ـَا	ـَا	ָ	â
6 Palatalis brevis	i	...	...	इ	𐬌	...	ـِ	ـِ	ִ	i
7 „ longa	î	(*i*)	...	ई	𐬍	ى	ـِي	ـِي	ִי	î
8 Dentalis brevis	*li*	...	...	ऌ	...	...	...	...	...	...
9 „ longa	*lî*	...	...	ॡ	...	...	...	...	...	...
10 Lingualis brevis	*ri*	...	...	ऋ	...	...	...	...	...	...
11 „ longa	*rî*	...	...	ॠ	...	...	...	...	...	...
12 Labialis brevis	u	...	...	उ	𐬎	...	ـُ	ـُ	ֻ	u
13 „ longa	û	(*u*)	...	ऊ	𐬏	ו	ـُو	ـُو	וּ	û
14 Gutturo-palatalis brevis	e	...	...	...	𐬈(e) 𐬉(*e*)	...	...	...	ֶ	e
15 „ longa	ê (ai)	(*e*)	...	ए	𐬆, 𐬇	ى	...	...	ֵ	ê
16 Diphthongus gutturo-palatalis	âi	(*ai*)	...	ऐ	...	...	ـَيْ	ـَيْ	...	âi
17 „ „	ei (ĕi)	...	...	...	...	...	...	...	...	ei, êi
18 „ „	oi (ŏu)	...	...	...	...	...	...	...	...	...
19 Gutturo-labialis brevis	o	...	...	...	𐬊	...	...	...	ָ	o
20 „ longa	ô (au)	(*o*)	...	ओ	𐬋	ו	...	...	וֹ	...
21 Diphthongus gutturo-labialis	âu	(*au*)	...	औ	𐬃𐬎 (*au*)	...	ـَوْ	ـَوْ	...	âu
22 „ „	eu (ĕu)	...	...	...	...	...	...	...	...	...
23 „ „	ou (ŏu)	...	...	...	...	...	...	...	...	...
24 Gutturalis fracta	ä	...	...	...	...	...	...	...	...	...
25 Palatalis fracta	ï	...	...	...	...	...	...	...	...	...
26 Labialis fracta	ü	...	...	...	...	...	...	...	...	ü
27 Gutturo-labialis fracta	ö	...	...	...	...	...	...	...	...	...

莊子

THE

SACRED BOOKS OF THE EAST

London

HENRY FROWDE

OXFORD UNIVERSITY PRESS WAREHOUSE

AMEN CORNER, E.C.

莊子

THE

SACRED BOOKS OF THE EAST

TRANSLATED

BY VARIOUS ORIENTAL SCHOLARS

AND EDITED BY

F. MAX MÜLLER

VOL. XL

Oxford

AT THE CLARENDON PRESS

1891

Oxford

PRINTED AT THE CLARENDON PRESS

BY HORACE HART, PRINTER TO THE UNIVERSITY

莊子

THE

SACRED BOOKS OF CHINA

THE TEXTS OF TÂOISM

TRANSLATED BY

JAMES LEGGE

PART II

THE WRITINGS OF *K*WANG-ȜZE

BOOKS XVIII—XXXIII

THE THÂI-SHANG TRACTATE OF ACTIONS AND THEIR RETRIBUTIONS

APPENDIXES I-VIII

Oxford

AT THE CLARENDON PRESS

1891

CONTENTS.

THE WRITINGS OF *K*WANG-ȜZE.

PART II.

PART III.

THE THÂI-SHANG TRACTATE OF ACTIONS AND THEIR RETRIBUTIONS.

海上絲綢之路文獻集成 科技與文化编

APPENDIXES.

THE TEXTS OF TÂOISM.

BOOK XVIII.

Part II. Section XI.

*K*ih Lo, or 'Perfect Enjoyment[1].'

1. Under the sky is perfect enjoyment to be found or not? Are there any who can preserve themselves alive or not? If there be, what do they do? What do they maintain? What do they avoid? What do they attend to? Where do they resort to? Where do they keep from? What do they delight in? What do they dislike?

What the world honours is riches, dignities, longevity, and being deemed able. What it delights in is rest for the body, rich flavours, fine garments, beautiful colours, and pleasant music. What it looks down on are poverty and mean condition, short life and being deemed feeble[2]. What men consider bitter experiences are that their bodies do not get rest and ease, that their mouths do not get food of rich flavour, that their persons are not finely clothed, that their eyes do not see beautiful colours, and that their ears do not listen to pleasant music. If they do not

[1] See vol. xxxix, pp. 149, 150.

[2] Of riches, dignities, longevity, and their opposites, enough is said, while the other two qualities are lightly passed over, and referred to only in connexion with 'meritorious officers.' I can only understand them as in the translation.

get these things, they are very sorrowful, and go on to be troubled with fears. Their thoughts are all about the body;—are they not silly?

Now the rich embitter their lives by their incessant labours; they accumulate more wealth than they can use:—while they act thus for the body, they make it external to themselves[1]. Those who seek for honours carry their pursuit of them from the day into the night, full of anxiety about their methods whether they are skilful or not:—while they act thus for the body they treat it as if it were indifferent to them[2]. The birth of man is at the same time the birth of his sorrow; and if he live long he becomes more and more stupid, and the longer is his anxiety that he may not die; how great is his bitterness!—while he thus acts for his body, it is for a distant result. Meritorious officers are regarded by the world as good; but (their goodness) is not sufficient to keep their persons alive. I do not know whether the goodness ascribed to them be really good or really not good. If indeed it be considered good, it is not sufficient to preserve their persons alive; if it be deemed not good, it is sufficient to preserve other men alive. Hence it is said, 'When faithful remonstrances are not listened to, (the remonstrant) should sit still, let (his ruler) take his course, and not strive with him.' Therefore when 3ze-hsü[3] strove with (his ruler), he brought on him-

[1] If they did not do so, they would be content when they had enough.

[2] Wishing to attach it more closely to them.

[3] Wû 3ze-hsü, the scourge of *Kh*û; and who perished miserably at last, when the king of Wû would no longer listen to his remonstrances;—in about B.C. 475.

self the mutilation of his body. If he had not so striven, he would not have acquired his fame:—was such (goodness) really good or was it not?

As to what the common people now do, and what they find their enjoyment in, I do not know whether the enjoyment be really enjoyment or really not. I see them in their pursuit of it following after all their aims as if with the determination of death, and as if they could not stop in their course; but what they call enjoyment would not be so to me, while yet I do not say that there is no enjoyment in it. Is there indeed such enjoyment, or is there not? I consider doing nothing (to obtain it) to be the great enjoyment[1], while ordinarily people consider it to be a great evil. Hence it is said, 'Perfect enjoyment is to be without enjoyment; the highest praise is to be without praise[2].' The right and the wrong (on this point of enjoyment) cannot indeed be determined according to (the view of) the world; nevertheless, this doing nothing (to obtain it) may determine the right and the wrong. Since perfect enjoyment is (held to be) the keeping the body alive, it is only by this doing nothing that that end is likely to be secured. Allow me to try and explain this (more fully):—Heaven does nothing, and thence comes its serenity; Earth does nothing, and thence comes its rest. By the union of these two inactivities, all things are produced. How vast and imperceptible is the process!—they seem to come from

[1] This is the secret of the Tâo.

[2] The last member of this sentence is the reading adopted by Wû *Kh*ăng towards the conclusion of the thirty-ninth chapter of the Tâo Teh *K*ing, instead of the common 致數車無車.

nowhere! How imperceptible and vast!—there is no visible image of it! All things in all their variety grow from this Inaction. Hence it is said, 'Heaven and Earth do nothing, and yet there is nothing that they do not do[1].' But what man is there that can attain to this inaction?

2. When *K*wang-ȝze's wife died, Hui-ȝze went to condole with him, and, finding him squatted on the ground, drumming on the basin[2], and singing, said to him, 'When a wife has lived with her husband, and brought up children, and then dies in her old age, not to wail for her is enough. When you go on to drum on this basin and sing, is it not an excessive (and strange) demonstration?' *K*wang-ȝze replied, 'It is not so. When she first died, was it possible for me to be singular and not affected by the event? But I reflected on the commencement of her being[3]. She had not yet been born to life; not only had she no life, but she had no bodily form; not only had she no bodily form, but she had no breath. During the intermingling of the waste and dark chaos[3], there ensued a change, and there was breath; another change, and there was the bodily form; another change, and there came birth

[1] Compare similar statements in the Tâo Teh *K*ing, ch. 48, et al.

[2] The basin or tub, not 'a basin.' The reference is, no doubt, to the basin of ice put down near or under the couch on which the body was laid. I suppose that *K*wang-ȝze was squatting so as to have this between his legs.

[3] Is the writer referring to the primal creation as we may call it, or development of things out of the chaos, or to some analogous process at the birth of his wife? However that be, birth and death appear to him to be merely changes of the same kind in the perpetual process of evolution.

莊子

and life. There is now a change again, and she is dead. The relation between these things is like the procession of the four seasons from spring to autumn, from winter to summer. There now she lies with her face up, sleeping in the Great Chamber[1]; and if I were to fall sobbing and going on to wail for her, I should think that I did not understand what was appointed (for all). I therefore restrained myself[2]!'

3. Mr. Deformed[3] and Mr. One-foot[3] were looking at the mound-graves of the departed in the wild of Khwăn-lun, where Hwang-Tî had entered into his rest. Suddenly a tumour began to grow on their left wrists, which made them look distressed as if they disliked it. The former said to the other, 'Do

[1] Between heaven and earth.

[2] Was it necessary he should fall singing to his drumming on the basin? But I subjoin a note here, suggested by the paragraph, which might have found, perhaps, a more appropriate place in the notice of this Book in vol. xxxix, pp. 149, 150.

In Sir John F. Davis' 'Description of the Empire of China and its Inhabitants (edition of 1857),' vol. ii, pp. 74–90, we have the amusing story of 'The Philosopher and his Wife.' The philosopher is *K*wang-ȝze, who plays the part of a magician; and of his wife it might be said, 'Frailty! thy name is woman!' Sir John Davis says, 'The story was translated into French by Père d'Entrecolles, and supplied the materials of Voltaire's Zadig.' I have not met in Chinese with Father d'Entrecolles' original. All of Zadig which can be supposed to have been borrowed from his translator is only a few sentences. The whole story is inconsistent with the account in paragraph 2 of the death of *K*wang-ȝze's wife, and with all which we learn from his writings of his character.

[3] We know nothing of these parties but what we are told here. They are called Shû, meaning 'uncle,' often equivalent in China to our 'Mr.' The lesson taught by them is that of submission to pain and death as merely phenomena in the sphere of change. For the phraseology of their names, see Bk. III, par. 3, and Bk. IV, par. 8.

you dread it?' 'No,' replied he, 'why should I dread it? Life is a borrowed thing. The living frame thus borrowed is but so much dust. Life and death are like day and night. And you and I were looking at (the graves of) those who have undergone their change. If my change is coming to me, why should I dislike it?'

4. When *K*wang-ȝze went to *Kh*û, he saw an empty skull, bleached indeed, but still retaining its shape. Tapping it with his horse-switch, he asked it, saying, 'Did you, Sir, in your greed of life, fail in the lessons of reason, and come to this? Or did you do so, in the service of a perishing state, by the punishment of the axe? Or was it through your evil conduct, reflecting disgrace on your parents and on your wife and children? Or was it through your hard endurances of cold and hunger? Or was it that you had completed your term of life?'

Having given expression to these questions, he took up the skull, and made a pillow of it when he went to sleep. At midnight the skull appeared to him in a dream, and said, 'What you said to me was after the fashion of an orator. All your words were about the entanglements of men in their lifetime. There are none of those things after death. Would you like to hear me, Sir, tell you about death?' 'I should,' said *K*wang-ȝze, and the skull resumed: 'In death there are not (the distinctions of) ruler above and minister below. There are none of the phenomena of the four seasons. Tranquil and at ease, our years are those of heaven and earth. No king in his court has greater enjoyment than we have.' *K*wang-ȝze did not believe it, and said, 'If I

莊子

could get the Ruler of our Destiny[1] to restore your body to life with its bones and flesh and skin, and to give you back your father and mother, your wife and children, and all your village acquaintances, would you wish me to do so?' The skull stared fixedly at him, knitted its brows, and said, 'How should I cast away the enjoyment of my royal court, and undertake again the toils of life among mankind?'

5. When Yen Yüan went eastwards to *Kh*î, Confucius wore a look of sorrow[2]. Ȝze-kung left his mat, and asked him, saying, 'Your humble disciple ventures to ask how it is that the going eastwards of Hui to *Kh*î has given you such a look of sadness.' Confucius said, 'Your question is good. Formerly Kwan-ȝze[3] used words of which I very much approve. He said, "A small bag cannot be made to contain what is large; a short rope cannot be used to draw water from a deep well[3]." So it is, and man's appointed lot is definitely determined, and his body is adapted for definite ends, so that neither the one nor the other can be augmented or diminished. I am afraid that Hui will talk with the marquis of *Kh*î about the ways of Hwang-Tî, Yâo, and Shun, and go on to relate the words of Sui-zăn and Shăn Năng. The marquis will seek (for the correspondence of what he is told) in himself; and, not finding

---

[1] I suppose the Tâo; but none of the commentators, so far as I have seen, say anything about the expression.

[2] Compare the long discourse of Confucius with Yen Hui, on the latter's proposing to go to Wei, in Bk. IV.

[3] Kwan Î-wû or Kwan *K*ung, the chief minister of duke Hwan of *Kh*î, whom he is supposed to have in view in his 'small bag and short rope.'

it there, will suspect the speaker; and that speaker, being suspected, will be put to death. And have you not heard this ?—Formerly a sea-bird alighted in the suburban country of Lû[1]. The marquis went out to meet it, (brought it) to the ancestral temple, and prepared to banquet it there. The *K*iû-shâo[2] was performed to afford it music; an ox, a sheep, and a pig were killed to supply the food. The bird, however, looked at everything with dim eyes, and was very sad. It did not venture to eat a single bit of flesh, nor to drink a single cupful; and in three days it died.

'The marquis was trying to nourish the bird with what he used for himself, and not with the nourishment proper for a bird. They who would nourish birds as they ought to be nourished should let them perch in the deep forests, or roam over sandy plains; float on the rivers and lakes; feed on the eels and small fish; wing their flight in regular order and then stop; and be free and at ease in their resting-places. It was a distress to that bird to hear men speak; what did it care for all the noise and hubbub made about it? If the music of the *K*iû-shâo[3] or the Hsien-*kh*ih[4] were performed in the wild of the Thung-thing[4] lake, birds would fly away, and beasts would run off when they heard it, and fishes would dive down to the bottom of the water; while men, when they hear it, would come all round to-

[1] Perhaps another and more ridiculous version of the story told in 'the Narratives of the States,' II, i, art. 7.

[2] The name of Shun's music;—see the Shû (in vol. iii), par. 2.

[3] Called also Tâ Shâo, in Book XXXIII, par. 2.

[4] Hwang-Tî's music;—see Bk. XIV, par. 3.—But the genuineness of the whole paragraph is called in question.

gether, and look on. Fishes live and men die in the water. They are different in constitution, and therefore differ in their likes and dislikes. Hence it was that the ancient sages did not require (from all) the same ability, nor demand the same performances. They gave names according to the reality of what was done, and gave their approbation where it was specially suitable. This was what was called the method of universal adaptation and of sure success.'

6. Lieh-ȥze (once) upon a journey took a meal by the road-side. There he saw a skull a hundred years old, and, pulling away the bush (under which it lay), he pointed to it and said, 'It is only you and I who know that you are not dead, and that (aforetime) you were not alive. Do you indeed really find (in death) the nourishment (which you like)? Do I really find (in life my proper) enjoyment? The seeds (of things) are multitudinous and minute. On the surface of the water they form a membranous texture. When they reach to where the land and water join they become the (lichens which we call the) clothes of frogs and oysters. Coming to life on mounds and heights, they become the plantain; and, receiving manure, appear as crows' feet. The roots of the crow's foot become grubs, and its leaves, butterflies. This butterfly, known by the name of hsü, is changed into an insect, and comes to life under a furnace. Then it has the form of a moth, and is named the *kh*ü-to. The *kh*ü-to after a thousand days becomes a bird, called the *k*an-yü-kû. Its saliva becomes the sȥe-mî, and this again the shih-hsî (or pickle-eater). The î-lo is produced from the pickle-eater; the hwang-kwang from the

*k*iû-yû; the mâu-zui from the pû-khwan. The ying-hsî uniting with a bamboo, which has long ceased to put forth sprouts, produces the *kh*ing-ning; the *kh*ing-ning, the panther; the panther, the horse; and the horse, the man. Man then again enters into the great Machinery (of Evolution), from which all things come forth (at birth), and which they enter at death[1].'

[1] A much larger paragraph from which this must have been abbreviated, or which must have been enlarged from this, is found in the first Book of Lieh-ȝze's works (pp. 4, 5). In no Buddhist treatise is the transrotation of births more fully, and, I must add, absurdly stated.

莊子

BOOK XIX.

PART II. SECTION XII.

Tâ Shăng, or 'The Full Understanding of Life[1].'

1. He who understands the conditions of Life does not strive after what is of no use to life; and he who understands the conditions of Destiny does not strive after what is beyond the reach of knowledge. In nourishing the body it is necessary to have beforehand the things (appropriate to its support)[2]; but there are cases where there is a superabundance of such things, and yet the body is not nourished[2]. In order to have life it is necessary that it do not have left the body; but there are cases when the body has not been left by it, and yet the life has perished[3].

When life comes, it cannot be declined; when it goes, it cannot be detained. Alas! the men of the world think that to nourish the body is sufficient to preserve life; and when such nourishment is not sufficient to preserve the life, what can be done in the world that will be sufficient? Though (all that men can do) will be insufficient, yet there are things which they feel they ought to do, and they do not try to avoid doing them. For those who wish to

[1] See vol. xxxix, pp. 150, 151.

[2] Wealth will supply abundantly the things that are necessary and fit for the nourishment of the body, but sudden death may render them unavailing.

[3] That is, the higher life of the spirit has perished.

avoid caring for the body, their best plan is to abandon the world. Abandoning the world, they are free from its entanglements. Free from its entanglements, their (minds) are correct and their (temperament) is equable. Thus correct and equable, they succeed in securing a renewal of life, as some have done[1]. In securing a renewal of life, they are not far from the True (Secret of their being). But how is it sufficient to abandon worldly affairs? and how is it sufficient to forget the (business of) life? Through the renouncing of (worldly) affairs, the body has no more toil; through forgetting the (business of) life, the vital power suffers no diminution. When the body is completed and the vital power is restored (to its original vigour), the man is one with Heaven. Heaven and Earth are the father and mother of all things. It is by their union that the body is formed; it is by their separation that a (new) beginning is brought about. When the body and vital power suffer no diminution, we have what may be called the transference of power. From the vital force there comes another more vital, and man returns to be the assistant of Heaven.

2. My master[2] Lieh-ʒze[2] asked Yin, (the warden) of the gate[2], saying, 'The perfect man walks under

[1] I think I have caught the meaning. The phrase signifying 'the renewal of life' has been used to translate 'being born again' in John's Gospel, ch. 3.

[2] We find here Lieh-ʒze (whose name has already occurred several times) in communication with the warden Yin, who was a contemporary of Lâo-ʒze, and we must refer him therefore to the sixth century B.C. He could not therefore be contemporary with our author, and yet the three characters of the text mean 'My Master, Lieh-ʒze;' and the whole of the paragraph is found in Lieh-ʒze's second Book (4a–5a) with a good many variants in the text.

海上絲綢之路文獻集成 科技與文化編

莊子

water without encountering any obstruction, treads on fire without being burned, and walks on high above all things without any fear; let me ask how he attains to do this[1]?' The warden Yin replied, 'It is by his keeping of the pure breath (of life); it is not to be described as an achievement of his skill or daring. Sit down, and I will explain it to you. Whatever has form, semblance, sound, and colour is a thing; how can one thing come to be different from another? But it is not competent for any of these things to reach to what preceded them all;—they are but (form and) visibility. But (the perfect man) attains to be (as it were) without form, and beyond the capability of being transformed. Now when one attains to this and carries it out to the highest degree, how can other things come into his way to stop him? He will occupy the place assigned to him without going beyond it, and lie concealed in the clue which has no end. He will study with delight the process which gives their beginning and ending to all things. By gathering his nature into a unity, by nourishing his vital power, by concentrating his virtue, he will penetrate to the making of things. In this condition, with his heavenly constitution kept entire, and with no crevice in his spirit, how can things enter (and disturb his serenity)?

'Take the case of a drunken man falling from his carriage;—though he may suffer injury, he will not

The gate was at the passage leading from the Royal Domain of those days into the great feudal territory of Ȝin;—from the north-west of the present province of Ho-nan into Shen-hsî.

[1] Lieh-ȝze puts an absurd question to the warden, which is replied to at length, and unsatisfactorily. We need not discuss either the question or the answer in this place.

die. His bones and joints are the same as those of other men, but the injury which he receives is different:—his spirit is entire. He knew nothing about his getting into the carriage, and knew nothing about his falling from it. The thought of death or life, or of any alarm or affright, does not enter his breast; and therefore he encounters danger without any shrinking from it. Completely under the influence of the liquor he has drunk, it is thus with him;—how much more would it be so, if he were under the influence of his Heavenly constitution! The sagely man is kept hid in his Heavenly constitution, and therefore nothing can injure him.

'A man in the pursuit of vengeance would not break the (sword) Mo-yê or Yü-*k*iang (which had done the deed); nor would one, however easily made wrathful, wreak his resentment on the fallen brick. In this way all under heaven there would be peace, without the disorder of assaults and fighting, without the punishments of death and slaughter:—such would be the issue of the course (which I have described). If the disposition that is of human origin be not developed, but that which is the gift of Heaven, the development of the latter will produce goodness, while that of the former would produce hurt. If the latter were not wearied of, and the former not slighted, the people would be brought nearly to their True nature.'

3. When *K*ung-nî was on his way to *Kh*û, as he issued from a forest, he saw a hunchback receiving cicadas (on the point of a rod), as if he were picking them up with his hand[1]. 'You are clever!' said he

[1] This paragraph is also found with variations in Lieh-ȝze,

莊子

to the man. 'Is there any method in it?' The hunchback replied, 'There is. For five or six months, I practised with two pellets, till they never fell down, and then I only failed with a small fraction[1] of the cicadas (which I tried to catch). Having succeeded in the same way with three (pellets), I missed only one cicada in ten. Having succeeded with five, I caught the cicadas as if I were gathering them. My body is to me no more than the stump of a broken trunk, and my shoulder no more than the branch of a rotten tree. Great as heaven and earth are, and multitudinous as things are, I take no notice of them, but only of the wings of my cicadas; neither turning nor inclining to one side. I would not for them all exchange the wings of my cicadas;—how should I not succeed in taking them?' Confucius looked round, and said to his disciples, '"Where the will is not diverted from its object, the spirit is concentrated;"—this might have been spoken of this hunchback gentleman.'

4. Yen Yüan asked *K*ung-nî, saying, 'When I was crossing the gulf of *Kh*ang-shăn[2], the ferryman handled the boat like a spirit. I asked him whether such management of a boat could be learned, and he replied, "It may. Good swimmers can learn it quickly; but as for divers, without having seen a boat, they can manage it at once." He did not

Bk. II (9[a]). The dexterity of the hunchback in catching the cicadas will remind some readers of the account given by the butcher in Book III of his dexterity in cutting up his oxen.

[1] The names of two small weights, used anciently for 'a fraction,' 'a small proportion.'

[2] This is another paragraph common both to our author and Lieh-ȝze, but in neither is there any intimation of the place.

directly tell me what I asked;—I venture to ask you what he meant.' *K*ung-nî replied, 'Good swimmers acquire the ability quickly;—they forget the water (and its dangers). As to those who are able to dive, and without having seen a boat are able to manage it at once, they look on the watery gulf as if it were a hill-side, and the upsetting of a boat as the going back of a carriage. Such upsettings and goings back have occurred before them multitudes of times, and have not seriously affected their minds. Wherever they go, they feel at ease on their occurrence.

'He who is contending for a piece of earthenware puts forth all his skill[1]. If the prize be a buckle of brass, he shoots timorously; if it be for an article of gold, he shoots as if he were blind. The skill of the archer is the same in all the cases; but (in the two latter cases) he is under the influence of solicitude, and looks on the external prize as most important. All who attach importance to what is external show stupidity in themselves.'

5. Thien Khâi-*k*ih[2] was having an interview with duke Wei of *K*âu[2], who said to him, 'I have heard that (your master) *K*û Hsin[2] has studied the subject of Life. What have you, good Sir, heard from him about it in your intercourse with him?' Thien Khâi-*k*ih replied, 'In my waiting on him in the courtyard with my broom, what should I have heard from my master?' Duke Wei said, 'Do not put the question off, Mr. Thien; I wish to hear what

[1] I think this is the meaning. 注 is defined by 射而賭物, 'to compete for anything by archery.'

[2] We have no information about who these personages and the others below were, and I have missed the story, if it be in Lieh-ȝze. The duke, it will be seen, had the appanage of *K*âu.

you have to say.' Khâi-*k*ih then replied, 'I have heard my master say that they who skilfully nourish their life are like shepherds, who whip up the sheep that they see lagging behind[1].' 'What did he mean?' asked the duke. The reply was, 'In Lû there was a Shan Pâo, who lived among the rocks, and drank only water. He would not share with the people in their toils and the benefits springing from them; and though he was now in his seventieth year, he had still the complexion of a child. Unfortunately he encountered a hungry tiger, which killed and ate him. There was also a *K*ang Î, who hung up a screen at his lofty door, and to whom all the people hurried (to pay their respects)[2]. In his fortieth year, he fell ill of a fever and died. (Of these two men), Pâo nourished his inner man, and a tiger ate his outer; while Î nourished his outer man, and disease attacked his inner. Both of them neglected whipping up their lagging sheep.'

*K*ung-nî said, 'A man should not retire and hide himself; he should not push forward and display himself; he should be like the decayed tree which stands in the centre of the ground. Where these three conditions are fulfilled, the name will reach its greatest height. When people fear the dangers of a path, if one man in ten be killed, then fathers and sons, elder brothers and younger, warn one another that they must not go out on a journey without a large number of retainers;—and is it not a mark of wisdom to do so? But there are dangers which

[1] Pay more attention to any part of their culture which they are neglecting.

[2] It served its purpose there, but had not been put in its place with any special object.

men incur on the mats of their beds, and in eating and drinking; and when no warning is given against them;—is it not a mark of error[1]?'

6. The officer of Prayer[2] in his dark and square-cut robes goes to the pig-pen, and thus counsels the pigs, 'Why should you shrink from dying? I will for three months feed you on grain. Then for ten days I will fast, and keep vigil for three days, after which I will put down the mats of white grass, and lay your shoulders and rumps on the carved stand;—will not this suit you?' If he had spoken from the standpoint of the pigs, he would have said, 'The better plan will be to feed us with our bran and chaff, and leave us in our pen.' When consulting for himself, he preferred to enjoy, while he lived, his carriage and cap of office, and after death to be borne to the grave on the ornamented carriage, with the canopy over his coffin. Consulting for the pigs, he did not think of these things, but for himself he would have chosen them. Why did he think so differently (for himself and) for the pigs[3]?

7. (Once), when duke Hwan[4] was hunting by a marsh, with Kwan *K*ung[5] driving the carriage, he saw a ghost. Laying his hand on that of Kwan

---

[1] This may seem to nourish the body, but in reality injures the life.

[2] Who had the charge also of the sacrifices.

[3] Lin Hsî-*k*ung says that the story shows the many troubles that arise from not renouncing the world. Ensnared by the world, men sacrifice for it their higher life, and are not so wise as pigs are for their life. The short paragraph bristles with difficulties.

[4] The first of the leading chieftains among the princes; B.C. 683–642.

[5] His chief minister.

莊子

*K*ung, he said to him, 'Do you see anything, Father *K*ung?' 'Your servant sees nothing,' was the reply. The duke then returned, talking incoherently and becoming ill, so that for several days he did not go out. Among the officers of *Kh*î there was a Hwang-ȝze Kâo-âo[1], who said to the duke, 'Your Grace is injuring yourself; how could a ghost injure you? When a paroxysm of irritation is dispersed, and the breath does not return (to the body), what remains in the body is not sufficient for its wants. When it ascends and does not descend, the patient becomes accessible to gusts of anger. When it descends and does not ascend, he loses his memory of things. When it neither ascends nor descends, but remains about the heart in the centre of the body, it makes him ill.' The duke said, 'Yes, but are there ghostly sprites[2]?' The officer replied, 'There are. About mountain tarns there is the Lî; about furnaces, the *Kh*ieh; about the dust-heaps inside the door, the Lei-thing. In low-lying places in the north-east, the Pei-a and Wa-lung leap about, and in similar places in the north-west there dwells the Yî-yang. About rivers there is the Wang-hsiang; about mounds, the Hsin; about hills, the Khwei; about wilds, the Fang-hwang; about marshes, the Wei-tho.' 'Let me ask what is the Wei-tho like?' asked the duke. Hwang-ȝze said, 'It is the size of the

[1] An officer introduced here for the occasion, by surname Hwang, and designation Kâo-âo. The Ȝze simply = Mr.

[2] The commentators have a deal to say about the folklore of the various sprites mentioned. 'The whole shows that ghostly sprites are the fruit of a disordered mind.' It is a touch of nature that the prince recovers as soon as he knows that the ghost he had seen was of good presage.

C 2

nave of a chariot wheel, and the length of the shaft. It wears a purple robe and a red cap. It dislikes the rumbling noise of chariot wheels, and, when it hears it, it puts both its hands to its head and stands up. He who sees it is likely to become the leader of all the other princes.' Duke Hwan burst out laughing and said, 'This was what I saw.' On this he put his robes and cap to rights, and made Hwang-ȝze sit with him. Before the day was done, his illness was quite gone, he knew not how.

8. *K*î Hsing-ȝze was rearing a fighting-cock for the king[1]. Being asked after ten days if the bird were ready, he said, 'Not yet; he is still vain and quarrelsome, and relies on his own vigour.' Being asked the same after other ten days, he said, 'Not yet; he still responds to the crow and the appearance of another bird.' After ten days more, he replied, 'Not yet. He still looks angrily, and is full of spirit.' When a fourth ten days had passed, he replied to the question, 'Nearly so. Though another cock crows, it makes no change in him. To look at him, you would say he was a cock of wood. His quality is complete. No other cock will dare to meet him, but will run from him.'

9. Confucius was looking at the cataract near the gorge of Lü[2], which fell a height of 240 cubits, and

[1] According to the Lieh-ȝze version of this story (Bk. II, 17^{b}), the king was king Hsüan, B.C. 827–782. The trainer's rule seems to have been that his bird should meet its antagonist, with all its vigour complete and undisturbed, and not wishing to fight.

[2] I think that there are two versions of this story in Lieh-ȝze. In Bk. VIII (4^{b}, 5^{a}), it appears that Confucius was on his way from Wei to Lû, when he stopped his carriage or cart at this spot to view the cataract, and the incident occurred, and he took the opportunity to give the lesson to his disciples.

the spray of which floated a distance of forty lî, (producing a turbulence) in which no tortoise, gavial, fish, or turtle could play. He saw, however, an old man swimming about in it, as if he had sustained some great calamity, and wished to end his life. Confucius made his disciples hasten along the stream to rescue the man; and by the time they had gone several hundred paces, he was walking along singing, with his hair dishevelled, and enjoying himself at the foot of the embankment. Confucius followed and asked him, saying, 'I thought you were a sprite; but, when I look closely at you, I see that you are a man. Let me ask if you have any particular way of treading the water.' The man said, 'No, I have no particular way. I began (to learn the art) at the very earliest time; as I grew up, it became my nature to practise it; and my success in it is now as sure as fate. I enter and go down with the water in the very centre of its whirl, and come up again with it when it whirls the other way. I follow the way of the water, and do nothing contrary to it of myself;—this is how I tread it.' Confucius said, 'What do you mean by saying that you began to learn the art at the very earliest time; that as you grew up, it became your nature to practise it, and that your success in it now is as sure as fate?' The man replied, 'I was born among these hills and lived contented among them;—that was why I say that I have trod this water from my earliest time. I grew up by it, and have been happy treading it;—that is why I said that to tread it had become natural to me. I know not how I do it, and yet I do it;—that is why I say that my success is as sure as fate.'

10. *Kh*ing, the Worker in Rottlera[1] wood, carved a bell-stand[2], and when it was completed, all who saw it were astonished as if it were the work of spirits. The marquis of Lû went to see it, and asked by what art he had succeeded in producing it. 'Your subject is but a mechanic,' was the reply; 'what art should I be possessed of? Nevertheless, there is one thing (which I will mention). When your servant had undertaken to make the bell-stand, I did not venture to waste any of my power, and felt it necessary to fast in order to compose my mind. After fasting for three days, I did not presume to think of any congratulation, reward, rank, or emolument (which I might obtain by the execution of my task); after fasting five days, I did not presume to think of the condemnation or commendation (which it would produce), or of the skill or want of skill (which it might display). At the end of the seven days, I had forgotten all about myself;—my four limbs and my whole person. By this time the thought of your Grace's court (for which I was to make the thing) had passed away; everything that could divert my mind from exclusive devotion to the exercise of my skill had disappeared. Then I went into the forest, and looked at the natural forms of the trees. When I saw one of a perfect form, then the figure of the bell-stand rose up to my view, and I applied my hand to the work. Had

[1] The 3ze or rottlera was and is a very famous tree, called 'the king of trees,' from its stately appearance and the excellence of its timber.

[2] The 'bell-stand' is celebrated in the Shih King, III, i, Ode 8. A complete peal consisted of twelve bells, suspended in two tiers one above the other.

莊子

I not met with such a tree, I must have abandoned the object; but my Heaven-given faculty and the Heaven-given qualities of the wood were concentrated on it. So it was that my spirit was thus engaged in the production of the bell-stand.'

11. Tung-yê *K*î[1] was introduced to duke *K*wang[2] to exhibit his driving. His horses went forwards and backwards with the straightness of a line, and wheeled to the right and the left with the exactness of a circle. The duke thought that the lines and circles could not be surpassed if they were woven with silken strings, and told him to make a hundred circuits on the same lines. On the road Yen Ho[3] met the equipage, and on entering (the palace), and seeing the duke, he said, '*K*î's horses will break down,' but the duke was silent, and gave him no reply. After a little the horses did come back, having broken down; and the duke then said, 'How did you know that it would be so?' Yen Ho said, 'The horses were exhausted, and he was still urging them on. It was this which made me say that they would break down.'

12. The artisan Shui[4] made things round (and square) more exactly than if he had used the circle

[1] *K*î would be the name of the charioteer, a gentleman of Lû, called Tung-yê, 'eastern country,' I suppose from the situation of his estate.

[2] Duke *K*wang would be the marquis Thung of Lû, B.C. 693–662.

[3] Yen Ho was probably the chief of the Yen family at the time. A scion of it, Yen Hui, afterwards became the favourite disciple of Confucius. He could hardly be the same Yen Ho who is mentioned in Bk. IV, par. 5. *K*î has had, and still has, his representatives in every country.

[4] Shui is mentioned in the Shû King, V, xxii, 19, as a famous maker of arrows. Some carry him back to the time of Shun.

and square. The operation of his fingers on (the forms of) things was like the transformations of them (in nature), and required no application of his mind; and so his Intelligence[1] was entire and encountered no resistance.

13. To be unthought of by the foot that wears it is the fitness of a shoe; to be unthought of by the waist is the fitness of a girdle. When one's wisdom does not think of the right or the wrong (of a question under discussion), that shows the suitability of the mind (for the question); when one is conscious of no inward change, or outward attraction, that shows the mastery of affairs. He who perceives at once the fitness, and never loses the sense of it, has the fitness that forgets all about what is fitting.

14. There was a Sun Hsiû[2] who went to the door of 3ze-pien *Kh*ing-ȝze, and said to him in a strange perturbed way, 'When I lived in my village, no one took notice of me, but all said that I did not cultivate (my fields); in a time of trouble and attack, no one took notice of me, but all said that I had no courage. But that I did not cultivate my fields, was really because I never met with a good year; and that I did not do service for our ruler, was because I did not meet with the suitable opportunity to do so. I have been sent about my business by the villagers, and am driven away by the registrars of the district;—what is my crime? O Heaven! how is it that I have met with such a fate?'

[1] Literally, 'Tower of Intelligence,'—a Tâoistic name for the mind.

[2] A weakling, of whom we know only what we read here.

莊子

Pien-ȝze[1] said to him, 'Have you not heard how the perfect man deals with himself? He forgets that he has a liver and gall. He takes no thought of his ears and eyes. He seems lost and aimless beyond the dust and dirt of the world, and enjoys himself at ease in occupations untroubled by the affairs of business. He may be described as acting and yet not relying on what he does, as being superior and yet not using his superiority to exercise any control. But now you would make a display of your wisdom to astonish the ignorant; you would cultivate your person to make the inferiority of others more apparent; you seek to shine as if you were carrying the sun and moon in your hands. That you are complete in your bodily frame, and possess all its nine openings; that you have not met with any calamity in the middle of your course, such as deafness, blindness, or lameness, and can still take your place as a man among other men;—in all this you are fortunate. What leisure have you to murmur against Heaven? Go away, Sir.'

Sun-ȝze on this went out, and Pien-ȝze went inside. Having sitten down, after a little time he looked up to heaven, and sighed. His disciples asked him why he sighed, and he said to them, 'Hsiû came to me a little while ago, and I told him the characteristics of the perfect man. I am afraid he will be frightened, and get into a state of perplexity.' His disciples said, 'Not so. If what he said was right, and what you

[1] This must have been a man of more note. We find him here with a school of disciples in his house, and sought out for counsel by men like Sun Hsiû.

said was wrong, the wrong will certainly not be able to perplex the right. If what he said was wrong, and what you said was right, it was just because he was perplexed that he came to you. What was your fault in dealing with him as you did?' Pien-ȝze said, 'Not so. Formerly a bird came, and took up its seat in the suburbs of Lû[1]. The ruler of Lû was pleased with it, and provided an ox, a sheep, and a pig to feast it, causing also the *K*iû-shâo to be performed to delight it. But the bird began to be sad, looked dazed, and did not venture to eat or drink. This was what is called "Nourishing a bird, as you would nourish yourself." He who would nourish a bird as a bird should be nourished should let it perch in a deep forest, or let it float on a river or lake, or let it find its food naturally and undisturbed on the level dry ground. Now Hsiû (came to me), a man of slender intelligence, and slight information, and I told him of the characteristics of the perfect man, it was like using a carriage and horses to convey a mouse, or trying to delight a quail with the music of bells and drums;—could the creatures help being frightened?'

[1] Compare par. 5, Bk. XVIII.

莊子

BOOK XX.

Part II. Section XIII.

Shan Mû, or 'The Tree on the Mountain[1].'

1. *K*wang-ȝze was walking on a mountain, when he saw a great tree[2] with huge branches and luxuriant foliage. A wood-cutter was resting by its side, but he would not touch it, and, when asked the reason, said, that it was of no use for anything. *K*wang-ȝze then said to his disciples, 'This tree, because its wood is good for nothing, will succeed in living out its natural term of years.' Having left the mountain, the Master lodged in the house of an old friend, who was glad to see him, and ordered his waiting-lad to kill a goose and boil it. The lad said, 'One of our geese can cackle, and the other cannot;—which of them shall I kill?' The host said, 'Kill the one that cannot cackle.'

Next day, his disciples asked *K*wang-ȝze, saying, 'Yesterday the tree on the mountain (you said) would live out its years because of the uselessness of its wood, and now our host's goose has died because of its want of power (to cackle);—which of these conditions, Master, would you prefer to be in?' *K*wang-ȝze laughed and said, '(If I said that) I would prefer to be in a position between being fit to be useful and wanting that fitness, that would

[1] See vol. xxxix, p. 151.

[2] Compare the accounts of great trees in I, par. 6; IV, par. 1; et al.

seem to be the right position, but it would not be so, for it would not put me beyond being involved in trouble; whereas one who takes his seat on the Tâo and its Attributes, and there finds his ease and enjoyment, is not exposed to such a contingency. He is above the reach both of praise and of detraction; now he (mounts aloft) like a dragon, now he (keeps beneath) like a snake; he is transformed with the (changing) character of the time, and is not willing to addict himself to any one thing; now in a high position and now in a low, he is in harmony with all his surroundings; he enjoys himself at ease with the Author of all things [1]; he treats things as things, and is not a thing to them:—where is his liability to be involved in trouble? This was the method of Shăn Năng and Hwang-Tî. As to those who occupy themselves with the qualities of things, and with the teaching and practice of the human relations, it is not so with them. Union brings on separation; success, overthrow; sharp corners, the use of the file; honour, critical remarks; active exertion, failure; wisdom, scheming; inferiority, being despised:—where is the possibility of unchangeableness in any of these conditions? Remember this, my disciples. Let your abode be here,—in the Tâo and its Attributes [2].'

2. Î-liâo [3], an officer of Shih-nan [3], having an in-

[1] The Tâo; called 衆父父, in Bk. XII, par. 5.

[2] But after all it comes to be the same thing in point of fact with those who ground themselves in the Tâo, and with others.

[3] The Î-liâo here was a scion of the ruling House of *Kh*û, and is mentioned fortunately in the Supplement to the Ȝo-*kh*wan, under the very year in which Confucius died (B.C. 479). His residence was in the south of the 'Market Place' of the city where he lived,

terview with the marquis of Lû[1], found him looking sad, and asked him why he was so. The marquis said, 'I have studied the ways of the former kings, and cultivated the inheritance left me by my predecessors. I reverence the spirits of the departed and honour the men of worth, doing this with personal devotion, and without the slightest intermission. Notwithstanding, I do not avoid meeting with calamity, and this it is which makes me sad.' The officer said, 'The arts by which you try to remove calamity are shallow. Think of the close-furred fox and of the elegantly-spotted leopard. They lodge in the forests on the hills, and lurk in their holes among the rocks;—keeping still. At night they go about, and during day remain in their lairs;—so cautious are they. Even if they are suffering from hunger, thirst, and other distresses, they still keep aloof from men, seeking their food about the *K*iang and the Ho;—so resolute are they. Still they are not able to escape the danger of the net or the trap; and what fault is it of theirs? It is their skins which occasion them the calamity.

'And is not the state of Lû your lordship's skin? I wish your lordship to rip your skin from your body, to cleanse your heart, to put away your desires, and to enjoy yourself where you will be

which is the meaning of the Shih-nan in the text. The description of his character is that no offer of gain could win him, and no threatening terrify him. We find him here at the court of Lû in friendly conference with the marquis, and trying to persuade him to adopt the ways of Tâoism, which he presents to him under the figure of an allegory, an utopia called 'the State of Established Virtue,' in the south of Yüeh.

[1] Probably known to us as 'duke Âi.'

without the presence of any one. In the southern state of Yüeh, there is a district called "the State of Established Virtue." The people are ignorant and simple; their object is to minimise the thought of self and make their desires few; they labour but do not lay up their gains; they give but do not seek for any return; they do not know what righteousness is required of them in any particular case, nor by what ceremonies their performances should be signalised; acting in a wild and eccentric way as if they were mad, they yet keep to the grand rules of conduct. Their birth is an occasion for joy; their death is followed by the rites of burial. I should wish your lordship to leave your state; to give up your ordinary ways, and to proceed to that country by the directest course.'

The ruler said, 'The way to it is distant and difficult; there are rivers and hills; and as I have neither boat nor carriage, how am I to go?' The officer from Shih-nan rejoined, 'If your lordship abjure your personal state, and give up your wish to remain here, that will serve you for a carriage.' The ruler rejoined, 'The way to it is solitary and distant, and there are no people on it;—whom shall I have as my companions? I have no provisions prepared, and how shall I get food?—how shall I be able to get (to the country)?' The officer said, 'Minimise your lordship's expenditure, and make your wants few, and though you have no provisions prepared, you will find you have enough. Wade through the rivers and float along on the sea, where however you look, you see not the shore, and, the farther you go, you do not see where your journey is to end;—those who escorted you to the shore will return, and after that you will feel yourself far away. Thus it is that he who owns men (as their ruler) is involved in troubles, and he who is owned by men (as their ruler) suffers from sadness; and hence Yâo would neither own men, nor be owned by them. I wish to remove your trouble, and take away your sadness, and it is only (to be done by inducing you) to enjoy yourself with the Tâo in the land of Great Vacuity.

'If a man is crossing a river in a boat, and another empty vessel comes into collision with it, even though he be a man of a choleric temper, he will not be angry with it. If there be a person, however, in that boat, he will bawl out to him to haul out of the way. If his shout be not heard, he will repeat it; and if the other do not then hear, he will call out a third time, following up the shout with abusive terms. Formerly he was not angry, but now he is; formerly (he thought) the boat was empty, but now there is a person in it. If a man can empty himself of himself, during his time in the world, who can harm him?'

3. Pei-kung Shê[1] was collecting taxes for duke Ling of Wei, to be employed in making (a peal of) bells. (In connexion with the work) he built an altar outside the gate of the suburban wall; and in three months the bells were completed, even to the suspending of the upper and lower (tiers). The king's son *Kh*ing-*k*î[2] saw them, and asked what

[1] Pei-kung, 'Northern Palace,' must have been the name of Shê's residence, and appears here as if it were his surname.

[2] A son, probably of king *K*ing of *K*âu (B.C. 544–529).—On the whole paragraph, see par. 10 of the preceding Book.

arts he had employed in the making of them. Shê replied, 'Besides my undivided attention to them, I did not venture to use any arts. I have heard the saying, "After all the carving and the chiselling, let the object be to return to simplicity." I was as a child who has no knowledge; I was extraordinarily slow and hesitating; they grew like the springing plants of themselves. In escorting those who went and meeting those who came, my object was neither to hinder the comers nor detain the goers. I suffered those who strongly opposed to take their way, and accepted those who did their best to come to terms. I allowed them all to do the utmost they could, and in this way morning and evening I collected the taxes. I did not have the slightest trouble, and how much more will this be the case with those who pursue the Great Way (on a grand scale)!'

4. Confucius was kept (by his enemies) in a state of siege between *Kh*ăn and 3hâi [1], and for seven days had no food cooked with fire to eat. The Thâi-kung *Z*ân [2] went to condole with him, and said, 'You had nearly met with your death.' 'Yes,' was the reply. 'Do you dislike death?' 'I do.' Then *Z*ăn continued, 'Let me try and describe a way by which (such a) death may be avoided.—In the eastern sea there are birds which go by the name of Î-îs [3]; they fly low and slowly as if they were deficient in power. They fly as if they were

[1] Compare Analects XI, ii.

[2] We might translate Thâi-kung by 'the grand-duke.' We know nothing about him. He tries to convert Confucius to Tâoism just as Î-liâo does the marquis of Lû in par. 2; and for a time at least, as *K*wang-ȝze makes it appear, with more success.

[3] Were these Î-îs swallows? So some of the critics say.

莊子

leading and assisting one another, and they press on one another when they roost. No one ventures to take the lead in going forward, or to be the last in going backwards. In eating no one ventures to take the first mouthful, but prefers the fragments left by others. In this way (the breaks in) their line are not many[1], and men outside them cannot harm them, so that they escape injury.

'The straight tree is the first to be cut down; the well of sweet water is the first to be exhausted. Your aim is to embellish your wisdom so as to startle the ignorant, and to cultivate your person to show the unsightliness of others. A light shines around you as if you were carrying with you the sun and moon, and thus it is that you do not escape such calamity. Formerly I heard a highly accomplished man say, "Those who boast have no merit. The merit which is deemed complete will begin to decay. The fame which is deemed complete will begin to wane." Who can rid himself of (the ideas of) merit and fame, and return and put himself on the level of the masses of men? The practice of the Tâo flows abroad, but its master does not care to dwell where it can be seen; his attainments in it hold their course, but he does not wish to appear in its display. Always simple and commonplace, he may seem to be bereft of reason. He obliterates the traces of his action, gives up position and power, and aims not at merit and fame. Therefore he does not censure men, and men do not censure him. The perfect man does not seek to be heard of; how is it that you delight in doing so?'

[1] A clause of uncertain meaning.

Confucius said, 'Excellent;' and thereupon he took leave of his associates, forsook his disciples, retired to the neighbourhood of a great marsh, wore skins and hair cloth, and ate acorns and chestnuts. He went among animals without causing any confusion among their herds, and among birds without troubling their movements. Birds and beasts did not dislike him; how much less would men do so!

5. Confucius asked 3ze-sang Hû[1], saying, 'I was twice driven from Lû; the tree was felled over me in Sung; I was obliged to disappear from Wei; I was reduced to extreme distress in Shang and *K*âu[2]; and I was kept in a state of siege between *Kh*ăn and 3hâi. I have encountered these various calamities; my intimate associates are removed from me more and more; my followers and friends are more and more dispersed;—why have all these things befallen me?' 3ze-sang Hû replied, 'Have you not heard of the flight of Lin Hui of *K*iâ[3];—how he abandoned his round jade symbol of rank, worth a thousand pieces of silver, and hurried away with his infant son on his back? If it be asked, "Was it because of the market value of the child?" But that value was small (compared with the value of the jade token). If it be asked again, "Was it because of the troubles

[1] Supposed to have been a recluse.

[2] I do not know the particulars of this distress in Shang and *K*âu, or have forgotten them. A still more full recital of the sage's misfortunes occurs in Lieh-ʒze, VII, 8[a].

[3] The text here appears to be somewhat confused. Lin Hui is said to have been a man of the Yin dynasty, and of a state which was called *K*iâ, and for the verification of such a state I have searched in vain. The explanation of his conduct put here into his mouth is very good.

莊子

(of his office)?" But the child would occasion him much more trouble. Why was it then that, abandoning the jade token, worth a thousand pieces of silver, he hurried away with the child on his back? Lin Hui (himself) said, "The union between me and the token rested on the ground of gain; that between me and the child was of Heaven's appointment." Where the bond of union is its profitableness, when the pressure of poverty, calamity, distress, and injury come, the parties abandon one another; when it is of Heaven's appointment, they hold in the same circumstances to one another. Now between abandoning one another, and holding to one another, the difference is great. Moreover, the intercourse of superior men is tasteless as water, while that of mean men is sweet as new wine. But the tastelessness of the superior men leads on to affection, and the sweetness of the mean men to aversion. The union which originates without any cause will end in separation without any cause.'

Confucius said, 'I have reverently received your instructions.' And hereupon, with a slow step and an assumed air of ease, he returned to his own house. There he made an end of studying and put away his books. His disciples came no more to make their bow to him (and be taught), but their affection for him increased the more.

Another day Sang Hû said further to him, 'When Shun was about to die, he charged[1] Yü, saying, 'Be

[1] The 眞冷 of the text here are allowed on all hands to be spurious, and 其命 have been substituted for them. What follows, however, from Shun to Yü, is far from being clear, in itself, or in its connexion.

upon your guard. (The attraction of) the person is not like that of sympathy; the (power of) affection is not like the leading (of example). Where there is sympathy, there will not be separation; where there is (the leading of) example, there will be no toil. Where there is neither separation nor toil, you will not have to seek the decoration of forms to make the person attractive, and where there is no such need of those forms, there will certainly be none for external things.'

6. *K*wang-ȝze in a patched dress of coarse cloth, and having his shoes tied together with strings, was passing by the king of Wei, who said to him, 'How great, Master, is your distress?' *K*wang-ȝze replied, 'It is poverty, not distress! While a scholar possesses the Tâo and its Attributes, he cannot be going about in distress. Tattered clothes and shoes tied on the feet are the sign of poverty, and not of distress. This is what we call not meeting with the right time. Has your majesty not seen the climbing monkey? When he is among the plane trees, rottleras, oaks, and camphor trees, he grasps and twists their branches (into a screen), where he reigns quite at his ease, so that not even Î[1] or Phăng Măng[1] could spy him out. When, however, he finds himself among the prickly mulberry and date trees, and other thorns, he goes cautiously, casts sidelong glances, and takes every trembling movement with apprehension;—it is not that his sinews and bones

---

[1] Î;—see Book V, par. 2. Phăng Măng was a contemporary of Î, learned archery from him, and then slew him, that he might himself be the foremost archer in the kingdom;—see Mencius IV, ii, 24.

莊子

are straitened, and have lost their suppleness, but the situation is unsuitable for him, and he cannot display his agility. And now when I dwell under a benighted ruler, and seditious ministers, how is it possible for me not to be in distress? My case might afford an illustration of the cutting out the heart of Pî-kan[1]!'

7. When Confucius was reduced to great distress between *Kh*ăn and *Kh*âi, and for seven days he had no cooked food to eat, he laid hold of a decayed tree with his left hand, and with his right hand tapped it with a decayed branch, singing all the while the ode of Piâo-shih[2]. He had his instrument, but the notes were not marked on it. There was a noise, but no blended melody. The sound of the wood and the voice of the man came together like the noise of the plough through the ground, yet suitably to the feelings of the disciples around. Yen Hui, who was standing upright, with his hands crossed on his breast, rolled his eyes round to observe him. *K*ung-nî, fearing that Hui would go to excess in manifesting how he honoured himself, or be plunged in sorrow through his love for him, said to him, 'Hui, not to receive (as evils) the inflictions of Heaven is easy; not to receive (as benefits) the favours of men is difficult. There is no beginning which was not an end. The Human and the Heavenly may be one

[1] 'A spurious paragraph, no doubt.' Lin Hsî-*k*ung thus concludes what he has to say on this paragraph; but it is not without its interest and lessons.

[2] I do not know who this was, nor what his ode or air was. Lû Teh-ming read the character 焱, and says that Piâo-shih was one of the old royal Tîs who did nothing. In all my texts it is wrongly printed with three 火.

and the same. Who, for instance, is it that is now singing[1]?' Hui said, 'I venture to ask how not to receive (as evils) the inflictions of Heaven is easy.' *K*ung-nî said, 'Hunger, thirst, cold, and heat, and having one's progress entirely blocked up;—these are the doings of Heaven and Earth, necessary incidents in the revolutions of things. They are occurrences of which we say that we will pass on (composedly) along with them. The minister of another does not dare to refuse his commands; and if he who is discharging the duty of a minister feels it necessary to act thus, how much more should we wait with ease on the commands of Heaven[2]!' 'What do you mean by saying that not to receive (as benefits) the favours of men is difficult?' *K*ung-nî said, 'As soon as one is employed in office, he gets forward in all directions; rank and emolument come to him together, and without end. But these advantages do not come from one's self;—it is my appointed lot to have such external good. The superior man is not a robber; the man of worth is no filcher;—if I prefer such things, what am I[3]? Hence it is said, "There is no bird wiser than the swallow." Where its eye lights on a place that is not suitable for it, it does not give it a second glance. Though it may drop the food from its

[1] This question arose out of the previous statement that man and Heaven might be one,—acting with the same spontaneity.

[2] Confucius recognises here, as he often does, a power beyond his own, 'his appointed lot,' what we call destiny, to which the Tâo requires submission. This comes very near to our idea of God.

[3] Human gifts had such an attraction, that they tended to take from man his heavenly spontaneity; and were to be eschewed, or received only with great caution.

莊子

mouth, it abandons it, and hurries off. It is afraid of men, and yet it stealthily takes up its dwelling by his; finding its protection in the altars of the Land and Grain [1].

'What do you mean by saying that there is no beginning which was not an end?' Kung-nî said, 'The change—rise and dissolution—of all things (continually) goes on, but we do not know who it is that maintains and continues the process. How do we know when any one begins? How do we know when he will end? We have simply to wait for it, and nothing more [2].'

'And what do you mean by saying that the Human and the Heavenly are one and the same?' Kung-nî said, 'Given man, and you have Heaven; given Heaven, and you still have Heaven (and nothing more). That man can not have Heaven is owing to the limitation of his nature [3]. The sagely man quietly passes away with his body, and there is an end of it.'

8. As Kwang Kâu was rambling in the park of Tiâo-ling [4] he saw a strange bird which came from the south. Its wings were seven cubits in width, and

[1] What is said here about the swallow is quite obscure. Hsî-kung says that all the old attempts to explain it are ridiculous, and then propounds an ingenious one of his own; but I will leave the passage with my reader to deal with it as he best can.

[2] Compare with this how in Book XVIII we find Kwang-ȝze singing by the dead body of his wife.

[3] That man is man and not Heaven is simply from the limitation of his nature,—his 'appointed lot.'

[4] Tiâo-ling might be translated 'Eagle Mount.' Where it was I do not know; perhaps the name originated with Kwang-ȝze, and thus has become semi-historical.

its eyes were large, an inch in circuit. It touched the forehead of *K*âu as it passed him, and lighted in a grove of chestnut trees. 'What bird is this?' said he, 'with such great wings not to go on! and with such large eyes not to see me!' He lifted up his skirts, and hurried with his cross-bow, waiting for (an opportunity to shoot) it. (Meanwhile) he saw a cicada, which had just alighted in a beautiful shady spot, and forgot its (care for its) body. (Just then), a preying mantis raised its feelers, and pounced on the cicada, in its eagerness for its prey, (also) forgetting (its care for) its body; while the strange bird took advantage of its opportunity to secure them both, in view of that gain forgetting its true (instinct of preservation)[1]. *K*wang *K*âu with an emotion of pity, said, 'Ah! so it is that things bring evil on one another, each of these creatures invited its own calamity.' (With this) he put away his cross-bow, and was hurrying away back, when the forester pursued him with terms of reproach.

When he returned and went into his house, he did not appear in his courtyard[2] for three months[2]. (When he came out), Lan Ʒü[3] (his disciple) asked him, saying, 'Master, why have you for this some time avoided the courtyard so much?' *K*wang-ȝze replied, 'I was guarding my person, and forgot myself; I was looking at turbid water, till I

[1] *K*wang-ȝze might now have shot the bird, but we like him the better for letting it alone.

[2] So then, masters of schools, like *K*wang-ȝze, received and taught their disciples in the courtyard of their house;—in China as elsewhere. For three 'months,' it is conjectured, we should read three 'days.'

[3] The disciple Lan Ʒü appears here, but not, so far as I know, elsewhere.

莊子

mistook the clear pool. And moreover I have heard the Master say[1], "Going where certain customs prevail, you should follow those customs." I was walking about in the park of Tiâo-ling, and forgot myself. A strange bird brushed past my forehead, and went flying about in the grove of chestnuts, where it forgot the true (art of preserving itself). The forester of the chestnut grove thought that I was a fitting object for his reproach. These are the reasons why I have avoided the courtyard.'

9. Yang-ȝze, having gone to Sung, passed the night in a lodging-house, the master of which had two concubines;—one beautiful, the other ugly[2]. The ugly one was honoured, however, and the beautiful one contemned. Yang-ȝze asked the reason, and a little boy of the house replied, 'The beauty knows her beauty, and we do not recognise it. The ugly one knows her ugliness, and we do not recognise it.' Yang-ȝze said, 'Remember it, my disciples. Act virtuously, and put away the practice of priding yourselves on your virtue. If you do this, where can you go to that you will not be loved[3]?'

[1] Who was this 'Master?'

[2] The story here is found in Lieh-ȝze II, 15[a, b]. The Yang-ȝze is there Yang *K*û, against whom Mencius so often directed his arguments.

[3] See the greater part of this paragraph in Prémare's 'Notitia Linguae Sinicae,' p. 200, with his remarks on the style.

BOOK XXI.

PART II. SECTION XIV.

Thien Ȝze-fang[1].

1. Thien Ȝze-fang, sitting in attendance on the marquis Wăn of Wei[2], often quoted (with approbation) the words of *Khî* Kung[3]. The marquis said, 'Is *Khî* Kung your preceptor?' Ȝze-fang replied, 'No. He only belongs to the same neighbourhood. In speaking about the Tâo, his views are often correct, and therefore I quote them as I do.' The marquis went on, 'Then have you no preceptor?' 'I have.' 'And who is he?' 'He is Tung-kwo Shun-ȝze[4].' 'And why, my Master, have I never heard you quote his words?' Ȝze-fang replied, 'He is a man who satisfies the true (ideal of humanity)[5]; a man in appearance, but (having the mind of) Heaven. Void of any thought of himself, he accommodates himself to others, and nourishes the true ideal that belongs to him. With all his purity, he is forbearing to others. Where they are without the Tâo, he rectifies his demeanour, so that they understand it, and in consequence their own ideas melt

[1] See vol. xxxix, pp. 151, 152. [2] B.C. 424–387.

[3] Some well-known worthy of Wei.

[4] A greater worthy still. He must have lived near the outside suburban wall of the capital, and his residence became a sort of surname.

[5] The Human and the Heavenly were blended in his personality.

莊子

away and disappear. How should one like me be fit to quote his words?'

When 3ze-fang went out, the marquis Wăn continued in a state of dumb amazement all the day. He then called Lung Lî-*kh*ăn, and said to him, 'How far removed from us is the superior man of complete virtue! Formerly I thought the words of the sages and wise men, and the practice of benevolence and righteousness, to be the utmost we could reach to. Since I have heard about the preceptor of 3ze-fang, my body is all unstrung, and I do not wish to move, and my mouth is closed up, and I do not wish to speak;—what I have learned has been only a counterfeit of the truth[1]. Yes, (the possession of Wei) has been an entanglement to me.'

2. Wăn-po Hsüeh-3ze[2], on his way to *Kh*î, stayed some time in Lû, where some persons of the state begged to have an interview with him. He refused them, saying, 'I have heard that the superior men of these Middle States[3] understand the (subjects of) ceremony and righteousness, but are deplorably ignorant of the minds of men. I do not wish to see them.' He went on to *Kh*î; and on his way back (to the south), he again stayed in Lû, when the same persons begged as before for an interview. He then said, 'Formerly they asked to see me, and now again they seek an interview. They will afford me

[1] So the Khang-hsî dictionary defines the phrase;—'a wooden image made of earth,' says Lû Shû-*k*ih.

[2] A Tâoist of note from some region in the south, perhaps from *Kh*û, having his own share of the Tâoistic contempt for knowledge and culture.

[3] Probably Lû and the northern states grouped closely round the royal domain.

some opportunity of bringing out my sentiments.' He went out accordingly and saw the visitors, and came in again with a sigh. Next day the same thing occurred, and his servant said to him, 'How is it that whenever you see those visitors, you are sure to come in again sighing?' 'I told you before,' was the reply, 'that the people of these Middle States understand (the subjects of) ceremony and righteousness, but are deplorably ignorant of the minds of men. Those men who have just seen me, as they came in and went out would describe, one a circle and another a square, and in their easy carriage would be like, one a dragon and another a tiger. They remonstrated with me as sons (with their fathers), and laid down the way for me as fathers (for their sons). It was this which made me sigh.'

*K*ung-nî saw the man, but did not speak a word to him. ȝze-lû said, 'You have wished, Sir, to see this Wăn-po Hsüeh-ȝze for a long time; what is the reason that when you have seen him, you have not spoken a word?' *K*ung-nî replied, 'As soon as my eyes lighted on that man, the Tâo in him was apparent. The situation did not admit of a word being spoken.'

3. Yen Yüan asked *K*ung-nî, saying, 'Master, when you pace quietly along, I also pace along; when you go more quickly, I also do the same; when you gallop, I also gallop; but when you race along and spurn the dust, then I can only stand and look, and keep behind you[1].' The Master said, 'Hui, what do you mean?' The reply was, 'In saying that "when you, Master, pace quietly along, I also pace

[1] They are both supposed to be on horseback.

莊子

along," I mean[1] that when you speak, I also speak. By saying, "When you go more quickly, I also do the same," I mean[1] that when you reason, I also reason. By saying, "When you gallop, I also gallop," I mean[1] that when you speak of the Way, I also speak of the Way; but by saying, "When you race along and spurn the dust, then I can only stare, and keep behind you," I am thinking how though you do not speak, yet all men believe you; though you are no partisan, yet all parties approve your catholicity; and though you sound no instrument, yet people all move on harmoniously before you, while (all the while) I do not know how all this comes about; and this is all which my words are intended to express[2].'

Kung-nî said, 'But you must try and search the matter out. Of all causes for sorrow there is none so great as the death of the mind;—the death of man's (body) is only next to it. The sun comes forth in the east, and sets in the extreme west;—all things have their position determined by these two points. All that have eyes and feet wait for this (sun), and then proceed to do what they have to do. When this comes forth, they appear in their places; when it sets, they disappear. It is so with all things. They have that for which they wait, and (on its arrival) they die; they have that for which they wait, and then (again) they live. When once I receive my frame thus completed, I remain unchanged, awaiting the consummation of my course.

[1] In these three cases the 也 of the text should be 者.

[2] So Hui is made to represent the master as a mental Thaumaturgist, and Confucius is made to try to explain the whole thing to him;—but not to my mind successfully. Still a distinction is maintained between the mind and the body.

I move as acted on by things, day and night without cessation, and I do not know when I will come to an end. Clearly I am here a completed frame, and even one who (fancies that he) knows what is appointed cannot determine it beforehand. I am in this way daily passing on, but all day long I am communicating my views to you; and now, as we are shoulder to shoulder you fail (to understand me);—is it not matter for lamentation? You are able in a measure to set forth what I more clearly set forth; but that is passed away, and you look for it, as if it were still existing, just as if you were looking for a horse in the now empty place where it was formerly exhibited for sale. You have very much forgotten my service to you, and I have very much forgotten wherein I served you. But nevertheless why should you account this such an evil? What you forget is but my old self; that which cannot be forgotten remains with me.'

4. Confucius went to see Lâo Tan, and arrived just as he had completed the bathing of his head, and was letting his dishevelled hair get dry. There he was, motionless, and as if there were not another man in the world[1]. Confucius waited quietly; and, when in a little time he was introduced, he said, 'Were my eyes dazed? Is it really you? Just now, your body, Sir, was like the stump of a rotten tree. You looked as if you had no thought of anything, as if you had left the society of men, and were standing in the solitude (of yourself).' Lâo Tan replied, 'I was enjoying myself in thinking about the commencement

[1] He was in the Tâoistic trance, like Nan-kwo Ȝze-*kh*î, at the beginning of the second Book.

莊子

of things[1].' 'What do you mean?' 'My mind is so cramped, that I hardly know it; my tongue is so tied that I cannot tell it; but I will try to describe it to you as nearly as I can. When the state of Yin was perfect, all was cold and severe; when the state of Yang was perfect, all was turbulent and agitated. The coldness and severity came forth from Heaven; the turbulence and agitation issued from Earth. The two states communicating together, a harmony ensued and things were produced. Some one regulated and controlled this, but no one has seen his form. Decay and growth; fulness and emptiness; darkness and light; the changes of the sun and the transformations of the moon:—these are brought about from day to day; but no one sees the process of production. Life has its origin from which it springs, and death has its place from which it returns. Beginning and ending go on in mutual contrariety without any determinable commencement, and no one knows how either comes to an end. If we disallow all this, who originates and presides over all these phenomena?'

Confucius said, 'I beg to ask about your enjoyment in these thoughts.' Lâo Tan replied, 'The

[1] This 'commencement of things' was not the equivalent of 'our creation out of nothing,' for Lâo Tan immediately supposes the existence of the primary ether in its twofold state, as Yin and Yang; and also of Heaven and Earth, as a twofold Power working, under some regulation and control, yet invisible; that is, under the Tâo. In the same way the process of beginning and ending, growth and decay, life and death go on, no one knows how, or how long. And the contemplation of all this is the cause of unceasing delight to the Perfect man, the possessor of the Tâo. Death is a small matter, merely as a change of feature; and Confucius acknowledges his immeasurable inferiority to Lâo-ȝze.

comprehension of this is the most admirable and the most enjoyable (of all acquisitions). The getting of the most admirable and the exercise of the thoughts in what is the most enjoyable, constitutes what we call the Perfect man.' Confucius said, 'I should like to hear the method of attaining to it.' The reply was, 'Grass-eating animals do not dislike to change their pastures; creatures born in the water do not dislike to change their waters. They make a small change, but do not lose what is the great and regular requirement (of their nature); joy, anger, sadness, and delight do not enter into their breasts (in connexion with such events). Now the space under the sky is occupied by all things in their unity. When they possess that unity and equally share it, then the four limbs and hundred members of their body are but so much dust and dirt, while death and life, their ending and beginning, are but as the succession of day and night, which cannot disturb their enjoyment; and how much less will they be troubled by gains and losses, by calamity and happiness! Those who renounce the paraphernalia of rank do it as if they were casting away so much mud;—they know that they are themselves more honourable than those paraphernalia. The honour belonging to one's self is not lost by any change (of condition). Moreover, a myriad transformations may take place before the end of them is reached. What is there in all this sufficient to trouble the mind? Those who have attained to the Tâo understand the subject.'

Confucius said, 'O Master, your virtue is equal to that of Heaven and Earth, and still I must borrow

莊子

(some of your) perfect words (to aid me) in the cultivation of my mind. Who among the superior men of antiquity could give such expression to them?' Lâo Tan replied, 'Not so. Look at the spring, the water of which rises and overflows;—it does nothing, but it naturally acts so. So with the perfect man and his virtue;—he does not cultivate it, and nothing evades its influence. He is like heaven which is high of itself, like earth which is solid of itself, like the sun and moon which shine of themselves;—what need is there to cultivate it?'

Confucius went out and reported the conversation to Yen Hui, saying, 'In the (knowledge of the) Tâo am I any better than an animalcule in vinegar? But for the Master's lifting the veil from me, I should not have known the grand perfection of Heaven and Earth.'

5. At an interview of *K*wang-ȝze with duke Âi[1] of Lû, the duke said, 'There are many of the Learned class in Lû; but few of them can be compared with you, Sir.' *K*wang-ȝze replied, 'There are few Learned men in Lû.' 'Everywhere in Lû,' rejoined the duke, 'you see men wearing the dress of the Learned[2];—how can you say that they are few?' 'I have heard,' said *K*wang-ȝze, 'that those of them who wear round caps know the times of heaven; that those who wear square shoes know the contour of the ground; and that those who saunter about with semicircular stones at their

[1] Duke Âi of Lû died in B.C. 468, a century and more before the birth of *K*wang-ȝze. On that, as well as on other grounds, the paragraph cannot be genuine.

[2] Compare the thirty-eighth Book of the Lî *K*î, where Confucius denies that there was any dress peculiar to the scholar.

girdle-pendents settle matters in dispute as they come before them. But superior men who are possessed of such knowledge will not be found wearing the dress, and it does not follow that those who wear the dress possess the knowledge. If your Grace think otherwise, why not issue a notification through the state, that it shall be a capital offence to wear the dress without possessing the knowledge.' On this the duke issued such a notification, and in five days, throughout all Lû, there was no one who dared to wear the dress of the Learned. There was only one old man who came and stood in it at the duke's gate. The duke instantly called him in, and questioned him about the affairs of the state, when he talked about a thousand points and ten thousand divergences from them. *K*wang-ȝze said, 'When the state of Lû can thus produce but one man of the Learned class, can he be said to be many?'

6. The ideas of rank and emolument did not enter the mind of Pâi-lî Hsî[1], and so he became a cattle-feeder, and his cattle were all in fine condition. This made duke Mû of *Kh*in forget the meanness of his position, and put the government (of his state) into his hands. Neither life nor death entered into the mind of (Shun), the Lord of Yü, and therefore he was able to influence others[2].

7. The ruler Yüan[3] of Sung wishing to have a map

[1] Pâi-lî Hsî, a remarkable character of the seventh century B.C., who rose to be chief minister to Mû, the earl (or duke) of *Kh*in, the last of the five Leading Princes of the kingdom. Mû died in B.C. 621. Mencius has much to say of Pâi-lî Hsî.

[2] Shun's parents wished to kill him; but that did not trouble his mind; his filial piety even affected them.

[3] His first year as duke of Sung was B.C. 530. The point of the story is not clear.

莊子

drawn, the masters of the pencil all came (to undertake the task). Having received his instructions and made their bows, they stood, licking their pencils and preparing their ink. Half their number, however, remained outside. There was one who came late, with an air of indifference, and did not hurry forward. When he had received his instructions and made his bow, he did not keep standing, but proceeded to his shed. The duke sent a man to see him, and there he was, with his upper garment off, sitting cross-legged, and nearly naked. The ruler said, 'He is the man; he is a true draughtsman.'

8. King Wăn was (once) looking about him at Ȝang[1], when he saw an old man fishing[2]. But his fishing was no fishing. It was not the fishing of one whose business is fishing. He was always fishing (as if he had no object in the occupation). The king wished to raise him to office, and put the government into his hands, but was afraid that such a step would give dissatisfaction to his great ministers, his uncles, and cousins. He then wished to dismiss the man altogether from his mind, but he could not bear the thought that his people should be without (such a) Heaven (as their Protector). On this, (next) morning, he called together his great officers, and said to them, 'Last night, I dreamt that I saw a good man, with a dark complexion and a

[1] Where Ȝang was cannot be told.

[2] The old fisherman here was, no doubt, the first marquis of *Kh*î, after the establishment of the dynasty of *K*âu, known by various names, as Lü Shang, Thâi-kung Wang, and *K*iang Ȝze-yâ. He did much for the new rule, but his connexion with kings Wăn and Wû is a mass of fables. The fishing as if he were not fishing betokened in him the aimlessness of the Tâo.

beard, riding on a piebald horse, one half of whose hoofs were red, who commanded me, saying, "Lodge your government in the hands of the old man of 3ang; and perhaps the evils of your people will be cured."' The great officers said eagerly, 'It was the king, your father.' King Wăn said, 'Let us then submit the proposal to the tortoise-shell.' They replied, 'It is the order of your father. Let not your majesty think of any other. Why divine about it?' (The king) then met the old man of 3ang, and committed the government to him.

The statutes and laws were not changed by him; not a one-sided order (of his own) was issued; but when the king made a survey of the kingdom after three years, he found that the officers had destroyed the plantations (which harboured banditti), and dispersed their occupiers, that the superintendents of the official departments did not plume themselves on their successes, and that no unusual grain measures were allowed within the different states[1]. When the officers had destroyed the dangerous plantations and dispersed their occupants, the highest value was set on the common interests; when the chiefs of departments did not plume themselves on their successes, the highest value was set on the common business; when unusual grain measures did not enter the different states, the different princes had no jealousies. On this king Wăn made the old man his Grand Preceptor, and asked him, with his own face to the north, whether his government might be extended to all the kingdom. The old

[1] That is, that all combinations formed to resist and warp the course of justice had been put an end to.

man looked perplexed and gave no reply, but with aimless look took his leave. In the morning he had issued his orders, and at night he had gone his way; nor was he heard of again all his life. Yen Yüan questioned Confucius, saying, 'Was even king Wăn unequal to determine his course? What had he to do with resorting to a dream?' *K*ung-nî replied, 'Be silent and do not say a word! King Wăn was complete in everything. What have you to do with criticising him? He only had recourse (to the dream) to meet a moment's difficulty.'

9. Lieh Yü-khâu was exhibiting his archery[1] to Po-hwăn Wû-ȥăn[2]. Having drawn the bow to its full extent, with a cup of water placed on his elbow, he let fly. As the arrow was discharged, another was put in its place; and as that was sent off, a third was ready on the string. All the while he stood like a statue. Po-hwăn Wû-ȥăn said, 'That is the shooting of an archer, but not of one who shoots without thinking about his shooting. Let me go up with you to the top of a high mountain, treading with you among the tottering rocks, till we arrive at the brink of a precipice, 800 cubits deep, and (I will then see) if you can shoot.' On this they went up a high mountain, making their way among the tottering rocks, till they came to the brink of a precipice 800 cubits deep. Then Wû-ȥăn turned round and walked backwards, till his feet were two-

[1] This must be the meaning of the 爲, 'for.' The whole story is found in Lieh-ȥze, II, p. 5. From Lieh's Book VIII, p. 2, we learn that Lieh-ȥze's teacher in archery was Yin Hsî, the warden of the pass famous in the history of Lâo-ȥze.

[2] Mentioned in Book V, par. 2.

thirds of their length outside the edge, and beckoned Yü-khâu to come forward. He, however, had fallen prostrate on the ground, with the sweat pouring down to his heels. Then the other said, 'The Perfect man looks up to the azure sky above, or dives down to the yellow springs beneath, or soars away to the eight ends of the universe, without any change coming over his spirit or his breath. But now the trepidation of your mind appears in your dazed eyes; your inward feeling of peril is extreme!'

10. *K*ien Wû asked Sun-shû Âo[1], saying, 'You, Sir, were thrice chief minister, and did not feel elated; you were thrice dismissed from that position, without manifesting any sorrow. At first I was in doubt about you, (but I am not now, since) I see how regularly and quietly the breath comes through your nostrils. How is it that you exercise your mind?' Sun-shû Âo replied, 'In what do I surpass other men? When the position came to me, I thought it should not be rejected; when it was taken away, I thought it could not be retained. I considered that the getting or losing it did not make me what I was, and was no occasion for any manifestation of sorrow;—that was all. In what did I surpass other men? And moreover, I did not know whether the honour of it belonged to the dignity, or to myself. If it belonged to the dignity, it was nothing to me; if it belonged to me, it had nothing

[1] Sun-shû Âo;—see Mencius VI, ii, 15. He was, no doubt, a good and able man, chief minister to king *K*wang of *Kh*û. The legends or edifying stories about him are many; but *K*wang-ȝze, I think, is the author of his being thrice raised and thrice dismissed from office.

莊子

to do with the dignity. While occupied with these uncertainties, and looking round in all directions, what leisure had I to take knowledge of whether men honoured me or thought me mean?'

Kung-nî heard of all this, and said, 'The True men of old could not be fully described by the wisest, nor be led into excess by the most beautiful, nor be forced by the most violent robber. Neither Fû-hsî nor Hwang-Tî could compel them to be their friends. Death and life are indeed great considerations, but they could make no change in their (true) self; and how much less could rank and emolument do so? Being such, their spirits might pass over the Thâi mountain and find it no obstacle to them[1]; they might enter the greatest gulphs, and not be wet by them; they might occupy the lowest and smallest positions without being distressed by them. Theirs was the fulness of heaven and earth; the more that they gave to others, the more they had.'

The king of Khû and the ruler of Fan[2] were sitting together. After a little while, the attendants of the king said, 'Fan has been destroyed three times.' The ruler of Fan rejoined, 'The destruction of Fan has not been sufficient to destroy what we had that was most deserving to be preserved.' Now,

[1] It is difficult to see why this should be predicated of the 'spirits' of the True men.

[2] Fan was a small state, held at one time by descendants of the famous duke of Kâu;—see the 3o Khwan, I, vii, 6; V, xxiv, 2. But we do not know what had been the relations between the powerful Khû and the feeble Fan, which gave rise to and could explain the remarks made at the entertainment, more honourable to Fan than to Khû.

if the destruction of Fan had not been sufficient to destroy that which it had most deserving to be preserved, the preservation of *Kh*û had not been sufficient to preserve that in it most deserving to be preserved. Looking at the matter from this point of view, Fan had not begun to be destroyed, and *Kh*û had not begun to be preserved.

莊子

BOOK XXII.

PART II. SECTION XV.

*K*ih Pei Yû, or 'Knowledge Rambling in the North[1].'

1. Knowledge[2] had rambled northwards to the region of the Dark Water[3], where he ascended the height of Imperceptible Slope[3], when it happened that he met with Dumb Inaction[2]. Knowledge addressed him, saying, 'I wish to ask you some questions:—By what process of thought and anxious consideration do we get to know the Tâo? Where should we dwell and what should we do to find our rest in the Tâo? From what point should we start and what path should we pursue to make the Tâo our own?' He asked these three questions, but Dumb Inaction[2] gave him no reply. Not only did he not answer, but he did not know how to answer.

Knowledge[2], disappointed by the fruitlessness of his questions, returned to the south of the Bright

[1] See vol. xxxix, p. 152.

[2] All these names are metaphorical, having more or less to do with the qualities of the Tâo, and are used as the names of personages, devoted to the pursuit of it. It is difficult to translate the name *Kh*wang *Kh*ü (狂屈). An old reading is 詘, which Medhurst explains by 'Bent or Crooked Discourse.' 'Blurter,' though not an elegant English term, seems to express the idea our author would convey by it. Hwang-Tî is different from the other names, but we cannot regard him as here a real personage.

[3] These names of places are also metaphorical and Tâoistic.

Water[1], and ascended the height of the End of Doubt[1], where he saw Heedless Blurter, to whom he put the same questions, and who replied, 'Ah! I know, and will tell you.' But while he was about to speak, he forgot what he wanted to say.

Knowledge, (again) receiving no answer to his questions, returned to the palace of the Tî[2], where he saw Hwang-Tî[3], and put the questions to him. Hwang-Tî said, 'To exercise no thought and no anxious consideration is the first step towards knowing the Tâo; to dwell nowhere and do nothing is the first step towards resting in the Tâo; to start from nowhere and pursue no path is the first step towards making the Tâo your own.'

Knowledge then asked Hwang-Tî, saying, 'I and you know this; those two did not know it; which of us is right?' The reply was, 'Dumb Inaction[3] is truly right; Heedless Blurter has an appearance of being so; I and you are not near being so. (As it is said), "Those who know (the Tâo) do not speak of it; those who speak of it do not know it[4];" and "Hence the sage conveys his instructions without the use of speech[4]." The Tâo cannot be made ours by constraint; its characteristics will not come to us (at our call). Benevolence may be practised; Righteousness may be partially attended to; by Ceremonies men impose on one another. Hence it

---

[1] See note 3, on preceding page.

[2] Tî might seem to be used here for 'God,' but its juxtaposition with Hwang-Tî is against our translating it so.

[3] See note 2, on preceding page.

[4] See the Tâo Teh *K*ing, chaps. 56 and 2. *K*wang-ȝze is quoting, no doubt, these two passages, as he vaguely intimates I think by the 夫, with which the sentence commences.

莊子

is said, "When the Tâo was lost, its Characteristics appeared. When its Characteristics were lost, Benevolence appeared. When Benevolence was lost, Righteousness appeared. When Righteousness was lost, Ceremonies appeared. Ceremonies are but (the unsubstantial) flowers of the Tâo, and the commencement of disorder[1]." Hence (also it is further said), "He who practises the Tâo, daily diminishes his doing. He diminishes it and again diminishes it, till he arrives at doing nothing. Having arrived at this non-inaction, there is nothing that he does not do[1]." Here now there is something, a regularly fashioned utensil;—if you wanted to make it return to the original condition of its materials, would it not be difficult to make it do so? Could any but the Great Man accomplish this easily[2]?

'Life is the follower of death, and death is the predecessor of life; but who knows the Arranger (of this connexion between them)[3]? The life is due to the collecting of the breath. When that is collected, there is life; when it is dispersed, there is death. Since death and life thus attend on each other, why should I account (either of) them an evil?

'Therefore all things go through one and the same experience. (Life) is accounted beautiful because it is spirit-like and wonderful, and death is accounted ugly because of its foetor and putridity. But the foetid and putrid is transformed again into the spirit-like and wonderful, and the spirit-like and wonderful is transformed again into the foetid and

[1] See the Tâo Teh *K*ing, chaps. 38 and 48.

[2] This sentence is metaphorical of the Tâo, whose spell is broken by the intrusion of Knowledge.

[3] This 'Arranger' is the Tâo.

putrid. Hence it is said, "All under the sky there is one breath of life, and therefore the sages prized that unity [1].'"

Knowledge [2] said to Hwang-Tî [2], 'I asked Dumb Inaction [2], and he did not answer me. Not only did he not answer me, but he did not know how to answer me. I asked Heedless Blurter, and while he wanted to tell me, he yet did not do so. Not only did he not tell me, but while he wanted to tell me, he forgot all about my questions. Now I have asked you, and you knew (all about them);—why (do you say that) you are not near doing so?' Hwang-Tî replied, 'Dumb Inaction [2] was truly right, because he did not know the thing. Heedless Blurter [2] was nearly right, because he forgot it. I and you are not nearly right, because we know it.' Heedless Blurter [2] heard of (all this), and considered that Hwang-Tî [2] knew how to express himself (on the subject).

2. (The operations of) Heaven and Earth proceed in the most admirable way, but they say nothing about them; the four seasons observe the clearest laws, but they do not discuss them; all things have their complete and distinctive constitutions, but they say nothing about them [3].

The sages trace out the admirable operations of Heaven and Earth, and reach to and understand the distinctive constitutions of all things; and thus it is that the Perfect Man (is said to) do nothing and the Greatest Sage to originate nothing, such language showing that they look to Heaven and Earth as

[1] I have not been able to trace this quotation to its source.

[2] See note 2, p. 57. [3] Compare Analects XVII, xix, 3.

莊子

their model[1]. Even they, with their spirit-like and most exquisite intelligence, as well as all the tribes that undergo their transformations, the dead and the living, the square and the round, do not understand their root and origin, but nevertheless they all from the oldest time by it preserve their being.

Vast as is the space included within the six cardinal points, it all (and all that it contains) lies within (this twofold root of Heaven and Earth); small as is an autumn hair, it is indebted to this for the completion of its form. All things beneath the sky, now rising, now descending, ever continue the same through this. The Yin and Yang, and the four seasons revolve and move by it, each in its proper order. Now it seems to be lost in obscurity, but it continues; now it seems to glide away, and have no form, but it is still spirit-like. All things are nourished by it, without their knowing it. This is what is called the Root and Origin; by it we may obtain a view of what we mean by Heaven[2].

3. Nieh *Kh*üeh[3] asked about the Tâo from Phei-î[3], who replied, 'If you keep your body as it should be, and look only at the one thing, the Harmony of Heaven will come to you. Call in your knowledge, and make your measures uniform, and the spiritual (belonging to you) will come and lodge with you; the Attributes (of the Tâo) will be your beauty, and the Tâo (itself) will be your dwelling-place. You will have the simple look of a new-born calf, and

[1] Compare the Tâo Teh *K*ing, ch. 25.

[2] The binomial 'Heaven and Earth' here gives place to the one term 'Heaven,' which is often a synonym of Tâo.

[3] See his character in Book XII, par. 5, where Phei-î also is mentioned.

will not seek to know the cause (of your being what you are).' Phei-î had not finished these words when the other dozed off into a sleep.

Phei-î was greatly pleased, and walked away, singing as he went,

'Like stump of rotten tree his frame,
Like lime when slaked his mind became[1].
Real is his wisdom, solid, true,
Nor cares what's hidden to pursue.
O dim and dark his aimless mind!
No one from him can counsel find.
What sort of man is he?'

4. Shun asked (his attendant) *Kh*ăng[2], saying, 'Can I get the Tâo and hold it as mine?' The reply was, 'Your body is not your own to hold;—how then can you get and hold the Tâo?' Shun resumed, 'If my body be not mine to possess and hold, who holds it?' *Kh*ăng said, 'It is the bodily form entrusted to you by Heaven and Earth. Life is not yours to hold. It is the blended harmony (of the Yin and Yang), entrusted to you by Heaven and Earth. Your nature, constituted as it is, is not yours to hold. It is entrusted to you by Heaven and Earth to act in accordance with it. Your grandsons and sons are not yours to hold. They are the exuviae[3] entrusted to you by Heaven and Earth. Therefore when we walk, we should not know where we are going; when we stop and rest, we should not know what to occupy ourselves with;

[1] See the account of Nan-kwo Ȝze-*kh*î in Book II, par. 1.

[2] Not the name of a man, but an office.

[3] The term in the text denotes the cast-off skin or shell of insects, snakes, and crabs. See the account of death and life in par. 1.

莊子

when we eat, we should not know the taste of our food;—all is done by the strong Yang influence of Heaven and Earth[1]. How then can you get (the Tâo), and hold it as your own?'

5. Confucius asked Lâo Tan, saying, 'Being at leisure to-day, I venture to ask you about the Perfect Tâo.' Lâo Tan replied, 'You must, as by fasting and vigil, clear and purge your mind, wash your spirit white as snow, and sternly repress your knowledge. The subject of the Tâo is deep, and difficult to describe;—I will give you an outline of its simplest attributes.

'The Luminous was produced from the Obscure; the Multiform from the Unembodied; the Spiritual from the Tâo; and the bodily from the seminal essence. After this all things produced one another from their bodily organisations. Thus it is that those which have nine apertures are born from the womb, and those with eight from eggs[2]. But their coming leaves no trace, and their going no monument; they enter by no door; they dwell in no apartment[3]:—they are in a vast arena reaching in all directions. They who search for and find (the Tâo) in this are strong in their limbs, sincere and far-reaching in their thinking, acute in their hearing, and clear in their seeing. They exercise their minds without being toiled; they respond to everything aright without regard to place or circumstance. Without this heaven would not be high, nor earth

[1] It is an abstruse point why only the Yang is mentioned here, and described as 'strong.'

[2] It is not easy to see the pertinence of this illustration.

[3] Hû Wăn-ying says, 'With this one word our author sweeps away the teaching of Purgatorial Sufferings.'

broad; the sun and moon would not move, and nothing would flourish:—such is the operation of the Tâo.

'Moreover, the most extensive knowledge does not necessarily know it; reasoning will not make men wise in it;—the sages have decided against both these methods. However you try to add to it, it admits of no increase; however you try to take from it, it admits of no diminution;—this is what the sages maintain about it. How deep it is, like the sea! How grand it is, beginning again when it has come to an end! If it carried along and sustained all things, without being overburdened or weary, that would be like the way of the superior man, merely an external operation; when all things go to it, and find their dependence in it;—this is the true character of the Tâo.

'Here is a man (born) in one of the middle states[1]. He feels himself independent both of the Yin and Yang[2], and dwells between heaven and earth; only for the present a mere man, but he will return to his original source. Looking at him in his origin, when his life begins, we have (but) a gelatinous substance in which the breath is collecting. Whether his life be long or his death early, how short is the space between them! It is but the name for a moment of time, insufficient to play the part of a good Yâo or a bad *K*ieh in.

'The fruits of trees and creeping plants have their distinctive characters, and though the relation-

[1] The commentators suppose that by 'the man' here there is intended 'a sage;' and they would seem to be correct.

[2] Compare the second sentence in the Tâo Teh *K*ing, ch. 42.

ships of men, according to which they are classified, are troublesome, the sage, when he meets with them, does not set himself in opposition to them, and when he has passed through them, he does not seek to retain them; he responds to them in their regular harmony according to his virtue; and even when he accidentally comes across any of them, he does so according to the Tâo. It was thus that the Tîs flourished, thus that the kings arose.

'Men's life between heaven and earth is like a white[1] colt's passing a crevice, and suddenly disappearing. As with a plunge and an effort they all come forth; easily and quietly they all enter again. By a transformation they live, and by another transformation they die. Living things are made sad (by death), and mankind grieve for it; but it is (only) the removal of the bow from its sheath, and the emptying the natural satchel of its contents. There may be some confusion amidst the yielding to the change; but the intellectual and animal souls are taking their leave, and the body will follow them:—This is the Great Returning home.

'That the bodily frame came from incorporeity, and will return to the same, is what all men in common know, and what those who are on their way to (know) it need not strive for. This is what the multitudes of men discuss together. Those whose (knowledge) is complete do not discuss it;—such discussion shows that their (knowledge) is not complete. Even the most clear-sighted do not meet

[1] Why is it the colt here is 'white?' Is it to heighten the impression made by his speedy disappearing? or is it merely the adoption of the phrase from the Shih, II, iv, 2?

(with the Tâo);—it is better to be silent than to reason about it. The Tâo cannot be heard with the ears;—it is better to shut the ears than to try and hear it. This is what is called the Great Attainment.'

6. Tung-kwo Ȝze[1] asked *K*wang-ȝze, saying, 'Where is what you call the Tâo to be found?' *K*wang-ȝze replied, 'Everywhere.' The other said, 'Specify an instance of it. That will be more satisfactory.' 'It is here in this ant.' 'Give a lower instance.' 'It is in this panic grass.' 'Give me a still lower instance.' 'It is in this earthenware tile.' 'Surely that is the lowest instance?' 'It is in that excrement[2].' To this Tung-kwo Ȝze gave no reply. *K*wang-ȝze said, 'Your questions, my master, do not touch the fundamental point (of the Tâo). They remind me of the questions addressed by the superintendents of the market to the inspector about examining the value of a pig by treading on it, and testing its weight as the foot descends lower and lower on the body[3]. You should not specify any particular thing. There is not a single thing without (the Tâo). So it is with the Perfect Tâo. And if we call it the Great (Tâo), it is just the same. There are the three terms,—"Complete," "All-embracing," "the Whole." These names are differ-

[1] Perhaps the Tung-kwo Shun-ȝze of Bk. XXI, par. 1.

[2] A contemptuous reply, provoked by Tung-kwo's repeated interrogation as to where the Tâo was to be found, the only question being as to what it was.

[3] We do not know the practices from which our author draws his illustrations here sufficiently to make out his meaning clearly. The signification of the characters 正 and 獲 may be gathered indeed from the Î Lî, Books 7-9; but that is all.

莊子

ent, but the reality (sought in them) is the same; referring to the One thing[1].

'Suppose we were to try to roam about in the palace of No-where;—when met there, we might discuss (about the subject) without ever coming to an end. Or suppose we were to be together in (the region of) Non-action;—should we say that (the Tâo was) Simplicity and Stillness? or Indifference and Purity? or Harmony and Ease? My will would be aimless. If it went nowhere, I should not know where it had got to; if it went and came again, I should not know where it had stopped; if it went on going and coming, I should not know when the process would end. In vague uncertainty should I be in the vastest waste. Though I entered it with the greatest knowledge, I should not know how inexhaustible it was. That which makes things what they are has not the limit which belongs to things, and when we speak of things being limited, we mean that they are so in themselves. (The Tâo) is the limit of the unlimited, and the boundlessness of the unbounded.

'We speak of fulness and emptiness; of withering and decay. It produces fulness and emptiness, but is neither fulness nor emptiness; it produces withering and decay, but is neither withering nor decay. It produces the root and branches, but is neither root nor branch; it produces accumulation and dispersion, but is itself neither accumulated nor dispersed.'

7. A-ho Kan[2] and Shăn Năng studied together

[1] The meaning of this other illustration is also very obscure to me; and much of what follows to the end of the paragraph.

[2] We can hardly be said to know anything more of the first and third of these men than what is mentioned here.

under Lăo-lung *Kî*. Shăn Năng[1] was leaning forward on his stool, having shut the door and gone to sleep in the day time. At midday A-ho Kan pushed open the door and entered, saying, 'Lâo-lung is dead.' Shăn Năng leant forward on his stool, laid hold of his staff and rose. Then he laid the staff aside with a clash, laughed and said, 'That Heaven knew how cramped and mean, how arrogant and assuming I was, and therefore he has cast me off, and is dead. Now that there is no Master to correct my heedless words, it is simply for me to die!' Yen Kang, (who had come in) to condole, heard these words, and said, 'It is to him who embodies the Tâo that the superior men everywhere cling. Now you who do not understand so much as the tip of an autumn hair of it, not even the ten-thousandth part of the Tâo, still know how to keep hidden your heedless words about it and die;—how much more might he who embodied the Tâo do so! We look for it, and there is no form; we hearken for it, and there is no sound. When men try to discuss it, we call them dark indeed. When they discuss the Tâo, they misrepresent it.'

Hereupon Grand Purity[2] asked Infinitude[2], saying, 'Do you know the Tâo?' 'I do not know it,' was the reply. He then asked Do-nothing[2], who replied, 'I know it.' 'Is your knowledge of it de-

[1] Shăn Năng is well known, as coming in the chronological list between Fû-hsî and Hwang-Tî; and we are surprised that a higher place is not given to him among the Tâoist patriarchs than our author assigns to him here.

[2] These names, like those in the first paragraph of the Book, are metaphorical, intended, no doubt, to set forth attributes of the Tâo, and to suggest to the reader what it is or what it is not.

莊子

termined by various points?' 'It is.' 'What are they?' Do-nothing[1] said, 'I know that the Tâo may be considered noble, and may be considered mean, that it may be bound and compressed, and that it may be dispersed and diffused. These are the marks by which I know it.' Grand Purity took the words of those two, and asked No-beginning[1], saying, 'Such were their replies; which was right? and which was wrong? Infinitude's saying that he did not know it? or Do-nothing's saying that he knew it?' No-beginning said, 'The "I do not know it" was profound, and the "I know it" was shallow. The former had reference to its internal nature; the latter to its external conditions. Grand Purity looked up and sighed, saying, 'Is "not to know it" then to know it? And is "to know it" not to know it? But who knows that he who does not know it (really) knows it?' No-beginning replied, 'The Tâo cannot be heard; what can be heard is not It. The Tâo cannot be seen; what can be seen is not It. The Tâo cannot be expressed in words; what can be expressed in words is not It. Do we know the Formless which gives form to form? In the same way the Tâo does not admit of being named.'

No-beginning (further) said, 'If one ask about the Tâo and another answer him, neither of them knows it. Even the former who asks has never learned anything about the Tâo. He asks what does not admit of being asked, and the latter answers where answer is impossible. When one asks what does not admit of being asked, his questioning is in (dire)

[1] See note 2 on last page.

extremity. When one answers where answer is impossible, he has no internal knowledge of the subject. When people without such internal knowledge wait to be questioned by others in dire extremity, they show that externally they see nothing of space and time, and internally know nothing of the Grand Commencement[1]. Therefore they cannot cross over the Khwăn-lun[2], nor roam in the Grand Void.'

8. Starlight[3] asked Non-entity[3], saying, 'Master, do you exist? or do you not exist?' He got no answer to his question, however, and looked stedfastly to the appearance of the other, which was that of a deep void. All day long he looked to it, but could see nothing; he listened for it, but could hear nothing; he clutched at it, but got hold of nothing[4]. Starlight then said, 'Perfect! Who can attain to this? I can (conceive the ideas of) existence and non-existence, but I cannot (conceive the ideas of) non-existing non-existence, and still there be a non-existing existence. How is it possible to reach to this?'

9. The forger of swords for the Minister of War had reached the age of eighty, and had not lost a hair's-breadth of his ability[5]. The Minister said to

[1] The first beginning of all things or of anything.

[2] The Khwăn-lun may be considered the Sacred Mountain of Tâoism.

[3] The characters Kwang Yâo denote the points of light all over the sky, 'dusted with stars.' I can think of no better translation for them, as personified here, than 'starlight.' 'Non-entity' is a personification of the Tâo; as no existing thing, but the idea of the order that pervades and regulates throughout the universe.

[4] A quotation from the Tâo Teh *K*ing, ch. 14.

[5] Compare the case of the butcher in Bk. III, and other similar passages.

莊子

him, 'You are indeed skilful, Sir. Have you any method that makes you so?' The man said, 'Your servant has (always) kept to his work. When I was twenty, I was fond of forging swords. I looked at nothing else. I paid no attention to anything but swords. By my constant practice of it, I came to be able to do the work without any thought of what I was doing. By length of time one acquires ability at any art; and how much more one who is ever at work on it! What is there which does not depend on this, and succeed by it?'

10. *Z*ăn *Kh*iû[1] asked *K*ung-nî, saying, 'Can it be known how it was before heaven and earth?' The reply was, 'It can. It was the same of old as now.' *Z*ăn *Kh*iû asked no more and withdrew. Next day, however, he had another interview, and said, 'Yesterday I asked whether it could be known how it was before heaven and earth, and you, Master, said, "It can. As it is now, so it was of old." Yesterday, I seemed to understand you clearly, but to-day it is dark to me. I venture to ask you for an explanation of this.' *K*ung-nî said, 'Yesterday you seemed to understand me clearly, because your own spiritual nature had anticipated my reply. To-day it seems dark to you, for you are in an unspiritual mood, and are trying to discover the meaning. (In this matter) there is no old time and no present; no beginning and no ending. Could it be that there were grandchildren and children before there were (other) grandchildren and children[2]?'

[1] One of the disciples of Confucius;—Analects VI, 3.

[2] Hû Wăn-ying says, 'Before there can be grandsons and sons there must be grandfathers and fathers to transmit them, so before

*Z*ăn *Kh*iû had not made any reply, when *K*ung-nî went on, 'Let us have done. There can be no answering (on your part). We cannot with life give life to death; we cannot with death give death to life. Do death and life wait (for each other)? There is that which contains them both in its one comprehension[1]. Was that which was produced before Heaven and Earth a thing? That which made things and gave to each its character was not itself a thing. Things came forth and could not be before things, as if there had (previously) been things;—as if there had been things (producing one another) without end. The love of the sages for others, and never coming to an end, is an idea taken from this[2].'

11. Yen Yüan asked *K*ung-nî, saying, 'Master, I have heard you say, "There should be no demonstration of welcoming; there should be no movement to meet;"—I venture to ask in what way this affection of the mind may be shown.' The reply was, 'The ancients, amid (all) external changes, did not change internally; now-a-days men change internally, but take no note of external changes. When one only notes the changes of things, himself continuing one and the same, he does not change. How should there be (a difference between) his changing and not changing? How should he put himself in contact with (and come under the influence of) those external changes? He is sure, however,

there were (the present) heaven and earth, there must have been another heaven and earth.' But I am not sure that he has in this remark exactly caught our author's meaning.

[1] Meaning the Tâo. [2] An obscure remark.

to keep his points of contact with them from being many. The park of Shih-wei[1], the garden of Hwang-Tî, the palace of the Lord of Yü, and the houses of Thang and Wû;—(these all were places in which this was done). But the superior men (so called, of later days), such as the masters of the Literati and of Mohism, were bold to attack each other with their controversies; and how much more so are the men of the present day! Sages in dealing with others do not wound them; and they who do not wound others cannot be wounded by them. Only he whom others do not injure is able to welcome and meet men.

'Forests and marshes make me joyful and glad; but before the joy is ended, sadness comes and succeeds to it. When sadness and joy come, I cannot prevent their approach; when they go, I cannot retain them. How sad it is that men should only be as lodging-houses for things, (and the emotions which they excite)! They know what they meet, but they do not know what they do not meet; they use what power they have, but they cannot be strong where they are powerless. Such ignorance and powerlessness is what men cannot avoid. That they should try to avoid what they cannot avoid, is not this also sad? Perfect speech is to put speech away; perfect action is to put action away; to digest all knowledge that is known is a thing to be despised.'

[1] This personage has occurred before in Bk. VI, par. 7,—at the head of the most ancient sovereigns, who were in possession of the Tâo. His 'park' as a place for moral and intellectual inquiry is here mentioned;—so early was there a certain quickening of the mental faculties in China.

BOOK XXIII.

Part III. Section I.

Kăng-sang *Kh*û[1].

1. Among the disciples[2] of Lâo Tan there was a Kăng-sang *Kh*û, who had got a greater knowledge than the others of his doctrines, and took up his residence with it in the north at the hill of Wei-lêi[3]. His servants who were pretentious and knowing he sent away, and his concubines who were officious and kindly he kept at a distance; living (only) with those who were boorish and rude, and employing (only) the bustling and ill-mannered[4]. After three years there was great prosperity[5] in Wei-lêi, and the people said to one another, 'When Mr. Kăng-sang first came here, he alarmed us, and we thought him strange; our estimate of him after a short acquaintance was that he could not do us much good; but now that we have known him for years, we find him a more than ordinary benefit. Must he not be near being a sage? Why should you not

[1] See vol. xxxix, p. 153.

[2] The term in the text commonly denotes 'servants.' It would seem here simply to mean 'disciples.'

[3] Assigned variously. Probably the mount Yü in the 'Tribute of Yü,'—a hill in the present department of Tăng-*k*âu, Shan-tung.

[4] The same phraseology occurs in Bk. XI, par. 5; and also in the Shih, II, vi, 1, q. v.

[5] That is, abundant harvests. The 壤 of the common text should, probably, be 穰.

莊子

unite in blessing him as the representative of our departed (whom we worship), and raise an altar to him as we do to the spirit of the grain[1]?' Kăng-sang heard of it, kept his face indeed to the south[2], but was dissatisfied.

His disciples thought it strange in him, but he said to them, 'Why, my disciples, should you think this strange in me? When the airs of spring come forth, all vegetation grows; and, when the autumn arrives, all the previous fruits of the earth are matured. Do spring and autumn have these effects without any adequate cause? The processes of the Great Tâo have been in operation. I have heard that the Perfect man dwells idly in his apartment within its surrounding walls[3], and the people get wild and crazy, not knowing how they should repair to him. Now these small people of Wei-lêi in their opinionative way want to present their offerings to me, and place me among such men of ability and virtue. But am I a man to be set up as such a model? It is on this account that I am dissatisfied when I think of the words of Lâo Tan[4].'

2. His disciples said, 'Not so. In ditches eight cubits wide, or even twice as much, big fishes cannot turn their bodies about, but minnows and eels find them sufficient for them[5]; on hillocks six or

---

[1] I find it difficult to tell what these people wanted to make of *Kh*û, further than what he says himself immediately to his disciples. I cannot think that they wished to make him their ruler.

[2] This is the proper position for the sovereign in his court, and for the sage as the teacher of the world. *Kh*û accepts it in the latter capacity, but with dissatisfaction.

[3] Compare the Lî *K*î, Bk. XXXVIII, par. 10, et al.

[4] As if he were one with the Tâo.

[5] I do not see the appropriateness here of the 制 in the text.

seven cubits high, large beasts cannot conceal themselves, but foxes of evil omen find it a good place for them. And moreover, honour should be paid to the wise, offices given to the able, and preference shown to the good and the beneficial. From of old Yâo and Shun acted thus;—how much more may the people of Wei-lêi do so! O Master, let them have their way!'

Kăng-sang replied, 'Come nearer, my little children. If a beast that could hold a carriage in its mouth leave its hill by itself, it will not escape the danger that awaits it from the net; or if a fish that could swallow a boat be left dry by the flowing away of the water, then (even) the ants are able to trouble it. Thus it is that birds and beasts seek to be as high as possible, and fishes and turtles seek to lie as deep as possible. In the same way men who wish to preserve their bodies and lives keep their persons concealed, and they do so in the deepest retirement possible. And moreover, what was there in those sovereigns to entitle them to your laudatory mention? Their sophistical reasonings (resembled) the reckless breaking down of walls and enclosures and planting the wild rubus and wormwood in their place; or making the hair thin before they combed it; or counting the grains of rice before they cooked them[1]. They would do such things with careful discrimination; but what was there in them to benefit the world? If you raise the men of talent to office, you will create disorder; making the people strive with one

[1] All these condemnatory descriptions of Yâo and Shun are eminently Tâoistic, but so metaphorical that it is not easy to appreciate them.

莊子

another for promotion; if you employ men for their wisdom, the people will rob one another (of their reputation)[1]. These various things are insufficient to make the people good and honest. They are very eager for gain;—a son will kill his father, and a minister his ruler (for it). In broad daylight men will rob, and at midday break through walls. I tell you that the root of the greatest disorder was planted in the times of Yâo and Shun. The branches of it will remain for a thousand ages; and after a thousand ages men will be found eating one another[2].'

3. (On this) Nan-yung *Kh*û[3] abruptly sat right up and said, 'What method can an old man like me adopt to become (the Perfect man) that you have described?' Kăng-sang Ȝze said, 'Maintain your body complete; hold your life in close embrace; and do not let your thoughts keep working anxiously:—do this for three years, and you may become the man of whom I have spoken.' The other rejoined, 'Eyes are all of the same form, I do not know any difference between them:—yet the blind have no power of vision. Ears are all of the same form; I do not know any difference between them:—yet the deaf have no power of hearing. Minds are all of the same nature, I do not know any difference between them;—yet the mad cannot make the minds of other men their own. (My) personality is indeed like (yours), but things seem to separate

[1] Compare the Tâo Teh *K*ing, ch. 3.

[2] *Kh*û is in all this too violent.

[3] A disciple of Kăng-sang *Kh*û;—'a sincere seeker of the Tâo, very much to be pitied,' says Lin Hsî-*k*ung.

between us[1]. I wish to find in myself what there is in you, but I am not able to do so[1]. You have now said to me, "Maintain your body complete; hold your life in close embrace; and do not let your thoughts keep working anxiously." With all my efforts to learn your Way, (your words) reach only my ears.' Kăng-sang replied, 'I can say nothing more to you,' and then he added, 'Small flies cannot transform the bean caterpillar[2]; Yüeh[3] fowls cannot hatch the eggs of geese, but Lû fowls[3] can. It is not that the nature of these fowls is different; the ability in the one case and inability in the other arise from their different capacities as large and small. My ability is small and not sufficient to transform you. Why should you not go south and see Lâo-ʒze?'

4. Nan-yung *Kh*û hereupon took with him some rations, and after seven days and seven nights arrived at the abode of Lâo-ʒze, who said to him, 'Are you come from *Kh*û's?' 'I am,' was the reply. 'And why, Sir, have you come with such a multitude of attendants[4]?' Nan-yung was frightened, and turned his head round to look behind him. Lâo-ʒze said, 'Do you not understand my meaning?' The other held his head down and was ashamed, and then he lifted it up, and sighed, saying, 'I forgot at the moment what I should reply to your

[1] The 辟 in the former of these sentences is difficult. I take it in the sense of 譬, and read it phî.

[2] Compare the Shih, II, v, Ode 2, 3.

[3] I believe the fowls of Shan-tung are still larger than those of *K*ih-*k*iang or Fû-*k*ien.

[4] A good instance of Lâo's metaphorical style.

莊子

question, and in consequence I have lost what I wished to ask you.' 'What do you mean?' 'If I have not wisdom, men say that I am stupid[1], while if I have it, it occasions distress to myself. If I have not benevolence, then (I am charged) with doing hurt to others, while if I have it, I distress myself. If I have not righteousness, I (am charged with) injuring others, while if I have it, I distress myself. How can I escape from these dilemmas? These are the three perplexities that trouble me; and I wish at the suggestion of *Kh*û to ask you about them.' Lâo-ȝze replied, 'A little time ago, when I saw you and looked right into your eyes[2], I understood you, and now your words confirm the judgment which I formed. You look frightened and amazed. You have lost your parents, and are trying with a pole to find them at the (bottom of) the sea. You have gone astray; you are at your wit's end. You wish to recover your proper nature, and you know not what step to take first to find it. You are to be pitied!'

5. Nan-yung *Kh*û asked to be allowed to enter (the establishment), and have an apartment assigned to him[3]. (There) he sought to realise the qualities which he loved, and put away those which he hated. For ten days he afflicted himself, and then waited again on Lâo-ȝze, who said to him, 'You must purify yourself thoroughly! But from your symptoms of

[1] In the text 朱愚. The 朱 must be an erroneous addition, or probably it is a mistake for the speaker's name 趎.

[2] Literally, 'between the eye-brows and eye-lashes.'

[3] Thus we are as it were in the school of Lâo-ȝze, and can see how he deals with his pupils.

distress, and signs of impurity about you, I see there still seem to cling to you things that you dislike. When the fettering influences from without become numerous, and you try to seize them (you will find it a difficult task); the better plan is to bar your inner man against their entrance. And when the similar influences within get intertwined, it is a difficult task to grasp (and hold them in check); the better plan is to bar the outer door against their exit. Even a master of the Tâo and its characteristics will not be able to control these two influences together, and how much less can one who is only a student of the Tâo do so!' Nan-yung *Kh*û said, 'A certain villager got an illness, and when his neighbours asked about it, he was able to describe the malady, though it was one from which he had not suffered before. When I ask you about the Grand Tâo, it seems to me like drinking medicine which (only serves to) increase my illness. I should like to hear from you about the regular method of guarding the life;—that will be sufficient for me.' Lâo-ȝze replied, '(You ask me about) the regular method of guarding the life;—can you hold the One thing fast in your embrace? Can you keep from losing it? Can you know the lucky and the unlucky without having recourse to the tortoise-shell or the divining stalks? Can you rest (where you ought to rest)? Can you stop (when you have got enough)? Can you give over thinking of other men, and seek what you want in yourself (alone)? Can you flee (from the allurements of desire)? Can you maintain an entire simplicity? Can you become a little child? The child will cry all the day, without its throat becoming hoarse;—so perfect is the harmony (of

莊子

its physical constitution). It will keep its fingers closed all the day without relaxing their grasp;—such is the concentration of its powers. It will keep its eyes fixed all day, without their moving;—so is it unaffected by what is external to it. It walks it knows not whither; it rests where it is placed, it knows not why; it is calmly indifferent to things, and follows their current. This is the regular method of guarding the life[1].'

6. Nan-yung *Kh*û said, 'And are these all the characteristics of the Perfect man?' Lâo-ȝze replied, 'No. These are what we call the breaking up of the ice, and the dissolving of the cold. The Perfect man, along with other men, gets his food from the earth, and derives his joy from his Heaven (-conferred nature). But he does not like them allow himself to be troubled by the consideration of advantage or injury coming from men and things; he does not like them do strange things, or form plans, or enter on undertakings; he flees from the allurements of desire, and pursues his way with an entire simplicity. Such is the way by which he guards his life.' 'And is this what constitutes his perfection?' 'Not quite. I asked you whether you could become a little child. The little child moves unconscious of what it is doing, and walks unconscious of whither it is going. Its body is like the branch of a rotten tree, and its mind is like slaked lime[2]. Being such, misery does not come to it, nor happiness. It has

[1] In this long reply there are many evident recognitions of passages in the Tâo Teh *K*ing;—compare chapters 9, 10, 55, 58.

[2] See the description of Ȝze-*kh*î's Tâoistic trance at the beginning of the second Book.

neither misery nor happiness;—how can it suffer from the calamities incident to men[1]?'

7. [2] He whose mind[3] is thus grandly fixed emits a Heavenly light. In him who emits this heavenly light men see the (True) man. When a man has cultivated himself (up to this point), thenceforth he remains constant in himself. When he is thus constant in himself, (what is merely) the human element will leave him[4], but Heaven will help him. Those whom their human element has left we call the people of Heaven[4]. Those whom Heaven helps we call the Sons of Heaven. Those who would by learning attain to this[5] seek for what they cannot

[1] Nan-yung *Kh*û disappears here. His first master, Kăng-sang *Kh*û, disappeared in paragraph 4. The different way in which his name is written by Sze-mâ *Kh*ien is mentioned in the brief introductory note on p. 153. It should have been further stated there that in the Fourth Book of Lieh-ȝze (IV, 2^b–3^b) some account of him is given with his name as written by *Kh*ien. A great officer of *Kh*ăn is introduced as boasting of him that he was a sage, and, through his mastery of the principles of Lâo Tan, could hear with his eyes and see with his ears. Hereupon Khăng-ȝhang is brought to the court of the marquis of Lû to whom he says that the report of him which he had heard was false, adding that he could dispense with the use of his senses altogether, but could not alter their several functions. This being reported to Confucius, he simply laughs at it, but makes no remark.

[2] I suppose that from this to the end of the Book we have the sentiments of *K*wang-ȝze himself. Whether we consider them his, or the teachings of Lâo-ȝze to his visitor, they are among the depths of Tâoism, which I will not attempt to elucidate in the notes here.

[3] The character which I have translated 'mind' here is 宇, meaning 'the side walls of a house,' and metaphorically used for 'the breast,' as the house of the mind. Hû explains it by 心胸.

[4] He is emancipated from the human as contrary to the heavenly.

[5] The Tâo.

learn. Those who would by effort attain to this, attempt what effort can never effect. Those who aim by reasoning to reach it reason where reasoning has no place. To know to stop where they cannot arrive by means of knowledge is the highest attainment. Those who cannot do this will be destroyed on the lathe of Heaven.

8. Where things are all adjusted to maintain the body; where a provision against unforeseen dangers is kept up to maintain the life of the mind; where an inward reverence is cherished to be exhibited (in all intercourse) with others;—where this is done, and yet all evils arrive, they are from Heaven, and not from the men themselves. They will not be sufficient to confound the established (virtue of the character), or be admitted into the Tower of Intelligence. That Tower has its Guardian, who acts unconsciously, and whose care will not be effective, if there be any conscious purpose in it[1]. If one who has not this entire sincerity in himself make any outward demonstration, every such demonstration will be incorrect. The thing will enter into him, and not let go its hold. Then with every fresh demonstration there will be still greater failure. If he do what is not good in the light of open day, men will have the opportunity of punishing him; if he do it in darkness and secrecy, spirits[2] will inflict the punishment. Let a man understand this—his relation both to men and spirits, and then he will do what is good in the solitude of himself.

[1] This Guardian of the Mind or Tower of Intelligence is the Tâo.

[2] One of the rare introductions of spiritual agency in the early Tâoism.

He whose rule of life is in himself does not act for the sake of a name. He whose rule is outside himself has his will set on extensive acquisition. He who does not act for the sake of a name emits a light even in his ordinary conduct; he whose will is set on extensive acquisition is but a trafficker. Men see how he stands on tiptoe, while he thinks that he is overtopping others. Things enter (and take possession of) him who (tries to) make himself exhaustively (acquainted with them), while when one is indifferent to them, they do not find any lodgment in his person. And how can other men find such lodgment? But when one denies lodgment to men, there are none who feel attachment to him. In this condition he is cut off from other men. There is no weapon more deadly than the will[1];—even Mû-yê[2] was inferior to it. There is no robber greater than the Yin and Yang, from whom nothing can escape of all between heaven and earth. But it is not the Yin and Yang that play the robber;—it is the mind that causes them to do so.

9. The Tâo is to be found in the subdivisions (of its subject); (it is to be found) in that when complete, and when broken up. What I dislike in considering it as subdivided, is that the division leads to the multiplication of it;—and what I dislike in that multiplication' is that it leads to the (thought of) effort to secure it. Therefore when (a man)

[1] That is, the will, man's own human element, in opposition to the Heavenly element of the Tâo.

[2] One of the two famous swords made for Ho-lü, the king of Wû. See the account of their making in the seventy-fourth chapter of the 'History of the Various States;' very marvellous, but evidently, and acknowledged to be, fabulous.

莊子

comes forth (and is born), if he did not return (to his previous non-existence), we should have (only) seen his ghost; when he comes forth and gets this (return), he dies (as we say). He is extinguished, and yet has a real existence:—(this is another way of saying that in life we have) only man's ghost. By taking the material as an emblem of the immaterial do we arrive at a settlement of the case of man. He comes forth, but from no root; he re-enters, but by no aperture. He has a real existence, but it has nothing to do with place; he has continuance, but it has nothing to do with beginning or end. He has a real existence, but it has nothing to do with place, such is his relation to space; he has continuance, but it has nothing to do with beginning or end, such is his relation to time; he has life; he has death; he comes forth; he enters; but we do not see his form;—all this is what is called the door of Heaven. The door of Heaven is Non-Existence. All things come from non-existence. The (first) existences could not bring themselves into existence; they must have come from non-existence. And non-existence is just the same as non-existing. Herein is the secret of the sages.

10. Among the ancients there were those whose knowledge reached the extreme point. And what was that point? There were some who thought that in the beginning there was nothing. This was the extreme point, the completest reach of their knowledge, to which nothing could be added. Again, there were those who supposed that (in the beginning) there were existences, proceeding to consider life to be a (gradual) perishing, and death a returning (to the original state). And there they stopped,

making, (however), a distinction between life and death. Once again there were those who said, 'In the beginning there was nothing; by and by there was life; and then in a little time life was succeeded by death. We hold that non-existence was the head, life the body, and death the os coccygis. But of those who acknowledge that existence and non-existence, death and life, are all under the One Keeper, we are the friends.' Though those who maintained these three views were different, they were so as the different branches of the same ruling Family (of *Kh*û)[1],—the *K*âos and the *K*ings, bearing the surname of the lord whom they honoured as the author of their branch, and the *K*iâs named from their appanage;—(all one, yet seeming) not to be one.

The possession of life is like the soot that collects under a boiler. When that is differently distributed, the life is spoken of as different. But to say that life is different in different lives, and better in one than in another, is an improper mode of speech. And yet there may be something here which we do not know. (As for instance), at the lâ sacrifice the paunch and the divided hoofs may be set forth on separate dishes, but they should not be considered as parts of different victims; (and again), when one is inspecting a house, he goes over it all, even the adytum for the shrines of the temple, and visits also the most private apartments; doing this, and setting a different estimate on the different parts.

Let me try and speak of this method of appor-

[1] Both Lâo and *K*wang belonged to *Kh*û, and this illustration was natural to them.

莊子

tioning one's approval:—life is the fundamental consideration in it; knowledge is the instructor. From this they multiply their approvals and disapprovals, determining what is merely nominal and what is real. They go on to conclude that to themselves must the appeal be made in everything, and to try to make others adopt them as their model; prepared even to die to make good their views on every point. In this way they consider being employed in office as a mark of wisdom, and not being so employed as a mark of stupidity, success as entitling to fame, and the want of it as disgraceful. The men of the present day who follow this differentiating method are like the cicada and the little dove[1];—there is no difference between them.

11. When one treads on the foot of another in the market-place, he apologises on the ground of the bustle. If an elder tread on his younger brother, he proceeds to comfort him; if a parent tread on a child, he says and does nothing. Hence it is said, 'The greatest politeness is to show no special respect to others; the greatest righteousness is to take no account of things; the greatest wisdom is to lay no plans; the greatest benevolence is to make no demonstration of affection; the greatest good faith is to give no pledge of sincerity.'

Repress the impulses of the will; unravel the errors of the mind; put away the entanglements to virtue; and clear away all that obstructs the free course of the Tâo. Honours and riches, distinctions and austerity, fame and profit; these six things produce the impulses of the will. Personal appearance

[1] See in Bk. I, par. 2.

and deportment, the desire of beauty and subtle reasonings, excitement of the breath and cherished thoughts; these six things produce errors of the mind. Hatred and longings, joy and anger, grief and delight; these six things are the entanglements to virtue. Refusals and approachments, receiving and giving, knowledge and ability; these six things obstruct the course of the Tâo. When these four conditions, with the six causes of each, do not agitate the breast, the mind is correct. Being correct, it is still; being still, it is pellucid; being pellucid, it is free from pre-occupation; being free from pre-occupation, it is in the state of inaction, in which it accomplishes everything.

The Tâo is the object of reverence to all the virtues. Life is what gives opportunity for the display of the virtues. The nature is the substantive character of the life. The movement of the nature is called action. When action becomes hypocritical, we say that it has lost (its proper attribute).

The wise communicate with what is external to them and are always laying plans. This is what with all their wisdom they are not aware of;—they look at things askance. When the action (of the nature) is from external constraint, we have what is called virtue; when it is all one's own, we have what is called government. These two names seem to be opposite to each other, but in reality they are in mutual accord.

12. Î[1] was skilful in hitting the minutest mark, but stupid in wishing men to go on praising him without end. The sage is skilful Heavenwards, but stupid

[1] See on V, par. 2.

莊子

manwards. It is only the complete man who can be both skilful Heavenwards and good manwards.

Only an insect can play the insect, only an insect show the insect nature. Even the complete man hates the attempt to exemplify the nature of Heaven. He hates the manner in which men do so, and how much more would he hate the doing so by himself before men!

When a bird came in the way of Î, he was sure to obtain it;—such was his mastery with his bow. If all the world were to be made a cage, birds would have nowhere to escape to. Thus it was that Thang caged Î Yin by making him his cook[1], and that duke Mû of *Kh*in caged Pâi-lî Hsî by giving the skins of five rams for him[2]. But if you try to cage men by anything but what they like, you will never succeed.

A man, one of whose feet has been cut off, discards ornamental (clothes);—his outward appearance will not admit of admiration. A criminal under sentence of death will ascend to any height without fear;—he has ceased to think of life or death.

When one persists in not reciprocating the gifts (of friendship), he forgets all others. Having forgotten all others, he may be considered as a Heaven-like man. Therefore when respect is shown to a man, and it awakens in him no joy, and when contempt awakens no anger, it is only one who shares in the Heaven-like harmony that can be thus. When he would display anger and yet is not angry, the anger comes out in that repression of it. When he would put forth action, and yet does not do so,

[1] See Mencius V, i, 7. [2] Mencius V, i, 9.

the action is in that not-acting. Desiring to be quiescent, he must pacify all his emotions; desiring to be spirit-like, he must act in conformity with his mind. When action is required of him, he wishes that it may be right; and it then is under an inevitable constraint. Those who act according to that inevitable constraint pursue the way of the sage.

莊子

BOOK XXIV.

PART III. SECTION II.

Hsü Wû-kwei[1].

1. Hsü Wû-kwei having obtained through Nü Shang[2] an introduction to the marquis Wû of Wei[3], the marquis, speaking to him with kindly sympathy[4], said, 'You are ill, Sir; you have suffered from your hard and laborious toils[4] in the forests, and still you have been willing to come and see poor me[5].' Hsü Wû-kwei replied, 'It is I who have to comfort your lordship; what occasion have you to comfort me? If your lordship go on to fill up the measure of your sensual desires, and to prolong your likes and dislikes, then the condition of your mental nature will be diseased, and if you discourage and repress those desires, and deny your likings and dislikings, that will be an affliction to your ears and eyes

[1] See vol. xxxix, pp. 153, 154.

[2] A favourite and minister of the marquis Wû.

[3] This was the second marquis of Wei, one of the three principalities into which the great state of Ȝin had been broken up, and which he ruled as the marquis *Kî* for sixteen years, B.C. 386–371. His son usurped the title of king, and was the 'king Hui of Liang,' whom Mencius had interviews with. Wû, or 'martial,' was *Kî*'s honorary, posthumous epithet.

[4] The character (勞) which I thus translate, has two tones, the second and fourth. Here and elsewhere in this paragraph and the next, it is with one exception in the fourth tone, meaning 'to comfort or reward for toils endured.' The one exception is its next occurrence,—'hard and laborious toils.'

[5] The appropriate and humble designation of himself by the ruler of a state.

(deprived of their accustomed pleasures);—it is for me to comfort your lordship, what occasion have you to comfort me?' The marquis looked contemptuous, and made no reply.

After a little time, Hsü Wû-kwei said, 'Let me tell your lordship something:—I look at dogs and judge of them by their appearance[1]. One of the lowest quality seizes his food, satiates himself, and stops;—he has the attributes of a fox. One of a medium quality seems to be looking at the sun. One of the highest quality seems to have forgotten the one thing,—himself. But I judge still better of horses than I do of dogs. When I do so, I find that one goes straightforward, as if following a line; that another turns off, so as to describe a hook; that a third describes a square as if following the measure so called; and that a fourth describes a circle as exactly as a compass would make it. These are all horses of a state; but they are not equal to a horse of the kingdom. His qualities are complete. Now he looks anxious; now to be losing the way; now to be forgetting himself. Such a horse prances along, or rushes on, spurning the dust and not knowing where he is.' The marquis was greatly pleased and laughed.

When Hsü Wû-kwei came out, Nü Shang said to him, 'How was it, Sir, that you by your counsels produced such an effect on our ruler? In my counsellings of him, now indirectly, taking my subjects from the Books of Poetry, History, Rites, and Music; now directly, from the Metal Tablets[2], and the six Bow-cases[2], all calculated for the service (of the

[1] Literally, 'I physiognomise dogs.'

[2] The names of two Books, or Collections of Tablets, the former

state), and to be of great benefit;—in these counsellings, repeated times without number, I have never seen the ruler show his teeth in a smile:—by what counsels have you made him so pleased to-day?' Hsü Wû-kwei replied, 'I only told him how I judged of dogs and horses by looking at their appearance.' 'So?' said Nü Shang, and the other rejoined, 'Have you not heard of the wanderer[1] from Yüeh? when he had been gone from the state several days, he was glad when he saw any one whom he had seen in it; when he had been gone a month, he was glad when he saw any one whom he had known in it; and when he had been gone a round year, he was glad when he saw any one who looked like a native of it. The longer he was gone, the more longingly did he think of the people;—was it not so? The men who withdraw to empty valleys, where the hellebore bushes stop up the little paths made by the weasels, as they push their way or stand amid the waste, are glad when they seem to hear the sounds of human footsteps; and how much more would they be so, if it were their brothers and relatives talking and laughing by their side! How long it is since the words of a True[2] man were heard as he talked and laughed by our ruler's side!'

2. At (another) interview of Hsü Wû-kwei with the marquis Wû, the latter said, 'You, Sir, have been dwelling in the forests for a long time, living

containing Registers of the Population, the latter treating of military subjects.

[1] Kwo Hsiang makes this 'a banished criminal.' This is not necessary.

[2] Wû-kwei then had a high opinion of his own attainments in Tâoism, and a low opinion of Nü Shang and the other courtiers.

on acorns and chestnuts, and satiating yourself with onions and chives, without thinking of poor me. Now (that you are here), is it because you are old? or because you wish to try again the taste of wine and meat? or because (you wish that) I may enjoy the happiness derived from the spirits of the altars of the Land and Grain?' Hsü Wû-kwei replied, 'I was born in a poor and mean condition, and have never presumed to drink of your lordship's wine, or eat of your meat. My object in coming was to comfort your lordship under your troubles.' 'What? comfort me under my troubles?' 'Yes, to comfort both your lordship's spirit and body.' The marquis said, 'What do you mean?' His visitor replied, 'Heaven and Earth have one and the same purpose in the production (of all men). However high one man be exalted, he should not think that he is favourably dealt with; and however low may be the position of another, he should not think that he is unfavourably dealt with. You are indeed the one and only lord of the 10,000 chariots (of your state), but you use your dignity to embitter (the lives of) all the people, and to pamper your ears, eyes, nose, and mouth. But your spirit does not acquiesce in this. The spirit (of man) loves to be in harmony with others and hates selfish indulgence[1]. This selfish indulgence is a disease, and therefore I would comfort you under it. How is it that your lordship more than others brings this disease on yourself?' The marquis said, 'I have wished to see you, Sir, for a long time. I want to love my people, and by the exercise of righteous-

[1] Wû-kwei had a high idea of the constitution of human nature.

莊子

ness to make an end of war;—will that be sufficient?' Hsü Wû-kwei replied, 'By no means. To love the people is the first step to injure them[1]. By the exercise of righteousness to make an end of war is the root from which war is produced[1]. If your lordship try to accomplish your object in this way, you are not likely to succeed. All attempts to accomplish what we think good (with an ulterior end) is a bad contrivance. Although your lordship practise benevolence and righteousness (as you propose), it will be no better than hypocrisy. You may indeed assume the (outward) form, but successful accomplishment will lead to (inward) contention, and the change thence arising will produce outward fighting. Your lordship also must not mass files of soldiers in the passages of your galleries and towers, nor have footmen and horsemen in the apartments about your altars[2]. Do not let thoughts contrary to your success lie hidden in your mind; do not think of conquering men by artifice, or by (skilful) plans, or by fighting. If I kill the officers and people of another state, and annex its territory, to satisfy my selfish desires, while in my spirit I do not know whether the fighting be good, where is the victory that I gain? Your lordship's best plan is to abandon (your purpose). If you will cultivate in your breast the sincere purpose (to love the people), and so respond to the feeling of Heaven and Earth, and not (further) vex yourself, then your people will already have escaped death;—what

[1] Tâoistic teaching, but questionable.

[2] We need more information about the customs of the feudal princes fully to understand the language of this sentence.

occasion will your lordship have to make an end of war?'

3. Hwang-Tî was going to see Tâ-kwei[1] at the hill of *K*ü-ȝhze. Fang Ming was acting as charioteer, and *Kh*ang Yü was occupying the third place in the carriage. *K*ang *Z*o and Hsî Phăng went before the horses; and Khwăn Hwun and Kû *Kh*î followed the carriage. When they arrived at the wild of Hsiang-*kh*ăng, the seven sages were all perplexed, and could find no place at which to ask the way. Just then they met with a boy tending some horses, and asked the way of him. 'Do you know,' they said, 'the hill of *K*ü-ȝhze?' and he replied that he did. He also said that he knew where Tâ-kwei was living. 'A strange boy is this!' said Hwang-Tî. 'He not only knows the hill of *K*ü-ȝhze, but he also knows where Tâ-kwei is living. Let me ask him about the government of mankind.' The boy said, 'The administration of the kingdom is like this (which I am doing);—what difficulty should there be in it? When I was young, I enjoyed myself roaming over all within the six confines of the world of space, and then I began to suffer from indistinct sight. A wise elder taught me, saying, "Ride in the chariot of the

[1] Tâ (or Thâi)-kwei (or wei) appears here as the name of a person. It cannot be the name of a hill, as it is said by some to be. The whole paragraph is parabolic or allegorical; and Tâ-kwei is probably a personification of the Great Tâo itself, though no meaning of the character kwei can be adduced to justify this interpretation. The horseherd boy is further supposed to be a personification of the 'Great Simplicity,' which is characteristic of the Tâo, the spontaneity of it, unvexed by the wisdom of man. The lesson of the paragraph is that taught in the eleventh Book, and many other places.

莊子

sun, and roam in the wild of Hsiang-*Kh*ăng." Now the trouble in my eyes is a little better, and I am again enjoying myself roaming outside the six confines of the world of space. As to the government of the kingdom, it is like this (which I am doing);—what difficulty should there be in it?' Hwang-Tî said, 'The administration of the world is indeed not your business, my son; nevertheless, I beg to ask you about it.' The little lad declined to answer, but on Hwang-Tî putting the question again, he said, 'In what does the governor of the kingdom differ from him who has the tending of horses, and who has only to put away whatever in him would injure the horses?'

Hwang-Tî bowed to him twice with his head to the ground, called him his 'Heavenly Master[1],' and withdrew.

4. If officers of wisdom do not see the changes which their anxious thinking has suggested, they have no joy; if debaters are not able to set forth their views in orderly style, they have no joy; if critical examiners find no subjects on which to exercise their powers of vituperation, they have no joy:—they are all hampered by external restrictions.

Those who try to attract the attention of their age (wish to) rise at court; those who try to win the regard of the people[2] count holding office a glory; those who possess muscular strength boast of doing what is difficult; those who are bold and daring exert themselves in times of calamity; those who are able

[1] This is the title borne to the present day by the chief or pope of Tâoism, the representative of *K*ang Tâo-ling of our first century.

[2] Taking the initial *k*ung in the third tone. If we take it in the first tone, the meaning is different.

swordmen and spearmen delight in fighting; those whose powers are decayed seek to rest in the name (they have gained); those who are skilled in the laws seek to enlarge the scope of government; those who are proficient in ceremonies and music pay careful attention to their deportment; and those who profess benevolence and righteousness value opportunities (for displaying them).

The husbandmen who do not keep their fields well weeded are not equal to their business, nor are traders who do not thrive in the markets. When the common people have their appropriate employment morning and evening, they stimulate one another to diligence; the mechanics who are masters of their implements feel strong for their work. If their wealth does not increase, the greedy are distressed; if their power and influence is not growing, the ambitious are sad.

Such creatures of circumstance and things delight in changes, and if they meet with a time when they can show what they can do, they cannot keep themselves from taking advantage of it. They all pursue their own way like (the seasons of) the year, and do not change as things do. They give the reins to their bodies and natures, and allow themselves to sink beneath (the pressure of) things, and all their lifetime do not come back (to their proper selves):—is it not sad[1]?

5. *K*wang-ȝze said, 'An archer, without taking aim beforehand, yet may hit the mark. If we say that he is a good archer, and that all the world may

[1] All the parties in this paragraph disallow the great principle of Tâoism, which does everything by doing nothing.

莊子

be Î[1], is this allowable?' Hui-ȝze replied, 'It is.' *K*wang-ȝze continued, 'All men do not agree in counting the same thing to be right, but every one maintains his own view to be right; (if we say) that all men may be Yâos, is this allowable?' Hui-ȝze (again) replied, 'It is;' and *K*wang-ȝze went on, 'Very well; there are the literati, the followers of Mo (Tî), of Yang (*K*û), and of Ping[2];—making four (different schools). Including yourself, Master, there are five. Which of your views is really right? Or will you take the position of Lû *K*ü[3]? One of his disciples said to him, "Master, I have got hold of your method. I can in winter heat the furnace under my tripod, and in summer can produce ice." Lû *K*ü said, "That is only with the Yang element to call out the same, and with the Yin to call out the yin;—that is not my method. I will show you what my method is." On this he tuned two citherns, placing one of them in the hall, and the other in one of the inner apartments. Striking the note Kung[4] in the one, the same note vibrated in the other, and so it was with the note *K*io[4]; the two instruments being tuned in the same way. But if he had differently tuned them on other strings different

[1] The famous archer of the Hsiâ dynasty, in the twenty-second century B.C.

[2] The name of Kung-sun Lung, the Lung Li-*kh*ăn of Bk. XXI, par. 1.

[3] Only mentioned here. The statement of his disciple and his remark on it are equally obscure, though the latter is partially illustrated from the twenty-third, twenty-fourth, and other hexagrams of the Yih *K*ing.

[4] The sounds of the first and third notes of the Chinese musical scale, corresponding to our A and E. I know too little of music myself to pronounce further on Lû *K*ü's illustration.

from the normal arrangement of the five notes, the five-and-twenty strings would all have vibrated, without any difference of their notes, the note to which he had tuned them ruling and guiding all the others. Is your maintaining your view to be right just like this?'

Hui-ȝze replied, 'Here now are the literati, and the followers of Mo, Yang, and Ping. Suppose that they have come to dispute with me. They put forth their conflicting statements; they try vociferously to put me down; but none of them have ever proved me wrong:—what do you say to this?' *K*wang-ȝze said, 'There was a man of *Kh*î who cast away his son in Sung to be a gate-keeper there, and thinking nothing of the mutilation he would incur; the same man, to secure one of his sacrificial vessels or bells, would have it strapped and secured, while to find his son who was lost, he would not go out of the territory of his own state:—so forgetful was he of the relative importance of things. If a man of *Kh*û, going to another state as a lame gate-keeper, at midnight, at a time when no one was nigh, were to fight with his boatman, he would not be able to reach the shore, and he would have done what he could to provoke the boatman's animosity[1].'

6. As *K*wang-ȝze was accompanying a funeral, when passing by the grave of Hui-ȝze[2], he looked

[1] The illustrations in this last member of the paragraph are also obscure. Lin Hsî-*k*ung says that all the old explanations of them are defective; his own explanation has failed to make itself clear to me.

[2] The expression in the last sentence of the paragraph, 'the Master,' makes it certain that this was the grave of *K*wang-ȝze's friend with whom he had had so many conversations and arguments.

莊子

round, and said to his attendants, 'On the top of the nose of that man of Ying[1] there is a (little) bit of mud like a fly's wing.' He sent for the artisan Shih to cut it away. Shih whirled his axe so as to produce a wind, which immediately carried off the mud entirely, leaving the nose uninjured, and the (statue of) the man of Ying[1] standing undisturbed. The ruler Yüan of Sung[2] heard of the feat, called the artisan Shih, and said to him, 'Try and do the same thing on me.' The artisan said, 'Your servant has been able to trim things in that way, but the material on which I have worked has been dead for a long time.' *K*wang-ȝze said, 'Since the death of the Master, I have had no material to work upon. I have had no one with whom to talk.'

7. Kwan *K*ung being ill, duke Hwan went to ask for him, and said, 'Your illness, father *K*ung, is very severe; should you not speak out your mind to me? Should this prove the great illness, to whom will it be best for me to entrust my State?' Kwan *K*ung said, 'To whom does your grace wish to entrust it?' 'To Pâo Shû-yâ[3],' was the reply. 'He will not do. He is an admirable officer, pure and incorruptible, but with others who are not like himself he will not associate. And when he once hears

[1] Ying was the capital of *Kh*û. I have seen in China about the graves of wealthy and distinguished men many life-sized statues of men somehow connected with them.

[2] Yüan is called the 'ruler' of Sung. That duchy was by this time a mere dependency of *Kh*î. The sacrifices of its old ruling House were finally extinguished by *Kh*î in B. C. 206.

[3] Pâo Shû-yâ had been the life-long friend of the dying premier, and to him in the first place had been owing the elevation of Hwan to the marquisate.

of another man's faults, he never forgets them. If you employ him to administer the state, above, he will take the leading of your Grace, and, below, he will come into collision with the people;—in no long time you will be holding him as an offender.' The duke said, 'Who, then, is the man?' The reply was, 'If I must speak, there is Hsî Phăng[1];—he will do. He is a man who forgets his own high position, and against whom those below him will not revolt. He is ashamed that he is not equal to Hwang-Tî, and pities those who are not equal to himself. Him who imparts of his virtue to others we call a sage; him who imparts of his wealth to others we call a man of worth. He who by his worth would preside over others, never succeeds in winning them; he who with his worth condescends to others, never but succeeds in winning them. Hsî Phăng has not been (much) heard of in the state; he has not been (much) distinguished in his own clan. But as I must speak, he is the man for you.'

8. The king of Wû, floating about on the *K*iang, (landed and) ascended the Hill of monkeys, which all, when they saw him, scampered off in terror, and hid themselves among the thick hazels. There was one, however, which, in an unconcerned way, swung about on the branches, displaying its cleverness to the king, who thereon discharged an arrow at it. With a nimble motion it caught the swift arrow, and the king ordered his attendants to hurry forward and shoot it; and thus the monkey was seized and killed. The king then, looking round, said to his friend Yen

[1] For a long time a great officer of *Kh*î, but he died in the same year as Kwan *K*ung himself.

莊子

Pû-î[1], 'This monkey made a display of its artfulness, and trusted in its agility, to show me its arrogance;—this it was which brought it to this fate. Take warning from it. Ah! do not by your looks give yourself haughty airs!' Yen Pû-î[1], when he returned home, put himself under the teaching of Tung Wû[1], to root up[2] his pride. He put away what he delighted in and abjured distinction. In three years the people of the kingdom spoke of him with admiration.

9. Nan-po Ȥze-*kh*î[3] was seated, leaning forward on his stool, and sighing gently as he looked up to heaven. (Just then) Yen *Kh*ăng-ȥze[3] came in, and said, when he saw him, 'Master, you surpass all others. Is it right to make your body thus like a mass of withered bones, and your mind like so much slaked lime?' The other said, 'I formerly lived in a grotto on a hill. At that time Thien Ho[4] once came to see me, and all the multitudes of *Kh*î congratulated him thrice (on his having found the proper man). I must first have shown myself, and so it was that he knew me; I must first have been selling (what I had), and so it was that he came to buy. If I had not shown what I possessed, how should he have known it; if I had not been selling (myself), how should he have come to buy me? I pity

[1] We know these names only from their occurrence here. Tung Wû must have been a professor of Tâoism.

[2] The text here is 助, 'to help;' but it is explained as = 鋤, 'a hoe.' The Khang-hsî dictionary does not give this meaning of the character, but we find it in that of Yen Yüan.

[3] See the first paragraph of Bk. II.

[4] 田禾 must be the 田和 of Sze-mâ *Kh*ien, who became marquis of *Kh*î in B.C. 389.

the men who lose themselves[1]; I also pity the men who pity others (for not being known); and I also pity the men who pity the men who pity those that pity others. But since then the time is long gone by; (and so I am in the state in which you have found me)[2].

10. *K*ung-nî, having gone to *Kh*û, the king ordered wine to be presented to him. Sun Shû-âo[3] stood, holding the goblet in his hand. Î-liâo of Shih-nan[3], having received (a cup), poured its contents out as a sacrificial libation, and said, 'The men of old, on such an occasion as this, made some speech.' *K*ung-nî said, 'I have heard of speech without words; but I have never spoken it; I will do so now. Î-liâo of Shih-nan kept (quietly) handling his little spheres,

[1] In seeking for worldly honours.

[2] That is, I have abjured all desire for worldly honour, and desire attainment in the Tâo alone.

[3] See Mencius VI, ii, 15. Sun Shû-âo was chief minister to king *Kh*wang who died in B.C. 591, and died, probably, before Confucius was born, and Î-liâo (p. 28, n. 3) appears in public life only after the death of the sage. The three men could not have appeared together at any time. This account of their doing so was devised by our author as a peg on which to hang his own lessons in the rest of the paragraph. The two historical events referred to I have found it difficult to discover. They are instances of doing nothing, and yet thereby accomplishing what is very great. The action of Î-liâo in 'quietly handling his balls' recalls my seeing the same thing done by a gentleman at *Kh*ü-fâu, the city of Confucius, in 1873. Being left there with a companion, and not knowing how to get to the Grand Canal, many gentlemen came to advise with us how we should proceed. Among them was one who, while tendering his advice, kept rolling about two brass balls in one palm with the fingers of the other hand. When I asked the meaning of his action, I was told, 'To show how he is at his ease and master of the situation.' I mention the circumstance because I have nowhere found the phrase in the text adequately explained.

and the difficulties between the two Houses were resolved; Sun Shû-âo slept undisturbed on his couch, with his (dancer's) feather in his hand, and the men of Ying enrolled themselves for the war. I wish I had a beak three cubits long[1].'

In the case of those two (ministers) we have what is called 'The Way that cannot be trodden[2];' in (the case of *K*ung-nî) we have what is called 'the Argument without words[2].' Therefore when all attributes are comprehended in the unity of the Tâo, and speech stops at the point to which knowledge does not reach, the conduct is complete. But where there is (not)[3] the unity of the Tâo, the attributes cannot (always) be the same, and that which is beyond the reach of knowledge cannot be exhibited by any reasoning. There may be as many names as those employed by the Literati and the Mohists, but (the result is) evil. Thus when the sea does not reject the streams that flow into it in their eastward course, we have the perfection of greatness. The sage embraces in his regard both Heaven and Earth; his beneficent influence extends to all under the sky; and we do not know from whom it comes. Therefore though when living one may have no rank, and when dead no honorary epithet; though the reality (of what he is) may not be acknowledged and his name not established; we have in him what is called 'The Great Man.'

A dog is not reckoned good because it barks well; and a man is not reckoned wise because he speaks

[1] This strange wish concludes the speech of Confucius. What follows is from *K*wang-ȝze.

[2] Compare the opening chapters of the Tâo Teh *K*ing.

[3] The Tâo is greater than any and all of its attributes.

skilfully;—how much less can he be deemed Great! If one thinks he is Great, he is not fit to be accounted Great;—how much less is he so from the practice of the attributes (of the Tâo)[1]! Now none are so grandly complete as Heaven and Earth; but do they seek for anything to make them so grandly complete? He who knows this grand completion does not seek for it; he loses nothing and abandons nothing; he does not change himself from regard to (external) things; he turns in on himself, and finds there an inexhaustible store; he follows antiquity and does not feel about (for its lessons);—such is the perfect sincerity of the Great Man.

11. Ȝze-*kh*î[2] had eight sons. Having arranged them before him, he called *K*iû-fang Yăn[3], and said to him, 'Look at the physiognomy of my sons for me;—which will be the fortunate one?' Yăn said, 'Khwăn is the fortunate one.' Ȝze-*kh*î looked startled, and joyfully said, 'In what way?' Yăn replied, 'Khwăn will share the meals of the ruler of a state to the end of his life.' The father looked uneasy, burst into tears, and said, 'What has my son done that he should come to such a fate?' Yăn replied, 'When one shares the meals of the ruler of a state, blessings reach to all within the three branches of his kindred[4], and how much more to his father and mother! But you, Master, weep when you hear this;—you oppose (the idea of) such happiness. It is the good fortune of your son, and

1 See note 3 on previous page.

2 This can hardly be any other but Nan-kwo Ȝze-*kh*î.

3 A famous physiognomist; some say, of horses. Hwâi-nan Ȝze calls him *K*iû-fang Kâo (皐).

4 See Mayers's Manual, p. 303.

you count it his misfortune.' Ȝze-*kh*î said, 'O Yăn, what sufficient ground have you for knowing that this will be Khwăn's good fortune? (The fortune) that is summed up in wine and flesh affects only the nose and the mouth, but you are not able to know how it will come about. I have never been a shepherd, and yet a ewe lambed in the south-west corner of my house. I have never been fond of hunting, and yet a quail hatched her young in the south-east corner. If these were not prodigies, what can be accounted such? Where I wish to occupy my mind with my son is in (the wide sphere of) heaven and earth; I wish to seek his enjoyment and mine in (the idea of) Heaven, and our support from the Earth. I do not mix myself up with him in the affairs (of the world); nor in forming plans (for his advantage); nor in the practice of what is strange. I pursue with him the perfect virtue of Heaven and Earth, and do not allow ourselves to be troubled by outward things. I seek to be with him in a state of undisturbed indifference, and not to practise what affairs might indicate as likely to be advantageous. And now there is to come to us this vulgar recompense. Whenever there is a strange realisation, there must have been strange conduct. Danger threatens;—not through any sin of me or of my son, but as brought about, I apprehend, by Heaven. It is this which makes me weep!'

Not long after this, Ȝze-*kh*î sent off Khwăn to go to Yen[1], when he was made prisoner by some robbers on the way. It would have been difficult to sell him if he were whole and entire, and they thought

[1] The state so called.

their easiest plan was to cut off (one of his) feet first. They did so, and sold him in *Kh*î, where he became Inspector of roads for a Mr. *Kh*ü[1]. Nevertheless he had flesh to eat till he died.

12. Nieh *Kh*üeh met Hsü Yû (on the way), and said to him, 'Where, Sir, are you going to?' 'I am fleeing from Yâo,' was the reply. 'What do you mean?' 'Yâo has become so bent on his benevolence that I am afraid the world will laugh at him, and that in future ages men will be found eating one another[2]. Now the people are collected together without difficulty. Love them, and they respond with affection; benefit them, and they come to you; praise them, and they are stimulated (to please you); make them to experience what they dislike, and they disperse. When the loving and benefiting proceed from benevolence and righteousness, those who forget the benevolence and righteousness, and those who make a profit of them, are the many. In this way the practice of benevolence and righteousness comes to be without sincerity and is like a borrowing of the instruments with which men catch birds[3]. In all this the one man's seeking to benefit the world by his decisions and enactments (of such a nature) is as if he were to cut through (the nature of all) by one operation;—Yâo knows how wise and superior men can benefit the world, but he does not

[1] One expert supposes the text here to mean 'duke *Kh*ü;' but there was no such duke of *Kh*î. The best explanation seems to be that *Kh*ü was a rich gentleman, inspector of the roads of *Kh*î, or of the streets of its capital, who bought Khwăn to take his duties for him.

[2] Compare in Bk. XXIII, par. 2.

[3] A scheming for one's own advantage.

also know how they injure it. It is only those who stand outside such men that know this[1].'

There are the pliable and weak; the easy and hasty; the grasping and crooked. Those who are called the pliable and weak learn the words of some one master, to which they freely yield their assent, being secretly pleased with themselves, and thinking that their knowledge is sufficient, while they do not know that they have not yet begun (to understand) a single thing. It is this which makes them so pliable and weak. The easy and hasty are like lice on a pig. The lice select a place where the bristles are more wide apart, and look on it as a great palace or a large park. The slits between the toes, the overlappings of its skin, about its nipples and its thighs,—all these seem to them safe apartments and advantageous places;—they do not know that the butcher one morning, swinging about his arms, will spread the grass, and kindle the fire, so that they and the pig will be roasted together. So do they appear and disappear with the place where they harboured:—this is why they are called the easy and hasty.

Of the grasping and crooked we have an example in Shun. Mutton has no craving for ants, but ants have a craving for mutton, for it is rank. There was a rankness about the conduct of Shun, and the people were pleased with him. Hence when he thrice changed his residence, every one of them became a capital city[2]. When he came to the wild

[1] I suppose that the words of Hsü Yû stop with this sentence, and that from this to the end of the paragraph we have the sentiments of *K*wang-ȝze himself. The style is his,—graphic but sometimes coarse.

[2] See note on Mencius V, i, 2, 3.

of Tăng[1], he had 100,000 families about him. Yâo having heard of the virtue and ability of Shun, appointed him to a new and uncultivated territory, saying, 'I look forward to the benefit of his coming here.' When Shun was appointed to this new territory, his years were advanced, and his intelligence was decayed;—and yet he could not find a place of rest or a home. This is an example of being grasping and wayward.

Therefore (in opposition to such) the spirit-like man dislikes the flocking of the multitudes to him. When the multitudes come, they do not agree; and when they do not agree, no benefit results from their coming. Hence there are none whom he brings very near to himself, and none whom he keeps at a great distance. He keeps his virtue in close embrace, and warmly nourishes (the spirit of) harmony, so as to be in accordance with all men. This is called the True man[2]. Even the knowledge of the ant he puts away; his plans are simply those of the fishes[3]; even the notions of the sheep he discards. His seeing is simply that of the eye; his hearing that of the ear; his mind is governed by its general exercises. Being such, his course is straight and level as if marked out by a line, and its every change is in accordance (with the circumstances of the case).

13. The True men of old waited for the issues of events as the arrangements of Heaven, and did not by their human efforts try to take the place of Heaven. The True men of old (now) looked on

---

[1] Situation unknown.

[2] The spirit-like man and the true man are the same.

[3] Fishes forget everything in the water.

success as life and on failure as death; and (now) on success as death and on failure as life. The operation of medicines will illustrate this:—there are monk's-bane, the *k*ieh-kăng, the tribulus fruit, and china-root; each of these has the time and case for which it is supremely suitable; and all such plants and their suitabilities cannot be mentioned particularly. Kâu-*k*ien[1] took his station on (the hill of) Kwâi-*kh*î with 3,000 men with their buff-coats and shields:—(his minister) *K*ung knew how the ruined (Yüeh) might still be preserved, but the same man did not know the sad fate in store for himself[1]. Hence it is said, 'The eye of the owl has its proper fitness; the leg of the crane has its proper limit, and to cut off any of it would distress (the bird).' Hence (also) it is (further) said, 'When the wind passes over it, the volume of the river is diminished, and so it is when the sun passes over it. But let the wind and sun keep a watch together on the river, and it will not begin to feel that they are doing it any injury;—it relies on its springs and flows on.' Thus, water does its part to the ground with undeviating exactness; and so does the shadow to the substance; and one thing to another. Therefore there is danger from the power of vision in the eyes, of hearing in the ears, and of the inordinate thinking of the mind; yea, there is danger from the exercise of every power of which man's constitution is the depository.

---

[1] See the account of the struggle between Kâu-*k*ien of Yüeh and Fû-*kh*âi of Wû in the eightieth and some following chapters of the 'History of the various States of the Eastern *K*âu (Lieh Kwo *K*ih).' We have sympathy with Kâu-*k*ien, till his ingratitude to his two great ministers, one of whom was Wăn *K*ung (the *K*ung of the text), shows the baseness of his character.

When the danger has come to a head, it cannot be averted, and the calamity is perpetuated, and goes on increasing. The return from this (to a state of security) is the result of (great) effort, and success can be attained only after a long time; and yet men consider (their power of self-determination) as their precious possession:—is it not sad? It is in this way that we have the ruin of states and the slaughtering of the people without end; while no one knows how to ask how it comes about.

14. Therefore, the feet of man on the earth tread but on a small space, but going on to where he has not trod before, he traverses a great distance easily; so his knowledge is but small, but going on to what he does not already know, he comes to know what is meant by Heaven[1]. He knows it as The Great Unity; The Great Mystery; The Great Illuminator; The Great Framer; The Great Boundlessness; The Great Truth; The Great Determiner. This makes his knowledge complete. As The Great Unity, he comprehends it; as The Great Mystery, he unfolds it; as the Great Illuminator, he contemplates it; as the Great Framer, it is to him the Cause of all; as the Great Boundlessness, all is to him its embodiment; as The Great Truth, he examines it; as The Great Determiner, he holds it fast.

Thus Heaven is to him all; accordance with it is the brightest intelligence. Obscurity has in this its pivot; in this is the beginning. Such being the

[1] This paragraph grandly sets forth the culmination of all inquiries into the Tâo as leading to the knowledge of Heaven; and the means by which it may be attained to.

莊子

case, the explanation of it is as if it were no explanation; the knowledge of it is as if it were no knowledge. (At first) he does not know it, but afterwards he comes to know it. In his inquiries, he must not set to himself any limits, and yet he cannot be without a limit. Now ascending, now descending, then slipping from the grasp, (the Tâo) is yet a reality, unchanged now as in antiquity, and always without defect:—may it not be called what is capable of the greatest display and expansion? Why should we not inquire into it? Why should we be perplexed about it? With what does not perplex let us explain what perplexes, till we cease to be perplexed. So may we arrive at a great freedom from all perplexity!

BOOK XXV.

Part III. Section III.

Ȝeh-yang[1].

1. Ȝeh-yang having travelled to *Kh*û, Î *K*ieh[2] spoke of him to the king, and then, before the king had granted him an interview, (left him, and) returned home. Ȝeh-yang went to see Wang Kwo[3], and said to him, 'Master, why do you not mention me to the king?' Wang Kwo replied, 'I am not so good a person to do that as Kung-yüeh Hsiû[4].' 'What sort of man is he?' asked the other, and the reply was, 'In winter he spears turtles in the *K*iang, and in summer he rests in shady places on the mountain. When passers-by ask him (what he is doing there), he says, "This is my abode." Since Î *K*ieh was not able to induce the king to see you, how much less should I, who am not equal to him, be able to do so! Î *K*ieh's character is this:—he has no (real) virtue, but he has knowledge. If you do not freely yield yourself to him, but employ him to carry on his spirit-like influence (with you), you will certainly get upset and benighted in the region of riches and honours. His help will not be of a virtuous character, but will go to make your virtue

[1] See vol. xxxix, pp. 154, 155.

[2] A native of *Kh*û, and, probably, a parasite of the court.

[3] An officer of *Kh*û, 'a worthy man.'

[4] A recluse of *Kh*û, but not keeping quite aloof from the court.

莊子

less;—it will be like heaping on clothes in spring as a protection against cold, or bringing back the cold winds of winter as a protection against heat (in summer). Now the king of *Kh*û is of a domineering presence and stern. He has no forgiveness for offenders, but is merciless as a tiger. It is only a man of subtle speech, or one of correct virtue, who can bend him from his purpose [1].

'But the sagely man [2], when he is left in obscurity, causes the members of his family to forget their poverty; and, when he gets forward to a position of influence, causes kings and dukes to forget their rank and emoluments, and transforms them to be humble. With the inferior creatures, he shares their pleasures, and they enjoy themselves the more; with other men, he rejoices in the fellowship of the Tâo, and preserves it in himself. Therefore though he may not speak, he gives them to drink of the harmony (of his spirit). Standing in association with them, he transforms them till they become in their feeling towards him as sons with a father. His wish is to return to the solitude of his own mind, and this is the effect of his occasional intercourse with them. So far-reaching is his influence on the minds of men; and therefore I said to you, "Wait for Kung-yüeh Hsiû."'

2. The sage comprehends the connexions between himself and others, and how they all go to constitute him of one body with them, and he does not know how it is so;—he naturally does so. In fulfilling his constitution, as acted on and acting, he

[1] Much of the description of Î *K*ieh is difficult to construe.

[2] Kung-yüeh Hsiû.

(simply) follows the direction of Heaven; and it is in consequence of this that men style him (a sage). If he were troubled about (the insufficiency of) his knowledge, what he did would always be but small, and sometimes would be arrested altogether;—how would he in this case be (the sage)? When (the sage) is born with all his excellence, it is other men who see it for him. If they did not tell him, he would not know that he was more excellent than others. And when he knows it, he is as if he did not know it; when he hears it, he is as if he did not hear it. His source of joy in it has no end, and men's admiration of him has no end;—all this takes place naturally[1]. The love of the sage for others receives its name from them. If they did not tell him of it, he would not know that he loved them; and when he knows it, he is as if he knew it not; when he hears it, he is as if he heard it not. His love of others never has an end, and their rest in him has also no end:—all this takes place naturally[1].

3. When one sees at a distance his old country and old city, he feels a joyous satisfaction[2]. Though it be full of mounds and an overgrowth of trees and grass, and when he enters it he finds but a tenth part remaining, still he feels that satisfaction. How much more when he sees what he saw, and hears what he heard before! All this is to him like a tower eighty cubits high exhibited in the sight of all men.

[1] That is, 'he does so in the spontaneity of his nature.' The 性 requires the employment of the term 'nature' here, not according to any abstract usage of the term, but meaning the natural constitution. Compare the 性之 in Mencius VII, i, 30.

[2] So does he rejoice in attaining to the knowledge of his nature.

莊子

(The sovereign) *Z*ăn-hsiang[1] was possessed of that central principle round which all things revolve[2], and by it he could follow them to their completion. His accompanying them had neither ending nor beginning, and was independent of impulse or time. Daily he witnessed their changes, and himself underwent no change; and why should he not have rested in this? If we (try to) adopt Heaven as our Master, we incapacitate ourselves from doing so. Such endeavour brings us under the power of things. If one acts in this way, what is to be said of him? The sage never thinks of Heaven nor of men. He does not think of taking the initiative, nor of anything external to himself. He moves along with his age, and does not vary or fail. Amid all the completeness of his doings, he is never exhausted. For those who wish to be in accord with him, what other course is there to pursue?

When Thang got one to hold for him the reins of government, namely, Măn-yin Tăng-hăng[3], he employed him as his teacher. He followed his master, but did not allow himself to be hampered by him, and so he succeeded in following things to their completion. The master had the name; but that name was a superfluous addition to his laws, and the twofold character of his government was made apparent[4]. *K*ung-nî's 'Task your thoughts to the utmost' was his expression of the duties of a

[1] A sage sovereign prior to the three Hwang or August ones.

[2] See the same phraseology in Book II, par. 3.

[3] I have followed Lin Hsî-*k*ung in taking these four characters as the name of one man.

[4] There was a human element in it instead of the Heavenly only; but some critics think the text here is erroneous or defective.

master. Yung-khăng said, 'Take the days away and there will be no year; without what is internal there will be nothing external[1].'

4. (King) Yung[2] of Wei made a treaty with the marquis Thien Mâu[3] (of *Kh*î), which the latter violated. The king was enraged, and intended to send a man to assassinate him. When the Minister of War[4] heard of it, he was ashamed, and said (to the king), 'You are a ruler of 10,000 chariots, and by means of a common man would avenge yourself on your enemy. I beg you to give me, Yen, the command of 200,000 soldiers to attack him for you. I will take captive his people and officers, halter (and lead off) his oxen and horses, kindling a fire within him that shall burn to his backbone. I will then storm his capital; and when he shall run away in terror, I will flog his back and break his spine.' *K*î-ȝze[5] heard of this advice, and was ashamed of it, and said (to the king), 'We have been raising the wall (of our capital) to a height of eighty cubits, and the work has been completed. If we now get it thrown down, it will be a painful toil to the convict builders. It is now seven years

[1] Said to have been employed by Hwang-Tî to make the calendar.

[2] B.C. 370–317.

[3] I do not find the name Mâu as belonging to any of the Thien rulers of *Kh*î. The name of the successor of Thien Ho, who has been before us, was 午, Wû, for which 牟, Mâu, may be a mistake; or 'the marquis Mâu' may be a creation of our author.

[4] Literally, 'the Rhinoceros' Head,' the title of 'the Minister of War' in Wei, who was at this time a Kung-sun Yen. See the memoir of him in Sze-mâ *Kh*ien, Book IX of his Biographies.

[5] I do not know that anything more can be said of *K*î and Hwâ than that they were officers of Wei.

since our troops were called out, and this is the foundation of the royal sway. Yen would introduce disorder;—he should not be listened to.' Hwâ-ȝze[1] heard of this advice, and, greatly disapproving of it, said (to the king), 'He who shows his skill in saying "Attack *Kh*î" would produce disorder; and he who shows his skill in saying "Do not attack it" would also produce disorder. And one who should (merely) say, "The counsellors to attack *Kh*î and not to attack it would both produce disorder," would himself also lead to the same result.' The king said, 'Yes, but what am I to do?' The reply was, 'You have only to seek for (the rule of) the Tâo (on the subject).'

Hui-ȝze, having heard of this counsel, introduced to the king Tâi Ȝin-zăn[2], who said, 'There is the creature called a snail; does your majesty know it?' 'I do.' 'On the left horn of the snail there is a kingdom which is called Provocation, and on the right horn another which is called Stupidity. These two kingdoms are continually striving about their territories and fighting. The corpses that lie on the ground amount to several myriads. The army of one may be defeated and put to flight, but in fifteen days it will return.' The king said, 'Pooh! that is empty talk!' The other rejoined, 'Your servant begs to show your majesty its real significance. When your majesty thinks of space—east, west, north, and south, above and beneath—can you set any limit to it?' 'It is illimitable,' said the king; and his visitor went on, 'Your majesty knows

[1] See note 5 on preceding page.

[2] Evidently a man of considerable reach of thought.

how to let your mind thus travel through the illimitable, and yet (as compared with this) does it not seem insignificant whether the kingdoms that communicate one with another exist or not?' The king replies, 'It does so;' and Tâi ʒin-zǎn said, finally, 'Among those kingdoms, stretching one after another, there is this Wei; in Wei there is this (city of) Liang[1]; and in Liang there is your majesty. Can you make any distinction between yourself, and (the king of that kingdom of) Stupidity?' To this the king answered, 'There is no distinction,' and his visitor went out, while the king remained disconcerted and seemed to have lost himself.

When the visitor was gone, Hui-ʒze came in and saw the king, who said, 'That stranger is a Great man. An (ordinary) sage is not equal to him.' Hui-ʒze replied, 'If you blow into a flute, there come out its pleasant notes; if you blow into a sword-hilt, there is nothing but a wheezing sound. Yâo and Shun are the subjects of men's praises, but if you speak of them before Tâi ʒin-zǎn, there will be but the wheezing sound.'

5. Confucius, having gone to *Kh*û, was lodging in the house of a seller of Congee at Ant-hill. On the roof of a neighbouring house there appeared the husband and his wife, with their servants, male and female[2]. ʒze-lû said, 'What are those people doing,

---

[1] Liang, the capital, came to be used also as the name of the state;—as in Mencius.

[2] 'They were on the roof, repairing it,' say some. 'They had got on the roof, to get out of the way of Confucius,' say others. The sequel shows that this second interpretation is correct; but we do not see how the taking to the roof facilitated their departure from the house.

莊子

collected there as we see them?' *K*ung-nî replied, 'The man is a disciple of the sages. He is burying himself among the people, and hiding among the fields. Reputation has become little in his eyes, but there is no bound to his cherished aims. Though he may speak with his mouth, he never tells what is in his mind. Moreover, he is at variance with the age, and his mind disdains to associate with it;—he is one who may be said to lie hid at the bottom of the water on the dry land. Is he not a sort of Î Liâo of Shih-nan?' Ȝze-lû asked leave to go and call him, but Confucius said, 'Stop. He knows that I understand him well. He knows that I am come to *Kh*û, and thinks that I am sure to try and get the king to invite him (to court). He also thinks that I am a man swift to speak. Being such a man, he would feel ashamed to listen to the words of one of voluble and flattering tongue, and how much more to come himself and see his person! And why should we think that he will remain here?' Ȝze-lû, however, went to see how it was, but found the house empty.

6. The Border-warden of *Kh*ang-wû[1], in questioning Ȝze-lâo[2], said, 'Let not a ruler in the exercise of his government be (like the farmer) who leaves the clods unbroken, nor, in regulating his people, (like one) who recklessly plucks up the shoots. Formerly, in ploughing my corn-fields, I left the clods unbroken, and my recompense was in the rough unsatisfactory crops; and in weeding, I destroyed and tore up (many good plants), and my recompense was in the scantiness of my harvests. In subse-

[1] Probably the same as the *Kh*ang-wû Ȝze in Book II, par. 9.

[2] See Analects IX, vi, 4.

quent years I changed my methods, ploughing deeply and carefully covering up the seed; and my harvests were rich and abundant, so that all the year I had more than I could eat.' When *K*wang-ȝze heard of his remarks, he said, 'Now-a-days, most men, in attending to their bodies and regulating their minds, correspond to the description of the Border-warden. They hide from themselves their Heaven(-given being); they leave (all care of) their (proper) nature; they extinguish their (proper) feelings; and they leave their spirit to die:—abandoning themselves to what is the general practice. Thus dealing with their nature like the farmer who is negligent of the clods in his soil, the illegitimate results of their likings and dislikings become their nature. The bushy sedges, reeds, and rushes, which seem at first to spring up to support our bodies, gradually eradicate our nature, and it becomes like a mass of running sores, ever liable to flow out, with scabs and ulcers, discharging in flowing matter from the internal heat. So indeed it is!'

7. Po *K*ü[1] was studying with Lâo Tan, and asked his leave to go and travel everywhere. Lâo Tan said, 'Nay;—elsewhere it is just as here.' He repeated his request, and then Lâo Tan said, 'Where would you go first?' 'I would begin with *Kh*î,' replied the disciple. 'Having got there, I would go to look at the criminals (who had been executed). With my arms I would raise (one of) them up and set him on his feet, and, taking off my court robes, I would cover him with them, appealing at

[1] We can only say of Po *K*ü that he was a disciple of Lâo-ȝze.

the same time to Heaven and bewailing his lot, while I said[1], "My son, my son, you have been one of the first to suffer from the great calamities that afflict the world[2]."' (Lâo Tan) said[1], '(It is said), "Do not rob. Do not kill." (But) in the setting up of (the ideas of) glory and disgrace, we see the cause of those evils; in the accumulation of property and wealth, we see the causes of strife and contention. If now you set up the things against which men fret; if you accumulate what produces strife and contention among them; if you put their persons in such a state of distress, that they have no rest or ease, although you may wish that they should not come to the end of those (criminals), can your wish be realised?

'The superior men (and rulers) of old considered that the success (of their government) was to be found in (the state of) the people, and its failure to be sought in themselves; that the right might be with the people, and the wrong in themselves. Thus it was that if but a single person lost his life, they retired and blamed themselves. Now, however, it is not so. (Rulers) conceal what they want done, and hold those who do not know it to be stupid; they require what is very difficult, and condemn those who do not dare to undertake it; they impose heavy burdens, and punish those who are unequal to them; they require men to go far, and put them to death when they cannot accomplish the distance. When the people know that the utmost of their

---

[1] There are two 曰 here, and the difficulty in translating is to determine the subject of each.

[2] The 離 of the text here is taken as = 罹.

strength will be insufficient, they follow it up with deceit. When (the rulers) daily exhibit much hypocrisy, how can the officers and people not be hypocritical? Insufficiency of strength produces hypocrisy; insufficiency of knowledge produces deception; insufficiency of means produces robbery. But in this case against whom ought the robbery and theft to be charged?'

8. When *K*ü Po-yü was in his sixtieth year, his views became changed in the course of it[1]. He had never before done anything but consider the views which he held to be right, but now he came to condemn them as wrong; he did not know that what he now called right was not what for fifty-nine years he had been calling wrong. All things have the life (which we know), but we do not see its root; they have their goings forth, but we do not know the door by which they depart. Men all honour that which lies within the sphere of their knowledge, but they do not know their dependence on what lies without that sphere which would be their (true) knowledge:—may we not call their case one of great perplexity? Ah! Ah! there is no escaping from this dilemma. So it is! So it is!

9. *K*ung-nî asked the Grand Historiographer[2] Tâ Thâo, (along with) Po *Kh*ang-*kh*ien and *Kh*ih-wei, saying, 'Duke Ling of Wei was so addicted to

[1] Confucius thought highly of this *K*ü Po-yü, and they were friends (Analects, XIV, 26; XV, 6). It would seem from this paragraph that, in his sixtieth year, he adopted the principles of Tâoism. Whether he really did so we cannot tell. See also Book IV, par. 5.

[2] We must translate here in the singular, for in the historiographer's department there were only two officers with the title of 'Grand;' Po *Kh*ang-*kh*ien and *Kh*ih-wei would be inferior members of it.

莊子

drink, and abandoned to sensuality, that he did not attend to the government of his state. Occupied in his pursuit of hunting with his nets and bows, he kept aloof from the meetings of the princes. In what was it that he showed his title to the epithet of Ling[1]?' Tâ Thâo said, 'It was on account of those very things.' Po *Kh*ang-*kh*ien said, 'Duke Ling had three mistresses with whom he used to bathe in the same tub. (Once, however), when Shih-ȝhiû came to him with presents from the imperial court, he made his servants support the messenger in bearing the gifts[2]. So dissolute was he in the former case, and when he saw a man of worth, thus reverent was he to him. It was on this account that he was styled "Duke Ling."' *Kh*ih-wei said, 'When duke Ling died, and they divined about burying him in the old tomb of his House, the answer was unfavourable; when they divined about burying him on Shâ-*kh*iû, the answer was favourable. Accordingly they dug there to the depth of several fathoms, and found a stone coffin. Having washed and inspected it, they discovered an inscription, which said,

"This grave will not be available for your posterity;
Duke Ling will appropriate it for himself."

[1] Ling (靈), as a posthumous epithet, has various meanings, none of them very bad, and some of them very good. Confucius ought to have been able to solve his question himself better than any of the historiographers, but he propounded his doubt to them for reasons which he, no doubt, had.

[2] We are not to suppose that the royal messenger found him in the tub with his three wives or mistresses. The two incidents mentioned illustrate two different phases of his character, as some of the critics, and even the text itself, clearly indicate.

Thus that epithet of Ling had long been settled for the duke[1]. But how should those two be able to know this?'

10. Shâo *K*ih[2] asked Thâi-kung Thiâo[2], saying, 'What do we mean by "The Talk of the Hamlets and Villages?"' The reply was, 'Hamlets and Villages are formed by the union—say of ten surnames and a hundred names, and are considered to be (the source of) manners and customs. The differences between them are united to form their common character, and what is common to them is separately apportioned to form the differences. If you point to the various parts which make up the body of a horse, you do not have the horse; but when the horse is before you, and all its various parts stand forth (as forming the animal), you speak of "the horse." So it is that the mounds and hills are made to be the elevations that they are by accumulations of earth which individually are but low. (So also rivers like) the *K*iang and the Ho obtain their greatness by the union of (other smaller) waters with them. And (in the same way) the Great man exhibits the common sentiment of humanity by the union in himself of all its individualities. Hence when ideas come to him from without, though he

[1] This explanation is, of course, absurd.

[2] These two names are both metaphorical, the former meaning 'Small Knowledge,' and the latter, 'The Grand Public and Just Harmonizer.' Small Knowledge would look for the Tâo in the ordinary talk of ordinary men. The other teaches him that it is to be found in 'the Great man,' blending in himself what is 'just' in the sentiments and practice of all men. And so it is to be found in all the phenomena of nature, but it has itself no name, and does nothing.

莊子

has his own decided view, he does not hold it with bigotry; and when he gives out his own decisions, which are correct, the views of others do not oppose them. The four seasons have their different elemental characters, but they are not the partial gifts of Heaven, and so the year completes its course. The five official departments have their different duties, but the ruler does not partially employ any one of them, and so the kingdom is governed. (The gifts of) peace and war (are different), but the Great man does not employ the one to the prejudice of the other, and so the character (of his administration) is perfect. All things have their different constitutions and modes of actions, but the Tâo (which directs them) is free from all partiality, and therefore it has no name. Having no name, it therefore does nothing. Doing nothing, there is nothing which it does not do.

'Each season has its ending and beginning; each age has its changes and transformations; misery and happiness regularly alternate. Here our views are thwarted, and yet the result may afterwards have our approval; there we insist on our own views, and looking at things differently from others, try to correct them, while we are in error ourselves. The case may be compared to that of a great marsh, in which all its various vegetation finds a place, or we may look at it as a great hill, where trees and rocks are found on the same terrace. Such may be a description of what is intended by "The Talk of the Hamlets and Villages."'

Shâo Kih said, 'Well, is it sufficient to call it (an expression of) the Tâo?' Thâi-kung Thiâo said, 'It is not so. If we reckon up the number of things, they are not 10,000 merely. When we speak of them as "the Myriad Things," we simply use that large number by way of accommodation to denominate them. In this way Heaven and Earth are the greatest of all things that have form; the Yin and Yang are the greatest of all elemental forces. But the Tâo is common to them. Because of their greatness to use the Tâo or (Course) as a title and call it "the Great Tâo" is allowable. But what comparison can be drawn between it and "the Talk of the Hamlets and Villages?" To argue from this that it is a sufficient expression of the Tâo, is like calling a dog and a horse by the same name, while the difference between them is so great.'

11. Shâo *K*ih said, 'Within the limits of the four cardinal points, and the six boundaries of space, how was it that there commenced the production of all things?' Thâi-kung Thiâo replied, 'The Yin and Yang reflected light on each other, covered each other, and regulated each the other; the four seasons gave place to one another, produced one another, and brought one another to an end. Likings and dislikings, the avoidings of this and movements towards that, then arose (in the things thus produced), in their definite distinctness; and from this came the separation and union of the male and female. Then were seen now security and now insecurity, in mutual change; misery and happiness produced each other; gentleness and urgency pressed on each other; the movements of collection and dispersion were established:—these names and processes can be examined, and, however minute, can be recorded. The rules determining the order in which they follow one another, their mutual influence

莊子

now acting directly and now revolving, how, when they are exhausted, they revive, and how they end and begin again; these are the properties belonging to things. Words can describe them and knowledge can reach to them; but with this ends all that can be said of things. Men who study the Tâo do not follow on when these operations end, nor try to search out how they began:—with this all discussion of them stops.'

Shâo *K*ih said, '*K*î *K*ăn[1] holds that (the Tâo) forbids all action, and *K*ieh-ȝze[1] holds that it may perhaps allow of influence. Which of the two is correct in his statements, and which is one-sided in his ruling?' Thâi-kung Thiâo replied, 'Cocks crow and dogs bark;—this is what all men know. But men with the greatest wisdom cannot describe in words whence it is that they are formed (with such different voices), nor can they find out by thinking what they wish to do. We may refine on this small point; till it is so minute that there is no point to operate on, or it may become so great that there is no embracing it. "Some one caused it;" "No one did it;" but we are thus debating about things; and the end is that we shall find we are in error. "Some one caused it;"—then there was a real Being. "No one did it;"—then there was mere vacancy. To have a name and a real existence,—that is the condition of a thing. Not to have a name, and not

[1] Two masters of schools of Tâoism. Who the former was I do not know; but Sze-mâ *Kh*ien in the seventy-fourth Book of his Records mentions several Tâoist masters, and among them *K*ieh-ȝze, a native of *Kh*î, 'a student of the arts of the Tâo and its Characteristics, as taught by Hwang-Tî and Lâo-ȝze, and who also published his views on the subject.'

to have real being;—that is vacancy and no thing. We may speak and we may think about it, but the more we speak, the wider shall we be of the mark. Birth, before it comes, cannot be prevented; death, when it has happened, cannot be traced farther. Death and life are not far apart; but why they have taken place cannot be seen. That some one has caused them, or that there has been no action in the case are but speculations of doubt. When I look for their origin, it goes back into infinity; when I look for their end, it proceeds without termination. Infinite, unceasing, there is no room for words about (the Tâo). To regard it as in the category of things is the origin of the language that it is caused or that it is the result of doing nothing; but it would end as it began with things. The Tâo cannot have a (real) existence; if it has, it cannot be made to appear as if it had not. The name Tâo is a metaphor, used for the purpose of description[1]. To say that it causes or does nothing is but to speak of one phase of things, and has nothing to do with the Great Subject. If words were sufficient for the purpose, in a day's time we might exhaust it; since they are not sufficient, we may speak all day, and only exhaust (the subject of) things. The Tâo is the extreme to which things conduct us. Neither speech nor silence is sufficient to convey the notion of it. Neither by speech nor by silence can our thoughts about it have their highest expression.

[1] A very important statement with regard to the meaning of the name Tâo.

莊子

BOOK XXVI.

Part III. Section IV.

Wâi Wû, or 'What comes from Without[1].'

1. What comes from without cannot be determined beforehand. So it was that Lung-făng[2] was killed; Pi-kan immolated; and the count of *K*î (made to feign himself) mad, (while) O-lâi died[3], and *K*ieh and *K*âu both perished. Rulers all wish their ministers to be faithful, but that faithfulness may not secure their confidence; hence Wû Yün became a wanderer along the *K*iang[4], and *Kh*ang Hung died in Shû, where (the people) preserved his blood for three years, when it became changed into green jade[5]. Parents all wish their sons to be filial, but that filial duty may not secure their love; hence

---

[1] See vol. xxxix, p. 155.

[2] The name of Kwan Lung-făng, a great officer of *K*ieh, the tyrant of Hsiâ;—see Bk. IV, par. 1, et al.

[3] A scion of the line of *Kh*in whose fortunes culminated in Shih Hwang-Tî. O-lâi assisted the tyrant of Shang, and was put to death by king Wû of *K*âu.

[4] The famous Wû Ȝze-hsü, the hero of Revenge, who made his escape along the *K*iang, in about B. C. 512, to Wû, after the murder of his father and elder brother by the king of *Kh*û.

[5] See Bk. X, par. 2. In the Ȝo-*k*wan, under the third year of duke Âi, it is related that the people of *K*âu killed *Kh*ang Hung; but nothing is said of this being done in Shû, or of his blood turning to green jade! This we owe to the *Kh*un *Kh*iû of Lü.

Hsiâo-*k*î[1] had to endure his sorrow, and Ȝăng Shăn his grief[2].

When wood is rubbed against wood, it begins to burn; when metal is subjected to fire, it (melts and) flows. When the Yin and Yang act awry, heaven and earth are greatly perturbed; and on this comes the crash of thunder, and from the rain comes fire, which consumes great locust trees[3]. (The case of men) is still worse. They are troubled between two pitfalls[4], from which they cannot escape. Chrysalis-like, they can accomplish nothing. Their minds are as if hung up between heaven and earth. Now comforted, now pitied, they are plunged in difficulties. The ideas of profit and of injury rub against each other, and produce in them a very great fire. The harmony (of the mind) is consumed in the mass of men. Their moonlike intelligence cannot overcome the (inward) fire. They thereupon fall away more and more, and the Course (which they should pursue) is altogether lost.

2. The family of *K*wang *K*âu being poor, he went to ask the loan of some rice from the Marquis Superintendent of the Ho[5], who said, 'Yes, I shall be

[1] Said to have been the eldest son of king Wû Ting or Kâo Ȝung of the Yin dynasty. I do not know the events in his experience to which our author must be referring.

[2] The well-known disciple of Confucius, famous for his filial piety.

[3] The lightning accompanying a thunderstorm.

[4] The ideas of profit and injury immediately mentioned.

[5] In another version of this story, in Liû Hsiang's Shwo Yüan, XI, art. 13, the party applied to is 'duke Wăn of Wei;' but this does not necessarily conflict with the text. The genuineness of the paragraph is denied by Lin Hsî-*k*ung and others; but I seem to see the hand of *K*wang-ȝze in it.

getting the (tax-) money from the people (soon), and I will then lend you three hundred ounces of silver;—will that do?' *K*wang *K*âu flushed with anger, and said, 'On the road yesterday, as I was coming here, I heard some one calling out. On looking round, I saw a goby in the carriage rut, and said to it, "Goby fish, what has brought you here?" The goby said, "I am Minister of Waves in the Eastern Sea. Have you, Sir, a gallon or a pint of water to keep me alive?" I replied, "Yes, I am going south to see the kings of Wû and Yüeh, and I will then lead a stream from the Western *K*iang to meet you;—will that do?" The goby flushed with anger, and said, "I have lost my proper element, and I can here do nothing for myself; but if I could get a gallon or a pint of water, I should keep alive. Than do what you propose, you had better soon look for me in a stall of dry fish."'

3. A son of the duke of *Z*ăn[1], having provided himself with a great hook, a powerful black line, and fifty steers to be used as bait, squatted down on (mount) Kwâi *Kh*î, and threw the line into the Eastern Sea. Morning after morning he angled thus, and for a whole year caught nothing. At the end of that time, a great fish swallowed the bait, and dived down, dragging the great hook with him. Then it rose to the surface in a flurry, and flapped with its fins, till the white waves rose like hills, and the waters were lashed into fury. The noise was like that of imps and spirits, and spread terror

[1] I suppose this was merely a district of *Kh*û, and the duke of it merely the officer in charge of it;—according to the practice of the rulers of *Kh*û, after they usurped the title of King.

for a thousand lî. The prince having got such a fish, cut it in slices and dried them. From the *K*eh river[1] to the east, and from Ȝhang-wû[2] to the north, there was not one who did not eat his full from that fish; and in subsequent generations, story-tellers of small abilities have all repeated the story to one another with astonishment. (But) if the prince had taken his rod, with a fine line, and gone to pools and ditches, and watched for minnows and gobies, it would have been difficult for him to get a large fish. Those who dress up their small tales to obtain favour with the magistrates are far from being men of great understanding; and therefore one who has not heard the story of this scion of *Z*ăn is not fit to take any part in the government of the world;—far is he from being so[3].

4. Some literati, students of the Odes and Ceremonies, were breaking open a mound over a grave[4]. The superior among them spoke down to the others, 'Day is breaking in the east; how is the thing going on?' The younger men replied, 'We have not yet opened his jacket and skirt, but there is a pearl in the mouth. As it is said in the Ode,

"The bright, green grain
Is growing on the sides of the mound.

---

[1] The 制河 of the text = the 浙江, still giving its name to the province so called.

[2] Where Shun was buried.

[3] This last sentence is difficult to construe, and to understand.—The genuineness of this paragraph is also questioned, and the style is inferior to that of the preceding.

[4] I can conceive of *K*wang-ȝze telling this story of some literati who had been acting as resurrectionists, as a joke against their class; but not of his writing it to form a part of his work.

莊子

While living, he gave nothing away;
Why, when dead, should he hold a pearl in his mouth[1]?"'

Thereupon they took hold of the whiskers and pulled at the beard, while the superior introduced a piece of fine steel into the chin, and gradually separated the jaws, so as not to injure the pearl in the mouth.

5. A disciple of Lâo Lâi-ȝze[2], while he was out gathering firewood, met with *K*ung-nî. On his return, he told (his master), saying, 'There is a man there, the upper part of whose body is long and the lower part short. He is slightly hump-backed, and his ears are far back. When you look at him, he seems occupied with the cares of all within the four seas; I do not know whose son he is.' Lâo Lâi-ȝze said, 'It is *Kh*iû; call him here;' and when *K*ung-nî came, he said to him, '*Kh*iû, put away your personal conceit, and airs of wisdom, and show yourself to be indeed a superior man.' *K*ung-nî bowed and was retiring, when he abruptly changed his manner, and asked, 'Will the object I am pursuing be thereby advanced?' Lâo Lâi-ȝze replied, 'You cannot bear the sufferings of this one age, and are stubbornly regardless of the

[1] This verse is not found, so far as I know, anywhere else.

[2] Lâo Lâi-ȝze appears here as a contemporary of Confucius, and the master of a Tâoistic school, and this also is the view of him which we receive from the accounts in Sze-mâ *Kh*ien and Hwang-fû Mi. Sze-mâ says he published a work in fifteen sections on the usefulness of Tâoism. Some have imagined that he was the same as Lâo-ȝze himself, but there does not appear any ground for that opinion. He is one of the twenty-four examples of Filial Piety so celebrated among the Chinese; but I suspect that the accounts of him as such are fabrications. He certainly lectures Confucius here in a manner worthy of Lâo Tan.

evils of a myriad ages:—is it that you purposely make yourself thus unhappy? or is it that you have not the ability to comprehend the case? Your obstinate purpose to make men rejoice in a participation of your joy is your life-long shame, the procedure of a mediocre man. You would lead men by your fame; you would bind them to you by your secret art. Than be praising Yâo and condemning *K*ieh, you had better forget them both, and shut up your tendency to praise. If you reflect on it, it does nothing but injury; your action in it is entirely wrong. The sage is full of anxiety and indecision in undertaking anything, and so he is always successful. But what shall I say of your conduct? To the end it is all affectation.'

6. The ruler Yüan of Sung[1] (once) dreamt at midnight that a man with dishevelled hair peeped in on him at a side door and said, 'I was coming from the abyss of 3âi-lû, commissioned by the Clear *K*iang to go to the place of the Earl of the Ho; but the fisherman Yü 3ü has caught me.' When the ruler Yüan awoke, he caused a diviner to divine the meaning (of the dream), and was told, 'This is a marvellous tortoise.' The ruler asked if among the fishermen there was one called Yü 3ü, and being told by his attendants that there was, he gave orders that he should be summoned to court. Accordingly the man next day appeared at court, and the ruler said, 'What have you caught (lately) in fishing?' The reply was, 'I have caught in my net a white tortoise, sieve-like, and five cubits round.' 'Present the prodigy here,' said the ruler; and, when it came, once and

[1] Compare in Bk. XXI, par. 7.

莊子

again he wished to kill it, once and again he wished to keep it alive. Doubting in his mind (what to do), he had recourse to divination, and obtained the answer, 'To kill the tortoise for use in divining will be fortunate.' Accordingly they cut the creature open, and perforated its shell in seventy-two places, and there was not a single divining slip which failed[1].

*K*ung-nî said, 'The spirit-like tortoise could show itself in a dream to the ruler Yüan, and yet it could not avoid the net of Yü Ȝü. Its wisdom could respond on seventy-two perforations without failing in a single divination, and yet it could not avoid the agony of having its bowels all scooped out. We see from this that wisdom is not without its perils, and spirit-like intelligence does not reach to everything. A man may have the greatest wisdom, but there are a myriad men scheming against him. Fishes do not fear the net, though they fear the pelican. Put away your small wisdom, and your great wisdom will be bright; discard your skilfulness, and you will become naturally skilful. A child when it is born needs no great master, and yet it becomes able to speak, living (as it does) among those who are able to speak.'

7. Hui-ȝze said to *K*wang-ȝze, 'You speak, Sir, of what is of no use.' The reply was, 'When a man knows what is not useful, you can then begin to speak to him of what is useful. The earth for instance is certainly spacious and great; but what a

[1] The story of this wonderful tortoise is found at much greater length, and with variations, in Sze-mâ *Kh*ien's Records, Bk. LXVIII, q. v. The moral of it is given in the concluding remarks from Confucius.

man uses of it is only sufficient ground for his feet. If, however, a rent were made by the side of his feet, down to the yellow springs, could the man still make use of it?' Hui-ȝze said, 'He could not use it,' and *K*wang-ȝze rejoined, 'Then the usefulness of what is of no use is clear [1].'

8. *K*wang-ȝze said, 'If a man have the power to enjoy himself (in any pursuit), can he be kept from doing so? If he have not the power, can he so enjoy himself? There are those whose aim is bent on concealing themselves, and those who are determined that their doings shall leave no trace. Alas! they both shirk the obligations of perfect knowledge and great virtue. The (latter) fall, and cannot recover themselves; the (former) rush on like fire, and do not consider (what they are doing). Though men may stand to each other in the relation of ruler and minister, that is but for a time. In a changed age, the one of them would not be able to look down on the other. Hence it is said, "The Perfect man leaves no traces of his conduct."

'To honour antiquity and despise the present time is the characteristic of learners [2]; but even the disciples of *Kh*ih-wei [3] have to look at the present age; and who can avoid being carried along by its course? It is only the Perfect man who is able to enjoy himself in the world, and not be deflected from the right,

[1] See Bk. I, par. 6, and XXIV, par. 14. The conversations between our author and Hui-ȝze often turned on this subject.

[2] Does our author mean by 'learners' the literati, the disciples of Confucius?

[3] *Kh*ih-wei,—see Bk. VI, par. 7. Perhaps 'the disciples of *Kh*ih-wei' are those who in our author's time called themselves such, but were not.

莊子

to accommodate himself to others and not lose himself. He does not learn their lessons; he only takes their ideas into consideration, and does not discard them as different from his own.

9. 'It is the penetrating eye that gives clear vision, the acute ear that gives quick hearing, the discriminating nose that gives discernment of odours, the practised mouth that gives the enjoyment of flavours, the active mind that acquires knowledge, and the far-reaching knowledge that constitutes virtue. In no case does the connexion with what is without like to be obstructed; obstruction produces stoppage; stoppage, continuing without intermission, arrests all progress; and with this all injurious effects spring up.

'The knowledge of all creatures depends on their breathing[1]. But if their breath be not abundant, it is not the fault of Heaven, which tries to penetrate them with it, day and night without ceasing; but men notwithstanding shut their pores against it. The womb encloses a large and empty space; the heart has its spontaneous and enjoyable movements. If their apartment be not roomy, wife and mother-in-law will be bickering; if the heart have not its spontaneous and enjoyable movements, the six faculties of perception[2] will be in mutual collision. That

[1] There seems to underlie this statement the Tâoist dogma about the regulation of the 'breath,' as conducive to long life and mental cultivation.

[2] Probably what in Buddhist literature are called 'the Six Entrances (六入),' what Mayers denominates 'The Six Organs of Admittance, or Bodily Sensations,' the Shadâyatana, the eye, ear, nose, mouth, body, and mind,—one of the twelve Nidânas in the Buddhist system.

the great forests, the heights and hills, are pleasant to men, is because their spirits cannot overcome (those distracting influences). Virtue overflows into (the love of) fame; (the love of) fame overflows into violence; schemes originate in the urgency (of circumstances); (the show of) wisdom comes from rivalry; the fuel (of strife) is produced from the obstinate maintenance (of one's own views); the business of offices should be apportioned in accordance with the approval of all. In spring, when the rain and the sunshine come seasonably, vegetation grows luxuriantly, and sickles and hoes begin to be prepared. More than half of what had fallen down becomes straight, and we do not know how.

10. 'Stillness and silence are helpful to those who are ill; rubbing the corners of the eyes is helpful to the aged; rest serves to calm agitation; but they are the toiled and troubled who have recourse to these things. Those who are at ease, and have not had such experiences, do not care to ask about them. The spirit-like man has had no experience of how it is that the sagely man keeps the world in awe, and so he does not inquire about it; the sagely man has had no experience of how it is that the man of ability and virtue keeps his age in awe, and so he does not inquire about it; the man of ability and virtue has had no experience of how it is that the superior man keeps his state in awe, and so he does not inquire about it. The superior man has had no experience of how it is that the small man keeps himself in agreement with his times that he should inquire about it.'

11. The keeper of the Yen Gate[1], on the death of

[1] The name of one of the gates in the wall of the capital of Sung.

his father, showed so much skill in emaciating his person[1] that he received the rank of 'Pattern for Officers.' Half the people of his neighbourhood (in consequence) carried their emaciation to such a point that they died. When Yâo wished to resign the throne to Hsü Yû, the latter ran away. When Thang offered his to Wû Kwang[2], Wû Kwang became angry. When *K*î Thâ[3] heard it, he led his disciples, and withdrew to the river Kho, where the feudal princes came and condoled with him, and after three years, Shăn Thû-tî[4] threw himself into the water. Fishing-stakes[5] are employed to catch fish; but when the fish are got, the men forget the stakes. Snares are employed to catch hares, but when the hares are got, men forget the snares. Words are employed to convey ideas; but when the ideas are apprehended, men forget the words. Fain would I talk with such a man who has forgot the words!

[1] The abstinences and privations in mourning were so many that there was a danger of their seriously injuring the health;—which was forbidden.

[2] See Bk. VI, par. 3; but in the note there, Wû Kwang is said to have been of the time of Hwang-Tî; which is probably an error.

[3] See IV, par. 3; but I do not know who *K*î Thâ was, nor can I explain what is said of him here.

[4] See again IV, par. 3.

[5] According to some, 'baskets.' This illustration is quoted in the Inscription on the Nestorian Monument, II, 7.

BOOK XXVII.

Part III. Section V.

Yü Yen, or 'Metaphorical Language[1].'

1. Of my sentences nine in ten are metaphorical; of my illustrations seven in ten are from valued writers. The rest of my words are like the water that daily fills the cup, tempered and harmonised by the Heavenly element in our nature[2].

The nine sentences in ten which are metaphorical are borrowed from extraneous things to assist (the comprehension of) my argument. (When it is said, for instance), 'A father does not act the part of matchmaker for his own son,' (the meaning is that) 'it is better for another man to praise the son than for his father to do so.' The use of such metaphorical language is not my fault, but the fault of men (who would not otherwise readily understand me).

Men assent to views which agree with their own, and oppose those which do not so agree. Those which agree with their own they hold to be right, and those which do not so agree they hold to be wrong. The seven out of ten illustrations taken from valued writers are designed to put an end to disputations. Those writers are the men of hoary eld, my predecessors in time. But such as are un-

[1] See vol. xxxix, pp. 155, 156. [2] See Bk. II, par. 10.

莊子

versed in the warp and woof, the beginning and end of the subject, cannot be set down as of venerable eld, and regarded as the predecessors of others. If men have not that in them which fits them to precede others, they are without the way proper to man, and they who are without the way proper to man can only be pronounced defunct monuments of antiquity.

Words like the water that daily issues from the cup, and are harmonised by the Heavenly Element (of our nature), may be carried on into the region of the unlimited, and employed to the end of our years. But without words there is an agreement (in principle). That agreement is not effected by words, and an agreement in words is not effected by it. Hence it is said, 'Let there be no words.' Speech does not need words. One may speak all his life, and not have spoken a (right) word; and one may not have spoken all his life, and yet all his life been giving utterance to the (right) words. There is that which makes a thing allowable, and that which makes a thing not allowable. There is that which makes a thing right, and that which makes a thing not right. How is a thing right? It is right because it is right. How is a thing wrong? It is wrong because it is wrong. How is a thing allowable? It is allowable because it is so. How is a thing not allowable? It is not allowable because it is not so. Things indeed have what makes them right, and what makes them allowable. There is nothing which has not its condition of right; nothing which has not its condition of allowability. But without the words of the (water-) cup in daily use, and harmonised by the Heavenly Element (in our

海上絲綢之路文獻集成 科技與文化編

nature), what one can continue long in the possession of these characteristics?

All things are divided into their several classes, and succeed to one another in the same way, though of different bodily forms. They begin and end as in an unbroken ring, though how it is they do so be not apprehended. This is what is called the Lathe of Heaven; and the Lathe of Heaven is the Heavenly Element in our nature.

2. *K*wang-ȝze said to Hui-ȝze, 'When Confucius was in his sixtieth year, in that year his views changed[1]. What he had before held to be right, he now ended by holding to be wrong; and he did not know whether the things which he now pronounced to be right were not those which he had for fifty-nine years held to be wrong.' Hui-ȝze replied, 'Confucius with an earnest will pursued the acquisition of knowledge, and acted accordingly.' *K*wang-ȝze rejoined, 'Confucius disowned such a course, and never said that it was his. He said, "Man receives his powers from the Great Source[2] (of his being), and he should restore them to their (original) intelligence in his life. His singing should be in accordance with the musical tubes, and his speech a model for imitation. When profit and righteousness are set before him, and his liking (for the latter) and dislike (of the

[1] Compare this with the same language about *K*ü Po-yü in Bk. XXV, par. 8. There is no proof to support our author's assertion that the views of Confucius underwent any change.

[2] 'The Great Source (Root)' here is generally explained by 'the Grand Beginning.' It is not easy to say whether we are to understand an ideal condition of man designed from the first, or the condition of every man as he is born into the world. On the 'powers' received by man, see Mencius VI, i, 6.

former), his approval and disapproval, are manifested, that only serves to direct the speech of men (about him). To make men in heart submit, and not dare to stand up in opposition to him; to establish the fixed law for all under heaven:—ah! ah! I have not attained to that."'

3. 3ăng-ȝze twice took office, and on the two occasions his state of mind was different. He said, 'While my parents were alive I took office, and though my emolument was only three fû[1] (of grain), my mind was happy. Afterwards when I took office, my emolument was three thousand *k*ung[2]; but I could not share it with my parents, and my mind was sad.' The other disciples asked *K*ung-nî, saying, 'Such an one as Shăn may be pronounced free from all entanglement:—is he to be blamed for feeling as he did[3]?' The reply was, 'But he was subject to entanglement[4]. If he had been free from it, could he have had that sadness? He would have looked on his three fû and three thousand *k*ung no more than on a heron or a mosquito passing before him.'

4. Yen *Kh*ăng 3ze-yû said to Tung-kwo 3ze-*kh*î[5], 'When I (had begun to) hear your instructions, the first year, I continued a simple rustic; the second

---

[1] A fû = ten tâu and four shing, or sixty-four shing, the shing at present being rather less than an English pint.

[2] A *k*ung = sixty-four tâu; but there are various accounts of its size.

[3] This sentence is difficult to construe.

[4] But Confucius could not count his love for his parents an entanglement.

[5] We must suppose this master to be the same as the Nan-kwo 3ze-*kh*î of Bk. II.

year, I became docile; the third year, I comprehended (your teaching); the fourth year, I was (plastic) as a thing; the fifth year, I made advances; the sixth year, the spirit entered (and dwelt in me); the seventh year, (my nature as designed by) Heaven was perfected; the eighth year, I knew no difference between death and life; the ninth year, I attained to the Great Mystery[1].

'Life has its work to do, and death ensues, (as if) the common character of each were a thing prescribed. Men consider that their death has its cause; but that life from (the operation of) the Yang has no cause. But is it really so? How does (the Yang) operate in this direction? Why does it not operate there?

'Heaven has its places and spaces which can be calculated; (the divisions of) the earth can be assigned by men. But how shall we search for and find out (the conditions of the Great Mystery)? We do not know when and how (life) will end, but how shall we conclude that it is not determined (from without)? and as we do not know when and how it begins, how should we conclude that it is not (so) determined?

'In regard to the issues of conduct which we deem appropriate, how should we conclude that there are no spirits presiding over them; and where those issues seem inappropriate, how should we conclude that there are spirits presiding over them?'

[1] In illustration of the text here Lû Shû-*k*ih refers to the use of Miâo (妙), in the account of the term 'Spirit,' in the fifth Appendix to the Yî, par. 10, as meaning 'the subtle (presence and operation of God) with all things.' Ȝze-yû's further exposition of his attainments is difficult to understand fully.

莊子

5. The penumbrae (once) asked the shadow[1], saying, 'Formerly you were looking down, and now you are looking up; formerly you had your hair tied up, and now it is dishevelled; formerly you were sitting, and now you have risen up; formerly you were walking, and now you have stopped:—how is all this?' The shadow said, 'Venerable Sirs, how do you ask me about such small matters? These things all belong to me, but I do not know how they do so. I am (like) the shell of a cicada or the cast-off skin of a snake[2];—like them, and yet not like them. With light and the sun I make my appearance; with darkness and the night I fade away. Am not I dependent on the substance from which I am thrown? And that substance is itself dependent on something else! When it comes, I come with it; when it goes, I go with it. When it comes under the influence of the strong Yang, I come under the same. Since we are both produced by that strong Yang, what occasion is there for you to question me?'

6. Yang Ȝze-*k*ü[3] had gone South to Phei[4], while Lâo Tan was travelling in the west in *Kh*in[5]. (He thereupon) asked (Lâo-ȝze) to come to the border (of Phei), and went himself to Liang, where he met him. Lâo-ȝze stood in the middle of the way, and, looking up to heaven, said with a sigh, 'At first I thought that you might be taught, but now I see that you cannot be.' Yang Ȝze-*k*ü made no reply;

[1] Compare Bk. II, par. 11.
[2] Such is the reading of Ȝiâo Hung.
[3] No doubt the Yang *K*û of Lieh-ȝze and Mencius.
[4] See in XIV, 26 b.
[5] In the borders of Phei; can hardly be the great State.

and when they came to their lodging-house, he brought in water for the master to wash his hands and rinse his mouth, along with a towel and comb. He then took off his shoes outside the door, went forward on his knees, and said, 'Formerly, your disciple wished to ask you, Master, (the reason of what you said); but you were walking, and there was no opportunity, and therefore I did not presume to speak. Now there is an opportunity, and I beg to ask why you spoke as you did.' Lâo-ʒze replied, 'Your eyes are lofty, and you stare;—who would live with you? The purest carries himself as if he were soiled; the most virtuous seems to feel himself defective.' Yang ʒze-*k*ü looked abashed and changed countenance, saying, 'I receive your commands with reverence.'

When he first went to the lodging-house, the people of it met him and went before him. The master of it carried his mat for him, and the mistress brought the towel and comb. The lodgers left their mats, and the cook his fire-place (as he passed them). When he went away, the others in the house would have striven with him about (the places for) their mats[1].

---

[1] So had his arrogant superciliousness given place to humility.

BOOK XXVIII.

Part III. Section VI.

*Z*ang Wang, or 'Kings who have wished to resign the Throne[1].'

1. Yâo proposed to resign the throne to Hsü Yû, who would not accept it. He then offered it to 3ze-*k*âu *K*ih-fû[2], but he said, 'It is not unreasonable to propose that I should occupy the throne, but I happen to be suffering under a painful sorrow and illness. While I am engaged in dealing with it, I have not leisure to govern the kingdom.' Now the throne is the most important of all positions, and yet this man would not occupy it to the injury of his life; how much less would he have allowed any other thing to do so! But only he who does not care to rule the kingdom is fit to be entrusted with it.

Shun proposed to resign the throne to 3ze-*k*âu *K*ih-po[2], who declined in the very same terms as *K*ih-fû had done. Now the kingdom is the greatest of all concerns, and yet this man would not give his life in exchange for the throne. This shows how they who possess the Tâo differ from common men.

---

[1] See vol. xxxix, pp. 156, 157.

[2] We know nothing of this man but what is related here. He is, no doubt, a fictitious character. *K*ih-fû and *K*ih-po are supposed to be the same individual. See Hwang-fû Mî, I, 7.

Shun proposed to resign the throne to Shan *K*üan[1], who said, 'I am a unit in the midst of space and time. In winter I wear skins and furs; in summer, grass-cloth and linen; in spring I plough and sow, my strength being equal to the toil; in autumn I gather in my harvest, and am prepared to cease from labour and eat. At sunrise I get up and work; at sunset I rest. So do I enjoy myself between heaven and earth, and my mind is content:—why should I have anything to do with the throne? Alas! that you, Sir, do not know me better!' Thereupon he declined the proffer, and went away, deep among the hills, no man knew where.

Shun proposed to resign the throne to his friend, a farmer of Shih-hû[2]. The farmer, however, said (to himself), 'How full of vigour does our lord show himself, and how exuberant is his strength! If Shun with all his powers be not equal (to the task of government, how should I be so?).' On this he took his wife on his back, led his son by the hand, and went away to the sea-coast, from which to the end of his life he did not come back.

When Thâi-wang Than-fû[3] was dwelling in Pin[3], the wild tribes of the North attacked him. He tried to serve them with skins and silks, but they were not satisfied. He tried to serve them with dogs and horses, but they were not satisfied, and then

[1] Nor do we know more of Shan *K*üan, though Mî relates a visit of Yâo to him.

[2] Name of a place; where it was is very uncertain.

[3] An ancestor of the House of *K*âu, who about B.C. 1325 removed from Pin (in the present small department so called of Shen-hsî), and settled in the district of *Kh*î-shan, department of Făng-ʒhiang. He was the grandfather of king Wăn.

with pearls and jade, but they were not satisfied. What they sought was his territory. Thâi-wang Than-fû said (to his people), 'To dwell with the elder brother and cause the younger brother to be killed, or with the father and cause the son to be killed,—this is what I cannot bear to do. Make an effort, my children, to remain here. What difference is there between being my subjects, or the subjects of those wild people? And I have heard that a man does not use that which he employs for nourishing his people to injure them.' Thereupon he took his staff and switch and left, but the people followed him in an unbroken train, and he established a (new) state at the foot of mount *Kh*î[1]. Thus Thâi-wang Than-fû might be pronounced one who could give its (due) honour to life. Those who are able to do so, though they may be rich and noble, will not, for that which nourishes them, injure their persons; and though they may be poor and mean, will not, for the sake of gain, involve their bodies (in danger). The men of the present age who occupy high offices and are of honourable rank all lose these (advantages) again, and in the prospect of gain lightly expose their persons to ruin:—is it not a case of delusion?

The people of Yüeh three times in succession killed their ruler, and the prince Sâu[2], distressed by it, made his escape to the caves of Tan, so that Yüeh was left without a ruler. The people sought

[1] See note 3, p. 150.

[2] Sze-mâ *Kh*ien takes up the history of Yüeh at a later period, and we have from him no details of this prince Sâu. Tan-hsüeh was the name of a district in the south of Yüeh, in which was a valley with caves containing cinnabar;—the fabled home of the phœnix.

for the prince, but could not find him, till (at last) they followed him to the cave of Tan. The prince was not willing to come out to them, but they smoked him out with moxa, and made him mount the royal chariot. As he took hold of the strap, and mounted the carriage, he looked up to heaven, and called out, 'O Ruler, O Ruler, could you not have spared me this?' Prince Sâu did not dislike being ruler;—he disliked the evil inseparable from being so. It may be said of him that he would not for the sake of a kingdom endanger his life; and this indeed was the reason why the people of Yüeh wanted to get him for their ruler.

2. Han[1] and Wei[1] were contending about some territory which one of them had wrested from the other. 3ze-hwâ 3ze[2] went to see the marquis *K*âo-hsî (of Han)[3], and, finding him looking sorrowful, said, 'Suppose now that all the states were to sign an agreement before you to the effect that "Whoever should with his left hand carry off (the territory in dispute) should lose his right hand, and whoever should do so with his right hand should lose his left hand, but that, nevertheless, he who should carry it off was sure to obtain the whole kingdom;" would your lordship feel yourself able to carry it off?' The marquis said, 'I would not carry it off,' and 3ze-hwâ rejoined, 'Very good. Looking at the thing from this point of view, your two arms are of more value to you than the whole kingdom. But

[1] Two of the three states into which the great state of 3in was divided about the beginning of the fifth century B.C.

[2] A native, we may call him a philosopher, of Wei.

[3] Began his rule in B.C. 359.

莊子

your body is of more value than your two arms, and Han is of much less value than the whole kingdom. The territory for which you are now contending is further much less important than Han:—your lordship, since you feel so much concern for your body, should not be endangering your life by indulging your sorrow.'

The marquis *K*âo-hsî said, 'Good! Many have given me their counsel about this matter; but I never heard what you have said.' Ȝze-hwâ Ȝze may be said to have known well what was of great importance and what was of little.

3. The ruler of Lû, having heard that Yen Ho[1] had attained to the Tâo, sent a messenger, with a gift of silks, to prepare the way for further communication with him. Yen Ho was waiting at the door of a mean house, in a dress of coarse hempen cloth, and himself feeding a cow[2]. When the messenger arrived, Yen Ho himself confronted him. 'Is this,' said the messenger, 'the house of Yen Ho?' 'It is,' was the reply; and the other was presenting the silks to him, when he said, 'I am afraid you heard (your instructions) wrongly, and that he who sent you will blame you. You had better make sure.' The messenger on this returned, and made sure that he was right; but when he came back, and sought for Yen Ho, he was not to be found.

Yes; men like Yen Ho do of a truth dislike riches and honours. Hence it is said, 'The true

[1] Perhaps the Yen Ho of IV, 5.

[2] The same thing is often seen at the present day. The party in charge of the cow pours its prepared food down its throat from a joint of bamboo.

object of the Tâo is the regulation of the person. Quite subordinate to this is its use in the management of the state and the clan; while the government of the kingdom is but the dust and refuse of it.' From this we may see that the services of the Tîs and Kings are but a surplusage of the work of the sages, and do not contribute to complete the person or nourish the life. Yet the superior men of the present age will, most of them, throw away their lives for the sake of their persons, in pursuing their (material) objects;—is it not cause for grief? Whenever a sage is initiating any movement, he is sure to examine the motive which influences him, and what he is about to do. Here, however, is a man, who uses a pearl like that of the marquis of Sui[1] to shoot a bird at a distance of 10,000 feet. All men will laugh at him; and why? Because the thing which he uses is of great value, and what he wishes to get is of little. And is not life of more value than the pearl of the marquis of Sui?

4. 3ze[2] Lieh-3ze[2] was reduced to extreme poverty, and his person had a hungry look. A visitor mentioned the case to 3ze-yang, (the premier) of *K*ăng, saying, 'Lieh Yü-khâu, I believe, is a scholar who has attained to the Tâo. Is it because our ruler does not love (such) scholars, that he should be living in his state in such poverty?' 3ze-yang immediately ordered an officer to send to him a supply of grain.

[1] Sui was a small feudal state, a dependency of Wei. Its name remains in the Sui-*k*âu, Teh-an department, Hû-pei. The story is that one of its lords having healed a wounded snake, the creature one night brought him a large pearl in its mouth.

[2] The phraseology is peculiar. See Introductory Note on Bk. XXXII.

莊子

When Lieh-ȝze saw the messenger, he bowed to him twice, and declined the gift, on which the messenger went away. On Lieh-ȝze's going into the house, his wife looked to him and beat her breast, saying, 'I have heard that the wife and children of a possessor of the Tâo all enjoy plenty and ease, but now we look starved. The ruler has seen his error, and sent you a present of food, but you would not receive it; —is it appointed (for us to suffer thus)?' Ȝze Lieh-ȝze laughed and said to her, 'The ruler does not himself know me. Because of what some one said to him, he sent me the grain; but if another speak (differently) of me to him, he may look on me as a criminal. This was why I did not receive the grain.'

In the end it did come about, that the people, on an occasion of trouble and disorder, put Ȝze-yang to death.

5. When king *K*âo of *Kh*û[1] lost his kingdom, the sheep-butcher Yüeh followed him in his flight. When the king (recovered) his kingdom and returned to it, and was going to reward those who had followed him, on coming to the sheep-butcher Yüeh, that personage said, 'When our Great King lost his kingdom, I lost my sheep-killing. When his majesty got back his kingdom, I also got back my sheep-killing. My income and rank have been recovered; why speak further of rewarding me?' The king, (on hearing of this reply), said, 'Force him (to take the reward);' but Yüeh said, 'It was not through any crime of mine that the king lost his kingdom,

[1] B.C. 515–489. He was driven from his capital by an invasion of Wû, directed by Wû Ȝze-hsü.

and therefore I did not dare to submit to the death (which would have been mine if I had remained in the capital). And it was not through any service of mine that he recovered his kingdom, and therefore I do not dare to count myself worthy of any reward from him.'

The king (now) asked that the butcher should be introduced to him, but Yüeh said, 'According to the law of *Kh*û, great reward ought to be given to great service, and the recipient then be introduced to the king; but now my wisdom was not sufficient to preserve the kingdom, nor my courage sufficient to die at the hands of the invaders. When the army of Wû entered, I was afraid of the danger, and got out of the way of the thieves;—it was not with a distinct purpose (of loyalty) that I followed the king. And now he wishes, in disregard of the law, and violations of the conditions of our social compact, to see me in court;—this is not what I would like to be talked of through the kingdom.' The king said to 3ze-*kh*î, the Minister of War, 'The position of the sheep-butcher Yüeh is low and mean, but his setting forth of what is right is very high; do you ask him for me to accept the place of one of my three most distinguished nobles[1].' (This being communicated to Yüeh), he said, 'I know that the place of such a distinguished noble is nobler than a sheep-butcher's stall, and that the salary of 10,000 *k*ung is more than its profits. But how should I, through my greed of rank and emolument, bring on our ruler the name of an unlawful dispensation of his gifts? I dare not

[1] Literally, 'My three banners or flags,' emblems of the favour of the sovereign.

respond to your wishes, but desire to return to my stall as the sheep-butcher.' Accordingly he did not accept (the proffered reward).

6. Yüan Hsien[1] was living in Lû. His house, whose walls were only a few paces round, looked as if it were thatched with a crop of growing grass; its door of brushwood was incomplete, with branches of a mulberry tree for its side-posts; the window of each of its two apartments was formed by an earthenware jar (in the wall), which was stuffed with some coarse serge. It leaked above, and was damp on the ground beneath; but there he sat composedly, playing on his guitar. Ʒze-kung, in an inner robe of purple and an outer one of pure white, riding in a carriage drawn by two large horses, the hood of which was too high to get into the lane (leading to the house), went to see him. Yüan Hsien, in a cap made of bark, and slippers without heels, and with a stalk of hellebore for a staff, met him at the door. 'Alas! Master,' said Ʒze-kung, 'that you should be in such distress!' Yüan Hsien answered him, 'I have heard that to have no money is to be poor, and that not to be able to carry one's learning into practice is to be distressed. I am poor but not in distress.' Ʒze-kung shrank back, and looked ashamed, on which the other laughed and said, 'To act with a view to the world's (praise); to pretend to be public-spirited and yet be a partisan; to learn in order to please men; to teach for the sake of one's own gain; to conceal one's wickedness under the garb of

[1] A disciple of Confucius, called also Yüan Sze;—see Confucian Analects VI, iii, 3. With the description of his house or hut, compare in the Lî *K*î, XXVIII, 10.

benevolence and righteousness; and to be fond of the show of chariots and horses:—these are things which Hsien cannot bear to do.'

Ȝăng-ȝze was residing in Wei. He wore a robe quilted with hemp, and had no outer garment; his countenance looked rough and emaciated; his hands and feet were horny and callous; he would be three days without lighting a fire; in ten years he did not have a new suit; if he put his cap on straight, the strings would break; if he drew tight the overlap of his robe, his elbow would be seen; in putting on his shoes, the heels would burst them. Yet dragging his shoes along, he sang the 'Sacrificial Odes of Shang' with a voice that filled heaven and earth as if it came from a bell or a sounding stone. The Son of Heaven could not get him to be a minister; no feudal prince could get him for his friend. So it is that he who is nourishing his mind's aim forgets his body, and he who is nourishing his body discards all thoughts of gain, and he who is carrying out the Tâo forgets his own mind.

Confucius said to Yen Hui, 'Come here, Hui. Your family is poor, and your position is low; why should you not take office?' Hui replied, 'I have no wish to be in office. Outside the suburban district I possess fields to the extent of fifty acres, which are sufficient to supply me with congee; and inside it I have ten acres, which are sufficient to supply me with silk and flax. I find my pleasure in playing on my lute, and your doctrines, Master, which I study, are sufficient for my enjoyment; I do not wish to take office.' Confucius looked sad, changed countenance, and said, 'How good is the mind of Hui! I have heard that he who is con-

莊子

tented will not entangle himself with the pursuit of gain, that he who is conscious of having gained (the truth) in himself is not afraid of losing other things, and that he who cultivates the path of inward rectification is not ashamed though he may have no official position. I have long been preaching this; but to-day I see it realised in Hui:—this is what I have gained.'

7. Prince Mâu[1] of *K*ung-shan[1] spoke to *K*an-ȝze[2], saying, 'My body has its place by the streams and near the sea, but my mind dwells at the court of Wei;—what have you to say to me in the circumstances?' *K*an-ȝze replied, 'Set the proper value on your life. When one sets the proper value on his life, gain seems to him unimportant.' The prince rejoined, 'I know that, but I am not able to overcome (my wishes).' The reply was, 'If you cannot master yourself (in the matter), follow (your inclinations so that) your spirit may not be dissatisfied. When you cannot master yourself, and try to force yourself where your spirit does not follow, this is what is called doing yourself a double injury; and those who so injure themselves are not among the long-lived.'

Mâu of Wei was the son of a lord of ten thousand chariots. For him to live in retirement among crags and caves was more difficult than for a scholar who had not worn the dress of office. Although he

---

[1] Prince Mâu was a son of the marquis of Wei, and had been appointed to the appanage of *K*ung-shan,—corresponding to part of the present Ting *K*âu in Pei *K*ih-lî.

[2] A worthy officer or thinker of Wei. One is not sure that his advice was altogether good.

had not attained to the Tâo, he may be said to have had some idea of it.

8. When Confucius was reduced to extreme distress between *Kh*ăn and 3hâi, for seven days he had no cooked meat to eat, but only some soup of coarse vegetables without any rice in it. His countenance wore the appearance of great exhaustion, and yet he kept playing on his lute and singing inside the house. Yen Hui (was outside), selecting the vegetables, while 3ze-lû and 3ze-kung were talking together, and said to him, 'The Master has twice been driven from Lû; he had to flee from Wei; the tree (beneath which he rested) was cut down in Sung; he was reduced to extreme distress in Shang and *K*âu; he is held in a state of siege here between *Kh*ăn and 3hâi; any one who kills him will be held guiltless; there is no prohibition against making him a prisoner. And yet he keeps playing and singing, thrumming his lute without ceasing. Can a superior man be without the feeling of shame to such an extent as this?' Yen Hui gave them no reply, but went in and told (their words) to Confucius, who pushed aside his lute, and said, 'Yû and 3hze are small men. Call them here, and I will explain the thing to them.'

When they came in, 3ze-lû said, 'Your present condition may be called one of extreme distress.' Confucius replied, 'What words are these! When the Superior man has free course with his principles, that is what we call his success; when such course is denied, that is what we call his failure. Now I hold in my embrace the principles of benevolence and righteousness, and with them meet the evils of a disordered age;—where is the proof of my being

莊子

in extreme distress? Therefore looking inwards and examining myself, I have no difficulties about my principles; though I encounter such difficulties (as the present), I do not lose my virtue. It is when winter's cold is come, and the hoar-frost and snow are falling, that we know the vegetative power of the pine and cypress. This strait between *Kh*ăn and Ȝhâi is fortunate for me.' He then took back his lute so that it emitted a twanging sound, and began to play and sing. (At the same time) Ȝze-lû, hurriedly, seized a shield, and began to dance, while Ȝze-kung said, 'I did not know (before) the height of heaven nor the depth of the earth.'

The ancients who had got the Tâo were happy when reduced to extremity, and happy when having free course. Their happiness was independent of both these conditions. The Tâo and its characteristics!—let them have these and distress and success come to them as cold and heat, as wind and rain in the natural order of things. Thus it was that Hsü Yû found pleasure on the north of the river Ying, and that the earl of Kung enjoyed himself on the top of mount (Kung)[1].

9. Shun proposed to resign the throne to his friend, the Northerner Wû-*k*âi[2], who said, 'A strange man you are, O sovereign! You (first) lived among the channeled fields, and then your

[1] This takes us to the famous Kung-ho period (B.C. 842–828), but our author evidently follows the account of it found in the 'Bamboo Books;'—see the prolegomena to the Shû King, p. 154.

[2] We found, in Book XXI (see vol. xxxix, p. 133), Wû-*k*âi as the name of Thien Ȝze-fang. Here is the same name belonging to a much earlier man, 'a man of the north.'

place was in the palace of Yâo. And not only so:—you now further wish to extend to me the stain of your disgraceful doings. I am ashamed to see you.' And on this he threw himself into the abyss of *Kh*ing-lăng[1].

When Thang was about to attack *K*ieh, he took counsel with Pien Sui, who said, 'It is no business of mine.' Thang then said, 'To whom should I apply?' And the other said, 'I do not know.' Thang then took counsel with Wû Kwang, who gave the same answer as Pien Sui; and when asked to whom he should apply, said in the same way, 'I do not know.' 'Suppose,' Thang then said, 'I apply to Î Yin, what do you say about him?' The reply was, 'He has a wonderful power in doing what is disgraceful, and I know nothing more about him!'

Thang thereupon took counsel with Î Yin, attacked *K*ieh, and overcame him, after which he proposed to resign the throne to Pien Sui, who declined it, saying, 'When you were about to attack *K*ieh, and sought counsel from me, you must have supposed me to be prepared to be a robber. Now that you have conquered *K*ieh, and propose to resign the throne to me, you must consider me to be greedy. I have been born in an age of disorder, and a man without principle twice comes, and tries to extend to me the stain of his disgraceful proceedings!—I cannot bear to hear the repetition of his proposals.' With this he threw himself into the *K*âu[2] water and died.

[1] At the foot of a hill in the present department of Nan-yang, Ho-nan.

[2] The reading uncertain.

莊子

Thang further made proffer of the throne to Wû Kwang[1], saying, 'The wise man has planned it; the martial man has carried it through; and the benevolent man should occupy it:—this was the method of antiquity. Why should you, Sir, not take the position?' Wû Kwang refused the proffer, saying, 'To depose the sovereign is contrary to right; to kill the people is contrary to benevolence. When another has encountered the risks, if I should accept the gain of his adventure, I should violate my disinterestedness. I have heard it said, "If it be not right for him to do so, one should not accept the emolument; in an age of unprincipled (government), one should not put foot on the soil (of the) country:"—how much less should I accept this position of honour! I cannot bear to see you any longer.' And with this he took a stone on his back, and drowned himself in the Lü water[2].

10. Formerly, at the rise of the *K*âu dynasty, there were two brothers who lived in Kû-*k*û[3], and were named Po-î and Shû-*kh*î. They spoke together and said, 'We have heard that in the west there is one who seems to rule according to the Right Way; let us go and see.' (Accordingly) they came to the south of (mount) *Kh*î; and when king Wû heard of them, he sent (his brother) Shû Tan to see them, and make a covenant with them, engaging that their wealth should be second (only to that of the king), and that their offices should be of the first rank,

[1] Not elsewhere heard of, save in the same connexion.

[2] In the west of Liâo-tung.

[3] A small principality, in the present Lwan-*k*âu, department of Yung-phing *K*ih-lî.

and instructing him to bury the covenant with the blood of the victim after they had smeared the corners of their mouths with it [1]. The brothers looked at each other and laughed, saying, 'Ah! How strange! This is not what we call the Right Way. Formerly, when Shăn Năng had the kingdom, he offered his sacrifices at the proper seasons and with the utmost reverence, but without praying for any blessing. Towards men he was leal-hearted and sincere, doing his utmost in governing them, but without seeking anything for himself. When it was his pleasure to use administrative measures, he did so; and a sterner rule when he thought that would be better. He did not by the ruin of others establish his own power; he did not exalt himself by bringing others low; he did not, when the time was opportune, seek his own profit. But now *K*âu, seeing the disorder of Yin, has suddenly taken the government into its hands; with the high it has taken counsel, and with those below employed bribes; it relies on its troops to maintain the terror of its might; it makes covenants over victims to prove its good faith; it vaunts its proceedings to please the masses; it kills and attacks for the sake of gain:—this is simply overthrowing disorder and changing it for tyranny. We have heard that the officers of old, in an age of good government, did not shrink from their duties, and in an age of disorder did not recklessly seek to remain in office. Now the kingdom is in a state of darkness; the virtue of *K*âu is decayed. Than to join with it and

[1] According to the usual forms in which a covenant was made and established. The translation is free and diffuse.

莊子

lay our persons in the dust, it is better for us to abandon it, and maintain the purity of our conduct.'

The two princes then went north to the hill of Shâu-yang[1], where they died of starvation. If men such as they, in the matter of riches and honours, can manage to avoid them, (let them do so); but they must not depend on their lofty virtue to pursue any perverse course, only gratifying their own tendencies, and not doing service in their time:—this was the style of these two princes.

---

[1] In the present department of Phû-*k*au, Shan-hsî.

BOOK XXIX.

PART III. SECTION VII.

Tâo *K*ih, or 'The Robber *K*ih[1].'

1. Confucius was on terms of friendship with Liû-hsiâ *K*î[2], who had a brother named Tâo *K*ih. This Tâo *K*ih had 9,000 followers, who marched at their will through the kingdom, assailing and oppressing the different princes. They dug through walls and broke into houses; they drove away people's cattle and horses; they carried off people's wives and daughters. In their greed to get, they forgot the claims of kinship, and paid no regard to their parents and brethren. They did not sacrifice to their ancestors. Wherever they passed through the country, in the larger states the people guarded their city walls, and in the smaller the people took to their strongholds. All were distressed by them.

Confucius spoke to Liû-hsiâ *K*î, saying, 'Fathers should be able to lay down the law to their sons,

[1] See vol. xxxix, pp. 157, 158.

[2] Better known as Liû-hsiâ Hui, under which designation he is mentioned both in the Confucian Analects and in Mencius, but it is an anachronism to say that Confucius was on terms of friendship with him. He was a scion of the distinguished family of *K*an in Lû, and was called *K*an Hwo and *K*an *Kh*in. We find, in the 3o *K*wan, a son of his employed in an important expedition in B.C. 634, so that he, probably, had passed away before Confucius was born in B.C. 551, and must certainly have deceased before the death of 3ze-lû (480), which is mentioned in the Book.

and elder to instruct their younger brothers. If they are unable to do so, they do not fulfil the duties of the relationships which they sustain. You, Sir, are one of the most talented officers of the age, and your younger brother is this Robber *K*ih. He is a pest in the kingdom, and you are not able to instruct him better; I cannot but be ashamed of you, and I beg to go for you and give him counsel.' Liû-hsiâ *K*î replied, 'You say, Sir, that fathers must be able to lay down the law to their sons, and elder to instruct their younger brothers, but if sons will not listen to the orders of their fathers, nor the younger receive the lessons of their elder brothers, though one may have your powers of persuasion, what is to be done? And, moreover, *K*ih is a man whose mind is like a gushing fountain, and his will like a whirlwind; he is strong enough to resist all enemies, and clever enough to gloss over his wrong-doings. If you agree with him, he is glad; if you oppose him, he is enraged; and he readily meets men with the language of abuse. You must not go to him.'

Confucius, however, did not attend to this advice. With Yen Hui as his charioteer, and Ȝze-kung seated on the right, he went to see Tâo *K*ih, whom he found with his followers halted on the south of Thâi-shan, and mincing men's livers, which he gave them to eat. Confucius alighted from his carriage, and went forward, till he saw the usher, to whom he said, 'I, Khung *Kh*iû of Lû, have heard of the general's lofty righteousness,' bowing twice respectfully to the man as he said so. The usher went in and announced the visitor. But when Tâo *K*ih heard of the arrival, he flew into a great rage; his eyes became like blazing stars, and his hair rose up and touched his cap. 'Is not this fellow,' said he, 'Khung *Kh*iû, that artful hypocrite of Lû? Tell him from me, "You invent speeches and babble away, appealing without ground to (the examples of) Wăn and Wû. The ornaments on your cap are as many as the branches of a tree, and your girdle is (a piece of skin) from the ribs of a dead ox. The more you talk, the more nonsense you utter. You get your food without (the labour of) ploughing, and your clothes without (that of) weaving. You wag your lips and make your tongue a drum-stick. You arbitrarily decide what is right and what is wrong, thereby leading astray the princes throughout the kingdom, and making its learned scholars not occupy their thoughts with their proper business. You recklessly set up your filial piety and fraternal duty, and curry favour with the feudal princes, the wealthy and the noble. Your offence is great; your crime is very heavy. Take yourself off home at once. If you do not do so, I will take your liver, and add it to the provision for to-day's food."'

But Confucius sent in another message, saying, 'I enjoy the good will of (your brother) *K*î, and I wish and hope to tread the ground beneath your tent[1].' When the usher had communicated this message, Tâo *K*ih said, 'Make him come forward.' On this Confucius hastened forwards. Declining to take a mat, he drew hastily back, and bowed twice to Tâo *K*ih, who in a great rage stretched

[1] That is, I wish to have an interview with you, to see and speak to you face to face.

莊子

his legs apart, laid his hand on his sword, and with glaring eyes and a voice like the growl of a nursing tigress, said, 'Come forwards, *Kh*iû. If what you say be in accordance with my mind, you shall live; but, if it be contrary to it, you shall die.' Confucius replied, 'I have heard that everywhere under the sky there are three (most excellent) qualities. To be naturally tall and large, to be elegant and handsome without a peer, so that young and old, noble and mean, are pleased to look upon him;—this is the highest of those qualities. To comprehend both heaven and earth in his wisdom, and to be able to speak eloquently on all subjects;—this is the middle one of them. To be brave and courageous, resolute and daring, gathering the multitudes round him, and leading on his troops;—this is the lowest of them. Whoever possesses one of these qualities is fit to stand with his face to the south[1], and style himself a Prince. But you, General, unite in yourself all the three. Your person is eight cubits and two inches in height; there is a brightness about your face and a light in your eyes; your lips look as if stained with vermilion; your teeth are like rows of precious shells; your voice is attuned to the musical tubes; and yet you are named "The Robber *K*ih." I am ashamed of you, General, and cannot approve of you. If you are inclined to listen to me, I should like to go as your commissioner to Wû and Yüeh in the south; to *Kh*î and Lû in the north; to Sung and Wei in the east; and to Ȝin and *Kh*û in the west. I will get them to build for you a great city several hundred lî in size, to

[1] To take the position of a ruler in his court.

establish under it towns containing several hundred thousands of inhabitants, and honour you there as a feudal lord. The kingdom will see you begin your career afresh; you will cease from your wars and disband your soldiers; you will collect and nourish your brethren, and along with them offer the sacrifices to your ancestors[1]:—this will be a course befitting a sage and an officer of ability, and will fulfil the wishes of the whole kingdom.'

'Come forward, *Kh*iû,' said Tâo *K*ih, greatly enraged. 'Those who can be persuaded by considerations of gain, and to whom remonstrances may be addressed with success, are all ignorant, low, and ordinary people. That I am tall and large, elegant and handsome, so that all who see me are pleased with me;—this is an effect of the body left me by my parents. Though you were not to praise me for it, do I not know it myself? And I have heard that he who likes to praise men to their face will also like to speak ill of them behind their back. And when you tell me of a great wall and a multitudinous people, this is to try to persuade me by considerations of gain, and to cocker me as one of the ordinary people. But how could such advantages last for long? Of all great cities there is none so great as the whole kingdom, which was possessed by Yâo and Shun, while their descendants (now) have not so much territory as would admit an awl[2]. Thang and Wû were both set up as the Sons of Heaven, but in after ages (their posterity) were cut

[1] It is said near the beginning that *K*ih and his followers had ceased to offer such sacrifices;—they had no religion.

[2] The descendants of those worthies were greatly reduced; but they still had a name and a place.

off and extinguished;—was not this because the gain of their position was so great a prize[1]?

'And moreover I have heard that anciently birds and beasts were numerous, and men were few, so that they lived in nests in order to avoid the animals. In the daytime they gathered acorns and chestnuts, and in the night they roosted on the trees; and on account of this they are called the people of the Nest-builder. Anciently the people did not know the use of clothes. In summer they collected great stores of faggots, and in winter kept themselves warm by means of them; and on account of this they are called the people who knew how to take care of their lives. In the age of Shăn Năng, the people lay down in simple innocence, and rose up in quiet security. They knew their mothers, but did not know their fathers. They dwelt along with the elks and deer. They ploughed and ate; they wove and made clothes; they had no idea of injuring one another:—this was the grand time of Perfect virtue[2]. Hwang-Tî, however, was not able to perpetuate this virtuous state. He fought with *Kh*ih-yû[3] in the wild of *K*o-lû[4] till the blood flowed over a hundred lî. When Yâo and Shun arose, they instituted their crowd of ministers. Thang banished his lord. King Wû killed *K*âu. Since that time the strong have oppressed the weak, and the many tyrannised over the few. From Thang and Wû downwards, (the

[1] See note 2, p. 170.

[2] Compare the description of this primeval time in Book X, par. 4.

[3] Commonly spoken of as 'the first rebel.' See Mayers's Manual, p. 36.

[4] Perhaps in the present Pâo-an *K*âu, department of Hsüan-hwâ, *K*ih-lî.

rulers) have all been promoters of disorder and confusion. You yourself now cultivate and inculcate the ways of Wăn and Wû; you handle whatever subjects are anywhere discussed for the instruction of future ages. With your peculiar robe and narrow girdle, with your deceitful speech and hypocritical conduct, you delude the lords of the different states, and are seeking for riches and honours. There is no greater robber than you are;—why does not all the world call you the Robber *Kh*iû, instead of styling me the Robber *K*ih?

'You prevailed by your sweet speeches on ʒze-lû, and made him your follower; you made him put away his high cap, lay aside his long sword, and receive your instructions, so that all the world said, "Khung *Kh*iû is able to arrest violence and repress the wrong-doer;" but in the end, when ʒze-lû wished to slay the ruler of Wei, and the affair proved unsuccessful, his body was exhibited in pickle over the eastern gate of the capital;—so did your teaching of him come to nothing.

'Do you call yourself a scholar of talent, a sage? Why, you were twice driven out of Lû; you had to run away from Wei; you were reduced to extremity in *Kh*î; you were held in a state of siege between *Kh*ăn and ʒhâi; there is no resting-place for your person in the kingdom; your instructions brought ʒze-lû to pickle. Such have been the misfortunes (attending your course). You have done no good either for yourself or for others;—how can your doctrines be worth being thought much of?

'There is no one whom the world exalts so much as it does Hwang-Tî, and still he was not able to perfect his virtue, but fought in the wilderness of

*K*o-lû, till the blood flowed over a hundred lî. Yâo was not kind to his son[1]. Shun was not filial[2]. Yü was paralysed on one side[3]. Thang banished his sovereign. King Wû smote *K*âu. King Wăn was imprisoned in Yû-lî[4]. These are the six men of whom the world thinks the most highly, yet when we accurately consider their history, we see that for the sake of gain they all disallowed their true (nature), and did violence to its proper qualities and tendencies:—their conduct cannot be thought of but with deep shame.

'Among those whom the world calls men of ability and virtue were (the brothers) Po-Î and Shû-*kh*î. They declined the rule of Kû-*k*û, and died of starvation on the hill of Shâu-yang, leaving their bones and flesh unburied. Pâo Ȝiâo vaunted his conduct, and condemned the world, but he died with his arms round a tree[5]. When Shăn-thû Tî's remonstrances were not listened to, he fastened a stone on his back, and threw himself into the Ho, where he was eaten by the fishes and turtles[6]. *K*ieh Ȝze-thui was the most devoted (of followers), and cut a piece from his thigh as food for duke Wăn. But when the duke afterwards overlooked him (in

[1] Referring to his setting aside his unworthy son, Tan-*k*û, and giving the throne to Shun.

[2] See in Mencius, V, i, 1. 3, 4.

[3] This, I think, is the meaning; the fact was highly honourable to Yü, and brought on by his devotion to his labours.

[4] In the present district of Thang-yin, department *Kh*ang-teh, Ho-nan. There king Wăn pursued his labours on the Yî King.

[5] A recluse of the time of Confucius, according to Han Ying (I, art. 27). After a dispute with Ȝze-kung, he committed suicide in the way described.

[6] See art. 26, in the same Book of Han Ying.

his distribution of favours), he was angry, and went away, and was burned to death with a tree in his arms[1]. Wei Shăng had made an appointment with a girl to meet him under a bridge; but when she did not come, and the water rose around him, he would not go away, and died with his arms round one of the pillars[2]. (The deaths of) these four men were not different from those of the dog that is torn in pieces, the pig that is borne away by a current, or the beggar (drowned in a ditch) with his alms-gourd in his hand. They were all caught as in a net by their (desire for) fame, not caring to nourish their life to its end, as they were bound to do.

'Among those whom the world calls faithful ministers there have been none like the prince Pî-kan and Wû 3ze-hsü. But 3ze-hsü's (dead) body was cast into the *K*iang, and the heart of Pî-kan was cut out. These two were what the world calls loyal ministers, but the end has been that everybody laughs at them. Looking at all the above cases, down to those of 3ze-hsü and Pî-kan, there is not one worthy to be honoured; and as to the admonitions which you, *Kh*iû, wish to impress on me, if you tell me about the state of the dead, I am unable to know anything about it; if you tell me about the things of men (alive), they are only such as I have stated, what I have heard and know all about. I will now tell you, Sir, my views about the condition of man. The eyes wish to look on beauty; the ears to hear music; the mouth to enjoy flavours; the will to be gratified. The greatest longevity man

[1] See Mayers's Manual, p. 80.

[2] Supposed to be the same with the Wei-shăng Kâo, mentioned in Analects, V, 23;—see Mayers's Manual, p. 251.

can reach is a hundred years; a medium longevity is eighty years; the lowest longevity is sixty. Take away sickness, pining, bereavement, mourning, anxieties, and calamities, the times when, in any of these, one can open his mouth and laugh, are only four or five days in a month. Heaven and earth have no limit of duration, but the death of man has its (appointed) time. Take the longest amount of a limited time, and compare it with what is unlimited, its brief existence is not different from the passing of a crevice by one of king Mû's horses[1]. Those who cannot gratify their will and natural aims, and nourish their appointed longevity, are all unacquainted with the (right) Way (of life). I cast from me, *Kh*iû, all that you say. Be quick and go. Hurry back and say not a word more. Your Way is only a wild recklessness, deceitful, artful, vain, and hypocritical. It is not available to complete the true (nature of man); it is not worth talking about!'

Confucius bowed twice, and hurried away. He went out at the door, and mounted his carriage. Thrice he missed the reins as he tried to take hold of them. His eyes were dazed, and he could not see; and his colour was that of slaked lime. He laid hold of the cross-bar, holding his head down, and unable to draw his breath. When he got back, outside the east gate of (the capital of) Lû, he encountered Liû-hsiâ *K*î, who said to him, 'Here you are, right in the gate. For some days I have not seen you. Your carriage and horses are travel-stained;—have you not been to see Tâo *K*ih?' Con-

[1] King Mû had eight famous horses, each having its own name. The name of only one—*Kh*ih-*k*i—is given here. See Bk. XVII, par. 5.

fucius looked up to heaven, sighed, and said, 'Yes.' The other went on, 'And did he not set himself in opposition to all your views, as I said he would do?' 'He did. My case has been that of the man who cauterised himself without being ill. I rushed away, stroked the tiger's head, played with his whiskers, and narrowly escaped his mouth.'

2. Ȝze-*k*ang[1] asked Mân Kâu-teh[2], saying, 'Why do you not pursue a (righteous) course? Without such a course you will not be believed in; unless you are believed in, you will not be employed in office; and if not employed in office, you will not acquire gain. Thus, if you look at the matter from the point of reputation, or estimate it from the point of gain, a righteous course is truly the right thing. If you discard the thought of reputation and gain, yet when you think over the thing in your own mind, you will see that the scholar should not be a single day without pursuing a (righteous) course.' Mân Kâu-teh said, 'He who has no shame becomes rich, and he in whom many believe becomes illustrious. Thus the greatest fame and gain would seem to spring from being without shame and being believed in. Therefore if you look at the matter from the point of reputation, or estimate it from the point of gain, to be believed in is the right thing. If you discard the thought of fame and gain, and think over the thing in your own mind, you will see that the scholar in the course which he pursues is (simply) holding fast his Heavenly (nature, and gaining nothing).'

[1] We are told (Analects, II, 18) that Ȝze-*k*ang 'studied with a view to official emolument.' This is, probably, the reason why he appears as interlocutor in this paragraph.

[2] A fictitious name, meaning, 'Full of gain recklessly got.'

莊子

Ȝze-*k*ang said, 'Formerly *K*ieh and *K*âu each enjoyed the honour of being the sovereign, and all the wealth of the kingdom was his; but if you now say to a (mere) money-grabber, "Your conduct is like that of *K*ieh or *K*âu," he will look ashamed, and resent the imputation:—(these two sovereigns) are despised by the smallest men. *K*ung-nî and Mo Tî (on the other hand) were poor, and common men; but if you say to a Prime Minister that his conduct is like that of *K*ung-nî or Mo Tî, then he will be put out and change countenance, and protest that he is not worthy (to be so spoken of):—(these two philosophers) are held to be truly noble by (all) scholars. Thus it is that the position of sovereign does not necessarily connect with being thought noble, nor the condition of being poor and of common rank with being thought mean. The difference of being thought noble or mean arises from the conduct being good or bad.' Mân Kâu-teh replied, 'Small robbers are put in prison; a great robber becomes a feudal lord; and in the gate of the feudal lord your righteous scholars will be found. For instance, Hsiâo-po [1], the duke Hwan, killed his elder brother, and took his sister-in-law to himself, and yet Kwan *K*ung became his minister; and Thien *Kh*ang, styled *Kh*ăng-ȝze, killed his ruler, and usurped the state [2], and yet Confucius received a present of silks from him. In their discussions they would condemn the men, but

[1] The name of duke Hwan.

[2] Compare the account of the same transaction in Book X, par. 1. See also Analects, XIV, 22. But there is no evidence but rather the contrary, that Confucius ever received a gift from Thien or *Kh*ăn Hăng.

in their conduct they abased themselves before them. In this way their words and actions must have been at war together in their breasts;—was it not a contradiction and perversity? As it is said in a book, "Who is bad? and who is good? The successful is regarded as the Head, and the unsuccessful as the Tail."'

Ʒze-*k*ang said, 'If you do not follow the usual course of what is held to be right, but observe no distinction between the near and remote degrees of kin, no difference between the noble and the mean, no order between the old and the young, then how shall a separation be made of the fivefold arrangement (of the virtues), and the six parties (in the social organisation)?' Mân Kâu-teh replied, 'Yâo killed his eldest son, and Shun banished his half-brother[1]:—did they observe the rules about the different degrees of kin? Thang deposed *K*ieh; king Wû overthrew *K*âu:—did they observe the righteousness that should obtain between the noble and the mean? King *K*î took the place of his elder brother[2], and the duke of *K*âu killed his[3]:—did they observe the order that should obtain between the elder and the younger? The Literati make hypocritical speeches; the followers of Mo hold that all should be loved equally:—do we find in them the separation of the fivefold arrangement (of the

[1] Exaggerations or misrepresentations.

[2] King *K*î was the so-called king *K*î-lî, the father of king Wăn. His elder brother, that the state of *K*âu might descend to him, left it, and withdrew south to what was then the wild region of Wû. See Analects, VIII, 1; the Shih King, III, i, Ode 7. 3, 4.

[3] Who had joined with Wû-kăng, son of the tyrant of Yin, in rebellion, thus threatening the stability of the new dynasty of *K*âu.

莊子

virtues)[1], and the six parties (in the social organisation)[2]? And further, you, Sir, are all for reputation, and I am all for gain; but where the actual search for reputation and gain may not be in accordance with principle and will not bear to be examined in the light of the right way, let me and you refer the matter to-morrow[3] to the decision of Wû-yo[4].'

(This Wû-yo) said, 'The small man pursues after wealth; the superior man pursues after reputation. The way in which they change their feelings and alter their nature is different; but if they were to cast away what they do, and replace it with doing nothing, they would be the same. Hence it is said, "Do not be a small man;—return and pursue after the Heavenly in you. Do not be a superior man;—follow the rule of the Heavenly in you. Be it crooked, be it straight, view the thing in the light of Heaven as revealed in you. Look all round on every side of it, and as the time indicates, cease your endeavours. Be it right, be it wrong, hold fast the ring in yourself in which all conditions converge. Alone by yourself, carry out your idea; ponder over the right way. Do not turn your course; do not try to complete your righteousness. You will fail in what you do. Do not haste to be rich; do not follow after your perfection. If you do, you will lose the heavenly in you."

---

[1] Probably what are called 'the five constant virtues.'

[2] The parties in the 'Three Bonds of Society,' or Three Cardinal Objects of Duty.

[3] So Lû Shû-kih (日 = 明日).

[4] If we take Wû-yo as a name, which is the simplest construction, we must still recognise its meaning as denoting 'one who is unbound by the conventionalities of opinion.' Much of what he is made to say is in rhyme, and might also be so translated.

'Pi-kan had his heart cut out; Ȝze-hsü had his eyes gouged out:—such were the evil consequences of their loyalty. The upright person[1] bore witness against his father; Wei Shăng was drowned:—such were the misfortunes of good faith. Pao-ȝze stood till he was dried up; Shăn-ȝze would not defend himself[2]:—such were the injuries brought on by disinterestedness. Confucius did not see his mother[3]; Khwang-ȝze[4] did not see his father:—such were the failures of the righteous. These are instances handed down from former ages, and talked about in these later times. They show us how superior men, in their determination to be correct in their words and resolute in their conduct, paid the penalty of these misfortunes, and were involved in these distresses.'

3. Mr. Dissatisfied[5] asked Mr. Know-the-Mean[5], saying, 'There is no man after all who does not strive for reputation and pursue after gain. When men are rich, then others go to them. Going to them, they put themselves beneath them. In that position they do honour to them as nobler than themselves. But to

[1] See the Analects, XIII, 18.

[2] The reading of the name here is not certain. The best identification perhaps is with Shan Shăng (申生), the eldest son of duke Hsien of Ȝin, who was put to death on a false charge of having put poison into his father's food, from which he would not defend himself.

[3] A false charge.

[4] The Khwang *K*ang of Mencius, IV, ii, 30, q.v.

[5] Both of these names are fictitious. About the meaning of the first, there can be no difference of opinion. I have given that of the second according to my understanding of it,—see in the Lî *K*î, Book XXVIII, section I.

莊子

see others taking that position and doing honour to us is the way to prolong life, and to secure the rest of the body and the satisfaction of the mind. You alone, Sir, however, have no idea of this. Is it that your knowledge is deficient? Is it that you have the knowledge, but want the strength to carry it into practice? Or is it that your mind is made up to do what you consider right, and never allow yourself to forget it?' Know-the-Mean replied, 'Here now is this man judging of us, his contemporaries, and living in the same neighbourhood as himself, that we consider ourselves scholars who have abjured all vulgar ways and risen above the world. He is entirely without the thought of submitting to the rule of what is right. He therefore studies ancient times and the present, and the differing questions about the right and wrong, and agrees with the vulgar ideas and influences of the age, abandoning what is most important and discarding what is most honourable, in order to be free to act as he does. But is he not wide of the mark when he thinks that this is the way to promote long life, and to secure the rest of the body and the satisfaction of the mind? He has his painful afflictions and his quiet repose, but he does not inquire how his body is so variously affected; he has his apprehensive terrors, and his happy joys, but he does not inquire how his mind has such different experiences. He knows how to pursue his course, but he does not know why he does so. Even if he had the dignity of the Son of Heaven, and all the wealth of the kingdom were his, he would not be beyond the reach of misfortunes and evils.' Dissatisfied rejoined, 'But riches are in every way advantageous to man.

With them his attainment of the beautiful and mastery of every art become what the perfect man cannot obtain nor the sagely man reach to; his appropriation of the bravery and strength of others enables him to exercise a powerful sway; his availing himself of the wisdom and plans of others makes him be accounted intelligent and discriminating; his taking advantage of the virtues of others makes him be esteemed able and good. Though he may not be the holder of a state, he is looked to with awe as a ruler and father. Moreover, music, beauty, with the pleasures of the taste and of power, are appreciated by men's minds and rejoiced in without any previous learning of them; the body reposes in them without waiting for the example of others. Desire and dislike, avoidance and pursuit, do not require any master;—this is the nature of man. Though the world may condemn one's indulgence of them, who can refrain from it?' Know-the-Mean replied, 'The action of the wise is directed for the good of the people, but they do not go against the (proper) rule and degree. Therefore when they have enough, they do not strive (for more); they have no further object, and so they do not seek for one. When they have not enough, they will seek for it; they will strive for it in every quarter, and yet not think of themselves as greedy. If they have (already) a superfluity, they will decline (any more); they will decline the throne, and yet not think of themselves as disinterested:—the conditions of disinterestedness and greediness are (with them) not from the constraint of anything external. Through their exercise of introspection, their power may be that of the sovereign, but they will not in their nobility be arrogant to others; their wealth may be that of the whole kingdom, but they will not in their possession of it make a mock of others. They estimate the evils to which they are exposed, and are anxious about the reverses which they may experience. They think how their possessions may be injurious to their nature, and therefore they will decline and not accept them;—but not because they seek for reputation and praise.

'Yâo and Shun were the sovereigns, and harmony prevailed. It did so, not because of their benevolence towards the people;—they would not, for what was (deemed) admirable, injure their lives. Shan *K*üan and Hsü Yû might have been the sovereigns, but they would not receive the throne;—not that they declined it without purpose, but they would not by its occupancy injure themselves. These all followed after what was advantageous to them, and declined what was injurious, and all the world celebrates their superiority. Thus, though they enjoy the distinction, they did what they did, not for the sake of the reputation and praise.'

Dissatisfied (continued his argument), saying, 'In thus thinking it necessary for their reputation, they bitterly distressed their bodies, denied themselves what was pleasant, and restricted themselves to a bare sustenance in order to sustain their life; but so they had life-long distress, and long-continued pressure till their death arrived.' Know-the-Mean replied, 'Tranquil ease is happiness; a superfluity is injurious:—so it is with all things, and especially it is so, where the superfluity is of wealth. The ears of the rich are provided with the music of bells, drums, flageolets and flutes; and their mouths are stuffed with the flesh of fed beasts and with wine of the richest flavour; so are their desires satisfied, till they forget their proper business:—theirs may be pronounced a condition of disorder. Sunk deeply in their self-sufficiency, they resemble individuals ascending a height with a heavy burden on their backs:—their condition may be pronounced one of bitter suffering. They covet riches, thinking to derive comfort from them; they covet power, and would fain monopolise it; when quiet and retired, they are drowned in luxurious indulgence; their persons seem to shine, and they are full of boasting:—they may be said to be in a state of disease. In their desire to be rich and striving for gain, they fill their stores, and, deaf to all admonition, refuse to desist from their course. They are even more elated, and hold on their way:—their conduct may be pronounced disgraceful. When their wealth is amassed till they cannot use it, they clasp it to their breasts and will not part with it; when their hearts are distressed with their very fulness, they still seek for more and will not desist:—their condition may be said to be sad. In-doors they are apprehensive of pilfering and begging thieves, and out-of-doors they are afraid of being injured by plundering robbers; in-doors they have many chambers and partitions, and out-of-doors they do not dare to go alone:—they may be said to be in a state of (constant) alarm.

'These six conditions are the most deplorable in the world, but they forget them all, and have lost their faculty of judgment. When the evil comes, though they begged it with all the powers of their nature, and by the sacrifice of all their wealth, they could

莊子

not bring back one day of untroubled peace. When they look for their reputation, it is not to be seen; when they seek for their wealth, it is not to be got. To task their thoughts, and destroy their bodies, striving for (such an end as) this;—is it not a case of great delusion?'

BOOK XXX.

Part III. Section VIII.

Yüeh *K*ien, or 'Delight in the Sword-fight[1].'

Formerly, king Wăn of *K*âo[2] delighted in the sword-fight. More than three thousand men, masters of the weapon, appeared as his guests, lining the way on either side of his gate, and fighting together before him day and night. Over a hundred of them would die or be (severely) wounded in the course of a year, but he was never weary of looking on (at their engagements), so fond was he of them. The thing continued for three years, when the kingdom began to decay, and other states to plan measures against it.

The crown-prince Khwei[3] was distressed, and laid the case before his attendants, saying, 'If any one can persuade the king, and put an end to these swordsmen, I will give him a thousand ounces of

[1] See vol. xxxix, pp. 158, 159.

[2] Probably king Hui-wăn (B.C. 298–265) of *K*âo, one of the states into which the great state of Ȝin was subdivided, and which afterwards all claimed the sovereignty of the kingdom. In this Book *K*wang-ȝze appears as a contemporary of king Wăn, which makes the 'formerly' with which the paragraph commences seem strange.

[3] Sze-mâ *Kh*ien says nothing of king Wăn's love of the sword-fight, nor of this son Khwei. He says that in 265 Wăn was succeeded by his son Tan (丹), who appears to have been quite young.

莊子

silver.' His attendants said, '(Only) *K*wang-ȝze is able to do this.' Thereupon the prince sent men with a thousand ounces of silver to offer to *K*wang-ȝze, who, however, would not accept them, but went with the messengers. When he saw the prince, he said, 'O prince, what have you to say to *K*âu, and why would you give me the silver?' The prince replied, 'I have heard that you, master, are sagacious and sage. I sent you respectfully the thousand ounces of silver, as a prelude to the silks and other gifts[1]. But as you decline to receive them, how dare I now tell you (what I wished from you)?' *K*wang-ȝze rejoined, 'I have heard, O prince, that what you wanted me for was to wean the king from what is his delight. Suppose that in trying to persuade his Majesty I should offend him, and not fulfil your expectation, I shall be punished with death;—and could I then enjoy this silver? Or suppose that I shall succeed in persuading his Majesty, and accomplish what you desire, what is there in the kingdom of *K*âo that I might ask for which I would not get?'

The crown-prince said, 'Yes; but my (father), the king, will see none but swordsmen.' *K*wang-ȝze replied, 'I know; but I am expert in the use of the sword.' 'That is well,' observed the prince; 'but the swordsmen whom his Majesty sees all have their hair in a tangle, with whiskers projecting out. They wear slouching caps with coarse and unornamented tassels, and their coats are cut short behind. They have staring eyes, and talk about the hazards of

[1] This, I think, is the meaning. It may possibly mean 'for presents to your followers in attendance on you.'

their game. The king is delighted with all this; but now you are sure to present yourself to him in your scholar's dress, and this will stand greatly in the way of your success.'

*K*wang-ȝze said, 'I will then, with your leave, get me a swordsman's dress.' This was ready in three days, and when he appeared in it before the prince, the latter went with him to introduce him to the king, who then drew his sword from its scabbard and waited for him. When *K*wang-ȝze entered the door of the hall, he did not hurry forward, nor, when he saw the king, did he bow. The king asked him, 'What do you want to teach me, Sir, that you have got the prince to mention you beforehand?' The reply was, 'I have heard that your Majesty is fond of the sword-fight, and therefore I have sought an interview with you on the ground of (my skill in the use of) the sword.' 'What can you do with your sword against an opponent?' 'Let me meet with an opponent every ten paces, my sword would deal with him, so that I should not be stopped in a march of a thousand lî.' The king was delighted with him, and said, 'You have not your match in the kingdom.' *K*wang-ȝze replied, 'A good swordsman first makes a feint (against his opponent), then seems to give him an advantage, and finally gives his thrust, reaching him before he can return the blow. I should like to have an opportunity to show you my skill.' The king said, 'Stop (for a little), Master. Go to your lodging, and wait for my orders. I will make arrangements for the play, and then call you.'

The king accordingly made trial of his swordsmen for seven days, till more than sixty of them were killed, or (severely) wounded. He then selected five or six men, and made them bring their swords and take their places beneath the hall, after which he called *K*wang-ȥze, and said to him, 'To-day I am going to make (you and) these men show what you can do with your swords.' 'I have long been looking for the opportunity,' replied *K*wang-ȥze. The king then asked him what would be the length of the sword which he would use; and he said, 'Any length will suit me, but I have three swords, any one of which I will use, as may please your Majesty. Let me first tell you of them, and then go to the arena.' 'I should like to hear about the three swords,' said the king; and *K*wang-ȥze went on, 'There is the sword of the Son of Heaven; the sword of a feudal prince; and the sword of a common man.'

'What about the sword of the Son of Heaven?'

'This sword has Yen-*kh*î[1] and Shih-*kh*ang[2] for its point; *Kh*î and (Mount) Tâi[3] for its edge; Ȥin and Wei for its back; *K*âu and Sung for its hilt; Han and Wei for its sheath. It is embraced by the wild tribes all around; it is wrapped up in the four seasons; it is bound round by the Sea of Po[4]; and its girdle is the enduring hills. It is regulated by the five elements; its wielding is by means of Punishments and Kindness; its unsheathing is like that of

[1] Some noted place in the state of Yen, the capital of which was near the site of the present Peking.

[2] A wall, north of Yen, built as a barrier of defence against the northern tribes.

[3] Mount Thâi.

[4] A region lying along the present gulf of *K*ih-lî, between the Pei-ho and the *Kh*ing-ho in Shan-tung.

the Yin and Yang; it is held fast in the spring and summer; it is put in action in the autumn and winter. When it is thrust forward, there is nothing in front of it; when lifted up, there is nothing above it; when laid down, there is nothing below it; when wheeled round, there is nothing left on any side of it; above, it cleaves the floating clouds; and below, it penetrates to every division of the earth. Let this sword be once used, and the princes are all reformed, and the whole kingdom submits. This is the sword of the Son of Heaven[1].'

King Wăn looked lost in amazement, and said again, 'And what about the sword of a feudal lord?' (*K*wang-ȝze) replied, 'This sword has wise and brave officers for its point; pure and disinterested officers for its edge; able and honourable officers for its back; loyal and sage officers for its hilt; valiant and eminent officers for its sheath. When this sword is thrust directly forward, as in the former case, there is nothing in front of it; when directed upwards, there is nothing above it; when laid down, there is nothing below it; when wheeled round, there is nothing on any side of it. Above, its law is taken from the round heaven, and is in accordance with the three luminaries; below, its law is taken from the square earth, and is in accordance with the four seasons; between, it is in harmony with the minds of the people, and in all the parts of the state there is peace. Let this sword be once used, and you seem to hear the crash of the thunder-peal. Within

[1] By this sword *K*wang-ȝze evidently means the power of the sovereign, supported by the strength of the kingdom, and directed by good government.

莊子

the four borders there are none who do not respectfully submit, and obey the orders of the ruler. This is the sword of the feudal lord.'

'And what about the sword of the common man?' asked the king (once more). (*K*wang-ȝze) replied, 'The sword of the common man (is wielded by) those who have their hair in a tangle, with whiskers projecting out; who wear slouching caps with coarse and unornamented tassels, and have their coats cut short behind; who have staring eyes, and talk (only) about the hazards (of their game). They hit at one another before you. Above, the sword slashes through the neck; and below, it scoops out the liver and lungs. This is the sword of the common man. (The users of it) are not different from fighting cocks; any morning their lives are brought to an end; they are of no use in the affairs of the state. Your Majesty occupies the seat of the Son of Heaven, and that you should be so fond of the swordsmanship of such common men, is unworthy, as I venture to think, of your Majesty.'

On this the king drew *K*wang-ȝze with him, and went up to the top of the hall, where the cook set forth a meal, which the king walked round three times (unable to sit down to it). *K*wang-ȝze said to him, 'Sit down quietly, Great King, and calm yourself. I have said all I wished to say about swords.' King Wăn, thereafter, did not quit the palace for three months, and the swordsmen all killed themselves in their own rooms[1].

[1] *K*wang-ȝze's parables had had their intended effect. It was not in his mind to do anything for the swordsmen. The commentators say:—'Indignant at not being treated as they had been before, they all killed themselves.'

BOOK XXXI.

Part III. Section IX.

Yü-fû, or 'The Old Fisherman[1].'

Confucius, rambling in the forest of Ȝze-wei[2], stopped and sat down by the Apricot altar. The disciples began to read their books, while he proceeded to play on his lute, singing as he did so. He had not half finished his ditty when an old fisherman stepped

[1] See vol. xxxix, p. 159.

[2] A forest or grove in the neighbourhood of the capital of Lû. Ȝze-wei means 'black silken curtains;' and I do not know why the forest was so denominated. That I have correctly determined its position, however, may be inferred from a quotation in the Khang-hsî dictionary under the character thân (='altar') to the effect that 'Confucius, leaving (the capital of) Lû by the eastern gate, on passing the old apricot altar, said, "This is the altar reared by Ȝang Wăn-*k*ung to solemnise covenants."' Dr. Morrison under the same thân defines the second phrase—hsing thân—as 'The place where Confucius taught,' which Dr. Williams, under hsing, has amplified into 'The place where Confucius had his school.' But the text does not justify so definite a conclusion. The picture which the Book raises before my mind is that of a forest, with a row or clump of apricot trees, along which was a terrace, having on it the altar of Ȝang Wăn-*k*ung, and with a lake or at least a stream near to it, to which the ground sloped down. Here the writer introduces us to the sage and some of his disciples, on one occasion, when they were attracted from their books and music by the appearance of the old fisherman. I visited in 1873, not far from the Confucian cemetery, a ruined building called 'the College of *K*û-Sze,' which was pointed out as the site of the School of Confucius. The place would suit all the demands of the situation in this Book.

down from his boat, and came towards them. His beard and eyebrows were turning white; his hair was all uncombed; and his sleeves hung idly down. He walked thus up from the bank, till he got to the dry ground, when he stopped, and, with his left hand holding one of his knees, and the right hand at his chin, listened. When the ditty was finished, he beckoned to Ȝze-kung and Ȝze-lû, who both responded and went to him. Pointing to Confucius, he said, 'Who is he?' Ȝze-lû replied, 'He is the Superior Man of Lû.' 'And of what family is he?' 'He is of the Khung family.' 'And what is the occupation of this Mr. Khung?' To this question Ȝze-lû gave no reply, but Ȝze-kung replied, 'This scion of the Khung family devotes himself in his own nature to leal-heartedness and sincerity; in his conduct he manifests benevolence and righteousness; he cultivates the ornaments of ceremonies and music; he pays special attention to the relationships of society; above, he would promote loyalty to the hereditary lords; below, he seeks the transformation of all classes of the people; his object being to benefit the kingdom:—this is what Mr. Khung devotes himself to.'

The stranger further asked, 'Is he a ruler possessed of territory?' 'No,' was Ȝze-kung's reply. 'Is he the assistant of any prince or king?' 'No;' and on this the other began to laugh and to retrace his steps, saying as he went, 'Yes, benevolence is benevolence! But I am afraid he will not escape (the evils incident to humanity). By embittering his mind and toiling his body, he is imperilling his true (nature)! Alas! how far removed is he from the proper way (of life)!'

ʒze-kung returned, and reported (what the man had said) to Confucius, who pushed his lute aside, and arose, saying, 'Is he not a sage?' and down the slope he went in search of him. When he reached the edge of the lake, there was the fisherman with his pole, dragging the boat towards him. Turning round and seeing Confucius, he came back towards him and stood up. Confucius then drew back, bowed to him twice, and went forward. 'What do you want with me, Sir?' asked the stranger. The reply was, 'A little while ago, my Master, you broke off the thread of your remarks and went away. Inferior to you, I do not know what you wished to say, and have ventured here to wait for your instructions, fortunate if I may but hear the sound of your words to complete the assistance that you can give me!' 'Ah!' responded the stranger, 'how great is your love of learning!'

Confucius bowed twice, and then rose up, and said, 'Since I was young, I have cultivated learning till I am now sixty-nine years old; but I have not had an opportunity of hearing the perfect teaching;—dare I but listen to you with a humble and unprejudiced mind?' The stranger replied, 'Like seeks to like, and (birds) of the same note respond to one another;—this is a rule of Heaven. Allow me to explain what I am in possession of, and to pass over (from its standpoint) to the things which occupy you. What you occupy yourself with are the affairs of men. When the sovereign, the feudal lords, the great officers, and the common people, these four classes, do what is correct (in their several positions), we have the beauty of good order; and when they leave their proper duties, there ensues the greatest disorder. When the officials attend to their duties, and the common people are anxiously concerned about their business, there is no encroachment on one another's rights.

'Fields running to waste; leaking rooms; insufficiency of food and clothing; taxes unprovided for; want of harmony among wives and concubines; and want of order between old and young;—these are the troubles of the common people.

'Incompetency for their charges; inattention to their official business; want of probity in conduct; carelessness and idleness in subordinates; failure of merit and excellence; and uncertainty of rank and emolument:—these are the troubles of great officers.

'No loyal ministers at their courts; the clans in their states rebellious; want of skill in their mechanics; articles of tribute of bad quality; late appearances at court in spring and autumn; and the dissatisfaction of the sovereign:—these are the troubles of the feudal lords.

'Want of harmony between the Yin and Yang; unseasonableness of cold and heat, affecting all things injuriously; oppression and disorder among the feudal princes, their presuming to plunder and attack one another, to the injury of the people; ceremonies and music ill-regulated; the resources for expenditure exhausted or deficient; the social relationships uncared for; and the people abandoned to licentious disorder:—these are the troubles of the Son of Heaven and his ministers.

'Now, Sir, you have not the high rank of a ruler, a feudal lord, or a minister of the royal court, nor are you in the inferior position of a great minister, with his departments of business, and yet you take

O 2

it on you to regulate ceremonies and music, and to give special attention to the relationships of society, with a view to transform the various classes of the people :—is it not an excessive multiplication of your business?

'And moreover men are liable to eight defects, and (the conduct of) affairs to four evils; of which we must by all means take account.

'To take the management of affairs which do not concern him is called monopolising. To bring forward a subject which no one regards is called loquacity. To lead men on by speeches made to please them is called sycophancy. To praise men without regard to right or wrong is called flattery. To be fond of speaking of men's wickedness is called calumny. To part friends and separate relatives is called mischievousness. To praise a man deceitfully, or in the same way fix on him the character of being bad, is called depravity. Without reference to their being good or bad, to agree with men with double face, in order to steal a knowledge of what they wish, is called being dangerous. Those eight defects produce disorder among other men and injury to one's self. A superior man will not make a friend of one who has them, nor will an intelligent ruler make him his minister.

'To speak of what I called the four evils :—To be fond of conducting great affairs, changing and altering what is of long-standing, to obtain for one's self the reputation of meritorious service, is called ambition; to claim all wisdom and intrude into affairs, encroaching on the work of others, and representing it as one's own, is called greediness; to see his errors without changing them, and to go on

莊子

more resolutely in his own way when remonstrated with, is called obstinacy; when another agrees with himself, to approve of him, and, however good he may be, when he disagrees, to disapprove of him, is called boastful conceit. These are the four evils. When one can put away the eight defects, and allow no course to the four evils, he begins to be capable of being taught.'

Confucius looked sorrowful and sighed. (Again) he bowed twice, and then rose up and said, 'I was twice driven from Lû. I had to flee from Wei; the tree under which I rested was cut down in Sung; I was kept in a state of siege between *Kh*ăn and Ȝhâi. I do not know what errors I had committed that I came to be misrepresented on these four occasions (and suffered as I did).' The stranger looked grieved (at these words), changed countenance, and said, 'Very difficult it is, Sir, to make you understand. There was a man who was frightened at his shadow and disliked to see his footsteps, so that he ran to escape from them. But the more frequently he lifted his feet, the more numerous his footprints were; and however fast he ran, his shadow did not leave him. He thought he was going too slow, and ran on with all his speed without stopping, till his strength was exhausted and he died. He did not know that, if he had stayed in a shady place, his shadow would have disappeared, and that if he had remained still, he would have lost his footprints:—his stupidity was excessive! And you, Sir, exercise your judgment on the questions about benevolence and righteousness; you investigate the points where agreement and difference touch; you look at the changes from movement to rest and from rest to movement; you have mastered the rules of receiving and giving; you have defined the feelings of liking and disliking; you have harmonised the limits of joy and anger:—and yet you have hardly been able to escape (the troubles of which you speak). If you earnestly cultivated your own person, and carefully guarded your (proper) truth, simply rendering to others what was due to them, then you would have escaped such entanglements. But now, when you do not cultivate your own person, and make the cultivation of others your object, are you not occupying yourself with what is external?'

Confucius with an air of sadness said, 'Allow me to ask what it is that you call my proper Truth.' The stranger replied, 'A man's proper Truth is pure sincerity in its highest degree;—without this pure sincerity one cannot move others. Hence if one (only) forces himself to wail, however sadly he may do so, it is not (real) sorrow; if he forces himself to be angry, however he may seem to be severe, he excites no awe; if he forces himself to show affection, however he may smile, he awakens no harmonious reciprocation. True grief, without a sound, is yet sorrowful; true anger, without any demonstration, yet awakens awe; true affection, without a smile, yet produces a harmonious reciprocation. Given this truth within, it exercises a spiritual efficacy without, and this is why we count it so valuable. In our relations with others, it appears according to the requirements of each case:—in the service of parents, as gentle, filial duty; in the service of rulers, as loyalty and integrity; in festive drinking, as pleasant enjoyment; in the performance

莊子

of the mourning rites, as sadness and sorrow. In loyalty and integrity, good service is the principal thing; in festive drinking, the enjoyment; in the mourning rites, the sorrow; in the service of parents, the giving them pleasure. The beauty of the service rendered (to a ruler) does not require that it always be performed in one way; the service of parents so as to give them pleasure takes no account of how it is done; the festive drinking which ministers enjoyment does not depend on the appliances for it; the observance of the mourning rites with the proper sorrow asks no questions about the rites themselves. Rites are prescribed for the practice of the common people; man's proper Truth is what he has received from Heaven, operating spontaneously, and unchangeable. Therefore the sages take their law from Heaven, and prize their (proper) Truth, without submitting to the restrictions of custom. The stupid do the reverse of this. They are unable to take their law from Heaven, and are influenced by other men; they do not know how to prize the proper Truth (of their nature), but are under the dominion of ordinary things, and change according to the customs (around them):—always, consequently, incomplete. Alas for you, Sir, that you were early steeped in the hypocrisies of men, and have been so late in hearing about the Great Way!'

(Once more), Confucius bowed twice (to the fisherman), then rose again, and said, 'That I have met you to-day is as if I had the happiness of getting to heaven. If you, Master, are not ashamed, but will let me be as your servant, and continue to teach me, let me venture to ask where your dwelling is. I will then beg to receive your instructions there, and finish my learning of the Great Way.' The stranger replied, 'I have heard the saying, "If it be one with whom you can walk together, go with him to the subtlest mysteries of the Tâo. If it be one with whom you cannot walk together and he do not know the Tâo, take care that you do not associate with him, and you will yourself incur no responsibility." Do your utmost, Sir. I must leave you,—I must leave you!' With this he shoved off his boat, and went away among the green reeds.

Yen Yüan (now) returned to the carriage, where 3ze-lû handed to him the strap; but Confucius did not look round, (continuing where he was), till the wavelets were stilled, and he did not hear the sound of the pole, when at last he ventured to (return and) take his seat. 3ze-lû, by his side in the carriage, asked him, saying, 'I have been your servant for a long time, but I have never seen you, Master, treat another with the awe and reverence which you have now shown. I have seen you in the presence of a Lord of ten thousand chariots or a Ruler of a thousand, and they have never received you in a different audience-room, or treated you but with the courtesies due to an equal, while you have still carried yourself with a reserved and haughty air; but to-day this old fisherman has stood erect in front of you with his pole in his hand, while you, bent from your loins in the form of a sounding-stone, would bow twice before you answered him;—was not your reverence of him excessive? Your disciples will all think it strange in you, Master. Why did the old fisherman receive such homage from you?'

Confucius leant forward on the cross-bar of the

carriage, heaved a sigh, and said, 'Difficult indeed is it to change you, O Yû! You have been trained in propriety and righteousness for long, and yet your servile and mean heart has not been taken from you. Come nearer, that I may speak fully to you. If you meet one older than yourself, and do not show him respect, you fail in propriety. If you see a man of superior wisdom and goodness, and do not honour him, you want the great characteristic of humanity. If that (fisherman) did not possess it in the highest degree, how could he make others submit to him? And if their submission to him be not sincere, they do not attain to the truth (of their nature), and inflict a lasting injury on their persons. Alas! there is no greater calamity to man than the want of this characteristic; and you, O Yû, you alone, would take such want on yourself.

'Moreover, the Tâo is the course by which all things should proceed. For things to fail in this is death; to observe it, is life. To oppose it in practice is ruin; to conform it, is success. Therefore wherever the sagely man finds the Tâo, he honours it. And that old fisherman to-day might be said to possess it;—dared I presume not to show him reverence?'

BOOK XXXII.

PART III. SECTION X.

Lieh Yü-khâu[1].

1. Lieh Yü-khâu had started to go to *Khî*, but came back when he was half-way to it. He met Po-hwăn Wû-zăn[2], who said, 'Why have you come back?' His reply was, 'I was frightened.' 'What frightened you?' 'I went into ten soup-shops[3] to get a meal, and in five of them the soup was set before me before (I had paid for it)[4].' 'But what was there in that to frighten you?' (Lieh-ȝze) said, 'Though the inward and true purpose be not set forth, the body like a spy gives some bright display of it. And this outward demonstration overawes men's minds, and makes men on light grounds treat one as noble or as aged, from which evil to him will be produced. Now vendors of soup supply their commodity simply as a matter of business, and however much they may dispose of, their profit is but little,

[1] See vol. xxxix, pp. 160–162.

[2] The same teacher, no doubt, who is mentioned in II, par. 2, and XXI, par. 2, though the Wû in Wû-zăn is here 瞀, and there 無.

[3] Like the tea and congee shanties, I suppose, which a traveller in China finds still on the road-side.

[4] The meaning is not plain. There must have been something in the respect and generosity of the attendants which made Lieh-ȝze feel that his manner was inconsistent with his profession of Tâoism.

and their power is but slight; and yet they treated me as I have said:—how much more would the lord of ten thousand chariots do so! His body burdened with (the cares of his) kingdom, and his knowledge overtasked by its affairs, he would entrust those affairs to me, and exact from me the successful conduct (of its government). It was this which frightened me.' Po-hwăn Wû-žăn replied, 'Admirable perspicacity! But if you carry yourself as you do, men will flock to you for protection.'

Not long after, Po-hwăn Wû-žăn went (to visit Lieh-ȝze), and found the space outside his door full of shoes[1]. There he stood with his face to the north, holding his staff upright, and leaning his chin on it till the skin was wrinkled. After standing so for some time, and without saying a word, he was going away, when the door-keeper[2] went in, and told Lieh-ȝze. The latter (immediately) took up his shoes, and ran barefoot after the visitor. When he overtook him at the (outer) gate, he said, 'Since you, Sir, have come, are you going away without giving me some medicine[3]?' The other replied, 'It is of no use. I did tell you that men would flock to you, and they do indeed do so. It is not that you can cause men to flock to you, but you cannot keep them from not so coming;—of what use is (all my warning)? What influences them and makes them glad is the display of your extraordinary (qualities); but you must also be influ-

[1] See the Lî Kî (vol. xxvii, pp. 70, 71). It is still the custom in Japan for visitors to leave their shoes outside, in order not to soil the mats.

[2] Whose business it was to receive and announce the guests.

[3] Good advice.

enced in your turn, and your proper nature be shaken, and no warning can be addressed to you. Those who associate with you do not admonish you of this. The small words which they speak are poison to a man. You perceive it not; you understand it not;—how can you separate yourself from them?

'The clever toil on, and the wise are sad. Those who are without ability seek for nothing. They eat to the full, and wander idly about. They drift like a vessel loosed from its moorings, and aimlessly wander about[1].'

2. A man of *K*ăng, called Hwan, learned[2] his books in the neighbourhood of *Kh*iû-shih[3], and in no longer time than three years became a Confucian scholar, benefiting the three classes of his kindred[4] as the Ho extends its enriching influence for nine lî. He made his younger brother study (the principles of) Mo[5], and then they two—the scholar and the Mohist—disputed together (about their respective systems), and the father took the side of the younger[6]. After ten years Hwan killed himself. (By and by) he appeared to his father in a dream, saying, 'It was I who made your son become a

[1] Was this then Wû-zăn's idea of how the Tâoist should carry himself? From 'those who associate with you' Wû-zăn's address might be rhymed.

[2] Read them aloud, and so committed them to memory;—as Chinese schoolboys do still.

[3] The name of a place, or, perhaps, of Hwan's schoolmaster.

[4] Probably, the kindred of his father, mother, and wife;—through his getting office as a scholar.

[5] Or Mih Tî;—Mencius's heresiarch.

[6] Literally, 'of Tî,' as if that had been the name of the younger brother, as it was that of the heresiarch.

Mohist; why did you not recognise that good service[1]? I am become (but) the fruit of a cypress in autumn[2].' But the Creator[3], in apportioning the awards of men, does not recompense them for their own doings, but recompenses them for the (use of the) Heavenly in them. It was thus that Hwan's brother was led to learn Mohism. When this Hwan thought that it was he who had made his brother different from what he would have been, and proceeded to despise his father, he was like the people of *Kh*î, who, while they drank from a well, tried to keep one another from it. Hence it is said, 'Now-a-days all men are Hwans[4].' From this we perceive that those who possess the characteristics (of the Tâo) consider that they do not know them; how much more is it so with those who possess the Tâo itself! The ancients called such (as Hwan) 'men who had escaped the punishment of Heaven.'

3. The sagely man rests in what is his proper rest; he does not rest in what is not so;—the multitude of men rest in what is not their proper rest; they do not rest in their proper rest[5].

4. *K*wang-ȝze said, 'To know the Tâo is easy; not to say (that you know it) is difficult. To know it and not to speak of it is the way to attain to the

---

[1] The character for this in the text (良) is explained as meaning 'a grave,' with special reference to this passage, in the Khang-hsî dictionary.

[2] The idea of a grave is suggested by the 'cypress,' and we need not try to find it in 良.

[3] The creator was, in *K*wang-ȝze's mind, the Tâo.

[4] Arrogating to themselves what was the work of the Tâo.

[5] The best editions make this sentence a paragraph by itself.

Heavenly; to know and to speak of it, is the way to show the Human. The ancients pursued the Heavenly (belonging to them), and not the Human.'

5. *K*û Phing-man[1] learned how to slaughter the dragon[2] from *K*ih-lî Yî, expending (in doing so) all his wealth of a thousand ounces of silver. In three years he became perfect in the art, but he never exercised his skill.

6. The sage looks on what is deemed necessary as unnecessary, and therefore is not at war[3] (in himself). The mass of men deem what is unnecessary to be necessary, and therefore they are often at war (in themselves). Therefore those who pursue this method of (internal) war, resort to it in whatever they seek for. But reliance on such war leads to ruin.

7. The wisdom of the small man does not go beyond (the minutiae of) making presents and writing memoranda, wearying his spirits out in what is trivial and mean. But at the same time he wishes to aid in guiding to (the secret of) the Tâo and of (all) things in the incorporeity of the Grand Unity. In this way he goes all astray in regard to (the mysteries of) space and time. The fetters of embodied matter keep him from the knowledge of the Grand Beginning. (On the other hand), the perfect man directs the energy of his spirit to what was before the Beginning, and finds pleasure in the mysteriousness

[1] These are names fashioned by our author.

[2] 'Slaughtering the dragon' means 'learning the Tâo,' by expending or putting away all doing and knowledge, till one comes to the perfect state of knowing the Tâo and not speaking of it.

[3] Being 'at war' here is not the conflict of arms, but of joy, anger, and desire in one's breast. See 3iâo Hung in loc.

belonging to the region of nothingness. He is like the water which flows on without the obstruction of matter, and expands into the Grand Purity.

Alas for what you do, (O men)! You occupy yourselves with things trivial as a hair, and remain ignorant of the Grand Rest!

8. There was a man of Sung, called Ȝhâo Shang, who was sent by the king of Sung on a mission to *Kh*in. On setting out, he had several carriages with him; and the king (of *Kh*in) was so pleased with him that he gave him another hundred. When he returned to Sung, he saw *K*wang-ȝze, and said to him, 'To live in a narrow lane of a poor mean hamlet, wearing sandals amid distress of poverty, with a weazen neck and yellow face[1];—that is what I should find it difficult to do. But as soon as I come to an understanding with the Lord of a myriad carriages, to find myself with a retinue of a hundred carriages,—that is wherein I excel.' *K*wang-ȝze replied, 'When the king of *Kh*ăn is ill, the doctor whom he calls to open an ulcer or squeeze a boil receives a carriage; and he who licks his piles receives five. The lower the service, the more are the carriages given. Did you, Sir, lick his piles? How else should you have got so many carriages? Begone!'

9. Duke Âi of Lû asked Yen Ho, saying, 'If I employ *K*ung-nî as the support of my government, will the evils of the state be thereby cured?' The

[1] The character for 'face' generally means 'ears;' but the Khang-hsî dictionary, with special reference to this paragraph, explains it by 'face.'—The whole paragraph is smart and bitter, but Lin Hsî-*k*ung thinks it too coarse to be from *K*wang-ȝze's pencil.

reply was, '(Such a measure) would be perilous! It would be full of hazard! *K*ung-nî, moreover, will try to ornament a feather and paint it; in the conduct of affairs he uses flowery speeches. A (mere) branch is to him more admirable (than the root); he can bear to misrepresent their nature in instructing the people, and is not conscious of the unreality of his words. He receives (his inspiration) from his own mind, and rules his course from his own spirit:—what fitness has he to be set over the people? Is such a man suitable for you (as your minister)? Could you give to him the nourishment (of the people)? You would do so by mistake (but not on purpose, for a time, but not as a permanency). To make the people leave what is real, and learn what is hypocritical—that is not the proper thing to be shown to them; if you take thought for future ages, your better plan will be to give up (the idea of employing Confucius). What makes government difficult, is the dealing with men without forgetting yourself; this is not according to the example of Heaven in diffusing its benefits. Merchants and traffickers are not to be ranked (with administrative officers); if on an occasion you so rank them, the spirits (of the people) do not acquiesce in your doing so. The instruments of external punishment are made of metal and wood; those of internal punishment are agitation (of the mind) and (the sense of) transgression. When small men become subject to the external punishment, the (instruments of) metal and wood deal with them; when they become liable to the internal punishments, the Yin and Yang[1] con-

[1] Compare the use of 'the Yin and the Yang' in XXIII, par. 8.—Yen Ho does not flatter Confucius in his description of him.

莊子

sume them. It is only the true man who can escape both from the external and internal punishment.'

10. Confucius said, 'The minds of men are more difficult of approach than (the position defended by) mountains and rivers, and more difficult to know than Heaven itself. Heaven has its periods of spring and autumn, of winter and summer, and of morning and evening; but man's exterior is thickly veiled, and his feelings lie deep. Thus the demeanour of some is honest-like, and yet they go to excess (in what is mean); others are really gifted, and yet look to be without ability; some seem docile and impressible, but yet they have far-reaching schemes; others look firm, and yet may be twisted about; others look slow, and yet they are hasty. In this way those who hasten to do what is right as if they were thirsty will anon hurry away from it as if it were fire. Hence the superior man looks at them when employed at a distance to test their fidelity, and when employed near at hand to test their reverence. By employing them on difficult services, he tests their ability; by questioning them suddenly, he tests their knowledge; by appointing them a fixed time, he tests their good faith; by entrusting them with wealth, he tests their benevolence; by telling them of danger, he tests their self-command in emergencies; by making them drunk, he tests their tendencies[1]; by placing them in a variety of society, he tests their chastity:—by these nine tests the inferior man is discovered.'

11. When Khâo-fû, the Correct[2], received the first

[1] Is this equivalent to the adage 'In vino veritas?'

[2] A famous ancestor of Confucius in the eighth century B.C.,

grade of official rank, he walked with head bowed down; on receiving the second, with bent back; on receiving the third, with body stooping, he ran and hurried along the wall:—who would presume not to take him as a model? But one of those ordinary men, on receiving his first appointment, goes along with a haughty stride; on receiving his second, he looks quite elated in his chariot; and on receiving the third, he calls his uncles by their personal names;—how very different from Hsü (Yû) in the time (of Yâo of) Thang!

Of all things that injure (men) there is none greater than the practising of virtue with the purpose of the mind, till the mind becomes supercilious. When it becomes so, the mind (only) looks inwards (on itself), and such looking into itself leads to its ruin. This evil quality has five forms, and the chief of them is that which is the central. What do we mean by the central quality? It is that which appears in a man's loving (only) his own views, and reviling whatever he does not do (himself).

Limiting (men's advance), there are eight extreme conditions; securing (that advance), there are three things necessary; and the person has its six repositories. Elegance; a (fine) beard; tallness; size; strength; beauty; bravery; daring; and in all these excelling others:—(these are the eight extreme conditions) by which advance is limited. Depending on and copying others; stooping in order to rise; and being straitened by the fear of not equalling others:—

before the Khung family fled from Sung. See the account of him, with some verbal alterations, in the 3o *Kh*wan, under the seventh year of duke *K*âo.

莊子

these are the three things that lead to advancing. Knowledge seeking to reach to all that is external; bold movement producing many resentments; benevolence and righteousness leading to many requisitions; understanding the phenomena of life in an extraordinary degree; understanding all knowledge so as to possess an approach to it; understanding the great condition appointed for him, and following it, and the smaller conditions, and meeting them as they occur:—(these are the six repositories of the person)[1].

12. There was a man who, having had an interview with the king of Sung, and been presented by him with ten carriages, showed them boastfully to *K*wang-3ze, as if the latter had been a boy. *K*wang-3ze said to him, 'Near the Ho there was a poor man who supported his family by weaving rushes (to form screens). His son, when diving in a deep pool, found a pearl worth a thousand ounces of silver. The father said, "Bring a stone, and break it in pieces. A pearl of this value must have been in a pool nine *kh*ung deep[2], and under the chin of the Black Dragon. That you were able to get it must have been owing to your finding him asleep. Let him awake, and the consequences to you will not be small!" Now the kingdom of Sung is deeper than any pool of nine *kh*ung, and its king is fiercer than the Black Dragon. That you were able to get the

[1] These eight words are supplied to complete the structure of the paragraph; but I cannot well say what they mean, nor in what way the predicates in the six clauses that precede can be called 'the stores, or repositories of the body or person.'

[2] = in a pool deeper than any nine pools. Compare the expression 九重天.

chariots must have been owing to your finding him asleep. Let him awake, and you will be ground to powder[1].'

13. Some (ruler) having sent a message of invitation to him, *K*wang-ʒze replied to the messenger, 'Have you seen, Sir, a sacrificial ox? It is robed with ornamental embroidery, and feasted on fresh grass and beans. But when it is led into the grand ancestral temple, though it wished to be (again) a solitary calf, would that be possible for it[2]?'

14. When *K*wang-ʒze was about to die, his disciples signified their wish to give him a grand burial. 'I shall have heaven and earth,' said he, 'for my coffin and its shell; the sun and moon for my two round symbols of jade; the stars and constellations for my pearls and jewels; and all things assisting as the mourners. Will not the provisions for my burial be complete? What could you add to them?' The disciples replied, 'We are afraid that the crows and kites will eat our master.' *K*wang-ʒze rejoined, 'Above, the crows and kites will eat me; below, the mole-crickets and ants will eat me:—to take from those and give to these would only show your partiality[3].'

The attempt, with what is not even, to produce what is even will only produce an uneven result; the attempt, with what is uncertain, to make the uncertain certain will leave the uncertainty as it

[1] Compare paragraph 8. But Lin again denies the genuineness of this.

[2] Compare XVII, par. 11.

[3] We do not know whether *K*wang-ʒze was buried according to his own ideal or not. In the concluding sentences we have a strange descent from the grandiloquence of what precedes.

was. He who uses only the sight of his eyes is acted on by what he sees; it is the (intuition of the) spirit, that gives the assurance of certainty. That the sight of the eyes is not equal to that intuition of the spirit is a thing long acknowledged. And yet stupid people rely on what they see, and will have it to be the sentiment of all men;—all their success being with what is external:—is it not sad?

BOOK XXXIII.

PART III. SECTION XI.

Thien Hsiâ[1].

1. The methods employed in the regulation of the world[2] are many; and (the employers of them) think each that the efficiency of his own method leaves nothing to be added to it.

But where is what was called of old 'the method of the Tâo[2]?' We must reply, 'It is everywhere.' But then whence does the spiritual[3] in it come down? and whence does the intelligence[4] in it come forth? There is that which gives birth to the Sage, and that which gives his perfection to the King:—the origin of both is the One[5].

Not to be separate from his primal source constitutes what we call the Heavenly man; not to be separate from the essential nature thereof constitutes what we call the Spirit-like man; not to be separate from its real truth constitutes what we call the Perfect man[6].

---

[1] See vol. xxxix, pp. 162, 163.

[2] All the methods of educational training and schemes of governmental policy, advocated by 'the hundred schools' of human wisdom in contradistinction from the method or art of the Tâo. Fang Shû has little more meaning than our word 'nostrum.'

[3] Which forms the sage.

[4] Which forms the sage king.

[5] Or, one and the same.

[6] Compare the three definitions in Book I, par. 3.

莊子

To regard Heaven as his primal Source, Its Attributes as the Root (of his nature), and the Tâo as the Gate (by which he enters into this inheritance), (knowing also) the prognostics given in change and transformation, constitutes what we call the Sagely man[1].

To regard benevolence as (the source of all) kindness, righteousness as (the source of all) distinctions, propriety as (the rule of) all conduct, and music as (the idea of) all harmony, thus diffusing a fragrance of gentleness and goodness, constitutes what we call the Superior man[2].

To regard laws as assigning the different (social) conditions, their names as the outward expression (of the social duties), the comparison of subjects as supplying the grounds of evidence, investigation as conducting to certainty, so that things can be numbered as first, second, third, fourth (and so on): —(this is the basis of government). Its hundred offices are thus arranged; business has its regular course; the great matters of clothes and food are provided for; cattle are fattened and looked after; the (government) stores are filled; the old and weak, orphans and solitaries, receive anxious consideration:—in all these ways is provision made for the nourishment of the people.

How complete was (the operation of the Tâo) in the men of old! It made them the equals of spiritual beings, and subtle and all-embracing as heaven and earth. They nourished all things, and produced

[1] Here we have five definitions of the 'Man of Tâo.'

[2] Still within the circle of the Tâo, but inferior to the five above.

harmony all under heaven. Their beneficent influence reached to all classes of the people. They understood all fundamental principles, and followed them out to their graduated issues; in all the six directions went their penetration, and in the four quarters all things were open to them. Great and small, fine and coarse;—all felt their presence and operation. Their intelligence, as seen in all their regulations, was handed down from age to age in their old laws, and much of it was still to be found in the Historians. What of it was in the Shih, the Shû, the Lî, and the Yo, might be learned from the scholars of 3âu[1] and Lû[1], and the girdled members of the various courts. The Shih describes what should be the aim of the mind; the Shû, the course of events; the Lî is intended to direct the conduct; the Yo, to set forth harmony; the Yî, to show the action of the Yin and Yang; and the *Kh*un *Kh*iû, to display names and the duties belonging to them.

Some of the regulations (of these men of old), scattered all under heaven, and established in our Middle states, are (also) occasionally mentioned and described in the writings of the different schools.

There ensued great disorder in the world, and sages and worthies no longer shed their light on it. The Tâo and its characteristics ceased to be regarded as uniform. Many in different places got

[1] These scholars were pre-eminently Confucius and Mencius. In this brief phrase is the one recognition, by our author, of the existence and work of Mencius, who was 'the scholar of 3âu.' But one is not prepared for the comparatively favourable judgment passed on those scholars, and on what we call the Confucian classics. The reading 3âu has not been challenged, and can only be understood of Mencius.

莊子

one glimpse of it, and plumed themselves on possessing it as a whole. They might be compared to the ear, the eye, the nose, or the mouth. Each sense has its own faculty, but their different faculties cannot be interchanged. So it was with the many branches of the various schools. Each had its peculiar excellence, and there was the time for the use of it; but notwithstanding no one covered or extended over the whole (range of truth). The case was that of the scholar of a corner who passes his judgment on all the beautiful in heaven and earth, discriminates the principles that underlie all things, and attempts to estimate the success arrived at by the ancients. Seldom is it that such an one can embrace all the beautiful in heaven and earth, or rightly estimate the ways of the spiritual and intelligent; and thus it was that the Tâo, which inwardly forms the sage and externally the king[1], became obscured and lost its clearness, became repressed and lost its development. Every one in the world did whatever he wished, and was the rule to himself. Alas! the various schools held on their several ways, and could not come back to the same point, nor agree together. The students of that later age unfortunately did not see the undivided purity of heaven and earth, and the great scheme of truth held by the ancients. The system of the Tâo was about to be torn in fragments all under the sky.

2. To leave no example of extravagance to future generations; to show no wastefulness in the use of

[1] Compare 'the spiritual' and 'the intelligence' near the commencement, and the notes 3 and 4.

anything; to make no display in the degree of their (ceremonial) observances; to keep themselves (in their expenditure) under the restraint of strict and exact rule, so as to be prepared for occurring emergencies;—such regulations formed part of the system of the Tâo in antiquity, and were appreciated by Mo Tî, and (his disciple) *Kh*in Hwa-lî[1]. When they heard of such ways, they were delighted with them; but they enjoined them in excess, and followed them themselves too strictly. (Mo) made the treatise 'Against Music,' and enjoined the subject of another, called 'Economy in Expenditure,' on his followers. He would have no singing in life, and no wearing of mourning on occasions of death. He inculcated Universal Love, and a Common Participation in all advantages, and condemned Fighting. His doctrine did not admit of Anger. He was fond also of Learning, and with it all strove not to appear different from others. Yet he did not agree with the former kings, but attacked the ceremonies and music of the ancients.

Hwang-Tî had his Hsien-*kh*ih; Yâo, his Tâ *K*ang; Shun, his Tâ Shâo; Yü, his Tâ Hsiâ; Thang, his Tâ Hû; king Wăṇ, his music of the Phi-yung[2]; and king Wû and the duke of *K*âu made the Wû.

---

[1] Thus Mohism appears as an imperfect Tâoism. Mo (or Meh) Tî was a great officer of the state of Sung, of the period between Confucius and Mencius. He left many treatises behind him, of which only a few, but the most important, survive. *Kh*in Hwa-lî seems to have been his chief disciple. He says, in one place, '*Kh*in Hwa-lî and my other disciples,—300 men.'

[2] The name of the great hall built by king Wăn, and still applied to the examination hall of the Han-lin graduates in Peking.

In the mourning rites of the ancients, the noble and mean had their several observances, the high and low their different degrees. The coffin of the Son of Heaven was sevenfold; of a feudal lord, fivefold; of a great officer, threefold; of other officers, twofold. But now Mo-ȝze alone, would have no singing during life, and no wearing of mourning after death. As the rule for all, he would have a coffin of elaeococca wood, three inches thick, and without any enclosing shell. The teaching of such lessons cannot be regarded as affording a proof of his love for men; his practising them in his own case would certainly show that he did not love himself; but this has not been sufficient to overthrow the views of Mo-ȝze. Notwithstanding, men will sing, and he condemns singing; men will wail, and he condemns wailing; men will express their joy, and he condemns such expression:—is this truly in accordance with man's nature? Through life toil, and at death niggardliness:—his way is one of great unkindliness. Causing men sorrow and melancholy, and difficult to be carried into practice, I fear it cannot be regarded as the way of a sage. Contrary to the minds of men everywhere, men will not endure it. Though Mo-ȝze himself might be able to endure it, how can the aversion of the world to it be overcome? The world averse to it, it must be far from the way of the (ancient) kings.

Mo-ȝze, in praise of his views, said, 'Anciently, when Yü was draining off the waters of the flood, he set free the channels of the *K*iang and the Ho, and opened communications with them from the

What the special music made for it by Wăn was called, I do not know.

regions of the four Î and the nine provinces. The famous hills with which he dealt were 300, the branch streams were 3000, and the smaller ones innumerable. With his own hands he carried the sack and wielded the spade, till he had united all the streams of the country (conducting them to the sea). There was no hair left on his legs from the knee to the ankle. He bathed his hair in the violent wind, and combed it in the pelting rain, thus marking out the myriad states. Yü was a great sage, and thus he toiled in the service of the world.' The effect of this is that in this later time most of the Mohists wear skins and dolychos cloth, with shoes of wood or twisted hemp, not stopping day or night, but considering such toiling on their part as their highest achievement. They say that he who cannot do this is acting contrary to the way of Yü, and not fit to be a Mohist.

The disciples of *Kh*in of Hsiang-lî [1], the followers of the various feudal lords [2]; and Mohists of the south, such as Khû Hu [3], *K*i *Kh*ih [3], and Tăng Ling-ȝze [3], all repeated the texts of Mo, but they differed in the objections which they offered to them, and in their deceitful glosses they called one another Mohists of different schools. They had their disputations, turning on 'what was hard,' and 'what was white,' what constituted 'sameness' and what 'difference,' and their expressions about the difference between 'the odd' and 'the even,' with which they answered one another. They regarded

[1] Some say this *Kh*in was the preceptor of Mo Tî.

[2] Easily translated; but the statement has not been historically illustrated.

[3] Known only by the mention of them here.

莊子

their most distinguished member as a sage, and wished to make him their chief, hoping that he would be handed down as such to future ages. To the present day these controversies are not determined.

The idea of Mo Tî and *Kh*in Hwa-lî was good, but their practice was wrong. They would have made the Mohists of future ages feel it necessary to toil themselves, till there was not a hair on their legs, and still be urging one another on; (thus producing a condition) superior indeed to disorder, but inferior to the result of good government. Nevertheless, Mo-ȝze was indeed one of the best men in the world, which you may search without finding his equal. Decayed and worn (his person) might be, but he is not to be rejected,—a scholar of ability indeed!

3. To keep from being entangled by prevailing customs; to shun all ornamental attractions in one's self; not to be reckless in his conduct to others; not to set himself stubbornly against a multitude; to desire the peace and repose of the world in order to preserve the lives of the people; and to cease his action when enough had been obtained for the nourishment of others and himself, showing that this was the aim of his mind;—such a scheme belonged to the system of the Tâo in antiquity[1], and it was appreciated by Sung Hsing[2] and Yin Wăn[2].

[1] It is difficult to understand the phases of the Tâo here referred to.

[2] Both these men are said to have been of the time of king Hsüan of *Kh*î. In the Catalogue of the Imperial Library of Han, Yin Wăn appears, but not among the Tâoist writers, as the author

When they heard of such ways, they were delighted with them. They made the Hwa-shan cap, and wore it as their distinguishing badge[1]. In their intercourse with others, whatever their differences might be, they began by being indulgent to them. Their name for 'the Forbearance of the Mind' was 'the Action of the Mind.' By the warmth of affection they sought the harmony of joy, and to blend together all within the four seas; and their wish was to plant this everywhere as the chief thing to be pursued. They endured insult without feeling it a disgrace; they sought to save the people from fighting; they forbade aggression and sought to hush the weapons of strife, to save their age from war. In this way they went everywhere, counselling the high and instructing the low. Though the world might not receive them, they only insisted on their object the more strongly, and would not abandon it. Hence it is said, 'The high and the low might be weary of them, but they were strong to show themselves.'

Notwithstanding all this, they acted too much out of regard to others, and too little for themselves. It was as if they said, 'What we request and wish is simply that there may be set down for us five pints of rice;—that will be enough.' But I fear the Master would not get his fill from this; and the disciples, though famishing, would still have to be mindful of the world, and, never stopping day or night, have to say, 'Is it necessary I should preserve

of 'one Treatise.' He is said also to have been the preceptor of Kung-sun Lung.

[1] I cannot fashion the shape of this cap or of the Hwa mountain in my own mind,—'flat both above and below.'

莊子

my life? Shall I scheme how to exalt myself above the master, the saviour of the age?'

It was moreover as if they said, 'The superior man does not censoriously scrutinize (the faults of others); he does not borrow from others to supersede his own endeavours; when any think that he is of no use to the world, he knows that their intelligence is inferior to his own; he considers the prohibition of aggression and causing the disuse of arms to be an external achievement, and the making his own desires to be few and slight to be the internal triumph.' Such was their discrimination between the great and the small, the subtle and the coarse; and with the attainment of this they stopped.

4. Public-spirited, and with nothing of the partizan; easy and compliant, without any selfish partialities; capable of being led, without any positive tendencies; following in the wake of others, without any double mind; not looking round because of anxious thoughts; not scheming in the exercise of their wisdom; not choosing between parties, but going along with all;—all such courses belonged to the Tâoists of antiquity, and they were appreciated by Phăng Măng[1], Thien Phien[1], and Shăn Tâo[1]. When they heard of such ways, they were delighted with them. They considered that the first thing for them to do was to adjust the controversies about different things. They said, 'Heaven can cover, but it cannot sustain; Earth can contain, but it can-

[1] Thien Phien is mentioned in the Han Catalogue, among the Tâoist writers, as a native of *Kh*î, and an author of twenty-five phien. Shăn Tâo also appears among the legal writers, as author of forty-two phien. He is mentioned by Han Fei.

not cover. The Great Tâo embraces all things, but It does not discriminate between them.'

They knew that all things have what they can do and what they cannot do. Hence it is said, 'If you select, you do not reach all; if you teach some things, you must omit the others; but the Tâo neglects none.' Therefore Shăn Tâo discarded his knowledge and also all thought of himself, acting only where he had no alternative, and pursued it as his course to be indifferent and pure in his dealings with others. He said that the best knowledge was to have no knowledge, and that if we had a little knowledge it was likely to prove a dangerous thing. Conscious of his unfitness, he undertook no charge, and laughed at those who valued ability and virtue. Remiss and evasive, he did nothing, and disallowed the greatest sages which the world had known. Now with a hammer, now with his hand, smoothing all corners, and breaking all bonds, he accommodated himself to all conditions. He disregarded right and wrong, his only concern being to avoid trouble; he learned nothing from the wise and thoughtful, and took no note of the succession of events, thinking only of carrying himself with a lofty disregard of everything. He went where he was pushed, and followed where he was led, like a whirling wind, like a feather tossed about, like the revolutions of a grindstone.

What was the reason that he appeared thus complete, doing nothing wrong? that, whether in motion or at rest, he committed no error, and could be charged with no transgression? Creatures that have no knowledge are free from the troubles that arise from self-assertion and the entanglements that spring from the use of knowledge. Moving and at

莊子

rest, they do not depart from their proper course, and all their life long they do not receive any praise. Hence (Shăn Tâo) said, 'Let me come to be like a creature without knowledge. Of what use are the (teachings of the) sages and worthies?' But a clod of earth never fails in the course (proper for it), and men of spirit and eminence laughed together at him, and said, 'The way of Shăn Tâo does not describe the conduct of living men; that it should be predicable only of the dead is strange indeed!'

It was just the same with Thien Phien. He learned under Phăng Măng, but it was as if he were not taught at all. The master of Phăng Măng said, 'The Tâoist professors of old came no farther than to say that nothing was absolutely right and nothing absolutely wrong.' His spirit was like the breath of an opposing wind; how can it be described in words? But he was always contrary to (the views of) other men, which he would not bring together to view, and he did not escape shaving the corners and bonds (of which I have spoken). What he called the Tâo was not the true Tâo, and what he called the right was really the wrong.

Phăng Măng, Thien Phien, and Shăn Tâo did not in fact know the Tâo; but nevertheless they had heard in a general way about it.

5. To take the root (from which things spring) as the essential (part), and the things as its coarse (embodiment); to see deficiency in accumulation; and in the solitude of one's individuality to dwell with the spirit-like and intelligent;—such a course belonged to the Tâo of antiquity, and it was appre-

ciated by Kwan Yin[1] and Lâo Tan[2]. When they heard of such ways, they were delighted with them. They built their system on the assumption of an eternal non-existence, and made the ruling idea in it that of the Grand Unity. They made weakness and humility their mark of distinction, and considered that by empty vacuity no injury could be sustained, but all things be preserved in their substantiality.

Kwan Yin[1] says, 'To him who does not dwell in himself the forms of things show themselves as they are. His movement is like that of water; his stillness is like that of a mirror; his response is like that of the echo. His tenuity makes him seem to be disappearing altogether; he is still as a clear (lake), harmonious in his association with others, and he counts gain as loss. He does not take precedence of others, but follows them.' Lâo Tan[2] says, 'He knows his masculine power, but maintains his female weakness,—becoming the channel into which all streams flow. He knows his white purity, but keeps his disgrace,—becoming the valley of the world. Men all prefer to be first; he alone chooses to be last, saying, "I will receive the offscourings of the world." Men all choose fulness; he alone chooses emptiness. He does not store, and therefore he has a superabundance; he looks solitary, but has a multitude around him. In his conducting

[1] Kwan Yin;—see Book XIX, par. 2, and vol. xxxix, p. 35. In the Catalogue of the Han Library there is an entry of a work by Kwan Yin in nine phien; and there is still a work current in China, called *K*wan Yin-ʒze in one *k*üan, but it is not generally received as genuine.

[2] See the account of Lâo-ʒze in vol. xxxix, pp. 34–36.

of himself he is easy and leisurely and wastes nothing. He does nothing, and laughs at the clever and ingenious. Men all seek for happiness, but he feels complete in his imperfect condition, and says, "Let me only escape blame." He regards what is deepest as his root, and what is most restrictive as his rule; and says, "The strong is broken; the sharp and pointed is blunted[1]." He is always generous and forbearing with others, and does not encroach on any man;—this may be pronounced the height (of perfection).'

O Kwan Yin, and Lâo Tan, ye were among the greatest men of antiquity; True men indeed!

6. That the shadowy and still is without bodily form; that change and transformation are ever proceeding, but incapable of being determined. What is death? What is life? What is meant by the union of Heaven and Earth? Does the spiritual intelligence go away? Shadowy, where does it go? Subtle, whither does it proceed? All things being arranged as they are, there is no one place which can be fitly ascribed to it. Such were the questions belonging to the scheme of Tâo in antiquity, and they were appreciated by Kwang Kâu. When he heard of such subjects, he was delighted with them. (He discussed them), using strange and mystical expressions, wild and extravagant words, and phrases to which no definite meaning could be assigned. He constantly indulged his own wayward ideas, but did not make himself a partisan, nor look at them as peculiar to himself. Considering that men were

[1] From the 'Lâo Tan says' down to this, may be said to be all quotation, with more or less exactness, from the Tâo Teh King. See chaps. 28, 22, et al.

sunk in stupidity and could not be talked to in dignified style, he employed the words of the cup of endless application, with important quotations to substantiate the truth, and an abundance of corroborative illustrations. He chiefly cared to occupy himself with the spirit-like operation of heaven and earth, and did not try to rise above the myriads of things. He did not condemn the agreements and differences of others, so that he might live in peace with the prevalent views. Though his writings may seem to be sparkling trifles, there is no harm in amusing one's self with them; though his phraseology be ever-varying, its turns and changes are worth being looked at;—the fulness and completeness of his ideas cannot be exhausted. Above he seeks delight in the Maker; below, he has a friendly regard to those who consider life and death as having neither beginning nor end. As regards his dealing with the Root (origin of all things), he is comprehensive and great, opening up new views, deep, vast, and free. As regards the Author and Master (the Great Tâo Itself), he may be pronounced exact and correct, carrying our thoughts to range and play on high. Nevertheless on the subject of transformation, and the emancipation of that from (the thraldom of) things, his principles are inexhaustible, and are not derived from his predecessors. They are subtle and obscure, and cannot be fully explained [1].

[1] The question of the genuineness of this paragraph has been touched on in vol. xxxix, p. 163. Whether from himself or from some disciple, it celebrates *K*wang-ȝze as the chief and most interesting of all ancient Tâoist writers.

莊子

7. Hui Shih[1] had many ingenious notions. His writings would fill five carriages; but his doctrines were erroneous and contradictory, and his words were wide of their mark. Taking up one thing after another, he would say:—'That which is so great that there is nothing outside it may be called the Great One; and that which is so small that there is nothing inside it may be called the Small One.' 'What has no thickness and will not admit of being repeated is 1000 lî in size[2].' 'Heaven may be as low as the earth.' 'A mountain may be as level as a marsh.' 'The sun in the meridian may be the sun declining.' 'A creature may be born to life and may die at the same time.' '(When it is said that) things greatly alike are different from things a little alike, this is what is called making little of agreements and differences; (when it is said that) all things are entirely alike or entirely different, this is what is called making much of agreements and differences.' 'The south is unlimited and yet has a limit.' 'I proceed to Yueh to-day and came to it yesterday.' 'Things which are joined together can be separated.' 'I know the centre of the world;—it is north of Yen or south of Yueh.' 'If all things be regarded with love, heaven and earth are of one body (with me).'

Hui Shih by such sayings as these made himself

[1] Introduced to us in the first Book of our author, and often mentioned in the intervening Books. He was not a Tâoist, but we are glad to have the account of him here given, as enabling us to understand better the intellectual life of China in Kwang-ȝze's time.

[2] It is of little use trying to find the answers to these sayings of Hui Shih and others. They are only riddles or paradoxes.

very conspicuous throughout the kingdom, and was considered an able debater. All other debaters vied with one another and delighted in similar exhibitions. (They would say), 'There are feathers in an egg.' 'A fowl has three feet.' 'The kingdom belongs to Ying.' 'A dog might have been (called) a sheep.' 'A tadpole has a tail.' 'Fire is not hot.' 'A mountain gives forth a voice.' 'A wheel does not tread on the ground.' 'The eye does not see.' 'The finger indicates, but needs not touch, (the object).' 'Where you come to may not be the end.' 'The tortoise is longer than the snake.' 'The carpenter's square is not square.' 'A compass should not itself be round.' 'A chisel does not surround its handle.' 'The shadow of a flying bird does not (itself) move.' 'Swift as the arrowhead is, there is a time when it is neither flying nor at rest.' 'A dog is not a hound.' 'A bay horse and a black ox are three.' 'A white dog is black.' 'A motherless colt never had a mother.' 'If from a stick a foot long you every day take the half of it, in a myriad ages it will not be exhausted.'—It was in this way that the debaters responded to Hui Shih, all their lifetime, without coming to an end.

Hwan Twan[1] and Kung-sun Lung[2] were true members of this class. By their specious representations they threw a glamour over men's minds and altered their ideas. They vanquished men in argument, but could not subdue their minds, only keeping them in the enclosure of their sophistry. Hui Shih daily used his own knowledge and the arguments of others to propose strange theses to all debaters;—

[1] Elsewhere unknown.

[2] See Book XVII, par. 10.

such was his practice. At the same time he would talk freely of himself, thinking himself the ablest among them, and saying, 'In heaven or earth who is my match?' Shih maintained indeed his masculine energy, but he had not the art (of controversy).

In the south there was a man of extraordinary views, named Hwang Liâo [1], who asked him how it was that the sky did not fall nor the earth sink, and what was the cause of wind, rain, and the thunder's roll and crash. Shih made no attempt to evade the questions, and answered him without any exercise of thought, talking about all things, without pause, on and on without end; yet still thinking that his words were few, and adding to them the strangest observations. He thought that to contradict others was a real triumph, and wished to make himself famous by overcoming them; and on this account he was not liked by the multitude of debaters. He was weak in real attainment, though he might seem strong in comparison with others, and his way was narrow and dark. If we look at Hui Shih's ability from the standpoint of Heaven and Earth, it was only like the restless activity of a mosquito or gadfly; of what service was it to anything? To give its full development to any one capacity is a good thing, and he who does so is in the way to a higher estimation of the Tâo; but Hui Shih could find no rest for himself in doing this. He diffused himself over the world of things without satiety, till in the end he had only the reputation of being a skilful debater. Alas! Hui Shih, with

[1] Elsewhere unknown.

all his talents, vast as they were, made nothing out; he pursued all subjects and never came back (with success). It was like silencing an echo by his shouting, or running a race with his shadow. Alas!